W9-AEF-533

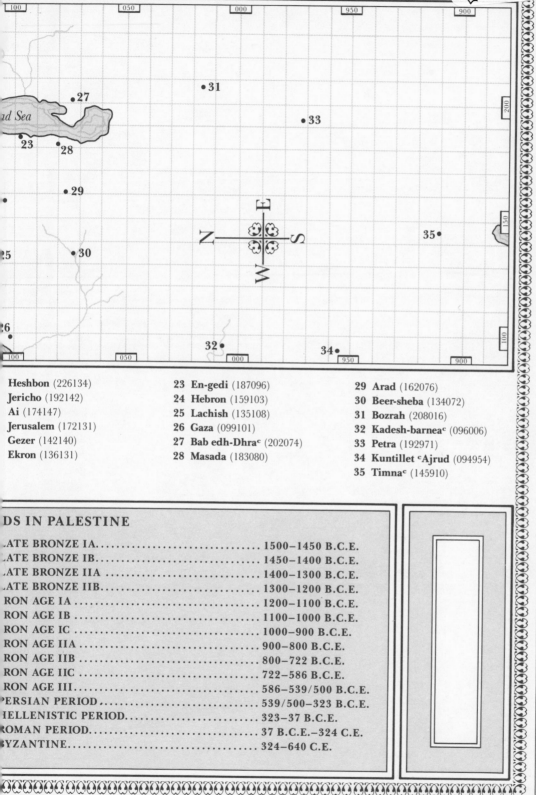

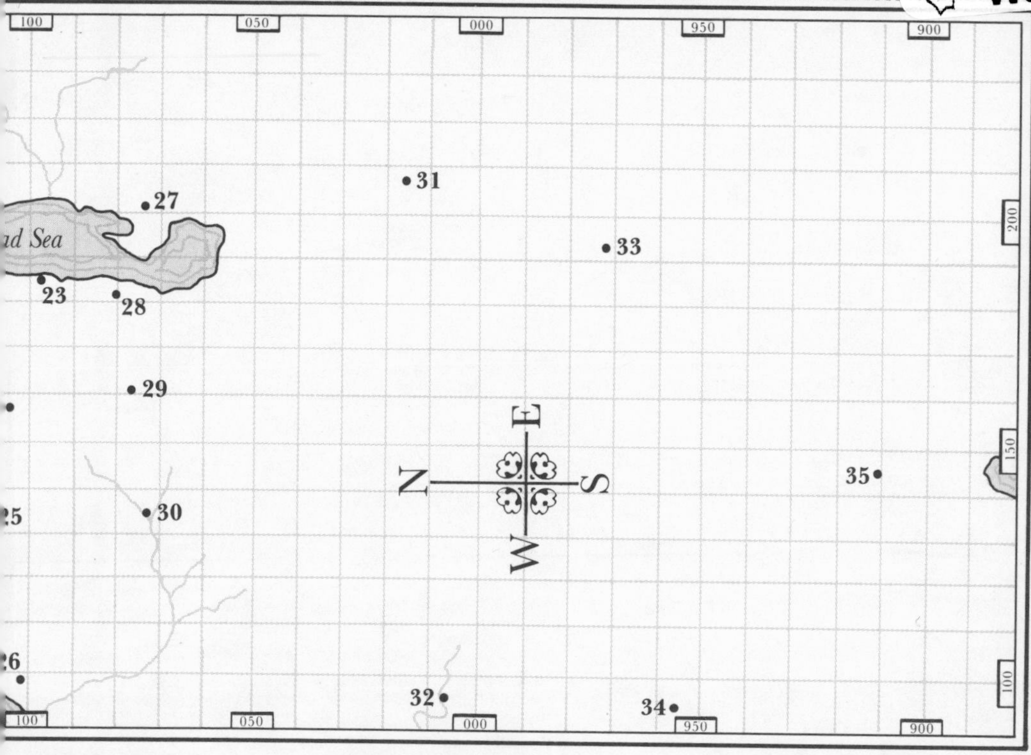

Heshbon (226134)
Jericho (192142)
Ai (174147)
Jerusalem (172131)
Gezer (142140)
Ekron (136131)

23 **En-gedi** (187096)
24 **Hebron** (159103)
25 **Lachish** (135108)
26 **Gaza** (099101)
27 **Bab edh-Dhra^c** (202074)
28 **Masada** (183080)

29 **Arad** (162076)
30 **Beer-sheba** (134072)
31 **Bozrah** (208016)
32 **Kadesh-barnea^c** (096006)
33 **Petra** (192971)
34 **Kuntillet ^cAjrud** (094954)
35 **Timna^c** (145910)

DS IN PALESTINE

ATE BRONZE IA	1500–1450 B.C.E.
ATE BRONZE IB	1450–1400 B.C.E.
ATE BRONZE IIA	1400–1300 B.C.E.
ATE BRONZE IIB	1300–1200 B.C.E.
RON AGE IA	1200–1100 B.C.E.
RON AGE IB	1100–1000 B.C.E.
RON AGE IC	1000–900 B.C.E.
RON AGE IIA	900–800 B.C.E.
RON AGE IIB	800–722 B.C.E.
RON AGE IIC	722–586 B.C.E.
RON AGE III	586–539/500 B.C.E.
ERSIAN PERIOD	539/500–323 B.C.E.
IELLENISTIC PERIOD	323–37 B.C.E.
OMAN PERIOD	37 B.C.E.–324 C.E.
YZANTINE	324–640 C.E.

THE ANCHOR BIBLE DICTIONARY

THE ANCHOR BIBLE DICTIONARY

VOLUME 3
H–J

David Noel Freedman
EDITOR-IN-CHIEF

ASSOCIATE EDITORS
Gary A. Herion • David F. Graf
John David Pleins

MANAGING EDITOR
Astrid B. Beck

ABD

DOUBLEDAY
NEW YORK • LONDON • TORONTO • SYDNEY • AUCKLAND

220.3
FrA-3

THE ANCHOR BIBLE DICTIONARY: VOLUME 3
PUBLISHED BY DOUBLEDAY
a division of Bantam Doubleday Dell Publishing Group, Inc.
666 Fifth Avenue, New York, New York 10103

THE ANCHOR BIBLE DICTIONARY, DOUBLEDAY,
and the portrayal of an anchor with the letters ABD
are trademarks of Doubleday,
a division of Bantam Doubleday Dell Publishing Group, Inc.

DESIGN BY Stanley S. Drate/Folio Graphics Company, Inc.

Library of Congress Cataloging-in-Publication Data
Anchor Bible dictionary / David Noel Freedman, editor-in-chief;
associate editors, Gary A. Herion, David F. Graf, John David Pleins;
managing editor, Astrid B. Beck.
—1st ed.
p. cm.
Includes bibliographical references.
1. Bible—Dictionaries. I. Freedman, David Noel, 1922– .
BS440.A54 1992
220.3—dc20 91-8385
CIP

Vol. 1 ISBN 0-385-19351-3
Vol. 2 ISBN 0-385-19360-2
Vol. 3 ISBN 0-385-19361-0
Vol. 4 ISBN 0-385-19362-9
Vol. 5 ISBN 0-385-19363-7
Vol. 6 ISBN 0-385-26190-X

Copyright © 1992 by Doubleday,
a division of Bantam Doubleday Dell Publishing Group, Inc.
All Rights Reserved
Printed in the United States of America

10 9 8 7 6 5 4 3 2 1

FIRST EDITION

CONSULTANTS

HANS DIETER BETZ (Greco-Roman Religion)
Shailer Mathews Professor of NT Studies, University of Chicago

JAMES H. CHARLESWORTH (Apocrypha and Pseudepigrapha)
George L. Collord Professor of NT Language and Literature, Princeton Theological Seminary

FRANK MOORE CROSS (Old Testament)
Hancock Professor of Hebrew and Other Oriental Languages, Harvard University

WILLIAM G. DEVER (Archaeology)
Professor of Near Eastern Archaeology and Anthropology, University of Arizona

A. KIRK GRAYSON (Mesopotamia and Assyriology)
Professor, University of Toronto

PETER MACHINIST (Bible and Ancient Near East)
Professor of Near Eastern Languages and Civilizations, Harvard University

ABRAHAM J. MALHERBE (New Testament)
Buckingham Professor of New Testament Criticism and Interpretation, The Divinity School, Yale University

BIRGER A. PEARSON (Early Christianity)
Professor of Religious Studies, University of California at Santa Barbara

JACK M. SASSON (Bible and Ancient Near East)
Professor in Religious Studies, University of North Carolina

WILLIAM R. SCHOEDEL (Early Christian Literature)
University of Illinois at Urbana-Champaign

EDITORIAL STAFF

EDITOR-IN-CHIEF:
David Noel Freedman

ASSOCIATE EDITORS:
Gary A. Herion
David F. Graf
John David Pleins

MANAGING EDITOR:
Astrid B. Beck

ASSISTANT EDITOR:
Philip C. Schmitz

PRODUCTION EDITOR:
Leslie Barkley

ASSISTANTS TO THE EDITOR:
Mark J. Fretz
Herbert Grether
John Huddlestun
John Kutsko
Dale Manor
Paul Mirecki
James Mueller
David R. Seely
William Ward
Harry Weeks

PRODUCTION ASSISTANTS:
Carol Herion
Dennis Moser

LIST OF ABBREVIATIONS

1 Apoc. Jas.	*First Apocalypse of James* (NHC V,*3*)
1 Chr	1 Chronicles
1 Clem.	*1 Clement*
1 Cor	1 Corinthians
1 En.	*1 Enoch (Ethiopic Apocalypse)*
1 Esdr	1 Esdras
1 John	1 John
1 Kgdms	1 Samuel (LXX)
1 Kgs	1 Kings
1 Macc	1 Maccabees
1 Pet	1 Peter
1 Sam	1 Samuel
1 Thess	1 Thessalonians
1 Tim	1 Timothy
1Q, 2Q, 3Q, etc.	Numbered caves of Qumran, yielding written material; followed by abbreviation of biblical or apocryphal book
1QapGen	*Genesis Apocryphon* of Qumran Cave 1
1QH	*Hōdāyôt (Thanksgiving Hymns)* from Qumran Cave 1
1QIsa$^{a, b}$	First or second copy of Isaiah from Qumran Cave 1
1QM	*Milḥāmāh (War Scroll)*
1QpHab	*Pesher on Habakkuk* from Qumran Cave 1
1QS	*Serek hayyaḥad (Rule of the Community, Manual of Discipline)*
1QSa	Appendix A *(Rule of the Congregation)* to 1QS
1QSb	Appendix B *(Blessings)* to 1QS
1st	first
2 Apoc. Jas.	*Second Apocalypse of James* (NHC V,*4*)
2 Bar.	*2 Baruch (Syriac Apocalypse)*
2 Chr	2 Chronicles
2 Clem.	*2 Clement*
2 Cor	2 Corinthians
2 En.	*2 Enoch (Slavonic Apocalypse)*
2 Esdr	2 Esdras
2 John	2 John
2 Kgdms	2 Samuel (LXX)
2 Kgs	2 Kings
2 Macc	2 Maccabees
2 Pet	2 Peter
2 Sam	2 Samuel
2 Thess	2 Thessalonians
2 Tim	2 Timothy
2d	second
3 Bar.	*3 Baruch (Greek Apocalypse)*
3 Cor.	*3 Corinthians*
3 En.	*3 Enoch (Hebrew Apocalypse)*
3 John	3 John
3 Kgdms	1 Kings (LXX)
3 Macc.	*3 Maccabees*
3d	third
3Q15	Copper Scroll from Qumran Cave 3
4 Bar.	*4 Baruch*
4 Ezra	*4 Ezra*
4 Kgdms	2 Kings (LXX)
4 Macc.	*4 Maccabees*
4QFlor	*Florilegium* (or *Eschatological Midrashim*) from Qumran Cave 4
4QMess ar	Aramaic "Messianic" text from Qumran Cave 4
4QPhyl	Phylacteries from Qumran Cave 4
4QPrNab	Prayer of Nabonidus from Qumran Cave 4
4QTestim	*Testimonia* text from Qumran Cave 4
4QTLevi	*Testament of Levi* from Qumran Cave 4
5 Apoc. Syr. Pss.	*Five Apocryphal Syriac Psalms*
5 Macc.	*5 Maccabees*
11QMelch	*Melchizedek* text from Qumran Cave 11
11QtgJob	*Targum of Job* from Qumran Cave 11
A	Codex Alexandrinus
ÄA	Ägyptologische Abhandlungen
AA	*Archäologischer Anzeiger,* Berlin
AAL	*Afroasiatic Linguistics,* Malibu, CA
AANLM	*Atti dell'Accademia Nazionale dei Lincei, Memorie, Classe di scienze morali, storiche e filologiche,* ser. 8
AANLR	*Atti dell'Accademia Nazionale dei Lincei, Rendiconti, Classe di scienze morali, storiche e filologiche,* ser. 8

AARAS	American Academy of Religion Academy Series
AARASR	American Academy of Religion Aids for the Study of Religion
AARCRS	American Academy of Religion Classics in Religious Studies
AARSR	American Academy of Religion Studies in Religion
AARTT	American Academy of Religion Texts and Translations
AASF	Annales Academiae Scientarum Fennicae, Helsinki
AASOR	Annual of the American Schools of Oriental Research
ÄAT	Ägypten und Altes Testament
AAWLM	*Abhandlungen der Akademie der Wissenschaften und der Literatur Mainz*
AB	Anchor Bible
ABAW	Abhandlungen der Bayerischen Akademie der Wissenschaften
AbB	Altbabylonische Briefe in Umschrift und Übersetzung, ed. F. R. Kraus. Leiden, 1964–
abbr.	abbreviated, abbreviation
ABD	*Anchor Bible Dictionary*
ABIUSJH	*Annual of Bar-Ilan University Studies in Judaica and the Humanities*
ABL	*Assyrian and Babylonian Letters,* 14 vols., ed. R. F. Harper. Chicago, 1892–1914
ABLA	M. Noth. 1971. *Aufsätze zur biblischen Landes- und Altertumskunde,* ed. H. W. Wolff. Neukirchen-Vluyn
ʿAbod. Zar.	*ʿAboda Zara*
ʾAbot	*ʾAbot*
ʾAbot R. Nat.	*ʾAbot de Rabbi Nathan*
Abr	Philo, *De Abrahamo*
ABR	*Australian Biblical Review*
ABRMW	H. Graf Reventlow. 1985. *The Authority of the Bible and the Rise of the Modern World.* Trans. J. Bowden. Philadelphia
AbrN	*Abr-Nahrain*
absol.	absolute
AcApos	*Acta Apostolorum Apocrypha.* 3 vols. Hildesheim, 1959
ACF	*Annuaire du Collège de France,* Paris
ACNT	Augsburg Commentary on the New Testament
AcOr	*Acta orientalia*
AcOrASH	*Acta orientalia Academiae Scientiarum Hungaricae*
ACR	*American Classical Review*
AcSum	*Acta Sumerologica*
act.	active
Acts	Acts (or Acts of the Apostles)
Acts Andr.	*Acts of Andrew*
Acts Andr. Mth.	*Acts of Andrew and Matthias*
Acts Andr. Paul	*Acts of Andrew and Paul*
Acts Barn.	*Acts of Barnabas*
Acts Jas.	*Acts of James the Great*
Acts John	*Acts of John*
Acts John Pro.	*Acts of John (by Prochorus)*
Acts Paul	*Acts of Paul*
Acts Pet.	*Acts of Peter*
Acts Pet. (Slav.)	*Slavonic Acts of Peter*
Acts Pet. 12 Apost.	*Acts of Peter and the Twelve Apostles* (NHC VI,*1*)
Acts Pet. Andr.	*Acts of Peter and Andrew*
Acts Pet. Paul	*Acts of Peter and Paul*
Acts Phil.	*Acts of Philip*
Acts Phil. (Syr.)	*Acts of Philip (Syriac)*
Acts Pil.	*Acts of Pilate*
Acts Thad.	*Acts of Thaddaeus*
Acts Thom.	*Acts of Thomas*
ActSS	*Acta Sanctorum*
ACW	Ancient Christian Writers
A.D.	*anno domini* (year)
ad loc.	*ad locum* (at the place)
ADAIK	Abhandlungen des deutschen archäologischen Instituts, Kairo
ADAJ	*Annual of the Department of Antiquities of Jordan*
Add Dan	Additions to Daniel
Add Esth	Additions to Esther
ADFU	Ausgrabungen der Deutschen Forschungsgemeinschaft in Uruk-Warka
adj.	adjective
ADOG	*Abhandlungen der Deutschen Orient-Gesellschaft,* Berlin
ADPV	Abhandlungen des Deutschen Palästina-Vereins
adv.	adverb
AE	*L'année épigraphique* [cited by year and no. of text]
AEB	*Annual Egyptological Bibliography*
Aeg	*Aegyptus: Revista italiana di egittologia e papirologia*
AEHE IV	*Annuaire de l'École pratique des Hautes Études,* IVe section, Sc. hist. et philol., Paris
AEHE V	*Annuaire de l'École pratique des Hautes Études,* V^{e} section, Sc. relig., Paris
AEHL	*Archaeological Excavations in the Holy Land,* ed. A. Negev. Englewood Cliffs, NJ, 1980
AEL	M. Lichtheim. 1971–80. *Ancient Egyptian Literature.* 3 vols. Berkeley
AER	*American Ecclesiastical Review*
AESH	B. Trigger, B. J. Kemp, D. O'Connor, and A. B. Lloyd. 1983. *Ancient Egypt: A Social History.* Cambridge
Aet	Philo, *De aeternitate mundi*
Aev	*Aevum: Rassegna di scienze storiche linguistiche e filologiche*

ÄF	Ägyptologische Forschungen
AFER	*African Ecclesiastical Review,* Eldoret, Kenya
AfL	*Archiv für Liturgiewissenschaft,* Regensburg
AFNW	*Arbeitsgemeinschaft für Forschung des Landes Nordrhein-Westfalen,* Cologne
AfO	*Archiv für Orientforschung,* Graz
AfrTJ	*Africa Theological Journal,* Arusha, Tanzania
AgAp	Josephus, *Against Apion (= Contra Apionem)*
ʾAg. Ber.	*ʾAggadat Berešit*
AGJU	Arbeiten zur Geschichte des antiken Judentums und des Urchristentums
Agr	Philo, *De agricultura*
AGSU	Arbeiten zur Geschichte des Spätjudentums und Urchristentums
AH	*An Aramaic Handbook,* ed. F. Rosenthal, 2 vols. Wiesbaden, 1967
Ah.	*Ahiqar*
AHAW	Abhandlungen der Heidelberger Akademie der Wissenschaften
AHG	B. Albrektson. 1967. *History and the Gods.* ConBOT 1. Lund
AHR	*American Historical Review*
AHW	*Akkadisches Handwörterbuch,* ed. W. von Soden. 3 vols. Wiesbaden, 1965–81
AI	Arad Inscription [cited according to Y. Aharoni. 1981. *Arad Inscriptions,* Jerusalem]
AION	*Annali dell'Istituto orientali di Napoli*
AIPHOS	*Annuaire de l'Institut de philologie et d'histoire orientales et slaves*
AIR	*Ancient Israelite Religion: Essays in Honor of Frank Moore Cross,* ed. P. D. Miller, P. D. Hanson, and S. D. McBride. Philadelphia, 1987
AIS	I. Finkelstein. 1988. *The Archaeology of the Israelite Settlement.* Jerusalem
AJA	*American Journal of Archaeology*
AJAS	*American Journal of Arabic Studies*
AJBA	*Australian Journal of Biblical Archaeology*
AJBI	Annual of the Japanese Biblical Institute, Tokyo
AJP	*American Journal of Philology*
AJSL	*American Journal of Semitic Languages and Literatures*
AJT	*American Journal of Theology*
Akk	Akkadian
AKM	*Abhandlungen zur Kunde des Morgenlandes (Leipzig)*
AL	*The Assyrian Laws,* ed. G. R. Driver and J. C. Miles. Oxford, 1935
ALBO	Analecta lovaniensia biblica et orientalia
ALGHJ	Arbeiten zur Literatur und Geschichte des hellenistischen Judentums
Allogenes	*Allogenes* (NHC XI,*3*)
Altertum	*Das Altertum,* Berlin
ALUOS	Annual of Leeds University Oriental Society
Am	*America,* New York
AmBenR	*American Benedictine Review*
AMI	Archäologische Mitteilungen aus Iran
Amos	Amos
AMT	R. C. Thompson. 1923. *Assyrian Medical Texts.* Oxford
AN	J. J. Stamm. 1939. *Die akkadische Namengebung.* MVÄG 44. Berlin
AnBib	Analecta Biblica
AnBoll	*Analecta Bollandiana*
AncIsr	R. de Vaux, 1961. *Ancient Israel: Its Life and Institutions.* Trans. J. McHugh. London. Repr. New York, 1965
ANE	Ancient Near East(ern)
ANEP	*Ancient Near East in Pictures Relating to the Old Testament,* 2d ed. with suppl., ed. J. B. Pritchard, Princeton, 1969
ANET	*Ancient Near Eastern Texts Relating to the Old Testament,* 3d ed. with suppl., ed. J. B. Pritchard, Princeton, 1969
ANF	The Ante-Nicene Fathers
Ang	*Angelicum,* Rome
ANHMW	*Annalen des Naturhistorische Museum in Wien*
Anim	Philo, *De animalibus*
Anon. Sam.	*Anonymous Samaritan Text*
AnOr	Analecta orientalia
ANQ	*Andover Newton Quarterly*
ANRW	*Aufstieg und Niedergang der römischen Welt,* ed. H. Temporini and W. Haase, Berlin, 1972–
AnSt	*Anatolian Studies*
Ant	Josephus, *Jewish Antiquities (= Antiquitates Judaicae)*
AntCl	*L'antiquité classique*
ANTF	Arbeiten zur neutestamentlichen Textforschung
ANTJ	Arbeiten zum Neuen Testament und Judentum
Anton	*Antonianum*
Anuario	*Anuario de Filología,* Barcelona
ANVAO	Avhandlinger utgitt av det Norske Videnskaps-Akademi i Oslo
AO	Der Alte Orient
AOAT	Alter Orient und Altes Testament
AOATS	Alter Orient und Altes Testament Sonderreihe
AÖAW	*Anzeiger der Österreichischer Akademie der Wissenschaften,* Vienna

*AOB*²	*Altorientalische Bilder zum Alten Testament,* 2d ed., ed. H. Gressman. Berlin and Leipzig, 1927
AOBib	Altorientalische Bibliothek
AoF	*Altorientalische Forschungen*
AOS	American Oriental Series
AOSTS	American Oriental Society Translation Series
*AOT*²	*Altorientalische Texte zum Alten Testament,* 2d ed., ed. H. Gressman. Berlin and Leipzig, 1926
AP	*L'année philologique*
Ap. Ezek.	*Apocryphon of Ezekiel*
Ap. Jas.	*Apocryphon of James* (NHC I,*2*)
Ap. John	*Apocryphon of John* (NHC II,*1*; III,*1*; IV,*1*)
APAACS	American Philological Association American Classical Studies
APAPM	American Philological Association Philological Monographs
APAT	*Die Apokryphen und Pseudepigraphen des Alten Testaments,* 2 vols., ed. E. Kautzch. Tübingen, 1900. Repr. 1975
APAW	*Abhandlungen der Preussischen Akademie der Wissenschaft*
APEF	*Annual of the Palestine Exploration Fund*
APNM	H. B. Hoffman. 1965. *Amorite Personal Names in the Mari Texts.* Baltimore
Apoc. Ab.	*Apocalypse of Abraham*
Apoc. Adam	*Apocalypse of Adam* (NHC V,*5*)
Apoc. Dan.	*Apocalypse of Daniel*
Apoc. Dosith.	*Apocalypse of Dositheus*
Apoc. El.	*Apocalypse of Elijah*
Apoc. Ezek.	*Apocalypse of Ezekiel*
Apoc. Messos	*Apocalypse of Messos*
Apoc. Mos.	*Apocalypse of Moses*
Apoc. Paul	*Apocalypse of Paul* (NHC V,*2*)
Apoc. Pet.	*Apocalypse of Peter* (NHC VII,*3*)
Apoc. Sedr.	*Apocalypse of Sedrach*
Apoc. Thom.	*Apocalypse of Thomas*
Apoc. Vir.	*Apocalypses of the Virgin*
Apoc. Zeph.	*Apocalypse of Zephaniah*
Apoc. Zos.	*Apocalypse of Zosimus*
Apocr.	*Apocryphal, Apocrypha*
Apol Jud	Philo, *Apologia pro Iudaeis*
Apos.	Apostolic, Apostles
Apos. Con.	*Apostolic Constitutions and Canons*
APOT	*Apocrypha and Pseudepigrapha of the Old Testament,* 2 vols., ed. R. H. Charles. Oxford, 1913
Ar	Arabic
AR	Archaeological Reports
ᶜArak.	*ᶜArakin*
Aram	Aramaic
ArbT	*Arbeitzen zur Theologie,* Stuttgart
Arch	*Archaeology*
ArchEleph	B. Porten. 1968. *Archives from Elephantine.* Berkeley
ArchPal	W. F. Albright. 1960. *The Archaeology of Palestine.* 3d rev. ed. Harmondsworth. Repr. Gloucester, MA, 1971
ARE	*Ancient Records of Egypt,* 5 vols., ed. J. H. Breasted. Chicago, 1906. Repr. New York, 1962
ARET	Archivi reali di Ebla, Testi
ARG	*Archiv für Reformationsgeschichte*
ARI	W. F. Albright. 1968. *Archaeology and the Religion of Israel.* 5th ed. Baltimore
Aris. Ex.	*Aristeas the Exegete*
Aristob.	*Aristobulus*
ARM	Archives royales de Mari
ARMT	Archives royals de Mari: transcriptions et traductions
ARNA	*Ancient Records from North Arabia,* ed. F. V. Winnett and W. L. Reed. Toronto, 1970
ArOr	*Archiv orientální*
art.	article
Art.	*Artapanus*
ARW	*Archiv für Religionswissenschaft*
AS	Assyriological Studies
ASAE	*Annales du Service des antiquités de l'Egypte*
ASAW	*Abhandlungen der Sächsischen Akademie der Wissenschaften in Leipzig*
Asc. Jas.	*Ascents of James*
Ascen. Is.	*Ascension of Isaiah*
Asclepius	*Asclepius 21–29* (NHC VI,*8*)
ASNU	Acta seminarii neotestamentici upsaliensis
ASORDS	American Schools of Oriental Research Dissertation Series
ASORMS	American Schools of Oriental Research Monograph Series
ASP	American Studies in Papyrology
ASS	*Acta sanctae sedis*
AsSeign	*Assemblées du Seigneur*
ASSR	*Archives des sciences sociales des religions*
Assum. Mos.	*Assumption of Moses*
Assum. Vir.	*Assumption of the Virgin*
Assur	*Assur,* Malibu, CA
ASTI	*Annual of the Swedish Theological Institute*
ASV	American Standard Version
ATAbh	Alttestamentliche Abhandlungen
ATANT	Abhandlungen zur Theologie des Alten und Neuen Testaments
ATAT	Arbeiten zu Text und Sprache im Alten Testament
ATD	Das Alte Testament Deutsch
ATDan	Acta theologica danica
ATG	*Archivo Teológico Granadino,* Granada

ATJ	*Ashland Theological Journal,* Ashland, OH
ATR	*Anglican Theological Review,* Evanston, IL
Aug	*Augustinianum,* Rome
AulaOr	*Aula Orientalis,* Barcelona
AuS	G. Dalman. 1928–42. *Arbeit und Sitte in Palästina.* 7 vols. BFCT 14, 17, 27, 29, 33, 36, 41. Gütersloh, 1928. Repr. Hildesheim, 1964
AusBR	*Australian Biblical Review*
AUSS	*Andrews University Seminary Studies,* Berrien Springs, MI
Auth. Teach.	*Authoritative Teaching* (NHC VI,*3*)
AUU	Acta universitatis upsaliensis
AV	Authorized Version
AW	*The Ancient World,* Chicago
AWEAT	Archiv für wissenschaftliche Erforschung des Alten Testaments
B	Codex Vaticanus
b. (Talm.)	Babylonian (Talmud) = "Babli"
B. Bat.	*Baba Batra*
B. Meṣ.	*Baba Meṣiʿa*
B. Qam.	*Baba Qamma*
BA	*Biblical Archaeologist*
Bab.	Babylonian
BAC	Biblioteca de autores cristianos
BAEO	Boletín de la asociación españala des orientalistas
BAfO	*Beihefte zur Archiv für Orientforschung,* Graz
BAGD	W. Bauer, W. F. Arndt, F. W. Gingrich, and F. W. Danker. 1979. *Greek-English Lexicon of the New Testament.* 2d ed. Chicago
BAIAS	*Bulletin of the Anglo-Israel Archaeological Society,* London
BANE	*The Bible in the Ancient Near East,* ed. G. E. Wright. Garden City, NY, 1961. Repr. Winona Lake, IN, 1979
Bar	Baruch
BAR	*Biblical Archaeologist Reader*
Bar.	*Baraita*
BARev	*Biblical Archaeology Review*
BARIS	British Archaeological Reports, International Series
Barn.	*Epistle of Barnabas*
BASOR	*Bulletin of the American Schools of Oriental Research*
BASORSup	BASOR Supplement
BASP	*Bulletin of the American Society of Papyrologists*
BASPSup	Bulletin of the American Society of Papyrologists Supplement
BAss	Beiträge zur Assyriologie und semitischen Sprachwissenschaft
BAT	Die Botschaft des Alten Testaments
BBB	Bonner biblische Beiträge
BBC	Broadman Bible Commentary
BBET	Beiträge zur biblischen Exegese und Theologie
BBLAK	*Beiträge zur biblischen Landes- und Altertumskunde,* Stuttgart
B.C.	before Christ
BC	Biblical Commentary, ed. C. F. Keil and F. Delitzsch. Edinburgh.
B.C.E.	before the common (or Christian) era
BCH	*Bulletin du correspondance hellénique*
BCNHE	Bibliothèque copte de Nag Hammadi Section Études
BCNHT	Bibliothèque copte de Nag Hammadi Section Textes
BCPE	*Bulletin de Centre Protestant d'Études,* Geneva
BDB	F. Brown, S. R. Driver, and C. A. Briggs. 1907. *A Hebrew and English Lexicon of the Old Testament.* Oxford
BDF	F. Blass, A. Debrunner, and R. W. Funk. 1961. *A Greek Grammar of the New Testament and Other Early Christian Literature.* Chicago
BDR	F. Blass, A. Debrunner, and F. Rehkopf. 1984. *Grammatik des neutestamentlichen Griechisch.* 16th ed. Göttingen
BE	*Bulletin epigraphique,* ed. P. Gauthier. Paris
BE	Bibliothèque d'étude (Institut français d'Archéologie orientale)
BEFAR	Bibliothèque des Écoles françaises d'Athènes et de Rome
Bek.	*Bekorot*
Bel	Bel and the Dragon
Bened	*Benedictina,* Rome
BeO	*Bibbia e oriente,* Bornato
Ber.	*Berakot*
Berytus	*Berytus,* Beirut, Lebanon
BES	*Bulletin of the Egyptological Seminar,* Chico, CA
Beṣa	*Beṣa (= Yom Ṭob)*
Beth Mikra	*Beth Mikra,* Jerusalem
BETL	Bibliotheca ephemeridum theologicarum lovaniensium
BEvT	Beiträge zur evangelischen Theologie
BFCT	Beiträge zur Förderung christlicher Theologie
BGBE	Beiträge zur Geschichte der biblischen Exegese
BGU	*Berlin Griechische Urkunden*
BHG	*Bibliotheca Hagiographica Graeca.* Brussels, 1909
BHH	*Biblisch-Historisches Handwörterbuch,* ed. B. Reicke and L. Rost. Göttingen, 1962

BHI	J. Bright. 1981. *A History of Israel.* 3d ed. Philadelphia
BHK	*Biblia hebraica,* 3d ed., ed. R. Kittel
BHNTC	Black's/Harper's New Testament Commentaries
BHS	*Biblia hebraica stuttgartensia*
BHT	Beiträge zur historischen Theologie
BIATC	*Bulletin d'information de l'Académie de Théologie Catholique,* Warsaw
Bib	*Biblica,* Rome
BibAT	*Biblical Archeology Today: Proceedings of the International Congress on Biblical Archaeology, Jerusalem, April 1984.* Jerusalem, 1985
BibB	Biblische Beiträge
BibBh	*Biblebhashyam,* Kerala, India
bibliog.	bibliography
BibOr	Biblica et orientalia
BibS(F)	Biblische Studien (Freiburg, 1895–)
BibS(N)	Biblische Studien (Neukirchen, 1951–)
BIES	*Bulletin of the Israel Exploration Society (= Yediot)*
BIFAO	*Bulletin de l'institute français d'archéologie orientale,* Cairo
Bij	*Bijdragen: Tijdschrift voor Filosofie en Theologie,* Amsterdam
Bik.	*Bikkurim*
BiMes	Bibliotheca Mesopotamica
BIN	*Babylonian Inscriptions in the Collection of James B. Nies,* New Haven, 1917–54
BiOr	*Bibliotheca Orientalis,* Leiden
BIOSCS	*Bulletin of the International Organization for Septuagint and Cognate Studies*
BJPES	*Bulletin of the Jewish Palestine Exploration Society (= Yediot;* later *BIES)*
BJRL	*Bulletin of the John Rylands University Library of Manchester*
BJS	Brown Judaic Studies
BK	*Bibel und Kirche,* Stuttgart
BK	E. Bresciani and M. Kamil. 1966. Le lettere aramaiche di Hermopoli. *AANLM* 12/5: 357–428
bk.	book
Bk. Barn.	*Book of the Resurrection of Christ by Barnabas the Apostle*
Bk. Elch.	*Book of Elchasai*
Bk. Noah	*Book of Noah*
BKAT	Biblischer Kommentar: Altes Testament
BLE	*Bulletin de littérature ecclésiastique,* Toulouse
BLe	H. Bauer and P. Leander. 1918–22. *Historische Grammatik der hebräischen Sprache.* Halle, Repr. Hildesheim, 1962
BLit	*Bibel und Liturgie,* Klosterneuburg
BMAP	E. G. Kraeling. 1953. *The Brooklyn Museum Aramaic Papyri.* New Haven. Repr. 1969
BMMA	*Bulletin of the Metropolitan Museum of Art*
BMQ	*British Museum Quarterly*
BMS	*The Bible in Modern Scholarship,* ed. J. P. Hyatt. Nashville, 1965
BN	*Biblische Notizen,* Bamberg
Bo	Unpublished Boğazköy tablets (with catalog number)
BOSA	*Bulletin on Sumerian Agriculture,* Cambridge
B.P.	before (the) present (time)
BR	*Biblical Research,* Chicago
BRev	*Bible Review*
BRevuo	*Biblia Revuo,* Ravenna
BRL	K. Galling. 1937. *Biblisches Reallexikon.* Tübingen
BRM	*Babylonian Records in the Library of J. Pierpont Morgan,* ed. A. T. Clay, New York, 1912–23
BSac	*Bibliotheca Sacra*
BSAW	*Berichte über die Verhandlungen der Sächsischen Akademie der Wissenschaften zu Leipzig,* phil.-hist. Kl.
BSC	Bible Study Commentary
BSFE	*Bulletin de la Société française d'égyptologie*
BSOAS	*Bulletin of the School of Oriental and African Studies*
BTAVO	Beihefte zum Tübinger Atlas des Vorderen Orients
BTB	*Biblical Theology Bulletin*
BTF	*Bangalore Theological Forum,* Bangalore
BTNT	R. Bultmann. 1955. *Theology of the New Testament.* 2 vols. Trans. K. Grobel. New York and London
BToday	*Bible Today,* Collegeville, MN
BTrans	*Bible Translator,* Aberdeen
BTS	*Bible et terre sainte*
BTZ	*Berliner Theologische Zeitschrift*
BU	Biblische Untersuchungen
BuA	B. Meissner. 1920–25. *Babylonien und Assyrien.* 2 vols. Heidelberg
Burg	*Burgense,* Burgos, Spain
BurH	*Buried History,* Melbourne, Australia
BVC	*Bible et vie chrétienne*
BWANT	Beiträge zur Wissenschaft vom Alten und Neuen Testament
BWL	W. G. Lambert. 1960. *Babylonian Wisdom Literature.* Oxford
ByF	*Biblia y Fe,* Madrid, Spain
BZ	*Biblische Zeitschrift,* Paderborn
BZAW	Beihefte zur *ZAW*
BZNW	Beihefte zur *ZNW*
BZRGG	Beihefte zur *ZRGG*
BZVO	Berliner Beitrage zum Vorderen Orient

C	Codex Ephraemi
C&AH	*Catastrophism and Ancient History,* Los Angeles
ca.	*circa* (about, approximately)
CaByr	*Cahiers de Byrsa*
CAD	*The Assyrian Dictionary of the Oriental Institute of the University of Chicago*
CaE	*Cahiers Evangile,* Paris
CAH	*Cambridge Ancient History*
CahRB	Cahiers de la Revue biblique
CahThéol	Cahiers Théologiques
CaJ	*Cahiers de Josephologie,* Montreal
Cant	Song of Songs (or Canticles)
CaNum	*Cahiers de Numismatique,* Bologna
CAP	A. E. Cowley. 1923. *Aramaic Papyri of the Fifth Century B.C.* Oxford [cited by document number]
CAT	Commentaire de l'Ancient Testament
Cath	*Catholica,* Münster
Cav. Tr.	*Cave of Treasures*
CB	*Cultura biblica*
CBC	Cambridge Bible Commentary on the New English Bible
CBQ	*Catholic Biblical Quarterly,* Washington, DC
CBQMS	Catholic Biblical Quarterly Monograph Series
CBSC	Cambridge Bible for Schools and Colleges
CC	*Cross Currents,* West Nyack, NY
CCath	Corpus Catholicorum
CCER	*Cahiers du Cercle Ernest Renan,* Paris
CChr	Corpus Christianorum
CD	Cairo (Genizah), Damascus Document [= S. Schechter, *Documents of Jewish Sectaries,* vol. 1, *Fragments of a Zadokite Work,* Cambridge, 1910. Repr. New York, 1970]
CdÉ	*Chronique d'Égypte,* Brussels
C.E.	common (or Christian) era
Cerinthus	*Cerinthus*
cf.	*confer,* compare
CGTC	Cambridge Greek Testament Commentary
CGTSC	Cambridge Greek Testament for Schools and Colleges
CH	*Church History*
CH	Code of Hammurabi [cited according to G. R. Driver and J. C. Miles, eds. 1952–55. *The Babylonian Laws.* 2 vols. Oxford]
CHAL	*A Concise Hebrew and Aramaic Lexicon of the Old Testament,* ed. W. L. Holladay. Grand Rapids, 1971
chap(s).	chapter(s)
CHB	*The Cambridge History of the Bible,* 3 vols., ed. P. R. Ackroyd, G. W. M. Lampe, and S. L. Greenslade. Cambridge, 1963–70
CHD	Chicago Hittite Dictionary
Cher	Philo, *De cherubim*
CHI	*Cambridge History of Iran*
CHJ	*The Cambridge History of Judaism,* ed. W. D. Davies and L. Finkelstein. Cambridge, 1984–
CHR	*Catholic Historical Review*
CHSP	*Center for Hermeneutical Studies Protocol Series,* Berkeley, CA
CIG	*Corpus inscriptionum graecarum*
CII	*Corpus inscriptionum indicarum*
CIJ	*Corpvs inscriptionvm ivdaicarvm,* ed. J. B. Frey. Sussidi allo studio delle antichità cristiane, pub. per cura del Pontificio istituto di archeologia cristiana 1, 3. Vatican City, 1936–52
CIL	*Corpus inscriptionum latinarum*
CIS	*Corpus inscriptionum semiticarum*
CiuD	*Ciudad de Dios,* Madrid
CJ	*Concordia Journal,* St. Louis, MO
CJT	*Canadian Journal of Theology*
CL	*Communautés et Liturgies,* Ottignies, Belgium
CL	Code of Lipit-Ishtar [R. R. Steele. 1948. The Code of Lipit-Ishtar. *AJA* 52: 425–50]
Cl. Mal.	*Cleodemus Malchus*
CLA	*Canon Law Abstracts,* Melrose, Scotland
cm	centimeter(s)
CMHE	F. M. Cross. 1973. *Canaanite Myth and Hebrew Epic.* Cambridge, MA
CMIB	*Canadian Mediterranean Institute Bulletin,* Ottawa
CNFI	*Christian News From Israel,* Jerusalem, Israel
CNS	*Cristianesimo nella Storia,* Bologna, Italy
CNT	Commentaire du Nouveau Testament
CO	*Commentationes orientales,* Leiden
Col	Colossians
col(s).	column(s)
Coll	*Collationes,* Brugge, Belgium
Colloquium	*Colloquium,* Auckland/Sydney
ColT	*Collectanea Theologica,* Warsaw
comp.	compiled, compiler
ComViat	*Communio Viatorum,* Prague
ConBNT	Coniectanea biblica, New Testament
ConBOT	Coniectanea biblica, Old Testament
Concilium	Concilium
Conf	Philo, *De confusione linguarum*
Congr	Philo, *De congressu eruditionis gratia*
conj.	conjunction; conjugation
ConNT	*Coniectanea neotestamentica*
constr.	construction; construct

ContiRossini	K. Conti Rossini. 1931. *Chrestomathia Arabica meridionalis ephigraphica,* Rome
COut	Commentaar op het Oude Testament
CP	*Classical Philology*
CPJ	*Corpus papyrorum Judicarum,* ed. A. Tcherikover. 3 vols. Cambridge, MA, 1957–64
CQ	*Church Quarterly*
CQR	*Church Quarterly Review*
CR	*Clergy Review,* London
CRAIBL	*Comptes rendus de l'Académie des inscriptions et belles-lettres*
CRBR	*Critical Review of Books in Religion*
CRINT	Compendia rerum iudaicarum ad novum testamentum
CRRA	*Compte Rendu de . . . Recontre Assyriologique Internationale*
Crux	*Crux,* Vancouver, BC
CS	*Chicago Studies,* Mundelein, IL
CSCO	Corpus scriptorum christianorum orientalium
CSEL	Corpus scriptorum ecclesiasticorum latinorum
CSR	*Christian Scholars Review,* Houghton, NY
CT	*Cuneiform Texts from Babylonian Tablets . . . in the British Museum,* London, 1896–
CT	*The Egyptian Coffin Texts,* ed. A. de Buck and A. H. Gardiner. Chicago, 1935–47
CTA	A. Herdner. 1963. *Corpus des tablettes en cunéiformes alphabétiques découvertes à Ras Shamra-Ugarit de 1929 à 1939.* MRS 10. Paris
CTAED	S. Ahituv. 1984. *Canaanite Toponyms in Ancient Egyptian Documents.* Jerusalem
CTH	E. Laroche. 1971. *Catalogue des textes hittites.* Paris
CThM	Calwer Theologische Monographien
CTJ	*Calvin Theological Journal,* Grand Rapids, MI
CTM	*Concordia Theological Monthly*
CToday	*Christianity Today,* Carol Stream, IL
CTQ	*Concordia Theological Quarterly,* Fort Wayne, IN
CTSAP	*Catholic Theological Society of America Proceedings,* New York
CTSSR	College Theology Society Studies in Religion
CU	Code of Ur-Nammu [J. J. Finkelstein. 1960. The Laws of Ur-Nammu. *JCS* 14: 66–82; F. Yildiz. 1981. A Tablet of Codex Ur-Nammu from Sippar. *Or* 58: 87–97]
CurTM	*Currents in Theology and Mission,* Chicago
D	"Deuteronomic" source; or Codex Bezae
DACL	*Dictionnaire d'archéologie chrétienne et de liturgie*
DAGR	*Dictionnaire des antiquités grecques et romaines d'après les textes et les monuments,* ed. C. Daremberg and E. Saglio. 4 vols. Paris, 1877–1919
Dan	Daniel
DB	*Dictionnaire de la Bible,* 5 vols., ed. F. Vigouroux. Paris, 1895–1912
DBAT	*Dielheimer Blätter zum Alten Testament*
DBM	*Deltion Biblikon Meleton,* Athens
DBSup	*Dictionnaire de la Bible, Supplément,* ed. L. Pirot, A. Robert, H. Cazelles, and A. Feuillet. Paris, 1928–
DBTh	*Dictionary of Biblical Theology,* 2d ed., ed. X. Léon-Dufour. Trans. E. M. Stewart. New York, 1973
DC	*Doctor Communis,* Vatican City
DD	*Dor le Dor,* Jerusalem
DDSR	*Duke Divinity School Review*
Dec	Philo, *De decalogo*
Dem.	*Demetrius (the Chronographer)*
Dem.	*Demai*
Deo	Philo, *De Deo*
Der. Er. Rab.	*Derek Ereṣ Rabba*
Der. Er. Zuṭ.	*Derek Ereṣ Zuṭa*
Deut	Deuteronomy
DH	Deuteronomistic History/Historian
DHRP	Dissertationes ad historiam religionum pertinentes
Diakonia	*Diakonia,* Vienna
Dial. Sav.	*Dialogue of the Savior* (NHC III,5)
Dial. Trypho	Justin, *Dialogue with Trypho*
Did	*Didaskalia,* Portugal
Did.	*Didache*
Diogn.	*Epistle to Diognetes*
Direction	*Direction,* Fresno, CA
Disc. 8–9	*Discourse on the Eighth and Ninth* (NHC VI,6)
DISO	C.-F. Jean and J. Hoftijzer. 1965. *Dictionnaire des inscriptions sémitiques de l'ouest.* Leiden
diss.	dissertation
div.	division
Div	*Divinitas,* Vatican City
DivT	*Divus Thomas,* Piacenza, Italy
DJD	Discoveries in the Judean Desert
DL	*Doctrine and Life,* Dublin
DMOA	Documenta et Monumenta Orientis Antiqui
DN	divine name
DÖAW	*Denkschriften der Österreichischer Akademie der Wissenschaften,* Vienna
DOSA	J. Biella. 1982. *Dictionary of Old South Arabic: Sabaean Dialect.* HSS 25. Chico, CA

DOTT	*Documents from Old Testament Times,* ed. D. W. Thomas. Edinburgh, 1958. Repr. New York, 1961
DRev	*The Downside Review,* Bath
DS	Denzinger-Schönmetzer, *Enchiridion symbolorum*
DTC	*Dictionnaire de théologie catholique*
DTT	*Dansk Teologisk Tidsskrift,* Copenhagen
DunRev	*Dunwoodie Review*
E	east(ern); or "Elohist" source
EA	Tell el-Amarna tablets [cited from J. A. Knudtzon, O. Weber, and E. Ebeling, *Die El-Amarna Tafeln,* 2 vols., VAB 2, Leipzig, 1915; and A. F. Rainey, *El-Amarna Tablets 359–379: Supplement to J. A. Knudtzon, Die El-Amarna Tafeln,* 2d rev. ed., AOAT 8, Kevelaer and Neukirchen-Vluyn, 1970]
EAEHL	*Encyclopedia of Archaeological Excavations in the Holy Land,* 4 vols., ed. M. Avi-Yonah, 1975
EAJET	*East Africa Journal of Evangelical Theology,* Machakos, Kenya
EAJT	*East Asia Journal of Theology,* Singapore
EB	Early Bronze (Age); or Echter Bibel
EBib	Études bibliques
Ebr	Philo, *De ebrietate*
Ec	*The Ecumenist,* New York, NY
Eccl *or* Qoh	Ecclesiastes or Qoheleth
EcR	*The Ecumenical Review,* Geneva
Ecu	*Ecumenismo,* Ravenna, Italy
ed.	editor(s); edition; edited by
ED	Early Dynastic period
ʿEd.	*ʿEduyyot*
EDB	*Encyclopedic Dictionary of the Bible,* ed. and trans. L. F. Hartman. New York, 1963
e.g.	*exempli gratia* (for example)
Eg	Egyptian
ÉgT	*Église et Théologie,* Ottawa
EHAT	Exegetisches Handbuch zum Alten Testament
EHI	R. de Vaux. 1978. *The Early History of Israel.* Trans. D. Smith. Philadelphia
EHS	Einleitung in die Heilige Schrift
EI	*Eretz Israel*
EJ	*Encyclopedia Judaica,* 10 vols., ed. J. Klutzkin and I. Elbogen. Berlin, 1928–34
EKKNT	Evangelisch-katholischer Kommentar zum Neuen Testament
EKL	*Evangelisches Kirchenlexikon*
El. Mod.	*Eldad and Modad*
EM	*Ephemerides Mexicanae,* Mexico City
Emm	*Emmanuel,* New York
EncBib	*Encyclopaedia Biblica,* ed. T. K. Cheyne. London, 1800–1903. 2d ed. 1958
EncBibBarc	*Enciclopedia de la Biblia,* ed. A. Diez Macho and S. Bartina. Barcelona, 1963–65
EncBrit	*Encyclopaedia Britannica*
EnchBib	*Enchiridion biblicum*
EncJud	*Encyclopaedia Judaica* (1971)
EncMiqr	*Entsiqlopēdiā Miqrāʾīt-Encyclopaedia Biblica,* Jerusalem, 1950–
EncRel	*Encyclopedia of Religion,* 16 vols., ed. M. Eliade. New York, 1987
Eng	English
Entr	*Encounter,* Indianapolis, IN
Ep Jer	Epistle of Jeremiah
Ep. Alex.	*Epistle to the Alexandrians*
Ep. Apos.	*Epistle to the Apostles*
Ep. Barn.	*Epistle of Barnabas*
Ep. Chr. Abg.	*Epistle of Christ and Abgar*
Ep. Chr. Heav.	*Epistle of Christ from Heaven*
Ep. Lao.	*Epistle to the Laodiceans*
Ep. Lent.	*Epistle of Lentulus*
Ep. Paul Sen.	*Epistles of Paul and Seneca*
Ep. Pet. Phil.	*Letter of Peter to Philip* (NHC VIII,2)
Ep. Pol.	*Epistles of Polycarp*
Ep. Tit. (Apoc.)	*Apocryphal Epistle of Titus*
Eph	Ephesians
Eph.	see *Ign. Eph.*
EphC	*Ephemerides Carmelitica,* Rome
Ephem	M. Lidzbarski. 1900–15. *Ephemeris für semitische Epigraphik.* 3 vols. Giessen
EphLit	*Ephemerides Liturgicae,* Rome
EphMar	*Ephemerides Mariologicae,* Madrid
EPRO	Études préliminaires aux religions orientales dans l'Empire romain
ER	*Epworth Review,* London
ErbAuf	*Erbe und Auftrag*
ERE	*Encyclopaedia of Religion and Ethics,* 12 vols., ed. J. Hastings. Edinburgh and New York, 1908–22
ErFor	Erträge der Forschung
ErfThSt	Erfurter Theologische Studien
ErJb	*Eranos Jahrbuch*
ERT	*Evangelical Review of Theology,* Exeter
ʿErub.	*ʿErubin*
Escr Vedat	*Escritos del Vedat,* Torrente
esp.	especially
EspVie	*Esprit et Vie.,* Langres
EstBib	*Estudios Bíblicos,* Madrid
EstEcl	*Estudios Eclesiásticos,* Barcelona
EstFranc	*Estudios Franciscanos,* Barcelona
Esth	Esther
EstTeo	*Estudios Teológicos,* São Leopoldo, Brazil
ET	English translation
et al.	*et alii* (and others)
etc.	*et cetera* (and so forth)

Eth	Ethiopic
ETL	*Ephemerides Theologicae Lovanienses,* Louvain
ETOT	W. Eichrodt. 1961–67. *Theology of the Old Testament.* 2 vols. Trans. J. A. Baker. Philadelphia
ÉTR	*Études théologiques et Religieuses,* Montpellier, France
Études	*Études,* Paris
Eugnostos	*Eugnostos the Blessed* (NHC III,*3*; V,*1*)
EuntDoc	*Euntes Docete,* Rome
Eup.	*Eupolemus*
EV(V)	English version(s)
EvJ	*Evangelical Journal,* Myerstown, PA
EvK	Evangelische Kommentare
EvQ	*Evangelical Quarterly,* Derbyshire
EvT	*Evangelische Theologie,* Munich
EWNT	*Exegetisches Wörterbuch zum Neuen Testament,* ed. H. Balz and G. Schneider
Ex	*Explor,* Evanston, IL
ExB	Expositor's Bible
Exeg. Soul	*Exegesis on the Soul* (NHC II,*6*)
Exod	Exodus
ExpTim	*Expository Times,* Surrey
Ezek	Ezekiel
Ezek. Trag.	*Ezekiel the Tragedian*
Ezra	Ezra
f(f).	following page(s)
FAS	Freiburger Altorientalische Studien
FB	Forschuung zur Bibel
FBBS	Facet Books, Biblical Series
FC	Fathers of the Church
fc.	forthcoming (publication)
fem.	feminine; female
FFNT	Foundations and Facets: New Testament
FGLP	Forschungen zur Geschichte und Lehre des Protestantismus
FGrH	F. Jacoby. *Die Fragmente der griechischen Historiker.* 2d ed. 3 vols. in 10 pts. Leiden, 1957–64 [cited by fragment no.]
FH	*Fides et Historia,* Grand Rapids
fig(s).	figure(s)
FKT	*Forum Katholische Theologie,* Aschaffenburg
fl.	*floruit* (flourished)
Flacc	Philo, *In Flaccum*
FoiVie	*Foi et Vie,* Paris
Fond	*Fondamenti,* Bresica
Forum	*Forum,* Bonner, MT
FOTL	Forms of Old Testament Literature
FR	Freiburger Rundbrief
Fran	*Franciscanum,* Bogotá
Frg. Tg.	*Fragmentary Targum*
Frgs. Hist. Wrks.	*Fragments of Historical Works*
Frgs. Poet. Wrks.	*Fragments of Poetic Works*
FRLANT	Forschungen zur Religion und Literatur des Alten und Neuen Testaments
Frm.	*Fragments* (NHC XII,*3*)
FSAC	W. F. Albright. 1957. *From the Stone Age to Christianity.* 2d ed., repr. Garden City, NY
FTS	Freiburger Theologische Studien
FuF	*Forschungen und Fortschritte,* Berlin
Fuga	Philo, *De fuga et inventione*
Fund	*Fundamentum,* Riehen, Switzerland
Furrow	*Furrow,* Maynooth
FWSDFML	*Funk and Wagnall's Standard Dictionary of Folklore, Mythology and Legend*
FZPT	*Freiburger Zeitschrift für Philosophie und Theologie,* Fribourg
GAG	W. von Soden. 1969. *Grundriss der akkadischen Grammatik samt Ergänzungsheft.* AnOr 33/47. Rome
Gaium	Philo, *Legatio ad Gaium*
Gal	Galatians
GARI	A. K. Grayson. 1972. *Assyrian Royal Inscriptions.* RANE. Wiesbaden
GB	D. Baly. 1974. *The Geography of the Bible.* 2d ed. New York
GBS	Guides to Biblical Scholarship
GCS	Griechischen christlichen Schriftsteller
Gem.	*Gemara*
Gen	Genesis
GesB	W. Gesenius. *Hebräisches und aramäisches Handwörterbuch,* 17th ed., ed. F. Buhl. Berlin, 1921
GGR	M. P. Nilsson. *Geschichte der griechische Religion.* 2 vols. 2d ed. Munich, 1961
GHBW	R. R. Wilson. 1977. *Genealogy and History in the Biblical World.* YNER 7. New Haven
Gig	Philo, *De gigantibus*
Giṭ.	*Giṭṭin*
GJV	E. Schürer. 1901–9. *Geschichte des jüdisches Volkes im Zeitalter Jesu Christi.* Leipzig. Repr. Hildesheim, 1970
Gk	Greek
GK	*Gesenius' Hebräische Grammatik,* 28th ed., ed. by E. Kautzsch. Leipzig, 1909. Repr. Hildesheim, 1962
Gk. Apoc. Ezra	*Greek Apocalypse of Ezra*
GKB	G. Bergsträsser. 1918–29. *Hebräische Grammatik mit Benutzung der von E. Kautzsch bearbeiteten 28. Auflage von Wilhelm Gesenius' hebräischer Grammatik.* 2 vols. Leipzig. Repr. Hildesheim, 1962
GKC	*Gesenius' Hebrew Grammar,* 28th ed., ed. E. Kautzsch. Trans. A. E. Cowley. Oxford, 1910
GLECS	*Comptes Rendus du Groupe Linguistique d'Études Chamito-Sémitiques,* Paris
GM	*Göttinger Miszellen*

GN	geographical name
GNB	Good News Bible
GNC	Good News Commentary
GNS	Good News Studies
GNT	Grundrisse zum Neuen Testament
GO	Göttinger Orientforschungen
Gos. Barn.	*Gospel of Barnabas*
Gos. Bart.	*Gospel of Bartholomew*
Gos. Bas.	*Gospel of Basilides*
Gos. Bir. Mary	*Gospel of the Birth of Mary*
Gos. Eb.	*Gospel of the Ebionites*
Gos. Eg.	*Gospel of the Egyptians* (NHC III,*2*; IV,*2*)
Gos. Eve	*Gospel of Eve*
Gos. Gam.	*Gospel of Gamaliel*
Gos. Heb.	*Gospel of the Hebrews*
Gos. Inf.	*Infancy Gospels*
Gos. Inf. (Arab)	*Arabic Gospel of the Infancy*
Gos. Inf. (Arm)	*Armenian Gospel of the Infancy*
Gos. John (Apocr.)	*Apocryphal Gospel of John*
Gos. Marcion	*Gospel of Marcion*
Gos. Mary	*Gospel of Mary*
Gos. Naass.	*Gospel of the Naassenes*
Gos. Naz.	*Gospel of the Nazarenes*
Gos. Nic.	*Gospel of Nicodemus*
Gos. Pet.	*Gospel of Peter*
Gos. Phil.	*Gospel of Philip* (NHC II,*3*)
Gos. Thom.	*Gospel According to Thomas* (NHC II,*2*)
Gos. Trad. Mth.	*Gospel and Traditions of Matthias*
Gos. Truth	*Gospel of Truth* (NHC I,*3*; XII,*2*)
GOTR	*Greek Orthodox Theological Review,* Brookline, MA
GP	F. M. Abel. 1933. *Géographie de la Palestine,* 2 vols. Paris
GRBS	*Greek, Roman and Byzantine Studies,* Durham, NC
Great Pow.	*The Concept of Our Great Power* (NHC VI,*4*)
Greg	*Gregorianum,* Rome
GSAT	*Gesammelte Studien zum Alten Testament,* Munich
GTA	Göttinger theologische Arbeiten
GTJ	*Grace Theological Journal,* Winona Lake, IN
GTT	*Gereformeerd Theologisch Tijdschrift,* Netherlands
GTTOT	J. J. Simons. 1959. *The Geographical and Topographical Texts of the Old Testament.* Francisci Scholten memoriae dedicata 2. Leiden
GuL	*Geist und Leben,* Munich
GVG	C. Brockelmann. 1903–13. *Grundriss der vergleichenden Grammatik der semitischen Sprachen.* 2 vols. Berlin. Repr. 1961
ha.	hectares
Hab	Habakkuk
HAB	*Harper's Atlas of the Bible*
HÄB	Hildesheimer ägyptologische Beiträge
HAD	*Hebrew and Aramaic Dictionary of the OT,* ed. G. Fohrer. Trans W. Johnstone. Berlin, 1973
Hag	Haggai
Ḥag.	*Ḥagiga*
HAIJ	J. M. Miller and J. H. Hayes. 1986. *A History of Ancient Israel and Judah.* Philadelphia
Ḥal.	*Ḥalla*
HALAT	*Hebräisches und aramäisches Lexikon zum Alten Testament,* ed. W. Baumgartner et al.
HAR	*Hebrew Annual Review*
HAT	Handbuch zum Alten Testament
HAW	Handbuch der Altertumswissenschaft
HBC	*Harper's Bible Commentary*
HBD	*Harper's Bible Dictionary,* ed. P. J. Achtemeier. San Francisco, 1985
HBT	*Horizons in Biblical Theology,* Pittsburgh, PA
HDB	*Dictionary of the Bible,* 4 vols., ed. by J. Hastings et al. Edinburgh and New York, 1899–1904. Rev. by F. C. Grant and H. H. Rowley, 1963
HDR	Harvard Dissertations in Religion
HDS	Harvard Dissertation Series
Hdt.	Herodotus
Heb	Hebrew; Epistle to the Hebrews
Heb. Apoc. El.	*Hebrew Apocalypse of Elijah*
Hec. Ab	*Hecataeus of Abdera*
Hel. Syn. Pr.	*Hellenistic Synagogal Prayers*
Hen	*Henoch,* Torino, Italy
Heres	Philo, *Quis rerum divinarum heres*
Herm	*Hermathena,* Dublin, Ireland
Herm. Man.	*Hermas, Mandate*
Herm. Sim.	*Hermas, Similitude*
Herm. Vis.	*Hermas, Vision*
Hermeneia	Hermeneia: A Critical and Historical Commentary on the Bible
Ḥev	Naḥal Ḥever texts
HeyJ	*The Heythrop Journal,* London
HG	J. Friedrich. 1959. *Die hethitischen Gesetze.* DMOA 7. Leiden
HGB	Z. Kallai. 1986. *Historical Geography of the Bible.* Leiden
HHI	S. Herrmann. 1975. *A History of Israel in Old Testament Times.* 2d ed. Philadelphia
HibJ	*Hibbert Journal*
HIOTP	H. Jagersma. 1983. *A History of Israel in the Old Testament Period.* Trans. J. Bowden. Philadelphia
Hist. Eccl.	Eusebius, *Historia ecclesiastica (= Church History)*

Hist. Jos.	*History of Joseph*
Hist. Jos. Carp.	*History of Joseph the Carpenter*
Hist. Rech.	*History of the Rechabites*
Hit	Hittite
HJP[1]	E. Schürer. *The History of the Jewish People in the Time of Jesus Christ,* 5 vols., trans. J. Macpherson, S. Taylor, and P. Christie. Edinburgh, 1886–90
HJP[2]	E. Schürer. *The History of the Jewish People in the Age of Jesus Christ,* 3 vols., ed. and trans. G. Vermes et al. Edinburgh, 1973–87
HKAT	Handkommentar zum Alten Testament
HKL	R. Borger. 1967–75. *Handbuch der Keilschriftliteratur.* 3 vols. Berlin
HKNT	Handkommentar zum Neuen Testament
HL	Hittite Laws [*ANET,* 188–97]
HM	*Hamizrah Hehadash/Near East,* Jerusalem
HNT	Handbuch zum Neuen Testament
HNTC	Harper's NT Commentaries
HO	Handbuch der Orientalistik
Hokhma	*Hokhma,* La Sarraz, Switzerland
Hor	*Horizons,* Villanova, PA
Hor.	*Horayot*
Hos	Hosea
HPR	*Homiletic and Pastoral Review,* New York
HPT	M. Noth. 1981. *A History of Pentateuchal Traditions.* Trans. B. Anderson. Chico, CA
HR	*History of Religions,* Chicago
HS	*Hebrew Studies,* Madison, WI
HSAO	*Heidelberger Studien zum Alten Orient.* Wiesbaden, 1967
HSAT	*Die heilige Schrift des Alten Testaments,* 4th ed., ed. E. Kautzsch and A. Bertholet. Tübingen, 1922–23
HSCL	Harvard Studies in Comparative Literature
HSCP	*Harvard Studies in Classical Philology,* Cambridge, MA
HSM	Harvard Semitic Monographs
HSS	Harvard Semitic Studies
HTKNT	Herders theologischer Kommentar zum Neuen Testament
HTR	*Harvard Theological Review*
HTS	Harvard Theological Studies
HUCA	*Hebrew Union College Annual,* Cincinnati
Ḥul.	*Ḥullin*
Hymn Dance	*Hymn of the Dance*
Hyp. Arch.	*Hypostasis of the Archons* (NHC II,*4*)
Hypo	Philo, *Hypothetica*
Hypsiph.	*Hypsiphrone* (NHC XI,*4*)
IB	*Interpreter's Bible*
IBC	Interpretation: A Bible Commentary for Teaching and Preaching
ibid.	*ibidem* (in the same place)
IBS	*Irish Biblical Studies,* Belfast
ICC	International Critical Commentary
IDB	*Interpreter's Dictionary of the Bible,* ed. G. A. Buttrick. 4 vols. Nashville, 1962
IDBSup	*Interpreter's Dictionary of the Bible Supplementary Volume,* ed. K. Crim. Nashville, 1976
IEJ	*Israel Exploration Journal,* Jerusalem
IG	*Inscriptiones Graecae*
IGRR	*Inscriptiones Graecae ad res Romanas pertinentes,* ed. R. Cagnat, J. Toutain, et al. 3 vols. Paris, 1901–27. Repr. Rome, 1964
Ign. Eph.	*Ignatius, Letter to the Ephesians*
Ign. Magn.	*Ignatius, Letter to the Magnesians*
Ign. Phld.	*Ignatius, Letter to the Philadelphians*
Ign. Pol.	*Ignatius, Letter to the Polycarp*
Ign. Rom.	*Ignatius, Letter to the Romans*
Ign. Symrn.	*Ignatius, Letter to the Smyrnaeans*
Ign. Trall.	*Ignatius, Letter to the Trallians*
IGLS	Jalabert, L., and Mouterde, R. 1929–. *Inscriptions grecques et latines de la Syrie.* 6 vols. Paris.
IGSK	Inschriften griechischer Städte aus Kleinasien
IJH	*Israelite and Judean History,* ed. J. Hayes and M. Miller. OTL. Philadelphia, 1977
IJT	*Indian Journal of Theology,* Calcutta
IKirZ	*Internationale Kirchliche Zeitschrift,* Bern
ILS	*Inscriptiones Latinae selectae,* ed. H. Dessau. 3 vols. in 5 pts. Berlin, 1892–1916. Repr.
Imm	*Immanuel,* Jerusalem
impf.	imperfect
impv.	imperative
inf.	infinitive
Inf. Gos. Thom.	*Infancy Gospel of Thomas*
INJ	*Israel Numismatic Journal,* Jerusalem
Int	*Interpretation,* Richmond, VA
Interp. Know.	*Interpretation of Knowledge* (NHC XI,*1*)
IOS	*Israel Oriental Studies*
IOTS	B. S. Childs. 1979. *Introduction to the Old Testament as Scripture.* Philadelphia
IPN	M. Noth. 1928. *Die israelitischen Personennamen.* BWANT 3/10. Stuttgart. Repr. Hildesheim, 1966
Iraq	*Iraq*
Irénikon	*Irénikon*
IRT	Issues in Religion and Theology
Isa	Isaiah
ISBE	*International Standard Bible Encyclopedia,* 2d ed., ed. G. W. Bromiley
ISEELA	*Instituto Superior de Estudios Eclesiasticos Libro Anual,* Mexico City
Istina	*Istina,* Paris

ITC	International Theological Commentary
ITQ	*Irish Theological Quarterly*, Maynooth
ITS	*Indian Theological Studies*, Bangalore
IvEph	*Die Inschriften von Ephesos*, ed. H. Wankel. 8 vols. IGSK 11–15
j. (Talm.)	Jerusalem (Talmud)
J	"Yahwist" source
JA	*Journal asiatique*
JAAR	*Journal of the American Academy of Religion*
JAC	*Jahrbuch für Antike und Christentum*
Jan. Jam.	*Jannes and Jambres*
JANES	*Journal of the Ancient Near Eastern Society of Columbia University*, New York
JAOS	*Journal of the American Oriental Society*, New Haven
JAOSSup	Journal of the American Oriental Society Supplement
JARCE	*Journal of the American Research Center in Egypt*, Boston
Jas	James
JAS	*Journal of Asian Studies*
JB	Jerusalem Bible
JBC	*The Jerome Biblical Commentary*, ed. R. E. Brown, J. A. Fitzmyer, and R. E. Murphy. 2 vols. in 1. Englewood Cliffs, NJ, 1968
JBL	*Journal of Biblical Literature*
JBR	*Journal of Bible and Religion*, Boston
JCS	*Journal of Cuneiform Studies*
JDAI	*Jahrbuch des deutschen archäologischen Instituts*
JDS	Judean Desert Studies
Jdt	Judith
JEA	*Journal of Egyptian Archaeology*, London
Jeev	*Jeevadhara*, Kottayam, Kerala, India
JEH	*Journal of Ecclesiastical History*, London
JEnc	*The Jewish Encyclopaedia*, 12 vols., ed. I. Singer et al. New York, 1901–6
JEOL	*Jaarbericht Vooraziatisch-Egyptisch Gezelschap "Ex Oriente Lux"*
Jer	Jeremiah
JES	*Journal of Ecumenical Studies*, Philadelphia
JESHO	*Journal of the Economic and Social History of the Orient*, Leiden
JETS	*Journal of the Evangelical Theological Society*
JFA	*Journal of Field Archaeology*
JFSR	*Journal of Feminist Studies in Religion*, Atlanta
JHNES	Johns Hopkins Near Eastern Studies
JHS	*Journal of Hellenic Studies*, London
JIBS	*Journal of Indian and Buddhist Studies*
JIPh	*Journal of Indian Philosophy*
JITC	*Journal of the Interdenominational Theological Center*, Atlanta
JJS	*Journal of Jewish Studies*, Oxford
JLA	*The Jewish Law Annual*, Leiden
JMES	*Journal of Middle Eastern Studies*
JMS	*Journal of Mithraic Studies*
JNES	*Journal of Near Eastern Studies*, Chicago
JNSL	*Journal of Northwest Semitic Languages*, Stellenbosch
Job	Job
Joel	Joel
John	John
Jonah	Jonah
Jos	Philo, *De Iosepho*
Jos. or Joseph.	Josephus
Jos. Asen.	*Joseph and Asenath*
Josh	Joshua
JPOS	*Journal of Palestine Oriental Society*, Jerusalem
JPSV	Jewish Publication Society Version
JPT	*Journal of Psychology and Theology*, La Mirada, CA
JQR	*Jewish Quarterly Review*
JQRMS	Jewish Quarterly Review Monograph Series
JR	*Journal of Religion*, Chicago
JRAI	*Journal of the Royal Anthropological Institute*
JRAS	*Journal of the Royal Asiatic Society*
JRE	*Journal of Religious Ethics*
JRelS	*Journal of Religious Studies*, Cleveland, OH
JRH	*Journal of Religious History*
JRS	*Journal of Roman Studies*, London
JRT	*Journal of Religious Thought*, Washington, DC
JSHRZ	Jüdische Schriften aus hellenistisch-römischer Zeit
JSJ	*Journal for the Study of Judaism*, Leiden
JSNT	*Journal for the Study of the New Testament*, Sheffield
JSNTSup	Journal for the Study of the New Testament Supplement Series
JSOT	*Journal for the Study of the Old Testament*, Sheffield
JSOTSup	Journal for the Study of the Old Testament Supplement Series
JSP	*Journal for the Study of the Pseudepigrapha*
JSPSup	Journal for the Study of the Pseudepigrapha Supplement
JSS	*Journal of Semitic Studies*, Manchester
JSSEA	*Journal of the Society for the Study of Egyptian Antiquities*, Mississauga, Ontario
JSSR	*Journal for the Scientific Study of Religion*
JTC	*Journal for Theology and the Church*
JTS	*Journal of Theological Studies*, Oxford

JTSoA	*Journal of Theology for Southern Africa,* Cape Town, South Africa
Jub.	*Jubilees*
Judaica	*Judaica: Beiträge zum Verständnis . . .*
Judaism	*Judaism,* New York
Jude	Jude
Judg	Judges
JW	Josephus, *The Jewish War (= Bellum Judaicum)*
JWH	*Journal of World History*
K	Kethib
K	Tablets in the Kouyunjik collection of the British Museum [cited by number]
KAI	*Kanaanäische und aramäische Inschriften,* 3 vols., ed. H. Donner and W. Röllig, Wiesbaden: Otto Harrassowitz, 1962
Kairos	*Kairos,* Salzburg
KAJ	*Keilschrifttexte aus Assur juristischen Inhalts,* ed. E. Ebeling. WVDOG 50. Leipzig, 1927
Kalla	*Kalla*
KAR	*Keilschrifttexte aus Assur religiösen Inhalts,* ed. E. Ebeling. WVDOG 28/34. Leipzig, 1919–23
KAT	Kommentar zum Alten Testament
KAV	*Keilschrifttexte aus Assur verschiedenen Inhalts,* ed. O. Schroeder. WVDOG 35. Leipzig, 1920
KB	*Keilschriftliche Bibliothek,* ed. E. Schrader. Berlin, 1889–1915
KB	L. Koehler and W. Baumgartner. 1953. *Lexicon in Veteris Testamenti libros.* Leiden; *Supplementum ad Lexicon in Veteris Testamenti libros.* Leiden, 1958
KBANT	Kommentare und Beiträge zum Alten und Neuen Testament
KBo	*Keilschrifttexte aus Boghazköi.* WVDOG 30/36/68–70/72– . Leipzig, 1916–23; Berlin, 1954–
KD	*Kerygma und Dogma,* Göttingen
KEHAT	*Kurzgefasstes exegetisches Handbuch zum Alten Testament,* ed. O. F. Fridelin, Leipzig, 1812–96
Kelim	*Kelim*
Ker.	*Keritot*
Ketub.	*Ketubot*
KG	H. Frankfort. 1948. *Kingship and the Gods.* Chicago. Repr. 1978
KHC	*Kurzer Handcommentar zum Alten Testament,* ed. K. Marti. Tübingen
Kil.	*Kilʾayim*
KJV	King James Version
KK	*Katorikku Kenkyu,* Tokyo, Japan
Klosterman	E. Klosterman. 1904. *Eusebius Das Onomastikon der Biblischen Ortsnamen.* Leipzig. Repr. 1966
KlPauly	*Der Kleine Pauly,* ed. K. Zeigler–W. Sontheimer, Stuttgart, 1964
KlSchr	*Kleine Schriften* (A. Alt, 1953–59, 1964 [3d ed.]; O. Eissfeldt, 1963–68; K. Ellinger, 1966)
KlT	Kleine Texte
km	kilometer(s)
KRI	K. Kitchen. 1968– . *Ramesside Inscriptions, Historical and Biographical.* 7 vols. Oxford
KRI	Y. Kaufmann. 1960. *The Religion of Israel.* Trans. M. Greenberg. New York
KTR	*King's Theological Review,* London
KTU	*Keilalphabetischen Texte aus Ugarit,* vol. 1, ed. M. Dietrich, O. Loretz, and J. Sanmartín. AOAT 24. Kevelaer and Neukirchen-Vluyn, 1976
KUB	Staatliche Museen zu Berlin, Voderasiatische Abteilung (later Deutsche Orient-Gesellschaft) *Keilschrifturkunden aus Boghazköi,* 1921–
LÄ	*Lexikon der Ägyptologie,* eds. W. Helck and E. Otto, Wiesbaden, 1972
L. A. B.	*Liber Antiquitatum Biblicarum*
Lad. Jac.	*Ladder of Jacob*
LAE	*The Literature of Ancient Egypt,* ed. W. K. Simpson. New Haven, 1972
L. A. E.	*Life of Adam and Eve*
Lam	Lamentations
Lane	E. W. Lane. 1863–93. *An Arabic-English Lexicon.* 8 vols. London. Repr. 1968
LAPO	Littératures anciennes du Proche-Orient
LAR	D. D. Luckenbill. 1926–27. *Ancient Records of Assyria and Babylonia.* Chicago
LÄS	Leipziger ägyptologische Studien
LAS	D. D. Luckenbill. 1924. *Annals of Sennacherib.* OIP 2. Chicago
LASBF	*Liber Annuus Studii Biblici Franciscani,* Jerusalem
Lat	Latin
Lat	*Lateranum,* Vatican City
Laur	*Laurentianum,* Rome
LavTP	*Laval Théologique et Philosophique,* Quebec
LB	Late Bronze (Age)
LB	*Linguistica Biblica,* Bonn
LBAT	*Late Babylonian Astronomical and Related Texts,* ed. T. G. Pinches and A. Sachs. Providence, RI, 1955
LBHG	Y. Aharoni. 1979. *The Land of the Bible,* 3d ed., rev. and enl. by A. F. Rainey. Philadelphia, 1979
LBS	Library of Biblical Studies
LCC	Library of Christian Classics
LCL	Loeb Classical Library
LD	Lectio divina
LE	Laws of Eshnunna [A. Goetze. 1956. *The Laws of Eshnunna.* AASOR 31. New Haven; *ANET,* 161–63]

Leg All I–III	Philo, *Legum allegoriae* I–III
Leš	*Lešonénu*
Let. Aris.	*Letter of Aristeas*
Lev	Leviticus
Levant	*Levant,* London
LexLingAeth	A. Dillmann. 1865. *Lexicon linguae aethiopicae.* Leipzig. Repr. New York, 1955; Osnabruck, 1970
LexSyr	C. Brockelmann. 1928. *Lexicon Syriacum.* 2d ed. Halle. Repr.
LHA	F. Zorrell. 1966. *Lexicon Hebraicum et Aramaicum Veteris Testamenti.* Rome
Life	Josephus, *Life (= Vita)*
List	*Listening: Journal of Religion and Culture,* River Forest, IL
lit.	literally
Liv. Pro.	*Lives of the Prophets*
LL	*The Living Light,* Washington, DC
LLAVT	*Lexicon Linguae aramaicae Veteris Testamenti documentis antiquis illustratum.* E. Vogt. 1971. Rome
loc. cit.	*loco citato* (in the place cited)
Lost Tr.	*The Lost Tribes*
LPGL	G. W. H. Lampe. 1961–68. *A Patristic Greek Lexicon.* Oxford
LQ	*Lutheran Quarterly*
LR	*Lutherische Rundschau*
LS	*Louvain Studies,* Louvain
LSJM	H. G. Liddell and R. Scott. 1968. *A Greek-English Lexicon.* rev. ed., ed. H. S. Jones and R. McKenzie. Oxford
LSS	Leipziger Semitistische Studien
LTJ	*Lutheran Theological Journal,* Adelaide, S. Australia
LTK	*Lexikon für Theologie und Kirche*
LTP	*Laval Théologique et Philosophique*
LTQ	*Lexington Theological Quarterly,* Lexington, KY
LUÅ	Lunds universitets årsskrift
Luc	Lucianic recension
Luke	Luke
LumVie	*Lumière et Vie,* Lyons, France
LumVit	*Lumen Vitae,* Brussels
LW	*Lutheran World*
LXX	Septuagint
m	meter(s)
MA	Middle Assyrian
Maarav	*Maarav,* Santa Monica, CA
Maʿaś.	*Maʿaśerot*
Maʿaś. Š.	*Maʿaśer Šeni*
MABL	*The Moody Atlas of Bible Lands,* ed. B. J. Beitzel. Chicago, 1985
Magn.	see *Ign. Magn.*
MaisDieu	*Maison-Dieu,* Paris
Mak.	*Makkot*
Makš.	*Makširin (= Mašqin)*
Mal	Malachi
MAL	Middle Assyrian Laws
MAMA	*Monumenta Asiae Minoris Antiqua,* vol. 1, ed. W. M. Calder and J. M. R. Cormack. Publications of the American Society for Archaeological Research in Asia Minor. Manchester, 1928. Vol. 3, ed. J. Keil and A. Wilhelm, 1931. Vol. 4, ed. W. H. Buckler, W. M. Calder, W. K. C. Guthrie, 1933. Vol. 5, ed. C. W. M. Cox and A. Cameron, 1937. Vol. 6, ed. W. H. Buckler and W. M. Calder, 1939
Man	*Manuscripta,* St. Louis, MO
MANE	*Monographs on the Ancient Near East,* Malibu, CA
Mansrea	*Mansrea,* Madrid
MAOG	Mitteilungen der Altorientalischen Gesellschaft, Leipzig
Marianum	*Marianum,* Rome
Mark	Mark
Marsanes	*Marsanes* (NHC XI,*1*)
MarSt	*Marian Studies,* Dayton, OH
Mart. Bart.	*Martyrdom of Bartholomew*
Mart. Is.	*Martyrdom of Isaiah*
Mart. Mt.	*Martyrdom of Matthew*
Mart. Paul	*Martyrdom of Paul*
Mat. Pet.	*Martyrdom of Peter*
Mart. Pet. Paul	*Martyrdom of Peter and Paul*
Mart. Phil.	*Martyrdom of Philip*
Mart. Pol.	*Martyrdom of Polycarp*
Mas	Masada texts
MÄS	Münchner Ägyptologische Studien
masc.	masculine
Matt	Matthew
May	*Mayéutica,* Marcilla (Navarra), Spain
MB	Middle Bronze (Age)
MB	*Le Monde de la Bible*
MBA	Y. Aharoni and M. Avi-Yonah. 1977. *The Macmillan Bible Atlas.* Rev. ed. New York
MC	*Miscelánea Comillas,* Madrid
MCBW	R. K. Harrison. 1985. *Major Cities of the Biblical World.* New York, 1985
McCQ	*McCormick Quarterly*
MD	E. S. Drower and R. Macuch. 1963. *Mandaic Dictionary.* Oxford
MDAIK	Mitteilungen des deutschen archäologischen Instituts, Kairo
MDOG	Mitteilungen der deutschen Orient-Gesellschaft
MDP	Mémoires de la délégation en Perse
MedHab	Epigraphic Expedition, *Medinet Habu.* OIP 8 (1930), 9 (1932), Chicago
Meg.	*Megilla*
Meʿil.	*Meʿila*

Mek.	*Mekilta*
Melch.	*Melchizedek* (NHC IX,*1*)
Melkon	*Melkon*
MelT	*Melita Theologica,* Rabat, Malta
Mem. Apos.	*Memoria of Apostles*
Menaḥ.	*Menaḥot*
MEOL	*Medeelingen en Verhandelingen van het Vooraziatisch-Egyptisch Gezelschap "Ex Oriente Lux,"* Leiden
Mer	*Merleg,* Munich
MeyerK	H. A. W. Meyer, Kritisch-exegetischer Kommentar über das Neue Testament
MGWJ	*Monatsschrift für Geschichte und Wissenschaft des Judentums*
mi.	mile(s)
Mic	Micah
Mid.	*Middot*
Midr.	*Midraš;* cited with usual abbreviation for biblical book; but *Midr. Qoh.* = *Midraš Qohelet*
MIFAO	Mémoires publiés par les membres de l'Institut français d'archéologie orientale du Caire
Migr	Philo, *De migratione Abrahami*
MIO	*Mitteilungen des Instituts für Orientforschung,* Berlin
Miqw.	*Miqwaʾot*
Mird	Khirbet Mird texts
misc.	miscellaneous
MM	J. H. Moulton and G. Milligan. 1914–30. *The Vocabulary of the Greek Testament Illustrated from the Papyri and other Non-Literary Sources.* London. Repr. Grand Rapids, 1949
MNTC	Moffatt NT Commentary
ModChurch	*Modern Churchman,* Leominster, UK
Moᶜed	*Moᶜed*
Moᶜed Qaṭ.	*Moᶜed Qaṭan*
Month	*Month,* London
MPAIBL	*Mémoires présentés à l'Académie des inscriptions et belles-lettres*
MPAT	*A Manual of Palestinian Aramaic Texts,* ed. J. A. Fitzmyer and D. J. Harrington. BibOr 34. Rome, 1978
MRR	*The Magistrates of the Roman Republic,* ed. T. R. S. Broughton and M. L. Patterson. 2 vols. Philological Monographs 15. 1951–52. Suppl., 1960
MRS	Mission de Ras Shamra
ms (pl. mss)	manuscript(s)
MScRel	*Mélanges de science religieuse,* Lille
MSD	Materials for the Sumerian Dictionary
MSL	*Materialen zum sumerischen Lexikon,* Rome, 1937–
MSR	*Mélanges de Science Religieuse,* Lille
MSU	Mitteilungen des Septuaginta-Unternehmens
MT	Masoretic Text
MTS	Marburger Theologische Studien
MTZ	*Münchner theologische Zeitschrift*
Mur	Wadi Murabbaᶜat texts
Mus	*Le Muséon: Revue d'Études Orientales,* Paris
MUSJ	*Mélanges de l'Université Saint-Joseph*
Mut	Philo, *De mutatione nominum*
MVAG	Mitteilungen der vorder-asiatisch-ägyptischen Gesellschaft
N	north(ern)
n(n).	note(s)
NA	Neo-Assyrian
NAB	New American Bible
Nah	Nahum
NARCE	*Newsletter of the American Research Center in Egypt*
NASB	New American Standard Bible
Našim	*Našim*
NAWG	*Nachrichten der Akademie der Wissenschaften in Göttingen*
Nazir	*Nazir*
NB	Neo-Babylonian
N.B.	*nota bene* (note well)
NBD	*The New Bible Dictionary,* 2d ed., ed. J. D. Douglas and N. Hillyer. Leicester and Wheaton, IL
NCBC	New Century Bible Commentary
NCCHS	*New Catholic Commentary on Holy Scripture,* ed. R. D. Fuller et al.
NCE	*New Catholic Encyclopedia,* ed. M. R. P. McGuire et al.
NCH	M. Noth. 1986. *The Chronicler's History.* Trans. H. G. M. Williamson. JSOTSup 51. Sheffield [translates chaps. 14–25 of *ÜgS*]
NClBC	New Clarendon Bible Commentary
NDH	M. Noth. 1981. *The Deuteronomistic History.* Trans. H. G. M. Williamson. JSOT-Sup 15. Sheffield [translates chaps. 1–13 of *ÜgS*]
NDIEC	*New Documents Illustrating Early Christianity,* ed. G. H. K. Horsley. Macquarie University, 1976– [= 1981–]
NE	northeast(ern)
NE	M. Lidzbarski. 1898. *Handbuch der nordsemitischen Epigraphik.* 2 vols. Weimar
NEB	New English Bible, Oxford, 1961–70
NEBib	Neue Echter Bibel
Ned.	*Nedarim*
NedTTs	*Nederlands Theologisch Tijdschrift,* The Hague
Neg.	*Negaᶜim*
Neh	Nehemiah
Neot	*Neotestamentica,* Stellenbosch

NETR	*The Near East School of Theology Theological Review,* Beirut
neut.	neuter
Nez.	*Neziqin*
NFT	New Frontiers in Theology
NGTT	*Nederduits Gereformeerde Teologiese Tydskrif,* Stellenbosch
NHC	Nag Hammadi Codex
NHI	M. Noth. 1960. *The History of Israel.* 2d ed. Trans. S. Godman, rev. P. R. Ackroyd. London
NHL	*The Nag Hammadi Library in English,* 3d ed., ed. J. M. Robinson. San Francisco, 1978
NHS	Nag Hammadi Studies
NHT	S. R. Driver. 1913. *Notes on the Hebrew Text and the Topography of the Books of Samuel.* 2d ed. Oxford
NICNT	New International Commentary on the New Testament
NICOT	New International Commentary on the Old Testament
Nid.	*Niddah*
NIDNTT	*New International Dictionary of New Testament Theology,* 3 vols., ed. C. Brown. Grand Rapids, 1975–78
NIGTC	New International Greek Testament Commentary
NIV	New International Version
NJB	New Jerusalem Bible
NJBC	*New Jerome Bible Commentary*
NJPSV	New Jewish Publication Society Version
NKJV	New King James Version
NKZ	*Neue kirchliche Zeitschrift*
no.	number
Norea	*The Thought of Norea* (NHC IX,*2*)
NorTT	*Norsk Teologisk Tidsskrift,* Oslo, Norway
NovT	*Novum Testamentum,* Leiden
NovTG^{26}	*Novum Testamentum Graece,* ed. E. Nestle and K. Aland. 26th ed. Stuttgart, 1979
NovTSup	Novum Testamentum Supplements
NPNF	Nicene and Post-Nicene Fathers
NRSV	New Revised Standard Version
NRT	*La nouvelle revue théologique*
n.s.	new series
NSSEA	*Newsletter of the Society for the Study of Egyptian Antiquities*
NT	New Testament
NTA	*New Testament Abstracts*
NTAbh	Neutestamentliche Abhandlungen
NTApocr	E. Henneke. *New Testament Apocrypha,* ed. W. Schneemelcher. Trans. R. McL. Wilson. 2 vols. Philadelphia, 1963–65
NTC	B. S. Childs. 1985. *The New Testament as Canon: An Introduction.* Philadelphia, 1985
NTCS	*Newsletter for Targumic and Cognate Studies,* Toronto
NTD	Das Neue Testament Deutsch
NTF	Neutestamentliche Forschungen
NTHIP	W. G. Kümmel. 1972. *The New Testament: The History of the Investigation of Its Problems.* Trans. S. M. Gilmour and H. C. Kee. Nashville
NTL	New Testament Library
NTM	New Testament Message
NTOA	Novum Testamentum et Orbis Antiquus
NTS	*New Testament Studies,* Cambridge, MA
NTT	*Nieuw theologisch Tijdschrift*
NTTS	New Testament Tools and Studies
Num	Numbers
Numen	*Numen: International Review for the History of Religions,* Leiden
NV	*Nova et Vetera,* Geneva
NW	northwest(ern)
NWDB	*The New Westminster Dictionary of the Bible,* ed. H. S. Gehman. Philadelphia, 1970
OA	Old Assyrian
OAkk	Old Akkadian
OB	Old Babylonian
Obad	Obadiah
OBO	Orbis biblicus et orientalis
ÖBS	Österreichische biblische Studien
OBT	Overtures to Biblical Theology
OC	*One in Christ,* London
OCA	Orientalia christiana analecta
OCD	*Oxford Classical Dictionary*
OCP	*Orientalia Christiana Periodica,* Rome
Odes Sol.	*Odes of Solomon*
OECT	*Oxford Editions of Cuneiform Texts,* ed. S. Langdon, 1923–
OED	*Oxford English Dictionary*
OG	Old Greek
OGIS	*Orientis graeci inscriptiones selectae,* ed. W. Dittenberger. 2 vols. Leipzig, 1903–5
Ohol.	*Oholot*
OIC	Oriental Institute Communications
OIP	Oriental Institute Publications
OL	Old Latin
OLA	Orientalia Lovaniensia Analecta
OLP	*Orientalia lovaniensia periodica*
OLZ	*Orientalistische Literaturzeitung,* Berlin
OMRO	*Oudheidkundige Medeelingen uit het Rijks-Museum van Oudheden te Leiden*
Onomast.	Eusebius, *Onomasticon*
Op	Philo, *De opificio mundi*
OP	*Occasional Papers on the Near East,* Malibu, CA

op. cit.	*opere citato* ([in] the work cited)
Or	*Orientalia*
ʿOr.	*ʿOrla*
OrAnt	*Oriens antiquus*
OrBibLov	Orientalia et biblica lovaniensia
OrChr	*Oriens christianus*
Orig. World	*On the Origin of the World* (NHC II,*5*; XIII,*2*)
OrSyr	*L'orient syrien*
o.s.	old series
OstStud	*Ostkirchliche Studien,* Würzburg
OT	Old Testament
OTA	*Old Testament Abstracts*
OTE	*Old Testament Essays,* Pretoria
OTG	Old Testament Guides
OTG	*The Old Testament in Greek according to the Text of Codex Vaticanus,* ed. A. E. Brooke, N. McLean, and H. St. J. Thackeray. Cambridge, 1906–40
ÖTK	Ökumenischer Taschenbuch-Kommentar
OTL	Old Testament Library
OTM	Old Testament Message
OTP	*Old Testament Pseudepigrapha,* 2 vols., ed. J. Charlesworth. Garden City, NY, 1983–87
OTS	*Oudtestamentische Studiën*
p	Pesher (commentary)
P	"Priestly" source
p(p).	page(s); past
PÄ	*Probleme der Ägyptologie,* Leiden
PAAJR	*Proceedings of the American Academy for Jewish Research,* Philadelphia
Pal.	*Palestinian*
Pal. Tgs.	*Palestinian Targums*
PalCl	*Palestra del Clero*
par(s).	paragraph(s); (gospel) parallel(s)
Para	*Para*
Paraph. Shem	*Paraphrase of Shem* (NHC VII,*1*)
part.	participle
pass.	passive
passim	throughout
PBA	*Proceedings of the British Academy,* Oxford
PBS	University Museum, University of Pennsylvania, *Publications of the Babylonian Section,* Philadelphia
PCB	*Peake's Commentary on the Bible,* rev. ed., ed. M. Black and H. H. Rowley. New York, 1962
P.E.	Eusebius, *Praeparatio evangelica*
Peʾa	*Peʾa*
PEFA	Palestine Exploration Fund Annual
PEFQS	*Palestine Exploration Fund Quarterly Statement*
PEGLAMBS	*Proceedings of the Eastern Great Lakes and Midwest Biblical Societies*
PEGLBS	*Proceedings of the Eastern Great Lakes Biblical Society*
PEQ	*Palestine Exploration Quarterly,* London
perf.	perfect
Pers	Persian
Pesaḥ.	*Pesaḥim*
Pesiq. R.	*Pesiqta Rabbati*
Pesiq. Rab Kah.	*Pesiqta de Rab Kahana*
PG	J. Migne, *Patrologia graeca*
PGM	*Papyri graecae magicae,* 3 vols., ed. K. Preisendanz. Leipzig, 1928–41
Ph. E. Poet	*Philo the Epic Poet*
PhEW	*Philosophy East and West*
Phil	Philippians
Phil.-hist. Kl.	Philosophische-historische Klasse
Phld.	see *Ign. Phld.*
Phlm	Philemon
PHOE	G. von Rad. 1966. *The Problem of the Hexateuch and Other Essays.* Trans. E. Dicken. Edinburgh and New York
Phoen	Phoenician
PhönWest	*Phönizier im Westen,* ed. H. G. Neimeyer. Madrider Beiträge 8. Mainz, 1982
PhRev	*Philosophical Review*
PI	J. Pedersen. 1926–40. *Israel: Its Life and Culture.* 2 vols. Copenhagen
PIBA	*Proceedings of the Irish Biblical Association,* Dublin
PIOL	Publications de l'Institut orientaliste de Louvain
PIR	*Prosopographia imperii Romani saec. I.II.III,* 3 vols., ed. E. Klebs, H. Dessau, and P. von Rohden. Berlin, 1897–98
PIR^2	*Prosopographia imperii Romani saec. I.II.III,* 2d ed., ed. E. Groag, A. Stein, and L. Petersen. 5 vols. Berlin and Leipzig, 1933–
Pirqe R. El.	*Pirqe Rabbi Eliezer*
P. J.	*Paraleipomena Jeremiou*
PJ	*Palästina-Jahrbuch*
PL	J. Migne, *Patrologia latina*
pl.	plural
pl(s).	plate(s)
Plant	Philo, *De plantatione*
Plato Rep.	*Plato: Republic 588B–589B* (NHC VI,*5*)
PMR	Charlesworth, J. H. 1976. *The Pseudepigrapha and Modern Research.* SCS 7. Missoula, MT
PN	personal name
PN A	Pottery Neolithic A
PN B	Pottery Neolithic B
PNPI	J. K. Stark. 1971. *Personal Names in Palmyrene Inscriptions.* Oxford
PNPPI	F. Benz. 1972. *Personal Names in the Phoenician and Punic Inscriptions.* Studia Pohl 8. Rome

PNTC	Pelican New Testament Commentaries
PO	Patrologia orientalis
Pol.	see *Ign. Pol.*
Post	Philo, *De posteritate Caini*
POTT	*Peoples of Old Testament Times,* ed. D. J. Wiseman. Oxford, 1973
POuT	De Prediking van het Oude Testament
PPN A	Pre-Pottery Neolithic A
PPN B	Pre-Pottery Neolithic B
Pr Azar	Prayer of Azariah
Pr. Jac.	*Prayer of Jacob*
Pr. Jos.	*Prayer of Joseph*
Pr Man	Prayer of Manasseh
Pr. Mos.	*Prayer of Moses*
Pr. Paul	*Prayer of the Apostle Paul* (NHC I,*1*)
Pr. Thanks.	*The Prayer of Thanksgiving* (NHC VI,7)
Praem	Philo, *De praemiis et poeniis*
Praep. Evang.	Eusebius, *Praeparatio evangelica*
Pre. Pet.	*Preaching of Peter*
Presbyterion	*Presbyterion,* St. Louis, MO
Prism	*Prism,* St. Paul, MN
Pro	*Proyección,* Granada, Spain
Prob	Philo, *Probus*
Procl	Proclamation Commentaries
Proof	*Prooftexts: A Journal of Jewish Literary History*
Prot. Jas.	*Protevangelium of James*
Prov	Proverbs
Provid I–II	Philo, *De providentia* I–II
PRS	*Perspectives in Religious Studies,* Macon, GA
PRU	*Le Palais Royal d'Ugarit,* ed. C. F. A. Schaeffer and J. Nougayrol. Paris
Ps(s)	Psalm(s)
Ps-Abd.	*Apostolic History of Pseudo-Abdias*
PSB	*Princeton Seminary Bulletin,* Princeton, NJ
PSBA	*Proceedings of the Society of Biblical Archaeology*
Ps-Clem.	*Pseudo-Clementines*
Ps-Eup.	*Pseudo-Eupolemus*
Ps-Hec.	*Pseudo-Hecataeus*
Ps-Mt.	*Gospel of Pseudo-Matthew*
Ps-Orph.	*Pseudo-Orpheus*
Ps-Philo	*Pseudo-Philo*
Ps-Phoc.	*Pseudo-Phocylides*
Pss. Sol.	*Psalms of Solomon*
PSt	*Process Studies,* Claremont, CA
PSTJ	*Perkins (School of Theology) Journal,* Dallas, TX
PT	*Perspectiva Teológica,* Venda Nova, Brazil
pt.	part
PThS	*Pretoria Theological Studies,* Leiden
PTMS	Pittsburgh Theological Monograph Series
PTU	F. Gröndahl. 1967. *Die Personennamen der Texte aus Ugarit.* Studia Pohl 1. Rome
Pun	Punic
PVTG	Pseudepigrapha Veteris Testamenti graece
PW	A. Pauly–G. Wissowa, *Real-Encyclopädie der classischen Altertumswissenschaft,* Stuttgart, 1839–; supplements, 1903–56, 11 vols.; 2d series, 1914–48
PWCJS	*Proceedings of the . . . World Congress of Jewish Studies*
PWSup	Supplement to PW
Pyr	K. Sethe. 1908–32. *Die altägyptischen Pyramidentexte.* 4 vols. Leipzig. Repr. Hildesheim, 1969
Q	Qere; "Q"-source; Qumran texts (e.g., 4QTestim)
Qad	*Qadmoniot,* Jerusalem
QD	Quaestiones disputatae
QDAP	*Quarterly of the Department of Antiquities in Palestine*
QHBT	*Qumran and the History of the Biblical Text,* ed. F. M. Cross and S. Talmon. Cambridge, MA, 1975
Qidd.	*Qiddušin*
Qinnim	*Qinnim*
QL	Qumran Literature
Qod.	*Qodašin*
Qoh or Eccl	Qoheleth or Ecclesiastes
Quaes Ex I–II	Philo, *Quaestiones et solutiones in Exodum* I–II
Quaes Gen I–IV	Philo, *Quaestiones et solutiones in Genesin* I–IV
Ques. Ezra	*Questions of Ezra*
Quod Det	Philo, *Quod deterius potiori insidiari soleat*
Quod Deus	Philo, *Quod deus immutabilis sit*
Quod Omn	Philo, *Quod omnis probus liber sit*
R	H. C. Rawlinson. 1861–1909. *The Cuneiform Inscriptions of Western Asia.* London
RA	*Revue d'Assyriologie et d'Archéologie orientale,* Paris
RAB	J. Rogerson. 1985. *Atlas of the Bible.* New York
Rab.	*Rabbah* (following abbreviation for biblical book: *Gen. Rab.* = *Genesis Rabbah*)
RAC	*Reallexikon für Antike und Christentum,* 10 vols., ed. T. Klauser, Stuttgart, 1950–78
RANE	Records of the Ancient Near East
RÄR	H. Bonnet. 1952. *Reallexikon der ägyptischen Religionsgeschichte.* Berlin
RArch	*Revue archéologique*
RasT	*Rassegna di Teologia,* Naples
RAT	*Revue Africaine de Théologie,* Kinshasa Limete, Zaire

RazFe	*Razón y Fe,* Madrid
RB	*Revue biblique,* Paris
RBén	*Revue bénédictine,* Maredsous
RBI	*Rivista biblica italiana,* Brescia
RBR	*Ricerche Bibliche e Religiose*
RCB	*Revista de Cultura Biblica,* São Paulo, Brazil
RCT	*Revista Catalana de Teología,* Barcelona, Spain
RDAC	*Report of the Department of Antiquities, Cyprus,* Nicosia
RdÉ	*Revue d'égyptologie*
RdM	*Die Religionen der Menschheit,* ed. C. M. Schröder, Stuttgart
RE	*Realencyklopädie für protestantische Theologie und Kirche,* 3d ed., ed. A. Hauck. Leipzig, 1897–1913
REA	*Revue des études anciennes*
REAug	*Revue des études augustiniennes,* Paris
REB	*Revista Eclesiástica Brasileira,* Brazil
RechBib	Recherches bibliques
RefRev	*Reformed Review,* Holland, MI
RefTR	*Reformed Theological Review,* Melbourne
REJ	*Revue des études juives,* Paris
RelArts	Religion and the Arts
RelLond	*Religion,* London, 1971–
RelNY	*Religion,* New York
RelS	*Religious Studies,* London
RelSoc	*Religion and Society*
RelSRev	*Religious Studies Review*
Renovatio	*Renovatio,* Bonn
repr.	reprint, reprinted
RES	*Revue des études sémitiques,* Paris
RES	*Répertoire d'épigraphie sémitique* [cited by number]
ResABib	Die Reste der altlateinische Bibel
ResQ	*Restoration Quarterly,* Abilene, TX
Rev	Revelation
Rev. Ezra	*Revelation of Ezra*
Rev. Steph.	*Revelation of Stephen*
RevExp	*Review and Expositor,* Louisville, KY
RevistB	*Revista Bíblica,* Buenos Aires
RevistEspir	*Revista de Espritualidad,* Madrid
RevQ	*Revue de Qumran,* Paris
RevRef	*La Revue Réformée,* Aix en Provence
RevRel	*Review for Religious,* St. Louis, MO
RevScRel	*Revue des sciences religieuses,* Strasbourg
RevSém	*Revue sémitique*
RevThom	*Revue thomiste,* Toulouse
RGG	*Religion in Geschichte und Gegenwart*
RGTC	*Répertoire géographique des textes cunéiformes,* 8 vols., ed. W. Röllig. BTAVO B7. Wiesbaden
RHA	*Revue hittite et asianique*
RHE	*Revue d'histoire ecclésiastique,* Louvain
RHLR	*Revue d'histoire et de littérature religieuses,* Paris
RHPR	*Revue d'histoire et de philosophie religieuses,* Strasbourg
RHR	*Revue de l'histoire des religions,* Paris
RIC	*The Roman Imperial Coinage,* ed. H. Mattingly et al. London, 1923–81
*RIC*²	*The Roman Imperial Coinage,* 2d ed., ed. C. H. V. Sutherland and R. A. G. Carson. London, 1984–
RIDA	*Revue internationale des droits de l'antiquité*
RIH	J. de Rouge. 1877–78. *Inscriptions hiéroglyphiques copiées en Egypte.* 3 vols. Études égyptologiques 9–11. Paris
RivArCr	*Rivista di archeologia cristiana,* Rome
RivB	*Rivista biblica,* Bologna
RLA	*Reallexikon der Assyriologie,* ed. G. Ebeling et al. Berlin, 1932–
RLT	*Revista Latinoamericana de Teologia,* San Salvador
RNAB	see *RAB*
RNT	Regenesburger Neues Testament
RocTKan	*Roczniki Teologiczno-Kanoniczne,* Lublin
Rom	Romans
Rom.	see *Ign. Rom.*
Roš Hš.	*Roš Haššana*
ROTT	G. von Rad. 1962–65. *Old Testament Theology.* 2 vols. Trans. D. M. G. Stalker. New York
RP	*Revue de philologie*
RQ	*Römische Quartalschrift für christliche Altertumskunde und Kirchengeschichte,* Vatican City
RR	*Review of Religion*
RS	*Ras Shamra*
RSLR	*Rivista di storia letteratura religiosa,* Turin
RSO	*Rivista degli studi orientali*
RSPT	*Revue des sciences philosophiques et théolgiques,* Paris
RSR	*Recherches de science religieuse,* Paris
RST	*Religious Studies and Theology,* Edmonton, Alberta
RSV	Revised Standard Version
RT	*Recueil de travaux relatifs à la philologie et à l'archéologie égyptiennes et assyriennes*
RTAM	*Recherches de Theologie Ancienne et Médiévale*
RTL	*Revue théologique de Louvain*
RTP	*Revue de théologie et de philosophie,* Lausanne
RUO	*Revue de l'université d'Ottawa*
Ruth	Ruth
RV	Revised Version
RVV	Religionsgeschichtliche Versuche und Vorarbeiten

Ry	G. Ryckmans. 1927–59. Inscriptions sudarabes I–XVII. *Mus* 40–72 [cited by no. of text]
S	south(ern)
S. ᶜOlam Rab.	*Seder ᶜOlam Rabbah*
Šabb.	*Šabbat*
SacDoc	*Sacra Doctrina,* Bologna
SacEr	*Sacris Erudiri: Jaarboek voor Godsdienstwetenschappen,* Brugge, Belgium
Sacr	Philo, *De sacrificiis Abelis et Caini*
SAHG	A. Falkenstein and W. von Soden. 1953. *Sumerische und akkadische Hymnen und Gebete.* Zurich
SAK	*Studien zur Altägyptischen Kultur,* Hamburg
Sal	*Salesianum,* Rome
Salman	*Salmanticensis,* Salamanca
Sam. Pent.	Samaritan Pentateuch
Sam. Tg.	*Samaritan Targum*
SamOstr	Samaria Ostracon/Ostraca
SANE	*Sources From the Ancient Near East,* Malibu, CA
Sanh.	*Sanhedrin*
SANT	Studien zum Alten und Neuen Testament
SAOC	Studies in Ancient Oriental Civilization
Sap	*Sapienza,* Naples
SAQ	Sammlung ausgewählter kirchen-und dogmengeschichtlicher Quellenschriften
SAT	*Die Schriften des Alten Testaments in Auswahl,* ed. and trans. H. Gunkel et al. Göttingen
SB	Sources bibliques
SBA	Studies in Biblical Archaeology
SBAW	Sitzungsberichten der (königlichen) bayerischen Akademie der Wissenschaften
SBB	Stuttgarter biblische Beiträge
SBibB	*Studies in Bibliography and Booklore,* Cincinnati, OH
SBJ	La sainte bible de Jérusalem
SBLABS	Society of Biblical Literature Archaeology and Biblical Studies
SBLAS	Society of Biblical Literature Aramaic Studies
SBLASP	Society of Biblical Literature Abstracts and Seminar Papers
SBLBAC	Society of Biblical Literature The Bible in American Culture
SBLBMI	Society of Biblical Literature The Bible and Its Modern Interpreters
SBLBSNA	Society of Biblical Literature Biblical Scholarship in North America
SBLDS	Society of Biblical Literature Dissertation Series

SBLMasS	Society of Biblical Literature Masoretic Studies
SBLMS	Society of Biblical Literature Monograph Series
SBLNTGF	Society of Biblical Literature: The New Testament in the Greek Fathers
SBLRBS	Society of Biblical Literature: Resources for Biblical Study
SBLSBS	Society of Biblical Literature: Sources for Biblical Study
SBLSCS	Society of Biblical Literature: Septuagint and Cognate Studies
SBLSP	*Society of Biblical Literature Seminar Papers*
SBLSS	Society of Biblical Literature: Semeia Studies
SBLTT	Society of Biblical Literature: Texts and Translations
SBLWAW	Society of Biblical Literature: Writings of the Ancient World
SBM	Stuttgarter biblische Monographien
SBS	Stuttgarter Bibelstudien
SBT	Studies in Biblical Theology
SC	Sources chrétiennes
SCCNH	*Studies on the Civilization and Culture of Nuzi and the Hurrians,* 2 vols., ed. D. I. Owen and M. A. Morrison. Winona Lake, IN, 1981–87
ScEccl	*Sciences ecclésiatiques*
ScEs	*Science et esprit,* Montreal
SCHNT	Studia ad corpus hellenisticum novi testamenti
Scr	*Scripture*
SCR	*Studies in Comparative Religion*
ScrB	*Scripture Bulletin*
ScrC	*Scripture in Church,* Dublin
ScrHier	*Scripta Hierosolymitana,* Jerusalem
Scrip	*Scriptorium,* Brussels
Scriptura	*Scriptura,* Stellenbosch
ScrT	*Scripta Theologica,* Barañain/Pamplona
SCS	Septuagint and Cognate Studies
ScuolC	*Scuola Cattolica,* Milan
SD	Studies and Documents
SDB	*Smith's Dictionary of the Bible,* ed. H. B. Hackett. Boston, 1880
SE	southeast(ern)
SE	*Studia Evangelica I, II, III* (= TU 73 [1959], 87 [1964], 88 [1964], etc.)
SEÅ	*Svensk Exegetisk Årsbok*
Search	*Search,* Dublin
Šeb.	*Šebiᶜit*
Šebu.	*Šebuᶜot*
sec.	section
Sec. Gos. Mk.	*Secret Gospel of Mark*
SecondCent	*Second Century,* Macon, GA
Sef	*Sefarad,* Madrid

SEG	*Supplementum Epigraphicum Graecum,* ed. J. J. E. Hondius. Leiden, 1923–
Sem	*Semitica,* Paris
Ṣem.	*Ṣemaḥot*
Semeia	*Semeia,* Chico, CA
SemiotBib	*Sémiotique et Bible,* Lyon
Semitics	*Semitics,* Pretoria
Sent. Sextus	*Sentences of Sextus* (NHC XII,*1*)
Šeqal.	*Šeqalim*
Seux	J. M. Seux. 1968. *Epithètes Royales Akkadiennes et Sumériennes.* Paris
SGL	A. Falkenstein. 1959. *Sumerische Götterlieder.* Heidelberg
SGV	*Sammlung gemeinverständlicher Vorträge und Schriften aus dem Gebiet der Theologie und Religionsgeschichte,* Tübingen
SHAW	Sitzungsberichte der Heidelberger Akademie der Wissenschaften
Shep. Herm.	*Shepherd of Hermas*
SHIB	R. M. Grant and D. Tracy. 1984. *A Short History of the Interpretation of the Bible.* 2d ed. Philadelphia
Shofar	*Shofar,* West Lafayette, IN
SHR	Studies in the History of Religions
SHT	Studies in Historical Theology
Sib. Or.	*Sibylline Oracles*
SICV	*Sylloge inscriptionum Christianorum veterum musei Vaticani,* ed. H. Zilliacus. Acta instituti Romani Finlandiae 1/1–2. Rome
SIDÅ	Scripta Instituti Donneriana Åboensis, Stockholm
SIDJC	*Service International de Documentation Judéo-chrétienne,* Rome
SIG[3]	*Sylloge Inscriptionum Graecarum,* ed. W. Dittenberger. 3d ed. Leipzig
SII	*Studies in Islam,* New Delhi
sing.	singular
Sipra	*Sipra*
Sipre	*Sipre*
Sir	Ecclesiasticus *or* Wisdom of Jesus Ben-Sira
SIRIS	*Sylloge inscriptionum religionis Isiacae et Serapicae,* ed. L. Vidman. RVV 28. Berlin, 1969
SJ	Studia Judaica
SJLA	Studies in Judaism in Late Antiquity
SJOT	*Scandinavian Journal of the Old Testament*
SJT	*Scottish Journal of Theology,* Edinburgh
SkrifK	*Skrif en Kerk,* Pretoria
SLAG	*Schriften der Luther-Agricola-Gesellschaft* (Finland)
SLJT	*Saint Luke's Journal of Theology,* Sewanee, TN
SMEA	*Studi Micenei ed Egeo-Anatolici*
SMS	*Syro-Mesopotamian Studies,* Malibu, CA
SMSR	*Studi e materiali di storia delle religioni*
Smyrn.	see *Ign. Smyrn.*
SNT	Studien zum Neuen Testament
SNTSMS	Society for New Testament Studies Monograph Series
SNTU	*Studien zum Neuen Testament und seiner Umwelt,* Linz
SNVAO	*Skrifter utgitt av det Norske Videnskaps-Akademi i Oslo*
SO	Symbolae osloenses
SÖAW	*Sitzungsberichte der Österreichen Akademie der Wissenschaften*
Sobr	Philo, *De sobrietate*
Somn I–II	Philo, *De somniis* I–II
SonB	Soncino Books of the Bible
Sop.	*Soperim*
Soph. Jes. Chr.	*Sophia of Jesus Christ* (NHC III,*4*)
Soṭa	*Soṭa*
SOTSBooklist	*Society for Old Testament Study Booklist*
SOTSMS	Society for Old Testament Study Monograph Series
Sou	*Soundings,* Nashville
SPap	*Studia papyrologica*
SPAW	Sitzungsberichte der preussischen Akademie der Wissenschaften
SPB	Studia postbiblica
Spec Leg I–IV	Philo, *De specialibus legibus* I–IV
SPhil	*Studia Philonica,* Chicago
SPIB	*Scripta Pontificii Instituti Biblici,* Rome
SpT	*Spirituality Today,* Dubuque, IA
SQAW	Schriften und Quellen der alten Welt
SR	*Studies in Religion/Sciences religieuses,* Waterloo, Ontario
SS	Studi semitici
SSAOI	*Sacra Scriptura Antiquitatibus Orientalibus Illustrata,* Rome
SSEA	Society for the Study of Egyptian Antiquities
SSN	*Studia Semitica Neerlandica,* Assen
SSS	Semitic Study Series
St	*Studium,* Madrid
ST	*Studia theologica*
STÅ	*Svendk teologisk årsskrift*
StadtrChr	P. Lampe. 1987. *Die stadtrömischen Christen in den ersten beiden Jahrhunderten.* WUNT 2/18. Tübingen
StANT	*Studien zum Alten und Neuen Testament,* Munich
StBT	*Studien zu den Boğazköy-Texten,* Wiesbaden
StDI	Studia et Documenta ad Iura Orientis Antiqui Pertinenti
STDJ	Studies on the Texts of the Desert of Judah
StEb	*Studi Eblaiti,* Rome
StEc	*Studi Ecumenici,* Verona, Italy

Steles Seth	*Three Steles of Seth* (NHC VII,5)
StFS	*Studia Francisci Scholten,* Leiden
STK	*Svensk teologisk kvartalskrift,* Lund
STL	Studia theologica Ludensia
StLtg	*Studia Liturgica,* Rotterdam
StMiss	*Studia Missionalia,* Rome
StOr	*Studia Orientalia,* Helsinki
StOvet	*Studium Ovetense,* Oviedo
StPat	*Studia Patavina,* Padua, Italy
StPatr	*Studia Patristica*
StPhilon	*Studia Philonica*
Str	*Stromata,* San Miguel, Argentina
Str-B	H. L. Strack and P. Billerbeck. 1922–61. *Kommentar zum NT aus Talmud und Midrasch.* 6 vols. Munich
STT	*The Sultantepe Tablets,* 2 vols., ed. O. R. Gurney, J. J. Finkelstein, and P. Hulin. Occasional Publications of the British School of Archaeology at Ankara 3, 7. London, 1957–64
StTh	*Studia Theologica*
StudBib	Studia biblica
StudBT	*Studia biblica et theologica,* Guilford, CT
Studium	*Studium,* Madrid
StudNeot	Studia neotestamentica, Studia
StudOr	Studia orientalia
StudPhoen	Studia Phoenicia [I–VIII]
STV	*Studia theologica varsaviensia*
Sukk.	*Sukka*
Sum	Sumerian
SUNT	Studien zur Umwelt des Neuen Testaments
suppl.	supplement
Sus	Susanna
SVF	*Stoicorum veterum fragmenta,* ed. J. von Arnim. 4 vols. Leipzig, 1903–24. Repr. Stuttgart, 1966; New York, 1986
SVTP	Studia in Veteris Testamenti pseudepigrapha
SVTQ	*St. Vladimir's Theological Quarterly,* Tuckahoe, NY
SW	southwest(ern)
SWBA	Social World of Biblical Antiquity
SwJT	*Southwestern Journal of Theology,* Fort Worth, TX
SWP	*Survey of Western Palestine:* *SWP* 1 = C. R. Conder and H. H. Kitchener. 1881. *Galilee.* London. *SWP* 2 = C. R. Conder and H. H. Kitchener. 1882. *Samaria.* London. *SWP* 3 = C. R. Conder and H. H. Kitchener. 1883. *Judaea.* London. *SWP* 4 = E. H. Palmer. 1881. *Arabic and English Name Lists.* London. *SWP* 5 = C. Wilson and C. Warren. 1881. *Special Papers.* London. *SWP* 6 = C. Warren and C. Warren, 1884. *Jerusalem.* London. *SWP* 7 = H. B. Tristram. 1884. *The Fauna and Flora of Palestine.* London.
SymBU	Symbolae biblicae upsalienses
Syr	Syriac
Syr	*Syria: Revue d'Art Oriental et d'Archéologie,* Paris
Syr. Men.	*Syriac Menander*
SZ	*Stimmen der Zeit,* Munich
T. 12 P.	*Testaments of the Twelve Patriarchs*
T. Ab.	*Testament of Abraham*
T. Adam	*Testament of Adam*
T. Ash.	*Testament of Asher*
T. Benj.	*Testament of Benjamin*
T. Dan.	*Testament of Daniel*
T. Gad	*Testament of Gad*
T. Hez.	*Testament of Hezekiah*
T. Isaac	*Testament of Isaac*
T. Iss.	*Testament of Issachar*
T. Jac.	*Testament of Jacob*
T. Job	*Testament of Job*
T. Jos.	*Testament of Joseph*
T. Jud.	*Testament of Judah*
T. Levi	*Testament of Levi*
T. Mos.	*Testament of Moses*
T. Naph.	*Testament of Naphtali*
T. Reu.	*Testament of Reuben*
T. Sim.	*Testament of Simeon*
T. Sol.	*Testament of Solomon*
Ṭ. Yom	*Ṭebul Yom*
T. Zeb.	*Testament of Zebulun*
TA	*Tel Aviv,* Tel Aviv
Taᶜan.	*Taᶜanit*
TAD	B. Porten and A. Yardeni. 1986. *Textbook of Aramaic Documents from Ancient Egypt.* Jerusalem *TAD* A = vol. 1, *Letters* *TAD* B = vol. 2, *Contracts* *TAD* C = vol. 3, *Literature and Lists* *TAD* D = vol. 4, *Fragments and Inscriptions*
TAik	*Teologinen Aikakauskirja,* Helsinki
Talm.	*Talmud*
TAM	*Tituli Asiae Minoris*
Tamid	*Tamid*
TAPA	*Transactions of the American Philological Association*
TAPhS	*Transactions of the American Philosophical Society,* Philadelphia
TBC	Torch Bible Commentary
TBei	*Theologische Beiträge,* Wuppertal
TBl	*Theologische Blätter*
TBT	*The Bible Today,* Collegeville, MN
TBü	Theologische Bücherei
TCGNT	B. M. Metzger. 1971. *A Textual Commentary on the Greek New Testament,* United Bible Societies

TCL	*Textes cunéiforms du Musée du Louvre,* Paris, 1910–
TCS	Texts from Cuneiform Sources: TCS 1 = E. Sollberger. 1966. *Business and Administrative Correspondence Under the Kings of Ur.* Locust Valley, NY. TCS 2 = R. Biggs. 1967. *ŠÀ.ZI.GA: Ancient Mesopotamian Potency Incantations.* TCS 3 = Å. Sjöberg, E. Bergmann, and G. Gragg. 1969. *The Collection of the Sumerian Temple Hymns.* TCS 4 = E. Leichty. 1970. *The Omen Series šumma izbu.* TCS 5 = A. K. Grayson. 1975. *Assyrian and Babylonian Chronicles.*
TD	*Theology Digest,* St. Louis, MO
TDNT	*Theological Dictionary of the New Testament,* 10 vols., ed. G. Kittel and G. Friedrich. Trans. G. W. Bromiley. Grand Rapids, 1964–76
TDOT	*Theological Dictionary of the Old Testament,* ed. G. J. Botterweck, H. Ringgren, and H. J. Fabry. Trans. J. T. Willis, G. W. Bromiley, and D. E. Green. Grand Rapids, 1974–
TE	*Theologica Evangelica,* Pretoria
Teach. Silv.	*Teachings of Silvanus* (NHC VII,*4*)
Tem.	*Temura*
Temenos	*Temenos: Studies in Comparative Religion,* Helsinki
Ter	*Teresianum,* Rome
Ter.	*Terumot*
Test	*Testimonianze,* Florence
Testim. Truth	*Testimony of Truth* (NHC IX,*3*)
TEV	Today's English Version
TextsS	Texts and Studies
TF	*Theologische Forschung*
Tg. Esth. I	*First Targum of Esther*
Tg. Esth. II	*Second Targum of Esther*
Tg. Isa.	*Targum of Isaiah*
Tg. Ket.	*Targum of the Writings*
Tg. Neb.	*Targum of the Prophets*
Tg. Neof.	*Targum Neofiti I*
Tg. Onq.	*Targum Onqelos*
Tg. Ps.-J.	*Targum Pseudo-Jonathan*
Tg. Yer. I	*Targum Yerušalmi I*
Tg. Yer. II	*Targum Yerušalmi II*
TGI	K. Galling. 1950. *Textbuch zur Geschichte Israels.* 2d ed. Tübingen
TGl	*Theologie und Glaube,* Paderborn
Thal.	*Thallus*
ThArb	*Theologische Arbeiten,* Berlin
THAT	*Theologisches Handwörterbuch zum Alten Testament,* 2 vols., ed. E. Jenni and C. Westermann. Munich, 1971–76
ThEd	*Theological Educator,* New Orleans
ThEH	*Theologische Existenz Heute,* Munich
Them	*Themelios,* Madison, WI
Theod.	*Theodotus*
Theology	*Theology,* London
THeth	Texte der Hethiter
ThH	*Théologie historique*
THKNT	Theologischer Handkommentar zum Neuen Testament
Thom. Cont.	*Book of Thomas the Contender* (NHC II,7)
Thomist	*Thomist,* Washington, D.C.
ThPh	*Theologie und Philosophie,* Freiburg
ThStud	Theologische Studien
Thund.	*The Thunder: Perfect Mind* (NHC VI,*2*)
ThV	*Theologische Versuche,* Berlin
ThViat	*Theologia Viatorum,* Berlin
TijdTheol	*Tijdschrift voor Theologie,* Nijmegen
Titus	Titus
TJ	*Trinity Journal,* Deerfield, IL
TJT	*Toronto Journal of Theology*
TLZ	*Theologische Literaturzeitung*
TNB	*The New Blackfriars,* Oxford
TNTC	Tyndale New Testament Commentary
Tob	Tobit
Ṭohar.	*Ṭoharot*
TOTC	Tyndale Old Testament Commentary
TP	*Theologie und Philosophie*
TPNAH	J. D. Fowler. 1988. *Theophoric Personal Names in Ancient Hebrew.* JSOTSup 49. Sheffield
TPQ	*Theologisch-Praktische Quartalschrift,* Austria
TQ	*Theologische Quartalschrift*
TR	P. Lucau. *Textes Religieux Égyptiens,* 1, Paris
Trad	*Tradition,* New York
Traditio	*Traditio,* New York
Trall.	see *Ign. Trall.*
TRE	*Theologische Realenzyklopädie*
Treat. Res.	*Treatise on Resurrection* (NHC I,*4*)
Treat. Seth	*Second Treatise of the Great Seth* (NHC VII,*2*)
Treat. Shem	*Treatise of Shem*
TRev	*Theologische Revue*
Tri. Trac.	*Tripartite Tractate* (NHC I,*5*)
Trim. Prot.	*Trimorphic Protennoia* (NHC XIII,*1*)
TRu	*Theologische Rundschau,* Tübingen
TS	*Theological Studies,* Washington, DC
TSK	*Theologische Studien und Kritiken*
TSSI	J. C. L. Gibson. 1971–82. *Textbook of Syrian Semitic Inscriptions.* 3 vols. Oxford
TT	*Teologisk Tidsskrift*
TTKi	*Tidsskrift for Teologie og Kirke,* Oslo, Norway
TTKY	*Türk Tarih Kurumu Kongresi Yayĭnlari.* Ankara
TToday	*Theology Today,* Princeton, NJ

TTS	Trierer Theologische Studien
TTZ	*Trierer theologische Zeitschrift*
TU	Texte und Untersuchungen
TUAT	Texte aus der Umwelt des Alten Testaments
TV	*Teología y Vida,* Santiago, Chile
TvT	*Tijdschrift voor Theologie,* Nijmegen, The Netherlands
TWAT	*Theologisches Wörterbuch zum Alten Testament,* ed. G. J. Botterweck, H. Ringgren, and H. J. Fabry. Stuttgart, 1970–
TWNT	*Theologisches Wörterbuch zum Neuen Testament,* 8 vols., ed. G. Kittel and G. Friedrich. Stuttgart, 1933–69
TynBul	*Tyndale Bulletin*
TZ	*Theologische Zeitschrift,* Basel, Switzerland
UBSGNT	*United Bible Societies Greek New Testament*
UCPNES	University of California Publications in Near Eastern Studies
UCPSP	University of California Publications in Semitic Philology
UET	Ur Excavations: Texts
UF	*Ugarit-Forschungen*
Ug	Ugaritic
UGAÄ	Untersuchungen zur Geschichte und Altertumskunde Aegyptens
ÜgS	M. Noth. 1967. *Überlieferungsgeschichtliche Studien.* 3d ed. Tübingen
UNT	Untersuchungen zum Neuen Testament
ᶜUq.	*ᶜUqṣin*
Urk. IV	*Urkunden des ägyptischen Altertums.* Abt. IV, *Urkunden der 18. Dynastie,* ed. K. Sethe and W. Helck. 22 fasc. Leipzig, 1903–58
US	*Una Sancta*
USQR	*Union Seminary Quarterly Review,* New York, NY
UT	C. H. Gordon. 1965. *Ugaritic Textbook.* AnOr 38. Rome; suppl. 1967
UUÅ	*Uppsala universitets Årsskrift*
v(v)	verse(s)
VAB	*Vorderasiatische Bibliothek,* Leipzig, 1907–16
Val. Exp.	*A Valentinian Exposition* (NHC XI,*2*)
VAT	Vorderasiatische Abteilung, Thontafelsammlung, Staatliche Musee zu Berlin
VC	*Vigiliae christianae*
VCaro	*Verbum caro*
VD	*Verbum domini*
VE	*Vox Evangilica*
VetChr	*Vetera Christianum,* Bari
VF	*Verkündigung und Forschung*
Vg	Vulgate
Vid	*Vidyajyoti,* Delhi
VigChrist	*Vigiliao Christianae*
VIO	Veröffentlichung der Institut für Orientforschung
Virt	Philo, *De virtutibus*
Vis. Ezra	*Vision of Ezra*
Vis. Is.	*Vision of Isaiah*
Vis. Paul	*Vision of Paul*
Vita	*Vita Adae et Evae*
Vita C	Eusebius, *Vita Constantini*
Vita Cont	Philo, *De vita contemplativa*
Vita Mos I–II	Philo, *De vita Mosis* I–II
VKGNT	*Vollständige Konkordanz zum griechischen Neuen Testament,* ed. K. Aland
VL	Vetus Latina
vol(s).	volume(s)
Vorsokr.	*Fragmente der Vorsokrater,* 4th ed., ed. H. Diels. Berlin, 1922
VR	*Vox Reformata,* Geelong, Victoria, Australia
VS	Vorderasiatische Schriftdenkmäler der königlichen Museen zu Berlin
VSpir	*Vie spirituelle,* Paris
VT	*Vetus Testamentum,* Leiden
VTSup	Vetus Testamentum Supplements
W	west(ern)
WA	["Weimar Ausgabe," =] *D. Martin Luthers Werke: Kritische Gesamtausgabe,* ed. J. K. F. Knaake et al. Weimar, 1883–
Way	*The Way,* London
WbÄS	A. Erman and H. Grapow. 1926–31. *Wörterbuch der ägyptischen Sprache.* 7 vols. Leipzig. Repr. 1963
WBC	World Bible Commentary
WBKL	Wiener Beitrage zur Kulturgeschichte und Linguistik
WbMyth	*Wörterbuch der Mythologie,* ed. H. W. Haussig, Stuttgart, 1961
WC	Westminster Commentaries, London
WD	*Wort und Dienst*
WDB	*Westminster Dictionary of the Bible*
Wehr	H. Wehr. 1976. *A Dictionary of Modern Written Arabic,* 3d ed., ed. J. M. Cowen. Ithaca
WF	Wege der Forschung
WGI	J. Wellhausen. 1878. *Geschichte Israels.* Berlin [see also *WPGI* and *WPHI*]
WHAB	*Westminster Historical Atlas of the Bible*
Whitaker	R. E. Whitaker. 1972. *A Concordance of the Ugaritic Literature.* Cambridge, MA
WHJP	*World History of the Jewish People*
Wis	Wisdom of Solomon
WLSGF	*The Word of the Lord Shall Go Forth: Essays in Honor of David Noel Freedman,* eds. C. L. Meyers and M. O'Connor. Winona Lake, IN, 1983

WMANT	Wissenschaftliche Monographien zum Alten und Neuen Testament
WO	*Die Welt des Orients*
WoAr	*World Archaeology*
Wor	*Worship,* Collegeville, MN
WordWorld	*Word and World,* St. Paul, MN
WPGI	J. Wellhausen. 1895. *Prolegomena zur Geschichte Israels.* 4th ed. Berlin
WPHI	J. Wellhausen. 1885. *Prolegomena to the History of Israel.* 2 vols. Trans. J. S. Black and A. Menzies. Edinburgh. Repr. Cleveland 1957; Gloucester, MA, 1973
WS	*World and Spirit,* Petersham, MA
WTJ	*Westminster Theological Journal,* Philadelphia, PA
WTM	J. Levy. 1924. *Wörterbuch über die Talmudim und Midraschim.* 5 vols. 2d ed., ed. L. Goldschmidt. Leipzig. Repr. 1963
WTS	E. Littmann and M. Höfner. 1962. *Wörterbuch der Tigre-Sprache.* Wiesbaden
WuD	*Wort und Dienst,* Bielefeld
WUNT	Wissenschaftliche Untersuchungen zum Neuen Testament
WUS	J. Aistleitner. 1974. *Wörterbuch der ugaritischen Sprache.* 4th ed., ed. O. Eissfeldt. BSAW 106/3. Berlin
WuW	*Wissenschaft und Weisheit,* Mönchengladbach
WVDOG	*Wissenschaftliche Veröffentlichungen der Deutschen Orient-Gesellschaft*
WW	*Word & World,* Fort Lee, NJ
WZ	*Wissenschaftliche Zeitschrift*
WZKM	*Wiener Zeitschrift für die Kunde des Morgenlandes*
WZKSO	*Wiener Zeitschrift für die Kunde Süd- und Ostasiens*
Yad.	*Yadayim*
Yal.	*Yalqut*
Yebam.	*Yebamot*
Yem. Tg.	*Yemenite Targum*
YES	Yale Egyptological Studies
YGC	W. F. Albright. 1969. *Yahweh and the Gods of Canaan.* Garden City, NY. Repr. Winona Lake, IN, 1990
YJS	*Yale Judaica Series,* New Haven
YNER	Yale Near Eastern Researches
Yoma	*Yoma (= Kippurim)*
YOS	Yale Oriental Series
y. (Talm.)	Jerusalem (Talmud) = "Yerushalmi"
ZA	*Zeitschrift für Assyriologie*
Zabim	*Zabim*
ZAH	*Zeitschrift für Althebräistic*
ZÄS	*Zeitschrift für Ägyptische Sprache und Altertumskunde*
ZAW	*Zeitschrift für die alttestamentliche Wissenschaft,* Berlin
ZB	Zürcher Bibelkommentare
ZDMG	*Zeitschrift der deutschen morgenländischen Gesellschaft*
ZDPV	*Zeitschrift des deutschen Palästina-Vereins*
Zebaḥ.	*Zebaḥim*
Zech	Zechariah
ZEE	*Zeitschrift für evangelische Ethik*
Zeph	Zephaniah
Zer.	*Zeraᶜim*
ZHT	*Zeitschrift für historische Theologie*
ZKG	*Zeitschrift für Kirchengeschichte*
ZKT	*Zeitschrift für katholische Theologie,* Innsbruck
ZMR	*Zeitschrift für Missionskunde und Religionswissenschaft*
ZNW	*Zeitschrift für die neutestamentliche Wissenschaft*
Zost.	*Zostrianos* (NHC VIII,*1*)
ZPE	*Zeitschrift für Papyrologie und Epigraphik*
ZPKT	*Zeitschrift für Philosophie und Katholische Theologie*
ZRGG	*Zeitschrift für Religions- und Geistesgeschichte,* Erlangen
ZST	*Zeitschrift für systematische Theologie*
ZTK	*Zeitschrift für Theologie und Kirche*
ZWT	*Zeitschrift für wissenschaftliche Theologie*
ZycMysl	*Zycie i Mysl*

H

H. The abbreviation used by biblical scholars to represent the Holiness Code in pentateuchal source criticism. See HOLINESS CODE.

HA-ELEPH (PLACE) [Heb *hāʾelep*]. A Benjaminite town listed between Zela and Jerusalem (Josh 18: 28). The name is problematic. LXX^B omits the name altogether; and LXX^A conflates it with Zela, reading *Sēlaleph.* On identification, see ZELA (PLACE).

Gary A. Herion

HAAHASHTARI (PERSON) [Heb *hāʾăḥaštārî*]. The eponymous ancestor of a family of Judah known as the "Ahashtarites" (1 Chr 4:6, cf. Noth *IPN,* 236). The genealogy traces Haahashtari's lineage back to Ashhur, the father of Tekoa through his wife Naarah. Immediately preceding the Ahashtarites in the list are three sons of Ashhur and Naarah: Ahuzzam, Hepher, and Temeni. Whether the Ahashtarites are descended from one of these three or represent a line through a fourth son is unclear. A derivation of the name from a Persian root *ḫšaça,* meaning "kingdom," "power," "rule" has been sought (*HALAT* 1: 36; cf. Myers *1 Chronicles* AB, 28). That the name is a corruption of *hāʾašḥûrî,* the "Ashhurites," and describes the preceding names (*ISBE* [1939] 2: 1311) is unnecessary. This emendation lacks manuscript support. Further, the name of the family may have been derived from a name in an intervening generation between Ashhur and the families of the Ahashtarites that were in existence at the time of the list's compilation.

Kenneth H. Cuffey

HABAIAH (PERSON) [Heb *ḥŏbayyâ*]. Var. HOBAIAH. The head of a family of priests which is listed among those exiles of uncertain descent returning from Babylon to Jerusalem and Judah (Ezra 2:61 = Neh 7:63; 1 Esdr 5:38). This priestly family, along with two others, was excluded, at least temporarily, from the priesthood as being unclean for lack of documentation of their priestly lineage. The name is theophoric and derives from the Heb root *ḥb* which means "withdraw," "hide." The *Qal* impv., *ḥăbî,* is used in Isa 26:20 thus suggesting that this name was formed with the imperative, not an unusual occurrence, according to Albright (1928: 234), in hypocoristic formations. Since the Heb root *ḥbʾ,* which in the causative means "hide," is used in the sense of "protect" elsewhere (Josh 6:17, 25; 1 Kgs 18:4, 13; Isa 49:2), the name, which Noth (*IPN,* 178) understands as "Yahweh has hidden," could also mean "Yahweh has protected" or "Protect, O Yahweh." The several Greek transliterations of this name account for the variety of its spelling in translation: Ezra—*hobaia* (A), *labeia* (B), *ōdouia* (Luc); Neh—*hebeia* (A, B), *abia* (S, Luc); 1 Esdr—*hobbeia* (B), *obdia* (A), *ōdouia* (Luc).

Bibliography

Albright, W. F. 1928. The Egyptian Empire in Asia in the Twenty-first Century B.C. *JPOS* 8: 223–56.

Rodney H. Shearer

HABAKKUK, BOOK OF. The eighth book of the Minor Prophets. Medieval and early modern exegetes derived the name from the Hebrew root *ḥbq,* "to embrace." Most modern scholars follow Noth (*IPN,* 231), who derives it from Akk *ḫabbaqūqū/ḫambaqūqū,* which refers to a type of garden plant (*AHW* 1: 304).

A. The Prophet
B. Text and Versions
C. Literary Issues and Authorship
   1. The Book as a Whole
   2. The Pronouncement of Habakkuk
   3. The Prayer of Habakkuk
D. Significance in Later Jewish and Christian Tradition

A. The Prophet

The book of Habakkuk provides little information concerning the identity and historical background of the prophet on whom it is based. He is identified simply as "Habakkuk the prophet" in 1:1 and 3:1 with no indication of his lineage, provenance, or dates. Consequently, a number of apocryphal traditions concerning Habakkuk appear in postbiblical literature. The apocryphal Bel and the Dragon (2d century B.C.E.) portrays him as a contemporary of Daniel during the Babylonian exile and identifies him as "Habakkuk, the son of Jesus, of the tribe of Levi" (Bel 1:1 = LXX Dan 14:1). The pseudepigraphic *Lives of the Prophets* (1st century C.E.) follows this dating but identifies him as a member of the tribe of Simeon (*Life of Habakkuk* 1–9). The midrashic historical treatise *Seder ʿOlam Rabbah* (2d–3d century C.E.) places him in the reign of Manasseh (*S. ʿOlam Rab.* 20). Clement of Alexandria (2d–3d century C.E.) identifies him as a contemporary of

Jeremiah and Ezekiel, but he also states that Jonah and Habakkuk are contemporaries of Daniel (*Str.* 1:21). Finally, the medieval kabbalistic commentary *Sefer ha-Zohar* (ca. 1300 C.E.) identifies him as the son of the Shunammite woman saved by the prophet Elisha (*Zohar* 1:7; 2:44–45).

Although most modern scholars reject these traditions as the product of later legend, the absence of personal information about Habakkuk continues to confound attempts to identify his historical background. A wide range of dates have been proposed, from Sennacherib's invasion of Judah in the late 8th century (Betteridge 1903) to Alexander the Great's conquest of the Near East in the 4th century (Duhm 1906; Torrey 1935). On the basis of Hab 1:6, which mentions the establishment of the Chaldeans, most contemporary scholars maintain that Habakkuk lived during the rise of the Neo-Babylonian Empire in the latter part of the 7th century, from the latter years of Josiah (640–609) to the reign of Jehoiakim (609–598) or perhaps Jehoiachin (598). A recent study by Haak (1986) maintains that Habakkuk was a pro-Babylonian supporter of King Jehoahaz, who was removed from the Judean throne and exiled to Egypt by Pharaoh Neco in 609. It should be kept in mind, however, that decisions concerning Habakkuk's dates and the relation of his message to the historical events of his time are dependent on a literary assessment of the book and the identification of several key references including the "righteous" (1:4, 13; 2:4), the "wicked" (1:4, 13; 3:13), the subject of the "woe" oracles (2:6–20), and the Chaldeans (1:6). These issues will be discussed below.

The question of the prophet's vocation is likewise dependent on the assessment of the book's literary genre. Many scholars follow Mowinckel (1921–24: 3. 27–29), who argued that Habakkuk was a temple cult prophet on the basis of the liturgical forms found in the book (cf. Sellin KAT [1930]; Eaton TBC [1961]; Watts CBC [1975]; Széles ITC [1987]). This view is supported by Jeremias (1970: 103–7), who notes the parallels between Habakkuk's watch station (2:1) and those of the postexilic Levites and priests in the Temple (Neh 13:30; 2 Chr 7:6; 8:14; 35:2; cf. Isa 21:8) as well as the temple context of the terms *nābîʾ*, "prophet," *maśśāʾ*, "pronouncement" (RSV 'oracle'), and *ḥāzâ*, "to see" (i.e., have a vision). A dissenting view sees Habakkuk as a visionary prophet without cultic connections (Rudolph KAT [1975]; Jöcken 1977). Others stress his wisdom background (Gowan 1968, 1976; Uffenheimer 1987) or his concern as an individual with the troubling events of his day (Keller CAT [1971]; 1973). Finally, a number of scholars note his connections with the Isaiah tradition (Brownlee 1971; Janzen 1982; Peckham 1986).

B. Text and Versions

The text of Habakkuk presents scholars with a number of problematic readings, not only because of the difficulties presented by the MT, but also because of the many variant readings found in ancient manuscripts and versions. Consequently, many scholars consider the MT of Habakkuk to be quite corrupt (e.g., Delcor 1961: 399). Earlier scholars generally assumed that these manuscripts and versions represented variant Hebrew originals and corrected the MT accordingly (Lachmann 1932; Good 1958). Recent advances in text-critical methodology which emphasize the interpretative character and intent of many text witnesses call this judgment into question (Sanders 1979). At present the issue is divided; some studies show great confidence in the MT (e.g., Haak 1986), whereas others rely heavily on textual emendation (e.g., Hiebert 1986).

A critical edition of the MT appears in *BHS*. This edition contains notes concerning the various medieval Masoretic mss and other textual versions. In addition to the Masoretic mss, the principal Hebrew, Greek, and Aramaic text witnesses are as follows:

The Habakkuk Pesher from Qumran (1QpHab) (Burrows, Trever, and Brownlee 1950; Trever 1972) dates to the 1st century B.C.E. and contains the text of Habakkuk 1–2 together with a commentary that interprets Habakkuk in relation to the early history of the Qumran sect. The text was thoroughly studied by Brownlee (1959), who examined over 160 variants from the MT. Most were minor orthographic, grammatical, and spelling changes or Aramaicisms which had crept into the text. There were a number of substantial changes, however, including *wyśm* for *wĕʾāšēm*, "guilty men," in 1:11; *ḥrbw* for *ḥermô*, "his net," in 1:17; *hwn wbgd* for *hayyayin bôgēd* (RSV: "wine is treacherous") in 2:5; *mwʿdyhm* for *mĕʿôrêhem*, "their shame," in 2:15.

The Scroll of the Minor Prophets from Wâdī Murabbaʿat (*Mur* 88) dates to the 2d century C.E., some decades after the fixing of the Textus Receptus. Within its text of the Minor Prophets, it contains Hab 1:3–2:11 and 2:18–3:19. Apart from orthographic changes, there are a few variant readings or corrections. Most notable is the substitution of *zrmw mym ʿbwt* from Ps 77:18 for *zerem mayim ʿābār* ("the raging waters swept on") in Hab 3:10.

The LXX and other Greek versions (Aquila, Theodotion, Symmachus) are represented in a critical edition (by J. Ziegler 1943) of the Greek text together with notes on the various readings found in the manuscripts. Cothenet (*DBSup* 45: 793) notes that its variations from the MT are due to a number of causes: variant consonantal texts, revocalized consonantal texts, and attempts at reinterpreting the text.

The Greek Scroll of the Minor Prophets from Naḥal Ḥever (8 Ḥev XIIgr) was apparently hidden during the Bar Kokhba revolt against Rome (Barthélemy 1963). The text contains Hab 1:5–11; 1:14–2:8; 2:13–20; 3:9–15. Barthélemy (1963: 144–57) attributes this text to Jonathan ben Uzziel, known in Greek as Theodotion (1st century C.E.). It represents a revision of the LXX made in Judea, based on a Hebrew consonantal text which is nearly identical to the MT.

The Barberini Greek version of Habakkuk 3 appears in six medieval manuscripts dating from the 8th to the 13th century (Good 1958, 1959). It does not correspond to any other known Greek version; but it appears to have a close relationship with the Coptic versions, especially the Achmimic. It has affinities with North African Latin texts, the Palestinian Syriac version, and the Peshitta. It is a free translation which employs paraphrase and is deliberately exegetical. Good (1959: 28–30) maintains that this translation was made for liturgical purposes. Its provenance is Alexandria, and it dates to the early 2d century C.E. at the latest.

Targum Jonathan ben Uzziel on the Prophets, an Aramaic version, presupposes a Proto-MT Hebrew text (Sperber 1962). It is contemporary with Targum Onqelos but preserves traditions from the Palestinian Targum. Brownlee (1956) has noted the affinities between the interpretations found in this Targum and those of 1QpHab.

Critical editions of the Peshitta (Peshitta Institute 1980; cf. Gelston 1987) and the Vulgate (Weber 1975) have also been published.

C. Literary Issues and Authorship

The history of critical scholarship on Habakkuk through the mid-1970s has been exhaustively surveyed and evaluated by Jöcken (*Habakkuk* BBB). Van der Wal (1988) has published a complete bibliography of works through 1987.

1. The Book as a Whole. Most scholars maintain that the book of Habakkuk contains three major literary units: a dialogue between the prophet and God in 1:1–2:4/5; a section containing a series of woe oracles in 2:5/6–20; and a psalm in chap. 3 (Childs *IOTS,* 448). This view raises problems, however, in that there is little agreement concerning the interrelationship of these units. An alternative proposal (Széles *Habakkuk, Zephaniah* ITC; Sweeney *HBC,* fc.) maintains that the book of Habakkuk comprises two distinct sections: Habakkuk 1–2, the Pronouncement *(maśśāʾ)* of Habakkuk, and Habakkuk 3, the Prayer *(tĕpillâ)* of Habakkuk. These sections are demarcated formally by their respective superscriptions in 1:1 and 3:1; the technical terms in 3:1, 3, 9, 13, 19, which identify Habakkuk 3 as a psalm; the distinctive mythological background of Habakkuk 3; and their respective generic characters.

The distinctive characteristics of the sections that comprise Habakkuk, however they are defined, together with the literary tensions within and between them, have raised the question of literary integrity and authorship. Many critics followed the lead of Stade (1884), who argued that 2:9–20 and chap. 3 were later additions, in arguing that Habakkuk did not constitute a unified, coherent literary work (Jöcken 1977: 116–240 surveys the history of scholarship). Under the influence of form-critical studies of the Psalms, chiefly by Mowinckel (1921–24) and Gunkel (1933), and the lexical study of Habakkuk by Humbert (1944), scholars have currently reached a consensus that although the book was probably not entirely written by a single author (contra Eissfeldt 1965 and Brownlee 1971), its present form constitutes a coherent literary unity (Jöcken 1977: 241–519). In this respect a number of scholars see the book as a liturgical or cultic composition (Mowinckel; Sellin KAT; Humbert 1944; Elliger ATD; Nielsen 1953; Eaton TBC; Jeremias 1970; Watts CBC; Haak 1986; Széles ITC) or a prophetic imitation of a cultic liturgy (Fohrer 1985). Others see it as a composition which is concerned with the prophet's visionary experience (Rudolph KAT; Janzen 1982; Peckham 1986). A third view maintains that the book is organized around the question of theodicy (Keller 1973; Gowan 1976; Bratcher 1984; Otto 1985; Gunneweg 1986; Sweeney *HBC,* fc.). Consequently, there is no consensus as to the nature of the final form of the book.

2. The Pronouncement of Habakkuk. In the present form of the book, the superscription in 1:1 identifies chaps. 1–2 as "The Pronouncement which Habakkuk the prophet saw." The Hebrew term *maśśāʾ,* "pronouncement," "burden," refers to a type of prophetic oracle, but its precise meaning has been an enigma. A recent investigation by Weis (1986) demonstrates that *maśśāʾ* refers to a specific type of prophetic discourse that attempts to explain the manner in which God's intention will be manifested in human affairs. It is generally based on a vision or other revelatory experience and is spoken by a prophet in response to a particular situation in human events. An alternative view maintains that these chapters are an expanded form of the complaint genre (Haak 1986).

The pronouncement contains four major sections. Hab 1:2–4 is a complaint by the prophet to God concerning the oppression of the "righteous" by the "wicked." Neither party is identified. Hab 1:5–11 is God's response to this complaint, announcing the coming threat of the Chaldeans. Hab 1:12–17 is a second complaint by the prophet to God concerning the oppressive nature of the Chaldeans. Hab 2:1–20 constitutes the prophet's report of God's second response in Hab 2:1–4 together with his explanation of the meaning of God's response in Hab 2:5–20.

The Pronouncement of Habakkuk raises three major problems which have been the subject of scholarly discussion. The first concerns the identity of the "righteous" *(ṣaddîq)* and the "wicked" *(rāšāʿ)* in 1:4, 13, and 2:4 and the role of the Chaldeans mentioned in 1:6. Most scholars maintain that the purpose of the Chaldeans is to punish the "wicked" oppressors of the "righteous" mentioned in 1:2–4. Two possibilities have been put forward for understanding this oppression. The first identifies the "wicked" as an external enemy which is threatening righteous Judah. Assyria, Egypt (Bič 1968), Chaldea (Wellhausen 1892; Sellin KAT), Greece (Duhm 1906; Torrey 1935), or an unidentified enemy (Horst HAT [1956]) have all been proposed. The second possibility identifies the oppression as a reference to an inner Judean conflict in which a "wicked" party is opposed to a "righteous" group. Scholars who hold this view argue that the language used to describe oppression in 1:2–4 refers to internal social tensions and identify the "wicked" very generally as the wicked in Judean society (Gowan 1976; Achtemeier *Nahum-Malachi* IBC; Gunneweg 1986) or specifically either as those who allowed the Josianic reform to lapse (Janzen 1982; Johnson 1985) or King Jehoiakim and his supporters (Ward *Habakkuk* ICC; Humbert 1944; Nielsen 1953; Rudolph KAT). Others argue that the prophet's complaint was originally directed against a Judean group but was later reapplied against Chaldea in light of historical experience (Jeremias 1970; Otto 1985; Peckham 1986; Haak 1986). Elliger (ATD) maintains that the book was originally directed against Egypt but was later reapplied against Chaldea.

Because each of these identifications presents problems, there is no consensus on the issue. A recent study by Johnson (1985) may resolve the impasse. The primary issue is to explain why Chaldea is used to correct oppression in 1:5–11 but then becomes the oppressor in 1:12–17. Johnson notes that 1:5–11 does not portray Chaldea in a positive light. He therefore concludes that the establishment of Chaldea should not be viewed as a solution to the oppression described in 1:2–4. Hab 1:5–11 does not therefore solve the old problem of theodicy but constitutes a heightened form of the complaint in 1:2–4 concerning the Chaldean oppression. Not only does this view resolve the difficulties of the text, it explains the reference to the treachery of the Chaldeans in 1:13 (cf. 2:5) in light of the long history of alliance between Judah and Babylon from the time of Hezekiah and King Josiah's death in battle supporting Babylonian interests.

The second problem concerns the meaning of Hab 2:4 and the relation of 2:1–4 to its context. Scholars generally view 2:1–4 in relation to the preceding dialogue between Habakkuk and God and maintain that 2:1–4 is God's response to Habakkuk's second complaint in 1:12–17. The prophet describes his waiting for the divine response in 2:1 and reports that response in 2:2–4, where he is instructed to write his vision clearly on tablets (Holt 1964) and to wait for its fulfillment.

Scholars agree that Hab 2:4 contains the core of God's answer to Habakkuk, but there is no consensus as to its meaning because of its grammatical and lexical problems. The verse reads, "Behold, he whose soul is not upright in him shall fail [a correction of MT 'is puffed up'] but the righteous shall live by his faith [or 'faithfulness']" (RSV). Emerton's study of the issue (1977) summarizes the problems of the first half of the verse. First, the translation of the Hebrew verb *ʿuppĕlâ* as "is puffed up" lacks support in the versions and appears nowhere else in the Hebrew Bible. Second, the antecedents of the pronouns "he" and "him" are not clear. Third, although the portrayal of a conceited and unjust (puffed up) figure in v 4a contrasts well with the righteous *(ṣaddîq)* of v 4b, there is no antithesis to the statement that the righteous shall live. These problems have prompted scholars to advance numerous textual emendations and interpretations (e.g., van der Woude 1966, 1970; Emerton 1977; Janzen 1980; Scott 1985), but none has gained general acceptance.

The text can be understood without resort to emendation. Hab 2:4 must be understood in relation to 2:5–20, which describes the downfall of an unsated oppressor because of excessive greed (cf. Schreiner 1974; Humbert 1944: 150–51; van der Woude 1966: 367). The vocabulary and syntax of 2:4 contrast the instability and impending fall of an arrogant oppressor with the righteous victim who will survive; the "wicked" oppressor is Chaldea and the "righteous" victim is Judah.

The third major problem presented by Habakkuk 1–2 concerns the identity of the oppressor presupposed by the woe oracles of 2:5–20. Because the crimes specified in these oracles are localized, some scholars suggest that the woes were originally directed against an internal Judean group, such as the ruling class of Jerusalem (Otto 1977; Jeremias 1970), before being reapplied against Chaldea by later editors (cf. Jer 22:13–23, where Jeremiah condemns Jehoiakim for such crimes). Others maintain that Chaldea was the intended subject of these oracles (Janzen 1982; Peckham 1986). In this respect it is important to recognize Coggins' observation (1982) that Habakkuk may represent a different prophetic tradition from that of Jeremiah. Prophets are known for using local imagery to condemn international crimes (e.g., Amos 1:3, 11, 13; Isa 10:14; Nah 3:5–7). Furthermore, statements in the woe oracles suggest an international situation, such as the references to peoples and nations (vv 6a, 8a, 10b, 13b), the earth, humankind, and the sea (vv 8b, 14, 17b), and the violence of Lebanon (v 17a). A supporting example is Nebuchadnezzar's report that he took Lebanon from an unnamed ruler and transported its wood back to Babylon to build a palace for the ruler of heaven and earth (*ANET,* 307). Such an act well suits the crimes mentioned in these oracles, which speak of extortion and plundering nations (vv 6b–8), unjust gain used to protect one's house (vv 9–11), bloodshed to build a city (vv 12–14), and the rape of a land (vv 15–17). The prophet concludes by stating that the oppressor will fall by its idolatry (vv 18–20), which corresponds to the Chaldeans' crime in 1:11 and 1:16 (cf. 2:13a).

3. The Prayer of Habakkuk. Habakkuk 3 begins with the superscription, "The Prayer of Habakkuk the Prophet concerning *šigyōnôt.*" The term *šigāyôn,* which has been associated with the Akk *šegû,* "song of lament" (Mowinckel 1921–24: 4.7; rejected by Seux 1981; see also MUSIC AND MUSICAL INSTRUMENTS) also appears in Psalm 7, a Psalm of Lament. This superscription, the technical music notations in 3:3, 9, 13, 19, and the situation of distress presupposed in the psalm have prompted many scholars to argue that Habakkuk 3 is a cultic song of lament sung as part of the temple liturgy (Sellin; Nielsen 1953; Eaton 1964; Margulis 1970). On the basis of its mythic themes of divine combat against the forces of cosmic chaos (cf. Cassuto 1975; Irwin 1942, 1956), others view it as a song of triumph (Albright 1950) or a song of victory (Hiebert 1986). Although many of these studies presuppose that the psalm was originally an oral composition because of its affinity with Ugaritic prosody (e.g., Albright 1950), Floyd (1980) disputes this view. Finally, a number of scholars have noted its associations with other theophanic texts in the Bible as well as a relationship between its framing verses (3:2, 16) and the reference to Habakkuk's vision in 2:1–4. Consequently, they define it as a vision report (Fohrer 1985) which contains a description of a theophany (Jeremias 1965; Rudolph; Achtemeier IBC).

In its present form the prayer in vv 2–19a is a petition addressed by the psalmist to God to manifest divine power in the world in order to deliver the land from invaders (v 16). It includes an introductory section (v 2), which petitions God to manifest divine acts in the world (cf. 1:5), and a concluding section (vv 16–19a), which expresses the psalmist's confidence that God will answer the petition. These sections bracket a description of a theophany in vv 3–15, which consists of two parts (cf. Jeremias 1965). Verses 3–6 describe the deity's approach, and verses 7–15 depict God's victory over the enemy in mythological terms. The theophany expresses the psalmist's confidence that God will deliver the land (v 13), demonstrating the steadfast faith of the righteous in 2:4. Instructions to the choirmaster in v 19b follow the psalm.

Because of its distinctive character many early scholars argued that Habakkuk 3 was an independent psalm that was originally not a part of the book of Habakkuk (Stade 1884; Wellhausen 1892; Nowack HAT [1897]; Marti KHC [1904]). Although the absence of Habakkuk 3 from 1QpHab might lend support to this view (Taylor *IB,* 974), most scholars maintain that this is irrelevant (Eissfeldt 1965; Fohrer 1985) because the reasons for its omission are unclear (Brownlee 1971). Contemporary scholars have identified a number of reasons for associating Habakkuk 3 with Habakkuk 1–2, including the same general theme that God will bring the oppression of the people to an end;

similarity of language, particularly the references to the "wicked" *(rāšāʿ)* in 3:13 and 1:4, 13; and the relationship between 3:2, 16, which indicate that the psalmist is waiting for God to bring about deliverance, and 2:1–5, which instruct the prophet to wait for the fulfillment of the vision (Eissfeldt 1965; Fohrer 1985). Others maintain that the unity of the book is to be found in its cultic character. This argument is based on the correspondence of the vocabulary of Habakkuk 1–2 and Habakkuk 3 with cultic psalms (Humbert 1944) or the association of the genres of lament/complaint and response in Habakkuk 1–2 with the liturgical character of Habakkuk 3 (Mowinckel 1921–24 vol. 3; Sellin; Eaton). Consequently, most scholars view the book as a unity. A number of contemporary scholars maintain that Habakkuk was the author of the psalm (Eissfeldt 1965; Fohrer 1985; Brownlee 1971; Rudolph). Hiebert (1986) employs textual and motif considerations, together with evidence pertaining to the Kuntillet Ajrud inscriptions, to argue that the psalm was composed in the premonarchic period and later added to Habakkuk 1–2. Although the question of authorship cannot be settled decisively for lack of an adequate text base (cf. Peckham 1986), it is clear that in the context of the book as a whole Habakkuk 3 functions as a corroborating conclusion which responds to the issues raised in Habakkuk 1–2. The poem expresses confidence that the vision mentioned in 2:1–4 will be fulfilled and that God's righteousness will be vindicated with the deliverance of the people from oppression.

D. Significance in Later Jewish and Christian Tradition

The book of Habakkuk has played an important role in both Jewish (Baumgartner 1885; Coleman 1964–65) and Christian (Cothenet *DBSup* 45: 791–811) traditions. As noted above, Habakkuk 1–2 served as the basis of a commentary which interpreted the text in relation to the early history of the Qumran community. In the NT, Hab 2:4 serves as the major textual basis for the doctrine of "justification by faith" in Rom 1:17; Gal 3:11; and Heb 10:38–39 (Sanders 1959; Feuillet 1959–60; Strobel 1964; Fitzmyer, 1981). The Talmudic Rabbi Simlai likewise identified Hab 2:4 as a summary of all 613 commandments of the Torah (*b. Mak.* 23b–24a). In Jewish tradition Habakkuk 3 is understood as a description of the revelation at Sinai and is read as the Haphtarah section for the second day of the Festival of Shavuot, which commemorates the revelation of the Torah at Sinai (*b. Meg.* 31a).

Bibliography

Albright, W. F. 1950. The Psalm of Habakkuk. Pp. 1–18 in *Studies in OT Prophecy,* ed. H. H. Rowley. Edinburgh.

Barthélemy, D. 1963. *Les devanciers d'Aquila: Première publication intégrale du texte des fragments du Dodékapropheton.* VTSup 10. Leiden.

Baumgartner, A. J. 1885. *Le prophète Habakuk.* Leipzig.

Betteridge, W. R. 1903. The Interpretation of the Prophecy of Habakkuk. *AJT* 7: 647–61.

Bič, M. 1968. *Sophonie. Nahum. Habaquq.* LD 48. Paris.

Bratcher, D. 1984. *The Theological Message of Habakkuk.* Richmond, VA.

Brownlee, W. H. 1956. The Habakkuk Midrash and the Targum of Jonathan. *JJS* 7: 169–86.

———. 1959. *The Text of Habakkuk in the Ancient Commentary From Qumran.* SBLMS 11. Philadelphia.

———. 1963. The Placarded Revelation of Habakkuk. *JBL* 82: 319–25.

———. 1971. The Composition of Habakkuk. Pp. 255–75 in *Hommages à André Dupont-Sommer.* Paris.

———. 1979. *The Midrash Pesher of Habakkuk.* SBLMS 24. Missoula, MT.

Burrows, M.; Trever, J.; and Brownlee, W. H. 1950. *The Dead Sea Scrolls of St. Mark's Monastery.* Vol. 1. New Haven.

Cassuto, U. 1975. Chapter III of Habakkuk and the Ras Shamra Texts. Vol. 2, pp. 3–15 in *Biblical & Oriental Studies.* Jerusalem.

Coggins, R. 1982. An Alternative Prophetic Tradition? Pp. 77–94 in *Israel's Prophetic Tradition,* ed. R. Coggins, A. Phillips, and M. Knibb. Cambridge.

Coleman, S. 1964–65. The Dialogue of Habakkuk in Rabbinic Doctrine. *AbrN* 5: 57–85.

Delcor, M. 1961. Habacuc. Pp. 389–433 in *Les Petits Prophètes,* by A. Deissler and M. Delcor. Vol. 8/1 in *La Sainte Bible,* ed. L. Pirot and A. Clamer. Paris.

Duhm, B. 1906. *Das Buch Habakuk.* Tübingen.

Eaton, J. H. 1964. The Origin and Meaning of Habakkuk 3. *ZAW* 76: 144–71.

Eissfeldt, O. 1965. *The OT: An Introduction.* Trans. P. R. Ackroyd. New York.

Emerton, J. A. 1977. The Textual and Linguistic Problems of Habakkuk II.4–5. *JTS* 28: 1–18.

Feuillet, A. 1959–60. La citation d'Habacuc II,4 et les premiers chapitres de l'épître aux Romans. *NTS* 4: 52–80.

Fitzmyer, J. A. 1981. Habakkuk 2:3–4 and the NT. Pp. 236–46 in *To Advance the Gospel.* New York.

Floyd, M. H. 1980. Oral Tradition as a Problematic Factor in the Historical Interpretation of the Poems in the Law and the Prophets. Ph.D. diss., Claremont.

Fohrer, G. 1985. Das "Gebet des Propheten Habakuk" (Hab 3,1–16). Pp. 159–67 in *Mélanges bibliques et orientaux en l'honneur de M. Mathias Delcor,* ed. A. Caquot, S. Légasse, and M. Tardieu. AOAT 215. Kevelaer and Neukirchen.

Gelston, A. 1987. *The Peshitta of the Twelve Prophets.* Oxford.

Good, E. M. 1958. *The Text and Versions of Habakkuk 3: A Study in Textual History.* Ph.D. diss., Columbia University.

———. 1959. The Barberini Greek Version of Habakkuk III. *VT* 9: 9–30.

Gowan, D. E. 1968. Habakkuk and Wisdom. *Perspective* 9: 157–66.

———. 1976. *The Triumph of Faith in Habakkuk.* Atlanta.

Gunkel, H. 1933. *Einleitung in die Psalmen.* 4th ed. Göttingen. Repr. 1985.

Gunneweg, A. H. J. 1986. Habakuk und das Problem des leidenden *ṣaddîq. ZAW* 98: 400–415.

Haak, R. 1986. Habakkuk Among the Prophets. Ph.D. diss., University of Chicago.

———. 1988. "Poetry" in Habakkuk 1:1–2:4? *JAOS* 108: 437–44.

Hiebert, T. 1986. *God of My Victory: The Ancient Hymn in Habakkuk 3.* HSM 38. Atlanta.

Holt, J. M. 1964. So He May Run Who Reads It. *JBL* 83: 298–302.

Humbert, P. 1944. *Problèmes du Livre d'Habacuc.* Neuchâtel.

Irwin, W. A. 1942. The Psalm of Habakkuk. *JNES* 1: 10–40.

———. 1956. The Mythological Background of Habakkuk, Chapter 3. *JNES* 15: 47–50.

Janzen, J. G. 1980. Habakkuk 2:2–4 in the Light of Recent Philological Advances. *HTR* 73: 53–78.

———. 1982. Eschatological Symbol and Existence in Habakkuk. *CBQ* 44: 394–414.
Jeremias, J. 1965. *Theophanie: Die Geschichte einer alttestamentlichen Gattung.* WMANT 10. Neukirchen-Vluyn.
———. 1970. *Kultprophetie und Gerichtsverkündigung in der späten Königszeit Israels.* WMANT 35. Neukirchen.
Jöcken, P. 1977. War Habakuk ein Kultprophet? Pp. 319–32 in *Bausteine Biblischer Theologie,* ed. H.-J. Fabry. BBB 50. Bonn.
Johnson, M. D. 1985. The Paralysis of Torah in Habakkuk I 4. *VT* 35: 257–66.
Keller, C. A. 1973. Die Eigenart der Prophetie Habakuks. *ZAW* 85: 156–67.
Lachmann, J. 1932. *Das Buch Habbakuk: Eine Textkritische Studie.* Aussig.
Margulis, B. 1970. The Psalm of Habakkuk. *ZAW* 82: 409–42.
Mowinckel, M. 1921–24. *Psalmenstudien.* 6 vols. Kristiana.
Nielsen, E. 1953. The Righteous and the Wicked in Hăbaqqūq. *ST* 6: 54–78.
Otto, E. 1977. Die Stellung der Wehe-Worte inder Verkündigung des Propheten Habakuk. *ZAW* 89: 73–107.
———. 1985. Die Theologie des Buches Habakuk. *VT* 35: 274–95.
Peckham, B. 1986. The Vision of Habakkuk. *CBQ* 48: 617–36.
Peshitta Institute. 1980. *The OT in Syriac According to the Peshitta Version.* Vol. 3/4. Leiden.
Sanders, J. A. 1959. Habakkuk in Qumran, Paul, and the OT. *JR* 39: 232–43.
———. 1979. Text and Canon: Concepts and Method. *JBL* 98: 5–29.
Schreiner, S. 1974. Erwägungen zum Text von Hab 2,4–5. *ZAW* 86: 538–42.
Scott, J. M. 1985. A New Approach to Habakkuk II 4–5A. *VT* 35: 330–40.
Seux, M.-J. 1981. *Šiggayôn = šigû?* Pp. 419–38 in *Mélanges bibliques et orientaux en l'honneur de M. Henri Cazelles,* ed. A. Caquot and M. Delcor. AOAT 212. Kevelaer and Neukirchen-Vluyn.
Sperber, A. 1962. *The Latter Prophets according to Targum Jonathan.* Vol. 3 of *The Bible in Aramaic.* Leiden.
Stade, B. 1884. Habakuk. *ZAW* 4: 154–59.
Strobel, A. 1964. *Untersuchungen zum eschatologischen Verzögerungsproblem auf Grund der späjüdisch-urchristlichen Geschichte von Habakuk 2,2ff.* NovTSup 2. Leiden.
Sweeney, M. A. fc. Structure, Genre, and Intent in the Book of Habakkuk. *VT* 41.
Torrey, C. C. 1935. The Prophecy of Habakkuk. Pp. 565–82 in *Jewish Studies in Memory of George A. Kohut,* ed. S. Baron and A. Marx. New York.
Trever, J. 1972. *Scrolls from Qumran Cave I.* Jerusalem.
Uffenheimer, B. 1987. Habakkuk from Shutter to Step: Observations on Habakkuk 1–2. Pp. 69–92 in *Studies in Bible Dedicated to the Memory of U. Cassuto,* ed. S. Loewenstamm. Jerusalem (in Hebrew).
Wal, A. van der. 1988. *Nahum, Habakkuk: A Classified Bibliography.* Amsterdam.
Weber, R. 1975. *Biblia sacra iuxta Vulgatam versionem.* Rev. ed. Stuttgart.
Weis, R. D. 1986. *A Definition of the Genre Maśśā᾿ in the Hebrew Bible.* Ph.D. diss., Claremont, CA.
Wellhausen, J. 1892. *Die Kleinen Propheten.* Berlin. Repr. 1963.
Woude, A. S. van der. 1966. Der Gerechte Wird Durch Seine Treue Leben: Erwägungen zu Habakuk 2:4–5. Pp. 367–75 in *Studia Biblica et Semitica Theodoro Christiano Vriezen.* Wageningen.
———. 1970. Habakuk 2,4. *ZAW* 82: 281–82.
Ziegler, J. 1943. *Duodecim prophetae.* Göttingen.

MARVIN A. SWEENEY

HABAZZINIAH (PERSON) [Heb *ḥăbaṣṣinyāh*]. The grandfather of the Rechabites who were tested by Jeremiah (Jer 35:3). Habazziniah's grandson Jaazaniah and his household are taken by Jeremiah to the Jerusalem temple. They are offered wine but citing the command of their ancestor Jonadab (2 Kgs 10:10–15) refuse to drink it (Jer 35:6–7). While the narrative in Jeremiah 35 concerns Habazziniah's grandson's generation, Habazziniah is likely included to underscore the continuity of the Rechabite tradition and family. In Jeremiah 35 the faithfulness of the Rechabites to Yahweh for many generations is contrasted with King Jehoiakim's failure to heed Yahweh's word in Jeremiah 36. Thus the Rechabites are promised descendants (Jer 35:18) while Jehoiakim is warned "he shall have none to sit upon the throne of David" (Jer 36:30). The Rechabites were noted for their zealous devotion to Yahweh, and this is perhaps reflected in the *yāh* endings of the three names in Jer 35:3—Jaazaniah, Jeremiah, and Habazziniah (Orelli 1889: 264). A variety of connections have been suggested between Habazziniah and the Akk *ḫabāṣu* ('the Lord has made me abundant'), though how this bears upon the text is not clear. Alternatively, it may mean "Yahweh has made me joyful" (*TPNAH,* 96, 178).

Bibliography

Orelli, C. von. 1889. *The Prophecies of Jeremiah.* Trans. J. E. Banks. Edinburgh.

JOHN M. BRACKE

ḪABIRU, ḪAPIRU. Often considered to be the Akkadian equivalent of Heb *ʿibrî.* See HEBREW.

A. The Identity of the *ḫabiru/ḫapiru*

Ever since this Akkadian expression was first recognized in A.D. 1888, viz., in the Amarna Letters written by Abdi-Ḫepa of Jerusalem around 1375 B.C. (EA 286–90; Greenberg 1955: 47–49) scholars have discussed the significance of the *ḫabiru/ḫapiru* for the origin of the Israelites. In this discussion the etymology of the word has played a significant part since it was soon recognized that a W Semitic word must lie behind the Akkadian expression. In Akkadian cuneiform writing the consonant *ḫ* represents at least three different W Semitic gutturals (notably *ḥ, ḫ,* and *ʿ*), and it was therefore proposed that the *ḫabiru* mentioned in Abdi-Ḫepa's letters were Israelite tribesmen who were then forcing their way into Palestine in the course of the Israelite conquest. The fact that these *ḫabiru/ḫapiru* (or *ʿabiru/ʿapiru*) were only mentioned by the king of Jerusalem was, however, considered a serious obstacle to this identification, because—according to the OT—Jerusalem was not attacked by the Israelites until the early days of King David, ca. 1000 B.C.

Only when the German orientalist Hugo Winckler succeeded in A.D. 1895 in identifying the *ḫabiru/ḫapiru* of Abdi-ḫepa's letters with the SA.GAZ people, who figure far more frequently in the Amarna Letters, did scholars in general incline to accept the identification of the *ḫabiru* with the Hebrews (Loretz 1984: 60). This seemingly obvious identification was soon challenged by other discoveries which showed that the *ḫabiru/ḫapiru* were present in sources from all over the ANE in the 2d millennium B.C. Especially when they appeared in the Hittite archives from Boghazköy (Ḫattušaš) it became doubtful whether they could in fact be identical with the early Israelites. Evidently the expression covered an ethnic entity which could not be equated with the forefathers of the Israelites in a simple way. The confirmation that it was necessary to disassociate the problem of the *ḫabiru* from the early history of the Israelites first became apparent in Egyptian sources and later in Ugaritic documents, which made it clear that the second consonant should most properly be read *p* instead of *b*; the same also proved that the first consonant actually was an ᶜ (in Eg *ᶜpr.w,* in Ug *ᶜpr*). Doubt also arose as to the ethnic content of the expression, especially because of the German Egyptologist Wilhelm Spiegelberg (1907: 618–20), who believed that the term designated a social group of some sort. According to Spiegelberg the term was most properly applied to nomads who lived on the fringe of the Syrian desert (including the Proto-Israelites).

Today the mainly social content of the expression is only occasionally disputed (e.g., by de Vaux 1968), but the interpretation of its social content has changed, most notably thanks to Benno Landsberger, who showed that the expression *ḫabiru/ḫapiru* should actually be translated "fugitives" or even "refugees" (in Bottéro 1954: 160–61). That such an understanding lies near at hand is confirmed by the Sumerian equivalent of *ḫabiru/ḫapiru,* SA.GAZ (variant spellings SAG.GAZ, or simply GAZ), as this Sumerogram is in fact merely a transcription of the Akk *šaggašum,* "murderer." Moreover, SAG.GAZ is occasionally, in the Akkadian lexicographical lists translated as *ḫabbatum* "brigand." Today most orientalists consider that the expression *ḫabiru/ḫapiru* encompassed fugitives who had left their own states either to live as refugees in other parts of the Near East or outlaws who subsisted as brigands out of reach of the authorities of the states (Bottéro 1980).

B. The Etymology of *ḫabiru/ḫapiru*

The etymology of the expression has never been fully explained; nor has the discussion about the correct spelling of the word ever ceased. The Semitic root on which the expression is based may be either *ᶜbr* or *ᶜpr* depending on the correct reading of the second consonant. If the term should actually be read *ḫabiru* then the most obvious etymological explanation must be that it is a derivation from the verbal root *ᶜbr* meaning "to pass by," "trespass" (e.g., a border, a river, or the like), a meaning which would suit the notion of the *ḫabiru* as fugitives/refugees excellently. If the correct rendering of the Akkadian cuneiform is *ḫapiru,* a derivation from the noun *ᶜpr* meaning "dust" or "clay" would be likely; and *ᶜapiru* might then have been a popular way of designating people of low social standing. Both Egyptian and Ugaritic evidence seems to favor a rendering of the cuneiform syllabic writing *(ḫa-bi/pí-ru)* by *ᶜapiru.* However, as several scholars have maintained, none of these sources is conclusive. The Egyptian writers in particular were inconsistent as to the rendering of the Semitic labials *b* and *p,* and also the Ugaritic writers seem to have been uncertain how to render the same labials (Weippert 1971: 76–79). The evidence in favor of the rendering *ḫabiru* proposed by Jean Bottéro (*RLA* 4/1:22) is perhaps more rewarding. Some of it dates from the Middle Babylonian period and includes a series of occurrences where the word is spelled *ḫa-bir-a-a* (*ḫabirāyu,* cf. Greenberg 1955: 78; cf., however, also Borger 1958: 126). Another part comes from the Hittite archives where the cuneiform sign *bi* always seems to represent a *bi* and never a *pí* (according to Bottéro *RLA* 4/1:22). Whether Bottéro's conclusions are fully justifiable is, however, still under debate. Therefore, although the rendering of the cuneiform writing as *ḫabiru* seems most likely at the moment, we cannot exclude the reading *ḫapiru.*

C. The Sources for the *ḫabiru/ḫapiru*

The total number of occurrences of the word *ḫabiru/ḫapiru* in the ANE documents is today just above 250 (total listing until ca. A.D. 1970 in *RLA* 4/1:15–21, supplemented and corrected by Bottéro 1980: 211 [no. 2]; English translation of most passages in Greenberg 1955). Practically all examples belong to the 2d millennium B.C. although there are certain indications that the expression was not totally unknown before that date. The latest occurrences are from Egyptian sources (from the reign of Rameses IV, ca. 1166–1160 B.C.) although a few literary texts from the 1st millennium mention the *ḫabiru/ḫapiru* (Bottéro 1954: 136–43; Greenberg 1955: 54–55). As a social and political force the *ḫabiru* seem to have disappeared just before the end of the 2d millennium B.C. The geographic distribution of the *ḫabiru/ḫapiru* covers most of the Near East, from Anatolia in the N, Egypt in the S, and W Iran (Susa) to the E. The *ḫabiru/ḫapiru* were found all along the Fertile Crescent, from Palestine to Sumer.

The oldest sources which for practical reasons tell us anything about the status of the *ḫabiru/ḫapiru* come from Kaniš, the Assyrian trading station in Anatolia (19th century B.C.) and from the Sumerian area during the Neo-Sumerian epoch. Whereas doubt may be cast over the last mentioned examples (the Sumerogram SA.GAZ is always used, although the spelling may differ), the evidence from Anatolia at the beginning of the 2d millennium B.C. is more promising. The information we gain from this is, however, not totally in accordance with later sources, because the persons named *ḫabiru/ḫapiru* here may at the same time be called *awīlu,* that is "Sir," "Mr." The derogatory content of the expression is conspicuous because the persons called *ḫabiru/ḫapiru* are at that time in jail, although in possession of sufficient funds to pay for their own release. Finally, these persons were members of the staff of the palace. More important is, on the other hand, that so far it has not been possible to decide whether they were foreigners in this Old Assyrian society or belonged to the local population.

During the following era, the Old Babylonian period, the *ḫabiru/ḫapiru* are mentioned more often. There is some indication of these people being employed as mercenaries in the pay of the state administration, whereas in the archival reports from the royal palace of Mari we are confronted with the first known examples of *ḫabiru/ḫapiru* as outlaws or brigands. One document mentions that they had even conquered a city belonging to the kingdom of Mari and caused serious trouble there (Greenberg 1955: 18). The documents from Mari and elsewhere also show that the *ḫabiru/ḫapiru* were considered a highly mobile population element.

The evidence of the presence of the *ḫabiru/ḫapiru* becomes far more extensive in the LB Age, during the second half of the 2d millennium B.C. The centers of gravity of this documentation are Nuzi, in NE Mesopotamia (15th century B.C.); Alalakh (15th century B.C.) and Ugarit, two coastal states in N Syria; Ḫattušaš (Boghazköy) in Anatolia; and Palestine and Lebanon as documented by the Amarna Letters (beginning of the 14th century B.C.). Most evidence originates in official state archives; only at Nuzi are private references to the *ḫabiru/ḫapiru* frequent. At Nuzi the *ḫabiru/ḫapiru* are most often mentioned in private contracts according to which persons called *ḫabiru/ḫapiru* bind themselves to the service of Nuzi citizens. The documents in question show that the *ḫabiru/ḫapiru* were not themselves citizens of Nuzi but foreigners without any juridical rights at Nuzi. By binding themselves through these service contracts they obtained a sort of social security so long as they remained in the service of a citizen of Nuzi. The analogy between these contracts and the OT law of the Hebrew slave (Exod 21:2–11) seems obvious (see HEBREW).

In Alalakh the *ḫabiru/ḫapiru* are normally mentioned in administrative documents listing persons of foreign origin. These foreigners seem to have been kept apart from the ordinary population of this state, maybe as servants of the royal palace administration (Greenberg 1955: 19–22). One inscription from Alalakh, however, shows that the *ḫabiru/ḫapiru* also operated as bands of brigands or outlaws outside the control of the state. In the autobiography of King Idrimi we are told how the young Idrimi during his exile lived for seven years among *ḫabiru/ḫapiru* out of reach of the authorities from whom he had escaped (*ANET,* 557–58). The same distinction between *ḫabiru/ḫapiru* as foreigners in the service of the state and *ḫabiru/ḫapiru* as outlaws is apparent in the sources from Ugarit and Ḫattušaš. Most important is, however, a passage in a treaty between the king of Ugarit and his overlord, the Hittite king, according to which the two monarchs promise to extradite citizens who have deserted their own state to seek refuge in territories known as *ḫabiru/ḫapiru* land. Such entries in the political treaties become quite frequent in this period; the phenomenon testifies to a growing concern because of the increasing number of persons who chose to live as *ḫabiru/ḫapiru* (Liverani 1965; cf. also, for the connection between *ḫabiru/ḫapiru* and the fugitives in Akk *munnabtu,* Buccellati 1977).

Most important, however, are the testimonies as to the activities of the *ḫabiru/ḫapiru* in the Amarna Letters, although the evaluation of the content of the expression *ḫabiru/ḫapiru* is subject to discussion. Generally two different hypotheses as to the content of the expression in the Amarna Letters prevail. The first (and more popular) maintains that their situation was not much different from their situation elsewhere in the ANE. The second argues that the mentioning of the *ḫabiru/ḫapiru* in the Amarna Letters does not normally indicate a sociological phenomenon, but that it is just as often used in an exclusively pejorative sense to denote opponents of the official community, that is, the Egyptian suzerainty (thus Mendenhall 1973: 122–35; Liverani 1979). In favor of the first option is the fact that the occurrence of the term *ḫabiru/ḫapiru* is unevenly distributed over the Palestinian/Lebanese area. It is seemingly concentrated in areas in or close to the mountains, the most obvious *ḫabiru/ḫapiru* territory (cf. below), whereas the number of sources mentioning the *ḫabiru/ḫapiru* becomes more restricted in other places. This distribution indicates that the expression was not just a derogatory term in the Amarna age but reflected a real social problem of the Palestinian and Lebanese societies. In favor of the second option is the fact that persons styled *ḫabiru/ḫapiru* in the Amarna Letters are in general neither foreigners nor fugitives, but heads of states or citizens of states. When a king of one of the Palestinian petty states calls his neighbor king a *ḫabiru/ḫapiru,* it is certainly not because this other king has left his country to become a *ḫabiru/ḫapiru* but because he is considered by his fellow king to be a public enemy. When we hear that the citizens of a certain city have joined the *ḫabiru/ḫapiru* and given their city over to them, this does not necessarily mean that they themselves have become *ḫabiru* or that they have in a physical sense left their city at the mercy of the *ḫabiru/ḫapiru.* It simply means that the rulers or the citizens of the neighboring city-states look upon them as enemies. That we cannot exclude the second possibility is proven by an Amarna Letter in which even the Egyptian governor residing at Hazor is accused of making alliances with the *ḫabiru/ḫapiru.* On the other hand, although this second hypothesis about the content of the expression in the Amarna Letters certainly limits the amount of actual references to the activities of the *ḫabiru/ḫapiru* people properly speaking, the derogatory use may be considered indirect evidence of the importance of the *ḫabiru/ḫapiru* phenomenon as such. If there had not been a considerable element of these people, the derogatory use of the expression itself would have been meaningless.

Perhaps the Amarna Letters cannot be taken to prove that gangs of *ḫabiru/ḫapiru* as well as *ḫabiru/ḫapiru* fugitives roamed Palestine proper. Their presence is, however, proved by an Egyptian inscription from the end of the 14th century B.C., which mentions an Egyptian campaign against some *ḫabiru/ḫapiru* living in the mountainous area around Beth-shan in Palestine (translation *ANET*, 255; cf. Albright 1952). In the Egyptian sources the *ḫapiru/ḫapiru* from Syria/Palestine are, however, mentioned as early as during the reign of Amenophis II (ca. 1440 B.C.), when they appear alongside the *ḫurri* people (i.e., the settled population of Asia) and the *šasu* nomads in a list counting the prisoners of a Palestinian campaign led by this pharaoh (*ANET,* 247). According to Egyptian documents mentioning the presence of *ḫabiru/ḫapiru* in Egypt proper, they seem to have been employed by the Egyptians as an unskilled labor force, used among other things for work on public building projects.

D. Factors Behind the *ḫabiru/ḫapiru* Movement

Although it is impossible to present a detailed history of the *ḫabiru/ḫapiru*, it should, nevertheless, be possible to delineate some of the conditions which contributed to the development of the phenomenon during the 2d millennium and to indicate some general reasons both for the seemingly increasing importance of the phenomenon especially in the LB Age and for its disappearance at the beginning of the Iron Age.

The etymology of the word is W Semitic and points toward an origin among the W Semitic- or Amorite-speaking population of the ANE, although the phenomenon as such was in no way confined to the areas inhabited by this population. Nor would it be correct to think that the *ḫabiru/ḫapiru* were generally of W Semitic origin. To the contrary, the available evidence shows that a variety of ethnic groups could be listed under this heading in any society of that time, as was the case at Alalakh, where the *ḫabiru/ḫapiru* groups encompassed foreigners bearing W Semitic as well as Ḫurrian names. Accordingly, the expression must already at an early date have been separated from any specific ethnic background and become a purely social designation. Since the *ḫabiru/ḫapiru* whose names are preserved in the source material are always considered foreigners in the societies where they lived and where they were excluded from normal civil rights, they were obviously intruders who had arrived from some other parts of the region. Though their presence was noted, their status in the society was invariably low; they were almost slaves, as at Nuzi, or else they were employed by the state as unskilled laborers or ordinary mercenaries. Finally, their affinity to groups of outlaws outside the control of the political centers of that period is evident from the fact that they shared their name or designation with the brigands. Therefore both the *ḫabiru/ḫapiru* living in state societies and *ḫabiru/ḫapiru* living on their own as outlaws must be seen as representatives of one and the same general social phenomenon, that is, they were refugees or fugitives who had left their own country to find a way of survival in other parts of the Near East.

The reasons for this wave of fugitives, which, according to the available sources, seems to have increased in force during the MB and especially the LB, may have varied, and it may be futile to attempt any easy explanation. However, such a factor as debt—resulting in regular debt slavery—may have induced many impoverished peasants of the ancient states to find a living out of reach of the authorities who were going to enslave them as debtors. The actual extent of such conditions which led to the enslavement of presumably a considerable part of (especially) the rural populace may only be surmised. On the other hand, the practice, common in the Old Babylonian period, of issuing at regular intervals royal grants which annulled debt as well as debt slavery and which released mortgages on landed property (see esp. Kraus 1958; Finkelstein 1961), demonstrates that the problem was very real. Such measures, however, may not have continued beyond the period of the Amorite dynasty in Babylonia proper; and edicts of that kind may not have been issued in other places, at least not to the same extent as in Mesopotamia proper (Lemche 1979). The burden of debt may have increased because of the growing centralization of the state administration, especially in the LB, when the so-called "palatinate" type of states developed into a despotic system with ever-diminishing rights of the ordinary population (on this system Liverani 1974 and 1975). It may be an indication of the juridical organization of this type of state that no law codices have survived from those regions of W Asia where, seemingly, the *ḫabiru/ḫapiru* movement grew to unprecedented dimensions in the LB Age, because all juridical power was vested in the centralized state authorities symbolized by the person of the king residing in his palace.

Two additional factors contributed to the development of the *ḫabiru/ḫapiru* movement. First of all, the region was subdivided into numerous petty states which evidently facilitated the possibility of escaping the authorities in one's own state. Second, and more important for the refugees who decided to live as outlaws, was the extent of territories especially suitable for the life of such brigands, that is, territories which could in no way be controlled by the tiny forces of the petty states of the area. Such territories were normally to be found in the mountains or in the steppes between the desert and the cultivated areas (on this see Rowton 1965: 375–87 and 1967; cf. also Rowton 1976). The extent of the movement and the problems which it caused transpire from a series of international treaties trying to regulate the traffic of the refugees by impeding their freedom in states other than their own. The reciprocity of the extradition of the *ḫabiru/ḫapiru* between states testifies to a deeply felt concern because of the movement of the refugees. The acme of these endeavours on the part of the communities is the paragraphs included in the great international treaty between Egypt and Ḫatti at the beginning of the 13th century B.C. (*ANET,* 199–203; cf. Liverani 1965).

Irrespective of whether this sketch of the development of the *ḫabiru/ḫapiru* movement is true or not, the movement lost its impetus after the breakdown of the palatinate system at the end of the LB; and although the problem of refugees and fugitives has always been endemic to the Near East, the *ḫabiru/ḫapiru* disappeared. One may only guess at the specific reasons, but the possibility exists that the ideological foundation of the new states which arose during the Iron Age, not least in W Asia, promoted a better understanding of social responsibility among the leading class, since many of the states were founded on the basis of former tribal societies. It may be that the egalitarian ideology of these tribal societies lived on, although it cannot be assumed that debt slavery disappeared in the Iron Age. To the contrary, debt slavery was very much in evidence; but it was perhaps softened by an ideology which proclaimed brotherhood among all members of the new states (on the egalitarianism of the Iron Age using Israel as an example see Gottwald 1979; cf., however, also Lemche 1985: 202–44, including criticisms of Gottwald for not distinguishing between ideology and real life).

In conclusion it must be maintained that after 1000 B.C. no reference to the activities of the *ḫabiru/ḫapiru* is known. References to *ḫabiru* in later sources are literary reflections of the past.

Bibliography

Albright, W. F. 1952. The Smaller Beth-Shan Stela of Sethos I (1309–1290 B.C.). *BASOR* 125: 24–32.

Borger, R. 1958. Das Problem der ʿapīru ("Ḫabiru"). *ZDPV* 74: 121–32.

Bottéro, J. 1954. *Le problème des Ḫabiru à la 4e rencontre assyriologique internationale.* Cahiers de la Société asiatique 12. Paris.
———. 1980. Entre nomades et sédentaires: Les Ḫabiru. *Dialogues d'histoire ancienne* 6: 201–13.
Buccellati, G. 1977. *ʿapirū* and *Munnabtūtu*—the Stateless of the First Cosmopolitan Age. *JNES* 36: 145–47.
Finkelstein, J. J. 1961. Ammiṣaduqa's Edict and the Babylonian "Law Codes". *JCS* 15: 91–104.
Gottwald, N. K. 1979. *The Tribes of Yahweh.* Maryknoll, NY.
Greenberg, M. 1955. *The Ḫab/piru.* AOS 39. New Haven.
Kraus, F. R. 1958. *Ein Edikt des Königs Ammi-Ṣaduqa von Babylon.* Studia et Documenta ad Iura Orientis Antiqui Pertinentia 5. Leiden.
Lemche, N. P. 1979. *Andurārum* and *Mīšarum:* Comments on the Problems of Social Edicts and their Application in the ANE. *JNES* 38: 11–22.
———. 1985. *Early Israel: Anthropological and Historical Studies on the Israelite Society Before the Monarchy.* SVT 37. Leiden.
Liverani, M. 1965. Il fuoruscitismo in Siria nella Tarda Etá del Bronzo. *Rivista Storica Italiana* 55: 315–36.
———. 1974. La royauté syrienne de l'âge du bronze récent. Pp. 329–56 in *Le palais et la royauté.* 19e Rencontre assyriologique internationale, ed. P. Garelli. Paris.
———. 1975. Communautés de villages et palais royal dans la Syrie du IIème millénaire. *JESHO* 18: 146–64.
———. 1979. Farsi Ḫabiru. *Vicino Oriente* 2: 65–77.
Loretz, O. 1984. *Habiru-Hebräer. Eine sozio-linguistische Studie über die Herkunft des Gentiliziums ʿibrî vom Appellativum ḫabiru.* BZAW 160. Berlin.
Mendenhall, G. E. 1973. *The Tenth Generation.* Baltimore.
Rowton, M. B. 1965. The Topological Factor in the *ḥapiru* Problem. *AS* 16: 375–87.
———. 1967. The Woodlands of Ancient Western Asia. *JNES* 26: 261–77.
———. 1976. Dimorphic Structure and the Problem of the *ʿapirû-ʿIbrîm. JNES* 35: 13–20.
Spiegelberg, W. 1907. Der Name der Hebräer. *OLZ* 10: 618–20.
Vaux, R. de. 1968. Le problème des Ḫapiru après quinze années. *JNES* 27: 221–28.
Weippert, M. 1971. *The Settlement of the Israelite Tribes.* SBT 2d ser. 21. London.

NIELS PETER LEMCHE

HABOR (PLACE) [Heb *ḥābôr*]. A river along which the Assyrians resettled some of the N Israelites after they had captured Samaria in 721 B.C. (2 Kgs 17:6; 18:11; cf. 1 Chr 5:26). The Habor was a tributary of the Euphrates river, attested in Assyrian sources as *ḫabûr*; today it still retains the name al-Khābûr. The biblical designation of the Habor as "the river of Gozan" was apparently unique to the Israelites. Assyrian documents recovered at Gozan (Akk *Guzana*, modern Tell Halaf on the Khābûr at the Turkish-Syrian border) contain some Israelite personal names which undoubtedly belonged to some of the exiles deported there from Samaria (see Cogan and Tadmor *2 Kings* AB, 197).

The "upper Habor" originates E of the Euphrates in the mountainous region of SE Turkey and flows SE into Syria. This "upper Habor" region (above Al-Hasakah [36°29′N; 40°54′E]) is within the 10-inch rainfall line; the agricultural fertility of this region (as well as its cultural vitality) is attested by the plethora of still-unexcavated mounds. Below Al-Hasakah the Habor flows due S where it joins the Euphrates at Buṣayrah (35°09′N; 40°26′E), about 60 miles upriver from Mari. This "lower Habor" region is within the 4-inch rainfall line, meaning that it was better suited for sustaining pastoral rather than agricultural activities. In the Old Babylonian period (esp. ca. 1900–1700 B.C.) numerous tribal groups considered the steppe-land bounded by the Habor, Balikh, and Euphrates rivers to be their territory. The Benē Sim'al tribes apparently pastured their flocks more along the upper Habor; the Yaminite tribes, which were actually quite wide-ranging, apparently centered their pastoral activities more to the S (along the Balikh and Euphrates rivers); the tribes of Khana (centered around Terqa) seem to have pastured their flocks more along the lower Habor as far SE as Mari (*CAH*³ 2/1: 24–27).

GARY A. HERION

HACALIAH (PERSON) [Heb *ḥăkalyāh*]. The father of Nehemiah (Neh 1:1), Hacaliah is mentioned only here and in Neh 10:2—Eng 10:1. It is often suggested that the name means "Wait for Yahweh," but the use of an imperative form runs counter to the way in which Hebrew proper names are usually formed (Brockington *Ezra, Nehemiah and Esther* NCBC, 124; Cohen *IDB* 2: 507; *TPNAH*, 125–26), and the root *ḥkl* has no attested verbal form in biblical Hebrew (*TPNAH*, 125). Apart from a brief reference to family sepulchers (Neh 2:3, 5), which may suggest a certain measure of wealth or social standing, nothing else is known about Nehemiah's father or his family (Brockington, 124).

FREDERICK W. SCHMIDT

HACHILAH (PLACE) [Heb *ḥăkîlâ*]. A hill in the Judean hill country where David found refuge from Saul (1 Sam 23:19; 26:1) and on which Saul encamped in his pursuit of David (1 Sam 26:3). Located on the hill of Hachilah (1 Sam 23:19) was HORESH, a site in the Wilderness of Ziph (1 Sam 23:15), and its strongholds. While the hill of Hachilah remains unidentified, the association of Horesh with Khirbet Khoreisa (*IDB* 2: 644) perhaps provides a clue. Accounts in the OT locate it "south of Jeshimon" (1 Sam 23:19), "east of Jeshimon" (1 Sam 26:1), and "beside the road on the east of Jeshimon" (1 Sam 26:3).

LAMOINE F. DEVRIES

HACHMONI (PERSON) [Heb *ḥakmônî*]. HACHMONITE. Since this name ends with *î*, which frequently occurs as a formal element indicating a gentilic name, it is possible in both passages in which the name occurs to read either a personal name, "Hachmoni," or a gentilic name, "a Hachmonite."

1. The father or ancestor of Jashobeam, one of David's champions (1 Chr 11:10–47, v 11; = 2 Sam 23:8–39, see v 8, where the variant Tahchemonite occurs). Here the name has generally been read as a gentilic designation with reference to some unidentified place or people: "son of a Hachmonite" or simply, "a Hachmonite" (Noth *IPN*, 232). If "Tahchemonite" is a corruption for "the Hachmonite" (Driver *NHT,* 364), then the form in 2 Samuel also supports reading with the gentilic name. Also, apparently the same Jashobeam, as well as 11 other men from this passage, is mentioned again in 1 Chr 27:2–15, where he is designated as the "son of Zabdiel" (v 2), a name, which formally cannot be other than a personal name. Caution, however, must be exercised before attempting to harmonize these two passages and reaching the conclusion that Jashobeam both was the son of Zabdiel and was a Hachmonite. Differences between the two lists in 1 Chronicles suggest that the composition of neither was dependent upon the other (Williamson *1 and 2 Chronicles* NCBC, 174). Further, there appears to be a convention in these lists of using personal names in the formula "a son of (personal name)" and gentilic references in the formula "the (gentilic name)." Note that the discrepancies to this rule found in the parallel text in 2 Sam 23:8–39 are resolved in Chronicles (see Hebrew texts: 2 Sam 23:11 and 2 Chr 11:27; 23:34 and the possible parallel 11:36; 23:30 and 11:31; 23:36 and 11:38). Also, two other names ending in *i* occur in the Chronicles text in the "son of" formula. The interpretation of the first, "the son of HAGRI" (v 38) may be open to debate; however, the second, "the son of SHIMRI" (v 45), designates a personal name, since the text goes on to mention his brother and give his gentilic reference, "JOHA his brother, the TIZITE." Given this convention, it appears that the author of our text understood Hachmoni to be a personal name for the father or ancestor of Jashobeam.

2. The father or ancestor of Jehiel, an official of the court who served as a counselor or tutor to David's sons (1 Chr 27:32). This name, if derived from *ḥkm,* "to be wise," would have an appropriate symbolic value (i.e., "Jehiel the son of 'the wise one' ") and raises the issue of the name being an artificial construction. Again, although it is possible to read this phrase as "son of a Hachmonite," the author appears to have followed the convention mentioned above and to have understood Hachmoni to be a personal name.

RODNEY K. DUKE

HADAD (DEITY) [Heb *hădad*]. The ancient Semitic storm god, the deity of rain, lightning (his weapon), and thunder (his voice). "Hadad" perhaps means "thunderer" (cf. Heb *hêdād,* "shout"). His name was Hadad among the Amorites and Arameans, Adad among the Mesopotamians, and Haddu among the Canaanites. He is the god Baal, well-known from the Ras Shamra texts and the OT. Hadad/Haddu was most probably the proper name of Baal ("Baal" means "lord," a word used to designate the deity, as a title for other gods, and in secular contexts). Hadad also was known as Ramman or Rimmon (2 Kgs 5:18).

The name Hadad may have been brought E to Mesopotamia by the Amorites toward the end of the 3d millennium B.C. Among the Mesopotamians Hadad/Adad was revered as the god who gave the life-sustaining rains but feared as the one sending storms causing destruction and loss of life. He was a god of oracles and divination (so, too, at Aleppo in Syria). The Assyrians in particular venerated him also as a war divinity.

Among the W Semites the dominant characterization of Hadad/Haddu, as seen especially in the Ras Shamra texts (and as reflected in the OT), was as the storm god who was the fertility deity par excellence. Baal-Haddu sent the all-important, fertilizing rains; he overcame the dark forces of chaos and death.

This divinity, when he is mentioned in the OT, is never designated as "Hadad" ("Baal" is used), with one possible exception ("Hadad-rimmon" of Zech 12:11). However, "Hadad" does appear as a theophoric element in OT personal names. Since Hadad was the chief deity of the Arameans of Syria, a number of kings from this area had the name Ben-hadad (Aram Bir-hadad), "son of Hadad" (e.g., 1 Kgs 15:18 [cf. the name Tabrimmon, "Rimmon/Ramman is good"]; 2 Kgs 13:3). An Aramean king of Zobah, defeated by David, was named Hadadezer, "Hadad is help" (e.g., 2 Sam 8:3, 5; 10:16, 19; 1 Chr 18:3). A prince of Hamath had the name Hadoram, "Hadad is high/exalted" (1 Chr 18:10; see also Gen 10:27; and 2 Chr 10:18). "Hadad" occurs by itself as a personal name (e.g., 1 Kgs 11:14; 1 Chr 1:30, 46–47, 50–51), which is probably an abbreviation of a compound or sentence name containing "Hadad" as theophoric element.

Concerning iconography, the bull was the symbolic animal of Hadad. The god himself is depicted in certain representations as wearing a headpiece with horns protruding from the front and grasping the thunderbolt.

The worship of Hadad persisted into the Hellenistic era and beyond. Lucian (or Pseudo-Lucian), giving his own eyewitness description of the religion of Hierapolis in his *The Syrian Goddess* (2d century A.D.), identifies "Zeus" as the consort of the Syrian goddess (Atargatis). It is generally agreed that this Zeus is actually Hadad.

See also BAAL (DEITY); HADADRIMMON (DEITY); RIMMON (DEITY); UGARIT (TEXTS AND LITERATURE).

WALTER A. MAIER III

HADAD (PERSON) [Heb *hădad; ḥădad*]. Var. HADAR. In addition to being the name of one of the sons of Ishmael (Heb *ḥădad*), Hadad (Heb *hădad*) is also the personal name of three rulers of Edom, only two of which are attested in the Edomite King List (Gen 36:31–39). Opinions vary as far as the date of the Edomite King List is concerned. Suggestions range from the 11th century B.C. (Weippert 1982: 155), through the 8th to 6th centuries B.C. (Bennett 1983: 16), to the 6th–5th centuries B.C. (Knauf 1985). Scholars tend to agree, however, that the succession scheme of this list is artificial and that, in all likelihood, the rulers listed in it were contemporaries (Bartlett 1972: 27; Weippert 1982: 155).

As a personal name, Hadad is only attested for Edom, ancient S Arabia (*hdd^m* CIS IV 55) and ancient N Arabia (Safaitic and South Safaitic *hdd,* to be vocalized *Hadād, Hudaid,* or *Haddād* according to the Classical Arabic; Knauf 1985: 246). According to these parallels it is not necessary to assume that Hadad is a hypocoristic name containing the name of the Syrian weather god, Hadad, without a predicative element. Certainly, however, Hadad, both as a name of a deity and of a person, conveys the same basic meaning: "The one who smashes."

1. The eighth son of Ishmael (Gen 25:15). The MT

here and in the parallel 1 Chr 1:30 reads *ḥădad*, while other mss read *hdd* and *ḥdr*. See also HADAR (PERSON).

2. The son of Bedad and fifth ruler of the Edomite King List (Gen 36:35f. = 1 Chr 1:46f.). For the name of his father, one may compare *bd* and *bdʾl* in Safaitic and Thamudic, Thamudic *bddt*, and Classical Arabic *Budaid*. This Hadad is said to have defeated Midian in the country of Moab. The historical value of this statement is doubtful; it may derive from an unjustified synchronism with the major judges of Israel in their present order, which made Hadad I contemporary with Gideon (Knauf 1985: 251f.). The name of his "capital" (a village, tower/castle, or encampment?), Avith, may reflect an Arabic **Ghuwaith*. The place is not yet identified (Knauf 1985: 250).

3. The eighth ruler of the Edomite King List (1 Chr 1:50f.). In the Gen 36:39 parallel the RSV translates HADAR, following MT *hădar*. His filiation is not recorded; instead, the name of his wife (Mehetabel) is given. This could indicate that he was a man of no family who owed his status to a marriage into the Edomite nobility. His "capital", Pau (Arabic **Faghw?*), remains unidentified (Knauf 1985: 250).

4. The adversary of Solomon (1 Kgs 11:14–22). The biblical narrative presents a number of problems: it is unclear what kind of "kingly stock" existed in Edom when David conquered the country (that is, probably the N part of what later became the Edomite state); and it is unclear how successful Hadad III was in organizing Edom against its occupation by Israel (Bartlett 1976). There was no "united monarchy" in Edom prior to the end of the 9th century B.C. (Bartlett 1972). That the name of the father of this Hadad remained unrecorded, too, indicates that his lineage was unknown to the biblical author. Remarkably, no name of a ruler of Edom is given in the account of David's subjugation of this country (2 Sam 8:14). It can be doubted, however, that Solomon would be overly concerned about the revolt of Hadad; Israel, at that time, was probably content to control the communication lines to Elath/Ezion Geber on the gulf of Aqaba, and had no interest in a permanent occupation of the Edomite plateau (and probably also lacked the means to do so). The basic outlines of the story of Hadad III, however, need not be questioned. He was a member of the Edomite nobility and fled from the Israelite onslaught to Egypt via Midian (NW Arabia), crossed the gulf of Aqaba and the Sinai peninsula via Pharan (Wâdī Feiran), and found political asylum in Egypt, where he was kept and taken care of as a potential card to play off against Israel when it would suit Egypt. At the same time the Israelite rebel, Jeroboam, was similarly treated by Egypt (1 Kgs 11:40).

Bibliography

Bartlett, J. R. 1972. The Rise and Fall of the Kingdom of Edom. *PEQ* 104: 26–37.

———. 1976. An Adversary against Solomon, Hadad the Edomite. *ZAW* 88: 205–26.

Bennett, C.-M. 1983. Excavations at Buseirah (Biblical Bozrah). Pp. 9–17 in *Midian, Moab and Edom*. Ed. J. F. A. Sawyer and D. J. A. Clines. Sheffield.

Knauf, E. A. 1985. Alter und Herkunft der edomitischen Königsliste Gen 36, 31–39. *ZAW* 97: 245–53.

Lemaire, A. 1988. Hadad l'Édomite ou Hadad l'Araméen? *BN* 43: 14–18.

Weippert, M. 1982. Remarks on the History of Settlement in Southern Jordan during the Early Iron Age. Pp. 153–62 in *Studies in the History and Archaeology of Jordan I*, ed. A. Hadidi. Amman.

ERNST AXEL KNAUF

HADADEZER (PERSON) [Heb *hădadʿezer*]. Aramean king defeated by David as reported in 2 Sam 8:3, 5 (= 1 Chr 18:3, 5); and 10:16 (= 1 Chr 19:16). According to the 2 Samuel 8 passage he was the son of REHOB, king of ZOBAH, located N of Damascus. In the 2 Samuel 10 passage his territory is unnamed. 1 Kgs 11:23 mentions him as king of Zobah from Davidic on through Solomonic times.

The exact location of the territory controlled by Hadadezer is not certain. While 2 Sam 8:3 and 1 Kgs 11:23 designate him as king of Zobah, which is generally located N of Damascus, 2 Sam 10:16 describes him as controlling the Aramean territory "beyond the river (i.e., the Euphrates)" (Malamat 1958), which suggests territory E of the Ammonite range and not N of Syria.

In the unit preceding 2 Sam 10:16 there is mention of Arameans from Beth-rehob and Arameans from Zobah functioning as mercenaries for the Ammonites. Though Hadadezer is not mentioned in this unit while there is in the unit mention of other kings, it would appear that an Aramean Empire controlled Syrian and Mesopotamian territory.

There is also a question as to the number of times Hadadezer and David met in battle. While on the surface the narratives of 2 Sam 8:3–8; 10:6–15, 16–19 suggest three such occasions, there is much disagreement as to whether the references to these battles between David and Hadadezer are to the same or different battles, and if the latter, as to the sequence in which they occurred.

First, the description of the battle in 2 Sam 10:16–19 ends with the claim that the Arameans thereby became subject to David. Since this is also the result of the battle described in 2 Samuel 8, other scholars argue that these are references to the same battle (Wellhausen 1891; Ackroyd 1981; Soggin 1984).

On the other hand, according to the 2 Samuel 8 account Hadadezer and his army are totally defeated and his territory subjugated. In the 2 Samuel 10 account, however, there is no sense that he is leader of a vassal state under Davidic control. Rather the state of affairs appears to be that his territory is independent of any foreign control and that he commands large mercenary troops. Thus the question arises as to how he could be so soundly defeated in chap. 8 and so independent in chap. 10. For this reason some scholars argue that the battle in 2 Samuel 10 must have preceded that in 2 Samuel 8 (Bright *BHI*; McCarter *2 Samuel* AB; Noth *NHI*).

Finally in the 2 Samuel 10 accounts as noted above Hadadezer is not mentioned in the unit which describes the coalition of Arameans hired by the Ammonites to attack David (2 Sam 10:6b–15 [= 1 Chr 19:6–15]). Rather his name appears in a subsequent unit (2 Sam 10:16–19a [= 1 Chr 19:16–19a]), where his army appears to be in battle along with other Arameans against David. Interestingly, there is no mention at all of Ammonites in this unit. This is surprising since the battle described there is used as the basis for an etiology on the break in the military relationship between the Ammonites and Arameans. Thus the question arises as to whether these war stories in chap. 10 relate to a two-stage operation or to totally different wars.

Bibliography

Ackroyd, P. 1981. The Succession Narrative (So-called). *Int* 35: 383–97.

Malamat, A. 1958. The Kingdom of David and Solomon in its Contact with Egypt and Aram Naharaim. *BA* 21: 96–102.

Soggin, J. A. 1984. *A History of Ancient Israel From Beginning to the Bar Kochba Revolt, A.D. 135.* Philadelphia.

Wellhausen, J. 1891. *Sketch of the History of Israel and Judah.* 3d ed. London.

RANDALL C. BAILEY

HADADRIMMON (DEITY) [Heb *hădad-rimmôn*]. The ancient Semitic storm god. Zech 12:11 states that in the future there will be great mourning in Jerusalem, "as great as the mourning for Hadadrimmon in the plain of Megiddo" (RSV). Hadad is the god Baal (well known from the Ras Shamra texts and the OT), "Hadad" probably being the proper name (perhaps meaning "thunderer") of Baal ("lord"). "Rimmon" is an epithet of Hadad (Adad in Mesopotamia); the Akk form is Ram(m)an. It has been suggested that Heb Rimmon *(rimmôn),* which is identical to the Heb word for "pomegranate," is a deliberate mispointing of an original Ram(m)an, *ram(m)ān* (or something similar), to disparage the deity. This epithet Rimmon/Ramman is best understood as "thunderer" (cf. Akk *ramāmu,* "to roar," hence, "to thunder"). Accordingly, the name Hadadrimmon means "Hadad is Rimmon" or "Hadad is the thunderer." Hadad, or Rimmon/Ramman, was the chief deity of the Arameans of Syria, and his worship there is mentioned in 2 Kgs 5:18 (cf. the name Tabrimmon, "Rimmon/Ramman is good," in 1 Kgs 15:18).

Concerning the mourning referred to in Zech 12:11, there are two main positions seen in the scholarly literature (for other interpretations of the passage, see the summaries of Baldwin *Haggai, Zechariah, Malachi* TOTC, 192–93 and Smith *Micah–Malachi* WBC, 278–79). The first, and older position, is that the verse should be translated, "the mourning *of* Hadadrimmon," Hadadrimmon being regarded as a village or town (named after the deity) in the plain of Megiddo. Reference is made to Jerome, who said that this Hadadrimmon was a town called in his day Maximianopolis, SE of Megiddo, close to Jezreel and Taanach (and later identified by some scholars with a village named Rummaneh). The lamentation "of Hadadrimmon," which took place in the village and/or throughout Judah, was, it is explained, for the good king Josiah (see 2 Chr 35:20–25, esp. v 25), because Hadadrimmon was the location either of Josiah's being mortally wounded or of his death. However, that this village actually existed is uncertain; that it was the spot of Josiah's being wounded by the archers is even more questionable. As to where the king died, 2 Chr 35:24 indicates he expired in Jerusalem (cf. 2 Kgs 23:29–30, to be understood as saying "Neco" fatally wounded Josiah, who was brought "dying" from Megiddo to Jerusalem?).

The second main position, preferable to the first, is that Zech 12:11 speaks about mourning rites for the deity Hadadrimmon. Devotees of the god believed that it was he who sent the rains necessary for abundant crops and the preservation of life. Conceivably this mourning took place at times of drought, when rain from Hadad would be sorely missed. Comparison can be made to the Baal cycle in the Ugaritic literature, which describes the mourning of El (the head of the pantheon) and Anath (Baal's consort) when Baal dies (later Baal revives), and a subsequent struggle between Baal and Death, which neither combatant wins. One should also note Ezek 8:14, which depicts annual, ritual mourning for the Mesopotamian fertility deity Tammuz (Dumuzi). Lamentation for Hadadrimmon is mentioned in Zech 12:11 as a point of comparison since it would have been a (or the) striking example from the ANE milieu of bitter mourning shared by many people. This grief would have been particularly intense in the broad, fertile plain of Megiddo, a choice agricultural area. See also BAAL (DEITY); HADAD (DEITY); RIMMON (DEITY); UGARIT (TEXTS AND LITERATURE).

WALTER A. MAIER III

HADAR (PERSON) [Heb *hădar*]. Var. HADAD. A masculine name found in the OT.

1. The eighth ruler listed on the Edomite King List (Gen 36:39). In the 1 Chr 1:50–51 parallel the MT reads *hădad.* See HADAD (PERSON).

2. The Syriac version and the Bomberg (Venice) edition (1524–25), followed by the KJV, read *ḥădar* as the name of the eighth son of Ishmael in Gen 25:15. The RSV here and the 1 Chr 1:30 parallel read Hadad. He is said to have dwelt with his brothers in the region from Havilah to Shur, in the area of the Sinai and NW coast of Arabia. The names of six of these brothers are mentioned in Assyrian inscriptions from the 8th and 7th centuries B.C.E., but Hadar is one of four names which do not appear elsewhere.

VICTOR H. MATTHEWS

HADASHAH (PLACE) [Heb *ḥădāšâ*]. Town situated in the Shephelah, or lowland, of Judah (Josh 15:37), within the same district as Lachish. This settlement, the name of which perhaps means "new town," is listed among the towns within the tribal allotment of Judah (Josh 15:21–62). It may be the same place as Adasa, which 1 Macc 7:40–45 identifies as the location of the victory of Judas Maccabeus over Nicanor. Although a general location somewhere between Lachish and Gath is called for by the context, no suitable candidate for the ancient town has been identified.

WADE R. KOTTER

HADASSAH (PERSON) [Heb *hădassâ*]. The name given to Esther when she is first introduced by the narrator of the book of Esther (2:7). He tells us that Mordecai, a Jew resident in Susa, was "raising Hadassah, that is Esther, his (i.e., Mordecai's) niece." The most natural understanding of this appositive construction is that her given name was Hadassah, but she subsequently became more commonly known by the name Esther. In this interpretation Hadassah would be her Hebrew name (the view adopted by the Targum, see Paton *Esther* ICC, 170; Moore *Esther* AB, 20), belonging to that class of male and female names in the OT drawn from the names of plants. "Hadassah" would be the feminine form of *hădas,* "myrtle" (cf. Isa 49:19; 55:13; Neh 8:15; see Noth *IPN*, 230–31). An earlier view held that the book of Esther was historicized Babylonian mythology in which "Esther" is Ishtar, the Babylonian goddess of love; and hence "Hadassah" was the Hebrew form of Akk *ḫadaššatu,* "bride," an epithet of Ishtar (Jensen 1892: 209; cf. Paton, 88). Such an etymology is belied not only by the fact that this view of the book is today given no credence, but also by the fact that it is highly improbable that Akk *ḫ* would be rendered by Heb *h*, i.e., Akk *ḫădaššatu* would appear in Hebrew as *ḥădassâ* (with *ḥet*), not *hădassāh* (with *he*).

Bibliography

Jensen, P. 1892. Elamitische Eigennamen: Ein Beitrag zur Erklärung der elamitischen Inschriften. *WZKM* 6: 47–70, 209–26.

FREDERIC W. BUSH

HADES, HELL. The Greek word Hades *(hądēs)* is sometimes, but misleadingly, translated "hell" in English versions of the NT. It refers to the place of the dead but not necessarily to a place of torment for the wicked dead. In Greek religious thought Hades was the god of the underworld; but more commonly the term referred to his realm, the underworld, where the shades or the souls of the dead led a shadowy existence, hardly conscious and without memory of their former life. In early times it seems Hades was usually conceived as a place of sadness and gloom (but not punishment) indiscriminately for all the dead. However, as early as Homer the notion existed that some individuals experienced endless punishment in Hades, and later, especially through the influence of Orphic-Pythagorean ideas, belief in postmortem rewards and punishments in Hades became common. While Greek ideas about the afterlife probably did not influence the origins of Jewish expectations of retribution after death, later Jewish writers sometimes incorporated particular terms and concepts from the Greek and Roman Hades into their own pictures of the afterlife.

The old Hebrew concept of the place of the dead, most often called Sheol *(šĕʾôl)* in the Hebrew Bible, corresponded quite closely to the Greek Hades. Both were versions of the common ancient view of the underworld. Like the old Greek Hades, Sheol in the Hebrew Bible is the common fate of all the dead, a place of darkness and gloom, where the shades lead an unenviable, fading existence. In the LXX therefore Sheol is usually translated as Hades, and the Greek term was naturally and commonly used by Jews writing in Greek. This Jewish usage explains the ten NT occurrences of the word *Hades.*

The rise of Jewish belief in resurrection and eternal life had a significant impact on ideas about Sheol/Hades. Resurrection was understood as God's eschatological act of bringing the dead from Hades back to life. Probably the earliest, simplest idea was that the shades will return from Hades to bodily life. Sometimes they were expected to be raised as spirits to dwell with the angels in heaven. According to a more dichotomous view of human nature, the soul will be brought from Hades, the body raised from the grave, and body and soul reunited in resurrection. Whichever view of resurrection was adopted, Hades became the *temporary* abode of the dead, between death and the general resurrection at the end of the age; but there was not *necessarily* any other change in the understanding of Hades.

In most early Jewish literature Hades or Sheol remains the place to which all the dead go (2 Macc 6:23; *1 En.* 102:5; 103:7; *Sib. Or.* 1:81–84; *Ps.-Phoc.* 112–113; *2 Bar.* 23:4; *T. Ab.* A 8:9; 19:7) and is very nearly synonymous with death (Wis 1:12–16; 16:13; *Pss. Sol.* 16:2; Rev 6:8; 20:13), as well as actually synonymous with other OT terms for the place of the dead ("the earth," "the dust," Abaddon: *1 En.* 51:3; Ezra 7:32; *Ps.-Philo* 3:10; *2 Bar.* 42:8; 50:2). At the resurrection Hades will return what has been entrusted to it (*1 En.* 51:3; 4 Ezra 4:42; 7:32; *2 Bar.* 42:8; 50:2; *Ps.-Philo* 3:10; 33:3; cf. Rev 20:13)—a notion which expresses God's sovereignty over Hades (cf. 1 Sam 2:6; Tob 13:2; Wis 16:13). The dead have been temporarily entrusted by God to the safekeeping of Hades; at the resurrection he will demand them back. Thereafter death will no longer happen, and so the mouth of Hades will be sealed so that it can no longer receive the dead (*2 Bar.* 21:23; *Ps.-Philo* 33:3), or, in an alternative image, Death and Hades will be thrown into the lake of fire (Rev 20:14). Thus Hades retains its close association with death and is not confused with the place of eternal torment for the wicked after the day of judgment, which was usually known as Gehenna. Even when Hades is portrayed as the fate for which the wicked are heading, in contrast to the eternal life to which the righteous are destined, the traditional characteristics of the place of the dead—darkness and destruction—are often in mind (*Pss. Sol.* 14:9–10; 15:10, 13; 16:2; *Jub.* 7:29; 22:22).

However, the picture of Hades was affected by the expectation of resurrection and eternal destiny in a further way. The notion of resurrection was connected with that of the judgment of the dead. At the day of judgment, the righteous will receive the reward of eternal life and the wicked the judgment of eternal destruction or eternal torment. This ultimate distinction between the righteous and the wicked was often held to be anticipated during the temporary abode of the dead in Hades. The earliest example is *1 Enoch* 22, where Enoch is shown four "hollow places" in which four different classes of the dead are kept until the day of judgment. The early character of this concept is shown by the fact that one of the two classes of the wicked, those who have already been punished for their sins in this life, will apparently be neither rewarded nor punished on the day of judgment, whereas sinners who have not been punished in this life will then receive their judgment. But for all classes Hades is essentially a place of waiting for judgment: the righteous are refreshed with a spring of water while they await the joys of paradise, but the wicked are not said to be punished. They are simply held in detention awaiting trial and condemnation.

In later conceptions the classes of the dead are reduced to two. The places where they wait came to be called the chambers or treasuries of the souls (*Ps.-Philo* 32:13; *2 Bar.* 21:33; 30:1; 4 Ezra 4:35, 41; 7:32, 80, 85, 95, 101, 121; cf. *Ps.-Philo* 15:5: "chambers of darkness" for the wicked; *Ps.-Philo* 21:9: "the secret dwelling places of souls"; the terminology of chambers may derive from Isa 26:20; cf. *1 Clem.* 50:3).

In the extended account of the intermediate state in 4 Ezra 7:75–101, it is explained that after death the souls of the dead have seven days of freedom, during which they see the rewards awaiting the righteous and the torments awaiting the wicked. The wicked are therefore sad in anticipation, and the righteous rejoice in anticipation of the destiny awaiting them, but the rewards and punishments themselves are reserved for the last day. After the seven days the righteous enter their chambers, where they rest in quietness, guarded by angels (7:85, 95). In this account the wicked do not have chambers at all but continue to wander around in tormented awareness of their doom (7:80, 93).

The idea that the eternal punishment of the wicked has already begun in Hades, even before the last judgment, begins to be found occasionally in Jewish literature of the NT period. In this case Hades sometimes becomes the scene not only of darkness and gloom, but also of fire (cf. Sir 21:9–10), which had traditionally been reserved for the torment of the wicked in Gehenna after the last judgment. (*1 En.* 63:10 seems to be an exceptional case where Sheol itself is the scene of final punishment in fire after the last judgment; cf. perhaps 103:7–8.) Thus in the surviving fragments of *Jannes and Jambres* we seem to have the first instance of the many stories (later popular in Christianity) in which someone is brought back temporarily from Hades in order to warn the living of the fate of the wicked (it is this possibility which is requested and refused in Luke 16:27–31). The Egyptian magician Jannes explains to his brother that he is being punished in the fires of the underworld. In the *Apocalypse of Zephaniah* Hades is equated with the abyss (6:15; 7:9; 9:2), and the seer sees in it the sea of fire and other forms of punishment for the wicked (6:1–2; 10:3–14). (However, neither of these works is certainly of pre-Christian Jewish origin.) Josephus claims that the Pharisees believed there are post-mortem rewards and punishments "under the earth" (*Ant* 18.14).

In a final development Hades sometimes becomes exclusively the place of punishment for the wicked, while the righteous go at death to paradise or heaven. This may be the case in the *Apoc. Zeph.* However, we should not expect too much consistency in eschatological concepts. Older images often survive alongside later developments. Thus the *Testament of Abraham* (Recension A) clearly refers to Hades as the fate of all the dead (8:9; 19:7); but it is not easy to reconcile this with its account of the separation of the souls, who at death go through two distinct gates, one leading to eternal punishment and the other to paradise (11), which is located in heaven (20:12, 14). In Jesus' story of the rich man and Lazarus (Luke 16:19–31), which reflects popular conceptions of the afterlife, it seems that only the rich man goes to Hades (though this is not entirely clear), where he is tormented in fire, while Lazarus goes to "Abraham's bosom" in paradise (cf. *T. Ab.* A 20:14). The two locations are within sight of each other (cf. 4 Ezra 7:85, 93); but this need not imply that both are in the underworld, since even after the last judgment paradise and Gehenna are said to be within sight of each other (4 Ezra 7:36–38; *1 En.* 108:14–15; *Apoc. El.* 5:27–28).

Other NT references to Hades also reflect Jewish usage. In Acts 2:27, 31, which directly reflect OT usage, Hades is the abode of all the dead before the resurrection. Also directly dependent on OT usage is Matt 11:23 = Luke 10:15 (cf. Isa 14:13–15). The image in Rev 20:18 is a traditional apocalyptic one (*1 En.* 51:3; *4 Ezra* 4:42; 7:32; *2 Bar.* 42:8; 50:2; *Ps.-Philo* 3:10; 33:3), while the personification of Hades, along with death, there and in Rev 6:8, derives from OT usage continued by later writers (for death and Sheol both personified, see Ps 49:14; Isa 28:15; Hos 13:14).

The gates of Hades (Matt 16:18) are traditional. Both the Babylonian Underworld and the Greek Hades had gates, but the image more immediately reflects the OT (Isa 38:10; cf. "gates of death" in Job 38:17; Pss 9:14; 107:18) and later Jewish writings (Wis 16:13; *3 Macc.* 5:51; *Pss. Sol.* 16:2; cf. *Ap. Pet.* 4:3). The gates of Hades keep the dead imprisoned in its realm. Only God can open them (cf. Wis 16:13; *Ap. Pet.* 4:3, which probably reflects a Jewish description of resurrection; Ps 107:16 may have been interpreted in this way). Whatever the precise meaning of Matt 16:18, its reference must be not to the powers of evil, but to the power of Hades to hold the dead in death. A related image is that of the keys of Hades (Rev 1:18), which open its gates (cf. *2 En.* 42:1): the risen Christ, victorious over death, has acquired the divine power to release from the realm of death (cf. also *b. Sanh.* 113a). For bibliography see DESCENT TO THE UNDERWORLD.

RICHARD BAUCKHAM

HADID (PLACE) [Heb *ḥādîd*]. Town in the territory of Benjamin. Scholars maintain that Hadid is already mentioned in the Thutmose III town list, no. 76 *"h(u)dit(i)i" (h-d-t),* after a place in the Shephelah and before a place in the Sharon. Hadid is also mentioned as one of a cluster of towns, the two others of which are Lod (Lydda) and Ono, to which the Babylonian exiles returned (Ezra 2:33; Neh 7:37; 11:34). From this text one may infer that Hadid was settled during the First Temple period, in the time when the tribe of Benjamin expanded W, perhaps during the reign of Josiah. See also Alt 1925: 11–15.

Hadid had strategic significance during the Hasmonean period, after Jonathan had fortified Jerusalem. Simeon, who encamped near Hadid, had fortified the town and installed gates during the Trypho's campaign (1 Macc 12:38; 13:13). In a clash near Hadid, Alexander Jannaeus was defeated by the Nabatean king, Aretas III, who invaded Judea (*Ant* 13.392). Later Vespasian conquered it and built a camp there (*JW* 4.486). According to the Mishnah, Hadid was among the cities surrounded by walls since the times of Joshua (*m. ʿArak.* 9:6). See also Abel 1926, 35: 218; Boree 1930: 29.

Josephus describes the city as being situated on a mountain overlooking the plains of Judea (*Ant* 13.203). Eusebius locates it E of Lydda (*Onomast.* 24:24; see also Beyer 1933:

233). It also appears on the Madeba Map (no. 59; Yeivin 1954: 149) and is mentioned by the Jewish traveler Astori Haparchi ca. 1322. The city is identified with a mound named al-Haditha, 6 km E of Lod. Archaeological surveys there yielded sherds of pottery dating from the LB and Iron Ages (Alt 1928: 71). A mosaic pavement with Nilotic scenes, dating from the 6th century C.E., was discovered there in 1940. See also Noth *Joshua* HAT, 93; *Historical Encyl. of Palestine* 2: 248 (in Hebrew).

Bibliography

Abel, F. M. 1923–26. Topographie des campagnes Machabéennes. *RB* 32: 485–521; 33: 210–17; 34: 194–216; 35: 206–22.
Alt, A. 1925. Judas Gaue unter Josia. *PJ* 21: 100–117.
———. 1928. Das Institut im Jahre 1927. *PJ* 24: 5–74.
Avi-Yonah, M. 1953. The Madeba Mosaic Map. *EI* 2: 129–56.
Beyer, G. 1933. Die Stadtgebiete von Diospolis und Nikopolis im 4. Jahrh. n. Chr. und ihre Grenznachbarn. *ZDPV* 56: 218–53.
Boree, W. 1930. *Die alten Ortsnamen Palaestinas.* Leipzig.
Yeivin, S. 1954. The Short List of the Towns in Palestine and Syria Captured by Thutmosis III during His First Campaign. *EI* 3: 32–38 (in Hebrew).

RAMI ARAV

HADLAI (PERSON) [Heb *ḥadlāy*]. The father of Amasa, one of the leaders of the tribe of Ephraim during the time of Pekah, ruler of the N kingdom, Israel (2 Chr 28:12). This patronymic could also refer to the extended family of Hadlai, rather than to the biological father of Amasa. The name belongs to a class of nontheological Semitic personal names having to do with the body (Noth *IPN*, 226). The precise determination of the meaning of the name is an illustration of the history of the Hebrew language. There are two meanings to the Heb root *ḥdl*, either "to stop," "forbear" or "to be fat," "successful" (*HALAT*, 280–81). The lack of a close semantic connection between the two meanings may be explained by the fact that the earliest form of the Semitic language from which Hebrew later developed had two closely related consonants, the voiceless, fricative, pharyngeal *ḥ* and the voiceless, fricative, velar *ḫ*. Hebrew used the one letter *ḥet* to represent both sounds (Moscati et al. 1969: 38, 41). Thus there are two roots represented with two separate meanings; and, according to Kutscher (1984: 18), they were pronounced by the ancient Hebrews differently from each other. Of the two choices Hadlai probably means "fat one" *(ḫdl)* rather than "forbearer" *(ḥdl)*, since fat is also used metaphorically in Hebrew to mean "successful" and a personal name is most likely to be complimentary or hopeful.

Bibliography

Calderone, P. J. 1961. HDL-II in Poetic Texts. *CBQ* 23:451–60.
Kutscher, E. Y. 1984. *A History of the Hebrew Language.* Ed. R. Kutscher. Jerusalem.
Moscati, S.; Spitaler, A.; Ullendorff, E.; and Soden, W. von. 1969. *An Introduction to the Comparative Grammar of the Semitic Languages.* Porta Linguarum Orientalium. n.s. 6. Wiesbaden.
Thomas, D. W. 1957. Some Observations on the Hebrew Root *ḥdl.* Pp. 8–16 in *Volume du Congrès, Strassbourg 1956.* VTSup 4. Leiden.

KIRK E. LOWERY

HADORAM (PERSON) [Heb *hădôrām; hădorām*]. **1.** A son of Joktan (Gen 10:27; 1 Chr 1:21) and hence the name of a S Arabian locality or of the tribe residing in it. E. Glaser (1980: 434) juxtaposed the biblical *hădôrām* and Yemenite *Dauram.* Epigraphically *dwrm* is attested in two Old Sabean inscriptions, RES 3945,15 from Ṣirwāḥ and CIS IV 603b,12 from Našq in the Jauf. In the first text it is listed along with several towns which the Sabean king Karibʾil Watar (probably in the 7th century B.C.) incorporated into his realm. The context of the other places mentioned in both inscriptions suggests that *dwrm* is to be identified with *Dauram* at the upper part of the Wâdī Ḍahr about 16 km NW of Ṣanʿāʾ. Probably because of its strategically important location, al-Hamdānī in the 10th century A.D. refers to *Dauram* as a pre-Islamic fortress of the Wâdī Ḍahr (1979: 123). The ruins of the ancient town are situated on the flat-topped mountain Ṭayba bordering on the SW part of the fertile valley, which still bears the name *Dauram* today. A clan name *(ḏ)dwrm*, which could be read *(Ḏū-) Dauram*, i.e., "(he of) *Dauram*," is attested in two votive inscriptions which are kept in the Museum of Aden (AM 840 = NAM 418,2; AM 343,1.3); both inscriptions had been dedicated to the Sabean god Almaqah in two different temples in the region of the oasis of Mārib. The reason why the name *Dôrām* is not attested in the biblical text, as one might expect, assuming that *Dauram* and *hădôrām* are to be identified, may be that the Arabian name was adapted to the NW Semitic name *hădôrām* borne by two different persons in the OT (see #2 and #3 below). The identification of *hădôrām* with the *Ahl al-Hadara*, a designation used by the inhabitants of Oman for certain bedouin tribes, was proposed by B. Thomas (1932: 48) and was taken over by Koehler-Baumgartner (*HALAT*, 229). This equation is, however, unacceptable, because the correct form is *Ahl al-Ḥadara* with the literal meaning "tribes of the down country." Likewise to be rejected because of the inaccurate correspondence of the consonants is the identification of biblical *hădôrām* with the tribe of the *Ḥaḍūr* (A. von Kremer 1866: 25), whose name survives in the *miḫlāf Ḥaḍūr* to the W of Ṣanʿāʾ.

Bibliography

al-Hamdānī. 1979. *al-Iklīl.* Vol. 8. Ed. M. al-Alwaʿ. Damascus.
Glaser, E. 1980. *Skizze der Geschichte und Geographie Arabiens.* Vol. 2. Berlin.
Kremer, A. von. 1866. *Über die südarabische Lage.* Leipzig.
Thomas, B. 1932. *Arabia Felix.* London.

W. W. MÜLLER
Trans. Phillip R. Callaway

2. Son of Tou, king of Hamath, who was sent by Tou with gifts to thank King David for defeating their mutual adversary Hadadezer (1 Chr 18:9–10; MT *hădôrām*; LXX *hidouraam*). The Israelite form of the name, Joram (Heb *yôrām*; an abbreviated form of "Jehoram"), is used in the parallel account (2 Sam 8:9–10; note LXX reads *ieddouran* here, and *Ant* 7.5.4 reads *adōramon*), replacing the theophoric element Hadad ("Hadad is exalted") with Jehu ("Yahweh is exalted"). According to Malamat (1963: 6–7) this is a second (diplomatic?) name taken by Hadoram and reflects Israel's influence in Hamath, which had been at least geographically part of the Hittite Empire (see also

Malamat 1958: 101; McCarter *2 Samuel* AB, 244, 250). Thus, rather than assuming there is a textual corruption and emending Joram to Hadoram in 2 Sam 8:10, both names can be considered authentic references to the son of Tou.

3. The taskmaster under Rehoboam who was stoned to death by the enraged Israelites, who heard Rehoboam vow to increase their burden of forced labor (2 Chr 10:18; MT *hădōrām*; LXX *adōniram*; but Codex Alexandrinus reads *adōram*; *Ant* 8.8.3 reads *adōramos*). Various spellings of the name create some confusion about the identity of Hadoram. The parallel account spells his name Adoram (1 Kgs 12:18; MT *ʾădōrām*; LXX *adōniram*; but Codex Vaticanus reads *aram*). The person responsible for forced labor under Solomon was named Adoniram, the son of Abda (1 Kgs 4:6; 5:28—Eng 5:14; MT *ʾădōnîrām*; LXX *adōniram*), and previously under David was named Adoram (2 Sam 20:24; MT *ʾădōrām*; LXX *adōniram*). It is reasonable to assume that the person in charge of forced labor could have remained in office from the time of David until the beginning of the reign of Rehoboam. Based on the shared office and similar spellings of their names, Hadoram can be identified with Adoniram and Adoram, as the LXX already did by standardizing the spelling to Adoniram. His brutal death stands as a symbol of the break between the N (Israel) and the S (Judah), and foreshadows the turmoil yet to come in their history.

Bibliography

Malamat, A. 1958. The Kingdom of David and Solomon in its Contact with Egypt and Aram Naharaim. *BA* 21: 96–102.

———. 1963. Aspects of the Foreign Policies of David and Solomon. *JNES* 22: 1–17.

Mark J. Fretz

HADRACH (PLACE) [Heb *hadrāk*]. A place, probably an Aramean city-state, located in N Syria on the Orontes river S of Hamath and N of Damascus. The city may be identified with the present day Tell Āfis, located about 20 miles (45 km) SW of Aleppo. It is mentioned only once by Zechariah along with Damascus and Hamath in connection with a prophecy concerning "the cities of Aram" (Zech 9:1), which were enemies of Israel. In 1908 the stele of Zakir, king of Hamath and Luʿash (ca. 800 B.C.), was discovered here. Zakir had withstood a siege of Hadrach by an Aramean coalition led by Ben-hadad III. Tiglath-pileser III named Hadrach in his annals as one of the "19 districts of Hamath" that had allied to support Azariah of Judah (742 B.C.) and was later made an Assyrian province. Zech 9:1–6 may be the record of an unsuccessful revolt by Hadrach against Sargon II (720 B.C.).

Ray L. Roth

HADRIAN (EMPEROR). Hadrian, who became emperor on 11 August 117, was born in Rome of a family whose ancestors, originally Italian colonists, had long been resident at Italica (near Seville) in Spain. After his father's death in 85, he was brought to Rome under the guardianship of the future emperor Trajan (to whom he was related) and the future praetorian prefect Attianus. The link with Trajan was further strengthened in 100 when he married Vibia Sabina, also an imperial relative. His official career began late in Domitian's reign with military service in Germany and Moesia and progressed rapidly once Trajan became emperor. He took part in the first Dacian War, commanded a legion (*I Minervia*) in the second, governed Pannonia in 107, became consul in 108 (when only 32), held a number of priesthoods, and, toward the end of the reign, was appointed governor of Syria. At the time of Trajan's death, Hadrian was designated to his second consulship, which he held in 118. His support in the imperial court was widespread, but not universal; and while his popularity with Trajan (and especially with his wife Plotina) is well attested, neither he nor anyone else received any of the honors usually granted to heirs apparent. However, on the day after Trajan's death at Selinus in Cilicia (8 August 117), a letter of adoption, allegedly written by Trajan, reached Hadrian at Antioch, followed on the eleventh by the news of Trajan's death. The same day, the troops proclaimed him emperor.

Despite the controversial circumstances surrounding his accession, the Senate immediately voted him the usual imperial powers; but he never managed to establish a successful relationship with that body, mainly because of the initial decision (which may not have been his) to execute four of Trajan's leading generals. They were accused of planning Hadrian's assassination, found guilty, and promptly executed. Possibly they had opposed his decision to abandon some of Trajan's E conquests. But the damage was done; and, when he reached Rome, he had to strive to attain some degree of popularity: he was obliged to dismiss Attianus, now prefect (responsibility for the executions was assigned to him); to distribute largess to the people on three occasions by January 119; to cancel debts; and to provide expensive gladiatorial displays. Yet his efforts were not without success. Throughout his reign of 21 years, he was away from Rome for about 12 (121–125; 128–134); and no serious attempts were made to take advantage of these absences. On the other hand, he was never popular with the Senate.

He worked hard. For him it was an emperor's duty to familiarize himself with the entire empire. So "he personally viewed and investigated absolutely everything" (Dio Cass. 69.9.1). He visited armies everywhere, drilled the soldiers himself, lived as they did (Dio Cass. 69.9.3), and even published an assessment of their efficiency (*CIL* VIII 2532, 18042: N Africa, July 128). But he did not limit himself to military matters; for he seems to have regarded it as his responsibility to become aware of a province's problems, to inspect its administration, to attend official and religious festivals—and, as well, to indulge in hunting and sight-seeing. The emperor was no longer a remote or vague figure.

Hadrian withdrew from some of the newly acquired provinces (e.g., those beyond the Euphrates) and consolidated Rome's gains in others (e.g., Dacia). Almost certainly his reasons were economic. He sought prosperity and security for the empire through a policy that was essentially defensive; and, in the main, he was successful, though there were uprisings on the lower Danube, in Britain, in Mauretania, and in Judea. But the most outstanding example of his policy, without parallel in Roman times, was seen in Britain, where, on the Tyne-Solway line to which Trajan had already withdrawn, Hadrian erected a massive wall some 70 miles long, more than half of it in stone. It was at least 15 feet high and 7.5 feet thick, with a deep ditch in front and substantial earthworks behind. As well, there were 16 garrison forts, a fortlet every mile, and a turret every third of a mile. Consistent with this was the considerably less expensive timber barrier linking the Rhine and the Danube.

He had least success in dealing with the Jews. Severe riots had occurred in Jewish areas throughout the east toward the end of Trajan's reign (Dio Cass. 68.32.1–2), and they continued under Hadrian until 119 (*Annee Epigraphique* 1928, Nos. 1 and 2). Later his insistence on having a shrine in Jerusalem dedicated to Jupiter Capitolinus and built on the site of the temple resulted in the revolt of 132–135, led by Bar Kokhba and ruthlessly suppressed by Hadrian (Dio Cass. 69.12.1–14.3). As a consequence, "From that time on, the entire race has been forbidden to set foot anywhere in the neighborhood of Jerusalem" (Eutropius *Historia Ecclesiastica* 4.6). His policy toward Christianity was, like Trajan's, one of toleration, as is evident from his much-discussed letter in 122/123 to the proconsul of Asia, Minicius Fundanus: Christians would be punished only "if someone prosecutes them and proves them guilty of any illegality" (Eutropius *Historia Ecclesiastica* 4.9).

In administration his aim was consolidation and centralization rather than innovation, as has sometimes been argued. Leading bureaucrats were now almost always equestrians and not freedmen. Attempts were made to improve control of the empire's finances, but whether they were introduced by Hadrian or Trajan is uncertain; and similarly with the development of a pay and career structure for equestrian officials. Again, legal reforms were introduced, soldiers' conditions improved, and their weapons standardized. In essence he tried to systematize existing practices rather than introduce new ones.

Hadrian was enlightened and intelligent, taking an active part in the empire's literary and cultural life. His architectural achievements included the villa at Tivoli, the mausoleum in Rome, and the rebuilding of the Pantheon. He was, nonetheless, an autocrat; and in 136, he executed his only relatives, his 90-year-old brother-in-law, Julius Ursus Servianus, and his grandson Pedanius Fuscus Salinator, then adopted one of the consuls for 136, Ceionius Commodus, who took the name L. Aelius Caesar. But when he died on 31 December 137, Hadrian chose another senator, Aurelius Fulvus (later the emperor Antoninus Pius), who was required to adopt both Aelius' son (later the emperor Commodus) and the grandson of another senator, Annius Verus (later Marcus Aurelius). On 10 July 138 Hadrian died at Baiae and was buried in his mausoleum. The Senate still detested him and deified him only at the insistence of Antoninus Pius.

Bibliography

Barnard, L. W. 1968–69. Hadrian and Judaism. *JRH* 5: 285–98.

Garzetti, A. 1974. *From Tiberius to the Antonines: A History of the Roman Empire A.D. 14–192.* London.

Syme, R. 1958. *Tacitus.* Oxford.

———. 1981. Hadrian and the Vassal Princes. *Athenaeum* 59: 273–83.

———. 1984. Hadrian and the Senate. *Athenaeum* 62: 31–60.

———. 1986. *Fictional History Old and New: Hadrian.* Oxford.

Brian W. Jones

HAGAB (PERSON) [Heb *ḥāgāb*]. A temple servant who was the progenitor of a family which returned from Babylon with Zerubbabel (Ezra 2:46 = 1 Esdr 5:30). The omission of Hagab in the parallel text in Nehemiah 7 appears to be a result of haplography, due to the similarity of the name Hagabah in Ezra 2:45 = Neh 7:48 = 1 Esdr 5:29 (Williamson *Ezra, Nehemiah* WBC, 26). Differences such as this raise questions about the sources of and literary relationships among 1 Esdras, Ezra, and Nehemiah.

Michael David McGehee

HAGABAH (PERSON) [Heb *hăgābâ*]. Head of a family of Nethinim (temple servants) who are listed as returnees from Babylonian exile under the leadership of Zerubbabel and others (Ezra 2:45 = Neh 7:48 = 1 Esdr 5:29). For further discussion, see AKKUB.

Chaney R. Bergdall

HAGAR (PERSON) [Heb *hāgār*]. According to Genesis 16; 21:8–21; 25:12, Hagar was the handmaiden of Sarah (Gen 16:1) with whom Abraham fathered his son Ishmael. See also ISHMAEL (PERSON); ISHMAELITES. Genesis 16 is a short story of high literary standing: human attempts to implement the divine promise (Gen 15:4) prove counterproductive; they lead to the anarchy of the desert (Gen 16:12). When the promised child, Isaac, finally is born, it is against human expectations (Gen 18:10–15; 21:6–7). From Gen 16:15–16 (usually attributed to the P source), the author of Gen 21:8–21 must have concluded that Hagar had returned to Abraham's house in order to give birth to Ishmael; accordingly, his story of Hagar's expulsion aims at bringing Ishmael back to the desert, where he belongs (Thompson 1987: 89–97; Knauf 1989: 16–35). As a sophisticated theological construct, the stories Genesis 16 and 21 do not necessarily reflect oral traditions about Hagar (and Ishmael) except for a general knowledge that Ishmael was the name of a bedouin tribe (or tribes; Gen 16:12; 20:20–21) and that Hagar was the legendary ancestress of the Ishmaelites (see below).

Hagar's Egyptian nationality (Gen 16:1; 21:9, 21; 25:12) is a literary device to connect the story in Genesis 16 with Gen 12:10–20 (cf. Gen 12:16). If the first story about Hagar was written at the time of Hezekiah, Hagar's nationality may veil the author's opposition to Hezekiah's foreign policy (cf. Isa 30:1–5; 31:1–5; Görg 1986).

As a female personal name, Hagar is well attested in ancient Arabia (Palmyrene and Safaitic *hgr*, Nabatean *hgrw*; to be distinguished from the male name *Hâjir* in Arabic, Minaean, and Nabatean; Knauf 1989: 52, n. 253). The name can be explained by Sabean and Ethiopic *hagar*, "town, city" (from an original meaning "the splendid" or "the nourishing"?); it is unlikely that there is any connection with *hajara,* "to emigrate," in more recent Arabian languages.

Just as Ishmael represents a large N Arabian tribal confederacy of the 8th and 7th centuries B.C. (see ISHMAELITES), so also can his mother be expected to have been of similar importance and antiquity. Therefore Ishmael's mother, Hagar, should not be connected with the Hagrites, a relatively small Syrian and N Arabian tribe of the Persian and Hellenistic periods, attested in 1 Chr 5:19 and in Greek and Roman geographers (Knauf 1989: 49–53; and see also HAGRITES).

A cuneiform inscription found on Bahrain and dating to the second half of the 2d millennium B.C. mentions "the palace of Rimum, servant of (the god) Inzak, the one of *A-gar-rum*" (Butz 1983). Hagar is then mentioned as a country and/or people by Darius I in an Egyptian hieroglyphic inscription from Susa (Roaf 1974: 135). The name, spelled *hgrw,* is accompanied by a representation of a typical Hagrean, whose hairdress distinguishes him from the central Arabian bedouin. This ethnographic feature suggests that Darius' "Hagar" refers to the E Arabian country and not to a central Arabian tribe (Knauf 1989: 144–45). In the 3d century B.C. a king of Hagar issued his own coins; at the same time, trade between Hagar, the Minaeans, and the Nabateans flourished. As D. T. Potts has most convincingly shown, Hagar is nothing else but the Gk *Gerrha* and can be identified with the present ruins of T̲âj (Potts 1984). Both Christian and Muslim authors used "Hagar" for E Arabia well into the Middle Ages (Knauf 1989: 54).

The available documentation, in spite of a gap between the LB Age and the Persian period, is more likely to connect Ishmael's mother with Hagar in E Arabia than with another Hagar (of which there is no lack, given the meaning of the word in Old S Arabic). For the prophet Jeremiah there were only two political entities in Arabia (with the exception of the caravan cities of NW Arabia): the Qedarites (see KEDAR), surviving from the Ishmaelite confederation, and Buz, which was the designation of E Arabia current in the 7th century B.C. See BUZ (PLACE).

Bibliography

Butz, K. 1983. Zwei kleine Inschriften zur Geschichte Dilmuns. Pp. 117–25 in *Dilmun. New Studies in the Archaeology and Early History of Bahrain,* ed. D. T. Potts. Berlin.

Görg, M. 1986. Hagar die Ägypterin. *BN* 33: 17–20.

Knauf, E. A. 1989. *Ismael.* 2d ed. ADPV. Wieşbaden.

Potts, D. T. 1984. Thaj and the Location of Gerrha. *Proceedings of the Seminar for Arabian Studies* 14: 87–91.

Roaf, M. 1974. The Subject Peoples on the Base of the Statue of Darius. *Cahiers du Délégation archéologique francaise en Iran* 4: 73–159.

Thompson, T. L. 1987. *The Origin Traditions of Ancient Israel.* Vol. 1. JSOTSup 55. Sheffield.

ERNST AXEL KNAUF

HAGGADAH. A noun derived from the Hebrew root *ngd,* "to show," "to announce," "to tell," "to testify" (Jastrow 1903: 871). In contemporary scholarship the word (also spelled *aggadah*) carries several meanings: (1) nonlegal material in rabbinic literature (*EncJud* 2: 354; 6: 141; Moore 1927: 161; Cohen 1975: 24); (2) narrative, story, legend, folktale, fairy tale, or the like (*EncJud* 2: 356; 6:141; Bacher 1892: 408); (3) biblical exegesis or an amplification of the Bible (*EncJud* 2: 354, 358–59; 6:410–11; Bacher 1892: 418); (4) discourses which are assumed to have followed the Torah readings in the ancient synagogues (*EncJud* 2: 358–59; Cohen 1975: 26); and (5) one segment of midrash, distinguishing between legal exegesis (halakic midrash) and nonlegal exegesis (haggadic midrash; *EncJud* 2: 354; 6:141; Cohen 1975: 25; *HJP*² 2: 346; Bacher 1892: 425; Vermes 1961: 1–8).

Approaching the meaning of Haggadah from the point of view of its role in rabbinic culture, several scholars underscore the fact that Haggadah was not authoritative, while the Halakah (legal discourse) was binding (*EncJud* 2: 354; Moore 1927: 162; Cohen 1975: 24; *HJP*² 2: 497). Therefore Haggadah is much more imaginative, freewheeling, and varied than Halakah (*EncJud* 2: 354–59; Cohen 1975: 25; *HJP*² 2: 346, 353–54, 497; Slomovic 1988: 65). Haggadah is often described as that segment of rabbinic literature which (1) deals with morals, ethics, and daily life; (2) provides the motivation and the will to follow YHWH and to perform his commandments; (3) includes the discussions of YHWH's attributes; or (4) contains words of comfort (Halivni 1986: 509; *EncJud* 2: 355–56, 360–62; 6: 141; Moore 1927: 161–62; Cohen 1975: 25; *HJP*² 2: 346; Halivni 1986: 509).

These varied meanings of Haggadah also appear in the rabbinic texts. In Mishnah *Ned.* 4:3 Haggadah probably refers to a nonlegal biblical exegesis. In Sipre Numbers the word conveys the sense of (1) tales and events, or (2) biblical exegesis (Kosovsky 1973: 1280). A review of the references to Haggadah in the concordance to the Babylonian Talmud reveals that Haggadah carries the meaning of (1) utterance, (2) giving evidence or testimony, (3) biblical exegesis, or (4) the nonlegal segment of rabbinic thought. Haggadah is set in opposition to (1) *ḥokmâ,* wisdom, (2) *šĕmûʾôt,* oral legal teachings, and (3) Halakah, law. The Talmud refers to books of Haggadah; however, their content is unknown, except for one which reportedly contained discussions of the laws concerning the execution of a gentile and another which included biblical terms and the ways in which they were to be treated in exegesis. References to books of Haggadah appear, even though there is a ruling that such collections should not be written down (Kasowski 1971: 1024–25).

Contrary to much speculation it seems likely that Haggadah did not derive solely from biblical exegesis (*EncJud* 2: 356; Moore 1927: 161–62). Also, the non-halakic nature of Haggadah has been exaggerated (*EncJud* 2: 359). There is a Jewish tendency to classify and categorize the phenomena in the world (Cooper 1987), and the distinction between Haggadah and Halakah probably results from this inclination. The difference between Halakah and Haggadah is artificial and perhaps too precise, and it may merely be literary convention for expressing a supposed binary division of rabbinic thought. The sages to whom Haggadah, in its variety of meanings, is attributed also are rabbis to whom halakic statements are assigned (*EncJud* 2: 363). Furthermore, the theological presuppositions which stand behind the Halakah—there is one God, who created the world according to a plan, who revealed that plan to Israel, and who will reward or punish Israel and all humankind commensurate with their adherence to that plan—also serve as the underpinning for the haggadic texts. Many haggadic passages serve to illustrate halakic statements, and there appear to be instances in which general halakic rules are derived from haggadic pericopes. While Halakah teaches by enumerating rules and principles, Haggadah enlightens by means of stories and examples (Safrai 1987: 127). The latter appeals to human imagination, while the former results from strict adherence to the intellectual processes. In expressing the complementary nature of Halakah and Haggadah, Bialik stated that "Halakhah is the crystallization, the highest quintessence of aggadah, while aggadah is the refinement of halakhah" (*EncJud* 2: 354). Cohen writes that Halakah ". . . stands for the rigid authority of the law, for the absolute importance of theory, the law and theory which the Haggadah illustrates by public opinion and the dicta of common-sense morality" (1975: 25).

Bibliography

Bacher, W. 1892. The Origin of the word Haggada (Agada). *JQR* 4: 406–29.

Cohen, A. 1975. Gemara and Midrash. Pp. 21–26 in *Understanding the Talmud,* ed. Alan Corré. New York.

Cooper, S. 1987. The Laws of Mixture: An Anthropological Study of Halakhah. Pp. 55–75 in *Judaism Viewed from Within and From Without,* ed. H. E. Goldberg. Albany.

Halivni, D. W. 1986. *Midrash, Mishnah, and Gemara: The Jewish Predilection for Justified Law.* Cambridge, MA.

Jastrow, M. 1903. *A Dictionary of the Targumim, the Talmud Babli and Yerushalmi, and the Midrashic Literature.* New York. Repr. 1971.

Kasowski, B. 1971. Haggadah. Vol. 25, pp. 1024–25 in *Thesaurus Talmudis Concordantiae Verborum quae in Talmude Babylonico Reperiuntur.* Jerusalem.

Kosovsky, B. 1973. Haggadah. Vol. 4, p. 1280 in *Oztar Leshon Hatannaʿim Thesaurus "Sifrei" Concordantiae Verborum quae in ("Sifrei" Numberi et Deuteronomium) Reperiuntur.* Jerusalem.

Moore, G. F. 1927. *Judaism in the First Centuries of the Christian Era: The Age of the Tannaim.* Cambridge, MA. Repr. 1966.

Safrai, S. 1987. Halakha. Pp. 121–209 in *The Literature of the Sages,* pt. 1, *Oral Tora, Halakha, Mishna, Tosefta, Talmud, External Tractates,* ed., S. Safrai. CRINT 2/3/1. Assen and Philadelphia.

Slomovic, E. 1988. Patterns of Midrashic Impact on the Rabbinic Midrashic Tale. *JSJ* 19: 61–90.

Vermes, G. 1961. *Scripture and Tradition in Judaism: Haggadic Studies.* Leiden.

GARY G. PORTON

HAGGAI, BOOK OF. The tenth book in the Masoretic ordering of the Book of the Twelve (or Minor Prophets). It contains oracles alluding to the harsh socio-economic conditions that dominated the tiny province of Yehud (Judah) during the reign of Darius I. Two factors had influenced Judean identity at this time: the Persian mandate to rebuild the temple, and the dyarchic structure of governor and high priest approved by the Persian authorities. The temple still lay in ruins when Haggai began to prophesy on 29 August 520 B.C.E. (Hag 1:1); but enormous progress had been made by the time he concluded his brief ministry, some three and a half months later, on 18 December 520 (Hag 2:10, 20). The book of Haggai itself provides vivid testimony to the effect of the prophet's words on the people as they began the task of rebuilding the temple (Hag 1:12–13), supplementing the cursory notes provided by Ezra (5:1; 6:14).

Because Haggai's ministry overlapped with that of Zechariah and since Zechariah presupposed that temple work had already recommenced, the decision to rebuild the temple, which dates back to the first return in 538 (Ezra 1:8–16; 3:6–4:4), was evidently reactivated as the result of Haggai's eloquent exhortations. Haggai was greatly concerned with the reluctance of the Judeans to respond to the Persian mandate to rebuild the temple. In urging them to begin reconstruction, he also supported the pattern of high priestly and gubernatorial joint rule as permitted by the authorities in Ecbatana (Hag 1:1). Zechariah's subsequent focus on the meaning and symbolism of the temple as a legitimate expression of the new dyarchy that accompanied it complements Haggai's program.

A. Dyarchic Pattern of Rule in Judah

Although Haggai's utterances were for the most part addressed to the whole community of Judeans, many of whom had only recently returned from Babylon (Hag 1:12; 2:2), it is clear that his words were directed mainly toward the two leaders, Zerubbabel, the Davidic governor, and Joshua, the high priest. The province of Yehud no longer had a Davidic king; and Zerubbabel, the governor, was officially in charge of the liaison in all matters requiring Persian attention. Joshua held an office of ecclesiastical authority that had clearly been upgraded in the restoration (see Zech 3:1ff.). The priesthood in the early postexilic period began to assume much of the internal political, economic, and judicial administration that previously had resided with the royal house, although the presence of the Davidic scion Zerubbabel as the governor of Yehud encouraged occasional eschatological outbursts that focused on the future role of the Davidide (Hag 2:21–23; Zech 4:6b–10a). These future-oriented oracles suggest a belief among the Judeans that this dyarchic pattern was only temporary. The lineage of Joshua, however, was no less impressive than Zerubbabel's, though from a Persian perspective such an arrangement was permanent except in case of rebellion, when any kind of home rule would be removed. Persia's motives in appointing both a Davidic governor and a legitimate priestly officer thus cannot be divorced from political purposes: establishing a loyal following in Yehud that would guarantee control of the major roadways that skirted the Mediterranean and that gave Persia access to the W portion of its far-flung empire.

B. Literary Considerations

The book of Haggai may be divided into two major parts containing five literary subunits. The first part, Restoration of the Temple (1:1–15), consists of two subunits: "Prophetic call to work on the temple" (1:1–11) and "Response of the leaders and people" (1:12–15a). The second part, Oracles of Encouragement (2:1–23), is divided into three subunits: "Assurance of God's presence" (1:15b–2:9), "Priestly ruling with prophetic interpretation" (2:10–19), and "Future hope" (2:20–23). Each of the units is associated with one of the five chronological notations in the book, indicating the separate moments in the second year of the reign of Darius when certain prophetic materials emerged. Although there is an integrity to each subunit with respect to content, there is also a continuity and flow from beginning to end, which gives the book a sense of unity and a vivid rhetorical style.

Although Haggai and Zechariah each have their distinct style and message, there are many literary similarities and connections between the two chapters of Haggai and Zechariah 7–8. Some 18 correspondences in literary form and language may be isolated for these four chapters (Meyers and Meyers, *Haggai, Zechariah 1–8* AB, xlix), indicating that Haggai and Zechariah 7–8 form an envelope construction tying together the elements of a composite work, Haggai–Zechariah 1–8. Because it makes no reference to the rededication of the temple in 516 or 515 B.C.E., this composite work probably was finished well in advance of that event. The latest date mentioned in either Haggai or First Zechariah is 7 December 518 (Zech 7:1). Hence, the compilation of the composite work, probably intended to be presented at the temple rededication, would have been completed between 518 and 516–15.

The following is a list of the chronological data in the book of Haggai and First Zechariah:

Chronological Data in Haggai–Zechariah 1–8

Passage No.	Passage	Year of Darius	Month	Day	Date of New Moon	Equivalent Date B.C.E.	Date No.
1	Hag 1:1	2nd	6th	1st	29 Aug.	29 Aug. 520	1
2	Hag 1:15	2nd	6th	24th	29 Aug.	21 Sept. 520	2
3	Hag 2:1	2nd[a]	7th	21st	27 Sept.	17 Oct. 520	3
4	Hag 2:10[b]	2nd	9th	24th	25 Nov.	18 Dec. 520	4
5	Hag 2:20	2nd	9th	24th	25 Nov.	18 Dec. 520	4
6	Zech 1:1[c]	2nd	8th	—[d]	27 Oct.	Oct. (Nov.) 520	5
7	Zech 1:7	2nd	11th	24th	23 Jan.	15 Feb. 519	6
8	Zech 7:1	4th	9th	4th	4 Dec.	7 Dec. 518	7

[a]The year appears at the end of the preceding date, Hag 1:15.
[b]This date is repeated, without the year, in 2:18 as a summary of the 2:10–18 section.
[c]This date breaks the sequence, being earlier than the previous two dates in Haggai.
[d]The formula omits the day.

The date formulas in Haggai, unlike comparable material in Kings, Chronicles, or other prophets, are tied to the realm of a foreign power. As such, they indicate the extent to which Judean policies and thinking were geared towards Persia. They also suggest prophetic awareness of the imminent conclusion of the 70 year period of desolation referred to in Jeremiah (Jer 25:11–12; 29:10). Reckoned from the destruction of the First Temple in 587–586, the approaching year 517–516 apparently signaled a new era for Judah. This careful reckoning of dates is unique in prophecy and accentuates Haggai's views regarding Yahweh's purposeful control over history. The date formulas, which mirror each other by virtue of the chiastic arrangement of year–day–month language, also constitute another literary device by which the overall unity of Haggai and First Zechariah is established.

1. Prophetic Call to Work on the Temple (1:1–11). Because of the adverse economic and political conditions in Judah at the time, the prophet was acutely aware of the disparity between present conditions and future hope. Temple language and ideology are utilized in trying to convince the populace to build God's house (1:8, 14). Haggai succeeded in rousing the spirit of Yahweh in the two leaders who, together with the people of Judah, rebuilt the temple. By providing centralized management for the limited resources to which the leadership had access, the temple became the cornerstone of the new administrative organization. In the first literary unit (1:1–11), the word "house" is used for God's dwelling in vv 2, 4, 8, and twice in 9, and for individual households in vv 4 and 9. This repetition highlights the contrast and the connection between the personal welfare of the people and the plight of the temple.

2. Response of the Leaders and People (1:12–15a). Haggai uses a clear and powerful argument to advance his case: the difficult circumstances of the present and the misfortunes of the past are directly related to the neglect of the temple, which represents God's presence in the community. The only escape from such a predicament lay in rebuilding the temple. Only then could appropriate blessings flow and the just rewards of human labor be realized, according to the promise of the covenant.

The description of the positive Judean response to this exhortation ends with a date formula (1:15), which gives the day and the month (21 September) of the year 520 B.C.E., Darius' second regnal year, less than a month after Haggai's initial address on 29 August (1:1). The people had wasted little time in beginning the temple project. The several weeks involved may have been the time required for community deliberation, although that deliberation may have been immediate. The decision was made, materials were secured, and the preliminary work on the temple site began immediately.

3. Assurance of God's Presence (1:15b–2:9). The next date (in 2:1) is built upon the regnal year given in 1:15b, indicating that within a month (17 October) enough progress had already been made on the building so that the people could already compare it to the preexilic one. Thus, after less than a month, Haggai had once again spoken in the name of Yahweh.

As in the previous section, he addressed the civil leader Zerubbabel, the priestly leader Joshua, and the people

(2:2). These three are then each commanded to "take courage" for the task at hand (vv 3–5), although the terminology used for the third group is altered ("all the remnant of the people" becomes "people of the land"). The full listing of the prophet's audience twice in this section emphasizes once more the prophetic role as intermediary between God and the people.

The dual concerns of this oracle of reassurance—economic well-being and political structure—come together in its final statement; "in this place I will grant well-being" (2:9). The well-being for which the people yearn will become available to them, but not only to them. In the future time, when all the nations recognize Yahweh's universal rule, those nations too will achieve well-being. The power of Yahweh as universal ruler will not be exploitative. In contrast to human emperors, Yahweh will establish universal plenty. This eschatological vision accords Yahweh the position of king. It is Yahweh's house (the temple) that is to be exalted with treasures, and Yahweh will give his blessings from there. The temple is a symbol of divine kingship, and no political king shares Yahweh's rule. The eschatological imagery of this passage, like that of Isa 2:2, is surely derived from the short-lived zenith of the Israelite empire under David and Solomon, when glory and wealth filled Jerusalem (1 Kings 4 and 10). But even that empire was a God-given structure in its Deuteronomistic formulation, and so its ideal replication in the future naturally shifts the focus to God's kingship.

4. Priestly Ruling with Prophetic Discourse (2:10–19). The arcane priestly language and the agricultural terminology of 2:10–19 are linked to the specificities of the prophet's immediate situation, making this passage in Haggai more difficult than most for the modern reader to comprehend. No passage, however, is more indicative of the transformation of prophecy itself than this. A complex priestly ruling has become the vehicle for conveying the message that work on the temple is related to the fortunes of the people. The prophet utilizes the ruling to expand on its meaning in God's design. Although this passage ends with an oracle (indicating Haggai's prophetic role), the situation involves priestly decisions and reveals the authoritative position of the priesthood even prior to the completion of the Second Temple.

The heart of the priestly ruling itself concerned the concepts of sanctity and defilement. Haggai asserted that sanctity is nontransferable but that defilement is; or rather, that sanctity can be transmitted only through direct contact with a sacred substance or person and not via a third party or object, whereas contamination can be transmitted both directly and indirectly. This distinction reveals something about the nature of holiness and purity, and about their opposites, defilement and impurity. Because these categories have contrasting properties, sanctity, which surrounds God, is much more difficult to contract than is uncleanness, which is apparently very contagious.

The sequence of conditions set forth in 2:15–19 amplifies Haggai's assertions of 2:14—that the sacrifices offered prior to the restoration of God's house were not acceptable. God's favor was not forthcoming because the people were tainted by sinful behavior, which had inevitably caused the pervasive impurity. Before temple restoration began, the people were experiencing economic deprivation; but now, however, God is offering them material blessings (2:19). God's power to do so is implicit in the dramatic change of fortunes. By drawing attention to God's power being used in the present for economic purposes, the stage was set for Haggai's final oracle, which portrayed Yahweh's exercise of power in the future and in the political realm.

5. Future Hope and Zerubbabel (2:20–23). This oracle, like the preceding one, was delivered on the 24th day of the 9th month (18 December 520). This time, however, Haggai's audience consisted of a single individual, Zerubbabel. Although a royal figure (as the final verse of the oracle makes clear), Zerubbabel is addressed as governor and his Davidic lineage is downplayed by the omission of his patronymic. This private oracle is addressed to a civil leader who, along with the high priest, shared the ceremonial aspects of temple refoundation. That event marked a restoration of the high priestly role that had been associated with tabernacle and temple in the Pentateuch and in Ezekiel's visions; but what implications did it have for the monarchic role? The rebuilding of the temple meant the reestablishing of the kingship of God, and not of man.

The eschatological idea evoked by the temple restoration appears in terms of political imagery: a political ruler such as had existed in the days of Israel's greatest grandeur would once again appear on the world scene. Yet there would be a difference. David as royal prototype first had to conquer many lands before establishing imperial domination. In contrast, this oracle asserts that Jerusalem's future universal role will be inaugurated first by God's overthrowing foreign kingdoms (2:22). Yahweh will assume the military tasks essential to the overthrow of lands that do not acknowledge his sovereignty. The Davidic model of a human warrior king is absent. Only divine intervention can bring about the universal kingdom. Because it is Yahweh who will one day overthrow the powers that dominate the world, it is Yahweh whose sovereignty will be established. The role of a Davidide cannot be the same as it was in the past. Having overturned the world order, Yahweh will then reign with the Davidide as his "servant" and his "signet." These two terms relegate the Davidide to a vice-regency, a participant in God's administration of the nations of the world, but not the initiator or leader in that task. The oracle is not only eschatological but also theocratic.

The monarchic potential contained in the figure of a Davidide has thus been made a component of theocratic rule; he is an instrument of Yahweh's dominion and not a political monarch of an independent kingdom. The accession of a Davidide to a special relationship with Yahweh in the future signifies the centrality of Jerusalem but not of a monarchy. Rather than being a "messianic" figure, an active participant in the struggle to bring about the new age, he will be a token earthly symbol of divine sovereignty.

The mention of Zerubbabel by name has occasioned all manner of speculation about political developments in Yehud. Did the Judeans perhaps expect Zerubbabel's status to change abruptly from governor to king? Does this oracle reveal stirrings of nationalism or even of rebellion against Persian rule? The answer to these questions, in the light of the preceding discussion, is negative. Zerubbabel is governor now, and his future role could only be a subsidiary one in a theocratic scheme. The naming of Zerubbabel is secondary to the choosing of Zion, which is the place where the locus of universal well-being will be established. That Zerubbabel's name appears in this eschatological vision testifies to Haggai's intense awareness of Judean uncertainty about rebuilding a temple without also restoring the palace; it does not testify to an expectation of some change in Yehud's status from Persian province to independent kingdom. The Jerusalem temple and priestly establishment had always accompanied, and indeed had legitimized, a royal house. That royal house was not ignored during this period of rebuilding, as Haggai's oracles indicate. The prophet deeply believed that the rebuilding of the temple accompanied the return of Yahweh's power as an active presence in the world. Could the overthrow of nations and the universal rule of Yahweh with his Davidic assistant be far behind? It is no wonder that with such a view of the temple, Haggai's words display a sense of imminence.

Subsequent generations felt that the eschatological force of this last oracle was weakened by its specific reference to a particular Davidic descendant who came and went without any noticeable change in world history. At the same time, pinpointing Haggai's utterance in this crucial transition period in Judean history has merit of another kind: it links the present moment, concretized by Zerubbabel's name, with the future. It inserts a contemporary figure into the age when God's benign and universal rule will prevail. Haggai, by using a living individual in his future vision, bridges the gap between present and future. Although he does not make the future imminent, he presents a view of time in which eschatology is not distinguished from history. Haggai's oracles inspired the rebuilding of the temple; and his words of encouragement ensured that the Judean restoration would begin in a framework that was true to its ancient heritage, with both priest and prophet as contributors to the organization of the affairs of the people of Israel.

(For bibliography see Meyers and Meyers, *Haggai, Zechariah 1–8* AB, lxxiii–xcv. See also Peterson, *Haggai and Zechariah* OTL.)

CAROL MEYERS
ERIC M. MEYERS

HAGGEDOLIM (PERSON) [Heb *haggĕdôlîm*]. Presumably the father of Zabdiel, a priest and contemporary of Nehemiah (Neh 11:14 RSV, NEB, AB). His supposed son, Zabdiel, is described as an overseer of the priests then engaged in the work of the house of God. "Haggedolim," however, as a personal name is very suspect, as it structurally appears to be a Hebrew masculine plural adjective used substantively, meaning "great ones" *[gĕdôlîm]*, prefaced by a definite article "the." Accordingly, BHS has proposed reducing the present word to its masculine singular counterpart *haggādôl,* "the great one," seeing in the present text's final two Hebrew consonants a case of mistaken dittography with the immediately succeeding Hebrew word in the next verse [*ûmin,* Neh 11:15]. As a consequence, Zabdiel may then be viewed as a person of high priestly descent, i.e., the son of the great (= high) priest (cf. the *terminus technicus* for "high priest," *hakkōhēn haggādôl* in Nehemiah [3:1; 3:20] and elsewhere [Lev 21:10]). Katzenstein believes that the title *(hak-)kōhēn (hā-)rōʾš* was the title of the chief priest in the time of the First Temple with the title *kōhēn gādôl* appearing only after its destruction. See Katzenstein 1962: 377–78, nn. 3, 4. The strong likelihood that we are not dealing here with a personal name is further strengthened by the LXX, where the end of the verse is omitted in the major mss; and in those remaining LXX mss which do have some addition one reads "son of (one of) one of the great men" *[huios tōn megalōn]*). Compare also the Vg's "son of the mighty ones" *[filius potentium]* and the KJV's "and their overseer was Zabdiel, the son of one of the great men." In closing, one may note the absence of the name Haggedolim as well as any reference whatsoever to Zabdiel as overseer in Neh 11:14's own synoptic parallel, 1 Chr 9:13.

Bibliography

Katzenstein, H. J. 1962. Some Remarks on the Lists of the Chief Priests of the Temple of Solomon. *JBL* 81: 377–84.

ROGER W. UITTI

HAGGI (PERSON) [Heb *ḥaggî*]. A son of Gad, grandson of Zilpah and Jacob, and ancestral head of the Haggites. His name is entered second among the seven sons of Gad mentioned in the list of the descendants of Israel that went to Egypt (Gen 46:16; so also *Jub.* 44:20). In the census reported in Numbers 26, he is again the second mentioned of the seven descendants of Gad whose names were adopted as clan names (Num 26:15—LXX 26:24).

RICHARD W. NYSSE

HAGGIAH (PERSON) [Heb *ḥaggiyâ*]. A Levite, a descendant of Merari and father of Asaiah (1 Chr 6:15—Eng 6:30). Noth (*IPN,* 222) argued that the last portion of the name is hypocoristic, not theophoric, so instead of meaning "Feast of Yah" it would mean "Born on a feast day."

TOM WAYNE WILLETT

HAGGITH (PERSON) [Heb *ḥaggît*]. A wife of David and mother of Adonijah (2 Sam 3:4 = 1 Chr 3:2). Haggith is the fourth wife/mother mentioned in two lists of David's sons born in Hebron (2 Sam 3:2–5 = 1 Chr 3:1–3). Her name also appears in the epithet "son of Haggith" as a designation for Adonijah (1 Kgs 1:5, 11; 2:13). Used three times, the phrase alerts the reader to the rivalry between Solomon/Bathsheba and Adonijah/Haggith.

The list of wives and sons in 2 Sam 3:2–5 serves both a genealogical and literary function. 2 Sam 3:1 notes that David grew "stronger and stronger," while his enemy Saul grew "weaker and weaker." This general statement about David's strength is made specific by the genealogical list in vv 2–5. The increase of David's strength is mirrored in the increase of his wives (i.e., Haggith) and sons. See also DAVID; ITHREAM.

LINDA S. SCHEARING

HAGRI (PERSON) [Heb *hagrî*]. According to 1 Chr 11:38 Hagri was the father of Mibhar, one of David's mighty men. In place of "the son of Hagri," the parallel passage at 2 Sam 23:36 reads "Bani the Gadite," indicating textual confusion between *bn hgry* (1 Chr 11:38) and *bny hgdy* (2 Sam 23:36). For a discussion of the variant forms see MIBHAR.

STEPHEN PISANO

HAGRITES [Heb *hagrî*]. Name of a pastoralist tribe residing in the region E of Gilead during the period of the early Monarchy. In the time of King Saul, the tribe of Reuben, assisted by the other Transjordanian tribes of Gad and Manasseh, subjected the Hagrites and took control of their territory "until the [Assyrian] exile" (1 Chr 5:10, 19–22). Since the Hagrites are listed with other Transjordanian enemies of Israel during the preexilic period—Edom, the Ismaelites, and Moab (Ps 83:7—Eng 83:7)—it appears that the hostilities continued even afterwards. King David later seems to have won the loyalty of at least some of the tribe, as Jaziz the Hagrite was given oversight of the royal flocks in the organization of his kingdom (1 Chr 27:30).

Since this information is derived entirely from later traditions, it has been suspected that it reflects the later Transjordanian ethnography at the time of the Chronicler in the postexilic or Persian period (Knauf 1985: 49–52). The earlier sources of Samuel and Kings are silent in regard to the Hagrites (cf. 1 Sam 15:47). The account of the Chronicler also contains some exaggerations and anachronisms that create suspicion the Hagrite material is a fabrication, e.g., the numbers provided for the booty and captives taken in the campaign seem incredible (1 Chr 5:21); the mention of Jetur (= Ituraeans?), Naphish, and Nodab with the Hagrites (5:19) appears to be a tradition no "earlier than the 8th century B.C." (Ephʿal 1982: 239). However, there is a possible reference to the Hagrites in the roster of David's soldiers from an earlier source (2 Sam 23:8–39). In v 36, the name of "Igal the son of Nathan" is followed by the phrase "of Zobah, Bani the Gadite" (MT *mṣbh bny hgdy*). This may be a corruption of the reading "Igal son of Nathan, the commander of the army of the Hagrites" *(rb ṣbʾ bny hgry),* as suggested by McCarter (*2 Samuel* AB, 493–94). The proposed emendation agrees both with the context and the parallel passage of 1 Chr 11:37, "Mibhar the son of Hagri" (*mbḥr bn hgry,* MT 11:38; but cf. LXX and Knauf 1985: 49, n. 235). This phrase also appears in a context with other foreign soldiers (23:36–39) who served in David's professional army at Jerusalem (Naʾaman 1988). The putative Hagrite may be another one of the mercenaries recruited during David's Transjordanian conquests. It is then possible that the references to the Hagrites in the Chronicler preserve an older tradition stemming from the early Monarchy, not a postexilic addition. Nevertheless, any ethnographic relationship of the Hagrites to Hagar and the Ismaelites is uncertain (Gen 16:15–16); and they definitely should be disassociated from the later *Agraioi/Agraei* mentioned by the Greek and Latin geographers (Str. 16.4.2 [767C]; Ptol. *Geog.* V.19.2; and Plin. *NH* VI.159–61). The latter are probably the inhabitants of Hofuf-Thaj located in the al-Hasa oasis in NW Arabia, on the Persian Gulf (Potts 1984: 111–12).

Bibliography

Ephʿal, I. 1982. *The Ancient Arabs.* Leiden and Jerusalem.
Knauf, E. A. 1985. *Ismael.* Wiesbaden.
Naʾaman, N. 1988. The List of David's Officers *(Šālîšîm). VT* 38: 71–79.
Potts, D. 1984. Northeastern Arabia in the Later Pre-Islamic Era. Pp. 85–144 in *Arabie orientale, Mésopotamie et Iran méridional de l'Age du Fer au début de la période islamique,* ed. R. Boucharlat and J.-F. Salles. Editions Recherche sur les Civilisations 37. Paris.

DAVID F. GRAF

HAIRNET. Hairnets, sometimes even made of gold, were worn by women in Palestine during the Roman period. See DRESS AND ORNAMENTATION.

HAKKATAN (PERSON) [Heb *haqqatan*]. A descendant of Azgad and the father of the returning exile Johanan. Johanan returned under Ezra with 110 other descendants of Azgad (Ezra 8:12 = 1 Esdr 8:38). Williamson (*Ezra, Nehemiah* WBC, 111) suggests that the list of twelve in Ezra 8 is indicative of the author's theology that the remnant is the true heir of Israel. According to the table in Ezra 2:12, 1222 other descendants of Azgad (Neh 7:17 reads 2322) had returned earlier to the land under Zerubbabel.

GARY S. SHOGREN

HAKKOZ (PERSON) [Heb *haqqôṣ*]. Var. KOZ; ACCOS. **1.** A Judahite, the father of Anub and Zobedah (1 Chr 4:8). Koz' abrupt entry into the Judahite genealogy in 1 Chr 4:8 may have resulted from the accidental or intentional omission of the name at the end of v 7 (Curtis and Madsen *Chronicles* ICC, 107). Scholars currently tend to argue that Koz represents an actual preexilic person whose name was embedded in a source that the Chronicler employed (Weinberg 1981: 104). This view diverges from an earlier generation which argued that Koz and his compatriots of 1 Chr 4:5–8 originated at an artificial construct, formed from postexilic familial names (Rudolph *Chronikbücher* HAT, 32–33).

2. A priest who received the seventh position in the priestly order of the temple during the reign of David (1 Chr 24:10). An evaluation of the historical reliability of his existence in the time of David depends ultimately on the literary context of 1 Chr 24:1–19. Though there is general agreement that the priestly list originated after the Exile, its exact date remains debated. J. Liver (1968: ix, 29–32) associates the 24-course priestly organization to the reforms of Nehemiah, while H. G. M. Williamson (1979: 262–68) assigns it to the late Persian period. Because of genealogical connections between 1 Chr 24:7–18 and the Hasmonean priestly claims, L. Dequecker (1986: 94–106) dates the list to the Hasmonean era. The stylistic characteristics of the list, however, seem to link the list to the time of the composition of Chronicles. Whatever the exact date of the composition of the list, Hakkoz does not seem to represent an individual from the time of David. The Chronicler may have transformed the name of an important postexilic family into the name of an individual for his priestly list in 1 Chronicles 24.

3. A prominent postexilic family, who returned from Babylon with Zerubbabel (Ezra 2:61 = Neh 7:63 = 1 Esdr 5:38). Upon their return to Jerusalem the family of Hakkoz were not able to produce the necessary genealogical records to prove their priestly lineage (Ezra 2:62 = Neh 7:64 = 1 Esdr 5:39). They thus had to wait upon the outcome of the casting of the Urim and Thummim. The outcome of this process is unknown. Only 1 Chr 24:10 suggests that the family may have been permitted to enter the priestly ranks. Other references to the family do not regard the family as priestly; nevertheless, they did obtain a certain degree of social prominence. A member of this family, Meremoth, constructed a section of Jerusalem's wall during Nehemiah's refortification of the city (Neh 3:21). The family seems to have retained its prominence well into the Hellenistic era. A certain Eupolemus, "the son of John, from [the family of] Accos," served as a special Judean ambassador to Rome in order to solicit Roman aid against the Syrians during the Maccabean War (1 Macc 8:17).

Bibliography

Dequecker, L. 1986. 1 Chr xxiv and the Royal Priesthood of the Hasmoneans. *OTS* 24: 94–106.

Liver, J. 1968. *Chapters in the History of Priests and Levites.* Jerusalem (in Hebrew).

Weinberg, J. 1981. Das Wesen und die funktionelle Bestimmung der Listen in 1 Chr 1–9. *ZAW* 93: 91–114.

Williamson, H. G. M. 1979. The Origins of the Twenty-Four Priestly Courses, A Study of 1 Chronicles xxiii–xxvii. Pp. 251–68 in *Studies in the Historical Books of the OT,* ed. J. A. Emerton. VTSup 30. Leiden.

John W. Wright

HAKUPHA (PERSON) [Heb *ḥăqûpā*ʾ]. Head of a family of Nethinim (temple servants) who are listed as returnees from Babylonian exile under the leadership of Zerubbabel and others (Ezra 2:51 = Neh 7:53 = 1 Esdr 5:31). For further discussion see AKKUB.

Chaney R. Bergdall

HALAH (PLACE) [Heb *ḥălaḥ*]. 2 Kgs 17:1–6 narrates Israel's revolt against Assyria and the Assyrian conquest of Israel. In v 3 the Assyrian king is Shalmaneser V (727–722); but the capture of Israel's capital, Samaria, is historically credited to his brother, the Assyrian monarch, Sargon II (721–705). Isa 20:1 refers to the conquests of Sargon. According to Sargon's archives he captured Samaria and deported 27,290 people (*ANET,* 284). According to 2 Kgs 17:6, "He carried the Israelites away to Assyria, and placed them in Halah, and on the Habor, . . . and in the cities of the Medes." 2 Kgs 18:9 states that Shalmaneser captured Samaria after a three-year siege and in v 11, "the king of Assyria carried the Israelites away to Assyria, and put them in Halah. . . ." In 1 Chr 5:26 we read that the two tribes of Reuben and Gad and half of the tribe of Manasseh in the Transjordanian region (Gilead) were deported by Pul (his personal name), better known by his throne name, Tiglath-pileser (745–727), "to Halah, Habor, Hara, and the river Gozan. . . ." In 2 Kgs 15:29 this same king had captured Gilead, Galilee, etc. and deported the people to Assyria. Obadiah 20 says "the exiles in Halah who are of the people of Israel shall possess Phoenicia as far as Zaraphath" (RSV emending Heb *haḥēl-hazzeh,* "this army," to *Halah*). While it is unclear exactly who deported them to Halah, the site seems distinct from Habor (the city or river), Hara, and Media. The LXX considered Halah a river, possibly the Balikh, which flows from Haran to the Euphrates 100 miles W of the Khabur. The Balikh, Khabur, and Media combination would have the sense of geographic spread, i.e., Sargon spread the Israelites across the N part of the Assyrian Empire.

However, the exact location of Halah is still debated. Gehman (1970: 358) calls Halah a district to which captives of the ten tribes, i.e., not just those of the city of Samaria, were taken as exiles. This combines the exiles of Pul and Sargon and assumes the ten tribes were still distinct entities. Gehman identifies Halah with the later Chalchitis (Ptolemy 5.18.4) in Mesopotamia near Gozan (the later Gausanitis—Tell Halaf on the river bank) in the basin of the Habor or Khābûr river. Another source says Ptolemy's Chalkitis [sic] is near Gozan, on the Balikh river. Halah has also been identified as Akkadian Halahhu on the W bank of the Tigris near the mouth of the Lower Zab river S of the capital of Ashur, 70 miles S of Nineveh, 250 miles from the Balikh, which is W of Ashur and Nineveh (Gray *Kings* OTL, ²1970: 644). Millard (1980: 602) identifies Halah with the Assyrian site of Halahhu, both a town and a district NE of Nineveh. Sennacherib's inscriptions refer to a gate of Nineveh named "the gate of the land of Halahhi." Halakku has been located near Kirkuk, 9 miles E of Nuzi, and 60 miles E of Ashur. An unidentified Halhu is related to Strabo's Calachene, a plain of N Assyria, E of the Tigris. There is a Chalonitis in Pliny and Strabo, NE of Assyria (cf. Millard), called Halah by Syrians. Halah has also been identified with Assyrian Kalah, biblical Calah (Gen 10:11), Nimrud, 18 miles S of Nineveh. Hilakku has been identified with Cilicia (Turkey). Pinches (*ISBE* 2: 1321–22 [1939 ed]) lists these various identifications, but considers all more or less improbable for philological reasons except Assyrian *Halahhu,* which (except for the doubling and the case ending) is the same as Halah, letter for letter. It is mentioned in *Western Asia Inscriptions* (2, pl. 53, 1. 35), between Arrapha (Arrapachitis) and Rasappu (Reseph). Tablet K. 123 calls it *mat Halahhi,* "the land of Halahhu." It apparently included the towns of Se-bise, Se-irrisi, and Lu-ammu[ti?], which were centers for the Assyrian government. The first quote implies that Halah was near or in Gausanitis and had chief towns of these names. Of the eight personal names in K. 123, five are Assyrian; and the remainder are Syrian rather than Israelite.

Bibliography

Gehman, H. S. 1970. Halah. P. 358 in *New Westminster Dictionary of the Bible.* Philadelphia.

Millard, A. R. 1980. Halah. P. 602 in *Illustrated Bible Dictionary,* vol. 2, ed. J. D. Douglas, et al. Leicester.

Henry O. Thompson

HALAK, MOUNT (PLACE) [Heb *hāhār heḥālāk*]. A mountain in the central Negeb, the identity of which is uncertain. It is sometimes thought to be the same as Jebel Halaq on the NW side of the Wâdī Marra, N of ʿAbdeh. The Bible describes it in fair detail. It is probably located close to the ascent of Akrabbim (Num 34:4; Josh 15:3). It is a range in between the Wilderness of Zin and the wooded slopes of Seir (Josh 11:17). The ancient towns of Tamar, at the S tip of the Salt Sea (Ezek 47:18–19), and Kadesh-barnea flanked it on either side. It formed the boundary of Judah and Edom (Josh 15:1) and indicated the S limits of the land conquered by Joshua (Josh 11:17; 12:7). The Deuteronomistic History, by its reference to Mount Halak, stresses an important theological point. The Lord, just as he promised to Moses (Josh 1:3; 11:23) and the fathers (Josh 1:6; 21:43), gave to Israel the whole land, Mount Halak being a prominent landmark in the wilderness in the S.

PAUL BENJAMIN

HALAKAH. A noun derived from the Hebrew root *hlk.* "to walk." It is usually translated as "law" and denotes a specific ruling, a legal statement or discussion, the general category of legal material, or that portion of rabbinic literature which is not Haggadah. Halakah focuses on activity, specifically that activity in which primarily Jews should be engaged in personal, social, national, and international relationships, as well as in all other practices and observances of Judaism (*EncJud* 7: 1156; Safrai 1987: 121–22; Finkelstein 1975: 261; Ginzberg 1970a: 166).

Moore believed that "Jewish ethics are impressed upon the Halakah as well as expressed in the Haggadah" (1927: 141). However, the Halakah is not independent of the ethical categories of Judaism, and it "expresses" Jewish ethics as much as does the Haggadah (Ginzberg 1970a). In theory at least, there was no hierarchical ranking among matters which we today might label as ethical laws, civil laws, or ritual laws because all of them play the same essential role in God's design of the universe (*m. ʾAbot* 2:1; *j. Qidd.* 1:1). Based on their reading of Genesis, the rabbis believed that God created a highly structured and ordered world and that the Torah, with its laws, commandments, proscriptions, and prohibitions provided the blueprint of this order (*Midr. Gen. Rab.* 1:1). It was the task of all Jews to study the Torah, so that they might understand God's plan and ascertain what they were expected to do in order to align themselves with the cosmic and social order God had designed. Because properly observing the entire Halakah was viewed as being essential to life on earth, the study of Torah in its broadest sense became the primary religious activity of rabbinic Judaism (Viviano 1978).

It has often been said that the Halakah is a set of rigid rules or commandments which were imposed upon the Jewish people by God (Moore 1927) or, in a pejorative sense, by the rabbis (Schürer *HJP*² 1:69; 2 §25,iii). While the rabbis would agree that God is the ultimate source of the Halakah, they did not view the commandments or the Halakah as an imposition: "Beloved are the Israelites, for God has encompassed them with commandments: Phylacteries on head and arm, fringes on their garments, *mezuzot* on their doors" (*b. Men.* 43b).

The Halakah, however, developed as much from within the life of the Jewish community as it did within the rabbinic academies. Local customs frequently took on the force of Halakah (*EncJud* 7: 1160; Safrai 1987: 121, 128, 175–77; Zeitlin 1975: 294, 305). If the majority of the people could not follow a particular law or if its implementation would cause a substantial loss, it was rejected (*b. B. Bat.* 60b; *b. Moʿed Qat.* 2a; *EncJud* 7: 1159; Safrai 1987: 125, 132; Zeitlin 1975: 305, 311). Because the laws were given to the Jews so that they might live by them, almost any specific rule could be abrogated in a time of emergency (*Sipra* 86b and parallels; *Mek. Ish.* on Exod 31:16). If there were uncertainty about a specific practice, one need only to observe how the common people acted in order to discover what was acceptable (Safrai 1987: 177–79; Zeitlin 1975: 290).

From the rabbinic point of view, the major source of the Halakah was the written Torah, the first five books of the Hebrew Bible—Genesis, Exodus, Leviticus, Numbers, and Deuteronomy. The importance of the written Torah is illustrated by the fact that laws designated as *dĕʾôraytâ,* "from the Torah," were viewed as superior to those which were *dĕrabbānān,* "from our rabbis" (*EncJud* 7: 1157–59). Alongside the written Torah was the oral Torah, the most important part of which is its legal as against its nonlegal portions.

It is likely that the designation of something as part of the oral Torah did not necessarily mean that it was created or transmitted orally; rather, it denoted that part of the Halakah which was not explicitly contained in the written Torah (Brüll 1876: 5–6). Some held that the injunctions in the "Prophets" and the "Writings" were the earliest portions of the oral Torah (*EncJud* 7: 1157). In any event part of the Halakah in the oral Torah derives directly from interpretations of Scripture, by whatever definition (*EncJud* 7: 1158). Many consider biblical exegesis to be the earliest source of the Halakah in the oral Torah, but the arguments over the origin of biblical exegesis, midrash, continue today. Some hold that biblical exegesis was the original route by which postbiblical Halakah was created, while others claim that biblical exegesis postdates the nonexegetical statements of law contained in the Mishnah, considered by many to be the first written compilation of the oral Torah (Lauterbach 1951; Halivni 1986: 38–65; Safrai 1987: 153–55).

Another view of the oral Torah argues that it contains legal materials which were transmitted orally from God through Moses, Joshua, the elders, the Prophets, the men of the Great Assembly, and the rabbis (*m. ʾAbot* 1:1). While these materials supplement, complement, and complete the material in the written Torah, they are not considered to be the product of actual biblical exegesis. A number of legal injunctions from the oral Torah are designated as "torah given to Moses at Sinai." These may be ancient traditions for which there is no scriptural support or at the most very faint support, but which are considered to be of equal authority with those which are specifically mentioned in the Torah (*EncJud* 7: 1158; Safrai 1987: 183). Some legal traditions are said to derive from "the words of the scribes" (*EncJud* 7: 1158–59), but this is an ambiguous phrase, for "scribes" existed throughout late antiquity, and their exact activity is unknown (*EncJud* 7: 1160; Safrai 1987: 128, 175–76; Zeitlin 1975: 305; Saldarini 1988: 241–76; Bickerman 1962: 54–71). Decrees and ordinances also serve as sources for acceptable activity (Ginzberg 1970b: 79; Safrai 1987: 128, 163; Zeitlin 1975: 302–4). In addition, case law and precedent also form an important source for legal decisions (Safrai 1987: 164, 178–79). It appears that most of the legal traditions derive from individual sages and discussions within rabbinic academies, not from formal national institutions, such as the Sanhedrin or court, *bêt dîn* (Safrai 1987: 168; Neusner 1981). A large number of these traditions have little or no support in the Bible; for example, we read that "the rules about the Sabbath, festival-offerings, and sacrilege are as mountains hanging by a hair, for Scripture is scanty and the rules are many" (*m. Hag.* 1:8; Safrai 1987: 155–56). Halakot may deal with practical matters or may be totally abstract and theoretical; however, seldom is this distinction made clear in the rabbinic documents. While the statements of Halakah are essential elements within the oral Torah, the methods by which the injunctions were to be derived are also carefully delineated and are also viewed as part of the oral Torah (*EncJud* 7: 1158; Safrai 1987: 153–55; Halivni 1986). Judaism seems to favor justificatory law, so that the reasons given for a specific Halakah were frequently assessed and debated (Halivni 1986).

Because Judaism does not have a hierarchal structure of authority, in principle each sage and each court has equal authority, so that the pronouncements of all sages are theoretically of equal value. For this reason, the rabbinic legal discussions are characterized by differences of opinions, disputes, and debates (Safrai 1987: 168–75; Neusner 1971). However, the rabbinic documents do contain some guidelines concerning which sage is more authoritative on a particular subject (*EncJud* 7: 1164). Similarly, the rulings of one court may supersede the rulings of another only if it is composed of sages of superior intellect and ability (*EncJud* 7: 1159).

Bibliography

Bickerman, E. 1962. *From Ezra to the Last of the Maccabees.* New York.

Brüll, J. 1876. *Mabo haMishnah.* Frankfurt-am-Main.

Finkelstein, L. 1975. Life and Law. Pp. 261–74 in *Understanding the Talmud,* ed. A. Corré. New York.

Ginzberg, L. 1970a. Jewish Thought as Reflected in the Halakhah. Pp. 163–73 in *The Jewish Expression,* ed. J. Goldin. New York.

———. 1970b. The Significance of the Halakhah for Jewish History. Pp. 77–124 in *On Jewish Law and Lore.* New York.

Halivni, D. W. 1986. *Midrash, Mishnah, and Gemara: The Jewish Predilection for Justified Law.* Cambridge, MA.

Lauterbach, J. Z. 1951. Midrash and Mishnah. Pp. 163–256 in *Rabbinic Essays by Jacob Z. Lauterbach,* ed. L. H. Silberman. Cincinnati.

Moore, G. F. 1927. *Judaism in the First Centuries of the Christian Era: The Age of the Tannaim.* Cambridge. Repr. 1966.

Neusner, J. 1971. *The Rabbinic Traditions About the Pharisees Before 70.* Leiden.

———. 1981. *Judaism: The Evidence of Mishnah.* Chicago.

Safrai, S. 1987. Halakha. Pp. 121–209 in *The Literature of the Sages,* pt. 1, *Oral Tora, Halakha, Mishna, Tosefta, Talmud, External Tractates,* ed., S. Safrai. CRINT 2/3/1. Assen and Philadelphia.

Saldarini, A. 1988. *Pharisees, Scribes and Sadducees in Palestinian Society.* Wilmington.

Viviano, B. T. 1978. *Study as Worship: Aboth and the NT.* SLA 26. Leiden.

Zeitlin, S. 1975. The Halaka. Pp. 290–312 in *Understanding the Talmud,* ed. A. Corré. New York.

GARY G. PORTON

HALAKHIC LETTER FROM QUMRAN. See MIQSAT MAᶜASE HATORAH (4QMMT).

HALAM, KHIRBET EL-. See ARUBBOTH (PLACE).

HALHUL (PLACE) [Heb *ḥalḥûl*]. Town situated in the N-central hill country of Judah (Josh 15:58), within the same district as Beth-zur. This settlement is listed among the towns within the tribal allotment of Judah (Josh 15:21–62). During Roman times this town was known as Alulus. Josephus records that the Idumeans assembled here in A.D. 68 (*JW* 4.9 §6). The ancient name is preserved at modern Halhul, located approximately 6 km N of Hebron (M.R. 160109). The ruins of the ancient town are surely located here or in the immediate vicinity.

WADE R. KOTTER

HALI (PLACE) [Heb *ḥălî*]. The second town listed in the description of the territory of the tribe of Asher (Josh 19:25). As such, it is to be sought in the S section of the tribal territory. Abel (*GP,* 2: 341) suggested it be identified with Tell el-Aly (M.R. 160235), which, however, is a natural hill and not an ancient ruin. Aharoni (*LBHG,* 377) proposed Khirbet Ras ᶜAli (Tel ᶜAlil; M.R. 164241) on a spur close to the coastal plain, S of the Naḥal Sipori gorge. This site was occupied during the EB and LB periods and during the first stages of the Iron Age. Gal (1982: 22, 107) has suggested that Ras ᶜAli retains the ancient name but that the actual location of biblical Hali was at a site on the other side of the gorge (Tel ᶜAlil West; M.R. 164242), which shows evidence of having been occupied from the 10th to 8th centuries B.C.E. and again in the Persian period. If this identification and those of Beten with Tell al-Far and of Achsaph with Tell el-Harbaj (Aharoni *LBHG,* 371) are correct, then these three places listed in Josh 19:25 are located in the same vicinity and appear in the text in geographic order, but from N to S.

Bibliography

Gal, Z. 1982. *The Lower Galilee in the Iron Age.* Diss., Tel Aviv (in Hebrew).

RAFAEL FRANKEL

HALICARNASSUS (PLACE) [Gk *Alikarnassos*]. The principal city of Caria in Asia Minor located on the coast opposite Cos on the N bank of the Sinus Ceramicus (37° 02' N; 27° 26' E). The ancient city had two ports protected by a small island called Zephyrion (or Arconnesus). The historians Herodotus and Dionysius and the elegiac poet Heraclitus came from the city of Halicarnassus. It was also the site of the famed tomb of King Mausolus. The city is mentioned in passing as a recipient of a letter from Lucius in support of the Jews (1 Macc 15:23).

Halicarnassus was probably established prior to 2200 B.C.E. by an unknown tribe belonging to a language family the most vivid testimony of which was the -ssos/-nthos place name suffixes scattered throughout W Anatolia and parts of Greece. Halicarnassus was later populated by Mycenaeans (compare with Strabo 14.2.6). A continuity of the pottery at Halicarnassus from the close of the Bronze Age through the Greek Dark Ages appears to suggest that the site was continuously occupied by the same people during a period otherwise marked by population shifts and political upheaval.

During the Dark Ages the city was revitalized by Dorians and Ionians from Troezen in the Argolis (Strabo 8.6.14; and 14.2.6; Vitr. 2.8; Paus. 2.30; and Hdt. 7.99). Later epitaphial evidence shows that the city had a mixed population of Greeks and Carians who apparently used the Ionic dialect as their official language (see Meiggs and Lewis 1969: no. 32). Halicarnassus was part of a six-state Dorian confederation but was expelled from the league because a champion athlete from the city supposedly refused to dedicate a victory tripod to Triopian Apollo, the god in whose honor the games were held (Hdt. 1.144).

In the 6th century B.C.E. a citizen by the name of Lygdamis (I) usurped authority in Halicarnassus and was succeeded by his daughter Artemisia (I). Artemisia (I) supplied five ships to the Persian fleet and fought valiantly at the Battle of Salamis (see Hdt. 7.99; 8.88; 8.93; and an interesting tradition about her death in Ptolemy Hephaestion 190). Artemisia (I) transmitted the rule to her son Lygdamis (II). Herodotus opposed Lygdamis (II) and was exiled to Samos during his reign. Lygdamis (II) later ordered the execution of the historian's uncle, the epic poet Panyassis. Herodotus, however, returned to lead a conspiracy which drove the tyrant from power. Shortly after this, the city came under Athenian control for a brief time (Thuc. 2.9; and 8.42).

In the early 4th century the Carian cities were subjugated by Hecatomnus from Mylasia (395–377 B.C.E.). Hecatomnus had three sons, Mausolus, Hidrieus, and Pixodarus, and two daughters, Artemisia and Ada, who married their two older brothers. Mausolus succeeded his father and changed his capital to Halicarnassus. When Mausolus died in 353 B.C.E., he was buried in an elaborate tomb that was completed by his wife and successor Artemisia (II).

The so-called Mausoleum at Halicarnassus, one of the Seven Wonders of the ancient world, was rediscovered by C. T. Newton in 1857 using descriptions found in Vitruvius and Pliny the Elder. Some architectural and sculptural fragments are now housed at the British Museum. Pliny described the tomb as a circular structure 140 feet high and 410 feet in circumference. It was surrounded by 36 columns and covered by a pyramidal dome. According to Vitruvius the tomb was behind the agora, which was situated along the seashore. Still further away from the agora behind the tomb was a temple of Mars. The agora was flanked by the palace of Mausolus and the temples of Venus and Mercury.

Artemisia (II) was succeeded by Hidrieus, who died without leaving an heir. The crown passed to Hidrieus' wife, Ada, who was deposed by her youngest brother Pixodarus with the assistance of Orontobates, a Persian satrap and son-in-law of Pixodarus. Alexander the Great laid siege to Halicarnassus; defeated Memnon, the Persian general who was defending the city; and restored Ada to authority. Halicarnassus was later rebuilt and six towns were annexed to it as compensation for its losses (Pliny 6.29). The city suffered again during the Mithradatic War but was restored to its former prosperity by Cicero's brother Quintus (Cicero, *QFr* 1.8).

A number of Jews lived in Halicarnassus, and in the year 139 B.C.E. a letter was written by the Roman Senate on their behalf (1 Macc 15:23). A decree was issued in the 1st century B.C.E. granting the Jews of Halicarnassus the freedom to worship and to construct a "place of prayer" near the seaside, according to their ancestral customs (Jos. *Ant* 14.10.23).

Bibliography

Meiggs, R., and Lewis, D., eds. 1969. *A Selection of Greek Historical Inscriptions to the End of the Fifth Century B.C.* Oxford.

SCOTT T. CARROLL

HALIF, TELL

HALIF, TELL (M.R. 137087). A site on the N fringe of the Negeb, between Beer-sheba and Lachish.

A. Identification

Tell Halif (Tell Khuweilifeh) has been identified with biblical Ziklag, the city ceded to David by the Philistines (1 Sam 27:6–7). This suggestion was first made by M. Abel in 1938 on the basis of its proximity to Horvat Rimmon (Khirbet Umm er-Rammamin), which lies less than 1 km to the S (Abel, *GP* 2, 318). Already in the 19th century, C. R. Conder and H. H. Kitchener had identified this latter site with biblical En-rimmon. Both sites are mentioned in the territorial lists of Judah in Josh 15:31–32 and as part of the inheritance of the tribe of Simeon in Josh 19:5–7.

Tell Halif has also been identified with the later Byzantine settlement called Tilla. According to the *Onomasticon* of Eusebius, two large Jewish villages, Tilla and Rimmon, were located just 16 miles S of Beit Guvrin, which places them exactly in the Halif area.

More recently E. Oren has suggested that Tell Seraʾ, on the Philistine plain 18 km W of Tell Halif, is Ziklag (Oren 1982). At the same time A. Kloner has argued that Tell Halif was the original site of Rimmon, its name having been taken and preserved at nearby Horvat Rimmon by the first Roman-Byzantine reoccupants of the area in the 2d century A.D. (Kloner 1980).

B. Location

Tell Halif is a prominent mound in the easternmost part of the high Shephelah at the N fringe of the Negeb. It faces the Hebron mountains to the E and overlooks the plain of Philistia to the W. Modern Kibbutz Lahav is located on its SE shoulder. The mound lies in a marginal and potentially erratic subsistence zone but occupies a strategic position astride the westernmost ridge of the Judean foothills. Its position commands the main S route from Egypt and the Mediterranean coast eastward into the Hebron area.

C. Excavations

Serious investigations at and around Tell Halif began only in the 1950s following the establishment of Kibbutz Lahav. Initial efforts included informal survey work and intermittent salvage operations (Biran and Gophna 1970; Gophna 1972; Seger 1972; and Alon 1974).

In 1975 the Lahav Research Project, a private consortium of American scholars and institutions, was formed by Joe D. Seger to undertake an integrated study of the region focused on excavation of the ancient remains at Tell Halif. During Phase I, through 1980, five major seasons of field investigations were conducted (see Seger 1984a; Seger and Borowski 1977). Phase II work was initiated in 1983 (see Jacobs 1984). From the start excavation efforts were accompanied by complementary investigations of the region surrounding Lahav, its ancient environments and human ecology, as well as by an ethnographic study of the area's more recent bedouin and village Arab occupants. Primary excavation work has been concentrated in three major fields on the mound summit (Fields I–III), with satellite projects in Cave Complex A, just below Field I, and on Sites 101 and 301 of the lower town area to the NE. In addition, an intensive site survey of the region within a 10-km radius of the site is being undertaken.

D. History of Settlement

Researches in the Lahav area have documented a long history of habitation stretching from the Chalcolithic period in the late 4th millennium B.C. to modern times (see Table 1). The earliest settlement was on the NE terrace (Sites 101 and 301), where Chalcolithic and EB I occupants lived in open villages. During the EB II the settlement shifted onto the higher ridge to the W, and a well-fortified town was established overlooking both the E valley and the W coastal plain. Four substantial strata of EB II and III remains have been identified with a history roughly coterminous with the Old Kingdom period in Egypt. Excavated remains in Field I include major Stratum XV fortification walls with an outlying glacis. The site suffered a major destruction ca. 2550 B.C. after which occupation resumed and continued until ca. 2300 B.C. From this time and until the very end of the MB in the mid-2d millennium, the tell was abandoned.

However, following the 16th century B.C. Egyptian resurgence under the early 18th Dyn. pharaohs and the associated destruction of Stratum D occupation at Tell Beit Mirsim, located just 8 km to the N, settlement at Halif resumed. During the LB I reoccupation included the construction of a substantial "residency" type Egyptian house suggesting that the area was firmly under Egyptian control. Analysis of faunal remains from associated Stratum X remains in Field I shows a frequent occurrence *equus assinus* (donkey), suggesting that Halif may have served as a trading outpost or way station during this time. Following a major destruction at ca. 1400 B.C., the residency house was partially reconstructed and reused during the Amarna age; but during the LB IIB (Stratum VIII) the area of the house was completely transformed into a storage facility with a succession of stone-lined pits.

Table 1
TELL HALIF—MAJOR STRATA

Stratum	*Period*	*Date*
I	Modern Arab	A.D. 1800–1948
II	Islamic-Crusader	A.D. 700–1500
III (Site 66)	Roman-Byzantine	A.D. 100–600
(gap)	Early Roman	100 B.C.–A.D. 100
IV	Hellenistic	300–100 B.C.
V	Persian	500–300 B.C.
(gap)	Late Iron II	650–500 B.C.
VIA	Iron II	700–650 B.C.
——— destruction		
VIB (Site 72)	Iron II	900–700 B.C.
VII	Iron I	1200–900 B.C.
VIII	LB IIB	1300–1200 B.C.
IX	LB IIA	1400–1300 B.C.
——— destruction		
X	LB IB	1475–1400 B.C.
XI	LB IA	1550–1475 B.C.
(gap)	MB II	1850–1550 B.C.
(gap)	EB IV	2300–1850 B.C.
XII	EB III	2400–2300 B.C.
XIII	EB III	2450–2400 B.C.
XIV	EB III	2550–2450 B.C.
——— destruction		
XV	EB II–III	2650–2550 B.C.
XVI (Site 101, 301)	EB I–II	3200–2650 B.C.
XVII (Site 101, 301)	Chalcolithic	3500–3200 B.C.

Aside from the abandonment of use of the storage area in Field I, only minor shifts in domestic architecture document the Stratum VIII–VII transition to the Iron Age I period in the early 12th century. In general, traces of 12th and 11th century occupation are limited. However, continuity through the period is indicated; and late 11th century settlement is inferred from the presence of degenerate-style Philistine potsherds and other late Philistine period artifacts. While the site clearly was not a major Philistine center, evidence, nonetheless, indicates that it was within the orbit of Philistine influences during the period of David's exile just before 1000 B.C. and thus may in fact have been Ziklag (see Seger 1984a).

During the 10th century and continuing into the Iron Age II period after 900 B.C., the site once more enjoyed an era of growth and expansion and was developed as one of Judah's frontier outposts. Perhaps as early as the reign of Jehoshaphat (874–849 B.C.), the mound was massively refortified with substantial walls and by an outlying glacis paved with a flagstone surface. The 9th–8th century is well marked on the mound by Stratum VIB occupation and by an extensive cemetery on the Site 72 hillside to the S. In both Fields II and III substantial late 8th-century domestic remains were found sealed by a massive destruction of the city. This has been associated with the 701 campaign of the Assyrian king Sennacherib against S Judah and Lachish. Iron Age II occupation was resumed by squatters for a brief time in the early 7th century, but by 650 B.C.

the site was completely abandoned and remained so until the Persian period after 500 B.C.

In the 5th century the E summit of the mound was again resettled. The remains of a substantial Stratum V building that probably served as a barracks or storage facility for a Persian military outpost were excavated in Field II. Above the Persian building two occupation phases of a subsequent Hellenistic domestic structure were found. A Ptolemaic coin from below its final-phase surface indicates that this Hellenistic occupation persisted at least into the late 3d century.

During the early Roman period between 100 B.C. and A.D. 100, the site once more lay abandoned. However, a dramatic recovery took place following the Roman destruction of Jerusalem and especially in the wake of the Second Jewish Revolt under Bar Kokhba in the 2d century A.D. Both Halif (Tilla) and nearby Horvat Rimmon (En-rimmon) were resettled. At Halif substantial remains of this occupation are found both on the mound and down its NE slopes on Site 101, and the occupation is documented also by presses and other installations throughout the surrounding countryside.

Site 101 continued to be occupied well into the early Islamic period. During the time of the Crusades, in A.D. 1192, a significant battle between Saladin and Richard the Lion Hearted took place at Beer Bustan, the area's main well just below the tell to the NW. In the 18th and early 19th century the site developed into the bedouin and village Arab market settlement of Khuweilifeh, which provides the Arabic name for the site.

Bibliography

Alon, D. 1974. Lahav-Tel Halif. *Hadashot Archaeologiot* 51: 28–29 (in Hebrew).

Biran, A., and Gophna, R. 1970. An Iron Age Burial Cave at Tel Halif. *IEJ* 20: 151–69.

Borowski, O. 1977. A Corinthian Lamp at Tell Halif. *BASOR* 227: 63–65.

Gophna, R. 1972. Egyptian Ceramics of the First Dynasty Period from the Tel Halif Terrace. *Haʾaretz Museum Bulletin* 14: 47–56.

Jacobs, P. 1984. Tell Halif, 1983. *IEJ* 34: 197–200.

Kloner, A. 1980. Hurvat Rimmon, 1979. *IEJ* 30: 226–28.

Oren, E. D. 1982. Ziklag—A Biblical City on the Edge of the Negev. *BA* 45: 155–66.

Seger, J. D. 1972. Tell Halif (Lahav). *IEJ* 22: 161.

———. 1981. Lahav Research Project: Excavations at Tell Halif, 1980. *BA* 44: 183–86.

———. 1984a. The Location of Biblical Ziklag: An Archaeological Identity Crisis. *BA* 47: 47–53.

———. 1984b. Lahav Research Project: Investigations at Tell Halif Israel, 1976–80. *BASOR* 252: 1–23.

Seger, J. D., and Borowski, O. 1977. The First Two Seasons at Tell Halif. *BA* 40: 156–66.

Joe D. Seger

HALL OF JUDGMENT. See JUDGMENT, HALL OF.

HALL OF PILLARS. See JUDGMENT, HALL OF.

HALL OF THE THRONE. See JUDGMENT, HALL OF.

HALL OF TYRANNUS. See TYRANNUS (PERSON).

HALLEL. A designation for a small grouping of psalms. The word comes from the Heb verb *hālal,* "to praise," since many of the psalms contain the phrase "Praise the Lord!" It has been variously used to describe the following psalm groups: 104–106, 111–118, 120–136, and 146–150.

Israel used the Hallel Psalms regularly in her three great feasts: Passover, Pentecost, and Tabernacles. Hallel Psalms 113–118 are called the "Egyptian Hallel"; in part, they recount the saving deeds of Yahweh from the time of the Exodus from Egypt under the leadership of Moses (to whom the authorship of these psalms was traditionally attributed). They were sung or recited at these feasts, the later Feast of Dedication (or Lights, the modern holiday Hanukkah), and the New Moon assemblies. They were not used at the more solemn occasions of the New Year and the Day of Atonement, where confession and self-examination predominated.

The celebration of Passover particularly utilized the Hallel Psalms 113–118. Jewish pilgrims sang these psalms on their way to Jerusalem. Bowman (1962: 743) relates that Psalm 118 was sung responsively by pilgrims and the Levites as the former approached to enter the temple and worship. The popular response to Jesus' entry into Jerusalem on Palm Sunday was the ritual welcome accorded to all pilgrims.

Jewish families sang Psalms 113–114 before the Seder meal and 115–118 afterward. In the Synoptic Gospels (Matt 26:17–29 [= Mark 14:12–25; Luke 22:7–20]), Jesus and his disciples ate a Seder (Passover) meal and sang a hymn before departing for the Mount of Olives (Matt 26:30). Thus, in all likelihood, they sang all or parts of Psalms 115–118 (or, less probably, Psalms 135–36).

The "Great Hallel" was identified with Psalms 120–136, 135–136, or 136 alone. It contains Israel's praise for Yahweh's provisions in the past and present. Along with Psalms 146–150, it was used in the daily morning service of the synagogue. See also PSALMS, BOOK OF.

Bibliography

Bowman, J. W. 1962. The Life and Teachings of Jesus. Pp. 733–47 in *Peake's Commentary on the Bible,* ed. M. Black and H. H. Rowley. London.

Steven R. Swanson

HALLELUJAH. See PSALMS, BOOK OF.

HALLOHESH (PERSON) [Heb *hallôḥēš*]. The father of Shallum, ruler over half the district of Jerusalem, and one of those who, with his daughters, assisted in making repairs to the city wall (Neh 3:12). Hallohesh is also described as one of the chiefs of the people and a signatory to the covenant established by Ezra (10:24).

FREDERICK W. SCHMIDT

HAM (PERSON) [Heb *ḥām*]. The name of the second son of Noah, and the brother of Shem and Japheth. The name appears 17 times in the Bible (Gen 5:32; 6:10; 7:13; 9:18 (twice), 22; 10:1, 6, 20; 14:5; 1 Chr 1:4, 8; 4:40; Pss 78:51; 105:23, 27; 106:22). It is either etymologically related to the word *ḥm,* "warm," "hot" (from *ḥmm,* "to become warm, hot"), or derived from the Egyptian Keme, "the black land" (a name for ancient Egypt). In support of the former, the descendants of Ham appropriately occupy the warmer or hotter lands of the S regions of the ancient world. In support of the latter, the name Ham is used in some of the later psalms in apposition to Egypt (78:51; 105:23, 27; 106:22).

A. Biblical Data

Ham's sons are Cush, Misraim, Put, and Canaan. The descendants of three of these—the Cushites (Ethiopians), the Egyptians, and the Canaanites—and their respective lands are mentioned hundreds of times throughout the Bible. The fourth son Put—Libya according to some, the Horn of Africa according to others—and his descendants figure less prominently. According to the biblical ethnographic conceptions, the descendants of Ham occupy chiefly the lands to the S and W of Israel. Some of his descendants, however, may have controlled part of Asia (cf. 10:6–20).

Ham is one of Noah's three sons who joined him in the Ark and thereby escaped the Flood (6:9, 13; 9:1–18). It was he who reported to his brothers that Noah, who had become a tender of vineyards after the Flood, was drunk and naked. His brothers walked carefully backward and covered their father (9:22–23). The disgrace of a drunken father, according to Ugaritic epic poetry, was a crime; and "looking upon the nakedness" of one's father, mother, or closest relatives was prohibited in Israelite tradition (Lev 18:7–19; 20:11–21).

Related to this episode, Ham is also distinguished as being the father of Canaan (9:18, 22) whom Noah, after he woke up from his drunken sleep, condemned to servitude (9:20–27) and after whom the land of Israel was named (9:18; 11:36; 13:12; 17:8). The text reads, "And Noah awoke from his wine, and knew what his younger son had done to him. And he said, 'Cursed be Canaan; a servant of servants [or, the bottom-ranked servant] shall he become to his brothers. . . .' " (9:24–25). This statement has been misinterpreted by medieval Jewish, Christian, and Muslim theologians, transferring the curse of Canaan on to Ham. Such an interpretation has no basis in the biblical text or in early Jewish thought. According to one postbiblical Jewish oral tradition (see B below), Canaan was actually Noah's *fourth* and youngest son—hence, he was Ham's brother, not his son. This and such phrases as "his younger son" and "to his brothers" in Gen 9:24–25 (the passage concerning Canaan) have led some exegetes to theorize that there was an earlier story separate from the flood story, with another list of Noah's sons as Shem, Japheth, Ham, and Canaan, and that a later tradition harmonized the two stories, making Ham the father of Canaan.

B. Later Jewish Tradition

Very few references are made to Ham in the so-called Apocrypha or Pseudepigrapha, or in the literature of Qumran (*Jub.* 4:33; 8:10, 22–24; 9:19; *L. A. B.* 1:22; 4:6; *T. Sim.* 6:4; *T. Isaac* 3:15). The most important references are found in the book of *Jubilees.* According to one of these, it was Ham who, together with his other sons Cush and Misraim, cursed his son Canaan, because Canaan violated the divine ordinance of land distribution and usurped the dwelling and inheritance of the children of Israel, the land of Canaan (*Jub.* 10:28–34). According to another the land given to Ham is hot, to Japheth cold, to Shem neither hot nor cold (18:12–30). See Fig. GEO.05.

The first world empire, the building of cities, and particularly the building of the Tower of Babel are attributed to Ham's grandson Nimrod, the son of Cush (*b. Ḥul.* 89a and *ʿAbod. Zar.* 53b; *Pirqe R. El.* 24; cf. also *3 Enoch* 1; *L. A. B.* 4:6–8; 5:1). According to a 13th-century ethical work called *Sefer ha-Yashar* (Noah 22), Ham stole from Noah the garments which God had originally made for Adam and Eve and which had been in the possession of Enoch and Methuselah and gave them to Nimrod. The quasi-Jewish Hellenistic *Sibylline Oracles,* in which the sons of Noah are given the names of Greek gods (3:110–15), and the gnostic Sethian *Apocalypse of Adam* (V, 5 72:17; 73:14, 25; 74:11; 76:134) mention Ham in the context of the division of the world and empires among the sons of Noah.

Few biblical stories are as enigmatic as Noah's curse of one of his descendants, popularly but erroneously known as "the Curse of Ham." Some later Jewish traditions speak about the punishment of Ham personally (Tanhuma Noah 13) or his immediate family (*Pesiq. R.* 21:22 [ed. Friedmann]) on account of "his sin." That Ham committed a sin is not questioned (*b. Sanh.* 70a; 108b). The expression "sin of Ham" is also found once in *Jubilees* (22:21). But the popular expression "curse of Ham" is found neither in biblical nor postbiblical Jewish literature.

Most later Jewish sources make it clear that Canaan, not Ham, suffered the curse (*Bek.* 13a; *Qidd.* 7a; 67b; *Lev. Rab.* 17:5; *Midr. Tadshe* 17; etc.). In their speculation as to why Canaan was cursed instead of the guilty Ham, some rabbis went as far as to assert that God wanted to spare the other members of his family which naturally included Cush, Misraim, and Put (*Midr. Ha-Gaggdol* Bereshith, Noah 25). Others, however, not content with this answer alone, chose to speculate that Noah, stopped by Ham from having a fourth son, in accordance with the law of retaliation cursed Canaan, his fourth son (*Gen. Rab.* 36:5–7). Still others, not being satisfied with this answer, propose the syllogism that since God had already bestowed a blessing upon Ham (Gen 9:1) and since a blessing cannot be retracted nor can a curse be substituted in its place, Noah put the curse on his grandson. None of these explanations seeming adequate, others suggest that not Ham but Canaan himself must have been the real culprit, ascribing to him varieties of sins which he might have committed against Noah—whether it was seeing and reporting Noah's nakedness or being involved in a disgraceful act of castration or sexual assault against Noah (cf. also *Gen. Rab.* 36:5–7; *Tanhuma* (Buber)

49–50; *Tanhuma* Noah 13–15; *b. Sanh.* 70a and *Pesaḥ* 113b; *Targum Jonathan; Genesis Apocryphon* 19:13).

It is not until the Middle Ages that the curse of Canaan became attributed directly to Ham by Jewish, Muslim, and Christian writers equally (see, e.g., Saadia Gaon, *Perush Rabbenu Saadia Gaon al ha-Torah* [ed. Y. Gafah, p. 21]; Rashi on Kiddushin 22b, *sade niqneth;* cf. also Benjamin of Tudeal, the 12th-century traveler, who speaks about the sons of Ham being black slaves [*Maasot Benyamin* or *The Itinerary of Benjamin of Tudela,* 1625]).

C. Christian Tradition

Early Christian exegesis was not kind to Ham. Augustine called him the "wicked brother," and said that "Ham (that is hot) who as the middle son of Noah, and as it were, separated himself from both, and remained between, neither belonging to the first family of Israel nor to the fullness of the gentiles, what does he signify but the tribe of heretics, hot with the spirit, not of patience, but of impatience, with which the breasts of heretics are wont to blaze, and with which they disturb the peace of the saints?" (*City of God,* Book 16: 2). Elsewhere he compared Ham with Cain.

Chrysostom likewise spoke about the sons of Noah who received good reports because they loved their father "whereas the other was cursed because he had no love for his father" *(Homilies on I Thess 4).* According to Clement of Rome, *"Tertia decima generatione cum ex tribus filiis suae ex maledicto conditionem servitutis induxit"* (*Recognitiones,* Book 1, 30; cf. also *Cave of Treasures,* fol. 19b [Budge's edition, p. 121]).

The objective of the early Christian theologians was primarily exegetical exposition, wrong as it may be, for homiletic purposes. Beyond that, they did not propound the slavery of African people on the ground that they are descendants of Ham. On the other hand, their rationalization of the biblical curse of Canaan, especially in the medieval period, contributed to the later justification of slavery and colonialism: the "Curse of Ham" was coined and the punishment transferred from Canaan and his descendants to Ham's whole family systematically (see, e.g., Jobson's *The Golden Trade* [1623], ed. C. Kingsley [Teignmouth, 1904], 65ff.; cf. also Pernal 1940).

D. Islamic Tradition

Ham is not mentioned by name in the Quran but is alluded to as the unbelieving son who refused to follow his father at the time of the Flood and who consequently drowned (11:44[42]–49[47]). Extra- and post-Quranic Islamic traditions are acquainted with the biblical story of Gen 9:18–27 concerning the curse of Ham's son, Canaan, and with later Jewish and Christian legends. Muslim historians repeat versions of a certain spurious Jewish haggadic tradition that Ham's sin was carnal relations in the Ark; and they add to his offense an assault against his father; they claim that, although born white, he turned black as a result of his father's curse.

According to al-Tabari Jesus brought Ham back to life. Ham related episodes of life in the Ark and the end of the Flood to the apostles. Al-Tabari meliorates the fate of Ham—although he was reduced to servitude, his brothers were lenient. The historian al-Masude, a contemporary of Saadia Gaon writing in the first part of the 10th century, obstinately misrepresents Gen 9:25 quoting it: "And he said, 'Cursed be Ham. . . .' "

Bibliography

Pernal, A. 1940. La Race Negre et la Malediction de Cham. *Revue de l'Universite d'Ottawa* 10: 157ff.

Ephraim Isaac

HAM (PLACE) [Heb *hām*]. In Gen 14:5 the locality at which CHEDORLAOMER and his allies defeated the Zuzim. It is listed between Ashteroth-karnaim (in Bashan) and Shaveh-kiriathaim (in Moab). Ancient interpreters were uncertain about its location. The Qumran text 1QapGen 21:29, which has *zwmzmyʾ* instead of Zuzim, accordingly replaced Ham with *ʿmn.* The LXX, *Tg. Neof.,* and Vg understood *bhm* of the Heb text as *bāhem* "among them" (i.e., among the Rephaim), rather than *bĕ-hām,* "in Ham." The *Tg. Onq.* and *Tg. Ps.-J.* rendered Ham by *hmtʾ* (Hemtā or Hamettā), as though they knew of a place so named in the appropriate region. But no such toponym appears in the Talmudic literature, unless it is a deliberate alteration of *ḥammeṯa dĕ-pĕḥal,* a place with hot springs near Pella in Transjordan mentioned in the Jerusalem Talmud. Ham is believed to appear as *hum* in the Palestine List of Thutmose III, No. 118; but its place in the enumeration provides no clues as to the area of its location. It has been suggested that Ham was identical with the small mound (37 × 34 m at the top) at the modern village of Hām, 5.5 km S-SW of the city of Irbid in N Jordan. See BETH-ARBEL. The surface survey of the mound by N. Glueck revealed great numbers of medieval and Roman sherds, a considerable number of Iron Age I–II sherds, a small quantity of EB I–II sherds, but no MB and LB sherds. Unless excavations prove differently, this gap in the occupation of the site excludes its identity with Hum of Thutmose III's list, though not necessarily with Ham of Genesis 14. A. Bergman (1934: 176) thought to have discovered another mention of Ham in the Bible by emending *ḥwtyhm* (*ḥawwōṯêhem,* "their villages") in Num 32:41 to *ḥwt-hm* (*ḥawwōt-hām,* "the villages of Ham") as the earlier name of Havvoth-Jair. However, the biblical passages on the latter disagree about their location (in Bashan or in Gilead); and in any case Tell Hām was too insignificant a site to have given its name to a cluster of 30 or 60 fortified cities.

Bibliography

Aḥituv, S. 1984. *Canaanite Toponyms in Ancient Egyptian Documents.* Jerusalem.
Albright, W. F. 1929. New Israelite and Pre-Israelite Sites: The Spring Trip of 1929. *BASOR* 35:1–14.
Bergman, A. 1934. The Israelite Occupation of Eastern Palestine in the Light of Territorial History. *JAOS* 54: 169–77.
Glueck, N. 1951. *Explorations in Eastern Palestine,* vol. 4, pt. 1. AASOR 25–28. New Haven.
Neubauer, A. 1868. *La géographie du Talmud.* Paris.

Michael C. Astour

HAMAN (PERSON) [Heb *hāmān*]. A nobleman, promoted to the rank of vizier by King Ahasuerus, and mortal enemy of the Jews in the book of Esther. After being made vizier by the king, Haman became enraged at Mordecai, who ministered at the king's gate, for not obeying a royal command to bow down and show proper respect to Haman (Esth 3:2–5). Haman decided therefore not only to eradicate Mordecai but also every Jew in the realm (3:6). He convinced the king that the Jews were disobedient to his rule and deserved to be eliminated (3:7–11). He received the authority to send out a decree ordering the elimination of all Jews and the confiscation of their property (3:12–14). In the meantime he built a gallows especially for Mordecai and was planning to ask the king's permission to hang him from it (5:9–14). This plan, however, was foiled when Queen Esther turned Ahasuerus against Haman at the second of two feasts she had prepared for the two men. When Haman accidentally fell on Esther's couch pleading for mercy, Ahasuerus thought he was trying to assault her. Thus he had him hanged from the same gallows that Haman had prepared for Mordecai (7:5–10).

This story portrays Haman as the adversary par excellence of the Jews. The MT tradition links him with AGAG, the ancient king of the Amalekites, who were enemies of the Hebrews (Esth 3:1, 10; 8:3, 5; 9:10, 24; cf. 1 Samuel 15; Num 24:7; Exod 17:8–16; Deut 25:17–19). Moreover, Mordecai is portrayed as a relative of King Saul, who was in turn the enemy of Agag, Haman's ancestor (Esth 2:5; 1 Sam 9:1–2). Thus the ancient conflict between Israel and Amalek is portrayed as continuing in the contest between Mordecai and Haman (McKane 1961; Clines 1984: 14–15; Berg 1979: 66–67). This interpretation of the person of Haman is continued by Josephus, the Targums of Esther, as well as the Talmud. These sources consistently describe Haman as a descendant of Amalek (Paton *Esther* ICC, 194–95; Thornton 1986; Moore *Esther* AB, 35). The LXX treats the figure of Haman in a similar way. He is never described as an Agagite but rather as either a "Bugaean" (Gk *Bougaios;* cf. LXX 3:1; 9:10; A:17), perhaps a reference to a famous friend of Alexander the Great, or as a "Macedonian" (Gk *ho Makedōn;* cf. LXX 9:24). Either way Haman would be seen as a hated Greek by later Jewish audiences who still remembered the atrocities of Greek rule (Moore 35–36; Clines 1984: 44).

This does not mean that Haman was a purely fictitious character. The name *agag* may be derived from *agazi,* a Mesopotamian tribe mentioned in Sargon's annals (Paton, 69–70). (Although it is difficult to explain how the final *g* in Heb *agag* has shifted to *z* in Akk *agazi.*) In addition, *hāmān* may be a Persian name derived from Old Persian *hamanā,* "illustrious," or perhaps *homa,* "a sacred drink." Several link it with *omanes,* a Persian name mentioned by Greek authors (Paton, 69; Moore, 35). Moreover, the ten sons of Haman (Esth 9:7–10) also appear to have genuine Persian names (Clines 1984: 323; Gehman 1924: 327–28). What we seem to have then in the character of Haman is a historical figure whose lineage has been reshaped and reinterpreted by the various traditions in a symbolic way (Clines 1984: 293).

Bibliography

Berg, S. B. 1979. *The Book of Esther.* SBLDS 14. Missoula, MT.
Clines, D. J. 1984. *The Esther Scroll.* JSOTSup 30. Sheffield.
Gehman, H. S. 1924. Notes on the Persian Words in the Book of Esther. *JBL* 43: 321–28.
McKane, W. 1961. A Note on Esther IX and 1 Samuel XV. *JTS* 12: 260–61.
Thornton, T. C. 1986. The Crucifixion of Haman and the Scandal of the Cross. *JTS* 37: 419–26.

JOHN M. WIEBE

HAMATH (PLACE) [Heb *ḥămāt*]. HAMATHITES. A city in Syria, the S border of which often became part of the formula for the N idealized border of Israel (cf. 1 Kgs 8:65; 1 Chr 13:5). The city was an object of the Assyrian conquest (Isa 36:19), and some of its inhabitants were exiled and settled in Israel (2 Kgs 17:24). The site has a long history, from early prehistoric through modern times. It was known as *Ematu* in the Ebla texts, and in the Syro-Hittite (Luwian) hieroglyphic inscriptions it is called *Amatu.* During the classical period its name was *Epiphaneia Syriae* or *Epiphaneia ad Orontem.* The non-classical name is thought to mean the "warm place" or "fortress." The modern name of the site is Hama.

A. Location and Excavations
B. Results of the Excavations
  1. Prehistoric Finds
  2. Early Bronze Age
  3. Middle and Late Bronze Ages
  4. Iron Age
  5. Hellenistic Hamath
  6. Roman Period

A. Location and Excavations

Hamath is situated in central Syria (M.R. 312503) where the main road from the N first crosses the river al-ʿĀsī, the ancient Orontes, 214 km N of Damascus. The river flows through the town from SE to NW, in the form of an S. The greater and older part of the town lies on the left bank and is dominated by the Citadel Mound, ca. 45 m high and ca. 400 × 300 m. From 1931 through 1938 the site was excavated by a Danish expedition, which opened a total area of 18,000 m^2, to a depth varying between 4 and 29 m. In addition, 48 smaller excavations were made in the modern town and a few in the neighborhood. The excavations on the Citadel Mound revealed a long series of cultural layers, numbered from the top, M marking the earliest, those of the Neolithic period, 6th millennium B.C., and A, the top layers containing remains from the Middle Ages.

B. Results of the Excavations

1. Prehistoric Finds. The earliest signs of human presence in the area are the so-called pebble tools from the Pluvial A period corresponding to the earliest two glacial periods of Europe, Günz and Mindel; they were found by Dutch geologists at Šarya in the E outskirts of Ḥamā. Somewhat later, from the First Interpluvial, the Second Interglacial period of Europe, are artifacts of Acheulean and Levalloisian types collected near Ḥamā. Seven Neolithic layers were distinguished on the tell, bearing witness of a culture related to that in the ʿAmq at the lower Orontes.

In Chalcolithic times, in layer L (ca. the 5th and most of the 4th millennium B.C.), there was a strong cultural influence from N Mesopotamia, probably because of intensive barter. This layer, however, also comprised obsidian from Asia Minor. In layer L 3 Ḥalāfian pottery appeared together with local imitations of pottery from Samarra. At the end of the 5th millennium, the influence from the SE was stronger, as is shown by a local variety of the ʿUbaiḍ ware. Houses at that time often had one large room with a hearth in the middle. The dead were buried under the floors. Board-shaped idols and animal figures of clay indicate the emergence of artistic development, as do stamp seals of stone or clay with incised geometric patterns. Some of the seals must have been personal identification marks like those of Mesopotamia in the 4th millennium, when the first attempts of writing developed. About 3300 B.C. full urbanization was a reality in Syria.

2. Early Bronze Age. The K layers belong to the earliest Bronze Age. Already in K 10, the potter's wheel appeared; and a terrace wall may be part of a true town wall; but houses were soon constructed beyond it. Seals and figurines of Mesopotamian types and primitive local sculptures have been discovered. About 2600 B.C. more primitive tribes from Asia Minor made their way into central Syria as inferred from a new, mottled reddish or yellow and black, polished pottery, the so-called KHIRBET KERAK WARE; at Ḥamā it turned up in K 5, from which period dates also the earliest-found casting mold for bronze tools. Interments under the houses became rarer; and a large space was reserved for round structures, which were probably grain silos.

Layer K 1 had signs of a destruction, which was followed by a rebuilding in J 8. Layer J is the fully developed EB. Apparently burials no longer occurred in the town, which had become a densely built-up area with narrow streets or alleys. From K to J the pottery did not change very much, but a tall goblet was the leading characteristic all through J 8–1, and "Goblet" or "Chalice Culture" has become a popular denomination of this period's Syrian civilization. In J 5 a spade-like rope-traction ard was used for tilling the ground, but soon the ard-plough gained predominance. Botanical finds indicate cultivation of barley, wheat, probably emmer, horsebean, lentil, a plant with seeds resembling peas, wine, cherry, and olive. Oil lamps were flat bowls with pinched rims to produce a spout for the wick. The wheeled carriage, and perhaps the horse, were known. Husbandry comprised at least donkeys, oxen, sheep, goats, pigs, and dogs. The town of J 5 suffered a violent destruction followed by a slow decadence in J 4–1. The J 5 pottery corresponds completely to that in the destruction layer of Ebla, modern Tell Mardikh, the center of a wealthy kingdom which reached its highest peak in the 24th century B.C. Evidently the same catastrophe hit both sites in the 23rd century, probably a consequence of the Akkadian conquest of N Syria; the date is confirmed by a C_{14} analysis of material from Hamath.

3. Middle and Late Bronze Ages. Nomads from the N part of the Euphrates valley, in Akkadian named "Amurru," (i.e., "West"), caused much trouble in Syria about 2000 B.C. In the 19th century these so-called Amorites established their own states, and the finds in H 5 actually present a new picture. In the middle of the town, enormous cylindrical grain silos were constructed; the dead were buried in rock-cut chambers outside the urban area; and the ceramic repertoire was simple and monochrome with combed or ropelike patterns and with a carinated bowl as the leading type. Between the MB layer H and the LB layer G, no real difference in culture can be proved; but H 1 showed signs of a great destruction, perhaps caused by the Hittites, who invaded N Syria ca. 1375 B.C. At that time the frontier of the Egyptian Empire was only about 50 km S of Hamath, the Bronze Age name of which, *Ematu,* may be identical with the *Imat* or *Amata* of Egyptian texts. Sherds of imported Cypriot and Mycenaean vases date the layers of the G period to the 14th and 13th centuries B.C. Some buildings were more spacious and had corridor-like storerooms resembling those of palaces elsewhere. However, the LB town may have been administratively subject to the neighboring, more wealthy city of Qatna.

4. Iron Age. According to the Bible the king of Hamath, Toi, sent his son, Joram, with gifts and congratulations after David had defeated Hadadezer, ca. 975 B.C. (2 Sam 8:9–10; cf. 1 Chr 18:9–10). Solomon, however, is said to have built fortresses and grain stores in part of Hamath's territory (2 Chr 8:4); Jeroboam II also is said to have defeated Hamath (2 Kgs 14:28). Nevertheless, the Assyrian records reveal that in 853–845 B.C. the Hamathite king, Urhilina, played an important role in the great coalition which for a time was able to stop the Assyrian advances toward the W. Stone blocks with Luwian inscriptions in Syro-Hittite hieroglyphs found at Ḥamā in the 19th century refer to Urhilina's renewal of a temple dedicated to Baʿalat and to his son, Uratamis, fortifying the town; the temple had been somewhat neglected under Urhilina's father, Paritas, and under his anonymous grandfather. In the first half of the 8th century B.C., under King Zakkur, from whom a victory stele inscribed in Aramaic is kept in Paris, Hamath apparently reached its greatest power, dominating most of Syria from the Amanus to the Lebanon and from the Mediterranean to the desert. But in 738 ʿEnel of Hamath was forced to surrender 19 provinces to the Assyrians, i.e., the coast and the N part of the Orontes valley. In 720 a usurper, Iaubiʾdi, perhaps of Palestinian origin, tried to regain the lost territory but was defeated and killed; and a number of the inhabitants were deported and the whole country incorporated in the Assyrian Empire.

The remains of biblical Hamath were discovered in the so-called Syro-Hittite or Early Iron Age layers F 2–1 and E 2–1 and are supplemented by the cemeteries found outside the mound. In the troubled times around 1200 B.C., several profound changes took place. A new burial rite, that of urn fields with cremation, was introduced; weapons and tools of iron appeared among which was the cut-and-thrust sword. The fibula replaced the dress pin, and the pottery developed new shapes and patterns in a "geometric" style showing influence from the Mycenaean culture in Greece and Cyprus.

The Royal Quarter was found on the SE part of the mound. See Fig. HAM.01. Its ruins, called Buildings I–IV, spread over an area of at least 160 × 160 m around an open central space with a small sanctuary. Toward the SE was a towered gate (I); toward the NE a temple, probably

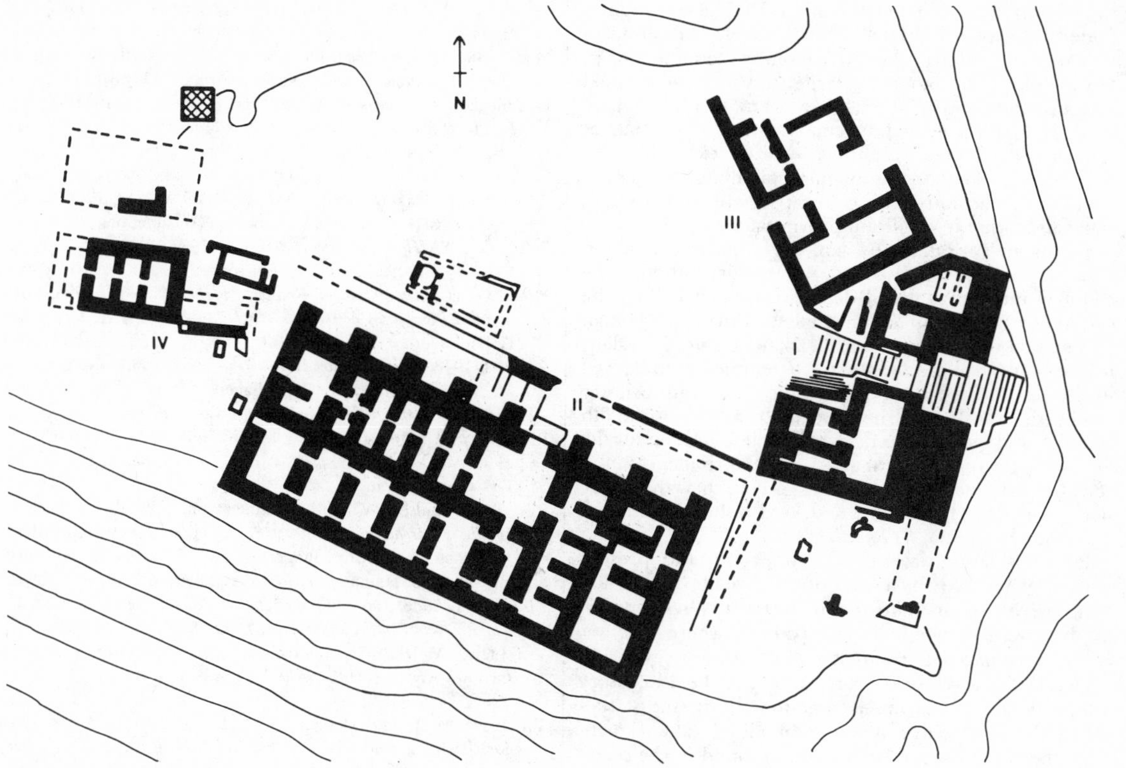

HAM.01. Plan of the Royal Quarter at Hamath, showing buildings I–IV. *(Adapted from Fugmann 1958: 151, fig. 185)*

that of Baᶜalat (III); in the W, a small gate (IV) led to the other quarters of the town; and to the S was a palace (II). The palace had a large reception hall, many storerooms, and an upper story, which seems to have been the royal residence. The entrances to the buildings were guarded by lion sculptures half in relief, and the front of the palace was guarded by colossi in the round. The fittings of the central sanctuary comprised a huge stone basin and two stone altars, one of which had the shape of an empty throne with armrests representing sphinxes. The basin and the throne obviously correspond to the Copper Sea and the cherubim-borne mercy seat in the contemporary temple of Jerusalem. A relief stele of ca. 900 B.C. was reused as a threshold in the supposed Baᶜalat temple. The front of the stele has a representation of a seated god served by a smaller person, most likely the king; below this is a monster with two lion heads and the body of an eagle, a creature which in Mesopotamia was the symbol of the war god Ningirsu. The storerooms of the palace contained jars for grain, wine, and oil, and included tools, weapons, horse trappings, and much more. A foundation document with the impression of a cylinder seal in the style of the first half of the 8th century was found under the E wing of the palace, and in front of the building were bricks with incised Aramaic inscriptions mentioning the *major domus* Adanlaram. Scanty remains of clay tablets inscribed in cuneiform writing, ritual texts, and a letter to king Uratamis were discovered in the temple.

Among the funerary offerings the most spectacular are a gold-plated bronze statuette of a seated god with beard and horns and an ivory goblet with a handle in the shape of a wild goat.

Other fine works of art were found in a small palace, Building V, in the SW part of the town (e.g., ivory reliefs from furniture, which seem to be local products). Several cylinder and stamp seals were brought to light, both in the cemeteries and in the town, including reused items, and sealings, among which was one with the name of Adanlaram. The cremation burials ceased about 700 B.C., and everywhere in the town indisputable signs of the Assyrian ravages were visible. The buildings perished in a conflagration which was so vehement that even some basalt sculptures and bowls partly melted. After the catastrophe most of the site was abandoned; but the literary sources report that Hamath still existed in the 7th and 6th centuries B.C.; and they are corroborated by a few remains from that period, now labeled E/D.

5. Hellenistic Hamath. Under the Seleucids the town revived and was named Epiphaneia, presumably after Antiochus IV Epiphanes, who reigned from 175 to 164 B.C. The excavations have shown that all over the mound a new settlement was laid out according to a rectangular plan with the streets orientated N-S and E-W. The coins found under the constructions date from the 3d and 2d centuries B.C. and thus confirm the attribution to the monarch. In the middle of the mound, a large ruin was transformed into a podium measuring ca. 20 × 20 m, which may have supported the principal sanctuary. Most of the names scratched or painted on pottery were Greek; only a few were Semitic. No doubt, Epiphaneia was almost completely included in the European cultural sphere; but it was a small and rather insignificant provincial town.

6. Roman Period. In 64 B.C. the Romans conquered Syria, and in 52–50 and 40 B.C. the Parthians invaded the country. But a coin hoard dated to the first half of the century betrays nothing of these events. During the Roman domination the town gradually expanded into the valley, where remains of a 3d-century A.D. temple are preserved in the present Great Mosque. In the 4th or 5th century A.D. it was transformed into a church, rebuilt in the 6th century; and recent finds nearer to the mound (under the Greek Orthodox cathedral and Episcopal residence) indicate the existence of another large church with mosaic floors (ca. A.D. 415); the earliest local bishop known was Mauritius about 325.

Probably large waterwheels similar to the present *nawaʿīr* or norias (which a tradition attributes to the Romans) were a dominant feature in the town's physiognomy, as they were in neighboring Apameia, where one was represented in a mosaic. Roman tombs were discovered in the rocks to the W. In the largest one, of the 2d century A.D., funerary plaster masks, limestone busts, and statues portray the deceased. Although of modest local workmanship, they are closely related to those found in the cemeteries of the important caravan town Palmyra. That the tomb was still used in the Christian period is established by the inscriptions and crosses on the walls. A few marble sculptures have survived in the town, hidden away by a faithful pagan worshipper. Two of them are busts of the Greco-Egyptian god Serapis, respectively a copy and a variant of Bryaxis's famous colossal cult statue from the 4th century B.C. in Alexandria. Compared with biblical Hamath, the Greco-Roman town marked both a step backward insofar as it had lost the characteristics of a capital in an independent state and an advance since it profited from participation in the culture of a world empire. The care of the central government is shown by the fact that a fortification wall was built under Constantine the Great, or more likely Justinian the Great, to avert the danger of Sassanian attacks.

After the Muslim conquest in A.D. 636, the ancient name of the town was resurrected.

Bibliography

Bezinger, I. 1907. Epiphaneia 3. *PW* 6/1: 192.

Dussand, R. 1927. Hama et son territoire jusqu'à la conquête assyrienne. Pp. 233–45 in *Topographie historique de la Syrie antique et médiévale*. Paris.

Fugmann, E. 1958. *Hama, Fouilles et Recherches 1931–1938*. Vol. 2, pt. 1, *L'architecture des périodes pré-hellénistiques*. Copenhagen.

Hawkins, J. D. 1975. Hamath. *RLA* 4: 67–70.

Ingholt, H. 1934. *Rapport préliminaire sur la première campagne des fouilles de Hama*. Copenhagen.

———. 1940. *Rapport préliminaire sur sept campagnes de fouilles à Hama en Syrie (1932–1938)*. Copenhagen.

Modderman, P. J. R. 1964. On a Survey of Palaeolithic Sites near Hama. *Les Annales Archéologiques de Syrie* 14: 51–66.

Papanicolaou-Christensen, A., and Friis-Johansen, C. 1971. *Hama, Fouilles et Recherches 1931–1938*. Vol. 3, pt. 2, *Les poteries hellénistiques et les terres sigillées orientales*. Copenhagen.

Papanicolaou-Christensen, A.; Thomsen, R.; and Ploug, G. 1986. *Hama, Fouilles et Recherches 1931–1938*. Vol. 3, *The Graeco-Roman Objects of Clay, the Coins, and the Necropolis*. Copenhagen.

Ploug, G. 1985. *Hama, Fouilles et Recherches 1931–1938*. Vol. 3, pt. 1, *The Graeco-Roman Town*. Copenhagen.

Ploug, G., et al. 1969. *Hama, Fouilles et Recherches 1931–1938*. Vol. 4, pt. 3, *Les petits objets médiévaux sauf les verreries et poteries*. Copenhagen.

Riis, P. J. 1948. *Hama, Fouilles et Recherches 1931–1938*. Vol. 2, pt. 3, *Les cimetières à crémation*. Copenhagen.

———. 1965. *Temple, Church and Mosque*. Copenhagen.

Riis, P. J., and Buhl, M.-L. 1987. *Hama, Fouilles et Recherches 1931–1938*. Vol. 2, pt. 2, *Les objets de la période dite syro-hittite (Age du Fer)*. Copenhagen.

Riis, P. J.; Poulsen, V.; and Hammershaimb, E. 1957. *Hamma, Fouilles et Recherches 1931–1938*. Vol. 4, pt. 2, *Les verreries et poteries médiévales*. Copenhagen.

Sourdel, D. 1965. Ḥamāt. *Encyclopaedia of Islam* 3: 119–21.

Thuesen, I. 1988. *Hama, Fouilles et Recherches 1931–1938*. Vol. 1, *The Pre- and Protohistoric Periods*. Copenhagen.

Van Liere, W. J. 1966. The Pleistocene and Stone Age of the Orontes River. *Annales Archéologiques Arabes Syriennes* 16/2: 7–29.

Van Liere, W. J., and Hooijer, D. A. 1961–62. A Paleo-Orontes Level with archidiskodon meridionalis (Nesti) at Hama. *Les Annales Archéologiques de Syrie* 11–12: 165–72.

Zaqzouq, A. 1983. Fouilles préliminaires à Hama. *Annales Archéologiques Arabes Syriennes* 33/2: 141–78 (in Arabic).

MARIE-LOUISE BUHL

HAMATH, ENTRANCE OF (PLACE) [Heb *lĕbōʾ ḥămat*]. A geographic location in modern Syria which is specifically mentioned as a part of the N boundary for the land promised to Israel (Num 34:7–9; Josh 13:5; Ezek 47:16). The land of HAMATH, with which Lebo-Hamath is associated, was well-known and may explain the function of Lebo-Hamath as a boundary marker. However, Lebo-Hamath itself may also have been well-known (*RLA* 6: 410).

The question of the exact location of Labo-Hamath has not been decisively answered. Some propose that the whole phrase *lĕbōʾ ḥămat* must be taken together as the name of a city. Riblah has been one possible site because of the association of Lebo-Hamath with Zedad and Hazar-enan (see Num 34:7–9). More strongly supported, however, is modern Lebweh, located below Riblah at the source of the Orontes river (attested in Assyrian texts as *La-da/ab-ʾu-u*). Lebo occurs in some Egyptian inscriptions (*rwbj* in the Execration Texts, *la-bi-ʾu* in the syllabic orthography of the New Kingdom) in reference to a city S of Hamath in the Lebanon valley, corresponding to modern Lebweh.

Others (including RSV) analyze *lĕbōʾ ḥămat* as a construct noun phrase. The infinitive *lĕbōʾ*, "to enter," "to approach," is taken together with the place name Hamath, specifying a particular geographic area of Hamath. Three suggestions have been given for the location of a possible area known as Lebo-Hamath. The Orontes valley, between Antioch and Seleucia, is one proposal. Also, an area near Wâdī Nahr el-Barid has been suggested. These first two ideas, however, are not well substantiated. More likely is the last notion of the lower part of the valley of Coele-Syria between the Lebanon and the Anti-lebanon mountains (see Josh 13:5; Judg 3:3; Num 13:21; see also CANAAN).

TOM F. WEI

HAMATH-ZOBAH (PLACE) [Heb *ḥămāt ṣôbâ*]. A compound place name found only once in the Bible (2 Chr 8:3). It occurs in an account of Solomon's fortification program throughout his empire (8:1–10). Verses 3–4 briefly state that Solomon captured Hamath-zobah in a military expedition and went on to fortify the great Syrian oasis of Tadmor and to build store cities in Hamath. These events are not mentioned in 1 Kgs 9:10–22, the passage that is roughly parallel to 2 Chr 8:1–10.

The exact referent of this name is not clear. Some scholars identify the name with the combined regions of the ancient states of Hamath and Zobah, suggesting that the Chronicler is using Persian period (i.e., his contemporary) terminology for that area, since during the Persian period Zobah was part of the province of Hamath (Noth 1937: 45–47; Myers *2 Chronicles* AB, 47–48). Others, however, propose that Hamath-zobah was the name of a city in the kingdom of Zobah. Eissfeldt (1975: 592–93) suggested that it was the capital of Zobah, a city quite distinct from the Hamath which was capital of the state of Hamath. Lewy (1944: 443–54) also viewed it as a city of Zobah and identified it with Baalbek/Heliopolis in Lebanon.

Another proposal has been made by Y. Aharoni (*LBHG,* 319, n. 54), who noted that the major manuscripts of the LXX read *Baisōba* instead of Hamath-zobah in 2 Chr 8:3. Arguing that the Greek reading represents Heb *Beth-zobah,* he proposed that the Greek reflects the original text, that the current Hebrew reading is the result of a scribal error, and that the town referred to here had no connection with the name Hamath.

Unfortunately, little certainty can be reached on these matters, although a few comments are worth making. The wording of 2 Chr 8:3 slightly favors the interpretation of Hamath-zobah as a city name, since similar occurrences of the verb "to go" in the sense of a military campaign normally appear in accounts of attacks against cities (cf. Judg 9:1; 1 Kgs 22:6 = 2 Chr 18:5; 1 Kgs 22:15 = 2 Chr 18:14). But even assuming that it is a city name, no further evidence is available which would allow one to determine whether the Hebrew or the Greek text preserves the name more accurately.

The question of the historical accuracy of this account of a military campaign by Solomon is also unsettled. The differing opinions on this passage are largely based on the varying evaluations of the historical reliability of Chronicles as a whole and particularly of the material in Chronicles that is not found in Kings. Those who generally accept the assertion in 1 Kgs 5:1(—Eng 4:21) that Solomon controlled the Levant as far N as the Euphrates usually assume some historical accuracy for the account of the campaign against Hamath-zobah (e.g., Eissfeldt 1975: 592–93; Malamat 1963: 7; Aharoni, *LBHG,* 319, n. 54). Others (e.g., Miller and Hayes, *HAIJ,* 197–98, 208–10) are much more skeptical about the extent of Solomon's empire in the N in general and about this passage in particular, arguing that the account occurs in the middle of a passage (8:2–4) that seems to be a serious distortion of what is found in 1 Kgs 9:10–18. In 1 Kgs 9:10–14 Solomon gives 20 cities to King Hiram of Tyre, while in 2 Chr 8:2 Hiram gives the cities to Solomon. 1 Kgs 9:15–18 makes no reference to Hamath at all and mentions Tamar, a small town in Judah, instead of Tadmor, the great oasis city in Syria referred to in 2 Chr 8:4. On the issue of the historical reliability of Chronicles, see CHRONICLES, BOOK OF.

Bibliography

Eissfeldt, O. 1975. The Hebrew Kingdom. *CAH*³ 2/2: 537–605.
Lewy, J. 1944. The Old West Semitic Sun-God Ḥammu. *HUCA* 18: 429–88.
Malamat, A. 1963. Aspects of the Foreign Policies of David and Solomon. *JNES* 22: 1–17.
Noth, M. 1937. Das Reich von Hamath als Grenznachbar des Reiches Israel. *PJ* 33: 36–51.

WAYNE T. PITARD

HAMID (PLACE). See ABU HAMID, TELL.

HAMMATH (PERSON) [Heb *ḥammat*]. Apparently a descendant of Hur, son of Caleb; and also the father of the Rechabites (1 Chr 2:55). It is possible that this Hammath is to be identified with the city of Hammath in Naphtali (Josh 19:35, where LXX A reads *hamatha,* but B reads *hamath*). In 1 Chr 2:55, however, the LXX reads *mesēma.* Talmon (1960) suspects that here *ḥmt* should be understood as "family-in-law." Apparently this is the idea that underlies the NEB: "These were Kenites who were connected by marriage with the ancestor of the Rechabites." The entire passage (1 Chr 2:42–50a, 50b–55) is problematic (see Braun *1 Chronicles* WBC, 42–43).

Bibliography

Talmon, S. 1960. 1 Chronicles 2:55. *IEJ* 10: 174–80.

CRAIG A. EVANS

HAMMATH (PLACE) [Heb *ḥammat*]. Var. HAMMOTH-DOR; HAMMON. One of the fortified cities of the tribe of Naphtali (Josh 19:35). Aharoni has suggested that Hammath was #34 in the hypothetical original list of Levitical cities on which the Joshua 21 and 1 Chronicles 6 lists were based (*LBHG,* 304), although in those lists it appears in its variant forms HAMMOTH-DOR (Josh 21:32) and HAMMON (1 Chr 6:61—Eng 6:76). The name Hammath—and that of its variants—means "hot springs," and at least since the time of Josephus (who referred to it as Emmaus) the place was renowned for its healing power (*Ant* 18.2.3 §36; *JW* 4.1.3 §11). Hammath was apparently well-known in the early rabbinic period, and it is referred to numerous times in Jewish writings of that period. These writings make it clear that Hammath was a suburb just outside Tiberias, the site of a major Jewish academy (*Talm.*

Meg. 2.2; *t. ʿErub.* 7.2, 146); consequently, ancient Hammath/Hammoth-Dor/Hammon can be confidently identified with Hammam Tabariyeh (M.R. 201241), a hot springs 3 km S of Tiberias on the W shore of the Sea of Galilee. Apparently the hot springs provided a sufficiently stable economic base to enable the town to last well beyond the abolition of the Jewish Patriarchate in A.D. 429. See also TIBERIAS (PLACE).

Excavations there, however, have thus far failed to yield Iron Age remains (see *EAEHL* 4: 1178–84). In 1921 Slouschz excavated a synagogue about 500 m N of the city's S wall, which has since been dated to the 4th century A.D. A contemporaneous cemetery was found nearby. In the early 1960s M. Dothan excavated a portion of the city wall and one of its towers, which were dated to the Byzantine period (although they apparently rested on the remains of earlier fortifications). Coins indicate that the site was occupied at least as early as the 1st century B.C. Dothan's excavations near the hot springs themselves uncovered three occupation levels. In the lowest (level III, early 2d century A.D.?) was found the remains of a public building the function of which is unknown. Above it, in levels IIB, IIA, IB, and IA, were found the remains of a synagogue that went through four successive construction phases between the 4th and the mid-8th centuries A.D. Among the finds associated with the level IIA synagogue (4th century A.D.) were important Greek and Aramaic inscriptions and well-preserved mosaics (of the Torah shrine and the zodiac) exemplifying superb Hellenistic-Roman artistic style.

Bibliography

Dothan, M. 1983. *Hammath Tiberias.* Jerusalem.

Shanks, H. 1984. Synagogue Excavation Reveals Stunning Mosaic of Zodiak and Torah Ark. *BARev* 10: 32–44.

GARY A. HERION

HAMMEDATHA (PERSON) [Heb *hammĕdātāʾ*]. The father of Haman. He is mentioned in several places in the book of Esther (3:1, 10; 8:5; 9:10, 24) as well as in the Additions to Esther contained in the LXX (Add Esth 12:6; 16:10, 17). He is never spoken of apart from being the father of Haman and as such has no independent existence as a character in the Esther story. Nothing further is known about him, but he appears to have a bona fide Persian name. A contemporary Aramaic ritual text found at Persepolis contains a proper name that could be the Aramaic equivalent to his name, spelled *ʾmdt.* In addition, in the Persepolis fortification tablets this name or one like it appears to be spelled out in cuneiform writing as *ha-ma-da-da* (Millard 1977: 484). Millard suggests that the Persian name from which these names are derived would be *amadāta,* "strongly made" (1977: 484). Other suggested Persian etymologies include *hāma-dāta,* "given by (the god) *Hāma,*" or *mâh-dāta,* "given by the moon." On the other hand, some see this name as a variant form of the name Haman (Paton *Esther* ICC, 69).

Bibliography

Gehman, H. S. 1924. Notes on the Persian Words in the Book of Esther, *JBL* 43: 321–28.

Millard, A. R. 1977. The Persian Names in Esther and the Reliability of the Hebrew Text. *JBL* 96: 481–88.

JOHN M. WIEBE

HAMMOLECHETH (PERSON) [Heb *hammōleket*]. A Manassite mother of three, who is mentioned only in 1 Chr 7:18. Her name means "she who reigns" and may have originally served as a divine title. The form of the name in the LXX, *Malecheth,* reflects the translator's interpretation of the initial *ha* in Hammolecheth as the Hebrew article. Ishhod, Abiezer, and Mahlah were her children. While all three are usually regarded as sons, the last name may be a feminine form and so designate a daughter (cf. Josh 17:3). Morgenstern (1931: 58), however, has suggested that *hammōleket* was not a proper noun at all but simply indicated the authoritative position that the woman held in one of the clans of Manasseh. In this way it preserves evidence of the matriarchate in Israel. This suggestion, though, has won little support, and most continue to regard *hammōleket* as a proper noun. (Rudolph *Chronikbücher* HAT, 70)

Two problems arise in the passage that introduces Hammolecheth. The first concerns the designation of her as "his sister." The preceding verse contains the name of five men, the last of whom is Manasseh. While the antecedent of "his" therefore is by no means certain, most interpreters have favored Gilead (Myers *1 Chronicles* AB, 50). In this case Hammolecheth's father would have been Machir and her grandfather Manasseh.

Additional problems arise in connection with Hammolecheth's children. While genealogies in the Hebrew Bible usually trace ancestry from father to son, in this case the husband of Hammolecheth is unnamed. The reason for this is not obvious. Moreover, Joshua 17 lists Abiezer and Mahlah, the second and third of Hammolecheth's children, as the first son of Gilead (17:2) and the first daughter of Zelophahad (17:3) respectively. This may reflect multiple uses of the same names, or it may indicate confusion in the genealogical tradition. Finally, Curtis and Madsen (*Chronicles* ICC, 152) have suggested that Shemida (1 Chr 7:19), who is not related to the rest of the genealogy of Manasseh in 1 Chronicles 7, was the fourth son of Hammolecheth. This proposal has found little support among other interpreters. See SHEMIDA.

Bibliography

Morgenstern, J. 1931. Additional Notes on "*Beena* Marriage (Matriarchat) in Ancient Israel." *ZAW* 49: 46–58.

M. PATRICK GRAHAM

HAMMON (PLACE) [Heb *ḥammôn*]. Var. HAMMATH; HAMMOTH-DOR(?). **1.** A town in the territory of Asher (Josh 19:28). The portion of the list in which Hammon occurs seems to refer to cities in the N area of the tribe, much of which today is in Lebanon. While some scholars (*GTTOT,* 191; *HGB,* 432) doubt that the city was located on the coast, the site is generally identified with Khirbet Umm el-Awamid (M.R. 164281) in the Wâdī el-Hamul near the spring of En-Hamul. Both the name of the wadi and the name of the spring suggest the preservation of the name Hammon.

Two Hellenistic period Phoenician inscriptions support this identification (*TSSI* 3: 188–121); one was excavated at Umm el-Awamid, and a second was purchased nearby, and both refer to an *ʾl ḥmn,* which can be read as "god of

Hammon" and to the *bʿl ḥmn,* "the citizens of Hammon." While the inscriptions are not conclusive given their Hellenistic date, on balance, the names of the spring and wadi, combined with the inscriptions, support the identification of Umm el-Awamid with Hammon.

2. A town in the tribal territory of Naphtali assigned to the Gershomite clan of the Levites as a Levitical city (1 Chr 6:61—Eng 6:76). Another list of Levitical cities is preserved in Joshua 21, where in v 32 Hammon is replaced by Hammath-dor. Most researchers have concluded that the two OT lists of Levitical cities were derived from a single original, which dated to the time of the United Monarchy (Albright 1945: 49–55). Aharoni (*LBHG,* 304) has suggested that both Hammon and Hammath-dor developed because of scribal errors from an original Hammath, which is located at modern Hammam Tabariyeh (M.R. 201241), springs to the S of modern Tiberias. See also HAMMATH (PLACE). Albright (1945: 55) argued that both Hammon and Hammath-dor were independent toponyms but suggested a location for neither.

Bibliography

Albright, W. F. 1945. The List of Levitical Cities. Pp. 49–73 in *Louis Ginzberg Jubilee Volume.* Philadelphia.

MELVIN HUNT

HAMMOTH-DOR (PLACE) [Heb *ḥammōt dōʾr*]. Var. HAMMATH; HAMMON. A town in the tribe of Naphtali which, along with its pasture lands, was set aside for the Levites (Josh 21:32). In 1 Chr 6:61—Eng 6:76, the second city in the parallel list is Hammon *(ḥammōn).* Albright (1945: 64) has argued that Hammoth-dor and Hammon are different cities and should not be understood to be the same. He based his argument on the readings of Joshua 21, observing that although the LXX offers variant readings, a comparison shows that the original text is preserved in the Greek. Albright's position has not been widely accepted. Aharoni (*LBHG,* 105) argued that Hammoth-dor and Hammon are an example of a "double list" and that the differences in the list may be interpreted as a variation on the same name. In his listing of the Levitical cities, he maintains the 34th city is Hammoth-dor/Hammon while Dor (unidentified in either Joshua 21 or 1 Chronicles 6) is the 35th city in the supposed original list. A problem with that reconstruction arises from the fact that there is no record of any city named Dor in Naphtali. Van Beek (*IDB* 2: 517) suggested that this Levitical city is almost certainly known as Hammon in 1 Chr 6:61—Eng 6:76 and Hammoth-dor in Josh 21:32. Hammoth-dor appears once outside the Levitical city listing as Hammath *(ḥammat)* in the allotment to Naphtali in Josh 19:35. Hammon is mentioned only in the list in 1 Chronicles 6. Outside the OT it is possible that the Hamath mentioned in the papyrus Anastasi I, a document from the time of Rameses II, is Hammath on the Sea of Galilee, i.e., Hammath-Dor. See also Thomas 1934: 147–48.

Hammoth-dor has been identified as Hamman Tabariyeh (M.R. 201241), a hot spring just S of Tiberias on the W shore of the Sea of Galilee (Dothan 1962: 153–54). It is located on a trade route that starts at Hazor and goes along the W coast of the Sea of Galilee. From there it goes into the Rift valley extending S to the Red Sea. A secondary route breaks off from this trade route a few km S of Hamman Tabariyeh. That road goes past Mt. Tabor on its way to Acco. Hammoth-dor is famous for its hot baths that date back to the period of the Second Temple; however, one of the problems of identifying Hamman Tabariyeh with Hammath is that there are no remains there earlier than the Roman period. Albright (1926: 26–27) argued that a Bronze Age town at the hot springs of Tiberias is not likely. He suggested that Hammath was probably on Iron Age foundations since there was no trace of a mound near the site. Because there are no early remains at Hamman Tabariyeh, its identification with biblical Hammoth-dor must be questioned. Just N of Tiberias is a site called Tell Raqqat. Peterson (1977: 95) in his survey has suggested this identification, and Boling (1985: 24) has accepted his proposal. At Tell Raqqat there is evidence that the site was occupied from the Early Bronze to Iron II inclusively. See also *EncJud* 7: 1242–44; 12: 818–21.

Bibliography

Albright, W. F. 1926. The Jordan Valley in the Bronze Age. *AASOR* 6: 26–27.
———. 1945. The List of Levitical Cities. Pp. 49–73 in *Louis Ginzberg Jubilee Volume.* New York.
Boling, R. 1985. Levitical Cities: Archaeology and Texts. Pp. 23–32 in *Biblical and Related Studies.* Winona Lake, IN.
Dothan, M. 1962. Hammath—Tiberias. *IEJ* 12: 153–54.
Peterson, J. L. 1977. *A Topographical Surface Survey of the Levitical "Cities" of Joshua 21 and I Chronicles 6.* Th.D. diss., Seabury-Western Theological Seminary.
Robinson, E. 1841. *Biblical Researches in Palestine.* Vol. 2. Boston.
Thomas, D. W. 1934. The Meaning of the Name Hammath-Dor. *PEQSup* 65: 147–48.

JOHN L. PETERSON

HAMMUEL (PERSON) [Heb *ḥammûʾēl*]. A descendant of Simeon (1 Chr 4:26). The various genealogies for Simeon differ in the number of sons attributed to Simeon. Gen 46:10 and Exod 6:15 list six and comment that Shaul (the last listed) was born to a Canaanite mother. Num 26:12–13 and 1 Chr 4:24–27 list only five, omiting Ohad and the comment on Shaul's mother. In 1 Chr 4:24–27 Simeon's line is traced seven generations beyond him through Shaul with only one name given for each generation and usually without notation on their activities. Hammuel is named the fifth generation descendant. He is not otherwise known. His grandson Shimei, however, did draw the notice that he outdistanced his unnamed siblings in producing offspring, 26 sons and 6 daughters; but none is named; and the genealogy ends with Shimei.

In 1 Chr 4:26 the LXX reads *amouēl,* suggesting a Hebrew spelling with only one *mem.* Such a spelling is commonly present in the versions outside the MT for Hamul, a son of Perez (Gen 46:12; Num 26:21; 1 Chr 2:5).

RICHARD W. NYSSE

HAMMURAPI (PERSON). The sixth and best attested of 11 kings in the so-called First Dynasty of Babylon (also known as Hammurabi), whose extensive collection of laws provides numerous correspondences with biblical law. During his 43-year reign the city of Babylon for the first time rose to prominence as the hub of a short-lived but extensive empire, which declined after his death. Although each of the 42 years following his accession year is identified sequentially with an event considered significant (building projects, pious royal donations to temples, wars), like other events in the early 2d millennium B.C. the absolute dates of Hammurapi remain uncertain. Astronomical data narrow the likely date for Hammurapi's first year to the years 1848 or 1792 or 1736 (the so-called high, middle, and low chronology respectively).

A. The First Dynasty of Babylon

Hammurapi is part of a wave of rulers in S Mesopotamia who began to appear at this time bearing Amorite names; some of the kings of the First Dynasty of Babylon who preceded Hammurapi still bore Akkadian names; but beginning with Hammurapi all of the rulers of this dynasty after him had Amorite names. The Amorites had long before begun to infiltrate the urban centers of Mesopotamia, and the reign of Hammurapi marks the apex of this culture shift. The tribal origins of Hammurapi's dynasty were not forgotten when the Amorites became thoroughly urbanized and ultimately wielded the scepter of the kingdom (see Finkelstein 1966), a situation with some similarity to Israel's tradition of a transfer from a tribal hegemony to a monarchic state. During the 300 years which passed from the founder of the First Dynasty of Babylon (Sumuabum) to the last king (Samsuditana), no king reigned longer than Hammurapi. The five kings of Babylon in the 100 years which preceded Hammurapi give little evidence of ambitions beyond the confines of the city-state of Babylon itself, and they may indeed have often been vassals of more powerful neighbors. Hammurapi's father and predecessor, Sin-muballiṭ, seems to have begun the inertia of expansion which his son brought to fruition. But Hammurapi's son and successor, Samsuiluna, already began to experience the consequences of an overextended empire confronted with numerous enemies (among them the Kassites—who eventually would rule Babylonia—and other foes formerly fought by Hammurapi). The decline which followed Hammurapi climaxed 155 years later in the reign of the final king (Samsuditana), who saw the dynasty brought to an end by a Hittite invasion.

B. Military Expansion

Before Hammurapi consolidated all of Mesopotamia under the dominion of Babylon, the balance of power was succinctly portrayed in a letter written by a contemporary who noted that "there is no king who is mighty by himself." The writer proceeds to clarify this generalization by identifying five primary coalitions: 10 to 15 kings follow Hammurapi of Babylon, a like number of kings each following Rim-Sin of Larsa, Ibal-pi-el of Eshnunna, and Amut-pi-el of Qatana, while Yarim-Lim of Yamhad stands out with 20 kings following him (*ANET*, 628). This balance began to shift when, according to Hammurapi's 30th-year date formula, he fought and protected his borders against Elam, Assyria, Gutium, Eshnunna, and Malgium; the following year he defeated Rim-Sin of Larsa. In order to defeat Rim-Sin, Hammurapi exploited the combined power of the above-noted royal coalitions by soliciting military support from the kings of Mari and Eshnunna (*ARM* 2. 33). Kings with foresight advised, "Don't provide the man of Babylon with auxiliary troops!" (*ARM* 6. 27); for Hammurapi eventually turned against even those to whom he once turned for help, a notable case being the king of Mari, who had commemorated his assistance in his own year date formula: "The year Zimri-Lim went to the aid of Babylon."

The year following Rim-Sin's defeat began an eight-year period of persistent attacks by Hammurapi to the N, beginning with his defeat of the armies of Eshnunna, Assyria, and Gutium. This N campaign was repeated in the following year when he this time defeated Mari and Malgu, returning two years later to demolish their walls. The 37th-, 38th-, and 39th-year date formulas record Hammurapi's victories against his foes to the N.

C. Administration of the Kingdom

Hammurapi's rule was not exclusively preoccupied with military exploits, for the 18 middle years of his 42 year reign (his 12th through 29th date formulas) are exclusively identified by domestic activities. The incorporation of S Mesopotamian cities into a single political unit under the leadership of Babylon was perceived as the legitimate continuation of an old tradition where the kingship of Sumer and Akkad was transferred from city to city. Not only does Hammurapi style himself the king of Sumer and Akkad, but in the prologue and epilogue to his collection of laws he appears as the one who benevolently restored the land's prosperity following a period of decline: "the Shepherd . . . who gathers the scattered people of Isin . . . who causes justice to appear . . . who causes the light to shine for the land of Sumer and Akkad, . . . I uprooted the enemies above and below, I extinguished strife, I promoted the welfare of the land, . . . I tolerated no trouble-makers . . . that the strong might not oppress the weak, to guide properly the orphan and the widow." Such imagery is related to that later employed by Israel's prophets in their descriptions of Yahweh's future restoration and gathering of his scattered people.

In addition to Hammurapi's official inscriptions, which are designed typically to publicize his regal grandeur to observers and future generations, eyewitness accounts of Hammurapi in action in his court in Babylon have been preserved, providing candid glimpses into the behavior of a Babylonian monarch. We have preserved the claims of a man who insists that "whatever subject occupies Hammurapi's mind, he always sends me word and wherever he is I go to him so that whatever troubles him he can tell me" (*ARM* 2. 31); and several such encounters are preserved (e.g., *ARM* 2. 21, 22, 24, 25). Hammurapi is represented by these sources as actively involved in all affairs of his kingdom, easily approachable, and hardly aloof. Another witness testifies that when Amorite messengers from the N once received an audience with Hammurapi, an inequality in gifts of garments on this occasion was perceived as an insult. Hammurapi was reported to have replied curtly to the messengers as he insisted on his absolute sovereignty: "You always cause trouble for me. Now you are harassing my palace about garments. I clothe those whom I wish; and if I don't wish, I don't provide garments!" (*ARM* 2. 76). Hammurapi is heard elsewhere imperiously insulting visiting dignitaries: "I'll return the Elamite messengers to their lord without escort!" (*ARM* 2. 73). On the other hand, Hammurapi's vassal rulers of what is now Tell-Rimah received a report from their son, who notes: "I reached Babylon safely and have seen the king Hammurapi in a good mood" (Dalley et al. 1976: 135).

Some of the correspondence in which Hammurapi was an active communicator is preserved. Of his international correspondence, there remains evidence of letters passing between Babylon and Mari (*ARM* 2. 33–34, 51–54, 67–68) and reputed quotes from correspondence between Hammurapi and Rim-Sin of Larsa (*ARM* 2. 72). Scores of letters from Hammurapi himself are also preserved in the archives of two of Hammurapi's administrators in Larsa toward the end of his reign, and these documents are helpful in discerning the structure of Babylonian society and Hammurapi's remarkably active role in the maintenance of the kingdom (*AbB* 2, 4, 9).

There is also a letter which gives a hint as to the eventual demise of Hammurapi. His son Samsuiluna wrote a letter now in our possession in which he notes: "The king my father i[s ill(?)] . . . . I have taken [my seat] on the throne of [my father's] house" (*ANET,* 627). He proceeds to relate how he has canceled debts in the land, a typical action of monarchs when they began their reigns.

The reign of Hammurapi, with its expanding horizons for Babylon, facilitated the enhancement of enriched cultural and cosmopolitan dimensions in Babylonian society. The flourishing of scribal activity is evident not only in the numerous administrative documents from this period, but also in the quantity of OB literary texts (themselves already heirs to a long tradition), which were to set the standard for future literary activity into the 1st millennium B.C.

D. Hammurapi and the Bible

Hammurapi's original significance for biblical studies derived from two facts. First was the discovery in 1901 of a corpus of laws which was promulgated by Hammurapi (*ANET,* 163–80). The 8-foot-high diorite stele (now in the Louvre) originally containing 282 laws was discovered not in Babylon (where it was erected by Hammurapi) but in Susa, where it had been taken as booty by the Elamites, who raided Babylon six centuries after the time of Hammurapi (many of the laws were effaced from the stone by the Elamites). In addition to that discovery, numerous copies and fragments of these laws have been found at other sites throughout Mesopotamia; and the stone was copied by scribes even down into the first millennium B.C. The portrait of Hammurapi on the stele depicts the deity Shamash granting to Hammurapi the symbols of justice (scepter and ring), appropriately corresponding to the content of the stone, which relates the laws which Hammurapi promulgated.

The relevance for society in general of the collection and standardization of Hammurapi's laws is perplexing. Prices, fines, and penalties do not always correspond with actual data from the same period; and records of actual court cases do not cite the collection of laws as a basis or rationale for adjudication. This is a problem similar to that which confronts the biblical scholar with regard to the antiquity of the civil laws in Exodus and Deuteronomy which were often ignored in narratives (e.g., Deut 24:16; Josh 7:24–25; 2 Sam 21:1–9; cf. 1 Kgs 21:1 with 2 Kgs 9:26). Likewise, the Laws of Hammurapi and the laws in the Pentateuch are incomplete and leave many subjects untreated. It is likely that Hammurapi's laws are to be understood as part of his amalgamation of diverse traditions in a newly unified domain, and he is therefore not to be pictured as an innovator of new legislation. Hammurapi was not the first patron of an edition of laws, for he stands in a tradition of legal editors as is seen in smaller and less well-preserved law collections sponsored by kings before the time of Hammurapi. A continuity among legal collections makes it clear that even the internal arrangement of laws was not haphazard but followed certain conceptual patterns, a feature which seems to be reflected in biblical law as well (Kaufman 1987).

In the epilogue of his laws, the public nature of this collection is underscored by an appeal to their non-elitist, universal availability to all: "Let any oppressed man who has a cause come into the presence of the statue of me, the king of justice, and then read carefully my inscribed stele, and give heed to my precious words; and may my stele make the case clear to him; may he understand his cause; may he set his mind at ease!" Only a minority could read the cuneiform inscription, making the appeal itself an exaggerated one. But the old tribal justice once achieved by recourse to tribal leaders was compromised by the reality of an extensive kingdom where, although Hammurapi continued to involve himself in mundane affairs to an amazing degree, a vast administration and bureaucracy stifled the active involvement of the king in every legal dispute. Such stone steles inscribed with laws distributed throughout the kingdom functioned as Hammurapi's surrogates—if not in fact, at least symbolically—in asserting a non-arbitrary and coherent stability to the justice administered by the kingdom's bureaucrats.

The format of engraving legal norms in stone finds an echo in Deuteronomy (5:22; 9:9–11; 10:3), where the laws given to Moses at Mt. Sinai are depicted as also being engraved in stone. Words in stone are not subject to easy manipulation, and the explicit words of Hammurapi's epilogue clarify the permanence which the medium presumes: "In the days to come, for all time, let the king who appears in the land observe the words of justice which I wrote on my stele; let him not alter the law of the land which I enacted." Numerous curses are inscribed for the person who "has abolished the law which I enacted, has distorted my words, has altered my statutes."

The second significance of Hammurapi for biblical studies lies in a now abandoned proposal that the biblical Amraphel from Shinar (appearing in a story about Abraham in Gen 14:1, 9) was the famous Hammurapi of the First Dynasty of Babylon. Although Shinar is defensible as a designation for Babylon, the Hebrew form of the name Amraphel seems to presuppose a name of Amorite background such as ʾAmar-pi-ʾel or Emudbal (Schatz 1972).

The name Hammurapi is not unusual, being attested elsewhere not only of other kings (e.g., of kings of Yamhad, Hana, or Kurda also in the early second millennium B.C.) but also of nonroyal figures. In the 13th century B.C., the last king of Ugarit of whom we have information bears the same name as well. The spellings of these names presume an initial element *ʿammu,* "paternal uncle" and a second element *rapiʾ,* "healer" or "hale," pointing to a name which signifies that the deceased divinized kinsman is the one who invigorates (perhaps bearing some connection to the Rephaim).

Bibliography

Dalley, S.; Walker, C. B. F.; and Hawkins, J. D. 1976. *The Old Babylonian Tablets from Tell al Rimah.* London.

Driver, G. R., and Miles, J. C. 1952–55. *The Babylonian Laws.* 2 Vols. Oxford.

Finet, A. 1973. *Le Code de Hammourabi.* Paris.

Finkelstein, J. J. 1966. The Genealogy of the Hammurapi Dynasty. *JCS* 20: 95–118.

———. 1981. The Ox That Gored. *TAPhS* 71: 5–47.

Kaufman, S. A. 1987. The Second Table of the Decalogue and the Implicit Categories of ANE Law. Pp. 111–16 in *Love and Death in the ANE,* ed. J. Marks and R. Good. Guilford, CT.

Klengel, H. 1976. *Hammurapi von Babylon und seine Zeit.* Berlin.

Leemans, W. F. 1985. Hammurapi's Babylon. *Sumer* 41: 91–96.

Schatz, W. 1972. *Genesis 14: Ein Untersuchung.* Frankfurt.

SAMUEL A. MEIER

HAMON-GOG (PLACE) [Heb *hamôn-gôg*]. The name, translated as "the multitude of Gog," of a valley described in Ezek 39:11, 15. Of uncertain location, Hamon-Gog was prophesied as a place for the massive burial of Gog, chief prince of Meshech and Tubal, and the multitudes that followed him. See also GOG (PERSON). Verse 11 reports that the extensive burial would deter traveling through this pass, even though it would also be called the "valley of Oberim" ("travelers"), perhaps a reference to a well-traveled highway or suggesting a connection with the Abarim mountain range of Num 33:47, located in NW of Moab, NE of the Dead Sea. Mt. Nebo is the dominant feature in this portion of land.

JEFFREY K. LOTT

HAMONAH (PLACE) [Heb *hămônâ*]. The name of the city in the valley in Ezek 39:16 where the armies of Gog will be buried after their destruction. This is the only occurrence of the name, and its location is unknown.

The name derives from the noun *hmôn,* "sound," "murmur," "roar," "crown," "abundance," from *hmh,* "murmur," "growl," "roar," "be boisterous," i.e., the roaring of a crowd, multitude (BDB, 242). The LXX has *Poluandrion,* "multitude" and uses the same term for Hamon-Gog (Ezek 39:11, 15) and as generic for multitude (Ezek 39:11; Jer 2:23; 19:2, 6). BDB (242) notes the reading as dubious, as does Kittel *(BHK),* for *wĕgam šem-ʿîr hămônâ,* literally "and also the name of the city Hamonah." RSV says the city is there (taking *šem,* "name," as *šam,* "there") while KJV supplies "shall be," i.e., will be built to commemorate the defeat, or a current city's name will be changed to Hamonah. Eichrodt (*Ezekiel* ET, OTL, 517–18) leaves the phrase out of the text, translates vv 11 and 15 as "the valley of the pomp of Gog," and footnotes v 16, "MT: 'And also the name of one city is Hamona' (i.e. pomp); and archaeological note, explaining the name of a city, Hamona, by the 'pomp of God.' "

The city is in the valley of the Travelers, called the valley of Hamon-gog, E of the sea (39:11). May (*IB* 6:28) interprets "sea" as the Dead Sea. The Hebrew for "travelers" is repointed by some following the Coptic version to read Abarim (*haʿăbārîm* for *hāʿōbĕrîm*), i.e., the mountains of Abarim, which included Mt. Nebo, N of Wâdī Zerqa Maʾin (Nahaliel; Num 27:12; 33:47–48; Deut 32:49) above the NE corner of the Dead Sea. One notes that the troops will die on the mountains of Israel (39:4); and God is quoted as saying, "I will give to Gog a place for burial in Israel." The people of Israel will spend seven months burying the dead (39:12). All this suggests the valley and its city are in Israel, i.e., Cisjordan. There were, of course, times when Israel controlled the Nebo area, which was also controlled by the Ammonites at times, though it seems most often to have been part of Moab. Thus it seems more natural to interpret "sea" as Mediterranean Sea and the burial and the city as in Israel proper, with the cleansing of the land meaning burial, and not removal of the bodies to another land.

Zimmerli (*Ezekiel 2* Hermeneia, 291–93, 317–19) also sees v 16a as an obvious addition. He translates v 11 as Oberim(?) valley, but acknowledges the reading Abarim. "Sea" may then mean Dead Sea, but he notes that this is not Israel. The sea may be the Mediterranean or the Sea of Galilee. The former might suggest the valley of Jezreel, while the latter might indicate the valley of the Wanderers, the Wâdī Fejjas, as cited by several scholars. Beth-shan, Megiddo, and Emmaus (Ammaoun in 1 Macc 3:40) have been suggested as the city that will be renamed Hamonah. He notes the identifications "remain in the realm of free speculation." For his own speculation Zimmerli raises a question about the loose assonance between the valley of Hamonah ("hordes") and the valley of Hinnom. This associates the valley of abomination with Gog. "That an etymological etiology is intended here is in any case probable."

Of course, the entire context in Ezekiel is metaphoric and symbolic, or legendary to use Eichrodt's phrase (*Ezekiel* ET, OTL, 529); so it may not be a literal city or place at all. The term "multitude" is a common metaphor as is another valley in the famous line in Joel 4:14 [—Eng 3:14], "Multitudes, multitudes in the valley of decision."

HENRY O. THOMPSON

HAMOR (PERSON) [Heb *ḥămôr*]. The father of Shechem (Gen 33:19). When Jacob returned from Paddan-aram, he purchased from the sons of Hamor a piece of land, upon which he erected an altar (33:19–20). Presumably the sale happened in the presence of the representatives of the place (cf. chap. 23). Joseph was later buried there at Shechem (Josh 24:32) when his remains were removed from Egypt to Canaan. Stephen jumbled two stories when he said that "Jacob and our fathers" were buried at Shechem in a plot bought by Abraham from the sons of Hamor (Acts 7:16). Actually Jacob was buried at Machpelah in a plot bought by Abraham from the "sons of Heth" (Gen 50:13).

Hamor's son Shechem raped Jacob's daughter Dinah

(34:2). At Shechem's request, Hamor, without mentioning the violation, asked for Dinah to be given in marriage to his son (vv 4–8). Both agreed to the condition of circumcision, only to be killed in that weakened state by Simeon and Levi three days later out of revenge (vv 13–29).

Hamor was the prince or chief of the region around the city (v 2). However, the textual tradition appears confused about whether the tribe of which Hamor was head was Hivite (MT) or Horite (LXX)—cf. Josh 9:7; also note Gen 36:2, 20. These terms seem to overlap to some extent, a circumstance which was historically grounded in contacts between the two groups to the N of Canaan proper (Boling *Joshua* AB, 251, 264–65; Blenkinsopp 1971: 275, esp. n. 38). The Hamor clan remained dominant at Shechem into the time of the judges. According to Judg 9:28, depending on how one understands the passage, either Abimelech and his deputy were put in office by the Hamorite aristocracy or the Shechemites were being urged back to traditional ways—viz., those of serving the "men of Hamor." Since the name Hamor means "(he-)ass," the MB practice among Amorites at the W Mesopotamian city-state Mari of ratifying a treaty by sacrificing an ass comes to mind. Some (e.g., Albright *ARI,* 113; Willesen 1954: 216–17) have supposed that the expression, "sons of the ass/Hamor," applied to the Shechemites several times, might have designated "members of a confederacy." Others (e.g., Kidner *Genesis* TOTC, 173; Davidson *Genesis 12–50* CBC, 191) have objected that although sacredness of the animal may account for the name, Hamor was an individual.

Bibliography

Blenkinsopp, J. 1971. The Prophetic Reproach. *JBL* 90: 267–78.

Willesen, F. 1954. Die Eselsöhne von Sichem als Bundesgenossen. *VT* 4: 216–17.

EDWIN C. HOSTETTER

HAMRAN (PERSON) [Heb *ḥamrān*]. Var. HEMDAN. A clan name mentioned in the genealogy of Seir the Horite in 1 Chr 1:41. Hamran is listed as the first of four sons of DISHON, son of Anah, and he is therefore a great-grandson of Seir. The name Hamran, which appears as "Amran" in the KJV, is found only in 1 Chr 1:41; but it is equivalent to HEMDAN (the Gk Lucian and Alexandrinus form) also found in the parallel genealogical clan list in Gen 36:26. For discussion of the Horite clans, see JAAKAN.

VICTOR H. MATTHEWS

HAMUL (PERSON) [Heb *ḥāmûl*]. The younger son of Perez (Gen 46:12; 1 Chr 2:5), one of the twin sons of Judah and Tamar (Gen 37:27–30). His name appears as Hamuel in the Samaritan Pentateuch and in the LXX, in which case it means "God protects" (*TPNAH,* 138). In the record of Jacob's family, Jacob's children and grandchildren are listed by families, according to their mother and order of birth (Gen 46:8–27). Hamul was the grandson of Jacob and Leah by their fourth son, Judah (Gen 46:12). None of Hamul's descendants is mentioned in the OT although the descendants of his brother Hezron are fully given (1 Chr 2:5–24). Hamul was the head of the family of the Hamulites (Num 26:21). The name may mean "spared" (*IDB* 2: 519).

CLAUDE F. MARIOTTINI

HAMUTAL (PERSON) [Heb *ḥămûṭal*]. Daughter of Jeremiah of Libnah; wife of King Josiah; and mother of Johoahaz and Zedekiah, kings of Judah (2 Kgs 23:31; K *ḥămîṭal,* Q *ḥămûṭal* in 2 Kgs 24:18 and Jer 52:1). The name of this individual perhaps means "my father-in-law is protection" (*HALAT,* 313b) or "my father-in-law is the dew" (*BDB,* 327b); if *waw/yod* expresses the vocative (see Dahood 1977: 218; 1978: 190), it may mean "become warm, O Dew."

Bibliography

Bauer, H. 1930. Die hebräischen Eigennamen als sprachliche Erkenntnisquelle. *ZAW* 48: 73–80.

Dahood, M. 1977. Vocative *waw* in Psalm 30,9. *Bib* 58: 218.

———. 1978. New Readings in Lamentations. *Bib* 59: 174–97.

ROBERT ALTHANN

HANA (PERSON) [Gk *Anan*]. Var. HANAN. A temple servant who was the progenitor of a family which returned from Babylon with Zerubbabel (1 Esdr 5:30) and clearly a variant of HANAN (Heb *ḥānān*) in Ezra 2:46 = Neh 7:49.

MICHAEL DAVID MCGEHEE

HANAMEL (PERSON) [Heb *ḥănamʾēl*]. The son of Jeremiah's uncle Shallum (Jer 32:6, 8, 9) and the cousin whose field at Anathoth the prophet purchases. This incident, widely held to be authentic, occurred during the Babylonian invasion of Jerusalem (587 B.C.E.) while Jeremiah was imprisoned. Included in that part of the book of Jeremiah known as the "Book of Consolation" (Jeremiah 30–33), the purchase of Hanamel's field expresses hope for Yahweh's restoration of Judah following the Exile: "Houses and fields and vineyards shall again be bought in this land" (Jer 32:15). The purchase of Hanamel's field occurs according to the right of redemption (Lev 25:25); so the event has been of particular interest because the detail of the text provides a glimpse into the social, economic, and legal practices of ancient Israel. It is widely held (*TPNAH,* 82) that Hanamel's name derives from *hnn ʾl,* "God is gracious," though how this bears upon Jer 32:6–15 is uncertain.

JOHN M. BRACKE

HANAN (PERSON) [Heb *ḥānān*]. Var. HANA. The name of nine men in the Hebrew Bible. Hanan is a shortened form of names such as Elhanan, "God is gracious," and Johanan or Hananiah, "YHWH is gracious." The root *ḥnn,* "to be gracious," is a common element in many biblical and extrabiblical Hebrew names from various periods (*IPN,* 187; Shiloh 1986: 29; Avigad 1986: 57–58, 74, 97; *TPNAH,* 345); the shortened form Hanan, however, is only known from late preexilic (Jer 35:4; Avigad 1986: 58) through postexilic sources. The name's prominence in the postexilic period suggests that the returnees were either thankful to God, who had restored them to Zion, or were hoping that God would soon complete the promised ideal restoration.

1. According to Jer 35:4 Jeremiah brought the Rechabites to "the chamber of the sons of *[bĕnê]* Hanan the son of Igdaliah, the man of God" in the Jerusalem temple. This Hanan is never mentioned elsewhere. The plural *bĕnê,* "sons of," is odd, especially since temple chambers are usually occupied by a single person. Carrol (*Jeremiah* OTL, 652) has suggested that *bĕnê* is being used as a technical term for a guild member and the verse refers to "the prophetic guild of Hanan . . . the prophet." A similar use of *bĕnê* plus a personal name for guild members is attested to in the names of psalmists' guilds, as in "the sons of Korah" (e.g., Psalm 42), namely, members of the Korahite guild. Thus Jeremiah brought the Rechabites to the chamber of a prophetic guild at the temple, probably since he thought they might be sympathetic to the anti-Jerusalem component of this prophecy (v 17). Several LXX mss read a longer form for the name Hanan; there are several similar cases within the MT where the full and abbreviated names of the same person alternate (*TPNAH,* 150–52).

2. One of the families of the NETHINIM, "temple servants," which returned from the Exile according to the lists in Ezra 2:46 and Nehemiah 7:49, which are almost identical. The list of returnees is probably composite and its original purpose and date remain uncertain (Williamson *Ezra, Nehemiah* WBC, 28–32; Blenkinsopp *Ezra Nehemiah* OTL, 83). According to the tradition of Josh 9:23 and 27, the temple servants were non-Israelite in origin; and this explains the many non-Israelite names in the temple servant list (Williamson *Ezra, Nehemiah* WBC, 36; Blenkinsopp, 90). In this case it is possible that Hanan should not be interpreted as an abbreviation of a specifically Israelite name like Yohanan but should be connected to the name Hanan, which was commonly used by other Semitic peoples (*HALAT,* 321), and to seals of probable Ammonite or Edomite origin which use the names Hananel and Elhanan (*TPNAH,* 345).

3. A prominent Levite who played a role in the reforms of Ezra according to Neh 8:7 and 10:11—Eng 10:10. Nehemiah 8:7 describes the public reading of the Torah by Ezra on the first day of the seventh month at the Water Gate in Jerusalem (Neh 7:72 [—Eng 7:73]–8:8). Hanan is listed as one of the 13 Levites who instructed the people in the meaning of the Torah. The MT reads *wĕhalwiyyîm,* "and the Levites," possibly suggesting that 13 people plus the Levites participated; however, *wĕhalwiyyîm* should either be emended with the LXX to *halwiyyîm* (BHS; Blenkinsopp, 284), or the *waw* should be understood explicatively. The exact role of these Levites remains unclear because of the unique technical vocabulary in v 8 (Fishbane 1985: 108–9), but the connection of the Levites to teaching or to liturgical reading and singing is consistent with what we know elsewhere of their role in the postexilic community (Cody 1969: 187–90). In Neh 10:11 (—Eng 10:10), Hanan appears on a list of Levites in vv 10–14 (—Eng 9–13) among the signers of the *ʾămānâ,* "compact," on the 24th of the first month (Neh 9:1). There is approximately a 50 percent overlap between the list of Levites in Neh 8:7 and 10:10–14 (—Eng 10:9–13); this might suggest that the list in Nehemiah 10 is largely artificial (Williamson, *Ezra, Nehemiah* WBC, 325–30), or it might suggest that the Hanan of 8:7 should probably be identified with that of 10:11 and indicates that Hanan was among the more important Levites of the period.

4 and 5. Two people listed in Neh 10:23 and 27 (—Eng 10:22 and 26), in a list of "the chiefs of the people" (vv 10:15–28—Eng 10:14–27). Both the list as a whole and the appearance of Hanan twice on the list may be problematic. In v 27—Eng 26 the Peshitta reads Hanani for Hanan, and Rudolph (*Esra und Nehemia* HAT, 172; so BHS) would change one of the Hanan's to Hanani. This is not compelling; this list is a compilation of various lists, and the doubling of Hanani probably reflects two separate Hananis in the author's source material. Williamson (*Ezra, Nehemiah* WBC, 325–30; and Blenkinsopp, 313) have shown persuasively that much of this list is an artificial creation since it incorporates lists known elsewhere in Nehemiah. In that case the overlap between the list of Levites in vv 10–14 (—Eng 9–13) and the list of chiefs in 15–28 (—Eng 14–27) should be pointed out (Bani in vv 10 [—Eng 9] and 15 [—Eng 14]; Hodayah in 10, 14, and 19 [—Eng 9, 13, and 18]; possibly Binui [10—Eng 9] = Buni [16—Eng 15]; and Hashaviah [11—Eng 10] = Hasub [24—Eng 23] or Hashabiah [26—Eng 25]), in which case the name(s) Hanan might have been borrowed from the levitical list to the list of chiefs. Thus it remains unclear how many, or indeed if any, people named Hanan were actually among the chiefs of the people who signed the compact.

6. Son of Zaccur, son of Mattaniah, one of the four people entrusted with the proper distribution of tithes upon Nehemiah's return from his visit to Persia according to Neh 13:13. The verse states that these four distributed tithes "to their brethren." This suggests that this Hanan was a Levite; perhaps he could be identified with the Hanan of 8:7 and 10:11. Williamson (*Ezra, Nehemiah* WBC, 388) and Blenkinsopp (356) suggest that this Hanan's grandfather, Mattaniah, should be identified with the Mattaniah the precentor mentioned in 11:17 and 12:35. This is possibly supported by the inclusion of Hanan's grandfather's name (Mattaniah) in Neh 13:13, since these name lists in Nehemiah sometimes give genealogical information to connect someone to a well-known ancestor (e.g., 12:35).

7. According to 1 Chr 8:23 a Benjaminite, the son of Shashak (v 25); Hanan among the clans who resided in Jerusalem (v 28). It is not clear how this entire section of the Benjaminite genealogy should be related to the rest of the chapter and when this Hanan supposedly lived (Williamson *1 and 2 Chronicles* NCBC, 82–83). The presence of the names Anthothijah and Penuel in vv 24–25, which are related to geographic locations, suggests that one of the functions of this genealogy is to relate clans living in various places (Demsky 1971; see ALEMETH and MOZA). In this case Hanan here might be related to the town Beth-hanan mentioned in 1 Kgs 4:9.

8. According to 1 Chr 8:38 and 9:44 one of the six sons of Azel, son of Moza, a descendant of Benjamin and Saul. Hanan's name within this list is a bit odd, since it is the only hypocorism among the six children. Given the tendency of v 36 in this genealogy to connect clans through geographic locations (Demsky 1971; see ALEMETH), this Hanan might be related to the Beth-hanan mentioned in

1 Kgs 4:9. The genealogy in chap. 9 ends with Hanan, while that in chap. 8 contains additional information (see ESHEK). On the repetition of the genealogy in chaps. 8 and 9, see AHAZ (PERSON) #1.

9. Son of Maacah and one of the warriors of David (Mazar 1963) according to 1 Chr 11:43. The list of David's warriors in 1 Chr 11:26–47 is derived from various sources; the first section (until the middle of v 41) is derived from 2 Sam 23:24–39. The second part differs in form from the first and probably reflects an additional preexilic source that was available to the Chronicler (Williamson *1 and 2 Chronicles* NCBC, 103–4). If it were a fabrication, it would probably follow the previous section's style more closely. The purpose of 1 Chronicles 11 is to glorify David by showing the extent of the military power that supported him, thus reinforcing the divine promise to David (see 1 Chr 11:10); this idea probably motivated the chapter's editor to go beyond his usual source and to find additional lists of David's warriors.

Bibliography

Avigad, N. 1986. *Hebrew Bullae from the Time of Jeremiah.* Jerusalem.

Cody, A. 1969. *A History of OT Priesthood.* AnBib 35. Rome.

Demsky, A. 1971. The Genealogy of Gibeon (1 Chronicles 9:35–44): Biblical and Epigraphic Considerations. *BASOR* 202: 16–23.

Fishbane, M. 1985. *Biblical Interpretation in Ancient Israel.* Oxford.

Mazar, B. 1963. The Military Élite of King David. *VT* 13: 310–20.

Shiloh, Y. 1986. A Group of Hebrew Bullae from the City of David. *IEJ* 36: 16–38.

MARC Z. BRETTLER

HANANEL, TOWER OF (PLACE) [Heb *migdal hănanʾēl*].

A tower in the N part of exilic and postexilic Jerusalem, mentioned in Jer 31:38; Zech 14:10; Neh 3:1; and 12:39. The tower's exact location is not certain. The fullest information for locating the tower comes from the topographical details in Nehemiah 2, 3, and 12. These passages indicate that the tower was at the NW corner of the wall surrounding the Temple Mount. Neh 3:1 specifies the tower as the farthest point in Nehemiah's restored wall to be consecrated by the high priest (or, following Williamson, to be boarded). It has been proposed that this tower, together with the Tower of the One Hundred, guarded the NW approach to the Temple Mount. Possibly they flanked the Fish Gate (Avi-Yonah 1954: 240–42). These towers were perhaps related to the temple's fortress mentioned in Neh 2:8 (Williamson *Ezra, Nehemiah* WBC, 204). The later citadel of 1 Macc 13:52 and the Antonia Fortress of Herod may correspond to the Tower of Hananel (Avi-Yonah 1954: 242) or mark the spot on which it had stood earlier. Zech 14:10 has led some to suppose that the Tower of Hananel was a prominent landmark for the N boundary of the city at that time (Williamson *Ezra, Nehemiah* WBC, 204).

It is striking that the Tower of Hananel appears in texts that stress the completion of some important, at times eschatological, event. In Jer 31:38–40 the reference to the Tower of Hananel appears at the climactic conclusion of the Book of Consolation (Jer 30:1–31:40). Here, in the last of three oracles about the coming days, Jeremiah speaks of the full restoration of the city for all time. The Tower of Hananel is one of several landmarks indicating the large scope of the restoration. Could the references in Neh 3:1 and 12:29 allude to this promise in Jeremiah? In Zechariah the Tower of Hananel also appears at a concluding section, in a sequence of proclamations concerning the coming Day of the Lord (Zech 14:1). Here nature itself will be transformed (Zech 14:6). God's kingship will be manifest (Zech 14:9), and Jerusalem will be literally elevated. The Tower of Hananel marks the N limit of this newly elevated and secure Jerusalem. Such references suggest that the Tower of Hananel represented more than a stronghold and a recognizable landmark. It may have become a symbol for a fulfillment of certain eschatological hopes (Eskenazi 1988: 85–86).

Bibliography

Avi-Yonah, M. 1954. The Walls of Nehemiah—A Minimalist View. *IEJ* 4: 239–48.

Blenkinsopp, J. 1988. *Ezra-Nehemiah.* OTL. Philadelphia.

Eskenazi, T. C. 1988. *In An Age of Prose: A Literary Approach to Ezra-Nehemiah.* SBLMS 36. Atlanta.

TAMARA C. ESKENAZI

HANANI (PERSON) [Heb *ḥănānî*].

The name of five individuals in the Hebrew Bible. The name is a shortened form of Hananiah, which means "YHWH has taken pity" (Noth *IPN*, 187).

1. The father of the prophet Jehu (1 Kgs 16:1, 7; 2 Chr 19:2; 20:34 [LXX *anani*]) and a seer during the reign of Asa (2 Chr 16:7). The Deuteronomistic Historian records only Jehu's prophecy against Baasha, king of Israel (900–877 B.C.E.). That Hanani is consistently named as Jehu's father might indicate either that Hanani was a well-known figure, thus helping to identify Jehu, or that "Jehu son of Hanani" is to be clearly distinguished from "Jehu son of Jehoshaphat" (2 Kgs 9:2). The Chronicler records a prophecy by Hanani himself against King Asa of Judah (913–873 B.C.E.) in the 36th year of his reign (2 Chr 16:1–10). This story is theologically motivated and follows the tradition of later prophets, e.g., Isaiah 7 and Zech 4:6 (Myers *2 Chronicles* AB, 94). Hanani's prophecy also shows the lessons of Asa's downfall just as Azariah's sermon in 15:2–7 explains the good years of his reign (Williamson *Chronicles* NCBC, 274). The Chronicler goes on to relate two prophecies of his son Jehu against Jehoshaphat of Judah (873–849 B.C.E.). The dates of these prophecies do not preclude the possibility that all the accounts are based on authentic memories of historical persons and their activity.

2. A postexilic family of levitical singers within the Heman group (1 Chr 25:4, 25 [LXX *ananias*]). 1 Chronicles 25 describes the selection of 288 Levites from the families of Asaph, Jeduthun, and Heman, who were to "prophesy with lyres, with harps, and with cymbals" (v 1). (The Chronicler seems to have replaced the cultic prophets with Levites [Myers *1 Chronicles* AB, 171; see 2 Chronicles 20, and compare 2 Kgs 23:2 with 2 Chr 34:30].) Lots were cast to determine the specific duties of each family. The 18th lot fell to the family of Hanani, but the text does not specify what duty was assigned to them. Although the Chronicler alleges a random selection process, the lots seem to fall in a regular pattern based on the order of names listed in vv 1–6. Myers believes the names listed in v 4b (of which Hanani is one) are actually incipits of hymns interpreted by the Chronicler as personal names, filling out the needed number for the 24 lots (Myers *1 Chronicles* AB, 172–73). Williamson asserts that these five families were named, "perhaps playfully, after the openings of Psalms which they were regularly accustomed to sing" (Williamson *Chronicles* NCBC, 167). In either case it seems likely that this "personal name" was originally a word in the opening line of a psalm.

3. A member of the priestly family of Immer and one of the returned exiles who was required by Ezra to divorce his foreign wife (Ezra 10:20 [LXX *anani*] = 1 Esdr 9:21 [LXX *ananias*]). Hanani was a member of a family from which a group of exiles returned with Zerubbabel (Ezra 2:37; Neh 7:40). For further discussion, see BEDEIAH.

4. A brother of Nehemiah who brought news to Nehemiah of Jerusalem's state of disrepair (Neh 1:2 [LXX *anani*]; 7:2 [LXX *anania*]). While the word "brother" (ʾaḥ) has a broad meaning within Nehemiah's memoirs, this is the only use of the term referring to a specific individual; so we can assume that Hanani was Nehemiah's blood brother. Noting the seemingly casual conversation between Nehemiah and Hanani, Fensham suggests that Hanani was merely on a family visit to Susa (*Ezra Nehemiah* NICOT, 151). Alternatively, Myers raises the discussion that Hanani was part of a delegation sent directly to Artaxerxes in order to bypass unfriendly Samaritans who had blocked attempts at rebuilding Jerusalem (*Ezra, Nehemiah* AB, 94–95). Neh 7:2 shows that Hanani held a position of power in Jerusalem under Nehemiah's governorship as one of two people responsible for opening and closing the gates during a time of political tension. (It is possible that "Hananiah" is in apposition with "Hanani my brother," but note "I said to them" in v 3.) Much has been made of a possible identification of Hanani with an individual named in the edict of Arsames to Elephantine. However, the reading of the name is questionable, and the probable reconstruction is "Hananiah" (Sachau 1911: pl. 4). Thus our knowledge of Hanani is limited to Nehemiah's memoirs.

5. A postexilic musician who assisted in the ceremony rededicating the newly reconstructed walls of Jerusalem (Neh 12:36). Neh 12:27–43 lists the persons who accompanied Ezra in a circumambulation of the walls of Jerusalem in a dedicatory service; however, the LXX omits Hanani and the five names preceding his, and there are other differences from the Hebrew text. Hanani is listed as a trumpeter who "went to the right" (12:31) around the wall while another group of celebrants "went to the left" (12:38). The inclusion of rituals of purification (v 30) underscores the importance of this rite. It is possible that this is the same Hanani mentioned in Ezra 10:20 or Nehemiah's own brother (Neh 1:2). However, Hanani was a popular name in the postexilic community (in addition to the above texts, note 1 Chr 25:4); and the missions of Ezra and Nehemiah may have been separated by several decades; therefore such an identification seems unlikely.

Bibliography

Sachau, E. 1911. *Aramäische Papyrus und Ostraka, Tafeln.* Leipzig.

JEFFREY A. FAGER

HANANIAH (PERSON) [Heb *ḥănanyāhû; ḥănanyāh*].

Eleven individuals in the Hebrew Bible bear this name, which means "Yahu is gracious" (Noth *IPN,* 187). The name is found three times in the Gibeon inscriptions (#'s 22, 32, 51. See *TSSI* 1: 56). It also occurs in a 2d-century A.D. fragment, probably from the Herodium (Puech 1980: 121 [line 5], 125).

1. Commander of a military unit under King Uzziah of Judah (2 Chr 26:11).

2. Father of the Zedekiah, who was a high official under King Jehoiakim and who was among those who listened to the scroll of Jeremiah's oracles being read by Baruch (Jer 36:12).

3. Son of Azzur, a false prophet from Gibeon who contradicted the prophet Jeremiah's warning that Judah should continue to accept the rule of Nebuchadrezzar, king of Babylon (Jeremiah 28; cf. chap. 27). In the fourth year of the reign of Zedekiah, king of Judah (594/593 B.C.), in the fifth month, Hananiah declared publicly in the temple that Yahweh had broken Babylon's yoke and that within two years the exiles of 597 B.C., including King Jehoiachin, would return (28:1–4). This optimistic view is probably to be understood in relation to the plans of Judah and her neighbors to rebel against Nebuchadrezzar. The moment might have seemed opportune for in 595/594 B.C. Nebuchadrezzar had to deal with a revolt in Babylon, which he rather quickly suppressed (Wiseman 1956: 36–37). Hopes may also have been pinned on the accession in 594 B.C. of a new pharaoh in Egypt, Psamtik (Gk Psammetichus), who might restore Judah's former boundaries (*BHI,* 328). The division between pro-Babylonian and pro-Egyptian parties will in any case have ensured continual ferment, which the royal government, weakened by the deportations and torn in different directions, will have been unable to control.

In 594/593 B.C. ambassadors from Edom, Moab, Ammon, Tyre, and Sidon came to Jerusalem, perhaps at Zedekiah's instigation. Jeremiah warned them to accept Babylonian rule. According to the MT (Jer 27:2–3) Yahweh tells the prophet to put on yokes and send them to the kings as a sign that they should submit. Jeremiah himself is still wearing the yoke when Hananiah meets him in the temple, and he replies to Hananiah that prophets who prophesy good fortune can be judged authentic spokesmen of Yahweh only when their words are fulfilled (28:6–9; cf. Deut 18:21–22). In a symbolic action Hananiah then takes off the wooden yoke Jeremiah wears around his neck and breaks it, reiterating his prophecy (vv 10–11). After an interval Yahweh informs Jeremiah that he has placed an iron yoke on the neck of Nebuchadrezzar's subjects, that is one that cannot be broken. Jeremiah then tells Hananiah that he has been misleading the people and preaching rebellion against Yahweh. For this he will die (cf. Deut 18:20), a prophecy that was fulfilled that same year in the seventh month (vv 12–17; cf. Ezek 11:1–13).

4. Father of Shelemiah and grandfather of Irijah, the sentry who arrested Jeremiah at the Benjamin Gate on the grounds that he was deserting to the Babylonians when the prophet was about to leave Jerusalem for Anathoth during a break in Nebuchadrezzar's siege of the city (Jer 37:13). (For a discussion of the spelling of Nebuchadrezzar, see NEBUCHADNEZZAR.)

5. A son of Zerubbabel and descendant of David (1 Chr 3:19, 21), perhaps born ca. 545 B.C. (Myers *1 Chronicles* AB, 21).

6. A postexilic person of the tribe of Benjamin (1 Chr 8:24).

7. A descendant of Heman (1 Chr 25:4, 23), a postexilic member of a family of temple singers established by David (v 1).

8. Member of the family of Bebai; he put away his foreign wife in the time of Ezra (Ezra 10:28; 1 Esdr 9:29).

9. A perfumer who helped renovate the walls of Jerusalem under Nehemiah (Neh 3:8).

10. Son of Shelemiah and among those who repaired the walls of Jerusalem under Nehemiah (Neh 3:30).

11. Governor of the castle, whom Nehemiah put in charge of Jerusalem (Neh 7:2). The Hebrew of the verse could mean "my brother Hanani, that is Hananiah, the governor of the castle." "Hanani" is a short form of "Hananiah."

12. A head of the people who signed Ezra's covenant (Neh 10:23; cf. McCarthy 1982: 34).

13. The head of the priestly family of Jeremiah in the time of the high priest Joiakim (Neh 12:12). He was a trumpeter at the dedication of the wall of Jerusalem (v 41).

14. Ancestor of a Levite family which returned from the Exile with Ezra (1 Esdr 8:48; cf. Ezra 8:19).

15. One of the four young men of the tribe of Judah who figure in the stories of the book of Daniel (1:6–7, 11, 19; 2:17) and the Alexandrian additions (see also 1 Macc 2:59). The chief of the eunuchs gave him the name Shadrach.

Bibliography

McCarthy, D. J. 1982. Covenant and Law in Chronicles-Nehemiah. *CBQ* 44: 25–44.

Puech, E. 1980. Abécédaire et liste alphabétique de noms hébreux du début du IIes. A.D. *RB* 87: 118–26.

Wiseman, D. J. 1956. *Chronicles of Chaldean Kings (626–556 B.C.) in the British Museum.* London.

ROBERT ALTHANN

HANDBREADTH. See WEIGHTS AND MEASURES.

HANDPIKE. See WEAPONS AND IMPLEMENTS OF WARFARE.

HANDS, LAYING ON OF.

HANDS, LAYING ON OF. The laying on of hands is a ritual gesture attested in both the OT and the NT.

OLD TESTAMENT

The laying on of hands is a gesture which, in the context of sacrifice, shows ritual attribution of a sacrificial animal to the one performing the gesture, or which, in a nonsacrificial context, demonstrates who the object of ritual action is.

The majority of examples of this gesture is found in the Priestly literature (P) described with the Hebrew verb *sāmak,* "lean on," "support." Outside of P the gesture is found only twice: in 2 Chr 29:23 with *sāmak* and in Gen 48:14, 17, 18 described by the verbs *śîm* and *šît* (both meaning "place," "put"). It has been thought that the verb *sāmak* indicates a form of the gesture where pressure is applied to the recipient (*m. Beṣa* 2:4; *m. Ḥag.* 2:2–3; Daube 1956: 225), as opposed to the gesture with *śîm/šît,* which would not entail pressure. But this distinction in the form is hard to sustain on the meager evidence. The verb *sāmak* in the Priestly writings may be only idiomatic and not indicate that pressure was applied.

The instances occurring with the verb *sāmak* can be sorted out into two categories distinguished by context of the rite, its physical form, and its meaning (Wright 1986):

(A) The majority of the cases of the gesture occurs in the context of sacrifice. Here the one who brings an offering (and only this person, not someone else in the person's behalf; cf. *m. Menaḥ.* 9:9) puts *one* hand on the head of the animal being offered (cf. Lev 1:4; 3:2, 8, 13; 4:4, 24, 29, 33). If a group of people perform the gesture together, they presumably each lay one hand on the head of the animal (Exod 29:10, 15, 19; Lev 4:15; 8:14, 18, 22; Num 8:12; 2 Chr 29:23).

This one-handed form of the gesture in sacrifices is best explained as ritually attributing the animal to the offerer; it indicates that the entire sacrificial rite pertains to him or her, even though others (priests and other auxiliaries) participate in making the offering later in the rite. This interpretation is confirmed by the fact that it makes sense of the lack of the gesture with birds and cereal offerings (Lev 1:14–17; 2; 5:7–13). These offerings are small and can be carried by the offerer in the hands. The simple presentation of these offerings is sufficient ritually to attribute them to the offerer; no hand placement is therefore necessary.

Other interpretations of the gesture in sacrifice, such as viewing the rite as the means of transferring the offerer's evil, personality, or emotion to the animal and through which the animal serves as the offerer's substitute (suffering punishment vicariously) or as a vehicle for carrying the personality or emotion to God, do not easily fit every case of sacrificial hand placement and do not explain the lack of the gesture with birds and cereal offerings.

The hand placement on the Levites in Num 8:10 is to be understood under the principle of attribution just explained (note that the surrounding terminology is sacrificial in nature). By this gesture the Israelites show that the Levites are their "offering" to God and that benefits from the Levites' service will accrue to them.

From a comparative perspective Hittite ritual has a hand placement gesture very similar in form and meaning to the gesture in biblical sacrifice. This rite occurs most frequently in contexts of sacrifice or offering. It is performed by placing one hand on or at a distance from some offering material (e.g., bread, cheese, wine, meats, a live animal). And it ritually attributes the offering material to the one performing the rite. This allows other persons to distribute the offering material while the credit goes to the one who placed the hand.

(B) Three cases of the gesture in the Bible described with *sāmak* are nonsacrificial and appear to be performed with *two* hands, rather than one (Peter 1977; Janowski

[1982] is more cautious in his assessment of the evidence). The clearest example is Lev 16:21. Here the text explicitly prescribes that Aaron place his two hands on the head of the scapegoat. (Note that the scapegoat is not a sacrifice; it is merely a bearer of impurity.) The other two cases are less clear in regard to how many hands are used. In Num 27:18 God tells Moses to place his hand (singular) on Joshua's head and set him apart as the new leader of Israel. In the fulfillment section (v 23), however, Moses places both his hands on Joshua's head (note that the parallel text, Deut 34:9, has the plural). The LXX reads a plural in both cases (though the Samaritan reads a singular in both cases). The final example is ambiguous. Witnesses of blasphemy are to place their hands on the head of a blasphemer before he is stoned (Lev 24:14). Since the subject of the action is plural, it is impossible to determine from the text how many hands were used.

A conclusion from the foregoing evidence is difficult and can only be tentative. Numbers 27, despite the conflict between prescription and fulfillment, indicates that two hands could be used in the ritual of succession. Hence it and Leviticus 16 provide two examples of a two-handed gesture outside of sacrifice. The ambiguous example in Leviticus 24, since it is also outside the context of sacrifice, may also be intended to occur with two hands.

Proceeding under the hypothesis that these three examples all use a two-handed form of the gesture, it is possible that a single meaning fits all of them. The meaning that suits all of them is *demonstrating* who or what is the focus of the ritual action. This is evident in three key texts. (1) The rite in Leviticus 24 is the means the witnesses have of demonstrating who the guilty party is, thereby confirming their testimony and emphasizing their responsibility in the death of the blasphemer. This meaning is suggested by the parallel action of witnesses in Deut 13:10; 17:7; and the hand placement gesture in Susanna 34. The interpretation that by this gesture the witnesses transfer the pollution of blasphemy that has attached to them back to the blasphemer is not supported by the what is known about impurities elsewhere in the priestly writings of the Bible. (2) In Leviticus 16 Aaron demonstrates what object is the recipient of the sins of the people. The rite here is not strictly a means of transfer; sins do not travel through Aaron's arms to the goat. It merely points out where the sins confessed by Aaron are to alight. (3) In Numbers 27 the rite demonstrates who Moses' successor will be. Again here, in view of the preceding examples, authority is not passed through Moses' arms to Joshua. Moses by the gesture merely points out who the recipient of his authority is and demonstrates to the community that Joshua is his legal successor.

Finally, hand placement in Gen 48:14–18, described with *śîm* and *šît,* can be understood like the last three examples as a means of designating who the recipients of blessing are. A gesture related to hand placement for blessing is Aaron's stretching of his hands out over the people in Num 9:22.

Bibliography

Daube, D. 1956. *The NT and Rabbinic Judaism.* London.

Janowski, B. 1982. *Sühne als Heilsqeschehen.* Neukirchen-Vluyn.

Peter, R. 1977. L'imposition des mains dans l'Ancien Testament. *VT* 27: 48–55.

Wright, D. P. 1986. The Gesture of Hand Placement in the Hebrew Bible and in Hittite Literature. *JAOS* 106: 433–46.

DAVID P. WRIGHT

NEW TESTAMENT

"Laying on of hands" is regularly the translation of the Gk phrases *(epi-)tithenai tas cheiras (epi)* and *epithesis tōn cheirōn,* which depend on the Heb *sāmak yad ʿal,* "to press or lean the hand on," or *šît (śîm) yad ʿal,* "to place the hand on." This Greek terminology is rather set, although Mark interchanges *epitithenai tas cheiras* and *haptesthai* (cf. Mark 7:32–35; 8:22–26; 10:13–16; cf. 16:18); and *cheirotonein* (Acts 14:23) should be viewed as part of this verbal pattern. The OT application of laying on of hands is followed in the NT, except that there is no sacrificial use and that the association with healings and with baptism and the Holy Spirit is added. Thus in the NT laying on of hands relates to healing, blessings, baptism and the Spirit, and assignment to a given task. There are underlying unifying characteristics. The context is always religious, as the frequent mention of prayer demonstrates; and obviously the laying on of hands is a symbolic action. Yet in each instance something is achieved (Adler 1951: 63, 67–68).

In the OT and rabbinic tradition the laying on of hands is never associated with healing (cf. 1QapGen 20:28–29), and surely this gesture is not an essential part of miracles (*TDNT* 9: 428, 431). According to Mark and Luke, Jesus did heal through the laying on of hands (Mark 5:23; 6:5; 7:32; 8:22–26; Luke 4:40; 13:13); and so did Christians (Mark 16:18) like Ananias (Acts 9:12, 17) and Paul (Acts 28:8; New 1933: 137–38). Of course, healing is communicated through this laying on of hands.

Jesus also blessed children through the laying on of hands (Mark 10:13–16 and parallels). The passage views children as having the correct attitude for reception into the kingdom. Luke 24:50, "and lifting up his hands he blessed them *(kai eparas tas cheiras autou eulogēsen autous),*" should be noted here, although the Greek is not that of "laying on of hands."

In Acts laying on of hands is related to the reception of baptism and the Holy Spirit. Acts 19:5–6 state this most clearly. In a scene reminiscent of Pentecost, Paul laid hands on those who had received only John's baptism and were now baptized in Jesus' name, and the Holy Spirit came upon them, and they spoke with tongues and prophesied. According to Acts 9:17 through Ananias' laying on of hands Paul not only regains his sight but is filled with the Holy Spirit. Acts 8:16–19, likewise, report the reception of the Holy Spirit through the laying on of hands. However, Luke in this passage is less interested in distinguishing the laying on of hands and the reception of the Spirit from baptism in the name of the Lord Jesus than in stressing the significance of the Church in Jerusalem's (and, hence, God's) approval of what has happened in Samaria (O'Toole 1980: 860–62). Finally, most scholars understand Heb 6:2 in terms of the laying on of hands connected with baptism (Parratt 1969: 211; cf. Attridge *Hebrews* Hermeneia).

Jesus himself did not ordain the apostles through the

laying on of hands, nor is Matthias through the laying on of hands assigned Judas' place among the Twelve. However, in the NT, ordination is associated with the laying on of hands and should probably be linked to the ordination of rabbis, the evidence for which comes from the second half of the 1st century. Daube (1956: 229–33; but see *TRE* 14: 418–20) holds that the rabbis confined *sāmak yad ʿal,* "to press or lean the hand on," to the sacrificial cult and to the ordination of a rabbi. Whether Daube is correct or not, it does not seem unreasonable to assume that the ordination of rabbis originated earlier than A.D. 50, with the development of the scribes as a specific group (*m. Sanh.* 1:3; *t. Sanh.* 1:1; *TDNT* 9: 429). But Christian ordination would also include recognition of apostolic authority and be accompanied by prayer (Knoch 1983b: 232).

Of the passages to be considered here, Acts 13:3 is really more of a commissioning of Barnabas and Paul for the task to which the Holy Spirit has called them, than an ordination (Barrett 1985: 51). Although it is difficult to uncover the historical background, most scholars hold that Acts 6:6 (cf. Num 8:10; 27:15–23) is an ordination (*TRE* 14: 418). For Vanhoye (Vanhoye and Crouzel 1982: 730) Acts 6:1–6 provide indications of how ministries were established in the Church. The passage distinguishes between ecclesial authority and "the multitude of the disciples." The Twelve call the meeting and explain what seems good to do and why. The assembly agrees, holds an election, and presents those elected to the Twelve, who confer on them their ministry through prayer and the imposition of hands. But some scholars feel that all the disciples laid hands on the Seven.

Paul and Barnabas, with prayer and fasting, appointed (*cheirotonein*) elders in Lystra, Iconium, and Antioch (Acts 14:21–23; *TDNT* 9: 437). Other passages refer to Timothy's ordination. According to 1 Tim 4:14 (cf. 1:18) Timothy is not to neglect the gift given him by the prophetic utterance when the council of elders laid their hands on him, while 2 Tim 1:6 again records the gift of God, but through the laying on of Paul's hands. Whether one sees a contradiction between these verses, or a "fiction" in the second (*TRE* 14: 420), or simply explains that Paul along with the council of elders could have ordained Timothy depends in part on the date given the Pastorals. On the other hand, Daube's (1956: 244–46) proposed translation of *meta epitheseōs tōn cheirōn tou presbyteriou* (1 Tim 4:14) as "ordination to the eldership" is not justified because it does not respect the context or the genitive case of *tou presbyteriou.* However, Timothy's ordination is designated a grace or a gift (Knoch 1983a: 160); and prophecy played a part in his being chosen for this ministry.

In 1 Tim 5:22 Paul advises Timothy not to be hasty in the laying on of hands. Since the context (vv 17–21) considers Timothy's treatment of elders and since the "laying on of hands" parallels 1 Tim 4:14 and 2 Tim 1:6, the author is speaking of Timothy's ordination of elders (Grelot 1983: 225).

Bibliography

Adler, N. 1951. *Taufe und Handauflegung: Eine exegetisch-theologische Untersuchung von Apg 8, 14–17.* Ed. M. Meinertz. NTAbh 19/3. Münster Westfalia.

Barrett, C. K. 1985. *Church, Ministry and Sacraments in the NT.* The 1983 Didsbury Lectures. Exeter.

Daube, D. 1956. The Laying on of Hands. Pp. 224–46 in *The NT and Rabbinic Judaism.* Jordan Lectures 1952. Repr. 1984, ed. J. B. Agus. Salem, NH.

Grayston, K. 1970. The Significance of the Word *Hand* in the NT. Pp. 479–87 in *Mélanges biblique en hommage au R.P. Béda Rigaux,* ed. A. Descamps and A. de Halleux. Gembloux.

Grelot, P. 1983. *Eglise et ministères: Pour un dialogue critique avec Edward Schillebeeckx.* Paris.

Knoch, O. 1983a. Charisma und Amt: Ordnungselemente der Kirche Christi. Pp. 124–61 in *SNTU* A, 8. Ed. A. Fuchs. Linz, Austria.

———. 1983b. Die Funktion der Handauflegung im Neuen Testament. *Liturgisches Jahrbuch* 33: 222–35.

New, S. 1933. The Name, Baptism, and the Laying on of Hands. Pp. 121–40 in *The Beginning of Christianity V: Additional Notes to the Commentary,* ed. K. Lake and H. J. Cadbury. London.

O'Toole, R. F. 1980. Christian Baptism in Luke. *RevRel* 39: 855–66.

Parratt, J. K. 1969. The Laying on of Hands in the NT: A Reexamination in the Light of the Hebrew Terminology. *ExpTim* 80: 210–14.

Schillebeeckx, E. 1985. The Practice and Theology of Ministry in the Early Communities of Christian Believers. Pp. 40–73 in *The Church with a Human Face.* Trans. J. Bowden. New York.

Vanhoye, A., and Crouzel, H. 1982. Le ministère dans l'Eglise. *NRT* 104: 722–48.

ROBERT F. O'TOOLE

HANES (PLACE) [Heb *hānēs*]. In Isa 30:1 the prophet condemns the rebellious people who seek protection from pharaoh (Shabaka of the 25th Dyn.). That protection will turn to shame, and v 4 notes "for though his officials are at Zoan and his envoys reach Hanes, every one comes to shame." Gold (1965: 857) notes this is an embassy sent to Egypt ca. 703 B.C. seeking support for Hezekiah's rebellion against Assyria (others see these as pharaoh's envoys). Gold identifies Hanes with Anusi, 80 km S of Memphis (at the S end of the delta), probably Heracleopolis, ca. 100 km S of Cairo. The site is known as Ahnas el-Medina, just S of the Fayyum, on the W bank of the Nile. Kyle (*ISBE* 2: 1335 [1939 ed]) says it was a large city on an island between the Nile and Bahr Yuseph (a branch of the Nile that leads into the Fayyum), opposite the modern town of Beni Suef. Simons (*GTTOT,* 440) describes it as on the right bank of the Bahr Jusuf and W of Beni Suef. Lambdin (*IDB* 2: 522) derived the Hebrew from Eg *Hwt-nn-nsw,* "the House of the royal child." Simons says its ancient Egyptian name *(h)nni* continued in Anysis (Herodotus) and as Khininshi in the annals of Ashurbanipal (ca. 668–631/627). The name now survives in the Coptic *ahnas* or *ahnasijeh el-medinah.* Its local name *ahnasijeh umm el-kiman* means "of the heaps of ruins," a reflection of the extensive remains of the ancient city. It is also the Egyptian Hunensuten, abridged Hunensu and Arabic Ahmeysa.

The Greeks identified the local deity, the ram-headed Herishef, with Hercules and called the city Heracleopolis, the city of Heracles. This was Heracleopolis Magna. Besides being the capital of the 20th nome of Upper Egypt, Hanes was the home of the 22d Dyn. (ca. 935–735 B.C.) and remained a city of great importance. In the reign of

Psammetichus I (ca. 663–609, 26th Dyn.), Hanes was the center of government for Upper Egypt. Griffith (*HDB,* 363) noted that in the 25th–26th Dyn. (ca. 715–600 B.C.) the standard silver of Egypt was that of the treasury of Harshafe. Shabaka, the Ethiopian, established the 25th Dyn. in 715 and wiped out the short-lived Saitic Dyn. and their Delta state. While Isaiah's oracle says Judean efforts at alliance with Egypt were useless, Scott (*IB* 5: 330) notes the reasonableness of it. The Ethiopian Dynasty had come N to Middle Egypt in Hanes and controlled Lower Egypt as well. Thus it might very well be strong enough to defeat Assyria. But it was not.

Hanes has also been identified with Heracleopolis Parva in the E delta in Lower Egypt. Spiegelberg derived such a site from Herodotus' (2.166.137) reference to Anysis in the delta (Kitchen *NBD,* 452–53). Griffith (363) says the LXX translators did not recognize the name of the city in Isa 30:4, so they tried to translate the word. There is a wide divergence of readings but "in vain," *hinnam,* seems to have been read instead of Hanes. One translation is "for there are in Tanis (Zoan) princes, wicked messengers." Kitchen suggested "mansion of the king" as the name of pharaoh's palace in Zoan/Tanis itself. The Aramaic Targum of Isaiah has Tahpanes, the Egyptian fortress on Egypt's E frontier, near Zoan, in the N delta. Kyle notes Dumichen's view that the hieroglypic name of Tahpanes is Hens. This could have influenced the Targum translation. He thought the plain meaning of Isa 30:4 points to a city in the delta nearer to Jerusalem than Tanis. Kitchen sees v 4 as a parallelism so that the second line refers to the first, either as the mansion of the king noted above, or as Heracleopolis Parva. But this is not necessary if the intent of v 4 is to show how far the embassy traveled in contrast to how little good it did.

Bibliography

Gold, V. R. 1965. Notes to Isaiah. In *Oxford Annotated Bible with the Apocrypha,* ed. H. G. May and B. M. Metzger. New York.

HENRY O. THOMPSON

HANGING. See PUNISHMENTS AND CRIMES.

HANGINGS [Heb *qelāʿîm*].

Fabrics that were part of the construction of the tabernacle court as described in the books of Exodus and Numbers (Exod 27:9–18; 35:17; 38:9–18; 39:40; Num 3:26; 4:26). The tabernacle was situated inside an enclosure measuring 50 × 100 cubits. This court was demarcated by a series of five-cubit-high (ca. 7.5 ft) pillars: 20 pillars on the two long sides, 10 pillars on the W end, and 6 on the E end. The fewer number on the E is the result of the 20-cubit-wide (ca. 30 ft) gate to the courtyard at that end. The gate had its separate fabric "screen" (RSV; also called "hangings" in the KJV). See also TABERNACLE.

The hangings were evidently stretched or draped from the pillars that marked the perimeter of the courtyard (Exod 27:9–18; 38:9–18). They thereby formed the courtyard walls, extending a total distance of 280 cubits (ca. 420 ft). Like the "walls" of the tabernacle itself, the hangings were fabric and thus part of the movability associated with all components of the tabernacle, which was a portable shrine. The hangings were among the tabernacle's components carried by the levitical family of Gershon (Num 3:26; 4:26).

The nature of the fabric from which they were made, along with their position as the outer boundary of the tabernacle precincts, makes the hangings the least sacred among the various furnishings and construction materials (fabrics and planks or pillars) that constituted the tabernacle complex. These materials exhibit a range of quality and workmanship, from ornate and costly to plain and less costly. The gradations correspond to levels of sanctity, with the richest items, and the ones most complicated to craft, being the most sacred.

The hangings were made of "fine twined linen," which was a much simpler fabric than the multicolored and mixed linen and wool weaves, some with decorative embroidery, that characterized other tabernacle fabrics. Four levels of complexity and thus of sanctity can be identified for the cloth used in the tabernacle (Haran 1978: 167); and the hangings belong to the fourth, or least elaborate, level. The only other fabrics described in the tabernacle texts of Exodus that are like those of the hangings are the four basic undergarments worn by all the priests. The word for the linen fabric of the hangings and the priestly garb is *šēš,* which is probably an Egyptianism and should be considered evidence of very early literary material, perhaps going back to an Egyptian environment, preserved in the priestly writings (Hurvitz 1967).

Two other Hebrew words are translated "hangings" in the RSV. One (*bāttîm,* 2 Kgs 23:7) apparently refers to woven garments or drapings made for the Asherah that stood in the temple in Jerusalem at the time of Josiah's reform. The other (*tĕkēlet,* "blue hangings," Esth 1:6) is a word for some sort of blue fabric that, along with white cotton material, was stretched on marble pillars in the garden of the Persian king Ahasuerus.

Bibliography

Haran, M. 1978. *Temples and Temple Service in Ancient Israel.* Oxford.
Hurvitz, A. 1967. The Usage of *šš* and *bwṣ* in the Bible and Its Implication for the Date of P. *HTR* 60: 117–21.

CAROL MEYERS

ḤANINA BEN-DOSA.

There are more rabbinic references to Rabbi Ḥanina ben-Dosa than to Ḥoni and Ḥilkiah. He was from Galilee and lived during the middle of the 1st century C.E.; he was thus a near contemporary of Jesus of Nazareth. A pupil of Joḥanan ben Zakkai, he was a Tannaitic sage of the first generation, and was revered as a wise teacher (*b. Ber.* 34a; *Pirqe R. El.* 204–5; *y. Ber.* 4, 5, 6; *b. Ber.* 34b). He is quoted in the Mishnah: "R. Ḥanina b. Dosa said, 'He whose fear of sin precedes his wisdom, his wisdom endures; but he whose wisdom precedes his fear of sin, his wisdom does not endure. . . .' " (*m. ʾAbot* 3:10). He was righteous, denied being a prophet, and was probably an ascetic. A voice from heaven is reputed to have commended his devotion and self-sacrifice (*b. Taʿan.* 24b–25a; *b. B. Bat.* 74b; *b. Ber.* 17b): "The whole world is sustained for the sake of my son Ḥanina (Heb *ḥnynʾ bny*), and Ḥanina my son *(bny)* has to subsist on a *qab* of carobs from one sabbath evening to the next sabbath evening" (*b. Ber.* 17b). He was a wonder-worker, and like Ḥoni and Ḥilkiah he was able to cause rain to fall (*b. Taʿan.* 24b). Like Jesus of Nazareth he was famous for his healing miracles. He is alleged to have healed not only R. Gamaliel's son but also R. Joḥanan ben Zakkai's son (*b. Ber.* 34b).

Like Ḥoni and Jesus of Nazareth, Ḥanina's life was embellished with legends (*Midr. Rab. Qoh.; y. Dem.* 1:22a; *t. Ber.* 3). His empty oven fills miraculously with bread; he sees his goats return home with bears on their horns and extends the beams of a neighbor's house (*b. Taʿan.* 25a).

Bibliography

Simon, M. 1984. *Berakoth: Translated into English with Notes, Glossary and Indices.* London.

Vermes, G. 1975. Ḥanina ben Dosa. Pp. 178–214 in *Post-biblical Jewish Studies.* Studies in Judaism in Late Antiquity 8. Leiden.

JAMES H. CHARLESWORTH

HANNAH (PERSON) [Heb *ḥannâ*]. The first, and doubtless the favorite, of the two wives of Elkanah (cf. 1 Sam 1:2, 5). Barren for many years, Hannah may have prompted Elkanah to take a second wife (a similar rationale explains the actions of Sarai, Gen 16:2; Rachel, 30:3; Leah, 30:9). To be infertile was the ultimate tragedy for a married woman, since only by bearing a son to her husband could she provide a means of perpetuating his name and securing the orderly transfer of his estate upon his death (cf. e.g., 11:30; 15:2–4; 16:1–2; 17:15–16; 21:1–2; 25:5).

Hannah's shrewish rival, Peninnah, became the mother of many children and made constant fun of Hannah, apparently unaware that her infertility was caused by the Lord (1 Sam 1:5–6; cf. similarly Gen 15:3; 16:2; 20:18; 30:2). So merciless and continuous was the provocation that Hannah not only often wept and refused to eat but also became "resentful" (1 Sam 1:8; literally, had a "bad/angry heart"; for the only other precise parallel cf. Deut 15:10, where the same phrase means "grudging[ly]"). On such occasions Elkanah would attempt to console her with the thought that he was better for her than ten sons.

But Hannah refused to resign herself to a life of barrenness, and her sadness and "bitterness of soul" led her to pray and make a vow to the Lord (1 Sam 1:10–11). While at Shiloh on one of her family's annual pilgrimages (probably to celebrate the Feast of Tabernacles; cf. Judg 21:19–21), she promised that if God would give her a son, she would give the child back to him as a perpetual Nazirite (1 Sam 1:11). Although the term *Nazirite* does not appear in the account, it is clearly presupposed (as demonstrated by 4QSam[a]; the Hebrew text of Sir 46:13; Jos. *Ant* 5.10.3 §347; and *m. Nazir* 9:5).

Eli, priest at Shiloh, observed Hannah moving her lips as she prayed silently, and he misinterpreted her action as a display of drunkenness. It is understandable that he should do so, since prayer in the ancient world was almost always audible (cf. e.g., Dan 6:10–11; Pss 3:4; 4:1; 6:9; etc.) and excessive drinking was a common accompaniment of festal occasions (including especially the Feast of Tabernacles; *AncIsr:* 496).

But Hannah justly protested that she had not been drinking; on the contrary, she had been pouring out her soul (1 Sam 1:15) to the Lord, a vivid figure of speech for praying earnestly (Pss 42:4; 62:8; Lam 2:19) to him. Her explanation satisfied Eli, who expressed his hope that God would grant her request. Sensing divine assurance in Eli's response, Hannah broke her self-imposed fast and in due course returned, expectantly, with Elkanah to their hometown. There the Lord "remembered" her (1 Sam 1:19)—as she had asked him to (1:11)—and enabled her to conceive and eventually bear a son to her husband. She named the boy Samuel.

After Samuel's birth Hannah decided not to make the annual pilgrimage to Shiloh until he was weaned so that, on her next trip, she could leave him there to serve the Lord for the rest of his life. Since the breast-feeding of a child lasted for two or three years in the ancient world (2 Macc 7:27), Samuel would have been considered old enough to spend an extended period of time away from home after his weaning. Accompanied by a three-year-old bull to be sacrificed to the Lord, Elkanah and his family made what was to be their most fateful journey to Shiloh. There Hannah affirmed to Eli that she was the woman whom he had first met a few years earlier; there she introduced him to Samuel as the son whom God had given to her; and there, as she had promised, she gave her son back to the Giver.

Although 1 Sam 2:1–10, the so-called Song of Hannah, may have originated as a royal song of triumph (Willis 1973) at the Shiloh sanctuary in connection with Israel's victory over an enemy, such songs would then have been taught to worshippers. This one would have perhaps become a personal favorite of Hannah and would have been used by her to express her gratitude and praise to God as well as her "victory" over Peninnah (see esp. 2:10, where Hannah declares that the Lord will "thunder against" all who oppose him, just as Peninnah's intention had been to "irritate"—literally, "thunder against"—Hannah; 1:6). The first three lines of 2:8 are almost identical to Ps 113:7–8a. If Psalm 113 is later than Hannah's song, the psalmist has added an exquisite touch in the light of Hannah's situation: "[The Lord] settles the barren woman in her home / as a happy mother of children" (113:9; cf. also the mention in 1 Sam 2:21 of additional children later born to Hannah). Since the Song of Hannah is commonly dated to the 11th or 10th century B.C. on the basis of stylistic phenomena as well as the divine names and titles it contains (cf. e.g., Freedman 1976: 55, 96), there would seem to be no compelling reason to deny that Hannah's song is contemporary with her.

Appearing near the beginning of 1 Samuel, its closest parallel in the OT is the Song of David (2 Samuel 22), which appears near the end of 2 Samuel. These two remarkably similar hymns frame the main contents of the books and remind us that the two books were originally one. Both songs begin by using "horn" as a figure of speech for "strength," by referring to God as the "Rock," and by reflecting on divine deliverance (1 Sam 2:1–2; 2 Sam 22:2–3). Both end by paralleling "his king" with "his anointed" (1 Sam 2:10; 2 Sam 22:51).

Hannah's song is generally conceded to have provided the main inspiration for Mary's *Magnificat* (Luke 1:46–55). The two hymns, both commemorating miraculous pregnancies, begin similarly; and certain themes in the Song of Hannah recur in the *Magnificat* (cf. 1 Sam 2:4, 7–8 with Luke 1:52; 1 Sam 2:5 with Luke 1:53). These two songs and their contexts have in turn influenced the *Protevangelium of James,* a 2d-century A.D. pseudepigraphic work that tells the story of Mary's elderly parents' prayers for a child. The old woman vows that the child will be "a gift to the Lord my God" (cf. 1 Sam 1:11). Mary is born in response to the prayers, and at the age of three she is presented by her parents to the priests in the temple at Jerusalem. Mary's aged mother is named Anna, the same as that of Samuel's aged mother, Hannah (see JAMES, PROTEVANGELIUM OF).

As for the name Hannah itself (*ḥannâ,* "Grace/Gracious"), it is found only in 1 Samuel 1–2 in the OT. But a Hebrew seal from the Lachish area dating to ca. 725–675 B.C. displays the name *ḥnh* (Bartlett 1976: 59–61). And in the NT, Luke 2:36–37 mentions an aged widow named Hannah. Unfortunately, the KJV spelling "Anna" in that verse has become conventional. In any case the NT Hannah is called a prophetess—as, coincidentally, is the OT Hannah in Jewish tradition as enshrined in the Targum of Jonathan ben Uzziel as well as in *Meg.* 14a.

Bibliography

Bartlett, J. R. 1976. The Seal of *Ḥnh* from the Neighborhood of Tell ed-Duweir. *PEQ* 108: 59–61.

Freedman, D. N. 1976. Divine Names and Titles in Early Hebrew Poetry. Pp. 55–107 in *Magnalia Dei: The Mighty Acts of God. Essays on the Bible and Archaeology in Memory of G. Ernest Wright,* ed. F. M. Cross, W. E. Lemke, and P. D. Miller, Jr. Garden City.

Willis, J. T. 1973. The Song of Hannah and Psalm 113. *CBQ* 25/2: 139–54.

RONALD YOUNGBLOOD

HANNATHON (PLACE) [Heb *ḥannātōn*]. A city on the N boundary of the territory of Zebulun (Josh 19:14). Situated on the Darb el-Hawarneh—the major highway connecting the Hauran and N Transjordan with coastal Palestine—Hannathon was one of the major Canaanite centers of the lower Galilee (Oded 1971). The town figures in two of the Amarna Letters, that of the king of Babylon (EA 8), who describes the robbing of a Babylonian caravan near Hannathon by the kings of Shimʿon and Acre, and that of Biridiya, king of Megiddo, who tells of the release of Labayu of Shechem at Hannathon, following the payment of a ransom or bribe to Zurata, king of Acre, who was to escort him to the custody of the pharaoh. Hannathon appears once more in the extrabiblical record in the annals of Tiglath-pileser III of Assyria who, in 733/732 B.C.E., campaigned in N Palestine. Hannathon, along with several other Galilean towns, fell to the Assyrians during this campaign (*ANET,* 283; cf. 2 Kgs 15:29).

Tel Hannaton (Tell Badawiya; M.R. 174243) is a large site (5 hectares) which dominates the SW part of the Bet Netofa valley. Systematic surveys of the site (Gal 1982: 24) have revealed evidence of settlements in the Chalcolithic period, the EB, MB, and LB, the Iron Age I, and in the 10th–8th centuries B.C.E. Traces of several fortification lines are visible on the site.

Bibliography

Gal, Z. 1982. Lower Galilee in the Iron Age. Ph.D. diss., Tel Aviv (in Hebrew).

Oded, B. 1971. Darb el-Hawarneh—An Ancient Route. *EI* 10: 191–97 (in Hebrew).

RAPHAEL GREENBERG

HANNIEL (PERSON) [Heb *ḥannîʾēl*]. Two persons mentioned in the Hebrew Bible have this name. The name Hanniel has been explained variously but is derived in one case from the root *ḥnn,* "to be gracious," "to show favor." This produces a meaning "god has been gracious." One suggestion (*EncMiqr* 3: 215–16) is that Hanniel is similar in form to Hannibaʿal, a name known from Punic (Benz 1972: 313) and which came into Latin as Hannibal. Another explanation of the name uses the root *ḥen,* "favor," "pity," as a noun and would suggest that "god is *ḥen* [pity]" or that "god is my *ḥini* [my pity-taker]."

Note that the Samaritan reads *ḥanaʾel* and that similar names occur in the Samaria ostraca and the Elephantine documents.

1. The son of Ephod and the member of the tribe of Manasseh selected to oversee the distribution of the land of Canaan (Num 34:23).

2. The father of a clan from the tribe of Asher (1 Chr 7:39).

Bibliography

Benz, F. 1972. *Personal Names in the Phoenician and Punic Inscriptions.* Studia Pohl 8. Rome.

RAPHAEL I. PANITZ

HANOCH (PERSON) [Heb *ḥănōk; ḥănôk*]. HANOCHITES. **1.** Third son of Midian (Gen 25:4). For the meaning of the name, see ENOCH, which shares the same Heb spelling *(ḥănôk).* As with the other offspring of Keturah and Abraham, this "grandson's" name may have been related to an Arabian town or oasis on the international trade routes (Ephʾal 1982: 231–33, 240), perhaps even the city Cain named after his son Enoch (Gen 4:17; Winnett 1970: 192–93).

2. First son of Reuben (Gen 46:9) and ancestor of the Hanochites (Num 26:5). The proximity of Reuben's tribal area to Midian may suggest a relationship between the peoples represented by the two Hanochs (Skinner *Genesis* ICC, 352).

Bibliography

Ephʾal, I. 1982. *The Ancient Arabs.* Jerusalem and Leiden.

Winnett, F. V. 1970. The Arabian Genealogies in the Book of Genesis. Pp. 171–96 in *Translating and Understanding the OT,* ed. H. T. Frank and W. L. Reed. Nashville.

RICHARD S. HESS

HANUKKAH. See DEDICATION, FEAST OF.

HANUN (PERSON) [Heb *ḥānûn*]. A personal name formed from the *Qal* passive participle of the root *ḥnn* meaning "favored." The implied source of favor is a deity (*IPN,* 169, n. 4; 187).

1. An Ammonite king, the son of Nahash (2 Sam 10:1–4; 1 Chr 19:1–4) and brother of Shobi (2 Sam 17:27). Hanun was a contemporary of David's, and is reported to have succeeded to the throne upon his father's death (2 Sam 10:1; 1 Chr 19:1). Following usual dynastic principles, he would have been the eldest son of Nahash. Upon the advice of his court, Hanun was to have rebuffed and humiliated David's envoys, who were sent to reaffirm the preexisting alliance between Israel and Ammon, which needed the ratification of the new king. Some were suspicious that David's messengers had been sent as spies to scout out the capital city's weaknesses in preparation for its capture (2 Sam 10:2–4; 1 Chr 19:2–4). The reference to loyal behavior *(ḥesed)* in v 2 designates the mutual relationship of rights and duties between allies (Glueck 1967: 46–47) and is frequently used in parity and vassal treaties. War was to have ensued as a result of Hanun's failure to ratify a new treaty, with an eventual victory by David's troops (2 Sam 10:6–12:31; 2 Chr 19:6–20:3). The historical reliability of the biblical account is questionable since the Israelite historiographer would not have been privy to the private consultations at the Ammonite court; nevertheless, the narrative would seem to be based on a reliable tradition about Ammon's refusal to continue treaty relations with Israel at Hanun's succession.

After the capture of the capital city of Rabbath Ammon, David is reported to have donned the crown of the king or the national god Milcom (O'Ceallaigh 1962), thereby signaling his assumption of direct control over Ammon. He was to have put the Ammonites to labor with saws, and iron picks, and axes (2 Sam 12:31; 2 Chr 20:3). According to tradition then Ammon lost its ally status soon after Hanun's accession to the throne; and Hanun was deposed. It is commonly argued that David took personal control of the throne of Ammon, joining it to Israel and Judah through a personal union, but assigning it a lower status (i.e., Alt *KlSchr,* 70; Noth *NHI,* 194; Bright *BHI,* 198; Herrmann *HHI,* 157–58). Two alternate views have been suggested. According to one, Ammon was made a vassal state (Soggin 1985: 59). According to the other, it was directly incorporated into the Davidic state, with a governor in charge (Ahlström fc.).

The subsequent report in 2 Sam 17:27 concerning Shobi ben Nahash indicates that after the capture of Rabbath Ammon, David reinstated a member of its ruling family to serve as titular head of state. Shobi was another son of Nahash, evidently a younger brother of Hanun's. His office tenure tends to rule out the general view that David became king in Ammon, unless he ruled only briefly and then decided to step down in favor of a new arrangement involving Shobi. Nor is it likely that David would have appointed a member of the former royal family to be a governor in annexed Ammonite territory; he would have served as a rallying point for rebellion by the local population in a bid to reestablish statehood. It is most likely that Shobi was set on the Ammonite throne personally by David, to be a loyal vassal, sometime after Hanun's deposition. David may have given Shobi his throne name, which means "captive." Shobi's status as a vassal is strongly implied by both his name and by his offering aid to his distressed overlord during Absalom's rebellion, demonstrating his resolve not to side with the overlord's enemy, following common vassal treaty requirements (McCarthy 1963: 182, 191, 194, 200). Even if one would choose to dismiss the reference in 2 Sam 17:27 about the aid supplied by the three Transjordanian vassals as fictional elaboration aimed at stressing David's legitimacy and status as king even in exile, the names of the three individuals depicted may well derive from official Davidic court records that indicated their status as vassals to David.

2. A member of the postexilic community who participated in the rebuilding of the walls of Jerusalem in the time of Nehemiah (Neh 3:13, 30). He appears to have worked on two different sections of the project, with different cohorts, as did a number of other individuals. In one assignment he worked alongside the inhabitants of the town of Zanoah to rebuild the Valley Gate, on the W side of the settlement, near the present-day Jaffa Gate (Burrows 1934: 129, 134–36; Simons 1952: 124–27), restoring its masonry, doors, bolts, and bars. In addition, the group repaired a segment of the old wall that ran S from the Valley Gate for about 1000 cubits, or 1500 ft, to the Dung Gate. Since this was a comparatively large section of wall and the only one the length of which is specified in the entire account of the wall rebuilding in chap. 3, it is suggested either that Hanun and the Zanoahites represented a large work force or that most of the wall was still standing and required only nominal repairs (Keil 1873: 197; Batten *Ezra, Nehemiah* ICC, 214; Williamson *Ezra, Nehemiah* WBC, 207). When the Neo-Babylonians destroyed the city in 587/586 B.C.E. (2 Kgs 15:4–10), they probably would not have broken down the entire wall, an act which would have been unnecessarily time-consuming. Instead, they probably would have breached at intervals segments of the wall that remained after the direct assault. Only certain segments would have required rebuilding from the foundation level. Hanun worked on another segment with Hananiah ben Shelemiah N of the Horse Gate, just S of the area where the temple servants and merchants resided.

Debate continues over whether or not the two Hanuns in vv 13 and 30 are a single individual or two separate people (i.e., Batten, 214; Keil 1873: 193; Myers *Ezra, Nehemiah* AB, 119). Hanun appears in v 13 without a patronymic or hometown identification, which has led some to conclude that he was a chief, ruler, or another inhabitant of Zanoah, the home of the group with which he was working (i.e., Batten, 214; Keil 1873: 183). In v 30 Hanun is identified as the sixth son of Zalaph. Because it is very unusual to denote birth order in a patronymic, it has been suggested that the consonants of the Hebrew word "sixth" *(hššy)* may have once represented Hanun's hometown (Guthe 1901: 44): Hanun, the son of Zalaph, the ". . . ite."

In favor of identifying the two Hanuns is the reference in v 30 to the work constituting a "second section," which implies that one or both of the individuals had already completed a section elsewhere (pace Burrows 1934: 127–28). There are seven instances where the text refers to work representing a second section. Of those occurrences, details of both sets of constructions are given for Meremoth, son of Uriah, son of Hakkoz; the Tekoites; and

Binnui/Bavvai, son of Henedad; while details are lacking for the first repair work completed by Malchijah, son of Harim, and Hasshub, son of Pahath-Moab; Ezer son of Jeshua; and Baruch son of Zabbai. Possible details about the first work assignments completed by both Hanun and his companion Hananiah may be provided in vv 8 and 13 respectively if one is willing to identify the individuals without patronymics with their namesakes with patronymics. It seems likely that the report of rebuilding in chap. 3, which follows a sequential arrangement for the entire circumference of the city, has been based on actual records of the repair process but has been simplified and pieced together from a nonsequential list for narrative flow and easy audience understanding (Myers, 112–13; contrast Williamson, 199–200). Work on many sections was almost certainly undertaken simultaneously, to speed completion of the project. It is possible that the first assignment Hanun completed was the one at the Horse Gate, so that his name was listed with patronymic in the records in this first occurrence and that he was listed by first name only under the second entry.

Bibliography

Ahlström, G. W. fc. *The History of Ancient Palestine.* Winona Lake, IN.

Burrows, M. 1934. Nehemiah 3:1–32 as a Source for the Topography of Ancient Jerusalem. *AASOR* 14: 115–40.

Glueck, N. 1967. *ḤESED in the Bible.* Trans. A. Gottschalk. Cincinnati.

Guthe, H. 1901. *The Books of Ezra and Nehemiah.* The Sacred Books of the OT, pt. 19. Baltimore.

Keil, C. F. 1873. *The Book of Ezra, Nehemiah and Esther.* Trans. S. Taylor. Edinburgh.

McCarthy, D. J. 1963. *Treaty and Covenant.* AnBib 21. Rome.

O'Ceallaigh, G. C. 1962. And *So* David Did to *All the Cities* of Ammon. *VT* 12: 179–89.

Simons, J. 1952. *Jerusalem in the OT: Researches and Theories.* Studia Francisci Scholten memoriae dicata, vol. 1. Leiden.

Soggin, J. A. 1985. *A History of Ancient Israel.* Trans. J. Bowden. Philadelphia.

Diana V. Edelman

HAPAX LEGOMENA. Words (other than proper names) which occur only once in the Bible. This originally Greek term, which means "once said," was first used by Alexandrian grammarians in the 3d century B.C.E. to mark unique terms in classic Greek works.

Rare biblical words have attracted attention for centuries, usually because they are believed more difficult to understand or more susceptible to scribal confusion than other words. However, the criteria used to identify such words have differed according to the varied concerns of those who study them. The Masoretes marked many phrases and spellings found only once in the Hebrew Bible with the letter *lamed,* as an abbreviation for the Aramaic word *lêtaʾ* ("there is no other"), presumably to warn scribes that, although unusual, these forms were not mistakes.

As is common in the early stages of linguistic study, medieval Jewish Bible scholars were particularly aware of difficult words, drawing special attention to those they described as having "nothing similar" (Heb *dômeh*). The 12th-century Spaniard Abraham ibn Ezra was especially fond of pointing out linguistic rarities, identifying such words with a variety of phrases, including "it has no mother or father" and "it is one, and there is no second," which Jewish tradition had used to describe God, often in anti-Christian contexts.

Whereas the Masoretes were concerned with avoiding scribal error, the medievals' concern was more linguistic. Committed to the accuracy of the traditional Hebrew text, they recognized that the Bible did not preserve all of ancient Hebrew. As a result, words which occurred only a limited number of times seemed particularly difficult to understand. Whereas some interpreters, such as the 10th-century Spanish lexicographer Menahem ibn Saruq, chose to rely on biblical context alone, his near-contemporary, the philosopher and exegete Saʿadia Gaon, proposed that one could use rabbinic literature as a source for additional attestations of such terms. His list of 90 (though the title of his work refers to only 70) words for which this approach was useful thus anticipates modern scholarship's reliance on cognate literatures where the biblical evidence is insufficient. However, Saʿadia's motive was not academic. Concerned with the Karaite movement's claim that Judaism should rely on the Bible alone, he saw such words as demonstrating the need for rabbinic literature.

Although the widening horizons of modern biblical scholarship have provided a host of new resources, the problem with hapax legomena is still generally perceived as resulting from the limited evidence available for their interpretation. This etymological focus is particularly apparent in the importance ascribed to a subcategory which I. Casanowicz (*JEnc* 6: 226–28) called "absolute" hapax legomena, those words which not only occur only once in the Bible, but are also unrelated to any other words found there. The fact that published lists differ as to which words belong in this class demonstrates inconsistency as to how the definition should be applied. One reason for this is uncertainty as to whether to include words which occur several times, but in only one context (for example, a single verse or a passage repeated verbatim in two different parts of the Bible). Although in itself a relatively minor disagreement, this reflects differing assumptions as to the significance of certain words being rare and disagreement as to their difficulty.

Scholars usually seek ways to link rare words with more common terms so as to make them less difficult to understand. In earlier times this often involved showing that certain pairs of consonants can interchange or that the order of letters can be reversed so that seemingly rare words can be correlated with more common terms. Arguing that unique words are incorrect, perhaps because of scribal errors resulting from their unfamiliarity, modern scholars have sometimes proposed textual emendations, preferably on the basis of some sort of credible evidence. Others accept the likely accuracy of the text, seeing such words as an accidental result of the Bible's relatively small size, the limited number of topics which it contains, and the paucity of surviving texts in ancient Hebrew. To compensate for the limited information available within the Bible itself, they have followed Saʿadia's lead in seeking evidence from other Semitic languages. During the Middle Ages the resources available for this approach, which can be traced back to antiquity, were extended beyond Aramaic and rabbinic literature to include Arabic and sometimes even unrelated languages, such as Berber and Greek. With the wealth of additional resources now available, modern scholars have found Akkadian and Ugaritic texts particularly valuable.

Noting that related words can have different meanings in different languages, H. Cohen (1978) has urged caution in the use of such materials. To avoid mistakes, he suggests that cognates must appear in at least one context that is identical with that of their biblical counterparts before information about one should be used to illuminate the meaning of the other. Although intellectually appealing, this method has proven possible in only a handful of cases.

An alternative approach looks upon hapax legomena as a statistical rather than a philological phenomenon. Numerous studies of word frequency have shown that about half of any work's vocabulary is likely to occur only once. The comparable proportion for the Hebrew Bible is closer to one-third. There are several possible explanations for this relative paucity. One is that because the Bible is substantially larger than the other texts studied, it offers more opportunities for words to recur. The nature of Hebrew grammar, in which different meanings can be generated by conjugating the same verbal root according to different patterns, may also play a role. In any event such evidence raises serious questions for those who have questioned the biblical text's reliability because of the supposedly large number of hapax legomena it contains.

A word's frequency is dependent on the nature of the text in which it occurs. For example, animal names are less likely to be found in military passages than in those devoted to farming. Words which are rare in the Bible may not therefore have been difficult for ancient readers or listeners. However, statisticians have also demonstrated that certain words are inherently more common than others. This is supported by the fact that the Bible's hapax legomena occur significantly more often in poetic passages than in prose, a result of poets' preference for less ordinary words as well as of the parallelism characteristic of biblical poetry, which relies heavily on synonyms. The concentration of uncommon words is also a function of style; some authors use a more esoteric vocabulary than others. One can find variation even within individual books. For example, God's speeches in the book of Job include markedly more rare words than those of other characters, a phenomenon which can be paralleled in the literatures of other traditions.

Bibliography

Allony, N. 1958. *Kitāb al-sabʿin Lafza Lerav Saʿadia Gaʾon.* Vol. 2, pp. 1–47 in *Ignace Goldziher Memorial Volume,* ed. S. Löwinger. Jerusalem.

Cohen, H. R. 1978. *Biblical Hapax Legomena in the Light of Akkadian and Ugaritic.* Missoula, MT.

Chude, F. 1954. *Hapax Legomena: A Linguistic Study of Words Occurring Only Once.* Ph.D. diss., Radcliffe.

Greenspahn, F. E. 1984. *Hapax Legomena in Biblical Hebrew.* Chico, CA.

Herdan, G. 1959. The Hapax Legomena: A Real or Apparent Phenomenon? *Language & Speech* 2: 26–36.

Martinazzoli, F. 1953–57. *Hapax Legomenon.* Rome.

Yahuda, A. S. 1902–3. Hapax Legomena im Alten Testament. *JQR* 15: 618–714.

Zelson, L. G. 1927. Les Hapax Legomena du Pentateuque Hébraique *RB* 36: 243–48.

Frederick E. Greenspahn

HAPHARAIM (PLACE) [Heb *ḥapārayim*]. A town located in the territory of the tribe of Issachar, mentioned only in Josh 19:19. Yeivin (1957: 590) equated Hapharaim with both Number 53 *(ʿpr wr)* and Number 54 *(ʿpr šri)* in the List of Thutmose III at Karnak. However, Kallai (*HGB,* 422) has noted that the Egyptians did not usually confuse the letters *ḥet* and *ʿayin* and that therefore the names in the Thutmose III list are not to be associated with Hapharaim. The toponym had also been connected with Number 18 *(ḥprm)* in the Conquest List of Shishak I at Karnak (see *ANET,* 242), which, while linguistically acceptable, is rejected by many researchers Aharoni (*LBHG,* 327) who believe the site Shishak mentioned was located E of the Jordan river.

Hapharaim is sometimes located (*RAB,* 146) at Khirbet el-Farriyeh (M.R. 160226), based in part on the similarity of the ancient and modern names. However, this site, located NW of Megiddo, is far outside the territorial boundaries of Issachar determined by the other sites in the passage. Albright (1926: 227–28) suggested the location of Hapharaim at the village of et-Ṭaiyibeh (M.R. 192223). While superficially the name is not similar, by the Islamic period Hapharaim had changed to a root of *ʿpr,* (*HGB, 423), which has negative connotations in Arabic, resulting in the substitution of a "good"* *(ṭyb)* name. Albright's identification has been generally accepted, although Kallai (*HGB,* 203) has noted that Afula (M.R. 177223) remains another possibility.

Bibliography

Albright, W. F. 1926. The Topography of the Tribe of Issachar. *ZAW* 44: 225–36.

Yeivin, S. 1957. Thotmoses III's Shorter List of Conquered Palestino-Syrian Towns. Pp. 586–98 in *Proceedings of the XXIInd International Congress of Orientalists,* Leiden.

Melvin Hunt

HAPIRU. See HABIRU, HAPIRU.

HAPPIZZEZ (PERSON) [Heb *happiṣṣēṣ*]. A priest who received the 18th position in the priestly order of the temple during David's reign (1 Chr 24:15). 1 Chronicles 24 is the only place where Happizzez appears in the OT. It seems highly unlikely that he was a historical priest contemporaneous with David. Instead, Happizzez may represent a familial name, a clan located at Beth-pazzez (Josh 19:21). An evaluation of the historical reliability of his appearance, however, depends ultimately on the literary context of 1 Chr 24:1–19. For questions regarding the date of this list of priests, see HAKKOZ. See BETH-PAZZEZ.

John W. Wright

HAR HARIF (M.R. 107989). A set of prehistoric sites located at the highest elevations of the central Negeb highlands adjacent to Sinai, ca. 900–1000 m above sea level. It was first investigated by an expedition under the direction of A. E. Marks from 1969 through 1974. More extensive excavations were conducted by A. N. Goring-Morris and A. Gopher in 1980 and 1981.

This area, at the S boundary of the Irano-Turanian vegetation zone, contained relatively abundant plant and animal food resources during the Late and Terminal Pleistocene and so provided an attractive focus for local hunter-gatherer bands. Various open-air campsites of Upper Paleolithic and Epipaleolithic groups (especially of the local "Ramonian" industry) have been investigated on the loess-covered plateau. These camps usually comprise limited (20–150 m^2) scatters of flint artifacts in which organic materials have not been preserved and presumably represent ephemeral hunting camps.

A large Natufian site complex of the 10th millennium B.C., Rosh Horesha, is located in an adjacent shallow valley; extending over at least 4 dunams, it is the southernmost Natufian base camp known in the Negeb. Many bedrock mortars in the vicinity indicate that plant resources (probably pistachio nuts, but perhaps also barley) were major staples in addition to meat from hunted prey. The associated lithic assemblage was abundant.

The Epipaleolithic Harifian industry is named after a series of sites found on Har Harif, the best documented of which are Abu Salem and Ramat Harif. These sites, well dated by C^{14} determinations to the second half of the 9th millennium B.C., apparently represent the summer base camps of a local group. These camps, each extending over ca. 600 m^2, comprise no more than three or four separate (family?), semi-subterranean, circular dwellings up to 3 m in diameter and a few additional smaller structures, such that there would have been no more than 30 occupants. The economy was based upon vegetal resources, processed on grinding slabs (barley? or other cereals) and by pounding with mortars and pestles, as well as upon hunting (especially gazelle, ibex, and wild goat), seemingly with the newly developed bow and arrow. An abundant flint industry (more than 5000 tools and 80,000 pieces of waste in one structure alone) is distinctive but reminiscent of the preceding Natufian. Exotic ornamental elements are quite common, especially sea shells, most from the Red Sea (as opposed to the Mediterranean orientation at Rosh Horesha), turquoise beads, malachite, and other rare minerals.

During the winter months the Harifians apparently separated into smaller (family?) units and moved to nearby lower regions, especially the dune fields of N Sinai and the W Negeb, where small transient campsites without architectural remains have been documented, and perhaps also E to the shelter of the Maktesh Ramon.

This transhumant Harifian adaptation was disrupted by increasing desiccation, leading to the virtual abandonment of the Negeb during the first half of the 8th millennium B.C. The region was only subsequently reoccupied some 1000 years later at Abu Salem, where the remains of a Pre-Pottery Neolithic B campsite with a few small structures were found.

Bibliography

Butler, B.; Tchernov, E.; Hietala, H.; and Davis, S. 1977. Faunal Exploitation during the Late Epipalaeolithic in the Har Harif. Pp. 327–46 in Marks 1977.

Davis, S.; Goring-Morris, A. N.; and Gopher, A. 1982. Sheep Bones from the Negev Epipalaeolithic. *Paleorient* 8: 87–93.

Goring-Morris, A. N. 1985. Terminal Pleistocene Hunter/Gatherers in the Negev and Sinai. Ph.D. diss., Hebrew University, Jerusalem.

Goring-Morris, A. N., and Gopher, A. 1981. Har Harif, 1980. *IEJ* 31: 133–34.

———. 1982. Har Harif, 1981. *IEJ* 32: 71–73.

Horowitz, A. 1977. Pollen Spectra from Two Early Holocene Prehistoric Sites in the Har Harif (West Central Negev). Pp. 323–26 in Marks 1977.

Larson, P. 1978. Ornamental Beads from the Late Natufian of Southern Israel. *JFA* 5: 120–21.

Marks, A. E., ed. 1977. *Prehistory and Paleoenvironments in the Central Negev, Israel.* Vol. 2, *The Avdat/Aqev Area, Part 2, and the Har Harif.* Dallas.

Marks, A. E., and Larson, P. A. 1977. Test Excavations at the Natufian Site of Rosh Horesha. Pp. 191–232 in Marks 1977.

Marks, A. E., and Scott, T. R. 1977. Abu Salem: the Type Site of the Harifian Industry of the Southern Levant. *JFA* 3: 43–60.

Marks, A. E., and Simmons, A. H. 1977. The Negev Kebaran of the Har Harif. Pp. 233–70 in Marks 1977.

Mienis, H. K. 1977. Marine Molluscs from the Epipalaeolithic and Harifian of the Har Harif, Central Negev (Israel). Pp. 347–54 in Marks 1977.

Scott, T. R. 1977. The Harifian of the Central Negev. Pp. 271–322 in Marks 1977.

NIGEL GORING-MORRIS

HAR-HERES (PLACE) [Heb *har-ḥeres*]. The toponym Har-heres, which means "scurfy mountain(s)," appears in the OT only in Judg 1:35. It was the name of a mountain range on the E or SE edge of the valley of Aijalon (cf. Josh 10:12), in the transition zone between the mountains and the hill country. In certain periods there may have been a settlement on the mountainside. In any case a site on the S slope of the bare hills running NW about 2 miles SE of Yalo bears the name *ḫirbet ḫirša;* another, on the W slope of a range slightly farther S is called *ḫirbet ḫarsīs*. It is reasonable to assume that one of these names preserves the OT toponym Har-heres.

Judg 1:35 mentions Har-heres in conjnction with Aijalon (Yalo) and Shaalbim (Selbiṭ), which are clearly villages; in the past the toponym has likewise been understood as the name of a village. It has usually been interpreted as a variant of the familiar Beth-shemesh (Tell er-Rumeileh near En-shems), since Heb *ḥeres,* like *šemeš,* can also mean "sun" (cf. Job 9:7). This identification is contradicted, however, by the initial element *har,* which in the OT always means "mountain (range)." The apparent exception in Josh 15:10, where Har-jearim is equated with the village Chesalon, is based on a mistaken secondary identification: Chesalon was located on the N slope of Har-jearim. Furthermore, the LXX of Judg 1:35 translates *har* as *oros,* whereas it always transliterates the names of villages (e.g., *baithsamys* for Beth-shemesh).

According to Judg 1:34–35 Har-heres, like the nearby

villages of Aijalon and Shaalbim, remained in the hands of the Amorites when the small band of Danites tried to enter the fertile valley of Aijalon before migrating to Laish (Judg 18:27–29) from their encampment at Kiriath-jearim (Judg 18:12). The house of Joseph, more precisely the tribe of Ephraim, considered this territory as part of its sphere of influence and finally acquired sovereignty over it.

Bibliography

Kallai, Z. 1952. Mount Heres. *EncMiqr* 2: 853.
———. 1987. *Historical Geography of the Bible.* Leiden.
Niemann, H. M. 1985. *Die Daniten.* FRLANT 135. Göttingen.
Schunck, K.-D. 1980. Wo lag Har Heres. *ZDPV* 96: 153–57.

K.-D. SCHUNCK
Trans. David E. Green

HARA (PLACE) [Heb *hārāʾ*]. A place of exile for some of the Israelites or at least the people of the capital city of Samaria. The word means "mountain" or "highland." It is omitted in LXX AB and Syr. In 1 Chr 5:26 Hara is listed with Hala, Habor, and the river Gozan, as the place of exile by Assyrian King Pul (his personal name) or Tilgath-pileser (more accurately, Tiglath-pileser III, his throne name, 745–727 B.C.). In 2 Kgs 17:6 and 18:11 the RSV records that the king took the people of Samaria (the city) to Assyria and put them in Halah; on the Habor, the river of Gozan; and in the *cities* of the Medes. Instead of Hara, Heb has "cities of Media." The LXX has "mountains of Media." Perhaps Hara is a corruption of *har,* "mountain," or *haʿir,* "city." Gozan (Ptolemy's Gauzanitis, modern Tell Halaf) is in N Mesopotamia. Curtis (*Chronicles* ICC) claimed it was a district, the Assyrian *Gu-za-na.* The Habor is the modern river Khābûr, the ancient Chaboras, which rises in Karabjab Dagh (ancient Mons Masius), runs for 200 miles through the Gozan district, and empties into the Euphrates SE of the modern town of ed-Deir, which some identify as Hara. Some suggest that Hara should be read Hara on the Balikh 100 miles to the W. Others understand Hara as a local designation of Mons Masius. But a similar attraction is found in the mountain district E of the Tigris river. Arabs called these highlands El Gebal "the Mountain." It is less likely, but possible, that Hara is a corruption of Harhar, a Median city conquered by Sargon and colonized by him with captives from other countries. Tobit (1:14–15) communicated with fellow Jews in Media (Bowman *IDB* 2: 523–24), lending some support to a location in Media. Many commentators see "mountains" or "cities" as original with the Chronicler, mistaking the term for a place called Hara. However, Keil (n.d.: 111) suggested the Chronicler was drawing on a separate authority. *Cities* is a more general term while Hara is the specific name of the district (El Jebel) in Aramaic, for Heb *har,* "mountain" a name which he knew through his separate authority. It is a name which could only have been handed down by the exiles who lived there. Keil identified Halah with Strabo's Calachene, E of the Tigris near Adiabene, N of Nineveh on the Armenian frontier. The Habor is not the Chaboras in Mesopotamia, but a district in N Assyria where Jakut mentions there is both a mountain Chaboras on the Assyria-Media frontier and a river Khābûr Chasaniae, which starts near the Upper Zab, near Amadijeh, and enters the Tigris below Jezirah. Thus Halah, Habor, and Hara are E and N of the Assyrian capital, further removed from Israel than the upper Euphrates and further removed as troublemakers for the Assyrian occupation of Israel.

Bibliography

Keil, C. F. n.d. The Books of the Chronicles. In *Biblical Commentary on The OT,* ed. C. F. Keil and F. Delitzsch. Grand Rapids. Repr. 1966.

HENRY O. THOMPSON

HARADAH (PLACE) [Heb *harādâ*]. The ninth encampment of the Israelites after leaving the Wilderness of Sinai as listed in Num 33:24–25, placed between Mt. Sepher and Makheloth. The name, which means "fear," "trembling," or "anxiety," gives no clue as to its possible location, though it may suggest a place where the Israelites met some misfortune (compare this with Kibroth-hattaavah, in Num 11:4–6 and 31–35, where a story relates the origin of a similar name). Suggested locations for this site include the Wâdī Lussan (*GP,* 215; M.R. 085985) and Jebel ʾAradeh (Palmer 1872: 253, 419; M.R. 099843). For a discussion of the location of any of the places associated with the journey of the Israelites from Egypt through Sinai see DOPHKAH.

Bibliography

Beit-Arieh, I. 1988. The Route Through Sinai—Why the Israelites Fleeing Egypt Went South. *BARev* 15/3: 28–37.
Palmer, E. H. 1872. *The Desert of the Exodus.* New York.

JEFFREY R. ZORN

HARAN (PERSON) [Heb *hārān; ḥārān*]. **1.** Son of Terah; brother of Abram and Nahor; and father of Lot, Milcah, and Iscah (Gen 11:27–29). Haran died in Ur of the Chaldeans while his father was still alive. Haran as a personal name is to be distinguished from Haran, the place name (Heb *ḥārān*). The personal name is composed of two elements: *hr,* the Hebrew word for "mountain"; and a W Semitic suffix which appears on proper names *-ānu/i/a* (Sivan 1984: 97–98). (For another use of the *-ān* ending in personal names of Genesis 1–11, see KENAN.) In personal names from Mari and Alalakh, the spellings *ḫa-ri-* and *ḫa-ru-* occur, but their relation to the *hr* element is not certain (cf. Sivan 1984: 222; but Huffmon *APNM,* 204). Such an element has not been recognized in Amorite; and the only example of the W Semitic noun, *hr,* in cuneiform, appears in a gloss in an Amarna Letter from Byblos (EA text 74, line 20), where it occurs in a geminate form *ḫa-ar-ri.* More certain is the initial element in both the later Phoenician personal name, *hr-bʿl* (Benz *PNPPI,* 303), and the Israelite personal name, *hryhw,* from Gibeon (Pritchard 1962: 119).

2. A son of Shimei, of the sons of Gershon, of the tribe of Levi (1 Chr 23:9).

3. Son of Caleb and his concubine, Ephah; brother of Moza and Gazez; and father of Gazez (1 Chr 2:46).

Bibliography

Pritchard, J. B. 1962. *Gibeon, Where the Sun Stood Still.* Princeton.

Sivan, D. 1984. *Grammatical Analysis and Glossary of the Northwest Semitic Vocables in Akkadian Texts of the 15th–13th C. B.C. from Canaan and Syria.* AOAT 214. Kevelaer and Neukirchen-Vluyn.

RICHARD S. HESS

HARAN (PLACE) [Heb *ḥārān*]. The place to which Terah and his family (including Abram) migrated from Ur and where the descendants of Abram's brother Nahor dwelt and Terah died (Gen 11:31, 32).

A. Name and Location

The Sumerian word KASKAL, which Akkadians read as *ḫarrānu,* "road," was adapted as the name of the city of Haran. The determinative signs URU or KUR attached before the name of the city of Haran indicated it either as (1) city (or town, or village), or (2) country (or land, or region). The Akkadian city name *Ḫarrānu* was transcribed into Hebrew as *Ḥārān.* The Babylonian and Assyrian word *ḫarrānu* as a feminine noun (rarely as masculine word) denoted (1) "highway," "road," "path"; (2) "trip," "journey," "travel"; (3) "business trip"; (4) "caravan"; (5) "business venture"; (6) "business capital"; (7) "military campaign," "expedition," "raid"; (8) "expeditionary force," "army"; (9) "corvée work"; (10) "service unit" from the OAkk period onwards. The city of Haran, probably located at the "junction of trade routes," was named after the crossroads.

Some consider that this city, Haran, was named after Terah's son Haran (Gen 11:26–28), but the Hebrew spelling of the names is different. Since Haran was born at Ur and died there before the migration of the Terahide family from Ur, it is inconceivable that the city of Haran was named after him.

Haran may be identified with Padan (Gen 48:7). The Akk *padānu* and *paddānu* both mean "road" (like *ḫarrānu*) and "the biliary ducts of the liver." The expression Padan Aram appears more often than the simple Padan but only ten times in Genesis. Some consider the expression "the field of Aram" (Hos 12:12) as the Hebrew translation of Padan Aram. However, most probably the expression "the field of Aram" may be another way of referring to the plain between two rivers (either Euphrates and Tigris or Euphrates and Khâbûr) corresponding to the name Aram-naharaim. In the Targumic Aramaic the word *paddĕnāʾ* means "yoke," "span of oxen." The Akk *paddānu* "road," and the Aram *paddĕnāʾ* "span of oxen," share the common idea of "spanning two regions," for the road is considered as the bridge between two or more regions.

Haran is situated about 100 km N from the confluence of the Euphrates and the Balikh (a tributary of the Upper Euphrates) and 80 km E of the city of Carchemish on the winding upper Euphrates river. It is located at the confluence of the wadis which join the Balikh in winter, also at 80 km W of the city of Guzana or Gozan (Tell Halaf) and halfway between Guzana and Carchemish on the E-W road which links Nineveh on the Tigris and the E Mediterranean countries, at the point where the N-S route along the Balikh crosses.

"The city of Nahor" in Gen 24:10, mentioned as the place where Rebekah's parents lived, may be identified with "Nakhur," which is often mentioned in the Mari tablets as well as in the Middle Assyrian documents of the 7th century B.C. According to Albright it is located below Haran in the Balikh valley, judging from the name of a town Til-Nakhiri, "the Mound of Nakhur," in the above documents (*FSAC* 115, 236–237). It was probably another town, different from the city of Haran, but still in the Haran district. In Assyrian documents we see more names of towns similar to the names of the people in Terah's family: e.g., Til-Turakhi, "Mound of Terah," probably also located on the S Balikh like Til-Nakhiri, and Serugi "Serug," modern Seruj, some 55 km W of Haran.

B. History

The OA Cappadocian tablets (Kültepe texts), business letters and legal documents of Assyrian merchants (working in the E portion of Asia Minor in the 19th and 18th century B.C.), and an itinerary and a letter addressed to Yasmah-Adad (the Assyrian viceroy at Mari of the OB period belonging to the 18th century B.C.) mention Haran as an important crossroads. The main temple, È-ḪULḪUL, at Haran was a center for the worship of Sin, the Mesopotamian moon-god.

The Israelite's confession that "my father was a wandering Aramean" (Deut 26:5) suggests that their ancestors were either Aramean nomadic people or non-Semitic nomadic people who came to live in an Aramean environment in the Haran district. Terah and his family genealogically belonged to the Hebrew (or perhaps ʿApiru), who are the descendants of Eber in Gen 10:21, 25; but they had a close association with Arameans before or after coming to Aram-naharaim "Aram of two rivers (= Mesopotamia)." Terah and his family settled there for a considerably long time, so that Abraham could call the Haran region "my country" (Gen 24:4).

At the time of Terah and Abram, the culture of the people of NW Mesopotamia, in the region around Haran, was a mixture of Hurrian and Amorite elements on a Sumero-Akkadian foundation defined and illustrated by the Cappadocian tablets, the Mari documents, the Code of Hammurapi, the OB letters from Babylon, and the Nuzi tablets of the 15th century B.C. There is no positive evidence for defining the time of the earlier migration from Ur of the Chaldees to Haran. Moreover, the Chaldeans during the patriarchal periods seem to be rather nomadic raiders (Job 1:17) who lived near Haran or Edom; so the traditional site of Ur in S Mesopotamia may be reexamined as some seek the location near Haran; but the place is not identified yet.

After Terah's death Abraham migrated from Haran to Canaan when he was 75 years old (Gen 12:4–5), but the family of Nahor remained there, and his wife Milcah bore 8 children: Uz, Buz, Kemuel, Chesed, Hazo, Pildash, Jidlaph, and Bethuel (Gen 22:20–22). Eliezer brought Rebekah, daughter of Bethuel, from there (Genesis 24); and later Jacob fled there to live with Laban; there he married Laban's two daughters, Leah and Rachel; and there his 11 children were born.

At the time of Hammurapi (1728–1686 B.C.) Haran was

under an Amorite king, Asdi-takim. The alliance between this king of Haran and the kings of Zalmaqum and sheikhs and elders of the Benjaminites (mentioned in one of the Mari Letters), was concluded in the temple of the moon-god at Haran. In the MA period Adad-nirari I (1307–1275 B.C.) fortified the citadel of Haran, and Tiglath-pileser I (1115–1077 B.C.) embellished the temple É.ḪULḪUL of the moon-god. Because of its rebellion the city of Haran was destroyed by Asshur-dan III in 763 B.C., which event Sennacherib (704–681 B.C.) mentioned to intimidate Jerusalem (2 Kgs 19:12; Isa 37:12). The city was restored by Sargon II (721–705 B.C.), and the temple was repaired by Esarhaddon (675 B.C.) and by Ashurbanipal (668–627 B.C.). A letter to Ashurbanipal says that Esarhaddon "saw in the region of Harran a temple of cedarwood. Therein the god Sin was leaning on a staff, with two crowns on his head" (*ANET,* 450). After the fall of Nineveh (612 B.C.), Haran became the last capital of the NA Empire until its capture by the Babylonians in 609 B.C. The NB Empire restored the temple of the moon-god at Haran and appointed Nabonidus' mother as the high priestess of the temple. In the book of Ezekiel, Haran is mentioned as one of the famous commercial cities trading with Tyre (Ezek 27:23), but after then the city existed without particular relation to the biblical account until several centuries after the NT period when it fell into ruin. For further discussion, see *EncJud* 7: 1328–30; *NBD,* 504.

YOSHITAKA KOBAYASHI

HARARITE [Heb *hahărārî*]. A gentilic adjective describing the location or clan from which a number of David's mighty men came (2 Sam 23:11, 33). Most scholars feel that the adjective designates a location, although it has not been identified with certainty. On the basis of the appearance of the term *A-ra-ri* in the Amarna Letters, it has been identified with either a town in the S district of Judah near Hebron (Elliger *KlSchr,* 98) or the biblical Aroer in the Negeb (Albright 1943: 14). Others have argued that the location is in the Shephelah, since a Hararite led a battle against the Philistines (2 Sam 23:11–12; *HDB* 2: 301). This assumes that the battle was fought near the border of Philistia and Israel and also that the Hararite's place of origin was in the same general area. Perhaps the simplest explanation is that of Gesenius, who argues that Hararite means "mountain dweller" (Heb *har* = mountain) (*BDB,* 251).

Three of David's mighty warriors were Hararites, one belonging to the group distinguished as "The Three" and two to the one known as "The Thirty." Shammah was a member of the former group. His father, Agee, was known as a Hararite (2 Sam 23:11; Heb *hārārî* is a contraction for *hahărārî*), and presumably he was too. Shammah played an important role in defeating the Philistines in a significant battle. The other two members were Shammah's son, Jonathan (reading with LXX: *huios* in 1 Chr 11:34; cf. LXX in 2 Sam 23:33), and Ahiam, whose father, Sharar (1 Chr 11:35 = *śākār*), is called the Hararite (Heb *hā*ʾ*rārî* in 2 Sam 23:33 is a variant of *hahărārî*). See also DAVID'S CHAMPIONS.

Bibliography

Albright, W. F. 1943. Two Little Understood Amarna Letters from the Middle Jordan Valley. *BASOR* 89: 7–17.

Stenning, J. F. 1899. The Hararite. *Hastings Dictionary of the Bible* 2: 301–2.

STEPHEN G. DEMPSTER

HARBONA (PERSON) [Heb *ḥarbônâ; ḥarbônā*ʾ]. See MEHUMAN (PERSON).

HARE. See ZOOLOGY (FAUNA).

HAREPH (PERSON) [Heb *ḥarep*]. Son of Hur and "father of Beth-gader" (1 Chr 2:51). Beth-gader is a town, not a person. Hareph possibly means "autumn" or "maturity" (or "to scorn"). In the LXX it appears as *hari[e]m.* Reflecting the uncertainties of the textual tradition, the Peshitta reads "Abi, who was born in Gader" (see also the KJV). The name Hareph occurs in a fragment of a Calebite genealogy that the Chronicler (or the tradition before him) has broken up (1 Chr 2:18–20, 24, 50b–55; 4:4b). This name occurs nowhere else in biblical literature, and the town of which this person was supposedly the father is unidentified. Most interpreters think that it was in the vicinity of Bethlehem, a town which Salma, another son of Hur, also supposedly founded (Braun *1 Chronicles* WBC, 42).

CRAIG A. EVANS

HARHAIAH (PERSON) [Heb *ḥarĕhāyâ*]. The father of Uzziel, one of those who worked on the wall of Jerusalem following the return from Babylonian exile (Neh 3:8). See UZZIEL. Since the root and meaning of the name are unknown (BDB, 354) and the word as it stands creates an awkward phrase, an emendation to *ḥeber* has been proposed, in which case this would be no proper name. The emendation would alter the phrase to "Uzziel, a son (member) of the guild of the goldsmiths" (cf. *IDB* 2: 525). Clines (*Ezra, Nehemiah, Esther* NCBC, 153) finds the proposed emendation attractive, since it would account for the plural form "goldsmiths." One hindrance in accepting the emendation is that in this same verse Hananiah is identified as "a son of the perfumers" and in 3:32 Malchijah is named as "a son of the goldsmiths," in both cases without the word *guild* being interjected.

MICHAEL L. RUFFIN

HARHAS (PERSON) [Heb *ḥarḥas*]. Var. HASRAH. Grandfather of Shallum, husband of the prophetess Huldah (2 Kgs 22:14). The name is unusual and may have resulted from metathesis. In the parallel text in 2 Chr 34:22, Shallum's grandfather is *Ḥasrâ,* which may be the proper form of the name.

PAULINE A. VIVIANO

HARHUR (PERSON) [Heb *ḥarḥûr*]. The name of a family of temple servants (Nethinim) who returned to Palestine with Zerubbabel shortly after 538 B.C.E., the end of the Babylonian exile. The name appears in Ezra 2:51 in the phrase "the sons of Harhur," where the temple servants are distinguished from the people of Israel, the priests, and the Levites. The parallel passage Neh 7:46–56 also lists "the sons of Harhur" (Neh 7:53).

In another parallel passage, 1 Esdr 5:29–32, it appears that the names Asur and Pharakim have replaced Harhur (1 Esdr 5:31). However, there are a sufficient number of discrepancies between the Ezra-Nehemiah and 1 Esdras lists to suggest that the absence of Harhur is not due to an intentional replacement; there is no known connection between Harhur and these other names which would occasion the suggested substitution.

STEVEN R. SWANSON

HARIF, HAR. See HAR HARIF (M.R. 107989).

HARIM (PERSON) [Heb *ḥārim*], Var. ANNAN; REHUM. **1.** Name of one of the 24 divisions of the priests in the time of David (1 Chr 24:8). Although the Chronicler attributes this division of the priests to David, most scholars regard the list as reflecting priestly organization from a later time, with estimates ranging from the late preexilic period (Myers *1 Chronicles* AB, 165–66) to ca. 300 B.C. (Williamson 1979: 251–68). See 3 below.

2. Name of a family of priests in the postexilic period who are listed as returnees from Babylonian exile under the leadership of Zerubbabel and others (Ezra 2:39 = Neh 7:42 = 1 Esdr 5:25). Some from this family married foreign wives and later agreed to divorce them in response to Ezra's reform (Ezra 10:21). In both of these contexts, Harim is one of four priestly families listed. For discussion of the list in Ezra 2, see AKKUB.

3. Name of one of the priestly divisions in the postexilic period (Neh 12:15), whose representative signed the covenant document of Nehemiah in Neh 10:6—Eng 10:5. In both of these contexts, Harim is one of more than 20 priestly names listed. The virtual identity between the priestly divisions of Neh 12:12–21 and Neh 12:1–7 indicates that REHUM (Neh 12:3) is a variant of Harim caused by the transposition of the first two consonants. The priestly lists in Ezra 2:36–39; 10:18–22; Neh 10:3–9—Eng 10:2–8; 12:1–7, 12:21; and 1 Chr 24:7–19 provide evidence for tracing the development of 24 priestly divisions in the postexilic period. (See Myers *Ezra-Nehemiah* AB, 196; Kidner *Ezra-Nehemiah* TOTC, 122; Clines *Ezra, Nehemiah and Esther* NCBC, 223–24; Williamson *Ezra-Nehemiah* WBC, 359–61.)

Many do not regard the list and covenant of Nehemiah 10 as belonging originally in this context. Williamson (*Ezra-Nehemiah* WBC, 325–30) surveys various views about the origins of this list. He concludes that it was compiled from other lists in Ezra and Nehemiah in order to be attached to the terms of an agreement drawn up by Nehemiah following his reforms of Nehemiah 13. This document was then kept in the temple archives until being inserted into its present position. (See also Clines, 199–200; Myers *Ezra-Nehemiah* AB, 174–75; Jepsen 1954: 87–106.)

4. Name of a family of laypeople who are listed as returnees from Babylonian exile under the leadership of Zerubbabel and others (Ezra 2:32 = Neh 7:35). The presence of Harim in a section with many geographic names (Ezra 2:21–35) raises the possibility that this family's name was derived from a place rather than a person. (See Batten *Ezra and Nehemiah* ICC, 81; *IB* 3: 581; Williamson *Ezra-Nehemiah* WBC, 33–34.) Some from this family married foreign wives and later agreed to divorce them in response to Ezra's reform (Ezra 10:31 = 1 Esdr 9:32). 1 Esdras gives ANNAN as the name of the family, which could be the personal name by which it was known.

A member of this family assisted Nehemiah in rebuilding the walls of Jerusalem (Neh 3:11). That the list of builders is a partial one is evident from the reference in this verse (and also vv 19, 20, 30) to a "second section" without any previous notation of a first section (compare 3:4 and 21; 3:5 and 27). There is widespread agreement that the list came from independent archives, perhaps in the temple, and was incorporated into the Nehemiah memoirs by Nehemiah himself or by some other editor. (See Batten, 206–7; Clines, 149; Williamson *Ezra-Nehemiah* WBC, 199–202.)

The leader of this clan affixed the family name to the covenant document of Nehemiah in Neh 10:28—Eng 10:27.

Bibliography

Galling, K. 1951. The Gōlā-List According to Ezra 2 and Nehemiah 7. *JBL* 70: 149–58.

———. 1964. Die Liste der aus dem Exil Heimgekehrten. Pp. 89–108 in *Studien zur Geschichte Israels im persischen Zeitalter*. Tübingen.

Jepsen, A. 1954. Nehemia 10. *ZAW* 66: 87–106.

Williamson, H. G. M. 1979. The Origins of the Twenty-four Priestly Courses, A Study of 1 Chronicles xxiii–xxvii. Pp. 251–68 in *Studies in the Historical Books of the OT*, ed. J. A. Emerton. VTSup 30. Leiden.

CHANEY R. BERGDALL

HARIPH (PERSON) [Heb *ḥārîp*]. The head of an important Judahite family who returned after the Exile (Neh 7:24). He was one of those who sealed the covenant of reform (Neh 10:20—Eng 10:19), and the men of his family are said to have numbered 112 (Neh 7:24; cf. 1 Esdr 5:16).

There appears to be some confusion among the OT versions of the list of returnees. In Ezra 2:18 the name Jorah corresponds to Hariph. 1 Esdr 5:16 variants read Arseiphoureth (Gk *arsiphouris;* cf. *hariphou*). In each case the family is recorded as numbering 112 "sons." The name Hariph may have some connection with the gentilic (RSV Haruphite) of 1 Chr 12:6 (Heb K *hărîpî,* Q *hărûpî*). A possibly related name is known from Ugarit (Ug *ḫrpn*).

NORA A. WILLIAMS

HARMON (PLACE) [Heb *harmôn*). A place to which the leading women of Samaria are to be carried away (Amos

4:3). All efforts to discover the place named in only this one text have failed. Many modern scholars will repoint the word to read Hermon (Wolff *Joel, Amos* Hermeneia, 207). Mt. Hermon lies beyond Bashan (famed for the cattle used to characterize the apparently voluptuous women of 4:1), far to the N of Israel in the general direction of Damascus, but by virtue of its great height is easily seen from most higher elevations within Israel. To be cast here, it may be argued, is but another way of saying that they will be deported by enemies from the N. This argument is much more convincing that those suggesting other place names like the mountain of Remmon (LXX), the mountains of Armenia (Targums), or such specific places as the palace (KJV) or dunghill (NEB), and certainly more than those that would turn the place into an otherwise unknown goddess by the name Rimmonah. See also Harper *Amos and Hosea* ICC.

ELMER H. DYCK

HARMONY OF GOSPELS. A gospel harmony is a narrative life of Jesus constructed by combining or otherwise harmonizing the four different canonical gospel accounts of Matthew, Mark, Luke, and John. A gospel harmony rests on the proposition that the four canonical gospels are in fundamental or absolute substantive agreement *(consensus evangelistarum)* in their presentation of the life of Jesus.

The earliest known gospel harmony is that of Tatian, who wrote his *Diatessaron* in the latter part of the 2d century (Eus. *Hist. Eccl.* 4.29.6). Many of the basic questions associated with the text remain in dispute, including the original language (Greek or Syriac), its place of composition (Rome or E Syria), and the sources Tatian used (simply the four canonical gospels or an additional noncanonical source). Attempts to settle these and other issues have been hampered by the fact that Tatian's text survives in but one small Greek fragment (Kraeling 1935). Most of our knowledge of the text comes from the partially preserved Syriac text in Ephrem's *Commentary on the Diatessaron* (ed. Leloir), and various later translations and versions, including texts in Armenian, Arabic, Middle Persian, Old Latin, and Italian (for a concise listing of the relevant manuscripts, see Wünsch *TRE* 10, 628–29).

Though Tatian's *Diatessaron* continued to be translated, summarized, or otherwise adapted for popular readership (so, for example, the *Gesta Christi* of John Hus, or the medieval Jesus epic *Heliand*), no new gospel harmony seems to have appeared before the 15th century, when the reformer Johannes Gerson wrote his *Monotessaron*. Gerson's method was to follow the narrative outline of John, inserting harmonized versions of synoptic pericopes into contexts which he thought to be appropriate (Wünsch 1983: 15–20). Gerson's work marks the beginning of a period in which this genre enjoyed immense popularity. The next two centuries saw the publication of over 40 different gospel harmonies, including those of Lucinius (1525), Beringer (1526), Alber (1532), Osiander (1537), Jansen (1549), and perhaps the most ambitious effort within the genre, the *Harmonia evangelica,* begun by Chemnitz but finished and published by P. Leyser and J. Gerhard between 1593 and 1652. Chemnitz' plan, like that of Gerson, was to follow the outline of John, filling in the interstices with harmonized versions of synoptic pericopes. Thus each chapter begins with an explanation of the relative placement of each pericope. This is followed by the parallel gospel texts themselves, in both Greek and Latin, then a harmonized version of the text with explanatory notes to the harmonization, and finally a commentary upon the particular section under consideration (Wünsch *TRE* 10, 633–34).

The popularity of gospel harmonies continued for another century, but with the Enlightenment and the advent of more critical approaches to the life of Jesus, the scholarly energy required to produce a work on the level of the *Harmonia evangelica* was channeled to newer methods of reconstructing the life of Jesus that were not so intent upon producing accounts in absolute literal conformity with the canonical texts.

In the modern period the comparative function performed by gospel harmonies was taken up by various gospel synopses, which present the canonical gospels in parallel columns or lines but do not necessarily presume the dogmatic position that all four gospel accounts must be in substantive agreement. The most popular of these has been the *Synopsis Quattuor Evageliorum* compiled by the German scholar Kurt Aland. It presents the three Synoptic Gospels in parallel columns, as well as the Johannine parallels where such exist. The basic plan of the Aland synopsis is based upon the Markan order, including the longer sections in which Matthew and Luke create their own order as detours within this overall framework. Robert Funk's *New Gospel Parallels,* on the other hand, seeks to arrange the material in such a way that preserves the narrative sequence of each of the primary texts. It thus presents each of the gospels (including John and several extracanonical texts) consecutively, first Matthew in its entirety, with parallels from other gospel texts given in parallel vertical columns located to the right of the primary text, then Mark in its entirety with parallels, then Luke, and so forth. The result is a longer, more repetitious work, but one which may prove more useful for persons interested in a more literary-critical approach to the gospels.

Bibliography

Aland, K., ed. 1985. *Synopsis Quattuor Evangeliorum.* 13th rev. ed. Stuttgart.

Funk, R. W., ed. 1985. *New Gospel Parallels.* 2 vols. Philadelphia.

Grant, R. M. 1957. Tatian and the Bible. Pp. 297–305 in *Studia Patristica 1,* ed. K. Aland and F. L. Cross. TU 63. Berlin.

Kraeling, C. H. 1935. *A Greek Fragment of Tatian's Diatessaron from Dura.* SD 3. London.

Leloir, L. 1966. *Éphrem de Nisibe. Commentaire de l'Évangile concordant ou Diatessaron.* SC 121. Paris.

Wünsch, D. 1983. *Evangelienharmonien im Reformationszeitalter. Ein Beitrag zur Geschichte der Leben-Jesu-Forschung.* Arbeiten zur Kirchengeschichte 52. Berlin.

STEPHEN J. PATTERSON

HARNEPHER (PERSON) [Heb *ḥarneper*]. A descendant of Asher, known only from the segmented genealogy of Asher in 1 Chr 7:30–40. The name appears in v 36 as a son of Zophah, as a fifth-generation descendant of the eponymous tribal ancestor Asher. Although the genealogy suggests that Harnepher was a person, other names in the list, such as Shual, Zophah, Japhlet, and Shelesh/Shilshah, are known from their appearances elsewhere in the Bible to have been clan names and/or geographic designations. The summary in v 40 would seem to indicate that the names used to create the genealogy were derived from administrative lists used for purposes of army conscription and possibly also taxation. Accordingly, the names probably represent clans, villages, or regions associated with clans rather than historical individuals. The entire Asherite genealogy in 1 Chronicles 7 reflects groups living in the Asherite enclave in S Mt. Ephraim, not those inhabiting the Galilean territory of Asher (Edelman 1988; see ASHER; ASHURITES).

Harnepher is an Egyptian name meaning "(the deity) Horus is good." According to the legend of the winged disk written on the walls of the temple of Horus at Edfu, Horus was the champion of the sun-god Ra and was symbolized in the winged solar disk. Thus he was especially associated with war and the conquest of foreign enemies. Pharaoh was believed to be Horus incarnate and as such became Ra's champion whenever he undertook military campaigns (Watterson 1984: 107).

The most plausible explanation for the appearance of an Egyptian name in an administrative list that would have been derived from Judahite archival records is that Harnepher represents an Egyptian military garrison that was built within Judahite territory sometime during the brief period of Egyptian domination of Palestine under Psammetichus I and his successor, Neco II (Edelman 1988: 19). 2 Kgs 23:33–35 indicates that Judah was a vassal to Neco II; and as overlord, the pharaoh would have been free to establish garrisons within Judahite territory in S Mt. Ephraim to secure his interests. Judah's vassal status may already have been established during Psammethicus' reign (Miller and Hayes *HAIJ*, 388–90, 402). The underlying administrative list that included Harnepher as a part of the Judahite taxation/military conscription base therefore can probably be dated within the last four decades of Judah's existence as an independent state, ca. 630–587 B.C.E., during the reign of Josiah or one of his successors.

Bibliography

Ahlström, G. 1990. *The History of Ancient Palestine.* Winona Lake, IN.

Edelman, D. 1988. The Asherite Genealogy in 1 Chronicles 7:30–40. *BR* 33: 13–23.

Watterson, B. 1984. *The Gods of Ancient Egypt.* London.

DIANA V. EDELMAN

HARNESS. See ZOOLOGY (FAUNA).

HAROD (PLACE) [Heb *ḥărod*]. **1.** The name of the spring by which Gideon made his camp before his battle against the Midianites (Judg 7:1). The name of the spring means "trembling," which is related to the first test to which Gideon subjected his men. It was at the spring that Gideon conducted his final test, excusing those who knelt down to drink. Traditionally, the spring is identified with that which flows today at Ain Jalud (M.R. 184217). At this site Gideon's camp would have overlooked the Midianites, who camped below the hill of Moreh.

2. The hometown of two of David's mighty men, Shammah and Elika (2 Sam 23:25). In this instance Harod should be understood as a town, not a physical feature. Given David's links with the S, most scholars (McCarter, *2 Samuel* AB, 497; *GTTOT,* 338) have suggested Khirbet el-Haredan (M.R. 178126), a few km SE of Jerusalem, as the location of this Harod. The question is complicated by the parallel list of the mighty men of David's army in 1 Chr 11:27, where Shammoth of Haror replaces Shammah and where Elika is dropped entirely. However, the final *reš* in Haror may be easily emended to *dalet;* however, it remains possible that Harod and Haror are distinct toponyms.

MELVIN HUNT

HAROEH (PERSON) [Heb *hārōʾeh*]. Son of Shobal, founder of Kiriath-jearim (1 Chr 2:52). Haroeh means "the seer." Although the LXX apparently supports this reading *(haraa),* Curtis and Noth, followed by others (Williamson *Chronicles* NCBC, 55; Braun *1 Chronicles* WBC, 38), believe that the original reading was Reaiah [Heb *rĕʾāyāh*], as in 1 Chr 4:2. This is likely the case. The Peshitta also attests the corrupt state of the textual tradition (compare the KJV). 1 Chr 2:50b–55 is probably a fragment of a Calebite genealogy that the Chronicler (or the tradition before him) has broken up (see 1 Chr 2:18–20, 24; 4:4b). Reaiah probably means "vision of the Lord." Although the name occurs elsewhere in biblical literature (Ezra 2:47; Neh 7:50), nothing is known of this Reaiah, the son of Shobal.

CRAIG A. EVANS

HAROSHETH-HAGOIIM (PLACE) [Heb *ḥărošet haggōyim*]. The place where Sisera, the army commander of Jabin of Hazor, dwelt; the place from which his chariots went forth before the battle at Mt. Tabor; and the place toward which they fled after their defeat (Judg 4:2, 13, 16). The precise location of this site has never been established. Indeed, serious questions have been raised whether Harosheth-Hagoiim was a town at all. The LXX translates the term as "forests of the nations"; so Maisler (1953: 83) and Aharoni (*LBHG,* 221–23) have argued that, like the term *gĕlîl haggôyim* "Galilee of the nations," it refers to a forested region of N Israel which Sisera "ruled" (an alternative translation of the verb *yšb b*) on behalf of Jabin, controlling the seminomadic Israelite inhabitants (see GOIIM). This explanation, while superficially plausible, requires a chronological reversal of the battles of Deborah and Barak with those of Joshua and overlooks the statements (Judg 4:13–16) that Sisera marshaled his forces at Harosheth-Hagoiim and fled there after the battle.

However, it remains puzzling why Harosheth-Hagoiim is mentioned only here in all the ancient sources available to us, if in fact it was an important power in antiquity. Attempts to link Harosheth-Hagoiim with the *Muḫrashti* of the Amarna archives (Boling, *Judges* AB, 94) are not convincing. Proposed identifications with Khirbet el-Harityye

(M.R. 161236) and Tell Amr/Tel Geva Shemen (M.R. 159237) (*GTTOT,* 288; *RAB,* 147) are not supported by the archaeological evidence from the sites.

Recent archaeological studies (Gonen 1984; Oren 1984) have shown that beginning in the LB and continuing into Iron I, urban activity in Palestine declined, while Egyptian influence as far N as Beth-shan remained strong. It seems unlikely that the remaining Iron I Canaanite strongholds, although they were strong enough to resist the Israelites, retained the economic or social capacity to field major chariot forces on their own. Yet the OT makes no explicit reference to Egyptian activity in Palestine during the period of the judges. It may be possible that the dilemma posed by the enigmatic Harosheth-Hagoiim is an oblique reference to an Egyptian presence in the Jezreel valley.

Bibliography

Gonen, R. 1984. Urban Canaan in the Late Bronze Age. *BASOR* 253: 61–73.

Maisler, B. 1953. Beth Sheᶜarim, Gaba, and Harosheth of the Peoples. *HUCA* 24: 75–84.

Oren, E. 1984. "Governor's Residences" in Canaan under the New Kingdom: A Case Study in Egyptian Administration. *JSSEA* 14: 37–56.

MELVIN HUNT

HARP. See MUSIC AND MUSICAL INSTRUMENTS.

HARSHA (PERSON) [Heb *ḥaršāʾ*]. Var. CHAREA. A temple servant who was the progenitor of a family which returned from Babylon with Zerubbabel (Ezra 2:52 = Neh 7:54). Although 1 Esdras is often assumed to have been compiled from Ezra and Nehemiah, the name of this family's ancestor appears as "Charea" (Gk *Charea*) in 1 Esdr 5:32. Differences such as this raise questions about the sources of and literary relationships among 1 Esdras, Ezra, and Nehemiah.

MICHAEL DAVID MCGEHEE

HARSHA, TEL. See TEL-HARSHA (PLACE).

HART. See ZOOLOGY (FAUNA).

HARUM (PERSON) [Heb *hārûm*]. A Judahite, the father of Aharhel and ancestor of the families of Aharhel (1 Chr 4:8; cf. Noth *IPN,* 241). Harum was apparently descended from Koz. Rudolph (*Chronicles* HAT, 30) concluded that the text is in disorder—since the line of Aharhel is traced back to Koz, how could the family also be descended from Harum? This objection is ungrounded, however, as Koz did not father the families *(mišpěḥôt)* of Aharhel in one generation. In genealogies the concepts of *father* and *son* are used to refer to descent over varying numbers of generations. Harum, then, might have been a prominent descendant of Koz in the line which gave rise to the families of Aharhel. The Greek has *Iarim.*

KENNETH H. CUFFEY

HARUMAPH (PERSON) [Heb *ḥărûmap*]. The father of Jedaiah, one of those who worked on the wall of Jerusalem following the return from Babylonian exile (Neh 3:10). See JEDAIAH. Batten (*Ezra and Nehemiah* ICC, 212) notes the suggestion of Bertholet (*Esra und Nehemia* KHC, 100) that the name means "with a split nose" but maintains that it would have been a nickname. This translation sees the name as a combination of *ḥāram* and *ʾp.* Lev 21:19 provides an example of *ḥāram* being used to describe a facial disfiguration.

MICHAEL L. RUFFIN

HARUPHITE [Heb K *ḥărîpî,* Q *ḥărûpî*]. A descriptive adjective designating either the ethnic or family affiliation of Shephatiah, one of the ambidextrous warriors from the tribe of Benjamin who joined David during the period of his fleeing from Saul (1 Chr 12:6—Eng 12:5). The term probably designates an otherwise unknown locality, but it could be associated with the Calebite clan of Hareph (1 Chr 2:51) or the clan of Hariph (Neh 7:24; 10:20—Eng 10:19). The Chronicler has doubled the list of warriors who supported David (1 Chr 11:41b–12:40) beyond what was contained in the parallel narrative (2 Sam 23:8–39 = 1 Chr 11:10–41a); the source for these additional lists can only be a matter of conjecture. The long list reflects his concern to show "all Israel" united in support for David, a characteristic theme of the Chronicler's history. Within the immediate context (1 Chr 12:1–8—Eng 12:1–7) the Chronicler is concerned to show the support David enjoyed among Saul's kinsmen before Saul's death; the 23 Benjaminite warriors named here joined David while he was at Ziklag, the Philistine city given to David by Achish, king of Gath (1 Chr 12:1; 1 Sam 27:6). Ambidexterity or left-handedness among Benjaminites is also noted in Judg 3:15; 20:16.

Bibliography

Williamson, H. G. M. 1981. We Are Yours, O David. *OTS* 21: 164–76.

RAYMOND B. DILLARD

HARVESTS, HARVESTING [Heb *qāṣîr*]. Harvesting (ingathering) is the culmination of the agricultural cycle followed immediately by the processing of crops and fruit into foodstuffs such as grain, wine, oil, and dried fruit. In a good year the season of ingathering was time for merrymaking (Judg 9:27; Isa 9:3; 16:9–10; Ps 126:5). A good agricultural year would have been one in which one ingathering activity did not end before another started (Amos 9:13).

The Gezer calendar, an ancient record of agricultural activities, designates five periods totaling seven months for ingathering activities, beginning with the harvesting of cereals. The first period, *yrḥ qṣr śᶜrym* (a month of harvesting barley), is named in the Bible *qěṣîr śěᶜorîm* (Ruth 2:23) and lasted from the spring equinox in mid-March to mid-April. This was followed by *yrḥ qṣr wkl* (a month of harvesting [wheat] and measuring [grain for taxes]) ending at the autumnal equinox in mid-May and mentioned in the Bible as *qěṣîr ḥiṭṭîm* (Gen 30:14; Judg 15:1). The time of cereal harvesting, referred to in the Bible as *qāṣîr* (Gen 8:22; Exod 34:21), opened with the festival of *pesaḥ/maṣṣôt* (Passover/Unleavened Bread) and ended with the festival of *šābuʿôt* (Weeks). These two periods of harvesting cereals were followed by *dayiš* (Lev 26:5), threshing and winnowing to separate the grain from the chaff.

Cereals were harvested during a hot period—an activity well described in Ruth 2. The ripe crops were either pulled out whole by hand or cut with a sickle (*maggāl* [Jer 50:16; Joel 4:13] or *ḥermēš* [Deut 16:9; 23:26]). At times, only the top of the stalk was cut, leaving the rest of the plant standing in the field for grazing animals. At other times, when straw was needed, more of the stalk was cut. Sickles were made either of segments of sharp flint chips attached with some adhesive to a bone or wooden frame or were made of metal (bronze, iron) with a wooden handle. The stalks were bound into sheaves and transported to the threshing floor for threshing and winnowing. From there the clean grain was transferred for storage in specially constructed pits or other facilities where it was stored in jars.

According to the Gezer calendar the two periods of cereal harvest were followed by a third period, *yrḥw zmr* (two months of grape harvesting [and wine making]), from mid-May to mid-July, mentioned in the Bible as *bāṣîr* (Lev 26:5; Isa 24:13). The fourth period in the Gezer calendar, *yrḥ qṣ* (a month of [ingathering] summer fruit), extended into August and is referred to simply as *qayiṣ* in the Bible (Jer 40:10, 12; Amos 8:1–2). This was followed by *yrḥw ʾsp* (two months of ingathering [olives and pressing oil]), referred to as *ʾāsîp* in the Bible (Exod 23:16; 34:22). If it is correct that the Gezer calendar is a product of the N, then this period lasted there for two months, while in Judah it lasted only one month. The agricultural year closed with the autumn festival of *ʾāsîp/sukkôt* (Booths, or Tabernacles).

Part of these latter harvest periods entailed the processing and storage of the harvest produce. Thus wine making was part of grape harvesting. Because of the nature of grapes that disallows their transport over long distances, most winepresses were hewed in bedrock near the vineyard (Isa 5:2). After treading the grapes, the wine makers stored the juice in jars, which were kept in a cool place for fermentation. Dried fruits such as raisins, dates, and figs were made by simply placing them in the sun. When ready, they were pressed into cakes or strung on a string to facilitate storage and transport. Olive oil was produced by first crushing the olives by mortar and pestle and then placing them in wicker baskets on top of a collection basin with pressure applied from on top. The beam press, invented in the Iron II period, made oil pressing a profitable venture. The oil was then placed in jars for storage and transport.

Bibliography

Borowski, O. 1987. *Agriculture in Iron Age Israel.* Winona Lake, IN.

ODED BOROWSKI

HASADIAH (PERSON) [Heb *ḥăsadyāh*]. The name of two men in the Bible. It means "God is kind" (*TPNAH,* 76, 161).

1. The sixth son of ZERUBBABEL, mentioned in 1 Chr 3:20. Hasadiah is part of a distinct list of Zerubbabel's offspring contained in v 20. Verse 19 lists his first two sons and a daughter. The distinctness of the list of *five* sons in v 20 is reinforced by the "tally" number, five, at the end of the verse. It is possible that the first three children listed in v 19 were born in Babylon and the following five in Palestine after the return, thus two lists (see Williamson *Chronicles* NCBC, 57).

2. The son of Hilkiah and the ancestor of Baruch, the son of Neriah and scribe of the prophet Jeremiah mentioned in Baruch 1:1.

RUSSELL FULLER

HASHABIAH (PERSON) [Heb *ḥašābĕyāh*]. Var. ASIBIAS. **1.** The ancestor of Ethan, the Levite musician under David (1 Chr 6:30—Eng 6:45); he was a descendant of Merari, son of Levi (called Asebi in the LXX).

2. A Levite, the son of Jeduthun (1 Chr 25:3). 1 Chronicles records that David established 24 divisions of singers for the worship of the Lord, headed by the 24 sons of Asaph, Heman, and Jeduthun. Hashabiah with his sons and brothers, 12 men in all, received the 12th lot (1 Chr 25:19). He was also the ancestor of Shemaiah (1 Chr 9:14; Neh 11:15).

3. A prominent Hebronite ruler. At the time of David's death, he with his brothers ("men of ability") was ruling Israel W of Jordan on behalf of King David and on behalf of the cult in Jerusalem (1 Chr 26:30).

4. A leader of the tribe of Levi at time of David's death (1 Chr 27:17). He was the son of Kemuel (LXX ms B reads "the son of Samuel").

5. A chief of the Levites during the reign of Josiah. He and other leading Levites gathered and turned over to the other Levites lambs, kids, and bulls for the Great Passover under Josiah (2 Chr 35:9). In 1 Esdr 1:9 he and his fellows are called "captains over a thousand."

6. A leading priest in the time of Ezra, he is usually linked with Sherebiah (Ezra 8:19, 24; 1 Esdr 8:54—AV Assanias, NEB Assamias). He later set his seal on the renewal of the covenant (Ezra 10:11). Neh 3:17 lists a Hashabiah, the ruler of half the district of Keilah, who with his fellow Levites repaired part of the wall of Jerusalem. This individual is likely the same prominent Levite mentioned in 1 Esdr 8:48—Eng 8:48; and Neh 12:24.

7. An Israelite descended from Parosh who returned from Exile and put away his foreign wife under Ezra (1 Esdr 9:26; Ezra 10:25, an emendation of Malchijah based on the LXX reading). His name is spelled Asibias or Asabeias in 1 Esdr 9:26.

8. An Asaphite, the ancestor of Uzzi. Uzzi was the overseer of the Levites in Jerusalem during the time of Nehemiah (Neh 11:22).

9. The head of the priestly house of Hilkiah (Neh 12:21) under the high priest Joiakim, the son of Jeshua, who officiated after the return from Exile.

GARY S. SHOGREN

HASHABNAH (PERSON) [Heb *ḥăšabnâ*]. One of the chiefs of the people and a signatory to the covenant established by Ezra (Neh 10:26—Eng 10:25). An attenuated form of Hashabneiah, the name probably means "Yahweh has taken account of (me)" (Brockington *Ezra, Nehemiah and Esther* NCBC, 182).

FREDERICK W. SCHMIDT

HASHABNEIAH (PERSON) [Heb *ḥăšabnĕyāh*]. **1.** A man known only through association with his son Hattush (Neh 3:10). Hattush helped rebuild the walls of Jerusalem during the time of Nehemiah.

2. A Levite (Neh 9:5) who participated in the ceremonies preceding the "sealing" of the new covenant (Neh 9:38). These ceremonies included both communal confession and worship. According to Neh 9:5 Hashabneiah and other selected Levites called the assembly to join in a liturgical blessing of Yahweh prior to Ezra's prayer.

In Neh 9:5 the Syriac reads Hashabiah. Such a reading suggests that Hashabneiah might be identical with a certain Hashabiah mentioned elsewhere during this time (Ezra 8:19, 24; Neh 10:12—Eng 10:11; 11:22; 12:24).

TERRY L. BRENSINGER

HASHBADDANAH (PERSON) [Heb *ḥašbaddānâ*]. One of the men who stood on Ezra's left during the great public reading of the Law (Neh 8:4). Hashbaddanah was not designated as a Levite; his position at this event suggests that he was an influential or representative member of the Israelite laity.

TERRY L. BRENSINGER

HASHEM (PERSON) [Heb *hāšēm*]. One of David's mighty men of war (1 Chr 11:34) named in a list of warriors which the Chronicler adapted from 2 Sam 23:32. This earlier text, however, contains a slightly altered spelling of the name: JASHEN (Heb *yāšēn*). Mazar (1986: 95, n. 49) considers both these forms "to be corruptions of *ḥšm*, a name which appears in the genealogies of both Dan and Benjamin." Most scholars agree that "sons" (Heb *bĕnê*) should be omitted from the MT of 1 Chr 11:34 (and 2 Sam 23:32) as dittography, since it simply repeats the final consonants of the preceding word (Heb *hsʿlbny*). Moreover, LXX (Lucianic) omits "sons of" here, simply reading (Gk *iassai*) (McCarter *2 Samuel* AB, 492). However, LXX codices Vaticanus and Sinaiticus interpret the Heb *bĕnê* of 1 Chr 11:34 as a personal name, Gk *bennaias,* possibly from the Heb root *bny(h),* which may reflect the omission of the appellative "son of" (Heb *bn*) in the hypothetical line Heb **bny bn hšm,* "Bani son of Hashem." Perhaps the list originally read "Jashen," as one of David's mighty men who supported his reign, beginning in Hebron and the Judean region.

Bibliography

Mazar, B. 1986. The Military Elite of King David. Pp. 83–112 in *The Early Biblical Period.* Ed. S. Ahituv and B. Levine. Jerusalem.

JOHN C. ENDRES

HASHMONAH (PLACE) [Heb *ḥašmonâ*]. The 14th encampment of the Israelites, after leaving the Wilderness of Sinai, as listed in Num 33:29–30, where it is placed between Mithkah and Moseroth. The meaning of the site's name is unknown and does not contribute to determining its location. Suggestions advanced for its location include Qeseimeh on the Wâdī el-Hashim (Abel *GP,* 215; Simons *GTTOT,* 255–56; M.R. 099008), though the area NW of Kadesh-barnea has also been suggested (Palmer 1872: 419–20; M.R. 145025). Palmer (419–20) also suggested identifying it with the Heshmon of the Negeb of Judah in Josh 15:27.

For a discussion of the location of any of the places associated with the journey of the Israelites from Egypt through Sinai, see DOPHKAH.

Bibliography

Beit-Arieh, I. 1988. The Route Through Sinai—Why the Israelites Fleeing Egypt Went South. *BARev* 15/3: 28–37.
Palmer, E. H. 1872. *The Desert of the Exodus.* New York.

JEFFREY R. ZORN

HASHUBAH (PERSON) [Heb *ḥăšūbâ*]. The third son of ZERUBBABEL. Hashubah appears in 1 Chr 3:20 at the head of the second group of Zerubbabel's children, who may have been born in Palestine (see Williamson *Chronicles* NCBC, 57). The name is based on the root *ḥšb* which means "to value," "consider," "think." Hashubah thus means "consideration." Note the related verbal element Hashub from the same root, which occurs frequently in names in levitical families in the postexilic period (e.g., HASHABIAH). Names formed on this root are frequent in Nehemiah and Chronicles. Newman (*IDB* 2: 536) considers Hashub a shortened form of the theophoric name Hashubyah—"Yah(weh) has considered." It is likely that Hashubah should also be related to these names.

The *BHS* suggests that *ḥăšūbâ* may be a corrupt rendering of *ʾaḥărê šûbô,* "after his return," meaning that the children of Zerubbabel in v 20 are "after his return," to Palestine, and that Hashubah is not one of them. If Hashubah is a name, then the *BHS* indicates that the form is doubtful and proposes *ḥăšābâ,* following the LXX^A *Aseba.*

RUSSELL FULLER

HASHUM (PERSON) [Heb *ḥašum*]. A postexilic name present throughout Ezra, Nehemiah, and 1 Esdras, whose occurrences suggest the identification of two separate individuals.

1. The progenitor of a family which returned from Babylon with Zerubbabel (Ezra 2:19 = Neh 7:22). His name is missing in the parallel account in 1 Esdr 5:17. He may be the same Hashum whose descendants divorced their foreign wives during Ezra's reform (Ezra 10:33; 1 Esdr 9:33 [Gk *asom*]).

2. The above instances of Hashum as an eponym suggest that it is another individual who participated in the assembly of the returned exiles when Ezra read the law of Moses to the people (Neh 8:4). In the parallel account of 1 Esdr 9:44, Lothsubus (Gk *Lōthasoubos*) occurs in place of Hashum. It also seems probable that the same Hashum present at the reading of the law subsequently signed the pledge to keep the law (Neh 10:19—Eng 10:18). The difficulties in identifying individuals such as Hashum and his family raise questions about the sources of and literary relationships among Ezra, Nehemiah, and 1 Esdras.

MICHAEL DAVID MCGEHEE

HASIDEANS [Gk *Asidaioi*]. The name of a group of pious Jews noted for their loyalty to the Torah, some of whom united with the priest Mattathias and his sons in their resistance to the practices of the Seleucid rulers of Judah (1 Macc 2:42). The event which precipitated their joining Mattathias was the slaughter of a thousand Jews who had hidden in caves outside Jerusalem so they could practice their faith and who refused to fight on the Sabbath (even when attacked) for fear of breaking the law (2:29–38). Mattathias offered them a new principle, namely, that defensive action in the face of death was allowable, even on the Sabbath (2:41).

The importance of the Hasideans to the Maccabean Revolt can be seen in the report of the aspiring high priest Alcimus, who exaggerated their role by telling Demetrius I Soter (Seleucid ruler 162–150 B.C.E.) that the Hasideans, with Judas as their leader, had carried out the Jewish Revolt (2 Macc 14:6). Demetrius named Alcimus high priest and sent him along with Bacchides, the new governor of the area W of the Euphrates, with instructions to take vengeance on Israel for revolting. Perhaps the Hasideans were willing to accept Alcimus as high priest because he was an Aaronite, or perhaps they simply misread the political situation, thinking the time was right to get good terms. Either way they believed Alcimus when he promised them safe conduct for a conference and stood in the forefront of a group of scribes who sued for peace. Their trust proved ill founded, for Alcimus killed 60 of their number (1 Macc 7:12–16). They hastily returned to Judas to continue the war.

The origin of the Hasideans is obscure. The name derived from the Heb word *ḥăsîdîm,* usually translated "saints" (e.g., 1 Chr 6:41) or "faithful ones" (e.g., 1 Sam 2:9), which appears frequently in the OT, especially in the book of Psalms (e.g., Pss 30:5—Eng 30:4; 31:14—Eng 31:23; 37:28; 50:5; 52:11—Eng 52:9; 97:10; 149:1, 5, 9). Scholars agree that the Hasideans as a group preceded their withdrawal to the caves in the wilderness outside Jerusalem (1 Macc 2:29), even though the term does not appear in earlier literature as a designation for a particular group. Beckwith (1982: 17–22) hypothesizes that the movement originated ca. 330 B.C.E. in a Proto-Pharisaic reaction against the marriage of Manasses, brother of the high priest Jaddua, to a Samaritan princess, when a lay revolt forced Jaddua to remove his brother from office. A subsequent revolt in 251 resulted in the addition to the Hasideans of a priestly group, which eventually separated into Essenes and Sadducees (Beckwith, 41–42).

In any case the Hasideans formed a recognizable group at the time of the persecution by Antiochus Epiphanes. The name Hasidean does not appear subsequently as a title for a group. Instead, during the time Jonathan was the high priest, one finds mention of three distinct groups: Pharisees, Sadducees, and Essenes (see Jos. *Ant* 13.6.9 §171). Scholars are divided about which group descended from the Hasideans. Older scholars saw the Hasideans as the forerunners of the Pharisees, but never writers, acquainted with the Dead Sea Scrolls, often see the Essenes as their descendants (see Milik 1959: 80). Hengel (1974: 1.224–28) thinks both groups derived from the Hasideans, while Beckwith argues (41) that all three parties originated in a common movement against the negligence of the common people as well as the overt syncretism of the Hellenists.

Most writers agree that the split among the Hasideans occurred because of a dispute over the legitimacy of Jonathan's claims to the office of high priest. This dispute apparently stands behind the negative tone of 1 Macc 7:12–17, whose author sided with Jonathan against the Hasideans, whom he considered naive for trusting Alcimus. Modern scholars often conclude from this passage that the Hasideans were only concerned with religious law and not Jewish nationalism, but that conclusion overlooks the partisan nature of the passage, the political nature of the split among the parties involved, and the lengthy involvement of the Hasideans in the Maccabean Revolt.

Bibliography

Beckwith, R. T. 1982. The Pre-history and the Relationship of the Pharisees, Sadducees and Essenes: a Tentative Reconstruction. *RevQ* 11: 3–46.

Hengel, M. 1974. *Judaism and Hellenism.* 2 vols. Philadelphia.

Milik, J. T. 1959. *Ten Years of Discovery in the Wilderness of Judea.* SBT 26. London.

PAUL L. REDDITT

HASIDIM [Gk *Asidaioi*]. The name of a group of participants in the Maccabean Revolt mentioned in 1 Macc 2:42; 7:14; and 2 Macc 14:6 (RSV "Hasideans"). The Greek appellation is a transliteration of the Hebrew *ḥăsîdîm* (Hasidim) or the Aramaic *ḥasîdayyāʾ*. While the name is rooted in the use of the term *ḥasîd* in the Hebrew Scriptures it is doubtful that Ps 149:1 or other references to *ḥăsîdîm* in the Psalms should be used as evidence of the group mentioned in 1 and 2 Maccabees. The appearance of the name in Gk transliteration does suggest that at least the translator of 1 Maccabees and the author of 2 Maccabees understood the term as a proper noun; hence any argument that claims these references merely allude to pious Jews in general must be rejected.

Any serious study of the Hasideans in antiquity must begin with an examination of the three passages in Maccabees where they receive mention (Davies 1977: 128; Collins 1977: 201–5). On the basis of a literary analysis, it has been demonstrated that the Hasideans of 1 Macc 2:42 are not the same persons as those who fled to the desert seeking righteousness and justice in 1 Macc 2:29. This connection has sometimes been used as evidence of the ascetic nature of the Hasideans, thereby providing justification for the hypothesis that the Essenes are one of the groups which arose out of the Hasideans (Black 1961: 16). The Hasideans in 1 Macc 2:42 are rather included as part of a description of the growth of the Hasmonean movement that begins with v 39 and ends with v 48, the major subject of which is Mattathias and his friends. The Hasideans are included with others who join this popular revolt.

In 1 Macc 2:42 the Hasideans are described as a *synagōgē* (company) which consisted of "mighty warriors of Israel, every one who offered himself willingly for the law." While the Gk *ischyroi dynamei* is almost certainly a translation of the Heb *gibbôrê ḥayil,* it is not as clear that the RSV "warriors" is the proper translation. It is just as possible that this phrase should be translated "mighty men," with the author of this text wishing to point out that these Hasideans were a group of leading citizens of Judea who joined the forces of Mattathias in revolt. This company of leading citizens was devoted to that law which in 1 Macc 1:41–50 Antiochus IV had ordered the Jews to forget. Among the activities prohibited by the king were circumcision as well as the sacrifices and festivals which constituted the temple cult.

The purpose of the story concerning the Hasideans in 1 Macc 7:12–18 is to discount their significance. While Judas Maccabeus refuses to listen to the "peaceable but treacherous words" (7:10) sent by the messengers of Bacchides because they are accompanied by a large force, the Hasideans are prepared to negotiate, presumably in order to avert the catastrophe that Bacchides could perpetrate. Since this governor and friend of the king is accompanied by Alcimus, "a priest of the line of Aaron," the company of Hasideans, here said to be scribes, thinks that they can be trusted in negotiations. Bacchides swears an oath to them, "We will not seek to injure you or your friends." When the Hasideans trust him, he seizes 60 of them and kills them in one day. Having already invoked in 1 Macc 1:37 and 3:45 images of the gentile pollution and destruction of the sanctuary through allusions to Ps 79:1–3, the author of the Hasmonean history, citing Ps 79:2b–3 as Scripture, equates the Hasideans with those leaders of Jerusalem who in 1 Macc 1:30 believed the peaceable words of Antiochus IV's tax collector, who "suddenly fell upon the city, dealt it a severe blow, and destroyed many people in Israel." This historian wishes to discount the influence of this company of leading citizens, whom he calls scribes, by portraying them as naive. According to the Hasmonean historian, their viewpoint did not provide a credible basis for the future development of the Jewish state. This means that any simplistic presentation of the Hasideans as either pacifists who deviated from their basic ideology in 1 Macc 2:42 or as the religious wing of the revolution that broke ranks with the Hasmoneans when their religious objectives had been accomplished does not find support in these sources.

In 2 Macc 14:6 the Hasideans are described as a seditious group led by Judas Maccabeus. Since these charges are placed in the mouth of Alcimus, who wishes to be appointed to the high priesthood by Demetrius, the epitomist of this history is probably making positive statements about Judas and the Hasideans in a negative way (Doran 1981: 68–70). Since Judas is the hero of this work, which emphasizes his piety and his purity, we can see that the Hasideans are incorporated into the work to augment that portrait. His leadership of that body is meant to provide further evidence of Judas' pious persona.

While this group has frequently been considered to be the forerunner of both the Essenes and the Pharisees, there is no evidence in these references to support the Essene connection, even though those who in 1 Macc 2:29 flee to the desert in search of righteousness and justice could be from such a group. There is, furthermore, no evidence in these references which would support a hypothesis that the Hasideans were the authors of apocalyptic literature (cf. Plüger 1968: 8; Hengel 1974: 1.80, 175–80). The treatment of the Hasideans in this work does coincide with what we would expect the attitude of a Hasmonean historian to be toward the Pharisees.

In Talmudic literature there are also references to *ḥăsîdîm* (Hasidim) as well as to individuals who are designated *ḥasîd,* such as Honi and Hillel. Resolution of the extensive debate over whether any of these references applies to the body mentioned in 1 and 2 Maccabees should begin with an analysis of the passages which refer to the *ḥăsîdîm hāriʾšonîm* (the "early" or "first" Hasidim). An examination of *m. Ber.* 5:1; *t. B. Qam.* 2:6; *b. Nid.* 38ab; *b. Ned.* 10a; and *B. Menah.* 40b–41a shows that this group was used in the Talmudic tradition as example rather than as evidence of a divergent legal tradition (cf. Safrai 1977, 1985). The examples cited from these early Hasidim could reflect the way of life of a group of the Maccabean period prior to the formation of some of the major legal traditions. In Talmudic literature other stories concerning individuals designated as *hasîd* were added to the traditions concerning these early Hasidim.

Bibliography

Berman, D. 1979. Hasidim in Rabbinic Traditions. *SBLSP* 2: 15–33.

Black, M. 1961. *The Scrolls and Christian Origins.* BJS 48. Chico, CA.

Büchler, A. 1922. *Types of Jewish Palestinian Piety from 70 B.C.E. to 70 C.E.: The Ancient Pious Men.* London. Repr. 1968, New York.

Collins, J. J. 1977. *The Apocalyptic Vision of the Book of Daniel.* HSM 16. Missoula, MT.

Davies, P. 1977. Ḥasidim in the Maccabean Period. *JJS* 28: 127–40.

Doran, R. 1981. *Temple Propaganda: The Purpose and Character of 2 Maccabees.* CBQMS 12. Washington.

Hengel, M. 1974. *Judaism and Hellenism.* 2 vols. Trans. J. Bowden. Philadelphia.

Jacobs, L. 1957. The Concept of *Ḥasid* in the Biblical and Rabbinic Literatures. *JJS* 8: 143–54.

Kampen, J. 1988. *The Hasideans and the Origin of Pharisaism.* SCS 24. Atlanta.

Plüger, O. 1968. *Theocracy and Eschatology.* Trans. S. Rudman. Richmond.

Safrai, S. 1977. The Pharisees and the Hasidim. *Sidic* 10: 12–16.

———. 1985. The Pious *(Ḥassidim)* and the Men of Deeds. *Zion* 50: 133–54.

John Kampen

HASMONEAN DYNASTY. A family of high priests and kings descended from Mattathias, the father of JUDAS MACCABEUS. They were prominent in Judea from 165 until 37 B.C. and controlled it as rulers between 142 B.C. and 63 B.C. The name derives, according to Josephus, from that of the great-grandfather of Mattathias, in Gk *Asamōnaios* (*Ant* 12.263); and its original version, in Hebrew or Aramaic, is now generally held to reflect a place name, either Heshmon or Hashmonah. The name does not appear in the books of the Maccabees, but it is used several times in Josephus in slightly varying forms (*Ant* 14.490; 16.187; 20.189; 20.238; *Life* 4); and it is also found in Talmudic literature (*m. Mid.* 1:6; *b. Sabb.* 21b). The emergence of a name for the dynasty drawn from that of an early progenitor may be due to Hellenistic influence. The family belonged to the priestly course of Joarib (= Jehoiarib, 1 Chr 24:7; Joiarib, Neh 11:10), originated in Jerusalem, but had settled before the time of Mattathias in Modein, near Lydda (1 Macc 2:1).

Under the Hasmoneans, Judea became, in the period of Seleucid decline and before the rise of Rome, an independent power with a considerable influence on the politics of the region; her dimensions equaled those of the kingdom of David. The impact of their national experience under the Hasmoneans continued for the Jews through the classical era, and, indeed, far beyond. However, long-term stability was not secured. Externally, her geographic position made Palestine vulnerable; internally, the conflict between profane and sacred values was ever present; and major religious and political differences opened up within the community. The formation of parties and sects within Judaism is a major feature of the Hasmonean period; and although this made the period fruitful in cultural and religious terms, politically it was often deeply troubled. There were significant elements which found the hardening authority, the wealth, the sacrilegious habits and perhaps the Hellenizing style of the Hasmoneans wholly unacceptable. In the end the ruling family, too, fell prey to conflict and brought civil strife upon the nation.

The basis of Hasmonean ascendancy lay in Mattathias' act of rebellion in 167 B.C. against the anti-Jewish decrees of Antiochus IV Epiphanes, when the old man resisted the demand by an officer of Antiochus IV for pagan sacrifice at Modein and then escaped to the hills with his five sons. By the time of Mattathias' death in the next year, the family had drawn all the rebels to itself and organized resistance throughout the country. The military successes of Judas (the "Maccabee"), whose increasingly well-organized fighting force overcame several Syrian armies before meeting defeat, and his reoccupation and rededication of the temple in 165 B.C. made him and his surviving brothers the unchallenged leaders of the majority of the nation, apart from the Hellenists. *See also* MACCABEAN REVOLT.

A. The Powers and Titles of the Hasmoneans

1. The Emergence of the Dynasty. No official title is associated with Judas Maccabeus. The death-bed instructions ascribed to Mattathias have him declare Judas, in biblical style, to be the people's commander who would fight their battles for them; and another son, Simon, was to act as adviser. In fact, it is obvious that Judas' overall responsibility for the nation took on both military and political aspects: he appointed "leaders of the people, commanders of thousands, of hundreds, of fifties and of tens" (1 Macc 3:55); and after 164 B.C. he organized the priests to serve in the rededicated temple service. Yet in the documents from 2 Maccabees which record the dealings of Lysias, Antiochus IV's viceroy, after the king's death (chap. 11), there is no acknowledgement of Judas at all. Perhaps it was this very absence of formal position which led Josephus to the belief that Judas actually became high priest on the death of the Seleucid nominee, Alcimus (*Ant* 12.415, 419, 434). Yet this is not only unsupported by 1 Maccabees, where Alcimus is shown to have died *after* Judas (1 Macc 9:54–56), but contradicts Josephus' own statements elsewhere that the high priesthood was vacant for seven years at the end of Alcimus' tenure (*Ant* 20.237; *Life* 4). In any case Judas himself was killed in battle within a year.

Judas had been the third of Mattathias' five sons (1 Macc 2:4–5); the survivors put the youngest, Jonathan, in charge of rescuing the situation after Judas' death and defeat at Eleasa in 161–160 B.C. Jonathan, now, was to be "our ruler and commander and to fight our battles for us" (1 Macc 9:30). The decision to continue the struggle, with the ultimate aim of ousting both the Seleucid general Bacchides and the Jewish Hellenizers who still held Jerusalem, was entirely in the spirit of Judas' activities since 164. The new element in the position of the leader was the registering of a popular vote in his favor. Jonathan, though tried and tested in war, was an instinctive politician just as Judas had been a natural general, and the younger brother may well have seen the value of securing a popular mandate by way of substitute for Judas' charisma.

When, around 155 B.C., the Syrian general Bacchides came to terms with Jonathan, Jerusalem remained with the Hellenizers; yet Jonathan was not prevented from establishing himself at Michmash, a small place N of the city; there he "began to judge the people" (1 Macc 9:73). This probably amounts to recognition by the Seleucid monarch Demetrius I of a local fiefdom. Subsequent developments were startlingly rapid. Jonathan had fully grasped what opportunities the moment held for fishing in the troubled Seleucid waters to enhance his own position; the continuing rivalries among the Seleucids led them to vie with one another in offering privileges to Jonathan. The Hasmoneans' influence in Judea was evidently now such that Jonathan could deliver better support than could the "Hellenizers," and Demetrius was especially in need of troops. Once authorized to raise a proper army, Jonathan was able, in 152, to occupy and fortify Jerusalem, though the Akra (which we should understand therefore to have been a sealed-off section of the city rather than a mere fort) was still in the hands of Hellenizers and Seleucids. It remained for Jonathan's supreme position in Jerusalem and in the country to be signaled with the high priesthood. During the disturbances of the 20 years before Jonathan, there had been either Hellenizing high priests or none, and the appointment of one of the rebel Maccabeus brothers was a momentous development. After the death of Demetrius, Jonathan received further grants, notably the position of provincial governor *(meridarch)*. Thus, the Maccabees, once the most unremitting of rebels, became willing dependents of one Seleucid after another, governing Judea by their favor.

Jonathan was careful also to look further afield, sending ambassadors to Rome to renew the friendship and alliance between Jews and Romans originally negotiated through Judas' envoys. Jonathan's ambassadors also gave expression to Judea's new self-consciousness as a Hellenistic state by visiting Sparta and securing letters that claimed kinship and ancient ties between the two peoples (see 1 Macc 12:1–23).

2. Simon. The work done by Jonathan made possible a formal declaration of independence under his successor, Simon (nicknamed Thassis). Here the history of the Hasmoneans as a dynasty may be said to begin. In the year 142, as 1 Macc 13:41–42 has it, "The yoke of the gentiles was taken away from Israel. And the people began to write on their records and their contacts, 'in the first year of Simon, the great high priest, general, and leader of the Jews.'" Simon had taken over directly from his elder brother and had been drawn into a similar course of action—a show of strength, followed by well-judged diplomatic feelers. Even before his brother's death, Trypho, a pretender to the Seleucid throne, had invaded Palestine from the NW. Negotiation with the usurping Trypho's rival, Demetrius II, had been the obvious move. From him, it would appear, came by letter the offer of peace, immunity from tribute, and remission of taxes or of tax arrears (it is not clear which). Simon's high priesthood was implicitly recognized by Demetrius; it may or may not have been a Seleucid grant in the first place. The freedom from tribute, in any case, now marked the autonomous status of Judea; it possessed a symbolic significance well captured in Josephus' accounts (*JW* 1.53; *Ant* 13.211). The announcement of the new chronological era was a statement of this, even if the era does not seem to have survived as a lasting basis of reckoning.

Simon was an excellent propagandist. He imprinted his achievement on the public mind with festival and ceremony. The literary record, which derives at least in part from a history of Simon's son and successor, John Hyrcanus, is tinged with flattery. Therefore, while Simon's achievement was an important one, the situation in Judea was by no means yet wholly resolved. Given the unsettled state of the Seleucid monarchy, Demetrius II's declaration did not guarantee the abandonment of future claims; it was not until the death of Antiochus VII Sidetes (in 129 B.C.) that claims to Jerusalem and the demand for tribute were finally abandoned. We may even doubt whether all the promises made to Simon actually bore fruit; for the right to issue coins, granted to him in a letter from Antiochus VII, after Demetrius II's imprisonment in 140/139 (1 Macc 15:6), seems never to have been exercised at all. There is a telling absence of any coinage of Simon's from the archaeological record.

What Simon accomplished was to impose his authority on the whole country and on Jerusalem as its capital. An early move, made in 141 B.C., was therefore to secure the surrender of the surviving garrison from the Akra, the city's Hellenistic base, which was probably on the W hill, though its location is still uncertain. From there, "They had sallied forth and polluted the precinct of the Temple" (Avigad 1984: 64–65). Since Jonathan had sealed off the zone with a wall, in an attempt to starve it out, his successor's task was to manage the expulsion. Choruses, hymns, and instruments as well as the traditional waving of palm branches accompanied the grand entry; and an annual festival was declared to commemorate the historic moment. The Hellenists as a faction were never heard of again. The reconstruction and walling of the city, begun by Jonathan, could now be pushed on (1 Macc 10:10–11; 13:10); and we should probably ascribe to Simon the inclusion, for the first time since the days of the First Temple, of the W hill as a living area within the city and of much of the completed circumference of the so-called "first wall." The planning of a spacious capital, its expansion over a difficult site, and the building of the wall are the enterprises of a self-confident ruler with substantial resources.

The year 140 saw another great moment: the assembled people declared Simon high priest, commander and ethnarch—head of the nation—of the Jews, "forever, until a trustworthy prophet shall arise" (1 Macc 14:41). The amalgam of powers was not new, but the change lay in the manner of their conferment; they were now internally sanctioned, and external approval was not deemed necessary. The Parthian invasion of Iran under Mithradates I probably emboldened the Jews to assert themselves, and it is possible that by the time of the people's decree Demetrius II was already in Parthian captivity. Simon's powers were as monarchic as the purple robe and gold clasp which he was to wear, even though the title king was avoided. His orders were not to be opposed, assemblies were not to be convened without his consent, all on pain of punishment if disobeyed; the unanimity of the popular decision was emphasized. On this Simon's position ultimately rested. It was endorsed by the new king, Antiochus VII, in a letter of 138 B.C. but not shaken by that king's rapid volte-face, his demands for the return of the Jerusalem citadal and other towns or else for the payment of tribute on them, or by his threat of war (1 Macc 15:2–9, 26–35).

The form of rule set up by the decree for Simon drew on traditional Jewish conceptions. Nonetheless, the people of Hasmonean Jerusalem were sufficiently influenced by the prevailing style in public affairs to have their declaration inscribed in bronze, just as a Greek city might do, and to display it in no less a place than the temple precinct and also in its treasury. The new Jewish state was thus visibly Hellenistic in at least some of its public forms. The mores of the ruler were also affected by this spirit, as is revealed by the manner of his death: the aged Simon was to be murdered within five years of the decree, together with two of his sons, as he feasted and drank in a fortress near Jericho. The assassin was his son-in-law, the wealthy and interestingly named Ptolemy, son of Abubus (Aboub), who was commander of the plain of Jericho (1 Macc 16:11) and had sought to involve other army officers in his conspiracy. This man does not appear to have been a Jew (*Ant* 13.234–

5); and on the failure of his attempt to gain the support of Antiochus VII for his coup, he fled to the court of a local dynast, Zenon Cotylas of the partly Hellenized city of Philadelphia (Amman).

3. John Hyrcanus. John Hyrcanus, Simon's third son, who had already been governor of the important fortified town of Gezer, assumed the high priesthood on his father's death. This suggests that the latter post was designated as hereditary by the "forever" of Simon's investitute decree; and John was presumably already high priest when he sacrificed before setting out to attack Ptolemy. However, Josephus (*Ant* 13.230) does not clarify the mechanism of succession.

There would always be uneasiness and often contention surrounding the definition of Hasmonean sovereignty. The Jews more often than not nursed doubts about the fitness of any man's holding power of a kingly type. We may point to various ways in which Hyrcanus' rule was hedged about or challenged. Yet, in the first place, we should stress the very real importance of a 31-year tenure (135–104 B.C.), followed by an accepted dynastic succession. John is described as the nation's secular authority as well as the high priest; and his regime is named an *arche,* or "rule." Under John too we see an independent coinage, albeit limited to bronze; it is now established that these are the first coins to be minted by any Hasmonean. While Tyrian silver was confirmed in its role as the principal major currency in the area, filling the gap left by the Seleucid withdrawal, everyday needs were henceforward supplied by successive large issues of aniconic *pĕrûtôt,* their craftsmanship varying in precision and quality. Hyrcanus' coins carry two types of formulas, both written in an archaizing paleo-Hebrew script which visibly evoked the days of the First Temple. One group has "Johanan the high priest and the council (or community, Heb *ḥeber*) of the Jews" and another group has "Johanan the high priest head of the *ḥeber* of the Jews." Their relative dating is uncertain, but it may be reasonable on historical grounds to posit an initial reluctance by John to take on any title beyond the traditional high priesthood, followed later by the emergence of a cautious formula, which still gave the assembled people a high visibility in its wording. This caution, did not, however, prove sufficient to curb the strictures of the more punctilious religious elements.

4. Alexander Jannaeus. The political style of the later Hasmoneans acquired, in due course, further Hellenistic traits. Jannaeus called himself king, as well as high priest, in a juxtaposition quite unsanctioned by Jewish tradition; and he feasted in public with his concubines in a manner perhaps not totally alien to David and Solomon, but quite unacceptable in the Jewish high priesthood (*Ant* 13.380). The testamentary choice of his widow, Salome Alexandra, as successor, in preference to either of his sons, may also reflect Hellenistic influence.

Jannaeus was the next after Hyrcanus to issue a major coinage. He was less conservative, using Greek and Aramaic as well as Hebrew, and, on some types, openly advertising his kingship, either in words or with the star and diadem symbols. On his Hebrew coins, he gave his Hebrew name, Jonathan, rather than Alexander; and there were others on which he employed Hyrcanus' form of legend, referring only to the high priesthood and to the Jewish *ḥeber.* A group of overstruck coins, where "Jonathan the high priest and the *ḥeber* of the Jews" obliterates the earlier text on the obverse, is plausibly associated with the major crisis surrounding the Pharisees which occurred in his middle years (Meshorer 1982). The Greek and Aramaic coinage, on the other hand, may well have been designed largely with the king's non-Jewish subjects in view, and first and foremost, for his mercenary soldiers. An undated lead issue and the light weight of most of Jannaeus' coins have been related to difficulties in meeting the troops' requirements for payment during the major campaigns (Ariel 1982).

B. The Hasmoneans as Conquerors

Simon's end in a soldiers' conspiracy had revealed, among other things, how the military base of Maccabean authority, far from diminishing with the end of the struggle for survival, had become institutionalized. Almost to the end the dynasty would remain a warrior dynasty. Peace was something to hope for; but even then, it was the security born of victory that was spoken of. Under Simon, it was said "each man sat under his own vine and under his own fig tree. The enemies in those days left their land and the enemy kings were crushed" (1 Macc 14:12–13). The dynasty's chronicler (as 1 Maccabees may fairly be dubbed) speaks with pride of the young men's appearance in their dazzling uniforms, and leaves us in no doubt that the regime's ideology contained a strong dose of militarism.

The largest territorial gains were to be made under Simon's successors. But the map had already changed significantly before the death of Simon. The Jewish entity of the Persian and early Hellenistic periods might be described as a small temple state. Now, with a strong army and enlarged aspirations, it had outgrown that model. Defensive needs had shaded imperceptibly into aggressive or punitive policies.

From the beginning the war against the Seleucids brought with it enmity with those local gentiles who lived beside the Jews, both within and outside Judea. The culmination came after Jonathan's kidnapping, when the surrounding peoples are said to have been enchanted with the possibility of destroying Judaism root and branch (1 Macc 12:53). The Maccabean wars are seen at this point quite simply as a struggle against the heathen; and it is impossible to distinguish in the leaders' activities between the vision of a holy and cleansing war, conceived of in biblical terms, and the real strategic need to weaken a threatening force. We can at any rate be sure that not all the local tribes were unfriendly during this period, for the Nabatean Arabs across the Jordan gave the Maccabees useful information more than once.

1. Jonathan. Jonathan's campaigns were undoubtedly well conceived and skillfully executed (see 1 Maccabees 10–11). Attacking the coastal strip, in the name first of Alexander Balas and then of Trypho, he mounted ferocious assaults on cities that did not open their gates, such as Ashdod, Joppa, and Gaza; though Askalon, which did, was unharmed. The Philistine city of Ekron with its territory came to Jonathan by way of reward. Other lasting results of his activities were the permanent garrisoning of Beth-zur, on Judea's S line, the area's last remaining Seleu-

CHRONOLOGY OF THE HASMONEAN DYNASTY (165–4 B.C.)

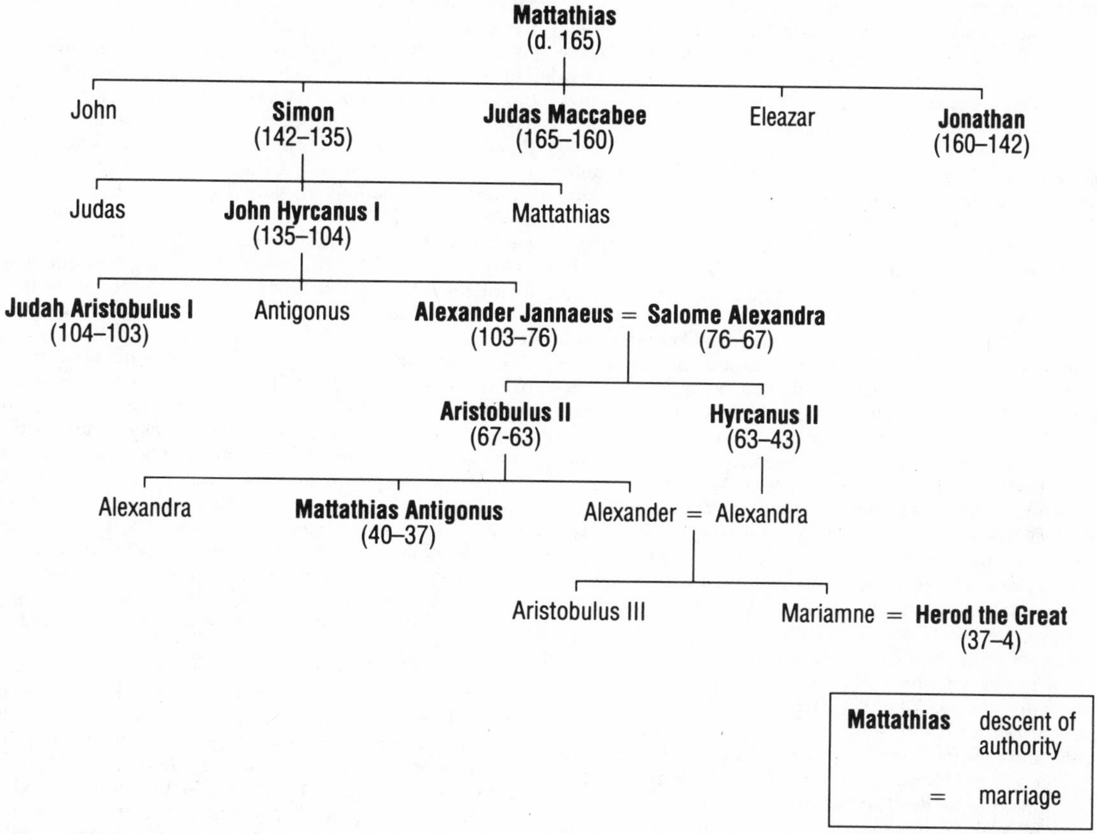

HAS.01. Genealogy chart of Hasmonean dynasty. See also Fig. HER.04.

cid fortress apart from the Akra in Jerusalem; and, to the N, the gain by royal grants of three districts which had previously been reckoned part of Samaria. Moreover, quite apart from acquisition, Jonathan's geographic and economic horizons were expanded by far-flung campaigns against Demetrius II, which took him through the northernmost part of Galilee and into Lebanon.

2. Simon. It was left to Simon, as one of his first acts, permanently to settle Jews in Joppa, expelling the "idolatrous" inhabitants (1 Macc 13:11), or at any rate some part of them. This secured for his state a dependable outlet to the sea, as was amply appreciated at (or near) the time (cf. 1 Macc 12:43–48). Gezer (= Gazara), strategically placed at the edge of the Judean foothills and controlling Jerusalem's access to Joppa, was treated in the same way as that city (1 Macc 13:43–48). Recent archaeological information to emerge from Gezer suggests that occupation was abandoned around 100 B.C. (Reich and Geva 1981). The same pattern was revealed with the excavation of Beth-zur, similarly a town fortified by the Seleucids and taken over by the Maccabees, where there are signs of vigorous growth under Jonathan and Simon, with settlement spreading outside the old walls, but soon afterwards coming to an end altogether.

The territorial claims of Jonathan and Simon did not go untested. As soon as the new king, Antiochus VII, had disposed of the usurper Trypho, Simon's assistance became less important to him than the restoration of his lost revenues and of his authority in Palestine. His general, Cendebeus, was told to regain possession of the coastal strip and to attack Judea from Jamnia (1 Macc 15:38–40). Josephus, who is here independent of 1 Maccabees, has the commander under instruction also to seize the person of Simon (*Ant* 13.225). Simon is said to have put 20,000 men into the field and to have held the day.

3. John Hyrcanus. Simon's success against Cendebeus prompted Antiochus to invade and ravage the country; he then laid Jerusalem under the strongest of blockades (*JW* 1.61; *Ant* 13.236–46). Both Josephus and a parallel account in the Greek historian Diodorus (which contains a notably hostile account of the Jewish cult) indicate that Sidetes terminated the siege in an unexpected and generous manner, with conduct very different from that of Epiphanes some 30 years earlier. No garrison was installed in Jerusalem; only a symbolic section of wall was taken down; and Joppa, Gazara, and the other cities held by Simon were made subject to tribute, but not removed from Jewish control. Hyrcanus, who, according to Josephus (*JW* 1.61; *Ant* 13.249), had equipped himself with funds by rifling David's tomb, soon afterward set off with his army to accompany Sidetes into Parthia, where he was treated with courtesy. The collapse of the expedition, Sidetes' death in battle, the Seleucid abandonment of Iran, and the renewal of wars within the Seleucid dynasty finally left the Jewish king a free agent. It is on record that the payment of tribute now ceased permanently (*Ant* 13.273).

At the very moment, however, when the Hasmoneans' dependence upon the Seleucids came to an end, a rising power was looking with intensified interest toward Judea. A senatorial decree cited out of context in Josephus' *Antiquities* suggests that Antiochus Sidetes' abrupt withdrawal from Jerusalem was encouraged by a behind-the-scenes move of the Roman Senate (Rajak 1981). The possibility of a Seleucid revival at this stage will hardly have been welcome to Rome; and the document, responding to the complaints of a Jewish embassy about Antiochus' seizure of various territories in contravention of a previous decree, reiterates Rome's long-standing friendship and alliance with the Jews. It is the diplomatic activity accompanying this statement which will have had the desired effect, delivering a stiff warning to Antiochus.

Judas' famous treaty of 161 B.C. (there is no reason to doubt its historicity) had been renewed and widely publicized under Jonathan and again under Simon. During Hyrcanus' period of rule, there were altogether three reassertions of the relationship. It is probable that in the early days no more than a token gesture, based upon a limited conception of her advantage, had been intended by Rome; but by the 130s her interest in the E was much greater. And for the time being she could look indulgently on what the Hasmoneans were doing. This phase lasted until the end of Hyrcanus' rule, after which we hear of no more renewals (Rappaport 1968).

The extension of Jewish territory was vigorously pursued under Hyrcanus; and the dynasty's military capacity grew, especially after he introduced the practice of hiring foreign mercenaries. Nonetheless, it is important to point out that, of all the rulers, only Jannaeus pursued patently aggressive policies. Hyrcanus, to be sure, paved the way; but his activities were restricted to carefully judged campaigns with limited targets; and there were long periods when he was not at war.

Josephus gives a résumé of Hyrcanus' early wars, beginning in 129 B.C.: "As soon as he had heard of the death of Antiochus [Sidetes], Hyrcanus marched out against the cities of Syria, expecting to find them devoid of soldiers and of anyone able to rescue them, which was indeed the case" (*Ant* 13.254). This sweeping sentence heralds several important conquests (*Ant* 13.255–58): the capture of Medeba in Moab (S Jordan), together with the neighboring town of Samoga (or Samega); the Samaritan city of Shechem and the shrine on Mt. Gerizim; and, lastly, the Idumean cities of Adora and Marisa, to the S of Judea. The Idumeans are said to have accepted circumcision and adopted the Jewish law in order to retain their homeland.

Toward the end of his life, Hyrcanus returned to the Samaritan region; this time two of his sons laid siege to the Hellenized city of Samaria (*Ant* 13.275–83). The siege lasted a year; but neither the Samaritan population, nor Antiochus IX (Cyzicenus) who came to their aid, nor the two generals whom he later left behind there, nor even the troops supplied to Antiochus by Ptolemy Lathyrus could shake off Hyrcanus. In the end he effaced the whole settlement by the method, if this can be believed, of undermining its foundations. Scythopolis, the Greek city situated at the key point where the valley of Jezreel meets the Jordan valley, was taken immediately afterward. According to Josephus (*JW* 1.66) the city was razed to the ground and its inhabitants reduced to slavery, a rare case of enslavement being mentioned as a consequence of Hasmonean seizure.

The precise motivation behind these different campaigns is for the most part lost to us. To increase his resources may well have been a priority for Hyrcanus, given on the one hand, the agriculturally unproductive character of his homeland and, on the other, the demands of a new aristocracy in an enlarged city. Trading interests might help to explain the conflict with the Nabateans, formerly a friendly people, since they had long operated by controlling the roads, and Medeba was situated on the King's Highway, the great trade route which skirted the desert and linked the Red Sea with Damascus. The Samaritans had cut Judea off on the N, as the Idumeans had done on the S.

Hyrcanus' treatment of conquered territory followed, for the most part, the unremitting severity learned by his family through bitter necessity during their early struggles. Special vindictiveness was reserved for the Samaritans of Shechem. The book of *Jubilees,* thought by some to belong to this period (Mendels 1987), highlights the biblical story of the rape of Dinah and of her brothers' brutal punishment of the Shechemites; this interpretation of the text may well have been meant to justify Hyrcanus' treatment of Samaria/Shechem.

It is often asserted that destruction and expulsion were the preordained lot of all those who would not convert and that Hyrcanus (and equally his successor, Jannaeus) were seeking to secure for the entirety of their holdings a purely Jewish occupation. But our evidence does not justify this extreme view. The Judaization of Edom had its own special story. In the light of indications in the ancient narratives that this transformation was at least partly voluntary and of the attachment of the Idumeans to the Jewish cause at the time of the great revolt of A.D. 66–74, a certain affinity between the Jews and a significant element within Idumea seems probable. Unfortunately, we cannot know what caused the removal to Egypt of a community of persons with obvious Idumean names revealed to us in papyri (Rappaport 1977).

4. Aristobulus. During the single year of his rule, Aristobulus managed one enterprise. The outcome in this case too was the circumcision of at least a part of a defeated people, this time, the Ituraeans of the N, who were ordered to become Jewish or to move (*Ant* 13.318). This policy was perhaps determined by the preexistence of a

Jewish population in upper Galilee. Strabo, the Greek writer whom Josephus mentions by name at this point, actually praises Aristobulus for having served his nation well by its enlargement.

5. Alexander Jannaeus. Jannaeus overran numerous towns in the course of a stormy career, with dramatic advances and equally dramatic setbacks. He has gone down in history as the destroyer of Greek cities, as a ruthless opponent of paganism and indeed of Hellenism. Josephus, however, lists the conquered cities as ones belonging to Syrians, Idumeans, and Phoenicians (*Ant* 13: 395). What is involved is, simply, the achievement of Hasmonean control over the remaining parts of Palestine and over its surroundings—the coastal strip, Idumea, Samaria, Carmel, the Perea, Gaulanitis (the Golan), and Moab. Certainly, recalcitrant cities were not spared brutality: Josephus (*JW* 1.87) speaks of Jannaeus' reducing Gaza, Raphia, and Anthedon to servitude. But this brutality was matched by that of the other side and seems to have been more a means of reducing opposition or punishing the obdurate than a bid to Judaize whole populations by the sword. So, for example, Amathus in S Jordan was demolished because its ruler, Theodorus, would not meet Jannaeus in combat. Only in the case of the Transjordanian city of Pella do we hear that Jannaeus' troops wrecked the city because the inhabitants rejected the customs of the Jews (*Ant* 13.397). That vague phrase may be taken as referring to an attempt formally to transfer political control to a Jewish element. In general, ancient (and modern) allegations about the root and branch destruction of Greek cities by Jannaeus must be viewed as exaggerated, since many of those mentioned rapidly revived (Kasher 1988a: 133–62), while the context of those statements in Josephus shows that they originated in the propaganda surrounding the subsequent refoundation of the cities by Pompey and Gabinius: Pompey, the new Alexander, was to arrive as the savior of the "Greeks" of Syria and of Palestine.

The wars of King Alexander Jannaeus were dominated by pragmatic rather than by religious considerations. The coastal strip and the E bank of the Jordan, from Moab to the Golan, were now the central areas of attention: here his predecessors had established a limited foothold. The determining factor of the advance was a complex interaction, scarcely avoidable, with other rising powers in the region. With this came, perhaps, the lure of new commercial possibilities.

Thus, Jannaeus' opening venture was a major assault on the important port of Ptolemais (Akko). This went well, until it was cut short by the intervention from Cyprus of the deposed Egyptian king, Ptolemy Lathyrus. Jannaeus reached an accommodation with Lathyrus, which, in turn, was soon nullified by Jannaeus' own double-dealing: he was caught in secret negotiations with Lathyrus' mother, now ruling as Queen Cleopatra III (*Ant* 13.324–37). Lathyrus went on to inflict two major defeats on Jannaeus, one in the lower Galilee and one in the Jordan valley and then to invade Judea. Only Cleopatra's military intervention halted his advance. In Josephus' narrative Jannaeus' initial assault on Akko remains unexplained; but it is not improbable that Lathyrus had already before nursed hopes of using the city as a springboard into Palestine and thence back to his own kingdom, while Jannaeus, for his part, had seen the advantages of gratifying Cleopatra by forestalling her son (Stern 1981).

Lathyrus was eventually, though as it turned out temporarily, deflected by Cleopatra; and some time before her death in 101 B.C., she signed a treaty with Jannaeus at Scythopolis (*Ant* 13.355). That observers were struck by the queen's subsequent disengagement from the affairs of Palestine is revealed by a story in Josephus which tells how a prominent Egyptian Jew in her army flatly refused to cooperate with her unless she undertook to leave the Jews alone. Whatever her real considerations, her decision was an invitation to Jannaeus to move in and onward; and in the succeeding years he took not only the towns of the tyrants, but also, notably, Gadara, which was becoming a genuine center of Greek culture, and Gaza. The latter was the key to the S sector of the coastal strip; it was also an established ally and outlet of the Nabateans, whose trade was threatened by Jannaeus, not only at Gaza, but also, and perhaps more so, by his activities across the Jordan. During some eight or nine years the Nabateans, with the help of the Seleucid monarch, Demetrius III, fought with unexpected tenacity to retain their sphere of influence; and in battle they inflicted a serious defeat on the Hasmoneans deep inside Judea. But in the last years of his reign (83–76 B.C.), Jannaeus was able to redress the balance, so that he finished master of most of what lay between the Golan (in the N) and Moab (in the S), including such places of importance as Gerasa, and Gamala, and, as already mentioned, Pella. The country was secured by a network of virtually impregnable fortresses, of which Josephus names three: Hyrcania, Alexandreion, and Machaerus, all of them overlooking Transjordanian territory (*Ant* 13.417).

The new areas were an integral part of the kingdom which on his death the king bequeathed to his widow and successor, Salome Alexandra. The queen retained her husband's kingdom intact during her nine years of rule (76–67 B.C.), and she substantially increased the army; but Judea's power across the Jordan was to prove short-lived and to be replaced almost immediately by a very different arrangement, the group of cities founded or refounded by Pompey, which together became known as the Decapolis. The mixed character of these places had probably persisted throughout, and the enhanced Jewish presence of the Hasmonean period will have served in equal measure to Hellenize the Jews and to Judaize the region.

C. Opposition to the Hasmoneans

The Hasmoneans may have acted on behalf of the people, but this did not mean that they were acceptable to all. The shifting patterns of support and opposition to the ruling house are now in large part lost to us. We are, however, able, by combining with caution reports in Josephus, recollections in the Talmudic literature, and allusions in the Qumran texts to form some impression of the connections between various groupings and political events. Overall, the emergence of a military monarchy was bound to have social and religious repercussions in a tightly knit society, as Judea had been. The formation of sects which dissociated themselves to a greater or a lesser extent from other Jews, begun under the impact of earlier pressures, was undoubtedly accelerated by the political changes of this period.

It is in connection with the rule of Jonathan that Josephus first mentions the three major divisions, which he calls *haireseis* (sects) or "philosophies," that were in existence "at this time"—the Pharisees, the Sadducees, and the Essenes; he then offers a brief account of them (*Ant* 13.171–73). We may take it therefore that Josephus' view, derived perhaps from tradition, was that these groupings had come into their own during the early Hasmonean period; and this is wholly plausible. It is a pity that the author then goes on to describe the bone of contention between them in terms which have nothing to do with the context from which they emerged, because he has chosen at this point to focus on what might interest his Greek readers, that is to say, differences of philosophical standpoint.

1. The Essenes. We are fortunate that the evidence from Qumran bears witness to a more direct (though enigmatically expressed) response to contemporary affairs, on the part, at least, of the community which possessed the scrolls that were found in the caves near that site. In the present state of research there are few who still deny the identification of this community as a branch of the Essene sect (see ESSENES). The specifically sectarian documents found in the Qumran library (which include, in fact, some of the best known of all the Dead Sea Scrolls) energetically castigate the sect's enemies and emphatically justify its members' withdrawal from the main body of the nation. None of the encoded allusions to persons, times, or places is unequivocal. But among the many reconstructions that have been made, some have a fair degree of probability (Vermes 1981).

Three hundred and ninety years after the Exile to Babylon, a "plant root," sprung from "Aaron and Israel," made it their purpose to cast off the iniquity around them in what they perceived as an "age of wrath." After they had groped "like blind men" for 20 years (the round number looks like a symbolic one), the drama began to unfold with the appearance of the "Teacher of Righteousness," a certain priest who made them understand the nature of the gulf between themselves and that "congregation of traitors" which was firmly set in its unacceptable ways. By this time the public evils had greatly increased, under the influence of a "scoffer," who dealt in lies, abolished the moral boundaries, and misled the people by detaching them from the traditions of their forefathers, thus calling forth on them all the curses contained in the covenant. His followers, "seekers of smooth things," turned on the righteous few, persecuting and killing them. If we are also to attach to the Teacher of Righteousness the hymns of thanksgiving (*Hōdāyôt*) from the somewhat damaged *Hymn Scroll* (1QH), then it emerges that his own former friends and companions had been among those who rebelled. There was one powerful persecutor, a "Wicked Priest," who, though "called by the name of truth when he first arose," had betrayed God and defiled himself and the cult out of greed and pride so as to "build a city of vanity with blood" and to rob the poor of their possessions. He had in the end been put to death by his enemies. The elect saw themselves not only as guardians of the Law, but as priests, "sons of Zadok," who were ultimately to protect the temple from the utter defilement which those in charge had wrought in it. However, they had been driven for a period into exile, described again, it would seem, symbolically, as located in Damascus. There they lived a life based upon the new covenant, interpreting the Law punctiliously, in its ritual and its compassionate requirements. Living in perfect purity, they had to remain separate from the community and, especially, to avoid all contact with the temple cult as it existed. They looked forward to the imminent punishment of the traitors and rebels and to their own salvation.

It has been observed that the date of 390 years from the Exile, even if we take it as an approximation accommodated to traditional reckonings, takes us to the beginning of the Hellenizing crisis, early in the 2d century. The withdrawal to "Damascus"—that is to say, perhaps, to Qumran and similar places beside the Dead Sea—would seem, then, to happen at about the time of the Hellenistic reform in Jerusalem. An identification of the Wicked Priest with Jonathan the Hasmonean, who did indeed die at the hands of his gentile enemies, is plausible. The archaeological evidence offered by the community's installations at Qumran cannot confirm this chronology but is consistent with it to the extent of revealing one stratum which precedes that of the Hyrcanus-Jannaeus era. That there is no known historical personage with whom we can identify the Teacher of Righteousness is not wholly surprising: the bitter quarrels which were all-important to the history of the sect had no real claim to attention in the Hasmonean record; and both Teacher and followers had conveniently taken themselves out of sight of Jerusalem, probably without causing much disruption to public life. This should not, of course, stand in the way of our recognizing the historical importance of their action.

The sect's abhorrence of the ruling house did not come to an end with the withdrawal from Jerusalem; but when the Commentary on Nahum (4Q169) points the finger at a peculiarly cruel ruler, seemingly Jannaeus, who is dubbed "the furious young lion," it is made clear that the lion's prey consisted not, now, of the Qumran sectaries, but, instead, of the "seekers of smooth things," reasonably interpreted as the Pharisees. The damaged text seems to suggest that the crucifixion of the seekers by the king, by way of reprisal, shocked the sect, and added a new note of revulsion to their long-standing criticism of the Hasmoneans for the familiar vices of accumulating wealth, abusing power, and polluting all that was holy. It is noteworthy that, even from their exile, these Essenes kept an eye on Jerusalem; indeed, the Nahum Commentary's public awareness extends to a unique reference to the doings of a King Antiochus (apparently Epiphanes) and a King Demetrius (most likely Jannaeus' adversary, Demetrius III). In this respect, the sectaries cannot be described as disengaged. Nor did the sad fate of the "seekers of smooth things" under Jannaeus (if indeed he was the culprit) reduce any of the sectaries' animus against that group.

The *Temple Scroll* (11QT) presents the temple legislation from the Pentateuch with a number of additions, and within this context it finds room for a theory of Jewish kingship (Hengel, Charlesworth, and Mendels 1986). Here a Bible-based reaction to the Hasmonean style of rule stands out plainly (the document is most usually dated, from its description of the Jewish monarch, to the period of Hyrcanus): the king must be Jewish; he must not have many horses; he must not make war in Egypt; he must not be polygamous; he must not acquire much silver and gold; his army must consist of Godfearers and is to protect him against foreigners; he must make all decisions in consultation with a council of 12 Israelites, 12 priests, and 22 Levites; he must marry a Jewish wife; his conduct in war must follow certain set patterns and must be preceded by a consultation by the high priest of the Urim and Thummim. The conclusion is a resounding warning, the contemporary meaning of which is undeniable: "The king whose heart and eyes have gone astray from my commandments shall never have one to sit on the throne of his fathers, for I will cut off his posterity forever so that it shall no more rule over Israel. But if he walk after my rules and keep my commandments and do that which is correct and good before me, no heir to the throne of the kingdom of Israel shall be cut off from among his sons forever" (col. 59).

2. The Pharisees. The nature of the other major groupings within Judaism and their relation to political developments is in some ways even more elusive. But it is clear that unlike the Essenes, the Pharisees did not turn their backs on Jerusalem, to criticize from afar; and there is great interest in the picture in Josephus of their regular involvement in direct opposition to the rulers. It is understandable, in the light of this opposition, that their influence should have spread through society. Josephus claims that by his day they had won wide popularity among the people and that their scholarly interpretations, as embodied in an oral law supplementing the Torah, dominated public practice. Throughout the Hasmonean period that influence was in the making.

The dynasty, whose authority would always depend on its beginnings as Israel's savior, showed understandable reluctance to break irrevocably with those who stood for piety and purity. Hyrcanus was in his early days a pupil and favorite of the Pharisees (*Ant* 13.289). His quarrel with them is couched in an anecdote which figures also in the Talmud (*b. Qidd.* 66a). The core of this story is the Pharisaic demand that Hyrcanus give up the high priesthood and retain only the temporal leadership. The underlying reason for the demand could be that the two functions had traditionally been separated or else that the Hasmonean house lacked the correct, Zadokite descent, or, again, that Hyrcanus outward-looking activities were polluting the temple. Josephus reports drastic results: Hyrcanus canceled the Pharisees' religious ordinances (to which he had evidently accorded binding force), punished their followers, and took up with the Sadducees. Josephus, furthermore, believed that the breach was never healed. Yet the hazy recollections of this ruler in Talmudic literature are favorable, and Josephus himself proceeds to sum him up as a man both fortunate and charismatic. It may well be that the image of special spirituality was one adopted by Hyrcanus to counter Pharisaic disapproval and that the historian reflects this projection when he says that Hyrcanus was honored by God in three separate ways: with the leadership, with the high priesthood, and with a prophet's power to make predictions (*Ant* 13.300). This last ability was exemplified in an episode, found in both Josephus (*Ant* 13.282) and Talmudic texts, which tells how Hyrcanus was busy about his high priestly duties when a voice from above *(bat-qôl)* brought him the news of his sons' victory over Antiochus Cyzicenus. While all three of Hyrcanus' roles are neatly united in this tale, the religious capacity has pride of place.

With Alexander Jannaeus the conflicts intensified greatly and gave rise to mass slaughter and to civil war. This time not the Pharisees but the Jewish masses in general are given as the king's opponents, and the reconstruction which puts the Pharisees at the forefront of the reaction rests on no more than a plausible conjecture. The Talmudic accounts of the flight of Simeon ben Shetah, one of the leading scholars of the era, may go some way to confirm that Jannaeus' quarrel was primarily with elements rigorous about the law, both written and oral, as we know the Pharisees to have been, and to show that politics and religion were not distinguishable spheres of activity (Efron 1987: 176–90). At this time objections seem, once again, to have been directed at the Hasmonean tenure of the high priesthood; in addition, since one popular outburst was the pelting of the king with the citrons carried at the Festival of Tabernacles, there would appear also to have been controversies about his holy day observances. For the rest it is hard for us to envisage how the slaughter of 6000 citizens could follow from the pelting, or what could have been the character of the ensuing troubles in which, between about 90 B.C. and 85 B.C., 50,000 people perished, while their surviving associates had to seek the protection of King Demetrius III (Eukairos). Six thousand of his subjects apparently changed sides twice before Jannaeus took his most appalling revenge of all, crucifying 800 of them in public and massacring their wives and children while, it was said, he feasted openly with his concubines. That this act sent ripples even to Qumran is hardly surprising. Josephus' assurance that the king, having disposed of all the troublemakers, "reigned thereafter in complete tranquility" (*Ant* 13.383), is not wholly believable, though he did recover somewhat from the military setbacks which also accompanied his middle years and which, no doubt, had been partly a consequence of the uprising within his own borders.

Yet even the dreadful deeds described by Josephus did not finally rupture the link between the Pharisees and the dynasty. Jannaeus, with striking pragmatism, concluded from his own extensive experience that the Pharisees were now a power in the land, without whom one could not govern securely. He allegedly left his widow and successor, the queen Salome Alexandra, with the instructions to placate them and to share power with them in the future (*Ant* 13.400–404). These concessions made them prepared, apparently, to go so far as honoring the corpse of Jannaeus.

D. The End of the Hasmoneans

During Alexandra's nine-year rule, the Pharisees are said by Josephus to have come to dominate public life. Talmudic tradition remembered the reign with affection, valuing it especially as the heyday of Simon, son of Shetah. But the Pharisees became, in their turn, objects of public resentment. Elements hostile to them rallied to the side of Alexandra's younger son, Aristobulus; and during her last illness they organized themselves to take over the country. His supporters included much of the priesthood (*Ant* 14.24); and it was that show of violence which persuaded the elder brother, Hyrcanus, formally to cede the throne to the younger shortly after the queen's death. However, under the impact of the Roman presence in the area and of his Idumean adviser, Antipater (the father of Herod the Great), Hyrcanus' claim was soon revived and was eventually endorsed by Pompey when he arrived.

We cannot judge which sector of the population it was that presented itself to Pompey at Damascus in the spring of 63 B.C. and requested the restoration of the traditional system of rule under a high priest (*Ant* 14.41). Josephus describes this as the view of the "nation." Whatever the case, the sad day had arrived when these people preferred to deal with Rome rather than with either of the aspiring Hasmonean rulers. Those hopes in a solution from the outside very rapidly faded, however, once Pompey had wrested the Temple Mount from the forces of Aristobulus after a three month siege, had marched into the holy of holies, had imposed Roman tribute, and had taken many into slavery. Some of the *Psalms of Solomon* express the horror of the pious at that act of desecration, voicing the feelings of those people who had been repelled, like the Qumran settlers, by the greed, lawlessness, and arrogance of their own leaders. Here, too, we read of some who had at first welcomed Pompey, the invader from the west, "a man alien to our race" (*Pss. Sol.* 2:1–2).

This was the end of the Hasmoneans as a ruling dynasty. The sequel is known to us almost entirely from book 14 of Josephus' *Jewish Antiquities*. Aristobulus was taken to Rome as a prisoner, to be displayed in Pompey's triumph. Hyrcanus was allowed to remain as high priest and receive the title "ethnarch." Between 57 and 55 B.C. the reduced entity of Judea was divided by Gabinius, the Roman proconsul of Syria, into five administrative and fiscal districts. During this period several revolts were organized, either by Aristobulus or by one or more of his sons, who seemed to have little difficulty in escaping from their Roman captivity; but these were fielded, on behalf of Rome, by Hyrcanus with his increasingly energetic minister, Antipater. A further rebellion, under Pitholaus, was crushed by Cassius, in 51 B.C.

During the 40s the upheavals in Roman politics consigned Judea to constant instability, for the civil wars were fought out largely in the E. Julius Caesar, maneuvering against Pompey, released Aristobulus and perhaps hoped to reinstate him; but Aristobulus' sudden death necessitated a rapprochment between the dictator and the party of Hyrcanus, which now included Antipater's sons, the younger of whom was Herod. Hyrcanus' ethnarchy and high priesthood were confirmed. This state of affairs did not change during the ascendancy of Marc Antony, though Antipater himself was killed in disturbances.

But the Parthian invasion of Rome's E provinces in 40 B.C., which brought a Parthian army into Jerusalem, again reversed the situation. Hyrcanus was taken prisoner and had his ear mutilated to disqualify him from the high priesthood, while Herod fled to Rome. Antigonus, son of Aristobulus, was installed as king; and the Hasmonean dynasty was for a brief moment revived. He issued coins with Greek on the reverse and Hebrew on the obverse, styling himself, in Greek, King Antigonus, and, in Hebrew, Mattathias the high priest. One issue makes mention in the Hebrew also of the community *(ḥeber)* of the Jews. The iconography is associated with the temple. Syria was torn between Romans and Parthians during the next three years, allowing Herod to engage in the reconquest of Palestine with Roman support. In 37 B.C. Jerusalem fell to Herod together with Sosius, the Roman general; and Antigonus was beheaded at Antioch on the orders of Antony. Earlier in the year, Herod had married Mariamne (Mariamme I), granddaughter of Aristobulus (through her father) as well as of Hyrcanus (through her mother), thus uniting and also superseding the two branches of the Hasmonean dynasty. Mariamne's death at the hands of her jealous husband occurred in 29 B.C., and the two sons of this marriage, Alexander and Aristobulus, fell under suspicion and were executed in the year 7 B.C.

That the dynasty was remembered with admiration by at least some sections of the Jewish aristocracy is shown by the pride with which the historian Josephus speaks of his Hasmonean ancestry in the introduction to his autobiography, a work published as late as the A.D. 90s (*Life* 2).

Bibliography

Ariel, D. T. 1982. A Survey of Coin Finds in Jerusalem. *LASBF* 32: 273–307.

Avigad, N. 1984. *Discovering Jerusalem.* Oxford.

Bickerman, E. 1962. *From Ezra to the Last of the Maccabees.* New York.

Efron, J. 1987. *Studies on the Hasmonean Period.* Leiden.

Hengel, M.; Charlesworth, J. H.; and Mendels, D. 1986. The Polemical Character of "On Kingship" in the Temple Scroll: An Attempt at Dating 11Q Temple. *JJS* 37: 28–38.

Jagersma, H. 1986. *A History of Israel from Alexander the Great to Bar Kochba.* Philadelphia.

Kasher, A. 1988a. *Canaan, Philistia, Greece and Israel: Relations of the Jews in Eretz Israel with the Hellenistic Cities (332 B.C.E.–70 C.E.).* Jerusalem (in Hebrew).

———. 1988b. *Jews, Idumaeans and Ancient Arabs.* Texte und Studien zum Antiken Judentum 18. Tübingen.

Mendels, D. 1987. *The Land of Israel as a Political Concept in Hasmonean Literature.* Texte und Studien zum Antiken Judentum 15. Tübingen.

Meshorer, Y. 1982. *Ancient Jewish Coinage.* 2 vols. New York.

Murphy-O'Connor, J. 1974. The Essenes and their History. *RB* 81: 215–44.

Rajak, T. 1981. Roman Intervention in a Seleucid Siege of Jerusalem? *GRBS* 22: 65–81.

Rappaport, U. 1968. La Judée et Rome pendant le règne d'Alexandre Jannée. *REJ* 127: 329–45.

———. 1977. Les Iduméens en Egypte. *Revue de Philologie* 43: 73–82.

Reich, R., and Geva, H. 1981. Archaeological Evidence of the Jewish Population of Hasmonean Gezer. *IEJ* 31: 48–52.

Stern, M. 1981. Judaea and her Neighbours in the Days of Alexander Jannaeus. *Jerusalem Cathedra:* 22–46.

Tcherikover, V. 1969. *Hellenistic Civilization and the Jews.* Philadelphia.

Tsafrir, Y. 1975. The Location of the Seleucid Akra in Jerusalem. *RB* 82: 501–21.

Vermes, G. 1981. The Essenes and History. *JJS* 32: 18–31.

TESSA RAJAK

HASRAH (PERSON) [Heb *ḥasrā*]. Var. HARHAS. **1.** Grandfather of Shallum, the husband of Huldah the prophetess (2 Chr 34:22 [LXX *chellēs*]). Harhas, a variant form of the name, appears in the parallel text of 2 Kgs 22:14.

2. A temple servant who was the progenitor of a family which returned from Babylon with Zerubbabel (1 Esdr 5:31 [Gk *Asara*]). He may be the same "keeper of the wardrobe" mentioned in 2 Chr 34:22 (= 2 Kgs 22:14). Although 1 Esdras is often assumed to have been compiled from Ezra and Nehemiah, the family of Hasrah does not appear among their lists of returning exiles (see Ezra 2:49; Neh 7:52). Omissions such as this raise questions about the sources of and the literary relationship among 1 Esdras, Ezra, and Nehemiah.

MICHAEL DAVID MCGEHEE

HASSENUAH (PERSON) [Heb *hassĕnûʾâ*]. The father of Judah, a Benjaminite and second in command over postexilic Jerusalem (Neh 11:9). In a related list Hassenuah is also described as the father of Hodaviah (1 Chr 9:7), but some scholars have argued that the record in 1 Chronicles has been corrupted (Curtis and Madsen *Chronicles* ICC, 171).

FREDERICK W. SCHMIDT

HASSHUB (PERSON) [Heb *ḥaššûb*]. The name of several different persons mentioned in the OT.

1. The father of Shemalah, one of 284 Levites who agreed to settle in postexilic Jerusalem (Neh 11:15). His name appears in the parallel account in 1 Chr 9:14. According to the latter account he was a member of the Merari clan, but Nehemiah omits this information. This, like other differences in the two lists, suggests that there is no direct literary relationship between the two lists (contra Kellermann 1966: 208–27; and Mowinckel 1964: 146–47). Some, however, have conjectured that both writers were dependent upon common archival materials (Schneider *Esra und Nehemia* HSAT, 42–43; Brockington *Ezra, Nehemiah and Esther* NCBC, 187; cf. Myers *Ezra, Nehemiah* AB, 185). In any event the differences at this point between the accounts provide no further evidence of use in resolving the problem. The name may be a shortened form of the name, *ḥšbyh*, meaning "Yahweh has considered" (*IDB* 2: 536).

2. The name of two men given responsibilities in the rebuilding of postexilic Jerusalem (Neh 3:11, 23). The first, described as the son of Pahath-moab, was charged with responsibility for rebuilding the wall "as far as" or, perhaps, "by" the Furnace Tower. (On the ambiguities of the Hebrew at this point, see Ehrlich 1914: 190; and Williamson *Ezra, Nehemiah* WBC, 197.) He may have already been responsible for reconstruction of other parts of the wall, since the writer describes this as the second section for which he (along with others) was responsible (Brockington, 138). The second Hasshub was charged with responsibility for rebuilding the wall in front of the dwelling he shared with someone named Benjamin (v 23). It is possible that the two men are actually one with two assignments, but it is impossible to be certain (*IDB* 2: 536).

3. A leader of the people and a signatory to the covenant established by Ezra (Neh 10:24).

Bibliography

Ehrlich, A. 1914. *Randglossen zur hebräischen Bibel.* Vol. 7. Leipzig.

Kellermann, U. 1966. Die Listen in Nehemia 11 eine Dokummentation aus den letzien Jahren des Reiches Juda? *ZDPV* 82: 209–27.

Mowinckel, S. 1964. *Studien zu dem Buche Ezra-Nehemia I: Die nachchronistische Redaktion des Buches. Des Listen.* Skrifter utgitt av Det Norske Videnskaps-Akademi i Oslo. Oslo.

FREDERICK W. SCHMIDT

HASSOPHERETH (PERSON) [Heb *hassōperet*]. The form in Ezra 2:55 for Sophereth. It is also the RSV rendering of the Gk *Assaphiōth* in 1 Esdr 5:33. See SOPHERETH (PERSON).

HASUPHA (PERSON) [Heb *ḥăśûpāʾ*]. A temple servant who was the progenitor of a family which returned from Babylon with Zerubbabel (Ezra 2:43 = Neh 7:46 = 1 Esdr 5:29).

MICHAEL DAVID MCGEHEE

HAT. See DRESS AND ORNAMENTATION.

HATHACH (PERSON) [Heb *hătāk*]. One of the eunuchs of King Ahasuerus appointed to attend to Queen Esther (Esth 4:5–12). Distressed with Mordecai's behavior when he learned of Haman's decree against the Jews in the empire, Esther sent her eunuch for some explanation. Mordecai returned her servant with a request urging the queen to go to the king and intercede for her people. Thus the Jews were delivered from Haman's plots against them. The deliverance was compared in the Targum to that of Daniel (Grossfeld 1984), and evidently some think that Hatach is called Daniel by the rabbi (Moore, *Esther* AB, 98). It has been claimed that the eunuch may have been a Jew (Haupt 1982), but his name has been assigned Persian origins meaning "the Good One" (*hataka* is *hat* plus *ka;* Gehman 1924) or "courier."

Bibliography

Gehman, H. S. 1924. Notes on the Persian Words in the Book of Esther. *JBL* 43: 321–28.

Grossfeld, B. 1984. *Concordance of the First Targum to the Book of Esther.* SBLAS 5. Chico, CA.

Haupt, P. 1982. Critical Notes On Esther. Pp. 1–79 in *Studies In the Book of Esther,* ed. C. A. Moore. New York.

JOHN MCKENNA

HATHATH (PERSON) [Heb *ḥătat*]. A Judahite, the son of Othniel and grandson of Kenaz (1 Chr 4:13). Hathath's name appears in a list of descendants or relatives of Caleb (1 Chr 4:11–13). The exact nature of his relationship to Caleb remains unclear. 1 Chr 4:15 apparently traces back from Kenaz to ELAH to Caleb, making Hathath at least Caleb's great-great-grandson. Yet Josh 15:17 refers to "Othniel, the son of Kenaz, the brother of Caleb" (cf. Judg 1:13), thus indicating that Hathath is Caleb's grandnephew (assuming that "the brother of Caleb" describes Kenaz and not Othniel). One could simply posit the existence of separate traditions. However, Myers (*1 Chronicles* AB, 26) suggests that a transposition of the "sons of Kenaz" with *ʾlh* (not as a name, "Elah," *ʾēlâ,* but the demonstrative pronoun, "these," *ʾēlleh*) may have occurred in 1 Chr 4:15, with the original text reading "these were the sons of Kenaz." However, this only accounts for the latter of the two occurrences of Elah in the verse. It is also possible that the name Kenaz was given to two people in the clan over a period of several generations, thus meaning that Caleb's grandson Kenaz, the son of Elah, was the grandnephew of another Kenaz, the brother of Caleb and grandfather of Hathath. The name probably meant "weakness," "weakling" (Noth *IPN,* 227; cf. *HALAT* for etymology). Both G[L] and Vg insert a Meonothai as Hathath's brother (1 Chr 4:13).

KENNETH H. CUFFEY

HATIPHA (PERSON) [Heb *ḥăṭîpāʾ*]. A temple servant who was the progenitor of a family which returned from Babylon with Zerubbabel (Ezra 2:54 = Neh 7:56 = 1 Esdr 5:32).

MICHAEL DAVID MCGEHEE

HATITA (PERSON) [Heb *ḥăṭîṭāʾ*]. A gatekeeper at the temple who was the progenitor of a family which returned from Babylon with Zerubbabel (Ezra 2:42 = Neh 7:45 = 1 Esdr 5:28).

MICHAEL DAVID MCGEHEE

HATTIL (PERSON) [Heb *ḥaṭṭîl*]. A servant of Solomon who was the progenitor of a family which returned from Babylon with Zerubbabel (Ezra 2:57 [LXX *atil*] = Neh 7:59 [LXX *etēl*] = 1 Esdr 5:34 [LXX *agia*]).

MICHAEL DAVID MCGEHEE

HATTUSH (PERSON) [Heb *ḥaṭṭûš*]. **1.** The son of Shemaiah and a descendant of Zerubbabel who is mentioned in the list of exilic and postexilic descendants of David in 1 Chr 3:22. If, as seems likely, the phrase; ". . . sons of Shemaiah . . ." is to be deleted as a dittography in v 22 (see Williamson *Chronicles* NCBC, 58), then Shemaiah becomes the first son of Shecaniah and Hattush is his second son. The root *ḥṭš* is otherwise unattested in biblical Hebrew.

2. A descendant of David who accompanied Ezra on his return to Jerusalem (Ezra 8:2). The text of Ezra 8:2 is a disturbed reading; ". . . of the sons of David, Hattush, of the sons of Shecaniah, of the sons of . . ." The superior reading is preserved in LXX[A] of 1 Esdr 8:29, which reads, "Hattush the son of Shecaniah." This reading agrees with the corrected text of 1 Chr 3:22, which deletes the phrase "sons of Shemaiah" in MT, and makes Hattush the second son of Shecaniah. It is uncertain whether the Hattush mentioned in Ezra 8:2 is identical to (1), because of the uncertainty of the date of Ezra's mission as well as the disturbed text of both Ezra 8:2 and 1 Chr 3:22; but it is quite possible.

3. The son of Hashabneiah (Heb *ḥăšabnĕyāh*), a man of Jerusalem who repaired a part of the walls under Nehemiah (Neh 9:5).

4. One of the priests who put his seal to the covenant of the postexilic community recorded in Nehemiah 10. He may be identical to the Hattush mentioned in Neh 12:2 who returned to Jerusalem with Zerubbabel and Jeshua.

RUSSELL FULLER

HATULA (M.R. 148137). A Natufian and Pre-Pottery Neolithic A (PPNA) site in the Shephelah near Latrun monastery. The site of Hatula is located on the S bank of Naḥal Nahshon close to its entrance to the plain of Aijalon. Its name is derived from the ruins of Hatula on a hill ca. 2.5 km to the E. The prehistoric remains are embedded in a brown alluvium covering an old river terrace 15 m above the present bed. The remains occupy an E-W orientation some 100 × 25 m along the lower edge of the rocky slope bodering the valley.

The site was discovered by Father Claude of Latrun monastery and was excavated during six seasons from 1980 by M. Lechevallier and A. Ronen. It contains two layers: Natufian and PPNA. The excavations have concentrated on the upper, PPNA layer, of which some 80 m^2 were uncovered. The underlying Natufian was reached in limited test pits which exposed approximately 10 m^2.

A. The Natufian

The Natufian remains occupy the lower half of the deposits covering the terrace, about 1 m of dark brown silty clay with small stones or calcareous fragments, with few stones larger than 3 cm. The archaeological remains are sparsely distributed in the entire thickness of the layer; but a major concentration exists at the bottom, near the calcareous crust *(nari)* which constitutes the local bedrock. Here is a rich living floor, 10 cm thick, with abundant flint industry and animal bones. A considerable length of time separated the Natufian and PPNA settlements, during which the site was unoccupied. The top of the Natufian bed served as the foundation of the Neolithic settlement; hence at this point the remains of the two periods may have mixed, with no way to distinguish them.

Among the lithics, flakes constitute some 66 percent of the knapping products, blades/bladelets form ca. 25 percent, and the remainder are cores and waste products. The cores are rather small; a good number among them were prepared by breaking a nodule into halves or quarters. The scarcity of nodules at the site indicates that prepared cores were imported from a flint source, probably from one of the conglomerates along the Nahshon river. Chief among the retouched tools are the microliths (57 percent), with lunates largely dominating. At Hatula, borers (ca. 9 percent) are the most numerous among all known Natufian sites. The borers have especially delicate, needlelike tips generally placed at an angle. Similar borers become very numerous in the PPNA. Other tools include retouched blades and flakes, grattoirs, burins, truncations, and a small number of sickle blades with sheen (0.2 percent). The size and shape of the lunates indicate a Late Natufian phase.

Nonlithic artifacts include a bone sickle fragment with a

groove 2.5 mm deep, a few bone awls (one with a pierced end), and a few pieces of ornament: beads, perforated seashell, and dentalium.

No structures or stone mortars have yet been discovered in the Natufian phase of Hatula. One burial, a female ca. 12 years old, without accompanying objects may belong to either the Natufian or Neolithic.

Table 1
Major Tool Types of Hatula (%)

	Natufian (*N = 517*)	*Khiamian* (*N = 705*)	*Sultanian* (*N = 610*)
Grattoirs	1.7	2.1	1.3
Burins	6.3	2.5	2.9
Borers	8.7	17.4	28.6
Backed blades	1.9	0.1	0.6
Truncatures	2.9	2.6	2.6
Denticulates & Notches	5.4	2.6	3.6
Sickle blades	0.19	1.4	1.8
Retouched pieces	13.0	18.8	27.9
Backed bladelets	22.0	8.8	9.1
Geometric Microliths	35.3	36.0	7.2
El Khiam Points	——	3.1	4.2
Celts	——	——	0. 8

B. The Neolithic

The layer of Neolithic remains is about 1 m thick and differs clearly from the underlying one. It is soft, of light brown color with white pockets. It is rich in stones of various sizes, dominated by those of 5–10 cm in diameter. Many of the stones are broken river pebbles, in our opinion, man-made breaks. The composition of the Neolithic layer and its structure closely resemble the deposits of a tell and likewise denote a strong anthropogenic influence. The upper part of the Neolithic layer was eroded, as indicated by the large number of artifacts found on the surface and by several Neolithic burials, which were originally dug to a certain depth but were found almost at surface level.

Two structures were unearthed in the Neolithic layer. Both are oval and were dug to form a shallow depression in the underlying sediment. One of the oval structures measures ca. 4 × 3 m. The depression was filled by a fine, loess-like yellow sediment, which seems to have been imported. In the yellow sediment were numerous concretions, yellow or orange in color, perhaps the remains of bricks or plaster from the roof or walls of this apparently adobe structure. The oval structure was subsequently (perhaps after a fire) filled with a 30-cm-thick, gray, ashy, soft sediment. In it a concentration of broken pebbles and numerous faunal remains was found.

The second structure measures ca. 5.5 × 4 m and was dug about 50 cm into the underlying deposit. The outer wall had a stone base, made of large cobbles in the S end and smaller ones in the rest of the periphery. The entrance, 1.4 m wide, was in the center of the E wall. The N end of the structure suffered from erosion. About 1 m W of this stone structure was a depression filled with a yellow deposit overlain by a gray, ashy layer rich in large bone fragments, similar to the situation described in the former structure. This depression was only partly excavated. Its precise relation to the stone structure is unclear—perhaps it was an adjacent working area (butchery or kitchen?).

Inside the stone structure and in the space separating the two depressions were numerous grinding implements, mortars and pestles made of limestone or basalt. The mortars and lithic concentrations indicate at least two superimposed floors.

The lithics are very similar to the Natufian ones, both in types and technique of manufacture. The major technical components—flakes, blade/bladelets, cores and waste—are represented in similar ratios to the Natufian series. The main differences are the presence of newly introduced El-Khiam arrowheads or points, the introduction of celts, and the considerable augmentation of borers (from 9 to 29 percent).

After the microliths (45 percent) borers constitute the most numerous tool type in the Neolithic of Hatula (29 percent). They are the same types as the Natufian ones. The El-Khiam points (4 percent) were made on carefully selected, thin blades with a width closely ranging around 10 mm. The notches which separate the stem from the top have a standard size around 5.5 mm. The butt is truncated, frequently concave. The presence of numerous El-Khiam points determines this assemblage as Khiamian. However, a few celts were also found at Hatula, specially located in the stone structure, an arrangement which gives a local Sultanian aspect to the industry. It remains to establish the precise chronological relationship between the "Sultanian" stone structure and the "Khiamian" adobe structure; this will determine whether these lithic facies denote functional or chronological differences.

Bone tools, mainly awls, are of the same type, but more abundant than in the Natufian. There are fine greenstone beads, with biconical perforations exceeding 40 mm in length. A few perforated seashell and dentalium beads are present here, as in the Natufian. Mortars and pestles are numerous in the Neolithic. The mortars are large slabs (ca. 30 × 30 × 20 cm) with a ca. 10-cm-deep depression and a diameter of 10 cm. The pestles are 10–15 cm long, with one end rounded and the other flat; the latter was held in the hand.

Four Neolithic inhumations were uncovered, all in flexed position. Only one had an accompanying object: a round, perforated, limestone bead near the chest.

Natufian fauna is largely dominated by gazelle (95 percent). Wild cattle and wild boar come next as food resources, followed by a few hares and sea fishes. Possibly mole rats and reptiles were also consumed, since several of these remains were charred; and test excavations failed to reveal mole rat and reptile bones outside the occupied area. Few carnivore remains were found in Hatula (fox and cat). Dog remains were not found, but their presence may be inferred from the small bones which were corroded in a way typical of a partial digestion by a dog. Isolated examples of deer, badger, polecat, and hedgehog were also present. A large quantity of birds, including aquatic species which require year-round water, completes the faunal remains.

The Neolithic has a faunal composition similar to that

of the Natufian but with a decreasing role of gazelle and an increase of fish and fowl in the diet.

C. Summary

The open-air site of Hatula was a permanent, or semipermanent, village during the Late Natufian (ca. 12,000 years ago) and PPNA (9500 years ago). The almost total reliance on gazelle as staple food in the Natufian indicates highly specialized hunting strategies, if not a form of seasonal control. The situation changed in the Neolithic when the gazelle population seems to have diminished, with a correspondingly greater dependence on smaller game, mostly birds and fish. In many ways the PPNA material culture seems a direct continuation of the Natufian—an "Epi-Natufian." The scarcity of forest-dweller game and the presence of such humidity lovers as polecat, badger, and ducks constitute somewhat contradictory evidence, implying a large treeless country with a nearby lake or marsh. But we should remember that at this stage man was capable of altering his environment, and our evidence does not necessarily reflect solely natural conditions.

AVRAHAM RONEN
MONIQUE LECHEVALLIER

HAUSTAFELN. The German word *Haustafeln* ("tables of household rules") is a technical term used to designate lists of duties for members of a household. These lists were widely used in antiquity as part of the moral instruction given to individuals in regard to proper behavior toward the gods, the state, friends, fellow members of the household, and others. Examples of the lists, which vary widely in form and function, occur in the "unwritten laws" of popular Greek ethics (e.g., Aesch. *Supp.* 701–9; ps-Arist. *Rh. Al.* 1421b 37–40; ps-Isoc. *Demonicus* 16; Lycurg. *Leoc.* 15; Xen. *Mem.* 4.4.18–24), philosophical traditions (e.g., Cic. *Off.* 1.17.58; 3.15.63; Dio Chrys. *Or.* 4.91; DL 7.108, 119–20; 8.22–23; Epict. *Diss.* 2.10.1–23; 14.8; 17.31; Hierocles *apud* Stob. [cf. Malherbe 1986: 85–104]; Hor. *Ars P.* 312–16; ps-Plut. *De liberis educandis* 7E; Sen. *Ep.* 94.1), Hellenistic Judaism (Joseph. *AgAp* 2.190–210; Philo *Dec* 165–67; *Deo* 17, 19; *Hypo* 7.3, 14; *Post* 181; ps-Phocylides *Gnom.* 175–227), and early Christian literature.

The earliest, most complete Christian examples are Eph 5:21–6:9; Col 3:18–4:1; and 1 Pet 2:13–3:12. The principal interest of these NT *Haustafeln* is in the relationships between husbands and wives, parents and children, and masters and slaves. Wives are exhorted to be submissive to their husbands (Eph 5:22–24, 33; Col 3:18; 1 Pet 3:1, 5–6), children to be obedient to their parents (Eph 6:1–3; Col 3:20), and slaves to be subject to their masters (Eph 6:5–8; Col 3:22–25; 1 Pet 2:18–25). Husbands (Eph 5:25–33; Col 3:19; 1 Pet 3:7), fathers (Eph 6:4; Col 3:21), and masters (Eph 6:9; Col 4:1) are exhorted to be considerate and just and not to abuse the power of their dominant position. Later material that belongs to this tradition of instruction or is related to it includes 1 Tim 2:1–2, 8–15; 5:1–8; 6:1–2; Titus 2:1–10; 3:1–2; *1 Clem.* 1:3; 21:6–9; *Ign. Pol.* 4:1–6:1; Pol. *Phil.* 4:2–6:3; *Did.* 4:9–11; and *Barn.* 19:5–7. Some of the preceding texts (such as Pol. *Phil.* 4:2–6:3) are frequently called *Gemeindetafeln* ("tables of church rules") because they include instructions for groups within the church, "the household of God" (1 Tim 3:15).

Scholarly debate has centered on the issue of the origin and function of these lists of social duties. Whereas early research on the NT *Haustafeln* sought their origin in Stoicism (Weidinger 1928; Dibelius *Kolosser, Epheser, and Philemon* HNT, 48–50), Hellenistic Judaism (Crouch 1972), or even early Christianity itself (Schroeder 1959), recent studies derive them principally from the Hellenistic discussion of the topic "concerning household management" *(peri oikonomias)*, especially as outlined by Aristotle (*Pol.* 1.1253b 1–14; cf. also *Eth. Nic.* 8.1160b, 23–1161a, 10) and developed by the Peripatetics and Neo-Pythagoreans (Lührmann 1975, 1980; Thraede 1977a, 1977b, 1980; Balch 1981, 1988). The function of the NT household codes is highly debated. Dibelius (48), for example, argues that the *Haustafeln* are parenetic in function and that they were adopted by early Christians when the hope for an imminent parousia began to wane. Crouch, on the other hand, argues that the Christian *Haustafel* reflects the nomistic tendencies of Deutero-Pauline Christianity and that it was formed to deal with the problem of social unrest within the Church occasioned by the egalitarian actions of women and slaves; it functioned therefore to combat the threat "to the stability of both the Church and the social order" (1972: 151). Elliott (1981: 208–20; 1986) contends that the *Haustafel* in 1 Peter is part of a sectarian strategy to foster the distinctive identity and solidarity of the Christian community as the household of God over against a hostile world that it still hopes to convert; that is, the code has an internal integrative function within the Church as well as an external missionary goal. Balch (1981, 1986), by contrast, maintains that the domestic code in 1 Peter represents an apologetic response to outsiders' criticisms that Christianity was socially irresponsible and domestically disruptive; the Petrine *Haustafel* encourages the Church's integration into Greco-Roman society by promoting the adoption of certain values of that culture. Balch's position is bolstered by the fact that the *Haustafeln* in Philo and Josephus have a similar apologetic function (cf. also Malherbe 1983: 50–53; 1989: 17).

Historically, the appearance of the *Haustafeln* in 1st-century Christianity reflects the theological conviction that the new life in Christ is to be lived within the framework of existing natural and social orders (Dahl 1965: 69). Modern Western society, however, differs markedly from the Greco-Roman culture that the household codes presuppose. These differences raise acute hermeneutical questions about the *Haustafeln* and their present theological relevance, especially in regard to the codes' acceptance of slavery as an institution (Laub 1982: 83–98) and their espousal of women's subordinate position (Schüssler Fiorenza 1984: 65–92; cf. also Müller 1983). In this regard it is important to interpret each of the *Haustafeln* individually; some of the codes do not simply assume the authority of the paterfamilias but also criticize aspects of it. For example, the *Haustafel* in 1 Peter rejects the ancient tradition that a wife was to fear her husband and acknowledge only his gods. In this tradition a wife was guilty of insubordination if she adopted a religion other than her husband's. 1 Peter (3:1–6) rejects these ideas, exhorting wives to maintain their Christian faith and not to be intimidated by their husbands (cf. Balch 1984). See also HOUSEHOLD CODES.

Bibliography

Balch, D. L. 1981. *Let Wives be Submissive: The Domestic Code in 1 Peter.* SBLMS 26. Chico, CA.

———. 1984. Early Christian Criticism of Patriarchal Authority: 1 Peter 2:11–3:12. *USQR* 39: 161–74.

———. 1986. Hellenization/Acculturation in 1 Peter. Pp. 79–101 in *Perspectives on First Peter,* ed. C. H. Talbert. NABPR Special Studies 9. Macon.

———. 1988. Household Codes. Pp. 25–50 in *Greco-Roman Literature and the NT.* SBLSBS 21. Atlanta.

Crouch, J. E. 1972. *The Origin and Intention of the Colossian Haustafel.* FRLANT 109. Göttingen.

Dahl, N. A. 1965. Bibelstudie über den Epheserbrief. Pp. 7–83 in *Kurze Auslegung des Epheserbriefes,* by N. A. Dahl et al. Göttingen.

Elliott, J. H. 1981. *A Home for the Homeless: A Sociological Exegesis of 1 Peter, Its Situation and Strategy.* Philadelphia.

———. 1986. 1 Peter, Its Situation and Strategy: A Discussion with David Balch. Pp. 61–78 in *Perspectives on First Peter,* ed. C. H. Talbert. NABPR Special Studies 9. Macon.

Karris, R. J. 1971. The Function and Sitz im Leben of the Paraenetic Elements in the Pastoral Epistles. Th.D. diss., Harvard University.

Laub, F. 1982. *Die Begegnung des frühen Christentums mit der antiken Sklaverei.* SBS 107. Stuttgart.

Lührmann, D. 1975. Wo man nicht mehr Sklave oder Freier ist: Überlegungen zur Struktur frühchristlicher Gemeinden. *WD* 13: 53–83.

———. 1980. Neutestamentliche Haustafeln und antike Ökonomie. *NTS* 27: 83–97.

Malherbe, A. J. 1983. *Social Aspects of Early Christianity.* 2d ed. Philadelphia.

———. 1986. *Moral Exhortation: A Greco-Roman Sourcebook.* Library of Early Christianity 4. Philadelphia.

———. 1989. Greco-Roman Religion and Philosophy and the NT. Pp. 3–26 in *The NT and Its Modern Interpreters,* ed. E. J. Epp and G. W. MacRae. Philadelphia and Atlanta.

Müller, K. 1983. Die Haustafel des Kolosserbriefes und das antike Frauenthema. Pp. 263–319 in *Die Frau im Urchristentum,* ed. G. Dautzenberg, H. Merklein, and K. Müller. QD 95. Freiburg.

Samply, J. P. 1971. *'And The Two Shall Become One Flesh': A Study of Traditions in Ephesians 5:21–33.* SNTSMS 16. Cambridge.

Schrage, W. 1974. Zur Ethik der neutestamentlichen Haustafeln. *NTS* 21: 1–22.

Schroeder, D. 1959. Die Haustafeln des Neuen Testaments. Ph.D. diss., Hamburg.

Schüssler Fiorenza, E. 1984. *Bread Not Stone: The Challenge of Feminist Biblical Interpretation.* Boston.

Schweizer, E. 1977. Die Weltlichkeit des Neuen Testamentes: die Haustafeln. Pp. 397–413 in *Beiträge zur Altestamentlichen Theologie,* ed. H. Donner, R. Hanhart, and R. Smend. Göttingen.

Thraede, K. 1977a. Ärger mit der Freiheit: Die Bedeutung von Frauen in Theorie und Praxis der alten Kirche. Pp. 31–182 in *"Freunde in Christus werden . . .": Die Beziehung von Mann und Frau als Frage an Theologie und Kirche,* ed. G. Scharffenorth and K. Thraede. Kennzeichen 1. Gelnhausen and Berlin.

———. 1977b. Frauen im Leben frühchristlicher Gemeinden. *US* 32: 286–99.

———. 1980. Zum historischen Hintergrund der 'Haustafeln' des NT. Pp. 359–68 in *Pietas: Festschrift für Bernhard Kötting,* ed. E. Dassmann and K. S. Frank. JAC Ergänzungsband 8. Münster.

Verner, D. C. 1983. *The Household of God: The Social World of the Pastoral Epistles.* SBLDS 71. Chico, CA.

Weidinger, K. 1928. *Die Haustafeln: Ein Stück urchristlicher Paränese.* UNT 14. Leipzig.

JOHN T. FITZGERALD

HAVILAH (PERSON) [Heb *ḥawîlâ*]. Two individuals with this name, whose identities are closely associated with the place which bears this name, appear in the Bible. See also HAVILAH (PLACE).

1. A son of Cush listed in the so-called Table of Nations (Gen 10:7; 1 Chr 1:9).

2. A son of Joktan listed in the so-called Table of Nations (Gen 10:29; 1 Chr 1:23).

Havilah is the biblical form of the name of the large and old tribal federation of *Ḫaulān* in SW Arabia, which is divided into two or three branches. The identification originates from Niebuhr (1772: 292f.), who associated Ḫaulān to the SE of Ṣanʿāʾ with Havilah, the son of Joktan, and Ḫaulān to the W of Ṣaʿda with Havilah, the son of Cush. He found it remarkable that two tribal districts in different regions of Yemen have the same name and are also mentioned twice in the Table of Nations (Gen 10:7, 29).

Two tribal groups of Ḫaulān continue to exist today. The E (or S) branch are the Ḫaulān al-ʿĀliya or Ḫaulān al-Ṭiyāl, the territory of which extends from the E of Ṣanʿāʾ over Tanʿim to Ṣirwāḥ and into the Wâdī Ḏana just before reaching the oasis of Mārib. The N branch is the federation of the Ḫaulān bin ʿAmr or Ḫaulān Quḍāʿa, the territory of which lies to the NW of Ṣaʿda. The Ḫaulān were probably originally one single tribe, the territory of which was later separated when the Minaean realm arose and the Ḥāšid and Bakīl invaded the Yemenite highland and settled there. Place names in the region of these two tribes still indicate the former presence of the Ḫaulān. Also, in other parts of Yemen, dispersed groups of the Ḫaulān are encountered at a later date.

The earliest epigraphic attestation of Ḫaulān is to be found in the Old Sabean record of the ruler Karibʾil Watar, set up at Ṣirwāḥ, RES 3946,3, where vassals of a certain Yaʿṯuq of Ḫaulān *(ʾdm yʿṯq ḏḫwln ḏyrrt)* are mentioned. In the Minaean inscription M̄ 247 = RES 3022,2 from Barāqiš from the time about 340–330 B.C., the donors of the text give thanks to their gods for having saved them and their possessions from the raids which Sabaʾ and Ḫaulān undertook against them on the caravan route between Maʿīn and Ragmatum (Nagrān). Also in the Qatabanian inscription RES 4274,1 a member of Ḫaulān *(ḏḫwln)* is attested as a person who makes a dedication to the goddess Aṯirat.

In the Sabean inscriptions from the time of the kings of Sabaʾ and Ḏū-Raydān there are numerous references to Ḫaulān, which can be subdivided into three different groups. The E branch is the tribe which settles around Ṣirwāḥ and is called the tribe Ḫaulān Ḫaḍilim (*šʿbn ḫwln ḫḍlm;* e.g., Iryānī 28,1); through common leaders it is closely connected with the tribe of Ṣirwāḥ and Hainān (*šʿbn ṣrwḥ wḫwln ḫḍlm whynn;* e.g., Fakhri 3,2). In the genealogy of the N Ḫaulān around Ṣaᶜda, which in Islamic times are the Ḫaulān bin ᶜAmr, the older name Banū Ğudād or al-Aǧdūd is still quoted by al-Hamdānī (1965: 143–45). In the inscriptions these are the tribe Ḫaulān Gudādim (*šᶜbn ḫwln gddm;* Ja 577,8) or the tribe Ḫaulān Gudādān (*šᶜbn ḫwln gddn;* Umm Lailà 1,1–2) or the groups of Ḫaulān ʾAgdūdān (*ᶜšr ḫwln ʾgddn;* Ja 658,13); the largeness of Ḫaulān is sometimes expressed by the plural *ʾšᶜbn* placed in front of the name ("the tribes of Ḫaulān"; Ja 601,10) or by the designation "the tribes and groups of Ḫaulān Gudādim" (*ʾšᶜb wᶜšr ḫwln gddm;* Ja 616,12); their territory is the land of Ḫaulān Gudādim (*ʾrḍ ḫwln gddm;* Ja 2109,4) or Ḫaulān Gudādān (*ʾrḍ ḫwln gddn;* Ja 601,5) respectively, or the land of Ḫaulān ʾAgdūdān (*ʾrḍ ḫwln ʾgddn;* Ja 658,10). Once the term Ḫaulān Gudādatān (*ḫwln gddtn;* Ja 671,5) is found. In pre-Islamic times there existed in SE Yemen around the town of Waᶜlān in the ancient district of Radmān a further branch of Ḫaulān, which is often attested in the inscriptions of the 2d and 3d centuries A.D., namely, the tribe of Radmān and Ḫaulān, the leaders of which came from the clan Maᶜāhir and Ḏū-Ḫaulān (*bn mᶜhr wḏḫwln qyl rdmn wḫwln;* e.g., RES 3958,1–2). See also HAVILAH (PLACE).

Bibliography

al-Hamdānī. 1965. *al-Iklīl.* Vol. 1/2. Ed. O. Löfgren. Uppsala.

Niebuhr, C. 1772. *Beschreibung von Arabien.* Copenhagen.

W. W. MÜLLER

HAVILAH (PLACE) [Heb *ḥăwîlâ*]. The rich land surrounded by the river Pishon according to the story of the Garden of Eden (Gen 2:11). Its richness derives from the gold, resin bdellium, and onyx stones present there. All three of these products point to S Arabia as the location of Havilah, since S Arabia is the homeland of valuable resins and precious stones. According to Pliny (*HN* 12.23), the tree which yields bdellium also grows in Arabia, and the resin from *Commiphora mukul,* Arabic *muql,* is up to now a Yemenite product (cf. Schopen 1983: 176f.). Onyx (Arabic *ğazᶜ*) is found at all times in various places in Yemen; and among the sorts which were usually named after the places where they were found, there was also a "Ḫaulānite onyx" (al-Hamdānī 1884: 202–3). Among the gold mines of the Arabian peninsula, the mine of ᶜAšam in the region of the Quḍāᶜa is attested, the gold of which is red and excellent; also attested are the mines of al-Qufāᶜa in the land of Ḫaulān, which yield gold of a superior quality (cf. al-Hamdānī 1968: 138–41). J. Halévy reports that, as an eyewitness in 1870 in Ṣirwāḥ in Ḫaulān, he saw Arabs washing gold and noted that gold was found in small grains in the sand and in the river bed (1872: 54). Since in Old South Arabic *ḏhb* does not only mean gold but also a type of incense, it is possible that *zāhāb ṭōb* in Gen 2:12 does not refer to "good gold" but rather to a fragrant resin (cf. de Langhe 1959: 493).

In Gen 25:18 *ḥăwîlâ,* which by the Israelites might have been connected with Heb *ḥôl,* "sand," designates presumably the SE desert border of the region where the Ishmaelites settled. From this fact and from the reference to the *Chaulotaîoi* by Eratosthenes (Strabo, *Geog.* 16.4.2), H. von Wissmann (1970: 905–80, esp. 947–54) concluded that there must have existed a colonial Sabean Ḫaulān in NW Arabia along the incense road before or perhaps still during the Minaean period in the oasis of Dedan. Probably this N Arabian *ḥăwîlâ* is to be distinguished from the S Arabian Ḫaulān and perhaps to be compared with the tribe of *ḥwlt,* which is repeatedly mentioned in the Safaitic inscriptions and which might be identified with the *Avalitae* of Pliny (*HN* 6.157) and the later Arabian tribe of *Ḥawāla.* Possibly the old biblical name of this region survives in the name of the N Arabian town of Ḥāʾil (cf. Knauf 1985: 64). The borders of the Ishmaelites in Gen 25:18 with the local destination *ḥăwîlâ* have also been taken over in 1 Sam 15:7 and transferred to the Amalekites.

It should also be noted that other less convincing identification of *ḥăwîlâ* have been proposed, e.g., in the central Arabian Yamāma, in NE Arabia at the Persian Gulf, or even with *Avalitēs* (*Periplus maris Erythraei* 7; Ptolemy, *Geog.* 4.7.10), the later Zaylaᶜ at the NE African coast. For further bibliography, see Westermann (1984: 214–15).

Bibliography

al-Hamdānī. 1884. *Ṣifat ğazīrat al-ᶜArab.* Ed. D. H. Müller. Leiden.

———. 1968. *Kitāb al-Ğauharatayn al-ᶜatīqatayn al-māʾiᶜatayn aṣṣafrāʾ waʾl-bayḍā. Die beiden Edelmetalle Gold und Silber.* Ed. and trans. C. Toll. Uppsala.

Halévy, J. 1872. Rapport sur une mission archéologique dans le Yémen. *JA* (6th ser.) 19: 54.

Knauf, E. A. 1985. *Ismael.* ADPV. Wiesbaden.

Langhe, R. de. 1959. L'autel d'or du temple de Jérusalem. *Bib* 40: 476–94.

Robin, C. 1982. *Les hautes-terres du Nord-Yémen avant l'Islam.* I. Recherches sur la géographie tribale et religieuse de Ḫaulān Quḍāᶜa et du pays de Hamdān. Uitgaven van het Nederlands Historisch-Archaeologisch Instituut the Istanbul 50. Istanbul-Leiden.

Schopen, A. 1983. *Traditionelle Heilmittel in Jemen.* Wiesbaden.

Westermann, C. 1984. *Genesis 1–11: A Commentary.* Trans. J. J. Scullion. Minneapolis.

Wissmann, H. von. 1970. Ōphīr und Ḥawīla (Maᶜmal und Ḫaulān), das westarabische Goldland; Dedan und Hegra. PWSup 12: 905–80.

W. W. MÜLLER

HAVVOTH-JAIR (PLACE) [Heb *ḥawwōt yāʾîr*]. A region E of the Sea of Galilee comprising a group of Amorite cities granted by Moses to the half-tribe of Manasseh. The name Havvoth-jair occurs in six OT passages (Num 32:41; Deut 3:14; Josh 13:30; Judg 10:4; 1 Kgs 4:13; 1 Chr 2:23). The noun *ḥawwâ,* "village" (?), is found only in the six passages listed above and in all but one (Num 32:41) of its six occurrences only in the phrase *ḥawwōt yāʾîr,* "Havvoth-jair." The lexical isolation of the phrase places its Israelite origin in question.

The name has been appropriated in Hebrew by means of conflicting etiologies. The two pentateuchal instances of Havvoth-jair incorporate an etiology which derives the toponym from the capture of these villages by *yāʾîr ben-mĕnaššê,* "Jair the son of Manasseh" (Num 32:41; cf. "the Manassite," Deut 3:14 [RSV]), in the course of the Israelite acquisition of land E of the Jordan. The etiology interprets *ḥawwōt yāʾîr* as "villages of [the person] Jair." A similar etiology (Judg 10:4) attaches the name to a Gileadite judge named Jair (on the text see Boling 1966: 295–96).

Just as the etiologies of the name differ, so also the number of cities included in the region, and its geographic associations, are variously given in the biblical texts. The etiologic narratives in the Pentateuch (Num 32:33; Deut 3:10–11, 13) and the topographic list in Joshua (13:30) associate Havvoth-jair with the kingdom of Og, the realm of which encompassed BASHAN. Deuteronomy (3:13–14) and the Deuteronomistic tradition (1 Kgs 4:13) further specify that the Bashan region overlapped "the whole region *(ḥebel)* of Argob" (Deut 3:4). The *ḥebel ʾargōb,* "region of Argob," is specified as the area captured by Jair and renamed eponymously (Deut 3:14). *See also* ARGOB (PLACE).

The Deuteronomistic traditions (Deut 3:13–14; Josh 13:30; 1 Kgs 4:13) agree that 60 cities comprised the region called Havvoth-jair, whereas Judg 10:4 presumes 30 cities, associated with the 30 sons of the judge Jair (the political significance of the kinship language is stressed by Boling *Judges* AB, 188). The Chronicler allots 23 cities to Jair (1 Chr 2:23); the cities of Havvoth-jair together with KENATH and its dependencies total 60 cities *(ʿîr)* taken by Geshur and Aram. The Solomonic administrative district centered at Ramoth-gilead included Havvoth-jair (1 Kgs 4:13), and 1 Chr 2:22 places the cities "in the land of Gilead." In the etiologic narratives Havvoth-jair seems to be distinguished from Gilead (see Aharoni *LBHG,* 209).

Bibliography

Boling, R. G. 1966. Some Conflate Readings in Joshua-Judges. *VT* 16: 293–98.

Kallai, Z. 1983. Conquest and Settlement of Transjordan. *ZDPV* 99: 110–18.

PHILIP C. SCHMITZ

HAWK. See ZOOLOGY (FAUNA).

HAZAEL (PERSON) [Heb *ḥăzā(h)ʾēl*]. Powerful king of Aram-Damascus between ca. 842–800 B.C.E., remembered by the Israelites as one of their most brutal enemies. Hazael is known from biblical and Assyrian sources, from an inscribed ivory fragment found at Arslan Tash (among booty seized by the Assyrians) which refers to him as "our lord, Hazael," and from a cylinder seal found at Aššur which mentions booty taken from Mallaḫu, one of his royal cities.

Hazael was a usurper to the throne of Aram. 2 Kgs 8:7–15 portrays him as a high official in the royal court who, after being told by the prophet Elisha that he was to become king of Aram, murdered the ailing king Ben-hadad and seized the throne. The annals of Shalmaneser III also indicate Hazael's status, calling him "the son of a nobody," i.e., a usurper. There is some question concerning the identity of the king that Hazael assassinated, and it is likely that the latter's name was Hadad-ʿizr, rather than Ben-hadad (see BEN-HADAD).

Following his seizure of the throne, Hazael began a campaign of aggression against Israel that was to characterize his entire reign. Before 841 B.C.E. Hazael and Joram of Israel were in conflict in Gilead (2 Kgs 8:28–29), and it was during these hostilities near Ramoth-Gilead that Joram was wounded and that Jehu began his revolution that resulted in the overthrow of the Omride dynasty (2 Kings 9).

The years between 841 and 836 were a period of serious trouble for Aram and Hazael. The powerful Syro-Palestinian coalition headed by Aram and Hamath, which had held back the advances of the Assyrian army of Shalmaneser III four times between 853 and 845, fell apart shortly after Hazael came to power. Hamath apparently made a separate peace with Shalmaneser, and the other partners appear to have pulled away from the alliance as well, leaving Aram alone to face the attack when Shalmaneser returned to Syria in 841. Hazael met the Assyrian army at Mt. Senir but was defeated. He withdrew into Damascus, which Shalmaneser besieged briefly but did not capture, although he devastated the orchards and farmland in the Damascus oasis. The Assyrians returned in 837 and perhaps also in 836 (cf. Pitard 1987: 149–50), but Aram held its own in these battles as well. After 836 Assyrian pressure abated; and Hazael recovered very quickly, turning his attention to the conquest of his S neighbors.

Biblical accounts indicate the extent of Hazael's attacks on Israel and Philistia. It appears that he annexed Israelite holdings E of the Jordan (2 Kgs 10:32–33) and decimated Israel's army, almost certainly making Israel into a vassal state. He also attacked Philistia (2 Kgs 12:17; 13:22 LXX) and Judah (2 Kgs 12:17–18), both of which also appear to have become vassals. There is no information on his relations with Ammon, Moab, and Edom; but it is likely that they too came under his sway. Although some scholars have suggested that Hazael was also able to subdue the major states in central and N Syria, there is actually no evidence of this. But the empire which he built in S Syria and Palestine was significant enough to make Aram-Damascus one of the leading states, and perhaps the dominant political power, of Syria during this period.

Few explicit details are known of the latter part of Hazael's reign besides the fact that he continued to dominate Israel through both Jehu's and Joahaz' reigns. Some scholars have identified the king of Aram called Marʾi in the inscriptions of Adad-nirari III (ca. 810–783 B.C.E.) with Hazael. These inscriptions describe Adad-nirari's attack on Damascus, which resulted in the surrender of Marʾi and the payment of a large tribute to the Assyrians. This campaign against Damascus, however, appears to have taken place in 796 B.C.E., some years after the death of Hazael, so that Marʾi should be identified with Hazael's son, Ben-hadad. Hazael appears to have died toward the end of the 9th century, in the last years of the reign of Joahaz of Israel (2 Kgs 13:22).

Hazael was one of the two most powerful kings of Aram-Damascus (along with Hadad-ʿizr, who ruled just before him), and he had a substantial impact on Israelite history. Israel's vivid memories of his harsh treatment of their people are well illustrated in the story of Elisha's fateful meeting with him (see esp. 2 Kgs 8:12).

Bibliography

Jepsen, A. 1941–45. Israel und Damaskus. *AfO* 14: 153–72.

Mazar, B. 1962. The Aramaean Empire and its Relations with Israel. *BA* 25: 98–120.

Pitard, W. T. 1987. *Ancient Damascus.* Winona Lake, IN.
Puech, E. 1981. L'ivoire inscrit d'Arslan-Tash et les Rois de Damas. *RB* 88: 544–62.

WAYNE T. PITARD

HAZAIAH (PERSON) [Heb *ḥăzāyāh*]. The father of Colhozeh and an ancestor of Maaseiah, a descendant of Judah, and a provincial leader who agreed to settle in Jerusalem (Neh 11:5). Although a shortened or corrupt form of Maaseiah (i.e., Asaiah) is mentioned in the parallel list found in 1 Chronicles 9 (cf. v 5), Hazaiah is not. This, like other differences in the two lists, suggests that there is no direct literary relationship between the two lists (contra Kellermann 1966: 208–27; and Mowinckel 1964: 146–47). Some, however, have conjectured that both writers were dependent upon common archival materials (Schneider *Esra und Nehemia* HSAT, 42–43; Brockington, *Ezra, Nehemiah and Esther* NCBC, 187; cf. Myers *Ezra-Nehemiah* AB, 185). In any event the presence of Hazaiah in the list provides no further evidence of use in resolving the problem. Apart from the probable significance of the name itself ("Yahweh has seen"), nothing is known about this Judean patriarch (Brockington, 188).

Bibliography

Kellermann, U. 1966. Die Listen in Nehemia 11 eine Dokummentation aus den letzten Jahren des Reiches Juda? *ZDPV* 82: 209–27.
Mowinckel, S. 1964. *Studien zu dem Buche Ezra-Nehemia I: Die nachchronistische Redaktion des Buches. Des Listen.* Skrifter utgitt av Det Norske Videnskaps-Akademi i Oslo. Oslo.

FREDERICK W. SCHMIDT

HAZAR-ENAN (PLACE) [Heb *ḥăṣar ʿênān*]. Var. HAZAR-ENON. The northernmost town on the idealized border of the promised land (Num 34:9–10). As such it also figures in Ezekiel's eschatological vision of the boundaries of the restored Israel, and Ezekiel confirms its location in the vicinity of "the entrance to Hamath" (Ezek 47:17–18; 48:1). Some scholars (*IDB* 2: 538) identify it with the modern village of Hadr (M.R. 228299) at the foot of Mt. Hermon 11 miles E-NE of Dan. However, Aharoni (*LBHG*, 73, 486, see map 4) and Simons (*GTTOT*, 283f.) identify it with the important desert oasis of Qayatein (M.R. 360402), about 70 miles NE of Damascus and 60 miles E of Lebo-Hamath (modern Lebwe). The differences between the two identifications are significant. The latter identification envisions an idealized Israelite territory about 80 percent larger than what it would be if Hazar-enan were identified with Hadr (see also *MBA*, map 50).

GARY A. HERION

HAZAR-GADDAH (PLACE) [Heb *ḥăṣar gaddâ*]. A town in the tribal territory of Judah (Josh 15:27). Its location is unknown.

HAZAR-SHUAL (PLACE) [Heb *ḥăṣar šuʿāl*]. A settlement of the tribe of Simeon. Hazar-shual appears in Josh 15:28, where it is listed as part of the tribe of Judah, and in Josh 19:3, where it is a Simeonite settlement. It is also listed as a town in Simeon in 1 Chr 4:28. Since Simeon assimilated to Judah at an early date, it is recorded under both tribes. Though the present literary context of the Judean town list is set in the period of Joshua, its original setting was as part of a post-Solomonic administrative division of the S kingdom. The date for the establishment of this system is debated, with suggestions ranging from the early 9th to the late 7th centuries B.C. Hazar-shual is in the southernmost district of Judah, the Negeb. It is also included in the list of settlements S of Jerusalem occupied by the exiles returning from Babylon in Neh 11:27.

The location of Hazar-shual is problematic. Its name, "the enclosure of the fox," is of no help in locating it. Hazar-shual occupies the same position in all three lists, between Moladah and Baalah/Balah/Bilhah (the latter three being variant spellings for the same site). This places it in the vicinity of Beer-sheba. Abel placed it at Khirbet el-Watan 4 km E of Beer-sheba (*GP*, 89.344; M.R. 137071), though Aharoni believes this site to be Moladah (*LBHG*, 410).

Bibliography

Albright, W. F. 1924. Egypt and the Early History of the Negeb. *JPOS* 4: 131–61.
Cross, F. M., and Wright, G. E. 1956. The Boundary and Province Lists of the Kingdom of Judah. *JBL* 75: 202–26.
Naʾaman, N. 1980. The Inheritance of the Sons of Simeon. *ZDPV* 96: 136–52.

JEFFREY R. ZORN

HAZAR-SUSAH (PLACE) [Heb *ḥăṣar sûsāh*]. Var. HAZAR-SUSIM. A settlement of the tribe of Simeon. Hazar-susah appears once in Joshua (19:5), where it is listed as being one of the settlements occupied by the tribe of Simeon in the aftermath of the Conquest. 1 Chr 4:31 has the variant Hazar-susim. Since the tribe of Simeon was assimilated to that of Judah at an early date and most of the Simeonite towns are listed again clearly in the record of the Judean settlements in Josh 15:21–32, an explanation for its absence there is necessary.

In 19:5–6a the text reads: Ziklag, Beth-marcaboth, Hazar-susah, Beth-lebaoth; the parallel passage in 15:31–32a has: Ziklag, Madmannah, Sansannah, Lebaoth. Since these short sections of the list begin and end with the same towns (Lebaoth being a variant for Beth-lebaoth), it is very likely that the towns in between are also to be equated. An explanation for this difference is that Sansannah is the earlier name for the site. The name Hazar-susah, meaning "the enclosure of the mare," may have been given to it under Solomon, who is known to have trafficked in chariots and horses (1 Kgs 10:28–29).

If the equation of Hazar-susah and Sansannah is accepted, the older name for the site may be preserved at Khirbet esh-Shamsaniyat (Abel *GP*, 447; Aharoni *LBHG*, 439), 16 km NW of Beer-sheba (M.R. 140083), though commentators who do not accept this identification locate it at Sbalat Abu Susein (M.R. 103074), 4 km to the E of Tell el Farah (Abel, 344; Albright 1924: 158). Aharoni reconstructs, with some plausibility, [Hazar]-susah on Ostracon 32 from Arad (*AI*, 60).

Bibliography

Albright, W. F. 1924. Egypt and the Early History of the Negeb. *JPOS* 4: 131–61.

Cross, F. M., and Wright, G. E. 1956. The Boundary and Province Lists of the Kingdom of Judah. *JBL* 75: 202–26.

JEFFREY R. ZORN

HAZARMAVETH (PERSON) [Heb *ḥăṣarmāwet*]. A son of Joktan (Gen 10:26; 1 Chr 1:20) and hence the name of a S Arabian tribe (*šʿbn/ḥḍrmwt:* Ja 643,6) and of the country Ḥaḍramaut (*ʾrḍ/ḥḍrmwt:* YM 349,5) inhabited by it. The S Arabian genealogies, too, follow the biblical tradition in making Ḥaḍramaut a person and a son of Qaḥṭān, the ancestor of all S Arabs (al-Hamdānī 1954, 1: 51–52). On the other hand, however, taking into account the political situation of pre-Islamic Arabia, a younger Ḥaḍramaut as brother of Ḥimyar and son of Sabaʾ is inserted in the genealogy of Sabaʾ the younger one (al-Hamdānī 1954, 2: 105). In the Old South Arabic inscriptions of Ḥaḍramitic dialect, the name is always written in the form *ḥḍrmt* (e.g., RES 2693,1), likewise in Minaean (RES 2775,1; etc.); in the Sabean texts, however, it is mainly written *ḥḍrmwt* (CIS IV 540,65; etc.), rarely *ḥḍrmt* (e.g., BR-M.Bayḥān 5,7). Both forms occur also in Qatabanian (*ḥḍrmt* in the older text RES 4932,4; *ḥḍrmwt* in the late text RES 4336,3); once also the form *ḥḍrmtm* is found (in CIS IV 547,5 from Haram).

The pronunciation of the name in the country itself continues up to the present day in Ḥaḍramūt or Ḥaḍramōt respectively; this is in accordance with the forms of the name transmitted by Greek and Latin authors: *hadramuta* in Theophrast (*Hist. Pl.* 9.4.2), *chatramōtitai* in Strabo (*Geog.* 16.4.2), *Chatramotitae* and *Atramitae* in Pliny (*Nat. hist.* 6.154f.), *chatramōnitai* and *hadramitai* in Ptolemy (*Geog.* 6.7.25 and 10), *hatramitai* in Uranios (*Arabica* III), and *chatramōtai* in Stephanos of Byzanz (*Ethnika* 689,12). In Arabic the name is, apart from dialectal variants, vocalized *Ḥaḍramaut,* which might also have been the pronunciation of the Sabean form *ḥḍrmwt.* This form has certainly been influenced by the popular etymology of the name as "abode of death," a new interpretation which arose from legends widespread in antiquity and deterring from the frankincense-growing region, since according to some records "this place was fearfully unhealthy and always fatal to those who work there" (*Periplus maris Erythraei* 29). Hebrew, too, followed this popular new interpretation, whereby **ḥăṣarmôt* postulated by the LXX *asarmoth* became *ḥăṣarmāwet* in the MT (cf. a parallel alteration of the vocalization of *ṣalmūt,* "darkness," to *ṣalmāwet,* "shadow of death"). A satisfying etymology of *ḥadramūt/ḥadramōt* could hitherto not be given; it is, however, certain, that *-ūt/-ōt* must be considered a suffix which occurs quite frequently in the toponymy of SE Arabia. The form of the relative adjective (Arabic *nisbah*) is in Sabean in the singular *ḥḍrmyn* (BR-Yanbug 47bis,2), which is equivalent to Arabic *al-Ḥaḍramī,* "the one from Ḥaḍramaut"; in the plural *'ḥḍrn, 'Aḥḍūrān* (YM 390,7; etc.), and *ḥḍrmn* (CIS IV 140,5) are equivalent to Arabic *al-Ḥaḍārim.*

According to present-day usage the name Ḥaḍramaut, strictly speaking, designates the deeply incised valley which is approximately 170 km away from the S Arabian coast and extends from the confluence of the Wâdī Kasr until just E of the town of Tarīm. In the most comprehensive sense, however, as the name also was understood in antiquity, Ḥaḍramaut comprises the plateau and the coastal strip in the S of the large valley and in the W the catchment area of the tributary valleys of the Wâdī Ḥaḍramaut to the old capital Shabwa. In the N it included the range of mountains running into the large central Arabian desert, and in the E the region around the Wâdī Masīla, the continuation of Wâdī Ḥaḍramaut, as far as the country of the Mahra. While in the Old South Arabic inscriptions that whole region of the ancient kingdom of Ḥaḍramaut is designated as Ḥaḍramaut, the Wâdī Ḥaḍramaut properly speaking is called, at least in the Sabean inscriptions, *srrn, Sarīrān* (e.g., Iryānī 32,37f.: *kl/hgr/ḥḍrmwt/wsrrn,* "all towns of Ḥaḍramaut and Sarīrān").

Hardly anything is known about the earliest history of Ḥaḍramaut; numerous prehistoric findings, however, indicate that ancient settlements existed in the wadis, in which artificial irrigation may have been used as early as the end of the 2d millennium B.C. A dense population is to be assumed for the Wâdī Ḥaḍramaut and its tributary valleys, for the Wâdī Gurdān and Wâdī Maifaʿa as well as for the capital Shabwa and for the seaport Qanaʾ. Special importance was due to Ḥaḍramaut because of the possession of the frankincense-producing regions, which especially lay in present-day Dhofār, the ancient Saʾkalān, from where the valuable resin was brought either by an overland route or by sea via Qanaʾ to Shabwa, where the proper incense road to the Mediterranean Sea started.

The first attestation of Ḥaḍramaut is to be found in the Old Sabean inscription RES 3945,12f., a record of Karibʾil Watar, probably from the 7th century B.C., in which the Ḥaḍramite king Yadaʿʾil is mentioned as ally of the Sabean king. When in the 4th century B.C. the Minaeans started to control the caravan route to the N the king of Ḥaḍramaut had become (probably because of commercial interests) a confederate of Maʿīn, as the Minaean inscription M 30 (= RES 2775) testifies. The Ḥaḍramitic inscription RES 2687, which had been engraved on the wall barrier of al-Bināʾ at the communication road between the harbor Qanaʾ and the capital Shabwa toward the end of the 1st century B.C., gives account of the efforts which Ḥaḍramaut made at that time to defend its territory against the Himyarites, who had gained ground on the S coast. Otherwise the local inscriptions give us only scanty information about the political history of Ḥaḍramaut. The Ḥaḍramite kingdom reached its largest expansion after it had annexed the remaining parts of the former Qatabān in the W in the second half of the 2d century A.D. The following period is marked by continuous warfare and hostilities with the Sabeans and Himyarites, in the course of which in the first quarter of the 3d century the Sabean king Šaʿirum Autar even succeeded in capturing the Ḥaḍramite capital Shabwa. Toward the end of the 3d century, the Himyarite king Šammar Yuharʿiš conquered Ḥaḍramaut and united S Arabia to a large realm; henceforth he and his successors also bore the designation "king of Ḥaḍramaut" in their titles. Efforts of indigenous princes in the following decades to regain the independence of Ḥaḍramaut met with failure.

Bibliography

al-Hamdānī. 1954. *al-Iklīl.* Vol. 1/1, ed. O. Löfgren. Uppsala. Vol. 2, 1966. Ed. M. al-Akwaᶜ. Cairo.

Bochow, K.-H., and Stein, L. 1986. *Hadramaut. Geschichte und Gegenwart einer südarabischen Landschaft.* Leipzig.

Breton, J.-F.; Badre, L.; Audouin, R.; and Seigne, J. 1982. *Wâdī Ḥaḍramawt. Prospections 1978–1979.* Aden.

Müller, W. W. 1981. Das Ende des antiken Königreichs Ḥaḍramaut. Die sabäische Inschrift Schreyer-Geukens = Iryani 32. Pp. 225–56 in *Al-Hudhud: Festschrift Maria Höfner zum 80 Geburtstag,* ed. R. G. Stiegner. Graz.

Petrácek, K. 1980. Ḥaḍramōt—Versuch einer Etymologie. *Mélanges offerts à M. Werner Vycichl. Société d'Égyptologie, Genève. Bulletin* 4: 73–76.

Thompson, G. C. 1944. *The Tombs and Moon Temple of Hureidha (Hadramaut).* Oxford.

van Beek, G. W.; Cole, G. H.; and Jamme, A. 1964. An Archaeological Reconnaissance in Hadhramaut, South Arabia—A Preliminary Report. Pp. 521–45 in *Annual Report of the Smithsonian Institute for 1963.* Washington.

Westermann, C. 1984. *Genesis 1–11: A Commentary.* Trans. J. J. Scullion. Minneapolis.

Wissmann, H. von. 1968. *Zur Archäologie und antiken Geographie von Südarabien. Ḥaḍramaut, Qatabān und das ᶜAden-Gebiet in der Antike.* Uitgaven van het Nederlands Historisch-Archaeologisch Instituut te Istanbul 24. Istanbul.

W. W. Müller

HAZAZON-TAMAR (PLACE) [Heb *ḥaṣăṣōn tāmār*]. In Gen 14:7 the locality at which the Amorites were defeated by Chedorlaomer and his allies. (See below on its mention in 2 Chr 20:2.) In the intinerary of those kings, it stands between "Enmishpat" (that is, Kadesh) and the valley of Siddim (that is, "the Salt Sea"). This should be compared with the tracing of the S border of the future land of Israel in Ezek 47:19–19; and 48:28: the E boundary, which runs along the Jordan and the Eastern Sea (Dead Sea), ends at Tamar, thence it turns to the waters of Meribath-kadesh and to the Great Sea, forming the S boundary of the land. This points to the identity of Hazazon-Tamar with Tamar, as believed, among others, by Aharoni (*LBHG,* 140, 142), who had located it at ᶜAin Ḥuṣb, 32 km (20 miles) S-SW of the southernmost point of the Dead Sea (Aharoni 1963; *LBHG,* 55, 70). The author of Genesis 14, following his predilection for composite place names, called the site *ḥaṣăṣōn tāmār,* "the pebbly terrain of Tamar" (Borée 1968: 89, §23:12).

2 Chr 20:2, in a different connection identified Hazazon-Tamar with En-gedi, an oasis on the W shore of the Dead Sea, about halfway between its N and S points. This identification was probably caused by an association of *tāmār,* "date palm," with the renowned palm groves at Engedi. It was followed by *Tg. Onq.,* which rendered Hazazontamar by *ᶜēn-gĕdî,* and by *Tg. Neof.,* which has *ᶜn gdy tmryʾ,* "En-gedi of the palms." But En-gedi lies too far N from the line of the march as understood by the author of Genesis 14.

Bibliography

Aharoni, Y. 1963. Tamar and the Roads to Elath. *IEJ* 13: 30–42.

Borée, W. 1968. *Die alten Ortsnamen Palästinas.* 2d ed. Hildesheim.

Michael C. Astour

HAZER-HATTICON (PLACE) [Heb *ḥāṣēr hattîkôn*]. The NE corner of Ezekiel's ideal boundary of Israel, located in the Hauran (Ezek 47:16). The unusual form coupled with the context of the passage has suggested to several scholars that this is another name for "Hazarenon," (Ezek 47:17). Aharoni identifies the latter site with Qaryatein (M.R. 360402), a desert oasis E of Zedad (*LBHG,* 73).

Randall W. Younker

HAZEROTH (PLACE) [Heb *ḥăṣērôt*]. The book of Numbers records the departure of Israel from Mt. Sinai (chaps. 1–10), the journey from Sinai to Kadesh (chaps. 10–21), and the journey from there to Transjordan (21–36). The Israelites were led by the ark and the pillar of cloud. At Taberah, they complained about their misfortunes (11:1–3). Then chap. 11 records the strong craving of the people for meat. The wind brought quail for them to eat, and they were struck with a great plague. The dead were buried at a place called Kibroth-hattavah, "Graves of Craving" (11:34). This has been identified with Rueiss el-Ebeirig. From there they journeyed on to Hazeroth and remained there (11:35). It was at Hazeroth that Miriam and Aaron spoke against Moses (chap. 12) because he had married a Cushite woman; and they asked if God's word was limited to Moses, claiming it came through themselves as well. Miriam got leprosy, but Aaron pleaded with Moses to pray for her. Moses did pray and Miriam was healed. After that the people traveled to the Wilderness of Paran (12:16), from which Moses sent spies to reconnoiter the land of Canaan in preparation for an invasion. Numbers 33 lists many stopping places. After Hazeroth (33:17) Israel traveled to Rithmah (site unknown), Rimmon-perez (possibly Naqb el-Biyar, W of Aqaba), Ezion-geber (v 35), and Kadesh (v 36).

If Mt. Sinai is in the S end of the Sinai peninsula (Jebel Musa) and if the Wilderness of Paran stretches from the Gulf of Aqaba NW into the N center of the peninsula, one would expect Hazeroth to be on the E side of the peninsula, where it is located by Wright and Filson (*WHAB,* 40, map V). They show Kadesh-barnea in the Wilderness of Zin, N-NW of Aqaba, ancient Ezion-geber, though Deut 1:19–23 says the spies were sent from Kadesh-barnea and Num 13:26 says they returned to Kadesh in Paran (Num 33:36 mentions Zin instead of Paran). Hazeroth is also listed in Deut 1:1, between Laban and Dizahab, both locations unknown. Hazeroth is usually identified with ʾAin el-Khadra or Hudra (Abel *GP* 2: 214), 35 km NE of Jebel Musa (Simons, *GTTOT,* 255–56). The identification was first suggested by Burckhardt, favorably entertained by Robinson (1856: 151), defended by Palmer (1872: 213–17), and adopted by others (Gray *Numbers* ICC, 119–20). Earlier, Keil and Delitzsch (n.d., 3: 74–75) noted the identification, Hazeroth = Bir et-Themmed, based on the hypothesis that the Israelites went from Sinai to Canaan by the most direct route, through the desert from the Wâdī es-Sheikh into the Wâdī ez-Zuranuk. Gray cautions that identification based on the similarity of the names is inadequate. Hazeroth simply means enclosures, parks, settlements, courts, or villages. Aharoni (*LBHG,* 109) says courts are especially typical of the Negeb.

Bibliography

Keil, C. F., and Delitzsch, F. n.d. *Biblical Commentary on the Old Testament,* vol. 3, *The Pentateuch.* Repr. Grand Rapids.
Palmer, E. H. 1872. *Desert of the Exodus.* New York.
Robinson, E. 1856. *Biblical Researches in Palestine.* Vol. 1. Boston.

HENRY O. THOMPSON

HAZIEL (PERSON) [Heb *ḥăzîʾēl*]. A Gershonite Levite, presumably the son of Shimei and the brother of Shelomoth and Haran (1 Chr 23:6–7, 9a). Yet, oddly enough, when the four sons of Shimei are listed in the very next verse (1 Chr 23:10), Haziel and his two brothers are not among them. What is more, Haziel and his two brothers are curiously encaptioned as "the heads of the fathers' houses of Ladan" (1 Chr 23:9b), the latter clearly Shimei's brother (1 Chr 23:7; 26:21), although elsewhere the name Libni enters the picture (Exod 6:17; Num 3:18, 21; 1 Chr 6:2—Eng 6:17). Possibly the Shimei of 1 Chr 23:7, 10 and the Shimei of 1 Chr 23:9 are not the same person (Williamson *1 and 2 Chronicles* NCBC, 161). However, the caption itself in 1 Chr 23:9b may be a secondary gloss inserted to escape the difficulty raised by the twofold reference to Shimei. In this view the second Shimei of 1 Chr 23:10 is to be interpreted as a textual error for the once original name "Shelomoth," as the name "Jahath" (1 Chr 23:10–11) reoccurs as a son of Shelomoth in 1 Chr 24:22, although unfortunately this time from the line of Kohath through Izhar (see 1 Chr 6:3—Eng 6:18) and not from Gershon (Curtis *Chronicles* ICC, 264). On the other hand, the name Shimei earlier in 1 Chr 23:9a may represent a scribal error for one of the three sons of Ladan given in 1 Chr 23:8, justifying then the presence and current position of the aforementioned caption in 1 Chr 23:9b. In this regard, interestingly, the NEB regards the whole of the problematic phrase "The sons of Shimei: Shelemoth, Haziel, and Haran, three" as corrupt enough to be omitted completely. Still, the LXX traditions retain the name Haziel, in its present location, as either *(e)i(e)iel* or *aziel;* and so does the Vg, in the name Ozihel. If authentic to its position, the name Haziel refers to one of the Gershonite levitical courses (1 Chr 23:7–11) important to the postexilic situation. The Chronicler or possibly even a later redactor wished to attribute the origin and assignment of these postexilic courses, among others, to the authority and initiation of King David (Braun *1 Chronicles* WBC, 228, 231).

ROGER W. UITTI

HAZO (PERSON) [Heb *ḥăzô*]. A son of Nahor by Milcah (Gen 22:20–22). More precisely he was the fifth of eight from the union of Milcah and Nahor, although the latter had others from a concubine. Hazo was also a nephew of Abraham, who was a brother of Nahor. Hazo was possibly the eponym of a Nahorite family or clan. The genealogy of which he is part shows an Aramean band of 12 whose home territory was in the area NE of the Jordan and who apparently belonged to "Nahor" as a summarizing generic term (von Rad *Genesis* OTL, 245). Thus a league of 12 Aramean tribes is introduced, just as 25:13–16 lists 12 Ishmaelite tribes and Jacob/Israel becomes the father of 12 tribes in 35:23–26. While "Hazo" was a personal name and while it cannot be proven that it was the name of a place or region as well (Westermann 1985: 368), some believe it should probably be identified with the mountainous, uninviting region of Hazu in N Arabia. An inscription of Esarhaddon's Arabian campaign describes *Ḫazû* as hill country consisting of bluish *sangilmud*-stone and extending over a space of 20 miles (*RA* 1: 440). The region of Hazu is the coastal district of al-Ḥasā, located opposite the island of Bahrain (Simons *GTTOT,* 15).

Bibliography

Westermann, C. 1985. *Genesis 12–36: A Commentary.* Trans. J. J. Scullion. Minneapolis.

EDWIN C. HOSTETTER

HAZOR (PLACE) [Heb *ḥāṣôr*]. **1.** A fortified town in N Galilee at the SW corner of the Huleh plain and N of the Sea of Galilee (M.R. 203269). Hazor stood at the crossroads of the main trade routes from Sidon to Beth-shan and from Damascus to Megiddo. It thus occupied the most strategic position in the region.

This strategic position is indicated by the prominence which Hazor receives in the story of the settlement of the land. Joshua 11 describes the "northern campaign" of Joshua, provoked by the coalition of the N cities under the leadership of Jabin, the king of Hazor, to oppose the Israelites. Hazor is said to be "the head of all those kingdoms" (Josh 11:10) and is destroyed by Joshua, the only one of the N cities said to receive such retribution (Josh 11:13). Hazor appears in the list of conquered cities (Josh 12:19) and is assigned to the tribe of Naphtali (Josh 19:36).

Hazor resurfaces as a source of trouble for Israel in Judges 4, where "Jabin, king of Canaan" threatens Israel by means of his army led by Sisera (Judg 4:2, 17). This threat was overcome by the prophetess and judge, DEBORAH, and her military counterpart, BARAK. This episode is recounted by Samuel in his farewell address to the nation (see 1 Sam 12:9). On the difficulties posed by the presence of Jabin in both the Joshua and Judges accounts, see JABIN.

Later Hazor is refortified by Solomon (1 Kgs 9:15) and is destroyed by Tiglath-pileser III of Assyria ca. 733 B.C.E. during the reign of Pekah (2 Kgs 15:29). Finally, the Maccabean warrior, Jonathan, defeated the Seleucid governor Demetrius II on the "plains of Hazor" (1 Macc 11:67).

The ruins of Hazor at modern Tell el-Qedah were first excavated by J. Garstang in 1928 and more thoroughly under the leadership of Y. Yadin over the course of several seasons from 1955 to 1969. The site is comprised of two areas: a mound of about 25 acres and a large area next to it of about 170 acres, the latter enclosed by steep slopes and earthworks. The large enclosed area was destroyed in the 13th century B.C.E., about the time of the Israelite settlement (and never reoccupied), as was the mound next to it. On the debate about the identity of the ones who caused this destruction, see Gray 1966 and the articles by Yadin (who attributes the destruction to the Israelites), Fritz 1973 (who attributes the destruction to the Sea Peoples), and Aharoni 1970 (who believes the destruction reflects the events of Deborah, Barak, Jabin, and Sisera). The excavations at Hazor have also unveiled on the smaller mound building projects which date from the time of Solomon. On the dates of the various layers of settlement at Hazor, see conveniently the chart at Yadin 1976: 495. See also QEDAH, TELL EL-.

2. Another Hazor is mentioned in an oracle by Jeremiah (Jer 49:28–33), though it was apparently located in the desert. Nothing further is known about this Hazor.

3. Josh 15:23–25 mention several towns with the name "Hazor" in the Negeb region. Nothing further is known about these locations.

4. The returnees from the Exile are said to have settled in a "Hazor" in the tribal region of Benjamin (Neh 11:33). This is the only mention of such a location, and nothing further is known about it.

Bibliography

Aharoni, Y. 1970. New Aspects of the Israelite Occupation in the North. Pp. 254–67 in *Near Eastern Archaeology in the Twentieth Century*, ed. J. A. Sanders. Garden City.

Fritz, V. 1973. Das Ende der Spätbronzenzeitlichen Stadt Hazor Stratum XIII und die Biblische Überlieferung im Joshua 11 und Richter 4. *UF* 5: 123–39.

Gray, J. 1966. Hazor. *VT* 16: 26–52.

Malamat, A. 1960. Hazor 'The Head of All Those Kingdoms'. *JBL* 79: 12–19.

Yadin, Y. 1956. Excavations at Hazor. *BA* 19: 2–11.

———. 1957. Further Light on Biblical Hazor: Results of the Second Season, 1956. *BA* 20: 34–47.

———. 1958. The Third Season of Excavations at Hazor. *BA* 21: 30–47.

———. 1959. The Fourth Season of Excavations at Hazor. *BA* 22: 2–20.

———. 1969. Excavations at Hazor, 1968–1969: Preliminary Communiqué. *IEJ* 19: 1–19.

———. 1976. Hazor. *EAEHL* 2: 474–95.

JEFFRIES M. HAMILTON

HAZOR-HADATTAH (PLACE) [Heb *ḥāṣôr ḥădattāh*].

A settlement of the tribe of Judah. Hazor-hadattah is only mentioned once, in Josh 15:25, where it is listed among the settlements occupied by Judah in the aftermath of the Conquest. Though the present literary context of the Judean town list is set in the period of Joshua, its original setting was as part of a post-Solomonic administrative division of the S kingdom. The date for the establishment of this system is debated, with suggestions ranging from the early 9th to the late 7th centuries B.C. Hazor-Hadattah is in the southernmost district of Judah, the Negeb.

The location of Hazor-hadattah is problematic. In the list it is placed between Bealoth and Kerioth-hezron. The second element of the name may be Aramaic for "new," and Hazor-hadattah would mean "New Hazor." Kerioth-hezron is qualified by "that is, Hazor." It seems that the author intended to make clear that he was referring to two towns in the same region with similar names. Even if this suggestion is correct, it does not explain why an Aramaic word was used in the town's name. Abel suggested a location in the region of el-Hudeira, 11.5 km NE of Arad (*GP,* 345; M.R. 170086). Eusebius placed it near Ashkelon, but this is too far to the W (*Onomast.* 20:4).

Bibliography

Cross, F. M., and Wright, G. E. 1956. The Boundary and Province Lists of the Kingdom of Judah. *JBL* 75: 202–26.

JEFFREY R. ZORN

HAZOROTH (PLACE). See HAZEROTH (PLACE).

HAZZELELPONI (PERSON) [Heb *haṣṣĕlelpônî*].

A woman listed in the genealogy of the tribe of Judah (1 Chr 4:3). She was the sister of Jezreel, Ishma, and Idbash. The LXX identifies Etam as their father ("these are the sons of Etam," *houtoi huioi Aitam*), while MT begins the verse with the statement "these are the father (singular) of Etam" (*wĕʾēlleh ʾăbî ʿêtām).* Myers (*1 Chronicles* AB, 28) suggests that something has fallen out between "these" and "the father of Etam." Whatever was originally there provided the name(s) of the ancestor(s) of the people living at Etam to parallel the mention of Penuel, "the father of Gedor," and Ezer, "the father of Hushah" in v 4. Myers identifies Gedor, Hushah, and Etam as places in the vicinity of Bethlehem (cf. the designation of their father as "Hur, the first-born of Ephrathah, the father of Bethlehem" in v 4). Were this the case, Etam would not necessarily have been the father of Hazzelelponi (possibly a brother?). The *BHS* proposes that Hazzelelponi does not represent a name, but rather the letters are a garbled rendering of a gloss on the sequence of the names of the two wives in vv 5b and 6–7 (MT: *wĕšēm ʾăḥôtām haṣṣĕlelpônî;* proposed: *hūṣṣab lipnê šēm ʾăḥôtāh*). However, this is not likely in that it lacks manuscript support, requires changing the consonants and word order, and is too distant from the text of vv 6–7. Her name is missing entirely from the Syriac versions. Evidently the text of 1 Chr 4:3 has suffered some corruption Noth (*IPN,* 241).

The name probably means "he shades my face," incorporating the *Hipʿil* of *ṣll* and *pānîm* (*HALAT* 244). The Vg has *Asalelphuni.*

KENNETH H. CUFFEY

HE. The fifth letter of the Hebrew alphabet.

HEAD COVERING. See DRESS AND ORNAMENTATION.

HEADDRESS. See DRESS AND ORNAMENTATION.

HEALING. See MEDICINE AND HEALING.

HEALING, GIFTS OF [Gk *charismata iamatōn*]. Literally rendered, "gifts of healings," *charismata iamatōn* occurs three times in the NT, 1 Cor 12:9, 28, 30. The phenomenon is indicated by other terms elsewhere in Paul and in the NT.

A. Pauline References

1. The Corinthian Context. The noun used here for "healing," *iama,* is not used elsewhere in the NT. No reason has been advanced for understanding anything other than the usual meaning of the Gk word: healing, physical cure (BAGD 368). The other noun used in the NT for healing, *iasis,* also occurs only three times, in Luke 13:32 and in Acts 4:22 and 4:30, where the Lukan contexts illustrate the meaning with the miraculous physical restorations of the stooped woman (Luke 13:10–17), the dropsical man (Luke 14:1–6), and the lame beggar (Acts 3:1–10, the referent of 4:22 and model for 4:30, picking up on the "wonders and signs" motif of 2:19, 22, 43). Given Paul's association of *charismata* with *charis* (the grace of God; see Koenig 1972: 48–70), *charismata iamatōn* are precisely experienced as gifts of God, not simply as human abilities.

The peculiar double plural form of Paul's phrase, "gift*s* of healing*s*," might suggest that he refers to the repeated phenomena of physical cures rather than an enduring personal gift for healing. However, since his point is that different persons have been given different gifts for the good of the community, the implication is that certain Christians have been given the special capacity to mediate physical cures on a regular basis. Hence *charismata iamatōn* is a stock phrase referring to a charism parallel to the eight other *charismata* (see 1:7; 7:7; 12:4,31) or *pneumatika* ("spiritual gifts"; 12:1; 14:1) listed by Paul in 1 Cor 12:8–10, or to the seven others listed (twice) at vv 28–31, or to the seven listed at Rom 12:6–8 (there described as *charismata* deriving from the *charis* ["favor"] "bestowed upon each of us"). Unlike glossolalia or prophecy (see 1 Corinthians 14), the gift of healing is simply alluded to as a fact of Christian life, and it never becomes a focus of Paul's pastoral concern.

2. Other Pauline References to the Gift. Scholars (see Gatzweiler 1961; Furnish *2 Corinthians* AB, 555–56) have recognized similar references to the experience of the gifts of healing in Pauline communities in Gal 3:5, Rom 15:19, and 2 Cor 12:12. As in 1 Corinthians 12, these contexts understand the healings as the work of the Spirit of God.

B. Non-Pauline References

1. Luke-Acts. Although all strata of the gospel tradition (Q, Mark, Matthew, Luke, John) witness to healing as a component of the activity of Jesus, it is Luke who comes closest to Paul in presenting that healing activity as a divine gift, as, for example, in 4:14–44, where Jesus' ministry is interpreted as an expression of divine endowment of the Spirit. When the verb *iaomai* ("I heal") is first used of Jesus, it is to say that "the power of the Lord [God] was with him to heal" (5:17). This Lukan interpretation of Jesus' healing as a kind of prophetic gift is most explicit at Acts 10:38, where the healing work is an effect of divine anointing with the Holy Spirit and power. Luke also understands healings in the ministry of the disciples according to the same model of prophetic gift. The healing activities of both Jesus and his disciples are called "signs and wonders" (Acts 2:19, 22, 43; 4:30; 5:12; 6:8; 14:3; 15:12), a stock OT phrase recalling the signs and wonders accompanying the first exodus (Acts 7:36; see Exod 7:3; Deut 4:34; 6:22; 26:8).

2. Hebrews. This letter summarizes Christian experience of God in language resonating with both Paul and Luke: ". . . God also bore witness by signs and wonders and various miracles *[dynameis]* and by gifts [*merismoi,* lit. "distributions"] of the Holy Spirit" (Heb 2:4).

3. James. James 5:14–16 is notable in that it describes prayer for physical healing without implying that it is a "charismatic" gift given to certain individuals. Rather it is occasioned by community prayer led by elders.

C. Contemporary Approaches

NT accounts of Jesus' healing activity and the gift of healing in the Christian community have been approached in a variety of ways in modern scholarship: in continuity with OT traditions of divine healing (e.g., Richardson 1941, Fuller 1963, and Brown 1971); from the historical perspective (van der Loos 1965, Kee 1986); form-critically (e.g., Achtemeier 1970, 1972); from the history-of-religious perspective (Smith 1971, Tiede 1972, Kee 1973 and 1986, Hull 1974); in continuity with later church history (Kelsey 1973); from the redaction-critical perspective (e.g., Held 1963 and Achtemeier 1975); as narratives with symbolic dimensions (Hamm 1986); and, increasingly, from the perspectives of the various social sciences (McCasland 1951, Hollenback 1981, Theissen 1983, and Pilch 1988).

Bibliography

Achtemeier, P. 1970. Toward the Isolation of Pre-Markan Miracle Catenae. *JBL* 89: 265–91.

———. 1972. The Origin and Function of the Pre-Markan Miracle Catenae. *JBL* 91: 198–221.

———. 1975. The Lukan Perspective on the Miracles of Jesus: A Preliminary Sketch. *JBL* 94: 547–62.

Brown, R. E. 1971. Jesus and Elisha. *Perspective* 12: 85–104.

Fuller, R. 1963. *Interpreting the Miracles.* Philadelphia.

Gatzweiler, K. 1961. La conception paulinienne du miracle. *ETL* 37: 813–46.

Hamm, D. 1986. Sight to the Blind: Vision as Metaphor in Luke. *Bib* 67: 457–77.

Held, H. J. 1963. Matthew as Interpreter of the Miracle Stories. Pp. 165–299 in *Tradition and Interpretation in Matthew.* Ed. G. Bornkamm. London.

Hollenbach, P. W. 1981. Jesus, Demoniacs, and Public Authorities: A Socio-Historical Study. *JAAR* 49: 567–88.

Hull, J. M. 1974. *Hellenistic Magic and the Synoptic Tradition.* SBT n.s. 28. Naperville, IL.

Kelsey, M. T. 1973. *Healing and Christianity.* New York.

Kee, H. C. 1973. Aretalogy and the Gospel. *JBL* 92: 402–22.

———. 1986. *Medicine, Miracle and Magic in New Testament Times.* New York.

Koenig, J. 1972. *Charismata: God's Gifts for God's People.* Philadelphia.

Loos, H., van der. 1965. *The Miracles of Jesus.* SNT, 9. Leiden.

McCasland, S. V. 1951. *By the Finger of God: Demon Possession and Exorcism in Early Christianity in the Light of Modern View of Mental Illness.* New York.

Pilch, J. 1988. Understanding Biblical Healing. *BTB* 18: 60–65.

Richardson, A. 1941. *The Miracle Stories of the Gospel.* New York.

Smith, M. 1971. Prolegomena to a Discussion of Aretalogies, Divine Men, the Gospels and Jesus. *JBL* 90: 174–99.
Theissen, G. 1983. *The Miracle Stories of the Early Christian Tradition.* Philadelphia.

M. Dennis Hamm

HEAVE OFFERING. See SACRIFICE AND SACRIFICIAL OFFERINGS.

HEAVEN [Heb *šāmayim;* Gk *ouranos*]. In the Bible the word "heaven" is used to describe both a physical part of the universe and the dwelling place of God. In Hebrew the word for heaven is plural; the LXX usually translates the Hebrew word by a singular noun. In the NT both the singular and plural forms occur with no difference in meaning.

A. Heaven as a Physical Reality

In the Hebrew Bible "heaven" is sometimes used as a synonym for "firmament" (Heb *rāqîaʿ*) to describe the dome-shaped covering over the earth that separated the heavenly waters above from the earthly waters beneath (Gen 1:6–8; Ps 148:4). Heaven, or the firmament, was thought to be supported by pillars (Job 26:11) and had foundations (2 Sam 22:8) and windows. When the windows of heaven were opened, the waters above the firmament fell upon the earth as rain (Gen 7:11; 8:2; Isa 24:18). Through these windows God also poured out blessings upon the earth (Mal 3:10). The birds fly across the firmament (Gen 1:20; Deut 4:17) and the sun, moon, and stars were set in the firmament (Gen 1:14–18).

Whereas the firmament referred specifically to the canopy covering the earth, heaven often had a broader meaning, referring to all that was above the earth, including the firmament. Rain, snow, hail, and thunder come from heaven (Exod 9:22–35; Isa 55:10; Josh 10:11; Rev 11:19). Heaven contained the storehouses of the winds, the snow, and the hail (Job 37:9; 38:22; Ps 135:7; Jer 10:13).

Heaven is also a place for signs. God placed the rainbow in the heavens as a sign to Noah of the covenant which God made with him (Gen 9:12–17). God's power is displayed in the signs and wonders which are performed in heaven and on earth (Dan 6:27). Signs in the heavens also portend God's judgment on the earth, particularly the eschatological judgment (Joel 2:30–31; Matt 24:30; Luke 21:11, 25; Acts 2:19; Rev 15:1).

The phrase "heaven and earth" was used to denote the entire universe, the totality of God's creation (Gen 1:1; Deut 4:26; Ps 121:2; 146:6; Mark 13:31; Acts 17:24). Because heaven is a part of the created order, it too suffers the judgment of God. The heavens are shaken by the anger of God (2 Sam 22:8); the sun and moon will be darkened (Amos 8:9; Jer 4:23, 28; Isa 51:6; Mark 13:24–26; Rev 8:12); heaven and earth will pass away (Matt 24:35; Luke 16:17; 2 Pet 3:10; Rev 21:1). Eschatological hope envisioned a new heaven and earth (Isa 65:17; 66:22; 2 Pet 3:13; Rev 21:1).

B. Heaven as the Dwelling Place of God

Whereas the Israelites could speak of God as dwelling on Mount Sinai (Deut 33:2; Ps 68:17), in the temple (1 Kgs 8:12–13; Ps 68:17–18; Ezek 43:7), or in Zion (Ps 74:2; Isa 8:18; Joel 3:17, 21), the supreme abode of God was in heaven. In the heavenly palace or temple is God's throne, from which God reigns as king over heaven and earth (Isa 6:1; Ps 11:4). Heaven is God's throne and the earth God's footstool (Isa 66:1). From heaven, "above the circle of the earth," God looks down upon the earth, where the people appear as grasshoppers (Isa 40:22; Ps 102:19).

To describe God as dwelling in heaven is to recognize the transcendence of God, God's separateness from the created order. At times, some individuals within Israel wondered if the clouds of heaven shielded the earth from God; God was shut up in the heavens. Eliphaz accuses Job of thinking, "Is not God high in the heavens? See the highest stars, how lofty they are! Therefore you say, 'What does God know? Can he judge through the deep darkness? Thick clouds enwrap him, so that he does not see, and he walks on the vault of heaven' " (Job 22:12–14; cf. Lam 3:44). The author of Isa 64:1 calls on God to "rend the heavens and come down" in order to make God's power known.

Even the vast expanse of heaven, however, is not large enough to contain God (1 Kgs 8:27). The "God of heaven" (2 Chr 36:23; Ezra 1:2; Jonah 1:9) is also the God of earth, who on occasions was described as coming down from heaven to visit the earth (Gen 11:5, 7; Exod 19:18; Isa 64:3). Moreover, even with the belief in Yahweh's transcendence, Israel always saw God as one who was involved in the world which God had created. The whole history of God's dealing with the people of Israel and Judah demonstrated God's activity in the world. God dwelt not only in heaven, but also among God's people (Exod 29:45–46; 1 Kgs 6:13; Zech 2:10–11). The NT, which also speaks of God as residing in heaven (Matt 5:16; 6:9; Mark 11:25; Rev 3:12; 4:2), likewise emphasizes the presence of God in the world, with special emphasis given to God's dwelling in the Church, God's temple (1 Cor 3:16; Eph 2:21–22).

Since heaven is the abode of God, heaven is also the source and locus of salvation. The bread which fed the Israelites in the wilderness came from heaven (Exod 16:4). Blessings upon God's people come from heaven (Gen 49:25; Deut 33:13). Elijah is taken up into heaven in a whirlwind (2 Kgs 2:11). When the idea of life after death developed within Judaism, the location of such existence was often situated in heaven with God (*T. Ab.* 11:10; 2 Esdras 7; cf. Dan 12:2–3). The idea of heaven as the place of eternal reward for the faithful is well attested in the NT, which describes heaven as having many rooms (John 14:2), as containing the believer's eternal house (2 Cor 5:1–10), and as being the location of the believer's commonwealth (Phil 3:20; see also Heb 11:16; Rev 11:12).

Postexilic Jewish literature manifests an intense curiosity about the contents of heaven. Various writings describe heavenly visions or journeys of revered individuals such as Enoch, Abraham, and Baruch *(1 Enoch, 2 Enoch, Testament of Abraham, 3 Baruch).* The topography of heaven, the inhabitants of heaven, the places of judgment, as well as other heavenly secrets are revealed to these persons. Many of these writings describe heaven as containing various levels, referred to as different heavens. The most popular number of heavens was seven. (Compare Paul's statement in 2 Cor 12:2 concerning the third heaven.) The various heavens contain not only the throne room of God, paradise (the intermediate reward for the righteous), and the eternal abode of the righteous, but in many cases one or more of the heavens also contain the places of punishment for the wicked.

Certain non-canonical Christian writings also contain elaborate descriptions of heaven (*The Apocalypse of Peter, The Apocalypse of Paul, The Ascension of Isaiah* 6–11). In the NT book of Revelation, John of Patmos describes his vision of God seated on the heavenly throne surrounded by various members of the heavenly court (Revelation 4–5). John's description of the New Jerusalem, which comes "down out of heaven from God" (Rev 21:1–22:5), has been the source for many later popular ideas about heaven.

MITCHELL G. REDDISH

HEAVEN, ASCENT TO. The motif of the journey to heaven is a vitally important phenomenon of ancient Mediterranean religions. There are five figures in the Bible who, according to standard Jewish and Christian interpretation, are reported to have ascended to heaven: Enoch (Gen 5:24); Elijah (2 Kgs 2:1–12); Jesus (Luke 24:51; Acts 1:9); Paul (2 Cor 12:2–4); and John (Rev 4:1). There are also four related accounts in which individuals behold the throne, or heavenly court, of Yahweh: Moses, Aaron, and the elders of Israel (Exod 24:9–11); Micaiah (1 Kgs 22:19–23); Isaiah (Isa 6:1–13); and Ezekiel (Ezekiel 1, 10). Finally, there is the scene in which an otherwise unidentified "son of man" comes before the throne of God in an apocalyptic vision of Daniel (Dan 7:11–14). The notion that mortals enter into, or behold, the realm of the immortal God (or gods) undergoes various complicated developments from the earlier ANE periods into the Hellenistic period. It is closely related to a number of other topics such as the descent or journey to the underworld of the dead (see DESCENT TO THE UNDERWORLD), the heavenly destiny of the immortal soul, the apotheosis or divinization of selected mortals (rulers, philosophers, divine men), and aspects of Greco-Roman, Jewish, and Christian mysticism. Sorting through this complex conceptual web and trying to understand these biblical texts with their contexts and complicated traditional development has occupied historians of ancient religions for the past 150 years (Bousset 1901; *ANRW* 23: 1333–94).

The motif of the heavenly journey can be divided into four basic types or categories, based upon the fundamental purpose or outcome of the ascent as reported in a given text. Generally speaking, the first two categories are more characteristic of the ANE or archaic period, which would include most texts of the Hebrew Bible (OT). The latter two categories are more typical of the Hellenistic period, which reflects the perspective of the NT.

A. Ascent as an Invasion of Heaven
B. Ascent to Receive Revelation
C. Ascent to Immortal Heavenly Life
D. Ascent as a Foretaste of the Heavenly World

A. Ascent as an Invasion of Heaven

In the cosmology reflected throughout most of the Hebrew Bible, mortal humankind belongs on earth, not in heaven, and at death descends below to the netherworld known as Sheol. Psalm 115 expresses this succinctly:

> The heaven's are the LORD's heavens,
> but the earth he has given to the sons of men.
> The dead do not praise the LORD,
> nor do any that go down into silence.
> But we will bless the LORD
> from this time forth and for evermore.

Generally speaking, just as there is no coming back from the dead, there is no idea or expectation that humans can go to heaven, a place reserved for God and his angelic attendants. This means that any report of a human being ascending to heaven would be seen as not only extraordinary, but often even as an intrusion or invasion of the divine realm. In an Akkadian text, Adapa, the son of Ea, attempts to ascend to heaven to obtain eternal life but is cast back down to earth (*ANET,* 101–3). A somewhat similar story is told of Etana, one of the legendary rulers of the Sumerian dynasty of Kish (*ANET,* 114–18). A direct protest against such an ascent is found in Isa 14:12–20 (compare Ezek 28:11–19). There the prideful King of Babylon, who wants to ascend to heaven and become like God, is cast down to the netherworld of worms and maggots (v 11). The ironic language of Prov 30:2–4 (compare Job 26; 38:1–42:6), though not a tale of ascent, emphasizes the contrast between the human and divine realms. A similar idea lies behind Deut 29:29 and 30:11–14. There is no need for one to ascend to heaven to learn the "secret things" which belong to God (compare Sir 3:21–22). Lucian's tale, *Icaromenippus,* though from the Roman imperial period, typifies this understanding of ascent to heaven as an invasion of the realm of the gods.

The accounts of Enoch and Elijah are best understood in this context. First and foremost, they are extraordinary. The normal fate, even of great heroes of the Hebrew Bible such as Abraham, Moses, and David, is death or "rest" in Sheol (Gen 25:7–9; Deut 34:6; 1 Kgs 2:10, cf Acts 2:29–34). Furthermore, both texts, particularly the one about Enoch, are ambiguous. Gen 5:24, from the P source, in lieu of recording Enoch's death, simply says "Enoch walked with God; and he was not, for God took him." The text does not say where he was taken. Though the bulk of later Jewish and Christian tradition understood this text as an ascent to heaven (*OTP* 1: 3–315; Tabor 1989), this was not universally the case (compare Heb 11:5, 13–16). The author might have had in mind a journey "beyond," to some special region on this earth (e.g., "Isles of the Blessed"), as in the cases of Gilgamesh's Utnapishtim or Menelaus in Homer. Such might also be the case with Elijah. Though it is clear he is taken from the earthly scene in a chariot of fire that rises to heaven like a whirlwind, the author might well have had in mind his removal or "retirement" to some remote area. If so, "heaven" in this text is equivalent to "sky," and the author does not intend to imply that Elijah joined Yahweh as an immortal in the heavenly court. This appears to be the understanding of the Chronicler, who reports that much later, Jehoram, king of Judah, receives a letter written by Elijah (2 Chr 21:12–15).

B. Ascent to Receive Revelation

This type of ascent involves a "round trip" from earth to heaven and back again, or some visionary experience of the heavenly court from which one returns to normal experience (ascent/descent). In contrast to the previous type, the journey or experience is appraised most positively. The earth, not heaven, is still understood as the proper human place, so that the ascent remains a "visit," though not an intrusion, into the divine realm.

The complex literary traditions surrounding the ascent of Moses on Mount Sinai, now found in Exodus 24, though not explicitly referring to a journey to heaven, are closely related to this category. Moses (or alternatively Moses, Aaron, and the seventy elders), in ascending the mountain, enter the presence of God, the realm of the divine. He is given revelation in the form of heavenly tablets, then descends back to the mortal realm. Though he is not explicitly deified or enthroned, he becomes a semi-divine figure, eating and drinking in the divine presence and returning from the mountain with his face transformed like an immortal (Exod 24:11; 34:29–30). In later interpretation this was understood as full deification (see Philo, *vita Mos* 2.290–91; *virt.* 73–75; *Ezekiel the Tragedian* 668–82). The prophetic call of Isaiah is a further example of this same pattern (Isa 6:1–3). Since there is no specific reference to Isaiah being "taken up," this is a "visionary ascent," though the distinction between the two types is not always clear (see 2 Cor 12:2–4). He sees "The LORD sitting on a throne, high and lifted up . . ." (v 1). He is then given a message with a corresponding prophetic commission. As a mortal, he is out of place in the divine realm; he cries out "Woe is me! For I am lost; for I am a man of unclean lips . . . for my eyes have seen the King, the LORD of hosts!" (v 5). The throne visions of Ezekiel (Ezekiel 1, 10) should be compared here, as well as the scene before the throne of the "Ancient of Days" in Dan 7:14 where a "son of man" is given cosmic rulership over all nations. Micaiah's vision of the heavenly court also belongs under this category (1 Kgs 22:19–23). In all these texts the ascent or vision of the heavenly throne serves as a way of claiming the highest and most direct heavenly authority for the message. Such experiences are clearly evaluated as more noteworthy than the epiphany of an angelic messenger or receipt of a prophetic "word of the LORD."

Widengren (1950) has traced this motif of royal or prophetic enthronement (ascent, initiation into heavenly secrets, receipt of a divine commission) into later Jewish traditions involving kingship, prophetic commissions, and the revelation of secret heavenly lore. This understanding of ascent dominates one of the oldest sections of *1 Enoch*, the Book of the Watchers (chaps. 1–36). The legendary figure Enoch is taken through the heavenly realms and shown cosmic secrets, even appearing before God's lofty throne. The Greek version of the *Testament of Levi* (2d century B.C.E.) draws upon the ascent motif in a similar way, as does the Latin *Life of Adam and Eve* (1st century C.E.) and the *Apocalypse of Abraham.* In each of these texts the ascent to heaven functions as a vehicle of revelation, offering divine authority to the cosmological and eschatological lore the authors were expounding.

The closest non-Jewish, or Greek, parallel to this notion of ascent is probably Parmenides' *prooemium,* which survives in only a few fragments (Taran 1965). He tells of being taken in a chariot through the gate leading to daylight, where he is received and addressed by a goddess. On the whole, for Greeks in the archaic period, revelations came through epiphanies, oracles, dreams, omens, and signs of various sorts, not by being taken before the throne of Zeus. The fair number of Jewish (and Jewish-Christian) texts which make use of the ascent to heaven motif as a means of legitimating rival claims of revelation and authority is likely due to the polemics and party politics that characterized the Second Temple period. It became a characteristic way, in the Hellenistic period, of claiming "archaic" authority of the highest order, equal to a Enoch or Moses, for one's vision of things.

C. Ascent to Immortal Heavenly Life

This type of ascent to heaven is final or "one way": a mortal obtains immortality, or release from mortal conditions, through a permanent ascent to the heavenly realms. Broadly, there are two overlapping ideas involved here, both of which have been extensively investigated: first, that a hero, ruler, or extraordinary individual has obtained immortal heavenly existence (Farnell 1921; Guthrie 1950; Bieler 1935–36; Smith 1971; Gallagher 1982); and second, the more general idea that the souls of humankind, bound by mortal conditions, can obtain release to immortal heavenly life (Rhode 1925; Bousset 1901; Burkert 1985). The second is not merely a later democratization of the first; rather, the two exist side by side throughout the Hellenistic period. While they are distinct from one another, both are related to a fundamental shift in the perception of the proper human place. Increasingly in this period one encounters the notion that humans actually belong in heaven, with life on earth seen as either a "fall" or temporary subjection to mortal powers (Nilsson 1969: 96–185; *EncBrit* 8: 749–51).

The only candidates for such immortalization in the Hebrew Bible are Enoch and Elijah, though, as noted above, both texts are ambiguous. As early as the Maccabean period (2d century B.C.E.) Daniel speaks of the righteous dead being resurrected and "shining like the stars forever and ever," having obtained immortality (12:3). A similar notion is found in the Wisdom of Solomon, where the "souls of the righteous" are promised immortal life (3:1–9). Gradually, in Jewish and Christian texts of the Hellenistic period, the older idea of the dead reposing in Sheol forever is replaced with either a notion of the resurrection of the dead or the immortality of the soul or some combination of the two (Nickelsburg 1972). Both ideas involve the notion of a final ascent to heaven.

The NT reflects this Hellenistic perspective in which mortals can obtain heavenly immortality. Matthew 13:43, reflecting the language and influence of Daniel, asserts that "the righteous will shine like the sun in the kingdom of their Father." Eternal life is promised to the righteous throughout the NT corpus (Mark 9:42–48; Q [Matt 10:32–33 = Luke 12:8]; Matt 25:46; Acts 13:48; John 3:16; 14:1–3; Rom 6:23; Col 3:1–4; 1 Tim 1:16; Heb 12:22–23; Jas

1:12; 1 Pet 1:4; 2 Pet 1:4; 1 John 5:11; Jude 21; Rev 20). In most cases this involves ascent to heaven and life before the throne of God (1 Thess 4:13–18; Rev 7:9–17). According to the NT, the righteous of the OT, such as Abraham, Moses, and the prophets, are included in this promised resurrection to immortal heavenly life (Hebrews 11).

In the NT the ascent of Jesus to heaven is the paradigm for all those righteous mortals who follow. Just as he was raised from the dead, made immortal, and ascended to the Father, so will followers experience the same at his return (John 14:1–3; 1 Cor 15:20–28; Rom 8:29–30). The state of the righteous souls who have died prior to the time of the end and the resurrection and ascent to heaven is not always clear. Paul seems to prefer the metaphor of "sleep," which parallels the Hebrew Bible notion of Sheol (1 Thess 4:13; 5:10; 1 Cor 15:18–20). But in two places he might imply that these "souls" or "spirits" depart immediately at death and ascend to the presence of Christ in heaven (Phil 1: 21–24; 2 Cor 5:1–10). In Revelation the "souls of the martyrs" are pictured as under the altar, presumably in heaven, longing for their time of vindication (6:9–11). In distinction to both of these views, the story of the rich man and the beggar Lazarus, unique to Luke, pictures the Hadean world of the dead, which is below, not above, as a place in which rewards and punishments are already being experienced prior to the final resurrection and judgment (Luke 16:19–31). This latter text is more in keeping with other Jewish materials of the period which see the "dead" as conscious, but in the Hadean world below, awaiting the resurrection and last judgment (cf. Rev 20:11–15). There is no uniform NT view of the "state of the dead."

Surprisingly, an actual narrative account of the ascent of Jesus to heaven occurs only in Luke (24:51, but see textual variants; Acts 1:9). It is assumed in Matthew and Mark and spoken of in John (20:17) and Paul (Rom 8:34). A similar resurrection from the dead followed by bodily ascension to heaven is prophesied for the "two witnesses" in the book of Revelation (11:7–12). They are God's final prophets before the return of Christ and the last judgment.

The contrast between the NT and the Hebrew Bible regarding this expectation of ascent to heaven could not be more striking. Other than the doubtful examples of Enoch and Elijah, it is not until the book of Daniel, which is perhaps the latest text in the canon of the Hebrew Bible, that one finds any reference to mortals ascending to heavenly life (some would include Isa 26:19; Job 14:14–16 is a longing, not an affirmation). The NT is fully a part of the process of Hellenization in which notions of resurrection from the dead, immortality of the soul, and ascent to heaven were the norm rather than the exception.

D. Ascent as a Foretaste of the Heavenly World

This type of ascent involves a journey or "visit" to heaven which functions as a foretaste or anticipation of a final or permanent ascent to heavenly life. Though related to the second category, ascent to receive revelation, it is fundamentally different. For example, when Isaiah is taken before God's throne, though he receives a commission and experiences the glories of the heavenly world, there is no idea that he will return to that realm. He remains a mortal who dies and descends to Sheol with all the other dead.

The earliest example of this notion of ascent is in the Similitudes of Enoch (*1 Enoch* 37–71), probably dating from the 1st century B.C.E. In chapter 39 Enoch relates how he was taken to heaven. The experience transforms him (39:14) and he is told that he will later ascend to heaven permanently and receive glory and immortal heavenly life (chaps. 70–71). *2 Enoch* (Slavonic) also reflects a similar pattern. Enoch's journey through the seven heavens, which lasts 60 days (chaps. 1–20), is followed by a return to earth. The experience transforms him and functions in anticipation of his final translation to heaven. Christians later took up and elaborated this understanding of ascent from such Jewish models, as seen in texts such as the *Ascension of Isaiah.*

In the NT we have the striking firsthand account of Paul's own experience of ascent to Paradise (2 Cor 12:2–4). This text provides evidence for the actual "practice" of ascent to heaven in Jewish-Christian circles during this period, in contrast to a purely literary motif adopted to lend heavenly authority to a text. Obviously Paul's experience functions as a highly privileged foretaste of the heavenly glorification which he expected at the return of Christ (Tabor 1986).

There are definite links from the language and ideas of these Jewish texts from Second Temples times and the testimony of Paul to and the Tannaitic and Amoraic *Merkabah* (and later *Hekhalot*) traditions (Scholem 1960; Gruenwald 1980; Halperin 1980).

There are also examples of this type of ascent to heaven in non-Jewish/Christian materials. Perhaps the clearest is Cicero's report of the "Dream of Scipio Africanus" in his *Republic* (6. 9–26). The text was highly influential and functions as a kind of universal declaration of the gospel of astral immortality (Luck 1985). Scipio travels to the heavenly world above and returns with a revelation that all humans are immortal souls, trapped in mortal bodies, but potentially destined for heavenly life above. The gnostic text *Poimandres,* found in the *Corpus Hermeticum,* also fits this category of ascent. There is also an important text in the *Greek Magical Papyri,* mistakenly called the "Mithras Liturgy" (*PGM* 4. 624–750). It provides the initiate who desires to ascend to heaven with an actual guide for making the journey with all its dangers and potentials. There are Jewish texts such as *Hekhalot Rabbati* which have strong parallels with such magical materials, showing that we are dealing here with an international phenomenon of late antiquity (Smith 1963). It is also likely that the rites of initiation into certain of the so-called "mystery religions," such as that of Isis, involved such proleptic experiences of ascent to heaven (see Apuleius, *Metamorphoses* 11, and discussion of Tabor 1986: 89–92).

It is noteworthy that Paul's testimony in 2 Cor 12:2–4 remains our only firsthand autobiographical account of such an experience from the Second Temple period.

Bibliography

Betz, H. D., ed. 1986. *The Greek Magical Papyri.* Vol. 1: *Texts.* Chicago.

Bieler, L. 1935–36. *THEIOS ANER: Das Bild des "Göttlichen Menschen" in Spätantike und Frühchristentum.* 2 Vols. Vienna.

Bousset, W. 1901. Die Himmelsreise der Seele. *ARW* 4: 136–69.

Burkert, W. 1985. *Greek Religion.* Trans. J. Raffan. Cambridge, MA.

Dieterich, A. 1923. *Eine Mithrasliturgie,* 3d ed., Ed. O. Weinreich. Leipzig.

Farnell, L. R. 1921. *Greek Hero Cults and Ideas of Immortality.* Oxford.

Gallagher, E. V. 1982. *Divine Man or Magician?: Celsus and Origen on Jesus.* SBLDS 64. Missoula.

Gruenwald, I. 1980. *Apocalyptic and Merkavah Mysticism.* AGSU 14. Leiden.

Guthrie, W. C. K. 1950. *The Greeks and Their Gods.* Boston.

Halperin, D. J. 1980. *The Merkabah in Rabbinic Literature. AOS* 62. New Haven.

Luck, G. 1985. *Arcana Mundi.* Baltimore.

Nickelsburg, G. W. E., Jr. 1972. *Resurrection, Immortality and Eternal Life in Intertestamental Judaism.* HTS 26. Cambridge, MA.

Nilsson, M. 1969. *Greek Piety.* Trans. J. J. Rose. New York.

Reitzenstein, R. 1978. *Hellenistic Mystery-Religions: Their Basic Ideas and Significance.* Trans. J. E. Steely. PTMS 15. Pittsburgh.

Rohde, E. 1925. *Psyche: The Cult of Souls and Belief in Immortality Among the Greeks,* trans. W. B. Hillis. 8th ed. New York.

Scholem, G. 1960. *Jewish Gnosticism, Merkabah Mysticism and the Talmudic Tradition.* 2d ed. New York.

Smith, M. 1963. Observations on Hekhalot Rabbati. Pp. 142–60 in *Biblical and Other Studies,* ed. A. Altmann. Cambridge, MA.

———. 1971. Prolegomena to a Discussion of Aretologies, Divine Men, the Gospels and Jesus. *JBL* 90: 174–99.

Tabor, J. D. 1986. *Things Unutterable: Paul's Ascent to Paradise in its Greco-Roman, Judaic, and Early Christian Contexts.* Lanham, MD.

———. 1989. Returning to the Divinity: Josephus's Portrayal of the Disappearance of Enoch, Elijah, and Moses. *JBL* 108: 225–38.

Taran, L., ed. 1965. *Parmenides: A Text with Translation, Commentary, and a Critical Essay.* Princeton.

Widengren, G. 1950. *The Ascension of the Apostle and the Heavenly Book.* UUÅ 7. Uppsala.

James D. Tabor

HEAVEN, NEW. See NEW EARTH, NEW HEAVEN.

HEAVEN, QUEEN OF. See QUEEN OF HEAVEN (DEITY).

HEBER (PERSON) [Heb *ḥeber*]. **1.** A son of Beriah, grandson of Asher, and ancestral head of the Heberites (Gen 46:17; Num 26:45; 1 Chr 7:31–32). Heber and his brother Malchiel are listed in the genealogies of Asher in Gen 46:17, Num 26:44–46—LXX 26:28–30, and 1 Chr 7:30–39. These lists vary in the number of sons of Asher mentioned, but all of them mention his daughter Serah and trace the next generation only through Beriah. Heber is not otherwise known, but apparently he was an important figure in the history of the tribe of Asher. In 1 Chr 7:30–39, which may have been drawn from a military census (Williamson *1 & 2 Chronicles* NCBC, 82), both Heber and Malchiel are listed as the sons of Beriah and grandsons of Asher, but the genealogy of Asher is continued only through Heber. Heber has three sons, Japhlet, Shomer, and Hotham, and a daughter, Shua. Grandchildren of Heber are listed for each of his sons: three sons through Japhlet (v 33), four sons through Shemer (= Shomer, v 34), and four sons through Helem (= Hotham, v 35). Heber's line is not traced further through Japhlet and Shermer/Shomer, but it is continued at least into a third generation of descendants through Zophah (vv 36–37), one of the four sons of Helem/Hotham, and perhaps even into a fourth generation if Ithran, one of eleven sons of Zophah, is the same as Jether (v 38), who has three sons. In 1 Chr 7:40 the summary statement on the descendants of Asher indicates considerable military importance, but there is no indication if this was true for all the generations listed or only some.

2. The Kenite ("smith") husband of Jael, and thus a descendant of Hobab (Jethro), the father-in-law of Moses (Judg 4:11). According to Judg 4:11, Heber had separated from the main group of the Kenites who were in the south (Judg 1:16) and moved his household to the "Oak in Zaanannim" near Kedesh (perhaps to be distinguished from the Kedesh of v 10). Judg 4:17 notes that while there he allied himself with Jabin, the king of Hazor, who had been harassing Israel for twenty years (Judg 4:3). Significantly, Jael is not mentioned in the reporting of either the movement or the alliance. Elsewhere in Judges 4–5, Heber is regularly subordinate to Jael, if he is mentioned at all ("Jael, wife of Heber" in 4:17, 21; 5:24, and simply "Jael" in 4:18, 22, and 5:6). From the viewpoint of Judges 4, Jael is treasonous to her husband, but in Judges 5 the narrator portrays Heber's actions as treasonous to Israel. As the battle unfolded, Sisera, Jabin's general, retreated to an allied household, but Jael's loyalties were elsewhere. She lavished attention on Sisera, providing milk when he asked for water, but, once asleep, she killed him inside her/Heber's tent. The narrator condemns Heber through silence, but in Deborah's song, where she is ironically termed the wife of Heber the Kenite, Jael is twice called blessed (Judg 5:24).

3. The father of Socoh, son of Mered and grandson of Ezrah the Judahite (1 Chr 4:18). This segment of the Judahites is not connected to the larger genealogy (1 Chr 4:1–20). Ezrah's father is not stated and the genealogy is extended only one generation beyond Heber. 1 Chr 4:17 mentions that Mered had married an Egyptian (Bithiah) who bore three children, and v 18 begins, "And his Judahite wife." The pronoun presumably refers to Mered. The Judahite wife is unnamed, but she bore three children: Jered, Heber, and Jekuthiel. The textual difficulty of having no subject in v 17 for "and she conceived" (Heb *wattahar*) may be solved by transposing v 186 to follow v 17a as in the RSV (Williamson *1–2 Chronicles* NCBC, 60).

4. The fourth of seven sons of Elpaal the Benjaminite. This Heber is mentioned only 1 Chr 8:17. His connection through his father Elpaal to the larger group is not clear, for the relationship of the Elpaal in vv 17–18 to the Elpaal of vv 11–12 is ambiguous. This segment of the Chronicler's genealogies appears to start with Shaharaim in 1 Chr 8:8. Shaharaim married Hushim, Baara, and Hodesh and divorced the first two, and from the union of Shaharaim and Hushim came Abitub and Elpaal (v 11). The genealogy continues through Elpaal, but the number of his sons is not entirely clear. Verse 12 lists Eber, Misham, and Shemed, and v 13 mentions Beriah and Shema, but their connection to Elpaal is interrupted by comments on Shemed's enterprises at the end of v 12. Presumably Beriah and Shema are to be included among the sons of Elpaal, for all the other names in the context are attached to a parent. The ambiguity is, however, compounded in subsequent verses, for offspring are listed for Beriah (14–16), Elpaal (17–18, where Heber is listed), and Shimei (= Shema, 19–21). On this basis some commentators (see Williamson, *1–2 Chronicles* NCBC, 84–85) would insert Elpaal in v 13 between the references to Beriah and Shema, thus assuming that Elpaal named one of his sons Elpaal and that the total number of sons was six. In short, Heber's grandfather is not known clearly.

RICHARD W. NYSSE

HEBREW [Heb *ʿibrî*]. In English, generally synonymous with "Jew," but in the Hebrew Bible it mostly designates members of the Israelite nation.

The use of this expression is confined to certain parts of the OT, the story of Joseph (Genesis 37–50), the history of Israel in Egypt (Exodus 1–15), and 1 Samuel. Apart from these major narrative compositions the Hebrews are mentioned in a few other passages, notably in Gen 14:13, where Abraham is called a Hebrew; in the Book of the Covenant, Exod 21:2–11, which regulates the service of Hebrews who had been enslaved; and in texts dependent on this law (Deut 15:12; Jer 34:8–20; see Lemche 1976: 43–45, 51–53). Finally, in Jonah 1:9 the prophet describes himself as a Hebrew who has run away from his country. The last mentioned example is the only one where a person describes himself as a Hebrew, in all other instances they are described as such by other peoples, in the story of Joseph and in Exodus by the Egyptians, in 1 Samuel by the Philistines.

The etymology of the expression is not yet totally clear (see proposals in Loretz 1984: 235–48) and the possible derivation from the Akkadian expression *ḫabiru/ḫapiru*, thought to mean a population element of fugitives and outlaws, remains a subject of discussion. See HABIRU, HAPIRU. This discussion about the connection between Hebrews and *ḫabiru/ḫapiru* is, however, fundamental for understanding the ethnic term "Hebrew" in the OT. If this derivation is correct, it would hardly be reasonable to deny the significance of the more general ḫabiru/ḫapiru-movement in the ANE in the 2d millennium B.C. for the population processes in Palestine and adjacent areas which led to the formation of the Israelite society in the early Iron Age, just before 1000 B.C. (against Loretz 1984; cf. already Mendenhall 1962, and 1973: 122–41). Therefore the rise of the Israelite nation cannot be separated from the social upheavals during the Late Bronze Age, of which the ḫabiru/ḫapiru-movement is evidence. According to this view we shall have to reckon with a considerable element of ḫabiru/ḫapiru in Late Bronze Age Palestinian society as one of the single major factors behind the emergence of Israel.

Since the expression *ḫabiru/ḫapiru* evidently covers a social phenomenon, whereas Hebrew in the OT, with perhaps one exception (Exod 21:2–11, the law concerning Hebrew slaves), always stands for members of the Israelite people, a certain shift of meaning has taken place. It is, however, interesting to note how some aspects of the former social meaning of the expression have survived almost everywhere in the OT where the expression is used (Lemche 1979; see also Naʾaman 1986). Thus in the story of Joseph and in Exodus, the word "Hebrew" is always used to refer to the Israelite refugees in Egypt, in contradistinction to the local population or authorities, and in 1 Samuel only the Philistines speak about Hebrews, normally in a derogatory sense, to indicate runaway slaves or renegades (David, who is considered to have deserted his own master, King Saul, is thus styled by his Philistine superiors in 1 Sam 29:3). Even in such late texts as Gen 14:23 and Jonah 1:9, relicts of the former sociological meaning of the expression may be supposed to be behind the present usage.

Irrespective of the relative age of those texts in the OT which mention the Hebrews, it is therefore true to maintain that the OT usage is based on an old and historical tradition. On the other hand, it is hardly possible to argue that all instances are postexilic, or that the use of the expression also derives from such a late period as maintained by O. Loretz (1984: 271–75). First and foremost, in the postexilic and pre-Hellenistic periods, "Hebrew" was never understood as a general term denoting ordinary Israelites or Jews. Moreover, in Exod 21:2–11 we have a testimony of the survival in Israel of an age-long societal connection; here two distinct terms are used which in the Late Bronze Age indicated two different though interrelated social categories (the ḫabiru/ḫapiru and the ḫupšu [Heb *ḥopšî*] respectively, i.e., "peasants" according to general opinion [a variant interpretation is mentioned by Lemche 1975: 139–42, "copyholders," or simply "clients"]). These distinctions disappear completely from Near Eastern documents after the collapse of the Bronze Age social system.

Only in the Greco-Roman tradition did Gk *Ebraios* become the ordinary way of indicating Jews, and thereafter this tradition was taken over by the Christian Church and became a general way of designing members of the Jewish people. The three passages using the term Hebrew in the NT (2 Cor 11:22; Phil 3:5; Acts 6:1) do not enlarge the meaning of the expression. In 2 Corinthians and Philippians, Paul calls himself a Hebrew, thus indicating that he is a Hebrew-speaking Jew in contrast to those Jews whose language is Greek, or perhaps he wanted to distinguish between himself as a Jew and the Gentiles. In Acts the expression is applied to characterize the so-called Jewish Christian congregation.

Bibliography

Lemche, N. P. 1975. The "Hebrew Slave." Comments on the Slave Law Ex. xxi 2–11. *VT* 25: 129–44.

———. 1976. The Manumission of Slaves—the Fallow Year—the Sabbatical Year—the Jobel Year. *VT* 26: 38–59.

———. 1979. "Hebrew" as a National Name for Israel. *ST* 33: 1–23.

Loretz, O. 1984. *Habiru-Hebräer. Eine sozio-linguistische Studie über die Herkunft des Gentiliziums ʿibrî vom Appellativum ḫabiru.* BZAW 160. Berlin.

Mendenhall, G. E. 1962. The Hebrew Conquest of Palestine. *BA* 25: 66–87.

———. 1973. *The Tenth Generation.* Baltimore.

Naʾaman, N. 1986. Ḫabiru and Hebrews: The Transfer of a Social Term to the Literary Sphere. *JNES* 45: 271–88.

NIELS PETER LEMCHE

HEBREW LANGUAGE. See LANGUAGES (HEBREW).

HEBREW NARRATIVE. See NARRATIVE, HEBREW.

HEBREW SCRIPTS. The study of the alphabetic scripts used to write the Hebrew language is a specialized field of palaeography, the study of ancient writing. To prevent confusion and to establish a common terminology, the definitions proposed by F. M. Cross (1961b: 189–90, nn. 4–5) have been adopted.

Hebrew script refers to the original Hebrew letter forms derived from the Phoenician alphabet and used throughout the First Temple Period. *Palaeo-Hebrew script* refers to the continued use of the Hebrew script after the loss of national sovereignty and in particular to the revived official use of the Palaeo-Hebrew script first noted in the late Persian period and continued into the Second Temple Period. Its last documented use is on the coins of the Bar Kokhba Revolt or the Second Jewish War against Rome (A.D. 132–135). However, Palaeo-Hebrew script survives until this day in the collateral branch known as the Samaritan script. *Jewish script* refers to the national script which developed from the Persian Aramaic script employed for official use throughout the Persian empire. This Jewish script is still used today.

A. Hebrew Script

The surviving examples of the Hebrew script were inscribed on durable materials such as stone, gems used for seals, jar handles, or clay bullae impressed by seals or written on ostraca with a carbon or iron salt ink. At present there is only one example of Hebrew script written on papyrus, found at the Wadi Murabbaᶜât. It is dated on the basis of palaeographic evidence to the mid-7th century B.C.

Some of the more important inscriptions include the Gezer Stone, the Siloam Inscription, and the tomb of the Royal Steward. The Gezer Stone is an agricultural calendar from the 10th century B.C. inscribed on limestone. It lists the months of the year by the tasks to be performed in that time period. The Siloam Inscription (late 8th century B.C.) records the joining of the tunnel of the aqueduct dug by Hezekiah to provide water for Jerusalem in the event of siege. The tomb inscription of the Royal Steward is from the same period and records the plea of the Steward to would-be grave robbers to leave his tomb alone as it contained no treasures, but simply the bones of him and his handmaiden.

Several collections of invoices or letters written on ostraca provide a base of evidence upon which palaeographic research depends. These include the Samaria Ostraca (8th century B.C.), the Arad Ostraca (8th to 6th century B.C.), and the Lachish Ostraca (6th century B.C.).

B. Palaeo-Hebrew Script

Aside from the discoveries in the caves of the Judean Desert, the bulk of surviving Palaeo-Hebrew inscriptions are found on stone, ostraca, and most extensively on the coins of the Hasmonaean rulers (circa 100–37 B.C.), the First Jewish War against Rome (A.D. 66–70), and the Second Jewish War against Rome (A.D. 132–135).

The importance of the manuscripts found at Qumran (the Dead Sea Scrolls) for the study of the biblical text, not to mention the history, culture, politics, and religion of Judea in 1st century B.C. and 1st century A.D., would be hard to overstate. This is especially true for the field of palaeography. Aside from manuscripts written exclusively in Palaeo-Hebrew Script or in Jewish Script, a number of manuscripts written in both Palaeo-Hebrew and Jewish Script have provided palaeographers with a key for developing a relative chronology for the evolution and use of the Palaeo-Hebrew script found in the manuscripts and in the nationalistic coinage of the Hasmonaean rulers and that of the leaders of the First and Second Jewish Wars against Rome.

Bibliography

Avigad, N. 1958. The Palaeography of the Dead Sea Scrolls and Related Documents. *Aspects of the Dead Sea Scrolls.* ScrHier 4. Jerusalem.

Birnbaum, S. 1971. *The Hebrew Scripts.* 2 vols. Leiden.

Burrows, M.; Trevor, J.; and Brownlee, W. 1950. *The Dead Sea Scrolls of St. Mark's Monastery.* New Haven.

Cross, F. M. 1961a. *The Ancient Library of Qumran and Modern Biblical Studies.* 2d ed. Garden City, NY.

———. 1961b. The Development of the Jewish Scripts. *The Bible and the Ancient Near East,* ed. G. E. Wright. Garden City, NY. Repr Winona Lake, IN, 1979.

———. 1975. The Contributions of Qumran Discoveries to the Study of the Biblical Text. *QHBT.*

Fitzmyer, J. A. 1977. *The Dead Sea Scrolls: Major Publications and Tools for Study.* SBLSBS 8. Missoula, MT.

Hanson, R. S. 1976. Jewish Palaeography and Its Bearing on Text Critical Studies. Pp. 561–76 in *Magnalia Dei, The Mighty Acts of God,* ed. F. M. Cross, W. Lemke, and P. D. Miller. Garden City, NY.

———. 1985. Palaeography. Pp. 15–23 in *The Palaeo-Hebrew Leviticus Scroll (11QpaleoLev),* by D. N. Freedman, and K. A. Mathews. Winona Lake, IN.

Herr, L. G. 1978. *The Scripts of Ancient Northwest Semitic Seals.* HSM 18. Missoula, MT.

Hestrin, R. et al. 1973. *Inscriptions Reveal.* Israel Museum Catalog 100. Jerusalem.

Jongeling, B. 1971. *A Classified Bibliography of the Finds in the Desert of Judah 1958–1969.* Leiden.

Kadman, L. 1954. The Hebrew Coin Scripts. *IEJ* 4: 150–67. Repr. in *Recent Studies and Discoveries on Ancient Jewish and Syrian Coins.* Numismatic Studies and Researches 1. Jerusalem, 1954.

Kanael, B. 1963. Ancient Jewish Coins and Their Historical Importance. *BA* 26: 38–62.

Kindler, A. 1958a. The Coinage of the Bar-Kokhba War. Pp. 62–80 in *The Dating and Meaning of Ancient Jewish Coins and Symbols,* ed. L. Kadman et al. Numismatic Studies and Researches 2. Jerusalem.

———. 1958b. The Coinage of the Hasmonaean Dynasty. In *The Dating and Meaning of Ancient Jewish Coins and Symbols,* ed. L. Kadman et al. Numismatic Studies and Researches 2. Jerusalem.

LaSor, W. S. 1958. *Bibliography of the Dead Sea Scrolls 1948–1957.* Fuller Library Bulletin 3. Pasadena.

McLean, M. D. 1981. The Initial Coinage of Alexander Jannaeus. *American Numismatic Society Museum Notes* 26: 153–61, pl. 26.
———. 1982. *The Use and Development of Palaeo-Hebrew in the Hellenistic and Roman Periods.* Ph.D. diss. Harvard.
Meshorer, Y. 1967. *Jewish Coins of the Second Temple Period.* Trans. I. H. Levine. Tel-Aviv.
———. 1981. *Sylloge nummorum graecorum.* Pt 6, *Palestine-South Arabia.* New York.
———. 1982. *Ancient Jewish Coinage.* 2 vols. Dix Hills, New York.
Naveh, J. 1970. *The Development of the Aramaic Script.* Jerusalem.
———. 1971. Hebrew Texts in Aramaic Script in the Persian Period? *BASOR* 203: 27–32.

MARK D. MCLEAN

HEBREW VERSION OF MATTHEW. See MATTHEW, HEBREW VERSION OF.

HEBREWS, EPISTLE TO THE. This product of the mature early Christian movement offers an impressive attempt to revitalize commitment to Christ through an imaginative reinterpretation of traditional Christological affirmations which undergirds an appeal to continued fidelity.

A. Authorship
B. Date
C. Addressees
D. Genre Structure, and Style
  1. Genre
  2. Structure
  3. Style
E. The Aim of Hebrews
F. The Christology of Hebrews
  1. The Eternal and Exalted Son
  2. The Suffering Son
  3. The High Priest
  4. The High Priest's Sacrifice
G. The Soteriology of Hebrews
H. The Use of Scripture
I. Hebrews and First-Century Religion
  1. Hebrews and Philo
  2. Hebrews and Qumran
  3. Hebrews and Gnosticism
  4. Hebrews and the New Testament
J. Canonization
K. Conclusion

A. Authorship

Although Hebrews is included in the Pauline corpus and was part of that corpus in its earliest attested form (P^{46}), it is certainly not a work of the apostle. This fact was recognized, largely on stylistic grounds, even in antiquity. Some patristic authors defended the traditional Pauline attribution with theories of scribal assistants such as Clement of Rome or Luke, but such hypotheses do not do justice to the very un-Pauline treatment of key themes, particularly those of law and faith. Numerous alternative candidates for authorship have been proposed. The most prominent have been Barnabas, to whom Tertullian assigned the work; Apollos, defended by Luther and many moderns; Priscilla, suggested by von Harnack; Epaphras; and Silas. Arguments for none are decisive, and Origen's judgment that "God only knows" who composed the work is sound.

B. Date

The latest possible date of composition is provided by the virtual citation of portions of Hebrews in *1 Clement,* conventionally dated to around 95 C.E. The earliest possible date is more difficult to determine. Several data suggest that a date prior to 60 C.E. is most unlikely. The author describes himself as among those who have received the message of salvation at second hand (2:3). His addressees have been believers for a considerable time (5:12). They have previously experienced persecution, reproach, and imprisonment (10:32–34). All of this indicates that some time has elapsed since their initial conversion (6:4).

Within the broad range of the years 60–95 C.E., various conjectures have been made about a more precise dating. References to the Jewish sacrificial cult in the present tense (9:6–10; 10:1–4), along with the lack of any mention of the destruction of the temple, have been taken as evidence of a date prior to 70 C.E., when the Jerusalem temple was destroyed. This argument, however, is inconclusive, since our author is not at all concerned with the Herodian temple. Rather, he deals with the desert tabernacle and argues exegetically from biblical data. Moreover, authors writing after 70 C.E., such as Josephus, Clement of Rome, and the compilers of the Mishnah, often refer to the temple as a present reality.

Attempts have been made to date the work by identifying the persecution mentioned. Thus, if the addressees were in Rome, the references to affliction and material loss (10:32–34), coupled with the remark that the addressees have not yet "resisted unto blood" (12:4), could indicate a date between the expulsion of Jews and Jewish Christians from Rome under Claudius and the bloody persecution under Nero. Yet even if the hypothesis of a Roman destination is accepted, the text could have been aimed at a segment of the community which did not bear the full brunt of Nero's persecution.

Attempts have also been made to date the work on the basis of its position within the development of early Christian doctrine. Unambiguous evidence for post-apostolic, "early Catholic" doctrinal or organizational principles are, however, lacking. Hence only a general time frame, from 60 to 90 C.E. can, with any degree of certainty, be determined as the date for Hebrews.

C. Addressees

The work itself gives no explicit indication of its intended readers. The title "To the Hebrews" is probably a later conjecture. The implication of that title, that the work was addressed to Jewish Christians, has often been defended, but that position is by no means certain. The extensive reliance upon the OT and the elaborate exegetical arguments which characterize the work indicate something about the author's background, but need say little about the addressees. Pauline letters such as Galatians or 1 Corinthians are certainly addressed to predominantly Gentile congregations but make extensive use of the OT and employ subtle exegesis. A major reason for assuming a Jewish-Christian readership is the assessment of the problem which the author addresses, but the judgment that the work is an apology for Christianity designed to prevent a relapse to Judaism is dubious.

The location of the addressees is also problematic. Many ancient and some modern commentators have assumed that the intended recipients were in Jerusalem. Others have argued for Corinth, Asia Minor (particularly the Lycus valley), and Rome. The only relevant internal datum is the final greeting to the addressees by "those from Italy" (13:24). The phrase is commonly taken to mean that Italians living away from home send greetings to their place of origin. The phrase could, however, mean that "those of Italy," i.e., Italians at home, send their greetings someplace else. The former construal is somewhat more natural. Moreover, there are other indications of a connection with Rome, particularly the citation by *1 Clement* and a series of close parallels in theme and vocabulary with 1 Peter which was probably written from Rome (1 Pet 5:13). It is likely then that Hebrews was sent to the Roman Christian community or a segment of it by someone familiar with that community's theological traditions.

D. Genre, Structure, and Style

1. Genre. The literary riddle of Hebrews arises from the fact that it concludes in standard epistolary form (13:22–25) but lacks any epistolary introduction with greetings and indications of sender or recipients. Various attempts to explain this anomaly have been proposed, including the accidental loss or intentional deletion of the prescript or the secondary addition of the conclusion. Either alteration could have been occasioned by a desire to make Hebrews suitable for inclusion in the Pauline letter corpus. Deletion of the prescript could have eliminated embarrassing evidence of non-Pauline authorship. An added conclusion with its reference to a Timothy (13:23) could, on the other hand, have suggested Pauline authorship. Such hypotheses are, however, unconvincing. The elaborately structured rhetorical prologue (1:1–3) makes a suitable beginning to the work, and the casual reference to Timothy is too subtle a device for a pseudepigraphist. If this Timothy is indeed Paul's companion and collaborator, the reference indicates some loose connection between the author and the Pauline circle. The concluding greetings may well be an addition made by the author, in order to render his text suitable as an address to a distant congregation, but suspicions about the integrity of Hebrews, and especially of chap. 13, are unfounded.

In those concluding remarks the work is described as a "word of exhortation" (13:22). This designation aptly describes the bulk of the text and suggests that the most appropriate generic identification is a homily. This homily, with its regular alternation between expository argument and exhortation, includes well-defined segments which probably exemplify homiletic patterns and may be based upon independent sermons. Chaps. 3 and 4 provide a good instance. An introduction (3:1–6) announces the major theme to be treated. A scriptural text from Psalm 95 is cited (3:7–11). Expository comments follow, culminating in an exhortation (3:12–4:11). A rhetorical flourish on God's word rounds off the treatment (4:12–13). Precisely the same pattern is evident in chapters 8–10. An introduction (8:1–6) articulates a basic opposition between the "heavenly" and the "earthly" which will dominate what follows. A lengthy citation of Jer 31:31–34 suggests other important thematic oppositions. The themes enunciated in the introduction and citation are explored and carefully interwoven (9:1–10:10). A concluding flourish triumphantly summarizes the basic affirmation of the sermonette (10:11–18) while recalling the quotation from Jeremiah. In each case the text continues with a formula indicating what the author and addressees "have" (4:14; 10:19–21), which in turn serves as the basis for further hortatory remarks (4:14–16; 10:22–25). Other less well-defined units of scriptural exposition (2:5–18; 7:1–28; 12:1–13) replicate major elements in this homiletic pattern.

2. Structure. Analyzing the overall structure of the text is made difficult by the elaborate foreshadowing and interconnecting devices which the author uses and various proposals highlight one or another of these literary techniques. The following outline attempts to convey some of the work's complexity while suggesting the function of its various segments:

1:1–4: Exordium

I. 1:5–2:18 Christ exalted and humiliated, a suitable High Priest
- A. 1:5–14 Christ exalted above the angels
- B. 2:1–4 Paraenetic interlude: hold fast
- C. 2:5–18 Christ the savior, a faithful and merciful High Priest

II. 3:1–5:10 Christ faithful and merciful
- A. 3:1–4:13 A homily on faith
  - i. 3:1–6 Introduction: the faithful Christ and Moses
  - ii. 3:7–11 Citation of scripture: the faithless generation
  - iii. 3:12–4:11 Exposition
    - a. 3:12–19 The failure of faithlessness
    - b. 4:1–5 The nature of the promised "rest"
    - c. 4:6–11 Faithfully enter the rest "today"
  - iv. 4:12–13 Concluding flourish: God's powerful Word
- B. 4:14–5:10 Christ the merciful High Priest
  - i. 4:14–16 Paraenetic prelude: hold fast and approach
  - ii. 5:1–5 The characteristics of high priests
  - iii. 5:6–10 Christ as High Priest "According to the Order of Melchizedek"

III. 5:11–10:25 The difficult discourse
- A. 5:11–6:20 Paraenetic prelude
  - i. 5:11–6:3 Progress to "maturity"
  - ii. 6:4–12 Warning and consolation
    - a. 6:4–8 The danger of failure
    - b. 6:9–12 Hopeful assurance
  - iii. 6:13–20 God's oath: a sure ground of hope
- B. 7:1–28 Christ and Melchizedek
  - i. 7:1–3 Introduction and scriptural citation
  - ii. 7:4–25 Exposition
    - a. 7:4–10 Melchizedek superior to the Levites
    - b. 7:11–19 The new priest and the new order
    - c. 7:20–25 The priesthood confirmed with an oath
  - iii. 7:26–28 Concluding flourish on the eternal High Priest

- C. 8:1–10:18 An exegetical homily on Christ's sacrificial act
  - i. 8:1–6 Introduction: earthly and heavenly sanctuaries
  - ii. 8:7–13 Citation of scripture: a new, interior covenant
  - iii. 9:1–10:10 Thematic exposition
    - a. 9:1–10 The old, earthly sacrifice
    - b. 9:11–14 The new, heavenly sacrifice
    - c. 9:15–22 The new covenant and its sacrifice
    - d. 9:23–28 The new, heavenly, unique sacrifice
    - e. 10:1–10 The new, earthly-heavenly sacrifice
  - iv. 10:11–18 Concluding flourish on Christ's sacrifice
- D. 10:19–25 Paraenetic application: have faith, hope, and charity

IV. 10:26–12:13 Exhortation to faithful endurance
- A. 10:26–38 Paraenetic prelude
  - i. 10:26–31 A new warning against failure
  - ii. 10:32–38 Recollection of faithful endurance
- B. 11:1–40 An encomium on faith
  - i. 11:1–2 Introductory definition
  - ii. 11:2–7 Faith from creation to Noah
  - iii. 11:8–22 The faith of the patriarchs
    - a. 11:8–12 The faith of Abraham and Sarah
    - b. 11:13–16 Faith's goal: a heavenly home
    - c. 11:17–22 The faith of Isaac, Jacob, and Joseph
  - iv. 11:23–30 The faith of Moses and followers
  - v. 11:31–38 The faith of prophets and martyrs
  - vi. 11:39–40 Summary: faith perfected in Christians
- C. 12:1–13 A homily on faithful endurance
  - i. 12:1–3 Jesus, the inaugurator and perfecter of faith's race
  - ii. 12:4–6 Citation of scripture
  - iii. 12:7–11 Suffering as discipline
  - iv. 12:12–13 Brace for the race

V. 12:14–13:21 Concluding exhortations
- A. 12:14–17 Paraenetic prelude: a final warning against failure
- B. 12:18–29 The serious, but encouraging situation
  - i. 12:18–24 Not Sinai, but a Heavenly Zion
  - ii. 12:25–30 An unshakable kingdom
- C. 13:1–21 The life of the covenant
  - i. 13:1–6 Mutual responsibilities
  - ii. 13:7–19 The implications of Christ's sacrifice

13:20–25 Concluding benediction and greetings

3. Style. Within this carefully structured work the author deploys an abundance of rhetorical fitures, including alliteration (1:1; 2:1–4; 4:16; 10:11, 34; 11:17; 12:21); anaphora (chap. 11); antithesis (7:18–20; 7:23–24; 7:28; 10:11–12); assonance (1:1–3; 6:20; 10:26; 12:90); asyndeton (6:3; 7:26; 12:25); chiasm (2:8–9; 2:18; 4:16; 7:23–24; 10:38–39; 12:19); ellipse (7:19; 12:25); hendiadys (2:21; 5:2; 8:5; 12:18); hyperbaton (12:25); isocolon (1:3; 6:3; 7:26); litotes (4:15; 6:10; 7:20; 9:7); and paronomasia (9:16–18; 13:2). Various metaphors, derived from the standard rhetorical repertoire, grace the discourse. These include images taken from the sphere of education (5:12–14); agriculture (6:7–8; 12:11); seafaring (6:9; cf. 2:1); law (2:3–4; cf. also 6:16; 7:12, 22, 9:16–17); athletics (5:14; 12:1–3, 11–13); and sacrifice (4:12–13). Common rhetorical formulas of citation (2:6) and transition (5:11; 11:32) are used. Inferential particles, "for," "wherefore," "therefore," and "hence," are exceedingly common and lend a veneer of consequential argumentation, although the author operates more on the level of symbolic and verbal association than on that of logic.

The pace of the discourse is modulated, and there is a harmonious balance between lapidary, sometimes sententious phrases (2:16; 3:19; 4:9; 7:19; 9:16; 10:4, 18, 31; 11:1; 12:29; 13:1, 8); series of staccato questions (3:16–18) or exempla (chap. 11); and complex periods (1:1–4; 2:2–4, 8–9, 14–15; 5:7–10; 7:1–3; 9:6–10; 10:19–25; 12:1–2). The author deploys an extensive vocabulary, including a large number of terms (150, excluding proper names) not found elsewhere in the NT and many others (92) which appear in only one other text. Our author avoids monotony in his exhortations, where he alternates between hortatory subjunctives (4:1, 11, 14, 16; 6:1; 10:22–24; 12:1, 28; 13:13, 15) and imperatives (3:12, 13; 10:32, 35; 12:3, 7, 12, 14, 25; 13:1, 2, 3, 7, 9, 6, 17, 18, 24). The general tone of the discourse is similarly variegated, ranging from the solemnity of festive, quasi-poetic passages (4:8–9; 7:11–12; 10:2), to the playfulness of suggestive exegesis (7:9–10; 9:16–17).

E. The Aim of Hebrews

This subtle and elusive text has been construed in a variety of ways. Many of these construals focus on one or another element of the text to the exclusion of others and reconstruct the problem being addressed on the basis of a partial and selective reading of the data. A prominent feature of Hebrews is its frequent comparative arguments which contrast Christ or aspects of the dispensation which he inaugurated to individuals or institutions of the old covenant. Thus Christ as Son is shown to be "better" than the angels (1:5–14), Moses (3:1–6), Aaron (5:1–10), and the Levitical priests (7:1–28). His sacrifice is better than the sacrifices of the old sanctuary (9:1–14) and the covenant which he inaugurated is better than the first (8:7–13; 9:15–22; 12:24). Such comparisons have often been seen as the heart of the work, which would then be construed as a polemical or apologetic tract arguing for the superiority of Christianity to Judaism, its "fleshly ordinances" (7:18; 9:10), and its "diverse and strange teaching" (13:9). The major problem with this construal is that it ignores the parenetic sections of the text which evidence little, if any, concern with the attractions of traditional Judaism. The problem addressed would thus seem to be in inner-Christian one.

The expository sections of Hebrews have been construed to provide evidence for various doctrinal problems. The insistence on a high Christology (1:3; 7:3; 13:8) might suggest that the addressees had too "low" a view of Christ, and an inadequate comprehension of his heavenly, mediatorial role. Yet Hebrews insists quite as strongly on the genuine humanity of Christ (2:6–18; 5:7–8). One could argue with equal plausibility that Hebrews attempts to correct too "high" a Christology. All such attempts to find a doctrinal problem behind Hebrews, which distantly reflect patristic use of Hebrews in Christological controversies, are equally unconvincing and rely on tendentious and one-sided interpretations of the work's doctrinal affirmations.

The same may be said of attempts to see Hebrews dealing with a sacramental problem. There are in the work vague references to baptism (6:4; 10:22) and even more vague allusions to the eucharist (13:10). Despite such meager material, allegorical readings of the discussion of Christ's sacrifice (9:11–10:10) have suggested that the author is advancing an apologetic interpretation of the eucharist. At the same time, the insistence on the unique quality of Christ's sacrifice (7:27; 9:26–28; 10:12) and the metaphorical use of cultic categories (13:15) have been construed as anti-sacramental polemic. These construals, which mirror debates about the Mass in the post-Reformation period, again find little support in the extensive parenetical sections of the work, and these sections must be considered in assessing its overall aims.

The parenetic sections contain a few rather general bits of information about the addressees and a series of interconnected exhortations which suggest what the author, at least, thought their problems to be. It is clear that they had undergone persecution (10:32–34) and likely that similar persecution was continuing or threatening (13:3). A major aim of Hebrews is to strengthen a community of believers in Christ in the face of opposition. This is certainly the major function of the exposition on faith in the final chapters. Faith is closely linked with "endurance" (10:36–39; 12:1–3). The catalogue of those who exemplified this virtue highlights the alienation which they experienced (11:9, 13–16, 26), culminates in a graphic description of the sufferings they endured (11:35–38), and prepares for the final dramatic portrait of Jesus as the martyr who inaugurated and perfected faith by his endurance (12:1–3). On the basis of this strand of Hebrews it might be fair to characterize the work not as the first *adversus Judaeos* tract but as the first exhortation to martyrdom.

Another datum on the addressees provided by the author's parenetic remarks is the notice that some members of the community addressed have withdrawn from fellowship (10:25; cf. 3:12). The extent and precise causes of such disaffection are not indicated, and it may well be that the author was not fully informed about them. Several elements in his parenesis, in addition to the external fact of persecution, suggest influences which may have been at work. The author's insistence on the assurance of a coming judgment (2:2–3; 6:8; 10:25, 29–31; 12:18–24, 26–29) and on the final revelation of Christ's lordship (2:8; 10:13) might indicate a weakening of faith due to the delay of the parousia. If this is indeed part of the perceived problem, it is addressed obliquely and indirectly. Other remarks by the author suggest that he is attempting to deal with a disaffection which has more diffuse roots. He thus refers to a potential neglect of the message of salvation (2:3) and, perhaps with a certain irony, argues that the addressees have through the course of time become sluggish or dull (5:11; 6:12). If such remarks reflect the actual situation of the addressees, a major element of their perceived problem would be the diminishing of the initial ardor of their Christian commitment. Such growing disaffection would be readily comprehensible in a community which had for some time accepted Jesus as the Christ, but was subject to external pressure and the disappointment of their first hopes.

Whatever the precise causes of the problem confronted by the author and whatever his perception of that problem, he is engaged in Hebrews in an attempt to revitalize the faith of his addressees and put their commitment on a more solid footing. To this end he deploys several parenetic devices, both negative and positive. On the one hand he issues a series of severe warnings, illustrating the dire consequences of apostasy (6:4–6; 10:26–31; 12:15–17; cf. 13:19–19; 4:11). These passages, which are regularly balanced by more positive, hopeful sentiments, are not so much condemnation of what has taken place as they are hypothetical sketches of where the community's tendencies could lead.

The more positive exhortations revolve around two related poles. On the one hand the author urges his addressees to "hold on," in particular to their "confession" (3:6, 14; 10:23; cf. 2:1). On the other, he urges movement, an approach either to the ultimately reliable source of support (4:16; 6:18–20; 10:19–22); to a deeper apprehension of their own faith (6:1); or to the "external" realm, where faith will be manifested in suffering (13:13). Characteristic of such faith will be both hope (3:6; 6:11; 7:19; 10:23) and a "boldness of speech" exercised before God and humanity (3:6; 4:16; 10:19, 35).

Although understanding the parenetic program of Hebrews is essential to comprehending the work's aims, the exhortations ought not to be seen in isolation. The author does not simply admonish his addressees and encourage them to a firmer commitment. He also attempts to secure that commitment through a deepened understanding of the person and work of the one who makes faith possible.

F. The Christology of Hebrews

1. The Eternal and Exalted Son. Woven into the first five chapters of Hebrews are several strands of Christological tradition which stand in some tension with one another. These strands probably reflect beliefs of the community addressed and constitute what the author refers to as its "confession" (3:1; 4:14; 10:23), that is, the faith which it professed in a variety of liturgical forms and settings. In the exordium there is a clear statement of a "high" Christology. Christ is affirmed to be the eternal Son, the agent of God's creative and sustaining activity and the final bearer of his word (1:1–4). These affirmations, like other high Christologies of the early Church, utilize imagery of the Wisdom tradition. That derivation is even clearer here than elsewhere in the NT, since the images of "effulgence" and "imprint" (1:3) are ultimately derived from Wis 7:25. Our author is probably not directly dependent on that work, but rather cites a modified form of an early Christian hymn. The forcefully stated high Christology is not confined to the exordium but is reflected at several points in the course of the text (7:3; 13:8). Nonetheless it is not the focal point of the Christology of Hebrews.

Immediately following the exordium stands another, probably traditional block of material with a different Christological perspective. In 1:5–13 is found a catena or florilegium of scriptural citations, the original function of which was probably to celebrate the exaltation of Christ and his "session at the right hand" (Ps 110:1, Heb 1:13). How our author reconciled the eternality of the Son with his eschatological "begetting" (Ps 2:7, Heb 1:5) is unclear. It is likely that he interprets the exaltationist language of the catena in terms of the three-stage Christology of the exordium, but his concern is not to systematize and render coherent such diverse traditions. Rather, his effort is to make all these traditions more vital. As they stand, the Christological statements of the exordium and the catena together highlight the heavenly status of Christ.

2. The Suffering Son. The next block of Christological material (2:10–18) derives from yet other sources. Here Christ is presented as the leader of a new humanity who blazes the way for his brethren, with whom he shares "blood and flesh" (2:14), to the heavenly glory to which God has destined them (2:10). He accomplishes this through undertaking suffering and death, whereby he defeats the satanic forces who control death and make it fearsome (2:10, 14–15). The imagery of combat with the powers of hell and liberation of their captives is rooted in widespread classical myths of heroic deliverers. This imagery was adapted by Hellenistic Jews and appropriated by early Christians. As in the case of the other Christological patterns of the first two chapters, Hebrews will not further exploit the details of this imagery. In the perspective of the whole work this pericope serves to balance the affirmations of the exordium and the catena and to highlight the humanity of Christ. This focus is made clear by the introductory exegesis of Ps 8:5–7 (Heb 2:6–9), which may originally have been part of the traditional catena of chap. 1. Its language of "man" and "Son of man" could have evoked in antiquity, as in the history of exegesis, numerous Christological affirmations. For our author it serves to emphasize that the one who was Son from the first and who is exalted at God's right hand is a human being, whose exalted status results from the fact that he was "for a little while made lower than the angels."

3. The High Priest. At the conclusion of chap. 2 the author introduces a new Christological element. The eternal, exalted Son who suffered is, because of that suffering, a "merciful and faithful high priest" (2:17). This is the first intimation of the Christological category which will dominate the central expository section of Hebrews. As a title for Christ, it is unique to Hebrews among the writings of the NT. It is, however, unlikely that it was invented by the author. Scattered references to Christ as high priest in later Christian literature may attest to a traditional use. In Judaism there was widespread speculation on angelic figures who exercised priestly functions in the heavenly sanctuary. This speculative tradition, which also underlies Philo's elaborate allegories of the high priest and his presentation of the Logos as chief intermediary between God and humankind, was probably adopted in some Christian circles as a way of portraying Christ's role as heavenly intercessor. The title of high priest first deployed in Hebrews 2:17 is probably rooted in such a Christian appropriation of Jewish tradition. The image of Christ as heavenly intercessor (4:16; 7:25) reflects that traditional usage. The author builds his Christological exposition on this basis, but his treatment of Christ's priesthood is not confined to the dimensions of the traditional title.

The next development of the high priest motif (5:5–10) highlights the human suffering and resultant exaltation of Christ. At this point yet another Christological strand is interwoven. Here the author cites another verse from one of the traditional exaltation texts, Ps 110:4, the use of which verse is unattested elsewhere in the NT or in other early Christian literature not dependent on Hebrews. This verse, with its reference to a priesthood "after the order of Melchizedek," forms the basis for the exposition of chap. 7. Its citation here, however, raises the question of when Christ became high priest. The problem is analogous to that of the differing Christological perspectives of chaps. 1 and 2 and is to be resolved in a similar fashion. The author has inherited a tradition of Christ as high priest which focuses on Christ's heavenly status. The citation from Psalm 110 gives expression to that understanding of Christ's priesthood. For the author, however, the decisive priestly act is a very earthly one; hence Christ's priesthood is not confined to heaven. The tradition will undergo modification in the course of the exposition, and that modification begins here (5:7–10) with its graphic portrait of the human Christ at prayer, a portrait inspired not by accounts of the agony in Gethsemane, but by the language of the psalms developed in Hellenistic Jewish circles.

The next stage in the Christological development is the explanation in chap. 7 of what it means to be a high priest "according to the order of Melchizedek." The chapter interprets data from Psalm 110 and the only other scriptural reference to Melchizedek. Gen 14:17–20, and argues that Christ, as a priest of this order, is eternal and hence superior to Levitical priests. Only such an eternal or heavenly priest can provide "perfection" (7:11). The chapter may be influenced by the widespread speculation on the mysterious Melchizedek found in various sources, including Qumran fragments (11QMelch), apocrypha *(2 Enoch)*, Philo, and Gnostic sources (NHC IX,1 *Melchizedek: Pistis Sophia*), but Hebrews is restrained and limited in its use of the figure.

4. The High Priest's Sacrifice. The climax of the Christological development occurs in the complex exposition of the nature of Christ's "once for all self sacrifice" (7:27) which occupies chaps. 8–10. Here the death of Christ, which had often been understood as an atoning sacrifice, is presented as analogous to a specific sacrifice, that of the high priest on Yom Kippur (Day of Atonement). Employing categories which probably derive from popular Platonism used to interpret Jewish cultic institutions, the author presents Christ as effecting real atonement for sin by entering "through the spirit" (9:14) into the realm of the "true" and "heavenly" or ultimately real (8:2; 9:11–12; 9:23–24) where God himself is present. This imagery does not stand uninterpreted but is ultimately taken to be a symbolic expression of the conformity of Christ to God's will (10:5–10). The "heavenly" act is paradoxically, an earthly one, done in a body (10:10), but is heavenly because of its intentionality.

The model of the Yom Kippur ritual is dominant in chaps. 8–10, but it is not the only device used to interpret Christ's sacrificial death. His sacrifice is also seen to be a covenant-inaugurating event (9:15–22), which fulfills the prediction of a new covenant made by Jeremiah (8:7–13; 10:16–17). The value of the victim guarantees the effective forgiveness promised under the covenant (8:12; 9:14; 10:17), while the disposition which makes Christ's sacrifice effective fulfills the promise of a new interior covenant (8:10; 10:10; 10:16). Furthermore, because Christ's death inaugurates a new covenant, it has direct implications for the behavior of members of that covenant who are called upon to follow Christ's exemplary self-sacrifice through their fidelity (12:1–3). Thus the Christological exposition is intimately related to the parenetic program of Hebrews.

G. The Soteriology of Hebrews

No other topic receives as much attention in the expository sections of Hebrews as does Christology. Other elements of early Christian belief are suggestively presented in images derived from the OT as they had been developed in Hellenistic Judaism, apocalyptic literature, and early Christian traditions.

The ultimate result of Christ's work is "salvation" (1:14; 2:3, 10; 5:9; 6:9; 9:28). This consists, negatively, of preservation from the fearful judgment (10:29–31) which will be manifested on the "day" (10:25) when heaven and earth will be removed (1:12; 12:26–28) by the God who is a "consuming fire" (12:29). More positively, salvation is a process of obtaining or inheriting God's "promises" (4:1; 6:17; 9:15; 10:36), which are to be fully realized in the "world to come" (2:5) when Christ's victory is complete (1:13; 2:8; 10:13), but can already be "tasted" now (6:5) in the "time of correction" (9:10). Such a foretaste is experienced in the life of the new covenant, where worshippers have their consciences cleansed (9:14; 10:2), experience "sanctification" (10:10) and thus, at least in a preliminary way, attain "perfection" (10:14). Yet as Christ's own perfection through suffering (5:8–9) was a process which culminated only in his exaltation (2:9), so the perfection of his followers is fully realized only when they too are led to glory (2:10). The nature and the goal of the salvific process find expression in the evocative image of the wandering people of God, aliens and sojourners on earth who seek for a "heavenly homeland" (11:13–16), a heavenly "city" founded by God himself (11:10); 12:22–24). That goal is further described with the image of "rest" (3:11; 4:3–6, 11), a designation derived from biblical accounts of Canaan, but widely interpreted in Jewish texts (*4 Ezra;* Philo) and Christian and Gnostic sources as an image of the heavenly realm or state which is the goal of the saved. The author's exegesis of Psalm 95 (4:3–10) offers a similar interpretation and equates the rest, which believers are promised, with a share in God's own festive sabbatical repose.

H. The Use of Scripture

The text with which the author works is clearly a form of the LXX. This is abundantly clear in the cases where his version differs markedly from the MT, and those differences are due to obvious translation errors or alternative readings attested in the LXX, such as "body" for "ears" in Ps 40:7 (Heb 10:5) or "staff" for "bed" in Gen 47:31 (Heb 11:21). In many cases the OT version cited in Hebrews does not correspond exactly to any extant witness to the LXX. This may be due to loose citation (cf. the varying citations of Jer 31:33–34 at 8:10–12 and 10:16–17), intentional alteration by the author (Ps 21:23 at 2:12 and Ps 95:7–11 at 3:9–10), or an otherwise unattested LXX text. Evidence for use of a Hebrew text is slender at best.

As consideration of Hebrews' Christology and soteriology indicates, the OT and its interpretation play a major role in developing the doctrinal perspectives of the work. The theoretical basis for that importance resides in the estimation of scripture as the word of God (1:1; 4:12–13) or of his holy spirit (3:7; 10:15). As such it has decisive significance for the contemporary listener (3:13; 4:7; 12:5–7). The key to understanding that word is the recognition that the God who spoke through the prophets has spoken eschatologically in his Son (1:2; 2:3). As for most other early Christians, the experience of and belief in Christ is the matrix within which the author's hermeneutic develops. Yet within that general framework, Hebrews displays remarkable boldness, subtlety, and technical sophistication in handling OT passages.

The Christological referent of scripture is clear in the traditional catena of 1:5–13, where common proof texts such as Ps 2:7 and 110:1 are taken not as addresses to an Israelite king but as divine oracles directed at Christ. The same principle underlies the application of the other, less common citations in the catena. A rather different Christological presupposition is evident in the citations from psalms and prophets at 2:12–13 and 10:5–10, where words of scripture are set on the lips of Jesus to give expression to fundamental aspects of his mission. These citations in fact are the only "sayings of Jesus" recorded in Hebrews. While the Jesus of "blood and flesh" (2:14), of the tribe of Judah (7:14), is of prime importance, traditions of his teaching play no explicit role. The conceit used here of attributing OT passages to Christ is not confined to Hebrews, but appears also in synoptic materials, particularly in the passion narratives. There is no explict development of a theory that Christ himself inspired the writers of the OT or that he spoke through them. Such theories, found in the second century, are rooted in elements of texts such as Hebrews, with its pre-existence Christology and attribution of OT texts to Christ.

Application of OT passages to Christ or to the contemporary situation usually involves taking them out of their original literary or historical contexts and construing them within a framework of the author's own devising (Ps 8:5–7 at 2:6–8; Ps 110:4 at 7:21; Ps 40:7–9 at 10:5–7). Yet occasionally the assumed original context plays a part in interpretation (3:7; 7:10).

Many texts are simply cited and given an interpretation from their new context in this discourse. For others, the author pays special attention to the vocabulary and syntax of the passage and argues exegetically. Thus in treating Ps 8:5–7, he exploits ambiguity to find a new referent for the "man" involved (2:8–9). In explicating the meaning of "rest" in Psalm 95, he employs the technique of "inference by analogy," utilizing Gen 2:2 (Heb 4:4–5); the argument, incidentally, works only on the basis of the Greek texts. In indicating the significance of Ps 110:4 and its references to Melchizedek, he again argues through appeal to another text (Gen 14:17–20) which is initially explicated both through etymology (7:2b, 3a) and through an argument from silence (7:3b). Comparative and a fortiori arguments are common (1:4; 2:2–3; 7:22; 8:6; 9:14; 12:9–11). An important exegetical device is the discovery and resolution of oppositions either in scriptural texts or implied by them. Thus the promise of a new priesthood after the order of Melchizedek implies the rejection of the Levitical priesthood and its laws (7:11–12). The antithesis between eternal sacrifice and interior conformity to God's will is evident in Ps 40:7–9, and the enunciation of the latter is taken to be a principle which abrogates the former (10:8–9). The complex exposition of Jeremiah 31 in chaps. 8–10 is based in part on the oppositions between new and old, interior and external suggested by the citation from the prophet.

In addition to explicit citations of and exegetical arguments from scriptural texts, Hebrews frequently makes allusive use of scripture. This is most obvious in the case of Psalm 110, which surfaces throughout the text (1:13; 5:6; 8:1; 10:12; 12:2). The lengthy encomium on faith (chap. 11) has few actual citations but is throughout based on OT narratives and their legendary elaborations. The word of exhortation which is Hebrews is above all an attempt to make the word of God "living, active, and sharper than any two-edged sword" (4:12).

I. Hebrews and First-Century Religion

Numerous attempts have been made to understand Hebrews and its peculiar conceptuality on the basis of its affinities with various religious traditions, particularly within Judaism. The author has been seen as a disciple or opponent of Philo and the sort of sophisticated Hellenistic Judaism which he represents, as a thoroughgoing apocalyptist, and as an interpreter utilizing gnostic patterns of thought to make Christianity comprehensible in a Hellenistic environment. Each of these appraisals can find evidence within the discourse which points in the appropriate direction. None, however, provides a satisfactory overall evaluation of Hebrews.

1. Hebrews and Philo. Hebrews does share with Philo not only his Greek Bible but also a number of exegetical concerns, perspectives, and traditions. Most interesting and least noticed of these commonalities is the way in which the author uses cultic images to symbolize both ontological and psychological elements (chaps. 8–10). Another telling indication of affinity with Philo are certain halachic or legal positions, mentioned only in passing in Hebrews. Such, for example, is the remark that the high priest must offer daily sacrifice for himself and the people (7:27; cf. Philo, *Spec Leg* 1.131). Insofar as philosophical presuppositions affect the argument of Hebrews, here too the author displays some affinities with Philo and his Platonic interpretation of Judaism. Hebrews, however, is at most a distant cousin of Philo. The philosophical elements of this text are much more superficial and unsystematic than anything in Philo. In his handling of Scripture, the author of Hebrews does not represent the same degree of consistent and complex allegorization found in Philo. He does not try to develop, nor does he presuppose, the same elaborate theology or anthropology as does the Jewish philosopher and exegete. What most distinguishes him from Philo is the seriousness with which he treats eschatology, a subject which Philo generally avoids.

2. Hebrews and Qumran. The eschatological dimensions of Hebrews have often been taken as evidence of a relationship between the author and Jewish apocalyptists, especially the Essenes of Qumran. Other elements in his discourse point in this direction, including the eschatological presuppositions of some of his exegesis of the OT (1:2) and his priestly Messianism, which has some remote parallels in the doctrine of the two Messiahs at Qumran (1QS 9:11; 1QSa 2:12–15). Yet here again the parallels are often superficial. Hebrews' hermeneutics cannot simply be reduced to a Christianized version of the Qumran pesher, nor is the text's Christology merely a unified and baptized version of the expectation of the two Messiahs. Its roots are more complex and its elaboration more subtle. While Hebrews does maintain a lively eschatological expectation, it differs from that of Jewish apocalypticism in general and Qumran literature in particular in several important respects. Like most early Christians, the author understands the decisive eschatological event to have occurred already in the death and exaltation of Christ. As a result of that event salvation is understood not only as a future reality with cosmic or political dimensions, but as a process under way in the present as Christians, through faith, hope, and charity (10:22–24), follow the "new and living way" to God's presence opened by Christ (10:19–21). The primary implications of this eschatology are a life of prayer, service, and suffering in an alien world (13:13–16), rather than anxious withdrawal in expectation of final vindication.

3. Hebrews and Gnosticism. There are obvious dualisms in the work, an eschatological dualism of the two ages (2:5; 6:5) and the more metaphysical dualism of flesh and spirit (7:16; 9:9–10) which is connected with the dualism of earth and heaven (8:5; 9:11; 11:13–16). Such sharp contrasts have been taken as evidence of the author's gnostic background. To do so is to construe Gnosticism in far too broad a sense. In such passages the author displays his acceptance of various common elements of 1st-century Jewish and Christian cosmology. He is not, however, radically anti-cosmic in his perspectives as is classical Gnosticism. Neither does his Christology, even at its most mythic (2:10–16), have gnostic roots. What affinities there are between Hebrews and Gnosticism result from their common heritage in the Hellenistic Judaism of the 1st century.

Attempts to anchor the author of Hebrews in one or another strand of 1st-century religious history are generally unsatisfactory because they fail to recognize that the work is fundamentally the product of a Jewish-Christian rhetor, an individual who draws freely on a broad spectrum of legends, theological and philosophical patterns, scriptural interpretations, liturgical formulas, and oratorical commonplaces. He reshapes many of these and combines them in an imaginative way, not in order to effect a new systematic synthesis on any doctrinal issue, nor to reproduce in Christian terms the conceptual scheme of another religious tradition, but to affect the heart and will of his addressees.

4. Hebrews and the New Testament. This homilist displays affinities with many of his Christian contemporaries, but as he is not simply a representative of some general religious tradition, neither is he easily classified within the spectrum of the 1st-century Church. We have noted a possible indication of relationship with the Pauline circle, but the author is hardly a member of a Pauline "school" as were the authors of Ephesians, Colossians, or the Pastoral Epistles. Unlike those texts, there is no appeal in Hebrews, either explicitly or through the device of pseudepigraphy, to the authority of the Apostle to the gentiles. Nor is there any intellectual indebtedness. The priestly Christology of Hebrews is quite different from anything in Paul. Like Paul, our author criticizes the Law (7:16–19), but on quite different grounds. For Paul the Law is either temporally limited (Gal 3:15–29) or an instrument of sin (Rom 6:20). For Hebrews the Law, conceived primarily in cultic terms, is simply ineffective. Like Paul, our author requires faith in order to attain salvation, but faith is not, as in Paul, the acceptance of God's gracious gift of righteousness (Rom 3:21–31) attained through the "faith of Jesus Christ" (Gal 2:16), but the hopeful fidelity which enables those who "participate in a heavenly calling" (3:1) to endure as Christ did (12:1–3). While faith in Hebrews has a Christological content expressed in the maintenance of the "confession," it is, more clearly than in Paul, an imitation of the faith imputed to Christ himself. If the author of Hebrews is indeed in the Pauline circle, he is a very independent member of that circle.

There are parallels between Hebrews and certain deutero-Pauline texts. The author of Colossians addressed a community in which some ill-defined objectionable belief or practice involving angels was at work (Col 2:18). Many scholars have found a similar problem behind the argument about Christ's superiority to angels in chap. 1 of Hebrews. Yet nothing in the hortatory portions of Hebrews suggests a problem of this sort in the community addressed. The argument of the first chapter is best understood as an expansion of the common imagery of Christ's exaltation, designed to highlight his heavenly status.

With Johannine Christianity Hebrews shares only the most general features. Attempts have been made to find the sources of Hebrews' Christology in the Fourth Gospel's overall conception of Christ as the mysterious revealer is far removed from Hebrews' high priest.

Many of the closest links to any other NT document are found in 1 Peter, another message of "exhortation" (5:12). Its Christology also combines traditions of the exaltation based on Psalm 110 (3:22) with an understanding of Christ's death as an atoning sacrifice (1:2, 19; 2:12–15) which cleanses conscience (3:16) and provides access to God (3:18). Hebrews (13:20) and 1 Peter (2:25; 5:5) also share the image of Christ as shepherd. The soteriological framework is also similar. Salvation for 1 Peter is the eschatological (4:7) attainment of a promised heavenly inheritance (1:4–5) which involves the glorification (1:11; 4:13; 5:4) of Christians. That glorification is to be attained through faithful endurance (1:6–9; 2:20), sharing the sufferings of Christ (4:13) and bearing the reproach of being Christian (4:14; Heb 11:26). The life of faith is also seen to involve many of the same particular virtues represented in Hebrews, including hospitality (4:9; Heb 13:2) and submission to authority (5:5; Heb 13:7, 17). Further parallels could be cited, but these suffice to show the extensive common tradition shared by both texts. While Hebrews is distinctive within the NT, it is clearly rooted in Christian traditions and in particular the traditions at home in the Roman community.

J. Canonization

Hebrews was accepted as Pauline in the Greek east, particularly among the Alexandrians (Pantaenus, Clement of Alexandria, and Eusebius) from the 2d century on. In the west, doubts about Pauline authorship, expressed by Tertullian, Hippolytus, and Irenaeus, contributed to a general neglect of the text in the first three centuries, and it is not mentioned in the Canon Muratori. By the end of the 4th century, however, the Pauline authorship and authoritative, canonical status of Hebrews became generally recognized in both east (Athanasius) and west (Lucifer of Cagliari, Prisicllian, and Ambrose). Jerome and Augustine both recognized that there had been doubts about the status and authorship of the text in the west; but primarily on the authority of the eastern tradition, they acknowledged Pauline authorship and accepted Hebrews as authoritative. That status remained unchallenged until the Reformation, when doubts were again expressed about Pauline authorship by Erasmus, Luther, and Calvin, but by that time the canonical status of the work was secure.

K. Conclusion

Despite its many enigmas and idiosyncrasies and a conceptuality and style of argument which is quite foreign to modern sensibilities, Hebrews is an elegant, sophisticated, and indeed powerful presentation of the Christian message. It is perhaps the most self-consciously rhetorical discourse of the NT and its unknown author one of the most imaginative figures of the early Church.

Bibliography

Commentaries on Hebrews are listed in:

Attridge, H. W. 1988. *Hebrews.* Hermeneia. Philadelphia.

The following works are special studies:

Cody, A. 1960. *Heavenly Sanctuary and Liturgy in the Epistle to the Hebrews.* St. Meinrad, IN.

Demarest, B. 1976. *A History of Interpretation of Hebrews VII, 1–10 from the Reformation to the Present.* BGBE 19. Tübingen.

Dey, L. K. K. 1975. *The Intermediary World and Patterns of Perfection in Philo and Hebrews.* SBLDS 25. Missoula, MT.

Feld, H. 1985. *Der Hebräerbrief.* Beiträge der Forschung. Darmstadt.

Filson, F. V. 1967. *"Yesterday": A Study of Hebrews in the Light of Chapter 13.* SBT 4. Naperville, IL.

Grässer, E. 1965. *Der Glaube im Hebräerbrief.* Marburg.

Greer, R. A. 1973. *The Captain of our Salvation: A Study in Patristic Exegesis of Hebrews.* BGBE 15. Tübingen.

Hagen, K. 1981. *Hebrews Commenting from Erasmus to Beza 1516–1598.* BGBE 23. Tübingen.

Hay, D. M. 1973. *Glory at the Right Hand: Psalm 110 in Early Christianity.* SBLMS 18. Nashville.

Hofius, O. 1970. *Katapausis: Die Vorstellung vom endzeitlichen Ruheort im Hebräerbrief.* WUNT 11. Tübingen.

———. 1972. *Der Vorhang vor dem Thron Gottes.* WUNT 14. Tübingen.

Horton, F. L. 1976. *The Melchizedek Tradition.* SNTSMS 30. Cambridge.

Hughes, G. 1979. *Hebrews and Hermeneutics.* SNTSMS 36. Cambridge.

Käsemann, E. 1984. *The Wandering People of God,* trans. R. A. Harrisville and I. L. Sandberg. Minneapolis.

Kobelski, P. J. 1981. *Melchizedek and Melchireša*ʿ. CBQMS 10. Washington, DC.
Laub, F. 1980. *Bekenntnis und Auslegung.* BU 15. Regensburg.
Loader, W. R. G. 1981. *Sohn und Hoherpriester.* WMANT 53. Neukirchen.
Peterson, D. 1982. *Hebrews and Perfection.* SNTSMS 47. Cambridge.
Schierse, F.-J. 1955. *Verheißung und Heilsvollendung.* Munich.
Schröger, F. 1968. *Der Verfasser des Hebräerbriefes als Schriftausleger.* BU 4. Regensburg.
Swetnam, J. 1981. *Jesus and Isaac: A Study of the Epistle to the Hebrews in the Light of the Aqedah.* AnBib 94. Rome.
Theissen, G. 1969. *Untersuchungen zum Hebräerbrief.* SNT 2. Gütersloh.
Thompson, J. W. 1982. *The Beginnings of Christian Philosophy.* CBQMS 13. Washington, DC.
Thurén, J. 1973. *Das Lobopfer der Hebraäer.* AAAbo ser. A, vol. 47, no. 1; Åbo.
Vanhoye, A. 1969. *Situation du Christ: épître aux Hébreux 1–2.* LD 58. Paris.
———. 1976. *La structure litteraire de l'Épître aux Hébreux.* StudNeot 1. 2d ed. Paris.
Williamson, R. 1970. *Philo and the Epistle to the Hebrews.* ALGHJ 4. Leiden.
Zimmermann, H. 1977. *Das Bekenntnis der Hoffnung.* BBB 47. Cologne.

HAROLD W. ATTRIDGE

HEBREWS, GOSPEL OF THE. The title ascribed in antiquity to at least one and probably two Jewish-Christian narrative gospels that are extant in fragmentary form in a few quotations preserved in early church writings. Because of the scantiness of the citations and the uncertainty of their patristic source attributions, assessing these fragments is one of the most vexing problems in the study of early Christian literature. Determining the precise number of these gospels, identifying which fragments may plausibly belong to which text(s), appraising the nature and extent of those texts, and establishing the relationship of one gospel to another are extremely problematic tasks that continue to challenge scholars.

Jerome has preserved the most numerous references to and apparent quotations of *Gos. Heb.* In a series of writings that date from 386–415 C.E., he repeatedly maintained the view that there was only one Jewish-Christian gospel in existence, assigning all quotations known to him to this one document. When referring to this document Jerome regularly used variants of the title *Gos. Heb.,* which he regarded as the original "Hebrew" or Aramaic Gospel of Matthew. However, critical scholarship has determined that Jerome almost certainly never saw an actual copy of this document but most likely knew of its existence from citations he had taken from other early Christian writers. Moreover, it is quite certain that Jerome never translated such a gospel into Greek and Latin, as he avers, for he misquotes certain texts that he allegedly had translated and assigns to this gospel several pericopes whose wording and construction are manifestly impossible in a Semitic language. Thus, in spite of himself, Jerome attests to the existence both of a Greek *Gos. Heb.* and another Jewish-Christian gospel, one which appears to be closely related to or identical with an expanded version of Matthew's Gospel that was translated from Greek into Aramaic or Syriac. This expanded version of Matthew is customarily referred to today as the *Gospel of the Nazoreans,* a document whose original title is unknown but which seems to have been used since the 2d century C.E. by the Nazoreans, a group of Jewish Christians in W Syria. Although it is extremely difficult to identify with confidence which patristic quotations may belong to which gospel, it is not possible to assign all of the extant quotations to only one text. In fact there can be no doubt that another, completely different Jewish-Christian gospel was in circulation in the early Church, for Epiphanius (late in the 4th century) has preserved a few quotations of the so-called *Gospel of the Ebionites,* a harmony, composed in Greek, of the Gospels of Matthew and Luke (and, probably, the Gospel of Mark as well). Therefore, the testimony of Jerome notwithstanding, there were at least two and most likely three Jewish-Christian narrative gospels in antiquity, one of which was composed in Greek and entitled *Gos. Heb.*

Although the existence of *Gos. Heb.* is not in question, identifying its fragments and appraising its character remains difficult. In quoting the sources of this gospel, early Church writers repeatedly cited those texts incorrectly, attributed quotations to the wrong gospels, and interpreted what they did record in a biased manner. Jerome, for example, only exacerbates the confusion when he introduces a quotation that he alone has preserved as follows: "In the Gospel which the Nazoreans and Ebionites use, which we have recently translated from Hebrew into Greek, and which is called by most people the original (Gospel) of Matthew . . ." (*Comm. in Matt.* 2). Mistakes such as this have led to countless difficulties in our attempts to isolate and verify the gospel(s) in which these fragments belong. Nevertheless, if one distinguishes the fragments on the basis of their original language of composition, their form and content, their relationship to the gospels of the NT, and the groups said to have used a particular gospel, one can reconstruct a number of sayings and stories which may plausibly be ascribed to *Gos. Heb.* The discussion that follows is based on such a reconstruction, though it must remain tentative pending the discovery of new manuscripts.

Gos. Heb. is a syncretistic, Jewish-Christian document, composed in Greek, which presents traditions of Jesus' preexistence and coming into the world, his baptism and temptation, some of his sayings, and a resurrection appearance to his brother, James the Just. This is the Jewish-Christian gospel most frequently mentioned by name in the early Church; it is also the only one whose original title has been transmitted from antiquity. The title seems to indicate the identity of the group who used this gospel, and suggests that this was the gospel of predominantly Greek-speaking Jewish Christians. *Gos. Heb.* appears to have no connection with the so-called *Gospel of the Nazoreans* or *Gospel of the Ebionites,* for it displays no kinship with the Gospel of Matthew. It is instructive to note that the earliest and most important witnesses to the text of *Gos. Heb.* come from quotations in the writings of persons who lived in Alexandria, Egypt.

Although Eusebius (early in the 4th century) reports that Papias of Hierapolis (ca. 100–150 C.E.) expounded a story contained in *Gos. Heb.* (*Hist. Eccl.* 3.39.17), the absence of any citations of *Gos. Heb.* in the extant writings of Papias does not permit this reference to be used as a witness to the existence of the text. The first certain attestation of *Gos. Heb.* by name is documented in the late 2d century by Hegesippus (Eus. *Hist. Eccl.* 4.22.8), whose extracts from the text are no longer preserved. Eusebius lists this gospel among the "spurious" writings rejected by some members of the Church (*Hist. Eccl.* 3.25.5), though he does not quote from the text. If the reference to a *Gos. Heb.* in the recently discovered *Commentary on the Psalms* by Didymus the Blind (in the mid to late 4th century) can be properly assigned to our text and not to some other Jewish-Christian gospel, then Didymus provides additional testimony of an acquaintance with this gospel in Alexandrian circles. Fragmentary quotations are preserved in the writings of Clement of Alexandria (late in the 2d century), Origen (early in the 3d century), and, apparently, Cyril of Jerusalem (in the mid 3d century). Jerome (ca. 400 C.E.) also preserves several fragments, most if not all of which he probably reproduced from the writings of Origen. The extent of *Gos. Heb.* is no longer known. According to the list of "canonical" and "apocryphal" books drawn up by Nicephorus (Patriarch of Constantinople, 806–818 C.E.), *Gos. Heb.* contained 2200 lines, only 300 fewer than Matthew.

The report of a resurrection appearance of Jesus to his brother, James the Just (Jerome *De vir. inl.* 2), indicates the position of authority assigned to James in *Gos. Heb.* James was regarded as a leading figure of the Jewish-Christian church in Jerusalem (Gal 1:19; 2:9, 12; Acts 12:17; 15:13; 21:18), one of those named in Paul's list of persons accredited for having seen a vision of the risen Jesus (1 Cor 15:7). According to the account in *Gos. Heb.*, James was the first witness of the resurrection and thus its principal guarantor. He is so distinguished that he is said even to have taken part in the Last Supper of Jesus. The esteem in which James is held in this gospel may be used to locate the authority and secure the identity of the tradition of those communities which appealed to him as their leader.

The accounts of Jesus' preexistence and coming (Cyr. H. *Discourse on Mary Theotokos* 12a), baptism (Jerome *Comm. in Isa.* 4), and temptation (Origen *Jo.* 2.12.87) are abbreviated mythological narratives. They presuppose a myth of the descent of divine Wisdom, embodying herself definitively in a representative of the human race for the revelation and redemption of humankind (Sir 24:7; Wis 7:27). If it is proper to correlate those narratives with the most prominent saying in *Gos. Heb.* (Clem. *str.* 2.9.45.5; 5.14.96.3), then this gospel announces that Wisdom's "rest" can be found in Jesus and attained by those who seek her (Sir 6:28; 51:27; Wis 8:16). The fact that a variant of this saying is also preserved in the *Gospel of Thomas* (saying 2) indicates that it was a tradition at home in Egypt as well as in Syria. The other two sayings ascribed to *Gos. Heb.* (Jerome *Comm. in Eph.* 3; *Comm. in Ezek.* 6) permit the suggestion that a majority of the sayings in this gospel had the same parenetic character as those in the synoptic gospels.

The extant fragments of *Gos. Heb.* display no dependence on the NT or other early Christian literature. Unfortunately there is no way to determine the (in)dependent status of those portions of the text that are no longer preserved. The earliest possible date of the composition of *Gos. Heb.* would be in the middle of the 1st century, when sayings of and stories about Jesus began to be produced and collected in written form. The latest possible date would be the middle of the 2d century, shortly before the first recorded reference to this gospel by Hegesippus and attested quotations of it by Clement and Origen. Based on the parallels in the morphology of the tradition, an earlier date of composition seems more likely than a later one. Identifying the provenance of *Gos. Heb.* is difficult, though external attestations make Egypt an attractive option. For further discussion see *ANRW* 2/25/5: 3997–4033.

Bibliography

Cameron, R. 1982. The Gospel of the Hebrews. Pp. 83–86 in *The Other Gospels*, ed. R. Cameron. Philadelphia.

Funk, R. W. 1985. Gospel of the Hebrews. Vol. 2, pp. 372–77 in *New Gospel Parallels*, ed. R. W. Funk. Philadelphia.

Harnack, A. 1958. Das Hebräer- und das Ebionitenevangelium. Pp. 625–51 in *Die Chronologie der Literatur bis Irenäs nebst einleitenden Untersuchungen*. Vol. 2, pt. 1 of *Geschichte der altchristlichen Literature bis Eusebius*, 2d ed. Leipzig.

Klijn, A. F. J., and Reinink, G. J. 1973. *Patristic Evidence for Jewish-Christian Sects*. NovTSup 36. Leiden.

Klostermann, E. 1929. Hebräerevangelium (Nazaräerevangelium). Pp. 5–10 and 12 in *Apocrypha II: Evangelien*, 3d ed., ed. H. Lietzmann. Kleine Texte für Vorlesungen und Übungen 8. Berlin.

Lührmann, D. 1987. Das Bruchstück aus dem Hebräerevangelium bei Didymos von Alexandrien. *NovT* 29: 265–79.

Preuschen, E. 1905. Reste des Hebräerevangeliums. Pp. 4–5 and 8–9 in *Antilegomena: Die Reste der ausserkanonischen Evangelien und urchristlichen Überlieferungen*. 2d ed. Giessen.

Santos Otero, A. de. 1985. Evangelio de los Hebreos. Pp. xv, 29–42, and 45 in *Los Evangelios apócrifos*. 5th ed. Madrid.

Schmidtke, A. 1911. *Neue Fragmente und Untersuchungen zu den judenchristlichen Evangelien*. TU 37/1. Leipzig.

Vielhauer, P. 1963. Jewish-Christian Gospels. *NTApocr* 1: 117–65.

Vielhauer, P., and Strecker, G. 1987. Judenchristliche Evangelien. Vol. 1, pp. 114–47 in *Neutestamentliche Apokryphen in deutscher Übersetzung*, ed. W. Schneemelcher. 5th ed. Tübingen.

Waitz, H. 1937. Neue Untersuchungen über die sogenannten judenchristlichen Evangelien. *ZNW* 36: 60–81.

Ron Cameron

HEBRON (PERSON) [Heb *ḥebrôn*]. HEBRONITE. Of the seventy-two references to "Hebron" in the OT (there are none in the NT) and one in the Apocrypha (1 Macc 5:65), nine refer to a person rather than a place. The related patronymic "Hebronite(s)" [Heb *ḥebrônî*] appears six times.

1. The third son of Kohath and grandson of Levi (Exod 6:18; Num 3:19; 1 Chr 5:28,6:3—Eng 6:2,18; 1 Chr 23:12. Hebron was the brother of Amram, Izhar, and Uzziel, and the uncle of Moses, Aaron, and Miriam. Hebron's son Eliel, with eighty of his brethren, is numbered among the levitical families summoned by David to arrange for the transfer of the ark to Jerusalem (1 Chr 15:9). Four Hebronite family heads, of which Jeriah was chief, appear in the series of chapters in Chronicles (1 Chronicles 23–27) which ascribe to David's ingenuity the levitical patterns in place in the postexilic period (1 Chr 23:19; 24:23; 26:31). There it is reported how the Hebronites Hashabiah and his brethren were given the oversight of Israel west of the Jordan "for all the work of the Lord and for the service of the king" (1 Chr 26:30). In David's last year as king a search was presumably conducted to find more Hebronites, and a sizable number were found in the levitical city of Jazer in Gilead (Josh 21:39; 1 Chr 6:66—Eng 6:81; 26:31; 29:27). David is said to have appointed Jerijah (variant of Jeriah above) and his number to have supervision over the tribes settled in Transjordan "for everything pertaining to God and for the affairs of the king" (1 Chr 26:32). Especially noteworthy here is the Chronicler's witness to a broader definition of and function of Kohathite Levites than the usual more sacral activities performed within the temple complex.

2. A Judahite, the son of Mareshah and grandson of Caleb (1 Chr 2:42 RSV). This manner of entry presupposes the adoption by the RSV of the textual emendation "Mareshah" [Heb *mārēšâ*] supplied from the second half of the verse, with the LXX *[marisa],* in place of the name "Mesha" *[mêšāʿ]* in the MT, which reads literally: "And the sons of Caleb, the brother of Jerahmeel, were Mesha his firstborn—he was the father of Ziph—and the sons of Mareshah, the father of Hebron." The phrase "the father of" may actually refer to the founding of the cities Ziph and Hebron, as the NEB so interprets it (cf. also the use of the same phrase with respect to Ashhur, Shobal, Salma, and Hareph in the same context in 1 Chr 2:24; 2:50–52). There was indeed a nearby city by the name of Ziph (Josh 15:55), and the link between Caleb and the city of Hebron is well attested (Josh 14:13; 15:13; Judg 1:20). However, the "Hebron" in the very next verse (1 Chr 2:43) who is ascribed four sons (Korah, Tappuah, Rekem, and Shema) appears to be a person. Still another reconstruction of the text of 1 Chr 2:42 has been to make Caleb the father of "Mesha his firstborn son who was the father of Ziph whose son was Mareshah the father of Hebron" (Myers *1 Chronicles* AB, 11). By this more conjectural reconstruction, Hebron, while still the son of Mareshah, becomes the grandson of Ziph and the great-great-grandson of Caleb.

Roger W. Uitti

HEBRON (PLACE) [Heb *ḥebrôn*]. An important city located on the crest (ca. 3350 ft. elev.) of the Judean mountain ridge ca. 19 mi. SSE of Jerusalem and ca. 23 mi. NE of Beer-sheba.

The ancient site (M.R. 159103) is strategically located on Jebel er-Rumeidah near where two routes coming from the Shephelah in the W, one via Lachish up the Adoraim ridge, and another following the Nahal Guvrin and ascending a ridge, intersect with the main N-S ridge route connecting Jerusalem and points N with Beer-sheba in the S. Another route leaves Hebron to the SE passing Carmel and Maon and then descending to Arad, the administrative center in the W Negeb.

The Canaanite city, which was built seven years prior to the establishment of Zoan (Gk. Tanis) in Egypt (Num 13:22), is also called Kiriath-arba (Gen 23:2, etc.) possibly after a notable ancestor of the Anakim (Josh 14:15; 15:13). Another suggested etymology assumes four villages connected with the city, hence, "City-of-Four" (Heb *ʾarba,* "four") (see Josh 15:54; 2 Sam 2:3). Kiriath-Arba was both the earlier as well as a later name for Hebron (see Neh 11:25).

Abraham lived in the vicinity for some time and eventually purchased a cave at Machpelah in the valley below in order to bury Sarah (Genesis 23). Later Abraham himself was buried there in the cave (Gen 25:9–10), as was Isaac (Gen 35:27–29).

Hebron was one of the cities which the twelve Israelites spies reconnoitered in Num 13:22. The biblical narrative indicates that the area just to the N of Hebron, the valley of Eshcol, was extraordinarily lush and fertile. Later, Hebron, under the leadership of king Hoham, joined a coalition of Amorite cities from the Shephelah and hill country headed by Adonizedek, king of Jerusalem. This coalition was formed against the Gibeonites, who had entered into an alliance with Israel after the fall of Ai (Josh 9–10). Under siege, the people of Gibeon invoked their treaty with Joshua and in response Israel marched all night, 3360 ft., up from Gilgal (Khirbet el-Mafjar?), surprising this Amorite coalition and routing them down the other side of the mountain by way of Beth Horon to the valley of Aijalon and beyond. In the aftermath of the battle of Aijalon, Hebron was conquered by Joshua (10:36–37). Joshua then deeded the city to his fellow veteran spy, Caleb (Josh 14:13). However, the city was later assigned to the Kohathites, who were Aaronic priests, as a levitical city (21:11–13) and designated a city of refuge (20:7; 21:13).

During Saul's reign, the people of Hebron were sympathetic toward David, who had cultivated a relationship with them (1 Sam 30:26–31). After Saul's death, the Lord instructed David to establish his rule in Hebron (2 Sam 2:1ff) where David reigned as king of Judah for seven and a half years (2:11; 5:5). By the end of that period David had proven his ability to consolidate the twelve tribes behind him. As a result the people of the northern tribes came to David at Hebron along with their tribal elders, and David was anointed king over all twelve of the tribes (5:1–4; 1 Chr 11:1–3). After this, David moved his capital to a more "neutral" site on the border of Benjamin: Jerusalem, a city which he had captured from the Jebusites and therefore called "the city of David" (5:7–12; 1 Chr 11:4–9).

Some years later, David's rebellious son Absalom established his base at Hebron and from there attempted a coup d'état and claimed the throne (2 Samuel 15).

The strategic location of Hebron is indicated yet again in 2 Chr 11:5–12, which reports that Rehoboam, concerned with protecting the southern flank, fortified a number of cities to the S and W of Jerusalem, including the administrative center, Hebron.

After the fall of Jerusalem to Nebuchadnezzar in 586 B.C., the Edomites (or Idumeans) extended their control almost to Beth-Zur, some 5 miles N of Hebron (1 Macc 24:33). After the return from Exile in Babylon, Jews moved back into many of the towns of Judah, then a Persian province, as well as Hebron and other towns in Idumea (Neh 11:25). By the end of the second century B.C. the Hasmoneans had conquered Idumea, including Hebron (1 Macc 5:65), and Judaized it (Josephus, *Ant* 13.257–

58) and named Antipater, who would be Herod the Great's grandfather, as governor.

On recommendation from Mark Antony, the Roman senate named the Idumean, Herod, "king of the Jews." Herod the Great (37–4 B.C.) built the beautiful enclosure which surrounds the cave of Machpelah to this day. This enclosure, or "haram," as it is called in Arabic, is of special interest because its architectural features, such as its large ashlar masonry (the largest stone is more than 24 ft long) and its pilasters, as well as its architectural proportions are almost identical to Herod's "haram" at the Temple Mount in Jerusalem (Vincent and Mackay 1923). The church structure on the "haram" over the caves was built during the Byzantine period.

Bibliography

Jacobson, D. M. 1981. The Plan of the Ancient Haram el-Khalil in Hebron. *PEQ* 113: 73–80.

Vincent, L.-H., and Mackay, E. J. H. 1923. *Hebron—Le Haram el-Khalil—Sépulture des Patriarches.* Paris.

PAUL WAYNE FERRIS JR.

HECATAEUS, PSEUDO-. The designation used to refer to one or more Jewish authors who are thought to have written pseudepigraphs attributed to the pagan author Hecataeus of Abdera.

Hecataeus of Abdera was a Hellenistic ethnographic historian who flourished around the time of Ptolemy I Soter (ca. 300 B.C.E.). He is credited with having written the grammatical work *On the Poetry of Homer and Hesiod,* as well as two ethnographic works, *On the Hyperboreans,* and *On the Egyptians.* Substantial portions of this last work are preserved in Diodorus Siculus' *World History* (Book 1). In other sections preserved by Diodorus (Book 40), Hecataeus treats various aspects of Jewish history and culture, including the emigration from Egypt and certain features of the Mosaic law. The treatment is remarkably accurate and generally positive in its assessment. It is also notable for containing the first documented reference to Moses in pagan literature.

It is widely believed that this material treating the Jews is from the hand of the pagan author Hecataeus. The major point of dispute has been whether it should be attributed to an earlier pagan author, the geographer Hecataeus of Miletus (ca. 500 B.C.E.), a position favored by Photius (9th century). This view, however, has not won acceptance, and consequently this material is reliably attributed to Hecataeus of Abdera.

In addition to these passages, however, there are other passages treating Jewish topics that are also attributed to Hecataeus but whose authenticity is disputed. Essentially, two such works are mentioned in ancient sources: *On the Jews* and *On Abraham (and the Egyptians).* Whether these were formal titles of the works or merely phrases describing their contents is not clear; probably the former.

A work devoted exclusively to the Jews, perhaps entitled *On the Jews,* attributed to Hecataeus of Abdera is first mentioned by Josephus (*AgAp* 1.22 §§183; 1.23 §214; cf. §205; later repeated in Eusebius *Praep. Evang.* 9.4.1) and later attested (perhaps independently) by Origen (*Cel.* 1.15). Clement possibly alludes to the work when he mentions "Hecataeus who composed histories . . ." (*Strom.* 5.14.113.1).

The content of this work is generally thought to be reflected in two passages from Josephus: *AgAp* 1.22 §§184–204 (portions of which are repeated in Eusebius *Praep. Evang.* 9.4.2–9) and *AgAp* 2.4 §§42–43 (extended by some scholars through §47).

In the first passage Josephus summarizes portions of the work and provides excerpts. He tells us that Hecataeus flourished in the time of Alexander the Great and Ptolemy I Soter and wrote a book devoted entirely to the Jews. Among the items selected from Hecataeus' account by Josephus are the following: the emigration of the Jews to Egypt after the battle of Gaza in 312 B.C.E.; an account of an elderly (high) priest Ezechias, otherwise unattested, who promotes emigration to Egypt as a good policy; the Jews' tenacious fidelity to their laws in the face of resistance and persecution, illustrated by specific examples from the time of Alexander; the populousness and population shifts resulting from the Jews' deportation to Babylon and subsequent migrations to Egypt and Phoenicia; a geographical description of Judea, Jerusalem, and the temple; the Jews' participation in the military campaigns of Alexander and his successors; and the account of Mosollamus, a shrewd Jewish archer, who bests a pagan diviner.

In the second passage (which Josephus attributes to Hecataeus without identifying the title of the work), Hecataeus is said to have reported that Alexander the Great gave the Jews the district of Samaria free of tribute in appreciation of their faithful service to him. This occurrence is not mentioned elsewhere.

Josephus also attributes to Hecataeus what appears to have been a separate work devoted to Abraham (*Ant* 1.2 §159; this passage is also repeated in Eusebius *Praep. Evang.* 9.16.3). Clement seems to refer (independently) to the same work, although he provides a longer title: *According to Abraham and the Egyptians* (*Strom.* 5.14.113.1; also repeated in Eusebius *Praep. Evang.* 13.13.40).

While Josephus only refers to the work, Clement provides an excerpt: a poetic passage attributed to Sophocles in which he confesses faith in the one true Creator God and concedes the error of idol worship and pagan sacrifice.

Besides the aforementioned references to actual works written by Hecataeus, there are other references that mention the figure Hecataeus, and his treatment of Jewish topics, yet without reference to a particular work, most notably *Let. Aris.* 31 (also quoted in Josephus *Ant* 12.4 §38 and Eusebius *Praep. Evang.* 8.3.3). Although ambiguous, this passage suggests that Hecataeus recognized the sacred character of the biblical writings and perhaps used this to account for the failure of other Greek authors to refer to them.

Assessments of the Pseudo-Hecataeus corpus (i.e., these several references to Hecataeus of Abdera, works attributed to him, and the summaries and excerpts from these works) have been numerous and widely divergent.

One point in which there is widespread agreement, however, is the pseudonymity of *On Abraham.* There is substantial agreement among scholars that such a work attributed to Hecataeus did exist in antiquity, but that it was written by a Jewish author. The author is variously designated as Pseudo-Hecataeus (*FrGrHist;* Collins 1983:

42–43, 137–41), Pseudo-Hecataeus II (Walter JSHRZ 1/2: 144–60), and Pseudo-Hecataeus III (Wacholder 1974: 263–73). Though only brief fragments survive, it certainly contained a pseudonymous poetic text attributed to Sophocles, and perhaps similar texts attributed to other Greek poets. Given the prominence of Hecataeus of Abdera, and the undisputed fact that he dealt with Jewish topics, the motivation for a Jewish author to write under his name is clear. Because of the brevity of the fragments, it is very difficult to suggest a date and provenance for this work. It is only known for certain that it predates Josephus, though it may have originated as early as the 1st century B.C.E.

If scholars are generally agreed about the pseudonymity of *On Abraham,* there is widespread disagreement about the authenticity of the statements summarized or quoted from *On the Jews.*

On the one hand, there is a well-established tradition of interpretation that finds it impossible to attribute these statements to the pagan author Hecataeus of Abdera. Even in antiquity, questions about the authenticity of the Hecataeus fragments were raised. According to Origen (*Cel.* 1.15), Herennius Philo found it difficult to believe that a pagan author could speak so positively about the Jews. Similar doubts continued into the modern period and led scholars to argue that *On the Jews* is a pseudonymous work written by Jewish author best designated Pseudo-Hecataeus. Among the reasons for seeing the work as pseudonymous are alleged anachronisms, including references to Jewish martyrdom, to the high priest Ezechias, to the practice of paying tithes to priests, and to Alexander's transfer of the district of Samaria to Jews. In various ways these have been seen to reflect a setting in the mid-2d century B.C.E. or later. Many modern scholars favor this view.

On the other hand, however, those defending the authenticity of the fragments insist that the evidence is ambiguous. Those who see no difficulty in attributing these passages to the pagan Hecataeus insist that there is no reason, in principle, that Jewish martyrdom could not have occurred during the late 4th and early 3d century, even if not with the frequency that it did during the Maccabean period. Moreover, certain numismatic evidence has been cited that points to the existence of a Jewish high priest named Hezekiah at a much earlier period. It is also argued that the precise details about the administration of the tithing system are not altogether clear. Certain other references that seem unlikely for a pagan author to make, e.g., the passage praising Jews for destroying pagan temples, are explained as later redactions by a Jewish author. Scholars who defend the passages as authentically Hecataean include Lewy, Tcherikover, Gager, Stern, Doran, and Collins.

Those who dispute the authenticity of the fragments and attribute *On the Jews* to a Jewish author have made several proposals concerning its authorship. One position sees a distinction in content, tone, and seriousness between *On the Jews* and *On Abraham.* The former work belongs to the genre of encomiastic ethnography and was probably written by a Palestinian Jewish priest who emigrated to Egypt in the aftermath of Antiochus IV Epiphanes' arrival in Palestine in 170–168 B.C.E. The references to Ezechias are regarded as thinly veiled references to Onias IV, who established the temple at Leontopolis. This is the work alluded to in *Let. Aris.* 31 and should be dated prior to the mid-2d century B.C.E.

This position is further refined by Walter, who attributes the work to a Jewish author whom he designates Pseudo-Hecataeus I. Walter sees no connection, however, between this work and the reference in *Let. Aris.* 31. Instead, he regards the latter as likely based on Hecataeus' *On the Egyptians.* Because of the probable anachronistic references in the surviving excerpts of *On the Jews,* Walter dates Pseudo-Hecataeus I towards the end of the 2d century B.C.E. The attention given to the Ptolemies leads him to propose an Alexandrian provenance for the work.

A further refinement is proposed by Wacholder (1974), who thinks the references in Josephus ordinarily attributed to a single work point to two separate works: an earlier work *On the Jews* written toward the end of the 4th century B.C.E. by Pseudo-Hecataeus I, a Jewish priest from Jerusalem, and a second work by a Jewish author whom he designates Pseudo-Hecataeus II, written sometime after *Let. Aris.* yet prior to Josephus (see further *HJP*² 3/1: 671–77).

Bibliography

Collins, J. J. 1983. *Between Athens and Jerusalem.* New York.

Gager, J. G. 1969. Pseudo-Hecataeus Again. *ZNW* 60: 130–39.

Holladay, C. R. 1983. "Pseudo-Hecataeus." Pp. 277–335 in *Fragments from Hellenistic Jewish Authors.* Vol. 1 *Historians.* SBLTT 20. Pseudepigrapha Series 10. Chico, CA.

Lewy, H. 1932. Hekataios von Abdera *peri Ioudaion.* ZNW 31: 117–32.

Schaller, B. 1963. Hekataios von Abdera über die Juden: Zur Frage der Echtheit und der Datierung. *ZNW* 24: 15–31.

Wacholder, B. Z. 1974. *Eupolemus: A Study of Judaeo-Greek Literature.* Cincinnati.

Walter, N. 1964. *Der Thoraausleger Aristobulus.* TU 86. Berlin.

CARL R. HOLLADAY

HEGAI (PERSON) [Heb *hēgay; hēgeʾ*]. A eunuch in charge of one of the harems of king Ahasuerus (Esth 2:3, 8, 15). His specific office, "the keeper of the women" (Heb *šōmēr hannāšîm*), entailed the supervision of a harem of virgin girls within the royal palace, in order to prepare them for eventual marriage to Ahasuerus as concubines. Their preparation consisted of a proper diet and continual bathings in aromatic substances (Esth 2:9–14). These bathings are said to have gone on for a full year (Esth 2:9–12), but this detail may be a satirical exaggeration on the part of the author. When Esther and the other virgins who were selected as possible replacements for the deposed queen Vashti were sent to Susa, they were placed in Hegay's care (Esth 2:8). Esther immediately became his favorite, and she received special treatment as well as advice on how to please the king (Esth 2:9, 15). The Heb *hēgay/hēgeʾ* appears to be a rendering of a Persian proper name derived from either the Sanskrit root, *āga,* meaning "eunuch," or Bactrian, *hugāo,* "one possessing beautiful cows," or perhaps Avestan, *haēk,* "the sprinkler" (Gehman 1924: 326 and Paton *Esther* ICC, 69). This name has been falsely equated by some to the contemporary name of *hēgias,* cited in Herodotus (9.33) and Ctesias (*Persians* 24)

(Gehman 1924: 326 and Paton, 69). Herodotus was referring to a Greek who was an enemy of Persia at the battle of Platea while Ctesias wrote of an Ephesian military officer of Ahasuerus. In both cases this name appears to be Greek and not Persian, and in any case the two sources mentioned are not making reference to the same *hēgay* of the book of Esther.

Bibliography

Gehman, H. S. 1924. Notes on the Persian Words in the Book of Esther. *JBL* 43: 321–28.

JOHN M. WIEBE

HEGEMONIDES (PERSON) [Gk *Hēgemonidēs*]. In 2 Macc 13:24 Hegemonides is left as governor over the area of Judea and its environs by Antiochus V Eupator (164–162 B.C.E.) as he rushes off to Ptolemais on the way to quell the revolt of Philip in Antioch. The absence of other uses of this term has caused many scholars to question whether it was the name of an actual person or even a proper noun (PW 14: 2598; Abel 1949: 456). It now seems quite probable that inscriptions from Dyme in Achaia on a monument to Antiochus IV, Queen Laodice, and the son Antiochus erected by *Hagēmonidas*, son of Zephorus, are a reference to the same person (Habicht 1958). The rare name on these inscriptions, dated between 170 and 164 B.C.E., suggests he was in a military position, perhaps a commander of Greek mercenaries, in Achaia prior to his appointment as governor in 162 B.C.E.

The area over which he was appointed as governor continues to be a matter of debate. While Ptolemais is readily identifiable as the biblical Acco, the land of the Gerrhenes *(tōn gerrēnōn)* is not as simple. While most commentators, following Grimm (1853: 191), propose Gerar in the Sinai SE of Gaza as the site, Abel points to Gerrha near Pelusium (1949: 456), and Goldstein suggests an area called Gerrha in the valley of Lebanon, later called Chalkis (*II Maccabees* AB, 468–69).

Bibliography

Abel, F.-M. 1949. *Les Livres des Maccabées.* EBib. Paris.
Grimm, C. L. W. 1853. *Kurzgefasstes exegetisches Handbuch zu den Apokryphen des Alten Testaments.* Leipzig.
Habicht, C. 1958. Der Stratege Hegemonides. *Historia* 7: 376–78.
———. 1976. *2. Makkabäerbuch.* JSHRZ 1/3. Gütersloh.

JOHN KAMPEN

HEGESIPPUS (PERSON) [Gk *hēgēsippos*]. A 2d-century Christian writer (b. before A.D. 130; d. between 180 and 192). Author of a work in five books (surviving only in fragments) entitled *Hypomnēmata ekklēsiastikōn praxeōn,* "Memoirs of the Acts of the Church," completed when Eleutherus was bishop of Rome (between 175 and 189). He set down oral traditions about the early 1st century Jerusalem Christian community and the earliest gnostic heretics, along with observations about other ecclesiastical matters down to his own time. He referred to Hadrian's favorite Antinous (d. 130) as someone who had lived during his own lifetime (Eus. *Hist. Eccl.* 4.8.2). The *Chronicon Pascale* says Hegesippus died during the reign of Commodus, that is, between 180 and 192 (Telfer 1960). At some time between ca. 154, when Anicetus became bishop of Rome, and the death of Eleutherus in 189, he traveled by sea to Rome—via Corinth, indicating that his home must have been in the E end of the Mediterranean world—and his *Memoirs* were completed at some time after this trip.

The actual passage in Hegesippus describing the visit (Eus. *Hist. Eccl.* 4.22.3) is ambiguous as to the time and length of the stay in Rome. The 4th century church historian Eusebius (*Hist. Eccl.* 4.11.7) interpreted it to mean that he came during the reign of Anicetus (ca. 154–166) and remained until that of Eleutherus (175–189), making a quite extended residency in the capital, but the odd construction of the passage could well mean instead that Hegesippus simply visited Rome briefly when Anicetus was bishop, took notes on the succession up to that point, then added the names of Soter and Eleutherus years later, after he had returned home and was preparing his final draft. Yet another interpretation of the peculiar syntax could be that Hegesippus had come and gone during the bishopric of Eleutherus, who had supplied information orally about his predecessors Anicetus and Soter, but that he wished his readers to know that obtaining an accurate list of the names of the earlier bishops had required independent research. The unanswerable question is whether Hegesippus's stay in Rome occurred during the time of Justin Martyr (fl. ca. 155–165), or Irenaeus (fl. ca. 177–190), or both.

The complete work survived in several Greek monasteries as late as the 16th–17th centuries, but only fragments exist today, nearly all preserved in Eusebius of Caesarea's *Church History* (see especially the quotations and paraphrases in Eus. *Hist. Eccl.* 2.23.4–18, parts of 3.5.2–3, 3.11.1–12.1, 3.16.1, 3.20.1–6, 3.32.1–8, 4.8.2, and 4.22.1–9).

Although some have attempted to call Hegesippus, rather than Eusebius of Caesarea, the Father of Church History, his work does not seem likely to have been a true continuous historical narrative. The account of the death of James the brother of the Lord, for example, was in the fifth and last book, far too late for a genuinely chronological presentation. Since *ekklēsiastikos* at that time frequently meant "orthodox" as opposed to heretical, the title of Hegesippus's work could equally well be translated as "Memoranda" or "Notes" (Turner 1918; Telfer 1960) "on an Orthodox Acts," with the target of attack being the various apocryphal acts of the apostles which began appearing in the 2d century (cf. Eus. *Hist. Eccl.* 4.22.9). Eusebius regarded it basically as a work defending "the orthodox kerygma" against heretical interpretations (Eus. *Hist. Eccl.* 4.7.15–8.2), both those of the apocryphal acts and those of the early gnostic theologians, from Simon to Marcion and Valentinus (*Hist. Eccl.* 4.22.5). A fragment of the *Memoirs* found in Photius seems clearly antignostic (Telfer 1960).

Hegesippus had access to certain traditions deriving from the early Jerusalem church. He described the death of James the brother of the Lord (Eus. *Hist. Eccl.* 2.23.4–18) and said that the Jerusalem community decided that the next leader of their church also had to be a blood relative of Jesus—Simon, the son of Joseph's brother Clopas, eventually being chosen (Eus. *Hist. Eccl.* 3.11–12, 4.22.4). Two grandsons of Jesus' brother Judas also played important roles (Eus. *Hist. Eccl.* 3.20.1–6, 3.32.5–6). This suggests something like a Muslim caliphate in its conception (Stauffer 1952 gives Jewish and Roman antecedents for the dynastic approach), but Hegesippus in addition seems to have stressed that these leaders were not only related to Jesus but also, by that fact, were of the line of David (Eus. *Hist. Eccl.* 3.12, 3.20.1–2, 3.32.3–4). These early "bishops" of Jerusalem seem therefore to have been regarded as the Davidic dynasty of the end time. The oral traditions which Hegesippus recorded described the central kerygma preached by these kinsmen of the Lord: Jesus was the Messiah and the Son of Man, who would return to establish his earthly kingdom at the apocalyptic end of this world (Eus. *Hist. Eccl.* 2.23.10, 2.23.13, 3.20.4).

Hegesippus was the first Christian historiographer to introduce the (usually pernicious) notion of the fall of the church from its apostolic purity at a particular point in its history. In his case, he chose the death of the last blood relatives of Jesus during the reign of Trajan. Until then, he said, "they called the church virgin, for it had not been corrupted" (Eus. *Hist. Eccl.* 4.22.4, 3.32.7). Later theologians and church historians have dated the ravishing of the "pure and uncorrupted virgin" to the rise of *Frühkatholizismus,* the triumph of Constantine, or (in Pope Leo XIII's *Aeterni Patris*) to the Protestant Reformation.

Eusebius believed that Hegesippus was a convert from Judaism, because of his knowledge of Hebrew and Syriac and of the unwritten Jewish tradition, and because of his use of the Gospel according to the Hebrews (Eus. *Hist. Eccl.* 4.22.8). He might instead have been brought up in a kind of traditional E Mediterranean Christianity of still slightly Jewish slant, though certainly not the sort represented by the Judaizers whom Paul combatted, for he acknowledged the teachings of the church of Corinth and of Rome as identical to his own in all true essentials (Eus. *Hist. Eccl.* 4.22.1–3) and Eusebius regarded him as totally orthodox (*Hist. Eccl.* 4.7.15–8.2). He also used the LXX rather than the Hebrew text for the prophecy of James's martyrdom (Eus. *Hist. Eccl.* 2.23.15; Telfer 1960). Hegesippus did however describe the Sadducees, Pharisees, Samaritans, Essenes, and so on as those "among the children of Israel" who opposed "the tribe of Judah and the Messiah" (Eus. *Hist. Eccl.* 4.22.7), indicating that his version of Christianity preserved a strong sense of Jewish identity—members quite specifically of the tribe of Judah, who had been led originally by a Davidic episcopacy.

The passage preserved in Eus. *Hist. Eccl.* 4.22.3 has drawn much discussion. Hegesippus said that while in Rome, "*diadochēn epoiēsamēn* [literally, 'I made a succession'] until Anicetus, whose deacon was Eleutherus; Soter *diadechetai* ['succeeded'] Anicetus, and after him came Eleutherus." The older scholarship interpreted this to mean simply that Hegesippus researched and drew up a list of all the bishops of Rome, from Peter to Eleutherus. The more modern scholarship points out that "succession" in that context referred to continuity of teaching and identity of doctrines (Turner 1918). That Hegesippus put this in the form of a list of "bishops" in chronological order seems likely, however, given his treatment of the early Jerusalem church, so the older scholarship had a point, but it would be anachronistic to regard this as having been intended by him as a sacramental guarantee of an "apostolic succession" of ordination to the priesthood and the episcopacy. When pagan philosophers represented continuity of teaching by listing the noted leaders of a philosophical school in a chronological "succession" list, the issue was not sacramental efficacy but an attempt to show that the same philosophical positions had continued to be held through the entire history of that school.

The fragments of Hegesippus are important, in spite of the fact that he wrote fairly late in the second century, because he seems to represent contact with an oral or written tradition and a conservative Christian community that preserved many archaic features going back to the first century.

Bibliography

For all extant fragments see:

Lawlor, H. J. 1912. *Eusebiana: Essays on the Ecclesiastical History of Eusebius, Bishop of Caesarea.* Oxford.

Preuschen, E. 1905. *Antilegomena: die Reste der ausserkanonischen Evangelien und urchristlichen Überlieferungen,* 2d ed. Giessen.

Zahn, T. 1900. *Forschungen zur Geschichte des neutestamentlichen Kanons und der altkirchlichen Literatur* 6:228–73. Erlangen.

Modern literature:

Caspar, E. 1926. *Die älteste römische Bischofsliste.* Berlin.

Hyldahl, N. 1960. Hegesipps Hypomnemata. *StTh* 14:70–113.

Quasten, J. 1963–64. *Patrology.* Vol. 1. Utrecht and Antwerp.

Stauffer, E. 1952. Zum Kalifat des Jacobus. *ZRGG* 4: 193–214.

Telfer, W. 1960. Was Hegesippus a Jew? *HTR* 53: 143–53.

Turner, C. H. 1918. Pp. 115–120 and 207 in *Essays on the Early History of the Church and the Ministry,* ed. H. B. Swete. London.

Glenn F. Chesnut

HEGESIPPUS, PSEUDO-. The name given the anonymous author of a Latin account of the Jewish revolt against Rome in 66–73. Ambrose is most commonly assumed to be the author, but the arguments are not convincing. The title and author's name are missing from the earliest extant mss. (6th century), but internal evidence suggests a date of composition of ca. 370 C.E. and the probability that the author was a bilingual Antiochene, perhaps Evagrius, the translator of Athanasius' *Vita Antonii* and close friend of Jerome. His history, which seems to have been originally titled *De excidio Hierosolymitano,* relies heavily on Josephus without being a mere translation. The author also draws information from Livy, Suetonius, Tacitus, and other appropriate Greek and Roman sources to produce what E. M. Sanford called "substantially an independent book." In five books instead of Josephus' seven, it was often cited as a co-equal authority with Josephus in the Middle Ages, which read Josephus in Rufinus' translation. It contains apocryphal material about Peter, including some Simon Magus narratives and an early version of the "Quo vadis?" story (*De excid.* 3.2). The text of this story differs so dramatically from Ambrose's account (*Ser. contra Auxent.* 13) that the two could not have been written by the same author. This apocryphal material led to the association of this work with the Hegesippus (mentioned by

Eusebius) who wrote a history of the Church in the mid-2d century.

The author's main purpose is to show that God had withdrawn his favor from the Jews and that the destruction of the Temple in 70 C.E. was irreversible, the *supremum excidium* (this perhaps prompted by Julian the Apostate's abortive effort to rebuild the temple in 363). In his prologue, which is original and bears no resemblance to that of Josephus, he announces his intention to make "clear to the whole world—and this is an indication of the depravity of the race—that they brought their misfortunes on themselves." This theme reflects the 4th century church's claim to be the new Israel, heir to the OT promises. It is echoed in Ambrose, Jerome, John Chrysostom, and other Christian authors of the period.

Pseudo-Hegesippus supports his reinterpretation of history with biblical proof-texts. In 400 pages of printed text there are over 270 biblical quotations or allusions, some in the most unlikely or inappropriate places. In a speech put in the mouth of Titus as he besieged Jerusalem, there are allusions to Abraham's sacrifice of Isaac and Jephthah's sacrifice of his daughter (*De excid.* 4.41,2). In his speech urging the Jews not to begin the rebellion, Herod Agrippa reminds them to "let what is owed to Caesar be paid to Caesar" (2.9,1). Josephus, in his role as a character in the story, also quotes the NT when he urges his comrades not to commit suicide (3.17).

At other points the author makes additions to the biblical accounts. He refers (5.32) to Naboth as a prophet, a view shared by Jerome (*Comment. in Matt.* 21.35) and Ambrose (*Expos. in Lucam* 9.25). He also heightens the shame of Herodias' marriage to Herod Antipas by noting that she was carrying the child of her first husband Philip, Herod's brother, at the time (2.5,3). No other patristic source makes that claim.

These citations provide some insight into the thinking of the 4th century church and also a long-neglected textual witness. Comparison with the pre-Vulgate texts reveals that pseudo-Hegesippus' biblical quotations follow no single version. Since, as his use of Josephus demonstrates, he was capable of translating Greek, it seems most likely that he was working from a Greek text and not an early Latin version. His biblical citations could thus be considered a version in themselves, one dating from about the time Jerome was beginning the Vulgate. From Jerome's own writings (*Ep.* 5.3; *De vir. illus.* 125; *Vita Malchi* prol.) it is clear that he was in frequent and close contact with Evagrius at this time, even staying in his home for a while. Further study of pseudo-Hegesippus is needed to identify him; if he should prove to be Evagrius, comparison of his biblical citations with the Vulgate text could also prove illuminating.

Bibliography

Hegesippus, Pseudo- 1932. *Historiae libri v*, ed. by V. Ussani. CSEL 66/1, with notes and indexes prepared by K. Mras in pt. 2 (1960).

Bardy, G. 1940. Traducteurs et adaptateurs au ive siècle. *RSR* 28: 257–306.

Bell, A. A., Jr. 1980. Classical and Christian Traditions in the Work of Pseudo-Hegesippus. *Indiana Social Studies Quarterly* 33: 60–64.

Morin, G. 1914/1919. L'Opuscule perdu du soi-disant Hégésippe sur les Macchabées. *RBén* 31: 81–87.

Mras, K. 1959. Die Hegesippus-Frage. *AÖAW* 95: 143–53.

Sanford, E. M. 1935. Propaganda and Censorship in the Transmission of Josephus. *TAPA* 66: 127–45.

ALBERT A. BELL, JR.

HEGLAM (PERSON) [Heb *heglām*]. A proper name equated with Gera in the RSV (1 Chr 8:7). Of the modern biblical translations only the RSV recognizes this verbal form as a proper name. Beck (*IDB* 2: 577–78) seemingly incorrectly identifies *heglām* as an ". . . alternative for the hypocoristic name Gera." The *Hipʿil* perfect form plus pronominal suffix can mean "caused them to be removed" or "carried them away into exile." The verbal form is used with *hu(w)ʾ* in the MT following a listing of three sons of Ehud in 1 Chr 8:7, Naaman, Ahijah, and Gera. These three sons are described as heads of families of the ones residing in Geba (8:6). They are given credit in this obscure reference, with Gera receiving chief emphasis, of deporting a group of Benjaminites from Geba to Manahath (8:6–7). Geba was one of the levitical cities of Benjamin as mentioned in Josh 21:17; 1 Chr 6:60; and Josh 18:24. It was located between Ai and Jerusalem some 6 miles NNE of the city of David close to Judah's N boundary. The city was an important site in the conflicts with the Philistines. The traditional site of Manahath is considered to be Malah, some 3 miles SW of Jerusalem (1 Chr 2:52–54).

The text is obviously difficult at this point. Scholars are divided as to whom, what, and where is actually being referred in vv 6–7 of 1 Chronicles 8. Slotki (1952: 47–48) suggests that perhaps Ehud is the subject of the verb *heglām* with the three sons as the objects. Myers (*1 Chronicles* AB, 60) speaks of the verses as defying explanation, but calls them a possible "garbled" version of the tradition reflected in Judges 20. Rudolph (*Chronikbücher* HAT, 79) considers that it is a reference to a movement of a portion of the Benjamin tribe to a site in Edom (1 Chr 1:40) in the postexilic period. Williamson (*Chronicles* NCBC, 83) points out that even though the sections of the Benjaminite genealogy move toward the postexilic time frame, not all material present must hail from this later period. Bartel (1969: 24–27) sees the narrative as being compressed and referring to the Benjaminites forcing indigenous inhabitants of Geba to relocate to Manahath in Judah (cf. 1 Chr. 2:52–54). Braun (*1 Chronicles* WBC, 127) suggests that a better translation of the verbal form *heglām* is "to emigrate." He states that this removes the difficulty of the exiler not being properly identified. He further suggests that the problem of period and circumstance remain at best obscure. However, he does suggest a possibility associated with Ehud, son of Gera, in Judg 3:12–4:11 in which action is taken against the Moabites. Braun feels that an event in the period of the Judges is the likely reference. This seems to be a situation in which one is forced to choose between a variety of speculative offerings. Given the current available options it may seem best to consider an emigration of some 9 miles from Geba to Malah associated with some military campaign at a time before the exile and likely as early as the period of the Judges.

Bibliography

Bartel, A. 1969. Tradition regarding the fate of the Gibeonites in I Chr. 8, 6f. *Beth Mikra* 39: 24–27.

Slotki, I. W. 1952. *Chronicles.* Soncino Books of the Bible 10. London.

G. Edwin Harmon

ḤEGRA (26°47'N; 38°14'E). An ancient Nabatean settlement of the Roman era located in the Ḥijāz of Saudi Arabia. It is mentioned only rarely by classical authors, who locate it in the territory of the Nabatean king Obodas III on the Red Sea coast (Strabo 16.4.24 [782]); associate it with the Laeanitae, i.e., the Liḥyanites of Dedan (Pliny, *HN* 6.156), and in Arabia Felix (Ptolemy, *Geog.* 6.7.29). The site is identified with the ruins just S of the village of Madāʾin Ṣāliḥ about 15 km N of al-ʿUla (Dedan) and 110 km SW of Taymaʾ. It is generally assumed that a nearby port of similar name to the inland ruins once existed on the Red Sea coast, but it has never been located. During the late 19th century, the ruins were visited by C. M. Doughty, J. Euting, and C. Huber.

Recent surveys of the site have provided additional evidence of the history of the area (Winnett and Reed, *ARNA,* 42–53; Parr, Harding, and Dayton 1972), but the definitive study of the monuments and inscriptions of the settlement remains that of Jaussen and Savignac (1909; 1914). The only possible mention of the site in the Bible is Paul's reference to Hagar as representing "Mount Sinai in Arabia" (Gal 4:25); this has been interpreted as a cryptic allusion to the Nabatean settlement of Ḥegra (Gese 1967), but the proposal is not convincing (see Davies 1972).

The settlement remains unexcavated, and its ruins are disappointing, with only a few traces of the city walls and towers barely visible. Far more impressive is the spectacular necropolis surrounding the settlement, which rivals even that of Petra. It consists of some 79 tombs cut into the adjacent mountains, 31 of which have inscriptions dating from A.D. 1 to A.D. 75. They reveal the names and professions of their owners, most of whom represent a civic and military elite. Attempts to arrange the various types of tombs in a chronological scheme from the simple to the complex are defied by the information contained in the dedication inscriptions about their construction. The names of the artisans and stonecutters are mentioned in 16 of the inscriptions; most of them are members of a single family, that of ʿAbdʿObodat, which also possibly operated at Petra and Wadi Ramm (Schmidt-Colinet 1983). This artisan family's repertoire included different types of styled facades to satisfy the demands of the individuals who commissioned them; the elaborate and ornated types are reflections of social status and are contemporary with the simpler types. The architectural style of the facades has been associated with that of Ptolemaic Alexandria (Schmidt-Colinet 1980; McKenzie and Phippen 1987).

The first appearance of the village in ancient sources is in connection with the Arabian expedition of Aelius Gallus' Roman expedition in 26/25 B.C. The Roman enterprise was supported by 1000 Nabatean troops and 500 Jews. A Nabatean official named Syllaeus, the ambitious chancellor *(epitropos)* of the Nabatean king Obodas II (30–9 B.C.), served as guide for the forces that accompanied the Roman commander. After the disastrous campaign, the forces stopped at the port of Egra, located within the territory of Obodas' kingdom (Strabo 16.4.22–24). Later, at the death of the Nabatean king in 9 B.C., Syllaeus seized control of Nabatea with the approval of the Roman emperor Augustus. The challenge of his rule by Herod the Great's envoy, Nicolaus of Damascus, and the opposing Nabatean claimant, Aretas (IV), saw his prompt removal. It recently has been conjectured that Syllaeus was from the Ḥijāz and even owned property at Ḥegra. The single uncompleted facade of Qasr al-Bint at Ḥegra also has been associated with him, its unfinished state being explained by his execution in Rome in 6 B.C. (Schmidt-Colinet 1987: 147). If correct, this would make it earlier than any of the tombs dated by inscriptions, but the hypothesis is dependent on a chain of assumptions lacking any explicit evidence.

There is a unique Nabatean coin inscribed with the name *ḥgrʾ* evidently referring to the city. It has the head of a long-haired Aretas IV on the obverse, and a bell-like object with a handle on the reverse, just above the inscription. The coin has been interpreted as a commemoration issue for the founding of the city (Meshorer 1975: 53–54, no. 87). It is possible that Aretas IV developed the site in conjunction with the harbor village of the same name. Earlier evidence for the settlement is minimal (Parr, Harding, and Dayton 1972: 23). The cosmopolitan atmosphere of the settlement is reflected in inscriptions from the site by inhabitants from Aela (Aqaba), perhaps Edom (JS no. 138), Petra (no. 152), Moab (386), and S Syria (no. 226). One of the tombs (A8) is also for a Jew (no. 4 = CIS II, 219), and a sundial found at the settlement also dating from the 1st century A.D. is inscribed *mnsʾ br nṭn,* "Mannaseh son of Nathan" (Healey 1989). The Diwan sanctuary or cultic center in the Siq of Jabal Ith̲lib at Ḥegra contains graffiti petitioning the Nabatean gods of Dushara and Allāt, and also the Edomite Qos, and the Syrian deity Shaiʾ al-Qaum; there is also a reference to "Aʿara, god of Rabbel, who is in Boṣra," the city in the Ḥaurān that later became the capital of the Arabian province. Since the settlement is located on the incense route, Ḥegra was originally interpreted as a commercial entrepôt, but recently emphasis has been placed on its strategic importance as a military frontier settlement on the S borders of Nabatea (Negev 1976; Bowsher 1986).

During the accession year of the Nabatean king Rabbel II (A.D. 71–106), a rebellion against the royal house of Petra was led by Damasī, one of the scions of a prominent family at Ḥegra. The tribes of the Ḥaurān known from Safaitic inscriptions and probably former subjects of the Nabatean realm also supported the rebel cause (Winnett 1973). Both his father, Rabibʾel, and uncle, Ganimū, the sons of a Damasippos, served as governors of Ḥegra and are known from inscriptions near Jauf (Dumat al-Jandal) in the Wadi Ṣirḥan (J. Milik and Starcky in Winnett and Reed *ARNA,* 142), explaining perhaps the N support for the rebel Damasī. The revolt appears to have been precipitated when Malikū, the younger brother of Damasī, was appointed governor of Ḥegra (JS no. 34) instead of him. The phrase "he who brought life and deliverance to his people" in the royal titulary of Rabbel II perhaps refers to the quelling of the rebellion by the young monarch.

After A.D. 75, Ḥegra falls into obscurity. Its fate after the Roman annexation of Nabatea in A.D. 106 is equally difficult to determine. The hypothesis of R. Dussaud that Ḥegra was the center of a truncated Nabatean kingdom under the rule of a putative dynast named Malichus III, the son of Rabbel II, must now be rejected on the basis of new documentary evidence (Graf 1988: 176–77). The family of Damasippos continued to dwell at the Ḥegra until at least the 2d century A.D. Rabbinic sources appear to refer to the site in conjunction with Petra.

In the 2d and early 3d century, Roman auxilia—the *ala Gaetulorum* and an *ala dromedariorum*—and even a detachment of the Arabian legion of the *III Cyrenaica* served in the region. It is generally assumed that the settlement was abandoned during Diocletian's reorganization of the E frontier, but it is possible that it was never formally annexed after the Roman acquisition of Nabatea (Graf 1988). The silence about the Ḥijāz in official Roman documents such as the Peutinger Table and *Notitia Dignitatum* is noteworthy. The last datable Nabatean inscription indicates that Ḥegra was ruled by a man named ʿAdnon, whose brother ruled Taymaʾ, descendants perhaps of a Jewish family (Stiehl 1970). Islamic sources provides the reason for the change in the name of the site to "Ṣāliḥ's villages." The Quran indicates that it was the Thamud who carved their houses out of the rock at the site. Other Arab sources characterized them as an idolatrous and rebellious people who rejected the prophet Ṣāliḥ, even slaying the camel he had conjured from the adjacent rocks to convince them of his divine mission. God then is said to have sent an earthquake to destroy the town and its inhabitants (Vidal 1971: 366). The ruins have never been excavated, but the Saudi Arabian Department of Antiquities has conducted several recent surveys of the environs and sponsored a preservation project for the ruins.

Bibliography

Bowsher, J. 1986. The Frontier Post of Medain Saleh. Pp. 23–29 in *Defence of the Roman and Byzantine East,* ed. P. Freeman and D. Kennedy. BARIS 297/i. Oxford.

Davies, G. I. 1972. Hağar, El-Ḥegrā and the Location of Mount Sinai. *VT* 22: 152–63.

Gese, H. 1967. Now Hagar is Mount Sinai in Arabia (Gal 4, 25). Pp. 81–94 in *Das ferne une nahe Wort,* ed. F. Maass. Berlin.

Graf, D. F. 1988. Qura ʿArabiyya and Provincia Arabia. Pp. 171–211 in *Géographie historique au Proche-Orient.* Notes et Monographies Techniques 23. Paris.

Healey, J. F. 1989. A Nabataean Sundial from Madain Salih. *Syr* 66: 331–36.

Jaussen, A., and Savignac, R. 1909. *Mission archéologique en Arabie.* Vol. 1. Paris.

———. 1914. *Mission archéologique in Arabie.* Vol. 2. Paris.

McKenzie, J., and Phippen, A. 1987. The Chronology of the Principal Monuments at Petra. *Levant* 19: 145–65.

Meshorer, Y. 1975. *Nabatean Coins.* Qedem 3. Jerusalem.

Negev, A. 1976. The Nabatean Necropolis at Egra. *RB* 83: 203–36.

Parr, P. J.; Harding, G. L.; and Dayton, J. E. 1972. Preliminary Survey in N.W. Arabia, 1968. *Bulletin of the Institute of Archaeology, University of London* 10: 23–61.

Schmidt-Colinet, A. 1980. Nabatäische Felscarchitekur. *Bonner Jahrbücher* 180: 189–230.

———. 1983. A Nabatean Family of Sculptors at Hegra. *Berytus* 31: 95–102.

———. 1987. The Mason's Workshop of Ḥegrā, Its Relations to Petra, and the Tomb of Syllaios. Pp. 143–50 in *Studies in the History and Archaeology of Jordan* 3, ed. A. Hadidi. Amman.

Stiehl, R. 1970. A New Nabataean Inscription. Vol. 2, pp. 87–90 in *Beiträge zur alten Geschichte und deren Nachleben: Festschrift für Franz Altheim.* Berlin.

Vidal, F. S. 1971. al-Ḥidjr. *Encyclopedia of Islam* 3: 365–66.

Winnett, F. V. 1973. The Revolt of Damasī. *BASOR* 211: 54–57.

DAVID F. GRAF

HEIFER.

A young cow, primarily one which has not given birth to a calf. This term is the usual translation of Hebrew *ʿeglâ* and occasionally of *pārâ.* A more precise translation of *ʿeglâ* would be "young cow," since an *ʿeglâ* may be a three year old animal (Gen 15:9) and may even be producing milk (so apparently in Isa 7:21–22; see Z. Zevit 1976: 384). Also, though contexts of certain passages suggest that *pārâ* may be translated "heifer," it should be kept in mind that this term indicates generally an adult female bovine (see R. Peter 1975).

The term *ʿeglâ* is found is several contexts in the OT.

(1) Young cows appear in agricultural contexts in capacities of plowing, threshing, and producing milk. Most of the instances in this category are metaphorical. Samson's party guests found out his riddle by "plowing with [his] young cow" (Jud 14:18). Babylon "gamboled like a young cow treading grain" when it spoiled Jerusalem (Jer 50:11). Ephraim was a trained young cow that "loved to thresh" (Hos 10:11). According to Isa 7:21–22, a young cow and two flock animals are to provide an abundance of milk.

(2) Young cows appear in various ritual contexts. Samuel was to take a young cow for a sacrifice at which David would be anointed king (1 Sam 16:2).

This type of animal is used in more unique ritual situations. Abraham divides a three year old young cow, along with other animals, in a covenant ceremony (Gen 15:9). A torch, probably representing God, passes between the pieces of the animals to establish the covenant with the patriarch.

In Deut 21:1–9 a unworked young cow is brought to a perennially flowing wadi where it is killed in a rite to remove pollution caused by a murder in which the culprit is not known. The killing of the cow has been interpreted as a sacrifice to the victim's ghost or underworld powers, the symbolic execution of the murderer, the representation of the penalty of the elders will suffer if their testimony that they had no part in the murder is false (cf. vv. 3–4, 6–8), the means of preventing the animal beset with guilt and pollution from returning to the community, or a reenactment of the murder which transfers blood pollution to an uninhabited area. The latter interpretation is preferable (see Wright 1987: 387–403; also Zevit 1976).

Also in a ritual context the term in the plural is used of bovine idols at Bethel (Hos 10:5).

(3) In miscellaneous contexts, "young cow" is found as a metaphor for Egypt (Jer 46:20). It is found as a constituent in the geographical name Eglath-shelishiyah (Isa 15:5; Jer

48:34; see EGLATH-SHELISHIYAH). Eglah was also the name of one of David's wives (2 Sam 3:5; 1 Chr 3:3).

The term *pārâ* has been construed occasionally as "heifer": (1) Many translate *pārâ ădummâ* in Num 9:2 (cf. vv. 5, 6, 9, 10) as "red heifer" rather than "red cow" because the context requiring an unworked animal suggests that the animal was young. Cf. the AV, RSV, JB and Greek.

(2) *Pārâ* in Hos 4:16, which compares Israel to a rebellious cow, has also been taken as "heifer" or "young cow" (see the translations mentioned above). This translation may be ultimately due to the influence of Hos 10:11 where Ephraim is metaphorically called a "young cow" (*ʿeglâ*).

(3) The LXX translates *pārôt* in Amos 4:1 as *damaleis* "young cows" or "heifers."

Bibliography

Peter, R. 1975. *Pār* et *šôr:* Note de lexigraphie hébraïque. *VT* 25: 486–96, 691.

Wright, D. P. 1987. Deuteronomy 21:1–9 as a Rite of Elimination. *CBQ* 49: 387–403.

Zevit, Z. 1976. The *ʿeglâ* Ritual of Deuteronomy 21:1–9. *JBL* 95: 377–90.

David P. Wright

HEIFER, RED. The animal slaughtered and burned to make ashes for purifying persons and objects from pollution by human corpses (Num 19). Though the context requiring an unworked animal for the rite implies that the animal is young (a "heifer"; cf. LXX *damalis*), the Heb. term *pārâ ădummâ* (v 2) literally means "Red Cow" (see HEIFER).

The rite of the Red Cow, found among the Priestly regulations of the Pentateuch, is unique in the OT. The legislation in Num 19:2–10, presented in terms of a revelation to Moses and Aaron, prescribes that the Israelites provide a perfect, unblemished red cow which has not been agriculturally worked. The cow is given to Eleazar, a priest, and Aaron's son who is next in line to become high priest, who takes it outside the camp. An anonymous slaughterer kills the animal under Eleazar's supervision. Eleazar then takes some of the blood and sprinkles it seven times in the direction of the front of the tent of meeting. An anonymous person, probably the same person who did the slaughtering, then burns the entire cow under Eleazar's supervision. When this is being done the priest throws cedar wood, hyssop, and scarlet thread into the fire. Finally, a pure person (this is someone other than the priest and the slaughterer/burner, since these are now impure; see below) then gathers the resulting ashes and stores them in a pure place outside the camp.

A main problem surrounding this rite is whether it is to be considered a sacrifice or an act of ritual slaughtering distinct from sacrifice. Certain features indicate that it is sacrificial. First, it is in fact called a *ḥaṭṭāʾt* (vv 9, 17), that is, a purgation sacrifice (otherwise known as a "sin offering"). Also, the sacrificial nature of the rite is underscored by the supervision and involvement of the priest Eleazar. His sprinkling of blood seven times toward the tent, which appears to be the means of initiating the ritual and consecrating the animal and its blood, particularly emphasizes the sacrificial nature of the ritual. Furthermore, the requirement of a female animal fits well with the requirement elsewhere that a *ḥaṭṭāʾt* of a lay individual be a female (Lev 4:28, 32; 5:6; Num 6:14; 15:27; the Red Cow, though provided by the community, is for lay individuals).

But though this evidence indicates that the rite is theoretically a sacrifice, other details show that it is very exceptional as such. Instead of being slaughtered at the altar at the sanctuary, the cow is killed outside the camp, apparently without an altar, in direct contradiction to general Priestly law (cf. Lev 17). The qualifications that the cow be perfect and unblemished are found in sacrificial rules (cf. Lev 22:17–25), but the additional qualification that it should not have had a yoke placed on it is not. This is found in cases which are not properly sacrifices (Deut 21:3; 1 Sam 6:7; Deut 15:19 has a similar requirement perhaps limited to firstborn sacrificial animals). That the cow is totally burnt is reminiscent of the total burning of a burnt offering (Lev 1:6–9, 12–13) or of the incineration of *ḥaṭṭāʾt* carcasses, whose blood is used in the Tent (Exod 29:14; Lev 4:11; 8:17; 9:11; 16:27, note the similarity of the list of parts here to that in Num 19:5; see also Lev 6:23; 10:18). But on second inspection it is really quite different. The burning of the holocaust is the means of making the offering, and the burning of *ḥaṭṭāʾt* carcasses is for the purpose of disposing of a impure sanctum. In Numbers the burning of the cow serves to provide ashes which will then later be used; it is not a means of offering or disposal. Finally the use of cedar, hyssop, and scarlet material is not found in sacrifice. The only other place where these three elements appear together is in the nonsacrificial rite for purification from scale disease (*ṣāraʿat;* see LEPROSY) in Lev 14:5–7, 51–52. There they are used as an instrument for applying purifying liquid, not burned, as in Numbers 19. These items certainly had symbolic meaning, but that meaning is unrecoverable (see Wefing 1981: 350 and Milgrom [1981] for explanation of these irregularities).

The goal of this unusual sacrificial procedure is to provide ashes for purifying persons and things from corpse contamination. Corpse contamination is one of the major impurities in the Priestly system of impurities. Persons or objects so polluted are impure for seven days and can pollute other persons and objects of a profane or common (i.e., nonholy) nature. See UNCLEAN AND CLEAN (OT). To purify from corpse contamination, the ashes obtained from the Red Cow rite are mixed with spring water (*mayim ḥayyîm;* Num 19:17). This water-ash mixture is called in vv 9, 13, 20, 21 *mê (han)niddâ* "water for purgation." See WATER FOR IMPURITY. A pure person dips hyssop in the water and sprinkles it on the corpse-contaminated persons or objects (v 18) once on third day of the period of impurity and again on the seventh day (v 19). In addition to sprinkling with the water for purgation, persons need to bathe and launder (in regular water) on the seventh day, and wait for evening, when they become pure (v 19). Noteworthy is the fact that Numbers 19 prescribes no seventh day ablutions for corpse contaminated objects that correspond to the laundering and bathing of people. Priestly legislation regularly has parallel purification procedures for persons and objects. This gap in the prescriptions was sensed by later editors who consequently supplemented the law with Num 31:19–24 to provide the missing ablutions. According to this passage, objects that can endure fire (such as those of metal) are to be passed through fire. Other objects that cannot endure fire (organic items) are simply immersed in water (see Wright 1985).

One of the most striking things about the rite of the Red Cow and the ashes is that while they lead to the purification of those polluted by a corpse, they pollute pure people who participate in the preparing of the ashes or who touch the ashes or the water for purgation. The priest who supervises the burning of the cow is impure for one day and needs to launder and bathe (v 7). The one who burns the cow and the one who gathers its ashes are similarly impure (vv 8, 10). One who sprinkles the water for purgation or one who otherwise touches it becomes impure for one day (v 21). This paradox is explained by character of the Red Cow rite as a *ḥaṭṭāʾt* (see above). The purpose of other *ḥaṭṭāʾt* sacrifices is to purify; their blood is applied to various sancta in order to remove impurity from those sancta. The *ḥaṭṭāʾt* carcass and blood as a result become impure, even to the extent that they can pollute other persons and things (cf. Lev 6:20–21; 16:28). This explains the impurity of the Red Cow and its ashes. As a *ḥaṭṭāʾt* sacrifice it is impure and can pollute others (here it does so prospectively, before actual use in purification), but as an agent of purification it can purify those who are corpse contaminated (see Milgrom 1981).

Recent discussion has focused on the nature of the rite before its incorporation in the Priestly legislation in its final form. S. Wefing (1981) has argued mainly through a literary critical approach that originally the rite was a non-Israelite burnt offering. This was eventually incorporated into Israelite liturgy, not as a legitimate sacrifice, but as a sort of ordeal inveighing against pagan sacrifice. The *mê (han)niddâ,* which were added at this stage, were perhaps like the drinks for ordeal in Num 5:17–24 and Exod 32:20. Finally, late in the exilic period, the rite received its present form. The *mê (han)niddâ* lost their significance of ordeal and came to mean simply "water against impurity" or "water for purification." J. Milgrom argues from a more traditio-historical point of view that an earlier, non-Israelite, purgation rite for corpse defilement was taken over into the Priestly corpus and assimilated, as much as it could be, to its sacrificial system, particularly to that of the *ḥaṭṭāʾt* sacrifice. In this assimilation of the Red Cow rite to the *ḥaṭṭāʾt* scheme there was also a move made to reduce somewhat the strength of corpse contamination: according to Numbers 19 the impure person needs no first-day ablutions (contrast the scale diseased person's rite in Lev 14:8); the corpse-defiled person does not need to leave the camp (cf. a different law in Num 5:2–3); and no sacrifice is required (contrast Num 6:9–12; Ezek 44:25–27).

Later Jewish tradition devoted two tractates of the Mishnah to the issues of this ritual *(Para, Oholot).* The Temple Scroll developed the laws of corpse contamination in cols 49:5–50:19. For discussion of the Red Cow in postbiblical traditions, see Bowman 1958.

Bibliography

Bowman, J. 1958. Did the Qumran Sect Burn the Red Heifer? *RQ* 1: 73–84.

Milgrom, J. 1981. The Paradox of the Red Cow (Num. XIX). *VT* 31: 62–72.

Wefing, S. 1981. Beobachtungen zum Ritual mit der roten Kuh (Num 19:1–10a). *ZAW* 93: 341–64.

Wright, D. P. 1985. Purification from Corpse-Contamination in Numbers XXXI 19–24. *VT* 35: 213–23.

David P. Wright

HEILSGESCHICTE. See THEOLOGY (BIBLICAL), HISTORY OF.

HEIR. See FAMILY.

HELAH (PERSON) [Heb *helʾâ*]. One of two wives of Ashhur, listed in the family line of Judah (1 Chr 4:5, 7). Ashhur is identified as the ancestor of the people of Tekoa (v 5). Helah bore him Zereth, Izhar, and Ethnan (v 7). The other wife of Ashhur was Naarah. Her sons are listed in 4:6. In 1 Chr 4:5, Helah is named first, while in 4:6–7, Naarah's sons are recorded before Helah's (a chiastic arrangement).

Both wives' names are omitted in the Syriac of v 5. The name Helah apparently means "necklace." Noth (*IPN* 223; cf. *HALAT* 2: 302) points to *ḥălî* (pl. *ḥălāʾîm*) and *ḥelyâ,* both of which refer to ornaments. See HAZZELELPONI regarding a proposed reading (in the *BHS* apparatus) of the end of v 3 as a gloss on the sequence of the names in vv 5–7.

Kenneth H. Cuffey

HELAM (PLACE) [Heb *hêlām*]. A town in Transjordan ca. 40 miles E of the Sea of Galilee. In 2 Sam 10:1–10 we read that King David sent messengers to Hanun, king of the Ammonites, to comfort Hanun when his father Nahash died. Hanun insulted David's messengers. In preparation for war, Hanun hired Syrian mercenaries from Beth-rehob, Zobah, Maacah, and Tob. The Israelites under Joab defeated them all (vv 6–14). The Syrians regrouped. Hadadezer, king of Zobah (8:3), brought other Syrians from beyond the Euphrates and came to Helam (10:16). David and his troops went to Helam (v 17) and fought the Syrians. The army commander Shobach was struck and died and the Syrians were again defeated. They made peace with Israel and became subject (tribute payers?) to Israel. The same story is told in 1 Chronicles 19, but there is no mention of Helam. McCarter (*2 Samuel* AB, 269) notes Thenius' view of the Heb *hylm* as meaning "their army" (cf. Vulgate), but the LXX, Syr and Targ render it as a proper noun identical with *hlʾmh* in v. 17. McCarter understands chapter 10 as a unit, though other commentators separate the Ammonites from the Aramaean wars and the vv 6–14 battle from the Helam battle. These views do not seem to affect the identification of Helam. Helam appears also in the LXX of Ezek 47:16 and 48:1 (Gk *Eliam*), but not in the Hebrew. In Ezekiel, the site is between Damascus and Hamath, not far from Hadadezer's main cities, Tebah and Berothai (2 Sam 8:8), from which David had taken large quantities of bronze as war loot.

Hoffmann identified Helam with Haleb, the city of Aleppo (Smith *Samuel* ICC, 316). Ewald connected it with Alamatha on the Euphrates as in Ptolemy's *Geography* 5.15 (Keil and Delitzsch, n.d.: 380). Ottosson (1969: 207) claims the Arameans would not have been threatened unless Helam was in Aramean territory. But McCarter (p. 273) and others consider this too far N. Shobach was invading Israelite territory or planning to, rather than waiting for David to come to Aramean territory.

The town of Alema, modern Alma, NE of Derʾa in the plain of Hauran on the S border of Syria in N Transjordan is mentioned in 1 Macc 5:26, 35. Judas Maccabeus burned it after having liberated its Jewish prisoners. McCarter notes that in the Greek, Alema is preceded by *en,* "in," rather than *eis,* "at," which appears with the preceding places. The other places are "in" Helam, i.e., Helam is the name of a district in which the battle took place, rather than the actual siege of a city. The preceding site of Bosor is identified with Busr el-Hariri, 45 mi east of the Sea of Galilee. From an earlier date, the city name appears as *Hlʾm* in the Egyptian Execration texts from ca. 1850 B.C., on a figurine now in Brussels (Albright 1941: 33).

Bibliography

Albright, W. F. 1941. The Land of Damascus between 1850 and 1750 B.C. *BASOR* 83: 30–36.

Keil, C. F., and Delitzsch, F. n.d. *Biblical Commentary on the Books of Samuel.* Grand Rapids. Repr. 1967.

Ottosson, M. 1969. *Gilead: Tradition and History.* Lund.

HENRY O. THOMPSON

HELBAH (PLACE) [Heb *ḥelbâ*]. One of the towns from which the tribe of Asher failed to drive the Canaanite inhabitants (Judg 1:31). Earlier in the same verse the town of Ahlab is mentioned, and many scholars (*GP* 2:67; Boling, *Judges* AB, 455) argue that Helbah is either a dittographic error for or a variant spelling of Ahlab, the *Maḫalliba* of Sennacherib, which they locate at Kh. el-Mahaḷib (M.R. 172303). See AHLAB (PLACE).

Kallai argues that Helbah is an independent location, which he links with the *mēḥebel* of Josh 19:29 (RSV "Mahalab"), also mentioned in a description of the territory of Asher (*HGB*, 222). He argues that the initial *mem* of *mēḥebel* is really the preposition "from," so that the two names (Helbah and *Hebel) share the same consonants. On balance, it seems more probable that Helbah, Ahlab, and *mēḥebel* are all variants of the same name. See also MAHALAB (PLACE).

MELVIN HUNT

HELBON (PLACE) [Heb *ḥelbôn*]. A place mentioned in Ezekiel's lamentation over Tyre (Ezek 27:18). According to Ezekiel, Damascus traded wine from Helbon (as well as wool, and wine from Uzal) for Tyrian merchandise. There is almost universal agreement that this place is to be identified with modern Helbûn, located 11 miles N of Damascus (33°38'N; 36°15'E), an area where even today viticulture plays a prominent role in the local economy. Contemporaneous with Ezekiel, a Babylonian text indicates that Nebuchadnezzar had a predeliction for the wine from *mât helbûnim* (*ISBE* 2: 676). Strabo, in discussing the customs of the Persian kings (*Geog.* 15.3.22), notes how they adopted a fondness for "Chalymonian wine from Syria." The Gk *chalumōnion* perhaps reflects the original Semitic *ḥlbwn* (note the *b/m* interchange).

GARY A. HERION

HELDAI (PERSON) [Heb *ḥelday*]. Var. HELEB; HELED. **1.** One of twelve commanders supervising monthly courses of 24,000 men in the armed service of the king (1 Chr 27:1–15), Heldai was in charge of the course of the twelfth month (v 15). A Netophathite, that is, one from the town of Netophah in the hill country of Judah (1 Chr 2:54; Ezra 2:21–22), he is said to be "of Othniel," probably a reference to a family name, possibly descendants of the deliverer of the Israelites in Judg 3:7–11. This list of commanders and their functions is possibly a construct of its composer, since (a) no such monthly, conscripted, civilian army is mentioned elsewhere during David's reign; (b) the large figure of 288,000 men seems improbable; and (c) one of the commanders, Asahel (v 7), was dead before David had rule over all Israel (Williamson *1 and 2 Chronicles* NCBC, 174–75). However, the author/redactor's thesis, that David made preparations for the proper ongoing cultic and national life of Israel, as illustrated throughout chapters 23-27, draws on the fact that David took a census (cf. vv 23–24; chap 21) which could have been utilized for designing a monthly plan of conscription, a plan which would have been analogous to Solomon's monthly courses for his provision (1 Kgs 4:7–19).

Because the names of the other eleven commanders appear again in the list of David's champions in 1 Chr 11:10–47 (= 2 Sam 23:8–39), it is probable that this Heldai is to be equated with Heled of 1 Chr 11:30 and Heleb of 2 Sam 23:29 and, therefore, was a member of this select class of warriors directly attached to the king for special assignments. ("Heldai" can be explained as an Aramized form of "Heled," while the name "Heleb" is probably a textual variant which arose because of the similarity of "b" *[bet]* with "d" *[dalet]* in the old Hebrew script; Meyers *Haggai and Zechariah* AB, 340).

2. A returned Babylonian exile who, according to an oracle to the prophet Zechariah, was to participate with the prophet in the symbolic crowning of the priest Joshua, a representative of a Messianic figure who would build the temple and rule upon the throne (Zech 6:9–15; vv 10 and 14). Due to the difficult language of the text, it is unclear if Heldai, along with Tobijah and Jedaiah, was to be taken along by Zechariah as a witness to this prophetic gesture (Mitchell *Haggai* ICC, 183–85) or if he was one from whom silver and gold were to be received in order to make the crowns which were used (Meyers *Haggai* AB, 337–38). The latter interpretation, which makes sense of the passage's stylistic difficulties rather than emending the text as the former interpretation does, is to be preferred. Reading with the latter interpretation, Heldai still probably functioned as a witness to the prophetic act, since the crown placed in the temple is to serve as a reminder to him and the others (v 14). Verse 14 in the Hebrew text has the name *ḥēlem,* "Helem," rather than Heldai. However, because of the presence again of Tobijah and Jedaiah, it is evident that "Helem" is either another name for Heldai or a spelling that arose due to textual corruption (see the variations for Heldai in 1. above). In the LXX, perhaps because of the symbolic nature of Zechariah's act, these names were read as appellatives.

Heldai is probably a secular name taken from the animal realm, meaning "mole" (*IPN,* 230).

RODNEY K. DUKE

HELEB (PERSON) [Heb *ḥēleb*]. See HELDAI (PERSON).

HELECH (PLACE) [Heb *ḥêlēk*]. Ezekiel 27 records an oracle against the city of Tyre, and in the oracle are references to foreign nationalities in Tyre's army—men from Persia, Lud, and Put, and men of Arvad (the island of Aradus, 125 miles N of Tyre) and Helech. These are usually taken to be foreign mercenaries, hired by Tyre to defend the city—"mercenaries from every country and allegiance to guard her walls and towers" says Eichrodt (*Ezekiel,* ET, OTL, 1970: 386) with some hyperbole. The RSV translates Helech as a place name, while LXX, Syriac, KJV, and ASV translate "thine army" from Heb *ḥyl,* "strength," "army" with the final letter understood as the feminine form of the pronoun "you" (Keil n.d.: 384; Eichrodt *Ezekiel,* ET, OTL, 1970: 379; Zimmerli 1983: 46). Simons' (*GTTOT,* 455) preference is that Ezekiel did not refer to a geographical or topographical name. Helech, like the Gamad or men of Gamad of v 11b in parallel, is also more like an appellative noun. With support from the LXX and Syriac and only a slight change in text, one can translate "the men of Arvad were your army (*ḥêlēk,* cf. v. 10) on your walls round about and watchmen (*šômrîm* instead of *gammādîm*) on your towers." In contrast to Simons, Cooke (*Ezekiel* ICC, 300) thinks a proper noun is necessary.

If Helech is a place, it is probably the Assyrian *Hilakku,* the original "Cilicia" N of the Taurus mountains in SE Asia Minor, today's Turkey. These Cilicians were noted for their warlike character and would fit as mercenaries of Tyre. Hilakku is found in the records of Shalmaneser III (858–824). The Cilicians were conquered ca. 720 by Sargon II (721–705). The area revolted against Sennacherib in 696 and also against Esarhaddon (680–669), but ca. 668/7 they sent tribute to Assurbanipal (Mellink, *IDB* 2: 578).

The name appears later on coins of Tarsus in the 4th century. Cooke (*Ezekiel* ICC, 300) credits Halevy with the Helek/Hilakku identification, but thinks "the context implies a town nearer to Phoenicia." He notes Cornill's suggestion of Hethlon (Ezek 47:15; 48:1) near Hamath. Simons claimed the identification of *ḥêlēk* as Chalcis is only a guess based on assonance. Chalcis ad Belum (near Qinnesrin, SW of Aleppo) as well as Chalcis ad Libanum in the Syrian Beqaʾ (now ʾAngarr) are suggested sites, but they are too late in origin for this recognition in Ezekiel.

Bibliography

Keil, C. F. n.d. *Biblical Commentary on the Prophecies of Ezekiel.* Grand Rapids. Repr. 1966.

Zimmerli, W. 1983. *Ezekiel 2.* Hermeneia. Philadelphia.

HENRY O. THOMPSON

HELED (PERSON) [Heb *ḥēled*]. See HELDAI (PERSON).

HELEK (PERSON) [Heb *ḥēleq*]. HELEKITES. In Num 26:30 (RSV) Helek translates *ḥēleq,* which there appears as the name of a person, a son of Gilead (son of Machir, son of Manasseh). In Josh 17:2 (RSV), part of a description of the allotment of land to the tribe of Manasseh, Helek translates the phrase *bĕnê ḥēleq* ("children of Helek"), which is described in the text as a "clan" (*mišpāḥâ,* RSV "family"). In Joshua Helek is not identified as a son of Gilead but is a part of the tribe of Manasseh independent of Gilead.

In Num 26:30 Helek is named as part of a listing of the "sons of Joseph according to their families" (Num 26:28–37), and is specifically associated with a clan group of the same name (RSV: "the family of the Helekites" *[mišpaḥat haḥelqî]*). OT genealogies, such as that underlying the census report in Numbers 26, are often descriptions of the relations among social and ethnic groups under the guise of individual kinship relations. Perhaps then none of the references to Helek should be thought of as referring to an individual of that name, but rather to a clan group described as an individual to meet the needs of genealogical form.

This view is supported by the occurrence of the name Helek in five of the SamOstr (Reisner, Fisher, and Lyon 1924: 229–40). In these records Helek is not the name of a person. It is either the name of a clan, or, as Naʾaman (1986: 159) asserts, the name of an administrative district, albeit derived from an earlier clan name.

According to Boling (*Joshua* AB, 406–15), Joshua 17 places Helek among the clans of Manasseh located W of the Jordan. The Samaria Ostraca are widely seen to point to a location west of the Jordan for Helek (e.g., *LBHG,* 315–27). Num 26:30, on the other hand, by associating Helek with Gilead, suggests a location east of the Jordan. That Helek was located west of the Jordan is widely accepted, however. The genealogy in Numbers is usually explained as a result of literary development of the genealogical texts (Noth *Numbers* OTL, 206–207), or a combination of literary development and changes in the societal relations mirrored in the genealogies (*LBHG,* 222).

Although Helek in the OT probably refers to a group, not an individual, the use of Helek as a personal name in ancient Israel is attested on three bullae (clay document seals) from late 7th or early 6th century B.C.E. Judah (Avigad 1986: 56, 73, 96). As a personal name it is probably a shortened form of the theophoric name Hilkiyahu (HILKIAH).

Bibliography

Avigad, N. 1986. *Hebrew Bullae from the Time of Jeremiah.* Jerusalem.

Naʾaman, N. 1986. *Borders and Districts in Biblical Historiography.* Jerusalem Biblical Studies 4. Jerusalem.

Reisner, G. A.; Fisher, C. S.; and Lyon, D. G. 1924. *Harvard Excavations at Samaria: 1908–1910.* Vol. 1. Cambridge, MA.

RICHARD D. WEIS

HELEM (PERSON) [Heb *hēlem*]. **1.** An Asherite, the father of Zophah, Imna, Shelesh, and Amal (1 Chr 7:35). BHS suggests that the MT of 1 Chr 7:35a "and the son of

Helem his brother" should be amended to read "and the sons of Hotham his brother." The context (1 Chr 7:32–35) and some textual witnesses (several medieval Heb mss, LXX Lucian recension, Vg) support this significant change, which, incidentally, is adopted totally by the NEB but only partially by the RSV (no name change). With the acceptance of this proposed textual emendation, "Helem" of 1 Chr 7:35 becomes the same person as "Hotham" in 1 Chr 7:32. See HOTHAM. In some early editions of the RSV (1952/53) the name was erroneously printed as "Heler."

2. An exile who returned from Babylon (MT Zech 6:14), also called Heldai (RSV, Zech 6:10, 14; see n. i). See HELDAI. He was one of at least three prime donors from whom the prophet Zechariah took silver and gold, either to make a "crown" for Joshua, the postexilic high priest (RSV), or perhaps more originally for Zerubbabel, the governor of Judah and descendant of the house of David (see ZERUBBABEL), whose name was then subsequently expunged in the face of political realities (see also NEB 1 Chr 6:11, n. g). Still, as the present MT reads the noun in the plural, "crowns," perhaps even the idea of two crowns, a silver crown for Joshua and a gold crown for Zerubbabel, should be seriously entertained (Cohen 1957: 292). To be sure, Zech 4:1–6a, and 10b–14, if not also 6:12–13, envision the postexilic community as reconstituted under a dual leadership, an idea still fully present in the later Essene Jewish community uncovered at Khirbet Qumran. In MT Zech 6:10 Heldai, Tobijah, and Jedaiah contribute the metals which were then taken to the house of Josiah, the son of Zephaniah; in MT Zech 6:14, when the same persons are noted again, two of the former names turn out differently, viz., as "Helem and Hen (= Josiah), the son of Zephaniah." Nevertheless, since both these variants, Hen and Helem, are shorter than their counterparts in 6:10, the suggestion has been made to understand the names Helem and Hen as nicknames rather than as inexplicable textual deviations (Petersen *Haggai and Zechariah* OTL, 278). Oddly, in the LXX, though, except for the name Josiah, there is no mention of any proper names in this context whatsoever. The citation of the name Helem and the other names in the text has served to document for posterity the wholesome participation of those newly returned from exile in the important work of postexilic cultic reconstruction and in the recognition of the validity of Zechariah's own ministry and word of promise. In this vein, one recent interpreter of Zech 6:9–15 has gone so far as to view the making and placing of a crown on Joshua's head and then in the temple as one comprehensive prophetic symbolic action: in her view, the three returnees from Babylon were taken as witnesses to the house of Josiah where the precious metals were fashioned into a single "double-ringed" royal tiara, which prior to its being deposited in the rebuilt temple was placed symbolically upon Joshua's head as a temporary "stand-in" for the longed-for Branch from the house of David who would come one day to wear it (Achtemeier *Nahum-Malachi* IBC, 130–32).

Bibliography

Cohen, A., ed. 1957. *The Twelve Prophets.* London.

Roger W. Uitti

HELENA (PERSON). Flavia Iulia Helena (*CIL* VI 1134) is said to have been born, probably in the year 248, in a place called Drepanum in Bithynia (Proc. *Aedif.* 5. 2, 1–5), renamed after her death Helenopolis (*Chron. Pasch.* 527). She was of humble origin (Eutropius, *Brev.* 10. 2; Zosimus, *Hist. Nova* 2.8.2) and may have been working as a serving girl at an inn (Ambrosius, *De Obitu Theodosii,* 42) when Constantius Chlorus met her. The difference in their social status was probably the reason that there is no unequivocal evidence of a formal marriage. Of their union was born, in 273, the future emperor Constantine the Great. Their relationship probably came to an end in 289, when, for political reasons, Constantius married Theodora, daughter of the Augustus Maximian. From 289 until Constantine's rise to power in 306 the sources are silent about Helena. From about the year 306 she lived as a *nobilissima femina* (*RIC* VII, 493–94) at or in the neighborhood of Constantine's court. Her first residence was in all likelihood the northern capital of the Empire, Trier. The vast corpus of medieval legends seems to go back to an early tradition attesting the connection between Helena and Trier (Ewig 1956–58; Linder 1975: 84–93). Frescoes found on a ceiling underneath the cathedral of Trier after the Second World War, in a part of the imperial palace known as the *domus Helenae,* allows a similar inference (Weber 1984). One of the paintings is in fact a portrait of Helena herself. Some time after Constantine's victory over Maxentius (312) Helena moved to Rome, where she lived in the *Palatium Sessorianum* in the SE part of the city. This palace, including its neighboring extramural territory, the *fundus Laurentus* (*Lib. Pont.* 1, 183, Deichmann and Tschira 1957: 66–81), was her personal property. Inscriptions (*CIL* VI 1134; *CIL* VI 1135; *CIL* VI 1136) found near the *Palatium* provide evidence for Helena's presence and activities in Rome. One inscription of special interest states that Helena had *thermae* repaired which had been damaged by fire (*CIL* VI 1136).

Following her son, Helena acquired an interest in the Christian faith and was converted by Constantine (Eus. *Vita C.* 3. 47). She was sympathetic to Arianism (Athanasius, *Hist. Ar.* 4. 1–2). Literary sources are not the only proof of her conversion: the transformation of one of the rooms of the *Palatium Sessorianum* into a chapel in the 320s is another strong indication (Krautheimer 1967: 130). This *basilica Heleniana quae dicitur Sessorium* (*Lib. Pont.* 1. 196) later became known as S. Croce in Gerusalemme. When Constantine had become sole ruler after his victory over Licinius in 324, he bestowed on his mother the title *Augusta* (*RIC* VII, 45, 69). By doing this he made her one of the most important and prestigious women of the Empire. After Fausta's murder by her imperial husband (326), Helena became the most influential woman at Constantine's court. In the same year she undertook a journey to the eastern provinces of the Empire. Eusebius, bishop of Caesarea, informs us well about her activities in Palestine (*Vita C.* 3. 42–47). Her travels through the Holy Land are represented by Eusebius as a pilgrimage. He is full of praise for her piety and her charity. She gave lavishly to cities, to certain groups of soldiery, and to the naked and the helpless poor: obviously she could spend as much money from the public treasury as she thought fit. She naturally donated large amounts of money to the churches she frequented, even to those in the tiniest places. Prisoners and forced laborers in the mines were freed at her orders, and exiles were recalled. She is most famous for the dedication of two churches in the Holy Land, the Church of Nativity in Bethlehem, built over the very cave where Christ was born, and the Church of Ascension on the Mount of Olives. At the end of the year 327 or early in 328, shortly after her return from the Holy Land, Helena died, at the age of about eighty years, in the presence of her son, probably in Nicomedia (Eus. *Vita C.* 3. 46). Accompanied by a large military escort her corpse was transported to Rome, where she was buried in a porphyry sarcophagus (now in the Vatican Museum) in a mausoleum at the Via Labicana not far from her palace in Rome (Eus. *Vita C.* 3. 47; Deichmann and Tschira 1957).

Whereas the historical evidence for Helena is scanty, the legendary data are abundant. Already at the end of the 4th century and in the first half of the 5th century several versions of a legend had emerged in which the discovery of the true Cross was ascribed to Helena. The legend probably originated in Jerusalem. Since the 340s at least the Cross was venerated there, and parts of it had already been distributed over the world (Frolow 1961: 155–65), but its discovery was not attributed to anybody until in 395 Ambrosius mentioned Helena as the finder of the Cross. Shortly afterward the legend is recorded by several other Latin writers (Rufinus, *Hist. Eccl.* 10. 7–8; Paulinus of Nola, *Epist.* 31. 4–6; Sulpicius Severus, *Chron.* 2. 33–34) and some time later by Greek church-historians (Theodoretus, *Hist. Eccl.* 7. 18; Socrates, *Hist. Eccl.* 1. 17; Sozomenus, *Hist. Eccl.* 2. 1).

A divine vision urges Helena to go to Jerusalem in search of the Cross. A sign from heaven shows her the place where the Cross is buried. Excavations at Golgotha result in the discovery of three crosses: that of Christ and those of the two criminals. The *titulus,* reading in Greek, Latin, and Hebrew: "Jesus of Nazareth, King of the Jews," which Pontius Pilatus had attached to Jesus' cross (John 19: 19–20) is also found, but it had become detached from the Cross. The three crosses lie in a heap, and it is impossible to identify the true one. Macarius, bishop of Jerusalem, inspired by a divine message, helps to reveal which is Christ's Cross. By bringing the crosses into contact with a dead or dying person the true Cross is identified. The touch of two of these crosses has no effect, but on the contact with the third cross the person is healed/resurrected. This is a miracle that could be performed only with the true Cross. Later on Helena also found the nails by which Christ had been fixed to the Cross. She sent them to Constantine to be used in a diadem and a bridle and so fulfilled Zacharias' prophecy (Zacharias 14:20). This is briefly the main version of the legend of Helena, as told by the various Latin and Greek authors.

Another version, transmitted in Syriac, Greek, and Latin, introduces a Jew called Judas who, with some initial reluctance, helps Helena to find the Cross and the nails. Impressed by the power of the Christian God, Judas is converted and adopts the name Cyriacus. Eventually he is to become a bishop of Jerusalem and dies a martyr's death in the reign of Julian the Apostate (Straubinger 1912: 1–81). This version became very popular in the Middle Ages.

A third version of the legend of the discovery of the Cross, the so-called Protonike legend, is of Syrian origin. It was inserted in the Edessan *Doctrina Addai* but continued also to circulate independently or in connection with the Judas-Cyriacus version. It relates events that are supposed to have taken place in the 1st century A.D. In this version the Cross was found by Protonike, wife of the emperor Claudius (Nestle 1889; Lipsius 1880: 67–92). Although Helena does not figure in this version, there are such striking similarities between the two legends that the legend of Protonike should be regarded as a derivative of that of Helena.

The attribution to Helena of the discovery of the Cross has made her one of the most famous women of early Christianity. Her journey to Palestine served as a model for future pilgrims (Hunt 1984: 49) and the legends of her devotion provided an example for many a Byzantine empress. The Church canonized her for her pious deeds. Her commemoration is on August 18.

Bibliography

Deichmann, F. W., and Tschira, A. 1957. Das Mausoleum der Kaiserin Helena und die Basilika der heiligen Marcellinus und Petrus an der Via Labicana vor Rom. *JDAI* 72: 44–110.

Drijvers, J. W. 1989. *Helena Augusta: Waarheid en legende.* Groningen.

Ewig, E. 1956–58. Kaiserliche und apostolische Tradition in mittelalterlichen Trier. *TTZ* 24–26: 147–86.

Frolow, A. 1961. *La Relique de la Vraie Croix.* Paris.

Heid, S. 1989. Der Ursprung der Helenalegende im Pilgerbetrieb Jerusalems. *JAC* 32: 41–71.

Hunt, E. D. 1984. *Holy Land Pilgrimage in the Later Roman Empire AD 312–460.* Oxford.

Krautheimer, R. 1967. The Constantinian Basilica. *Dumbarton Oaks Papers* 21: 115–40.

Linder, A. 1975. The Myth of Constantine the Great in the West. *Studi Medievali,* 3d ser. 16: 43–95.

Lipsius, R. A. 1880. *Die Edessenische Abgarsage.* Braunschweig.

Nestle, E. 1889. *De Sancta Cruce. Ein Beitrag zur christlichen Legendengeschichte.* Berlin.

Straubinger, J. 1912. *Die Kreuzauffindungslegende.* Forschungen zur Christlichen Literatur- und Dogmengeschichte. Paderborn.

Weber, W. 1984. *Constantinische Deckengemälde aus dem römischen Palast unter dem Dom.* Trier.

JAN W. DRIJVERS

HELEPH (PLACE) [Heb *ḥēlep*]. The first place mentioned in the description of the territory of Naphtali (Josh 19:33). Both the LXX rendering of the name (Gk *meeleph*) and the explanation in the Talmud (*j. Meg.* 1:1, 70a) imply that the prefixed *mem* is part of the name. The context, however, shows that this *mem* has its usual meaning (MT *mēḥēlep,* "from Heleph"), and that Heleph is the starting point of Naphtali's S border, which is described E from the Mt. Tabor area to the Jordan (while Aznoth-Tabor is the starting point of the W border described from Mt. Tabor northward). Saarisalo (1927: 98, 122) has suggested identifying Heleph with Kh. ʿIrbadah (M.R. 189236) 4 km NW of Mt. Tabor. Pottery of the 9th–8th centuries B.C.E. has been found at the site (Gal 1982: 19), situated at the point where the E-W route, "Darb el-Hawarneh" (Oded 1971), meets the main N-S route, often called the "Way of the Sea." Located close to this site is Kh. et-Tuggar, which contains remains of caravanseries from Turkish and earlier periods.

Bibliography

Gal, Z. 1982. *The Lower Galilee in the Iron Age.* Diss., Tel Aviv (in Hebrew).

Oded, B. 1971. Darb el-Hawarneh: An Ancient Route. *EI* 10: 191–97 (in Hebrew).

Saarisalo, A. 1927. *The Boundary Between Issachar and Naphtali.* Helsinki.

RAFAEL FRANKEL

HELEZ (PERSON) [Heb *ḥeleṣ*]. **1.** One of David's champions, a select class of warriors directly attached to the king for special assignments, named in the parallel lists of 2 Sam 23:8–39 (v 26) and 1 Chr 11:10–47 (v 27). Although of high repute, he is distinguished from the more elite warriors (vv 8–23 and 11–25, respectively) listed before his grouping. In 2 Sam 23:26 he is called a Paltite, often assumed to refer to Beth-pelet in the Negeb of Judah (*NHT,* 369), whereas in 1 Chr 11:27 he, as well as Ahijah (v 36), is designated a Pelonite, either a gentilic name with an unidentified referent or a textual corruption.

The same Helez appears to be mentioned in a list of commanders found in 1 Chr 27:1–15 (v 10), since this list mentions eleven other mighty men found in 1 Chr 11:10–47. (However, here Helez, "the Pelonite," is also said to be "of the sons of Ephraim," a designation which would conflict with the interpretation that Helez of 2 Sam 23:26 is from Beth-pelet in Judah.) These commanders were each in charge of a monthly course of 24,000 men in the armed service of the king; Helez being in charge of the seventh month. This list of commanders and their functions is possibly a construct of its composer, since (a) no such monthly, conscripted civilian army is mentioned elsewhere during David's reign; (b) the large figure of 288,000 men is improbable; and (c) one of the commanders, Asahel (v 7) was dead before David had rule over all Israel (Williamson *Chronicles* NCBC, 174–75). However, the thesis that David made preparations for the proper ongoing cultic and national life of Israel, as illustrated throughout chap. 23–27, draws on the fact that David took a census (cf. vv 23–24; chap 21) which could have been utilized for designing a monthly plan of conscription, a plan which would have been analogous to Solomon's monthly courses for his provision (1 Kgs 4:7–19).

2. The son of Azariah and father of Eleasah, occurring in the diverse genealogical material of the tribe of Judah (1 Chr 2:3–4:23; 2:39) in the introductory lists and genealogies of the books of Chronicles (1 Chronicles 1–9).

Helez is possibly an abbreviated form, missing a theophoric element, for, "Yahweh has drawn out *(Qal)* / delivered *(Piᶜel)*" as in the extrabiblical *ḥlṣyhw* (*TPNAH,* 94) or the Phoenician *ḥlṣbᶜl,* "Baal has drawn out" (*IPN,* 180).

RODNEY K. DUKE

HELI (PERSON) [Gk *Hēli*]. The father of Joseph and son of Matthat, according to Luke's genealogy tying Joseph, the "supposed father" of Jesus, to descent from Adam and God (Luke 3:23). D omits Heli, substituting a genealogy adopted from Matt 1:6–15 for Luke 3:23–31. Heli (some mss and versions read Gk *ēli,* as well as an *-ei* ending), as the father of Joseph, occurs nowhere else in the biblical documents, including Matthew's genealogy, as a relative of Jesus, although the name is found elsewhere in the OT as Gk *ēli* and Heb *ᶜly* (1 Sam 1:3 etc.) (Fitzmyer *Luke 1–9* AB, 500). Kuhn (1923: 208–209, 211) argues that two seemingly parallel lists of names—Luke 3:23–36 (Jesus to Mattathias) and 3:29–31 (Joshua/Jesus to Mattatha)—were originally identical, the first perhaps reflecting a Hebrew context and the second, in an Aramaic context, tracing Mary's line of descent (since it does not mention Joseph as Jesus' father). Heli in the first list corresponds to Eliezer in the second list. Kuhn posits that Eliezer perhaps is derived from Heli appearing as Heb *zrᶜ ᶜly,* meaning "of the seed of Eli," but later misunderstood and corrupted to Heb *ʾlyᶜzr,* with the result that Eli was named as an ancestor of Jesus in both lines. Few scholars have found this suggestion plausible. Strack and Billerbeck (Str-B 2:155; cf. Kuhn 1923: 209–10 n. 1) cite a Miriam the daughter of Eli in *j. Hag.* 2:77d, 50, who could have been identified with Mary, Jesus' mother, making Eli Joseph's father-in-law. But this is rightly rejected (see also Marshall *Luke* NIGTC, 162). More attention has been directed toward harmonizing Matthat as the father of Heli in Luke 3:23–24 with Matthan as the father of Jacob in Matt 1:15. See MATTHAT #2 for discussion. A few late mss include "of Jacob" after Joseph and before "of Heli" in Luke 3:23.

Bibliography

Kuhn, G. 1923. Die Geschlechtsregister Jesu bei Lukas und Matthäus, nach ihrer Herkunft untersucht. *ZNW* 22: 206–228.

STANLEY E. PORTER

HELIODORUS (PERSON) [Gk *Hēliodōros*]. According to 2 Maccabees 3, Heliodorus, an official of the Seleucid court, was sent by Seleucus IV Philopater to confiscate funds from the Temple in Jerusalem. Simon, the administrator of the Temple, conspired with the Seleucid governor of Coele Syria and Phoenicia, Apollonius, to convince Seleucus to seek funds deposited in the Temple. While in the Temple treasury, Heliodorus encounters an apparition in the form of a rider wearing golden armor on a horse and two youths who strike Heliodorus repeatedly. Heliodorus is saved by the prayers of the high priest Onias III. Admonished by the reappearance of the two youths to show gratitude for his life, Heliodorus offers sacrifice to God and returns to Seleucus with news of the power of the Jewish God. Appian mentions Heliodorus as an officer of the Syrian court who masterminded the conspiracy to assassinate Seleucus and install himself as king (*Sur* 45). In Appian's history Heliodorus' conspiracy is thwarted by Eumenes and Attalus, who make Antiochus Epiphanes king. With respect to the account of 2 Maccabees 3, Bickerman identified two separate versions which were merged (1939: 21–35). Version A contains the story of the horse and rider (vv 24–25) and version B includes the account of the two youths who flog Heliodorus (vv 26–28). *4 Macc.* 3:19–4:14 roughly parallels Bickerman's version A although it is not Heliodorus but Apollonius who enters the Temple and is attacked by several figures on horseback. It is noteworthy that the account in 2 Maccabees 3 deems Heliodorus' attempted appropriation of Temple funds reprehensible, but not his presence in the Temple. Zeitlin noted that as *4 Macc.* 3:11 relates that Apollonius collapsed in the Court of the Gentiles (which did not exist), the author of *4 Maccabees* was more sensitive to the issue of the defilement of the Temple, whereas 2 Maccabees focuses on the attempted theft (1954: 122, n. 12 and 126, no. 27). Goldstein suggests that the Temple treasury was located on the Temple mount but was not part of the complex forbidden to gentiles (*II Maccabees* AB, 209). This thesis is supported by Josephus, who indicates that the outer court of the Temple was open to all individuals, including foreigners (*AgAp* 2.103). That Heliodorus offered sacrifice to God was also not unknown. Josephus records that Alexander the Great also made sacrifice (*Ant.* 11.8.5 §336). It is possible that as Heliodorus was contemplating a political coup, he found it politic to curry favor with the Jewish high priest.

Bibliography

Bickerman, E. 1939. "Héliodore au Temple de Jérusalem." *AIPHOS* 7: 5–40. Repr. Vol. 2, pp. 159–91 in *Studies in Jewish and Christian History*. Leiden. 1980.

Zeitlin, S. 1954. *The Second Book of Maccabees*. Trans. S. Tedesche. New York.

MICHAEL E. HARDWICK

HELIOPOLIS (PLACE) [Heb *bêt šemeš*]. A city of Egypt mentioned by Jeremiah in an oracle of doom directed against the Egyptians (Jer 43:13). The Hebrew here (lit. "house of the sun [which is in the land of Egypt]") clearly echoes the Gk form *Heliopolis*, "city of Helios (the sun)," so called from the worship of solar deities peculiar to the city. In Egyptian the town was called *Iwnw*, "pillar town," a form reflected in Akk *Āna*, Coptic *Ōn*, and Heb *ʾôn*/*ʾāwen* (Ezek 30:17), which LXX renders *Helioupoleus*). The ancient city is now identified with Tell Hisn in Matariyeh, a N suburb of Cairo. See also SUN, CITY OF THE.

Heliopolis was the metropolis of the 13th nome of Lower Egypt, occupied as early as predynastic times (Debono 1954), with extensive building operations carried out throughout the Old Kingdom. Although never a center of political power, the local high priesthood ("the greatest of seers") became influential early in the Old Kingdom and maintained itself throughout most of Egyptian history (Moursi 1972; Daressy 1916). The principal deity was Re-harakhty (*RÄR*, 269), but Atum figured more prominently in Heliopolitan theology (Myśliwiec 1978). Attached to the figure of Atum were the "Nine" (Ennead), i.e., Atum himself and the eight deities descended from him, the whole providing both the framework of solar creation and the mythological genealogy of the king. By the end of the 4th Dyn. Pharaoh had become "son of Re," and the theology of Heliopolis had involved itself in the legitimation of kingship (Anthes 1954; 1959). In the Pyramid Texts (see *AEL* I: 29–50) of the late 5th through 8th Dynasties (ca. 2450–2180 B.C.) the dominance of the cult of Re was complete (Faulkner 1969), and (at one level) its antipathy to Osiris and his cycle most marked (Griffiths 1980: 99–107). This theological importance of the town and its gods continued through the Middle Kingdom when the solar cult was clearly the informing principle behind the Coffin Texts. Likewise in the fields of art and architecture, style, repertoire, and construction techniques seem to have owed a great deal to Heliopolitan prototypes (Gasse 1981).

During the 2d millennium B.C. royal construction was lavished upon the site. Senwosret I rebuilt the temple of Re-Harakhty and contributed an obelisk and a palace (El-Banna 1981). Whether the Hyksos built the earthen embankment there is a moot point (Kemp, *AESH*, 157) but they certainly continued the worship of Re. Under Thutmose III two obelisks (now in London and New York) were erected, the enclosure wall was restored, and various gates were added (Radwan 1981); Amenophis II and Thutmose IV contributed some decoration, and Amenophis III erected a temple to Horus (Bakry 1967). Akhenaten built a temple called *Wṯs-itn* ("Elevating the Sun disc") somewhere on the site (Habachi, 1971). The Ramesside kings built extensively at Heliopolis: temples (Sety I, Rameses II, Merenptah, Rameses III, and Rameses IV; see Saleh 1981–83; Bakry 1967), chapels for Mnevis (Rameses II, Rameses VII), royal mortuary installations (Rameses IX), and storehouses (Rameses III). During the 20th Dyn. the city reached its apogee in material wealth, owning 12,963 chattels, 45,544 head of cattle, 64 plantations, over 100,000 acres of farmland, and 103 Egyptian towns.

Geography dictated that Heliopolis' main orientation should be S towards Kher-aha (modern Fustat), whence proceeded the Heliopolis canal which passed W of the town. The topography of the site itself centers upon the main enclosure, 1100 × 475 m. The principal and most ancient temple belonged to the sun-god Re (-Harakhty) and was associated with an artificial mound of sand and a sacred lake. Adjacent thereto stood the "Mansion of the *benben*-stone" (a truncated obelisk sacred to the sun-god; *KG*, 380) focusing upon a monumental staircase and window for viewing the sun. Of equal antiquity, and particularly concerned with the legitimation of kingship (Anthes 1959: 192–93; Griffiths 1980: 178–9), was the "Great Mansion," or the "Mansion of the Prince," associated with the creator Atum (El-Banna 1985: 149–63; Mysliwiec 1978). Here stood the *išd*-tree, on the leaves of which the king's name and annals were inscribed (Redford 1986: 82), while acacia and willow trees were also revered in their own shrines. On the N side of the site stood some sort of installation dedicated to the "Souls of Heliopolis," divine manifestations of the powers of the place, while on the S, west of the canal, was the temple of Saosis and Hathor, mistress of Hetpet. Sacred animals associated with the solar cults and worshipped at Heliopolis included the phoenix, *bnw*, revered in the "Mansion of the Phoenix," and the black bull Mnevis, "Re's replica, who elevates Truth to Atum" (Myšliwiec 1978, I: 33ff, 78–79). The latter possessed a formal burial ground NE of the city.

Throughout the New Kingdom, Heliopolis occupied a prominent place in the theology of kingship. Kings were considered the image of the sun-god on earth. The coronation was supposed to take place at Heliopolis, and the well-known motif of Atum affixing the crown in the presence of the *išd*-tree is of Heliopolitan inspiration (Myśliwiec, 1980). Princes might enjoy appointment as high priest of Re, while kings could assume the appellative

"Heliopolitan ruler" in imitation of Atum (Myśliwiec 1978, II: 99).

Heliopolis suffered in the foreign invasions of the 20th Dyn., and before the close of the New Kingdom it had already begun to decline (Osing 1983). At the end of the 20th Dyn. (ca. 1080 B.C.) are reports of lawless acts perpetrated by the inhabitants (Caminos 1977). Although Osorkon I (ca. 900 B.C.) lavished gifts on its temples, a century later Heliopolis had sunk to a mere dependency of neighboring Athribis as an appendage of the crown prince. With the visit of Piankhy in the late 8th century, the fortunes and reputation of Heliopolis revived, and the Saite period (664–525 B.C.) marked its last brief restoration, a period contemporaneous with the oracles of Jeremiah and Ezekiel. It was then that the priests of Heliopolis gained a reputation for intellectual and "scientific" pursuits (cf. Strabo xvii.1.29). Solon is supposed to have studied under Psenophis of Heliopolis (Plut. *Sol.* 113) and Pythagoras with an Oinouphis from the same town. The tradition to which Strabo and Apion fell heir made Moses a priest of Heliopolis (Redford 1986: 284–88), and the same late prominence of the city may account for its presence in the Pentateuch (Gen 41:45, 50; 46:20; Exod 1:11 [LXX]).

Strabo found Heliopolis mostly deserted in his day (1st cent. B.C.), the temples in ruins and only a few priests performing the cult (xvii.1.27–29). Allusions in Chaeremon and Plutarch, both 1st cent. A.D., undoubtedly derive from earlier sources. In 640 A.D. Heliopolis was the site of one of the decisive battles in the Islamic conquest of Egypt.

Bibliography

Anthes, R. 1954. Note Concerning the Great Corporation of Heliopolis. *JNES* 13: 191–92.

———. 1959. Egyptian Mythology in the Third Millennium B.C. *JNES* 18: 169–212.

Bakry, H. 1967. Was there a Temple of Horus at Heliopolis? *MDAIK* 22: 53–60.

Balboush, M. 1976. General Soundings in Heliopolis in 1971. *GM* 22: 65–70.

Caminos, R. 1977. *A Tale of Woe.* Oxford.

Daressy, G. 1916. La nécropole des grands prêtres d'Héliopolis sous l'ancien empire. *ASAE* 16: 193–220.

Debono, F. 1954. La nécropole prédynastique d'Héliopolis. *ASAE* 42: 625–52.

El-Banna, E. 1981. L'obélisque de Sésostris Ier a Héliopolis. *RdÉ* 33: 3–9.

———. 1985. Deux études héliopolitaines. *BIFAO* 85: 149–72.

Faulkner, R. 1969. *The Ancient Egyptian Pyramid Texts.* Oxford.

Gasse, A. 1981. Une influence héliopolitaine dans la science de la construction? *RdÉ* 33: 23–28.

Griffiths, F. 1980. *The Origin of Osiris and His Cult.* Leiden.

Habachi, L. 1971. Akhenaten in Heliopolis. *Beiträge zur ägyptischen Bauforschung und Altertumskunde* 12: 135–45.

Moursi, M. 1972. *Die Hohenpriester des Sonnengottes von der Frühzeit Ägyptens bis zum Ende des Neuen Reiches.* Munich.

Myśliwiec, K. 1978. *Studien zum Gott Atum.* Hildesheim.

———. 1980. Die Rolle des Atum in der išd-baum Szene. *MDAIK* 36: 349–54.

Osing, J. 1983. Die Wörte von Heliopolis. Pp. 347–61 in *Fontes atque Pontes.* Wiesbaden.

Radwan, A. 1981. Zwei Stelen aus dem 47. Jahre Thutmosis' III *MDAIK* 37: 403ff.

Redford, D. B. 1986. *Pharaonic King Lists, Annals, and Daybooks.* Toronto.

Saleh, A. 1981–83. *Excavations at Heliopolis.* Vols. 1–2. Cairo.

DONALD B. REDFORD

HELIOS (DEITY). Although the Gk sun-god *(Helios)* was not one of the great Olympian deities, it rose by way of the history and politics of religion to become, as the focus of a philosophical theology, an imperial god. In this latter form lies its significance for Judaism and Christianity.

A. Classical Greece

The sun was the object of only marginal veneration by Greeks, although the sun enjoyed respect as a symbol of life. Socrates is said to have called upon the sun each morning (Plato *Symp.* 220d). Metaphorically the sun often represents life, and death represents the sun's departure; injustice is brought by the sun into "the light of day." The seasons, day and night, and nature all originate from the sun. Love, happiness, and freedom can be referred to as "sun." Goodness and truth are related to it. The Greeks were aware that the sun was the object of worship by non-Greeks, i.e., the barbarians (Plato *Leg.,* 10.887 e; *Cra.* 397c). As a deity the sun-god functioned for the Greeks primarily as a witness to oaths (Hom. *Il.* 11.30; *Od.* 5. 184) and as a patron of justice and law (already characteristic of the sun-god in the ancient East). The sun's universal presence promises protection and security. Offerings made as part of an oath were accompanied by prayer to Zeus, the sun, the waters, and the earth (Hom. *Il.* 3.268ff.) and Zeus, the earth, and the sun were frequently addressed in this context. For Aeschylus, the sun is the witness to the trials of Prometheus (*PV* 5.88ff.). Yet another function of the sun-god was healing, especially for blindness. The sun was the god of the vision given at birth; at the same time, the sun could send blindness as a penalty.

The cult of Helios was centered especially in Rhodes, where the sun-god (Helios) was considered the "Lord of the Island" (Pindar *Isthm.* 7). A temple to the sun was found there, and "sun-festivals" (Gk *Aleieia* or *Aleia*), with games, competitions, sacrifices, and processions, were celebrated. The Colossus of Rhodes was the sun. Additional cult centers are known to have been located in Laconia, Argolis, Elis, Athens (as god of oaths), Apollonia (Illyria), and Crete. In Corinth the sun was considered the main deity of the fortress, which was known as the City of the Sun and minted coins showing the sun-god as a charioteer driving four horses. The kiss of the hand, prostration, and sacrifices of white sheep and horses were cultic acts associated with the sun cult.

The legends and myths associated with the sun-god are largely of late origin. The deity's father was said to have been the Titan Hyperion (but also Zeus and Hephaestus); his mother was the Titan Theia or Europhaessa; his sister was Selene (the Moon). His spouse was variously given as Perse, Antiope, and Selene (!); his lover as Leukothea, Clytia; his children as Selene (!), Eos (Dawn), and Circe (according to Homer). The sacred sheep and cattle of the sun were known already to Homer (*Od.* 1.8–9; 11.108ff.; 12.127ff., 260ff.) In late antiquity the Phoenix legend was linked to the sun (cf. *1 Clem.* 25). In literature and art the sun-god is initially portrayed as a "wanderer" (Homer), then as riding on a chariot drawn by horses. Originally symbolized by the sun-disk above his head, the Sun was later identified by a wreath of rays (from about the 5th century B.C. until the end of the ancient world). Because, possibly under Egyptian influence, the sun's nightly journey from the west back to the east was portrayed as taking place in a ship (in the form of a kettle or chalice), a boat or a bowl also served as an emblem for Helios.

B. Hellenistic Era and Late Antiquity.

The late antique sun cult had its antecedents in the Hellenistic era. Both foreign, oriental sun-worship and astrological teachings, on the one hand, and new philosophical ideas (especially in Stoicism), on the other, contributed to the emergence of the sun-god (Helios) as a universal deity (Aion). The ancient image of the sun owed much to these, above all his being considered equal to other deities, especially Apollo (himself an oriental sun-god), Pluto, Dionysos (through Orphism), and the oriental deities Sarapis and Mithras. Cleanthes (331/30–232/31 B.C.) was the first to mention the sun as the director (Gk *Hegemon*) of the cosmos (cf. Diog. Laert. 7.139). In this way the sun became the highest principle, the prime source for the world of matter and spirit (cf. Poseidonios and Pliny). Helios originated as a fiery substance, the intellect *(nus)* and soul of the cosmos from which all human souls have arisen like rays of the sun. This "theologia solaris" had monotheistic tendencies (in the utopian sun-state of Jambulos only the sun was worshipped) but remained primarily on the level of philosophy and theology until, probably through the Julian calendar reform carried out by Augustus (46 B.C.), it became a cultic religion (according to Nilsson 1933). The sun-god then began to play a larger role in popular religion. This is indicated by magical texts, which cite a number of hymns to the sun that illustrate the "syncretistic" spirit of the cult (*PGM* [ed. Preisendanz] 1.315–25 [Betz 11]; 3.198–229 [Betz 23–24]; 4.436–61 [Betz 46]; 4.939–48 [Betz 56–57]; 4.1957–89 [Betz 72]; 8.74–81 [Betz 47]). The public role of sun-worship was augmented by the expansive penetration of the Syrian-Arabic sun cult (especially Bel of Emesa) that was firmly established in Rome by the Severan dynasty (193–235). The final step was the creation of the imperial cult of the *Sol Invictus* by Aurelian in 274. The calendar firmly established the festival of the *dies natalis Solis invicti* (Dec. 25) in the Roman Empire.

A variety of evidence for growing veneration of the sun since the 1st and 2d centuries can be cited: Plutarch considered Apollo/Helios as the highest god; Apollonius of Tyana (1st century) prayed regularly to Helios; Mesomedes, one of Hadrian's freedmen, composed hymns to the sun; the Hermetic writings, drawing on ancient Egyptian tradition, are familiar with the sun as the ruling director of the world (especially Tractate XVI); Helios and Apollo dominate the well known novel "Aithiopica" of Heliodorus (3d century), the son of a priest of the sun-god from Emesa (Homs). The 31st Homeric hymn, probably also dating from this period, is dedicated to the sun-god and concludes with the petition, "Hail to you, Lord! Freely bestow on me substance that cheers the heart." The Orphic hymn to the sun (no. 8) is also probably best understood as coming from this period. In it the sun-god is addressed as lord of light, life, and the seasons and as the cosmic, all-encompassing eye of justice, "immortal Zeus," "Lord of the World," and "Light of Life" (ed. and trans. A. Athanassakis).

The time was ripe for the identification of other gods with the sun, a sort of "solarization" of the Pantheon. In this process Apollo and Dionysos followed the path already taken by the Egyptian deity Sarapis and the pseudo-Iranian god Mithras. The Roman emperors began to add "New Sun" to their titles, beginning with Caligula (37–41), then Nero (54–68), who had a statue to the sun placed in front of his palace and minted the first coins carrying an image of the emperor crowned by rays of the sun. Caracalla (211–17) and Elagabalus (218–22) were called *Helioi.* All of this pointed to the victory of the *Sol invictus* as the focal point of the political imperial ideology as described above. Emperor Julian (360–63) was a firm adherent of the sun cult, as his famous speech to "King Sun" (*Or.* 4) makes clear. The monotheistic trend in Julian owed something to both resistance to and influence by Christian ideas. The sun is the highest being, binding the invisible (intellectual) and visible world together, and has salvific significance as the creator of humans and the refuge of souls that originated from him.

The 4th and 5th centuries brought what was probably the height of the solar religion. The late- or neoplatonic philosophy owed as much to it as did the (heathen) emperors. In his *Saturnalia* (1.17–23), Macrobius (ca. 400) developed a monotheistic teaching on the sun-god that had a pantheistic tint: Helios/Apollos is not only the supreme Lord, power, and inner mover of the intellectual and material world, but he is also linked to all the old and new gods. Such neoplatonists as Libanius, Iamblichus, and Proclus (who wrote a hymn to the sun-god) were likewise taken in by this sun cult, as were most of the contemporary intellectuals. Indeed, Christianity in the west understood its *Soter Christus* as *Sol Salutis* and, in contrast to the Greek east, retained the sun-day of the ancient solar calendar. Churches were thus oriented toward the east in a manner corresponding to the Helios temples. What was being lost in the sun cult, however, was restored by the new religion: a more popular orientation, which was missing in the politically abstract sun theology.

C. Judaism

The so-called OT (in the form of the LXX) refers to apostasy into worship of the sun (LXX: *Helios*), e.g. Deut 4:19, 17:3; Ezek 8:16; 2 Kgs 23:5 (Baal = *Helios*), but uses the word "sun" solely metaphorically or symbolically. God is not directly described as sun, but his eyes are brighter than the sun (Sir 23:28) and his throne is like the sun (Ps 89[88]:37). God's wisdom *(Sophia)* is greater than the sun (Wis 7:92). God established the sun and thus brought light into being (1 Kgs 8:12; Ps 18[19]:5, 73[74]:16; Gen 1:3–4). With God's help Joshua was able to interrupt the sun's journey (Josh 10:12–13). Sun and moon (Selene) are called upon to praise God in Dan 3:62 (LXX). In Mal 3:20 (LXX) the promise of salvation to God's people is called the "sun of righteousness" (*helios dikaiosyne;* see also Isa 30:26).

This situation helps explain why a mosaic with the sun

and the planets has been found in the 3d-century synagogue at Hammath-Tiberius (Levine 1982: 8, 66). If this is to be interpreted as an indication of how Judaism, at least in terms of art, could not ignore the sun cult, then an even earlier indication of the way the sun had entered the terminology of a Greek-speaking and -thinking Jew of this era is found in Philo of Alexandria (1st century). Philo gives the sun the title "Great King" (*Op* 56), corresponding to contemporary royal ideology and portrays it as the center of the planets (*Heres* 222–23) as found on the aforementioned mosaic. The "flaming sword" of Gen 3:24 in one instance is interpreted allegorically as applying to the revolution of the heavens, in another instance is applied to the sun (*Cher* 21–25). Philo even goes beyond the scriptures to compare God, the Lord *(Hegemon)* of the world, with the sun (*Somn.* I.87), whose rays go forth to enlighten humans (*Somn.* I.112–14). In the same way that God separated light from darkness, so the sun creates day and night. Allegorically the Bible is placed in the service of the solar theology by describing human understanding *(nus)*, sense-perception *(aisthesis)*, and also the "Word" *(logos)* of God" as sun (*Cher.* 1.77–86, commenting on Gen 28:11, 32:31; 19:23–24). It is not suprising then that Philo ascribes a sort of sun-worship to the Therapeutae (*Vita Cont* 89]. Josephus writes similarly of the Essenes (*JW* 2.8.5). Finally, an entire Greek prayer to the sun-god (Helios) is included in the magical "Book of Secrets" (*Sefer ha-Razim* 99–100).

D. Christianity

Early Christian writings, like the OT, make no mention of sun-worship. "Sun" is used metaphorically, allegorically, or symbolically for "light" and "brightness" (Rev 12:1, 19:7). Here it is the natural sun that is playing a role. The end of the world brings with it the extinguishing of the sun (Acts 2:20; Rev 6:12; Mark 13:24; and elsewhere). In the New Jerusalem no sun will be needed (Rev 21:23, 22:5; *Ep. Barn.* 15:5). Christ is the Light of the World (John 8:12), but his divine appearance is brighter than the sun (Acts 26:13, cf. *Ep. Barn.* 5:10; Matt 17:3). The star of Bethlehem is also brighter than the sun (*Ign. Eph.* 19:2). The righteous shall shine like the sun (Matt 13:43), i.e., they will be transformed into light (cf. Matt 17:3 on Christ).

The Apostolic writings and those of the Church Fathers emphasize the createdness of the heavenly bodies (cf. *1 Clem.* 20:3). The sun's divinity is denied on the basis of scripture and reason (*LPGL*, 605–606). In metaphors and allegories "sun" is a favored word, used figuratively for the most diverse matters of early Christian faith: for God himself; for the Trinity (the sun and its rays as a proof of the unity of the Trinity); for the "Father," the "Son" (with reference to Mal 3:20 and/or 4:2), and the "Holy Spirit"; for the Church (as proof of her endurance); for Mary and the apostles; and for spiritual life in general. The passion of Christ is interpreted as sunset, the resurrection as dawn. Christ is the *sol salutis,* the sun of salvation, who takes up the ancient sun piety and returns it to its "natural" foundations. In Christianity the Helios cult has been overcome, although this does not mean that the pagan role of the sun does not from time to time reappear (in astrology, magic, alchemy). It survives in our planetary week and the eastward orientation of many churches even today.

Bibliography

Altheim, F. 1939. Sol invictus. Vol. 5 pp. 290–303 in *Welt als Geschichte.*

———. 1943. *Die Krise der Alten Welt im 3. Jahrhundert u. Zw. und ihre Uhrsachen.* Berlin.

Altheim, F., and Stiehl, R., eds. 1966. *Die Araber in der Alten Welt.* Vol. 3. Berlin.

Betz, H. D. ed. 1986. *The Greek Magical Papyri in Translation.* Chicago.

Boll, F. 1922. *Die Sonne im Glauben und in der Weltanschauung der alten Völker.* Stuttgart.

Cumont, F. 1909. *La Théologie Solaire du Paganisme Romain.* MPAIBL 12/2. Paris.

———. 1949. *Lux perpetua.* Paris.

Dölger, F. 1929. *Sol Salutis, Gebet und Gesang im Christlichen Altertum.* 2d ed. Münster.

Halsberghe, G. H. 1972. *The Cult of Sol Invictus.* EPRO 23. Leiden.

Heitsch, E. 1960. Die Helioshymnen. *Hermes* 88: 139–58.

Jessen, O. 1912. Helios. *Real-Encyclopädie der classischen Altertumschaft* 15:58–93.

Kerényi, K. 1943. Vater Helios. *ErJb* 10: 81–124.

———. 1944. *Töchter der Sonne.* Zurich.

Levine, L. 1982. *Ancient Synagogues Revealed.* Jerusalem.

Mau, G. 1907. *Die Religionsphilosophie Kaiser Julians und seine Reden auf König Helios und die Göttermutter.* Leipzig.

Nilsson, M. P. 1933. Sonnenreligion und Sonnenkalender. *ARW* 30: 141–73.

———. 1961. *Geschichte der Griechischen Religion.* Vol. 2. 2d ed. Munich.

Schauenburg, K. 1955. *Helios: Archeologisch-Mythologische Studien über den Antiken Sonnengott.* Berlin.

Smith, M. 1982. Helios in Palestine. *EI* 16: 199–214.

Stähli, M.-P. 1985. *Solare Elemente in Jahweglauben des Alten Testaments.* Freiburg and Göttingen.

Usener, H. 1911. Sol invictus. *Rheinisches Musem* 60: 465–91. Repr. in *Religionsgeschichtliche Untersuchungen I: Das Weihnachtsfest.* 2d ed. Bonn, 1972.

KURT RUDOLPH
Trans. Dennis Martin

HELKAI (PERSON) [Heb *ḥelqāy*]. A priest who is of the House of Meraioth in the days of the High Priest Joiakim, son of Jeshua (Neh 12:15). The name means "My portion is Yahu" and perhaps is contracted from *ḥelqāyyâhû.*

GARY C. AUGUSTIN

HELKATH (PLACE) [Heb *ḥelqāt*]. The third city in the tribe of Asher given to the Levites. In Josh 21:31 the name of the city is *ḥelqāt,* but that name does not appear in the parallel 1 Chr 6 list. Instead, the third city given to the Levites in Asher is *ḥûqōq* (6:60) (—Eng 6:75). There is no other reference to Hukok in the OT. Albright (1945: 71) explains the two readings by maintaining there was confusion in the consonantal text which later also occurred in the vocalization. Besides occurring in the Levitical city list, Helkath also appears in the Joshua allotment list to Asher (19:25). The first extrabiblical reference to Helkath is in the Thutmose III list of towns. Helkath *ḫ-r-q-t* is 112 on the topographical list of conquered cities on the temple wall at Karnak. There is no agreement concerning the identification of Helkath, although it is usually associated with either Tell el-Qassis or Tell el-Harbaj.

Tell el-Qassis (M.R. 160232) has been identified as Helkath by Aharoni (1959: 151) and most recently by Boling (*Joshua* AB, 494). It is located on an outlying spur of the Galilean foothills at the extreme NW end of the Esdraelon Plain. The Kishon flows through a narrow corridor just E of Qassis into the Plain of Acco. At Qassis, the river is a small stream, but throughout history it has provided a life support for the Esdraelon Plain. Tell el-Qassis is located on a significant trade route between Acco and Jokneam/Megiddo/Taanach/Beth-shan. This trunk road is important in Palestinian geography, for nowhere is the land higher than 110 m above sea level, and the slopes are gradual. The importance of this pass cannot be overemphasized in the history of ancient Israel.

The 19th century geographer M. V. Guérin (1880: Map) did not visit Tell el-Qassis, but he identified "Tell el Kasis" on his map. Robinson (1874: 114) makes only passing reference to "Tell Kusis" as it stood in relationship to Tell esh-Shemmâm. The first geographer to write of his experiences at Qassis was G. A. Smith (1899: 380–81). Smith was intrigued by the location of "Tell el Kasis" in the Plain of Esdraelon and carefully described its history.

Numerous surveys, soundings, and excavations have been conducted at Tell el-Qassis. A long occupational history has been reconstructed starting in the EB and extending to the Arabic period. Periods in evidence at Tell el-Qassis include EB, MB, LB, Iron I, Iron II, Hellenistic, Roman/Byzantine, and Arabic. The Yokneam Regional Project (Ben-Tor et al. 1981: 137–64) has found evidence of EB I, EB III (when the entire site was occupied), MB, Iron Age I, Iron Age II, Persian, and Hellenistic periods. The pottery that became the corpus of the Levitical city survey contained EB, LB, Iron I, Iron II, Hellenistic, Roman, Byzantine, and Arabic sherds.

The alternative identification for Helkath is Tell el-Harbaj (M.R. 158240). This site has been identified as the Levitical city Helkath by Alt (1929: 39), Abel (*GP* 2: 66), and Wright (*WHAB,* 128). Harbaj is located on a tributary which joins the Kishon 2 km to the W of the tell. It is just N of the narrow corridor separating the Plain of Acco and Plain of Esdraelon. It stood on one of the major roads in ancient Israel, the route from Egypt towards Acco, which followed the inland route around Carmel. Although the Plain of Acco was important as a major trade route, the forces which controlled it belonged to Galilee. The tell lies near the S border of the Plain of Acco, some 18 km S of the ancient harbor at Acco.

Harbaj is a low mound that has a gentle uniform slope rising decidedly on all sides from the relatively flat valley floor. One of the first geographers to visit the tell was Guérin in 1875. In 1922, Garstang directed an excavation at Tell el-Harbaj, in which he found only Bronze Age occupation (1922: 10–14). In a brief campaign in 1923, Garstang (1924: 45–46) found some Neolithic and early Iron Age material. In the 1930s many surface surveys were conducted at el-Harbaj, but the only pottery identified was from the Iron and Medieval Ages.

The next survey was conducted by the Levitical City Survey in 1971 (Peterson 1977: 37–55). They found pottery from the 10th–7th centuries, Hellenistic, Roman, and Arabic periods. Although Tell el-Harbaj has been identified by some as biblical Harosheth, the geographical evidence points to Harbaj as biblical Helkath. The fact that Harbaj is one of the most southern tells in the Plain of Acco, located just N of the pass connecting the Plain of Acco with the Esdraelon Plain, supports its identification as a Levitical city in the tribe of Asher.

Bibliography

Aharoni, Y. 1959. Zephath of Thutmose. *IEJ* 9: 110–22.

Albright, W. F. 1945. The List of Levitic Cities. Pp. 49–73 in *Louis Ginzberg Jubilee Volume on the Occasion of his Seventieth Birthday.* New York.

Alt, A. 1929. Die Reise (Helkath, Kitron und Nahalol). *PJ* 25: 38–42.

Ben-Tor, A.; Portugali, Y.; and Avissar, M. 1981. The First Two Seasons of Excavations at Tel Qashish, 1978–1979: Preliminary Report. *IEJ* 31: 137–64.

Garstang, J. 1922. Geography of the Plain of Acre (S). *British School of Archaeology in Jerusalem.* 2: 16.

———. 1924. El Harbaj: Notes on Pottery found at El-Harbaj, Summer 1923. *British School of Archaeology in Jerusalem Bulletin* 4: 45–46.

Guerin, M. V. 1880. *Description Géographique, Historique et Archaeologique de la Palestine,* 3. Paris.

Peterson, J. L. 1977. A Topographical Surface Survey of the Levitical "Cities" of Joshua 21 and I Chronicles 6. Th.D. diss. Evanston, IL.

Robinson, E. 1874. *Biblical Researches in Palestine,* vol. 3. 11th ed. Boston.

Smith, G. A. 1899. *Historical Geography of the Holy Land.* 6th ed. New York.

John L. Peterson

HELKATH-HAZZURIM (PLACE) [Heb *ḥelqaṯ haṣṣūrîm*].

The name of a piece of ground close to the pool of Gibeon where soldiers of David and Ishbosheth, twelve representative warriors from each side, met and fought in one-to-one combat. Abner, commander of Saul's army, said to Joab, "Now let the young men arise and make sport before us." And Joab, general of the army of David, consented to it. If it really meant "making sport," they really were "treacherous" combatants (as translated in LXX). If it was a delegate combat, like that of David and Goliath, it was certainly not the cause célèbre. The battle continued because neither side won the combat.

This place name is found in 2 Sam 2:16, but its meaning is unclear and problematic because there are many interpretations for it, even if there is a story of etymological derivation. Young translated this GN as the "field of rocks," but its meaning is unlikely to be "field of rocks" because it is difficult to seek the reason why "the rocks" are related to the story of this one-to-one group combat. Some see a possibility of "(sharp) rocks" in the sense of "flint (knives)," but *haṣṣūrîm* probably does not mean "flint"; the Hebrew word for "flint" is regularly *ḥallāmîš* (Deut 8:15; 32:13; Ps 114:8; Isa 50:7). Even if *ṣōr,* "sharp stone" (Exod 4:25), which Zipporah used for the traditional circumcision may actually be "flint stone knife," the twenty-four warriors of Joab and Abner probably did not use such flint knives because they were good for cutting, but not so much for thrusting or piercing the human body. It is doubtful that they all used flint knives as daggers at the time of David because they are easily broken.

Some see the possibility to translate "field of (sword)-edges," but this interpretation is also less likely. The common word for the sword-edge is *peh,* literally "mouth."

A slight change of a vowel makes a translation of "the place of opposers" or "the portion of adversaries" *(ḥelqat haṣṣārîm).* By an emendation of a consonant *ḥelqat haṣṣiddîm* offers another plausible interpretation "the place of the sides." The LXX translation "the portion of the treacherous ones" and the Syriac transcription *ḥaqlat-ṣadan* suggest the original Hebrew as *ḥelqat haṣṣādîm* "the field of the hunters," but it is difficult to find the meaning of "treacherousness" in "hunting."

YOSHITAKA KOBAYASHI

HELL. See HADES, HELL; and GEHENNA.

HELLENISM. From its first usage, the term "Hellenism" has meant a variety of things generally pertaining to Greek culture and its impact on the non-Greek world after the conquests of Alexander the Great (ca. 333–323 B.C.). The Judeans were not immune to this impact, and consequently Hellenism had some impact upon Jewish religion.

A. The Concept and Its Definition
B. In the OT/Hebrew Bible
  1. Greek Translations
  2. Hellenistic Influences
  3. Confrontation with Hellenism
  4. Subsequent Literary History
C. In the NT
  1. Application of the Concept
  2. The History of Research
  3. Early Christianity and Hellenism
  4. The NT Becoming Literature

A. The Concept and Its Definition

The concept of Hellenism originated in modern historiography; it must be distinguished from its usage in antiquity *(hellenismós).* The modern historiographical concept has its own history since Joseph Justus Scaliger (1540–1609) identified the "Hellenists" of Acts 6:1 as Jews who used Greek as the language in their synagogue. Similarly, Claudius Salmasius (1588–1653) called the language of the Greek Bible *lingua hellenistica* (see Laqueur 1925; Momigliano 1977: 307–323). Taking his clues from J. G. Herder (1744–1803) and J. G. Hamann (1730–1788), J. G. Droysen (1808–1884) made the term "Hellenism" *(Hellenismus)* a historiographical technical term to designate an epoch ranging from Alexander the Great (356–323 B.C.E.) to Roman Imperial rule (ca. 30 B.C.E.). Droysen understood Hellenism to be the mixture of the world of Greece with that of the Orient, a mixture that became the preparation for Christianity. Julius Kaerst (1857–1930), on the other hand, emphasized the expansion of Greek culture in the Mediterranean as a phenomenon of intellectual history *(Geistesgeschichte).* Richard Laqueur (1881–1959) took Hellenism to be the transformation of the ethnic-national culture of Greece into a universal culture and civilization. According to him, "hellenistic man" transcended the traditions of his people: "hellenistic man" became the bearer and promoter of a world culture believed to be identical with progress. As a program of cultural expansion Hellenism held the potential for new cultural creativity as well as for deep-seated conflicts with the older national cultures.

In the late 20th century, scholarship turned from grand concepts to specialized research. The work of M. Rostovtzeff was devoted to the developments of social history. Carl Schneider's informative but problematic survey (1967–69) treated the history of culture (see the critical review by Murray, 1969). Imaginative overviews were contributed by Toynbee (1959) and Adorno (1977). Whereas the standard work of Will (1966–1967) is concerned with political history, other scholars focused their attention on special areas such as the history of culture, art, philosophy, and religion (see Bickerman 1976–85; 1985a; Grimal 1968; Préaux 1978; Long and Sedley 1987, with bibliography).

Present research is especially interested in the explorations of the history of Hellenistic religion and, closely connected with it, that of Hellenistic philosophy. Based on the foundational studies by Hermann Usener (1834–1905), Albrecht Dieterich (1866–1908), and Richard Reitzenstein (1861–1931), this research has produced a wealth of publications (see the monograph series RVV, EPRO, and also *ANRW*). For Hellenistic religions no up-to-date survey exists, after the comprehensive works by Prümm (1954) and Nilsson (1974) have become outdated. The steady increase in textual materials and artifacts attributable to excavations makes it difficult to stay abreast of the advancements of scholarship (see for American scholarship Danker [1988, with bibliography]; for journal articles, reports, surveys, and lexica especially, PW, *KlPauly, RAC* [with its supplements and *JAC*], *ANRW,* and the bibliographies in *Gnomon* and *L'Années philologiques*).

B. In the OT/Hebrew Bible

The problem of Hellenism in regard to the OT/Hebrew Bible must be distinguished from the NT. By far the largest part of the OT is pre-Hellenistic in origin and character; it is written in Hebrew or Aramaic. Confrontation with Hellenism, however, had occurred even before the final formation of the canon. Reflections of this encounter with Hellenism can be seen in linguistic, redactional, and thematic phenomena.

1. Greek Translations. The Greek translations of the LXX originated over a considerable period of time, contrary to the legend contained in the *Epistle of Aristeas* (see *HJP*[2] 3/1: 677–87), according to which the whole translation of the Hebrew Bible was accomplished by 72 translators in 72 days. It was known even at the time of the *Epistle of Aristeas* (see sections 312–16) that such a translation carried with it the dangers of illegitimate Hellenization. The fact is that at numerous places the LXX is not merely a translation of the Hebrew or Aramaic text, but a transformation into Gk language and thought. Only later translators such as AQUILA, SYMMACHUS, and THEODOTION were concerned with a systematic approach to close literal rendering (see Goshen-Gottstein 1983; *HJP*[2] 3/1: 142–49, 470–504; Tov, *ANRW* 2/20/1: 121–89).

2. Hellenistic Influences. Presently scholarship is divided on the question to what extent Hellenistic influences have determined the *composition* and *redaction* of OT literature (see Smith 1971). At any rate, from the beginning the intellectual and religious confrontation between Judaism and Hellenism has led to the composition or revision of entire books. This literary confrontation begins with the book of Daniel and includes the entire corpus of the Apocrypha and the Hellenistic-Jewish literature.

3. Confrontation with Hellenism. Thematically, the confrontation with Hellenism can be seen from the preferred literary genres. These include the proverbial collections (see PROVERBS, BOOK OF; ECCLESIASTES, BOOK OF; WISDOM OF BEN-SIRA; SOLOMON, WISDOM OF), the apocalyptic literature, and historiographical works (Hengel 1974; 1976; Momigliano 1975; 1977; Nickelsburg 1981; Kaiser 1982; Collins 1983; *HJP*[2]; *ANRW* 2/20/1–2; Hoffmann 1988).

Present scholarship has frequently discussed the possibility of Hellenistic influences, especially those of Gk philosophy, but these discussions have often been hampered by conceptional limitations such as merely external takeover of terms or doctrines. While such takeovers can be identified, the confrontation with Hellenistic ideas went much deeper and found foremost expression indirectly in allusions and theological counterproposals.

A classic example of this debate has been the investigation of the Wisdom of Solomon, esp. 2:1–20; 7:1–6; 13–15, as the studies by Larcher (1969; 1983–85), Reese (1970), Gilbert (1978), Georgi (1980), and Winston (*Wisdom of Solomon* AB) have shown. The differences between these scholars can to a large extent be explained from their differing methodological presuppositions (see also the careful account of the evidence in Theiler 1982: 2.283–85). The increased interest in the individuality of authors is characteristically Hellenistic also (see, e.g., Braun 1973 on Qoheleth; Stadelmann 1980 on Ben Sirach).

A further phase of development was initiated in Hellenistic-Jewish literature, when the "hebraic peripatetic" Aristobulus (see ARISTOBULUS) attempted to harmonize the holy scriptures with Gk philosophy; he was indeed convinced that the Gk philosophers depended on the "philosophy of the Hebrews" (Aristobulus, Fragment 3, preserved in Eusebius, *Praep. ev.* 13.12.1–2; see Walter 1964; Hengel 1974; *HJP*[2] 3/1: 579–87; Droge 1989).

4. Subsequent Literary History. The presence of the OT in the post-OT literature (see APOCRYPHA and PSEUDEPIGRAPHA) and in the NT literature (see below, section C) must be seen in the light of these general presuppositions as well as in accordance with the theological ideas of the individual authors of those writings. On the whole it can be said that the post-OT literature, including the NT, does *not* presuppose the closing of the canon, although its authority is acknowledged. Quotations and other references to the OT in the later literature represent a complicated and very diverse phenomenon. There are not only explicit quotations, but also a broad stream of traditions drawn upon in written and oral form (e.g., traditions of proverbs and maxims, stories, liturgical materials). This literature has its original purpose to a large degree in the debates with Hellenism about the question of the Jewish religion.

Consequently, the presence of the OT in the NT is not a direct but a mediated one: it is mediated through the Judaism at the time of Jesus and the early Church. Although the NT interprets OT passages differently and not uniformly, the authority of the OT is in principle acknowledged. This acknowledgment can be stated in formulaic expressions such as "the law and the prophets" (Matt 5:17; 7:12; etc.) or by the concept of "Scripture" *(graphē)*. References to the OT in the NT include explicit quotations (see NEW TESTAMENT, OT QUOTATIONS IN) and a very diversified stream of doctrinal and liturgical traditions. The quotations are always according to the LXX, although the text often differs from the LXX versions known to us. The Heb text is declared binding only in Matt 5:16 (= Luke 16:17), coming from an early layer of tradition showing Christian confrontation with Hellenism (see below, section C.3.b.). Hellenistic as it certainly is, the NT uses the OT as a tool in the debates with Hellenism as it pertains to issues of theological thought, religious and ethical practice, and general cultural customs and behavior.

C. In the NT

1. Application of the Concept. When the concept of Hellenism is applied to the NT, several aspects should be distinguished. In regard to the historical epoch, the NT is as such Hellenistic. Droysen's interpretation of Hellenism as mixture should be applied first to Judaism in the Hellenistic environment (see Tcherikover; Hengel). Early Christianity, however, was not simply an extension of Hellenistic Judaism. Granting that there was high degree of continuity, the NT was the product of a new mixture. On the other side, the NT itself proved to be a powerful agent furthering the expansion of Hellenism. Thus all NT authors were Hellenistic people as Laqueur had characterized them. The expansion of Christianity, however, could not simply ride on the waves of an expanding world culture. As Momigliano put it (1975: 10–11):

> What accentuates the peculiar physiognomy of Hellenistic civilization is the special role two foreign groups—Jews and Romans—came to play in it. The Jews basically remained convinced of the superiority of their beliefs and ways of life and fought for them. Yet they continuously compared their own ideas with Greek ideas, made propaganda for their own beliefs, absorbing many Greek notions and customs in the process—and ultimately found themselves involved in that general confrontation of Greek and Jewish values which we call Christianity. The Romans never took their intellectual relations with Hellenism so seriously. They acted from a position of power and effortlessly preserved a strong feeling of their own identity and superiority. They paid the Greeks to teach them their wisdom and often did not have to pay because they were their slaves.

Christianity thus became the intellectual and spiritual battleground on which the confrontation between Judaism and Hellenism was fought with unprecedented intensity. In the NT the earliest and most decisive phase of this confrontation had become literature. The texts are documents indicating not only the beginning of a long historical struggle but also containing the main principles, goals, and limits which determined the Christian transformation of Hellenism and the formation of a new European culture as well as the history of Christianity.

2. The History of Research. a. The Language. The language of the NT was the primary reason that the study of Hellenism was connected with the NT from the very beginning. This peculiar language became the first object of scholarship, that is, the grammar, the idioms, and the lexicology of the so-called *koinē.* Of special importance were the works of Adolf Deissmann (1866–1937).

The most important NT grammars in use today are those by Radermacher (1925) and Blass, Debrunner, and Rehkopf (BDR). *A Greek-English Lexicon to the New Testament* has found international recognition. The monumental *TDNT* was started by G. Kittel in 1933 and completed by G. Friedrich in 1979. Despite its unevenness and tendentiousness, this lexicon has proved to be an irreplaceable source of information. The *EWNT,* edited by H. Balz and G. Schneider (1979, 1981, 1983), and C. Spicq's *Notes de lexicographie néotestamentaire* (Fribourg and Göttingen, 1978–1982) are to be used as supplements to Bauer's *Lexicon* and the *TDNT.*

b. The Observations Literature. In the 17th and 18th centuries an entire literature often called "observations literature" was devoted to investigating the relations between Hellenism and the NT. These studies, following the example of the great Hugo Grotius (1583–1645), collected parallel passages from Greek and Latin literature for the illumination of NT texts (see Delling 1963; van Unnik 1973–83, 2: 194–214). The most important work of this genre is the critical edition of the NT, supplied with a vast collection of parallel materials, by J. J. Wettstein (1693–1754), published in 1751–52. References to classical parallels began in the NT itself (Acts 17:28; 5:29; 26:14; 1 Cor 15:33). Comparative studies and the interpretation of parallels was a concern also throughout the patristic period, but it was the era of encyclopedias that was characterized by systematic attempts at collection. At the time of Wettstein a similar work by G. D. Kypke (1755) appeared. Older contributions were collected in the seven volumes of the *Critici Sacri* 1660 (excerpts from Laurentius Valla, Desiderius Erasmus, Joseph Justus Scaliger, Isaac Casaubonus, Hugo Grotius, and others). In the 19th century there was only one more work of this kind, *Spermaticós Logos* by Edmund Spiess, in 1871.

c. Paul's Rhetoric. For the question of the relationship between the NT and Hellenism, investigations of the rhetoric of the Apostle Paul played a major role. This question was discussed by Paul himself in his confrontations with his Corinthian adversaries (see Betz 1972; 1985; 1986), but commentators have taken the matter up continuously until modern times.

In antiquity, Augustine commented on Paul's rhetoric in his *De doctrina Christiana* (4.31–47), and in the Reformation period it was Melanchthon (see Betz, *Galatians* Hermeneia, 14). In the 18th century, systematic studies appeared, e.g., Karl Ludwig Bauer (1782) and Herman Johan Royaard's Utrecht dissertation (1818; for references see Betz, *2 Corinthians 8–9* Hermeneia, 129–130; 1986: 16–21); in the 19th century this type of study ceased. The end of the century, however, witnessed the strange controversy between the philologist E. Norden (1868–1941) and the NT scholar G. Heinrici (1844–1915). Heinrici, who knew his classical authors well, has pointed to a wealth of classical parallels in his commentary on 2 Corinthians (1887), which Norden sharply attacked (1898), a standard work still today. Norden's aim was to put the Apostle Paul into Judaism, which he described as "unhellenic" and "educationally impoverished." Norden's pathetic and resentful attack, quite in conformity with the Zeitgeist, became influential in NT circles. This fact was not altered by Heinrici's rebuttal, well documented and convincing, in the 2d edition of his commentary (*2 Corinthians* Meyer, 436–58). Norden had found little support among other scholars and tried to amend things (Norden 1898: 3–4 of the supplement). The subsequent investigations by J. Weiss (1863–1914) and R. Bultmann (1884–1976), later also of H. Windisch (1881–1935) finally refuted Norden, but the question is still alive today (see Betz 1986; Schmeller 1987).

d. The Corpus Hellenisticum. The study of the relationships between Hellenism and early Christianity became the objective of the international research project of the Corpus Hellenisticum Novi Testamenti. This project was first suggested by Heinrici shortly before his death in 1915. In the course of the century the project has undergone vast changes in method and outlook attributable to shifts in scholarship generally. While the project is still being continued, its objective is being pursued in many other forms as well (see Betz, *TRE* 15: 23–24; see also CORPUS HELLENISTICUM NOVI TESTAMENTI). In principle, there is no longer any question about the necessity of this research. The NT and other early Christian literature cannot be interpreted in a scholarly justifiable way unless it is understood in its relationships with the language, literature, religion, culture, and civilization of its Hellenistic (including the Jewish) environment.

The problems, however, which make this research so difficult, should not be underestimated. The fields of study relevant to the enterprise have expanded since World War II in unprecedented measures; simultaneously the methods have become extremely diversified and refined, not only in NT studies but in the study of antiquity as a whole. All this has occurred at a time when theological education has seriously deteriorated in quality, so that there are fewer and fewer researchers qualified for the tasks at hand. Therefore the number of workers in this vineyard is small while the tasks are many. Moreover, the idea held at earlier times that NT scholars should merely exploit the results of scholarship in the fields of classical antiquity has to be given up. Rather, NT scholars have to make genuine contributions to these fields, and they have to learn to collaborate with scholars in the fields of classical antiquity. This collaboration, which had led to the great scholarly production in the 18th and 19th centuries, has in fact been resumed, and the first benefits have become apparent.

Another idea to be shelved is that of the mechanical

gathering of raw data. Rather, the data to be collected must be studied in the contexts of larger phenomena and problems, within which the NT literature will then be seen in its specific contours. Given these presuppositions, the assembling of data and their interpretation continue to present exciting challenges to NT scholarship. These investigations of course form the foundations for the problems of hermeneutics in the contemporary situation.

3. Early Christianity and Hellenism. a. The Languages of the Early Christians. The primary characteristic for Hellenism is the language; secondarily it is the way of life, education, and ethos mediated through that language. Typical is the description of a Hellenized Jew in Josephus (*AgAp* 1.180), by way of a quotation from Clearchus of Soli: "He was a Greek not only by his language but also by his soul." With regard to its language, the NT is certainly Greek. By contrast, earlier hypotheses, according to which parts of the NT were taken to be translations from the Hebrew or Aramaic, have not been substantiated. Even in view of peculiar linguistic phenomena in NT Greek, Semitic influences are difficult to prove and less frequent than one would expect (see Fitzmyer 1979). Influences of a Semitic background are also difficult to distinguish from peculiarities of *koinē* Greek attributable to regional dialect. And the Latinisms, stemming from the language of the military, the law-courts and commerce, are signs of Hellenization.

One of the most intractable problems is that of determining which language was spoken by the early Christians. For the NT, even in its oldest layers of tradition, it is taken for granted that Jesus and his disciples spoke Greek in their daily life. Whether this assumption is merely naiveté on the part of the NT writers or whether it conforms to actual facts is no longer discernible. Among the NT authors it is only the Gk historian Luke who is interested in the language problem. According to him, Paul spoke Greek with the Roman authorities (Acts 21:37) but Hebrew with the people of Jerusalem (Acts 21:40; 22:2). Even the heavenly voice occurring to Paul (Acts 26:14) was in Hebrew. The Church, however, is, thanks to the gift of the Holy Spirit (Acts 2:8–11), pluralistic in its use of languages. This view is the result of Luke's interests as a Christian Hellenist.

The evidence coming from the NT and from extra-NT sources reveals that in 1st-century Palestine, while Aramaic was still the preferred language, Greek was also widely used, not only in the Hellenized cities but also among farmers and craftsmen in the countryside. The knowledge and use of Hebrew was clearly on the retreat and limited to smaller circles (see Lieberman 1962; 1965; Sevenster 1968; Rabin 1976; Mussies 1976: 1040–64; Fitzmyer 1979; *HJP*² 2: 20–28, 74–80).

In regard to the NT, two special problems must be faced. First, did Jesus of Nazareth speak only Aramaic, or did he speak Greek as well? In view of the fact that Greek was widely spoken in Palestine at the time, its knowledge cannot be denied to Jesus, who came from the bilingual area of Galilee (see Freyne 1988: 171–72). Such knowledge must not, however, be confused with one's preference in daily life. If Jesus taught in Aramaic or in mishnaic Hebrew, which has been assumed but cannot be proved, his teachings must have been translated into Greek even at the earliest level of the tradition (see Barr 1970; Jeremias 1971: 1–37; Rabin 1976: 1036–39; *HJP*² 2: 79–80). The second main problem is, which language did the so-called Hellenists in Acts speak (Acts 6:1; 9:29; 11:20)? Most likely these Hellenists were Hellenized and therefore Greek-speaking Jews. Does that mean that they spoke only Greek? Such a conclusion would be hard to prove (see Fitzmyer 1979: 36–37; Hengel 1983: 3–11).

b. The Conflict with Hellenism. If the NT is a Hellenistic document with regard to its language, the question remains whether it is Hellenistic also according to its "soul." To a certain degree this question is one of definition, and one of whose definition it is. The definition given in Ps.-Clementine *Homilies* 11.6 (a Greek is everyone who does not observe the Torah, no matter whether he or she is of Jewish or Greek origin) merely reflects the particular situation of Jewish Christianity. The question raised in the NT as the decisive issue however, is what it really means to observe the Torah.

(1) Judaism in the NT Period. In the NT period, Judaism consisted of a large variety of different groups and movements of a partly political and partly religious nature. All of these groups and movements took positions with regard to Hellenism, whereby the range of possibilities was considerable. Whereas, e.g., Philo of Alexandria went as far as he could in accommodating himself to Hellenism, the Qumran sect tried to isolate itself from it. Between these extremes many different compromises existed. The question of the limits of Jewish accommodation was raised, but no unanimous answer was given. See HERESY AND ORTHODOXY IN THE NT.

(2) The Jesus Movement. The movement initiated by Jesus of Nazareth was anti-Hellenistic. So much at least seems to be clear in spite of the dearth of reliable data. Even the little we know about John the Baptist suggests his anti-Hellenistic tendencies. His opposition against Herod Antipas, his death as a martyr, and his messianic-apocalyptic message were reactions against Hellenization of Judaism. The ritual of baptism, the origin of which has not yet been sufficiently clarified, served as a means of demarcation between faithful Jews and those whose religion had been corrupted as a result of Hellenism. On the whole, the historical Jesus appears to have shared the anti-Hellenistic sentiments of his mentor. In the eyes of Jesus, Hellenism was represented in Palestine by the Roman occupation and by the Jewish authorities imposed on the Jews by Rome. Although the Christian gospel writers who were Hellenists themselves have done their best to tone down these anti-Hellenistic sentiments, Jesus' rejectionist attitudes are clearly stated in the tradition (see, e.g., Mark 12:15–22 and parallels, and the Passion Narratives as a whole). Jesus' rejection of the Hellenized Jewish authorities is well attested in old source materials (e.g., Mark 8:15; 12:13; Luke 13:31–33). Jesus' critique of other Jewish movements follows tendencies of John the Baptist and other anti-Hellenistic movements (see, e.g., Matt 11:2–19; the laments over the towns of Galilee [Matt 11:20–23] and over Jerusalem [Matt 23:37–38]). The fact that Jesus was crucified as a messianic revolutionary is a sure indication of his anti-Roman and thus anti-Hellenistic attitude (on the inscription on the cross, see Mark 15:26 and parallels; John 19:19–22; Blinzler 1969: 367–68; Sanders 1985: 294–

318). The gospel writers, however, have correctly maintained that Jesus did not see himself as a militant revolutionist (see Cullmann 1970; Hengel 1971). He probably reacted to the external superiority of the Roman power by the conviction of his religious and moral superiority as a Jew. He may have avoided contacts with Gentiles whenever possible. The title of Messiah when applied to Jesus in the gospels is always the result of Christian interpretation and accompanied by a rejection of political and military ambitions and expectations (see Luke 24:19–27; John 6:14–15; and the Passion Narratives entirely).

(3) The Origin of Hellenistic Christianity. The question then arises: how, given this anti-Hellenistic attitude of Jesus, could Hellenistic Christianity have come into existence? Historically, it is improbable that Jesus himself had initiated the opening toward the Gentiles, although the gospel writers suggest it (see Mark 7:24–30 and parallels; Matt 8:5–13 and parallels; Luke 10:30–38; 17:16; John 4:4–26, 39–40; 8:48). While these suggestions reflect later retrospective construction, the sources themselves indicate that the early Christian mission to the Gentiles was a new phase in the history of the Church. This new mission, however, had some connection with the historical Jesus. His openness toward the *am hāʾāreṣ* and the so-called "sinners and tax collectors" (Matt 11:19 and parallels; see Braun 1969, 2: 18–23, 38 n. 1; *TDNT* 8: 103–105; *EWNT* 3: 835–38) seems to have prepared the mission toward the non-Jewish world. This corresponds also with Jesus' anti-Pharisaic understanding of the Torah. His rejection of asceticism, his reinterpretation of purity concepts (see esp. Mark 7:15) and sabbath observances, and his rejection of esotericism and ritual formalism will have made it easier for his disciples to establish relations with non-Jews. If Jesus' understanding of the Torah could be interpreted by his disciples partly as intensification and partly as relaxation, the roots for both interpretations should be seen in his teaching and conduct.

The sources also reveal that the mission to the Gentiles was not the result of careful planning, but it was characterized by erratic developments and confusion, while planning occurred mostly in hindsight. For the transition to Gentile Christianity, the fringe areas of Galilee, Decapolis, Samaria, Syria, and Nabatea (Arabia) seem to have played an important role (Acts 1:8; 2:9–11). There is also the question whether in these areas Jews were always clearly distinguished from non-Jews. Moreover, the sources mention again and again the role of military personnel (Mark 15:39–40 and parallels; Matt 8:5–13; Acts 10:1–2; etc.). Whatever the role of the "Hellenists" (Acts 6:1; 9:29; 11:20), it must have been an important one (see Hengel 1983: 1–29; Schneider 1979: 215–40). They were most likely Greek-speaking Jews from the Diaspora who had settled in Jerusalem and had joined (in their entirety?) the Christian Church. The fact that they were forced out of the city (Acts 8:1–3) is evidence that they were Hellenized. Stephen's speech (Acts 6:13–14; 7:1–53), even if not historical, may at least provide the general contours of their views. Caution is, however, needed in view of the tendency of Acts to attribute to the "Hellenists" all of the mission to the Gentiles. Hengel's hypothesis that the "Hellenists" were responsible for the translation of Jesus' message into Greek has no support in the sources (Hengel 1983: 26–29).

(4) The Gentile-Christian Mission. The Christian mission to the Gentiles must be seen in connection with the phenomenon of missionary religions typical of Hellenism. Especially, non-Christian religions such as those of Isis and Osiris or Mithras deliberately set out to gather devotees and build worldwide reputation. Membership in "world religions" based on voluntary association became customary alongside participation in local, ethnic, and national cults. In Judaism especially the Hellenistic Diaspora carried out its mission among non-Jews. In conjunction with it, an entire propaganda literature developed which applied the commonplace of the superior "wisdom of the barbarians" to Judaism and offered it as the religion that fits best the conditions of the Hellenistic world (see *HJP*[2] 3/1: 150–76). This mission also resulted in a transformation of Judaism itself. By emphasizing monotheism, law, ethics, and eschatology, this literature accommodated itself and responded to demands made by Gk philosophers for the reformation of religion. While the conversations with Gk philosophy occurred mostly indirectly, Hellenistic Jewish wisdom was most sympathetic to the Socratic, the middle-Platonic, and the Stoic traditions. By contrast, Epicureanism was almost unanimously rejected. Compared with Diaspora Judaism, Palestinian Judaism joined the proselyte movement only hesitantly; later it became more and more anti-Hellenistic and isolationistic. The tensions thus arising between the different branches of Judaism also entered into early Christianity, which at the early stages of its history was connected with the proselyte movement. The gentile Christian mission was therefore mostly a matter of the Diaspora (Acts 2:11; 6:5; 13:43). The mission kerygma (1 Thess 1:9–10) addressed in particular the so-called "god-fearers" (Acts 13:43, 50; 16:14; etc.; see *TDNT* 6: 727–44; *HJP*[2] 3/1: 162–76).

In Palestinian Jewish Christianity the mission to the gentiles remained disputed. No doubt its critics could appeal to the example of Jesus himself (cf. Matt 15:24; 23:15). On the other hand, the Jewish missionaries going to the Gentiles referred to experiences of miracles and ecstatic enthusiasm, experiences the problems of which would soon become manifest.

The inner Christian tensions can be seen in the Sermon on the Mount (Matt 5:3–7:27; see SERMON ON THE MOUNT), a source from the middle of the 1st century C.E. reflecting Jewish-Christian theology. In the Sermon, the gentile world is presented negatively, and assimilation is rejected (5:47; 6:7, 32). Law-free gentile Christianity is repudiated (5:17; 7:21–23). At the time, however, a separation between the Jesus movement and gentile Christianity is not yet seen as an ecclesiological problem, but only the threat to the salvation of the Gentiles is underscored.

The conference at Jerusalem (Gal 2:1–10; Acts 15) presupposes, on the one hand, a deepening of the conflict but, on the other hand, the recognition of the unity of the church as a demand implicit in the gospel itself. The conflict reached the point of crisis when Jewish-Christian particularists insisted on Torah and circumcision as Jewish (and Christian) symbols of identity. By contrast the gentile Christians defended the missionary kerygma, faith in Jesus Christ, baptism, and the new Christian ethos as sufficient for salvation. The basic question was whether the purpose of the mission to the Gentiles was their incorporation as converts into Judaism or whether gentile Christianity possessed their own status due to the salvation in Christ. The particularists must have designated as evils of Hellenization precisely those achievements which the Gentiles were so proud of. On the other hand, the gentile Christians rejected the demands of the Jewish rigorists as forms of judaization. Faced with this threat of split, the idea of the unity of the church, taken apparently to be the consequence of monotheism (Gal 2:8), proved to be the antidote and led to the division of only the mission fields, not the Church itself. Barnabas and Paul were sent to the Gentiles, Peter to the Jews—this was the formula negotiated in Jerusalem (Gal 2:8–9; cf. the mission instruction Matt 10:5–6; also Betz, *Galatians* Hermeneia, 97–101).

Clearly, dividing the mission fields was a compromise. Paul interpreted it in the sense that the gentile mission was in principle recognized as legitimate and that only for reasons of ethnic sensitivity a special status was granted to the Jews. The result was that gentile Christianity was finally separated from Judaism. The particularist party, called "false brothers" by Paul (Gal 2:4), refused to support the compromise. The so-called "pillars" (James, Peter, and John), however, attempted to steer a kind of middle course, the duration of which was short. Jewish Christianity had to make a choice between Judaism and gentile Christianity (called by Paul the "Israel of God" [Gal 6:17]). The choice became final during the famous Antioch episode (Gal 2:11–14). This inner Christian conflict continued throughout the history of the ancient Church as the opposition between the Catholic Church and Jewish-Christian "heresies" (see Lüdemann 1983).

(5) Pauline Christianity. After the conflict with Peter in Antioch (Gal 2:11–14; see *Galatians* Hermeneia, 103–112) Paul became the key figure in gentile Christianity, the "apostle of the Gentiles" (Rom 11:13; see Lüdemann 1984). Paul's background was the Hellenistic-Jewish diaspora. According to Acts, he inherited from his ancestors the citizenship of Tarsus in Cilicia (Acts 9:11, 30; 11:25; 21:39; 22:3; see *HJP*[2] 3/1: 33–34). The *cognomen* Paulos, most probably given him at birth (cf. Acts 7:58; 8:1, 3 etc.) points to the family's civic pride and consciousness which no doubt expressed itself also in giving young Paul a respectable education. *Religiously,* however, the family as well as Paul himself must have belonged to those who were opposed to a Hellenizing of the Jewish religion, the so-called "Hebrews" (Phil 3:5–6; Gal 1:14; Acts 22:3; 26:6). The claim, however, that he studied at Jerusalem under Gamaliel (Acts 22:3; 26:4; see *HJP*[2] 2: 367–68) and that he had a knowledge of Hebrew (Acts 21:40; 22:2; 26:14) cannot be sustained. The extant letters of the apostle do not contain signs of a knowledge of Hebrew; the occurrence of loanwords such as *abba, maranatha,* etc., cannot be used as evidence for the knowledge of Hebrew (a similar situation exists for Philo of Alexandria, while that of Josephus is different (see *HJP*[2] 2: 80; 3/1: 479, n. 27; 3/2: 873–74). These loanwords came to Paul through the liturgy and tradition of early Christianity. It should also be remembered that we possess practically no information about the cultural milieu and educational facilities of diaspora Pharisees.

In his pre-Christian period, Paul's "zeal" was concerned about the strict observance of the Torah (Phil 3:5–6; Gal 1:14; 5:3; Acts 22:3; 23:6); it thus was directed against Hellenizing tendencies to abolish the Torah. Because early Christian communities had opened themselves up to these Hellenizing tendencies, Paul persecuted them (Gal 1:13, 23; Phil 3:6; 1 Cor 15:9; Acts 8:3; 9:1–2; 22:4–5, 19; 26:10–11; see *HJP*[2] 3/1: 119). His persecution seems to have been limited to the law-free diaspora Christianity (at Damascus, Acts 9:2; 22:5; 26:12, 20) and it did not extend to the law-abiding Christians in Judea (differently Acts 8:1–3; 22:19–20; 26:10–11). Paul's so-called "conversion" (Gal 1:15–16; 1 Cor 9:1; 15:8; see *Galatians* Hermeneia, 62–72) also fundamentally changed his attitude toward Hellenization. From the anti-Hellenistic Pharisees Paul turned to the Hellenizing Jewish Christians of the Diaspora. Even his descriptions of his conversion and vocation as a missionary to the Gentiles are characteristically Hellenistic; the same is true in the somewhat different accounts in Acts 9:3–29; 22:3–21; 26:9–20. Further interpretations of his experience by Paul himself employ concepts characteristic of Hellenistic mystery cults (e.g., Phil 3:7–11; 2 Cor 4:4–6). Yet Paul did not simply embrace Hellenism while ignoring the problems. Rather, his own theology was shaped by confrontations with Christian developments which in his view were illegitimate forms of Hellenization. The decisive points of these debates are reflected in Paul's letters, in which he argues against opponents of various persuasions, some of them at least based on misinterpretations of his own message.

In the eyes of his Jewish-Christian rivals and opponents Paul was doubtless an apostate. See HERESY AND ORTHODOXY IN THE NT. In fact, Paul himself had to struggle hard to steer his churches away from becoming "paganized." Paganizing tendencies were carried on by people who took Paul's message and pushed it further toward extreme Hellenization, which would in the final analysis destroy the very gospel he was preaching. The struggle proved difficult because in its nascent state the formation of gentile Christian identity possessed no firm and agreed standards yet. Paul himself did not enter into these controversies with his ideas completely worked out, but his theology took shape gradually as he attempted to come to grips with ever-changing new experiences and oppositional viewpoints. See PAUL. Unquestionably the greatest challenge for Paul resulted from his founding of the church in Corinth. In Corinth he had succeeded in carrying the Christian mission to the cultured and wealthy citizens of this prosperous and cosmopolitan city. Their acceptance of the gospel went hand in hand with their consistent assimilating it to and melting it in with Hellenistic religiosity. Thus, baptism and eucharist became transformed in analogy to Hellenistic mystery rituals (1 Cor 1:13–17; 15:29; 11:17–34). The traditional Jewish-Christian ethos was replaced by the big-city lifestyle. Besides material wealth, the congregation enjoyed a plethora of spiritual gifts (1 Cor 1:5; 2 Cor 8:7–9; 9:11; see Betz 1986). Ecstatic and enthusiastic experiences provided a new set of values. The relationship between Christianity and other religions was regulated in the spirit of Hellenistic enlightenment and polytheistic practice (1 Cor 8:1–11:1). In regard to morality there seems to have been an attitude of "live and let live": libertinism was tolerated (1 Corinthians 5–6) just as was radical asceticism (1 Corinthians 7). Setting aside the older ethical catalogs (1 Cor 5:9–11; 6:9–10; 2 Cor 12:20; see *Galatians* Hermeneia, 281–88) was justified by appealing to the notion of "freedom" (1 Cor 7:21–22; 9:1–23; 10:29; 2 Cor 3:17): where there is freedom, "everything is permitted to me" (1 Cor 6:12; 10:23). The basic assumption for this "freedom" was of course that liberation from the old religions was taken to mean also the end of the myth of the last judgment (1 Cor 6:9; 15:12, 50).

The fact that factions existed in the community (1 Cor 1:10–17; 3:3–23) shows, however, that extreme Hellenization of the Christian faith was not acceptable to all members. The center of the problem was the conflict between the older Jewish-Christian heritage and the newly forming Hellenistic-Christian identity.

The significance of Paul for the question of Hellenism was that he was the first to understand the problems raised by the Corinthians in their deeper theological dimensions and that he had the courage to face those problems. He felt confronted by the alternatives of either integrating the new Corinthian experiences and insights into a conception of Christian existence and lifestyle, or having to witness the disintegration of the churches founded by him. The Corinthian letters are the literary fixation of this profound encounter with the central issues of Hellenistic religiosity and morality. These letters testify to the emergence of Paul's theology (at least prior to Romans).

Paul addresses the Corinthians programmatically as Greeks (1 Cor 1:22). As Greeks they are accustomed and indeed expected to ask for "wisdom." What does the gospel yield in terms of wisdom? His answer is that a rich intellectual inventory (1 Cor 1:5) is not by itself wisdom, but that it is first of all important to distinguish the "wisdom of this world," which is no wisdom at all but folly, from the "wisdom of God," which to the superficial appears as folly. Real wisdom, and that is indeed what the "wisdom of God" is, becomes evident in its application to the concrete problems of life. The argument for this claim is carried through in 1 Corinthians. Its main thrust is to convince the Corinthians that *agapē* is the foundation and content of the Christian faith and as such, true wisdom, which is able to stand the tests of daily life (1 Cor 8:1, 13:1–13; 14:1–5; etc.). Paul does not identify himself with any of the Corinthian parties, but by taking up the major Corinthian problems case after case he demonstrates in what way Christian love is also the wisdom of God. An entire course of education can be seen to run through the letters of 1 and 2 Corinthians, a course that passes through tumultuous confrontations before it is resolved and reconciliation is achieved. The completion of the collection for the church of Jerusalem (1 Cor 16:1–4; 2 Corinthians 8 and 9; Rom 15:25–32) plays a major role in these developments (see Betz, *2 Corinthians 8–9,* Hermeneia).

(6) Paul's Opponents. As one would expect, Paul's opponents spread the accusation that he not only abolished the law but also negated the reality of sin (Rom 3:5–8:31; 6:1; Matt 5:17; 7:21–23). Behind this defamation is again the claim of illegitimate Hellenization and indeed "paganization": as a result of Paul's teaching, gentile Christianity would be doomed to fall back into paganism and would, as unredeemed, again be juxtaposed to Judaism. Paul confronted these objections in his letter to the Romans. He began his defense of his gospel (Rom 1:16–17) with an incisive critique of Hellenistic religion, culture, and morality (1:18–32) as well as of non-Christian Judaism (2:1–29), in order then to turn to the unfolding of the notion of a "true Judaism," which he had introduced already in Gal 6:17. In this argument Christianity is shown to be the universal church, in which the law is not abolished (7:12) and sin is not negated (7:13–25), but in which the world is defeated (8:31–39). In chapters 9–11 Paul demonstrates that the church is not opposed to but rooted in Judaism, and that both will find their eschatological fulfillment through God's grace and mercy.

(7) Developments After Paul. The conflicts concerning Hellenization in the Deutero-Pauline Epistles and the Pastoral Epistles continued after Paul. In these letters the debates about Hellenism coincide with those about heresy versus orthodoxy. Each of these texts discusses in its own way the problems of accommodation to and separation from Hellenism.

(8) The Gospels and the Book of Acts. The Gospels and the book of Acts originated in connection with the problem of how best to communicate the life and teaching of Jesus as well as the beginnings of the church to the Hellenistically oriented. In this literature the christology of Jesus as "divine man," contained already in the pre-synoptic miracle-story tradition, was reinterpreted in accordance with the theology of the evangelists (see Betz, *RAC* 12: 234–312). In the Gospel of Mark the teachings, miracles, and crucifixion of Jesus are presented as a "mystery" (Mark 4:11), a concept familiar to Hellenistic religious thinking. The Gospel of Matthew combines the gentile Christian Gospel of Mark with traditions derived from older Jewish Christianity. The Gospel of John debates the issues of Hellenism in its confrontation with Gnosticism. In the Gospel of Luke and the book of Acts the author recommends Christianity as the religion best suited for the Hellenistic world.

4. The NT Becoming Literature. Part of the phenomenon of Hellenism as it applies to the NT is the way in which it became literature. This process can be studied in the NT itself, but investigations have long been hampered by outdated ideas and concepts. Most important in this regard is the application of the category of literature to the NT (see Aune 1987; 1988). For a long time scholarship was influenced by Franz Overbeck's distinction between Christian "primitive literature" *(christliche Urliteratur)* and patristic literature, with only the latter to be properly called "literature." This concept of literature, the history and problems of which have yet to be studied adequately, has shaped subsequent NT scholarship, especially form criticism, redaction criticism, and genre research. Even the recent comprehensive history of early Christian literature by Vielhauer (1975) is based on Overbeck.

In regard to the epistolary literature, the distinction between "real letter" and "artistic, literary letter" (which has been common since Adolf Deissmann) is no longer usable (see Doty 1973; Aune 1988: 85–105; Malherbe 1988). The authentic letters of Paul include Romans, 1 and 2 Corinthians, Galatians, Philippians, 1 Thessalonians, and Philemon; in the case of Romans, 2 Corinthians, and Philippians, many scholars assume combinations of fragments by later redactors. The interpretation of Paul's letter writing in the context of ancient epistolography and rhetoric is still in its beginning stages, but detailed analyses have been presented by Betz (*Galatians* Hermeneia; *2 Corinthians 8–9* Hermeneia) and others that demonstrate formal composition in accordance with Gk epistolography and rhetoric (see also Hübner 1984; Aune 1987: 158–225). The pseudepigraphical letters include 2 Thessalonians, Colossians, Ephesians, the Pastoral Epistles, Hebrews, the Catholic Epistles, and the letters contained in Acts 15:23–29 and Rev 2:1–3:22. 2 Thessalonians, Colossians, and Ephesians imitate Paul's letter writing and therefore presuppose that his letters have become literary prototypes. (See Holland 1987 on 2 Thessalonians and Donelson 1986 on the Pastoral Epistles.)

The Gospels were interpreted in terms of ancient literature first by K. L. Schmidt, M. Dibelius, and R. Bultmann, but their main interest was directed toward the smaller literary forms; redaction criticism later focused on the overarching work of the gospel writers. Recent attention shows renewed interest in the question of the gospel as literary genre (see Aune 1987: 17–76; 1988: 107–26; Talbert 1977; 1988: 53–73 with bibliography). It was Dibelius' aim to interpret the book of Acts as part of ancient literature. He was followed by many others, so that today scholarship agrees that the author of Luke-Acts must be regarded as one of the major historians of the Hellenistic age, along with Polybius, Plutarch, Josephus, and Tacitus. The book of Revelation has also been studied in terms of its literary nature, composition, and genre. (For the state of this research and bibliography see Collins 1983; Hellholm 1989).

Bibliography

Adorno, F., ed. 1977. *La cultura ellenistica.* 2 vols. Milan.

Aune, D. E. 1987. *The New Testament in Its Literary Environment.* Philadelphia.

Aune, D. E., ed. 1988. *Greco-Roman Literature and the NT.* SBLSBS 21. Atlanta.

Barr, J. 1970. Which Language Did Jesus Speak? Some Remarks of a Semitist. *BJRL* 53: 9–29.

Bengtson, H. 1958. Der Hellenismus in alter und neuer Sicht. Von Kaerst zu Rostovtzeff. *HZ* 185: 88–95.

Betz, H. D. 1972. *Der Apostel Paulus und die sokratische Tradition.* BHT 45. Tübingen.

———. 1985. *Essays on the Sermon on the Mount.* Philadelphia.

———. 1986. The Problem of Rhetoric and Theology according to the Apostle Paul. Pp. 16–48 in *L'Apôtre Paul: Personnalité, style et conception du ministère.* Ed. A. Vanhoye. BETL 73. Leuven.

Bichler, R. 1983. *"Hellenismus." Geschichte und Problematik eines Epochenbegriffs.* Impulse der Forschung 41. Darmstadt.

Bickerman, E. 1976–85. *Studies in Jewish and Christian History.* 3 vols. Leiden.

———. 1985a. *Religion and Politics in the Hellenistic and Roman Periods,* edited by E. Gabba and M. Smith. Como.

Blass, F.; Debrunner, A.; Funk, R. W. 1961. *A Greek Grammar of the NT and Other Early Christian Literature.* Trans. and ed. R. W. Funk. Chicago.

Blinzler, J. 1969. *Der Prozess Jesu.* 4th edition. Regensburg.

Braun, H. 1969. *Spätjüdisch-häretischer und frühchristlicher Radikalismus.* 2d edition. 2 vols. BHT 24/1–2. Tübingen.

Braun, R. 1973. *Kohelet und die frühhellenistische Popularphilosophie.* BZAW 130. Berlin.

Clemen, C. 1924. *Religionsgeschichtliche Erklärung des NT.* 2d edition. Giessen.

Collins, J. J. 1983. *Between Athens and Jerusalem.* New York.

Corssen, P. 1908. Über Begriff und Wesen des Hellenismus. *ZNW* 9: 81–95.

Cullmann, O. 1970. *Jesus and the Revolutionaries.* New York.

Danker, F. 1988. *A Century of Greco-Roman Philology.* Atlanta.

Delling, G. 1963. Zum Corpus Hellenisticum Novi Testamenti. *ZNW* 54: 1–15.

———. 1974. Perspektiven der Erforschung des hellenistischen Judentums. *HUCA* 45: 133–76.

———. 1987. *Die Bewältigung der Diasporasituation durch das hellenistische Judentum.* Berlin.

Donelson, L. R. 1986. *Pseudepigraphy and Ethical Argument in the Pastoral Epistles.* HTU 22. Tübingen.

Doty, W. G. 1973. *Letters in Primitive Christianity.* Philadelphia.

Downing, F. G. 1988. À bas les aristos. The Relevance of Higher Literature for the Understanding of the Earliest Christian Writings. *NT* 30: 213–30.

Droge, A. J. 1989. *Homer or Moses?* HUT 26. Tübingen.

Droysen, J. G. 1877–78. *Geschichte des Hellenismus.* 3 vols. 2d edition. Tübingen.

Feldman, L. H. 1977. Hengel's Judaism and Hellenism in Retrospect. *JBL* 96: 371–82.

Fitzmyer, J. A. 1979. *A Wandering Aramean.* Missoula, MT.

Freyne, S. 1988. *Galilee, Jesus and the Gospels.* Philadelphia.

Fuchs, H. 1938. *Der geistige Widerstand gegen Rom in der antiken Welt.* Berlin.

Georgi, D. 1980. *Weisheit Salomos.* JSHZ III/4. Gütersloh.

Gilbert, M., ed. 1978. *La Sagesse dans l'Ancien Testament.* BETL 51. Gembloux.

Grimal, P., ed. 1968. *Hellenism and the Rise of Rome.* London.

Goshen-Gottstein, M. H. 1983. The Textual Criticism of the Old Testament Rise, Decline, Rebirth. *JBL* 102: 365–99.

Hatch, E. 1891. *The Influence of Greek Ideas and Usages upon the Christian Church.* London.

Hellholm, D., ed. 1989. *Apocalypticism in the Mediterranean World and the Near East.* 2d edition. Tübingen.

Hengel, M. 1971. *Was Jesus a Revolutionist?* Philadelphia.

———. 1974. *Judaism and Hellenism.* 2 vols. Trans. J. Bowden. Philadelphia.

———. 1976. *Juden, Griechen und Barbaren.* SBS 76. Stuttgart.

———. 1983. *Between Jesus and Paul.* Philadelphia.

Hoffmann, C. 1988. *Juden und Judentum im Werk deutscher Althistoriker des 19. und 20. Jahrhunderts.* Leiden.

Holland, G. 1987. *The Tradition that You Received from Us: 2 Thessalonians in the Pauline Tradition.* HUT 24. Tübingen.

Hommel, H. 1983–84. *Sebasmata. Studien zur antiken Religionsgeschichte und zum frühen Christentum.* WUNT 31–32. Tübingen.

Horsley, G. H. R. 1981–87. *New Documents Illustrating Early Christianity.* 4 vols. North Ryde, NSW, Australia.

Hübner, H. 1984. Der Galaterbrief und das Verhältnis von antiker Rhetorik und Epistolographie. *TLZ* 109: 241–50.

Jeremias, J. 1971. *New Testament Theology.* Trans. J. Bowden. London.

Kaerst, J. 1926–27. *Geschichte des Hellenismus.* 2 vols. 3d edition. Leipzig.

Kaiser, O. 1982. Judentum und Hellenismus. *VF* 27: 68–88.

Krüger, P. 1908. *Hellenismus und Judentum im neutestamentlichen Zeitalter.* Leipzig.

Kypke, G. 1755. *Observationes sacrae in Novi Foederis libros ex auctoribus potissimum Graecis et antiquitatibus.* 2 vols. Wratislaviae.
Laqueur, R. 1925. *Hellenismus.* Giessen.
Larcher, C. 1969. *Études sur le livre de la Sagesse.* Paris.
———. 1983–85. *Le livre de la Sagesse ou la Sagesse de Salomon.* 3 vols. Paris.
Lieberman, S. 1962. *Hellenism in Jewish Palestine.* 2d edition. New York.
———. 1963. How Much Greek in Jewish Palestine? Pp. 123–41 *Biblical and Other Studies,* ed. A. Altmann. Vol. 1, Cambridge, MA.
———. 1965. *Greek in Jewish Palestine.* 2d edition. New York.
Long, A. A., and Sedley, D. N. 1987. *The Hellenistic Philosophers.* 2 vols. Cambridge.
Lüdemann, G. 1983. *Paulus, der Heidenapostel.* Vol. 2. FRLANT 130. Göttingen.
———. 1984. *Paul, Apostle of the Gentiles.* Trans. F. S. Jones. Philadelphia.
Malherbe, A. J. 1988. *Ancient Epistolary Theorists.* SBLSBS 19. Atlanta.
Momigliano, A. 1970. Review of Martin Hengel, *Judentum und Hellenismus* (1969). *JTS* 21: 149–53.
———. 1975. *Alien Wisdom. The Limits of Hellenization.* Cambridge.
———. 1977. *Essays in Ancient and Modern Historiography.* Oxford.
Murray, O. 1969. Review of C. Schneider, Kulturgeschichte. *ClR* 19: 69–72.
Mussies, G. 1976. Greek in Palestine and the Diaspora. Pp. 1040–1064 in *The Jewish People in the First Century.* CRINT 2. Ed. S. Safrai and M. Stern. Assen/Philadelphia.
Nickelsburg, G. W. E. 1981. *Jewish Literature Between the Bible and the Mishnah.* Philadelphia.
Nilsson, M. P. 1974. *Geschichte der griechischen Religion.* Vol. 2. 3d edition. Munich.
Norden, E. 1898. *Die antike Kunstprosa.* 2 vols. Leipzig.
Pippidi, D. M., ed. 1976. *Assimilation et résistance à la culture gréco-romaine dans le monde ancien.* Paris.
Préaux, C. 1978. *Le monde hellénistique.* 2 vols. Paris.
Prümm, K. 1954. *Religionsgeschichtliches Handbuch für den Raum der altchristlichen Umwelt.* Rome.
Rabin, C. 1976. Hebrew and Aramaic in the First Century. Pp. 1007–1039 in *The Jewish People in the First Century.* Ed. S. Safrai and M. Stern. Assen/Philadelphia.
Radermacher, L. 1925. *Neutestamentliche Grammatik.* Tübingen.
Reese, J. 1970. *Hellenistic Influence on the Book of Wisdom and Its Consequences.* AnBib 41. Rome.
Sanders, E. 1985. *Jesus and Judaism.* Philadelphia.
Schmeller, T. 1987. *Paulus und die "Diatribe".* NTAbh NF 19. Münster.
Schneider, C. 1967–69. *Kulturgeschichte des Hellenismus.* 2 vols. Munich.
Schneider, G. 1979. Stephanus, die Hellenisten und Samaria. Pp. 215–40 in *Les Actes des Apôtres,* ed. J. Kremer. BETL 48. Louvain.
Sevenster, J. N. 1968. *Do You Know Greek? How Much Greek Could the First Christians Have Known?* NovTSup 19. Leiden.
Smith, M. 1971. *Palestinian Parties and Politics That Shaped the OT.* New York.
Stadelmann, H. 1980. *Ben Sira als Schriftgelehrter.* WUNT 2/6. Tübingen.
Talbert, C. 1977. *What is a Gospel? The Genre of Canonical Gospels.* Philadelphia.
———. 1988. Once Again: Gospel Genre. *Semeia* 43: 53–73.
Tarn, W. W., and Griffith, G. 1952. *Hellenistic Civilization.* 3d ed. London.
Tcherikover, V. 1959–66. *Hellenistic Civilization and the Jews.* Philadelphia.
Theiler, W. 1982. *Poseidonios, Die Fragmente.* 2 vols. Berlin.
Toynbee, A. J. 1959. *Hellenism: The History of a Civilization.* London, New York.
Unnik, W. C. van. 1973–83. *Sparsa collecta: Collected Essays.* 3 vols. NTS 29–31. Leiden.
Vielhauer, P. 1975. *Geschichte der urchristlichen Literatur.* Berlin.
Walter, N. 1964. *Der Thoraausleger Aristobulos.* TU 86. Berlin.
Wendland, P. 1912. *Die hellenistisch-römische Kultur nach ihren Beziehungen zu Judentum und Christentum.* HNT 1/2. 3d edition. Tübingen.
Wettstein, J. 1751–52. *He Kainē Diathēkē.* 2 vols. Amsterdam.
Will, E. 1966–67. *Histoire politique du monde hellénistique (323–30 av. J.-C.).* 2 vols. Nancy.
Will, E., and Orrieux, C. 1986. *Ioudaïsmos-Hellènismos. Essai sur le Judaïsme judéen à l'époque hellénistique.* Nancy.

HANS DIETER BETZ

HELLENISTIC SYNAGOGAL PRAYERS. See PRAYERS, HELLENISTIC SYNAGOGAL.

HELLENISTS [Gk *hellēnistai*]. The term used in Acts (6:1; 9:29) to designate Jews living in Jerusalem but originally connected with Diaspora Judaism and characterized by the use of Greek as their principle language, especially for worship and scripture.

The traditional understanding of the Hellenists as Greek-speaking Jews is first found in Chrysostom (*Hom. 14 in Acts* 6:1 and *Hom. 21 in Acts* 9:29). This has been expanded in recent years to an understanding of them as Diaspora Jews, acculturated in the Greek language, who returned to live in Jerusalem, forming their own synagogues and community relationships. There remained a degree of separation from Aramaic-speaking Jews even though the boundaries were not rigid, as some Greek-speaking Jews may have known Aramaic, and Aramaic-speaking Jews almost certainly knew some Greek. Some of these Jews, returning with a sense of awe for their ancestral customs, had staunchly conservative attitudes toward the Law and Temple, e.g., Acts 6:8–9 and 9:29. Others experienced dissonance between Diaspora theological emphases and the ethos of Palestinian legal observance and the Temple cult. They may have found Christian preaching attractive. Some of these Greek-speaking Jews were converted along with Jews who spoke Aramaic, perhaps as early as Pentecost, forming parallel Christian worshipping communities that reflected the distinctions known in the larger Jewish community.

That Luke understood the term in this manner seems certain. The Seven (6:5), usually taken to be representatives of the Hellenists, are Jewish Christians (Hengel 1983: 6). When dispersed (11:19) the Hellenists preach at first only to Jews. The conversion of the gentile Cornelius (Acts 10), is a unique event which is the precedent for the conversion of all gentiles (Acts 15). For Luke the Hellenists in Acts 6:1 are Christian Jews, while in 9:29 they represent the larger group of Diaspora Jews who have not converted.

Since *hellēnistēs* does not occur in any extant literature before Acts and does not occur again with regularity outside of literature influenced by Acts, until the 3d century it is the context of Acts which must be the primary determinant in establishing its meaning. But what can be gleaned from the etymological derivation of the term appears to confirm the meaning "Greek-speaking." *Hellēnistēs* is formed from the verb *hellēnizō,* which usually means "speak Greek" (Hengel 1983: 9). But it must be recognized that most verbs derived from national names mean to live by that group's national customs; e.g., *Ioudaïzō,* "live by Jewish customs," Gal 2:14.

It seems historically implausible that there could have been a gentile segment of the Christian community in Jerusalem at this early date large enough to have caused problems with daily food rations or to have been in a position to attempt to kill Paul (9:29). Luke's theology does not in this case obscure a different historical reality.

There are three main dissenting opinions. Cadbury (1933: 59–74) argued that the Hellenists were gentiles. Most of his points have been answered above, except for the variant reading at 11:20. Here *hellēnistas,* the majority reading, clearly means "Greeks." Thus most commentators and versions adopt the minority reading *hellēnas.* But it is possible that a scribe, having gotten used to Luke's uncommon *hellēnistēs,* repeated it here when the original read *hellēnas,* "Greeks" (Hengel 1983: 8). If the majority reading is original it may still attest to the meaning "speak Greek," but with a variable racial connotation which must be taken from the context. Blackman (1937: 524–25) argued that the Hellenists were proselytes, but in the list of the Seven only Nicolaus is designated as such. Others have argued that the Hellenists represent a syncretistic fringe group in Judaism, but this fails to account for the archconservatism of Stephen's (6:9) and Paul's (9:29) opponents.

It is important that in the consensus of recent scholarship the Hellenists of Acts 6:1 acquire an immense significance in the development of the early Church. Robin Scroggs (1968: 177) has termed their community "the mother of Western Christianity." Of course Palestine had been subject to a process of Hellenization at least since its conquest by Alexander. But the local persistence of Aramaic as the primary language of acculturation means that it is still useful to distinguish between a Palestinian sphere and the larger Hellenistic world. Thus it is now thought that it was this community of Christian Hellenists who accelerated the transferal of the Jesus tradition from Aramaic into Greek, who helped bring Christian theology fully into the realm of Greek thought freed from Aramaic pre-acculturation, who were instrumental in moving Christianity from its Palestinian setting into the urban culture of the larger Empire, who first saw the implications of Jesus' resurrection for a Law-free Gospel for the gentiles (and for Jews), and who were the bridge between Jesus and Paul. These Christian Hellenists were the founders of Christian mission outside Palestine, and a theological tradition capable of articulating a gospel for the Greco-Roman world.

Bibliography

Blackman, E. C. 1937. The Hellenists of Acts vi. 1. *ExpTim* 48: 524–25.

Cadbury, H. J. 1933. The Hellenists. Vol. 5, pp. 59–74 in *The Beginnings of Christianity,* ed. Kirsopp Lake and H. J. Cadbury. London.

Ferguson, E. 1969. The Hellenists in the Book of Acts. *ResQ* 12: 159–80.

Hengel, M. 1983. Between Jesus and Paul: The 'Hellenists,' the 'Seven' and Stephen. Pp. 1–29 in *Between Jesus and Paul.* Trans. J. Bowden. London.

Scroggs, R. 1968. The Earliest Hellenistic Christianity. In *Religions in Antiquity,* ed. J. Neusner. Leiden.

Walter, N. 1983. Apostelgeschichte 6.1 und die Anfänge der Urgemeinde in Jerusalem. *NTS* 29: 370–93.

THOMAS W. MARTIN

HELMET. See WEAPONS AND IMPLEMENTS OF WARFARE.

HELON (PERSON) [Heb *ḥēlōn*]. The father of the chief (*nāśîʾ*, Num 2:7) Eliab of the tribe of Zebulon. Of the five times that Helon is mentioned in the OT, each occurs in a tribal list where his mark of distinction is his status as the father of Eliab. Under the leadership of Helon's son Eliab, the tribe of Zebulon participated in the census of Israelite fighting men carried out by Moses (Num 1:9, 30–31), presented its offerings on the third day of the twelve-day celebration of the dedication of the altar (Num 7:24, 29), took its proper place on the E side of the tabernacle in the Israelite camp (Num 2:7), and assumed its position in the order of march at the Israelites' departure from Mt. Sinai (Num 10:16). The name "Helon" means "the strong one," which appears simply to refer to the bodily strength of the one bearing the name (*IPN,* 225).

DALE F. LAUNDERVILLE

HEM. See DRESS AND ORNAMENTATION.

HEMAN (PERSON) [Heb *hêmān*]. Var. HOMAM. The name of three men in the OT.

1. A clan name in the genealogy of Seir the Horite mentioned in Gen 36:22. If Heman is read here, then his origin would be among the clans of the earliest known inhabitants of this region of Seir (Edom). However, this reading of the name appears in the RSV, GNB, and Douay versions. The MT, KJV, NEB, NAB, and many others read, more correctly, Hemam *(hêmām),* who is identified in the Horite genealogy as a son of Lotan. The name "Hemam" only appears in Gen 36:22; however, in the parallel genealogical list of 1 Chr 1:39, the name is written Homam. Unlike the clans of Israel, the Horite clans did not permanently inherit a dwelling place. They were ultimately dispossessed from the land of Seir (Edom) by the encroaching "sons of Esau" (Deut 2:12–22). This conquest is paired in the text with the conquest of Canaan by the Israelite tribes.

2. One of the three sons of Mahol in 1 Kgs 5:11 (Eng 4:31). This designation may not reflect family relationship, but rather serve as a title, "sons of the dance" (compare "daughters of music" in Eccl 12:4), reflecting their role in the temple worship. Heman, and his brothers Calcol and

Darda, plus Ethan the Ezrahite, were proverbial wisemen of Israel. The unsurpassed wisdom of king Solomon was demonstrated by comparison with that of the sages of the east, of Egypt, and of these four men. In the Judahite genealogical list of 1 Chr 2:6 these four are described as the sons of Zerah. This connection may be the result of the Chronicler identifying the name Zerah with Ezrahite in the superscriptions to Psalms 88 and 89.

3. A son of Joel in the genealogical list of the temple guild in 1 Chr 6:18–32 (Eng 6:33–38). Twenty-two generations of this family are traced through the Levite tribe. Such attention to detail added authority to their leadership in the Second Temple period as well as providing a sense of continuity of service back to the origins of the covenant with God. In 1 Chr 15:16–17, David instructed the "chiefs of the Levites" to appoint musicians to perform during religious celebrations. It is noted that Heman the son of Joel was so appointed, and in 6:19 he is said, along with Asaph and Ethan, to be among those who "sound bronze cymbals." In 1 Chr 16:41–42, Heman and Jeduthun are described as sounding trumpets and cymbals in accompaniment to sacred songs. Similarly, 2 Chr 5:12 describes a grand procession taking the ark of the covenant into the temple accompanied by ranks of priests and the levitical singers and musicians including Heman, Jeduthun, and Asaph.

An expanded role for Heman and the other musicians is found in 1 Chr 25:1. Here they are said to "prophesy with lyres, with harps, and with cymbals" (compare Elisha's use of a musician in 2 Kgs 3:15). This role as prophet is further enhanced in 25:5 where Heman is described as the "king's seer" (see the parenthetical insertion regarding "the seer" in 1 Sam 9:9 and the designation of Gad as the "visionary of David in 2 Sam 24:11). It may be that originally the guild of musicians associated with Heman, Asaph, and Jeduthun began as a prophetic group and later was absorbed into the corps of temple musicians. However, Wilson (1980: 294) suggests that the Chronicler recognized prophecy as a regular part of the Levites' cultic role. "Visionaries" were thus not to be assigned to just one period of Israelite history.

Bibliography

Wilson, R. R. 1980. *Prophecy and Society in Ancient Israel.* Philadelphia.

VICTOR H. MATTHEWS

HEMDAN (PERSON) [Heb *ḥemdān*]. Var. HAMRAN. A son of Dishon (Gen 36:26; 1 Chr 1:41), which makes him a grandson of "Seir, the Horite" (Gen 36:20). See also HORITES. The genealogical list Gen 36:20–28 belongs to the most ancient traditions in Genesis 36 (Weippert 1971). Together with Gen 36:10–14, the list describes the Edomite tribal system in the 7th century B.C. (Knauf 1989: 10–11, n. 45, 61–63). The name is attested in Sabaic (Harding 1971: 200) and Arabic (*Ḥamdân;* Littmann 1921: 9). It can be interpreted as "object of desire" (cf. Dan 11:37). In 1 Chr 1:41, *ḥmdn* is misspelled as *ḥmrn,* a name that occurs in Safaitic and Qatabanian (Harding 1971: 201).

Bibliography

Harding, G. L. 1971. *An Index and Concordance of Pre-Islamic Arabian Names and Inscriptions.* Toronto.

Knauf, E. A. 1989. *Ismael.* 2d ed. ADPV. Wiesbaden.

Littmann, E. 1921. Beduinen- und Drusennamen aus dem Haurân-Gebiet. *Nachrichten von der Königlichen Gesellschaft der Wissenschaften zu Göttingen, Philologisch-historiche Klasse 1921:* 1–20.

Weippert, M. 1971. *Edom. Studien und Materialien zur Geschichte der Edomiter auf Grund schriftlicher und archäologischer Quellen.* Ph.D. diss., Tübingen.

ERNST AXEL KNAUF

HEMORRHAGE. See SICKNESS AND DISEASE.

HEMORRHOIDS. See BIBLE, EUPHEMISM AND DYSPHEMISM IN THE; SICKNESS AND DISEASE.

HEMP. See DRESS AND ORNAMENTATION.

HENA (PLACE) [Heb *hēnaᶜ*]. Assyria under Shalmaneser V (726–722) and Sargon II (721–705) conquered Samaria and took tribute from Judah's king Ahaz (733–727). Hezekiah (727–698) continued the tribute, but when Sargon died, Hezekiah rebelled against Assyria. The Assyrian King Sennacherib (704–681) attacked Judah and captured many cities (2 Kgs 18:13). He sent three Assyrian officials to confer with the leaders of Judah. One, the Rabshakeh, argued that the situation was hopeless. To illustrate his point, he asked (v 34), "Where are the gods of Hamath and Arpad? Where are the gods of Sepharvaim, Hena, and Ivvah?" The officials returned to Sennacherib, who sent them back with another message, including the words of 19:13, "Where is the king of Hamath, the king of Arpad, the king of the city of Sepharvaim, the king of Hena, or the king of Ivvah?" The story is repeated in Isa 36–37 where 37:13 records the same question of 2 Kgs 19:13. These were apparently places the Assyrians had conquered and the city gods had been unable to save them; the city kings were gone, presumably dead. Hena may have been in upper Mesopotamia, judging by the listing with Hamath (modern Hama, on the Orontes River, 120 miles N of Damascus), Arpad (Arfad, Tell Rif'at, 19 miles N of Aleppo), Sepharvaim (Ezek 47:16, Sibraim between Hamath and Damascus, near Homs; but Astour, *IDBSup,* 807, suggests Saparda in Media). Simons (*GTTOT,* 367) says the site is unknown.

The name simply means "low land." Scholars have pointed out that Hena and Ivvah do not appear in Isa 36:19, a parallel to or a repetition of 2 Kgs 18:34. After the question about the gods of Sepharvaim is the question, "Have they delivered Samaria out of my hand?" Hena and Ivvah do not appear in a somewhat similar list in 2 Kgs 17:24, which says the king of Assyria brought colonists (exiles) from Babylon, Cutha, Avva, Hamath, and Sepharvaim. This has led some scholars to claim that Hena and Ivvah are not geographical places at all. Astour claims there are no traces of toponyms of Hena and Ivvah anywhere in the ancient Near East. The "names" are due to dittography in the original phrase about the perverse king of the Sapardians. Gray (*Kings* OTL, [2]1970: 677) omits the *hēnaᶜ wĕᶜiwwâ* of MT with the Greek (BL) and Isaiah 36. The Targum takes them as the *Hipᶜil* of *nuaᶜ* and *Piᶜel* of *ᶜawa,* meaning "He sent them wandering and caused them to stray." Symmachus in the parallel passage in Isa 37:13 reads "displaced and humiliated them," reading *ᶜinna* for MT *ᶜiwwâ.* G(L) and L read *wĕᵓayyēh ᵓĕlōhê ᵓereṣ šōmrôn,* "and where are the gods of the land of Samaria," which is suggested by the immediate sequel. A reference to Samaria is natural after its recent fall rather than a reference to more distant places. Gray (p. 684) translated v 34, "Where are the gods of Hamath and Arpad? Where are the gods of Sibraim and where were the gods of the land of Samaria that they should deliver Samaria from my hand?" The gods of these Syrian peoples could not be expected to deliver Samaria; hence Lucian's reading "where are the gods of Samaria?" is demanded before the final phrase (unless, of course, Hena and Ivvah are actual places). In 2 Kgs 19:13, Gray (p. 686) omits *sĕparwāyim hēnaᶜ wĕᶜiwwâ* as a mere echo of 18:34.

Earlier Cheyne (*EncBib* 2: 2016) claimed Hena and Ivvah were imaginary names. "Underlying this is a witty editorial suggestion that the existence of cities called *hnᶜ* and *ᶜwh* respectively has passed out of mind (cf Ps 9:6[7]), for [Hena and Ivah] clearly means 'he has driven away and overturned' (so Tg, Sym)." He would drop Hena out of the text. Hommel (1898: 330–31) though that these were divine names. Hena is the Arabic star-name al-hanᶜa, and Ivvah is al-ᶜawwa, the 6th and 13th stations of the moon. Delitzsch (1877: 97) noted also that if Hena and Ivvah are words, the phrase means "he has taken away and overthrown," but he thought they were the names of cities whose location is unknown. Hena is hardly the well-known Avatho on the Euphrates as Gesenius, Niebuhr, and others supposed. Gehman (1970: 378) noted the common identification with Anah on the Euphrates at 42° E longitude. Ivvah (2 Kgs 18:34; 19:13 RSV) may be the same as Avva in 2 Kgs 17:24, which was a town and has been identified with Tell Kafr 'Aya on the Orontes, SW of Homs. Thus Hena would be in the same vicinity, i.e., somewhere near Damascus, an area familiar to the inhabitants of Jerusalem. Thus the Rabshakeh's analogy makes sense—Jerusalem will be destroyed; her God will not help her; her king will be killed—just like Hena and these cities near Damascus, whose fate was already known to the people of Jerusalem.

Bibliography

Delitzsch, F. 1877. *Biblical Commentary on the Prophecies of Isaiah.* Vol. 2. 3d ed. Grand Rapids. Repr. 1967.

Gehman, H. S. 1970. *New Westminster Dictionary of the Bible.* Philadelphia.

Hommel, F. 1898. Hena and Iwwa. *ExpTim* 9/7: 330–31.

HENRY O. THOMPSON

HENADAD (PERSON) [Heb *ḥēnādād*]. This name means literally, "the grace of Hadad," Hadad being the West Semitic storm-god (cf. Benhadad of Syria). Similar names are found in Ugaritic, such as *ḥnbᶜl,* "the grace of Baal," and *ḥnil,* "the grace of El." Henadad was the patronym of a family group among the Levites. The "sons of Henadad," i.e., members of this family group, were among those charged with overseeing the repairs of the house of the Lord (Ezra 3:9). Henadad, mentioned in connection with the restoration of Jerusalem under Nehemiah (Neh 3:18, 24; cf. also Ezra 3:9), and with the sealing of Nehemiah's covenant (Neh 10:10—Eng 10:9), was of this same family group.

D. G. SCHLEY

HENNA. See PERFUMES AND SPICES; FLORA.

HEPHER (PERSON) [Heb *ḥēper*]. HEPHERITES. Three people in the OT bear this name. The noun is probably related to the West Semitic root *ḥpr,* meaning "to dig, search for" (cf. Ar *ḥafara,* Aram *ḥĕpar*), hence *ḥēper* would refer to something dug, such as a well. In post-biblical Hebrew *ḥēper* refers to "grave digging," an obvious later restriction to one kind of hole (cf. Jastrow 1903: 493 for references).

1. The head of the clan (properly Heb *mišpaḥâ,* which is midway between a family and a clan) of the Hepherites (Heb *haḥeprî*) in the tribe of Manasseh. He is also identified as the father of Zelophehad, whose daughters were given their father's inheritance in the absence of a male heir (see Num 26:32, 33; 27:1; 17:2, 3). See HEPHER (PLACE).

2. One of the sons of Naarah, a clan of Judah (1 Chr 4:6).

3. One of the mighty men (Heb *gibbôrîm*) of David in 1 Chr 11:36. Note that the parallel passage in 2 Samuel 23 differs in some respects from the Chronicler's list, including omitting any mention of Hepher. Some textual corruption of either or both passages is possible (cf. the discussion in Hertzberg *I and II Samuel* OTL, 402–408; Williamson *1 and 2 Chronicles* NCBC, 101–4), although it also seems possible that the two lists come from different sources representing the composition of David's mighty men at different times.

Bibliography

Jastrow, M. 1903. *A Dictionary of the Targumim, the Talmud Babli and Yerushalmi, and the Midrashic Literature.* New York. Repr. 1985.

H. ELDON CLEM

HEPHER (PLACE) [Heb *ḥēper*]. A town located in the tribal territory of Manasseh, first appearing alongside Tappuah in the list of defeated Canaanite kings (Josh 12:17). Hence, the editor of the book of Joshua testifies that Hepher was a Canaanite city-state. But the credibility and dating of this list has been questioned and debated by different scholars (Noth 1935; Aharoni 1976). Most scholars place the origin of the list within the context of the Iron I period, but Fritz (1969) has suggested a date in the United Monarchy. The appearance of the sites in the list in pairs, usually in the same geographic vicinity, and the identification of Tappuah in the Manassite territory in the central mountain region may serve as a preliminary guideline for locating the city of Hepher nearby. The term "the land of Hepher," which appears in the Solomonic district list (1 Kgs 4:10), apparently refers to a geographic definition of the area of jurisdiction of a Canaanite city-state. In this sense the Hebrew term *ʾereṣ* (land) is similar to the Akkadian term *mat,* which also appears as a definition for the territorial area of cities, families, and tribes. The Bible contains some examples of this term, in reference to Canaanite cities: "the land of Shechem" (Gen 34:1–2; 10:21); "the land of Tappuah" (Josh 17:8); "the land of Cabul" (Josh 19:27; 1 Kgs 9:13).

These two references define Hepher as a city-state, a description typical of the LB period. Its location should be sought within the bounds of the 3d Solomonic district, of which "the land of Hepher" is a part. According to Albright (1925), the district belonged to the Manassite inheritance in the hill country. However, Alt (1932) and Aharoni (1976) placed it in the Sharon plain of the coastal region. Following this latter placement Mazar suggested identifying Hepher with Tel Ifshar (M.R. 141197) in the central Sharon, while Alt suggested that Arubboth, the capital of the district, was located at Tel Assawir (M.R. 151210) in the N part of the same plain. From the outset these identifications presented great difficulties: Tel Ifshar is a small site, unfit to have been a Canaanite city-state; and Tell Assawir contained no remains from the 10th century. Another problem with placing the 3d district in the Sharon plain is the fact that the territories of the granddaughters of Hepher—the daughters of Zelophehad, according to the genealogical lists—were located in the NE of the Manasseh hill country; thus the "land of Hepher," if in the Sharon, is too far W from his "granddaughter's" allotments.

In 1978 a detailed archaeological survey of the Manassite allotment W of the Jordan was begun. With the identification of Arubboth at Kh. el-Hamam (M.R. 163201) near the Dothan valley, it became apparent that Hepher and the "land of Hepher" should be sought in the hill-country nucleus of Manasseh. As a result of the survey, Zertal (1984) suggested a new identification for the city-state of Hepher at Tell el-Muhaffar (M.R. 170205), located at the N fringes of the Dothan valley. The survey established that settlement on this large tel, which lies upon a good water source and near the international route which connected the coast and the valley of Jezreel (cf. Gen 37:25; *ANET,* 235), began during the EB I–II period. The settlement dwindled during the MB and LB periods, but an additional flourishing of the settlement was during the Iron I–II periods.

The name of the fortified tell was also well preserved. In the British PEF maps, the site is named Umm el-Haffeh, whereas in later maps it appears with its full name, Mu-Haffar. The rarity of the root *ḥpr/ḥfr* in the lexicon of Palestinian place-names supports the idea that the original name was preserved in the above. Therefore it seems that the original territory of the "land of Hepher" included the area of the Dothan valley, originally the area belonging to the Canaanite city-state of Hepher.

In the genealogical lists of Manasseh (Josh 17:2), the Canaanite Hepher appears as the son of Manasseh, along with Shechem, Shemida, Helek, Asriel, and Abiezer. See HEPHER (PERSON). The list continues with Zelophedad, son of Hepher, and his daughters: Milka, Mahla, Hogla, Noah, and Tirza. The Samaria Ostraca indicate that all these were subdivisions within Manassite territory; therefore, the term "the land of Hepher" during the Israelite settlement period apparently expanded to include all the territories in the NE area of Manasseh, from Wadi Fariʿah and S of it to the Gilboa range in the N, including the E valleys of the Shechem Sincline. Lemaire (1977) and others have suggested identifying these areas as the territories of the daughters of Zelophohad. The archaeological survey conducted by Zertal showed that the earliest Iron I settlements in Manasseh were located in the desert fringe and the E valleys near the Jordan. This conclusion is based upon the presence of the early cooking pot type A, which is dated to the 14–13th centuries B.C.E., from which developed the later "Israelite" cooking pot type B, typical to the 12–11th centuries B.C.E.

In light of the results of the survey, Zertal suggested identifying the territory of Tirzah at Wadi Fariʿah, of Mahlah in Wadi Malih, of Milcah in the Sanur Valley (10 miles N of Nablus) of Hoglah in the vicinity of Yasid (M.R. 176189), and of Noah possibly in the Zebabde valley (7 miles N of Tirzah; already suggested by Lemaire). This division appropriately defines the final development of the term "the land of Hepher" during the period of the United Monarchy, as it appears in the Solomonic district list.

Bibliography

Aharoni, Y. 1976. The Solomonic Districts. *TA* 3: 5–15.

Albright, W. F. 1925. The Administrative Division of Israel and Judah. *JPOS* 5: 17–54.

Alt, A. 1913. Israels Gaue unter Salomo. Pp. 1–19 in *Alttestamenliche Studien Rudolf Kittel zum 60.* Leipzig.

———. 1932. Die Reise. *PJB* 28: 34–57.

Fritz, V. 1969. Die Sogennante Liste der Besiegten Konige in Josua 12. *ZDPV* 85: 136–161.

Lemaire, A. 1977. *Inscriptions Hebraiques.* Vol. 1. Paris.

Maisler, B. 1935. Die Westliche Linie des Meerweges. *ZDPV* 58: 78–84.

Noth, M. 1935. Studien zu den Historisch-Geographischen Dokumenten des Josuabuches. *ZDPV* 58: 185–225.

Zertal, A. 1984. *Arubboth, Hepher and the Third Solomonic District.* Tel Aviv (in Hebrew).

ADAM ZERTAL

HEPHZIBAH (PERSON) [Heb *ḥepṣî-bāh*]. Mother of Manasseh, king of Judah (2 Kgs 21:1). Hephzibah's name occurs in her son's regnal formula in 2 Kings but is omitted from the parallel account in 2 Chr 33:1. She is the only queen mother for whom no information is given concerning either her father or her place of origin. Her name, which means "my delight is in her," appears in Isa 62:4 as a symbolic name for the restored Zion. See also MANASSEH, KING OF JUDAH; QUEEN.

LINDA S. SCHEARING

HEPTAPEGON (M.R. 200251). A term (Gk *Heptapegon*), which specifically refers to several still-existing springs near the NW bank of Lake Kinneret. These springs flow between the foot of the hills of the Mount of Beatitudes and the bank of the lake in a rocky area that is situated 2 miles to the SW of Talhum-Capernaum and on the NE side of Tell ᶜOreimeh (i.e., the ancient city of Kinneret, from which the name of the lake is derived). Between Tell ᶜOreimeh and the springs, Wadi Jamus widens out, forming a small plain.

The name "Heptapegon," which means "seven fountains," does not occur in the writings of the NT and is attested only beginning from the 9th century, although the name is implied in the Latin texts of the 4th century *(Septem Fontes)*. The Arabic pronunciation et-Tabgha derives directly from "Heptapegon," where *hep* has been changed into *et* by assimilation with the following consonant, and *tapegon* is contracted to *tabgha* with the normal shift of *p* to *b;* the *a* ending probably derives from the plural feminine substantive *heptapegai* instead of from the neuter singular of the substantive adjective *heptapegon*. The Arabic name et-Tabgha, or simply TABGHA is still in use, along with the modern Hebrew name ᶜEin Sheba, and is a safe assurance of the identification of the site.

According to Josephus, the spring (*pege* in the singular) was commonly called Capernaum ("the inhabitants call it Capernaum": *JW* 3.519). This designation, the most ancient, is explained by the fact that Capernaum was in the 1st century A.D. the installation closest to the springs. It is also recorded in the Middle Ages that the limited area around the springs was called Tabula (cf., the Florentine map of the 13th century).

A. Research and Excavations

Many travelers and topographers of the past century, in their impassioned research on Capernaum, have stopped at et-Tabgha and have described in particular the springs and the hydraulic installations connnected with them, ignoring, however, the existence of the sacred Christian buildings. The systematic excavations since 1932 have revealed the presence of three churches built by the Byzantines in memory of three important events of the gospel accounts—the multiplication of loaves and fishes (Matt 14:13–21), the Sermon on the Mount (Matt 5:1–11), and the appearance of the resurrected Jesus (John 21:1–24).

The three sanctuaries were constructed in the late 4th century and were of modest proportions. Toward the end of the 5th century the little Church of the Multiplication of Loaves and Fishes was replaced by a much larger church which had mosaic pavements with scenes of exceptional artistic merit. The mosaic of the Chapel of the Sermon on the Mount was also partially remodeled. With the Persian invasion at the beginning of the 7th century, the Church of the Multiplication and the Church of the Sermon on the Mount fell gradually into ruins, and only the rustic little chapel on the traditional site of the appearance of the resurrected Jesus remained functional until the period of the Crusades.

B. The Heptapegon at the Time of the Gospels

The Heptapegon is of interest to biblical scholars because the site was near, and directly dependent upon Capernaum, "the city of Jesus" (Matt 9:1), and because the Christian communities located at this place the three important events mentioned above. The reliability of these traditions cannot be quickly dismissed, especially after the recent excavations of Capernaum have indicated both the uninterrupted presence there of a strong community of Jewish Christians in the first centuries of the Christian era, and their pronounced interest for the preservation of traditions. Furthermore, archaeological research, and especially that of 1968, not only has uncovered in the limited area of the springs certain elements consonant with the topographical data in the gospel accounts, but it has helped further to re-create the physical environment.

One thing is clear: in the area of the springs of et-Tabgha, there has never been a village, much less an urban center, in spite of what some explorers of the last century have suggested. According to them the Heptapegon was at the time of Jesus an industrial suburb of Capernaum, or even the place of Bethsaida of Galilee. Only in one place have some silos been found excavated in the rock presupposing a farmhouse. Although the initial date of its construction escapes us, it must date before the 2d century A.D. In addition, the Heptapegon was separate from the urban centers: between the Heptapegon and the entrance of the Jordan river at the N of the lake, the only village was Capernaum, two miles away from the Heptapegon, while along the W shore of the lake there existed no installations between the Heptapegon and Magdala (with the possible exception of Tell Hunud where, however, the pottery gathered on the surface does not predate the 3d century A.D.).

Besides being a "solitary" place, the Heptapegon consists of a vast area of land that is completely rocky and inadequate for agriculture but much more adapted for an assembly of a great multitude. The rocks on the surface were exploited, beginning in the 2d century A.D., as a source of white limestone, much more precious than the basalt which is abundant in the area of the lake. The small plain however, along the Wadi Jamus, to the W of the springs, lent itself well to cultivation. It is to this arable area that the pilgrims refer to when they spoke of a level field where many olives and palms grew.

At the time of the Jesus, the abundant springwater flowed in the lake and was utilized only in part to irrigate the fertile valley of Ginnosar through canals which now are very difficult to locate. These waters still attract a great quantity of fish so that the shores of the lake between the Heptapegon and Capernaum are the richest for fishermen. Only in the 4th century A.D. was a more rational and efficient system of irrigation created: several springs in fact were channeled into gigantic cisterns from which canals carried the water in various directions. In more recent times the springwater has been used to propel many mills, some of which have remained in use until as recently as fifty years ago.

The Heptapegon, although it is a solitary place and for the most part rocky, was easily accessible both by the lake it bordered and by land, since it was crossed by a very important imperial road; this road passed from Beth-shan to Damascus, turning from Tell ᶜOreimeh toward et-Tabgha. This road was still functional in the 4th century and is recorded by the pilgrim Eteria.

All evidence seems to corroborate the events of the gospels and the ancient Christian tradition which located them in the restricted area of the Heptapegon.

Bibliography

Bagatti, B. 1937. La Cappella sul Monte Delle Beatitudini: Scavi della Custodia di Terra Santa. *Rivista di Archeologia Cristiana* 14: 1–49.

Gauer, B. 1938. Werkbericht uber die Istandsetzung der Boden-Msaiken von Heptapegon. *JPOS* 18: 233–53.
Loffreda, S. 1970a. *Scavi di Et-Tabgha*. Jerusalem.
———. 1970b. Sondaggio nella Chiesa della Moltiplicazione dei Pani a Tabgha. *LASBF* 20: 370–80.
Mader, U. E. 1934. Die Ausgrabung der Brotvermehrungskirche auf dem deutschen Besitz et-Tabgha am See Genesareth. *Das Helige Land* 78: 1–15, 41–44, 89–103, 131–49.
Schneider, A. M. 1937. *The Church of the Multiplying of the Loaves and Fishes*. London.

STANISLAO LOFFREDA

HERAKLES (DEITY). The most popular and the most complex of the ancient Greek heroes, Herakles (a theophorous name meaning "glory of Hera") was reportedly the son of Zeus and the mortal woman Alcmene. Herakles was prominent in four areas of Greek and Roman culture: folklore, cult, art, and literature. He is mentioned several times in the oldest extant Greek compositions, the *Iliad* and the *Odyssey* (Galinsky 1972: 9–22). Archaeologists have discovered artistic representations of his exploits which date to the 8th century B.C. According to Nilsson (1932: 187–220), the Herakles cycle (along with the other major Greek mythological cycles) can be traced back to the Mycenaean period (ca. 1550–1150 B.C.). Iconographic evidence from the ANE, dating as far back as the 3d millennium B.C., provides evidence for the popularity of such Herakles-like figures as Ninurta, the son of the storm god Enlil (Burkert 1979: 80–83). A hero with club, bow, and lionskin (the traditional costume of the Greek Herakles, which appears after ca. 650 B.C.) is depicted on Sumerian cylinder seals. Burkert traces the figure of Herakles back even further to a neolithic and EB age figure who is not primarily a warrior fighting other warriors but rather a "master of animals" (Burkert 1979: 83–98). According to the *interpretatio Graeca* ("Greek interpretation") which prevailed from the 5th century B.C., in which certain barbarian deities were seen as Greek gods under various aliases, Herakles was identified with the Tyrian god Melgart, whose worship spread to the Decapolis, Cyprus, Egypt, and Carthage (Herodotus 2.44; 2 Macc 4:19; Joseph. *AgAp* 1.118–19; *Ant* 8.146; Arr. *Anab.* 2.16.1–8; Arist. *Or.* 40.10; cf. Teixidor 1977: 34–35). At Palmyra, Herakles was identified with the Mesopotamian ruler of the dead Nergal (Seyrig 1945). In one of the surviving fragments of Cleodemus or Malchus (Holladay 1983: 245–59), possibly a Jew or a convert to Judaism, the author claims that two of the sons of Abraham by Keturah, Aphran and Apher, joined Herakles to fight Antaeus in Libya, one of Herakles traditional *parerga* (Diod. Sic. 4.17.4–5). Herakles later married the daughter of Aphran, who bore a son named Diodorus.

Herakles differed from other Greek heroes (such as Perseus, Theseus, Odysseus, Oedipus, and Amphiaraus) in that he had no tomb which might serve as a center for his cult. This feature was quite unusual, since the Greek term *heros* (usually simply transliterated into English as "hero") was a term for a mortal who received worship at his tomb as a local earth deity after death. In part the widespread popularity of Herakles was due to the fact that his worship was not localized by not being limited to the site of a tomb. Despite the fact that he had particular associations with Tiryns and Thebes, neither city ever claimed to possess his remains.

The worship of Herakles had two quite different forms, each characterized by a distinctive sacrificial protocol (Guthrie 1950: 229–31). In some places he was honored as a hero, while at other places he was worshipped as an Olympic god (Herodotus 2.44). Pindar combined these two perceptions by describing Herakles as a "hero-god" (*Nem.* 3.22), by which he meant a hero who had become an Olympic deity as a reward for his labors. The dual nature of Herakles is also reflected in a famous passage in *Odyssey* 11.601f., where Odysseus sees, during his tour of Hades, "the phantom of mighty Herakles; but he himself is with the immortal gods." Another reason for Herakles' enormous popularity was the fact that he was a mortal who through his own striving had become a god, thereby breaking the barrier between mortality and immortality so rigidly maintained in ancient Greek religious thought (Guthrie 1950: 239).

The most extensive ancient syntheses of Herakles legends are found in Diodorus Siculus 4.8–53 and Apollodorus 2.4.5–2.8.5. These and other ancient mythographers divided the adventures of Herakles into three categories. First came the Twelve Labors (Brommer 1986), the so-called canonical tasks assigned to Herakles by king Eurystheus of Tiryns (to purify him for killing his wife Megara and her children during an insane rampage), which can be subdivided geographically into a *Peloponesian group* (of six): (1) The Nemean Lion, (2) The Lernaean Hydra, (3) The Erymanthian Boar, (4) The Ceryneian Hind, (5) The Stymphalian Birds, and (6) The Stables of Augeas; an *eastern group* (of three): (7) The Cretan Bull, (8) The Thracian Horses (Mares of Diomedes), and (9) The Girdle of Hippolyta; and a *western group* (of three): (10) The Cattle of Geryon, (11) The Apples of Hesperides, and (12) Cerberus (descent and return from Hades).

Second came the *Parerga,* or "subsidiary activities," the so-called "noncanonical" adventures, some of which punctuate the Twelve Labors; others were narrated after the completion of the Twelve Labor, but all were considered incidental to them (Brommer 1984).

Third came military expeditions during which Herakles both conquered and civilized the world. It was this final type of activity which made Herakles popular as a paradigm of the king and victorious conqueror with whom many Hellenistic kings and Roman emperors and generals identified.

These three types of adventures were framed by stories of Herakles' birth and youth on the one hand and death by self-immolation on the other. Shortly after Zeus had impregnated Alcmene disguised as her husband (compressing three nights into one), Amphitryon himself arrived home and also had sexual relations with Alcmene. Consequently she bore twins, Alcides (the original name of Herakles), son of Zeus, and Iphicles, son of Amphitryon. Hera, a patron of Eurystheus and adversary of Herakles, sent a serpent to destroy the infant Herakles, but the infant hero strangled it. By the 5th century B.C., Herakles' labors were understood allegorically, and as tasks which he took on voluntarily. In line with this understanding Prodicus (a contemporary of Socrates) lectured on the allegory of Herakles' Choice (Xenophon 2.1.34), presented as a testing or temptation scene. Two women, personifications of Vice and Virtue, appeared to Herakles. The former tried to persuade him to follow the easy road of ease and pleasure, while the latter urged him to take the rough road of hardship and struggle. Herakles chose the latter, and so became an example for Stoics and Cynics, as well as others. Herakles' death was the result of a tragic accident. His wife Deianira gave him a garment which had been anointed with the blood of the dying centaur Nessus. Though she thought the blood was an aphrodisiac, in reality it was a poison. Suffering greatly, Herakles had a funeral pyre constructed on Mount Oeta. According to the version of the myth in Apollodorus (2.7.7; trans. Simpson), "While the pyre was burning a cloud is said to have enveloped Heracles and to have raised him up to heaven with a crash thunder. Thenceforth he was immortal" (cf. Sen. *Her. O.* 1966–69).

Samson (as a theophorous name meaning "man of the sun"), an Israelite leader with superhuman strength, performed many fantastic feats, many of which have parallels in Greek and Mesopotamian legends of figures like Herakles, Ninurta, and Gilgamesh. In a series of articles, O. Margalith has argued that the Biblical figure of Samson is associated with a pastiche of adventures drawn from a LB Age cycle of Herakles legends as well as other Greek mythical themes and motifs (1986a; 1986b; 1987). The Herakles legends, he argues, were mediated to the Israelites by their Philistine neighbors. Samson's slaying of a lion barehanded to win the favor of a maiden (Judg 14:5–9), for example, is a motif missing from the ancient Near East but common in Greek folklore (Margalith 1987). The birth story of Samson in Judg 13:2–24 consists of three motifs common in Greek myth: a barren mother, the intervention of a supernatural being, and a miraculous birth (Margalith 1986b). Some of Margalith's parallels are weak, such as his contention that the sacrifice of Samson's parents in Judg 13:15–20, in which they supposedly see Samson's divine father ascend to heaven in flames, was influenced by the story of Herakles' fiery apotheosis on Mount Oeta (Margalith 1986b). Augustine provides evidence that early Christians also connected Samson with Herakles (*Civ. Dei* 18.19), and Samson is depicted as Herakles in the frescoes of the Via Latina catacomb (Simon 1981: 86–96; Malherbe *RAC* 14: 581–83).

Early Christians recognized parallels between Herakles and Jesus but considered the former to be based on the imitation of the latter (Just. *1 Apol.* 21.1; *Dial.* 69.3; Or. *Cels.* 3.22, 42). Several modern scholars have noted the striking similarities between the legends of Herakles (and other Greek heroes) and the life of Jesus as presented in the canonical Gospels (surveys in Simon 1955: 49–74 and Malherbe *RAC* 14: 568–72). Pfister (1937) proposed that the author of the "Urevangelium," from which the Synoptic Gospels were derived (in itself an improbable hypothesis), was heavily influenced by a Cynic-Stoic life of Herakles. Pfister's proposal received a devastating critique by Rose (1938), who nevertheless conceded that the legendary features of the Gospels (virgin birth, miracles, resurrection, ascension) in many cases were influenced by ancient conceptions of the divine hero or divine man. Toynbee listed twenty-four parallels between Herakles and Christ (1939: 465–76), yet suggested that the influence of the former upon the latter was through "folk memory."

There is evidence which suggests the possible influence of Herakles imagery on the formation of aspects of the Christology of Hebrews (Aune 1990). Though Jesus was the Son of God, he learned obedience through suffering (Heb 5:8) and provides an example for Christians (Heb 12:3–4). Similarly Aelius Aristides heard a divine voice exhorting him "to endure the present circumstances, since Herakles also endured his, although he was the son of Zeus" (*Or.* 40.22; trans. Behr), and others considered Herakles' divine sonship as a metaphor referring to his "education" in toil and suffering (Dio Chrys. *Or.* 2.78; Epict. 2.16.14). Since Jesus has passed through the heavens and experienced human weakness, he is able to help those who pray to him (Heb 4:14–16). Similarly Dio Chrysostom is critical of the many common people "who pray to him [Herakles] that they may not themselves suffer—to him who in his labours suffered exceedingly great" (*Or.* 40.16; LCL trans. with modifications). Both Jesus (Heb 5:8–9; 10:5–10) and Herakles (*DL* 6.2; Diod. Sic. 4.11.1; Epict. 2.16.44) are hailed as examples of obedience to their divine fathers. Finally, just as Jesus' heavenly enthronement is achieved through his suffering and death (Heb 2:9; 12:2), so the apotheosis of Herakles is seen as the consequence of his life of obedience, suffering, and virtue (Lucian *Deor. conc.* 6; Dion. Hal. *Ant. Rom.* 1.40). These and other parallels suggest that the author of Hebrews thought that many of the functions of Herakles as a Hellenistic savior figure were even more applicable to the mission and achievement of Jesus. See also HERCULES (DEITY).

Bibliography

Aune, D. E. 1990. Herakles and Christ: Herakles Imagery in the Christology of Early Christianity. *Greek, Romans and Christians: Essays in Honor of Abraham J. Malherbe,* ed. D. L. Balch, E. Ferguson and W. A. Meeks. Minneapolis.

Brommer, F. 1984. *Herakles II: Die unkanonischen Taten des Helden.* Darmstadt.

———. 1986. *Heracles: The Twelve Labors of the Hero in Ancient Art and Literature.* New Rochelle.

Burkert, W. 1979. *Structure and History in Greek Mythology and Ritual.* Berkeley.

Galinsky, G. K., 1972. *The Herakles Theme.* Oxford.

Guthrie, W. K. C. 1950. *The Greeks and Their Gods.* Boston.

Höistad, R. 1948. *Cynic Hero and Cynic King.* Lund.

Holladay, C. R. 1983. *Fragments from Hellenistic Jewish Authors.* Vol. 1, *Historians.* Chico, CA.

Margalith, O. 1986a. Samson's Riddle and Samson's Magic Locks. *VT* 36: 225–34.

———. 1986b. More Samson Legends. *VT* 36: 397–405.

———. 1987. The Legends of Samson/Heracles. *VT* 37: 63–70.

Nilsson, M. P. 1932. *The Mycenaean Origin of Greek Mythology.* Berkeley.

Pfister, F. 1937. Herakles und Christus. *ARW* 34: 42–60.

Rose, H. J. 1938. Heracles and the Gospels. *HTR* 31: 113–42.

Seyrig, H. 1945. Heracles-Nergal. *Syria* 24: 62–80.

Simon, M. 1955. *Hercule et le Christianisme.* Paris.

———. 1981. Remarques sur la Catacombe de la Via Latine. *Le Christianisme antique et son contexte religieux: Scripta Varia.* Tübingen.

Simpson, M. 1976. *Gods and Heroes of the Greeks: The Library of Apollodorus.* Amherst, MA.

Teixidor, J. 1977. *The Pagan God: Popular Religion in the Graeco-Roman Near East.* Princeton.

Toynbee, A. J. 1939. *A Study of History.* Vol. 6. Oxford.

D. E. AUNE

HERBS. See FLORA.

HERCULES (DEITY) [Gk *Hēraklēs*]. The Greek figure who is honored in quadrennial games at Tyre to which Jason in 2 Macc 4:19–20 sends a delegation with three hundred drachmas of silver to offer sacrifices in the opening ceremonies. While the Greek term *pentaetērikou* literally would mean quinquennial, an inclusive method of counting was employed (Goldstein *II Maccabees* AB, 232). Known in Greek texts as "Heracles," Hercules is the Roman name given to this figure regarded in Greek literature as both hero and god. See also HERAKLES (DEITY). Heracles cults were spread throughout almost all the Greek world (Burkert 1985: 208–211). Both Strabo (16.2.23) and Arrian (2.16.2; 2.24.5; 3.6.1) give ample attestation to the major importance of this cult at Tyre. By the time of Herodotus (2.44) this Greek divinity is already connected with the Phoenician god Melqart.

While the wording of the account varies considerably in the manuscripts, the essential elements of the event remain the same. The 300 drachmas of silver mentioned in the story were a sufficient amount to buy an ox for sacrifice (Habicht *2 Makkabäerbuch* JSHRZ, 218), so later Latin and Syriac versions which read "3,300" reflect the inflation rate (Goldstein, 233). Goldstein is probably correct to argue that Jason viewed the sacrifice as a non-religious "admission fee" (pp. 232–33). Jason sent the envoys because King Antiochus IV Epiphanes (175–164 B.C.E.) was present and to establish Jerusalem's reputation as a Hellenistic city. In this chapter on the conflict over the Hellenization of Jerusalem, the envoys of Jason are used as an example of Jewish resistance to its religious demands. The Jewish delegation has some qualms about offering a sacrifice to a Greek god; they use the money given them for the purchase of an offering to pay for the construction of galleys *(triēreōn)* for the king instead. There is no indication that this decision presented a problem for the Hellenistic officials in Tyre.

Josephus (*Ant* 1.240–41) notes that Cleodemus Malchus in his history of the Jews says that the sons of Abraham aided Heracles in his battle against Libya, and that Heracles later married Abraham's granddaughter. From Menander he gets the information that Hiram, King of Tyre, erected new temples to Heracles (*Ant* 8.146, *AgAp* 1.118–19). Megasthenes is cited as arguing that the accomplishments of Nebuchadnezzar were greater than those of Heracles (*Ant* 10.227, *AgAp* 1.144).

Bibliography

Burkert, W. 1985. *Greek Religion.* Trans. J. Raffan. Cambridge.

JOHN KAMPEN

HERDSMAN [Heb *nōqēd*]. A term that denotes the work of shepherding small cattle (sheep and goats), and possibly specified the care of a choice breed of sheep. The Ar *naqad* refers to a species of small sheep producing abundant wool, and the shepherd of this animal was a *naqqad.* The Akk *nāqidu* was used of shepherds of cattle, sheep, and goats, and even of mankind; sometimes the term was used of the overseers of herdsmen. The word *nōqēd* is used twice in the OT: "King Mesha of Moab was a sheep breeder" (*nōqēd;* 2 Kgs 3:4) and Amos was "among the shepherds *(nōqĕdîm)* of Tekoa" (Amos 1:1). As a *nōqēd* Mesha operated a profitable business; his annual tribute to the king of Israel was 100,000 lambs and the wool of 100,000 rams (2 Kgs 3:4). The care of such large numbers of sheep would have required many shepherds serving under Mesha. At Ugarit the *nqd* was a known functionary appearing in lists with priests and others of the nobility, and he presumably held an official position (*ANET,* 141b; see *UT,* 78, 447). The Ugaritic material raises the question of whether Amos should be regarded as different from the ordinary shepherd, as more like Mesha, a prosperous businessman. He may have occupied a professional status under the king or the temple which obligated him to supply them with flocks, to pay taxes, or even to fulfill a military role; he would have also enjoyed certain privileges that came with employment by the royal house (Hammershaimb 1970: 17–18; Cutler and Macdonald 1977: 25–27; Craigie 1982: 30–33). It has also been proposed that the title *nōqēd* as applied to Amos meant he held a position as some kind of cult functionary, even a hepatoscoper (see Bic 1951; cf. Murtonen 1952).

Bibliography

Bic, M. 1951. Der Prophet Amos—Ein Hepatoskopos. *VT* 1: 293–96.

Craigie, P. 1982. Amos the Nōqēd in the Light of Ugaritic. *SR* 11/1: 29–33.

———. 1983. *Ugarit and the Old Testament.* Grand Rapids.

Cutler, B., and Macdonald, J. 1977. The Unique Ugaritic Text UT 113 and the Question of 'Guilds.' *UF* 9: 13–30.

Hammershaimb, E. 1970. *The Book of Amos.* Trans. J. Sturdy. Oxford.

Murtonen, A. 1952. The Prophet Amos—A Hepatoscoper? *VT* 2: 170–71.

JACK W. VANCIL

HERES, ASCENT OF (PLACE) [Heb *maʿălēh heḥāres*]. The place E of the Jordan River by which Gideon returned from capturing the Midianite kings Zebah and Zalmunna (Judg 8:13). The text is problematic. First the presence of the definite article before *ḥeres* argues against Heres being a proper last name, but perhaps the word "sun" (BDB, 357); thus Gideon returned from the battle "before the sun arose" (although *maʿălēh* is not the normal word to indicate the path of the sun). Second, both Aquila and Symmachus presuppose *millĕmaʿlâ hĕhārîm,* "from up on top of the mountains."

GARY A. HERION

HERESH (PERSON) [Heb *ḥereš*]. A Levite who lived in Jerusalem after the return from Babylonian exile (1 Chr 9:15). Heresh is listed in 1 Chr 9:15 as a descendant of Asaph, the head of one of the three families of levitical singers appointed by David (1 Chr 15:16–17, 25:1–8) and the author of several Psalms (Psalms 50, 73–83). Heresh probably followed in his ancestor's footsteps as a levitical singer. The parallel passage in Nehemiah (11:15–18) does not list Heresh but does indicate that other descendants of Asaph lived in Jerusalem at that time (11:17). Braun (*1 Chronicles* WBC, 136) has suggested that the author of 1 Chronicles 9 may have had access to other traditions than did the author of Nehemiah; or he may have updated the list in Nehemiah 11 by adding the names of prominent families of his own day.

ROBERT C. DUNSTON

HERESY AND ORTHODOXY IN THE NT. The issue of whether or not particular religious expressions conformed to established norms and/or doctrines was certainly important within early Judaism and early Christianity. However, it is important to note that at early stages "established norms" by definition did not exist. For early Judaism of the Greco-Roman period, diversity was prevalent, with various forms of Judaisms each understanding themselves to be the true successor to biblical "Israel." See JUDAISM (GRECO-ROMAN PERIOD).

The origins of Christianity are bound up with theological controversies surrounding true and false doctrine, controversies occurring first within Judaism and subsequently within Christianity. The NT as a literary manifestation is the result of these debates. See CANON (NT). Debates about true and false doctrine are thus presupposed in the NT, although the recorded material is only a cross-section of what must have occurred in the real life of the early Church.

A. Concept and Terminology
B. History
   1. John the Baptist
   2. Jesus of Nazareth
   3. Paul and his Opponents
C. Literature
   1. The Sermon on the Mount
   2. The Letters of Paul
   3. Pauline Pseudepigrapha
   4. The Gospels
   5. The Book of Revelation

A. Concept and Terminology

Complementary to orthodoxy, the concept of heresy includes authoritative doctrines both theoretical (interpretations of Scripture; theology) and practical (rituals, ethics, organization) in content. The decision about what should be accepted as orthodox or rejected as heretical depended to a large extent on the viewpoint of the respective author(s) of a given text, that is, on doctrinal presuppositions and traditions as well as on concrete situations. The traditional definition of heresy as an arbitrary deviation by a minority from a doctrinal norm represented and safeguarded institutionally by a majority cannot be applied to primitive Christianity, a caveat correctly recognized in 1934 by Walter Bauer (Bauer 1971; see *TRE* 5: 317–19). The facts, however, are considerably more complicated than Bauer had presupposed and cannot be abstracted into one formula or rule.

The notion of heresy in the Christian sense of the word did not exist at the beginning; its gradual inception and development can be seen in the NT. Acts knows the notion of *hairesis* ("party," "sect") in the neutral sense, used by and derived from the Greek philosophical schools (see Glucker 1978: 166–225). According to Acts, the Jewish religious parties of the Sadducees (5:17) and the Pharisees (15:5; 26:5) are to be classified under this name. For the Jews in Acts, the Christian movement is nothing but another *hairesis* (24:5, 14; 28:22). Paul is shown to have changed parties from the Pharisees (26:5) to the "Nazoraeans" (24:14; 28:22). In the eyes of the Jews, the term *hairesis* takes on the connotation of "heresy" (24:5); but for the author of Acts, the early Church was "orthodox" in both Christian and Jewish terms. In the letters of Paul, the use of the terminology vacillates between the two meanings "heresy" and "schism," and he thereby introduces these terms into early Christian language and thought: *hairesis* points to divisive parties within the congregations, but at times it can also mean "heresy" (Gal 5:20; 1 Cor 11:18–19). In the post-apostolic period, the word always designates "heresy," in opposition to the "right" doctrine advocated by the author of the text (Titus 3:10; 2 Pet 2:1; Ign *Eph.* 6:2; Ign *Trall.* 6:1; *1 Clem.* 14:2; etc.). See *EWNT* 1: 96–97; *TRE* 14: 313–318; *RAC* 13: 248–97; *TDNT* 1: 180–85.

B. History

1. John the Baptist. Although there is little reliable information, the movement of John the Baptist apparently originated from debates in Judaism on true and false doctrine pertaining to the very essence of the Jewish religion. The phenomenology of John the Baptist, his message of repentence *(tĕšûbâ),* and his ritual of baptism had their origin and purpose in a return to "true" Judaism, not simply in political opposition to the ruling authorities. When Jesus had himself baptized by John (Mark 1:9–11 and par.), the act itself was a confession by Jesus that he had accepted John's message as orthodox in the Jewish sense. At some point (after the arrest and death of the Baptist), Jesus proceeded on his own (Mark 1:14; 6:17–29) and called disciples, among whom were former disciples of John. Since Jesus' own message and conduct were, despite a large degree of agreement, considerably different from John's, debates over the issues must have ensued. Such debates may also have been the reason why not all of John's disciples jointed Jesus: in fact, the Baptist's movement continued to exist parallel to and in competition with Christianity. This competition is reflected in the NT, where differences between the Christian conduct and doctrines and those of the Baptists's followers are settled (Mark 1:7–8 par.; Mark 2:18–22 par.; Acts 13:24–25; 19:1–7), or where literary sources and traditions from the Baptist's own movement are taken over and integrated into the gospels (Matthew 1–2; Luke 1; John 1). Thus was John the Baptist given the place as a legitimate forerunner of Jesus.

2. Jesus of Nazareth. From the beginning, the appearance of Jesus was a matter of controversy. Jesus was a self-conscious and conscientious Jew. His understanding of the Torah and of God's will and activity was in his view orthodox, but in the eyes of his opponents it was heretical (Braun 1969). Jesus' preaching of repentence (Mark 1:14–15 par.) was directed against other practices of Torah obedience ("pseudo-orthodoxy") and, by implication, against an erroneous understanding of the Jewish religion as such (see Matt 21:28–31; Luke 13:1–5). Jesus' critique focused on the teaching of the scribes and Pharisees, whereas other Jewish movements received little attention. This rather one-sided approach seems to imply that Jesus agreed with much of what those whom he attacked espoused. In his critique against current practices of Temple worship, he largely shared the view of the Qumran sect; yet contrary to Qumran and other rigorists in Judaism, Jesus held a positive view of the religion of the ordinary Jewish person. The controversies over Jesus seem to have targeted his combination of Torah observance and love of neighbor (see Mark 12:28–34 par.), an emphasis resulting in the different positions he took on cultic purity, observance of the Sabbath, prayer, marriage, and possessions. Moreover, on this basis he also strongly opposed the summary expulsion of the so-called tax collectors and sinners (Mark 2:15–16; Matt 11:19 par.; Luke 15:1–2, 18:9–14) as well as of the prostitutes (Matt 21:31–32; cf. Luke 15:30).

The condemnation of Jesus as a heretic by other Jewish parties is not reported by the earliest layers of the synoptic tradition. The accusation, however, that John the Baptist was possessed by a demon (Matt 11:18–19) was also turned against Jesus. Statements such as "he has the Beelzebul" or "through the prince of the demons he expels the (lower) demons" (Mark 3:22 par.; Matt 10:25; cf. Mark 11:27–33 par.) classify Jesus as a magician and thus initiate a kind of "negative christology" that has its advocates even in the present (see Smith 1978; Betz, *RAC* 12: 235–36, 251).

That Jesus was regarded to be a heretic is reflected first in Jewish-Christian sources or layers of NT tradition; the accusation apparently stems from a developed christology and soteriology. The Jewish-Christian Sermon on the Mount defends the theology of Jesus against the charge of apostasy (Matt 5:17–20; 7:21–23). In the synoptic controversy stories, Jesus appears in debates with opposing Pharisees, each charging the other with heresy (see Bultmann 1968: 39–55). The confession of Jesus as Messiah and Son of God (Mark 14:61–62 par.; Matt 22:41–46 par.) is, in the eyes of his opponents, evidence of heresy not only on the part of the Church but also on Jesus' part (see the summary in John 7–8). It is in these traditions that we first encounter the explanation that Jesus was crucified because he was a heretic (Mark 14:63–64 par.; John 10:33; 19:7; cf. Acts 7:54–60). This explanation also justified the expulsion of the Christians from the Synagogue (John 9:22; 12:42; 16:2).

3. Paul and his Opponents. Paul began as an orthodox Pharisee (Phil 3:5; Acts 23:6; 26:5; cf. Gal 1:13–14) who persecuted early Christian groups for their heresy (Gal 1:13, 23; 1 Cor 15:9; Phil 3:6; Acts 8:3; 9:1, 21; 22:4, 19; 26:10–11). See PAUL. Subsequent to his vision of Christ (Gal 1:16; 1 Cor 9:1; 15:8), Paul joined a Jewish-Christian community; soon, however, he and his gospel free of the law became suspect in the eyes of more conservative Jewish-Christians. Yet Paul and Barnabas succeeded at the Conference at Jerusalem (Gal 2:1–10) in clearing themselves from suspicion and obtaining approval of the so-called "pillars" of the Jerusalem church, although a conservative minority (the so-called "false brothers") remained among the opposition (Betz, *Galatians* Hermeneia, 81–103; Dunn 1982; Lüdemann 1980–83, vol. 2). In other words, the inner-Jewish problem of heresy and orthodoxy had become an inner-Christian problem.

The Conflict at Antioch (Gal 2:11–14; see *Galatians* Hermeneia, 103–12; Kieffer 1982; Dunn 1983; Holtz 1986) indicates that the dilemma of the Jewish Christians associated with Paul and Peter surrounded the necessity to decide between orthodoxy in the Jewish sense or orthodoxy in the Christian sense. The majority at Antioch decided against Paul, and, as a result, those Jewish Christians who so decided declared him a heretic. The inevitable resultant split in the Church remained associated with Paul's name. Later Jewish Christianity persisted in a somewhat stereotyped anti-Paulinism (see Lüdemann 1980–83, vol. 2), but the main Church (*Grosskirche*) secured Paul's orthodoxy (see Lindemann 1979), in particular by publishing his letters.

C. Literature

1. The Sermon on the Mount. The Sermon on the Mount (Matt 5:3–7:27) originated in Jewish Christianity and presents the teachings of Jesus in the form of an epitome. Sayings of Jesus are critically selected and arranged so as to ward off the accusation that they reflect what is believed to be gentile Christian heresy. The teaching of Jesus is defended as orthodox in the Jewish sense (5:17–20; 7:12). See SERMON ON THE MOUNT/PLAIN.

2. The Letters of Paul. The letters of Paul owe their existence to the threat of heresy in his churches. The letters presuppose a situational context in which debates occurred on appropriate and inappropriate Christian doctrine and conduct. In all his letters Paul struggles against suspicion and actual accusations of heresy to prevent his churches from drifting into heresy and to defend his theology and conduct as right. Paul himself is therefore responsible for initiating what later became orthodox Paulinism.

In Galatians, the apostle defends himself and his gospel against competing Jewish-Christian missionaries who have tried with astonishing success to persuade the Galatians that his message and status are inferior. His apology before the Galatians is the first known attempt to demonstrate the orthodoxy of the Pauline gospel in the Christian sense of the term (see *Galatians*, Hermeneia).

In Romans, Paul presents this defense again in a much expanded and changed form. These changes apparently stem from a number of factors: anti-Pauline propaganda in Rome (Rom 3:5–8, 31; 6:1–2), internal discussions among both Paul's collaborators and other Christian communities about Paul's theological positions, the fact that Paul addressed a church which he did not found and which subscribed to non-Pauline theological ideas, and the forthcoming journey to Jerusalem to deliver the collection for the poor. As Paul had indicated in Gal 6:16 ("the Israel of God"), for him, orthodoxy in both the Christian and the Jewish sense are one and the same; this assumption he points out in greater detail in Rom 2:17–29. Non-Christian Judaism, however, must not simply be written off as a loss; the apostle presents coexistence between the two religions as the new challenge for the Church (especially Romans 9–11) to demonstrate its own orthodoxy.

The letters to the Corinthians present an apparently confusing situation. In 1 Corinthians, Paul reacts to the problems in the Church caused by party factions (1 Cor 1:10; 11:18; 12:25). There can be little doubt that the parties named have had their own theological outlook, but not much can be inferred concerning their peculiar theologies. Paul assumes a mediating position, identifying himself with none of the parties, not even the Pauline party. It should no longer be denied that some of the theological tendencies of the parties tend toward Gnosticism.

The letter fragments assembled in 2 Corinthians indicate a conflict markedly inflamed since the writing of 1 Corinthians. The issue has shifted from party factionalism to alleged inadequacies on the part of Paul and his apostolate. In all probability the anti-Pauline opposition in 2 Corinthians has been reinforced, or even taken over, by other adversaries who have invaded the Corinthian church (see Georgi 1986), and these adversaries may have contributed a new assessment of Paul's alleged inadequacies (2 Cor 10:10; 11:6; 12:1–10). The apostle defends himself without success in a first apology, fragments of which are extant in 2 Cor 2:14–6:13; 7:2–4. A second apology, replete with irony and satire (2 Cor 10:1–13:10), connected with a visit from Titus, changes the Corinthians' mind.

A letter of reconciliation (2 Cor 1:1–2:13; 7:5–16; 13:11–13) follows the second apology. Here Paul expresses his joy over the resolution of the conflict and justifies his taking a hard line in the previous letter. The letter fragments 2 Corinthians 8 and 9, designed to reorganize the financial collection for Jerusalem which had collapsed because of the crisis, followed the reconciliation (see Betz, *2 Corinthians 8–9* Hermeneia). 2 Cor 6:14–7:1 is an interpolated fragment of non-Pauline origin and is anti-Pauline in tendency; it is a succinct statement of a theology Paul's opponents might have held (see Betz 1973). Apparently the redactor of the letter corpus of 2 Corinthians, who seems to represent a Pauline orthodoxy of a later time, took the fragment 6:14–7:1 as Pauline, thereby reflecting the decline in perception regarding the finer points of the apostle's theology. Similar developments must be assumed for the collection of the letter fragments in Philippians (see Köster 1961–62).

3. Pauline Pseudepigrapha. Continued battles against heretics and the establishing of a Pauline orthodoxy was the preoccupation and goal of Paul's disciples who authored the pseudepigraphical letters of Colossians, Ephesians, 2 Thessalonians, and the Pastorals (1 and 2 Timothy, Titus). This literature is at the same time distinguished by new developments and new confrontations in theology and Church life.

Colossians develops Paul's concept of the Church as the body of Christ into a speculative cosmology in order to refute as heretical a cult of astral mysteries which called itself "philosophy" (Col 2:8). Also involved in a debate with heretics (Eph 4:14–19), Ephesians emphasized the historical and cosmic nature of the universal Church; here the epistle reveals points of contact with Acts, from which it otherwise differs fundamentally. 2 Thessalonians is a commentary on 1 Thessalonians in epistolary form; its author reinterprets the authentic letter of 1 Thessalonians in terms of a later Paulinism committed to an apocalyptic time schedule and opposed to rival Paulinists perhaps inspired by Gnosticism (see Holland 1987). In second-generation Christianity, Christian apocalypticism, once the product of heretical developments seen from the perspective of non-Christian Judaism, became an important weapon used by the Church against the threat of Gnosticism. Evidence for this development is found in later writings of the NT, especially in 2 Peter and in Epistles of John.

4. The Gospels. Each in its own way, the Synoptic Gospels are the products of early Christian debates about heresy and orthodoxy. At least this much can be said, although precise information is extremely limited. The Gospel of Mark combines in a work of intriguing literary quality heterogeneous traditions and sources showing incipient heretical tendencies, interpreting them to fashion a new statement of Christian orthodoxy, entitled "the gospel" (see Weeden 1968; on the titles, see Hengel 1984). The Gospel of Matthew preserves the traditions of an older Jewish Christianity and secures their orthodoxy by embedding them in an ecumenical theology (Matt 28:18–20). The Gospel of John contains evidence of diverse controversies about orthodox and heretical interpretations of the Jesus tradition and the Christian faith. What these debates were we can only guess from the texts, just as the beginning of the Johannine church, from which this gospel came, remains obscure because of lack of information. Conflicts with the Jews, however, as well as with gnostic tendencies, and points of contact with other early Christian church branches can still be recognized. Perhaps the redactor of the Fourth Gospel is identical with the author of the First Epistle of John, an antidocetic polemic identifying and refuting heretical points of doctrine (see especially 1 John 2:18–27; 4:1–5); 2 John 7; 3 John 9–10). The Gospel of Luke, together with the Acts of the Apostles, is marked by strong apologetic tendencies. According to Luke, the beginning period of the Church was free from heresies, presumably in contrast to the situation in his time.

5. The Book of Revelation. The Apocalypse of John takes issue against heretics at several points (Rev 2:6, 9, 14–15, 20–24; 3:9), but concrete information concerning these heresies (Nicolaitans, the prophetess Jezebel, the "synagogue of Satan") is almost completely lacking. As an apocalyptic book, the Apocalypse of John is itself the product of conflicts with Jewish apocalypticism and perhaps Gnosticism. In later Church history the Revelation of John became the preferred text for new apocalyptic movements inside as well as outside the established institutions of Christianity.

Bibliography

Bauer, W. 1971. *Orthodoxy and Heresy in Earliest Christianity*, ed. A. Kraft and G. Krodel. Philadelphia.

Betz, H. D. 1965. Orthodoxy and Heresy in Primitive Christianity. *Int.* 19: 299–311.

———. 1968. Jesus as Divine Man. Pp. 114–33 in *Jesus and the*

Historian, Festschrift Ernest C. Colwell, ed. F. T. Trotter. Philadelphia.
———. 1973. 2 Cor 6:14–7:1: An Antipauline Fragment? *HTR* 92: 88–108.
Braun, H. 1969. *Spatjüdisch-häretischer und frühchristlicher Radikalismus. Jesus von Nazareth und die essenische Qumransekte.* BHT 24/1–2. 2d ed. Tübingen.
Bultmann, R. 1968. *The History of the Synoptic Tradition.* Trans. J. Marsh. Oxford.
Campenhausen, H. von. 1979. Einheit und Einigkeit in der Alten Kirche. Pp. 1–10 in *Urchristliches und Altkirchliches.* Tübingen.
Conzelmann, H. 1981. *Heiden, Juden, Christen.* BHT 62. Tübingen.
Dunn, J. D. G. 1977. *Unity and Diversity in the NT.* Philadelphia.
———. 1982. The Relationship between Paul and Jerusalem according to Galatians 1 and 2. *NTS* 28: 461–78.
———. 1983. The Incident at Antioch (Gal 2:11–18). *JSNT* 18: 3–57.
Elze, M. 1974. Häresie und Einheit der Kirche im 2. Jahrhundert. *ZTK* 71: 389–409.
Georgi, D. 1986. *The Opponents of Paul in Second Corinthians.* Philadelphia.
Glucker, J. 1978. *Antiochus and the Late Academy.* Göttingen.
Harrington, D. J. 1980. The Reception of Walter Bauer's *Orthodoxy and Heresy in Earliest Christianity* during the Last Decade. *HTR* 73: 289–98.
Hengel, M. 1984. *Die Evangelienüberschriften.* SHAW phil.-hist. kl. 3. Heidelberg.
Holland, G. S. 1987. *The Tradition That You Received from Us: 2 Thessalonians in the Pauline Tradition.* Hermeneutische Untersuchungen zur Theologie 24. Tübingen.
Holtz, T. 1986. Der antiochenische Zwischenfall (Galater 2.11–14). *NTS* 32: 344–61.
Kieffer, R. 1982. *Foi et justification à Antioche. Interpretation d'un conflit (Ga 2, 14–21).* LD 111. Paris.
Köster, H. 1961–62. The Purpose of a Pauline Fragment (Phil. III). *NTS* 8: 317–32.
———. 1964. Häretiker im Urchristentum als theologisches Problem. Pp. 61–76 in *Zeit und Geschichte, Dankesgabe an R. Bultmann.* Tübingen.
Lindemann, A. 1979. *Paulus im ältesten Christentum.* BHT 58. Tübingen.
Lüdemann, G. 1980–83. *Paulus, der Heidenapostel.* Vols. 1–2. FRLANT 123, 130. Göttingen.
———. 1984. *Paul, Apostle to the Gentiles. Studies in Chronology.* Trans. F. S. Jones. Philadelphia.
Paulsen, H. 1982. Schisma und Häresie. Untersuchungen zu 1 Kor 11, 18.19. *ZTK* 79: 180–211.
Rudolph, K. 1972. Einige grundsätzliche Bemerkungen zum Thema 'Schisma und Häresie' unter religionsvergleichendem Gesichtspunkt. Vol. 2, pp. 326–39 in *Ex Orbe Religionum, Studia G. Widengren oblata.* Leiden.
———. 1979. Wesen und Struktur der Sekte. *Kairos* 21: 241–54.
Sanders, E. P., ed. 1980–1982. *Jewish and Christian Self-Definition.* 3 vols. Philadelphia.
Sanders, E. P. 1985. *Jesus and Judaism.* Philadelphia.
Schmithals, W. 1971. *Gnosticism in Corinth: An Investigation of the Letter to the Corinthians.* Trans. J. E. Steely. Nashville.
———. 1972. *Paul and the Gnostics.* Trans. J. E. Stelley. Nashville.
Simon, M. 1979. From Greek *Hairesis* to Christian Heresy. Pp. 101–16 in *Early Christian Literature and the Classical Greek Tradition, Festschrift Robert M. Grant.* Paris.
———. 1986. *Verus Israel: A Study of the Relations between Christians and Jews in the Roman Empire (A.D. 135–425).* Trans. H. McKeating. Oxford.
Smith, M. 1973a. *Clement of Alexandria and a Secret Gospel of Mark.* Cambridge, MA.
———. 1973b. *The Secret Gospel: The Discovery and Interpretation of the Secret Gospel according to Mark.* San Francisco.
———. 1978. *Jesus the Magician.* San Francisco.
Vielhauer, P. 1975. *Geschichte der urchristlichen Literatur.* Berlin.
Weeden, T. 1968. The Heresy That Necessitated Mark's Gospel. *ZNW* 59: 145–69.
———. 1971. *Mark-Traditions in Conflict.* Philadelphia.
Wengst, K. 1976. *Häresie und Orthodoxie im Spiegel des 1. Johannesbriefes.* Gütersloh.
Woll, D. B. 1981. *Johannine Christianity in Conflict: Authority, Bank, and Succession in the First Farewell Discourse.* SBLDS 60. Chico, CA.

HANS DIETER BETZ

HERETH (PLACE) [Heb *ḥāret*]. Hereth is mentioned only once in the Bible, as the forested place to which the fugitive David goes after he departs the stronghold of Moab on the advice of Gad the prophet. This occurs as David is leaving his parents in Moab, out of harm's way, as he flees from Saul. One version of the LXX renders the place as *sareik.* Its site is unknown, though some (*IDB* 2: 583 and McCarter *1 Samuel* AB, 357) propose modern Kharas as the location of Hereth. This identification is strengthened by the fact that subsequent events in the narrative occur at the town of Keilah, where David defeats the Philistines and is pursued by Saul (1 Sam 23:1–13). Keilah is identified with modern Khirbet Qīlā (McCarter *1 Samuel* AB, 370), which is near Kharas (*IDB* 2: 583). In any case, David's removal to Hereth in Judah at the urging of Gad can be taken as a divine reassurance that David is under the protection of YHWH even in the heart of Saul's Judah (so Hertzberg *1 and 2 Samuel* OTL, 185).

JEFFRIES M. HAMILTON

HERITAGE. See FAMILY.

HERMAS (PERSON) [Gk *Hermas*]. A Roman Christian who received greetings from Paul in Romans 16:14. He was probably a gentile Christian (Lampe *StadtrChr,* 58) because Paul usually made specific mention of persons in the list of Romans 16 who were Jewish-Christian "kins(wo)men" (Rom 16: 7, 11, 21). The latter term is absent from his other letters, but in Romans, after chaps. 9–11 (cf. 9:3), Paul shows interest in emphasizing Christians' ties to Israel. It therefore can be assumed that he applied and omitted the label "kins(wo)man" purposefully in Romans 16. (The only exception is Aquila at the beginning of the list; so many other characteristics were reported about him that his Jewish background was passed over. See also MARY (PERSON) #7 and RUFUS.)

A member of a Roman house-church, Hermas, and four other members were quoted by name, while the other participants in the house-church were mentioned only generally as "brethren who are with them." The five persons therefore may have played leading roles in the house-church. The name "Hermas" occurs only six times according to the epigraphical and literary sources from the city of Rome (Lampe *StadtrChr,* 139–41). Since the name was not common there, it probably indicates that Hermas had immigrated to Rome.

PETER LAMPE

HERMAS' THE SHEPHERD. The early Christian document *Hermas,* or *Shepherd of Hermas,* was known to the early Church Fathers. The Muratorian canon, a list of canonical books from about the 3d century, says Hermas was written by the brother of Pius, Bishop of Rome, about 140–154. Despite much speculation, the author remains unknown. It was written in Rome and involves the Roman church. The document was composed over a longer period of time. Visions I–IV were composed during a threatened persecution, probably under Trajan (the Clement of 8:3 could be Clement of Rome). Vision V–Similitude VIII and Similitude X were written perhaps by the same author to describe repentance to Christians who were wavering. Similitude IX was written to unify the entire work and to threaten those who had been disloyal. This last phase must have occurred before Irenaeus (ca. 175). A preferred date would be 140. On the basis of this internal analysis multiple authorship seems necessary (Giet 1963), though the work could have been composed by one person over a long period of time (Joly 1958).

There are no complete Greek texts of Hermas. The great 4th-century manuscript of the Greek Bible, Codex Sinaiticus, contains only the first fourth of Hermas (to 31:6). Codex Athous, a 15th-century copy, lacks 107:3–114:5, while Papyrus 129, a 3d-century papyrus at the University of Michigan, contains most of the Similitudes (51:8–82:1). When all the texts are put together, 107:3–114:5 is still missing and must be supplied by the Latin text in the Vulgate.

Hermas consists of five Visions, twelve Mandates, and ten Similitudes. In the first Vision, Hermas has a desire for a certain woman, Rhoda, and then is accosted by an elderly woman (the Church) about his sin. In the second Vision, Hermas receives a revelation in the form of a book. When the meaning of writing is revealed to Hermas, he learns repentance is possible. Hermas sees the Church as a tower in the third Vision. The tower is built on a foundation of apostles, bishops, teachers, and deacons, though a variety of stones reflects the diversity of the Church. The fourth Vision takes the form of an apocalypse in which the Church is threatened by an unusual beast which foreshadows a great tribulation. The first four visions involve the elect lady as the revelator. In the fifth vision a shepherd appears to Hermas in order to introduce the Mandates and Similitudes. This vision introduces the work entitled "Shepherd." All of the visions are written in the form of a Jewish apocalypse, with the presence of a revelator, a mysterious revelation and explanation, and an unworthy or foolish recipient.

The twelve Mandates consist of admonitions regarding faith, innocence, truthfulness, chastity, repentance, patience, ill temper, self-control, doublemindedness, grief, cheerfulness, and evil desire. The Mandates take the form of a Jewish-Hellenistic homily, with a revelator (the Shepherd), the diminutivized recipient (Hermas), a commandment, a homily on the commandment, and appropriate blessings and curses.

The ten Similitudes are analogies or parables with similar concerns. The Similitudes build analogies on two cities, trees, vineyards, shepherds, sticks, mountains, a tower, and a garment. The parables are unlike the NT parables. They resemble more those of *Enoch:* the revelator tells a parable, the recipient asks for an explanation, and the revelator responds with an interpretation.

Hermas reflects a local type concern for morality much like the *Epistle of Barnabas* and the *Didache.* Like them, Hermas contains a Two-Way theology (36–39), though his system depends on two angels rather than two impulses (36:1) and he stresses self-control more than right choice. As in other Two-Way systems doublemindedness *(dipsuchia)* and doubt are the primary sins (39:1–12).

From the beginning Hermas was caught in a struggle over repentance. Hermas speaks for the possibility of one postbaptismal repentance. Even within the document some argue against any repentance for the Christian (31:1), while others count on the continuing mercy of God (43:4). Hermas holds to both—a strict morality with a merciful God (31:2–7).

The christology of Hermas has often been called adoptionist (see chap. 59). There is little christological reflection in the book. Most NT christological functions are performed by angels or the Holy Spirit (12:1; 25:2). The complete dwelling of the Spirit in the Son so pleased God that the Son was taken as a divine partner (59:5–7).

The *Shepherd of Hermas* paints a remarkable picture of the 2d-century church at Rome (Osiek 1983). We find among the Christians good and evil, faith and hypocrisy, wealth and poverty—all the qualities of everyday Christian life. The Church is not in danger, but it has reached certain interior accommodations. In addition to postbaptismal repentance, for example, in the parable of the elm and the vine (Similitude II) the elm tree, representing the wealthy of the congregation, gives financial support to the congregation, while the vine, supported by the elm, represents the poor, who pray for the congregation.

The form of Visions, Mandates, and Similitudes share much with similar Jewish material, yet direct use of either Hebrew Scriptures or NT can only be lightly attested. Many of the analogies, such as the garment, the willow, the elm and vine, and the empty jars, have no biblical counterpart. A number of significant details, such as the elderly woman of Vision II, or the virgins of Similitude IX, come from the Greco-Roman milieu.

Bibliography

Giet, S. 1963. *Hermas et les pasteurs: Les trois auteurs du Pasteurs d'Hermas.* Paris.

Joly, R. 1958. *Hermas le Pasteur.* SC 53. Paris.

Osiek, C. 1983. *Rich and Poor in the Shepherd of Hermas.* CBQMS 15. Washington, DC.

Pernveden, L. 1966. *The Concept of the Church in the Shepherd of Hermas.* STL 27. Lund.

Quasten, J. 1950. *Patrology.* Vol. 1. Westminster, MD. Repr. 1953.

Reiling, J. 1973. *Hermas and Christian Prophecy.* NovTSup 37. Leiden.

GRAYDON F. SNYDER

HERMENEUTICS. In the most general terms, hermeneutics can be described as the "art of understanding." Used in its narrower sense, hermeneutics can refer to the method and techniques used to interpret written texts. In a wider sense, it can refer to the conditions which make understanding possible and even to the process of understanding as a whole. In theology, it is usually used in contrast to exegesis—the former is understood as the theory, the latter as the practice of interpretation.

The etymology of the term "hermeneutics" is uncertain. The verbs "say" and "speak" seem to convey the basic connotations. It is contained in the name of Hermes, who in Greek mythology acts as the messenger and spokesman of the gods. He is seen as the inventor of speech and writing, and from this association a variety of meanings developed. The most important of these are "speech" as the faculty of logical formulation and articulate expression, "translation" as the ability to channel meaning from one medium or context to another, and "commentary" as the clarification of the obscure or unfamiliar.

A. General and Specific Hermeneutics
B. Development of Biblical Hermeneutics
C. Elements of an Effective Hermeneutic for Biblical Texts
D. The Hermeneutical Process

A. General and Specific Hermeneutics

Hermeneutics as a general philosophical enterprise should be distinguished from specialized forms like legal and theological hermeneutics, which were designed to interpret a specific corpus of texts or to meet a special need. General hermeneutics traces its origins back to antiquity. In his *Peri hermeneias* (On interpretation), Aristotle deals with the logic of statements. This approach, which treats hermeneutical problems as belonging to the domain of logic, dominated the sporadic treatment of the subject up to the 18th century. It was only with the work of Schleiermacher that a truly general hermeneutics emerged.

Instead of concentrating on technical rules governing the interpretation of texts, Schleiermacher shifted the focus to the preconditions which make understanding possible. Misunderstanding is a universal problem which threatens all forms of communication and therefore calls for a general hermeneutical theory. The root cause for misunderstanding lies in the individuality of the writer or reader. Although language presupposes shared conventions between persons, the unique experience of the individual cannot be expressed adequately through this medium. The receiver therefore needs help to reproduce the meaning of the sender in his or her own consciousness. The task of hermeneutics is to provide this help. Schleiermacher distinguishes between grammatical and technical (or psychological) interpretation. The former is only a preparatory step for the latter, which represents understanding in the full sense of the word.

The idea of a general hermeneutics for all forms of communication was taken a step further by Dilthey when he applied it to the phenomenon of history. Understanding has to do not only with linguistic communication, but with historical consciousness. Both the possibility and problems of understanding are rooted in this consciousness. On the one hand it provides a link with the past, on the other hand it causes an experience of alienation. Understanding requires a conscious effort to overcome this historical distance. The interpreter must transpose himself or herself out of the present time frame to that of the past. Understanding is a *Nacherleben* (re-experience) of an original *Erlebnis* (experience). The re-experience is never identical with the original, but it is co-determined by the interpreter's own historical horizon. Nonetheless through historical consciousness the interpreter has access to the past as expressed in the tradition and cultural manifestations of the past. The text to be interpreted is not only that of linguistic communication, but of the whole of humanity's cultural heritage in which is contained the interpretive experience of the past. To interpret this heritage, the social and human sciences require a distinctive method—that of *Verstehen* (understanding) in contrast to *Erklären* (explaining), the method of the natural sciences.

The horizon of hermeneutics is expanded further by Heidegger. For Schleiermacher the focus is still on the individual and problems related to interpersonal communication. Dilthey takes it a step further by introducing an epistemological perspective and includes history and tradition as part of his reflection in an effort to explore the hermeneutical dimensions of historical consciousness. For Heidegger the hermeneutical problem is even more encompassing and fundamental; it is essentially ontological in nature. Interpretation is the modus in which reality appears; it is constitutive for being itself. A person's existence comes into being by an act of interpretation. Reality is the text which is to be interpreted and this reality includes a person's own existence. The hallmark of the interpretation process is historicity, which is ongoing in nature. In this historical context, Heidegger develops his concept of the hermeneutical circle. To begin with, interpretation never starts with a clean slate. The interpreter brings a certain pre-understanding to the process. This pre-understanding is challenged when new possibilities for existence are exposed through the event of understanding, which leads to a modification or revision of the interpreter's self-understanding. Finally, the modified understanding becomes the new pre-understanding in the next phase of the process. In conjunction with the hermeneutical circle, Heidegger posits that the communication of existential possibilities through language is fundamental to human existence. Consequently the notion of language as the house of being is developed. The attempt to understand, to discover possibilities for existence, is therefore one of the driving forces behind human history.

From its traditional meaning as the technical rules governing interpretation, the scope of hermeneutics has thus widened to include communicative, epistemological, and finally ontological dimensions. To mark this transition, "hermeneutics" is sometimes reserved for the narrower meaning, while "hermeneutic" is used to indicate the wider sense of the term.

For Gadamer, the insight of Heidegger that propositional truth should be counterpoised with a different kind of truth, that of disclosure, has important consequences. Hermeneutics cannot be only a question of method, striving for objectively secured knowledge, but must open up a dialogical process through which possibilities for existence are acknowledged. Thus a dialogue unfolds between present and past, between text and interpreter, each with its own horizon. The goal of interpretation is the fusion of these horizons; the medium through which this takes place is language. Language is not an objectification of thought but that which speaks to us. In this sense our very existence is linguistic. The implication is that the interpreter always finds himself or herself in the stream of tradition, for here past and present are constantly fused. Tradition and the related concept of "effective history" thus represent important aspects of Gadamer's hermeneutics.

Habermas and Apel's critique of Gadamer starts at this point. For them Gadamer's uncritical acceptance of tradition as authoritative and his ontological understanding of language obscure the fact that language may be used as medium of domination. They develop a "critical hermeneutics" based on the experience of manipulation and propaganda and fed by a suspicion regarding the truth claims of tradition. The aim is to reveal the suppressed interests underlying the apparent normal interaction with the past. Hermeneutics thereby becomes a social science in the form of a critique of ideology.

In the dispute between philosophical and critical hermeneutics, the mediating role of Ricoeur is of special significance. In drawing together hermeneutics, phenomenology, and structuralism, he displays his ability to mediate between what at first sight seem to be mutually exclusive approaches. But through his theory of the conflict of interpretations, Ricoeur demonstrates that hermeneutical philosophy, more directed toward understanding the past and its significance for the present, and critical hermeneutics, more directed toward the future and changing the present, are both one-sided when maintained as absolute positions. In directing his attention to biblical hermeneutics, Ricoeur develops a hermeneutic which grafts an existential interpretation on a structural analysis. He demonstrates how an analysis of the narrative by means of the metaphorical process can open up the world in front of the text.

In close association with the ideas of Gadamer and Ricoeur, Tracy designs his interpretation theory for Christian theology by reemphasizing the underlying hermeneutical nature of Christian theological articulation. At the same time he demonstrates the need for a special hermeneutics for the interpretation of biblical material.

Apart from understanding as a universal problem and hermeneutics as a general theory, a particular hermeneutics may become necessary, depending on the nature of the material to be interpreted and the purpose for which it is done. The revival of interest in Roman law during the 12th century led to the development of a special hermeneutics of jurisprudence, continued in its contemporary form as the interpretation of statutes. Likewise the need for a special hermeneutics for the interpretation of biblical texts was soon recognized which led to various attempts to establish a sacred or biblical hermeneutics in contrast to a profane or secular hermeneutics. But the difference does not lie in different methods and techniques required for biblical texts, but rather in the specific nature of these texts and the interpretative community in which they are read. General and particular hermeneutics have always influenced each other and continue to do so. Major shifts in general hermeneutics are always reflected in specialist applications. For its part, biblical hermeneutics has also been responsible for important developments in general hermeneutics.

B. Development of Biblical Hermeneutics

Insofar as biblical texts form part of a dynamic communication process, their essential hermeneutical nature is undeniable. Interpretation is essential to discerning the will of God. Numerous examples from the origin, collection, and preservation of these documents attest to this need. Individuals (e.g., Moses and the prophets) and even a whole class of people (scribes in postexilic Israel) act as interpreters of God's will. The temptation story is a classic example of a hermeneutical debate. According to Luke, Jesus' first public appearance begins with an interpretation of Isaiah 61 (Luke 4:21)—a style which characterizes the rest of his ministry (cf. the antitheses in the Sermon on the Mount, the parables, the discourses). Paul's mission to the gentiles is in essence a reinterpretation of the gospel in a Hellenistic context. Apocalyptic literature reveals the same hermeneutical tendencies. In a broader sense, the NT can be understood as an interpretation of the OT.

Even after the formation of the canon, the need for interpretation continued. The early Church drew on its Jewish heritage, using the techniques of proof texts, typology, and allegory. While a grammatical-historical approach was favored in Antioch, allegory thrived in the environment of Alexandria, where Origen continued the hermeneutical tradition of Philo. The ensuing plurality of meaning eventually required some kind of norm or authority to distinguish between acceptable and unacceptable interpretations. For Tertullian, this authority was vested in the church and more specifically in the doctrine of the rule of faith *(regula fidei)*. In the process, exegesis was subordinated to dogma and lost its critical function. Consequently, no hermeneutical innovation of significance took place during the Middle Ages.

The Reformation represented a fundamental change in hermeneutical thinking. Luther's insistence that the Bible should first of all be understood as the living word (Lat *viva vox*) of God, in which Christ himself is present, reintroduced the existential dimension of the text. The Bible is not a historical document in the first place, but a text for preaching. Philological and historical research should serve this end. The Bible's central theme is Christ, and from this perspective the rest of Scripture is to be interpreted. Hermeneutics is more than rules or techniques; it concerns the problem of understanding as a whole. Luther's position had two important consequences: multiplicity of meaning is replaced by the central scopus of the text, and the priority of the Word over against any other authority is confirmed.

If tradition and ecclesiastical authority no longer serve as controlling forces in the interpretation process, heavy responsibility is placed on exegesis itself. The Reformation, therefore, also marks the beginning of intense hermeneutical and exegetical activity which has shaped subsequent hermeneutical developments. The post-Reformation era is characterized by at least four consequences which are related to the historical, existential, structural, and pragmatic aspects of the interpretation process.

The emphasis on the independence and priority of exegesis in relation to dogma and tradition had two different results. It led to an attempt to strengthen scriptural authority by the doctrine of verbal inspiration, but, it also resulted in the discovery of the historically determined nature of the Bible. The second development was influenced decisively by the Enlightenment spirit of emancipation and the emerging rationalism of the post-Reformation era. A critical attitude toward all forms of (external) authority was made possible by the discovery of the historical and therefore relative nature of these institutions. The implication was that the Bible should also be read as a historical document. Thus began the long tradition of historical criticism, which appeared subsequently in various forms: text criticism, form criticism, historical background studies, redaction criticism. The basis for all these methods is the genetic principle: the idea that insight into the origins and development of a phenomenon contains the key to its understanding.

In the course of the 19th century, the relativizing effect of historical criticism was countered by the idealistic view of a universal spirit and unchanging ethical values underlying the fluctuations of history. This made it possible to pursue rigorous historical criticism and also to preserve the universal ethical message contained in the biblical texts. On the hermeneutical level, the result was the dichotomy between "scientific" and "practical" exegesis which characterized liberal theology at the turn of the century. This position was challenged only when Schweitzer again emphasized the unmistakable eschatological nature of biblical texts.

The existential dimension of biblical hermeneutics became prominent through the development of dialectical theology, first by Barth and then more extensively by Bultmann and his pupils. The devastating effect of World War I (1914–18) was a severe blow to the spirit of liberal optimism in Europe. A search for existential meaning followed, which in the churches resulted in a crisis for preaching. Barth's theology is an attempt to meet this challenge. With his concept of a "theological exegesis" his goal was to bridge the division between scientific and practical exegesis and to regain the supposed unity of biblical interpretation. From the perspective of the incarnation, the Bible is to be understood as the unity of God's and man's word. Historical exegesis is therefore unavoidable, but should serve the better understanding of the real subject matter of the text, Jesus Christ. Completely objective exegesis is impossible, and real understanding requires the interpreter's personal input.

At this point, Bultmann is in agreement with Barth—exegesis without presuppositions is an illusion. Bultmann therefore takes up Dilthey's suggestion of a special hermeneutics for the human sciences in order to include the subjective element in hermeneutical reflection. Thus the biblical text is the result of an existential encounter between God and man, and the subsequent interpretation of the text is aimed at making a similar encounter possible in the present. Bultmann's whole hermeneutical program is motivated by the need to communicate the *kerygma,* the existential message of the NT, to a modern audience. In doing so he develops a remarkable dialectic between the historical and existential dimensions of the text. The existential encounter inherent in the *kerygma* cannot be objectified in any full sense of the word. The written text represents only an incomplete rendering. This opens the possibility for Bultmann to apply the full range of historical-critical operations on the text without endangering its essential *kerygma.* The latter rests on the fact *(Dass)* of Jesus' life, not on its historical details *(Was).*

Fuchs and Ebeling further refined Bultmann's hermeneutical program, especially with regard to the existential analysis of the text. Trivial questions will render only trivial information. In terms of Heidegger's existentialia, the real questions to be put to the text are those in which the very existence of the reader is put on line. Only in this way can the self-understanding *(Selbstverständnis)* of the reader be challenged. Thus the hermeneutical circle is set in motion, which eventually leads to a new self-understanding.

Advances in linguistic and literary theory during the seventies focused attention on the structural dimension of biblical hermeneutics. A seminal influence in this context was the work of the early 20th-century Swiss linguist Ferdinand de Saussure, but Russian formalism, the school of Prague, French structuralism, and various other streams contributed to this development as well. In fact, the formative influences are so diverse that it would be misleading to talk of structuralism as a unified movement. Semiotics, the science of signs, did achieve a greater degree of coherence by distinguishing three dimensions of the communication process in terms of the relationship between signs: (1) syntactics (relation between sign and sign), (2) semantics (relation between sign and reference), (3) and pragmatics (relation between sign, reference, and action).

For the interpretation of biblical texts, several basic concepts of the structural approach are of special significance. First and foremost is the insistence on the autonomy of texts as analytical objects. In reaction to historicism, which views texts as the product of historical forces and explains them in terms of their origins, they should be understood as autonomous structures in their own right. A text constitutes a self-contained unit, and its different parts should be explained in terms of their relation to each other and not in terms of some external cause or authority. Second, the emphasis is on synchronic rather than diachronic relations. It is not the history of the text which holds the key to its meaning but the relations of the textual elements as they stand. Furthermore the author's intention cannot be used as some external criterion for evaluating the interpretation; it is discernible only in the text. The need is therefore for a "text-immanent" exegesis which takes the text seriously as a network of relations. Third, the structure of the text and techniques for its analysis become an important consideration. Different types can be distinguished: linguistic, literary, narrative, discursive, rhetorical, or thematic structures, each requiring its own form of analysis. The structural approach is therefore a conscious effort to eliminate subject, history, and intentionality as factors in the interpretation of texts.

Finally, in recent hermeneutical reflection, the pragmatic aspect of texts has gained in importance. Various factors contributed to this development. Speech act theory focused attention on the effect of verbal communication.

Similarly, the revival of rhetorical criticism is directly linked to an interest in the persuasive potential of biblical material. Up to this point the role and situation of the receiver hardly formed part of hermeneutical reflection. But the advance of reader theories in literature and the appearance of contextual theologies (black, liberation, feminist), made it imperative to include the context of reception in any effective hermeneutical design. Deconstruction and post-modern theories pose a challenge to the structural and new critical concept of the autonomy of the text and attempt to move beyond what is seen as the foundationalism of reader studies and the modernist position.

C. Elements of an Effective Hermeneutic for Biblical Texts

If hermeneutics is taken in its wider sense, that is, not merely as the formal rules controlling the practice of exegesis, but as something concerned with the total process of understanding, biblical hermeneutics can only be developed as part of an encompassing theory of communication. Because interpretation in this case is mainly directed to written texts, such an overall theory must of necessity include an adequate text theory.

In its most basic form, communication can be described as the relationship between sender, message, and receiver (SENDER ⟶ MESSAGE ⟶ RECEIVER). This basic model can be expanded in various directions to provide for the different functions of language and for the full spectrum factors determining the communication process (Gülich and Raible 1977; Plett 1975).

Although communication takes place via different channels (visual, auditive, intuitive), in the case of biblical texts the medium is the written word. As such, the text represents the solidification of a preceding communication event. It is the deposit of a prior encounter between sender (e.g., Moses or Jesus) and receiver (e.g., Israel or the disciples). In the process of becoming a written text, the message may pass through various stages (oral tradition, pre-literary forms), but the text represents also the first stage in the process of reinterpretation. The latter has as its aim a new communication event, this time between text and contemporary receiver. The challenge of interpretation is the fusion of the horizons (Gadamer) of sender and receiver. In the case of biblical texts, the original sender is no longer present and interpretation becomes the interaction between text (and its horizon) and receiver. See Fig. HER.01.

The text therefore forms the meeting point of two axes (Hernadi 1976): the rhetorical axis of communication, which reflects the diachronic movement from sender to receiver via implied author and implied reader, and the mimetic axis of representation, which reflects the synchronic selection from the available reservoir of signs and codes to form a "world"—that of the sender, text, or receiver. See Fig. HER.02.

In terms of this greatly simplified outline, it is possible to locate the main elements of the hermeneutical process. The multiplicity of methods currently available for biblical exegesis is confusing and can tempt the interpreter to focus on method(s) rather than on the dynamics of the process of understanding. When the full scope of the problem (including its "ontological" dimensions) is taken as the point of departure, it becomes possible to classify methods in terms of the specific aspect they address and to select the most suitable method in each case.

The historical aspect of the problem has mainly to do with the relationship between sender and message. From

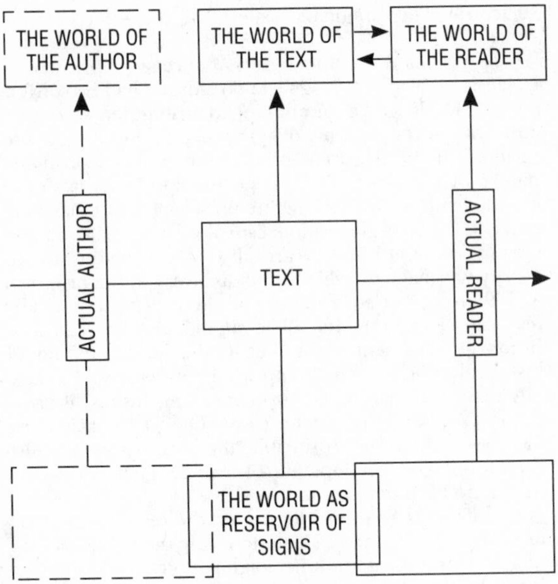

HER.01. Textual interpretation—relationship of the worlds of the author, text, and reader.

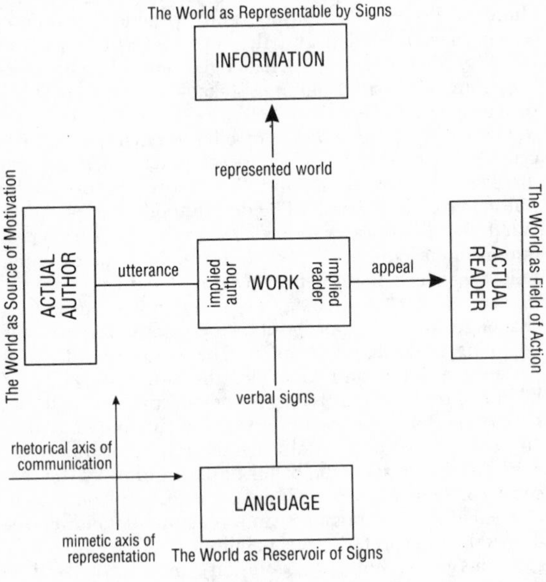

HER.02. Textual interpretation—intersection of communication and representation.

this important area of research a number of specialized techniques evolved. Background studies *(Zeitgeschichte)* focus on the historical environment from which the text emerged. FORM CRITICISM assumes an oral tradition behind the written text and is interested in its transition from the pre-literary form to the literary form. SOURCE CRITICISM studies the relationship between individual texts in a wider literary context and their dependence on sources. REDACTION CRITICISM proceeds from the assumption that the individual authors of biblical books had a strong influence on their eventual form and analyzes the composition of these texts from the perspective of the final redactor. TEXTUAL CRITICISM is a specialized and technical discipline aimed at restoring the presumed original form of the text as accurately as possible. Questions of authorship, the history of individual books, and the formation of the canon all have to do with the historical aspect of the relationship between sender and message. See CANONICAL CRITICISM, REDACTION CRITICISM, RHETORIC AND RHETORICAL CRITICISM, and STRUCTURALISM.

The structural component is concerned with the message itself, understood as an autonomous and self-contained entity, without taking the relation with sender and receiver into consideration. Also, structural features are constitutive at both the micro- and macro-level. Several types of synchronic analysis have been developed for biblical material, usually adapted from linguistic and literary theory. At the linguistic level, discourse analysis is used to reveal detail of the surface structure of the text; syntactic and semantic markers play an important part in this respect. On the literary level, stylistic features offer a clue to the communicative intention of the text. These may include metaphors, rhetorical devices, and point of view, but also narrative and theological structures.

The pragmatic dimension deals with the relationship between message and receiver. Speech act theory focuses on the desired effect of an utterance. Closely related is the growing recognition of the rhetorical nature of biblical texts and their persuasive power. Interest in the reader led to the development of reader response studies—both as a theoretical endeavor and as a form of empirical research. Awareness of the context of the receiver is an important key in the analysis of contextual theologies (black, liberation, feminist). Recognition of the creative input of the reader has relativized the objective status of the text, especially in post-modern thought. It is believed that all statements about the text depend on a prior reading of the text; consequently, the relationship between experience and thought is again a focal point in hermeneutical reflection.

D. The Hermeneutical Process

In practice, the text mediates between two events of understanding: the one which produced the text and the one flowing from interaction with the text. When dealing with biblical material, a variety of considerations are important.

First, the present reader is not the first reader or even one intended to read the text. In most cases, the reader is dealing with an "enriched text." Jesus' command to Levi, "Follow me!" (Luke 5:26), is not merely repeated by the evangelist, but enriched by Levi's response, Jesus' comments, and a description of the context. This enriched text (and not merely the original command) becomes the text for interpretation. In the extended history of the biblical tradition, more than one enrichment is possible, as the Abraham story in its many versions illustrates.

Second, clarity concerning the purpose and the context in which reading takes place is important. While the text can be read to gather linguistic data or to study literary features, the *kerygmatic* or proclaiming nature of the text presupposes a new event of understanding as the ultimate goal of reading. Although a variety of audiences are possible, it is the interpretive community of believers which constitutes the context of such a reading.

Third, although what we understand as a text is dependent on a prior reading of the text, thus making it impossible to speak of the objective status of the text in absolute terms, the text does function as a separate entity within the interpretation process. The horizon of the text forms the counterpoint of the horizon of the reader and the tension between the two opens the possibility of a new understanding.

Fourth, because the original authors of biblical texts are no longer participants in the process, the interpretive interaction takes place between text and (present) reader, thus making the text the natural point of departure for the subsequent hermeneutical process.

The text is thus both the end of the process of text production and the beginning of the process of interpretation. In its written form, it is the static record of a preceding event of understanding, and its text-immanent features are important clues for its interpretation. An analysis of the surface structure makes it possible to discern the syntactic arrangement and cohesion and the way in which the smaller units combine to form the macrostructure of the text. Syntactic analysis also provides the basis for discovering the literary features of the text and its narrative or argumentative structure. In this way, the distinctive "world" of the text comes into view, with its own "sociology," its own point of view, representative of a specific set of beliefs. This world is not an imitation, but an interpretation of reality—with important implications for the mediating function of the text.

However, the text is a self-contained entity only up to a certain point. It inevitably points beyond itself, to its past and to its future. The syntagmatic relationships between signs in the text have semantic implications, that is, implications for the relationship between these signs and to what they refer. Reference may be text-immanent, linking internal elements with each other, or text-external, pointing to realities outside the text. As a whole, this referential capacity highlights the historical dimension of the text.

Biblical texts are historical in a double sense, though. They are historical documents in their own right, with their own history of composition, tradition, and preservation. But they also refer to specific historical events, for example, in the history of Israel, the life of Jesus, or the ministry of Paul. For an adequate understanding of the text, analysis of its structure has to be complemented by the historical study of the world behind the text. For this task, the full range of historical methods is at the disposal of the interpreter. Not all methods are relevant for all texts or parts thereof, and the nature of a specific segment will determine the appropriate method(s).

Finally, the text refers to the world in front of itself. The contribution from the structural and historical dimensions converge at this point to activate the pragmatic potential of the text. Understanding the original speech event is the prerequisite for its appropriation in the contemporary situation. Rhetorical analysis and speech act theory are important tools to reveal the persuasive strategies used by the author. The concept of the implied reader sharpens the eye for directions given on all levels for the realization of the text. But not only is the reader as textual construct at stake, the interpreter has to take the real receptor and his or her existential situation into account. It is in this context that the world of the text plays a mediating role. What the text offers is an alternative way to look at reality, a "proposed world," a world which "we may inhabit" (Ricoeur). Thus the self-understanding of the reader is challenged. Between the horizon of the text and that of the reader a creative tension develops which calls for the affirmation of the status quo or for the openness and courage to accept a new self-understanding.

Bibliography

Barthes, R. 1988. *Das semiologische Abenteuer.* Frankfurt.

Berger, K. 1977. *Exegese des Neuen Testaments.* Heidelberg.

Bernstein, R. J. 1983. *Beyond Objectivism and Relativism: Science, Hermeneutics, and Praxis.* Philadelphia.

Betti, E. 1976. *Allgemeine Auslegungslehre als Methodik des Geisteswissenschaften.* Tübingen.

Bleicher, J. 1980. *Contemporary Hermeneutics.* London.

Bultmann, R. 1950. Das Problem der Hermeneutik. *ZTK* 49: 47–69.

———. 1969. *Faith and Understanding.* London.

Dilthey, W. 1968. *Gesammelte Schriften.* Vol. 7. Göttingen.

Ebeling, G. 1963. *Word and Faith.* London.

Eco, U. 1976. *A Theory of Semiotics.* Bloomington, IN.

Egger, W. 1987. *Methodelehre zum Neuen Testament.* Freiburg.

Frör, K. 1967. *Biblische Hermeneutik.* Munich.

Fuchs, E. 1968. *Marburger Hermeneutik.* Tübingen.

Funk, R. W. 1966. *Language, Hermeneutic and the Word of God.* New York.

Gadamer, H.-G. 1975. *Truth and Method.* New York.

Gülich, E., and Raible, W. 1977. *Linguistische Textmodelle.* Munich.

Habermas, J. 1973. *Theory and Practice.* Boston.

Heidegger, M. 1962. *Being and Time.* New York.

Hellholm, D. 1980. *Das Visionenbuch des Hermas als Apokalypse I.* Lund.

Hernadi, P. 1976. Literary theory: A compass for critics. *Critical Enquiry* 3: 369–86.

Hirsch, E. D. 1967. *Validity in Interpretation.* New Haven.

Jeanrond, W. G. 1986. *Text und Interpretation als Kategorien theologischen Denkens.* Tübingen.

Lührmann, D. 1984. *Auslegung des Neuen Testaments.* Zurich.

Lundin, R.; Thiselton, A. C.; and Walhout, C. 1985. *The Responsibility of Hermeneutics.* Grand Rapids.

Marshall, I. H., ed. 1977. *New Testament Interpretation: Essays on Principles and Methods.* Exeter.

McKnight, E. V. 1978. *Meaning in Texts: The Historical Shaping of a Narrative Hermeneutics.* Philadelphia.

———. 1988. *Postmodern Use of the Bible.* Nashville.

Mueller-Vollmer, K., ed. 1985. *The Hermeneutics Reader.* Oxford.

Palmer, R. O. 1969. *Hermeneutics: Interpretation Theory in Schleiermacher, Dilthey, Heidegger, and Gadamer.* Evanston.

Patte, D. 1976. *What is Structural Exegesis?* Philadelphia.

Petersen, N. R. 1978. *Literary Criticism for New Testament Critics.* Philadelphia.

———. 1985. *Rediscovering Paul: Philemon and the Sociology of Paul's Narrative World.* Philadelphia.

Plett, H. F. 1975. *Textwissenschaft und Textanalyse: Semiotik, Linguistik, Rhetorik.* Heidelberg.

Ricoeur, P. 1975. Biblical Hermeneutics. *Semeia* 4: 27–148.

———. 1976. *Interpretation Theory: Discourse and the Surplus of Meaning.* Fort Worth, TX.

———. 1981. *Hermeneutics and the Human Sciences.* Cambridge.

Robinson, J. M., and Cobb, J. B., eds. 1964. *The New Hermeneutic.* New York.

Rousseau, J. 1986. *A Multidimensional Approach towards the Communication of an Ancient Canonized Text.* Pretoria.

Stuhlmacher, P. 1979. *Vom Verstehen des Neuen Testaments.* Göttingen.

Thiselton, A. C. 1980. *The Two Horizons.* Exeter.

Tracy, D. 1981. *The Analogical Imagination: Christian Theology and the Culture of Pluralism.* New York.

Van Dijk, T. A. 1977. *Text and Context: Explorations in the Semantics and Pragmatics of Discourse.* London.

Weder, H. 1986. *Neutestamentliche Hermeneutik.* Zurich.

BERNARD C. LATEGAN

HERMENEUTICS, EARLY RABBINIC. The early rabbis inherited a long tradition of scriptural interpretation beginning in the Bible itself (Kugel and Greer 1986: 11–106). Following biblical precedent, they continued to interpret Scripture for the needs of their communities, particularly following the destruction of the Jerusalem temple and its levitical cult in 70 C.E. Interpretation included oral traditions passed down from generation to generation about the meaning of a verse or the particular way in which to carry out a biblical command. At the same time there was an active tradition of scriptural exegesis based on hermeneutic norms, many of which could be inferred from the Bible.

Rabbinic traditions as early as the 3d century present both types of scriptural exegesis as being known to Hillel the Elder before the destruction of Jerusalem. In a disagreement with the elders of Batayra he uses both exegetic norms and relies on the tradition of his teachers (*t. Sanh.* 7, end; intro. to *Sipra; t. Pesah.* 4; *y. Pesah.* 33a; *ʾAbot R. Nat.* A. 37). The versions of this tale attribute to Hillel from three to seven hermeneutic devices.

Other rabbinic texts from the 3d century and later attribute more extensive hermeneutic norms to the two Jabnean (viz. late 1st to early 2d century) masters Rabbi Akiba and Rabbi Ishmael. Akiba's methods seem to be more far reaching, and although not organized in a given list, include the principle of exclusion and inclusion (e.g. *m. Šebu.* 3.5; *Midr. Gen. Rab.* 1.14, 53.15) learned from his teacher Naḥum of Gimzo. Akiba is also presumed to make inferences from juxtapositions of scriptural verses (*Sipre* 131) and doublets in the Bible (*m. Soṭa* 5.1).

Rabbi Ishmael's hermeneutic norms (Heb *mîddôt* = Aram *mĕkîlatā* = Gk *kanones,* "measures") have been collected in a list of thirteen devices (intro. to *Sipra, Mek. Rabbi Šimʿon ben Yoḥai* to Exod 21:1; for a full exposition see *EncJud* 8:366–72). Examples of some of the devices on Rabbi Ishmael's list include inference from minor to major, the construction of analogous sets based on one or two verses, and the resolution of scriptural contradictions by the introduction of a third verse to tilt the balance.

The differences between these sages' methods may be explained in part by a generally different hermeneutic outlook toward the Bible. Akiba apparently perceived Scripture as a code which hermeneutic rules could crack. Thus Scripture could be atomized into constituent words or even individual letters, and doublets could be profitably exploited for interpretation since the divine authority of the text could tolerate such unusual exegeses. Rabbi Ishmael disagreed, tersely stating his principle that the Torah speaks in human discourse (*Sipre* 112).

Rabbi Ishmael's list of hermeneutic norms also discloses that he, his colleagues, and his predecessors were comfortable using some of the hermeneutic devices known to the Greco-Roman rhetorical schools (Lieberman 1950; Daube 1949). Whether these norms were directly borrowed from the Hellenistic schools or only the organizing principles of the rhetors were used to canonize already existent rabbinic devices is still open to question. It is not surprising, however, that in rabbinic circles which perceived and presented themselves as Hellenistic "schools" such norms would have found a home.

All of the hermeneutic rules discussed thus far pertain to inferring halakic (behavioral) rules from Scripture. The rabbis also engaged in aggadic (nonbehavioral) exegesis aimed at the exposition of the narrative text as well as for didactic, ethical, and moral purposes. This hermeneutic involved a much broader range of midrashic techniques which were freely employed given the non-binding nature of aggada. A medieval collation of techniques, attributed to the 2d-century sage Rabbi Eliezer, son of Rabbi Yose the Galilean, lists from thirty-two to thirty-six such norms, depending on the manuscript (see the edition of H. Enelow [1933]). These rules include patently Hellenistic devices such as *notarikon* (which assumes a word is really shorthand for other words). Elaborate codes may be employed for the sake of aggadic exegesis (e.g., *ʾatbaš,* which presumes substitution of letters of the alphabet for one another while interpreting), and in rabbinic circles puns were a favorite means of deriving a homiletical message from Scripture.

As time went on and the rabbinic communities grew ever farther from the cultic religion outlined in the Bible, in some places hermeneutical technique became more and more radical. Where early rabbis knew that their interpretations were on a continuum with the apparent meaning of Scripture, some later rabbis seemed startled to learn that Scripture cannot lose its plain *(pěšat)* sense (*b. Šabb.* 63a). It seems that hermeneutic allegorization *(děraš)* had pushed the interpretation of text so far that any original sense of Scripture was obliterated. This parallels certain tensions regarding scriptural interpretation found in the Church (Visotzky 1988). In the rabbinic community, a reaction to this extreme was an uneasy marriage of two kinds of hermeneutics. Contextual and consentual meaning *(pěšat)* now coexisted with readings of Scripture that solely served the halakic and aggadic needs of the community *(děraš).* This dual hermeneutic of Scripture kept faith with a long tradition of a given understanding of a biblical text while affording an elasticity to interpretation which allowed that text to speak afresh to every generation of rabbinic Jews.

Bibliography

Daube, D. 1949. Rabbinic Methods of Interpretation and Hellenistic Rhetoric. *HUCA* 22: 239–64.

Enelow, H., ed. 1933. *The Mishna of Rabbi Eliezer.* New York.

Kugel, J. L., and Greer, R. A. 1986. *Early Biblical Interpretation,* Philadelphia.

Lieberman, S. 1950. Rabbinic Interpretation of Scripture. Pp. 47–82 in *Hellenism in Jewish Palestine.* New York.

Visotzky, B. L. 1988. Jots and Tittles: On Scriptural Interpretation in Rabbinic and Patristic Literatures. *Proof* 8: 1–13.

BURTON L. VISOTZKY

HERMES (DEITY)

HERMES (DEITY). The Hellenic deity identified by the Romans with Mercury, he was born on Mt. Cyllene in Arcadia, the son of Zeus and the Titan nymph Maia. Such was the lineage myth conferred on the anthropomorphic Hermes.

His actual origins were far more humble, for he began his divine career as the power of spirit residing in the roadside cairn, the stone heap, or *herma,* which served throughout Greece as a marker of boundaries, entrances, and graves. He then arose from the rocks that held him fast and came to surmount them in the form of a herm, a stone pillar endowed with an erect phallus and a bearded head. The Athenians especially worshipped him in this form and were filled with consternation when his herms, which stood at the entrances to both temples and houses, were ominously mutilated in 415 B.C., virtually on the eve of the departure of the great armada that would be annihilated in its attempt to conquer Sicilian Syracuse.

Long before this, however, popular imagination, magnificently assisted by art and literature, particularly the Homeric poems, had released Hermes from the stone heap and transformed him into one of the Olympians, though he lacked the grandeur of the others and was commonly their servant. By the time his new configuration was complete, he had become the inventor of the lyre (see the Homeric *Hymn to Hermes*), Zeus' envoy (see, e.g., *Od.* 1.32–95, 5.28–148, *Prometheus Bound* 941–1093), the deity responsible for conducting the souls of the dead to Hades (see, e.g., *Od.* 24.1–204), and the patron of travelers, herdsmen, merchants, and servants. He was also a clever trickster with an amoral strain to his character, and he granted his patronage to thieves and perjurers (see, e.g., *Od.* 19.392–98); in fact, perhaps his most famous mythological exploit, recounted in the Homeric hymn in his honor, was his theft of his half-brother Apollo's cattle on the very day of his birth.

There is a single reference to Hermes in the NT at Acts 14:8–18, where the inhabitants of Lystra respond to Paul's healing of the cripple by identifying him with Hermes and Barnabas with Zeus. Two factors account for these particular identifications: the story that Zeus and Hermes once appeared in the region of Lystra "in the likeness of men" (Acts 14:11), to bestow blessings on the hospitable Philemon and his wife Baucis (see Ov. *Met.* 8.611–724); and the fact that by this time Hermes had become the patron of eloquence, for the Lystrians noted that Paul "was the chief speaker" (Acts 14:12).

Bibliography

Athanassakis, A. N. 1976. *The Homeric Hymns.* Baltimore.
Burkert, W. 1985. *Greek Religion.* Trans. J. Raffan. Cambridge, MA.
Guthrie, W. K. C. 1954. *The Greeks and Their Gods.* Boston.
Nilsson, M. P. 1961. *Greek Folk Religion.* New York.
———. 1967. *Geschichte der griechischen Religion.* Vol. 1, 3d ed. Munich.
Otto, W. F. 1954. *The Homeric Gods.* Trans. M. Hadas. New York.

HUBERT M. MARTIN, JR.

HERMES (PERSON) [Gk *Hermēs*]. A Roman Christian who received greetings from Paul in Rom 16:14. He was probably a gentile Christian (Lampe *StadtrChr,* 58), because Paul usually mentioned specifically if persons in the list of Romans 16 were Jewish-Christian "kins(wo)men" (Rom 16:7, 11, 21). While the latter term is absent in his other letters, Paul, in Romans, after chaps. 9–11 (cf. 9:3), was interested in emphasizing Christians' ties to Israel. It therefore can be assumed that he applied and omitted the label "kins(wo)man" purposefully in Romans 16. (The only exception is Aquila at the beginning of the list; so many other characteristics were reported about him that his Jewish background was passed over. See also MARY (PERSON) #7 and RUFUS.) A member of a Roman house-church, Hermes was quoted by name, as were four other members, while other participants were mentioned only generally as "brethren who are with them." The five persons therefore may have played leading roles in the house-church. Hermes' Greek name indicates that he probably was a slave or freedman. As the inscriptions in the city of Rome show, Greek names were mostly carried by (freed) slaves; "Hermes" was even preferred for slaves (see Lampe *StadtrChr* 142, 144–45, 152–53).

PETER LAMPE

HERMES TRISMEGISTOS. The name of a Greco-Egyptian deity influential from Late Antiquity through the Middle Ages. The syncretistic nature of the god is apparent from the name: Hermes, Greek god of eloquence and science, was identified with his Egyptian counterpart Thot, who contributed the epithet "thrice-greatest" (Gk *trismegistos*).

A. Hermetic Literature

Hermes Trismegistos is best known because of his association with the so-called Hermetic literature, in particular the Corpus Hermeticum (abbreviated *CH*). The Corpus Hermeticum is a collection of 17 philosophical/theological tractates written in Greek probably between the 2d and 5th centuries C.E., and most are ascribed to Hermes Trismegistos. The Latin (Pseudo-Apuleius) *Asclepius* (an apocalypse attributed to the god Asclepius), the Hermetic fragments assembled by Ioannes Stobaeus (5th century), and Hermetic texts recently discovered at Nag Hammadi are usually studied alongside the Corpus Hermeticum under the categories of philosophical or religious Hermetism. In addition, numerous references to and excerpts from Hermetic works, many of which are no longer extant, are found in the Church Fathers. All these texts are of interest to biblical studies because they provide a window onto the religious and philosophical milieu of Late Antiquity, and thus partly reflect the religious world in which the NT and other early Christian literature arose.

The earliest known manuscript of the Corpus Hermeticum (tractates 1–14) probably goes back to the 11th century and was brought from Macedonia to Cosimo de Medici in Florence, who asked Marcilio Ficino to prepare a Latin translation (1463). The reasons for the tractates' being collected together, as well as questions about their provenance, are still largely unresolved. The best critical edition of the entire corpus, along with the Latin *Asclepius* and the Stobaeus fragments, is by A. D. Nock and A.-J. Festugière (1945–1954). The older edition by Walter Scott (1924–1936) contains highly speculative textual reconstructions, but it is still useful because of its notes and an introduction to the history of textual transmission. Jean-Pierre Mahé (1978) has published a critical edition of the Coptic Hermetic texts found at Nag Hammadi.

B. Date and Provenance of the Corpus Hermeticum

Isaac Casaubon (1559–1614) was the first scholar to recognize that the Corpus Hermeticum did not pre-date Plato, as Ficino and other 16th century scholars had believed, but rather dated from the first centuries of the common era (Scott 1924–36, 1: 31–34). This understanding reversed Ficino's view that the doctrines of Plato and even of Moses had derived from these teachings of Hermes Trismegistos. Subsequently the corpus came to be understood as a mixture of later Platonic, Stoic, Neo-Pythagorean, and some Jewish ideas. Scholars have almost unanimously accepted a 2d- to 5th-century dating as the time when most of the tractates in their present forms took shape, while the Hermetic traditions they contain are assumed to have older roots in Greco-Egyptian syncretism. This dating is given credence by references in the early Church Fathers Athenagoras (ca. 180), Tertullian (ca. 200), and Cyprian (ca. 250) to Hermes Trismegistos as an ancient teacher of wisdom. While it is unclear whether these writers know specific documents attributed to Hermes, the early 4th-century writer Lactantius quotes from such writings; some of his references may be to our "Corpus Hermeticum," while others are to presumably lost works.

The religious and philosophical ideas contained in the tractates can be described as an amalgam of the Greek philosophical schools which is given an Egyptian dress, or alternatively as Hellenized Egyptian religion in a Greek philosophical garb. Thus, the works reflect the adaptation of Greek philosophy to late Egyptian religious thought, and they therefore reflect the influence of Egyptian gods and cults. One difficult question is whether the tractates are the products of a functioning cultic community or school. *CH* I *(Poimandres)* hints at the life of a worshipping community in chapter 29, while Arnobius' *Adv. Nat.* 2.13 (late 3d century) speaks of "those who follow Mercury" (Hermes; see Grese 1979: 40–43). While each tractate has a distinctive message, the similarity in terminology and thought among the tractates probably does indicate a number of authors with a common religious and philosophical outlook.

C. Points of Contact with Early Christian Literature

The affinities of the Corpus Hermeticum with Pauline and Johannine literature, as well as with Christian and non-Christian gnostic sources, are striking. Speculative cosmologies, various types of dualism, the devaluation of the empirical world, the idea of the body as evil, individual salvation, the *Urmensch* myth, sacraments, and revelation dialogues, to name only the most obvious, all constitute points of contact. See GNOSTICISM. Verbal parallels abound, as God is identified as "light and life" (*CH* 1.12 and 13.18–19; John 1:4, 9), and the theme of *CH* 13 is "rebirth" (*paliggenesia,* John 3:3, Titus 3:5, and 1 Pet 1:23). Although there is no direct mention of Christianity in the Corpus Hermeticum, there may be points at which the Hermetic authors are taking deliberately anti-Christian positions (Büchli 1986): death does not enter the world on account of sin (*CH* 1.20; Rom 5:12), and "it is impossible for the incorporeal (God) to become manifest in a body" (*CH* 4.9).

The relationships between Hermetic and early Christian thought have been studied by C. F. G. Heinrici (1918), Richard Reitzenstein (1904), C. H. Dodd (1935; 1953) and William Grese (1979), among others. The general consensus is that there are few, if any, literary dependencies either way, but that some early Christian (especially Johannine) texts and the Hermetic texts are representative of a common religious milieu. Parallels are also found between the Hermetica and the 2d-century Christian work the *Shepherd of Hermas.*

While each treatise is characterized by its own particular concerns, the main point of the Hermetic texts generally is to provide a way for human salvation from the empirical world. The empirical world is viewed as the result of developments due to tragic errors on the part of divine beings in the primordial past (especially *Poimandres* and *Kore Kosmou,* Stobaeus Fragment 23). Acquiring knowledge about this past and the resultant human predicament is the essential step toward salvation (Betz 1966). Unlike some forms of Gnosticism, the Hermetica do not attribute the empirical world to an evil creator god in opposition to the Highest God. In some of the tractates, the created world is even pronounced good; only human involvement with matter, the result of tragic error without evil intent, created the situation which requires salvation (*CH* 1.12–15; *CH* 13; *Kore Kosmou*). According to *Poimandres,* the individual must recognize the divine element within himself or herself; such recognition leads to ultimate divinization. *CH* 4 calls for a dipping (baptism) into the "basin of mind" (Gk: *nous*) sent down from heaven, and *CH* 13 takes the reader through a complete regeneration and rebirth of the individual which are necessary for true understanding and salvation to take place. The disclosure of knowledge about the nature of the universe and salvation occurs in the form of a dialogue in most of the tractates. Usually Hermes is the hierophant (*CH* 2, 4, 5, 6, 8, 9, 12, 13, 14, and *Asclepius*), and Hermes' son Tat (Eg. Thot) or Asclepius serves as the receiver of the knowledge. In *CH* 1, the instruction proceeds directly from the highest God to an unnamed recipient. In *CH* 9, God himself imparts knowledge to Hermes, and in *CH* 16 and 17, Tat and Asclepius take over the role of instructor. *CH* 7 and 18 have no role assignments. While influences of Greek philosophical speculation can readily be seen in the Hermetica, some scholars have also argued for Jewish influences, particularly B. Pearson (1981) and, earlier, C. H. Dodd (1935), who argued that the cosmogony of *Poimandres* utilized the Genesis account. For an understanding of the religious world of Late Antiquity, including Gnosticism and early Christianity, especially Johannine Christianity, the Hermetica are an invaluable resource. See further *EncRel* 6: 287–93; *ANRW* 2/17/4: 2240–81.

Bibliography

Betz, H. D. 1966. Schöpfung und Erlösung im hermetischen Fragment "Kore Kosmou." *ZTK* 63: 160–87.

Büchli, J. 1986. *Der Poimandres-ein heidnisches Evangelium.* Zürich.

Delatte, L.; Govaerts, S.; and Denooz, J. 1977. *Index du Corpus Hermeticum.* Rome.

Dodd, C. H. 1935. *The Bible and the Greeks.* London. Repr. 1954.

———. 1953. *The Interpretation of the Fourth Gospel.* Cambridge.

Festugière, A.-J. 1949–54. *La Révélation d'Hermès Trismégiste.* Vols. 1–4. Paris.

———. 1967. *Hermétisme et mystique païenne.* Paris.

Grese, W. 1979. *Corpus Hermeticum XIII and Early Christian Literature.* Studia ad Corpus Hellenisticum Novi Testamenti 5. Leiden.

———. 1983. The Hermetica and New Testament Research. *BR* 28: 37–54.

Heinrici, C. F. G. 1918. *Die Hermes-Mystik und das Neue Testament,* ed. Ernst von Dobschütz. Leipzig.

Mahé, J.-P. 1978–82. *Hermès en Haute-Égypte: Les Textes hermétiques de Nag Hammadi et leur parallèles grecs et latins.* 2 vols. Québec.

Moorsel, G. van. 1955. *The Mysteries of Hermes Trismegistos.* Utrecht.

Nock, A. D., and Festugière, A.-J., eds. and trans. 1945–54. *Hermès Trismégiste: Corpus Hermeticum.* 4 vols. Paris.

Pearson, B. A. 1981. Jewish Elements in *Corpus Hermeticum* I (Poimandres). Pp. 336–48 in *Studies in Gnosticism and Hellenistic Religions. Festschrift for Gilles Quispel,* ed. R. van den Hoeck and M. J. Vermaseren. EPRO 91. Leiden.

Reitzenstein, R. 1904. *Poimandres.* Leipzig. Repr. 1966.

Scott, W. 1924–1936. *Hermetica: The Ancient Greek and Latin Writings which Contain Religious or Philosophic Teachings Ascribed to Hermes Trismegistos.* Oxford. Repr. 1985.

Windisch, H. 1918. Urchristentum und Hermesmystik. *Theologische Tijdschrift* 52: 186–240.

J. A. Trumbower

HERMOGENES (PERSON) [Gk *Hermogenēs*] Hermogenes, along with Phygelus, is singled out for mention in 2 Tim 1:15 as being among "all (those) in Asia" who had turned away from Paul, presumably because of or during his imprisonment. A contrast is drawn between these Asians and another, Onesiphorus of Ephesus, who upon arrival in Rome had found Paul and "was not ashamed of (his) chains" (1:16). The contrast implies that Hermogenes and Phygelus indeed were ashamed of Paul's incarceration, but what their turning away meant (total apostasy? desertion of Paul?) or what it led to is hard to assess. Dibelius and Conzelmann (*The Pastoral Epistles,* Hermeneia, 106) judge that the phrase "all . . . turned away from me," because it is compartively mild terminology, should not be taken to imply apostasy. But Fee (*1 and 2 Timothy, Titus* GNC, 186) counters that the same wording argues for a rejection of the gospel since "it means that they have abandoned their loyalty to Paul . . . [and] for him that would mean they have also abandoned his gospel, since that is about the only way one could desert the apostle."

Also difficult to interpret are the "all . . . in Asia." It is hardly likely that the phrase is meant to imply that every Asian Christian had defected. Perhaps it means a number of Asians had come to Rome and all but Onesiphorus had deserted Paul. Or perhaps the reference is to a great wave of defections in Asia even among Paul's friends, including Hermogenes and Phygelus. It has also been suggested that the desertion had to do with the refusal of certain Asians to go to Rome to help Paul as Onesiphorus had done. In any case, Hermogenes and Phygelus are portrayed by the author of 2 Timothy as having deeply disappointed the Apostle, and their case functions as a warning to Timothy to be ashamed neither of the Lord nor of his prisoner Paul (1:8).

The issue may be raised as to whether characters in the Pastoral Epistles such as Hermogenes and Phygelus are merely fictitious creations of the deutero-Pauline authorship who function to combat various heresies. While that possibility ought not too readily be dismissed, the very intentions of the Pastoral writer(s), presumed to be Paul, argue that those referred to could well be historical persons known from the Pauline tradition. Also, the appearance of some of the same characters in apocryphal literature about Paul, insofar as that literature may be independent of the Pastorals, likewise suggests at least some historical basis for such persons.

Hermogenes, for example, is also mentioned in the apocryphal *Acts of Paul* (3.1, 4, 12–16). He and Demas travel with Paul from Antioch to Iconium. According to these Acts, they "were full of hypocrisy and flattered Paul as if they loved him" (3.1). The same text identifies Hermogenes as a coppersmith, depicting Hermogenes and Demas as turning against the apocryphal Paul's teaching on celibacy and the future resurrection. Both teach that resurrection "has already taken place in the children whom we have, and . . . we are risen again in that we have come to know the true God" (*Acts Paul* 3.14).

If the *Acts of Paul* is primarily an elaboration on 2 Timothy, as has often been supposed (MacDonald 1983: 62–64), then the apocryphal Hermogenes and Demas could be judged a conflation of such texts as 2 Tim 1:15; 2:17–18, 4:10. But if, as is more likely (MacDonald 1983: 65–66), the apocryphal writer drew independently from the same oral traditions as did the Pastorals, then the *Acts of Paul* may supply a piece of information lost to 2 Timothy, namely that the Hermogenes (and Phygelus) of 2 Tim 1:15, as well as Demas in 2 Tim 4:10, broke with Paul in a dispute concerning the resurrection.

Bibliography

MacDonald, D. R. 1983. *The Legend and the Apostle: The Battle for Paul in Story and Canon.* Philadelphia.

FLORENCE MORGAN GILLMAN

HERMON, MOUNT (PLACE) [Heb *har hermôn*]. A mountain mentioned in the Bible as marking the N border of the territory conquered by Moses and Joshua E of the Jordan river (Josh 11:17; 12:1, 4–5), and the N border of the half tribe of Manasseh (1 Chr 5:23). Mt. Hermon is located above the valley of Lebanon (Josh 11:17) and above the land of Mispeh or the valley of Mispeh, where Joshua chased the kings of the Canaanites in the battle of the waters of Merom (Josh 11:1–8). Prior to the Israelite conquest, it was mentioned as the place where the Hivite resided (Judg 3:3, Hurites according to the LXX), under the reign of Og king of Bashan (Josh 12:4, 5), Sihon king of the Amorite (Josh 13:10, 11), and the Gebalites (Josh 13:5).

The toponym Hermon derives from *hrm,* which in many Semitic languages means a ban, taboo or consecrated (*al-Haram* means in Arabic a sacred enclosure). ANE beliefs associated high peaks and mountains with the dwelling places of gods. Hittite and biblical records support the use of Hermon as a dwelling place of gods. Muršiliš II (1344–1320 B.C.E.) called to witness his peace treaty with the Amorite Duppi-Tessub, the gods of *Sariyana,* a synonym for Hermon (KBO. V, #9, *ANET,* 205). The Bible mentions the mountain, along with other places, where the name of God is rejoiced (Ps 89:12). Ritual centers were located at the foot of Hermon: Baal-gad (Baal of the Oracle ?) in the valley of Lebanon under Mt. Hermon (Josh 11:17), and Baal-hermon (1 Chr 5:23).

The Hermon is praised for its dew, which flows over the mountains of Zion (Ps 133:3). It was known for its lions and leopards (Cant 4:8), as well as for its cypresses (Ezek 27:5). It is mentioned in reference to the might of God (Ps 29:6), to other high mountains (Ps 89:13), and to the Jordan river (Ps 42:7).

The term "Hermon" is not found in ANE texts. It is juxtaposed in the Bible with other toponyms known also from epigraphical records. "Which Hermon the Sidonians call Sirion and the Amorite call Senir" (Deut 3:9). Scholars debate whether all three toponyms refer to the entire Anti-Lebanon range or only to its S spur, known today as Hermon or Jabal ash-Shaykh. The name "S[iri]on" is recorded in the Egyptian Execration texts dating from the 18th century B.C.E. (Helck 1962: 57). However, no MB settlements have been found thus far on this range. Hermon is contrasted to Lebanon in an Ugaritic text: "[Le]banon and its trees, Sirion and its precious cedars" (UH, 51, VI, 18–21; *ANET,* 134), as well as in the Hittite text mentioned above, and a few times in the Bible (Ezek 26:5; Ps 29:6). Mt. Senir, on the other hand, is mentioned once in the Assyrian records. In the campaign of Shalmaneser III to Damascus in 841 B.C.E., Hazael fortified "Mount Senir (Sa-ni-ru), a mountain facing Lebanon," (*LAR,* 672; *ANET,* 280). This obviously refers to the N section of the Anti-Lebanon range, known today as Jabal ash-Sharqi. This identification was also known to Medieval Arab geographers. Ibn Hokal (10th century) maintains that Snir is the source of the river Barada (biblical Pharpar [?] 2 Kgs 5:12), which springs from the mid Anti-Lebanon. The book of *Enoch* contributes to this identification. It tells of an assembly of angels on the top of Mt. Hermon. "They call it Hermon because they vowed and took an oath" to marry human wives (1 *En.* 6:6). Enoch tells of reading and sleeping on the river Dan, "which is southwest of Hermon." He then awakened and went to the angels who gathered "between Lebanon and Senir" (1 *En.* 13:9). It seems, however, that the Bible differs from other sources over the boundaries of Hermon. While the Bible sometimes includes the Anti-Lebanon range within its understanding of Hermon, other sources call the N range Senir, while they leave unnamed the S spur. It is also possible that the names Senir, Sirion, and Hermon are general names pertaining to the entire Anti-Lebanon range, while the name Hermon also relates specifically to the S section. Another name that is associated with the Hermon, or one of its peaks, is śîʾōn (Deut 4:48).

Josephus does not use the term Hermon, but rather Mount Lebanon (*Ant* 5.3.1). Sirion and Senir, on the other hand, are well documented in the Talmudic literature as places where sacred wine was produced (*b. [Talm.] Sukk.* 12; *Soṭa* 48). One phrase states that "Senir and Sirion are among the mountains of the land of Israel" (*Ḥul.* 60).

Eusebius relates the toponym Hermon only to the S range and testifies that: "until today the mount in front of Panias and Lebanon is known as Hermon and it is respected by nations as a sanctuary" (*Onomast.* 20.12). Hieronymus comments that "the Hermon is close to Paneas, which formerly was inhabited by the Hivites and the Amorites, from which summer snow was carried to Tyre for indulgence" (Hieron. *De Locis*).

Today the Hermon is identified only with the S spur of the Anti-Lebanon range. It is known by the names Jabal ash-Shaykh, (Arabic, "the mountain of the chieftain") and Jabal al-Thalj (Arabic, "the snow mountain"). In Aramaic translations of the Bible, Hermon is identified as *Tur Talga* ("Mountain of snow"; *Tg. Onq.,* Deut 3:9 and Cant 4:8), because the mountain is covered with snow most of the year.

Mt. Hermon is a large convex block that rises above its surroundings as a result of the Syro-African rift. It extends over 50 km along a NE–SW axis, and is 25 km at its widest point. The Hermon range is mainly Jurassic limestone which leads into Karstic landscape. Its highest peak reaches 2814 m and slopes steeply toward the E. The W slope descends in a series of several terraces, where precipitation (dew, rain, and snow) is more abundant. The Barada brook divides it from the N Anti-Lebanon range. In the E it borders the Damascus tableland, in the S the basalt tableland of the Golan, and in the W the valley of the Senir (Ar Hasbani) and its continuation Wadi al-Taym.

The flora of the Hermon on the W slope is similar to that of the Lebanon mountains. The terrain up to 1440 m is dominated by vines, beyond which are oak trees and bushes. Between 1150 and 1650 m are fruit trees, including plums, cherries, pears, and almonds. For this reason the area is also called "the almond slope," (ʿAqabat el-Loz). There are, in addition, a few types of pines. Above this altitude, bushes and low plants dominate the landscape. The S and E slopes are different. Up to the altitude of 1200 m the vegetation is similar to that of the Galilee and is dominated by Mediterranean forest. From 1200 m to ca. 1900 m the forest becomes thinner. The upper part is covered with low bushes and is mostly bare. Most of the year the peak of the mountain is covered with snow. Until recently it was customary to bring snow to the foothill villages to cool foods and drinks. This custom, which was recorded by Hieronymus, was perhaps followed in biblical times.

The view from the top of the mountain is magnificent and covers a large part of N Israel and Syria. In the S, the view covers the Gilead mountains, the Jordan valley, the Ḥuleh, and the Sea of Galilee. The scene in the W covers the Galilee, the Carmel range, the Mediterranean coast, Tyre, and the mountains of Lebanon. In between are the Litani depression (identified with *Nsn,* in an Egyptian source, according to Aharoni 1958: 295; Papyrus Anastasius I, *ANET,* 477; and identified with Leontis according to Avi-Yonah 1966: map 49) and its river. The view extends from Klaʿat ash-Shaqif through the Biqaʿ valley ("the Valley of Lebanon," Josh 11:17). In the N, the Anti-Lebanon peaks are visible. To the NE, lies Damascus, and to the SE, the Golan and the Bashan.

The summit of the Hermon has three peaks, in the N, E, and SW. On the highest of these peaks, the SW, there are the remains of a temple known as Qasr ʿAntar or Qasr ash-Shabib. The temple contains an enclosure, a large basin carved in rock, and a building that measures 10 by 11 m. A Greek inscription was found that, on behalf of the "Greatest and Holiest God," addresses all those "who had not taken the oath to stay away." Scholars interpret this as an order preventing the uninitiated from reaching the sacred temple. Other scholars refer to the belief of keeping the temple pure from the angels who swore to take human wives. The temple dates from the 1st to the 4th centuries C.E. Surveys yielded a few Iron Age sherds on the summit indicating probable early use. The temple is perhaps mentioned by Hieronymus (*Onomast.* 21.13–14), and by a Jewish traveler in 1624, Rabbi Gershon Berabbi Ĕliezer.

More than twenty temples have been surveyed on Mt. Hermon and its environs. This is an unprecedented number in comparison with other regions of the Phoenician coast. They appear to be the ancient cult sites of the Mt. Hermon population and represent the Canaanite/Phoenician concept of open-air cult centers dedicated, evidently, to the celestial gods. During the 2d century B.C.E., chapels carved out of rock were incorporated within the enclosures. In the 1st century C.E., temples built in Classical style were added to the complex. The pottery collected from these temples shows an affiliation to that attributed to the Iturean repertoire. The Itureans were the inhabitants of the mountain from the 2d century B.C.E. until the 7th century C.E.

Since Mt. Hermon is juxtaposed with Mt. Tabor (Ps 89:13), biblical exegesis from the medieval period sought to place Hermon next to Tabor. Consequently, the mountain S of Tabor, the hill of Moreh, was called "Hermon Minor" (Burchardus de Monte Sion (1283) in Laurent 147, Baldi 1982: 342).

Bibliography

Aharoni, Y. 1958. Hermon. *EncMiqr* 3: 294–98 (in Hebrew).

Avi-Yonah, M. 1966. *Carta's Atlas of the Period of the Second Temple, the Mishnah, and the Talmud.* Jerusalem (in Hebrew).

Baldi, D. 1982. *Enchiridion Locorum Sanctorum.* Jerusalem.

Dar, S. 1985. The Temples of Mount Hermon and its Environs. In *Abstracts of a Conference on Greece and Rome in Eretz Israel.* Haifa (in Hebrew).

Dar, S., and Mintzker, J. 1987. A Roman Temple at Senaim, Mount Hermon. *EI* 19: 30–45 (in Hebrew).

RAMI ARAV

HEROD ANTIPAS (PERSON) [Gk *Antipas*]. The son of Herod the Great who, in 4 B.C., inherited from his father the territory of Galilee and Perea, which he governed as Tetrarch until A.D. 39. Antipas is named simply "Herod"—not "Antipas" or "Herod Antipas"—in Josephus, in the NT, and on his own coins (Hoehner 1972: 105–106). The NT gospels mention him in two important contexts. First, because his marriage to Herodias (see below) was harshly criticized by John the Baptist (who preached in the Perea area), Antipas had John arrested and beheaded (Matt 14:1–12 = Mark 6:14–28 = Luke 9:7–9; cf. also *Ant* 18.5.2 §§117–119). Second, because he was ruler of Jesus' home province of Galilee, Antipas was given an opportunity to question and ridicule Jesus during his trial before Pontius Pilate (Luke 23:6–12).

Although the Bible says nothing more about Herod Antipas than this (cf. *HJP*² 1: 345–51), the Jewish historian Josephus provides us with some detailed information. Antipas and Archaelaus, Herod's two sons by Malthace, a Samaritan, were raised in Rome (*Ant* 17.20). Although initially he had been favored as the principal beneficiary under Herod's will, Antipas received only prosperous Galilee and Perea under Herod's final will ratified by Augustus in 4 B.C. (see ARCHELAUS). His title, "tetrarch," is attested in inscriptions dedicated in his honor on Cos and Delos, which were erected respectively by a certain Philo and by the Athenian people (*HJP*² 1: 341 n.1).

In Galilee he rebuilt Sepphoris and surrounded it with strong walls: he re-named it Autocratoris, evidently in honor of the emperor, who in Greek might be called *autocrator*. In Perea he fortified Betharamphtha and renamed it Livias (and subsequently Julius) in honor of Livia, wife of the emperor Augustus (*Ant* 18.27). He also built a new city in Galilee which he named after Augustus' successor, Tiberius, using forced migration to populate it. While Josephus stresses the impiety entailed in the creation of Tiberias, which was founded on the site of tombs (*Ant* 19.36–38; with Schürer *HJP*² 1: 342–343), Antipas could also show considerable respect for Jewish traditions, as when he sympathized with complaints over votive shields which offended many Jews (Philo *Leg. ad Gaium* 38), when he would attend holy feasts at Jerusalem (cf. Luke 23:7), and when he would mint aniconic coins.

Antipas had first been married to the daughter of Aretas, king of neighboring Nabatea. When Antipas divorced her and married HERODIAS, trouble ensued. First, the marriage to Herodias apparently was considered unlawful by some traditionalists, including John the Baptist (Matt 14:4). Herodias was Antipas' niece (daughter of Aristobulus and sister of Agrippa I); in order to marry Antipas, she had first to divorce another uncle (Antipas' half brother), by whom she had had a daughter, Salome. (On the problematic identity of this first husband, see HEROD PHILIP.) Second, Antipas' divorce enraged his former father-in-law, the king of Nabatea; but since a disputed boundary was also at issue, we cannot be entirely sure whether the divorce was a cause or a symptom of the quarrel between the two rulers (*Ant* 18.109–13). Aretas attacked, and in the subsequent battle Antipas' forces were soundly defeated. Antipas appealed to Tiberius for assistance, and the emperor instructed Vitellius, Roman governor of Syria, to capture Aretas dead or alive (*Ant* 18.113–15; see ARETAS). The defeat was all the more serious for Antipas since some of the Jews considered it to be divine retribution for his execution of John the Baptist (*Ant* 18.116–20).

Vitellius' expedition against Aretas had scarcely begun when Tiberius died on March 16, A.D. 37. Vitellius, probably no great friend of Antipas, halted the campaign and awaited instructions from the new emperor, Gaius; consequently Aretas escaped punishment (*Ant* 18.120–26). Although the chronology is uncertain (Schürer *HJP*² 1: 351), it was about this time that Antipas hosted a feast for Vitellius and Artabanus, king of Parthia, who wished to make peace with the Romans. Antipas wrote to the emperor (whether Tiberius or Gaius) to report this good news, preempting Vitellius' own official report and earning his considerable displeasure (*Ant* 18.101–105).

Josephus implies that a vengeful Vitellius subsequently played a role in Antipas' downfall (*Ant* 18.105); however, Agrippa I's old quarrel with Antipas probably played a more central role in Antipas' decline (*Ant* 18.149–50; see AGRIPPA). Gaius' appointment of Antipas' nephew Agrippa as "king" encouraged Antipas to seek the same title for himself. Allegedly spurred on by his nagging wife Herodias (Agrippa's sister), Antipas sailed to Italy to present this request. But at the same time envoys from Agrippa arrived to denounce Antipas to the emperor, accusing him of treasonous dealings with the discredited Sejanus and now with Artabanus, king of Parthia. Gaius believed these accusations (Antipas could not deny that he had amassed a great quantity of weapons, even though he may well have done so for use against Nabatea, not Rome), and consequently he deposed Antipas and annexed his tetrachy into Agrippa's kingdom. Antipas was exiled to the W (probably to Lyons, although N Spain is also possible). Although Gaius offered to pardon Herodias because she was Agrippa's sister, she chose instead to follow her husband into exile (*Ant* 18.240–55 with Braund 1983: 241–42). It is not known whether Antipas and Herodias had any children.

Bibliography

Braund, D. C. 1983. Four Notes on the Herods. *Classical Quarterly* 33: 239–42.

Hoehner, H. W. 1972. *Herod Antipas*. SNTS Monograph 17. Cambridge. Repr. 1980.

DAVID C. BRAUND

HEROD PHILIP. A name some scholars have adopted for one of the sons of Herod the Great, who would have been Herodias' first husband and, therefore, father of her daughter Salome. It is important to note that there is no single source attesting to a person by this name, and that the name is a scholarly construction resulting from the combined evidence of two unrelated sources.

The first source is the NT pericope recounting the death of John the Baptist. In Mark 6:17 (= Matt 14:3; cf. Luke

3:19), Herodias' first husband (and presumably the father of Salome) was named "Philip," the brother of Herodias' second husband, Herod (= HEROD ANTIPAS). This "Philip" therefore would have been a son of Herod the Great. The second source is Josephus' account of the quarrel between Herod Antipas and Aretas, king of Petra (*Ant* 18.5.1 §109). In it, Josephus recounts that Herodias' first husband was named "Herod," and that he was the half-brother of Herod Antipas; therefore he was a son of Herod the Great by Mariamme (see also *Ant* 18.6.2 §148). Josephus explicitly identifies him as the father of Salome (*Ant* 18.5.4 §136). By assuming that these two sources refer to the same son of Herod the Great (albeit under different names), some scholars have combined the two and posited the existence of a "Herod Philip."

While some insist that the Gospels and Josephus each accurately preserve a separate element of an original double-name (*ISBE* 2: 695), others feel that the Gospels (particularly Mark) have used the name erroneously. The name "Philip" is omitted in the best mss of Luke 3:19, as it is in codex D and the Latin versions of Matt 14:3. This omission has caused some to argue that Mark confused Herodias' first husband with Philip the Tetrarch, the son of Herod the Great by Cleopatra. See PHILIP (PERSON) #5. The confusion may have resulted from the fact that this Philip was the *husband* (not the father) of Salome, and therefore the *son-in-law* (not the husband) of Herodias (*Ant* 18.5.4 §157). On balance, however, the existence of a "Herod Philip" (and the compatibility of Mark and Josephus) resolves more problems than it creates (Mann *Mark* AB, 296).

GARY A. HERION

HEROD THE GREAT (PERSON) [Gk *Hērōdēs*]. The king who, by arrangement with Rome, ruled Jewish Palestine from 37 B.C.E. to 4 B.C.E. According to the NT (Matt 2:1–19; cf. Luke 1:5), Jesus was born during the reign of this king.

A. Introduction
B. The Period of Consolidation
C. The Herodian Kingdom at its Peak
  1. The Political Dimension
  2. Herod's Domestic Policy
  3. Herod's Building Program
  4. Hellenistic Influence on Herod and in Jerusalem
D. The Last Years
E. Conclusion

A. Introduction

Herod was born in the late 70s B.C.E. into an aristocratic Idumean family that had converted to Judaism a half century earlier, in the reign of John Hyrcanus I. His father, Antipater, was adviser to Hyrcanus II and later held office in his own right when he was appointed *epitropos* (overseer) of Judea in 47 B.C.E. The rise to power of both Antipater and Herod was predicated first and foremost on their unswerving loyalty to Rome. Both father and son were convinced that, following the conquest of Judea by Pompey in 63 B.C.E., nothing could be achieved without the consent and aid of Rome. This principle was inviolable, and it guided their actions under all circumstances and at any price. At the age of 25 Herod was appointed governor of Galilee by his father and gained a reputation as a vigorous ruler by his aggressive campaign against brigands in the area.

By the late 40s, however, Herod's political fortunes took a turn for the worse. The murder of his father in 42 B.C.E. put him on the defensive with regard to Jerusalem's aristocracy. Taking revenge on what it considered a tyrannical usurper, this nobility attempted to have Herod removed through Roman intervention, only to be thwarted by the steadfast loyalty of the Romans to Antipater's memory and Herod's proven abilities. Nevertheless Herod was finally forced to flee Judea in 40 B.C.E. when the Hasmonean Mattathias Antigonus joined with the Parthian invaders to oust both Herod and the Romans. Herod then made his way to Rome, where he was formally crowned King of Judea. He returned to Judea in 39 B.C.E., and in the summer of 37, after a stay of some two years during which Herod and the Romans were pitted against Antigonus and the Parthians, Herod was finally able to claim his kingdom. He proceeded to rule for the next 33 years.

Herod's reign can be divided into three periods. The first was one of consolidation, lasting from 37 to 27 B.C.E. The second, from 27 to 13 B.C.E., was a period of peace and prosperity, marked by Herod's close relationship with Rome and her leaders on the one hand and an ambitious building program on the other. The third period, from 13 to 4 B.C.E., was marked by domestic strife and misunderstandings with Rome, and was capped by Herod's physical and emotional deterioration.

B. The Period of Consolidation

Herod's conquest of Jerusalem in 37 did not bring his problems to an end. Inheriting a divided city, he moved swiftly and decisively to thwart all opposition. Forty-five leaders of the pro-Antigonus faction in the city were executed (*Ant* 15 §5) and others were forced into hiding (*Ant* 15 §264). The wealthy were despoiled, and the revenue gained was used to pay Herod's debts to his Roman patrons and his army. Having established ties with one branch of the Hasmonean family through his marriage to Mariamme (Mariamne), grand-daughter of Aristobulus (*JW* 1 §344; *Ant* 14 §467), Herod attempted to cement this relationship further by returning Hyrcanus II from exile in Babylonia and according him an esteemed position (*Ant* 15 §18–21). Josephus claims, however, that Herod's prime motivation for having Hyrcanus nearby was more out of fear than honor; proximity would allow Herod to control Hyrcanus' whereabouts and, if necessary, eliminate him.

In the years following his ascension, Herod was almost obsessively concerned about the security of his rule. Thus he appointed an old friend, Hananel, a Babylonian, to assume the high priesthood (*Ant* 15 §22–40, 56). Alexandra, daughter of Hyrcanus II and mother of Mariamme, was incensed at the slight to her son, Aristobulus III, who was next in line to assume the duties of high priest. She appealed to Cleopatra, who in turn solicited the aid of Antony; he succeeded in persuading Herod to appoint Aristobulus. Herod agreed reluctantly, with good reason. Little time elapsed before he realized the extent of Aristobulus' popularity and the potential danger he posed (*Ant*

15 §52). Herod ordered the young man drowned in a swimming pool at his Jericho palace (*Ant* 15 §54–56).

Herod's moves to forestall any Jewish uprising are noted by Josephus on a number of occasions. It was for this reason that Antigonus was beheaded in Antioch (*Ant* 15 §8–9) and that the king kept the young Aristobulus homebound despite Antony's request, at one point, for the lad to join him (*Ant* 15 §28–30). Even as late as the year 30, before leaving for a fateful rendezvous with Octavius, Herod executed Hyrcanus II and placed Alexandra in a fortress under guard. He feared that in his absence either of them might foment a rebellion or assert his right to leadership (*Ant* 15 §174–78, 183–86). Similarly, Herod justified the execution of his wife Mariamme two years later, claiming that a popular disturbance might have broken out had she lived (*Ant* 15 §231).

The focus of anti-Herodian sentiment at this time lay close to home. Alexandra, both fearing and detesting the Idumean king, strongly opposed the appointment of Hananel as high priest and became totally distraught upon her son's murder. Herod's suspicion of her intensified, moving him to place her under house arrest. On Cleopatra's advice, Alexandra attempted to flee Jerusalem in a coffin but was apprehended in the act (*Ant* 15 §46–48). Herod was forced to overlook this incident for fear of Cleopatra's possible retaliation (*Ant* 15 §42–49). Alexandra informed Cleopatra of Herod's guilt in the drowning of Aristobulus, leading Antony to summon him to Laodicea. The king, however, succeeded in exonerating himself of all charges (*Ant* 15 §62–67, 74–79).

Cleopatra's association with such anti-Herodian machinations was not fortuitous. She indeed wished to incorporate Judea, S Syria, and Arabia into her kingdom. Despite the fact that Antony resisted her ultimate demands, much as he had refused to respond to her initiatives with regard to Alexandra, Cleopatra was not entirely unsuccessful. She succeeded in gaining the whole coastal region of Phoenicia and Judea ("the cities between the Eleutherus River and Egypt with the exception of Tyre and Sidon"—*Ant* 15 §95). The lucrative palm and balsam groves of the Jericho Plain were also transferred to her, although here she agreed to lease the territory to Herod for 200 talents a year (*Ant* 15 §132).

Despite these intrigues, Herod kept both his kingdom and relations with Rome on an even keel. In 31, three crises of major proportions beset the king—a war, an earthquake, and the defeat of his Roman patron. Charged by Antony and Cleopatra to collect the revenues owed by the Nabatean king, Herod was forced to resort to arms when the former refused to honor his debts. Although Herod was victorious in his first battle near Dion, E of the Jordan, he suffered a serious defeat at Canatha in the Hauran and was forced to disband his army due to heavy losses of men and equipment (*Ant* 15 §108–20). To make matters worse, a disastrous earthquake struck Judea about the same time, claiming, according to Josephus, some 30,000 lives and a considerable loss of cattle (*Ant* 15 §121–22). However, the most decisive event of the year 31 was Antony's defeat at Actium (*Ant* 15 §161–62). Octavius now stood as sole ruler of the Roman Empire. At first glance Herod's previous loyalties and ties to Antony were not the most auspicious credentials for winning the support of the new ruler.

Yet Herod emerged from these crises stronger than ever. Avoiding open warfare for a time, he finally engaged the Nabateans in battle near Amman (Philadelphia) in 31 and twice inflicted heavy casualties on them (*JW* 1 §380–85; *Ant* 15 §147–60). Spurred by this victory, Herod next addressed himself to the post-Actium political situation. It was to his benefit that the Nabatean war had engaged his attention at the time, leaving him no opportunity to dispatch troops in support of Antony. Herod was thereby spared the embarrassment of having actually backed the losing side. On learning of the outcome at Actium he immediately declared his loyalty to Octavius and demonstrated it by helping prevent gladiators in the service of Antony from joining him in Egypt for a last stand (*JW* 1 §386–92; *Ant* 15 §194–96). Herod in the spring of 30 B.C.E. proceeded to Rhodes, where Octavius had made public his decision to support, wherever possible, existing client kings. He realized that the loyalty shown Antony—who had been the legitimate Roman ruler in the East—was natural and commendable. The main concern of the new emperor (in 27 B.C.E. to be officially so named and given the title "Augustus") was to guarantee efficient, effective, and loyal rulers. As Herod met these qualifications it is not surprising that he was immediately ratified as King of Judea and awarded other honors as well. Soon after, when Augustus was passing through Judea on his way to Egypt for the final battle against Antony, Herod met him at Ptolemais and provided his army with elaborate provisions and gifts, including abundant wine and water for their march across the desert. In a demonstration of munificence designed to win gratitude and support, Herod also gave Octavius 800 talents of silver (*JW* 1 §394–95; *Ant* 15 §187–201).

Octavius received Herod in Egypt after his final victory and awarded him the 400 Gauls who previously had served as Cleopatra's bodyguards. It was then that he restored to Herod the territory confiscated by Cleopatra (Jericho) in addition to the coastal cities of Gaza, Anthedon, Joppa, Strato's Tower, Samaria, and the Transjordanian cities of Gadara and Hippos (*Ant* 15 §217). When Octavius passed through Judea upon his return to Rome, he was once again lavishly received by Herod, who even accompanied him as far as Antioch.

This recognition, in addition to the newly acquired territory, fortified Herod's determination to put to rest the remaining vestiges of domestic opposition. Having already eliminated Hyrcanus II just prior to his journey to Rhodes, Herod then executed Alexandra: the king had fallen ill, and Alexandra, finding this to be a propitious opportunity for insurrection, moved to capture the Jerusalem fortress. Apprised of the situation, and having recovered from his illness, Herod immediately ordered her execution (*Ant* 15 §247–51). A year or so later Herod's sister Salome sought to divorce Costobar who, together with others, was plotting a revolt. She also told Herod that Costobar had provided refuge for his enemy, the Baba family, during the conquest of Jerusalem a decade earlier. Already aware of Costobar's seditious proclivities, Herod now moved quickly to execute him and his companions (*Ant* 15 §253–66).

All this was but a prelude to the most tragic—and, in the

long run, the most significant—execution of all. Despite the extraordinary love he felt for his wife, Mariamme, Herod's relationship with her had seriously deteriorated. Precisely owing to his passionate attachment, and dreading the thought that his beloved might be wedded to another, Herod on two separate occasions had ordered her death should he fail to return from a fateful encounter. Mariamme, however, misjudged his intentions and was incensed at such plans. Salome's machinations against her only added fuel to the fire, as did Mariamme's own intemperate remarks and actions vis-à-vis the king. Imbued with a sense of familial superiority because of her Hasmonean lineage, she often treated her husband and sister-in-law with contempt and arrogance. In 29, under the incessant prodding of Salome, Herod finally ordered her execution (*Ant* 15 §222–39).

The murder of Mariamme thrust Herod into a distraught state. He would call out to her, lament her absence, and absentmindedly tell the servants to summon her. Herod sought distraction through banquets, parties, and hunting expeditions, but to no avail. The king became seriously ill with an inflammation and constant pain in the back of the head, and a temporary loss of reason. No medicine seemed to have any effect, and at one point there was fear for his life (*Ant* 15 §240–46).

The specter of Mariamme returned to haunt Herod during the last decade of his life. His sons by her, Alexander and Aristobulus, could not forgive their father for this deed, and the tensions and intrigues in Herod's court became unbearable and ultimately proved disastrous. On a deeper level, Mariamme's fate and the circumstances surrounding it reflected Herod's inability to exercise control over the many and disparate members of his family. Each strove to further his own interests and ambitions and sought ways—with more or less success—to manipulate the king according to his desires. The irony of events was such that Herod's political fortunes were on the rise while his personal life was the scene of much anguish and pain.

C. The Herodian Kingdom at Its Peak (27–13 B.C.E.)

1. The Political Dimension. By 27 B.C.E., and for the next 14 years, Herod's prosperity and accomplishments were practically unsullied. The territory under his rule continued to expand, there were no wars, and domestic unrest was almost nonexistent. Whatever tensions arose were limited and short-lived and do not seem to have affected the kingdom as a whole.

Herod's ties with Rome remained the backbone of his policy. His successful meetings with Augustus provided a firm basis on which these ties were to develop; as a result, Herod's kingdom was further augmented in 23 with the inclusion of the territories of Trachonitis, Batanea, and the Hauran to the NE. These lands had formerly been under the control of Zenodorus who, aware of the local population's predilection for brigandage, encouraged it to plunder its neighbors, particularly the inhabitants of Damascus, thus enabling him to increase his revenues. When complaints from Damascus reached Octavius (who since 27 was titled Augustus), he ordered Varro, the governor of Syria, to strip Zenodorus of his territories and eliminate the bandits. Augustus subsequently conferred these lands upon Herod in order to prevent similar disruptions in the future. Operating with his customary zeal, Herod abruptly aborted all unlawful acts and restored order to the area (*Ant* 15 §343–48).

Zenodorus, however, refused to accept this demotion and continually attempted to undermine Herod's position. He brought charges against the king and on several occasions encouraged the residents of Gadara to do likewise. On each occasion the Romans rejected these charges out of hand. Three years later, upon Zenodorus' death, Augustus awarded Herod his remaining territory, which included the Golan and Ḥulah areas, including the towns of Ulatha and Panaeas (*Ant* 15 §349–60). Thus, by the year 20 Herod had regained practically all the territory which had once comprised the Hasmonean kingdom, and in some areas much more.

As a sign of his newly acquired status, Herod was recognized as a "friend and ally" (*philos kai symmachos; Ant* 17 §246) as well as "friend of the Romans" (*philorōmaios*—Dittenberger, *OGIS,* no. 414) and "friend of Caesar" (*philokaisar*—Meshorer, *IEJ* 20 [1970]: 97–100). Moreover, Augustus issued a directive to his procurators (i.e., financial officials) in Syria to obtain Herod's authorization for their activities which, if indeed carried out, would have given him extensive power throughout Syria (*Ant* 15 §360). In addition, in as early as 23, Caesar granted Herod the privilege of choosing his successor, requiring only the confirmation of the emperor.

Herod lost no opportunity to express loyalty and gratitude to his Roman patrons. Augustus was undoubtedly impressed with the lavish reception accorded him by Herod before and after his Egyptian campaign against Antony. The Jewish king was again in attendance when Augustus visited Syria in 20 B.C.E., not only to further solidify his friendship with the emperor, but to answer charges brought against him by the people of Gadara. Herod also obtained an appointment for his brother Pheroras as tetrarch of Perea (*Ant* 15 §354–62). On three occasions in subsequent years Herod traveled to Rome in order to visit the emperor.

Herod also forged close personal relations with the second-in-command in Rome, Augustus' son-in-law, Marcus Vipsanius Agrippa. He visited Agrippa at Lesbos (an island off the coast of Asia Minor) during the years 23–21 (*Ant* 15 §350) and on another occasion, in 15 B.C.E., invited Agrippa to visit Judea, where the latter was warmly welcomed by the king and populace at large. Agrippa visited Herod's newly founded cities Sebaste and Caesarea, as well as the Judean desert fortresses of Alexandreion, Herodium, and Hyrcania. His stay in Jerusalem bore special significance, for it was here that he received the acclamation of the people. Agrippa expressed his appreciation by offering a sacrifice at the temple and by feasting the populace (*Ant* 16 §12–14). The following spring Herod joined Agrippa in Asia Minor on an expedition to Crimea. Upon the conclusion of the expedition, Herod accompanied Agrippa throughout much of Asia Minor, distributing gifts and helping those who presented petitions to Agrippa (*Ant* 16 §16–26). Herod also took this opportunity to plead the cases of a number of Jewish communities in Asia Minor.

Within his own realm Herod wielded absolute authority. One method of assuring this support was through an oath of loyalty; on one occasion, dated to about 20 B.C.E. (*Ant* 15 §368–70), he demanded an oath of fidelity to his own rule, on another—during the last years of his reign—to Caesar as well (*Ant* 17 §42). The anniversary of Herod's accession was declared an official holiday (*Ant* 15 §423), and there is some evidence that his non-Jewish subjects erected statues of him in his honor; later on the same was done for the daughters of Agrippa I at Caesarea (*Ant* 19 §357). Herod's royalty is regularly proclaimed on his coins, as is evidenced by the legends "of Herod the King" or simply "Herod the King."

Herod exercised complete control over his realm by dominating all key institutions. No matter was beyond his scrutiny. The highest tribunal (Sanhedrin), whatever its composition and authority in the previous era, was now merely a rubber stamp for the king's wishes. In effect, this judicial body was similar to the privy councils of other Hellenistic kings. Summoned whenever it suited the king, this group consisted primarily, if not exclusively, of Herod, his friends, and his relatives, and it was convened, for example, to condemn Pheroras' wife (*JW* 1 §571) and later Antipater (*Ant* 17 §93). It was before such a council that Herod announced the appointment of Aristobulus III as high priest (*Ant* 15 §41) and reviled Hyrcanus II's alleged treason several years later (*Ant* 15 §173). Following the execution of his sons, Alexander and Aristobulus, Herod convened this body to hear plans for the marriages of his grandchildren. In a speech purportedly delivered on that occasion, Herod personally addressed several members of that body, his brother Pheroras, and his son Antipater (*JW* 1 §556–58).

The high priesthood was another institution manipulated by Herod for his own purposes. Herod realized from the outset that control of this office was crucial for a successful reign, and it is for this reason that he immediately installed his long-time friend Hananel of Babylonia as high priest (*Ant* 15 §22, 40). The rise and fall of Aristobulus III, as already noted, clearly exemplify the threat perceived by Herod if that office were to fall to the hands of a potentially inimicable person. He appointed a series of high priests, several of whom apparently came from Egypt—Jesus, son of Phiabi, and Simon, son of Boethus (*Ant* 15 §320–22). The appointment of relatives to high positions was likewise a Hellenistic practice fully embraced by Herod. Simon was appointed high priest in 23 after Herod fell in love with his daughter, also named Mariamme, and he remained in office almost until Herod's death; Simon's son Joazar succeeded to the high priesthood in the year 4, following a brief ministry of one Matthias, son of Theophilus, a native of Jerusalem (*Ant* 17 §78, 164–67).

The army, too, was tightly controlled by Herod. It was comprised of Jews and non-Jews alike, and although precise information on the composition of his troops is unavailable, it would seem that the pagan element was crucial—if not in numbers, then at least in the importance of their position. The elite troops, those closest to the king and charged with personally protecting him, appear to have been of non-Jewish origin. Between 40 and 37 this foreign element was apparently dominant in the makeup of Herod's troops (*Ant* 14 §394; *JW* 1 §290, 301). Following the battle at Actium, Augustus had presented Herod with 400 Gauls who had served as Cleopatra's bodyguards (*Ant* 15 §217). The cortege at Herod's funeral was headed by his bodyguards, then the Thracians, Germans, and Gauls, and they were followed by the rest of the army (*JW* 1 §672; *Ant* 17 §198). Prominent among Herod's soldiers were those recruited from the cities of Sebaste and Caesarea, who numbered some 3,000 in all.

The expenses involved in maintaining an army and a court as lavish as those of Herod, as well as the need to finance his ambitious building program, required an enormous outlay of money. Herod's sources of income were many and varied. First and foremost he depended on the revenue from taxes, which were certainly levied on agricultural produce and included taxes on public purchases and sales (*Ant* 17 §205). Tax revenue figures mentioned at the deposition of Herod's will approached the not inconsequential sum of 1,000 talents (*Ant* 17 §317–21). Herod himself brought significant personal wealth to the throne, and this was augmented by his despoliation of political enemies. Moreover, his appropriation of Hasmonean property, which included large tracts of land throughout the country, added vast new sources of income. Thus Herod came into possession of fertile lands near Jericho, the coastal plain, and the Jezreel Valley. Furthermore, the vast tracts of land to the NE (Trachonitis, Batanea, the Hauran, and the Golan) were awarded to him by Augustus in 23 and 20 B.C.E. The customs duties derived from his control of lucrative trade routes, Nabatean trade from the Arabian peninsula, and maritime trade through his ports, especially Caesarea, and the revenue accrued from his Cyprus copper mines (*Ant* 16 §128) all provided significant sources of income. On occasion Herod resorted to less savory means of acquiring money. For example, he once opened the tomb of David and stole some 3,000 talents (*Ant* 16 §179–82).

These sources of revenue undoubtedly operated with relative efficiency during years of peace and tranquility, from the time of the battle of Actium to Herod's death. Broken by only a few skirmishes with the Nabateans, this era allowed the Judean agricultural economy to flourish. The blessings of the *pax Romana* were felt in the country's commerce as well; trade prospered throughout the Mediterranean world and extended as far as Parthia, Arabia, India, and beyond.

Moreover, the peaceful conditions throughout the Roman world strengthened the ties between Judea and the Diaspora. Pilgrimages to the Holy City and donations by Jews everywhere to the temple were of enormous benefit to the Jerusalem economy. Rome protected the rights of Diaspora Jews to send contributions, no matter how substantial, and upon reaching their destination these funds were earmarked for the repair and development of Jerusalem, its walls, and its aqueducts, as well as for ritual purposes.

There were, on occasion, famines and plagues in Judea, and the need to reduce taxes temporarily (*Ant* 15 §365), but such crises appear to have been the exception. The complaints of the citizenry following Herod's death with regard to the enormous tax burdens undoubtedly bear much truth, but we must be careful not to emphasize their significance unduly. Rarely have people, no matter how prosperous, *not* complained about tax measures. However heavily assessed, the population does not seem to have suffered any serious consequences. Despite the devastating wars under Alexander Jannaeus (103–76), the civil war between Aristobulus II and Hyrcanus II (67–63), and the cases of rapacity and exploitation during the first years of Roman rule (under Pompey, Crassus, Cassius, and Antony), the Herodian period—for all its royal expenditures and financial pressures—was a distinct improvement over its predecessors. When all is said and done, Herod's reign appears to have brought significant economic prosperity.

2. Herod's Domestic Policy. Despite Herod's apparently successful political fortunes throughout much of his reign, the king never felt secure in his position. His sense of insecurity (and here we must be careful not to exaggerate, for most Hellenistic-Roman rulers shared these same apprehensions) stemmed from a number of factors. Since he came from a family which until the not-too-distant past had been entirely outside the Jewish fold, it is understandable that some Jews might have looked askance at Herod's lineage; they might have been upset that an "outsider" assumed the title of king that was historically associated with the Davidic lineage. For others, his ascension was objectionable as it came at the expense of the Hasmonean Dynasty. Moreover, Herod's rule was repugnant to some, owing to his dependence upon and identification with a foreign power, and many were undoubtedly dismayed, if not enraged, by the high-handed methods and cruel tactics employed as Herod rose to power. Undoubtedly much of the resentment toward Antipater in the previous generation was now transferred to Herod. Finally, some Jews were clearly offended by the markedly increased tempo at which Hellenistic customs and practices were being introduced and absorbed into Judea. Although this process had been going on since the time of Alexander the Great (336–323), the extent and intensity of this process in Herodian Judea dramatically increased.

Herod's relations with his non-Jewish population were also problematic. Although of Idumean stock, Herod was considered by the pagans a Jew in all respects. It is difficult to imagine that the pagan population would take kindly to Jewish rule, since tensions between Jewish and non-Jewish segments of the population had become quite exacerbated during the Hasmonean era. When Pompey liberated the pagan cities from Jewish rule, their inhabitants undoubtedly breathed a sigh of relief; now, however, with their reincorporation into Herod's realm, many of the old antagonisms surfaced once again.

In light of this situation, Herod adopted a wide range of measures to assert his control over the native populations. Meetings of citizens were prohibited, as was any kind of mass assembly. Spies were ubiquitous both in the city and in rural areas. Herod is said to have disguised himself and to have mingled with the people in order to assess their attitude toward his rule. Anyone showing objection to his regulations or violating any law was severely punished; this included the death penalty, which was often carried out at Hyrcania (*Ant* 15 §365–68). Attempted assassins of the king were put to death, but only after being tortured. At times whole families were punished for crimes committed by one of its members (*Ant* 15 §289–90). According to Josephus, the entire network of fortresses, starting with the Antonia in Jerusalem through Sebaste and Caesarea and culminating with Gaba and Heshbon, was intended to provide a bulwark against any possible Jewish uprising. Together these fortress-cities were meant to monitor seditious activity and, if necessary, to suppress any insurrection originating in the main centers of Jewish population, Judea, the Galilee, and Perea.

Herod, however, was far too shrewd a politician to settle for such preventative measures. He actively sought to mollify negative attitudes and win the allegiance and support—if not the love and affection—of his people. On one occasion (ca. 24 B.C.E.) when a particularly severe drought and plague struck the country, Herod moved quickly to relieve the crisis. He converted his personal ornaments into silver and gold coinage and sent the money to Egypt in return for a large shipment of grain. He also helped the aged and infirm by providing bakers to prepare their food. Clothes were distributed to the needy, and when the time came for the harvest, Herod sent tens of thousands of people to the fields at his own expense to help. He likewise distributed grain to the people of Syria, although Josephus makes it clear that the king distributed eight times more grain within his own kingdom. The generosity and timeliness of these benefactions apparently made a profound impression on the populace and did much not only to neutralize existing antagonisms, but also to build up a reservoir of goodwill (*Ant* 15 §299–316).

Around the year 20/19 the crops again failed, and this time Herod remitted one third of the taxes due (*Ant* 15 §365). On his return from visiting Agrippa in 14 B.C.E., Herod jubilantly reported to the people of Jerusalem his triumphs and their good fortune. He then remitted one fourth of their taxes for the previous year (*Ant* 16 §64).

Another way of winning the respect and loyalty of the people was through the popular assemblies called by the king from time to time. These meetings were advantageous to the king in that they enabled him to establish direct communication with his subjects and to win their approval for acts already accomplished or about to be undertaken. We know that such assemblies were convoked at Caesarea, Jerusalem, and Jericho, where Herod announced grandiose plans (such as the building of the temple—*Ant* 15 §380–87), reported on his trips abroad (in 12—*Ant* 16 §132–35), or used the occasion to gain popular support for intended executions, as at the convocation at Caesarea regarding the imminent deaths of his sons, Alexander and Aristobulus (*Ant* 16 §393).

The above measures were aimed at winning the support of the inhabitants of his kingdom generally. Certain undertakings, however, were intended for specific groups. The large populations residing in Sebaste and Caesarea were indebted to the king for the generosity and benefactions bestowed upon their cities. The character and institutions of these urban centers went a long way toward reducing fears that a Jewish king was, by definition, inimicable to pagans and paganism. That Herod succeeded in gaining the loyalty of these local populations is reflected decades later in Caesarea. In a polemic against the Jews there (ca. 60 C.E.) the pagans praised Herod as the founder of their city (*JW* 2 §266).

Moreover, Herod sought to win the loyalties of the pagans in his realm by incorporating them into his administration. As noted, many non-Jews held high positions in his court and army. Finally, Herod strengthened his ties with this sector of the population by closely identifying himself with Roman rule. The close contacts maintained with Augustus and Agrippa, along with the building of temples and other Hellenistic institutions, were designed not only as a general expression of support for Rome, but also as a message to his pagan subjects that Jewish rule could be supportive of local pagan interests and was not necessarily at odds with their way of life.

Herod's relationship to his Jewish subjects was far more complex. In part, it was related to their conception of Jewish political leadership, the roots of its legitimacy and authority, and its relationship to a number of well-established institutions (the council of elders and the high priesthood). For much of the Second Temple period political and religious leadership was epitomized in the figure of the high priest. He was the political spokesman and the central religious figure of his people. This symbiosis reached its peak under the later Hasmoneans when the high priest was also king. On Hasmonean coinage the Hebrew name and the title "high priest" in ancient Hebrew script appeared, as did the ruler's Greek name and the title *basileus,* "king" in Greek.

Herod, however, sought to end the dual nature of Hasmonean leadership. For him, political power was the "be-all and end-all," while religious leadership (of the priestly or non-priestly variety) was of no interest. Whether this was because his unsuitable origins would preclude any chance of holding such a position or whether he simply was not interested in this religious aspect is a moot point. Herod was indeed keen to separate the functions of religion from those of the state, and he left no doubt as to the superior status he accorded the latter.

3. Herod's Building Program. a. With Rome in Mind. As was customary among client kings at the time, Herod named buildings and even whole cities in honor of his patrons. The two wings of his Jerusalem palace he called Caesareum and Agrippeum, and around the theater built by him in Jerusalem he placed inscriptions in honor of the emperor (*Ant* 15 §272). In Caesarea Paneion, near the source of the Jordan, Herod erected a temple of white marble in honor of Augustus (*JW* 1 §404). The coastal town of Anthedon was renamed Agrippeum, and Agrippa's name was inscribed on one of the gates of the Jerusalem temple. Moreover, Agrippa was often the namesake of Herod's progeny. Josephus speaks of a complex of buildings erected in the vicinity of Jericho in honor of his two Roman patrons, noting, in addition and perhaps with some exaggeration, that there were few landmarks in all his realm which did not bear tributes to Caesar (*JW* 1 §407).

However, the pièce de résistance of Herod's building projects in honor of the emperor was the construction of two cities he named Sebaste and Caesarea. The former, Herod's first major project, begun in 27 and completed in 25, was built in Samaria, on the site of the ancient Israelite capital. The newly founded city of Sebaste was intended to afford the king a strong measure of security. It was fortified by a wall some two miles in circumference and settled by a contingent of veteran soldiers, local inhabitants, and people brought from the surrounding areas—all told, some 6000 colonists were settled there (*JW* 1 §403; *Ant* 15 §296–98). Situated in the center of the country, about a day's journey from Jerusalem, Sebaste afforded an ideal location for an urban center whose *raison d'être* included security considerations. The carefully selected population was to provide a contingent whose loyalty to the king was unquestionable.

An even more ambitious project initiated by Herod was the building of Caesarea, located on the site of Strato's Tower, the Phoenician colony which had long since fallen into a destitute state. Herod invested enormous sums to construct a magnificent city and an impressive port. The city itself boasted a theater, an amphitheater, a stadium or hippodrome, palaces (including one for Herod and his family), an effective sewage system, and other buildings characteristic of Greco-Roman cities (a forum, a basilica, baths, etc.).

Herod's various tributes to the emperor in numerous cities throughout the empire were not merely expressions of adulation from a client king to his patron. In a deeper sense they expressed Herod's commitment to and identification with the *pax Romana,* the vision of the new world order which Rome was then offering the entire *oikumene.* The list of pagan cities that benefited from his generosity is impressive (*JW* 1 §422–28; *Ant* 15 §326–30; 16 §18–19, 24–26, 146–49). He built baths, fountains, and colonnades in Ascalon, gymnasia in Ptolemais (Acco), Tripoli, and Damascus, and theaters in Damascus and Sidon. In Tyre and Berytus Herod built halls, porticoes, temples, and marketplaces, in Byblos a wall, in Laodicea an aqueduct, and in Antioch he constructed colonnades and laid stone or marble pavement for its main street which, according to Josephus, stretched for some 4 km.

Somewhat further afield, Herod rebuilt, on a grander scale than before, the Pythian temple at Rhodes, which had burned down, and on several occasions he contributed to the shipbuilding industry of the city. Herod is reputed to have built most of the public buildings in Nicopolis, a city founded by Augustus following the battle of Actium, and when visiting Chios he restored the collapsed local basilica. Athens and Sparta could boast of his gifts as well. Josephus claims that in Asia Minor, as in Judea, no district was bereft of some sort of Herodian benefaction. See also HEROD'S BUILDING PROGRAM.

b. The Private Needs and Pleasure of Herod. Herod expressed his royal prerogatives liberally through the extensive building activities undertaken for his own pleasure. Foremost among his palaces were those erected in Jerusalem. The Antonia, situated at the NW corner of the Temple Mount, and a much larger and more sumptuous palace in the Upper City served as Herod's palaces in the city during the first 15 years of his rule.

Josephus informs us that royal palaces existed throughout the country (*Ant* 17 §274). He specifically mentions those in Ascalon (*Ant* 17 §321), Ammatha in Perea (*Ant* 17 §277), Jericho (*Ant* 17 §274), Herodium (*Ant* 17 §323–25), Masada (*JW* 7 §286–94), and perhaps Sepphoris (*Ant* 17 §271). Acts 23:35 notes a palace of Herod in Caesarea.

c. Herodian Jerusalem: The Temple and the City. Herod's ambitious building plans were also aimed at winning Jewish support, especially his rebuilding of the temple on a scale and magnitude heretofore unknown. Herod's convocation of a Jerusalem assembly for the purpose of announcing these plans is an indication of the importance he attached to this undertaking (*Ant* 15 §380–425). This is described as his noblest achievement, one which would guarantee his immortality. Herod's plans were ambitious indeed: he intended to double the size of the Temple Mount by extending the artificial podium to the S, W, and N. Only the E portico, associated in popular memory with Solomon, remained more or less untouched. The Temple Mount was to resemble closely other *temenoi* (sacred areas) in the early empire, which were all constructed on a foundation and augmented by an artificial podium surrounded on three sides by porticoes and on the fourth by a large basilica. The temple in these *temenoi* was a free-standing building erected in the center.

The sacred area of the Temple Mount contained a series of courts which only Jews—and only those Jews who were ritually pure—were allowed to enter. The first—called the "women's court"—seems to have been open to all; the second was primarily intended for men, although women bringing sacrifices (for instance, following birth) might also enter; the innermost court was designated exclusively for priests. Here were to be found the main altar, the site for slaughtering sacrifices, and other installations required by the priests for carrying out their daily functions.

The temple building itself was divided into three rooms. The first was an empty porch that was wider than the other two rooms; it had no entrance door. Beyond the porch was the *hêkal,* which contained the *mĕnôrôt* (candelabra), a priestly altar, and a table for the sacred bread. Beyond this was the Holy of Holies, to be entered only by the high priest, and then only on Yom Kippur. Originally, in the days of the First Temple, the Holy Ark and the tablets of the Covenant were kept here, but these were lost following the destruction of the First Temple in 586 B.C.E. Throughout the Second Temple period the Holy of Holies remained empty.

Indeed, the rabbinic saying "whoever has not beheld Herod's building (i.e., the temple) has not seen anything beautiful in his life" (*b. B. Bat.* 4a) attests to the magnitude and magnificence of his enterprise at the Temple Mount. Given the sanctity and centrality of the site to all Jews, it is easy to understand why this was Herod's principal gift to his people; "for he believed that the accomplishment of this task would be the most notable of all the things achieved by him, as indeed it was . . ." (*Ant* 15 §380). Popular imagination even saw a divine blessing in this undertaking. It was said that throughout the period of construction rain fell only at night so as not to interrupt the work (*Ant* 15 §425; *b. Taʿan.* 23a).

Herod's building projects extended beyond the Temple Mount and were noticeable throughout all of Jerusalem. It seems likely that the second of the city's three walls was built in Herod's reign, although its date remains problematic. This wall ran from the vicinity of the three towers near Herod's palace to the Antonia fortress, adjacent to the Temple Mount, and probably included the Damascus Gate area (*JW* 5 §146). It enclosed much of the Christian and Muslim quarters of today's Old City, about 60 acres (including the enlarged Temple Mount), and probably contained some 10,000 additional inhabitants within the city walls. The city's population was thus augmented by about 25 percent, bringing it to somewhere in the vicinity of 40,000. These numbers, in themselves somewhat speculative, did not include the many homes built outside the walls (later to be enclosed by the third wall), nor the villages which existed in the Jerusalem environs.

Mention has already been made of Herod's splendid palace situated in the Upper City of Jerusalem and the three towers named after his brother (Phasael), wife (Mariamme), and friend (Hippicus). These towers were reputedly unparalleled in terms of their beauty, strength, and magnitude (*JW* 5 §156–75). Every Roman city of note boasted a theater, an amphitheater, and a hippodrome, and Herod had these three major entertainment institutions built in Jerusalem as well. The theater was the scene of dramatic and musical presentations, the hippodrome of chariot and horse races, and the amphitheater of gladiatorial spectacles featuring wild animals. Remains of these buildings in Jerusalem have to date eluded archaeologists. See also TEMPLE, JERUSALEM.

4. Hellenistic Influence on Herod and in Jerusalem. In light of archaeological remains and literary sources, it is evident that Hellenistic influence on Jerusalem was considerable under Herod. The extent and nature of this influence is, however, not entirely clear. Were we to depend only upon Josephus' accounts, the dominant impression would be that circles close to Herod's court were largely Hellenized, while others were unreservedly opposed or even indifferent to this foreign culture. Such a conclusion, however, would be superficial and at best only partially true. Indeed, Herod's court appears to have been very highly Hellenized: his non-Jewish advisers, the almost universal use of Greek names, the Greek education accorded his sons in Rome, and the style of the buildings he constructed are but a few indications of the king's Hellenistic proclivities. Herod's enthusiasm for Hellenistic-Roman culture was second only to his loyalty and faithfulness to the Roman political system.

Yet Herod himself set definite bounds to his adoption of Greek norms. He scrupulously avoided any human or animal representations on the coins he minted, and it seems that he pursued the same strict line in his private life as well: in none of Herod's buildings discovered to date is there any trace of figural representation. Nothing which smacked of idolatrous practices was introduced into Jewish society at the time, and the construction of any temple for the glory of Caesar was carried out for the benefit of the pagan population only. Moreover, Herod was careful regarding intermarriage: whenever a member of his family wished to marry a non-Jewish male, he insisted on circumcision. His sister Salome was unable to dissuade him of this prescription, and he prevented her from marrying the Arab Syllaeus when the latter refused to be circumcised (*Ant* 16 §225). Moreover, Herod's cordial relations with some Pharisees and Essenes and his concern for the Jewish Diaspora communities (whatever his motivations) reflect this fundamental identification and sympathy with Jewish matters.

Just as we must see Herod's Hellenistic proclivities in proper perspective, so too we should be careful not to overemphasize Jewish aversion to Hellenism. Although such aversion is noted on several occasions by Josephus, or, more exactly, by his Jewish sources of information, we do not know how accurate such sources are in this regard.

Just as Josephus' primary source, Nicolaus of Damascus, is clearly tendentious in his praise of Herod, so too we may assume that his other sources concerning the Jewish people were biased in the opposite direction. Judging by what actually happened—and not by the evaluation of events related by these sources—we are witness to the emergence of an interesting pattern. The popular reaction of the Jews to the eagle being fixed above the temple gate was indeed violent, but given the general Jewish prohibition regarding figural representation, the placement of an eagle in such a spot was probably as insensitive and as irrational a step as could be imagined (*Ant* 17 §146–63). Herod's decision in this regard was so completely out of step with everything we know of his cautious religious policy that we must ascribe this action to the king's last years, a time when he was far from being in rational control of affairs.

Of equal interest is the response of the people to the major entertainment arenas built by Herod in Jerusalem. After emphasizing the impious non-Jewish nature of this activity, Josephus (or his source) notes that the only reaction involved the dispatch of a delegation which demanded to know if there were figural representations decorating the theater premises. Interestingly enough, no objections were registered concerning the erection of the theater itself, and no grievances were aired against the building of the hippodrome and the amphitheater. In fact, when Herod showed the delegation that there were only trophies of war, and not images, in the theater, everyone laughed at the misunderstanding (*Ant* 15 §267–79). Following the report of these events, Josephus remarks that a few people (ten in all), alarmed and overwrought by the events taking place and by the degree of acculturation in their midst, attempted to assassinate the king (*Ant* 15 §280–91).

The foregoing does not necessarily imply that the people at large liked Herod. As mentioned, we have ample evidence of spies, outlawed meetings, and the building of fortresses to indicate the antipathy of many toward the king or, at the very least, of Herod's fears of such hatred. However, it would be a mistake to attribute this animosity simply to an aversion to Hellenistic practice per se. There were other reasons to dislike Herod on political, economic, and social grounds without assuming that religious-cultural issues constituted the main point of contention. It is not without significance that the delegation to Rome following Herod's death requested annexation to Syria because of the reign of terror and economic hardship imposed upon them (*Ant* 17 §299–314). There were no complaints of religious and cultural crisis, nor was there any demand for the removal of offensive Hellenistic buildings and institutions. The absence of such statements is certainly not because the Romans would have been averse to such requests; in fact, Roman officials, both in Judea and the Diaspora, were invariably sensitive and responsive to Jewish claims of a religious nature. We can only conclude that such issues either did not exist or were not all that critical, at least for the Jews of this delegation.

D. The Last Years (13–4 B.C.E.)

The latter years of Herodian rule were ignominious. The intrigues and manipulations initiated by various family members were widespread, and Herod displayed little ability to control this depraved behavior. Such circumstances were not new, just more intensive and extensive than before. As will be recalled, even during Herod's early years the struggles between the Hasmonean (Alexandra and Mariamme) and Idumean (Salome and Cypros) branches of his house were severe and often deadly. However, with the deaths of Mariamme and Alexandra a respite ensued. Mariamme's sons, Alexander and Aristobulus, were too young (about seven years old at the time) to instigate any serious trouble. Yet with their return from Rome ca. 17 B.C.E. the intrigues resumed. At first Herod made it very clear that these young men would enjoy a special status. He himself went to Rome to escort them back to Judea, and he arranged for Alexander to marry Glaphyra, daughter of King Archelaus of Cappadocia, and for Aristobulus to marry Berenice, daughter of his sister Salome (*Ant* 16 §6–11). The handsome appearance and royal carriage of these two young men won them much popularity with the public at large as well as with the army.

However, the brothers carried a heavy burden of antagonism vis-à-vis their father. They left no doubt that they did not forgive those responsible for their mother's death and that in due time they would seek revenge. Moreover, their royal bearing was often interpreted as contempt for others, such behavior serving only to enhance opposition by Salome, Pheroras, and Antipater, Herod's eldest son by Doris. The poison spread by Salome had its effect, and Herod's ambivalence regarding the Hasmonean family again resurfaced. Already by 14–13 he had recalled Antipater, once repudiated, and sent him to Rome to foster ties with imperial circles (*Ant* 16 §66–86). The situation became exacerbated by the brothers' antipathy toward their father and his suspicions of their patricidal plans. By the year 12 he decided to accuse them formally before the emperor in Rome. A reconciliation, however, was effected, but on his return to Jerusalem, Herod informed a popular assembly that he was bequeathing the throne to Antipater, with Alexander and Aristobulus next in line (*Ant* 16 §130–35).

Matters degenerated in the following years, and the brothers' fate was sealed by the discovery of a number of alleged plots to murder the king. Herod believed the evidence presented by Antipater, Salome, and Pheroras, and following a trial in Berytus with the participation of Roman officials, Alexander and Aristobulus were executed in 7 B.C.E.

Removal of the brothers, however, did not put an end to the family's intrigues. The situation at court had become much more complicated even earlier because of friction between the king on the one hand and both Salome and Pheroras on the other. In both cases the issue was marriage: Salome deeply resented the king's decision to prevent her intended marriage to the Arab Syllaeus, when the latter refused to become circumcised, and Pheroras insisted upon marrying a slave girl with whom he was in love, thereby rejecting Herod's request that he marry the king's daughter (*Ant* 16 §188–219).

Herod's domestic problems at this time were further exacerbated by external political crises. Unruly inhabitants of Trachonitis gained refuge with Syllaeus, who then refused to hand them over to Herod. Thereupon the king marched on the Nabateans, having gained the approval of Saturninus, the Roman governor of Syria, and Syllaeus went to Rome to accuse Herod of unlawful initiation of a war. With Augustus unaware of the circumstances (at least as far as Josephus would have us believe), he reproached Herod and refused to receive his delegation. Only a second embassy, led by Nicolaus of Damascus, managed to have a hearing and duly rectified the situation (*Ant* 16 §271–99).

Following the brothers' demise, Antipater's position as successor appeared unassailable. He strove hard to strengthen his support at Rome and among Roman officials in Syria and drew especially close to Pheroras at home. Salome viewed this relationship with alarm and proceeded to arouse Herod's suspicions against their brother. When Pheroras died, poison that was allegedly intended for the king himself was found, and after an investigation Antipater was implicated, recalled from Rome, put in chains, tried, and condemned (*Ant* 17 §52–145).

By this time Herod had fallen seriously ill. He was moved to make a new will naming Antipas, son of the Samaritan Malthace, his successor (*Ant* 17 §146). News of the king's incurable disease incited two sages, Judah, son of Sariphaeus, and Matthias, son of Margalothus, to provoke their disciples into destroying the eagle erected by the king over a temple gate. The deed was accomplished, but the perpetrators were apprehended and sentenced to death (*Ant* 17 §149–67). Realizing his end was imminent, Herod ordered that upon his death the men whom he had locked up in the Jericho hippodrome should be executed, thus ensuring general mourning at the time of his death (*Ant* 17 §173–75). He ordered Antipater killed and once again altered his will by naming Archelaus, the older son of Malthace, successor to the throne, Antipas tetrarch of the Galilee and Perea, and Philip, son of Cleopatra, tetrarch of Gaulanitis, Trachonitis, Batanaea, and Panaeas (*Ant* 17 §188–90). Finally, in 4 B.C.E., five days after the execution of Antipater, Herod himself succumbed. A solemn prearranged funeral procession, featuring his troops and private bodyguard, accompanied his body from Jericho to Herodium, where he was interred (*Ant* 17 §199).

E. Conclusion

To evaluate Herod's life and reign is well nigh impossible. Most primary sources either vilify or extol him. He is described both as a consummate politician and as clumsy and ineffective, as adroit in his use of power and as blindly cruel. Love and hate, strength and weakness, grandiose plans, and petty concerns were all a part of his personality and behavior. There can be no doubt that contemporary attitudes toward Herod were as complex and varied as they are today. Some despised and others respected him; most were probably ambivalent. But above the personal likes and dislikes, Herod offered the Jews an unwavering political policy which advocated cooperation and integration within the *pax Romana*. When conditions led to the collapse of that policy some seventy years after his death, the consequencces proved to be catastrophic and tragic for the Jewish people.

Other general surveys of Herod the Great may be found in *WHJP* ("The Herodian Era"; "Society and Religion in the Second Temple Period"); *HJP*^{2} 1: 287–329; PW 7/2: 1–158; and *CAH* 10: 316–36.

Bibliography

Avigad, N. 1980. *Discovering Jerusalem.* Jerusalem.

Jeremias, J. 1969. *Jerusalem in the Time of Jesus.* Trans. F. H. and C. H. Cave. London.

Naor, M., ed. 1985. *The King Herod and His Era.* Jerusalem (in Hebrew).

Schalit, A. 1969. *König Herodes: der Mann und sein Werk.* Berlin.

Stern, M. 1974. The Reign of Herod and the Herodian Dynasty. In *The Jewish People in the First Century,* vol. 1. Ed. S. Safrai and M. Stern. CRINT. Assen.

———. 1982. Social and Political Realignments in Herodian Judaea. In *The Jerusalem Cathedra,* vol. 2. Ed. L. I. Levine. Jerusalem.

L. I. LEVINE

HEROD'S BUILDING PROGRAM.

Herod the Great's building projects in W Palestine constitute the most prominent in the country, for any single specific period or personality. One of the significant characteristics of his projects is their variety—he initiated the construction of towns, fortifications, fortresses, palaces (and palatial fortresses), temples, gymnasia, theaters, stadia, hippodromes, monuments, harbors, irrigation projects, and other buildings. The building activity virtually never stopped during the years of his reign (37–4 B.C.).

The main sources for our knowledge of these building projects are Josephus' books (mainly *Wars* and *Antiquity*) and archaeological excavations. These sources complement one another to provide an impressive picture.

Herod excelled in choosing the sites for his buildings (e.g., Masada's N palace, the third winter palace at Jericho, and the harbor city of Caesarea). Another characteristic of his projects was the multi-functional design (of which the HERODIUM is the best example). Herod's logical and practical approach, as well as economic factors, influenced this multi-functional strategy. For a map showing locations and distributions of these sites, see Fig. HER.03.

A. Building Projects in Jerusalem

Naturally, most of Herod's important projects were built in his capital, Jerusalem. On the other hand, because of the destruction that occurred during the Roman sack in A.D. 70 and the intensive building activities of later periods, most of these buildings have nearly totally disappeared.

1. Antonia Fortress. Herod's first building in the capital was named to honor Mark Antony. Except for minor remains, our knowledge depends mostly on Josephus. Antonia combined a palace and a fortress (controlling the Temple Mount which was just to its S). It was a high square or rectangular building surrounded by steep walls and a moat, and was crowned with four towers, one at each corner, three of the same height, but the SE corner tower was much higher.

2. The Central Palace. Situated at the W edge of the upper city, this palace is almost totally missing. Josephus describes it as being encircled with ramparts and towers. While nothing else is known except from Josephus' descriptions, it was probably the biggest and most elaborate of Herod's palaces; it had two huge, elaborate reception halls to entertain hundreds of guests and was named to honor Augustus and Marcus Agrippa. It also included many bedrooms and peristyled courtyards (some of which were rounded) with gardens and fountains.

The three multistoried towers—Phasael, Hippicus, and Mariamne—were all integrated near one another into the city wall N of the central palace (now the site of "The Citadel"). From Josephus' careful descriptions, it is known that these towers ranged from 35–45 m high. All had solid foundations with palatial facilities on top. Only one solid foundation (22 × 18 × 20 m, probably Phasael's) has survived from these unique towers.

3. Theater and Amphitheater. Although these are mentioned by Josephus, they have not yet been located.

4. Fortifications. Data unearthed in excavations indicate city walls and towers either built or reinforced in Herod's day.

5. The Temple Mount. Herod's most prestigious building project was the rebuilding of the Jewish temple in Jerusalem and the enlargement of the sacred temenos around it. Josephus and the Mishna are our main sources concerning the temple itself. The new temple followed the ancient plan but no doubt was more elaborate and perhaps even higher. A major effort was given to the enlargement of the Temple Mount toward the NW, and mainly to the S. Archaeological investigations complement Josephus' description of the various gates, the doubled stoas which surrounded the temenos on three of its sides, and especially the royal basilica (Herod's most monumental building), which adorned the Temple Mount on its S. The royal basilica, no doubt, was built to compensate for Herod's inability, since he was not a priest, to enter the temple itself. The excavations have exposed not only major parts of the W and S walls, but also many details of the adjacent roads, the monumental stairway at the SW corner (Robinson's arch), the Hulda gates on the S, and the adjacent monumental stairways and plaza.

B. Samaria/Sebaste

Samaria, the ancient capital of the Israelite kingdom, was rebuilt by Herod to settle veteran soldiers. The prominent building was the Augusteum, the temple built on the acropolis to honor Augustus. Foundations have survived not only of the temple (34 × 24 m), but also of the large forecourt (ca. 82 × 70 m with its surrounding stoas); both are described by Josephus. Herod also built a circling wall (ca. 3.5 km long) with towers (also described by Josephus), and a large rectangular stadium (about 200 × 60 m) which was surrounded by stoas. See SAMARIA.

C. Caesarea Maritima

Caesarea was one of Herod's most important projects and the biggest planned town built by him (replacing the ancient Phoenician "Migdal Straton"). Josephus' detailed description (already partially attested by archaeology) focuses on the harbor as Herod's main effort and achievement.

Most of the harbor was built in the open sea. It was surrounded by massive breakwaters built with huge concrete blocks cast *in situ* in special wooden forms. Six monuments decorated the entrance into the harbor. Walls, towers, and promenades circled the harbor. Only the podium has survived from the temple which Herod built opposite the harbor; this temple was also in honor of Augustus.

The city was well planned, with streets intersecting at right angles, and with impressive underground drainage systems. Both a theater (which is still preserved) and a hippodrome were built to accommodate the games which were held every five years in honor of Augustus.

Herod's palace should probably be identified with the ruins exposed on the promontory W of the theater.

The earliest of the three aqueducts which exist at the site was probably part of Herod's activity. See CAESAREA.

D. The Desert Fortresses

In all the desert sites, Herod followed the Hasmoneans, who had been the first to build palatial fortresses. All these projects were described by Josephus (with special attention to Masada and Machaerus).

1. Masada. Masada was situated on top of a prominent rocky plateau W of the Dead Sea. It seems that Herod continued to use the buildings, first built by the Hasmoneans (including the nucleus of the Western Palace, the three small palaces, and a few other buildings), but he added many more buildings besides constructing an impressive water system.

The most outstanding building was the Northern Palace, built on three natural rocky terraces. The upper terrace

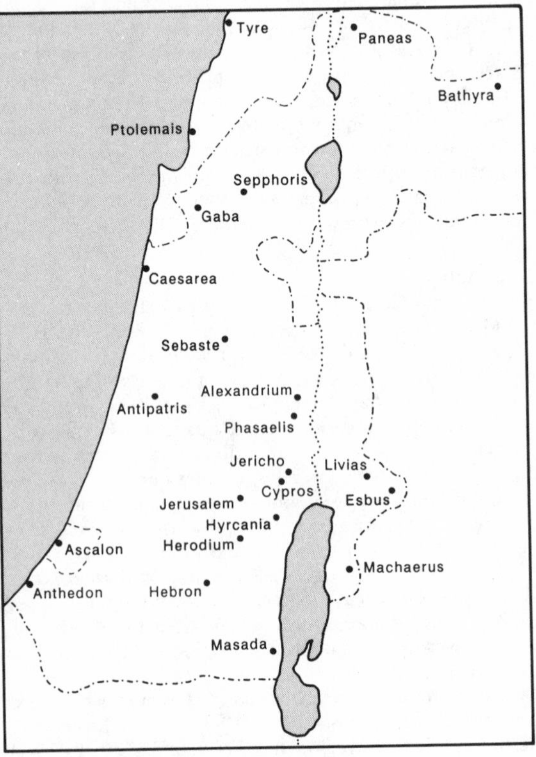

HER.03. Map of Herod's building projects.

was the dormitory wing; the main structure on the central level was a rounded building, probably a *tholos*-shaped hall; the lower terrace consisted of a square hall surrounded by colonnades and a small bathhouse in the Roman style at its basement. Another much larger bath installation was built close to the Northern Palace. Around the latter was exposed the large storeroom complex built by Herod. The whole mountain was fortified with a casemate wall and towers (intensively used during the first Jewish revolt against the Romans).

Twelve huge cisterns were also built on the NW cliff to store water from the occasional flash floods. At the same time, additional cisterns were built on top of the hill. See MASADA.

2. Machaerus. Built to the E of the Dead Sea, Herod's palatial fortress replaced the Hasmonean one. It consisted of walls and towers, dwelling and storage rooms, and a bathhouse in the Roman style. It also included a lower town just outside the summit. See MACHAERUS.

3. Hyrcania. This desert fortress which is W of the Dead Sea is virtually unexcavated.

4. Cypros. This was a desert fortress W of Jericho built on top of a ruined Hasmonean one. It included many palatial rooms and two bathhouses in the Roman style. Herod built a water channel from the Qelt springs especially to feed this site.

5. Alexandrium. The site is located on a high hill W of the Jordan, between Jericho and Beth-shan. Only one peristyled courtyard has been excavated of Herod's royal fortress. This fortress was also built on top of a Hasmonean one.

E. The Plain of Jericho

Because of the proximity of Jericho to Jerusalem, and because of the abundance of water and land, as well as the mild climate, Jericho was a favored location for Herod. At "Tulul Abu el-Alayiq," near Wadi Qelt, he followed the Hasmoneans and built in succession three palaces which ultimately were merged to function as one. On another part of the plain, Herod built a unique multipurpose structure, the "Hippodrome."

The first palace was a rectangular building (85 × 45 m) built S of Wadi Qelt. It was initially misinterpreted as a gymnasium by its excavator, but more recent investigations have clarified its function.

The second palace was built later, N of the wadi, on top of the Hasmonean palace which had probably been destroyed in the 31 B.C. earthquake. It had a large entertainment wing (including a swimming pool and a bathhouse in the Roman style), another swimming pool surrounded by gardens, and what appears to have been an elevated wing on top of an artificial mound.

The most outstanding palace was the third one, covering 3 hectares on both sides of the wadi. Its construction implemented Roman techniques, such as *opus reticulatum* stonework. It comprised a large entertainment wing N of the wadi (with a huge triclinium hall 29 × 19 m), and S of the wadi a large exotic formal garden, a huge pool (90 × 70 m), and a round hall (16 m in diameter) built on top of an artificial mound. It seems that the two halls were also named after Augustus and Marcus Agrippa. See JERICHO.

The hippodrome was built about a mile N of the palaces and was a unique combination of a 350 × 85 m racing course, a 70 × 70 m building (perhaps a gymnasium) built on top of an artificial mound, and a theater built on the mound's S slope, facing the course. In the context of the political events near the death of Herod, Josephus refers probably to these structures which were unique in the whole Classical world (*Ant* 17 §161, 194; *JW* 1 §659).

F. Herodium

The Herodium was one of the most important sites built by Herod, and the only one to carry his name. Situated about 10 miles S of Jerusalem, in Herod's most crucial battlefield, Herodium was a unique combination of a huge summer palace complex, a district capital, a fortress, a monument, and the royal tomb estate. The 25-hectare site, well planned with one grid system, combined a unique elevated building situated on top of a mountain, and a lavish lower campus.

The mountain fortress had a palace at its center surrounded by walls which were laid out in a circle. Along the walls were four towers, three of which were apsidal, while the fourth was completely round and much higher. This outstanding building was half buried and surrounded by an artificial, cone-shaped mountain.

The lower campus, at the bottom of the mountain, included a huge pool (70 × 46 m) surrounded by gardens, colonnades, and various buildings. These buildings laid in a "rug pattern" included palatial edifices, a large bathhouse in the Roman style, and service facilities. Not far from the pool are remains of a 130 × 60 m building which was probably the campus' main palatial wing.

Although Herod's tomb has yet to be located, it probably existed in the lower campus. Hints of such are a 250 m long "course" (the funeral track?), a monumental building at its end, and a group of beautifully curved stones, characteristic of contemporaneous funerary monuments at Jerusalem. Stones which are reused in a nearby Byzantine church probably came from the facade of the missing tomb monument itself. See HERODIUM.

G. Other Building Projects

More building projects are mentioned by Josephus: a harbor at Antedon (S of Gaza); a royal estate at Phasael (N of Jericho) named after Herod's brother; a palace at Beth Haramtha E of the Dead Sea and other fortifications further E at Heshbon; a royal residency, perhaps a governor's palace, at Sepphoris; and two veterans' settlements, one near Mt. Carmel (Geva Haparashim) and the other one E to the Golan (Biethura).

Archaeological evidence exists for a pagan temple at Banias (Panion), situated at one of the sources of the Jordan river. On the other hand, the only complete monument dated to Herod's days (and attributed by all scholars to this king) is the temenos built above the Patriarchs Tombs at Hebron, which was never mentioned by Josephus.

H. Building Projects Outside Herod's Kingdom

Josephus speaks of widespread building activity outside Herod's kingdom, not only in nearby places like Ashkelon, Ptolemais (Acco), Tyre, Sidon, Beirut, and Damascus, but also at more remote sites such as Antioch, Rhodes, Chios, and even Nikopolis, in W Greece. Of all of these projects, including theaters, gymnasia, markets, etc., only one (what appears to be a colannaded street in Antioch) has archaeological attestation. However, these projects manifest Herod's ambition, ability, and political orientation which tried to maintain good relations with various parts of the Roman Empire.

No doubt Herod had a deep understanding for building and architecture. The wide range of original ideas, the buildings' outstanding locations, and the unique combination of functions (such as at Herodium and Jericho's hippodrome) are clear evidence of Herod's personal role in the initiative as well as the implementation of these vast building activities.

EHUD NETZER

HERODIAN ARMY. We are relatively well informed about the army of Herod the Great, especially through the *Jewish History* and *Jewish Antiquities* of the historian Josephus, who was writing in the late 1st century A.D. However, our knowledge of the development of the army, its composition, and its tasks remains fragmentary.

First an appreciation of how Herod came to the throne is necessary. He owed his position, as a client-king of the Roman Empire, to his father, Antipater, who, although not a member of the Hasmonean house, the Jewish royal family, had gained real power and positions of influence for his sons through services to great Romans like Julius Caesar. After his father's death in 43 B.C., Herod was driven from Judea by the Parthians in a world stricken by civil war. He went to Rome and through influence had himself appointed king of the Jews. But he had to fight to make his title a reality against his Hasmonean rival, Antigonus. When he arrived in Judea in 39 B.C., his forces already included foreigners as well as his own countrymen, and it was not until 37 B.C. that, with the help of the Roman forces of M. Antonius, Jerusalem was taken and Herod made himself king in fact. From this date Herod enjoyed the support of a legion based at Jerusalem until its withdrawal in 30 B.C.

The military tradition that Herod inherited derived from the world of the successor states of Alexander the Great: Herod's Hasmonean predecessors had used mercenaries—we hear of Greeks, Pisidians and Cilicians—in his armed forces, as well as Jews he could rely on, trained and commanded on the Seleucid model. But Herod had collaborated with Roman officers in the 30s and even commanded Roman troops, and it is likely that he was influenced by these experiences in building up his own army. His professional forces were supplemented when necessary by a popular levy from his own kingdom.

Herod's use of the forces at his disposal in this period is illustrated by the hostilities in which he was embroiled by Cleopatra in 32 B.C. at the time of the outbreak of civil war between Octavian and Antonius. The war was against Malichus, ruler of the Nabatean kingdom. Herod was defeated at Canatha, modern Qanawat in the Jebel Hauran, but successfully crushed an Arab invasion of Judea in 31 B.C. at Philadelphia.

We see here Herod acting within the Hasmonean tradition. Josephus describes Herod's forces simply as "the Jews," who are opposed to "the Arabs." Herod has taken advantage of his prerogative as king to raise an army from his subjects which he is leading against a hostile neighboring kingdom.

After the defeat of Herod's patron, M. Antonius, in 31 B.C., Herod was confirmed in his position as king by Octavian, who took over Antonius' role and increased Herod's territory. A new phase in Herod's reign began as king under the strict supervision of Octavian, who in 27 B.C. took the cognomen Augustus.

His main military duties in this capacity were to keep the peace with his neighbors and refrain from aggression himself. Augustus sternly disapproved of major military action by client-kings unless they had received his permission. He was angered by punitive action taken by Herod against the Nabatean king later in his reign, in 10–9 B.C., even though Herod was severely provoked by incursions into his territory.

Herod, however, was compelled to base his rule on force. This was directed mainly against his own subjects. The kingdom included troublesome areas like Auranitis, the modern Jebel Hauran, and Trachonitis-el Lejah, whose inhabitants resented being forced to live peaceably from agriculture. Herod also had little support either from the Greek cities who disliked being ruled by a Jew or from the Jews, who hated Herod as an Idumean and as an instrument of their oppressors, the Romans. His lack of popularity is emphasized by the plot to assassinate him in the theater, which came to light in 25 B.C.

The army was thus Herod's main means of maintaining his power. After the departure of the Roman legion from Jerusalem, Herod had to rely on a professional army loyal to himself. His troops included his own countrymen, Idumeans, recruits from his own settlements like Sebaste, or from the wild tribes from the NE of his kingdom. A unit of Trachonites took part in the disturbances after Herod's death in 4 B.C. But the best elements of his standing army came from the fighting men of the west. Herod's funeral procession was led by élite corps of Gauls, Thracians and Germans. Early in his reign, Herod's guard had been reinforced by 400 Gauls, formerly Cleopatra's, who were presented to Herod by Octavian.

Among the officers serving in the army were Roman citizens, possibly from Italy. We meet, for example, a Volumnius as military tribune, and Rufus and Gratus in charge of the royal cavalry and infantry, respectively. As large numbers of soldiers who had fought in the civil wars were demobilized, Herod should easily have been able to find suitably qualified recruits to command and train his forces.

How large was Herod's standing army? Precision is impossible. We hear in 4 B.C. of 3,000 Sebastenes going over to the Romans while the bulk of the royal troops joined the rebels. This gives a minimum of 6,000 men. It is tempting to compare with this the garrison of the Roman province under the emperor Vespasian. A legion and the auxilia in the discharge diploma of A.D. 86 suggest a minimum garrison of 9,000 men. Conditions were by then different, but the figures are perhaps helpful in providing a rough idea of the scale of the garrison.

What were the dispositions of the army? Much of it was

based in fortresses throughout the kingdom. Because of the distrust and hostility felt toward him by his subjects, Herod had to hold them down harshly and ruthlessly. Strongpoints, as Josephus notes, were built throughout the country so that Herod could find out about, and quickly nip in the bud, any trouble that was brewing. A strong garrison was based at Jerusalem, where Herod rebuilt the citadel dominating the temple early in his reign—its name, Antonia, dates it to before Antonius' demise in 31 B.C.. He also constructed a second citadel in the upper citadel, completed by 29 B.C. Then Josephus, in his survey of Herod's means of controlling his kingdom, mentions major fortresses at Caesarea, Gaba in Galilee, Heshbon-Esbonitis in Perea, and Sebaste-Samaria. Areas of strategic importance were similarly strongly held. We know of a cluster of forts dominating the region E of Jerusalem: Cyprus overlooking Jericho, Herodium 7 miles S, Hyrcania 8 miles SE of Jerusalem, and Alexandrium in the Jordan valley 15 miles N of Jericho. They would all no doubt have contained garrisons and were supplemented by sites like Masada, kept in readiness in case of an emergency.

But Herod did not rely only on his standing army. He followed the practice of Hellenistic kings in building up a reserve army by granting plots of land on condition of military service in time of need. Such a settlement of reservists was established at Heshbon-Esbonitis, E of the Dead Sea. Another body was settled in the fortress at Gabae, N of Mount Carmel. The duty of these colonists was to hold Galilee in check, as they attempted to do later at the time of the rebellion that broke out in A.D. 66. But the most important military settlement was at Samaria, where Herod granted plots of land to six thousand men. He refounded the city and renamed it Sebaste in 27 B.C.: it was a day's march from Jerusalem and was useful for controlling both those in the city and those in the country.

In the unruly NE provinces of his kingdom Herod planted two colonies to police the area after a serious revolt by the inhabitants. The first colony was composed of three thousand Idumeans, fellow countrymen of Herod. The colony was destroyed during a second revolt in 10–9 B.C. The second colony was more unusual. Zamaris, a wealthy Babylonian Jew, migrated from Parthian to Roman territory ca. 10–6 B.C. Herod offered him a permanent home in his kingdom, in Batanea, a region centering on the modern town of Deraa, on very favorable terms. In return for policing the area Zamaris and his followers were granted land free of taxation. Zamaris accepted the offer, built the village of Bathyra, and fortified the area. He was clearly a man of some substance. He came from Babylon with 500 cavalry, all of them horse archers, and a group of 100 relatives. The Babylonian Jews, living in an alien country, out of touch with the Jews of Palestine and dependent on the Herodian house for their favored position, flourished under Herod and remained loyal to the dynasty.

One particular section of Herod's frontier line has been examined with the aid of archaeological evidence. This is in the south, in Idumea. Herodian pottery has been found at seven sites between the mouth of the Zohar valley in the E and Ber Shema (Bersama) in the W. Fortified settlements with Herodian occupation have also been noted, for example, at Arad. On the basis of this evidence, Professor Gichon has argued for a defensive line based on the E–W running valleys of the Besor, Beer-sheba, and Malhata-Zohar. Forts, watchtowers, and fortified settlements gave, it is maintained, depth to this line. However, the interpretation of this evidence is open to some doubt. Josephus does not record any serious incursions into this area during Herod's reign. Indeed, the interests of Herod and the Nabatean king at Petra were similar: both wished to ensure that caravans to and from Arabia journeyed unmolested. The archaeological evidence is thus compatible with small-scale occupation, possibly temporary, involved in the protection of traffic and travelers passing through the region. The fortified settlements in Idumea can then be seen as serving to protect the local inhabitants from the occasional raiding expeditions from the Negeb which were to be expected in the desert borderlands. A substantial presence of Herod's troops in this region thus remains questionable.

The importance to Herod of his armed forces throughout his reign is clear. After receipt of an empty title from the Roman senate at Antonius' urging in 40 B.C., Herod had to make himself king by armed force. His rule was at first buttressed by Antonius' legion, but after 30 B.C., under Augustus' stricter suzerainty, he had to depend on his own resources: most important was his standing army. A large garrison was based at Jerusalem, and other troops garrisoned fortresses strategically placed throughout the kingdom. His grip was strengthened by means of colonies of veterans, loyal subjects, and outsiders like Zamaris. So Herod both protected and held down his difficult and rebellious subjects.

For further reading, see also PW 7/2: 1–158 and *HJP*^{2} 1: 287–324.

Bibliography

Gichon, M. 1967. Idumaea and the Herodian Limes. *IEJ* 17: 27–42.

Jones, A. H. M. 1938. *The Herods of Judea.* Oxford.

Schalit, A. 1969. *König Herodes: der Mann und sein Werk.* Berlin.

M. H. GRACEY

HERODIAN DYNASTY. The Herodian "dynasty" properly begins with ANTIPATER, the grandfather of Herod the Great, who won acclaim as Alexander Jannaeus' governor in Idumea around the turn of the 2d century B.C. (*Ant* 14.10). His son, also named Antipater, was an energetic supporter of Hyrcanus II; he was especially skilled at winning and exploiting friendly connections with powerful Romans, from Pompey onward (e.g. *Ant* 14.37). He also helped the Romans in their dealings with the Nabateans; his wife was a Nabatean (*Ant* 14.80–84). The ability to work with Rome was the basis of the success of the Herodian dynasty; Antipater II set this pattern, and it was by and large followed by his descendants. Yet that particular political strategy was fraught with danger, especially when the interests and values of the essentially Greco-Roman culture of the Roman Empire conflicted with Jewish tradition.

In 48 B.C., when Rome was still caught up in the civil war between Caesar and Pompey which had erupted the year before, Antipater II astutely realigned his loyalties. Caesar was in mortal danger in Alexandria. Antipater, who had hitherto supported the Pompeian cause, judged that that cause was lost now that Pompey was dead; he therefore sought and won the favor of the likely victor by raising troops and bringing them to Caesar's aid (*Ant* 14.127–39). As a reward, Caesar gave Antipater and his family Roman citizenship in 47 B.C.: his full name was now presumably Gaius Julius Antipater. The administration of Judea was put in his hands; Phasael and Herod, his sons, administered Jerusalem and Galilee respectively. The abilities of Herod, who was to become HEROD THE GREAT, were soon obvious (*Ant* 14.140ff.).

In 43 B.C., shortly after the assassination of Caesar, Antipater was poisoned while collecting money for Cassius (*Ant* 14.280ff.). In 40 B.C., with Hyrcanus II captured and Jerusalem in Parthian hands, Herod made his way to Rome, where he was appointed king of Judea by the Roman Senate, thanks to the combined efforts of Antony and Octavian. But it was not until 37 B.C. that Roman forces made it possible for Herod to enter Jerusalem. Herod's position could only have been uneasy: he had no dynastic claim to rule, and there was some resistance among the Jews toward the establishment of any king at all.

As the Roman world divided in civil warfare once more, with Octavian in the W and Antony in the E, Herod had little choice but to support Antony's cause; his links with Antony were stronger. After Octavian's victory, Herod deftly won his pardon in 30 B.C. Under Octavian (later known as Caesar AUGUSTUS) Herod proceeded to build up his kingdom. His reconstruction projects are especially noted for their elaborate foundations. He also developed a reputation throughout the empire for his generous beneficence. Despite the occasional rift, Herod's relations with the imperial family were notably warm, yet Herod's dealings with non-Jewish communities and his flirtation with Greco-Roman culture won him some displeasure at home. His position became ever more uncomfortable in the latter years of his reign, thanks largely to the opposition of Jewish traditionalists, who abhorred this Idumean king with gentile ways.

Herod's difficulties found expression within his family: he was led to execute a wife, Mariamme I, in 29 B.C., and later, three sons—Alexander and Aristobulus in 7 B.C., and Antipater in 4 B.C. His several and significant changes to his will further indicate the unsettled nature of his last years. He died, some 70 years old, in 4 B.C. Consequent social disorder also points to the extent of problems in Herod's reign.

Augustus was free to enact Herod's will as he saw fit: he divided Herod's property, partly to ensure the future of each of Herod's dependents. The bulk of the kingdom was divided between Herod's three sons—ARCHELAUS, HEROD ANTIPAS, and Philip the Tetrarch (see PHILIP [PERSON] #5). Archelaus, given the title of ethnarch, had the core of Herod's kingdom (Judea), but he could not maintain order and only made himself unpopular in the attempt. He was removed by Augustus in A.D. 6 at the request of his subjects and replaced by a Roman governor. Antipas and Philip each received smaller territories to the N and the title tetrarch, but were more successful in retaining control. Antipas was deposed in A.D. 39 by the emperor Gaius (alias Caligula), largely through the machinations of his nephew and brother-in-law Agrippa, who received his tetrarchy (later AGRIPPA I). Philip died in A.D. 33/4, and ultimately his tetrarchy also passed to Agrippa.

In A.D. 41 Agrippa helped Claudius to power at Rome. A grateful Claudius gave him the province of Judea; thus the original domain of Herod's kingdom was restored for Agrippa. Agrippa had made astute use of the connections he had formed with the imperial family during his youth in Rome. Earlier, Herod had sent his sons to Rome for just this purpose, but they seem to have derived less advantage from their sojourn than did Agrippa. Agrippa used his contacts to protect Jewish interests from the worst excesses of Roman power; he also gained the territory of Chalcis for his brother Herod (of Chalcis).

Upon the death of Agrippa I in A.D. 44, Claudius appointed a Roman governor to his kingdom, since his son (Agrippa II) was considered too young for such a responsibility. The young Agrippa lived at the court of Claudius in Rome until about A.D. 50, when Chalcis became available through the death of his uncle Herod (of Chalcis). In A.D. 53 he received an extended version of Philip's old tetrarchy while exercising certain religious prerogatives in Jerusalem.

Agrippa II owed everything to Rome and seems to have thought that the best future for the Jews lay in acquiescence in Roman rule, which was to be coaxed and tempered rather than thwarted. Together with his sister, BERNICE, Agrippa opposed the Jewish revolt of A.D. 66, first with words and then with arms. Agrippa's royal forces fought beside the Romans to suppress the revolutionaries, who, it must be said, were also fighting among themselves. Such cooperation was the essence of Herodian rule; the book of Acts clearly shows the essentially amicable and everyday dealings of Roman governors with Antipas and Agrippa II. The latter's other sister, DRUSILLA, even married the Roman governor FELIX.

After the revolt had been crushed, Agrippa and Bernice were duly rewarded by the Romans with honors and territory. It was thought that Bernice might even marry into the new imperial family of Rome, the Flavians (A.D. 69–96), but she did not. By the end of the 1st century A.D. Agrippa died. Drusilla's son by Felix had been killed in the volcanic eruption of Mt. Vesuvius in A.D. 79. The rest of the family faded from history, though occasional glimpses survive of possible descendants of the Herodian dynasty (Sullivan *ANRW* 2/8: 344–45 with Braund 1983: 242). (See also *HJP*² 1: 243–454.)

Bibliography

Braund, D. C. 1983. Four Notes on the Herods. *Classical Quarterly* 33: 239–42.

———. 1984. *Rome and the Friendly King.* New York.

Jones, A. H. M. 1967. *The Herods of Judaea.* 2d ed. Oxford.

Schalit, A. 1969. *König Herodes.* SJ 55. Berlin.

DAVID C. BRAUND

HERODIAS (PERSON) [Gk *Herodias*]. The daughter of Aristobulus (son of Herod the Great) and Bernice (daughter of Herod the Great's sister, Salome). She was probably born between 9 and 7 B.C., shortly before Aristobulus died in 7 B.C. According to Josephus (*Ant* 17 §14) she was

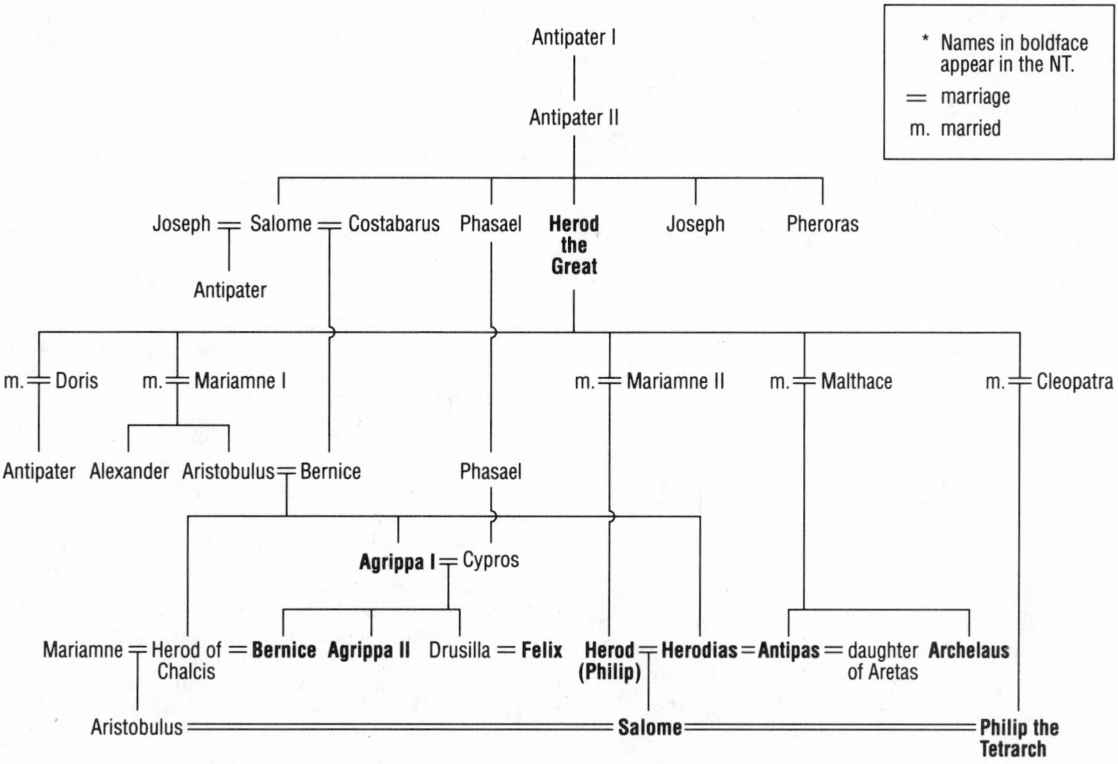

HER.04. Genealogy chart of the Herodian family. See also Fig. HAS.01.

betrothed about 6 B.C. to Herod the Great's son Herod, whose personal name seems to have been Philip. Apparently Herodias bore to her first husband a daughter, whom Josephus says was named Salome (*Ant* 18 §136). While Herod Antipas was visiting the residence of his half-brother Herod Philip, Herodias became interested in Antipas and agreed to divorce Philip for Antipas (*Ant* 18 §110).

Herodias was the niece of Herod Antipas and was nearing her fortieth birthday at the time of her second marriage. This second marriage would have been judged incestuous by the OT laws (Lev 18:13) and definitely forbidden (Lev 20:21; 18:16). It is probable, considering Jesus' close relationship to John the Baptist and the fact that John apparently lost his life for condemning the relationship of Antipas and Herodias, that Jesus made indirect reference to this relationship in his discussion of marriage (Mark 10:12, but especially Matt 19:1–9 [Witherington 1985: 571–76]).

The Synoptic Gospels give attention to the relationship of Antipas to Herodias because of its effect on the Baptist's career and life (Mark 6:17–29; Matt 14:3–12; Luke 3:19–20). Luke explicitly says that John was imprisoned because he criticized the incestuous and unlawful marriage between Herodias and Antipas. Thus, this comment provides a plausible explanation why we find Herodias biding her time, "nursing a grudge against the Baptist and wanting to kill him" (Mark 6:19), and finally forcing Antipas to execute John. It must be remembered that Josephus' version of this affair was written some 60 years later by one who focused on the political rather than the personal aspects of the story. Thus it is not surprising to hear Josephus say that John was executed because Herod perceived him to be a political threat (*Ant* 18 §116–19).

Some believe that the story in Mark 6 (and any parallel) is legendary in character, that it would be unlikely for a Jewish princess like Salome to dance a lascivious dance. Yet elsewhere in Josephus (*JW* 2.2.5) we hear of this same sort of revelry and drinking within the Herodian household, which was thoroughly Hellenized (Windisch 1917: 73–81). Furthermore, the machinations of Herodias in this story are true to form, the Herodian household being infamous for plots to bring about an opponent's downfall. The most probable reading of the text in Mark 6:22 is not "his daughter" but "her daughter," a reading supported by many and varied sorts of manuscripts (Taylor 1966: 314–15). Thus it is unlikely that Mark was ill informed about the actual state of relationships among Herodias, Salome, and Antipas.

The picture of Herodias derived from the Gospels is in fundamental agreement with Josephus. In both works she is seen as a scheming, clever woman who would stop at nothing to achieve her ends (Mark 6:19–29, *Ant* 18 §111, 136). There is also no counterhistorical evidence to suggest that either Mark or Josephus was pursuing some antifeminist agenda in his respective portrayals of Herodias. Indeed, there is some evidence to suggest that Mark was sympathetic to the plight of women in his era (Witherington 1988: 158–66). Notice too the story in *Ant* 18 §240–55, where Herodias is jealous of her brother Agrippa I receiving the title of king and insists on Antipas going to Rome and asking for a similar title, an act which leads to the downfall of Antipas and Herodias, both banished by the Emperor Gaius either to Spain or the Lyons in Gaul (*Ant* 18 §252–53; *JW* 2 §183; there are divergent traditions about their final location).

Bibliography

Hoehner, H. W. 1980. *Herod Antipas.* Grand Rapids.
Taylor, V. 1966. *The Gospel According to St. Mark.* 2d ed. New York.
Windisch, H. 1917. Kleine Beitrage zur evangelischen Uberlieferung. *ZNW* 18: 73–81.
Wink, W. 1968. *John the Baptist in the Gospel Tradition.* Cambridge.
Witherington, B. 1985. Matthew 5.32 and 19.9—Exception or Exceptional Situation? *NTS* 31(4): 571–76.
———. 1988. *Women in the Earliest Churches.* Cambridge.

BEN WITHERINGTON, III

HERODION (PERSON) [Gk *Hērōdiōn*]. A Roman Jewish-Christian who received greetings from Paul in Rom 16:11. His name, unique in the Roman Empire at that time, was likely the Greek equivalent of the Lat "Herodian(us)." In the 1st century C.E. this latter name identified former Herodian slaves who had been sold to a second master (in most cases slaves with this type of name were sold to the public or to the household of the emperor), and they usually were freed later (Lampe *StadtrChr*, 67, 68, 148, 153, 296; cf. *CIL* 6: 9005). It is therefore possible that Herodion was an imperial freedman and had Roman citizenship (cf. Phil 4:22; Christians in the emperor's household). As a former Jewish slave of Herod, Herodion probably had immigrated to Rome. Other former Herodian slaves had gone the same way from the east to the capital: the inscription in *CIL* 6: 9005 (1st century C.E.) mentions a former slave of Herod the Great, Coetus Herodianus, who had become an imperial freedman in Rome. The inscription in *CIJ*, no. 173 even proves the existence of a Roman "Synagogue of the Herodians" ([*syna*]*gōgē* [*Hē*]*rodiōn*), which apparently had been founded by several former Jewish Herodian slaves.

It may not be coincidence that just one verse earlier (Rom 16:10), Paul greeted the servants of Aristobulus. Aristobulus was probably a member of the Herodian family; Herodion may therefore have had connections to Aristobulus' household.

The Greek form *Hērōdiōn* was first used by an Alexandrian veterinarian (*Hippiatrica* 82); as far as we know, the name was not used again until the 4th century C.E.

Bibliography

Oder, E., and Hoppe, K., eds. 1924. *Corpus Hippiatricorum Graecorum.* Vol. 1. Leipzig.

PETER LAMPE

HERODIUM (M.R. 173119). A palace-fortress built by Herod the Great on the site known in Arabic as Jebel el-Fureidis. It is situated 13 km S of Jerusalem, 6 km SE of Bethlehem (N of the biblical Tekoa), on the edge of the Judean desert. No settlement earlier than the days of Herod the Great (37–4 B.C.) is known at the site, which comprises a steep conical artificial mountain into which is integrated a building; to its N are additional substantial ruins (including a huge pool). The final identification of the site as Herodium, following Josephus and Pliny (*JW* 1.13.8 §625; 1.21.10 §419; 1.33.9 §673; *Ant* 14.13.9 §360; 15.9.4 §323–25; 17.8.3 §199; Pliny *HN* 5.14.70) is attributed to E. Robinson, who visited the site in 1838. Herodium was surveyed later by F. de Saulcy, in 1850 and 1863, who excavated a small trench in the center of the large pool in an effort to locate Herod's tomb; by M. V. Guerin in 1868; by C. R. Condor and H. H. Kitchener on behalf of the Palestine Exploration Fund in 1873, 1881, and 1883; and by C. Schick in 1879. The first excavations at the site were carried on by V. Corbo in four seasons (1962–1967). Corbo exposed a major part of the interior structure which is surrounded by the artificial mountain. Corbo's work was followed by minor additional work by G. Foerster (1969). E. Netzer was the first to excavate Lower Herodium—the ruins below and to the N of the mountain (1972, 1973–78, and 1980–87).

According to Josephus a crucial battle occurred in 40 B.C. at the site where Herod later built the Herodium. The battle was between Herod, son of Antipater (of Edomite origin), who had just escaped from Jerusalem, and Mattathias Antigonus (a Hasmonean prince). The event was a result of an agreement between Antigonus and the Parthians (following their occupation of Syria in the same year) to displace John Hyrcanus II and the Romans, who had dominated Judea since 63 B.C.

According to Josephus, during the same flight from Jerusalem, Herod tried to commit suicide after his mother fell under the wheels of her cart. Herod, however, won the battle and managed ultimately to reach Rome, where he was nominated to be the king of Judea.

The two successive events were no doubt traumatic for Herod, and it seems that much before Herodium was actually built (around 23 B.C.), Herod had determined it to be his burial place instead of his capital.

As inferred from Josephus and the archaeological material finds, Herodium served various functions: it was a large, countryside summer palace (his winter palace was at Jericho); it served as a monument to Herod's name, since it is the only site to perpetuate his name (although a second Herodium is mentioned in *JW* 1.21.10 §419, it cannot be confirmed either from textual or archaeological evidence); it was a monument to the battle which occurred here; it became Herod's burial estate (although his tomb has not yet been found); it was the capital of the toparchy (which Herod probably moved from Beth-zur); and it served as a fortress. The fortress, as inferred from the remains, was only in the mountain and was probably only to secure Herod and his family during their assumed long visits to this substantial palace. Some scholars understand Herodium to be part of the wider range of palatial fortresses. Since there was no water source in the vicinity, Herod built a 6-km water channel from a spring S of Bethlehem; it is documented by Josephus and confirmed by archaeological surveys.

A. The Mountain Palace-Fortress

The Mountain Palace-Fortress is bounded by two concentric walls forming a "cylinder" 63 m in diameter. See Fig. HER.05. The space between the two walls, filled today by debris, was originally divided into galleries, each about 5 m high, which were probably used as corridors and for storage. Inside the cylinder, well protected by the surrounding towers and artificial steep slopes, was a luxurious villa. The round space was divided into two equal parts. The W half consisted of dwelling quarters and the E half contained a large peristyle courtyard surrounded by colonnades on three sides. The columns were in the Corinthian style, similar to those found at Masada, Jericho's winter palaces, and Cypros. Semicircular excedras adorned the courtyard on both its narrow sides. The entrance to this inner building was located at the NE corner of the courtyard.

The W half consisted of a large triclinium (10.5 × 15 m; this was used as a synagogue during the first Jewish revolt against the Romans); dormitories on either side of a cross-shaped central corridor; and a bathhouse in the Roman style. The bathhouse included one or two *apoditeria* rooms, a small *frigidarium,* a large *caldarium,* and a small rounded *tepidarium* with a fully preserved cupola, one of the oldest found in the Holy Land. Many of the inner building's rooms had walls covered with frescoes, which depicted only geometrical patterns. The triclinium was originally paved with *opus sectile* tiles, and the bathhouse's rooms were paved with mosaics.

Of the four towers which surrounded the cylinder, the one to the E was round (18.3 m in diameter) and the other three, to the N, W, and S, were semicircular (16.5 m in diameter). The semicircular towers were divided into floors, each having four rooms, which probably served as dwellings for soldiers and servants. Of the E round tower only a massive stone-built structure (about 20 m high) is preserved. Apart from a water cistern and two small cellar-like rooms on its top, it appears to have been completely solid. This tower resembles the so-called "David's tower" in Jerusalem, the only remnant of Herod's three famous towers (named Phasael, Hippicus, and Mariamme) mentioned by Josephus.

The mountain complex was approached by a steep, 6.5 m wide stairway (about 120 m long), in a straight line to the NE of the mountain. Adjacent to the stairway, at the foot of the hill, three large water cisterns were revealed with a total capacity of about 2500 m^3.

Once the rounded structure was completed (according to Netzer's reconstruction, the cylinder reached the height of 30 m above the original hill), huge quantities of soil and

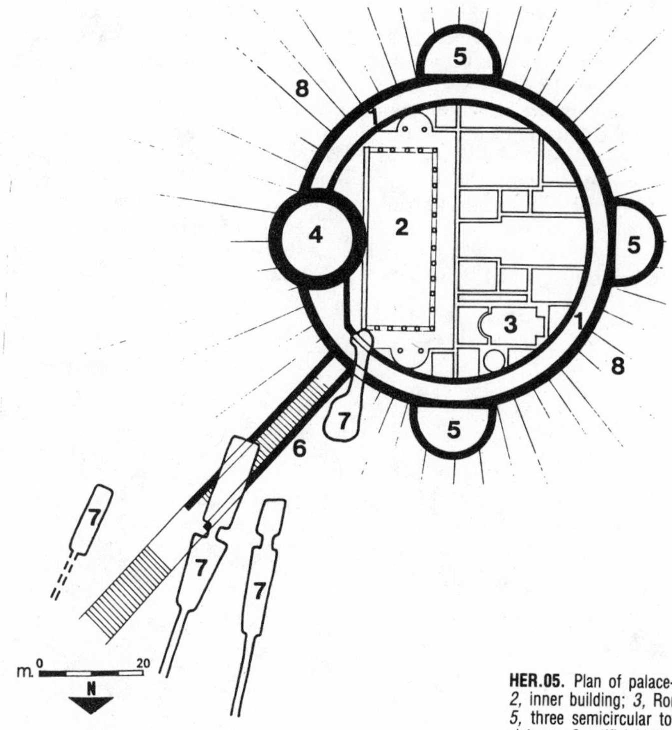

HER.05. Plan of palace-fortress at Herodium. *1,* cylinder; *2,* inner building; *3,* Roman bathhouse; *4,* E round tower; *5,* three semicircular towers; *6,* main staircase; *7,* water cisterns; *8,* artificial hill. *(Courtesy of E. Netzer)*

gravel were dumped around it. Thus the cone-shaped hill was created. The fill covered about ⅔ of the building (15–20 m above the original height of the hill) but also continued down the slopes for another 20 m.

The Mountain Palace-Fortress combined at the same time three major functions: it was an exotic villa, an outstanding monument to be seen from afar, and a fortress. According to the excavator's reconstruction, the cylinder consisted of a two-level barrel-vaulted foundation, above which were five stories. See Fig. HER.06. It protruded close to 10 m above the steep artificial slopes, thus serving as the fortress's wall. The semicircular towers were either slightly higher or perhaps lower than the cylinder, but the round E tower had probably about five stories above the solid base (an estimated height of about 15 m above the cylinder). It was used, it seems, not only as an observation post, but also to house palatial rooms, from which to enjoy the superb landscape and breezes, which otherwise were hidden by the cylinder inside the inner building.

Scholars have seen the prototype for this unique building in Augustus' mausoleum in Rome. Others postulate the Antonia Fortress (probably Herod's first building project, which was a large palace built in Jerusalem surrounded by four towers).

B. Lower Herodium

About 100 m below the Mountain Palace-Fortress, Lower Herodium was built as a complex of buildings and gardens spread over an area of about 15 hectares. See Fig. HER.07. This complex was well planned and had one homogeneous grid system. Large-scale earthworks preceded the construction of the campus, built along both sides of a small valley. It consisted of two major sections: (1) the "large palace" directly below the mountain; and (2) the "pool complex" at the center of the lower site. The pool site had rows of buildings to its S, W, and mainly to its N (all built in a kind of a "rug pattern" design). Another outstanding feature was a long artificial terrace, the "course," measuring 350 × 25 m, which lay N and parallel to the large lower palace.

The "large palace" (its function is postulated) was the largest and most prominent building at Lower Herodium. It was 130 m long and about 55 m wide, and was built on a relatively steep slope. This rectangular building shares the same E–W axis with the Mountain Palace-Fortress. Only the substructure has survived, including remains of two long halls (each about 130 × 5 m) probably used as storage spaces.

The "pool complex" combined a huge rectangular pool (70 × 46 m and 3 m deep) within a garden 125 m long and 105 m wide. In the pool's center are the foundations of a round structure, probably a *tholos*-shaped pavilion. The garden, which encircled the pool, extended 18 m on the N, W, and S, but 60 m on the E. The garden probably was bounded on three sides by colonnades 5–6 m wide which were elevated 1.2–1.5 m above the garden level with access via about 5 steps. Two long halls, at least 9 m wide and 110 m long, lay E and W of the garden. The hall to the W lay behind the W colonnade and the E hall (of which only its substructure has survived) was built next to the wide section of the garden. The purpose of these halls, however, remains unknown. Most of the structures to the S, W, and N of the pool complex remain unexposed. Among the few that are exposed are the central bathhouse, a storage and service wing, and the remains of two luxurious villas.

The "central bathhouse" to the SW of the garden was built in the Roman manner; it was relatively well preserved and included some decorated mosaic floors and frescoed walls. Its *caldarium* measured about 16 × 9 m, twice the size of the ones exposed in the Mountain Palace-Fortress or at Masada. It also included a round heated *laconicum*.

The "service and storage wing," to the NW of the garden, had a long barrel-vaulted hall which collapsed in the middle of the 1st century A.D. An adjacent hall may have been a stable.

The two luxurious villas, situated one beside the other in the area N of the garden, included in each a small Roman style bathhouse. These villas probably served the officers in charge of the local toparchy since Herod had moved the capital to Herodium.

An intriguing group of structures have been exposed in the Lower Herodium S of the pool complex, at the W end

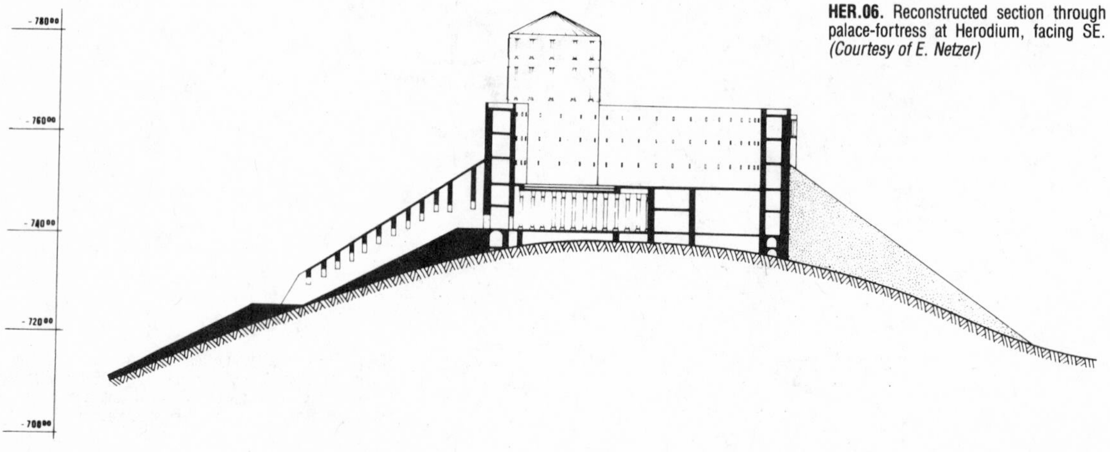

HER.06. Reconstructed section through palace-fortress at Herodium, facing SE. *(Courtesy of E. Netzer)*

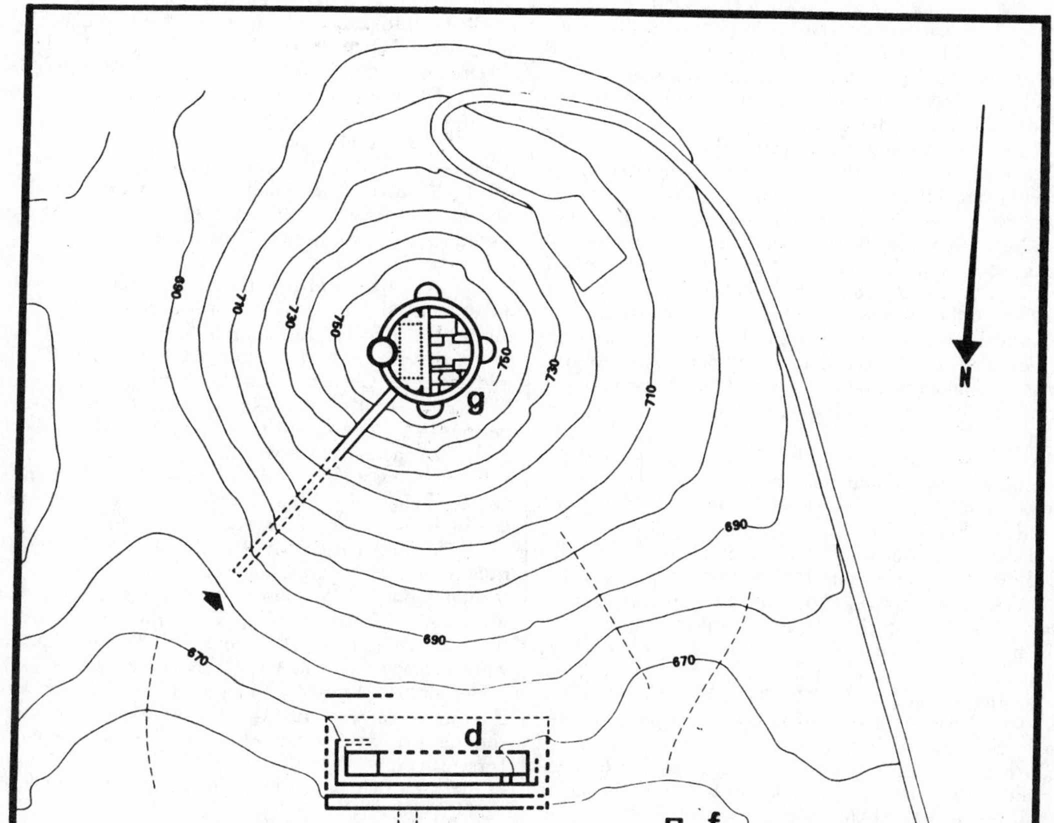

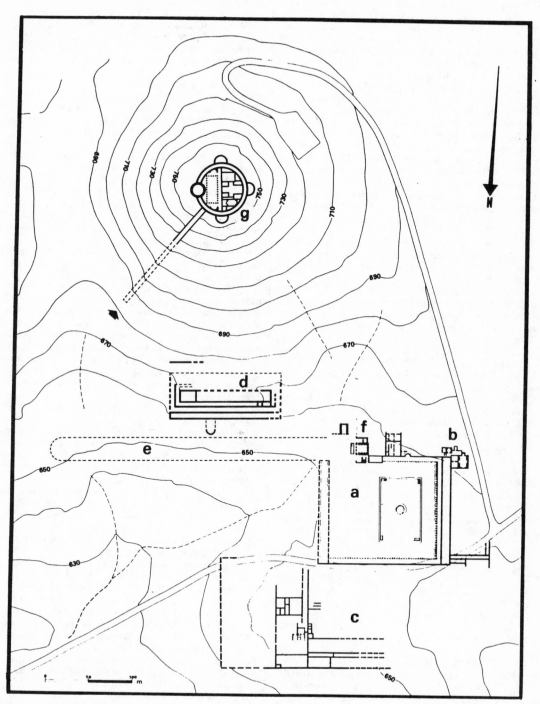

HER.07. Site plan of Greater Herodium, *a,* pool complex; *b,* central bathhouse; *c,* northern area; *d,* large palace; *e,* course; *f,* monumental building; *g,* palace-fortress (see Fig. HER.05 for detail). *(Courtesy of E. Netzer)*

of the long "course." The main building is the monumental building (14 × 15 m) which faces the "course." Inside is an elaborate hall (8 × 10 m) surrounded by niches separated by half columns based on pedestals. The hall, which originally had a barrel-vaulted ceiling, had probably five entrances and probably was surmounted with a monumental roof. A long but narrow (reflecting?) pool was found in front of the building.

Evidence of a second monument, which was probably nearby, was found in a group of well-carved and decorated ashlar blocks. These were reused in a Byzantine church, which was exposed just S of the monumental building. Some of these stones belonged to a Doric frieze (in the Roman style) and others carried floral patterns, both often used in Jewish tomb monuments in Judea. The monument that yielded these stones could be the yet-unlocated tomb monument of Herod. Perhaps the long course was built for Herod's funeral procession (as described by Josephus), whereas the monumental building may have been a related triclinium (similar to ones integrated into burial complexes at Petra).

A ceremonial ritual bath with a double entrance was also exposed near the monumental building and could relate to this group of structures. However, only the discovery of Herod's tomb in this vicinity will prove such a hypothesis.

Following the death of Archelaus, Herod's son who ruled over Judea after him, Herodium was controlled for 60 years by the Roman procurators except for a short interval (42–45 A.D.) when Agrippa I was in power.

In 66 A.D., the site was occupied by the Jewish rebels, but probably surrendered a short time after the destruction of Jerusalem (*JW* 7.163). The rebels settled in the Mountain Palace-Fortress and turned its large triclinium into a synagogue similar to the one exposed at Masada.

During the Second Jewish Revolt against the Romans, the site was occupied again by Jewish warriors (the site is mentioned in Bar Kokhba's letters found in the Judean desert caves). These warriors built an intricate and sophisticated system of tunnels into the hill under the palace-fortress.

The site was abandoned until the 5th and 6th centuries, when a Byzantine community settled inside and beside the ruins. Three churches were exposed here during the excavations at Lower Herodium in addition to a chapel exposed by Corbo on the mountain. The site was finally abandoned at the beginning of the Early Arabic Period.

Bibliography

Corbo, V. 1963. L'Herodion di Gjebal Fureidis. *LASBF* 13: 219–77.

———. 1967. L'Herodion di Gjebal Fureidis. *LASBF* 17: 65–121.

Netzer, E. 1981. *Greater Herodium.* Qedem 13. Jerusalem.

Netzer, E., and Arzi, S. 1985. The Tunnels of Herodium. *Qad* 18/1–2: 33–38 (in Hebrew).

EHUD NETZER

HERODOTUS (PERSON) [Gk *Hērodotos*]. Herodotus (b. 484 B.C.) of Halicarnassus was "The father of History," the first important prose writer of Classical Greece. He wrote his famous *History of the Persian Wars* at Athens ca. 445 B.C. He then took part in the colonization of Thurii in southern Italy, where he died and was buried.

Herodotus traveled broadly in the Persian Empire after the Peace of Callias in 449 B.C. He is not only our chief source for Median and Persian history, but also gives us invaluable information about ancient Mesopotamia, Egypt, and Scythia (Yamauchi 1982).

Herodotus was above all a raconteur of entertaining stories. The fact that he himself did not believe an account did not deter him from relating an interesting tale. At times he gives several contradictory stories.

Herodotus' veracity was contested in antiquity by Ctesias and by Plutarch. It was challenged early in the 20th century by scholars who questioned whether Herodotus even visited Egypt or Babylonia (Yamauchi 1966: 10).

Few scholars now doubt that Herodotus visited Egypt (but cf. Armayor in *JARCE* 15: 59–73 for a more cautious assessment), though he does not mention the Sphinx nor the hypostyle hall at Karnak. He does transmit the name of the first pharaoh Menes and the builders of the pyramids at Giza: Cheops (Khufu), Chephren (Khofre), and Mycerinus (Menkaure). He knows very little about the early periods of Egyptian history, but he is our most important source for the 26th Dynasty (6th century B.C.).

With the exception of errors as to the size of the city and the height of the wall, Herodotus' descriptions of the city of Babylon have been remarkably vindicated by the excavations of that city by R. Koldewey from 1899–1917 (Ravn 1942). Herodotus, however, gives us very little information about Babylonian or Assyrian history (Baumgartner 1959). His story about Semiramis may reflect the Assyrian Sammuramat (Thompson 1937) and that about Nitocris may reflect the Assyrian Naqiʾa (Lewy 1951).

Herodotus claims that Deioces first unified the Medes. This name corresponds with the Assyrian Daiukku. Herodotus preserves accurately a number of Median and Persian names (Schmitt 1967; 1976). Herodotus' account of the rise of Cyrus can be confirmed by cuneiform texts. See ASTYAGES (PERSON).

His narrative of Cambyses' invasion of Egypt was based on anti-Persian Egyptian sources. His claim that Cambyses stabbed the Apis bull is directly contradicted by a sarcophagus which was dedicated to the Apis by Cambyses.

Herodotus gives us a full account of the accession of Darius and the overthrow of the usurper, Pseudo-Smerdis (3.66–88). He describes Darius' satrapies (3.88–96), his invasion of European Scythia (4.1–142), the Ionian Revolt from 499 to 494 (5.23–6.27), the punitive expedition shipwrecked at Mount Athos in 492 (6.42–44), and the famous battle of Marathon in 490 (6.112–17).

There are some passages in Herodotus which classicists have rejected as entirely fabricated, such as the celebrated "Constitutional Debate" (3.80–88), during which three conspirators discussed the respective merits of three forms of government: (1) Otanes argued for democracy, (2) Megabyzus for oligarchy, and (3) Darius for monarchy. Though these ideas and the mode of presentation are thoroughly Greek (Bringmann 1976), some Iranologists have argued that there may be elements in the passage which go back to Persian traditions (Gschnitzer 1977: 31; Dandamaev 1976: 145, 163; Schmitt 1977: 243–44).

When it comes to the account of the overthrow of the usurper Gaumata/Bardiya/Pseudo-Smerdis by Darius and his six colleagues, Herodotus reveals an impressive correspondence with the information which we can derive from Darius' Behistun Inscription (Wiesehöfer 1978: 96–97). He transmitted with remarkable accuracy all but one of the six names of Darius' colleagues. And even in that one case he gave us a genuine Persian name which may be explained as a later substitution (Schmitt 1977: 243–44). Among those who could have been able to supply Herodotus with such accurate information, passed down in their families, could have been the descendants of the six coconspirators (Wells 1907). Other descendants of these ruling families could have been contacted by Herodotus in western Asia Minor (Drews 1973: 82–83).

Though the correspondence of Herodotus with Darius' Behistun Inscription is undeniable, there are scholars who suspect that Darius was lying and that Herodotus was simply gullible in accepting the king's propaganda. This view was held by Olmstead (1948: 108–9) and has been followed by Dandamaev (1976: 116–21) and Balcer (1987). But despite difficulties in reconciling the Old Persian and the classical sources, the official version remains more credible than revisionist theories (see How and Wells 1912: vol. 1, 393; Altheim and Stiehl 1960: 75–105; Hinz 1979; Frye 1984: 99).

Herodotus grossly exaggerates the size of Xerxes' forces. But archaeological evidences, topographical surveys (Pritchett 1962a; 1963; 1969), and linguistic studies have for the most part vindicated the honesty and credibility of much in Herodotus' account of Xerxes' invasion of Greece in 480, such as his accounts of the battles of Thermopylae (7.205–26), of Salamis (8.78–97), and of Plataea (9.28–75).

The newly discovered Themistocles' Decree contradicts Herodotus on the nature of the evacuation of Athens before Xerxes' advance. In this case scholars are divided as to whether Herodotus or the inscription is more trustworthy. Pritchett (1962b: 43) argues: "Herodotus has in fact been proven to be correct in so many cases where he had earlier been doubted, that when a late document is found which flatly contradicts him, this document has to be considered *a priori* suspect."

Unfortunately for a history of Xerxes, Herodotus provides little information on the king after the battles of 479 B.C. See AHASUERUS (PERSON).

Bibliography

Altheim, F., and Stiehl, R. 1960. *Die aramäische Sprache unter den Achämeniden.* Frankfurt.

Balcer, J. M. 1987. *Herodotus and Bisitun.* Stuttgart.

Baumgartner, W. 1959. Herodots babylonische und assyrische Nachrichten. Pp. 282–331 in *Zum Alten Testament und seiner Umwelt.* Leiden.

Bringmann, K. 1976. Die Verfassungsdebatte bei Herodot 3, 80–82 und Dareios' Aufstieg zur Königsherrschaft. *Hermes* 104: 266–79.

Brown, T. S. 1965. Herodotus Speculates about Egypt. *AJP* 86: 60–76.

Dandamaev, M. A. 1976. *Persien unter den ersten Achämeniden.* Wiesbaden.

Drews, R. 1973. *The Greek Accounts of Eastern History.* Cambridge, MA.

Evans, J. A. S. 1968. Father of History or Father of Lies: The Reputation of Herodotus. *Classical Journal* 64: 11–17.

Fornara, C. 1971. *Herodotus: An Interpretive Essay.* Oxford.

Frye, R. N. 1984. *The History of Ancient Iran.* Munich.

Gammie, J. G. 1986. Herodotus on Kings and Tyrants. *JNES* 45: 171–95.

Godley, A. D., trans. 1960. *Herodotus.* LCL. 4 vols. Cambridge, MA.

Gschnitzer, F. 1977. *Die sieben Perser und das Königtum des Dareios.* Heidelberg.

Hegyi, D. 1973. Historical Authenticity of Herodotus in the Persian "Logoi." *Acta Antiqua* 21: 73–87.

Hinz, W. 1979. *Darius und die Perser II.* Baden-Baden.

How, W. W., and Wells, J. 1912. *A Commentary on Herodotus.* 2 vols. Oxford.

Hurt, J. 1982. *Herodotus and Greek History.* London.

Lewy, H. 1951. Nitokris-Naqî-a. *JNES* 10: 264–86.

Momigliano, A. 1958. The Place of Herodotus in the History of Historiography. *History* 43: 1–13.

Myres, J. L. 1953. *Herodotus.* Oxford.

Olmstead, A. T. 1948. *History of the Persian Empire.* Chicago.

Pritchett, W. K. 1962a. Xerxes' Route over Mount Olympus. *AJA* 65: 369–75.

———. 1962b. Herodotos and the Themistokles Decree. *AJA* 66: 43–47.

———. 1963. Xerxes' Fleet at the "Ovens." *AJA* 67: 1–6.

———. 1969. *Studies in Ancient Greek Topography.* Pt 2. Battlefields. Berkeley.

Ravn, O. E. 1942. *Herodotus' Description of Babylon.* Copenhagen.

Schmitt, R. 1967. Medisches und persisches Sprachgut bei Herodot. *ZDMG* 117: 119–45.

———. 1976. The Medo-Persian Names of Herodotus in the Light of the New Evidence from Persepolis. *Acta Antiqua* 24: 25–35.

———. 1977. Die Verfassungsdebatte bei Herodot 3, 80–82 und die Etymologie des Dareios-Namens. *Historia* 26: 243–44.

Selincourt, A. de. 1962. *The World of Herodotus.* London.

Sourdille, C. 1910. *Hérodote et la religion de l'Egypte.* Paris.

Spiegelberg, W. 1927. *The Credibility of Herodotus' Account of Egypt in the Light of the Egyptian Monuments.* Oxford.

Thompson, R. C. 1937. An Assyrian Parallel to an Incident in the Story of Semiramis. *Iraq* 4: 35–43.

Waters, K. H. 1972. *Herodotus on Tyrants and Despots.* Wiesbaden.

Wells, J. 1907. The Persian Friends of Herodotus. *JHS* 27: 37–47.

Wiesehöfer, J. 1978. *Der Aufstand Gaumātas und die Anfänge Dareios' I.* Bonn.

Yamauchi, E. 1966. *Composition and Corroboration in Classical and Biblical Studies.* Philadelphia.

———. 1982. *Foes from the Northern Frontier.* Grand Rapids.

EDWIN M. YAMAUCHI

HERON. See ZOOLOGY (FAUNA).

HESHBON (PLACE) [Heb *ḥešbôn*]. A town on the central plateau E of the Jordan River, mentioned 38 times in the Bible. For geographical and linguistic reasons it is identified with Tell Hesban (M.R. 226134), a mound which rises 895 m above sea level, guarding the NW edge of the rolling Madaba (Moabite) plain where a southern tributary to the Wadi Hesban begins to cut down sharply toward the Jordan River about 25 km to the W. It is about 55 km E of Jerusalem, 20 km SW of Amman, 6 km NE of Mount Nebo, and 185 m higher than ʿAin Hesban, the perennial spring with which it is associated.

Between 1968 and 1976 Andrews University sponsored five seasons of excavation; in 1978 Baptist Bible College (Pennsylvania) continued the excavation of a Byzantine church. These six seasons of archaeological excavation at Tell Hesban did not uncover any remains antedating about 1200 B.C. This poses a problem for the location of Sihon's Amorite capital referred to in Num 21:21–25 (cf. Deut 2:16–37, reiterated in Judg 11:12–28). Evidence of Amorite occupation may not have been found either because it is elsewhere on the site (unlikely) or because its (seminomadic) impermanent nature left no trace to be discovered (most likely). The most extreme options are to consider the biblical account unhistorical or at least anachronistic (now favored by such OT scholars as Miller and Van Seters) or to seek the Amorite capital at another location; e.g., Jalul (a view favored by Horn). Most scholars would identify Tell Hesban with Greco-Roman Esbus, based on coin and milestone evidence coupled with such geographical specifications as required by Ptolemy and Eusebius. If Cross' reading of an Ammonite ostracon found at the site in 1978 is accepted, it as well would support such an identification for Iron Age Heshbon. During this period it was alternately Reubenite, Gadite, Levite, Moabite, and finally Ammonite (Num 32:1–7; Josh 13:15–28; 21:34–40; 1 Chr 6:81; Isaiah 15, 16; Jeremiah 48, 49). Altogether, the Andrews University expedition has reconstructed 19 superimposed strata from the excavated remains, covering a period from about 1200 B.C. to A.D. 1500.

A. Iron Age Remains

The Iron Age remains (ca. 1200–500 B.C.) are very fragmentary due to periodic removals of earlier strata on top of the hill by later builders; nevertheless evidence for at least four strata remains. Stratum 19 (12th–11th century) represents probably a small unfortified village dependent on an agrarian-pastoral economy. In its earlier phase its most notable installation was a long (15 m exposed) 3.6 m-deep trench crudely carved out of bedrock on the tell's S shelf. There is no real clue as to its purpose though suggestions have included a moat for defense, storage, or cultic activity, subterranean habitation, or a water channel if not a narrow reservoir itself. In its later phase this installation was filled with soil and into it were built both the cobbled floor of a room and a 2.5 m-wide "filler" wall. An egg-shaped cistern may also be associated with this phase; this produced so many loom weights that we infer the presence of a cottage industry. Stratum 18 (10th century) left no *in situ* remains but its typologically later pottery was found in deep dump layers outside the contemporary settlement on the W slope; it may have been a continuation of the stratum 19 village. Stratum 17 (9th–8th centuries) is also represented by sloping debris layers dumped to the W. During this phase was the initial construction, on the tell's S shelf, of a nearly 2-million-liter-capacity reservoir, 15 m to a side (its thrice-plastered E wall supplemented a bedrock cut with a header-stretcher retaining wall), and 6 m deep. Could this be the pool referred to in Cant 7:4? Though several channels carved out of adjoining bedrock funneled rainwater to the reservoir, its capacity appears to exceed the normal amount of winter rain that would fall on the catchment area; perhaps it was intended that extra water be transported up to the reservoir from below the mound. If so, perhaps this stratum is what is left of Mesha's attempt to fortify his N border with Israel. (The Mesha Stone from the 9th century does not mention Heshbon but since Medeba, Nebo, and Jahaz all came back into Moabite hands at that time, presumably Heshbon did as well. At least by the close of the 8th century and into the 7th, Heshbon appears to be under firm Moabite control, because it figures in both extant recensions of a prophetic oracle against Moab [Isa 15:4; 16:8, 9; and Jer 48:2, 34, 35], where its fields, fruit, and harvest are mentioned. By this time it may have been a steep *tell,* for fugitives stop in its shadow [Jer 48:45].) Stratum 16 (7th–6th century) was the best preserved Iron Age stratum; its remains indicate a general prosperity and that the settlement continued to grow, probably clustered around a fort. A few scattered domestic units came to light on the W slope and the reservoir continued in use—perhaps a part of a way station or supply depot on the King's Highway. It was probably controlled by the Ammonites, to judge from the pottery and several ostraca found in the reservoir fill. (These ostraca have already been important in enlarging a knowledge of the Ammonite dialect and script.) Stratum 16 may have come to a violent end, considering the great quantity of ash in the debris scraped from the abandoned town into the reservoir by the (Maccabean?) rebuilders in the 2d century B.C.

B. Hellenistic and Roman Remains

According to the post–Hebrew Bible literary sources (mostly Josephus), the site should have been occupied in the following periods: *Hellenistic* (2d–mid 1st century)—perhaps moving from Ptolemaic/Tobiad control to Maccabean; *Early Roman* (late 1st century B.C.–early 2d century A.D.)—Herodian fortress populated with veterans, later sacked by Jews at the beginning of the Jewish War (A.D. 66); *Late Roman* (2d century)—Ptolemy giving site's exact location; (3d century)—locally mined coins during reign of Elagabalus; (4th century)—Eusebius' *Onomasticon's* site location; and all through this period—milestone finds counted from Esbus along the road down to Livias. This literary evidence was confirmed by excavation. After about a 300-year abandonment of the site, Tell Hesban was reoccupied in the Late Hellenistic period. The remains from the Hellenistic and Roman periods (ca. 200 B.C.–A.D. 365) comprise at least five strata. Stratum 15 (ca. 200–63 B.C.) consisted primarily of a rectangular military fort at the site's summit probably surrounded by the dwellings of dependents, often in association with bell-shaped subterranean store silos. In stratum 14 (ca. 63 B.C.–A.D. 130) Esbus came under the control of Herod the Great, probably as a border fort against the Nabateans. There is abundant evidence for extensive underground dwellings on the mound and characteristic Herodian period family tombs in the cemetery where two such tombs were found sealed by rolling stones. The town of stratum 14 was destroyed by an earthquake so stratum 13 (A.D. 130–ca. 193) contained much new building. A new inn with an enclosed courtyard S of the fort testifies to the increased traffic past the road junction (*Via Nova* and Esbus-Livias) at which Roman Esbus was located. In stratum 12 (ca. A.D. 193–284) the inn was partially rebuilt and well used. On the acropolis, earlier masonry was incorporated into what has been interpreted as a small temple—perhaps the one depicted on the Elagabalus coin minted for Esbus, a very fine example of which was found at the site in 1973. Access to the temple from the S was by a ramp. Stratum 11 (ca. A.D. 284–365) continued to demonstrate a modest level of prosperity. A porch was added to the temple and a double colonnade built eastward from it. The inn to the S of the acropolis platform was demolished and a wide monumental stairway replaced the earlier earth ramp. The stratum came to an abrupt end with the severe earthquake of A.D. 365.

C. Byzantine and Early Arab Remains

Apart from the earthquake the transition from the Roman to the Byzantine periods was a gradual one. The Roman cemetery continued to be used. At least six strata encompass the Byzantine and Early Arab remains at Tell Hesban (A.D. 365–ca. 1000). In stratum 10 (A.D. 365–408) the growing Christian community was apparently significant enough to prevent the rebuilding of the temple that had been destroyed by the earthquake but not quite strong enough to immediately construct a church. In the 4th century, Esbus appeared for the first time as an episcopal seat when Gennadius, its bishop, is mentioned twice in the Acts of the Council of Nicea. Stratum 9 (A.D. 408–551) saw the construction of a slightly asymmetrical basilica-type church on the acropolis (plaster apparently coming from a large subterranean lime kiln to the S). The stratum may have been brought to a close by the earthquake of 551. Again, we know from literary sources that Esbus sent its bishop to the councils of Ephesus (A.D. 431) and Chalcedon (A.D. 457). In addition to reconstruction activity, possibly necessitated by the 551 earthquake, stratum 8 (A.D. 551–614) also witnessed the construction of another basilica-type church with well-preserved mosaic floors to the N of the acropolis. The reconstructed acropolis church had a much less ornate mosaic floor than its predecessor. After the close of stratum 8, probably brought on by the invasion of the Sassanid Persians, stratum 7 remains (A.D. 614–661) are very scant. Occupation seems to have centered S of the acropolis church within the acropolis circumvallation wall. Some correspondence of Pope Martin I (A.D. 649) shows that Esbus was still an important bishopric, however, in the middle of the 7th century. The coming of Islam in the Umayyad period coincided with a slight increase in activity in stratum 6 (A.D. 661–750). A large oven was constructed in the mosaic floor of one of the anterooms of the Late Byzantine acropolis church which by then was probably already in ruins since there is no evidence for an Umayyad destruction. With the move of the center of Islamic rule to the E in the Abbasid period, there was a sharp decline in population in stratum 5 (A.D. 750–ca. 1000). No architectural remains from the period were uncovered so the tell may have been occupied by a seminomadic population before subsequent apparent abandonment. Indeed, after the 7th century, the name Esbus disappears from literary sources, reappearing only centuries later in its Arabic form *Ḥesbân*. Its mention in the Abbasid period by ᶜAbu-Djaᶜfar Muhammad at-Tabari' (839–923) in reference to Israelite history does not make it clear whether a Jabal Ḥesban (the *tell*?) existed in his time or not.

D. Ayyubid/Mamluk Remains

Although a village of no particular significance during the earlier periods of Islamic rule, after a gap in sedentary occupation, Hesban flourished again immediately after the Crusades. The first clear literary reference to Hesban as an inhabited place comes in 1184 in connection with a campaign of Saladin recorded by Beha ed-Din. In the Arabic geographical literature originating from before the time of the Mamluks (ca. 1260–1456), Hesban is not mentioned. By the 14th century, however, it even replaced ᶜAmman as the capital of the Belqa' district of central Transjordan and is mentioned by Ibn Fadl Allah al-Umari (1301–1348), Dimishqi (died 1327), Abu el-Feda (died 1331), and several others. Its excavated remains comprise at least three strata (ca. 1200–1456) which were relatively well preserved compared to earlier remains. Stratum 4 (ca. 1200–1260) represents an Ayyubid village's occupational surfaces and terracing around two cisterns on the mound's summit. Stratum 3 (ca. 1260–1400) is characterized by a large number of soil and architectural loci which reflect extensive new Early Mamluk construction activity using the existing Roman-Byzantine ruins as a base: at the tell's summit was an elaborate U-shaped building complex (including a bathhouse) reached by a stairway from the S. A number of vaulted rooms opened onto a central courtyard created by clearing the debris of the collapsed Byzantine church. Because the postal route from Karak to Damascus passed through the town, these remains may be interpreted as an inn complex to care for travelers and their animals. The mound was surrounded by numerous domestic dwellings and cisterns which covered most of the slopes above terraces used for agriculture. Stratum 2 (ca. 1400–1456) began with a general collapse of the town in the Late Mamluk period (due probably to plague or warfare) and is characterized by gradual abandonment leading, apparently, to the tell's desertion until the late 19th century when stratum 1 marks the gradual return to limited occupation in the Ottoman and modern periods. Several Western travelers and explorers visited Hesban, particularly during the 19th and 20th centuries, from Seetzen in 1806 to Glueck in the early 1930s, many of them recording for posterity what they saw.

Bibliography

Boraas, R. S., and Geraty, L. T. 1976. *Heshbon 1974*. Berrien Springs, MI.

———. 1978. *Heshbon 1976*. Berrien Springs, MI.

———. 1979. The Long Life of Tell Hesban, Jordan. *Archaeology* 32/1: 10–20.

Boraas, R. S., and Horn, S. H. 1969. *Heshbon 1968*. Berrien Springs, MI.

———. 1973. *Heshbon 1971*. Berrien Springs, MI.

———. 1975. *Heshbon 1973*. Berrien Springs, MI.

Bullard, R. G. 1972. Geological Study of the Heshbon Area. *AUSS* 10/2: 129–41.

Cross, F. M., Jr. 1986. An Unpublished Ammonite Ostracon from Hesban. Pp. 475–89 in *The Archaeology of Jordan and Other Studies Presented to S. H. Horn*, ed. L. T. Geraty and L. G. Herr. Berrien Springs, MI.

Ibach, R. D., Jr. 1987. *Archaeological Survey of the Hesban Region (Hesban 5)*, ed. Ø. S. LaBianca. Berrien Springs, MI.

Lacelle, L., and LaBianca, Ø. S., et al. 1986. *Environmental Founda-*

tions: Studies of Climatical, Geological, Hydrological, and Phytological Conditions in Hesban and Vicinity (Hesban 2). Berrien Springs, MI.
Lawlor, J. I. 1980. The Excavation of the North Church at Hesban, Jordan: A Preliminary Report. *AUSS* 18/1: 65–76.
Lugenbeal, E. N., and Sauer, J. A. 1972. Seventh–Sixth Century B.C. Pottery from Area B at Heshbon. *AUSS* 10/1: 21–69.
Miller, J. M. 1977. The Israelite Occupation of Canaan. Pp. 213–84 in *IJH*.
Sauer, J. A. 1973. *Heshbon Pottery 1971.* Berrien Springs, MI.
Terian, A. 1971. Coins from the 1968 Excavations at Heshbon. *AUSS* 9/2: 147–60.
———. 1974. Coins from the 1971 Excavations at Heshbon. *AUSS* 12/1: 35–46.
———. 1980. Coins from the 1976 Excavations at Heshbon. *AUSS* 18/2: 173–80.
Van Seters, J. 1983. *In Search of History.* New Haven.
Vyhmeister, W. K. 1968. The History of Heshbon from Literary Sources. *AUSS* 6/2: 158–77.
Vyhmeister, W. K.; Ferch, A. J.; and Russell, M. B. 1989. *Historical Foundations: Studies of Literary References to Hesban and Vicinity (Hesban 3),* ed. L. T. Geraty and L. G. Running. Berrien Springs, MI.

LAWRENCE T. GERATY

HESHMON (PLACE) [Heb *ḥešmôn*]. Judging from its position in the list of Negeb settlements assigned to the tribe of Judah (Josh 15:21–29), the town of Heshmon (Josh 15:27) was situated somewhere between Hazargaddah and Beth-pelet in the vicinity of Beer-sheba, though its precise location has not been identified. The name Heshmon is lacking in the LXX's rendering of the list, an omission which some scholars (Boling *Joshua* AB, 379) attribute to haplography, while others (Aharoni *EncMiqr* 3: 316) suggest that the name was a later addition. Heshmon is also missing from the list of Simeonite settlements (Josh 19:2–9), which closely parallels the list of Josh 15:21–29 in many respects (Cross and Wright 1956: 214). The term "Hasmonean," a designation for the Maccabees used by the Mishna, Talmud, and occasionally Josephus, is frequently derived from "Heshmon," but the sources themselves do not confirm such a conjeccture, and other derivations are possible. See HASHMONAH (PLACE).

Bibliography

Cross, F. M., and Wright, G. E. 1956. The Boundary and Province Lists of the Kingdom of Judah. *JBL* 75: 202–26.

STEVEN WEITZMAN

HESHVAN [Heb *ḥešwān*]. The eighth month of the modern Hebrew calendar, roughly corresponding to October and November, and equivalent to the ancient month of MARCHESHVAN. See CALENDARS.

HESI, TELL EL- (M.R. 124106). A site in the S Shephelah whose biblical identification is a matter of dispute. It was, however, essentially the first Palestinian site to be excavated (by William Flinders Petrie in 1890) using a scientific method.

A. Location and Topography
B. Identification
C. History of Excavations
D. History of Occupation

A. Location and Topography

Tell el-Hesi is located in the SE coastal plain, 23 km from the Mediterranean coast and 26 km NE of Gaza and occupies a cluster of barchan sand dunes on the W bank of the Wadi Hesi (Nahal Shiqma). The site is comprised of a 25-acre, roughly rectangular lower city, with a small acropolis at its NE corner. The base of the acropolis is about 4 acres, while it narrows to only 0.69 acres at its summit. The acropolis, about 150 m above sea level, was originally a sand dune 17 m high. Occupational remains have added 21 m to its height. Three sand dunes form the S border of the lower city, and on the E, W, and N perimeter, the site is bordered by deep wadis.

Hesi's location at the SE limit of the "Philistine Plain" was too far inland to influence the coastal highway, although Hesi was able to control some of the internal road systems, in particular a branch of the *Via Maris* which turned E a short distance N of the site. Its position also allowed Hesi to exert control over the S approaches to the Shephelah. In addition, the site is located at a natural border. Immediately to the S, the semi-arid Negeb region begins. This places Hesi in a location of fluctuating rainfall which makes agricultural production unpredictable.

B. Identification

The ancient name of the site is unknown. Conder (1878: 20) was the first to identify Hesi with Lachish. This identification was reinforced by Bliss' discovery, in his 1891 excavations, of an Amarna tablet which mentioned Lachish (1894: 184). It was not until 1924 that Albright rejected the identification of Hesi with Lachish. He pointed out the small size of the site and the fact that its location did not fit Eusebius' placement of Lachish in the Shephelah, seven Roman miles S of Eleutheropolis (Beth Jibrin). Albright concluded (1924: 8) that Hesi was "almost certainly Eglon," a Canaanite city-state conquered by the Israelites (Josh 10:34; 15:39). Excavations at Tell ed-Duweir in the 1930s revealed written materials which confirmed that site's identity as Lachish. The identification of Hesi with Eglon was maintained by Wright (1971). More recently, however, some scholars have argued that Tell Aitun may be identified with Eglon (Rainey *IDBSup*, 252). The biblical accounts locate Eglon in the Shephelah. Hesi's location several km W of these foothills probably disqualifies Hesi as a contender. Hesi's ancient identity remains uncertain.

C. History of Excavations

Hesi holds a unique place in the history of Near Eastern archaeology. It was at Hesi, in 1890, that the site's first excavator, Sir Flinders Petrie, developed the foundations of modern archaeological method in applying the principles of stratigraphic excavation and ceramic chronology. For the first time, pottery was used as a chronological indicator based on its stratigraphic location. His publication of the Hesi excavation (1891) was the first to present architecture and ceramics in a sequential manner, to correlate pottery and artifacts with stratigraphy, and to illustrate pottery in section drawings.

Petrie excavated at Hesi for six weeks, and in this short time was able to formulate an occupational history of the site. He identified three major occupational periods: Amorite (ca. 1700 B.C.E.), Phoenician (1350–850 B.C.E.) and Jewish (ending 450 B.C.E.). His Amorite period can now be identified with the EB Age, his Phoenician with the LB and Iron ages, and his Jewish primarily with the Persian and Hellenistic periods.

Excavations continued in 1891 and 1892 with a new director, Frederick Jones Bliss. His strategy was to excavate a large portion of the site stratigraphically to virgin soil. At the conclusion of his work, Bliss had removed almost one third of the acropolis, and "Bliss' Cut" has remained a distinguishing feature of the site ever since.

Bliss identified eleven layers of architectural features and grouped them into eight strata or "cities." City I belonged to Petrie's Amorite occupation, Cities II, III, and IV to the Phoenician, and Cities V through VIII to the Jewish. Bliss' publication of these "cities" in 1894 was the first attempt to present large-scale architectural remains in a stratigraphic context.

Following an 80-year hiatus, excavations resumed at Hesi in 1970, when the Joint Archaeological Expedition began its work. The expedition carried out eight field seasons (1970, 1971, 1973, 1975, 1977, 1979, 1981, 1983). Its goals were: (1) to investigate in more detail, and with more refined methods, the structures found by Petrie and Bliss; (2) to integrate scientific disciplines for the purpose of achieving a broader data base and interpretive results; and (3) to provide a carefully structured educational experience for participating volunteers. During its eight seasons of excavation, the expedition investigated the acropolis (Field I), its S slope (Field III) and the lower city (Fields II, IV, V, VI, VII, VIII, and IX).

D. History of Occupation

Excavation has confirmed that the site was occupied almost continuously from the Chalcolithic through the Hellenistic periods. Unstratified Roman pottery was also found. Following a gap of several centuries, the site was again in use during the 16th to 18th and 20th centuries C.E. See the following table.

A. STRATIGRAPHIC CHART FOR FIELD I (ACROPOLIS) AND FIELD III

Stratum	*Date*	*Cultural Period*	*Characteristics*
I	After C.E. 1900	Modern	Military trenching
II	ca. C.E. 1600–1900	Turkish	Muslim cemetery
III	Yet to be determined	Late Arabic	Fragmentary walls and surfaces
IV	4th–3d centuries B.C.E.	Hellenistic	Three phases, Bliss City VIII
V	6th–4th centuries B.C.E.	Persian	Four phases, Bliss City VII
VI	6th century B.C.E.	Iron II	Poor construction of houses
VII	9th–6th centuries B.C.E.	Iron II	Four phases, Bliss City VI
VIII	11th (?) century B.C.E.	Iron I	Probably same phase as Petrie's Pilaster Building
pre-VIII	34th–15th centuries B.C.E.	Iron I, Late Bronze, EB III, Chalco	Twelve phases of occupation, unexcavated

B. STRATIGRAPHIC CHART FOR FIELD VI

Phase	*Date*	*Cultural Period*	*Characteristics*
1	After C.E. 1900	Modern	Military trenching
2	ca. C.E. 1600–1800	Turkish	Muslim cemetery
3	Yet to be determined	Late Arabic	Fragmentary pits and surfaces
4	28th or 27th to 24th centuries B.C.E.	EB III (and EB II?)	Five phases, Bliss City I

1. Chalcolithic Period. Evidence indicates that use of the site began during the Chalcolithic Period. Although a good quantity of pottery has been found on the acropolis and in the lower city, stratified remains are confined to two pits at the base of the S slope of the acropolis (Toombs 1974: 31). Probably more Chalcolithic remains exist at the unexcavated base of occupation on the acropolis.

2. Early Bronze Age. The EB was the only period when occupation at Hesi covered the entire 25 acres of the site. On the acropolis, remains of seven EB phases were identified and were associated with pottery from EB I and II; EB III pottery was characteristic of the lower city.

Probes by all three excavators in the lower city indicated a shallow depth of domestic occupation. On the S ridge of dunes, the Joint Expedition uncovered the EB city wall in Fields V, VI, and IX and traced it for 82 m along the S and 95 m along the E sides. The wall was about 5 m wide, with towers placed at intervals. One tower found by Bliss in City I (1894: 26) and one found by the Joint Expedition were almost identical in shape and each contained two long chambers connected by a narrow passageway. Along the outer face of the city wall was a deep deposit of water-and-wind-sorted ash with a heavy organic content. At the SE corner of the site, where the city wall turns to the N, a glacislike deposit of crushed limestone was laid against the outer face of the wall and extended to the N for 60 m. Its unusually wide (9 m), horizontal exposure suggests that it served primarily for erosion control. Inside the city wall, remains of domestic and industrial activity were found. Five phases were identified, and all belonged to EB III (Toombs 1983: 35–44; Doermann and Fargo 1985: 13–22).

The EB city wall was constructed of mold-made mud bricks of varying colors and composition. Many of the bricks were made of a humus-filled clay no longer available in the region. Also present in the remains was *Gryaulus piscinarum*, a snail which lives in sluggish streams and swamps. The presence of pistachio in the ash deposits adds to the evidence that the climate at Hesi was noticeably more moist in the EB than it is today.

It is likely that the earliest settlement at Hesi began in late Chalcolithic or EB I and centered on the acropolis. In late EB II–EB III, the population increased and the site expanded to 25 acres. At some point during EB III, Hesi appears to have been abandoned. There is no evidence of destruction. The contents of the ash layers suggest an economy based on the raising of cattle, sheep, and goats, and the production of emmer wheat. There is strong evidence for progressive desiccation which extended northward from Egypt during the EB. This climatic change, coupled with the exhaustion of natural resources to accommodate an increasing population, proved too much of a strain for the environment. As with most other sites in the area, Hesi was abandoned for the rest of the millennium.

3. Middle Bronze Age. Following the abandonment during EB III, there is a gap in occupation at Hesi. None of the excavators has found any structural remains of the MB, although occasional MB sherds have been identified. The nearby site of Tell en-Nagila, 5.5 km SSE of Hesi, experienced a period of prosperity during MB II–III, but occupation at Hesi was not resumed.

4. Late Bronze Age. Bliss' Cities II, III, and IV contained LB material. Cities II and IV had large public buildings. Of particular note was an Amarna tablet found in City III (1894: 184). The Joint Expedition did not reach the LB levels on the acropolis. During exposure of later strata, three phases of structures containing Late Bronze pottery were encountered. In the lower city, significant quantities of LB sherds were found in Field V, but any associated structures had suffered erosion.

5. Iron Age I. The Joint Expedition reached the Iron Age I level (Stratum VIII) only in one probe. Fragments of a wall and floor were covered with destruction debris. The associated pottery was dated to the 11th century (Doermann and Fargo 1985: 8–9). Petrie's "Pilaster Building" is probably to be dated to this stratum (Petrie 1891: 23). This stratum also corresponds to City V of Bliss.

6. Iron Age II. A major engineering project was undertaken in the 9th century (Stratum VIId). Portions of a structure had been identified by Petrie as the "Manasseh Wall" and a "long range of chambers." Bliss also had excavated a small portion of this construction in City VI. Stratum VIId was constructed to raise the S half of the acropolis by 6–7 m, to provide a platform on which occupational structures could be built and to defend the site by means of two large mud-brick walls, one at the crest and the other at the base of the acropolis. This construction surrounded the acropolis on all sides, although erosion has removed much of the E portion. See Fig. HES.01.

The foundation for the entire system was a mud-brick wall, 12 m wide, at the base of the slope. A series of four terraces consolidated the slope. Above the terraces stood the Upper Wall (Petrie's Manasseh Wall; 3 m wide). A chamber and fill system was constructed on the summit. This structure consisted of chambers composed of parallel walls connected by cross walls (see structure A on Fig. HES.01). This system was what Petrie identified as a long range of chambers. The space between the chambers and the area enclosed by the rows of chambers was filled with earth to form a solid platform of walls and fill (Toombs 1983: 25–33; Doermann and Fargo 1985: 1–6).

The structures of the Iron II occupation were built directly on the platform created by the chamber and fill system. The first phase in the 9th century consisted of a large courtyard building. Above this were several smaller

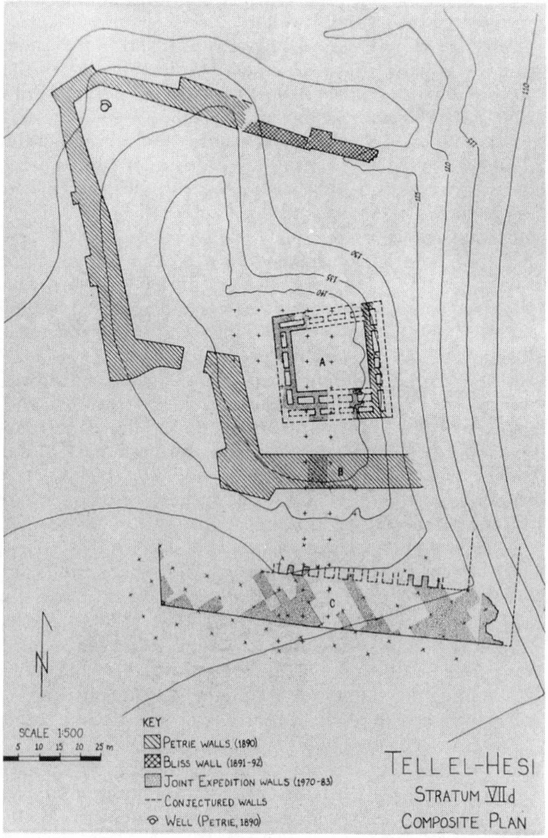

HES.01. Composite site plan of Tell el-Hesi—Stratum VIId, Iron II. *A*, chamber and fill system; *B*, upper wall; *C*, lower wall. *(Drawing by N. Clark and J. Blakely, courtesy of V. M. Fargo)*

structures which belonged to the 8th–6th centuries. A heavy layer of ash and destruction debris covered the 6th-century occupation. Above this was a poorly built mud-brick house (Stratum VI), which probably represents a relatively brief resettlement by a poor population during the time of the Exile. Its transitory nature may explain why this stratum was not identified by Bliss (O'Connell, Rose, and Toombs 1978: 78–80).

The massive constructions of Stratum VIId and VIIc were most likely preparations for Hesi's use as a military outpost. A group of small Iron Age sites extends along the E edge of the coastal plain: Bornat, Areini, Sheqef, Hesi, Quneitirah, and Muleihah. These probably served as the outer perimeter of defense for Lachish and SW Judah. After a number of Egyptian raids, Rehoboam established a new network of outposts to protect the S and W borders of Judah (2 Chr 11:5–12). At this time, the important fortress at Lachish was constructed. This fortress is almost identical in plan to that at Hesi. Rehoboam's defensive system continued in use through the 8th century until it was destroyed during the Assyrian conquest of Judah. In the 7th and 6th centuries, the Hesi occupation was no longer military, but residential and industrial. The Iron II occupation came to an end with a destruction in the 6th century, very probably associated with the Babylonian conquest (Fargo 1987).

7. Persian Period. Hesi regained its position as a military/governmental outpost during the Persian period. Once again, a massive building project produced a large platform on which a sizable mud-brick building was placed. The large building served as a small citadel and had casemate walls surrounding a courtyard (Rose and Toombs 1976: 43–46).

In contrast with earlier periods, there was a sizable quantity of imported pottery, in particular Greek wares. There was no evidence of residential dwellings on the acropolis, although there were signs of domestic activities. Characteristic of the Persian occupation were large, deep pits 1 to 2 m wide and equally deep. These pits, probably originally used for grain storage and later for garbage, contained vast quantities of broken pottery, seeds, bones, and a variety of implements and weapons which imply a range of activities (O'Connell and Rose 1980: 77; Toombs 1983: 33–35).

The large quantity of amphorae and transport vessels suggests storage or transport of materials, probably grain grown in the fields around the site. The lack of permanent housing structures may indicate a mobile population. Beginning around 500 B.C.E. and for about a century (a date based on the Attic ceramics), Hesi probably became a semipermanent depot and storehouse for the Persian military. It may also have been converted temporarily into a staging area and supply dump for Persian military raids into Egypt around 460–455 B.C.E. and 404–401 B.C.E. On the S slope of the acropolis was a small cemetery of the Persian period which contained burials of men, women, and children. This may imply a more permanent population to oversee the grain business. At the end of the 5th century, Persian troops began to focus their attention on areas farther to the N and no longer needed a depot at Hesi. This allowed Egypt to regain control of S Palestine, and in 401 B.C.E. the Persian occupation at Hesi ended (Blakely and Horton 1986; Bennett and Blakely fc.).

8. Hellenistic Period. The Hellenistic occupation at Hesi had three phases, all of which were of a domestic nature. Bliss' plan for City VIII was a composite of all three phases. Unusual in this period was the use of stone for walls, as foundations for brick walls, and in a stone-lined drain and basin. In the latest phase there was little architecture, but instead a large number of pits, full of pottery, artifacts, and faunal and botanical material. Remains of this period were fragmentary, because burials from the Muslim cemetery (Stratum II) had badly disturbed the Hellenistic stratum (Rose and Toombs 1976: 46–47; Rose, Toombs, and O'Connell 1978: 126–28).

9. Late Arabic Period. Following the end of the Hellenistic occupation, the summit of the site was roughly leveled, and it may have been used sporadically for agriculture. On the acropolis, there was virtually no evidence for the Roman, Byzantine, or early Arabic periods. A few remains such as pits, hearths, surfaces, and fragmentary walls (Stratum III) apparently belong to the Turkish period and probably were associated with agriculture and stock raising (Rose, Toombs, and O'Connell 1978: 128–29).

10. Muslim Cemetery. Bliss had noted the presence of burials immediately below the surface. He identified them as Arab and suggested that they were 200 to 300 years old. This date has been confirmed, and the burials of Stratum II have been dated to about C.E. 1600–1800. The cemetery is located on the acropolis and along the dunes on the S rim of the site. The S dunes were probably used because of the presence of a shrine of a minor Muslim saint. The Joint Expedition excavated over 800 burials. The burials were simple earth graves, and the bottoms of the shafts were sometimes lined with stone slabs. Stone slabs also were used as capstones. The body was placed so that the eyes were directed toward Mecca. There were few grave goods, but some jewelry (Toombs 1985).

11. Military Trenching. The most recent use of the site occurred after C.E. 1900. At various times in this century, military confrontations have taken place in the Hesi area. Because of the excellent view of the surrounding area, troops have been stationed at Hesi and have dug trenches and machine gun emplacements (Toombs 1985).

Bibliography

Albright, W. F. 1924. Researches of the School in Western Judaea. *BASOR* 15: 2–11.

Bennett, W. J., Jr., and Blakely, J. A. fc. *Tell el-Hesi: The Persian Period (Stratum V),* ed. K. G. O'Connell. Excavation Reports of the American Schools of Oriental Research: Tell el-Hesi 3.

Blakely, J. A., and Horton, F. L., Jr. 1986. South Palestinian Bes Vessels of the Persian Period. *Levant* 18: 111–19.

Bliss, F. J. 1894. *A Mound of Many Cities or Tell el Hesy Excavated.* London.

Conder, C. R. 1878. Notes from the Memoir. *PEFQS* 18–22.

Doermann, R. W., and Fargo, V. M. 1985. Tell el-Hesi, 1983. *PEQ* 117: 1–24.

Fargo, V. M. 1987. Hesi in the Iron II Period: A Judean Border Fortress. Pp. 157–64 in *Archaeology and Biblical Interpretation,* ed. L. G. Perdue; L. E. Toombs; and G. L. Johnson. Atlanta.

O'Connell, K. G., and Rose, D. G. 1980. Tell el-Hesi, 1979. *PEQ* 112: 73–91.

O'Connell, K. G.; Rose, D. G.; and Toombs, L. E. 1978. Tell el-Hesi, 1977. *PEQ* 110: 75–90.

Petrie, W. M. F. 1891. *Tell el-Hesy (Lachish).* London.

Rose, D. G., and Toombs, L. E. 1976. Tell el-Hesi, 1973 and 1975. *PEQ* 108: 41–54.

Rose, D. G.; Toombs, L. E.; and O'Connell, K. G. 1978. Four Seasons of Excavation at Tell el-Hesi: A Preliminary Report. Pp. 109–49 in *Preliminary Excavation Reports: Bab edh-Dhra*ᶜ*, Sardis, Meiron, Tell el-Hesi, Carthage (Punic),* ed. D. N. Freedman. AASOR 43. Cambridge, MA.

Toombs, L. E. 1974. Tell el-Hesi, 1970–71. *PEQ* 106: 19–31.

———. 1983. Tell el-Hesi, 1981. *PEQ* 115: 25–46.

———. 1985. *Tell el-Hesi: Modern Military Trenching and Muslim Cemetery in Field I, Strata I–II,* ed. K. G. O'Connell. Excavation Reports of the American Schools of Oriental Research: Tell el-Hesi 2. Waterloo, Ontario.

Wright, G. E. 1971. A Problem of Ancient Topography: Lachish and Eglon. *BA* 34: 76–86.

VALERIE M. FARGO

ḤET. The eighth letter of the Hebrew alphabet.

HETH (PERSON) [Heb *ḥēt*]. A son of Canaan, grandson of Ham and great-grandson of Noah (Gen 10:15; 1 Chr 1:13). His descendants settled in the area of Hebron, in the hill country south of Jerusalem. Early in the 2d millennium, at the time of the death of his wife Sarah, Abraham negotiated the purchase of a cave site for her burial from descendants ("sons") of Heth (Genesis 23). The transaction shows some of the legal procedures of the period. Tradition holds that Abraham himself is also buried there (25:10), as is his grandson Jacob (50:13). Rebekah, Jacob's mother, does not consider these descendants of Heth suitable for marriage to her son (27:46) because they are not ethnically related to Abraham's immediate family, though her son Esau does marry two of their women (26:34).

These people continued to occupy the land through the Conquest under Joshua and the settlement of Israel (Deut 7:1; Josh 3:10; Judg 3:5). This is evident when Solomon also takes a Hittite wife (1 Kgs 11:1) and David commits adultery with Bathsheba, the wife of Uriah who is called a Hittite (2 Sam 11; 12:9–10). All of the names given, apart possibly from Uriah, are Semitic.

These people are apparently distinct from the larger group of Hittites or *bĕnē ḥēt,* "sons of Heth." These were an Indo-European people who established an empire in Asia Minor in the middle half of the 2d millennium B.C. They continued in international politics as city-states until the 8th century B.C.

Bibliography

Hoffner, H. A. 1969. Some Contributions of Hittitology to Old Testament Study. *TynBul* 20: 27–37.

———. 1973. The Hittites and the Hurrians. Pp. 225–26 in *POTT.*

DAVID W. BAKER

HETHLON (PLACE) [Heb *ḥetlôn*]. A place mentioned in one of Ezekiel's visions as located on the N boundary of restored Israel (Ezek 47:15; 48:1). Its location was apparently somewhere between the Mediterranean coast and the "entrance of Hamath" at the N end of Lebanon, or it may be identical to the "entrance of Hamath" (Num 34:8; Ezek 47:15 [LXX]; 48:1). Some have identified Hethlon as Heitela, NE of Tripoli on the Lebanon coast; others with ʿAdlûn, along the Lebanon coast halfway between the mouth of the Litani River and Sarepta. Its precise location is not known.

RAY L. ROTH

HEXAPLA OF ORIGEN, THE. One of the great achievements of textual criticism, Origen's six-columned presentation of various Gk versions of the OT was begun in Alexandria either in 230 or in 238, and was finished in Caesarea in about 245. Origen's aim was to establish a relationship between the Septuagint (LXX) and Hebrew texts of the OT. His motivation was not purely text-critical, although his writings show that he obviously enjoyed textual study, and he could hardly have got to the end of such an undertaking without an aptitude for it. But he had also a reason of a somewhat different character—he wished to establish for the Church a sound basis in its dialogue with Judaism. As will become clear, the Hexapla showed those passages which were accepted either only by Jews or only by Christians. Origen's approach is set out in his reply to a letter from Julius Africanus (ca. 240). He writes, "I make it my endeavour not to be ignorant of their [LXX's] various readings, lest in my controversies with the Jews I should quote to them what is not found in their copies, and that I may make some use of what is found there, even although it should not be in our Scriptures."

To achieve his aim, Origen brought together all available materials relating to the Hebrew and to the Greek versions. He set out the Hebrew and the various Greek versions in parallel columns. These contained, from left to right:

1. The Hebrew text, in Hebrew characters
2. A transliteration of this into Greek characters
3. The version of Aquila
4. The version of Symmachus
5. The LXX
6. The version of Theodotion (at least in some books, though not in the Psalms or Minor Prophets)

In addition, three other versions were used. These are known as *Quinta, Sexta,* and *Septima.* None of them was complete (*Quinta* contained at least 4 Kingdoms [2 Kings], Job, Psalms, and the Minor Prophets; *Sexta* at least Job, Psalms, the Song of Songs, and Habakkuk). It seems that the terms "Heptapla" and "Octapla" were used to describe portions of the work that contained seven or eight columns, where one or more of the three additional versions was available. There is dispute about the meaning of another term, "Tetrapla." In the past, it has been generally believed that after completing the Hexapla, Origen later compiled a Tetrapla, consisting of columns 3–6 of the larger work. This has been challenged by Orlinsky, who argued that the Hexapla was preceded by an attempt at revision, before Origen came to possess *Quinta, Sexta,* and *Septima.* According to this theory, the Hexapla itself was begun in about 238. The matter is rendered complex by the imprecise and contradictory statements of ancient witnesses, and by the fact that the term "Hexapla" does not seem to have been used by Origen himself.

A fragment of the Hexapla has been found as the lower script of a palimpsest in Milan. It has columns 2–6, the sixth being *Quinta.* Each line has just a couple of words—partly to facilitate comparison between the columns, partly because even the largest parchment leaf can contain only narrow columns when there are so many of them. This palimpsest is quite extensive, containing 35 folios and about 150 verses.

A much smaller fragment, of Psalm 22, was found in the Cairo Genizah. This contains all six columns.

The comparison of the Hebrew and the LXX revealed both additions and omissions in the latter. Origen indicated these by means of the symbols developed by Alexandrian classical scholarship (the Aristarchian symbols). Words in the LXX but not in the Hebrew were embraced by an obelus (÷ or ÷) and metobelus (/. or ⁒). Where the LXX lacked material found in the Hebrew, Origen added it from another version (usually Theodotion), between asterisk (※) and metobelus. However, such signs are totally absent from the Milan fragments. This has led Kahle to challenge the traditional view that they were used in the Hexapla. In his opinion, Origen used the Hexapla as the basis for a critical edition of the LXX, in which these signs were used. Against this, it has been suggested that by the time the Milan copy was written in the 10th century, the symbols had dropped out of the text.

Kahle also draws attention to the fact that in all columns of the Milan palimpsest, the Divine Name is written with the letters of the Hebrew tetragrammaton. This leads him to conclude that all the manuscripts used by Origen, including those of the LXX, were of Jewish origin.

The effect of the Hexapla on the text of the LXX was not altogether good. Origen believed that the original text of the LXX was the one closest to the Hebrew text of his own day, which he supposed to be itself original (this Hebrew text was very similar to the Masoretic text). Actually, there are many readings where the LXX preserved an older and purer form of the Hebrew text (evidence from Qumran has established some of these). Origen's work tended to hold in low esteem such variants from the current Hebrew text. The study of the Hexapla in its original form would have made the situation clear to a competent scholar. However, copies that were made generally only contained the fifth column. The critical signs cannot have made much sense on their own, and as a consequence were gradually obliterated. The result was a form of the LXX which contained supplementary passages from other versions where it had omitted material found in the Hebrew. Study of the Hexapla, and the recovery of the Aristarchian symbols, is a vital stage in our recovery of the Old Greek, pre-Origenic, text of the LXX.

The Hexapla itself, an enormous compilation of 6,500 or more pages, in a good 15 volumes, stayed in Caesarea. It was never copied in its entirety. Certain eminent scholars took the trouble to consult it—one thinks especially of Pamphilus, Eusebius of Caesarea, and Jerome. The volumes are presumed to have been destroyed with the rest of the library in the Arab invasions of the early 7th century. Our knowledge of it is therefore fragmentary. Manuscripts which preserve the critical symbols are of great importance. The most valuable of these are the manuscripts G (Codex Sarravianus), M (Coislianus), both containing the Pentateuch and some historical books, and 86 and 88 (the Chigi manuscript) of the prophets. There are also highly significant versional materials—the Syro-Hexapla and the Armenian.

Editions of the Hexaplaric remains have been made by Montfaucon (1713), Bahrdt (1769–70), and Frederick Field (1875).

In conclusion, the reader must be warned that the attempt made by this article to achieve clarity may be misleading: there is almost no question which may be asked about the Hexapla that could receive a simple answer. For text see *PG* 11: 41–48.

Bibliography

Primary texts:

Cox, C. E. 1986. *Hexaplaric Materials Preserved in the Armenian Version.* SBLSCS 21. Atlanta.

Field, F. 1875. *Origenis Hexaplorum quae supersunt.* 2 vols. Oxford.

Mercati, G. 1958. *Psalterii Hexapli Reliquiae . . . Pars Prima. Codex rescriptus Bybliothecae Ambrosianae O 39 SVP. Phototypice Expressus et Transcriptus.* Vatican City.

———. 1965. *Pars Prima. "Osservazioni": Commento critico al testo dei frammenti esaplari.* Vatican City.

Taylor, C. 1900. *Hebrew-Greek Cairo Genizah Palimpsests.* Cambridge.

Secondary works:

Hanson, R. P. C. 1959. *Allegory and Event.* London.

Jellicoe, S. 1968. *The Septuagint and Modern Study.* Oxford.

Kahle, P. 1960. The Greek Bible Manuscripts used by Origen. *JBL* 79: 111–18.

Mercati, G. 1896. D'un palimpsesto ambrosiano contenente i Salmi esapli. *Atti della Accademia Reale delle Scienze di Torino* 31: 655–76.

Orlinsky, H. M. 1952. Origen's Tetrapla—a Scholarly Fiction? *PWCJS* 1: 173–82.

Swete, H. B. 1914. *An Introduction to the Old Testament in Greek.* 2d ed. Cambridge.

D. C. Parker

HEZEKIAH (PERSON)

HEZEKIAH (PERSON) [Heb *ḥizqîyāhû; ḥizqîyāh; yĕḥizqîyāhû; yĕḥizqîyāh*]. The name of three persons in the Hebrew Bible. The root of the name is *ḥzq*, "to be strong, to strengthen."

1. King of Judah. See HEZEKIAH KING OF JUDAH.

2. The great-great-grandfather of the prophet Zephaniah (Zeph 1:1). Zephaniah prophesied during the brief reign of Amon ca. 640 B.C.E. Assuming 20–25 years per generation, this Hezekiah would have been alive during the latter years of the 8th century B.C.E. Indeed, some have suggested that this ancestor of the prophet was none other than the famous king Hezekiah, and that Zephaniah was therefore of the royal family. See ZEPHANIAH, BOOK OF.

3. The older Heb name of the head of a family that returned from Babylonian exile (Ezra 2:16 = Neh 7:21 = 1 Esdr 5:15). This person affixed the family name to the covenant document of Nehemiah (Neh 10:18—Eng 10:17). See also ATER (PERSON).

Gary A. Herion

HEZEKIAH KING OF JUDAH

HEZEKIAH KING OF JUDAH. Hezekiah was king of Judah ca. 715–687 B.C.E., the son and successor of Ahaz. He came to the throne at the age of 25 and ruled 29 years (2 Kgs 18:2; 2 Chr 29:1). His mother's name was Abi (perhaps a hypocoristic of "Abijah," 2 Chr 29:1), daughter of Zechariah. His name is attested as *Ḥzqyhw* in a seal impression of a royal servant, *Yhwzrḥ* (Hestrin and Dayagi 1974: 27–29) and as *Ḫa-za-qi-a-ú* in the account of the third campaign of Sennacherib in 701 B.C.E. (*ANET,* 287–88).

Sources are inconsistent on the date of Hezekiah's accession. In 2 Kgs 18:9–10 the conquest of Samaria (722/1) is recorded as the sixth year of Hezekiah's reign, making his accession 727/6; however, in 2 Kgs 18:13 the mention of Sennacherib's conquest of 701 in Hezekiah's fourteenth year supports an enthronement in 716/5. Much of German scholarship has accepted the earlier date; most others assume the later (*IJH,* 678–83; cf. Hayes and Hooker 1988; Jenkins 1976) which has received independent support (Tadmor 1958: 22–40, 77–100; Hallo 1960: 55). The terminal date of Hezekiah's reign (687/6) is established by a combination of 2 Kgs 19:9, which chronicles a challenge to Sennacherib by Tirhakah of Egypt (ascent: ca. 690/89), and the 29 years of the sources.

Hezekiah's acts fall into two major, interlocking categories: his religious reform and his efforts to gain political independence from Assyria. Historiographically, his reign is noteworthy for the convergence of a variety of biblical sources and diverse extrabiblical evidence often bearing on the same events. Significant data concerning Hezekiah appear in the Deuteronomistic History, the Chronicler, Isaiah, Assyrian annals and reliefs, Israelite epigraphy, and, increasingly, stratigraphy.

A. Hezekiah's Reform
  1. The Deuteronomistic History
  2. The Chronicler's Depiction: Conflation or History?
  3. The Nehushtan's Omission
B. The Impact of Assyrian Events
C. Archaeology of Hezekiah's Reign
  1. Revisions in Stratigraphy
  2. The *lmlk* Stamps
  3. Jerusalem and Related Fortifications
  4. Sennacherib's Invasion

A. Hezekiah's Reform

The Chronicler's depiction of Hezekiah's reform (2 Chr 29:1–31:31) departs strikingly in length and detail from the Deuteronomistic History's brief version (2 Kgs 18:4, 16, 22). In both, Hezekiah is depicted as a king who "did right in the eyes of YHWH" and who inaugurated a religious reform which included the removal of the *bāmôt* ("high places" of decentralized worship and sacrifice), the shattering of the sacred pillars *(maṣṣēbôt),* the cutting down of the Asherah, and the refurbishing of the Jerusalem temple (to which 2 Kgs 18:16 gives only passing, backhanded acknowledgement). Chronicles depicts other major details of the reform (Passover celebration and invitation to remnants in the North, establishment of covenant), which are omitted by 2 Kings. On the other hand, the Deuteronomistic History alone (2 Kgs 18:4) credits Hezekiah with destroying the Nehushtan associated with Moses.

1. The Deuteronomistic History. The concept of the Deuteronomistic History (DH) first proposed by Noth *(NDH)* was refined by Cross (*CMHE,* 274–89) who suggested two Deuteronomistic editors: a Josianic one, Dtr_1; and an exilic one, Dtr_2. Subsequently, Smend (1978) and Veijola (1977; cf. 1975) posited new Deuteronomistic redactors, basing their conclusions on internal inconsistencies in the text. Weippert (1983), Peckham (1985a; 1985b), and Provan (1988) place the earliest Deuteronomistic redactor in the period of Hezekiah; Peckham discards a Josianic version entirely. Weippert (1985) adds a Josianic updating of the Hezekian version, thereby revising rather than rejecting Cross' original conclusions. In this Weippert is joined by Provan (1988), who independently confirms McKenzie's Josianic redactor (1985: 171–80). Halpern (1988: esp. 114–16, 134) supports a Hezekian document and seeks to harmonize Weippert and Cross (Halpern and Vanderhooft fc.). A Josianic revision and updating may explain the surprisingly short shrift given by 2 Kings to the reform of Hezekiah: the Josianic redactor may have feared the undermining influence of comparing his patron, Josiah, with Hezekiah's well-meaning but ultimately failed reform (Rosenbaum 1979).

2. The Chronicler's Depiction: Conflation or History? For more than a century the tendency of critical scholarship (e.g., *WPHI,* 222) was to dismiss the historicity of the Chronicler's sources (see Japhet 1985 for a summary of the literature). Support for the earlier position repudiating the historicity of preexilic accounts in Chronicles continued to be found in the writings of von Rad (1930) and Noth (*NHI,* 292–93, 296, though Noth [*NHI* 319–20] accepts the Chronicler's sources for his own period) and has recently received support from some scholars who dismiss the work on historiographical grounds (e.g., Welten 1973; Klein 1983; and Williamson, *1–2 Chronicles* NCBC, 15–23) and others who see the Chronicler's motivation as theological (Ackroyd 1967: 509; Gonçalves 1986: 95, 522).

While scholarly opinion is virtually unanimous that the Chronicler used the DH as a source, a wide range of scholars have begun to hold with Albright (1921) that the Chronicler possessed independent, accurate sources which he preserved without substantial amendment. Albright (1950: 62) went further, adding that archaeological evidence had begun to confirm the Chronicler's historical reliability. Authentic data could be found in tendentious as well as neutral stories since the Chronicler did not invent but selected the sources which suited his purposes. Recent surveys based on independent case studies (Halpern 1981: 35–54; Friedman 1980) have added significant evidence to these conclusions.

Because of the striking disproportion between the portrayal of Hezekiah's reform found in Chronicles (three chapters [2 Chr 29:1–33:31] totaling seventy-four verses) and Kings (three verses), the subject provides intriguing data to test the historicity of Chronicles. It is one of the few episodes where Chronicles supplies substantial information which differs in quantity and content from Kings. The disproportion cannot be dismissed by appeals to differences of viewpoint or emphasis, since although only one chapter of Chronicles (2 Chr 32:1–33) is devoted to Hezekiah's foreign policy (i.e., his rebellion and Sennacherib's response) versus three chapters in the DH (2 Kgs 18:7–20:20), virtually every element claimed by 2 Kings also appears in Chronicles' briefer version.

Sennacherib's invasion was indisputably a catastrophe for Judah and thereby undermined an acknowledged theme of the Chronicler's work (defense of the legitimate claims of the Davidic line; Freedman 1961: 438–41). Therefore, the Chronicler's detailed account of the Assyrian onslaught would be gratuitous if his history were pure invention anyway. Its inclusion would seem to lend support to the Chronicler's historicity regarding Hezekiah.

The Chronicler's history receives further support in its lack of bias in describing Hezekiah's reform itself. Though the priestly Chronicler was certainly committed to the centralization of the priesthood in Jerusalem, he acknowledges a rural priesthood in the time of Hezekiah (e.g., 2 Chr 31:15–19). Alt (*KlSchr* 2: 255–58) held that such a decentralized priesthood is also the accepted view of Deuteronomy and did not end until the centralization of the priesthood by Josiah, whose reform exceeded the Deuteronomic legislation. Thus, in this area, Hezekiah was more faithful to Deuteronomic legislation than Josiah. The fact that the Chronicler presents this point despite its potential for thwarting his own theological commitments to centralization in Jerusalem adds support to the assessment that his presentation is relatively impartial.

3. The Nehushtan's Omission. In light of the Chronicler's detailed accounts, the omission of any reference to the destruction of the bronze serpent (Nehushtan) attributed to Moses (Num 21:6–9) is odd. The act appears exclusively in DH (2 Kgs 18:4), which otherwise provides a minimal view of the reform. For this reason, even those scholars who have doubted the reform itself have tended to accept the eradication of the Nehushtan (e.g., Rowley 1961: 425). Similar images have been found at Megiddo, Gezer, Hazor, and Shechem (Joines 1968: 245–56). The reason for Chronicles' omission of the Nehushtan's obliteration may lie in the Mushite (i.e., descendants of Moses)–Aaronide competition identified by Cross (*CMHE,* 195–215) and ultimately won by the Aaronides. The Nehushtan's exclusive association with Moses may have been sufficient cause for the Aaronide Chronicler to delete the material.

B. The Impact of Assyrian Events

A precise date of Hezekiah's reform has not been established. It is generally assumed that the reform immediately preceded his rebellion since the reform entailed politically provocative actions such as appeals to the remnants of the exiled northern kingdom and centralization of the cult in Jerusalem (*BHI,* 282). Judah sagaciously avoided the wrath of Sargon II in 714 probably by refusing to participate in the Philistine revolt (Tadmor 1958: 80–84) and eluded his interest again in 710 at the height of the Assyrian king's military successes.

Though the reform fits most logically into the period after Sargon's death in battle in 705, its less provocative elements such as the rededication of the priesthood may have been inaugurated earlier in Hezekiah's reign while Sargon ruled Assyria (cf. 2 Chr 29:3). Even the centralization of the cult with its attendant destruction of local shrines may not have drawn Assyrian ire. This position gains additional credence in light of Cogan's demonstration (1974: 72–77; cf. Spieckermann 1982, for contrast) that religious syncretism was not an element of Assyrian domination. The altar which Ahaz accepted under Tiglath-pileser III (2 Kgs 16:10–18) was not Assyrian. Therefore, religious reform may have been possible for Hezekiah without making a major political statement as has been previously believed (e.g., *BHI,* 282).

While the reform's date is debatable, Hezekiah's rebellion undeniably arose in response to the shift in Assyrian power occasioned by Sargon's death and Sennacherib's assumption. The resulting opportunity for independence ignited revolts throughout the empire. Insurrection flared from Babylon, where Marduk-apal-iddina (Merodach-Baladan, 2 Kgs 20:12–19), a perpetual thorn in the Assyrian side since Sargon's early days, led a temporarily successful uprising, to Egypt, where the invigorating 25th Dynasty offered tempting if unreliable support to potential rebels.

C. Archaeology of Hezekiah's Reign

1. Revisions in Stratigraphy. Until the 1970s, those scholars who sought to dismiss Hezekiah's reform as fiction (e.g., Rowley 1961: 425) found complementary evidence in the Deuteronomistic sparseness regarding the events and the conclusions of the excavators of the most pertinent Judean sites. Albright's conclusions at Tell Beit Mirsim (1932; 1943: 39–45) attributed Stratum A2 to a 300-year period ending with the beginning of the Babylonian deportations. This schema was followed by Starckey (1937) at Lachish where he equated Stratum III to Tell Beit Mirsim A2 and dated it from Sennacherib's campaign in 701 to the first Babylonian invasion in 597. He placed Stratum II in the slim period between the first and second Babylonian campaigns (598/7–586 B.C.E.). These conclusions tended to dominate Judean stratigraphy in Iron IIC while leaving Sennacherib's successful invasion of 701 unidentified.

O. Tufnell (1953: 55–58), however, who published the major account of Iron Age Lachish, assigned the destruction of Stratum III to 701, thereby evoking a cacophony of criticism (on the scholarly debate, see Rosenbaum 1979: 30–31). She based her conclusions on ceramic analysis, the destruction of Stratum III, and the Assyrian bas-reliefs of Sennacherib's siege of Lachish (*ANEP,* 129–32, 293–94; cf. *ANET,* 288). Subsequent excavations by D. Ussishkin (e.g., 1980; 1982) have vindicated Tufnell. See also LACHISH (PLACE). Further, Y. Aharoni's major revision of Judean stratigraphy (Aharoni and Aharoni 1976), equating the end of Tell Beit Mirsim A2 and Beth Shemesh IIC with Sennacherib's 701 destruction, has now gained wide acceptance. These conclusions have a definite bearing on Hezekiah: artifacts and strata previously associated with Josiah must now be assigned to Hezekiah.

2. The *lmlk* Stamps. Significantly, the *lmlk* store jars must now be placed in Hezekiah's reign. Their distribution in the N along Judah's border with Assyrian Samaria and in the W of the country demonstrate careful preparations to counter Sennacherib's likely route of invasion (Naʾaman 1979; 1986). (Naʾaman 1988 forcefully counters a critique of his conclusions by Garfinkel 1988.) Further, they demonstrate a notable degree of royal control of towns and cities which would facilitate Hezekiah's destruction of rural sacrificial sites and his centralization of worship in Jerusalem. See also STAMPS, ROYAL JAR HANDLE.

3. Jerusalem and Related Fortifications. The capital city itself yields significant evidence of Hezekiah's preparation. The Siloam tunnel (2 Kgs 20:20; 2 Chr 32:30) with its famous inscription (*ANET,* 321) is the most obvious example, and later studies have documented the tunnel's sophistication. See also SILOAM INSCRIPTION; DAVID, CITY OF (PLACE). Hezekiah also probably began the Broad Wall (Avigad 1983: 49–59). Perhaps most impressive are the increasing data substantiating the expansion of Jerusalem's population under Hezekiah. Broshi (1978) has estimated that a census under Hezekiah would have revealed some 25,000 inhabitants, five times the population under Solomon. Excavations originally undertaken by N. Avigad in 1970 point to an enlargement of the city under Hezekiah, perhaps due to the influx of refugees from the N kingdom in agreement with 2 Chr 30:25. Such an influx may add support to the Chronicler's claim that Hezekiah invited the North to participate in his reestablished Passover ritual.

Excavations suggest that Hezekiah augmented fortifications in preparation for Sennacherib's assault and may have established administrative centers and command posts, which Halpern (fc) calls a " 'hedgehog' defense—a pattern of self-contained, fortified nodes." As part of the process, Hezekiah may have implemented a key element of his reform, destroying local altars (as excavations at Beer-sheba suggest). (Previous, similar conclusions regarding the altar at Arad must now be suspended, since scholarly debate on the subject continues.)

4. Sennacherib's Invasion. Despite the considerable preparations made by Hezekiah, the effect of Sennacherib's offensive was catastrophic. After stabilizing his eastern holdings in two initial campaigns, the Assyrian king embarked on a westward campaign which sought to suppress rebels and establish his unchallenged hegemony. The events are well documented in both the Assyrian annals (e.g., *ANET,* 287–88) and in the biblical sources (2 Kgs 18:13–19:37; 2 Chr 32:1–22; Isaiah 36–39). In addition, an echo of Sennacherib's failure to conquer Jerusalem may survive in Herodotus (2: 14–141), whom Josephus (*Ant* 10) followed.

Sennacherib utilized classic Assyrian military techniques to reduce Judah. Though the figure of 200,150 captives and the razing of 46 walled cities has been contested (see *BHI,* 286 n. 49), later scholarship has increasingly accepted the possible authenticity of the numbers (see Halpern fc. for a summary of the supporting data). Certain facts are uncontested: Sennacherib successfully captured the fortified towns of Judah (2 Kgs 18:13; 2 Chr 32:1), exacted spectacular tribute (2 Kgs 18:14–16), and failed to capture Jerusalem though he walled up Hezekiah "like a caged bird."

The seeming paradox that Hezekiah paid tribute but was never captured raised the possibility that the sources (biblical and Assyrian) refer to two separate invasions with different outcomes (*BHI,* 298–309; Horn 1966). This theory gains fundamental support from a reference to Tirhakah of Egypt, whose anticipated aid is mocked by Sennacherib's Rabshakeh (2 Kgs 19:9). Since Tirhakah did not reach the Egyptian throne until ca. 690 and since he would have been a child in 701, Bright (*BHI,* esp. 299–303) found the two-invasion theory especially persuasive. Subsequent work by Kitchen (1973a: 154–72; 1973b) showed that in 701 Tirhakah was old enough to command, thereby disabling the theory's main defense. Heavy tribute and survival in a well-fortified and well-supplied mountainous capital are not mutually exclusive; they may have been mandatory elements in Hezekiah's quest for Judah's perpetuation.

Recent studies suggest a greater acknowledgement of Hezekiah. His reform (previously doubted as a fictional reading back from Josiah) and his capacity as an administrator and strategist (denied because of erroneous stratigraphy which placed the *lmlk* stamps and considerable building in a later era) have gained acceptance as archaeological data have emerged to lend support. The literary activity of his reign already known through Micah and First Isaiah has been amplified by suggestions of a Hezekian redactor of the DH. Independent verification has also bolstered arguments for the historicity of the Chronicler and his use of sources independent of the DH. The bulk of this evidence suggests that rather than being a mere foreshadowing of Josiah's deeds, Hezekiah's accomplishments may have surpassed those of his great-grandson.

Bibliography

Ackroyd, P. 1967. History and Theology in the Writings of the Chronicler. *CTM* 38: 501–15.

Aharoni, Y. and Aharoni, M. 1976. The Stratification of Judahite Sites in the 8th and 7th Centuries B.C.E. *BASOR* 224: 73–90.

Albright, W. F. 1921. The Date and Personality of the Chronicler. *JBL* 40: 104–24.

———. 1932. The Seal of Eliakim and the Latest Preexilic History of Judah, with Some Observations on Ezekiel. *JBL* 51: 77–106.

———. 1943. *The Excavations at Tell Beit Mirsim.* Vol. 3. AASOR 21–22. New Haven.

———. 1950. The Judicial Reform of Jehoshaphat. Pp. 61–82 in *Alexander Marx Jubilee Volume.* New York.

Avigad, N. 1983. *Discovering Jerusalem.* Jerusalem.

Broshi, M. 1978. Estimating the Population of Ancient Jerusalem. *BARev* 4/2: 10–15.

Cogan, M. 1974. *Imperialism and Religion: Assyria, Israel, and Judah in the Eighth and Seventh Centuries B.C.E.* SBLMS 19. Missoula, MT.

Freedman, D. N. 1961. The Chronicler's Purpose. *CBQ* 23: 436–41.

Friedman, R. 1980. The Tabernacle in the Temple. *BA* 43: 241–48.

Garfinkel, Y. 1988. 2 Chr 11:5–10 Fortified Cities and the *lmlk* Stamps—Reply to Nadav Naʾaman. *BASOR* 271: 69–73.

Gonçalves, F. 1986. *L'expédition de Sennachérib en Palestine dans la littératre hebraï ancienne.* EBib ns 7. Paris.

Hallo, W. 1960. From Qarqar to Carchemish: Assyria and Israel in the Light of New Discoveries. *BA* 23: 34–61 (= *BAR* 2: 152–88).

Halpern, B. 1981. Sacred History and Ideology: Chronicles' Thematic Structure—Indications of an Earlier Source. Pp. 35–54 in *Creation of Sacred Literature: Composition and Redaction of the Biblical Text,* ed. R. E. Friedman. Berkeley.

———. 1988. *The First Historians.* San Francisco.

———. fc. Jerusalem and the Lineages in the 7th Century B.C.E.: Kinship and the Rise of Individual Moral Liability. In *Law in Its Social Setting in the Ancient Mediterranean World,* eds. B. Halpern and D. W. Hobson. ASOR.

Halpern, B. and Vanderhooft, D. fc. Observations on the Redactional Development on the Book of Kings.

Hayes, J. H. and Hooker, P. K. 1988. *A New Chronology for the Kings of Israel and Judah and Its Implications for Biblical History and Literature.* Atlanta.

Hestrin, R. and Dayagi, M. 1974. A Seal Impression of a Servant of King Hezekiah. *IEJ* 24: 27–29.

Horn, S. 1966. Did Sennacherib Campaign Once or Twice Against Hezekiah? *AUSS* 4: 1–28.

Japhet, S. 1985. The Historical Reliability of Chronicles. *JSOT* 33: 83–107.

Jenkins, A. 1976. Hezekiah's Fourteenth Year. *VT* 26: 284–98.

Joines, K. 1968. The Bronze Serpent in the Israelite Cult. *JBL* 87: 245–56.

Kitchen, K. 1973a. *The Third Intermediate Period in Egypt (1100–650 B.C.).* Warminster.

———. 1973b. Late Egyptian Chronology and the Hebrew Monarchy. *JANES* 5: 225–33.
Klein, R. 1983. Abijah's Campaign Against the North (1 Chr. 13)—What Were the Chronicler's Sources? *ZAW* 95: 210–17.
McKenzie, S. L. 1985. *The Chronicler's Use of the Deuteronomistic History.* HSM 33. Atlanta.
Naʾaman, N. 1979. Sennacherib's Campaign to Judah and the Date of the LMLK Stamps. *VT* 29: 61–86.
———. 1986. Hezekiah's Fortified Cities and the LMLK Stamps. *BASOR* 261: 5–21.
———. 1988. The Date of 2 Chronicles 11:5–10—A Reply to Y. Garfinkel. *BASOR* 271: 74–77.
Peckham, B. 1985a. *The Composition of the Deuteronomistic History.* HSM 35. Atlanta.
———. 1985b. The Deuteronomistic History of Saul and David. *ZAW* 97: 190–209.
Provan, I. 1988. *Hezekiah and the Books of Kings.* BZAW 172. Berlin.
Rad, G. von. 1930. *Das Geschichtsbild des chronistischen Werkes.* BWANT 54. Stuttgart.
Rosenbaum, J. 1979. Hezekiah's Reform and the Deuteronomistic Tradition. *HTR* 72: 23–43.
Rowley, H. H. 1961. Hezekiah's Reform and Rebellion. *BJRL* 44: 395–431.
Smend, R. 1978. *Die Entstehung des Alten Testaments.* Stuttgart.
Spieckermann, H. 1982. *Juda unter Assur in der Sargonidenzeit.* FRLANT 129. Göttingen.
Starckey, J. 1937. Lachish as Illustrating Bible History. *PEQ* 69: 176–77.
Tadmor, H. 1958. The Campaigns of Sargon II of Assur: A Chronological-Historical Study. *JCS* 12: 22–40, 77–100.
Tufnell, O. 1953. *Lachish III: The Iron Age.* London.
Ussishkin, D. 1980. The Battle of Lachish, Israel. *Arch* 33: 56–59.
———. 1982. *The Conquest of Lachish by Sennacherib.* Tel Aviv University Publications of the Institute of Archaeology 6. Tel Aviv.
Veijola, T. 1975. *Die ewige Dynastie.* Helsinki.
———. 1977. *Das Königtum in der deuteronomistischen Historiographie.* Helsinki.
Weippert, H. 1983. Die Ätiologie des Nordreiches und seines Königshauses (I Reg. 11, 29–40). *ZAW* 95: 344–75.
———. 1985. *Beiträge zur prophetischen Bildsprache in Israel und Assyrien.* OBO 64. Göttingen.
Welten, P. 1973. *Geschichte und Gesichtsdarstellung in der Chronikbüchern.* WMANT 42. Neukirchen.

JONATHAN ROSENBAUM

HEZION (PERSON) [Heb *ḥezyôn*]. Grandfather of Ben-Hadad I, king of Syria (1 Kgs 15:18). Scholars have sometimes identified Hezion with Rezon, who became king of Damascus during the reign of Solomon (1 Kgs 11:23–24), but there is no convincing evidence for this nor does it solve any pressing chronological or historical problem. Formerly, Hezion's name (Aram *ḥazyān*) was sometimes included in the Bir-Hadad Stela, but more recent studies have proposed other readings. If Hezion was himself king of Syria, something implied but not explicitly stated by the biblical text, he probably reigned in the late 10th century B.C.E.

Bibliography

Pitard, W. 1987. *Ancient Damascus.* Winona Lake, IN.

RICHARD D. NELSON

HEZIR (PERSON) [Heb *ḥēzîr*]. The name of two men in the OT. It may mean "swine" (*IPN* 230).

1. A priest who received the seventeenth position in the priestly order of the temple during David's reign (1 Chr 24:15). An evaluation of the historical reliability of his existence in the time of David depends largely upon the literary context of 1 Chr 24:1–19. Though generally agreed that the priestly list originated after the Exile, its exact date remains debated. See HAKKOZ (PERSON). The consensus agrees, at any rate, that Hezir represents a name from the postexilic period, rather than an individual who was contemporaneous with David.

2. A member of the Judean aristocracy who signed a document that forbid intermarriage between Judeans and other ethnic groups, insured the observation of Sabbath, and provided for the maintenance of the temple and its staff (Neh 10:21—Eng 10:20). While some commentators have thought the signees reflect authentic historical persons from the time of Nehemiah (Rudolph *Ezra Nehemiah* HAT, 173–75), the names of Neh 10:2–27—Eng 10:1–26 seem to represent "an artificial literary compilation, based on other material in Ezra and Neh" (Williamson *Ezra Nehemiah* WBC, 329).

The ultimate source of the name Hezir remains a mystery, as both occurrences appear in artificially constructed lists. It may represent a common familial name from Judah in the late Persian period.

JOHN W. WRIGHT

HEZRO (PERSON) [Heb *ḥeṣrô*]. One of the members of "the Thirty," the distinguished group of warriors who fought for David (2 Sam 23:35, Heb *ḥeṣrô; ḥeṣray,* LXX *asarai;* 1 Chr 11:37, Heb *ḥeṣrô*). He is known as the Carmelite, a noun describing his origin, the town of Carmel, seven miles southeast of Hebron in southern Judah. This town produced not only a rich landowner like Nabal, who hated David, but also a poor person like Hezro, who was devoted to him (Elliger 1966: 114–15). It is tempting to think of Hezro as a runaway slave of Nabal who joined David in the wilderness of Judah (1 Sam 25:10–11, cf. 1 Sam 22:2). His name appears toward the end of the list of "the Thirty" in 2 Samuel, an indication that he may have had a lesser rank among the group (McCarter *II Samuel* AB, 501).

Bibliography

Elliger, K. 1966. Die dreissig Helden Davids. *KlSchr,* 72–118.

STEPHEN G. DEMPSTER

HEZRON (PERSON) [Heb *ḥeṣrôn*]. **1.** The third son of Reuben (Gen 46:9; Exod 6:14; 1 Chr 5:3). In the enumeration of the family of Jacob who migrated to Egypt (Gen 46:8–27), Jacob's sons are listed by family, according to their mothers. The family of Reuben was listed first because he was Jacob's and Leah's firstborn. Hezron also was the eponymous head of the family of the Hezronites (Num 26:6). According to Noth (*NHI,* 64), the Hezronite clan of Reuben became the Judean Hezronite clan when the Reubenites, who lived in the vicinity of Judah, were assimilated into the tribe of Judah. In 1 Chr 4:1 the genealogy of

Judah may provide some evidence for this assimilation. Hezron appears as the brother of Carmi and both are the sons of Judah, while in Gen 46:9 both are brothers but the sons of Reuben.

2. The son of Perez and the grandson of Judah by his daughter-in-law Tamar (Gen 38:29; 46:12). Hezron is included in the list of the family of Jacob who migrated to Egypt. Hezron and his brother Hamul are counted among the sons of Leah in order to complete the list of seventy people who descended with Jacob to Egypt. Hezron was the eponymous father of the Hezronites, a southern Judean clan (Num 26:6; Josh 15:3).

Hezron was an important clan in Judah. From the descendants of Hezron came the Calebites (1 Chr 2:18–24) and the Jerahmeelites (1 Chr 2:25–33), two great clans in Judah. The family of David came from Hezron through his son Ram (1 Chr 2:10–15; Ruth 4:18–19). Hezron also appears in the genealogy of Christ (Matt 1:3; Luke 3:33).

The genealogy of Hezron found in 1 Chronicles 2 presents serious problems in interpretation (Braun *Chronicles* WBC, 25–35). 1 Chr 2:9 says that Hezron had three sons, Jerahmeel, Ram, and Chelubai. 1 Chr 2:18 states that Caleb was the son of Hezron. Caleb probably was the Chelubai mentioned in 2:9. However, Caleb in another passage is said to be the son of Jephunneh the Kenizzite. According to 1 Chr 2:24 (RSV), the wife of Hezron was Ephrathah. However, the translation in the RSV depends on an emendation of the MT. The KJV translates 1 Chr 2:24 as follows: "And after that Hezron was dead in Caleb-ephratah, then Abiah, Hezron's wife bare him Ashur, the father of Tekoa." If Abiah was Hezron's wife, then the expression "and the wife of Hezron" should be read as a gloss to 1 Chr 2:21 as Williamson (1979: 355) has proposed.

Bibliography

Williamson, H. G. M. 1979. Source and Redaction in the Chronicler's Genealogy of Judah. *JBL* 98: 351–59.

Claude F. Mariottini

HEZRON (PLACE) [*ḥeṣrôn*]. Station named in the description of the extreme S border of the tribal allotment of Judah (Josh 15:3). This place, whose name seems to mean "enclosure," is located between Kadesh-barnea and Addar. Alt (1953) has persuasively argued that the border list of Joshua 15 is derived from an ancient legal document delineating the territorial claims of the tribes during the period of the judges. The parallel nature of the S border descriptions in Numbers 34 and Joshua 15 suggests that both depend on a single, presumably premonarchical, tradition. It is possible that "Hazar-addar" in Num 34:4 represents a mistaken combination of "Hezron" and "Addar" from Josh 15:3. Ancient Hezron may perhaps be located at or near Ain Qedeis (Aharoni *LBHG*, 65; M.R. 100999), one of three small wells in the vicinity of the oasis of Ain el-Qudeirat (Kadesh-barnea?). This S border station is not to be confused with Kirioth-Hezron.

Bibliography

Alt, A. 1953. Das System der Stammesgrenzen im Buche Josua. *KlSchr* 1: 193–202.

Wade R. Kotter

HIDDAI (PERSON) [Heb *hidday*]. Var. HURAI. At 2 Sam 23:30 Hiddai "of the brooks of Gaash" is listed as one of David's thirty mighty men. In the parallel at 1 Chr 11:32 he is called Hurai. Thenius (*Die Bücher Samuels* KEHAT, 253), Wellhausen (1871: 215), and Smith (*Samuel* ICC, 387f.) preferred this alternate reading as the more original and indeed it is found in Origen's text (Field 1875: 586) as well as in several Greek mss. The OG, however, has *haddai* (attested in mss b o c_2 e_2) and the original reading of cod. B is *hadaoi,* which was later modified to *hadroi.* The strength of the OG reading, along with the possibility of the confusion of the letters *dalet* and *reš,* suggests that "Hiddai" was the original form.

Hiddai's home, the brooks, or the valleys, of Gaash, would be at the base of Mount Gaash, which is found in the hill country of Ephraim (Josh 24:30; Judg 2:9). Thus in this verse two Ephraimites, Benaiah of Pirathon and Hiddai, are mentioned together (Budde, *Samuel* KHC, 325).

Bibliography

Field, F. 1875. *Origenis Hexaplorum Quae Supersunt.* 2 vols. Oxford.
Wellhausen, J. 1871. *Der Text der Bücher Samuelis.* Göttingen.

Stephen Pisano

HIDDEKEL (PLACE) [Heb *ḥiddeqel*]. The Hebrew name for one of the four branches of the river which flowed out of the Garden of Eden (Gen 2:14). The etymology of the name can be traced as follows: Sum *Idiglat, Idigna,* Akk *Idiqlat,* Arab and Aram *Diglath,* Pers *Tigra,* Gk *Tigris.* The only other OT occurrence is in Dan 10:4 where some see possible universal connotations, in contrast to limitations tied with the Abrahamic covenant connected with the Euphrates river.

Zdravko Stefanovic

HIEL (PERSON) [Heb *ḥîʾēl*]. A citizen of Bethel who rebuilt Jericho when Ahab reigned as king of Israel (1 Kgs 16:34). It is stated that he laid the foundation of Jericho with Abiram, his eldest son, and the city gates with Segub, his youngest son. The meaning of this statement is not clear. Some suggest that it indicates Hiel used his sons as foundation sacrifices; others take it to mean that Hiel's sons died of natural causes at the time that the city was being rebuilt. Though archaeologists have discovered bodies of infants buried in homes, it is not certain whether these infants were sacrificed to lay the foundation of the home or if they simply died of natural causes and were subsequently buried in the home. Whether Hiel's sons died a natural death or were sacrificed, the incident is taken as the fulfillment of the curse against the rebuilding of Jericho in Josh 6:26.

Pauline A. Viviano

HIERAPOLIS (PLACE) [Gk *Hierapolis*]. A city in the Lycus valley of SW Phrygia, probably originated as a settlement attached to the sanctuary of the Anatolian mother goddess, worshiped locally under the name Leto.

A. The Hellenistic City
B. Jewish Settlement
C. The Church of Hierapolis

A. The Hellenistic City

It has commonly been supposed that Hierapolis received its city status from Eumenes II of Pergamum (197–159 B.C.); to his reign belongs the earliest known inscription on the site, recording a decree in honor of his mother Apollonis (*OGIS* 308). But the character of tribal names in a theater inscription points to its being a Seleucid foundation (Kolb 1974: 255–70), dating perhaps from the reign of Antiochus I (281–261 B.C.).

Hierapolis stood on a road which left the main Iconium-Ephesus highway at Laodicea and led NW to Philadelphia, Sardis, and the Hermus valley—the road along which Xerxes marched after leaving Colossae in 481 B.C. (Hdt. 7.31). It looks across to Laodicea from a terrace 300 feet high on the north bank of the Lycus (modern Çürük-su); in the plain beneath the terrace the Lycus flows into the Maeander. Behind the site a hot mineral spring wells up (one of several lime-charged springs in the neighborhood), filling the "sacred pool" and overflowing so as to cover the rocks beneath with white deposits of lime, which give the appearance of a frozen cascade. It is to these formations probably that the Turkish name Pamukkale ("Cotton Castle") is due. The medicinal properties of the hot water attracted visitors in antiquity, as they do today. On coins of Hierapolis, Asklepios and Hygieia feature either separately or together.

Hierapolis honored Apollo as its divine founder *(Apollo Archēgetēs);* the temple of Apollo which is still to be seen is a structure of the 3d century A.D., but an early temple may once have stood on the site, where his oracle was available for consultation. To the S of this temple was a cave, called the Plutonium, which was believed to be an entrance to the underworld. The *galli,* the eunuch-priests of the Magna Mater, were said to be the only living beings not to be asphyxiated by the carbon dioxide generated in the cave. The cave was filled in at the beginning of the 4th century A.D., but has been rediscovered by Italian excavators. W. C. Brice (1978: 226–27) describes his visit in 1950 to a similar cave at Hierapolis which also emitted carbon dioxide.

Hierapolis long maintained its importance as a cult center: Caracalla (A.D. 211–218) conferred on it the title *neōkoros,* "temple warden" (compare the Ephesian pride in the same title, attested in Acts 19:35). But shortly after its foundation it became a commercial center also: in particular, it was noted for the quality of its textile products. Perhaps the local water imparted a special richness or stability to the purple dye which was manufactured there from the juice of the madder root (Strabo 13.4.14). There is epigraphic evidence of a guild of purple dyers; a guild of carpet weavers and "the most august gild of wool washers" are similarly attested (*IGRR* 4.816, 818, 821, 822), all suggesting Hierapolis was a center for textile production.

Hierapolis belonged to the judicial circuit of cities called the Cibyratic *conventus,* from Cibyra, a city between 50 and 60 miles to the S (although from the 1st century B.C. on the central headquarters of the circuit were at Laodicea).

In the history of human thought the city's chief claim to fame lies in its being the birthplace of the Stoic philosopher Epictetus (A.D. ca. 50–117).

The ruined buildings on the site are all Roman; the earthquake which flattened Laodicea in A.D. 60 may also have devastated Hierapolis. The city was constructed on the grid system. One can see sections of the city walls and the main colonnaded street running NW and SE, with a monumental gateway at either end and with other streets crossing it at right angles. Down the center of each street was a channel for the disposal of sewage. Other channels carried water from the springs to various points in the city.

From 1957 onward excavation and restoration work has been carried on by Italian archaeologists, particularly on the temple of Apollo, the agora (notable for the fine locked stone of its arches), the nymphaeum, the Roman baths with gymnasium attached, and especially the theater, overlooking the city and the Lycus valley, with seating accommodation for up to 15,000 persons. The necropolis contains some 1,200 tombs, 300 of which have epitaphs.

B. Jewish Settlement

Like other cities of SW Phrygia, Hierapolis had a Jewish community, called a *katoikia,* "colony" (*CIJ* 2.775), from its earliest days as a city. Some members of this community have left epigraphic records, like the 2d-century A.D. "Marcus Aurelius Alexander, also called Asaph, of the people of the Jews" (*CIJ* 2.776), and Jewish members of some of the craft guilds (*CIJ* 2.777).

C. The Church of Hierapolis

There was a Christian group in Hierapolis about A.D. 60 (Col 4:13). It probably came into existence during the missionary campaign of Paul and his associates in proconsular Asia in A.D. 52–55 (Acts 19:10). With the other churches of the Lycus valley, the church of Hierapolis was evidently founded by Paul's colleague Epaphras (Col 1:7; 4:12).

Some time before A.D. 70 the Palestinian Christian leader Philip and his daughters settled in Hierapolis: their tombs were pointed out there toward the end of the 2d century (Eus. *Hist. Eccl.* 3.31.2–5; 3.39.9; 5.24.2). Eusebius or his sources show some confusion between Philip of Bethsaida, the apostle, and Philip of Caesarea, the evangelist (Acts 21:8–9); it is not impossible that they were the same person (Hengel 1983: 14). A local inscription (Ramsay 1897: 552) indicates the existence of a church dedicated to "the holy and glorious apostle and divine, Philip." Above the city to the NE, just outside the walls, stands the early-5th-century *martyrion* (monument) of Philip, an octagonal chamber set within a square comprising a series of rectangular chambers.

Papias, bishop of Hierapolis ca. A.D. 125, compiler of five volumes of *Exegeses of the Dominical Oracles* (no longer extant), is an important figure in the history of postapostolic tradition. Irenaeus says Papias was a hearer of "John the disciple of the Lord" (*Haer.* 5.33.4); Eusebius questions this (*Hist. Eccl.* 3.39.2).

In A.D. 172 a later bishop of Hierapolis, Claudius Apollinaris, addressed a defense of the Christian faith to Marcus Aurelius. This work, with several others ascribed to him, is lost (Eus. *Hist. Eccl.* 4.26.1; 4.27.1; 5.5.4; 5.16.1; 5.19.1–2).

The church of Hierapolis was represented at the councils of Nicaea (A.D. 325), Ephesus (431) and Chalcedon (451). Under Justinian, before the Second Council of Constantinople (553), Hierapolis became a metropolitan see, with jurisdiction over churches in the NW of the province Phrygia Pacatiana.

Bibliography

Bean, G. E. 1971. *Turkey beyond the Maeander.* London.

Brice, W. C. 1978. A Note on the Descent into the Plutonium at Hierapolis of Phrygia. *JSS* 23: 226–27.

Hengel, M. 1983. *Between Jesus and Paul: Studies in the Earliest History of Christianity.* Trans. J. Bowden. London.

Jones, A. H. M. 1971. *The Cities of the Eastern Roman Provinces.* 2d ed. Oxford.

Kolb, F. 1974. Zur Geschichte der Stadt Hierapolis in Phrygien. *Zeitschrift für Papyrologie und Epigraphik* 15: 255–70.

Magie, D. 1950. *Roman Rule in Asia Minor.* Princeton.

Ramsay, W. M. 1895. *The Cities and Bishoprics of Phrygia.* Vol. 1, pt. 1. Oxford.

———. 1897. *The Cities and Bishoprics of Phrygia.* Vol. 1, pt. 2. Oxford.

Verzone, P. 1960. Il martyrium ottagono a Hierapolis di Frigia. *Palladio* 10: 1–20.

———. 1961–62, 1963–64. Le campagne a Hierapolis di Frigia. *Annuario della Scuola Archeologica di Atene* 23–24: 633–47; 25–26: 352–70.

Yamauchi, E. 1980. *The Archaeology of New Testament Cities in Western Asia Minor.* Grand Rapids.

F. F. BRUCE

HIEROGLYPHICS. See LANGUAGES (EGYPTIAN LANGUAGE AND WRITING).

HIERONYMUS (PERSON) [Gk *Hierōnymos*]. One of five military governors of the Jews in the time of Antiochus V Eupator, 164–162 B.C.E. (2 Macc 12:2). The five governors have Greek names, which seems to imply that the Jews fought with local Macedonian officials, whereas 1 Maccabees 5 shows that they fought with neighboring peoples. There is no further specific information about Hieronymus himself, but the governors mentioned in the text are designated by the Greek term *strategos.* This term might refer to a commander of any rank from general to commander of a small tactical unit. Here they are set over "local" places, which likely indicates that they are commanders of lesser rank. They would not let the Jews live quietly and in peace, but whether their harassment resulted from orders from the central government or from their own initiative is not known.

BETTY JANE LILLIE

HIGH PLACE (Heb *bāmâ*). A type of cultic installation in ancient Israel. The precise architecture and purpose of high places has been a subject of considerable disagreement.

A. History of Interpretation
  1. Etymological Inferences
  2. Archaeological Influences
  3. Generalizing Tendencies
B. The Biblical Picture
  1. Language Usage
  2. Location
  3. Appearance

A. History of Interpretation

The traditional interpretation of Heb *bāmâ* begins with the Vg's *excelsus,* whence Eng "high place" (conventional since the 1535 Coverdale Bible; cf. Wycliffe's *high things* and Luther's *Höhe*). The LXX, although generally using *hupsēlon,* approached the word very differently (see Daniel 1966: 33–53). The modern era of biblical scholarship inherited this understanding of *bāmâ* as signifying physical elevation, as well as an etymological explanation for it. The word has no known verbal root in Hebrew, but on the basis of the irreducible *qāmes* the hypothetical root **bûm* (cf. *qûm: qāmâ*), meaning "to be high," had been advanced (e.g., Pagninus 1578: 30; GKC 187). Nineteenth-century lexicographers took the newly discovered Akk topographical pl. *bamātu* as cognate to *bāmâ* and defined it accordingly (e.g., Norris 1868: 104; Delitzsch 1896: 177); this datum, in turn, entered Hebrew lexica (e.g., BDB, 119) and biblical encyclopedias (e.g., *JEnc,* 387) as confirmation that *bāmâ* must be a topographical term denoting high ground. This meaning was applied to Ug *bmt* when that word became known in the 1930s (Virolleaud 1932: 136), but almost immediately gave way to Albright's suggestion that *bmt* is an anatomical term comparable to Akk *bamtu,* "back, trunk (of animal or man)" (1934: 120 n. 86). This anatomical sense has rightly been claimed for *bāmâ* in several biblical and extrabiblical passages (Deut 33:29; Isa 14:14; Job 9:8; 1QM 12:10 and 19:3; Sir 9:2 [Heb]) and is cited in current Hebrew lexica as one of the standard meanings of the word (*HALAT,* 130–31; *CHAL,* 42).

The prevailing consensus holds, therefore, that *bāmâ* can refer both to a part of the body ("back," although the exact reference is disputed) and to a part of the landscape (a "high place"). Its Akk cognate evidently shares this semantic duality, but thus far only the anatomical sense is certain in Ugaritic. To reconcile these meanings, a common proto-Semitic ancestor capable of generating both has been posited by Albright: **bahmatu,* the medial *h* having quiesced to produce *ā* in the first syllable in the attested forms. This should have become *ō* in Hebrew (cf. **qahlu* > **qāl* > *qōl*), and suffixed forms of *bāmâ* with an initial *o*-vowel are found in the Qumran literature (1QIsa[a] 14:14; 53:9; 58:14); thus, Albright reasons, the familiar *a* spelling "may be due to dialectal phenomena, *ah* being preserved in some places until after the principle that an accented *ā* became *ō* had ceased to operate" (1957: 245, 256). The *h* is preserved in such derivatives as Heb *bĕhēmâ* ("animal, beast") and Ug *bhmt* ("cattle") in which the anatomical idea has expanded from a bodily part to the entire creature, and obscure Ar *buhmatun* ("mass of rock"), which develops the topographical idea. The basic semantic nexus, however, is high-ness or, in de Vaux's words, "something which stands out in relief from its background" (*AncIsr,* 284).

1. Etymological Inferences. Over four-fifths of the some 100 occurrences of *bāmâ* in the MT refer to places where cultic acts were performed, i.e., to cultic installations of some sort. Speculation about the nature of these installations has proceeded from the aforementioned etymological considerations: whatever a bamah might be, it must somehow exhibit high-ness because that is the root meaning of the word. As Hirsch observed in 1904, "the only point in doubt is whether the bamah originally received its name from the circumstance that it was located on a towering elevation or from the possible fact that independently of its location, it was itself a raised construction" (*JEnc,* 387). These alternatives underlie virtually all subsequent efforts to describe or further identify these installations with any specificity. These efforts have produced two basic images: (1) a primitive open-air hilltop precinct, with altars, maṣṣeboth (cultic stones), and asherim (wooden cultic objects; cf. Day 1986), scattered throughout the Palestinian countryside; and (2) some sort of constructed elevation, such as a raised platform or mound. (Albright's view that bamoth were funerary installations [1957: 242–58], a variation of the platform hypothesis, is entirely without foundation: see Barrick 1975.)

Despite its pervasiveness, this etymological approach to the question is methodologically problematic. Etymologizing reveals the past history of a word and its past meaning(s), which may provide clues as to its possible (or even probable) sense in a given text, but "it cannot impose a sense authoritatively upon known usage" (Barr 1961: 158). Known usage of the word *bāmâ* suggests that it refers to built constructions of urban provenance and without a noticeable locational preference for high ground (see below). The few texts that do seem to place them in mountainous locales do not warrant the common presumption that there is a pronounced "biblical tradition that the bamoth were built on hills" (Albright 1957: 249), nor do they justify positing an evolutionary development of the bamah phenomenon itself to explain why some bamoth—virtually all of them, to judge from the biblical record—were in fact not built on hills (e.g., BDB, 119). If, on the other hand, a bamah was an artificial elevation upon which cultic acts were performed, a view much favored in recent scholarship (e.g., *AncIsr,* 284–88; Conrad 1968: 85–100; Haran 1978: 18–25), this should be reflected in the verbs and prepositions used in the texts to locate the worshipper relative to the bamah. But this is not the case. For example, the preposition routinely used in biblical reports of bamah usage is not *ʿal* as one should expect, but *b-,* suggesting *prima facie* that a bamah was something *within* which cultic acts took place. When this most embarrassing incongruity is acknowledged, appeal usually is made to the principle of prepositional "ambiguity" whereby *ʿal* and *b-* could be semantically equivalent (so, e.g., Vaughan 1974: 31). While this is a possibility to be considered (see below), the appeal amounts to circular reasoning since *b-* need be "ambiguous" in these passages only if bamoth were mounds or altars. In both cases, etymologically inspired presuppositions have been imposed onto textual evidence which otherwise would lead the interpreter in a very different direction.

2. Archaeological Influences. Vaughan's study (1974) departs from the traditional understanding of the word. From the Akk and Ug materials he deduces that the semantic origin of *bāmâ* is *anatomical* ("rib-cage, chest, back, flank, etc.") and that "there is no idea of *height* inherent in this concept at all" (10; cf. already Vincent 1948: 276). This anatomical sense is applied figuratively in the expression *bomŏtê-ʾāreṣ* (Deut 32:13; Isa 48:14; Amos 4:3; Mic 1:3), lit. "flanks of the land," the topographical nuance being supplied by *ʾereṣ.* Vaughan sees this phrase as a "stock poetic formula" originating in an ancient theophanic myth and referring to the mountainous terrain astride which Yahweh manifests himself in symbolic possession of the land. The mythological site of the theophany, according to Vaughan, was realized architecturally as a mound or platform which took its name from its mythic prototype (1974: 9, 11–12, 25). That the specialized technical use of the word to designate a cultic installation should have derived from a mythological image is an intriguing possibility, but Vaughan's claim that bamoth were cultic platforms does not hinge on that hypothesis. For him, the consistent semantic factor is the hill-like *shape* of the objects to which the word refers: mythological mountains or cultic platforms representing them; actual mountains (2 Sam 1:19, 25; but the word may carry an anatomical sense here: see e.g., McCarter, *2 Samuel* AB, 74–75); and grave-mounds (Isa 53:9 and Job 27:15 [both emended]) having no connection whatever with either the myth or its cultic symbolism. Implicit in Vaughan's argument is a semantic assumption not unlike the traditional etymological one.

Vaughan's conclusions are heavily influenced by recent archaeological discoveries in the Levant. A number of platformlike structures have come to light over the years and are in need of interpretation (Vaughan 1974: 37–54). A reliance upon archaeological materials is characteristic of 20th-century speculation about the bamah phenomenon. Too often, however, the relevance of these artifacts is presupposed rather than demonstrated, and the burden of proof for a particular understanding of the bamah phenomenon is shifted (as in Vaughan's case) from the texts to the artifacts (cf. Fowler 1982: 210–11). This too is methodologically questionable. A cultic installation called a "bamah" is known to have existed at all only from references to it in the Hebrew Bible (and in the inscription of the Moabite king Mesha). Archaeology has revealed the context into which those references must be placed if we are to move beyond the heavily theologized and imperfectly controlled literary traditions of the Bible to the actual life of people in biblical times (*WLSGF,* 572–87). But for something known from archaeology to be identified as a "bamah" there must be a demonstrable correspondence between the artifact and the literary descriptions. And, as one reviewer of Vaughan's monograph cautiously observes, "given our present very incomplete knowledge of what a bamah really was and looked like, we need to find an edifice actually labelled 'bamah' before we can be sure" (Ap-Thomas 1975: 107).

3. Generalizing Tendencies. Whitney's study (1979) moves in a very different direction. He maintains that "fundamentally *bāmâ* meant 'shrine' and was used of the whole cult complex, which may or may not have contained a platform" (134). Most commentators would agree that the word is such a generic designation in at least some of its occurrences. That the bamoth of the Bible were common Canaanitish cult places is a view omnipresent in the secondary literature. Typically, a categorical distinction is drawn between bamoth—understood as open-air rustic sanctuaries—and more architecturally sophisticated urban temples (e.g., Noth 1966: 177–78; Ringgren 1966: 156–58). The fact that archaeologically known cult places in Syria-Palestine do not conform to such a sharp dichotomy has not lessened the popularity of this view (cf. Schunck 1971: 132–40, and Welten 1972: 19–37; Wright 1971: 17–32). But for Whitney *bāmâ* does not carry any specific architectural or functional connotations; bamoth were "different things in different places at different times" (147). The earliest references may be to cult places located on high ground, but by the late monarchy (whence most of the references come) the word had become an all-purpose label for "local shrines" in general (138). This view also has a wide following and, in fact, underlies the normative reconstruction of Israel's religious history: worship was conducted at "local shrines" throughout the land until the erection of Solomon's temple (cf. 1 Kgs 3:4); thereafter those sanctuaries remained the loci of popular religiosity until their final illegitimation in the reign of Josiah (e.g., *WPHI,* chap. 1). This reconstruction, anticipated already in the Talmud (*Zeb.* 14:4–8), assumes that the orders in Deuteronomy 12 to destroy the cult places "upon the high mountains and upon the hills and under every green tree" (v 2) and to worship only at "the place which Yahweh will choose" (v 5) coincide with Josiah's actions as recorded in 2 Kings 23, specifically the centralization of worship in the temple at Jerusalem and the concomitant elimination of all other sanctuaries in the country. The only non-temple sanctuaries mentioned in 2 Kings 23 are called "bamoth" and, as Whitney points out, more than one type of installation seems to be so identified: small gate shrines, royal chapels dedicated to foreign gods, large public sanctuaries, and rustic local sanctuaries (137–38). Since Josiah's reform was "Deuteronomic," these "bamoth" must be equated with the cult "places" *(ham-mĕqōmôt)* proscribed in Deuteronomy 12. In at least "Deuteronomistic" vocabulary, therefore, *bāmôt* is synonymous with *mĕqōmôt* as a generalization with distinctly pejorative overtones (see, e.g., *AncIsr,* 288).

This generalizing approach to the question also is methodologically problematic, for it makes the meaning of *bāmâ* in a given passage contingent upon other exegetical judgments which may be neither correct nor germane. For example, the supposed open-air rusticity of a bamah installation stems from a romanticized conception of "primitive" religious practice, buttressed by dubious ethnographical analogies and biblical passages which "though not expressly mentioning any bamah, certainly have the same type of religion in mind" (*AncIsr,* 285). Relevance is assumed, but not demonstrated. Similarly, Israel's religious history *may* have unfolded in the way supposed, or later biblical writers *may* have presented this as an idealization, but it is by no means a certainty and should not be accepted uncritically as the basis for solving all other exegetical puzzles. Reconstructing history of Israelite religion and literature by linking the cult "places" of Deuteronomy 12 with the "bamoth" of 1–2 Kings and then using that reconstruction as the basis for interpreting the "Deuteronomistic" meaning of the word is a circular argument which excludes other exegetical options at the outset; the possibility that a specific architectural or functional type of installation may be referred to even in "Deuteronomistic" passages is not seriously considered (cf. Fowler 1982: 212).

B. The Biblical Picture

The OT evidence, meager and fragmentary as it is, does yield a consistent if sketchy picture of those installations called "bamoth" by the ancient writers.

1. Language Usage. Bamoth appear to have been man-made installations. They are "built"/*bnh* (1 Kgs 11:7; 14:23; 2 Kgs 17:9; 21:3; 23:13; Jer 7:31; 19:5; 32:35; 2 Chr 33:3, 19; MI 3–4[?]) or "made"/*ʿśh* (Ezek 16:16; 2 Chr 21:11; 28:25; MI 3), "torn down"/*ntṣ* (2 Kgs 23:8, 15; 2 Chr 31:1) or "burned"/*śrp* (2 Kgs 23:15). These verbal actions do not suggest ephemeral sacred precincts or crudely augmented natural phenomena. While this does not prove that all bamoth were man-made structures, there is no evidence that any bamah was not.

The verb *ʿlh* (in Qal) is used of bamoth in four biblical passages (1 Sam 9:13, 14, 19; Isa 15:2). This verb can express movement up to a position upon something, and also movement up to something. When upward movement resulting in superimposition is the intended sense, the destination is always subordinated to the verb by means of the preposition *ʿal:* e.g., "You shall not go up upon my altar by steps" (Ex 20:26, and 20 other examples). When *ʿlh* is used of bamoth, however, the subordination is thrice by means of the "accusative" and once by the "terminative" *h.* In none of the 35 other *ʿlh* + accusative constructions does the one "going up" demonstrably conclude his journey upon his destination. In a great many cases superimposition is obviously impossible: e.g., "the king went up (to) the House-of-Yahweh" (2 Kgs 23:2, and 10 other passages with *bayit*). When the nature of the destination will admit superimposition, the passage makes as good or better sense without this nuance. The situation with the 14 other *ʿlh* + terminative constructions is identical. Language usage suggests, therefore, that one does not climb up a bamah (as one would a hill or a stepped altar or platform), but rather climbs up to (and descends from: 1 Sam 9:25; 10:5) a bamah.

When the OT writers speak of bamah worship, they regularly use the verbs *zbḥ* and *qṭr,* plus the preposition *b* (20 occurrences). In each of the 15 other occurrences of these two verbs plus *b-* in the OT, the nature of the prepositional object or the context of the passage or (in most cases) both leave no doubt that the "ritual slaughtering" and "burning of food offerings" (so Edelman 1985) is being done within something. When this activity is conducted upon something, the preposition *ʿal* is always used. There is no evidence of "ambiguity" or semantic overlapping between *b-* and *ʿal* with these two verbs. To interpret *babbāmôt* in these passages as anything other than "in the bamoth" would be completely contrary to attested Hebrew usage.

The preposition *b-* is used of bamoth in three other passages as well: Samuel is expected to preside at a sacrifice to be held *babbāmâ* (1 Sam 9:12), and the Chronicler reports that during David's reign the tabernacle and altar of burnt offerings were *babbāmâ* at Gibeon (1 Chr 16:39–

40; 21:29). There is no reason why *b-* should not mean "in" in all three. This is consistent with the use of *bāʾ*, primarily "to enter," in reference to bamoth in 1 Sam 10:13 (although the text is uncertain) and Ezek 20:29, the latter a lame pun purporting to explain the meaning of the term *bāmâ* (cf. Greenberg, *Ezekiel 1–20* AB, 370–71).

On the basis of the biblical writers' use of the term, therefore, it would appear that a bamah is something within which cultic acts were performed—not a piece of cultic furniture (like a platform or altar), but an installation within which cultic furniture could be housed and used. Only Isa 16:12 suggests otherwise: *wĕhāyâ kî-nirʾâ kî-nilʾâ môʾāb ʿal-habbāmâ, ûbāʾ ʾel-miqdāšô lĕhitpallēl welōʾ yûkāl.* Assuming that a bamah was a platform or hill, *ʿal-habbāmâ* obviously would mean "upon the bamah." But since this passage is the sole textual basis for that assumption and contradicts the unanimous testimony of the passages just reviewed, its meaning may not be so obvious. The parallelism with *ʾel-miqdāšô* (cf. Amos 7:9) and the well-documented incidence of semantic overlapping (or scribal confusion) between *ʾel* and *ʿal* in biblical Hebrew (e.g., Ps 90:16, also with *rʾh* in *Nipʿal*) suggest that *ʿal* here might actually mean "in" (cf. Isa 28:22) or simply "at."

2. Location. The most complete description of a bamah in the OT is given in 1 Sam 9:1–10:16. This one is associated with an unnamed "city" *(ʿîr)* in "the land of Zuph." The present arrangement of the text gives the impression that the installation lay somewhere outside the city wall. Vv 14 and 18a conflict on this point, and commentators have long sought to harmonize the two through an arbitrary emendation of v 14 (recently, e.g., McCarter, *1 Samuel* AB, 169). Recognition that the story as a whole is composed of two distinct strata of material (Schmidt 1970: 53–102; Miller 1974: 157–61; Birch 1976: 29–42; McCarter *1 Samuel* AB, 185–87) provides a more defensible solution. In v 14 Saul and his servant are "entering into the midst of the city" *(bāʾîm bĕtôk hāʿîr)* and there meet Samuel as he was "coming out" of some unspecified location (presumably his residence) within the city en route "up (to) the bamah"—all exactly as predicted by the girls at the well in v 13. A second version of this encounter is given in vv 12 and 18a: here Samuel is walking on the road up to the city some distance ahead of Saul; the girls point him out, and Saul overtakes him "in the midst of the gate" *(bĕtôk haššāʿar)* as both men are entering the city. In both accounts the subsequent activity at the bamah would have taken place inside the city wall. The fact that this bamah actually lay somewhere within the city was obscured when the two versions of the story were combined, and Samuel's "coming out" (v 14) juxtaposed with the meeting "in the gate" (v 18)—yet it was recognized by the LXX and 4QSam[a] which harmonize the two by reading "city" in place of "gate" in v 18a (just the reverse of the usual solution today).

This is by no means an exceptional case. The preponderance of texts which specify the location of bamoth also give them an urban setting. They are said to have been "in" *(b-)* "the cities of Judah" (2 Kgs 23:8; cf. v 5 and 2 Chr 14:4), the city of Gibeon (1 Chr 16:39; 21:29; 2 Chr 1:3, 13), and all the cities of northern Israel (2 Kgs 17:9). Mesha of Moab made a bamah "in Qarhoh," probably the royal quarter or citadel of his capital city (MI. 3). "Bamoth houses" *(bāttê-bāmôt)* were found "in the cities of Samaria" (1 Kgs 13:32; 2 Kgs 17:29; 23:19); "bamoth priests" *(kōhănê-bāmôt)* were stationed "in (the city of) Bethel" (1 Kgs 12:32) and apparently also in "the cities of Judah" (2 Kgs 23:8–9). The bamoth built by Solomon "in the mountain east of Jerusalem" to serve the religious needs of some of his foreign wives (1 Kgs 11:7–8 and 2 Kgs 23:11; cf. 1 Kgs 16:32) and the bamah installation(s) in the Ben Hinnom Valley (Jer 7:31; 19:5; 32:35 [the number is text-critically uncertain]; cf. 2 Kgs 23:10 which, oddly, does not use the term) were certainly part of the cultic life of the capital city, their extramural location probably due to political considerations, and perhaps (especially for the second) the special character of the cultus conducted there (cf. Heider 1985). Ezek 6:3 speaks of the ubiquity of the bamoth, not their specific location (v 6 nonetheless does indicate an urban setting), and so too 2 Chr 21:11.

It is commonly supposed that bamoth are the object of the frequent polemic against worship conducted in the countryside "upon every high hill and under every green tree" (especially Deut 12:2; cf. Holladay 1961). But 2 Kgs 16:4 (= 2 Chr 28:4) argues against the identification: Ahaz is said to have "slaughtered animals and burned food offerings in the bamoth *and* upon the hills and under every green tree." Similarly, 2 Kgs 17:9–11 apparently distinguishes urban bamoth from hilltop installations featuring (only?) maṣṣeboth and asherim (cf. 1 Kgs 14:23 which seems defective; one does not "build"/*bnh* maṣṣeboth and asherim). The firmest evidential basis for the identification is Ezek 20:28–29 where, however, many commentators regard the pun in v 29 as a secondary or tertiary gloss (e.g., Zimmerli, *Ezekiel 1* Hermeneia, 412).

3. Appearance. The biblical record says little about what a bamah may have looked like or how it was furnished. Since sacrificial activities were conducted there, bamoth would have contained altars of one sort or another (cf. 1 Chr 16:35–40; 21:29). Some undoubtedly also possessed maṣṣeboth and/or asherim. Each bamah undoubtedly was furnished with the special paraphernalia of the cultus conducted there, the details of which are no longer extant.

In terms of architecture, 1 Sam 9:1–10:16 provides a clue. The "sacrifice" to be held "in the bamah" (v 12) is not mentioned further in the story. We are told, however, that "Samuel took Saul and his servant and brought them to the *liškâ*" (v 22a) where a meal was consumed. According to the traditional view, a *liškâ* was a supplementary structure (a shelter or dining hall; cf. LXX, Targ, Vg) not intrinsically part of the bamah phenomenon. Elsewhere, however, the term is used exclusively in reference to architectural components of the temple complex in Jerusalem, "chambers" used to house temple personnel, cultic equipment, and offerings. The Gk version of 1 Sam 1:18b (which may be textually superior to the MT) reports that the "temple" *(hêkāl)* at Shiloh also had a *liškâ*, to which Hannah retired to eat. This associational consistency and functional variety indicate that *liškâ* (possibly a Mediterranean loanword) may be the technical term for the more utilitarian architectural elements of the category of sanctuary we call "temples"—as illustrated by the Israelite temple complex at Arad, with its cult building, courtyard, and adjoining "chambers" (see Aharoni 1968; Herzog et al. 1984).

The occurrence of the term *liškâ* in 1 Sam 9:1–10:16 suggests that at least this bamah was a sanctuary of some architectural sophistication, not too different in its essentials from the sanctuary complex at Arad or, for that matter, the sanctuary complex in the royal quarter of Jerusalem—which one climbed up to and descended from, within which cultic acts were performed, which possessed *liškōt* (as well as altars, and even an asherah [2 Kgs 23:6]), which was "built" and "burned" (and, although the term is not used, was certainly capable of being "torn down")—which, in fact, meets all the criteria which the ancient writers have given us to identify a bamah.

Bibliography

Aharoni, Y. 1968. Arad: Its Inscriptions and Temple. *BA* 31: 2–32.
Albright, W. F. 1934. The North-Canaanite Poems of Al'eyan Ba'al and the "Gracious Gods." *JPOS* 14: 101–40.
———. 1957. The High Place in Ancient Palestine. *SVT* 4:242–58.
Ap-Thomas, D. R. 1975. Review of Vaughan 1974 in *PEQ* 107: 166–67.
Barr, J. 1961. *The Semantics of Biblical Language.* London.
Barrick, W. B. 1975. The Funerary Character of "High Places" in Ancient Palestine: A Reassessment. *VT* 25: 565–95.
Birch, B. C. 1976. *The Rise of the Israelite Monarchy: The Growth and Development of 1 Samuel 7–15.* SBLDS 27. Missoula, MT.
Conrad, D. 1968. *Studien zum Altargesetz (Ex. 20:24–26).* Marburg.
Daniel, S. 1966. *Recherches sur le Vocabulaire du Culte dans la Septante.* Etudes et Commentaires 41. Paris.
Day, J. 1986. Asherah in the Hebrew Bible and Northwest Semitic Literature. *JBL* 105: 385–408.
Delitzsch, F. 1896. *Assyrisches Handwörtebuch.* Baltimore.
Edelman, D. 1985. The Meaning of *Qitter. VT* 35: 395–404.
Fowler, M. D. 1982. The Israelite *bāmâ:* A Question of Interpretation. *ZAW* 94: 203–13.
Haran, M. 1978. *Temples and Temple Service in Ancient Israel.* Oxford.
Heider, G. C. 1985. *The Cult of Molek.* JSOTS 43. Sheffield.
Herzog, Z.; Aharoni, M.; Rainey, A. F.; and Moskovitz, S. 1984. The Israelite Fortress at Arad. *BASOR* 254: 1–34.
Holladay, W. L. 1961. On Every High Hill and Under Every Green Tree. *VT* 11: 170–76.
Miller, J. M. 1974. Saul's Rise to Power: Some Observations concerning 1 Sam 9:1–10:16; 10:26–11:15 and 13:2–14:46. *CBQ* 36: 157–74.
Norris, E. 1868. *Assyrian Dictionary.* London.
Noth, M. 1966. *The Old Testament World.* Trans. V. I. Gruhn. Philadelphia.
Pagninus, S. 1578. *Epitome Thesauri Linguae Sanctae.* 3d ed. Antwerp.
Ringgren, H. 1966. *Israelite Religion.* Trans. D. E. Green. Philadelphia.
Robinson, G. L. 1914. High Place. *ERE* 6: 678–81.
Schmidt, L. 1970. *Menschlicher Erfolg and Jahwes Initiative.* WMANT 38. Neukirchen-Vluyn.
Schunck, K. D. 1971. Zentralheiligtum, Grensheiligtum, and "Hohenheiligtum" in Israel. *Numen* 18: 132–40.
Vaughan, P. H. 1974. *The Meaning of "bāmâ" in the Old Testament.* SOTSMS 3. Cambridge.
Vincent, L. H. 1948. La Notion biblique du Haut-Lieu. *RB* 55: 245–78, 438–45.
Virolleaud, C. 1932. Un nouveau Chant du Poeme d'Alein-Baal. *Syria* 13: 113–63.
Welten, P. 1972. Kulthöhe and Jahwetemple. *ZDPV* 88: 19–37.
Whitney, J. T. 1979. "Bamoth" in the Old Testament. *TynBul* 30: 125–47.
Wright, G. R. H. 1971. Pre-Israelite Temples in the Land of Canaan. *PEQ* 103: 17–32.

W. Boyd Barrick

HILEN (PLACE) [Heb *ḥîlēn*]. Var. HOLON. A levitical town in Judah (only slightly to the east of Debir) assigned to the sons of Aaron (1 Chr 6:58). The same place appears as "Holon" in a second list of such towns (Josh 15:51). The difference in spelling could be due either to mechanical error or, as Williamson (*Chronicles* NCBC, 75) suggests, to the likelihood that the Chronicler had access to another (and better preserved?) recension of the list than that preserved in Joshua. This town, along with a number of other towns in the list, probably came under Israelite control during the time of David. The prophet Jeremiah includes a Moabite town by the name of Holon in his oracle against that nation (Jer 48:21).

Bibliography

Pritchard, J. B. ed. 1987. *The Harper Atlas of the Bible.* New York.

Elmer H. Dyck

HILKIAH (PERSON) [Heb *ḥilqîyāhû*]. **1.** A Levite, the son of Amzi, and father of Amaziah (1 Chr 6:30—Eng 6:45). He was a descendant of Levi through Merari. His name occurs in the middle of a list justifying Ethan's rightful place as a levitical singer in the time of David. Oddly enough, his name is one among many others (see 1 Chr 6:29–33—Eng 6:44–47) not paralleled in the list of Merari's descendants given earlier in 1 Chronicles 6 (see 1 Chr 6:4—Eng 6:19; 6:14–15—Eng 6:29–30). In view of the fact that one of the unparalleled names, Hashabiah (1 Chr 6:30—Eng 6:15), occurs in connection with Ezra's activities (Ezra 8:19, 24; see also **7.** below) the second Merari list in 1 Chronicles 6 need not be the literary creation of the Chronicler, but rather a reflection of the levitical guild structure of his own day, whose very legitimacy he was seeking to underscore (Williamson *1 and 2 Chronicles* NCBC, 74).

2. A levitical gatekeeper, the second son of Hosah of the sons of Merari (1 Chr 26:11). His name appears in a chapter which attributes to the efforts of King David the elaborate levitical organization at work in a much later age. On the historicity of David's relationship to the Levites, see Hauer 1982: 41–44. It seems David had appointed Hilkiah's father, Hosah, as one of the gatekeepers in the days of the tent of the ark of the covenant in Jerusalem (1 Chr 16:38; 17:1). But in anticipation of the construction of the Solomonic temple, the Chronicler reports how the lot for the keeping of the gate of Shallecheth fell to Hosah and his sons (1 Chr 26:16). This gate was located apparently on the western side of the temple complex (yet cf. LXX B).

3. The father of Eliakim (2 Kgs 18:18 = Isa 36:3; 2 Kgs 18:26; 18:37 = Isa 36:22). He was the major-domo during the reign of King Hezekiah. In the oracle of Isa 22:20 it is said that Eliakim ben Hilkiah would succeed the arrogant Shebna as the king's major-domo. Understandably, in 701

B.C., he was one of the officials sent out from Hezekiah to parley with the Assyrian Rabshakeh during the invasion and siege of Jerusalem by King Sennacherib.

4. A levitical priest, the father of the prophet Jeremiah (Jer 1:1). Possibly he was a descendant of Abiathar, the last chief priest of the house of Eli, as he resided in the priestly town of Anathoth in the land of Benjamin, whither Abiathar centuries before had been exiled by Solomon (1 Kgs 2:26–27). This possible Shiloh connection may also be noted in Jeremiah's "temple sermon" (Jer 7:12, 14; 26:9).

5. A levitical high priest, the son of Shallum, and father of Azariah (III?), and grandfather of Seraiah (1 Chr 5:39–40—Eng 6:13–14; 9:11; Ezra 7:1–2). He was active during the reign of King Josiah (2 Kgs 22:4 = 2 Chr 34:9). It was he who found "the Book of the Law" in the temple which helped play a role in Josiah's far-reaching reform movement (2 Kgs 22:8, 10, 12, 14; 23:4, 24; 2 Chr 34:14, 15, 18, 20, 22) and this king's celebration of the Passover (2 Chr 35:8; 1 Esdr 1:8). See JOSIAH (PERSON). Interestingly, in both Neh 11:11 and 1 Chr 9:11 he is called the son of Meshullam (= Shallum?). While 1 Chr 9:11 entitles this Hilkiah the father of Azariah, Neh 11:11 dubs him the father (not the grandfather) of Seraiah. He is also regarded as the progenitor of Ezra the priest (Ezra 7:1; 1 Esdr 8:1; 2 Esdr 1:1). In the apocryphal book of Baruch this same high priest (LXX *chelkios*) is evidenced. Here Hilkiah is described as the son of Shallum, but he is also named as the father of an otherwise unknown priest named Jehoiakim who supposedly was the recipient of a gift of money collected among the exiles and sent to Jerusalem (Bar 1:7).

6. The father of Gemariah, the envoy of King Zedekiah to King Nebuchadnezzar (Jer 29:3). While on his mission he carried a letter from the prophet Jeremiah to the Jews in Babylon who had been exiled by Nebuchadnezzar in 597 B.C.

7. One of the priests who returned from exile with Zerubbabel and Jeshua in 536 B.C. (Neh 12:7). He is one of twenty-two leaders cited in Neh 12:1–7. As four major phratries are known to have accompanied Zerubbabel and Jeshua (Ezra 2:36–39 = Neh 7:39–42 = 1 Esdr 5:24–25) the mention of these twenty-two leaders here must refer to leaders of subgroupings within the same four larger phratries (Clines *Ezra* NCBC, 223). This Hilkiah became the progenitor of Hashabiah, the head of one of the important priestly families in the time of Joiakim (Neh 12:21), the high priest who succeeded Jeshua (Neh 12:10) and who became the father of Eliashib, the contemporary of Nehemiah (Neh 3:1).

8. A contemporary of Ezra (Neh 8:4). He may be the same person as **7.** above. He is named as one of a number of individuals who stood at the right hand of Ezra the priest as he read "the law of God" to the people. The closest that the parallel verse in 1 Esdr 9:43 comes to repeating his name is in its reference to the name Hezekiah [LXX *ezekias*].

9. The father of Susanna, Joakim's virtuous wife who was falsely accused of adultery and vindicated by the apocryphal Daniel (Sus v 2).

10. A progenitor of Baruch, the son of Neraiah (Bar 1:1). Baruch was the secretary of the prophet Jeremiah (Bar 1:1; Jer 36:4). The name occurs in the very first verse of Baruch, the apocryphal book purported to have been written by Baruch while in Babylonian captivity. The book of Jeremiah seems to support at least the latter part of the full ancestry given in Bar 1:1, when it calls Baruch "the son of Neriah the son of Mahseiah" (Jer 32:12). What is more, the historical Baruch seems to have had a brother by the name of Seraiah who is likewise described as "the son of Neriah, son of Mahseiah" (Jer 51:59). See BARUCH (PERSON) #1.

11. The son of Eliab and father of Elijah and grandfather of Ahitub. He is named as an ancestor of the apocryphal Judith, the pious widow who delivered her people from Holofernes (Jdt 8:1).

Bibliography

Hauer, C. 1982. David and the Levites. *JSOT* 23: 33–54.

ROGER W. UITTI

HILKIAH THE HASID. Abba Ḥilkiah is an obscure Jew. He was "a great Hasid" (*hyh Ḥsyd gdwl; b. Taʿan.* 23a), but that description does not necessarily place him among the Hasidim. He lived in the second half of the 1st century B.C.E., since he was the grandson of Ḥoni Ha-Meaggel. Through the power of prayer he was able, like his famous grandfather, to control the fall of rain. While Ḥoni was asked by crowds to cause the rain to fall, Abba Ḥilkiah once received scholars sent by the rabbis who wanted him to influence God to send rain. He was exceedingly poor and had to seek work as a laborer and to borrow a cloak. It is reported that he performed numerous mysterious acts and had penetrating insight. Although a renowned miracle worker, he is never reported to have performed healing miracles.

Bibliography

Hyman, A. 1910. *Toldoth Tannaim Veʾamoraim.* 3 vols. London.
Rabbinowitz, J. 1938. *Taʿanith: Translated into English with Notes, Glossary and Indices.* London.

JAMES H. CHARLESWORTH

HILLEL (PERSON) [Heb *hillēl*]. The father of the Israelite judge Abdon (Judg 12:13, 15).

HILLEL THE ELDER. Pharisaic leader of the late 1st century B.C.E., eponym and perhaps founder of the school of Pharisaic rabbinic leaders that ultimately shaped the Jewish tradition.

Precisely on account of the importance that came to be attached to Hillel's name, the task of extracting biographical information from the legends that surround him is extremely difficult. Hillel came to be remembered as the ideal sage (see Urbach 1971: 128), and stories recounting his acts and teachings are sometimes demonstrably didactic rather than historical in origin (Neusner 1971: 286). Even if the facts of the matter therefore cannot always be ascertained, however, the image of Hillel that was created by his successors can be described with some clarity.

Hillel is said to have immigrated as a young adult from Babylonia to Jerusalem (his Davidic ancestry was almost certainly a later invention; see Levi 1895); some traditions describe him as having arrived already possessing great learning (*y. Pesaḥ.* 6:1, 33a; *t. Neg.* 1:16; *Sipra Tazria* 9:16), others place him in the chain of Pharisaic (i.e., Jerusalem) tradition as the disciple of Shemaiah and Abtalyon (e.g., *m. ʾAbot* 1:12; *Ḥag.* 2:2) without reference to any previous teachers. He quickly rose to prominence, and according to tradition after solving a problem concerning the Passover offering that no one else could settle he became the leader (*nāśîʾ*) of the entire movement (*y. Pesaḥ.* 6:1, 33a; *b. Pesaḥ.* 66ab; *t. Pesaḥ.* 4:13). Later generations identified him with other great founders or refounders of the tradition (Moses: *Sipre Ve-Zot Ha-Berakhah* 357; Ezra: *b. Sukk.* 20a; *Soṭa* 48b); of his successors, only Yoḥanan b. Zakkai and Akiba were considered his equals.

The enactment most commonly associated with Hillel's name is the *pĕrôzbûl* (from the Gk *prosboulē*), a procedure whereby creditors could avoid the cancellation of debt every seven years; this innovation is said to have been ordained because lenders would refuse to make loans as the sabbatical year grew closer (*Šeb.* 10.2–4; *Sipre Reeh* 113; see Neusner 1971: 217–23).

Hillel's reported teachings, especially the series of sayings included in the Mishnaic tractate *ʾAbot* ("Ethics of the Fathers") embody a number of fundamental rabbinic conceptions, such as "Do not separate yourself from the community" (2:4), "If I am not for myself who will be for me, but if I am for myself alone what am I?" (1:14), or "Be among the disciples of Aaron, who loved peace and pursued it" (1:12). Similarly, his behavior in numerous situations is portrayed as that of the ideal sage or scholar of Torah: when he could not afford the fee to a public lecture, he hid on the roof of the building and listened through a skylight even though he wound up covered by snow (*b. Yoma* 35b), and when badgered by a would-be convert who would accept Judaism only under impossible conditions he replied, "Do not do to another what you would not wish done to yourself; that is the whole Torah. The rest is commentary; go and study" (*b. Šabb.* 31a).

The earliest known list of rules (*mîddôt*) for proper exegesis of the Torah is attributed to Hillel, though it is nowhere suggested that Hillel actually invented the procedures in question or formulated their enumeration. These procedures appear in the story about the Passover offering already mentioned, and are also listed in his name at *t. Sanh.* 7:11.

Bibliography

Goldenberg, R. 1986. Hillel/Hillelschule. *TRE* 15: 326–30.

Levi, I. 1895. De l'origine davidique de Hillel. *REJ* 31: 202–11; 32: 143–46.

Neusner, J. 1971. *The Rabbinic Traditions about the Pharisees before 70.* Vol. 1. Leiden.

Urbach, E. E. 1971. The Talmudic Sage, Character and Authority. *Jewish Society through the Ages,* ed. H. H. Ben-Sasson and S. Ettinger. New York.

ROBERT GOLDENBERG

HIN [Heb *hîn*]. See WEIGHTS AND MEASURES.

HINNOM VALLEY (PLACE) [Heb *gê hinnôm*]. A narrow gorge curving along the W and S sides of Jerusalem. The valley begins near the modern Jaffa Gate as a shallow valley, turns S at the gate for approximately a half mile, and winds to the E, deepening to become a gorge as it reaches the Kidron Valley. Besides the designation "Valley of Hinnom" (Josh 15:8; Neh 11:30), the valley is also referred to as "valley of the son of Hinnom" (*gê ben-hinnôm;* Josh 15:8 [var.]; 18:16; 2 Chr 28:3; 33:6; Jer 7:31–32; 19:2, 6; 32:35; Q in 2 Kgs 23:10), "valley of the sons of Hinnom" (*gê bĕnê-hinnôm;* K in 2 Kgs 23:10), and "the valley" (*haggayʾ;* 2 Chr 26:9; Neh 2:13, 15; 3:13; Jer 2:23; cf. 31:40). These forms of "son" or "sons of" suggest that Hinnom is a personal name.

A. Hinnom in the Biblical Record

The Valley of Hinnom was accessed from Jerusalem through the Potsherd Gate (Jer 19:2) and the Valley Gate (Neh 2:13, 15; 3:13). The valley marked the E to W boundary between the tribal holdings of Judah and Benjamin (Josh 15:8; 18:16).

During the Monarchy, the valley was the site of idolatry. It was there that kings Ahaz and Manasseh burned incense and sacrificed their own sons as burnt offerings to Molech (2 Chr 28:3; 33:6). As a reform measure to prevent the Israelites from such practices, Josiah defiled the Topheth, the junction of the Hinnom, Kidron, and Tyropoeon valleys below Siloam near Jerusalem (2 Kgs 23:10).

By the time of Jeremiah the Valley of Hinnom was infamous for Baal worship, so much so that Jeremiah could simply refer to it as "the valley" (Jer 2:23). Jeremiah prophesied that because of judgment for the sacrifice of children in Hinnom, there would be so many dead on the Day of the Lord that the valley would be renamed the Valley of Slaughter (Jer 7:31–32; 19:5–6). The valley was the N limit of the postexilic settlements of the tribe of Judah (Neh 11:30).

In light of passages which speak of the judgment upon Israel's enemies in a valley near Jerusalem (Isa 30:29–33; 66:24; Joel 3:2, 12, 14) and the worship of underworld deities (Molech) in the Valley of Hinnom, the valley became a fiery place of judgment known by the transliteration "Gehenna." Gehenna was both a place of eschatological judgment in the environs of Jerusalem and an otherworldly place of judgment for the wicked. See GEHENNA (PLACE).

B. The Location of Hinnom

The location of the valley has been identified with any of the three valleys outside Jerusalem: the Kidron Valley E of Jerusalem, the Wâdī er-Rabâbi to the W of Jerusalem, and the Tyropoeon Valley which lies in between these two valleys. The identification which emerged at the turn of the century and still enjoys scholarly consensus is the Wâdī er-Rabâbi.

The Kidron Valley was the identification popular with early Christian, Moslem, and Jewish writers. The Kidron probably became a candidate when the location of the Valley of Hinnom was uncertain, but yet associated with fiery judgment. In light of Isa 66:24 which describes a scene of fiery judgment of Israel's enemies visible from the Temple Mount, the Kidron Valley probably was associated with Hinnom because it lies the closest to the Mount. This identification is questionable because the Kidron is never called a *gayʾ* (valley without a winter brook, a gorge), as is Hinnom, but a *naḥal* (a valley with a winter brook, a wadi). Also, the Valley Gate which opened into the Valley of Hinnom did not lie on the E of Jerusalem before the Kidron, but on the W over either the Tyropoeon or Wâdī er-Rabâbi near the present Jaffa Gate.

The Tyropoeon Valley is usually no longer associated with the Valley of Hinnom. During the Monarchy, in the period of Ahaz and Manasseh, the Tyropoeon lay within the walls of Jerusalem and child sacrifice would have been practiced outside the walls of the city. The Wâdī er-Rabâbi is the best identification, fitting the data of Joshua that the Valley of Hinnom ran E and W and lay outside the city walls. According to Joshua, the valley began in En-rogel. If the modern Bîr Ayyûb is correctly identified as En-rogel, then the Wâdī er-Rabâbi which begins there is the Valley of Hinnom.

Bibliography

Bailey, L. R. 1986. Gehenna: The Topography of Hell. *BA* 49: 187–91.

Dalman, G. 1930. Jerusalem und sein Gelände. *Schriften des Deutschen Palästina-Instituts* 4: 199–208.

Smith, G. A. 1907. *Jerusalem: The Topography, Economics and History from the Earliest Times to A.D. 70*. London.

DUANE F. WATSON

HIRAH (PERSON) [Heb *ḥîrâ*]. The Adullamite mentioned in Genesis 38, the Tamar and Judah interlude of the Joseph story, with whom Judah was staying (Gen 38:1) when he married the Canaanite woman, the daughter of Shua. In vv 12 and 20–23, he is described as Judah's friend who accompanied him to Timnah for sheep shearing, and who was sent by Judah with a kid to pay the prostitute (the disguised Tamar) for her sexual favors and to redeem the pledges (his staff and seal) which Judah had left with her. In these verses, the LXX and Vg call him Judah's shepherd *(poimēn, pastor, opilio)* rather than his friend, which probably resulted from a reading of *rōʿēhû*, "his shepherd," for *rēʿēhû*, "his friend." Some scholars have seen Hirah as an elder of a particular tribal group in the Shephelah or as representing a tribal designation.

GARY H. OLLER

HIRAM (PERSON) [Heb *ḥîrām*]. Var. HURAM, HURAMABI. The name of two persons in the Hebrew Bible, both associated in some way with Tyre.

1. A king of Tyre (ca. 969–936 B.C.E.) who was involved in commercial relations with David and Solomon (2 Sam 5:11; 1 Kgs 5:15—Eng 5:1). There is some confusion over the spelling of Hiram's name. It is usually found in the form *ḥîrām* (2 Sam 5:11 and 1 Kgs 5, 9 and 10), except in 1 Kgs 5:24—Eng 5:10 and 5:32—Eng 5:18 where it is spelled *ḥîrôm*. The Chronicler (2 Chr 1:18–2:15—Eng 2:1–16) invariably uses a variant form, *ḥûrām*. Josephus *(Antiquities; Contra Apionem)* uses the form "Hirom" *(Eiromos)*. The biblical name Hiram is a shortened version of the Phoenician "Ahiram" *(ʾahiram)*, which is found as the name of a king of Byblos on an inscribed sarcophagus at Byblos (ANET, 661).

Our information about Hiram and Tyre during this period is dependent upon the biblical traditions and the Jewish historian Josephus. Katzenstein (1973: 75–115) provides a discussion of some of the problems of interpreting and correlating these sources. According to Josephus (*AgAp* 1.106–11), Tyre kept very detailed chronicles of its internal affairs and foreign relations. Josephus draws upon the biblical account and two other historians, Dius and Menander of Ephesus, using the no longer extant history of Dius (*AgAp* 1.112–15; *Ant* 8.147–49), "an accurate historian of Phoenicia," in outlining the main achievements of Hiram's reign. Dius reportedly credits Hiram with the construction of embankments to level the eastern part of the city, the enlargement of the city, the creation of a causeway to the temple of Zeus (Baal) and the logging of timber from Lebanon for the construction of temples. Dius also reports that Hiram and Solomon used to set riddles for each other as part of a wager: Hiram, it seems, lost a large part of his wealth gambling with Solomon until Abdemun ("Abdemon" in *Ant* 8.149) solved them and recuperated even more money from Solomon, who was unable to solve the riddles he posed. Josephus claims (*AgAp* 1.111) that much of this correspondence was still preserved in the Tyrian archives during his own time. His other source, Menander of Ephesus, adds further information about Hiram (*AgAp* 1.116–121; *Ant* 8.144–460). He reports that Hiram succeeded his father Abibaal *(Abibalos)*, lived for fifty-three years and reigned for thirty-four years. Apart from the general building program mentioned by Dius, Menander recounts that Hiram also demolished a number of temples, built shrines to Heracles (Melkart) and Ashtarte, and conducted a successful campaign against Utica for its refusal to pay tribute. The reliability of Josephus' information is difficult to assess without further independent evidence, particularly in light of the apologetic nature of his writings.

The strategic position of Tyre, modern-day Ṣûr ca. 40 km south of Sidon, on the Mediterranean littoral was enhanced by its location on a small island offshore which protected it against siege and contributed to its rise as one of the most important maritime powers in the eastern Mediterranean. The Phoenician colony of Carthage in North Africa was founded in the 9th century B.C.E. along with other trading colonies in Spain. The biblical account of Hiram's relations with David and Solomon, not unnaturally, concentrates on their major commercial activities. Hiram is said to have supplied workmen and raw materials for the palace of David (2 Sam 5:11) shortly after the capture of Jerusalem. Soggin (1984: 56) believes that since Hiram was a contemporary of Solomon any overlap ought to come at the end of David's reign, not the beginning. He is not able to offer a convincing explanation for this reference except to say that the sources were probably confused over the chronology. Garbini (1986: 22–25) also questions the veracity of 2 Sam 5:11 since the biblical chronology would mean that Hiram reigned for a minimum of fifty-four years, which conflicts with Josephus' information on his life and reign. This problem has been noted by McCarter (*2 Samuel* AB, 145–46), who thinks that it is chronologically misplaced and is to be attributed to the Deuteronomist.

The two biblical accounts (1 Kgs 5:15–32—Eng 5:1–18 and 2 Chr 1:18–2:15—Eng 2:1–16) differ considerably with regard to Solomon's relationship with Hiram. 1 Kgs 5:15 (Eng 5:1) reports that Hiram made the initial contact after Solomon's accession to the throne. He then agreed to Solomon's request for timber and labor for his massive building projects in return for an annual shipment of wheat and oil. The Chronicler (2 Chr 2:1—Eng 2:3), however, credits Solomon with initiating the transaction for raw materials and skilled labor necessary for the building of the temple. The wheat, barley, wine, and oil was to be given to the workers rather than sent to Tyre to feed its population. This account appears to have been edited in line with the Chronicler's idealization of Solomon. It is generally concluded that Solomon's temple was designed by Phoenician craftsmen in accord with Syro-Palestinian models (Bright *BHI,* 218), presumably adapted to fit the Israelite milieu.

Kings and Chronicles also report important commercial activities during the reigns of Hiram and Solomon (Peckham 1976). Hiram is said to have supplied Solomon with ships and sailors for the commercial fleet at Ezion-geber on the Red Sea (1 Kgs 9:26–28; 10:11, 22; 2 Chr 8:17–18; 9:10, 21). The exact details of this commercial relationship and the precise extent of the trade network are not easy to determine. It is not clear whether Solomon or Hiram owned the fleet (1 Kgs 9:26–28; cf. 10:11–12) or whether they combined their ships as part of the commercial operations (1 Kgs 10:22). It seems that this fleet operated along the African and Arabian coasts of the Red Sea, dealing in high-cost and low-bulk luxury items such as gold, silver, ivory, and exotic animals. The location of Ophir and Tarshish are uncertain. Ophir is variably placed in India, Somaliland, and Arabia, while Tarshish is thought to have been in Spain or Cilicia (Dillard *2 Chronicles* WBC, 66, 73). Ophir is mentioned on ostraca from Tell Qasile dating from the 9th or 8th centuries. The Chronicler's reference to Solomon and Hiram's fleet visiting Tarshish (2 Chr 9:21) is usually viewed as a misunderstanding of the term "ships of Tarshish" (1 Kgs 10:22). It is hardly feasible that a fleet would circumnavigate Africa in order to trade in the Mediterranean. This phrase is taken to refer to a particular type or class of ships (Gray *Kings* OTL, 267). The two locations have also been understood to refer to a mythical or symbolic geography indicating that the fleet traded far and wide (Soggin 1984: 78). Israel and Phoenicia sat astride the major overland trade routes between Africa, Asia, and Europe and with the development of maritime activities along the African and Arabian coasts must have been able to fully exploit their strategic position. Hiram's trade relations appear to have been cemented by marriage since Solomon is reported to have married a Sidonian princess (1 Kgs 11:1). Clement of Alexandria (*Strom.* 1.114) quotes Menander of Pergamum that Hiram's daughter was married to Solomon when Menelaus visited Phoenicia after the capture of Troy.

The report that Solomon ceded twenty cities "in the land of Galilee" to Hiram (1 Kgs 9:10–14) is often interpreted as inferring that his trading operations ran into serious trouble and he was forced by debt or by the need to raise capital to give Hiram these cities (Bright *BHI,* 222; Miller and Hayes *HAIJ,* 216). Donner (1982) has argued that Hiram exploited commercial advantages to the detriment of Solomon's kingdom. Gray (*Kings* OTL, 240) argues that the term *ʿîr,* "city," refers rather to "villages." Their exact location is uncertain. The phrase "the land of Cabul" (cf. Josh 19:27) would suggest the vicinity of Acco. Gray (*Kings* OTL, 241) rejects the popular etymology and understands the term as a passive participle from the Arabic cognate *kabala,* meaning "mortgaged." Josephus (*Ant* 8.141–42) refers to the "land of Chabalon" *(chabalon)* and states that this is the Phoenician for "not pleasing." The Chronicler's version of this episode (2 Chr 8:1–2) presents a different picture in which Solomon rebuilt the cities given to him by Hiram and settled Israelites in them. Once again this would appear to be a reflection of the theological idealization of Solomon in the work of the Chronicler. Willi (1972: 75–78), however, believes that the Chronicler based his report on a text of Kings that was corrupt. Miller and Hayes (*HAIJ,* 216) conclude that Hiram controlled the Mediterranean coast and a large area of the Jezreel Valley by the end of Solomon's reign.

2. A skilled craftsman and metalworker responsible for the decoration of Solomon's temple, including the erection of Jachin and Boaz (1 Kgs 7:13–47). He is called Hiram *(ḥîrām)* in 1 Kgs 7:13, 45, Hirom in 1 Kgs 7:40 *(ḥîrôm;* LXX *cheiram),* Huram *(ḥûrām)* in 2 Chr 4:11, and Huramabi *(ḥûrāmʾābî)* in 2 Chr 2:13; 4:16. The addition of the element *ʾabî* may be part of the name or it has been explained as a title, "my master (craftsman)" (Dillard *2 Chronicles* WBC, 20).

The details of his parents are also confused. In 1 Kgs 7:14 he is said to be the son of a Tyrian father and a woman of Naphtali. However, in 2 Chr 2:12 his mother is remembered as a Danite. Dillard (*2 Chronicles* WBC, 4–5) believes that the Chronicler changed Huramabi's descent to that of a Danite in order to draw a parallel with Oholiab and the construction of the tabernacle. The Chronicler draws a parallel between the construction of the temple and the making of the tabernacle by comparing Solomon with Bezalel and Huramabi with Oholiab. The addition of the element *ʾab* to the end of his name has also been explained as making the parallel with Oholiab more explicit. The timing of the introduction of Huram in the Chronicler's account draws out the parallel further since in 1 Kgs 7:13–47 he is introduced only after the completion of the temple and palace (1 Kgs 6:38–7:1) and is responsible only for the bronze work (1 Kgs 7:13–47). In the Chronicler's account Huram arrives at the very beginning of the building of the temple and is responsible for extensive craftwork corresponding to the timing and range of work carried out by Oholiab on the tabernacle.

Bibliography

Donner, H. 1982. The Interdependence of Internal Affairs and Foreign Policy during the Davidic-Solomonic Period (with Special Reference to the Phoenician Coast). Pp. 205–14 in *Studies in the Period of David and Solomon and other Essays,* ed. T. Ishida. Tokyo.

Garbini, G. 1986. *History and Ideology in Ancient Israel.* Trans. J. Bowden. London.

Katzenstein, H. J. 1973. *The History of Tyre. From the Beginning of the*

Second Millennium B.C.E. *until the Fall of the Neo-Babylonian Empire in 538* B.C.E. Jerusalem.
Peckham, B. 1976. Israel and Phoenicia. Pp. 224–48 in *Magnalia Dei,* ed. F. M. Cross. New York.
Soggin, J. A. 1984. *A History of Israel.* London.
Willi, T. 1972. *Die Chronik als Auslegung.* Göttingen.

KEITH W. WHITELAM

HIRI, RUJM EL-. See RUJM EL-HIRI (M.R. 225257).

HISTORIOGRAPHY. Because a main component of biblical writings is narrative about past persons and events, "historiography" (the recounting of the past) is a major element in biblical literature. This entry consists of three articles that attempt to put biblical historiography in context. The first explores history writing in the great cultures of Mesopotamia; the second focuses specifically upon Israelite historiography especially as this is attested in the Old Testament; and the third surveys historiography in the Greco-Roman world.

MESOPOTAMIAN HISTORIOGRAPHY

Ancient Mesopotamian civilization was made up of three major peoples, the Sumerians, the Babylonians, and the Assyrians, and the cultural continuity from the Sumerians to the Assyrians and Babylonians is a vital factor in the genius of Mesopotamian civilization and certainly in the attitude of these people toward the passage of time and past events, which is reflected in what are called "historiographical texts." The Babylonians and Assyrians were the cultural heirs of the Sumerians and despite the fact that they spoke a language which was entirely different from the Sumerians their ideas and customs were very much conditioned by the earlier civilization. Since Mesopotamian civilization endured for over 3000 years inevitably some changes did take place and new developments appeared after Sumerian times; nevertheless the innovations in Assyrian and Babylonian times were surprisingly few and limited at least in their view of world events. It is also a fact that although Assyrian and Babylonian civilizations were contemporaneous and had a common heritage, there were some differences in the way they wrote about their past and about the passage of time in general. Babylonian historians were much closer in their views to Sumerian historians than were Assyrians. Assyrian royal scribes were much more concerned with the image of the king and his activity as a warrior whereas Sumerian and Babylonian scribes were more interested in the religious and peaceful activities of their rulers. This fundamental difference comes out very strongly in their writing about the past.

The historiographical texts, with which we are concerned here, form part of what has been called the "stream of tradition," that is, texts which were preserved in Ancient Mesopotamian libraries. There is some evidence of an oral tradition in Sumer, Babylonia, and Assyria in historical times which has survived in later literature about such figures as Semiramis and Ahiqar, and this is an indication that contemporaneous with the official records of past events there were popular tales being passed down in the vernacular. Toward the end of Mesopotamian civilization, just after the conquest of Alexander the Great, a Babylonian priest, Berossos, wrote a history of Babylonia in Greek in order to educate the Greeks about what a real civilization was like, for the Babylonians regarded the Greeks as barbarians with no history or culture.

Let us first describe briefly the various types of historiographical texts and then conclude with a discussion of Mesopotamian ideas of the past. There were three major types of historiographical texts: royal inscriptions, chronographic texts, and historical-literary texts. Royal inscriptions in Sumer, Babylonia, and Assyria were originally written as pious reports by the ruler to a god that he had performed some deed to honor his commitment as representative of the god on earth. This usually involved a building enterprise such as the excavation of an irrigation canal or the construction of a temple. Thus in origin, royal inscriptions were building inscriptions. From this original purpose royal inscriptions developed into elaborate records of royal achievements written not only as reports to the god but for future peoples to read and admire. In Sumer and Babylonia the chief content of these inscriptions, in addition to the description of the building projects, concerned religious matters. Military events, even in the heyday of the NB Empire, were rarely mentioned. This is in contrast to Assyrian royal inscriptions where the major part of the narrative concerned the military campaigns of the Assyrian kings. In fact in Assyria, a special type of royal inscription, annals, developed; that is, year-by-year accounts of the royal campaigns in chronological sequence.

The term "chronographic texts" covers a wide variety of compositions, most of which could be characterized as either king lists or chronicles. Among the many documents belonging to this general category were the Sumerian King List, the Assyrian King List, various lists of Babylonian kings, and the Babylonian Chronicle series. The feature all of these texts have in common is an attempt to narrate or list information in chronological sequence.

The category "historical-literary texts" is very amorphous and includes a number of compositions which are really unique. Among these were the historical epics, the prophecies (see also APOCALYPSES AND APOCALYPTICISM [AKKADIAN]), and pseudo-autobiographies. The feature which all of these individual texts have in common is that they present a description of historical events in a highly developed literary style.

Now let us turn to Mesopotamian ideas of the past and the passage of time in general as these ideas appear in the compositions described above as well as in some other sources. The most prominent feature is that Sumerians, Babylonians, and Assyrians were intensely interested in their past and conscious that their civilization had a long history. This comes out very strongly at the end of their civilization when Berossus set about the task of educating the Greeks on what an ancient civilization was all about. This fundamental interest in their history was intuitive and in many ways as essential to them as eating or drinking. This is apparent in the Babylonian Chronicle series, which is a series of cuneiform tablets upon which the history of Babylonia in the late period is succinctly described year by year. Inevitably events had to be selected according to what the scribes regarded as "important" and all events revolved around the king of Babylonia. Nevertheless within these restrictions the presentation of events was quite objective and so, for example, the Babylonian chroniclers recorded impassively Babylonian defeats on the battlefield. In other words they simply wanted to record each year the most important events in Babylonian history for the sake of recording them.

Ancient Mesopotamians were not above using history for other purposes, however. Causes could be furthered and ideas disseminated by means of compositions about former times. There are many chronographic texts which were written in order to justify institutions and promote theories. Thus an Assyrian document called the Synchronistic History, a brief description of Assyro-Babylonian relations over several centuries, was written to prove that whenever Babylonia attacked Assyria, Babylonia was in the wrong and lost; this text was written in a period when Assyria in fact was losing on the battlefield to Babylonia and was an attempt to stir up Assyrian morale. In the same vein the Cuthean *Legend of Naram-Sin* was written in the late period to revive interest at the royal court in divination by extispicy, the examination of animal entrails, in contrast to the increasing popularity of divination by astrology.

The ancient Mesopotamian view of the passage of time and of the past in particular is, after several decades of modern scholarship, reasonably clear. To the Sumerian, Assyrian, and Babylonian past, present, and future were all part of one continuous stream of events in heaven and earth. There was a beginning in the distant past but there was no middle or end; gods and men continued *ad infinitum.*

Bibliography

Carena, O. 1989. *History of the Near Eastern Historiography and Its Problems. 1852–1985. Part 1: 1953–1945.* AOAT 218/1. Neukirchen.

Finkelstein, J. J. 1963. Mesopotamian Historiography. *Proceedings of the American Philosophical Society* 107: 461–72.

Grayson, A. K. 1980. History and Historians of the Ancient Near East: Assyria and Babylonia. *Or* 49: 140–94.

Güterbock, H. G. 1934. Die historische Tradition und ihre literarische Gestaltung bei Babyloniern und Hethitern, Part 1. *ZA* 42: 1–91.

Kramer, S. N. 1953. Sumerian Historiography. *IEJ* 3: 217–32.

Michalowski, P. 1983. History as Charter. *JAOS* 103/1: 237–48.

Speiser, E. 1955. Ancient Mesopotamia. Pp. 37–76 in *The Idea of History in the Ancient Near East,* ed. R. C. Denton. New Haven.

Van Seters, J. 1983. *In Search of History.* New Haven.

A. Kirk Grayson

ISRAELITE HISTORIOGRAPHY

Since the mid–19th century, under the influence of the historicism of Herder and Hegel and in reaction to the empiricism of French and English scholarship, the genre of historiography has been increasingly used to describe biblical narrative. Although throughout the history of its use in biblical scholarship, and in modern usage generally, the term "historiography" often loosely refers to any of the many genres of prose narrative including tale and story, imaginary or real, the ancient and particularly the classical Greek genre of historiography used the term in a much narrower, more restrictive sense. This more distinctive meaning has been maintained also in its present usage, namely, as a specific literary genre relating to critical descriptions and evaluations of past reality and events, in contrast to more fictional varieties of prose.

A. Nonbiblical Historiographic Traditions
   1. Hittite Historiography
   2. Greek Historiography
B. The Content of Biblical Historiography
   1. Ordered Chronology
   2. Source Criticism
   3. Form Criticism
C. The Form of Biblical Historiography
   1. Historiographical Genres
   2. Antiquarianism
D. Historiography As an Intellectual Tradition
   1. "Salvation History"
   2. The Prophetic Tradition
   3. The Narrative Tradition
E. Collapse of the "Salvation History" and "Bible History" Movements

---

A. Nonbiblical Historiographic Traditions

1. Hittite Historiography. An essential aspect of early Hittite historiographical texts is that the truth of statements about historical or mythical time is explicitly maintained or challenged (Cancik 1970: 7–8). The concepts of truth, facticity, and historicity comprise a central pivotal concept in the writing of the annals of Hattusili I and especially of Mursili II (Cancik 1976: 101–84). Similarly, the Babylonian Chronicle (747–539 B.C.), in contrast (for example) to the religiously tendentious Assyrian annals, also seems to hold historicity as a central structural value (Van Seters 1983: 79–80). It is certainly from such annals and chronicles that ancient Near Eastern historiography develops, separate and independent of the epical and literarily fictive narrative traditions.

2. Greek Historiography. Within Greek literary traditions, a similar concern for historicity developed among the *logographoi* ("prose writers") who considered their task one of *historía* ("research") seeking to offer a true and correct version of both the traditional past and of mythology. The first to systematically evaluate and criticize traditional Greek folk narrative with logic and rationality was Hecataeus of Miletus, who had a wide personal experience of travel and a considerable knowledge of both geography and ethnography. While much of the work of his successors, including Herodotus, was ethnographic, archival, and antiquarian in nature, the critical task which Hecataeus established with *historía* became the dominant factor in the "scientific" history of Thucydides' account of the Peloponnesian War.

Early Greek historiographers, like their ANE counterparts, developed the genre of *historía* in terms of rational critical research and as an evaluative science, in contrast to the more imaginative literary and poetic traditions of epic and mythology. The criterion for this discipline of historiography was historicity: the truth of the events recounted.

In sharp contrast to this extensive historiographical tradition of Greece from the early 5th century B.C. on, and to some extent, even to that of the Hittites of a much earlier age, biblical tradition does not present us with any critical historiographical production prior to the Hellenistic work of Jason of Cyrene, which has been summarized in 2 Maccabees (2 Macc 2:23). Certainly it is most likely that from the time of the Assyrian Empire, the minor political courts of Syria-Palestine, and those of Samaria and Judah among them, maintained the kinds of lists, inscriptions, and annals, and even perhaps court chronicles, which we find in Assyrian and Mesopotamian records. However, such early historical forms we know only by way of later reference (e.g., of Tyre: Josephus *Ant* 7.144–46; 9.283–85; *AgAp* 1.155–57; of Byblos: Philo of Byblos [Attridge and Oden 1986]; of Israel: 1 Kgs 14:19, etc.; of Judah: 1 Kgs 14:29, etc.) and such references may either have been invented, or like perhaps the Books of Jashar (Josh 10:13), of the Wars of Yahweh (Num 21:14), of the Acts of Solomon (1 Kgs 11:41), of the Toledoth of Mankind (Gen 5:1), and of the Law of Moses (Josh 8:31) have been non-historiographical sources for the biblical tradition.

Although it is commonplace today to refer to "the historical books," to Deuteronomistic and even Yahwistic "histories," to "patriarchal biographies" and a "court history" of David, an equivalent of the word "history" does not exist in Hebrew, and a developed genre of historiography is particularly difficult to associate with the kind of prose narratives collected in the Hebrew Bible. Historiography proper seems unlikely to have been part of the Palestinian literary culture prior to the Hellenistic period. Both 2 Maccabees and Josephus stand fully within the tradition of Greek historiography, in striking contrast to Hebrew prose narrative.

The role of historiography in biblical literature is an issue of wide disagreement among biblical scholars. This debate has taken quite distinct but closely interrelated directions. The definition of historiography has been broadened to include a wider range of narrative prose. Dominant examples of this tendency are both the common perception of biblical narrative as an account of Israel's past, ordered chronologically, and the adoption of J. Huizinga's more theoretical definition of history writing as "the intellectual form in which a civilization renders account to itself of its past" (*apud* Van Seters 1983: 1). Such broader views of early Israelite historiography allow many modern scholars to understand the documentary sources of the Pentateuch, the final editions of the "Former Prophets," and the compilations of 1–2 Chronicles, Ezra, and Nehemiah as historiographies, and to speak of their authors as historians. In this they define a genre and tradition which stands in direct contrast to the genre and traditions of Mesopotamian, Hittite, and Greek historiography (*contra* Van Seters 1983; Hallo 1980).

Closely related to this broadening of the genre of historiography is the understanding of biblical historiography as an intellectual tradition of morally and religiously critical commentary on Israel's past, reflected in the biblical texts. This intellectual tradition, most notably centering on themes of "promise," "covenant," and various forms of "divine providence," has been seen to inform a wide range of literature. In terms of "salvation history," it is seen to form the core of the Pentateuch; especially, for example, of the so-called "Yahwistic theology." It has also strongly influenced both the content and collection of the prophetic books and has been seen as the motivating force behind the formation of the so-called Deuteronomistic History. Similar theological *Tendenz* is recognizable in almost all of Hebrew narrative: in Ruth, Jonah, Chronicles, Ezra, and Nehemiah. The recognition of an ever-recurrent concern for and judgment about Israel's past is so marked in this scholarship that Israel's faith is commonly understood as preeminently a historical faith. This is a theory or philosophy of history, making of biblical historiography not so much a genre as a frame of mind.

These tendencies to understand historiography as playing a decisive role in the form (genre) and content (themes) of biblical tradition have been strongly influenced by two related developments within critical scholarship: The "biblical theology" movement, which until the 1960s understood "salvation history" not as a literary subgenre within the tradition but as a viable historical view about Israel's past, centered the focus of the Bible's theological content on assumptions about both the historicity and the historiographical intent of the traditions. Similarly, the long-standing efforts of historical-critical scholarship since Wellhausen and Meyer has attempted to reconstruct a criticial modern history of Israel by using biblical narrative as its primary source.

B. The Content of Biblical Historiography

1. Ordered Chronology. Prose narratives, whether historical or fictional, typically proceed through successive actions or events; that is, they speak chronologically. Both fictional and historical narratives speak from the historical context of the narrator in terms of what has happened, whether real or imagined; that is, they speak of a past. What distinguishes them, and what distinguishes historiography from other narrative genre, is neither their content nor mode of speech, and certainly not such tangential issues as their plausibility and verisimilitude, but rather their referent as perceived by their author. The referent of historiography lies within *a world of the past understood as true and real, and as probable in terms of evidence.* The referent of fictional literature, on the other hand, lies within a *conceptional realm, understood as valid and possible, in terms of the author's own making.* The distinction between the two lies within the intentionality of the authors and in their assumptions regarding the reality of the past of which they write. There is little difficulty in distinguishing historical from fictional literature when the author's intention is clear and explicit. However, such is rarely the case with biblical literature. Moreover, when the received tradition presents itself in large complexes of interrelated units of tradition, extending themselves over enormous reaches of time, the interplay of the motives of multiple authors necessarily precludes any simple or indeed any comprehensive designation of genres based on authorial intention.

2. Source Criticism. For most of the last two centuries, the larger tradition complexes, such as the Pentateuch and the Former Prophets, have been understood to contain smaller units of tradition with single narratives and complexes of narratives, as well as extensive narrative frameworks which hold the smaller units together in a more or less continuous chain of narration from the creation story (Genesis 1) to the story of the deportation into Babylon (at the end of 2 Kings). This understanding has led to extensive research into both the history of traditions and into compositional theory. By the end of the first decade of the 20th century, compositional theory was dominated by the Graf-Kuenan-Wellhausen Documentary Hypothesis of source criticism, which understood the formation of the Pentateuch in terms of four chronologically successive parallel strands of tradition. Not only did the Documentary Hypothesis establish a relative chronology for the pentateuchal source documents, but this same framework has served several generations of scholars as a much-needed basis for Israel's intellectual history. The earliest source of the Yahwist ("J") was seen to reflect the Jerusalem court of the united monarchy. The Elohist ("E") was associated with the period of the divided monarchy and the thought-world of the northern kingdom. Deuteronomy ("D") was linked with the Josianic reforms of 2 Kings and was dated to the late 7th century; and the Priestly Document ("P") was tied to the exilic, and ultimately post-exilic, period, marking the transition to what Protestant scholarship saw as the legalistic and xenophobic world of Ezra's and Nehemiah's Judaism.

Once the Documentary Hypothesis was firmly in place, not only could the Pentateuch be understood within an historical-critical perspective, but most of the rest of early biblical narrative could be cataloged within associated contexts, forming mutually supportive interpretive matrices of considerable explanatory potential for the entire pre-Hellenistic biblical tradition. Among the least popular implications of Wellhausen's history of pentateuchal thought was the necessary collusion between the historical contexts of his documents and their referents in a now seemingly only literary past. The sources were understood as mere refractions of the world of their authors.

3. Form Criticism. It was the work of the historian Eduard Meyer (1896) and the pioneering form-critical work of Herman Gunkel (*Genesis* HKAT[3]) and Hugo Gressmann (1910), concentrating on the orality of the smaller units of tradition within a framework of comparative religion, which finally established for most of the individual Pentateuch narratives a context within ANE and world literature, providing a network of analogies of both content and form. This work became significant in issues of biblical historiography in its implied repudiation of Wellhausen's axiom that the historical context of the traditions must needs be understood as consonant with their literary fixation. Rather, a substantial oral tradition was seen as responsible for much of the content of Wellhausen's written pentateuchal documents, having had a considerable history prior to their final and secondary written context, perhaps long antedating even the united monarchy of J. The implicitly conservative thrust of this research was not apparent in the early Gunkel or in Gressmann, who both frequently expressed what threatened to become a dominant assumption that Israel's earliest stories had originated as oral folktales and as wholly imaginative works of entertainment. Only over time, it was at first thought, through the influence of the ideological and at times theological and historiographical thrust of a growing literary tradition, had these original folktales become historicized in the manner described by the Documentary Hypothesis. Rather, it was the brilliant and prolific Otto Eissfeldt who, in the Gunkel Festschrift itself, transposed Gunkel's arbitrary assumption about the fictive origination of the tradition, and asserted a historical rootedness of the traditions in terms of such then seemingly pervasive genres as *"Stammessage"* and *"Menschheitserzählungen."* Eissfeldt argued that the referents of the tradition were, in their origin, refractions of the sociopolitical associations of earliest Israel. Historical realities lay at the core of the traditions and gave them their earliest *raison d'être* as historical memories. The pentateuchal traditions had their roots in history. Real events lay behind their narration. However, over time, Eissfeldt admitted, the narratives had undergone a folkloric mutation which often hid this essential historical quality from modern perception. With such arguments, the working assumption was established which formed the basis for an ever-uneasy marriage of source and form criticism: that ultimately historical events lay under the hoary accretions of pentateuchal tradition. It is hardly surprising that Martin Noth in the development of his *Überlieferungsgeschichte* and *Traditionsgeschichte* took for granted that originating tradition was consonant with originating event, allowing Tradition History to become the primary tool of his historical research. Noth also held as a corollary that the mutations which occurred during the process of tradition accumulation inherently reflected comparable historical experiences of the tradent. It is from such assumptions that his confidence in describing a premonarchic period of early Israel, and his belief in the historicity of the peaceful settlement of an original Israel as reflected in the book of Judges, grew. Noth rejected the historicity of most of the patriarchal period only because he could not identify any convincingly coherent tradent which might be identified as the tradition's implicit referent at any time prior to Israel's emergence in Palestine, other than a very undefined association with migratory movements of early West Semitic groups which he referred to as "proto-Aramaeans."

C. The Form of Biblical Historiography

1. Historiographical Genres. The adoption of Huizinga's definition by biblical scholars (Hallo 1980; Van Seters 1983: 1) understands historiography in essentially fictive categories, placing the early forms of ANE historiography, such as lists, inscriptions, annals, and the like, into the category of mere record-keeping, and preserving the category of historiography for *history interpreted.* Such a definition also ignores the origins of Greek and Hittite historiography specifically as a critical discipline, and blurs the distinctions of a wide variety of literary and narrative genres from etiology to propaganda. The adoption of this understanding of historiography for the biblical traditions is dependent on a perception of the larger blocks of prose narrative as substantially unitary and historiographically motivated productions of literary authors, and denies both the fragmentary nature and the potentially oral and folkloric roots of the smaller units collected within the literary contexts of the larger frameworks. Moreover, while moral, ideological, and theological tendentiousness is a common trait of these larger frameworks which collect Israel's traditions, to understand such literary perspectives in terms of Israel seeking self-understanding not only confuses categories, but also attributes to a peripheral and occasional characteristic of only some historiography the essence of the genre itself. A definition centering on a nation's self-understanding is far more appropriate to ethnography, to genealogies and constitutional narratives, to origin stories, and to much mythology, than it is to historiography.

To define the genre of historiography one must of necessity distinguish in prose narrative traditions a considerable number of discrete formal types: etiologies, traditional tales, fables, parables, legends, myths, *Standesgeschichte, Stammesgeschichte* (tribal histories), genealogical tales, romances, geographical tales, biographies, constitutional tales, origin stories, ethnographies, and historiographies. One must also distinguish simple from compound tales, and these from various forms of chains of narratives. Similarly, occasional historiographical tales (Genesis 14?) must be sharply distinguished from identifiable historiographic intentionality that has informed the collection and transmission process of the tradition (Exodus 1–15), and both of these must be distinguished from those greater literary works of tradition collection which may or may not have assumed that the tradition sources had reflected a real or only a usable past. When dealing with the biblical tradition on the level of the specific units of the tradition, the genre of historiography is rare. Only very few Hebrew narratives involve historiography at a primary level. This genre is rather most notably present in the larger redactions and the final forms of composition. However, even there, a comprehensive historiographically motivated critical perspective only very occasionally surfaces in biblical literature (Gen 11:26–12:5?) and is nowhere dominant.

2. Antiquarianism. Of greater importance is the observation that the redactional techniques of the comprehensive traditions reflect the antiquarian efforts of curiosity and preservation. Such intentionality is specifically inimical to that of historiography. Historians ask the question of historicity and critically distinguish and evaluate their sources. They "understand" history, and therefore at times slip into tendentious ideologies and theologies. The antiquarian on the other hand shows the more ecumenically pluralistic motivations of the librarian: classifying, associating, and arranging a cultural heritage that is greater than the compiler or any single historiographical explanation. So, for example, we notice that in the larger blocks of tradition, narrative development has only the appearance of chronological progression. The progress is rather plot-oriented, as in the Torah story of Exodus 16–23 or most clearly in Abraham's travels from story to story allowing (among other things) Sarah to be an old woman in Genesis 18 and 21 but a young, marriageable beauty in Genesis 20. The recounting of such passages as Genesis 6–9, Exodus 1–12, Exodus 14–15, and especially Exodus 19–21, which collect so many different seemingly disharmonious tale variations is inimical to historiographical narration, for these collections present not accounts (whether critical or uncritical) of what is understood as past events, but rather they narrate variations existing within a tradition, self-consciously rendering *accounts* (not events) past, and in doing so, clearly reflecting the intentionality of our collector and redactor: to preserve what is old. The antiquarian intentionality is both pluralistic and in its own way objective. A similarly non-historiographical motivation is also noticeable in some of the compositional links of the larger redactions. So, for example, the genealogical structure of Genesis encloses this extensive composition through a patterning of such episodes as deathbed scenes, burials, genealogies, introductory and closing formulas, and post-introductory inclusions, as well as by the conjunction of motifs (Exodus 16–17), themes (Genesis 10 and 1:1–9), and parallel narratives (5 genealogies of Esau: Gen 36:1–5, 9–43). Indeed, disjunction is such a common phenomenon in what is only apparently a chronological progression of tradition from Genesis to 2 Kings that one must view this appearance of historical development and change as late and secondary, if not entirely accidental.

This extended tradition is structured very loosely as a succession of heroic biographies: Adam-Cain-Noah-Abraham-Isaac-Jacob-Joseph-Moses-Joshua-Judges-Samuel-Saul-David-Solomon-Kings. This structure, however apparent, clearly stands at a distance from the narratives themselves, and is for the greater part a very secondary ordering of stories which are individually wholly independent of this structure. Genesis–2 Kings is structured as a succession of great periods: Origins-Patriarchs-Exodus-Wilderness-Conquest-Judges-United Monarchy-Divided Monarchy-Destruction. But the existence of such anomalies as conquest stories set in the wilderness and patriarchs such as Judah among the Judges shows this process of structuring to be both secondary and subsequent to the traditions collected. It is extremely difficult to see any historiographical motivation in this collection, or indeed any purpose beyond general classifying or cataloging. The post-compositional and peripheral significance of this progression of texts of necessity excludes this aspect of the tradition from any such self-conscious literary genre as historiography.

D. Historiography As an Intellectual Tradition

1. "Salvation History." An understanding of the intellectual tradition of judgments or critical commentaries on Israelite tradition reflected in the biblical text has been closely associated with scholarly efforts to trace the history of the formation of the Bible and to identify the ideological and theological biases of the larger compositional sources contained within the various biblical books (Whybray 1976). Central to this discussion has been the elucidation of what was understood to be a particularly biblical view of Israel's past, commonly referred to as *Heilsgeschichte* or "salvation history." This concept of "salvation history" was one of the primary issues on the agenda of the Biblical Theology movement. However, considerable confusion was introduced by its use both to designate the biblical view of history (a form of theologically motivated *Tendenz* in Israel's view of its past) and as a concept of revelation (a view of the history of Israel itself as salvific). In this latter, modern theological sense, the concept today has been largely discredited, because, as a view of history and an affirmation about the past it is open in every way to historical-critical research and can neither be equated with revelation nor seen as an object of faith alone (Gnuse 1989: 23, Barr 1962: 66–69). Moreover, by associating revelation with the events of Israel's history, this tendency of the "biblical theology movement" implicitly rejected the Bible as the foundation of "biblical theology" in understanding the Bible as "revelatory" only to the extent that it recounted the external historical events of the past in which revelation was understood to have occurred (Thompson 1974: 327).

As an understanding of a *biblical* view of history, however, the concept of "salvation history" can be seen to epitomize a significant aspect of ancient Israel's intellectual perception of its tradition. In this perspective, scholarly discussion of "salvation history" has concentrated above all on the identification and description of the theological *Tendenz* of the collectors and redactors of biblical narrative, most notably in the understanding of the Yahwist (of the Pentateuch's Documentary Hypothesis) as a theologian, who developed his narrative about the origins of Israel and of all humanity in a theologically motivated historiographical framework of progression from sin to grace and from promise to fulfillment (von Rad 1948). This interpretation grew out of the understanding of the Yahwist as an historian. Nevertheless, the understanding of the Yahwist as a theologian, and indeed as an independent source of the Pentateuch at all, has undergone serious criticism over the past decade (Rendtorff 1977; Schmid 1976; Blum 1984; Thompson 1987) and continues to be an issue of serious debate today (Van Seters 1987).

Also closely associated with the biblical theology movement's use of the concept of "salvation history" has been an effort to create a special value of Israel's historical understanding as unique in the ANE, in light of the biblical concepts of time, as well as in the understanding of an unparaleled relationship which Israel was seen to have had with its God, who was viewed as guiding Israel's destiny as well as controlling and acting in history. The Israelite concept of time was thought to be dynamic and linear, a fundamentally historiographical perspective in which events occurred, definitely establishing causal chains of unrepeated results through time. In contrast, the ANE understanding of time was described as static and circular, not historiographical but mythical, creating an understanding of the past as ever recurring in the present. Such stereotypes of both ANE and biblical thought have been thoroughly discredited today, and it is now widely recognized that substantial portions of ANE thought understood linear progression of time and established considerable causally oriented historiographies. Moreover, the concept of time as circular is no more characteristic of ANE literature than it is of biblical. Rather, the biblical tradition shares a literary and conceptual mode of typology and analogy. Its writers frequently describe the past and its traditions in terms of *patterns of recurrence,* a technique by which one tradition or event might be seen as a commentary on another, rendering both meaningful. Similarly, the recurrent biblical motif of God guiding Israel, playing an active role in historical events, and controlling world history is a motif in no way unique to Israel, but is a typical description of divine action found throughout ANE historical records, and is a dominant motif from the Assyrian period onward (*AHG*; Cancik 1970; 1976; Saggs 1978; Van Seters 1983).

Finally, it is difficult to maintain an understanding of the motif of "salvation history" in the Pentateuch as an intellectual view of Israel's *past.* Unlike the Deuteronomistic tradition and Chronicles, the Pentateuch is essentially an origin tradition and holds as its primary referent not any Israel of the past so much as an Israel contemporary with its own self-formation as a tradition of origins, defining Israel's essence and significance as an ethnic community of faith. The motifs of promise and fulfillment are not elements from past history so much as they are assertions meaningful in the tradition's contemporary world (Thompson 1974: 329). As such, the genre of the Pentateuch is not historiographical but rather constitutional narrative, a complex subgenre of etiology, which uses stories and traditions from the past in what is essentially an illustrative and paradigmatic mode.

2. The Prophetic Tradition. Central to what might be described as a biblical view of Israel's past is the critical commentary of the prophetic collections and redactions. Illustrating the more-than-a-millennium-old West Semitic tradition of the prophet and seer as a moral and political critic of the government and the populace (Ellermeier 1977), the books of the classical prophets collect many early exilic and preexilic poems and oracles which condemn the governments of Israel, Judah, and neighboring states, as well as their populaces, for a variety of major crimes such as war atrocities, injustices, moral indifference, and cultic hypocrisies. The exilic and postexilic redactions and collections compare these earlier traditions in terms of radical and final judgment—Israel has committed *unforgivable* crimes—condemning the totality of Israel's political and ethnic history as religiously and morally bankrupt. They understand the destruction of the states of Israel and Judah by the Assyrians and Babylonians respectively as a divinely guided punishment. This analysis of the past laid the foundation for a future-oriented religious understanding of divine mercy and forgiveness. This prophetic tradition cast a trajectory toward a new Jerusalem of peace and justice in which Israel would finally carry out the destiny which had been established for it by Yahweh from Israel's earliest beginnings.

Historiographically, the focus of the redactions of the prophetic traditions is not so clearly directed toward the past except insofar as it serves as a justification for the moral and cultic reorientation demanded by the composite tradition in the postexilic world. That the critical judgment involved in this literature relates more to the genres of religious interpretation, ideology, and propaganda (Garbini 1988) than to the sort of criticial judgment normally associated with historiography is indicated in the idealistic and futuristic orientation of the redactions of prophetic collections. Comparable to the pentateuchal narrative's preference for an heroic past to illustrate the meaning of Israel in constitutional etiologies, the exilic and postexilic redactions of Israelite prophecy create a revolutionary future by reference to the failed past as a paradigm of glory shattered.

The intellectual assumption at the core of the West Semitic prophetic traditions (which biblical prophecy continues), is that gods interfere in human affairs and control the political and military events of history, as well as of the cult, of fertility and other aspects of reality. Divinities use their control of events to reward or punish their subjects for good or ill. With the help of this common ANE perspective (Saggs 1978; *AHG*), the redactors of the books of the prophets were able to salvage a religious understanding and continuing identity out of disaster.

The images of Assyria and Babylonia as conquerers subsequently humiliated, Israel's punishment under the wrath and anger of Yahweh, and the role of Cyrus as messiah and savior of a chastised remnant are not historical reflections analyzing what happened in Israel's past so much as they are explanations of piety, illustrative of future demands. This judgment about the past is not drawn from reflection about past events. Rather, the past, in the form of collected tradition, stands both as warning and basis for hope in the future. It is this hope for the future which selected the past remembered.

3. The Narrative Tradition. Comparably pious explanations of tradition are found occasionally in the Pentateuch. Fulfillment confirms promises cast yet in the future (Gen 22:17–18 and 28:13b–15); the wilderness-murmuring motif operates as a pattern of Israel's recurrent history (Exod 24:2–8); the self-conscious anachronism of the Passover festival bridges past and present (Exod 12:3, 14, 17, 24, 26, 27). Even more frequently in the collections of the traditions of Joshua–2 Kings, the criticism of Israel for immorality, injustice, and loss of cultic integrity becomes a recurrent leitmotiv. In 2 Kings this critical judgment becomes indistinguishable from the redactional framework itself. The motifs of the divine control of Israel's destiny by Yahweh, of Yahweh's anger at Israel's unfaithfulness and the ever-recurrent need for reform, are didactic and moralizing theological reflections on the traditions from the past. They echo motifs from many nonbiblical texts, for example the Mesha stele and the Assyrian texts (*AHG*, 106–7), but ideologically they belong to the same exilic and postexilic circles which were responsible for the redactions of the prophetic works. Instead of prophetic oracles, traditional tales and other early traditions are being used as narrative illustrations of ideology and theology (Rogerson 1974: 182–83).

National self-understanding is claimed by some today to be essential to the genre of historiography, and it is a central concern of prophetic and narrative collections in the Hebrew Bible. But this intellectual tradition in its entirety neither presents nor has an abiding interest in history. It deals, rather, with what one might better describe as ethnographic or ethnocentric etiology, those intellectual efforts which created the *ethnos* of Israel, reflecting a literary motivation which is characteristic of Persian-period literary works throughout the ancient world. Historiography proper does not have the goal of self-understanding so much as that of a critical reconstruction or representation of the past, eschewing etiology along with legend and mythology.

The biblical tradition brings together three distinct tendencies which should not be confused with historiography: (a) an understanding of Israel's deity as providential and as determining historical events; (b) a West Semitic prophetic tradition which judges the morality of historical events and is critical of the action of king and state; and (c) the theological and moralizing *Tendenz* of the exilic and postexilic collectors of traditional narrative who applied the prophetic judgments to the events of the tradition.

E. Collapse of the "Salvation History" and "Bible History" Movements

After the early 1960s, the biblical theology movement, which had linked understanding of the Bible as a theology of events to an understanding of revelation as history, and thus faith to historicity, collapsed. By the mid-seventies the Documentary Hypothesis and the investigations into the history of biblical narrative traditions had come under increasing attack (Mayes 1973; Van Seters 1975; Rendtdorff 1977; Blum 1984; Whybray 1974), undermining confidence in the ability of modern historiography to recreate Israel's historical past from its traditions. The challenge to the historicity of the patriarchs in the mid-seventies (Thompson 1974; Van Seters 1975) was quickly extended to the remainder of the so-called "historical" books of the Bible (*IJH;* Miller and Hayes 1986), leading to recent efforts to develop a history of Israel—and especially of its earliest beginnings—independently of the biblical tradition (Coote and Whitelam 1987; Ahlstrom fc.; Thompson 1987 and fc.).

The historicity of the greater units and of the larger redactions of the tradition is no longer widely accepted. Rather, historicity is an issue to be tested with each of the primary units of the tradition, not with the larger secondary constructs. A contemporary history of Israel no longer takes its starting point (with the tradition) at some point in the past at which Israel began. Rather, a critical history of Israel takes its starting point from the Israel formed by the tradition: the Israel of the exilic and postexilic periods. In this way modern historiography achieves an independence from the tradition itself.

Bibliography

Ahlström, G. fc. *The History of Palestine.* Winona Lake, IN.

Attridge, H. W., and Oden, R. A. 1986. *Philo of Byblos.* CBQMS 9. Washington, D.C.

Barr, J. 1962. *Biblical Words for Time.* SBT 33. Naperville, IL.

Blum, E. 1984. *Die Komposition der Vatergeschichte.* WMANT 57. Neukirchen.

Cancik, H. 1970. *Mythische und historische Wahrheit.* SB 48. Stuttgart.

———. 1976. *Grundzuge der Hethitischen und altestamentlichen Geschichtschreibung.* ADPV. Wiesbaden.

Childs, B. 1962. *Memory and Tradition in Israel.* SBT 37. Naperville, IL.

Coote, R., and Whitelam, K. 1987. *The Emergence of Early Israel in Historical Perspective.* Sheffield.

Eissfeldt, E. 1923. Stammessage und Novelle in den Geschichten von Jakob und von seinen Sohnen. Vol. 1, pp. 56–77 in *Eucharisterion: Festschrift von H. Gunkel.* Berlin.

Ellermeier, F. 1977. *Prophetie in Mari und Israel.* Theologische und Orientalische Arbeiten aus Göttingen 1. Göttingen.

Garbini, G. 1988. *History and Ideology in Ancient Israel.* Trans. J. Bowden. New York.

Gnuse, R. 1989. *Heilsgeschichte as a Model for Biblical Theology.* CTSSR 4. New York.

Graf, K. H. 1867–69. *Die sogenannte Grundschrift des Pentateuchs.* AWEAT 1.

Gressman, H. 1910. Sage und Geschichte in dem Patriarchenerzählungen. *ZAW* 30: 1–34.

Hallo, W. W. 1978. Assyrian Historiography Revisited. *EI* 14: 1–7.

———. 1980. Biblical History in Its Near Eastern Setting: The

Contextual Approach. Pp. 1–26 in *Scripture in Context.* New Haven.
Halpern, B. 1988. *The First Historians.* San Francisco.
Kukenen, A. 1887. *Historisch-kritische Einleitung in die Bücher des alten Testaments hinsichtlich ihrer Entstehung und Sammlung.* Leipzig.
Mayes, A. D. H. 1973. Israel in the Pre-Monarchy Period. *VT* 23: 151–70.
Meyer, E. 1896. *Die Entstehung des Judentums.* Halle.
Miller, J. M., and Hayes, J. H. 1986. *A History of Israel and Judah.* Philadelphia.
Noth, M. 1948. *Uberlieferungsgeschichtlich des Pentateuch.* Stuttgart.
Rendtorff, R. 1977. *Das uberlieferungsgeschichtliche Problem des Pentateuch.* BZAW 147. Berlin.
Rad, G. von. 1948. Theologische Geschichtsschreibung im Alten Testament. *TZ* 4: 166–76.
Rogerson, J. W. 1974. *Myths in Old Testament Interpretation.* BZAW 134. Berlin.
Saggs, H. W. F. 1978. *Encounter with the Divine in Mesopotamia and Israel.* London.
Schmid, H. H. 1976. *Der Sogenannte Jahwist.* Zurich.
Schmitt, R. 1982. *Abschied von der Heilsgeschichte.* EHS 195. Frankfurt.
Schulte, H. 1972. *Die Entstehung der Geschichtsschreibung im alten Israel.* BZAW 128. Berlin.
Soggin, J. A. 1984. *The History of Israel.* London.
Thompson, T. L. 1974. *The Historicity of the Patriarchal Narratives.* BZAW 133. Berlin.
———. 1987. *The Origin Tradition of Ancient Israel.* Vol. 1. JSOTSup 55. Sheffield.
———. fc. *Biblical Archaeology and the History of Israel's Origins.*
Van Seters, J. 1975. *Abraham in History and Tradition.* New Haven.
———. 1983. *In Search of History.* New Haven.
———. 1987. *Der Jahwist als Historiker.* ThStud 134. Zurich.
Whybray, N. 1976. *The Intellectual Tradition in the Old Testament.* BZAW 135. Berlin.
Wright, G. E. 1952. *God Who Acts: Biblical Theology as Recital.* SBT 8. London.

THOMAS L. THOMPSON

GRECO-ROMAN HISTORIOGRAPHY

Oral and written literature—epic, lyric, rudiments of drama, even primitive prose—existed in Greek by 550 B.C.E., but accounts of past events and institutions and their intelligible causes and contingent explanations of subsequent and present circumstances were yet to come. Near Eastern histories either did not extend beyond campaign summaries and accession narratives (Persian, Hittite) or were limited to skeletal lists of royal names and regnal dates, when not blatant propaganda and invented fantasy (Assyrian, Egyptian). Rational, critical knowledge of the notable past based on evidence and testimony had no function or audience in largely illiterate and unfree societies.

A. Greek Origins
B. The Creative Geniuses
C. Hellenistic Historiography
D. Rome from Origins to Early Empire
E. The Later Imperial Period
F. Methodology and Conclusions

A. Greek Origins

Greco-Roman historiography arose from an acute sense of life's brevity in an indifferent world. From the earliest 8th-century Homeric meditations on time and the human condition, the only survival of the individual to be hoped for was human recollection and the memorial of literary celebrity. The modern idea of historiography, as practiced in the European tradition, owes its largest debt to the choice of subjects (war and peace, administration of public affairs, growth of a nation, imperialism), the narrative rhetoric, and the analytical categories of two late 5th-century Hellenes and one Italian: Herodotus, Thucydides, and Livy. The Greeks introduced objectivity and verification of facts into historiography, anticipating the modern concept of critical historical research and interpretation.

A survey of ancient historiography can reconstruct the major habits, concerns, ideas, and themes of this discipline, despite the fact that no ancient critic seems to have composed a formal analysis of it and no rigorous definition of historiography emerged. The historical materials have been divided by Felix Jacoby, the most knowledgeable student of Greek historiography, into five categories: genealogy and mythography, ethnography, chronography, horography or local history, and history proper. Stimuli included familial and local civic pride, the diffusion of literacy, commercial contacts, and military conflicts with foreign peoples both more and less civilized. Certain orientations for these writers followed from a social and economic order in which some free males had the leisure and liberty to reflect on change, human variety, and the challenges faced by a peculiar civilization. Historical discourse ever since has been produced by private individuals in an attempt based on a unique Greek experience to craft meaning and legitimacy in the midst of serial, unvalidated human and natural occurrences.

The Greeks by 700 B.C.E. had learned to write from the Phoenicians and to memorialize in stone from the Egyptians. Anaximander of Miletus (the leading commercial power and colonial mother city in the Aegean) is the first known Greek prose writer (ca. 560). He made a map and wrote up the relevant geography, the basis of later ethnology and history in Ionian lands, the exclusive place of origin of the first historians, the meeting place and battleground of West and East. Fifty years later, Hecataeus of Miletus, a prominent politician under the Persian dispensation, wrote *Genealogies* (family histories often attached to rationalized legends), traveled extensively, and made another map. For this he composed his *Periēgēsis,* a companion ethnology organized by location around the Mediterranean and inland, e.g., the Celts. He referred to distant places and events, although his attempts to explain phenomena seem to have been limited to crude rationalizations. No historical event or events gave focus to Hecataeus' collection of biological curiosities, exotic customs, and sporadic comparative inquiries about past generations. Hecataeus, and later Herodotus, were led to recover the Greek past by their encounters with the oral traditions of the Orient (travels to Egypt, Phoenicia, Scythia, etc.). Hecataeus and Herodotus wrote to disabuse their compatriots of provincial attitudes. Their polemics against popular delusions and received tradition, their groping toward methodical rigor, and their criticisms of their predecessors' inconsistencies and dogmatic beliefs are healthy signs of *historía* or "investigation" from the beginning.

B. The Creative Geniuses

Herodotus produced the first systematic narrative of a battle, a campaign, a war, an empire's growth, and comparative political systems. His ethnographies of Greek and many barbarian (e.g., Lydian, Egyptian, Persian, Scythian) societies encompass economies, social customs, and geography as well as marvels and annalistic information. Herodotus incorporates many personal stories from Persian and other "native" informants and quotes from translations of Persian documentary sources. His narratives of decisive historical events in the Aegean basin during the previous century re-create the issues by borrowing the mimetic techniques of earlier genres, particularly Homer's epics but also Attic tragedy and oratory.

The first historian is aware of many of historiography's central problems. He shrewdly discusses the bias, conflicts, and prejudices of sources oral and written, the frequent failure of information to satisfy minimal criteria of probability or human experience, the need to select and omit phenomena (such as myth, theology), and the uses and problems of chronology (2.43–44; 3.122).

The latter half of the *Histories* seeks to explain how and why some Greeks after 500 B.C.E. decided to resist the Achaemenid Empire. That is, Herodotus first leapt, as all historians hence must, from oral tradition and record to explanation, to relations of cause and effect, interpretations of individual and communal behavior, and the significance of choices, acts, and events. Overlapping systems of explanation include occasional references to supernatural causes, but these are few, vague, and subordinated to mundane political and strategic considerations and to observed historical patterns. Herodotus' influential invention, an objective account of the human past in its ordinary and extraordinary but always human dimensions, a story based on empirical evidence and sifted testimony, incorporates into the narrative and speeches an analysis of the significance and effect of those events. He produced a clearer identity for his Hellenic audience and his *Histories* created the essential tool for historical consciousness.

Thucydides offers a narrower yet deeper kind of historiography of war and political conflict. He largely eschews events before his lifetime, he generally ignores the past and present of all states and peoples that played no part in the Peloponnesian War (431–404 B.C.E.), and austerely limits his study to that war, its real and alleged long- and short-term causes, its battles and their consequences, the imperial administration of Sparta, Persia, and especially Athens.

He lived to see the imposed peace but his account breaks off in 411. Stripped of genealogy, ethnography, local history, biography and anecdote, his *History* retains many dramatic elements including paired, opposing, highly wrought speeches in legislative, battlefield, diplomatic, and judicial assemblies, descriptions of near-disaster (Lesbian genocide, Syracusan defeat), and rhetorically dry but emotionally intense accounts of sea and land battles and other devastating catastrophes such as the Athenian plague.

Thucydides less successfully ascribes motives to leading individuals and even to armies, political factions, and mobs (3.82; 8.1). The acquisition and abuses of political and military power over other states provide a central theme in both his paradigmatic opening essay on past empires and in the body of his text on Athens' experience. Thucydides absolutely excludes the supernatural from his account except insofar as men are motivated by perceptions of divine interference (e.g., the superstitious response to the eclipse at Syracuse in 413 B.C.E.). He expects future events to resemble past and present occurrences, not because of a cyclical metaphysic but because he has seen that humans tend to respond in similar ways to similar problems. Omission, compression, a false psychological omniscience, and a knotty style mar his excellence but cannot trouble the claim of his being the ancient historian who best approaches the 19th century's concept of historiography.

Thucydides criticizes predecessors (Herodotus, Hellanicus, Ion of Chios) for sloppy chronology, false criteria of prosperity and significance (1.10), too easy acceptance of partial, plausible, and traditional reports, and failure to dig into data to discover the decisive causes in national self-interest and charismatic individuals. On the whole, however, he reinforced the criteria of Herodotus' genre rather than redirecting it. His own rigid chronological scheme is ill-suited to any theme other than a narrow one. He has high standards of evidence and does not supply answers when information does not warrant. He endorses certain traditional moral values (e.g., 2.51, 3.82–83) without any moralizing, while neutrally recording their inefficacy in the stress of international power conflicts.

C. Hellenistic Historiography

An anonymous writer, known as the Oxyrhynchus historian (from the find spot of the 40-page fragment of his *Histories*), possessed Thucydides' dry but accurate manner of battle description without apparently his psychological skills or interest in political analysis. Xenophon also continued Thucydides' narrative in 7 books down to 362 B.C.E., but different capacities and interests produced a very unlike result. The title of his work, *Hellenica,* implies a comprehensive coverage, not a topic limited in time or theme. Painstaking research comes second to explicit historical moralizing (2.3.56, 7.2.1), propaganda for Panhellenism, and an analysis of character that shows traces of his friend Socrates' influence. Xenophon's work begins and ends in the middle of crises, an indication of his weakness in historical conception and literary architectonics. Chronology, motivation, and causation similarly suffer in an innovative writer for whom history was only a sideline. The *Anabasis,* his journalistic account of the pretender Cyrus' campaign against the Persian king (in which Xenophon participated), provides both a more dependable record and more vivid presentation.

After Thucydides, Greek historiography turned to the exotic and the sensational (Duris' *Hellenica,* Ctesias' fantastic *Persica*), to the emotional scene more fictional than factual and intended to arouse fear and pity (Duris again, Phylarchus' *Histories*), and to a moralistic education in elegant rhetoric that Isocrates conceptualized (Ephorus,

Theopompus). These 4th-century historians channeled the main current of ancient historiography for the next half-millennium.

Ephorus of Cyme (405–330 B.C.E.) was first to try to include all Mediterranean history in one work of 30 volumes; his emphasis remained nonetheless Hellenocentric and contemporary. Moral edification by example and platitudes are evident in his fragments. Trivial in his etiologies of war, uncritical of his sources for myth and legend, superficial in political understanding, and derivative at best, he was essentially a synoptic compiler and popularizer. Diodorus the Sicilian composed a 40-volume world history between 60 and 30 B.C.E. He drew from many authors, but Ephorus was his historiographical model as well as a principal authority.

Theopompus of Chios (380–305 B.C.E.) admired Sparta, the Macedonian Philip's strategic policies, and oligarchy, while he railed against Athens, democracy and demagogues, and previous historians. He digressed often and at whim in his 12-volume *Hellenica,* a competitor of Xenophon's. He devoted 58 volumes of *Philippica* to the colossus of the mid–4th century, Philip of Macedon, including Philip's remarkable achievements but also castigating his sexual profligacy, chronic drunkenness, and spending habits. He enjoyed debunking popular views. Moral indignation, inconsistently applied, replaces political analysis. Shocking description, coarse and violent opinions, made his work popular and influential on certain techniques of Hellenistic historiography. Fifth-century confidence in rational analysis, the political process, and human abilities is replaced by emphasis on personality, telling anecdotes, and a fatalistic pessimism.

Histories of individual Greek cities and larger territories were produced in ancient Greece only after Herodotus' general history. They were designed to establish the antiquity and dignity of a Greek community, they presented the rulers and constitutional changes in chronological sequence, and they showed the results of antiquarian research on topography, local myth, monuments, cultic and social customs. The Atthidographers provided a political account in chronical form for Athens, but other subgenres also existed for studying the past of this political, cultural, and intellectual capital. Hellanicus of Lesbos produced at least 12 regional chronicles and ethnological surveys before the earliest and paradigmatic *Atthis,* ca. 400. After 350, nostalgia for former glory produced at least 6 other local chronicles for Athens, several from men holding Athenian priestly office. Antiquarian studies also were valued for the piquancy of their obscure details and implications of former greatness. Craterus of Macedon was unusual in collecting and publishing verbatim primary sources, inscriptions.

Early in the 3d century, two barbarian priests presented improved accounts of their nations' accomplishments to generally uninformed Greeks. Berossus of Babylon transmitted ancient Mesopotamian traditions about the creation and the kings of Babylon; Manetho of Heliopolis then did the same for Egypt. These important compilations of authentic national traditions were later to serve as sources for Jewish and Christian chronographers.

Socrates, the spiritual gadfly, was the first individual in history to have his daily life recorded (ca. 469–399 B.C.E.), but Alexander the Great has forced even historians hostile to hero-worship to acknowledge the power of personality to affect the lives of millions. The revolution wrought in East-West relations, the instant legends, manufactured and natural, the problems of an incomprehensible success and spiritual impact made and make the short-lived Macedonian (356–323 B.C.E.), like Jesus, an insoluble historical enigma.

At least 20 contemporaries wrote accounts of Alexander's life and campaigns. There were hostile pasquinades and encomiastic essays, but after his death 40 years passed before his general and successor as ruler of Egypt, Ptolemy, wrote the first complete narrative. Five full accounts survive today, from the earliest—Diodorus' (300 years later)—to the latest—Arrian's sober military account (450 years later). Alexander's career forced Hellenic historiography to reopen the geographic boundaries of history and raised new questions about historical forces. Also, both sane geographers like Aristobulus and recorders of fantastic beasts and peoples like Onesicritus attached their projects to his deeds. Marvel books and even the genre of the novel resulted from these parahistorical efforts.

Timaeus of Tauromenium in Sicily (355–260 B.C.E.) produced a history in 38 books of the Greek West, Carthage, and Italy (including Rome) down to 264. He tried to synchronize these nations' pasts. Polybius criticizes him severely for the consequences of his inexperience in public affairs, failure to visit battle sites, and naive acceptance of myth and etymological explanations, but he honors him by beginning where his predecessor ended and by often arguing with his method and results. Although Timaeus' work has perished, later Greek historians of Rome owed much to this diligent western Greek pioneer who introduced Rome and the Celts to the historiography of Western Europe. Polybius and Posidonius continued his explorations of primitive and non-European peoples.

Polybius (200–155 B.C.E.) had extensive personal experience of war and politics (39.5). After his efforts for the Achaean league, as an official hostage in Rome and friend of Scipio Aemilianus, he found unusual opportunities to produce a 40-volume history of the Roman unification of previously separate nations. The Roman conquest required only about 140 years (264–146 B.C.E.); Polybius presents this astonishing feat with unusual impartiality, conscientious topographical research, examination of witnesses, accuracy of narrative detail, study of original documents (3.22, 33; 16.15), and with the presentation of the causes of each particular conflict (12.25E).

Like Herodotus and Thucydides, Polybius begins with a long introduction explaining his plan and providing the background necessary for understanding his chosen events in their proper context. His accounts of war are more perceptive than his analyses of political organizations and success (cf. the etiology of Rome's victories: they were due to the armies, moderation in victory, the constitution, and the attitudes of the ruling class [book 6]). He is critical of many historians and schools for their literary sensationalism, their ignorance of geography and warfare (book 34), their inflated rhetoric and credulity toward myths, and their self-glorification (29.12.3), but most of all for their inadequate grasp of etiological factors. His frequent digressions on theory are polemical and his own practice can differ from his precepts.

Polybius' determined intentions were to train men of public affairs in practical politics (9.1–7; 10.21.2–4) and to enable readers to understand power and its consequences. He felt comfortable with Roman values and political wisdom. *Tyche,* Fortune, appears frequently not so much as a cause but as a convenient non-explanation when no one can have foreseen outcomes. He displays Gibbon's two preconditions for the historian: diligence and accuracy; but his style is dreary.

D. Rome from Origins to Early Empire

Roman historiography suffered from the start from the eminence of its senatorial authors and from the dominance of oratorical education over most of its practitioners. Contemporary political issues were retrojected onto remote ages; the desire to glorify one's family made historiography a branch of rhetorical skill; plausibility outweighed evidence, or the frequent absence of any. As Cicero too plainly states, historians were expected to dress up the exploits of their "heroes" (*Fam.* 5.12).

The historians of the Republic patriotically reconstructed the rise of Rome from insignificance to Mediterranean hegemony by friendship, treaty, war, and conquest. But the historiography of the Roman Empire, initiated by Sallust, elaborates a perceived pattern of moral degeneration, the decline of liberty, the extension of autocracy, a long battle more against internal dissolution than external attack (Ammianus 31.5.14).

Roman senators first kept records as officials (e.g., pontifices), to produce a public record of a year's events that mattered to Rome, such as consuls, triumphs, famines, and omens (Gellius 2.28.6, from Cato). They first wrote history as politicians of notable lineage to glorify their own families, and to gain literary repute in the cultural efflorescence that followed the 2d-century conquest of the Greek world. History-writing came late to Rome, and began in the Greek language with Fabius Pictor's ambitious *Annales* retelling the founding of Rome, summarizing the following centuries, and then giving a more detailed yet anecdotal account of the First Punic War. From the few fragments, one can conclude that he wrote in order to explain Rome to the Hellenistic world, and perhaps to educated Carthaginians and Romans. History was an extension of diplomacy as well as of patriotic didacticism: the Romans owed their initial success and recent expansion to perseverance, good faith, and strict moral values. Antiquarians, of whom Varro (115–27 B.C.E.) was to be the greatest, researched the names, origins, and functions of religious rites, the calendar, public places, and state offices. But even Roman antiquarians often had moral improvement in mind.

The elder Cato wrote his Latin *Origines* covering both Rome's legendary history and the imperial expansion from the First Punic War down to nearly the beginning of the Third (264–149 B.C.E.). He provided a prose parallel to the poet Ennius' earlier historical epic.

Cato's 7 volumes were not only didactic and political but also polemical and apologetic. He defended Roman achievements for Romans, as a plebeian senator he stripped the famous political names from Rome's communal victories, and in the last section he used the account of the past to promote his own considerable achievements as a senatorial and military leader. He included his own speeches and denigrated his political opponents (Livy 34.15.9, 35.25.1; Cic. *De Or.* 1.53). Historiography in the hands of active statesmen naturally showed partisan distortions.

Later writers imaginatively filled in the poorly known epoch between regal Rome and the Punic Wars. Distortion and invention helped to give shape to the void, sometimes to sate antiquarian curiosity about customs and holidays, often, to be sure, to promote a moral and political agenda. Official records were scant, the demand considerable, so the result was more coherent than true. The upheavals of the Gracchan age (145–120 B.C.E.) produced propagandistic accounts by factional leaders, and the next generation produced several senatorial memoirs, for instance, those of Aemilius Scaurus and the dictator Cornelius Sulla. Strictly contemporary accounts and historical monographs (e.g., Sisenna's *Histories* to 78 B.C.E.) become the fashion of the ambitious politician and historian.

Annalists for the distant past are now less prominent persons often at work in their studies remembering what had never happened. Valerius Antias, for example, notorious even in antiquity (Livy 30.19.11, 33.10.8), sought to edify and to entertain connoisseurs of rhetoric—even if this purpose required the invention of speeches and factitious documents. The personal researches of Varro and others were disdained and their results ignored. Cicero, who names most of these writers, judges them chiefly by their style and rhetoric rather than by their mendacity, and this Roman standard, a result of rhetorical education, was all too common.

Cicero's letter to the senatorial historian Lucceius (*Fam.* 5.12 [56 B.C.E.]) requested a history that would celebrate in a dramatic and eulogistic manner his own vicissitudes from his repulse of Catiline to his return from exile. The cajoling purveys a slippery description of Hellenistic-Roman historiography. Later, imperial historians justly feared to offer an honest account of their own times (Livy *Praef.*; Tac. *Hist.* 1.1; Pliny *Ep.* 5.8.12–13).

Julius Caesar (100–44 B.C.E.) wrote not history but elaborate *commentarii, aides-mémoire* of his military campaigns with no political framework or explicit historical introduction or rationale. The year-by-year summaries of the *Gallic* and *Civil Wars* in 10 books constitute a public record, hastily compiled but purposefully slanted, by the commander in the field. As consul, pontifex maximus, orator, and faction leader, Caesar took serious risks in politics, war, and literature, the continuation of politics by other means. The *commentarii* justify his self-aggrandizing and illegal actions. He notoriously speaks of himself in the third person, conveying a tone of passionless objectivity. Suppression, severe compression, and false suggestion elegantly promote a favorable view of the author. The memoirs are covert propaganda; they demonstrate Caesar's skill in war and diplomacy as well as literary subtlety. The aggressive imperialist tone employed to justify war atrocities in the *Gallic Wars* is abandoned for the delicate subject of the *Civil Wars* and Caesar's self-exculpation. In the imperial period, one can compare Augustus' autobiographical yet magisterial *Res Gestae,* cast in bronze and carved in stone around the Mediterranean.

Sallust (85–35 B.C.E.) grew up in Sabine Italy between the Civil Wars. He became a senator but was expelled in 50, joined Caesar, was accused of extortion in Africa, and retired from "public service" to write his historical essays, *Catiline's Conspiracy* and *Jugurtha's War,* and an annalistic History of Rome from 78 to 66 B.C.E. in 5 books, now largely lost.

His theme was the political and moral decline of the senate through venality and incompetence. This prejudice resulted from both his own experience and his sources' bias. His archaistic diction and vengeful rhetoric is highly colored, censorious, pointed, and not unearned. He dislikes popular champions as much as greedy oligarchs. He wrote between Caesar and Augustus when pessimism and cynicism had a warrant as the only realism. Much detail is excised in the service of the dramatic scene, the impressionistic analysis. Tacitus found his corrosive tone congenial, even necessary (*Ann.* 3.30), although Asinius Pollio, who wrote *Histories,* covering 60–42 B.C.E., criticized him and Livy for their stylistic excesses. Sallust crafted the thenceforth canonical presentation of Roman history as a tale of degeneration and breakdown.

Livy (59 B.C.E.–17 C.E.) wrote a history of Rome from the founding of the city to his own day comprising 142 books, of which 34 survive. He conducted almost no independent research and depended on authorities whose accuracy he could judge only by the criterion of their inherent probability. Like other ancient historians, he had not developed the critical method of source criticism and his own acumen was vulnerable to any plausible invention that fit his presuppositions and didactic purpose of spiritual regeneration. Too often he innocently accepts his predecessors' fabrications. As with many of his forerunners, history turns out to be moral biography; his heroes embody the characteristics that built Rome. Economic, social, and political issues are seen as personal contests, institutions are downplayed. The annalistic framework and the focus on dramatic episodes smother inquiries into structural problems and analysis of intellectual change. Livy is weak on geography, military matters, and factional politics.

Livy met Cicero's criteria of elegant style, dramatic construction, dignified yet graphic presentation, variety of tone, edifying themes with implicit judgments of character. His idealistic patriotism made him uncritical of Roman "manifest destiny" and racial superiority. His history offers magnificent examples and warnings and a record of moral decline from a primitive yet robust simplicity. He explains Rome's unique success as compromise among citizen groups, dedication to the common welfare, plain living, and honest dealings with foreign governments. Heroes such as Scipio are made perfect; bad qualities or ignoble acts are distorted or suppressed. Divinity has only a trivial role compared to Roman virtues such as *fides, clementia,* and *pietas;* his organic central metaphor is *crescere,* Roman growth.

Livy had an antiquarian dimension. He explains the origins of customs, names, particular holy sites. His complete narrative and his scale had no predecessor. His success was immediate and long lasting (cf. Pliny *Ep.* 2.3.8; 6.20), indeed, the model for modern national historiography. One of his pupils was the future emperor Claudius, who wrote in Greek on Etruscan and Carthaginian history and in Latin on events following the civil wars (after 27 B.C.E.; Suet. *Claud.* 41–42).

E. The Later Imperial Period

Tacitus (50–120 C.E.) was a Gallic provincial senator, a noted orator, a successful officer of the emperors who lucidly anatomized and deeply disliked the autocratic system that he served. Exigencies of survival under Domitian and after led him to cultivate obliquity (*Hist.* 1.1), an epigrammatic and asymmetrical style, and an elevated and cryptic manner of expression in which the significant meaning is rarely obvious. He minded the experience of the historian Cremutius Cordus, who had been led to suicide in 25 C.E. and whose *Annals* of the Civil Wars had been burnt by the Aediles for their Republican sympathies (*Annals* 4.34). His work stems from the same hostile, pro-Republican, senatorial tradition. Ironic juxtaposition, tendentious emphasis, and malicious insinuation permeate both the *Annals* and the *Histories,* originally 30 books covering 14–96 C.E., the relatively recent Julian and Flavian dynasties of the New Testament epoch.

The psychology of personality attracts the energies of Tacitus, the historian of seemingly all-powerful emperors. His pessimism drives him to reveal the internal political lies and shams of the imperial administration and to indict more often than praise the Roman exploitation of the Mediterranean world (*Hist.* 1.11; *Agr.* 30). His accounts of military strategy and battles are perfunctory, but he does connect the dynastic quarrels, frontier wars, provincial complaints, constitutional changes, and disturbances at Rome. Tacitus tends to present characters in clear categories—the victim, the tyrant, the freedmen opportunists. He provides posterity with examples of morality, acts to avoid and imitate. *Fama* as public reputation, rumor and renown, and *memoria* are his concern (*Ann.* 3.65; 4.35).

Tacitus' demolitionary account of emperors such as Tiberius and Domitian and their propaganda follows from his view that accounts of recent history must witness and memorialize a tale of debasement and ceaseless woe (*Ann.* 4.32; 16.16, 25). Even the record of acts of memorable courage and justifiable prudence further darken the portrait of unlimited power; rare (but significant) are the acknowledgments of the Empire's achievement (*Ann.* 3.55; *Hist.* 1.1; 4.74).

Tacitus' claims to objectivity (e.g., *Ann.* 1.1; *Hist.* 1.1) are puzzling, yet he strove to report names, dates, and events correctly, even if his inveterate psychologism, with its invention of motives and his extreme version of the Roman nostalgic model of degeneration from ancient virtue, colors his partial account of a century of despotism (*Ann.* 4.33). A dramatic focus on Rome and its aristocracy, natural and traditional for a man of his status but still profoundly misleading, could hardly lead to any other result. His own career's circumspection led him to identify virtue with the bureaucrat Agricola's unostentatious and courageous service to the state, and to write an account of his father-in-law's life and death.

In the 4th century B.C.E., a greater political dependence on individuals rather than on collectives emerged, and the individual became increasingly alienated from communal social and religious values. The spectacle of Alexander had promoted a focus on character and an interest in idiosyncracy digestibly packaged in anecdotes. In Greece biography began as collections of illustrative stories from the lives of influential men (Socrates, Philip); in Rome, it began as accounts of famous ancestors (*laudationes*) and retained that character (see, for example, Plutarch *Cimon* 2.2–5; Tacitus *Agricola*). Chronological arrangement (Plutarch generally; cf. *Alexander* 1) often jostled against topical inventories (Suetonius *Augustus* 9), because ethical concerns outweighed historical. Plutarch's generous "comparisons" of Greeks and Romans (perhaps Varro's innovation) reflect his purpose of describing constructive behavior—deliberate, rational choices—by historical examples. Plutarch rarely chose protagonists to condemn them (*Per.* 1–2; *Tim. Pref.; Demet.* 1), while his contemporary Suetonius, the private secretary of the emperors, elected to emphasize coolly the scandalous facets of his subjects, the Caesars from Julius to Domitian.

Biography was considered a separate genre (Polyb. 10.24; Plut. *Alex.* 1.2), but the northern Italian Cornelius Nepos (100–25 B.C.E.), the Boeotian Plutarch (50–120 C.E.), and the African bureaucrat Suetonius (70–130 C.E.) require mention as reporters of lost historical sources. Furthermore, the generic barrier between history and biography was more permeable than some modern critics have supposed.

In both writers, unique examples of behavior serve to substantiate noble and criminal tendencies. Coherence of character leads Plutarch to suppress or downplay exceptions; Suetonius sacrifices such coherence to the juicy anecdote. Political analysis is largely absent, not safe or even interesting. The problematical *Historia Augusta*—author(s) unknown—constitutes a contradictory and often fraudulent collection of imperial biographies continuing Suetonius from Hadrian to Numerianus (117–284 C.E.). Ancient biography was a kind of moral essay organized to illustrate one man's character, his great and trivial deeds. We get certified heroes and villains. Biography's popularity and influence have often exceeded those of history proper.

Compilers of the imperial age depend more on other compilations than on earlier researchers. In this encyclopaedic and anthologizing epoch, we have, for example, the naive contemporary of Augustus, Dionysius of Halicarnassus (*Roman Antiquities* in 20 books), the compendious and inelegant Appian of Alexandria (*Roman Wars* in 24 books), the rhetorical consul Cassius Dio of Nicaea (*Roman History* in 80 books to 229 C.E.), and the Syrian Herodian (8 books, 180–238 C.E.). Derived from these already secondary sources are epitomators who dutifully record consuls and portents and excerpt crises without fleshing out their material with spiritual causes and context. For examples, consider Florus, and his 4th-century followers Eutropius, Justin, and Aurelius Victor. These authors often present similar summaries of the canonical main events of Roman history rather than intelligently compact the historical vision of Livy or the Gallic "universal" historian Trogus. Their gullibility and erratically sensationalist tendencies, qualities also found in other sometimes parasitic genres such as literary dialogues, biography, and utopian "histories," make them treacherous sources for us, however indispensable.

Lucian of Samosata (115–200 C.E.) wrote a satire on historians of the Parthian War entitled *How to Write History*. The essayist's dogmatic advice is conventional (34–39); the model to imitate is Thucydides; or rather, Thucydides is the stick with which Lucian beats his generation's sloppy research, exotic descriptions, servile imitations, inappropriate emphasis, and adulatory rhetoric (7, 15, 20, 28, 59, 61). In general, Greek nostalgia for the pre-Roman era, Greek ambivalence toward the Roman peace, and flattering treatments of the indecisive Parthian Wars dominate the historiography of the later 2d century.

Flavius Josephus (35–115 C.E.), a Hellenized Pharisee, fought against and for the Roman government of Palestine. Thus both Jews and Romans distrusted him. His *Jewish War* (7 books, 66–73 C.E.) as well as *Against Apion* defends his career and political acts. Josephus had represented Jewish interests in Rome under Nero and, after failing to hold Galilee in the rebellion, he lived in Rome from 70 on. Josephus advocated the Jewish community's accommodation to Hellenistic culture under Roman rule. Resistance to Rome was hopeless and Jews would do better to suppress nationalism (he blamed the Zealots for the ruin of the Jews) and to enjoy their culture and faith under the invincible Roman peace (*JW* 5.367). The Stoic Posidonius (135–50 B.C.E.) from Syrian Apamea had similarly vindicated Roman imperialism in his *Histories* (52 books).

Josephus' *Jewish War* provides our fullest history of any Roman provincial rebellion (with information from both sides). For once, a subject from the periphery, even a prisoner of war (although a Roman citizen and an intimate flatterer of the Flavians in the years to come), wrote the eyewitness account. Josephus describes the horrible fate of the Jerusalem Jews in detail. He is the first extant historian to present Jewish history from a Jewish point of view in Hellenic terms and in decent Greek; he is also the first to refer to Jesus and his sect (see *Jewish Antiquities,* which draw on Hebrew Scripture and Greek sources; 18.63–64; 20.200). His historiography is largely conventional by Greco-Roman standards ("this was the greatest war of all time"), but his circumstances and the subject justify inclusion here.

Eusebius (260–340 C.E.) of Caesarea, a Christian bishop and confessor to the emperor Constantine, produced a panegyrical biography of his patron, and harmonized pagan and biblical chronologies in the *Chronica.* He wrote the *Ecclesiastical History* (10 books, down to 324 C.E.), the first such history and a model for all his churchly successors. Hellenistic principles of biography and historiography (including the example of Josephus) informed the history of the origin, growth, tribulations, and triumph of Christianity. Martyrdoms, persecutions, battles over doctrine and heresy, and miracles required a new kind of history (8.9), a new subgenre, institutional and "fulfillment" history.

Eusebius may be derivative in his political and military narrational methods, but his record of the Church's development is radically different for its profuse documentation, inclusion of verbatim quotation, and absence of invented speeches. Eusebius made the form and substance of classical historiography accessible to Christian writers, although his work has a slovenly style and little conceptual structure. Like Josephus he uses history to justify faith; unlike his predecessor, he has a sensational success to narrate (10.4.9) rather than a tragic failure to explain. He included Greek and Roman pagan achievements as part of the preparation for the triumph of the Christian Church in the vast lands already, providentially, under Roman control. Conceptually the peoples of the East and their mystery cults have moved from the periphery to the center of Greco-Roman history and historiography.

Ammianus Marcellinus (330–395 C.E.), an Antiochene Greek officer of the military elite (15.5.22; 19.8.6) and a man of wide reading, served under Julian and other commanders in the East and West. Thirty-one books in forceful Latin covered the years 96–378. The extant and more detailed portion, beginning in 353 C.E., records wars with barbarians, internal dynastic struggles, and the rapacious administration of the Empire (16.8.11; 29.1.21; 31.16.9). He hopes the Empire can be salvaged, endorses an indispensable absolutism, and analyzes the internal and external crises of his age.

Ammianus argues for the truth, impartiality, and thoroughness of his account, which he based on personal observation, examination of witnesses, and public records (15.1.1). He disparages historians who criticize selective, ungossipy writers, who strive to include every trivial fort or praetor, or who industriously invent motives (26.1.1). This soldier-historian recognizes the limitations of his accuracy and will not supply false figures (31.5.10).

In an oppressive epoch for writers of any creed he shows unusual humanity, tolerance, and even admiration for both Christianity (22.11.5, 10; 21.16.18) and traditional pagan beliefs (divination: 23.6.25; 30.9.5; cf. the attitudes of Eunapius or Orosius). He digresses into scientific and social topics (14.6.2; 22.15.1). His wide travels and active military career aid his topographical explanations and geographical notices (16.10.14–17; 27.4.2). Ammianus takes fair measure of Julian (25.4) and provides succinct if exaggerated summary epilogues for each emperor, highlighting their characteristic traits of remarkable cunning and violence (e.g., 14.27–8; 30.7.1, 8–9; 31.14.2–7). He proclaims Roman values in an age that justly fears impending chaos, and dislikes the Germans because of the threat they pose to civilization. Nevertheless he forgoes the usual deference to the wisdom of the Roman senate, he criticizes rampant peculation by officials, and he admires valiant and astute enemies. His dependable concern for facts leads him to avoid unjustified generalizations (27.11.1) in an age of dogma, fear, and brutality.

F. Methodology and Conclusions

Local records, the Homeric epics, and a rationalism critical of mythical tradition gave the preconditions for historical research. The Greek genre is eclectic in its sources and scope, secular and humanistic in purpose. A rational method and a literary genre were constructed by Herodotus to solve a particular historical puzzle and to legitimate his demonstrably eccentric society. History of politics, public administration, and war remained central but sociocultural history emerged already with Herodotus. The best historians limited themselves to an extended narrative of the period within living memory; the preeminence of recent history was a consequence of methodology's failure to produce reliable evidence for earlier periods.

To record with honesty and after determined research the recent past, especially its changes with no norm postulated, to comprehend the rational, continuous, and earthly connections among things, to inform not a dynasty but all those (of the dominant class) who cared to understand contingent but decisive forces in human societies: these were the ancient historian's professed intentions. The impulse varied as of course did the style, the diligence, and perceptivity of the explanations. Some authors delight in the trivial deed revelatory of personality, many have a moral purpose. Some have a theory of historical causation (cyclical, pendular, linear), but rarely is it applied systematically. Sudden change and contingency were explanations more often invoked than gradual evolution and inevitability. The best of the ancient historians express surprise over outcomes, a sense that things could have gone forward differently, and their historical reconstructions preserve that three-dimensional quality.

The superior historians identified problems of time, change and cause, bias, evidence, individual and group interests, culture, nation, myth, and power. They downplayed the gods, giving them at most the job of keeping the show running, not proving their power. They sought to render events intelligible in human, not providential terms. To instruct and to entertain readers with true examples were goals (cf. Pliny *Ep.* 5.8). Their narrative histories of events were not as analytical as ours. The causes of war were not profoundly discussed, success was measured by duration rather than by ethical notions, evidence was inadequately evaluated and sometimes fabricated. Metaphors, models, and ideological assumptions were rarely considered: narrative history did not question the rights of power, the aim of dominion, or slavery.

Writers of history competed less frequently to unearth new material than to extend the scope of political discourse or to delight their audience with drama, passion, and elegant prose. The chief theoretic was rhetoric; the motive of inciting the reader's virtue and condemning vicious behavior tempted writers to persuade unscrupulously more often than to strive for accuracy. Neither Greek nor Roman historians bothered to learn foreign languages in order to search native resources. Quotation of sources was rare, testing their authorities' accuracy occurred to few of them, and the disinterested weighing of conflicting material evidence was uncommon.

Greek ethnic bias did not lead historians to see history as proof of their nation's favor or disfavor before a god or as a fulfillment of divine promises. Greek historians were often from, but no longer of, their city's power elite. Herodotus, Thucydides, Xenophon, and Polybius all wrote in exile, a political limbo. This reduces parochial favoritism, but not class prejudices. Many Romans deploy history to explain and justify Rome's growth and supremacy. Some subordinate disinterested curiosity to apologetic, polemical, and didactic ends. The great Roman achievement in historiography is the transformation of Greek antiquarian local history in annalistic form into Roman national history. This relocation of focus became the precursor of most modern historiography.

The story of particular men and contingent events has

always been insufficiently logical for philosophers and scientists, but the ancient historians did create a beachhead for systematic research into past human activities. Ancient classical historians generally find and leave men in the historical process, responsible for their choices and acts. The genre maintained a recognizable, if profitably fluid, profile for 750 years in Greek hands, for 500 years in Roman.

Bibliography

Studies of Ancient Historiography:

Badian, E. 1966. The Early Historians. Pp. 1–39 in *Latin Historians,* ed. T. A. Dorey. London.

Bury, J. B. 1908. *The Ancient Greek Historians.* Repr. New York, 1958.

Drews, R. 1973. *The Greek Accounts of Eastern History.* Cambridge, MA.

Fornara, C. 1983. *The Nature of History in Ancient Greece and Rome.* Berkeley.

Grant, M. 1970. *The Ancient Historians.* New York.

Jacoby, F. 1949. *Atthis.* Repr. New York, 1973.

Laistner, M. L. W. 1947. *The Greater Roman Historians.* Berkeley.

Momigliano, A. 1966. *Studies in Historiography.* New York.

———. 1971. *The Development of Greek Biography.* Cambridge, MA.

———. 1977. *Essays in Ancient and Modern Historiography.* Oxford.

Pearson, L. 1960. *The Lost Histories of Alexander the Great.* London.

———. 1983. *Selected Papers,* eds. D. Lateiner and S. Stephens. Chico, CA.

Studies of Individual Historians:

Adcock, F. E. 1969. *Caesar as a Man of Letters.* Cambridge.

Blockley, R. C. 1975. *Ammianus Marcellinus: A Study of His Historiography and Political Thought.* Latomus 141. Bruxelles.

Connor, W. R. 1984. *Thucydides.* Princeton.

Gomme, A. W.; Andrewes, A.; and Dover, K. J. 1956–81. *A Historical Commentary on Thucydides.* 5 vols. Oxford.

Jacoby, F. 1956. *Griechische Historiker.* Stuttgart.

Lateiner, D. 1989. *The Historical Method of Herodotus.* Toronto.

Martin, R. 1981. *Tacitus.* Berkeley.

Rajak, T. 1983. *Josephus.* London.

Syme, R. 1958. *Tacitus.* 2 vols. Oxford.

———. 1967. *Sallust.* Berkeley.

Walbank, F. W. 1957–79. *A Historical Commentary on Polybius.* 3 vols. Oxford.

Walsh, P. G. 1970. *Livy: His Historical Aims and Methods.* Cambridge.

Wardman, A. E. 1974. *Plutarch's Lives.* London.

Donald Lateiner

HISTORY OF JOSEPH. See JOSEPH, HISTORY OF.

HITTITE HISTORY. The Hittites were a people of Indo-European origin who penetrated into Asia Minor probably before or around 2000 B.C. and in the subsequent period became one of the greatest powers of the ANE.

A. The Name "Hittite"
B. Geography
C. Form of Government
D. Excavations and Discoveries
E. Hittite History
F. Economy
G. Languages
H. Religion
I. Literature
J. Culture

A. The Name "Hittite"

The name is derived from the indigenous *ḫatti,* while the modern designation is based on the Hebrew *ḥēt/ḥittī.* In the Old Assyrian texts, *ḫatti* is used as the geographical term for (central) Anatolia and hence is not a gentilic. At that time (19th to 18th century B.C.), *Ḫattuš* was the name of the later Hittite capital, where there was an Assyrian trading post. (In the Hittite language the name of the town becomes an *a*-stem, giving the well-known Ḫattuša.) During the New Kingdom or Empire (from about 1425 to 1180 B.C.), in addition to the expressions "the land" or "the people of [the town of] Ḫattuša," the name Ḫattuša alone was used as a gentilic. From the end of the 2d millennium, Assyrian texts use the term *ḫattû* (Hittite) usually in a pejorative sense—in a way which corresponds to the term *ḥēt/ḥittī* in the later books of the OT.

Numerous passages in the OT refer to Hittites as forming part of or even as actually constituting the original population of Canaan. References to Hittites in the books of the Pentateuch are likely to reflect Canaanite and Hebrew traditions concerning the political reality of the Hittite state during the stage of the Old Hittite kingdom or the initial phase of the Empire period. References in later books (1 and 2 Samuel, 1 and 2 Kings, 1 Chronicles) usually refer to the symbiosis of the Neo-Hittite and Aramaic states in more northern regions as well as to individuals stemming from the north. From a Hittitological point of view, Palestine does not belong to those countries which at any given time belonged to the Hittite sphere of influence. However, this does not preclude that in isolated cases persons or even groups may have crossed the borderline which separated the Hittite from the Egyptian sphere of influence. See also HITTITES IN THE OT.

B. Geography

The geography of Hittite Asia Minor is still a strongly contested area of Hittitology. In the SE lay Kizzuwatna, which comprised sections of the later Roman provinces of Cilicia and Cappadocia. In the NW, later known as Paphlagonia, lay Palā. In the W and SW of Asia Minor lay Luwiya (from ca. 1400 B.C. onward called Arzawa).

C. Form of Government

It has been postulated that an Indo-European trait can be discerned in the character of Hittite kingship, which originally was less absolutist and despotic than elsewhere in the ANE, and in the position of authority held by the *pangus,* or council of able-bodied (?) men. There was a clear relationship between the Hittite queen and the sun goddess of Arinna, the leading female figure of their pantheon, while in a religious text which, as far as its contents are concerned, stems from Old Hittite times, the Hittite king is designated "the governor" of the storm god, the most important male figure in their pantheon. According to Hittite terminology, the Hittite kings "became gods" when they died. It would seem that in the 13th century B.C. the Hittite king and queen were, to an extraordinary degree, assimilated with the gods, whom they appear to have represented on earth and with whom they were perhaps identified after death.

The Hittites formed what was essentially a federatively organized state which during the New Kingdom or Empire was second only to Egypt in the ANE. At first the kingdom manifested certain feudal traits, but gradually it developed into a state ruled by officials.

D. Excavations and Discoveries

The existence of the Hittite kingdom during the 2d millennium B.C. and the later continuance of Hittite traditions in the so-called Neo-Hittite states in the region around modern Kayseri, SE Anatolia, and N Syria in the period from 1180 to 700 B.C. have gradually been pieced together as a result of numerous archaeological excavations. In 1834 the earliest surface exploration resulted in the discovery by the Frenchman C. Texier of the extensive ruins of Boghazköy/Boğazkale about 150 km E of Ankara, and the nearby rock sanctuary Yazılıkaya. In 1905 the German Assyriologist H. Winckler first visited the site, and in 1906 regular excavation work began and continued in 1907, 1911, and 1912. After a long hiatus as a consequence of World War I and its aftermath, excavation work was resumed in 1931 by the German prehistorian K. Bittel. The same thing happened in 1952 after World War II, but work finally resumed and is still going on.

From the beginning of the excavations at Boghazköy large numbers of clay tablets were found near the great Temple I in the lower city, at Büyükkale, the citadel, the Palace of the Hittite "Great Kings," and the so-called "House on the Slope." The presence of Akkadian and Sumerian texts among the collections of tablets was very quickly discerned. Soon, too, a tentative reconstruction of the succession of Hittite kings during the period of the New Kingdom (ca. 1425–1180 B.C.) was formulated, and only later did it become clear that the texts are preponderantly of an administrative and religious character. For some periods of Hittite history the texts reveal a surprisingly clear picture of how the upper stratum of the Hittite population lived and worked. Written on clay tablets in an adapted version of the cuneiform writing system used in Mesopotamia, the texts comprise a variety of genres: royal inscriptions, religious documents, diplomatic correspondence, and treaties.

The Hittite hieroglyphic script had been previously rediscovered. This system of writing, typologically affiliated (as a syllabary) with cuneiform script, but with a closer resemblance to pictography in its sign forms, was especially used (beginning in the late 18th and 17th centuries?) for official documents. Numerous seals and seal impressions have been preserved together with longer or shorter texts inscribed on (natural) stone, mostly stemming from the late 14th and 13th centuries B.C. Statements on clay tablets reveal that this type of script was also used for lower administrative purposes within the palace, the temple and the army, and was in these contexts inscribed on wax-covered wooden tablets. The hieroglyphic script and wax as a writing material were presumably used by broader layers of the population, and they continued to be used in the period of the Neo-Hittite states, from about 1180 to 700 B.C. Stone, lead, and probably wood continued in use as writing materials. The first example was discovered in Hama(th) in Syria in 1812 by the Swiss explorer J. L. Burckhardt, was published in 1822, and was rediscovered together with other examples in 1870.

Turkish archaeologists were already closely involved in the earliest excavations at the Hittite capital. A second important site in the central region within the bend in the Halys River, Alaca Höyük (1907, 1935, and 1937–39), was excavated solely by Turkish scholars. German archaeologists sponsored by American institutions excavated Alişar (= Ankuwa?) in 1927–32. Both sites have proved especially important for the earlier periods of Hittite history. However, the main new developments in the field of Hittite archaeology since World War II are without doubt the Turkish excavations in Inandık led by R. Temizer and K. Balkan (1966–68). There they discovered an important Old Hittite temple, an exceptionally important relief vase and a donation deed (published by Balkan in 1973). Since 1973, the Turks have been conducting excavations in Maşat led by T. Özgüç and S. Alp. In Maşat a large palace dating from the beginning of the Empire period was excavated and an important local archive of 125 letters on 94 clay tablets, 16 lists, and 1 oracle text was found. These two excavations filled in sizable lacunae in the archaeological documentation of Ḫattuša, while the letters from Maşat, when finally published, will prove of great historical, linguistic, and paleographical significance. The period in question, the last decades before the accession of Suppiluliumas I (ca. 1350–1325 B.C.), is rather poorly attested in the text collections of the Hittite capital.

During the first stage of the study of the hieroglyphic script and again since 1974 English scholars in particular have been intensely occupied with this Anatolian method of writing. Between 1872 and 1884 and on the basis of the find spots of the hieroglyphic script, W. Wright and A. H. Sayce succeeded in drawing a rough map of the extent of the Hittite New Kingdom or Empire. The find spots are dispersed over a wide area, from the Sipylos inscription near Smyrna (= Izmir) on the west coast, via Boghazköy in the heart of Turkey, and on to Carchemish (= Çerablus) on the Turkish-Syrian border near the Euphrates (after Boghazköy the largest tell in the whole country; English excavations in 1878, 1881, 1911–14, and 1920). The unity of the script was correlated with the textual data on the kingdom of the Hittites in inscriptions of the pharaohs of the Egyptian New Kingdom, of the Assyrian king Tiglath-pileser I (1115–1077 B.C.) and the OT.

The discovery of the so-called Arzawa letters in the Archive of Amarna (1887) led to the surmise that in view of the two systems of writing, cuneiform and hieroglyphic, in use there, Boghazköy must have been the capital of the Kingdom of Arzawa. Now Arzawa is known to have been located on the SW coast of Turkey. Only after the work of H. Winckler and the other German and Turkish researchers in Boghazköy and after the deciphering (or rather the analysis) of cuneiform Hittite by the Czech scholar B. Hrozný (1915–17; cuneiform had already been deciphered, so that the script could be read) was it conclusively established that the site represented Ḫattuša, the Hittite capital, and that a new branch of the Indo-European family of languages had been discovered. In 1926 the Swiss scholar E. O. Forrer made available the most important historical text material for both the Old Hittite Kingdom (17th–15th centuries B.C.) and the Empire period (approx. 1425–1180 B.C.). In about 1952 paleographic research began to make headway with the work of the American scholar H. G. Güterbock and the German epigrapher H. Otten. Specific forms of signs much used during the Old Hittite period and the first half of the Empire period were distinguished as such, making it also possible, therefore, to date more precisely the religious texts of earlier periods, especially those written in the Old and Middle Hittite scripts.

E. Hittite History

In a surprisingly quick succession of events, the first three kings of the Old Hittite dynasty of Ḫattuša, Labarnas, Ḫattusilis I, and Mursilis I, succeeded in establishing a realm in Anatolia and later add to it large parts of present-day northern Syria. According to the historical prologue of a legal and administrative edict of the later Hittite king Telepinus, who in this prologue gives a tendentious survey of Old Hittite history up to his time (beginning of the 15th century), Labarnas already held considerable regions in S Turkey. Either Labarnas himself or Ḫattusilis I, his successor (and probably his grandson), must have penetrated far into the NW. Kizzuwatna, reached by way of the famous "Cilician Gate," was probably annexed to the kingdom during the reign of Ḫattusilis I.

It was under this same king that conflict began with Aleppo, the capital of the Yamḫad kingdom in Syria, which at that time was perhaps the most powerful state in W Asia. Yamḫad prevented the Hittites from entering Syria. According to the bilingual (Akkadian and Hittite) annals of Ḫattusilis I (found in 1957), the Hittites attacked the coalition of city-states (which included Emar, Ebla, and Zalpa) from two directions: by the way of Kizzuwatna, specifically that part later known as the Cilician plain (around present-day Adana), and from the N after crossing the Euphrates. It appears from one of the two edicts dating from the end of his reign (but perhaps not of his life), in which Ḫattusilis I probably again appointed a grandson, Mursilis I, as his successor, that Aleppo had not as yet been defeated. The text suggests that this was to be the task of the new, young king when he had attained the age to undertake campaigns independently. This latter detail derives, however, from the second edict, likewise bilingual, dealing with the succession to the throne. During the reign of Ḫattusilis I the Hittites penetrated deep into the Hurrian country in N Mesopotamia. The Hurrians, on their part, invaded Anatolia in the early part of his reign and advanced far into Hittite country.

After capturing Aleppo, Mursilis I undertook the gamble of sending a military expedition to the then weakened Babylon, an event known not only from Hittite sources but also from Akkadian texts. Mursilis I probably joined battle with the Hurrians both before and after the expedition against Babylon, which was carried out with foot soldiers and charioteers and resulted in a temporary occupation of the city. The same period of his reign (about 1600 B.C. according to the "Middle Chronology" or in the second half of the 16th century according to the "Low Chronology") also yielded a number of important texts. These include the Old Hittite version of "The Laws" and several interesting and original historical texts, one of which describes the conflict with Aleppo during his reign and the reign of his predecessor and another text which would seem to be devoted to the conflicts with the Hurrians. It is this latter composition which, in addition to another "contemporary" fragment, alludes to the predatory raid on Babylon. A third text contrasts instances of corruption in official conduct and military action with the description of a meal at court at which sat the "good" dignitaries from the reign of Ḫattusilis I.

This period of prosperity was followed by a long one of decline, attributed by Telepinus to dissent within the royal family concerning the rights of succession and initiated by the murder of Mursilis I by his brother-in-law Hantilis I. About 1425 B.C. a new dynasty arose, perhaps with the transfer of power to a secondary branch of the reigning royal family. The Hurrian names of the new queens (Nikalmati and Asmunikal, but also Taduhepa and Henti) and the originally Hurrian birthnames of a number of its male princes (Manninni, Tulpi-Tešub, and Tasmisarri), two of whom later became kings under traditional Hittite names, strongly suggest connections with Kizzuwatna. Little is known about the period between Telepinus and the New Kingdom or Empire period. Recent archaeological discoveries in the Upper Town of Ḫattuša have confirmed the historical reality of Hantilis II, Zidanza II, and Huzziyas II, whose existence had been doubted by some scholars, and even added a final Old Hittite or Early Empire king, Muwattallis I, whose claims to sovereignty had not yet been recognized by modern scholarship (Houwink ten Cate 1987). At least five and possibly six kings need now be reckoned with; they must have succeeded each other quickly, and certainly did not represent separate generations.

The advancing Gasga nomads of the N must have made their proximity felt, at the latest under Hantilis II, but perhaps already under the reign of Hantilis I. In the course of later centuries they several times threatened or actually attacked Ḫattuša, located dangerously near the north zone. The first incursion was during the reign of Tudḫaliyas II (?), the direct predecessor of Suppiluliumas I (1350–1325 B.C.), when not only the palace of Maşat but also large sections of the capital itself were laid waste. Less than a hundred years later, at the beginning of the 13th century, the threat of the Gasga nomads was likely one of the reasons Muwattallis II removed the royal residence to Tarhuntassa. His successor, Urḫi-Tešub (= Mursilis II) returned the palace to Ḫattuša. Some scholars ascribe the ultimate devastation of Ḫattuša (ca. 1180 B.C.) to the Gasga nomads. A recently found hieroglyphic inscription concerning Suppiluliumas II, the last known Hittite "Great King," may contain information regarding the actual causes for the final disaster.

The beginning of the New Kingdom can be dated to about 1425 B.C. There is uncertainty, however, as to the number and succession of the kings of the first part of this period. A genealogical reconstruction of this first stage reckons with four or five kings belonging to three generations, and provides an historical sequence whereby under Tudḫaliyas I extensive annexations were made: land on the west coast and later Isuwa, East of the Euphrates, and territory around present-day Elaziğ was added to the realm. This king is the same Tudḫaliyas who, according to the later Aleppo treaty, conquered both Aleppo and Mitanni. It would seem that even Wašukanni, the as yet unidentified capital of Mitanni, was held temporarily by the Hittites. In all reconstructions, the reign of Ḫattusilis II, presumably a son and direct successor of Tudḫaliyas I, witnessed the first signs of a decline which became acute during the reign of Arnuwandas I, now assumed to have been the brother-in-law of Ḫattusilis II (Arnuwandas I was married to Asmunikal, the daughter of Tudḫaliyas I and Nikalmati). This rapid decline, which continued during the beginning of the reign of Tudḫaliyas II, led to a situation in which, when the enemies of the kingdom were pressing on all sides, the Hittite king was driven back to the core of his realm, the region around Ḫattuša within the bend of the Halys River. There is evidence that during a later stage of his reign, Tudḫaliyas II was able to recapture Kizzuwatna. But the success of the second attempt to expand the kingdom beyond the frontier of present-day Turkey was of short duration.

It was the third attempt at expansion, during the reign of Suppiluliumas I, that had longer success and resulted in a firmly demarcated sphere of influence. This hegemony was maintained for almost a century and a half. Suppiluliumas I concentrated initially on the consolidation of the kingdom in Anatolia itself; later, during the second stage of his reign, he put an end to the independent existence of the Hurrian kingdom of Mitanni (perhaps with Babylonian assistance) and captured important towns and regions which lay within the sphere of Egyptian influence. The superiority of Suppiluliumas I lay in the combination of cautious diplomatic maneuvering and strong military action at the opportune moment. Ugarit and Amurru were removed practically forever from the Egyptian realm and added to the Hittite Empire. In domestic and foreign affairs he made frequent use of the well-known strategem of dynastic marriage. He arranged the marriages of one sister and of two daughters with vassal princes; he himself married a Babylonian princess before he began his more internationally orientated career; and the widow of the Egyptian pharaoh Tutanhkamen asked him for a son to be her husband and future pharaoh of Egypt. The latter marital project was not, however, realized. The prince Zannanzas was killed *en route*, and this led to new military and political complications.

The administrative consolidation of the new realm was expressed in the installation of two princes, sons of Suppiluliumas I, as viceroys in Aleppo and Carchemish respectively. In particular the dynasty of Carchemish, strategically located at the point where the Assyrian and Hittite spheres of influence adjoined, thereafter played an important role in the governance of the Syrian provinces of the empire. Four generations of kings of Carchemish were contemporaneous with the four generations of Hittite "Great Kings" who ruled the realm after the death of Suppiluliumas I. It is likely that the fifth king of Carchemish, Kuzi-Tešub (recently attested in two seal impressions found at Lidar Höyük [see Hawkins 1988]), outlived the disastrous end of the Hittite Empire. In the second half of the 13th century the city of Tarḫuntassa played an equally important role in the defense against western invaders. The recently published "Bronze Tablet," an official copy of a treaty between Tudḫaliyas, the son and successor of Ḫattusilis III, and Kuruntas, son of Muwattallis II, and the later treaty that Tudḫaliyas concluded with his brother Ulmi-Tešub prove that during this period the kings of this SW border province functioned on a par with their contemporary, the king of Carchemish. Both were preceded in rank by the Hittite "Great King" and the heir apparent to the Hittite throne.

The rapprochement with Egypt in the course of the 13th century B.C. undoubtedly took place under Assyrian pressure. The New Kingdom came to an end around 1180 B.C., in the period of the migrations of the so-called "Sea Peoples." Ḫattuša was captured, plundered, and razed, a fate which—with the likely exception of Carchemish—also befell towns in other parts of the empire. That the "Sea Peoples" should be held responsible for the destruction of the Hittite capital is not thought to be very probable; the Hittite Empire was too much of a continental power and most of the important settlements lay far away from the coast. Disastrous occurrences within Anatolia itself are likely to have played an important role in this downfall.

The Neo-Hittite states in the region around modern Kayseri, SE Anatolia, and N Syria thereafter carried on the Hittite-Luwian traditions for another five centuries. Since the references in the Neo-Hittite hieroglyphic texts to different ethnic components—Luwian and Hurrian, but also Northwest Semitic—are indicative of the continuation of a pattern which already existed in the late 14th and 13th centuries B.C., no large-scale migrations need be assumed. As far as the regions outside of Anatolia proper are concerned, one might also evoke the picture of former colonies outlasting the political existence of their mother country. Recent research has indicated that Neo-Hittite kings in the Malatya region claim descent from a "Great King" of Carchemish named Kuzi-Tešub, who is said to have been their grandfather. If this Kuzi-Tešub turns out to be the king now known to have been fifth in line in our listing of Carchemish rulers, the long-sought piece of evidence for continuity between the Hittite Empire and the Neo-Hittite kingdoms would now have been found (Hawkins 1988: 101–3). In a more general sense, vestiges of the glorious past can be discerned in the continued use of the titulature "Great King, Hero," not only in Malatya and Carchemish but also in Karahöyük (Elbistan) and in the group of presumably early Neo-Hittite inscriptions found in the W (Karadağ-Kızıldağ southeast of Konya and Burunkaya in the vicinity of Aksaray). In Tabal (the region around Kayseri) the titles were still adhered to in the late 9th and 8th centuries B.C. Also the more general recurrence of famous Hittite king names, Labarnas, Ḫattusilis, Mursilis, Arnuwandas, and Muwattallis, in the whole region for which Neo-Hittite inscriptions are attested suggests a tradition rooted in the older Hittite dynasties.

In the 9th century B.C. the Neo-Hittite states became involved in renewed Assyrian expansion toward the NW. After a short intermediary period in the first half of the 8th century when Urartu was exceptionally powerful, the Neo-Hittite states were gradually, one by one, incorporated into the Assyrian Empire. At that time, from the middle of the 8th century onward, the Phrygians ruled W

Anatolia. In the E, Urartu was still an important power. During the last stage of their independent existence, the Neo-Hittite states of SE Turkey endeavored in vain to gain the support of the Phrygians and Urartu against Assyria. In the 7th century there was again unrest and apparently intervention from both the Greeks and Phoenicia. After the fall of the Assyrian Empire, the coastal region of the Mediterranean fell under the political influence of the Neo-Babylonian Empire. The further course of events forms part of the more traditional classical ancient history. All that remains to be said is that Luwian population groups would appear to have continued to exist in broad zones of the S coast and in particular in the lands of Lycia and Cilicia Aspera down into the Hellenistic age.

A number of factors make it difficult to give a broad description of Hittite history. For some periods, however, there is an abundance of historical material, both in volume and in genres. Moreover, the historiography of the Hittites is of a relatively high level. This obtains in particular for the reign of Mursilis II (ca. 1321–1298 B.C.). The earliest example of Hittite historiography, the "Text of Anittas," recorded for a king of Kaneš/Nesa (near Kültepe in the vicinity of Kayseri) who belonged to a local dynasty and lived approximately seventy-five years before Labarnas, describes lucidly events which may encompass more than one reign, sometimes even long periods. The presentation is seldom exclusively centered around the main personage, the Hittite king. The achievements of other leaders are fittingly described. Later examples of historiographic texts contain geographical digressions and historical transitions when a change is made to another location or another subject. Letters are cited and sometimes events in the enemy camp are described at length. Often an important opponent is allowed to speak. All this results in an easily readable description of events. Setbacks and defeats are hardly ever mentioned, however, and important omissions are merely ascribed to royal predecessors; these historical texts definitely give a biased account.

The Hittite annals, intended as self-justifying reports to the gods, but also as accounts of personal achievements recorded for the benefit of future successors and probably also for contemporaries of the ruling class, reach a level of sophistication unparalleled in those days. Their notable character as compared with examples from elsewhere in the ANE is probably due to the different administrative structure, by which rights and duties were more evenly spread over a larger number of people.

F. Economy

Hittite economy was clearly based on crop and cattle raising, carried on by farmers who were either independent or belonged to one of the two "Great Organizations" (palace and temple), or to the larger unit of a private estate. The limited number of land grant deeds and of cadastral texts shows that an estate or a farm could comprise dispersed parcels of lands. In the so-called land grant deeds (Old Hittite end Early Empire) in which were registered the royal grants of estates, a distinction is made between arable, horticultural, and pasture land. The horticultural land was divided into vineyards and orchards and mention is also made of forestland. The work of cultivation was done by resident families of farmers (also working on their "own" plots) assisted by slaves. It is remarkable that craftsmen are sometimes listed in the descriptions of these estates. The king was undoubtedly the largest landowner. Oxen (used for plowing), cows and goats (for milk), sheep (for wool), and also pigs and donkeys are mentioned. Horses are already referred to in the Cappadocian texts and also in the texts of the Old Kingdom. The art of metalworking (mines were the greatest asset of Anatolia and apparently continued to attract the Assyrian interest) and the manufacture of textiles must have reached a high degree of perfection, as is evidenced by the archaeological finds and the data in the texts.

G. Languages

Very soon after Hrozný's "decipherment" (1919), it was noted that no less than eight different languages were represented on the roughly 10,000 clay tablets and fragments of tablets found thus far. Although the obvious interpretation of this phenomenon is that it is the first formal indication of the composite nature of Hittite civilization, it could also indicate that the administrative system was less rigid and monolithic than in other parts of the ANE. Only Hittite, the language of the central region within the bend of the Halys River, Luwian, used in the S and W, and Hurrian, spoken in the SE and especially E of the Euphrates, were still living languages at the time of the New Kingdom. The most remarkable aspect of this phenomenon is, therefore, that the texts and linguistic products of six centuries appear to have been kept in a rather large number of places in the administrative and religious center of the kingdom when the capital was devastated about 1180 B.C. Apparently the Hittites were strongly oriented toward the past. To this must be added that Sumerian and Akkadian were included in the teaching of cuneiform, since practically every written Hittite sentence contains Sumerian and Akkadian logograms. Hence the use of cuneiform script implied at least a passive knowledge of some Sumerian and Akkadian. Recent research has revealed that scribes with Akkadian names were employed at the beginning of the New Kingdom and Hurrian scribes in the 14th and 13th centuries B.C. Moreover, two of the extinct languages, Hattic and Palaic, are mainly found in scattered passages in religious texts called "festival texts" or "festival descriptions" where Hattic and Palaic gods are addressed.

The eighth language attested was in all likelihood extinct as well. It can be detected in the scattered evidence for a form of Indo-Aryan among the numerous Hurrian personal names found not merely in Ḫattuša but in a great number of archives which came to light in a broad northern zone of the ANE. The Hurrians, like the Urartians later, spread out from a region between Lake Van and Lake Urmia and took possession of large tracts of present-day SE Turkey, N Syria, and N Iraq during the final phase of the 3d and the subsequent first half of the 2d millennium B.C. The Hurrians reached the pinnacle of their political power in the Mittanni Kingdom (16th–14th centuries B.C.). Originally it was thought that among the Hurrians there was an upper stratum of Indo-Aryans who forced their way in from the N at the beginning of the 2d millennium. The data from the collections of texts from Ḫattuša which provided important new clues are the occurrence of a number of Indo-Aryan divine names in a state treaty between Suppiluliumas I and his son-in-law Sattiwaza, at that time vassal king of Mitanni under Hittite sovereignty and protection, and the likewise Indo-Aryan technical terms in the training manual of Kikkulli, the horse trainer from the land of Mitanni. Nowadays the presence of these Indo-Aryan names of gods and persons and these technical terms has been reduced to a minor element in Hurrian studies. See also LANGUAGES (HITTITE).

H. Religion

The Hittite texts speak of the "thousand gods" of the Hatti kingdom. In addition to the Indo-European types of divinities (the storm god of heaven and the male sun god of heaven may be compared to Zeus and Helios respectively) and the numerous divine figures derived from the Hattic substratum who retained their Hattic names, many Hurrian deities also occur in the Hittite pantheon, especially from the beginning of the New Kingdom. Within this Hurrian group some, like Enlil and Ea, ultimately go back to Mesopotamia. The beginning of the New Kingdom period also witnessed the introduction of the state cult calendar with the two main festivals of Spring and Autumn, both lasting originally for 35 days or more. During both festivals the king and the queen visited the sanctuaries in the capital and the temples of the most important towns in the vicinity of Ḫattuša. After the "Upper Town" had become the main terrain for archaeological work, no less than 21 additional temples were uncovered. During the course of the Empire period, Hurrian influence increased steadily, and consequently with regard to the 13th century B.C. use is often made of the term *interpretatio hurritica* of the Hittite pantheon, best illustrated in the rock sanctuary Yazılıkaya near the Hittite capital. The hieroglyphs added show that reference is made to Hurrian deities. On the main panel Tešub, leading the procession of gods, and Hepat, leading the goddesses, stand facing each other. They are here apparently identified with the storm god of Hatti and the sun goddess Arinna, the two leading deities of the Hittite pantheon. In the capital itself, both deities shared a double temple, the "Great Temple" located in the "Lower Town" of the old city.

A group of Hittite mythological tales are indigenous to Anatolia, and the Hattic deities figuring in them probably go back to Old Hittite times. Another group is predominantly Hurrian and belongs to the period of the New Kingdom. All of the epic texts (in the introductions and in the colophons, often added to the texts, characterized as "Songs") go back to the Hurrians or to Mesopotamia (presumably through Hurrian mediation; e.g., the Hittite version of the Gilgamesh Epic). A few Northwest Semitic deities and myths also penetrated as far as Ḫattuša. The Hittite royal prayers, particularly the numerous prayers of Mursilis II, are of great historical importance. Most large collections contain many rituals and festival texts. See also ANATOLIA (MYTHOLOGY).

I. Literature

It is of importance to realize that the concept of literature is more limited for the 20th-century reader than for the ANE. Hittite literature comprises everything that was deemed worthy of being recorded in writing. The findspots of the tablets are both "archives" and "libraries" (or, for that matter, "scriptoria") in the later usages of these terms. Even a term like "chancellery" might be applied to the collections found at Büyükkale (buildings A, E, and K). Many genres are represented already among the Old Hittite texts. Unrepresented genres—instructions, oracle texts, and royal prayers—may have been disregarded for highly practical reasons. Historiography is the literary genre that was most productive. The scribe's training was based on Mesopotamian texts, which were traditional in this respect (see Beckman 1983). The high esteem attached to the ability to write in cuneiform is evident from the two groups of persons for whom genealogies are available: the kings of the second half of the Empire period and a fairly large number of scribes.

J. Culture

The Hittite civilization was manifestly composite. Much was derived or borrowed from the autochthonous Hattic population, particularly in matters of religion, court ceremonies, and iconographic traditions in art. Hurrian influence became significantly evident during the New Kingdom or Empire. The most important achievements of the Hittites in the cultural sphere lie in the field of historiography (compositions on a central theme) and in law. The political talent of the Hittites was great. They have sometimes been characterized as the Romans of the East. Such a comparison can also be made on account of their interests in architecture and warfare in addition to historiography and legal matters. It is also applicable to the way in which they, like the Romans, assimilated and incorporated cultural achievements from their predecessors and from elsewhere. See *CAH* 2/1: 228–55; 659–83; 2/2: 252–73. See also ANATOLIA (HISTORY).

Bibliography

Alkim, U. 1968. *Anatolia*. Vol. 1. Trans. J. Hogarth. Archaeologica Mundi. Cleveland.

Beckman, G. 1982. The Hittite Assembly. *JAOS* 102: 435–42.

———. 1983. Mesopotamians and Mesopotamian Learning at Hattuša. *JCS* 35: 97–114.

Carruba, O. 1977. Beiträge zur mittelhethitischen Geschichte I–II. *Studi Micenei ed Egeo-Anatolici* 18: 137–95.

Goetze, A. 1940. *Kizzuwatna and the Problem of Hittite Geography*. YOS 22. New Haven. Repr. 1980.

———. 1964. State and Society of the Hittites. Pp. 23–33 in *Neuere Hethiterforschung*, ed. G. Walser. Historia Einzelschriften 7. Wiesbaden.

Gurney, O. R. 1981. *The Hittites*. 2d rev. ed. London.

Güterbock, H. 1954. The Hurrian Element in the Hittite Empire. *Journal of World History* 2: 383–94.

———. 1957. Toward a Definition of the Term Hittite. *Oriens* 10: 233–39.

Hawkins, J. D. 1988. Kuzi-Tešub and the "Great Kings" of Karkamiš. *AnSt* 38: 100–8.

Hoffner, H. 1980. Histories and Historians of the Ancient Near East: The Hittites. *Or* 49: 283–332.

Houwink ten Cate, P. H. J. 1974. The Early and Late Phases of Urhi-Tesub's Career. Pp. 123–50 in *Anatolian Studies Presented to Hans Gustav Güterbock on the Occasion of His 65th Birthday*, ed. K. Bittel; P. H. J. Houwink ten Cate; and E. Reiner. Uitgaven van het Nederlands Historisch-Archaeologisch Instituut 35. Istanbul.

———. 1987. Recent Archaeological Research in Turkey. *AnSt* 37: 179–223.

Lehmann, J. 1977. *The Hittites.* Trans. J. M. Brownjohn. London.

Macqueen, J. G. 1975. *The Hittites.* London.

PHILO H. J. HOUWINK TEN CATE

HITTITE LANGUAGE. See LANGUAGES (HITTITE).

HITTITE RELIGION. The Hittite royal archives, known since 1907, cover the 18th to the 13th centuries B.C. They constitute one of the richest archives of the ancient Near East, and contain the most religious documents of any archive. These archives are the oldest evidence of an Indo-European language and religion.

A. Sources

These documents were written in cuneiform script on clay tablets, following Mesopotamian practice. The majority of the texts are of religious content, containing myths, hymns, and prayers, cultic inventories, divinatory texts, and descriptions of festivals and magic rituals (Laroche 1971: 321–720). The myths indirectly furnish precious facts about the origins of the kingdom (Laroche 1965: 62–176; Gonnet 1987a, fc.); the hymns and the prayers enlighten us as to the specific character of the relationships that existed between the king and the god (Laroche 1964–65; Houwink ten Cate 1969; Lebrun 1980). The prayers contain promises made by the king to a god in exchange for desired divine favors, while detailed descriptions of the festivals (Güterbock 1960; 1969; Darga and Dinçol 1969–70; Singer 1983–84; Popko and Taracha 1988), rituals (Goetze 1938; Otten 1958; Kümmel 1967; 1987; Neu 1970), and the cultic inventories (Brandenstein 1943; Jacob-Rost 1963; Carter 1962; Güterbock 1983), apprise us not only of divinity lists and the organization of cults (Archi 1973b), but also of the juncture of the human universe with the world of deities. Certain of these rituals are closely linked to mythological texts, of which they give a kind of synchronic equivalent; this circumstance permits both the myths as well as the rituals to be understood (Gonnet fc.).

B. General Characteristics

If one were to name three general and specific traits of the Hittite religion, one would say that it was characterized by the contractual nature of its relationship between the Hittites and their gods, by the importance played by rituals, and by the role played by the king.

In fact, the Hittite god was less attached to a place than to a cult: one could attract him with the promise of giving him a particularly elaborate cult; a god might leave his sanctuary and the country if his cult was not attended to according to the ritual (through negligence, insufficient offerings, or omissions from the cultic calendar), and might take with him everything necessary for life (Gonnet 1988). This departure would bring catastrophies regarded as divine punishments. Mobility is one of the original characteristics of the Hittite gods, and the strength of the Hittite Empire was directly linked to the number of gods that it was able to attract, appropriate, and hold on to. The Hittite land was not in and of itself sacred; it was so only to the degree that it sheltered numerous gods for each of whom a cult was conducted according to tradition: tradition is the very essence of the sacred.

Among the Hittites, proper conduct of a cult is essentially conforming to an archaic ritual, carefully transcribed on tablets found in libraries by scribes, meticulously faithful to their model: the ritual is a succession of *acts* that ends in a *sacrifice* offered, at a *moment* dictated by the liturgical calendar, to a particular *god.*

The importance of the king in the religion is linked to two facts: the king is the head of the clergy, and he becomes a god at his death. When the son of a king evokes the death of his father, he says: "when my father became a god" and this expression is only used for kings and their queens. Like the gods, dead kings have images that receive offerings (Otten 1951; Gonnet 1987b). It is the same for the queen, the king's wife (Bin-Nun 1975). Although the king, while alive, is only human, he is the "favorite of the gods" (Gonnet 1979: 23–24; 1987a). That is to say, he was elected by the gods to exercise royal power in a country and in a capital—Ḫattuša (Boghazköy)—that had likewise been chosen by them (*KUB* II 2: 42–43: "the gods have allotted the nations, they have established the capital at Ḫattuša for the king to rule there"; *KUB* XXIX 1: 17–18: "it is on me, on the king, that the gods, the Sun and the god of Storms have conferred the country and my house"). One of the major aspects of the royal function is directly linked to the divine election: it is the king himself who, seconded by numerous clergy (Güterbock 1975: 129–32; Gurney 1977: 25–43), enacts the cult on behalf of the gods. He is responsible for the proper execution of the cults, a condition for prosperity; and this fact explains the important role of rituals and more generally of religion in the society.

C. Deities

From the beginning, Hittite religion combined two traditions. The one is called Hattic; it was pre-Hittite, non–Indo-European, named for a people located in the Halys River valley; the other was called *nesite,* properly Hittite, from the name of the town of Neša (Kaneš), in Cappadocia. In the course of time, gods of other populations were adopted; those of the Palaites in Paphlagonia and those of the Luwians in the region of Tyane, two Indo-European groups; then a little later, the gods of the Hurrians (a non–Indo-European people of Cilicia/Kizzuwatna; Güterbock 1949; Gurney 1977; Laroche 1980). With all these disparate elements, the Hittites assembled a vast pantheon that they designated as "the thousand Hittite gods." It is in the organization of this pantheon that they left the specific mark of their culture.

In the middle of the 13th century B.C., under the influence of Queen Puduhepa, of Hurrian origin, the Hittite pantheon was founded upon the Hurrian pantheon, which had become official. This pantheon is well known thanks to the rupestral sanctuary of Yazīlīkaya (Bittel 1975), located 2 km from Ḫattuša. More than fifty divinities are represented there in relief, wearing above their arm their

Horite name written in hieroglyphic Luwian. It is the oldest representation of a pantheon.

A Hittite god was never isolated (Laroche 1967); he was always part of a divine grouping (Laroche 1952) that one honored according to the hierarchical order of the divinities (Puhvel 1984: 129–35). The place where all the gods assembled was above all, Ḫattuša, called "the city of the gods." But other sacred cities, such as Arinna, Nerik, and Zippalanda, (Tischler and Del Monte 1979) were designated as "places of the Assembly and of the Judgement of the gods" (Beckman 1982; Houwink ten Cate 1987). Outside of Ḫattuša, seat of the state pantheon, each Hittite city possessed its own pantheon, comprising gods, goddesses, mountains, rivers, and springs. In the longest royal prayer known, that of the king Muwattalli (Lebrun 1980: 256–85), there are more than fifty enumerations of provincial pantheons.

The lists of gods are known to us above all from two types of documents: texts that describe the royal offerings during the cults and the festivals, and treaties concluded between the Hittite king and a neighboring country (Weidner 1923; Friedrich 1926–30; Laroche 1980). The difference between these divinity lists is in general slight; they always begin with the sun (^{d}UTU) and his group, followed by three groups of gods: the storm god (^{d}U/IM) and his circle, the protector gods (^{d}KAL) and the group of gods of war (^{d}ZABABA). This tripartition recalls the distribution of functions recognized in other civilizations by Georges Dumézil (1966: 68–74; 77), although among the Hittites, the group of war gods is found in the third position. In the lists of royal offerings, before the sun one finds an entity whose nature is still unclear, Tauri(t), a divine concept associated with a tree.

The sun is a complex divinity: when feminine, she can be the solar goddess Arinna, consort of the head of the pantheon, the storm god; or even the solar goddess of the earth (Lelwani), an infernal goddess (Otten 1950). But when the sun is a male god (*Ištanu*) like the Mesopotamian Šamaš, a sort of assimilation takes place between the king and the god (Houwink ten Cate 1987), as the principal royal title, "My Sun" (= My Majesty), indicates. In the Anatolian hieroglyphic system this is represented by a winged solar disk (Laroche 1960 no. 190; Gonnet 1979). Relief number 34 of the Yazīlīkaya Sanctuary reflects this ambiguity: the person represented wears a royal costume; he has the royal title "My Sun" above his head but also the name of the sun god above his arm (Bittel 1975: Tafel 22, 1). The Hittite sun seems to be outside the three groups of gods cited above. He floats above these categories, like a guardian angel.

The lists of divinities end with the enumeration of secondary divinities, of which some are only hypostases of the principal divinities mentioned above. The "(favorable) day," deified among the Hittites, often appears at the end of the lists (Otten 1958: 77–78).

D. The Cult

Worship was offered to a divine image. This could be a statuette (Puhvel 1984: 313–15), a stele (Darga 1969), or an object symbolizing the god (a rython or statuette in the form of an animal, for example: a bull for the storm god, a deer for the protector gods, a lion for the gods of war).

A god's cult was initiated by a royal decision. It was the king who decided to have the image made, who fixed the date, the place, and the form of the cult, and endowed the temple with houses for the clergy and temple personnel, lands, vineyards, and storehouses for the harvests (*CTH* 81 II: 79–82; Archi and Klengel 1980; Gonnet 1987a: 91, 96). The clergy assisted the king in the celebration of the cult. The priests and priestesses of the temple took care of and prepared the sacrifices. A priest was elected by lot. After his enthronement, he carried the image of the god to the altar of the temple dedicated to him (Gonnet 1985–86). It is necessary to distinguish the clergy proper from the temple personnel, who were responsible for all the necessary elements for the preparation and the execution of the cult: chefs, bakers, cupbearers, potters, singers, instrumentalists, dancers, etc. At the head of the administrative services was the overseer, who managed the goods and furniture of the temple.

The cult took place in a temple or outdoors, in a "pure" place, "in the mountains where there is water." The cult image and the cultic equipment (throne, hearth, portable altar) were transported to the chosen spot where they were set in place on a rock.

As the excavations at Boghazköy have shown (Neve 1975; Klengel 1975), a temple was located in a sacred enclosure in which other buildings have also been found (library, storehouse). A temple could be dedicated to one or two divinities at a time (Güterbock 1975: 127). In the temple, several sacred places received offerings as well as the divine image: the throne (Archi 1966; Starke 1979), the hearth, the altar, the keyhole (symbolizing the door), and the window (Popko 1978).

Most often the cult of the gods was integrated with a seasonal festival that lasted several weeks. The most important festivals were those of autumn and spring. That of autumn, *nuntariyšhaš,* called the "festival of speed," lasted 21 days (*CTH,* 626; Košak 1976). The spring festival, which bore the name of a plant, AN.TAH.ŠUM., numbered 38 days (*CTH,* 604–25; Güterbock 1960; 1964; Gonnet 1981; 1982; Houwink ten Cate 1986; Popko and Taracha 1988). Both were agrarian festivals. They were centered around the opening (in the spring) and the closing (in the autumn) of the grain jar (Archi 1973a). During the last cultic season, winter, other festivals were celebrated, for example the festival of the winter solstice or that of the New Year (*CTH,* 597–600; Hoffner 1967: 39–41; Carter 1962: 180–83; Neu 1982: 125–27).

The rituals that ended with sacrifices offered to the gods of beverages, bread, and meat (Kammenhuber 1971; Archi 1973b; Rosenkranz 1973) often included the burning of incense; the manipulation of objects pertaining to the throne, the king, and the symbols of power; foot races; horse races; simulated combat (Archi 1978); a banquet (Archi 1979) in which the royal couple and the principal officers of the empire took part; vocal and instrumental music (Kümmel 1973); dances; recitations, and acrobatics. The sequence of these traditional and seemingly very ancient rituals evidently carried significance, but nothing obliges one to think that it was always perceptible during the time of the empire.

Bibliography

Akurgal, E. 1962. *The Art of the Hittites.* London.
Archi, A. 1966. Trono regale e trono divinizzato nell'Anatolia ittita. *SMEA* 1: 76–120.
———. 1973a. Fêtes de printemps et d'automne et réintégration rituelle d'images de culte en Anatolie hittite. *UF* 5: 7–27.
———. 1973b. L'organizzazione ammistrative ittita e il regime delle offerte cultuali. *OrAnt* 12: 217–26.
———. 1978. Note Sulle Feste ittite I. *RSO* 52: 19–26.
———. 1979. Das Kultmahl bei den Hethitern. *TTKY* 8: 197–213.
Archi, A., and Klengel, H. 1980. Ein hethitischer Text über die Reorganisation des Kultes. *AoF* 7: 143–51.
Beckman, G. M. 1982. The Hittite Assembly. *JAOS* 102: 435–42.
———. 1983. *Hittite Birth Rituals. StBT* 29. Wiesbaden.
Bin-Nun, S. R. 1975. *The Tawannanna in the Hittite Kingdom.* Texte der Hethiter 5. Heidelberg.
Bittel, K. 1975. *Boğazköy-Hattusa IX. Das hethitische Felsheiligtum Yazīlīkaya.* Berlin.
Brandenstein, C.-G. 1943. *Hethitische Götter nach Bildbeschreibungen in Keilschrifttexten.* MVAG 46/2.
Carruba, O. 1966. *Das Beschwörungsritual für die Göttin Wisuriyanza. StBT* 2. Wiesbaden.
Carter, C. W. 1962. *Hittite Cult Inventories.* Diss. Chicago.
Darga, M. 1969. über das wesen des huwasi-stein nach Hethitischen Kultinventaren. *RHA* 84–85: 5–24.
Darga, M., and Dinçol, A. 1969–70. Die Feste von Karahna. *Anatolica* 3: 99–118.
Dumézil, G. 1966. *La religion romaine archaïque.* Paris.
———. 1968–74. *Mythe et épopée.* 3 vols. Paris.
———. 1977. *Les dieux souverains des indo-européens.* Paris.
Friedrich, J. 1926–30. *Statsverträge des Hatti-Reiches, in hethitischer Sprache.* MVAG 31/1; MVAG 34/1.
Goetze, A. 1938. *The Hittite Ritual of Tunnawi.* AOS 14. New Haven.
Gonnet, H. 1979. La titulature royale hittite au IIe millénaire avant J.C. *Hethitica* 3: 3–108.
———. 1981. Remarques sur un geste du roi hittite lors des fêtes agraires. *Hethitica* 4: 79–94.
———. 1982. La grande fête d'Arinna. Pp. 43–71 in *Mémorial Atatürk.* Paris.
———. 1985–86. Aspects de la religion hittite. *AEHE V* 289–93.
———. 1987a. L'institution d'un culte chez les Hittites. *Anatolica* 14: 89–100.
———. 1987b. Notes additionnelles. *Anatolica* 14: 69–71.
———. 1987c. Tabarna, favori des dieux ? *Hethitica* 8: 177–85.
———. 1988. Dieux captés, dieux fugueurs chez les Hittites. *RHR* 4: 385–98.
———. fc. Telibinu et l'organisation de l'espace chez les Hittites.
Gurney, O. R. 1940. Hittite Prayers of Muršili II. *Annals of Archaeology and Anthropology* 27: 3–163.
———. 1958. Hittite Kingship. Pp. 105–21 in *Myth, Ritual and Kingship.* Oxford.
———. 1977. *Some Aspects of Hittite Religion.* Oxford.
Güterbock, H. G. 1949. Hittite Religion. *Forgotten Religions.* New York.
———. 1960. Outline of the Hittite AN.TAH.ŠUM festival. *JNES* 19: 80–89.
———. 1964. Religion und Kultus der Hethiter. *Neuere Hethiterforschung.*
———. 1969. Some Aspects of Hittite Festivals. *CRRA* 18: 475–80.
———. 1975. The Hittite Temple According to Written Sources. *CRRA* 20: 125–32.
———. 1983. Hethitische Götterbilder von Kultobjekte. Pp. 203–17 in *Festschrift K. Bittel.*
Haas, V. 1970. *Der Kult von Nerik: Ein Beitrag zur hethitischen Kulturgeschichte.* Studia Pohl 4. Rome.
Hoffner, H. A. 1967. An English-Hittite Glossary. *RHA* 25/80: 2–99.
———. 1969. Some Contributions of Hittitology to Old Testament Study. *TynBul* 20: 27–55.
———. 1974. *Alimenta Hethaeorum.* AOS 55. New Haven.
Houwink ten Cate, P. H. 1969. Hittite Royal Prayers. *Numen* 16: 81–98.
———. 1986. Brief Comments on the Hittite Cult Calendar: The outline of the AN.TAH.ŠUM festival. Pp. 95–110 in *Kaniššuwar. A Tribute to H. G. Güterbock on his Seventy-Fifth Birthday.* Chicago.
———. 1987. The Sun God of Heaven; the Assembly of Gods and the Hittite King. Pp. 13–34 in *Effigies Dei. Essays on the History of Religions.* Leiden.
Jacob-Rost, L. 1963. Zu den hethitischen Bildbeschreibungen. *MIO* 8: 161–217; 9: 175–239.
———. 1972. *Das Ritual des Malli aus Arzawa gegen Behexung.* Texte der Hethiter 2. Heidelberg.
Jacob-Rost, L., and Haas, V. 1984. Das Festritual des Göttes Telibinu in Hanhana und Kašha. *AoF* 11: 10–91.
Kammenhuber, A. 1971. Heth. *haššus 2-e ekuzi* 'Der König trinkt zwei'. *SMEA* 14: 143–59.
Kellerman, G. 1980. *Recherches sur les rituels de fondation hittites.* Diss. Paris.
Klengel, H. 1975. Zur ökonomischen Funktion des Hethitischen tempel. *SMEA* 16: 181–200.
Košak, S. 1976. The Hittite Nuntarrijashas-Festival. *Linguistica 16. In Memoriam Stanko Škerlj Oblata.* Lublijana.
Kronasser, H. 1961. Füng hethitische Rituale. *Die Sprache* 7: 140–67.
———. 1963. *Die Umsiedlung der schwarzen Gottheit. Das hethitische Ritual KUB XXIX 4.* Vienna.
Kümmel, H. M. 1967. *Ersatzrituale für den hethitischen König. StBT* 3. Wiesbaden.
———. 1973. Gesang und Gesanglosigkeit in der Hethitischen Kultmusik. Pp. 169–78 in *Festschrift H. Otten.*
———. 1987. Rituale in hethitischer Sprache. *TUAT* 2: 282–92.
Laroche, E. 1949. La bibliothèque de Hattuša. Pp. 7–23 in *Mélanges B. Hrozny.*
———. 1952. Tešub, Hebat et leur cour. *JCS* 2: 113–36.
———. 1960. *Les hiéroglyphes hittites I. L'Ecriture.* Paris.
———. 1964–65. La prière hittite: vocabulaire et typologie. *AEHE V* 3–29.
———. 1965. *Textes mythologiques hittites en transcription.* Paris.
———. 1967. Les noms anatoliens du dieu et leurs dérivés. *JCS* 21: 174–77.
———. 1971. *Catalogue des textes hittites.* Paris.
———. 1974. Les dénominations des dieux antiques dans les textes hittites. Pp. 175–86 in *Anatolian Studies presented to H. G. Güterbock.*
———. 1975. La réforme religieuse du roi Tudhaliya IV et sa signification politique. Pp. 87–95 in *Les syncrétismes dans les religions de l'Antiquité, Colloque de Besançon (1973).* Leiden.
———. 1980. *Dictionnaire des mythologies.* Paris.

———. 1983. Notes sur les symboles solaries hittites. Pp. 309–12 in *Festschrift K. Bittel.*
Lebrun, R. 1980. *Hymnes et prières hittites.* Louvain-la-Neuve.
Neu, E. 1970. *Ein althethitisches Gewitterritual. StBT* 12. Wiesbaden.
———. 1982. Studi über den Gebrauch von Genetivformen auf "-was" des hethitichen Verbalsubstantius -war. Pp. 125–27 in *Festschrift H. Kronasser.*
Neve, P. 1975. Der Grosse Tempel in Boğazköy-Hattusa. *CRRA* 20: 73–79.
———. 1987. Bogazköy-Hattusa. Ergebnisse der Ausgrabungen in der Oberstadt. *Anatolica* 14: 41–88.
Orthmann, W. 1971. *Untersuchungen zur späthethitischen Kunst.* Bonn.
Otten, H. 1942. *Die überlieferungen des Telipinu-Mythus.* MVAG 46/1.
———. 1950. Die Göttheit Lelwani des Boğazköy-Texte. *JCS* 4: 119–36.
———. 1951. Die hethitischen "Königlisten" und die altorientalische Chronologie. MDOG 83: 47–71.
———. 1953. Pirva- der Gott auf dem Pferde. *JKF* 2: 62–73.
———. 1956. Ein Text zum Neujahrfest aus Boğazköy. *OLZ* 51: 102–5.
———. 1958. *Hethitische Totenrituale.* Berlin.
———. 1959. Ritual bei Erneuerung von Kultsymbolen hethitischer Schutzgottheiten. Pp. 351–59 in *Festschrift J. Friedrich.*
———. 1964. Die Religionen des alten Kleinasien. *Handbuch der Orientalistik* 8/1.
———. 1965. Der Gott Akni in den hethitischen Texten und seine indoarische Herkunft. *OLZ* 60: 545–51.
———. 1971. *Ein hethitische Festritual. StBT* 13. Wiesbaden.
———. 1987. *Das hethitische Könighaus im 15.Jahrhundert.* Vienna.
Otten, H., and Souček, V. 1965. *Gelübde des königin Puduhepa an die Göttin Lelwani. StBT* 1. Wiesbaden.
———. 1969. *Ein althethitiches Ritual für das Königspaar. StBT* 8. Wiesbaden.
Popko, M. 1978. *Kultobjekte in der Hethitisehen Religion.* Warsaw.
Popko, M., and Taracha, P. 1988. Der 28. und 29. Tag des hethitischen AN.TAH.ŠUM-Festes. *AoF* 15: 82–113.
Puhvel, J. 1984. *Hittite Etymological Dictionary.* Berlin.
Rosenkranz, B. 1973. Kultisches Trinken und Essen bei den Hethitern. Pp. 283–89 in *Festschrift H. Otten.*
Rost, L. 1953. Ein hethitisches Ritual gegen Familienzeit. *MIO* 1: 345–79.
Singer, I. 1975. Hittite *hilammar* and Hieroglyphic Luwian **hilana.* *ZA* 65: 69–103.
———. 1983–84. The Hittite KI.LAM festival. *StBT* 27–28. Wiesbaden.
Starke, F. 1979. Halmašuit im Anitta-Text und die hethitische ideologie vom Königtum. *ZA* 69: 47–120.
Szabo, G. 1971. *Ein hethitisches Entsühnungritual für das Königspaar Tudhaliya und Nikalmati.* Texte der Hethiter 1. Heidelberg.
Taracha, P. 1985. Ritual *taknaz da. AoF* 12: 278–82.
Tischler, J., and Del Monte, G. 1979. *Répértoire géographique des textes cunéiformes.* Tübingen.
Vieyra, M. 1939. Rites de purification hittites. *RHR* 119: 121–53.
———. 1961. Les nom du *mundus* en hittite et en assyrien et la pythonesse d'Endor. *RHA* 69: 47–55.
Weidner, E. 1923. *Politische Dokumente aus Kleinasien.* Boghazköi-Studien 8–9. Leipzig.

HATICE GONNET
Trans. Stephen Rosoff

HITTITE TEXTS AND LITERATURE. In discussing Hittite texts one must first specify how the term "Hittite" is to be understood. Modern scholars distinguish between two major groups: (1) the Hittite kingdom with its capital at Ḫattuša, modern Boğazkale (Boghazköy), which existed ca. 1750–1200 B.C., and (2) the Neo-Hittite kingdoms of S Anatolia and N Syria, small city-states which carried on some aspects of the Hittite culture after the central administration at Ḫattuša had collapsed with the destruction of the city. The Hittite kingdom used both a distinctively Hittite cuneiform script and a hieroglyphic script. Cuneiform was used for all types of texts, while the hieroglyphs are restricted primarily to seals and monumental inscriptions. Cuneiform texts have not been found at the Neo-Hittite sites; these kingdoms continued the use only of the hieroglyphic script.

A. Terminology
B. Types of Texts
  1. Historical Texts
  2. Administrative Texts
  3. Law
  4. Lexical Texts
  5. Mythological Texts
  6. Hymns and Prayers
  7. Rituals
  8. Divination
  9. Festivals
C. Hittite Literature
D. Hieroglyphic Luwian Texts

A. Terminology

The term "Hittite (abbrev. "Hit") text" can be somewhat ambiguous because of the multilingual nature of the corpus. We may include under this rubric not only texts written in Hit, but also those composed or copied down by the Hittites in other languages such as Akkadian (Akk). There are eight languages attested in the corpus of cuneiform tablets at Boghazköy (Gurney 1981: 119–30): (1) Hittite, the Indo-European language of the founders of the Hittite kingdom. The early Hittites borrowed the cuneiform script of Mesopotamia and adapted it to their own language, allowing them to develop their own literary traditions and to translate the literature of other cultures into Hit. The majority of the Ḫattuša archive is written in Hit. (2) Luwian, a related Indo-European language of southern Anatolia. The Luwian of the cuneiform tablets consists of passages within the context of Hit-language ritual texts, usually incantations to be recited in Luwian. Luwian is also the language of the Hittite hieroglyphic inscriptions. (3) Palaic, another Indo-European language of the Anatolian group, attested only in fragments from the Ḫattuša archives. (4) Akkadian, the Semitic language of Mesopotamia and the language of international correspondence in the Near East of the 2d millennium. The Hittites not only borrowed the cuneiform script of Mesopotamia but also learned to write Akk, using it especially for treaties and letters intended for non-Hit speakers. The influence of the Mesopotamian scribal tradition on early Hittite literature may be seen in the historical texts from the Old Hittite period written in Akk or bilingual Akk and Hit (Güterbock 1964: 108). Texts borrowed from the Mesopotamian tradition, such as omens, epics, and proverbs, also tend to be written in Akk, although they were also frequently translated into Hit. In addition Akk words occur throughout texts written in Hit, used logographically for Hit words. (5) Sumerian (Sum), the ancient language of Mesopotamia and the first to be written down by the inventors of cuneiform. Sum words occur as logograms throughout Hit texts (as they do in Assyrian and Babylonian texts). Sum also occurs in the Hittite lexical texts, most of which are in three languages: Sum, Akk, and Hit. (6) Hurrian, the language of the Hurrians of northern Mesopotamia and Syria, including the kingdom of Mitanni. An agglutinative language unrelated to any other known language except Urartian, Hurrian occurs at Ḫattuša primarily in passages meant to be recited in rituals, in loan words (especially in divination), and in a few texts written totally in Hurrian, including fragments of the Gilgamesh Epic. The Hurrian material from Boghazköy presently forms the bulk of that language's corpus, as the capital of the Hurrian-speaking kingdom of Mitanni, Waššukanni, has not yet been discovered. (7) The Aryan language of Mitanni's rulers, preserved in some technical terms in a Hurrian-inspired horse training treatise. (8) Hattic, the language of the pre-Hittite inhabitants of Anatolia. This language is preserved only in the Hittite tablets from Ḫattuša. There are some purely Hattic texts, including poetry (Güterbock 1964: 104) as well as Hattic material preserved in bilingual Hattic-Hit texts, and in Hattic passages meant to be recited in rituals and festivals.

The great majority of the Hittite texts come from the capital at Ḫattuša. The Hittites housed their tablets primarily in a large archive in the palace, a major archive in the main temple, and in a building of uncertain function situated on the slope of the acropolis. Additional tablets have been discovered throughout the site of Ḫattuša, especially in the smaller temples.

There are a few Hittite texts extant from areas outside Ḫattuša. From Tell el-Amarna in Egypt comes diplomatic correspondence written in Hit (Hoffner 1980: 283 n. 4). A few tablets from Alalaḫ also are in Hit, and at Ugarit (Ras Shamra) a few Hit texts have been found. The only major archive outside the capital has been found at the Turkish site of Maşat (Hittite Tapikka), a provincial administrative center. Correspondence between Tapikka and Ḫattuša figures prominently in the Maşat archive, although other kinds of texts not specifically related to Maşat's administrative role have been found at the site.

The texts of the Hittite corpus are published in the form of copies made by experienced Hittitologists, who render as exactly as possible the form of the tablet and of each individual sign. Thus scholars all over the world may work with the material without having to travel to the Turkish museums where the actual tablets are housed. Perhaps 30,000 tablets or tablet fragments have been discovered at Boghazköy to this point, of which most of the major texts and perhaps half of the total corpus has been published in copy. A number of Hittite texts in English translation are collected in Pritchard, *ANET.*

B. Types of Texts

Hittitologists profit greatly from the comprehensive (when it was published) *Catalogue des Textes Hittites* of Emmanuel Laroche, which categorizes all published texts from the Boghazköy archives. The following sketch of Hittite text genres depends on this fundamental work. For each section the reader may refer to the appropriate category in Laroche for specific bibliography.

1. Historical Texts. See Hoffner 1980 for an extensive analysis of Hittite historiography and types of historical texts. The Hittites are to be credited with the earliest known examples of annals, a form of historical writing later used extensively by the Assyrian kings. For the Hittites this type of text is perhaps best exemplified by the various versions of the annals of Muršili II, in which each year of the reign is carefully documented with a record of its campaigns. A unique historical document is the "Political Testament" of Ḫattušili I, a bilingual Akk-Hit text in which the dying king describes to his assembled nobles the provisions for his succession. A series of early texts grouped by Laroche under the title "Palace Chronicle" are anecdotes of events in the royal palace in the early days of the Hittite state.

The "Telepinu Proclamation" is an especially important text for the Old Hittite period. In it the king, Telepinu, describes the period of anarchy characterizing the later Old Hittite era and details new rules for succession to the throne designed to reduce dynastic intrigue. The Hittite king not only records in writing his measures to enhance stability, but includes the historical context in which the need for such a proclamation arose. The Hittite corpus contains other royal edicts or decrees as well. An unusual historical text is the "Apology of Ḫattušili III," in which one of the later Hittite kings justifies his usurping of the throne from his nephew. As in the case of the Telepinu Proclamation much of the text is historical background to provide the context and reasons for Ḫattušili's actions.

A major type of historical text is the treaty, of which a number have been discovered at Ḫattuša. The best known of these is the treaty between Ḫattušili III and Rameses II of Egypt, of which both versions are extant, one from Ḫattuša and the other from Karnak. Many of the Hittite treaties are in Akk, as one would expect from documents which by their nature are international. Treaties with local, Hit-speaking Anatolian vassals are usually in Hit. Unique among the treaties is a recently discovered tablet made not of clay but of bronze, with the cuneiform signs carefully chiseled into the metal. It is the only bronze cuneiform tablet ever discovered. The text is a treaty between the king at Ḫattuša and a king in the south, at Tarḫuntašša.

One other major category within the historical genre is letters. These are royal letters, written to or by the Hittite kings in correspondence with other great kings of Assyria, Babylon, and Egypt, or with lesser princes. As with the treaties some of the letters are in Akk, some in Hit.

2. Administrative Texts. Like the historical text category, a number of different kinds of texts may be grouped under this rubric. One type of administrative text is the land donation, in which the king or king and queen make a grant of land to a subject. Other administrative texts include lists of officials, of personnel, or of towns, and inventories of resources, manufactured goods, or tribute.

The "instructions" form a major group of administrative texts. Each instructions text is a written description, developed by the Hittite bureaucracy, of the duties of various government officials. The instructions are addressed to officials such as the majordomo of the palace, the mayors of provincial towns, the border guards, and temple personnel. They are quite specific, detailing day-to-day duties, overall responsibilities, and the necessity of upright behavior and loyalty to the king in administering his resources.

There are attested from Boghazköy a number of shelf lists or catalogs of tablets, a kind of index system to facilitate finding tablets in the archives. The tablets are described in these catalog texts by author, tablet number if part of a multitablet text, and some descriptive phrase for the tablet by which it may be identified. Thus did the librarians of Ḫattuša organize their archives.

One subset of the administrative texts are the cult inventories, records of the religious resources of the kingdom. These include lists of cult equipment, cult statues, and religious personnel by town, and reflect the importance which the Hittites placed on maintaining local cults in the provinces. The festivals which are to be celebrated for each god are also detailed in these inventories, so that a record is kept not only of each town's cult resources, but also the festivals for which it is responsible.

3. Law. The Hittites, like many ANE peoples, had a written set of laws. The Hittite code comprises 200 individual laws; the many copies and versions of these texts show their importance in Hittite culture. The laws are formulated as hypothetical cases of the type "if a man does *x* . . . ." Most punishments are monetary fines, although for some offenses corporal punishment is prescribed.

In addition to this comprehensive codification of the Hittite principles of justice, there are extant several interesting records of actual court cases. The best known of these involves charges brought against GAL-^{d}U and his father Ukkura, palace attendants of some responsibility accused of misappropriating palace equipment and livestock. The court recorder has set forth both the charges of the accusers and the attempts of the defendants to defend themselves and explain the disappearance of the articles in question.

4. Lexical Texts. There are several series of lexical texts, or vocabularies, from Boghazköy. These texts are normally 3-column tablets, one column each for Sum, Akk, and Hit equivalents, with sometimes a fourth column to indicate the pronunciation of the Sum. They are the ancient version of our foreign-language dictionaries, designed to be used by the scribes for looking up words in foreign languages. This type of text is borrowed from Mesopotamia, where the texts are 2-column lists of Sum and Akk equivalents.

5. Mythological Texts. For this genre, see ANATOLIA (MYTHOLOGY).

6. Hymns and Prayers. The Hittites wrote down prayers to their gods, of which approximately 14, plus other fragments, have survived. These prayers sometimes include hymns of praise. They are almost always of royal authorship. Some are addressed to a specific god, some pertain to a particular crisis, and at least one, of Muršili II, addresses all of the gods. They contain elements of praise, confession of sins, and supplication. Perhaps the best known prayers are those of Muršili II petitioning the gods for relief from the plague which was ravaging the Hittite homeland. They are a poignant expression of a monarch's concern for his people as well as his theological speculation on the causes for such a disaster.

7. Rituals. The Hittites distinguished between rituals and festivals, a distinction which Hittitologists maintain in their terminology for these texts. Ritual texts record the magical procedures performed by a professional magician, usually designated as a "seer" or an "old woman." Each ritual text identifies the name of the practitioner and his place of origin, what the ritual is intended to cure, and often a list of required ingredients. The magicians are frequently foreigners coming from areas outside the Hittite homeland, especially from Kizzuwatna in southern Anatolia and Arzawa in the west. Rituals were performed on behalf of individuals suffering from various ills such as black magic, impurity, or impotence. Rituals utilize various kinds of sympathetic magic and may or may not involve offerings to invoke the power of the gods.

A particular type of ritual, in Hit *mugawar,* is a kind of attraction magic, designed to draw back to Hatti a god who has disappeared. See ANATOLIA (MYTHOLOGY) for a discussion of the myths that accompany these rituals.

8. Divination. Under this heading several distinct text types may be discerned. A number of omen texts are extant, some in Akk, some in Hit, but all borrowed from the Mesopotamian tradition of divination. The texts are records of ominous events in the form of protasis, e.g., "If the moon eclipses . . ." and apodosis, "Then *x* will occur . . . ." Omens may be astral or lunar, or involve unusual events or malformed births. A major type of omen involves examination of the entrails of animals, again relying on the tradition of extispicy developed in Mesopotamia. A number of liver models, with the omen texts written in Akk (or, rarely, partially in Hit) near the appropriate parts of the organ, have been discovered at Boghazköy.

A distinctively Hittite type of divination text from Boghazköy is the oracle. These texts represent a different approach to divination from the omens. The omen texts record a divination which is not sought, but is rather an observation of unusual phenomena, while Hittite oracles involve a deliberate attempt to learn the will of the gods. The texts describe the process involved, the questions put to the gods, and the answers received. The Hittites employed several methods of oracular investigation, including: (1) "Lot," in which symbolically named objects (lots) moved about among symbolically named locations by a mechanism not yet understood. (2) "Bird," in which the flight of birds, described in bewildering detail in the texts, was interpreted as the response of the gods to the questions put to them. (3) "Snake," in which a water snake was observed swimming about a large basin with symbolically named regions. (4) "Flesh," in which the exta of slaughtered sheep were examined for signs supposed to reveal divine responses.

Matters about which oracles might be consulted to determine the will of the gods included the health of the king, where the king should campaign, or the changing of part of a festival. Since each oracle could only provide a yes or no answer, deciding the will of the gods on questions such as these required a long process of elimination with a correspondingly large number of individual oracles taken to arrive at the answer.

Dreams represent another way in which the Hittites communicated with the divine. In the dream texts the king or queen recorded what he or she had seen in a dream.

The texts also record the vows usually made by the person during the visitation of the god in a dream. Some Hittite rituals involve having the client sleep in the presence of the deity (the cult image) to encourage that deity to reveal himself to him in a dream (Hoffner 1987: 282).

9. Festivals. The most numerous type of Hittite text is the festival text, that is the texts describing how a particular religious festival was to be performed. Such texts detail the cultic equipment, personnel, and offering materials required for the festival, and provide a detailed account of the various ceremonies and where, when, and how they are to be performed. Some festivals lasted for several days and involved travel by the king and priests to surrounding cult centers outside the capital. From the thousands of festival tablets discovered at Boghazköy dozens of distinct festivals have been identified, all part of a well-defined religious calendar. Festivals may be devoted to a particular deity or be associated with a certain season of the year.

C. Hittite Literature

One cannot draw sharp distinctions in the ancient texts between literary and nonliterary texts, and the question of what among these texts may be considered literature must be left to the individual reader of the Hittite tablets. For a careful consideration of this by a scholar thoroughly familiar with these texts, see Güterbock 1964. The mythological texts are certainly literary compositions, as are the Hattic poems. There is some wisdom literature from this area, showing a mixture of Hittite and Mesopotamian elements. The hymns addressed to the gods may also be seen as literary compositions. Some of the historical documents, such as the story recounting the Hittite siege of the city of Urša, or the palace anecdotes could also be considered literary.

D. Hieroglyphic Luwian Texts

The Hittites of the Empire period and the Neo-Hittite states used a hieroglyphic system of writing which includes both logographic and syllabic signs. The language of the hieroglyphs is a dialect of Luwian. The Hittites of the Empire period used the cuneiform and hieroglyphic systems simultaneously, as may be seen on many of their seals, which give the name of the owner in both scripts. The Neo-Hittite states did not use cuneiform, although they did use other writing systems besides the hieroglyphs, as may be seen in the long inscription at Karatepe, a bilingual text in hieroglyphic Luwian and alphabetic Phoenician.

Texts in hieroglyphic Luwian are mostly seals, which give little information beyond the name of the owner, and the monumental inscriptions of kings and princes. The Nişantaş inscription at Ḫattuša, authored by the last Hittite king, Šuppiluliuma II, is the longest hieroglyphic text from the Empire period. It recounts the deeds of the king's predecessor Tudḫaliya IV, but unfortunately its poor state of preservation makes it almost illegible. Hieroglyphic inscriptions often accompany reliefs, as at Yazılıkaya, the rock sanctuary where the figures of the gods are identified by hieroglyphic renderings of their names. There is a rich corpus of Hittite rock reliefs, on orthostats or carved onto living rock, dating from the Empire and Neo-Hittite periods. Many of these reliefs are accompanied by hieroglyphic captions or short inscriptions. Longer inscriptions such as that at Karatepe, a Neo-Hittite site, provide more text and historical information. However, the hieroglyphic corpus does not show the same rich diversity of text genres which makes the Hittite cuneiform archives such a valuable source for so many aspects of Hittite history and culture.

Bibliography

Gurney, O. R. 1981. *The Hittites.* 2d ed. New York.

Güterbock, H. G. 1964. A View of Hittite Literature. *JAOS* 84: 107–15.

Hoffner, H. A. 1980. Histories and Historians of the Ancient Near East: The Hittites. *Or* 49: 283–332.

———. 1987. Paskuwatti's Ritual against Sexual Impotence (CTH 406). *AulaOr* 5: 271–87.

Laroche, E. 1971. *Catalogue des Textes Hittites.* Paris.

GREGORY MCMAHON

HITTITES IN THE OT.

This entry surveys the OT references to "Hittites."

A. Hebrew Terms for "Hittite"
B. The Hittites in OT History
C. Who Were the Hittites?

A. Hebrew Terms for "Hittite"

Several different Hebrew words or phrases in the OT are usually translated "Hittite" or "Hittites." Occurring only in passages concerning Abraham's purchase of the field and cave in which to bury Sarah, especially Genesis 23, is the phrase *bĕnê Ḥet,* "sons [or children] of Heth." Heth is listed in Gen 10:15 and the parallel passage in 1 Chr 1:13 as one of the sons of Canaan, along with other ethnic groups who consistently occur with the Hittites as peoples of Canaan. The analogous phrase *bĕnôt Ḥet,* "daughters of Heth," translated "Hittite women" in RSV and NIV, occurs twice in Gen 27:46, describing the native women from whom Rebekah fears Jacob will take a wife. These phrases reflect the patriarchs' perception of the Hittites as early inhabitants of Canaan, "Canaanites" in the broad sense of the term.

The more common Hebrew word used to denote the Hittites, *ḥittî,* is also based on the name Heth and formed with the regular gentilic *yod.* This form always occurs with the definite article and is used in only two distinct ways. One of these is to designate the ethnicity of an individual, for instance Gen 23:10, *ʿEprôn haḥattî,* "Ephron the Hittite." The passage in Genesis 23, in which *ʿEprôn haḥittî* occurs with many examples of *bĕnê Ḥet,* confirms the identification of the children of Heth with the term "Hittite." Four individuals, Ephron, Zohar (Ephron's father), Beeri, and Elon, are identified as Hittites from the time of the patriarchs, while from the time of David two more, Ahimelech and Uriah, are so identified.

The much more common use of the phrase *haḥittî* is in the lists of the peoples of the promised land. This singular form used in a generic sense is translated in the plural, "the Hittites," in most modern versions of the OT. The Hittites usually occur in first or second position in the "standard" list of the seven major peoples of Palestine: the

Hittites, Girgashites, Amorites, Canaanites, Perizzites, Hivites, and Jebusites (e.g. Deut 7:1).

Two examples of a feminine singular form *ḥittît* exist in the OT, in analogous passages in Ezekiel 16. In Ezek 16:3 and 16:45, in language full of imagery, Jerusalem is castigated with the charge that its mother was a Hittite. There is one attested example of the form *ḥittiyyot* (1 Kgs 11:1), the plural feminine form. This occurs in a list of the foreign (non-Israelite) women admired by Solomon. These singular and plural forms are regular formations of the feminine based on the gentilic *ḥittî*.

There are also five occurrences of a masculine plural, *ḥittîm*. This form differs from the others in that it is used in widely varying contexts. In Josh 1:4 it occurs in the phrase *ʾereṣ haḥattîm*, "land of the Hittites," in the description of the land promised by God to Moses. In Judg 1:26, we again have the phrase *ʾereṣ haḥattîm* in the story of the man who betrayed Bethel to the Hebrews and then went to the land of the Hittites to found a new city. In 1 Kgs 10:29 and the parallel 2 Chr 1:17 we have *malkê haḥittîm*, "kings of the Hittites," to whom Solomon was exporting chariots and horses. Finally in 2 Kgs 7:6 the Syrians lift their siege of Samaria because they think that the "kings of the Hittites and the kings of Egypt" have been hired by Israel to attack their camp.

The LXX does not consistently follow the Hebrew forms, showing both singular and plural forms for the Hebrew singular *ḥittî*. It does not have the reference to the land of the Hittites in Josh 1:4, and it translates the 2 Kgs 7:6 plural *ḥittîm* with a plural form *chettaiōn*. In Judg 1:26 it reads *chettin*, and in 1 Kgs 10:29 and 2 Chr 1:17 *chettiin*, for the plural *ḥittîm*.

There is of course a people known to us as Hittites from their own rich archaeological and epigraphic record in Asia Minor and north Syria. The Anatolian Hittite kingdom flourished ca. 1650–1200 B.C., while its Neo-Hittite successor states lasted down to the 7th century. These people referred to their kingdom as the land of Ḫatti, and to themselves as the people of Ḫatti. In the Bronze Age the land of Ḫatti is primarily Anatolia, while 1st-millennium Assyrian records refer to north Syria in general as the land of Ḫatti *(māt Ḫatti)*, reflecting the presence of the Neo-Hittite states in that area after the fall of the Hittite Empire.

B. The Hittites in OT History

The Hittites were settled in Palestine before Abraham arrived, as may be seen from references to them in the patriarchal narrative. When God described to Abraham the land which he was going to give him (Gen 15:20), the Hittites were already settled there. When Sarah died, Abraham was living among the Hittites as a foreigner and bought the field and cave in which to bury her from Ephron the Hittite in the presence of the Hittite community. Later, while Isaac's family was living around Beer-sheba, Esau took two Hittite women as wives. Rebekah's concern that Jacob would also take a wife from the Hittite women was so great that Isaac specifically forbade Jacob to marry a Canaanite woman, where "Canaanite" must be understood in a general sense to include all the inhabitants of the area.

Several centuries later, when the Hebrews returned from Egypt and conquered the land which God had promised to them, the Hittites were still one of a number of local ethnic groups of Palestine. Both in God's description of the land before they entered it and in the cataloging of the peoples against whom the Israelites fought in the Conquest the Hittites almost invariably occur in the somewhat standardized list of the local inhabitants of the land. When the spies return and make their report at Kadesh Barnea (Num 13:29), they locate the Hittites, Jebusites, and Amorites in the hill country, while other groups live on the coast or in the Negeb. This is corroborated in Josh 11:3, in which the same three peoples plus the Perizzites are described as living in the hill country. That the Hittite territory is in the heart of the promised land which the Israelites are to conquer is made clear in Deut 20:16–18, where God includes them in the list of peoples of the promised land who must be utterly destroyed. They must have been organized politically, as Josh 9:1–2 talks of the coalition of the Canaanite peoples to defend themselves, which included the kings of the Hittites, Amorites, Canaanites, etc.

The patriarchs encountered the Hittites around Hebron (Genesis 23) and Beer-sheba (Gen 26:34; 27:46), and most of the evidence as to their location at the time of the Conquest is consistent with that location. The exception to this is Josh 1:4, in which the area around the Euphrates is described as the land of the Hittites. This does not fit with the other references to the Hittites as one of the local peoples of southern Palestine, and probably refers to the Neo-Hittite principalities of northern Syria. After Joshua's death the tribe of Joseph received the assistance of a man who betrayed Bethel to them and then fled to the land of the Hittites and founded a new city. Unfortunately no indication is given of where this land of the Hittites was.

The Israelites never completely conquered the peoples they were supposed to have eradicated, and they thus left themselves open to the ever-present danger of Canaanite influence. The Hittites are one of the Canaanite peoples in the period of the judges whom the Israelites continued to encounter in areas which they had conquered and settled. Judg 3:5–6 specifically indicates that the Hebrews had failed to eradicate the Hittites and had in fact now begun to intermarry with them and adopt Canaanite religions.

This failure of the Hebrews to eliminate the Hittites of Palestine can be seen in the continued contact between Hittites and Hebrews in the period of the monarchy. One of David's comrades while he was being pursued by Saul was Ahimelech the Hittite, whom David trusted sufficiently to ask if he would accompany him into Saul's camp at night (1 Sam 26:6). Ahimelech's Hebrew name is an index of how completely he had been integrated into Hebrew society. The story of David and Uriah the Hittite in 2 Samuel 11–12 indicates the presence of Hittites in Jerusalem. Although Uriah, a Hittite, was sufficiently integrated into Hebrew society to serve in the king's army, marry a Hebrew woman, and be listed among David's mighty men, the distinction between Hebrews and other ethnic groups was still maintained, and his ethnicity was an essential part of his identity.

Under Solomon the Hebrews were still in active contact with the Hittites; they were among the Canaanite women whom that king admired and took in marriage or concubinage (1 Kgs 11:1–2) even though they were one of the peoples with whom marriage had been specifically forbidden by God. They are also listed among the descendants of the early peoples of Canaan whom the Israelites had not exterminated, but who had been made subject and were forced by Solomon to work on his building projects (1 Kgs 9:20–21, 2 Chr 8:7–8).

Two other references to the Hittites in the time of the monarchy reflect a very different relationship between Hebrew and Hittite and must refer to a different people. In 1 Kgs 10:29 (and the parallel 2 Chr 1:17) we learn that Solomon was importing chariots from Egypt and horses from Cilicia, and exporting them to the kings of the Hittites and the Arameans. These Hittites cannot be the same people whom Solomon conscripted for forced labor, but rather a politically independent group of kings. These kings of the Hittites and of the Arameans must be located in the city-states of north Syria, which were Neo-Hittite and/or Aramean. Solomon's geographical location made him an ideal middleman for the shipping of Egyptian chariots to north Syria. However, we must wonder how he could export Cilician horses to the Neo-Hittite states, as they were located between Cilicia and Jerusalem. Did the horses come by sea to Palestine, whence they were then sold to the Neo-Hittite kings?

The Hittites, or at least their reputation, played a major role in the fate of Israel during the divided monarchy. In 2 Kgs 7:6, the Syrians who had been besieging Samaria fled their camp when they thought they heard the sound of a great army, telling themselves that the king of Israel had hired kings of the Hittites and kings of the Egyptians to attack them. Again this powerful group whose very name can terrorize an army can hardly be the Hittites of Solomon's enslavement, but must rather be the Neo-Hittite kingdoms.

Even in the exilic and postexilic periods, the Hebrews remembered or actually encountered the Hittites in Palestine. In one of Ezekiel's prophecies, he refers to the parentage of Jerusalem: "your mother was a Hittite and your father an Amorite" (Ezek 16:45, 16:3 similar, RSV). When the Hebrews returned from Babylon in the 5th century, Ezra encountered the same crisis of intermarriage with the Hittites that had caused problems for Isaac and Rebekah and for Solomon. In Ezra 9:1–3, Ezra is horrified by the information that the Hebrews have taken as wives the women of all the local tribes of Palestine, including the Hittites. As in the period of the Conquest, this is perceived as disastrous to the religious purity of the Israelites. In Neh 9:8, Nehemiah, in recounting the promises of God to Abraham, describes the land promised to Abraham as that of the Canaanites, Hittites, Amorites, etc.

C. Who Were the Hittites?

In the biblical references to the Hittites two different groups may be discerned. One is a local people of Palestine, settled in the area around Hebron before Abraham's arrival, the descendants of Canaan through the eponymous ancestor Heth. They lived in the heart of the land promised to the Israelites, so that God had to expressly command the Israelites to destroy them. That they were not eradicated but continued to inhabit southern Palestine, including the area around Jerusalem, may be seen in the references to Hittites in the Hebrew army, as forced labor conscripts, or as possible wives for the Hebrews, all the way through to the return from the Babylonian exile. Almost all of the references of Hittites in the OT fit into this picture of a local Canaanite people never quite eradicated in the Hebrew conquest of Canaan.

There are, however, five references to Hittites which do not fit with this picture (*IDB* 2: 613–14). The reference in Josh 1:4 to the area around the Euphrates as the Hittite country cannot be the Hittites of Hebron, but rather, depending on the dating of the Conquest, either the Hittite Empire's territories in north Syria or the successor Neo-Hittite kingdoms in that region. See Boling, Wright *Joshua* AB, 122–23 for a different view. The reference in Judg 1:26 to the man who after betraying Bethel goes to the "land of the Hittites" could refer to southern Palestine or to north Syria. In view of the use of the phrase *ʾereṣ haḥattîm,* "land of the Hittites," the only other occurrence of this phrase besides the Josh 1:4 passage, it is quite possible that the Neo-Hittite area is meant. Boling *Judges* AB, 59, indirectly implies his understanding of his phrase as the area of the Anatolian-Syrian Hittites.

The references to the "kings of the Hittites" in 1 Kgs 10:29 and 2 Chr 1:17, where they are importing horses and chariots from Solomon, and 2 Kgs 7:6, in which their very name causes the Syrian army to flee, again imply a powerful and wealthy group of kings, not a local Canaanite people who had been reduced by the Conquest and enslaved by Solomon. Again the Neo-Hittite kingdoms fit perfectly; the chronology is right, they were in the same area as the Syrians and thus known to them, and the plural "kings" fits very well with the nature of these states, which were not unified into one polity, but consisted of a number of small kingdoms.

These five references to the Hittites which on the basis of context may be understood as the Hittites of north Syria, that is, the Neo-Hittites, are also the only five occurrences of the plural form *ḥittîm* in the OT. This may mean nothing, but it could be some indication of a distinction made in the text between the Hittites of Palestine, descendants of Heth, and the Hittites of Anatolia and north Syria, the men of Ḫatti.

We must then distinguish between the "sons of Heth" of Palestine and the "men of Ḫatti" of Anatolia and northern Syria (see already *IDB* 2: 614; *POTT,* 213–14; Speiser *Genesis* AB, 169–70). The similarity of "Heth" and "Hatti" may have led to the use of *ḥittî* to refer to both (*POTT,* 214). This is not to say that these two groups called "Hittites" in the OT may not be related ancestrally from some period antedating our earliest records. Nor do we imply that there was never any confusion between the Canaanite Hittites and Hittites of the Anatolian or north Syrian kingdoms who may have migrated into Palestine and settled there. For the period covered by the OT, however, it is clear that the terms usually translated "Hittites" referred to two distinct groups of people.

Bibliography

Hoffner, H. A. 1969. Some Contributions of Hittitology to Old Testament Study. *TynBul* 20: 27–55.

Kempinski, A. 1979. Hittites in the Bible: What Does Archaeology Say? *BAR* 5: 21–45.

GREGORY MCMAHON

HIVITES [Heb *ḥiwwî*]. In the Table of Nations (Gen 10:17) and the corresponding genealogy in 1 Chr 1:15, the Hivites are descended from Ham, one of the three sons of Noah, through the Canaanites. They are therefore not a Semitic people, in spite of the Semitic names given to certain of them in the Bible (e.g., Gen 36:2). Most often, the Bible mentions these people along with others, that is, the Amorites, Hittites, Perizzites, Canaanites, and Jebusites. They are the indigenous inhabitants of the land promised by God to the Israelites. They were to be dispossessed by Israel under Joshua during the Conquest, to fulfill the promises of land made earlier to the patriarchs (Exod 3:8; 23:23; Josh 9:1; 24:11). Contact with them was strictly forbidden to Israel, who had to put them under the ban lest they lead her astray into the worship of their deities (Deut 20:17). This policy was not adhered to, however (Judg 3:5), since even Solomon was able to exploit the yet undestroyed peoples as conscripted labor in his building projects (1 Kgs 9:20–21). One explanation Scripture gives about why God allowed them to remain was to serve as a training field for the Israelites in the art of warfare, and also as a test to see if Israel would finally obey God's command, presumably by exterminating these predecessors of Israel (Judg 3:3–4).

Israel unwittingly made a pact with the Hivite (LXX "Horite") inhabitants of Gibeon, a village just north of Jerusalem, who through trickery were able to escape the eradication God had decreed (Joshua 9, especially v 7; 11:19). Geographically, the Hivites appear to inhabit the central and N regions of the land, ranging from Gibeon, just N of Jerusalem (Josh 9:7; 11:19), through Shechem, where a Hivite raped Jacob's daughter Dinah (Gen 34:14), up toward Lebanon and Mount Hermon (Josh 11:3; Judg 3:3; 2 Sam 24:7). They also seem to have some contacts in Transjordan (Gen 36:2).

Textual variants occur in several of the biblical passages. In Josh 9:7, the MT reads "Hivite" while the LXX reads "Horite." This variant could arise from a simple misreading of two Hebrew letters, *reš* and *waw*, which are physically similar not only in the later, square script, but also at earlier stages in the development of the Hebrew script. The same process in reverse, with one additional step of scribal error, could be evident in Isa 17:9. There the LXX reads "Hivites" while the MT has *ḥrš*, from a suggested *ḥry*, "Horite" (BHS; Kaiser *Isaiah 13–39* OTL, 80). Within one passage in the MT itself are both variants: a certain Zibeon is designated a Hivite in Gen 36:2 but a Horite in v 20.

Scribal error could account for these discrepancies, though the number seems somewhat high for this to explain all of them adequately. Another, more attractive suggestion, though itself without any objective evidence, is that a historico-geographical shift such as the incursion of a new group into the area of Canaan caused a change of nomenclature. It has been suggested that an original Semitic Horite group, possibly cave dwellers (from the Hebrew *ḥōr*, "cave"; Speiser 1933: 30) living in Edom (Seir, Genesis 36) were displaced by the ethnically distinct, non-Semitic Hurrians, who took over not only territory but also the name Horite. "Horite" could then have referred to two distinct ethnic groups which shared the same territory. "Hivite" could have arisen from a textual error, or more possibly as another designation of the Horites (Westermann 1985: 562) or of a subgroup within them (Speiser 1933: 30).

Bibliography

Speiser, E. A. 1933. Ethnic Movements in the Near East in the Second Millennium B.C.: The Hurrians and Their Connections with the Habiru and the Hyksos. *AASOR* 13: 13–54.

Westermann, C. 1985. *Genesis 12–36: A Commentary*. Minneapolis.

DAVID W. BAKER

HIZKI (PERSON) [Heb *ḥizqî*]. Son of Elpaal appearing in the extended genealogy of Benjamin (1 Chr 8:17). The name occurs in no other place in this form—Apocrypha or the deuterocanonical literature. The name is possibly a shortened form of the name Hezekiah or Ezekiel and means "my strength is [Yah or El]." The family of Hizki is associated with Ono and Lod according to 8:12. This association is well preserved in the work of the Chroniclers with other references in Ezra 2:33, Neh 7:37, and 11:35. However, this association proves very interesting since these cities and their surrounding villages are located in the maritime plain in what is traditionally considered to be Danite territory (Adams and Callaway 1965: 55). Myers (*1 Chronicles* AB, 60) suggests that this location may have been settled by Benjamin during the reign of Rehoboam. He also points out that the names in this section of the genealogy occur in the list of Thutmose III but not in the MT until Chronicles-Ezra-Nehemiah. Perhaps, since there is so little mention of Dan in 1 Chronicles (2:2; 27:22), the inheritance had probably been absorbed by Judahite and Ephraimite tribes. The fact that Hizki and others associated with Lod and Ono are called "chiefs living in Jerusalem" (v 28) might further reflect a mixing of the tribal groups of Judah and Benjamin from the time of the division of the kingdom. Coggins (*Chronicles* CBC, 54) points out that this mixing resulted in some areas never being fully absorbed into certain tribal holdings. He considers that the reference to "chiefs living in Jerusalem" shows that Jerusalem itself was never fully absorbed into Judah. References making these two entities distinct are abundant and Judg 1:8, 21 show attempts to control the city by both Judahite and Benjaminite groups.

Bibliography

Adams, J. M., and Callaway, J. A. 1965. *Biblical Backgrounds*. Nashville.

G. EDWIN HARMON

HIZKIAH (PERSON) [Heb *ḥizqîyāhû*]. The second son of Neariah in the list of postexilic descendants of David in 1 Chr 3:23. His name is identical to that of Hezekiah. The name may mean "Yahweh is strength" or some variant (*TPNAH*, 153).

RUSSELL FULLER

HOBAB (PERSON) [Heb *ḥōbāb*]. A Midianite/Kenite whom Moses asked to guide the Israelites through the wilderness from Mount Sinai to the promised land (Num

10:29–32). Hobab was either Moses' father-in-law or his brother-in-law. In Judg 4:11, Hobab the Kenite is identified as Moses' father-in-law; however, in Num 10:29, Hobab the Midianite is referred to as Moses' brother-in-law while Reuel is mentioned as Moses' father-in-law. Contending that Hobab was Moses' father-in-law, Noth (*Numbers* OTL, 77) claims that the father-son relationship between Reuel and Hobab in Num 10:29 is a later harmonization and that even in the Yahwist's version of Num 10:29 Hobab would have been identified as Moses' father-in-law. Nevertheless, a further difficulty in identifying Hobab as Moses' father-in-law is that Jethro, the priest of Midian, frequently receives this designation (Exod 3:1; 4:18; 18:1–2, 5–6, 12).

Hobab's acceptance of Moses' invitation to guide the Israelites is not recorded in Num 10:29–32. However, evidence that Hobab consented to guide the Israelites may be present in Judg 1:16 which states that the Kenites and Judahites together went up and settled in the wilderness of Judah near Arad. If Hobab was the leader of the Kenites at the time of this concerted action, then he probably forged an alliance between the Kenites and the Judahites (*AIR,* 307). The absence of a response by Hobab in Num 10:29–32 to Moses' invitation to guide the Israelites may be a consequence of the tradition's emphasizing the divine guidance of the Lord from the Ark (Num 10:33–34) and its downplaying of the human guidance which Hobab would have provided. Evidence that the Israelites believed that they received guidance in the wilderness not only from the Lord enthroned on the Ark but also from Hobab may be found in Deut 33:2–3 if Weinfeld's revocalization of v 3a is accepted, reading *ʾap ḥōbāb ʿimām,* "also Hobab was with them," in place of *ʾap ḥōbēb ʿammîm,* "indeed, he loved his people" (*AIR,* 308). So while the Lord's guidance of the Israelites in the wilderness was primary, Hobab provided such guidance on the earthly level.

Dale F. Launderville

HOBAH (PLACE) [Heb *ḥôbâ*]. In Genesis 14, Abraham and Lot separated their herds and flocks. Lot went to the Jordan Valley and camped near Sodom. The area was raided by four kings, perhaps from Mesopotamia (14:1). The kings took loot and apparently captives. Among the latter was Lot and his goods (v 12). When the news reached Abraham, he gathered his fighting men and pursued the raiders as far as Dan (v 14). He routed the enemy and pursued them then to Hobah, N of Damascus (v 15). Some claim this chapter is not historical, though it is written in historical fashion. One may, therefore, argue that Hobah was not a place at all, but Damascus was and presumably Dan was. So it is possible that Hobah was also. The LXX *Chōba* appears in Gen 14:15 and Judith 4:4; 15:5; and maybe 15:4. The first reference in Judith is a list that includes Samaria, Jericho, Choba, and Jerusalem. This would seem to be a Judean or Israelite site, perhaps el-Marmaleh in the Jordan Valley, 30 miles S of Beth-shan, or el-Mekhubbi between Beth-shan and Tubas. But Abel (*GP* 1: 299) identified it with Hobah in Gen 14:15 (Moore *Judith* AB, 149). In chapter 15, after Judith cut off the head of their general, Holofernes, the enemy army panicked and fled. Uzziah, the chief magistrate of Judith's beseiged city of Bethuliah, sent (v 4) for reinforcements to Chobai (Choba, LXX N), etc. This too would seem to be a Judean or Israelite site. However, in v 5, the Israelites pursued the enemy and cut them down as far as Choba, even beyond Damascus and its border. This sounds more like Gen 14:15 and could, of course, be a conscious repetition of Gen 14:15. But whether it is or not, the description is similar, and no more helpful in locating the site.

There are a number of proposed identifications of Hobah. Genesis describes it on the left of Damascus, i.e., to one facing E, and hence Hobah would be to the N. The additional phrase "on the left of Damascus" has been compared with three other explanatory topographical glosses, Siddim (v 3), Enmishpat (v 7), and the King's Valley (v 17), all of which may be of doubtful value. Wetzstein thought it was Hoba, about 20 hours' journey N of Damascus (Skinner *Genesis* ICC, 267). Another Hoba (or the same?), a spring, is ca. 50 miles N of Damascus, on the road to Palmyra; and yet another Hoba is a village mentioned by Troilo as .25 miles N of Damascus (Keil and Delitzch n.d.: 206). Sellin and others have related Hobah to Ubi or Ube, which appears in the 1850 B.C. Execration Texts (*ANET,* 329) and in the Tell el-Amarna tablets (EA 53; 139:63; 146:12; 189) of the 13th century. Here it is the district around Damascus (Skinner *Genesis* ICC). EA Letter 53 is one from Akizzi of Qatna to the Egyptian pharaoh Amenhotep III which says Ube no longer belongs to my lord (53:23, 27, 28, 37, 57, 59; Mercer 1939: 229). The name also appears in letter 189: reverse 12. Haldar (*IDB* 2: 615) considered Amarna Ube a territory with its capital at Damascus; Damascus is unknown before the 16th century. Thus another town was the center of settlement. He suggests this is represented by the mound of Tell el-Salihiye, ca. 10 miles E of Damascus. It is the largest mound found in the region, which may favor the view that this was the capital in the early periods. Accordingly Hobah was probably the name of this place. It was settled in prehistoric times, and in the Old Babylonian period it was a fortified town.

Bibliography

Keil, C. F., and Delitzsch, F. n.d. *Biblical Commentary on the Old Testament: Vol. 1. The Pentateuch.* Grand Rapids. Repr.

Mercer, S. A. B. 1939. *Tell el-Amarna Tablets.* Toronto.

Henry O. Thompson

HOBAIAH (PERSON) [Heb *ḥŏbayâ*]. An alternate spelling of *Habaiah* in Neh 7:63. See HABAIAH (PERSON).

HOD (PERSON) [Heb *hôd*]. One of the eleven sons of Zophah in the genealogy of Asher (1 Chr 7:37). Although Hod is placed within the dominant line of the Asherite genealogy (Beriah-Heber-Hotham/Helem-Zophah), this figure appears neither in parallel lists in Numbers 26 and Genesis 46 nor elsewhere in the Hebrew Bible.

Based upon the military terminology used in 1 Chr 7:40, scholars have suggested that the Asherite genealogy reflects military census lists which were organized in genealogical form (for example, Johnson 1969: 64–66). In keeping with this interpretation, the name Hod ("splendor, vigor") may bear a military connotation.

Bibliography

Johnson, M. D. 1969. *The Purpose of the Biblical Genealogies.* Cambridge.

JULIA M. O'BRIEN

HODAVIAH (PERSON) [Heb *hôdawyāhû, hôdawyâ*]. Var. SUDIAS. **1.** The first of seven sons of Elioenai named in a list of King Solomon's descendants (1 Chr 3:24). The Qere of the MT (Heb *hwdwyhw*) reverses the letters *wy* from the Kethib letter sequence (Heb *hdywhw*); thus, the Massoretes read the long theophoric ending (Heb *-yhw*). The LXX variously renders the Heb form (Gk *hodolia, ōdouia, ōdia,* and *ouadia*), but the NT may have substituted *iōda* (Luke 3:26). See JODA (PERSON). Noth (*IPN,* 194) reconstructs Heb *hôdûyâ (based on the LXX variant *ōdouia*), and explains the name as the combination of Heb *hwd* + *yhwh* with a *waw* connector (cf. Heb *hôdû lyhwh,* "O give thanks to the Lord," Ps 105:1; etc.). He claims that Heb *hwdwyh,* "Hodaviah," and Heb *hwdyh,* "Hodiah," do not share the same root, yet, as Kuhn notes (1923: 212, n. 1), their forms are frequently confused.

Since Hodaviah is a postexilic descendant of Solomon (ca. 420 B.C.E.), the Heb *-yhw* ending of his name is an exception to the almost exclusive absence of this form in postexilic names (Zevit 1983: 3). The name Hodaviah (Heb *hwdwyh*) occurs once in an extrabiblical source from Palestine (Lachish Ostracon 3 [*ANET* 322], ca. 589 B.C.E.), as well as in documents from Egypt (Elephantine Papyri, ca. 5th century B.C.E.; *CAP* 4, 30–31, 56, 58–59, 70–72, 170). This demonstrates the popular usage of this name by Jews before, during, and after the Exile.

2. Head of his father's household within the half-tribe of Manasseh (1 Chr 5:24). Along with his half-tribe and two other tribes, Hodaviah was carried into captivity by "Tilgathpilneser king of Assyria" (Tiglath-pileser III, ca. 744–727 B.C.E.) because his people sinned against God (1 Chr 5:25–26). This historical note, which concludes a list of tribal leaders and settlements, explains what happened to these tribes (1 Chronicles 5).

3. A Benjaminite whose grandson Shallu was among the first to live in his ancestral city after returning from exile (1 Chr 9:7). In a parallel list (Neh 11:7), the corresponding name is Joed (Heb *yôʿēd;* LXX *iōad;* cf. Syriac *jwdʿ*, which corresponds to Gk *iōda*). See JODA (PERSON). This occurrence of the abbreviated form of the name Hodaviah (the Heb *-yh* ending is missing) in a postexilic list of returnees (1 Chronicles 9) is predictable based on the absence of the Heb *-yh* ending in postexilic biblical material (see Zevit 1983).

4. A Levite forefather of 74 returnees from Babylon (Ezra 2:40; LXX variants include *sodouia* and *ōdouia*). In one parallel list (Neh 7:43), the corresponding name is Heb *hôdĕwâ,* "Hodevah" (LXX variants include *thoudouia, oudouia,* and *ōdouia*), which is a variant of either *hôdawyâ,* or *hôdîyâ.* See HODIAH (PERSON). The parallel in 1 Esdr 5:26 mentions "Sudias" (Gk *soudiou*), which corresponds to a LXX variant of "Hodaviah" in Ezra 2:40, and likely resulted from a scribal misreading of the Hebrew exemplar (see Myers *1 & 2 Esdras* AB, 60). From these parallel lists of returnees it is clear that Hodaviah was an important Levite in the exilic and postexilic community.

Bibliography

Kuhn, G. 1923. Die Geschlechtsregister Jesu bei Lukas und Matthäus, nach ihrer Herkunft untersucht. *ZNW* 22: 206–28.

Zevit, Z. 1983. A Chapter in the History of Israelite Personal Names. *BASOR* 250: 1–11.

MARK J. FRETZ

HODESH (PERSON) [Heb *ḥōdeš*]. A wife of Shaharaim, a Benjaminite (1 Chr 8:9). Shaharaim was one of the Benjaminites who dwelt in Jerusalem (1 Chr 8:28). The Heb word *ḥōdeš* means "new" and thus "Hodesh his wife" might be translated "his new wife" (Meyers *1 Chronicles* AB, 57; see also Curtis and Madsen *Chronicles* ICC, 159–60). "Hodesh" is also the word commonly used for "month" or "new moon."

TOM WAYNE WILLETT

HODIAH (PERSON) [Heb *hôdîyāh*]. **1.** The husband of the sister of Naham, and ancestor of "Keilah the Garmite and Eshtemoa the Maacathite" (1 Chr 4:19). Since the name Hodiah appears in this misplaced and fragmentary list of names (1 Chr 4:16–20), and his descendants appear nowhere else, it is difficult to identify him. Given the preponderance of female subjects in vv 17–18, and the resemblance of v 18 (*wĕʾištô hayhûdîyâ,* "and his Jewish wife") to v 19 (*ûbĕnê ʾēšet hôdîyâ,* "and sons of the wife of Hodiah"), it is possible to emend v 19 to read "and the sons of his Jewish wife" (Rudolf *Chronikbücher* HAT, 34). While this suggestion eliminates the problem of identifying Hodiah by changing the proper name into an adjective, such emendation is not necessary; the name is part of a damaged and incomplete list, and it may have been intelligible in its original context.

2. A leader of the Levites who lived in Palestine during the time of Ezra (ca. late 5th century B.C.E.). Within the books of Nehemiah and 1 Esdras Hodiah appears as one of the Levites who explained the Torah to the people when Ezra read it publicly (Neh 8:7 = 1 Esdr 9:48; only the Ethiopic version of the LXX of Neh 8:7 reflects the name *Hudia,* while variants of 1 Esdr 9:48 read either *hautaias* or *ōdouia*). Hodiah also helped lead the people in blessing the Lord after they confessed their sins (Neh 9:5; the LXX generally omits the name, although a few mss read *ōdouias*). In the list of those who pledged to keep the Law with Ezra, there are two Hodiahs listed (Neh 10:10, 14—Eng 10:9, 13). Since a patronymic is normally used to distinguish two individuals with the same name, and since neither Hodiah is listed with such, some scholars (Rudolf *Esra und Nehemia* HAT, 172; Williamson *Ezra, Nehemiah* WBC, 324) emend one of the names to "Hodaviah" (the LXX renders Heb *hôdîyâ* in Neh 10:14—LXX 10:13 variously as *ōdoum, ōdouia,* or *ōdoua;* cf. Ezra 2:40). See HODAVIAH (PERSON). Noth (*IPN,* 194) suggests emending one occurrence to Heb *hôdûyâ which is not related to the root of "Hodiah" (Heb *hwd*). It is likely that the name

Hodiah is used as a personal name, rather than as a gentilic in this list.

3. A chief of the people listed with others who pledged to keep the Law (Neh 10:19—Eng 10:18). This Hodiah was not a Levite, hence he cannot be identified with Hodiah #2 above.

MARK J. FRETZ

HOGLAH (PERSON) [Heb *ḥoglâ*]. One of the five daughters of Zelophehad son of Hepher of the tribe of Manasseh (Num 26:33; 27:1–11; 36:1–12; Josh 17:3–6; cf. 1 Chr 7:15). The five daughters petitioned to receive legal status as heirs because their father had no sons. Their request to inherit their father's property was judged to be valid. A divine injunction to marry within their father's tribe in order that their inheritance remain in the tribe of Manasseh was given. Hoglah and her sisters followed the divine ruling on their case and married cousins on their father's side. Many have posited a relationship between Zelophehad's daughter Hoglah and the town Beth-hoglah W of the Jordan (Josh 15:6; cf. the Samaria Ostraca 45, 46, 47 and 66 [3876] which refer to Hoglah as a district). Beth-hoglah has been identified with a certain degree of surety as Yaṣid. Lemaire (1972) locates the district of Hoglah N of Shechem, NE of Samaria and S of Noah. Budd (*Numbers* WBC) suggests that the author of Numbers might have transformed the names of towns with feminine endings into the daughters of Zelophehad in order to make the point that women are entitled to inheritance. Others would want to argue that a veritable historical tradition lies behind the present narrative. See MAHLAH (PERSON); MILCAH (PERSON); TIRZAH (PERSON); ZELOPHEHAD (PERSON).

Bibliography

Lemaire, A. 1972. Le "Pays de Hépher" et les "filles de Zelophehad" à la lumière des Ostraca de Samarie. *Sem* 22: 13–20.

MARION ANN TAYLOR

HOHAM (PERSON) [Heb *hôham*]. The Amorite King of Hebron at the time of Joshua who (along with Piram of Jarmuth, Debir of Eglon, and Japhia of Lachish) joined the coalition led by Adoni-Zedek of Jerusalem against Gibeon, after the Gibeonites had made peace with Joshua (Josh 10:1–5). This coalition was defeated and its five kings were subsequently captured and hanged (10:16–27).

D. G. SCHLEY

HOLIDAYS. See CALENDARS.

HOLINESS. This entry surveys the subject of "holiness" as it presented in the Hebrew Bible and in the Christian New Testament.

OLD TESTAMENT

In the OT, holiness is a positive cultic or moral condition of God, people, things, places, and time. It may be an inherent condition or achieved through ritual means. It is defined on the one hand as that which is consistent with God and his character, and on the other as that which is threatened by impurity. See D.1. and UNCLEAN AND CLEAN (OT). In the Hebrew Bible, the most extensive material about holiness is in the Priestly writings (= P) of the Pentateuch. Hence the discussion below will focus on this corpus, though non-P evidence will be discussed more completely when possible.

A. Terminology
B. Major Loci and Degrees of Holiness
  1. Divine Beings
  2. Humans
  3. Objects
  4. Places
  5. Time
  6. Miscellaneous
C. Methods of Sanctification and Desanctification
  1. Legitimate Sanctification and Desanctification
  2. Unintentional or Illegitimate Sanctification and Desanctification
D. Theoretical Concerns
  1. Relationship of Holy, Profane, Pure, Impure
  2. Sanctification Rituals and Ritual Time
  3. Ritual Place

A. Terminology

The main Hebrew root denoting holiness is *qdš*, "to be holy; sanctify," which appears as a verb, noun, and adjective over 850 times (with cognates in Akk, Ar, Aram, Eth, Phoen, Punic, Syr). Other roughly synonymous Heb roots include *bdl*, "to divide" (*Hipʿil* verb); *ḥnk*, "to dedicate" (*Qal* verb and noun); *ḥrm*, "severely dedicate; put under ban" (*Hipʿil* verb and noun); *rwm*, "contribute, devote" (*Hipʿil* verb and noun); *nzr*, "separate, consecrate" (verbs and nouns); *ʿbr*, "devote" (*Hipʿil* verb). The main Heb antonym is *ḥll*, "profane, desecrate" (verbs, nouns, and adjectives; cognates in Akk, Ar, Aram, and Syr) with the approximate synonyms *gʾl*, "desecrate" (verbs); *mʿl*, "betray; commit sacrilege" (*Qal* verb and noun); and the noun *piggûl*, "desecration." See below for discussion of verbs and nouns from these roots. See also UNCLEAN AND CLEAN (OT) for a treatment of terms relating to purity and impurity; Milgrom 1970: 23–24, n. 78; 1976: 16–21, 35–44, 86–89 (and word indexes under the foregoing roots); Haran (1978) under his word index; and Bettenzoli 1979.

B. Major Loci and Degrees of Holiness

We will first review the major loci or bearers of holiness as represented mainly in P and secondarily in other OT literature. This review when possible will discuss gradations of holiness which has been a recurring concern of some recent scholarship (e.g., Haran 1978; Milgrom 1970; 1976; 1983b). Miscellaneous carriers of holiness will be discussed in B.6 below.

1. Divine Beings. a. God. The P and non-P writings both consider God the ideal manifestation, indeed the source, of holiness. Holiness is not inherent in creation but comes by God's dictates. He sanctifies or sets apart the Sabbath (Gen 2:3; Exod 20:11), Israel and its priests (Exod 29:44; 31:13; Lev 21:8, 15; 22:9, 16; Ezek 20:12; 37:28;

cf. also Exod 29:43), classes of creation like the firstborn (Num 3:13; 8:17; cf. also Exod 29:43), and sanctuaries (Exod 29:44; 1 Kgs 9:3, 7; 2 Chr 7:16, 20; 30:8; 36:14). But if he is the source of holiness for creation, creation—specifically his people—must maintain God's holiness and his name's holiness which, in this context, are nearly synonymous with his honor, reputation, and glory. This is mainly a duty of the people's leaders (Lev 10:3; 22:32; Num 20:12–13; 27:14; Deut 32:51). Should the people sin, God or his name becomes desecrated (see sec. C. 2. b.) and his holy spirit, an aspect of his character, is grieved and may abandon them (Isa 63:10, 11; Ps 51:13). In addition to obedience, people bless, sanctify, and rejoice in God and his name (Isa 29:23; Ps 30:5; 97:12; 99:3, 5, 9; 103:1; 105:3; 106:47; 145:21; 1 Chr 16:10, 35; cf. Ps 22:4; 29:2; 96:9; 1 Chr 16:29; 29:16; 2 Chr 20:21; even divine beings: Isa 6:3). The people, too, are charged to emulate God's holiness by keeping the commandments (Lev 11:44, 45; 19:2; 20:26; cf. 20:26). Inscriptions may declare and recall his sacred character (Exod 28:36; 39:30; Zech 14:20). For his own part God sustains and displays his sanctity through miraculous acts and punishments (Isa 5:16; Ezek 20:41; 28:22, 25; 36:23; 38:16, 23; 39:7, 25–27; Hab 3:3; Ps 111.9; cf. God's "holy arm" in Isa 52:10; Ps 98:1). God, as holy, is above any competitors and is eternal (Exod 15:11; 1 Sam 2:2; Isa 40:25; 57:15; Hos 11:9; Hab 1:12) and is to be the sole object of Israel's devotion (Isa 8:13–14; Ps 33:21; cf. Ezek 11:16; Hos 12:1; Job 6:10; Prov 9:10; 30:3). The title "Holy One of Israel" reflects this supremacy (Isa 1:4; 5:19, 24; 10:20; 12:6; 17:7; 29:19; 30:11, 12, 15; 31:1; 37:23 [= 2 Kgs 19:22]; Isa 41:14, 16, 20; 43:3, 14; 45:11; 47:4; 48:17; 49:7; 54:5; 55:5; 60:9, 14; Jer 50:29; 51:5; Ps 71:22; 78:41; 89:19; cf. Isa 10:17; 29:23; 40:25; 43:15; Ezek 39:7). Paradoxically, this high holiness may make it difficult for people to worship him (Josh 24:19; cf. 1 Sam 6:20). On the holiness of God's word or promise, see Jer 23:9; Ps 105:42.

b. Lesser Divine Beings. Subordinate divine beings are also described as holy (Zech 14:5; Ps 16:3; 89:6, 8; Job 5:1; 15:15; Dan 4:10, 14, 20; 8:13; cf. Deut 33:2; some read this as a place-name). From the point of view of Nebuchadnezzar, the spirit of the "holy gods" is in Daniel (Dan 4:5, 6, 15; 5:11; some take this as a plural of majesty for Israel's God).

2. Humans. Not discussed here are so-called cultic prostitutes whose Hebrew designation is formed from the root *qdš* (cf. Gen 38:21, 22; Deut 23:18; 1 Kgs 14:24; 15:12; 22:47; 2 Kgs 23:7; Hos 4:14; Job 36:14).

a. Priests. In P, there are two classes of priests, high and undistinguished. Several points indicate the high priest has a higher degree of holiness than undistinguished priests. First, he is called a *high* priest (Lev 21:10; Num 35:25, 28). Second, there is only one high priest at a time. Third, the high priest has a more elaborate consecration ritual (Exod 29:5–8, 20–21; Lev 8:7–9, 12, 23–24, 30; see also Exod 28:41; 30:30; 40:13–15; Lev 4:3, 5, 16; 6:15; 21:10, 12; Num 35:25; Ps 133:2 and see sec. D. 2.). Fourth, each high priest is newly consecrated (Exod 29:29; Lev 6:15; 16:32; 21:10, 12; Num 35:25; cf. Num 20:25–28) while the undistinguished priests apparently are not, the initial consecration of Aaron's sons sufficing for all generations to come (Exod 40:15). Fifth, only the high priest can enter the adytum (the most holy place) of the tabernacle (Lev 16:3–4, 11–16) and is designated to perform the regular (Heb *tāmîd*) rites within the shrine (the holy place; Exod 27:20–21; 30:7–8; Lev 24:1–4, 5–8; Num 8:1–3; cf. also Exod 25:37; 30:10; Lev 4:3–12 and 13–21; 16:1–28). Ordinary priests generally officiate in the court at the altar outside the tent sanctuary (cf. Leviticus 1–7, passim) and enter the shrine only to aid the high priest in his duties or to perform other auxiliary work (cf. Exod 27:21; 28:43; 30:19–20; 40:31–32; Lev 10:9; 16:17; Num 4:5–20; see Haran 1978: 205–29). Finally, the high priest has more severe marriage, purity, and mourning restrictions than other priests (Lev 21:1–15; cf. Ezek 44:22).

A less holy class of priests among the descendants of Aaron are those with physical defects. While they are still holy enough to eat most holy offerings, they are prohibited from serving at the altar or in the tent (Lev 21:16–23).

Non-P literature distinguishes between high and undistinguished priests (2 Kgs 22:4, 8; 25:18; Hag 1:1, 12, 14; Zech 3:1, 8; Ezra 7:5; Neh 3:1, 20; 1 Chr 9:11; 2 Chr 19:11; 24:11; 34:9, 14; etc.; cf. Ps 106:16). It also mentions deputy priests (2 Kgs 25:18; Jer 52:24) and elders of the priests (2 Kgs 19:2; Isa 37:2; Jer 19:1) which may, but not certainly, indicate further distinctions in holiness. The Chronicles designate Aaron and his sons as "most holy" (1 Chr 23:13), in apparent contrast to the Levites whom it calls "holy" (2 Chr 23:6; 35:3; see sec. B. 2. d.). The priests' holiness allows them access to the temple, to offer incense, and to attend to and guard the sanctums (1 Sam 7:1; Ezra 8:28; 1 Chr 23:13; 2 Chr 23:6; 26:18). See sec. B. 4. a. and LEVITES AND PRIESTS.

b. Israelites. In P, lay Israelites do not share the same holy status as priests. The story of the Korah's rebellion emphasizes this point (cf. Num 16:3, 5, 7). Yet though they are denied priestly holiness attained through inaugural rites and genealogical right, they are charged to achieve another type of holiness: that which comes by obedience. This obligation is the result of Yahweh's separating them from the other nations and redeeming them from Egypt whereby he became their God. As their God, he enjoins them to be holy as he is holy (Lev 11:44–45; 19:2; 20:7–8, 24–26; 22:32–33; Num 15:40–41; cf. Exod 31:13; Ezek 20:12).

While in P holiness is a responsibility ensuing from God choosing Israel, in Deuteronomy it is the resultant state of God's choosing the Israelites which they must attain. Deuteronomy calls the people holy in the present tense (Deut 7:6; 14:2, 21). In the related P passages only God is called holy in the present, not the people (Lev 11:41, 45; 19:2; 20:26). Deut 26:19 and 28:9 (apparently referring back to JE's statement in Exod 19:6) do not necessarily contradict this. As in P, holiness is connected with observing dietary laws (Deut 14:21; cf. Lev 11:44–45 and [JE's] Exod 22:30). Other passages reflect a notion similar to Deuteronomy's (Isa 63:18; Jer 2:3; Ps 34:10; Ezra 9:2). Those who suffer or survive punishment or have been redeemed are often called holy (Isa 4:3; 6:13; 62:12; Obad 17; Dan 7:18, 21–22, 25, 27; 8:24; 12:7). The people's holiness can also derive from the presence of the sanctuary among them (Ezek 37:28; see also Deut 33:3; Isa 43:28).

c. Nazirites. Though, according to P, laypersons cannot

share in priestly holiness, they could for a period of time imitate it by taking upon themselves the vow of a Nazirite (Num 6:1–21). Literature outside P describes lifelong Nazirites; presumably a condition of sacredness attached to them, but perhaps not as high (Judg 13:5, 7; 16:17; cf. Amos 2:11–12). By taking this vow, the person (Num 6:8) or specifically the head, is consecrated (vv 5, 11). The Nazirite, like a high priest, is restricted from all corpses (Num 6:7–8; cf. Lev 21:10–12; note the similarity between Num 6:7 and Lev 21:12). Like priests on duty, the Nazirite is not to drink wine or other strong drink (Num 6:3; Judg 13:4–5; 1 Sam 1:11 [LXX]; Amos 2:12; cf. Lev 10:9–10; Ezek 44:21). The mother of the Nazirite Samson was to avoid unclean food like priests (Judg 13:4, 7, 14; cf. Lev 22:8; Ezek 44:31). See sec. D. 2.

d. Levites and Firstborn Humans. Firstborn humans are holy: God dedicated them to himself in Egypt (Num 3:13; 8:17; cf. Exod 13:2) and they must be redeemed as is required with other holy items (Num 18:15–16; cf. 3:44–51). From this, one would expect the Levites, the cultic substitutes for the firstborn (Num 3:44–51), to be holy. But P never calls them such, even in the long prescription for their installation (Num 8:5–22; on the elevation rites, see C. 1. a. [1]). That they are restricted from the sanctums shows they have not risen in holiness much above the status of lay Israelites (Num 4:4–20; 18:2–4). If one grants them some degree of holiness, it must be strictly distinguished from that of the priests (cf. Milgrom 1970: 29, n. 103).

In contrast to P, the Chronicler designates the Levites as holy (2 Chr 23:6; 35:3; Milgrom 1970: 71, n. 257). For a possible similar perception of Levites in Ezekiel, see Milgrom 1981: 291–94. In other passages, all firstborn are described as belonging or being devoted to God, which intimates they are holy (Exod 13:12–13; 22:28; 34:19–20; see sec. C. 1. b. [1]).

e. Prophets. Only non-P literature speaks of the holiness of prophets, and what it says is meager: Elisha is called a "holy man of God" (2 Kgs 4:9) and God set Jeremiah apart as a prophet (Jer 1:5). The anointing of prophets, understood literally or figuratively, may also imply holiness (1 Kgs 19:16; Isa 61:1; cf. Ps 105:15 = 1 Chr 16:22).

3. Objects. a. Offerings. Offerings fall into two main groups, most holy and lesser. Those called most holy (Heb *qōdeš [haq]qŏdāšîm*) are the sin or purgation offering, the reparation offering, and the cereal offering, which includes the bread of presence in the tabernacle (Lev 2:3, 10; 6:10, 18, 22; 7:1, 6; 10:12, 17; 14:13; 21:22; 24:9; Num 18:9). A mark of most holy offerings is that only the priests may eat them (see foregoing references and Lev 6:11) and then only in the sanctuary court (called a "holy place" or the "place of the sanctuary": Lev 6:9, 19; 7:6; 10:13, 17; 24:9; Num 18:10 appears to refer to eating in a *state* of most holiness). The burnt offering, though not called most holy, must be included in this class by analogy (cf. Lev 14:13; cf. the hint in Num 18:9 with the Heb preposition *min,* "from/of"). The priestly consecration offering was probably also considered most holy since priests were to eat it in the sanctuary court (Exod 29:31–34; Lev 8:31–32).

Lesser holy offerings include well-being offerings (Lev 3:1–17; 7:11–36); firstborn of clean animals (Num 18:15–18); the Passover (Exod 12:3–11, 43:50); the produce tithe (see below; Lev 27:30–31; Num 18:25–32); the animal tithe (Lev 27:32–33); items put under "severe dedication" (Heb *ḥērem;* Lev 27:28; Num 18:14); first-ripe produce (Lev 19:24; 23:10–11; Num 18:13); and first-processed products (Lev 2:12; 23:17–20; Num 15:20–21; 18:12). Some passages technically distinguish these from most holy offerings by calling them simply "holy offerings" (Heb *qŏdāšîm:* Lev 21:22; Num 18:9, 11, 19; note the contrast in Lev 10:12–16). Other passages use this term without contrast (Lev 22:2–4, 6–7, 12, 15–16; Num 18:32) as well as the singular Heb *qōdeš* (Lev 12:4; 22:10, 14; 23:20; Num 18:17). But *qōdeš* and *qŏdāšîm* can include most holy offerings (Exod 28:38; Lev 5:15–16; 23:20; Num 5:9–10; 18:8, 10). The related noun *miqdāš* infrequently refers to lesser holy offerings (cf. Num 18:29). Apart from terminology, the fact that these offerings may be eaten by nonpriests outside the sanctuary precincts shows their distinction from most holy offerings. In connection with this, the designation of things under Heb *ḥērem* as most holy (Lev 27:28) is probably to emphasize their irredeemable nature and not to characterize them technically as most holy. That nonpriests may eat or use *ḥērem* shows its lesser holy character (Num 18:14 and context).

A main subdivision of the holiness of lesser holy offerings is perceptible. The Israelites eat only the well-being sacrifice (excluding portions given the priests) and the Passover (Exod 12:1–14; Lev 7:15–18; 19:5–8; 22:29–30). Because of their restriction to the priests' households, there priests and their households (Lev 22:10–13; Num 18:11, 13, 19) are entitled to the breast and right thigh from the well-being offerings (Exod 29:26–28; Lev 7:31–36; 10:14–15; Num 18:11) and all of the other offerings listed above. The portions of the priests' households presumably are more holy than the Israelites' portions. The prohibition that laypersons not eat the priestly portions supports such a valuation (Lev 22:10–16). A subdivision of the holiness of the well-being offering is detectable also. One type, brought for a vow or a freewill offering, may be eaten over two days and the leftover meat destroyed on the third (Lev 7:16–17; 19:6). Another type, the thank offering, may only be eaten on one day (7:15; 22:30). The shorter period for eating suggests a slightly higher degree of holiness for the latter type (note that most holy offerings can only be eaten for one day; cf. Exod 29:34; Lev 8:32; 10:16–20; see Wright 1987: 139). The Passover offering which can only be eaten for one day may have had a degree of holiness similar to that of the thank offering (Exod 12:10; Num 9:12).

Ezekiel labels the cereal, purgation, and reparation offerings most holy (42:13; cf. Ezra 2:63; Neh 7:65; 2 Chr 31:14). The term *qŏdāšîm,* introduced above, is used for offerings that are lesser holy in P (Deut 12:26; 2 Chr 29:33; 31:6, 12; 35:13; and perhaps Ezek 36:38; 1 Chr 26:20), but it is also used for all offerings (Ezek 20:40; 22:8; 26; Neh 10:34; 1 Chr 28:12) and Ezek 44:13 uses this term to refer to most holy offerings. The singular *qōdeš,* "holy thing(s)," may be used of lesser holy offerings as well (Deut 26:13; 1 Chr 23:28; 2 Chr 30:19; cf. Jer 2:3). Sacrificial meat can be called Heb *bĕśar qōdeš,* "holy flesh" (Jer 11:15). In Hag 2:12 it refers to meat of offerings that P calls most holy. The bread of presence at the sanctuary of Nob, which in P is most holy, is called Heb *leḥem qōdeš,* "holy bread," or simply *qōdeš,* "a holy thing" (1 Sam 21:5, 7).

A way to distinguish relative degrees of holiness of offerings outside P may be to determine who received them. For example, in Deuteronomy, officiating priests receive the shoulder, cheeks, and stomach from the "sacrifice" (Heb *zebaḥ;* equivalent to the well-being offering in P; 18:3) and the gifts of agricultural produce and wool (18:4; 26:2–11). Lay Israelites, their households, and nonofficiating Levites receive other portions of *zebaḥ* offerings, the firstborn animal, Passover, tithes, and various contributions at the sanctuary (12:6–7, 11–12, 17–18, 26; 14:22–27; 15:19–20; 16:2–7; cf. 16:10–17). The fatherless, widows, resident aliens, and nonofficating Levites receive the third-year tithe in the Israelite towns (14:28–29; 26:12–15; called *qōdeš* in 26:13). However, exegetical problems cloud the conclusiveness of these observations.

b. Sanctuary Furniture. Six pieces of cultic furniture are designated most holy: the ark, the incense altar, lamp stand (or menorah), bread table, the outer or burnt-offering altar, and laver (Exod 29:37; 30:10, 26–29; 40:10; Num 4:4, 19). The base of the laver and the utensils listed for some of these items may also be most holy, like the main furniture pieces (see Exod 30:26–29; but cf. Exod 40:9–11). The furniture may simply be labeled *qōdeš* (Exod 40:9; Num 3:28, 31, 32; 4:15, 16, 20; 7:9; 18:3, 5) or *miqdāš* (Lev 21:23; Num 10:21; 18:1; perhaps included in 3:38), both meaning "holy object(s); sanctums." An auxiliary to the outer altar is the cover made from the censers of Korah and his rebels (17:2–5—Eng 16:37–40).

Location, materials, lethality, and the cultic importance of the pieces suggest a gradation of holiness, with the ark being the highest, the outer altar and laver being the lowest. The ark is located in the adytum; the table, lamp stand, and incense altar in the shrine; and the burnt-offering altar and laver in the court. The ark, table, lamp stand, and incense altar are all made of pure gold, while the burnt-offering altar and laver are made of copper (Exod 25:11, 17, 24, 31, 36, 39; 27:2; 30:3; 37:2, 6, 11, 17, 22, 23, 24, 26; 38:2, 30). When transported the ark is wrapped in the tabernacle veil, a skin cover, then a completely blue cloth; the table is wrapped in a regular blue cloth, a scarlet cloth, then a skin cover; the lamp and incense altar are wrapped in a regular blue cloth and a skin cover; and the outer altar in a purple cloth, then a skin cover (Num 4:5–14). The gold furniture is lethal by sight to nonpriests (Num 4:18–20) but the copper pieces are not (they are on public display). Lastly, the ark is the most important piece of furniture: it is the place where God manifests himself (Exod 25:22; 30:36; Num 7:89; cf. Exod 29:42) and it may be the sole piece of sanctum which was not to be seen at all (cf. Lev 16:2, 12–13). The holy vessels taken into battle in Num 31:6 probably include the ark and the Urim and Thummim, which again shows the ark's importance.

This furniture appears to be more holy relative to the tent structure's planks, columns, bars, footings, lower cover (Heb *miškān*), and entrance hanging, which are also most holy (cf. Exod 30:26–29). The pieces of furniture are made of or covered with pure gold (see above), while the planks, columns, and bars are covered with plain gold (Exod 26:29, 32, 37; 36:34, 36, 38). The furniture pieces are prohibited to the touch and sight of the Levites on the pain of death; they are carefully wrapped by the priests, while the planks, columns, bars, footings, cover, and entrance hanging are not so lethal, nor are they covered (Num 4:4–20 versus vv 24–28, 31–33). The furniture pieces are carried on the Levites' shoulders while the planks, covers, and other items are transported in wagons (Num 7:7–9).

Outside of P, the ark and other holy furniture are brought to Solomon's new temple (1 Kgs 8:4; 1 Chr 22:19; 2 Chr 5:5; see sec. B. 4. a.). As in P, these articles are guarded and carried by priests and Levites (Ezra 8:24–29; 1 Chr 9:29; 23:32; 2 Chr 35:3). Deutero-Zechariah (Zechariah 9–14) hoped for the time that every vessel in the temple, Jerusalem, and Judah would increase in holiness (14:20–21). In addition to these articles, independent altars, pillars (Heb *maṣṣēbôt*), and other legitimate cult objects would be considered holy.

c. Priestly Clothing. All priestly clothing is holy, but that of the high priest has an elevated degree of holiness. First of all, it is more elaborate. Priests wear a fine linen tunic, waistband, headdress, and breeches (Exod 28:40, 42–43; 39:27–28). The high priest wears linen breeches, a tunic with a fancier weave (28:4, 39); a waistband of colored wool and fine linen (28:4, 39; 39:29); a headdress which is designated differently than the regular priest's (Heb *miṣnepet* versus Heb *[paʾărê ham]migbaʿōt;* 28:4, 39; 39:28) and to which was attached an inscribed golden plate (28:36–38; 39:30–31); a robe worn over these items made out of blue wool with golden bells and pomegranates made of colored wool and fine linen (28:4, 31–35; 39:22–26; cf. Haran 1978: 169, n. 44); and on top of all this the ephod made of colored wool, fine linen, and strips of gold, all woven together, with two framed stones inscribed with the names of the Israelite tribes attached to shoulder straps and a pouch—also with stones with the tribal names inscribed—fastened to the ephod and hanging over the chest (28:4, 6–13, 15–30; 39:2–21). The high priest's clothing is also holier because it consisted of a mixture of wool and linen, a holy mixture (see sec. B. 3. f below). It may be considered holier, too, since it is specifically required for working in the shrine (Exod 28:29, 30, 35, 38). Finally, only the high priest's clothing is called Heb *bigdê (haq)qōdeš,* "holy clothing" (Exod 28:2, 4; 29:29; 31:10; 35:19 [cf. v 21]; 39:1 [cf. vv 27–29]; 41; 40:13; the golden plate is called holy in Exod 29:6; Lev 8:9). Aaron's sons' clothing is only categorized thus once (Exod 28:4), but the context shows that the high priest's clothing is mainly in mind.

Two other sets of priestly clothing are prescribed in P. When removing ashes from the burnt-offering altar a priest is to dress in a plain linen robe and plain linen breeches (Lev 6:3–4). These may be utilitarian to prevent soiling of regular priestly clothing while at the same time to befit the holiness of the altar. After the work at the altar the priest puts on other, perhaps profane, clothing to take the ashes to the ash dump. When performing the blood rites in the adytum, shrine, and court on the Day of Atonement the high priest wears a plain linen tunic, breeches, waistband, and headdress (Lev 16:4, 32; called holy). The reason for the simpler plain linen clothing may also have been utilitarian, to prevent the soiling of the regular high priestly clothing with blood, which is sprinkled in abundance in this ceremony.

Ezekiel has the most extensive information about priestly clothing but only speaks, it appears, of that of regular priests. It is completely linen, including a headdress, breeches, and, implicitly, a waistband (44:17–18). A tunic is necessarily included. Hence Ezekiel's clothing is exactly like that of regular priests in P. But in contrast to P, Ezekiel calls this clothing holy (42:14). This designation reflects a conception about the clothing not found in P: it has the power to render laypersons who touch it holy (42:14; 44:19). The only piece of high priestly clothing mentioned outside of P is the ephod. While it sometimes appears to be a garment, it often has a character different than P's ephod (Judg 8:27; 17:5; 18:14–20; 1 Sam 2:18, 28; 14:3; 21:10; 22:18; 23:6, 9; 30:7; 2 Sam 6:14; Hos 3:4; 1 Chr 15:27).

d. Real Estate. People may dedicate their houses or inherited land (Lev 27:14–25). Doing so makes them "holy to the Lord," i.e., the property of the sanctuary and priests (v 14). Inherited land which is not redeemed and is sold to another becomes "holy to the Lord" in the jubilee year (v 21). It is then like a field dedicated as Heb *ḥērem* and becomes a priestly holding (cf. v 28).

e. Money and Precious Metals and Stones. Money used to redeem land in the foregoing cases is "holy to the Lord" (Lev 27:23). Analogically, all money or precious metals given to the sanctuary would be holy (Exod 25:3; 30:11–16; 35:5, 22, 24; 38:24–26; Lev 5:15, 18; 27:2–8, 12–13, 27, 31; Num 3:44–51; 7:1–88; 18:15–16; 31:48–53). If not used for constructing the tabernacle, these metals would have been kept in the sanctuary and used for maintaining the structure and supporting the priests (cf. Exod 30:16; Num 3:51, 54).

The holiness of dedicated money and booty is well attested outside of P. These items were put into sanctuary treasuries (Josh 6:17, 19, 24; 2 Sam 8:10–12; 1 Kgs 7:51; 15:15; 2 Kgs 12:5–17; 1 Chr 18:9–11; 2 Chr 5:1; 15:18; 2 Chr 24:5–14; cf. Ezra 8:24–29). The accumulated wealth became vast and was a source for maintenance of the temple and priests (2 Kgs 22:3–7; 1 Chr 26:26–28; 2 Chr 34:8–11; cf. Isa 23:18), paying tribute to invaders or allies (1 Kgs 15:17–22; 2 Kgs 12:19; 2 Chr 16:1–6), or spoil for the enemy (1 Kgs 14:25–28; 2 Kgs 14:11–14; 24:13; Jer 15:13; 17:3; Dan 1:2; 2 Chr 12:2–12; 36:18). Cf. Judg 17:3.

Precious stones were also dedicated to the temple treasury (cf. 1 Chr 29:8; 2 Chr 32:27). Perhaps Lam 4:1 has such stones in mind. Also recall that the high priest's clothing incorporated precious stones.

f. Mixtures. Certain mixtures are prohibited: crossbreeding animals, plowing with an ox and ass together, sowing a field or vineyard with two different types of seeds, and making or wearing a Heb *šaᶜaṭnēz* garment, i.e., one made of wool and linen (Lev 19:19; Deut 22:9–11). The reason seems to be that mixtures are holy (Deut 22:9). This explains in part the holiness of the high priest's clothing and of the fabric wall and hangings of the tabernacle which employ a mixture of wool and linen. Israelites are allowed to use mixtures in one case. They are to wear fringes on the edges or corners of their clothing, normally made of linen, and with a thread of blue, implicitly of wool, attached (Num 15:37–41; Deut 22:12; see Milgrom 1983a; 1983c).

g. Oil. Oil used for anointing priests, the tabernacle, and its furniture had a special and restricted composition and was holy (Exod 30:22–33; 37:29; Num 35:25). One would expect this oil to be most holy since it confers a status of most holiness on the sanctuary furniture (cf. the incense below). Oil used on cereal offerings would be most holy as part of the offering (Lev 2:1, 4, 6–7; etc.). The elevated and sprinkled oil in the ritual for purification from Heb *ṣāraᶜat* (so-called leprosy) would be holy, but not most holy (Lev 14:12, 15–18, 24–29; see sec. C. 1. a. [1]). The beaten pure oil for the tabernacle lamp may have had a lesser holy status as a dedicated item (Exod 27:20; Lev 24:2). Outside of P, holy oil is used to anoint kings (1 Kgs 1:39; figuratively, Ps 89:21; see sec. C. 1. a. [1]).

h. Incense. Like anointing oil, incense (Heb *qĕṭōret hassamîm*) used on the incense altar and on the Day of Atonement has a unique restricted formula (Exod 30:34–38; cf. Lev 16:12–13). The text calls it "holy" (Exod 30:35, 37), but once calls it "most holy" which is technically more correct (v 36). Relatively less holy, but still most holy, would be the frankincense (Heb *lĕbōnâ*) used on cereal offerings (Lev 2:1–2, 15, etc.). The degree of holiness of plain incense (Heb *qĕṭōret*) offered in censers by priests is unclear (this offering implied in Lev 10:1; Num 7:14, 20, etc.; 16:7, 17–18, 35; 17:5, 11–12—Eng 16:40, 46–47).

i. Water. Holy water is mentioned in the ordeal for a woman suspected of committing adultery (Num 5:17; probably taken from the laver). Water libations (1 Sam 7:6; cf. 2 Sam 23:16) and the river flowing from the temple in Ezekiel's vision (Ezek 47:12; cf. Joel 4:18; Zech 14:8) may be considered holy. Spring water for certain rituals (Lev 14:5–6, 50–52; 15:13; Num 19:17) and that of the Jordan (as in 2 Kgs 5:10–14) are probably not to be considered holy.

4. Places. a. Sanctuaries. P's wilderness tabernacle is marked off by a linen fence 100 by 50 cubits which forms a court whose entrance faces eastward. In the front half of the court is the open-air altar for burnt offerings. In the back half of the court is the tent structure—30 cubits long, about 10 wide, and 10 high—which is divided into two rooms: a foreroom, the shrine; and a back room, the adytum.

Terminology shows a gradation of different parts of the tabernacle. Technically the adytum is called Heb *qōdeš haqqŏdāšîm*, "the most holy place" and the shrine simply Heb *haqqōdeš*, "the holy place" (Exod 26:33–34; 1 Chr 6:34; cf. Heb *miqdāš haqqōdeš* of the adytum in Lev 16:33). But the entire tent structure could be called "most holy" which indicates its collective holiness is greater than the rest of the sanctuary area (Exod 30:26, 29). Less technically, both rooms could be called *haqqōdeš*, "the holy place" (the adytum: Lev 4:6 [unless this refers to both rooms]; 16:2–3, 16–17, 20, 23, 27; the shrine: 28:29, 35; 29:30; 31:11; Lev 6:23; 10:18 [first occurrence]; Num 4:12; both rooms together: Exod 38:24, 27). The sanctuary area in general or the court could be called *haqqōdeš*, "the holy place" (Exod 28:43; 35:19; 36:1, 3, 4, 6; 39:1, 41; Lev 10:4, 18 [2d occurrence]; Num 8:19; 28:7; see Haran 1978: 171–73; cf. Heb *mĕqôm haqqōdeš*, "place of the sanctuary" Lev 10:17; 14:13; Heb *šeqel haqqōdeš*, "sanctuary shekel" Exod 30:13, 24; etc.), Heb *(ham)miqdāš,* "(the) holy place/area" (Exod 25:8; Lev 12:4; 19:30; 20:3; 21:12; 26:2; Num 3:38; 19:20; plural in Lev 26:31; cf. Milgrom 1970: 23–24, n. 78), and Heb *māqôm qādôš,* "holy place" (Exod 29:31; Lev 6:9, 19, 20; 7:6; 10:13; 16:24; 24:9; Wright 1987: 232–35).

The distribution of furniture, the extent of access to the different parts of the sanctuary, the materials used in the tabernacle, and anointing rites also display the structure's graded holiness. The ark, the most important piece of furniture, is in the adytum; the incense altar, lamp stand, and bread table are in the shrine; and the burnt-offering altar and laver, the least holy of the most holy furniture, are in the court. Similarly, only the high priest, the holiest of the Israelites, is allowed in the adytum; the high priest aided by regular priests performs daily and weekly rites in the shrine; and the Levites and Israelites, both profane, have access only to the court. Some argue the Israelites were even restricted to the area between the burnt-offering altar and the entrance, which would indicate a subdivision in the court's holiness (Haran 1978: 187–87; Milgrom 1970: 17–18). As for materials, the wall planks of the tabernacle and the columns supporting the veil and the entrance hanging are overlaid or covered with gold (Exod 26:29, 32, 37; 36:24, 36, 38) while the columns holding up the fence of the court and the hanging to the court entrance are covered with silver (27:10–11, 17; 38:10–12, 17, 19). The footings for the planks of the tabernacle and for the columns of the veil are made of silver (26:19, 21, 25, 32; 36:24, 26, 30, 36; 38:27) while those for the columns of the tent entrance, of the sanctuary entrance, and of the perimeter of the court are copper (26:37; 27:10–11, 17; 36:38; 38:10–11, 17, 19, 30–31). The tent structure itself is made of four layers: an elaborate underlayer of costly materials (the Heb *miškān,* "tabernacle"; 26:1–6; 36:8–13), another layer made of simple goat hair (Heb *ʾōhel,* "tent"; 26:7–13; 36:14–18), and a top cover of tanned ram skins, and then one of Heb *tĕḥāšîm* skins (26:14; 36:19; 39:34). The veil and bottom layer of the tabernacle is made of blue, purple, and scarlet wool, and fine linen, with cherubim designs (26:1, 31; 36:8, 35; the listing of materials for the bottom layer may indicate it has more linen than the veil), while the hangings to the entrances of the tabernacle and court have blue, purple, and scarlet wool, fine linen, and carry designs but not cherubim (26:36; 27:16; 36:37; 38:18). The fence surrounding the entire court is of fine linen (Exod 27:9, 18; 38:9, 16). The clasps holding the two sections of the bottom layer of the tabernacle together are gold (26:6; 36:13), while those of the overlying goat-hair layer are copper (26:11; 36:18). Finally, when the sanctuary is dedicated only the tent structure, the burnt-offering altar, and the laver are anointed; the court itself is not.

Non-P literature mentions cult places and sanctuaries in towns such as Beer-sheba, Bethel, Gibeon, Gilgal, Hebron, Mizpah (of Benjamin), Nob, Ophrah (of Abiezer), Ramah (Ramathaim), Shechem, Shiloh, as well as in undefined places. These cult places would have been considered holy—if not by a particular biblical book or tradition, which may treat them as illegitimate, at least by worshipers there. Solomon's and Ezekiel's temples, whose descriptions are more complete, exhibit degrees of holiness like those of P's tabernacle. The entire area of Solomon's temple, including courts, was called a Heb *miqdāš,* "holy/sanctuary area" (clearly, Ezek 9:6; 23:39; see also Isa 63:18; Jer 17:12; Ezek 5:11; 8:6; 23:38; 24:21; 25:3; Ps 74:7; 78:69; Lam 1:10; 2:7, 20; 1 Chr 22:19; 2 Chr 20:8; 26:18; 29:21; 30:8; perhaps 1 Chr 28:10; cf. Heb. *bêt miqdāš* in 2 Chr 36:17; for the Second Temple: Isa 60:13; Dan 8:11; 9:17; 11:31; Neh 10:40; of other sanctuaries: Exod 15:17; Josh 24:26; Amos 7:9, 13; Ps 96:6). The plural in Jer 51:51 probably refers to sacred areas of the temple (cf. Ezek 7:24; 21:7; Ps 68:36; 73:17). The entire area was also called a Heb *qōdeš,* "holy place" (Ps 74:3; 1 Chr 24:5; 2 Chr 29:5, 7; 35:5; cf. Ps 20:3; 60:8; 63:3; 68:25; 108:8; 134:2; cf. Isa 64:10; Ps 24:3; 1 Chr 29:3; Heb *har haqqōdeš,* "holy mountain" and variants: Isa 56:7; Ezek 20:40; Ps 3:5; 15:1; 43:3; 99:9; cf. Isa 27:13; 65:11; *qōdeš* for the Second Temple: Dan 8:13, 14; 9:26; cf. Isa 62:9). The temple building itself had two main rooms, but with a vestibule added in front. The adytum can be called the "most holy place" (1 Kgs 6:16; 7:50; 8:6; 2 Chr 3:8, 10; 4:22; 5:7; cf. Ps 28:2; Second Temple: Dan 9:24). The shrine can be called the *qōdeš,* "holy place" (1 Kgs 8:8, 10; 2 Chr 5:11). The adytum, overlaid with gold, contains the ark underneath the wings of gold-covered cherubim (1 Kgs 6:20, 27–28, 31–32; 8:6–9); the shrine, also overlaid with gold, contains a gold incense altar, a gold bread table, and gold lamp stands (1 Kgs 6: 21–22, 30, 33–35; 7:48–50); and the court contains a copper altar, a large copper laver, and ten smaller copper lavers (1 Kgs 7:27–39, 43–45; 8:64; on Ahaz's altar: 2 Kgs 16:10–16). The two pillars standing in front of the temple were of copper (1 Kgs 7:13–22). Only priests, not Levites (2 Chr 29:16) nor laypersons (2 Chr 26:16–21), had access to the building (cf. 1 Kgs 8:6, 10–11; see also Ps 93:5; Eccl 8:10; 2 Chr 2:3).

Ezekiel's visionary temple, described in Ezekiel 40–48 (cf. Ezek 20:40; 37:26–28), has a walled-off area 500 cubits square. This entire area is called a *miqdāš,* "holy area" (37:26, 28; 43:21; 44:1, 5, 7–9, 11; 45:3–4; 47:12; 48:8, 10, 21) and a *qōdeš,* "holy place" (45:2). In a relative sense the sanctuary area is holy *(qōdeš)* while the area outside of it is profane (Heb *ḥōl;* see Ezek 42:20). Calling the sanctuary area "most holy" vis-à-vis the rest of the land also reflects its holier status (Ezek 43:12; cf. 45:3). The sanctuary area has an outer and inner court. The latter is called *qōdeš,* "holy place" (Ezek 42:14; 44:27) and perhaps also *miqdāš,* "holy place" (44:15–16; 45:18–19). The inner court contains the burnt-offering altar and the temple building. The temple building has two main rooms: the adytum or most holy place (41:4; simply *qōdeš,* "holy place" in 41:21, 23), and the shrine. It also has a vestibule at the front. The inner court has an implicit higher holiness. Only priests have access to it (44:15–19, 27; cf. 40:44–46; 42:13–14; 46:19–20). Not even the civic leader, the "prince" (Heb *nāśîʾ*), can enter (46:1–3, 8, 12). The Levites have access only to the outer court and gates of the inner court (44:10–14; cf. 40:38–43). Israelites are restricted to the outer court. Uncircumcised foreigners are restricted from the sanctuary area altogether (44:9). Priests, furthermore, are not to wear their official robes in the outer court (42:14; 44:17–19). Most holy offerings are to be eaten in holy chambers adjoining the inner court (42:13; 46:20), while lesser holy offerings are cooked in the outer court (46:21–24). See D. 3.

For foreign sanctuaries, see Isa 16:12; Ezek 28:18. For a temple plan reflecting a more complicated gradation of holiness see the Temple Scroll (11QTemple; Yadin 1983). See also TABERNACLE; TEMPLE, JERUSALEM; TEMPLES AND SANCTUARIES.

b. Places of Theophany. Moses was told to remove his shoes on Sinai because the ground was holy (Exod 3:5; cf. Josh 5:15). The mountain's hallowed state was due to God's presence there (Exod 19:9–25; 24:16–17; Deut 4:10–5:29)—it was "God's mountain" (1 Kgs 19:8; cf. vv 8–14). Rules that the people purify themselves for the theophany there (Exod 19:10, 14–15, 22) and not encroach on the mountain's boundaries on the penalty of death (vv 12–13, 17, 21, 23–24) also evidence its sacred character. Milgrom (1970: 44–46) has argued that the mount had a tripartite gradation of holiness similar to that of the tabernacle: the summit where God's presence was and to which only Moses has access, the area below the summit covered by a cloud, and the area below the cloud, the "bottom of the mountain," where the altar was set up (Exod 24:4) and where the people gathered (cf. Ps 68:18).

Other places where God's presence is manifested are implicitly holy, such as Israel's war camp (Deut 23:10–15; cf. Num 5:2–3; 1 Sam 21:6) and the Garden of Eden (Gen 3:8). Tyre, figuratively a man in Eden, lived on the "holy mountain of God" (Ezek 28:14). Places where God or angels appeared to the patriarchs and others, and where they, in consequence, set up altars or pillars, may be considered sacred (e.g., Shechem: Gen 12:6–7; Bethel: 28:10–22; 35:1–5, 9–15; Gideon in Ophrah: Judg 6:20–24).

c. Land of Israel and Jerusalem. Though some of the P laws perhaps hint that the land of Israel is holy (Lev 18:25–28; Num 35:33–34), only the non-P literature explicitly calls it or its cities such (Exod 15:13; Isa 64:9; Zech 2:16; Ps 78:54; cf. Zech 14:20–21; Ps 114:2; Ezra 9:8; perhaps Josh 5:15). The Heb term *har haqqōdeš,* "the holy mountain," and its variations often refers to the entire land of Israel (Isa 11:9; 57:13; 65:25; Jer 31:23; Obad 16; Zeph 3:11; cf. Isa 27:13; Joel 2:1; Ps 87:1). Other passages imply the holiness of the land (Josh 22:19; 2 Kgs 5:17; Ezek 4:14; Hos 9:3–4; Amos 7:17; Ps 137:4; Ezra 6:21).

More specifically, the city of Jerusalem is called holy (Isa 48:2; 52:1; Ps 46:5; Dan 9:24; Neh 11:1, 18), and the term *har haqqōdeš:* "the holy mountain" (and variants) can refer particularly to it (Isa 66:20; Joel 4:17; Zech 8:3; Ps 2:6; 48:2; Dan 9:16, 20; 11:45; cf. Isa 27:13; 56:7; 65:11; Joel 2:1). Jeremiah speaks in detail of a promised increase of holiness to be experienced by the city (Jer 31:38–40; cf. Zech 14:20–21). Because of its holiness, the uncircumcised, foreigners, and the defiled would not be found in the city (Isa 52:1; Joel 4:17). On the dedication or sanctification of Jerusalem's walls, see Neh 3:1; 12:27.

d. Ezekiel's Teruma. Ezekiel's future map (45:1–8; 48:8–22) has a section of land 25,000 cubits square called the *tĕrûmâ* ("contributed portion," 48:8, 12, 20–21). This *tĕrûmâ* contains three horizontal strips for (1) the priests and sanctuary, (2) the Levites, and (3) the city (i.e., Jerusalem) and its outlying area. The northernmost strip, 25,000 by 10,000 cubits, apparently belongs to the Levites. It is called the Levites' *ʾăḥuzzâ,* "possession" (45:5; 48:22). Adjoining on the south is an area of the same dimensions for the priests with the sanctuary at the center (45:3; 48:10, 21), called *qōdeš qodāšîm,* "most holy" (45:3; 48:12); a *qōdeš,* "holy portion" (45:4; cf. 45:1); a *miqdāš,* "holy area" (45:4); *hamĕquddāš,* "the dedicated portion" (48:11; but see commentaries), the *tĕrūmiyyâ,* "special contribution" (48:12); and probably *tĕrûmat haqqōdeš,* "the holy contribution" (48:21b). The levitic and priestly areas together are called *tĕrûmat haqqōdeš,* "the holy contribution" (45:6–7; 48:10, 18, 20–21a); the "first fruit of the land" which is *qōdeš lyhwh,* "holy to Yahweh" (48:14); and, if emendations are followed, *qōdeš,* "holy portion" (45:1), and *hattĕrûmâ . . . lyhwh,* "the contribution . . . to Yahweh" (48:9). Bordering the priestly land on the south is the *ʾăḥuzzat hāʿîr,* "possession of the city" (45:6–7; 48:20–21) which is *ḥōl,* "profane" (48:15). Despite some overlap of terminology for the priestly area and the priestly and levitic areas combined, a configuration of degrees of holiness is found: the holiest land with the sanctuary and priests, the lesser holy land with the Levites, and the profane land with the city. That these degrees are not arranged more systematically, e.g., in a concentric order, may be due to geographic and historical realities influencing the vision. That the city lies in a profane area, separated from the sanctuary, is striking in view of other prophetic expectations that Jerusalem would be holy.

e. Heaven. As God's dwelling on earth, namely the sanctuary, is holy, so his dwelling in heaven is holy. Various Heb terms are used: *mĕʿôn qodšô/qodšĕkā,* "his/your holy habitation" (Deut 26:15; Jer 25:30; Zech 2:17; Ps 68:6; 2 Chr 30:27); *mĕrôm qodšô,* "his holy height" (Ps 102:20; a Qumran text has *mĕʿôn*); *šĕmê qodšô,* "his holy heavens" (Ps 20:7); *zĕbûl qodšĕkā,* "your holy elevation" (Isa 63:15); and perhaps *qodšô/qodšî/haqqōdeš,* "his/my/the (heavenly) sanctuary" (Amos 4:2; Ps 60:8; 77:14; 89:36; 108:8; 150:1); *miqdāš,* "holy place" (Ps 68:36; 73:17); and some of the instances of *hêkal qodšô,* "his holy temple" (Jonah 2:5, 8; Mic 1:2; Hab 2:20; Ps 11:4; some refer clearly to the earthly temple: Ps 5:8; 79:1; 138:2; cf. 65:5). See also Isa 57:15, and for God's throne, Ps 47:9.

5. Time. a. Sabbath. The OT generally calls the Sabbath sacred and describes or prescribes its sanctification by abstaining from work (Exod 16:23; 20:8; 31:14–15; 35:2; Deut 5:12; Isa 58:13–14; Jer 17:22, 24, 27; Ezek 20:20–21; 44:24; Neh 9:14; 13:22).

b. Holidays. P designates certain holidays as Heb *miqrāʾ qōdeš,* perhaps meaning "declaration of, call for, summoning to holiness" rather than "holy convocation" (cf. Lev 23:2, 4, 37). These days include the first and seventh days of the Feast of Unleavened Bread (Exod 12:16; Lev 23:7–8; Num 28:18, 25); the Feast of Weeks day (Lev 23:21; Num 28:26); the first day of the seventh month (Lev 23:24; Num 29:1); the Day of Atonement (Lev 23:27; Num 29:7); the first and eighth days of the Feast of Tabernacles (Lev 23:35, 36; Num 29:12). The phrase *miqrāʾ qōdeš* is accompanied by a prohibition of work on these days which evidently serves as the means of hallowing these times (cf. the use of the phrase for the Sabbath in Lev 23:3). Observance of ritual requirements at the sanctuary would have also led to the days' sanctification. Degrees of holiness are apparent: the Sabbath and Day of Atonement are the holiest since they require complete rest; other days, designated *miqrāʾ qōdeš,* are less holy since they require abstinence only from laborious work; and other special days, such as new moons (apart from that in the seventh month), are least holy since they require no abstention (see Milgrom 1970: 80–81, and n. 297). The differences in sacrificial requirements in Leviticus 23 and Numbers 28–29 also imply more minute degrees of holiness.

Festivals were holy periods outside P, too (Ezra 3:5). A specific indication of this is the idiom of "sanctifying" a festival (Isa 30:29; a fast: Joel 1:14; 2:15; a festival for the god Baal: 2 Kgs 10:20). Holy days require abstention from work or unseemly behavior (Neh 8:9–11; Neh 10:32).

c. Jubilee and Sabbatical Year. The jubilee year is to be sanctified by not sowing or harvesting (Lev 25:10–12). The sabbatical year is not called holy but the requirement to not sow or harvest would indicate it has a holiness similar to the jubilee (Lev 25:2–7; note the terminology with *šabbāt* and *šabbātôn;* cf. Exod 23:10–11). The restrictions enforcing rest indicate that these periods of time are holy.

6. Miscellaneous. a. War. Several passages speak of "sanctifying" or inaugurating war (Jer 6:4; Joel 4:9; Mic 3:5). While the verb may simply mean to "prepare," it may refer to performing preparatory rites, including purification (cf. Jer 22:7; 51:27–28). Like the holiness associated with theophany, it may be the divine presence that makes a war holy.

b. Covenant. A covenant can be called holy (Dan 11:28, 30; here meaning Israel's religion) and can be desecrated (Mal 2:10; Ps 55:21; 89:35; Neh 13:29).

C. Methods of Sanctification and Desanctification

Since holiness is fraught with danger, the movement into or out of it is of great prescriptive concern. Such movement may be legitimate, or unplanned and illegitimate.

1. Legitimate Sanctification and Desanctification. a. Sanctification. Some beings, places, objects, or times are inherently holy (e.g., God, the firstborn) and others become such through the people's proper behavior (e.g., the people through obedience, the Sabbath through cessation of work). Two other means of attaining a holy state require further elucidation: ritual procedures and theophany.

(1) Ritual Procedures. Persons or things made holy by special anointing oil (see sec. B. 3. g.) in P include high and common priests and their clothing (Exod 29:7, 21; Lev 8:12, 30) and the tabernacle and the most holy furniture (Exod 29:36; 30:26–29; 40:9–11; Lev 8:10–11; Num 7:1, 10–11, 84, 88). Pouring of oil on *maṣṣēbôt,* "pillars," may have consecrated them (Gen 28:18; 31:13; 35:14). The anointing of prophets, if this was really done, may have imparted holiness (see sec. B. 2. e.). Anointing a person recovered from scale disease (Lev 14:10–29), kings (1 Kgs 1:39; cf. Ps 89:21), and shields (2 Sam 1:21; Isa 21:5) did not sanctify them (cf. Ps 110:3).

Offerings often accompany sanctuary dedications (e.g., Exodus 29; Leviticus 8–9; Numbers 7; 1 Kgs 8:5, 62–64; Ezek 43:18–27; 2 Chr 5:6; 7:1–10; 29:20–36). The purgation sacrifice in particular cleanses and sanctifies the outer altar, readying it for ensuing sacrificial activity (Exod 29:36–37; Lev 8:15; Ezek 43:18–22, 25–26) and is used in recurring purgation rites to maintain sanctity (Leviticus 16, esp. v 19 and Ezek 45:18–20). Consecration-offering blood is placed on the priests and sprinkled on them and on their clothing (Exod 29:21; Lev 8:30).

Priests at their consecration donned special clothing (Exod 28:3, 41; 29:1, 5–9; Lev 8:7–9, 13). When Eleazar became high priest, he was dressed in Aaron's clothing (Num 20:25–28). For Ezekiel, the contagious character of priestly clothing may contribute to the priests' holiness (42:14; 44:19; cf. the tassels in sec. B. 3. f.).

Objects may be dedicated by elevating them (literally or symbolically) in the sanctuary. Sanctification is specifically mentioned in the case of the shoulder of the Nazirite's well-being offering with accompanying bread (Num 6:19–20), and the two well-being lambs and the two firstfruits loaves offered on the Feast of Weeks (Lev 23:17–20). Other cases where it is implicit are the breast of the well-being and priestly-consecration offerings (Exod 29:26–27; Lev 7:30, 34; 8:29; 9:21; 10:14–15; Num 6:20; 18:18), thigh and fat of the consecration offering with accompanying bread (Exod 29:22–24; Lev 8:25–27), the thigh of the well-being offering (Lev 9:21; 10:14–15), the reparation offering and log of oil for a recovered *mĕṣōrāʿ* (Lev 14:12, 24), the barley *ʿōmer* (Lev 23:11–15), the cereal offering of a suspected adulteress (Num 5:25), and gold and copper for the sanctuary (Exod 35:22; 38:24, 29). The Levites are "elevated" (Num 8:11, 13, 15, 21) but this does not necessarily make them holy (see sec. B. 2. d., and Milgrom 1983b: 139–70).

A substance presumably increases in holiness when brought in direct or indirect contact with a most holy sanctum. This is implicit in the cases of putting consecration-offering blood on the altar before sprinkling it on the priests and their clothing (Exod 29:21; Lev 8:30), sprinkling oil "before the Lord" before it is placed on a recovered *mĕṣōrāʿ* (Lev 14:16, 27), and sprinkling red cow blood toward the sanctuary (Num 19:4). It is also the case with the portions of most holy offerings, which can communicate holiness apparently only after their blood or initial portions have come in contact with the altar (Lev 6:11, 20; Milgrom 1981; see sec. C. 2. a.).

An offerer may verbally declare something holy or dedicate it by physically setting it apart. This dedication generally occurs outside the sanctuary precincts and includes sacrificial animals (Exod 28:38; Lev 22:2–3, 15; 27:9; cf. 2 Chr 30:24; 35:7–9; not the firstborn in P, Lev 27:26, but cf. Deut 15:19), firstfruits and first-processed materials (Num 15:20; 18:12–13), the tithe (Lev 27:32; cf. Num 18:24–32; Neh 12:47), a house or land (Lev 27:14–16, 18–19, 22), the half-shekel (Exod 30:13–15), building materials (Exod 25:2–3; 35:5, 21, 24; 36:3, 6), booty (Num 31:28–29, 41, 52), and oneself as a Nazirite (Num 6:2–21). See in general Lev 22:12, 15; Num 5:9; 18:8, 11, 19; Deut 12:6, 11, 17; Ezek 20:40; 44:30; 45:13, 16; Mal 3:8; Neh 10:38, 40; 12:44, 47; 13:5; 2 Chr 30:17; 31:10, 12, 14; figuratively, Jer 12:3. Verbal dedication or setting apart in the sanctuary precincts presumably occurs with the breads of the thank offering and the right thigh of the well-being offering (Lev 7:14 and Exod 29:27–28; Lev 7:32, 34; 10:14, 15; Num 6:20). Judg 17:3 and perhaps Prov 20:25 show how verbal dedications are made (see Milgrom 1983b: 159–72).

A special form of dedication is Heb *ḥērem,* "severe dedication; ban." This is found mainly in contexts of war (Josh 6:17–21; 8:26; 10:1, 28, 35, 37, 39, 40; 11:11, 12, 20, 21; etc.) but may apply to one's own property (cf. Lev 27:28, "field of one's inheritance"; cf. v 21). Things placed under *ḥērem* include persons, their buildings, animals, precious objects and metals, and land. Objects, animals, and land so dedicated would be destroyed or become sanctuary property to be used by the priests (Num 18:14; Josh 6:19, 24; Ezek 44:29). Humans would be put to death (Lev 27:29). As with regular dedication, *ḥērem* can take the form of an unconditional declaration or a vow (Num 21:2–3).

(2) Theophany. In addition to the cases discussed in sec. B. 4. b., stories about the major sanctuaries describe God's manifestation at the time of dedication: the desert tabernacle (Exod 40:34–35; Num 9:15 and Lev 9:4, 6, 23–24); Solomon's temple (1 Kgs 8:10–11; 2 Chr 5:11–14; cf. the Chronicler's addition in 7:1–3); Ezekiel's temple (43:1–5; cf. 44:1–3; 46:1–3, 8, 12). These theophanies have not only a sanctifying effect but also show that God accepts the structures and their cult. God's presence or appearance at a sanctuary at other times in its existence would have a continuing sanctifying effect.

b. Desanctification. The prevailing rule in most cases is: Whatever is not offerable on the altar may be desanctified (Milgrom 1976: 52–53). The two main methods are redemption and ritual. A unique example is in Ezra 2:61–63 (= Neh 7:63–65) where priests are "disqualified" (Heb *wayĕgōʾălû;* the verb carries "the notion of desanctification) and not allowed to eat the most holy offerings.

(1) Redemption. Money or, in some cases, another item of equal worth may be paid or given to redeem or purchase a sanctum. The sanctum loses its holiness while the money or other item becomes holy (cf. Lev 27:23). In P, the main method of desanctifying is paying the principal value of an item, assessed by a priest, plus one fifth. This is found in the case of a dedicated or vowed unclean sacrificial animal (Lev 27:11–13), a firstborn unclean animal (vv 26–27; cf. Num 18:15), produce tithe (Lev 27:30–31), a dedicated house (vv 14–15), and a dedicated field of one's inheritance (vv 16–19). A dedicated field of one's inheritance and unredeemed unclean firstborn may be sold at the assessed price, apparently without the added fifth (vv 20–21, 27). Firstborn humans were redeemed at first by being replaced by the Levites, and the extra Israelites and later firstborn were redeemed by paying five shekels (Num 3:44–51; 18:15–16). Outside of P, a firstborn ass, an unclean animal, may be redeemed by a sheep or goat (Exod 13:13; 34:20). Firstborn people must also be redeemed, but no means is prescribed (Exod 13:13; 34:20); perhaps a sacrificial redemption is intended. An object designated as *ḥērem* is not redeemable according to P (Lev 27:29). Jonathan's redemption, if he was under *ḥērem* after eating honey in violation of Saul's oath, could be legitimate since his violation was unintentional (1 Sam 14:24, 27, 45).

(2) Ritual Procedures. The removal of a holy portion from a batch desanctifies the rest. The tithe given to the Levites at first is holy (Num 18:32). When they give a tithe of the tithe to the priests, itself called holy (v 29), the remaining nine tenths becomes profane (cf. v 31). The same desanctification process may be seen in the selection of the animal tithe (Lev 27:32), the implicit donation of the fourth-year produce of a new tree to God before personal consumption can begin in the fifth (Lev 19:23–25; cf. Deut 20:6; 28:30; Jer 31:5), and the separation of firstfruits and first-produced materials from a large batch.

Some sanctums are unusable and cannot be redeemed. To prevent desecration they are disposed of or destroyed. The Nazirite's hair and leftover portions of sacrifices are burned (Num 6:18–19 and Exod 12:10; 29:34; Lev 7:17; 10:16–20; 19:6; cf. Lev 7:19). Altar ashes and the crop and plumage of a burnt-offering bird are taken outside the camp to the ash dump (Lev 1:16; 6:3–4). Carcasses of inedible purgation sacrifices are also taken to the ash dump and burned (Exod 29:14; Lev 4:11–12, 21; 6:23; 8:17; 9:11; 16:27; cf. Ezek 43:21). The blood of purgation and other sacrifices is collected or poured at the base of the altar where it will sink into the ground (Exod 29:12; Lev 4:7, 18, 25, 30, 34; 5:9; 8:15; 9:9; cf. Exod 29:16, 20; Lev 1:5, 11: 3:2, 8, 13; 7:2; etc.). Outside of P, persons and things under *ḥērem* are killed and burned, or otherwise destroyed (Deut 13:17; Josh 6:24; 7:15, 25; 8:28; 11:11, 13). Necks of unredeemed firstborn of asses could be broken (Exod 13:13; 34:20; see Wright 1987: 129–59, 284–90).

At the successful completion of their vows Nazirites bring sacrifices which mark their departure from a holy status (Num 6:13–20; see sec. D. 2.). The high priest's bathing in Lev 16:24 may be for desanctification after working in the most holy place of the sanctuary. The washing or disposal of pots in which purgations offerings were cooked may be due to impurity rather than for desanctification (Lev 6:20–21; Wright 1987: 93–113, 129–31).

2. Unintentional or Illegitimate Sanctification and Desanctification. a. Sanctification. Four times P says "anyone/thing that touches *x* becomes holy" (Exod 29:37; 30:29; Lev 6:11, 20). The sanctums specified in these verses are the Tent of Meeting, the six most holy pieces of furniture, and the portions of the cereal, reparation, and purgation sacrifices. Objects becoming holy in this way perhaps may be redeemable or become property of the sanctuary and priests. It is arguable whether people are included in this rule (Milgrom 1981; Haran 1978: 179). At any rate, the consequence for contact with the furniture for nonpriests is death (by divine agency; Num 4:15, 19–20; 18:3). The tent structure, however, is not lethal, at least for the Levites, who may touch it (Num 4:24–33). In Ezekiel the priestly clothing and most holy offerings can sanctify persons and objects (42:14; 44:19; 46:20). See also Hag 2:12; 2 Chr 8:11 and perhaps Isa 65:5 (reading a *Piʿel*).

Another form of unplanned and detrimental consecration is *ḥērem* contagion. If a person misappropriates a cult object that is under *ḥērem,* the person acquires that status (Deut 7:25; Josh 6:18; cf. Exod 22:19). A person having this status would be put to death (cf. Achan in Josh 7, esp. v 12; cf. 1 Kgs 20:42).

b. Desanctification. It is in the case of illicit desanctification—desecration—that the dramatic character of holiness appears. Such profanation rouses God's destructive ire against malefactors and the community at large. Any impurity threatens the sanctity of any holy place, object, being, or occasion (e.g., Lev 7:19–21; 12:4; 21:1–4, 10–12; Num 6:9–12; 9:6–13). Desecration—making something profane but not necessarily impure—is often implied. It occurs when someone of a profane or even holy status infringes upon what is holy or misuses it. Sanctuaries or holy places are desecrated by encroachment of those unauthorized (Lev 16:2; 21:21, 23; Num 1:51; 3:10, 38; 16:1–35; 17:5—Eng 16:40; 18:7, 22; outside P: Exod 19:12–13, 16, 21–24; Ezek 44:7; 2 Chr 26:16–18 = 2 Kgs 15:5), priests' misdeeds (Exod 28:35, 43; 30:20–21; 40:32; Lev 10:1–6, 9; 21:12; cf. Zeph 3:4); and enemy incursions (outside P: Ezek 7:22, 24; 24:21; 25:3; Ps 74:7; Dan 11:31). Sanctum desecration occurs by mishandling holy furniture (Num 4:15, 20; 18:3; outside P: 1 Sam 6:19; 2 Sam 6:6–7); eating a well-being offering outside its proper time (Lev 7:16–18; 19:7–8); mishandling the tithe (Num 18:32); a layperson eating sacrificial portions of the priestly households (Lev 22:14); substituting sacrificial animals (Lev 27:10, 33); eating sacrificial blood and fat (Lev 7:25–27; 17:10–14); and outside P, working a firstborn ox or shearing a firstborn sheep (Deut 15:19); misappropriating *ḥērem* (Josh 7:1; 22:20; 1 Chr 2:7); and using iron on an altar (Exod 20:25). Priests are profaned by illicit mourning rites and harlot daughters (Lev 21:6, 9), and a high priest's lineage by marrying a prohibited woman (21:15). The people are profaned through harlotry (Lev 19:29), mixed marriages (outside P: Ezra 9:2, 4; 10:2, 6, 10, 19; Neh 13:27, 29; cf. Mal 2:10, 11), and enemy assault (outside P: Ezek 22:16). God or his name are desecrated by various sins: false swearing and breaking an oath (Lev 5:21–26; 19:12; Num 5:6; cf. 30:3; outside P: Ezek 17:20); idolatry and improper worship (Lev 18:21; 20:3; Num 31:16; cf. 25:1; outside P: Josh 22:16, 22, 31; Ezek 13:19; 20:39; Mal 1:7–12; 1 Chr 10:13; 2 Chr 28:2–4, 19, 22–24; 29:6, 19; 33:19); improper priestly impurity (Lev 21:6); not sanctifying God (outside P: Deut 32:51); misuse of sanctums (Lev 22:2; outside P: 2 Chr 26:16–18; cf. Ezek 43:7–8); enslaving freed slaves (non-P: Jer 34:16); sexual sins (non-P: Amos 2:7); general sins (Lev 22:32; 26:40; Num 5:6; outside P: Isa 48:11; Ezek 14:13; 15:8; 18:24; 20:27; 22:26; 39:23, 26; Dan 9:7; Neh 1:8; 1 Chr 9:1; 2 Chr 12:2; 30:7; 36:14); and God's necessary punishment of his people (non-P: Ezek 20:9, 14; 36:20–23; 39:7). The land is profaned by idolatry and enemy attack (non-P: Jer 16:18 and Isa 47:6). Holy occasions are profaned by work (Exod 31:14; outside P: Isa 56:2, 6; Ezek 20:13, 16, 21, 24; 22:8; 23:38; Neh 13:18) and not observing prescriptions (cf. Exod 12:15, 19; Lev 23:29–30; Num 9:13). Covenants and commandments may be profaned by not abiding them (outside P: Mal 2:10; Ps 55:21; 89:32, 35; cf. Ezek 7:21; 28:18).

Desecration carries penalties (these have been fully discussed by Milgrom 1970; 1976). In P, inadvertent profanation, when one does not know of the desecration until after the fact, can be required by restoring the price of the sanctum plus one fifth, and bringing a reparation offering (Lev 5:16–18; cf. 5:20–26; 22:14; Num 5:5–8; Ezra 10:19). For suspected sanctum trespass a reparation offering is brought (Lev 5:17–19; cf. Num 6:12). Even if people do not intend desecration, but are conscious of their act, death may ensue (Num 4:15, 20; 18:3; 2 Sam 6:6–7). Intentional sacrilege is perilous. Only in the case of a false oath, where God's name has been desecrated, does P prescribe rectification procedures (Lev 5:20–26; cf. Num 5:6–8). Death by deity, however, is the usual consequence (described with the Heb *Qal* form *mût,* "die": Exod 28:43; 30:20–21; Lev 10:6, 9; 16:2, 13; 22:9; Num 4:15, 19–20; 17:28; 18:3, 22, 32; or with Heb *kārēt,* "be cut off": Exod 12:15, 19; 31:14; Lev 7:18, 20–21, 25, 27; 17:4, 9–10, 14; 19:8; 20:2–5; 22:3; 23:29–30; Num 4:18; 9:13; 19:13, 20; see Wold 1979). Some cases of sanctum trespass involve execution after judgment or preemptory execution by sanctuary guards to prevent God's fury from being poured out on the community (Exod 19:12–13; 31:14–15; 35:2; Lev 20:2; 24:16; Num 1:51; 3:10, 38; 15:35; 18:7; 2 Chr 23:6–7; cf. Judg 6:25–32; and see the passages in the previous paragraph). It is the danger inherent in the holy that lies behind fear of the divine presence (Gen 28:17; Exod 20:18–19; 24:11; 33:3, 5, 20; 34:30; Num 17:27–28—Eng 17:12–13; Deut 5:24–27; Judg 6:22–23; 13:22).

D. Theoretical Concerns

In addition to the foregoing observations about gradations of holiness, some additional general comments are in order. Much can be said about holiness from a more comprehensive theoretical perspective (see bibliography). Here we discuss the relationship of the conception of purity/impurity to holiness/profaneness and some recent contributions from anthropology and the theoretical study of religion to the understanding of sanctification rituals, sacred time, and ritual place.

1. Relationship of Holy, Profane, Pure, Impure. P and Ezekiel expressly view the states of holiness, profaneness, purity, and impurity in terms of two pairs of opposites: pure vs. impure and holy vs. profane (Lev 10:10; 11:47; Ezek 22:26; 42:20; 44:23; cf. 1 Sam 21:5). While it is true that impurity is a state opposed and detrimental to holiness, profaneness is its technical antonym. The presence or lack of a dynamic quality distinguishes the opposites from one another: profaneness is the lack of holiness; and purity is the lack of impurity. Any object, place, or person bears one state from each of the pairs at the same time (time is not called pure or impure). Four states, all of which are legitimate in certain contexts, are possible: profane and pure, profane and impure, holy and pure, and holy and impure. "Profane and pure" is a neutral and basic state since it lacks dynamic elements of holiness and impurity. Most laws that talk about becoming holy or impure assume a person or object starts with this combined state. Being profane and impure is the concern of most purity legislation. "Holy and pure" is the state of most persons, objects, and places considered holy. Only the last, ostensibly contradictory pairing of holiness and impurity demands attention. While this is not an expected or desired state, it is legitimate, even demanded, in cases of purgation offerings. A regular purgation offering removes impurity adhering to sanctums in the sanctuary. That it can pollute others after it is used for purification indicates it has become impure (Lev 16:27–28), but the requirement that it be eaten by the priests or be burned at the pure ash dump where other sanctuary materials are disposed indicates it is holy as well (Lev 6:19–23; see sec. C. 1. b. (2) on disposal). Similarly the scapegoat, part of a purgation offering complex (16:5), becomes impure when loaded with the community's sins while apparently remaining holy (cf. v 26). And the red cow, also a purgation offering (Num 19:9), pollutes those who prepare it (vv 7–

8, 10), yet it is still holy as suggested by the rule that the water made from the resulting ash can only be handled by a pure person (v 18).

J. Milgrom recognizes the two pairs of opposites above, but treats them in terms of their dynamic *interactions* and the consequences involved (1970: 1; *Leviticus* AB). He distinguishes between most and lesser holy, assumes that these holy states and the profane state are pure, eliminates the cases where same states would interact with one another, and treats the impure state without regard to whether it is in addition holy or profane. He then posits five interactions: (a) most holy with profane, (b) lesser holy with impure, (c) lesser holy with profane, (d) profane with impure, and (e) most holy with impure. One regularity Milgrom observes is that the interactions of (a), (b), and (e) are illicit and lead to dire consequences while those in (c) and (d) are not necessarily so. Profane Levites who touch, even look at most holy sanctums, are liable to death (Num 4:15, 19–20) and those who pollute a well-being offering (which is lesser holy) are liable to *kārēt,* "cutting off" (Lev 7:19–21), while the profane can legitimately contact what is lesser holy (but not misuse it), and the profane can generally contact what is impure (cf. sec. C. 2). If a spectrum of holiness and impurity strength be set up (most holy—lesser holy—profane—impure) only contact between noncontiguous categories poses a threat. This exhibits the systematic character of P's rules about holiness and purity.

2. Sanctification Rituals and Ritual Time. The anthropologist Edmund Leach (1976: 77–93) has developed insights proposed by van Gennep (1960) and has applied them to the priestly consecration ritual in Leviticus 8–9. He argues that many rituals involve a movement in social status and often have a threefold division: (1) rites of separation where the subject is demarcated from his or her surroundings by actual removal or symbolic rites (disrobing-clothing; purification; etc.), (2) a marginal or liminal period—of "social timelessness"—of long or short duration which often continues the subject's separation with prohibitions to be observed and which may be accompanied by rites, and (3) rites of aggregation or incorporation where persons return to their previous state or, at least, having a new social status, to a state of integration with society. To this scheme he adds a structuralist perspective that ritual is a type of language: not one which communicates in detail like speech, but which communicates more abstractly and generally like art and music. The parts of each ritual derive their meaning in relationship to one another, and a ritual complex derives its meaning in relationship to other complexes. Though not everything he says about the biblical material is acceptable, his approach generates many insights into biblical sanctification rituals. Following Leach's leads, we can offer the following abbreviated analysis of the priestly consecration ceremony and the Nazirite vow and desanctification. These two rites which raise the status of persons are actually quite different and convey thereby different ritual messages.

In the priestly consecration ritual the rites of separation cover almost all of Leviticus 8. Aaron and his sons are brought forward from the congregation, a physical separation (v 6). Though all are washed at first, Aaron is treated differently: he is dressed first (vv 7–9) and uniquely anointed (v 12). Aaron's special treatment, which continues throughout the rite, marks him as holier than his sons. After the sons are dressed and Moses offers sacrifices (vv 13–28), he places blood on Aaron's extremities first, and then on those of his sons (vv 23–24). Later, anointing oil and consecration-offering blood from the altar is sprinkled upon Aaron's clothes and perhaps Aaron, and then on his sons and their clothes (v 30). At this point the rite of separation has come to an end. The initiates now have a holy character (vv 12, 30). As vv 2–6 indicate the congregation has been present during this entire ritual segment. Their presence is not incidental but actually part of the ritual itself. The separation of the priests from the group and the latter's observation signifies or communicates the advancement of the priests' status. The period or rites of marginality or transition immediately ensue: the priests remain in the sanctuary area for seven days (vv 32–36; cf. Exod 29:35b–37). After this week of separation, rites of incorporation begin (Leviticus 9). On the eighth day offerings of the priests and the people are brought (vv 2–6). Though Moses instructs what is to be done, it is Aaron and his sons, not Moses, who now perform the sacrifices (7–20). Aaron, too, blesses the people (v 22). All this reveals the extent and nature of the priests' reintegration. While they can deal again with society, they are not on the same level as they were before. They are now the community's cultic representatives: they are holy. The appearance of God's glory gives closure and sanction to the entire tripartite ritual (v 24; cf. vv 4, 6).

To be compared, and contrasted, is the Nazirite vow and desanctification. The Nazirite period is simply initiated by a vow, a statement of intent (cf. Num 6:2). The "rite" of separation if therefore quite simple in comparison with the priestly ritual. The marginal or transitional period is one of restrictions (vv 3–8). The rite of aggregation consists of bringing offerings (vv 13–20) and cutting the hair (v 18–19). After this the Nazirite "may drink wine" (v 20). The cutting of the hair is a reversal of the initiation of the rite. As opposed to the priestly rites, this brings the person back to the profane status where he or she began. The Nazirite ritual is also private: there is no assembly when the vow is made and apparently none when the offerings are brought at the end. This is one of the great differences between this and the priestly ritual. Though both of them increase the holiness of the subjects, only the sanctification of the priests has broad social significance and relevance.

Leach's model is a temporal one. Ritual complexes such as those of the priests and Nazirite take place over and in time. As Leach notes, these rituals break up social time: they give meaning, direction, and order to an otherwise undifferentiated and homomorphous temporal continuum. There is thus a similarity between the rituals just discussed and the regular holy festival times of Israel. The regular recurrence of Sabbath and holidays also gives definition to Israelite time. These days punctuate it with focal points to which the group orients itself and works toward and from. Such orientation brings social unity and solidarity. Holy days, moreover, are periods of marginality or, better, timelessness, when the everyday is set aside for the unique; they are periods of restriction. If we had enough evidence we might find that these days or times were preceded by rites of separation or inauguration and rites of incorporation or termination which returned the people to regular time, as are found, for example, in postbiblical Judaism for the Sabbath (cf. Lev 25:9–10).

3. Ritual Place. Leach also offers a model for understanding ritual space (1976: 81–93). For the human mind, reality consists of the real world and another, metaphysical world where things are the reverse of the real world: gods live there, they are immortal, power which can ultimately be beneficial to humans exists there, etc. Sacred space is where these two worlds are brought into contact with one another through various rituals. Religious specialists, e.g., priests, serve as intermediaries between the two worlds in these places, and purity and other restrictions prevail. For the P material specifically, Leach sees the adytum as symbolic of the other world, the veil being what separates the real from the other world. Inside the rest of the sanctuary area are graded intermediate zones. His model includes the area outside the sanctuary: the camp is the area of "tame culture" and the area outside the camp is that of "wild nature."

While Leach's model explains why sacred space exists functionally, it does not explain why societies have different conceptions of sacred space. Scholars argue that specific ideas about ritual space derive in part from social structure and other social concerns. Recently J. Z. Smith (1987) has applied some of these ideas to the verbal maps of the temple and land in Ezekiel 40–44. He suggests that the social hierarchies of a particular society determine its gradation of ritual space and the access that groups have to its different parts. One may disagree with his interpretation of some of the verses (particularly with the view that the Levites had access to the inner court), but his theoretical ideas are worthy of consideration and development.

To review, in Ezekiel's temple God's residence is the adytum; undistinguished priests have access to the inner court; Levites have access only up to the gates of the inner court; the civil ruler is barred from the inner court but allowed to enter the hall of the east inner gate from the outside; and laypeople have access to the inner court. The supposition is that the more access one has, the higher is one's social rank. This seems a fair supposition; Ezekiel's style in particular substantiates it. The book's gradation is not descriptive but prescriptive; yet not just prescriptive, but revisionist. It is a polemical reformulation of social and religious relationships. The Zadokite priests are exalted while the Levites are demoted and castigated. Civic leaders—kings—are criticized for their breach of purity rules and are restricted in the future from access much beyond laypersons and Levites. Compare the redefinitions in 43:7–9, 19; 44:1–16; 45:8–9; 46:16–18. By changing access to the temple, the prophet is changing the constitution and organization of society.

P's access rules are similar to Ezekiel's: God's place is the adytum; the high priest has access to the adytum; the high priest aided by undistinguished priests has access to the shrine; the priests mainly work in the court and the Levites and people have access only to this area; more specifically, the people may be restricted to the area between the altar and the entrance to the court. (P does not clearly define how a civil ruler would fit in.) P's rules are not polemic like Ezekiel's, but the social tensions underlying them and in part giving rise and justification to them are visible in narratives about Levites vying for power (Numbers 16) or about priests committing sacrilege (Lev 10:1–5). The access laws in P and elsewhere do not just protect the sanctuary from encroachment and sacrilege, they sustain the borders between categories of persons in society. To carry it further, encroachment prohibitions (see C. 2. b.) do not just protect potential encroachers and the community from God's wrath, they protect the group from the confusion of social boundaries and thereby from social dissolution.

Finally, a case of ritual redundancy. Within a ritual corpus, practices and rules often symbolically articulate the same or similar messages of other practices and rules. Such is found with Ezekiel's Teruma (see B. 4. d.). The Teruma, we recall, consists of three portions: the holiest portion in the center where the sanctuary was and where the priests resided, a lesser holy section on the north for the Levites, and a southern profane section containing the city (i.e., Jerusalem). On the east and west of the Teruma was the land of the civic leader (Ezek 45:7–8; 48:21–22). This map repeats the same hierarchical relationships of the temple, with the priests at the top and with Levites and civic leader below them. One refinement is perhaps perceptible. In the temple map, it is difficult to determine whether the civic leader has a greater status than the Levites. If the Teruma is a deciding factor, the Levites seem to have a higher status since they are closer to the sanctuary. But this conclusion is confounded by the facts that the Levites are cultic officials and hence expected to have some proximity to the sanctuary and that the civic leader, though further from the sanctuary, is given more land.

Bibliography

Bettenzoli, G. 1979. *Geist der Heiligkeit: traditionsgeschichtliche Untersuchung des QDŠ-Begriffes im Buch Ezechiel.* Quaderni di Semitistica 8. Florence.

Cohn, R. L. 1981. *The Shape of Sacred Space.* AARSR 23. Chico, CA.

Eliade, M. 1959. *The Sacred and the Profane.* New York.

Gennep, A. van. 1960. *The Rites of Passage.* Chicago.

Girard, R. 1977. *Violence and the Sacred.* Baltimore.

Hänel, J. 1931. *Die Religion der Heiligkeit.* Gütersloh.

Haran, M. 1978. *Temples and Temple-Service in Ancient Israel.* Oxford.

Leach, E. R. 1976. *Culture and Communication.* Cambridge and New York.

Levine, B. A. 1974. *In the Presence of the Lord.* SJLA 5. Leiden.

Milgrom, J. 1970. *Studies in Levitical Terminology, I: The Encroacher and the Levite; The Term ʿAboda.* UCPNES 14. Berkeley.

———. 1976. *Cult and Conscience: The Asham and the Priestly Doctrine of Repentance.* SJLA 18. Leiden.

———. 1981. Sancta Contagion and Altar/City Asylum. *VTSup* 32: 278–310.

———. 1983a. Of Hems and Tassels. *BARev* 9/3: 61–65.

———. 1983b. *Studies in Cultic Theology and Terminology.* SJLA 36. Leiden.

———. 1983c. The Tassels Pericope, Numbers 15:37–41. *Beth Mikra* 92: 14–22.

Otto, R. 1923. *The Idea of the Holy.* London.

Schmidt, W. 1962. Wo hat die Aussage: Jahwe "Der Heilige" ihren Ursprung? *ZAW* 74: 62–66.

Smith, J. Z. 1987. *To Take Place: Toward Theory in Ritual.* Chicago.

Turner, V. 1977. *The Ritual Process: Structure and Anti-Structure.* Ithaca, NY.
Wold, D. J. 1979. The *Kareth* Penalty: Rationale and Cases. *SBLSP* 1: 1–45.
Wright, D. P. 1987. *The Disposal of Impurity: Elimination Rites in the Bible and in Hittite and Mesopotamian Literature.* SBLDS 101. Atlanta.
Yadin, Y. 1983. *The Temple Scroll.* Jerusalem.

DAVID P. WRIGHT

NEW TESTAMENT

In the NT, holiness is an attribute of God that the people of God are urged to reflect in their lives (Luke 1:75; 2 Cor 7:1; Eph 4:24; etc.).

A. Introduction
1. Terminology
2. General Definitions
B. *Hagios* and Cognates in the NT
1. Jesus
2. Synoptic Sayings Source
3. Mark
4. The Special Material in Matthew and Luke
5. Acts of the Apostles
6. Paul
7. The School of St. Paul
8. Gospel of John
9. The School of St. John
10. Hebrews
11. The Catholic Epistles
C. *Hagios* and Cognates in Early Christian Literature
1. Apostolic Fathers
2. The Apocryphal NT
D. Summary

A. Introduction

1. Terminology. The language of holiness in the NT and other early Christian literature is almost entirely represented by a word family that is rare in Attic Greek: *hagios,* "holy," *hagiazein,* "to make holy," and cognates (possibly derived from the Sanskrit *yaj,* "sacrifice"). The few instances of *hagios* in classical writers occur chiefly among the historians (Herodotus 2.41, 44; Xenophon, *HG* 3.2.19), rhetoricians (Demosthenes, *Ep.* 25.11), philosophers (Plato, *Criti.* 116c; *Cri.* 51a; *Lg.* 729e; 904e; Aristotle, *Mir.* 834b 11), and comedians (Aristophanes, *Av.* 522; *Nu.*, 304). For the historians it is temples or shrines that are holy, while for Demosthenes and Aristophanes it is the rites of the mysteries. In the philosophical tradition oaths (Aristotle) and contracts (Plato, *Lg.* 729e) as well as the moral life (*Lg.* 904e) and fatherland (*Cri.* 51a) count as holy.

Among the Hellenistic writers in which *hagios* occurs Lucian (*Syr. D.* 13) and Appian (*Syr.* 50) may be named. The latter identifies Jerusalem as a holy city.

Greek *hagios* corresponds with *sanctus* in Latin, *ouaab* in Coptic, and *qdš* in Syriac. Other Greek words occasionally express holiness or the related idea of purity (*hosios* in Acts 2:27 and *2 Clem.* 1:3; *hosiotēs* in Eph 4:24 and *1 Clem.* 29:1; *hagnos* in 2 Cor 7:11 and Pol. *Phil.* 5:3; *hagnotēs* in 2 Cor 6.6 and *Herm. Vis.* 3:7; *hieros* in 1 Cor 9:13 and *1 Clem.* 43:1). But their association with Hellenistic religions of the period prevented any widespread use among NT and early Christian authors. Also the preponderance of *hagios* in the LXX as a translation for the Hebrew *qdš,* "holy," made this word group ready at hand for early Christian writers.

It is in the LXX, in fact, that *hagios* developed luxuriantly (ca. 700 occurrences), spawning a full family of cognates: *hagiazein,* "to make holy" (ca. 200 occurrences); *hagiasma,* "holy place" (ca. 64 occurrences); *hagiasmos,* "holiness" (10 occurrences); *hagiastērion,* "holy place" (4 occurrences); *hagiōsynē,* "holiness" (4 occurrences). Lev 19:2, "you shall be holy, for I, the Lord your God, am holy" (cf. 1 Pet 1:16; 1 Thess 4:3); Ps 2:6, "I have set my king on Zion, my holy hill"; and Wis 1:5, "For a holy and disciplined spirit will flee from deceit," illustrate the breadth of usage: ontology and theology, social description, cult, and ethics.

2. General Definitions. Schleiermacher (1955: 19–82) and Durkheim (1968: 37) placed the idea of holiness at the center of the study of religion, and since then a variety of biblical and theological disciplines has unfolded its general meaning. For the psychology of religion, holiness is a category of interpretation and valuation which describes the numinous (Otto 1958: 5–8); holiness reveals itself in encounters with a *mysterium tremendum,* evoking feelings of creatureliness, awe, and fascination.

For the phenomenology of religion the holy reveals itself in whatever is not profane (Eliade 1959: 14). It is experienced in hierophanies or manifestations of power (Van der Leeuw 1963 1: 23–36). In principle everything may disclose the holy: time, space, action, word, plant, animal, or person (Eliade 1963: 1–4). For the sociology of religion holiness marks status within a community, maintains boundaries vis-à-vis outsiders, and creates group identity (Hodgson 1986: 65–91). For traditional scholastic philosophy holiness remains a fundamental ontological category, designating what belongs to or is united with God and the divine will.

B. *Hagios* and Cognates in the NT

1. Jesus. To the extent that Jesus' sayings can be distilled from the faith of the early Church and the editorial work of the evangelists, one sees that Jesus rarely, but deliberately, spoke of holiness. The Lord's Prayer invokes the Father with the petition "hallowed [*hagiazesthai*] be thy name" (Matt 6:9, Luke 11:2, *Did.* 8:2). The holiness of God's name, a common motif in Hebrew prayer (Ps. 30:4; 97:12; Tob 3:11), evolved into a powerful symbol and rallying point for Christian life and faith (cf. Luke 1:49; John 17:11; *1 Clem.* 58:1; 64:1; 9:1; *Did.* 10:2). Apart from the Lord's Prayer, the word "holy" turns up in four sayings attributed to Jesus. At Mark 8:38 (cf. Matt 16:27 and Luke 9:26) Jesus speaks of the *hagioi angelloi,* "holy angels," who will accompany the Son of Man upon his return. An important part of Jewish and early Christian faith was the belief in holy angels (Ps 89:7; Zech 14:5; Acts 10:22; *1 Clem.* 39:7; *Herm. Vis.* 2.2.7; 3.4.1–2; *Herm. Sim.* 5.5.3). By the mid–2d century C.E. this concept had grown to include the idea that the just were the holy angels (*Herm. Vis.* 2.2.7; *Herm. Sim.* 9:25; *Mart. Pol.* 2.3) who would return with Jesus (*Did.* 15:7; cf. 1 Thess 3:13).

In another saying (Matt 7:6; cf. *Did.* 9:5 and *Gos. Thom.* 93) Jesus declares, "Do not give dogs what is holy *(to hagion).*" If this meant for Jesus that his mission did not include gentiles, then so too in Matthew. In the *Didache* the saying becomes a rationale for excluding the catechumens from the Eucharist. In each case holiness serves to fix a boundary that restrains the outsider.

In the Synoptic apocalypse only Matthew reports that the desolating sacrilege will stand in the "holy place" *(hagios topos)* or temple (Matt 24:15; cf. Mark 13:14).

And finally, in Matthew's Woes against the Pharisees one reads at 23:17, "What is then greater, the gold or the temple which sanctified *(hagiazein)* the gold?" Presupposed in this saying is the dialectic of holiness (Eliade 1963: 12) or the belief that the holy (temple) can raise ordinary things (gold) to the level of the sacred.

2. Synoptic Sayings Source. Apart from the Lord's Prayer there is only one other occurrence of the idea of holiness in the synoptic sayings source: "The devil took him to the holy city, and set him on the pinnacle of the temple" (Matt 4:5; cf. Luke 4:9).

3. Mark. In Mark, holiness is twice attributed to a person. Once (Mark 1:24) a demoniac recognizes Jesus as "the holy one of God" *(ho hagios tou theou),* that is, as one removed from the profane order of things for the service of God (cf. Luke 4:34; John 6:69; Exod 22:31; Lev 11:44–45; 19:2; 20:7; 26; 21:6; Num 15:40; 1 Sam 7:1; 1 Esdr 8:58; Hab 3:3; Isa 4:3; Jer 1:5). In the second instance (Mark 6:20; cf. Matt 14:5; Luke 9:7–9) Herod Antipas fears to put John the Baptist to death because he was a righteous and holy *(hagios)* man.

4. The Special Material in Matthew and Luke. Apart from the four sayings of Jesus discussed above Matthew's special material refers only once more to holiness. Matt 27:52–53 narrates that upon the death of Jesus "the tombs also were opened, and many bodies of the holy who had fallen asleep were raised, and coming out of the tombs after his resurrection they went into the holy city and appeared to many." Whatever the origin of this tradition, whether in a saying of Jesus (cf. John 5:25) or in Jewish-Christian apocalypticism (cf. Dan 7:18–27), the holy ones became in the course of the 2d century C.E. identified with the Hebrew prophets (Ign. *Phld.* 5:2), thus expanding again already existing conceptions of who constituted the holy ones of the end time.

In Luke's special material holiness is an attribute of God's name or of those set apart for his service. The texts appear only in the infancy narrative (Luke 1:35, 49, 70, 72; 2:23). At the Annunciation Luke writes, for example, that "the child to be born will be called holy [*hagios*]." The view that the summons to holiness takes place through a "calling" *(kalein)* in traditional (cf. Isa 4:3; 35:8; 62:12; *klētē hagia,* "holy assembly": Ex 12:16; Lev 23:2; passim). Mary's hymn of praise, the Magnificat, celebrates God's holy name *(hagion to onoma autou),* and if Ps 110:9 LXX lies behind this verse (Fitzmyer, *Luke* AB, 368), then "holy" is equivalent here to "awe-full" *(phoberon).*

5. Acts of the Apostles. The 14 occurrences of *hagios* and cognates in Acts (apart from its use in the "Holy Spirit") reflect conventional Jewish usage. Eight belong to kerygmatic and sermonic material (3:14, 21; 4:27, 30; 7:33; 20:32; 26:10, 18); three to the traditions of Peter in Lydda, Joppa (9:32, 41), and the seacoast city of Caesarea (10:22); and three to the charges raised against Paul (9:13; 21:28) and Stephen (6:13). In Peter's sermon at Solomon's portico Jesus is identified as the holy and righteous one (3:14: *ho hagios kai dikaios;* cf. 4:27, 30; otherwise of John the Baptist at Mark 6:20). Among the earliest christological titles, "the holy and righteous one" and "the holy servant" *(pais)* combine traditional Jewish designations for Moses (Wis 11:1), the Suffering Servant (Isa 53:11), and Elijah (2 Kings 4:9) and apply them to Jesus (Fuller 1965: 48).

In another sermon Peter calls the prophets of old holy (3:21; cf. Luke 1:70), while the charge against Stephen is that he "never ceases to speak words against this holy place" (6:13; cf. Matt 24:15; in ancient Jewish piety a favorite circumlocution of God's name was *hammāqôm* "the place," while the graves of saints in late antiquity were known simply as *ho topos,* "the place" [cf. *1 Clem* 5:7]).

In Paul's farewell discourse at Miletus and in his defense speech before Herod Agrippa II, holiness becomes a category of social and religious identity. Paul commends the assembled Miletians to God and his word, who will give them "the inheritance among all those who are made holy" (20:32). Likewise, before Agrippa, Paul says that it is "the holy ones" (26:10; cf. 9:13) whom he formerly persecuted, before God called him to preach the gospel to the gentiles so "that they receive a portion among those who are made holy by faith in me" (26:18). Here Paul identifies faith as the social and religious wellspring of holiness.

At Joppa Peter seeks out believers described as the holy ones and the widows (9:41; cf. 9:32), a designation which suggests that while "the holy ones" serves as a blanket designation for "believers," there are also nuances to be considered, since the category of "holy" may from time to time mark a special role or function in early Christianity (cf. Eph 4:11–12; Heb 13:24; Rev 11:18).

6. Paul. Of the undisputed letters of Paul, Romans, 1 Corinthians, 2 Corinthians, and Philippians begin and end by addressing themselves to Christian communities whose members are designated as holy. Among the disputed letters, Ephesians and Colossians open in this manner. Philemon and the Thessalonian letters do not use this form of opening address, and *hagios* and cognates are completely wanting in Galatians. In Rom 1:7 and 1 Cor 1:2 the addressees are "those called to be holy" *(klētoi hagioi).* According to 1 Cor 1:2 the addressees enjoy this status because they are "made holy in Christ."

For Paul, Jesus incarnates holiness (*hagiasmos;* cf. 1 Cor 1:30). A pre-Pauline formula says that Jesus was designated son of God at his resurrection "according to the Spirit of holiness" (*kata pneuma hagiōsynēs,* Rom 1:4).

At the end of Romans Paul encourages the Church to receive Phoebe the deaconess in a manner "worthy of the holy ones" (16:2), and to "greet Philologus . . . and all the holy ones" (16:15). Similarly at the end of 1 Corinthians (16:15), 2 Corinthians (13:13), and Philippians (4:21) Paul uses the designation "the holy ones" as an epithet for the faithful.

Within the general designation of all believers as the holy ones there are special usages that derive from Paul's own theological and pastoral concerns. There is first the special status accorded the Jerusalem Church, most visible in the collection for its benefit. Everywhere except in Galatians, where the word "holy" is missing and the collection is a "remembering of the poor," the subscriptions of the gentile churches are earmarked for the holy ones. Paul prays at Rom 15:16 that the Holy Spirit will render holy the gifts of the gentile churches. From Corinth, Paul traveled to Jerusalem "to relieve the holy ones (Rom 15:25)," bringing Macedonia and Achaia's donation "for the poor among the holy ones at Jerusalem" (15:26) in the hope that his ministry to Jerusalem will be acceptable to the holy ones (15:31; cf. 12:13). Similarly, in the Corinthian correspondence Paul appeals on behalf of the holy ones in Jerusalem (1 Cor 16:1; 2 Cor 8:4; 9:1,12). Their vulnerability to economic and political distress gives their status as the impoverished holy ones a special sense of urgency and connects them with the tradition of the pious and persecuted poor of Hebrew scriptures and intertestamental literature (Osiek 1983: 15–24).

Secondly, there is the conception of the eschatological holy ones: those who join Christ at his second coming. Only 1 Thess 3:13 and 2 Thess 1:10 (this latter often reckoned among the disputed letters) articulate this role of the holy ones clearly, although it is assumed in other texts (e.g. 1 Cor 6:2; cf. above on Mark 8:38 and Matt 27:53). 1 Thess 3:13 envisions the holy ones appearing with Jesus at his second coming, at which time their holiness will be completed. At 2 Thess 1:10, it is the holy ones *in whom* Jesus' final glory is encompassed. At the end of time the holy ones will judge the world (1 Cor 6:2). To the extent that the end has already begun for Paul, the holy ones already incur certain obligations within their communities, and this leads to a third special usage, the ethical.

Rom 12:1, "present yourselves as holy and living sacrifices," opens the ethical section of a letter which sets forth the day-to-day dimension of holiness in a series of exhortations on brotherly love, civil obedience, and tolerance (Rom 12:3–15:6). Elsewhere the holy ones serve as arbiters at internecine suits (1 Cor 6:1) and persevere even in marriage with an unbeliever, since "the unbelieving husband is made holy by his wife, and the unbelieving wife by the husband" (1 Cor 7:14). Thanks to the holy marriage partner, the unclean *(akathartos)* children of such a marriage become holy (1 Cor 7:14b). The search for holiness in body and spirit informs the life of the single woman (1 Cor 7:34). At 1 Thess 4:1–12 Paul frames his earliest set of ethical instructions in concepts that derive ultimately from the holiness code of Leviticus 17–26 and from Hellenistic popular philosophy.

Loyalty to moral, doctrinal, and liturgical traditions both precede and deepen the "holiness of the spirit" (2 Thess 2:13–15). The churches of the holy ones are invoked as precedents for the silence of women (1 Cor 14:33). In his discussion of dying and rising with Christ Paul points to righteousness as the ethical and theological ground of holiness: "Yield your members to righteousness for holiness" (Rom 6:19; cf. 6:22). Holiness, Paul boasts, is a benchmark of apostolic life (2 Cor 1:12), and in a section with close ties to the ideology of the Essenes Paul envisions the life of holiness as a wearing down of defilement in order to "make holiness perfect" (2 Cor 7:1).

Fourth, Paul knows that the following are holy: Scripture (Rom 1:2); law and commandment (Rom 7:12); firstfruits, root, and branches (in the allegory of ancient Israel; Rom 11:16); and the temple (1 Cor 3:17). Finally, Christian liturgical and prayer life set off certain traditional rituals as holy. In 1 Cor 6:11 baptism is explicated as a moment of holiness (*hagiazein;* Dinkler 1967: 226–27), while Paul recognizes the holy kiss as a fitting greeting among Christians (Rom 16:16; 1 Cor 16:20; 2 Cor 13:12; 1 Thess 5:26; cf. 1 Pet 5:14; *Gos. Phil.* II,*3*:59,5; Asting 1930: 148). The prayers of the holy ones rise up to God on the intercession of the Spirit (Rom 8:27).

7. The School of St. Paul. In Colossians, Ephesians, and the Pastorals, holiness has a distinctive trait which lies in its application to the routine life of Christians both individually and corporately. Almost completely lacking are the more specialized usages characteristic of the undisputed letters which associate holiness with eschatology, ritual, and the special position of the Jerusalem church. Col 1:2 and Eph 1:1 address themselves to the holy and faithful ones whose hallmark is the love of the holy ones (Col 1:4; Eph 1:15). To a life without blemish God has set apart (*eklegein* not *kalein,* "to call"; cf. 2 Tim 1:9) his holy ones individually (Eph 1:4) and corporately (Eph 2:21; 5:27; cf. Col 1:22) in order that they will acquire "a share in the inheritance of the holy ones in the light" (Col 1:12; cf. Eph 1:18; Acts 20:32; *Gos. Eg.* III, *2*:51,3). The holiness of the faithful stems from possessing the long-hidden but now-revealed mystery of Christ's presence to the world (Col 1:26; cf. Eph 3:5 [where the mystery is revealed to the holy apostles and prophets] and 3:18). The routinization of holiness is evidenced in Col 3:12 where a conventional list of virtues *(Tugendkatalog)* discloses the ethical duties of "God's chosen ones, holy and beloved." Fornication, impurity, and covetousness belong to the vices which the holy ones avoid (Eph 5:3; cf. 1 Thess 4:1–12). Positively, "the work of ministry, for building up the body of Christ" and "prayer" contribute to the day-to-day agenda of the holy ones (Eph 4:12; 6:18). Lists of household duties *(Haustafel)* further domesticate holiness by lifting up the ideal ancient household, managed by husband and wife in a spirit of love, as an analogy for that love between Christ and the Church which makes the Church holy (Eph 5:26; cf. 1 Cor 7:14). Such lists also provide a strategy through which the "ignoble vessels" in a great household, that is the servants, can become holy and useful (2 Tim 2:21). Even more concretely, a woman is saved by childbearing, if she perseveres in "holiness" (*hagiasmos;* 1 Tim 2:15). Mention should be made, too, of the test with which 1 Tim 5:8–10 discerns the authentic widow. Full of good deeds, a mother of children, hospitable, she has also washed the feet of the holy ones (cf. John 13:4).

Although it is more characteristic of pre-Pauline and Pauline writings to say that holiness creates identity and status in the Church, this idea nonetheless shines faintly through in the self-designation of the author of Ephesians as the "least of all the holy ones" (Eph 3:8). Eph 2:19 belongs here as well: the gentile Christian readers of the letter are no longer "strangers and sojourners" but "fellow citizen with the holy ones and members of the household of God."

8. Gospel of John. In the gospel of John there are only five occurrences of "holy" *(hagios)* and its cognates, although in the apocalyptic side of the subsequent school the Revelation of John owes a substantial debt to the concept of holiness. The Father is the foremost bearer of holiness in John. In his high priestly prayer Jesus prays to the Father as "Holy Father" (17: 11; cf. Matt 6:9; Luke 11:2) that he "make them holy in the truth" (17:17; cf. v 19). As the Holy Father sanctifies (or sets apart) through truth, so too Jesus becomes the "Holy One of God" by speaking the "words of eternal life" (John 6:69; cf. Mark 1:24; Luke 4:34; Acts 3:14; 4:27). At John 10:36, Jesus advances the "works of God" which he performs as evidence that God has sanctified him, that is, has set him apart as son of God.

9. The School of St. John. Within the Johannine letters only 1 John 2:20 mentions holiness: "You have been anointed by the Holy One." In the Revelation of John, however, there are some twenty-two instances of "holy" and cognates. The most distinctive feature is the belief that the holy ones, along with the apostles and prophets, constitute the martyrs who await in heaven their final vindication.

At the blast of the seventh trumpet (Rev 11:18) the elders announce (cf. Ps 2:1) that the time has come for rewarding "the servants, prophets, and holy ones." The holy ones belong to those against whom the beast raged (13:7) but whose sterling qualities of "endurance and faith" (13:10), that is their ability to "keep the commandments of God" (14:12; cf. John 8:51; 14:15, 21, 23; 15:10; 17:6; 1 John 2:3, 5; 3:22, 24; 5:3) helped them persevere.

The spilling of the third bowl of wrath occasions a heavenly hymn which laments the blood of the holy ones and prophets (16:6). Of the great harlot it is said that she is drunk with the blood of the holy ones and martyrs (17:6). Babylon's doom is sealed because an angel laments that the blood of the prophets and holy ones runs within her walls (18:24). This same angel celebrates the vindication of the "holy ones, apostles, and prophets" (18:20) whose "righteous deeds" *(dikaiōmata)* are symbolized by the linen worn by the Lamb at his marriage (19:8; cf. 22:11; Rom 6:19) and whose prayers are to God as incense (5:8; 8:3, 4). The holy ones participate in the first resurrection (20:6) that opens the thousand-year reign of Christ after which Satan will surround the camp of the holy ones for a time (20:9; cf. Matt 27:52–53).

In Relevation God is the holy one whose heavenly court resounds with the epithet "holy" (4:8; 6:10; cf. *1 Clem.* 34:6). His angels are holy (14:10) as is his city Jerusalem (11:2; 21:2, 10; 22:19).

10. Hebrews. Hebrews borrows the idea of holiness from Hellenistic Judaism at a time when Platonism and the Roman destruction of Jerusalem and its temple in 70 C.E. impelled 1st century C.E. Judaism (e.g., Philo) to moralize and idealize the language of the Jewish cult, including the idea of holiness. Hebrews 9 and 10 represent in this regard the classic NT statement of the ideal, heavenly cult over against the earthly one. The earthly sanctuary *(hagion kosmikon)* belongs to the first covenant (9:1; cf. 13:11; *Gos. Phil.* II, *3*:69,15–36), while the heavenly sanctuary is the one into which Christ entered to render his sacrifice (9:10–11; cf. 9:24–25). The high priests of old entered the earthly sanctuary repeatedly in order to "make holy for the purification of the flesh" (9:13), but Christ entered the heavenly sanctuary once, and immolated himself to "purify the conscience" (9:14). Inspired by the prophetic and sapiential criticism of sacrifice, Christ's will was that "we be made holy through the offering of the body of Jesus Christ once for all" (10:10; cf. 10:14; 13:12).

The blood of Jesus, shed for his followers, gives them confidence that they too can enter the same sanctuary (10:19). Sharing in Jesus' heavenly call *(klēseōs epouraniou metochoi;* cf. 2:11), these followers acquire the status of holy associates *(adelphoi hagioi)* of the new apostle and high priest, Jesus Christ (3:1; cf. *1 Clem.* 64:1; Ign. *Phld.* 9:1).

Occasionally the more primitive Christian connotations of holiness stand out. At 6:10 the readers are praised (cf. Rom 12:13) because they have loved the vulnerable holy ones. At 13:24 the author of Hebrews greets two groups, the leaders and the holy ones. Holiness *(hagiasmos)* and peace are the presupposition and goal, respectively, of the moral life (12:14; cf. 1 Thess 5:23). Holiness *(hagiotēs)* represents, too, the crown toward which God's discipline directs his people (12:10).

11. The Catholic Epistles. 1 Peter, 2 Peter, and Jude combine traditional Jewish views of holiness (the concept is missing in James) with an ecclesiological emphasis. Echoing the language and levitical sources that Paul drew upon, 1 Peter urges that the holiness of God issue in the holiness of his people (1 Pet 1:15–16; cf. 1 Thess 4:1–12; Lev 11:44 passim), and that they consider themselves a "holy priesthood." The readers are a "holy nation" (1 Pet 2:9; cf. Exod 19:5–6), and are "made holy by the Spirit for obedience to Jesus Christ and for sprinkling with his blood" (1 Pet 1:2; cf. Heb 10:19). In a traditional list of domestic duties, the holy women of old serve as a model for submission within the Christian household (1 Pet 3:5). Persecution calls for "revering as holy the Lord Christ in your heart" (1 Pet 3:15; cf. 1 Thess 3:13; *Ep. Barn.* 6:15). For 2 Peter, holiness is a property of the mountain on which Jesus was transfigured (1:18) and the commandments from which the apostates have turned (2:21). It is also an attribute of the prophets (Christian? Hebrew?) whose predictions have come true (3:2), and the life which Christians lead (3:11). For Jude the holy ones are those to whom the faith was once entrusted (v 3; cf. v 20). When the Lord returns, his holy myriads will accompany him (v 14).

C. *Hagios* and Cognates in Early Christian Literature

Since some noncanonical early Christian literature is older than or contains traditions older than the canonical writings, scholarship increasingly turns to it for illumination of the NT.

1. Apostolic Fathers. Among the Apostolic Fathers it is principally in 1 Clement and Hermas that holiness plays a significant role in theology and exhortation. The most notable feature is the appropriation of the category of holiness for purposes of Church order. *1 Clem.* 46:2 exhorts the rebellious Corinthians, "Cling to the holy ones, for those who cling to them will be themselves made holy" (cf. 1 Cor 7:14; *Herm. Vis.* 3.6.2; *Herm. Sim.* VIII. 8.1). God's holy words *(hagioi logoi)* set the course for Christian life and require obedience (*1 Clem.* 13:3; cf. 56:3; on God's holy name cf. 58:1; 64:1; 59:3). God's wisdom chastens those who flaunt the holiness of God (*1 Clem.* 58:1; cf. 39:6). As God's holy portion (*hagia meris;* cf. Col 1:12, Eph 1:18, Acts 20:32), Christians do all holy things (*1 Clem.* 30:1; *ta tou hagiasmou panta*). In the interests of Church order, one prays to God and the holy ones (*1 Clem.* 56:1;

angels? heavenly saints? living Christians?; cf. Fischer 1970: 95, n. 332).

The apocalyptic theology of *1 Clem.* 22:8–29:3 teaches that God as the Holy One will return suddenly, and as the Holy of Holies he will step forth from his people (*1 Clem.* 23:5 and 29:3). The traditional common prayer of the Roman liturgy which *1 Clem.* 59:3 quotes reveres God as the Holy One who reposes among his holy people (cf. 34:6).

Familiar associations of holiness also include the designation of the readers as those called to be holy (*klētoi hēgiasmenoi; 1 Clem.* Salutation; cf. Rom 1:7; 1 Cor 1:2) and of Paul's final resting place as the holy place (*1 Clem.* 5:7; cf. Matt 24:15; Acts 7:33; John 14:2). The Scripture is holy (*1 Clem.* 45:2; cf. Rom 7:12), and an ancient creedal formula states that God has sanctified his people through his servant Jesus (*1 Clem.* 59:3; cf. Acts 4:27; 26:18; John 10:36; 17:17,19; 1 Pet 1:2; 1 Cor 1:2,30; 2 Tim 1:9; Heb 2:11; 10:10; 13:12). Increasingly, however, holiness becomes a property of God's spirit (*1 Clem.* 2:2; 8:1; 13:1 passim).

In Hermas' Mandates, the spirit alone is declared holy (5.1.2–3; 2.5; passim), while Christians evince reverence (*semnotēs;* 4.4.3; 5.2.8; *1 Clem.* 41:1; cf. 1 Tim 2:2; 3:4; Titus 2:7). In the Similitudes, holiness is also a property exclusively of God's spirit (5.6.5; passim) or angels (5.4.4; cf. 9.13.2) except for a single text in which the holy ones are the believers to whom the apostates no longer cleave (*Herm. Sim.* 8.8.1; cf. *Herm Vis.* 3.6.2; cf. *1 Clem.* 46:2). Like the Mandates, the Similitudes prefer reverence (*semnotēs*) to indicate the quality of the Christians' interior life (cf. 5.6.5; 8.3.8).

In the Visions, by contrast, social description, an apocalyptic ecclesiology, and ethics as well as early Christian pneumatology are the frames of reference for holiness. The Church is holy (1.1.6), because God in his wisdom and forethought created it holy (1.3.4; cf. 4.1.3). Individually the members of the Church are holy, both in this life (3.3.3; 8.8.9, 11) and in the next (1.3.2). Holiness especially means separation from sin (3.9.1; cf. 1 Cor 6:11), although—here a new note is sounded in the development of holiness' relationship to sin—postbaptismal sin is forgivable once (2.2.4; cf. 1.1.9) but not twice (2.2.5). The Visions also teach that God (3.2.1) and the angels (3.4.1, 2) are holy.

Barnabas, for all its OT citations, allusions, and images, shows little interest in the idea of holiness. In *Barn.* 6:16, the churches of the holy appear in a composite quotation of Ps 31:23 and 107:4 (cf. *Barn.* 14:6), and once the heart is depicted as a holy temple for God (cf. 1 Pet 3:15). Allegorizing Deut 14:6, *Barn.* 10:11 determines that the cloven hoof means that the just live in this age but await the holy time. Teaching the two ways, *Barn.* 19:10 exhorts the readers to search out the holy ones for right counsel (cf. *Did.* 4:2). Only a lengthy section on the correct understanding of the Sabbath appeals regularly to the idea of holiness (15:1, 3, 6, 7).

In the Didache, one traditional saying (cf. Matt 7:6 with *Did.* 9:5) and two traditional prayers (cf. Matt 6:9 with *Did.* 8:2; cf. John 17:11 with *Did.* 10:2) include holiness. At *Did.* 9:5 and 10:2 Jesus' words belong to the ancient Eucharistic ritual and theology of the Church. (Wengst 1984: 28, 81). Older apocalyptic traditions appear at 16:7 where the holy ones return with the Lord at the end of time (cf. 1 Thess 3:13). And finally, the holy ones are those of special rank whom readers should daily seek out (4:2; cf. *Barn.* 19:10).

For Ignatius, holiness is above all a property of God's spirit (*Eph.* 9:1; 18:2). It is also the reward for obedience to bishops (*Eph.* 2:2), Paul's crown for martyrdom (*Eph.* 12:2), and the mark of presbyters (*Magn.* 3:1) and of the Church (*Trall.* salutation). Prophets (*Phld.* 5:2; 9:2) are holy, as well as believing Jews and gentiles (*Smyrn.* 1:2).

The use of holiness in *2 Clement* is restricted to the spirit of God (14:3, 5). There are no instances of holiness in Polycarp's Letter to the Philippians, Diognetus, or Quadratus.

2. The Apocryphal NT. The theological and philological opulence of the apocryphal NT make broad statements about the use of holiness risky. Nonetheless some general observations are possible. In the surviving literature of late Jewish Christianity (e.g., *Gospel of the Nazoreans, Gospel of the Hebrews, Gospel of the Ebionites, Protoevangelium of James,* the *Apocryphon of James*) holiness is chiefly the property of God's spirit: *Gos. Heb.* 2 (Cameron 1982: 85); *Gos. Naz.* 15a,b (Cameron 1982: 100); *Gos. Eb.* 4 (Cameron 1982: 105); *Prot. Jas.* 14:2; 19:1; 24:4 (Cameron 1982: 116, 118, 121). The nascent Mariology of *Prot. Jas.* 13:2 and 14:2 teaches that Mary grew up in the holy of holies within the Jerusalem Temple, and that Jesus already at conception was a "holy thing" (11:3; cf. Luke 1:35; Cameron 1982: 115–16).

In the sapiential sayings tradition, the Coptic *Gospel of Thomas* reports traditional sayings of Jesus about blaspheming against the Holy Spirit (*appna etouaab*) (logion 44 = Mark 3:28–29 and parallels) as well as against throwing what is holy (*petouaab*) to the dogs (logion 93 = Matt 7:6; *Did.* 9:5).

Within the older portions of the apocryphal Johannine literature ("John's Preaching of the Gospel" from the *Acts John; Ap. John*) the spirit of God is designated as holy (*Acts John* 96 and—in a complex mythological drama typical of Sethian gnosticism—*Ap. John* II,*1*:3,19; 5,8; 7,16 passim). Otherwise God is the holy one (*Acts John* 94) whose will is that holy souls (*psychai hagiai*) be prepared for him (*Acts John* 96; cf. *Ap. John* II, *1*:9,17).

The literature of Christian gnosticism makes varied but incisive use of the concept of holiness, especially in the construction of an elaborate story of creation, fall, and redemption. Taking the Sethian Gnostic literature as representative (without any discussion of its complex literary and ideological history [Turner 1986: 279–312]) one may note that the ineffable high God is holy (*Hyp. Arch.* II,*4*: 92,34; *Melch.* IX,*1*:16,16–18,4). In one text he praises his holy warrior Melchizedek-Jesus (cf. Heb 7:3) for triumphing in the great eschatological battle (*Melch.* IX, *1*:26,2–9; Pearson 1981: 33). God's dwelling place and all the heavenly citizens who dwell within it (thus the pleroma and aeons) are holy (*Ap. John* II,*1*.25:14–15). Naturally, God's spirit is holy as well (*Hyp. Arch* II, *4*:93,6 passim). Through holy books (*Gos. Eg.* III,*2*:69,7,16) and decrees (*Ap. John* II,*1*:19,19), God signals to the temporarily estranged race of the Sethians their ultimate restoration to him.

Apart from its use in the ontology and mythology of Sethian gnosticism, holiness is part of the self-designation of the Sethians. They spring from a holy seed (*Apoc. Adam* V,5:85,30) and are set apart through a holy baptism (*Apoc. Adam* V,5:85,25) as a holy race (*Gos. Eg.* III,2:68,21; cf. 1 Pet 2:9). They are the holy men of the great light (*Gos. Eg.* III,2:51,3; cf. Col 1:12).

D. Summary

Distinctive features of the Synoptic use of holiness include its use as a category for describing the awesomeness of God (or his name), and the marking of others (Jesus, John the Baptist, Hebrew prophets, angels) for his service. As a quality of things, actions, time, and place, it plays only a modest role. Holiness in Acts, as in the Synoptic tradition, identifies Jesus as one set apart by God, but it also describes the temple precincts in Jerusalem. The idea that the followers of Jesus share in God's holiness and become the "holy ones" originated according to Acts in earliest Jewish Christianity, but Paul popularized the idea.

Paul used the designation "holy ones" for early Christians in general, although he uses the expression in more particular ways to call attention to the special status of the Jerusalem Church or to speak of those who would accompany the Lord upon his return. The holy life is, for Paul, one in conformity with established moral and ethical norms of the Hellenistic Jewish world. Paul borrows from contemporary Judaism the view that Temple, Law, Scripture, certain forms of ritual, and God's spirit are holy. In the school of Paul the depth and breadth of the Pauline view of holiness have given way to a more stereotyped use of holiness to describe a preeminent quality of day-to-day Christian life.

In the gospel of John and the subsequent school that formed around it holiness plays a leading role only in the theological life of Revelation, designating especially in the martyrs whose keeping of the commandments constitutes their peculiar form of testimony *(martyria)*. In Hebrews, holiness is the paramount quality of the ideal, heavenly world, whose high priest Jesus, by means of a once-and-for-all self-sacrifice, established a new heavenly covenant. The holy ones are those whom the covenant has set apart with a fresh identity and moral purpose. Ecclesiology provides the chief frame of reference for holiness in 1 Peter. 2 Peter and Jude use holiness to describe an important feature of the common life and faith of God's people.

In the Apostolic Fathers holiness is increasingly associated with God's spirit. When the Holy Spirit dwells in believers the interior transformation is described more and more in the language of Hellenistic popular philosophy and ethics. Naturally conceptions of holiness originating in prophetic, levitical, and apocalyptic thought, as well as in early Christian self-understanding, still persist. The apocryphal NT, like the Apostolic Fathers, assigned holiness increasingly to God and his spirit. Although holiness in this sense predominates, other traditional usages such as the social, phenomenological, and psychological persevere.

Bibliography

Asting, R. 1930. *Die Heiligkeit im Urchristentum.* FRLANT 46. Göttingen.

Cameron, R., ed. 1982. *The Other Gospels.* Philadelphia.

Colpe, C. 1977. *Die Diskussion um das Heilige.* Darmstadt.

Dinkler, E. 1967. Zum Problem der Ethik bei Paulus—Rechtsnahme und Rechtsverzicht (1 Kor 6:1011). Pp. 204–40 in *Signum Crucis: Aufsätze zum Neuen Testament und zur Christlichen Archäologie.* Tübingen.

Durkheim, E. 1968. *The Elementary Forms of the Religious Life.* Trans. J. W. Swain. London.

Eliade, M. 1959. *The Sacred and the Profane.* Trans. W. R. Trask. New York.

———. 1963. *Patterns in Comparative Religion.* Trans. R. Sheed. Cleveland.

Fischer, J. A., ed. 1970. *Die Apostolischen Vaeter.* Schriften des Urchristentums 1. Darmstadt.

Fuller, R. H. 1965. *The Foundations of NT Christology.* Great Britain. Repr. 1976.

Hodgson, R., Jr. 1986. The Social Setting of Holiness in Intertestamental Judaism and Early Christianity. Pp. 65–91 in *Reaching Beyond: Studies in the History of Perfectionism,* ed. S. Burgess. Peabody, MA.

Osiek, C. 1983. *Rich and Poor in the Shepherd of Hermas.* CBQMS 15. Washington, D.C.

Otto, R. 1958. *The Idea of the Holy.* Trans. J. W. Harvey. New York.

Pearson, B. 1981. *Nag Hammadi Codices IX and X.* NHS 15. Leiden.

Schleiermacher, F. D. E. 1955. *On Religion: Speeches to Its Cultured Despisers.* Trans. J. Oman. New York.

Turner, J. 1986. Sethian Gnosticism: A Literary History. Pp. 279–312 of *Nag Hammadi, Gnosticism, and Early Christianity,* ed. C. W. Hedrick and R. Hodgson, Jr. Peabody, MA.

Van der Leeuw, G. 1963. *Religion in Essence and Manifestation.* 2 vols. Trans. J. E. Turner. New York.

Wengst, K. 1984. *Didache, Barnabasbrief, Zweiter Klemensbrief, Schrift an Diognet.* Schriften des Urchristentums 2. Darmstadt.

ROBERT HODGSON, JR.

HOLINESS CODE. The label conventionally assigned to Leviticus 17–26 (*Heiligkeitsgesetz,* and abbreviated as H), generally thought to contain an originally independent legal corpus which was later edited from the perspective of the Priestly School.

A summary of the contents will outline the sections, and thereby the issues of H. Lev 17:1–9 contains two apodictic laws concerning illegitimate sacrifice. Vv 10–12 form a third apodictic law prohibiting the consumption of blood (cf. Deut 12:16, 23–25; 15:23), while vv 13–14 and 15–16 prescribe the proper treatment of the blood of nonsacrificial animals, and the ritual treatment for one who eats an animal carcass. Lev 18:6–23 prohibit a variety of sexual crimes for which vv 1–5 and 24–30 form a parenetic framework. The absence of a prohibition against sexual relations between a man and his daughter (cf. also Lev 20:10–21; Deut 27:20–23) is usually explained as a textual (copyist) error but it may be deliberate (cf. Bassett 1971; Rattray 1987). Chap. 19 contains a variety of texts which illustrate the call to "be holy" (v 2). Chap. 20 prescribes the death penalty for a father who offers his son or daughter to Molek (vv 1–5), for one who consults a soothsayer (vv 6–8 = v 27), for one who curses his parents (v 9), and for the violation of many of the sexual crimes prohibited in chap. 18 (vv 10–21). Vv 22–26 form a parenetic appeal to obey the law, and v 25 recalls Lev 11:43–45. Chaps. 21–22 contain texts dealing with a variety of concerns related to the priestly office and its conduct. Chap. 23 details a festival calendar (cf. also Exod 23:14–19; 34:22–26; Numbers 28–29; Deut 16:1–16; Ezek 45:21–25). Lev 24:1–9 prescribes the manipulation of certain elements of the Priestly tabernacle, while vv 10–14, 23 form an illustrative narrative for the apodictic law concerning blasphemy (vv 15–16; vv 17–22 are unrelated to this topic though similar in form). Lev 25:1–7 prescribes a fallow year every seventh year (cf. Exod 23:10–11) while vv 8–17, 23–55 treat a variety of topics related to jubilee redemption. (Verses 18–22 do not indicate knowledge of the jubilee year prohibitions of v 11.) After two prohibitions (26:1) and commands (26:2), and based upon obedience and disobedience (cf. Deut 28), Lev 26:3–45 promises rewards and threatens punishments. Lev 26:46 is a subscript, but the extent of the corpus is disputed. Eerdmans (1912: 121) argues for a connection with chap. 25, and Wagner (1974) wishes to relate it to chap. 11, whereas scholarly consensus generally takes it back to chap. 17. The corpus as a whole is often thought to be theologically unified around the notion of holiness (purity, cleanliness, etc.), both of Yahweh and consequently of Israel. See LEVITICUS, BOOK OF.

Among the genres contained in H, one may mention especially the following. The prohibition uses the negative adverb *lōʾ* plus a 2d person (sing. or pl.) impf. verb to prescribe certain types of behavior which must be avoided, as in Lev 18:8: "The nakedness of your father's wife you must not uncover" (Gerstenberger 1965 defines the genre; see also Richter 1966; Knierim 1989). Apodictic law combines the definition of a crime (using principal or relative syntax) with a prescribed punishment in a singlar sentence: "The man who sleeps with his father's wife . . . shall surely be executed" (20:11; Liedke 1971: 101–53). Traditiohistorically, prohibitions and apodictic laws are intimately connected, the prohibition constituting the (customary) ethical basis for the penalties prescribed in apodictic form (Schultz 1969). Although it is often thought that the series of ten prohibitions or apodictic laws constitutes an ancient genre, recent research more and more sees such decalogues as late combinations of small groups of laws (Gerstenberger 1965). The casuistic "if you" laws contain a protasis which sets forth a legal situation in the second person followed by its apodosis (19:5–8, 9–10; Gilmer 1975). The priestly Heb *daʿat* is the genre in which professional, priestly knowledge and lore is transmitted (chaps. 21–22; cf. Begrich 1936). The exhortation and admonition appeal to the audience's will and volition in an attempt to persuade or dissuade certain kinds of behaviors; together, the exhortation and admonition constitute a parenesis (Tiffany 1978). Pure casuistic law (the typical form of ancient Near Eastern legislation) is not found in H (though cf. Lev 25:25, 35–37, 47–54); Lev 19:20–22 is a late mixture of the casuistic and apodictic form. See LAW. The name "Holiness Code" was coined by A. Klostermann (1893: 385), though Leviticus 17(18)–26 had already been isolated as a separate unit (e.g., Graf 1866: 75–83; Wellhausen 1963: 149–72). Early research concentrated on the literary-historical identification of the original legislation and later (Priestly and non-Priestly) redaction (Horst 1881; Baentsch 1893; Paton 1894; Bertholet *Leviticus* KHC) and the relationship between H and Ezekiel (Horst 1881; cf. Haran 1979; Zimmerli *Ezekiel 1* Hermeneia, 46–52). Both Eerdmans (1912: 83–87) and Küchler (1929) denied the existence of an independent legal corpus behind these chapters, while Rabast (1948; cf. von Rad 1953) studied the prohibitions in H and Deuteronomy, and Kornfeld (1952) concentrated especially on the laws concerning sexual ethics. Reventlow (1961), using form-critical and traditiohistorical methods, proposed that H is a legal document whose setting from start to finish was the ancient Israelite covenant (renewal) festival. According to Reventlow, much of this material reaches back to the very beginnings of Israel's historical existence, being pre- or non-Israelite in origin. Kilian (1963), using mostly literary-critical methods, attempted to reconstruct the literary process which produced the present shape of the original H (essentially Leviticus 18–25). He concluded that Leviticus 17 is not part of H proper. Feucht (1964) proposed the reconstruction of two corpora which were later combined into H: H 1 (= chaps. 18–23A [= vv 9–22]; Num 15:37–41) and H 2 (chaps. 25–26). At the same time, he considered chaps. 17, 23B (= vv 4–8, 23–37), and 24 to be later additions. Elliger (*Leviticus* HAT) denied the existence of an originally independent legal corpus, positing instead two main redactional hands (Ph^1 and Ph^3) with two related supplementary layers (Ph^2 and Ph^4) which took independent legal texts and brought them into their present literary context (with some textual relocation during this literary process). For Elliger, no independent legal corpus can be detected in this material. Thiel (1969) argued that both a homiletic (originally oral) and a priestly redaction are reflected in H. The later homiletic material presupposes the Deuteronomistic preaching, as its affinity with Ezekiel and its priestly redaction shows. Thiel therefore dates the composition of H to the exilic period. Wagner (1974) rejected the identification of Leviticus 17–26 as a distinct corpus. In its place, Wagner sees several themes treated in Exodus 25–Leviticus 25: (1) the sanctuary, Exodus 25–31; (2) rituals, Leviticus 1–7; (3) cultic impurity, Leviticus 11–22, and (4) calendric concerns, Leviticus 23, 25, for which Leviticus 26 forms the conclusion. Using redaction-critical methods Cholewinski (1976) reconstructed a highly complex composition process involving several compositional strata, some of which involve more than one redactional hand. He too denied the existence of H as an originally independent legal corpus (following Elliger). Knohl (1987) isolates a Holiness School (distinct from the Priestly and Deuteronomistic schools) whose redactional activities are also found in the legislation of Exodus, Leviticus, and Numbers.

A number of critical issues emerge from the history of research. The most important is the question, does an originally independent legal corpus lie beneath Leviticus 17–26 in its present shape, and if so, what is its date of composition? The arguments in favor of such a view are linguistic, formal, and theological in nature. Linguistically, there are numerous words and phrases which are found only (or mostly) here, and on this basis other texts (notably Exod 31:12–17; Lev 11:1–23, 41–47; Num 15:37–41) are sometimes assigned to the original corpus (Wurster 1884: 123–27; Driver 1913: 59). Formally, the subscription in 26:46 clearly brings a corpus of some kind to a close, and it is often argued on the basis of analogy with Deuteronomy 12 and Exod 20:24–26 that Leviticus 17 is the opening section of the code which 26:46 concludes, though the connection between chap. 17 with chaps. 18–26 is often denied (e.g., Kilian 1963: 176–79). Some scholars hold that 17:2 ("This is what Yahweh commands") constitutes the original superscription for this unit, but this is doubtful. Theologically, the content of some of the legislation appears to contradict other Priestly texts. The date of this originally independent corpus is hotly debated, with pre-Deuteronomic and post-Deuteronomic dates (some as late as the exilic period) finding their advocates. The lack of any structural integrity to the reconstructed corpus, acknowledged by virtually all interpreters, does not bolster the case for this view. Klostermann puts it well: "Lev. 18–26 preserves only fragments of a more comprehensive legislation" (1893: 378). Moreover, assuming the originally independent status of the legislation contained in these chapters, one would expect to find at least one redactional stratum which cuts through or presupposes the existence of an originally independent corpus; but attempts to identify such a layer have not resulted in any consensus. The following formal considerations are not suggestive of an originally independent legal corpus: (1) the plurality of speech report formulae (17:1; 18:1; etc.); (2) the two compliance reports (21:24; 23:44); (3) the repetition of material within the corpus (e.g., 19:3 = 19:30; 19:4, 30 = 26:1–2; 19:5–8 = 22:29–30 [cf. Lev 7:15–18]; 19:9–10 = 23:22; 19:27–28 = 21:5; 19:31 = 20:6; 19:34 = 24:22; 20:6–8 = 20:27; 25:18–19 = 26:4–5). From a historical perspective, the fact that the earliest recoverable literary layer of some of the laws may be relatively old (e.g., chaps. 18, 19), while others are demonstrably post-Deuteronomistic or Priestly (see below) is also problematic for the assumption that an originally independent legal corpus lies beneath this material. Finally, the subscription in 26:46 mentions "laws" (Heb *tôrōt*), but the word *tôrâ* does not appear in Lev 17:1–26:45, though it appears with some frequency in other portions of Leviticus (chaps. 6–7; 11–15). No consensus has as yet been reached, but the arguments against seeing an original independent legal corpus are compelling. Second, the relationship between H and the preaching of the prophet Ezekiel (one part of the larger question of the relationship between Ezekiel and P; cf. Haran 1979) is striking, so much so that earlier interpreters identified the author (Graf 1866: 81–83) or compiler (Horst 1881: 69–95) of H as Ezekiel, though Klostermann (1893: 385–416) argued that Ezekiel's preaching is wholly dependent on H. Some vocabulary is found only (or mostly) in these two corpora (cf. Horst 1881: 72–79). More importantly, Ezekiel appears to know some of the legislation presently contained in H (cf. especially Ezek 14:1–11; 18:5–17; chap. 20; 22:6–12; 34:25–31). Pfeiffer (1948: 241–46; cf. Zimmerli *Ezekiel 1* Hermeneia, 52) argued that the relationship moves in two directions: Ezekiel knows the legislation while the compiler (to whom Pfeiffer assigned the parenetic sections) knows Ezekiel, and this appears to be the consensus of recent scholarship. The third critical problem concerns the relationship between the (parallel) legislation of H and Deuteronomy 12–26 (Cholewinski 1976; Bettenzoli 1984). (Traditiohistorically, both corpora harken back to the Covenant Code of Exodus 21–23, the oldest legal corpus preserved from ancient Israel.) Thus, Lev 17:1–9 is often thought to presuppose the Deuteronomic demand for cult centralization which here takes the form of the Tent of Meeting. The earliest form of the festival calendar of chap. 23 already appears to be later than Deut 16:1–16 (and closer to Numbers 28–29), while the Sabbatical Year legislation of Lev 25:2–7 presupposes the seven-year cycle of Deut 15:1. The nature of the historical relationship between Leviticus 26 and Deuteronomy 28 (within the context of similar ANE rewards and punishments) remains a subject of dispute.

Bibliography

Baentsch, B. 1893. *Das Heiligkeits-Gesetz Lev XVII–XXVI: Eine historisch-kritische Untersuchung.* Erfurt.

Bassett, F. W. 1971. Noah's Nakedness and the Curse of Canaan: A Case of Incest? *VT* 21: 232–37.

Begrich, J. 1936. Die Priesterliche Tora. Pp. 63–88 in *Werden und Wesen des Alten Testament,* ed. P. Volz, F. Stummer, and J. Hempel. BZAW 66. Berlin.

Bettenzoli, G. 1984. Deuteronomium und Heiligkeitsgesetz. *VT* 34: 385–98.

Cholewinski, A. 1976. *Heiligkeitsgesetz und Deuteronomium.* AnBib 66. Rome.

Cortese, E. 1981. L'esegesi di H (Lev. 17–26). *RivB* 29: 129–46.

Driver, S. R. 1913. *An Introduction to the Literature of the Old Testament.* 9th ed. Edinburgh.

Eerdmans, B. D. 1912. *Alttestamentliche Studien 4: Das Buch Leviticus.* Giessen.

Elliot-Binns, L. E. 1955. Some Problems of the Holiness Code. *ZAW* 67: 26–40.

Feucht, C. 1964. *Untersuchungen zum Heiligkeitsgesetz.* ThArb 20. Berlin.

Gerstenberger, E. S. 1965. *Wesen und Hekunft des "apodiktischen Rechts."* WMANT 20. Neukirchen.

Gilmer, H. W. 1975. *The If-You Form in Israelite Law.* SBLDS 15. Missoula, MT.

Graf, K. H. 1866. *Die Geschichtlichen Bücher des Alten Testaments.* Leipzig.

Haran, M. 1979. The Law Code of Ezekiel XL–XLVIII and Its Relation to the Priestly School. *HUCA* 50: 45–71.

Horst, L. 1881. *Leviticus XVII–XXVI und Hezekiel: Ein Beitrag zur Pentateuchkritik.* Colmar.

Kilian, R. 1963. *Literarkritische und formgeschichtliche Untersuchung des Heiligkeitsgesetzes.* BBB 19. Bonn.

Klostermann, A. 1893. Ezechiel und das Heiligkeitsgesetzes. Pp. 368–418 in *Der Pentateuch: Beiträge zu seinem Verständnis und seiner Entstehungsgeschichte.* Leipzig.

Knierim, R. P. 1989. The Problem of Ancient Israel's Prescriptive Legal Traditions. *Semeia* 45: 7–25.

Knohl, I. 1987. The Priestly Torah Versus the Holiness School: Sabbath and the Festivals. *HUCA* 58: 65–117.

Kornfeld, W. 1952. *Studien zum Heiligkeitsgesetz (Lev 17–26).* Vienna.

Küchler, S. 1929. *Das Heiligkeitsgesetz. Lev. 17–26: Eine literarkritisch Untersuchung.* Königsberg.

Liedke, G. 1971. *Gestalt und Bezeichnung alttestamentlicher Rechtssätze.* WMANT 39. Neukirchen.

Paton, L. B. 1894. The Relation of Lev. XX to Lev. XVII–XIX. *Hebraica* 10: 111–21.

———. 1897. The Original Form of Leviticus XVII–XIX. *JBL* 16: 31–77.

———. 1898. The Original Form of Leviticus XXI, XXII. *JBL* 17: 149–74.

———. 1899. The Original Form of Leviticus XXIII, XXV. *JBL* 18: 35–60.
Pfeiffer, R. H. 1948. *Introduction to the Old Testament.* New York.
Rabast, K. 1948. *Das apodiktische Recht im Deuteronomium und im Heiligkeitsgesetz.* Hermsdorf.
Rad, G. von. 1953. Form Criticism of the Holiness Code. Pp. 25–36 in *Studies in Deuteronomy.* SBT 1st ser. 9. London.
Rattray, S. 1987. Marriage Rules, Kinship Structures and Family Structure in the Bible. *SBLSP,* 537–44.
Reventlow, H. Graf. 1961. *Das Heiligkeitsgesetz: Formgeschichtlich untersucht.* WMANT 6. Neukirchen.
Richter, W. 1966. *Recht und Ethos: Versuch einer Ortung des weisheitlichen Mahnspruches.* SANT 15. Munich.
Schultz, H. 1969. *Das Todesrecht im Alten Testament.* BZAW 114. Berlin.
Thiel, W. 1969. Erwägungen zum Alter des Heiligkeitsgesetzes. *ZAW* 81: 40–73.
Tiffany, F. C. 1978. *Parenesis and Deuteronomy 5–11 (Deut. 4:45; 5:2–11:29).* Claremont, CA.
Wagner, V. 1974. Zur Existenz des sogenannten »Heiligkeitsgesetzes«. *ZAW* 86: 307–16.
Wellhausen, J. 1963. *Die Composition des Hexateuchs.* 4th ed. Berlin.
Wurster, P. 1884. Zur Charakteristik und Geschichte des Priestercodex und Heiligkeitsgesetzes. *ZAW* 4: 112–23.

HENRY T. C. SUN

HOLOFERNES (PERSON) [Gk *Olophérnēs*]. The arch-enemy of the Jews in the book of Judith. Though ms evidence fluctuates between *holo-* (= Vg) and *olo-,* the latter is clearly original to the Greek text. Likewise original is *olo-* as opposed to *oro-,* the more correct Persian form of the name. Inscriptional and numismatic evidence from Priene and Knidos of the 2d century B.C. gives both spellings, and literary evidence likewise attests some fluctuation. Polybius (3, 5.2; 32, 10; 33, 6) and Aelian (*Var. Hist.* 2, 41) support *oro-,* while Appian (*Syr. Wars* 47) and Diodorus (31, 19.2–3, 7) read *olo-*. Because of uncertainty in the mss, editions vary on the aspiration of *olo-*.

Second in command to Nebuchadnezzar, "king of Assyria," Holofernes was sent to wreak vengeance on "the entire western region" for failure to obey a royal call to arms against "Arphaxad king of the Medes." The punitive expedition is said to have taken place shortly after the Jews' return from exile. Part of its alleged purpose was the destruction of local cults in order to promote the worship of Nebuchadnezzar.

When Holofernes stood poised to capture the (unknown) Jewish town of Bethulia, the reputed gateway into Judea, with its inhabitants suffering from lack of water and contemplating surrender, Judith, a pious widow, set out for the enemy camp. Armed with piety, beauty, and cunning, she killed the great general, whose severed head was carried to Bethulia as a trophy and hung from its wall.

How the author came by Holofernes as the name for one of the protagonists in his romance is not clear. No general of the historical Nebuchadnezzar is likely to have borne a Persian name. A broad consensus of modern scholarship, however, assigns the book to Maccabean times and sees it as a reflection of Jewish altercations with the Syrian government. Interesting parallels have been noted between the Seleucid general Nicanor (cf. 1 Macc 7:26–49) and Holofernes. Connection with Orofernes, a Cappadocian prince who in 159/58 B.C. usurped the throne with the assistance of Demetrius I Soter of Syria (who sent Nicanor against the Jews), seems not unlikely. The new king lost no time in making himself odious on account of his avarice. Moreover, almost two hundred years earlier (341 B.C.) another Cappadocian prince by the same name had assisted Artaxerxes III Ochus in his reconquest of Egypt. Our author may have fused the two Cappadocian princes as a basis for his Holofernes.

Bibliography

Dumont, A. 1872. *Inscriptions céramiques de Grèce.* Paris.
Hicks, E. L. 1885. Judith and Holofernes. *JHS* 6: 261–74.
Sherk, R. K. 1969. *Roman Documents from the Greek East.* Baltimore.

ALBERT PIETERSMA

HOLON (PLACE) [Heb *ḥōlôn*]. One of the most obscure levitical cities in the Judah/Simeon list. There are numerous textual variations, which present some difficulties when reconstructing the text. The Hebrew name in Josh 21:15 is *ḥōlōn,* while 1 Chr 6:43—Eng 6:58 reads *ḥîlēn.* See HILEN (PLACE). Albright (1945: 66) has suggested that the original vocalization was *ḥîlôn* which later became *ḥîlên* by dissimilation, which is closer to the form presented in the MT of the Chronicler. The different LXX texts also show variations in the spelling of the name. These variations indicate that this city was either not well known or not known at all by the copyists of the Scripture. Besides the references to Holon/Hilen in the levitical city lists, the city's name appears in only one other text. Holon was assigned to Judah as one of the villages in the hill country district of Debir (Josh 15:51). There are no references to Holon/Hilen in any ancient nonbiblical texts.

Biblical Holon has been identified with Khirbet ʿAlîn (M.R. 152118) by scholars such as Albright (1924: 10–11) Simons (*GTTOT,* 201) and Wright (*WHAB,* 124). Khirbet ʿAlîn is bordered on the immediate W and NW by a narrow valley, which in turn is separated from a major valley by a fairly broad ridge. To the E the mound slopes gently into a saddle which then rises to another hill, higher than ʿAlîn. S of ʿAlîn there are also mountains directly blocking the view; however, SW of the tell the valley basin continues. Directly to the N are low rolling hills and a wadi; 2 km to the N the high mountains begin. Khirbet ʿAlîn can be described as a mound completely surrounded by hills to the N and S with a valley on the W and, to the E, hills except for the wadi pass. The terrain indicates that the tell was isolated from the normal flow of traffic found on major or secondary roads. See Peterson 1977: 509–16.

At Khirbet ʿAlîn there appears to be virtually no artificial mound resulting from accumulation of habitation debris. Although Guérin (1869: 340) was the first geographer to visit the site, he made no identification. It was Albright (1924: 11) who first argued for its identification as Holon on philological grounds and the following year he (1925: 9) found Early Iron pottery from the second phase (10th–6th centuries) and Byzantine sherds.

Cross and Wright (1956: 220) reinstituted interest in the identification of biblical Holon with Khirbet ʿAlîn in their boundary and province list study. They pointed out the one serious difficulty of associating ʿAlîn with this biblical city: it had been "displaced" from Province VIII (Beth-zur) into Province V (Debir). However, because of the inexactness of the references to the city there are no other "candidates" for the site on philological grounds in Province VIII. The "movement" that occurred must be one of the reasons why the LXX had such a difficult time with this city. Not only was Holon out of its province, but Khirbet ʿAlîn was an obscure town, very difficult to visit.

Bibliography

Albright, W. F. 1924. Researches of the School in Western Judea. *BASOR* 15: 2–11.

———. 1925. Topographical Researches in Judea. *BASOR* 18: 6–11.

———. 1945. The List of Levitic Cities. Pp. 49–73 in *Louis Ginzberg Jubilee Volume.* New York.

Cross, F. M., and Wright, G. E. 1956. The Boundary and Province Lists of the Kingdom of Judah. *JBL* 75: 202–26.

Guérin, M. V. 1869. *Description géographique, historique et archéologique de la Palestine.* Vol. 3: Judee. Paris.

Peterson, J. L. 1977. *A Topographical Surface Survey of the Levitical "Cities" of Joshua 21 and I Chronicles 6.* Diss. Seabury-Western Theological Seminary.

JOHN L. PETERSON

HOLY OF HOLIES. See TEMPLE, JERUSALEM.

HOLY ONE

HOLY ONE [Heb *qādoš*]. A title used in the Hebrew Bible for God. The most frequent use of the title is in the book of Isaiah, where the phrase occurs thirty times as a reference to Yahweh. The term appears also in the writings of some of the other prophets (Hosea, Jeremiah, Ezekiel, and Habakkuk), in the book of Psalms, and in Job. To speak of God as "the Holy One" is to emphasize God's separateness, God's otherness, God's mystery. This idea is expressed in Hos 11:9 when Yahweh says, "I am God and not man, the Holy One in your midst." Likewise, Deutero-Isaiah reports the words of "Yahweh your God, and of the Holy One of Israel," who says, "My thoughts are not your thoughts, neither are your ways my ways" (Isa 55:8). In the NT, Jesus is called the Holy One (Gk *hagios,* Mark 1:24; Luke 4:34; John 6:69; Acts 3:14; Rev 3:7; cf. 1 John 2:20 where "the Holy One" could be God or Jesus).

MITCHELL G. REDDISH

HOLY PLACE. See TEMPLE, JERUSALEM.

HOLY SEPULCHER, CHURCH OF THE.

HOLY SEPULCHER, CHURCH OF THE. The Gospels agree that Jesus was buried in a tomb belonging to Joseph of Arimatheia (Matt 27:57; Luke 23:50–51; John 19:38) and that after his burial the entrance to the tomb was blocked with a stone (Matt 27:60; Mark 15:46; Luke 24:2; John 20:1). Luke explicitly says (23:53) that the tomb was hewn from stone, and Matthew (27:60) and John (19:41) indicate that it was new; Matthew adds that Joseph had meant it for himself. John (19:41–42) states that the tomb was in a garden near the place where Jesus was crucified and that the place of execution was "nigh to the city" (19:20). This was known as the place of the skull (Luke 23:33, translated as Calvary) or in Hebrew, Golgotha (Matt 27:33; Mark 15:22; John 19:17). From the Epistle to the Hebrews it is clear that it was outside the walls of Jerusalem at the time: Jesus suffered "without the gate" (13:12—an analogy is being drawn with the sin offerings made by the priests as in Exodus 29:14).

The site at Jerusalem which has been venerated since at least the reign of Constantine the Great (306–37) as the place of Christ's death on Golgotha-Calvary and his burial in the tomb in the garden is now covered by the Church of the Holy Sepulcher where worship is offered by various Orthodox Churches and by the Roman Catholics. The history of the building is complex. A comprehensive account was given earlier in this century by Fathers Vincent and Abel (1912–26), but restoration work between 1960 and 1980 made possible important archaeological investigations, which have resulted in lectures by Father Coüasnon (1974) and a comprehensive report by Father Corbo (1981). Problems remain in understanding the history of the buildings, but the excavations suggest nothing on the site at the time of Christ that is incompatible with the gospel stories.

According to the Gospels, Christ was crucified and buried outside the city. Although the Holy Sepulcher is within the present Old City of Jerusalem, it stands on ground which at the time of Christ was outside the walls; the "second wall" of Jerusalem built by Herod the Great (37–4 B.C.) was not supplemented by the "third wall" until the reign of Herod Agrippa (A.D. 41–44). The distinction between the old wall and the outer wall was still apparent to a writer of the mid–4th century A.D. (Cyril H. *Catech.* 14.9). Outside the present Damascus Gate, which stands above a gate in the "third wall," is a cave known as the Garden Tomb, which was identified as the tomb of Christ by the zealous General "Chinese" Gordon during a visit to the city in 1882–83; his reasoning is reproduced by Wilkinson (1978: 198–200). Archaeology has established the chronology of the walls more firmly since the time of Gordon and his identification is no longer credible.

The excavations under the present Church have shown that between the 7th and 1st centuries B.C., the site of the Holy Sepulcher was a quarry for malaky stone. When this was abandoned at the beginning of the Christian era, the area was given over to burials and gardens: "we can picture to ourselves some patches of fertile ground among rocky cliffs" (Corbo 1981: II, plate 67). Two tombs of the period survive at the site, the traditional Tomb of the Lord and that known to the excavators as Tomb 28 (Corbo 1981: I, 31–32). The latter is of the *kokh* type, designed to hold several burials in *kokhim* (ovens) radiating from a central passage. The Tomb of the Lord, now surmounted by an aedicule and severely damaged in 1009, was a cave with a rock-cut bench intended to accommodate a single body. It seems that it originally had, like other tombs of this type, a rock-cut antechamber, destroyed in the 4th century during the process of Christian adornment (Cyril H. *Catech.* 14.9). At the same time the cliff from which the Tomb of the Lord had originally been carved was cut down to ground level to leave it in freestanding splendor. At a stone's throw from the tomb is a rocky eminence, venerated as Golgotha-Calvary, the site of the Crucifixion; this was similarly isolated in the 4th century by having the rock around it cut back. However, parts of the present church do still rest on the cuttings of the quarry (Corbo 1981: III, photo 11, 12, 29, 37, 54–55).

The site remained unbuilt upon until the time of the emperor Hadrian, who in A.D. 135 put down a Jewish revolt, expelled the Jews from their homes, and refounded Jerusalem as a Roman *colonia* named, after himself, Aelia Capitolina (Eus. *Hist. Eccl.* 4.6.3; Dio Cass. 69.12–13). The area immediately contiguous to the Holy Sepulcher was laid out as the forum and the site of the sepulcher itself became sacred to Jupiter and Venus (Hieron. *Ep.* 58. 3; Eus. *Vita C.* 3.26 mentions only Aphrodite). The Hadrianic construction involved considerable filling-in of the former quarry, thereby preserving the configuration of the land beneath the temple. Stretches of wall from Hadrian's temple survive, for instance under the Crusader façade of the present church (Corbo 1981: II, plate 68).

Hadrian's temple survived until after the emperor Constantine (306–37) became master of the eastern half of the Roman Empire in 324, when it was replaced by a great church. The earliest surviving reference to Constantine's constructions is made by a pilgrim from Bourdeaux who made a visit in 333; his summary account mentions Golgotha, the tomb a stone's throw from it and the basilica built by Constantine with its font (*Itin. Burdig.* 593.4–594.4). The fullest account is in Eusebius's *Life of Constantine* (3.25–40), which also reproduces a letter of the emperor to Macarius, Bishop of Jerusalem (*Vita C.* 3.30–32); this *Life* was left unfinished by Eusebius when he died in 339 and combines the characteristics of a history and a panegyric (Barnes 1981: 265–71). The oration given by Eusebius on the occasion of the dedication of the church in 335 survives in his *Triaconteterieus* or *Praise of Constantine* (*l.C.* 11–18). Further evidence comes from the *Catechetical Orations* ascribed to Cyril, Bishop of Jerusalem, in the third quarter of the 4th century, and from the description of her pilgrimage by Egeria, who spent three years in Jerusalem in the early 380s (*Itin. Egeriae*). The accounts of the Bourdeaux Pilgrim and Egeria have been translated with copious annotation by Wilkinson (1981).

Eusebius describes Constantine's intention as the removal of Hadrian's temple from the traditional site of Christ's death and resurrection (*Vita C.* 3.25–27). It came as a surprise that once the overburden had been removed the "most holy cave" of the Tomb of the Lord was revealed (*Vita C.* 3.28); Eusebius understands the event as a type of the resurrection itself. The letter of Constantine expresses similar wonder (*Vita C.* 3.29) and gives the bishop facilities to build a magnificent church on the spot (*Vita C.* 3.31–32). It is not possible to look behind Eusebius's narrative at Constantine's intentions. In other places the emperor had temples destroyed simply to eliminate pagan cults (e.g., *Vita C.* 3.54–58), but at the Holy Sepulcher he is said explicitly to have wanted to purify the place which had seen the Resurrection. Though the substantial survival of the tomb was a wonder, there was, Eusebius implies, no difficulty about where to look for it.

Eusebius also describes the visit to the Holy Land of Constantine's mother, the empress Helena, in 326–27, but does not associate her with the Holy Sepulcher; he ascribes to her only two foundations in the Holy Land, those over the "sacred caves" of the Nativity at Bethlehem and at the place of the Ascension on the Mount of Olives (*Vita C.* 3.41–45). See HELENA (PERSON). Egeria in the 380s is the first to associate her with the buildings at the Holy Sepulcher (*Itin. Egeriae* 25.9).

Though he says that Constantine's constructions were "sacred to the Saving Sign" (*l.C.* 9.16), Eusebius does not mention the Invention of the Cross. However the relic of the True Cross was venerated already in the mid–4th century (Cyril H. *Catech.* 10.19) and Egeria describing the kissing of the cross during the Good Friday ceremonies says that it was closely guarded by the clergy because on a previous occasion one of the faithful had bitten off and carried away a mouthful of it. It is not until the end of the 4th century that stories are told associating Helena with the Invention (Gel. Caes. *fr.* 20; Amb. *In ob. Theod.* 46).

By the end of the 4th century there were two principal buildings at the site of the Holy Sepulcher, which came to be known as the Martyrium and the Anastasis. The entrance from the street was from the east; a courtyard gave onto a large five-aisled basilica, the Martyrium. The apse of this basilica was at its west end. Beyond it was a further courtyard from which eight doors led into a rotunda, the Anastasis, in the center of which, surrounded by columns, was the profusely decorated Tomb of the Lord. In the SE corner of the second courtyard rose the stony outcrop of Golgotha-Calvary (Corbo 1981: I, 94–100). The chronology of these buildings raises difficulties. The solemn dedication by many bishops, with costly offerings of gold and silver, at which Eusebius spoke, took place in September 335 (Eus. *Vita C.* 4.43–47). The Martyrium was clearly by this time complete; Eusebius describes the glittering sea of its gilded ceiling (*Vita C.* 3.36). Eusebius mentions also the adornment of the Tomb of the Lord and the highly polished courtyard in front of it (*Vita C.* 3.34–35). Father Coüasnon (1974: 15) suggested that although "the Rotunda over the Tomb was, indeed, part of the original project of Constantine," the lengthy works involved in quarrying the cliffs around the tomb for the blocks from which the rotunda was built meant that it was not completed in the lifetime of Constantine or his biographer. Father Corbo, on the other hand, has argued that there was not only a single program of work but that it was carried out all at one time (1981: I, 51). There is also disagreement between reconstructions of details of the building, such as the half-columns which form a circle around the Tomb of Christ. What is certain is that when Egeria frequented the Holy Sepulcher in 381–84 both the Martyrium and the Anastasis were being used for worship and continued to be the focus of great devotion throughout Late Antiquity.

Liturgy evolved in and around the holy places. Lectures given to catechumens in the middle of the 4th century at the Holy Sepulcher (Cyril H. *Catech.* 4.10) show how the drama of baptism during the Easter vigil fitted into a larger program of observances (19.32–33); they also suggest the deeper levels of meaning to be found in the physical relics which had witnessed the Resurrection: "the Holy Sepulcher is his witness and the stone which lies there to this day" (10.19). Egeria gives a vivid account of the Holy Week ceremonies, and also of the regular worship. She describes the Anastasis in the early morning ablaze with lamps, and the incense offered with prayers and psalms "so that the whole Anastasis basilica is filled with the smell." Then the bishop, standing at the door of the cave, read the story of the Resurrection from the gospel: "at the beginning of the reading the whole assembly groans and laments at what the Lord underwent for us and the way that they weep would move even the hardest heart to tears" (24.9). The Armenian liturgy published by Dom A. Renoux (1969) gives details of what was done in the early 5th century.

Golgotha came to be thought the center of the world (Cyril H. *Catech.* 13.28). Even before Constantine, Christians had come to Palestine "for the purpose of prayer and investigation of the sacred places" (Eus. *Hist. Eccl.* 6.11.2); subsequently their numbers increased and in the circuit of their visits, the Holy Sepulcher customarily came first (Wilkinson 1976: 95–101). Those who left accounts of their visits include the Bourdeaux Pilgrim of 333; Egeria, an abbess from Spain or Gaul; a pilgrim from Piacenza in Italy of ca. 570; and Arcult, a Gallic bishop whose observations were recorded by Adamnan, Abbot of Iona (died 704). These have all been edited in *Itineraria et alia geographica* (1965), and the last two translated by Wilkinson (1977).

Some visitors came to stay; by the end of the 4th century these included Christians from the Greek east, such as Euthymius from Melitene near the Persian frontier; fashionable Roman ladies such as Melania the Elder and the religious friends of Jerome; and, for eighteen years in the mid–5th century, the empress Eudocia herself. It is typical that Euthymius's first visit was to the True Cross and the Anastasis (Cyril of Scythopolis *Life of Euthymius* 14.1).

From Jerusalem relics spread across the Christian world. Already in the mid–4th century pieces of the True Cross had been "distributed piecemeal to all the world" (Cyril H. *Catech.* 13.4; cf. 4.10; 10.19 and Frolow 1961). Pilgrims took home flasks of oil which had been blessed by being placed against the cross—the oil boiled on contact (*Itin. Antonini Placentini* 20). Some of these flasks survive, and some bear engravings of the Tomb of the Lord; Weitzmann (1974) discusses these and other artifacts he considers to be associated with the holy places. Stories also spread, especially about Constantine and the True Cross; a tale from Egypt has been published, with references to other legends, by Orlandi, Pearson and Drake (1980).

The buildings of the Holy Sepulcher were burnt by the Persians in 614 (Antiochus Strategus 510), but did not suffer irreparable damage. When the Caliph ʾUmar received the surrender of Jerusalem on behalf of the Muslims in 637, the patriarch Sophronius showed him around the Holy Sepulcher. Christians were left in undisturbed possession until 1009 when the eccentric Fatimid Caliph Hakim gave orders to destroy the church and even to dig up its foundations. Demolition was thorough, the Tomb of the Lord was attacked with pickaxes and hammers, but parts of the Anastasis, including walls up to a height of over 30 feet, survived. The Byzantine emperor Constantine IX Monomachus eventually provided funds for restoration of the rotunda, which was completed in 1048, and when the Crusaders occupied Jerusalem in 1099 they added to the east of it a church in the Romanesque style. These buildings substantially survive, though they have been damaged at various times, notably by a fire in 1808. Restoration was carried out under the auspices of the Orthodox and Roman Catholic guardians between 1960 and 1980. Pilgrimage and devotion have also been continuous. Pilgrims from the Christian East came to see a visit to Jerusalem in somewhat of the same way as their Muslim neighbors regarded the Haj, and in the years before the revolution, large numbers of simple pilgrims from Russia journeyed to the holy places. The modern pilgrim will find Wilkinson (1978) a convenient guide.

Bibliography

Barnes, T. D. 1981. *Constantine and Eusebius.* Cambridge, MA.

Conybeare, F. C. 1910. Antiochos' Account of the Sack of Jerusalem by the Persians in A.D. 614. *English Historical Review* 25: 502–17.

Corbo, V. C. 1981. *Il Santo Sepolcro di Gerusalemme (The Holy Sepulchre in Jerusalem).* 3 pts. Studium Biblicum Franciscanum 29. Jerusalem.

Coüasnon, C. 1974. *The Church of the Holy Sepulchre in Jerusalem.* Schweich Lectures of the British Academy 1972. London.

Cyril of Scythopolis. 1962. *Life of Euthymius.* Trans. A. J. Festugiere. Les moines d'Orient 3/1: Les moines de Palestine. Paris.

Frolow, A. 1961. *La rélique de la vrai croix.* Archives de l'Orient 7. Paris.

Geyer, P., and Cuntz, O. 1965. *Itineraria et alia geographica.* CChr Series Latina 175–176. Turnhout.

Orlandi, T.; Pearson, B. A.; and Drake, H. A. 1980. *Eudoxia and the Holy Sepulchre: A Constantinian Legend in Coptic.* Testi e documenti per lo studio dellʾ antichita 67. Milan.

Renoux, A. 1969. *Le Codex Arménien Jerusalem 121.* PO 35/1 no. 163. Turnhout.

Vincent, H., and Abel, F. M. 1912–26. *Jerusalem: Recherches de topographie, d'archéologie et d'histoire.* 2 vols. Paris.

Weitzmann, K. 1974. *Loca Sancta* and the Representational Arts of Palestine. *Dumbarton Oaks Papers* 28: 31–55.

Wilkinson, J. 1976. Christian Pilgrims in Jerusalem during the Byzantine Period. *PEQ* 108: 75–101.

———. 1977. *Jerusalem Pilgrims before the Crusades.* Warminster.

———. 1978. *Jerusalem as Jesus Knew It.* London.

———. 1981. *Egeria's Travels to the Holy Land.* Rev. ed. Warminster.

OLIVER NICHOLSON

HOLY SPIRIT. The manifestation of divine presence and power perceptible especially in prophetic inspiration. The concept was only incidental in late biblical thought, but developed in early Judaism and Christianity to a fundamental dogma. Theological conceptions or teachings concerning the spirit are referred to as *pneumatology.*

A. Concept and Occurrence
   1. Concept
   2. Occurrence
B. Secular Greek Usage
   1. Meaning of the Term
   2. History of the Concept
C. Spirit in the OT
   1. Meaning of the Term
   2. History of the Concept

A. Concept and Occurrence.

1. Concept. The combination of the terms "holy" (Heb *qōdeš* [lit. "holiness"]; Gk *hagios*) and "spirit" (Heb *rûaḥ,* Gk *pneuma*) does not occur in Greek literature, and in the OT only in two historically late texts. The juxtaposition of *rûaḥ* and *qōdeš* is oxymoronic in that a concept of dynamic power beyond human control, *rûaḥ,* has been combined with a word of static character, *qōdeš* (Westermann 1981: 224). The combination becomes a technical expression in Christian usage first through the evangelist Luke and in rabbinic literature.

2. Occurrence. The only OT instances of the combination are Isa 63:10, 11; and Ps 51:13. Belonging in the postexilic period, they probably presuppose the foretelling of the gift of the spirit (Ezek 36:26–27), but understand the bestowal of the holy spirit as an individual gift, as do also the following references from the LXX: Ps 142:10; Dan 5:12; 6,4 (Sym); 4:8, 18 (Th); Wis 1:5; 9:17; Sus 45 (Th); Ps Sol 17:37; Sir 48:12. The Apocrypha and Pseudepigrapha likewise contain few instances of the phrase: *Jub.* 1:21 (cf. Ps 51:12, 13); 4 Ezra 14:22; *Ascen.Is.* 5:14 (post-Christian); *Test Lev* 18:11. Philo and Josephus do not attest the combination *pneuma hagion,* but prefer *pneuma theion.* In the pre-NT period it is the scrolls of Qumran which first mention "holy spirit" in this way: 1QS 3:7; 4:20, 21; 8:16; 1QH 7:6; 9:32; 16:2, 3, 12; 18:26; CD 2:12; 5:11; 7:4 and others.

Most NT writings attest the combination (*to*) *pneuma* (*to*) *hagion* or *to hagion pneuma* (both meaning "the holy spirit"). In the earliest NT writings, the letters of Paul (1 Thessalonians, 1–2 Corinthians, Galatians, Romans, Philippians, Philemon), *pneuma hagion* is used only 13 times, as compared with *pneuma* alone, which occurs 113 times. In order to understand Paul's pneumatology, it is primarily the absolute usage (*to pneuma*) or adverbial constructions (*en pneumati*) which must be considered.

In the remaining NT writings likewise, a technical usage of *pneuma hagion* is not yet apparent (see Mark 1:10; cf. Luke 3:22; Matt 3:16; 1 Cor 12:3). Only Luke and John manifest a considered use of the phrase. Luke makes an effort to subsume his broadly developed pneumatology under the expression *to pneuma to hagion,* "the holy spirit." John avoids the phrase *pneuma hagion* in his gospel. Only the Transfigured One imparts the spirit to the community (John 20:22; anticipated in 14:26).

Outside biblical texts, the expression *pneuma hagion* is encountered in the Greek Magical Papyri, which come from the post-NT period (*PGM* 2:69; 3:289; 4:510).

Why, during the NT period, does *pneuma hagion* evolve as a specific element of Christian theology? On the one hand, a borrowing from Qumran usage is probable. On the other hand, it must be noted that in pre-NT times *pneuma* was often qualified in order to clarify a contrast; for instance, in *T. Jud.* 20 "spirit of truth" is contrasted with "spirit of error"; 1QS 3:18–19 contrasts spirits of truth and of blasphemy (cf. *T. Naph.* 10:9 [Heb]). Hence it has been conjectured that *pneuma hagion,* "holy spirit," represents an ethical concept contrasting with *pneuma akatharton,* "unclean spirit" (*TDNT* 6: 396).

The use of this concept provides distance, factually and terminologically, from the neutral use of *pneuma* in Greek-Hellenistic usage. The qualifier *hagion* also implies the beginnings of a personal understanding of spirit analogous to the development of conceptions of the holiness of God (Schmidt 1981). Thus *pneuma hagion* may be understood as a relatively new construction emphasizing the transcendence of the spirit in contrast to the Hellenistic notion of immanence (Kremer 1973: 77). The later rabbinate also speaks of *rûaḥ haqqōdeš,* using this construction to link the spirit with the God manifest in the sanctuary (*TRE* 12: 175).

A survey of references to "holy spirit" in the NT reveals that despite its frequent use in Luke–Acts, the concept remains peripheral compared with the absolute use of *pneuma,* "spirit." Not until the post-NT period, and as a result of the formulation of pneumatological dogma in 381 C.E., does the concept of "holy spirit" move to the center of Christian theology.

The interpretation of the biblical understanding of "spirit," therefore, cannot start with the use of the concept "holy spirit" alone, but must also take into account the semantic field of "spirit" in its entirety, including its derivatives and synonyms. Since the biblical authors in their application of the concept borrow from secular usage both linguistically and with respect to content, it is imperative that the history of religions be considered in any attempt to understand the biblical statements.

B. Secular Greek Usage

1. Meaning of the Term. The Gk noun *pneuma* derives from the verb **pnewo* and denotes air in movement, experienced as wind, breeze, or breath. Even "breath" and "wind" express only a part of the more comprehensive sense of movement implicit in *pneuma.* The concept itself involves a surplus of meaning which must have abetted its spiritualization and metaphorical extension. Contemplation of the animating effect of breathing might have suggested the psychological phenomenon of inspiration (PWSup 14: 387). Notwithstanding such extension, the basic sense of natural energy is retained.

In classical Greek texts the word *pneuma* is used with four discernible meanings: wind, breath, life, and metaphorical extensions of these.

a. Wind. From at least the time of Aeschylus and Herodotos, *pneuma* is used as a synonym for *pnoe/pnoie,* used previously by Homer and Hesiod for "wind" and its reduced and refined materiality (Aesch. *PV* 1086: *anemon pneumata;* further evidence in Leisegang 1922: 35).

b. Breath. The phenomenon of wind in the macrocosm (the natural world) is paralleled physiologically in the microcosm of the human being by the phenomenon of breathing, which can be discerned and measured according to its strength (Eur. *Or* 277). It can even animate inanimate objects such as wind instruments (Eur. *Bacch.* 128).

c. Life. "Spirit" in its connotation of animating power is itself occasionally characterized as life or living being (Aesch. *Pers.* 507: *pneuma biou,* "breath of life"; Polyb. 31.10.4). This is the starting point for the occasional synonymous use of *pneuma* and *psyche,* "breath, life, spirit, soul." But *pneuma* is to be sharply distinguished from *nous,* "mind"; the latter, with its implications of reason, differs practically and theoretically from the dynamic-enthusiastic sense of *pneuma* (Arist. *Metaph.* 11.7 1072b.21).

d. Metaphorical Uses. The word *pneuma* is used metaphorically because the phenomena to which it directly refers are invisible but nonetheless perceptible in their effects; this dichotomy generates a surplus of meaning. A distinction should be made, however, between an initial spiritualization and later religious and mythical metaphysics. The word *pneuma* is used to characterize human-to-human relations and political sentiments (Soph. *OC* 611; Aesch. Supp. 29, 30). In Greek *manticism* (divination), *pneuma* is seen as divine breath inspiring enthusiasm; as *hieron pneuma,* "sacred spirit" (Democr. frg. 18); *mantikon pneuma,* "prophetic spirit" (Plut. *De def. or.* 40); *enthousiastikon pneuma,* "inspired spirit" (Strab. 9.3.5). This *pneuma* imparts knowledge of transcendent events to occasional prophets, priests, and artists.

2. History of the Concept. The earliest evidence of a religious understanding of *pneuma* is found in connection with the inspiration of the oracle of Apollo at Delphi. The god Apollo fills the priestess with his spirit during the cultic event (Eur. *IA* 760–61). The noun *pneuma,* however, does not occur until the 1st century B.C.E. in the context of the somatic-psychic divination of Pythia via the spirit which rises up into her from the earth and enables her to prophesy (Leisegang 1922: 32–34). This Apollinian inspirational mantic was remarkably popular and appears even in the Greek magical papyri of the post-NT period (*PGM* 289). A characteristic feature of the mantic spirit is the circumvention of the individual's rationality and the ecstatic-enthusiastic possession of the person for a limited time (Cic. *Div.* 1.31, 49; *N.D.* 2.6).

Alongside the mantic use, early Greek philosophy employs the term *pneuma* scientifically. According to Anaximenes, macrocosm and microcosm correspond by means of the correlation guaranteed by the spirit (Anaximen. *Vorsokr.* 13 B 2). *Pneuma* moves with the blood through the human veins (Diog. *Apoll. Vorsokr.* 64 B 5). Its seat—here the Sicilian and Hippocratic schools diverge—is either in the heart or in the brain.

Stoicism developed the medical schools' scientific theory of *pneuma* into a comprehensive philosophical theory. Spirit, a sublime material substance superior to the four basic elements, encompasses and permeates the whole cosmos (Chrysipp. *Stoic. SVF* frg. 473; 479; 1027) and is at the same time its rational soul (Zeno *SVF* frg. 88). It is the substance of the godhead and of the individual soul. Spirit represents the god within the human being; indeed, humankind participates in the divine *nous,* "reason" (Seneca *Ep.* 41.2). Here, the distinction between *pneuma* and *nous* upheld by Aristotle is abandoned. In Stoicism, finally, there is frequent evidence of an identification of "spirit" and "god" (Chrysipp. *Stoic. SVF* frag. 310; 913; *TDNT* 6: 356).

C. Spirit in the OT

1. Meaning of the Term. In the OT *rûaḥ* occurs 378 times in Hebrew texts and 11 times in Aramaic passages. Its basic meaning is "wind, moving air," and "breath." Between the latter and the two former there is no strict distinction (Johnson 1964; Lauha 1983: 57–58; *THAT* 2: 727–28). Accordingly, *rûaḥ* may be an onomatopoeic word (Lys 1962: 19–21) connoting the power of wind to move objects. Nominal qualifiers indicate the direction or origin of winds (Jer 13:24; Exod 10:19; Prov 25:23; Ezek 5:10). Verbs reinforce the aspect of its movement (Num 11:31; Ps 103:16) or effect (Isa 7:2; Ps 48:8).

Beyond this essentially physical meaning, *rûaḥ* is used to refer to qualities of human beings, God, and—less frequently—animals and supernatural spirits. Anthropologically (*THAT* 2: 734–42; Wolff 1984: 57–67; Lauha 1983: 57–64), it denotes breath (Jer 2:24; Job 8:2) and psychic states (Ps 76:13; Ezek 3:14). In this context, *rûaḥ* often overlaps *lēb,* "heart, mind" (Josh 2:11; Ezek 21:12). Its intimations of a vitality that expresses itself dynamically attenuate with time, and this trend continues in postexilic literature even as the term comes to stand for the breath of life which God imparts (Isa 42:5) or creates (Isa 57:16). As intimated in Ezekiel 37 and Isa 57:14–21 (in adumbrations of redemption for the exiled community), the gift of the spirit is understood as analogous to creation. Thus *rûaḥ* came to be understood as a term for life itself (*THAT* 2: 736–37).

In the context of demonology, likewise, the basic dynamic meaning "wind, breath" gradually disappears. Originally the focus was on sudden experiences ("spirit of jealousy" [Num 5:14]; "unclean spirit" [Zech 13:2]; "evil spirit from God" [1 Sam 18:10]), but in Judaism this usage eventually devolves into demonology (Bietenhard 1951).

It is not always possible to distinguish theological from profane usage (Wolff 1984: 57; Lys 1962: 336). It was reasonable to associate *rûaḥ* with God in view of the wind's immateriality on the one hand and its palpable power on the other. Furthermore, *rûaḥ* was understood as a means of divine judgment (Exod 14:21; Jonah 4:8): God commands the wind (Ps 104:4), which accompanies God's self-manifestation (Ezek 1:4) or symbolically heralds God's coming (Jer 4:11; Ezek 17:11–13; Hos 4:19).

2. History of the Concept. References to the power of the spirit of God in the OT period occur first with the charismatic judges and ecstatic prophets. Here we seem to be dealing with a temporally limited gift of the spirit for the purpose of executing an extraordinary task (Schunck [1979: 7–30] sees a permanent gift of the spirit). God's spirit touches the charismatic person without human intervention (e.g., a Judge) and he/she in turn inspires a small group of people opposing a large inimical power (Judg 3:10; 11:29; 13:25; 14:6, 9; 15:14; 1 Sam 11:6).

In parallel fashion, early ecstatic prophecy likewise seems to have led to conferral of the spirit to a group (1 Sam 10:10; 19:23). In this context, the reference to the *rûaḥ ʾĕlōhîm*, "spirit of God," points to Canaanite origins of ecstatic prophecy (Schmitt 1977: 270). Ecstasy can be induced (1 Sam 10:5–6 mentions music). As far as the oldest strata of tradition indicate, the spirit does not facilitate words or actions, nor is it related to history. The emphasis, rather, is on ecstasy as manifestation of religious inspiration (Westermann 1981: 226–27). In addition to ecstatic prophets, visionaries also appeal to the *rûaḥ Yhwh*, "spirit of the Lord," or the *rûaḥ ʾĕlōhîm*, "spirit of God" (1 Sam 23:2; Num 24:2). Here, as in the Elijah/Elisha tradition, the gift of the spirit appears for the first time as simultaneously dynamic and static (2 Kgs 2:9).

With the exception of Ezekiel, scriptural prophecy of the 8th–7th centuries does not appeal to the spirit of Yahweh (concerning the exceptions Hos 9:7; Mic 3:8; Isa 30:1; 31:3, see *THAT* 2: 747–48). The classical prophet disappears completely behind his task as messenger and is precisely not characterized by proofs of spiritual power. Not until the exilic and postexilic period is prophecy viewed in retrospect as wrought by the spirit (Neh 9:30; Zech 7:12).

The transition from charismatic leadership to kingship changes the perception of the spirit of God. The dynamic aspect gives way to a static understanding of spirit as related to office. The spirit of Yahweh is bestowed (Num 11:25, 29) and rests on the blessed one (2 Kgs 2:15), who is thus filled with the spirit (Deut 34:9). The rite of anointing (1 Sam 16:13, 14) as well as the laying on of hands (Deut 34:1) symbolizes this change of perception. The gift of spirit and blessing become related concepts. The narrative of 1–2 Kings consistently refers to the "spirit of God" only in the context of royal accession or rule, never as an indication of special deeds or words (Westermann 1981: 227). Though it cannot always be determined with certainty whether this static understanding of spirit has been introduced retroactively from a later time, the notion is clearly present in the expectation of the Messiah king. His actions derive solely from the spirit bestowed on him (Isa 11:2; 42:1; 61:1). See MESSIAH. Alongside the gift of the spirit to the Messiah, we find in the exilic and postexilic writings the announcement of the gift of the spirit to the whole people—chiefly in the form of a word of Yahweh. Here, too, the spirit appears as a permanent gift. The verbs employed indicate this by suggesting a substance in liquid form ("pour out" [Ezek 39:29; Joel 3:1, 2]; "be emptied out" [Isa 44:3; 32:15]). According to Ezekiel, the gift of the spirit enables the people to live according to the commandments (36:27); it creates new life (37:5, 14; cf. Gen 2:7; Eccl 12:7). In addition, there is reference to the "gift of prophecy" (Joel 3:1–5), the end of social inequalities (Joel 3:2 and Jer 31:34), understanding and learning (Isa 29:24), growth in nature (Isa 32:15), peace and community (Isa 32:17), and immediate relation to God (Ezek 39:29).

The LXX translates *rûaḥ* predominantly as *pneuma*. Even though both words originally describe the selfsame reality of moved and moving air, the LXX participates in the completed philosophical extension of the concept. In terms of the history of its impact, the reception of OT statements concerning the spirit concentrates on Ezek 36:26, 27; 37:5–6, 9–10, 14 and Joel 3:1–5, the proof texts for the eschatological gift of the spirit in Judaism and Christianity.

Confronted with the deep depression felt by the exiled community (Ezek 33:10; 37:11), Ezekiel announces over the field of dry bones the gift of the spirit which causes revivification (37:5–6, 14). Whereas Ezek 37:9 suggests the winds from the four points of the compass and 37:5 anthropologically implies the breath, 37:14 unequivocally specifies the "spirit of God" which is given to the dead and animates them. In Ezek 36:26–27a the bestowal of the spirit of God is related to the gift of a new heart (Heb *lēb*) and a new spirit (*rûaḥ*). The gift of the spirit makes Torah obedience possible (36:27b). A subsequent passage (Ezek 39:29) harks back to these statements and at the same time prepares the way for Joel 3:1–5 (Zimmerli *Ezekiel* Hermeneia, 2.321; Wolff *Joel and Amos* Hermeneia, 66).

Joel 3:15 presupposes the traditions of Ezekiel and Deutero-Isaiah. The interest in establishing historical periods for the eschatological events (2:23b, 25; 3:1, 2, 4—Eng 2:28, 29, 31) represents rudiments of apocalyptic thinking. The pouring out of the spirit is the beginning of the day of Yahweh, who passes over converted Israel (2:12, 13). This will be followed by the judgment of the gentiles (4:1–8—Eng 3:1–8) and by cosmic signs (3:3–4—Eng 2:30–31). The consequences of the pouring out of the spirit are prophetic utterances and dreams and visions. The gift of the spirit—a sign, not the content, of the approaching end of time (Volz 1910: 93–94)—establishes a direct relation to God. In concurrence with Zech 12:10 and Ezek 39:29, Joel 3:1–5 (Eng 2:28–32) locates the expectation of the eschatological community of faith not in the cultic restoration according to Torah but in the prophetic relationship to God manifested in God's immediate call (Wolff *Joel and Amos* Hermeneia, 69).

D. Spirit in Judaism

1. Occurrence. a. Doctrine of the Prophetless Era. In rabbinic theology, "spirit of God" and "spirit of prophecy" are used almost synonymously (*y. Sanh.* 10; 28b, 51: if no prophets, then, no holy spirit). This synonymity led to the formation of the rabbinic doctrine stating that after the time of the last prophets, Haggai, Zechariah, and Malachi, the spirit abandoned Israel (*t. Soṭa* 13:2ff); or that since the destruction of the First Temple the spirit left Israel and would be absent from the Second Temple (*b. Yoma* 21b; in detail, Schäfer 1972: 89–111). Historically, however, it is the period of the Maccabeans which manifests a relative absence of prophecy (1 Macc 4:46; 9:27), a situation presumed also by primitive Christianity (Acts 2:17–21; John 7:39; Mark 1:8). Pneumatics, prophets, and an awareness of individual spirit endowment are documented, however, for the intertestamental period (Leivestad 1972–73; Foerster 1961–62). Not until the collapse of the Second Temple and the loss of this cultic center as the locus of God's presence, however, did the notion of a prophetless-spiritless era become a possibility. The decisive stimulus for the formation of this dogma lies in the establishment of the canon. Ezra was the last inspired prophet. The normative period for Israel, therefore, is the time governed by the Law, which ends with Ezra (Smend 1984: 13–20; Barton 1986: 105–16).

There are two further motives contributing to the formation of the doctrine: *2 Bar.* 85:3; 1 Macc 4:46; 9:27; and 14:41 already intimate a tripartite historical schema (prophecy at the time of the First Temple, prophetless present, prophecy of the end-time). Since nomism had prevailed, it needed to disclaim the spirit as a present medium of revelation to the point of asserting that prophecy was dormant.

Concepts in Hellenistic and Palestinian Judaism provide the immediate presuppositions for NT pneumatology. In view of the multiple strata of evidence, only an illustrative understanding can be provided here.

b. Spirit in Philo Judaeus. Philo represents an exponent of Jewish theology of the Hellenistic synagogue of the Diaspora at Alexandria. In an apologetic proselytizing effort, he attempts to square the Stoic-Platonic theory of *pneuma* with the OT statements in the LXX, or rather, to find the former in the latter. See PHILO OF ALEXANDRIA. Consonant with Hellenistic Jewish literature, *pneuma,* according to Philo, denotes wind, air, breath, the human spirit, the spirit of God, and supernatural beings (itemization by Isaacs 1976: 150–52). Cosmologically, *pneuma* is the substance which pervades matter and holds it together (*Aet* 125; *Op* 131; *Heres* 242; cf. Wis 1:7). Anthropological reflection repeatedly refers to Gen 2:7. The natural human being had the gift of *nous,* "reason," but it is *geōdēs,* "earthlike," and *phthartos,* "corruptible" (*Leg All* 1: 32, 37). The inspiration of *pneuma theion,* "divine spirit" (*Op* 135, 144), also provided the *nous* (*Gig* 27) and thus distinguishes the human soul from that of the animal. Thus, humankind is allowed to share in the divine spirit. This qualification reveals the dichotomized view of humanity: the human being consists of *pneuma theion,* "divine spirit," and *geōdēs ousia,* "earthlike being" (*Op* 135; *Heres* 55). Nevertheless, Philo's statements containing the tradition-historical and religio-historical disparities are not consistent within themselves. Animistic and dynamistic notions are intermingled. The Philonic notion that *pneuma prophetikon,* "prophetic spirit," represents the highest gift derives from both Hellenistic and OT-Jewish notions of spirit (Wolfson 1948: 2.26). In analogy to the Platonic critique of inspiration manticism, *pneuma theion* facilitates higher insight than does *nous* (*Heres* 265). Moses is the interpreter gifted with *pneuma theion* and serves as Philo's model.

c. Spirit in the Qumran Texts. Multiple uses of *rûaḥ* are evident also in the Dead Sea Scrolls. Frequently the referent of *rûaḥ* is "human spirit," and the word can often designate the self or a person's attitude. Theologically *rûaḥ* denotes both evil spirits and the holy spirit of God. It also has the meaning "breath" and, far less frequently, "wind" (see Anderson 1962; Nötscher 1957).

The original traditional material of the Qumran community includes the so-called "doctrine of the two spirits" presented in 1QS 3:13–4:26 as basic doctrine (Lichtenberger 1980: 123–42). It postulates that from the outset human behavior is determined by two kinds of spirits which are appointed by God, the spirits of truth and the spirits of wickedness. *Rûaḥ* thus appears to be the predestined existence of humanity. The sons of righteousness and the sons of wickedness are subject to the domination of those spirits. At present, the sons of light are in danger of perdition (1QS 3:24); only the judgment ordained by God will bring future purification when God will pour out his spirit on a part of humankind and thus cleanse it (1QS 4:20, 21).

The work of God's spirit on humanity takes place in three ways according to the Qumran texts: (1) with the gift of the spirit during creation (1QS 9:12; 1QH 9:32); (2) when initiants become part of the community (1QH 13:19; 16:11; 17:17); (3) in the outpouring of the spirit during the end-time (1QS 4: 18–23). However, there is no causal connection between the bath of purification and the gift of the spirit (O. Betz 1960: 133–34; Schreiner 1965: 176–77). It is in character with the exclusive self-consciousness of the community that it claims the presence of the spirit in its midst (and within at least some individuals; note the formula *rwḥ ʾšr ntth by,* "the spirit which you placed in me" [1QH 12:11; 13:19; 16:11; 17:17, etc.; see Kuhn 1966: 130–36]). A specifically eschatological understanding of the presence of the spirit should not be inferred from this, however. Only the end-time will bring the full outpouring of the spirit (1QS 4:2–23 with reference to Exod 36:25–26).

d. Spirit in Rabbinism. A systematic itemization of the particular statements on "holy spirit" in rabbinic literature will schematize the source material. Thus, salient aspects of the rabbinic literature spanning several centuries can be listed together (Goldberg 1969; Schäfer 1972). The construction *rûaḥ haqqōdeš,* lit. "spirit of holiness," implies the divine origin of the spirit. Yet this does not mean that the holy spirit was regarded as a hypostasis distinct from the divine presence (*šĕkînâ*). The holy spirit is a mode of God's self-revelation (Goldberg 1969: 462; *TRE* 12: 174) and is imparted primarily in the sanctuary, the place of God's presence. The high priest has the gift of the spirit qua office (*Lev. Rab.* 21:12; *Yoma* 73). The destruction of the First Temple caused the dormancy of the spirit (*t. Soṭa* 13:2ff). In the interim, the *bat qôl* (lit. "daughter of a voice"; audible divine speech) is a poor substitute. Not until the end-time will the spirit return to the sanctuary (*Num. Rab.* 15:10) as a national charism (*TRE* 12:175). Both the Messiah (*Gen. Rab.* 2:3) and the just will then be spirit bearers. The expectations of salvation follow Ezekiel 36–37 and Joel 3.

In rabbinic literature there is no systematic theory concerning the spirit's presence. Alongside the official charisma of the high priest, there are gifts of the spirit for good works, study of Torah, and keeping the commandments (Schäfer 1972: 127–34).

2. Conclusions. a. The Semantic Field. Under the influence of theological reflection and philosophical speculation, both the Hebrew term *rûaḥ* and the Greek term *pneuma* underwent a semantic development from a concrete, material meaning in everyday language to a metaphysical meaning. The physical sense of the word persisted alongside the new meaning. Thus, *pneuma* is "a word into whose mythical depths everyone has deposited all that fit into his range of ideas, and out of which everyone heard what he could or would, according to the level of his own understanding" (Leisegang 1919: 16). Anthropological and theological use cannot always be strictly distinguished. With Philo, Stoic influence prompted their synonymous use. Thus, the concept of *pneuma* approaches a generic abstraction to which the addition of qualifiers provides specificity. These qualifiers include prepositional expressions (*en pneumati,* "in [the] spirit"), genitival constructions (*to pneuma tou kosmou,* "the spirit of the world"; *to pneuma theou,* "the spirit of God"); coordination of nearly synonymous terms (*pneuma kai dynamis,* "spirit and power"); and antithetical pairs (*pneuma/sarx* "spirit/flesh"; *pneuma/gramma* "spirit/letter"). In the imagination, obvious substances such as water (Sir 24:33; Philo *Op* 135) or fire (frequent in Stoicism; cf. *TDNT* 6: 930) were used increasingly alongside wind, because they were able to convey and promote not only the aspect of external and independent power, but also an understanding of spirit as substance within the sacramental act. Given this OT and Greek-Hellenistic history, it is natural that animistic and dynamistic statements are used interchangeably. Even in the NT a conception of a unique and visible manifestation of the spirit in baptism (1 Cor 12:13) is juxtaposed with instances of intervention and empowerment by the spirit for a specific action (Acts 13:4). The exact meaning of *pneuma* in the NT period can be discovered only by observing the larger context.

b. Anthropology. The contrast between *sōma,* "body," and *psychē,* "soul," in Hellenistic Judaism was enhanced through the influence of Greek-Hellenistic anthropology. The body is of earthly origin, the soul of heavenly origin. No consistent conceptual differentiation between *nous, psychē,* and *sōma* is evident. In the Greek-Hellenistic arena, the Platonic tripartition of the person into *nous, psychē,* and *soma* was normative. Popular usage in the pre-NT period, however, had led to such a generalization of the concept of *pneuma* that its meaning was no longer precisely set (*RAC* 9: 503–4). *Pneuma* could now be used in its anthropological sense to the exclusion of a metaphysical dimension; the juxtaposition of *sarx,* "body," and *pneuma,* "spirit" (Col 2:5), could describe the totality of the human being. The word *pneuma* alone can designate the self (Rom 8:16; *PMG* 12:327).

c. Demonology. In contrast to the idealist concept of "spirit" in F. C. Baur, history-of-religions research into NT pneumatology discovered demonology as a common myth within popular belief (Everling 1888; Dibelius 1909; Weinel alluded directly to demonology in the title of his work *The Effects of the Spirit and of the Spirits* [1899]). NT demonology corresponds to that of ancient Judaism. Good and evil spirits confront each other in their allegiance to the archangel Michael and the devil respectively (*1 Enoch* 19; *Jub.* 10; 22:17; 1QS 3:13–4:26). The evil spirits are often linked to the fallen angels (Genesis 6), or considered fathered by them in intercourse with human women (*1 Enoch* 15). In the Greek-Hellenistic arena, likewise, contrary powers may be called pneumata (*CIG* 3: 5858b; *PMG* 13: 198; 36: 160). The use of terms for the world of the spirits in the NT is as varied as in the Hellenistic Jewish sources: *to pneuma to akatharton,* "the unclean spirit" (Mark 1:23, 26; *T. Benj.* 5:2); *to pneuma to ponēron,* "the evil spirit" (Acts 19:15–16; *1 En.* 99:7); or absolutely ("the spirit[s]"), Mark 9:20; Luke 10:20, to denote evil spirits. In addition, *daimonia* and *daimones* are used frequently. On the other hand, "pneumata" can also denote benign spirits: Acts 23:8, 9; Jos *Ant* 4: 108; Heb 1:14; Rev 1:4.

d. Eschatology. In OT texts, the gift of the spirit to the Messiah (Isa 11:2; 28:5; 42:1; 61:1) and to the people (Ezek 36:27; 37:14; 39:29; Joel 3:1, 2; Isa 32:15; Zech 12:10; Hag 2:5) occur together. Before the NT period, both strands are transmitted independently alongside each other and only in late NT writings are they combined to state that a spirit-endowed Messiah will transmit the spirit to the elect on behalf of God. Sectarian believers claim individual and collective anticipation of the eschatological spirit in the present (*1 En.* 91:1; 4 Ezra 5:22; 14:22; 1QH 7:6, 7; 17:26).

The following texts affirm the gift of the spirit to the Messiah during the end-time: *Pss. Sol.* 17:37; 18:7; *1 En.* 49:3; 62:2; *T. Levi* 18:7; *T. Jud.* 24:2 (the latter passages are a Christian postscript); *Tq. Isa.* 11:2; 42:1–4; 1QS Sb 5:24, 25; 11QMelch 18.

The concept of the latter-day gift of the spirit to the elect relies primarily on Joel 3:1–5 and Ezek 36:27; 37:14, and is extensively attested in the rabbinic literature. Testimony to spirit endowment of the Messiah, conversely, is strikingly rare in the same sources. A few intertestamental texts, moreover, are suspected of having been reworked by Christian redaction: 4 Ezra 6:26; *Jub.* 1:23; *T. Levi* 18:11; *T. Jud.* 24:3; *1 En.* 61:11; 1QS 4: 20–22. *T. Levi* does not witness to the agency of the Messiah in the gift of the eschatological spirit, but rather of God's agency; by contrast *Sib. Or.* 3:528 and *T. Jud.* 24:2 do associate the Messiah with an eschatological gift of the spirit. Both latter texts, however, reasonably suggest Christian interpolation (Becker 1980: 76), so that this whole idea becomes understandable only as a theme of Christian theology.

E. Spirit in the NT

1. Terminology. Of the 379 occurrences of the substantive *pneuma,* only John 3:8, Heb 1:7, and 2 Thess 2:8 reflect the original meaning "wind/breath," the latter two being influenced by OT quotations. In approximately 275 instances *pneuma* must be understood as "spirit of God"; of these, 149 are absolute; *pneuma hagion,* "holy spirit," 92 times; *pneuma hagiosynes,* "spirit of holiness," once (Rom 1:4); *pneuma theou,* "spirit of God," 18 times; *pneuma tou patros,* "spirit of the Father," once. Referring to *Christos* it is used 3 times; as *pneuma tou huiou autou,* "the spirit of his Son," once; and as *pneuma Iesou,* "spirit of Jesus," once. *Pneuma* is used roughly 47 times in the anthropological sense, mostly with reference to breath (Matt 27:50; John 2:26). *Pneuma* may describe the whole human being, like *sōma* and *psychē* (2 Cor 7:1; 1 Thess 5:23), also in rhetorical pathos within the final greetings (Gal 6:18; Phil 4:23; Phlm 25; 2 Tim 4:22) and thus approaches the meaning of "I." Therefore *pneuma* may also be interpreted, under the aspect of the acting and thinking "I," as *pneuma praytētos* (1 Cor 4:21), as the locus of feelings (Luke 1:47), intellect (Luke 1:80), and, in a single instance, as reason (1 Cor 2:11).

Used either absolutely or with modifiers, *pneuma* denotes evil spirits approximately 38 times. Jesus and the disciples attack the *pneumata akatharta,* "unclean spirits" (Mark 1:23); *ponēra,* "evil [spirits]," (Luke 7:21); *alala,* "dumb [spirit]," (Mark 9:17) and exorcise them, since the power of the spirit of God in them overcomes the power of Satan. Unique uses of *pneuma* are Luke 24:37 (ghost); Heb 12:33; 1 Pet 3:19 (souls); Heb 1:14; Rev 1:4; 3:1; 4:5 and 5:6 (angels). Heb 12:9 calls God *pater ton pneumaton* "Father of spirits." The adjective *pneumatikos*, "spiritual," is used 23 times in the NT, and the adverb *pneumatikōs*, "spiritually," 3 times. Beyond its use in contrast to words for the flesh and carnality (*sarkikos/sarkinos/psychikos;* Rom 7:14; 1 Cor 1:15; 3:1; 9:11; 15:44, 46), or its substantival use in reference to things spiritual (Rom 15:27; 1 Cor 9:11) or spiritual persons (1 Cor 14:37; Gal 6:1), the adjective *pneumatikos* is used as a qualifier for the law (Rom 7:14), prayer (Eph 1:3; 5:9; Col 3:16), the Church (1 Pet 2:5), the resurrected body (1 Cor 15:44–46), and sacrifice (1 Pet 2:5).

2. Preliminary Methodological Reflections. In exilic and postexilic Jewish literature, some writings manifest expectation of the future outpouring of the spirit. On the other hand, the NT writings generally regard the gift of the spirit as a present eschatological event. This demarcates the historical location of the NT era. Here we trace the NT evidence for early Christian pneumatology. A review of the history of research will conclude with methodological reflections.

F. C. Baur and H. Gunkel significantly influenced the perception of primitive Christian pneumatology. Baur (1831; 1845) saw in Pauline thought a parallel to his own understanding of existence (which he derived from Hegel; concerning the following see *BTNT* 2: 244–45). Accordingly, he disregarded the lexical content and semantic field of *pneuma*, or rather, he understood it a priori as "spirit" in the sense of absolute self-consciousness. This "spirit" stands in fundamental contrast to what is finite, to flesh, insofar as "spirit" is identical with "spirit of God." This view set forth by Baur could be applied to the understanding of the history of early Christianity at a time when Baur was still uninfluenced by Hegel and when his historical studies had led him to recognize the compelling contrast between Paulinism and Judaism, between pneumatism and nomism.

Baur's idealist view of the NT concept of "spirit" was shaken by Gunkel's phenomenological approach (1888; 3d ed. 1909). To Gunkel, speculation concerning spirit is secondary compared to experiences of, and encounters with, the spirit (1909: 8). Thus he made it his task to describe and sensitively interpret. In the mysterious effects of power and unexplained phenomena, according to Gunkel, we encounter not the subsequent conclusions regarding the power of God by a disinterested outsider, but the immediate experience of one inspired (1909: 3–4). Therefore, according to Gunkel, the exegete must "in some way put himself in the place of the pneumatic to empathize with his experience"; indeed, "he who clings to the letter cannot see the life" (1909: 4, 6).

Even though Gunkel's slogan would soon be passionately contradicted (Bousset 1901; Harnack 1899), the characterization of the NT concept of *pneuma* as a supernatural power which affects life has nevertheless met with appreciation to this very day.

For the present understanding of the NT concept of *pneuma* with its derivatives and related concepts, a survey of its uses in the respective historical contexts of the earliest Christian writings is essential. In contrast to Gunkel, we must not begin with phenomena of the spirit. In so doing we would neglect the religiohistorical parallel phenomena in Judaism and Hellenism, as Gunkel later conceded to Bousset's critique (1909: 5–6). When one disregards these connections, the particularity of NT pneumatology is sought solely in the realm of phenomena. But phenomena themselves are ambiguous and cannot be interpreted unequivocally. And since the conceptual framework evaluates phenomena and experiences, it must be given particular attention in the early Christian tradition.

3. Primitive Christian Preconditions for the Consciousness of Spirit Endowment. All NT writings present the Christian community as a spirit-endowed entity. Late communal theology has anchored this claim in history via a narrative of the event in which the spirit was bestowed. In terms of the history of its impact these ideas represent not the primary form, but the most significant form, of the consciousness of spirit-endowment.

a. Pre-Easter Gift of the Spirit. The redaction of the Gospels has viewed the synoptic mission narrative (Mark 6:6b–13 par) also as a communal missionary etiology. This is reflected in the dramatic framework (Mark 6:6b, 7, 12): the inspired actions of the community reflect the pre-Easter spirit endowment of the disciples through Jesus. The gift of exousia empowers the disciples to subjugate the demons, as was the case with Jesus. Vv 11 and 12 develop the content of this gift, in keeping with the typical spheres of activity of the communal theology. Functions of this spirit endowment are the preaching of repentence (Acts 2:38; Rom 2:4), exorcisms (Acts 19:11, 12; *Acts John* 37), anointing with oil (John 5:14) and healings (Acts 5:16; 8:7; cf. also the lists of charisms 1 Cor 12:9, 28, 30).

b. Gift of the Spirit at Easter. In the Fourth Gospel's account of post-resurrection appearances, Easter and Pentecost are collapsed (John 20:19–23). Jesus appears to the band of disciples and imparts his spirit to them on the evening of the day of resurrection. Comparison with Luke 24:36–49 suggests that John 20:19–23 represents a pre-Johannine tradition which presupposes the Lukan text (Dauer 1984: 207–96). John 20:20–22 combines the act of transmission of the spirit with the explication and function of the gift.

The act by which Jesus imparts the spirit to his disciples is itself a significant biblical allusion. In its use of the verb *enephysēsen*, "he breathed on them" (John 20:22), the gospel tradition recalls the same form in the creation narrative (Gen 2:7 LXX). This would contradict an animistic interpretation of the action. The word of explication ("receive the *pneuma hagion* [Holy Spirit]" John 20:22) likewise suggests a substratum of earliest Christian terminology. The motifs of gift of the spirit and forgiveness of sins are likewise attested together in earliest Christianity (1 Cor 6:11; Titus 3:4–11); John 20:19–23 manifestly represents a stage of communal theological reflection which combines earliest Christian statements and incorporates them into the history of Jesus. This applies to both its content and its place in the history of tradition.

c. Post-Easter Gift of the Spirit. More influential was the position that the post-Easter gift of the spirit occurred on the first Pentecost after Easter (only Acts 2:1–4 in the NT). According to the Lukan construction these events, the outpouring of the spirit, enabled the disciples to preach in foreign languages. Peter's speech following the account (Acts 2:14–36) explains the event as an eschatological fulfillment of Joel 3:1–5 (Eng 2:28–32), but attributes the gift of the spirit to the Exalted One himself (2:33).

Inconsistencies in the text suggest fragments of pre-Lukan tradition. An immediate result of the gift of the spirit is the ability *lalein heterais glōssais,* "to speak in other tongues" (Acts 2:4). Luke interprets this as empowerment to speak in foreign languages, to judge from the observation that each member of the multitude heard the disciples speaking *idią dialektǭ,* "in his own language" (vv 6, 8). Should Luke have also inserted the word *heterais* into this tradition in keeping with this line of interpretation (note that *heteros* appears 52 times in Luke, in Mark and John only once each), and thus critically altered the stock phrase *glōssais lalein,* "to speak in tongues" (Mark 16:17; 1 Cor 12:30; 14:2, 45), then his tradition was probably concerned only with spirit endowment and glossolalia. If v 8 likewise represents an allusion to a miracle of hearing, then it, too, would have fundamentally misunderstood the tradition of a glossolalic phenomenon.

It is therefore conceivable that a fragment of tradition spoke of a glossolalic event, possibly in connection with a house (v 2 differing from v 5). Further details of this event cannot be inferred from the pre-Lukan substance of this text. It is very unlikely, however, that the Jerusalem community could have regarded an outbreak of glossolalia as the advent of the spirit. Glossolalia does not figure among the anticipated phenomena of the eschaton. Apart from isolated remarks (*T. Job* 48–50), it is a phenomenon totally rooted in the Hellenistic world.

The association of this event with the festival of Pentecost in Jerusalem has possibly been influenced by the reinterpretation (after 70 B.C.E.) of Pentecost as the covenant-renewal festival. It is conceivable that the reestablishment of the band of disciples took place on the first festival day after the crucifixion. But this cannot be demonstrated decisively, even with reference to the undated appearance to the 500 (1 Cor 15:6) (see also Dunn 1975: 144–46). The association with Pentecost, in any case, reinforces the universal and public importance which Luke attaches to the Christ event. It is specifically this festival which repeatedly had been the occasion of outbreaks of political rioting (Roloff *Apostelgeschichte* NTD, 40). The three quoted theories, without exception late formations, manifest the need of the community to explain the gift of the spirit within a theory of transmission. However, the fact that all three accounts present Jesus rather than God as the bestower of *pneuma* indicates the late NT location of the notion.

The community's awareness of having received the spirit is not based on one basic event of spirit transmission. It is rather the theological consequence of primitive Christian theology and arises from definite presuppositions about the nature and activity of the spirit.

d. The Spirit and the Raising of the Dead. The conviction that God raised Jesus from the dead (1 Thess 1:10; Gal 1:1; 1 Cor 6:14; Rom 4:24; 8:11; 2 Cor 4:14; Acts 2:32; 3:15) is expressed in some of the oldest Christian formulas (Becker 1976: 14–15; Hoffmann 1982: 14–15).

Because the resurrection of both Jesus (Rom 1, 3, 4; 8:11) and Christians (1 Cor 6:14; 15:45; 2 Cor 3:6; Phil 3:10) is linked to the spirit in early NT tradition, it must be asked whether the eschatological notion implied in the resurrection formula allowed room for the anticipated outpouring of the spirit.

Ezek 37:5, 9–10 had already envisioned the revivification of the dead as an effect of the gift of the spirit. In an altered form this idea is picked up in 2 Macc 7:23; *Jos. Asen.* 8:9; *Soṭa* 9:15; *Exod. Rab.* 48 (102d); *Midr. Ps* 104:30; Rev 11:11. The second of the Eighteen Benedictions offers a direct parallel, in both form and content, for the combination of resurrection and spirit. In the older Palestininan version (which recalls Ezek 37:5; Isa 26:19) it reads : "you make the spirit return . . . which cares for the living and makes alive those who are dead" (Müller 1980: 25–30). Admittedly, the integrity of the text has been questioned. If it is presumed to be intact here, the statement may be seen as the interpretive framework for the resurrection event on the basis of its familiarity in the NT period. The raising of Jesus from the dead is an act of God and, at the same time, evidence of the activity of his spirit (Rom 1:3–4; 8:11).

e. The Spirit and the Activity of Jesus. The primary basis of the believed efficacy of the spirit lies in the Easter experience. The attention of the community is initially focused on the ascended Messiah whose return they anticipate without immediately interpreting his earthly activity as messianic. Gradually however, the community appropriates the OT-Jewish tradition of the spirit-filled Messiah and applies this perception to the earthly activity of Jesus. The redaction of the Gospels gives purposeful expression to this conviction by placing the spirit-baptism at the beginning of the story of Jesus as fulfillment of the messianic prophecies of Mal 3:1 and Isa 40:3 (Mark 1:2–11 par); by the inclusion of Isa 42:1 within the fulfillment quotation Matt 12:18; and by the interpretation of Isa 61:1 implicit in Jesus' inaugural sermon (Luke 4:16–30). Beyond the Easter event, Jesus' claim and activity themselves are likely to have formed the matrix for this application of the tradition of the spirit-filled Messiah to Jesus. Admittedly, not one synoptic word concerning the spirit (Mark 3:29 par; 13:11 par; Matt 12:28; Luke 4:18, 19; 11:13; Matt 28:19; Luke 11:2) can be positively claimed as Jesus' own. Nor does he himself seem to have explicitly appealed to the spirit of God to substantiate his claim. The exorcisms by themselves were ambivalent and certainly did not prove the presence of the spirit (cf. Luke 11:19). On the other hand, isolated images (Luke 10:18; 11:20) can be regarded as veiled metaphorical references to the presence of the spirit (Jeremias 1973: 81–84). Finally, the portrayals of the exorcisms of Jesus as conflicts with satanic powers (Mark 3:27 par); the working of miracles and the proclamation of the kingdom (Luke 6:20 par; Mark 1:15); and the authoritative interpretation of the law attributed to Jesus under the rubric *egō de legō hymin,* "but I say to you" (Matt 5:21 etc.) together yield a total impression which approaches an implicitly pneumatic self-consciousness. Even though Jesus neither declared his deeds as evidence of the spirit nor held out the prospect of a universal gift of the spirit for the future, the community was able to see, retrospectively in the light of the Easter event, confirmation of the working of the spirit in the activity of Jesus.

f. The Eschatological Self-Consciousness of the Church. The factors mentioned so far permitted belief in the present working of the spirit, but not yet awareness of a universal gift of the spirit. Faith in Christ placed Christians in a special position within Judaism, comparable to the sect of Qumran or the groups around baptizers.

It is likely that in the context of this eschatological self-consciousness the anticipated bestowal of the spirit for the end-time was thought to be taking place (Kuhn 1966: 138–39). In the OT tradition itself, the relation between the present and future eschatological spirit was not precisely established (Volz 1910: 93, 94 A1). The reception of Joel 3:1–5—Eng 2:28–32 (Acts 2:17–21; Rom 10:13, etc.) within the Christian community identifies the gift of the spirit as an event preceding the Day of the Lord (Acts 2:20b).

g. Phenomenological Proofs of the Spirit. E. Schweizer has steadfastly maintained as "historically assured" that the primitive Church experienced an outpouring of the spirit in some form (1952: 5; *TDNT* 6: 408; in agreement, Lohse *TDNT* 6:51–52; Goppelt 1978: 298; Kremer 1973:59). Historical analysis, however, demands the following verdict: "All such hypotheses have too little definite evidence in their support to ever become more than interesting possibilities" (Foakes Jackson and Lake 1933: 1.5.121). It has been shown above that in the Palestinian region glossolalia (Acts 2:1–13) would not have been perceived as proof of the anticipated spirit of the end-time. It is a counsel of despair to suspect a different ecstatic experience behind the event described in Acts 2:1–13 (Goppelt 1978: 298). None of the stated phenomena is unequivocal proof of the gift of the spirit. Experiences can only be interpreted in the context of a preexisting self-consciousness or framework of expectation. Historically, a process of interpretation moving back and forth between faith and experience is likely. At the same time, the group situation of the primitive Church and its eschatological ethos (mission, community, expectation of the Messiah, etc.) posed a situation where certain experiences could be understood as the workings of the spirit. In view of the overwhelming number of reports of pneumatic experiences within the early Christian literature of the first two centuries C.E., however, it should be noted that reports of pneumatic experiences do not necessarily always reflect real experiences but could very well have served other purposes as literary inventions (Harnack 1899: 515).

Once these preconditions are appreciated, belief in the outpouring of the holy spirit at or after Easter becomes plausible. Now we trace the development of this notion.

4. The Hellenists. Their eschatological claim to possess the spirit places the group of Hellenists in opposition to the Jewish-Christian community of Jerusalem. Although it is hardly possible to reconstruct an Antiochian source for Acts 6–7, we must nevertheless retain the notion of a preexisting tradition.

The reasons which led to the separation of the Christian Hellenists from the original Aramaic-speaking community probably were linguistic in nature. (Note that the body of leaders elected from among the Hellenists comprises men with exclusively Greek names [Acts 6:5].) The formation of a community for the sole purpose of worship is a common and perfectly legitimate process within Judaism (Hengel 1975: 178).

Historically it is likely that along with the linguistically motivated separation of the Hellenists, a simultaneous theological dispute took place, a dispute which can still be detected below the surface of the Lukan redaction. In the Lukan account, Stephen is portrayed as an early Christian pneumatic. His speech is characterized by "wisdom" and "the Spirit" (Acts 6:10); his deeds, known to all (v 8), are possible because he is filled with the spirit, a fact which the list of names (v 5) emphasizes by setting him apart from the other apostles. Luke linguistically adapted this image of Stephen to that of other pneumatics: *plērēs pneumatos,* "full of (the) Spirit" (Acts 6:3, 5, 8; 7:55; cf. Luke 4:1; Acts 11:24). Moreover, the combination of motifs, wisdom/spirit/working of miracles (Acts 2:22, 43; 7:36), expresses the Hellenistic ideal of the Christian pneumatic. The emphasis on the gift of the spirit is inseparably linked with references to criticism of the law (Acts 6:11, 13, 14; 7:51–53). Acts 6:11 raises the charge of blasphemy provoked by Stephen's utterances against Moses (= Torah) and God. Verse 13 attributes similar charges to false witnesses, but pointedly places criticism of the Temple first. Verse 14 has Stephen say further that Jesus will destroy the Temple and alter the ceremonial law which originated with Moses (*ethē*). The source, or tradition, is presumed by most to be contained in the general statements (v 11) (Conzelmann *Apostelgeschichte* HNT, 51; Hengel 1975: 187). Verse 14, however, is a deliberate variation of the Temple saying in Mark 14:58. It lacks the promise that a new temple will be built and is expanded to include an announcement of the future alteration of the ceremonial law. Roloff (*Apostelgeschichte* NTD, 112–13) surmises that these alterations in the Temple saying represent the interest and bias of the Hellenists. Critique of the Temple and the Temple saying of Jesus have been included, and with them have been combined a criticism and modification of the ceremonial law. That all this is still far from Paul's rejection of the law is perfectly clear to Luke, who renders the anti-Pauline accusations more brusquely (Acts 21:21, 18; 24:5). It can be presumed that the intended effect of this cultural critique was a focus on the true will of God in view of the end-time, similar to Jesus' critique of Temple and culture. The Hellenists, as returned Jews of the Diaspora, hold a more conservative view that separates them from Hellenistic enlightenment theology.

Mention of possession of the spirit in the Stephen narrative cannot be attributed exclusively to martyriological motives (Acts 7:55) but is part of the tradition. This is made plausible by the following considerations: (1) besides Stephen, Philip also belongs to the Seven; he too, the tradition stresses, had pneumatic characteristics (Acts 8:6, 13; 21:8–9); (2) the Temple saying of Jesus (Mark 14:58) omits reference to the building of a new temple. It is likely that among the Hellenists the Church was already spoken of as the new temple.

The mob justice for Stephen (Acts 7:56–57) culminates the persecution of the Hellenistic Christians, who subsequently embark on a mission to the gentiles in Phoenicia, Cyprus, and Antioch (Acts 11:19).

Pauline theology is rooted primarily in the Hellenistic

community of Antioch (Gal 1:21; Acts 11:19–20; 13:1). Since no direct sources for its theology are extant, only sketches of its ideas can be inferred from the traditions of Paul's letters (Köster 1982: 2.91–93). It must be remembered, however, that the community continued to produce original theology independent of Paul, and that all traditions and accounts do not point to Antioch. If one subscribes to the early date of 1 Thessalonians (Lüdemann 1980) it is likely that this letter most closely reflects Antiochian theology and the founding sermon in Corinth.

It is with the Hellenists and in the Hellenistic community that we must look for the roots of primitive Christian pneumatology. Early Palestinian Christianity, by contrast, maintained a basic aloofness toward the pneumatology evolving there.

5. Pneumatology in Pre-Pauline and Non-Pauline Communities. The primary sources of Antiochian pneumatology are formulas and formulaic statements in Paul's letters.

a. The Community and the Spirit: Formulaic Traditions. (1) "God had given us the spirit" (Acts 5:32; 15:8; Rom 5:5; 11:8; 2 Cor 1:22; 5:5; 1 Thess 4:8; 2 Tim 1:7; 1 John 3:24; 4:13). The following features are evidence for formulaic crystallization: (a) the author of the gift of the spirit is always God; (b) the gift is always described in the aorist tense (except 1 Thess 4:8; 1 John 4:13); (c) the gift of *pneuma* is described with minimal grammatical variation, e.g., articles, addition of adjectives, or in combination with appositions; (d) the object is predominantly *hēmin,* "us."

This suggests that a relatively fixed phrase, probably a formula (*ho theos edoken to pneuma hēmin,* "God has given us the spirit"), circulated in the communities. The phrase is older than the Pauline letters since Paul makes use of it secondarily, or rather, interprets it and in each case incorporates it into his own line of argument.

In the LXX, beyond the related statements of 1 Kings 22:23; 2 Kings 19:7; Isa 42:1; Ezek 11:19, particularly Ezek 36:26–27 and 37:5, 14, two passages deserve mention: *pneuma kainon (mou) dosō en hymin,* "I will put (my) new spirit in you (pl.)" (Ezek 36:26–27); *dosō pneuma mou eis hymas,* "I will put my spirit in you" (37:5, 14; both of these are 1st-person prophetic pronouncements of God).

A similar formula expressing assurance that God has given his spirit appears in hymns from Qumran (1QH 12:11–12; 13:18–19; 16:11; 17:17, 26). It is probable that the NT and Essene formulas each make independent use of the OT, since the respective contexts of the formulas differ (Kuhn 1966: 139). What is consistent, however, is that the gift of the spirit, a future gift in Ezekiel, is here a present occurrence which facilitates an eschatological outlook.

(b) "You have received the spirit" (John 20:22; Acts 2:33, 38; 8:15, 17, 19; 10:47; 19:2; Rom 8:15; 1 Cor 2:12; 2 Cor 11:4; Gal 3:2, 14; 1 John 2:27). It is the Pauline evidence which most likely displays the original formula (verb always in the aorist). The formula is used by Paul in his reference to the ongoing dispute with his antagonists.

The succinct, thematic character of both formulas suggests a social setting of proclamation, possibly baptismal catechesis (Paulsen 1974). The use of this formula in the Qumran hymns could suggest its origin within the Palestinian community. It is more probable, however, that it originated in a reflection on Scripture within the Greek-speaking community, because all the NT passages are found in the area of Hellenistic Christianity, and a positive relation between spirit endowment and fulfillment of the law—in contrast to the OT tradition—is missing.

(c) "The spirit of God dwells within you" (1 Cor 3:16; 6:19; Rom 8:9, 11; Eph 2:21; 1 Pet 2:5; *Ep. Barn.* 16:10). The formulaic origin of this sentence is still evident despite its secondary use and its combination with additional motifs. In 1 Cor 3:16; 6:19, for instance, Paul calls to mind a familiar subject of Christian preaching by using the rhetorical question "Do you not know?" The interpretation of this formula must not be based on its treatment in the Pauline context (in connection with the temple motif in 1 Cor 3:16; 6:19; antithesis of spirit/flesh in Rom 8:9). However, since the motifs of indwelling and temple are not consistently linked in Paul, we must insist on an independent origin of the formula.

As Paul's rhetorical question suggests, the social setting of this formula is probably early Christian catechesis and proclamation. The history of the motif points more clearly to the Hellenistic community than does the history of the two former formulas. The concept of the indwelling of God in the believer (Wis 3:14; 2 Macc 14:35; Philo *Somn* I 148–49) as well as that of the indwelling of the spirit (Philo *Heres* 264; Seneca *Ep.* 41:2; Lactantius *Inst. Div.* 6 25:3; *Corpus Hermeticum* 1:6, par. 329) have precedents in the Hellenistic world. This indwelling of the spirit, a first interpretation of the concept of spirit endowment, must be understood in terms of a substance. This is likewise suggested by its secondary connection with the temple motif. The return of the spirit to the eschatological temple anticipated in OT theology has become present reality within the community as the temple of God.

Thus, on the one hand, the temple motif is likely to refer to the OT Jewish expectation of the new eschatological temple (Ezekiel 40–48; Mal 3:1–4). On the other hand, the generally similar use of the motif in Qumran (1QS 8:4–8; 9:3–6; 11:8; CD 3:18–20) raises the question (with Klinzing 1971: 92–93), whether the decisive impetus for the motif's spiritualization was the separation from the Jerusalem Temple.

(d) 1 Cor 6:11. This Hellenistic Jewish-Christian, pre-Pauline baptismal tradition refers to a primary locus of the conveyance of the spirit (for form-critical classification, see Schnelle 1986b: 39). This tradition does not yet approach the later, mystery-like baptismal theology of the main Pauline letters (Reitzenstein 1977: 261) but does manifest a degree of liturgical crystallization (Plummer *1 Corinthians* ICC, 120) which makes it unsuitable for explaining the primary early Christian concept of baptism. The tradition contrasts the present state of salvation with the past, describing the former effectively as washing, sanctification, and justification. The adverbial construction *en tǭ onomati tou kyriou Iēsou Christou kai en tǭalo pneumati,* "in the name of our Lord Jesus Christ and in the Spirit" (1 Cor 6:11), describes the means by which transition to the state of salvation is effected. This means is the invocation of the name of the exalted Lord over the baptizand, and the baptizand's dedication. The second adverbial construction, *en tǭ pneumati,* "in the Spirit," corresponds quite naturally, because originally the naming had an exorcistic function and cleared the way for the baptizand to receive the spirit (Bultmann *Johannes* MeyerK, 142). In that sense 1 Cor 6:11 indirectly also suggests a conveyance of the spirit. Primarily, however, it is the power of the spirit of God to cleanse the baptizand which is emphasized, a function which originally was part of the rite itself.

b. The Function of the Spirit for the Community. Since there are no primary sources, and the tradition analysis of the letters is controversial, there can be no far-reaching hypotheses regarding the theology of the pre-Pauline Hellenistic Jewish-Christian community of Antioch. This community consisted of Jewish and gentile Christians who knew themselves called to render service to God in anticipation of the Messiah's imminent return, as the pre-Pauline tradition of 1 Thess 1:9 records. Their service to God also includes mission to the gentiles. Thus Paul, with his roots in Antiochian theology, emphasizes the pneumatic character of his mission in Thessalonica and Corinth (1 Thess 1:5–6; 1 Cor 2:4–5) and identifies his ministry to the gentiles as a sacrifice made holy by the holy spirit. As Luke reports (Acts 11:19–20), the Hellenists in Antioch, banished from Jerusalem, had formerly begun a mission to the Greeks. Historically, this probably refers to previous mission activity in Samaria and the coastal area of Palestine-Phoenicia (cf. the legendary tradition of Philip [Acts 8]). While the Jewish Christians in Palestine, having adopted the synoptic mission tradition, for the time being continue with their mission to Israel specifically (Matt 10:6; 15:24), the Hellenistic Jewish Christians approach the gentiles, in likely continuity with the orientation of their precursor, the Synagogue of the Diaspora (Hahn 1963: 15–18). The gift of the spirit is here perceived as empowerment for this service. The messengers thereby validate their eschatological claim to being empowered for a mission to the gentiles, a mission which, according to OT-Jewish tradition, was reserved for God's own eschatological action (Hahn 1963: 46; Käsemann 1970a: 87).

c. Christ and the Spirit. This Hellenistic Jewish-Christian community speaks of the gift of the spirit to the Messiah as well as to the community. Rom 1:3b–4 has long been recognized as a formulaic tradition of Jewish Christianity (Wilckens *Brief an die Römer* EKKNT, 56) which has undergone secondary redaction. With the first words of the sentence the community acknowledges the messianic descent "from the seed of David" (cf. *Pss. Sol.* 17:21; John 7:42; 2 Tim 2:8). However, in keeping with the kerygmatic tradition of resurrection (1 Cor 15:3–5(4), it emphasizes that only his resurrection from the dead is evidence of Jesus' sonship. This presumably is the prototype of the formula "designated Son of God . . . by his resurrection from the dead" (Rom 1:3b). Redaction-critical analysis of the passage warrants the conclusion that the contrast "according to the flesh"/"according to the Spirit" represents Paul's christological redaction of the older formula. In Hellenistic Jewish discourse, exaltation into the heavenly realm indicates only transformation into and participation in spirit-substance (Vos 1973: 80).

6. Jewish Christianity of Palestine. The Lukan portrait of the original Jerusalem community cannot be taken as evidence of the universal spirit-endowment of the early Palestinian community. Historical inquiry leads no further than a theologically shaped tradition. This point is highly controversial in the history of research: Goguel (1954: 113–14), Bultmann (*Johannes* MeyerK, 41), and others see the evolution of primitive Christian pneumatology as a product of the Hellenistic community. On the other hand, Käsemann (1970a; 1970b), Vielhauer (*NTApocr* 2: 426), and others, on the basis of form- and tradition-historical considerations, regard Palestinian Jewish Christianity as a pneumatically determined entity. It must be remembered, however, that the Jewish-Christian community in Palestine does not share the claim of its Hellenistic sister community of possessing the spirit of God, a claim, morevoer, which the gentile-Christian community broadens into the contention that they are actually living in the spirit (1 Cor 12:13; Gal 5:25).

In the Jerusalem community, according to von Campenhausen (1963: 196–98), even the form of community leadership by the Twelve, or rather by James and his successors, became a hindrance to a spiritual understanding of community. Later sources, moreover, never mention a spirit endowment of James (Lohmeyer 1936: 76, 98). The reference to Agabus (Acts 11:28; 21:10–11) in no way proves a universal spirit endowment of the Jerusalem community. It shows, rather, that as an occasional phenomenon, prophecy had not ceased in Jerusalem (*TDNT* 6: 819–28). The following observation is significant: the primary source of anti-Paulinism is the Jewish-Christian community of Jerusalem (Lüdemann 1983). Paul's adversaries accuse him (1 Cor 10:1, 10; 13:1–3) of not being endowed with the spirit. It is unlikely that they raise this charge in comparison with their own behavior; they rather seek to disprove Paul's own claim (1 Cor 7:40) and thereby to undermine his apostolic authority. This specific charge of lacking spirit endowment seems to originate primarily with the Corinthian enthusiasts and to have been seized upon by the Jerusalemites as an additional point of argument (Windisch *Der zweite Korintherbrief* MeyerK, 107; Lüdemann 1983: 125). In his reply Paul himself does not reflect a proven spirit endowment of the anti-Paulinists. Furthermore, in 2 Cor 11:4 he intimates that the preaching of his opponents does not impart the spirit which distinguishes Paul's communities. Paul's boast of ecstatic experiences (2 Cor 12:1) is proof of his own spirit endowment (Lüdemann 1983: 136–37); yet here, too, the only thing clear is the point of the debate: the "visions and revelations" which Paul's Jewish-Christian opponents deny he ever had (cf. 1 Cor 1:22). The point of contention is not the positive reference to these manifestations in Paul's self-characterization. On the contrary, Paul substantiates his apostolate as pneumatic and it is this basic position that the Jerusalem antagonists do not share. Their own authority is established by the letter of commendation and by their origin in Jerusalem (2 Cor 3:1, 10, 12; 11:22) (Käsemann 1969: 490).

In Luke 7:22 (= Matt 11:4–5) and 6:20 (= Matt 5:3; allusions to Isa 61:1), Q speaks implicitly (and in Luke 11:20 [= Matt 18:28] explicitly [pneuma in Matt is secondary]) of a functional spirit endowment of Jesus for his messianic office. In Luke 12:12 (= Matt 10:20) Christians are promised the spirit in the event of a trial. All further references to the spirit in Q are probably a result of retroactive influence of the Mark tradition on Q and thus are presumably located later in time and written in the context of Hellenistic redaction.

In Luke 3:16 *en pneumati hagiō* (cf. Mark 1:8) is inserted into the image of the future baptism by fire. Luke 4:1 par may be prompted by Mark 1:12. The final clause of the prohibition against blaspheming the spirit (Luke 12:10 = Matt 12:32) conforms largely to Mark 3:29. While in Mark the phrase referred to the Beelzebul controversy (Mark 3:30), the Q version introduces a salvation-historical periodization (time of the Son of Man/time of the holy spirit) which sees the present as a time marked by the spirit. The parallels in Mark suggest that the quoted references to "spirit" were secondarily introduced into the Q tradition. Beyond that there is the form-critical aspect of the genres of the "disputation" and the "miracle story" in Luke 11:14–23 = Matt 12:22–30 = Mark 3:22–27, which are typical for Mark but atypical for Q. Therefore, there is no positive, unequivocal statement concerning a universal spirit endowment of the Christians and the Christ in the basic material of Q prior to Hellenistic redaction.

Schulz (1972: 63–64) concurs but proceeds on the assumption that the Q community lives in the knowledge of the being endowed with the spirit of Jesus, not of God (!). This spirit, according to Schulz, intensifies the apocalyptic expectation into prophetic enthusiasm which manifests itself in the use of "but I say to you" in the beatitudes and "woe" in the *ius talionis,* and the amplification of Torah (1972: 57–66). However, inferring a consciousness of participation in the spirit of Jesus from an intensification of traditional prophetic forms of speech is a dubious undertaking. Tradition-historically, an association with prophecy is questionable (Polag 1877: 26–27). And the attribution of the body of sayings to either Palestinian or Hellenistic communities also has to be reexamined (cf. Berger 1970; Boring 1982). Enthusiasm is based on the present activity and expected imminent return of the Son of Man. While the spirit is experienced as power in special situations (Luke 4:1; 12:12), the Q community does not anticipate fire- and spirit-baptism until the Son of Man returns as judge (Matt 3:11 = Luke 3:16). The prophetic post-Easter enthusiasm described by Käsemann and Schulz does not have its basis in pneumatology as in the Hellenistic communities (Corinth), but is the result of proclamation and of the anticipation of the return of the Son of Man as judge.

Palestinian Jewish Christianity seems to have maintained a distance from a distinctly pneumatic Christianity. Thus, Matt 7:22–23 relegates prophets and miracle workers to the periphery and inveighs against a lack of work righteousness (cf. Strecker 1985: 171–75). Mark 9:38–40 knows of exorcisms in the name of Jesus which do not take place in accordance with following Jesus, that is to say here with following the apostles (Bultmann 1979: 23). In 2 Corinthians, Galatians, and Philippians, Paul must defend his pneumatic gospel against the nomism of Jewish Christians which appears unconscious of spirit endowment. On the contrary, the Judaizing Christians seek to establish a position of authority over the universal community which undermines its charismatic character.

The sources for post-NT Jewish Christianity likewise lack positive evidence concerning the relative significance of the spirit within the community (cf. Strecker 1981: 203–4; Lohmeyer 1936: 76; von Campenhausen 1963: 196–98). The reasons for this situation are probably basic. Christological differences between Palestinian and Hellenistic Christianity could have led to differences in the understanding of spirit. Whereas Hellenistic Christianity was open to perceiving paranormal phenomena as spirit-caused (Volz 1910: 198), Palestinian Christianity was more reluctant to see enthusiastic states as manifestations of the spirit (Schlatter 1927: 27). These differences soon coalesce with other disagreements (mission to the gentiles, question of circumcision, doctrine of justification).

7. Spirit in Paul. a. 1 Thessalonians. This letter assumes a special place as a document of early Pauline theology (Schade 1984: 115–16) and must be seen as removed in time from the later Pauline letters.

Beyond the anthropological use of *pneuma* (5:23), there are the following three aspects which characterize early Pauline theology:

(1) The gentile-Christian community of Thessalonica belongs among the *eklogē,* "chosen," as brethren "beloved by God" (1:4) (customarily, *eklogē* refers to Israel: Rom 9:10; 11:5, 7, 28; however, see 1 Cor 1:27–28). Historically, their calling is based on the proclamation of the gospel which, through the mediation of the word, revealed the power of God, the holy spirit, and confident hope (concerning the contrast logos/dynamis, see 1 Cor 2:2, 4; 4:13). The *eklogē* of the community, wrought by the spirit, in turn leads to imitation of the apostle and of the Lord, and to joy wrought by the spirit. The condition of the gentile-Christian community is the work of the manifest spirit of God (in principle, later, Rom 15:16–20).

(2) The ethical precept, the will of God, is described as "sanctification," as such behavior is manifested in the renunciation of immorality and dishonesty (4:3–6). Because of their calling, the members do not continue in the previous condition of "uncleanness" but enter into "sanctification" (4:7). Human and divine aspects of sanctification are not sharply distinguished (4:3–6 stresses the aspect of demand, 5:23 that of gift). Both aspects are pneumatologically linked in 4:8. God continuously pours his spirit into the faithful (reminiscent of Ezek 36:27; 37:14). The gift of the holy spirit is related to the goal of sanctification.

(3) 1 Thess 5:19–22 forms a sayings unit separable from its surrounding context. Structurally, two prohibitions (vv 19–20) and two commandments (vv 21b–22) frame an admonition to "nevertheless weigh everything" (*RAC* 11: 130–32). The statement of Paul reads: prophets are to be highly esteemed if they occur within the community as a work of the spirit. The admonition to weigh everything is not to be limited to the problems inherent in prophecy. As a form of rhetorical conclusion, it urges the rejection of everything evil (*RAC* 11: 131) and leaves this task to the judgment of the whole community rather than individual members (1 Cor 12:10). Paul commends prophecy as the essential gift of the spirit knowing that in the Hellenistic community it was held in low esteem when compared with glossolalia (cf. 1 Cor 14; on the topic see *RAC* 11: 131).

The pneumatology of 1 Thessalonians can be distinguished from the pneumatology of the later Pauline letters. The characteristic contrasts in these later writings (*pneuma/sarx,* "spirit/flesh," *pneuma/gramma,* "spirit/letter," *pneuma/nomos,* "spirit/law") are not yet present. The spirit as "spirit of God" is still separate from the later christological qualification (1 Cor 15:45; 2 Cor 3:17; Rom 8:9). Spirit endowment via baptism is not mentioned (the imperfective aspect of the verb *didonta* "gives" [1 Thess 4:8], furthermore, would contradict the notion of a single event of impartation). It is true, however, that in this earliest letter of Paul there is an association of spirit and mission (1:5–6), ethics (4:8) and prophecy (5:19–20). The concept of spirit in 1 Thessalonians shows strong OT and Jewish influence (imitation of Ezek in 4:8).

Romans 8 is a precis of Pauline pneumatology. The statements of this chapter are the product of a twofold dispute with an enthusiastic interpretation of spirit endowment as something sacramentally conferred which lifts believers out of the secular realm and promises them participation in the heavenly glory (1 Cor) and with a Jewish-Christian nomistic reaction to the Pauline mission, which includes the relation of spirit to letter and law (2 Corinthians; Galatians; Philippians).

b. Dispute with Pneumatic Enthusiasm. The textual basis is primarily 1 Corinthians; 2 Corinthians reflects influence of Jewish-Christian agitation against Paul within the Corinthian community and refers to a different situation. 1 Thessalonians interpreted spirit endowment functionally as the power of proclamation and sanctification for the time prior to the Parousia. In the environment of the Corinthian community a view emerged which saw "spirit" as a salutary substance which is conveyed to the believer, or rather into which the believer is transplanted. This is where the self-characterization *pneumatikos* appears (1 Cor 2:13; 3:1; 12:1; 14:37), where believers are conscious of having the spirit of God (7:40). If 15:46 reflects a view held by the community, it highlights a consciousness of living in the spirit rather than in the flesh (see Sellin 1986: 175–81). Slogans which evidence this eschatological consciousness of participation in the spirit are conspicuous: "all things are lawful" (6:12; 10:23); "all of us possess knowledge" (8:1); "there is no resurrection of the dead" (15:12). The intellectual slogans are congruent with a communal practice which turns out to be enthusiastic pneumatism: devaluation of bodily existence (6:12–20), libertinistic or ascetic marriage ethics (7:1–40), an individualistic conception of liberty (10:23; 11:1) and emphasis on an individual's gifts as manifestations of spirit endowment (14:1–40). Paul's evaluations ironically confirm the self-definition of the community: "Already you are filled! Already you have become rich!" (4:8); they are puffed up, Paul accuses (4:6, 18–19; 5:2; 8:1). Superimposed on this condition is a factious spirit (1:10–17; 3:3) which threatens the unity of the community. The factions are probably based on a high esteem of the baptizers Apollos and Cephas (1:12). Paul gives thanks, on the other hand, that his own practice, hardly one of baptizing, could not lead to schism (1:14–17). The contrast between his preaching and that of his opponents is stated in terms of *logos tou staurou* versus *en sophia logou* (1:18–2:16).

The material concept of *pneuma* is evident in an essentially pre-Pauline baptismal tradition, 1 Cor 12:13: baptism incorporates the baptizand into the body of Christ and nourishes him with the spirit. Baptism works a substantive transformation through transferral into the sphere of the *Kyrios,* "Lord" (pre-Pauline baptismal tradition may be inferred from Rom 6:4 and Col 2:12). A further pre-Pauline baptismal tradition in 1:30 locates the existence of the community within the sphere of the *Kyrios.* Salvation consists in the sacramental incorporation into the pneumatic *Kyrios* and does not require a bodily resurrection yet to come (15:12).

In order to explain this Corinthian pneumatology, researchers have proposed primarily external influences and have pointed to the influence of mystery religions (Reitzenstein 1977), gnosis (Schmithals 1969), Hellenistic materialistic thinking (*TDNT* 6: 415–16) and Greek orgiastic practices (Leisegang 1922: 120). The reference to Apollos who, as an Alexandrian (Acts 18: 24–25) had combined Christian theology and Alexandrian philosophy—a precursor of later gnostic practice—suggests an intermediate position between external and local influences (Sellin 1986). It must be granted immediately, however, that our knowledge of Apollos is minimal (Acts 18:24; 19:1; 1 Cor 1:12; 3:4–22; 4:6; 16:12) and that his dependence on Alexandrian philosophy is mere speculation. Accordingly, introduction of this philosophy into Corinth can hardly be demonstrated.

Rather than explaining pneumatic enthusiasm in Corinth through external influences, Vielhauer (1978: 139), adopting Lütgert's position (1908), correctly views this pneumatism as primarily an internal development in the theology of the community and only secondarily as external influence. This raises the question of Paul's own role in this development (likewise PWSup 14: 399; *TRE* 12: 191; Lüdemann 1983: 125). Here the baptismal rite is interpreted for the first time as an efficacious event which imparts justification, sanctification, and salvation and, beyond 1 Cor 6:11 (baptismal tradition), places the baptizand *en Christō,* "in Christ" (1:30). This is of fundamental significance for understanding the pneumatology of the Corinthian community. Since 1 Thessalonians shows no trace of this baptismal theology, its origin at Corinth is probable (Holtzmann 1911: 451; Bultmann *Johannes* MeyerK, 42; Käsemann 1970a: 121–25; Becker 1976: 61–65; comprehensively, Schnelle 1986b: 34–53). This may have been the social setting of the parting formula of Rom 8:9c. This baptismal theology may also be understood as a solution to the problem of the death of members of the community. While 1 Thessalonians 4, in anticipation of the impending second coming (4:17), emphasizes the future aspect of being "with the Lord" for both the living and the dead, this baptismal theology by contrast includes both the living and the dead of the present in the body of the Lord and can therefore assert that there is no resurrection of the dead (1 Cor 15:12). The effects of this new existence are knowledge (1 Cor 8:1), participation in the reign of God (4:8), suspension of former customs (11:1–16), and speaking in the heavenly language (14:1–40).

This sacramentally mediated incorporation into the Christ who was himself exalted into the sphere of the spirit is the determinant factor in explaining pneumatism. It does not derive directly from Paul, who baptized only in exceptional cases, as 1 Cor 1:13–17 attests, and who explicates his baptismal theology only through retrospective reference to Corinth (Romans 6). Other Pauline concepts, however, have been incorporated. The indwelling of the spirit was one of the subjects of his founding sermon (1 Cor 3:16; 6:19). Most importantly, Paul does not dispute a spirit endowment of the community. In principle he commends their spiritual riches (1:49) and admonishes them to continue striving for the gifts of the spirit (12:31; 14:1, 12). In Romans 6, the baptismal theology itself is the starting point for Paul's exposition.

Pre-Christian enthusiasm (1 Cor 12:2) and the Hellenistic concept of *pneuma* as substance may certainly be considered secondarily as external factors. The application of the idea "as Christ, so the Christians" to the baptismal rite (Rom 6:3–4; Col 2:12), finally, points to the influence of the mystery religions.

c. Pauline Dispute with Pneumatic Enthusiasm. Pauline criticism is aimed primarily at refuting an enthusiasm of transcendence. In opposition to the latter, 1 Corinthians 15 develops a theology of the resurrection of the dead by analogy to God's raising of Jesus (6:14; 15:20–22); but it is a future hope yet to be realized. The Corinthian position is simply reversed in 15:46: "it is not the spiritual which is first but the physical." This future cannot be experienced in this world but only *ex ouranou,* "from heaven" (v 47). The gift of a "spiritual body" is a transference into the future of the "last Adam" (1 Cor 15:45), who is raised into the heavenly sphere and made a spiritual body. By thus maintaining an apocalyptic-eschatological perspective, Paul dealt a vital blow to transcendence enthusiasm. And further statements now have to take on the soteriology of the ontological baptismal statements, the anthropology of the satisfied, the libertines' ethic, and the ecclesiology of the individualists. In principle, Paul affirms the baptismal theology: baptism is the occasion of the bestowal of the spirit and of the incorporation into the salvific sphere *en Christō,* "in Christ." Yet the eschatological reservation does not invalidate the ethical demand. It is especially in the realm of physical existence that the spiritual life manifests itself. Thus, in 6:19 Paul inserts *soma,* "body," into the traditional statement and designates it as the place of the temple, even though the believers are already "members of Christ" (6:15). Into the pre-Pauline baptismal formula Paul inserts the purpose clause "so that . . . we too might walk in newness of life" (Rom 6:4), which recurs in slightly altered wording: "walk . . . according to the Spirit" (Rom 8:4; cf. Gal 5:25). In opposing enthusiasm, Rom 8:11 includes mortal bodies in the hope of the resurrection. In contrast to the ontological claims of the baptismal theology, this also indicates that the believer is at the same time both old and new human being. The claim of *gnosis* by the "spiritual" is likewise deflated (2:10–16; cf. Wilckens *Römer* EKKNT). Despite the gift of *pneuma,* a person can still turn out to be *psychikos,* "unspiritual, worldly," or *sarkikos,* "carnal." In early Pauline theology the relationship between Christ and the spirit had remained unclear. Here, however, Paul defines the ascended Christ himself as *pneuma zōopoioun,* "a life giving spirit" (1 Cor 15:45).

Even though the Corinthian enthusiasm of transcendence proved to be divisive for the community (1:10; 3:1–5; 8:12; 10:24; 11:18), Paul validates the spirit manifestations of the community as genuine gifts; but they are differing apportionments of the spirit and subject to critical evaluation (12:10) and to the supreme test of that love whose constant intention is the edification of the body, the Church (3:9; 14:3, 4, 12, 26). With the Church seen as one body with many members (12:12), baptism leads to the service of the one body, rather than to freedom from constraints (pre-Pauline in Gal 3:26–28; 1 Cor 12:13). It is not individual pneumatics who represent the community: rather, the community as a whole has received the spirit in baptism and is part of, and subordinate to, the body of Christ (10:17; 12:27). Finally, the concept of edification becomes the critical norm, and self-aggrandizing gifts such as the glossolalia, prized in Corinth, where uninterpreted are to be subordinated to prophecy (14:4, 39).

d. Dispute with Jewish-Christian Nomism. *2 Corinthians.* It is likely that Paul's opponents in 2 Corinthians were of Jewish-Christian origin (2 Cor 11:22–23; 11:5; and 12:11; Lüdemann 1983: 125–43), even though it seems they did not demand circumcision and Torah obedience. In the biographical statement of 12:1–10, Paul answers his opponents' chief accusation (10:1, 10; 13:3) that he did not demonstrate himself to be the spirit-endowed person he claimed to be. He disdains the immediate use of letters of commendation (3:1; 5:12; 10:12) in favor of vindicating the pneumatic character of his apostolate (2 Cor 3). Of even greater importance is the passage in which he describes his apostolic office (2:13–7:4). The personal statement in 2:16b–3:6 refers to Paul's sincerity (2:16b–17), to the existence of the community as a letter of commendation (3:1–3), and to his divinely endowed qualification for ministry (3:4–6). Verse 3c extends the metaphor of the letter of recommendation by an allusion to the historical antithesis "old covenant/new covenant" (referring to Jer 31:33) which v 6 employs to intensify the contrast of "letter" with "spirit."

The verses which follow, 7–18, have long been recognized as a "Christian midrash" on Ezek 34:29–35 (Windisch *Der zweite Korintherbrief* MeyerK, 112). In contrast to Schulz (1958), our task here is not to discover, through literary criticism, a prototype which might shed light on the theology of the opponents (for a critique, see Luz 1968: 130). The contrast of "letter" and "spirit" (also Rom 2:27–29; 7:5), appearing here for the first time in Pauline writings, denotes both two contrasting powers and two opposing sides. The consequence of "the letter" is death (v 6), but the consequence of "the spirit" is life (v 6; cf. vv 7, 9). The ministry of the apostle constitutes a fulfillment of the promise of Exod 34:34: his ministry is directly from God and lacks the separating "veil" (v 16). This is the way the apostle is different from Moses (v 13), and the Christian community from Israel (v 18); Israel is "veiled" in its reading of the OT (v 14). The removal of the veil through Christ (v 14) makes it possible to enter the sphere of *pneuma* and exit the deadly sphere of *gramma.* Acceptance of this "Lord" (v 16 harks back to v 14, Christ) places the believer in immediate eschatological relation to God, the sphere of the life-creating *pneuma.*

Galatians. The gentile-Christian community which Paul founded in Galatia exists in the spirit. Six times within his *probatio* 3:1–4:31 (Betz *Galatians* Hermeneia, 16–23), and always at critical points, Paul reminds the community of this new existence. In 3:1–5 he refers to their reception of the spirit as a result of their obedience in faith (3:2–3) and to God who, since the time of that spirit endowment, continuously grants the spirit and works miracles (3:5).

Gal 3:14 summarizes the arguments of the first part of the Abraham example with a Christian interpretation: the promise of blessing given to Abraham is made universally inclusive (3:14a) and its content is the gift of the spirit. The explication of sonship (4:1–5) is framed by two traditional passages which corroborate the pneumatic existence of the community: the baptismal tradition in Gal 3:26–28 (compare with 1 Cor 12:13) and the "Abba" saying in 4:6, which brackets present sonship, past bestowal of the spirit, and present effect (for the passage's traditional character see Luz 1968: 282). Both 3:14 and 4:6–7 demonstrate the fulfillment of the promise within the gentile-Christian Church through the gift of the spirit. In a similar way 4:29 contrasts birth "according to the flesh" with birth "according to the Spirit" in order to Christianize the present gentile-Christian community as a pneumatic entity.

After the apostle's departure, anti-Paulinists who insisted on observance of the Jewish law (4:21; 5:4), circumcision (5:2; 6:12–13), and observance of the Jewish religious calendar (4:10) infiltrated the community. (On the nature of Paul's opponents in 2 Corinthians, see CORINTHIANS, SECOND EPISTLE TO THE.) In dealing with these opponents, Paul formulates his doctrine of law and justification for the first time within a context of polemic (Strecker 1976: 257). The transferral of the community from the realm of the law to a condition of the liberty of the children of God has effected its participation in the spirit of God (3:14; 4:6). Thus, the actualization of faith can take place only in the sphere of this liberty and this spirit. A reintroduction of legal rules would betray this condition and would be tantamount to a return to slavery (4:9; 5:18). Refusal of a complementary relationship between law and spirit does not lead to unbridled libertinism. The boundaries of freedom are determined by the contrast between the spheres of "flesh" and "spirit" (5:16–25) which are temporally irreconcilable (5:17) since "law" itself leads back to the sphere of "flesh" (compare 5:17 and Rom 7:7–11, 15, 23). The tables of vices and virtues set out respectively the "works of the flesh" (5:19) and "fruits of the spirit" (5:22).

Betz (1974: 92) took the "naive trust in the spirit" as a basis for locating Galatians at the beginning of the apostle's work, certainly before the apostle's Corinthian experience (in agreement, Hübner 1982: 57; Köster 1982: 2.53; at variance, Lüdemann 1980: 273). In all phases of his work, however, Paul reiterates the fundamental exhortation to strive for the spirit (1 Thess 5:19; 1 Cor 14:1, 39; Gal 5:16–25; Rom 12:11). Moreover, it is especially the spirit references in Galatians 5 which most closely parallel Romans 8 (Paulsen 1974: 67), even though other differences clearly demonstrate a more considered approach for Romans.

Philippians. In the fragment of a letter to the Philippians which starts at 3:1b, Paul contends for the last time with opponents of a Judaizing Christian origin. The term *kakous ergatēs,* "evil-workers" (3:2), relates them to those agitators named in 2 Cor 11:13, but clearly makes the question of circumcision (3:2–4) central (Gnilka *Philipperbrief* HTKNT, 211–18).

The pointed reply of Paul (3:2) deprives the opponents of the distinction of as well as the demand for circumcision, and, interpreting it figuratively in a play on words, transforms it into a mark of the Christians ("we are the true circumcision" 3:3). The metaphorical extension of circumcision as an ethical symbol (Deut 10:16; Jer 4:4; 9:25; 1QS V 5:25) means that insistence on circumcision fails to appreciate the eschatological position of the community. Outward circumcision is set aside (Rom 2:28): circumcision of the heart is wrought by the spirit "inwardly" (Rom 2:29; Col 2:11). The opponents' demand that believers be circumcised would insist on linking the old and new condition of the community and merely revalidate "confidence in the flesh" (3:3). To counter this, Paul exhorts the community to reorient their thinking (Phil 3:15) toward their newly given Christian status.

Romans. Paul's doctrine of the spirit is most fully expounded in Romans. The body of primitive Christian formulas which surfaced in the dispute with enthusiasts and Pauline opponents has been incorporated in Romans as well. In the style of a dialogue (6:3; 7:1) addressing both Jewish and Christian interlocutors, the letter probes the relationship between law and spirit. In Romans, Paul values *nomos,* "law," more highly than he did even in Galatians (Hübner 1982).

Rom 7:1–6 describes the "change of regime" from "law," which brings enslavement to sin and flesh, to the service "in the new life of the Spirit" (7:5–6) which took place in baptism.

7:7–25 describes previous pre-Christian existence (7:5); 8:1–17, the new spiritual condition (7:6). 8:1–4 here explains for the Christian the meaning of the law which no longer enslaves to sin. In 8:5–8 Paul contrasts an orientation according to the flesh and an orientation according to the spirit. In 8:9–11, 12, and 13–17 he describes consequences of the new life in the spirit. Paul uses the opposition then-now to describe the present condition of the Christian as being dead to the law (7:4) and liberated from the law (7:6), in analogy to the images in 7:1–3. This basic notion is further developed in 7:7–8:17. Exegetes argue, however, whether *nomos,* "law," according to Paul, is completely abolished as a norm for the Christian (Käsemann *An die Römer* HNT, 181) or whether it is the power of the spirit which is supposed to facilitate the fulfillment of the *nomos* (Wilckens *Römer* EKKNT, 119).

While the image in vv 1–3 and the arguments in vv 7–11 are concerned with the individual command, in 7:6, Paul explains the liberation from *nomos* specifically as liberation from *gramma* "[the] letter." It is not the law, therefore, which is on the side of death, but sin which inhabits the human being as a power (7:23) and which has reference to the law (7:8, 11, 13). If, therefore, the human being is identified with *sarx,* "flesh," then the law is holy and the commandments are just and good (7:12); indeed, the law is "spiritual" (7:14) in contrast to the human carnality.

With Christ, redemption from the snare of law, sin, and flesh (7:23–25a) is accomplished. Consequently, the accusatory role of law is canceled. Liberation from the "law of sin and death" was brought about, as Rom 8:2 explains, by the "law of the Spirit of life in Christ Jesus." Many exegetes read this "law" in the figurative sense, as norm (Bultmann *Johannes* MeyerK, 260; Käsemann *An die Römer* HNT, 205; Paulsen 1974: 64; Räisänen 1979–80). Yet the figurative use of *nomos* is almost nonexistent in Greek literature and at best has parallels only within Pauline writings (Rom 3:27; 7:23; Gal 6:2). On the other hand, vv 2b–4 clearly speak of *nomos* as Torah, an unambiguous figure. The broader context should also be considered. According to Rom 7:2–4, until Christ the law was weak because of the flesh. Since *sarx,* "flesh," was judged in Christ, and Christ's mission consisted in freeing *nomos* from *sarx,* the demands of the law can now be fulfilled in the realm of life in the spirit.

Nevertheless, this does not reinstate the *nomos* as absolutely valid. The ethical statements in Paul's letters demonstrate that he concurs with the Hellenistic Jewish tradition in systematically applying the love commandment to the law (Gal 5:14; Rom 13:8–10), and that he is able to embrace the pagan ethic when it comes to portraying the content of the will of God (Strecker 1978).

In contrast to *sarx,* which works death (7:13; 8:6), *pneuma* effects "life and peace" (8:6). While in 8:5–8 "then and now" are contrasted once more, the following section (8:9–11) provides an ontological description of the state of salvation. Here Paul builds his argument exclusively with traditional formulations. The effect is that the statements here are not quite consistent, although their goal is: those who believe are in the sphere of the spirit; the spirit, Christ himself, dwells in the believer. Rom 8:10 may approximate early Pauline statements (1 Cor 5:5) which dualistically separate flesh and spirit. But v 11 adjusts this statement to reflect a more holistic theology of resurrection.

In congruence with the antienthusiastic arguments in 1 Cor 3:16 and 6:16, Paul concludes that the state of salvation "in the Spirit" is demonstrated in the sphere of the body, which indeed shall be accorded the high honor of resurrection. Flesh continues to exist as a contrary power. However, it can no longer misuse the letter of the law, from which the Christian has been liberated (Rom 7:6). At the same time, the Christian can combat it since it is no longer flesh which lives within him (Rom 7:17, 20), but Christ and the spirit. To return to "life according to the flesh" would be a manifestation of having left the sphere of Christ's rule, and its consequence would be future death (Rom 8:10).

e. Aspects of Pauline Pneumatology. The primitive Christian starting point is critical: the latter-day outpouring of the spirit which was anticipated in OT and Jewish theology has been realized in Christ and his community. Although Paul as a Jew shared this anticipation in a specific form, only traces of the pneumatology of a pre-Christian Paul can be inferred. It is also unlikely that at the inception of his mission Paul would have had at his disposal a fully formed pneumatology (according to Schnelle 1986a: 219; 1986b: 112). Paul's theology of the spirit rather expands from the primitive Christian doctrine of the eschatological gift of the spirit into his distinctive teaching. The development can be traced in the three phases discussed above: his early theology, represented in 1 Thessalonians; his dispute with pneumatic enthusiasm; his dispute with Jewish-Christian nomism.

The conclusions which Paul drew from the fundamental conviction that an endowment of the spirit had taken place remain unchanged in all three phases:

(1) Proclamation of the gospel is wrought by the spirit and (a) it is addressed to the gentiles (1 Thess 1:4–5; Gal 3:14; Rom 15:16); (b) it is accompanied by powerful phenomena (1 Thess 1:5; Gal 3:5; Rom 15:18–19); (c) it thus inspires faith (1 Thess 1:6–7; 1 Cor 2:9; Gal 5:22); alternatively, faith receives the spirit (Gal 3:2, 5, 14; 5:5).

(2) In all three phases of Pauline pneumatology the gift of *pneuma* is parallelled by a pledge "to walk according to the spirit." It is inaccurate to claim, however, that Paul was the first to propose a direct link between spirit and ethic (Gunkel 1909: 71). Even OT and Jewish thinking saw latter-day spirit endowment as also directed toward latter-day behavior (Bousset 1901: 760–61; Ezek 36:26–27; Ps 51:12–13). Hellenistic Judaism also emphasized the ethical significance of the spirit (Wis 1:5; 7:20; Philo *Leg All* I 34–35; *T. Benj.* 8:2). Finally, the pre-Pauline tradition of 1 Cor 6:11 already links liberation from a sinful past to orientation toward a new life. In 1 Thess 4:8 the gift of *pneuma* is related to the obligation of holiness. Physical existence is the locus of the spirit (1 Cor 3:16; 6:19) and leaves no room for immorality. Gal 5:16–25 and Rom 8:1–17 define the Christian life as walking in (or according to) the spirit.

(3) In all phases Paul stresses the gift of prophecy as a special gift of the spirit (1 Thess 5:19–20; 2 Cor 12:10; 13:2, 8; 14:3, 6, 21, 31; Rom 12:6). 1 Cor 12:28–29 and 14:37 suggest that the prophets of the community are resident rather than itinerant prophets. Their function as described in 1 Cor 14:3 is to speak to the community "for their upbuilding and encouragement and consolation," so that "all may learn and all be encouraged" (14:31). Prophecy is distinguished technically from glossolalia through its orderly procedure (4:29–33) and intelligible speech (4:19–20). Prophecy takes place in proportion to faith (Rom 12:6).

The dispute with pneumatic enthusiasm leads to clarification of the relationship between pneumatology and Christology, eschatology, anthropology, and ecclesiology.

The denial of physical resurrection resulted from an overvaluation of participation in *zoē,* "life," via possession of the spirit, and from an undervaluation of the difference between *soma psychikon,* "physical body," and *soma pneumatikon,* "spiritual body." The enthusiasts saw transformation in mystical terms as incorporation into the exalted body of Christ. Paul concurs that *zoopoioun,* "being made alive," does take place in the sphere of the Christ but maintains that it does so in the future resurrection. Accordingly, being in Christ is conceived historically. It has its beginning in baptism in Christ and is consummated in the resurrection with Christ. The polemic emphasis in 1 Cor 2:16 and the traditional departure formula of Rom 8:9c suggest that the correlation of Christ and the spirit first occurred in the context of pneumatic enthusiasm. Through an historical differentiation Paul distinguishes his interpretation from an identification of Christ and spirit. Further correlations of Christ and spirit in later letters (2 Cor 3:17; Gal 4:6; Phil 1:19) are not pivotal and are contingent in part on the larger context. This opposes Bousset's famous postulate (1926: 112) that 2 Cor 3:17 is the heart of Pauline christology.

(b) Since the gift of the spirit—existence *en pneumati*—does not implicitly include the *eschaton,* the "firstfruits of the Spirit" (Rom 8:23) and the "seal of the spirit" constitute a reservation (2 Cor 1:22; 5:5). The spirit is a down payment and sure indication of the redemption to come

(2 Cor 5:5; Rom 8:23) and is thus intended as gift for the time betwen baptism and redemption.

(c) In anthropological terms this means that the gift of the spirit achieves its object not merely in a transformation of consciousness, but through action in the present and in universal liberation in the future (Rom 8:21–23). Since human life is always determined by an indwelling power (Rom 6:12; 7:1, 17, 20; 1 Cor 3:16; 2 Cor 6:16), this power is manifested in the sphere of *soma* (Rom 6:13; 7:23–24; 1 Cor 6:17).

(d) Finally, the dispute with the enthusiasts yields some ecclesiological conclusions. The community is not composed solely of individual pneumatics (1 Cor 3:1; 14:37); spirit is related to body (1 Cor 6:13–17; 12:12–13), which takes its form as the body of Christ within the entire community (1 Cor 12:14, 27). In this way it is possible to appreciate the diverse gifts as charisms of the one spirit (1 Cor 12:7–11; Rom 12:6–8) insofar as they do not conflict with the norm of edification (1 Cor 14:5, 12). In order to counter enthusiasm by introducing the term *charismata,* "gifts," to replace *pneumatika,* "spiritual gifts (marg. persons)," a term which was probably more current in Corinth (12:1; 14:1), Paul also creates a conceptual distance between the cause and effect of the spirit.

The dispute with Jewish-Christian nomism deepened the insights previously gained. The results of that dispute are basically unrelated to pneumatology. As a consequence of the dispute that the doctrine of justification could be formulated on the basis of the pneumatic doctrine of redemption (Strecker 1976), a sharply defined concept of law in the context of anthropology was developed (Hübner 1982). The combination of indicative and imperative in formulaic statements (Gal 5:16, 25; Rom 8:4, 14) was employed by Paul as a vehicle for ethical argument.

Rom 8:26–27 ascribes to the spirit the function of intercessor which otherwise had been reserved for the Son (Heb 7:25; 1 John 2:1).

Beginning with the Corinthian correspondence, the view that life in its entirety is determined by Christ and the spirit is expressed in antitheses: "spirit"/"flesh" (Gal 3:2–5; 6:8; 4:29; 5:17; Rom 1:4; 8:4–5, 9, 13; Phil 3:3; cf. also 1 Cor 3:1); "spirit"/"letter" (2 Cor 3:6; Rom 2:19; 7:6); "freedom"/"slavery" (Rom 6:18; 8:21; Gal 5:1); "grace"/ "law" (Gal 5:4; Rom 6:14).

8. The Deutero-Pauline Letters. In Colossians, christology assumes a more prominent place in comparison with statements relating to the spirit (Schweizer 1982). Ephesians, however, though dependent on Colossians, places great weight on matters of the spirit but subordinates its testimony to a characteristic ecclesiological perspective (Schnackenburg 1973). When Col 2:18 is seen as the kerygmatic heart of the letter (Mussner *Brief an die Epheser* ÖTK, 88) then gentile and Jewish Christians are viewed as having access to the Father (note here the already triadic form!) through one spirit (probably christological rather than anthropological; *TDNT* 6: 443). The influence of the pre-Pauline and Pauline traditions is still seen in the emphasis on one spirit (Eph 4:4–5), the inclusion of the temple motif (2:22), and the model of "then/now" (3:5). Even though Ephesians specifically emphasizes the present nature of salvation specifically with the help of pneumatology (Mussner *Brief an die Epheser* ÖTK, 27), the ethic of the letter nevertheless manifests a notion of spiritual growth (1:17; 3:16; 4:23; 5:18). The spirit, accordingly, is both a past gift in baptism (1:13; 4:3c) and a present reality capable of decrease (4:30) or increase (5:18) in quantity. Ephesians does not relate spirit to the idea of ecstasy.

9. Hebrews. Most of the references to *pneuma* in Hebrews are dependent on Jewish or Christian tradition. The terminology is uneven. In 1:14, *pneumata,* "spirits," refers to angels; in 12:23, to the deceased. The name for God, "Father of spirits" (12:9), is formulaic and has an OT-Jewish history (Michel *Brief an die Hebräer* MeyerK, 442–43). In 3:7, 9:8, and 10:15 the holy spirit is considered the author of scriptural passages. Hebrews 2:4 names signs and miracles, powers and endowments as gifts proceeding from God. The formulaic character of the phrase argues against its being a direct reference to pneumatic experiences. Participation in the spirit is mediated through the sacraments (6:4–6). Apostasy precludes the possibility of second repentance. The contrast of sacrifice under the old covenant and sacrifice in the person of the mediator Jesus Christ illustrates the surpassing worth of the latter through the implicit antithesis between the sphere of flesh (v 13) and the sphere of *pneuma aionion* (v 14).

10. 1 Peter. For 1 Peter, spirit is primarily the power which inspires proclamation. The proclamation of the OT prophets was already determined by the "Spirit of Christ" (1:11)—a unique statement within the NT. Present proclamation of the gospel takes place through the power of the holy spirit (1:12), whose heavenly origin calls to mind Acts 2:2 (the Pentecost account). Christ himself, as the Risen One who is translated into the sphere of the spirit, preaches to the spirits. This is most likely a reference to the generation of the flood rather than to demons in general (Goppelt *Erste Petrusbrief* MeyerK, 246–54). 4:14, finally, is determined by the context of proclamation. The blessing praises particularly those who are reviled for their witness to Christ and promises them the succor of the God and the spirit of glory (cf. Mark 13:11). At the same time, 4:14 clearly indicates that "spirit" no longer connotes something which is given once for all and determines the life of the community as a whole, but identifies an extraordinary power which gives succor to the individual believer. By contrast, the statement of the prescript (1:1–2) which credits sanctification to the work of the spirit in the traditional manner of baptismal terminology remains isolated.

11. Apocalypse of John. In regard to the various uses of *pneuma,* four are particularly striking:

1. 1:4; 3:1; 4:5 and 5:6 mention the "seven spirits of God." They may be compared with the seven archangels and represent here the spirit of God in its all-encompassing form (Schweizer 1951–52).
2. The plural *pneumata* denotes demons (16:13–14; 18:2).
3. The spirit is the power of ecstasy (1:10; 4:2; 17:3; 21:10).
4. The formulaic warning (2:7, 11, 17, 29; 3:6, 13, 22) in the letters to the churches (cf. Müller *Offenbarung des Johannes* ÖTK, 93–94) has Christ himself speaking through the prophet in the spirit.

In Rev 19:10, the addendum concerning the "spirit of prophecy" may be taken as a marginal note (Müller *Offenbarung,* 310). The parallelism between bride and spirit in 22:17 places both on the side of the temporal church which invokes Christ (Müller, 371).

12. Johannine Writings. John takes over certain primitive Christian formulaic phrases of spirit transmission (John 3:24; 4:13) and shares the primitive Christian traditional notion that the gift of the spirit cannot be bestowed until after the glorification of Jesus (John 7:39; 20:22). The spirit and the two sacraments shepherd the Church (7:39; 19:34–35; 1 John 5:7–8; cf. Porsch 1974: 53–81) and remain with it (John 14:17); this is told the Church for its comfort (1 John 2:27; 3:9; cf. also Schnackenburg *Johannesevangelium* HTK, 41). The spirit manifests itself, however, not in ecstatic or charismatic phenomena, but in the area of the proclamation of the word, specifically in remembrance (14:26), doctrine (14:26), imitation (16:13), and prediction (16:13). *Pneuma* is the power which leads to the knowledge of Jesus Christ. Beyond this functional definition, the harsh antithesis of spirit/flesh in John 3:3–6 and 6:63 is conspicuous. 3:3–6 establishes a parallel between being born from above/anew (3:3), of water (3:5), of the spirit (3:5–6), and of the flesh (3:5). While this indicates a division between higher and lower spheres, baptism transfers (a person) into the sphere and substance of the spirit (3:6). Becker (*Evangelium nach Johannes* ÖTK, 1: 226) closely associates this assertion with the Corinthian sacramentalists. 6:63, likewise a Johannine tradition (Bultmann *Johannes* MeyerK, 34–35 n. 9), also points to this context of opposing spheres of influence of flesh and spirit. It was the life-creating function of *pneuma* which the pre-Pauline tradition in Rom 8:11; 1 Cor 15:45; 2 Cor 3:6; and 1 Pet 3:18 emphasized. Over against such a static ontology of salvation the evangelist champions a concept of the spirit as a power for proclamation (cf. even 6:63 as a recasting). It is the spirit who makes the revelation of Christ accessible. As the spirit of truth (14:17; 15:26; 16:13; 1 John 4:6; 5:6) he is the one who reveals the truth of God in contrast to the lie. In the farewell discourse this spirit of truth is termed *parakletos,* "Counselor" (except in 16:7). The paraclete, introduced as person in the farewell discourse, guarantees the abiding presence of the revelation of *zoē* as continuing the presence of Jesus (14:16). In this way the locus of the experience of the spirit is defined christologically—possibly countering Docetism (1 John 4:1–6)—without declaring Christ and the spirit to be identical (PWSup 14: 398–99).

The Johannine references to the spirit must be seen in relation to the overarching, divinely established contrasts to *kosmos,* "world," *skotia,* "darkness," *sarx,* "flesh" (Bultmann *Johannes* MeyerK, 98–100, n. 3; Schottroff 1970: 272–76). A comparison with Paul must take into account the authors' different settings within early Christianity. The view that the sphere of the spirit is the basis for action, a view so central to Paul, is also shared to some extent by 1 John 2:24; 4:12–13.

13. Luke–Acts. Luke is surely the theologian of the spirit, not only in terms of statistics (*pneuma* 106 times; *pneuma theou,* 75 times; *pneuma hagion,* 54 times) but also in terms of his reflection on primitive Christian testimony and ideas concerning the spirit from the perspective of a concept of salvation history. The action of the spirit is already evident in the birth and infancy narrative of Luke 1–2 (1:15, 35, 41, 67, 80; 2:25–27), especially as the creator power of God who effects the pregnancy of Mary (1:35). Tatum (1974) subsumes the references to the spirit in Luke 1–2 within Conzelmann's periodic schema of history by contrasting prophetic/creative to messianic spirit. It is nevertheless the prophetic spirit which remains central for Luke, so that the references to the spirit transcend periodization typical of historical thinking. In his baptism the spiritual origin of Jesus is manifest in the dove as the physical form of spirit endowment (3:21–22). Hellenistic substantive thinking and a tendency toward objectification accounts for the visible manifestation of the spirit's power both in this passage and in Acts 2:3–4; 4:31. In contrast to Mark there is a less animistic description of Jesus' spirit endowment here (cf. Mark 1:12; Luke 12:10 derives from the Lukan context); Jesus is Lord of the spirit and, until Pentecost, the only bearer of the spirit (Conzelmann 1977: 168). This is corroborated by Jesus' testimony about himself in 4:18–19, verses incorporating Isa 61:1. Thus, while the gospel presents Jesus as the paradigmatic spirit bearer (1:35; 3:21–22; 4:1, 11, 18–19), in Luke's view it is the task of the Messiah to pass on this spirit after Easter. That which the baptizer announces in Luke 3:16–17 (fire and spirit) is fulfilled in Acts 2:3–4 as the work of the Exalted One (Luke 24:49; Acts 2:33). This proximity of the spirit and the Exalted One—expressed also in their common functions (Luke 12:12 = 21:15; Acts 10:14, 19; Acts 7:55: the pneumatic sees the glory of God and of Jesus)—speaks against a notion of an interim between Easter and Pentecost which is devoid of the spirit (Conzelmann 1977: 26–27, 171).

The Pentecost account describes the spirit endowment of the Twelve (Acts 2:1–13). Even though Dietrich (1972: 294–95) speaks of a triple Pentecost in reference to the gift of the spirit to Jews (2:38–41), Samaritans (8:15, 17) and gentiles (Acts 10:44–45), the reference of 10:47, "just as we," places Jews and gentiles on the same level of spirit endowment. Obviously, therefore, as in 2:4 so also in 10:46, glossolalia is repeated for the gentiles as proof of the spirit. Although Luke is not opposed to associating ecstatic phenomena with the spirit (Accts 8:39; 2:4; 10:46) for both the time of Jesus and that of the Church, according to Luke the power of the spirit is manifested primarily in proclamation and prophecy. A fundamental connection between spirit and prophecy/preaching occurs in Luke 4:18–19 and Accts 2:17. The inaugural sermons of Jesus (Luke 4:16–21) and Peter (Acts 2:14–36) are each presented as the consequence of a preceding endowment with the spirit (Lampe 1967: 159).

The course of the Church is presented as determined by the spirit sent by Jesus and is often characterized in personal categories (Acts 8:29, 39; 20:39). The holy spirit is present at important decisions (2:1–4; 4:31; 8:17–18; 9:17–18; 10:44–45; 19:6), contributes to the formulation of the apostolic decree (15:28), and appoints the presbyters in their offices (20:28).

Acts 2:17–21 indicates the salvation-historical location of the works of the spirit. In contrast to Joel 3:1–5, Luke inserts *en tais hemerais,* "in those days," into the quotation, thus identifying the time before the end as the time of the

Church when the promises are fulfilled (2:17; cf. also 10:46; 19:6; 22:17–18).

According to Luke, the community is an entity endowed with the spirit and presently living in the power of the spirit (Luke 11:13; cf. Matt 7:11). The ecclesiological orientation of Lukan pneumatology is evident in such passages; but the issue, so critical for Paul, is absent here: the idea of the pneumatic body of Christ, the doctrine of the *charismata,* the pneumatic basis of faith and action (Horn 1986: 283–86). Contrasts between *pneuma* and *sarx/gramma/nomos* are also absent. On the other hand, other ecclesial aspects are evident. Prayer prepares for reception of the spirit (Luke 3:21; Acts 4:31; 9:9, 11; 13:1–3), but is not an effect of the spirit. Baptism and spirit are related (Acts 2:38; 8:14–17; 10:44–45; and 19:2–6 confirm these as valid exceptions; Haenchen *Apostelgeschichte* MeyerK, 147). The practice of the laying on of hands for transmission of the spirit surfaces once in Acts 8:14 and 17. The gift of the spirit as power to proclaim the gospel is predominant (positioned thematically at the beginning Acts 1:8).

14. Individual Passages. Matt 1:18, 20; and Luke 1:35 attribute Jesus' origin to the action of the *pneuma* as the creative power of God. Though Isa 7:14 was similarly interpreted in Hellenistic Judaism, the closest parallels to the NT statements are found in Hellenistic accounts of the supernatural origins of kings, philosophers, and other prominent persons (see Luz *Evangelium nach Matthäus* EKKNT, 98–107).

According to Matt 5:3, it is the poor "in spirit" who are blessed. In contrast to the original Q formulation (Luke 6:20) Matt adds *tǭ pneumati,* "in spirit," in order to attribute the beatitude to those who are humble in will and thereby distinguish themselves from the haughtiness of the Pharisees (Strecker 1985: 33).

Matt 28:19 along with 1 Cor 12:4–6 and 2 Cor 13:13 form the NT point of departure for later triadic formulations and theological constructions. Matthew receives as tradition the tripartite baptismal formula and combines it with the mission command. The notion of baptizing in "the name of the spirit" along with the Father and the Son is unique. Abramowski suspects an expansion of the unitary baptismal formula parallel to the blessing of Aaron (1984; cf. also Schaberg 1982 and Friedrich 1983).

For further developments, see Hauschild 1972; *TRE* 12: 96–217; Opitz 1960.

Bibliography

Abramowski, L. 1984. Die Entstehung der dreigliedrigen Taufformel—ein Versuch. *ZTK* 81: 417–46.

Anderson, A. A. 1962. The Use of "Ruah" in I QS, I QH, and I QM. JSS 7: 293–303.

Baer, H. von. 1926. *Der Heilige Geist in den Lukasschriften.* BWANT 3/3. Stuttgart.

Barrett, C. K. 1947. *The Holy Spirit and the Gospel Tradition.* London.

Barton, J. 1986. *Oracles of God.* London.

Baur, F. C. 1831. Die Christuspartei in der korinthischen Gemeinde, der Gegensatz des petrinischen und paulinischen Christenthums in der alten Kirche, der Apostel Petrus in Rom. *Tübinger Zeitschrift für Theologie* 61–206.

———. 1845. *Paulus, der Apostel Jesu Christi.* Repr. Osnabruck, 1968.

Beavin, E. L. 1961. Ruah Hakodesh in Some Early Jewish Literature. Ph.D. diss. Vanderbilt.

Becker, J. 1975. Das Gottesbild Jesu und die älteste Auslegung von Ostern. Pp. 105–26 in *Jesus Christus in Historie und Eschatologie,* ed. G. Strecker. Tübingen.

———. 1976. *Auferstehung der Toten im Urchristentum.* SBS 82. Stuttgart.

———. 1980. *Die Testamente der Zwölf Patriarchen.* 2d ed. JSHRZ 3/1.

Berger, K. 1970. *Die Amen-Worte Jesu.* BZNW 39. Berlin.

Betz, H. D. 1974. Geist, Freiheit und Gesetz: Die Botschaft des Paulus an die Gemeinden in Galatien. *ZTK* 71: 78–93.

Betz, O. 1960. *Offenbarung und Schriftforschung in der Qumransekte.* WUNT 6. Tübingen.

Beitenhard, H. 1951. *Die himmlische Welt im Urchristentum und Spätjudentum.* WUNT 2. Tübingen.

Boring, M. E. 1982. *Sayings of the Risen Jesus.* SNTSMS 46. Cambridge.

Bousset, W. 1901. Review of *Die Wirkungen des Geistes,* by H. Weinel. *Göttinger Gelehrte Anzeigen* 163: 753–76.

———. 1926. *Kyrios Christos.* 3d ed. FRLANT 21. Göttingen.

Brandenburger, E. 1968. *Fleisch und Geist.* WMANT 29. Neukirchen-Vluyn.

Bruce, F. F. 1977. Christ and Spirit in Paul. *BJRL* 59: 259–85.

Bultmann, R. 1979. *Die Geschichte der Synoptischen Tradition.* 9th ed. FRLANT 29. Göttingen.

Campenhausen, H. von. 1963. *Kirchliches Amt und geistliche Vollmacht in den ersten drei Jahrhunderten.* 2d ed. BHT 14. Tübingen.

Chevallier, M. A. 1958. *L'esprit et le Messie dans le bas-judaisme et le Nouveau Testament.* Etudes d'histoire et de philosophie religieuses 49. Paris.

———. 1966. Esprit de Dieu, paroles d'hommes. Diss. Strasbourg.

———. 1978. *Souffle de Dieu,* vol. 1. Paris.

Conzelmann, H. 1977. *Die Mitte der Zeit.* 6th ed. BHT 17. Tübingen.

Dauer, A. 1975. *Urchristliche Prophetie.* BWANT 104. Stuttgart.

———. 1984. *Johannes und Lukas.* FB 50. Würzburg.

Davies, W. D. 1980. *Paul and Rabbinic Judaism.* 4th ed. Philadelphia.

Dibelius, M. 1909. *Die Geisterwelt im Glauben des Paulus.*

Dietrich, W. 1972. *Das Petrusbild der lukanischen Schriften.* BWANT 5/14. Stuttgart.

Dietzfelbinger, C. 1985. *Die Berufung des Paulus als Ursprung seiner Theologie.* WMANT 58. Neukirchen-Vluyn.

Dunn, J. D. G. 1975. *Jesus and the Spirit.* London.

Everling, O. 1888. *Die paulinische Angelologie und Dämonologie.* Göttingen.

Foakes Jackson, F. J., and Lake, K., eds. 1933. *The Beginnings of Christianity.* Pt. 1, *The Acts of the Apostles,* vol. 5. London. Repr. Grand Rapids, 1979.

Foerster, W. 1961–62. Der heilige Geist im Spätjudentum. *NTS* 8: 117–34.

Friedrich, G. 1954. Das Gesetz des Glaubens (Röm 3,27). *TZ* 10: 401–19.

———. 1983. Die formale Struktur von Mt 28, 18–20. *ZTK* 80: 137–83.

Georgi, D. 1964. *Die Gegner des Paulus im 2. Korintherbrief.* WMANT 11. Neukirchen-Vluyn.

Goguel, M. 1954. *The Birth of Christianity.* Trans. H. C. Snape. New York.

Goldberg, A. M. 1969. *Untersuchungen über die Vorstellung von der Schekhinah in der frühen rabbinischen Literatur.* Studia Judaica 5.

Goppelt, L. 1978. *Theologie des Neuen Testaments,* ed. J. Roloff. 3d ed. Göttingen. ET 1981, Grand Rapids.

Gunkel, H. 1909. *Die Wirkungen des Heiligen Geistes.* 3d ed. Göttingen.

Hahn, F. 1963. *Das Verständnis der Mission im Neuen Testament.* WMANT 13. Neukirchen-Vluyn.

Harnack, A. von. 1899. Review of *Die Wirkungen des Geistes,* by H. Weinel. *TLZ* 24: 513–15.

Hauschild, W.-D. 1972. *Gottes Geist und der Mensch.* BevT 63. Munich.

Heinemann, I. 1920. Philons Lehre vom Heiligen Geist und der intuitiven Erkenntnis. *MGWJ* 64: 8–29; 101–22.

———. 1922–23. Die Lehre vom Heiligen Geist im Judentum und in den Evangelien. *MGWJ* 66: 169–80; 268–79; 67: 26–35.

Hengel, M. 1975. Zwischen Jesus und Paulus. *ZTK* 72: 151–206.

Hermann, I. 1961. *Kyrios und Pneuma.* SUNT 2. Göttingen.

Hoffmann, P. 1982. *Die Toten in Christus.* 3d ed. NTAbh 2. Münster.

Holtzmann, H. J. 1911. *Lehrbuch der neutestamentlichen Theologie.* 2 vols. 2d ed.

Horn, F. W. 1986. *Glaube und Handeln in der Theologie des Lukas.* 2d ed. GTA 26. Göttingen.

———. 1989. Das Angeld des Geistes. Habibilitationschrift. Göttingen.

Hübner, H. 1982. *Das Gesetz bei Paulus.* 3d ed. FRLANT 119. Göttingen.

Isaacs, M. E. 1976. *The Concept of Spirit and its Bearing on the NT.* Heythrop Monographs.

Jeremias, J. 1973. *Neutestamentliche Theologie.* Pt. 1, *Die Verkündigung Jesu.* 2d ed. Gütersloh.

Johnson, A. R. 1964. *The Vitality of the Individual in the Thought of Ancient Israel.* 2d ed. Cardiff, Wales.

Johnston, G. 1960. "Spirit" and "Holy Spirit" in the Qumran Literature. Pp. 27–42 in *New Testament Sidelights,* ed. H. K. McArthur. Hartford.

Käsemann, E. 1969. Die Legitimität des Apostels. Pp. 475–521 in *Das Paulusbild in der neueren deutsche Forschung,* 2d ed., ed. K. H. Rengstorf. WF 24. Darmstadt.

———. 1970a. Die Anfänge christlicher Theologie. Vol. 2, pp. 82–104 in *Exegetische Versuche und Besinnungen.* 3d ed. Göttingen.

———. 1970b. Sätze heiligen Rechts im Neuen Testament. Vol. 2, pp. 69–82 in *Exegetische Versuche.*

Klinzing, G. 1971. *Die Umdeutung des Kultus in der Qumrangemeinde und im Neuen Testament.* SUNT 7. Göttingen.

Köster, H. 1961–62. The Purpose of the Polemic of a Pauline Fragment. *NTS* 8: 317–32.

———. 1982. *Introduction to the New Testament.* 2 vols. Philadelphia.

Kremer, J. 1973. *Pfingstbericht und Pfingstgeschehen.* SBS 63–64. Stuttgart.

Kuhn, H.-W. 1966. *Enderwartung und gegenwärtiges Heil.* SUNT 4. Göttingen.

Lampe, G. W. H. 1967. The Holy Spirit in the Writings of St. Luke. Pp. 159–200 in *Studies in the Gospels. Essays in Memory of R. H. Lightfoot,* ed. D. E. Nineham. Oxford.

Laufen, R. 1980. *Die Doppelüberlieferungen der Logienquelle und des Markusevangeliums.* BBB 54. Bonn.

Lauha, R. 1983. *Psychophysischer Sprachgebrauch im Alten Testament.* AASF 35. Helsinki.

Leisegang, H. 1919. *Die vorchristlichen Anschauungen und Lehren vom pneuma und der mystisch-intuitiven Erkenntnis.* Vol. 1 in *Der Heilige Geist.* Leipzig.

———. 1922. *PNEYMA HAGION: Der Ursprung des Geistbegriffs der synoptischen Evangelien.* Veröffentlichungen des Forschungsinstituts für vergleichende Religionsgechichte an der Universität Leipzig 4. Leipzig.

Leivestad, R. 1972–73. Das Dogma von der prophetenlosen Zeit. *NTS* 19: 288–99.

Lichtenberger, H. 1980. *Studien zum Menschenbild in Texten der Qumrangemeinde.* SUNT 15. Göttingen.

Lohmeyer, E. 1936. *Galiläa und Jerusalem.* FRLANT 52. Göttingen.

Lüdemann, G. 1980. *Paulus der Heidenapostel.* Vol. 1, *Studien zur Chronologie.* FRLANT 123. Göttingen.

———. 1983. *Paulus der Heidenapostel.* Vol. 2, *Antipaulinismus im frühen Christentum.* FRLANT 130. Göttingen.

Lull, D. J. 1980. *The Spirit in Galatia.* SBLDS 49. Missoula, MT.

Lütgert, W. 1908. *Freiheitspredigt und Schwarmgeister in Korinth.* BFCT 12/3.

Luz, U. 1968. *Das Geschichtsverständnis des Paulus.* BEvT 49.

Lys, D. 1962. *"Ruach": Le souffle dans l'Ancien Testament.* Etudes d'histoire et de philosophie religieuses 56. Paris.

Montague, G. T. 1976. *The Holy Spirit.*

Moody, D. 1976. *Spirit of the Living God.* Philadelphia.

Moule, C. F. D. 1978. *The Holy Spirit.* Grand Rapids.

Müller, D. 1980. Geisterfahrung und Totenauferweckung. Diss. Kiel.

Nötscher, F. 1957. Geist und Geister in den Texten von Qumran. Pp. 305–15 in *Mélanges Bibliques rédigés en l'honneur de A. Robert.* Paris.

Opitz, H. 1960. *Ursprünge frühchristlicher Pneumatologie.* ThArb 15. Berlin.

Paulsen, H. 1974. *Überlieferung und Auslegung in Röm 8.* WMANT 43. Neukirchen-Vluyn.

Pearson, B. A. 1973. *The pneumatikos-psychikos Terminology in I Corinthians.* SBLDS 12. Missoula, MT.

Polag, A. 1977. *Die Christologie der Logienquelle.* WMANT 45. Neukirchen-Vluyn.

Porsch, F. 1974. *Pneuma und Wort.* FTS 16. Freiburg.

Räisänen, H. 1979–80. Das "Gesetz des Glaubens" (Röm 3,27) und das "Gesetz des Geistes" (Röm 8,2). *NTS* 26: 101–17.

Reinmuth, E. 1985. *Geist und Gesetz.* ThArb 44. Berlin.

Reitzenstein, R. 1977. *The Hellenistic Mystery Religions.* Trans. Philadelphia.

Rohde, E. 1898. *Psyche: Seelencult und Unsterblichkeitsglaube der Griechen.* 2d ed. Leipzig. ET 1925, London.

Schaberg, J. 1982. *The Father, the Son and the Holy Spirit.* SBLDS 61. Chico, CA.

Schade, H.-H. 1984. *Apokalyptische Christologie bei Paulus.* 2d ed. GTA 18. Göttingen.

Schäfer, P. 1972. *Die Vorstellung vom Heiligen Geist in der rabbinischen Literatur.* SANT 28. Munich.

Schlatter, A. 1927. *Die Geschichte der ersten Christenheit.* 4th ed. BFCT 2/11.

Schmid, H. H. 1974. Ekstatische und charismatische Geistwirkungen im Alten Testament. Pp. 83–100 in *Erfahrung und Theologie des Heiligen Geistes,* ed. C. Heitmann and H. Mühlen.

Schmidt, K. L. 1981. Das Pneuma Hagion bei Paulus als Person und als Charisma. Pp. 215–63 in *Neues Testament—Judentum—Kirche.* TBü 69. Munich.

Schmithals, W. 1969. *Die Gnosis in Korinth.* 3d ed. FRLANT 66. Göttingen.

———. 1965. *Paulus und die Gnostiker.* TF 35. Hamburg (ET 1972).

Schmitt, H.-C. 1977. Prophetie und Tradition: Beobachtungen zur Frühgeschichte des israelitischen Nabitums. *ZTK* 74: 255–72.

Schnackenburg, R. 1973. Christus, Geist und Gemeinde (Eph 4:1–16). Pp. 279–96 in *Christ and Spirit in the New Testament,* ed. B. Lindars and S. S. Smalley. Cambridge.

Schnelle, U. 1986a. Der erste Thessalonicherbrief und die Entstehung der paulinischen Anthropologie. *NTS* 32: 207–24.
———. 1986b. *Gerechtigkeit und Christusgegenwart.* 2d ed. GTA 24. Göttingen.
Schottroff, L. 1970. *Der Glaubende und die feindliche Welt.* WMANT 37. Neukirchen-Vluyn.
Schreiner, J. 1965. Geistbegabung in der Gemeinde von Qumran. *BZ* 9: 161–80.
Schulz, S. 1958. Die Decke des Moses: Untersuchungen zu einer vorpaulinischen Überlieferung in II Cor 3, 7–18. *ZNW* 49: 1–30.
———. 1972. *Q: Die Spruchquelle der Evangelisten.* Zurich.
Schunck, K.-D. 1979. Wesen und Wirken des Geistes nach dem Alten Testament. *SLAG.A* 18: 7–30.
Schweizer, E. 1951–52. Die sieben Geister in der Apokalypse. *EvT* 11: 502–17.
———. 1952. *Geist und Gemeinde im Neuen Testament und heute.* ThEH 32. Munich.
———. 1963. Röm 1,3f und der Gegensatz von Fleisch und Geist vor und bei Paulus. Pp. 180–89 in *Neotetamentica.* Zurich.
———. 1978. *Heiliger Geist.* TTSup. Berlin.
———. 1982. Christus und der Geist im Kolosserbrief. Pp. 179–93 in *Neues Testament und Christologie im Werden: Aufsätze.* Göttingen.
Sellin, G. 1986. *Der Streit um die Auferstehung der Toten.* FRLANT 138. Göttingen.
Smalley, S. S. 1973. Spirit, Kingdom and Prayer in Luke–Acts. *NovT* 15: 59–71.
Smend, R. 1984. *Die Entstehung des Alten Testaments.* 3d ed. Theologische Wissenschaft 1. Stuttgart.
Strecker, G. 1976. Befreiung und Rechtfertigung. Pp. 479–508 in *Rechtfertigung,* ed. J. Friedrich; W. Pöhlmann; and P. Stuhlmacher. Tübingen and Göttingen.
———. 1978. Strukturen einer neutestamentlichen Ethik. *ZTK* 75: 117–46.
———. 1981. *Das Judenchristentum in den Pseudoklementinen.* 2d ed. TU 70/2. Berlin.
———. 1985. *Die Bergpredigt.* 2d ed. Göttingen.
Tatum, W. B. 1974. Die Zeit Israels: Lukas 1–2 und die theologische Intention der lukanischen Schriften. Pp. 317–66 in *Das Lukas—Evangelium,* ed. G. Braumann. WF 280. Darmstadt.
Unnik, W. C. van. 1968. "Den Geist löschet nicht aus" (1. Thess. 5,19). *NovT* 10: 255–69.
Vielhauer, P. 1978. *Geschichte der urchristlichen Literatur.* Berlin.
Volz, P. 1910. *Der Geist Gottes und die verwandten Erscheinungen im AT und im anschliessenden Judentum.*
Vos, J. S. 1973. *Traditionsgeschichtliche Untersuchungen zur paulinischen Pneumatologie.* Assen.
Weinel, H. 1899. *Die Wirkungen des Geistes und der Geister im nachapostolischen Zeitalter bis auf Irenäus.*
Westermann, C. 1981. Geist im Alten Testament. *EvT* 41: 223–30.
Wilcken, U. 1979. Zu 1 Kor 2, 1–16. Pp. 501–37 in *Theologia Crucis—Signum Crucis,* ed. C. Andresen and G. Klein. Tübingen.
Winter, M. 1975. *Pneumatiker und Psychiker in Korinth.* MTS 12. Marburg.
Wolff, H. W. 1984. *Anthropologie des Alten Testaments.* 4th ed. Munich.
Wolfson, H. A. 1948. *Philo: Foundations of Religious Philosophy in Judaism, Christianity and Islam.* 2 vols. Cambridge, MA.

F. W. HORN
Trans. Dietlinde M. Elliott

HOMAM (PERSON) [Heb *hômām*]. A clan name in the genealogy of Seir the Horite in 1 Chr 1:39. Homam is listed as the second son of Lotan, son of Seir, and he is thus the grandson of Seir. The name in this form appears only in 1 Chr 1:39, but it is equivalent to the name Hemam (MT and KJV, while RSV reads incorrectly HEMAN) in the parallel genealogical listing in Gen 36:22. For discussion of these clans, see JAAKAN.

VICTOR H. MATTHEWS

HOMER [Heb *ḥōmer*]. See WEIGHTS AND MEASURES.

HOMICIDE. See PUNISHMENTS AND CRIMES.

HOMILY FORM (HELLENISTIC AND EARLY CHRISTIAN). Christian preachers of the 3d century and later had clearly adopted explicit forms and methods for their preaching. They inherited and adapted these homiletical techniques from their predecessors in the art of persuasion, namely the rhetoricians of Greek and Roman culture. The Greeks gave names to certain rhetorical techniques and organized speech and the art of persuasion into a system which was taught within schools of formal rhetoric (Kennedy 1984: 9). These schools produced rhetorical handbooks which were intended to train a student to speak effectively and to acquire the ability to move an audience. The primary arena for the use of these rhetorical techniques was the court of law, though formal rhetoric would not have been restricted solely to this setting. Plato's dialogue *Phaedrus,* Aristotle's *Rhetorica,* Cicero's *Brutus, De inventione, De oratore,* Cornificus' *Rhetorica ad Herennium,* and Quintilian's *Institutio oratoria* are the most important works from the Hellenistic and Roman period on the subject of rhetoric and persuasion. These works provide us with valuable early information concerning the nature and importance of formal rhetorical training and the art of persuasion in the period leading up to the development of a form of early Christian preaching.

By the 4th and 5th centuries C.E. the formal rhetorical techniques and forms employed by the orators of Greece and Rome had clearly influenced Christian writing and preaching. In the 4th century Gregory of Nazianzus, for example, gave a sermon precisely in the form of a Panegyricus, a form of speech intended originally for a pagan festival. At the end of the 4th and beginning of the 5th century Augustine wrote *On Christian Doctrine,* which is itself a major contribution to the history and theory of rhetoric, although now from a decidedly Christian perspective (Kennedy 1980: 39, 155). Even earlier in the common era, Clement of Alexandria, Tertullian, Jerome, John of Chrysostom, and Melito of Sardis all demonstrated familiarity with formal rhetorical forms and techniques, and their own sermons reflect the impact classical rhetoric had upon them.

However, when we move earlier into the 1st century C.E. and inquire about a homily or sermon form, the matter is less clear. The role and influence of Greek oratory and rhetoric have long been recognized within NT studies. Paul's letter to the Romans (Scroggs 1976), Philemon (Church 1978), and the Epistle to the Galatians (Betz 1975; cf. Vouga 1988) have all been studied within the context of, and according to, formal Greco-Roman rhetoric. The influence of other classical Greco-Roman conventions on Paul has also been recognized within Pauline studies. Prominent in this regard has been the influence of the cynic-Stoic diatribe (Bultmann 1910; Stowers 1981).

However, when looking for a distinctive homily form within Jewish or Christian preaching in the 1st century, scholars have heretofore found little. In fact, it has been said that "we know virtually nothing about the contours of such a genre in the first century" (Donfried 1974: 26). Recently attention has been drawn to a form of early Christian and Jewish preaching which seems to be an explicit homily form, and which appears to be indebted to the formal rhetoricians of the Greek and Roman periods (Wills 1984; Black 1988). However, it should be noted that the *degree* to which formal rhetoric influenced this homily form remains a matter of debate.

In 1984 L. Wills referred to the homily form within early Jewish and Christian preaching as a "word of exhortation." The word of exhortation typically has three parts: an *exempla,* which is a reasoned exposition of the points to be made, usually with examples from the past or scriptural quotations for support; this is followed by a *conclusion* based on the "facts" laid out in the exempla, and "therefore" the audience should respond or behave in such and such a manner. The conclusion is often introduced with a participle and *dia, dio, touto,* or some other Greek particle of conjunction. This is followed by an *exhortation,* usually expressed with an imperative or hortatory subjunctive (Wills 1984: 279).

Examples of this early Christian and Jewish homily form can be seen in Acts 2:14–40; 3:12–26; 13:14–41; 20:17–35; 1 Cor 10:1–14; Heb 1:1–2:1; 1 Pet 1:3–11; *1 Clem* 6:1–7:2; 42:1–44:6. Wills claims the pattern of "the word of exhortation" can also be found in Ignatius of Antioch's *Letter to the Ephesians* and the *Epistle to Barnabas* (1984: 291–92). Within Jewish sources the same pattern of exempla, conclusion, and exhortation can be seen in *Wisdom of Solomon* 13–15 and the *Testament of the Twelve Patriarchs* (*T. Reu.* 5:1–5; *T. Levi* 2:6–3:8; *T. Benj.* 2:5; 3:1; 6:6; 7:1; 8:1).

The structure and outline of this homily form, like formal rhetoric itself, are not concrete. The homily can be modified, broken up, or used in a cyclical fashion at the author's or speaker's discretion. The background for this early Christian and what seems to be Hellenistic Jewish homily form is formal Greek rhetoric. Wills finds this threefold form in the speeches of the Greek orators. Broadly speaking, there are three types of speeches, according to the handbooks: deliberative, forensic, and epideictic (Quintilian, *Inst.* 3.4.16). The deliberative speeches were intended for audiences before a governing or authoritative body, forensic speeches were given before the courts, and epideictic speeches were meant for public and honorary gatherings. Wills, having isolated this early homily form, and having suggested the background out of which the form developed, remains cautious about how directly one should connect it with the structure of speeches given within *formal* Greco-Roman rhetoric (1984: 298–99).

Building upon the work of Wills, C. C. Black has argued for a stronger correlation between this earlier homily form—the "word of exhortation" in the NT and other early Christian and Jewish documents—and classical rhetoric. Black maintains that the word of exhortation appears to be in fundamental agreement with the judicial (forensic), deliberative, and epidiectic address. This form of early Christian and Jewish homily is perfectly understandable in terms of the rhetorical conventions outlined in Aristotle's *Rhetorica* or Quintilian's *Institutio oratoria.* Viewed in such a way, 1st-century Jewish Hellenistic and Christian preaching can be located far more within the mainstream of classical rhetoric (Black 1988: 3, 10, 16).

It was not long after the 1st century that Christian preaching began explicitly to employ and engage classical rhetoric. It was precisely this influence of classical philosophy and rhetoric upon 2d-century Christians which provoked Tertullian to ask rhetorically, "What has Athens to do with Jerusalem?" What concord is there between the Academy and the Church?" (*De Praescr. Haeret.* 7). Jerome follows Tertullian in his concern over the influence of Greco-Roman rhetoric, saying, "What has Horace to do with the Psalms, Virgil with the Gospels or Cicero with the Apostles?" (*Ep.* 22.29). As early Christian preaching was more and more influenced by classical rhetoric and its techniques and conventions, certain Church Fathers began to feel a tension between rhetoric and Christian preaching. Ironically, however, both Jerome and Tertullian display significant ability and schooling where the same rhetoric is concerned. Perhaps, as Cicero said of Plato, it is when they are most concerned with orators that they themselves appear the consummate orators (*De oratore* 1.11.47).

Yet other early Christian preachers embraced the rhetorical forms and the techniques of persuasion taught and practiced by the classical orators. Lactantius (ca. 250–300 C.E., known as the "Christian Cicero") taught rhetoric prior to his conversion, and following it was made tutor to Emperor Constantine's son. In his *Divinae institutiones* he attempted to put in "literate style" the teachings of Christianity for pagans. Out of this work emerges a philosophical Christian rhetoric (Kennedy 1980: 148).

Gradually the Church began to employ more formal and classical rhetoric in order to address the culture and world of which they were becoming a part and which they were beginning to embrace with enthusiasm. The definitive expression of the coalescing of Christian doctrine and classical Greco-Roman rhetoric would be Augustine's *De doctrina christiana.* In this book Augustine tried to provide the preacher with the necessary skills of interpretation and homiletics. In the 4th book he is explicitly in dialogue with classical rhetoric. A teacher of rhetoric prior to his conversion, Augustine was largely dependent on Cicero for the writing of this "Christian Rhetoric" (Kennedy 1980: 156–57). This work represents the culmination of a process of enculturation and education of the early Christian orators and preachers which resulted finally in the synthesis of classical rhetoric and Christian doctrine and preaching.

The literature of the 1st century, and the NT in particular, evidences the influence of classical culture and rhetorical conventions. Out of this influence and sociocultural interaction a homily form emerged, "the word of exhortation." This form, it can be recognized, owes a significant degree of its shape and form to the conventions of classical rhetoric. The homily form seems to have been rather widespread, and is seen in both Jewish and Christian documents. Over the next century Christianity would begin explicitly to engage and employ the techniques and forms associated with Greek and Roman oratory. Classical rhetoric was a major contributor to the nature and form of Hellenistic Jewish and Christian preaching. Though some expressed concern about the influence of these "pagan" rhetorical practices upon Christians, it seems clear that the classical forms of persuasion and rhetoric, which played such an important role in the Greco-Roman period, did indeed influence Christian preaching and were finally adopted by Christians in order that they might speak persuasively to that same world.

Bibliography

Betz, H. D. 1975. The Literary Composition and Function of Paul's Letter to the Galatians. *NTS* 21: 353–79.

Black, C. C. 1988. The Rhetorical Form of the Hellenistic Jewish and Early Christian Sermon. *HTR* 81: 1–18.

Bultmann, R. 1910. *Der Stil der paulinischen Predigt und die kynisch-Stoische Diatribe*. Göttingen.

Church, F. F. 1978. The Rhetorical Structure and Design in Paul's Letter to Philemon. *HTR* 71: 17–33.

Donfried, K. 1974. *The Setting of Second Clement in Early Christianity*. Leiden.

Kennedy, G. 1980. *Classical Rhetoric and Its Christian and Secular Tradition from Ancient to Modern Times*. Chapel Hill, NC.

———. 1984. *New Testament Interpretation Through Rhetorical Criticism*. Chapel Hill, NC.

Scroggs, R. 1976. Paul as Rhetorician: Two Homilies in Romans 1–11. Pp. 271–98 in *Jews, Greeks and Christians: Religious Cultures in Antiquity*. Leiden.

Stowers, S. 1981. *The Diatribe and Paul's Letter to the Romans*. SBLDS 57. Chico, CA.

Vouga, F. von. 1988. Zur rhetorischen Gattung des Galaterbriefes. *ZNW* 79: 291–93.

Wilder, A. N. 1964. *Early Christian Rhetoric*. Cambridge, MA.

Wills, L. 1984. The Form of the Sermon in Hellenistic Judaism and Early Christianity. *HTR* 77: 277–99.

J. Andrew Overman

HOMOSEXUALITY. See PROSTITUTION; PUNISHMENTS AND CRIMES; ROMANS, EPISTLE TO THE; and SEX AND SEXUALITY.

HONI. A righteous Jew who received the name "Ḥoni the Circle-Drawer" because he once reportedly refused to leave a circle he had drawn until rain relieved the parched land (*m. Taᶜan.* 3.8; *y. Taᶜan.* 3.9 [8]; *b. Taᶜan.* 23). His Greek name is "Onias" (Joseph. *Ant* 14.22). He lived in the early 1st century B.C.E. and was stoned to death during the civil war between Hyrcanus II and Aristobulus II by fellow Jews (*Ant* 14.22). Josephus (writing in 93 or 94 C.E.) says that Ḥoni was righteous, was revered for his efficacious words—especially prayers—and was martyred outside the walls of Jerusalem, where Aristobulus and his men were being besieged, probably just before the Passover feast in April 65 B.C.E.

From rabbinic literature we also learn the following about Ḥoni: (1) he was a wise teacher and revered in the Beth Hamidrash (*b. Taᶜan.* 23a); (2) he was a righteous individual, but not an Essene as some scholars have stated (and certainly not the famous Righteous Teacher of Qumran); (3) he was able to do miraculous things through prayer, notably to cause rain to fall; (4) he apparently understood himself to be "son" of God in a special way, "like a son" in God's house (*m. Taᶜan.* 3.8); (5) he was honored by the masses and Sanhedrin (*b. Taᶜan* 23a), but grudgingly acknowledged by Simon ben Shetah, the most influential rabbi in his time (*m. Taᶜan.* 3.8); (6) legends subsequently developed about him, most notably that he slept for seventy years (*b. Taᶜan.* 23a; cf. *4 Bar.*), and that the violent wind that destroyed crops throughout Palestine (*Ant* 14.25–30) was God's punishment on the inhabitants for the murder of Ḥoni. Despite some scholarly attempts to prove otherwise (see Vermes 1981: 58–82), there is no unambiguous evidence that Ḥoni performed healing miracles; although it is also clear that our sources are late and selective and it is conceivable that he did cause miraculous cures as did another Palestinian, charismatic Ḥanina ben Dosa.

Bibliography

Green, W. S. 1979. Palestinian Holy Men: Charismatic Leadership and Rabbinic Tradition. *ANRW* 2/19/2: 614–47.

Neusner, J. 1988. The Sage, Miracle, and Magic. Pp. 13–30 in *Why No Gospels in Talmudic Judaism?* Brown Judaic Studies 135. Atlanta.

Vermes, G. 1981. *Jesus the Jew*. London.

James H. Charlesworth

HOOK. Several different Hebrew terms are rendered "hook" in the RSV. The various hangings of the tabernacle are suspended from hooks or pegs (*wāwîm*) attached to the pillars. Some of these were gold (as Exod 26:32), and others were silver (as Exod 27:4, for the courtyard pillars), the choice of material being related to the degree of holiness of the pillars involved. That is, hooks closest to the holiest zone of the tabernacle were made of gold, and those farther away were silver. See also TABERNACLE. A completely different term (*ḥaḥ* or *ḥôaḥ*) is translated "hook" and denotes a ring put in the nose of an animal (as Ezek 19:4, 9; 29:4) or a human taken captive (as 2 Kgs 19:28 = Isa 37:29).

Carol Meyers

HOOPOE. See ZOOLOGY.

HOPE (NT). Even if the noun "hope" (Gk *elpís*) is not found at all in the Gospels and the verb "to hope" (Gk *elpízein*) is found only five times in the Gospels—with the OT sense of "to trust" (Matt 12:21; John 5:45) or with a purely secular and nonreligious sense (Luke 6:34; 23:8; 24:21)—the idea of hope as confidence in God "whose goodness and mercy are to be relied on and whose promises cannot fail" (Barr 1950: 72) is everywhere presupposed in the NT (see also *TDNT* 2: 517–35 and *LTK* 5: 416–24).

In the Synoptic Gospels the notion of hope is conveyed through the sense of "expectation" (Gk *prosdechomai*) generated by Jesus' preaching of conversion in the face of the imminent arrival of the kingdom of God. Paul's theology, which is oriented around the twin poles of Christ's resurrection as the in-breaking of the kingdom and Jesus' parousia as its fulfillment, manifests the most fully elaborated theology of hope (1 Thessalonians, Romans, 1–2 Corinthians, Galatians, Philippians, Philemon). This line is continued with various additional nuances in Hebrews, in the Deutero-Paulines (Colossians, Ephesians, 2 Thessalonians), and in the Pastoral and Catholic Epistles. While a great deal has been made of the Johannine emphasis on "realized eschatology," there can be little doubt that John also speaks of the glory of the heavenly world as the goal of the believer's hope (John 13:33, 36). Finally, although Revelation also lacks the vocabulary of hope, the notion is manifestly conveyed by the call to "patient endurance," which undergirds the theology of the whole work.

A. The Gospels and the Acts
   1. The "Q" Source
   2. Mark and Matthew
   3. Luke-Acts
   4. John
B. The Pauline Epistles
   1. The "Faith-Love-Hope" Triad
   2. Being "with Christ"
   3. "Hoping against Hope"
C. The Deutero-Pauline and Pastoral Epistles
D. Hebrews, the Catholic Epistles, Revelation
   1. The Hope of "Seeing God"
   2. "The Anchor of Hope"
   3. Hope as "Patient Endurance"
E. Conclusion

A. The Gospels and the Acts

In the Synoptic Gospels the strong sense of assurance that the divine promises articulated in the OT are soon to be fulfilled in the Messiah, Jesus, calls forth from the reader sentiments of expectation and longing. The parenetic dimension of the gospels urges the community of believers to steadfast patience and to "keeping watch" (Mark 13:37).

1. The "Q" Source. In the Q source, which is comprised of the bulk of the Jesus sayings common to Matthew and Luke, Jesus' mode of proclaiming the kingdom implies the incarnate presence of divine wisdom (Luke 7:35 = Matt 11:19) and an implicit Christological claim that in his ministry God's salvation is offered. Just as the harvest is "already" implicitly present in the farmer's handful of seed though "not yet" gathered in (Luke 10:2 = Matt 9:37), so God's kingdom is near in the proclamation of the good news (Luke 10:9 = Matt 10:7), and finds an echo in the petition Jesus taught regarding the coming of God's reign (Luke 11:2 = Matt 6:10). Hope's tensile dynamic, stretching between the "already" and the "not yet," and found in Jesus' heralding of conversion, gets taken up by Paul in his proclamation that "by faith we wait for the *hope* of righteousness" (Gal 5:5) and "in *this hope* we were saved" (Rom 8:24).

2. Mark and Matthew. The "Little Apocalypse" of Mark 13 carefully interweaves strands of the tradition which assert that the end is "near" and still is "not yet." The disciples are informed by Jesus that they will follow the path of suffering (Mark 13:9, 11–12) already realized by John the Baptist (1:14; 9:13) and the OT prophets (12:3–4) and soon to be embarked upon by Jesus himself (14:21, 42). The negative cast given to the disciples elsewhere in Mark disappears here, indicating that Mark intends to present a proleptic portrait of the post-Easter Church—the only such depiction in this gospel, given the absence of resurrection appearances. This hopeful characterization of the disciples is attributed to the gift of the Holy Spirit (13:11), which enables them to save their souls by "enduring patiently" (13:13) and "keeping watch" (13:37).

For Matthew, the future appearance of the Son of Man in glory will reveal the true state of affairs; e.g., which members of the Church are "wheat" and which ones "tares" (Matt 13:41–43). Matthew is quite serene in encouraging members of the Church to face the future with hope, for Christ promises, "I am with you always" (28:20; cf. 1:23; 18:20). Only those who divorce their faith from their deeds need to be concerned about the future (7:21–23), for Matthew knows with the OT that "hope in the sense of confident expectation of future well-being proved to be ill-founded whenever it was divorced from the perfect and upright character and will of God and applied instead to merely self-regarding matters of well-being, escape from distress and so forth—even when these were dressed up in respectable, religious phrases" (Moule 1970: 10–11).

3. Luke-Acts. Luke stresses, in both the gospel and Acts, the continuity of Judaism and the Church, the piety of the OT and that of "the way," under the rubric of longing or expectation. Thus, in the infancy narrative, Simeon is said to be "looking for the consolation of Israel" (Luke 2:25), and Anna spoke of the child Jesus to all who were looking for the redemption of Jerusalem (2:38). When John the Baptist preached, people were "in expectation" (3:15), as they also were when they inquired of Jesus whether he were "he who is to come" (7:19–23). For Luke, this sense of hopeful expectation will characterize the Church in the end times (12:36, 46); though bringing fear to those unprepared, it bids confidence and peace to those who await their salvation (21:26–28). In Acts, except for an OT quotation (2:26) and two instances of hope used with a purely secular meaning (16:19; 27:20), Luke regularly places the word on Paul's lips (23:6; 24:15; 26:6–7; 28:20) to show that he shares with his people Israel's eschatological expectation of the resurrection of the dead (Grossouw 1954: 531).

4. John. Scholars have noted the juxtaposition in the Fourth Gospel of "futurist" and "realized" eschatologies ("the hour *is coming* and *now is*," John 4:23; cf. 16:32). This should not lead one to conclude that hope plays little or no role in the Johannine view. Texts which refer either to the final judgment or to the resurrection of the dead, taken together, manifest a strong futurist dimension (John 5:28–29; 6:39–40, 44, 54; 12:48) and the object of the Christian's hope is clearly mentioned in several texts

(12:25–26; 14:1–3; 17:24). What is clear is that John's focus is a double one: the present union of the disciple with Jesus the Revealer (realized eschatology) *and* the believer's continuing and future union with Christ in the father's glory (futurist eschatology). Human existence in this world (the possession of one's "soul" [Gk *psychē*]) will give way to the inheriting or gaining of "eternal life" (Gk *zoē aionios*). Of this hope Christ is simultaneously guarantor and mediator (Woschitz 1979: 705–7).

B. The Pauline Epistles

1. The "Faith-Love-Hope" Triad. Paul's well-known assertion that in the end "faith, hope, love abide" (1 Cor 13:13) has prompted speculation on the how, when, and by whom of their association. Since the three theological virtues appear listed in different orders—with hope and love alternating in the third position (e.g., 1 Thess 5:8)—one may surmise that at one time faith and love were found paired without hope, perhaps as a summary of the double commandment of love of God and of neighbor (cf. 1 Thess 1:3; Gal 5:5). Living the commandment of love within the "already/not yet" tension brings the Christian personal experiences, denominated "trials" or "tribulations." At this point, there enters upon the scene a gift of the Holy Spirit to sustain the believer amidst adversity, that of "hope" which is sometimes accompanied by "perseverance" (Gk *hypomonē*). Perseverance is so closely allied with hope that at times hope can even be called perseverance (1 Thess 1:3; Léon-Dufour 1980: 231). Indeed, in the post-Pauline literature, perseverance takes the place of hope as a characteristic of faithful discipleship (Titus 2:2; 1 Tim 6:11; 2 Tim 3:10; Rev 2:19).

2. Being "with Christ." The parallels noted between the death and resurrection of Christ and the sufferings undergone by believers led Paul to describe the object of Christian hope as a share in the glory of God (2 Cor 4:16–18), which marks the state of the risen Christ. In 2 Corinthians and elsewhere, when Paul describes his experience of tribulation, he uses the concept of "trust" or "confidence" in God to describe the hope that wells up in him (2 Cor 3:4, 12; cf. Philemon 21). Later, Paul describes all Christians as groaning in their anticipation of being clothed with the glory of the resurrection body (2 Corinthians 5). When, in Philippians, Paul contemplates the possibility of his own death, he describes his hope as one of going to be with Christ in that divine glory into which Jesus has already entered (Phil 1:23; cf. 3:20–21).

3. "Hoping against Hope." In Romans, Paul reflects on Christian hope as an attribute shared not only by human persons but, in some sense, also by the whole of creation, which "has been groaning in travail until now" (Rom 8:22). Léon-Dufour notes (1986: 233) that in Romans 8 Paul uses a series of Greek words to communicate the various tonalities of hope; these include *apekdechomai,* a violent waiting that he translates "spy out attentively," and *apokaradokia,* an attitude of craning one's neck to observe what is coming about, translated as "stalking." This vocabulary serves to underline not that creation "keeps hope" but that God does so by situating the created world on a firm foundation of hope.

Paul's vision extends as deeply into the past as it does into the future which God has reserved for the world in Christ. As he gazes into salvific history, Paul focuses on Abraham, his father in faith, whom he characterizes as *"hoping against hope"* (Rom 4:18) in order to stress how great was the trust Abraham put in the promises God had given him. Here Paul says that Abraham believed or trusted in God ("hoped") against all human evidence or odds ("against hope"). For Paul, Abraham's hope, as his own, was in the God "who gives life to the dead and calls into existence the things that do not exist" (Rom 4:17).

C. The Deutero-Pauline and Pastoral Epistles

The Deutero-Pauline and Pastoral Epistles continue the Pauline emphases, except that the tension between the "already" and the "not yet" has been diminished somewhat, possibly under the impact of the delay of the parousia.

1. Hope in the Person of Christ. What was looked to as future by Paul is somehow already given in Colossians and 2 Thessalonians. Thus God is said to have given the Thessalonians "eternal comfort and good hope through grace" and Christ is said now to be "in you," and this is, for the Christians of Colossae, their "hope of glory" (Col 1:27). Even so, the "hope of the gospel" (1:23) does have a future dimension, being "the hope laid up for you in heaven" (1:5). Ephesians contrasts the former condition of the pagan converts, who formerly were "without hope because without God" (Eph 2:12), with their present status in Christ, having the "one hope that belongs to your call" (4:4), the riches of Christ's "glorious inheritance" (1:18).

2. Hope in Eternal Life. The object of Christian hope is one of the themes of the Pastorals. In 1 Timothy we read that hope is not in "uncertain riches but on God" (1 Tim 6:17), who is further characterized as "the living God who is the Savior of all men, especially of those who believe" (4:10; cf. 5:5). Christ, too, is described as "our hope" (1 Tim 1:1), especially in his parousia which completes Christian hope (Titus 2:13). On two occasions "eternal life" is presented as the goal of hope (Titus 1:2; 3:7).

D. Hebrews, the Catholic Epistles, Revelation

The variety of ways of describing the object of Christian hope, begun in the Deutero-Paulines and continued in the Pastorals, continues in the later NT writings.

1. The Hope of "Seeing God." The context of suffering, which marks the later NT period, leads to the view that hope can be tested and found solid "in steadfastness" (Jas 1:2–4); also that if hope is alive it must be rooted in the living God and proclaimed to a world which may not share it but asks about it (1 Pet 1:3, 21; 3:15). Christians are called upon to be steadfast in bearing sufferings so that they not be put to shame on the day of judgment (1 Pet 4:14). The positive issue of hope is described in the Johannine tradition as "seeing God," for "when he appears we shall be like him, for we shall see him as he is" (1 John 3:2–3).

2. "The Anchor of Hope." The book of Hebrews as an extended exhortation to a community wavering in its commitment in time of persecution, introduces the anchor as the image that symbolizes hope (Heb 6:18–19). In effect, Hebrews summarizes the biblical teaching on hope, which it regards as rooted in God's promises and related to Christ (10:23). Just as Christ bore patiently with the shame of the cross to enter into God's glory (12:1–2), so the Christian is to keep focused on where Christ has gone as trailblazer, into God's heavenly presence. Belonging to Christ's household is the Christian's "pride in our hope" (3:6) and God's oath to Christ is one's surety of a "better hope" than was had even by Melchizedek, the high priest to whom Abraham paid tithes (7:19–22).

3. Hope as "Patient Endurance." In the book of Revelation, the letters to the whole Church (represented by the seven churches of Asia Minor) constitute a word of purification and judgment from the exalted Christ. Threats are addressed to believers to shock them into holding fast, turning back to youthful vigor or to waking up (Rev 2:1–3:22). This is the risen Christ's prophetic judgment which urges confidence and patient endurance; it is the other side of the apocalyptic manifestation of God's saving plan for the elect. It is the same God standing behind Revelation who makes possible the Church's "patient endurance," which, in this scheme, describes the same reality that elsewhere in the NT is described as "hope."

E. Conclusion

As in the Bible generally, so also in the NT, hope is rooted in God. For the Christian, God has revealed the way to salvation in Jesus' preaching of the kingdom and his call to conversion in light of its imminence. God has authenticated this saving design by raising Jesus from the dead, which at once ushered in the "end of the ages" and prefigures the believer's own hoped-for resurrection. Between Jesus' resurrection and his parousia, tension caused by the "already" and "not yet" dimensions of this salvation stirs the disciple to hope. Both the delay of the parousia and the outbreak of persecution against the Church challenged the NT authors to rethink the notion of hope and, to a degree, to spiritualize it. However, neither these nor other factors served to attenuate hope's role within the armor of the Christian life (Titus 2:13; cf. 1 Thess 5:8).

Bibliography

Barr, A. 1950. Hope *(elpís, elpízein)* in the New Testament. *SJT* 3: 68–77.

Groussouw, W. 1954. L'Espérance dans le Nouveau Testament. *RB* 61: 508–32.

Léon-Dufour, X. 1980. Hope. Pp. 231–32 in *Dictionary of the New Testament.* Trans. T. Prendergast. San Francisco.

———. 1986. *Life and Death in the New Testament.* Trans. T. Prendergast. San Francisco.

Morton, W. K. 1952. The Meaning of Hope in the Bible. *ER* 4: 419–26.

Moule, C. F. D. 1970. *The Meaning of Hope.* Philadelphia.

Nebe, G. 1983. *Höffnung bei Paulus.* Göttingen.

Nicolau, M. 1972. La Esperanza en la Carta a los Hebreos. Pp. 187–202 in *La Esperanza en La Biblia.* Semana Biblica Española 30. Madrid.

Spicq, C. 1931. *La Révélation de l'espérance dans le Nouveau Testament.* Paris.

Woschitz, K. M. 1979. *Elpis: Höffnung.* Vienna.

TERRENCE PRENDERGAST

HOPHNI (PERSON) [Heb *ḥopnî*]. Hophni is one of the sons of Eli, the priest. The name is probably from Eg *ḥfn(r)* meaning "tadpole," and thus suggests an Egyptian connection for Hophni. Hophni only appears in 1 Samuel and only in association with his brother PHINEHAS.

Hophni and Phinehas are first mentioned as priests and as the two sons (1 Sam 1:3) of Eli, who was also a priest (1 Sam 1:9). They all served at the temple at Shiloh (1 Sam 1:3, 7, 9, 24), where the "LORD of Hosts" (= YHWH *ṣĕbāʾôt* ["armies"]) was worshipped (1 Sam 1:3).

The attitude of this introduction of Hophni and Phinehas is neutral toward them, and it is set within the context of the story of the early years of Samuel. As the story continues, it becomes clear that the author, probably the Deuteronomistic Historian, is using Hophni and Phinehas as foils in contrast to Samuel. Samuel emerges as the true priest of Israel, and Eli's sons become examples of evil, greedy priests who have rejected Yahweh. This has larger implications for understanding the struggle between priestly factions, for the Elide faction is being rejected and the Zadokite group is being advocated.

The first indication of trouble for Hophni and Phinehas appears in 1 Sam 2:12–17. The brothers are described as "worthless men" ("sons of Belial") and as "not knowing" Yahweh (2:12). The phrase "sons of Belial" *(bĕnê bĕliyyaʾal)* suggests the degree of condemnation of Hophni and Phinehas by the writer. The phrase literally means "not *(bly)* of use *(yʿl),*" but implies the worship of gods other than Yahweh (Deut 13:14—Eng 13:13); Judg 19:22; 2 Sam 20:1). Later usage (*Liv. Pro.* 4:6, 21; 17:2; *T. Dan.* 1:7; *T. Levi* 3:2–3; 2 Cor 6:15) suggests that Belial is associated with Satan and that in this earlier instance evil is at least hinted at. See also BELIAL. In addition, there may be a wordplay between Belial *(bĕliyyaʿal)* and Baal *(baʿal),* which would also suggest the evilness of the two sons. A similar understanding of evil is implicit in the statement that they "did not know" ("had no regard for"—RSV) Yahweh. The clear implication is that their activities were evil, and that they had turned away from Yahweh.

This perspective is reinforced in 1 Sam 2:13–17, where the greed of Hophni and Phinehas is displayed in their demands for an excessive portion of the offering and in their threatening of violence (v 16) if the extra portion was not surrendered. Finally, in 2:22, Eli is told about his sons' "lying" *(škb)* with the women who guarded *(ṣbʾ)* the door of the "tent of meeting." Eli speaks to his sons (vv 23–24a), but they ignore him, and thus Yahweh "takes delight" *(ḥpṣ)* in slaying the sons.

The special relationship of Eli to Yahweh is rehearsed on the occasion of the appearance of "a man of God" (=a prophet). Eli's house was chosen in Egypt (1 Sam 2:27) to be priests (2:28), but since Eli's sons became greedy (2:29), Yahweh will destroy Eli and his house, and Eli's sons shall no longer serve as priests (2:30–34).

In place of Eli, Yahweh will raise up a faithful priest, for whom he will build a faithful house and who will forever stand before Yahweh's anointed (i.e., his king) (2:35). The statement in 1 Kgs 2:27 indicates that Solomon's expulsion of Abiathar from the priesthood in Jerusalem fulfills the prophecy concerning Eli (Abiathar is supposedly the great-great-grandson of Eli [1 Sam 4:19; 14:3; 22:20; 2 Sam 8:17]). In place of Abiathar, Solomon appoints Zadok (1 Kgs 2:35). By implication, then, this is support for worship in Jerusalem by the Zadokites and a rejection of the Elides and their worship in Shiloh. This, in turn, fits the Deuteronomistic Historian's perspective on history: only worship Yahweh, and only in Jerusalem. Anyone who violates these norms is not fit to be a priest and at best can only become servants of the faithful priests (1 Sam 2:36).

The last appearance of Hophni and Phinehas is connected with the battle of the Israelites against the Philistines at Ebenezer and Aphek. The first encounter was a victory for the Philistines. Seeking reinforcements, the Israelites bring the "ark of the covenant of the Lord of armies (hosts)" from Shiloh to the battle. Hophni and Phinehas accompany the ark on its journey, but neither they nor Eli are now identified as priests. The subsequent battle is a total disaster. The Israelites lose the battle in a great slaughter (1 Sam 4:10), the ark is captured, and Hophni and Phinehas are slain (4:11). Upon hearing of the disaster, Eli falls over in his chair, breaks his neck, and dies (4:18).

Given the ANE conceptualization of war, the loss of the ark would imply the defeat of the god of the ark. However, the power and efficacy of the ark persist after its capture, with plagues and evil events taking place among the Philistines (1 Sam 5:3–12). Since the power of the ark is not lost, there must be another reason for the defeat of the Israelites. That reason goes back to Hophni and Phinehas. Their faithless activities and subsequent coming into contact with the ark lead to the defeat. The fault is not in the god or the ark, but in the actions of the people. So like the conquest of Ai (Joshua 7–8), the story seeks to reinforce the necessity of the righteousness of the people in holy war. Any violation of that righteousness can lead to disaster.

So the story of Hophni and Phinehas serves three functions (1) it is a counterexample of the good, righteous priest, Samuel; (2) it explains the rejection of the Elide priesthood in favor of the Zadokites; and (3) it supports the necessity of ritual cleanliness for participating in holy war.

John R. Spencer

HOPHRA (PERSON) [Heb *ḥopraᶜ*]. The king of Egypt who opposed Nebuchadnezzar, king of Babylon, in the days of the prophet Jeremiah (Jer 44:30; cf. 37:5). In Egyptian, his name was *Ḥᶜᶜ-ib-rᶜ*, "Happy-hearted is Re" (Gk *Apriēs*), which should not be confused with his birthname, *w3ḥ-ib-rᶜ* (Gk *Oaphrēs*; LXX *Ouaphrēs;* Aram *wḥprᶜ;* and Akk *Uḫ-pa-ra* [Wiseman 1966: 155]).

Fourth king of the 26th (Saite) Dynasty, son and successor of Psamtek II, Hophra ascended the throne in mid-February 589 B.C. He actively pursued the policy of intervention in SW Asia begun by his grandfather Necho II and furthered by his father Psamtek II (Freedy and Redford 1970: 470–76). When Nebuchadnezzar appeared in the W in the spring of 588 and besieged Jerusalem, Hophra quickly led forth a relief army, but was obliged to withdraw in the face of superior Babylonian forces (Jer 37:5–11; Oded *IJH,* 473). A counterthrust in the form of a naval operation against Phoenicia, perhaps designed to undermine the Babylonian flank, was partly successful and Cyprus was reduced in the action (Diod. 1.68.1); however, it failed to avert the fate of Judah, which was soon annexed by Nebuchadnezzar.

In the aftermath Hophra received and settled Judean refugees (*IJH,* 486–87) and maintained the fortifications in the E delta (Oren 1984). Indeed, the delta seems to have captivated his whole attention, to judge from the fact that almost all his building operations are attested from there.

Internally the country remained stable and prosperous. Hophra resided at Memphis where his large palace has come to light (Petrie and Walker 1909; Kemp 1977; 1978). In 586 his sister Ankh-nes-neferibre was confirmed as Divine Adoratress (high priestess and regent) in Thebes, and in 578 an Apis bull was buried at Saqqara with the customary pomp (see also APIS). In the spring of the following year, Hophra endowed the temple of Ptah at Memphis with extensive tracts of land in the central delta (Gunn 1927); and similar endowments for other gods are widely attested from the reign (Drioton 1939; Jacquet-Gordon 1972).

In the military sphere, several of Hophra's native generals are known. Like his predecessors, Hophra relied heavily on foreign mercenaries, especially Carians and Ionian Greeks, but he suffered from poor liaison with his troops. On one occasion he was narrowly able to avert the wholesale defection of a foreign mercenary garrison stationed at Elephantine (Schäfer 1904). If Jeremiah's assessment is close to the truth (he derisively named Hophra the "overconfident one who misses the opportunity"; 46:17), Hophra may have gained a reputation for arrogance and indecision (Hoffmeier 1981).

Certainly the events which terminated his reign betray a lamentable lack of judgment. Perceiving a threat in the growing power of the Greek colony at Cyrene, Hophra directed his attention first to buffering the Kharga and Bahriya oases, finally to sending an expeditionary force against the town. This army, composed largely of native levies, was soundly defeated by the Cyreneans. At the news of this disaster, open revolt broke out back in Egypt, and despite a desperate effort to employ his Carians, Hophra was deposed in favor of one of his generals, Amasis, and was forced to flee (570 B.C.). Three years later, when Nebuchadnezzar attempted to take advantage of the stasis in Egypt to invade the land, Hophra threw in his lot with the foreigners. But the invading force was repulsed, and Hophra was captured and put to death. His tomb at Sais was still visible in Herodotus' day (Herod. 2.161–67; Diod. 1.68.1; Edel 1978).

Bibliography

Drioton, E. 1939. Un stele de donation de l'an XIII d'Apries. *ASAE* 39: 121–25.

Edel, E. 1978. Amasis und Nebukadrezar II. *GM* 29: 13–20.

Freedy, K. S.; and Redford, D. B. 1970. The Dates in Ezekiel in Relation to Biblical, Babylonian and Egyptian Sources. *JAOS* 90: 462–85.

Gunn, B. 1927. The Stela of Apries at Mitrahina. *ASAE* 27: 211–37.

Hoffmeier, J. K. 1981. A New Insight on Pharoah Apries from Herodotos, Diodorus and Jeremiah 46:17. *JSSEA* 11: 165–68.

Jacquet-Gordon, H. 1972. A Donation Stela of Apries. *RdÉ* 24: 84–90.

Kemp, B. J. 1977. The Palace of Apries at Memphis. MDAIK 33: 101–8.
———. 1978. A Further Note on the Palace of Apries at Memphis. *GM* 29: 61.
Oren, E. 1984. Migdol: a New Fortress on the Edge of the Eastern Nile Delta. *BASOR* 256: 7–44.
Petrie, W. M. F., and Walker, J. W. 1909. *The Palace of Apries at Memphis.* London.
Schäfer, H. 1904. Die Auswanderung der Krieger unter Psammetich I und der Söldneraufstand in Elephantine unter Apries. *Klio* 4: 152–63.
Wiseman, D. J. 1966. Some Egyptians in Babylonia. *Iraq* 28: 154–58.

DONALD B. REDFORD

HOR (PLACE) [Heb *hōr*]. **1.** A mountain on the border of Edom where Aaron died and was buried (Num 20:22–28; Deut 32:50). Since the name Hor always is given with the definite article it is suggested that it is a prominent mountain ridge. It is alleged that there are two conflicting traditions regarding the place where Aaron died and where he was buried. Deut 10:6 states that these events occurred at Moserah; however, Deut 20:27–28 records that Aaron died and was buried on Mt. Hor. There appears, however, to be no conflict since the name Moserah (Moseroth), meaning "chastisement(s)," was applied to the event, not to the location of Aaron's death. Aaron died in Edom on Mt. Hor as punishment for the Meribah incident (Num 20:24; Deut 32:51), while the people of Israel were encamped below. To commemorate this event, the incident and the campsite were called Moseroth (Num 33:30).

A tradition going back at least to the 1st century A.D. (*Ant* 4.4.7), identifies Mt. Hor with Jebel Nebī Harun ("mountain of Aaron") near Nabatean Petra; however, this two-topped sandstone mountain some 4800 ft (1460 m) high, is in the middle of Edomite territory rather than on the border. Its rugged summit is the location of a tomb allegedly belonging to Aaron, the upper portion of which is a Muslim mosque. The tomb, however, is more likely a reconstructed Christian church dating to the time of Justinian (A.D. 527–65). Any tradition placing Mt. Hor in the middle of Edomite territory rather than on its border (Num 20:22) would be open to serious question. Also, since the Edomites were able to prohibit the Israelites access to their land, and could do so with a powerful border force (Num 20:17–21), Israel could never have reached Jebel Nebī Harun without crossing Edom, which obviously was an impossibility. Again, such a location is too distant from Kadesh, and the mountain peak too lofty and inaccessible, for the Israelites to witness the ceremonies transferring the high priestly office from father to son (Num 20:22–29).

A more likely location would be Jabel Madurah, 15 miles (24 km) NE of Kadesh. This place stands at the extreme NW boundary of Edom yet outside Edomite territory. For topographical reasons it appears more suitable since Israel began its detour around Edom at Mt. Hor (Num 21:4), and the entire area was more accessible for the Israelites to witness the subsequent ceremonies conducted there. Positive identification of Mt. Hor is uncertain, owing to insufficient evidence, leaving Jabel Madurah the most widely accepted site.

2. A mountain mentioned only in Num 34:7–8 as a point of reference delineating the N boundary of Israel's promised land which they were about to conquer. The actual location is not identified. The Mediterranean was the W border; the first point was Mt. Hor, and the second point of reference was "the entrance to Hamath." It may describe a prominent peak in Lebanon. Suggested possibilities include Mt. Hermon and Jabel Akkar, a spur of the Lebanon range W of Tripoli. The reference may also refer to the whole Lebanon range of mountains.

RAY L. ROTH

HOR-HAGGIDGAD (PLACE) [Heb *hor-haggidgād*]. The seventeenth encampment of the Israelites, after leaving the wilderness of Sinai, as listed in Num 33:32–33, where it is placed between Bene-jaakan and Jotbathah. The meaning of the site's name is "Hollow of Gidgad," but LXX and the Vg understand this as *har,* instead of *hor,* rendering it as "Mountain of Gidgad." In Deut 10:6–7 the Israelites are said to have traveled from the wells of Bene-jaakan to Moserah (the reverse of the order in Num 33:31), and from Moserah to Gudgodah, which is evidently a variant of Gidgad. A suggested location is the wadi Ghadhaghedh (*GP,* 215–16; Simons 1959: 259 and map VI; M.R. 117094); though Robinson (1856: 181) camped in that area he did not mention it as a possible location. For a discussion of the location of any of the places associated with the journey of the Israelites from Egypt through Sinai, see DOPHKAH.

Bibliography

Beit-Arieh, I. 1988. The Route Through Sinai—Why the Israelites Fleeing Egypt Went South. *BARev* 15/3: 28–37.
Robinson, E. 1856. *Biblical Researches in Palestine.* Boston.
Simons, J. 1959. *The Geographical and Topographical Texts of the Old Testament.* Leiden.

JEFFREY R. ZORN

HORAM (PERSON) [Heb *hōrām*]. A king of Gezer who was slain by Joshua when he came to help the city of Lachish in its struggle against the Israelites at the time of Conquest (Josh 10:33). A king of Gezer is listed among the defeated kings of the land in Josh 12:12, but Gezer itself remained in the possession of the Canaanites (cf. Josh 16:10; Judg 1:29) until the time of Solomon when it was conquered by the Egyptian pharaoh and given as a dowry to his daughter, Solomon's wife (1 Kgs 9:16).

PAULINE A. VIVIANO

HOREB, MOUNT [Heb *ḥōrēb*]. See SINAI, MOUNT (PLACE).

HOREM (PLACE) [Heb *ḥŏrēm*]. A town in the allotment of Naphtali (Josh 19:38). Horem is mentioned with towns in N Galilee, such as Yiron. Thus, Horem is also thought to have been in upper Galilee. Its exact location, however, is unknown.

DAVID SALTER WILLIAMS

HORESH (PLACE) [Heb *ḥōreš*]. A place in the Judean hill country in the Wilderness of Ziph (1 Sam 23:15–19) equipped with strongholds and located on the hill of HACHILAH (v 19). It was used by David as a hiding place from Saul and is the location at which David and Jonathan made a covenant of friendship (v 18). Horesh has been identified with Khirbet Khoreisa (M.R. 162095) by many scholars, though the association between the two is still uncertain (*IDB* 2: 644; *MABL,* map 43; *RAB,* 30, 95). Some have questioned the interpretation that Horesh was an actual site name. Since the word Horesh means "forest" or "wood," it may have been a forest or thicket in the wilderness of Ziph, a place that would have provided ideal hiding conditions for David and his men as they continued to evade Saul (*RAB,* 103); however, limited rainfall in the area poses a problem for this theory.

LAMOINE F. DEVRIES

HORI (PERSON) [Heb *ḥōrî; ḥôrî*]. **1.** A son of LOTAN (Gen 36:22; 1 Chr 1:39) and grandson of "Seir, the Horite." See also HORITES. In at least one other case, the genealogy of Gen 36:20–28 seems to have entered the same "individual" twice (see DISHAN) without recognizing the identity. Hori means "Horite"; as a son of Lotan the son of Seir the Horite, Hori/"Horite" is the grandson of a Horite. Such a genealogy may reflect a struggle between two tribal groups for supremacy, each claiming its eponymous ancestor to have fathered the other, and/or a desperated scribe's attempt to deal with conflicting traditions.

2. The father of Shaphat, of the tribe of Simeon, one of the spies sent by Moses into Canaan (Num 13:5). The list of the spies' names in Num 13:3–16 is usually regarded as a late addition to the P source; i.e., it derives from a time when all the tribes except Judah (and Benjamin) had disappeared. It is unlikely that the list contains traditions of any sort. Thinking of Hori in Gen 36:20, 22, the compiler of the Numbers list may have attributed an "Edomite" father to his "Simeonite" spy because his source—the earliest scriptures—already had this tribe dwelling in the Negeb (which, in turn, seems to be the result of speculations about what happened to the tribe of Simeon rather than a reliable tradition; cf. Mittmann 1977: 217–19).

It is, therefore, doubtful whether a biblical personal name "Hori" ever existed; if it did, see HUR for a possible interpretation.

Bibliography

Mittmann, S. 1977. Ri. 1, 16f und das Siedlungsgebiet der kenitischen Sippe Hobab. *ZDPV* 93: 213–35.

ERNST AXEL KNAUF

HORITES [Heb *ḥōrî*]. A tribe or group of tribes in the mountains of Seir (Gen 14:6; 36:20–30; Deut 2:12, 22). According to Gen 14:6 and Deut 2:12, 22, the Horites inhabited the country of Seir until they were conquered and expelled by the Edomites. This, however, is a reconstruction of Edomite history which originates from a preconception of the Deuteronomistic school fashioned after the model of the Israelites' treatment of the Canaanites as commanded by Yahweh in Deut 7:1–2. The Deuteronomists and their successors learned from Gen 36:20 that Horites were the inhabitants of Seir. Because (like most of the biblical tradition) they regarded "Edom" and "Seir" as synonymous, they concluded that the Horites had been the Edomites' predecessors in the country of Seir. However, Seir and Edom originally referred to separate areas in S Transjordan. See also SEIR. The 7th-century B.C. coexistence of the "sons of Esau" in Edom (the agricultural land on the Transjordanian plateau) and the Horites in Seir (the wooded mountain slopes) is attested by the genealogical list in Gen 36:20–28 (its copy, 1 Chr 1:38–42, drops the Horites and retains only Seir). Together with Gen 36:10–14, this list belongs to the most ancient traditions in Genesis 36 (Weippert 1971; for a probable date in the 7th century B.C., cf. Knauf 1989: 10–11, n. 45; 61–63). As can be deduced from the name of the state, "Edom," and from the geographical factors, the more agricultural Edomite tribes eventually gained supremacy over the more pastoral Horite/Seirite tribes in the process of Edomite state formation.

Neither geography nor chronology favors the equation of the Horites (or Edomites) with the Hurrians of the 2d millennium B.C., as is sometimes suggested (e.g., Mendenhall 1973: 158). The tribal names in Gen 36:20–28 argue more decisively against such an assumption: they are easily explained by parallels within Semitic, but only laboriously brought into connection with Hurrian (Weippert 1971). This does not exclude the possibility that Hebrew scholars of the 1st millennium B.C. applied the term "Horite/Hurrian" to the tribes of Seir; comparably, the "Hittites" and the "Amorites" mentioned by biblical and neo-Assyrian authors do not refer to the same nations and areas who were known by these names in the 2d millennium B.C. See also AMORITES. One may as well, however, assume that "Horites" was the name by which these tribes referred to themselves. In this case, the name can be explained either by Heb *ḥōr,* "cave" (Ar *ḫaur* "bay, gulf"), and would denote "cave dwellers," troglodytes, in perfect accordance with geology and geography and the portrait of Esau in Gen 25:27; or it could be explained by Heb *ḥor,* Ar *ḥurr,* "free, noble."

Bibliography

Knauf, E. A. 1989. *Ismael.* 2d ed. ADPV. Wiesbaden.
Mendenhall, G. E. 1973. *The Tenth Generation.* Baltimore.
Weippert, M. 1971. *Edom. Studien und Materialien zur Geschichte der Edomiter auf Grund schriftlicher und archäologischer Quellen.* Ph.D. diss., Tübingen.

ERNST AXEL KNAUF

HORMAH (PLACE) [Heb *ḥormâ*]. A city or cluster of cities in the Negeb region of Judah. Hormah plays a role in the episode of the aborted S invasion of Canaan by the Israelites. When their invasion was repulsed by the Amorites, the fleeing Israelites were pursued as far as Hormah (Num 14:45; Deut 1:44). Another tradition speaks of a destruction of Arad by the Israelites on their way around the S part of Canaan (Num 21:1–3). The town was subsequently renamed Hormah ("destruction"). A third tradition holds that the name "Horman" was applied to the destroyed remains of a city formerly called Zephthah, taken after the initial conquest by Simeon and Judah together (Judg 1:17). Altogether, these traditions demonstrate the difficulties inherent in reconstructing the sequence of events which lay behind Israel's settlement in Canaan. Hormah appears in the list of conquered cities in Joshua 12 (14) and was allotted to the tribe of Judah (Josh 15:30), though technically part of Simeon's allotment (Josh 19:4; 1 Chr 4:30) which was incorporated into Judah's. Hormah is also listed as one of the cities to which David sent spoil after his defeat of the Amalekites at Ziklag (1 Sam 30:30).

Several sites have been proposed for Hormah, as one might imagine from the multitude of traditions attached to the name. Among them are Tell el-Milḥ (M.R. 152069), 7 miles NE of Beer-sheba (*IDB* 2: 645; Aharoni 1968: 31); Tell esh-Sheriᶜah, 12 miles NW of Beer-sheba (*IDB* 2: 645); Tell Masos (M.R. 146069; Boling *Joshua* AB, 327; Aharoni 1976: 71–73); and Tel Ira (M.R. 148071; Aharoni 1976: 73). All of these sites lie within the same general region, and the tradition-layer one counts as most authentic would determine which of them would seem most likely. The connection of Hormah with Arad (the Numbers 21 tradition) favors Tell el-Milḥ, while the listing of Arad and Hormah as separate cities in Josh 12:15 inclines one toward Tell Masos, and the identification of Zephthah and Hormah (Judg 1:17) favors Tell Ira. The possibility that the process of abandonment and resettlement at each of these sites, and hence their being renamed, complicates the picture enormously. See Aharoni 1976 (who settles on Tell Masos) for the most complete discussion of this issue.

Bibliography

Aharoni, Y. 1968. Arad: Its Inscription and Temple. *BA* 31: 2–32.

———. 1976. Nothing Early and Nothing Late. *BA* 39: 55–76.

JEFFRIES M. HAMILTON

HORN. See MUSIC AND MUSICAL INSTRUMENTS.

HORONAIM (PLACE) [Heb *ḥōrônayim*]. A name which occurs four times in the Hebrew Bible and once in the 9th-century B.C.E. inscription of the Moabite king Mesha (Isa 15:5; Jer 48:3, 5, 34; *ANET,* 321, lines 31–32). The biblical references are included in prophetic oracles against Moab; the inscriptional reference is unfortunately fragmented, but it occurs in the context of a revelatory word to the king to "go down to Horonaim and fight" *(rd hltḥm bḥwrnn).*

Most scholars have located Horonaim in central or S Moab between the Wadi Mujib and Wadi Hasa (respectively the Arnon and the Zered of the Hebrew Bible). This conclusion appears confirmed by extrabiblical sources that refer not to Horonaim but to a neighboring town, Luhith. Luhith is associated by parallelism with Horonaim in Isa 15:5 along an ascending roadway from Zoar at the S edge of the Dead Sea to the Moabite plateau. A further geographical indication is found in Isa 15:6, which refers to the waters of Nimrin. These waters should be identified with the modern Seil en Numera, a stream which cuts through the cliffs on the SW edge of the Moabite plateau to flow down to the Dead Sea. The extrabiblical sources—a Nabatean inscription from Madeba and a Hebrew contract from the time of Bar Kokhba—place Luhith in the SW quadrant of the Moabite plateau, probably along a Roman road that descends the plateau to circle around the S end of the Dead Sea.

Archaeological research has demonstrated the existence of a roadway that led to the Dead Sea from what is now the modern town of Kathrabba, SW of Kerak on the edge of the Moabite plateau. The roadway dates from the Roman/Nabatean period, and surface sherds suggest that Kathrabba itself was inhabited during this period. If this roadway follows the way of an earlier one from the Iron Age, then the sites of Horonaim and Luhith are most likely along it. Indeed, Ai (M.R. 211060), a town just E of Kathrabba, produced surface sherds from the Bronze, Iron, and Roman periods, suggesting that it and Kathrabba (M.R. 209061) would make good candidates for the sites of Luhith and Horonaim. Furthermore, there are Iron Age and Nabatean sites around these two towns, demonstrating the importance of this area in these periods. Khirbet Meidan, a twin site with remains from both periods, is located on a strategic hill W of Kathrabba overlooking the Dead Sea and approaches to the plateau from it. Tell el Mise, an outpost or small fort on a high hill just SE of Kathrabba, also has Iron Age and Nabatean pottery associated with it. This site arguably has the most strategic view in this section of the Moabite plateau. From the crumbled walls of the site one can see the Dead Sea to the W and traffic on the modern King's Highway to the E.

Other proposals for the location of Horonaim have been made. One candidate is the modern town of el-Iraq (M.R. 211055), 7 km S of Kathrabba at the head of the Seil en Numera. Two others located in the SW corner of the Moabite plateau near the Wadi Hasa are Medinet er Ras and Khirbet Dhubab. The former is a fort or outpost, the latter is a tell on the N bank of the Hasa with surface sherds suggesting almost continuous occupation from the EB period.

A recent suggestion equates Horonaim with the isolated, hilltop ruins of ed-Deir, a site SW of Rabba on the W edge of the plateau. Though clearly a strategic site, it is probably too far N to be identified with Horonaim. On the other hand, ed-Deir is located along a secondary Roman road that connected the Dead Sea with the plateau. Thus it cannot be ruled out as a possible location for Horonaim.

Bibliography

Mittmann, S. 1982. The Ascent of Luhith. Pp. 175–80 in *Studies in the History and Archaeology of Jordan I,* ed. A. Hadidi. Amman.

Schottroff, W. 1966. Horonaim, Numrim, Luhith und der Westrand des "Landes Ataroth." *ZDPV* 82: 163–208.

Worschech, U., and Knauf, E. A. 1985. Alte Strasse in der nordwestlichen Ard el-Kerak. *ZDPV* 101: 128–33.

———. 1986. Dimon und Horonaim. *BN* 31: 70–94.

J. ANDREW DEARMAN

HORSE. See ZOOLOGY.

HORSE GATE (PLACE) [Heb *šaʿar hassûsîm; ʾel-mĕbôʾ šaʿar-hassûsîm; derek-mĕbôʾ hassûsîm*]. Two separate entrances for horses in Jerusalem. The Horse Gate (Heb *šaʿar hassûsîm*) mentioned by Jeremiah (31:40) and Nehemiah (3:28) was a gate through the outer defensive wall on the E side of the city (not to be equated, however, with the East Gate of Neh 3:29 or Ezek 10:19; 43:1–5). The second Horse Gate, the "entrance of the gate for horses" (2 Chr 23:15 [Heb *ʾel-mĕbôʾ šaʿar-hassûsîm*]), and the "way of the entrance of the horses" (2 Kgs 11:16 [Heb *derek-mĕbôʾ hassûsîm*]) was an entrance for horses into the royal compound from the Horse Gate in the outer wall. Avi-Yonah suggests (1954: 240, fig. 1; 247) that this entrance was to the stables in the House of the Forest of Lebanon in the palace compound and was situated between the palace and the temple precints. It is this entrance that figures in the execution of Athaliah at the coronation of her grandson Joash (2 Kings 11; 2 Chronicles 23).

The Horse Gate mentioned by Nehemiah (3:28) was located N of the wall of Ophel opposite "the great projecting tower" that was a part of the SE corner of the royal compound (Avi-Yonah 1954: 240, fig. 1). This, coupled with the fact that Jeremiah (31:39) associated the Horse Gate with the sacred temple precincts and the priests repaired the walls from the Horse Gate N (Neh 3:28), indicates that the Horse Gate was in close proximity to the temple precincts and would place this gate near the SE corner of the present-day Haram esh-Sharif.

Bibliography

Avi-Yonah, M. 1954. The Walls of Nehemiah—A Minimalist View. *IEJ* 4: 239–48.

Simons, J. 1952. *Jerusalem in the Old Testament.* Leiden.

DALE C. LIID

HORVAT RIMMON (PLACE). See RIMMON, HORVAT.

HOSAH (PERSON) [Heb *ḥōsâ*]. A gatekeeper of the levitical family of Merari. According to 1 Chr 16:38, Hosah (whose name means "refuge"), along with Obed-edom, was one of two gatekeepers at the tent which David pitched for the ark in Jerusalem. However, the status of Hosah and his descendants appears considerably less significant in the more elaborate organization presented in 1 Chr 26:1–19. The mention of Hosah and his sons in vv 10–11 may be attributable to the Chronicler (Williamson *1 and 2 Chronicles* NCBC, 169) or to a later source (Rudolph *Chronikbücher* HAT, 173). Here they are the fewest in number (13) among the ranks of gatekeepers (compare 18 for Meshelemiah in 26:9 and 62 for Obed-edom in 26:10). In vv 12–18, attributable to a reviser of the Chronicler's work (Williamson, 170–71; Rudolph, 173), they were stationed at the W, or back, gate of the temple. According to this passage, Hosah and his sons were responsible for posting daily four men at the gate called Shallecheth (its meaning is unknown), and two men at the nearby PARBAR.

J. S. ROGERS

HOSAH (PLACE) [Heb *ḥosâ*]. A town located in the territory of the tribe of Asher (Josh 19:29). Hosah occurs immediately after the fortified city of Tyre, so some scholars (*GP* 2: 12; *LBHG,* 436) have suggested that the OT Hosah was identical to the Usu mentioned in extrabiblical texts as the mainland city which supplied Tyre. Usu had a long history, occurring in an Egyptian inscription of Seti I, the Amarna archives, the Papyrus Anastasi I, and in the Assyrian records of Sennacherib and Esarhaddon. During the Hellenistic period and later, Usu came to be called Palaityros, or "Old Tyre."

Most scholars (*LBHG,* 443) have located Hosah/Usu at Tell Rashidiyeh (M.R. 170293), but Dussaud (1927) suggested an identification with Kh. el-Hos (M.R. 172293). Kallai objects to the link between Hosah and Usu, noting that the Egyptians wrote the latter with an initial *i* rather than *ḫ* (*HGB,* 215–18). He also places Hosah at Kh. el-Hos, suggesting that Usu was located either at Rashidiyeh or at Tell Masuq (M.R. 170297).

Bibliography

Dussaud, R. 1927. *Topopgraphie historique de la Syrie antique et médiévale.* Paris.

MELVIN HUNT

HOSANNA [Gk *hōsanna*]. *Hōsanna* occurs five times in the gospels (Matt 21:9 *bis;* Mark 9:11; 11:10; John 12:13) as the cry raised by the crowd when Jesus entered Jerusalem the first day of the week ending with Passover and his crucifixion. The term is simply a transliteration of the Heb imperative *hôšaʿ*, "save," augmented by the enclitic precative particle *-(n)nā,* which adds a note of urgency, "save, now/please." The form *hôšaʿnnā* actually is not found in the Hebrew Bible, but the imperatives *hôšaʿ* and *hôšîʿāh,* without the precative particle *-nnā,* "please," occur 29 times, addressed to deity, mostly in the Psalter, and twice directed to royalty.

The cry "save" or "help" is elemental whether addressed to mortal, king, or deity. The long or so-called "emphatic" form of the imperative *hôšîʿāh* occurs only once in the Hebrew Bible with the precative particle *-nnā, hôšîʿā(h)-nnā,* in Ps 118:25 where the precative or pleading tone is doubly emphasized by introducing appeal with the sigh *ʿannā,* "Oh, please" (as in Gen 50:17 and elsewhere), and ending with an added note of urgency by means of the precative particle affixed to the imperative:

ʿannā YHWH hôšîʿā(h)nnā	"Oh, please, Lord, save (us), please!
ʿannā YHWH haṣlîḥā(h)nnā	Oh, please, Lord, prosper (us), please!"

This is followed by the *benedictus qui venit* liturgical formula which has been misunderstood because of poetic variation in the word order, but lately properly translated in the

New JPS Version: "May he who enters be blessed in the name of the Lord." It is obvious that this passage, Ps 118:25–26, is echoed with variations, additions, omissions, and distortions in all the gospel accounts of the cry of the crowd at Jesus' Palm Sunday entry into Jerusalem.

The imperative cry *hôšîᶜānnā* > *hôšaᶜnnā* in Jewish liturgy was a feature of the post-harvest celebration Sukkoth, or Booths/Tabernacle, concerned with the vital need for rain. Given the climatology of Palestine-Syria, similar rain rites must be very ancient. The seven-day celebration of Sukkoth ended with sevenfold cries of *hôšîāᶜnnā*, "save/help, please," i.e., by giving rain, the prayers accompanied by waving and beating the ground with branches of willow and palm (cf. Mishnah *Sukk.* 4:3–6). This is obscurely mentioned in Ps 118:27, "bind festival (with) branches as far as the horns of the altar." This climax was called the "Great Hosanna," *hôšaᶜnā rabbā*, the great "Save Please," whence the nominalization *hôšaᶜnā*, plural *hôšaᶜnôt*, came to be applied to these rain prayers and later to prayer(s) in general. Even the branches beaten on the ground were called Hosannas, hence the proverbial Hebrew and Yiddish expression "a beaten *hosanna*" for a person buffeted by misfortune.

There is, however, no evidence whatsoever that Hosanna in biblical or postbiblical Jewish usage was ever an acclamation of praise. It was Christian misapprehension of a well-known Hebrew term that has confused even scholars to this day. The difference between acclamation and a stark cry, "Help, please!" is too great to be glossed over. How could such misapprehension occur? Why did not the gospel writers look to the Gk of Ps 118:25 and some thirty other passages where the Hebrew imperative is duly rendered by the Gk imperative *sōson*, "save"? The crux of the problem lies in the nonsensical cries "*hōsanna to* the son of David" and "*hōsanna in* the highest" which indicates that the cry was not understood because of the Semitic particle *l-* before the addresses "Son of David" and "highest."

C. C. Torrey (1933) surmises that in the original cry the Aramaic use of the proclitic particle *l-* as the object marker was mistaken for dative sense, "to/for the Son of David," thus distorting the imperative cry for help: "Save the Son of David!" and "Give him help on high!" Recently a new and compelling clue has emerged from the oldest corpus of W Semitic poetry exhumed at Ugarit, dating to the middle of the 2d millennium B.C., wherein proclitic *l-* is a common vocative particle. Accordingly, Albright and Mann boldly translated Matthew 21:9, 15 "Hosanna, O son of David" and noted that "the meaning of vocative *la-* was misunderstood quite early, and the Gk translation therefore rendered the vocative *'O son of David'* as 'to the son of David,' because the Hebrew *la, lĕ* is also used to indicate 'to' as a dative. What we have, therefore, is an ancient liturgical text, a cry to the anointed king for deliverance" (*Matthew* AB, 252).

Albright and Mann, however, failed to apply the same logic to "Hosanna in the highest" and rendered it awkwardly "(Cry) Hosanna in the heavenly heights!" taking this as an echo of Ps 148:1. This appears to be precisely the flawed logic of the author of Luke 2:14 and 19:30 where the Gk noun *doxa*, "glory," is used instead of *hōsanna*, which was wrongly supposed to be equivalent in the sense to the "*hallĕlû-Yāh* in the heights" of Ps 148:1. Luke's errant surmise that *hōsanna* (which he avoids) means something like *hallĕlû-Yah* has misled readers of the gospels to this day. Even Albright, who perceived that "*hōsanna* to the son of David" misconstrued the ancient and long obsolete vocative *l-* as dative, failed to realize that in the nonsensical "*hōsanna* in the highest" we have also the original vocative particle *l-* similarly mistaken for the dative. "Highest" or "Most High" (Semitic *ᶜelyôn;* Gk *hypsistos*) was an ancient divine title applied to the first of the four great gods in the ancient tradition of divine succession (1) Elyon, (2) Heaven, (3) El/Kumarbi/Kronos, (4) the Weather-god Baᶜl/Hadd/Teshub/Zeus. The title "Highest" is used many times of God in both the OT and the NT. Accordingly, thanks to ancient W Semitic usage of vocative *l-*, we can finally explain how the cries *hôšaᶜnnā lĕ-ben dāwîd* and *hôšaᶜnnā lĕ-ᶜelyon*, "Save/help, please, O Son of David!" and "Save/help, please, O Highest!" came to be misunderstood.

It is manifest that the cry *hōsanna,* meaning "help, please!" addressed first to the carpenter from Nazareth as the Messiah and secondly to (God) the Highest, was politically and religiously provocative, to both Jews and the Roman rulers, especially at the paschal season celebrating the great rescue of the past and the hope of present liberation from Roman rule. There has long been puzzlement at the unseasonal use of elements of the autumnal rain rites of Sukkoth, especially the palms (cf. John 12:13) during the spring paschal celebration of liberation from political and religious oppression. The provocative impact of cries of "Help!" accompanied by palm waving can be appreciated by reference to 2 Macc 10:5–8, which tells us how the first Hanukkah celebrating hard-won but short-lived political and religious independence was actually a repeat performance of the crucial rain rites of Sukkoth given new political significance by coincidence with recent victory over foreign rule. Memories of this delivery some two centuries earlier made the cries of Hosanna, "help, please," a powerful appeal calculated to incite the oppressed and alarm the oppressors.

Bibliography

Blank, S. H. 1961. Some Observations concerning Biblical Prayer. *HUCA* 32: 75–79.

Freed, E. D. 1961. The Entry into Jerusalem in the Gospel of John. *JBL* 80: 329–38.

Miller, P. D. 1980. Vocative Lamed in the Psalter. *UF* 2: 617–37.

Petuchowski, J. J. 1955. Hoshi ᶜana in Psalm CXVIII, 25, a Prayer for Rain. *VT* 5: 266–71.

Pope, M. H. 1988a. Hosanna—What It Really Means. *BRev* 4: 16–25.

———. 1988b. Vestiges of Vocative L- in the Bible. *UF* 20: 201–7.

Torrey, C. C. 1933. *Four Gospels: A New Translation.* London and New York.

Werner, E. 1946. Hosanna in the Gospels. *JBL* 65: 97–122.

Marvin H. Pope

HOSEA, BOOK OF. The book of Hosea is the first of twelve prophetic books called the "minor prophets" not because of their insignificance when compared with the "major prophets," but because of their relative brevity. Chronologically, it is second only to Amos among the twelve. The prophet Hosea was the only one of the writing prophets who was a native of the northern kingdom who also prophesied there. His ministry extended from around the mid-eighth century to the fall of Samaria in 721 B.C.E.

A. Text
B. Literary History
C. The Prophet
D. Historical Context
E. Canaanite Religion
F. Structure
G. Theology

A. Text

With the possible exception of Job, the book of Hosea has the dubious distinction of having the most obscure passages of the entire Hebrew Bible. Apart from the frequent and sudden shifts in mood and subject, and the difficulty of establishing the historical contexts, the book is replete with linguistic peculiarities. The text is traditionally regarded as the most corrupt and poorly preserved of the Hebrew Bible. A little fragment containing parts of Hos 1:7–2:5 is found among manuscripts from Qumran (4Q XII). It is very similar to the MT and, hence, of little value for reconstruction of the text. The LXX is frequently literalistic and incomprehensible in part. The other versions are, likewise, garbled at critical junctures. It appears that the translators of the versions were themselves struggling to understand the texts before them. Sometimes the literalistic readings actually help us to reconstruct the consonants that the translators may have seen but not understood. The linguistic peculiarities in much of Hosea may be explained as dialectal idiosyncrasies, rather than errors or textual corruptions. Many of the difficulties one encounters in the book may be attributed not to the scribal process, but rather to our lack of familiarity with the N dialect of Hebrew. Hosea is, after all, the only one of the writing prophets who had his home in the N. And so, in this century, scholars have called on new understandings of Hebrew grammar in the light of epigraphic evidence, especially from Ugarit, to explain many linguistic problems in the book.

B. Literary History

As the different moods, styles, and historical allusions in the book suggest, the final form of the book has come to us through different hands and in several stages. Some commentators would attribute a major portion of the book to a Judean redactor in the Josianic period (late 7th century B.C.E.) or in the Babylonian exile (6th century). There is no reason to doubt, however, that Hosea was responsible for most of the oracles in the book, which appear to have been delivered in the second half of the 8th century. It is impossible to outline here the literary history of the entire book, but even a cursory examination of the first three chapters will show the complexity of the process. The autobiographical account of Hosea's call in 3:1–3 may have indeed come from the prophet himself. The woman is not named here and the children are not mentioned. She is said to be "the beloved of another" and an adulteress. But there is also an extended and somewhat different account written in the third person about Hosea's call and his misfortunes with his family (1:2–6, 8–9). The woman is named Gomer bat-Diblaim. She is called the wife of the prophet, is said to be a harlotrous woman, *ʾēšet zĕnûnîm.* The three children are given symbolic names. This biographical account may have been written by a disciple or some other close associate of the prophet. An editor (perhaps the author of the biographical account) collected the two accounts of Hosea's call and wove them together with an oracle of judgment against Israel for her unfaithfulness to Yahweh (2:4–15—Eng 2:2–13) and an oracle of hope (2:16–23—Eng 2:14–20). These Hoseanic oracles are framed by two short redactional units that link the unfaithfulness of Israel with Hosea's family (2:1–3, 23–25[—Eng 1:10–2:1, 21–23]). This redaction may be dated to the period after the fall of Samaria in 721 B.C.E., if one includes the call for reunification of Israel and Judah (2:2—Eng 1:11). The superscription for the entire book (1:1) is the work of editors in the exilic or postexilic period who were also responsible for the superscriptions on other prophetic books (cf. Joel 1:1; Mic 1:1; Zeph 1:1; Zech 1:1).

A similar process may be discernible in the rest of the book. While scholars are virtually unanimous that the book has a long history of transmission and that there is at least one Judean redaction, there is no agreement on the number and extent of the redaction. Major studies have appeared in recent years precisely on this question (Emmerson 1984; Yee 1987). The last verse of the book (14:10) is usually taken to be a late, perhaps postexilic, gloss by a scribe associated with wisdom circles. This conclusion, however, exaggerates the difference between prophetic and wisdom circles and fails to do justice to the vocabulary and thematic connections between this verse and the rest of Hosea (Seow 1982).

C. The Prophet

Nothing is known of the prophet Hosea ben-Beeri or his family outside this book. The name Hosea (properly Hoshea) is fairly common in the 8th and 7th centuries. Several seals and seal impressions bearing that name have been found from that period. The last monarch of the N kingdom, a younger contemporary of the prophet, was also called Hoshea (2 Kgs 17:1). The name is probably a shortened form of *hwšʿyh(w),* "YHWH has delivered," or "Deliver, O YHWH!" This name appears as an alternate of Joshua (Num 13:8; Deut 32:44).

In the opening chapter of the book, Hosea is called by YHWH to marry a certain Gomer bat-Diblaim. She is called a promiscuous woman *(ʾēšet zĕnûnîm).* Some say she was a cultic prostitute, but others suggest that she was or became a harlotrous woman, but was not a professional whore. She bore Hosea two sons, Jezreel ("God will sow") and *lōʾ ʿammî* ("Not my people") and a daughter, *lōʾ ruḥāmâ* ("Not pitied"). It is no surprise, given the shocking divine command to marry a harlot and the symbolic significance of the children's names, that many commentators through the ages have treated the first three chapters of Hosea as pure allegory, parable, vision, or dream. The medieval commentators Ibn Ezra, David Kimḥi, and Maimonides, for instance, regarded the whole experience as a prophetic vision. Finding the command morally offensive, many modern scholars have insisted that there was no real marriage with such a woman; Gomer bat-Diblaim is unfaithful Israel personified and nothing more (see the survey in

Rowley 1963). Others have conceded that Hosea did marry the harlotrous woman as a symbolic act. Still others argue that God did not in fact command Hosea to marry such a woman. Rather, the prophet interpreted his marriage as divinely arranged when he learned of his wife's adultery and saw in his own experiences the meaning of God's love and commitment. In this line of thinking, Hosea's firstborn Jezreel ("God will sow") was so named as a sign of impending doom for "Israel," specifically the Jehu dynasty (1:4–5) on account of its bloodshed at the valley of Jezreel (cf. 2 Kgs 9:17–26; 10:1–11). By the time the second child was born, Hosea had learned of his wife's unfaithfulness. Hence that child was named "Not pitied" and the third child "Not my people." In the third chapter of the book the prophet is asked to love a woman who is beloved of another and an adulteress. It is not certain if this woman is Gomer; many argue that this is a different woman here (Stuart *Hosea-Jonah* WBC, 11–12, 65–66). The adverb "again" (*ʿôd*) in 3:1 may be taken with the call (thus, "YHWH called to me again") or with the imperative ("love again!"). Some maintain that Hosea was asked to take another promiscuous woman after his marriage with Gomer had failed or, as others would have, after Gomer died. If Gomer is the woman of chap. 3, then she must have abandoned her family or been cast out. Eventually, she was put out for sale in the slave market where Hosea found her and bought her back (3:1–3).

According to the prophet himself, he was labeled "a fool" and "a crazy fellow" (9:7). The former is a technical term in the wisdom tradition, characterizing a person who is quarrelsome, hot-tempered, lacking self-control, promiscuous, or associating with promiscuous people. Perhaps in the eyes of Hosea's opponents his frequent tirades and his association with the promiscuous Gomer marked him as a fool, a simpleton who was easily seduced by the wicked temptress. It would be farfetched, however, to suggest that Hosea belonged to the class of the wise, or that he was educated in a wisdom school. Wisdom themes and vocabulary were known to the prophets of the 8th century, as studies of Isaiah, Amos, and Micah have borne out. Even though there are certain features in the book that would normally be associated with the wisdom tradition, Hosea's insistence on the certainty of divine intervention in history and his covenant theology place him firmly within the prophetic tradition. Yet, like his contemporaries in the 8th century, Hosea appears to have been familiar with the language and imagery of the sages, and so he uses them in his oracles and disputations. His central claim concerns Israel's lack of knowledge (Heb *daʿat*). The choice of "knowledge" is apt, for it is at home in both the wisdom and covenant traditions. Israel is portrayed consistently as a recalcitrant fool who has no understanding and makes foolish choices (Seow 1982). So the people will "come to ruin" like the typical fool (4:14; cf. Prov 10:8). They are drunk (4:1, 18; cf. 20:1) and gluttonous (4:8). They brag about not fearing YHWH (10:3). They are likened to stupid animals and birds that wander about aimlessly. The mention of foreigners who sap the strength of Israel (7:9) is reminiscent of the warning given to the simpleton regarding unsavory alliances with "foreigners" (Prov 5:10). Indeed, the foolish people have borne "foreign children" (5:7). Israel's reliance on foreign powers is deemed futile, and compared with the pursuit of wind (12:2 [1]). In the book, one also finds references to the use of false balances (12:7; cf. Prov 11:1; 16:11) and to the shifting of boundary markers (5:10), unjust practices against which the sages repeatedly warned (e.g., Prov 22:28; 23:10). The prophet considered Israel an unwise fetus that does not know its proper time—as the wise always did (13:13).

Hosea was thoroughly familiar with the prophetic and historical traditions. Although he condemned a certain prophet ("the prophet" in 4:5), Hosea held the prophetic office in highest regard. The prophets received their authority from YHWH. Through the prophets God dealt with humans (12:10; 6:5) and through them God delivered Israel (12:13). The prophet was a watcher of and a snare to the people (9:8). In this connection, Moses is regarded as the prophet to whom the prophetic office may be traced.

Hosea was apparently well schooled in the historical traditions. Wolff (1956) has proposed that Hosea was so well versed in the traditions because of his close associations with certain priestly families and Levites. He was able to use his knowledge of Israel's history to call his people back to a correct relationship with YHWH. So he refers to the tradition of Jacob, who grabbed the heels of his brother and strove with God (12:2–6).

The date of Hosea cannot be set with certainty, but the material in the book suggests at least the period from the end of Jeroboam's reign to the fall of Samaria, approximately 752–721 B.C.E. This makes Hosea a contemporary of Amos, who prophesied in the N kingdom, and of Isaiah, who prophesied in the S. When Amos prophesied at Bethel, he was confronted by Amaziah, the royal priest at the national sanctuary (Amos 7:10–17). Since Hosea was a contemporary of Amos, Andersen and Freedman (*Hosea* AB, 38, 351–53) have proposed that Amaziah was the wicked priest against whom Hosea prophesied (4:4; cf. Amos 7:10–12).

There is no mention of Hosea's hometown anywhere in the book, nor is anything said about Beeri's origin. Nevertheless, it is accepted by all scholars that Hosea prophesied in the N kingdom, probably in the vicinities of Samaria, the capital, and near the sanctuaries at Bethel and Gilgal.

D. Historical Context

Scholars are by no means agreed on the extent to which one can reconstruct the historical events that lie in the background of the book. Hosea rarely mentions his contemporaries by name. He may have intended to be vague in his oracles, or the details may have been eliminated by someone in a later period who sought to generalize the oracles for later generations. Several of the oracles may be placed in any number of historical situations. The specific details are usually not spelled out in the oracles. Hence, some scholars hold that at best only one or two passages may be pinned down historically, but others are more optimistic about historical reconstructions. Among the latter, it is commonly assumed that the present sequence of passages in the book corresponds roughly to the chronological sequence in Israel's history—with the earliest events in the earliest part of the book and the latest at the end.

The superscription (1:1) places the prophecies of Hosea in the reigns of the Judean kings Uzziah, Jotham, Ahaz, and Hezekiah, but only Jeroboam II is mentioned of the kings of Israel. This is peculiar, since Hosea was a N prophet preaching to the N kingdom. The priority given to the Judean kings and the inadequate reference to the N monarchy indicate that the superscription belongs to a Judean editor, following the fall of Samaria.

Some of the oracles of Hosea probably originated during the last years of the reign of Jeroboam II (786–746 B.C.E.), as the superscription suggests. Several passages in the book reflect the relative political stability and wealth in the Jeroboam era. The people were gluttonous, drunk, and far too complacent, if not arrogant (4:1–5:7). The atmosphere of Israel described here is very similar to that which Amos confronted in the days of Jeroboam. The sanctuaries of Gilgal and Beth-aven (Bethel) had been abused and foreign elements were introduced into the cult of YHWH (4:15–5:7; 9:15). The people had misplaced their trust on cultic acts (8:13; 6:6). They were more concerned about accumulating wealth than they were with justice (12:8–9—Eng vv 7–8). They had become overly confident in the military might of the nation (10:13–14; 8:14). The wealthier they became, the more readily sanctuaries multipled. This Hosea condemned, as the Deuteronomist(s) did. God would destroy their altars, their pillars, and their high places.

Even during the stable reign of Jeroboam, political intrigues threatened the Jehu dynasty. In such a climate, Amaziah accused Amos of plotting to assassinate Jeroboam (Amos 7:11). The oracles of Amos were too subversive and the country could not tolerate them. The possibility of sedition was certainly in the air. Indeed, from the death of Jeroboam in 746 till the fall of Samaria in 721 six kings ascended the throne in Israel; all except one died by violence. Assassination was the order of the day. Several of Hosea's oracles reflect this state of instability and confusion (5:1; 7:5–7; 8:4; 9:15; 13:10–11).

In 743, Tiglath-pileser III (745–727) of Assyria launched his infamous W campaign. The Syro-Palestinian states had to decide to acquiesce in the face of Assyrian threats or to join other states in a united front to stem the Assyrian tide. In this period Israel vacillated between submission and resistance, turning alternately between the rival powers of Assyria and Egypt (7:11). Israel's king Menahem (745–738) decided to submit in the face of Tiglath-pileser's superior military power. Israel paid a heavy tribute which was raised by a head tax levied on every landholder (2 Kgs 15:19–20; *ANET,* 283). Hosea alludes to the capitulation of Ephraim (*ʾprym*) to the Assyrians in this period, depicting Ephraim as a stupid dove (7:11) and a wild ass (*prʾ*) wandering alone (8:9).

Menahem was succeeded by his son Pekahiah, who was himself quickly assassinated by nationalistic elements headed by Pekah ben-Remaliah with a gang of fifty Gileadites (2 Kgs 15:23–26). Gilead is known in Hosea is a "a city of evil doers" (6:8; cf. 12:12 [11]). The mention of Gilead and bloodshed there may be a veiled reference to the murder of Pekahiah. Under Pekah, Israel joined the Arameans and the Philistines in an anti-Assyrian alliance. The coalition tried to persuade and then coerce Judah to join their ranks, thus initiating the Syro-Ephraimitic war (735–733). Albrecht Alt's thesis that this war lies in the background of 5:8–6:6 is accepted by most scholars. Against the pleading of the prophet Isaiah, King Ahaz of Judah turned to Tiglath-pileser, who gladly complied by seizing Galilee and some territories in the Transjordan. The prophecy concerning the "breaking of Israel's bow" at Jezreel (1:4–5) probably alludes to the decisive battle which Tiglath-pileser won in 733. Only Samaria and the hill country of Ephraim remained in Israelite control. Tiglath-pileser ravaged the land and deported a large segment of the population (5:13–14; 2 Kgs 15:29). Pekah was assassinated by a pro-Assyrian faction led by Hoshea ben-Elah, who quickly sued for peace and sent a tribute to the Assyrian king (2 Kgs 15:30). This triumph of Assyria is recorded in Akkadian in one of the annals of Tiglath-pileser:

> (Israel's) inhabitants (and) its possessions I led to Assyria. They overthrew their king Pekah *(Pa-qa-ḫa)* and I placed Hoshea *(A-u-si')* as king over them. I received from them 10 talents of gold, 1,000 (?) talents of silver as their [tri]bute and brought them to Assyria (*ANET,* 28).

As long as Hoshea was content to be a vassal of Assyria, there was some measure of peace in Israel. But Hoshea sought to cast off the Assyrian yoke by turning to Egypt (cf. 7:11). Thus, when Tiglath-pileser died in 727, Hoshea withheld tribute from the Assyrians (2 Kgs 17:4). These events may form the background of the references to Israel's "return to Egypt" in 9:3; 11:5; 12:1.

Succeeding Tiglath-pileser, Shalmaneser V launched his punitive expedition against Israel in 725. The oracles about the demise of Israel's king (10:7; 13:10–11) are commonly taken to be allusions to the punishment of Hoshea by the Assyrians. The mention of Shalman who destroyed Beth-arbel (10:14) is sometimes taken to be a reference to Shalmaneser V, who was supposed to have destroyed Beth-arbel (modern Irbid?) en route to Samaria. This would put the oracle sometime just before the fall of Samaria in 721 B.C.E. Others identify Shalman with the Moabite king Salamau who is mentioned in one of Tiglath-pileser's inscriptions (*ANET,* 282). No evidence is available, however, for the devastation of Beth-arbel, which was apparently widely known to Hosea's audience.

There are several probable allusions in the book to the last days of Samaria (9:1–9; 10:3–10; 11:5–7). But there is no mention of the actual destruction of Samaria anywhere. Indeed, in the conclusion of the book, Samaria is apparently still standing, but her end is nigh (14:1—Eng 13:16).

E. Canaanite Religion

The book of Hosea provides us with rare textual insights into N Israelite religion in the 8th century B.C.E. The Elijah stories (1 Kings 17–19) tell of the struggle in the N kingdom between the prophets of YHWH and the adherents of Baalism only a century before Hosea. In general, the picture is in accord with scholarly reconstruction from archaeological discoveries. Yahwism apparently did not dominate in the N kingdom as it did in Judah. By all accounts, Israel flirted with all manners of Canaanite religion. Many personal names on Hebrew seals discovered in Israel bear Canaanite theophoric elements, contrasting dramatically with the personal names of seals from Judah. The Samaria ostraca from this general period also contain numerous Baal names. At Kuntillet ʾAjrud in the Sinai, the site of an ancient Israelite (as opposed to Judean) colony has been discovered with evidence of a syncretistic Yahwistic cult. On one pithos one finds the drawing of a couple with bovine features, and above it is the inscription: *brkt . ʾtkm . lyhwh . šmrn . wlʾšrth,* "May you be blessed by YHWH of Samaria and by his Asherah" (Meshel 1979).

It is sometimes posited that Gomer bat-Diblaim was a cultic prostitute who participated in the ritual sexual acts of Canaanite religions (2:7–15—Eng 2:5–13). It has also been suggested that the name Diblaim, which may be taken to mean "Two Fig" or the like, is a veiled reference to Gomer's partaking of the "raisin cakes" (3:1). The latter is possibly an aphrodisiac associated with Canaanite fertility cults.

According to Hosea, the people consecrated themselves at Baal-peor, soon after they had made the covenant with YHWH (9:10; Num 25:1–18). They were brought by YHWH to the land which he had blessed, but they turned to the Canaanite gods instead, and attributed blessings and success to Baal (2:7, 10–11—Eng 2:5, 8–9). The polemic against Canaanite religion is clear here. Baal was thought to be the god of nature and fertility, but it was really YHWH who gave and took away.

Among the practices of Canaanite religion, none irked Hosea more than their attempt to induce fertility by sympathetic magic. Since fertility was thought to have been generated by sexual intercourse between the deities (specifically between Baal and Anat), certain men and women were set apart for cultic coitus. But Hosea insisted that the Canaanite gods could not deliver on their promise. The woman pursued them but she could not catch up; "she will seek them, but they will not be found" (2:5—Eng 2:7). The imagery of a woman pursuing her lover is known in other erotic contexts (Cant 3:1–4). Here it may have to do with a sexual ritual to bring about fertility. The people participated in such sexual rites to ensure rich harvests and fecundity, but they would "eat but not be satisfied, prostitute themselves but not multiply" (4:10).

Eventually Israel had to learn that only YHWH could grant the blessings of the land. Then, YHWH alone would have the allegiance of his bride, not Baal. The name of Baal would be removed forever; Israel would call YHWH "my husband" *(ʾîšî)* and not "my master" *(baʿălî)* as before.

No other Canaanite god is explicitly mentioned besides Baal, although it is sometimes supposed that the Hebrew of 14:9—Eng 14:8 contains an allusion to the goddesses Anat and Asherah. In 4:12 one finds mention of people seeking oracles from "wood." This is probably an allusion to the statue of the goddess Asherah and/or the sacred tree in the sanctuary. Hosea inveighed against the use of idols, but special mention is made of the "calf of Samaria" (8:5), the "calf of Beth-aven" (10:5), and certain calves that people kissed (13:2). These are probably the calves that Jeroboam I made to prevent his subjects from going down to the Jerusalem temple (1 Kgs 12:28; cf. Exod 32:1–10). They were probably nothing more than pedestals on which YHWH was supposed to have stood, but the polemics of Yahwistic prophets made these out to be idols made for worship.

F. Structure

It is clear that chap. 1–3 and 4–14 constitute two major divisions of the book. The first section (chap. 1–3) functions as the preface for the entire book. The preface represents the unfaithfulness of Israel in the person of Gomer, and the pain and love of God in the person of Hosea. The prophet is asked to marry the promiscuous Gomer because "the land" had gone awhoring, going after her Canaanite "lovers" (the gods), depending on these illegitimate lovers for sustenance, and performing rites that joined her to them. Judgment is proclaimed, but it is followed by a message of hope for a new beginning. Eventually, the recalcitrant wife would realize that life was much better with her first spouse. Thus, out of the troublesome valley of suffering (see ACHOR) there would, nevertheless, be a door of hope (2:17—Eng 2:15). YHWH would no longer be confused with Baal. Indeed, the names of the Baalism would be removed from Israel's lips, and a new relationship would be established by YHWH. Israel would be betrothed to YHWH once again. The same juxtaposition of judgment with hope and the theme of redemption is also found in chap. 3.

Reflecting the structure of the first three chapters, the major portion of the book also juxtaposes oracles of hope (11:1–11; 14:1–8) with oracles of judgment. As in the first three chapters, so in the oracles of 4–14 YHWH's relation with Israel is expressed in familial terms, as husband and wife and parent and child (11:1–4). YHWH is portrayed as the faithful lover and husband, Israel as the adulterous and recalcitrant wife. The theme of the wife's unfaithfulness is carried through the book. YHWH is also the patient parent bent on teaching Israel, the rebellious child (11:1–7). Although he resorted to discipline, his compassion and mercy for the child prevented the child from being destroyed.

The book may be outlined as follows:

- I. Preface: The Family of Hosea (chap. 1–3)
  - A. Hosea's Call and His Family (1:2–2:3—Eng 1:1–11)
  - B. God and the Wife (2:4–25—Eng 2:1–23)
  - C. Restoration (3:1–5)
- II. Faithful God and Unfaithful Israel (chap. 4–13)
  - A. Unfaithfulness of Israel (4:1–8:14)
  - B. Proclamation of Judgment (9:1–13:16)
- III. Restoration (chap. 14)
  - A. Call to Return (14:2–4—Eng 14:1–3)
  - B. Promise of Restoration (14:5–9—Eng 4–8)
  - C. Summary Call to Faithfulness (14:10—Eng 9)

G. Theology

Hosea stands firmly in the ancient Mosaic tradition of the conditional covenant, a tradition having its greatest influence in the N kingdom. Fundamental to this theological tradition is the understanding that the validity of the covenant was conditional upon the faithfulness of the covenant partners. This covenant has been compared with the suzerainty treaties of the ANE. Following this model, YHWH is seen as the benevolent suzerain and Israel as the vassal who owed allegiance to YHWH.

There are allusions in the book to the Sinai revelation. The very name *lōʾ-ʿammî,* "not my people," suggests the Mosaic tradition in which YHWH called Israel *ʿammî,* "my people" (cf. Exod 6:7; 3:7, 10). That relationship assumed that the nation would obey the command of YHWH and "keep the covenant" (Exod 19:5); failure to do so would result in covenant curses and invalidation of the relationship. According to Hosea, God used to call Israel *ʿammî,* "my people," but because of their unfaithfulness the Israelites will be called *lōʾ-ʿammî,* "not my people." At Sinai, the deity was revealed as the great *ʾehyeh,* "I am" (Exod 3:14), but now, because of Israel's unfaithfulness, the message from God is *lōʾ-ʾehyeh,* "I am not (your God)" (1:9). Hosea was interested primarily in Israel as a chosen people. Unlike his contemporary, Amos, he was not interested in the punishment or salvation of other nations. Because of his emphasis on the covenant relationship, he refers to the deity usually by the name YHWH (38 times); where *ʾĕlōhîm* is used, a pronominal suffix is used to imply that it is the God of the Exodus and Sinai of whom Hosea is speaking. As a divine name, *ʾĕlōhîm* occurs only 3 times in Hosea without suffixal or other specification. Thus, Hosea was concerned with YHWH, the God of Israel, who led the Israelites out of Egypt and preserved them in the wilderness (12:13, 14). Israel knew "no other God" but YHWH, there was no other savior (13:4; Exod 20:3).

Throughout the book there are specific references and allusions to the Exodus event (2:17—Eng 2:15; 11:1; 12:10, 14[—Eng 12:9, 13]; 13:4) and the wilderness experience (2:16[—Eng 2:14]; 9:10; 13:4). Hosea romanticized the early days of Israel's history as a time of Israel's faithfulness (2:15 [13]).

Against this background one must understand the sins of Israel. The vassal had betrayed the suzerain; the people of Israel had rebelled (5:7; 6:7; 7:1; 7:13, 14; 8:1–2; 9:15; 14:1—Eng 3:16). Israel (the figuration as a woman surfaces repeatedly) had transgressed the covenant and violated its stipulations (4:1–3; 6:7; 7:1; 8:1). This she did by showing allegiance to other gods, turning to foreign military power, and relying on her own military prowess. Sharing the same world view as the predecessors of the Deuteronomic school, Hosea condemned any deviation from the Yahwistic cult. The people had made molten images of silver and gold, just as they did in the days of Moses and Aaron (8:4–5; 13:2). Israel had violated her trust by turning to the Canaanite gods and participating in their sexual rituals (2:7b–15—Eng 2:5b–14; 9:10). The prophet described this unfaithfulness in sexual terms, as harlotry and adultery (1:2; 2:4–15—Eng 2:2–13; 4:10–19; 5:3–4; 6:10; 7:4; 9:1). Here again is an allusion to the covenant at Sinai where the proliferation of altars and the worship of other gods are regarded as acts of harlotry (Exod 34:12–16; cf. Judg 8:33). They have indeed rejected the love of Yahweh and turned to the Canaanite gods. They made idols and worshipped them (4:17; 8:4; 10:5; 11:2; 13:1–3; 14:9—Eng 14:8). Like the later Deuteronomists, Hosea condemned the proliferation of altars and local sanctuaries (10:1–2, 8; 12:11). He regarded the temple in Jerusalem as the sole legitimate sanctuary in which to worship YHWH, and he condemned those who worshipped at the N shrines at Gilgal and Bethel (4:15; 9:15). He attributed the apostasy of Israel to what the Deuteronomist called "the sin of Jeroboam," namely, the erection of the golden calf at Bethel (10:5).

In spite of YHWH's faithfulness as evident in history, Israel did not trust in YHWH's power to protect and deliver them. Instead, they turned to Assyria and Egypt (5:13; 7:8, 11; 8:9–10; 12:2—Eng 12:1), precisely the oppressive nations from which they had to be rescued. Thus Israel acted treacherously against YHWH her suzerain. Hence her sacrifices and offerings were of no use to YHWH (6:6; 8:13).

Because of Israel's violations of the covenant, YHWH brought a lawsuit against her (2:4 [—Eng 2:2]; 4:1; 5:1). YHWH charged that Israel lacked faithfulness *(ʾĕmet),* loyalty *(ḥesed),* and knowledge of God *(daʿat ʾĕlōhîm;* cf. 4:1). Knowledge and loyalty are two key theological concepts in Hosea. They occur together again in 6:6, where it is emphasized that YHWH preferred loyalty and knowledge of God to sacrifice.

Knowledge of God marked Israel's special relationship with YHWH. People and priest alike are rejected by YHWH because of their lack of knowledge (4:1, 6; 5:4). The verb *ydʿ* indicates intimate knowledge as of partners in a covenant or marriage. Israel's relationship with YHWH was once correct: they *knew* no other God but YHWH, and YHWH knew them in their wilderness wandering (13:4). But as soon as they were satiated with the nourishment that YHWH had provided them, they forgot the benevolence of YHWH (13:6). They claimed to know YHWH (8:2), but they had flagrantly broken the covenant with YHWH and violated the law (8:1). In fact, they did not know. They did not even know that it was YHWH who provided her with grain, wine, and oil (2:8). Instead, they attributed these products of the land to other gods (2:7 [—Eng 2:5]). They reckoned that vines and fig trees were their payment for their devotion to their "lovers" (2:14 [—Eng 2:12]). For the sake of grain and wine they participated in the fertility rites associated with Baal (7:14; cf. 1 Kgs 18:28). They gashed themselves even though it was explicitly forbidden for them to do so (Deut 14:28). It was YHWH who cared for them and healed, but they did not know it (11:3). They did not know YHWH because they were possessed by the "spirit of harlotry" (5:4). But YHWH knew them (5:3). They had rejected knowledge, the absence of which was evident in their violation of the commandments of God (4:1–3, 6). The lack of knowledge is taken to be synonymous with treachery (5:7; 6:6–7), and for this treachery she was to go into exile (4:1, 6). But beyond the judgment Hosea saw hope for a new relationship established by YHWH and based on faithfulness, loyalty, justice, and mercy. Then would Israel truly know YHWH (2:22—Eng 2:20). To that end, Hosea urged his audience to "know YHWH and pursue the knowledge of YHWH" (6:2).

For Hosea, "loyalty" *(ḥesed)* marked the covenant of mutuality. Both covenant partners were expected to demonstrate this quality. There was inequality. YHWH's reliability was likened to the predictability of dawn and the spring rain (6:1–3). Israel's loyalty, on the other hand, was as fleeting as the morning cloud and the dew that evaporates all too quickly (6:4). She must repent and sow righteousness in order to reap the fruits of *ḥesed* (10:12). The people must keep loyalty and justice (12:7). Israel will, indeed, be punished for the abandonment of her covenant responsibilities. But beyond judgment there is hope. Eventually, God will take Israel back as bride in righteousness, justice, mercy, faithfulness, and loyalty, and Israel will truly know YHWH (2:22–23—Eng 2:19–20).

It is for good reason that Hosea is often called the

prophet of love. The love of YHWH for Israel is substantiated and exemplified in Hosea's own relationship with his wife. Divine love is shown in the microcosm of Hosea's marriage. Love, indeed, is the central theme that unifies the book. The relationship between Hosea and his beloved (chap. 1–3) which mirrors the relationship between YHWH and Israel (chap. 4–14) is one of love on the part of the gracious husband. As with loyalty and knowledge, so love may be understood in terms of the covenant. In the ANE, the ties between the vassal and suzerain were said to be marked by "love." The vassal was supposed to "love" the suzerain by observing the treaty stipulations, honoring its responsibilities, and being loyal to the suzerain. Hosea was commanded to love a harlotrous woman as a symbol of YHWH's love for the people in spite of their unfaithfulness (3:1). God is also said to have loved Israel like a child, even though Israel kept gravitating toward other gods (11:1–4). That same love would be freely given with the eventual reconcilation (14:5 [—Eng 14:4]). By the same token, the invalidation of the covenant is expressed as the withdrawal of love (9:15).

For their transgressions, the people would be punished. Covenant curses would be upon them. They would be cursed with hunger (4:10; 9:2). Their threshing floors and wine vats would cease to be operational (9:2). Though they were engaged in all sorts of rites to bring fertility, they would experience barrenness and dryness of breasts instead (4:10; 9:11). They and their princes would die by the sword (7:16; 9:13; 11:6). Their children would be dashed in pieces and their pregnant women would be cut open (11:6; 14:11—Eng 13:16]). War would overtake them (10:9; 14). Their cities would be destroyed by fire (8:14). Parents would be bereft of their children (9:11–14, 16). Worst of all, there would be a reversal of the Exodus; they would be brought back to Egypt whence they had been delivered (8:13; 9:3; 11:5; 14:1–2) or be in exile (9:3, 17; 11:5, 11). Thus the unfaithful nation would receive the same punishment as the unfaithful Gomer: they would be cast out of their home (land) and left to fend for themselves in foreign territories. Through this experience of punishment Israel would learn, even as the unfaithful wife did, that life was better with her first husband, namely YHWH (2:9 [—Eng 2:7]).

Thus, Hosea's message is not entirely of doom. Punishment was inevitable. The situation was not hopeless because God's compassion for Ephraim the child was great (11:8–9), and God could not bear to see God's beloved destroyed. In the end, the children would "be pitied" (14:4 [—Eng 14:3]; cf. 1:6; 2:25 [—Eng 2:23]). Hence, the people were asked to return *(šûb)* to YHWH (6:1; 12:7 [—Eng 12:6]; 14:2–3—Eng 14:1–2) in order that they might be restored to their wealth and health. In accordance with Deuteronomistic covenant theology, the repentance of the offender would bring forgiveness and life. YHWH's affliction was only temporary; it was intended to cause Israel to see the foolishness of her ways. Eventually YHWH would heal the sickness and bind the wounds so that his people would live again (6:1–2). Their fortunes would be restored and they would be healed (6:11). The exiles would return home (11:10–11; 6:11; cf. 3:5). They would be healed (6:1, 11). YHWH would correct their apostasy and love them freely again (14:5—Eng 14:3). They would return and dwell under his shade (14:8 [—Eng 14:7]).

Bibliography

Anderson, B. W. 1954. The Book of Hosea. *Int* 8: 290–303.

Brueggemann, W. 1968. *Tradition for Crisis: A Study in Hosea.* Richmond, VA.

Buck, F. 1973. *Die Liebe Gottes beim Propheten Oseé.* Rome.

Buss, M. J. 1969. *The Prophetic Word: A Morphological Study.* BZAW 111. Berlin.

Craghan, J. F. 1971. The Book of Hosea: A Survey of Recent Literature on the First of the Minor Prophets. *BTB* 1: 81–100; 145–70.

———. 1975. An Interpretation of Hosea. *BTB* 5: 201–7.

Crotty, R. 1971. Hosea and the Knowledge of God. *AusBR* 19: 1–16.

Eichrodt, W. 1961. "The Holy One in Your Midst." The Theology of Hosea. *Int* 15: 259–73.

Emmerson, G. I. 1984. *Hosea: An Israelite Prophet in Judean Perspective.* JSOTSup. 28. Sheffield.

Ginsberg, H. L. 1961. Hosea's Ephraim, More Fool Than Knave: A New Interpretation of Hosea 12:1–14. *JBL* 80: 339–47.

Gordis, R. 1971. Hosea's Marriage and Message: A New Approach. Pp. 230–54 in *Poets, Prophets, and Sages: Essays in Biblical Interpretation.* Bloomington.

Kinet, D. 1977. *Baᶜal und Jahweh: Ein Beitrag zur Theologie des Hoseabuches.* Frankfurt am Main.

King, P. J. 1982. Hosea's Message of Hope. *BTB* 12: 91–95.

Kuhnigk, W. 1974. *Nordwestsemitischen Studien zum Hoseabuch.* BibOr 27. Rome.

May, H. G. 1931. The Fertility Cult in Hosea. *AJSL* 48: 73–98.

McDonald, J. R. B. 1964. The Marriage of Hosea. *Theology* 67: 149–56.

McKenzie, J. L. 1955. Divine Passion in Osee. *CBQ* 17: 167–79.

———. 1955. Knowledge of God in Hosea. *JBL* 74: 22–27.

McKenzie, S. 1979. Exodus Typology in Hosea. *ResQ* 22: 100–8.

Meshel, Z. 1979. Did Yahweh Have a Consort? The New Religious Inscriptions from the Sinai. *BARev* 5/2: 24–35.

North, F. S. 1957. A Solution to Hosea's Marital Problems by Critical Analysis. *JNES* 16: 128–30.

———. 1958. Hosea's Introduction to His Book. *VT* 8: 429–32.

Nyberg, H. S. 1935. *Studien zum Hoseabuch.* Uppsala.

O'Connor, M. P. 1982. The Deceptions of Hosea. *TBT* 20: 152–58.

Östborn, G. 1956. *Yahweh and Baal.* Lund.

Rowley, H. H. 1963. The Marriage of Hosea. Pp. 66–97 in *Men of God.* London.

Ruppert, L. 1982. Erwägungen zur Kompositions- und Redaktionsgeschichte von Hos 1–3. *BZ* 26: 208–23.

Seow, C. L. 1982. Hosea 14:10 and the Foolish People Motif. *CBQ* 44: 212–24.

Ward, J. M. 1969. The Message of Hosea. *Int* 23: 387–407.

Wolff, H. W. 1956. Hoseas geistige Heimat. *TLZ* 81: 83–94.

———. 1961. Guilt and Salvation: A Study of the Prophecy of Hosea. *Int* 15: 274–85.

Yee, G. A. 1987. *Composition and Tradition in the Book of Hosea.* SBLDS 102. Atlanta.

C. L. Seow

HOSHAIAH (PERSON) [Heb *hôšaᶜăyāh*]. **1.** Leader of the princes of Judah at the dedication of the wall of Jerusalem (Neh 12:32). The list of participants in vv 32–

36 has probably been spliced into a separate narrative about the procession (vv 27–31, 37–43) from the first-person accounts in Nehemiah known as Nehemiah's Memoirs (Williamson *Ezra, Nehemiah* WBC, 370), perhaps for the purpose of making a historical connection between Nehemiah and Ezra (whose name in v 33 may itself be a gloss on "Azariah").

2. Father of Jezaniah (Jer 42:1) or Azariah (Jer 43:2), a leader in Jerusalem after the assassination of Gedaliah and one of the "insolent men" (Heb *hazzādîm;* 43:2) who forced Jeremiah to flee with them to Egypt. Therefore, Hoshaiah was presumably also the Maacathite referred to in Jer 40:8. The LXX versions of Jer 49:1 (—Eng 42:1) and 50:2 (—Eng 43:2) both refer to Azariah as the son of MAASEIAH *(maasaiou)* instead of Hoshaiah. The reasons for these variations are unclear. The name Hoshaiah in its longer form, *hwšʿyhw,* is well attested in inscriptions outside of the Bible including the Lachish letters (Fowler *TPNAH,* 97). There is no certainty that the Hoshaiah of the Lachish correspondence is the same man referred to in Jeremiah, but this is a possibility. See JAAZANIAH and JEZANIAH.

STEVEN L. MCKENZIE

HOSHAMA (PERSON) [Heb *hôšāmāʾ*]. The sixth son of Jeconiah (Jehoiachin), king of Judah (598–597), who was exiled by Nebuchadnezzar. Hoshama is mentioned only in 1 Chr 3:18, as part of the list recording the postexilic descendants of David.

RUSSELL FULLER

HOSHEA (PERSON) [Heb *hôšēaʿ*]. **1.** The earlier name of Joshua, the son of Nun (Num 13:8; cf. Deut. 32:44), which Moses, for some unspecified reason, changed to Joshua (v 16). This Ephraimite was among the twelve scouts whom Moses, at Yahweh's command, dispatched N from the wilderness of Paran in order "to spy out the land of Canaan" (v 17). See JOSHUA.

2. The son of Azaziah and chief officer (*nāgîd,* 1 Chr 27:16) of Ephraim during the Davidic monarchy (1 Chr 27:20).

3. The last king of Israel (ca. 732–724 B.C.E.), the son of Elah (2 Kgs 15:30), and a contemporary of two Judean kings, Ahaz and Hezekiah. Though his ultimate fate is unknown, this murderer and successor of Pekah had a relatively short and troubled rule prior to being taken captive by Shalmaneser V, king of Assyria. Hoshea's career and its impact on the N kingdom will be considered under three categories: prelude, Hoshea's regal tenure, and aftermath.

a. Prelude. When the anti-Assyrian coalition that was headed by two politically unrealistic monarchs—Pekah of Israel and his ally, Rezin of Aram—proved ineffective, these small states in W Asia were slated for trouble. In 734 B.C.E. Assyria's king, Tiglath-pileser III (745–727), pressed westward. After an initial sweep down the Mediterranean coast, he directed his attention to interior regions in Syria-Palestine. Tiglath-pileser reached the climax of his campaign when he moved against Damascus in 733–732 B.C.E. He devastated the city, executed its king, Rezin, deported much of the population, and reorganized Aram into four Assyrian provinces. During or just prior to his siege against Damascus, Tiglath-pileser confirmed Hoshea's appointment as king of Israel (*ANET,* 284). Israel seems not to have suffered accutely from Assyrian visitation at this juncture, though some of its people were deported. Also the Assyrians took charge of Israelite territory in Galilee, the valley of Jezreel, and Transjordan that Rezin had seized for Aram some years earlier. In mounting the throne in Samaria, Hoshea would govern a small territory that did not range beyond the city of Samaria and the neighboring hill country of Ephraim.

b. Hoshea's Regal Tenure. Credited with a reign of nine years (2 Kgs 17:1), Hoshea presumably entered the regal office during the latter phase of Tiglath-pileser's W campaign. The precise manner whereby he displaced his predecessor Pekah is not known. On the one hand, the biblical text reports that "Hoshea the son of Elah made a conspiracy against Pekah the son of Remaliah, and struck him down, and slew him, and reigned in his stead" (2 Kgs 15:30). On the other hand, a first-person statement in the annals of Tiglath-pileser III discloses that the people "overthrew their king Pekah and I placed Hoshea as king over them" (*ANET,* 284). Though forthright initiative on Hoshea's part need not be questioned, surely the Assyrian endorsement of the one who would next govern the vassal Israelite state was a matter of import.

Whatever the exact circumstances may have been, pro-Assyrian sentiment momentarily prevailed in Samaria. It was not a moment too soon for Israel to make amends to the Assyrians, who surely would applaud Pekah's removal. If Israel's fate were not to replicate Aram's, Hoshea would need to provide visible tokens of his awareness that his relationship to Tiglath-pileser was that of vassal to overlord. Indeed, in 731 B.C.E., at an obviously early stage in his regal tenure, Hoshea dispatched tribute to Tiglath-pileser, who was currently involved in a campaign in distant Babylonia.

Though no details are available, we may assume that Hoshea's response to Shalmaneser V (727–722 B.C.E.), the son and successor of Tiglath-pileser III, was likewise submissive. Admittedly, the text in 2 Kgs 17:3 invites two distinct interpretations. Reporting that "against him [Hoshea] came up Shalmaneser king of Assyria; and Hoshea became his vassal, and paid him tribute," this verse could be perceived as a disclosure that Shalmaneser V found it necessary to pay Hoshea a personal visit in order to remind him of the requirements of Israelite vassaldom to Assyria. A second and more viable interpretation holds that, as Hoshea had placated Tiglath-pileser with tribute, he did no less for his new successor Shalmaneser.

In 724 B.C.E., however, Hoshea committed a costly political error by shifting his loyalty from Assyria to Egypt. He ceased making annual payments of tribute to Shalmaneser V and began to cultivate diplomatic ties with Egypt. Thus the biblical text states that "the king of Assyria found treachery in Hoshea; for he had sent messengers to So, king of Egypt, and offered no tribute to the king of Assyria" (2 Kgs 17:4). Owing to the lack of historiographic literature for the reign of Shalmaneser V, this laconic biblical text remains in the shadows. Perhaps an increasingly strong anti-Assyrian faction in Samaria induced Hoshea to shift his position. Moreover, Hoshea might have assumed that other Palestinian states were ripe for a mutual campaign against Assyria. In any event, Hoshea misread Egypt's capacity to help on this occasion. Currently fragmented into several insignificant rival kingdoms, Egypt was not about to spend its energies tending to some other nation's problems.

Also it is not clear to whom Hoshea directed his appeal. Egyptian records do not attest any pharaoh named So. Until 1960 it was commonplace for So (perhaps vocalized as Sewe) to be equated with Sibʾe, the Egyptian military commander often mentioned in the inscriptions of Sargon (*ANET*, 285). Since Borger (1960: 49–53) has demonstrated that the cuneiform sign in question must be read ideographically as Reʾe, the identification of So with Sibʾe has been abandoned. Kitchen (1986: 463) accepts So as an abbreviation of the name Osorkon IV, the last pharaoh of Egypt's 22d Dynasty. Since the identity of the pharaoh with whom Hoshea sought to establish diplomatic ties is not beyond dispute, another approach commends itself. This involves equating So with a *place* (the city of Sais in the Nile delta) rather than with a *person* (Goedicke 1963: 64–66). Thus Albright (1963: 66) argues that the Hebrew text originally stated that Hoshea sent "to So (i.e., to Sais), to the king of Egypt." Several years prior to 720 B.C.E., Pharaoh Tefnakht, who founded Egypt's 24th Dynasty, established an independent kingdom in Sais. Uncertainties surrounding the identity of So, however, in no way discount the fact that Hoshea's appeal to some Egyptian element went unanswered.

c. Aftermath. The Assyrian reprisal was prompt. In some manner, Shalmaneser V captured Hoshea and "bound him in prison" (2 Kgs 17:4). Perhaps Hoshea, choosing to break with Samaria's anti-Assyrian faction, appeared before his overlord to make amends. At any rate, Israelite resistance did not cease with the king's arrest. Only after a lengthy siege involving two calendar years did Samaria's stalwart population surrender to the Assyrians. Apparently Shalmaneser deployed only some of his forces against this city that was still being well served by superbly constructed defensive walls erected more than a century earlier by Omri and Ahab.

In the biblical text, Shalmaneser is credited with having captured Samaria. Since he died shortly before or after Samaria's citizens were forced to surrender, it is not surprising that his brother and successor, Sargon II (722–705), celebrated the conquest of Samaria as the outstanding event of his first year of rule (*ANET*, 284). Though during the early months of his rule Sargon's energies were devoted to settling problems in both Assyria and S Mesopotamia, by 720 B.C.E. he was able to reclaim Samaria, deport 27,290 of its citizens, and incorporate it into the expanding Assyrian provincial system.

Finally, whereas Hoshea is censured in the biblical text for having done "evil in the sight of the LORD" (2 Kgs 17:2), the judgment is softened by this additional statement: "yet not as the kings of Israel who were before him." Though no precise reason is available to explain why Hoshea is the one N monarch to receive a mitigated condemnation, perhaps he lacked time and energy to mount religious pursuits that the Deuteronomic author would have found objectionable. That he was treated with some respect in the light of his tragic role as the last king of the N kingdom is a possible, though not compelling, answer.

4. One of "the chiefs of the people" (*roʾšê hāʿām;* Neh 10:15—Eng 10:14), a lay leader who set his seal to the covenant in the time of Nehemiah (Neh 10:24—Eng 10:23). This deed is perceived as a solemn commitment that flowed naturally from the communal fasting and confession of sin that is the subject of Nehemiah 9. Presumably, by means of his own personal seal, Hoshea formally signed the document in question.

Bibliography

Albright, W. F. 1963. The Elimination of King "So." *BASOR* 171: 66.

Borger, R. 1960. Das Ende des ägyptischen Feldherrn Sibʾe = *sôʾ*. *JNES* 19: 49–53.

Cogan, M. 1974. *Imperialism and Religion: Assyria, Judah and Israel in the Eighth and Seventh Centuries B.C.E.* Missoula, MT.

Donner, H. 1977. The Separate States of Israel and Judah. *IJH*, 381–434.

Goedicke, H. 1963. The End of "So, King of Egypt." *BASOR* 171: 64–66.

Kitchen, K. A. 1986. *The Third Intermediate Period in Egypt.* 2d ed. Warminster.

J. KENNETH KUNTZ

HOSPITALITY [Gk *philoxenia*]. The practice of receiving a guest or stranger graciously was common to many social groups throughout the period in which the OT and NT were composed. But special nuances of hospitality, particularly with regard to the guest and host roles played by God or Christ, serve to distinguish the notions of the biblical writers from those of their contemporaries. The word most often associated with hospitality in the LXX and the NT is *xenos,* which literally means foreigner, stranger, or even enemy. In its derived sense, however, the term comes to denote both guest and host alike. Typically, the verb used to describe the extending of hospitality is *xenizein* (Sir 29:25; 1 Macc 9:6; Acts 10:23; Heb 13:2). In the NT one who receives visitors is said to be *philoxenos,* i.e., a "lover of strangers," or to be practicing the virtue of *philoxenia* (1 Tim 3:2; 1 Pet 4:9; Rom 12:13; Heb 13:2). All these terms occur in classical Greek literature as well.

The Hebrew Scriptures contain no single word for hospitality, but the activity itself is prominent, especially in the patriarchal stories and accounts in the book of Judges. In these narratives the practice usually illustrates bedouin traditions having to do with a resident's obligation to nourish and protect travelers who find themselves in hostile environments. Thus, in Gen 18:1ff. Abraham rushes out of his tent to greet three strangers who approach him "in the heat of the day." When a feast is set before them, these unknown visitors reveal how God's promise concerning the son to be born of Abraham and Sarah is at long last approaching fulfillment. By conveying their message, the guests return a favor to their host, thus setting in motion a numinous reciprocity which is typical of stories about table fellowship in the ancient world. A similar exchange occurs when Abraham's servant visits Mesopotamia to procure a wife for Isaac (Gen 24:1–49). Having reached his destination, the servant prays that God will make known the desired bride in the person of the first young woman who not only responds to his request for a drink of water but also offers, on her own initiative, to water his camels as well. This turns out to be Rebekah. Over dinner in the house of Rebekah's father the servant discloses his identity and tells of his mission, ending with an account of the answered prayer. In both of these patriarchal stories God's will comes to light through an act of hospitality.

A more direct encounter with the divine occurs in a meal scene recorded by the preexilic author of Exodus 24. Immediately following the ratification of the Sinai covenant Moses, Aaron, and 70 elders of Israel ascend the holy mountain at God's command. Still at some distance from the top, "they saw the God of Israel . . . and he did not lay his hand on the chief men of Israel; they beheld God, and ate and drank" (Exod 24:9–11). This connection between a meal and an extraordinary vision of the divine finds echos in rabbinic literature (*m. ʾAboth* 3:4; *m. Ber.* 17a) and in the NT (Luke 24:13–35; John 21:1–14). By contrast, the Sodom and Gomorrah story (Gen 19:1–11) and an account of the rape-murder of a Levite's concubine by some Benjaminites (Judg 19:16–30) depict abuses of hospitality which call down wrathful responses from God and the people of Israel.

Another feature of hospitality that emerges from the OT record is Israel's deep sense of God as its host. Conscious of its formation from descendants of a "wandering Aramean," Israel knew and treasured its identity as a pilgrim people (Deut 26:5–22), especially during the Exodus journey when it received manna from God in the wilderness (Exodus 16–17). Having taken possession of the promised land, Israelites nevertheless remembered that their home belonged to Yahweh (Lev 25:23) and that they, like their forebears, remained sojourners and passing guests in God's eyes (Ps 39:12). Precisely as inhabitants of the land, they pictured themselves being led into green pastures and feted at the table of the divine king in the presence of their enemies. The "house of the Lord" in which they hoped to dwell forever was essentially God's perpetual hosting (Psalm 23; see also Psalm 104 in which God is portrayed as feeding and sustaining the entire creation day by day). When Israel's prophets looked forward to an era of perfect righteousness and *shalom,* it was no accident that they envisioned God entertaining the people at an endless feast (Amos 9:13–15; Joel 3:18; Isa 25:6–8; see also *1 En.* 62:14; *Midr. Exod.* 25:7–8). According to Isaiah, this great banquet would be spread for everyone on earth: "On this mountain the Lord of Hosts will make for all peoples a feast of fat things, a feast of wine on the lees. . . . He will swallow up death forever, and the Lord God will wipe away tears from all faces. . . ." This passage may have formed the basis for Jesus' pronouncement that many would come "from east and west and sit at table with Abraham, Isaac, and Jacob in the kingdom of heaven" (Matt 8:11).

Even more than their Greco-Roman neighbors, Jews of the Second Temple and rabbinic periods prized hospitality as a virtue (*T. Zeb.* 6:4f.; Jos. *Ant* 1.250f.). Particularly in the synagogue, which could serve as a hostel or meeting place for travelers seeking accommodations, and at the sabbath eve meal visitors were welcomed. The extent to which gentiles were included in these acts of hospitality must have varied from community to community. Among the rabbis, scholars were to be given precedence in the receiving of food and lodging (*m. Abot* 3:4). For both Palestinian and Diaspora Jews one figure, the patriarch Abraham, emerged as a special exemplar of hospitality (*T. Ab.* 1–5; Philo, *Abr* 107–18; *ʾAbot R.N.* 7; *Tg. Yer.* on Gen 21:33; *Tg. Neof.* on Gen 18:1f.). The last text cited contains a midrash on the story of the three visitors in which God, having appeared to Abraham shortly after the advent of his messengers, is told by the patriarch to wait until he has attended to the needs of those who arrived first! In the NT, Abraham's role as archetypal host can be glimpsed in Matt 8:11 and the parable of the rich fool, where heaven is termed "Abraham's bosom" and is probably to be understood as a place of abundant eating and drinking (Luke 16:22–26). Other rabbinic stories portray Abraham as the founder of inns for travelers (*Gen. Rab.* 39:14), the inventor and teacher of grace after meals (*b. Soṭa* 10a–b), and the missionary host who insists that his guests praise the God of Israel for their meal or pay cash for it (*Gen. Rab.* 49:4).

As pictured by the Synoptic writers, the ministry of Jesus manifests the theme of hospitality in two basic ways. First, Jesus' proclamation of the kingdom is frequently symbolized by images of food and drink, especially at festive meals. Thus the kingdom is compared to a great banquet (Matt 8:11; 22:1–14 = Luke 14:16–24), and Jesus ends his ministry with a ceremonial meal at which words about eating and drinking in the kingdom are spoken (Mark 14:17–25 and parallels). In Luke's version of the Lord's Prayer the petitions for the coming of the kingdom and for daily bread are joined together (Luke 11:2–3). Moreover, teaching about the kingdom is implied in Jesus' pronouncements about feasting with the bridegroom and new wine (Mark 2:18–22 and parallels), in the promise that faithful servants will be invited to enter into the joy (i.e., feast) of their master (Matt 25:21–33), and in the conclusion to the parable of the prodigal son (Luke 15:20–32). Indeed, the majority of Jesus' parabolic sayings have to do with the production and use of food and drink or the providing of homelike refuge for God's creatures. What seems to lie behind this body of teaching is a conviction held by the Synoptic Jesus that God is revealing himself powerfully and eschatologically as Israel's host. The feast predicted by Isaiah (25:6–8) has already begun to appear in the present world order.

Second, the Synoptic record of Jesus' behavior shows that he intended to live in accordance with the coming feast of the kingdom. This is epitomized in a dominical saying about how Jesus' contemporaries were perceiving him. "John," he complained, "came neither eating nor drinking, and they say, 'He has a demon'; the Son of man came eating and drinking, and they say, 'Behold, a glutton and a drunkard, a friend of tax collectors and sinners!' " (Matt 11:18f. = Luke 7:33f.). If the substance of this saying is genuine, one may conclude that the various accounts of Jesus' eating with tax collectors and sinners (Mark 2:15ff. and parallels; Luke 19:1–10) or welcoming them (Luke 7:36–50; 15:1–2), though sometimes built up from the sayings tradition and always modified in their transmission and redaction, nevertheless have some basis in fact. It is difficult to determine what sort of event underlies the narratives of Jesus' feeding the 5000; but the fact that this is the only miracle story to appear in all four gospels suggests that the early Church considered it foundational for the interpretation of Jesus' mission. It has long been observed that Jesus' choice of twelve itinerant disciples constituted a claim that God had initiated the end-time restoration of Israel's dispersed tribes. But it should also be noted that Jesus' larger group of followers, which included residential supporters, seems to have functioned as a network for sharing God's eschatological abundance among themselves, and for inviting the broader population to join them in this new mutuality. The Jesus movement was itself both guest and host of the kingdom.

It is Luke especially who accents this theme in Luke-Acts. Only the third gospel contains the parables of the good Samaritan, the prodigal son, the rich man and Lazarus, the story of Zaccheus, and the Emmaus narrative, according to which two disciples come to recognize the risen Jesus "in the breaking of bread" (24:35). For its part, Acts may be read as a collection of guest and host stories depicting missionary ventures that have originated in circles associated with the earliest churches. Luke's special concern is to show how itinerant and residential believers can support one another in the worldwide mission of the Church. Through this mutuality, he believes, the Holy Spirit will bring about rich exchanges of spiritual and material gifts; and the Church will grow (Koenig 1985).

Paul writes that "the kingdom of God is not food and drink but righteousness and peace and joy in the Holy Spirit" (Rom 14:17). This statement appears to contradict the gospel traditions in which meals are seen as a primary locus for the appearance of the kingdom. But the context in Romans shows that Paul does not intend to separate meals as such from the impact of the gospel. Instead, he is trying to reconcile two factions of believers who disagree over which foods may be consumed and are thus prevented from sharing the common meals of the Church. Presumably, these would include the Lord's Supper. Paul's hope is that all groups in Rome will "welcome one another . . . as Christ has welcomed [them] for the glory of God" (Rom 15:7). This reciprocal welcoming, preeminently at meals, becomes both an act of worship and a display of unity that will attract outsiders. A similar point is made when Paul writes to correct abuses of the Lord's Supper in Corinth which have the effect of excluding or dishonoring certain believers, especially the poor. Paul insists that there must be no second-class citizens in this ritual proclamation of the crucified Christ and his world-reversing gospel (1 Cor 11:17–34). Much earlier in his ministry Paul had opposed Peter publicly in Antioch when the latter reneged on his practice of eating with gentile converts (Gal 2:11ff.). For Paul, the meals of the Church have become a critical arena for the revealing of God's righteousness in Christ and humanity's response to it. It is not surprising that the Pauline disciple who wrote 1 Timothy considered the talent for hospitality much to be desired in one who occupied the office of bishop (3:2).

In the Fourth Gospel exchanges of food or drink also function as occasions for the revelation of God's love in Christ (4:7ff.; chaps. 6 and 13–17). But the distinctive character of John's concern for hospitality shows itself in his christological statements. Jesus is not only the door to the sheepfold, the preparer of heavenly chambers, and the way to the Father (10:1ff.; 14:1–6). He is himself the place where believers worship (2:13–22) and dwell (14:20, 23; 15:1ff.). These images take on special meaning if members of the Johannine community have recently suffered expulsion from the synagogue. In the Johannine letters the presbyter-author urges his readers not to receive Christian travelers who do not abide in the doctrine of Christ (2 John 9f.). But he and his emissaries are themselves the objects of inhospitable treatment by a certain Diotrephes (3 John 9f.). Apparently the issue is one of conflict over authority.

Images of hospitality occur with some frequency in the general epistles. James exhorts the recipients of his epistle not to humiliate poor people by assigning them to inferior places in the public assemblies of the Church (2:1–7). The author of 1 Peter addresses his readers as aliens and exiles who were once "no people" but are now a "chosen race . . . built into a spiritual house to be a holy priesthood" (1:1; 2:4–10). As such, they are to "practice hospitality ungrudgingly to one another" (4:9). This terminology may reflect a real social-political situation in which the readers suffered from their status as resident aliens and transient strangers (Elliott 1981). Perhaps the most winsome of all reflections on hospitality by early Christian writers is found in Heb 13:2 where believers are urged to receive strangers graciously on the ground that "thereby some have entertained angels unawares." Clearly the allusion is to Abraham's enthusiastic reception of the three heavenly messengers. But Jesus too may come as a stranger. Matthew, Luke, and John all make this point (Matt 25:31–46; Luke 24:13–35; John 20:11ff.; 21:1–14). And so does the author of Revelation when he records the words of the Risen One to the church in Laodicea: "Behold, I stand at the door and knock; of any one hears my voice and opens the door, I will come in to him and eat with him, and he with me" (3:20). The context indicates that this meal with Jesus, like many of those narrated in the gospels, will be one of repentance and reconciliation.

Bibliography

Brown, R. E. 1979. *The Community of the Beloved Disciple.* New York.

Elliott, J. H. 1981. *A Home for the Homeless: A Sociological Exegesis of 1 Peter.* Philadelphia.

Koenig, J. 1985. *New Testament Hospitality: Partnership with Strangers as Promise and Mission.* Philadelphia.

Malherbe, A. 1983. *Social Aspects of Early Christianity.* 2d ed. Philadelphia.

Verner, D. C. 1983. *The Household of God: The Social World of the Pastoral Epistles.* SBLDS 71. Chico, CA.

Visotzky, B. L. 1986. The Image of Abraham in Rabbinic Literature. *Face to Face* 13: 9–12.

JOHN KOENIG

HOSTS, HOST OF HEAVEN. The term *ṣābāʾ*, pl. *ṣĕbāʾôt* (masc. pl. 2x; Pss 103:21; 148:2 [Q]), commonly translated "host," "hosts," denotes primarily a military retinue or army, a meaning consistent with its common Semitic etymology (cf. Akk. *ṣābu;* Old South Arabic *ḍbʾ;* Eth. *ḍabʾa/ṣabʾa;* Ug. *ṣbʾu*). The term occurs some 486 times in the Hebrew Bible, 315 of which are in the plural. The plural form, *ṣĕbāʾôt,* occurs as a divine epithet associated with Yahweh in 284 of those occurrences. The term is used in Hebrew to designate both human and divine armies, as well as to connote certain celestial bodies, a usage that is not uncommon within the mythopoeic conceptions of the ANE.

A. Hosts
B. Host of Heaven
   1. Yahweh's Military Retinue
   2. Yahweh's Council
   3. Objects of Worship
C. Yahweh *Ṣĕbāʾôt*
   1. Cultic Name
   2. Associations with Prophetic Speech

A. Hosts

Apart from its use with the divine name Yahweh, the word *ṣābāʾ* most commonly designates a military retinue or army (e.g., Exod 6:26; 12:51; Num 1:3, 52; 2:3, 4, 6, 8; 10:14, 15, 16, 18; 31:48; Deut 20:9; 24:5; Josh 4:13; Judg 4:2; 8:6; 1 Sam 12:9; 2 Sam 2:8; 8:16; 10:18; 1 Kgs 1:19; 2:35; 2 Kgs 4:13; Isa 13:4; Pss 44:10—Eng 44:9; 60:12—Eng 60:10; 108:12—Eng 108:11; etc.). By extension, the word also indicates warfare or military service (Num 1:3, 20, 22, 24; 26:2; 31:3, 4, 5, 6; Josh 22:12, 33; 1 Sam 28:1; 1 Chr 5:18; 12:26—Eng 12:25; etc.). Additionally, *ṣābāʾ* may be used to designate cultic service (Num 4:3, 23, 30, 35, 39, 43; 8:24, 25) as well as difficult or harsh service (Isa 40:2; Job 7:1; 14:14; Dan 10:1).

B. Host of Heaven

The phrase *ṣĕbāʾ haššāmayim,* "host of heaven," is used to denote the heavenly bodies, either as personified forces or as celestial bodies. In this usage, *ṣābāʾ* always occurs in the singular.

1. Yahweh's Military Retinue. *ṣābāʾ* is also used to designate the retinue of Yahweh, reflecting the Hebrew belief that Yahweh led the armies of Israel (Num 10:35–36; Deut 33:2–5, 26–29; Josh 5:13–15; Judg 5:23; Isa 13:1–5; Joel 4:11b—Eng 3:11b; Ps 68:8–13, 18—Eng 68:7–12, 17; etc.). This usage could be applied to the arena of human warfare (Exod 6:26; 7:4; 12:17, 41, 51). One of the clearest examples of this is found in David's exchange with Goliath, where the young Israelite notes that he has come out to fight in the name of "Yahweh *Ṣĕbāʾôt,* the god of the battle lines of Israel *(maʿarkôt yiśrāʾēl)*" (1 Sam 17:45). Additionally, the association of Yahweh war with the ark (cf. especially 1 Sam 4:1–7:2) further exemplifies the conception of Yahweh's involvement in military affairs.

In the cosmic arena, Yahweh is depicted as the one who musters the heavenly army (*ṣĕbāʾ milḥāmâ;* Isa 13:4). As the "host of the heights" (*ṣĕbāʾ hammārôm;* Isa 24:21), the celestial bodies are depicted as the heavenly corps under the command of Yahweh. This "host of heaven" is conceived as the creation of Yahweh, the members of which constitute his heavenly army (Isa 40:26; 45:12; Pss 33:6; 103:21; 148:2; Gen 2:1; Sir 17:32; 24:2; 43:8). Indeed, the sun, moon, and stars may be depicted as composing this heavenly retinue (Josh 10:12–13; Judg 5:20; Hab 3:11; Dan 8:10). While preparing for the conquest of Jericho, Joshua encountered his heavenly counterpart, "the commander of the army of Yahweh" *(śar-ṣĕbāʾ-yhwh),* who appeared in the guise of a warrior to deliver a message prior to the conquest of the land (Josh 5:14–15; see also Dan 8:11). In this function, the members of this heavenly army might be conceived as angels, i.e., "messengers" of Yahweh. In Ps 103:20–21 Yahweh's messengers *(malʾākāyw),* the mighty warriors *(gibbōrê kōaḥ),* are included among his host *(ṣĕbāʾāyw),* his ministers who do his will. When Jacob encounters the "messengers of God" *(mălʾăkê ʾĕlōhîm),* he responds by calling them "the army of God" *(maḥănēh ʾĕlōhîm),* providing an etiology for the place name Mahanaim (Gen 32:2–3—Eng 32:1–2). At Qumran the angelic figures are often designated as warriors (1QM 15: 14; 12: 8; IQH 3: 35–36; 5: 21; 8: 11–12; etc.), and in the NT, the "heavenly host" is depicted alongside the angels (Luke 2:13).

2. Yahweh's Council. In conjunction with this messenger function attributed to the members of Yahweh's heavenly armies, the "host of heaven" are also depicted as members of Yahweh's heavenly council. In 1 Kgs 22:19, the prophet Micaiah ben Imlah proclaims: "I saw Yahweh seated upon his throne and all the host of heaven were stationed about him *(wĕkol-ṣĕbāʾ haššāmayim ʿōmēd ʿālāyw* [cf. 2 Chr 18:18])." It was these figures who served to execute the will of the deity (1 Kgs 22:19–23 = 2 Chr 18:18–22; Isaiah 6). Within the context of the depictions of the divine council, these beings are called *bĕnê ʾēlîm,* "sons of god" (Pss 29:1; 89:7—Eng 89:6; compare *bĕnê [hā]ʾĕlōhîm,* Deut 32:8 [LXX; 4QDt]; Gen 6:2, 4; Job 1:6; 2:1; *bĕnê ʿelyôn,* Ps 82:6). More commonly, they are referred to as "holy ones" (*qĕdōšîm,* Deut 33:2–3; Job 5:1; 15:15 [Q]; Pss 16:3; 89:6, 8—Eng 89:5, 7; Zech 14:5; *qōdeš,* Exod 15:11; Pss 77:14—Eng 77:13; 93:5). These beings, while clearly assigned an inferior status (cf. Deut 3:24; 10:17; Jer 10:6; Pss 86:8; 95:3; 135:5; etc.), constituted the "host of heaven." The parallelism of "the morning stars" with "all the sons of god" (*kôkĕbê bōqer//kol-bĕnê ʾĕlōhîm;* Job 38:7), when coupled with those references to the heavenly bodies as participants in the wars of Yahweh (Josh 5:13–15; 10:12b-13a; Judg 5:20; Ps 148:2–3), clearly suggests the identity of the groups. As members of the assembly, they also serve to praise Yahweh in his court (Pss 29:1; 148:2–3).

3. Objects of Worship. Given the distinctive function of these heavenly beings, it should occasion no surprise that they were accorded special status by some and became the object of worship. The worship of "the host of heaven" *(ṣĕbāʾ haššāmayim)* is consistently condemned in the biblical materials. Such worship practices were equated with the worship of "other gods" (*ʾĕlōhîm ʾăḥērîm;* Deut 17:3), and they are often listed alongside "the sun, the moon, and the stars" (Deut 4:19; 17:3; Jer 8:2; 2 Kgs 23:4–5). In these instances, the *ṣĕbāʾ haššāmayim* seem to include the totality of the celestial bodies and the signs of the zodiac (2 Kgs 23:5), as did the militaristic application of the term. The practice of worshipping these beings constitutes the reason for part of the Deuteronomistic Historian's condemnation of both Israel and Judah; the historian condemns the worship of "the host of heavens" along with that of Baal and Asherah. Altars were built to the *ṣĕbāʾ haššāmayim,* to whom incense and libations were offered (2 Kgs 17:16; 21:3, 5 = 2 Chr 33:3, 5; Jer 19:13; Zeph 1:5). Though

Babylonian and Assyrian influences are often cited as motivating factors in such practices, a common Canaanite background seems more likely.

C. Yahweh *Ṣĕbāʾôt*

According to certain traditions contained in the Hebrew Bible, the god of Israel was called "Yahweh [the god] of Hosts," *yhwh [ʾĕlōhê] ṣĕbāʾôt,* for that was "his name" (Isa 47:4; 48:2; 51:15; Jer 10:16; 31:35; 46:18; Amos 4:13; 5:27). The plural form *ṣĕbāʾôt* occurs as part of the divine name 285 times in the Hebrew Bible. In 267 of these occurrences, *ṣĕbāʾôt* follows the name Yahweh immediately, while the longer phrase *yhwh ʾĕlōhê (haṣ)ṣĕbāʾôt* occurs 18 times. The precise meaning and grammatical explanations for the name and its various forms continue to be debated. The interpretation of the divine name Yahweh as well as the broad range of possible meanings for the epithet *ṣĕbāʾôt* heighten the difficulties involved in a resolution to the issue.

Three general approaches are characteristic of the attempts to resolve the problem. If the original form *yahweh* was a verb, possibly a causative form of "to be," then the phrase *yhwh ṣĕbāʾôt* might be interpreted as a part of a longer sentence name, perhaps an original epithet of the Canaanite god El. According to this explanation, the name would mean "he creates the heavenly armies." The longer form of the epithet, *yhwh ʾĕlōhê ṣĕbāʾôt,* "Yahweh, the god of hosts," might then be viewed as a secondary interpretation that developed when the name Yahweh was seen as only a proper name.

Though it is possible that the phrase *yhwh ṣĕbāʾôt* preserves the verbal force of the divine name, it is also clear that the divine name functions in most instances as a proper noun. If Yahweh is so interpreted, then the term *ṣĕbāʾôt* may be taken as an abstract or intensive plural noun, "might" or "mighty," used in apposition to Yahweh. Such an interpretation might be suggested by the common LXX translation of *yhwh ṣĕbāʾôt* as *kyrios pantokratōr,* "the Lord Almighty." This explanation avoids the problem of interpreting *yhwh* as a proper name in the construct state. The inscriptions discovered at Kuntillet ʿAjrud, which refer to *yhwh šmrn* and to *yhwh tmn,* may be relevant to this problem. If these are to be read as "Yahweh of Samaria" and "Yahweh of Teman" (cf. Hab 3:3), then these might furnish a Hebrew parallel for understanding *yhwh ṣĕbāʾôt* as a construct chain, hence "Yahweh of hosts." The LXX translation *kyrios tōn dynameōn* reflects such an understanding of the term.

1. Cultic Name. Despite the controversies surrounding the exact nature of the epithet *ṣĕbāʾôt,* there is general agreement that the origin of the name is to be found within the Israelite cultus, most probably in association with the militaristic qualities associated with the independent use of the term *ṣābāʾ*. The epithet *yhwh ṣĕbāʾôt* is not attested in the Pentateuch, Joshua, or Judges. The first occurrence of the phrase, according to the canonical arrangement of the Hebrew Bible, is in association with the ark of the covenant and the cult center at Shiloh. In 1 Sam 4:4 the ark is called "the ark of the covenant of *yhwh ṣĕbāʾôt,* who is enthroned on the cherubim" (cf. 2 Sam 6:2). The association of *yhwh ṣĕbāʾôt* with the ark and with the cultic shrine of Shiloh (1 Sam 1:3, 11) suggests that the origins of the epithet are to be found in the pre-Jerusalem cultus. The significance of the ark and the traditions associated with it is illustrated by David's establishment of the ark in his new cult center, with which it came to be associated (2 Sam 6:2, 18; 2 Sam 7:8, 26; Isa 6:3; etc.).

The premonarchical Israelite traditions which interpret the ark as a war palladium upon which the god of Israel was enthroned and from which he led the armies of Israel make explicit the association of the epithet "Lord of Hosts" with the ark and with its military functions (1 Sam 17:45). The warrior imagery of the Lord of the heavenly armies, marching victoriously from war over his enemies, is clearly portrayed in Ps 24:8, 10 where "Yahweh of Hosts," "Yahweh strong and mighty," the "mighty warrior," the "king of glory," is praised.

2. Associations with Prophetic Speech. Of the 285 occurrences of *ṣĕbāʾôt* as part of a divine epithet, 251 (88%) are to be found in the prophetic books. Additionally, 244 instances (97.2%) of the phrase *yhwh ṣĕbāʾôt* (or the variant *yhwh ʾĕlōhê [haṣ]ṣĕbāʾôt*) occur in the following six works: Isaiah 1–55 (62x); Jeremiah (82x); Amos (9x); Haggai (14x); Zechariah (53x); Malachi (24x). A major conceptual background for Hebrew prophecy was formed by the idea of the prophet as the messenger of Yahweh (Hag 1:13; Mal 3:1) who had been privy to Yahweh's council (Jer 23:18, 22; Amos 3:7). The frequent introduction of prophetic oracles with the phrase "thus says Yahweh" *(kōh ʾāmar yhwh)* suggests a further connection between the prophetic messenger role and the name *yhwh ṣĕbāʾôt.*

Regrettably, the connection of the epithet *ṣĕbāʾôt* with the formula *kōh ʾāmar yhwh* is not at all clear. Despite the attractiveness of the suggestion that the formula *kōh ʾāmar yhwh ṣĕbāʾôt* might have originated as part of a priestly oracle ritual associated with the ark, the use of the epithet with the messenger formula does not seem to support such a position. The inability to demonstrate that such a connection can be traced back to early traditions does not diminish the significance of the name *yhwh ṣĕbāʾôt* in Hebrew prophecy. For Isaiah, Yahweh *ṣĕbāʾôt,* "Yahweh of Hosts," was the god of Israel (5:16, 24; 21:10; 44:6), the one who mustered and commanded the heavenly armies (13:4; 34:4; 45:12). The abstract nature conveyed by the epithet might be indicated by the LXX's transliteration of *ṣĕbāʾôt* by *sabaōth* throughout the book of Isaiah (see also Rom 9:29; Jas 5:4). A connection between *ṣĕbāʾôt* and *kōh ʾāmar yhwh* may be demonstrated for Jeremiah, Haggai, Zechariah, and Malachi, however. While such might indicate that this is a late, postexilic prophetic development, the importance of the epithet as an expression of the power and majesty of Israel's god is not diminished. Additionally, with the possible exception of Amos, these prophetic works display a close association of one kind or another with Jerusalem and the temple establishment. For these prophetic voices, Yahweh *ṣĕbāʾôt,* envisioned as the leader of both the earthly and heavenly armies, directed the affairs of history, both earthly and cosmic, through the proclamation of his divine decree, delivered by either heavenly or prophetic messengers.

Bibliography

Albright, W. F. 1948. Review of *L'Épithète divine Jahvé Sᵉbaʾôt: Étude philologique, historique et exégétique,* by B. N. Wamdacq. *JBL* 67: 377–81.

Cross, F. M. 1973. *Canaanite Myth and Hebrew Epic*. Cambridge.
Eissfeldt, O. 1950. Jahwe Zebaoth. *Miscellanea Academica Berolinensia* 2: 128–50. Repr. *KlSchr* 3: 103–23.
Emerton, J. A. 1982. New Light on Israelite Religion: The Implications of the Inscriptions from Kuntillet ʿAjrud. *ZAW* 94: 1–20.
Freedman, D. N. 1960. The Name of the God of Moses. *JBL* 79: 151–56.
Janzen, J. G. 1973. *Studies in the Text of Jeremiah*. HMS 6. Cambridge.
Miller, P. E. 1973. *The Divine Warrior in Early Israel*. HMS 5. Cambridge.
Ross, J. P. 1967. Jahweh Ṣeb̲āʾôt̲ in Samuel and Psalms. *VT* 17: 76–92.
Tsevat, M. 1965. Studies in the Book of Samuel, IV: Yahweh Ṣeb̲aʾot̲. *HUCA* 36: 49–58.

E. THEODORE MULLEN, JR.

HOSTS, LORD OF. One of the most enigmatic divine names in the Hebrew Bible is *yhwh ṣĕbāʾôt* (here = YHWH Sebaʾot), commonly translated "LORD of Hosts," or "Yahweh of Hosts." The LXX usually renders it as *kyrios pantokratōr,* "Lord Almighty," or *kyrios tōn dynameōn,* "Lord of the Forces" (*dynamis* is used in the military sense in both Attic and Hellenistic Greek). Alternatively, one may simply get the transcription *sabaōth.* This is the form of the name quoted in the NT (Rom 9:29; Jas 5:4).

In addition to the name YHWH Sebaʾot, which occurs 261 times, we also get the forms *yhwh ʾĕlōhê ṣĕbāʾôt,* "YHWH God of Hosts," and *ʾĕlōhê ṣĕbāʾôt,* "God of Hosts." All told, variant forms of the epithet occur 284 times in the Hebrew Bible, twice in the NT.

A. The Host(s)
B. Origin
C. YHWH Sebaʾot as Divine Warrior
D. YHWH Sebaʾot as King
E. Significance

A. The Host(s)

The most obvious place to begin an examination of this divine epithet is the meaning of "hosts." The related Heb verb *ṣbʾ* occurs 14 times in the Bible, 9 times in clearly military contexts (Num 31:7, 51; 2 Kgs 25:19 = Jer 52:25; Isa 29:7 [2x], 8; 31:4; Zech 14:12). The occurrence in Isa 31:4 is especially noteworthy, since the verb occurs together with the name YHWH Sebaʾot.

The noun *ṣābāʾ* is used in a variety of ways, including (1) war or warfare, (2) an army celestial or terrestrial, (3) luminaries of the sky and, by extension, astral deities and other celestial beings, and (4) creation in general. It is found in predominantly military contexts, in numerous instances in connection with holy war. The commanders of the military are regularly called *śārê ṣĕbāʾôt,* "commanders of the hosts" (Deut 20:9; 1 Kgs 2:5; 1 Chr 27:3). A peculiar story in Joshua 5 tells of Joshua's encounter with a celestial military figure who is said to be *śar ṣĕbāʾ yhwh,* "the commander of YHWH's army" (Josh 5:14; cf. Dan 8:10). Clearly, the texts speaks of YHWH as the commander of some celestial host that fights on Israel's behalf (cf. 2 Sam 5:22–25). The heavenly host apparently is comprised of the luminaries, sometimes perceived as gods of the heavenly council, who fight at YHWH's command against the enemies of YHWH's people (Judg 5:11–21; Josh 10:12–14).

In Ps 148, the heavenly hosts are extolled to praise YHWH (vv 1–5):

> Praise YHWH from the heavens,
> Praise him from on high.
> Praise him, all his angels,
> Praise him all his host.
> Praise him, O Sun and Moon,
> Praise him, all you radiant Stars.
> Praise him, O heaven of heavens,
> You waters of high heavens.
> Praise the name of YHWH,
> For he commanded and they were created.

The heavenly host which YHWH created (cf. Gen 2:1; Ps 33:6; Isa 40:26; Neh 9:6) is perceived here as members of the celestial court. This view is evident also in Ps 103:19–21:

> YHWH has established his throne in heaven,
> His kingship rules over all.
> Bless YHWH, all his angels,
> Mighty ones who do his bidding,
> Obeying his every word.
> Bless him, all his hosts,
> His ministers who do his will.

The pl. noun *ṣĕbāʾôt* is used in reference to Israel as "the hosts of YHWH" (Exod 12:41; cf. Exod 7:4; 6:26; 12:17, 51). Israelite armies are called *ṣĕbāʾôt* (2 Kgs 2:5 = 1 Chr 27:3). Several psalms contain laments that God had failed to "go forth" with Israel's *ṣĕbāʾôt* (Pss 44:10—Eng 44:9; 60:12—Eng 60:10; 108:12—Eng 108:11). The implication is that YHWH's march with Israel's hosts was something to be expected.

It is not surprising, therefore, that *ṣĕbāʾôt* is taken to refer to YHWH's celestial and/or terrestrial hosts, the divine council, the luminaries of the sky, and the totality of creation. Some would take the name to mean "Militant YHWH," "Powerful YHWH," or the like. A few scholars stress the military aspect of the epithet; others deny it, or prefer to stress the royal aspects. No doubt the epithet denotes all these elements; they are not mutually exclusive.

B. Origin

The epithet YHWH Sebaʾot does not occur at all in the Pentateuch or in Joshua and Judges. It first appears in connection with the central sanctuary at Shiloh where the ark was located. Given the military connotations of the root *ṣbʾ* and the use of the ark as a war palladium (see ARK OF THE COVENANT), it is likely that the title was first used at Shiloh in association with the ark. In that period the ark was called by its full name, "the ark of YHWH Sĕbaʾot who sits enthroned upon the cherubim" (cf. 1 Sam 4:4; 2 Sam 6:2; 1 Chr 13:6; Isa 37:16).

The origin of the name *yhwh ṣĕbāʾôt* is not known. F. M. Cross posits plausibly that it was originally the epithet *par excellence* of the divine warrior in Israel (*CMHE,* 65–71). In its full and primitive form, the name may have been something like *ʾil d̲ū yahwi ṣabaʾōt, "the god who created the hosts," the divine name YHWH being originally a causative verb. As a proper name, YHWH would not have been put in the construct state, argues Cross. That is to say, the epithet *yhwh ṣĕbāʾôt* originally denoted the role of Israel's god as creator of the heavenly hosts, the luminaries that sit as lesser divine beings in the heavenly council. The name *yhwh ʾĕlōhê ṣĕbāʾôt* is actually secondary, according to Cross; *ʾĕlōhê* was inserted after YHWH came to be known as a personal name to ease the awkward construction. Nevertheless, the divine epithet is overwhelmingly *yhwh ṣĕbāʾôt;* the inserted form occurs only 21 times out of the possible 284, including 4 occurrences of the peculiar name *yhwh ʾĕlōhîm ṣĕbāʾôt.* The designation *ʾĕlōhê ṣĕbāʾôt*—without *yhwh*—occurs twice. If the juxtaposition of a proper name with another noun is indeed intolerable in Heb syntax, one may conclude that the name YHWH, whatever its origin, came to be understood as a virtual synonym for "god"—in the same way that the proper name El became a generic term in West Semitic. The inscriptions from Kuntillet ʾAjrud in the Sinai desert seem to confirm that YHWH could, in fact, be juxtaposed in this manner. There we find the names *yhwh šmrn* "YHWH (god) of Samaria," and *yhwh tmn* "YHWH (god) of Teman."

The close association of the name YHWH Sebaʾot with the expression *yōšēb hakkĕrūbîm,* "the one who sits enthroned on the cherubim," leads Cross and others to consider the representations of El in West Semitic texts and iconography. Mettinger, indeed, argues for the original epithet being **ʾēl ṣĕbāʾôt.* El was the chief god of the Canaanite pantheon. He is known in the Ugaritic texts as the ultimate king. In reliefs from the region, he is portrayed as one who is enthroned, frequently on seats supported by cherubim. He is known as the creator (Ug "creator of creatures") who formed all things, including the gods of the divine council. In Philo Bylius' account of Sanchuniathon's "Phoenician History" from around the 7th century B.C.E., Kronos (El) is a triumphant warrior-king surrounded by *symmachoi,* "allies," called *eloeim,* that is, *ʾĕlōhîm* "gods" (*Praep. Evang.* 1.10.17–21). The image of El as a warrior is supported by the appearance of an Ugaritic personal name *ʾilmhr,* "El is a Warrior" (cf. Heb *ʾēl gibbôr,* Isa 9:5; 10:21), as well as various West Semitic names indicating the might of El.

Even though El may have been regarded as a divine warrior in Canaanite myth, the paradigmatic warrior-god is Baal. According to Sanchuniathon's "history" reported by Philo, Baal was called Demaros (Ug *d̲mr,* "brave one"). In Ugaritic mythology, Baal was the god who fought the unruly waters Sea and River, and the monsters of the waters, Tannin (cf. Ps 74:13; Job 7:12), Lothan (=Leviathan), and "*Šlyṭ* with the seven heads." It was Baal who fought for his right to rule and to take possession of his temple in "the mount of victory."

If the name *yhwh ṣĕbāʾôt* is ultimately linked with the El traditions, the ties of the Shiloh cultus with El are noteworthy. There was apparently an annual festival at Shiloh to which Samuel's ancestor Elkanah went regularly "to offer sacrifices to YHWH Sebaʾot" (1 Sam 1:3; cf. Judg 21:19). The name Elkanah means "El has created," and recalls the epithet "El (God), the Highest One, who created Heaven and Earth" (Gen 14:19, 22). A similar name, "El (God), Creator of the Earth" is attested in several West Semitic inscriptions and is reflected in the name Ilkunirsa from a Hittite adaptation of a Canaanite myth. The creative function of El is clear in the Ugaritic texts where El is called by the gods "our creator *(qnyn).*" In all these cases the verb used of creation is the same as in the name Elkanah.

In any case, Elkanah is said to be the son of Jeroham. There is no theophoric element on the latter name, but one may conjecture from the El-names of both Jeroham's father (Elihu, but 1 Chr 6:27 has Eliel—i.e., "My God is El") and son (Samuel) that the unmentioned deity may have been El. The LXX renders the name as *Ieremeel,* that is, with the theophoric element El. The names Jerahmeel and Jerahmeeli are attested only in late biblical texts; the former also on a late 7th-century seal. In Amorite onomastica, however, we find the names *Ya-ar-ha-mu, Ya-ar-ha-am-AN (=Yarḫamʾil), Ir-ḫa-mi-AN (=Yirḫamʾil), Ir-ḫa-mi-la,* and *Ir-ḫa-mi-il-la*—all names expressing confidence in the compassion of El. This is in accord with the character of El, who is called "the kindly one" and "the Compassionate" in Ugaritic (cf. also the epithet *ʾēl raḥûm* "Compassionate God" in Exod 34:6; Deut 4:31; Ps 86:15).

The issue at hand in 1 Samuel 1 appears to be the childlessness of Hannah, one of Elkanah's two wives. She went to the Shiloh sanctuary year after year, and yet remained barren. She wept bitterly and prayed that YHWH Sebaʾot would give her a son. Certain facets of the story parallel the Ugaritic tales of Kirta and Aqhat. In the latter Ugaritic tale, a childless Danel performed a ritual, probably to induce a dream theophany. Subsequently he was blessed with fecundity by El. Kirta, too, became childless when all his seven children died. In a dream vision El descended to ask why Kirta was weeping and what it was that he desired. Kirta asked for nothing but the blessing of a son. In these stories, as elsewhere in West Semitic myths, El is the one who grants life and progeny.

The child who was born to Elkanah and Hannah was, of course, given the El-name Samuel. The boy ministered under the tutelage of Eli at the Shiloh sanctuary. There, as he slept before the ark, he received a dream vision. It is typical of El to communicate with an authoritative word through dreams, visions, or messengers. This is evident also in the tales of Kirta and Aqhat.

Yet the function of the ark in 1 Samuel 4–5 suggests a bellicose deity fighting to gain supremacy (note the mention of YHWH Sebaʾot in 1 Sam 4:4). As in the myth of Baal, it appeared for a time that the status of Israel's god was in question. The ark was captured and placed in the temple of Dagon. In a confrontation with the Philistine god, YHWH gained dominion. The statue of Dagon fell prostrate before the ark of YHWH, as if in obeisance. Eventually, the heads and hands (power) of Dagon were cut off. Clearly, YHWH had triumphed over his rival god.

In another battle with the Philistines at Baal-perazim, YHWH Sebaʾot's victory over his enemies is likened to the defeat of unruly waters: "YHWH has broken my enemies like the breaking of waters" (2 Sam 5:20; see the divine epithet in v 10). It was a victory scored over other gods. The divine images of the Philistines were abandoned and carted away by the Israelites. In the next chapter (2 Samuel 6), the emblem of triumphant YHWH Sebaʾot (v 2) was brought into the newly won mount and put in its place (v 17). A symbolic banquet was given in the name of YHWH Seba᾿ot (v 18).

It appears that the epithet YHWH Seba᾿ot combines themes and dominant imagery in the El and Baal traditions: of El a god enthroned, and of Baal a god in battle. The El tradition was certainly known at Shiloh, but it is uncertain precisely when that tradition might have been combined with motifs normally associated with Baal.

C. YHWH Seba᾿ot as Divine Warrior

The name YHWH Seba᾿ot is mentioned in the ancient Ark Narrative (1 Samuel 4–6), in the context of Israel's battle with the Philistines, near Ebenezer and Aphek. In the face of defeat, the Israelites brought forth from Shiloh "the ark of the covenant of YHWH Seba᾿ot who is enthroned upon the cherubim" (1 Sam 4:4). The expressed purpose of that act was to engage YHWH in the battle. The entry of the ark into the battlefield was understood as YHWH's participation in Israel's war. Ironically, through the ark's capture and subsequent sojourn in Philistine territory, the power of YHWH was demonstrated.

From the start, the epithet YHWH Seba᾿ot is understood in military terms—at least in part. The epithet appears later in connection with a holy war against the Amalekites (1 Sam 15:2). Even more poignantly, this divine name is invoked by David against Goliath: "You have come to me with sword and spear and lance, but I have come to you in the name of YHWH Seba᾿ot, the God of the armies of Israel" (1 Sam 17:45). Elsewhere, too, YHWH Seba᾿ot is linked with David's rise to power: "David became greater and greater because YHWH, the God of *ṣĕbā᾿ôt,* was with him" (2 Sam 5:10; cf. 1 Chr 11:9). The language of the deity's accompaniment of the king belongs with the oracles of holy war in some Akkadian and Hittite texts, and is found also in certain propagandistic inscriptions in Old Aramaic.

D. YHWH Seba᾿ot as King

The Ugaritic texts portray El as a king in the divine council, surrounded by the minor gods *(bn ᾿ilm).* This is also the view of YHWH Seba᾿ot. In Isaiah's inaugural vision, he saw the deity sitting enthroned in the *hêkāl,* "temple/palace" (Isaiah 6). YHWH's stature exceeded earthly dimensions by far. Around him stood a host of seraphim, winged creatures in the service of the cosmic king. One is reminded here of Sanchuniathon's description of divine creatures: "two wings for each on the shoulders in order that they may fly with Kronos" (Eusebius *Praep. Evang.* 1.10.37). As in Sanchuniathon, the deity is presented as the triumphant king in the heavenly court. Isaiah declared: "My eyes have seen the King, YHWH Seba᾿ot!" (Isa 6:5, cf. v 3). This vision should be compared with that of Micaiah ben-Imlah, for Michaiah, too, saw "YHWH sitting on his throne, with all the host of heaven standing beside him" (1 Kgs 22:19=2 Chr 22:18). The royal imagery is unmistakable, but here, as in Isaiah, the military significance of YHWH Seba᾿ot is evident. In both cases, war with the Arameans was imminent. The same is true of the picture painted in Ps 89:6–12—Eng 89:5–11:

> Let the heavens confess your wonder, O YHWH,
> Your fidelity in the assembly of the holy ones.
> For who in heaven is equal to YHWH,
> Or likened to YHWH among the *bĕnê ᾿ēlîm?*
> A god *(᾿ēl)* awesome in the council of the holy ones;
> Great is he, and feared above all around him.
> O YHWH, God of *ṣĕbā᾿ôt,* who is like you?
> Your might and your fidelity surround you.
> You rein the swelling of Sea;
> When its waves rise you calm them.
> You crushed Rahab like a carcass;
> With your mighty arm you scattered your enemy.
> The heavens are yours, yea, the earth is yours,
> The world which you created.

Again, the royal character of YHWH Seba᾿ot is combined with the martial character. The cosmic king is surrounded by his heavenly host. He is evidently enthroned by virtue of his defeat of Chaos in cosmogonic battle. Images of El and Baal are once again combined: YHWH is the God enthroned as heavenly king, but he is also the brave warrior who defeated the waters and the dragons of the sea.

The gods of the heavenly council are variously called *qĕhal qĕdōšîm,* "assembly of the holy ones" (v 6—Eng v 5), *bĕnê ᾿ēlîm,* "sons of God" (v 7—Eng v 6), *sôd qĕdōšîm,* "council of the holy ones" (v 8—Eng v 7), and *kol-sĕbîbâw,* "all who surround him" (v 8—Eng v 7). The expression *bn ᾿lm* is found also in Ps 29:1, various Ugaritic texts, Phoenician inscriptions from Karatepe and Arslan Tash, and in the Amman citadel inscription, where Milcom the patron god of the Ammonites is said to be "feared among the *bn ᾿lm.*" These divine beings are the hosts of heaven who fight at YHWH's command (Judg 5:20; cf. Josh 5:14–15; 10:12–14; Hab 3:10–11; Isa 40:26; 45:12) and are summoned to praise YHWH (Job 38:7; Pss 29:1–2; 103:19–22; 148:1–5). These luminaries were perceived as gods of the divine council. Hence the Israelites were commanded not to worship the hosts of heaven, for that was tantamount to worshipping other gods (Jer 19:13; Deut 4:19; 17:3; etc.).

E. Significance

The implication of the name YHWH Seba᾿ot is discernible in its conspicuously uneven distribution in the Hebrew Bible. It appears 82 times in MT of Jeremiah, but only 12 of these are reflected in the shorter and probably more authentic Greek version. Apart from this, the greatest number occur in texts deriving from the Zion tradition, or those in which the temple of Jerusalem was of utmost concern. The appellation occurs 56 times in Isaiah, 53 in Zechariah, 24 in Malachi, 14 in Haggai, and 15 in the Psalms. The contrast in the number of occurrences in First Isaiah (56 times) and Second Isaiah (6 times) is telling. The name does not appear at all in the Pentateuch, Ezekiel, or Third Isaiah, and it is relatively infrequent in the extensive histories of the Deuteronomist(s) and the Chronicler. The reason for this uneven distribution probably lies in the ideas of God associated with the name YHWH Seba᾿ot, namely God as warrior and God as king.

For Isaiah, YHWH Seba᾿ot is the great king (Isa 6:3, 5) who dwells on Mt. Zion (Isa 8:18). This is in accord with the view in the Zion psalms. In that tradition, Mt. Zion is called God's holy mountain and is equated with *yarkĕtê ṣāpôn,* "the far reaches of the north" (Ps 48:3—Eng 48:2).

This reference again reflects a conscious or unconscious merger of Baal and El traditions. Though Saphon is normally the abode of Baal, it is El who lives in the far reaches. It was there in his mountain abode that El convened the divine council (cf. Isa 14:12–14, the far north is the divine council where the "stars of El" are convened). Thus Zion is called "the city of the great king" and "the city of YHWH Seba᾽ot" (Ps 48:3, 9—Eng 48:2, 8). Therein is a river "whose streams make glad the city of God, the holy tabernacle of the Highest One"—that is, of the divine council (Ps 46:5—Eng 46:4). This again recalls the abode of El in the far north, "at the source of the two-rivers, in the midst of the double-deep" where the tabernacle of El was located (*CTA* 2.3.4; 4.4.21–22, etc.; Ezek 28:2, 16).

According to these Songs of Zion, the city cannot be successfully attacked because it is the dwelling place of YHWH Seba᾽ot. Thus the unruly nations may encroach upon Zion like the chaotic waters, but they will be held at bay because YHWH Seba᾽ot is in Zion (Pss 46:2–4, 7–8—Eng 46:1–3, 6–7; 48:1–12; cf. Isa 17:12–13). So YHWH Seba᾽ot is asked to rouse up and punish the unruly nations (Ps 59:6). At all events, YHWH Seba᾽ot is invoked at once as warrior and king to fight on Zion's behalf (Ps 80:3—Eng 80:2; cf. 84:4, 8—Eng 84:3, 7). Thus, in the face of Sennacherib's attack, Hezekiah went to the temple to pray (Isa 37:16 = 1 Kgs 19:15):

> O YHWH Seba᾽ot, who sits enthroned upon the
> cherubim,
> You alone are God of all the kingdoms of the earth.

The mention of YHWH's enthronement on the cherubim is a reference to YHWH as both warrior and king. All the explicit references to YHWH's enthronement on the cherubim are associated with his role as king and warrior (cf. 1 Sam 4:4; 2 Sam 6:2 = 1 Chr 13:6; Pss 80:2; 99:1; also 2 Sam 22:11 = Ps 18:11). At issue in Hezekiah's petition is the kingship of YHWH. Sennacherib had dared to call himself *hammelek haggādôl,* "the great king" (Isa 36:4, 13). In Zion theology, that was the title reserved for YHWH Seba᾽ot, who was perceived as the *ʿelyôn,* "the Highest One," in the divine assembly. Sennacherib had come to Jerusalem "to mock the living God." Hence YHWH was asked to vindicate his honor and deliver the city of his dwelling. For Isaiah, YHWH Seba᾽ot was at once king and warrior, who would fight *(liṣbō᾽* on Zion's behalf and protect the city (Isa 31:4–5).

Thus, in the Zion tradition, the name YHWH Seba᾽ot served to legitimate Jerusalem as YHWH's chosen city. The epithet is theologically loaded. Hence, even though Isa 9:6, 37:32, and 2 Kgs 19:31 all carry the same idiom, in the Deuteronomistic History the loaded term *ṣĕbā᾽ôt* is omitted (i.e., assuming the Hebrew consonantal text is correct). Such reticence in using this epithet is understandable, given the connotations that it carried. In the face of Judah's humiliation at the hands of the Babylonians, the name YHWH Seba᾽ot became theologically problematic. Thus, for example, Ezekiel and P (Priestly Writer) prefer to speak of God's presence in nonroyal and nonmilitary terms.

Isaiah 13 purports to be an oracle against Babylon. It is replete with literary and historical problems. Nevertheless, it is clear that it speaks with the idioms of the Zion tradition about a holy war, an eschatological battle on the Day of YHWH. The God of Zion has gathered "his consecrated ones" and his warriors for a holy war (Isa 13:3); YHWH Seba᾽ot is mustering a host for battle (Isa 13:4). The army will be comprised of troops from the nations, as well as from the ends of the heavens; celestial and terrestrial divisions of YHWH's hosts are gathered at YHWH Seba᾽ot's command.

The battle of YHWH Seba᾽ot is clearly waged not only in the historical realm but also in the end time. In the Isaianic apocalypse, YHWH Seba᾽ot is expected to punish "the host of heaven in heaven." Thereupon he will reign once again on Mt. Zion in his glory (Isa 24:21, 23). The victorious warrior will celebrate with an eschatological banquet for all peoples on Zion, the mount of his victory (Isa 25:6).

The eschatological battle is nowhere more emphatically articulated than in Zechariah 14, a chapter replete with the language of holy war. On that final day YHWH will go forth and fight against all nations, coming with "all the holy ones" *(kol-qĕdōšîm).* Then he will reclaim kingship over all the earth, and all nations will come to Jerusalem annually (cf. Judg 21:19; 1 Sam 1:3, 7, 21) "to worship the King, YHWH Seba᾽ot, and to keep the feast of Sukkoth" (Zech 14:16–17).

Thus the name YHWH Seba᾽ot denotes God as a victorious warrior enthroned as king of the divine council. He is ever ready to fight battles with the forces of chaos. As YHWH Seba᾽ot fought and won the cosmogonic battle, so he fights the battles of his people in the historical realm and will fight the ultimate battle in the end time.

Bibliography

Arnold, W. R. 1917. *Ephod and Ark.* HTS 3. Cambridge, MA.

Baumgartel, F. 1961. Zu den Gottesnamen in den Büchern Jeremia und Ezechiel. Pp. 1–29 in *Verbannung und Heimkehr,* ed. A. Kuschke. Tübingen.

Eissfeldt, O. 1963–68. Jahwe Zebaoth. *KlSchr* 3: 103–23.

Emerton, J. A. 1982. New Light on Israelite Religion; The Implications of the Inscriptions from Kuntillet Ajrud. *ZAW* 94: 2–20.

Görg, M. 1985. *Sb᾽wt*—ein Gottestitel. *BN* 30: 15–18.

Maier, J. 1965. *Das altisraelitische Ladeheiligtum.* BZAW 93. Berlin.

Mettinger, T. N. D. 1982a. YHWH Sabaoth—the Heavenly King on the Cherubim Throne. Pp. 109–38 in *Studies in the Period of David and Solomon and Other Essays,* ed. T. Ishida. Tokyo.

———. 1982b. *The Dethronement of Sabaoth.* Trans. F. H. Cryer. ConBOT 18. Lund.

Miller, P. D. 1973. *The Divine Warrior in Early Israel.* Cambridge, MA.

Ross, J. P. 1967. Jahweh *Ṣĕbā᾽ôt* in Samuel and Psalms. *VT* 17: 76–92.

Schmitt, R. 1972. *Zelt und Lade as Thema alttestamentlicher Wissenschaft.* Gütersloh.

Tsevat, M. 1980. YHWH *Ṣĕḇā᾽ôṯ.* Pp. 119–29 in *The Meaning of the Book of Job and Other Biblical Studies.* New York.

Wambacq, B. N. 1947. *L'Épithète divine Jahvé Ṣĕbā᾽ôt.* Rome.

C. L. Seow

HOTHAM (PERSON) [Heb *ḥôtām*]. Two persons appear in the Hebrew Bible with this name.

1. An Asherite, the son of Heber and brother of Japhlet, Shomer (=Shemer, 1 Chr 7:34?), and sister Shua, of the family of Beriah (1 Chr 7:30–32). He is apparently the same person as "Helem" [Heb *hēlem*] in 1 Chr 7:35, to whom is attributed four sons and at least eleven grandsons through his (firstborn?) son Zophah (1 Chr 7:36). His name occurs in a list of the heads of fathers' houses within the tribe of Asher (1 Chr 7:30–40), a list perhaps derived from some earlier military census. While the names in 1 Chr 7:30–31, up to "Malchiel," are paralleled in Gen 46:17 and Num 26:44–46, the rest of the list, Hotham included, is without parallel elsewhere. The numerous inconsistencies in the names in this Asher pericope point possibly to a collection of disparate notices loosely attached to the person of Heber, the son of Beriah the son of Asher (Braun *1 Chronicles* WBC, 119). That the Chronicler had an open mind on the extent and breadth of God's ideal people is evidenced here in his inclusion within that vision of so peripheral a tribe as Asher.

2. The father of Shama and Jeiel, two of David's famous military heroes (1 Chr 11:44b). In the KJV his name is given as Hothan and that of his second son as Jehiel. He is called an "Aroerite," and though it is possible that he came from Aroer in S Judah (1 Sam 30:28; *IDB* 1: 231), as the immediate context (1 Chr 11:41b–47) ostensibly singles out a number of warriors as hailing from Transjordan, he more probably had his residence either in Aroer in Gilead (Josh 13:25; Judg 11:33) or Aroer on the edge of the valley of the Arnon river (Deut 2:36; 3:12; 4:48). See AROER. While the upper portion of the complete list of David's mighty men or "officers" (if one is willing to read Heb *šālîšîm* in place of MT *sělōšîm* in 2 Sam 23:13, 23, and 24; cf. Naʾaman 1988: 79) is synoptic (2 Sam 23:8–17, 18–39 = 1 Chr 11:10–19, 20–41a), the additional sixteen names in 1 Chr 11:41b–47 are not. It is unlikely that this non-synoptic section is a postexilic invention, as there would seem to be no good reason for such a fabrication (see Williamson *1 and 2 Chronicles* NCBC, 104). The Chronicler evidently had access to a source beyond 2 Sam 23:8–39 and used it expeditiously to illustrate how supportive all Israel was to the rise of David as king (1 Chr 11:1–9; 12:1–41—Eng 12:1–40). While this support included men of valor mostly from Judah and Benjamin (*MBA*, map no. 94), some of it came even from Transjordan (1 Chr 11:10–41a, 41b–47). This emphasis upon the inclusiveness of Israel in the past was part of the Chronicler's theological agenda and hope for the Israel of his own day.

Bibliography

Elliger, K. 1935. Die dreissig Helden Davids. *PJ* 31: 29–75. Repr. *KlSchr*, 72–118.

Mazar, B. 1963. The Military Élite of King David. *VT* 13: 311–20.

Naʾaman, H. 1988. The List of David's Officers *(šālîšîm)*. *VT* 38: 71–79.

Williamson, H. G. M. 1981. "We are yours, O David": The Setting and Purpose of 1 Chronicles xii 1–23. Pp. 164–76 of *Remembering All the Way . . . A Collection of Old Testament Studies*. OTS 21. Leiden.

ROGER W. UITTI

HOTHIR (PERSON) [Heb *hôtîr*].

One of the fourteen sons of Heman who were appointed to prophesy with musical instruments under the direction of their father and the king (1 Chr 25:4). Hothir received the twenty-first lot cast to determine duties (1 Chr 25:28). Scholars have long suggested that the final nine names in 1 Chr 25:4 can be read as a liturgical prayer. For instance, Hothir is the *Hipʿil* perf. form of the verb *yātar*, "show excess, give plentifully." It would function as the verb in the final line of the liturgical prayer as it is reconstructed by scholars. For a reconstruction and translation of the prayer, a summary of interpretative possibilities, and bibliography, see ELIATHAH.

J. CLINTON MCCANN, JR.

HOUSE OF THE FOREST OF LEBANON.

See FOREST OF LEBANON, HOUSE OF THE.

HOUSE, ISRAELITE.

From the beginning of the Iron Age until the Babylonian Exile, two major types dominated Israelite domestic architecture: the larger is usually called the "four-room house," the smaller, the "three-room house." A "two-room" variant appears in exceptional settings. Through 1987, more than 155 examples of these houses have been discovered (Shiloh 1987: 3), with new examples being found in the excavation of almost every Israelite Iron Age site. Against this, few examples occur in patently non-Israelite sites of the same period. On this basis it seems appropriate, at our present stage of understanding, to refer to these as "Israelite" houses.

Despite their ubiquitousness in the archaeological record, no satisfactory functional interpretation of these plans presently exists, and the satisfactory development of needed analyses would exceed the permissible limits of a dictionary article. In lieu of a useful present consensus, the following discussion is based on theoretical approaches and findings reached in the author's own working paper on the subject, intended for future monographic publication (Holladay fc.).

A. Definition and Description
  1. Floor Plan
  2. Major Constructional Features
  3. Interaction between Houses and Fortifications
  4. Family Unit
  5. Origins of the House Type
B. Functional Analysis and Reconstruction
  1. Unsatisfactory Current Consensus
  2. An Alternative Interpretation
C. Toward a New Consensus
  1. Ethnoarchaeological Data
  2. Ethnoarchaeology and the Israelite House
D. Socioeconomic Analysis

A. Definition and Description

1. Floor Plan. With few exceptions, the "four-room house" is known only from its ground plan. See Figs. HOU.01 (A and C), and HOU.04(B). By Iron II times, the entry is usually in the center of the front wall, leading into a large central space generally floored with beaten earth (rarely covered with marly chalk plaster). To either side of this larger area are side aisles delimited by pillars, generally associated with a stub wall. These aisles often have stone paving: cobbles or flagstones. Farther back, the columns generally give way to stone walls and doorways leading into small rooms, generally with dirt floors; in fact, one side may lack columns altogether, having only walled rooms. Across the back stretches the "fourth" room, usually entered from the central space, and usually having a dirt floor. Not infrequently it is subdivided.

Three-room houses vary mainly in having only one row of pillars, generally off center. See Figs HOU.01(B); HOU.02; HOU.04(A). Variations in floor plans often occur, however, when space constraints do not allow for the realization of the plan's regular arrangement (House 581 of Fig. HOU.01B), or when the owner's requirement for additional space leads to additions. See the side room in Figs. HOU.01(C) and HOU.04(B).

2. Major Constructional Features. a. Pillars. Regional availability of materials dictated variability in details. The hallmark pillars, allowing for shared air space and visibility in the forepart of the interior, vary according to the geography. Many sites in the central hill country, the Shephelah, and the Galilee used monolithic pillars, hewn from the local caprock. These regularly were reused from one period to the next. In the Negeb, pillars were often built of blocks or "drums" of roughly trimmed chert or limestone. The coastal region (e.g., Tell Qasile: Mazar 1951: 76) and the Jordan valley (e.g., Tell es-Saᶜidiyeh: Pritchard 1964: 6) have examples of pillars built of mudbrick. The central hill country, Galilee, and the coastal plain also have examples of column bases on which apparently stood wooden pillars. In all cases, the load-bearing capacities of these pillars are in excess of that required to support a simple flat mud-plastered roof.

b. Wall Construction. Walls were usually founded upon at least a single course of stones, whether one or two stones wide, and in stone-rich areas several courses might be stone-built. Above this foundation the walls were built of mudbrick, plastered inside and out with a mud-chaff plaster. This was essential, and required at least yearly renewal to ward off the erosion of the mudbrick during the winter rains (see the prophetic reference to the dangers of shoddy maintenance in Ezek 13:10–18). Within spatially restricted fortified town sites, houses were regularly built adjacent to one another, often sharing their side wall(s) with their neighbors.

c. Roofing. As today in the Middle East, roofs were flat and served as important areas of domestic activity (cf. Josh 2:6–8; 2 Sam 11:2; Jer 19:13; 32:29). They were built upon beams and lintels over which were placed slats or poles (cf. Callaway 1976: 29), reeds, etc., which in turn were covered with mud and chaff plaster. This required regular compaction and resurfacing to maintain its waterproof qualities (cf. Eccl 10:18). Limestone cylinders (i.e., roof-rollers) are occasionally found in domestic contexts, but careful foot compaction is often used today. At Hasanabad, only two out of 43 active households owned stone roof-rollers, the landlord's agent owning a third (Watson 1979: 119–20). Deut 22:8 mandates the construction of parapets around house roofs. These are regularly depicted in Egyptian (Wreszinski 1935, pt. 2: pls. 35, 53, 54a, 56–58, etc.) and Assyrian (e.g., Ussishkin 1982: 80–85) representations of monumental Palestinian architecture. Since no houses have yet been found preserved to the roof line, house parapets cannot be demonstrated archaeologically. If they existed, waterspouts would have been required to remove water safely from the rooftops, but their remains would also be difficult to identify in the archaeological record (see, however, evidence for downspouts at Taanach [Lapp 1967: 21–22] and Gezer [Holladay 1971: 116, fig. 1]). No efforts seem to have been made as yet to discover erosional features around houses suggestive of drainage arrangements.

d. Other Features. Several other architectural and domestic features have been found in excavations, which can help to clarify the organization and functions of rooms and buildings. Shallow troughs are often found on top of the stubwalls between the characteristic pillars toward the front of the house. These are similar to the mud and stone mangers found in the stables at Beer-sheba and Hazor (Herzog 1973; Yadin et al. 1960: 6–9; pls. 4, 200–1; see STABLE, STABLES). Evidence of stairways (which are usually placed on the exterior) exists at many sites (e.g., Figs. HOU.01[C] and HOU.04[B]; Tell Beit Mirsim [Albright 1943: 51], Beer-sheba [Beit-Arieh 1973: 31, Fig. HOU.04(A) here], and Hazor [Yadin 1972: 184]), which in turn implies either the existence of upper stories (e.g., Shechem [Wright 1965: 161]; Jerusalem [Shiloh 1984: 14, 18–19]), or intensive use of the roof. Estimates of the heights of first stories, based upon the height of stairways or preserved stone lintels, etc., range from a low of 1.1 m (Tell en-Nasbeh [McCown 1947: 213]) to a more normal ca. 2.0 m (Tel Masos [Fritz and Kempinski 1983: 25]). Such heights are more in line with domestic stabling and storage functions than for areas of human habitation (below).

Ovens (cf. Gunneweg 1983: 106–12) are relatively frequent, generally in sheltered exterior settings, but also in the central space. Cooking hearths, on the other hand, are relatively infrequent (cf. Hazor [Yadin et al. 1960: pls. 7:3; 202 9/F], Mesad Hashavyahu [Naveh 1962: 92], Shechem [Wright 1965: 151–52; cf. also Figs. HOU.02 and HOU.04(B) here, the square, stone-lined heating and cooking hearths of Fig. HOU.03(A), and the round plastered heating hearths of Fig. HOU.03(B)]). Simple cooking pits also appear, e.g., in many of the central spaces of the Strata III-II houses at Tel Masos (Fritz and Kempinski 1983: 13), but they are by no means regularly present. The relative sparseness of these and similar facilities in the archaeological record suggests that cooking activities were regularly carried out in parts of the house not typically recovered archaeologically (below).

3. Interaction between Houses and Fortifications. The reference to Rahab, whose "house was in the wall of the city-wall" (Heb *bêtah bĕqîr haḥômâ;* Josh 2:15), may suggest that the passage dates to the later Iron II. Archaeologically attested city walls are in extremely short supply for the LB II (although that does not necessarily mean that there were none, since gates are known). Casemate walls would, in any case, not be expected. In the early Iron Age I, there is some evidence that houses were arranged around the perimeter of the town site in such fashion that the back rooms, together with connector walls, made up a sort of *ad hoc* casemate wall (Shiloh 1978: 45–46). This, however, does not seem to be what is implied by the account. Early Iron II casemate walls, as these are presently known, do not incorporate private houses, although palaces may be built in (Hazor, Megiddo; [Yadin et al. 1960: pls. 199–200; Yadin 1972: 154–58, fig. 40]). On the other hand, the casemate town walls characteristic of the later Judean Iron II period regularly incorporated private houses, the casemate often serving as the rear, transverse architectural element of the three- and four-room houses of the period (e.g., Fig HOU.04[A]).

4. Family Unit. Cross-cultural analysis strongly suggests that houses of this general size were occupied by nuclear families, i.e., typically a mother, father, and their dependent children, plus any resident servants or slaves (Shiloh 1980: 29; Stager 1985: 17–18). Clustering of houses around shared common space (e.g., Figs. HOU.02 and HOU.01[A] [?]) may be taken as evidence for patrilocal residence patterns, reflecting the extended family structure known in the Bible as the *bêt ʾab,* "House of the Father" (Stager 1985: 18–23), although such residential patterning may, in the long run, be incompatible with the realities of long-term land use in the constrained urban environment.

5. Origins of the House Type. Houses of this general plan were already common in the "Israelite" hill country settlements, beginning perhaps as early as ca. 1200 B.C. (A. Mazar 1982: 168–70; Stager 1985: 3; Finkelstein *AIS,* 30, 254–55, 315–23), but it is unclear whether the general plan was an independent innovation of these people, or an outgrowth of a rare earlier LB house type (cf. summaries by Stager 1985: 17; Finkelstein *AIS,* 254–59). The only reasonable LB antecedent is the "Burnt Building" from LB II Tell Batash Stratum VII (Kelm and Mazar 1982: 9–13). Appeal to Philistine prototypes seems counterproductive, since the only examples of these plans associated with Sea People's settlement come from late 10th-century contexts (Tell esh-Shariʾa, Tell Qasile; cf. Holladay 1990). On balance, the very general use of houses of the three- and four-room type in the early hill country settlements versus the extreme paucity of reasonable LB prototypes seems to argue in favor of a hypothesis of independent invention, though future discoveries could easily alter this balance of probability.

Particularly in the late 10th century B.C., a few houses of this type do appear at theoretically non-Israelite sites, and some explanation of this phenomenon must be sought. Assuming as a test hypothesis that houses of this general plan were as strong a marker for ethnic self-differentiation as the "Amarna"-style house (which has a much longer history than simply the Amarna period) may have been for Bronze Age Egyptian residents of Canaan, one may ask: "What sort of house did David (assuming there is any trace of truth in the traditions) occupy at Ziklag?" The answer, suitably adjusted for date and occupant (e.g., traders), could easily account for the evidence presently in hand. I.e., it is not improbable that there was a sizable "Israelite" component to Tell Esh-Shariʾa Stratum VIII and Tell Qasile Stratum X, etc. This would be expected within the Solomonic *koine.* The fact that this house form does not characterize later Iron II Ashdod or Tel Miqne/Ekron seems sufficient basis to suggest that considerations other than simple function or availability governed the later Philistine's choice of architectural styles, since, by then, the three- and four-room house had an unbroken use-history of some 400–500 years in the region.

B. Functional Analysis and Reconstruction

1. Unsatisfactory Current Consensus. In spite of the large body of archaeological data available, published archaeological analyses attempting to interpret either the plan or its constituent elements have been few (note, however, Stager 1985: 11–17; Holladay 1986: 153–54). The prevailing general understanding of these structures is summed up in evolutionary terms by Herzog (1984: 76–77):

> The sole fundamental and constant feature [of the four-room house is] the broadroom at the rear. Considering primarily the function of the room (which is a factor of its shape), it is obvious that it served as the main living and sleeping quarters of the household (Shiloh 1970: 186). [Over the course of time] a courtyard was added to the front of the broadroom. . . . Subsequently, this enlarged courtyard may have been subdivided and one or two units partitioned off as work or storage areas.

This view of the broadroom's function, which lies at the heart of most present treatments, simply will not work. The broadroom of Beer-sheba House 75 (Fig. HOU.04 [A]) measures ca. 1.15 × 4 m, or ca. 4.5 m^2 (ca. 3′9″ × 13′1.5″). A person leaning against one wall could completely block passage by holding out one arm, and only four sleeping pallets would occupy the entire floor space, leaving no room for furnishings or storage. While the above is one of the smaller rear rooms, a survey of Braemer's catalogue of houses (1982: 162–269) shows a median width of 1.98 m, a measurement which does not significantly improve the problem of domestic logistics.

2. An Alternative Interpretation. More reasonably, in terms of space, Braemer has suggested that the central space was, in fact, the living area. A significant problem with this interpretation (if one is limited to a single-story structure) is that it enforces a strong interaction between the inhabitants and their livestock, assuming that animals were stalled in the side aisles (below), since the main function of the pillared structure, as opposed to solid walls, is to provide for open communication between the side aisle(s) and the central space.

C. Toward a New Consensus

A useful starting point is the recognition of the strong similarities between operative aspects of the Israelite and Judean tripartite pillared stables and the smaller-scaled side aisle(s) of the domestic houses, including bench-type mangers and paved standings, together with pillared construction. See STABLE, STABLES. Together with semicircular ground-level mangers and typically low ceiling heights, these features imply that the provision of stalling and folding facilities were central concerns both of the original designers and of following generations (cf. Wright 1965: fig. 79; Holladay 1982; 1986: 153–54; Stager 1985: 11–15; *contra* Herzog 1984: 77; Fritz and Kempinski 1983: 27). Since this very specialized house type is already characteristic at the early subsistence-based settlements (e.g., Ai and Kh. Radannah, cf. Fig. HOU.02), one may infer that the design was either an indigenous innovation aimed at solving the needs of agriculturalist and horticulturalist peasants, or was soon adapted to those needs. While facil-

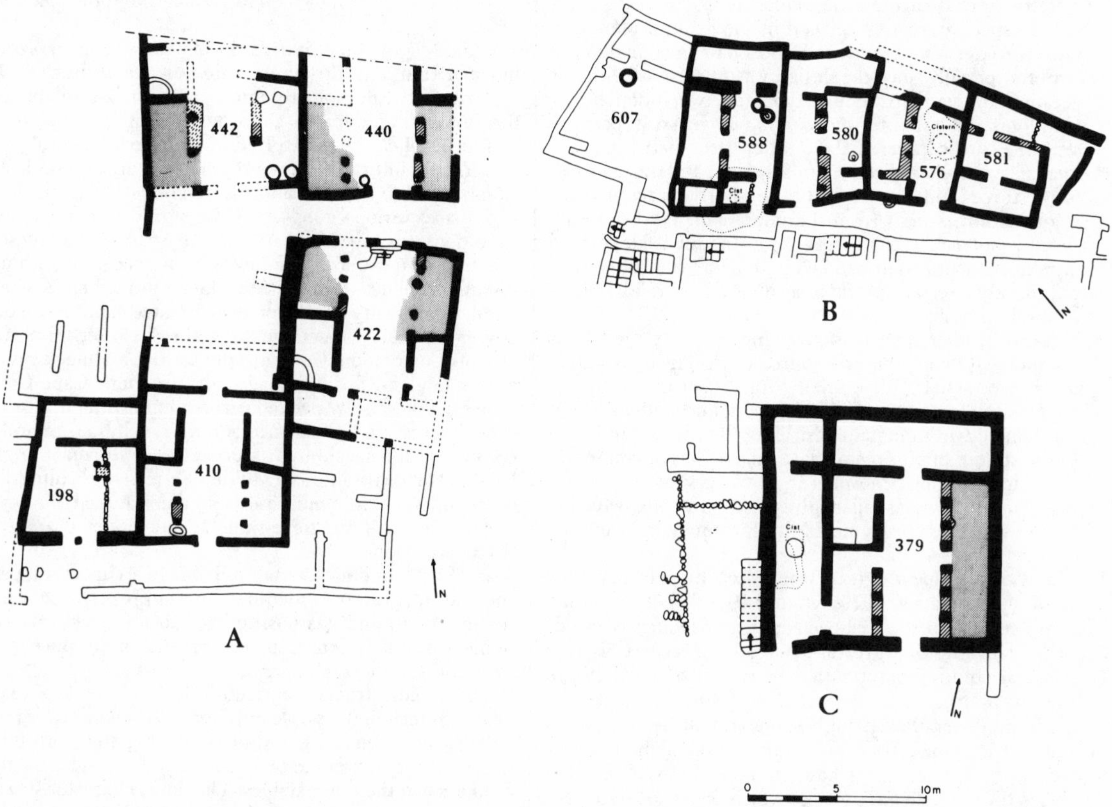

HOU.01. House plans. *A,* "four-room" houses from Tell el-Farᶜah (N), level 3, probably destroyed ca. 925 B.C.; *B,* "three-room" houses from Tell en-Nasbeh, Iron II; *C,* "four-room" house from Tell en-Nasbeh, probably destroyed ca. 586 B.C. *(Redrawn,* A, *from de Vaux 1952: pl. 10;* B *and* C, *from McCown 1947: survey map, courtesy of J. S. Holladay, Jr.)*

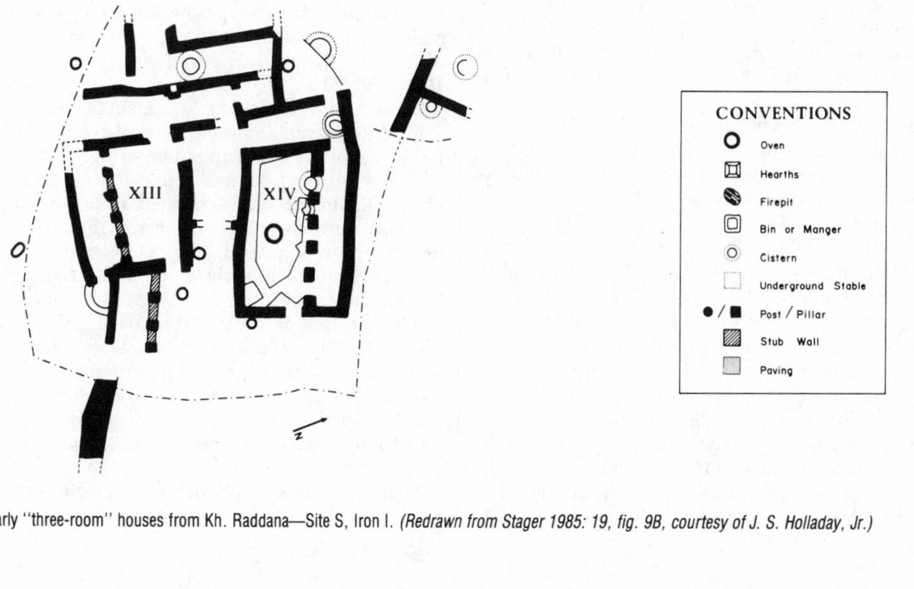

HOU.02. Early "three-room" houses from Kh. Raddana—Site S, Iron I. *(Redrawn from Stager 1985: 19, fig. 9B, courtesy of J. S. Holladay, Jr.)*

ities for animal care and agricultural storage can, from this perspective, readily be seen in the ground plan, one must consider what other needs must have been met in the layout, especially since the design was so successful that it became the standard house type for two independent kingdoms and lasted for more than 600 years. In particular, what can be inferred about other basic spatial requirements, layout, specialized room function, and overall form of the three- and four-room house—particularly of those elements not evident from the floor plan? And not only "what," but *how* can we reliably go about asking these questions about a vanished civilization? This is, of course, only another version of the basic question of valid archaeological inference.

As with other questions involving complex models of operating systems, the best source of insight is the study of similar systems in contemporary societies living at roughly the same stage of development and under most of the same environmental constraints. I.e., we should turn to the sphere of ethnology, particularly that of communities living in similar biospheres, keeping similar domesticates, and following similar subsistence strategies, which in the present case means mixed dry farming employing the simple plow.

1. Ethnoarchaeological Data. Recent ethnographic studies (e.g., Watson 1979; Kramer 1979; 1982), explicitly conducted from the perspective of archaeologists' needs (which involves far greater concern for aspects of the material culture complex than is typical of most ethnographic approaches), have provided valuable new data to assist in generating hypotheses about ancient material remains and their functional implications. Among other issues, these researchers have studied the areal requirements for domestic occupation, which prove to be surprisingly similar among widely varying societies. While the figure of 10 m^2 roofed dwelling area per person (Naroll 1962) is most frequently cited, a more significant figure is that involving total roofed area per person, which, for Iranian peasant societies living under conditions closely similar to those of ancient Israel, work out to ca. 21 m^2 per person (LeBlanc 1971). This figure includes not only living space but also stabling, storage, and other activity space, and is more truly reflective of total domestic needs than the former.

Data from the ethnoarchaeological study of Hasanabad (a pseudonymous village in W Iran) show that a typical household of 4.5–5 people lived in roofed space, including wall thickness, ranging from 94.5 to 105 m^2 (the 21 m^2/person cited above; Watson 1979; LeBlanc 1971). Of this, slightly more than half was devoted to economic activities such as stabling and storage. See Fig. HOU.03. Hasanabad basically was a single-storied, sprawling village. In the few houses there which had second stories, in all cases the second floors were used for living rooms and light storage. Elsewhere, in houses within walled enclosures (e.g., a fortified city where space was at a premium), ground floors typically were devoted to the stabling of herds and flocks and heavy storage, while the second story was typically devoted to human habitation and light storage, the warmth of the animals contributing significantly to human comfort during the winter's cold (Fig. HOU.03 [B]; cf. Stager 1985: 12). This pattern can be seen today all around the Mediterranean.

While few of the ethnographically attested plans from modern Iran and Turkey (or those of late 19th- to early 20th-century Palestine) resemble those of ancient Israel, the function and spatial characteristics of the individual architectural elements involved in a nontechnological pastoralist/agriculturalist economy's housing must have been closely similar. Various animals require certain facilities and space, various goods must be stored under varying conditions for varying parts of the year, and domestic functions require a certain amount of space and various essential facilities. What differs among individual societies (even villages) are the "mental templates" and aesthetics governing the arrangements, together with technical details of construction. Compare the relative architectures of a New England fishing village (e.g., wooden "Cape Cod" houses), a densely packed urban environment (brick "townhouses"), a New Mexico adobe "ranch house," and a classic California suburb (stuccoed "California bungalows"). For a traditional Middle Eastern agriculturalist community, these similarities may be grouped into two major functional categories: the "Living Domain" and the "Economic Domain."

a. The "Economic Domain." From an architectural perspective, this involves adequate and appropriate housing for the goods and chattels involved in the quest for economic survival: animals, stored agricultural produce, and tools and supplies.

The typical Iranian agriculturalist's house (e.g., Fig. HOU.03) included a stable area for traction and transport animals (cows, bullocks, and donkeys), together with folding space for an average of 21 sheep and goats. Cattle and donkeys had their own stables. The floors characteristically were unfinished and covered with accumulations of dung and decomposing fodder which was occasionally cleaned out and used for fuel (Kramer 1982: 106). Watson does not give ceiling or beam heights but describes stables as being typically "low" (1979: 160). Stables were usually fitted with adobe mangers. Both semicircular ground-level and rectilinear bench types were used, the latter predominating. Some stables for sheep/goats were subterranean, with ceiling heights ranging from 1.5 to 3.5 m (Watson 1979: 160–61).

Other rooms served either as utility or store rooms, storing items such as food; animal feed; chaff/straw for fodder, mudbrick making, plastering, and mixing with dung for fuel; agricultural implements; and seasonal furniture. Room use often changed with the seasons, or as contents were consumed (note that Fig. HOU.03[A] reflects usage as of 5 April 1960). Grain and milled flour was sometimes stored in sacks or large mud-plastered wicker baskets, but most often on the ground floor in mud bins or chests raised on short legs (Watson 1979: 295; Kramer 1982: 100, 102, 105). Grain pits, mostly bell-shaped and averaging ca. 1 m^3, were variously used for either wheat or barley, or, in some villages, for barley alone. Some villages did not practice underground storage. Grain pits could be located in ground-level living rooms (often in the corners), storerooms, or courtyards.

Stables averaged 12.25 m^2 in area (internal), and many families had more than one stable. Storerooms averaged

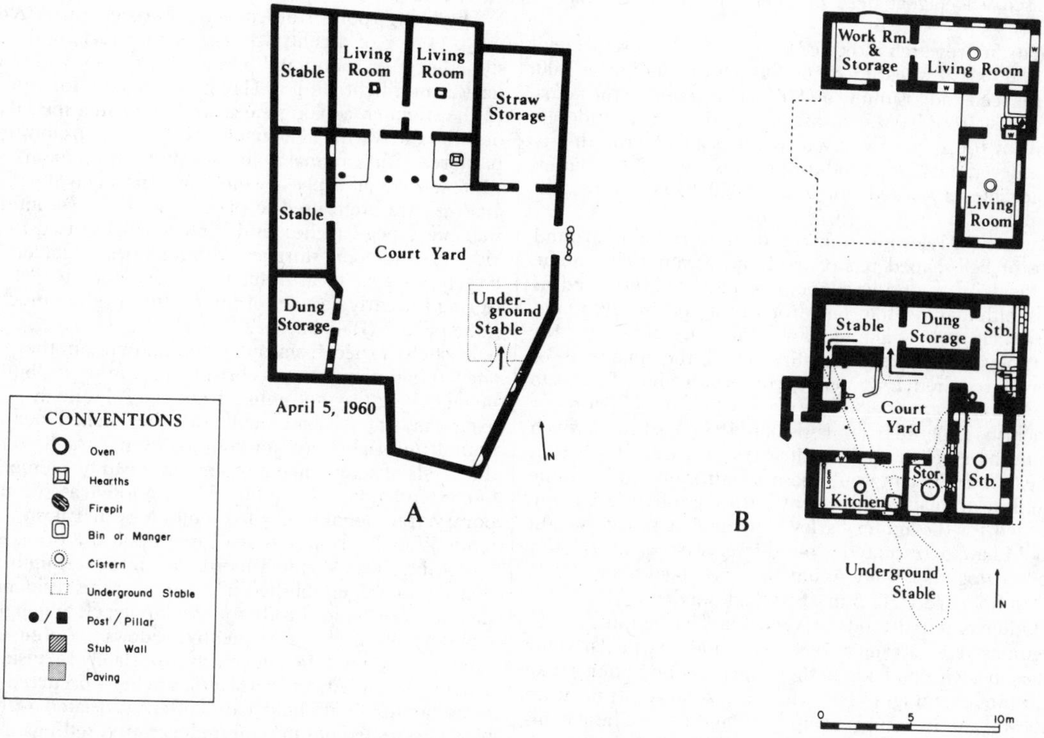

HOU.03. Archaeo-ethnographically documented agriculturalist peasant houses from W Iran. *A*, one-story house complex from "Hasanabad"; *B*, two-story compound from "Aliabad." *(Redrawn,* A, *from Watson 1979: fig. 5.16;* B, *from Kramer 1982: 96, fig. 4.7, courtesy of J. S. Holladay, Jr.)*

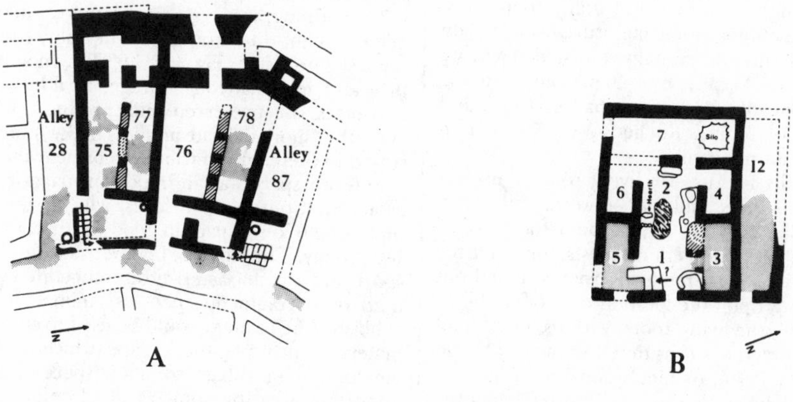

HOU.04. House plans. *A*, "three-room" houses with controlled "side alley" space, incorporating elements of the casemate town wall as their rear transverse room at Beer-sheba Stratum 2, destroyed 701 B.C.; *B*, "four-room" house with an attached side room at Shechem. The building is restored to its configuration as of its primary destruction, ca. 725 B.C. Note the industrial installations in the central space. This building employed wooden pillars upon tall stone pillar bases and had a grain silo in the rear transverse room. *(Redrawn,* A, *from Ussishkin 1977;* B, *from Wright 1965: fig. 76, courtesy of J. S. Holladay, Jr.)*

12.4 m^2. Folding space for the (at the time strongly depressed) sheep/goat herd probably would average ca. 20 m^2.

Watson's research indicated that a family of five needed ca. 1800 kg of wheat (=ca. 66 bushels), including ca. 300 kg for seed and assuming an 80% extraction rate for flour, to subsist from harvest to harvest. Barley was considered feed for the animals and was useful as a cash crop. It was considered starvation food for humans (1979: 291). Barley requirements worked out to ca. 1080 kg/year (=ca. 49 bushels).

In ancient Palestine grain was often stored in in-ground silos or bell-shaped pits (Currid and Navon 1989). Some features in ground-level rooms could be interpreted as bins, although twofold bins (for wheat and barley) would be anticipated. Grain was also stored in store jars. For purposes of concrete visualization of the quantities of storage required, if we were to convert the above figures to the average capacities of the typical Judean *lmlk* store jar (Lachish Type 484; cf. Ussishkin 1983: 161–63), which would have held a median capacity of ca. 1.277 bushels of wheat each, 55 jars would have been needed to hold one family's annual requirements, with another 36 being needed for the lighter barley. The total aggregate weight would have necessitated ground-level storage, and, closely packed together, they would have occupied about 22.75 m^2 of floor space (11.5 m^2 if stacked two deep).

Other required foodstuffs must be factored in, such as legumes (e.g., Kramer 1982: 34), and, particularly for Palestine, wine and oil. To these must be added dung-cake and wood storage, dried fodder, a large straw store (above), and furniture, equipment, and tools. These items constitute subsistence requirements alone. Obviously, additional space would be required for surplus production. In season, portions of storerooms (or even ground-level living rooms) were partitioned off for the keeping of baby animals.

b. The "Living Domain." This is the portion of the house reserved for human occupation and food preparation, together with lighter storage and utility rooms. See Fig. HOU.03. In the ethnographic literature (esp. Watson 1979; Kramer 1982), this space usually consisted of a living room (ranging from ca. 11 m^2 to over 40 m^2, but averaging ca. 19 m^2 at Hasanabad), an entrance hall or foyer, and storage and/or utility rooms. Kitchens were present in most communities, but not in all.

Each nuclear family had its own living room. This was where the family ate, slept, did indoor work, and entertained. Some families had two living rooms (a mark of wealth), one for the entertainment of guests, the other for family living. Families with three living rooms rented out the third. Depending upon the location of cooking facilities and local custom, the living room, with its hearth and vertical loom, was sometimes considered women's domain (Hasanabad; Watson 1979), or men's domain ("Aliabad"; Kramer 1982), the kitchen, in the latter setting, being the domain of the women (often of an extended family), the vertical loom being set up there (Fig. HOU.03[B]), or, occasionally, in the foyer, which looked out upon the courtyard and was a preferred location for spinning and women's socialization and tea drinking. At Hasanabad, the entrance hall served for the storage of men's goods and outer clothing but was not a setting for social activity.

The living rooms studied were always characterized by the presence of a central hearth, either rectangular and stone-lined, or round and plastered, which provided winter warmth, light, and, at Hasanabad, served for cooking. In the summer, cooking was usually done in a special area of the courtyard. The living area was invariably mud-plastered, with annual renewal. Most living rooms were whitewashed, and special white earth (probably the Arabic *huwwar*) was often used to plaster the floors. Around the walls were pegs, niches, and window ledges, used to provide off-the-floor storage. Although less detailed and largely wanting measurements, observations in Palestine during the early decades of this century present much the same picture (Dalman 1942).

Kitchens varied from one community to another. Hasanabad had none, nor was bread baked in ovens, but on a metal baking tray not unlike Iron Age Palestinian pottery exemplars; at Aliabad there was one kitchen per compound (invariably housing a bread oven), usually serving the needs of several living rooms, occupied by members of one extended family. (In the villages studied, as in contemporary traditionalist Arab communities in Palestine, extended family groupings are based upon the principle of virilocality, i.e., having subordinate nuclear family residence patterns established in relation to the residence of the father or senior brother in the family; cf. Stager 1985: 18–22; below). Not infrequently, widows, or even whole families, also used the kitchen, appropriately furnished, as a living room. At other villages, kitchens occurred on a household-by-household basis, often associated with stables, and sometimes in semi-underground settings. At still other sites, including late 19th- to early 20th-century (A.D.) Palestine, they were separate rooms, often totally detached, entered from the courtyard. Except at Aşvan (Turkey: Hall et al. 1973: figs. 3, 4, 7; 273), disused fireplaces at Hasanabad, and elite houses in Palestine, chimneys were unknown, simple holes in the roof or side wall allowing some smoke to escape.

The ethnographic studies demonstrated a consistent need for light-duty storage and/or utility rooms for various domestic needs (cf. Fig. HOU.03[B]). In addition to furniture and miscellaneous storage, a wide variety of dried and otherwise preserved milk products, fruits, produce, and other more delicate and less bulky foodstuffs could be stored in these, or in facilities in or near the kitchen.

Exterior space was an important part of the household economy. Courtyard surfaces, which were often used as nighttime folding space in good weather, were customarily swept daily. The surface, however, was uneven, with damp spots, and was characteristically embedded with potsherds, mud oven fragments, pebbles, animal dung, and other rubbish. The corners would be used to store various bulky materials, including dungheaps (which otherwise were often located in village common space and served as an important area for women's socialization, dung cakes being the standard domestic fuel). Fixtures (not all occurring at individual sites) were ovens, hearths, food preparation platforms or areas, unroofed animal pens, and, in one semisedentarized village, a platform for the black tent. Customary courtyard activities included shearing, milking, milk processing, cooking and baking, and various household manufacturing activities (e.g., felt making, horizontal looms). Kramer's (1982) data on 67 courtyards at Aliabad revealed great variability in size, with a mean of 103.3 m^2, but a median of only 74 m^2 and a standard deviation of 112.2 m^2.

Roofs were accessed either by stairs (including mudbrick staircases), ladders, or ramps. Roofs were important activity areas, generally within the women's domain, serving for socialization, the drying of clothes, food, and other agricultural products (including washed grain), and for the temporary storage of dried fodder, brush, wood, and wooden equipment. In densely settled towns, contiguous rooftops served as women's thoroughfares between households. Rooftops were also used in many locales for normal extensions of domestic activities, including sleeping during the summer months.

c. Summary Observations. Whatever the degree of observed virilocal residence association, each nuclear family occupied its own living room. The number of rooms associated with a house varied significantly, ranging from essentially one room to as many as nine. The mean number of rooms at Hasanabad was 4.55, the median being 5.0. Average total roofed space (including wall thickness) per individual at Hasanabad, the site best studied in this respect, was 21 m^2. The average number of individuals per rural household across the total sample studied ranged from 4.2 to 5.9 (Korosan and Ilam provinces, Iran; Sumner 1979: 169–70). Usage of grain pits varied between communities but never accounted for total grain storage space. Rooms for heavy storage, animal stables, and protected folding space were essential parts of the household complex. Where second stories existed, the upper story was invariably used for human occupation and light storage.

2. Ethnoarchaeology and the Israelite House. a. Spatial and Functional Determinants. For 43 households, Watson (1979: Table 5.2) recorded 56 living rooms, 12 entry halls, 32 stables, 11 utility rooms, 6 wood storage rooms, 7 dung storage rooms, 24 straw storerooms, 17 underground stables, and 25 courtyards (note that storeroom functions varied seasonally). Kramer lists 67 courtyards, 90 living rooms, 74 kitchens, 137 storerooms, and 33 stables (1979: Table 5.1). Assuming as average requirements, for the economic domain, one stable, one protected "folding area," and one storeroom, all necessarily at ground level, and, for the domestic domain, one living room, an entry hall, and one utility/store room, reference to the well-documented Hasanabad data set (Watson 1979: 119–61) yields a more or less generic requirement for the average household of ca. 83 m^2 of unencumbered floor space. A comparable figure for Aliabad is ca. 72 m^2, probably brought about by the shared use of kitchen facilities. Estimating on the basis of a family size of 4.5 to 5.0 individuals, an overall roofed space requirement (including walls, above) would stand at ca. 94.5–105 m^2.

Sheltered folding space would have been a necessity for wintering sheep in most of ancient Israel and all of Judah, except the Jordan valley and the Negeb. But one may wonder why a subsistence-level agricultural economy, such as that of the average Israelite town and village, should invest simultaneously in pastoralist activity. The answer for ancient times is the same as that which applies to traditionalist societies in the region today. Diversification of subsistence strategies is a significant means of spreading risk, and hence better insures the family unit's survival in otherwise marginally viable environmental zones, such as those characterizing most of ancient Israel (Ruthenberg 1976: 25; Hopkins 1985: 213–50).

Other figures gleaned from the ethnographic literature useful for archaeological reconstruction include the following: *ceiling heights* for kitchens and living rooms at Aliabad ranged from 2.0 to 2.6 m (Kramer 1982: 104); at Hasanabad they averaged ca. 2.55 m (Watson 1979: figs. 5.8–5.27); the narrowest and widest *living rooms* at Hasanabad were 2.42 m and 3.95 m respectively (the mean for 25 living rooms was 3.02); at Aliabad, the mean width of 7 illustrated living rooms was 2.78 m, the narrowest being 2.57 m, the widest being 2.95 m (Kramer 1982: figs. 4.6, 4.7, 4.12, 1.18).

b. Reconstructing the Three-Room House. Analysis of Beer-sheba House 75 (Fig. HOU.04[A]) yields ca. 29.5 m^2 of floor space, exclusive of walls. Including wall thickness, and assuming average walls in place of the fortification wall enclosing the casemate room, the total ground-plan area comes to ca. 42 m^2. The central space and side aisle (Loci 75 and 77) encompass only ca. 19 m^2—in the range of a Hasanabad living room. However, not only are the floors of these two areas unsuited to living-room functions, one has to ask where the necessary room can be found for the entire range of ground-level functions of the economic domain. Even allocating all the ground-floor space to stables, folding, and heavy storage, we find it necessary to suggest that the adjacent alleyway (Locus 28) probably was also incorporated as shelterable folding space, which need not have been as well protected as at sites in the hill country. This combination yields a usable total area of ca. 45 m^2, as compared with our theoretical requirement of ca. 44.7 m^2.

Reviewing other data, we note that the Beer-sheba excavations provided some evidence for casemates having served a storage function (Beit-Arieh 1973: 33; Sheffer 1973). The stalling facilities (Locus 77) are exceptionally narrow, and may have operated more as a narrow loosebox than as a proper set of stalls. Room 75 seems to have served store functions at the time of its destruction (Aharoni 1973: pottery pls. 64–65). An oven is situated in a screened location near an entrance, here beside the stairs at the entrance to the alleyway. It is typical in Israel and Judah for such facilities to be placed at points easy of access.

In this particular set of houses we have good evidence for a second story in the form of well-constructed exterior stairways. That they are not there simply to access the roof is self-evident from the lack of suitable living-room facilities on the ground floor. Adding a second story yields another 30 m^2 to the total house plan, the space required for an average-sized ethnographically attested living room plus light-storage/utility room. At these overall dimensions, including the use of alleyway, this house plan, realized in two stories, closely approximates the mean at Hasanabad and is slightly over the Aliabad mean. By any reckoning, this is an impressive degree of "fit" between an ethnographically based model and an archaeological reconstruction attained by simply extending the perimeter walls and columned interior structure upward for one more story, easily within the load-bearing capabilities of the walls and massive stone columns (cf. Beit-Arieh 1973: 32).

With respect to the relationship between houses and fortifications for a casemate-walled small site like Beer-sheba, the above would suggest a reasonable height for the top of the battlements of some 6.5 m above interior ground levels, with the broad rooftops of the houses affording excellent fighting platforms. Greater heights for the fortification walls would necessitate narrower fighting platforms and more difficult access arrangements.

c. Four-Room House. The ethnographically informed archaeological reconstruction of the medium-sized four-room house can be demonstrated through an analysis of House 1727 at Shechem (Fig. HOU.04[B]). Its overall dimensions, after the elimination of 7th-century rooms tacked onto its S side, are ca. 8.0 × 10.4 m (=83.2 m^2). With the addition of the N side room, the total ground-floor area increases to ca. 108.6 m^2, the internal area of the side room being ca. 17.5 m^2. The ground level of the main house block consists of two paved stable areas (Rooms 3 and 5) with both semicircular and bench-style mangers. Unpaved rooms (Rooms 4 and 6) stand behind each of the paved side rooms. The central space (Room 1-2) has two large grinding installations, a large industrial hearth and a smaller, possibly domestic, hearth, and, immediately to the left of the entrance, what may be the foundation platform for a flight of steps to an upper story. The lateral broadroom at the back (Room 7) measured 6.85 × 1.95 m and had a large horseshoe-shaped stone-lined pit (probably a grain silo) at the N end. The unencumbered internal ground-floor space totaled ca. 54 m^2. With the addition of the N side room, the total ground-floor space was 71 m^2.

As with the Beer-sheba house, if one assumes, with much of contemporary thinking, that this was a one-story house, the areal requirements are unrealistic to accommodate storage, stabling, folding (which, however, is adequately addressed by the added side room), and living. Furthermore, the central area, the only one large enough to be a typical living area (assuming conformity with the general outlines of the ethnographic data cited above), is restricted by the presence of the large industrial hearth. The back room is undersized for a living room, lacks an appropriate floor surface, and is significantly narrower than any of the attested peasant agriculturalist living rooms in the literature cited above. Significantly, even if the structure to the left of the main doorway is not the basis for an inner staircase, the house has yielded perhaps the strongest evidence yet for a second-floor living room: closely spaced split poles covered by a rough mud plaster layer which in turn was covered by a mud plaster finish coat characterized by a heavy concentration of calcite crystals, ground down on the upper surface to a remarkably close approximation of a terrazzo floor. Uncritical assessment suggesting that this might only be an unusual roof surface ignores the fact that the roofing material for this house, typically comprised of many layers of mud and chaff plaster well rolled out, was carefully observed and documented in the field (Wright 1965: fig. 80). Acting in accordance with the principles applied to the Beer-sheba house, if we simply carry the perimeter walls up for a second story, perhaps replacing some of the interior walls with pillar lines and continuing the first-floor columned structure into the second story, we will add some 55 m^2 to the overall house plan, making it ca. 126 m^2. This almost duplicates the area of one of the larger Hasanabad houses (125.5 m^2; Watson 1979: 139), in which six people resided. In that Hasanabad is a wretched poor isolated village, and Shechem was a thriving central place in the last half of the 8th century B.C., that seems a not improper order of magnitude for a medium-sized version of the larger model of standard Israelite house.

Much larger houses, of course, existed, e.g., the 9th-century elite houses flanking the "Citadel" at Hazor (Yadin et al. 1960: pl. 205), or the 7th–6th-century "West Tower" at Tell Beit Mirsim, styled along the lines of a typical four-room house with added side room (Shiloh 1970: 186), but these were houses of the governing elite. As with the analysis of "nonstandard" houses at Israelite sites (e.g., the "House of Makbiram," better, "House of the Servers" at Hazor; Yadin et al. 1960: 72–73; cf. Naveh 1981: 301–2; 85*), the effort would take us beyond the permissible limits of the present article.

D. Socioeconomic Analysis

1. "Israelite House" and the Populace. From the time of its emergence in force until its demise at the end of the Iron II Age, the economic function of the "Israelite House" seems to have been centered upon requirements for storage and stabling, functions for which it was ideally suited. While the design stabilized and became ubiquitous during the time of the open rural hamlet (i.e., Iron Age IA–B), its compact layout, neatly separating the domestic from the economic sphere, allowed for easy adaptation to the confinements and constraints of the urban or fortified village environment. Furthermore, its durability as preferred house type, lasting over 600 years throughout all the diverse environmental regions of Israel and Judah, even stretching down into the wilderness settlements in the central Negeb (Cohen 1979; Herzog 1983), testifies that it was an extremely successful design for the common—probably landowning—peasant. From the frequency of the appearance of this design, one may infer that individuals requiring facilities for managing mixed agricultural pursuits constituted the great majority of the population in ancient Israelite and Judean nucleated, as well as nonnucleated, settlements.

2. Israelite House, Settlement Hierarchy, and Social Stratification. It may be assumed that at sites with little architectural variation (e.g., Tell Beit Mirsim) the social organization was on a village level, with few specialized services being available. Although more detailed studies need to be carried out, it appears that the falloff of proportions of "Israelite Houses" (i.e., three- and four-room houses) in relation to other buildings (e.g., other types of domestic and/or public structures) seems to become progressively greater as one graduates from village to town (e.g., Beth-shemesh?), to city (central place), to major governmental center/regional capital (e.g., Lachish, Megiddo, probably Hazor), to the national/state capital (Jerusalem and Samaria). If one may assume a direct relationship between the magnitude and/or sophistication of domestic architectural features and wealth (note that Kramer 1982: 126–36 cautions against such conclusions on the village level), and if both the richest and the poorest lived in the urban environments, then, given the relatively narrow range of sizes of three- and four-room houses, it might be argued that—apart from those who lived in palaces (e.g., in Samaria, Ramat Rahel, Megiddo, Hazor, Gezer, Lachish, etc.)—the disparity in wealth between various households was not great.

The excavations at Tell Beit Mirsim have provided a fairly large horizontal exposure of the town plan. From it one may infer that, in many cases, the smallest and largest houses actually reflect the habitations of differing generations of the same extended family (Stager's *bêt ʾab,* above). The lack of significant intrasite architectural variability (as opposed to that which exists at Megiddo, Lachish, and Hazor) implies that Tell Beit Mirsim was not a "central place," but that it should be seen as a fortified expanded village (Amiran 1953: 70–73), instead of a "town" or "city" in any modern sense of the terms. There is only one large house, misnamed the "West Tower," and its location and structure seem to mark it off as the residence of the local town magistrate. Furthermore, as noted above, its plan is essentially that of an enlarged four-room house with additions.

Future study probably will demonstrate a discontinuity in ground-floor plan areas between normative three- and four-room houses (which probably form a continuum) and structures of the governmental elite like the Tell Beit Mirsim "West Tower" and the outsized "Elite Houses" at Hazor (above). The point to consider, however, is that—ideologically—the middle tier of rulers lived in houses comparable to those of their subjects, and the present evidence indicates that only governors and kings lived in architecturally distinct palaces or "citadels."

3. Fortified Farming Villages and Regional Security. The demographer D. Amiran (1953) has argued an inverse relationship between strong centralized government and site size in unstable peripheral regions. The security of a strong government fosters the budding-off of dispersed and smaller "daughter" settlements: farmers living farther afield from the population centers and nearer their fields. With governmental weakening or collapse, the dispersed settlements are abandoned and the landscape is dominated by a few very large villages, to which people relocate for greater mutual security, at the expense of convenient access to their fields (1953: 66–73; 205–8; 259–60).

Given this model, the size and occupational density of such largely undifferentiated fortified settlements as Tell Beit Mirsim, Beth-shemesh, and Tell en-Nasbeh, as well as the planned chariot city of Beer-sheba (the settlement of Strata III-II being partially or largely self-sustaining despite a heavy governmental investment in its construction—note the substantial quantities of cedar of Lebanon in its construction; Liphschitz and Waisel 1973: 99–108), speak volumes of the lack of security, not only of the Shephelah and the Negeb during the 8th–7th centuries, but also of the more exposed S reaches of the central hill country N of Jerusalem. The other side of such considerations, of course, is that population estimates based upon the supposed presence of a sizable extramural population in these regions (e.g., Shiloh 1980: 32b) may still be much too high (similarly for the central highlands, cf. Hopkins 1985: 164).

Bibliography

Albright, W. F. 1943. *Excavation of Tell Beit Mirsim.* Vol. 3. AASOR 21–22. New Haven.

Aharoni, Y. 1973. *Beer-Sheba I,* ed. Y. Aharoni. Tel Aviv.

Amiran, D. 1953. The Pattern of Settlement in Palestine. *IEJ* 3: 65–78; 192–209; 250–60.

Beit-Arieh, I. 1973. The Western Quarter. Pp. 31–37 in Aharoni 1973.

Braemer, F. 1982. *L'Architecture domestique du Levant a l'âge du Fer.* Éditions Recherche sur les civilisations 8. Paris.

Callaway, J. 1976. Excavating Ai (et-Tell): 1964–1972. *BA* 39: 19–30.

Cohen, R. 1979. The Iron Age Fortresses in the Central Negev. *BASOR* 236: 61–79.

Currid, J. D., and Navon, A. 1989. Iron Age Pits and the Lahav (Tell Halif) Grain Storage Project. *BASOR* 273: 67–78.

Dalman, G. 1942. *Das Haus, Hünerzucht, Taubenzucht, Bienenzucht.* Arbeit und Sitte in Palästina 7. Gütersloh. Repr. 1964.

Fritz, V. 1977. *Tempel und Zelt.* WMANT 47. Neukirchen-Vluyn.

———. 1980. Die Kulturhistoirische Bedeutung der früheisenzeitlichen Siedlung auf der Hirbet el-Mesas und das Problem der Landnahme. *ZDPV* 96: 121–35.

Fritz, V., and Kempinski, A. 1983. *Ergebnisse der Ausgrabungen auf der Hirbet el-Mšāš (Tēl Māśōś) 1972–1975.* Text, plates, and plans. Wiesbaden.

Gunneweg, J. 1983. The Ovens of the First Campaign. Pp. 106–12 in Fritz and Kempinski 1983.

Hall, G.; McBride, S.; and Riddell, A. 1973. Architectural Analysis. Pp. 245–69 in D. French et al., Asvan 1968–72, An Interim Report. *AnSt* 23: 71–309.

Herzog, Z. 1973. The Storehouses. Pp. 23–30 in Aharoni 1973.

———. 1983. Enclosed Settlements in the Negeb and the Wilderness of Beer-sheba. *BASOR* 250: 41–49.

———. 1984. *Beer-Sheba II.* Tel Aviv.

Holladay, J. S., Jr. 1971. Field III. Pp. 112–20 in W. G. Dever et al. Further Excavations at Gezer, 1967–71. *BA* 34: 94–132.

———. 1982. The Palestinian House: A Case Example of the Use of Ethnographic Analogy in Archaeological Reconstruction. Paper read at the annual meeting of the American Schools of Oriental Research. December 19. New York.

———. 1986. The Stables of Ancient Israel: Functional Determinants of Stable Reconstruction and the Interpretation of Pillared Building Remains of the Palestinian Iron Age. Pp. 103–65 in *Archaeology of Jordan and Other Studies,* ed. L. T. Geraty and L. G. Herr. Berrien Springs, MI.

———. 1990. Red Slip, Burnish, and the Solomonic Gateway at Gezer. *BASOR* 277: 23–70.

———. fc. *Israelite House: A Case study in Applied Archaeoethnographic Analogical Reconstruction.*

Hopkins, D. C. 1985. *Highlands of Canaan.* Sheffield.

Jacobs, L. 1979. Tell-i Nun: Archaeological Implication of a Village in Transition. Pp. 175–91 in *Ethnoarchaeology: Implications of Ethnography for Archaeology,* ed. C. Kramer. New York.

Kelm, G. L., and Mazar, A. 1982. Three Seasons of Excavations at Tell Batash—Biblical Timnah. *BASOR* 248: 1–36.

Kramer, C. 1979. An Archaeological View of a Contemporary Kurdish Village: Domestic Architecture, Household Size, and

Wealth. Pp. 139–63 in *Ethnoarchaeology: Implications of Ethnography for Archaeology*, ed. C. Kramer. New York.
———. 1982. *Village Ethnoarchaeology: Rural Iran in Archaeological Perspective.* New York.
Lapp, P. W. 1967. The 1966 Excavations at Tell Taᶜannek. *BASOR* 185: 2–39.
LeBlanc, S. 1971. An Addition to Naroll's Suggested Floor Area and Settlement Population Relationship. *American Antiquity* 36: 210–11.
Liphschitz, N., and Waisel, Y. 1973. Analysis of the Botanical Material of the 1969–1970 Seasons and the Climatic History of the Beer-Sheba Region. Pp. 97–105 in Aharoni 1973.
Mazar, A. 1982. Three Israelite Sites in the Hills of Judah and Ephraim. *BA* 45: 167–78.
Mazar, B. 1951. The Excavations at Tell Qasile: Preliminary Report. *IEJ* 1: 61–76, 125–40, 194–218.
McCown, C. C. 1947. *Tell en-Naṣbeh I.* Berkeley.
Naroll, R. 1962. Floor Area and Settlement Population. *American Antiquity* 27: 587–89.
Naveh, J. 1962. The Excavations at Meṣad Ḥashavyahu—Preliminary Report. *IEJ* 12: 89–113.
———. 1981. "Belonging to Makbiram" or "Belonging to the Food-Servers"? *EI* 15: 301–2; English summary, p. 85*.
Pritchard, J. B. 1964. Two Tombs of a Tunnel in the Jordan Valley: Discoveries at the Biblical Zarethan. *Expedition* 6/4: 2–9.
Ruthenberg, H. 1976. *Farming Systems in the Tropics.* 2d ed. Oxford.
Sheffer, A. 1973. An Object of Palm Frond. Pp. 47–51 in Aharoni 1973.
Shiloh, Y. 1970. The Four-Room House—Its Situation and Function in the Israelite City. *IEJ* 20: 180–90.
———. 1978. Elements in the Development of Town Planning in the Israelite City. *IEJ* 28: 36–51.
———. 1980. The Population of Iron Age Palestine. *BASOR* 239: 25–35.
———. 1984. *Excavations at the City of David I.* Qedem 19. Jerusalem.
———. 1987. The Casemate Wall, the Four Room House, and Early Planning in the Israelite City. *BASOR* 268: 3–15.
Stager, L. E. 1985. The Archaeology of the Family in Ancient Israel. *BASOR* 260: 1–35.
Sumner, W. M. 1979. Estimating Population by Analogy: An Example. Pp. 164–74 in *Ethnoarchaeology: Implications of Ethnography for Archaeology*, ed. C. Kramer. New York.
Ussishkin, D. 1977. The Destruction of Lachish by Sennacherib and the Dating of the Royal Judean Storage Jars. *TA* 4: 28–60.
———. 1982. *Conquest of Lachish by Sennacherib.* Tel Aviv.
———. 1983. Excavations of Tel Lachish 1978–1983: Second Preliminary Report. *TA* 10: 97–185.
Vaux, R. de. 1952. La Quatrième Campagne de fouilles à Tell el-Farᶜah, près Naplouse. Rapport préliminaire. *RB* 59: 551–83.
Watson, P. J. 1979. *Archaeological Ethnography in Western Iran.* Viking Fund Publications in Anthropology 57. Tucson.
Wreszinski, W. 1935. *Atlas zur altägyptischen Kulturgeschichte*, pt. 2. Leipzig.
Wright, G. E. 1965. *Shechem.* New York.
Yadin, Y. 1972. *Hazor, the Head of All Those Kingdoms.* London.
Yadin, Y.; Aharoni, Y.; Amiran, R.; Dothan, T. 1960. *Hazor II.* Jerusalem.

John S. Holladay, Jr.

HOUSEHOLD CODES. From the German *Haustafeln,* a word used by scholars to designate certain biblical texts that outline the duties and responsibilities associated with the proper or ideal management of private affairs. Significant advances have been made in understanding the form and function of these codes (Col 3:18–4:1; Eph 5:21–6:9; 1 Pet 2:11–3:12; 1 Tim 2:8–15; 5:1–2; 6:1–2; Titus 2:1–10; 3:1) since the mid-1970s. The following article surveys recent research, characterizes the relevant biblical and early Christian texts, suggests how the ethic functioned, and gives alternative evaluations of it.

A. Recent Research on the Source of the Form

Earlier in this century, Dibelius and his student, Weidinger, argued that these household codes were slightly Christianized versions of a code borrowed from the Stoics, e.g., from Hierocles (trans. in Malherbe 1986). Crouch (1972), however, argued that the Stoic influence was minimal compared to that of Oriental-Jewish values. Discussion of (1) social duties in reciprocal terms and (2) the distinction between subordinate and superior persons are non-Stoic features which characterize Hellenistic Jewish codes (Philo *Apol. Jud.* 7.14; Jos. *AgAp* 2.190–219). Therefore, NT codes mirror Jewish morality; they are one aspect of a nomistic tendency in Pauline churches over against the license allowed women in Hellenistic cults of Dionysus, Isis, and Cybele.

In the mid-seventies, three scholars—D. Lührmann, K. Thraede, and D. Balch—independently rejected both hypotheses, suggesting instead that the NT codes are related to the stereotypical Hellenistic discussion of "household management" *(peri oikonomias),* especially as formulated by Aristotle (*Pol.* 1.1253b.1–14). This Aristotelian text (cf. *Mag. Mor.* 1.1194b.5–28) is parallel to the form of Col 3:18–4:1 and Eph 5:21–6:9 in that (1) it outlines relationships among three pairs of social classes; (2) these classes are related reciprocally; and (3) it describes one social class in each of these three pairs as "being ruled."

Since the Aristotelian structure is found only in Colossians and Ephesians, Müller (1983: 266, 317) suggests restricting the designation "household code" *(Haustafel)* to these texts alone, but this poses two problems. (1) Modern categories would then be narrower than the classical Greek terms. The structured Hellenistic discussion of "household management" did not always, or even usually, have an Aristotelian outline. (2) Relationships in the "house" were discussed in the larger context of "city" management. Therefore the exhortation to be obedient to the emperor and his governors in 1 Pet 2:13–14 is consistent with the observation that 1 Pet 2:11–3:12 is also a household code, as is *1 Clem.* 21:4–9. However, the concerns reflected in 1 Pet 5:1–5 are combined with exhortations about domestic relationships in other codes, so that the designation "congregational code" is more appropriate for 1 Tim 2:8–15; 6:1–10; Titus 2:1–10; *Ign. Pol.* 4–6; and Polyc. *ep.* 4–6.

Verner (1983) focuses on the structure of individual exhortations within the code: (a) an address; (b) an imperative, grammatically expressed in various ways; (c) an amplification, often in the form "not . . . but . . ."; and (d) a reason clause. The sources of this "schema" (Verner's term) remain to be specified, but Verner is incorrect that it is exclusively Christian (cf., e.g., Epict. *Dis.* 3.12.10;

3.14.4–5; Tobit 4:3–21; Philo *Cher.* 48–49; *Spec. Leg.* 2.67–68; 3.137).

B. Biblical and Other Early Christian Texts

Many scholars (e.g., Crouch 1972; Müller 1983) assume that the Colossian code is the earliest. However, the code in 1 Peter may be just as early and is not literally dependent on the one in Colossians. Nor is the Colossian code a later interpolation (as suggested by Munro 1983). Colossians Christianizes institutional Greek values about managing households, and scholars sometimes exaggerate either the christological deepening or the new motivation involved in the editor's addition to the formula "in the Lord (Christ)" (Col 3:18, 20, 22, 23, 24; 4:1; see Müller 1983: 310–16).

On the other hand, the christological grounding is clear in 1 Peter and Ephesians. In 1 Peter the slaves are exhorted to patience in unjust suffering because Christ left them an example (2:21). They sing an early christological hymn which interprets Isaiah 53 of Christ (2:22–24), their shepherd and Episcopos (2:25).

Ephesians (5:21, 22–33; 6:5–8) transforms the Colossians code by specifically Christian motivation. Wives are exhorted to "be subject" to their "head," their husbands, who are to "love" their wives. The author employs a parallel christological model: the Church is "subject" to its "head," Christ, who "loves" it. This is founded on the confession that Christ is "Savior" of the Church, the body (5:23, 25). Further, as the baptized (5:26) are members of the body of Christ (5:30), so husband and wife are one body, one flesh (5:28–29), an emphasis on unity in marriage and in Christ.

The reformulation of these codes in 1 Timothy and Titus is not focused exclusively on the household: (a) more groups are included, e.g., community officers, widows, and the wealthy, and (b) the context of the exhortations changes, e.g., to men's roles and women's behavior in worship. Passages on the bishop and deacons emphasize qualifications for entering the office so that they will be models of behavior in a Church and society valuing prosperity and propriety.

Reciprocal exhortations to masters are absent in the Pastorals, as in 1 Peter. Whereas Colossians and Ephesians exhort slaves to noble character, the prosperous writer of Titus 2:9–10 wants slaves not to steal. Further, restriction of the leadership of wealthy women is evident in texts about "widows" (1 Tim 5:3–16; *Ign. Pol.* 4; Polyc. *ep.* 4). Laub (1982: 90–94) suggests that these growing patriarchal emphases are not characteristic; rather the distinctive, new elements are that (a) slaves are addressed, (b) various households are united in *ekklesiai,* "churches," and (c) slaves are integrated into these churches in ways unusual for Greco-Roman society. MacDonald (1983; and Verner 1983: 178), on the other hand, shows that the Pastorals were written to oppose oral traditions whose values are reflected in the *Acts of Paul and Thekla:* celibate women teach in public, baptize, and exercise leadership while male bishops, presbyters, and deacons remain unmentioned; i.e., the Pastorals do patriarchalize Pauline traditions over against socially marginal Christian groups which are disrupting pagan and Christian households.

C. The Function of These Codes

Following Roman and Jewish precedents, the author of 1 Peter adopts the domestic code, exhorting Christians to "apologize" (3:15, a technical term denoting both defense and eulogy of their faith and behavior). But in Colossians (Schweizer 1977 cites Col 3:11) the code opposes "false teaching," as does 1 Timothy, Ign. *Pol.* 3 (immediately preceding the duties of chaps. 4–6), and Polyc. *ep.* 7 (immediately following chaps. 4–6). Positively stated, these orthodox authors emphasize social duties as given in secular society.

D. Evaluation of the Ethic

Thraede (1980) insists that these codes do not represent general Greco-Roman ethics but take a partisan position over against other available options. Müller (1983) interprets this as a specific choice for a liberalizing, pragmatic, moderate, "middle," humane, sensible social-ethical orientation, not as a hard insistence on the existing order of authority.

More critically, Schweizer (1977) writes of the "paganization" of Christianity by these household codes. Eph 5:22–33 sanctions hierarchical order by salvation history. Whereas Col 3:22–23 distinguishes one's fleshly lord from the Lord, Eph 6:5 directly connects the two. One no longer fears God alone (Col 3:22; 1 Pet 2:17; 3:6), but also one's master (Eph 6:5). This suggests the misunderstanding that service to God is identical with service to the higher social classes. One no longer pleases the Lord alone (Col 3:20), but the master (Titus 2:9). *Didache* 4:11 says masters are a type of god for the slaves, so identifies social and divine orders! This becomes the divine cosmic order of Stoicism in *1 Clement* 20.

Schüssler Fiorenza (1984: 290–91) observes that the leadership and behavior of women and slaves become restricted and defined according to the patriarchal standards of Greco-Roman society so that outsiders will not take offense at their insubordinate behavior. The Pastorals merge the leadership of wealthy patrons with that of local male bishops, which patriarchializes Church order according to the model of the wealthy Greco-Roman household, a move which leads to the exploitation of slaves and women even within the Church community.

Balch agrees with Schüssler Fiorenza, with the qualification that the original adaptation of the household codes in 1 Peter and Colossians does contain critical elements. Whereas Aristotle (*Eth. Nic.* 5. 1134b.9–18; 8. 1060a.23–1661a.10) argues that the proper relationship between master and slave is one of "tyranny," not "justice," 1 Pet 2:19–20 reports that Christian slaves are suffering "unjustly," but unlike Roman masters, God judges "justly" (2:21–23). Col 4:1 exhorts masters to treat slaves "justly and fairly." A second critique is clear in 1 Pet 3:1; the wife is independent enough from her husband to choose her own God over against foolish, lawless pagans (1 Pet 1:18; 4:3). The earliest household codes reject the unjust treatment of slaves and the absolute subordination of wives to the religious inclination of their husbands. See also HAUSTAFELN.

Bibliography

Balch, D. L. 1981. *Let Wives Be Submissive.* SBLMS 26. Chico, CA.
———. 1984. Early Christian Criticism of Patriarchal Authority. *USQR* 39: 161–73.

———. 1986. Hellenization/Acculteration in 1 Peter. Pp. 79–101 in *Perspectives on 1 Peter,* ed. C. H. Talbert. Macon, GA.

———. 1988. Household Codes. Pp. 25–30 in *The New Testament and Graeco-Roman Literature,* ed. D. E. Aune. SBLSBS. Atlanta.

———. fc. Neopythagorean Moralists and the New Testament. *ANRW* 2/26/1.

Berger, K. 1984. Hellenistische Gattungen im NT. *ANRW* 2/25/2: 1078–86.

Bieritz, K.-H., and Kähler, C. 1985. Haus II–III. *TRE* 14: 478–92.

Crouch, J. E. 1972. *The Origin and Intention of the Colossian Haustafel.* FRLANT 109. Göttingen.

Elliot, J. H. 1981. *A Home for the Homeless: A Sociological Exegesis of 1 Peter, Its Situation and Strategy.* Philadelphia.

Fiedler, P. 1986. Haustafel. *RAC* 13: 1063–73.

Klauck, H.-J. 1981. *Hausgemeinde und Hauskirche im frühen Christentum.* SBS 103. Stuttgart.

Laub, F. 1982. *Die Begegnung des frühen Christentum mit der antiken Sklaverei.* SBS 107. Stuttgart.

Lührmann, D. 1980. Neutestamentliche Haustafeln und antike Okonomie. *NTS* 27: 83–97.

MacDonald, D. R. 1983. *The Legend and the Apostle.* Philadelphia.

Malherbe, A. J. 1986. *The Graeco-Roman Moral Tradition and Early Christianity.* Philadelphia.

Müller, K. 1983. Die Haustafel des Kolosserbriefes und das antike Frauenthema. Pp. 263–319 in *Die Frau in Urchristentum. QD* 95. Basel.

Munro, W. 1983. *Authority in Paul and Peter.* SNTSMS 45. Cambridge.

Sampley, J. P. 1971. *"And the Two Shall Become One Flesh": A Study of Tradition in Ephesians 5:21–33.* SNTSMS 16. Cambridge.

Schrage, W. 1975. Zur Ethik der neutestamentliche Haustafel. *NTS* 21: 1–22.

Schüssler Fiorenza, E. 1984. *In Memory of Her. A Feminist Reconstruction of Christian Origins.* New York.

Schweizer, E. 1977. Die Weltlichkeit des Neuen Testaments: die Haustafeln. Pp. 397–413 in *Beiträge zur alttestamentliche Theologie,* ed. H. Donner et al. Göttingen.

Selwyn, E. G. 1981. *The First Epistle of St. Peter.* 2d ed. Grand Rapids.

Thraede, K. 1980. Zum historischen Hintergrund der "Haustafeln" des NT. Pp. 359–68 in *Pietas, Festschrift für Bernhard Kötting,* ed. E. Dassmann and K. S. Frank. JAC Ergänzungsband 8. Munich.

Verner, D. C. 1983. *The Household of God: The Social World of the Pastoral Epistles.* SBLDS 71. Chico, CA.

DAVID L. BALCH

HOUSEHOLD GODS. See IDOL, IDOLATRY.

HOZAI (PERSON) [Heb *ḥôzāy*]. Apparently the author of a chronicle that included information about the reign of Manasseh, king of Judah (2 Chr 33:19). The text mentions nothing further about the man, nor have his writings survived. Some of the content of his work is specified, however. His chronicle told of Manasseh's prayer, God's answer, and Manasseh's sins, especially in setting up idols. The reference to the prayer inspired the later, apocryphal book the *Prayer of Manasseh.* The name Hozai means "my seers." Both his name and his activity in recording the story of the spiritual highlights of a king's reign may indicate that he was a prophet.

The Greek appears to be based on a Heb text that had *ḥôzîm (tōn horōntōn),* i.e., "the seers" (RSV). A proposal that we read *ḥôzāyw,* "his (Manasseh's) seers," has also been made (*BHS;* Myers *2 Chronicles* AB, 197). Nearly all modern translations prefer the rendering based on the Greek (thus RSV, KJV, AB, NEB, NAB). Very few (JB, NJPSV, Douay) consider Hozai to be the name of an individual. Nevertheless, several scholars believe that there is nothing that actually rules out a reference to a specific, otherwise unknown, historiographer/prophet (*IDB* 2: 658). McAllister (*ISBE* 2: 773) is of the opinion that the Gk "seers" is an error resulting from confusing v 19, *dibrê ḥôzāy* ("writings of Hozai"), with v 18, *wĕdibrê haḥōzîm* ("writings of the seers"). The Syr reads *(d)ḥnn nbj*ʾ = *ḥānān hannābî* ("favor [?] of the prophet).

KENNETH H. CUFFEY

HUKKOK (PLACE) [Heb *ḥûqōq*]. A town defining part of the border of the tribe of Naphtali (Josh 19:34). It is usually identified with Yaquq (M.R. 195254), 3 miles W of Chinnereth overlooking the Sea of Galilee. However, this identification is problematic, mainly because it is much too far E for a town that is apparently located near Aznoth-tabor (Kh. umm-Jubeil? M.R. 186237) and ostensibly along the S and W boundary shared with Zebulun and Asher. The Chronicler also mentions a levitical city by the same name (MT *ḥûqōq,* but RSV "Hukok"), but includes it among a list of towns belonging to Asher (1 Chr 6:60—Eng 6:75). See also HUKOK. It is possible that this is the same town mentioned in Josh 19:34 as having belonged to Naphtali. On the one hand, if the Chronicler's "Hukok" is indeed a variant for HELKATH, and if the Josh 19:34 "Hukkok" refers to this place, then the SW quadrant of Naphtali would include virtually all of the tribal territory of Zebulun. Aharoni, apparently assuming that Hukkok = Helkath (*LBHG,* 105, 271), correctly observes that this is incomprehensible (*LBHG,* 239). On the other hand, the Chronicler may have had in mind a town other than Helkath (which is just E of Mt. Carmel). Thus, some have suggested that Hukkok/Hukok be identified with Kh. el-Jemeija (M.R. 175252), 3 miles E of Cabul (see *MBA,* 179 and map 72). A line drawn from here to Aznoth-tabor would leave the territory of Zebulun intact and would be consistent with the general picture we have of Asher's E border (Josh 19:27–28).

GARY A. HERION

HUKOK (PLACE) [Heb *ḥûqōq*]. Var. HELKATH? A town in the tribe of Asher which, along with its pasture lands, was set aside for the Levites (1 Chr 6:60—Eng 6:75). In the parallel list of levitical towns in Joshua 21, the Asherite town listed between Abdon and Rehob is not Hukok but HELKATH. If Hukok here is a variant of Helkath, then it could be identified with either Kh. Harbaj (M.R. 158240), Tel el-Amar (M.R. 159237), or Tel Qashish (M.R. 160232), all along or close to the Kishon river just E of the Mt. Carmel range. If Hukok is not a variant of Helkath, it is possible that the Chronicler had in mind the same town listed in Josh 19:34 as lying along Naphtali's W border with Asher, possibly Kh. el-Jemeija (M.R. 175252). See also HUKKOK.

GARY A. HERION

HUL (PERSON) [Heb *ḥûl*]. According to the Table of Nations, the second son of Aram, the grandson of Shem and great-grandson of Noah (Gen 10:23). The corresponding genealogy in 1 Chr 1:17 places him as the seventh son of Shem and brother of Aram. This is probably due to the eye of an early scribe slipping from the first to the second of two lines each ending with the same word "Aram" when copying the text. This led to the loss of the line reading "the sons of Aram (are)" which is found in the Genesis genealogy. Originally the two genealogies were undoubtedly identical. Certain mss of the Sam. Pent. render the name *ḥûṣ*. Little else apart from his Semitic roots is known regarding the identity or geographical location of Hul and his descendants.

DAVID W. BAKER

HULDAH (PERSON) [Heb *ḥuldâ*]. A prophetess during the reign of Josiah, king of Judah (2 Kgs 22:14; 2 Chr 34:22). Nothing is known of her but that she is the wife of Shallum, "keeper of the wardrobe." It is not known whether he was in charge of the king's wardrobe or the vestments of the priests in the temple; thus it is not known whether she was the wife of a court official or one of the temple personnel. She is alternately identified as a cult or court prophet. From the role she plays in 2 Kings, court prophet is the more likely possibility. Her prophetic oracle is divided into two parts, 2 Kgs 22:16–17 and 22:18–20. The first part is a word of judgment against Judah, and the second a word of assurance to the king that he will die in peace before that judgment is carried out. The word of judgment is written in typically Deuteronomistic style and is fulfilled in subsequent chapters. The second part of the prophetic oracle is not fulfilled. Though the king dies before Judah is destroyed, he does not die in peace but in battle. Such unfulfilled prophecy is not characteristic of the Deuteronomistic Historian, and may be an indication of the authenticity of the second part of Huldah's oracle. Huldah is the only female prophet mentioned in the books of Kings. It is impossible to determine from this isolated case the characteristic roles of female prophets in Judah or their frequency, but we have evidence of the existence of female prophets in Mari and Assyria. These prophets, like their male counterparts, uttered oracles, some of which were addressed to kings on matters of safety and divine protection.

PAULINE A. VIVIANO

HUMANITY, NT VIEW OF. The human being (*anthrōpos*) is seen in the NT as a living being who is to be distinguished from animals as well as from God and other higher beings such as angels. To that extent the NT is in continuity with the OT and Judaism, as well as with much of the Greek tradition (Taylor 1981: 11–317).

Also in continuity with the OT, the *anthrōpos* is understood as a psychosomatic unity, over against much of the Greek world. The Greek language of the NT can be misleading, as utilization of Greek terms such as soul (*psychē*) and body (*sōma*) can incorrectly give the reader a dualistic view of anthropology, since the terms are used that way in the non-Christian Greek world. In the NT the terms are, however, used in a manifestly Hebrew/OT way; that is, not as ways to speak of different parts of the individual but as different ways to speak of the entire unified, integrated person (*BTNT* 1: 192–239). For that matter, there is no independent reflection on anthropology in the NT dealing with humanity's qualities, constituent parts, or nature, and therefore little definition of terms and no standardization of their usage. Rather, the *anthrōpos* is always understood in terms of the relationship with God. In relationship to God there is a dual perspective on who humanity is and who humanity is to become. In the present the *anthrōpos* is sinful (Synoptics) and enslaved under the power of sin (Paul and John). The individual person and humanity as a whole are weak, mortal, and sinful (Matt 16:23; Rom 1:18–3:20; 1 Cor 1:25.)

The relationship of humanity to God has, however, been changed in the Christ event (Rom 3:21–26; Eph 2:1–22; 1 Pet 1:18–2:10). Believing humanity has been reconciled to God in Christ and therefore, as the justified image of God, is destined to become a new humanity (Eph 2:14–16) because of the saving activity of the true *anthrōpos,* Jesus Christ (Rom 5:12–21). In the present the Christian person thus lives in the tension of having been freed of the past but not yet having reached the completed future. At the same time the identification of that future and of the eschatological significance of Jesus enabled the early Church to proclaim a Christ who had come not only for Jews but for all people. This-worldly distinctions between people were radically eliminated (Gal 3:26–28) as one unified Church was created from the variety of individual human lives.

A. Synoptic Gospels
B. John
C. Paul
D. Rest of the NT
E. Early Church Outside the NT

A. Synoptic Gospels

The Jesus of the Synoptic Gospels comes proclaiming the kingdom of God which is breaking into history by his sheer presence. That presence forces each person to make a decision about repentance and belief (Mark 1:14–15 [=Matt 4:17]; Matt 11:21–22, 12:41), calling on the individual to leave the wrong way and to enter the way of God's will (Luke 15:11–32).

Jesus evaluates humanity very highly, yet humanity is far from God. His high evaluation of humanity is illustrated not only by the fact that he brings God's message to humanity but also by his view, in tandem with the OT, that the *anthrōpos* is the crown of God's creation and therefore worth more than ravens, lilies, sparrows, and sheep (Matt 6:26–30 [=Luke 12:24–28]; Matt 10:29–31 [=Luke 12:6–7]; Matt 12:12). The human being is worth more even than the sabbath observance (Mark 2:27–28; 3:1–6 [=Matt 12:9–14; Luke 6:6–11]; Luke 13:10–17). Yet humanity lives in danger of gaining the world and losing the self (Mark 8:36–37 [=Matt 16:26; Luke 9:25]) by living as God's enemy. The enmity is expressed as "thinking what humanity thinks" rather than what God thinks (Mark 8:33 [=Matt 16:23]). Merely being religious is not the answer, as is illustrated by the scribes and Pharisees, whose human religious thinking seeks to replace the command of God with the statutes of people (Mark 7:5–13 [=Matt 15:2–9]; Matt 5:21–48). Humanity refuses to recognize God's care and is therefore unable to entrust itself to God (Matt 6:25–34 [=Luke 12:22–32]; Mark 4:35–41; 9:14–29 [=Matt 8:18, 23:27; Luke 8:22–25]). Part of the manifestation of that inability is humanity's concrete lack of care for the neighbor (Matt 25:31–46), which is set in the sharpest contrast to Jesus' radical definition of "neighbor" to include enemies and foreigners (Matt 5:43–48 [=Luke 6:27–28, 32–36]; Luke 10:29–37). All people are evil (Matt 7:11 [=Luke 11:13]) and are a sinful generation in God's eyes (Luke 11:29 [=Matt 12:39]; Matt 16:4). The heart of humanity is misdirected and needs to be turned around (Matt 5:28; Mark 7:21–23 [=Matt 15:19–20]).

The *anthrōpos* is, however, addressable and changeable, and so Jesus comes with his message of the kingdom, which sets in proper order the relationship of God and humanity. That proper order is one of master and slave (Luke 17:7–10), in which the human slave is called to glorify, by his or her life and good works, the Father who is in heaven (Matt 5:16). As Kümmel writes (1963: 29), "To Jesus, man is simply God's slave and as a created being is pledged to the service of God, who will call him to account." It is the failure to recognize the proper God-human relationship which results in the self-justifying schemes of the religious (Luke 14:7–14; 18:9–14), and thus the believer needs to realize the truth of what Jesus teaches: no one can serve two masters (Matt 6:24 [=Luke 16:13]). The one called to be a slave is also called to be a disciple (Mark 6:6–11) and thus to function as a light to others (Matt 5:16) and a fisher of people (Mark 1:16–20 [=Matt 4:18–22; Luke 5:1–11]), knowing that such commitment can lead to persecution and homelessness (Matt 5:10–12; Luke 6:20–23; Matt 8:20 [=Luke 9:58]).

In both his actions and his words, Jesus illustrates the meaning of fishing for people. He has table fellowship with tax collectors and sinners (Mark 2:15–17 [=Matt 9:10–12; Luke 5:29–32]; Matt 11:19 [=Luke 7:34]), he treats women with dignity and equality (Mark 1:29–31 [=Matt 8:14–15; Luke 4:38–39]; 5:21–43; Luke 10:38–42), he restores outcasts (Mark 1:40–45 [=Matt 8:2–4; Luke 5:12–16]), and he heals gentiles (Mark 5:1–20 [=Matt 8:28–34; Luke 8:26–39]; 7:24–30 [=Matt 15:21–28]), treating all as full human beings. He also speaks of a God who seeks even the single lost individual, especially the nonreligious (Luke 15:1–32). The God of Jesus is not, in fact, the God of the religious but the God of the lowly (Luke 18:9–14; see 1:52), who calls the followers of Jesus to take the gospel to all people regardless of race or nation (Matt 28:19; Acts 10:28; 15:8–9).

B. John

Just as Jesus in the Synoptics knows what is in the heart of humanity, so in John he knows and understands people (1:47–48; 2:24–25; 4:17–19). What he (and thus the author of John) understands about people is that they live in darkness *(skotia, skotos),* being blind and without understanding or knowledge (9:39–41; 12:40; 1 John 2:11). This condition is universal. All humanity sins (3:19; 7:19; 16:8–9; 1 John 1:8, 10) to such an extent that people cannot recognize their lack of freedom (8:34–45). The primary example of sin is humanity's refusal to believe the revelation of God in Jesus (8:24; 9:41; 15:22–25; 16:8–9; 1 John 4:3). Bultmann writes (*BTNT* 2: 18): "*Darkness,* then, means that a man does not seize this possibility—that he shuts himself up against the God revealed in the creation. Darkness is nothing other than shutting one's self up against the light." The humanity which lives in the darkness is equated with the world, or *kosmos* (1:10–11; 3:19), so that *kosmos* usually means the negative totality of humanity (1:29; 3:16; 1 John 2:2) to such an extent that it seems that mere existence in the *kosmos* results in alienation from God. Yet Jesus can resist praying that his followers be removed from the world (17:15), for existence in the world is not in and of itself negative. Sin means living *in* the world in such a way that one is *of (ek)* the world (3:31; 8:23; 15:19; 17:14–16; 18:36; 1 John 2:16; 4:5). To be *of* the world is to be not of God but to identify one's source of being and life with the world.

The division between those who are of God and those who are of the world seems insurmountable. On the one side are those who are of God (8:42, 47; 1 John 4:6) and of the truth (18:37). They are from above (3:3, 7). On the other side are the people who are from below (8:23). They are from this world (8:23) and are of the devil (8:44). The point of distinction between the two types is the reaction to the encounter with Jesus; by one's reaction to him one constitutes oneself as from above or below and shows one's true origin (3:20–21; 8:23). While close to a gnostic-metaphysical dualism in which some people seem by nature to be destined for salvation while others are destined for damnation, John's gospel ultimately avoids that position by its conception that the redeeming activity of God in the Son is directed toward the entirety of humanity (1:29; 3:16; 8:26; 1 John 2:2), with a universal call to decision (12:46–48). Each person who hears has the opportunity to be drawn by the Father (6:44; 12:32). The "dualism," if one uses that term, is more properly a dualism of decision rather than a dualism of nature (*BTNT* 2: 21). There is nothing inherent in any *anthrōpos* that necessarily saves or condemns.

C. Paul

"In the whole of the NT it is only Paul who expounds what we should call a thoroughly thought-out doctrine of man" (Käsemann 1971: 1). Yet one may well question how systematic Paul's anthropology really is. As Jewett (1971: 1–10) has shown, Paul's anthropology seems erratic because of his great sensitivity to the terminology being utilized by his partners in conversation. For that reason he can use different terms to mean the same thing, and he can use the same anthropological term to designate different things. Unfortunately, Paul did not develop a lexicon of anthropological terms to which he then slavishly adhered. So while on the one hand we can say with Betz (1972: 165) that "the apostle Paul was the first Christian theologian who developed and presented a well-conceived anthropology," we need also to admit with Betz that "Paul's lack of terminological systematization and his excessive intricacies appear overwhelming," for, "apparently, conceptual systematization was not the goal of Paul's anthropology." At the same time, anthropology is a pervasive concern in Paul's letters to such an extent that Bultmann (*BTNT* 1: 191) could write: "Every assertion about God is simultaneously an assertion about man and vice versa. For this reason and in this sense Paul's theology is, at the same time, anthropology."

For Paul, humans are historical beings who belong to the *kosmos* (Rom 1:8; 3:19; 11:12, 15; 1 Cor 1:20–22, 27–28; 4:13; 2 Cor 1:12). They are to be properly understood as creatures (Rom 9:19–21; 1 Cor 11:9) who are marked by weakness and mortality (Rom 7:13–20; 1 Cor 15:53–54). Humans, moreover, inevitably stand over against God (Rom 1:18, 21; 3:4; 14:18; 1 Cor 1:25; 2 Cor 5:11). There is nothing divine in the *anthrōpos* (1 Thess 2:4; 4:8).

In addition, human beings are inevitably and inexorably enmeshed in and ruled by sin, which in Paul is to be understood as virtually a hypostasized power (Rom 7:15–20) which takes over the life of the individual and rules his or her will. The universal sinfulness of all of humanity is a fundamental presupposition of Paul's anthropology and is painstakingly developed in Rom 1:18–3:20. In that section he turns first to the gentile who indeed might claim exemption from culpability, since God's revelation in the law had been given not to gentiles but to Jews. Paul dismisses that plea by means of an argument from a general revelation that has come to all people who, however, have rejected it and have "exchanged the glory of the immortal God for images resembling mortal humanity or birds or animals or reptiles" (Rom 1:19–23). He similarly removes any claim of the religious Jew (2:1, 18–24) and ends his lengthy discussion of sin with a chain of OT quotations that illustrates that "the whole world" is "held accountable to God" for its sin (3:10–20). From a negative perspective, the distinctions between people are removed, because "all have sinned and fall short of the glory of God" (3:23), whether they have the law or not. Sin is thus introduced through disobedience and it brings with it death (Rom 5:12; 6:23a).

When Paul wishes to speak of humanity from the perspective of its sinfulness, he uses the term "flesh" *(sarx)*. *Sarx* is what is opposed to God's spirit (Rom 7:14–25) but, in agreement with the OT, flesh and spirit do not refer to two parts of human nature but to two ways of carrying out one's life: one lives either according to the flesh or according to the spirit (Rom 8:4, 5, 9, 12, 13). *Sarx,* however, does not refer to the physical aspect of humanity as in some way separable from the mental or spiritual. Rather, *sarx* refers to the totality of a person's existence as understood from the perspective of humanity's fallenness. Indeed, *sarx* is the regular shorthand way in which Paul indicates the *anthrōpos* in his or her fallen, sinful condition. Flesh thus means the totality of the fallen individual, including the mind, and so both the physical and the mental are understood to be polluted and in need of cleansing (Rom 1:28).

To be distinguished from flesh is the term for body, *sōma.* As opposed to an important part of the Greek tradition running from Plato through Gnosticism, in which the body is viewed as the prison of an immortal soul, the body for Paul is not necessarily bad (soul in Paul should be understood in the Hebrew rather than the Greek sense, which means that the distinction between body and soul does not indicate opposition). Theoretically the body is neither good nor bad in itself, but its evaluation depends on whether sin or spirit rules it. When the body is misused, it "becomes" flesh. That is, when Paul writes of the body as it is misused by sinful humanity, he writes of it as flesh. Body as body, however, is not evil simply by being material. In fact, humanity falls and in fact the body has fallen victim to sin and death, but it is not the body that is constitutively bad. Flesh is the negative term which allows Paul to retain a potentially positive view of the body. Indeed, his view of the body is so positive that a body is required in the resurrection (1 Cor 15:35–44; Phil 3:20–21). At the same time Paul is skeptical of what happens in the reality of life in this world, in which the weak part of humanity, the *sarx,* becomes the beachhead in the body for the operation of sin. When the flesh is thus elevated and becomes the focus of life, that life is misdirected and opposed to the spirit. A life, therefore, that is oriented to the flesh serves the flesh and does its thinking (Rom 8:5–8, 12–13). Believers, however, no longer live in the flesh (Rom 7:5–6; 8:8–9), which signals not a putting aside of the body but a living in the body in a new way, namely, in relationship to God.

One obvious question to be addressed to Paul's anthropology is that of metaphysical dualism. Is the *anthrōpos* in Paul to be comprehended as having two parts (body and soul) or three parts (body, soul, and spirit) or is the *anthrōpos* a unified being who cannot properly be divided? Certainly there are sections which exhibit dichotomous or trichotomous thought (2 Cor 4:6; 5:1–9; 1 Thess 5:23), but in interpreting Paul at this point one has to deal with the fact of his Hebraic background, in which humanity is looked upon as a whole, rather than as assembled but discrete parts. The human being is seen as a psychosomatic unity there and in Paul as well (see *BTNT* 1; Kümmel 1963; Robinson 1963; Gutbrod 1934; Stacey 1956). A more accurate use of the term dualism would be for the sort of ethical dualism one sees in the anthropological dividedness Paul identifies in Rom 7:7–24. In his discussion of non-Christian humanity he points to the unresolved conflict between the ability of the nonbeliever to will the right and his or her inability to carry out the right (7:15–20).

A second obvious question for Paul is how humanity can move from the dividedness of Romans 7 and break the power that sin and flesh exert over the body. His answer is in part anthropological, for he identifies the solution to the anthropological dilemma in the One *Anthrōpos,* the One Man, Jesus (Rom 5:15, 17–19; 1 Cor 15:21, 47; see also 1 Tim 2:5). Jesus has redone correctly what the first *anthrōpos*/human did incorrectly (Rom 5:15–21). Humanity is thus confronted with two fundamental options: the humanity of the sinful Adam and the humanity of the redeemer Adam (Betz 1972: 166). By faith and through the ritual action of baptism the person is identified with both the redeeming activity of Christ and the body of that redeemer, the Church (Rom 6:3–6; 12:3–8; 1 Cor 12:12–31, especially vv 12–13). The transfer from one realm to another is such a dramatic one (Rom 5:12–6:11) that Paul expresses it in terms of dying and living. The transfer, moreover, is not a return to the beginning, where the first *anthrōpos* was, but a recreation and the bringing forth of a new person (Rom 6:4; 7:6; 12:2; 2 Cor 4:16; 5:17; Gal 2:19–20; 6:15). The new person lives in the confidence that God is the giver of life. Seeking life within one's self is thus given up, and the destructive direction seen in Rom 1:18–3:20 is reversed. The believer is freed from sin and death (Rom 6:15–23; Gal 5:1–16) to a life of service and love (1 Cor 7:22; 9:19). In addition, the reprobate mind of Rom 1:28 is being changed into the renewed mind of Rom 12:2, and the Christian is enabled to present his or her body as a living sacrifice to God (12:1).

Another way that Paul expresses his anthropology is by means of the concept of the image of God. Christ himself is the image of God (2 Cor 4:4, 6), in that uniquely in Christ God's presence is most fully revealed. Through the powerful message of that Christ, people are in turn being changed into the image of the Son (Rom 8:29; 1 Cor 15:48–49; 2 Cor 3:18). What needs to be noted is that the Christ Paul identifies as the image of God is the resurrected and exalted Christ; image of God is therefore an eschatological concept which points to the resurrection of the believer as the ultimate transformation (Childs 1978: 85–102). Thus Christ as the image of God is the final destiny of the humanity that is in Christ (1 Cor 15:23–28, 44–49; see also Eph 1:9–10). That final destiny is already in part realized in the elimination of the distinctions that separate people from each other; in Christ a united humanity is already effected in which racial, social, and sexual barriers are pronounced void (Gal 3:26–28; 1 Cor 12:12–13). In the present the Christian is called to a life of radical obedience, set free to love others (Rom 13:8–10; 1 Cor 8:1; 13:1–13; Gal 5:6, 13–14, 22; 1 Thess 3:12). Yet until the eschaton the Christian lives in the tension that exists between the future promised in the new Man and the sin inherited from the first (Rom 8:18–30; 2 Cor 12:5–10). While moving toward the future (Phil 3:12–14), the believer is always drawn backward by the past.

On the whole, the deutero-Pauline letters of Ephesians and Colossians move in the same direction as the historical Paul. Christ is the image of God (Col 1:15) through whom believers are being renewed in the image of God (Col 3:10). Formerly dead in their sins (Eph 2:1–3; Col 2:13; 3:7), Christians have been raised to a new life in Christ (Eph 2:4–10; Col 3:1–4) in which the divisions of this world are overcome (Col 3:11) as a new humanity is being created by God in Christ (Eph 2:14–16; 4:15–16, 22–24; Col 3:9–10).

D. Rest of the NT

On the whole the rest of the NT has a less highly developed anthropology, although the basic concepts of the gospels and Paul are essentially present, especially in terms of the sinfulness of humanity and the God-human alienation apart from Christ. Two exceptions are Acts 17:27–29 and 2 Pet 1:4. In the former text the kinship of every person with God is outlined; in the latter the goal of attaining divine nature is held out. The Acts passage is heavily Stoic and is unique in the NT; the 2 Peter passage is also strongly Hellenistic and quite uninfluenced by Hebraic thought, with its escape from the corruption of this world into divine nature. Indeed, as the later NT authors utilize even more frequently the Hellenistic concepts, they do tend to a more dichotomous and trichotomous view of the human person (1 Pet 1:9; 2:11; Heb 4:12). In the Pastorals humanity is viewed less in the individual anthropological sense that Paul had developed and much more in the direction of the person as a member of a Church which no longer expects the imminent end of the world but which is settling in for the indefinite future. Thus Church discipline, orthodox doctrine, and good works are emphasized, and so the Christian is understood as the man/person *(anthrōpos)* of God (2 Tim 3:17; cf. 2:21; 1 Tim 6:11 seems to reserve the phrase as a title [and office designation?] for Timothy). James continues the basic anthropology of the OT and NT, although he sharpens the negative evaluation of humanity with terms such as "empty" (2:20) and "double-hearted" (1:8; 4:8). The universal sinfulness of humanity is indicated in Hebrews (2:14–15; 10:22), and therefore humanity is destined for judgment (6:2). At the same time, for the believer God is the future (13:13; chaps. 11–12), and so the believer is called to live as a pilgrim (11:8) who realizes that persecution will come (11:32–40). The model for such living is the forerunner Jesus (6:20).

E. Early Church Outside the NT

In the Apostolic Fathers there are no extensive anthropological discussions as in Paul, but the writings continue many of the themes seen in the NT. There is thus a high view of the *anthrōpos* (*1 Clem.* 33:4) at the same time that humanity is also viewed as sinful (*2 Clem.* 1:6; 18:2).

While there is some continuity in the use of anthropological terms (*Diogn.* 5.8 uses *sarx* in a way quite similar to Paul in Rom 8:12–13, and *psychē* frequently refers to the whole life of the individual, as in *2 Clem.* 15:1; *Barn.* 19:5; *Did.* 2:7) and while flesh can designate that which is opposed to God (Ign. *Magn.* 3.2; *Rom.* 8.3), *sarx* in the Apostolic Fathers is consistently used in a positive way quite distinct from the usage of Paul. God can therefore be designated the God or Lord of all flesh (*1 Clem.* 59:3; 64:1). Jesus came in the flesh and gave his flesh for the flesh of humanity (*1 Clem.* 49:6; Ign. *Smyrn.* 1:2; *Barn.* 5:1, 6, 10, 11; 6:7, 9; 7:5; 12:10). Ignatius frequently referred to the eucharistic flesh of Jesus Christ (Ign. *Trall.* 8:1; *Rom.* 4:1; 7:3; *Smyrn.* 7:1; cf. *Phld.* 5:1; *Smyrn.* 12:2). Moreover, believers are to be pure in flesh (*1 Clem.* 38:2), guarding their flesh from impurities so that the flesh may be justified (*Herm. Sim.* 5.7.1–4). The flesh, in fact, can be understood as the temple of God (Ign. *Phld.* 7:2; *2 Clem.* 9:3), and the Church can be designated as flesh (*2 Clem.* 14:4). It is the flesh that will be resurrected (*2 Clem.* 9:1–2, 4–5; 14:5; *Herm. Sim.* 5.6.7) just as Jesus was in the flesh after the resurrection (Ign. *Smyrn.* 3:1–2). Flesh, in distinction from Paul, is constitutive of the human person, so that "flesh and spirit" becomes a way to refer to the *anthrōpos* (Ign. *Smyrn.* 1:1; *Pol.* 5:1; *Magn.* 13:2; *Rom.* Int; on Jesus as flesh and spirit, see Ign. *Eph.* 7:2). In general, it would be accurate to say that the Apostolic Fathers use "flesh" where Paul would have used "body"; "body" is therefore less important as an anthropological term, and the Pauline nuances of "flesh" are largely missing. Nor is the NT understanding of Jesus as the new *anthrōpos* very prominent. Only Ign. *Eph.* 20:1 speaks of the new man Jesus Christ (*Diogn.* 11:4).

At the same time the combination of a more positive view of flesh and a rigorous ethical stance led to a certain optimism about the ability of humanity, under God's grace, to be pure and attain salvation. If the flesh is kept pure, believers shall obtain eternal life (*2 Clem.* 8:4, 8:6). The Christian strives for perfection through the new law of Jesus Christ (*Barn.* 2:6; 4:10, 11; *Did.* 6:2–3), knowing that deeds are important for salvation (*2 Clem.* 8:4, 11:7, 19:1; *Barn.* 3:4–5, 4:12; *Herm. Vis.* 2.3.2; *Man.* 12.3.4–6). At the same time, sexual sins are especially highlighted (*Barn.* 10:6–8, 19:4; *Did.* 2:2; *Herm. Vis.* 1.1), and the ideal is sexual chastity (*1 Clem.* 38:2; Ign. *Pol.* 5:2). Thus, although there is a kind of optimistic view of the ability of redeemed humanity to live properly, there is need for repentance (*1 Clem.* 7:5–7; 8:2; 51:1 and 3; *2 Clem.* 8:1; 9:8; 13:1; 16:1; 17:1; Ign. *Phild.* 8:1; *Herm. Vis.* 1.1.9). On the other hand, the rigorism that continues to emerge in the 2d century begins to limit repentance to the beginning of the Christian life, for the baptized Christian should no longer sin (Ign. *Eph.* 14:2; *Herm. Vis.* 2.2.5). At the most, one postbaptismal repentance is allowed (*Herm. Man.* 4.1.8; 4.3.1–7).

There are elements of anthropological dualism in the Apostolic Fathers (*Diogn.* 6:1–10; *2 Clem.* 12:4), but the most consistent dualistic conception is that of *dipsychia* (dividedness, double-mindedness, literally "double-souledness"). The Christian is constantly tempted to be doubledminded, that is, to be split in loyalties (*1 Clem.* 23:2; *2 Clem.* 19:2; *Herm. Man.* 9; 10.1.1; 10.2.2 and 4; *Vis.* 2.2.4; 3.7.1; 3.10.9; 3.11.2; cf. the two angels in *Man.* 6). Dualism, however, is more accurately applied to the ethical perspective of the Apostolic Fathers, where two opposite ways of living are available to people (*Barn.* 5:4; 18:1–2, 19–21; *Did.* 1:1 and the rest of the document; *Herm. Sim.* 1).

Where anthropological dualism is quite evident in the 2d century is in developing Gnosticism, where anthropology is placed at the center. Because the physical world was created by an inferior, unstable, and capricious God, gnostics are to have nothing to do with this world, for they do not belong to it. While that view is expressed most clearly in "The Song of the Pearl" in *The Acts of Thomas* and the cosmogonies from Nag Hammadi, we find the beginnings of the later clarified dualism in the *Gospel of Thomas,* which in origin goes back well into at least the 2d century A.D. A key term is the Greek loan word *monachos,* which occurs in sayings 16, 49, and 75. Related Coptic terms occur in sayings 4, 11, 22, 23, and 106. Later the Greek term designated a monk, but at this earlier stage the term means "solitary one." In saying 16, Jesus comes "to throw divisions upon the earth." The divisions are those between the gnostics and the rest of the world. The gnostics are the separated ones—separated from the evil in their own bodies and separated from whatever binds them to the evil world, especially the family (sayings 55, 101, 105). Gnostics are also to separate themselves from such outward trappings of the world as clothing (saying 36) and the conventional forms of (Jewish) piety (saying 14). Yet, somewhat ironically, the relationship of the gnostics to the world can be summed up as one of fasting (sayings 27, 81, and 110). The world tries to invade the gnostics to take their "goods," that is, belief in their otherworldly origin and existence, which is the only thing of worth gnostics possess (saying 21). Put in other language, the goal of the life of gnostics in this world is to become passersby (saying 42) in relationship to this world, for gnostics are aliens or strangers who do not properly belong to this creation. Their origin is in the higher world of the true God, and the important part of gnostics, the soul, is therefore divine (sayings 13, 49, 50, 108). The goal of gnostics is to be independent of the fleshly body and ultimately free of it (sayings 87 and 112).

By the middle of the 2d century the stage was set for the ongoing battle with Gnosticism, which forced the emerging catholic theologians, who also appropriated non-Christian Greek anthropological understandings, to themselves take a more and more dualistic view of anthropology.

Bibliography

Betz, H. D. 1972. "Humanizing Man: Delphi, Plato, and Paul." Pp. 159–73 in *Religion and the Humanizing of Man,* ed. J. M. Robinson, Waterloo, Ontario.

Childs, J. M., Jr. 1978. *Christian Anthropology and Ethics.* Philadelphia.

Gundry, R. H. 1976. *Soma in Biblical Theology: With Emphasis on Pauline Anthropology.* Cambridge.

Gutbrod, W. 1934. *Die paulinische Anthropologie.* BWANT 4/15. Stuttgart.

Jewett, R. 1971. *Paul's Anthropological Terms: A Study of Their Use in Conflict Settings.* AGJU 10. Leiden.

Käsemann, E. 1971. "On Paul's Anthropology." Pp. 1–31 in *Perspectives on Paul.* Tran. M. Kohl. Philadelphia.

Kümmel, W. G. 1963. *Man in the New Testament.* Tran. J. J. Vincent. Rev. and enl. ed. London.

Robinson, J. A. T. 1963. *The Body: A Study in Pauline Theology.* London.

Stacey, W. D. 1956. *The Pauline View of Man in Relation to Its Judaic and Hellenistic Background.* London.

Taylor, W. F., Jr. 1981. *The Unity of Mankind in Antiquity and in Paul.* Ann Arbor.

WALTER F. TAYLOR, JR.

HUMOR AND WIT. Because humor requires a somewhat "playful" disposition and a willingness (at least temporarily) to suspend all seriousness, many people—especially those with strong and well-defined religious beliefs—may be reluctant to admit that portions of Scripture may be funny or may have been written by someone trying to be humorous. The assumption often is that religion is serious and that it demands a transformation of human nature—especially the eradication of that aspect of human nature that derives pleasure from "worldly" things. Yet in the past century this theological assumption has been abandoned by many people, some of whom point out that humor can be a powerful vehicle for making important points, while others go further and insist that even biblical writing may have been intended primarily to *entertain* the reader. Because humor is such a fundamental aspect of human nature, there can be little doubt that the ancients laughed at things that struck them as funny. Of course, because humor is so greatly dependent upon the cultural conventions of the moment, it is often difficult (and sometimes impossible) for the modern Western mind-set to appreciate what was humorous in ancient Israel or in the early Christian Church. Nevertheless, with the appropriate methodological cautions, something can be said about humor and wit in the ancient world from which the Bible emerged. This entry is intended to survey what is known about humor in antiquity and in the Bible. It consists of four articles, one surveying ancient Egypt, one surveying ancient Mesopotamia, one surveying the Hebrew Bible, and one surveying the NT.

GARY A. HERION

ANCIENT EGYPT

Anyone attempting to discuss the humor of an extremely different and distant culture will indubitably reveal much more about his/her sense of humor than about that of the people under study. Though cultural differences make it doubtful whether we can correctly identify all of the references which the ancient Egyptians intended as humorous without errors of both commission and omission, and more doubtful that we can grasp the import or impact of their humor on its intended audience, a profusion of representational as well as textual materials testifies to what we are likely justified in regarding as a pervasive vein of humor and wit (van de Walle 1969; *LÄ* 3:73–77; Mueller 1973; Guglielmi 1980).

A. Representations

The highly visual ancient Egyptian culture produced an untold number of representations on all scales and in a wide array of media (Saleh 1964; cf. Lesko 1986: 86).

1. Monumental Art. While much of Egyptian sculpture, relief, and painting belongs to cultic, mortuary, and display contexts involving a high degree of convention and motives other than the aesthetic, and while the conventions of Egyptian art are normally regarded as subordinating the individual/particular to the general/essential, Egyptian art often relishes observational detail and provides a "snapshot" which seems to freeze a moment or "frame" of activity. This includes many details which have attracted the modern observer, such as the calf and its mother bleating at each other (tomb of Ti, Old Kingdom; Westendorf 1968; 55), and some which seem humorous, e.g., two girls pulling each other's hair (tomb of Menna, New Kingdom; Smith 1981: 265). Some of these recur over long periods of time or are revived in periods of "archaism" (cf. Aldred 1985: 222). Some details, such as a huge baboon helping to press grapes (an Old Kingdom tomb; Lesko 1977: 19), baboons picking and eating figs (tomb of Khnumhotpe, Middle Kingdom; Aldred 1985: 120), or pet animals under the queen's throne (tomb of Anen, New Kingdom; Smith 1981: 260), strike the modern observer, at least, as humorous touches. One of the most celebrated humorous vignettes in monumental art is the relief of the immense queen of Punt and the little donkey she rides, in Hatshepsut's temple at Deir el-Bahri (Nims 1965: 36); the queen is also sketched on a Ramesside ostracon by a later artist who may have found her amusing (Peck 1978: 115).

These scenes can be accompanied by captions, comprising description and/or dialogue (see below).

2. Graffiti, Ostraca, Illustrated/Pictorial Papyri, etc. These media, especially the former two, lent themselves to humorous and perhaps more personal expression on the part of the artist.

Figured ostraca included some likely to be "practice sketches," some "doodles" or "cartoons," and are especially numerous from the artisans' community at Deir el-Medina during the New Kingdom. Humorous themes found on them include the "topsy-turvy" or *"mundus inversus"* type, cat-mouse reversals, etc. (cf. Vycichl 1983; Brunner-Traut 1977a; Peck 1978: 142–47). A unique object from Amarna is a children's toy depicting a family of monkeys in a chariot in obvious burlesque of the chariot theme so frequent in Amarna art depicting the royal family (Wilson 1956: 220).

Among graffiti is an erotic sketch in ink at Deir el-Bahri which has been regarded as a "political cartoon" of Hatshepsut and perhaps Senmut (Wente 1984; Romer 1982: 158–159). Erotic scenes are also found on ostraca (Peck 1978: 151–53), as well as on the great Turin erotic-satirical papyrus (Omlin 1973), which has one side devoted to the somewhat caricatured sexual encounters between a young woman and a priest, and the other to a group of "topsy-turvy" vignettes. These latter have been regarded by some as illustrations for animal stories which have not survived in writing (Brunner-Traut 1968; 1977b).

3. Hieroglyphic Writing System. The visual dimension of Egyptian culture is also found in its writing system, which, in its hieroglyphic form, is in a way an extension of artistic representation (cf. Meltzer 1980). This script lends itself to "sportive" writings based on puns and creative combinations/variations of signs, and scribes seem to delight in showing their erudition and ingenuity and, perhaps, matching wits with each other. Some such writings are found in standard hieroglyphic texts, while this tendency reaches its apex in "cryptographic" or "enigmatic" texts, often with religious importance, or sometimes display texts closely integrated with architectural decoration, and in the temple inscriptions of the Greco-Roman period at the tail end of the hieroglyphic tradition (cf. Derchain-Urtel 1978).

B. Texts

Wordplay is ubiquitous in Egyptian texts (Meltzer 1975; Morenz 1975). Frequently it is not humorous but religiously significant or characteristic of literary sophistication and elegance. There are cases in which, apparently, punning or polysemy can yield two readings of a passage (Fecht 1958; Williams 1981: 6), a procedure which, if deliberately employed as a literary device, certainly has humorous potential and was likely so employed.

The "satire" is well attested in Egyptian literature (Curto 1965; Seibert 1967; Wilson 1971; Millet 1988), especially in wisdom compositions and the curriculum of the scribal academy. The "Satire on the Trades," in which various occupations are compared disadvantageously with that of scribe (*AEL* 1: 184–92), begins a tradition elaborated in the Late Egyptian Miscellanies (*AEL* 2: 167–78). These latter compositions include the scathing description of the dissipated scribal student enjoying nightlife, and the "satirical letter" in which some basic facts about the Syro-Canaanite region and other things that every military scribe should know are livened up by being couched as a denunciation of the ignorant scribe Amenemope by the scribe

Hori (Fischer-Elfert 1983). In a similar vein is the description of the drunkard in the 18th Dynasty Instruction of Anii (*AEL* 2: 137), and, earlier, the well-known characterization of the hapless Asiatics in the Instruction for Merykare (*AEL* 1: 103–4). Turning to Demotic wisdom, there are undoubtedly humorous highlights, such as Papyrus Insinger's characterization of the plight of a sexagenarian (*AEL* 3: 199); a Demotic fragment of advice for "a little child who is very, very young," continuing with bawdy maxims (Williams 1976: 270–71), is also perhaps a comic piece.

Egyptian stories are sometimes predominantly humorous and frequently give considerable play to humor in a lively and sophisticated approach to composition. The classic Middle Egyptian story of Sinuhe features a scene which has always been regarded as humorous, the homecoming of the protagonist who has "gone native" as a Canaanite and is seen by an incredulous royal family (*AEL* 1: 231–33). The story of the "Petitioner of Memphis" or "King Neferkare and General Sisenet" features a petitioner whose suit is drowned out by musicians and who, investigating, discovers an apparent liaison between the king and a general (Posener 1971: 237–38). The interminable speechmaking of the Eloquent Peasant might have been facilitated, according to one suggestion, by the extremely generous beer ration provided by the high steward (Leprohon 1975). The tale of the Shipwrecked Sailor ends with a grim proverb: "What good is there in giving a drink to a goose on the eve of its slaughter?" (Gilula 1976). The entire story takes on a humorous cast in light of a recent suggestion according to which the sailor is an illustration of how to disobey all of the injunctions of the Wisdom Literature regarding etiquette—that is, how to be an overbearing, rude, arrogant boor (Bryan 1979). As such, it is part of a persistent thread of protagonists who can be regarded as "anti-heroes." One possible reading of the story as a whole is as a "tall tale," which, if justified, can represent another kind of humor. The episodes of the magicians in Papyrus Westcar (*AEL* 1: 215–22) feature a number of humorous touches. King Snofru is diverted by young women rowers dressed, if that is the right word, in nets; Khufu is entertained by the magician Djedi, who eats and drinks an immense quantity daily; a group of gods and goddesses assist at a birth and meet a distraught expectant father (though his tying his kilt upside down may rather be an example of "*Bindeszauber*"). It is possible to interpret the courtly conversation between Djedi and Prince Hardedef as a verbal display of elegant sarcasm and one-upmanship (for an opposite interpretation, see Goedicke 1986).

In Late Egyptian narrative, our attention is immediately caught by the "Contendings of Horus and Seth," a slapstick burlesque treatment of that narrative (which has a fragmentary Middle Kingdom predecessor; (*AEL* 2: 214–23; cf. Meltzer 1974; Redford 1973: 71–78). The picaresque misadventures of Wenamun, who makes himself *persona non grata* at Dor and Byblos and narrowly escapes being lynched in Alashiya (*AEL* 2: 224–30), have an appreciable element of humor; it has been suggested that this text is a documentary account rather than a tale. Among other documentary texts, one of the Late Ramesside Letters includes a rare example of an actual joke (Wente 1967: 80). The Late Egyptian love poetry's sensitive portrayal of young lovers includes a number of humorous touches (*AEL* 2: 181–93; cf. Foster 1974; Lesko 1986). The rather grim story of Apophis and Sekenenre, the missing conclusion of which is often linked with the hideously wounded mummy of Sekenenre, features the insulting message or challenge sent by the Hyksos king to his Theban opponent. While most Egyptologists have regarded that message as a provocation leading to war, an early suggestion recently revived is that it is part of a context of escalating verbal ripostes (Redford 1970: 36–39; 1973: 58–59). Outwitting by verbal cleverness provides the denouement of yet another Late Egyptian story, that of Truth and Falsehood (*AEL* 2: 211–14).

Demotic narrative richly repays the search for humor and wit. The two stories of Setna Khamwas (*AEL* 3: 125–51; cf. Posener 1971: 250) portray that formidable magician as being soundly upstaged by the dead sorcerer Naneferkaptah and the boy wonder Si-Osiri respectively. Naneferkaptah puts him in his place with several extremely grim practical jokes in the first story, while the second features the magical abduction of Pharaoh every night to Kush, where he is beaten in the public square. The Petubastis epic cycle includes the story of Prince Pedikhons and Queen Sarpot (*AEL* 3: 151–56), in which what begins as the combat between the Egyptian prince and the Amazon queen becomes a different kind of encounter by the fragmentary conclusion. The Demotic Chronicle includes the escapades of the tippling king Amasis (cf. Posener 1971: 250).

While instances of intended humor are hard to come by in royal and other commemorative or display inscriptions, the possibility can be considered that in the triumphal inscription of the Kushite king Piye ("Piankhy" formerly), if the ostensibly cheering Egyptians at the end are being quoted accurately, they are actually jeering the monarch and casting aspersions on his legitimacy (*AEL* 3: 80). If so, this might be one instance of the intercultural misunderstanding which characterizes the Kushite-Egyptian encounter. At an earlier period, the autobiographical inscription of an 18th Dynasty viceroy of Nubia, Usersatet, quotes a letter from King Amenhotep II, apparently reminiscing in his cups about foreign women, or foreign chieftains disparagingly characterized as such (Helck 1984: 1343–44). The conversations, exclamations, and songs or chants represented as spoken by workmen, fishermen, herdsmen, etc., in "daily life scenes" starting in Old Kingdom tombs ("*Reden und Rufe*"—Erman 1919; Guglielmi 1973; Montet 1925) contain a number of apparently lighthearted or jocular exchanges and sometimes seem to be humorous (e.g., the "herdsman's song").

It is difficult if not impossible to separate "religious" or "mythological" narrative from stories in general (cf. the Horus and Seth narrative cited above), but those which are designated *r3*, "utterance," or found in "magical" or mortuary contexts include some which could perhaps be considered humorous. Some commentators have seen humor in the "Myth of Re and Isis," in which the aged and doddering sun god must tell the goddess his secret name to stop the torment of a snakebite, and in the "Book of the Divine Cow" (commonly known as the "Destruction" or "Deliverance of Mankind") found in some New Kingdom royal tombs, in which the rampaging goddess is foiled in her intention to destroy mankind when she gets drunk on beer dyed red to resemble blood (Redford 1973: 69–71). Whether the Egyptians did, I cannot say.

Herodotus may have played a role in the dissemination of Egyptian humor to new audiences insofar as such episodes as Khufu's prostituting of his daughter and the racy story of Rhampsinitus have authentic roots in Egyptian tradition (cf. Posener 1971: 237–38).

Bibliography

Aldred, C. 1985. *Egyptian Art.* London.

Brunner-Traut, E. 1968. *Altägyptische Tiergeschichte und Fabel.* Darmstadt.

———. 1977a. Der Katzmäusekrieg—Folge von Rauschgift. *Göttinger Miszellen* 25: 47–51.

———. 1977b. *Tiergeschichten aus dem Pharaonenland.* Mainz.

Bryan, B. M. 1979. The Hero of the "Shipwrecked Sailor." *Serapis* 5/1: 3–13.

Curto, S. 1965. *La Satira nell'antico Egitto.* Turin.

Derchain-Urtel, M.-Th. 1978. Esna, Schrift und "Spiel." Kleine Bermerkunzen zu einem grossen Thema, I. *Göttinger Miszellen* 27: 11–21.

Erman, A. 1919. *Reden, Rufe und Lieder auf Gräberbildern des Alten Reiches.* APAW 15. Berlin.

Fecht, G. 1958. *Der Habgierige und die Maat in der Lehre des Ptahhotpe, 5. und 19. Maxime.* ADAIK 1. Glückstadt.

Fischer-Elfert, H.-W. 1983. *Die satirische Streitschrift des Papyrus Anastasi I. Textzusammenstellung.* Kleine ägyptische Texte. Wiesbaden.

Foster, J. L. 1974. *Love Songs of the New Kingdom.* New York.

Gilula, M. 1976. Shipwrecked Sailor, Lines 184–85. Pp. 75–82 in *Studies in Honor of George R. Hughes.* SAOC 39. Chicago.

Goedicke, H. 1986. Gentleman's Salutations. *Varia Aegyptiaca* 2: 161–70.

Guglielmi, W. 1973. *Reden, Rufe und Lieder auf altägyptischen Darstellungen der Landwirtschaft, Viehzucht, des Fisch- und Vogelfangs vom MR bis zur SpZt.* TÄB 1. Bonn.

———. 1980. Lachen und Weinen in Ethik, Kult und Mythos der Ägypter. *Chronique d'Égypte* 55: 69–86.

Helck, W. 1984. *Urkunden der 18. Dynastie.* Urkunden des ägyptischen Altertums 4/17022. Berlin.

Leprohon, R. J. 1975. The Wages of the Eloquent Peasant. *JARCE* 12: 97–98.

Lesko, B. S. 1986. True Art in Ancient Egypt. Pp. 85–97 in *Egyptological Studies in Honor of Richard A. Parker,* ed. H. Lesko. Hanover and London.

Lesko, L. H. 1977. *King Tut's Wine Cellar.* Berkeley.

Meltzer, E. S. 1974. Egyptian Parallels for an Incident in Hesiod's *Theogony* and an Episode in the Kumarbi Myth. *JNES* 33: 154–47.

———. 1975. A Possible Word-play in Khamaus I? *ZÄS* 102: 78.

———. 1980. Remarks on Ancient Egyptian Writing with Emphasis on Its Mnemonic Aspects. Pp. 43–66 in *Processing of Visible Language 2,* ed. P. A. Kolers et al. NATO Conference Series 3: Human Factors 13. New York.

Millet, N. B. 1988. Some Canopic Inscriptions of the Reign of Amenhotep III. *Göttinger Miszellen* 104: 91–93.

Montet, P. 1925. *Scènes de la vie privée dans les tombeaux égyptiens de l'Ancien Empire.* Strasbourg.

Morenz, S. 1975. Wortspiele in Ägypten. Pp. 328–42 in *Religion und Geschichte des alten Ägypten. Gesammelte Aufsätze.* Weiman.

Mueller, D. 1973. Review of Helck, W., *Die Lehre des Dw3-Htjj. BiOr* 30: 218–19.

Nims, C. F. 1965. *Thebes of the Pharaohs.* London.

Omlin, J. A. 1973. *Der Pap. 55001 und seine satirisch-erotischen Zeichnungen und Inschriften. Cat. del Mus. Eg. di Torino.* Turin.

Peck, W. H. 1978. *Egyptian Drawings.* New York.

Posener, G. 1971. Literature. Pp. 220–56 in *The Legacy of Egypt,* ed. J. R. Harris. 2d ed. Oxford.

Redford, D. B. 1970. The Hyksos Invasion in History and Tradition, *Or* 39: 1–51.

———. 1973. "And the Great God Laughed": The Egyptian Wit. Pp. 65–78 in *Papyrus and Tablet,* ed. A. K. Grayson and D. B. Redford. Englewood Cliffs.

Romer, J. 1982. *People of the Nile. Everyday Life in Ancient Egypt.* New York.

Saleh, ʿAbdel-ʿAziz. 1964. Humorous Representations in Ancient Egyptian Art. *Al-Migallah* 88: 33–42 (in Arabic).

Siebert, P. 1967. *Die Charakteristik. Untersuchungen zu einer altägyptischen Sprechsitte und ihren Ausprägungen in Folklore und Literature.* ÄgAbh 17. Wiesbaden.

Smith, W. S. 1981. *The Art and Architecture of Ancient Egypt.* Rev. ed., W. K. Simpson. Harmondsworth.

Vycichl, W. 1983. Histoire des chats et de souris. Un Problème de la littérature égyptienne. *Bulletin de la Société de Égyptologie de Genève* 8: 101–8.

Walle, B. van de 1969. *L'Humour dans la littérature et dans l'art de l'ancienne Égypte.* Leiden.

Wente, E. F. 1967. *Late Ramesside Letters.* SAOC 33. Chicago.

———. 1984. Some Graffiti from the Reign of Hatshepsut. *JNES* 43: 47–54.

Westendorf, W. 1968. *Painting, Sculpture and Architecture of Ancient Egypt.* Rev. ed., W. K. Simpson. Harmondsworth.

Williams, R. J. 1976. Some Fragmentary Demotic Wisdom Texts. Pp. 263–71 in *Studies Hughes.* SAOC 39. Chicago.

———. 1981. The Sages of Ancient Egypt in the Light of Recent Scholarship. *JAOS* 101: 1–19.

Wilson, J. A. 1956. *The Culture of Ancient Egypt.* Chicago.

———. 1971. Review of Seibert, *Die Charakteristik. JNES* 30: 79–81.

EDMUND S. MELTZER

MESOPOTAMIA

Humor, or the perception and expression of the ludicrous or amusing, is known in both Sumerian and Akkadian literary tradition, and was no doubt as much a part of everyday life in Mesopotamia as in contemporary societies. At its most basic, Mesopotamian humor was scatological and crass; at its most obvious, diverting and jocose; at its most subtle, refined and penetrating. As with all humorous literatures, the point lies in breaking a taboo, inverting or reversing expectations, drawing attention to the gap between what is and what is wished for, pretended, or ignored.

Humorous allusions to excretion and flatulence are commonplace. Here the point can lie in unappetizing imagery, such as an Akkadian parody on a menology that enjoins wild donkey dung in garlic as the diet for the month kislimu, and for shabat hot bread and donkey anus stuffed with dog turds and fly dirt (Foster 1974: 77–78; Römer 1975: 63–66). A spoof Akkadian incantation, to be recited by a person losing sleep to the bleating of a goat, has the Babylonian national god Marduk stuffing the offending goat's left ear with its own dung, in an "ear-for-an-ear" reprisal (Genouillac 1925: pl. 3, C1 [cuneiform text only]). Some errant Babylonian scholar offered a precative paradigm of the verb "to break wind" in the context of a Sumerian grammatical treatise, taking advantage of a graphic ambiguity in his original (Foster 1974: 84). Flatulence as an enemy of intimacy is alluded to in Babylonian "love lyrics": "Why did you break wind and feel mortified? Why did you stink up her boyfriend's wagon like a wi[ld ox]?" (Lambert 1975: 120–21). A Sumerian joke alludes to a bride's flatulence as an example of inconsequence; in another a boastful fox opines that when he urinated in the ocean he created it (Gordon 1959: 495; 222–23).

Humorous allusions to personal habits, appearance, and behavior abound in Sumerian debates and dialogues, wherein the interlocutors trade elaborately artificed but now often scarcely understandable insults. These reflect on the opponent's genealogy, appearance, intelligence, competence, and education, as in the following example: "(You) dog spawn, wolf seed, mongoose stench . . . hyena whelp, carapaced fox, addlepated mountain monkey of reasoning nonsensical" (Sjoberg 1972: 108). Likewise in Akkadian: "I saw my girl friend and was stunned: You are chalky like a gecko, your hide is swart like a cook[ing pot]!" (Lambert 1975: 120–21).

Sexual activity is, of course, a favored subject of jokes and double entendres in both Sumerian and Akkadian (examples in Farber 1986; Gordon 1959; Foster 1974). The infamous "love lyrics," for example, have the ardent man begging the women of "Babylon-town" for a rag to swab his girl friend's genitalia. He later plants a watchbird in her vulva, enjoining it not to peck at the fungus and to stay clear of the stench of her armpits (Lambert 1975: 104–5; 122–23).

Forsaking the bodily for the social, we find satirical quips on various trades and professions. The launderer, for example, is the butt of a Sumerian joke: "Men say, 'I'm dirty.' 'By god I'm dirty too!' says the laundryman" (Gadd 1963: 187). The singer of Sumerian cultic laments is pilloried for his absurd piety: if his boat sinks he wishes the river enjoyment of his cargo; if he slips and falls he is doubtful of the propriety of getting up since his mishap was a visitation from heaven (Gordon 1959: 248–49, 251–52, 483–84). An Akkadian parody of exorcism has the would-be exorcist burning down the haunted house to free it of its ghost (Foster 1974: 77).

Extended texts of a light or jocose nature include a Sumerian composition about three ox drivers from Adab, owners of an ox, cow, and wagon, who fall into a dispute as to who will fetch water. They solve it by going off together. Upon their return they find that the ox has mated with the cow, the cow has produced a calf, and the calf is suckling(?) on the wagon. They dispute now who shall be owner of the calf. They seek judgment from the king, whose dilemma is resolved by a "cloistered woman," perhaps the Sumerian equivalent of the "lady from Philadelphia." Her pronouncement is unclear, owing to damage to the unique manuscript (Foster 1974: 70–72).

A well-preserved Akkadian folktale is referred to as the "Poor Man of Nippur." This man sells his shirt to buy a ewe for a feast to ease his hunger pangs, ends up with a male goat instead, and, loath to share his repast with his relatives and neighbors, takes it to the mayor of Nippur. The mayor proceeds to dine on the goat himself, leaving the poor man only a bit of gristle and a quaff of cheap beer. The poor man's threefold revenge takes up the rest of the tale (Gurney 1956: 142–62; 1972: 149–58; Cooper 1975: 163–74; Jason 1979: 189–215). In another humorous Akkadian text, a sophomoric fop lectures a cleaner in detail as to how to clean his garments, whereupon the exasperated cleaner tells the youth to go and wash them in the canal himself. He then offers some good advice to the effect that no one would help such a self-important young man (Gadd 1963: 181–88; Livingstone 1988: 176–82).

In another, comparable text, a physician from Isin goes to Nippur, the center for Sumerian learning, to collect a fee. As he asks directions in the street, he is answered in Sumerian, which, as a man of letters, he is supposed to have mastered. The physician imagines that he is being cursed at and remonstrates. After several reprises of this situation, he learns that his client is not at home anyway, and the author apparently suggests that such an illiterate be run out of town forthwith (Reiner 1986: 1–6). A satirical Akkadian letter in the name of the hero Gilgamesh threatens and cajoles its addressee, and makes a series of gargantuan demands: "send . . . 100,000 mares whose bodies have markings like wild tree roots, 40,000 continually gambolling miniature calves, 50,000 fine calves with well-turned hooves and horns intact, 50,000 teams of dappled mules . . ." (Kraus 1980: 109–21). Sumerian epistolary literature includes a plaintive effort by a homesick monkey (Dunham 1985: 244–45).

Humor can show a more serious side in satire, and, if carried far enough, becomes bitter. Perhaps the best-known example is the "Dialogue of a Master and His Servant," wherein a seemingly capricious master sets forth a proposition, then its opposite, to each of which the servant has a glib reply: "Servant, listen to me!" "Yes, master, yes!" "I will fall in love with a woman." "[So], fall in love, master, fall in love! The man who falls in love with a woman forgets sorrow and care." "No, servant, I will certainly not fall in love with a woman." "[Do not] fall in love, master, do not fall in love. A woman is a pitfall, a hole, a ditch; a woman is a sharp iron dagger that slashes a man's throat" (Lambert 1960: 139–49).

Other satirical possibilities are exploited in narrative poems that are not primarily humorous or satirical in intent. In the Akkadian Gilgamesh Epic, for example, satirical passages include Ishtar's occasional use of colloquial speech; the pedantic scorpion woman correcting her mate concerning the genealogy of Gilgamesh; and the reversal of the irreversible curse of Enkidu upon the prostitute, where he concludes by wishing her an ardent, moneyed, and marriageable clientele (Foster 1987: 36–39). Sumerian narrative poems, even at the present level of understanding, teem with witty and satirical passage. In "Enmerkar and the Lord of Aratta," for example, the plot turns upon limitations of royal power, trickery, bluffing, and trials, and climaxes in an etiology for the origins of writing as a means of conveying messages too prolix to be memorized. Such texts presuppose an audience sure enough of itself to see its strategies and values parodied (Cohen 1973).

The vocabulary of humor in Sumerian and Akkadian seems rather sparse: Sumerian for "funny" (ZU-LILI) may mean something like "making the teeth flash," whereas Akk *sâḫu,* "laugh," may rather refer to the sound of laughter as a loud noise. The Akkadian word is mostly attested in contexts of ridicule or amusement at the discomfiture of others. An interesting Sumerian expression, ISIŠ-LÁ, refers to "breaking down" or "giving way" to either tears or laughter. For discussion and examples, see Foster 1974: 84–85; Römer 1975: 48–49.

The professional jester or clown seems to have existed in the profession called *aluzinnu.* The personage is known from Assyrian and Babylonian manuscripts that preserve what seem to be snatches of songs and routines. These deal with his gross appetites and sexuality, his inept performance of various trades, the revolting monthly diet alluded to above, and a heroic journey in the manner of the kings of old (Foster 1974: 74–79; Römer 1975: 53–68).

Pranks and practical jokes are best known from the "Poor Man of Nippur" alluded to above, where three tricks are worked on the mayor.

Wit and humor outside of literary contexts are more difficult to assess. Heavy sarcasm and irony can sometimes be read in letters, for example: "Do go on being such a good sister to me! Even though we grew up together, you didn't pay me two cents worth (text: ¼ shekel) of attention when you got your big break . . . if that big chief you're married to needs beams, let him write me; I'll send him five beams . . . send me (in return) a hundred locusts and a cent-and-a-half's worth (text: ⅓ shekel) of food, so I can see what sort of sister you are" (Stol 1981: 10–11). An Assyrian king allows himself a bit of "gallows" humor in a letter to the Babylonians (Lambert 1960: 281). In an inscription Sennacherib sneers at the incontinence of his enemies (Grayson 1963: 95). A Sargonic official lightheartedly invokes a magic spell in asking his correspondent to come see him (Thureau-Dangin 1926: 23–29).

Although some Mesopotamian humor was undoubtedly considered "vulgar" by the Mesopotamians themselves (Foster 1974: 85), one can be sure that, as always with humor, what was produced by the few was enjoyed by the many.

Bibliography

Cohen, S. 1973. Enmerkar and the Lord of Aratta. Diss. Pennsylvania.

Cooper, J. 1975. Structure, Humor, and Satire in the Poor Man of Nippur. *JCS* 27: 163–74.

Dunham, S. 1985. The Money in the Middle. *ZA* 75: 234–64.

Farber, W. 1986. Associative Magic: Some Rituals, Word Plays, and Philology. *JAOS* 106: 447–49.

Foster, B. 1974. Humor and Cuneiform Literature. *JANES* 6: 69–85.

———. 1987. Gilgamesh: Sex, Love and the Ascent of Knowledge. Pp. 21–42 in *Love & Death in the Ancient Near East,* ed. J. H. Marks and R. M. Good. Guilford, CT.

Gadd, C. 1963. Two Sketches from the Life at Ur. *Iraq* 25: 177–88.

Genouillac, H. de. 1925. *Premières recherches archéologiques à Kich.* Vol. 2. Paris.

Gordon, E. 1959. *Sumerian Proverbs.* Philadelphia.

Grayson, A. 1963. The Walters Art Gallery Sennacherib Inscription. *AfO* 20: 83–96.

Gurney, O. 1956. The Tale of the Poor Man of Nippur. *AnSt* 6: 145–62 + *AnSt* 7: 135–36.

———. 1972. The Tale of the Poor Man of Nippur and its Folktale Parallels. *AnSt* 22: 149–58.

Jason, H. 1979. The Poor Man of Nippur: An Ethnopoetic Analysis. *JCS* 31: 189–215.

Kraus, F. 1980. Der Brief des Gilgameš. *AnSt* 30: 109–21.

Lambert, W. 1960. *Babylonian Wisdom Literature.* Oxford.

———. 1975. The Problem of the Love Lyrics. Pp. 98–135 in *Unity and Diversity,* ed. H. Goedicke and J. J. M. Roberts. Baltimore.

Livingstone, A. 1988. "At the Cleaners" and Notes on Humorous Literature. Pp. 175–87 in *Ad bene et fideliter seminandum,* ed. G. Mauer and U. Magen. AOAT 220. Neukirchen-Vluyn.

Reiner, E. 1986. Why Do You Cuss Me? *Proceedings of the American Philosophical Society* 130/1: 1–6.

Römer, W. 1975. Der Spassmacher in alten Zweistromland, zum "Sitz im Leben" altmesopotamischer Texte. *Persica* 7: 43–68.

Sjoberg, Å. 1972. "He Is a Good Seed of a Dog" and "Engardu, the Fool." *JCS* 24: 107–19.

Stol, M. 1981. *Letters from Yale, Transliterated and Translated.* AbB 9. Leiden.

Thureau-Dangin, F. 1926. Une Lettre de l'époque d'agadé. *RA* 24: 23–29.

BENJAMIN R. FOSTER

OLD TESTAMENT

Humor appears in many forms and serves various functions in the Hebrew Bible, although there are those (notably the philosopher A. N. Whitehead) who question its presence there. Since humor is found to be a universal phenomenon, and it has been recognized in other literature of the ANE (see, e.g., Foster 1974; Rosenthal 1956; van de Walle 1969), one expects to find it in ancient Israelite literature, too, even in texts as serious in purpose as the Hebrew Scriptures.

A. Laughter and Humor

The Bible has no term for humor per se, but it has an etymologically related set of verbs for "to laugh" (*ṣāḥaq, śāḥaq;* e.g., Gen 18:12–13; Qoh 3:4), "to laugh at, scoff" (*śāḥaq;* e.g., Prov 31:25; Job 5:22), and "to laught at, mock" (*śāḥaq;* e.g., Job 30:1; Lam 1:7; *lāʿag;* e.g., Ps 2:4; 59:9; on the etymology see Steiner 1977: 111–12). Note also the *Piʿel* conjugation *śiḥēq/ṣiḥēq,* "to amuse" (e.g., 2 Sam 2:14; Judg 16:25), and *ṣiḥēq,* "to mock" (Gen 39:14, 17). Laughter, both harmless and that directed at a victim, is a sign of humor, reference to laughter in the Bible indicates the presence of humor.

It is instructive to examine the single elaborate episode of laughter. Gen 18:9–15, in which Sarah overhears an angel (or God) tell Abraham that his elderly wife will bear a son. Sarah laughs (v 12); when YHWH challenges Sarah's apparent disbelief (vv 13–14), she denies having laughed, only to be contradicted by YHWH (v 15). Sarah's laughter here can be explained handily by a common theory (cf., e.g., Paulos 1980; Williams 1978) according to which three factors together occasion humor: a sense of the incongruous, a relaxed or lightheaded mood or attitude, and an effect of suddenness or surprise. In conjunction with the third element one finds a characteristic technique of humor: economy of expression.

The episode of Sarah's laughter confirms the workability of the widely held theory of humor. The incongruity is the idea that a postmenopausal woman (v 11) can conceive; second, the mood of the scene is festive and Sarah is uninhibited, thinking she is unnoticed (she doesn't know how far God's ears reach); and third, the joke is unexpected—Sarah catches the conversation by accident. This episode is related to two nearby passages, Gen 17:15–17, where Abraham laughs at the prospect of Sarah conceiving, and 21:1–7, where Sarah says, after giving birth, "God has made laughter for me; every one who hears will laugh over me" (v 6). The implication is that Sarah's incongruous situation would be a source of humor to anyone. As for economy, Sarah laughs at the mere statement that she will give birth. A joke or humorous situation must be immediately perceived. Thinking about or analyzing it, as has been done here, kills the humor.

B. Types of Humor

Humor is notoriously difficult to classify, and definitions of types vary. The remarkably comprehensive treatment by Freud (1938) assumes complex categorization. One can distinguish, with Freud, wit in word from wit in thought and harmless wit from tendentious wit. In a discussion of biblical humor, it might be useful to divide tendentious wit between lowbrow burlesque and the more serious highbrow satire, such as one encounters frequently in the prophets. The categories below have been adopted from convention and for convenience and should not be viewed rigidly.

This is particularly so because biblical humor and wit often intermix a variety of types. Consider, for example, one of the Bible's few extended comical scenes, the Israelite judge Ehud's slaying of the Moabite king Eglon in Judg 3:15–30. Ehud exploits his abnormality, left-handedness, to trick the Moabite and stab him. Eglon, whose name suggests both "bovine" and "rotund," is described as "very fat" (v 17), a visually comic image. Ehud's dagger punctures the obese king blade, hilt, and all (v 22). In a moment of rare scatological humor in the Bible, the fatal blow causes Eglon's bowels to loosen, which, in a sense of high dramatic irony, allows Ehud to escape while the Moabite guards wait around judging by the odor that their king is relieving himself (vv 24–26). Ehud magnifies the comedy through verbal wit as well. In v 19 he tells Eglon he has a "word" (Heb *dābār,* "word, thing") for him—the dagger, of course. The pun involves another wordplay: the Heb expression for the weapon's two "edges" has the basic meaning of "mouths" (v 16; cf. Good 1965: 33). The dagger's "mouths" surely have a "word" to say to the king. The double entendre embodies the joke.

The scene vents hostility toward Moab through its satire of the royal court and its flawed security, and Ehud's role as deft trickster (cf. Niditch 1987) would no doubt entertain an Israelite audience. When comedy is aimed at a victim, it is only amusing to those who are aggressive or hostile toward the butt of the humor. The audience's attitude as well as motives (e.g., laughing with versus laughing at) are important to consider in identifying humor. Haman's parading Mordecai through Susa (Esther 6) may well have pleased the Jews, but it was more than a little distressing to Haman, his wife, and his friends (Esth 6:13).

C. Comedy and the Comical

In classical Greek comedy a dissembling "ironist" (Gk *eirōn*) undoes an overblown "imposter" (Gk *alazōn*). The Bible, in a general way, includes a number of comedies. YHWH through Moses and Aaron exposes Pharaoh as a false god and ironically drowns him in the sea (Exodus 14–15) as he had drowned Hebrew boys in the Nile (Exod 1:22; see further Robertson 1977: 16–32). In a perhaps more obvious example, Mordecai and Esther unmask Haman as the man who would annihilate the Jews, the very antithesis of what the king (now) wants. At the suggestion of the obsequious eunuch Harbona, the king orders that Haman be impaled on the stake he erected for hanging Mordecai, the epitome of poetic justice—and humor (Esth 7:10; see further Beet 1921).

Within such comedies and others are various comical moments. Pharaoh's magicians, who had displayed modest powers in earlier plagues, cannot assist their god-king with the boils because they themselves are afflicted (Exod 9:11). The wicked Ninevites, in Jonah 3, are so eager to repent—itself a ludicrous notion—that they dress their cattle in mourning clothes and force them to fast too (vv 7–8). Not every biblical comedy is comical; cf., e.g., the Tower of Babel (Gen 11:1–9), which is witty—note the play on Babel's name—but not necessarily funny.

The classical form of comedy, as in Aristophanes' plays, is farce. Pure farce would be hard to find in the largely high-minded religious literature of Scripture. There are, however farcical scenes, usually at the expense of an enemy. When Esther exposes Haman's plot to the king, the king storms out in an exaggerated rage. Upon his return he sees Haman fallen on his wife's divan. Although we know Haman was begging for mercy, the king assumes he was making a move on the queen (Esth 7:7–8). The outrage is compounded, and any idea of Haman's to appeal for clemency is quashed. Samson's tying torches to fox tails and burning down the Philistine crops, as well as his massacre of a thousand Philistines with the jawbone of an ass (Judges 15), might also have been farce were it not that these actions led to tragic consequences.

As Landy (1980: 14) has observed, biblical jokes often abort because they loop back into the continuing narrative. Nevertheless, certain characters exhibit comical traits, especially when they repeat a pattern of behavior without developing (cf. Bergson's theory of humor as mechanical conduct, in Sypher 1956: 61–190; cf. Exum and Whedbee 1984: 27). They are caricatured. Pharaoh repeatedly changes his mind the wrong way; Samson ever impetuous, is continually duped; Jonah insists on a theology at odds with God's.

Fables as a genre tend to feature the comical. Consider Balaam's talking ass, who halted at the sight of the angel in spite of Balaam's multiple beatings (Num 22:21–35); or Jotham's fable in which the trees by process of elimination choose the thornbush to be their king (Judg 9:7–15).

D. Forms of Irony

Irony underlies virtually all humor in the Bible, but it will be useful to enumerate some victim-directed types.

1. Sarcasm. Sarcastic speech is not common in the Bible, and, without hearing speech intonation, it is hard to detect. A clear example is Gen 37:19. When Joseph's brothers say, "Here comes this dreamer," lit., "master of dreams," they would seem to deride or deny his alleged talent. Note also Amos 4:4–5: "Come to Bethel, and transgress; to Gilgal, and multiply transgression; bring your sacrifices every morning, your tithes every three days . . . for so you love to do, O people of Israel!"

2. Ridicule. In the biblical ethos, the ignominious crushing of Abimelech's head by the woman of Thebez (Judg 9:53–54) is calculated ridicule; Abimelech had his aide run him through lest people say: "A woman killed him" (cf. 2 Sam 11:21 and Jael's murder of Sisera in Judges 4–5). The most oft-cited example of biblical humor is Elijah's mockery of the Baal prophets in 1 Kgs 18:27: "Cry aloud [i.e., louder, to Baal], for he is a god; either he is musing or he is gone aside, or he is on a journey, or perhaps he is asleep and must be awakened." The humor does not exclude Elijah's seriousness: gods in the ANE may be out of touch (cf. Ps 44:24, where YHWH is said to sleep), so the prophet wants to remove any possible excuses from his opponents when they inevitably fail.

3. Satire. Representation of a target such that the image becomes ironic or ludicrous is most common in the Hebrew Bible in prophetic and other attacks on foreign gods, cults, and kings (e.g., Isa 44:9–20; Ezekiel 29, 31; Nahum 2; Daniel 4). A notable example is the "taunt" of the king of Babylon in Isaiah 14; e.g., "your pomp is brought down to Sheol . . . maggots are the bed beneath you, and worms are your covering" (v 11). The description of the king's humiliating end is rather more vivid than expected and accordingly humorous. Human justice, or just being human, would seem to be satirized in the Garden of Eden when each character in turn passes the guilt to the next (Gen 3:9–13). Many (e.g., Burrows 1970; Ackerman 1981; Fisher 1977: 577) read the story of Jonah as a satire on a prophet.

4. Parody. Some (e.g., Miles 1974–75) interpret Jonah, whose values are the inverse of those of the real prophets, as a prophetic narrative, i.e., as parody. The account of Ahasuerus' silly, irreversible edicts in Esther 1–3 may parody Persian protocol (see, e.g., Greenstein 1987: 227–28).

5. Trickery. A trickster amuses when one is on his or her side. Laban's deceit of Jacob in Genesis 29 would not please an Israelite, but Jacob's "breeding trick" (Gen 30:29–43; cf. Good 1965: 101–3), by which he uses his wits to get rich from wily Laban, would. In the biblical context, Jacob's deception of his father Isaac in Genesis 27 is not humorous because of its moral ambiguity and our sympathy for Isaac (cf. Gammie 1979: 127–28). A gallery of tricksters figures in Judges: Ehud (chap. 3), Jael (chap. 4), Gideon (chaps. 7–8), and Samson (chaps. 14–16).

One can deceive through language, too, as in Samson's riddle (Judges 14) and Abraham's representation of his wife as his sister (Gen 12:10–20; 20)—she was his *half* sister, after all, as the patriarch explains (Gen 20:12; cf. Niditch 1987: 50).

6. Verbal Wit. While verbal trickery manifests wit, far more common is wordplay, especially punning (see WORDPLAY, HEBREW). When Jeremiah addresses the heavens and begins by saying, "Be appalled, O heavens . . ." (Jer 2:12), Heb *šōmmû,* "Be appalled," puns on Heb *šimʿû,* "Hearken," which opens a standard, innocuous formula (e.g., Isa 1:2). His bite is louder than his bark. Wit serves up so-called gallows humor in Gen 40:19. The Heb idiom "to lift the head" means "to elevate (to status)." Joseph announces to the baker his sorry fate by saying: "Within three days Pharaoh will lift up your head—from you!" No doubt the baker would have preferred the more figurative usage.

A contest of wits may characterize such scenes as Abraham's haggling with YHWH over the hypothetical righteousness of Sodom (Gen 18:23–33; see, e.g., Landy 1980: 16–17) and Delilah's deadly game with Samson (Judg 16:4–21).

7. Proverbial Humor. A special case of verbal wit, proverbs emblematize the typical biblical use of humor: occasionally proverbs are humorous—but they also make a serious point. Consider Prov 11:22: "Like a gold ring in a swine's snout/ is a beautiful woman without discretion." The grotesque hyperbole and surrealism of the simile produce the humor. In Prov 26:17 the situation in the simile is comical: "He who meddles in a quarrel not his own/ is like one who takes a passing dog by the ears." Prov 26:18–19 reads: "Like a madman who throws firebrands, arrows, and death,/ is the man who deceives his neighbor and says, 'I am only joking!' " As though following this advice, the Bible is careful with its humor.

Bibliography

Ackerman, J. S. 1981. Satire and Symbolism in the Song of Jonah. Pp. 213–46 in *Traditions in Transformation,* ed. B. Halpern and J. D. Levenson. Winona Lake, IN.

Beet, W. E. 1921. The Humorist Element in the Old Testament. *The Expositor* 22: 59–68.

Burrows, M. 1970. The Literary Character of the Book of Jonah. Pp. 80–107 in *Translating and Understanding the Old Testament,* ed. H. T. Frank and W. L. Reed. Nashville.

Chotzner, J. 1905. *Hebrew Humour and Other Essays.* London.

Crenshaw, J. L. 1978. *Samson.* Atlanta.

Exum, J. C. and Whedbee, J. W. 1984. Isaac, Samson, and Saul: Reflections on the Comic and Tragic Visions. Pp. 5–40 in *Tragedy and Comedy in the Bible,* ed. J. C. Exum and J. W. Whedbee. Semeia 32. Chico, CA.

Fisher, E. J. 1977. The Divine Comedy: Humor in the Bible. *Religious Education* 72: 571–79.

Foster, B. R. 1974. Humor and Cuneiform Literature. *JANES* 6: 69–85.

Freud, S. 1938. Wit and Its Relation to the Unconscious. Pp. 631–803 in *The Basic Writings of Sigmund Freud,* ed. A. A. Brill. New York.

Gammie, J. G. 1979. Theological Interpretation by Way of Literary and Tradition Analysis: Genesis 35–36. Pp. 117–34 in *Encounter with the Text,* ed. M. Buss. Philadelphia and Missoula.

Good, E. M. 1965. *Irony in the Old Testament.* Philadelphia.

Greenstein, E. L. 1987. A Jewish Reading of Esther. Pp. 225–43 in *Judaic Perspectives on Biblical Israel,* ed. J. Neusner et al. Philadelphia.

Landy, F. 1980. Humour in the Bible. *Jewish Quarterly* 29/1: 13–19.

Lang, D. B. 1962. On the Biblical Comic. *Judaism* 11/3: 249–54.

Lasine, S. 1984. Guest and Host in Judges 19: Lot's Hospitality in an Inverted World. *JSOT* 29: 37–59.

Miles, J. A. 1974–75. Laughing at the Bible: Jonah as Parody. *JQR* 65: 168–81.
Niditch, S. 1987. *Underdogs and Tricksters: A Prelude to Biblical Folklore.* San Francisco.
Paulos, J. A. 1980. *Mathematics and Humor: A Study of the Logic of Humor.* Chicago.
Robertson, D. 1977. *The Old Testament and the Literary Critic.* Philadelphia.
Rosenthal, F. 1956. *Humor in Early Islam.* Leiden.
Sandmel, S. 1972. *The Enjoyment of Scripture.* London.
Steiner, R. C. 1977. *The Case for Fricative-Laterals in Proto-Semitic.* AOS 59. New Haven.
Sypher, W., ed. 1956. *Comedy.* Baltimore.
Walle, B. van de. 1969. *L'Humour dans la littérature et dans l'art de l'ancienne Égypte.* Leiden.
Webster, G. 1960. *Laughter in the Bible.* St. Louis.
Williams, J. G. 1978. The Comedy of Jacob: A Literary Study. *JAAR* 46: 208.

EDWARD L. GREENSTEIN

NEW TESTAMENT

Humor exploits the observation of the absurd, the incongruous, and the comical, often poking fun at the foibles of human life. Wit is the quick perception of cleverness and ingenuity. Both humor and wit delight in deviations from what is expected or what is required in various social situations.

They are often expressed by means of verbal subtleties, indirection, and clever turns of phrases. Consequently, humor and wit do not translate well from one culture, age, or language to another. Context can also encourage or stifle our perception of humorous incongruity. When we read the biblical writings as sacred Scripture, enshrined by centuries of liturgical use and theological reflection, we often miss the light touches, sly remarks, witty expressions, and comical elements in them.

Jesus made use of incongruity, drawing pictures of a camel passing through the eye of a needle (Mark 10:25), a beam of wood in an eye (Matt 7:3–5; Luke 6:41–42), straining out a gnat and swallowing a camel (Matt 23:24), whitewashing tombs (Matt 23:27), and washing the outside of a cup while leaving the inside dirty (Matt 23:25). Jesus also applauded the quick repartee of the Syrophoenician woman (Mark 7:24–30). He himself outwitted the chief priests, scribes, and elders (Mark 11:27–33); the Pharisees and Herodians (Mark 12:13–17); and the Sadducees (Mark 12:18–27). While giving instructions on fasting, Jesus comments, "They disfigure *(aphanizousin)* their faces that they may figure *(phanōsin)* in public as fasting" (Matt 6:16).

2 Cor 1:21 plays on the words *Christ* and *christen.* John frequently employs double entendre and words that have multiple meanings: wind-spirit [*pneuma*] (3:8); flowing water-living water (4:11); asleep-dead (11:11–14). The NT also plays on the meaning of names. "Jesus" is derived from the verb "to save" (Matt 1:21). Jesus gives Simon a new name: "You are Peter [Gk *petros;* Aram *kepha*] and on this rock [Gk *petra;* Aram *kepha*] I will build my church" (Matt 16:18). Later, the leader of the early Church is left pounding on the door while the maid, Rhoda, runs to tell the others of his escape from prison (Acts 12:6–16). When the sons of the Jewish high priest Sceva attempt to exorcise demons in the name of Jesus, the unclean spirit answers, "Jesus I know, and Paul I know; but who are you?" (Acts 19:15).

Mark pokes fun at physicians, saying, "And there was a woman who had had a flow of blood for twelve years, and who had suffered much under many physicians, and had spent all that she had, and was no better, but rather grew worse" (Mark 5:25–26).

Zacchaeus, the short tax collector who climbed a sycamore tree to see Jesus, is a comical figure, and one can overhear the delight of early Christians laughing at a chief tax collector (Luke 19:2–5).

The story of the healing of the man born blind makes wonderful use of irony, wit, and sarcasm. When the Pharisees interrogate the man, they challenge him to praise God and discredit Jesus as a sinner. He answers, "Whether he is a sinner, I do not know; one thing I know, that though I was blind now I see" (John 9:25). When the Pharisees ask (for the second time) how the healing occurred, the man answers, "Why do you want to hear it again? Do you want to become his disciples?" (John 9:27). Later, when Jesus asks the man if he believes in the Son of Man, and he responds, "And who is he, sir?" Jesus answers, "You [a man born blind] have seen him!" (John 9:37). The story ends by underscoring the irony that those who could see have chosen blindness, while one who was born blind has received sight and come to faith.

Humor in the Bible celebrates the goodness of God, the world God created, and the life God gives. A foundational incongruity sustains the NT. God enters the world as a baby born to a peasant girl, is unrecognized by all but a few, and redeems the world by dying on a cross. Rejecting wisdom and signs, God chose to save those who believe through the foolishness of preaching (1 Cor 1:21).

Bibliography

Duke, P. D. 1985. *Irony in the Fourth Gospel.* Atlanta.
Hyers, C. 1987. *And God Created Laughter: The Bible as Divine Comedy.* Atlanta.
Trueblood, E. 1964. *The Humor of Christ.* New York.

R. ALAN CULPEPPER

HUMTAH (PLACE) [Heb *ḥumṭâ*]. Town situated in the central hill country of Judah (Josh 15:54), within the same district as Hebron. This settlement is listed among the towns within the tribal allotment of Judah (Josh 15:21–62). Although we know its general location, somewhere in the country between Hebron and Aphekah, a suitable candidate for the ancient town has not been identified.

WADE R. KOTTER

HUNCHBACK. See SICKNESS AND DISEASE.

HUNDRED, TOWER OF THE (PLACE) [Heb *migdal hammēʾâ*]. A tower in the outer wall of Jerusalem protecting the N approach to the city, E of the Fish Gate and the Tower of Hananeel. Nehemiah mentions these two towers in both the restoration (3:1) and procession (12:39) texts. Reference to the Tower of Hananeel by Jeremiah and Zechariah (Jer 31:38; Zech 14:10) affirms the location of the Tower of the Hundred as indicated by Nehemiah. The two towers (overlooking the fish market) were intended to protect the Fish Gate that opened to a ridge leading to the Benjamin Plateau and most likely correspond to the fortress (Heb *bîrâ*) of Neh 7:2 and the later "Hasmonaeon Baris" and Antonia Fortress. Avi-Yonah, on the other hand, places the two towers on either side of the Fish Gate (1954: 240, fig. 1, 241–42).

The name "Tower of the Hundred" suggests to some that a substantial garrison was stationed in the tower, while others would emend the texts to read *meʾâ*, "hundred," as a measurement. Critical issues raised by Vincent have prompted him to omit both of Nehemiah's references to the Tower of the Hundred (Vincent and Steve 1954: 240, 242) and likewise prompted Simons to discount the existence of the tower (1952: 343 and fn. 1).

Bibliography

Avi-Yonah, M. 1954. The Walls of Nehemiah—A Minimalist View. *IEJ* 4: 239–48.

Simons, J. 1952. *Jerusalem in the Old Testament.* Leiden.

Vincent, L.-H., and Steve, M.-A. 1954. *Jerusalem de l'Ancient Testament.* Paris.

DALE C. LIID

HUNTING. See ZOOLOGY.

HUPHAM (PERSON) [Heb *hûpām*]. Var. HUPPIM.

One of the descendants of Benjamin and ancestor of the Huphamites (Num 26:39). The descendants of Benjamin are listed in three geneaological tables: Gen 46:21; Num 26:38–40; and 1 Chr 7:6–12. Confusion from these lists concerning Hupham exists along two lines. First, the Genesis list establishes Hupham as a son of Benjamin, whereas Numbers and 1 Chronicles record him as a grandson or later descendant. The 1 Chronicles list appears more orderly; three sons of Benjamin are listed and their sons in order, Hupham being the son of Ir and grandson of Benjamin. A second difficulty centers in the name "Hupham." The Genesis and 1 Chronicles source uses the name "Huppim" while the Numbers source employs the name "Hupham." Both are supposed to be the same. Jacob Myers suggests that Huppim may be of Arabic origin (Myers *1 Chronicles* AB, 53). Others theorize that the same name has a different Hebrew form. Speiser, on the other hand, suggests that Huppim in the Genesis source should be corrected to Hupham as Numbers (*Genesis* AB, 343).

JOEL C. SLAYTON

HUPPAH (PERSON) [Heb *ḥūppâ*].

A priest who received the sixteenth position in the priestly order of the temple during David's reign (1 Chr 24:13). 1 Chronicles 24 is the only place where Huppah appears in the OT. Therefore, an evaluation of the historical reliability of his appearance depends upon the literary context of 1 Chr 24:1–19. Though generally agreed that this list of priests originated after the Exile, its exact date remains debated. See HAKKOZ. Huppah may represent a Judean individual or priestly family in the late Persian period that the Chronicler has retrojected into the reign of David.

JOHN W. WRIGHT

HUPPIM (PERSON) [Heb *ḥūppîm*]. See HUPHAM (PERSON).

HUR (PERSON) [Heb *ḥûr*].

The name of five persons in the OT.

1. A "king" of Midian (Num 31:8; Josh 13:21). Historically, the five Midianite kings in Numbers 31 may be drawn from a list of place names that form an itinerary through N Arabia and S Transjordan in the Persian period (Knauf 1988: 166–67). "Hur" can be identified, then, with the Nabatean town of Auara/*Ḥaurâʾ* (today al-Ḥumaymah; M.R. 180929).

2. A companion and assistant of Moses and Aaron during the battle against the Amalekites (Exod 17:10, 12), and, together with Aaron, a "substitute judge" while Moses stayed on the mountain of the Lord, Exod 24:14.

3. The grandfather of Bezalel, from the tribe of Judah; it was Bezalel who designed and crafted the paraphernalia of the Israelite cult, according to the P source (Exod 31:2; 35:30; 38:22; 2 Chr 2:1). According to 1 Chr 2:19–20, 50, this Hur was a Calebite, and grandfather of the town of Bethlehem; 1 Chr 4:1, 4 makes him a Judean, and father of Bethlehem. In the original genealogies of the tribe of Judah (1 Chr 2:50; 4:1, 4), the father of Bezalel is not mentioned among Hur's sons. This observation gives rise to the suspicion that Hur #2 (see above) and the "grandfather of Bezalel" both personify a claim to fame and dignity by this Calebite (later Judahite) clan.

4. The father of Rephaiah, head of half the district of Jerusalem (Neh 3:9). Since Heb *ben,* "son of," can precede a family/tribal name as well as a personal name, this Hur may be identical with Hur #3 above (i.e., the name of a prominent clan).

5. The father of Solomon's governor in Ephraim (1 Kgs 4:8). See also BEN-HUR. The note to Hur #4 also applies to this Hur, if one does not prefer Alt's explanation that "the son of Hur" is a designation for the holder of the hereditary fief of Hur (*KlSchr,* 211–12). However, the question of how "Canaanite" (and institutionalized) Solomon's principality actually was is disputed, as is the reliability of 1 Kgs 4:7–9 (*HAIJ,* 205–7).

For Hur #2, 4, and 5 above (if referring to persons), compare Ugaritic, Phoenician, and Aramaic names with *ḥr,* all of which can be connected with the Egyptian god Horus. For Hur #3, the Calebite clan, compare the name *ḥwr* in Sabaic, Minean, Thamudic, and Safaitic (Nabatean *ḥwrw*), meaning "a camel's kid" (Knauf 1988: 89).

Bibliography

Knauf, E. A. 1988. *Midian.* ADPV. Wiesbaden.

ERNST AXEL KNAUF

HURAI (PERSON) [Heb *ḥûray*]. See HIDDAI (PERSON).

HURAM (PERSON) [Heb *ḥûrām*]. **1.** A son of Bela and grandson of Benjamin (1 Chr 8:5). The lists of Benjamin's sons (Genesis 46; Numbers 26) exhibit considerable variations which are difficult to explain. The two lists of Bela's sons (1 Chr 7:7; 8:3–5) also differ quite considerably. The Syriac version of 1 Chr 8:5 reads Hupham, who in Num 26:39 is said to be one of Benjamin's sons. The LXX provides a further variant to the list by reading *Arouam.* Bela is said to have nine sons with Huram in ninth position. However, in Num 26:40 only two sons of Bela are recorded, with five named in 1 Chr 7:7; in both cases Huram is omitted. It is clear that the tradition of Benjamin's sons and their descendants showed considerable variation. Some of the names of Bela's sons (Num 26:39–40; 1 Chr 7:7; 8:3–4) are identical to names of Benjamin's sons in other lists (Gen 46:21; Num 26:38; 1 Chr 7:6; 8:1–2). These genealogical lists in 1 Chronicles are often dated to the postexilic period, which would help to explain their divergences over a long period of time (Braun *1 Chronicles* WBC, 122–28).

2. The king of Tyre. See HIRAM (PERSON).

KEITH W. WHITELAM

HURAMABI (PERSON) [Heb *ḥûrāmʾābî*]. See HIRAM (PERSON).

HURI (PERSON) [Heb *ḥûrî*]. A Gadite who was the father of Abihail, the father of the eleven (or ten; see SHAPHAT) sons named in 1 Chr 5:12–14. Although some have related his name to the cult of the Egyptian god Horus, others have seen a connection with the Heb *ḥāwar,* "to be or grow white," and interpreted it to mean "linen weaver." More likely, perhaps, is the connection with the Akk *ḫūru,* "child" (*IPN,* 38, 221). Neither Huri nor the others named in the Chronicler's genealogy for Gad (1 Chr 5:11–17) appear in other lists of Gadites (Gen 46:16; Num 26:15–18; 1 Chr 12:9–16—Eng 12:8–15).

M. PATRICK GRAHAM

HURRIAN LANGUAGE. See LANGUAGES (HURRIAN).

HURRIANS. An ethnic group attested in the ANE from the 3d to the 1st millennium B.C. During the second half of the 2d millennium B.C. they reached their greatest geographical extent and figured prominently in the history and culture of the Near East. The Hurrians may be the people referred to in the OT as *ḥōrî.* For all that is known concerning their significance, there are major difficulties in studying the Hurrians: (1) their language is imperfectly understood, largely because there are still relatively few extant Hurrian texts; (2) the chronology of the epigraphic and archaeological evidence relating to the Hurrians is not always clear; (3) much of the information concerning the Hurrians comes from non-Hurrian sources, i.e., their neighbors in Mesopotamia, Syria, Egypt, and Anatolia; (4) it is difficult to identify what is Hurrian and what is indigenous in the cultures in which they played a role, because they appear to have assimilated easily to the cultures that they joined. Nonetheless, it is possible to identify their language and many of its characteristics, to trace a general history of the Hurrians, and to discuss certain cultural features associated with Hurrians and Hurrian sites.

A. Hurrian Language
B. History before ca. 1550 B.C.
C. History after ca. 1550 B.C.
D. Hurrians in Mitanni
E. Hurrians of Syria
F. Hurrians in Anatolia
G. Hurrians in Canaan
H. Hurrian Culture
I. The Hurrian Participation in the ANE

A. Hurrian Language

Like many of the ethnic groups entering Mesopotamia, Syria, and Anatolia, the Hurrians chose the local language and script for their records. Thus, most of the records coming from sites known to have had Hurrian populations are written in Akkadian (often a Peripheral variety such as at Nuzi or Amarna), Hittite, or Ugaritic. However, some texts completely in Hurrian have been found at Boghazköy, Mari, Ugarit, and elsewhere. Furthermore, a great many Hurrian words appear in texts written in other ANE languages, and Hurrian personal names, which tend to be "sentence names," provide additional information. On the basis of the available evidence, it is clear that the Hurrian language is an agglutinative language of the Asianic group. Of the known languages of the ANE, it is most closely related to Urartian, which appears later in the history of the Near East, and a number of dialects within the Hurrian language may be discerned (Bush 1968; *SCCNH* 1: 77–89 and 1971; Speiser 1941; Gelb, Purves, and MacRae 1943).

B. History before ca. 1550 B.C.

The Hurrians may have originated in the S Caucasus and Armenia. Their history is normally divided into two phases: before and after ca. 1550 B.C. In the first, they are always somewhat shadowy figures who appear to have migrated S and W from their original homeland into the Near East. Evidence from geographical names places them in the N Transtigris region during the pre-Sargonic period (Astour *SCCNH* 2: 3–68). As early as the Sargonic period of the 3d millennium B.C. they may have been established at Urkiš near Diyarbakr if the letter of Tish-atal, king of Urkiš and Nawar, belongs in fact to the late Akkadian period (Hrouda 1958; Gelb 1956). In fact, Urkiš figures in Hurrian mythology as the seat of Kumarbi, one of the major Hurrian deities. During the Ur III period, Hurrian names appear on texts relating to the regions to the N and E of southern Mesopotamia—areas in which the Ur III kings campaigned and conquered. Some of the individuals with Hurrian personal names are high officials in conquered territories while others are prisoners of war (Gelb 1944). This evidence suggests that the Ur III kings engaged in what are called the "Hurrian Wars."

In the 19th and early 18th centuries B.C. Hurrians appear among the populations of Mari, Chagar Bazar, and

Šemšara. Indeed, some Hurrian texts were found at Mari. During the reign of Šamši-Adad, who consolidated an empire stretching from Assyria to Mari, Hurrians appear among the "hill people" raiding the territories N and E of Assyria as reported by Ishme-Dagan, who campaigned for his father in those regions. Furthermore, there is evidence for Hurrian states in the "High Country" in N Syria at this time. By the time of Zimri-Lim of Mari, Hurrians were well established N of Aleppo. After the fall of Mari to Hammurabi of Babylon the sources are scarce for the regions in which Hurrians are attested. By the 18th and 17th centuries B.C., however, significant numbers of Hurrians are found in the texts of Alalakh Level VII. Furthermore, Hurrian month names were in use in both Alalakh and Yamhad at that time. Thus, it appears that from the pre-Sargonic period through the OB period the Hurrian presence in the Near East grew and expanded S and W into Mesopotamia and Syria. This was possible, particularly during the later OB period, because Babylonian rule did not extend far enough N to encompass the Hurrian areas, the kingdom of Yamhad in Syria was concentrated W of the Euphrates, and Assyria was divided and weak. Therefore the way was clear for Hurrian settlement in upper Mesopotamia and Syria. Indeed, by the time of Ḫattušiliš I and Maršiliš I of the Hittite Old Kingdom in the later 17th century B.C., there are references to a Hurrian threat to the Hittites in Anatolia. Moreover, Muršiliš I fought a battle with the Hurrians on his return march from the sack of Babylon (Kupper *CAH* 2/1: 1–41).

C. History after ca. 1550 B.C.

In the second phase, after ca. 1550 B.C., the Hurrians in the ANE present a startlingly different picture. First, they are present in sizable numbers in upper Mesopotamia (Tepe Gawra, Arraphe, and Nuzi, for example), in Syria (Alalakh, Ugarit, Qatna, and Tunip), and in Anatolia (Kizzuwadna and in the Hittite lands). Hurrians, then, are attested in the area stretching at least from the Zagros Mountains to the Mediterranean and far into Anatolia. Moreover, their influence was felt in Cyprus and in Canaan, though the evidence in these cases is far from clear. Second, the Hurrian states of N Syria and Mesopotamia had unified. This "confederation" was known by a number of names, most famous of which is Mitanni, with its capital at Wašukanni (perhaps Tell Fakhāriyyah; see also MITANNI). Though the precise relationship between the two is not clear, one of the states within Mitanni was the kingdom of Hurri or the Hurri lands, apparently located in the N region of Mitanni, which may have had some claim to primacy within Mitanni. The exact process by which the Hurrians spread so quickly into new areas and Mitanni was formed is not known (Drower *CAH* 2/1: 417–525).

At the same time, a new element appears among Hurrian names. More than 100 Indo-Aryan names, most belonging to kings, princes, or high officials, appear in the records. The Indo-Aryan elements include the names of gods equated with the Vedic gods Indar, Soma, Vaya, the Devas, Svar, and Rta. Also a number of Indo-Aryan numerical terms and terms relating to horses and chariots appear as well in the records. Of particular importance, the nobility in Hurrian areas, those of the chariot-owning class, were called *maryannu,* which probably stems from Indo-European *marya,* "young man or warrior."

The Indo-Aryan element among the Hurrians has been linked to the "Indo-European migrations" of the 2d millennium B.C. The coincidence of the appearance of this element and the changes in Hurrian political organization have been interpreted as a takeover of the Hurrians by an Indo-Aryan ruling class with a chariot-based aristocracy who molded the Hurrians into an efficient military power. On the other hand, the percentage of Indo-Aryan names is very small, Hurrian states did exist before this time, and Mitanni and the other Hurrian centers remained essentially "Hurrian." Therefore it is possible that the Hurrians simply felt a strong Indo-European influence, particularly in the technology of warfare.

D. Hurrians in Mitanni

Mitanni (including the kingdom of Hurri) represents the most important Hurrian political entity in the later 2d millennium B.C. The history of Mitanni is discussed elsewhere; here it is sufficient to note that Mitanni, with its core Hurrian population, expanded rapidly to become the most powerful nation in Syria and Mesopotamia. After a period of hostilities with Egypt during the campaigns of the New Kingdom pharaohs, Mitanni and Egypt entered diplomatic relations during the Amarna period. So Mitanni became a principal participant in the great age of internationalism in the ANE. As a result, the Hurrians of Mitanni were in contact politically and culturally with Egypt, Mesopotamia, the Levant, the Aegean, and S Mesopotamia (Drower *CAH* 2/1: 417–525). The archaeological evidence from such sites as Nuzi and Alalakh demonstrates clearly the effect of these contacts in wall painting, pottery, and glyptic arts (Smith 1965).

After the fall of the kingdom of Mitanni (ca. 1350 B.C.) its territory and Hurrian populace were ruled at times by Assyrians in the E and Hittites in the W. Although the latter ultimately controlled Mitanni as a vassal state, the area was contested by the Assyrians and Hittites until the reign of Shalmaneser I of Assyria (1274–1245 B.C.), who annexed what remained of Mitanni to Assyria. Throughout this period of occupation and conflict, Hittite and Assyrian influence was keenly felt in the Hurrian territories of Mitanni, particularly in the city-states of N Syria that were early on absorbed by the Hittite Empire (Goetze *CAH* 2/2: 1–20; Munn-Rankin *CAH* 2/2: 274–306).

It is important to note that some of the "Neo-Hittite" states that grew up in N Syria and the Taurus Mountains in the wake of the Hittite Empire and the general confusion in the Near East after ca. 1200 were well within the old Mitannian territory. The extent to which the Hurrian population of Mitanni was still present in these areas and their contribution to the culture of the Neo-Hittite states are matters that require further evidence and research. However, it is reasonable to believe that the Hurrian presence was still alive in these areas, especially in light of certain scattered references to individuals with Hurrian personal names in Assyrian records after ca. 1100 B.C. (Gelb 1944).

E. Hurrians of Syria

Mitanni grew to include numerous city-states and territories in which Hurrians were only a part of the population. Moreover, Hurrians were present in areas never controlled by Mitanni, though such Hurrians may have been disposed politically to Mitanni. This was particularly true in Syria where earlier Semitic-speaking peoples still dominated. Evidence for the Hurrians in Syria comes from the records of the Egyptian campaigns in Syria during the New Kingdom and native sources. Repeatedly, the Egyptians met stiff resistance from Syrian cities with pro-Mitannian parties such as Kadesh, Tunip, and Qatna. References to captured *maryannu* warriors in the records of Thutmose III and Amenhotep II demonstrate at least the Hurrian influence in Syria. The actual presence of Hurrians is indicated in that Amenhotep II took booty including Hurrians and their wives during one of his Syrian campaigns (Drower *CAH* 2/1: 417–525).

At the site of Ugarit, Hurrians appear as soldiers and craftsmen. Tablets in Hurrian appear among the archives there along with bilingual glossaries and a lexical text containing four languages: Hurrian, Sumerian, Akkadian, and Ugaritic. Hurrian loan words, personal names, and divine names appear in Ugaritic and Akkadian texts found at Ugarit. Moreover, Hurrian divinities were worshipped at Ugarit (Drower *CAH* 2/2: 130–160; Gelb 1944).

Similarly at Alalakh (Level IV), where Hurrians were attested only minimally in the OB period, Hurrian names abound and Hurrian deities were worshipped. The Amarna texts and other sources provide Hurrian names from Amurru, Neya, Nuhasse, Qatna, and Tunip (Gelb 1944).

F. Hurrians in Anatolia

Kizzuwadna in Cilicia was a vassal state alternately of Mitanni and of the Hittites as the fortunes of the two nations changed in the later 2d millennium B.C. On the basis of personal names associated with Kizzuwadna, this state appears to have been predominantly Hurrian (Goetze 1940).

In the Hittite lands the Hurrians appear to have exerted considerable influence from the beginning of the empire period, and some of what became accepted as "Hittite" in religion, literature, and art may well have had Hurrian origins (Güterbock 1954). Indeed, the dynasty of the Hittites in the Empire period may have been Hurrian. King Urḫi-Tešup and Queen Pudu-ḫepa of that dynasty had Hurrian names. Moreover, the Boghazköy archives produced Hurrian texts, and Hurrian loan words abound in Hittite documents. Furthermore, Hurrian deities figured in the pantheon of the Hittites.

G. Hurrians in Canaan

The evidence for Hurrians in Canaan is far less clear than that for other ANE areas. Among the rulers of Egypt's Syro-Canaanite sphere of influence who appear in the Amarna Letters is one Abdi-Ḫepa of Jerusalem, whose name includes that of the Hurrian goddess Ḫepa (EA 280: 285–90). Other Hurrian names appear on tablets from Tell Ta'annek. The evidence of these personal names has been taken to reflect a Hurrian presence in Palestine (Gelb 1944; Albright *CAH* 2/2: 98–116 and 1935). The Egyptians used the term Khor or Khurri-land for Syria and Canaan, presumably because they perceived all or part of the land as occupied by Hurrians. By the 19th Dynasty Khor was used generally for Asia or "The North." Thutmose IV claimed to have taken "Hurrians" from Gezer and made them temple slaves in Egypt. Most famous of the supposed Hurrians in Palestine are the biblical Horites described as original occupants of the land of Canaan (Albright 1935). Certainly the existence of individuals with Hurrian names suggests at least a Hurrian influence in the region. However, it is far from clear whether the captives from Gezer and the Horites were Hurrians. Instead, their designation may derive from the Egyptian term for the area—"Khurri-land." That is, individuals from "Khurri-land" would be called "Khurri"—Hurrians.

H. Hurrian Culture

As noted above, it is difficult to separate what is Hurrian from what is native in the cultures where Hurrians were present, particularly in the second half of the 2d millennium B.C. when there was such cross-cultural activity among the nations of the Near East. A complex of cultural features is attested throughout known Hurrian areas, however, and these features are thereby associated with the Hurrians.

In religion, the pantheon is reasonably clear. Tešup, a storm god, was the chief male deity, often equated in Syria with Dagan, Adad, and Baal in Syria and Canaan. His consort was Ḫepet/Ḫepa and their son Šarruma. Šeriš and Hurri were two bull gods who were attributed of Tešup. Tilla was also a bull god related to Tešup. Simika was the sun god and Kušukh the moon god. Kumarbi, celebrated in the "Song of Ullikummi," was an elder god replaced by the storm god. In addition to these Hurrian gods, certain Vedic or proto-Indian gods attached to the Indo-Aryan element among the Hurrians appear occasionally (Drower *CAH* 2/1: 417–525; Kupper *CAH* 2/1: 1–41).

A number of the Hurrian texts and Hurrian portions of texts in other languages that survive are ritual and magic texts, attesting to the importance of Hurrian religious practices in areas such as Mari, Ugarit, and the Hittite lands. Apparently Hurrians carried their practices to Syria and Anatolia, where the original forms of the rituals were valued. The Hurrians also translated divination texts from Akkadian and appear to have transmitted their knowledge in this area to Syria and Hittite centers (Kupper *CAH* 2/1: 1–41; Drower *CAH* 2/1: 417–525).

In literature, the mythological text "The Myth of Kumarbi and the Song of Ullikummi" describes an epic cycle of the birth of the gods and their struggles for supremacy. This text is thought to have influenced both Canaanite and later Greek ideas about intergenerational conflict among the gods. The relationship between the Hurrian myth and the Mesopotamian *Enūma eliš* is, itself, unclear. The Hurrians also translated the Epic of Gilgamesh, as did the Hittites (Drower *CAH* 2/1: 417–525).

In the area of art it is far more difficult to identify anything specifically Hurrian. Truly remarkable ivory carvings and glyptic arts originate in sites associated with Hurrians (Ugarit, Alalakh, Ashur, Nuzi) but more of the motifs and crafts involved can be attributed to Hurrians. In both crafts, Syrian, Mitannian, Egyptian, Mesopotamian, and Aegean elements are mixed in the "International Style" of the Amarna period. The fine "Nuzi ware" pottery and Khabur ware are associated with Hurrian sites in the later 2d millennium B.C. (Drower *CAH* 2/1: 417–525; Smith 1965).

Another craft closely associated with Hurrian areas was metallurgy. Bronze, copper, gold, silver, and rarely iron tools and weapons are widely attested in the archaeological and epigraphic record. At least one style of weapon, that in which the blade seems to come out of the mouth of a lion, is found throughout the Hurrian areas (Drower *CAH* 2/1: 417–525).

Yet another craft closely linked to Hurrian areas is glassmaking. West Semitic *mekku* and synonymous Hurrian *eḫlipakku* both refer to "glass," specifically raw material used in making glass vessels. Though glazes were known from early times in the Near East and a recipe for glass-making dates to the end of the OB era, glass itself appears from the 15th century B.C. in Mesopotamia, throughout the Hurrian areas (Ashur, Nuzi, Chagar-Bazar, Ugarit, Alalakh) and in Egypt. Shapes and techniques are the same in all of these areas. The center for this industry appears to have been upper Syria, from which came both the raw materials and the craftsmen who spread glassmaking throughout the Amarna-age world.

In one area of expertise the Hurrians were the masters of the ANE: horse training. Clearly, their society held the chariotry in high esteem. The *maryannu* or "charioteer" class denoted the nobility and high officials throughout the predominantly Hurrian areas and beyond in the Syrian city-states. Not all of the individuals called "charioteers" actually owned and used chariots in war. Instead, the title evolved into an honorific term used for the elite of the society. It is not surprising, then, that hippic texts are found at Nuzi, Boghazköy, Ugarit, Alalakh, and Ashur. From Boghazköy in Anatolia are the famous Kikkuli texts named for their author, the Hurrian horse trainer from the land of Arraphe (where Nuzi was located) E of the Tigris (Drower *CAH* 2/1: 417–525; O'Callaghan 1948).

For discussion of typical Hurrian society, see also NUZI. Among the special characteristics worth noting here are the position of women and slaves. Women in Hurrian society enjoyed considerably more freedom than in other areas of the Near East. They could own property, enter into contracts, litigate, and participate independently in most areas of public life. Similarly, slaves, though bound to masters or households, had considerable economic and legal rights.

I. The Hurrian Participation in the ANE

Once considered the base population of the N part of the ANE, the Hurrians clearly entered the Near East at a comparatively late date. Their political influence was enormous, as they dominated N Mesopotamia and portions of Syria and Anatolia for three centuries and some areas for even longer. The cities and nations in which they lived were linked by trade and conquest during the late 2d millennium B.C., a crucial period in the cultural history of the Near East. However vague their own contribution to Near Eastern culture is, there is ample evidence for their role as transmitters of literature, art, and technology during this all-important era (Speiser 1953).

As for their role vis-à-vis the OT, the customs documented in the Nuzi tablets were long held forth as evidence for Hurrian influence, particularly on the patriarchal narratives. For a discussion of this issue, see also NUZI.

Bibliography

Albright, W. F. 1935. The Horites in Palestine. In *From the Pyramids to Paul.* New York.
Bush, F. W. 1968. *A Grammar of the Hurrian Language.* Diss. Brandeis.
Diakonoff, I. M. 1971. *Hurrisch und Urartaisch.* Munich.
Gelb, I. 1944. *Hurrians and Subarians.* SAOC 22. Chicago.
———. 1956. New Light on Hurrians and Subarians. In *Studi Orientalistici in onore di Giorgio Levi della Vida* 1. Rome.
Gelb, I.; Purves, P. M.; and MacRae, A. A. 1943. *Nuzi Personal Names.* OIP 57. Chicago.
Goetze, A. 1940. *Kizzuwadna and the Problem of Hittite Geography.* Yale Oriental Series Researches 22. New Haven.
Güterbock, H. 1954. The Hurrian Element in the Hittite Empire. *JWH* 2: 383–94.
Hrouda, B. 1958. *Wassukanni, Urkis, Šubat-Enlil.* MDOG 90. Berlin.
O'Callaghan, R. T. 1948. *Aram Naharaim.* AnOr 26. Rome.
Smith, W. S. 1965. *Interconnections in the Ancient Near East.* New Haven.
Speiser, E. A. 1941. *An Introduction to Hurrian.* AASOR 20. Cambridge, MA.
———. 1953. The Hurrian Participation in the Civilizations of Mesopotamia, Syria and Palestine. *JWH* 1: 311–27.

MARTHA A. MORRISON

HUSBAND. See FAMILY.

HUSHAH (PERSON) [Heb *ḥûšâ*]. Var. HUSHATHITE. The son of Ezer (1 Chr 4:4), who appears to have been one of the sons of Hur. The name Hushah is then eponymously applied to a town of Judah, which was possibly first settled as an Israelite town by Ezer the son of Hur. It was the home of two of David's notable men, Mebunnai (2 Sam 23:27) and Sibbecai (2 Sam 21:18). Sibbecai is described as having killed Saph, one of the descendants of the giants, and was eventually made a commander in David's army (1 Chr 27:1, 11).

The village of Hushah is strategically located about 6 km W of Bethlehem at the top of a ridge that gave access to Bethlehem and Jerusalem from the Elah valley in the Shephelah (M.R. 162124). While Bethlehem overlooked the wilderness to the E from the Judean ridge, Hushah overlooked the Shephelah or lower hill country to the W. Hushah was in the path of the Philistine expansion from the coast as the Philistines tried to penetrate into the Judean hill country, and it was probably down the Hushah ridge that David went to inquire about his brothers (who were facing the Philistines) and which ultimately led to David's confrontation with Goliath (1 Samuel 17).

Bibliography

Monson, J. 1983. *The Land Between.* Jerusalem.

DALE C. LIID

HUSHAI (PERSON) [Heb *ḥûšay*]. **1.** A member of the Archite branch of the tribe of Benjamin (2 Sam 15:32).

During the reign of David he served as the king's *rēʿeh,* commonly translated as "friend" or "companion" although those terms are perhaps too informal in tone (2 Sam 15:37; 16:16, 17). In 1 Chr 27:33 Hushai is listed with other officers in David's service (there termed *rēaʿ hammelek*). On the possible origin of his name and office, see McCarter (*2 Samuel* AB, 371–72).

Hushai played a prominent role in the unfolding of events surrounding Absalom's rebellion. With torn clothes and dirt on his head, he met David as the latter was fleeing the city (2 Sam 15:32). David did not allow him to flee with him, but instead requested that Hushai return to the city. There he was to swear allegiance to Absalom and, having gained Absalom's confidence, he was to frustrate the advice of Ahithophel and be an informant reporting to Zadok and Abiathar (2 Sam 15:33–37). Absalom mocked Hushai's lack of loyalty to David, but Hushai forcefully pledged his commitment to serve Absalom (2 Sam 16:16–19). Absalom was convinced, for he later requested Hushai to evaluate Ahithophel's plan to pursue David immediately. Hushai countered by suggesting a delay during which time Absalom could rally a larger military force to counter the skill of David as a military commander. His advice was accepted over that of Ahithophel. The narrator comments that this sequence of events was exactly what Yahweh had ordained (2 Sam 17:5–14). Hushai reported the proceedings to Zadok and Abiathar, and David was able to gain a strategic advantage (2 Sam 17:15ff.). Hushai's role, if any, in the rest of the events of Absalom's rebellion is not reported.

2. The father of Baana (1 Kgs 4:16). He is not connected with Hushai #1, but many commentators regard them as the same person. Hushai's son Baana was from the region of Asher and Bealoth, and is listed as one of twelve deputies Solomon appointed to raise the monthly provisions for the royal household.

RICHARD W. NYSSE

HUSHAM (PERSON) [Heb *ḥušām*]. The third ruler in the Edomite king list (Gen 36:34f.; 1 Chr 1:45f.). Opinions vary as to date of this list (Gen 36:31–39). Suggestions range from the 11th century B.C. (Weippert 1982: 155) through the 8th to 6th centuries B.C. (Bennett 1983: 16) to the 6th–5th centuries B.C. (Knauf 1985a). Scholars tend to agree, however, that the succession scheme of this list is artificial and that, in all likelihood, the rulers listed in it were contemporaries (Bartlett 1972: 27; Weippert 1982: 155). The name is attested in Arabic (*Ḥusām,* Safaitic and Classical) and means "sword" (Knauf 1985a: 246). One may also compare the Arabic names *Khushām/Khushaim,* "Little Nose" (Harding 1971: 189). This comparison, however, is less likely, since Arabic *š* would require to be represented by Hebrew *ś.*

Husham is said to stem "from the country of the Temanite" (Gen 36:34). A "Temanite" could be an inhabitant of Teman, or of the city of Tayma in NW Arabia. Since Teman as the name of a country seems to be another name for Edom, it is more likely that Husham immigrated into Edom from the territory of Tayma (Knauf 1985a: 249f.; 1987). This immigration may be reflected in Pliny's note (*Geog.* 6.28 [32]. 157): *Nabataeis Thimaneos iunxerunt veteres,* "The ancients linked the Temanites with the Nabateans," the Nabateans being the descendants of a Qedarite clan which gained control over Edom in the course of the late 6th to early 5th century B.C. (Knauf 1985b: 103–8).

Bibliography

Bartlett, J. R. 1972. The Rise and Fall of the Kingdom of Edom. *PEQ* 104: 26–37.

Bennett, C.-M. 1983. Excavations at Buseirah (Biblical Bozrah). Pp. 9–17 in *Midian, Moab and Edom,* ed. J. F. A. Sawyer and D. J. A. Clines. Sheffield.

Harding, G. L. 1971. *An Index and Concordance of Pre-Islamic Arabian Names and Inscriptions.* Toronto.

Knauf, E. A. 1985a. Alter und Herkunft der edomitischen Königsliste Gen 36, 31–39. *ZAW* 97: 245–53.

———. 1985b. *Ismael.* 1st ed. ADPV. Wiesbaden.

———. 1987. Supplementa Ismaelitica 10. Rehoboth ha-Nahar. *BN* 38/39: 44–49.

Lemaire, A. 1988. Hadad l'Édomite ou Hadad l'Araméen? *BN* 43: 14–18.

Weippert, M. 1982. Remarks on the History of Settlement in Southern Jordan during the Early Iron Age. Pp. 153–62 in *Studies in the History and Archaeology of Jordan 1,* ed. A. Hadidi. Amman.

ERNST AXEL KNAUF

HUSHATHITE [Heb *ḥūšātî*]. See HUSHAH (PERSON).

HUSHIM (PERSON) [Heb *ḥūšîm*]. Var. SHUHAM. **1.** The only descendant of Dan (Gen 46:23) mentioned in the genealogy of Jacob in Genesis 46. In Num 26:42 again, only one descendant of Dan is mentioned, but here he is called Shuham (possibly resulting from the transposition of the letters *ḥet* and *šin*).

2. Descendants or a descendant of Aher (1 Chr 7:12). The MT reads Heb *bĕnê,* "sons," but only mentions Hushim, which makes the plural form of the name itself ambiguous. The larger group to which these Hushites belong is a matter of dispute, too. As the MT stands, they are listed among the Benjaminites (1 Chr 7:6–12). In Genesis 46 the genealogy of Benjamin precedes that of Dan and is in turn followed by that of Naphtali, while in 1 Chronicles 7 Benjaminites precede the sons of Naphtali, which leads commentators to suggest that the text be emended to connect the Hushim to Dan. In that case, the Hushites named in 1 Chr 7:12 would be the same as #1 above. For contrasting views, see Braun (*1 Chronicles* WBC, 106–7) and Williamson (*1 & 2 Chronicles* NCBC, 78).

3. One of the wives of Shaharaim of the descendants of Benjamin (1 Chr 8:8, 11). Shaharaim divorced her as well as Baara before he had additional children in Moab, presumably with Hodesh, his third named wife. Hushim was the mother of Abitub and Elpaal. The genealogy is continued through Elpaal.

RICHARD W. NYSSE

HUSN, EL- (M.R. 232210). A cave site in Jordan containing remains of the EB of both domestic occupation and funereal activity.

A. Identification and Excavation of the Site

This cave site, situated some 22 km N of Jerash, Jordan, takes its name from the nearby modern town of el-Ḥuṣn. It lies just 1 km S of Tell el-Ḥuṣn, one of the largest mounds in Jordan. The mound remains unexcavated, although past surveys seem to indicate that it was important throughout the Bronze and Iron Ages. The cave itself is described as an amorphous hole in the ground whose roof had collapsed in antiquity. Thus, whether it was originally a cave or a shaft tomb is impossible to determine. The disturbance to the chamber was such that the excavation uncovered no stratification, although on the basis of the pottery it was clear that there were two periods of use. The tomb was excavated by G. L. Harding. A more extensive comparative analysis of the finds was done by B. S. J. Isserlin (Harding and Isserlin 1953).

B. History of the Site

There were two periods of use in this cave, a domestic EB I level (Harding thought it was EB II) and an EB IV burial interment. The former consisted entirely of sherds of two distinct pottery types: heavy, coarse storejars with "grain wash" decoration, plain ledge handles, and flaring rims; and undecorated storejars and gritty holemouth jars that may have been cooking pots (Harding and Isserlin 1953: fig. 5). Harding's postulation that this level represented a domestic usage of the cave is probably correct, on the basis of the cooking pots. The skeletal remains intermixed with the pottery must, therefore, reflect a burial interment in the EB IV period. The ceramic remains of the latter period consisted of intact vessels of a variety of types well known from other EB IV burial sites. Two copper pins with convoluted head and a flint implement round out the burial offerings.

The EB IV corpus comprised mostly storejars, amphoriskoi, and one-handled jugs, although it also included teapots, cups, bowls, and a four-spouted lamp (Harding and Isserlin 1953: figs. 1–4). Storejars were of both the round-based and flat-based type with the latter showing the typical envelope ledge-handle. There were about 50 vessels in all. What has always been notable about the el-Ḥuṣn assemblage is its distinctive style of vase painting. Generally referred to as "trickle-paint," this red paint and/or red slip decoration is characterized at el-Ḥuṣn by vertical and horizontal bands, as well as by vertical rows of wavy or straight lines on the upper shoulder.

The corpus under discussion has been variously categorized. R. Amiran (1960) assigned the el-Ḥuṣn assemblage to ceramic Families B (round-based jars and single-point incision) and C (red paint and slip). In Dever's geographical-cultural classification, el-Ḥuṣn belongs to Family (NC) North Central (1980: 45–47). Contrary to Amiran, it is clear that the red-slip and red-paint decoration continues a well-known EB tradition and is therefore the mark of early EB IV (Richard 1980). Although in a new schema (EB IVA-B-C) the el-Ḥuṣn assemblage was dated to the EB IVB period (Dever 1973; Richard 1980), it now appears highly likely that the several distinctive ceramic "families" in this period may well be more regional than chronological. There is in any case a great deal of overlap (Richard and Boraas 1988).

C. Sociocultural Considerations

Recent excavation and analysis suggest that "trickle-painted" ware may represent a "fine ware" produced at certain sites for dissemination to other villages in the region (Falconer 1987; Hess 1984). If so, then production and exchange of this product are indicated primarily in the following regions: from Tiberius to Beth-shan and Tel ʾArtal (W of the Jordan river), and E of the Jordan from el-Ḥuṣn S to the Jordan valley settlements (opposite Beth-shan) of Tell el-Hayyāt and Tell ʾAbu en-Niʾaj. "Trickle-paint" ware is an important diagnostic trait for cross-cultural comparisons. The discovery recently of this distinctive decorative type as far S as Khirbet Iskander (Richard fc.) not only provides a chronological link with the above sites but likewise widens exchange to an interregional orbit.

This evidence for trade among settlement sites in the EB IV may be added to a growing list of new elements to consider in any evaluation of the sociopolitical organization of the population. This "dark age" (ca. 2350–2000 B.C.) was once thought to be a nomadic interlude. It is now evident that cultural adaptation in the EB IV included a range of adaptive strategies. Following EB III, it is true, there was a shift from a complex urban society to a less specialized nonurban sociopolitical framework; however, the latter is characterized not only by seasonal settlements of pastoral nomads but likewise by permanent towns and villages (Richard 1987).

Bibliography

Amiran, R. 1960. The Pottery of the Middle Bronze I in Palestine. *IEJ* 10: 204–25.

Dever, W. G. 1973. The EB IV-MB I Horizon in Transjordan and Southern Palestine. *BASOR* 210: 37–63.

———. 1980. New Vistas on the EB IV ('MB I') Horizon in Syria-Palestine. *BASOR* 237: 35–64.

Falconer, S. A. 1987. Village Pottery Production and Exchange: A Jordan Valley Perspective. Pp. 251–68 in *Studies in the History and Archaeology of Jordan 3,* ed. A. Hadidi. Amman.

Harding, G. L., and Isserlin, B. S. J. 1953. An Early Bronze Cave at El Husn. *Palestine Exploration Fund Annual* 6: 1–13.

Hess, O. 1984. Middle Bronze I Tombs at Tel ʾArtal. *BASOR* 253: 55–60.

Richard, S. 1980. Toward a Consensus of Opinion on the End of the Early Bronze Age in Palestine-Transjordan. *BASOR* 237: 5–34.

———. 1987. The Early Bronze Age: The Rise and Collapse of Urbanism. *BA* 50: 22–43.

———. fc. Excavations at Khirbet Iskander, 1987: Fourth Preliminary Report. *BASORSup* 26.

Richard, S., and Boraas, R. S. 1988. The Early Bronze IV Fortified Site of Khirbet Iskander, Jordan: Third Preliminary Report, 1984 Season. *BASORSup* 25: 107–30.

SUZANNE RICHARD

HYDASPES (PLACE) [Gk *Hydáspēs*]. The name of a river mentioned in Jdt 1:6 along with the Euphrates, Tigris, and the plain of Elymais (Elam). However, no river by that name is attested in this region. In Greek literary sources the name renders (Sanskrit) *Vitasta* (=modern Jhelum), a tributary of the Indus in NW India, well known since Alexander's battle against Porus on its banks (cf. Arrian *Anab.* 5.9–18). Given the unconventional geography (and history) of the book of Judith, the above association is not unexpected. If the author had in mind more than the name of a river somewhere in the distant E, he may have meant the Choaspes (modern Karkheh), which flowed past Susa (Herodotus 1.188; 5.49). Corruption in the Gk text, though not impossible, seems unlikely.

Albert Pietersma

HYENA. See ZOOLOGY.

HYKSOS.

HYKSOS. The Greek form of an Egyptian word (Eg *ḥk3[w] ḫ3s[w]t*) meaning "ruler(s) of foreign land(s)," i.e., of alien origin (Redford 1970), used to refer to nonnatives who ruled over portions of Lower Egypt as the 15th Dynasty in the first half of the 2d millennium B.C. (the "Second Intermediate Period").

HISTORY

Folk etymology of the 4th–3d centuries B.C. incorrectly derived the Eg term from *š3sw*, "shepherd" (thus "shepherd kings"), and from *ḥ3k*, "plunder, captivity" (thus "captive shepherds"; *AgAp* 1.14 §§82–83). Neither of these latter writings occurs in contemporary New Kingdom sources, and are best attributed to the eisegesis of Judeo-pagan polemics in the Hellenistic period. The translation of Manetho's *anthrōpoi to genos asēmoi* (cited in *AgAp* 1.14 §75) as "men of obscure race" diverted earlier scholarship into a fruitless search for unlikely candidates: Arabs (Redford 1986b: 278, n. 77); Indo-Iranians (Albright 1957: 30–31; *YGC*, 57, n. 12); Hittites (Duncan 1931: 69–72); Hurrians (Engberg 1939; Helck 1972: 100–6); Hebrews (*AgAp* 1.14 §§91–92); or a mysterious horse-breeding aristocracy from Asia (Mayani 1956). In fact, *asēmoi* is simply the rendering of Eg *ẖsi*, "vile," in Manetho's Demotic source (Redford 1986b: 242).

A. Ethnic Composition
B. Advent and Extent of Rule
C. The Fifteenth Dynasty
D. Administration
E. Religion and Culture
F. Expulsion
G. Later Traditions

A. Ethnic Composition

Although human skeletal remains from excavations at Tel ed-Dabᶜa reportedly exhibit European traits (Jungwirth 1970), too few specimens have survived and the analysis is too premature to inspire confidence (Kemp *AESH*, 157). One is therefore thrown back on an attempt to establish the linguistic affiliation of the newcomers. Contemporary texts from Egyptian sources call them *ᶜ3mw*, a term roughly designating any "Asiatic," but used especially of those who spoke a W Semitic, "Amorite" tongue (Alt 1961; Redford 1986a); and for most of the score of "Hyksos" names surviving, a W Semitic, "Amorite" etymology may be convincingly proposed (Astour 1965: 94, n. 4; Van Seters 1966: 181–83; Ward 1975; Kempinski 1985). In corroboration may be viewed the notice in the Epitome of Manetho (*apud* Africanus) that the 15th Dynasty was "Phoenician" in origin (= Eg *Ḫ3rw/Fnhw*, general terms for the Levantine littoral; Waddell 1940: 90; Redford 1986b: 200, n. 249).

B. Advent and Extent of Rule

The sole, connected account of the Hyksos takeover of power in Egypt comes from Manetho (Waddell 1940: 78–81), who describes it in terms of a destructive invasion which took place under a king called Tutimaeus (plausibly identified with the Djed-mose of TC IX, 9 [Redford 1970: 2, n. 1; Helck 1975: 43]). Since World War II, new evidence has revealed that a sizable proportion of the Egyptian population in the 13th Dynasty comprised an immigrant Asiatic element, convincing a number of scholars to construe the Asiatic assumption of power as a peaceful fulfillment of self-determination on the part of the majority of the population of the E delta. The alleged violence associated with this rise to power could be attributed to the anti-Asiatic bias in Manetho's sources, a bias stemming from much later Assyrian and Persian invasions of Egypt (Säve-Söderbergh 1951; Van Seters 1964; 1966). On the other hand, that the Hyksos perpetrated wanton devastation was part of the record of the texts contemporaneous with their occupation (Kamose I, 4–5, 13); and their stubborn refusal to acculturate themselves militates against the postulate of a prior period of peaceful infiltration and assimilation (Redford 1970).

All sources agree that the Hyksos rulers established their headquarters (and later capital) at Avaris (= Egyptian *Ḥwt-wᶜrt*, "Mansion of the Desert Tract [or Department (?)]"; Kees 1961: 197) on the easternmost of the delta branches, a site already patronized by Egyptian kings (Habachi 1974; Helck 1975: 48; Bietak 1984a), now identified as Tell el-Dabᶜa, ca. 5 miles NNE of modern Faqus (Bietak 1975a; 1975b; 1979). The sources also agree that Memphis was also taken; a tradition in Eusebius (*Chron.* [ed. Helm] pp. 32, 44) credits Apophis (Epafus/Apis) with having founded Memphis, perhaps a recollection of his residence there. The environs of the old capital and Saqqara were pillaged for their monuments both to adorn Avaris and to be transported abroad (Weinstein 1975: 9–10; Helck 1976a). Find-spots of MB II A-B horizon (first half of 2d millennium B.C.) are confined to the E half of the delta (Tell el-Yehudiyeh, Heliopolis, Farash, Tell ed-Dabᶜa, Tell el-Maskhuta, El-Salhiya, Sahaba, etc.) and betray the presence of an unassimilated Asiatic population (Kemp *AESH*, 156–57), perhaps partly nomadic (Gardiner 1946: pl. 6:36ff.). But textual evidence indicated that Hyksos hegemony extended over Middle Egypt as far as Hermopolis (Kamose II, 16) and Kusae (Kamose I, 6). While it is questionable whether the Hyksos ever threatened or took Thebes (as Vernus 1982), inscribed objects found in Upper Egypt mentioning Sheshy (Edfu: Engelbach 1921), Khayan (Gebelein: Von Beckerath 1965: 271), and Apophis (Gebelein, Su-menu: Von Beckerath 1965: 273; James 1961) may indicate local acknowledgment of their authority. Certainly Kamose of the 17th Dynasty seems to confess to vassal status at the outset of his career (Kamose II, 1ff.).

The alleged "world-empire" of the Hyksos, postulated

by scholars of an earlier generation on the basis of small objects with royal names found in Crete, Baghdad, and Boghazköy, has long since been rejected. These undoubtedly must be construed as diplomatic gifts or as plunder from Levantine cities centuries later (Von Bissing 1936–37; Stock 1963; Helck 1979: 45–48). But the distribution of Hyksos inscriptions does demarcate a sphere of influence. In Asia scarabs and seal impressions are found sporadically along the Palestinian coast and as far N as Shikmona (Giveon 1965; 1974; 1981), but no farther (Vercoutter 1954: 78), while a passage in the second Kamose stela refers to "300 ships of new wood filled with . . . all the fine products of Retenu" (Kamose II, 13–15). Such evidence might betoken nothing but simple commerce, but Apophis' dedication to "[Seth], lord of Avaris" who had "placed all lands under his feet" sounds like a record of foreign conquest late in the Hyksos period (Helck 1975: 55). The same impression is conveyed by Apophis' epithets on the scribal palette of Atchu: "stout-hearted on the day of battle, with a name greater than any king's, one who protects strange lands which have never (even) seen him" (Helck 1975: 58). In Nubia numerous scarabs and seal impressions are found, especially in Kerma (Giveon 1983), evidence surely of a lively trade with the Sudan via the oases of the Sahara desert, with overtones of Hyksos suzerainty (Stadelmann 1965a; 1965b; Redford 1977). While some trade with Cyprus (Merrillees 1970; 1971; 1975) and diplomatic contacts with the Aegean (Helck 1979: 48–49) cannot be denied, to postulate Hyksos influence on the shaft graves at Mycenae is too daring (Huxley 1961: 36–37).

C. The Fifteenth Dynasty

With very few exceptions Hyksos royal names have come to us either on minor objects in contemporary hieroglyphic transcription or in garbled Greek forms from over one millennium later. Of the first, the number of Hyksos royal scarabs are too meager and their style too unreliable to establish a sequence of kings from such primary material. Moreover, no contemporary king-list has survived from the Hyksos period, and the six names in the Turin Canon of Ramesside times (13th century B.C.) are all missing except for the last, *H3mwdy*.

From the various versions of the Epitome of Manetho (Waddell 1940) the following names (with variants) emerge for the 15th Dynasty and can be compared with the 17th Dynasty names recounted by Manetho (see Table 1).

Table 1

15th Dynasty		17th Dynasty
Josephus' version	Africanus' version	Eusebius' version
Salitis 19 yrs	Saites 19 yrs	Saites 19 yrs
Bnon 44 yrs	Bnon 44 yrs	Bnon 40 yrs
Apachnan 36 yrs 7 mo	Pachnan 61 yrs	———
Apophis 61 yrs	Staan 50 yrs	———
Iannas 50 yrs 1 mo	Archles 49 yrs	Archles 30 yrs
Assis 49 yrs 2 mo	Apophis 61 yrs	Apophis 14 yrs

As can be clearly seen from the table, some of these names have been reduplicated in Manetho's 17th Dynasty, owing to his inability to accommodate contemporaneity in his linear king-list (Redford 1986b: 240). Common to all are the three personal names Salitis (Saites), Bnon, and Apophis. Of the five remaining, "Staan" can plausibly be derived from "Iannas" through an orthographic error, while "Archles," through position and length of reign, can be identified with "Assis." The total is thus reduced to six in agreement with the Turin Canon, but the only two which can with certainty be equated with contemporary royal names are Iannas (Bietak 1981) and Apophis. A major discrepancy concerns the position of Apophis (fourth *apud* Josephus, sixth *apud* Africanus); this can now be resolved in favor of Africanus as a result of the discovery of a doorjamb of Khayan from Tell el-Dabᶜa. It commemorates "the king's eldest son," whose name is very likely to be read *Ynss* (= Iannas). Iannas (Staan) thus occupies fourth position, and the fact that his father and predecessor was Khayan rules out the order in Josephus.

Of names surviving from earlier pharaonic times, "Sharek" (mentioned in an 8th-century genealogy used to date a high priest of Ptah) *may* be Salitis (Albright's attempt to identify the latter with a "Caludi" [= *Za-a-lu-ti*], chief of the Umman-manda in a 17th-century Hittite text [1957] has gained no acceptance). "Apep" in the same genealogy (appearing one generation later than Sharek) is clearly Apophis. The *ḫ3mwdi* who fills the sixth and only surviving line in the Turin Canon's list of Hyksos rulers remains problematical. The name occurs in none of the inscribed objects naming kings which come from the Hyksos period itself; and the only recourse, if one wishes to treat the name seriously, is to identify its bearer arbitrarily with one of the attested kings. But the question remains unresolved as to whether the Turin Canon recorded the throne names of the Hyksos kings or their birth names.

Contemporary finds have yielded large numbers of seals and a few stone monuments of the 15th Dynasty rulers. From these, the following cartouche-bearing names and their known titularies can be elicited (see in general Von Beckerath 1965; Helck 1975; Kempinski 1985):

1. The Good God, *M3ᶜ-ib-rᶜ*, the son of Re, Sheshy.
2. The Good God, *Mr-wsr-rᶜ*, the son of Re, Yaᶜḳob-har (Yeivin 1959; Giveon 1981).
3. Horus: He-who-encompasses-the-lands; the Good God, *Swsr.n-rᶜ*, son of Re, Khayan.
(4. The Eldest king's-son, Yansas-? [Bietak 1981; Kempinski 1985].)
5. The Good God, Lord of the Two Lands, Master of the cult, *ᶜ3-sḥ-rᶜ*, the son of Re [. . .] (but see Bietak 1984a).
6. The Good God, Lord of the Two Lands, *Nb-ḫpš-rᶜ*, the son of Re, Apophis.
7. Horus: who-pacifies-the-Two-Lands, the Good God, *ᶜ3-ḳnn-rᶜ*, the son of Re, Apophis.
8. The King of Upper and Lower Egypt, *ᶜ3-wsr-rᶜ*, the son of Re, Apophis.

The position of 1 and 2, although not their relative order, is guaranteed by the style of their scarabs, the lack of sophistication in their carving, and the absence of monumental inscriptions. The order 3–4 is confirmed by the doorjamb from Tell el-Dabᶜa (see above). That 8 is close to, or at the end of, the list is demonstrated by the fact that he was the opponent of Kamose of the 17th Dynasty, within a decade of the final expulsion of the Hyksos (Habachi 1972). Finally, it is very likely that 6 and 7, both rarely attested, are earlier forms of 8, and that we are dealing with a single Apophis (Redford 1967: 44, n. 90).

A relatively small number of scarabs provides a group of names, not in cartouche, but preceded by the title *ḥk3ḫ3s(w)t*, "foreign ruler":

1. Yat (?) (Giveon 1980: 90–91)
2. ᶜAper-ᶜanat (Martin 1971: no. 318)
3. ᶜAnat-har (Von Beckerath 1965: 279; Martin 1971: nos. 349–50)
4. User-ᶜanat (Petrie 1917: XXI, D 15.1)
5. Khayan (Von Beckerath 1965: 272)
6. Samḳuna (Martin 1971: no. 1453)

These are sometimes classed as "Lesser Hyksos," and are construed as a line of rulers either earlier than the 15th Dynasty (Hayes, *CAH* 2/2; Albright 1965: 448–49 [distinguishing 3 groups]; *YGC*, 153, n. 1) or following them (references in Redford 1967: 43). But in light of the unanimous tradition that Hyksos domination of Egypt began with Salitis and ended in the reign of Apophis or shortly thereafter, the hegemony of these rulers would have to be located outside Egypt (in contradiction of the provenience of the majority of their scarabs within Egypt). It is much more likely that this group is to be understood as chieftains of small enclaves within the delta, subservient in a quasi-feudal manner to the kings of the 15th Dynasty.

D. Administration

Very little is known about how the Hyksos kings governed their domain. The plethora of seals mentioning "treasurers" (*imy-r sḏ3t* [or *ḫtmt*]; Helck 1975: 57.83; Labib 1936: pl. 6; Säve-Söderbergh 1951: 65; Martin 1971: nos. 479–508, 904–912; Ward 1976) has suggested to some a continued strength in that branch of the government (Helck 1958: 79–80). While attractive, it remains unprovable whether native Egyptian dynasts, as well as Asiatic chiefs, were subordinated as a species of "feudal" vassal to the Hyksos king, modeling their names on his (Stadelmann 1965a: 65). Certainly there were many Egyptians who cooperated with the Hyksos (cf. Kamose II, 17–18) and allowed garrisons to be stationed in their towns (cf. Kamose I, 14).

E. Religion and Culture

Initially, it would appear, the ruling class among the invaders retained the religion and social customs they had brought with them, and the rank and file indeed probably never gave them up. Until the reign of Khayan there is a notorious carelessness in the transcription into Egyptian of Hyksos personal names (Giveon 1976; 1981), as though the conquerors cared little how the conquered represented them. At Avaris they maintained a royal ancestor cult of Amorite origin (Redford 1986b: 199–201), constructed temples on Asiatic, not Egyptian, patterns (Bietak 1979: 249–50), and continued to practice non-Egyptian inhumations, with sacrifices of the ass and sheep (Bietak 1979: pl. 15A; Leclant 1986: 245–46). Hyksos seals suggest the worship of a hero-god of the Baal type and a female deity of the Qodsu type (Stadelmann 1967: 14–20). The former came shortly to be identified with the Egyptian Seth, a god renowned locally for his physical strength and wild temperament, who had long been worshipped in Avaris and the E delta (Habachi 1974; Stadelmann 1965b; Helck 1975: 48) and was to be associated with the Hyksos in New Kingdom tradition and folklore (Gardiner 1931: 85–86; Redford 1970: 35–37). In contradiction to later New Kingdom propaganda (Gardiner 1946), the Hyksos kings did not eschew the worship of Re, the Egyptian sun god, suffering their prenomina to be constructed with Re-infixes, and modeling them on patterns of 13th Dynasty usage (Redford fc.). Again, in the tradition of the 13th Dynasty, the Hyksos maintained the important role assigned to the titular "king's (eldest) son," whether a physical offspring or a surrogate (Giveon 1976; Bietak 1981; Schmitz 1976: 203–57). "King's daughters (and sisters)" are also known (Simpson 1959; Van Seters 1966: 182; Gamer-Wallert 1978: 39–40); and the vivid description of the walls of Avaris recorded by Kamose apparently mentions the harem and its inmates (Kamose II, 9).

By the end of the period of Hyksos occupation the royal family at least appears to have come under the influence of Egyptian culture. Apophis dons the pharaonic image and mimics the sophistication of the true wearer of the Double Crown. Most of the Hyksos monumental texts come from his reign, and include dedications on offering tables (Kamal 1909: 61; Helck 1975: 55, 57), building texts mentioning flagstaves (Helck 1975: 56, no. 79; Simpson 1959); and folkloristic tradition remembers him for having built a temple to Seth and to have modeled part of the ritual on that of Re (Gardiner 1931: 85–86; Goedicke 1986b: 11–14). The Rhind Mathematical Papyrus dates to his 33d year (Peet 1923: pl. 4), and the Westcar papyrus may likewise have been copied at this time (*AEL* 1: 215). Apophis even had pretentions to literary activity in the hieroglyphic script, for he calls himself a "scribe of Re, taught by Thoth himself . . . multi-talented (?) on the day when he recited faithfully all the difficult (passages) of the writings . . ." (Berlin 7798).

F. Expulsion

The Thebaid was not initially, or directly, affected by the Hyksos incursion, and thither fled the remnants of the native regime ousted from the Middle Kingdom capital of Itj-towy (Hayes 1953). Here, shorn of its former Nubian (Säve-Söderbergh 1956) and N holdings, the 13th Dynasty withered away and was succeeded by an equally impoverished 16th Dynasty whose ephemeral kings were once listed in the final, surviving column (xi) of the Turin Canon. These in turn were supplanted during the first quarter of the 16th century B.C. by a 17th Dynasty, possibly of partly Nubian extraction (Redford 1967: 67–69; Harris and Weeks 1973: 123), and arguably in some way related to the movement into the Thebaid of "Pan-grave" mercenaries (Kemp, *AESH*, 169–71).

That Thebes, the savior of Egypt in the First Intermediate Period, would once again consider itself the instrument of the gods' will in initiating a war of liberation is understandable; still, the immediate cause of the outbreak of hostilities with the Hyksos dynasts remains obscure. (The Tale of Apophis and Seqnenre of the 19th Dynasty, which blames Apophis for having picked a quarrel over a fantastic and implausible charge, is to be discounted as pure folklore [Redford 1970: 35–38; Störk 1981a; Goedicke 1986a]). The mummy of Seqnenre Taᶜo shows signs of a violent death, and it is almost certain that he fell in battle with the Hyksos (Bietak and Strouhal 1974).

The fortunately surviving text of two stelae of Seqnenre's son and successor Kamose (Gardiner 1916; Habachi 1956; 1972; Smith 1976) strongly implies that, on Seqnenre's death, Kamose had been reduced to vassal status and bound by treaty (Störk 1981b). This he broke unilaterally by invading Hyksos territory N of Kusae. The fifteenth Upper Egyptian nome of Nefrusy was captured, and the seventeenth Upper Egyptian nome Cynopolis was destroyed; Apophis' attempt to raise Nubian support was thwarted by the timely capture of the Hyksos messenger on the oasis route. But while Kamose penetrated as far as Avaris and was able to destroy a merchant fleet in the harbor, he was unable to sustain a formal siege, and the lapse into vague generalizations at the end of his second stela may conceal a reverse.

His younger brother Ahmose succeeded him and pursued the war by recovering the lost ground and by capturing Memphis. From *obiter dicta* in contemporary biographies and daybooks it transpires that in the second month of summer in the 11th year of an unnamed Hyksos king (= Khamudy?) Heliopolis was taken, and two months later the border fort of Sile fell (Helck 1976a; Goedicke 1986b). Avaris itself suffered a series of assaults but must have been captured fairly soon afterward (Vandersleyen 1971). A series of attacks over three years on Sharuhen (perhaps Tell el-Ajjul; Kempinski 1974), apparently a base or residence of the Hyksos royal family, resulted in the reduction of this site also (Goedicke 1974: 40f.; 1986b: 42; *ANET,* 233–34). Thereafter the term *ḥḳ3(w) ḫ3swt* occurs sporadically during the 18th and 19th Dynasties (see *ANET,* 230–34), especially in the inscriptions of Thutmose III (*ANET,* 234–41); however, it is doubtful whether there was any blood or political relationship between the former 15th Dynasty and the king of Kadesh whose minions aimed at marching on Egypt during the reign of Thutmose III.

G. Later Traditions

The Hyksos invasion lived on in oral and written tradition, both in Egypt and the E Mediterranean littoral, long after their expulsion. In the 6th–5th centuries B.C. a reasonably accurate portrayal could still be written up in Demotic, based on surviving sources (Redford 1986b: 241–42). A more distorted recollection of the 15th Dynasty and its expulsion underlies the Greek legends about Io and Danaus (Berard 1952a; 1952b; Astour 1965: 91–94); while the "Canaanite" version of these events allegedly inspired the Hebrew "Descent" and "Exodus" legends (Redford 1987).

Donald B. Redford

ARCHAEOLOGY

Properly speaking, the term "Hyksos archaeology" refers only to the material remains associated with the Canaanite rulers of Egypt during Manetho's 15th Dynasty (ca. 1648–1540 B.C.). However, archaeologists generally use this phrase in a broader sense, i.e., to encompass all of the archaeological materials relating to the Asiatics living in Egypt during the Second Intermediate Period. Also coming under this heading are any sites and remains outside the Nile valley that are connected in some way to the Hyksos rule in Egypt.

A. Archaeological Sources in Egypt
B. Tell el-Dabᶜa and Other Hyksos Sites
C. Hyksos Fortifications
D. Hyksos Objects
E. Trade in the Hyksos Period
F. End of the Hyksos Period

A. Archaeological Sources in Egypt

The primary archaeological data for the Hyksos come from a small number of sites located E of the ancient Pelusiac branch of the Nile in the E delta (Bietak 1975b: 102, 165, fig. 35). These include Tell el-Yahudiyeh (Petrie 1906: 3–15; Tufnell 1978; Leclant and Clerc 1985: 344); Tell el-Maskhuta and a series of small pastoral sites along the Wadi Tumilat (Holladay 1982: 44–47, 50; Redmount 1986); Inshas (Anonymous 1949: 12); Tell Farasha (Yacoub 1983); and especially Tell el-Dabᶜa (Bietak 1968; 1970; 1975b; 1979; 1984b; 1989). Unpublished Asiatic remains have been reported from Tell Basta, Ghita, and Tell el-Sahaba (van den Brink 1982: 56–57). Tell el-Dabᶜa is the only urban settlement in this group. Tell el-Maskhuta had a small, seasonally occupied Asiatic village with associated burials, while Tell el-Yahudiyeh has yielded a cemetery and perhaps a large defensive enclosure (but see below). The remaining Asiatic sites have revealed only cemetery materials so far. Other important sources of archaeological data on the Hyksos include scarabs inscribed with Hyksos royal names (which have been found in Egypt, Nubia, and Palestine) and a small number of inscribed monuments (e.g., architectural blocks and metal artifacts inscribed with Hyksos names and the two stelae of King Kamose) from the delta, Nile valley, and outside Egypt.

B. Tell el-Dabᶜa and Other Hyksos Sites

The principal Hyksos site in Egypt is Avaris (Eg *Ḥwt-wᶜrt*), located in the Khatana-Qantir region of the NE delta. The ruins of this enormous city cover an area of about 2.5 km². Identification of this site as both the Hyksos capital and the later Ramesside residence called Piramesse was first made by Hamza (1930: 64–68). The largest surviving portion of Avaris is at Tell el-Dabᶜa, which has been under excavation since 1966. As the only Egyptian site where continuous occupation by Asiatics during the Second Intermediate Period can be traced, Tell el-Dabᶜa is the primary source of archaeological data and cultural information on the Hyksos.

The two principal areas of excavation at Tell el-Dabᶜa are Tell A and Area F/1. At Tell A, which has the best-documented sequence, the Second Intermediate Period strata are labeled G through D/2. The levels within this sequence that can be assigned to the Hyksos period are E/2, E/1, D/3, and D/2 (Bietak 1979: 236–37; 1984b: 37, table 1; 1989: 95–96, fig. 7). The chronological placement of these occupational levels is uncertain: Bietak (1984b: table 3) dates these strata to ca. 1660/1630–1540/1530 B.C., while Dever (1985: 78–79, fig. 2) opts for an earlier dating (ca. 1725–1550 B.C.). Stratum G represents an early 13th Dynasty occupation and includes a palace of Egyptian type in Area F/1. The excavator attributes the architectural and other cultural changes in the succeeding Stratum F to Asiatics arriving from the area of Byblos at the time of the 13th Dynasty. He construes this supposed movement to Avaris as providing the impetus for the rise of Hyksos rule in Egypt (Bietak 1987: 52). Whether there is any connection between this purported migration and the Manethonian account of the Hyksos takeover of Egypt as a violent event (Waddell 1940: 78–81) is unknown, but the absence of distinctively N Levantine architectural traditions, ceramic types, and funerary offerings in Stratum F requires a cautious approach to the theory of a Syrian influx. (For the claim of "material culture parallels" between Hyksos period sites in the Wadi Tumilat and N Syria, see Redmount 1986: 22.)

The religious architecture and burial practices at Tell el-Dabᶜa reflect the Levantine heritage of the Hyksos. The major religious structures at the site include an immense cult temple (Temple III) and two mortuary temples (Temples I and II), all of which are of Canaanite or mixed Egyptian-Canaanite types; these structures were erected during the time of Strata F and E/3 (Bietak 1989: 82–84). The principal tomb type at Tell el-Dabᶜa through most of the Second Intermediate Period is the vaulted mudbrick chamber tomb. Donkey sacrifices appear outside some of these tombs (Bietak 1979: 245–46, pl. 15A). Similar tombs, also with donkey sacrifices, are attested at Tell el-Maskhuta (Holladay 1982: 44, figs. 66–67) and at Inshas (Anonymous 1949: 12, unnumbered pl. at top of p. 9). Two tombs having mudbrick vaulting but no donkey burials were found in a small MB II–III cemetery at Tell el-Yahudiyeh; the pottery in this cemetery is comparable to that in Strata E/1, D/3, and D/2 at Tell el-Dabᶜa (Petrie 1906: 10–14, pls. 5–8, 12; Tufnell 1978: 101, n. 38). Vaulted MB II–III tombs have also been reported from Tell el-Sahaba, Tell Basta, and Ghita in the delta (van den Brink 1982: 56–57). Bietak (1987: 52), following van den Brink (1982), views these tombs as possibly Mesopotamian in origin, whereas Dever (1985: 82, n. 9) considers them a local adaptation of the Palestinian MB I rectangular cist tomb. The equine burials are paralleled in Palestine at Jericho, Lachish, and Tell el-ᶜAjjul (Stiebing 1971: 114–16).

The material culture of the Hyksos was an amalgam of Syro-Palestinian and Egyptian features. There was a gradual trend toward Egyptianization in the burial practices and ceramics at Tell el-Dabᶜa during the 17th and early 16th centuries B.C. (This development has also been observed at Hyksos period sites in the Wadi Tumilat: see Redmount 1986: 22–23.) Tombs in the later Hyksos phases (especially Strata D/3 and D/2) also sometimes contain Cypriot pottery and follow Egyptian rather than Asiatic funerary practices (Bietak 1989: 79–81). Among the metal objects in the burials at Tell el-Dabᶜa and at several of the other delta sites are bronze daggers and axheads of Levantine forms. Egyptian goods in these tombs include scarabs, jewelry, and alabaster vessels. No royal tombs have been discovered at Tell el-Dabᶜa, but a rich collection of funerary offerings, possibly from a Hyksos royal burial, is said to come from El Salhiya, 10 km SE of Tell el-Dabᶜa (Fischer 1969–70). The outstanding piece in this group, which is now in the Metropolitan Museum of Art in New York, is an electrum circlet with a magnificent stag's head at the front (Aldred 1971: 204–5, pl. 59).

C. Hyksos Fortifications

Data on Hyksos fortifications in Egypt are minimal. The high water table and activities of the *sebbākhin* have obscured all traces of the defensive system at Tell el-Dabᶜa (Bietak 1979: 268, 287). Large square embankments of sand with brick facing and rounded corners have been found at Tell el-Yahudiyeh (Petrie 1906: 3–10, pls. 2–4) and Heliopolis (Petrie and Mackay 1915: 3–4, pls. 1–3). The similarity of these two enclosures to embankments constructed in the Levant during the MB has led many archaeologists to identify them as Hyksos defense systems, but a growing number of scholars (mostly Egyptologists) feel that these embankments were retaining walls for Egyptian temple foundations (Ricke 1935; Wright 1968; cf. Kemp 1982: 744).

D. Hyksos Objects

Objects of substantial size inscribed with the names of Hyksos rulers are rare outside the delta (Giveon 1983). The southernmost occurrence of such finds is at Gebelein, where a granite block of Khyan (Daressy 1894: 42) and a limestone lintel of Awoserre Apophis (Daressy 1893: 26) were found. The paucity of Hyksos monuments and the lack of Asiatic settlements in the Nile valley suggest that the Hyksos maintained their authority in Middle Egypt and much of Upper Egypt through local vassals. This interpretation accords well with the reference in the "second stela" of the 17th Dynasty Theban king Kamose to Egyptians serving the Asiatics (Habachi 1972: 38, fig. 24, lines 17–18). The history of Hyksos expansion and rule in Egypt cannot be traced, since most Hyksos rulers are known solely from the appearance of their names on scarabs and other small objects. Some success has been achieved in arranging the Hyksos kings in chronological order by a typological analysis of the royal-name scarabs (Ward 1984). Numerous scarabs inscribed with the names and/or titles of officials who lived during this period and may have been Hyksos officials (e.g., the Chancellor Ḥar) have been found, but the rarity of non-Egyptian names on these scarabs (see, e.g., Giveon 1976: 127) makes it difficult to distinguish scarabs of Hyksos officials who adopted Egyptian names from scarabs belonging to contemporary Egyptian bureaucrats.

E. Trade in the Hyksos Period

The Asiatics in the E delta maintained an active commercial relationship with Cyprus, the Levant, and Nubia. This international trade appears to have been an important factor in the development of their wealth and power. The second stela of Kamose reports the seizure by the Theban king of hundreds of cargo ships in the harbor at Avaris (Habachi 1972: 37, fig. 23, lines 13–15). The goods aboard these ships included many substances originating in or traded through W Asia: gold, silver, bronze, lapis lazuli, turquoise, oil, incense, fat, honey, and precious woods. Stone and faience vessels, jewelry, amulets, scarabs, and other Egyptian merchandise were exported to the S Levant in exchange for such raw materials and finished products. Many Egyptian objects have been found at Tell el-ʿAjjul, Gezer, Tell el-Farʿah (South), Jericho, Megiddo, and other Palestinian sites. The widespread distribution of Tell el-Yahudiyeh ware in Egypt, Upper and Lower Nubia, the Levant, and Cyprus and the manufacture of this pottery in Egypt as well as the Levant provides further confirmation for the existence of an extensive trade network (Kaplan 1980; Kaplan, Harbottle, and Sayre 1982; Bietak 1987). The discovery of Middle Kingdom statuary in MB II–III and even later contexts in Palestine as well as in the Aegean and Nubia suggests that some of this trade consisted of items looted by the Hyksos from earlier Egyptian cemeteries (Weinstein 1974; Helck 1976a). The horse was first brought into Egypt from W Asia during the Second Intermediate Period (Boessneck 1976: 25; Dixon, Clutton-Brock, and Burleigh 1979), but it is unclear what part the Hyksos may have played in its introduction and dispersal up the Nile valley. The absence of occupational remains in N Sinai during the Second Intermediate Period indicates that Egyptian-Levantine trade went by sea rather than overland (Oren 1979).

F. End of the Hyksos Period

According to the autobiographical inscription of a naval officer from El Kab named Ahmose Son of Abana, the first king of the 18th Dynasty, Ahmose, besieged and plundered Avaris (Sethe 1961: 4, lines 13–14). Erosion and modern agricultural activity make it impossible to determine whether Avaris was destroyed by Ahmose, but occupation in the latest Hyksos stratum (D/2) at Tell el-Dabʿa ended abruptly, the tombs of this phase were looted, and the area was largely abandoned until the end of the 18th Dynasty (Bietak 1979: 268; 1989: 79). The Ahmose Son of Abana text reports that, after the taking of Avaris, Ahmose besieged and plundered Sharuhen (Sethe 1961: 4, lines 14–15). This town should be identified with Tell el-ʿAjjul in Gaza (Kempinski 1974), which has produced a large number of Hyksos royal-name scarabs and was probably a Hyksos stronghold and trading emporium (Weinstein 1981: 8; fc.). The lower city and Palace I at Tell el-ʿAjjul show evidence of a major destruction (Petrie 1931–32, 1: 3; 2: 4; Albright 1938: 348–51). Many other towns in S Palestine were destroyed and/or abandoned at the end of MB III or early in LB I. Dever (1985), Weinstein (1981; fc.), and the majority of Palestinian archaeologists attribute most or all of the devastation to the Egyptian army, while Redford (1973; 1979a; 1979b: 278, 286, n. 146; 1982: 117), Shea (1979), and Hoffmeier (1989) deny that the Egyptians were directly responsible for these events.

James M. Weinstein

Bibliography

Albright, W. F. 1938. The Chronology of a South Palestinian City, Tell el-ʿAjjûl. *AJSL* 55: 337–59.

———. 1957. Further Observations on the Chronology of Alalakh. *BASOR* 146: 26–34.

———. 1965. The Role of the Canaanites in the History of Civilization. Pp. 438–87 in *BANE*.

Aldred, C. 1971. *Jewels of the Pharaohs.* New York.

Alt, A. 1961. *Herkunft der Hyksos in neuer Sicht.* Leipzig.

Anonymous. 1949. Compte rendu de la séance du lundi 7 Mars 1949. *BSFE* 1: 11–22.

Astour, M. 1965. *Hellenosemitica.* Leiden.

Berard, J. 1952a. Les Derniers Hyksos et la legende d'Io. *BSFE* 10: 41–43.

———. 1952b. Les Hyksos et la legende d'Io. *Syr* 29: 1–43.

Bietak, M. 1968. Vorläufiger Bericht über die erste und zweite Kampagne der österreichischen Ausgrabungen auf Tell ed-Dabʿa im Ostdelta Ägyptens (1966, 1967). *MDAIK* 23: 79–114.

———. 1970. Vorläufiger Bericht über die dritte Kampagne des österreichischen Ausgrabungen auf Tell ed-Dabʿa im Ostdelta Ägyptens (1968). *MDAIK* 26: 15–42.

———. 1975a. Die Hauptstadt der Hyksos und die Remsesstadt. *Antike Welt* 6/1: 28ff.

———. 1975b. *Tell el-Dabʿa II.* Vienna.

———. 1979. Avaris and Pi-Ramesse. *Proceedings of the British Academy* 65: 225–90.

———. 1981. Eine Stelle des ältesten Königssohnes des Hyksos Chayan. *MDAIK* 37: 63ff.

———. 1984a. Zum Königsreich des *ʿ3-zẖRʿ* Nehesi. *SAK* 11: 59–76.

———. 1984b. Problems of Middle Bronze Age Chronology: New Evidence from Egypt. *AJA* 88: 471–85.

———. 1987. Canaanites in the Eastern Nile Delta. Pp. 41–56 in *Egypt, Israel, Sinai,* ed. A. F. Rainey. Tel Aviv.

———. 1989. The Middle Bronze Age of the Levant—A New Approach to Relative and Absolute Chronology. Pp. 78–120 in *High, Middle, or Low? Acts of an International Colloquium on Absolute Chronology Held at the University of Göthenburg 20th–22nd August 1987,* 3, ed. P. Åström. Göthenburg.

Bietak, M., and Strouhal, E. 1974. Die Todesumstände des Pharao Seqnenreʿ. *ANHMW* 78: 29–52.

Boessneck, J. 1976. *Tell el-Dabʿa III.* Vienna.

Brink, E. C. M. van den. 1982. *Tombs and Burial Customs at Tell el-Dabʿa.* Vienna.

Daressy, G. 1893. Notes et remarques. *RT* 14: 14–38.

———. 1894. Notes et remarques. *RT* 16: 42–60.

Dever, W. G. 1985. Relations between Syria-Palestine and Egypt in the "Hyksos" Period. Pp. 69–87 in *Palestine in the Bronze and Iron Ages,* ed. J. N. Tubb. London.

Dixon, D. M.; Clutton-Brock, J.; and Burleigh, R. 1979. The Buhen Horse. Pp. 191–95 in *The Fortress of Buhen: The Archaeological Report,* by W. B. Emery; H. S. Smith; and A. Millard. London.

Duncan, J. G. 1931. *Digging up Biblical History.* London.

Engberg, R. M. 1939. *The Hyksos Reconsidered.* Chicago.

Engelbach, R. 1921. Notes of Inspection, April 1921. *ASAE* 21: 18.

Fischer, H. G. 1969–70. Egyptian Art. *BMMA* 28: 69–70.

Gamer-Wallert, I. 1978. *Ägyptische und ägyptisierende Funde von der Ibirischen Halbinsel.* Wiesbaden.

Gardiner, A. H. 1916. The Defeat of the Hyksos by Kamose: the Carnarvon Tablet no. 1. *JEA* 3: 95–110.

———. 1931. *Late Egyptian Stories.* Brussels.

———. 1946. Davies' Copy of the Great Speos Artemidos Inscription. *JEA* 32: 43–56.

Giveon, R. 1965. A Sealing of Khyan from the Shephela of Southern Palestine. *JEA* 51: 202–4.

———. 1974. Hyksos Scarabs with Names of Kings and Officials from Canaan. *CdÉ* 49: 222ff.

———. 1976. New Egyptian Seals with Titles and Names from Canaan. *TA* 3: 127–32.

———. 1980. A New Hyksos King. *TA* 7: 90ff.

———. 1981. Ya^cqob-har. *GM* 44: 17–20.
———. 1983. The Hyksos in the South. Pp. 155–61 in *Fontes atque Pontes,* ed. M. Görg. Wiesbaden.
Goedicke, H. 1974. Some Remarks concerning the Inscription of Ahmose. *JARCE* 11: 31–41.
———. 1986a. The End of the Hyksos in Egypt. Pp. 37–47 in *Egyptological Studies in Honor of Richard A. Parker,* ed. L. H. Lesko. Hanover, NH.
———. 1986b. *The Quarrel of Apophis and Seqnenre.* San Antonio.
Gunn, B., and Gardiner, A. H. 1918. New Renderings of Egyptian Texts II: Expulsion of the Hyksos. *JEA* 5: 36–56.
Habachi, L. 1956. Preliminary Report on the Kamose Stela and Other Inscribed Blocks Found Re-used in the Foundations of Two Statues at Karnak. *ASAE* 53: 195–202.
———. 1972. *The Second Stela of Kamose and His Struggle against the Hyksos Ruler and His Capital.* Glückstadt.
———. 1974. Sethos I's Devotion to Seth and Avaris. *ZÄS* 100: 95–102.
Hamza, M. 1930. Excavations of the Department of Antiquities at Qantîr (Faqûs District) (Season, May 21–July 7, 1928). *ASAE* 30: 31–68.
Harris, J. E., and Weeks, K. R. 1973. *X-Raying the Pharaohs.* New York.
Hayes, W. C. 1953. Notes on the Government of Egypt in the Late Middle Kingdom. *JNES* 12: 31–39.
Helck, W. 1958. *Zur Verwaltung des mittleren und neuen Reichs.* Leiden.
———. 1972. *Die Beziehungen Ägyptens zur Vorderasien.* 2d ed. Wiesbaden.
———. 1975. *Historisch-biographische Texte der 2. Zwischenzeit und neue Texte der 18. Dynastie.* Wiesbaden.
———. 1976a. Ägyptische Statuen im Ausland—ein chronologischen Problem. *UF* 8: 101–14.
———. 1976b. Zum Datum der Eroberund von Auaris. *GM* 19: 33ff.
———. 1979. *Die Beziehungen Ägyptens und Vorderasien zur Agäis bis ins 7 Jahrhundert v. Chr.* Darmstadt.
Hoffmeier, J. K. 1989. Reconsidering Egypt's Part in the Termination of the Middle Bronze Age in Palestine. *Levant* 21: 181–93.
Holladay, J. S., Jr. 1982. *Tell el-Maskhuṭa.* Malibu.
Huxley, G. L. 1961. *Crete and the Luwians.* Oxford.
James, T. G. H. 1961. A Group of Inscribed Egyptian Tools. *BMQ* 24: 36–43.
Jungwirth, J. 1970. Die anthropologischen Ergebnisse der Grabungskampagne 1969 in Tell ed-Dab^ca, Unterägypten. *Annalen des Naturhistorische Museum in Wien* 74: 1959–66.
Kamal, A. 1909. *Tables d'offrandes.* Cairo.
Kaplan, M. F. 1980. *The Origin and Distribution of Tell el Yahudiyeh Ware.* Studies in Mediterranean Archaeology 62. Göteborg.
Kaplan, M. F.; Harbottle, G.; and Sayre, E. V. 1982. Multi-disciplinary Analysis of Tell el Yahudiyeh Ware. *Archaeometry* 24: 127–42.
Kees, H. 1961. *Ancient Egypt, a Cultural Topography.* London.
Kemp, B. J. 1982. Old Kingdom, Middle Kingdom, and Second Intermediate Period in Egypt. Pp. 658–769 in *The Cambridge History of Africa,* vol. 1, ed. J. D. Clark. Cambridge.
Kempinski, A. 1974. Tell el-^cAjjul—Beth Aglayim or Sharuhen? *IEJ* 24: 145–52.
———. 1985. Some Observations on the Hyksos (XVth) Dynasty and Its Canaanite Origins. Pp. 129–38 in *Pharaonic Egypt, the Bible and Christianity.* Jerusalem.
Labib, P. 1936. *Die Herrschaft der Hyksos in Ägypten und ihr Sturz.* Berlin.
Leclant, J. 1986. Fouilles et travaux en Égypte et au Soudan 1984–85. *Or* 55: 236–319.
Leclant, J., and Clerc, G. 1985. Fouilles et travaux en Égypte et au Soudan, 1983–1984. *Or* 54: 337–415.
Martin, G. T. 1971. *Egyptian Administrative and Private Name Seals.* Oxford.
Mayani, Z. 1956. *Les Hyksos et le monde de la Bible.* Paris.
Merrillees, R. S. 1970. Evidence for the Bichrome Wheel-made Ware in Egypt. *AJBA* 1/3: 3ff.
———. 1971. Syrian Pottery from Middle Kingdom Egypt. *AJBA* 2: 51–59.
———. 1975. Cypriote Black Slip Flasks. *Levant* 7: 141–45.
Oren, E. 1979. Land Bridge between Asia and Africa: Archaeology of Northern Sinai up to the Classical Period. Pp. 181–91 in *Sinai,* ed. Beno Rothenberg. Washington.
Peet, T. E. 1923. *The Rhind Mathematical Papyrus (B.M. 10057 and 10058).* London.
Petrie, W. M. F. 1906. *Hyksos and Israelite Cities.* British School of Archaeology in Egypt and Egyptian Research Account 12. London.
———. 1917. *Scarabs and Cylinders with Names.* London.
———. 1931–32. *Ancient Gaza.* 2 vols. I. British School of Archaeology in Egypt 53. London.
Petrie, W. M. F., and Mackay, E. 1915. *Heliopolis Kafr Ammar and Shurafa.* British School of Archaeology in Egypt and Egyptian Research Account 18. London.
Redford, D. B. 1967. *History and Chronology of the Egyptian 18th Dynasty. Seven Studies.* Toronto.
———. 1970. The Hyksos in History and Tradition. *Or* 39: 1–51.
———. 1973. Review of C. Vandersleyen, *Les Guerres d'Amosis, fondateur de la XVIIIe Dynastie. BO* 30: 223–25.
———. 1977. The Oases in Egyptian History to Classical Times. III. ca. 1650–1000 B.C. *JSSEA* 7, no. 3: 2–6.
———. 1979a. The Historical Retrospective at the Beginning of Thutmose III's Annals. Pp. 338–42 in *Festschrift Elmar Edel, 12 März 1979,* ed. M. Görg and E. Pusch. ÄAT 1. Bamberg.
———. 1979b. A Gate Inscription from Karnak and Egyptian Involvement in Western Asia during the Early 18th Dynasty. *JAOS* 99: 270–87.
———. 1982. Contact between Egypt and Jordan in the New Kingdom: Some Comments on Sources. Pp. 115–19 in *Studies in the History and Archaeology of Jordan I,* ed. A. Hadidi. Amman.
———. 1986a. Egypt and Western Asia in the Old Kingdom. *JARCE* 23: 125–43.
———. 1986b. *King-lists, Annals and Daybooks.* Toronto.
———. 1987. An Egyptological Perspective on the Exodus Narrative. Pp. 137–62 in *Egypt, Israel, and Sinai,* ed. A. F. Rainey. Tel Aviv.
———. fc. The Concept of Kingship in the 18th Dynasty.
Redmount, C. A. 1986. Wadi Tumilat Survey. *NARCE* 133: 19–23.
Ricke, H. 1935. Der "Hohe Sand in Heliopolis." *ZÄS* 71: 107–11.
Säve-Söderbergh, T. 1951. The Hyksos Rule in Egypt. *JEA* 37: 53–71.
———. 1956. The Nubian Kingdom of the Second Intermediate Period. *Kush* 4: 54ff.
Schmitz, B. 1976. *Untersuchungen zum Titel S3-Njswt, "Königssohn."* Bonn.
Sethe, K. 1961. *Urkunden der 18. Dynastie.* 4 vols. Repr. of 2d ed. Berlin.

Shea, W. 1979. The Conquests of Sharuḥhen and Megiddo Reconsidered. *IEJ* 29: 1–5.
Simpson, W. K. 1959. The Hyksos Princess Tany. *CdÉ* 34: 233–39.
Smith, H. S., and Smith, A. 1976. A Reconsideration of the Kamose Texts. *ZÄS* 103: 48ff.
Stadelmann, R. 1965a. Ein Beitrag zum Brief des Hyksos Apophis. *MDAIK* 20: 62–69.
———. 1965b. Die 400-Jahr Stele. *CdÉ* 40: 46–60.
———. 1967. *Syrisch-Palästinensische Gottheiten in Ägypten.* Leiden.
Stiebing, W. H., Jr. 1971. Hyksos Burials in Palestine: A Review of the Evidence. *JNES* 30: 110–17.
Stock, H. 1963. Der Hyksos Chian in Bogazköy. MDOG 94: 73–80.
Störk, L. 1981a. Er ist ein Gott, während ich ein Herrscher bin. Die Anfechtung der Hyksossuzeränität unter Kamose. *GM* 43: 63ff.
———. 1981b. Was störte den Hyksos Apophis am Gebrüll der thebanischen Nilpferde? *GM* 43: 67.
Tufnell, O. 1978. Graves at Tell el-Yehudiyeh: Reviewed after a Life-time. Pp. 76–101 in *Archaeology in the Levant,* ed. R. Moorey and P. Parr. Warminster.
Vandersleyen, C. 1971. *Les Guerres d'Amosis.* Brussels.
Van Seters, J. 1964. A Date for the "Admonitions" in the Second Intermediate Period. *JEA* 50: 13–23.
———. 1966. *The Hyksos.* New Haven.
Vercoutter, J. 1954. *Essai sur les relations entre les égyptiens et les prehellenes.* Paris.
Vernus, P. 1982. La Stèle du roi Sekhemsankhtowi Neferhotep Ikhernofret et la domination Hyksos. *ASAE* 68: 129–35.
Von Beckerath, J. 1965. *Untersuchungen zur politischen Geschichte der zweite Zwischenzeit in Agypten.* Glückstadt.
Von Bissing, W. 1936–37. Das angebliche Weltreich der Hyksos. *AfO* 11: 325–35.
Waddell, W. G. 1940. *Manetho.* Cambridge, MA.
Ward, W. A. 1975. Some Personal Names of the Hyksos Period Rulers and Notes on the Epigraphy of Their Scarabs. *UF* 8: 353–65.
———. 1976. A New Chancellor of the 15th Dynasty. *Or* 6–7: 589–94.
———. 1984. Royal-Name Scarabs. Pp. 151–92 in *Studies on Scarab Seals II.* Warminster.
Weinstein, J. M. 1974. A Statuette of the Princess Sobeknefru at Tell Gezer. *BASOR* 213: 49–57.
———. 1975. Egyptian Relations with Palestine in the Middle Kingdom. *BASOR* 217: 1–16.
———. 1981. The Egyptian Empire in Palestine: A Reassessment. *BASOR* 241: 1–28.
———. fc. Egypt and the Middle Bronze IIC/Late Bronze IA Transition in Palestine. *Levant* 22.
Wright, G. R. H. 1968. Tell el-Yehūdīyah and the Glacis. *ZDPV* 84: 1–17.
Yacoub, F. 1983. Excavations at Tell Farasha. *ASAE* 65: 175–76.
Yeivin, S. 1959. Yaᶜqobᶜel. *JEA* 45. 16–18.

DONALD B. REDFORD
JAMES M. WEINSTEIN

HYMENAEUS (PERSON) [Gk *Hymenaios*]. Hymenaeus was a heretical Christian, apparently living in Ephesus (cf. 1 Tim 1:3), mentioned in connection with Alexander in 1 Tim 1:20 and with Philetus in 2 Tim 2:17. That the references are to the same Hymenaeus is generally agreed since in each instance he is characterized as having deviated from the faith.

From 1 Tim 1:19 it is learned that Hymenaeus and Alexander "by rejecting conscience" had "made shipwreck of their faith." As a result, Paul "delivered [them] to Satan" that they might "learn not to blaspheme" (1:20). Although one's attention is often immediately captured by the vivid image of shipwreck, a metaphor used often in Greek philosophy (Dibelius and Conzelmann *The Pastoral Epistles* Hermenia, 33), most commentators focus on the deliverance. This is reminiscent of Paul's instruction to the Corinthians concerning the incestuous man in their community: "When you are assembled, and my spirit is present, with the power of our Lord Jesus, you are to deliver this man to Satan for the destruction of the flesh, that his spirit may be saved in the day of the Lord Jesus" (1 Cor 5:5). The author of 1 Timothy, presumably not Paul, must have known this text, yet he obviously does not intend for Hymenaeus and Alexander to experience "destruction of the flesh," i.e., death, in the same physical sense implied in 1 Cor 5:5. Nor does he envision deliverance to Satan as mere exclusion, putting them outside the Church, back into Satan's sphere. Rather, in 1 Timothy there is a nuance of potential reform before death through punishment. The author does, however, appear to expect physical consequences (1 Cor 11:32 and 2 Cor 6:9 may express a similar understanding). As Dibelius and Conzelmann (Hermenia, 34) note, "Since 'Satan' in 1 Tim 1:20 . . . can only refer to his function as the destroyer of body and of life, one has to think of sickness or the like." Thus it appears that great misfortune was wished upon Hymenaeus and Alexander with some thought, although the emphasis probably remains on punishment, that they might repent of their blasphemy, the precise content of which is never stated.

The author of 1 Timothy presupposes, unlike Paul in 1 Cor 5:5, that the apostle possessed magical powers enabling him to deliver the recalcitrant Hymenaeus and Alexander to Satan. Paul himself, however, understands such a deliverance to be a community action done in the "power of our Lord Jesus" (1 Cor 5:5). For this reason, commentators often draw parallels between 1 Tim 1:20 and various magical papyri (Collins 1980: 258). At the same time, it must be noted that a different stance is presupposed in 1 Timothy, where Paul presumably had carried out the excommunication of Hymenaeus and Alexander, while in 1 Cor 5:5 he instructs the Corinthians to carry out the action in his absence.

From 2 Tim 2:17, where Hymenaeus is linked with Philetus, it is learned that these two men had "swerved from the truth by holding that the resurrection is past already." Apparently they had embraced a gnostic-type doctrine of non-bodily resurrection which viewed that event as having merely a spiritual sense, i.e., the resurrection of a person from a sinful past. Hymenaeus and Philetus, since they were "upsetting the faith of some" (2:18), must have been teachers or leaders in the Ephesian church and rather effective ones at that. The author of 2 Timothy cites them as an example of those to be avoided in their "disputing about works, which does no good, but only ruins the hearers" (2:14). Timothy is warned that "such godless chatter . . . will lead people into more and more ungodliness, and their talk will eat its way like gangrene" (2:16–17). Unlike 1 Timothy, 2 Timothy does not suggest that Hymenaeus was excommunicated.

Given the convergence of names and ideas between the Pastorals and the later apocryphal *Acts of Paul,* one would expect to find Hymenaeus and Philetus in the apocryphal *Acts.* While they are not present (Alexander is present, probably the same as above), their position on resurrection is prominent and its proponents are DEMAS and Hermogenes. Regarding the possibility that characters in the Pastoral letters such as Hymenaeus, Alexander, and Philetus might be fictional creations of the deutero-Pauline author, see HERMOGENES.

Bibliography

Collins, A. Y. 1980. "The Function of 'Excommunication' in Paul." *HTR* 73: 251–63.

FLORENCE MORGAN GILLMAN

HYMN OF THE PEARL. *The Hymn of the Pearl* (also entitled *The Hymn of the Soul,* and *The Hymn of Jude Thomas the Apostle in the Country of the Indians*) is a mythological poem "which presents a Hellenistic myth of the human soul's entry into bodily incarnation and its eventual disengagement" (Layton 1987: 366). This myth of human salvation is not literally expressed but is conveyed in the form of an allegorical folktale, possibly originally oral, in which a young prince from the East (Parthia?) is sent on a westward mission to Egypt to rescue "the one pearl" from a dragon, is distracted and forgets his true identity and mission, is revived by a message of remembrance sent from his father the king, and finally returns home with his prize pearl amid great pomp and circumstance.

A. The Manuscript Tradition and the Acts of Thomas

The text of *Hymn Pearl* is only known as one part of a larger work in the early Christian literary tradition of the apocryphal acts of the apostles (MacDonald 1986: 1–6; Bovon and Junod 1986: 161–71) known as the *Acts of Thomas* (Klijn 1962). Considering the relationship between *Hymn Pearl* and *Acts Thom.,* researchers have yet to determine (1) whether or not *Hymn Pearl* existed prior to the composition of *Acts Thom.* and (2) whether it was included in the first edition of *Acts Thom.* or is a secondary addition to that text. As the "host text" for *Hymn Pearl, Acts Thom.* itself purports to transmit stories of the eastward journeys and miraculous activities of the ascetic apostle Didymus Jude Thomas and his divine twin brother Jesus. As is typical with many of the apocryphal acts of the apostles, *Acts Thom.* has a rich but complicated ms tradition (Poirier 1981). Although that tradition is limited to the Syriac (6 mss) and Greek (75 mss) languages, scholars have not reached a consensus concerning which of these two was the original language of composition. The *Hymn Pearl* is found in only two of the 81 extant mss containing *Acts Thom.:* a Syr ms dated to 936 C.E. and a Gk ms of ca. 1050 C.E. Also extant is an 11th-century epitome by Nicephoras of Thessalonica based on the Gk version (Lipsius and Bonnet 1903: 219–24; cf. Poirier 1981).

B. Time and Place of Composition

All indicators of time and place of composition are obscure and offer no easy solutions. The relevant data and most likely options have been discussed by Layton (367–69) and are reviewed here. First, the Syriac style and content of the story demonstrate that *Hymn Pearl* was composed independently of *Acts Thom.,* suggesting that it was either one of the author's sources which he incorporated into *Acts Thom.* or was interpolated into the text at a later time, from an unknown place, and by an unknown editor. The second option concerns the relationship between *Hymn Pearl* and the other literature from the Syrian Thomas tradition (see THOMAS, GOSPEL OF (NHC II,*2*) and THOMAS THE CONTENDER, BOOK OF) which employ the distinctive theological model of "divine twinship" (Layton, 359–64) reflected in the tripartite titular name *Didymus* (Gk title: twin) *Judas* (personal name) *Thomas* (Aram title: twin). If *Hymn Pearl* was composed in the general locale of the Thomas tradition (Syrian Edessa), one could argue that the strong similarity with Thomas theology (model of divine twinship) is due to the fact that *Hymn Pearl* either provided the model for the other Thomas texts (in which case *Hymn Pearl* would predate those texts) or it presupposed that model (in which case *Hymn Pearl* would postdate those texts). The chronological order of composition for these three texts is a crucial factor yet to be determined by researchers. But if *Hymn Pearl* was not composed in Syrian Edessa, then the interpretive framework of the text cannot be supplied by reference to the other texts in the Syrian Thomas tradition and their model of divine twinship. With this option, one would suppose that *Hymn Pearl* originated in another religious milieu, was secondarily introduced into the Syrian Thomas tradition, and was then adapted to the new religious context. Layton notes that the favorable mention (*Hymn Pearl* 38) of the Parthian dynasty of Persia (247 B.C.E.–224 C.E.), which lost control of Syrian Edessa in 165 C.E., strongly suggests that *Hymn Pearl* could have been composed in Syrian Edessa sometime before 165 C.E.

C. The Allegory

A résumé of the story line is presented in the introduction to this brief article and need not be expanded here (for recent English translation, see Layton, 371–75). The allegorical theme of a highly desirable pearl was a popular image in antiquity and is found in Christian form in the so-called "Parable of the Pearl of Great Price" (Matt 13:45–46 and *Gos. Thom.* 76; cf. Matt 13:44). Similarly, the theme of a young man's journey into personal loss, self-recognition, and final restoration is also known in the so-called "Parable of the Prodigal Son" (Luke 15:11–32; but cf. Phil 2:5–11).

The hermeneutical key which unlocks the deeper allegorical meaning of the myth is given at several points near the end of the story. The prince's garment (*Hymn Pearl* 76–78, 88, 98) is clearly shown to be an allegorical representation of his newly gained "self-recognition" (= gnosis?) which ushers him into the realm of authentic existence and peace. With these suggestive clues to the allegorical method of interpretation "an ancient reader could work back through the story at another level, retelling it as an account or model of the quest for self-knowledge and salvation" (Layton, 366).

The lack of any exclusively sectarian elements (whether Jewish, Christian, or other) is striking and suggests a popular allegorical story which was adaptable to any number of specific religious sects in numerous cultures. The general requirement for its adaptation was the presupposition in the receiving group that the human soul had its birth and true home in a spiritual realm, that the soul's present condition of material incarnation was negative, and that it could be rescued from this unfortunate fate only through a spiritual experience of self-recognition which would ultimately free the soul from the shackles of the fleshly body and the material world.

Bibliography

Bovon, F., and Junod, E. 1986. Reading the Apocryphal Acts of the Apostles. Pp. 161–71 in *The Apocryphal Acts of the Apostles,* ed. D. R. MacDonald. Semeia 38. Decatur, GA.

Klijn, A. F. J. 1962. *The Acts of Thomas.* NovTSup 5. Leiden.

Layton, B. 1987. *The Gnostic Scriptures.* ed. B. Layton. New York.

Lipsius, R., and Bonnet, M. 1903. *Acta Philippi et Acta Thomae Accendunt Acta Barnabae.* Acta academiae Aboensis 2/2. Leipzig.

MacDonald, D. R. 1986. The Forgotten Novels of the Early Church. Pp. 1–6 in *The Apocryphal Acts of the Apostles,* ed. D. R. MacDonald. Semeia 38. Decatur, GA.

Poirier, P.-H. 1981. *L'Hymne de la perle des Actes de Thomas.* HR 8. Louvain.

PAUL ALLAN MIRECKI

HYMN OF THE THREE YOUNG MEN.

See DANIEL, ADDITIONS TO.

HYMNS, EARLY CHRISTIAN.

The term "hymn" is derived from the Greek word *hymnos,* which in classical Greek from Homer on means a song of praise in honor of the gods, heroes, and conquerors. In the NT it is used in reference to songs of praise honoring the God of Israel (Matt 26:30; Mark 14:26; Acts 16:25).

A. Terminology

In certain passages in the Pauline Epistles (Eph 5:19; Col 3:16) the word *hymnos* is used with two other terms as well. One is *psalmos,* which was already used by the translators of the LXX for the Hebrew book of Psalms (Heb *tĕhillîm,* or "songs of praise"). In classical Greek the word *psalmos* meant "plucking musical strings with the fingers" and, later, a song sung to the accompaniment of a stringed instrument. (No doubt this was found by the translators to be the most satisfactory Greek equivalent because of the instrumental implications of the superscriptions to many of the psalms.)

The other term used by Paul is *ōdē pneumatikē* ("spiritual song"). The Greek word *ōdē* means a song, lay, or strain (from which derives the English word "ode"). In the plural it means "lyric poetry." While these terms might be considered synonymous, there must be some distinction, be it ever so slight.

B. Songs, Hymns, and Psalms in the Bible

1. Complete Hymns. The term *ōdē* (or song) seems to be generic. The fact that Paul feels the need to add the adjective *pneumatikē* ("spiritual") seems to corroborate this view. It was not an ordinary or secular, pagan, heathen song that they were to sing, but a spiritual one, that is, one that had Christian orientation.

The other two terms, *hymnos* and *psalmos,* then, are specific, the latter taking the characteristics of the OT psalms if not the psalms themselves. It is to be remembered that Jewish Christians were accustomed to using the biblical book of Psalms in the synagogue and gentile converts had the Psalter available in the LXX. Besides the psalms themselves there were other OT songs such as the song of Moses (Exod 15:1–18), the song of Deborah and Barak (Judges 5), and the song of Hannah (1 Sam 2:1–10), to name but a few. In addition there are the various NT songs (especially in Luke), such as the *Magnificat* (Luke 1:46–55), the *Benedictus* (Luke 1:68–79), and the *Nunc Dimittis* (Luke 2:29–32), which bear close resemblance to the psalms.

Hymnologists are agreed that these NT songs were inspired by older poems, for example, the *Magnificat* by the song of Hannah, and the *Benedictus* by the language used by the OT prophets and by the eighteen benedictions used in the temple service. Szövérffy (*NCE* 7: 287) indicates that "with few exceptions, early Christian hymns were not written down but were very often the product of sudden inspiration. They probably resembled Hebrew Psalms and Canticles, using parallelism in structure, long enumerations of the attributes of the Deity, Etc."

2. Fragmentary Hymns. Many hymnologists also believe that fragments of primitive hymns can be found throughout the NT. This certainly harmonizes with Szövérffy's assertion regarding momentary and sudden inspiration and an attempt to recapture the thought later. Most of these fragments seem to be found in the Pauline Epistles and one might conclude that he was quoting from them as he was writing to the various congregations he had founded, and he might even originally have heard them there.

In general these fragments fall into two categories. The first category includes those that are doctrinal, didactic, or liturgical in scope. Some examples of this first category can be found in Eph 5:14; 1 Tim 3:16 and 6:15–16; 2 Tim 2:11–13; Titus 3:4–7; Phil 2:6–11; and Rev 22:17. Many of the early teachings of the Christian Church seem to be found in some of these hymn fragments. It must be remembered that outside the OT there were no written documents in the Church of the apostolic age except those that appeared and were circulated either as general epistles (such as those of John, James, and Peter) or the specific letters of Paul; the gospels only began to appear later. It must also be kept in mind that many other documents were being circulated, and that controversy and conflict already appeared at this early time as a result of conflicting views being circulated by those who opposed the apostles. Paul, the great Jewish convert, zealous missionary, and champion of orthodoxy, seems to have an abundance of these primitive hymn fragments supporting and reflecting his views about the essence of the Christian gospel.

In the second category are those that are doxological in content. These are all found in the book of Revelation

(1:4–8; 4:8; 4:11; 5:9–10; 5:12; 11:15; 11:17–18; and 15:3–4).

While none of these fragments are strophic (as are later Greek and Latin hymns), they are nevertheless in metrical prose (as is the *Te Deum* of a later date), and they certainly meet the standards of good poetry; there is music in their very sound.

C. Extrabiblical References to Early Christian Hymns

We also gain a little information about early Christian hymnody from the famous letter of Pliny the Younger to the Emperor Trajan, written shortly after the close of the apostolic era (ca. A.D. 107–15). In asking the emperor how he should deal with the Christians, Pliny, governor of Bithynia and Pontus, briefly summarized their gatherings on the basis of information he had been able to glean through interrogation of witnesses. The pertinent portion of his letter states that "they were accustomed to come together on a regular day (probably Sunday) before dawn and to sing a song alternately to Christ as to a god."

Another early source, the *Apostolic Constitutions* (completed before the end of the 4th century), mentions a number of primitive Greek hymns which may very well have been the sort of "hymn to Christ" which Pliny refers to in his letter (Funk 1905: 7, 47, 454; 8, 13, 517).

One of these hymns is the *hymnos eothinos* or "morning hymn," which is also found in a number of other ancient sources, such as were appended to the Codex Alexandrinus (5th century). These "anonymous hymns" had considerable influence in shaping the liturgy of the early Church. The morning hymn is an expansion of the greater doxology ("Glory to God in the highest"). Another hymn mentioned in the *Apostolic Constitutions* is an "evening hymn" *(hymnos espirinos)*. There are three noteworthy sections to this hymn: (1) the beginning seems to be taken from Psalm 113: "Praise the Lord! Praise, O servants of the Lord, praise the name of the Lord!"; (2) the next portion paraphrases the "Gloria in Excelsis" section of the morning hymn; and (3) the last portion consists of the song of Simeon (Luke 2:29–32), the *Nunc Dimittis* (Funk 1905: 7; 8).

Numerous other hymns are to be found in these documents, but we shall restrict our discussion to those which have been retained in present-day liturgies. One of these is the *Tersanctus* or "Thrice Holy" taken from the opening verses of Isaiah 6 (the *qādôš* of the Hebrew liturgy). In the Clementine liturgy it appears in this form: "Holy, holy, holy is the Lord of Sabaoth. The whole creation is full of His glory. Praise to all ages. Amen." (Werner 1959: 284). The liturgies of St. Mark, St. James, and St. John Chrysostom have slight alterations to this basic text, the latter two including the "Hosanna" section: "Hosanna in the highest. Blessed is he that cometh in the Name of the Lord. Hosanna in the highest." (Brightman 1922: 43).

In passing we should also make mention of another trinitarian hymn which became important in the Eastern Church. This is the *Trisagion*, which should not be confused with the *Tersanctus*. In the Eastern liturgies it is a short hymn verse sung after the Little Entrance. The text is as follows: "Holy God, Holy Mighty, Holy Immortal, have mercy on us." It is also found in the old Roman Good Friday liturgy in both Latin and Greek, sung antiphonally by the choirs. (In the latter language it seems to be a vestigial remainder from the days when the liturgy was still recited in Greek.)

A final hymn is the lesser doxology, *Doxa Patri*, which is identical with the Latin *Gloria Patri* ("Glory be to the Father, and to the Son, and to the Holy Spirit: as it was in the beginning, is now, and ever shall be, world without end. Amen"). In Rome it was already in use at the time of Clement (ca. 91). In the Western usage of St. Benedict (ca. 480) the lesser doxology was to be used after each psalm, a practice which has persisted to the present day and gives a Christian trinitarian orientation to the OT psalms. The same applies to the three Lukan canticles *(Magnificat, Benedictus, Nunc Dimittis)* which do not themselves actually contain such an orientation.

The use of hymns not derived from Scriptural sources varied in certain locations throughout the Church and were used sparingly in the liturgy, mostly as paraliturgical devotions—this as late as the 4th and 5th centuries. Duchesne (1903: 452, n. 1) points out that down to the 9th century hymns were unknown at Rome, "chants, psalms, and other Scriptural canticles alone being used."

It was primarily because of the activity of certain heretical sects (such as Gnosticism) that some hymns found gradual acceptance in order to combat heresy with truth. In his interesting collection of heretical writings from the early Christian periods Grant (1961: 105, 115; 116–22) quotes a number of these gnostic hymns. On the other hand, Schalk (1978: 189) points up the fact that "a steady hymn production was maintained by the more orthodox hymnists." Among these is to be found the evening hymn *Phos hilaron hagias doxas* which has come down to us in translation as "O Gladsome Light, O Grace."

It would seem in order to conclude our discussion by making a brief comparison of Eastern and Western liturgies, the substantial lack of early non-Scriptural hymns notwithstanding.

The culmination of all Eastern rites is to be found in the Divine Liturgy of St. John Chrysostom (Brightman 1922), which is still in usage today. The elaborateness and richness of the Divine Liturgy with its numerous litanies and supplications make the Roman Tridentine Mass with its abbreviated ninefold *Kyrie* somewhat pale by comparison.

Bibliography

Bichsel, M. A.; Hueller, M. M.; and Selhorst, E. J. 1967. *NCE* 7: 29–304.

Brightman, F. E. 1896. *Liturgies Eastern and Western.* Oxford.

———. 1922. *The Divine Liturgy of St. John Chrysostom.* London.

Britt, M. 1922. *The Hymns of the Breviary and Missal.* New York.

Duchesne, L. 1903. *Christian Worship, Its Origin and Evolution.* London.

Funk, F. X. 1905. *Didascalia et Constitutiones Apostolorum.* Paderborn.

Grant, R. M. 1961. *Gnosticism.* New York.

Schalk, C. 1978. *Key Words in Church Music: New Testament Hymnology.* St. Louis.

Werner, E. 1959. *The Sacred Bridge.* London.

M. Alfred Bichsel

HYMNS, THANKSGIVING. See THANKSGIVING HYMNS (1QH).

HYPOCORISTIC NAMES. See NAMES, HYPOCORISTIC.

HYPOSTASIS OF THE ARCHONS (NHC II,*4*).

Cast in the form of a revelatory discourse, the *Hypostasis of the Archons* (NHC II,*4*) from the Nag Hammadi Library is a Sethian gnostic treatise in which an anonymous teacher offers secret knowledge *(gnosis)* to a gnostic Christian community. This knowledge clarifies both the origin and nature of the evil archons (rulers) who created and presently dominate the visible universe and the situation of the elect in their struggle against these archons.

Utilizing a clearly gnostic interpretation of the Genesis 1–6 story line, the author recounts the drama of salvation from the creation of the material universe by the blind Samael (alias laldabaoth), to the fabrication of Adam and Eve, to the births of Seth and Norea (sister of Seth), to the Flood and Noah's role (86.27–92.19). There follows a revelation to Norea by the great angel Eleleth of the ultimate banishment of the ignorant creator laldabaoth, the advent of the savior ("the true human being" [96.32]), the destruction of the evil archons, and the salvation of the "spirituals" (93.13–97.20). The final victory is achieved through the savior's gift of "gnosis" to the elect, informing them of their intrinsic, spiritual, immortal nature.

The presence in the text of Hellenistic-Jewish speculation on the figures of Sophia and Norea, the homiletic interpretation of Genesis 1–6, the influence of the early Church's christology, and the presence of religiously oriented Middle Platonic philosophical tradition focused on ontological and theological speculation—all have led most scholars to identify *Hyp. Arch.* with the Sethian cycle of texts found in the Nag Hammadi Library (e.g., Schenke 1981: 588–616; Bullard and Layton 1989: 220ff.; Layton 1974: 371–72). Also, comments in the text about Norea (91.34–94.2), daughter of Eve, reveal connections of *Hyp. Arch.* with a literary tradition about this figure found among the Sethian Ophites, Jewish apocryphal and rabbinical works, and *Orig. World* in NHC II,*5*. Indeed, the last-mentioned refers to a "Book of Norea" (102,11.24–25) to which Epiphanius alludes (*Haer.* 39.5.2). Some would identify *Hyp. Arch.* with this "Book," though convincing demonstration has not been made.

While some maintain *Hyp. Arch.* was originally a non-Christian gnostic text that has been subsequently Christianized (Hedrick 1986: 9; Barc 1981: 10ff.; Roberge 1980: 7–9), an increasing number of commentators view the work as Christian gnostic, the author drawing the structure and much terminology in the text from the only authority actually cited, the "spirit-inspired Apostle," Paul (Bullard 1970: 161; Pagels 1986: 258, 266; Layton 1974: 363f.).

Hyp. Arch. appears fourth among the seven tractates in Codex II. Apart from minor lacunae in the first 10 lines, the text is fairly well preserved. Written principally in Sahidic Coptic with significant incursions of Subachmimic forms, the tractate has clearly been translated from a Greek original. Though it undoubtedly contains earlier traditional material, *Hyp. Arch.* was probably composed in the 3d century C.E., perhaps in Egypt (cf. the Coptic puns in 86.30; 94.22; and reference to theriomorphic rulers in 87.29).

Bibliography

Texts and Translations:

Bullard, R. 1970. *The Hypostasis of the Archons.* Patristische Texte und Studien 10. Berlin.

Bullard, R., and Layton, B. 1989. NHC II,*4:* Hypostasis of the Archons: Introduction, Text, and Translation. Pp. 220–59 in *Nag Hammadi Codex II,2–7: Introductions, Texts, Translations, Indices,* Ed. B. Layton. NHS 20. Leiden.

Layton, B. 1974. The Hypostasis of the Archons or "The Reality of the Rulers." *HTR* 67: 351–425.

———. 1987. *The Gnostic Scriptures.* Garden City, NY.

Articles

Barc, B. 1981. *L'Hypostase des Archontes: Traité gnostique sur l'origine de l'homme, du monde et des archontes NH II,4.* BCNHE 1. Quebec.

Hedrick, C. W. 1986. Introduction: Nag Hammadi, Gnosticism, and Early Christianity—A Beginner's Guide. Pp. 1–11 in *Nag Hammadi, Gnosticism and Early Christianity,* ed. C. W. Hedrick and R. Hodgson, Jr. Peabody, MA.

Pagels, E. H. 1986. Exegesis and Exposition of the Genesis Creation Accounts in Selected Texts from Nag Hammadi. Pp. 257–85 in *Nag Hammadi, Gnosticism and Early Christianity,* ed. C. W. Hedrick and R. Hodgson, Jr. Peabody, MA.

Roberge, M. 1980. *Norea.* BCNHT 5. Quebec.

Schenke, H.-M. 1981. The Phenomenon and Significance of Gnostic Sethianism. Pp. 588–616 in *The Rediscovery of Gnosticism,* ed. B. Layton. Numen Sup 41. Leiden.

MALCOLM L. PEEL

HYPSIPHRONE (NHC XI,*4*).

Hypsiphrone, which means "high-minded one" or perhaps "she of exalted thought," is the fourth and last treatise of Codex XI of the Coptic Library from Nag Hammadi (NHC XI,*4:* 69.23–72.35). It presently consists of four large and two small fragments containing the lower portions of the inner and outer margins of two papyrus leaves, which must have originally contained the entirety of this short treatise. It is written in the same script as the much longer and better-preserved treatise of that codex, *Allogenes,* although there is no discernible further relationship beyond these two treatises. *Hypsiphrone* is written in an apparently standard Sahidic Coptic dialect, unlike the other treatises of Codex XI. It bears the superscript title "Hypsiph[rone]," the remainder of the title being restored from other occurrences within the treatise; since the conclusion of the treatise is not extant, it may or may not have borne a subscript title.

Apart from the poor condition of the treatise, even its cryptic title affords little insight into its content. The *incipit* "The book (or scroll) [of visions] which were seen [by Hypsiphrone; and] they [are revealed] in the place of [her] virginity" adds little more. Although there is mentioned a plurality of persons speaking with one another, the treatise does not appear to be a dialogue. Instead, the whole is presented as a speech of Hypsiphrone, who reports the receipt of certain revelations during her descent from the "place of her virginity" into the world. The only figure mentioned by Hypsiphrone is one Phainops, "he of the gleaming eye," who apparently presides over a fount of blood into which he breathes, and which seems to produce a fiery effect.

One may conjecture that Hypsiphrone represents some form of the personified thought of a high deity who leaves her dwelling in the transcendental realm, where there are no distinctions of gender, to descend to the earthly realm at the time of the creation of humankind. There she encounters Phainops, probably in the act of creating humankind, who apparently produces "a [man in the likeness] of blood" from his fiery fount of blood.

In spite of the paucity of text, what remains seems to have some affinity with the group of gnostic texts generally designated as "Sethian." To judge from the name "Hypsiphrone," one may have to do here with the Sethian figure of Eleleth, called Phronesis in *Hyp. Arch.* 93.8–97.21, one of the traditional Sethian Four Illuminators, whose name might be derived from Aramaic *Fillith,* "the tall one," which could be rendered by Gk *hypsiphrone.*

The fount of blood may refer to the heavenly Adamas or heavenly archetype of Adam, described in *Orig. World* (108.2–31) as the "enlightened bloody one" (based on the Hebrew pun on *Eadam,* "man," and *dam,* "blood"). In this case, Hypsiphrone would be the Illuminator Eleleth, who in some Sethian texts is regarded as the abode of Sophia and certain "repentant souls" and in others *(Trim. Prot.; Gos. Egypt.)* is held responsible for the act usually ascribed to Sophia: that of producing the demiurge Yaldabaoth. Eleleth/Hypsiphrone would also be responsible for the downward projection of the likeness of Adamas, the divine image after which the earthly Adam is modeled by the demiurge. In any case, Hypsiphrone is certainly a figure similar to that of the descending and restored Sophia. Phainops, "radiant-faced one," might then be a name for either the enlightened archetypal Adamas, or—since he seems to be distinguished from the "fount of blood"—for the fiery angel Sabbaoth, the brother of the evil demiurge produced by the breath of Zoe, Pistis Sophia's daughter, in an effort to imprison the demiurge (*Hyp. Arch.* 95.5–96.4). Thus, although it bears no trace of the traditional Sethian names for these figures, *Hypsiphrone* may in fact be very closely related to the other Sethian texts.

Bibliography

Turner, J. D. 1977. Hypsiphrone. P. 453 in *The Nag Hammadi Library in English,* ed. J. M. Robinson. San Francisco.

———. 1989. Hypsiphrone: NHC XI,*4:* 69.23–72.35. in *Nag Hammadi Codices XI, XII and XIII,* ed. C. W. Hedrick. Leiden.

JOHN D. TURNER

HYRAX. See ZOOLOGY.

HYRCANUS (PERSON) [Gk *Hyrkanos*]. **1.** The son of Tobias, a wealthy depositer to the temple treasury (2 Macc 3:11).

2. John Hyrcanus I ruled as high priest and ethnarch from 135/4 to 104 B.C.E. He succeeded Simon Maccabeus, his father, who was murdered with Hyrcanus I's two elder brothers by Ptolemy, Simon's son-in-law. Antiochus VII, king of Syria, laid siege to Jerusalem, forcing Hyrcanus I to pay heavy tribute (Jos. *Ant* 13.8.2–3), but the long struggle with Syria ended when Antiochus VII was succeeded by Demetrius II and internal strife. An embassy sent by Hyrcanus I received Roman confirmation of the Hasmoneans' independence.

Hyrcanus I conquered Shechem, destroyed the Samaritan temple on Mt. Gerizim, and invaded Idumea, forcibly circumcising many of the inhabitants (Jos. *Ant* 13.9.1). Hyrcanus I razed the city of Samaria (Jos. *Ant* 13.10.2–3) and occupied the Esdraelon valley to Mt. Carmel (Jos. *JW* 1.2.7). According to Josephus, Hyrcanus I employed foreign mercenaries for his campaigns paid with money plundered from King David's tomb (Jos. *Ant* 13.8.4).

Hyrcanus I was the first Jewish ruler to mint coins bearing his own name. The coins read on the obverse side, "John the High Priest, and the Community of the Jews," and on the reverse side was a horn of plenty with a poppy head inside (Greek symbols of prosperity and fertility). The Pharisees and Sadducees also rose to prominence during the reign of Hyrcanus I (Jos. *Ant* 13.10.5–7; but see also *Ant* 13.10.9).

3. Hyrcanus II was the irresolute son of Alexander Jannaeus and Alexandra Salome. He served as high priest during his mother's reign from 76 to 67 B.C.E. After his mother's death, his claim to the kingship was challenged by his younger brother Aristobulus II, embroiling the two in civil war. Hyrcanus II was reinstated in the office of high priest by Pompey and served from 63 to 40 B.C.E. He was executed by Herod the Great in 30 B.C.E. See also HASMONEAN DYNASTY.

SCOTT T. CARROLL

HYSSOP. See FLORA.

I

IBEX. See ZOOLOGY.

IBHAR (PERSON) [Heb *yibḥār*]. One of 13 sons of David listed as having been born to David's wives in Jerusalem (2 Sam 5:15; 1 Chr 3:6; 14:5), in addition to his six sons born at Hebron. His mother's name is unknown: four of the 13 sons born in Jerusalem were Bathsheba's sons; the remainder were born to unnamed wives. Besides these 13, David had numerous (unnamed) sons born to his concubines, according to 1 Chr 3:9. Ibhar is the first son listed after Bathsheba's four sons, but nothing further is known of him. See also DAVID, SONS OF.

David M. Howard, Jr.

IBLEAM (PLACE) [Heb *yiblĕʿām*]. Var. BILEAM. A town in the territory of Issachar, given to Manasseh, but from which Manasseh could not drive out the Canaanite inhabitants (Josh 17:11–12; Judg 1:27). Ibleam was an important city in the Bronze Age, mentioned as a royal city in Egyptian archives (*LBHG*, 152) and occurs in the conquest list of Thutmose III (*GP* 2: 357; *ANET*, 242). During the Iron Age (2 Kgs 9:27), Jehu mortally wounded Ahaziah, king of Judah, at the ascent of Gur, outside Ibleam. It is possible that in 2 Kgs 15:10 the Heb *qblʿm*, "before the people," should be read *byblʿm* as the Lucian version of the LXX renders it (Gk *en Ieblaam*) and that Zechariah, the king of Israel, was therefore killed "in Ibleam" (Cogan and Tadmor *2 Kings* AB, 170–71). Other scholars (Albright 1945: 69) restore Ibleam to the list of levitical cities, replacing Bileam in 1 Chr 6:55 (—Eng 6:70) and Gath-rimmon in Josh 21:25.

Ibleam is almost universally identified with Kh. Belʿameh (M.R. 177205), which guards the easternmost pass through the mountains of Ephraim into the Jezreel valley (*LBHG*, 436). The site has strong natural defenses (Phythian-Adams 1922: 143), which may have been supplemented by an ancient underground water system from Bir Senjar at the foot of the tell (Schumacher 1907: 107). Ibleam, along with Megiddo and Jokneam, was one of the fortress cities which guarded access to and from the S limits of the Jezreel valley.

Bibliography

Albright, W. F. 1945. The List of Levitical Cities. Pp. 75–104 in *Louis Ginzberg Jubilee Volume*. New York.

Phythian-Adams, W. J. 1922. The Site of Ibleam. *PEQ* 1922: 142–47.

Schumacher, G. 1907. The Great Water Passage of Khirbet Belʿameh. *PEQ* 1907: 107–12.

Melvin Hunt

IBNEIAH (PERSON) [Heb *yibnĕyāh*]. One of the Benjaminites who is listed in 1 Chr 9:8 as having returned from exile in Babylon to Jerusalem. Ibneiah is not listed in Neh 11:7–9, which is a parallel passage to 1 Chr 9:7–9. Although some have attempted to equate Ibneiah with Gabbai in Neh 11:8, Braun (*1 Chronicles* WBC, 140) has stated that this identification is doubtful. It is more likely that the author of 1 Chronicles 9 and the author of Nehemiah 11 simply had different traditions at their disposal. The name Ibnijah, which occurs later in 1 Chr 9:8, has the same consonants as the name Ibneiah *(ybnyh)*. Although Dahlberg (*IDB* 2: 671) has suggested that these two names in reality refer to the same person, the text presents them as two individuals separated by several generations.

Robert C. Dunston

IBNIJAH (PERSON) [Heb *yibnîyāh*]. A Benjaminite who returned to Jerusalem from exile in Babylon (1 Chr 9:8). The consonants in the name Ibnijah are identical to the consonants in the name Ibneiah *(ybnyh)*, which occurs earlier in 1 Chr 9:8. Dahlberg (*IDB* 2: 671) suggested that the two names referred to the same person but the text presents them as separate individuals from separate generations. Ibnijah does not appear in the parallel passage in Nehemiah (Neh 11:7–9) but 1 Chr 9:7–9 and Neh 11:7–9 vary at several points, which seems to indicate that the authors had different traditions from which to work.

Robert C. Dunston

IBRI (PERSON) [Heb *ʿibrî*]. One of the "remaining Levites" who, according to the Chronicler, casts lots before David, Zadok, and Ahimelek in order to receive his place among the levitical household leaders (1 Chr 24:27). Although only mentioned in 1 Chr 24:27, the Chronicler grants Ibri a levitical lineage as the son of Jaaziah, a descendant of Merari, along with his brothers, Shoham, Zaccur, and Beno (1 Chr 24:27). Although Liver (1968: 8. 29–32) believes that this list may have originated from an authentic source composed during the reign of David or Solomon, most commentators have attributed the list in which Ibri appears to a time later than the main composition of Chronicles, either to the late Persian period (Williamson 1979: 259–60, 265–68) or, more commonly, to the Maccabean era (Rudolph *Chronikbücher* HAT, 163–65). The style of the list, however, corresponds closely with the compositional techniques of the Chronicler. Ibri, a gentilic form meaning "a Hebrew" [Heb *ʿibrî*], may represent the

Chronicler's notion of a suitable name for a levitical household leader in the reign of David.

Bibliography

Liver, J. 1968. *Chapters in the History of Priests and Levites.* Jerusalem (in Hebrew).

Williamson, H. G. M. 1979. The Origins of the Twenty-Four Priestly Courses, A Study of 1 Chronicles xxiii–xxvii. Pp. 251–68 in *Studies in the Historical Books of the Old Testament,* ed. J. A. Emerton. VTSup 30. Leiden.

JOHN W. WRIGHT

IBSAM (PERSON) [Heb *yibśom*]. Ibsam was a descendant, perhaps grandson, of Issachar, according to the genealogy of 1 Chr 7:1–5. The sons of Issachar were Tola, Puah, Jashub, and Shimron and the sons of Tola were Uzzi, Rephaiah, Jeriel, Jahmai, Ibsam, and Samuel. Tola's "sons" were probably not immediate sons but descendants.

Other listings of the sons of Issachar are found in Gen 46:13 and Num 26:23–25. Neither passage mentions any of the sons of Tola; thus 1 Chr 7:2 is the only OT occurrence of Ibsam. However, Judg 10:1 names Tola, a man of Issachar, as one of the minor judges. He is son of Puah, son of Dodo, who resided in Shamir in Ephraim. Curtis (*Chronicles* ICC, 144–45) has theorized that all four names given as Issachar's sons can be obtained from this information in Judg 10:1.

Tola's sons are said to be "heads of their fathers' households," a phrase that has different usages in the OT but in genealogies refers to military commanders (Williamson *1 and 2 Chronicles* NCBC, 67). Assuming a military background for the Chronicles' genealogy, then "fathers' households" would have been the means of military conscription (*1 Chronicles* WBC, 7). Ibsam and the other sons of Tola are also called "mighty men of valor" *(gibbor ḥayil),* a term that usually means "warrior" or "soldier" in Chronicles, but could possibly be a technical term for the social class, "nobles," who bore arms for their king (Oswalt 1980: 148).

Bibliography

Oswalt, J. N. 1980. *gabar.* Vol. 1, p. 148 in *Theological Wordbook of the Old Testament,* ed. R. L. Harris; G. L. Archer, Jr.; and B. K. Waltke. Chicago.

M. STEPHEN DAVIS

IBZAN (PERSON) [Heb *ʾibṣan*]. One of the leaders who "judged Israel" in the premonarchic period and is mentioned only in Judg 12:8–10, immediately following the stories of Jephthah. The brief notice indicates that Ibzan, whose name means "swift" (if related to Ar *ʿabuṣun*), had 30 sons for whom he arranged exogamous marriages, bringing women from "outside," presumably from beyond the clan or protective association of villages. Similarly his 30 daughters were sent "outside" in marriage. Given the same round number in the notice about Jair (Judg 10:4), the kinship language most likely denotes sociopolitical affiliation. Ibzan's extended family was the regional subgroup of nuclear Israelite families over which he exercised direct leadership.

Ibzan's leadership lasted seven years. His place of residence and burial was Bethlehem. A tradition of interpretation as old as Josephus assumed this to be the famous Bethlehem in Judah; but the context of the Ibzan pericope makes it more likely that the reference is to a N Bethlehem close to the border of Asher (Josh 19:15). The book of Judges appears to be structured, at least in part, by the idea that each of the tribes had at one time or another produced a leader who "judged Israel." Whereas Elon of Zebulun comes next, Ibzan was possibly regarded as the leader who came out of Asher.

Ibzan is the third in a series of five such leaders about whom no warfare stories survive. He is preceded by Tola and Jair (10:1–5) and followed by Elon and Abdon (12:11–15). Each of them, like most of those whose achievements are recounted at some length, "judged Israel." If this implies military leadership, it is not described. With such scant information given about them, it may be that they represent two major interludes of relative peace, framing the crisis which generated the stories of Jephthah (10:6–12:7) and which are enclosed within the same rubrics that mark the so-called minor judges.

How far the leader's authority extended beyond clan or tribe is unclear. It is conceivable but not demonstrable that an archival list of persons who filled a central position in the early intertribal organization was the source of such information for the compiler of the book of Judges. With no difference in the formula indicating that each "judged Israel," it is more likely not a difference in the office filled by major and minor judges, but a difference of literary purpose, a quickening of the pace before and after the career of Jephthah (Mullen 1982: 196).

Bibliography

Mullen, E. T. Jr. 1982. The "Minor Judges": Some Literary and Historical Considerations. *CBQ* 44/2: 185–201.

ROBERT G. BOLING

ICHABOD (PERSON) [Heb *ʾîkābôd*]. Son of Phinehas, grandson of Eli (1 Sam 4:19–21; 14:3). His mother is shocked into a premature labor when she learns that the Ark has been captured by the Philistines and that her husband and father-in-law are dead. Before she dies she gives her child the name Ichabod, a name whose exact meaning is disputed. The Hebrew word *kābôd* means glory and refers to the radiant light that surrounds a deity. It had been thought that the particle *ʾī* was to be taken as a negation, thus Ichabod would mean "no glory." This would support Josephus' reading of the name as "Inglorious" (*adoxia, Ant* 5.360). More recently, however, it has been suggested that Ichabod is derived from the Ug *ʾiy* which means "where is . . ." or "alas" and *kbd,* glory. Accordingly Ichabod would mean "Where is the Glory?," or "Alas, (for) the Glory" and signifies the absence of the deity. Thus the name of the child is related to the departure of the glory of the Lord signified by the loss of the Ark, an association made explicit in 1 Sam 4:22.

Though in 1 Sam 14:3 Ichabod is said to be the brother of Ahitub, father of Ahimelech whose son is Abiathar, such a relationship seems unlikely. Verse 3, which relates Abiathar to the family of Eli, is probably a gloss.

PAULINE A. VIVIANO

ICONIUM (PLACE) [Gk *Ikonion*]. A city in S central Anatolia (modern Konya, Turkey [37°51′N; 32°30′E]) visited by Paul on his missionary journeys (Acts 13:51; 14:1, 19,21; 16:2). Located approximately 170 mi (280 km) S of Ankara (ancient Ancyra) on the border between mountainous Phrygia to the W and the broad plain of Lycaonia to the S and E, it lies on a high, fertile plateau (3,770 feet or 1,150 m). One of the oldest continually occupied cities in the world, it dates back at least to the 3d millennium B.C. According to local legend, it was the first city to be built following the great Flood. Its location caused it to be linked at various times with both Phrygia and Lycaonia. Founded as a Phrygian settlement and linked with Phrygia both geographically and culturally, the native people would have considered themselves Phrygians. As a part of the empire of the Seleucid successors to Alexander the Great, and later as a part of the Roman empire, it was linked with the cities of Lystra and Derbe (in Lycaonia). Those who were strongly attached to the Gk language and culture would have considered themselves Greeks, while a few would have identified with the vision of the Roman empire. For millennia, Iconium has been—and, as Konya, continues to be today—"a prosperous city of peace and commerce as well as a center of agriculture" (Hagner *ISBE* 2: 792). Located on an important crossroads linking Rome and the Greek cities of the Roman provinces of Asia, Macedonia, and Achaia with the luxuries of the Levant, Iconium was a large and wealthy city in NT times.

The city figures in Greek mythology as the place where Perseus cut off the head of the Gorgon Medusa (Hes. *Theog.* 270). An ancient tradition saw in the name of the city, connecting it with the Gk *eikōn* (image), an allusion to this event. The foundations of the city are, however, lost in the prehistory of antiquity. From the 3d century B.C. it was ruled variously by the Seleucids to the SE, who were responsible for its partial Hellenization, and by the kings of Galatia and Pontus to the N. It came under the influence of Rome in 65 B.C. and was later incorporated into the empire in 25 B.C. when Galatia became a province. During the time of the Emperor Claudius (A.D. 41–54), the city received the honorific imperial prefix and thus became known as Claudiconium. Under the Emperor Hadrian (117–138), Iconium became a Roman colony. In the time of Paul's 1st-century visits, the city became a center of early Christian vitality, a fact attested by numerous inscriptions, traditions, and legends, and remained so until the Islamic conquest in 708. In 235 a church council was held there. In 372 the city became the capital of the Roman province of Lycaonia. During the Middle Ages, Konya was the capital of the Seljuk empire of Roum and the center of a dynamic religious and cultural movement (11th–14th century) that produced great works of literature, beautiful art, and magnificent buildings. Marco Polo reported that the carpets made in Konya were the best and the most beautiful in the world. Perhaps its most famous son during this period was Maulana Jelal-uddin Rumi (1207–1273), the Islamic mystic and founder of the order popularly known as "the Whirling Dervishes." Even today the city continues in its importance—hence the continued popularity of the old Turkish proverb: "See all the world, but see Konya!"

The narrative of the Acts of the Apostles focuses on a visit of Paul and his missionary associate Barnabas to the cities of Pisidian Antioch, Iconium, Lystra, and Derbe (13:14–14:24) in A.D. 47–48. Having been expelled from Antioch as a result of their successful evangelistic endeavor, they found refuge in Iconium, 90 miles (150 km) away. Here history repeated itself: as a result of their witness, there were many conversions, which led, in turn, to hostility among both local Jews and gentiles. So Paul and Barnabas had to flee across the regional border into the Lycaonian cities of Lystra and Derbe. At the end of their mission they retraced their footsteps through the same cities for the purpose of "strengthening" or "confirming" (Gk *epiststerizō*) the new disciples and encouraging them to remain faithful to their commitment (14:22). Acts also says that they appointed elders for the churches at this time (14:23), though many interpreters would regard this as an anachronism introduced into the narrative as a result of later practice.

Later, during what is traditionally called his "second missionary journey" (A.D. 49), Paul, this time accompanied by Silas, visited these cities again to "strengthen/confirm" (Gk *epiststerizō*) the churches that had been founded earlier (Acts 15:36–16:6). It was on this trip that he was joined by a younger associate named Timothy, who was a native of this region. And it also seems likely that the author of Acts (18:23; so Bruce *Acts* NICNT, 357–58 and *Galatians* NIGTC, 13; Finegan 1981: 92; *ISBE* 2: 792–93; Hemer fc.) intends to suggest a further visit to this region for the same purpose on his way back to Ephesus on the so-called "third missionary journey" (A.D. 52). The consensus of recent scholarship is that these cities are to be identified with the churches addressed in the Epistle to the Galatians (Bruce *Galatians* NIGTC, 3–18). See GALATIANS, EPISTLE TO THE. In 2 Timothy 3:11 we have an independent reference to "persecutions [and] sufferings" experienced by Paul "in Antioch, Iconium, and Lystra." The intended recipient of the letter, Timothy, was, according to Acts, "well spoken of by the brethren of Lystra and Iconium" (16:2).

The apocryphal work entitled *The Acts of Paul*, dating from the second half of the 2d century, contains traditions and legends about Paul's missionary activity. It was written by an elder of the church in this very region, who, unfortunately, was disciplined by his compatriots for his labor of love (he said he had done his work "out of love for Paul"). One famous series of episodes focuses on Paul's friendship of a young woman by the name of Thecla and on her evangelism, teaching, and exploits for the Lord. The narrative tells us more about the late 2d century tendencies to asceticism, religious enthusiasm, and credulity than about the events of a century earlier. But it does contain this description of Paul, set in Iconium, that many scholars have regarded as historically trustworthy: "And [Onesiphorus] saw Paul coming, a man small of stature, with a bald head and crooked legs, in a good state of body, with eyebrows meeting and nose somewhat hooked, full of friendliness; for now he appeared like a man, and now he had the face of an angel" (*NTApocr* 2: 354). For further discussion see *HDB* 2: 443–45.

Bibliography

Bruce, F. F. 1977. *Paul: Apostle of the Heart Set Free.* Grand Rapids.
Finegan, J. 1981. *The Archaeology of the New Testament.* Boulder, CO.

Hemer, C. J. fc. *The Historical Value of the Acts of the Apostles,* ed. C. Gempf. Tübingen.
Johnson, S. E. 1987. *Paul the Apostle and His Cities.* Wilmington.
Ramsay, W. M. 1920. *St. Paul the Traveller and the Roman Citizen.* London.
———. 1953. *The Bearing of Recent Discovery on the Trustworthiness of the New Testament.* Grand Rapids.
———. 1960. *The Cities of St. Paul.* Grand Rapids.

W. WARD GASQUE

ICONOGRAPHY AND THE BIBLE.

The study of artistic subject matter or content (as opposed to artistic techniques and styles). Iconography therefore strives to describe the appearance, development, and disappearance of certain motifs and compositions, or the substitution of one artistic form by another.

A. Introduction
B. Iconography and History
C. Iconography and the Material Culture of Biblical Times
D. Iconography and the Culture of Concepts

A. Introduction

The relationship between iconography and iconology is somewhat similar to that between geography and geology. *Iconography* describes, e.g., the development of artistic representations of Christ from the triumphant Savior on the Cross to the man of sorrows depicted by Grünewald, or e.g., the depiction of the romanesque Virgin from the *sedes sapientiae* ("throne of wisdom") to the "Virgin of Lourdes" represented without the child at all. *Iconology* attempts to establish which movements of social and religious life and thought manifest themselves through the changes described by iconography (see Kaemmerling 1979).

The relationship between the Bible and iconography is not understood here as the edifying illustration of biblical texts by the arts, although this pictorial expression is a valuable contribution to the history of biblical exegesis. Many of the insights and results won in a century of research in this very broad field are compiled in the 8 volumes of the *Lexikon der christlichen Ikonographie* (Kirschbaum and Braunfels 1968–76). The relationship between the Bible and iconography is here understood as the influence of the contemporaneous art on the biblical texts in Israel itself (Schroer 1987) and in the neighboring countries, or as the scientific pictorial reconstruction of certain data given by the biblical texts (e.g., description of architecture).

Although innumerable biblical handbooks are illustrated with pictures from ANE sources, and each year sees the appearance of yet another volume of this kind (Lamp 1982–1983), the relationship between biblical texts and pictures contemporaneous to them remains neglected, in that it has never been studied in a systematically thought-out way, as is normal in the other disciplines of biblical research. These relationships are manifold: (1) A biblical text can explicitly describe a work of art, as e.g., the descriptions of drawings of Chaldean warriors in Ezek 23:14. (2) Descriptions can also be implicit. There are sound reasons for believing that Ezekiel was influenced by pictorial representations when describing the 4 living creatures supporting the sky (Ezekiel 1; Keel 1977: 125–273). (3) A text and a picture can independently deal with the same subject matter, as e.g., the appointment of an official or his being rewarded (Gen 31:37–45 and several Egyptian tomb paintings of New Kingdom date; Vergote 1959: 121–135).

What is the purpose of seeking and studying such pictures? First of all we usually want to see something of which we hear or read, or on the contrary, to have an explanation of what we visually behold. Our wish is to hear and to see. But what exactly is the advantage of seeing something which we have heard about? In his book on Giotto, M. Imdahl (1980) coined the term *Ikonizität,* describing the particular possibilities of a picture in contrast to words. The visual image is better adapted for the portrayal of complicated relationships. The proportions of a human face or body, or any other object, are far more easily conveyed by means of a picture than through the use of descriptive words; the relationships uniting family members are more easily understood by a family tree than by the use of mere words. Also, it would require an extraordinary number of words to provide information regarding the exact relationships between a large number of buildings, streets, rivers, etc. to each other—relationships that are more conveniently conveyed by a simple map. Conversely, a series of actions is more easily described by words than by pictures.

This is related to the second important characteristic of visual information. The figurative picture always maintains a certain affinity to the object represented. It has a natural relationship to it. A horse or a cow in an ancient Egyptian or Chinese painting is recognizable to every human being (familiar with horses and cows), despite the stylistic variations. It is, however, impossible to recognize the Chinese or Egyptian words for horse or cow without proper knowledge of these languages and their scripts, since language is wholly artificial. This artificiality permits differentiation *ad libitum.* You can give every human being a different name and even one to every different aspect of one individual human being (e.g., as father, son, husband, etc.). But language is equally capable of generalizing; pictures usually depict a man or woman, adult or child, black or white, standing or seated, etc., while language can easily create terms like "humanity." Language can easily distinguish one aspect of a thing; pictures lend themselves to the representation of clusters of aspects. The description of the cherubim in 1 Kgs 6:23–28 mentions a few aspects (the materials of which they are made, their measurements, the positions of their wings) but fails to furnish an all-around picture. Thus Josephus may claim, "as for the cherubim themselves, no one can say or imagine what they looked like" (*Ant* 8.73). If we had a picture, we would have fewer doubts concerning the appearance of the cherubim; and were there a god or goddess seated upon the cherubim, we would also be informed about the nature of the relationships between both, as well as the meaning of the arrangement as a whole.

The significance of pictorial representation in the realm of man-made objects (useful and artistic) has long been recognized. Iconography is also important—perhaps even more important—when considering entities with which we ourselves are familiar, such as the sun, moon, storms, earth, and trees. We far too readily assume that these phenomena possessed the same significance in the ANE as they do today. The merism "heaven and earth," for example, sounds quite natural to us, without any peculiar connotations. When looking at illustrations from the Egyptian *Book of the Dead,* where the sky is the figure of the goddess Nut arched over the extended figure of the earth god (e.g., *ANEP*, no. 542; Keel 1972: figs. 27–30, 32–33), it becomes quite clear that in ancient Egypt the concepts "heaven and earth" were associated with ideas and feelings very different from ours. Faced with words and ideas, the individual hearer quite often understands them in terms supplied primarily by his or her own cultural heritage. It is considerably more difficult for the terms of that cultural heritage to prevail when a concept is visually rendered, because we are then confronted with a cluster of aspects and not with a mere abstract pattern permitting arbitrary interpretations.

Iconography allows this influence of the cultural heritage considerably less latitude than does the abstract phoneme. It can thus emphasize a number of very common peculiarities in the reasoning and imagination of the ANE more quickly and effectively than can the written word. Iconography unavoidably compels us to see with the eyes of the ANE (Keel 1972: 8).

B. Iconography and History

Palestinian Judaism regarded the Bible as *Torah,* as "instruction." Josephus however presented it to the Greco-Roman world as a history book (cf. his *Antiquities* and *AgAp* 1.37f). Corresponding to this new historical understanding, a desire was awakened for historical pictures of biblical personalities and events, in a naturalistic style, preferably of "photographic" quality. Since the middle of the 5th century B.C., the Greek world had been cultivating a realistic type of portraiture which the Romans subsequently developed even further.

When the pilgrim Egeria (Etheria) visited the Lands of the Bible about 400 A.D., the Bishop of Arabia showed her a double statue of Moses and Aaron amid the ruins of Ramesses (Peregrinatio Etheriae 8.2; Wilkinson 1971: 217; Maraval 1982: 159). Most probably what she saw was a statue of Ramesses II (1279–1213 B.C.) with some Egyptian deity. When the famous English nobleman and traveller Sir Robert Ker Porter visited the Behistun (Bisutun) Mountain in 1812, encountering the relief of Darius I (*ANEP,* nos. 249 and 462) with 10 subjugated rebels before him, he was quite convinced that he was looking at a monument of the Assyrian King Shalmaneser before the 10 tribes of N Israel he had deported to N Syria and Media (2 Kgs 17:3–6). In Porter's view, the location of the relief in Median territory was intended to remind the deportees of their situation (Porter 1821–22, 2: 149–63).

J. G. Wilkinson (1878, 1: 479; see C below) thought that the well-known painting from Beni Hassan (*ANEP*, no. 3; Keel 1972: fig. 308) showing "Asiatic nomads" represented the arrival of the sons of Jacob in Egypt. A correct rendering of the inscriptions proved this interpretation to be misguided, since these "nomads" were connected with antimony (used as eye-paint) and equipped with a bellow, presenting desert game to the Egyptians but without any apparent flocks. They are perhaps best regarded as coppersmiths and hunters, together with their wives and children, who have come to Egypt as specialists to work in an antimony mine (Goedicke 1984; Kessler 1987). They are thus quite an inappropriate illustration of seminomads, such as the biblical patriarchs are generally represented.

H. Rosellini (1832–44, 2: tav. 49,1), who accompanied Champollion on his Egyptian expedition in 1828–29, labelled the brick makers in the Tomb of Rechmire (*ANEP*, no. 115), "The Hebrews who are making the bricks." Wilkinson (1878, 1: 343–345) argued, however, that the Israelites had not been detained at Thebes (where the inscription places the scene) and that in the course of the centuries, thousands of Asiatics—in addition to the Israelites—would have been compelled to fabricate bricks.

Rosellini (1832–44, 1: tav. 148A) and to a lesser degree also Champollion (1909, 2: 161f.) were convinced that they had found a portrait of Solomon's son, Rehoboam, in Shishak's reliefs at Karnak (*ANEP*, no. 349) because they had read one of the 150 names of conquered cities as *ywdh mr(= l)k,* "Judah's king." The 150 figures are all identical however, representing Asiatics in general—without individual traits—and, more importantly, they do not identify individuals, but represent place-names. The one referred to is perhaps *yd-hmlk,* "hand (= stronghold) of the King" (*CTAED,* 197).

It has often been stated that Jehu is the only historical personality of ancient Israel represented on an ANE monument (*ANEP,* nos. 351–54). What does this actually mean? The English explorer A. H. Layard, who in 1846 at Kalah discovered the Black Obelisk with the famous picture, thought that the 20 small images on the obelisk commemorated a victorious expedition to the East, perhaps as far as India. He was led to this conclusion by the 2-humped bactrian camels and the Indian (but in reality perhaps N Syrian) elephant (Layard 1849, 2: 433–37). Only the decipherment of the legends revealed that one of the two prostrate figures before the Assyrian king was "Jehu of the House of Omri." The costume and physiognomy of the figure representing him, unfortunately, appear to be identical to that of his counterpart, King Sua of Gilzanu. The figures are thus not portraits but mere "determinatives" for vassal kings paying homage to the Assyrian overlord (Smith 1977). Israel and Gilzanu were probably selected since they represented Shalmaneser III's most distant conquests, lying (respectively) far to the SW and NE of Assyria (Liebermann 1985).

In a lavishly illustrated volume, D. Ussishkin (1982) has attempted to demonstrate that the Lachish reliefs of Sennacherib (*ANEP,* nos. 371–74) give a realistic picture of the conquest of Lachish in 701 B.C. We can view a landscape with hills, fig trees, vineyards, and a city situated on a hill with a double wall (most probably representing the city walls and the acropolis) and square towers. Walls with square towers are conventionally used to represent the cities of the hilly and mountainous regions to the N and W of Mesopotamia. Since fig trees, vineyards, and cities built atop hills were common in these regions, the Assyrian scheme would fit many cities. W. M. F. Petrie (1891: 38) believed that Tell el-Hesi, which he excavated in 1890, was the ancient Lachish, thinking that the Sennacherib reliefs matched his finds. Ussishkin thinks the same today; however, he correctly identifies Lachish with Tell ed-Duweir, not with Tell el-Hesi. Apart from the general scheme, however, the reliefs do not bear much resemblance to the archaeologically based reconstruction of Lachish. There is no double wall and no traces of square towers have been found. The access road follows the W flank of the tell to a saddle, and does not zigzag down to the foot of the tell, as shown in the reliefs. Only the isolated gate tower before the city seems to be a specific feature of Lachish.

Thus, ANE art does not supply "historical photographs" as W. Keller suggests in his popular book, *The Bible as History*. Pictures had more or less the same function as Egyptian hieroglyphic determinatives: representing a class of objects, and not specific individual phenomena. (This is also true of medieval iconography; in the famous Nuremberg Chronicle of 1439, the same woodcut "illustrated" such very different cities as Syrian Damascus and Italian Mantua; Gombrich 1959: 59f.) Once this is recognized, it becomes clear that the entire section "Royalties and Dignitaries" in *ANEP* (nos. 376–463) is somewhat misleading. This section presents statues and heads of statues with the names of various rulers in the captions. This form of presentation reminds one of a modern encyclopedia with photographs of Churchill, Freud, Jung, and Kennedy, etc. But especially alarming is the caption of no. 419, "Statue of Tut-ankh-Amon usurped by Hor-em-heb." It sounds like "photograph of Kennedy used as photograph of Nixon." Even if Egyptian art occasionally attempted to portray certain individual features (especially in comparison to that of Mesopotamia), the custom of labeling older statues with the names of living kings, as Ramesses II was particularly inclined to do, reveals that they could not have been primarily intended as "portraits" in the modern sense, but rather intended to represent a *role* and not an individual.

History was conceived as the perpetually repeated fulfillment of divine decrees, a kind of ritual; history was a festival where the roles were more important than the individuals who filled them. In this manner, ANE art intended to emphasize the position and functions of the king and to a lesser extent individual kings and dignitaries. This was the approach selected by H. Frankfort and O. Keel (see D below).

Because the need for historical illustrations of the Bible will continue to remain strong, ancient oriental pictures will continue to be presented as such, regardless of what the scientific value of this practice might be. Ancient oriental iconography really cannot achieve more than to furnish the historical names and events of the Bible with contemporary clothes, weapons, etc., and to provide "portraits" of the various types of peoples (e.g., the Philistines, cf. *ANEP*, no. 341).

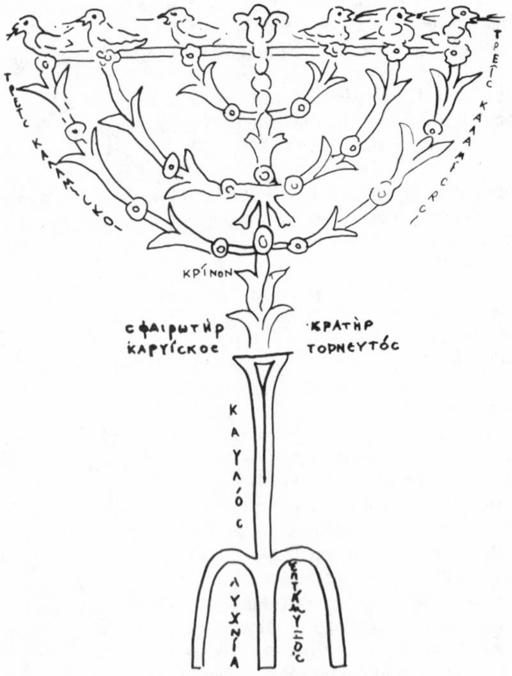

ICO.01. Seven-branched candelabrum as illustrated in the *Topographia Christiana* (ca. 550 A.D.). The illustrator was trying to depict word-for-word the almost incomprehensible technical terms of Exod 25:31–40. The use of doves instead of lamps goes back to the allegorical interpretation of the seven lamps as the gifts of the Holy Spirit. *(Codex Sinaiticus Graecus Nr. 1186, fol. 81 recto—11th century A.D. Redrawn from Wolska-Conus 1970: 61)*

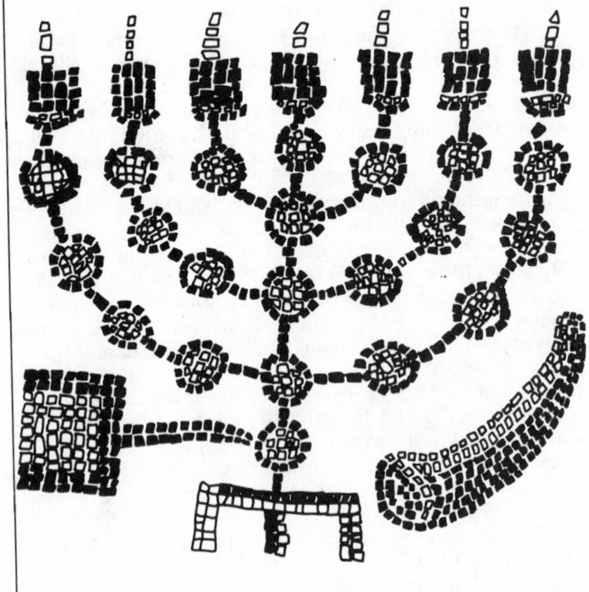

ICO.02. Mosaic from the synagogue in Hulda (550 A.D.). Note the three-legged base on the candelabrum which is typically found in the Byzantine period (as in Figs. ICO.01, ICO.03, and ICO.05). According to Josephus (*Ant* 3.145), the candelabrum had a solid base. Cf. Fig. ICO.10. *(Redrawn from Keel 1972: 319, fig. 458)*

C. Iconography and the Material Culture of Biblical Times

ANE iconography is suitable for the illustration of the typical and the institutional, but not for that of the individual person or the historical event. The interest in the actual appearance of certain objects and in the functioning of certain institutions was linked to a literal exegesis which already at an early date had attempted with the help of pictures to illustrate such things as the Tent of Meeting described in detail in Exodus 25–31 and the Temple of Solomon (described in less detail in 1 Kgs 5:15–6:37 and 7:17–51. In the Christian realm it was particularly Theodore of Mospsuestia who, influenced by the philological exegesis of Homer by the pagans (Schäublin 1974), in turn influenced the anonymous author of the *Topographia Christiana,* written around A.D. 550 and attributed since the 11th century to Kosmas Indicopleustes. In this work the author attempted to arrive at an illustration of the Tent of Meeting and its contents with the help of reconstructive sketches (Wolska-Conus 1968: 183–96; 1970: 38–65). See Fig. ICO.01. He was inspired not only by the biblical texts but also by pictures of the 7-branched candelabrum, the tables for the bread of offering, and similar furnishings which had frequently been reproduced in Jewish context since the 1st century B.C. (albeit for religious and political purposes rather than for scholarly ones). See Fig. ICO.02.

In the West, Cassiodorus (ca. A.D. 490–583) made a similar attempt. Influenced by the historicizing explanations of Josephus in his *Antiquities* (3.102–50; 8.61–98) and by the Jewish devotional art, he added a sketch of the Tent of Meeting (see Fig. ICO.03) and one of the temple to be added to his *Codex Grandior,* "so that which the text of the Holy Scriptures says about them might be more clearly laid before the eyes" (Adriaen 1958: 789; cf. 132). As was the case with the *Topographica Christiana,* Cassidorus was dependent not only on the biblical text but also on Jewish devotional art. See Fig. ICO.04. Cassidorus' reconstructive sketches found imitators far into the Middle Ages (Herrmann 1905: 148, fig. 49; 1926: 51, fig. 27).

ICO.03. Representation of the Tent of Meeting—Codex Amiatinus (ca. 690–712 A.D.). This codex provides a faithful copy of Cassiodorus' Codex Grandior. *(Biblioteca Laurenziana, Florence, Codex Amiatinus 1, fol. 2 verso, 3 recto, photograph by G. Sansoni, courtesy of O. Keel)*

ICO.04. Coin from the period of the Bar-Kokhba Revolt depicting the water basin. Exod 30:17–21 mentions a stand that is not depicted in the representation of the water basin *(labrum)* in Fig. ICO.03; nevertheless, note the striking similarity between the water basins in Figs. ICO.03 and ICO.04. *(Drawing by H. Keel-Leu from Meshorer 1967: pl. XXI, no. 169, courtesy of O. Keel)*

Another root of the literal exegesis was the philological Quran exegesis, which had an effect on the Karaïtes beginning in the 8th century A.D. In opposition to the ever increasing influence of the Talmud, this Jewish group held to a type of *sola scriptura* principle which stimulated rabbinic Judaism to a new and vigorous type of philologically oriented commentary. The most famous commentator of this school was Rabbi Shlomo ben-Izhaq, known as Rashi (A.D. 1040–1105). Parallel to this development, it became customary to begin the biblical manuscripts with 2 or more pages of illustrations of Jewish liturgical objects, in which the East and West (particularly Spain in the 13th–15th centuries) each may have had its own tradition (Gutmann 1978: 14, 16; cf. Roth 1953: 28; Schubert 1983: 81). In spite of the fact that this catalogue of liturgical objects had primarily the religious function of reminding one of the glory of God in the temple and of keeping alive the hope of its rebuilding, the painstaking, captioned illustrations of the individual objects oblige a scholarly curiosity. See Fig. ICO.05.

The Jewish literal exegesis first gained noticeable influence in Christian circles with members of the Victorine school in Paris (Smalley 1952: 83–195). In his commentary *In visionem Ezechielis* written before 1150, Richard of St. Victor (d. 1173) interpreted Ezek 1:5–10 and 40:1–45:5 in an exclusively literal way, and for the sake of better understanding he illustrated the interpretation with 13 diagrams (*PL* 196: cols. 527–600). Among other things he

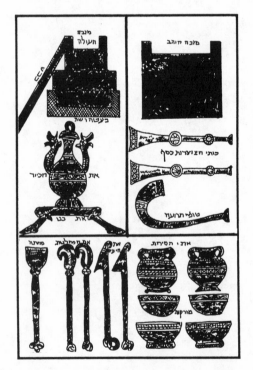

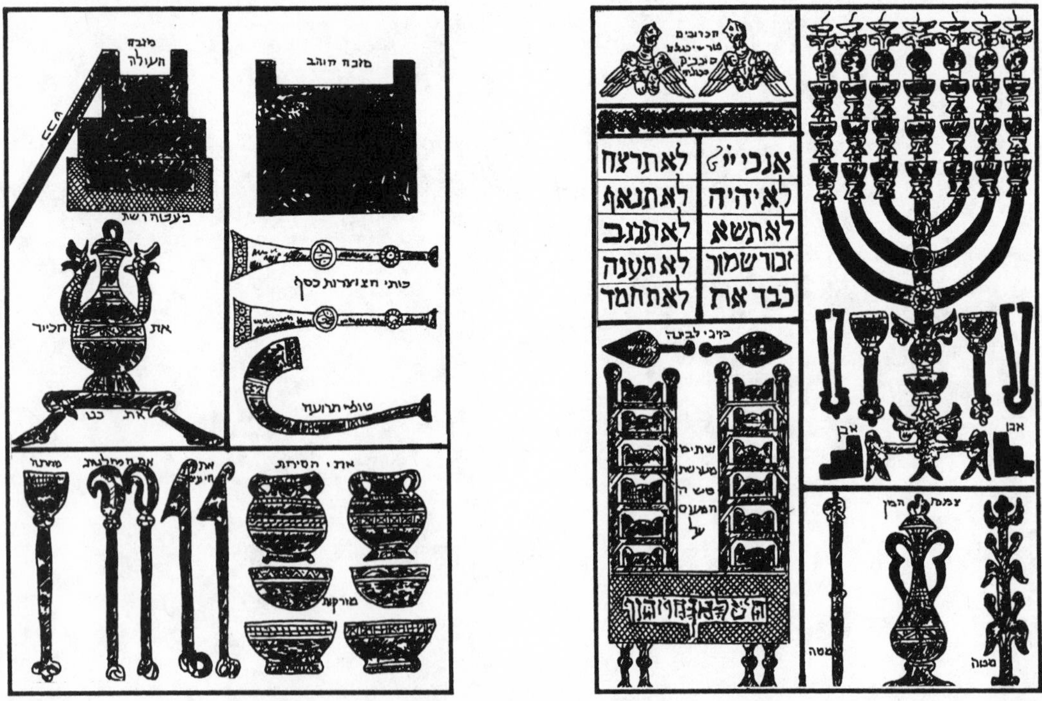

ICO.05. Two manuscript pages from a Hebrew Bible prepared by Salomo ben Raphael in Perpignan, France (ca. 1299 A.D.). Here each individual cult object is carefully rendered and identified with the help of labels. The influence of Jewish tradition is noticeable in the case of the steps flanking the menorah (extreme right), which are labelled *ʾeben*, "stone." The illustration of the basin (*hakkiyyôr*, extreme left) betrays the influence of Islamic art. *(Redrawn by G. Herion)*

offered an interesting reconstruction of the gateway designs, which strongly resemble the "four-entry type" gates excavated in Lachish, Megiddo, Hazor, etc. (Keel 1972: figs. 159–60, 174). See ICO.06. Richard of St. Victor showed that particularly architectural descriptions, if they want to be understood literally, hardly ever succeed without accompanying diagrams. A short time later, Maimonides added floor plans of the Herodian temple to his *Mishneh Torah,* finished in A.D. 1180 (Wischnitzer 1974: 16–27).

The Victorine reception of Jewish literal exegesis remained a prelude to the more-lasting reception through the N French Franciscan, Nicholas of Lyra. He wrote a tremendously successful literal commentary to all the books of the Bible *(Postilla Litteralis).* Between 1350 and 1450, 700 mss of this work were copied (some admittedly incomplete). The period of the first half of the 16th century saw the appearance of more than 100 printed versions. Lyra's work was illustrated with over 30 technical drawings, particularly with architectural plans, but also illustrating cultic furniture: e.g., the ark with the cherubim, the molten sea, and similar items. He took the architectural drawings in part from Richard of St. Victor. He did not stop with one reconstruction, but included, e.g., the ark of the covenant according to the opinion of Rashi as well as one according to the Christian exegetes. See Fig. ICO.07. Such a degree of objectivity is seldom found even in modern handbooks.

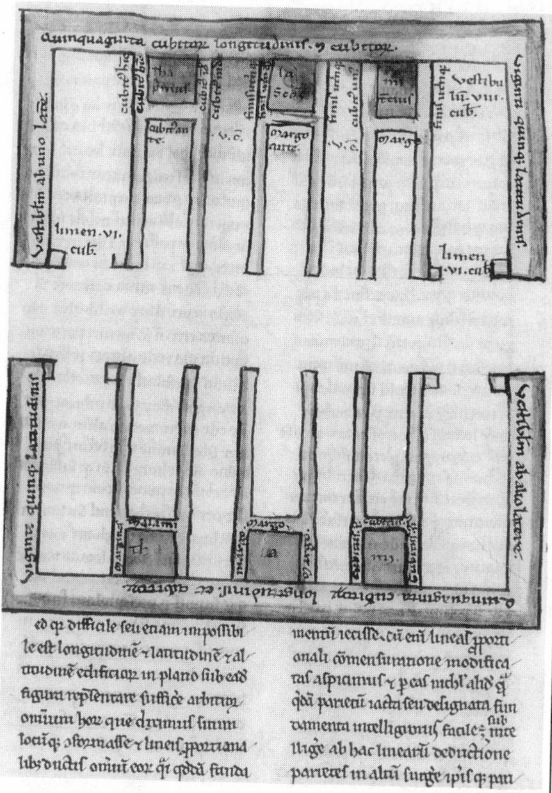

ICO.06. One of the 13 drawings with which Richard of St. Victor illustrated his tractate concerning the design of the temple in the book of Ezekiel. It shows the outline of a gate construction as it is described in Ezek 40:6–32. Modern excavations show that the tradition utilized by Richard succeeded surprisingly well in preserving authentic, archaic features. Cf. esp. Fig. FOR.03. *(Badische Landesbibliothek, Karlsruhe, Hs. Aug. CCXIV, courtesy of Badische Landesbibliothek)*

Through his literal exegesis but also through his graphic illustration Nicholas of Lyra exercised a great influence on Martin Luther. Already for his 1523 translation of the OT Luther adopted a number of Lyra's archaeological illustrations (Netter 1943; Schmidt 1962). In his foreword to Ezekiel from 1541, Luther expressly stated that it would be futile to understand Ezekiel 40–45 without the figures from Lyra (WA 11/1: 406). What is new about the illustrations of the Luther Bible is that they place the objects decidedly in a German Renaissance landscape so that an imaginary "biblical museum" results. In the previously mentioned preface to Ezekiel, Luther says that the best thing would be to have a 3-dimensional woodcut model of the temple. Exactly 100 years later the Dutch Jew, Jacob Jehuda da Leon, made a large (about 1 meter tall) wooden model of the temple and exhibited it with great success in many places (Herrmann 1967: 148).

The "archaeological" illustrations of the Luther Bible have also found their way into French Bibles. Sebastian Châtillon, who made a new translation of the Bible into Latin (1551) and French (1555, which was published by Oporin in Basel), provided it with an appendix "Annotationes" to which he added about 30 illustrations. Some of these come from the Luther Bible, others from Vatable's illustrations in Estienne's Bibles. Still others are original. In this way Châtillon presented the most exact reconstructions of the 4 beings in the vision in Ezekiel 1.

Other famous exegetes of the 16th century repeated the effort of Lyra to provide adequate visual reproductions of Noah's ark, the Tent of Meeting, the Temple of Solomon, and Ezekiel's temple (e.g., Francois Vatable for Robert Estienne's critical edition of the Vulgate published in Paris in 1540, and Benedictus Arias Montanus for the Archaeological treatises of vol. 8 of the *Antwerp Polyglot* published in 1572).

In the 17th century the proper conception of the temple in Jerusalem became the subject of a widespread debate in which the participants, including the best exegetes, were separated into the idealists and the historians. The idealists saw the Temple of Solomon as the prototype of all classical buildings, thinking that the Phoenicians had conveyed its proportions to the Greeks and Romans. The historians, however, reconstructed the temple strictly according to the textual descriptions and considered it to be a more modest and primitive building (Herrmann 1967).

This thought-provoking concern about the way things actually looked aroused interest in archaeological monuments. Perhaps the oldest evidence of this can be found in an addition to Moshe ben Naḥman's commentary on the Pentateuch. Driven out of Spain in A.D. 1267, he went to Acre where he was shown an Israelite shekel (from the time of the Jewish War, A.D. 66–70), which he then weighed with a money-changer's scales in order to determine its precise weight. He interpreted the images on the coin as

ICO.07. Nicholas of Lyra's drawings of the ark of the covenant. The drawings first appeared in his *Postilla litteralis* (ca. 1320–30) and subsequently were added as woodcuts to the first printed edition (1481). On the left is an "illustration of the ark and of the expiation according to rabbi Salomo" [i.e., Rashi]; on the right is an "illustration of the ark and of the expiation according to Catholic scholars." *(Drawings from Schramm 1934: taf. 1, Abb. 5–6; from the edition of Anton Koberger, Nuremberg 1481, courtesy of O. Keel)*

ירושלים הקדושה Ierufalaim halzedoffah.
Ierufalem fancta.
שקל ישראל Selzel Ifraël
Pondus feu numifma Ifraël:

Grammatica ipfa nil differt ab Hebraica,
ideo vbi characteres differentes habes, omnia
habes.

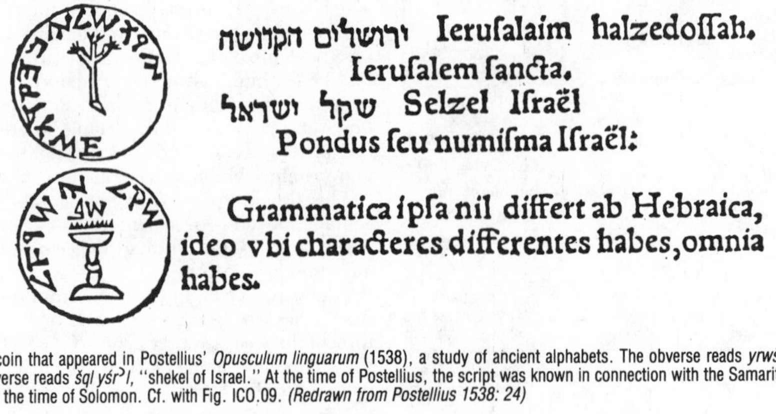

ICO.08. Drawing of a coin that appeared in Postellius' *Opusculum linguarum* (1538), a study of ancient alphabets. The obverse reads *yrwšlym hqdwš*, "Jerusalem the Holy," while the reverse reads *šql yśrʾl*, "shekel of Israel." At the time of Postellius, the script was known in connection with the Samaritans, and such coins were mistakenly attributed to the time of Solomon. Cf. with Fig. ICO.09. *(Redrawn from Postellius 1538: 24)*

being Aaron's rod and the vase of Manna (Chavel 1959: 507). The humanist Guilelmus Postellius seems to have been the first to have published such a coin; shown as an illustration in his *Opusculum Linguarum duodecium characteribus differentium Alphabetum* (Paris 1538). See Fig. ICO.08. Arias Montanus published another shekel from the first Jewish War in his treatise *Thubalcain sive de mensuris Sacris liber* which appeared in vol. 8 of the *Polyglot* published in Antwerp by Plantin in 1572. See Fig. ICO.09. There Arias celebrated the emergence of this coin as an act of divine providence. In the first serious work devoted not to weights and measurements in general but *exclusively* to Jewish coins, C. Waser (1605) recognized thoroughly the meaning of the iconography of the coins.

During the 17th century the debate revolved mainly around chronology and genuineness (since at the same time interest was budding a multitude of counterfeits were also in circulation). About half of the 13 coins published by B. Walton in the first volume of the *London Polyglot* in 1657 are counterfeits, although Walton had already taken out the crudest ones. At the end of the 17th century the question was for the most part cleared up, the counterfeits were separated out, and it was clear that there had been no Jewish coins before the exile (Kadman 1960: 155; Minc 1985). In addition to the Jewish coins, the 17th century also saw the rise into consciousness of the reliefs of the arch of Titus in Rome with its representations of the Jewish liturgical objects (Pfanner 1983). See Fig. ICO.10.

Regarding both Jewish coins and these reliefs, the most clear-sighted observations from this early period come from Hadrian Reland of Utrecht. His *Dissertationes V de nummis veterum hebraeorum, qui ab inscriptarum literarum forma samaritani appellantur* appeared in Utrecht in 1709. As the title implies, it had been known for quite a while that the Samaritan script was in reality the old Hebrew which was archaized and used on the Jewish coins. Reland paid attention not only to weights, legends, and dates, but also to the iconography. In his fifth dissertation, based upon the 2 trumpets *(ḥăṣōṣĕrôt)* on a coin of Simon Bar Kokhba (which he, however, dated to Simon the Hasmo-

ICO.09. A shekel from the First Jewish War, as published by Arias Montanus (1572). The inscription on the front (left) side reads *šql yśrʾl* ("Israelite shekel"), with the letter *ʾalep* in the center indicating year 1 of the revolt (A.D. 66). On the back (right), the inscription reads *yrwšlm qdšh* ("Jerusalem the Holy"). Cf. Fig. ICO.08. In order to be as exact as possible, Arius also depicted the thickness of the coin *(crassitudo)*. *(Drawing from Arius Montanus 1572: 16, courtesy of O. Keel)*

ICO.10. The arch of Titus in Rome as it looked at the beginning of the 18th century. The illustration is from Hadrian Reland's 1716 work about the pieces plundered from the Jerusalem temple. *(Drawing from Ugolinus 1748: frontispiece to vol. 9, courtesy of O. Keel)*

nean, 143–134 B.C.), Reland was able to conclude that the "trumpets" in Num 10:1 and 20:9 were straight, and should not be confused with the curved ram's horns *(šōpārôt)* of the New Year, as was done quite often. In another work, *De spoliis templi Hierosolymitani in arcu Titiano conspicuis* (Utrecht, 1716), a penetrating analysis of the representation of the 7-branched candelabrum demonstrated that this could hardly have been that of Moses, which was smaller and golden, aside from having been stolen—at the latest—by Antiochus IV. The thick branches of the candelabrum on the Titus Arch would have been those of the wooden lampstand which, according to Rabbi Jose (*b. Talm. ʿAbod. Zar.* 43a), the Hasmoneans had made; furthermore, the base showing mythological scenes must have been Roman since the representation of living creatures was prohibited by the Law.

Apart from the coins and reliefs mentioned, other monuments of antiquity played a relatively limited role. Nevertheless small collections began to emerge in the 17th and 18th centuries, containing mainly Egyptian antiquities (amulets, scarabs, statues, stele, relief fragments, coffins, and of course mummies). Only rarely were these used in connection with biblical texts. Athanasius Kircher collected, published, and interpreted all the then-known works of Egyptian art (including all the obelisks) in his monumental 3-volume work, *Oedipus aegyptiacus,* which was published in Rome between 1652 and 1654 by V. Mascardi. In his work a representation of the subterranean Egyptian burial vaults is also included (See Fig. ICO.11) as well as a fragment of a relief from such a vault with a slaughter scene containing legends in hieroglyphs (falcon, ibis, owl, etc.), which he interpreted as proof of a cult with gods in animal form, such as that attacked in Ezek 8:7. See Fig. ICO.12.

Both of Reland's tracts, along with numerous other works of a similar nature, were gathered together and published by Blas Ugolinus in the 34 volumes of the *Thesaurus antiquatatum sarcarum,* Venice 1744–69). Thus, the gleanings of these limited sources were all available towards the end of the 18th century.

The scholars who accompanied Napoleon on his military expedition to Egypt in 1798 broadened the horizons considerably with their monumental description of Egypt (Jomard 1809–13). Their interests were mainly in the realm of landscape and architecture, with iconography neglected and relations between Egypt and the Bible almost completely ignored. As a consequence of the atmosphere of the Revolution, the French were possessed by a quite distracted fascination for classical antiquity. Even Champollion (1845: 3, text concerning pl. 361f) was convinced that the "nomads" of Beni Hassan represented Greeks.

For biblical scholars, J. G. Wilkinson's work was far more important than Jomard's *Déscription de l'Égypte.* He spent more than a decade in Egypt (1821–33) studying and drawing the monuments. Unable to read the hieroglyphs properly, he relied merely on the pictorial evidence, the Bible, and classical authors for his *Manners and Customs of the Ancient Egyptians* (1837). Such titles were very popular at the time because the entire world was swarming with

ICO.11. A drawing of a subterranean Egyptian burial chamber, which Athanasius Kircher published between 1652 and 1654. He related these burial techniques with the chambers mentioned in Ezek 8:7–13. *(Drawing from Kircher 1654, vol. 3: 402, fig. I, courtesy of O. Keel)*

ICO.12. Relief from an Egyptian Old Kingdom burial chamber. Kircher interpreted the relief as Egyptians slaying a bull in the presence of their deities, which are represented as birds. Kircher did not realize that the "birds" were phonetic characters used in Egyptian hieroglypics. *(Drawing from Kircher 1654, vol. 3: 417, fig. 5, courtesy of O. Keel)*

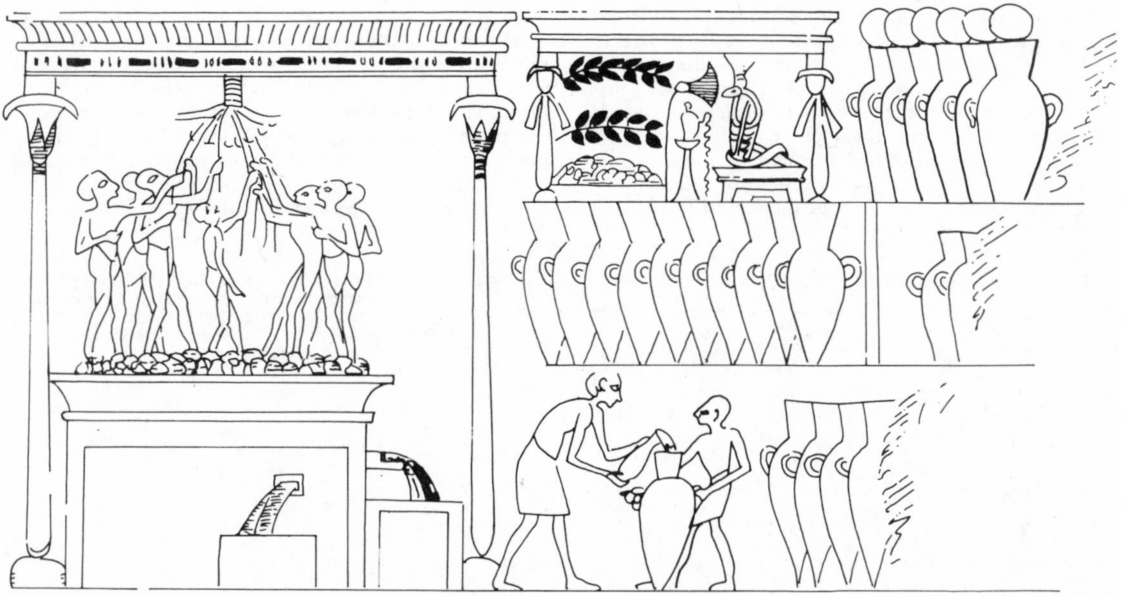

ICO.13. Agricultural scene from a New Kingdom Period tomb at Thebes. Wilkinson used this to explain why the word "treading" in the OT means "to press/squeeze out" (e.g., wine or oil—Judg 9:27; Neh 13:15; Isa 63:3). *(Redrawn from Wilkinson 1878, 1: 385)*

travellers and explorers. The innumerable illustrations of private life, agriculture (See Fig. ICO.13), technology, governmental institutions, warfare, etc. influence biblical dictionaries of all kinds until today.

The first person significantly to use the Egyptian materials supplied by Jomard (1809–13), by Wilkinson (1837; cf. 2d edition), by Champollion (1835–45), and by Rosellini (1832–44) was L. Philippson, a German rabbi who published the Hebrew text of the Bible, a German translation, and a commentary illustrated with woodcuts (1844–54). Of the 500 woodcuts, 211 were derived from Egyptian sources, the remainder consisting mainly of Greco-Roman antiquities and fanciful artistic reconstructions of biblical scenes with institutions, landscapes, flora, and fauna. This was the Bible that Sigmund Freud had known since childhood, and its illustrations may have been responsible for his convictions concerning the impact of Egypt on the Bible (Pfrimmer 1982). Philippson only sparingly employed material from Mesopotamia, claiming that such simply could not be found: Because the prophets had announced the demise of the Babylonian and Assyrian idols (Isa 21:9), it followed that they had all been completely destroyed (1848–54, 2: 783).

Actually Botta had already excavated at Khorsabad in 1843–44, and his success was documented in the 5 volumes of his *Monuments de Ninive* (Paris 1846–50). More important was Layard's work at Kalah (Nimrud, 1845–47 and 1849–51) and Nineveh (Kuyunjik, 1847 and 1849–50). The second volume of Layard's *Nineveh and its Remains* (London 1849) contained "An Enquiry into the Manners and Arts of the Ancient Assyrians," as a kind of Assyrian counterpart to Wilkinson's *Manners and Customs.* Layard's second work of this type, *Discoveries in the Ruins of Nineveh and Babylon* (London 1853) usefully supplemented the first with more material of this nature. In a fashion similar to Wilkinson's, Layard also connected only small sections of the reliefs with individual biblical verses. See Fig. ICO.14.

Wilkinson and Layard were the main sources from which the biblical dictionaries of the following decades, such as Smith's *Dictionary of the Bible* (2d ed. 1893) or Riehm's *Handwörterbuch des Biblischen Altertums* (2d ed. 1893–94), drew their Egyptian and Assyrian material. F. Vigouroux' *Dictionnaire de la Bible* (1895–1912) was the most comprehensive of them all since he made extensive use of additional sources. However, of the 338 illustrations relating to Assyria, 123 (or ca. 36 percent) still came from Layard. One hundred forty-four (34 percent) of the 502 pictures relating to Egypt were taken from R. Lepsius' colossal *Denkmäler aus Aegypten und Aethiopien* (12 volumes: Berlin 1849–59), the collection of the best and most accurate pictures then available, and Wilkinson still supplied 90 pictures (or ca. 18 percent).

Fragmentation, as initiated by Wilkinson and Layard and followed by many biblical scholars, is still typically the way in which Egyptian and Assyrian pictures are presented in illustrating biblical civilization. Very seldom is an entire relief or a complete wall painting reproduced. Usually particular kinds of agricultural activity, specific cult utensils, or single musical instruments are selected for illustration. This is legitimate for those interested in material culture in a narrow sense. For example, to illustrate "dress," individual figures are—as a space-saving measure—invariably removed from their contexts (as in Fig. ICO.14). Although technical aspects are thus clear, the social significance of a given dress is lost. Egyptian harvest scenes (Davies and Gardiner 1936: pl. 50f) show that the field workers wore a kilt (if anything at all), while the overseer wore a sleeved garment; Joseph's robe with "sleeves" (Gen 37:3) thus may not be a mere gown but a status symbol. As mentioned above, individual figures from Sennacherib's Lachish reliefs have been used repeatedly to illustrate contemporary Jewish dress. These figures were, however, unable to illustrate the several social classes present, as e.g., Ussishkin (1982) has done by examining the whole set of reliefs.

The arrival of the Hebrews and other refugees in Egypt is sometimes illustrated by a section only of the famous reliefs from the tomb of Haremhab in Memphis (e.g., Grollenberg 1957: fig. 128; *ANEP,* no. 5). In contrast to this fragment, the whole relief shows how the refugees are confronted with the sophisticated machinery of the Egyptian government at whose end is the unapproachable Pharaoh (cf. Gen 12:10–20). See Fig. ICO.15. With respect to the situation of minorities like the early Hebrews, the

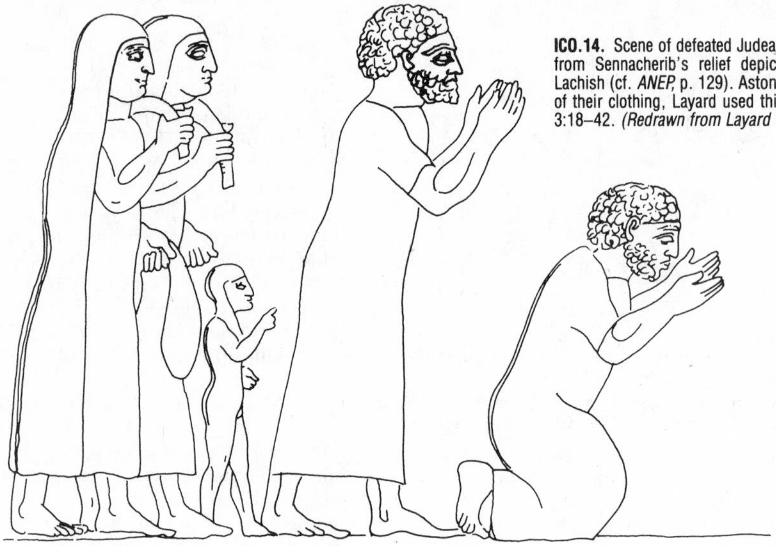

ICO.14. Scene of defeated Judeans begging for mercy, from Sennacherib's relief depicting the conquest of Lachish (cf. *ANEP,* p. 129). Astonished by the simplicity of their clothing, Layard used this scene to explain Isa 3:18–42. *(Redrawn from Layard 1853: 152)*

ICO.15. Relief of Haremhab graphically depicting the "distance" separating the Asiatic refugees from the Pharaoh. At the right, the crowd of Asiatics and Libyans (lying on the ground) appeal to a translator, who in a "second scene" (center) communicates their appeal to the vizier. In yet a "third scene" (left), the vizier presents the appeal to the king and queen, who are represented in gigantic dimensions. The point is that Asiatics have no direct access to the center of decision making. *(Redrawn from Hari 1965: 112–15, fig. 36–41, pl. 19–20; drawing by H. Keel-Leu)*

ICO.16. A relief of Assurbanipal depicting his soldiers ambushing a nomadic camp. In the upper two registers, the women left behind are being raped (?) and killed. In the lower register the tents in which the corpses have been piled are being burned. *(Reproduced by courtesy of the Trustees of the British Museum)*

pictures of nomads on Assurbanipal's reliefs in the British Museum are also of great interest (Barnett 1976: pl. 33). Aside from the shape of the tents (round!), they show that nomadic woman—in contrast to their urban sisters—were mercilessly abused and slaughtered. See Fig. ICO.16. This unusual behavior by the Assyrian army may reflect the opinion that nomads were somehow subhuman, or that their women were actively engaged in conflict (which is less likely since the women are not depicted defending themselves). If this very interesting relief was used at all, then it tended to be used only to illustrate how tents in biblical times may have looked (cf., e.g., Benzinger 1907: fig. 54).

Under such fragmentization the sociological aspect of the pictures is not revealed. For example, when the great relief of the conquest of Lachish by Sennacherib serves to illustrate "battering rams," "women's clothes," and "wagon types" (*BRL*, 39, 188, 356), that is indeed useful; but the picture's possibilities for information do not stop there. This method of presenting only fragments, characteristic of all the handbooks, pays no respect to the original message of these works, the purpose of which was not the illustration of perceptual material culture, but of concepts like divine rule, world order, kingship and the gods, etc. The same also holds for Yadin's very informative work on the art of war (1963), which indeed uses entire relief cycles and impressively presents the technical side of war with the help of numerous illustrations, but does not take into account the sociological and ideological aspects of warfare which are expressed in these relief cycles.

Because the Bible itself is no more concerned with material culture and its achievements than is the art of the ANE, it would be better to evolve a system of comparison identifying their common points. Since neither deals primarily with history in a modern sense nor with material culture, one needs to search at the conceptual level.

D. Iconography and the Culture of Concepts

Comparisons at this level reflect the influence of the Enlightenment and a liberal theology receptive to the notion that the basic tenets of one's own creed can also be found elsewhere. Comparative theology may also be employed within the framework of a relatively literal belief in the Revelation, assuming that an original revelation *(Uroffenbarung)* really did reach all the nations. Catholics, like F. Vigouroux, were particularly interested in interpreting the new discoveries in this way. That was already the case with Layard, who, after uncovering the gate genii *(Torgenien)* in Nimrud in the spring of 1846, assumed that Ezekiel was influenced by having seen these genii when describing his vision of the creatures in Ezekiel 1 (Layard 1849, 1: 69f; 2: 464f.)

G. Smith's *Chaldean Account of Genesis* is a famous case where pictures were exploited in this fashion. He was the first to suggest that the early chapters of Genesis might have been based on Babylonian concepts, and he published a cylinder seal which, in his opinion, represented a Baby-

ICO.17. Impression of a cylinder seal. For about 40 years this was the most discussed oriental scene, believed to illustrate the fall from creation as depicted by the Mesopotamians, with clear parallels to biblical traditions in Genesis 3 (note the man, the woman, the tree, the fruit, and the serpent). However, the scene probably should be viewed in the tradition of the divine banquet, possibly representing enhanced vitality. *(Redrawn from Smith 1876: 9)*

lonian version of the Fall (Genesis 3; Smith 1876: 91). See Fig. ICO.17. In 1902, F. Delitzsch presented a widely publicized lecture in which he considered this seal to be the nucleus of the whole Pauline teaching on sin and redemption (1903: 37, 67). This provoked a wave of protest, not only from the defenders of orthodoxy, but also from more sober contemporaries like Gressmann and Jeremias, whose research essentially pursued a similar line of thought, but in a more restrained fashion. The latest publication of the "Adam and Eve" seal places it in the tradition of Akkadian banquet scenes (Collon 1982: 124, no. 302; Collon 1987: 37, no. 112). In the first edition of Gressmann's *Altorientalische Bilder zum Alten Testament* (1909), 116 pages are devoted to illustrating the history of religion, with a mere 23 reserved for secular subjects. Admittedly, his selection was influenced by the overriding concern for material culture prevailing since the days of Layard and Wilkinson. Thus, sacred pillars, altars, and similar cultic furniture are well represented not only in the biblical dictionaries but also in Gressmann's work.

Exceptions to this general line were already to be found in works like Vigouroux' *Dictionnaire de la Bible,* where the entry on *âme* ("soul, spirit") uses an Egyptian painting with the judgment scene (see Fig. ICO.18) to illustrate a concept quite familiar to the 19th-century Catholic author (A. Vacant). This "hall of judgment" scene probably entered the Judeo-Christian world from ancient Egypt, and repeatedly came to be displayed prominently on Gothic Cathedrals and other important Christian monuments. Unaware of the probable Egyptian origin of this motif, Vacant understood it as an integral part of the true religion (about the immortality of the soul and the individual judgment at death), and he was surprised not at its presence in Egypt but rather at its absence from the Law of Moses. He was thus able to conclude that since Moses refrained from condemning this religious motif in particular while otherwise disparaging so many Egyptian superstitions, Moses must have believed in it.

Jeremias (1904), who further developed G. Smith's ideas, was less concerned with the uniqueness of the biblical revelation and Lutheran orthodoxy than the *Dictionnaire de la Bible* was with Catholic dogma; he also was less dominated by interest in material culture than was Gressmann. His work was the first to present the cosmic order as perceived by the ancients using their own pictures, and discussing the Bible's share in that world. He understood the peculiarities of ANE art better than did most of his contemporaries. He did not understand the pair on the "Adam and Eve Seal" (Fig. ICO.17) as the first couple, since he knew that their horned crowns identified them as deities. He also showed the connection between the "dragon combat" on Assyrian cylinder seals and Ps 74:13 and Isa 30:6 (1904: 53–60; cf 3d ed., pp. 9–21). Jeremias likewise saw the similarity between the temples depicted in Neo-Assyrian reliefs (a temple on a mountain with a park and rivers) and the descriptions of Paradise in Genesis 2 and Ezekiel 28 (3d ed., pp. 65–87). Along the same line as Jeremias, L. Dürr (1917) systematically used the ancient oriental iconography along with the texts to come to an appropriate understanding of the complex visions in Ezekiel 1 and 10.

In his first work which treated an ancient oriental theme, H. Gunkel (1895) still made no use of the ancient oriental iconography. In his commentary on the Psalms, however, he frequently cited ancient Mesopotamian and Egyptian pictures, particularly for the Royal Psalms (Psalms 2, 45, 110, etc.), identifying a number of common points. For example, he compared Ps 110:1, which speaks of making a footstool of enemies, to an Egyptian tomb painting depicting subjugated peoples beneath a royal footstool (*Psalms* HKAT, 481ff.; see Davies and Gardiner 1936, 1: pl. 29; Keel 1972: fig. 341). It is striking that his introduction refers only to "ancient oriental lyrics" with the intention to "clarify both the similarity and contrast to the singularity of the Bible" (*Psalms* HKAT, viii): Theory was limping behind practice.

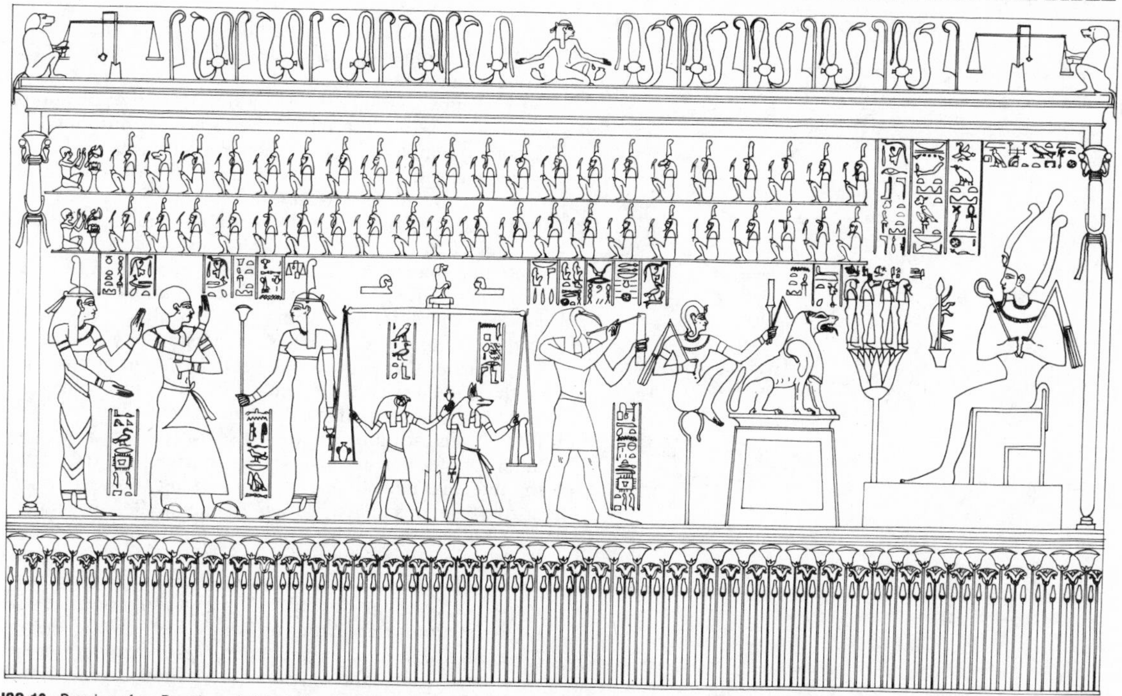

ICO.18. Drawing of an Egyptian relief depicting the Hall of Judgment. The relief was published in the *Dictionaire de la Bible* to illustrate the pre-Christian origin of concepts such as immortality of the soul and individual judgment after death. In this scene, Osiris (right) presides, while the heart of the deceased is weighed against an ostrich feather, symbolizing Maat (truth, justice). *(Drawing from Lepsius, vol. 9, Abtl. IV, Bl. 16b, courtesy of O. Keel)*

The comparative work done by Gressman, Jeremias, Gunkel, and other scholars was based on a liberal theology that assumed that any expression of the human spirit could contain potential insights into the nature and deeds of God *(revelatio generalis).* The danger, to which they often fell victim, was a leveling of biblical belief whenever it could not be completely integrated into the contemporaneous world. K. Barth led the dialectic theology which responded in the 1920's by asserting that the biblical revelation alone was totally different from everything conceivable in the religions of Egypt and Mesopotamia. Comparisons could merely demonstrate that the biblical message expressed serious doubts about everything of any significance in the entire ancient world. The best policy was to avoid all comparisons, lest the suspicion arise that analogies were advocated. Only Scripture could elucidate Scripture. All forms of nonbiblical comparison were thus brought to a halt. The a priori assertion of an absolute and total uniqueness for the Bible was, of course, not intellectually satisfying.

Archaeologists, after all, were nevertheless emphasizing the influence of the ANE on the Bible. In the 1950s, Parrot published a series of studies in the *Cahiers d'Archéologie Biblique,* where elements of ANE art were compared with biblical passages. In his 2 books dealing with the tower of Babel (1949; 1954) he criticized the restrictive view of the Bible which had failed to grasp the iconographically established significance of the ziggurat. He himself often showed a strong attraction to historicizing interpretations (cf., e.g., Parrot 1955). In *Babylone et l'Ancien Testament* (1956), half a dozen pictures for Ezekiel 1 were presented; the insights, however, do not go any farther than those of Dürr (1917). A year later (1957: 11) he illustrated the conception of Paradise in Genesis 2 (4 rivers, Cherubim, etc.) with the famous Mari wall painting (See Keel 1972: fig. 191; the scene is only partially reproduced in *ANEP*, no. 610). For the god gathering his foes in a net (Hab 1:14), he cited the Stele of Eannatum (*ANEP*, no. 298), and almost 50 pages are devoted to Canaanite divine images, with their correspondences in the Bible. Vanel's comprehensive study on the iconography of the weather god (1965) scrupulously avoided references to the Bible since a second volume (which has not appeared) was intended to show how these Canaanite concepts were adopted and adapted in biblical texts.

The 1950's also saw the appearance of 2 large pictorial works. The first is Pritchard's classic and still extremely useful collection *(ANEP)*, which is, however, dominated by an historico-cultural orientation; beside this, the reader must take the initiative in supplying the purported "relationship" to the OT. The second collection is that edited by Mazar, Avi-Yonah, and Malamat (1958). In this work, connections between the pictures and biblical texts are explicitly made, but in a partial, secular manner reflecting historical and semi-historical ideas that cannot do justice to ANE art, which was primarily conceptual in form and ideological or religious in content.

After the Second World War there arose a great deal of interest in other cultures (including the ancient ones). It was taken for granted that the different religions should

ICO.19. Late Babylonian and early Achaemenid porters of heaven, as depicted on early Persian seal impressions. These may have served as the models for the four living creatures in Ezekiel 1, which also had human bodies, four wings, the feet of bullocks, and several faces. *(Redrawn from Keel 1977: 214, Abb. 166; and 234, Abb. 182)*

be compared. The time was ripe to compare the ancient oriental iconography with the (ideal?) biblical conceptions, not in its historical character or in the context of the development of civilization, but in its primarily ideological-religious character. Building on efforts in the history of religions at the turn of the century (Jeremias, Gressmann), Keel (1972) attempted a systematic comparison of ideas about the world, the temple, the king, etc. found in the Psalms, with concepts represented in ANE art, identifying points of contact and divergence. The attempted comparison is that of thought with thought, and pictures are only one type of evidence, while words are another. For the representation of the world, Keel was inspired by H. Schaefer's study on the representation of the world by the ancient Egyptians, while the chapter on the king stood under the influence of H. Frankfort (1969). While Pritchard (*ANEP*, nos. 376–463) illustrates royalty almost exclusively with "portraits" (see, e.g., *ANEP*, no. 419), Keel (1972) illustrates the *role* of Pharaoh using relief cycles of the birth, enthronement, temple foundation, etc., stressing the role and functions of the king (not royal individualities) and comparing this role with that played by the Israelite king in the Royal Psalms.

In recent years Keel endeavored to show that certain of the motifs used in the Bible were to be found not only in Egyptian Temple reliefs, or their counterparts in the Assyrian palaces, etc., but also in the realm of miniatures, such as seals, amulets, ivories, textiles, etc. which were well distributed in Israel itself. He was able to interpret Isaiah 6, Ezekiel 1 and 10, and Zechariah 4 by drawing on contemporaneous glyptic art (1977). See Fig. ICO.19. A year later (1978) he interpreted the singular passage in Job 39 (where Yahweh refers to his dealings with lions, wild oxen, onagers, ostriches, etc.) as an exploitation of the "Lord of the Animals" motif, thus providing this part of the speech with a meaning, without being obliged to seek recourse in modern theological reasoning. See Fig. ICO.20. The advantage of a picture for the clear representation of stellar constellations was particularly useful for the interpretation of Job 38 (concerning the significance of constellations in general, see Assmann 1983: 54–60).

In his comprehensive work on women and goddesses, U. Winter (1983) compared the images of Syrian goddesses with the feminine ideals (and their negative counterparts) found in the Bible. In 2 contributions to the interpretation of the Song of Songs, Keel (1984; *Song of Songs* ZBK) has used Egyptian and Mesopotamian sources in order to isolate the Egyptian and Mesopotamian motifs in the love song. For example, the dove as the messenger of love (cf. Jesus' baptism, where the dove represents the words "You are my son, whom I love," Mark 1:10) is clearly a concept originating in W Asia (see Fig. ICO.21), while the lotus (as a symbol of regeneration) is thoroughly Egyptian.

S. Schroer (1987) has collected and critically analyzed all the accounts about representative art in the OT and related them to the finds of the archaeological work done in biblical lands. A global presentation of Canaanite-Israelite iconography (cf. Keel and Schroer 1985) presupposes a systematic treatment of the smaller works of art—especially the seals (Keel 1986a; 1986b; Keel, Keel-Leu, and Schroer 1989)—to provide material for further comparative work, the possibilities and methodology of which will demand more reflection in order to consolidate what has been hitherto achieved, and to assure a solid basis for additional possible results.

Bibliography

Adriaen, M. 1958. *Magni Aurelii Cassiodori Expositio Psalmorum.* CChr Series Latina 97–98. Vol. 1. Turnhout.

Ahituv, S. 1984. *Canaanite Toponyms in Ancient Egyptian Documents.* Jerusalem.

Arius Mantanus, B. 1572. *Thubalcain sive de mensuris sacris.* Antwerp.

Assmann, J. 1983. *Re' und Amun.* Freiburg.

Barnett, R. D. 1976. *Sculptures from the North Palace of Ashurbanipal at Nineveh (668–627 B.C.).* London.

Benzinger, I. 1907. *Hebräische Archäologie.* Grundriss der Theologischen Wissenschaften 2/1. 2d rev. ed. Tübingen.

Champollion, J. F. 1835–45. *Monuments de l'Egypte et de la Nubie.* 4 vols. Paris.

———. 1909. *Lettres et journaux de Champollion le Jeune,* ed. H. Hartleben. 2 vols. Bibliothèque égyptologique 30–31. Paris.

ICO.20. Scarab from Acco (left) and stamp seal from Beth-shemesh (right). These suggest that the motif of "the Lord of the Animals" was well known in Iron Age Israel. This motif probably underlies YHWH's association with the animals in Job 39. See also Fig. ART.35. *(Redrawn from Keel 1978: 93, fig. 19b; and 103, fig. 36)*

ICO.21. Old Syrian cylinder seal impression. This depicts the connection between the goddess of love and the dove. The goddess of love (left of center) apparently bares herself in front of the storm-god, who strides over the mountains. A dove, which flies from her toward him, symbolizes her love for him and her readiness to make love (cf. Song of Songs 1:15; 4:1; 5:12). *(Drawing courtesy of O. Keel)*

Chavel, H. B. 1959. *Piruše Ben Hathora Lerabbenu MoNahman (Ramban).* Vol. 2. Jerusalem (in Hebrew).

Collon, D., ed. 1982. *Catalogue of the Western Asiatic Seals in the British Museum.* Vol. 2. London.

———. 1987. *First Impressions: Cylinder Seals in the ANE.* London.

Davies, N. M., and Gardiner, A. H. 1936. Ancient Egyptian Paintings. 3 vols. Chicago.

Delitzsch, F. 1903. *Babel und Bibel.* Leipzig.

Dürr, L. 1917. *Ezechiels Vision von der Erscheinung Gottes (Ez. c. 1 und 10) im Lichte der vorderasiatischen Altertumskunde.* Würzburg.

Frankfort, H. 1969. *Kingship and the Gods.* 6th ed. Chicago.

Goedicke, H. 1984. Abi-Sha(i)'s Representation in Beni Hasan. *JARCE* 21: 203–10.

Gombrich, E. H. 1959. *Art and Illusion: A Study in the Psychology of Pictorial Representation.* Oxford.

Gressmann, H. 1927. *Altorientalische Bilder zum Alten Testament.* 2d ed. Berlin.

Grollenberg, L. H. 1957. *Bildatlas zur Bibel.* Gütersloh.

Gunkel, H. 1895. *Schöpfung und Chaos in Urzeit und Endzeit.* Göttingen.

Gutmann, J. 1978. *Buchmalerei in hebräischen Handschriften.* Munich and New York.
Hari, R. 1965. *Horemhab et la reine Moutnedjemet.* Geneva.
Hermann, H. J. 1905–26. *Beschreibendes Verzeichnis der illuminierten Handschriften in Oesterreich.* 2 vols. Leipzig.
Herrmann, W. 1967. Unknown Designs for the Temple of Jerusalem by Claude Perrot. In *Essays in the History of Architecture,* ed. D. Fraser. London.
Imdahl, M. 1980. *Giotto: Arenafresken: Ikonographie, Ikonologie, Ikonik.* Munich.
Jeremias, A. 1904. *Das Alte Testament im Lichte des Alten Orients.* (3d ed. 1916.) Leipzig.
Jomard, E. F., ed. 1809–13. *Déscription de l'Égypte.* 24 vols. Paris.
Kadman, L. 1960. *The Coins of the Jewish War of 66—73 C.E.* Corpus Nummorum Palestinensium 2/3. Tel Aviv and Jerusalem.
Kaemmerling, E., ed. 1979. *Bildende Kunst als Zeichensystem.* Vol. 1. DuMont Taschenbücher 83. Cologne.
Keel, O. 1972. *Die Welt der altorientalischen Bildsymbolik und das Alte Testament.* 4th ed. 1984. Zürich and Neukirchen. Trans. 1978.
———. 1977. *Jahwe-Visionen und Siegelkunst.* SBS 84/85. Stuttgart.
———. 1978. *Jahwer Entgegnung an Ijob.* FRLANT 121. Göttingen.
———. 1984. *Deine Blicke sind Tauben.* SBS 114/115. Stuttgart.
———. 1986a. Ancient Seals and the Bible. A Review Article. *JAOS* 106: 307–11.
———. 1986b. A Stamp Seal Research Project and a Group of Scarabs with Raised Relief. *Akkadica* 49: 1–16.
Keel, O., Keel-Leu, H., and Schroer, S. 1989. *Studien zu den Stempelsiegeln aus Palästina/Israel.* Vol. 2. OBO 89. Freiburg and Göttingen.
Keel, O., and Schroer, S. 1985. *Studien zu den Stempelsiegeln aus Palästina/Israel.* Vol. 1. OBO 67. Freiburg and Göttingen.
Kessler, D. 1987. Die Asiatenkarawane von Beni Hassan. *SAK* 14: 147–65.
Kircher, A. 1652–54. *Oedipus Aegyptiacus.* 3 vols. Rome.
Kirschbaum, E., and Braunfels, W. 1968–76. *Lexikon der christlichen Ikonographie.* 8 vols. Freiburg.
Lamp, H. F. 1982–83. An OT Index to Archaeological Sources. *TJ* 3: 170–94; 4: 44–71.
Layard, A. H. 1849. *Nineveh and Its Remains.* 2 vols. London.
———. 1853. *Discoveries in the Ruins of Nineveh and Babylon.* London.
Lepsius, C. R. 1849–59. *Denkmäler aus Aegypten und Aethiopien.* 12 vols. London.
Liebermann, S. J. 1985. Giving Directions on the Black Obelisk of Shalmaneser III. *RA* 79: 88.
Maraval, P. 1982. *Egérie: Journal de Voyage (Itinéraire) et Lettre sur la Bse Egérie.* SC 296. Paris.
Mazar, B.; Avi-Yonah, M.; and Malamat, A. 1958. *Views of the Biblical World.* 5 vols. Ramat Gan.
Meshorer, Y. 1967. *Jewish Coins of the Second Temple Period.* Chicago.
Minc, H. 1985. Ancient Jewish Coins in the Correspondence between John Locke and Nicolas Roinard. *BA* 48: 108–21.
Netter, M. 1943. *Die Postille des Nikolaus von Lyra in ihrer Wirkung auf die Bibelillustration des 15. und 16. Jahrhunderts.* Basel.
Parrot, A. 1949. *Ziggurats et Tour de Babel.* Paris.
———. 1954. *La tour de Babel.* Cahiers d'Archéologie Biblique 2. Neuchâtel.
———. 1955. *Déluge et Arche de Noé.* Cahiers d'Archéologie Biblique 1. Neuchâtel.
———. 1956. *Babylone et l'Ancien Testament.* Cahiers d'Archéologie Biblique 8. Neuchâtel.
———. 1957. *Le musée du Louvre et la Bible.* Cahiers d'Archéologie Biblique 9. Neuchâtel.
Petrie, W. M. F. 1891. *Tell el Hesy [Lachish].* London.
Pfanner, M. 1983. *Der Titusbogen.* Beiträge zur Erschliessung hellenistischer und kaiserzeitlicher Skulptur und Architektur 2. Mainz.
Pfrimmer, T. 1982. *Freud, lecteur de la Bible.* Paris.
Philippson, L. 1844–54. *Die Jisraelitische Bibel.* 3 vols. Leipzig.
Porter, R. K. 1821–22. *Travels in Georgia, Persia, Armenia, Ancient Babylonia etc.* 2 vols. London.
Postellius, G. 1538. *Opusculum linguarum duodecim characteribus differentium alphabetum.* Paris.
Rosellini, H. 1832–44. *Monumenti dell' Egitto e della Nubia.* 3 vols. Pisa.
Roth, C. 1953. Jewish Antecedents of Christian Art. *Journal of the Warburg and Courtauld Institutes* 16: 24–44.
Schäublin, C. 1974. *Untersuchungen zur Methode und Herkunft der antiochenischen Exegese.* Cologne.
Schmidt, P. 1962. *Die Illustration der Lutherbibel 1522–1700.* Basel.
Schramm, A. 1934. *Der Bilderschmuch der Frühdrucke.* Vol. 17. Leipzig.
Schroer, S. 1987. *In Israel gab es Bilder.* OBO 74. Freiburg and Göttingen.
Schubert, U., and K. 1983. *Jüdische Buchkunst.* Vol. 1. Graz.
Smalley, B. 1952. *The Study of the Bible in the Middle Ages.* Oxford.
Smith, C. C. 1977. Jehu and the Black Obelisk of Shalmaneser III. In *Scripture in History and Theology,* ed. A. Merrill and T. Overholt. Pittsburgh.
Smith, G. 1876. *The Chaldean Account of Genesis.* London.
Ugolinus, B. 1744–69. *Thesaurus antiquitatum sacrarum.* 34 vols. Venice.
Ussishkin, D. 1982. *The Conquest of Lachish by Sennacherib.* Tel Aviv.
Vanel, A. 1965. *L'iconographie du dieu de l'orage.* CahRB. Paris.
Vergote, J. 1959. *Joseph en Egypte: Chapitres 37–50 à la lumière des études égyptologiques récentes.* OrBibLov 3. Louvain.
Waser, C. 1605. *De antiquis numis Hebraeorum, Chaldaeorum et Syrorum.* Zürich.
Wilkinson, J. 1971. *Egeria's Travels.* London.
Wilkinson, J. G. 1837. *The Manners and Customs of the Ancient Egyptians.* 3 vols. (2d ed. 1878.) London.
Winter, V. 1983. *Frau und Göttin: Exegetische und ikonographische Studien zum weilblichen Gottesbild im Alten Israel und in dessen Umwelt.* OBO 53. Freiburg and Göttingen.
Wischnitzer, R. 1974. Maimonides' Drawings of the Temple. *Jewish Art* 1: 16–27.
Wolska-Conus, W. 1968–73. *Cosmas Indicopleustès: Topographie chrétienne.* 3 vols. SC 141, 159, 197. Paris.
Yadin, Y. 1963. *The Art of Warfare in Biblical Lands.* 2 vols. New York.

OTHMAR KEEL

IDALAH (PLACE) [Heb *yidʾălâ*]. A town located in the territory of Zebulun (Josh 19:15). Many scholars emend the name to Iralah (*GTTOT,* 183) on the basis of the reading of the Talmud. Kallai notes that the Jerusalem Talmud identifies Iralah with a site called Huriyah (*HGB,* 417). This site has been linked with the remains at Kh. el-Hurwarah (M.R. 167236) located SW of the Bethlehem in Zebulun and 9.5 miles N of Megiddo.

MELVIN HUNT

IDBASH (PERSON) [Heb *yidbaš*]. Idbash is listed in the OT as being related to Etam of the tribe of Judah in 1 Chr

4:3. The MT of this verse reads "And these the father of Etam: Jezreel and Ishma and Idbash; and the name of their sister was Hazzelelponi." Since this phrase apparently makes no sense, we would expect the versions to differ in their understanding of this passage, which is precisely what we have. The LXX reads "And these are the sons of Aitam: Jezrael (Gk *iezraēl*) and Jesman (Gk *iesman*) and Jebdas (Gk *iebdas*); and the name of their sister was Eselebbon." The LXX form of the name is easily accounted for as a metathesis of the labial *b* and the dental *d*. But which is the authentic reading: "father" or "son" of Etam? The Targum to Chronicles solves the problem by reading "And these are the chiefs who were dwelling in Etam: Jezreel and Ishma and Idbash; and the name of their sister was Hazzelelponi." The quite-unreliable (for Chronicles) Peshitta reads, "And these are the sons of Aminadab: Ahizarel (Syr *ʾăḥîzarʿēl*) and Neshma (Syr *nēšmāʾ*) and Dibash (Syr *dîbāš*)." The Vg interprets *ʾăbî* differently by reading "That too is the *stock* of Etam: Iezrahel and Iesema and Iedebos; and the name of their sister was Asalelphuni." The great diversity between the versions demonstrates their inability to understand the Hebrew text.

Probably the best solution is still that of C. F. Keil (1978: 86) who proposed that on the basis of the end of the preceding verse, *mišpaḥâ* should be supplied. The whole clause would then be elliptical for "And these are the [families/clans] of Abi Etam." The noun, *ʾăbî*, would then be part of the name of the individual. This reading has the principle of the *lectio difficilior* in its favor, as well as fitting more naturally with the expected connection to the previous verse (which the RSV lacks, as pointed out by Williamson *1 and 2 Chronciles* NCBC, 59). The name *yidbaš* is probably a verbal form cognate with the noun *debaš* meaning "honey," which was most likely named for its black or brown color (cf. *BDB* 185). It then would literally mean "he will be brown" or "may he be brown" (if a jussive).

Bibliography

Keil, C. F. 1978. *I & II Kings, I & II Chronicles, Ezra. Nehemiah, Esther.* Vol. 3 in *Commentary on the Old Testament in Ten Volumes.* Trans. J. Martin, A. Harper and S. Taylor. Grand Rapids.

H. Eldon Clem

IDDO (PERSON) [Heb *ʿiddô*]. Var. JADDAI; ADAIAH. The English translation of several different Hebrew names (*ʾiddô; ʿiddô; ʿiddoʾ; ʿiddôʾ; yiddô*), some etymologically related, others possibly not. The name seems to have arisen in Babylon during the 6th century B.C.E. and to have been relatively popular in postexilic Judah, expecially in priestly circles. The occurrence of the name in an authentic source from the time of the united monarchy seems to have resulted from Massoretic assimilation to this postexilic name (see #1). Found authentically within the book of Zechariah and the Ezra and Nehemiah memoirs, the Chronicler then employed the name anachronistically in order to fill out incomplete Levitical genealogies (see #2), to establish the administrative structure for the Davidic kingdom (see #3), and to provide prophetic legitimation for portions of his history (see #4).

1. The father of Ahinadab, a district governor under Solomon in the region of Mahanaim, the S half of the Transjordan (1 Kgs 4:14). 1 Kings 14 provides the only preexilic context where the name Iddo appears in the biblical writings. This statement, however, is slightly misleading. The name is embedded in what is generally regarded as an authentic source from the reign of Solomon (Mettinger 1971:111–27). Yet the identification of the Hebrew name here (*ʿiddoʾ*) with similar postexilic names is not without difficulties and is complicated further by the textual variations of the name in the various versions of 1 Kgs 4:14. The appearance of the name Iddo in 1 Kgs 4:14 may be the result of the Massoretic assimilation of a rare early name to a more common postexilic name than of onomastic continuity throughout the history of Israel.

2. According to 1 Chronicles, a Gershomite (1 Chr 6:6—Eng 6:21). Iddo (*ʿiddô*) first appears as a Levite in 1 Chr 6:6 (—Eng 6:21) as the son of Joah and the father of Zerah. He appears soon after in 1 Chr 6:26 (—Eng 6:41) within the genealogy of his kinsman Asaph, this time as Adaiah (*ʿadāyāh*), a Yahwistic form of the same name. This text still portrays him as the father of Zerah, but changes his father to Ethan. Such discrepancies within 2 genealogical lists have led to several hypotheses concerning the origin and nature of the Levitical genealogies in 1 Chronicles 5–6. See JAHATH. Yet the structure of the lists suggest that they were composed by the Chronicler himself for the purposes of his history (Williamson *1 and 2 Chronicles* NCBC, 68–72). Iddo the Gershomite, therefore, most likely represents the Chronicler's borrowing of a prominent name from the Second Temple period to complete artificial Levitical genealogies.

3. The prince over the half-tribe of Manasseh in Gilead during the reign of David, according to the Chronicler (1 Chr 27:21). The inclusion of both the sons of Levi and the sons of Aaron into the 12-tribe structure of Israel reveals the late, artificial nature of the list of the princes of Israel in 1 Chr 27:16–22. Iddo here appears as the son of Zechariah, reversing the genealogical relationship between Zechariah the prophet and Iddo his "father." The Chronicler thereby seems to have retrojected both Zechariah and Iddo anachronistically into the reign of David.

4. According to the Chronicler, the prophetic author of histories of the reigns of Jereboam (with pertinent information on the reign of Solomon, 2 Chr 9:29), Rehoboam (2 Chr 12:15) and Abijah (2 Chr 13:22). If the onomastic variation (compare, *yeʿddoy*, 2 Chr 9:29 with *ʿiddô*, 2 Chr 12:15 and 13:22) is inconsequential as is generally assumed, the Chronicler portrays Iddo as one of the most-prominent historians in the history of Israel, the author or coauthor of 3 different works: his "visions" (*ḥezôt*) concerning Jereboam the son of Nebat (2 Chr 9:29); a genealogical "record" (*dibrē*) coauthored with Shemaiah the prophet (2 Chr 12:15); and a "misdrash" (*midraš*) of Iddo the prophet (2 Chr 13:22). The Chronicler here transforms Iddo from a "seer" (*haḥozeh*) to a "prophet" (*hannābîʾ*), a change that suggests the prophet's special advisory role to the king in Chronicles (see Micheel 1983: 38). Whether the Chronicler actually knew of and drew upon such independent historical accounts is a matter of debate and largely contingent upon the presupposed historical accuracy of the non-synoptic materials in Chronicles. Literary analysis of similar references to the activities and writings of prophets and seers, however, suggests that the Chronicler invented such references to legitimate his portrayal of the history of Judah (see Micheel 1983: 79–80).

5. The grandfather of Zechariah the prophet (Zech 1:1). While the book of Ezra (Ezra 5:1 and 6:14) names Zechariah as the "son of Iddo," the introduction to the book of Zechariah ("Zechariah the son of Berechiah, son of Iddo," Zech 1:1) more accurately describes Iddo as the grandfather of Zechariah or possibly the name of Zechariah's family. While we cannot with certainty place Iddo, and thus Zechariah within a priestly family, it seems that the editor of Ezra-Nehemiah did. The editor of the Nehemiah Memoir found Iddo as a familial name in an authentic priestly list from the early 5th century B.C.E. (Neh 12:6) and erroneously portrayed him as a priestly participant in the repatriation of Judah under Zerubbabel (Neh 12:4; see Williamson *Ezra, Nehemiah* WBC, 358–61). This same editor, then, would have used Iddo as a best means to tie Zechariah into a priestly family and to identify him within the Ezra Memoirs (Ezra 5:1; 6:14).

6. A Judean community leader in Babylon, whom Ezra petitioned for Levitical personnel necessary for Ezra's Jerusalem temple reforms (Ezra 8:17). Iddo (*ʾiddô*) responded by releasing 38 Levites and 220 temple slaves to Ezra (Ezra 8:18–20). The narrative, embedded within the authentic Ezra Memoir, clearly presupposes Iddo's role as a leading person within the Judean diaspora community of Casiphia. Indications within the passage of the presence of a Judean temple in Casiphia (see Blenkinsopp *Ezra-Nehemiah* OTL, 165–66), Iddo's association with, but superior status to the temple slaves ("his brothers, the temple slaves," v 17), and the subsequent release of temple slaves to Ezra suggest that Iddo occupied a top administrative position within a Judean temple enclave in Babylon, a social structure commonly found within Achamenid Babylon (see Dandamaev 1984: 56–58; 506–8; and 522–24). Iddo of Casiphia, therefore, was most likely a priest, especially in light of the presence of a priestly familial name Iddo in Babylon (see #5).

7. A Judean, from the family of Nebo, who divorced his non-Judean wife under the threat of complete ostracism from the Jerusalem temple state under the reforms of Ezra (Ezra 10:43). See JERIMOTH.

Bibliography

Dandamaev, M. A. 1984. *Slavery in Babylonia.* Trans. V. A. Powell. DeKalb, IL.

Mettinger, T. N. D. 1971. *Solomonic State Officials.* ConBOT 5. Lund.

Micheel, R. 1983. *Die Seher- und Prophetenüberlieferungen in der Chronik.* BEvT 18. Frankfurt am Main.

JOHN W. WRIGHT

IDOL, IDOLATRY.

IDOL, IDOLATRY. An idol is a physical representation of a deity, usually used as an object of worship, though idols and images were used in a variety of ways throughout the ANE.

A. Images in the ANE
B. Images in Israel
C. Images in the NT

A. Images in the ANE

A major focus of worship in Mesopotamia from the Sargonic period on (Hallo 1983: 4–11; 1988: 54–66) and in Egypt was the cult image. While there are few extant examples of these statues, literary texts and artistic representations provide significant information as to their manufacture, appearance, and use in the ancient world. These statues varied in size, appearance, and method of manufacture (see *RLA* 6: 310–13), but cult statues in Mesopotamia were typically life-size and made of a wooden core overlaid with metal and precious stones. The statue played a central role in various cult festivals (*RLA* 3:480–83) and the proper care of the statue was an essential task of the priests. Hallo (1970) has suggested that many divine hymns were composed at the dedication of the cult statue and were used on important cult occasions involving the statue. Prayers were continually deposited before these images.

Akkadian texts give instructions for making these statues (Oppenheim 1977: 186). They were to be made of specific materials and detailed procedures were to be followed in their manufacture. In the Erra Epic, Erra points out to Marduk that his appearance and attire (i.e., that of his statue) have lost their luster, presumably because the people had neglected Marduk's cult. Marduk explains that after a previous disaster caused by him, he changed the location where *mesu* wood, lapiz lazulli, and the kind of gold needed to make cult statues could be obtained. Marduk's statue could not be properly restored without the specific materials and craftsmen required for the project.

In addition to the general requirements that prevailed for cult statues, some texts suggest that in Babylon images of particular deities had to be made in a specific way for the statue to be legitimate. A text describing Nabu-apla-iddina's restoration of the Šamaš cult at Sippar (9th cent. B.C.E.) reports that the statue of Šamaš had been taken in a raid by the Sutu, and consequently the Šamaš cult had been neglected. An earlier king had tried to restore the cult and had sought instruction from the gods as to how the statue was to be made. He did not receive the necessary instruction and was thus unable to make the statue. He was forced to reinstitute the cult using another symbol of Šamaš. In the course of Nabu-apla-iddina's general restoration, a priest found a clay model of Šamaš, and this made it possible to make a new cult image. According to Lambert (1957–58: 399), "The providential finding of the model alone made possible the manufacture of a totally new statue, for had one been made without the model, it would not have been Shamash." In Assyria and Egypt more flexibility as to how images of deities were made seems to have been permitted, but fairly fixed general conventions were followed.

Apart from the earliest periods, when deities were sometimes depicted theriomorphically (Jacobsen 1967: 14), and a number of minor deities were depicted as animals or as part-human, part-animal (Köcher 1953: 57–105), gods in Mesopotamia were depicted anthropomorphically. It seems clear that the basic purpose of the statues was not to describe the appearance of the god since there is little difference in how the various deities are depicted. Often the only basis for determining the god represented is the symbol or weapon characteristic of that particular god.

There is, in fact, little difference in size, shape, features, etc. between the way humans and deities are depicted in Mesopotamia, and many statues once thought to be gods are now recognized as votive statues of worshippers (Spycket 1968: 105) presented by them to the god. The criteria for distinguishing the image of a deity from that of a human being is that the gods are depicted wearing the horned crown and the flounced garment (Hallo 1983: 4–5). Occasionally a stone without any representation is called an image *(ṣalam)* of an individual. As Dalley (1986: 88) notes, "This shows that the noun [*ṣalmu*, 'image'] may also stand for an object that represents a person without bearing a picture of him."

In Egypt, too, "gods are recognized, not from their facial traits or bodily stature, but from the emblems they bear, or from the head of their sacred animal placed on a human body" (Bleeker 1973: 23). Often the face on Egyptian statues of gods is the face of the reigning monarch. Gods are depicted in various ways in Egypt (see Hornung 1982: 100–42), and the same god is often depicted in both human and animal form. Anthropomorphic depictions of gods are relatively rare in the early periods, but there is little evidence to suggest an evolutionary development. Certain gods like Min were from the earliest time only depicted anthropomorphically, and most gods were depicted in animal forms to the end of Egypt's independence. One way of representing a god did not replace other forms. Rather, different ways of depicting the same god existed side by side. In one example from the Louvre, 4 different ways of representing the goddess Hathor are presented next to one another (Hornung 1982: 113 n. 27). This makes it clear that images were not intended to describe the appearance of the god. Rather, they depict various ways in which the deity was thought to manifest himself or herself, and the images were meant to describe aspects of the function and attributes of the god. As Frankfort (1961: 12) has suggested the images were "probably pictograms rather than portraits."

While the incident about the statue of Dagan in 1 Samuel 5 makes it clear that cult statues were used by Israel's neighbors, representations of gods from Syria-Palestine are limited in number, and no cult statues are extant. There are, however, many figurines that have been identified as deities. It is likely, as Tigay (1986: 91) has noted, that some of these are in fact votive statues since they are lacking the distinctive symbols of divinity such as the Hathor headdress, papyrus stalks, and lotus blossoms or animals beneath their feet. At the same time certain statuettes and artistic representations have been plausibly identified as Baal. As Dever (1987: 226) points out, "The most common are rather standardized representations of a warlike Baal, often brandishing in his upraised arm a bundle of thunderbolts," representing his function as storm god. He is regularly depicted wearing a horned crown. In some instances he is represented as a bull or standing on the back of a bull. Several representations from Ugarit have been identified as El. They depict him as an old man with a thick beard seated on a throne and wearing a horned crown; as Caquot and Sznycer (1980: 12) note, "The representations of the god confirm and complete the descriptions given in the texts." Many female figurines, plausibly identified as Asherah (e.g., Maier 1986: 81–121) have been found. They are usually nude and with the reproductive aspects emphasized.

To the Egyptians and Mesopotamians—and almost certainly to the Canaanites as well—images were not the inanimate objects that the Hebrew prophets insisted they were; rather, they were living, feeling beings in which the deity was actually present. The primary significance of images lay in the fact that the life of the deity was thought to be present in the statue. The Egyptian view is expressed in a passage from the Memphite Theology which says, "He placed the gods in their shrines, He settled their offerings, He established their shrines, He made their bodies according to their wishes. Thus the gods entered into their bodies, Of every wood, every stone, every clay" (*AEL* 1:55). The gods were thought to manifest themselves in a variety of ways and to animate a variety of objects, but the cult image was a primary focus of the god's presence on earth. Numerous Egyptian texts (though coming mostly from the Greek and Roman periods) describe the god in the form of a bird descending from heaven to alight on his image. Morenz (1973: 157) says that this figure "represents the living substance of the deity which is imparted to the inanimate image." A similar view of images existed in Mesopotamia and appears to be an idea commonly associated with the use of images in religion (Bernhardt 1956). Oppenheim (1977: 184) says, "Fundamentally, the deity was considered present in its image. . . . The god moved with the image when it was carried off. . . . Only on the mythological level were the deities thought to reside in cosmic localities." It is this living presence of the deity in the statue that accounts for the Mesopotamian practice of taking away the gods of a conquered people and depositing them in the temple of the victorious deity. This demonstrated the power of the conquering god and removed the deity from the conquered area so that he or she would not be able to help the people overthrow the conqueror's authority. Certain literary compositions celebrate the return of the deity from exile to his or her city and the subsequent prosperity that the god's presence brings.

This living presence of the god in the image was magically accomplished through the "opening (or washing) of the mouth" ceremony, a ceremony that Jacobsen (1987: 15–32) suggests was a cultic reenactment of the birth of the deity in heaven. The presence of the deity in the statue was then maintained through offerings and the proper care of the statue. Morenz (1973: 155) says that "from early times onward Egyptians were not satisfied with just fashioning an image, i.e., with the creation of a work of art. On the contrary, a ritual was performed on the statues while they were still in the sculptor's workshop . . . , as a result of which the work of human hands was thought to come alive. This ceremony of 'opening the mouth' had the purpose of making all the organs serviceable and so vitalizing the image." An Akkadian text (Ebeling 1931: 120–21) dealing with the consecration of a sacred object (perhaps a statue, although the text is broken at the point where the object is mentioned) describes the purpose of the ceremony. It reads "this [statue ?] without the mouth-opening ceremony cannot smell incense, cannot eat food, and cannot drink water." Some texts suggest that the opening of the mouth ritual was performed on the statue periodically in order to maintain the vitality of the statue.

The daily care given to the statue reflects the belief that the statue was alive and thus needed the same attention and sustenance that any living individual would require. Two meals a day were provided for the images in the Uruk temple, and Oppenheim (1977: 188–89) has provided a composite picture of these meals. A table was brought in and placed before the image, and water for washing was provided. Various dishes including specific cuts of meat were presented to the statue and finally fruit was brought in an aesthetically attractive arrangement. Musicians played during the meal and curtains were drawn around the statue while the image partook of the food. The table was cleared and water was again provided for washing after the meal. Great attention was also given to proper and splendid attire for the image.

A similar situation prevailed in Egypt. Except for festive occasions when the image was carried in procession along the festival routes in a special shrine—where it was still normally hidden from the people—the cult statue was kept in a dark niche in the interior of the temple where it was accessible only to the officiating priest. Each day the priest opened the shrine containing the image, cleansed and perfumed it with incense, put a crown on it, and anointed and beautified it with cosmetics. According to Morenz (1973: 88) the purpose of this cultivation "was to furnish the image with vital force and to ensure that the deity—with whom it is not identical—lodges within it."

Among the numerous figurines used for apotropaic purposes are some that can be identified as deities, and perhaps some of these were household gods similar to the *tĕrāpîm* of Gen 31:30. The protective function of many of the Mesopotamian figures is clear from inscriptions like "that the foot of evil may not approach a man's house" or "overthrower of the evil *gallû* demons" found on some of them (see Rittig 1977: 185–208 for a collection of these inscriptions). They also probably served to promote good fortune and prosperity for those who possessed them.

B. Images in Israel

The position of official Israelite religion as defined in the Hebrew Bible stands in striking contrast to the thought and practice of their ANE neighbors. The Israelite view is clearly stated in Exod 20:4–5a, "You shall not make for yourselves a graven image *(pesel)* or any likeness *(tĕmûnâ)* of what is in heaven above or on the earth below or in the water under the earth. You shall not worship them or serve them; for I, the Lord your God am a jealous God." This prohibition of images is repeated in Exod 20:23; 34:17; Lev 19:4; 26:1; Deut 4:15–19, 25; 5:8, and is probably presupposed in Josh 24:18–23. The prohibition seems to underlie both the prophetic condemnation of Israel and Judah (e.g., Jer 11:10–13) and the prophetic contempt for images in passages like Jer 10:3–5.

The earliest date for the prohibition is difficult to establish without dispute (see Curtis 1984: 274–86) because of differences of opinion among critical scholars about the date of the various sources, and the various components of those sources generally assumed to underlie the Pentateuch. While some scholars argue for an origin of the prohibition that predates the conquest and provides a basis for the Israelites' resistance to assimilating their beliefs with those of the Canaanites, others would argue for a later date for the origin of the material. All would agree, however, that the prohibition was in place by the time of the 8th century prophets Isaiah, Hosea and Micah.

The negative attitude of Israel's official religion is clearly illustrated in the biblical vocabulary used for images. A number of words for images are descriptive of the way the image was made or the material from which it was made. The word *pesel* comes from a root that means "to hew, hew into shape" and the verb is used of shaping stones of various kinds. The word *ʿāṣāb* comes from a root that means "to shape or form." The words *massēkâ, nesek,* and *nasîk* are all probably related to the root *nāsak,* "to pour out," and the words refer primarily to molten images. Words such as *semel, ṣelem,* and *tĕrāpîm* are of uncertain etymology. A few words denote the resemblance between the image and that which it depicts or represents. The word *tabnît* means "copy" or "pattern," and it can refer to the pattern from which something is made (e.g., Exod 25:9; 2 Kgs 16:10) or that which resembles its prototype (e.g., Deut 4:16; Josh 22:28). Other words for images such as *dĕmût,* "likeness," and *tĕmûnâ,* "form, shape," belong in this category as well.

Another group of words constitutes a theological evaluation of images and the gods they represent (in general the biblical authors made little distinction between the two), and it is here that the contempt in which idols were held by the prophets is evident. Images were called *gillûlîm,* (e.g., Jer 50:2; Ezek 22:3–4); irrespective of etymology, it appears that the negative and derogatory associations of the word come from its similarity to the words *gēl* and *gālāl,* both of which mean "dung." Thus the idols are referred to as "dung pellets." The word *ʾĕlîlîm* sounds much like *ʾĕlōhîm,* "god," but it suggests rather an association with the adjective *ʾĕlîl,* "weak, worthless." The biblical authors declare that the "god" that the person thinks he is worshipping is in fact worthless and weak and impotent (e.g., Lev 26:1). Habakkuk calls the images made by the craftsman "dumb, worthless idols" (2:18–20). Another word for idol is *šiqqûṣ,* "detestable thing" (e.g., Ezek 20:7–8). The related noun *šeqeṣ* is used of various ritually unclean creatures that would render anyone eating them ceremonially unclean. Thus idols pollute anyone using them and render them unclean before God. The word *tôʿēbâ* refers to that which goes against established religious or ethical conventions, and more specifically to that which violates the moral and ritual standards of God's covenant with Israel. An idol is an abomination (Isa 44:19), and Jer 16:18 and Ezek 5:11 make it clear that idols are an abomination that pollutes the land.

Idols are *hebel,* "that which is insubstantial or worthless" (Jer 10:14–15); they are *šeqer,* "deception, falsehood" (Jer 10:14; 51:17); they are *šāwʾ,* "emptiness, vanity" (Ps 31:7; Jonah 2:9); and they are *mipleṣet,* "that which causes trembling" (1 Kgs 15:13).

The Bible does not give a clearly articulated basis for the prohibition of images, and in all probability there was not a single basis. From one perspective Israelite religion did not need an explanation for the prohibition: Yahweh had declared his sovereign will as to how he was to be worshipped, and no further justification was required (Faur 1978: 1). Deut 4:12–18 does provide an explanation, though it involves associative logic rather than formal linear logic. The passage declares that because at Sinai the people saw no shape *(tĕmûnâ)* but only heard a voice, they were not to make an image *(pesel)* in the shape *(tĕmûnat)* of any idol *(kōl samel)*. Since the context has to do with the way God chooses to manifest himself, the point of the passage seems to be that God makes himself known to his people through words rather than through a form. Other passages make it clear that God does sometimes assume a form, and Moses is said to have seen the form *(tĕmûnâ)* of God in Num 12:8; presumably Moses and the elders who looked at Yahweh (Exod 24:10–11) could have made a figure of what they saw. Yahweh, unlike the gods of Egypt, Mesopotamia, and Canaan, did not manifest himself through images. His self-disclosure came through a revelation in words, and the Sinai experience constituted a paradigm of God's self-disclosure to Israel; thus images were prohibited.

At a later time the author of Isa 40:18, 25 argued that Yahweh is incomparable and thus no form would be adequate to represent him. The prophets (e.g., Jer 10:3–5; 51:17; Isa 42:17) deny that idols are alive and thus ridicule the worship of a lifeless and impotent object made by a person. Finally an important pragmatic consequence of the prohibition was that it minimized the danger of assimilating foreign religious values and the resulting syncretism. The context in which the prohibition of images is given in the Ten Commandments suggests that its basic purpose was to prohibit images as a focus of worship rather than to eliminate the possibility of art (Gutmann 1961: 161–74).

Despite the prohibition of images in Israel's official religion and the contempt for images found throughout the prophets, a number of biblical passages make it clear that the problem of idolatry continued through much of Israel's history. It was only after the Babylonian Exile that the problem was effectively eradicated. The exact nature of what is described is often not clear since the authors do not normally distinguish between worshipping other gods (with or without images), the worship of images, and the worship of Yahweh using images. From the standpoint of the official religion described in the Bible all were equally repugnant.

Exodus 32–34 recounts the making of a golden calf by the Israelites in the wilderness as they grew impatient about Moses' delay in returning from the mountain. It is clear that they were attempting to insure god's/God's presence, and the calf was meant to accomplish that. It is not clear whether the calf was meant as an image of Yahweh or of another god (either Egyptian or Canaanite). See also GOLDEN CALF. It is possible that the calf was meant as a pedestal on which Yahweh (perhaps conceived as invisible) was enthroned since various Canaanite deities are often depicted standing on an animal typically associated with them. Uncertainties in understanding the details of Exodus 32–34 are compounded by (1) the similarities between this passage and the account of Jeroboam's dedication of the golden calves in 1 Kgs 12:28, and (2) the failure of scholars to reach a consensus concerning the chronological priority of the passages.

The story of Micah's image in Judges 17–18 describes the use of an idol during the period of the judges. The context does not make it clear how Micah or the Danites viewed the image, or even whether they understood it as an image of Yahweh, though that seems probable. It does seem clear that both the Danites and Micah viewed the use of the image and the private shrine in which it was used as legitimate. The editor of the book of Judges evaluates the incident from the perspective of the official religion, and the point of the story in its present context is that the incident illustrates how bad things were when "there was no king in Israel" and when "every man did that which was right in his own eyes."

The incident about Gideon's ephod (Judg 8:26–27)—whatever exactly the ephod was—may only make the point that an object that was not originally intended as an idol can become an object of worship and thus lead to idolatry, a point also illustrated by the bronze serpent that Moses made in the wilderness (2 Kgs 18:4; cf. Num 21:4–9).

A kind of thinking similar to that associated with the use of images outside Israel is found in 1 Samuel 4–6, but the focus is the ark rather than an idol. The Israelites attributed their defeat at the hands of the Philistines to the fact that the LORD was not with them. They brought the ark into the next battle in order to insure that the LORD would be present so as to assure their victory. It seems likely from vv 6–8 that the Philistines understood the Israelite strategy in terms of bringing a cult statue into battle. The Israelites were defeated and the ark was captured by the Philistines; as was commonly done with cult statues in Babylon and Assyria, the Philistines took the ark (the functional equivalent of an image) and presented it to Dagan (i.e., to his cult statue). The subsequent story of the cult image of Dagan falling broken before the ark and the problems encountered in each city to which the ark was taken made it clear to both Israel and the Philistines that Yahweh, despite the loss of the ark, is sovereign.

Gen 31:30–35 describes Laban's search for his household gods *(tĕrāpîm)*, which were small enough to be hidden under a saddle. Their use reflects the custom in Aram, and perhaps they were similar to the numerous figurines, many of them of deities, found throughout the Near East. Other passages indicate that teraphim were used in divination (Ezek 21:21; Zech 10:2). Their use is condemned in 1 Sam 15:23 and 2 Kgs 23:24, though some have taken Hos 3:4 to imply that the use of teraphim was considered legitimate in some circles. The mention of teraphim in David's house in 1 Sam 19:13 is problematic in that it appears to refer to an object that was the size of a person and thus much larger than both the teraphim described in the other texts or the figures known from archaeological excavations (see Pritchard 1943; Negbi 1976).

Many of the references to the use of images are connected with the court. Solomon permitted his foreign wives to bring the worship of their gods into the areas outside Jerusalem according to 1 Kgs 11:5–8, and this probably involved some physical representations of these deities. These syncretistic tendencies continued. Asa, Solomon's great-grandson, destroyed images made by his father and removed Maacah, the queen mother, because she set up an "object that caused trembling," apparently some sort of image to Asherah. Asa burned the object which was apparently made of wood (1 Kgs 15: 12–13). However, these practices remained in Judah until the fall of Jerusalem to the Babylonians, reaching their height during the time of Manasseh (2 Kgs 21:1–7).

Jeroboam I (1 Kgs 12:28–33) introduced a form of Yahweh worship into Israel that used images of bulls (perhaps as a pedestal for the invisible Yahweh), a form of worship that the prophets and religious leaders of Judah viewed as idolatry (e.g., 1 Kgs 13:33–34). Ahab's marriage to Jezebel brought the religion of Tyre into Samaria and began a period of regular confrontation between the prophets Elijah and Elisha and the devotees of Baal worship. It is probable that there was a statue of Baal along with a representation of Asherah in the Baal temple in Samaria (1 Kgs 16:32–33). Jehoram, son of Ahab "put away the pillar of Baal that his father made" (2 Kgs 3:2) and various representations appear to have been used throughout the history of the northern kingdom.

It is difficult to assess the extent of idolatry among the general population of Judah and Israel because the relevant biblical accounts are generally polemic in nature and make little attempt at statistical analysis; in addition the focus tends to be on the leadership rather than describing the practices of the common people. The texts describing the participation of the people in idolatry give a conflicting impression of its extent. The accounts of Baal worship during the time of Ahab suggest that the worship had a fairly extensive popular following. 1 Kgs 18:19 reports that there were 850 prophets of Baal and Asherah on Mt. Carmel with Elijah. In the midst of Elijah's discouragement, God declares that there were 7,000 who had not bowed down to Baal. If the number is not a figurative one, it would represent a fairly small portion of the population that had remained loyal to Yahweh. At the same time that Jehu killed all the worshippers of Baal—some 10 years after the death of Ahab—he gathered them together in one temple and had 80 soldiers kill the entire group (2 Kgs 10:18–28). The perspective of the prophets is that the people of both Israel and Judah were, at many points in their history, not deeply committed to strict obedience to the covenant; instead, they were involved, at least at a popular and superstitious level, in syncretistic religious practices, often influenced by their Canaanite neighbors whose religion seems to have retained many common features despite significant chronological, cultural, and geographical differences among those who practiced it (Oden 1976: 31–36).

Archaeological data from Israel have contributed significantly to reconstructing religious practices in Israel. Israelite personal names found on seals and inscriptions, most of which date to the 8th century B.C.E., suggest that the great majority of people worshipped Yahweh rather than other gods (Tigay 1986: 41). At the same time, Israelite shrines found at Arad, Kuntillet ʿAjrud, and other sites (Dever 1987: 232–33) make it clear that actual practice in the 8th century and before was much more varied than the Deuteronomic ideal demanded.

The sanctuaries at Arad (Aharoni 1969: 25–39) date between the time of Solomon (10th century B.C.E.) and the end of the First Temple period (ca. 600 B.C.E.), and correspond in a number of respects to the Temple in Jerusalem. Altars were found with evidence that sacrifices were offered at this sanctuary. In addition a stone pillar or *maṣṣēbâ* was found in the sanctuary. Excavations from Kuntillet ʿAjrud, a remote site in the NE Sinai, S of Beersheba, have revealed drawings of human and other figures along with graffiti and inscriptions which include the names Yahweh, Baal, Asherah, and El. The figures appear to be in violation of the commandment against making the likeness of anything in heaven, on earth, or under the earth (Deut 4:8). A large storage jar, dating to about 800 B.C.E., on which human and other figures were painted, includes the words *lyhwh šmrn wlʾšrth,* "to Yahweh of Samaria (or our keeper) and his *ʾšrt*." The inscription has been variously interpreted (see Tigay 1986: 26–29, 93; Emerton 1982:2–20; Dever 1984: 21–37; Holladay 1987: 258–59); some have argued that *ʾšrt* refers to a cult object of some sort while others have taken it as evidence that Yahweh was thought to have a consort (his asherah). Kuntillet ʿAjrud most likely was a border fortress frequented by various ethnic and religious groups, and in addition to the uncertainty in interpreting the meaning of the drawings and inscriptions, it is difficult to determine whether the evidence for practices that differ significantly from the Deuteronomic ideal are typical of practices throughout Israel, and are in any sense illustrative of the kinds of practices condemned by the prophets. The evidence pertaining to the use of idols in Israel is sparse and as Dever (1983: 573) notes, "No monumental Israelite art survives. No Israelite statuary or sculpture, large-scale iconographic representations, or paintings are known to us save two 10th-century cultic stands from Taʿanach, with fantastic representations of what appears to be Asherah as the 'Lion Lady'."

For the most part the numerous figurines of male and female deities come from Late Bronze and earlier levels and thus are earlier than the Israelite presence in Palestine. Many figurines of nude females often pregnant or with large breasts have been found in clearly Israelite contexts. However, the function of these figures is debated (see Tigay 1986: 91–92). As Dever (1983: 574) points out, "Obvious fertility aspects, usually exaggerated sexual characteristics, connect these figurines with the ancient Near Eastern cult of the 'Mother-goddess'." He concludes, "Since these figurines are found almost without exception in domestic or tomb contexts, they are undoubtedly talismans to aid in conception and childbirth rather than idols in the true sense, designed for sanctuary use." The statues probably reflect popular practice and superstition more than formal religion.

C. Images in the NT

Christianity had its origins out of a Judaism that had been purged of idolatry, and there is little mention of idolatry in the Gospels. The NT concerns about idolatry came from penetration into the gentile world where a variety of religions involved ideas and practices similar to those found in the ANE. Fertility cults, emperor worship, and the mystery religions were practiced throughout the Greek and Roman world (see Stambaugh and Balch 1986: 41–46; 138–67) and these involved both the use of images/statues and the worship of other gods, either of which constituted idolatry in the eyes of early church leaders whose roots were in Judaism. Paul found Athens to be a city full of idols (Acts 17:16). He confronted idolatry in Ephesus (Acts 19:24–41) and in keeping with the perspective of Judaism declared that "gods made with hands are no gods at all" (see Stambaugh and Balch 1986: 149–54). In some instances Paul seems to have argued that the idols have no real existence (1 Cor 8:4), while in others he suggests that there is a demonic reality that underlies the idolatrous practices (1 Cor 10:20). Paul explains the origin of idols as human rejection of God's revelation which replaces the worship of the Creator with the worship of a creature (Rom 1:18–23). The NT exhorts believers to flee idolatry (e.g., 1 Cor 10:14), and the Jerusalem Council advised all believers to avoid things sacrificed to idols (Acts 15:29). The NT also understands idolatry as putting anything in the place that God alone should occupy as the proper focus of obedience and worship (e.g., Col 3:5).

One example of the practical problems faced by believers living in a pluralistic and idolatrous society is addressed by Paul in 1 Corinthians 8 and 10 (see Willis 1985). There a dispute existed over the extent to which a believer could appropriately participate in eating meat that had been offered to idols in the pagan temples in Corinth, a practice condemned in Jewish tradition (see Orr and Walther *1 Corinthians* AB, 228–29). While Paul does not refute those who argued that because idols have no real existence, meat offered to them cannot harm the believer, he does strongly caution them of the danger that participation in these meals presents to both them (1 Cor 10:1–14) and others (1 Cor 8:7–12). The problem for believers was further complicated by the fact that meat offered in the pagan temples could be encountered, not only in communal meals in the temples, but also in various social settings throughout the community as well as in the market (see Stambaugh and Balch 1986: 158–59 and Willis 1985).

Bibliography

Aharoni, Y. 1969. The Israelite Sanctuary at Arad. Pp. 25–39 in *New Directions in Biblical Archaeology*, ed. D. N. Freedman and J. Greenfield. Garden City.

Bernhardt, K. 1956. *Gott und Bild.* Berlin.

Bleeker, C. J. 1973. *Hathor and Thoth.* Leiden.

Caquot, A., and Sznycer, M. 1980. *Ugaritic Religion.* Leiden.

Curtis, E. 1984. *Man as the Image of God in Genesis in the Light of Ancient Near Eastern Parallels.* Diss. University of Pennsylvania.

Dalley, S. 1986. The God Salmu and the Winged Disc. *Iraq* 48: 85–101.

Dever, W. G. 1983. Material Remains and the Cult in Ancient Israel: An Essay in Archaeological Systematics. Pp. 571–87 in *WLSGF.*

———. 1984. Asherah, Consort of Yahweh? New Evidence From Kuntillet Ajrud. *BASOR* 225: 21–37.

———. 1987. The Contribution of Archaeology to the Study of Canaanite and Early Israelite Religion. Pp. 209–47 in *AIR.*

Ebeling, E. 1931. *Tod und Leben nach den Vorstellungen der Babylonier.* Berlin.

Emerton, J. A. 1982. New Light on Israelite Religion: The Implications of the Inscriptions from Kuntillit 'Ajrud. *ZAW* 94: 2–20.

Faur, J. 1978. The Biblical Idea of Idolatry. *JQR* 69: 1–15.

Frankfort, H. 1961. *Ancient Egyptian Religion.* New York.

Gutmann, J. 1961. The "Second Commandment" and the Image in Judaism. *HUCA* 32: 161–74.

Hallo, W. W. 1970. The Cultic Setting of Sumerian Poetry. Pp. 116–34 in *Actes de la XVIIe Rencontre assyriologique internationale*, ed. A. Finet. Brussels.

———. 1983. Cult Statue and Divine Image: A Preliminary Study. Pp. 1–17 in *Scripture in Context II*, ed. W. Hallo, J. C. Moyer, and L. G. Perdue. Winona Lake, IN.

———. 1988. Texts, Statues and the Cult of Divine King. *VTSup* 40: 54–66.

Holladay, J. S., Jr. 1987. Religion in Israel and Judah Under the Monarchy: An Explicitly Archaeological Approach. Pp. 249–99 in *AIR.*

Hornung, E. 1982. *Conceptions of God in Ancient Egypt.* Trans. J. Baines. Ithaca, NY.

Jacobsen, T. 1967. *The Treasures of Darkness.* New Haven.

———. 1987. The Graven Image. Pp. 23–32 in *AIR.*

Köcher, F. 1953. Die babylonische Göttertypentext. *MIO* 1: 57–105.

Lambert, W. G. 1957–58. Review of F. Gössmann *Das Era Epos. AfO* 18: 395–401.

Maier, W. A., III. 1986. *Asherah: Extrabiblical Evidence.* HSM 37. Atlanta.

Mettinger, T. 1979. The Veto on Images and the Aniconic God in Israel. Pp. 15–29 in *Religious Symbols and Their Functions,* SIDÅ 10. Stockholm.

Morenz, S. 1973. *Egyptian Religion.* Trans. A. Keep. Ithaca, NY.

Negbi, O. 1976. *Canaanite Gods in Metal: An Archaeological Study of Ancient Syro-Palestinian Figurines.* Tel Aviv.

North, C. 1961. The Essence of Idolatry. Pp. 151–60 in *Von Ugarit nach Qumran,* ed. J. Hempel and L. Rost. BZAW 77. Berlin.

Oden, R. A., Jr. 1976. The Persistence of Canaanite Religion. *BA* 39: 31–36.

Oppenheim, A. L. 1977. *Ancient Mesopotamia.* 2d ed. Chicago.

Pritchard, J. B. 1943. *Palestinian Figurines in Relation to Certain Goddesses Known Through Literature.* AOS 24. New Haven.

Rittig, D. 1977. *Assyrisch-babylonische Kleinplastik magischer Bedeutung vom 13–6 Jh. v. Chr.* Munich.

Spycket, A. 1968. *Les statues de cult dans les textes Mesopotamiens des origines à le Ire Dynastie de Babylone.* CahRB 9. Paris.

Stambaugh, J. E., and Balch, D. L. 1986. *The New Testament in its Social Environment.* Philadelphia.

Tigay, J. 1986. *You Shall Have No Other Gods Before Me: Israelite Religion on the Light of Hebrew Inscriptions.* HSS 31. Atlanta.

Willis, W. L. 1985. *Idol Meat in Corinth.* SBLDS 68. Chico, CA.

EDWARD M. CURTIS

IDRIMI. The son of Ilimilimma who ruled Alalakh (Tell Atchana) in N Syria in the first half of the 15th century B.C. He is known (1) from documents found in level IV (ca. 1460–1400) of that site (although most of his reign should be seen as belonging to level V), and (2) from his 104 line "autobiography" inscribed on a statue found in a pit in the floor of a temple of level I (ca 1200 B.C.). Leonard Woolley, the site's excavator, thought that this statue, an object of veneration, was originally fitted into a throne flanked by lions (sphinxes have also been suggested) and that it had been preserved in a series of temples from the 14th century to the destruction of the site at the end of the LB Age.

The first section of the inscription describes the circumstances by which Idrimi, a younger son, came to power after his family was forced to flee from Aleppo, its original power base, following an unspecified "evil occurrence." He ultimately regained the kingdom with the assistance of his father's displaced supporters (*ḫapiru*) with whom he had lived for 7 years. His position as ruler of Alalakh was confirmed by an alliance making him a vassal to Barrattarna, a Hurrian king who previously had been his enemy (and who should be equated with a like-named ruler mentioned in the Nuzi documents). The second section notes major events in Idrimi's reign including a campaign through Hittite territory and the capture of 7 cities, the creation of a royal court, and the promotion of the welfare of his subjects. A final section presents curses against those who might efface the monument, and the unusual request of blessings for Sharruwa, the scribe responsible for the text.

This text has been used to shed light on Syria in the mid-2d millennium, a period about which little is known. For example, Barrattarna and his suzerainty over Idrimi have been related to the rise of the kingdom of Mitanni and its expansion into NW Syria. However, dangers exist in using the text uncritically as an historical source. The numerous literary and folkloristic aspects (the questing hero, the use of the number 7—elements which have led scholars to compare Idrimi's story to those of such biblical figures as Joseph and David) suggest a document wherein real events have been recast along traditional literary lines to glorify Idrimi and emphasize his legitimacy. Some scholars have also proposed that the text be seen as fictional or pseudo-historical, possibly based on fact, but created perhaps as late as the 13th century B.C.

Bibliography

Dietrich, M., and Loretz, O. 1981. Die Inschrift der Statue des Konigs Idrimi von Alalah. *UF* 13: 201–278.

Gates, M.-H. 1981. Alalakh Levels VI and V: A Chronological Reassessment. *SMS* 4/2: 11–50.

Longman, T. 1983. Fictional Akkadian Royal Autobiography: A Generic and Comparative Study. Diss. Yale.

Oller, G. 1977. The Autobiography of Idrimi: A New Text Edition with Philological and Historical Commentary. Diss. University of Pennsylvania.

Sasson, J. M. 1981. On Idrimi and Sarruwa the Scribe. Pp. 309–24 in *SCCNH.*

Smith, S. 1949. *The Statue of Idrimi.* London.

GARY H. OLLER

IDUEL (PERSON) [Gk *Idouēlos*]. See ARIEL.

IDUMEA (PLACE) [Gk *Idoumaia*]. IDUMEANS. A territory that during the Second Temple period stretched approximately from the S portion of the Judean hill country to the N part of the Negeb. To the N, the borders ran between Beth-Zur and Alouros (Ḥalḥūl), while the S border reached the height of the Arad-Malatha-Beersheba-Aroer line (cf. the so-called Limes of Herod and the Limes Palastinae; Gichon 1967; 1975). To the E, Idumea bordered the Judean desert or the Dead Sea (and perhaps the N tip of the Wadi Arabah), and its territory reached W into the provinces of the port cities Gaza, Ashkelon, and Ashdod. Among the most important Idumean cities mentioned in the literary texts are Hebron, Marisa (Tell Sandaḥanne), Adora (Dūrā), and Betabris (Bēt Gibrīn). Whoever ruled Idumea controlled a share of the profitable E–W trade between the Mediterranean coast and Transjordan as well as the N–S trade routes. They could also protect the hinterland against Nabatean and bedouin raids.

It cannot be unequivocally ascertained if the name "Idumea"—with Aramaic *ʾdwmy* as the link—can be derived from "Edom" (*ʾd[w]m,* Heb *ʾĕdôm,* "red land") or if it ought simply to be derived from *ʾdmh,* "earth/field." At any rate, the presence of the Edomites and their influence in the territories of the Negeb later belonging to Idumea is already verifiable at the end of the 7th and the beginning of the 6th century B.C. The evidence for this is literary (2 Kgs 24:2), epigraphic (Khirbet Ghazze, Tell el-Milḥ, Khirbet ʿArāʿir, Arad) and archaeological (Khirbet Ghazze, Ḥorvat Qitmit, etc.). The Edomites probably began emigrating increasingly into the S portions of the Judean territory following the destruction of Jerusalem by Nebuchadnezzar in 587 B.C. (cf. Jer 13:19; Ezek 25:12–14; 35:5, 10–12, 15; also *3 Esdras* 4:50; *Ant* 11.3.8 §61); even the downfall of Edom at the hands of Nabonidas did not effect this trend (see Myers 1971). At any rate, numerous Arabic personal names are attested in the Persian, Hellenistic, and Roman periods, as are theophoric names containing the name of the Edomite god Qaus (cf. Barkos in Ezra 2:53 = Neh 7:55). These names are also evidenced in the Aramaic ostraca from Tell es-Sebaʿ and Arad (4th century B.C.); the bilingual ostraca from Khirbet el-Qōm; the wall inscriptions from Marisa; and the name Costabaros by which the Herodian governor of Idumea and several Jews were designated (cf. *JW* 2.418, 556; *Ant* 15.7.9 §252).

Around the middle of the 5th century B.C., the whole of S Palestine, including the district that was later designated Idumea, fell under the dominion of the Qedar-Arab Geshem (Guśam b. Sahr; cf. Neh 2:19; 4:1; 6:1–6). Apparently, the Persians did not initially include this area in their administrative system (Herdotus III.4, 7, 9, 88, 97), but did so only toward the end of their sovereignty over Idumea. According to Diodorus (19.98.1), Idumea was included in the satrapy Syria-Phoenicia.

Beginning in the Hellenistic period and stretching into the Roman period, Idumea was firmly incorporated into the administrative system of the Diadochi, Hasmoneans, and Romans (see the Zenon-Papyri). Diodorus (19.95.2) documents Idumea as an "eparchy" in 311 B.C., while Josephus (*JW* 3.55 [see also Strabo 16.2.2 §749, 34 §760 and Ptolemy 5.16.10]) designates it a "toparchy" in the Roman period. A governor (Gk *stratēgos*), first attested during the Seleucid and Hasmonean period and then in the Herodian-Roman period (2 Macc 12:32; *Ant* 14.1.3 §8; 15.7.9 §253; *JW* 2.566), stood at its head. In post-Herodian times it appears that Idumea was divided into 2 smaller administrative units: a W (?) unit, "the so-called upper Idumea" (*JW* 4.552) or "greater Idumea" (*JW* 4.511); and an E unit called "East-Idumea," also attested as the toparchy En-gedi (cf. *JW* 3.55).

The population of Idumea consisted of Edomites/Arabs (cf. Strabo 16.23.34), Jews (Mark 3:8; *JW* 2.43), Sidonians (Marisa graves), Nabateans (Strabo 16.2.34; Marisa graves), and others. These inhabitants lived as farmers (Strabo 16.2.2), tradesmen (Strabo 16.2.2; Marisa graves), veterans (*JW* 2.55, 76–79), as well as soldiers and mercenaries of the ruling power (cf. Zenon-Papyri).

In the first military dispute with the Seleucids, Judas Maccabeus in 165 B.C. (?) defeated Gorgias and persued him into the borders of the hostile territory of Idumea (1 Macc 4:15; 2 Macc 10:15, 17; 12:32; *Ant* 12.7.4 §308). In the battles that followed, Lysias attacked the Hasmoneans from his base in Idumea but was finally defeated by Judas at Beth-Zur (1 Macc 4:29; 2 Macc 11:5–12; *Ant* 12.7.5 § 313). Judas fortified Beth-Zur to withstand attacks from Idumea (1 Macc 4:61). Not long afterwards he successfully renewed his attacks against the Idumeans (1 Macc 5:3; *Ant* 12.8.1 §328) and took Hebron (1 Macc 5:65; *Ant* 12.8.6 §353) as well as Marisa and Azotus (Ashdod) (*Ant* 12.8.6). However, under Lysias in 163 B.C.(?) the Seleucids renewed their attacks against Judea from Idumea (1 Macc 6:31, 50; *Ant* 12.9.4–5 §367), and did so again under Tryphon in 143 B.C.(?) (1 Macc 13:20; *Ant* 13.6.4 §207). (See also Fischer 1980: 62–63, 82, 136, 150, 205, 208.)

John Hyrcanus I conquered Idumea in 129 B.C. and forced the non-Jewish population to be circumcised (1 Macc 4:36–59; 2 Macc 10:1–8; *Ant* 13.9.1 §257; *JW* 1.63; cf. Strabo 16.2.34). This led to the eventual incorporation of Idumea into the Hasmonean empire (*Ant* 13.15.4 §395). Apparently an Idumean named Antipater was appointed to the position of governor of Idumea under Alexander Jannaeus (*Ant* 14.1.3 §8). Antipater's son, who also bore the same name, was probably appointed to the same position. Along with the Nabatean king Aretas III, he supported the Hasmonean Hyrcanus II against Hyrcanus' rival Aristobulus (*Ant* 14.1.3 §8; *JW* 1.123). The graves and burial practices in Marisa (Oren and Rappaport 1984) provide evidence of the increase in the population of Jewish inhabitants during the Hasmonean and Roman periods. A portion of the non-Jewish population seems to have emigrated to Egypt (Rappaport 1969). After the political reorganization of Palestine by Pompey in 63 B.C., Idumea (but without Marisa) remained part of the Roman province of Syria under the dominion of the Hasmoneans (*Ant* 14.4.4 §74–76; *JW* 1.156).

Idumea, homeland of Herod the Great, formed a vital starting point for and buttress of his power (Schalit 1969: 87–91, 142–45, 200–19). He and his troops fled from the Parthians into Idumea (*JW* 1.263–68; *Ant* 14.13.7 §353; 14.13.9 §361–64), which he had militarily secured shortly after he became king (*Ant* 14.15.3–4 §411, §413; *JW* 1.302–3). He gave his sister Salome in marriage to the Idumean Costabar (*Ant* 15.7.9–10 §252–57; *JW* 1.486) and appointed him to the governorship of Idumea (Ant 15.7.9–10 §253–55). He settled 3,000 Idumeans in the Trachonitis after there had been an uprising in that area (*Ant* 16.9.2–3 §285, §292).

When the kingdom of Herod was divided, Idumea fell to the ethnarch Archelaus (*Ant* 17.11.4–5 §319; *JW* 2.93–98). It belonged to the kingdom of Agrippa I from A.D. 41–44 (*Ant* 19.5.1 §275; cf. 18.6.2 §147; *JW* 2.215). Between A.D. 6–41 and after A.D. 44 Judea, as a part of the province of Syria, stood under the Roman administrative system of procurators; Idumea, as one of Judea's toparchies (*JW* 3.55) stood with her.

After the outbreak of the first Judean revolt, the rebels appointed their own commanders (Gk *stratēgoi*) over Idumea (*JW* 2.566; cf. 3.20). In the years A.D. 68 and 69 various Zealot groups, like that of Gischala (*JW* 4.224, 228–354, 566–68; 5.290, etc.), attempted to use Idumean troops to gain advantages for their own cause in Jerusalem. Others, like Simon bar Giora's group, descended into Idumea, plundered it, and forced portions of the population to "flee" to Jerusalem (*JW* 4.511–37, 556, 577; 5.248–49; 6.378–81; 7.267–68, etc.). During his subjugation of the uprising, Vespasian allowed Idumea to be devastated, while its population was decimated and placed under military occupation (*JW* 4.447–48). Following the destruction of Jerusalem in A.D. 70, Idumea was absorbed into the independent province of Judea. Soon after, all contemporary accounts about Idumea cease. Useful summary articles on Idumea are provided in PW 9/1: 913–18 and *TRE* 9: 291–99. (See also Alt 1964: 338–45; Bengston 1964: 36–37, 170–71, 187, 267; Eph'al 1982: 70, 197–214; de Geus 1979–80; Stern 1982: 249–50.)

Bibliography

Alt, A. 1964. *Judas Nachbarn zur Zeit Nehemias.* 3d ed. Munich.

Bengtson, H. 1964. *Die Strategie in der hellenistischen Welt.* Vol. 2. 2d ed. Munich.

Buhl, F. 1893. *Geschichte der Edomiter.* Leipzig.

Eph'al, I. 1982. *The Ancient Arabs.* Jerusalem and Leiden.

Fischer, T. 1980. *Seleukiden und Makkabäer.* Bochum.

Geus, C. H. J. de. 1979–80. Idumaea. *JEOL* 26: 53–74.

Gichon, M. 1967. Idumaea and the Herodian Limes. *IEJ* 17: 27–42.

———. 1975. The Sites of the *Limes* in the Negev. *EI* 12: 149–66 (in Hebrew).

Hengel, M. 1973. *Judentum und Hellenismus.* 2d ed. WUNT 10. Tübingen.

Kahrstedt, U. 1926. *Syrische Territorien in hellenistischer Zeit.* Berlin.

Knauf, E. A. 1989. *Ismael.* 2d ed. ADPV. Wiesbaden.

Myers, J. M. 1971. Edom and Judah in the Sixth-Fifth Centuries B.C. Pp. 377–92 in *Near Eastern Studies in Honor of William Foxwell Albright,* ed. H. Goedicke. Baltimore.

Oren, E. D. and Rappaport, U. 1984. The Necropolis of Maresha-Beth Govrin. *IEJ* 34: 114–53.

Rappaport, U. 1969. Les Iduméens en Égypte. *RP* 42: 73–82.

Schalit, A. 1969. *König Herodes. Der Mann und sein Werk.* Studia Judaica 4. Berlin.

Stern, E. 1982. *Material Culture of the Land of the Bible in the Persian Period 538–332 B.C.* Warminster and Jerusalem.

ULRICH HÜBNER

IEZER (PERSON) [Heb *ʾîʿezer*]. IEZERITES. A son of Gilead (Num 26:30). The name is probably a variant of ABIEZER.

IGAL (PERSON) [Heb *yigʾāl*]. The name held by 3 persons in the Hebrew Bible, Igal is a hypochoristic, or shortened theophoric name meaning "may El redeem." The name is attested in extrabiblical sources (Myers *Chronicles* AB, 21).

1. One of the 12 spies sent out by Moses to spy out the land with Joshua and Caleb (Num 13:7). He was the son of Joseph from the tribe of Issachar.

2. One of David's "mighty men" (2 Sam 23:36). The Hebrew Bible records them as the "thirty," although there is some inconsistency in the text regarding their number.

The parallel passage in 1 Chr 11:38 records the name as "Joel" as does the LXX for both 2 Sam 23:36 and for 1 Chr 11:38. This may possibly reflect a confusion of the Heb letters *gimel* and *waw* in the course of the text's transmission.

3. In the MT of 1 Chr 3:22, Igal is given as the second son of Shemiah son of Sheconiah, who was the grandson of Zerubbabel, if the genealogies in this section of 1 Chronicles 3 are to be connected to the line of Zerubbabel. There is disagreement among scholars on this question (see Williamson *Chronicles* NCBC, 57–58). A widely accepted emendation deletes the phrase "and the sons of Shemiah . . ." in v 22. This makes sense of the number 6 as the total number of sons given at the end of the verse. It would make Igal the third son of Sheconiah.

RUSSELL FULLER

IGDALIAH (PERSON) [Heb *yigdalyahû*]. In Jeremiah 35:4, when the prophet Jeremiah takes the Rechabites to the temple, they go to the chamber of the sons of Hanan son of Igdaliah. Hanan is called "the man of God"; if this title should also be applied to Igdaliah is not clear. In Israel's earlier history, "man of God" was a prophetic title applied to Samuel (1 Sam 10:6–10), Elijah (2 Sam 1:9–13), Elijah (2 Kings 4:16, 21), and various unnamed prophets (e.g. I Sam 9:6; 8:10, 1 Kgs 12:22; 13:1; 17:24; 20:20). The title "man of God" appears in Jeremiah only in Jer 35:4, and it is not known if this is still a prophetic title (late 7th century). Jer 35:4 indicates that Hanan had sons, and it has been proposed these may be "disciples" (Bright *Jeremiah* AB, 189). While it may be that Igdaliah is simply Hanan's biological father (cf. "Ezekiel the Priest, the son of Buzi" [Ezek 1:3]), it is at least possible he is Hanan's prophetic mentor and father to Hanan as Elijah is to Elisha (2 Kgs 3:12). Igdaliah means "great is Yahweh." The name has been found on at least one Hebrew seal (*TPNAH*, 340).

JOHN M. BRACKE

IGNATIUS, EPISTLES OF. Ignatius is known to us from seven letters which he wrote early in the 2d century (traditionally ca. A.D. 110) while en route to Rome as a prisoner destined to be thrown to wild animals in the arena.

A. Ignatius' Journey to Rome
B. The Recensions of Ignatius' Letters
C. The Form and Style of Ignatius' Letters
D. Ignatius' Theology
E. Ignatius, the NT, and Early Christian Literature
F. Ignatius' Conception of Ministry
G. Ignatius, Judaism, and Hellenism

A. Ignatius' Journey to Rome

Ignatius was conducted from Antioch in Syria across Asia Minor and on to Rome by a detachment of 10 Roman soldiers who grudgingly gave him leave to meet with other Christians along the way. He was especially well received in Smyrna by Polycarp, leader of the local church. There too he was visited by representatives from Ephesus, Magnesia, and Tralles and in return wrote a letter to each of these communities. He also took the opportunity to communicate with the Christians in Rome in order to proclaim to them his longing for martyrdom and to forestall any effort on their part to obtain his release.

The next stop was Troas where Ignatius wrote to the Christians in Philadelphia. He had visited Philadelphia before reaching Smyrna and had just received news about the church in that city from two messengers who had passed through it in an effort to catch up with Ignatius. From Troas Ignatius also sent two letters back to Smyrna. One of the letters to Smyrna was addressed to the church as a whole and the other to Polycarp in particular. The second letter, however, was evidently intended to be read publicly and was designed to reinforce the links between Ignatius and the Christians in Smyrna.

We hear about Ignatius for the last time from Polycarp, who in his letter to the Philippians recalls that Ignatius and two other Christians (who presumably had been added to the band of prisoners after the departure from Troas) had been well received by the Philippians (Pol. *Phil.* 1.1; 9.1). In the same letter (or, if Polycarp's letter is composite, in an earlier communication) Polycarp indicates that he was making a collection of Ignatius' letters at the request of the Philippians (Pol. *Phil.* 13.2).

The information about Ignatius contained in later accounts of his martyrdom is historically worthless.

B. The Recensions of Ignatius' Letters

Eusebius (*Hist. Eccl.* 3.36) places Ignatius' martyrdom in the reign of Trajan (A.D. 98–117), and a date in the second half of Trajan's reign or somewhat later seems to fit the picture of the conditions reflected in the letters. Arguments are still advanced (notably by Joly 1979) that call into question the authenticity of these documents, but the researches of Zahn (1873) and Lightfoot (1885, ²1889) and their followers continue to dominate the scholarship. Thus the authenticity of (a) what is now often, though misleadingly, called the "middle recension" is generally accepted. By the same token, (b) the so-called "long recension" is usually regarded as a 4th-century (perhaps Neo-Arian) revision (Hagedorn 1973:xxxvii–lii) consisting of interpolations into the original letters and the addition of 6 spurious letters. This recension is found in numerous Greek and Latin manuscripts and came to be the form in which Ignatius was most often known until Archbishop Ussher, in his *Polycarpi et Ignatii Epistolae* of 1644, brilliantly unearthed an earlier (Latin) form of the text akin to that quoted by Eusebius. Ussher had rediscovered the middle recension. The Greek of that recension (except for the letter to the Romans) became available with the publication of Ignatius' letters from *Codex Mediceo-Laurentianus* 57,7 by Isaak Voss in 1646. The Greek text of Ignatius' letter to the Romans had a separate history as part of an account of Ignatius' martyrdom (*Codex Parisiensis-Colbertinus* 1451), and this too was soon published by Th. Ruinart (1689). Our knowledge of the middle recension has been increased somewhat by the discovery of several important oriental versions: Coptic (fragments), Syriac (fragments), Armenian, Arabic. It should be noted that almost all of the collections of the letters of the middle recension in the manuscripts also include some or all of the spurious letters. Since the interpolations and the spurious letters are in all likelihood the work of one person, these collections represent a curious mixture of textual traditions. Finally, (c) what some have called the "short recension" proves to be no recension at all but merely an abridgment of a Syriac version of the middle recension. The term-short recension, then, would serve most accurately to describe the so-called middle recension and is often so used.

C. The Form and Style of Ignatius' Letters

Although the epistolography of the authentic letters of Ignatius owes something to Paul, Ignatius is more deeply indebted to the formulae of the Hellenistic letter; and he varies such formulae in ways that are distinctively his own. Thus he works up the greetings at the beginning and end of his communications from a wider range of conventional materials; he developes special forms of common transitional devices at the beginning of the body of the letter (where he avoids the thanksgiving) and elsewhere; and he reflects more directly the Hellenistic idea of the letter as a substitute for face-to-face encounter (Schoedel *Ignatius of Antioch* Hermeneia, 7). Perler (1949) has shown that the colorful, ornate, and sometimes reckless style of the letters has connections with a stream of popular and, in some quarters, suspect rhetoric known as "Asianism." Ignatius is saved from vacuity and bombast, however, by the fire and passion that fuses the elements of his style into a single, if somewhat dense, whole.

D. Ignatius' Theology

Ignatius' self-understanding as a martyr provides the most useful point of departure for appreciating his thought. His experience in this regard may be seen as a heightened form of the experience of all Christians (*Ign. Eph.* 10), and the special difficulties that he faced may be taken as extensions of the difficulties confronted by every bishop (*Pol.* 1–5). Among these was resistance from the bishop's own people and, in Ignatius' own case, a sense of possible unworthiness. More than conventional self-depreciation seems to be involved in the doubts that Ignatius expresses about his spiritual condition. His arrest may well have precipitated the crisis. But there is also a good possibility that he was shaken by a challenge to his authority in Antioch. This possibility depends on taking the "peace" restored in Antioch and reported to Ignatius by the two messengers on their arrival in Troas (*Phld.* 10.1; *Smyrn.* 11.2; *Pol.* 7.1) not as the cessation of persecution in Antioch but as the capitulation of those formerly opposed to their bishop (Harrison 1936: 79–106). In any event, Ignatius is gratified by those who see beyond his bonds and the apparent unworthiness that they symbolize (*Smyrn.* 10.2; *Pol.* 2.3); and it seems fair to suggest that his persistent call for unity in the churches and obedience to the bishop was at the same time a call for recognition and support and a search for the ratification of his own worthiness (Schoedel 1985: 10–14). Certainly the level of activity involved in terms of letters written, messengers sent on ahead, and representatives assembled (or yet to be assembled in Antioch) is extraordinary and suggests that more was involved than simply a spontaneous outpouring of sympathy for a persecuted fellow Christian.

Ignatius links his self-understanding as a martyr and his theology at one crucial point: He asks how his impending death can have any meaning if the Lord did not truly die (*Trall.* 10; *Smyrn.* 4.2). Anti-docetic themes are common in Ignatius and are found concentrated especially in the letters to Tralles and Smyrna. Ignatius probably responds also to a distinct Judaizing form of Christianity in his letters to Magnesia and Philadelphia (*Magn.* 8–10; *Phld.* 5–9). But it is significant that he tends to deal with it in terms drawn from his debate with docetism (*Magn.* 9.1; 11). Any threat to the authority of a bishop is naturally resisted by Ignatius. But at a deeper level he senses a connection between the reality of the incarnation and passion of the Lord (as well as his presence in the elements of the sacred meal) and a genuine commitment to concrete deeds of faith and love (*Smyrn.* 6.2–8.2); such faith and love, as Ignatius sees it, are to be found only in a community united under its bishop and not in an elitist conventicle.

Corollaries of Ignatius' emphasis on the incarnation include the relegation of the doctrine of creation to the periphery of his thought, the attentuation of eschatological themes, and a preoccupation with the worshipping community as the sphere of divine influence in the world. It is characteristic that when Ignatius turns his attention to the cosmos, it is to describe (in mythological terms that are far from clear) the mysterious events that surround the entrance of Christ into the world and his departure from it (*Eph.* 19). In doctrinal terms, Ignatius anticipates orthodox theology in seeing the incarnation as the paradoxical union of flesh and spirit in the God-Man (*Eph.* 7.2; *Smyrn.* 3.2). And this in turn presupposes a definition of the divine nature as timeless and changeless in good Hellenistic terms (*Eph.* 7.2; *Pol.* 3.2). The association of God (and bishops) with silence elsewhere in Ignatius (*Eph.* 6.1; 14.2–15.2; 19.1; *Magn.* 8.2; *Phld.* 1.1) may indicate that his conception of divine transcendence owes something to Gnosticism as well (Paulsen 1978: 110–22); but it is perhaps more likely that his language here has metaphorical significance (*Magn.* 8.2) and that it represents an extension of his insistence on the superiority of the silent deed over empty words (Schoedel, 56–57, 76–78, 91, 170–71).

An important feature of Ignatius' view of the incarnation is his teaching that flesh and spirit complement rather than oppose one another in the God-Man. Flesh and spirit in this context, however, refer to two spheres or two dimensions; and it is significant that Ignatius describes not only Christ but also redeemed humanity in terms of the complementarity of the two spheres (Martin 1971). Thus things fleshly become spiritual when done by those who are spiritual (*Eph.* 8.2). This reinterpretation and reversal of the NT formula opens up the way for a more-open attitude toward the things of this world and probably has something to do with the greater appreciation that Ignatius himself shows for the popular culture of the Greek city. It should be noted that when he speaks of the hatred shown Christians by the "world" (*Rom.* 3.3), he is thinking primarily of the exercise of Roman power. Pagans in the immediate vicinity of Christians, on the other hand, are to be dealt with as "brothers" (*Eph.* 10.2).

E. Ignatius, the NT, and Early Christian Literature

In developing his thought, Ignatius was in a position to draw on many strands of the theology reflected in the NT, and he absorbed much of the basic religious vocabulary of his sources (with a notable lack of attention to "sin" however). He had been particularly impressed by Paul, not least because he had found in the apostle a model for dealing with his sense of possible unworthiness (Ign. *Rom.* 9.2; cf. 1 Cor 15:8–9). In appropriating the earlier materials, Ignatius' thought seems to have been shaped especially by two somewhat antithetical yet ultimately reconcilable developments: the emergence of more "mystical" strands of Christianity (which the gospel of John and Ephesians also reflect); and a growing emphasis on the need for discipline and order (which Matthew and the Pastorals also reflect). It was a theology of the incarnation, as we have seen, that served to give coherence to these diverse tendencies in Ignatius.

The gospel material in the letters is reminiscent especially of Matthew, and one passage in particular (*Smyrn.* 1.1) suggests that Ignatius may in fact have had the gospel of Matthew before him (Köhler 1987: 73–96). That, however, is not certain (Koester 1957: 24–61). There is no real trace of Mark in Ignatius, and we find only one passage with special affinities with Luke (*Smyrn.* 3.2). And that passage (in which the resurrected Lord "came to those about Peter" and said, "Take, handle me, and see that I am not a bodiless demon") may well depend on tradition independent of the gospel. Some (Maurer 1949) argue that Ignatius knew the Gospel of John (*Rom.* 7.3; *Phld.* 7.1; 9.1), but that seems unlikely (Paulsen 1978: 36–37).

Of Paul's letters only 1 Corinthians can confidently be said to have been read with any care by Ignatius, though echoes of other letters of Paul are probably also discernible from time to time. Points of contact between Ignatius and Paul's (or Deutero-Paul's) Ephesians are sometimes striking, yet probably not sufficient to require a literary relation. That is even more obvious in the case of similarities between Ignatius and the Pastorals.

One striking parallel between Ignatius and 1 John is found (*Eph.* 14.2), but it provides no guarantee that the bishop had read that document. Equally problematic are parallels involving *1 Clement, 2 Clement, Hermas,* the *Preaching of Peter,* and the *Odes of Solomon.*

The numerous echoes in Ignatius of Rom 1:3–4 are likely to go back not to Paul himself but to a development of semi-credal material in the tradition. Other strands of tradition seem to stand behind formulized passages elsewhere in Ignatius, but it is not at all clear what accounts for the shape that they have. The prior crystallization around baptism of statements about the birth, ministry, and passion of Jesus seems possible at times (*Eph.* 18.2). Elsewhere such a listing of events reflects anti-docetic concerns more strongly and may represent in part a response to the immediate situation (*Trall.* 9). Certainly the series of Christological antitheses in one celebrated passage (*Eph.* 7.2; cf. *Pol.* 3.2) looks like a rhetorical elaboration of a few traditional elements created by Ignatius himself (von Campenhausen 1972: 241–53). Contact with apologetic themes in another passage (*Smyrn.* 1–3) suggests yet another context within which collections of statements about the ministry of Jesus once figured (Schoedel, 220–29).

F. Ignatius' Conception of the Ministry

Ignatius' conception of the local ministry consisting of a single bishop (overseer), presbyters (elders), and deacons goes beyond the NT but is close in spirit to the Pastorals. Ignatius apparently found the arrangement in place in the congregations of Asia Minor. He seems, however, to have emphasized the authority of the bishop in ways that appeared unusual to his contemporaries, and he no doubt assumed too readily that monarchic bishops were to be found everywhere in the church (*Eph.* 3.2). The threefold ministry reflected in the letters may represent a fusion of a Jewish-Christian system of elders and a gentile-Christian system of overseers and deacons (cf. Phil 1:1). In any event, there are hints that the arrangement is still somewhat in flux in Ignatius. Also still missing in Ignatius is any convincing evidence of the idea of apostolic succession, for episcopal authority is seen as derived directly from God or Christ. This in turn probably does not mean, as some have suggested, that Ignatius conceives of the bishop as embodying the presence of God or Christ in an extraordinary manner. Ministerial authority has been significantly enhanced by Ignatius, but it is difficult to show that it has been legitimated in a fundamentally new way. The elaborate and quite varied comparisons between the bishop and God or Christ, between the presbyters and the apostles, and between the deacons and divinely approved service seem to remain true comparisons and to express conventional ideas about receiving the one sent as the one who sent him (Schoedel, 112–14). It is also interesting to note in this connection that when Ignatius reflects on the words of inspired prophecy that he delivered in Philadelphia about the need to obey the bishop, he does not link the charisma of prophecy formally with the office of bishop (*Phld.* 7). In principle the Spirit still blows where it wills.

There is also no convincing evidence in Ignatius of an overarching ecclesiastical authority above the level of the local bishop. The preeminence accorded the Roman church in the address of his letter to them (the one letter that fails to draw attention to the bishop of the community) is a spiritual preeminence and is emphasized precisely because the Roman Christians form the last and presumably most important link in a chain of churches to whom Ignatius looks to give his martyrdom significance. It is the approval of the churches that will assure Ignatius of the value of his ministry and thereby confirm his worthiness to "become a disciple" and "to attain God" in martyrdom (*Eph.* 1.2). For the churches are made up of Christians who apparently realize their discipleship here and now (*Magn.* 9.1; 10.1; *Pol.* 2.1) and who walk united in the path marked out for them by the apostles (*Eph.* 11.2–12.2). In this connection Ignatius may well have been thinking of his own presumed failure to unite the church of Antioch until the turn of events announced to him by the messengers in Troas. In any event, Rome is the place where the reality of Ignatius' Christianity is to be decisively demonstrated, and the Roman Christians are the last in a line of well-wishers who will paradoxically show their love for their visitor by urging on the wild beasts.

G. Ignatius, Judaism, and Hellenism

The broader cultural horizons of Ignatius have proved difficult to define. He does little with the OT Scriptures (*Eph.* 5.3; *Magn.* 12; *Trall.* 8.2; cf. *Eph.* 15.1; *Magn.* 10.3; 13.1); and he regards "Judaism" as an entity distinct not only from "Christianity" but also from Scripture and the prophets (*Magn.* 8.1–2;9.2; 10.3). Important light on some points in Ignatius is shed by parallels from Philo and Josephus, however, and Ignatius met a group of Judaizers in Philadelphia who worked with a Hellenistic-Jewish conception of the Scriptures as "archives" (*Phld.* 8.2). The gnostic affinities of Ignatius were stressed by Schlier (1929) who took the mythological account in *Eph.* 19 as his point of departure. Daniélou (1964: 39–43) accepted Schlier's analysis as a whole but reclassified what emerged as "Jewish Christianity." And the importance of the *Ascension of Isaiah* as an item in the background reconstructed by Schlier lends plausibility to this shift of perspective. Bartsch (1940), on the other hand, chose to take the emphasis on oneness as the main indicator of Ignatius' indebtedness to gnostic and quasi-gnostic thought. But it now seems clear that more relevant parallels to such themes as "unity" and "concord" are to be found in less esoteric realms of Hellenism and Hellenistic Judaism (Schoedel, 51–55; 74; 116–17). As suggested above, this may well be true also for the theme of "silence" in Ignatius. The reflections of these and other features of popular culture in the letters go a long way to account for the literary and theological peculiarities of Ignatius.

Bibliography

Bartsch, H.-W. 1940. *Gnostisches Gut und Gemeindetradition bei Ignatius von Antiochien.* Gütersloh.

Campenhausen, H. F. von. 1972. "Das Bekenntnis im Urchristentum." *ZNW* 63: 210–53.

Daniélou, J. 1964. *The Theology of Jewish Christianity.* London and Philadelphia.

Hagedorn, D. 1973. *Der Hiobkommentar des Arianers Julian.* Patristische Texte und Studien 14. Berlin.

Harrison, P. N. 1936. *Polycarp's Two Epistles to the Philippians.* Cambridge.

Joly, R. 1979. *Le dossier d'Ignace d'Antioche.* Université libre de Bruxelles, Faculté de Philosophie et Lettres 69. Brussels.

Koester, H. 1957. *Synoptische Überlieferung bei den Apostolischen Vätern.* TU 65. Berlin.

Köhler, W.-D. 1987. *Die Rezeption des Matthäusevangeliums in der Zeit vor Irenäus.* WUNT, 2d ser. 24. Tübingen.

Lightfoot, J. B. 1889. *The Apostolic Fathers,* Part 2: *Ignatius, S. Polycarp.* 2d ed. 3 vols. London.

Martin, J. P. 1971. "La pneumatologia en Ignacio de Antioquia." *Sal* 33: 379–454.

Maurer, C. 1949. *Ignatius von Antiochien und das Johannesevangelium.* ATANT 18. Zurich.

Paulsen, H. 1978. *Studien zur Theologie des Ignatius von Antiochien.* Forschungen zur Kirchen- und Dogmengeschichte 29. Göttingen.

———. 1985. *Die Briefe des Ignatius von Antiochia und der Brief des Polkarp von Smyrna.* 2d ed. HNT 18. Tübingen.

Perler, O. 1949. Das vierte Makkabäerbuch, Ignatius von Antiochien und die ältesten Martyrerberichte. *RivArCr* 25: 47–72.

Rathke, H. 1967. *Ignatius von Antiochien und die Paulusbriefe.* TU 99. Berlin.

Schlier, H. 1929. *Religionsgeschichtliche Untersuchungen zu den Ignatiusbriefen.* BZNW 8. Giessen.

Smith, J. D. 1985. *The Ignatian Long Recension and Christian Communities in Fourth Century Syrian Antioch.* Diss. Harvard.

Zahn, T. 1873. *Ignatius von Antiochien.* Gotha.

William R. Schoedel

IIM (PLACE) [Heb *ʿiyyîm*]. A settlement of the tribe of Judah mentioned only once, in Josh 15:29, where it is listed among the settlements occupied by Judah in the aftermath of the conquest. This section of the list parallels passages in Josh 19:3 and 1 Chr 4:29 which record the towns of Simeon. In Josh 15:29 it is inserted between Baalah and Ezem; between Balah/Bihah and Ezem in the Simeonite list Iim is lacking. The tribe of Simeon was assimilated to Judah at an early date, and virtually all the towns in the two Simeonite lists have clear equivalents in the Judahite section. Albright suggested that Iim was a corrupt dittography for Ezem (1924: 160). It is also possible that Iim was dropped accidentally from the Simeonite list, and that the Chronicler worked from that same list. If not a textual corruption, Iim is in the southernmost district of Judah, the Negeb.

The location of Iim is problematic. Its name, "ruins," is of no help in determining its location. On the basis of the LXX reading, Aueim, Abel read it as ʿAwim and identified it with Deir el-Gawi, 19 km NE of Beer-sheba (*GP,* 352; M.R. 142086).

Bibliography

Albright, W. F. 1924. Egypt and the Early History of the Negeb. *JPOS* 24: 131–61.

Cross, F. M., and Wright, G. E. 1956. The Boundary and Province Lists of the Kingdom of Judah. *JBL* 75: 202–26.

Jeffrey R. Zorn

IJON (PLACE) [Heb *ʿiyyôn*]. A fortified town of Naphtali located at the northernmost end of the Huleh Valley, on the main highway leading from Palestine to Syria. The LXX in Kings renders Ijon as *Ain* or *Nain*; and in Chronicles as *Iōn* or *Aiōn.* Josephus (*Ant* 8.12.4) writes *Aiōn.*

Ijon is mentioned in the Bible as the first Israelite city to be captured by Ben-hadad king of Aram-Damascus at the instigation of Asa (1 Kgs 15:20; 2 Chr 16:4; ca. 885 B.C.E.). Since Ijon is mentioned before Dan and Abel-beth-maacah, the Aramean forces probably came around through the W, rather than the alternative route through the Upper Golan, S of Mt. Hermon (Monson 1983: 67–68). The town was again captured some 150 years later by Tiglath-pileser III during his campaign of 733 B.C.E. (2 Kgs 15:29). Both of these events illustrate the strategic role played by Ijon in helping to secure Israel's N approaches. It is possible that the name Dan-jaan (2 Sam 24:6), a town mentioned on the way to Sidon, is a corruption of Ijon (Abel *GP* 2: 352; Aharoni *EncMiqr* 6: 184). Simons (*GTTOT,* 347), though, considers an emendation of *yaʿan* to *ʿiyyôn* to be unwarranted.

During his travels in the early 19th century, E. Robinson noted how the name of Ijon probably survived in the Arabic name of *Merj ʿAyyûn,* "meadow of springs," a rich oval-shaped plain in modern-day Lebanon, about 12 km N of Metulla (Robinson 1856: 372–75). The valley is bounded on the W by the Līṭânī River and on the E by the Ḥaṣbanî River and Mt. Hermon. At its N end sits the tall mound of Tell ed-Dibbîn (M.R. 205308). Surface surveys have revealed remains of walls and pottery from the Bronze Age to the Arabic period (Aharoni *EncMiqr* 6: 185). A road leading E from Sidon to Damascus passed by the foot of the mound, placing Ijon at this important juncture of E–W and N–S traffic.

Posener (1940: 74) suggested that Ijon may already be mentioned in the 19th/18th century B.C.E. Execration Texts (No. 18) as *ʿynw* (= *ʿAyyānu*). Subsequent scholarly opinion, however, prefers an equation with Ḥayani in the land of the *GA<ŠU>RI,* mentioned in El Amarna letter 256: 28 (Ahituv *CTAED,* 120). This site has been identified with ʿAyyûn (M.R. 212235), 3 km N of Hammat on the Yarmuk River (Albright 1943). This same Ijon in the S Golan Heights (the biblical land of Geshur) appears during the Second Temple period as a village in the district of Hippos (Susita), E of the Sea of Galilee (*t. Šeb.* 4:10). The earliest mention of Galilean Ijon outside of the Bible is probably during the reign of Thutmose III (15th century B.C.E.) in his roster of 119 Canaanite towns (No. 95; Aharoni *LBHG,* 163; Ahituv *CTAED,* 120).

Bibliography

Albright, W. F. 1943. Two Little Understood Amarna Letters from the Middle Jordan Valley. *BASOR* 89: 7–17.
Monson, J. M. 1983. *The Land Between.* Jerusalem.
Posener, G. 1940. *Princes et pays d'Asie et de Nubie.* Brussels.
Robinson, E. 1856. *Biblical Researches in Palestine.* Vol. 3. London.

R. A. MULLINS

IKKESH (PERSON) [Heb *ʿiqqēš*]. The father or ancestor of Ira, one of David's champions, named in the parallel lists of 2 Sam 23:8–39 (v 26) and 1 Chr 11:10–47 (v 28), Ikkesh is said to be "of Tekoa" (lit. "the Tekoite"), that is, from the town of Tekoa in Judah, which lies about five miles south of Bethlehem. Father and son are mentioned again in 1 Chr 27:1–15, where Ira is listed as the commander in charge of the sixth monthly course of 24,000 men in the armed service of the king (v 9). Noth (*IPN* 228–29) supposes that "Ikkesh," probably from the root *ʿqš* ("twist"), is a secular name referring to one's character (i.e., "twisted," "wrong-headed"), although it just as likely might refer to a physical anomaly (see *HALAT*).

RODNEY K. DUKE

ILAI (PERSON) [Heb *ʿîlay*]. An Ahohite who was one of David's warriors (1 Chr 11:29). Since his name parallels that of Zalmon the Ahohite in 2 Sam 23:28, it is possible that Ilai is actually a corruption of the Hebrew *ṣîlay,* which may be a diminutive form of Zalmon. See ZALMON (PERSON). This corruption would have been possible because of the similarity between the Hebrew letters *ʿayin* and *ṣade,* beginning *ʿîlay* and *ṣîlay,* respectively.

D. G. SCHLEY

ILIADUN (PERSON) [Gk *Iliadoun*]. A Levite, the father of Joda, whose descendants helped rebuild the temple under Zerubbabel's leadership (1 Esdr 5:56—Eng 5:58). Although 1 Esdras is often assumed to have been compiled from Ezra and Nehemiah, this family does not appear in the list of returning Levites who rebuilt the temple (Ezra 3). Omissions such as this also raise questions about 1 Esdras being used as a source by Ezra or Nehemiah. Furthermore, problems associated with dating events and identifying persons described in 1 Esdras have cast doubt on the historicity of the text.

MICHAEL DAVID MCGEHEE

ILLYRICUM (PLACE) [Gk *Illyrikon*]. A Roman province where Paul affirms that he had preached the gospel (Rom 15:19). It was in the NW part of the Balkan peninsula along the E coast of the Adriatic Sea. Illyricum was one of four large provinces established by the Romans across the N part of the peninsula. These provinces—Illyricum, Moesia, Dacia, and Pannonia—covered the area from Vienna to the Black Sea and from Macedonia to the Carpathian Mountains. Illyricum was the westernmost and, in the early 1st century A.D., was divided into two sections: Pannonia in the N and DALMATIA in the S. The term Illyricum refers at times to Dalmatia and at other times to a larger area which includes Dalmatia. What is meant by Dalmatia in 2 Tim 4:10 is not clear, but it probably designates the S sector of Illyricum.

The boundaries of Illyricum are not easy to define, because they fluctuated through time. The Roman province seems to have extended from the Drina River (ancient Drilo) in the S to Istria, near the Austrian border, in the N; and from the Adriatic Sea on the W to the Sava River (ancient Savus) in the E. Suetonius stated that after Tiberius suppressed a rebellion in Illyricum (A.D. 6–9), he reduced "the whole of Illyricum," which Suetonius described as "enclosed by Northern Italy, Noricum, the Danube, Thrace, Macedonia, and the Adriatic Sea . . ." (*Tib.* 16). The struggles of Tiberius with Illyricum are recounted by Dio Cassius in his history of Rome (54.34; 55.28–34), written between A.D. 200 and 222.

Octavian had subjugated the Dalmatian tribe in 33 B.C., after a war which lasted several years, but it was not until after A.D. 9 that Dalmatia became a separate province. At that time Pannonia (Austria and W Hungary), which had been attached to the N part of Illyricum, was detached and made a separate province, while the S part of Illyricum (W Yugoslavia) was shortly thereafter renamed Dalmatia.

The Illyrians were probably an Indo-European people who settled in the W half of the Balkan peninsula around 1000 B.C. and consisted of numerous tribes, two of which were the Dalmatae and the Albani. These two tribes settled in the S part of Illyricum, the area now known as S Yugoslavia and Albania. Subsequently, some of the Illyrian tribes of S Albania spilled over into the area further S, where they came into contact with Greek culture and eventually established their own kingdom known as Epirus, which lies today in NW Greece.

When Paul spoke of his ministry as reaching from Jerusalem to Illyricum (Rom 15:19), it is unclear whether he meant the province as a whole, just the S portion of it (Dalmatia, 2 Tim 4:10), or perhaps just the border of it, near the city of Dyrrachium, which lay at the W end of the Ignatian Way.

It is quite possible that Paul himself did not actually preach in Illyricum. Contrary to most modern translations, the word "preach" does not occur in the text of Romans. It rather states that he "fulfilled" or "completed" the gospel of Christ in a geographical circle which stretched from Jerusalem to Illyricum. He may have viewed his ministry among the gentiles as a completion of the work begun among Jews in Jerusalem by the apostles before him, a work which reached W to Illyricum where some of his companions labored (e.g., Titus in Dalmatia, 2 Tim 4:10).

If Paul meant that he himself had preached all the way to Illyricum, we cannot determine when this occurred because the exact chronology of Paul's journeys is unclear, and Illyricum is not mentioned again in the letters of Paul or in Acts. A likely possibility would be the occasion of his third journey, when Luke describes his travels as taking him "through these parts," referring to Macedonia (Acts 20:2). It could not have been after his Roman imprisonment (Acts 28:16), because the Roman letter in which he refers to Illyricum was written in Corinth *before* this imprisonment.

Bibliography

Cary, M. 1962. *A History of Rome.* New York.

Finley, M. I. 1977. *Atlas of Classical Archaeology.* New York.

Metzger, B. 1964. Romans 15:14–33 and Paul's Conception of his Apostolic Mission. *JBL* 83: 1–11.

JOHN MCRAY

IMAGE. See IDOL, IDOLATRY; GRAVEN IMAGE.

IMAGE OF GOD (OT). Even though the statement of humanity's creation in the image of God appears to have had less importance in the biblical tradition than it assumed in later theological discussion, this statement clearly constitutes an important and positive affirmation about humanity's place in the created order. Man and woman are said to have been created in the *image/likeness* of God in only three passages in the early chapters of Genesis (Gen 1:26–28; 5:1–3; 9:6), all of which are assigned to the Priestly source of the Pentateuch as proposed by most modern scholars. The positive nature of this description is clear from the contexts in which it occurs, but the contexts are lacking the kind of explicit clues that would remove the ambiguity as to the exact meaning of the terms.

The etymology of the word *ṣelem,* "image," is uncertain. Some have suggested that it is related to a verb *ṣālam,* "to cut off," which does not occur in the Hebrew Bible. Apart from the "image of God" passages, the word is used twelve times. In ten instances the word refers to a physical representation of something (e.g., golden images of mice and tumors in 1 Sam 6:5, 11; images of Baal in 2 Kgs 11:18 and 2 Chr 23:17; molten images of Canaanite deities in Num 33:52; pagan images in Ezek 7:20, 16:17, and Amos 5:26; painted pictures of Babylonians in Ezek 23:14). *Ṣelem* has an abstract meaning in Ps 39:7 (—Eng 39:6), where it refers to the insubstantial nature of human life, and in Ps 73:20, where it refers to a dream image that a person retains upon waking. Westermann (*Genesis 1–11* BKAT, 146) is perhaps correct in suggesting that the basic meaning of *ṣelem* is "representation," a meaning sufficiently broad to include both the concrete and the abstract aspects of the word. The Akkadian cognate of the word (*ṣalmu*) is the common Akkadian word for statue/image, and it also includes an abstract aspect. The Aramaic cognate of *ṣelem* is a common word for image, and the word is used in the Aramaic portions of Daniel for the images/statues described in chapters 2 and 3. The word is also used of the attitude of the king (lit. "the appearance of his face") toward those who refused to bow down to the image that he was dedicating.

The second word used in these passages is *dĕmût,* an abstract noun from the verb *dāmâ,* which means "to be like." It is generally argued that this abstract term suggests approximation and weakens or blurs the meaning of the previous word *ṣelem* (Bird 1981: 139, n. 23), and this does seem to be the effect of the term in the visions of Ezekiel (e.g., 1:5, 26; 8:1; 10:1). The similarity indicated by *dĕmût* is not necessarily physical, as is clear from its use in Isa 13:4 to describe "the sound of a tumult on the mountains like (*dĕmût*) many people." *Dĕmût* clearly refers to a physical likeness in 2 Kgs 16:10, where Ahaz sent a likeness (*dĕmût*) and a model of an altar from Damascus to Jerusalem so that he could have a similar altar constructed for the temple. In 2 Chr 4:3, the figures of oxen that supported the molten sea in front of the temple are called *dĕmût bĕqārîm,* "figures/images of oxen." The Aramaic cognate of the word *dĕmût* is used in a similar way in a bilingual inscription on a statue from Tell Fekheriye (Millard and Bordreuil 1982: 137–38), in which the Akkadian word *ṣalmu,* "image/statue," is rendered into Aramaic as *ṣalma* in lines 12 and 16 and as *dĕmûta* in lines 1 and 15. Thus, while the term *dĕmût* indicates that the human being is in some sense "like God," the word seems to be virtually a synonym for the word *ṣelem.*

Gen 1:26 introduces the account of humanity's creation with God's statement, "Let us make man in our image (*bĕṣalmēnû*) according to our likeness (*kidmûtēnû*)." Gen 5:1 talks about humanity's creation "in the likeness of God" (*bidmût ʾĕlōhîm*), and this suggests that the prepositions used with the nouns "image and likeness" are interchangeable in meaning. It has been suggested by some that the preposition *b* is used as *bet essentiae,* and that it indicates identity. Thus, the meaning is that man and woman were created not "according to" the image of God but rather "as" the image of God. Many have denied that the preposition *k* ever has this meaning, though certain considerations suggest that this may be the meaning intended by the biblical author.

It is clear that a certain ambiguity is associated with the meaning of the terms "image and likeness of God" in these passages in Genesis. It is difficult to know whether the author of the material used expressions from the tradition that his audience would immediately understand in their cultural context, but which we in a vastly different cultural setting lack the contextual clues to understand precisely, or whether the author deliberately presented these ideas in a somewhat ambiguous way.

Because of this ambiguity, interpreters have had to look for clues in the context of these passages that might be decisive for determining the exact meaning of these descriptions of humanity. Unfortunately, commentators have not been able to agree on what the decisive clues are, and the interpretation of the image of God has often reflected the *Zeitgeist* and has followed whatever emphasis happened to be current in psychology, or philosophy, or sociology, or theology.

The contexts in which the image/likeness of God occur do provide certain clear indications as to the significance of these statements about humanity about which virtually all commentators agree.

The account of creation in Genesis follows a clearly established literary pattern whose general contours are quite evident. Each creative act begins with an announcement ("and God said"), followed by a command ("let there be . . ."), a report ("and it was so"), an evaluation ("God saw that it was good"), and a temporal framework ("the *n*th day"). The account of humanity's creation follows this general pattern, but it also departs from the other accounts in significant ways: It is introduced by the words, "Let us make man," and this rather startling statement, whatever its exact meaning, immediately calls attention to the creation of humanity, presumably the climax of God's creative activity. The greater length of the account of humanity's creation in comparison to descriptions of the other creative acts, the threefold repetition (in 1:27) of the word *bārā*ʾ, "to create" (a word reserved in the Hebrew Bible for God's creative activity), the fact that humanity is given dominion over the rest of creation, and the evaluation "very good" that follows the creation of man and woman make it clear that humanity is the climax of God's creative activity. It is man and woman alone who are said to be created in (or as) God's image, and this appears to account for humanity's preeminent position in the created order. The image of God sets man and woman apart from everything else that God made.

This point is also affirmed in Gen 9:6, which is part of the blessing given to Noah after the flood. Unlike God's instruction in 1:29–30, the human is given permission to kill animals for food. In addition to certain restrictions as to how the meat was to be eaten, it is specified that only animals may be killed. The life of another human being is not to be taken because "in the image of God (*bĕṣelem* ʾ*ĕlōhîm*) He made man." Thus, the image of God in man and woman gives dignity and worth to all people; it sets humankind apart from everything else that God made.

Gen 5:1–2 makes it clear that both male and female are included under the designation ʾ*adam* who was made in God's image. Gen 5:3 reports that Adam fathered a son "in his likeness, according to his image," and the verse employs the same nouns used in Gen 1:26–27, though the order of the nouns and the prepositions used with each are reversed in comparison to Gen 1:26. This suggests that the way in which a son resembles his father is in some sense analogous to the way in which the human is like God. Since this passage has made the point that it is both male and female who are in the image of God, it seems clear that the similarity, while not excluding the physical in the broadest sense, focuses on capacities such as personality, self-determination, and rational thought. It is probable that it is the whole person who is in the image of God rather than some specific aspect of that person to the exclusion of others, and this focus on the human being as a whole being is consistent with the way humanity is viewed throughout the Hebrew Bible. Even more fundamental than resemblance between Adam and his son was the relationship between them, and some have suggested that the image of God implies that the human was made with the capacity for relationship with God. It is also possible that the point of this analogy is that the son is the image of his father because he functions both like his father and on behalf of his father.

Apart from the question of what information may have been known to the various sources that underlie the present biblical text, the image of God passages, in their present canonical context, make it clear that humanity even after the Fall is still in the image of God.

The fact that man and woman were created in (or as) the image of God is clearly a positive statement affirming humanity's preeminence over everything else that God created. In view of the strong condemnation of idolatry and the unqualified prohibition of images in the Bible, this positive use of *ṣelem* is most unexpected, and even though this word is not used in the legislation that specifically condemns the use of images, the same negative connotations are almost certainly associated with the word. There seems to be nothing in the biblical understanding of images that would give content to the meaning of the image of God beyond that which the context of the passages suggests, and it appears that the basis for any further understanding of the image of God will have to be found outside the biblical material. This even raises the possibility that this is an idea that Israel borrowed from another culture.

Images were used in both Mesopotamia and Egypt, and the literature of those countries provides a basis for determining how those people understood images. Egyptian texts make it clear that images were not meant to depict what a god looked like, but represented attempts to describe certain qualities or attributes of the deity. The primary purpose of the image, though, was not to describe the god; rather, the image was one of the primary places where the god manifested himself. The presence of the deity in the statue was magically effected through a ceremony called the "Opening of the Mouth," and perhaps there are reflections of this in the description of humanity's creation in Genesis 2, where God forms a figure of the man out of dust from the ground and then animates that figure by breathing life into it. The significance of the image did not lie in the way it described or depicted the god (though that was not totally unimportant); rather, it lay in the fact that the statue was a place where the deity was present and manifested himself. Thus, the presence of the god and the blessing that accompanied that presence were effected through the image. It was the function of the image rather than its form that constituted its significance.

In both Egypt and Mesopotamia, people were sometimes referred to as images of god, and while there are occasional exceptions, it was usually the king who was referred to in this way. The focus for this seems to be Egypt, where, beginning with the New Kingdom, there are numerous examples of the king described as the image of a particular god; in contrast to this, only five examples are known from Mesopotamia (four of which date to the neo-Assyrian period). The pharaoh was described in these terms because he was believed to be the earthly manifestation of the deity, and thus he functioned on earth exactly as the image functioned in the temple. In Mesopotamia, where the idea of the deified king made a brief appearance in the Ur III period but died out thereafter, there was little basis for referring to the king in such a way. There are indications in Gen 1:26–28 that the "image of God" terminology perhaps had its origins in the royal ideology of the ancient Near East. The idea of dominion and the idea of subduing are most appropriate in the context of kingship. Psalm 8 uses similar royal terminology in its description of humanity's place in the created order, though it does not use the term "image of God."

It seems likely that the image of God idea was introduced into Israel through her contacts with Egypt, and the idea was emptied of content that was incompatible with Israelite theology and used to express the apparently uniquely Israelite idea that all persons, not just the king, occupy a preeminent place in the created order. There are several periods in Israel's history when this influence was possible, though the period of the Egyptian bondage and the Exodus would have provided a context where the Israelites would have taken great delight in affirming that the pharaoh, as magnificent and impressive as he may have been, was not the one who rightly deserved the title "image of god"; rather, all persons as the special creatures of God are made in/as His image. It should be noted that the fact that the "image of God" passages are all a part of what most modern biblical scholars identify as the Priestly source of the Pentateuch, which is normally assumed to date to the period of the Babylonian exile, does not preclude the possibility that the image of God idea had its origins in Egypt at a much earlier time, since scholars are becoming increasingly aware of ancient traditions that are a part of that material.

The image of God terminology clearly affirms the preeminent position of humanity in the created order and declares the dignity and worth of man and woman as the special creations of God. The ANE background that appears to stand behind the biblical idea provides an appropriate base for such a declaration about humankind. It is not as clear whether other elements of the Egyptian understanding of images are implied through the figure as well. Perhaps the image of God idea suggests that humankind is the primary place where God manifests Himself; perhaps the figure implies that it is humanity that stands in a special relationship to God and that should function both like God and on His behalf; it does seem clear, in the light of the Near Eastern parallels, that the term has less to do with form and appearance than with function and position in the created order of things.

This suggestion as to the origin of the image of God terminology suggests that a term that entered Israel's tradition at an early date remained somewhat isolated in that tradition without being developed elsewhere in the preexilic literature. It seems likely that the danger presented to Israel's religion by idolatry precluded that use until after the Exile had eliminated idolatry as a major problem. In the new religious context created by the Exile and return, the "image of God" motif was again taken up and developed both in the intertestamental period and in the NT.

Bibliography

Barr, J. 1967. The Image of God in Genesis—Some Linguistic and Historical Considerations. Pp. 5–13 of *Old Testament Papers Read at the Tenth Meeting of Die ou-Testamentiese Werkgemeenskap in Suid-Africa.* Pretoria.

———. 1968. The Image of God in the Book of Genesis—A Study in Terminology. *BJRL* 51: 11–26.

Bird, P. 1981. "Male and Female He Created Them": Gen 1:27b in the Context of the Priestly Account of Creation. *HTR* 74: 129–59.

Clines, D. J. A. 1968. The Image of God in Man. *TBl* 19: 53–103.

Curtis, E. M. 1984. Man as the Image of God in Genesis in the Light of Ancient Near Eastern Parallels. Diss. Pennsylvania.

Millard, A. R., and Bordreuil, P. 1982. A Statue from Syria with Assyrian and Aramaic Inscriptions. *BA* 45/3: 135–41.

Miller, M. 1972. In the "Image" and "Likeness" of God. *JBL* 91: 289–304.

Schmidt, W. H. 1967. *Die Schöpfungsgeschichte der Priesterschrift.* 2d ed. WMANT 17. Neukirchen-Vluyn.

Wildberger, H. 1965. Das Abbild Gottes. *TZ* 21: 245–59; 481–501.

EDWARD M. CURTIS

IMALKUE (PERSON) [Gk *Imalkoue*]. Imalkue is mentioned in 1 Macc 11:39 as an Arab ruler, with whom the Seleucid king Alexander Balas left his child Antiochus VI during his struggle with Demetrius II in 146 B.C.E. (cf. Jos. *Ant* 13.131–32; Diodorus 32.9d, 1.10). The Gk and Lat transcription is customarily written *Iam(b)licus* (e.g., Diodorus 33.4a; Jos. *Ant* 14.129; *JW* 1.129; 4a; Livy *Epit.* 52; *CIL* 13.7040). It is apparently an abbreviation of an ancient theophoric name such as *Ia-am-li-ik-el,* meaning "God will rule." Imalkue was a common name among Syrian Arabs near Palmyra and Emesa, and among Ituraeans in Lebanon (HJP^2, 183; Goldstein *1 Maccabees* AB, 436). Two Nabatean kings bore the name Malichus (*Ymlkw* in Arabic or Nabatean), which derived from the same root. A similar Hebrew name *Yamlek* is mentioned in the Bible (1 Chr 4:34), and several related Arabic forms date back to the same period (*EncMiqr* 3: 702). Diodorus (32.9d, 1.10) mentions Imalkue by the Gk name of Diocles, meaning "glory of Zeus," which was apparently a rather free equivalent of his Arabic name.

Although 1 Maccabees denotes Imalkue as "the Arab," neither his tribal identity nor the area of his rule can be precisely determined. Some believe that he was the son of Zabdiel, mentioned in 1 Macc 11:16–17 as the killer of Balas (Abel 1949: 212); this, in fact, could explain how Imalkue laid his hand on Antiochus VI (145 B.C.E.). It was Tryphon, one of Balas' chief officers, who persuaded Imalkue to place the young heir in his protection, in order to rule in his name and to foil Demetrius' plans (1 Macc 11:39–40; *Ant* 13.131–32). Imalkue cooperated with him and even permitted him to establish in his country a military base against Demetrius. As Diodorus locates this base near Chalcis, it seems that Imalkue ruled in the Lebanon Valley and probably headed one of the Ituraean tribes there. This impression is supported by the fact that two later Ituraean rulers were called Iamblicus, and that at least one of them "lived on Mount Lebanon" (*Ant* 14.129; Kasher 1988: 38, 120).

Bibliography

Abel, F.-M. 1949. *Les livres de Macchabées.* Paris.

Kasher, A. 1988. *Jews, Idumaeans and Ancient Arabs.* Tübingen.

ARYEH KASHER

IMITATE, IMITATORS [Gk *mimeomai, mimētēs*]. The term "imitator" is one link between the disciples of Jesus in the Gospels and the believers of the early Church. Although the word "disciple" (*mathētēs*) is curiously absent from the epistles, Michaelis' conclusion is representative of recent scholarship: "The *mathētēs* . . . and the *mimētēs* are one and the same" (*TDNT* 4: 673; cf. Betz 1967: 42–43; Schulz 1962: 332–35).

The nouns *mimētēs* (1 Cor 4:16; 11:1; Eph 5:1; 1 Thess 1:6; 2:14; Heb 6:12) and *summimētēs* ("fellow imitator"; Phil 3:17) are always joined in the NT with the verb *ginomai* ("be, become") and are thus similar in meaning to the simple verb *mimeomai* (2 Thess 3:7, 9; Heb 13:7; 3 John 11). Related concepts are found in the use of *tupos* ("type, example," which occurs in several contexts with "imitation" terms: Phil 3:17; 1 Thess 1:7; 2 Thess 3:9), *hupogrammos* ("example" cf. 1 Pet 1:21), and the adverbial forms *kathōs* ("just as," 2 Cor 1:5) and *hōs* ("like," Luke 6:40).

In classical and Hellenistic Greek, *mimeomai/mimētēs* designates (1) the simple act of mimicking what one sees another doing, (2) the joy of following and emulating another, and (3) the representation of reality in artistic activities (e.g., theater, painting, sculpture, poetry). Used in a derogatory manner, the terms indicate weak and unoriginal copying. In Platonic cosmology the present world is the visible, imperfect copy (*mimēma*) of the invisible archetype in the higher world of Ideas; therefore, "to imitate God" indicates ontological development—not an ethical personal decision (Morrison 1982: 3–31). In the mystery religions, the cultic and magical imitation of God becomes a central focus (Betz 1967: 48–84).

While the word group is absent from the canonical LXX, imitation of exemplary men and women is prominent in Jewish literature (e.g., *4 Macc* 9:32; 13:9; *T. Benj.* 4:1; Sirach 44–50; 1 Macc 2:49 ff., esp. v 61). In the Pseudepigrapha, *mimeomai/mimētēs* also indicates imitation of God (*T. Ash.* 4:3) and his characteristics (*Let. Aris.* 188, 210, 280–81). Philo regularly uses *mimēma* for the Platonic cosmological idea of original and copy (*Op* 3.877), and uses *mimeomai* for imitation of a model, including man (*Vita Mos.* I. 158) and God (e.g., *Dec* 111; *Leg All* I.48; *Op* 26.79). Josephus does not speak of the imitation of God, but does use the terms for conscious imitation of the qualities or acts of others (*mimeomai, Ant* 12.241; *mimētēs, Ant* 8.315).

Mimeomai/mimētēs in NT usage calls believers to imitate other believers, Christ, and God. Human objects are those most numerously given for imitation. Human imitation ranges from simple comparison with the conduct of other believers (1 Thess 2:14) to presentation of examples of conduct to imitate (Phil 3:17; 2 Thess 3:7, 9; Heb 6:12; 13:7). Paul gives himself as an example for imitation (1 Cor 4:16; 11:1; Phil 3:17; 2 Thess 3:7, 9), but he does not hold himself up as the ideal of mature perfection. On one occasion he deliberately confesses his own imperfection before he gives the call for them to imitate him (cf. Phil 3:13, 17). Imitation of Paul's ways (1 Cor 4:16–17) should bring believers to an appropriate understanding of the message of the cross and its implications for their life as a community (Sanders 1981: 363).

Human objects, therefore, ultimately point to Christ. Twice, Paul calls for his readers to imitate himself, but at the same time he names Christ as the final object of their imitation (1 Cor 11:1; 1 Thess 1:6). Only in Eph 5:1 are believers called to be imitators of God, but even here the example given is Christ: his forgiveness, love, and sacrificial service (Eph 4:32; 5:2). Christ is the incarnate example of God for believers to emulate in their daily experience.

Although certain aspects of Christ's earthly life are held up as examples for the believer to follow (e.g., suffering, 1 Thess 1:6; cf. 1 Pet 1:21: *hupogrammos*), this does not imply self-justification through emulation of his works. The NT use of *mimeomai/mimētēs* has a unique ethical dimension which stresses the contrast between the "indicative" and the "imperative" in the Christian life. Participation in Christ's cross and resurrection (the indicative which makes the believer a new creature in Christ [2 Cor 5:17]) is constituted in the life of the believer here and now by obedience to the imperatival call to imitation (Webster 1986: 106).

Bibliography

Abrahams, I. 1967. The Imitation of God. *Studies in Pharisaism and the Gospels.* 2d Series. New York.

Betz, H. D. 1967. *Nachfolge und Nachahmung Jesu Christi im Neuen Testament.* BHT 37. Tübingen.

Boer, W. P. de. 1962. *The Imitation of Paul: An Exegetical Study.* Kampen.

Morrison, K. F. 1982. *The Mimetic Tradition of Reform in the West.* Princeton.

Sanders, B. 1981. Imitating Paul: 1 Cor 4:16. *HTR* 74/4: 353–63.

Schulz, A. 1962. *Nachfolgen und Nachahmen: Studien über das Verhältnis der neutestamentlichen Jüngerschaft zur urchristlichen Vorbildethik.* SANT 6. Munich.

Stanley, D. M. 1959. Become Imitators of Me: The Pauline Conception of Apostolic Tradition. *Biblica* 40: 859–77.

Tinsley, E. J. 1960. *The Imitation of God in Christ: An Essay on the Biblical Basis of Christian Spirituality.* London.

Webster, J. B. 1986. The Imitation of Christ. *TynBul* 37: 95–120.

MICHAEL J. WILKINS

IMLAH (PERSON) [Heb *yimlâ*]. The father of the 9th-century Israelite prophet Micaiah, who prophesied against King Ahab (1 Kgs 22:8–9). See MICAIAH. Nothing more is known of the biblical Imlah. The name is spelled differently in 1 Kgs 22:8–9 (*ymlh*) and in 2 Chr 18:7–8 (*yml*ʾ), where the story of Micaiah's prophecy is repeated. This indicates that the text of Kings on which the Chronicler relied was not identical to the present MT (Coggins *1 and 2 Chronicles* CBC, 215). The Chronicler's form is more likely in Hebrew, and a similarly spelled name appears also in an Aramaic inscription from Palmyra.

JEROME T. WALSH

IMMANUEL (PERSON) [Heb *ʿimmānûʾēl*]. A symbolic name meaning "with us [is] God," found in Isa 7:14 and 8:8; it is alluded to in 8:10. Isaiah 7:14 is cited in Matt 1:23.

The use of the name in Isa 7:14 is the primary one of the four occurrences, but many elements of the interpretation of the passage within which it occurs (7:10–17) are disputed. Neither the etymological meaning of the name nor the historical context in which these words of Isaiah are spoken is in doubt. The occasion is the same as that of 7:1–9; namely, the invasion of Judah by Syria and Israel (the so-called SYRO-EPHRAIMITE WAR, 735–732 B.C.). Syria and Israel were in the process of revolting against Assyria, of which they were vassals; fearing to have a neutral or possibly hostile Judah to their S at the time of the expected retaliation from Assyria, they were trying to force Judah into their coalition or at least render it harmless by placing someone of their own choice and persuasion on the throne of Judah (7:6). In these circumstances Ahaz, king of Judah, appears to have seen joining the coalition or calling on Assyria for help (thus voluntarily submitting to vassalhood) as the only alternative. Isaiah sought to dissuade him from following either course with the assurance that Syria and Israel did not present a serious threat (v 4; cf. 8:1–4), giving the Lord's own assurance that their plans would not succeed (v 7), and challenging Ahaz to faith in the Lord's promise as a condition to his own continuation (v 9).

It is likely that Ahaz' circle of advisers were urging submission to Assyria as the course to follow. In any case, 7:10–17 opens with Isaiah seeking to dispel whatever doubts Ahaz may have had by telling him to ask for any sign he might choose as assurance that the Lord had spoken through the prophet. Ahaz may already have decided to turn to Assyria for help (which is what he did, according to 2 Kings 16:7–9), but, in any case, he refused to ask for a sign. The prophet responds by asserting that the Lord himself will give a sign; namely, that "the young woman (*hāᶜalmâ*)" will conceive (or: has conceived—the Hebrew does not clearly specify) and bear a son and call his name Immanuel. The child is to live on curds and honey so that he may learn (or: until he learns) to reject the evil and choose the good; before that, however, Syria and Israel will be devastated, but the Lord will bring upon Ahaz' dynasty and his people terrible times (which a gloss identifies, no doubt correctly, as the king of Assyria). The rest of the chapter (vv 18–25) consists of a series of shorter oracles relating to the same context, some of which may cast light upon the interpretation of vv 10–17.

As already indicated, many aspects of these verses are disputed. For example, Immanuel is said to be a royal child (H. Gressmann, E. Hammershaimb, A. S. Herbert, E. J. Kissane, J. Lindblom, J. L. McKenzie, S. Mowinckel, H.-P. Müller, H. Ringgren, J. J. Scullion, B. Vawter, W. Vischer, H. Wildberger, G. E. Wright), specifically Hezekiah (Hammershaimb, Kissane, Lindblom, O. Procksch, Wildberger), or Isaiah's son (R. E. Clements, N. Gottwald, T. Lescow, J. J. Stamm, H. M. Wolf), or any child conceived at this time (B. Duhm, G. Fohrer, G. B. Gray, O. Kaiser, L. Koehler, W. McKane, K. Marti, J. Mauchline), with "the young woman" being explained accordingly; he is the new Israel (L. G. Rignell); and some authors emphasize the difficulty of relating Immanuel to Isaiah's historical context in order to favor a more strictly messianic interpretation (T. E. Bird, J. Coppens, F. Delitzsch, J. Fischer, Gressmann, H. Junker, M. McNamara, F. L. Moriarity). Immanuel is said to be a favorable sign of salvation (S. Blank, Hammershaimb, Marti, Rignell, Scullion); he is purely a sign of disaster (K. Budde, H. W. Hertzberg, R. Kilian, Lescow); he is a double-edged sign (Fischer, Gressmann, Junker, Kaiser, Vischer, H. W. Wolff). Immanuel's food ("curds and honey") is ideal and luxurious food of abundance (Gray, Hammershaimb, Lindblom, Rignell, Scullion, J. Skinner, Wildberger, Wolff); his food is the nomad fare available in a land that has been devastated (Budde, Cheyne, Delitzsch, Duhm, Fischer, Fohrer, Herbert, Hertzberg, Kaiser, Kilian, McNamara, Marti, Mauchline, Stamm). Immanuel's coming to knowledge in v 15 is a temporal expression ("when he learns to reject . . . ," "by the time he learns . . ."—G. W. Buchanan, T. F. Cheyne, Duhm, Fohrer, Herbert, Hertzberg, Kaiser, Lindblom, McNamara, Marti, Mauchline [following LXX], Rignell, Skinner, Stamm); it expresses finality ("so that he may learn to reject . . ."—Budde, F. Dreyfus, P. G. Duncker, Junker, McKane, Mauchline [following MT], Müller, Scullion, Wildberger, Wolff). The age at which a child learns to reject evil and choose good means the age at which he can distinguish pleasant from unpleasant (usually set at 2 or 3 years—Clements, Duhm, Fohrer, Herbert, Kilian, Lescow, Lindblom, McKane, Marti, Mauchline, Skinner, Stamm); it means the age of moral discernment (often set at around 20 years—Budde, Buchanan, Cheyne, Delitzsch, Fischer [at age 3!], Herzberg, Kaiser, McNamara, Rignell, Scullion, Wolff); it means the age of sexual awareness or maturity (around age 13—R. Gordis, L. F. Hartman, B. Reike). Although most commentators agree that v 17 foretells devastation, there are some who take it as a prediction of future blessedness (Lindblom, Hammershaimb, McKane, Scullion). Some authors question the authenticity of certain words, phrases, or even verses of the passage; in fact, some of the positions listed above require the rejection of parts of the text.

In spite of the diversity of views just referred to, the majority of scholars would endorse an interpretation something like the following. The "young woman" referred to is a wife of Ahaz, and the son to be born would be a child of Ahaz; as such he would be a guarantee of the continuation of the Davidic dynasty, to which perpetuity has been promised (2 Samuel 7) and from which great things have been expected. For this reason the symbolic name "with us (is) God" could be given to the child, and, as the Lord had already promised, the threat from Syria and Israel would dissolve. Nevertheless, because Ahaz had refused to believe and to repose his faith in the Lord alone, the trust he had placed in Assyria would occasion terrible devastation for Judah. This interpretation is "messianic" (and sometimes characterized as dynastic messianism) in that the continuation of the dynasty preserves the channel for the promised blessings and leaves open the possibility of a future individual in whom these blessings will be realized in a unique way.

No critical scholar today holds that Isaiah directly foretold the birth of Jesus of a virgin, and this for a number of reasons. First, the sign of Immanuel was given to Ahaz and his contemporaries as part of Isaiah's message, and an event that occurred some seven hundred years later would not be relevant to them. Moreover, by his reference to the fate of "the land before whose two kings you stand in dread" (i.e., Syria and Israel), Isaiah clearly ties Immanuel to the contemporary scene. Second, the Hebrew term for "the young woman" (*hāᶜalmâ*) refers to a young woman of marriageable age, who may normally be supposed to be a virgin, but it is not the technical term for "virgin" (*bĕtûlâ*)—

which would have to have been used if that were the precise point intended. Third, there is also the fact that while a virgin birth may be the object of faith, it is not subject to the kind of observation that would make it a sign in any meaningful sense.

Those who hold that Immanuel is any child conceived at this time obviously do not relate the sign to the dynasty or to the promises to David; the import would be (though the view is proposed with many variations) that any young woman who conceived now could, by the time her child was born, bestow a name expressive of deliverance because the Syria-Israel threat would have evaporated by then (see 2 Kgs 7:2 for a conditional construction which begins with *hinnēh*). The objection often raised, that the definite article in *hāʿalmâ* ("*the* young woman") rules this out, should not be pressed; the use of the definite article in Hebrew is not always all that precise. There are, however, other reasons for rejecting it. An important part of the Syria-Israel threat is their intention of deposing Ahaz and placing their own king on the throne (v 6), so the fate of the dynasty comes prominently into the picture. There are, furthermore, references to "the house of David" in this context that are sufficiently unusual to require explanation (vv 2, 13; cf. v 17). Isaiah's assurance of safety and challenge to effective faith (vv 4, 7, 9) would relate well to the dynastic promises.

Those who see Immanuel as Isaiah's son sometimes identify him with Maher-shalal-hash-baz of 8:1–4 (or even with Shear-jashub—cf. 7:3) or sometimes see him as a separate sign-child. The arguments for this view are drawn partly from the alleged parallelism with 8:1–4, but it is also asserted that only the prospective parent can know what the child will be named; if Isaiah can assert that the child will be named Immanuel, it must be his child. The latter argument would appear to fail to take note of the obviously symbolic nature of the name. It is true that Isaiah imposed actual names of symbolic import on two of his sons (Shear-jashub and Maher-shalal-hash-baz—see above), but he had a particular penchant for consigning his teaching in names; the series of four names ascribed to the ideal king to come in 9:5—Eng 9:6 depict his qualities but are not to be understood as names that are actually bestowed. The naming of Maher-shalal-hash-baz in 8:1–4 occurs in a context which spells out the fate of Syria and Israel within a fairly precise chronological framework, i.e., the brief time between a child's conception and its first simple words; the time involved in Immanuel's coming to know how to reject evil and choose good involves far more (see below).

In many ways v 15 holds the key to the interpretation of the whole passage. It is true that many authors (including Wildberger) reject the verse in whole or in part, but there is no basis in textual criticism for this. The rejection of v 15 is usually dictated by the interpretation adopted for vv 10–17; but an interpretation that relies on emendations that have no warrant in the textual tradition is necessarily suspect. The reference to "curds and honey" as Immanuel's food is taken by a number of commentators to refer to idyllic circumstances (as in the phrase "a land flowing with milk and honey"—Exod 3:8, 17; 13:5; 33:3; Deut 6:3; etc.) or even to ambrosial nourishment provided for a divine infant in some myths. Neither would suit the threatening context of Isaiah's situation, and this is given as reason for the elimination of the verse—though it is sometimes rejected on other grounds, too. However, while a land "flowing with milk and honey"—even if that cliché were used here, instead of the relatively rare "curds and honey"—was an apt manner in which to describe an ideal land in Israel's nomad days, an Israel settled in its own land thought of the ideal in terms of corn and wine and oil. For these and other reasons, the majority of scholars see the expression as indicating a land that has been devastated; no agriculture is possible, and so the only food available is wild honey and the produce of the flocks. (Vv 21–25, separate compositions but probably closely related in historical context to vv 10–17, indicate tiny flocks and difficult times in a land where agriculture has been rendered impossible.) The meaning would thus be that, owing to Ahaz' misguided policy, Immanuel would grow up under difficult circumstances in a devastated land.

The majority of translators and commentators take the expression in v 15 that relates to Immanuel's coming to knowledge (*lĕdaʿtô*—preposition + infinitive + suffix) as temporal, and as referring to a relatively few years, the time needed for an infant to learn to distinguish pleasant from unpleasant (see above). Many are influenced to take this position by 8:1–4, where Isaiah gives the sign of Maher-shalal-hash-baz. There, the prophet speaks of the speedy evaporation of the threat of the Syria-Israel coalition: Before the child whose conception and birth there described is able to speak his first words, those two lands will have been devastated; and in each of the two texts the same expression "before the child knows . . ." occurs (cf. 7:16 and 8:4). However, there are also strong reasons for taking the expression in 7:15 in the causal sense. None of the OT references to the knowledge of "good and evil" can easily be applied to the knowledge that is proper to infants or very young children. Where the reference does indicate the stage of development, adulthood or something close to it seems to be required; for example, the knowledge attributed to David and Solomon for the office of judging is not that of infancy (2 Sam 14:17—cf. v 20; 1 Kgs 3:9). So also when Deut 1:39 designates "your children, who this day have no knowledge of good and evil" as the ones who will one day enter the promised land, it must have in mind approximately the same age as that in Num 14:29–30 (cf. 32:11), which excludes those "from twenty years and upward." The terminology in Isa 7:15 that speaks of Immanuel rejecting evil (*māʾôs bārāʿ*) also indicates adult discernment. For some scholars, such considerations argue for a rejection of a temporal sense for v 15 in favor of a causal sense, the more usual force of *lĕ* + the infinitive. The meaning would thus be "that he may learn to reject the evil and choose the good"; i.e., the difficult circumstances in which Immanuel was to grow up would be the occasion of a moral development that would make him very unlike Ahaz, to whom he seems to be deliberately contrasted. This interpretation goes somewhat beyond dynastic messianism in the importance it attributes to Immanuel in Isaiah's thought and leaves the way open to a connection between this figure and the ideal king depicted in 8:23–9:6—Eng 9:1–7 and 11:1–9.

The meaning of the oracle at 8:5–8 is again disputed. Clearly, Isaiah is saying that because Judah has rejected the Lord's call to faith by turning to Assyria for help, it will be overwhelmed by that nation; the reference to "outspread wings" may continue that threatening message, but such imagery more usually signals Yahweh's protection (cf. Pss 17:8; 36:7; 57:1). In any case, the address to Immanuel, the fate of whose land is at stake, though rejected by many as inauthentic, can very possibly be original. The same Hebrew expression, *ʿimmānû ʾēl,* though now not a proper name but literally "(for) God is with us," is found as the conclusion of 8:9–10, given as the reason that the hostile plans and behavior of the pagan nations against Judah will come to nought.

The citation of Isa 7:14 in Matt 1:23 follows the Greek of the LXX rather than the Hebrew of the MT; Matthew's citation varies from the LXX on a couple of minor points, either because these differences were already in the text he followed or because he adapted it for his own purposes. The most striking difference between the LXX and the Hebrew is the use of "virgin" (*parthenos* in Gk) instead of "young woman" (*ʿalmâ* in Heb). While the latter is not the normal designation for "virgin" (see above), the Gk *parthenos* does normally mean "virgin" and is the word regularly used to translate *bĕtûlâ,* the Heb term for "virgin." One would have expected *neanis* (the Gk term for "young woman"), which is the term normally used to render *ʿalmâ* in the LXX and which is, in fact, used for this text in the later, more literal, Greek translations of Aquila, Symmachus, and Theodotion. No certain explanation of why the LXX chose to render *ʿalmâ* by *parthenos* can be given. Some have supposed that in the period after Isaiah, his Immanuel oracle occasioned a development which posited a marvelous birth for the one who would fulfill it. However, since Isa 7:14 is not among the passages that later Jewish thought saw as "messianic," the suggestion is unsupported by the evidence. It is more likely that the translator was indicating that Immanuel's mother was a virgin at the time the oracle was spoken and would be until she conceived in the usual manner; unlike the Hebrew, the Greek clearly has the conception as future.

While Matthew was thus not constrained by any OT evidence that the Messiah would be born of a virgin, he clearly uses the Isaiah passage in support of his own presentation of the virginal conception of Jesus, a tradition that must have reached him from a different source. The Isaiah text is cited after Joseph's doubt has been countered by the assurance that Mary's conception is through the action of the Holy Spirit, and in this context the emphasis falls on "virgin," a point the Evangelist can see as foretold in prophecy. The meaning of the Hebrew name "Immanuel" would not have been evident to many of Matthew's readers, and so to the Isaiah citation he adds the explanation, "a name which means 'God with us,' " an interpretation probably taken from Isa 8:10. Thus, Matthew uses the text not only as prophecy, now fulfilled, of the coming of Jesus and of his virginal conception, but also to say something of the divine sonship of Jesus, through whom God is present in a very special way. On both points, Matthew goes well beyond anything envisioned in the OT text.

Bibliography

Bratcher, R. G. 1958. A Study of Isaiah 7:14. *BTrans* 9:97–126.
Brown, E. R. 1977. *The Birth of the Messiah.* Garden City, NY.
Gordis, R. 1957. The Knowledge of Good and Evil in the Old Testament and the Qumran Scrolls. *JBL* 76: 123–38.
Gottwald, N. K. 1958. Immanuel as the Prophet's Son. *VT* 8: 36–47.
Hammershaimb, E. 1951. The Immanuel Sign. *StTh* 3: 124–42.
Jensen, J. 1979. The Age of Immanuel. *CBQ* 41: 220–39.
Kissane, E. J. 1957. "Butter and honey shall he eat" (Is., 7:15). Pp. 169–73 in *L'Ancien Testament et L'Orient.* Louvain.
Lindblom, J. 1958. *A Study on the Immanuel Section in Isaiah: Isa. vii, 1–ix, 6.* Scripta Minora Regiae Societatis Humaniorum Litterarum Lundensis 4. Lund.
McKane, W. 1968. The Interpretation of Isaiah VII 14–25. *VT* 17: 208–19.
Scullion, J. J. 1968. An Approach to the Understanding of Isaiah 7:10–17. *JBL* 87: 288–300.
Stamm, J. J. 1960. Die Immanuel-Weissagung und die Eschatologie des Jesaja. *TZ* 16: 439–55.
Wolff, H. W. 1962. *Freiden ohne Ende: Jesaja 7, 1–17 und 9, 1–6 ausgelegt.* Neukirchen.

Joseph Jensen

IMMER (PERSON) [Heb *ʾimmēr*]. The LXX regularly transliterates the name as *emmēr* (1 Chr 9:12; 24:14; Ezra 2:37; 2:59; 10:20; Neh 3:29; 7:40; Jer 20:1; 1 Esdr 9:21) and once as *iemēr* (Neh 7:61). Cf. also 1 Esdr 5:24 LXX *emmērouth;* KJV Meruth; NEB Emmeruth; and 1 Esdr 5:36 LXX *amar; allar;* KJV Aalar; NEB Alar; AB Allar.

1. An Aaronide priest whose family, according to the Chronicler, by lot became the 16th course of priests in the time of David (1 Chr 24:1–6, 14). The name appears at the close of the Exile, when as many as 1,052 priests who claimed descent from Immer were able to return from Babylon to Jerusalem with Zerubbabel (Ezra 2:1–2, 37 = Neh 7:6–7, 40 = 1 Esdr 5:7–8, 24). This same Immer is cited as the ancestor of one of the prominent priestly families residing in Jerusalem, that of Amashsai (= Maasai in 1 Chr 9:12), in Nehemiah's time (Neh 11:13). According to Nehemiah 11, Immer was the progenitor of the line Meshillemoth-Ahzai-Azarel-Amashsai. In 1 Chr 9:12, this genealogy is expanded considerably, stating that Immer was the head of the lineage Meshillemith-Meshullam-Jahzerah-Adiel-Maasai. By comparison it would thus appear that Meshillemoth is the same person as either Meshillemith or Meshullam, and that Ahzai and Azarel are the equivalents of Jahzerah and Adiel in the 1 Chronicles 9 list. It is also known that, in Ezra's day, two of Immer's descendants, Hanani and Zebadiah, were found to have married foreign women and were subsequently moved to make a solemn pledge to divorce their wives (Ezra 10:19–20). What is more, the synoptic parallel, 1 Esdr 9:20–21, adds four additional violators to these two, namely Maaseiah, Shemaiah, Jehiel, and Azariah. In Ezra 10:21, in both the MT and LXX B, the four have become five (Maaseiah, Elijah, Shemaiah, Jehiel, and Uzziah), but these names are all attributed to the line of a man named Harim, not Immer.

2. The father of Pashhur, the priest who was chief officer in the last days of the temple and who as the opponent of the prophet Jeremiah beat him and put him in stocks overnight (Jer 20:1–2). If this person is the same as #1 above, then the word for "son" [Heb *ben*] would have to be understood in the broader sense of "descendant."

3. The father of Zadok, a person who is said to have repaired the wall of Jerusalem opposite his own house, near the Horse Gate, in the time of Nehemiah (Neh 3:28–29). The Horse Gate (2 Kgs 11:16; 2 Chr 23:15; Jer 31:40) is thought to have been located in the SE corner of the temple-palace complex. Working where he did, Immer was probably a priest. If the Immer intended here is #1 above, again the Hebrew word for "son" (*ben*) would have to be interpreted in the wider sense of "descendant."

4. One of the leaders who brought exiles from Telmelah and Telharsha back home to Judah (1 Esdr 5:36). These exiles were distinguished by their inability to show proof of their Israelite ancestry (1 Esdr 5:37). In the synoptic parallels to 1 Esdr 5:36, namely, Ezra 2:59 and Neh 7:61, it is worth noting that this same "Immer" is treated as a place name, not a personal name. However, "Immer" as a personal name should not be too quickly dismissed in this context, as the 1 Esdras–type text often preserves many older readings (Klein 1969: 107).

Bibliography

Klein, R. W. 1969. Old Readings in 1 Esdras: The List of Returnees from Babylon (Ezra 2/Nehemiah 7). *HTR* 62: 99–107.

Williamson, H. G. M. 1979. The Origins of the Twenty-four Priestly Courses. Pp. 251–68 in *Studies in the Historical Books of the Old Testament,* ed. J. A. Emerton. VTSup 30. Leiden.

ROGER W. UITTI

IMMER (PLACE) [Heb *ʾimmer*]. Unidentified Babylonian site from which Jewish exiles returned under Zerubbabel (Ezra 2:59; Neh 7:61; see also 1 Esdr 5:36, where the text is uncertain). These returnees were unable to prove their Israelite ancestry, which was needed as a crucial line of continuity between the restoration community and preexilic Israel (Johnson 1969: 42–44; Williamson *Ezra, Nehemiah* WBC, 39). Some scholars have taken "Immer" in the Ezra and Nehemiah references as a personal name, which may find support in 1 Esdr 5:36 (for arguments, see Batten *Ezra and Nehemiah* ICC, 96).

Bibliography

Johnson, M. D. 1969. *The Purpose of the Biblical Genealogies.* Cambridge.

BILL T. ARNOLD

IMNA (PERSON) [Heb *yimnāʿ*] A descendant of Asher, found in the segmented tribal genealogy in 1 Chr 7:30–40. The name occurs in the LXX as Imana, and in LXX^L as Iamna. In form, it is a verbal imperfect 3 m.s. *qal* conjugation of the root *mnʿ*, meaning "he will withhold," and may be a hypocoristicon for an original form that contained the name of a deity after the verb.

Imna appears in v 35 as a son of Helem, making him a fourth-generation descendant of the eponymous ancestor Asher. Since other names in the list such as Shual, Zophah, Japhlet, and Shelesh/Shilshah appear elsewhere in the Bible as names of clans and/or geographical regions, and the summary in v 40 indicates that the underlying source for the genealogy was an administrative list used for purposes of army conscription and possibly also taxation, it is likely that Imna is not the name of an individual but that of a clan or a village. All groups named in the Chronicles genealogy for Asher appear to have lived in the Asherite enclave located in southern Mt. Ephraim and not in the Galilean territory of Asher (Edelman 1988). See ASHER (PERSON); ASHURITES.

Imna probably is a variant spelling or textual corruption of Imnah, found in v 30, and of Imrah, found in v 36, of the same genealogy. In the first instance, the final *he* has interchanged with the final *ʿayin,* which would not have affected the name's pronunciation. In the second instance, in addition to the same alteration at the end of the name, a medial *nun* has been mistaken as a *reš*, a mistake that was possible to make in the square script, but not in the older archaic Hebrew script. Such a mistake could easily have occurred through a copyist's error during the centuries of transmission of the text of Chronicles. Imna/Imnah would accordingly represent an Asherite clan located somewhere in S Mt. Ephraim.

The appearance of the name three times within the genealogy has been understood in two ways. In accordance with the view that the genealogy is homogenous and derives from an administrative list of Asherite clans made at a single point in time, Imna in v 35 would be an intergenerational namesake of the Imnah in v 30, and Imrah in v 36 would be a corrupted reference to the Imna of v 35. The two names Beri and Imrah (*bry* and *ymrh*) would not be children of Zophah but rather would represent the corruption of an original reading *bny ymnh,* "sons of Imnah," which introduced Imnah's descendants in the continuing presentation of the fifth generation of descent in the segmented genealogy (Naʾaman fc.).

According to the alternate view, the instances of name repetition within the genealogy, including Beriah/Beri, Zophah, Shelesh/Shilshah, Shua/Shual, and Imnah/Imna/Imrah, are to be taken as indications of the composite nature of the genealogy. Three administrative lists deriving from different eras but naming the members of the Asherite enclave at three separate points in time would have been combined by the Chronicler to produce the final form of the genealogy. Following this understanding, the three Imnahs would represent the same clan at different points in time, or the final two would represent the same clan over time, while the first might represent a distant namesake within the Galilean region, before the splintering off of the enclave group (Edelman 1988).

Regardless of the structural approach taken to the genealogy, Imna can be further linked with the land of Yemini that Saul is reported to have traversed in his search for his father's lost asses in 1 Sam 9:4 (Curtis and Madsen *Chronicles* ICC, 155; Edelman 1989: 53–54). The gentilic of the lesser known Asherite clan of Imnah is so close to the gentilic of the tribe of (Ben)jamin, *ymny* vs. *ymyny,* that the medial *yod* in the MT text could easily have been added as a *mater lectionis* by a scribe or later copyist when the original reference to the Asherite group was no longer understood and one to the well-known Benjaminites was presumed. All four lands traversed by Saul in southern Mt. Ephraim can be identified with Asherite clans in the genealogy in 1 Chronicles 7; and based on Saul's following a sequential route, the land of the Yemnites can tentatively be situated in the region around Bethel and Ai (Edelman 1989: 53–54).

Bibliography

Edelman, D. 1988. The Asherite Genealogy in 1 Chronicles 7:30–40. *BR* 33: 13–23.

———. 1989. Saul's Journey through Mt. Ephraim and Samuel's Ramah (1 Sam 9:4–5; 10:2–5). *ZDPV* 104: 44–58.

Naʾaman, N. fc. *JBL*.

DIANA V. EDELMAN

IMNAH (PERSON) [Heb *yimnâ*]. Var. IMNA. IMNITES. **1.** The firstborn son of Asher (Gen 46:17; 1 Chr 7:30). In the genealogical list of Jacob's sons, which is listed by family and mother (Gen 48:8–27), Imnah appears as the grandson of Jacob and Leah through Asher. Asher was the second son of Zilpah, Leah's maid (Gen 37:12–13). Imnah was the father of the Imnites (Num 26:44). See also IMNA (PERSON).

2. A Levite, whose son Kore assisted Hezekiah in his religious reform (2 Chr 31:14). Nothing is known about this Imnah, but probably he exercised a prominent position in the temple. His son Kore was the keeper of the East Gate and was in charge of the freewill offerings presented in the temple. Kore also supervised the distribution of the portion to be given to the Levites and to the priests. For this reason, S. A. Cook (*EncBib,* 2688) has said that the name Imnah was probably written mistakenly by a scribe for Heman, a Levite who was associated with the Korahites and with the doorkeeper of the temple.

CLAUDE F. MARIOTTINI

IMPALEMENT. See PUNISHMENTS AND CRIMES (OT AND ANE).

IMPEDIMENT OF SPEECH. See SICKNESS AND DISEASE.

IMPURITY, WATER FOR. See WATER FOR IMPURITY.

IMRAH (PERSON) [Heb *yimrāh*]. The fifth son of Zophah in the genealogy of Asher (1 Chr 7:36). Although this name is similar to others found in the same genealogy (Imnah–7:30; Imna–7:35), it appears neither in parallel lists in Numbers 26 and Genesis 46 nor elsewhere in the Hebrew Bible. See also IMNA (PERSON). Speculation about the meaning of the name varies; if based upon the Hebrew root *mrh,* it may be translated "may he rebel." Such an interpretation of the name may be in keeping with the military character of the Asherite genealogy noted by scholars such as Johnson (1969: 66–68).

Bibliography

Johnson, M. D. 1969. *The Purpose of the Biblical Genealogies.* Cambridge.

JULIA M. O'BRIEN

IMRI (PERSON) [Heb *ʾimrî*]. **1.** An ancestor of one of the exiles who returned to Jerusalem from exile in Babylon (1 Chr 9:4). Imri was a descendant of Judah through Judah's and Tamar's first-born son Perez. The name Imri is an abbreviation of the name Amariah (Bowman *IB* 3: 684). In Neh 11:4, which is a parallel passage to 1 Chr 9:4, Amariah is listed as one of the ancestors of one from the tribe of Judah who returned to Jerusalem from Babylonian exile. Dahlberg (*IDB* 2: 691) suggested that Amariah might have been the same person listed in 1 Chr 9:4 as Imri. This is a possibility, but none of the names in 1 Chr 9:4 are identical to those in Neh 11:4 with the exceptions of Perez and Judah. It is possible that the author of 1 Chronicles 9 simply employed different traditions than did the author of Nehemiah 11 (Braun *1 Chronicles* WBC, 136). If the two authors did possess and employ different traditions, then Imri and Amariah might well have been two distinct individuals.

2. An ancestor of Zaccur who helped rebuild the walls of Jerusalem during the time of Nehemiah (Neh 3:2). Imri is presented as Zaccur's father, but Imri might have been an earlier, distinguished ancestor rather than Zaccur's biological father.

ROBERT C. DUNSTON

INCARNATION. "Incarnation" means literally "enfleshment" or, slightly more fully, "embodiment in flesh." The question of where the concept of incarnation is to be found in the biblical texts is to a large extent dependent on whether that definition is interpreted in a broader or a narrower sense.

A. Definition
B. Preliminary Clarifications
  1. Incarnation and Indwelling
  2. Incarnation and Inspiration
C. Antecedents
D. Jesus
E. Earliest Christianity
F. Paul
  1. Phil 2:6–11
  2. Col 1:15–20
G. Between Paul and John
H. John
I. Conclusions

A. Definition

The *Encyclopaedia Britannica* defines "incarnation" as "a central Christian doctrine that the eternal Word of God (Logos), the Son of God, the second Person of the Trinity, became man in Jesus Christ, who was then truly God and truly man." This certainly reflects what has been the dominant meaning of the term itself within Christian thought. But it is doubtful whether the concept in such a developed sense can be found anywhere within the Bible, since clearly presupposed therein is the full-blown Trinitarian doctrine as that came to expression in the 4th and 5th centuries of the Christian era.

The question then becomes whether the Christian concept is present in a less developed or undeveloped sense in the NT. Alternatively expressed, it becomes a question of defining the beginnings or foundations within the biblical writings of the doctrine as later formulated. To what extent can these early adumbrations or embryonic formulations be described as expressing a belief in "incarnation"?

In turn, this raises the question of how distinctive was that less clearly defined Christian teaching. Is "incarnation" a specifically "Christian doctrine" as such? Or in its earliest form, was the Christian doctrine of incarnation of a piece with a larger and vaguer understanding of incarnation or of incarnational possibilities? Can "incarnation" not be used quite properly for other forms of "embodiment in flesh"? And if so, what were the distinctive features of the early Christian use of this broader category which caused the Christian conception to stand out from that broader usage and in due course to become the dominant technical sense for the word itself?

B. Preliminary Clarifications

"Incarnation" could quite properly be used for any embodiment in any flesh. But we can limit the inquiry to *human* flesh most of the time, since that is the predominant range of reference. The incarnation of *what* is another question. Clearly implied is the assumption that the "what" is something other than flesh and something "higher" than flesh. It would be unwise, however, to limit the discussion to the idea of God or a god incarnate, even though that would give the most promise of finding an antecedent to the Christian doctrine; for the concept can apply quite properly to the incarnation of any spiritual entity or quality. More modern phrases, such as "an incarnate fiend" or "Liberty incarnate," should provide sufficient warning against narrowing the discussion prematurely. And it will soon become apparent that ancient usage was as broad.

It would of course be possible to define all humanity in incarnational terms—as offspring of the gods (cf. Acts 17:28), as sons of God by virtue of sharing the one divine reason, or as possessing a divine spark. But in such cases, the concept of incarnation has become so diluted as to require a quite different inquiry: What is the "divine" in humankind? What is "human"? A similar problem would arise where the embodiment was thought of in corporate terms—a nation or a large group embodying some ideal. Important as it is to bear in mind the continuity of conception among all these usages, this study will have to be limited to the sense of incarnation as denoting one individual or a number of individuals unusual in the degree or kind of their embodiment of the divine.

Can we bring our question to sharper focus by delimiting the concept of incarnation still further? The problems of conceptuality and definition can be highlighted by noting the overlap and difference between "incarnation/embodiment" on the one hand and "indwelling" and "inspiration" on the other. In both cases it is a question of how the gap or difference between the higher form of existence (spiritual, divine) and the lower (flesh) is perceived as capable of being overcome, so that the higher becomes embodied "in" the lower in some sense.

1. Incarnation and Indwelling. In a dualistic system, where spirit and flesh are seen as sharply and irreconcilably distinct and even antithetical, the resulting embodiment is probably more accurately described as indwelling than as incarnation. The point is that Hellenistic religion and philosophy, which determined the dominant worldview in the Mediterranean world during the period before and after the emergence of Christianity, was characteristically dualistic. The consequence was that in Hellenistic conceptuality the divine could manifest itself *in* the flesh but not *as* flesh. The axiomatic structures of thought made it literally unthinkable that the divine should *become* flesh, that the (by definition) eternal and unchanging should *become* that which (by definition) changed, decayed, and perished. Gods might appear *in the guise* of human beings, but they were still gods and not flesh. The divine reason was *part* of the human species, but as "the inner person," quite distinct from the material body.

The extent of the problem here for Hellenistic thought is clearly reflected subsequently in the Christian difficulty in correlating its own emerging doctrine of incarnation with the "given" of divine impassibility. Nor is it surprising that the option of Docetism (the divine Christ only seemed to be a man) proved so attractive to many Christians in the 2d century. And the gnostic systems of the 2d and 3d centuries simply serve to underline the fact that Hellenistic dualism could only cope with the concept of divine indwelling (the splinter of light imprisoned within the mud of matter), and not with incarnation as distinct from indwelling.

2. Incarnation and Inspiration. Here, the problem is more difficult than has usually been realized. What is the difference between these two categories?—incarnation and inspiration—the latter not dependent on Hellenistic dualism and very highly regarded in Jewish thought. After all, the phenomenon of inspiration could be described as "god-possession" (Gk *entheos, enthousiasmos*) or, in Jewish terms, as a being filled or possessed by the Spirit of God (as in Judg 6:34). An inviting distinction might be developed in terms of inspiration as esssentially a temporary phenomenon; a prophet would not be described as an incarnation of the Spirit, nor a demoniac as an incarnation of Satan. The difficulty arises, however, if one wants to speak of inspiration as continuous or unique—as indeed some Christians did (e.g., Acts 6:3, 5; Eph 5:18). John the Baptist was described as "filled with the Holy Spirit from his mother's womb" (Luke 1:15). And Jesus was accused of being possessed by Beelzebul (Mark 3:22 pars.).

The problem here is that incarnation and permanent inspiration would be indistinguishable phenomenologically. This is illustrated by the fact that the early Fathers of the Church did sometimes speak of incarnation in terms of the *Spirit* rather than of the Son (e.g., Hermas *Sim.* V6.5; Tertullian *Prax.* 26; Cyprian *Idol.* 11). Consequently, there is a question as to whether the distinction between the two can be maintained beyond the conceptual level—rather like the distinction between "the eternal generation of the Son" and "the procession of the Holy Spirit," that is, a confession that there is and must be an important difference, but we are not at all sure what it amounts to.

Such reflection serves to emphasize the fact that "incarnation" was neither a clearly conceived category ready to be used in reference to Jesus nor an empty concept ready to be filled with specifically Christian meaning. "Incarnation" evidently emerged within a world of meaning where other concepts lay close to hand but which were not seen as adequate to express the Christian perception regarding Jesus. In other words, if we may already draw a preliminary conclusion, it looks as though it is not the overlap of meaning between "incarnation" and other categories such as "indwelling" and "inspiration" which was important so much as it is the distinction between them: incarnation being developed as a distinctive category in order to express the distinctive way in which the divine and human were seen to have come together in Jesus—incarnation as a particular way of conceiving the embodiment, as the divine *becoming* human, rather than simply indwelling or inspiring the human. This becomes clearer when we look for antecedents to what became the later orthodox Christian concept.

C. Antecedents

A representative range of ideas and idiom, all of which could warrant the description "incarnation" in some sense at least, would include those shown below (fuller details in *TDNT* 8: 335–62; Boslooper 1962: 170–78; Hengel 1976: 21–56; Dunn 1980: 13–22). The categories are in no sense mutually exclusive and indicate overlapping usage along a more or less continuous spectrum of conceptuality:

(a) The gods themselves appearing in the form or guise of men, as recounted classically in Ovid's *Metamorphoses.*

(b) Descent from the gods, particularly legendary heroes like Dionysus and Heracles, sons of Zeus by mortal mothers.

(c) Pharaohs, kings, and then emperors as representatives of God/the gods, whether by descent or by adoption, and thus embodying divine presence/authority.

(d) The broad category often embraced by the phrase "divine men," as indicating individuals specially favored or empowered by God or the gods, who thus warranted the epithet "divine," Apollonius of Tyana being a much cited case in point.

(e) Poetic hyperbole, sometimes used in incarnational categories, as classically in the case of Augustus, represented by Virgil as Apollo come to earth (*Ecl.* IV.6–10) and by Horace as Mercury descended in the guise of a man (Odes I.2.41–52).

(f) Individuals understood as the embodiment of divine wisdom (Sophia), particularly as in Philo's portrayal of Abraham and Moses as archetypes of the wise man (*Leg All* III: 217, 244; *Cher* 10, 18, 31; etc.; *Leg All* II: 87; III: 45, 140–47; *Cher* 41; *Sacr* 9; etc.) and of Sarah as the embodiment of Wisdom herself (*Leg All* II: 82; *Cher* 9–10, 49; *Quod Det* 124; etc.).

In the light of sec. B above, however, we can put a question mark against most of these categories, if it is indeed antecedents to the concept of "incarnation" for which we are looking. Within Hellenistic conceptuality, the dualism which allowed the thought of gods appearing in the guise of men (*a* above) militates against the possibility of translating that into the idea of a god becoming man. And the questionable category of the "divine man" (*d* above) is anyway better set under the heading of "inspiration" (divine empowering).

It is equally doubtful whether the more intellectual circles of the time within the Hellenistic world would have recognized a category of "incarnation" as equivalent to other of the usages just listed. Whatever the popular view of such matters, about which we have only a few hints anyway, those who determined the intellectual climate of the day saw the myths about gods and demigods (*a* and *b*) as just that—myths and not factual truth. Likewise, talk of king or emperor as divine or as son of God (*c*) was largely a matter of political convention, and as such expressive of the symbolical power of the head of state and of an underlying desire for divine legitimation for the social and political structure; and as such regularly manipulated in bloody power struggles. And the poetic hyperbole of a Virgil lauding Augustus' success (*e*) was presumably seen as such—the exaggerated description quite proper in the eulogy of a remarkable man. Certainly, important attitudes and claims were embodied in all this language, but to use the word "incarnation" to describe them is at best of doubtful value and probably serves more to confuse than to help forward the discussion.

All this seems to indicate that while the "in"-put of the divine to the human was variously conceived within the wider Greco-Roman world, the idea of incarnation in the sense of the divine actually becoming human was nowhere formulated prior to Christianity. Whatever language might be proper within myth and poetic eulogy, the inherent dualism of the Hellenistic worldview was probably a decisive barrier which prevented such a narrower concept of incarnation from emerging.

Within the more specifically Jewish milieu, there is a similar range of usage:

(1) The anthropomorphism of early Hebrew thought facilitated the idea that God could appear in human form (cf. the appearance of "the angel of the Lord" in human form, as in Genesis 18; 32:24–30; Josh 5:13–15).

(2) Equivalent to Heracles (descent from the gods) are the "giants" of Gen 6:4.

(3) The king of Israel was occasionally called "son of God" or "god," particularly in the Psalms (Pss 2:7; 45:6; 82:6; 89:26–27).

(4) Fully equivalent to any "divine men" in wider Hellenistic thought were the charismatic leaders in the period of the Judges and the later prophets (e.g., Judg 14:19; 1 Kgs 18:46; Jer 20:9; Ezek 2:2), not to mention the righteous individual and charismatic rabbi (Wis 2:13–18; *m. Taʿan.* 3:8).

(5) As classic an example of Virgil's eulogy of Augustus would be the Wisdom of Solomon's description of the plagues of Egypt (Wis 18:15–16).

If parallels to or precursors of the subsequent Christian doctrine of incarnation are sought, similar qualifications would have to be made. Although later Christian thought took some of the anthropomorphisms as manifestations of the Son of God (already in the 2d century in Justin Martyr's *Dialogue with Trypho*), there is nothing of this in the NT itself; there is some christological use of angelomorphic language, particularly in the vision of Rev 1:13–16, but not as a description of Jesus on earth or of incarnation. In Jewish circles, the episode of Gen 6:1–4 was taken as one of the major sources to account for human sin (*Jub.* 5:1–10; *1 Enoch* 6:10; *T. Reu.* 5). Use of the language of deity to speak of the king was the idiom of representation and legitimation as much within Israel as beyond. Charismatic leadership or prophecy likewise belongs more to the category of inspiration than to that of incarnation. And the imagery of Hebrew poetry was as vivid and as vigorous as any of its Greek equivalents. There is nothing in all this which leads us to conclude that by a process of natural evolution any of these usages would have given rise to the more specifically Christian idea of incarnation.

The one exception, or nearest thing to an exception, would seem to be the talk of Wisdom noted previously under (f). Here, we cannot go into the question of whether Wisdom was understood as a divine being other than God, or as a hypostasis, or as a way of speaking (personification) of divine action and immanence within creation; in the framework of Jewish monotheism, the last of these seems most likely, with the concept of "hypostasis" a category which only emerged later in Christian theology, in large part at least as a *consequence* rather than as a *precursor* of the idea of "incarnation" (see Dunn 1980: 168–76). The point here, however, is that Wisdom certainly denotes the divine as over against the human, so that a concept of divine "in"-put or of incarnation in at least a broader sense is involved. Even so, Philo's portrayal of such a figure as Moses or Sarah as an embodiment of divine wisdom does not actually bring us much further forward, for it is an example of Philo's characteristic use of allegorizing in his handling of scriptural texts, and so remains within the broader range of poetic symbolism and hyperbole. Philo, himself, was too much influenced by Hellenistic philosophy for the antithesis between divine and human, rational and material, to be overcome so easily. Juxtaposed they were in the human mind, and identified in allegory they might be, but for the one to become the other or be identified with the other in actual fact was probably a step beyond what was yet thinkable.

If anything, the closer antecedent to the concept of "incarnation" is to be found in the idea of divine wisdom as given to Israel, embodied in the Torah, for in this case the language of actual identification seems to be used. The clearest examples are Sir 24:23 and Bar 4:1. In the former, the hymn where Wisdom praises herself in the first person is immediately followed by the comment: "All this is the book of the covenant of the Most High God, the law which Moses commanded us." And in the latter, a description of Wisdom is followed in just the same way by a similar comment: "She is the book of the commandments of God, and the law that endures for ever." Of course, we are still some way from a concept of incarnation, especially since we have restricted the definition of the term to embodiment in *human flesh.* Nonetheless, such usage of a word which so clearly betokens the divine, a usage which includes both the description of the unique inspiration of Moses and its identification with something as tangible as the law, is clearly not far from the idea of incarnation in the more specifically Christian sense. All it needed was for the two to come together, unique inspiration and identification, in reference to a single individual for the distinctive concept of "incarnation" to be born.

And this is what seems to have happened with regard to Jesus. But in what way, and why, and how soon? Despite the well-known difficulties of stratifying and dating the material, and although other ways of structuring the examination are of course quite possible, we shall seek to maintain a chronological approach as the one most appropriate to an attempt to trace a conceptuality in process of evolution.

D. Jesus

Is the word "incarnation" appropriate to describe Jesus' self-consciousness or claims he made regarding himself? Did Jesus think or speak of himself in terms of the divine embodied in human flesh, whether as a divine being or as God himself become man? The question, of course, is complicated by the usual problem of distinguishing what in the Jesus tradition goes back to Jesus himself and what expresses the later perspective of the earliest Christians or of the Evangelists themselves. The Johannine portrayal of Jesus is the most supportive of an affirmative answer, inviting the evangelistic-apologetic challenge: "He who so speaks of himself is either mad, bad, or God." But it is precisely at this point, Jesus' explicit claims to have preexisted with the Father, at which the Fourth Gospel differs consistently and strikingly from the other Gospels, so that it is precisely the overt incarnationalism of that gospel which is most likely to indicate a later perspective. As we shall also see later, there are some features of Matthew's portrayal which likewise seem to indicate a developed christology, but for the most part the words of Jesus in the Synoptic Gospels probably bring us closer to Jesus' own self-assertions.

Almost all of that material, however, fits most naturally under the heading of "possession" (whether indwelling or inspiration) rather than of "incarnation." This is certainly the case with the relatively strong use of prophet categories, as in Mark 6:4 and Luke 4:18–19; and the implication that Jesus saw himself as spokesman for God and emissary of divine Wisdom, as in Mark 9:37 and Luke 7:31–35. Even if Jesus occasionally spoke of himself as "the son (of God)" or God's "beloved son" (Matt 11:27; Mark 13:32), though the point is disputed, there would have been no implication in the category itself of any claim to preexistence, since divine and intimate sonship was already attributed to a messianic king and the righteous person within Israel (Ps 2:7; Isa 42:1; Wis 2:16–18). And Jesus' talk of himself as "the son of man," even where an allusion to Dan 7:13 is given, would not be understood as a claim to preexistence, since Dan 7:13 was evidently not yet interpreted as speaking of a divine individual. See CHRISTOLOGY.

Does the authority expressed by Jesus not carry with it an implicit claim to incarnation? The "But I say to you" of Matthew 5 seems to go beyond the prophets' "Thus says the Lord" and to set Jesus over, against, or above Moses. Even so, however, it is some way from the absolute claim of the Johannine "I am" formula, and it does not seem to have moved beyond the category of inspiration. The most striking expression of divine authority on the part of Jesus would seem to be his claim to forgive sins in Mark 2:5, 10, especially as in the narrative itself it prompts the response, "Who can forgive sins but God alone?" The issue here, however, seems to be that of authorization. After all, the priest was entitled to pronounce sins forgiven in the context of the cult, on the authority of Leviticus 5. The provocative feature of Jesus' pronouncement was that he spoke neither as priest nor in the context of the cult. To pronounce sins forgiven or even to forgive sins is not of itself an indication of incarnation, since according to John 20:22 Jesus' disciples can do the same (Matt 16:19; 18:18). Here again, we do not seem to have moved beyond the category of inspiration, or authorization.

It has been suggested that in Jesus' parables he applied OT imagery which depicted God to himself, indicating that Jesus thought of himself as in some sense God (Payne 1981). The flaw in this reasoning is the twofold non sequitur that Jesus consistently intended his parables to be understood allegorically and that he consistently intended to portray himself in them. For example, is the sower of Mark 4:3–8 a specific person or anyone who preaches the good news? And the farmer of Mark 4:26–29, who sleeps and rises night and day, is hardly to be understood as a portrayal of God. If any identification is intended by the figure of the father (as in Luke 15:11–32) or of the king (as in Luke 19:12–27), it is obviously God. The imagery of the shepherd (as in Luke 15:4–7) is certainly that of God, but in the same passages it is also that of those set over Israel by God (Jer 23:1–6; Ezek 34:10–16, 20–24). Most striking here is the use of wedding imagery (Mark 2:19; Matt 25:1–13), but even here it is by no means clear if Jesus intended to refer to himself as the bridegroom, as distinct from simply using the symbolism of the wedding to denote the new age of the kingdom (Isa 49:18; 62:5); and the parable of the king giving a marriage feast for his son (Matt 22:1–10) hardly suggests an identification between the bridegroom and God.

In short, within the earlier strata of the Jesus tradition there is substantive evidence that Jesus laid claim to speak with divine inspiration and authorization as in some sense the representative of God. But there is nothing of consequence to support the thesis that Jesus saw himself in some sense as God, as the incarnation of deity.

E. Earliest Christianity

Here, the issue resolves itself down to the significance implied or understood in the claim that Jesus had been raised from the dead and exalted to heaven. The claim was clearly fundamental from the beginning of Christianity proper. What were the incarnational corollaries of this claim?

It is quite often assumed that any affirmation of Jesus as exalted to heavenly status would inevitably have carried with it the implication that he had thereby been restored to or had resumed a status already previously enjoyed (e.g., Knox 1967: 11; Moule 1977: 138–40). Thus, it is argued that the assertion of Jesus' postexistence, after his life on earth, would have been seen to include as a corollary the assertion of his preexistence, before his life on earth. The more exalted the claims made regarding the risen Christ, or the more divine the functions attributed to the exalted Christ, the more unavoidable that corollary would have been. Consequently, even though the concept of incarnation as such was not yet formulated, its conceptualization must have been simply the outworking of that earliest belief in Jesus as raised from the dead. In which case, incarnation could be said to have been an integral part of Christian belief from the very first. So the argument runs.

The argument has power, and since the belief in Jesus as incarnate deity did emerge sooner or later within early Christianity, it can hardly be disputed that the doctrine of incarnation was in some sense a consequence of the Easter faith. But if our concern is to trace the emergence of the Christian idea of incarnation, the question to be asked is how soon that consequence was perceived and affirmed. The argument just stated sees it as an almost immediate consequence. But stated like that, it takes too little account of the range of belief and conceptuality at the time. In particular, 1st-century Judaism knew a good deal of speculation about hero figures who had been exalted to heaven and given some participation in God's judgment, e.g., Enoch, Abel, and the mysterious Melchizedek (*Jub.* 4:22–23; *T. Abr.* 13:1–6; 11QMelch 10). According to Matt 19:28 and 1 Cor 6:2–3, Christians themselves were to take part in the final judgment. None of this would have been understood to imply the deity or preexistence of the individuals named. The bestowal of the Spirit (as in Acts 2:33) may seem to take a step beyond anything affirmed of a human figure in pre-Christian Judaism (Turner, in Rowdon 1982: 183), but John the Baptist attributed some sort of bestowal of the Spirit to the "coming one" (Mark 1:8). Even the confession of Jesus as "Lord," which is certainly very early, did not carry with it a necessary implication that the one so confessed was thereby identified with God, since there were many "lords" (1 Cor 8:5), and since in Paul at least the confession of Jesus as Lord was bound up with the confession of God as one (1 Cor 8:6; Phil 2:9–11). See also CHRISTOLOGY.

It is unlikely, therefore, that the thought of incarnation was part of earliest Christian faith, or that the conviction regarding Jesus' exaltation to God's right hand would have been seen more or less from the first to carry that corollary within it.

F. Paul

The issue of whether Paul's christology included the thought of incarnation has been obscured for most of the 20th century by the debate regarding a pre-Christian gnostic redeemer myth. Bultmann especially had argued that there was already in existence before the emergence of Christianity the myth of a heavenly redeemer figure sent from on high to awaken to their true nature the sparks of light imprisoned within matter (1948: 1.175). According to Bultmann, early christology, including that of Paul, was indebted to this concept of a cosmic figure, a preexistent Son of the Father, who came down from heaven and assumed human form.

The fatal flaw in this whole thesis was that it read the fully developed form of the myth, first clearly attested in the 2d century A.D., back into the period before Christ. Elements of pre-Christian and early Christian thought, which are better seen as the building blocks from which the gnostic redeemer myth was later constructed, were assumed to be the broken fragments of an already existing myth whose fuller expressions have been lost to us—a highly questionable argument from silence. In particular, the Christian belief about Jesus probably provided one of the most important of these building blocks, since the actual redeemer figures of the 2d- and 3d-century gnostic systems seem to be modeled on this Christian belief rather than vice versa. The thesis is also basically unsatisfactory since the postulated myth is fundamentally dualistic in character; that is to say, it would have led if anything to a docetic rather than an incarnational christology; whereas, in the event, Docetism seems to have emerged as an attempt to translate a newly evolved concept of incarnation into the more characteristically dualistic categories of Hellenistic thought.

The passages in Paul on which the debate mostly focused are the Christ-hymns of Phil 2:6–11 and Col 1:15–20. And even when the pre-Christian redeemer myth has been dismissed from the debate, these passages seem to offer the clearest examples of a preexistence and so incarnational christology in Paul.

1. Phil 2:6–11. Here, the issue is largely reduced to the question of the christological imagery being used and its significance. More specifically, to what extent is the imagery that of Adam christology? The talk of being in God's form (or image), and of a grasping at equality with God (Phil 2:6), certainly seems to be intended as a portrayal of Jesus in Adamic terms (Gen 1:26–27 and 3:5 are clearly alluded to). But if that is the case, is it the preexistent Jesus who is in view (the heavenly Christ chose to humble himself to become a man), or is it the epochal significance of Jesus' ministry expressed in Adamic terms (Jesus refused the path of individual self-advancement and chose rather to identify himself completely with humankind in its enslavement to sin and to the death which is the consequence of that enslavement)?

Most commentators find the former more convincing. In which case, the talk of "taking the form of a slave, being/becoming in the likeness of men, and being found/having proved himself to be like man" (Phil 2:7) is probably to be reckoned the earliest expression of incarnation christology. On the other hand, Adam christology elsewhere in Paul focuses on Christ's death and resurrection, not on his birth, as the decisive moments of epochal significance (Rom 2:15–19; 1 Cor 15:20–22, 45–50). And the distinctiveness of Adam christology from gnostic redeemer myth lies precisely in the fact that the life, and death, of a historic individual (Jesus) is perceived as imbued with suprahistorical significance for humankind as a whole, rather than that a preexistent divine being entered the alien territory of the human form. (Adam, properly speaking, was prehistoric rather than preexistent.) Moreover, the regular link between Ps 110:1 and Ps 8:6 elsewhere in earliest christology (1 Cor 15:25–27; Eph 1:20–22; Heb 1:13–2:8; 1 Pet 3:22; cf. Phil 3:21) suggests that Christ's exaltation to lordship following his Adamic death was also seen in Adamic terms; that is, not as a restoration to a heavenly status previously enjoyed, but as the fulfillment of God's purpose in creating man in the first place ("to put all things under his feet"), "to the glory of God the Father" (Phil 2:11). So, perhaps the issue is not so clear-cut as is usually assumed to be the case.

The debate is the same in other expressions of Adam christology. In 1 Cor 15:47, "the second man, from heaven" is almost certainly the exalted Christ. Although some have argued along the lines of the gnostic redeemer myth that "the man from heaven" is the spiritual, preexistent prototype of Adam (the Primal Man), Paul explicitly denies this: the spiritual comes *after* the natural; it is the risen Christ who is the prototype of resurrected humankind (15:46–49). In 2 Cor 8:9, on the other hand, there is an ambivalence similar to that in Philippians 2. Is Christ's richness his preexistent state, and is Christ's becoming poor his incarnation? Or is the richness that of unbroken fellowship with God (such as Adam had enjoyed before the fall) and the poverty the state of separation from God, particularly in his death (cf. Mark 15:34)? The parallel with 2 Cor 5:21, if anything, suggests the latter.

In Gal 4:4 and Rom 8:3, the issue is again more open and depends on how the talk of God sending his Son is to be correlated with his description of the Son as "born of woman, born under the law," and as being sent "in the likeness of sinful flesh." Again, the emphasis seems to be on describing Christ's complete oneness with the human condition ("under the law," "sinful flesh"), which made redemption necessary so that the redemption achieved (on the cross) might be effective for that condition ("to redeem those under the law," "condemned sin in the flesh"). The language of "sending" may have been drawn from the idea of commissioning a prophet (e.g., Jer 1:7; Ezek 2:3; Mark 12:2–6), as in the case of Isaiah, conscious of his solidarity with the sinfulness of his people (Isa 6:5–8), or indeed of the Servant to bear the iniquity of his people (Isa 49:1–7; 53:4–6). Had Paul intended to evoke the thought of a sending from heaven, it is questionable whether he would have used the word "likeness" in Rom 8:3, since within Hellenistic thought the word could lend itself too readily to a docetic-type interpretation—not a genuine solidarity with human sinfulness, and so not an actual redemption.

2. Col 1:15–20. Here, the matter seems to be more straightforward. Christ is described as "the image of God, the first-born of all creation," as the one in, through, and for whom all things were created, the one who is "before all things" and in whom all things hold together (1:15–17). There is no reference to incarnation (a descent from heaven, or becoming man), but the language is clearly that of preexistence; and since the preexistence is predicated of Christ himself, the idea of incarnation, rather than that of indwelling or inspiration, must be implicit. Much the same could be said of 1 Cor 8:6: "one Lord, Jesus Christ, through whom all things . . ."

There are some difficulties even in this case, however: (1) The language is generally recognized to be that used of Wisdom in the Jewish wisdom literature (Prov 3:19; 8:22, 25; Sir 24:9; Wis 7:26). In the same passages, Wisdom is spoken of as God's first creation, which, if the language of personal preexistence is pressed, leaves us with a rather Arian understanding of "first-born of creation." (2) Equally awkward for subsequent classic credal christology would be the assertion of the personal preexistence of Christ, since in subsequent orthodoxy it is clear that Jesus Christ is the man whom preexistent Wisdom became. The preexistence is attributed to Wisdom; Jesus is the incarnation of preexistent Wisdom. (3) Within the Colossian hymn itself, there is the problem of the second half, often ignored in such discussions. There Christ's exalted preeminence is described as the result of his resurrection (1:18) and as the consequence of God having been pleased to dwell in him in all his fulness (1:19; cf. 2:9)—language more appropriate to the concept of indwelling, or of adoption, than to that of incarnation.

Once again, therefore, the thought does not appear to be so clear-cut as it first appeared. The hymn writer does not seem to have been attempting to achieve a consistent christological statement. If by reading the text as straightforward factual affirmation, we find ourselves with unlooked-for corollaries and contradictory assertions, that may be sign enough that we are reading the text with a different meaning than that the author intended, that the author was simply drawing on diverse theological imagery and language to describe the significance of Christ rather than to make a dogmatically coherent claim of incarnation. Even so, the use of Wisdom imagery and language for Christ in both 1 Corinthians 8 and Colossians 1 is striking. Never before, so far as we can tell, had such affirmations been made of a man who had lived and died within living memory. More is being said here of Jesus than Philo said of Moses or the wisdom writers said of the law; more than Virgil said of Augustus. At the very least, we have to say that Jesus' life, death, and resurrection were being seen to possess a divine significance, a revelation of the divine wisdom, a self-disclosure of God himself, so that it was taken as wholly proper to speak of him as that Wisdom, as the manifestation of the one God, with the death of Jesus in particular serving as a definitive expression of that Wisdom (1 Cor 1:22–25). The explicit concept of incarnation lies very close at hand in such language; and in the way that language is used here we may indeed even be able to observe the concept of "incarnation" on the point of emerging into conscious thought.

G. Between Paul and John

In the period following Paul, the conceptuality is more varied, but the same question as that posed by Paul's Wisdom christology remains of uncertain answer. Has the Christian understanding of Jesus begun to break through the older catgories, images, and hyperboles? The focus of such language on Jesus certainly indicates that he was seen as the focus of divine revelation for the first Christians. But has the conceptuality of indwelling and inspiration been stretched to express a new category, that of incarnation? Here again, the answer is more open than many have assumed to be the case.

For example, if the Pauline talk of the sending of the Son (Rom 8:3; Gal 4:4) is read as an expression of Wisdom christology, on the parallel of Wis 9:10, then it should also be read in parallel with Philo's description of Moses, sent by God "as a loan to the earthly sphere and suffered to dwell therein" (*Sacr* 9). If the latter is an expression of Philo's allegorical hyperbole (Moses as the archetype of the wise man; cf. above), what does that say of the former? Similarly, the talk of the appearing of the one predestined from the beginning of time, in passages such as 2 Tim 1:9–10, Heb 9:26, and 1 Pet 1:20, seems to be a fairly clear expression of preexistence and incarnation, until we remember that similar language is used of Moses in *T. Mos.* 1:14: "chosen and appointed, and prepared from the foundation of the world, to be the mediator of the covenant." The christology of Heb 1:1–3 is also dependent on Jewish wisdom language (e.g., Wis 7:26; Philo *Plant* 8–9, 18) and shares the same difficulty with Col 1:15–20 as to how its reference to Christ should be interpreted, particularly as later on (2:6–9; 5:7–10) we find one of the most fully developed expressions of Adam christology in the NT. The language of Heb 7:3 seems to envisage Melchizedek as an ideal type on the Platonic model, while 10:5 assumes that the Jewish idiom, "those who come into the world," is a circumlocution for human beings.

Even the idea of virginal conception (and birth?), which may be thought to have broken new ground, does not seem to have gone beyond Philo's talk of Zipporah as "pregnant through no mortal agency," and of Sarah as "ranked as a pure virgin" even after giving birth (*Cher* 47, 50). Of course, the birth narratives of Matthew 1–2 and Luke 1–2 are not allegories such as those that characterize Philo's exposition of the Pentateuch. But the problem of discerning where midrash and poetic imagery end and where literal claims begin in the birth narratives permits of no easy resolution. To be sure, the imagery of birth (the coming into existence of a new human being) does not immediately mesh with the idea of incarnation (the enfleshment of one already preexistent). But that is less of a problem if we recognize the metaphorical and midrashic character which such descriptions would be assumed to have within a 1st-century Jewish context. Whether fresh ground had in fact been broken would only become evident when the idea of virginal conception was subsequently integrated into the more powerful concept of incarnation.

Matthew, in fact, is not far off from doing just that. For not only does he make good use of the virginal conception tradition (Matthew 1–2), but he also goes beyond the earlier portrayal of Jesus as the emissary of Wisdom to a portrayal of Jesus as Wisdom herself (Matt 11:19, 25–30; 23:34–36; 37–39). Not only so, but he also takes up the language of divine presence and depicts Jesus as "God with us" (1:23; 18:20; 28:18, 20). Here is confirmation that Wisdom was not thought of as a divine being other than God (not even the Son of God in that sense), but as God himself in his active concern for and outreach to his creation and people. It is because Jesus was seen as the complete embodiment of that concern and outreach that he could be spoken of in such terms, with the function of the birth narratives used as much to underscore the point that he embodied this divine presence from the first. In this sense, at least, we can speak of a concept of incarnation in Matthew, even if it does not come to explicit expression as such.

H. John

In the Fourth Gospel, there is an extraordinary concentration of christological claims. Individually, they might be understood as still caught within the earlier categories and structure of thought; but together, they may well be judged to express a breakthrough into a different conceptuality and a bolder claim.

The claim is posed at once in the prologue. The subject is God's Word—another way of speaking of God's self-revelation, action upon, and communication with the world of humankind, along with Wisdom and Spirit (e.g., Pss 33:6; 107:20; Wis 9:1–2, 17; Philo *Somn* 1:65–69; Luke

1:2; Acts 10:36–38). So in John 1, the Word was in the beginning, was with God, and was God; all things were made through this Word (John 1:1–3). It was this Word which "became flesh" in Jesus Christ (1:14). The juxtaposing in this way of the two concepts, "Word" and "flesh," is very striking. For just as John is clear that the Word belongs wholly to the realm of the divine, is *theos* (God/god), so is he clear that flesh belongs wholly to this world, transient and corruptible and antithetical to the other (1:13; 3:6; 6:63). The choice of verb, therefore, is hardly accidental, and it cannot easily be diminished in significance or rendered unwarrantably as "appear" (despite Berger 1974). John evidently wanted to say "the Word *became* flesh." The concept of incarnation, as distinct from indwelling or inspiration, has come to explicit expression. Jesus is being presented as the incarnation of the divine Word.

In the light of this, John's other christological emphases gain a clearer perspective. The characteristic talk of Jesus as the Son sent from the Father is there to emphasize primarily that Jesus is the self-revelation of God, the only one who can make God fully known (1:18; 6:46; 14:9). The less prominent but equally striking talk of Jesus as the Son of Man descended from heaven is used to emphasize that Jesus is the authoritative spokesman of the mystery of God (1:47–51; 3:12–13; 6:60–62). The "I am" statements no doubt deliberately echo the "I am" of Exod 3:14 and Isa 43:10 (particularly John 8:58); Jesus is the glory of God visible to man (12:41, referring to Isa 6:1). Most striking of all is the uninhibited use of the title "God/god" to describe *Jesus* (1:18; 20:28). That the title was provocative to his fellow Jews was well known to the author (5:18; 10:33) and probably resulted within a few years in the rabbinic charge that the Christians had abandoned belief in the unity of God (early 2d century). This is probably sufficient evidence to confirm that the fourth Evangelist was aware that in pushing such a developed portrayal of Jesus, he was going beyond what had previously been acceptable or at least retainable within the hitherto accepted conventions of Jewish talk of God and his self-revelation. To speak of God's wisdom dwelling in Israel or embodied in the Torah was one thing; to portray the man Jesus as God's word incarnate was something else.

The matter seems to be put beyond doubt by the way in which John ties the thought of incarnation tightly to the cross. The whole gospel moves toward the climax of Christ's death. The glory of the Son is manifested particularly in his death (12:23–24; 13:31; cf. 21:19). The lifting up, which corresponds to his descent from heaven, is a lifting up on the cross (3:14; 12:32–33). Most striking of all is the emphasis in 6:53–58 that the flesh of the Son of Man must be chewed if it is to result in eternal life. The point of the incarnation is the death of the incarnate one (6:51). Here, too, John was probably aware that he was pushing into uncharted territory (6:60). A claim that God had revealed himself in king, prophet, sage, or righteous man could be expressed in a variety of hyperbolic language without breaching philosophic or theological conventions. But to claim that the Eternal had *become man* in order to *die* was a step beyond.

I. Conclusions

(1) It is difficult to draw a sharp line between a before and after in the emergence of the concept of incarnation. All we can say with some confidence is that before Christians began to express the significance of Jesus, the concept of incarnation as such is not yet attested; whereas at the end of the 1st century the concept has been deliberately and provocatively put forward. Arguably, the thought is implicit already in formulations used by Paul. But whatever we make of these formulations, it does look rather as though the concept of incarnation was the outcome of what seems with hindsight to have been an inevitable and logical evolution, as the first Christians found that previous ways of speaking of the revelation of God were inadequate to express the full significance of the divine revelation which was Jesus.

(2) The focal point of this being sent, coming under the law, as man, becoming flesh, in all cases seems to be the death and resurrection of Jesus. Within the NT there is no evidence of a concept of incarnation as itself the decisive act of salvation—flesh redeemed by being assumed. The moment of salvation remains decisively centered on the cross. At this point, incarnation and Adam christologies readily blend into each other.

(3) The recognition that Wisdom christology is the most obvious root of incarnation christology also has an important corollary, particularly when it is recalled that in Jewish thought Wisdom is not a being independent of God but is God's self-manifestation. The point is that Christ is the *incarnation* of this Wisdom/Word. To speak of *Christ* as himself preexistent, coming down from heaven, and so forth, has to be seen as metaphorical, otherwise it leads inevitably to some kind of polytheism—the Father as a person, just like Jesus was a person (Lampe 1977). Whereas, what a Wisdom/Word christology claims is that Jesus is the person/individual whom God's word *became*. Even to speak of the incarnation of the Son of God can be misleading, unless the Son christology of John is seen, as it was probably intended, as an expression of the same Wisdom/Word christology; otherwise, there is the danger of a too literal translation of Father-Son language once again into a form of polytheism—that very abandoning of the oneness of God of which Jew and Muslim accuse Christians. The incarnation doctrine which comes to expression in the NT is properly understood only if it is understood as the incarnation of God's self-revelation, in that sense as the incarnation of God himself. The issue which caused the breach with Jewish thought and with Judaism is the charge against the Johannine Jesus, that "you being a man, make yourself God" (John 10:33).

Bibliography See under CHRISTOLOGY.

JAMES D. G. DUNN

INCENSE. A Greek legend tells the story of the birth of the god Adonis, whose mother, Myrrha, fell in love with her own father, King Cinyras of Cyprus. Disguised, she succeeded in making love to him, but when he discovered that it was his own daughter he wanted to kill her. Myrrha fled, asking the gods for protection. They transformed her into a myrrh tree. Nine months later, the bark of the tree cracked and Adonis appeared. The naiads took care of him and anointed him with his mother's tears. Her tears are the incense myrrh (Ovid *Metamorphoses* LCL, 10.298–518).

This legend connects Greece with the Orient. Adonis is ultimately the dying and rising Semitic god Tammuz. And Myrrha is the personification of one of the most beloved incense substances, namely myrrh, which is a product of S Arabia.

The basic idea of the legend relates the origin of myrrh. Myrrh belongs to the divine world; it is the result of a divine creation. Thus, the legend legitimates the use of myrrh in divine worship, in which the deity just receives what already belongs to him. This belief is in harmony with the ethereal or "divine" qualities of the incense material, be it the sap, wood, bark, roots, or fruit of the special odoriferous plants, which became associated with the various incense rituals.

Burnt on charcoal, on special altars or burners, the smoke and odor of incense would please, elevate, mystify, and stupefy the mind of the user, and simultaneously have an effect on the divine sphere. Incense was a holy substance. Incense was powerful. Incense had "mana."

The ritual use of incense is an expression of man in an emotional state. It is a call upon the gods expressing helplessness, happiness, or gratitude. The basic role of incense is to persuade, to threaten, to remedy, to cure, to reveal, to defend, to please, to seduce. In other words, incense is always used with a purpose, be it the substance, its odor, or its smoke. The use of incense is a symbolic expression of man's yearning to understand himself in a dramatic world where odoriferous ritual is an indispensable part of the drama.

This article will partly focus on a phenomenological survey of the various functions and uses of incense in the ancient Near East, and partly describe the impact of incense trade on the trade routes.

A. Uses of Incense in the Nonbiblical World
   1. Incense at Funerals
   2. Incense in Divine Worship
   3. Incense in Rituals of Magic
   4. Incense as a Cosmetic
B. Uses of Incense in the Old Testament
   1. Incense in Divine Worship
   2. Incense as Cosmetic and Medicine
   3. Incense Trade and Trade Routes
C. Uses of Incense in the New Testament

A. Uses of Incense in the Nonbiblical World

1. Incense at Funerals. In Egypt, incense was an indispensable part of ritual life. In connection with funerals, the basic idea of the ritual use of incense was to preserve the dead, to prolong life, and to aid the passage beyond death. The Egyptians believed that incense possessed certain qualities which could be released in the performance of the rituals and which were a prerequisite for obtaining the purpose.

The Pyramid texts from the 3d millennium B.C. reveal an elaborate arrangement for the use of incense at the funeral or cult of the dead king. The texts inform us of the qualities of incense, which were necessary to obtain the noble purpose. Incense purifies. Physically, it removes the evil odor of putrefaction. And cultically and spiritually, it prepares the king for the entrance into eternal life as a god. Incense is an offering to the divine king. This offering also protects the king against evil. Purification and protection are two closely connected ideas in the use of incense all over the Near East. It is the burning of incense, the fumigation, which purifies and protects. During the fumigation, the good odor of incense is transferred from the burning material to the king. However, the burning of incense is also responsible for a third idea associated with incense rituals present in the Pyramid texts: the belief that the smoke of incense establishes communication between man and god. A Pyramid text, utterance 267, reads: "A stairway to the sky is set up for me that I may ascend on it to the sky, and I ascend on the smoke of the great censing . . ." (Faulkner 1969: 76). The use of incense at funerals was also commonplace for the man in the street. He hoped that incense could do the same for him as it was believed to do for the king.

Aromatic incense was also used in the embalmment of the dead body. This use of the substance without burning presupposes a belief in a continued corporeal existence, in which incense materially changes the dead body from a human body of decay and death into a divine body of everlasting life and endurance. Incense functions as a preservative for the body, keeping its identity in a new state of being.

At the root of this use of incense lies the belief that the incense material quite concretely represents the divine (consider the possible etymology of the frequent Egyptian word for incense, *sntr,* which may be a contraction of *sty ntr* = divine fragrance). The presence of the incense is the presence of the divine. The enchanting odor belongs to the gods. Its presence on earth is proof of the presence of the gods.

In Phoenicia, we find the same habit of embalmment, or at least the preparation of the dead body for future life by using myrrh and bdellium. On an inscription on a sarcophagus from Byblos, the dead person describes himself as lying in these two substances (Röllig 1974: 1–15).

In Ugarit, incense seems to be present in a ritual connected with the cult of the dead in *Aqhat* 17.1.28–29. In Mesopotamia, the dead were provided with food and drink at their funeral, and the same kind of offerings took place in the regular cult of the dead. There is reason to believe that aromata of various kinds were used at the time of the funeral, although it is difficult to determine their exact nature. An Assyrian king remembers the funeral of his father: "In royal oil I caused (him) to rest . . ." (Heidel 1967: 153). This oil was undoubtedly fragrant, and its purpose was to facilitate the entrance of the dead person into the afterlife.

2. Incense in Divine Worship. In Egypt, the daily cult of the gods varied from temple to temple. However, the cultic ritual at Medinet Habu, the temple of Ramesses III, may be symptomatic in its lavish use of incense. The day began with an incense offering to the Uraeus goddess, followed by the ritual of the opening of the door. After various incense rituals performed to purify the image of the god Amon-Re, the god finally received his meal. The incense rituals are enacted in order to persuade the god to enter the image. In other words, incense burning makes the deity descend from heaven and enter the temple and the image man has created to his honor.

At the great festivals, incense was burnt from the beginning to the end. At both the cultic festivals and the funerals, we find that incense burning and processions belong together. The fumigation of the participants of a procession purifies them, consecrates them for the special occasion, and protects them from evil. The association of incense and processions reappears much later in the early Christian Church.

In Mesopotamia, incense was part of the daily cult in various temples. A golden incense altar was erected in Marduk's temple Esagila in Babylon during Assurbanipal's reign. A copy of the original dedicatory inscription on the altar tells that the altar was going to be used for propitiatory incense offerings, i.e., to ask Marduk for forgiveness. Assurbanipal hoped that Marduk would hear his prayers, illustrating the belief that incense smoke carries man's prayer to heaven. Furthermore, the text tells that the incense burning took place for the sake of purification (*LAR* 2: 385–86).

The basic reason for using incense in Mesopotamia is clearly expressed in one of Assurbanipal's prayers to Shamash, which explicitly states that the gods inhale incense (*ANET,* 387). This belief is also illustrated in the Gilgamesh epic, where Utnapishtim after his rescue offers incense to the gods, who "smelled the sweet savor. The gods gathered like flies over the sacrificer" (Heidel 1967: 87).

Incense was also used at the great annual festivals. The New Year Festival in Babylon was celebrated with an elaborated incense ritual that embodied purificatory, apotropaic, and propitiatory ideas.

At the beginning of this article, the Greek god Adonis was mentioned as a counterpart of the Semitic god Tammuz. It is no surprise that incense was used in the annual festival to the latter's honor. When Ishtar returns from the Nether World with Tammuz, the lover of her youth, and the wailing company that has mourned Tammuz' disappearance, they are greeted on earth with the sweet smell of incense (*ANET,* 109).

3. Incense in Rituals of Magic. In the magic of both Egypt and Assyria-Babylonia, incense was used in ways similar to its function in divine worship. Magical rituals were used in various situations involving emotional, psychological, and medical problems believed to be caused by evil spirits. The function of incense in rituals aimed at exorcising evil spirits was to call upon the gods for help, to please the gods, and to protect the suppliant against the potential wrath of the gods. In particular, it seems to be the supposed purificatory quality of incense that was effective in magic rituals performed to restore human beings or even geographical places to their normal condition. At the same time, however, the fragrant smell or smoke protected the client from further attacks of the evil spirits.

In Assyria-Babylonia, we find a special idea connected with the use of incense smoke, namely libanomancy; i.e., omens read from the movement of the incense smoke.

4. Incense as a Cosmetic. All over the Near East, aromata of various kinds have been used to beautify men and women, their clothes, and the rooms of a house. Queen Hatshepsut adorned herself with what seems to have been myrrh oil or stacte (*ARE* 2: 113). Others used the incense as a kind of chewing gum to do away with bad breath. Incense was burnt at parties and banquets, and it beautified the union of man and woman. The use of incense as a cosmetic is intended first of all to impress, to please, and to seduce, be it the gods or a fellow person.

B. Uses of Incense in the Old Testament

Based on the Near Eastern background, one would expect incense to play an equally important role in the ritual life of ancient Israel. The archaeological evidence seems to support that expectation. Altars and burners of various forms that have been unearthed give the impression of the frequent use of incense in public worship, as well as in private homes.

However, the problem attached to these finds is the question, To whom did these vessels really belong—to "Israelites" or to "non-Israelites"? Another problem connected with the use of incense in ancient Israel is the relationship of these archaeological finds to the biblical text. Do the finds reflect the rituals which are described in the Hebrew Bible? Or does the Bible express theological reflections belonging to the clergy of Jerusalem, which are not in harmony with the vessels and practices found around the country? Was the use of incense introduced into the Israelite cult in early or late monarchical times? These questions are hard to answer, but are eagerly discussed in the scholarly literature on the subject.

1. Incense in Divine Worship. The OT makes a distinction between lawful and unlawful worship, the unlawful worship being either a wrong execution of Israelite tradition or a pagan cult. The lawful worship, in which incense is employed, prescribes Aaron to burn incense (*qĕṭōret,* based on the root *qṭr*, the meaning of which is discussed in Edelman 1985 and Nielsen 1986: 54–59) regularly on the golden incense altar in front of the holy of holies in the morning and in the evening according to the priestly tradition in Exod 30:7–8. It is emphasized that it is unlawful to burn unauthorized incense, i.e., an incense material different from the one prescribed for lawful use in Exod 30:34–35.

To understand this regular incense offering on the incense altar, it may be profitable to glance at the ritual which belongs to the Day of Atonement described in Leviticus 16. At this occasion (Lev 16:12–13), the high priest takes in one hand a shovel with charcoal and in the other hand some of the ritually correct incense. He enters the holy of holies, where he puts the incense onto the charcoal in the shovel to produce an incense cloud which prevents him from being killed while performing certain rites of expiation. This incense cloud provides the high priest with cover against the divine wrath or the divine "radiation." The incense smoke gives protection. In Lev 16:2, however, it seems that the incense being burnt produces a cloud, in which the deity appears; the incense cloud in v 2 is a symbol of the call upon the deity, a call which the deity answers favorably.

It is hardly a coincidence that the place of the incense altar in the Tent of Meeting, or the temple in Jerusalem, corresponds to the position of the incense altar or burner, which is used in the Assyro-Babylonian incantation rituals. It is always situated between the priest and the image of the deity. The Hebrew incense altar is likewise placed as close to the deity as possible so that it stands between the priest and Yahweh. Only on the Day of Atonement does the high priest dare to transgress this borderline between the human and the divine. The purpose of the regular morning and evening incense offerings at this altar is to secure the presence of God and his attention to man's prayer. The incense smoke carries the prayer to God, who is hopefully appeased when he smells the fragrant odor of the delicious incense.

The special incense called *lĕbōnâ,* "frankincense," is mentioned as an addition to certain meal offerings in Leviticus 2. The part of the flour that is burnt on the altar of burnt offerings together with the frankincense is called an *ʾazkārâ.* This expression may be based on the Heb root *zkr* in Hipʿil, which can mean to call upon the name of a deity; cf. the Akk *zakāru,* which also can refer to invoking the name of a deity. The frankincense of the *ʾazkārâ* facilitates the contact between the suppliant and God.

Several stories in the Torah may reflect a ritual use of incense which is no longer identifiable. In Leviticus 10, Nadab and Abihu appear to be performing a ritual with censers and *qĕṭōret.* The fire they use, however, presumably was not prescribed. The fire is called an *ʾeš zārâ,* i.e., an unconsecrated fire. Consequently, they are struck dead, "devoured" by the fire. The Korah incident in Numbers 16 is depicted as a rebellion against the Aaronite privilege to serve in general and to burn incense in particular in front of the Lord. The consequences are grave for the Korah group. These stories may indicate that there once were rituals with censers which the present Torah does not prescribe.

Num 17:11–13 (—Eng 16:46–48) relates the story of an apotropaic censer ritual, in which Aaron stops the plague from the Lord by placing himself with burning incense between the dead and the living. The text itself explains the purpose of this ritual as an expiation or atonement (v 11), both propitiating the deity and protecting the people. The Torah does not contain a law prescribing this ritual.

In the nonprescriptive literature, the use of incense in worship may be hinted at in 1 Sam 2:28, although its exact use is obscure. Isa 1:13 may be interpreted as describing the incense smoke of the *ʾazkārâ* (cf. Isa 40:23; Jer 27:26; 41:5).

In Ps 141:2, *qĕṭōret* may indicate the regular incense burning in the temple. The cloud which is present at the call of Isaiah (Isa 6:4) may be due to the daily incense offering as well. The reed and frankincense in Jer 6:20, however, show that there once were more incense offerings and rituals in the temple than those which the Torah mentions.

In connection with the polemic against unlawful cults (e.g., Jer 19:13; Isa 65:3; 1 Kgs 22:44), the root *qṭr* is often used to describe the specific worship. The meaning of this root, however, is unclear. Consequently, it is impossible to identify the activity with any certainty.

The use of incense at funerals (or its use in rituals of magic, which is so common in the nonbiblical Near East) is hardly mentioned in the OT as part of Israelite-Jewish culture. The medical doctors, who embalmed the bodies of Jacob and Joseph (Gen 50:2–3, 26), may have used incense material for their purpose (in Phoenician the root *ḥnṭ,* which in Hebrew designates the act of embalmment, is found in a term for "incense altar," *HAL,* 320). The embalmment of Jacob and Joseph is Egyptian in origin.

The OT does not reflect much upon the origin of the use of incense. Its use is simply based on the divine commandment in Exodus 30. Unlike the mythological literature of the surrounding peoples, the Hebrew Bible has no such speculation as to why God wants incense to be used.

2. Incense as Cosmetic and Medicine. The use of aromatic incense as a perfume and its use in medicine are closely connected. Some personal names such as *qĕṭûrâ* (Gen 25:1), *ṣĕrûyâ* (2 Sam 2:18), *bāśĕmat* (Gen 36:3), and *qĕṣîʿâ* (Job 42:3) all may refer to substances used for incense (*qĕṭōret, ṣŏrî, beśem,* and *qĕṣîʿâ*). A name like *qĕṭûrâ,* therefore, may refer to a girl that has been perfumed and purified by means of *qĕṭōret,* which brings joy to the heart (cf. Prov 27:9). The idea behind the fumigation may be exorcistic or apotropaic in nature. However, the names of the children may just express the joy and happiness of their parents.

The use of incense and other aromata for cosmetics is first of all to please, to seduce, and to stupefy. In Ruth 3:3, Ruth is asked to anoint herself for the meeting with Boaz. The perfume she uses is probably olive oil mixed with aromatic substances. In Prov 7:17, the adulteress sprinkles her bed with myrrh, aloe, and cinnamon to make it attractive. The king does the same to his clothes with myrrh, aloe, and cassia at the royal wedding (Ps 45:9); and in Esth 2:12, we are told that women who joined the Persian king's harem had to perfume themselves for twelve months.

This picture continues in the Song of Songs, where references to incense are both metaphors for the beauty of the beloved (4:6) and the result of a lavish use of incense materials as perfume (5:5).

The use of incense as a cosmetic may be a desire to elevate the relationship between man and woman into a sphere as close to the "divine" as possible. Incense and love belong together in the relationship between man and woman, just like incense and the worship of the divine belong together in the relationship betwen humans and God.

From Jer 8:22; 46:11; and 51:8, it appears that *ṣŏrî,* probably storax, was used as a medicine believed to be able to cure diseases and heal wounds.

3. Incense Trade and Trade Routes. The very names of biblical aromata and their possible identification with substances known today suggest a quite intensive traffic in these goods. To compound the holy incense of Exod 30:34–35 for temple use in Jerusalem, galbanum had to be imported from Syria and frankincense from S Arabia. To compound the anointing oil of Exod 30:23, Israel had to import cinnamon from China, myrrh from S Arabia, and sweet-smelling cane from Syria or N Mesopotamia. These biblical texts may date from the exilic or early postexilic period and presuppose an international trade in aromata, which can be further substantiated by the archaeological finds of, for example, the small originally S Arabian cubic incense altars found in Lachish, Gezer, Tell Jemmeh, Tell es-Saidiyeh, and Samaria, dating from the exilic period to Hellenistic times (Nielsen 1986: 47), and by the literary evidence of Theophrastus' *Historia Plantarum.*

Trade has always created riches. It is only to be expected that nations had a political and economic interest in controlling the trade that affected their geographical areas. Control of trade and trade routes meant income in the form of toll and taxes. This may have contributed to David and Solomon's interest in the districts E of the Jordan river through which the King's Highway passed and in the important land bridge of the Sinai desert.

South Arabia, itself, produced frankincense and myrrh. But it was also a bridge for goods from India and China. Some of these aromata along with other goods traveled N along the W mountain ridge of Arabia. Others traveled by sea northwards toward Egypt, as recorded in the beautiful reliefs on the walls of the temple at Deir al-Bahri, which depict the expedition that Queen Hatshepsut (mid-2d millennium B.C.) sent to Punt to collect incense. However, most of the goods from S Arabia that were destined for Palestine traveled by land. From the frankincense-producing areas like Dhufar, the incense route traveled through Wadi Hadhramaut to the myrrh-producing areas around Shabwah. From there, the incense road ran via Najrān to Tathlīth, where the road divided into two: the main road going N toward Medina (Yathrib), and a secondary road going E across the desert to ancient Gerrha on the coast of the Arabian Gulf (Groom 1981: 192). At Medina, the incense road split into three routes: one going E through the S part of the Nafūd desert via Hāʾil toward the S part of Babylonia, and another going more NE toward the oases of Taymaʾ (cf. Isa 21:14) and Al Jawf (Dumah; cf. Gen 25:14) and from there toward Babylon. The main road following the mountain ridge continued toward Al ʿUlā (Dedan; cf. Gen 25:3), Tabūk, Maʿān, Petra, Amman, and Damascus. From Damascus the route went E toward the oasis of Palmyra and on to the N part of Mesopotamia. At Maʿān or Petra, the route diverged toward Gaza and Elat. From these destinations, the commodities went to Egypt. From Amman there was a connection to Mesopotamia through Wadi Sirhān to Dumah and from there to Babylon (Eph'al 1982: 241). Naturally, these routes were used in both directions. From Syria the incense was carried to Palestine and Egypt, and the produce of Syria-Palestine was carried toward Arabia.

These routes seem to have been active in the first half of the 1st millennium B.C. In the 9th century the Arabs first appear in Assyrian inscriptions, and subsequently they occur frequently in Assyro-Babylonian records. It is quite obvious that the Assyrians and the Babylonians wanted to integrate the Arabs into their political structure to control them and their trade in incense and other commodities. The inscriptions mention ethnic groups which are well known from the Bible, for instance Sheba, Ephah, Kedar, Dedan, Dumah, and others which occur in the list of the sons of Keturah (Gen 25:1 ff.) and the list of the sons of Ishmael (Gen 25:13 ff.). These names designate various Arab tribal groups in the N part of the Arabian peninsula and the Sinai desert. As for Sheba, which from S Arabian sources is known to be the name of a kingdom in the S, its presence among ethnic groups living in N Arabia may be due to the fact that the S Arabian kingdom established trading stations in the N. The sons of Keturah and Ishmael designate Arabs in the N who traded in incense.

There are several biblical texts that record trade in incense and other aromata, such as the Joseph story (Gen 37:25), the visit to Solomon of the Queen of Sheba (1 Kgs 10:11), the oracle of Isaiah mentioning the Arab caravans from Dedan (Isa 21:13), and the mention of the camels and dromedaries from Midian and Ephah (Isa 60:6). The list of trade connections in Ezek 27:2ff. seems to indicate a growing Israelite involvement in international trade.

Finally, the various forms of incense altars and burners testify to the international incense trade. The small cubic altar or burner referred to earlier is S Arabian in origin and belongs especially to the Persian period. The ladle-shaped incense burner adorned with the relief of a hand seems to be of Egyptian origin and belongs to the monarchical period (Nielsen 1986: 38–42), whereas the so-called pottery shrine is of Mesopotamian origin and belongs to the early monarchical period (Nielsen 1986: 48–49).

To what extent Jews established themselves as international merchants in incense is difficult to assess. The longer trips through the desert probably continued to be dominated by Arab caravanners, who established themselves in Petra around 300 B.C. They dominated the traffic to Palestine throughout the Hellenistic period.

C. Uses of Incense in the New Testament

The few references to incense and fragrant odor in the NT conform to the general Jewish culture known from the OT.

Even though the texts of Matt 2:11 and Rev 18:13 are legendary and imaginative in nature, they indirectly testify to the existence of the traditional trade routes in incense in the time of the NT, whereas more direct literary evidence is found in Pliny's *Historia Naturalis,* in *Periplus Maris Erythraei,* and in Strabo's *Geographus.*

It is no accident that the priest Zechariah sees an angel of God at the time of the regular incense offering in the temple, since incense brings about the presence or appearance of the divine being or his messenger (Luke 1:8–13). In this passage, incense also brings the prayer of the people to heaven (v 10), as it does in Rev 8:3–4. The gifts of the wise men or astrologers in Matt 2:11 are those fit for a king (cf. 1 Kgs 10:2, 10).

In Mark 14:3–9, we are told about the anointing of Jesus by a woman in Bethany. This act is described as a preparation for his burial. The aromatic she uses is nard (cf. Matt 26:6–13; Luke 7:37–38; and John 12:1–8). In John 19:38–42, the burial of Jesus is performed by Joseph of Arimathaea and Nicodemus. They anoint Jesus' body with nearly a hundred pounds of myrrh and aloe (cf. Mark 16:1 and Luke 24:1).

As was the case in the OT, people in the NT anointed themselves on a regular daily basis (Matt 6:17). Unguents, probably mixed with aromatic substances, were used to cure diseases (Mark 6:13; Jas 5:14; Luke 10:34).

In the epistles and Revelation, incense and fragrance are used as metaphors. In 2 Cor 2:14–16, the knowledge of God or Christ is described as a fragrant odor; and the apostles themselves are compared to incense or fragrance offered to God by Christ (esp. NEB). The sacrifice of Christ himself is called a fragrant odor pleasing to God in

Eph 5:2 (cf. Gen 8:21). In Rev 5:8, incense is used to describe the prayers of the believers.

Finally the very title of Jesus, *ho christos,* which means "the anointed one," may have had an atmosphere of fragrant odor about it in the Greek-speaking world, even though the title was also used as a metaphor for the possession of the Holy Spirit (Luke 4:18; Acts 10:38).

Bibliography

Atchley, E. G. C. F. 1909. *A History of Incense in Divine Worship.* Alcuin Club Collections 13. London.

Brenner, A. 1983. Aromatics and Perfumes in the Song of Songs. *JSOT* 25: 75–81.

Edelman, D. 1985. The Meaning of *qiṭṭēr. VT* 35: 395–404.

Eph'al, I. 1982. *The Ancient Arabs.* Jerusalem and Leiden.

Faulkner, R. O. 1969. *The Ancient Egyptian Pyramid Texts.* Oxford.

Groom, N. 1981. *Frankincense and Myrrh.* London.

Heidel, A. 1967. *The Gilgamesh Epic and Old Testament Parallels.* Chicago.

Löhr, M. 1927. *Das Räucheropfer im Alten Testament.* Schriften der Königsberger Gelehrten Gesellschaft 4/4. Halle.

Neufeld, E. 1971. Hygiene Conditions in Ancient Israel (Iron Age). *BA* 34: 42–46.

Nielsen, K. 1986. *Incense in Ancient Israel.* VTSup 38. Leiden.

Röllig, W. 1974. Eine neue phoenizische Inschrift aus Byblos. *Neue Ephemeris fur semitische Epigraphik* 2: 1–15.

Kjeld Nielsen

INCENSE ALTARS. There can be no doubt that incense was featured prominently in Israelite ritual. Two words attested in biblical Hebrew may be rendered "incense": *lĕbōnâ* (actually translated "frankincense") and *qĕṭōret.* The extensive use of *qĕṭōret* as an element in Israelite ritual is attested in Exod 25:6; 35:8; and 37:29. In Exod 30:34–38, *lĕbōnâ* is named as one of the four ingredients of *qĕṭōret,* which was burned in the tabernacle.

Understandably, perhaps, the discovery of what is thought to have once been an incense burner often generates great excitement among archaeologists, for this is sometimes taken to be evidence of a cultic site. However, it is as well to remember that incense also had multifarious secular uses in ancient Israel. Throughout the ANE, disagreeable smells and pestilential insects abounded. The strong olfactory appeal derived from the combustion of incense and other aromatics would have encouraged their use as deodorants and insecticides. The application of incense and other aromatics to funeral pyres for fumigation is still evident in certain parts of the world today. The unnamed "various kinds of spices prepared by the perfumer's art" which filled the bier at Asa's funeral (2 Chr 16:14) may well have included *lĕbōnâ* and *qĕṭōret.* Nor was it unknown for blends of incense and other ingredients to be used as perfume (Exod 30:34–38): semantically, the words "incense" and "perfume" are the same. See also INCENSE.

A. Excavated "Incense Burners"

At Arad, two incense altars of stone 0.4 and 0.5 m high were found on the steps leading up to the holy of holies of the Israelite sanctuary. In these altars, the tops of which are concave, archaeology has been provided with material evidence of objects that played a part in ancient Israelite ritual. It is extremely doubtful, however, that every so-called incense burner was similarly employed.

The artifacts in question include round stands cut out of limestone, sometimes accompanied by a pottery bowl; similarly crowned tubular pottery stands; and pottery models, supposedly of shrines. The earliest examples are from the EB III sanctuary at et-Tell. They are in the form of rectangular clay stands with side openings (for air circulation or as a means of carrying the pot stand?) and a bowl on top. Together with a so-called clay incense altar from Iron Age Taanach and a bronze openwork stand of uncertain provenance from Megiddo, these have been identified as "cultic objects." It is just as likely that at least some may have been no more than braziers used for heating in the winter months (cf. Jer 36:22–23). Although incense could be dropped on any fire in a brazier, the discovery of one such object does not justify the classification "incense burner."

Many so-called "incense burners" show no signs of combustion whatsoever; this was particularly the case of the one found at Taanach. Indeed, the term "incense stand," common in archaeological literature, has no warrant, since their function was by no means confined to the burning of incense; among numerous possible alternatives are their use as plant holders, libation stands, and devices for keeping warm food and drink.

So-called pottery shrines, which may have featured in ANE cults, have also been identified as incense altars (the terra-cotta shrine from Achzib is one example), but it is as well to remember that not every pottery model of an edifice from ancient Palestine is evidence of a cultic object. Unlike the examples from Beth-shan, the pottery models from Megiddo, for instance, had no necessary cultic significance whatsoever.

B. Horned Altars

At Tell Arad and Tell Beer-sheba, large altars of burnt offerings from the First Temple period have been uncovered. Much smaller horned altars were also found in Iron Age Palestine, several in private houses, which have been identified as altars of incense.

In OT literature, "horns" symbolize strength and denote political power, imagery drawn from the force exerted by the bull's forward thrust (Deut 33:17). In prophetic symbolism, "horns" signify kings or military powers (Dan 7:8; 8:21). The reference in 1 Kgs 1:50; 2:28 attests that fugitives seeking asylum clung to "the horns of the altar." These were horn-shaped protuberances on the four corners of the altars, the original purpose of which is now lost to us.

The common assumption that the design was handed down to the altar of incense, where the horns served as a means of supporting the incense bowl, remains conjecture. There are no pictorial representations of horned altars supporting a bowl; no bowls have been uncovered in this position, nor has it been proved that bowls found nearby were used in this manner.

C. Later Altars

From the Babylonian and Persian periods, excavators in Palestine have recovered numerous so-called incense altars at, among other places, Lachish, Gezer, and Samaria. Many of these are small and cuboid in shape. They have four legs and are decorated with geometric or conventional designs. Some bear naturalistic representations of palm trees and animals. Despite their lateness and decoration, however, the problem of identification remains, and both Glueck (1970) and Albright (1974) expressed grave doubts over the cultic associations of several such objects.

On the above evidence, it is clear that many artifacts identified in scholarly literature as "incense burners" were probably nothing of the kind. Although there can be no doubt that incense featured prominently in Israelite ritual, in ancient Israel the burning of incense had different uses in different places, and the precise function of any particular object is seldom apparent.

Bibliography

Albright, W. F. 1974. The Lachish Cosmetic Burner and Esther 2:12. Pp. 25–32 in *A Light Unto My Path,* ed. H. N. Bream, R. D. Heim, and C. A. Moore. Gettysburg Theological Studies 4. Philadelphia.

Amiran, R. 1970. *Ancient Pottery of the Holy Land.* New Brunswick, NJ.

Culican, W. 1976. A Terracotta Shrine from Achzib. *ZDPV* 92: 47–53.

Fowler, M. D. 1984. Excavated Incense Burners. *BA* 47: 183–86.

———. 1985. Excavated Incense Burners: A Case for Identifying a Site as Sacred? *PEQ* 117: 25–29.

Glueck, N. 1970. Incense Altars. Pp. 325–29 in *Translating and Understanding the Old Testament,* ed. H. T. Frank and W. L. Reed. Nashville.

Groom, N. 1981. *Frankincense and Myrrh: A Study of the Arabian Incense Trade.* London.

Mazar, A. 1980. Cult Stands and Cult Bowls. *Qedem* 12: 87–100.

McCown, C. C. 1950. Hebrew High Places and Cult Remains. *JBL* 69: 205–19.

Neufeld, E. 1971. Hygiene Conditions in Ancient Israel (Iron Age). *BA* 34: 42–46.

Shea, M. O. 1983. The Small Cuboid Incense-Burners of the Ancient Near East. *Levant* 15: 76–109.

MERVYN D. FOWLER

INCENSE DISH [Heb *kap*]. The common word for the hollow part of the hand is used to indicate a shallow bowl used as a censer, for burning incense. The RSV renders this term "incense dish." Archaeological discovery of shallow stone bowls, with a hand carved on the bottom so that the vessel appears to be a cupped palm, provides artifactual evidence for these cultic objects. Incense dishes are mentioned in various priestly texts in the Pentateuch (e.g., Exod 25:29; Num 4:7) dealing with the tabernacle, and they appear in other parts of the Bible in relationship to temple equipment (see 1 Kgs 7:50; 2 Kgs 25:14). The incense dishes were made of gold and weighed ten shekels (Num 7:14). In the tabernacle, they were placed on the small golden table which held various other receptacles for food as well as the bread of the Presence; there were twelve such dishes according to Num 7:84, 86. Various other English versions render this term as "spoons" or "pans." See also CENSERS.

CAROL MEYERS

INCEST. See PUNISHMENTS AND CRIMES (OT AND ANE).

INDIA (PLACE) [Heb *hôddû;* Gk *Indikēs*]. The Hebrew word may be derived from the Old Persian *hidav* or the Avestan *hindav.* Both are derivations of the Sanskrit word *sindhu,* which has two meanings: the common usage of "stream" and the proper noun designated for the name of the ancient Indus river. The Indus river is approximately 1,900 miles long, flowing NW from its head in Tibet and eventually proceeding SW across what now is Pakistan. It finally empties out in the Arabian Sea. The area crossed by the Indus river may mark the boundary or main contact point for the large subcontinent of India, situated in S Asia. India is mentioned twice in Esther (1:1; 8:9) to describe the extent of the E boundary of King Ahasuerus' territory. In 1 Esdr 3:2 and Add Esth 13:1; 16:1, it is also used to state the geographical expanse of the Persian domain. There seems to have been no integral historical connection between ancient Israel and ancient India, although many desirable Indian products found their way into Palestinian markets, including ivory, ebony, sandalwood, assorted exotic animals, and other precious materials. These items were usually delivered by either the Arabian and Syrian trade routes or shipped by means of the Red Sea. Elephants, intended for use in warfare, and their drivers, were also traded, as referred to in 1 Macc 6:37.

JEFFREY K. LOTT

INDUS RIVER. See INDIA (PLACE).

INFANCY GOSPELS. See THOMAS, INFANCY GOSPEL OF.

INFANCY NARRATIVES IN THE NT GOSPELS. While Mark's gospel starts with the baptism where God's voice identifies Jesus as His Son and stops with the empty tomb proclamation, the other three canonical Gospels have additions at the end (resurrection appearances) and at the beginning. A christological aim dominates the three beginnings: John's introductory hymn (Prologue) identifies Jesus as the Word of God spoken before creation who has become flesh and dwelt among us as God's Only Son; Matthew and Luke associate the identity of Jesus as Savior and God's Son with his conception in Mary's womb by the Holy Spirit. Thus all three gospel beginnings prevent the interpretation (which was theoretically possible for Mark) that Jesus' identity stems from the baptism seen as adoption.

A. Evaluation of Contents
B. Theological Motifs
  1. Christology
  2. Imagery from Jewish Scriptures
  3. Relation to Gospel of Jesus Christ
C. Pre-Gospel Sources and Traditions
  1. Pre-Matthean Sources/Traditions
  2. Pre-Lucan Sources/Traditions

A. Evaluation of Contents

If we leave until later the story of Jesus at age 12 (Luke 2:41–52), the following features of the infancy narratives that constitute the gospel beginnings of Matthew and Luke (first two chapters in each) are important.

(1) They *agree* on these points: Chap. 1 deals with the prebirth situation; chap. 2 with the birth or postbirth situation. The parents of Jesus are Mary and Joseph, who are legally engaged or married but have not yet come to live together or have sexual relations. Joseph is of Davidic descent. There is an angelic announcement of the forthcoming birth of the child. The conception of the child by Mary is not through intercourse with her husband but through the Holy Spirit. There is a directive from the angel that the child is to be named Jesus. The roles of Savior (Matt 1:21; Luke 2:11) and Son of God (Matt 2:15; Luke 1:35) are given to Jesus. The birth of the child takes place at Bethlehem after the parents have come to live together. The birth is chronologically related to the reign of Herod the Great (Matt 2:1; Luke 1:5). Eventually, the child is reared at Nazareth.

(2) Matthew and Luke *disagree* on the following significant points. In chap. 1, the Lucan story of John the Baptist (annunciation to Zechariah by Gabriel, birth, naming, growth) is absent from Matthew. According to Matthew, Jesus' family live at Bethlehem at the time of the conception and have a house there (2:11); in Luke, they live at Nazareth. In Matthew, Joseph is the chief figure receiving the annunciation, while in Luke, Mary is the chief figure throughout. The Lucan visitation of Mary to Elizabeth and the Magnificat and Benedictus canticles are absent from Matthew. At the time of the annunciation, Mary is detectably pregnant in Matthew, while the annunciation takes place before conception in Luke. In chap. 2 in each gospel, the basic birth and postbirth stories are totally different to the point that the two are not plausibly reconcilable. Matthew describes the star, the magi coming to Herod at Jerusalem and to the family house at Bethlehem, the magi's avoidance of Herod's plot, the flight to Egypt, Herod's slaughter of Bethlehem children, the return from Egypt, and the going to Nazareth for fear of Archelaus. Luke describes the census, birth at a stable(?) in Bethlehem because there was no room at the inn, angels revealing the birth to shepherds, the purification of Mary and the presentation of Jesus in the temple, the roles of Simeon and Anna, and a peaceful return of the family to Nazareth.

(3) None of the significant information found in the infancy narrative of either gospel is attested clearly elsewhere in the NT. In particular, the following items are found only in the infancy narratives. (a) The virginal conception of Jesus, although a minority of scholars have sought to find it implicitly in Gal 4:4 (which lacks reference to a male role), or in Mark 6:3 (son of Mary, not of Joseph), or in John 1:13 ("*He* who was born . . . not of the will of man"—a very minor textual reading attested in no Gk ms). (b) Jesus' birth at Bethlehem, although some scholars find it implicitly in John 7:42 by irony. (c) Herodian knowledge of Jesus' birth and the claim that he was a king. Rather, in Matt 14:1–2, Herod's son seems to know nothing of Jesus. (d) Wide knowledge of Jesus' birth, since all Jerusalem was startled (Matt 2:3), and the children of Bethlehem were killed in search of him. Rather, in Matt 13:54–55, no one seems to know of marvelous origins for Jesus. (e) John the Baptist was a relative of Jesus and recognized him before birth (Luke 1:41, 44). Rather, later John the Baptist seems to have no previous knowledge of Jesus and to be puzzled by him (Luke 7:19; John 1:33).

(4) None of the events that might have been "public" find attestation in contemporary history. (a) There is no convincing astronomical evidence identifiable with a star that rose in the East, moved westward, and came to rest over Bethlehem. In Matthew's story this would have happened before the death of Herod the Great (4 B.C. or [Martin 1980] 1 B.C.). There have been attempts to identify the star with the supernova recorded by the Chinese records in March/April 5 B.C., or with a comet (Halley's in 12–11 B.C.), or with a planetary conjunction (Jupiter and Saturn in 7 B.C.; Jupiter and Venus in 3 B.C. [Martin 1980]). (b) Even though the Jewish historian Josephus amply documents the brutality in the final years of Herod the Great, neither he nor any other record mentions a massacre of children at Bethlehem. Macrobius' frequently cited pun (*Sat.* 2.4.11) on Herod's ferocity toward his sons is not applicable to the Bethlehem massacre. (c) A census of the whole world (Roman provinces?) under Caesar Augustus never happened, although there were three Augustan censuses of Roman citizens. It is not unlikely that Luke 2:1 should be taken as a free description of Augustus' empire-cataloguing tendencies. (d) Luke's implication that Quirinius was governor of Syria and conducted a "first census" (2:2) before Herod's death (1:5) has no confirmation. Quirinius became legate of Syria in A.D. 6 and at that time conducted a census of Judea, which was coming under direct Roman administration because Archelaus had been deposed (Brown 1977: 547–56; Benoit *DBSup* 9: 704–15). (e) Although this item differs somewhat from the immediately preceding one, Luke's idea that the *two* parents were purified ("their purification according to the Law of Moses": 2:22) is not supported by a study of Jewish law, whence the attempts of early textual copyists and of modern scholars to substitute "her" for "their" or to interpret the "their" to refer to other than the parents.

A review of the implication of nos. 1–4 explains why the historicity of the infancy narratives has been questioned by so many scholars, even by those who do not *a priori* rule out the miraculous. Despite efforts stemming from preconceptions of biblical inerrancy or of Marian piety, it is exceedingly doubtful that both accounts can be considered historical. If only one is thought to be historical, the choice usually falls on Luke, sometimes with the contention that "Those who were from the beginning eyewitnesses and ministers of the word" (Luke 1:2) includes Mary who was present at the beginning of Jesus' life. See Fitzmyer *Luke I–IX* AB, 294, 298, for the more plausible interpretation that it refers to the disciples-apostles who were eyewitnesses from the beginning of Jesus' public life (Acts 1:21–22) and were engaged in a preaching ministry of the Word. There is no NT or early Christian claim that Mary was the source of the infancy material, and inaccuracies about the census and purification may mean that Luke's infancy account cannot be judged *globally* as more historical than that of Matthew.

Such a general judgment, however, need not imply that there are not some historical elements in either or both accounts. The mutual agreement have an importance, for they probably represent points that were in a tradition antedating both Matthew and Luke. For instance, an intelligent case can be made that Jesus was truly descended from David and born at Bethlehem in the reign of Herod the Great. Arguments to the contrary are far from probative (Brown 1977: 505–16). In particular, the virginal conception (popularly but confusingly called the Virgin Birth) should be evaluated cautiously. Despite extremely limited attestation and inherent difficulties, no satisfactory nonhistorical explanation which could dispense with the virginal conception has been brought forward. The frequent approach to the virginal conception as a theologoumenon, whereby the common "Son of God" title of Jesus would have been translated into a (fictional) narrative in which he had no human father, could acquire plausibility only if there were a good antecedent or parallel for the idea of virginal conception. There is no good antecedent or parallel. While there were Greco-Roman and other examples of male gods impregnating earth women to produce a divine child, the NT contains no hint of such a sexual union. Within Judaism there was no expectation that the messiah would be born of a virgin. (The MT of Isa 7:14 does not clearly refer to a virgin, and even the LXX need mean no more than that one who is now a virgin will conceive through future intercourse. Matthew has not derived Jesus' conception from Isa 7:14, but interpreted the OT passage through Christian data.) A claimed Hellenistic-Jewish tradition that the patriarchal wives conceived from God without male intervention (Philonic allegory; Gal 4:23, 29) is far from certain. (On all this, see Boslooper 1962; Brown 1977: 517–33). In terms of historical catalysts behind the concept of a virginal conception, those worth noting are: (a) the agreement of Luke (implicit) and Matthew that Jesus was conceived before Joseph and Mary came to live together and hence that the birth might be noticeably early after cohabitation; (2) the 2nd-century Jewish charge that Jesus was illegitimate (Or. *Cels* 1.28, 32, 69), possibly reflected earlier in John 8:41. If there was a family tradition of a virginal conception, the pre-Gospel shaping of it into a narrative may reflect Christian pastoral needs in face of Jewish polemics.

B. Theological Motifs

The question of historical elements in the infancy narratives should not distract from the clearer theological intent to Matthew and Luke. The following major theological emphases are to be noted:

1. Christology. By referring to Jesus from his conception as descended from David through Joseph and as the Savior/Son of God through the Holy Spirit, the two Evangelists are adapting to this first stage of Jesus' life language that elsewhere in the NT is related to the resurrection or the baptism. Rom 1:3–4, for instance, refers to ". . . the gospel concerning God's Son who was born of the seed of David according to the flesh; designated Son of God in power according to a Spirit of Holiness [= Holy Spirit] as of *resurrection* from the dead." A combination of Holy Spirit, designation as Son of God, and divine power is found in relation to the *baptism* in Luke 3:22; 4:1, 14. The angelic annunciation at the time of conception in Luke combines Davidic descent in 1:32–33 with 1:35, where the Holy Spirit comes on Mary and the power of the Most High overshadows her so that the child is called Son of God. Thus, the conception and infancy of Jesus become the vehicle of the basic gospel message of Jesus' fundamental identity.

2. Imagery from Jewish Scriptures. Matthew begins his narrative with the genealogy of Jesus that includes the Hebrew patriarchs and the Judean kings. Matthew's story of Joseph, who receives revelation in dreams and goes to Egypt, clearly recalls the story of the OT Joseph, the dreamer or master of dreams (Gen 37:19) who went to Egypt. The wicked king Herod who kills the male children at Bethlehem evokes the pharaoh who killed the male children of the Hebrews in Egypt. Jesus, the one child who escapes to become the Savior of his people, offers a parallel to Moses. The words spoken to Joseph by the angel after Herod's death, "Go back to Israel, for those who were seeking the child's life are dead" (Matt 2:20) are almost verbatim the words to Moses in Midian, "Go back to Egypt, for all those who were seeking your life are dead" (Exod 4:19). When ultimately Moses went from Egypt through the desert toward the land of Canaan, he encountered another wicked king with homicidal tendencies. Balak of Moab summoned Balaam, a visionary or magus (Philo, *Vita Mos* 1.50 §276) who came from the East (LXX Num 23:7) with two servants (22:22). Balaam foiled the hostile plans of the king by delivering oracles seen in a vision (as of one who sees God in his sleep; LXX 24:4, 16). These predictions concerned a star coming forth from Jacob (24:17) and a king who would rule many nations (24:7). The Matthean magi echo this story. Indeed, the blending of the pharaoh and Balak into Herod may have been facilitated by developments of the Moses story attested in Josephus (*Ant* 2.9 §205–37) and in early midrashim, whereby the pharaoh was forewarned by his sacred scribes (or in a dream which had to be interpreted by magi) that a Hebrew child who would deliver his people was about to be born. At this news, the Egyptians were filled with dread (cf. Matt 2:3: "When King Herod heard this, he was startled and so was all Jerusalem with him."). The pharaoh's plan to forestall the work of the promised child by executing all the male Hebrew children was frustrated because God appeared in a dream to Amram (Moses' father), a Hebrew whose wife was already pregnant. Obviously, Matthew's infancy account is quite close to these midrashic developments of the Moses story.

To the genealogy of patriarchs and kings, and to this narrative evocative of Joseph, Moses, and the Exodus, Matthew has added five citations from the Hebrew prophets which are fulfilled by the infancy happenings. These citations echo the LXX (Isa 7:14 in Matt 1:22–23), the MT (Hos 11:1 in Matt 2:15), or other texts and combinations (Mic 5:1 [—Eng 5:2] and 2 Sam 5:2 in Matt 2:5–6; Jer 31:5 in Matt 2:18, 23). The fifth "prophetic citation" appears in Matt 2:23, but the source from which Matthew took that quotation is unknown: it may be from Isa 4:3 and Judg 16:7 (for extended discussion, see Brown 1977). Such eclecticism and combining of different prophets and versions have led some to describe Matthean composition as a school-like exercise, carefully comparing texts to find the most suitable way of interpreting Jesus (Stendahl 1968; see also Soares Prabhu 1976). The geographical motif that appears in the four citations of Matthew 2 may be a key to the development of the Matthean infancy message. If the genealogy and the annunciation plus Isa 7:14 in chap. 1 help to tell us *who* Jesus is (Son of David and Savior sent by God), *how* he is that (legal acknowledgment by the Davidide Joseph, and conception from a virgin through the Holy Spirit), then the magi/Herod/flight-to-Egypt story in chap. 2 commented on by four citations tells us *where* Jesus was born (Bethlehem) and *whence* he went subsequently (Egypt, Nazareth). The quotation in Matt 2:23 may be from Isa 4:3 and Judg 16:17 (Brown 1977; see Stendahl 1964).

Luke also makes good use of imagery drawn from the Jewish Scriptures but with a technique less obvious than Matthew's. (Luke's Davidic genealogy for Jesus [3:23–38—some names different from Matthew's] is placed after Jesus has been addressed by God from heaven and before he begins his mission, even as the genealogy of the tribes and of Moses in Exod 6:14–25 is given after Moses has been addressed by God but before he begins his mission of leading the tribes out of Egypt.) If Matthew's infancy narrative begins with Abraham begetting Isaac, Luke's narrative begins with Zechariah and Elizabeth, parents of John the Baptist, who resemble closely Abraham and Sarah (for these are the only two biblical couples whose childlessness is traced to both old age and barrenness; cf. Gen 18:11; Luke 1:7). The birth announcement only to the father, the response of Zechariah ("How am I to know this?" which is a verbatim quotation from Abraham in Gen 15:8), the rejoicing with Elizabeth of those who hear about the conception/birth (Luke 1:58, echoing Gen 21:6)—all these features show the extent to which for Luke too, the Abraham story is the gospel beginning.

The angel who speaks to Zechariah at the hour of incense is Gabriel, who appeared in Dan 9:20–21 at the time of liturgical prayer—his only other appearance in biblical literature. A comparison of Dan 10:7–15 with Luke's infancy account shows a number of similarities, including the visionary being struck mute. If the Abraham story of Genesis stands near the beginning of the collected Law and Prophets in the Hebrew Scriptures, Daniel would have had a place at or near the end of "the other Books" which terminated the collection (even if this last category was a fluid grouping in NT times). Gabriel interpreted for Daniel (9:24–27) the seventy weeks of years, including the end when "everlasting justice will be introduced, vision and prophecy will be ratified, and a Holy of Holies [a place or person?] will be anointed." (See Legrand 1981 for a strong apocalyptic motif in Luke's annunciation.) Thus, Luke's infancy opening has motifs ranging from the beginning to the end of the sacred story of God's people.

From the midst of that sacred story comes another parallel that helped to fashion a major part of the Lucan infancy narrative: conception by Hannah of the child Samuel. Luke's words, "Zechariah went back to his home; afterwards, Elizabeth his wife conceived," resemble strongly 1 Sam 1:19–20; Mary's Magnificat resembles Hannah's song of praise after she conceived and bore a son (1 Sam 2:1–10); the presentation of Jesus in the temple and his reception by the aged Simeon (Luke 2:22–40) echoes the presentation of Samuel at the central shrine in the presence of the aged Eli (1 Sam 1:21–2:11); the two descriptions of Jesus' growth in Luke 2:40, 52 resemble the two descriptions of Samuel's growth in 1 Sam 2:21, 26. Thus, while the Matthean infancy narrative was heavily influenced by the Joseph/Moses epic, the Lucan infancy narrative is heavily influenced by the Samuel epic, perhaps because of the liturgical setting of the Samuel story in the central shrine. For Luke, the Gospel of Jesus begins and ends (24:53) in the temple, and the continuity of Jesus with the cult as well as with the Law (2:22–24, 27, 39) is important. The Lucan narrative has minor reminiscences from the David story, e.g., the shepherds and the "City of David" (2:1–20).

The prophetic books of the OT are not neglected either, for a context of prophetic oracle and inspiration (1:67; 2:27) surrounds the Lucan canticles: the Magnificat (1:46–55), the Benedictus (1:68–79), the Gloria in Excelsis (2:14), and the Nunc Dimittis (2:29–32). Almost every line in these hymns echoes OT psalms or prophets, in the manner of Jewish psalmody attested in the last two centuries B.C. (Maccabean hymns; DSS Thanksgiving Hymns). In particular, the Benedictus is a paean of continuity, citing "our fathers, Abraham, the covenant, the House of David, and God's holy prophets." Luke's two-volume work culminates with the proclamation of Paul that God has sent this salvation to the gentiles and they will listen (Acts 28:29); the two-volume work opens with the insistence that this salvation stands in continuity with Israel.

In summary reflection on the two principal theological points common to Matthew and Luke, we see a strong affirmation of the identity of Jesus in common Christian terms (Son of David, Son of God) combined with a remarkable compendium of scriptural narratives and motifs. Thus, the infancy narratives become a bridge summarizing the story of Israel and anticipating the gospel of Jesus Christ.

3. Relation to Gospel of Jesus Christ. The reaction to that gospel is anticipated in the two infancy narratives, but in different ways. In Matt 1:19, Joseph is described as a just man in a context which implies that his justice consists in the observance of the Law of Moses. He accepts the divine revelation about Jesus' identity; and by being obedient to God's direction given by an angel, he protects Jesus and brings him ultimately to Nazareth. The magi are gentiles who receive revelation through a star and come eagerly to Jerusalem seeking the newborn King of the Jews; yet they cannot find him without the precise revelation in the Scriptures. When the prophet Micah is explained to them, they hasten to Bethlehem to worship. A third reaction is exemplified by Herod, the chief priests, and the scribes: they have and can read clearly the message of the Scriptures about the messiah. However, not only do they not come and worship, but they also seek to end Jesus' life (2:20: note the plural). Matthew's community has encountered or embodies all three reactions. The gentiles who eagerly become disciples are clearly part of Matthew's world (28:19). Joseph, who is just in his observance of the Law, and yet open to new divine revelation about Jesus, is the hero of the story because for Matthew he exemplifies the ideal reaction of Jews to Jesus. Elsewhere, the author praises a scribe who can combine the new with the old (13:52). Herod the king, the chief priests, and the scribes who would destroy the infant Jesus foreshadow Pilate the governor, the chief priests, and the elders who put Jesus to death (chap. 27). Almost surely, Matthew relates them to the Pharisees whom Jesus criticizes fiercely (chap. 23) and who find a conflict between Jewish traditions and Jesus. From the beginning, then, in Matthew's portrayal there has been a divided reaction to Jesus in Judaism—a just Joseph versus priests, scribes, and rulers.

Turning to Luke, we find a passing reference to a similar set of ideas in 2:32–34, where Jesus is a light to the gentiles, and a glory for the people of Israel—but not for all in Israel, since he is set for the fall and rise of many. This one Lucan infancy suggestion that many in Israel will not accept Jesus is overshadowed by the dramatic examples of Law-observant Jews who eagerly accept the new revelation given by God concerning Jesus, namely, Zechariah, the shepherds, Simeon, and Anna. The shadow of rejection is, therefore, not nearly so dark in Luke as it is in Matthew. A special emphasis is given to Mary's reaction to the proclamation of Jesus. The first one to hear about Jesus, Mary is a model disciple according to the criteria of Luke 8:21 and 11:28, namely, being willing to hear the word of God and keep or do it. This is exemplified in her response to the angel's annunciation: "Be it done to me according to your word" (1:38), a reaction praised by Elizabeth (1:45). Her interpretation of the significance of Jesus expressed in the Magnificat (scattering the proud; putting down the mighty; exalting the lowly; filling the hungry) is an anticipation of Jesus' own interpretation of his basic message in Luke 6:20–26 ("Blessed are you who are hungry. . . . Woe to you who are full now"). In the reiterated motif that "Mary kept with concern all these events, interpreting them in her heart" (2:19, 51), Luke is portraying Mary as one to whom God communicated gradually the interpretation of the mysterious revelatory events of Jesus' infancy in which she participated, and as one who was a receptacle of God-given wisdom (Brown 1986: 672).

C. Pre-Gospel Sources and Traditions

It is extremely difficult to determine the extent to which Matthew and Luke (1) composed freely through reflection on the Scriptures and on Jesus; (2) composed freely by combining such reflection with traditions they received about Jesus' infancy; and/or (3) reused verbatim already-existing narratives or sources (in Greek or Semitic). There is a particular problem in the instance of Luke/Acts, a work which employs different compositional styles, illustrating either the use of fixed sources or the skill of the author who employed a style most appropriate to the narrative at hand, e.g., a highly Semitized style in the infancy narrative, where all the characters are Jews and many of them clearly parallel to OT figures. Brown (1977: 246) stated that he abandoned "the thesis that by style and language one can decide the question of sources; the linguistic opponents have fought one another to a draw." Farris (1981) thinks it probable, however, that Luke used Hebrew sources. Two facts seem relatively clear: (1) both Matthew and Luke used earlier material, and (2) both authors reworked considerably the material they took over. The following treatment does not attempt to settle the question whether that material was freely used tradition (oral or written) or from already fixed sources.

1. Pre-Matthean Sources/Traditions. a. Matt 1:17 insists on a 3 × 14 pattern of the generations in the genealogy. (There are actually only 13 generations [14 male names] in the first part; 14 generations [14 new male names, but 4 royal generations and 6 ruling kings omitted] in the second part; and only 13 generations [13 new male names, with no other biblical attestation of any figure between Zerubbabel and Joseph] in the third part.) The Evangelist's air of discovering the marvelous in this design makes it difficult to think that he completely invented the genealogy. Yet, it is equally difficult to think that he has given us an exact copy of a family record. For the patriarchal period, Matthew may have drawn on a genealogy similar to that in Ruth 4:18–22 and 1 Chr 1:28, 34; 2:1–15. For the monarchical period, he may have drawn on a popular genealogy of the royal House of David—one in which there were accidental omissions because of similar sounding names. For the last part of the genealogy, Matthew himself may have added the names of Joseph, Mary, and Jesus to a list of uncertain derivation pertaining to putative descendants of Zerubbabel. The addition of the four OT women (all appearing in stories colored by the apparently scandalous or irregular, and yet women who showed initiative or played an important role in God's plan, three of them outsiders to Israel and the fourth married to an outsider) was Matthew's attempt to prepare for Mary's role (apparently scandalous but a unique vehicle of God's plan) and for the spread of the gospel to gentile outsiders.

b. A narrative centered on three stylized angelic dream appearances of Joseph, with Joseph's response to each (see Brown 1977: 109 for reconstruction). The basic-story theme would have been the forthcoming birth of a savior, Herod's jealous suspicions, the flight to protect the newborn child, and the ultimate return after Herod's death—a narrative based on the Moses story.

c. A narrative of magi from the East who saw the star of the King of the Jews at its rising and came to worship—a narrative based on the Balaam story.

d. An annunciation of birth that involved Jesus' identity as Son of David and Son of God, with conception through the Holy Spirit (rather than through a male parent) as part of that identity. This followed an OT pattern of birth annunciations with stereotyped features (Brown 1977: 156), including the appearance of an angel, fear by the visionary, a divine message, an objection by the visionary, and the giving of a sign. In the infancy narrative, the message was shaped in part by the christology of the early preaching now being applied to Jesus' conception.

2. Pre-Lucan Sources/Traditions. a. An annunciation similar to pre-Matthean *d*. The similarities between the two gospels on this item (amidst great dissimilarities on other items) is a reason for positing this as a once-separate element. Luke's annunciation pattern is even fuller than Matthew's, involving some elements of OT annunciations that commission divinely chosen figures like Moses (Exod 3:2–12) and Gideon (Judg 6:11–32). The added features reflect the Lucan use of the scene as also a call of Mary to be the first Christian disciple (see discussion in Legrand 1981: 90–96; Muñoz Iglesias 1984).

b. Tradition about John the Baptist, involving his priestly origins. (Luke is noteworthily accurate in his description of the temple courses of priestly service.) Some (like Fitzmyer *Luke I–IX* AB, 316, 320) posit a relatively fixed birth source from Baptist circles behind Luke 1:5–

25, 57–66. Indeed, this posited John the Baptist infancy narrative is often considered the pattern on which Luke constructed the story of Jesus' infancy, granted the clear parallelism between the two annunciations and the two accounts of birth. Others (Brown 1977: 266–69) think of some tradition about John the Baptist's family plus retroversion of John the Baptist material from the ministry (e.g., 1:15 compared with 7:28, 33; 1:42–45 compared with 11.27, 28), rather than a fixed source. The shaping of the annunciation of John the Baptist's birth may have been influenced by the already-circulating story of the annunciation of Jesus' birth.

c. The infancy narrative canticles discussed above, stemming from a Jewish-Christian group, perhaps from the Jerusalem community of temple-observant poor (*ᶜanawîm*), described with enthusiastic idealism in Acts 2:43–47. Scholars debate whether these canticles were originally composed in Semitic or in Greek (Brown 1986: 660–62).

d. Some traditions from Jesus' family about his birthplace, circumcision, and presentation. The extent and detail of such traditions are debated, depending in part on whether one thinks Mary was the ultimate source of Lucan information. The present writer judges that this cannot be shown and remains quite dubious, especially because of apparent inaccuracies about the census and Jewish customs.

e. A story of Jesus at age 12. Having the air of an appendage after the conclusion of 2:40, the narrative in 2:41–51 was probably once independent of the conception and infancy tradition. Read by itself, 2:47–50 gives no indication of what has preceded in Luke by way of the revelation of Jesus' divine identity. Probably this story is an example of a wider collection of boyhood-christology stories (see *Infancy Gospel of Thomas*), where the knowledge and power evident in the public ministry of Jesus appear in contexts of his youth as he worked miracles (on the Sabbath) and speaks with divine knowledge. This type of story was another way of demonstrating that Jesus did not become divine at the baptism; he was divine throughout his whole life, as could be seen in the first times he acted and spoke.

The infancy narratives of Matthew and Luke, once written, contributed to a wider efflorescence of infancy gospels, e.g., the *Protevangelium of James* and the *Arabic Gospel of the Infancy*. It is not always easy to determine the extent to which these subsequent infancy gospels draw only from the canonical narratives or from other oral traditions (however imaginative). See THOMAS, INFANCY GOSPEL OF.

Bibliography

Boslooper, T. 1962. *The Virgin Birth*. Philadelphia.

Brown, R. E. 1977. *The Birth of the Messiah*. Garden City, N.Y.

———. 1986. Gospel Infancy Narrative Research from 1976 to 1986. *CBQ* 48: 469–83, 661–80.

Farris, S. C. 1981. On Discerning Sources in Luke 1–2. Vol. 2. Pp. 201–37 in *Gospel Perspectives*, 2 vols., ed. R. T. France. Sheffield.

Legrand, L. 1981. *L'Annonce à Marie (Lc 1,25–38)*. LD 106. Paris.

Martin, E. L. 1980. *The Birth of Christ Recalculated*. 2d ed. Pasadena.

Muñoz Iglesias, S. 1984. El procedimiento literario del anuncio previo en la Biblia. *EstBib* 42: 21–70.

Soares Prabhu, G. M. 1976. *The Formula Quotations in the Infancy Narrative of Matthew*. AnBib 63. Rome.

Stendahl, K. 1964. Quis et Unde? Pp. 94–105 in *Judentum, Urchristentum, Kirche*, ed. W. Eltester. BZNW 26. Berlin.

———. 1968. *The School of St. Matthew*. 2d ed. Philadelphia.

Raymond E. Brown

INFANTRY. See MILITARY ORGANIZATION IN MESOPOTAMIA.

INGATHERING, FEAST OF. The Feast of Ingathering is the same as the Feast of Booths. See CALENDARS (ANCIENT ISRAELITE).

INGOTS. See COINAGE.

INHERITANCE (OT). See FAMILY.

INHERITANCE (NT). The Gk terms are *klēronomia*, "inheritance"; *klēronomein*, "to inherit"; *klēronomôs*, "heir"; *sugklēronomos*, "joint heir." In the NT the content of the terms can move all the way from a simple judicial concern for personal property (Luke 12:13) to a heavenly and imperishable inheritance beyond history (1 Pet 1:4). What is distinctive is the way NT writers relate their varied uses of inheritance language to Jesus Christ and to his followers.

A. Background

The uses of inheritance language in the OT vary widely within the context of the history of Israel. These contexts move from a concern for personal property to theological affirmations of Canaan as Israel's inheritance, of Israel as Yahweh's inheritance, and of Yahweh as Israel's inheritance.

Some later Jewish writings can view the Law as Israel's inheritance (e.g., Sir 24:23; *1 En.* 99:14). Some speak of inheriting life or eternal life (e.g., *Pss. Sol.* 14:7; *1 En.* 40:9; cf. *2 En.* 50:2; *2 Bar.* 44:13). Philo can see inheritance as a mystical unity with God (in *Heres*). This variety shows how different historical contexts produce a rich diversity in understandings of inheritance in the historical background to the NT.

B. Paul

Turning to the oldest NT writings, we find that Paul relates inheritance language to the covenant promise to Abraham (Gal 3:18; 4:30; Rom 4:13–14) and sees that promise fulfilled in Jesus Christ. However, unlike the OT, he never refers to the land of Canaan as Abraham's inheritance. For Paul, those with faith in Jesus Christ are Abraham's true heirs (Gal 3:29). Through God's gift, the gift of a new relationship in Christ, they are adopted (cf. Gal 4:5; Rom 8:15) as God's sons and heirs (Gal 4:7) and "fellow heirs with Christ" (Rom 8:17). Though Paul uses a legal understanding of inheritance that sees minor children as heirs (Gal 4:1), it is with Christ's coming that they enter into their inheritance. As the offspring of Abraham (Gal 3:16), Christ is the heir, but as the fulfilled promise of blessing to Abraham (Gal 3:14), he also is the inheritance.

Thus as heir and inheritance, he becomes both the means to and the content of the new life and of new relationships which believers have through their baptism into Christ (Gal 3:26–29).

Paul also can use the verb "inherit" futuristically regarding those who will not inherit the kingdom (1 Cor 6:9–10; Gal 5:21; cf. also the future use of inheritance language in the probable Paulinists: Col 3:24; Eph 5:5; Titus 3:7), as well as concerning the resurrection in which "flesh and blood cannot inherit the kingdom of God" (1 Cor 15:50). Thus, God's reign or kingdom is the final realization of that inheritance already inaugurated with the historical coming of Christ.

C. Ephesians

This author emphasizes a future-oriented inheritance (Eph 1:14, 18; cf. 5:5), which is the cosmic unity of all things in Christ (cf. Eph 1:9–10). Already however, the Holy Spirit is the "down payment" (*arrabōn;* cf. 2 Cor 1:22; 5:5) that anticipates the future. As in Paul, Christ is indeed the means to that inheritance; but unlike Paul, the emphasis does not fall on Christ as already its promised fulfillment. Given the writer's concern for Church unity, Ephesians refers to the gentiles as "fellow heirs" (Eph 3:6) and understands the unity of Jews and gentiles in the Church as already showing (cf. 3:4–6) and pointing to (cf. 3:10) the ultimate inheritance of cosmic unity through God's saving deed in Christ.

D. The Synoptic Gospels and Acts

In the story of the rich man who comes to Jesus, Matthew, Mark, and Luke all refer at some point to inheriting eternal life (Matt 19:29; Mark 10:17; Luke 18:18). Matthew, however, gives "inherit" a pronounced futuristic emphasis. Unlike Mark and Luke, he uses the term only after the story itself, relating it to the "new world" and the coming of the Son of man (Matt 19:28; cf. Dan 7:13; *1 En* 71:14–17). Matthew gives this future emphasis further support by using such phrases as "shall inherit the earth" (Matt 5:5; cf. Ps 37:11; *1 En.* 5:7b) and "inherit the kingdom" (Matt 25:34; cf. *2 En.* 9:1; Jas 2:5 strikes a similar note).

All three writers use "heir" and "inheritance" with special christological significance in the allegorized parable of the wicked tenants (Matt 21:38; Mark 12:7; Luke 20:14). The early Church Fathers understood Jesus as Son and heir, and with his death they viewed the inheritance (i.e., the vineyard; cf. Isaiah 5) as passing to them. Matthew sees the vineyard as God's kingdom (Matt 21:43), and with the death of God's Son and heir this inheritance now becomes the trust of those "producing the fruits of it."

In Acts, Luke denies any "inheritance" of land to Abraham, though it is promised to him and his descendants (Acts 7:5) and its historic connection to Canaan affirmed (13:19). Luke finally interprets the inheritance as given to "all those who are sanctified" (20:32), i.e., to the Church.

E. Hebrews

This writer depicts Christ as the Son and heir of all things (Heb 1:2; cf. 1:4 where *keklēronomēken* should be translated "inherited"). As high priest and mediator of a new covenant, Christ is the means to "the promised eternal inheritance" (9:15; cf. Syr. Enoch 10:6; 55:2; in Heb 1:14 *klēronomein* should be translated "inherit") for those who (6:12) through faith and patience "inherit the promises." The content of this promised inheritance is the heavenly city (11:8–10).

Hebrews relates inheritance language to Abraham (6:12, 17; 11:9; note also references to Noah and Esau in 11:7; 12:17), but his inheritance is not the land of Canaan; it is the city "whose builder and maker is God" (11:10).

Hebrews also includes a judicial perspective. Only through the death of the eschatological (cf. 1:2) Son and heir does the will or covenant *(diathēkē)* take effect (9:15–17). Thus, the death of Jesus becomes the covenantal means for persons to receive the promised eternal inheritance of the heavenly city.

F. 1 Peter

This writer also gives to inheritance a content that is beyond human history, "an inheritance which is imperishable, undefiled, and unfading, kept in heaven for you" (1 Pet 1:4). The crucial means to this "living hope" is the resurrection of Jesus Christ from the dead (1:3). Thus, the event of Jesus' resurrection makes the hope of future resurrection a present reality and becomes the basis for the future imperishable inheritance (cf. other uses of inheritance language in 3:7, 9; in the latter, *klēronomēsēte* should be translated "may inherit").

G. Conclusion

The theological use of inheritance language in the NT exhibits a tension between the present and the future. For Paul, Jesus Christ already fulfills the inheritance promised to Abraham and makes persons of faith heirs of God and joint heirs with Christ, even though there remains a kingdom to inherit in the future. Ephesians points to a future inheritance that is the cosmic unity of all things in Christ, while simultaneously Jews and gentiles already are joint heirs in the Church, and their unity witnesses already to that ultimate unity. The Synoptics speak futuristically of inheriting eternal life, with Matthew especially giving inheritance language a strong eschatological emphasis. For all synoptic writers, Jesus is the heir of the vineyard inheritance, now understood as the reign or kingdom of God. The reign of God is both present and future; it calls for present faithfulness, but its full realization is in the future. Unlike the other synoptic writers, Luke sees this realization as occurring already within the Church. For Hebrews, the content of the inheritance is the future heavenly city of God, and it is by the covenantal death of Jesus, the heir of all things, that this inheritance will be effected. In 1 Peter, the content also is future, "an inheritance . . . kept in heaven for you," a "living hope" made effective by the resurrection of Jesus Christ from the dead (cf. Rev 21:7 for an additional future reference to inheritance).

Bibliography

Denton, D. R. 1982. Inheritance in Paul and Ephesians. *EvQ* 54: 157–62.

Hammer, P. L. 1958. The Understanding of Inheritance *(klēronomia)* in the New Testament. Diss. Heidelberg.

———. 1960. A Comparison of *Klēronomia* in Paul and Ephesians. *JBL* 79: 267–72.

Hester, J. D. 1967. The "Heir and Heilsgeschichte: A Study of Galatians 4:1ff. Pp. 118–25 in *OIKONOMIA, Heilsgeschichte als Thema der Theologie,* ed. F. Christ. Hamburg-Bergstadt.

———. 1968. *Paul's Concept of Inheritance. SJT,* Occasional Paper No. 14. Edinburgh.

Lyall, F. 1981. Legal Metaphors in the Epistles. *TynBul* 32: 90–95.

PAUL L. HAMMER

INK. See WRITING AND WRITING MATERIALS.

INQUIRE OF GOD. The process of consulting the deity on some matter of individual and/or communal importance, generally through the offices of an intermediary. The Hebrew Scriptures use, with varying frequencies, three distinct verbs to designate the process, each referring to a somewhat different inquiry procedure. Least frequent in this connection is the term *biqqēš.* In Exod 33:7, it denotes the Israelites' asking for Yahweh's guidance through the mediation of Moses at a particular site, i.e., the "Tent of Meeting" outside the camp during the desert period. The subject matter of their inquiries is not specified. The context does, however, allude to the communication process between Yahweh and the mediator Moses: Yahweh, present in the "pillar of cloud" at the tent door, speaks "face to face" with Moses (Exod 33:9, 11).

Far more common as a designation for the inquiry process is the verb *šāʾal* (Num 27:21; 1 Sam 10:22; 14:37; 22:10, 13, 15; 23:2, 4; 28:6; 30:8; 2 Sam 2:1; 5:19 [= 1 Chr 14:10], 5:23 [= 1 Chr 14:14]; cf. Exod 28:30; 1 Sam 14:41). All but the first of these passages concern events of the early monarchical period, under Saul and David. From a piecing together of the indications provided by the texts, an approximate, composite picture of the particular sort of "inquiry" they envisage emerges: An Israelite politico-military leader—or on occasion the people as a whole (1 Sam 10:22)—put one or more *yes* or *no* questions to Yahweh. The mediator of Yahweh's response thereto is a priest, whose role is to manipulate—in some unspecified way—the sacred dice known as the Urim and the Thummim (1 Sam 14:41), one of which represented a positive answer, the other a negative one. The officiating priest carried these dice in a sort of pouch called the ephod (Exod 28:30). The inquiry might take place at a sanctuary (e.g., 1 Sam 22:10), but more often it transpired in the open air, e.g., in a military camp. Questions posed concerned significant projected political or military measures about whose outcome the inquirer especially felt the need of divine assurances. Omission of the procedure prior to such initiatives is denounced as culpable presumption (Josh 9:14; Isa 30:2). Yahweh remains free, however, presumably by causing the repeated rolls of the dice to produce inconsistent results, not to answer the inquiry in a particular case (1 Sam 14:37; 28:6). In any event, there is no mention of this particular form of inquiry being carried out subsequent to David's definitive triumph over the Philistines (2 Sam 5:17–25). This fact likely reflects the demand of later times for something more in the say of divine guidance/assurance than a simple *yes* or *no* answer could provide. There is, however, a NT echo of the practice in the account of Matthias' being selected to succeed Judas as apostle by means of lot-casting in Acts 1:26. Finally, the OT uses the verb *šāʾal* also in reference to an inquiry of some deity, whether by Israelites or non-Israelites, involving other (and illegitimate) intermediaries and/or devices (Deut 18:11; 1 Chr 10:13; Ezek 21:23; Hos 4:12).

The most frequent of the OT's three verbs for designating an inquiring of God is *dāraš* (Gen 25:22; Exod 18:15; 1 Sam 9:9; 1 Kgs 14:5; 22:5 [= 2 Chr 18:4], 7 [= 2 Chr 18:6]; 2 Kgs 3:11; 8:8; 22:13 [= 2 Chr 34:21]; Jer 21:2; 37:7; Ezek 14:3; 20:1–3). The inquirer is usually the Israelite king who, however, often puts his question indirectly, through a delegation dispatched by him. On occasion, the inquiry proceeds from other categories of persons: Rebekah (Gen 25:22), Moses (Exod 18:15), the (pagan) Syrian king Benhadad (2 Kgs 8:8), and the Jewish elders (Ezek 14:3; 20:1–3). The intermediary figure in these texts is, typically, not a priest but a prophet/seer (1 Sam 9:9), e.g., Ahijah (1 Kgs 14:5), Micaiah (1 Kgs 22:7), Elisha (2 Kgs 3:11; 8:8), Huldah (2 Kgs 22:13), Jeremiah, and Ezekiel. The inquiry takes place in a battlefield setting (e.g., 1 Kings 22; 2 Kings 3) or at the prophet's place of residence (e.g., 1 Kings 14; 2 Kings 22); it is never explicitly said to occur at a sanctuary. The questions addressed to Yahweh through the prophets cover a somewhat wider range than is the case in the *šāʾal*-type inquiry: legal disputes (Exod 18:15), lost property (1 Sam 9:6–9), outcome of a pregnancy (Gen 25:22) or sickness (1 Kgs 14:5; 2 Kgs 8:8), the upshot of a military crisis (1 Kgs 22:5, 7; 2 Kgs 3:11; Jer 21:2; 37:7), and the significance of a newly discovered book (2 Kgs 22:13). Unlike the priest in the foregoing texts, the prophetic intermediary in these passages is cited as being offered remuneration for his services on several occasions (1 Sam 9:7; 1 Kgs 14:3; 2 Kgs 8:9). Very little is recounted concerning the actual process by which the prophet relays the inquirer's question to Yahweh and receives the latter's reply—although see 2 Kgs 3:15, where Elisha prepares himself for a divine communication by having a minstrel play. In any case, Yahweh's answer as mediated by the prophet takes the form of a longer or shorter first-person divine speech which, depending on its content, constitutes an oracle of either salvation or doom. The latter type predominates. In terms of their historical referents, those passages cover an extended period, from patriarchal times down to shortly before the Exile. The greater expansiveness of the divine response which it allowed helps explain the perdurableness of the *dāraš* inquiry and its supplanting of the *šāʾal* type. Eventually, however, this form of inquiry also disappeared with the gradual tapering off of its prophetic practitioners in the postexilic period. Finally, two further similarities between the *dāraš* and *šāʾal* inquiries can be noted. Like the latter, the former term can also designate an illegitimate "inquiry," i.e., one directed to a divinity other than Yahweh (2 Kgs 1:2ff.: Ahaziah inquires of Baal-zebub), or utilizing a reprobate mantic figure (1 Sam 28:7: Saul inquires of a medium). Similarly, Yahweh is free in both forms of inquiry to withhold an answer to the questions posed (see Ezek 14:3; 20:1–3—*dāraš*).

By way of conclusion to this discussion, it should be pointed out that in the OT two of the above terms, i.e., *biqqēš* and *dāraš,* undergo an evaluation in which they progress from signifying a one-time "consulting" of Yahweh about a particular matter to designating a habitual stance of "seeking" God in fidelity and obedience. This development is observable in the prophetic writings (see e.g., Isa 65:1, 10; Hos 10:12; Amos 5:4, 6; Zeph 1:6; 2:3), and especially in Chronicles (see e.g., 1 Chr 22:19, etc.). It can likewise be noted in the NT's use of the term *zēteō*, "seek" (see e.g., Matt 6:32f.; 7:7ff.; Rom 10:20 = Isa 65:1; Gal 2:17; Col 3:1).

Bibliography

Begg, C. T. 1982. "Seeking Yahweh" and the Purpose of Chronicles. *LS* 9: 128–41.

Bonora, A., et al. 1980. *Quaere Deum.* Atti della XXV Settimana Biblica. Brescia.

Garcia de la Fuente, O. 1971. *La busqueda de Dios en el Antiguo Testamento.* Madrid.

Hunter, A. V. 1982. *Seek the Lord! A Study of the Meaning and Function of the Exhortations in Amos, Hosea, Isaiah, Micah and Zephaniah.* Baltimore.

Merino, L. D. 1982. Il vocabolario relativo alla'Ricerca di Dio' nell' Antico Testamento. *BeO* 24: 81–96, 129–45.

Turbessi, G. 1980. *Cercare Dio nell'ebraismo, nel mondo greco, nella patristica.* Rome.

Westermann, C. 1960. Die Begriffe für Fragen und Suchen im Alten Testament. *KD* 6: 2–30.

CHRISTOPHER T. BEGG

INSCRIPTIONS, SAFAITIC. The name "Safaitic" is conventionally given to a group of inscriptions in an ancient N Arabian language, expressed in a variety of the S Semitic script, written by the ancient bedouin and semi-nomads of the Syro-Arabian desert. The name is derived from the *Ṣafâ*, an area of basalt desert SE of Damascus, near which they were first discovered in 1857. The inscriptions have since been found over a wide area of S Syria, Jordan, and N Saudi Arabia, with isolated examples as far afield as Palmyra, Hâʾil, the Wadi Ḥaurân in W Iraq, and the Lebanon. However, the largest concentration appears to be in the *ḥarra*, or basalt desert, stretching S and E from the Jebal Druze. Some 14,000 have been published so far, but these represent the fruits of relatively few expeditions, and there are clearly scores of thousands of texts still awaiting discovery. With the exception of one large (Littmann 1943) and several small collections, all the Safaitic inscriptions found before 1950 were brought together in that year in Part 5 of the *Corpus Inscriptionum Semiticarum* (CIS), edited by G. Ryckmans. However, several major collections have appeared since (see the bibliography at the end of this article).

Work on the definitive decipherment of the script was begun by J. Halévy in 1877, refined by F. Praetorius in 1882–83, and completed in 1901 by E. Littmann, who was the first to recognize that the alphabet consisted of 28 letters, rather than 23 (the equivalents of the 22 letters of the Phoenician alphabet, plus *ḥ*), as had previously been thought.

A. Script

While it was clear from the beginning that the script was in some way related to that of the S Arabian and other N Arabian (Dedanite, Lihyanite, Thamudic) inscriptions (see Fig. INS.01), the exact details of this relationship have remained in dispute. The reasons for this are as follows. First, there is virtually no secure dating evidence for any of the types of N Arabian inscriptions, and it is therefore impossible to establish either an internal chronology for these texts or their chronological relationship to the S Arabian inscriptions. Second, the vast majority of N Arabian inscriptions are known only from hand-copies, in almost all of which scant attention has been paid to the exact shape of the letters. Thus, features taken as indicating development may in fact be merely copyists' errors. Finally, the letter-forms of monumental S Arabian and those of the Safaitic and Thamudic graffiti are in no way comparable, since the shapes in each have developed under completely different pressures and for quite distinct purposes. Thus, the view, which is implicit in many discussions of these texts, that there was an evolution from S Arabian, via Dedanite and the various script-types classed as "Thamudic," ending with Safaitic, in which each script developed out of its predecessor, can only be highly speculative and, on present evidence, seems unlikely to represent the true picture.

This view lies behind the term "Thamudic-Safaitic" used by H. Grimme (1929: 12; 17; 55) and E. Littmann (1940: 97) to describe two different types of text, which they thought contained a mixture of Thamudic and Safaitic letter-forms, and therefore considered early. However, some of Littmann's examples are in fact pure Thamudic B (see Fig. INS.01:4), and the letter-forms in the rest, and in Grimme's texts, are no different from those occurring in inscriptions which both scholars considered pure Safaitic.

The most striking variety of Safaitic is the so-called "square script" (see Fig. INS.01:1; Fig. INS.02:B) in which the letters are given a neat angular appearance. This has led a number of scholars to regard these letter-forms as more "monumental" than other types and, by a curious series of nonsequiturs, as therefore closer to S Arabian, and hence "the older type of Safaitic." In fact, it will be clear from Fig. INS.01 that it is merely the elegant appearance that invites comparison with monumental S Arabian, not the letter-forms themselves, which are in all important features identical to the common Safaitic shapes. There is also no evidence that it was a "monumental script," since virtually all the texts in which it is used are graffiti, and hardly any of the handful of inscriptions which could be called "monumental" employ it. It would appear to be contemporary with other Safaitic letter-forms, since there are square script and common script texts by the same authors.

B. South Safaitic

E. A. Knauf has argued that the style and onomastic content of many of the most northerly Thamudic texts (known as "Thamudic E" or "Tabuki Thamudic" [see Fig. INS.02:C]) have more in common with Safaitic than with other forms of Thamudic. He therefore suggested reclas-

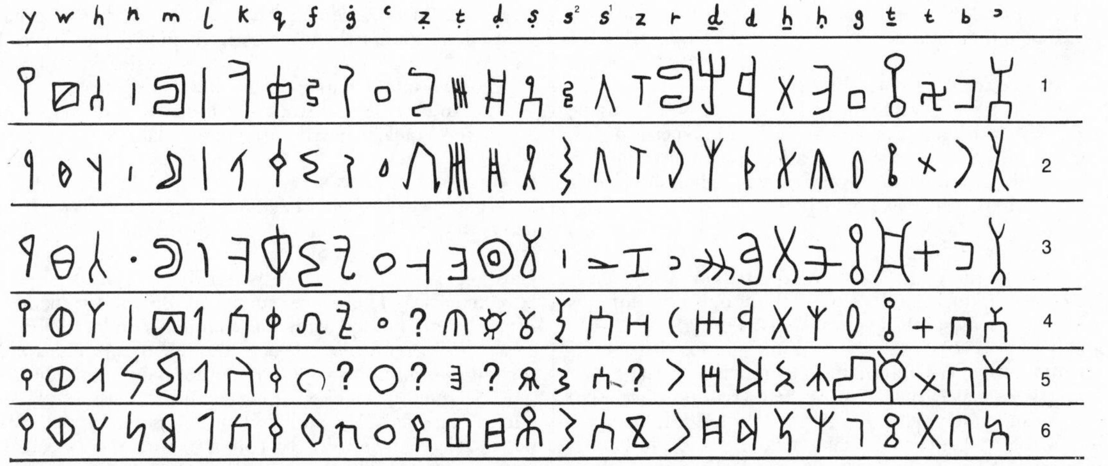

INS.01. Comparative chart of South Semitic alphabetic scripts. *1,* Safaitic "square script"; *2,* Safaitic; *3,* South Safaitic/Thamudic E; *4,* Thamudic B; *5,* Dedanite; *6,* Northern Minaic. All letters have been placed as if in a text reading right to left. The stance and shape of many letters in Safaitic and Thamudic may vary considerably. *(Courtesy of M. C. A. Macdonald)*

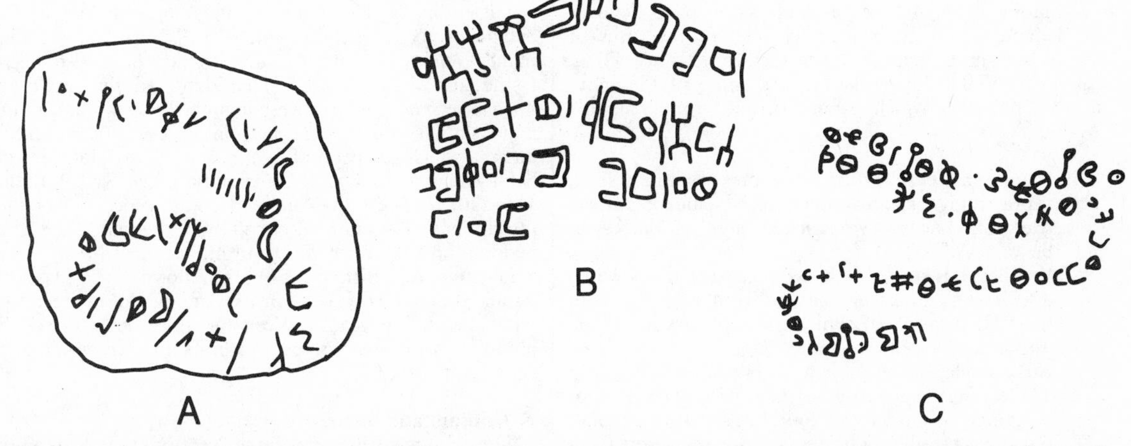

INS.02. Safaitic and Thamudic Inscriptions. *A,* a Safaitic inscription: starting in the top lefthand corner, it curves down and round upon itself. It reads: *l ʿty bn wqsʾ bn sʾlm w mlḥ f h lt sʾlm w ġnyt w mḥlt l ḏ yʿwr.* "By ʿty son of Wqsʾ son of Sʾlm. And he traded in salt. And so, O Lt, [grant] security and riches, and misfortune to whoever obliterates [the inscription]" (WH 24). Note the typical sequence of name–genealogy–statement–invocation–curse. The magic sign of 7 lines (see Littmann 1940: 120) is very common as is the cartouche enclosing the text.

B, a text in the Safaitic "square script": starting in the top right-hand corner and running boustrophedon, it reads: *l g̱rm bn dmṣy ḏʾl ʿmrt w ndm ʿl ʾbh w ʿl grm bn ʿqrb bn ʿm,* "By Grm son of Dmṣy of the tribe of ʿmrt. And he grieved for his father and for Grm son of ʿqrb son of ʿm" (Macdonald 1980: no. 36).

C, a South Safaitic/Thamudic E inscription: starting at the bottom and running upward boustrophedon. Note the variant forms of *ṯ, d,* and *ḏ.* It reads: *l km bn gmhr w ḏkrt lt ġt w ḥbk wʿrb w bkr w hlʾ w qnfd w wd w ḥmlg w qnfd w gmʿ,* "By Km son of Gmhr. And may Lt remember . . ." followed by a list of names (Harding and Littmann 1952: no. 58). The expression *ḏkrt lt* is characteristic of this type of text. *(Redrawn by M. C. A. Macdonald,* A, *from Winnett and Harding 1978: 659, pl. 1, no. 24;* B, *from Macdonald 1980: 337, pl. CXI, no. 36;* C, *from Harding and Littmann 1952: pl. IV, no. 58)*

sifying these inscriptions as "South Safaitic," while retaining the term "Tabuki Thamudic" for those texts in the same script but with a "non-Safaitic" content (1983: 589). At the same time, he demonstrated that South Safaitic and Tabuki Thamudic shared marked peculiarities of script and orthography which clearly distinguish them from other forms of Safaitic and Thamudic. Most notable among these was the use of the Safaitic *ṯ*-sign to represent etymological /g/. Following this, G. M. H. King (1988) showed that two other signs in this script had unexpected values; viz. the Safaitic *ḍ*-sign represented /t/ and a sign consisting of two concentric circles /d/ (see Fig. INS.01:3).

The majority of inscriptions of this type are to be found in S Jordan and N Saudi Arabia (e.g., most of those in Harding and Littmann 1952).

C. Abecedaries

Two ABCs have been found so far, one for South Safaitic arranged, with some exceptions, in the Phoenician order, and the other, in the common Safaitic script, arranged in a hitherto unknown order, apparently based on similarities of letter-shape (see Macdonald 1986).

D. Language

The most thorough survey of the Safaitic language is still that of Littmann (1943: 12–24), though for additions and corrections see Winnett and Harding (1978: 12–15) and Clark (1979: 112–24); and for an excellent brief account, Müller (1980). Safaitic is a branch of the language group known as early North Arabian (Frühnordarabisch) and is thus closely related to Arabic. Within this group, it is one of a number of dialects (along with Dedanite, Lihyanite, "Thamudic," and Hasaitic) distinguished by their use of *h-*, rather than *ʾal-*, for the definite article. The alphabet consists of 28 letters which, ethymologically at least, represent the same phonemes as those of Standard Arabic. The orthography is severely consonantal, leaving all vowels, diphthongs, and doubled letters unmarked (on possible exceptions, see Müller 1980: 68–69). Writing is continuous, with neither word-dividers nor spaces between words, and the direction depends solely on the whim of the author and the nature of the surface he is inscribing. See Fig. INS.02. The following are some of the more notable points in which Safaitic differs from Standard Arabic.

1. s^1 and s^2 are clearly still in Beeston's (1962) Phase II, representing [ʃ] and a lateralized sibilant respectively, and have not yet reached their Standard Arabic values of [s] and [ʃ].
2. Vowelless *n* is sporadically assimilated in many words (e.g., *bt*/*bnt*, "daughter," *m*/*mn*, "from") but always in the VIII form of *nẓr*, which thus appears as *ṭzr:* "he was on the look-out, he waited."
3. No examples of the X form have yet been identified.
4. The endings represented by *tâʾ marbûṭa* in later Arabic appear as *-t* in all positions, but see Müller (1980: 69) for a possible indication of the transition from *-at* to *-ah*.
5. Etymological *-y* is found in such words as *my*, "water," and *sʾmy*, "sky," where Standard Arabic has *-âʾ*.
6. The third radical is usually represented in verbs tertiae *w* and *y* suggesting that they were formed on the pattern of the strong verb, though there are apparent expectations (e.g., s^2t as against s^2ty, "to winter").
7. The relative pronoun is *ḏ* and the vocative particle *h-*.
8. Many of the words which lie at the heart of the Safaitic authors' way of life are better explained from NW Semitic cognates than from later Arabic. Thus *mdbr* (Heb *midbār*, Aram *madbĕrāʾ*), "open steppe, desert," as opposed to *ḥrt* (Ar *ḥarra*), the "basalt desert"; ms^1rt (Aram *mašrîtāʾ*), "encampment"; *nḫl* (Heb *naḥal*, Aram *naḥălāʾ*), "valley," as against Ar *naḫl*, "palm," *dd* (Heb *dôd*, Aram *dôdāʾ*), "paternal uncle," rather than Ar *ʿamm*, which in Safaitic is used for "grandfather." It is unlikely that these are words loaned into Safaitic; rather, they must represent part of an early lexical stock which has been displaced in later Arabic by words from other dialects.

E. Names

No complete study has been made of the names in these texts, though Littmann (1943: xxiv–xxviii) and Müller (1980: 72–73) have provided very useful discussions, and Harding (1971) gives an indispensable index with comparative material. There are numerous theophoric names, usually compounded with the common Semitic deity *ʾIl* (*ʿbdʾl*, *ʿbdl*) or *Lh* (*tmlh*, s^1*ʿdlh*), though these deities are seldom found in prayers. On the other hand, those deities most frequently invoked appear much more rarely in names (e.g., *Lt*, Ds^2r, and *Rḍw*/*y*); and some, apparently not at all (e.g., S^2*ʿhqm*). In common with the Nabatean texts of Sinai, Safaitic has a number of names prefixed by *bn-* (in Nabatean, *ʾbn*), where the name is never that of the father, when that can be established, e.g., *bnkbr bn mḥnn* (Winnett and Harding 1978: No. 1194). A number of names have the *-w* ending characteristic of Nabatean (e.g., *ḥyw*, *ʿbdw*), though all of them also occur without the *-w*. Müller (1980: 73) has suggested that the Aramaic emphatic ending *-ʾ* may occur on some names, parallel to the Safaitic prefixed article *h-* (e.g., *ʿbdʾ* beside *hʿbd*). The Latin names *Titus* (tts^1) and *Claudius* (*ʾqlds*^{1}) have also been found, and Müller (1980: 73) has identified *ʾftnyʾ* as Greek *Aphthonios*. *Tlmy* could represent either *Ptolemy* or a Semitic name similar to that of *Talmay*, king of *Gĕšûr* (2 Sam 3:3), an area which has been placed in or near the Ḥaurân (on Safaitic names in Greek transcription, see Sartre 1985: 161–276). At the same time as he was recording Safaitic inscriptions, Littmann also collected the names of the bedouin and Druze of the Ḥaurân, and noted that many Safaitic names, which are rare or unknown in the Classical Arabic onomasticon, were in use among the modern inhabitants of the area. However, far more work is needed before conclusions can be drawn from this apparently significant correlation.

F. Content and Structure

The vast majority of Safaitic inscriptions are graffiti. They are thus a form of self-expression rather than communication. They record the author's name and what he was doing or what he felt. There are *cris de coeur*, boasts and prayers, but no memoranda, messages, history, or literature. It seems probable that most were written as a way of passing the time while the authors were pasturing their herds or on the lookout either for enemies or for game, because their drawings show them to have been keen hunters.

Almost all the texts are expressed in a series of formulaic constructions (Petráček 1973; Voigt 1980). All but a handful of short prayers are introduced by the preposition *l* (the *lâm auctoris*), followed by the author's name and usually that of his father, with, very often, a more or less lengthy genealogy. Many authors also indicate the social group to which they belong, most commonly by placing *ḏʾl* plus the name of the group at the end of the genealogy. *D̲ʾl* is commonly translated "of the tribe of," but *ʾl* (Ar *ʾâl*) appears to have been used for all social groups from the family to the tribal confederation. Alternatively, the *nisba* form can be used, e.g., *h-ḍf-y,* "the Ḍaifite" (the vocalization is purely conventional), or the genealogy may be taken back to the eponymous ancestor of the group (Harding 1969: 13, No. 4). Many texts then continue with descriptions of the author's activities. Thus, they speak of seasonal migrations *(ʾs²rq)* E to the open steppe beyond the basalt, and of returning, often to the same spot *(h dr)* year after year *(ʿm f ʿm)* to spend the winter *(s²ty)* or the spring *(dt̲ʾ)*. They mention encampments *(ms¹rt)* and watering places *(wrd, brkt),* of pasturing their herds of camels *(ʾbl),* goats *(mʿzy),* and sheep *(ḏʾn)* and of shearing them *(qṣṣ)*. They go on raids (*ġzz,* a dialectical form of Ar *ġazâ*) and pray for booty *(ġnmt)*. The texts also abound with words of longing *(ts²wq)* and grief (*wgm, wlh, ndm, bʾs¹mẓll,* etc.), the distinct nuances of which are much disputed. Some follow the discovery of a relative's inscription (e.g., *w wgd ʾt̲r ʾbh f ngʿ,* "and he found his father's inscription [literally "traces"] and so he was sad"), a sequence reminiscent of the conventional opening passage of the pre-Islamic Arabic odes. Above all, however, these words occur in texts connected with the burial of the dead. Most corpses were probably buried, as they are today, in a simple grave covered with stones to keep off wild animals. However, over the graves of some men and women, presumably those of status, large cairns were erected. To such a cairn *(rgm),* the mourners brought stones inscribed with their names, their relationship to the deceased, and the fact that they were mourning *(wgm)* and/or building *(bny)* the cairn for him or her (Harding 1953).

The statement is often followed by a prayer of the form *f h lt* . . . ("and so, O Lt . . .") with a request, e.g., *s¹lm,* "security," *ġnmt,* "booty"; *rwḥ,* "relief"; *t̲ʾr,* "revenge," etc.; and the text may be completed with curses on those who would deface the inscription and blessings on those who leave it intact. Thus, the typical Safaitic inscriptions would consist of some, or all, of these elements, usually, but not always, in this order: *l N ± genealogy ± tribal marker ± statement ± invocation ± curse/blessing*. See Fig. INS.02: A–B.

We catch only fragmentary glimpses of the relations of the Safaitic authors with their neighbors. Several say that they were escaping from the Romans, or Byzantines *(nfr mn rm);* others seem to have been aware of, and some involved in, a war of the Nabateans *(ḥrb nbṭ)* and a rebellion by them against the Romans *(mrd nbṭ ʿl ʾl rm)*. Winnett (1973) has suggested that some Safaitic tribes were caught up in an unsuccessful revolt by a son of the Nabatean governor of Ḥegra (Medâʾin Ṣâliḥ) in ca. A.D. 71, but this is by no means certain. One or more Persian *(md̲y)* invasions of the Ḥaurân are mentioned, and there are enigmatic references to the Jews *(yhd)*. There are also some less easily identifiable peoples, e.g., those of *Rhy* (variously identified as Edessa, Ḥâʾil, and a subtribe of *Madḥiğ*), the *ʾhl khl* (possibly Qariyat al-Faw in central Arabia, the ancient name of which was *Qariyat D̲ât Kahl*) and *Ḥwlt* (possibly one of the places called *Ḥăwîlâ* in the OT).

G. Dating

The Safaitic texts are conventionally dated between the 1st century B.C. and the 4th century A.D., but the grounds for this are extremely insecure. A handful of texts can be assigned to precise dates in the 1st, 2d, and 3d centuries A.D., and several others which mention the Nabateans and Romans must fall within this period, but there is no clue as to the date of the vast majority. A number of them are dated by events of local importance (e.g., *snt ḥl d̲ʾl ḍf lg,* "the year members of the tribe of Ḍf camped in the Leğâ, Winnett and Harding 1978: 1025), but unfortunately none of these can be reconciled with the known historical record. Even such references as *snt mrdt nbṭ ʿl ʾl rm,* "the year the Nabateans rebelled against the people of Rome" (Winnett and Harding 1978: 2815) are difficult to relate to known events and are the source of much disagreement. There is no indication as to when the art of writing first reached these tribes, or when it disappeared. However, there is no trace of either Christianity or Islam in these texts, and the early Islamic historians have no recollection of these tribes or their script; nor the grammarians of their dialect. Thus, it would seem probable that the use of Safaitic must have ceased some considerable time before the rise of Islam for the memory of it to have been so effectively erased.

H. Religion

Grimme (1929: 24–30) believed that all Safaitic texts were of a religious nature. However, this position was based on such strained interpretations of the evidence that it has attracted no support (see Littmann 1940: 103–4). In fact, we know frustratingly little of Safaitic religion. Although there are some apparent references to religious practices (*d̲bḥ,* "sacrifice"; *ḥg,* "pilgrimage"; and possibly *ʿd,* "festival" (see Winnett and Harding 1978: 31–32), and a great many prayers addressed to a number of deities, they are all expressed in a limited range of formulae and are generally uninformative. Most of the deities invoked in Safaitic are also known from the texts of the settled peoples (see NABATEANS; PALMYRA) and some from classical writers. However, the information derived from these different sources is not always reconcilable. The two deities most often invoked in Safaitic are *Rḍw* (or *Rḍy*) and *Lt* (or *ʾlt*). *Rḍw/y* has been identified with Herodotus' *Orotal(t)* and the Jawfian deity *Ruldaiu* mentioned in the annals of Esarhaddon, as well as the Palmyrene *ʾArṣû* (Milik 1972: 49). The Safaitic texts give no clue as to the nature of this, or any other, deity since identical requests are made of all of them. The variation in spelling has suggested to some a pair of deities, male and female, representing the morning and evening star (Littmann 1940: 107). However, even this cannot be demonstrated from the texts, because the prayers are all in the form either of nouns (with a verb understood) or verbs in the imperative, in which the vowels marking masculine and feminine are not shown. Others (e.g., Dussaud 1955: 142–43) base a claim that both forms refer to the same, feminine, deity on a number of Safaitic drawings of a female figure with arms raised to her flowing hair. However, there is no reason to connect these drawings with *Rḍw/y,* and when they are identified in accompanying texts it is as *ġlmt,* "girl," or *qnt,* "female singer." On the other hand, Starcky (*DBSup* 6: 990–91) has argued strongly that *Rḍw/y* is male and is the deity behind the Nabatean divine epithet *Dushara*. A male *Rḍw/y* would certainly fit better with the known sex of *Orotal(t)* and

ʾArṣû, though variations in the sex of Semitic deities are, of course, well known.

The deity most frequently invoked in Safaitic is *Lt* or *ʾlt.* A third form, *hʾlt,* is also found, but so far only in theophoric names *(tmhʾlt),* where it parallels *hnʾlt* in Lihyanite and Hasaitic names. The exact relationship between the three Safaitic forms has yet to be satisfactorily clarified. Certainly *Lt* occurs over six times more often than *ʾlt;* and in texts such as CIS V 97 both forms are used, though in successive invocations. It is thus by no means certain that the three forms represented the same deity in the minds of the Safaitic authors. Again, the texts give no clue as to her nature. Whereas *Rḏw/y* is rarely found in multiple invocations, *Lt/ʾlt* is commonly associated with other deities in prayers.

The worship of the two other "Daughters of Allâh" (Qurʾân 53:19–21; 16:57), *Manât* and *al-ʿUzzâ* (in Safaitic *h-ʿzy*), is attested only in occasional theophoric names. The divine name represented in later Arabic by *Allâh* is also found in Safaitic in three forms, parallel to those of *Lt;* thus *Lh, ʾlh,* and *hʾlh.* All three forms occur both in theophoric names, where they are very common, and in prayers, where they are much rarer. The reasons for this uneven distribution are not entirely clear, but it is possible that while *Lt/ʾlt* had become a divine *name, Lh/ʾlh* (and possibly *ʿl/l*) was still regarded as the common name for "god" and could therefore be used with reference to any divinity in a theophoric compound. The situation is paralleled in Nabatean, where *-ʾl* and *-ʾlhy* are common elements in names, although there are no prayers or other references to them. The prayers to *Lh/ʾlh/hʾlh* in Safaitic are no different from those addressed to other deities, and he is often "associated with" other divinities in multiple invocations. Thus, the use of this divine name or epithet cannot be taken as an indication of monotheism.

The principal deity of the Nabateans, *Dushara,* also receives a considerable number of prayers from Safaitic devotees, most often in association with *Lt.* In the N, the name is usually spelled *ds*^{2}*r,* suggesting that it reached these authors via Aramaic. But in the texts from S Jordan, the etymologically correct form *ḏs*^{2}*ry* (equivalent to Ar *ḏû-Šarâ*) is more common. Another deity whose name occurs in Safaitic in its Aramaic form is *Bʿlsʾmn, Baʿal Šāmîn,* to whom a great temple was dedicated at Sîʿ. Indeed, one Safaitic text (Clark 1979: No. 424) calls him "the god of Sîʿ." The name is occasionally found in an arabized form *Bʿlsʾmy.* By contrast, the name of the third god shared by the Nabatean and Safaitic peoples is entirely Arabic in form. It appears as *Šyʿ-ʾl-qwm* among the former and *S*^{2}*ʿ-h-qm* among the latter. The name is generally interpreted as "Helper or leader of the people," and from this it has been assumed that he was a tutelary god of caravans (Sourdel 1952: 81–84; Teixidor 1977: 88–89). A famous Palmyrene inscription (by two Nabateans) calls him the "good and rewarding god who does not drink wine." From this he has been identified with Lycurgus and assumed both to be in conflict with Dushara-Dionysus and to be a deity considered by the nomads as their special god (Starcky *DBSup* 6: 996). However, Sourdel (1952: 84) and Dussaud (1955: 145–46) have questioned both the identification and the supposed conflict with Dushara. Certainly there is no evidence for such hostilities in Safaitic, where *Ds*^{2}*r* and *S*^{2}*ʿhqm* are invoked together. Nor is there any evidence that he was the particular god of the nomads. He receives relatively few prayers in Safaitic, certainly fewer than *Ds*^{2}*r,* the supposed god of the sedentaries, and in multiple invocations he stands sometimes with the ancient Arabian divinities (*Lt* and *Rḏw/y*), sometimes with the tutelary gods of the Safaitic tribes, sometimes with *Bʿlsʾmn* or *Ds*^{2}*r,* and sometimes with a selection from all three groups.

There are frequent invocations to *Yṯʿ* (also *ʾṯʿ,* with no apparent distinction between the forms), a deity found in theophoric names throughout North and South Arabian and in Nabatean, though rarely invoked outside Safaitic. Traditionally, *yṯʿ,* a root not found in later Arabic, has been held to be cognate with the Hebrew root *yšʿ* and so glossed *Sōtēr* "Savior." It has even been suggested (Winnett 1941) that *Yṯʿ* in North and South Arabian represented Heb *Yēšûaʿ,* Syr *Yešûʿ,* "Jesus," and that texts mentioning this deity were therefore Christian. However, the Christian South Arabian inscriptions do not use the name Jesus in any form, referring to him instead as *Ms*^{1}*ḥ* "Messiah" or *Krs*^{3}*ts*^{3} "Christ," while *Yṯʿ* in both North and South Arabian is frequently invoked in the company of other deities. Moreover, a divine name adopted by the Safaitic or South Arabian writers from a different language group (Hebrew or Aramaic) would appear as a loan-form (**ys*^{1}*ʿ*) not a cognate *(yṯʿ),* particularly since the root *yṯʿ* appears to have no independent existence in North Arabian, South Arabian, or later Arabic, outside the onomastic stock (see Müller 1979 for discussion).

Gd (probably *Gad*), equated with *Tychē* in Greek texts (Sourdel 1952: 49–52), and particularly common at Palmyra (Teixidor 1979: 88–100), is also found in Safaitic. Among the sedentaries of the Ḥaurân and at Palmyra, *Gad* appears to have "personified the especial providence reserved by a god or a goddess for an individual, a group of individuals, or a town" (Teixidor 1979: 89), a tutelary role which any deity could assume. It is probable, though alas unprovable, that this conception was shared by the nomads. Certainly *Gd* in Safaitic usually appears as *Gd-Ḍf* or *Gd-ʿwḏ,* i.e., the *Gd* of one or another of the two great tribal confederations (Knauf 1985), and they are most often found in multiple invocations where, in one text or another, they stand beside all the known Safaitic divinities.

For general surveys of the field, see Littmann 1943: vii–xxviii; Eissfeldt 1954; Dussaud 1955: 135–47; Oxtoby 1968: 1–30; and Müller 1980. Major collections of inscriptions are *Corpus Inscriptionum Semiticarum, Pars 5;* Littmann 1943; Winnett and Reed 1957; Winnett and Harding 1978; and Clark 1979. See also the smaller collections in Jamme 1971 (some of the most southerly texts), Harding 1953, and Oxtoby 1968.

Bibliography

Beeston, A. F. L. 1962. Arabian Sibilants. *JSS* 7: 222–33.

Clark, V. A. 1979. *A Study of New Safaitic Inscriptions from Jordan.* Diss. Melbourne.

Dussaud, R. 1955. *La pénétration des arabes en Syrie avant l'Islam.* Bibliothèque archéologique et historique 59. Paris.

Eissfeldt, O. 1954. Das Alte Testament im Lichte der safatenischen Inschriften. *ZDMG* 104: 88–118.

Grimme, H. 1929. *Texte und Untersuchungen zur ṣafatenisch-arabischen*

Religion. Studien zur Geschichte und Kultur des Altertums 16/1. Paderborn.

Harding, G. L. 1953. The Cairn of Haniʾ. *ADAJ* 2: 8–56.

———. 1969. The Safaitic Tribes. *Al-Abhath* 22: 3–25.

———. 1971. *An Index and Concordance of Pre-Islamic Arabian Names and Inscriptions*. Near and Middle East Series 8. Toronto.

Harding, G. L., and Littmann, E. 1952. *Some Thamudic Inscriptions from the Hashemite Kingdom of Jordan*. Leiden.

Jamme, A. 1971. Safaitic Inscriptions from the Country of ʿArʿar and Raʾs al-ʿAnânîyah. Vol. 1, pp. 41–109 and 611–37 in *Christentum am Roten Meer*, ed. F. Altheim and R. Stiehl. Berlin.

King, G. M. H. 1988. Some Inscriptions from Wadi Matakh. In *Arabian Studies in Honour of Mahmud Ghul*, ed. M. M. Ibrahim. Wiesbaden.

Knauf, E. A. 1983. Südsafaitisch. *ADAJ* 27: 587–96.

———. 1985. Nomadischer Henotheismus? Bemerkungen zu altnordarabischen Stammesgöttern. Pp. 124–32 in *XXII. Deutscher Orientalistentag vom 21. bis 25. März 1983 in Tübingen, ausgewählte Vorträge*, ed. W. Röllig. ZDMGSup 6. Stuttgart.

Littmann, E. 1940. *Thamûd und Ṣafâ: Studien zur altnordarabischen Inschriftenkunde*. AKM 25/1. Leipzig.

———. 1943. *Safaïtic Inscriptions*. Division 4, Section C in *Publications of the Princeton University Archaeological Expeditions to Syria in 1904–1905 and 1909*. Leiden.

Macdonald, M. C. A. 1980. Safaitic Inscriptions in the Amman Museum and Other Collections II. *ADAJ* 24: 185–208; 337–59.

———. 1986. ABCs and Letter Order in Ancient North Arabian. *Proceedings of the Seminar for Arabian Studies* 16: 101–68.

Milik, J. T. 1972. *Dédicaces faites par des dieux (Palmyre, Hatra, Tyr) et des thiases sémitiques à l'époque romaine*. Recherches d'épigraphie proche-orientale I. Bibliothèque archéologique et historique 92. Paris.

Müller, W. W. 1979. *Abyataʿ* und andere mit *yṯʿ* gebildete Namen im Frühnordarabischen und Altsüdarabischen. *WO* 10: 23–29.

———. 1980. Some Remarks on the Safaitic Inscriptions. *Proceedings of the Seminar for Arabian Studies* 10: 67–74.

Oxtoby, W. G. 1968. *Some Inscriptions of the Safaitic Bedouin*. AOS 50. New Haven.

Petráček, K. 1973. Zur semantischen Struktur der ṣafatenischen Inschriften. *ArOr* 41: 52–57.

Ryckmans, G., ed. 1950–51. *Corpus Inscriptionum Semiticarum, Pars V, Tomus 1*. Paris.

Sartre, M. 1985. *Bostra des origines à l'Islam*. Bibliothèque archèologique et historique 117. Paris.

Sourdel, D. 1952. *Les cultes du Hauran à l'époque romaine*. Bibliothèque archáologique et historique 53. Paris.

Teixidor, J. 1977. *The Pagan God*. Princeton.

———. 1979. *The Pantheon of Palmyra*. EPRO 79. Leiden.

Voigt, R. M. 1980. On the Structure of the Safaitic Inscriptions. *ADAJ* 24: 79–93.

Winnett, F. V. 1941. References to Jesus in Pre-Islamic Arabic Inscriptions. *Moslem World* 31: 341–53.

———. 1973. The Revolt of Damaṣî: Safaitic and Nabataean Evidence. *BASOR* 211: 54–57.

Winnett, F. V., and Harding, G. L. 1978. *Inscriptions from Fifty Safaitic Cairns*. Near and Middle East Series 9. Toronto.

Winnett, F. V., and Reed, W. L. 1957. *Safaitic Inscriptions from Jordan*. Near and Middle East Series 2. Toronto.

M. C. A. Macdonald

INSECTS. See ZOOLOGY (FAUNA).

INSTRUMENTS, MUSICAL. See MUSIC AND MUSICAL INSTRUMENTS.

INTEREST AND USURY IN THE GRECO-ROMAN PERIOD.

"Interest" (Gk *tokos*) is a charge for the use of invested capital, most typically money. From an economic perspective, interest is composed of four principal factors: the real cost of using the capital; a premium compensating the investor for the risk of not getting his capital back; an estimate of the likely inflation rate during the period of the investment; and the lender's expenses in negotiating and administering the investment. The interest rate of an investment should ultimately derive from these four factors, but in the ancient world it was also heavily affected by custom and convention.

"Usury," for which there is no exact equivalent in Greek and Latin, is the lending of money, especially at what society considers an exorbitant interest rate. Particularly under the Romans, usury laws often limited the form that interest could take and fixed a maximum interest rate, and law also often imposed other restrictions on interest-bearing loans.

The basic concept of interest is almost as old as organized societies; interest; interest-bearing loans of precious metals or commodities are found already in Hammurabi's Babylon (early 2d millennium B.C.E.). But the introduction of coined money in the Aegean (7th century B.C.E.) led to the practice becoming much more common. Greek interest-bearing loans are attested already in the early 6th century, and by the 4th century the charging of interest had become quite normal at Athens, as we know from many Greek private orations.

However, interest on money loans aroused disquiet, especially among Greek philosophers such as Plato (*Leg.* 11.921 c–d) and Aristotle (*Pol.* 1.10). As Aristotle reasoned, coined money had originated as a store of value and a medium of exchange; although coins struck in precious metals had an intrinsic worth, they served chiefly as a standard to make other goods commensurable. It therefore seemed "unnatural," contrary to the immanent characteristics of civilized society, that money could generate more money through payment of interest. This philosophical bias against interest, which later writers shared (e.g., Seneca *Ben.* 7.10.3), was to have a long history in cultures influenced by Greco-Roman civilization, especially after early Christian writers merged it with religious prohibitions against the taking of interest (e.g., Clement of Alexandria *Str.* 2.18; Tertullian *Adv. Marc.* 4.17).

Notwithstanding such philosophical doubts, Greek city-states, as also the Hellenistic states of the 3d to 1st centuries B.C.E., did not intervene to prohibit interest, and even statutory restraints on interest only became common slowly. Customary interest rates remained high; the prevailing annual interest rate was 12 to 18 percent in 4th-century Athens and 25 percent (the legal limit) in Ptolemaic Egypt of the 3d century. These rates prematurely reflected both continuing instability in the Levantine credit market and a relative scarcity of capital. Interest rates generally fell below 10 percent after 200 B.C.E., but unusually risky loans were sometimes made at much higher rates.

The picture changed in the 2d and 1st centuries B.C.E.,

as Rome became the master of the Mediterranean. Rome had, for internal political reasons, a long-standing tradition of attempting to limit or even prohibit interest; and the influx of capital that imperial Rome attracted made it possible to sustain lower interest rates than had prevailed in the Greek world. A Decree of the Senate in 51 B.C.E. (Cicero *Att.* 5.21.13) forbade interest higher than 12 percent per year, as well as compound interest and the accrual of unpaid interest above the amount of the initial capital. But market-determined interest rates at Rome had by that date already fallen to a level much lower than the legal maximum, with 6 percent being the most common rate for sound loans during peacetime. In general, this regime persisted into the early Roman Empire.

Although transfer of money over long distances was not easy in the ancient world, Rome's central government interposed no effective legal barriers to the flow of capital within the empire. As interest rates in Roman Italy dropped, capital was attracted to portions of the empire where higher rates persisted; provincial governors responded (with how much success is uncertain) by imposing usury laws reflecting accepted interest rates at Rome. Cicero, as proconsul of Cilicia in 51–50 B.C.E., had to deal with a virtually extortionate loan by Marcus Brutus to the city council of Salamis on Cyprus; Cicero's letters on this loan (*Att.* 5.21, 6.1–3) vividly illustrate the dynamics of credit in the later Roman Republic.

After the battle of Actium in 31 B.C.E., prevailing annual interest rates at Rome fell from 12 to 4 percent (Cassius Dio 51.21.3), demonstrating clearly the effect of domestic tranquility on credit. The ensuing centuries of imperial peace resulted in interest rates that throughout the empire normally fluctuated between 4 and 6 percent, approximately equivalent to the return that landowners could anticipate from farming. The charitable alimentary endowments instituted in Italy and elsewhere, especially during the 2d century C.E., usually envisaged an annual return on conservatively invested capital of 5 to 6 percent. Although higher rates were charged for delay in paying debt and for short-term or risky loans, the legal annual limit of 12 percent was only occasionally evaded and apparently caused slight inconvenience. Inflation did not significantly affect interest rates until the currency debasements of the 3d century C.E. and after.

Apart from occasional literary complaints, moneylending and interest-bearing loans were not visited with pronounced social or legal opprobrium during the early Empire. Roman law, building on previous Greek institutions, was particularly ingenious in developing ways to secure debts through personal suretyship or the pledge of property, thus further reducing the creditor's risk; the jurists showed no aversion to interest.

Distinct from the normal credit pattern was the interest on bottomry loans *(faenus nauticum);* these "loans," repayable only if the ship reached its destination, were actually a means of insuring ships or their cargoes against the dangers of long voyages, and the interest rates charged on them could be as high as the parties wished, depending on the timing and duration of the voyage. Loans of farm products were normally repaid with interest of up to 50 percent of kind (*Cod. Theod.* 2.33.1 pr.).

The economic difficulties of the later Empire evidently caused prevailing interest rates to edge upward against the limits set by usury laws, which the emperors then attempted to strengthen and enforce with greater vigor. In the 4th century, these largely economic measures merged with Christian attacks on interest as such.

Ancient authors, starting with Aristotle (*Pol.* 1.10), showed good intuitive understanding of the nature of interest. The Roman jurists distinguished interest on money from ordinary "fruits," such as the produce of farms, in that interest derived from a purely legal relationship (e.g., Pompon. *Dig.* 50.16.121).

Although attested interest rates suggested that capital was generally available and secure, especially in the early Empire, the primitiveness and fragility of the ancient credit market required stress. With but few exceptions, the Greco-Roman world did not know large-scale professional lenders; banks, in particular, did not serve as important financial institutions, but instead operated locally and with poor capital funding. At least in the private sector, large loans were typically provided (with or without interest) by wealthy individuals functioning as patrons, not as professional bankers or moneylenders. Correspondingly, loans were often not "productive," in the sense of being used to create new sources of wealth; instead, they were frequently used to sustain consumption among the upper classes. For discussion of the various types of interest mentioned in the Bible, see DEBTS.

Bibliography

Andreau, J. 1987. *La Vie Financière dans le Monde Romain.* Rome.
Billeter, G. 1898. *Geschichte des Zinsfusses im Griechisch-Römischen Altertum bis auf Justinian.* Leipzig.
Cervenca, G. 1969. *Contributo allo Studio delle 'Usurae'.* Mílan.
Duncan-Jones, R. 1982. *The Economy of the Roman Empire.* 2d ed. New York.
Heichelheim, F. 1930. *Wirtschaftliche Schwankungen der Zeit von Alexander bis Augustus.* Jena.
———. 1970. *An Ancient Economic History.* 2d ed. Leiden.
Jones, A. H. M. 1964. *The Later Roman Empire, 284–602; A Social, Economic and Administrative Survey.* Oxford.
Kühnert, H. 1965. *Zum Kreditgeschäft in den Hellenistischen Papyri Aegyptens bis Diokletian.* Diss. Freiburg.

BRUCE W. FRIER

INTERPRETATION OF KNOWLEDGE (NHC XI,*1*). See KNOWLEDGE, INTERPRETATION OF (NHC XI,*1*).

INTERPRETATION, HISTORY OF. Two articles appear under this heading. The first surveys the history of interpreting specifically the Hebrew Bible/OT, with a special emphasis on how this has been practiced within Christian circles. The second article surveys the history of biblical interpretation by focusing more on underlying philosophical issues associated with hermeneutic theory. See also HERMENEUTICS; HERMENEUTICS, EARLY RABBINIC; THEOLOGY (BIBLICAL), HISTORY OF.

HISTORY OF OT INTERPRETATION

A. OT Interpretation in the NT

Whatever else it may be, Christianity is a unique interpretation of the OT. A surface reading of the OT suggests that its writers did not expect God to become incarnate and did not envisage that a future servant of God would rise from the dead three days after his public execution, nor that he would combine in his life and death the roles of high priest and sacrificial victim. It is true that hints of some of these ideas may be found in the OT, and that these hints had begun to become trends in intertestamental Judaism. For example, a Qumran fragment from Cave 11 develops the idea of Melchizedek as a heavenly figure, the Wisdom of Solomon sees Wisdom as a preexistent "person" who was with God before the creation, and the "sacrifice" of Isaac in Genesis 22 gave rise to ideas about the atoning blood of Isaac; but the NT interpretation of the life and death of Jesus combined these and other ideas in a new way. This fact was to have profound significance for the way that the OT was interpreted until the 17th and 18th centuries.

In the NT, the most spectacular use of the OT is to be found in the letter to the Hebrews. It begins with a series of OT quotations designed to show that Jesus is the son of God and superior to the angels. The writer assumes that God was addressing Jesus when he said, in Ps 2:7, "Thou art my son, today I have begotten thee," or in Ps 45:6, "Thy throne, O God, is for ever and ever" (Heb 1:5, 8). The words of Ps 102:25, "Thou Lord, didst found the earth in the beginning," are also seen as addressed to Jesus, thus claiming that he was, in some sense, the creator of the universe (Heb 1:10). Later in the letter (7:17), the words of Ps 110:4 are understood in terms of Jesus: "Thou art a priest for ever, after the order of Melchizedek," and this enables the writer to present Jesus as a high priest, whose death once and for all fulfilled and rendered obsolete the sacrificial system given by God to Moses in the wilderness. In chap. 11 of Hebrews, the great OT figures are dealt with: Abel, Enoch, Noah, Abraham, Moses, the Judges, David, Samuel, and the prophets. These people all lived by faith—faith that they were journeying to a heavenly city whose God was the God who had spoken finally and decisively in Jesus.

The book of Hebrews is the most spectacular because it is the most daring and explicit attempt in the NT to interpret the OT in the light of the early Church's understanding of Jesus; but implicit throughout the whole of the NT is the conviction that the life, death, and resurrection of Jesus were in fulfillment of the Scriptures. The Gospels, and especially Matthew, make frequent reference to OT passages that the life of Jesus fulfilled (e.g., the Virgin Birth, the flight to Egypt of his parents, his growing up in Nazareth, the removal of his home to Capernaum during his public ministry, and the rejection of his message by the people). The account of the passion of Jesus contains many allusions to the OT, from his entry into Jerusalem upon an ass, through his betrayal, to the division of his garments by Roman soldiers and his cry from the cross: I thirst.

The Pauline writings struggled with the antithesis of faith and law, and did so by identifying figures such as Abraham as men of faith, and therefore as ancestors of a divine promise that would be fulfilled in Christ and would also be made available to non-Jews. Paul added two important features to the use of the OT, both of which subsequently influenced its interpretation. In Gal 4:21–31, he used the method of allegory to prove that Hagar, the mother of Ishmael, represented Mt. Sinai, the earthly Jerusalem, and (by implication) Christians who wanted to observe the Jewish law. He urged his readers to "cast out the slave and her son" (cf. Gen 21:10–12) as Abraham had done. This piece of exegesis became the main NT sanction for spiritualizing the OT (Paul did not, of course, invent allegorical interpretation), that is, not interpreting it at its surface level, but reading into it a deeper, spiritual, or moral or mystical meaning, In 1 Cor 10:1–4, Paul claimed that Christ was present in the OT in that he had been a Rock which followed the Israelites through the wilderness, from which Moses had struck water for the thirsty people. This exegesis, too, encouraged later interpreters to look for Christ in the OT.

B. Apostolic Fathers and Apologists

In the Apostolic Fathers (*1 Clement,* the *Didache,* the *Shepherd of Hermas,* and the *Epistle of Barnabas*), we find three main uses of the OT. The first involves the renunciation of Judaism, and thus of the legal parts of the OT. The latter are conspicuously absent from works such as the *Didache* and the *Shepherd,* both of which purport to show how the Christian life should be lived. Instead, and this is the second main use, the OT law is spiritualized in order to show that it points to Christ. The type of exegesis is especially prominent in *Barnabas.* The 310 men of Abraham's household indicate the name Jesus, and the cross (*Barnabas* 9:7–8); the red heifer (Numbers 19) and the scapegoat (Leviticus 16) are types of Christ, while the cross is foreshadowed when Moses crossed his hands during Israel's battle against Amalek (Exod 17:8–13). The third main type of interpretation was the appeal to OT heroes as examples of faith: Enoch, Noah, Abraham, Lot, Rahab, David, the prophets, Judith, and Esther are all cited.

It was the Apologists, Justin Martyr (ca. A.D. 114–165), Irenaeus (ca. A.D. 130–200), and Tertullian (ca. A.D. 160–225) who took OT interpretation to deeper levels, mainly because they found themselves in conflict with pagans, Jews, and sectarian Christians. In Justin's dialogue with the Jew Trypho, use is made of passages such as Genesis 18; 32:22–32, and Exod 3:1–16 to show that the OT speaks of a Lord who is not the Father above, yet who acts fully in accord with the will and purpose of the Father (*Dialogue with Trypho,* chaps. 56ff.) In each case, Justin exploits an ambiguity in the text. In Genesis 18, the mysterious visitors to Abraham are both human and angelic; in Gen 32:22–32, Jacob is told that he had wrestled with God, while in

Exod 3:12–16, the Lord both appears in the burning bush and speaks from heaven. Justin's interpretations are not the crude allegorizings of *Barnabas*. They depend as much upon a close reading of the text as upon an overtly christological hermeneutic.

Tertullian and Irenaeus were confronted not only with Jewish opponents, but also by Marcion, the founder of a type of Christianity which completely rejected the OT. Marcion read the OT mostly in a literal manner, and found there a God who was ignorant (e.g., he said to Adam, "Where are you?"), who changed his mind (e.g., Gen 6:1–5), and who made cruel and immoral demands upon Israel. Such a God could not be the God of Jesus. Therefore, Jesus was the son of a God who was different from the creator of the visible universe. He belonged to an unseen world, took human form (to be born as a man would have involved assuming what belonged to the God of the visible world), and died to free mankind from obligation to the God of the visible world.

The defense of Irenaeus against Marcion was an orthodox restatement of the Christian view of the unity of the OT and NT. Christ was foretold in the OT, and God's promise of salvation to Abraham was for all humanity. The OT law in its essence agreed with the "first and great commandment" affirmed by Jesus. Tertullian's defense was far more successful. He tackled head-on Marcion's literal reading of the text, and he argued that when the OT used the language of human passions and sensations regarding God, the language could not be taken literally. God had neither a "right hand" nor "eyes" in a human sense; similarly, his supposed ignorance or changes of mind were not to be evaluated as though he were human. Tertullian thus sought to undermine Marcion's accusation that the OT God was incompetent and immoral, and he turned the attack back against Marcion by pointing out that the latter had found it necessary not only to dispense with the OT but also to delete large parts of the NT from his Bible—all those passages that referred back to the OT.

C. The Exgetical Schools of Alexandria and Antioch

Alexandria and Antioch were two of the greatest centers of influence and learning in the Church of the late 2d to the 5th centuries. In Alexandria, a catechetical school was founded in the 2d century, and in Clement of Alexandria (ca. A.D. 180–215) and Origen (A.D. 185–253) it reached the height of its achievements. Clement was concerned to address the pagans of his day, arguing that Christ was the supreme source of knowledge who had spoken in the OT as well as in the NT, and was also the source for all that was best in Greek philosophy. Clement stressed the harmony of the OT and NT; but in order to do this he had to divide the Mosaic law into the historical, the legislative, and the sacrificial. Where possible, he used the literal method of interpretation, e.g., in historical sections relating to the history of Israel. Where laws could be taken at their face value, he also avoided spiritualizing them. For example, the humane laws in Deuteronomy 24 which make provision for the poor could be taken literally. But some laws were spiritualized: the division between clean and unclean animals was taken to refer to avoiding the company of certain types of people (this is already found in *Barnabas*) and to the distinction between the Church on the one hand and Jews and heretics on the other.

Origen went to much greater lengths to champion the spiritual senses of the OT. Although laws such as "honor thy father and mother" were obviously to be taken literally, this was not true of the many parts of the law that seemed to be impracticable. Origen was also worried about contradictions in the OT, such as the creation of the light before the sun in Genesis 1. Since a book whose author was God could not be contrary to common sense, Origen concluded that Genesis 1 was not intended to be read literally. The same was true of passages in which God appeared to make immoral demands on his people, and of those which ascribed to him human passions and activities.

A remarkable side to Origen's work concerned his interest in textual criticism. Jews and Christians disagreed about the text of the OT. The Greek versions used by Christians contained passages such as "from the wood" in Ps 96:10, which clearly pointed to the crucifixion. The Hebrew lacked these phrases, and the Jews were accused of deliberately omitting them. Origen set out to establish the truth. In so doing, he became aware of the great differences between the Greek and Hebrew versions of Job and Jeremiah; and he caused to be compiled the *Hexapla,* which set out the Hebrew text together with four or more Greek versions.

The tendency of the Alexandrian scholars to allegorize the OT no doubt owed something to the influence of Greek and Jewish scholarship there, of which a notable example would be Philo (30 B.C.–A.D. 40). In Antioch, an opposite influence existed, that of literal and historical exegesis. The school of Antioch was represented from A.D. 169 by its bishop Theophilus. His *To Autolychus* marked out a chronology from the creation of the world to his own day, and Theophilus stressed that the OT was an authentic history of God's dealings with the Jewish nation. However, Theophilus believed that the Logos of John 1 had spoken through Moses and was the source of the light created in Genesis 1 before the sun. He also used parts of the OT law as guidance for Christian life.

A second phase of the school of Antioch produced Diodore of Tarsus (A.D. 378) and Theodore of Mopsuestia (ca. A.D. 350–428). Diodore's commentary on the Psalms interpreted Psalm 2 of Jesus and how the Jews handed him over to Herod and Pilate. Diodore rejected, however, the view that Psalm 22 referred to Christ's passion, because the sufferings described in the psalm did not correspond to those of Christ. Theodore seems to have excluded from the category of inspired books the Wisdom Literature and Chronicles, Ezra, and Nehemiah. In his commentary on the minor prophets, he interpreted prophecies in terms of Christ only if this had also been done in the NT; otherwise, he sought a historical reference for the prophecies. Thus, while Theodore accepted that Joel 2:28–32 predicted the outpouring of the Holy Spirit because it was quoted in Acts 2:17–21, he rejected the view that the words of Mic 4:2 ("for out of Zion shall go the law, and the word of the Lord from Jerusalem") referred to Christ. Christ taught (John 4:21) that God did not require to be worshiped in a special place, while Mic 4:2 clearly referred to the reestablishment of Jewish law and worship in Jerusalem.

D. Jerome and Augustine

With Jerome (A.D. 331–420) and Augustine (A.D. 354–430), OT interpretation reached a high point that was not to be surpassed for the next 600 years. Jerome was a great linguist. Educated in Rome, he lived in a Greek-speaking household in Antioch until about A.D. 373, and he began to learn Hebrew around A.D. 374/5. From 386 to his death, he lived in Bethlehem, where he translated the OT from Hebrew into Latin and wrote philological works on the OT which remained standard works for centuries and became the main source of knowledge of OT Hebrew for many later interpreters. His commentaries, as opposed to his philological works, were influenced by Didymus the Blind, whom Jerome visited in Alexandria in A.D. 385. Didymus was a great exponent of spiritual meanings of the text, and this certainly affected Jerome. In his work on the Psalms, for example, he referred many details to Christ, such as the "holy hill" in Ps 3:4 from which God answers the psalmist. This could only mean the Son of God and the Church.

Augustine was no linguist; nor did he lead the life of a scholar-monk. He was a hard-pressed bishop; yet his works such as *On Christian Culture (de doctrina Christiana)* and the *City of God* made a profound contribution to OT hermeneutics. The *City of God* is notable for the way in which it handles the history contained in the OT. This history is the story of the two cities—the heavenly and the earthly, or the city of God and that of the devil—which exist in the present world and affect a person's ultimate destiny. The distinction is worked out with great skill. The city of God does not simply equal Israel and the Church; in both Israel and the Church, good and bad and members of both cities are mingled. On the other hand, the difference between the cities can be seen clearly in the story. Cain and Abel, for example, show the cities of earth and God, respectively, with the former persecuting the latter. The idea of seeing the Bible as the struggle between two cities gives it a unity which cuts across the two Testaments, and minimizes the way in which the OT becomes subordinate to the NT. The OT becomes revelatory history, that is, a story from the past which gives a clue to the meaning of the present and the future.

Along with this grand design, Augustine wrestled with many problems presented by the text: for example, the creation of light before the sun, the extremely long lives of the heroes prior to the Flood, the existence of giants before the Flood, and the apparent immorality of Abraham and others (e.g., Abraham's fathering a child through his wife's servant). Augustine did not try to spiritualize these difficulties. The light created before the sun was the angels; the years lived before the Flood were normal years, as a close reading of the text indicated; the existence of giants could be proved from colossal ancient monuments; Abraham's extramarital activities were performed without lust, and could be excused but were not to be imitated. It is true that Augustine spiritualized from time to time; e.g., the door in the side of the ark is the wound made in the side of Christ. But what is impressive about Augustine is his positive reading of OT history. It is not simply information about the past; nor is it a set of veiled allusions to the future coming of Christ. It contains a dialectic which provides the clue for the understanding of the present in terms of the divine purpose.

E. The 5th to the 15th Centuries

During this millennium the Church suffered great losses which had their effect upon biblical scholarship. Christian North Africa was lost soon after the death of Augustine, while the triumph of Islam in the 7th century meant the loss of large parts of the eastern Roman Empire. Origen's *Hexapla,* which was kept at Caesarea, was lost when Palestine became Muslim. In Europe there were many upheavals. Learning was kept alive in the monasteries and, from the 12th century, in the cathedral schools, the forerunners of the universities.

An important preoccupation in this period was with the status of the Mosaic law. The *Apostolical Constitutions* (possibly earlier than this period) drew upon the OT priestly orders to justify the hierarchy of bishops, priests, and deacons. This text also distinguished between the laws given after the incident of the Golden Calf (Exodus 32) and those given before, e.g., the Ten Commandments and those in Exodus 21:1–23:19. The post–Exodus 32 laws were held to have been given to Israel following its apostacy in making the Golden Calf: they dealt with sacrifices and were not binding on Christians. However, laws made prior to Exodus 32 were binding if they were not ceremonial laws. A type of "dispensationalism" can also be found in the work of Cyril of Alexandria (bishop from A.D. 412 to 444), who divided the OT into five periods. The first three, those of Moses, Joshua, and the Judges, are "impure" for Christians. In the fourth period, that of the prophets, the law is "purified," as the need for mercy and not sacrifice is stressed. The fifth period is that of Christ, who completes the work of purifying and spiritualizing the law.

The issue of the Mosaic law again came to the fore in the 12th–13th centuries. The revival of interest in Hebrew, especially in the school of St. Victor in Paris, resulted in greater sympathy among interpreters for the literal and historical sense of the law. Also, the translation into Latin of Maimonides' *Guide of the Perplexed* (about A.D. 1220) made available a powerful and rational defense of the literal sense of the OT. William of Auverne's *De legibus* (about A.D. 1230) defended the literal sense on the ground that if this was impracticable or absurd (as Origen had maintained), then Moses had deceived his people. In fact, the laws, while abolished by the coming of Christ, were well suited to a simple people such as the Israelites. This was seen by some as an extreme position. In the *Tractatus* of John of La Rochelle (written sometime between 1228 and 1249), the spiritual and allegorical interpretation of the law was reasserted.

Aquinas (ca. 1225–1274) reconciled the literal and spiritual approaches to the Mosaic law in a masterly fashion. Like many commentators before him, he divided the laws into three categories: moral, ceremonial, and judicial. The moral laws (e.g., the Ten Commandments) contained the obligations of natural law and were thus binding upon all people. The ceremonial and judicial laws of the OT were particular applications of the natural law to the specific circumstances of ancient Israel. They were therefore not binding upon all people.

Aquinas defended the rationality of the very complicated details of the sacrificial laws. The animals specified were not used by other people for idolatry. They were also the cleanest available for providing food. Although God did not in Himself need the sacrifices, as the OT made clear (Ps 50:13), the sacrifices served to focus the minds of the Israelites upon God, and to prevent idolatry. However, Aquinas also allowed that the sacrifices had a spiritual sense that pointed to Christ (*Summa Theologiae* vol. 29, pp. 114–5). Furthermore, the OT ceremonies enabled the faithful Israelites to benefit from the saving work of Christ. Of course, they knew nothing of Christ, but their faith in God, which the Mosaic law made possible, linked them to the work of Christ.

Mention has already been made of the revival of interest in the study of Hebrew, especially in the school of St. Victor. This school was founded in Paris in 1100, and was famous for Hugh (died 1141) and Andrew (who taught there until 1147 and from 1155 to 1163). Their concern was with the literal and historical sense of the text. Thus, we find them reluctant to refer prophecies to the coming of Christ unless this had already been done in the NT. Andrew, for example, understood Isaiah 53 not in terms of Christ, but as referring to the Babylonian exile of the Jews. Also, he explored the possibility that God had not directly revealed the past to Moses, but that Moses had used traditions handed down orally and in writing from the time of Adam.

Another feature of OT interpretation in this period was the dispensationalism and apocalypticism of Joachim of Fiore (ca. 1135–1204). This approach embodied the complete triumph of the spiritual interpretation of the OT over the literal and historical interpretation. Joachim posited three ages, those of the Father (the OT), the Son (the NT), and the Spirit, and he saw many links between the two Testaments, in persons and institutions. Thus Abraham, Isaac, and Jacob corresponded to Zechariah, John the Baptist, and Christ. Also, these trios referred to the Trinity and to the three ages. Joachim's writings were to influence many generations of apocalyptists.

Another feature of this period was the use made of philosophy in OT interpretation. Aquinas was, of course, deeply influenced by the rediscovery of Aristotle and by the use of Aristotle in Maimonides' *Guide of the Perplexed* (which Aquinas had studied). Abelard (1079–1142), on the other hand, had studied works such as Plato's *Timaeu,* from which he derived a framework within which he interpreted the Genesis account of creation. Thus, God had already ordered the world as an archetype through his reason before he created it. Also, the six days of creation represented six stages in the salvation history of mankind. Thus, the creation of light on day four signified the prophets who came after the law and who looked for the coming of Christ, while the creation of water creatures on day five looked forward to the renewal of those who received Christian baptism.

A quite different use of philosophy is apparent in the approach of Wycliffe. As a student of philosophy, he had been converted from nominalism to realism. Thus, he believed that the text of the Bible corresponded to what was true in the world and should be entirely in agreement with philosophical reasoning. If there were apparent contradictions in the OT, this was due to the ignorance of the interpreters. The names of things in the Bible, especially when studied via Greek and Hebrew, corresponded to metaphysical realities. In this way, Wycliffe developed his belief in the all-sufficiency of the Bible, and he then turned this belief against many aspects of the teaching of the Church of his day. However, Wycliffe's position was very different from that of Luther, even though both emphasized the all-sufficiency of Scripture.

During this period there developed the practice of copying the books of the OT together with glosses or *postilla.* The former were either in between the lines or in the margins, and the latter were blocks of commentary alternating with the text. The glosses and *postilla* were mainly citations from earlier commentators, with Jerome, Augustine, Bede, and Gregory the Great prominent among them. Thus, the text was not read except in conjunction with these annotations drawn from the great interpreters. A famous compiler of *postilla* was Nicholas of Lyre (1270–1349). He was notable in that he drew upon Jewish as well as Christian commentators, and in particular upon the work of Rashi (Rabbi Solomon ben Isaac of Troyes, died 1105). The latter's commentaries are among the most highly regarded within Judaism, and were made available to Christian interpreters via the collection of Nicholas.

F. The Reformation

At the end of the 15th century there was a revival of learning in Europe, accompanied by the dissemination of books thanks to the invention of the printing press. In 1506 there appeared the first Hebrew grammar written by a Christian, that of J. Reuchlin. This revival of learning paved the way for the Reformation, as did the commentary on the Psalms by Faber Stapulensis (ca. 1455–1536). The latter abandoned the medieval practice of dividing the meaning of Scripture into four senses—historical, christological, ethical, and mystical—and substituted two senses, a literal historical sense and a literal prophetic sense.

These developments form the background to the work of Martin Luther (1485–1546), the founder of the Reformation. His approach to the OT was complex. At one level, he championed the literal prophetic sense, and regarded as the key to the OT that which "leads to Christ." This did not mean that he necessarily read Christ arbitrarily into OT's pages; rather, where he saw God active on behalf of the people, or men and women responding in faith, or the nations being called upon to acknowledge God (as in the Psalms), there he saw the Gospel—and thus, implicitly, Christ. At the same time, Luther was not interested in parts of the OT where the Gospel was not apparent, i.e., in books such as Esther and in Joshua, Samuel, Kings, and Chronicles. Other schemes that Luther used as hermeneutical tools were those of Gospel and Law and of promise and fulfillment. The purpose of Law was to show the utter hopelessness of humankind without God, while Gospel was the total undeserved word of forgiveness and acceptance addressed to all people by God. Both Gospel and Law could be found in the OT where people were forgiven and responded to God in faith and hope. The dialectic of promise and fulfillment depended upon an analogy between Israel and the Church. The former looked forward to the coming of Christ, the latter to his coming again. Both communities therefore lived in the hope that God's promises would be fulfilled, and consequently the Church could learn much from the example of ancient Israel. Thus Luther found himself very much at home in the OT, and saw similarities between the situation of his own times and those of the OT. A favorite character of his was Samson, who had stood single-handedly against his enemies, and who, at the end of his life, had been granted abundant forgiveness by God in spite of his unfaithfulness. This was demonstrated by the return of his strength, with which he killed many enemies along with himself.

Luther's approach to the OT was intensely practical, and he had little time for abstract speculation. While he did not despise the study of the humanities and sciences as a means for attaining a better understanding of the world, he rejected metaphysical theological speculation. Commenting on Genesis, he maintained that all that was needed was to accept the existence of angels and the devil, and not to speculate about how their creation could be fitted into Genesis 1. He also refused to speculate about the metaphysical sense of humankind being created in the image of God: all that we needed to know was that, before the fall, the relationship of Adam and Eve with God was one that had no shame or sin. Since this was no longer the case, it was pointless to speculate about something beyond our experience. Luther believed that the fall had fundamentally altered the world from its original ideal to its present condition. Only the former had been considered "good" by God.

On the Mosaic law, Luther took a radical position. This law was not binding upon Christians. Even the Ten Commandments were not binding in their existing form, as indicated by the fact that the Church did not observe the Jewish Sabbath. Insofar as they were an expression of natural law they were binding, but not because they had been given by God to Moses. Luther's view of other moral or judicial laws of the OT was that they could be observed voluntarily if desired, but could not be demanded of Christians.

The greatest systematic commentator of the Reformation was John Calvin (1509–1564), who (except for a brief exile) worked in Geneva from 1536 until his death. His lectures and sermons were derived from his weekday and Sunday expositions of the Bible. His approach to the OT derived from his opposition to radical groups, such as Anabaptists on the one hand and Roman Catholics on the other. The former wanted to dispense with the OT altogether, while the latter, in Calvin's view, wanted to impose the ecclesiology of the OT upon the Church and its interpretation of Scripture. Calvin opposed both groups by insisting that the OT should be read in its historical and literal sense, but in the light of a hermeneutic that was supplied by the Reformation's understanding of Christianity. The Gospel was to be found in both Testaments; it was differently administered in the OT and not so apparent as in the NT; nevertheless, Christ was implicitly to be found in the OT because only through his saving work was reconciliation possible between God and humanity.

Calvin's commentaries lack the enormous profundity of Luther's ideas, but they are masterpieces of skillful exposition based upon secular and theological learning. In his commentary on Genesis, Calvin recognized the importance of the astronomy and physics of his day, and that the findings of those disciplines were at variance with Genesis 1. His view was that Genesis 1 was not a scientific account of the origin of the universe, but a description of it as visible to the naked eye of an Israelite: thus, according to Genesis 1, the moon was regarded as one of the two great lights, while astronomy showed that several of the planets were actually much larger than the moon.

Calvin's view of the OT law was more favorable toward its use by Christians than was the case with Luther. Indeed, this was generally true of the Reformed wing of the Reformation as a whole. In some writers this resulted in the almost wholesale reintroduction of the OT judicial law as binding upon Christians, while in Puritan circles the Christian Sunday was made to resemble the Jewish Sabbath.

An example of the rehabilitation of the OT judicial law can be found in the *De regno Christi* of the Strasbourg reformer Martin Bucer (1491–1551). This work was addressed to Edward VI of England. It took as its justification the reforming kings of the OT (such as Hezekiah and Josiah) and stressed the duty of the Christian monarch to order the life of the realm. The OT judicial laws, as the laws of God, were better than the laws of men; and although Bucer accepted that the circumstances of ancient Israel were different from those of 16th-century Europe, he nonetheless urged the following of OT precepts as strongly as he could. The king was to appoint magistrates, as Moses had done (Exod 18:21), and the death penalty was to be enforced for blasphemy, violating the Sabbath, adultery, rape, and giving false evidence.

Another Reformed approach to the OT was in terms of covenant theology, and can be found in the writings of the Zurich reformer Heinrich Bullinger (1504–1575). According to this view, Christianity is not a new covenant so much as a renewal of the original covenant made by God with Adam, and renewed with Noah and Abraham. This covenant was in abeyance from the time of Moses to John the Baptist, although many worthwhile institutions and practices were established during this interregnum, such as the appointment of magistrates and judges. The conversion of Constantine enabled the "new" (i.e., original) covenant to be administered under the conditions intended by God, while the Reformation allowed a return to the Constantinian situation following the apostasy of the pre-Reformation Church. The Christian monarch, through the magistrates, was to effect a reform of schools, courts, and economic matters, according to God's law.

Another type of Reformed covenant theology envisaged two covenants: a covenant of works, which God made with Adam at creation, and a covenant of grace, made with Adam after the fall. The covenant of works was required by God of all people even though sin made it impossible to fulfill. This defect was coped with by the covenant of grace; it both removed believers from the condemning power of the law and gave grace to enable the law to be observed. Under this type of covenant theology, OT laws came into their own indicating how God wished human society and daily life to be ordered.

The Lutheran wing of the Reformation was gradually forced to adopt a more practical attitude to the OT law than was implied in Luther's position; yet the Lutherans continued to stress their fear of falling back into what they saw as the legalism of both Judaism and the Roman Catholics. Melanchthon's *Loci communes,* first published in 1521, divided the Mosaic laws into the categories of moral, judicial, and ceremonial, and asserted that Christians were freed from obligation even to the moral laws. The OT laws remained, however, as guidelines to be adopted voluntarily by Christians; and Melanchthon did not conceal his preference for these laws over the laws of pagans or Roman Catholics. J. Gerhard (1582–1637) identified the Ten Commandments with the moral law, and in some areas under Lutheran influence the Commandments became the basis of civil legislation. Where the judicial law was concerned, some areas of Lutheranism preferred to adopt Roman law rather than OT judicial laws.

G. Beginnings of Biblical Criticism

Between 1640 and 1750 the bond between the OT and the NT was loosened to the point where the OT was no longer being interpreted according to hermeneutical schemes derived from the NT. This resulted in what is known as the "historical critical method." Its advent did not mean that scholars began for the first time to ask critical questions; they had been doing this for over a thousand years. The difference between the so-called "precritical" and "critical" eras lay in the way the critical questions were answered. For an Origen, critical questions were answered by recourse to allegorical interpretation, on the assumption that the OT in fact contained no errors or absurdities. An Augustine, who made the same basic assumption, would look for answers of a more rational and historical kind. But from the 1640s, scholars were more ready to say that the OT could be wrong or inconsistent, and that this did not matter since Christianity was based on the NT, of which the OT was mainly the background. Also in this period, traditional beliefs about the authorship of the books of the OT were challenged.

Much impetus for these new moves came from Holland, especially from circles loyal to Arminius. The *Annotata and Vetus Testamentum* of Hugo Grotius (1583–1645), published in Paris in 1644, advocated literal and historical interpretation solely in terms of the circumstances of the writers. Thus, the servant figure of Isaiah 53 was not Jesus, but Jeremiah. The OT law was set aside on the pragmatic grounds that it was archaic and incomplete (Grotius was a lawyer). Another important writer from Holland was the Jewish scholar Benedict Spinoza (1634–1677). His *Tractatus Theologico-Politicus* (1679) argued that the author of the Pentateuch was not Moses but Ezra. Ezra was also the probable writer of Joshua, Judges, Samuel, and Kings. Even so, the twelve books, Genesis to 2 Kings, were left incomplete by Ezra and were completed by later revisers, Chronicles had been written some time after 164 B.C. Spinoza pointed out many inconsistencies in the OT, and excused himself on the grounds that he wanted to focus attention on the many clear and uncorrupted passages, whose value was not at all affected by the fact that there were apparently faults in the OT.

An unexpected contribution to critical scholarship came from Catholic France, in the form of Richard Simon's *Histoire critique du Vieux Testament* (1678). This work argued strongly for a new translation of the OT based upon a critical edition of the Hebrew text; it was also an attack on Protestants, who were accused of basing their faith on a book whose text was in some parts lost or corrupted. Simon rejected many traditional views of the authorship of OT books. They had not been written by inspired individuals such as Moses, Joshua, Samuel, or David, but had been compiled by scribal schools. Simon's belief that a scholar could have freedom to investigate such matters critically so long as he accepted the teaching authority of the Catholic Church was not shared by his ecclesiastical superiors.

In England, the move toward critical scholarship came partly as a reaction against the Reformed view that a Christian king had the duty to order the affairs of the nation. For those who disliked such things as the Anglican attempt to make it compulsory to worship God according to the rites of the Book of Common Prayer, one method of opposition was to attack the OT model which sustained this view of the duty of the Christian king. This could be done by pointing out the immorality of David and the failings of Solomon. Further, the complex phenomenon of Deism went a long way toward diminishing the authority of the OT. Deism accepted the primacy of reason in matters of truth and faith, and believed in a universal religion of one God, the importance of good works, and immortality for the upright. Such a view found many parts of the OT to be barbaric and immature.

In Lutheran Germany, critical scholarship arose out of pietism, a religious movement that stressed individual experience at the expense of Reformation doctrine. At the University of Halle, itself a pietist foundation, the philosopher Christian Wolff stressed Leibniz' distinction between the necessary truths of reason and the contingent truths of history. This distinction had unpromising implications for the OT, given that so much of its witness was expressed via historical narratives. A scholar who was profoundly influenced by Wolff was S. J. Baumgarten (1706–1757). Although he believed that the OT was free from historical and other errors, he maintained that this conclusion had to be justified by scholarly research, not by appeal to inspiration. His pupil, J. S. Semler (1725–1791), took a different view. Basing his ideas upon what he believed to be Luther's position—that the purpose of the Bible was to assure believers that God had graciously accepted them—Semler felt able to handle matters of authorship freely and critically. Theologically, he valued only those parts of the OT that mirrored the spirit of the NT.

H. From 1750 to 1890

As critical and free inquiry into the authorship of OT books gathered momentum, there was established in Protestant Germany a body of critical scholars whose findings laid the foundation for modern scholarship. J. D. Michaelis (1717–1791) was, like Semler, a student of Baumgarten. He published many papers on the social world of ancient Israel and was especially well known for his *Commentaries on the Law of Moses* (1770–1775). J. C. Döderlein (1746–1792) is usually credited with the suggestion that Isaiah chaps. 40–55 were written not by the 8th-century Jerusalem prophet but by a 6th-century prophet-in-exile in Babylon. J. G. Eichhorn (1752–1827) studied under Michaelis and developed the Documentary Hypothesis of the composition of the Pentateuch along lines already indicated in

1753 by J. Astruc. Eichhorn published the first modern *Introduction to the Old Testament* in 1780–1785.

J. P. Gabler (1753–1826) delivered an inaugural lecture in Altdorf in 1785, which is usually held to mark the emergence of biblical theology as a discipline freed from the shackles of dogmatic theology. The task of biblical theology, according to Gabler, was to describe the history and development of theological ideas in the Bible, selecting those ideas that could command acceptance. This was a far cry from seeing the OT as providing proof texts for already-established dogmatic positions, and reflects the growing interest in the study of the development of OT religion.

In the 19th century, Protestant Germany greatly extended the lead that it had built up over other countries in the matter of critical scholarship. Britain and America were to accept critical scholarship only reluctantly from Germany. In both countries the Unitarians would be in the vanguard of critical scholarship, and in both countries critical OT scholars would face heresy trials before the century was out.

A turning point was reached in OT interpretation with the publication in 1806–1807 of the *Contributions to Old Testament Introduction,* by W. M. L. de Wette (1780–1849). De Wette was the first scholar to use criticism to put forward a view of the history of Israelite religion that was radically at variance with the picture presented in the OT itself. De Wette demonstrated that the books of Chronicles were dependent upon Samuel and Kings, and that the picture of Israelite religion contained in these latter books was at variance with the view that Moses had instituted a fully fledged sacrificial and priestly system. De Wette argued that Moses had instituted very little, that religion in the early monarchy lacked a centralized cult and priesthood, and that the fully developed Mosaic system owed much to the impetus of Josiah's cultic centralization and to his enforcement of the newly discovered Book of the Law (622 B.C.).

The position advocated by de Wette was taken up by scholars such as W. Gesenius (1786–1842), the father of the modern study of Hebrew grammar and lexicography, and it was further developed by C. P. W. Gramberg (1797–1830), J. F. L. George (1811–1873), and W. Vatke (1806–1882). Vatke's *Biblical Theology* of 1835 acknowledged its debt to the philosophy of Hegel, but it was nevertheless a deeply critical work which drew attention to problems raised by the OT text. Like de Wette, Vatke found little to attribute to Moses. Unlike him, however, Vatke saw the development of Israelite religion continuing through the Persian period. For de Wette, the postexilic religion of Israel was a falling away into "Judaism."

The triumph of the de Wettian view was prevented by a resurgence of Lutheran orthodoxy and neoconservativism that came to the fore from the 1830s, and was spearheaded by E. W. Hengstenberg (1802–1869). Hengstenberg worked in Berlin and was increasingly able to ensure that anticritical scholars were appointed in universities under the control of Prussia. De Wette's views were also opposed by H. Ewald (1803–1875), who was himself a critical scholar but who believed that much more of Israel's earliest history could be recovered than de Wette had supposed. Ewald produced, in 1843–1848, the first modern history of Israel, and he interpreted the patriarchal narratives as evidence for the movements of the tribes and subtribes that later constituted Israel. De Wette's criticism was also opposed by the Erlangen scholar J. C. K. Hofmann (1810–1877). He believed that biblical history was *Heilsgeschichte,* that is, the privileged account of God's direct interventions into human affairs via Israel. As such, biblical history was not open for critical study and could only be understood by those who had experienced new birth through the Church's proclamation of the Gospel.

From the late 1860s, the tide began to run in favor of the de Wettian position. His work on Chronicles was more or less reproduced in K. H. Graf's *The Historical Books of the Old Testament* (1866), while B. Duhm's *The Theology of the Prophets* (1875) stressed the importance of the prophets in the development of Israelite religion. It was left to J. Wellhausen (1844–1918) to bring together the various threads to produce a brilliant synthesis in his *Prolegomena to the History of Israel* (1883, 1st edition 1878). He drew upon the results of the Documentary Hypothesis in its newer form to correlate the presumed sources with differing eras of Israel's religious history. Thus, the J (Jahwist) and E (Elohist) documents of the early monarchy reflected the period of freedom in Israel's religion, when there was no centralized cult or priesthood. D (Deuteronomy) was the law book discovered in Josiah's reign that was written in the 7th century and became the basis for Josiah's centralization. P (Priestly Code) was written after the Exile, when Israel's religion had become the levitical and sacrificial system ascribed (wrongly) to Moses. From then on, OT interpretation could not avoid the Wellhausen synthesis, whether it accepted it or not.

In Britain, the Wellhausen position was accepted cautiously in the 1880s. The ground for its acceptance had been prepared by *Essays and Reviews* in 1860, in which seven essays by prominent members of the Church of England had welcomed critical scholarship of the Ewald type. From 1862 to 1879, J. W. Colenso, bishop of Natal, published a series of volumes on OT criticism that became increasingly competent, and which advocated a late (postexilic) date for the composition of the levitical and sacrificial material. The most brilliant advocate of German criticism, and of the Wellhausen position, was the Scot W. Robertson Smith. He was a fervent evangelical and believed that critical scholarship was the true product and continuation of the Reformation. His superiors in the Free Church of Scotland disagreed, and, after a heresy trial, Smith was dismissed in 1881 from his post in Aberdeen. His *Old Testament in the Jewish Church* (1881), written to justify his position in the face of the heresy charge, remains a classic. The Wellhausen position triumphed in Britain in 1891 with the publication of S. R. Driver's *Introduction to the Literature of the Old Testament.*

In the United States, German critical works were made known by Moses Stuart, a professor at Andover Seminary, in Massachusetts, from 1812, and by Theodore Parker, who translated de Wette's Old Testament introduction in 1843. Two prominent scholars, C. A. Briggs of Union Seminary, New York, and H. P. Smith of Lane Seminary, Cincinnati, were subjected to heresy trials in the 1890s. However, from the 1890s critical scholars on both sides of the Atlantic were joined together in two important projects: the Hebrew lexicon of Brown, Driver, and Briggs and the *International Critical Commentary,* to which Driver, Briggs, and Smith were contributors.

I. From 1890 to the Present

Opposition to the Wellhausen synthesis took two main forms that can be loosely described as "outflanking" and "confrontation." The "outflanking" drew upon the Assyriological materials that became ever more abundant from the 1870s. These not only brought to life at first hand the great empires of Assyria and Babylon, but they also settled once and for all the dispute between scientists and conservative biblical scholars about the scientific accuracy of the opening chapters of Genesis. This dispute had begun in the 1820s when geologists claimed that the world was much older than the 6,000 years implied by Archbishop Ussher's chronology, and it had received new life following publication of Darwin's *The Origin of Species* in 1859. Assyriological discoveries in the 1870s indicated that the OT account of creation and the flood had much in common with the traditions of neighboring peoples. The possibility of interpreting the OT in the light of Babylonian and Assyrian texts, combined with the form critical studies pioneered by H. Gunkel (which went behind the sources J and E to the individual units of narrative and their presumed social setting), produced a new synthesis which was championed by Scandinavian scholarship and accepted warmly by some British scholars.

A landmark in this new synthesis was the publication of S. Mowinckel's Psalm studies from 1921 to 1924. The synthesis concentrated upon the role of the king in the Jerusalem cult, in the light of the Babylonian New Year Festival. It stressed the importance of this festival for Israelite belief in the universal kingship of the God of Israel, his power as creator, and his ultimate victory over evil. Whereas the Wellhausen synthesis regarded the prophets as the creators of Israelite religion at its best, the cultic approach looked to the worship of the Jerusalem temple during the monarchy as the fountainhead, and even sought to subordinate the prophets to the Jerusalem cult. Wellhausen was accused of having ignored or overlooked the importance of the Assyriological material.

A similar charge was brought against Wellhausen by those who "confronted" him. Here, the protagonists were the American scholars who, under the leadership of W. F. Albright, believed that Palestinian archaeology together with Assyriology vindicated many of the details of the patriarchal traditions, as well as the biblical accounts of the Exodus and the conquest of Canaan. Their charge against the Wellhausen synthesis was that it was based purely on the literary criticism of the OT, and ignored the findings of Assyriology and archaeology.

The 20th century saw new developments in the study of OT theology. In the 19th century this had been undertaken either by the imposition of the categories of Systematic Theology upon the OT, or in terms of the history of Israelite religion. For a time in the 20th century, it seemed impossible to write more than a history of Israelite religion, given the evident similarities not only between the OT and the religion of Israel's neighbors but also between the OT and the religion of "primitive" peoples studied by anthropologists. However, the theological climate following World War I was that of a new orthodoxy that challenged the liberalism of the preceding decades. Further, the attempt of Nazi "Christians" in Germany to dispense with the OT called for a passionate defense of its distinctiveness.

In American scholarship, a new type of biblical theology developed from the Albright school. Convinced that archaeology vindicated the substantial historical accuracy of the OT, this approach saw in the acts of God, especially in the Exodus, a direct intervention of God into the affairs of Israel. This intervention had stamped upon the OT witness to the acts of God a uniqueness which biblical theology was supposed to elucidate. This uniqueness even extended to the grammatical and linguistic features of biblical Hebrew, so that the study of key OT concepts gave access to God's revelation to his people. G. E. Wright's *God Who Acts: Biblical Theology as Recital* (1952) is a fine statement of some of the points made in this paragraph.

In German-speaking scholarship, two approaches emerged. The Swiss scholar W. Eichrodt adopted in his *Old Testament Theology* (1933–1939) the simple idea that the organizing principle of the OT was the covenant between God and Israel. This covenant was the practical expression of the "irruption of the Kingship of God into this world and its establishment here," and it became the interpretative principle in terms of which Israel understood and expressed its history. The other approach in German-speaking scholarship was that of G. von Rad, whose *Old Testament Theology* of 1957–1960 was influenced by M. Noth's studies of the growth of tradition. Von Rad shared some of Noth's historical skepticism about the possibility of reconstructing the foundational events of Israel's faith, such as the Exodus. Instead, he focused upon OT traditions as confessions of faith in God, arising from communal celebrations of that faith. Israel's confession of faith took several different forms, and had to adapt to changing historical circumstances; thus, von Rad's *Theology* was a historical study of the rise and development of Israel's witness to faith as embodied in the Yahwistic, Deuteronomic, Priestly, and prophetic traditions.

Von Rad's was essentially a descriptive, historical, and genetic way of reading the OT. In the 1960s there arose a synchronic way of reading it. This was indebted to structuralism, a movement which had been slowly influencing linguistics, and which began to shape OT studies as scholars turned to these disciplines for new insights.

In 1961, James Barr's *Semantics of Biblical Language* attacked, among other things, one of the central ideas of the Biblical Theology Movement: that Hebrew linguistic structures were privileged vehicles for communicating divine reality. Barr showed that it was a mistake to understand Hebrew words always in terms of their supposed etymological "roots," that usage in context had to be studied, and that the basic unit of meaning was not words but sentences and larger aggregates of text.

At about the same time, the social anthropologist E. R. Leach was applying to the OT the structuralist reading of myths pioneered by the French anthropologist C. Levi Strauss. This involved denying to biblical texts any historical value, and reading them as "codes" whose meanings were expressed by the structural opposition within them. So understood, biblical texts were explorations of the problem of Israel's unique status versus its need to participate in cultural, economic, and social relationships with surrounding nations. In itself, structural anthropology made only a short-lived impact upon OT studies; but it prepared the ground for the arrival of literary structuralism, and for the study of the Bible in the light of literary theory.

This movement, which is in essence ahistorical, is concerned not with the world *behind* the text but with the world *within* the text. It is sometimes hostile to the attempt to discover the original intentions of the biblical writers, or to interpret biblical literature in its original historical and social setting. At its worst, it can result in totally subjective and idiosyncratic readings of OT texts. At its best, it can discover features in texts which, whether or not intended by the biblical writers, greatly illumine the encounter between text and readers.

A movement which, on the face of it, has totally conflicting aims with literary readings is that which employs modern social and anthropological theory to rediscover the social world of ancient Israel. This is, in effect, a renewal of long-established goals in OT studies with the help of more powerful and sophisticated methods. These include ethnoarchaeology, which investigates the settlement patterns, ecosystems, and economic geography of earliest Israel, and comparative studies of social and political systems of the ancient and modern worlds with a view to the better understanding of Israel's social organization and development. A massive, although controversial, contribution to this discussion has been Norman Gottwald's *The Tribes of Yahweh* (1979). There have also been valuable studies of the social dimensions of Israelite prophecy.

The apparent contradictory aims of literary and sociological approaches to the OT are indications of a methodological pluralism that has come to dominate the discipline in the past two decades, although in some cases special interests have brought an uneasy uniting of these divergent approaches. For example, women's studies have become a burgeoning field within OT study. In some instances, these have been sociological investigations of, for example, the role of women in the economy of ancient Israel. In other cases they have been purely literary, involving the reading of narratives from a feminist or female standpoint. The use of the OT by the liberation theologians of Latin America and southern Africa has put another set of ideas into the agenda. The very assumption that academics living in secure positions in the wealthy countries of the world can be authentic interpreters of the OT has been challenged; only the poor and the oppressed, it has been claimed, can hear in the OT the authentic voice of the God who liberated his people from actual physical slavery.

While the literary and sociological movements have engaged the energies of their proponents, there has also emerged a new attempt to see the OT theologically. This is the canonical approach expressed in B. S. Childs' *Introduction to the Old Testament as Scripture*. In some ways, this is almost the negation of von Rad's descriptive account of the history of Israel's narrative witness to faith. Instead of tracing how the traditions, as witnesses to faith, changed and developed over the centuries, the canonical approach as advocated by Childs is concerned with the canonical form of the text. And this is more than simply a literary final-form reading of the text. There is a "canonical intentionality" which can be discerned from the final form and which then provides guidance for a theological interpretation of texts. For example, whatever may have been the use made of the psalms in the preexilic cult in Israel, the book of Psalms in its canonical form knows little or nothing of those situations. The canonical intentionality of the collection as a whole is indicated by psalms such as Psalms 1 and 119, which imply that the psalms are to be used for meditation, and that what were originally words of worshippers addressed to God have become the word of God to worshippers. Although Childs has been heavily criticized, his approach has gained many adherents, and attempts have begun to anchor it in contemporary hermeneutical theory.

Childs' approach indicates clearly what has happened to OT interpretation since the link that bound it to the NT was snapped in the 17th and 18th centuries. If it is to be interpreted theologically, then the OT itself must provide the categories for such interpretation; but the "discovery" of these categories will be guided and shaped by concerns and movements in the arts and humanities in general.

J. W. Rogerson

HISTORY OF BIBLICAL HERMENEUTICS

The discipline that considers the theory of interpretation is usually called "hermeneutics." The concern of this article is to outline the principles of biblical interpretation and their historical development, thus to provide a systematic and historical discussion of biblical hermeneutics.

A. The Need for Biblical Hermeneutics
B. Development of Biblical Hermeneutics until Schleiermacher
   1. Greek Influence on Jewish and Christian Hermeneutics
   2. Principles of Rabbinic Interpretation
   3. Early Christian Hermeneutics
   4. Medieval Jewish Hermeneutics
   5. Medieval Christian Hermeneutics
   6. Biblical Hermeneutics in the Age of the Reformation
   7. Biblical Hermeneutics in the Period of "Orthodoxy"
   8. Biblical Hermeneutics in the Age of Enlightenment
   9. Schleiermacher's Hermeneutics
C. Philosophical Hermeneutics and Modern Biblical Interpretation
D. Theories of Biblical Hermeneutics in the 20th Century
   1. The Barth-Bultmann Controversy
   2. The "New Hermeneutic"
   3. Contemporary Biblical Hermeneutics
   4. Current Developments in Biblical Hermeneutics
E. Conclusion

A. The Need for Biblical Hermeneutics

Every act of text understanding operates, consciously or unconsciously, with a number of presuppositions. Text hermeneutics reflects not only on these general presuppositions of reading but also on more specific reader orientations, such as expectations of the text content, attitudes toward the communicative perspective of the text, attribution of authority to the text (e.g., the "sacredness" of a biblical text), and suspicion over against the text's claims. Hermeneutical reflection is conscious of the fact that every act of text understanding is characterized by a twofold "hermeneutical circle": the whole of a text can only be understood by understanding its parts, and vice versa, and every reader approaches a text with a certain preunderstanding which will be either confirmed or challenged in the act of reading.

It is the sign of *critical* text understanding that in every group or institution the general methodological presuppositions and the specific orientations of readers are discussed in a public theoretical discourse. In view of the particular hermeneutical implications of biblical interpretation, such a critical discourse (in which the modes and motivations of text understanding are reflected and which aims at improving human text understanding) has been developed and promoted by both Jewish and Christian thinkers. Here we refer to theoretical statements on biblical interpretation from both traditions, to their interrelatedness, to their historical development, and to their significance for the religious and academic communities involved.

B. Development of Biblical Hermeneutics until Schleiermacher

1. Greek Influence on Jewish and Christian Hermeneutics. There was, of course, a rich Jewish interpretive praxis long before Israelite hermeneutics met with the emerging Greek interpretation theory. The texts of the Hebrew Scriptures themselves witness to a number of ways of appropriating ancient texts in new contexts (liturgical, personal, social, political, etc.). In Israel, the appropriation of ancient religious writings was generally linked with particular religious persons or institutions, such as Moses, the Levites, the prophets, and the kings. These authorities were charged with the development of an authoritative interpretation of the texts of the Hebrew Scriptures in changing historical circumstances. Especially the texts proclaiming God's law (the Torah) needed to be understood and explained in order to be able to function as instructions for the people of God. The records of such appropriations point to the urgency of questions such as these: How can one arrive at a proper understanding of a text? How can one use a biblical text in order to solve nonbiblical questions? How many meanings does a text have, and how can we locate the proper one? In response to these questions, sets of hermeneutical principles have emerged which were meant to facilitate the exegetical task of the individual interpreter within the community. These principles always comprised both a philological approach to the text and the broader existential-theological interpretation of the text's sense in particular historical circumstances. See also PESHARIM, QUMRAN; TARGUM, TARGUMIM.

Similarly, the emerging Christian movement had to come to terms with the problem of biblical understanding. Respecting the same texts as authoritative as the Jews did, the Christians were faced with the question of whether their particular set of religious experiences concerning the life, death, and resurrection of Jesus Christ necessitated a new interpretive praxis. The Torah, for instance, continued to be a sacred text for the early Christians, but it was now understood in the light of Jesus of Nazareth's proclamation of God's reign, and thus was somewhat relativized in its authority. Some NT texts display a pneumatic approach toward the texts of the Hebrew Scriptures, spirited by the belief that in Jesus Christ the prophecies given to Israel and recorded in the Hebrew Scriptures were fulfilled (see Matt 1:22–23); other texts make use of such a prophecy-fulfillment scheme by identifying types in the OT which correspond to Jesus Christ (e.g., the Adam-Christ correlation in Romans 5). Apart from these new hermeneutical moves which resulted from the particular experiences of the people who gave rise to the NT texts, the NT not surprisingly attests to the fact that its originally Jewish authors worked within the tradition of rabbinic text understanding (see below).

The critical and systematic reflection on the process of biblical understanding as such began to develop in Hellenistic Judaism, particularly in such centers of learning as Alexandria, Antioch, and Jerusalem, where Greek thought and the needs of Jewish (and later Christian) interpretive praxis had met. Greek reflection on interpretation theory resulted in the development of proper modes of reading the foundational texts of Greek society, i.e., Homer's epics. Two schools had emerged in Hellenistic literary criticism: the grammatical-literal and the allegorical reading of texts. The first hermeneutical program, adopted by the theological school of Antioch, aimed at retrieving the "literal" meaning of the Homeric texts. "Literal" referred to the sense of the words which the interpreters understood as obviously intended by the text's author. The second hermeneutical program, defended by the Alexandrian School of theology, aimed at disclosing the meaning behind the text, namely, the deeper sense to which the words refer. This method emerged in response to the contradiction which existed between the authority of the Homeric texts and the ethos of a later generation of interpreters. Where the literal sense appeared to open such gaps, the search for a deeper or a hidden sense could bridge these gaps and thus rehabilitate the classical author from any suspicion of immorality, etc.

The allegorical method was applied to biblical interpretation and further developed by the Jewish scholar Philo of Alexandria. Philo argued for the necessity of an extratextual key through which the hidden sense of the biblical text could be unlocked. Moreover, the allegorical method proved to be the best way of preserving the sacredness and integrity of the biblical text against any critique of the Bible's crude or apparently nonsensical passages (esp. those which spoke of God in an anthropomorphic manner). Thus, the allegorical method must be seen as serving a particular set of theological convictions.

2. Principles of Rabbinic Interpretation. While it is not possible to measure precisely the amount of Greek influence on rabbinic interpretation theory before and after the destruction of the temple, it is more essential to note that both Greek and Jewish interpreters were united by a similar goal, namely, to understand and apply their classical but ancient texts in new cultural, linguistic, ethical, political, social, and economic contexts. Thus, hermeneutical similarities may have emerged not only because of geographical and cultural affinities, but also because of the similar necessities of interpretive practice.

The destruction of the temple generated a new hermeneutical challenge in Judaism: when this unique means of mediating the past and the present of Israelite religion was annihilated, the now canonical Scriptures came to represent more than ever before the spiritual essence of Jewish identity. Now, rabbinic interpreters were faced with a religious, linguistic, and social situation which required a sophisticated process of appropriating the Torah (i.e., the legal parts of the Hebrew Scriptures) in an alien world. The written law, however, did not provide all the answers required by the changing external and internal circumstances of Jewish religious existence. In this context, the Midrashim (the oral derivations and applications of the written Torah) developed. Different sets of principles, normally referred to as Heb *middôt,* emerged which guided the Midrashic interpreter in his difficult task. The best known among these hermeneutical principles are the seven rules associated with Rabbi HILLEL THE ELDER (ca. 20 B.C.–15 C.E.) and the thirteen rules of Rabbi ISHMAEL (see below). These rules themselves became the object of much hermeneutical discussion and were then amended accordingly. They concerned the possibility of deriving certain "oral" laws from one or more biblical passages with the help of logical procedures. It was necessary to demonstrate the biblical origins of any such "oral" law. Thus, the canonical, i.e., closed, written law was opened to new and unforeseen applications. The measure of "adequacy" in such applications, however, was not what we today would name historical accuracy; rather, it related to particular interpretive expectations and convictions which often had only some literal connection in the actual text. The differences in interpretative method can be seen from a look at the debate between two rabbis in the 2d century C.E., when the foundations for the new rabbinic praxis of biblical interpretation were laid. While Rabbi AKIBA favored a more creative approach to the biblical texts, Rabbi Ishmael insisted that the texts of the Torah must be interpreted according to traditional rules, i.e., an amended version of Rabbi Hillel's compendium. The difference between both approaches has been also interpreted as a reflection of the rabbis' different concepts of philological and theological thinking: Akiba was more mystically oriented, and Ishmael was more philologically oriented.

As far as the nonlegal texts in the Bible, the Haggadah, were concerned, rabbinic hermeneutics was much more open to a diversity of creative readings. Any aspect of the text could provide the foundation for a sophisticated interpretive treatment and application on a new context in the life of the faithful. The various interpretations of a passage were then collected in authoritative sources such as the Talmud and used not only in liturgical contexts but also as information for future interpreters. See also HERMENEUTICS, EARLY RABBINIC.

3. Early Christian Hermeneutics. In the early Church, the debate on the proper method of biblical interpretation resembled the outlined divisions in Greek and Jewish hermeneutics: Alexandrian Christian theologians such as Origen (d. 254) defended the allegorical method, whereas Antiochene theologians such as Diodorus of Tharsus (d. 394), Theoderet of Cyrrhus (d. 460), Theodore of Mopsuestia (d. 428), and Chrysostom (d. 407) protested against the allegorical "misuse" of the biblical texts and declared the literal reading to be the only proper method of biblical appropriation.

It is important for us today to appreciate the foundational nature of this hermeneutical debate. The rather philological orientation of Antiochene theology implied a basic openness toward a critical assessment of the content of each biblical text within the emerging biblical canon. The Song of Songs, for instance, was classified as an ancient wedding song without any theological significance. Hence, the Antiochene exegetes approached each text as a meaningful whole, while their Alexandrian colleagues viewed each biblical text as part of the overall body of sacred writings, i.e., the canon. The allegorical method made it easy for them to raise every text passage above philological suspicion and theological critique. However, both hermeneutical camps agreed that the Hebrew Scriptures ought to be approached typologically. That means, many of the biblical texts were assumed to contain already a *typus* of Christ (e.g., texts such as Amos 9:11–12 were interpreted typologically as pointing to the coming Christ). Thus, even the anti-allegorical theologians allow to some extent for the existence of a double meaning in the biblical text. Eventually, the allegorical method developed into the leading approach to the Bible in the early Church, both East (Greek) and West (Latin), while the Antiochene approaches which promoted a literal or historical reading of the Bible (such as Theodore's five books *Adversus Allegoricos*) disappeared altogether. But the influence of Antiochene hermeneutics would eventually re-emerge, especially in the Protestant Reformation (see B.6 below).

The leading allegorist in the early Church was ORIGEN. In the fourth and final book of his theological work *Peri Archon (On First Principles),* he addressed the problems of interpretation theory. *Theoria* meant for him allegory (for the Antiochenes *theoria* referred to the literal approach). Since the Scriptures contained the ultimate mystery of divine-human relationship, Origen considered the allegorical method to be the only adequate approach to these texts. It alone could provide the key to unlock the hidden sense of the texts so far as this was possible at all. Although in his theory, Origen distinguished between three dimensions of the textual sense (literal, moral, and spiritual), in his exegetical praxis he distinguished only between two levels of meaning (the "letter" and the "spirit"). It is also interesting to note that in spite of his allegorical orientation in exegesis, Origen must be counted among the most influential philologists in the early Church. He was thoroughly involved in text criticism and in the comparison of different traditions of textual variants (as evidenced by his *Hexapla*). This shows that the search for the most trustworthy textual traditions and a wholly allegorical approach to the text, thus critically retrieved, did not exclude each other.

Allegorical interpretation also proved useful in the fight against the gnostic heresy. Many gnostics employed a method of allegorical exegesis, or allegoresis. Church fathers, such as Irenaeus of Lyons (d. ca. 202), fought against this gnostic allegoresis while using their own allegorical "keys" in order to expose the gnostic "keys" as false or heretical. The fight against gnostic hermeneutics also led to the formation of ecclesiastical criteria which were to determine the adequacy of any particular exegesis: only those theologians who interpret the Bible from within the Church could hope to do justice to the texts.

The further development of Christian hermeneutical thought was mainly the work of Jerome and Augustine of Hippo. Jerome (ca. A.D. 347–420), generally known for his revision of the Latin text of the Bible (later called the Vulgate), favored the literal exegesis as practiced in the School of Antioch, where he once had been a student. Although in principle he recognized the legitimacy of spiritual interpretation of the Scriptures, he insisted that such spiritual reading must be firmly based on the literal understanding of the text. His own biblical commentaries displayed fewer and fewer allegorical moves as he grew older. He, too, used Origen's philological contributions, especially the *Hexapla,* in his own efforts to work out a proper textual basis for the literal interpretation of the Bible. Jerome's strong emphasis on literal interpretation makes him one of the forerunners of the growing interest in literal understanding of the Scriptures in later medieval hermeneutics.

While Jerome's contribution to the development of biblical hermeneutics has always been well appraised, the significance of the hermeneutical thought of Augustine of Hippo (354–430) and his influence on medieval theology have not always received adequate attention. In his work *De Doctrina Christiana* (427), we can see the mature development of Augustine's theological hermeneutics. Augustine's great achievement in the hermeneutical field lay, first, in his effort to combine both Antiochene and Alexandrian concerns for the benefit of the Christian community, and, second, in his semiotic reflections on which his own hermeneutics was based. For Augustine, the Bible fulfilled a communicative function: it enlightened the reader about God's salvific activity in the world. Thus, the biblical texts themselves are only significant for the Christian reader because of the realities to which they refer. The insight that signs are not what they refer to but rather operate as signifiers motivated Augustine to study the best ways of decoding what the signs constituting the biblical texts wish to say. So far one can see Antiochene influence. But unlike the Antiochene interpreters, Augustine in his own hermeneutics presupposed the christological content and the canonical integrity of the biblical texts as well as the ecclesial rootedness of their interpreter. Moreover, he concluded from his own biblical reading that the Bible is about faith, hope, and love: "A person who bases his life firmly on faith, hope and love, thus, needs the Scriptures only in order to teach others. Therefore we may find many people who live on this basis even without sacred texts" (*De Doc. Christ.* 1, 43). Hence, the need for intense philological study of these texts and for the interpretive effort was somewhat relativized, and a theological framework for allegorical, and especially for typological, reading was established. However, Augustine repeatedly warned against the excesses of allegorical text interpretation. Therefore, it would be wrong to count Augustine among the propagators of an uncritical allegorical method in biblical interpretation. As Bonner (*CHB* 1: 561) observes, the influence of Augustine on the later biblical exegesis of the Latin Middle Ages was enormous. With Jerome, Gregory the Great, and the Venerable Bede, he was one of the four great authorities, and would probably have been reckoned the greatest of the four.

In spite of Augustine's warnings against an uncontrolled allegorical reading of the Bible, the particular form of allegorical interpretation which was originally advanced by John Cassianus in the 5th century became very prominent in medieval theology. Cassianus had proposed a fourfold theory of interpretation. Following Origen, he distinguished between literal and spiritual interpretation, but then subdivided spiritual interpretation more sharply into (1) tropological (= moral), (2) allegorical, and (3) anagogical (= future-oriented) interpretation. However, occasionally this fourfold scheme was reduced to a triad, and in actual exegetical praxis we still often observe only the classical twofold distinction between literal and spiritual interpretation.

4. Medieval Jewish Hermeneutics. There was no one single center of Jewish hermeneutics after the destruction of the temple. By the medieval period, Jewish hermeneutics was characterized by local and theoretical diversity. In some parts of the world, especially in the Orient and in Spain, many Jewish thinkers adopted Arabic as their language (note the translation of the Bible into Arabic by Saadiah Gaon [882–942]) and also Arabic concerns of text interpretation; in other parts, such as France, Jewish teachers employed Hebrew as their language and were much more involved in an exchange with Christian approaches to the Scriptures.

The influence of the more Arabic strand within medieval Jewish hermeneutics can be seen in the very strong rejection of allegorical interpretation and the cultivation of literal reading and its philological presuppositions. The encounter with Arabic philosophy and the Arabic retrieval of Aristotelian thinking have also promoted an attempt to explain the Torah in more rational terms. Moreover, Arabic interest in poetry strengthened the sensitivity of Jewish interpreters for the respective passages of their own Scriptures. Philological studies, including grammar, lexicography, etymology, and accentuation, blossomed, particularly in Spain; while in France, a more traditional rabbinic hermeneutics was employed in text interpretation.

Among the outstanding representatives of medieval Jewish hermeneutics in Spain were Abraham ibn Ezra (1092–1167) and Moses ben Maimon, called Maimonides (1135–1204). Ibn Ezra approached the biblical texts through a combination of sophisticated philological methods and traditional rabbinic rules; while Maimonides interpreted the Bible through categories of Aristotelian metaphysics, stressing the human (linguistic) mode of Bible transmission, and thus arrived at some form of "demythologization." In France, Solomon ben Isaac, called Rashi (1040–1105), favored a literal reading of the biblical texts, claiming that the biblical text does not depart from its plain meaning. Rashi's very popular biblical commentary became the first Hebrew book printed in Italy (1475). His work had a profound influence on the School of St. Victor in Paris and thus on the whole of medieval Christian hermeneutics.

The struggles of medieval Jewish exegetes resembled those of their Christian counterparts. Both groups attempted to come to terms on the one hand with the problems of literal and allegorical understanding of their sacred texts, and with the relationship between philological and philosophical methods, and on the other with traditional forms of sacred or mystical reading.

5. Medieval Christian Hermeneutics. In the early medieval period, i.e., from the 6th to the 8th centuries, the development of biblical interpretation was the work mainly of monks. At that time, the exegetical praxis in the medieval Christian church was dominated by allegorical methods. Gregory the Great (ca. 540–604) was a master of this approach to the Bible and one of the chief illustrators of the advantage of allegoresis. Like other medieval interpreters, he compared the act of reading the Bible with the building of a house: upon the historical foundation we erect the walls with the help of our spiritual reading, and then we color the whole structure by the grace of moral teaching (Brinkmann 1980: 231–34). Thus, for Gregory, biblical interpretation reached a state of perfection when it led to a disclosure of the deeper sense of the text, because only in that disclosure do we gain insight into God's act of revelation in Christ. Like Augustine's, Gregory's hermeneutics was firmly rooted in a set of theological and ecclesial convictions.

While the popular piety in the later medieval period remained strongly influenced by allegorical interpretation, the development of interpretation theory followed a somewhat different path. In order to understand the increasing interest in the literal sense of the Bible, one must appreciate not only the influence of both Jerome and Augustine (which can be observed throughout the hermeneutical discussion in the Middle Ages) but also the impact of Jewish scholars such as Rashi and his followers. Although not explicitly acknowledged by Christian thinkers, this Jewish hermeneutical influence was significant, especially on the two major representatives of Christian hermeneutical thinking of the time, namely Hugh of St. Victor (d. 1141) and Nicholas of Lyra (d. 1349). Hugh was a master at the famous monastic school of the Victorines in Paris; Nicholas was a Franciscan teacher at the University of Paris. Thus, the place where Christian hermeneutics was discussed was now no longer the community of believers as such, but the academy. This change of framework also helps to explain the widening gap between popular biblical interpretation, which continued to be allegorical, and the academic treatment of the Bible, which now attended to the philological study of the text in order to retrieve its literal meaning. This academic interest in the literal meaning of the text did, however, not exclude the subsequent use of allegorical methods even in academic circles. With these qualifications in mind, one can say that the following verses are characteristic of the medieval method of biblical interpretation:

Littera gesta docet, quid credas allegoria,
Moralis quid agas, quo tendas anagogia.

("The letter shows us what God and our fathers did; the allegory shows us where our faith is hid; the moral meaning gives us rules of daily life; the anagogy shows us where we end our strife"; see Grant and Tracy 1984: 85.)

As a result of the rediscovery of Aristotle in Christian theology since the 12th century and the related growth of scholastic theology, biblical hermeneutics became very critical of allegorical interpretation and paid even more attention to the retrieval of the literal sense of the biblical text. The greatest scholastic theologian, Thomas Aquinas (1225–1274), upheld in principle the fourfold sense of Scripture, but at the same time he did not hesitate to question the scientific nature of allegorical interpretation and of theological thinking based on its results. Thomas demanded that proper theological thinking ought to be firmly based on the literal sense of the biblical text. "Nothing necessary for faith is contained under the spiritual sense which is not elsewhere put forward clearly by the Scripture in its literal sense" (*Summa Theologiae* 1a. 1, 10). However, Thomas' critique of allegorical interpretation and his promotion of a new academic ideal in biblical hermeneutics did not succeed in reforming the love for allegorical reading in the preaching of the Church and in the popular religious realm. In fact, here allegorical readings increased even further and continued to challenge theologians to fight back. Already since the 14th century—i.e., long before the Protestant Reformation—theologians such as Marsilius of Padua, William Ockham, John Wycliff, John Hus, Gabriel Biel, Wendelin Steinbach, and John Major attacked (though not with any immediate result) the widespread uncritical use of the Bible and tried to formulate new and more critical principles of biblical interpretation.

6. Biblical Hermeneutics in the Age of the Reformation. The Reformers' contribution to biblical hermeneutics (i.e., the *theory* of biblical interpretation) has at times been assessed in isolation from the overall development of biblical hermeneutics and thus has been perceived to be more original than it really was. Although Martin Luther (1483–1546), John Calvin (1509–1564), and Ulrich Zwingli (1484–1531) applied the interpretive methods which were prepared both by the critical academic tradition referred to above and by the great humanist thinkers (such as Reuchlin and Erasmus of Rotterdam), the Reformers' actual *praxis* of reading the biblical texts, in particular their fresh theological reading perspectives, differed greatly from their predecessors and led to the development of a new attitude in biblical reading. In that sense, one may be justified in describing the Reformation as a hermeneutical event. Its new interpretive praxis was also promoted by the translation of the Bible into the vernacular, facilitating a fresher look at the text itself. While the philological emphasis in humanist interpretation must be seen in the long tradition of interest in the literal meaning of the texts—which comprises the Antiochene concerns and those of Augustine, Aquinas, and their followers as well as those of the medieval Jewish thinkers—the most decisive differences between these interpretation theories and the humanists' approach to the Scriptures lay both in the new understanding of the authority and the function of the Scriptures and in the radically transformed self-understanding of the biblical interpreter. By contrasting the ecclesial status quo with the newly interpreted meaning of the Scriptures, the Reformers saw an urgent need to work for the necessary changes in the Christian community. For the Reformers, the ultimate criterion for such a reform of the Church was the Word of God as communicated in the Bible. They all agreed that the Bible alone *(sola scriptura)* represented the foundation of the Christian faith, and its content was perceived to be fully clear, or self-interpreting *(scriptura sui ipsis interpretes)*. But each of the Reformers added his own theological reading perspective to these formal criteria for biblical interpretation.

For Luther, this reading perspective consisted both in his belief in the justification by faith alone and in his corresponding negative view of human nature. Only through faith in God's salvific action in Jesus Christ can the biblical interpreter sharpen his perspective for the content of the text. However, unlike the later "Lutheran Orthodoxy," Luther himself never considered the Bible as a text system free of problems and contradictions. Rather, he applied philological means of critique in unison with his theological considerations. Even the occasional allegorical interpretation was accommodated. Like Augustine, whom he much admired, Luther felt free to apply his exegetical genius to the text even when his own hermeneutical maxims in fact did not sanction such a move. Thus, he did not refrain from a typological reading of the Hebrew Scriptures, either. But unlike Augustine, Luther's exegesis was not limited by a total acceptance of the canonical status of the whole Bible. Rather, the Reformer treated every text according to its own christological merits, thus reaching a negative verdict about the theological legitimacy of including the Epistle of James in the NT.

Other Reformers, such as Melanchton, Calvin, and Zwingli, contributed to the development of hermeneutics by offering their particular combination of humanist philological methodology and their specific theological approach to the overall content of the Scriptures.

Following the Reformers' hermeneutical concerns, Matthias Flacius Illyricus (1520–1575) attempted to provide a synthesis of reformational thinking on biblical interpretation. In his work *Clavis scripturae sacrae* (1567), Flacius particularly stressed the need of a grammatical interpretation, and he advanced the theory of the unity of the Scriptures as the necessary foundation of biblical hermeneutics.

Assessing the Reformers' hermeneutical initiatives, G. Ebeling (1967: 26) concludes that they were not sufficiently conscious of the distance between them and the time of early Christianity, and thus not sufficiently aware of the philosophical implications of text interpretation as such. In particular, "It remained unclear what the principle of *sola scriptura* meant for the theological method as such" (Ebeling 1967: 73). Hence, without further elaboration on the hermeneutical principles operative in the theology promoted by the Reformers, this theology remained uncritical and therefore open to misuse. However, before the hermeneutical discussion in Protestantism was advanced eventually by theologians such as Semler and Schleiermacher, the time of the Reformation was followed first by a period of uncritical biblicism—the so-called Lutheran Orthodoxy.

7. Biblical Hermeneutics in the Period of "Orthodoxy." None of the Reformers had ever defended the verbal inerrancy of Scripture. However, their theological successors, among them Johannes Andreas Quenstedt (1617–1688) and Abraham Calovius (1612–1686), defended the verbal inspiration of the entire Bible and developed the principle of biblical infallibility. For these thinkers, the Bible was identical with the Word of God and thus as text the infallible foundation of a set of dogmatic convictions. Although all these theologians reached dogmatic statements by using the same rationalistic method, these statements of "orthodoxy" often differed significantly.

For Roman Catholicism, the Council of Trent (1545–1563) formulated the "orthodox" conditions for biblical interpretation by confirming the two-source theory. That theory decreed that both the Bible and Christian tradition together represent the sources for authentic Christian faith and theology. This differed sharply from the Protestant theory that the Bible was a clear and sufficient source. In the ensuing controversy between both "orthodoxies," the Roman Catholic challenge of the Protestant principle of *sola scriptura* and the Protestant challenge of the Roman Catholic two-source theory were each met by the opposite side with an even stronger ideological defense. However, when the traditional biblical worldview which supported both "orthodoxies" was challenged by the emerging new worldview, Lutheran, Reformed, and Roman Catholic "orthodoxies" fought with the same kind of argument against this new and common enemy which opposed not only their hermeneutical foundations but also their particular methods of reading the Scriptures.

The discoveries of new parts of the world, the new insights into the laws of nature, and the emerging technological progress challenged the ancient set of convictions, (i.e., the traditional paradigm of biblical interpretation). The Western discovery of China and Chinese culture, for instance, challenged the belief in the biblical chronology of the world and the still widely cherished belief that Adam was the father of humankind. Moreover, the rationalistic demands by philosophers such as Spinoza and Descartes that reason should become the criterion of faith upset all "orthodoxies" alike. Their representatives now felt called to defend the Christian heritage against the new movements which were based on rational thought and experiment. While a few theologians working in Holland, among them Balthasar Bekker (1643–1698) and Christoph Wittich (1625–1687), accepted the challenge of the biblical worldview and tried to find ways of bridging the traditional faith and the new reason, their German Protestant colleagues in particular felt the need to harden their "orthodox" standpoint even further. Hence, biblical hermeneutics was reduced to the development of a set of rules which read the texts in such a literal way that the dogmatic preunderstandings of the "orthodox" theologians were confirmed. But this negative attitude toward the new philosophical and scientific challenges could not last forever.

Interestingly, a first critique of the "orthodox" literalism came from the Pietiest movement, which deplored the dogmatic and formalistic way of reading the Scriptures and demanded now a new hermeneutical emphasis on the personal experience of the biblical interpreter. Thus, the problem of the relationship between private and public understanding of the biblical texts was now added to the already existing problem of the relationship between faith and reason in biblical hermeneutics. It took a new generation of interpreters to attend to these questions with a fresh and critical mind.

8. Biblical Hermeneutics in the Age of Enlightenment.

The attitude of the Protestant Orthodoxy toward the revolutionary changes in the early modern period and its attempt to stick to its hermeneutical principles and horizons could not remain successful for long. Neither could the mere repetition of the doctrines of verbal inspiration and of the identity between Scripture and the Word of God stop the hermeneutical reflection in theology; nor did it impress the now independent disciplines of scientific research and of critical philosophical thinking. Moreover, in Roman Catholic theology a new interest in biblical interpretation arose which, in response to the Protestant claim of *sola scriptura,* tried to show the wider hermeneutical basis of Christian faith and the need for a thorough critique of the biblical text (cf. the work of Richard Simon). The combination of these challenges led to a new beginning in Protestant hermeneutics in the 18th century. This new movement in biblical interpretation was strengthened further by the now universal interest in philological methodology.

Among the centers of enlightened scholarship, the University of Halle (Germany) played a very significant role. Here Johann Salomo Semler (1725–1791), influenced by the philosopher Christian Wolff and the theologian Siegmund Jakob Baumgarten, developed a new biblical hermeneutics. This new approach was characterized more by its effort to prepare a new general foundation for biblical hermeneutics than by a set of detailed rules for the interpretation of biblical texts. Semler demanded both a critical reading of the Scriptures free from dogmatic presuppositions, and a multidisciplined approach to the text which included attention to questions of grammar, rhetoric, logic, history of the text, translations, criticism of editions, and exegesis proper. Although Semler did not yet penetrate deeply into the problem of historicity, he did help prepare such an insight by demanding both a critical study of the history of the text and a strong attention to the meaning intended by the biblical authors, that is, to the *sensus litteralis historicus* of the biblical text. Unlike either the Reformers or the representatives of Protestant Orthodoxy, Semler cultivated a sense of historical distance between modern reader and ancient text and understood the resulting need for hermeneutical procedures. He also questioned the legitimacy of typological interpretation of the OT.

A great admirer of Richard Simon, Semler began to develop a critical understanding of the traditions behind the biblical texts and to question the single authorship of certain biblical books. Moreover, he promoted a theory of "accommodation," which stated that the authors of biblical texts had to "accommodate" their literary style, etc., to the communicative capacity of their audience. With the help of this theory, Semler could explain both the linguistic differences and the doctrinal particularities in the Bible. Semler and his fellow theologians who propagated a critical study of the biblical texts, among them especially Johann August Ernesti and Gotthold Ephraim Lessing, helped to ensure that biblical hermeneutics again entered into a critical dialogue with the demands of reason, and thus participated in the universal search for principles of critical text understanding.

9. Schleiermacher's Hermeneutics. The enormous contribution of Friedrich Schleiermacher (1768–1834) to the development of hermeneutics can be assessed more adequately now since the critical edition and publication of some of his manuscripts on the subject (Schleiermacher 1977). Unlike his theological predecessors, Schleiermacher rejected all theological claims to a privileged access to the Bible and all demands for a prerogative of a special hermeneutics. Instead, he called for a general hermeneutics, because understanding was for him a universal process requiring the critical attention of all disciplines concerned with it. Theology, therefore, must abandon any hermeneutical prerogative, and, like any other effort to understand ancient texts, follow the general principles of hermeneutics in its attempt to understand the biblical texts. For instance, the belief that the Scriptures were divinely inspired must not guide biblical interpretation, but might be a possible result from actual interpretation itself. Thus, the theologian Schleiermacher was the first to promote the development of philosophical hermeneutics.

Developing such a philosophical hermeneutics, Schleiermacher distinguished between a general aspect of communicative performance, that is, the presence of conventional or grammatical patterns of discourse, and an individual aspect, that is, the particular application of such general patterns, in every act of expression. Accordingly, he demanded a twofold reconstruction of the sense of a text in the act of interpretation: grammatical and psychological (sometimes also called "technical") interpretation. In order to grasp the overall sense of the text through the combination of these two moves, Schleiermacher called for an act of "divination." Because of the necessary presence of the interpreter in this act of divination, no act of interpretation can ever be considered to be complete. Therefore, Schleiermacher described the aim of understanding as "approximation." Like Semler, Schleiermacher attempted ultimately to understand the author of a text, and because he knew that even authors are not always conscious of their creativity, he defined the goal of understanding accordingly as the effort of understanding a text first as well and then even better than its author had done.

Schleiermacher himself did not develop a special theory of biblical interpretation, though he pointed to some of its dimensions in his other theological writings. The full impact of his hermeneutical thinking on the development of interpretation theory is only felt today. His immediate influence was limited; and in the course of the 19th century interest in hermeneutics declined.

In the later 19th century, philological and historical concerns dominated biblical interpretation. Freed from dogmatic impositions on the texts, the quickly developing historical-critical study of the Bible achieved major insights into the nature and history of the biblical texts, but failed to appreciate the limits of its own capabilities. Moreover, in spite of all the insights into the philological nature and the historical character of the biblical texts, the reductionist view which treated the biblical texts as mere historical documents could not adequately grasp the theological intentions of these texts. Thus, both the deepening philosophical insight into the nature of understanding and the theological protest against such a historicist reading of the Bible had to lead to a radical challenge of a purely historical-critical approach to the Scriptures.

C. Philosophical Hermeneutics and Modern Biblical Interpretation

After Schleiermacher's death, interest in hermeneutical questions was minimal until the philosopher Wilhelm Dilthey (1833–1911) appropriated Schleiermacher's hermeneutical concerns for his own project of establishing a foundational theory for all the human sciences. Over against the natural sciences, whose primary task Dilthey identified as "explanation," he defined the aim of the human sciences as "understanding" different life expressions. Thus, at a time when biblical interpreters defined their task purely in historical-critical terms, Dilthey resumed Schleiermacher's project of a general hermeneutics, without, however, completing it. Nevertheless, he reemphasized the hermeneutical focus in the humanities. Moreover, his interest in understanding "life" through its expressions helped prepare the way for Edmund Husserl and the phenomenological movement, and thus also for the hermeneutical philosophy of Martin Heidegger (1889–1976).

Heidegger's work, especially his book *Being and Time* (1962; first published in 1927), has had a great impact on 20th-century theology and biblical interpretation. While some theologians, such as Karl Barth, rejected the imposition of philosophical thinking on theology, Rudolf Bultmann, Gerhard Ebeling, Ernst Fuchs, and other theologians have welcomed Heidegger's hermeneutical theory and applied it to biblical interpretation.

In particular, Heidegger's analysis of the hermeneutical circle, of the impossibility of an interpretation without presuppositions, and his criteria for authentic human existence have influenced biblical hermeneutics ever since. But also Heidegger's later move toward a philosophy based on the understanding of language (the language of the artist in particular) as a call to being has stimulated biblical interpretation.

More recently, the development of philosophical hermeneutics was promoted further by the philosophers Hans-Georg Gadamer (b. 1900), Jürgen Habermas (b. 1929), and Paul Ricoeur (b. 1913). All three philosophers are having a significant impact on biblical interpretation and contemporary theological thinking.

Continuing Heidegger's project of developing a universal theory of understanding (and in a sense also Schleiermacher's hermeneutical enterprise), Gadamer has investigated especially the conditions of aesthetic understanding. In his major work *Truth and Method* (1960), he advocates a theory of understanding in which "Understanding is not to be thought of so much as an action of subjectivity, but as the placing of oneself within a process of tradition, in which past and present are constantly fused. This is what must be expressed in hermeneutical theory, which is far too dominated by the idea of a process, a method" (1975: 258–89). Thus, instead of developing a method of interpretation, Gadamer wishes to describe what happens when we get involved in text interpretation. He emphasizes that we always approach a text through a set of questions which shape our preunderstanding. This preunderstanding, however, is always already conditioned in some way by the text's own history of effects. Therefore, Gadamer speaks of the "historically operative consciousness" [*Wirkungsgeschichte*] of a text and identifies the structure of that consciousness as language: "Being that can be understood is language" (1975: 432). Language, then, is the place of our disclosure of truth. And this disclosure is the aim of the hermeneutical experience and the characteristic of its universality.

Habermas (1971) protests against what he sees as the uncritical nature of Gadamer's universal hermeneutics, especially its trust in the undistorted flow of communication. Ricoeur criticizes Gadamer's total rejection of methodological moves in text interpretation and proposes a twofold program of interpretation which includes acts of understanding and explanation. Thus, he can incorporate formalist and structuralist methods of text explication without subscribing to structuralist and formalist ideologies. Unlike Gadamer and Habermas, Ricoeur also has contributed directly to the discussion on adequate biblical interpretation (Ricoeur 1980). Today, Ricoeur must be seen as the philosopher who exerts the greatest influence on the development of biblical interpretation. Thus, he has brought Schleiermacher's program of a general hermeneutics to a new height, while at the same time also contributing directly to the appropriation of such a general theory in applied biblical interpretation.

D. Theories of Biblical Hermeneutics in the 20th Century

1. The Barth-Bultmann Controversy. Karl Barth (1886–1968), Rudolf Bultmann (1884–1976), and the other representatives of the "dialectical theology" movement in German-speaking theology after World War I agreed that a mere historical-critical study of the biblical texts did not do justice to these texts' theological character and particular existential claims. They all wanted to overcome the historicism which had dominated biblical interpretation for almost a century. But these theologians could not agree on a new method of biblical interpretation. While Bultmann appropriated Heidegger's ontological hermeneutics for his own program of biblical interpretation, Barth advocated an interpretation of the Bible without the interference of philosophical methodology.

a. Barth. The question which shaped Barth's hermeneutical perspective with regard to the biblical texts was, What is the Word of God and who am I in relationship to God's Word? Barth never identified the Word of God with the biblical texts, but neither did he explain how an attentive reading of the Bible would arrive at a disclosure of God's Word. God must not become an object of our interpretation theory: "Revelation is not a predicate of history, but history is a predicate of revelation" (1956: 58). Thus, Barth's interpretation of the Bible was motivated by his theological insight into the nature of God's revelation. On the basis of this theological preunderstanding, he approached the biblical texts. In the famous second edition of his commentary on the Epistle to the Romans (1922—ET 1968), he challenged the historical-critical exegetes to become "more critical." By that he meant they should listen more carefully to the specific content of the Scriptures and become open to God's act of self-communication in the process of reading.

In his *Church Dogmatics*, Barth suggests three practical steps for an adequate interpretation of the Scriptures: (1) observation: to attend to the literary and historical presentation of the text; (2) reflection: to think along with the text without imposing one's own modes of thought on it; and (3) appropriation: applying the text to one's own situation, which meant for Barth that interpreters ought to subject themselves to God's purposes which are witnessed to by the biblical texts (1956: 722–38). Hence, Barth's hermeneutics is totally theological by nature.

b. Bultmann. Unlike Barth, Bultmann accepted and defended the necessity of a philosophical reflection on the contemporary existential condition and on the principles of biblical interpretation. His particular reflection was located within the Schleiermacher tradition of philosophical hermeneutics and was greatly influenced by Heidegger's existential philosophy. Like Schleiermacher, Bultmann insisted that biblical interpretation must follow the same principles as the reading of any other literary text; following Heidegger, Bultmann stated that there cannot be any "presuppositionless" understanding of the biblical texts, and he demanded therefore that biblical interpreters ought to become conscious of their preunderstandings. Distinguishing between prejudice and preunderstanding, Bultmann demanded that the first must be abandoned and the latter be made conscious. Moreover, there has to be a life relationship between the exegete and the text which produces the particular preunderstandings that in turn will be transformed by the existential encounter between the reader and the text. Given the subjective aspect of this encounter, no interpretation of a biblical text can ever claim to be the definitive one (cf. Schleiermacher above).

Bultmann's own hermeneutical framework was shaped by Heidegger's call for an existential understanding; thus, Bultmann attempted to interpret the biblical texts with the aim of disclosing authentic modes of existence in the world. However, because of the historical distance between text and reader and in view of the particular "mythological" nature of some NT texts, Bultmann suggested a program of "demythologization." This somewhat misleading concept did not imply that the modern interpreter was to get rid of the mythological parts of the NT; rather, Bultmann intended to offer a method of interpretation which was aware of the difference between the rather mythological worldview of the Bible and the rather scientific worldview of the contemporary biblical reader. He did not aim to replace the mythological worldview with the modern scientific one; instead, he wanted to highlight the fact "that faith itself demands to be freed from any worldview produced by man's thought, whether mythological or scientific" (Bultmann 1958: 83).

c. The Debate. The debate between Barth and Bultmann, which has both promoted and polarized the further discussion on biblical hermeneutics, concerned once again the role of philosophical thinking in biblical interpretation. While Barth rejected any dependence of biblical interpretation on philosophical hermeneutics, Bultmann not only accepted the need for philosophical hermeneutics in biblical interpretation but also adopted a particular philosophical system and terminology, namely, that of the early Heidegger, in order to facilitate appropriations of the biblical texts today. In the meantime, both poles in biblical interpretation have received much criticism: Barth's hermeneutics has been criticized for its positivistic nature, Bultmann's for its sometimes ahistorical character, especially of his existential appropriation (see Bartsch 1953: 62). Nevertheless, the fact that in spite of all its shortcomings Bultmann's hermeneutical program was open for a dialogue with philosophy and other hermeneutical disciplines made it a springboard for subsequent approaches to biblical interpretation.

2. The "New Hermeneutic." This is the name of a movement which comprised both American and European exegetes who responded positively, though not without critical reflection, to Bultmann's hermeneutical program (see Robinson and Cobb 1964). Its main protagonists, Ernst Fuchs (1903–1983) and Gerhard Ebeling (b. 1912), understood faith as speech event and thus committed their theological attention to the hermeneutical problem present both in biblical interpretation and in the related theological discourse. Influenced not only by the concerns of "dialectical theology" (especially by Barth, Bultmann, and Gogarten), but also by Heidegger's philosophical reflection on language, Fuchs developed a hermeneutics which emphasized first the hermeneutical condition of all biblical interpretation and then suggested some concrete moves in NT interpretation (Fuchs 1954; 1968). Over against Barth, he stressed the need to reflect on the process of the mediation of God's Word in the Bible. Modern man has to ask who he is and approach the biblical texts through such an existential question. The proper approach to the NT is characterized then by a neutrality with regard to faith (Fuchs 1954: 116). Thus, through his hermeneutical reflection, Fuchs reintroduced the problem of natural theology into theology. However, his commitment to and his use of philosophical hermeneutics were ultimately defined by their service to the particular retrieval of biblical thinking or more precisely NT thinking. (The OT was not an object of hermeneutical reflection for either Bultmann or Fuchs.) Viewed from this perspective, Fuchs' theological connection to Barth is stronger than his hermeneutical thinking, taken in isolation, would suggest.

Like no other contemporary theologian before, Gerhard Ebeling has devoted a great deal of energy to hermeneutical reflection. Recognizing the limits of methodological rigor in traditional reformational theology, Ebeling, too, has appropriated Heidegger's understanding of language in order to develop a new foundation of biblical interpretation whose ultimate goal is to free the way for the Word of God in the act of text interpretation (*RGG* 3: 242–62). For Ebeling, the context of adequate biblical interpretation is the faithful approach to the Scriptures. The only real correspondence in biblical interpretation is the one between Word and faith. Thus, Ebeling's hermeneutical thinking remains strictly bound to the Protestant tradition of the Word.

Thus, up to the 1960s, Protestant thinkers dominated the discussion on biblical hermeneutics. But since then, a new interconfessional climate of hermeneutical thinking has been established in which Jewish, Roman Catholic, and Protestant thinkers contribute to the discussion of both the universal aspects of hermeneutics and the particular application of such philosophical theories on biblical interpretation.

3. Contemporary Biblical Hermeneutics. Since the period of the Enlightenment, Jewish and Christian interpreters have been struggling to come to terms both with the demands of reason in biblical interpretation and with the changing horizon of biblical interpretation. In spite of the particularities of the different movements within either Judaism or Christianity, it can be said that the hermeneutical discussion in both religions has received an attention that is increasingly transconfessional. This development was, of course, strongly promoted by a hermeneutical program such as the one offered by Schleiermacher, but it has also been facilitated by the organization of biblical research in modern academic institutions. Thus, modes and theories of biblical interpretation emerging from either religious tradition have been discussed beyond the boundaries of these traditions and were allowed to influence one another (see Loretz and Strolz 1968). For example, approaching the Hebrew Scriptures through the horizon of modernity, 20th-century Jewish thinkers such as Franz Rosenzweig, Martin Buber, and Gershom Scholem have influenced new approaches to the Hebrew Bible within the Christian tradition. The question of whether or not the Hebrew Scriptures can be adequately understood only in a particular Jewish religious context has found as many and as diverse answers as the parallel question of whether or not an adequate interpretation of the Christian Bible requires the interpreter's active participation in a Christian ecclesial context.

The long hostility in the Roman Catholic teaching authority, the Magisterium, against any form of modern critical interpretation theory also has come to an end in the course of the 20th century. Even though the Magisterium continues to reserve for itself the ultimate right of judging the orthodoxy of a particular reading of the Scriptures, the previous ban on modern exegetical techniques has been lifted more and more, especially in Pius XII's encyclicals *Divino afflante Spiritu* (1943) and *Humani Generis* (1962). The documents of the Second Vatican Council (see in particular *Dei Verbum*) confirmed this development toward a more critical biblical hermeneutics and thus, *de facto,* abolished any formal difference in exegetical method between Roman Catholic, Protestant, and Jewish scholars.

4. Current Developments in Biblical Hermeneutics. The more recent discussion of hermeneutics in biblical studies has concentrated on several themes. We intend to survey these main topics by way of a brief overview.

a. Biblical Theology. Ever since positivistic and historicist approaches began to dominate biblical interpretation, a reaction against these methods could be witnessed from those scholars who defended either the religious importance of the biblical canon as a whole or the thematic unity of the Bible. Already in the 19th century, such attempts to develop a biblical theology were visible. Also, in a sense, all the representatives of dialectical theology were engaged in developing a biblical theology. Today, scholars such as Gerd Theissen (1978; 1985) and Brevard Childs (*NTC*; 1986) propagate a renewed interest in the Bible as a theological and canonical unity. See THEOLOGY (BIBLICAL), HISTORY OF.

b. The Bible as Literature. The recent application of literary critical methods in biblical interpretation may be seen as a natural consequence of Schleiermacher's and Bultmann's demands that the Bible be treated like any other piece of literature. While in the past, the historical-critical method originated in biblical scholarship itself, the spectrum of literary methods used in contemporary biblical interpretation has been developed mainly by literary theorists (e.g., structuralist and poststructuralist theory). Two strands in that movement may be distinguished: (a) those biblical interpreters who, in their search for a theological interpretation of the biblical texts, either apply literary methods themselves in order to do better justice to the particular genres of biblical writing or are at least open to such an interpretation; and (b) those who treat the biblical texts solely as literary documents without any consideration of a possible faith context. The recent attention to reader-response criticism and other theories of reading has allowed interesting insights into the phenomenon of reading and into the potential of the biblical texts themselves to direct their readers. At the same time, a deepening awareness of the textuality of the biblical texts suggests that the often atomistic treatment of textual passages ought to be overcome or at least balanced by a consideration of the text as a whole (Jeanrond 1988).

c. Historical, Sociological, and Psychological Approaches. In the current interdisciplinary climate of biblical research, the traditional historical-critical approaches to the Bible have been amended by sociological and psychological perspectives of reading. This interdisciplinary approach has already yielded some interesting insights into the very complex relationship between religious and nonreligious dimensions in the biblical texts (see, e.g., Theissen 1985; Drewermann 1985; Gottwald 1985).

d. Feminist Criticism. The continuing development of a feminist perspective in biblical interpretation has not only rediscovered forgotten dimensions within the biblical texts themselves but has also raised awareness in biblical interpretation of the traditionally male characteristics of the perspectives through which the biblical texts have been read until now (see Schüssler Fiorenza 1984).

e. Theory and Praxis. Johann Baptist Metz (1980), Matthew Lamb, Dermot Lane (1984), and other theologians have repeatedly questioned the overemphasis on theory in biblical interpretation and the accompanying neglect of the praxis of Christian experience in the light of which the texts should be read. In view of this deficit, Metz calls for a practical hermeneutics of Christian liberation. The impact which this debate on the emancipatory nature of praxis has had in biblical interpretation can be seen in the biblical readings offered by leading representatives of the liberation theology movement (e.g., Gustavo Gutiérrez 1988).

f. Ethics. Fuchs (1954), Jeanrond (1988), and Berger (1988) have called for a renewed ethical consciousness in biblical interpretation. Fuchs (1954: 155) demanded a moral seriousness *(sittlicher Ernst)* from every biblical interpreter; Jeanrond (1988: 123–28) has emphasized the ethical demand of attending and responding to the theological nature of the communicative perspectives and claims of the biblical texts; and Berger (1988: 17–28) has advocated an approach to the biblical texts based on an awareness of actual human experience.

g. Interreligious and Cultural Criticism. David Tracy (1981; 1987) has stressed the cultural role of the Bible by calling it a "classic" text which bears an excess and permanence of meaning, yet always resists definitive interpretation. As such, it can function as a means of "interruption" in the cultural process, provided its interpreters are open to disclosing the instances of truth contained in it. Paul Knitter (1985) and Hans Küng (1986) have advocated the perspective of the interreligious dialogue as a necessary complement to any inner-religious approach to understanding these texts. Such a wider approach to the Scriptures moved by questions of the history and the comparative study of religion will also be able to point out such ideological dimensions within the biblical texts as, for instance, anti-feminist and anti-semitic attitudes (see Sandmel 1978).

E. Conclusion

The theoretical reflection on the conditions, methods, and motivations of biblical interpretation may be helpful both for a reading of the Bible within a context of religious faith and for a critical examination of the Bible as a religious and historical document within the academy. In either case, hermeneutical reflection promotes a critical and self-critical consciousness of the interpreter, but also encourages critical attitudes toward the biblical texts themselves. Whatever method may be applied in biblical interpretation, the hermeneutical reflection will point to its particular opportunities and limitations, and thus encourage an open-ended and critical attitude to all possible approaches which promise to support an adequate disclosure of the biblical texts' sense. Moreover, hermeneutical thinking will provide a critical view of all forms of power, individual and institutional, which aim at controlling the process of biblical interpretations within the different communities of interpreters.

Bibliography

Barth, K. 1956. *Church Dogmatics.* Vol. 1. Pt. 2. Edinburgh.
———. 1968. *The Epistle to the Romans.* 6th ed. Oxford.
Bartsch, H.-W. 1953. *Kerygma and Myth.* Vol. 1. London.
———. 1962. *Kerygma and Myth.* Vol. 2. London.
Berger, K. 1988. *Hermeneutik des Neuen Testaments.* Gütersloh.
Brinkmann, H. 1980. *Mittelalterliche Hermeneutik.* Darmstadt.
Bultmann, R. 1933–65. *Glauben und Verstehen.* 4 Vols. Tübingen. (ET 1969–1984).
———. 1958. *Jesus Christ and Mythology.* New York.
Childs, B. 1986. *Old Testament Theology in a Canonical Context.* Philadelphia.
Drewermann, E. 1985. *Tiefenpsychologie und Exegese.* 2 Vols. Olten.
Ebeling, G. 1962. *Evangelische Evangelienauslegung: Eine Untersuchung zu Luthers Hermeneutik.* Darmstadt.
———. 1967. *Wort und Glaube.* Vol. 1. 3d ed. Tübingen.
———. 1969. *Wort und Glaube.* Vol. 2. Tübingen.
Feld, H. 1977. *Die Anfänge der modernen biblischen Hermeneutik in der spätmittelalterlichen Theologie.* Wiesbaden.
Fuchs, E. 1954. *Hermeneutik.* Bad Cannstadt.
———. 1968. *Marburger Hermeneutik.* Hermeneutische Untersuchungen zur Theologie 9. Tübingen.
Gadamer, H.-G. 1975. *Truth and Method.* New York.
Ganoczy, A., and Schild, S. 1983. *Die Hermeneutik Calvins.* Wiesbaden.
Gottwald, N. 1985. *The Hebrew Bible: A Socio-literary Introduction.* Philadelphia.
Grant, R., and Tracy, D. 1984. *A Short History of the Interpretation of the Bible.* 2d ed. Philadelphia.
Gutiérrez, G. 1988. *A Theology of Liberation.* Maryknoll, NY.
Habermas, J. 1971. Der Universalitätsanspruch der Hermeneutik. Pp. 120–59 in *Hermeneutik und Ideologiekritik.* Theorie-Diskussion. Frankfurt am Main.
Heidegger, M. 1962. *Being and Time.* Oxford.
Hornig, G. 1961. *Die Anfänge der historisch-kritischen Theologie.* Göttingen.
Jeanrond, W. G. 1988. *Text and Interpretation as Categories of Theological Thinking.* Dublin and New York.
Knitter, P. 1985. *No Other Name?* Maryknoll.
Krüger, F. 1986. *Humanistische Evangelienauslegung.* BHT 68. Tübingen.
Küng, H. 1986. *Christianity and the World Religions.* New York.
Lane, D. 1984. *Foundations for a Social Theology.* Dublin.
Longenecker, R. N. 1975. *Biblical Exegesis in the Apostolic Period.* Grand Rapids.
Loretz, O., and Strolz, W., eds. 1968. *Die hermeneutische Frage in der Theologie.* Schriften zum Weltgespräch 3. Freiburg.
Lubac, H. de. 1959–79. *Exégèse médiévale: Les quatre sens de l'Écriture.* 4 vols. Paris.
Metz, J. B. 1980. *Faith in History and Society.* New York.
Morgan, R., and Barton, J. 1988. *Biblical Interpretation.* Oxford.
Palmer, R. 1969. *Hermeneutics.* Evanston.
Ricoeur, P. 1980. *Essays on Biblical Interpretation,* ed. L. S. Mudge. Philadelphia.
———. 1981. *Hermeneutics and the Human Sciences,* ed. J. B. Thompson. Cambridge.
Robinson, J. M., and Cobb, J. B., Jr., eds. 1964. *The New Hermeneutic.* New York.
Sandmel, S. 1978. *Anti-semitism in the New Testament.* Philadelphia.
Schleiermacher, F. D. E. 1977. *Hermeneutics: The Handwritten Manuscripts,* ed. H. Kimmerle, trans. J. Duke and J. Forstman. AARTT 1. Atlanta.
Scholder, K. 1966. *Ursprünge und Probleme der Bibelkritik im 17. Jahrhundert.* Munich.
Scholem, G. 1970. *Über einige Grundbegriffe des Judentums.* Frankfurt am Main.
Schüssler Fiorenza, E. 1984. *Bread Not Stone.* Boston.
Stuhlmacher, P. 1979. *Vom Verstehen des Neuen Testaments.* Göttingen.
Theissen, G. 1978. *Sociology of Early Palestinian Christianity.* Philadelphia.
———. 1985. *Biblical Faith: An Evolutionary Perspective.* Philadelphia.
Tobin, T. H. 1983. *The Creation of Man: Philo and the History of Interpretation.* CBQMS 14. Washington, DC.
Tracy, D. 1981. *The Analogical Imagination.* New York.
———. 1987. *Plurality and Ambiguity.* San Francisco.

WERNER G. JEANROND

IOB (PERSON) [Heb *yôb*]. The third son of Issachar (Gen 46:13). In the list of the people who went down to Egypt (Gen 46:8–27), Jacob's sons and grandsons are listed by families, according to their mothers. Iob was the grandson of Jacob and Leah by their fifth son, Issachar. In the genealogical list of Issachar in 1 Chr 7:1, the Ketib lists his name as *yāšîb,* Jashib, but the Qere has *yāšûb,* Jashub. This latter reading is supported by the Samaritan Pentateuch, by the LXX, and by all the versions. Jashub is also listed in Num 26:24 as the eponymous leader of the clan of the Jashubites. Speiser (*Genesis* AB, 345) explains this textual error in Genesis by saying that the scribe dropped the *šin* from the name. According to Speiser, it is easier to explain the dropping of the consonant in Genesis than to explain its addition in the parallel passage. Westermann (1986: 153) believes that Iob is an abbreviation of the theophoric name Yahshub, in which case it means "May Yahweh return" (*TPNAH,* 168).

Bibliography

Westermann, C. 1986. *Genesis 37–50,* trans. J. J. Scullion. Minneapolis.

CLAUDE F. MARIOTTINI

IOTA.

The ninth letter of the Greek alphabet.

IOTAPE (PERSON)

IOTAPE (PERSON) [Gk *Iōtapē*]. This name designates no fewer than seven princesses or queens active in the late 1st century B.C. and for most of the 1st century A.D. It also refers to two towns. See IOTAPE (PLACE).

1. Iotape I. The young daughter of Artavasdes, king of Media Atropatene (modern Azerbaijan, lying between the Upper Tigris river and the Caspian Sea), who was betrothed to Alexander Helios, son of Marc Antony and Cleopatra (Dio Cass. 49.40; 49.44; Plut. *Ant.* 53.6). The marriage ended when Antony died. The girl had been taken to Alexandria, where Octavian discovered her in 30 B.C., and reunited her with her father (Dio 51.16.2).

She next appears in the record about 20 B.C., when King Mithradates III of Commagene acquired her as his wife, though he was "still a little boy" and she was at least in her late teens. Because she was queen of Commagene, her children were considered valuable intermarriage partners by the heads of neighboring states. Iotape I and Mithradates II became the ancestors of the remaining royal women named Iotape, and grandparents of two kings of Emesa.

2. Iotape II. The daughter of Iotape I and Mithradates II who married her own brother, King Antiochus III of Commagene, in a philadelphic marriage typical of that dynasty. She presumably ruled with him up to his death in A.D. 17. A crisis in Commagenian affairs occurred then, and Tacitus records disturbances (*Ann.* 2.42). The royal family was presumably taken to Rome, and the kingdom itself became a Roman province from A.D. 18 to 38 (see Sullivan *ANRW* 2/8: 783–85).

3. Iotape III. Another daughter of Iotape I and Mithradates II who married Sampsigeramus II of Emesa (a Syrian kingdom located between Commagene and Judea). This marriage may have occurred as early as 5 B.C. Inscriptions honor her husband widely, sometimes as "Great King" (Baalbek) or *"roi suprême"* (Palmyra), but Iotape III went largely unmentioned. She became the mother of two kings of Emesa: Sohaemus and Azizus (see Sullivan *ANRW* 2/8: 212–14).

4. Iotape IV. The daughter of Iotape III and Sampsigeramus II of Emesa, who married Aristobulus of Judea, grandson of Herod the Great. This marriage placed her close to the Judean throne, since her husband's brothers included Herod of Chalcis and King Agrippa I. But they and others (not Aristobulus) ruled instead, and Aristobulus died "a private citizen" (Jos. *JW* 2 §221; cf. *Ant.* 18 §135; Sullivan *ANRW* 2/8: 319).

5. Iotape V. The "mute" *(kophe)* daughter of Iotape IV and Aristobulus. Her father's death occurred while she was still alive, but nothing further is known of her. No children in the Judean or other dynasties can be traced to her. Her handicap might have prevented her from assuming the high position otherwise expected from her royal descent.

6. Iotape VI "Philadelphos." She presumably appeared along with her husband-brother, King Antiochus IV of Commagene, when Caligula restored the kingdom's royal family in A.D. 38. The marriage must have occurred during the twenty years when Commagene was a province, because by A.D. 44 their son, Epiphanes, was old enough for betrothal to the Jewish princess Drusilla, niece of Iotape IV. Besides the city named for her in Cilicia, we have other traces of her activity. For instance, an inscription from Chios honors "Great King Antiochus Philocaesar; Iotape, wife of King Antiochus." Her head appears on coins of the dynasty and its cities, especially in Tracheiam where Antiochus joined other kings in a considerable effort at pacification. Antiochus also participated in the wars of Nero for control of Parthia, and their sons engaged in the Jewish War.

Iotape reigned with Antiochus until A.D. 72, when after the "Commagenian War" of Vespasian, Antiochus decided to give up the struggle, departing his kingdom "in a chariot with his wife and children." The two sons escaped to Parthia, but eventually joined the family in Rome (Sullivan *ANRW* 2/8: 783–94).

7. Iotape VII. The daughter of Iotape VI and Antiochus IV. She became the last queen of Cilicia (or some part thereof) when her husband, the Judean king Alexander (great-grandson of Glaphyra of Cappadocia), went there. In the joint coinage they issued, her portrait takes the place of honor on the obverse. Eventually both apparently journeyed to Rome, where Alexander became a consul, as did Iotape's nephew, Philoppapus. Two of their sons and two grandsons are known, highly placed in Roman society (Sullivan *ANRW* 2/8: 794f.; 1978: 935–37).

Bibliography

Macurdy, G. H. 1936. Iotape. *JRS* 26: 40–42.
———. 1937. *Vassal Queens and Some Contemporary Women in the Roman Empire.* Baltimore.
Sullivan, R. D. 1978. Priesthoods of the Eastern Dynastic Aristocracy. Pp. 914–39 in *Studien zur Religion und Kultur Kleinasiens,* ed. S. Sahin, E. Schwertheim, and J. Wagner. Leiden.

RICHARD D. SULLIVAN

IOTAPE (PLACE)

IOTAPE (PLACE) [Gk *Iōtape*]. Var. IOTABE; JOTAPATA. Although not mentioned in biblical sources, several towns in antiquity were named after the popular royal name Iotape. See IOTAPE (PERSON).

1. A town in Cilicia Tracheia, named after Iotape VI and situated at the end of a spectacular promontory on the S coast of modern Turkey. The harbor and well-cut sarcophagi nearby hint at the vitality it had in the 1st century and for some time afterward. Coins bearing its name from as late as the reign of Valerian (A.D. 253–260) attest its survival. It appeared for centuries longer in the ecclesiastical records of Isauria (Jones 1971: Appendix 4, Table xxx).

2. An episcopal see in Syria during Byzantine times was named Iotabe, a name possibly related linguistically to the royal name Iotape. A connection stemming from the period of dynastic rule (late 1st century A.D.) seems possible, though it cannot be demonstrated (Jones 1971: 293, 469, n. 91). An "Iotabe" in Palestine III is listed as a participant at the Council of Jerusalem in A.D. 536 (Jones 1971: 547, Appendix 4, Table xli).

3. On the strength of its name, the town of Jotapata (Gk *Iōtapata*) deserves brief mention here since it may be connected with the royal name Iotape. The city was situated in lower Galilee and should probably be identified with Kh. Jifat (M.R. 176248), about 20 km inland from the Bay of Acre, E of modern Haifa. It is not mentioned in the OT, but it was well known to Josephus, who in fact claims to have been instrumental in its defense during the Jewish War (*JW* 3 §141–339). Vespasian had laid siege to it, and it fell in July, A.D. 67. See also JOTBAH (PLACE).

Bibliography

Jones, A. H. M. 1971. *Cities of the Eastern Roman Provinces.* 2d ed. Oxford.

RICHARD D. SULLIVAN

IPHDEIAH (PERSON) [Heb *yipdĕyāh*]. One of eleven sons of Shashak, a Benjaminite (1 Chr 8:25), a portion of the extended genealogy of Benjamin (1 Chr 8:1–40). This is the only occurrence of the name in the MT, and it does not appear in the Apocrypha or the deuterocanonical literature. The name means "Yah will liberate" or "May Yah set free." Braun (*1 Chronicles* WBC, 124) and Coggins (*Chronicles* CBC, 54) both point to the scarcity of material associated with the names found in 8:6–27. However, the text does state that Iphdeiah was a *roʾšê ʾābôt,* and one of the *tōlĕdôtām roʾšîm* living in Jerusalem. This points to a probable mixing of tribal groups which intensified after the divided monarchy. Myers (*1 Chronicles* AB, 61) cites pressures exerted on boundary cities and an emphasis on administrative continuity on the district level as reasons for this mixing. One might infer a high status for Iphdeiah politically, socially, and perhaps to an extent militarily because of his identification as the head of a family and head of a genealogy. In early Israel (Harmon 1983: 153), the *bêt ʾāb* would have been the primary social unit which further comprised the *mišpāḥâ,* the clan or protective association of families (Gottwald 1979: 258), and then the *maṭṭeh/šēbeṭ* or tribe. The *bêt ʾāb* housed the extended family which was patriarchal, polygynous, patrilocal, and endogamous at the level of the *mišpāḥâ.* This social pattern would have held without great change to the time of Iphdeiah.

Bibliography

Gottwald, N. K. 1979. *The Tribes of Yahweh.* Maryknoll, NY.
Harmon, G. E. 1983. *Floor Area and Population Determination.* Diss. Southern Baptist Theological Seminary.

G. EDWIN HARMON

IPHTAH (PLACE) [Heb *yiptāḥ*]. Town situated in the Shephelah, or lowlands, of Judah (Josh 15:43), within the same district as Libnah and Maresha. This settlement, whose name perhaps means "he opens" (from *ptḥ,* "to open"), is listed among the towns within the tribal allotment of Judah (Josh 15:21–62). The ancient town is most often identified with modern Terqumiyeh, located approximately 10 km NW of Hebron and 11 km SE of Beit Jibrin (Simons *GTTOT* 148; M.R. 151109). Given the lack of similarity between the ancient and modern names, and the absence of archaeological substantiation, this identification should be regarded as tentative.

WADE R. KOTTER

IPHTAHEL (PLACE) [Heb *yiptaḥ-ʾēl*]. A valley in lower Galilee that is mentioned in concluding the description of the border of the territory of Zebulun after it "passed north of Hannathon" (Josh 19:14); it is also listed in the description of the territory of Asher at the point where Asher's border touches that of Zebulun (v 27). Dalman (1923: 35) suggested that the valley be identified with Nahal Sippori (Wadi el-Malik) that drains the Beth Netofa valley and opens out into the coastal plain in a deep and imposing gorge. Gal (1985), however, has suggested that the valley of Iphtahel be identified with Nahal ʾEvlayim (Wadi ʾAbbelin) that is connected at its NW corner by a pass to the Beth Netofa valley. He based this on the settlement pattern, the geological structure, and the fact that the ancient route from Acco that crossed through lower Galilee entered the Beth Netofa valley through Nahal ʾEvlayim. See also YIFTAHEL (M.R. 171240).

Bibliography

Dalman, D. G. 1923. Nach Galilea. *PJ* 18/19: 10–80.
Gal, Z. 1985. Cabul, Jiphtah-El and the Boundary Between Asher and Zebulun in the Light of Archaeological Evidence. *ZDPV* 101/2: 114–27.

RAFAEL FRANKEL

IR (PERSON) [Heb *ʿîr*]. Descendant of Benjamin appearing in an unusual genealogy in 1 Chr 7:6–12. The name means "city" or "town." This is the only occurrence of this form as a proper name in the MT, and it does not appear in the Apocrypha or the deuterocanonical literature. Some scholars have equated Ir with the Iri, son of Bela, seen in 1 Chr 7:7 (*ISBE*[1], 1490; Odelain and Séguineau 1981: 170); however, this is not certain. Ir is said to be the father of Shuppim and Huppim. At this point, the Chroniclers may be following the Benjaminite genealogy from Numbers 26 since v 39 mentions sons Shephupham and Hupham as opposed to the occurrence of Muppim and Huppim in Gen 46:21 (Myers *1 Chronicles* AB, 53). Scholars are quite divided over the origin of 1 Chr 7:12, and which Israelite tribal head is actually the ancestor of the individuals mentioned. Myers (AB, 53) states that 12b is a Danite fragment. Curtis and Madsen (*Chronicles* ICC, 147) and Brunet (1953: 485f.) feel that the genealogy belongs to the tradition of Zebulun. Coggins (*Chronicles* CBC, 50) is quite adamant in saying that there is no Danite reference in v 12. He suggests that the additional Benjaminite names shown at this point are both surprising and without explanation. It seems difficult to recover Danite or Zebulunite material without doing violence to the text. So perhaps those are additional Benjaminite names added to a post-exilic military census list.

Bibliography

Brunet, A.-M. 1953. Le Chroniste et ses Sources. *RB* 60: 481–508.

Odelain, O., and Séguineau, R. 1981. *Dictionary of Proper Names and Places in the Bible.* Trans. M. J. O'Connell. Garden City, NY.

G. EDWIN HARMON

IR-SHEMESH (PLACE) [Heb *ʿîr šemeš*]. A town in the territory of Dan (Josh 19:41), which is also known as BETH-SHEMESH (M.R. 147128). The name of the site means "city of the sun."

RAPHAEL GREENBERG

IRA (PERSON) [Heb *ʿîrāʾ*]. **1.** Ira the Jairite, a priest *(kōhēn)* to David mentioned in a list of officials of David (2 Sam 20:23–26; v 26). If a Jairite, Ira is probably to be associated with Havvoth-Jair, a group of villages in Gilead, which were taken by Jair, the son of Manasseh (Num 32:41; Deut 3:14). However, instead of "Jairite," some versions apparently read either "of Jattir," a levitical city of Judah (Josh 21:14), or "Ithrite," which would probably identify this person with the Ira in #3 below (Lucianic and Symmachus [?], *ho Iether;* Syriac, *yt(y)r*). Because Ira is not called a Levite, question is raised as to whether he was actually a nonlevitical priest or some sort of secular official, a situation analogous to that of the sons of David who are also designated "priests" in 2 Sam 8:18, but "chief officials" *(riʾšōnîm)* in 1 Chr 18:17 (see Cody 1969: 103–5; Mettinger 1971: 8–9).

2. One of David's champions, a select class of warriors directly attached to the king for special assignments, named in the parallel lists of 2 Sam 23:8–39 (v 26) and 1 Chr 11:10–47 (v 28). He is called the son of Ikkesh of Tekoa (lit. "the Tekoite"); that is, from the town of Tekoa in Judah, which lies about 5 miles S of Bethlehem. Although of high repute, he is distinguished from the more elite warriors (vv 8–23 and 11–25, respectively) listed before his grouping. The same Ira appears to be mentioned in a list of commanders found in 1 Chr 27:1–15 (v 9), since this list draws on eleven other mighty men found in 1 Chr 11:10–47. These commanders were each in charge of a monthly course of 24,000 men in the armed service of the king; Ira being in charge of the sixth month. This list of commanders and their functions is possibly a construct of its composer, since (a) no such monthly, conscripted, civilian army is mentioned elsewhere during David's reign; (b) the large figure of 288,000 men seems improbable; and (c) one of the commanders, Asahel (v 7), was dead before David had rule over all Israel (Williamson *Chronicles* NCBC, 174–75). However, the author/redactor's thesis, that David made preparations for the proper ongoing cultic and national life of Israel, as illustrated throughout chaps. 23–27, draws on the fact that David took a census (cf. vv 23–24; chap. 21) which could have been utilized for designing a monthly plan of conscription, a plan which would have been analogous to Solomon's monthly courses for his provision (1 Kgs 4:7–19).

3. Another of David's champions (see #2 above), Ira the Ithrite (2 Sam 23:38; 1 Chr 11:40), is probably to be associated with the people of Kiriath-jearim (1 Chr 2:53). Other versions of 1 Chr 11:40 in the Gk mss Vaticanus and Sinaiticus as well as in the Syriac and Arabic apparently read "of Jattir," which would identify this person with the Ira in #1 above. "Ira" is possibly a secular name taken from the animal realm: *ʿayir,* "a young male donkey" (*IPN,* 230).

Bibliography

Cody, A. 1969. *A History of the Old Testament Priesthood.* AnBib 35. Rome.

Mettinger, T. N. D. 1971. *Solomonic State Officials.* ConBOT 5. Lund.

RODNEY K. DUKE

ʿIRA, TEL (M.R. 148071). A site in the N Negeb with occupation levels ranging from the EB III through the Arab period.

A. Location and Identification

Tel ʿIra (Kh. Gharra in Arabic) is located on a high, flat-topped hill in the Beer-sheba valley on one of the southernmost ridges of the Hebron Hills that juts deep into the heart of the valley. As the site is cut off from the ridge by a ravine and surrounded by steep scarps, the ascent to the top of the tell is extremely difficult. At approximate 100 m above the surrounding terrain (514 m above sea level), it commands a sweeping view over the wide expanses and road network in the valley below. The site (ca. 25 dunams) covers the entire chalky hilltop. Remnants of the thick stone wall around the upper perimeter, contoured like the sole of a shoe, were visible on the surface even prior to excavation. See Fig. IRA.01.

The site was first reported by D. Alon in the early 1950s. In 1956, Y. Aharoni surveyed it intensively, and the results were published in the same year. Aharoni, who was impressed by the size and strategic potential of the site in comparison to other settlements in the region, suggested that the capital of the Negeb was transferred there in the 7th century B.C.E. following the final destruction of Beer-sheba by Sennacherib in 701.

The biblical name of the town is uncertain. Aharoni, with some reservations, proposed identifying it with Kabzeel, which heads the list of Judean towns in the Negeb (Josh 16:21). Others (A. Lemaire, N. Naʾaman, A. F. Rainey) believe that it is "Ramah of the Negeb" (or "of the South"), listed in the inheritance of the sons of Simeon (Josh 19:8), a name that reflects its lofty topographical position. It should be noted, however, that the archaeological excavations did not encounter any settlement level that could be attributed to the 10th–9th centuries B.C.E., which should be present if it is indeed the Ramoth-negeb to which David sent part of the plunder taken in his wars with the Amalekites (1 Sam 30:27). But neither were remains of this period discovered at Tel Aroer, which casts some doubts on the authenticity of this list of towns in a Negeb context. Nevertheless, some evidence of early Israelite occupation was found in a number of places on the

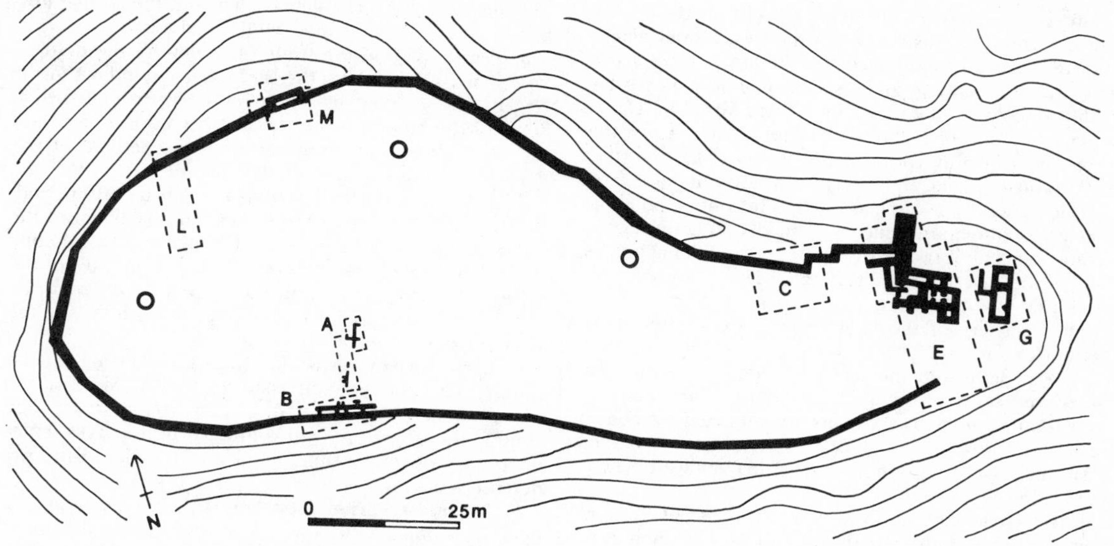

IRA.01. Site plan of Tel ʿIra—7th century B.C.E. *(Courtesy of I. Beit-Arieh)*

tell: sherds that date to the 10th–9th centuries were collected on the E escarpment, and there was also an earlier Iron Age burial in one of the graves belonging to the later Israelite settlement. Hence, it is possible that there was a small open village on the tell during this period. If so, the proposal to identify the site with Ramoth-negeb is worth consideration, although confirmation would require further excavation and discovery of the town itself.

Identification of the later settlements established on the tell (from the Hellenistic to Byzantine periods) is so far also unknown.

B. History of the Excavations

The excavations were directed by I. Beit-Arieh during six seasons, between 1979 and 1984. An additional season was conducted in 1979 in another sector of the site under the direction of A. Biran.

Nine strata, dating from the EB III to the Early Arab period, were exposed. The excavations unveiled a long history of settlement, showing that in certain periods (namely the Israelite, Hellenistic, and Byzantine periods) it was a city of major importance.

Chronological-Stratigraphical Chart

Strata/Period		Nature of Settlement
I	Early Arab (7th–8th centuries C.E.)	Small-scale occupation of Hellenistic structures.
II	Byzantine (5th–7th centuries C.E.)	City and monastery; reuse of Israelite city wall.
III	Early Roman (1st century C.E.)	City; reuse of Israelite city wall.
IV	Hellenistic (4th–2d centuries B.C.E.)	City; reuse of Israelite city wall.
V	Early Persian (5th–4th centuries B.C.E.)	Reoccupation of Israelite period buildings.
VI	Israelite II (second half of 7th century B.C.E.)	Fortified city.
VII	Israelite II (first half of 7th century B.C.E.)	Fortified city.
VIII	Israelite II (10th–9th centuries B.C.E.)	Pottery in fill of Stratum VII; burial in town's cemetery. Unwalled settlement (?)
IX	Early Bronze Age III (27th–23rd centuries B.C.E.)	Unwalled settlement; pottery scattered throughout site.

C. Results of the Excavations

1. Early Bronze Age. The tell was first occupied in the EB III and seems to have been a rural settlement of sporadic nature, the duration and reason for existence of which are unknown. Tel ʿIra is the southernmost known site to yield traces of EB III habitation, which in general was concentrated in the Shephelah; the closest EB III neighbor to Tel ʿIra was at Tel Halif.

2. Iron Age. Following a gap of some 1,500 years, the site was apparently resettled at the beginning of the second phase of the Israelite period, but because of the lack of architectural remains, it is impossible to determine the nature of this first occupation. However, the archaeological evidence implies an unwalled and materially poor village or hamlet.

However, in the 7th century B.C.E., Tel ʿIra was a large, fortified city of royal character that extended over the entire site. A massive, solid city wall (1.6-m thick), supported from the outside by retaining walls built against the steep scarps, surrounded the site almost completely. Large public buildings and a six-chambered gate passage with two towers of the type known from Megiddo, Hazor, and Gezer were erected in the E sector. A large tower that projected some 9 m from the N wall controlled the steep path to the city gate, and this strategically vulnerable area was defended by a casemate wall. The public buildings included a storehouse which contained a large number of pithoi. Remains of two superimposed occupational phases, both of the 7th century B.C.E. (Strata VII–VI), were uncovered inside the casemates.

The cemetery of the Israelite city was located at the bottom of the E slope, where more than twenty burial chambers hewn into the soft cretaceous limestone were discovered. Some of these were cleared by the excavators, who found dozens of skeletons accompanied by pottery vessels and jewelry. In one of these tombs there were at least thirty skeletons, a number that may indicate a large population.

The Israelite city was destroyed at the end of the First Temple period, either by the Babylonians in their campaign against Judah or perhaps somewhat earlier by the Edomites, who had been waiting for the chance to move in and take over these Negeb regions.

In view of the aridity of the area, a permanent water source was crucial for the existence of the city. Rock-hewn cisterns were the solution. Five large plastered cisterns for collection of runoff water from flash winter floods were discovered inside the settlement, one in the W sector, two in the center, and two in the E sector, creating a reservoir system that would have had sufficient capacity even in years of drought. Considering the location of the cisterns in relation to the buildings of the various periods, it is likely that the two cisterns in the E sector were hewn by the Byzantine population and the other three by the Israelites. Due to the topographical location of the settlement and its distance from any known springs or wells, such reservoirs were obviously the only means of ensuring a water supply.

Although the central government may have contributed to the subsistence of the city to a certain extent, the excavations have shown that the town had its own independent economic resources. The livelihood of the population was at least partially based on cultivation of field crops, and herding of cattle, sheep, and goats. Three agricultural terraces from the Israelite period can be distinguished in the small ravine N of the site. The only pottery from two probes near these terrace walls belongs to the 7th century B.C.E. Pollen samples taken from various depths of the soil showed that the principal crops were cereals. The fields of this large city undoubtedly extended over a large area, as testified by a small 7th-century B.C.E. farmstead that was discovered nearby. A ploughshare point and an iron sickle in one of the rooms of the settlement are further evidence of agricultural activity. Three silos were also found in the center of the town.

From the statistical study of the animal bones retrieved from the excavations, the livestock consisted mainly of sheep and goats (85 percent of the total faunal remains). These results are similar to those from other Israelite settlements in the Beer-sheba valley and the animal husbandry practices of the modern-day bedouin.

3. Persian Period (Stratum V). Following the destruction of the Israelite city, the site, like many others in the Negeb, was resettled by exiles returning from Babylon. Some of the houses of the Israelite city were reused, and silos were dug. Apparently the postexilic settlement was much smaller than that of the Israelite period.

4. Hellenistic Period (Stratum IV). During this period, the tell was the site of a populous city, probably one of the fortresses of the Seleucid defense line along the Edomite front. Remains of this city were unearthed in most of the excavated areas. Some new houses were built over the Israelite buildings that abutted the city wall, following the same orientation as their predecessors.

5. Early Roman Period (Stratum III). During the 1st century C.E., the site was sparsely settled. Most of the structures were concentrated in the E sector, where they abutted the city wall, which continued in use. This settlement was evidently a small outpost of the Herodian *limes* defense system.

6. Byzantine Period (Stratum II). Tel ᶜIra became a densely populated city once again during the Byzantine period, equaling the size of the earlier Israelite city. A large number of dwellings were built against the S segment of the Israelite city wall, which continued its defensive function. A monastery was erected in the E sector, superimposed over the Israelite gate and adjacent area, while a chapel with a decorated mosaic floor was built just E of it. Various small structures were crowded around the monastery. Tel ᶜIra seems to have served as the Byzantine administrative center of the E and central Negeb at this time.

7. Early Arab Period (Stratum I). Following the Muslim conquest of the country in the 7th century C.E., the Byzantine city became an Arab settlement. New rooms were built against the ancient city wall, and the monastery underwent extensive alterations, but the population seems to have been very small.

There is no doubt that Tel ᶜIra's largest populations were during the Israelite and Byzantine periods. Both were periods when the central authority invested the cities with regional administrative functions in addition to their primary defensive roles, guarding the S borders of the kingdom. Archaeological surveys indicate that these cities had an economic basis (reflected by the numerous small farmsteads and rural settlements scattered throughout the Negeb) that contributed to the security and economic viability of the cities.

Bibliography

Aharoni, Y. 1958. The Negeb of Judah. *IEJ* 8: 26–38.

Beit-Arieh, I. 1985. Tel ᶜIra—A Fortified City of the Kingdom of Judah. *Qad* 18/1–2: 17–25 (in Hebrew).

Gichon, M. 1975. The Sites of the *Limes* in the Negev. *EI* 12: 149–66 (in Hebrew).

Naʾaman, N. 1980. The Inheritance of the Sons of Simeon. *ZDVP* 96: 136–52.

ITZHAQ BEIT-ARIEH

IRAD (PERSON) [Heb *ᶜîrād*]. Son of Enoch and father of Mehujael, in the line of Cain (Gen 4:18). The LXX substitution of the "r" with a "d," rendering *Gaidad* (possibly reflecting the similarity of *rēš* and *dālet* in later Heb script), is not followed by the other versions. Various etymological explanations have been conjectured for the name (Gabriel 1959: 412–13). From the standpoint of comparative Semitics, *ʿrd* has been related variously to the (Ar, Akk, Heb, Ug) words for "wild ass, onager" (CAD 9: 88; *DISO*, 221; Huffmon *APNM*, 204; Dahood 1975), and to the (Ar) word for "cane huts" (where the initial *ʿayin* is read as a *ghayin;* Cassuto 1961: 231–32). Another approach, without textual evidence, has been to eliminate the final reference to Enoch in Gen 4:17, thereby relating the statement about the naming of the first city to Enoch's son, Irad. If separated from the rest of the name, the initial *îr* in Irad is the Hebrew word for city (cf. Jacob 1934: 148). Attempts have been made to identify Irad with the city of Eridu (Hallo 1970: 64; Sasson 1978: 174; Miller 1985: 241–42 n. 9; Wenham *Genesis 1–15* WBC, 111). The similarity of names in the genealogies of Genesis 4 and 5 has also led to comparison of Irad with Jared (Gen 5: 18–20).

Bibliography

Cassuto, U. 1961. *A Commentary on the Book of Genesis.* Pt. 1, *From Adam to Noah,* trans. I Abrahams. Jerusalem.

Dahood, M. 1975. Four Ugaritic Personal Names and Job 39 5.26–27. *ZAW* 87: 220.

Gabriel, J. 1959. Die Kainitengenealogie. Gn 4, 17–24. *Bib* 40: 409–27.

Hallo, W. W. 1970. Antediluvian Cities. *JCS* 23: 57–67.

Jacob, B. 1934. *Das Erste Buch der Tora. Genesis Übersetzt und Erklärt.* Berlin. Repr. New York.

Miller, P. D., Jr. 1985. Eridu, Dunnu, and Babel: A Study in Comparative Mythology. *HAR* 9: 227–51.

Sasson, J. M. 1978. A Genealogical "Convention" in Biblical Chronography? *ZAW* 90: 171–85.

RICHARD S. HESS

IRAM (PERSON) [Heb *ʿîrām*]. One of the eleven Edomite "tribal chiefs" (Heb *ʾallûpîm*) listed in Gen 36:40–43, a later appendix to the Edomite materials in Genesis 36 (probably originating with the Priestly source), and also listed in 1 Chr 1:51b–54, an abbreviated form of the Gen 36:40–43 list. This is the only place where Iram occurs, and therefore it is impossible to view the name as an authentic historical part of the Edomite tribal system. In Gen 36:43 the LXX reads *Zaphōim/Zaphōein,* while in 1 Chr 1:54 it reads *Eram/Zaphoein.* The interpretation of the name is uncertain; perhaps it can be understood as an animal name **ʿair-,* "donkey foal" (cf. Heb **ʿîr*) with the suffix *-ām.*

ULRICH HÜBNER

IRAM (29°34′N; 35°24′E). An ancient settlement of the Nabatean and Roman era located in Wadi Ramm, 40 km E of ʿAqaba. The ruins include a Nabatean temple dedicated to the goddess Allat, surrounded by a large settlement of the Nabatean-Roman era. A hydrological system is also constructed from the nearby spring and shrine of Allat at ʿAin Shellaly, which is nestled in the lofty heights of Jabal Ramm about 1 km S of the temple site. It consists of an aqueduct leading from the spring to a reservoir in the valley floor about 500 m from the settlement; the remains of another branch which led toward the settlement are also visible. More than a dozen other springs which exist in Wadi Ramm have undoubtedly been an attraction for visitors in various periods. Prehistoric remains are particularly abundant in the region, but only a few scattered Iron Age (II) sherds have been found in the valley. Although several Minean (S Arabian) graffiti in the vicinity of the settlement reflect activities in the Hellenistic period (G. Ryckmans in Savignac 1934: 590–91), most of the extant remains emanate from the Roman era.

The site was first discovered by G. Horsfield in 1930. The temple was later excavated by Savignac and Horsfield (1935), and more recently by D. Kirkbride (1960). The surrounding settlement was cleared in 1963 by Rida al-Rawwad. Hundreds of pre-Islamic Thamudic graffiti lining the bays of the adjacent mountains in the wadi have been collected (Harding 1952), and hundreds more await publication (D. F. Graf, W. L. Jobling, and G. King are currently preparing additional texts from the region). A number of these laconic texts include petitions to the goddess Allat. Nabatean texts from nearby ʿAin Shellaly and Umm al-Quseir about 7 km SE of the temple indicate that Allat was "the goddess who (dwells) at Iram" (Savignac 1932: 593). Other deities, namely Dushara, Baʿal-samin, al-ʿUzza (Savignac 1934: 576; 586–89), and al-Kutba' (Strugnell 1959), are also mentioned in Nabatean texts from the site.

The temple has been the focus of attention at the site. It consists of a columned hall (11 m × 13 m) with an E entrance; chambers also align the exterior walls. The initial date and possible phases of its construction remain controversial. The original excavaters postulated a date in the early 2d century A.D. for the entire complex, but Kirkbride (1960) argued for an evolutionary development of three stages for the construction of the temple: (1) under Rabbel II, the initial peripteral temple was erected; (2) in the 2d century, partitions were built between the columns to form an enclosed hall, and a rectangular cella was constructed in the interior of the court; and (3) during the 3d century, the walls of the temple were buttressed and annexes built, and the columns and walls were stuccoed and then painted in red, yellow, and blue. More recently, an earlier date for the initial construction of the temple has been advocated, either in the 1st century B.C. (Hammond 1973: 63) or in the time of Aretas IV (9 B.C.–A.D. 40). Nabatean temples from the time of Aretas IV at Petra ("the Winged Lion sanctuary") and at Kh. al-Dharih in N Edom offer close parallels to the temple at Iram. A fragmentary Nabatean text from the temple area ambiguously dated to the year of 41 or 45 (Savignac and Horsfield 1935: 268) also has been associated with the reign of Aretas IV based on the architectural and ceramic remains of the temple (Negev *ANRW* 2/8: 587). However, the paleography of the text implies a date of the Roman provincial era (cf. Starcky *DBSup* 7: 980), i.e., A.D. 147 or 151, rather than A.D. 31 or 36. The only other clearly dated inscription in the area is a Nabatean text from nearby ʿAin Shellaly from the time of Rabbel II, i.e., A.D. 71–106 (Savignac 1933: 408). Other datable materials are from the later period: a coin of

Marcus Aurelius, some Roman and Byzantine sherds, and a Latin inscription on a small altar discovered at the entrance to the temple, which probably is to be assigned to the 3d century A.D. (Sartre 1982: 24). Greek inscriptions to the goddess, which are also found at the spring of ʿAin Shellaly, are probably the product of local inhabitants and indigenous troops assigned to this corner of the Roman imperial frontier.

The ancient settlers at the oasis have been identified with the Arreni, an Arab tribe involved in the caravan trade (Pliny *HN* 6.32.157). In Ptolemy's 2d-century A.D. list of the inland villages of the Arabian peninsula, Aramaua is listed first, followed by Ostama and Thapaua (*Geog.* 6.7.27), which have been identified with the modern villages of Qurayya and Tabuk (cf. Graf 1983: 655). The village complex at Ramm has also been associated with the "many columned city of Iram" mentioned in the Quran (89:5–7). A tribe named Iram is also known in ancient pre-Islamic Arabic poems and mentioned with the tribes of ʿAd and the Thamud. The former is known from pre-Islamic texts from the region of Ramm (Harding 1952: no. 4) and the latter was centered in the adjacent land of Midian (Graf 1978). Ramm is also the location of one of the earliest pre-Islamic Arabic inscriptions known, a brief text that recently has been assigned to the 4th century A.D. (Bellamy 1988: 372). Arabic genealogies of the Islamic period identified Iram with Aram, the son of Shem (Gen 10:22 and 1 Chr 1:17), and interpreted other Arab tribes as the descendants of Iram (Watt 1971).

Bibliography

Bellamy, J. A. 1988. Two Pre-Islamic Arabic Inscriptions Revised: Jabal Ramm and Umm al-Jimal. *JAOS* 108: 369–78.

Graf, D. F. 1978. The Saracens and the Defense of the Arabian Frontier. *BASOR* 229: 1–26.

———. 1983. The Nabateans and the ḥisma: In the Footsteps of Glueck and Beyond. Pp. 647–664 in *WLSGF.* Winona Lake.

Hammond, P. 1973. *The Nabataeans—Their History, Culture and Archaeology.* Studies in Mediterranean Archaeology 37. Gothenburg.

Harding, G. L. 1952. *Some Thamudic Inscriptions from the Hashimite Kingdom of the Jordan.* Leiden.

Kirkbride, D. 1960. Le Temple Nabatéen de Ramm. *RB* 67: 65–92.

Sartre, M. 1982. *Trois études sur l'Arabie romaine et byzantine.* Brussels.

Savignac, R. 1932. Notes de Voyage: Le sanctuaire d'Allat à Iram. *RB* 41: 581–97.

———. 1933. Le sanctuaire d'Allat à Iram. *RB* 42: 405–22.

———. 1934. Le sanctuaire d'Allat à Iram. *RB* 43: 572–91.

Savignac, R., and Horsfield, G. 1935. Le Temple de Ramm. *RB* 44: 245–78.

Strugnell, J. 1959. The Nabataean Goddess 'Al-Kutba' and Her Sanctuaries. *BASOR* 156: 29–36.

Watt, W. M. 1971. Iram. *Encyclopaedia of Islam,* vol. 3, ed. B. Lewis et al. London.

DAVID F. GRAF

IRAN, PREHISTORY OF. The prehistoric period in Iran covers the period from the beginnings of human occupation in the Pleistocene to the beginning of the historic period, traditionally set on the plateau at 550 B.C. with the accession of Cyrus the Great. In the Khuzistan lowlands of SW Iran, however, writing developed at the end of the 4th millennium B.C. As a result, in this one corner of Iran the historical period begins in the 3d millennium B.C. when the sporadic local records are augmented by the ED texts of Mesopotamia (Carter and Stolper 1984).

The Pleistocene occupation of Iran by simple hunters and gatherers is documented by scattered finds of stone tools and by limited excavations in a number of caves, many of which contain Middle Palaeolithic Mousterian remains (Smith 1985).

With the end of the Ice Age and the amelioration of cold steppe conditions on the Iranian plateau, an environment conducive to the adoption of sedentary life was established between 9000 and 6500 B.C. This change is partly visible at a number of aceramic sites located around the lowland fringes of the plateau and in the lower valleys of the central W Zagros. These sites include Tepe Ali Kosh in the Deh Luran plain of NW Khuzistan (Hole et al. 1969), Tepes Guran and Ganj Dareh in nearby Luristan (Meldgaard et al. 1964; Smith 1976), Hotu and Belt Caves at the SE corner of the Caspian Sea (Coon 1957), pre-Jeitun sites in neighboring Soviet Central Asia (Kohl 1984), and Mehrgarh on the border of the Indus valley in SE Baluchistan (Lechavallier 1985). While differing in details, these aceramic occupations share various aspects of the transition to a sedentism based on a growing exploitation of domesticated plants and animals as a subsistence base. The hunting of wild animals was gradually superceded by the keeping of domesticated goats, sheep, and, later, cattle; while the collecting of wild seeds was replaced by the growing of wheat, barley, and legumes. Grinding stones for food preparation and the crushing of red ochre were common, while geometric microliths were mounted with bitumen as sickle blades and as transverse arrowheads, as shown at Mehrgarh. All of these settlements lack properly fired ceramics but show an early association with the use of clay as a plastic material for the making of quadruped animal and stylized human female figurines, sundried brick, and plaster for walls, floors, and storage silos. Houses with small rooms and blocks of storage bins were built—associated with hearths, small cooking ovens, and storage pits. Bricks were often long slabs of finger-impressed clay, and floor plaster was sometimes colored. Vessels of unbaked clay occur at Ganj Dareh. Horns of wild sheep attached to walls and elaborate human figures of clay at Ganj Dareh suggest religious practices. Other religious practices are suggested by the inclusion of red ochre in graves along with matting and simple offerings such as personal ornaments in the form of shell and stone bead necklaces and bracelets. In Deh Luran and at Mehrgarh, seashells (*Olivia* and *Conus*) suggest an early trade with the Persian Gulf–Indian Ocean area. At Ali Kosh, obsidian from Anatolia occurs in the earliest aceramic levels, while at Mehrgarh the use of turquoise, lapis lazuli (from the Chagai mountains near the frontier of Pakistan and Afghanistan), steatite, and calcite show the existence of an indirect long-distance exchange trade in exotic materials. These same materials remained popular luxury items throughout the Bronze Age. Rare stone vessels and bitumen-lined baskets provided containers before the appearance of pottery. The aceramic period was already one of extensive experimentation and innovation in technology and cultural practice.

Between 6500 and 5500 B.C. the population increased, so that by the end of this period settled villages are in evidence in nearly every part of the plateau (Hole fc.). Only a few have been sampled by excavation, and almost none have been excavated horizontally to provide complete building plans or settlement information. The most complete information comes from Hajji Firuz in Azerbaijan (Voigt 1983), Zagheh in central Iran (Malek Shahmirzadi 1979), Jeitun in Soviet Turkmenia (Kohl 1984), and, slightly later, Jaffarabad in Khuzistan (Dollfus 1983). Other important information comes from Ali Kosh, Chogha Sefid, and Chogha Mish (Khuzistan); Late Guran (Luristan); Sarab (Kirmanshah); Zagheh and Sialk (Central Iran); Sang-i Chakhmaq East (Gurgan); Tal-i Mushki and Tal-i Jari (Fars); Yahya (Kerman); and Mehrgarh (Baluchistan) (Voigt and Dyson fc.; Hole, fc.).

In addition to relying on a mixed economy of hunting, gathering, farming, and herding, these villages contained houses and other small structures of mud brick, sometimes built on mud-brick platforms or rows of stone. In the case of Hajji Firuz and Jeitun, houses were usually one- or two-room rectangular structures with outside alleys and open areas devoted to hearths, pottery kilns, and debris from stone, bone, and shell manufacturing processes. Occasional structures appear to have been used for special purposes; for example, the "Painted Building" at Zagheh (Negahban 1979), with red-, white-, and black-painted walls, which were further enhanced by the addition of animal skulls and horns. Human female figurines of clay were found inside this structure, which was equipped with benches. The purpose of the building thus appears to have been religious in nature. Its complexity suggests a development toward more formal religious practices in the community, perhaps under the direction of part-time specialists.

The ceramic technology now practiced in these villages was based on the firing of chaff-tempered clay at low temperatures. The handmade bowls and jars produced were often slipped red or buff, sometimes burnished, and often painted in red, brown, or black geometric designs derived from local decorative traditions (Mellaart 1975). Experiments with ceramics were continuous, and in Deh Luran and the nearby Zagros valleys, Black-on-Cream and Black-on-Red slipped ware appears, while at Zagheh a sand-encrusted ware was produced by covering the wet clay vessel with sand before firing.

Other widely distributed artifacts indicate intersite contact and shared customs across the plateau. These include grooved stone polishers, miniature cosmetic mortars and pestles, stone labrets, geometric microliths, and carved-bone sickle handles with animal (Mushki, Chakhmaq) or human (Sialk) motifs (Voigt and Dyson fc.). The dead were buried beneath the floors of houses or, in the case of Hajji Firuz, in bins or on platforms in the house. Simple gifts of pottery bowls, rare polished stone axes, or pieces of meat were placed in the graves. Red ochre continued to be scattered over the remains. While such practices were widespread, indicating perhaps shared concepts of life after death, the distinctiveness of the local decorative traditions shows that for the most part these settlements were largely independent of one another.

During the following millennium (5500–4500 B.C.), this independence began to break down due to two developments: one, the growing complexity of town life in neighboring Mesopotamia, which produced an increasing interest in foreign sources of raw materials for luxury consumption; and, second, the continuing development of craft activity in Iran itself, which gave rise to an increasing exchange between the source areas of raw materials and market centers. In the first half of this period, a very specialized form of pottery, Cheshmi Ali ware, appeared along the N trade route from Sialk and Zagheh in the W to the border of Khorasan and the SE Caspian shore in the E (Voigt and Dyson fc.). The pottery is brittle, thin, and orange colored and is decorated with birds, boars, and leaping ibex painted in thin black lines. Whether this distribution represents trade, the movement of potters or people, or some combination of these is not currently known. A probable movement of people is suggested in the middle of this period by the distribution of Dalma Monochrome, Painted and Impressed Ware from Azerbaijan S to the Kurdistan-Luristan border at Godin Tepe and smaller surrounding sites (Young and Levine fc.). This distribution follows the natural line of march along the parallel Zagros valleys. Toward the end of the period, an intensification of contacts between Khuzistan and Fars is seen in the painted pottery which shares geometric and naturalistic patterns. This pottery is highly developed in the Middle Bakun period of Fars (Langsdorf and McCowan 1942) with the appearance of stylized human beings, caprines, insects (ticks), flying birds, fish, and plants—all elements which reappear subsequently in Iranian art at frequent intervals (Porada 1965).

Combined with these regional spreads of ceramics is the appearance of evidence for the existence of locally specialized craft production. For example, at Chogha Mish, which was already a sizable town at this time, a burned structure yielded pots, flint nodules, and flint working debris in the main room. The flint materials were far in excess of local needs, indicating a production intended for export (Kantor 1976). At the village of Jaffarabad near the later urban center of Susa, the entire site was a potter's workshop in this period (Dollfus 1983). On the plateau, the site of Iblis in Kerman province was heavily engaged in copper working, as indicated by masses of crucible and copper ore fragments and a number of copper objects (Caldwell 1967).

Equally important at this time is the evidence for trade contacts in the S: numerous Persian Gulf and Indian Ocean shells, obsidian from Anatolia, and carnelian, turquoise, steatite, and ivory from other areas. At Yahya these occur in a major architectural complex of more than fifty rooms. Tools, ornaments, chisels, and pins and an ingot of copper show the importance of metallurgy. Clay and stone stamp seals, like those in Fars, show the gradual spread of the use of this device for the identification of ownership eastward from Mesopotamia by way of Khuzistan and Fars to Kerman. Similar indications of extended exchange occur at Sialk in Central Iran, where carnelian, turquoise, and copper all occur. It is probably not an accident that the evidence for the growth of this trade parallels the wider spread of ceramic traditions.

Beginning around 4000 B.C., the cultural dynamics of the lowland area underwent a significant change. Although in contact with the piedmont zone of E Mesopotamia since the aceramic period, Khuzistan became gradually more exposed to direct S Mesopotamian contact as Sumerian civilization developed. From 4000 B.C., the influence from Mesopotamia grew steadily stronger, leading at first to the introduction of Uruk pottery and glyptic to Deh Luran and then Susa (Rencontre 1979), and later, in the 3d millennium, to the direct military and political confrontations of the historic period (Carter and Stolper 1984). Probably in part from the stimulus of the growing complexity of Sumerian social and urban organization, the Susians, shortly after 4000 B.C., constructed a massive temple platform of mud brick decorated along the sides with rows of votive clay cones (Rencontre 1979). This temple apparently functioned as a cult center along the lines of similar centers in S Mesopotamia and, like these, attracted to itself a large cemetery. Burials were accompanied by stone vessels, copper celts, mirrors, and other objects and by extremely thin and elaborately painted pottery decorated with stylized animals, human figures, and geometric symbols. The labor and capital investment represented by this cult center indicates the rise of a religious and political hierarchy capable of carrying out such a monumental project. This cult function continued to develop and led to Susa's emergence as the chief administrative and religious center of Elam. As part of the process, perhaps under the influence of S Mesopotamia, a system of ownership identification using stamp and cylinder seals developed; and, in the middle of the 4th millennium B.C., a system for the notation of numbers and products by marking clay tablets was invented. The system of stamp seals spread eastward onto the plateau, where it is found in Fars at Tal-i Bakun in the Late Bakun period (Langsdorf and McCown 1942). Jar, packet, and door sealings show the existence of formal administrative control over goods being moved and stored (Langsdorf and McCown 1942). The basic agricultural wealth of Susiana combined with its unique geographical position between the Iranian plateau and its access to raw materials and the urban markets of the Mesopotamian plain undoubtedly explain the influential role it came to play in both areas.

Toward the end of the 4th millennium B.C., these various trends led to the first full-scale interregional intrusions through the establishment of extensive trade enclaves, intensive exchange, and actual migration. In the SW of Iran for the first time there is a virtual identity of ceramics associated with a pictographic "Proto-Elamite" script at Susa in Khuzistan and at Malyan (ancient Anshan) in Fars (Rencontre 1979). Malyan at this time was five times the size of contemporary Susa and was the largest known Proto-Elamite center. Since it is likely that the script records an early form of Elamite, these two sites may already represent two of the incipient polities of the later Elamite state (Carter and Stolper 1984). The third Elamite polity, Simashki, was probably located in Luristan, but has yet to be firmly located. Further E of Fars, in Kerman province, a late 4th millennium trading enclave was established at Tepe Yayha (Potts 1977). At this site a large structure containing impressions of Proto-Elamite cylinder seals, tablets inscribed in Proto-Elamite pictographic script, and monochrome and polychrome pottery of Sumerian type appear to indicate the establishment of a Proto-Elamite administrative center or trading enclave (Lamberg-Karlovsky and Tosi 1973). The purpose of this center seems to have been to exploit the sources of chlorite found around the site for the production of stone bowls, plaques, and other objects. The excavated area of the mound does not permit a firm conclusion as to whether the structure is simply an enclave or whether it represents a complete occupation of the site at this time. What it does indicate, however, is the direct presence in Kerman of individuals from Anshan or Susa. Whether this was a military or political presence or simply a trading arrangement on the order of the later Assyrian trading colonies in Cappadocia remains to be seen. Further E, the appearance of seal impressions and a single Proto-Elamite tablet in the earliest period at Shahr-i Sokhta in Sistan shows a remote extension of the contacts more strongly evidenced at Yahya (Lamberg-Karlovsky and Tosi 1973).

In W central Iran, a similar manifestation of Proto-Elamite interests is evidenced at Godin Tepe near Kangavar and at Tepe Sialk near Kashan on the edge of the central desert (Weiss and Young 1975). At Godin, it is very clear that a multi-roomed structure and compound in the center of the site, containing Proto-Elamite tablets, cylinder seals, and imported pottery (including beveled rim bowls, sometimes thought in Mesopotamia to have been used for measuring out grain rations), formed a self-contained enclave in the midst of an otherwise local community. Further E at Sialk, similar painted pottery, seals and sealings, and tablets also indicate direct contact with Susa (Ghirshman 1938). Unfortunately, the excavated area at Sialk is too limited to tell whether the material also occurs in an enclave or is more generally distributed. Whether these various enclaves of slightly differing dates represent peaceful trading arrangements or were forcefully imposed on these localities cannot yet be determined. If forceful occupation is the case, we may have the first evidence for the existence and expansion of an early state structure centered on Malyan (Anshan) and Susa in the Proto-Elamite period.

In this same period in NE Iran, the making of burnished gray pottery became widespread at the end of the 4th millennium. It is especially well known from Shah Tepe and Tureng Tepe just E of the Caspian Sea and at Tepe Hissar immediately S on the plateau (Schmidt 1937). The technique of reduced firing was developed well back in the painted-pottery period of the 4th millennium at these sites. By the end of the 4th millennium, gray pottery became the common ware, although at Tepe Hissar painted pottery continued to be made in small quantities into the early 2d millennium (Schmidt 1937). The development of decorative techniques and vessel shapes in gray pottery is largely distinct as seen between the Gurgan plain and the plateau, although trade contacts are clearly indicated. At Hissar, painted bowls on low hollow stems were gradually replaced by bowls on tall hollow or solid stems, beaker forms, and low-necked jars. By 3000 B.C., the town was full of craftsmen working lapis lazuli with an elaborate tool kit of flint drills and cutting blades. Extensive working of copper ore is also in evidence (Dyson and Howard fc.). Numerous stamp seals and small pottery "tokens" indicate linkages to the W, but few actual imports can be documented. One of these, however, is half a burned chlorite cylinder seal of a type known from Proto-Elamite contexts at Shahr-i Sokhta, Yahya, Malyan, and Susa. East of Hissar in this period, the first significant southward expansion of the Namazga painted-pottery culture of Soviet Turkmenia occurred, as shown by its presence in the earliest settlement at Shahr-i Sokhta in Sistan (Tosi 1979). By the late 3d millennium, a N–S cultural relationship extended from Mehrgarh on the edge of the Indus valley in Baluchistan to an Indus emporium at Shortugai on the S edge of the Bactrian plain in N Afghanistan (Jarriage 1985). The emergence of a knowledge of this N–S pattern and its strength is one of the major changes in our knowledge of Iranian prehistory in recent years.

Beginning around 3000 B.C., for the first time we can see the expansion of cultures originating beyond the N borders of Iran onto the plateau. In NW Iran, the N half of Azerbaijan province was occupied by the Early Bronze Age Transcaucasian Culture, also called the Yanik Culture in Iran after the site where it is best known (*CAH* 2/1: 686–715). This culture was characterized by round mud-brick buildings with a central pole supporting a roof of wattle and daub. Twenty-three structures have been excavated at Yanik Tepe (Burney and Lang 1972). Toward the end of the Early Bronze I period, a stone-based defensive wall 4-m to 6-m thick was built. In the following Early Bronze II period, the round structures were replaced by rectangular one- and two-room houses. The pottery of both periods was handmade and colored in black to gray with a high burnish (but of a different type from that in the NE). The Early Bronze I period pottery was decorated with incised and excised geometric and bird patterns. This cultural group appears to have spread southward through E Azerbaijan, arriving sometime in the second quarter of the 3d millennium at Godin Tepe in the Kangavar valley, where it makes up period IV (Young and Levine fc.). Further to the S only trade sherds are known to occur.

The latter half of the 3d millennium was a time of prosperity for all of the widespread trading towns. In the W, the painted pottery of Godin III and its analogues spread through the Zagros with the disappearance of the Transcaucasian intrusion (Young and Levine fc.); in the south an elaborate painted pottery characterized by rows of fat birds (Kaftari ware) spread over Fars and even reached Yahya in Kerman in small quantities; the gray burnished pottery of the NE continued in Gurgan, while the Namazga-derived pottery of Shahr-i Sokhta continued to be made at that site (Voigt and Dyson fc.). The towns continued as specialized manufacturing centers. Especially notable is the continuing production of chlorite objects and vessels at Yahya, but in the absence of evidence for any enclave from the W (Kohl 1979). The level of wealth of the period is seen in the richly furnished graves of Hissar and Shahdad, which contain a wide variety of copper, bronze, lead, gold, silver ornaments, tools, and vessels along with beads of agate, carnelian, lapis, and alabaster and pottery vessels (Schmidt 1937). At Shahdad a number of extraordinary painted clay busts have been recovered (Hakemi 1973). Many of the pots from the Shahdad graves, as well as those from Yahya, bear symbols originally incised or impressed into the wet clay. At least one inscription shows that a post–Proto-Elamite script existed in the area. Cylinder seals showing a vegetation goddess provide a glimpse of religious iconography (Hakemi 1973).

The long-range trade in raw materials that presumably provided much of this prosperity came to an unexpected halt at the end of the first quarter of the 2d millennium when most of the sites in E and S Iran were mysteriously abandoned. The cause of this abandonment provides the basis for much speculation, but the explanation remains unknown. In Turkmenia the population shifted eastward toward Bactria (Kohl 1984). Other elements from Turkmenia and perhaps NE Iran appear to have moved S toward the upper Indus valley. Yahya and Malyan appear to have been abandoned as well.

In central W Iran, on the other hand, the occupation of Godin and related sites in the early 2d millennium continued, while in N and W Azerbaijan painted pottery related to adjacent areas evidences a local occupation. After 1500 B.C., a change begins to occur in the NW with the appearance of a new cultural pattern marked by extramural cemeteries, distinctive architectural forms, and an entirely new assemblage of burnished gray pottery, many forms of which appear to copy metal prototypes. The origins of this new cultural pattern are unclear. It has been suggested that it represents the displaced gray-ware-using peoples of NE Iran arriving finally in the W (Young 1967). It has also been suggested that the source was the Turkish or Caucasian area in view of many similarities to objects in these areas and to Iron Age Europe. Perhaps both movements occurred (Ghirshman 1977) at the same time.

This cultural pattern, seen best in the burned settlement at Hasanlu, at the S end of Lake Urmia, and in the cemetery of Marlik on the Sefid Rud in Gilan province, contains the cultural inventory which characterizes NW Iran down almost to the historic period (Burney and Lang 1972). This gray-pottery period is commonly referred to as the "Iron Age," although very little iron existed prior to the 9th century B.C. The tombs at Marlik were built of stone and contained large quantities of bronze weapons, pottery animal effigy vases, and elaborate gold vessels decorated in repoussé (Negahban 1964). The style of these vessels suggests a temporal spread from the 2d into the 1st millennium B.C. A bronze fibula in one tomb should indicate that many of these items were hierlooms, since the fibula cannot be dated to before the 8th century B.C. on present evidence.

At Hasanlu, a complex of columned halls and auxiliary buildings was burned around 800 B.C. (Dyson 1972). It is believed on the basis of the occurrence of Urartian inscriptions in the area that this event took place when the kingdom of Urartu expanded southward under kings Menua and Ishpuini at a time when Hasanlu was probably allied with the Assyrians (Levine fc.). The ruins of this period yielded over 7,000 objects of copper, bronze, iron, lead, antimony, silver, gold, amber, glass, carnelian, alabaster, Egyptian blue, wood, ivory, and pottery. Some items, particularly cylinder seals and wall tiles, show a close relationship to Assyria and may even be imports, while others appear to be heirlooms several hundreds of years old. The site appears to have been an administrative and religious center, apparently defended by mounted horsemen, to judge by the equipment recovered. The building plans evolved from a simple plan involving an entry, a small stair, a main room with two center columns and raised fireplace, a raised platform at the rear, and a side storage room to large-scale structures, each with an open portico, an entry room and adjacent stair, a large columned hall (the largest being 18 m × 24 m) with raised central hearth and rear platform, and additional storerooms. This architectural development clearly ties into the background of the Median columned halls seen in the 8th–7th century buildings at Godin, Baba Jan, and Nushijan in central W Iran (Levine fc.). These settlements—a fortified palace at Godin, a fortified manor house and shrine at Babajan, and a fort, temple, and palace at Nushijan—represent the protohistoric occupation of the W Zagros by the Iranian Iron Age Median population. In the S, the buildings of Cyrus the Great at Pasargadae (Stronach 1979) remain the initial evidence of the Iranians at Fars, although some enigmatic remains at Susa in the so-called Ville Archaemenide-Perse may be earlier (Stronach 1974).

Bibliography

Burney, C., and Lang, D. M. 1972. *The Peoples of the Hills.* New York.

Caldwell, J. R., ed. 1967. *Investigations at Tal-i Iblis.* Illinois State Museum Preliminary Report 9. Springfield, IL.

Carter, E., and Stolper, M. W. 1984. *Elam.* Berkeley.

Coon, C. S. 1957. *The Seven Caves.* New York.

Deshayes, J. 1979. A propos des terasses hautes de la fin du lle millénaire en Iran et en Asia Centrale. Pp. 95–112 in *Le Plateau Iranien et l'Asie Centrale des Origines à la Conquête Islamique.* Paris.

Dollfus, G. 1983. Remarques sur l'organisation de l'espace dans quelques agglomerations de la Suisiane du Ve millénaire. Pp. 283–313 in *The Hilly Flanks.* SAOC 36. Chicago.

Dyson, R. H., Jr. 1972. The Hasanlu Project, 1961–1967. Pp. 39–58 in *The Memorial Volume of the Vth International Congress of Iranian Art and Archaeology.* Tehran.

Dyson, R. H., and Howard, S. M., eds. fc. *Tappeh Hesar.* Preliminary Reports of the Restudy Project, 1976. Mesopotamia, Sup.

Ghirshman, R. 1938. *Fouilles de Sialk, près de Kashan.* Vol 1. Paris.

———. 1977. *L'Iran et la migration des Indo-Aryens.* Leiden.

Hakemi, A. 1973. Prehistoric Discovery in East Iran. *Illustrated London News* July (6900): 63–66.

Hole, F. ed. fc. *Archaeological Perspectives on Western Iran.* Washington, DC.

Hole, F.; Flannery, K. V.; and Neely, J. A. 1969. *Prehistory and Human Ecology of the Deh Luran Plain.* Museum of Anthropology, Memoir No. 1. Ann Arbor.

Jarriage, J. F. 1985. Les relations entre l'Asie centrale méridionale, Le Baluchistan et la vallée de l'Indus à la fin du 3e et au debut du 2e millénaire. Pp. 105–24 in *Le Plateau Iranien et l'Asie Centrale.* Paris.

Kantor, H. 1976. The Excavations at Coga Mish 1974–75. *Proceedings of the IVth Annual Symposium on Archaeological Research in Iran:* 23–41. Tehran.

Kohl, P. W. 1979. The "world economy" of West Asia in the third millennium B.C. Pp. 55–86 in *South Asian Archaeology 1977,* ed. M. Taddei. Naples.

———. 1984. *Çentral Asia: Palaeolithic Beginnings to the Iron Age.* Editions Recherche sur les Civilisations 14. Paris.

Lamberg-Karlovsky, C. C., and Tosi, M. 1973. Shahr-i Sokhta and Tepe Yahya: Tracks on the earliest history of the Iranian Plateau. *East and West* 23 (1–2): 21–53.

Langsdorf, A., and McCown, D. E. 1942. *Tall-i-Bakun* OIP 59. Chicago.

Lechavallier, M. 1985. La Néolithique à Mehrgarh au Balouchistan et ses rapports avec l'Asie centrale. Pp. 57–62 in *L'archéologie de la Bactriane ancienne.* Paris.

Levine, L. D. fc. The Iron Age. In *Archaeological Perspectives on Western Iran,* ed. F. Hole. Washington, DC.

Malek Shahmirzadi, S. 1979. A Specialized Housebuilder in an Iranian Village of the VIth Millennium B.C. *Paleorient* 5: 183–92.

Meldgaard, J.; Mortensen, P.; and Thrane, H. 1964. Excavations at Tepe Guran, Luristan. *Acta Archaeologica* 34: 7–133.

Mellaart, J. 1975. *The Neolithic of the Near East.* New York.

Negahban, E. O. 1964. *Marlik.* Tehran.

———. 1979. A brief report on the painted buildings of Zaghe. *Paleorient* 5: 239–50.

Porada, E. 1965. *The Art of Ancient Iran.* New York.

Potts, D. T. 1977. Tepe Yayha and the end of the 4th millennium on the Iranian Plateau. Pp. 23–31 in *Le Plateau Iranien et l'Asie Centrale.* Paris.

Rencontre Internationale de Suse. 1979. La sèquence archéologique de Suse et du Sud-Ouest de l'Iran. *Paléorient* 1978/4: 133–244.

Schmidt, E. F. 1937. *Excavations at Tepe Hissar, Iran.* Philadelphia.

Smith, P. E. L. 1976. Reflections on Four Seasons of Excavations at Tappeh Ganj Dareh. Pp. 11–22 in *Proceedings of the IVth Annual Symposium on Archaeological Research in Iran.* Tehran.

———. 1985. *Paleolithic Archaeology in Iran.* The American Institute of Iranian Studies, Monograph 1. Philadelphia.

Stronach, D. 1974. Achaemenid Village I at Susa and the Persian Migration to Fars. *Iraq* 36: 239–48.

———. 1979. *Pasargadae.* Oxford.

Sumner, W. M. 1976. Excavations at Tall-i Malyan (Anshan) 1974. *Iran* 14: 103–15.

Tosi, M. 1979. The Proto-Urban Cultures of Eastern Iran and the Indus Civilization. Pp. 149–71 in *South Asian Archaeology 1977,* ed. M. Taddei. Naples.

Voigt, M. M. 1983. *Hajji Firuz Tepe, Iran: The Neolithic Settlement.* Monograph 50. Philadelphia.

Voigt, M. M., and Dyson, R. H., Jr. fc. The Chronology of Iran, ca. 8000–2000 B.C. in *Chronologies in Old World Archaeology,* ed. R. W. Ehrich. 3d ed. Chicago.

Weiss, H., and Young, T. C., Jr. 1975. The Merchants of Susa: Godin V and plateau-lowland relations in the late fourth millennium B.C. *Iran* 13: 1–18.

Young, T. C., Jr. 1967. The Iranian Migration into the Zagros. *Iran* 5: 11–34.

Young, T. C., Jr., and Levine, L. fc. A Summary of Ceramic Assemblages of the Central Western Zagros from the Middle Neolithic to the Late Third Millennium B.C. In *La Mesopotamie Pre- et Protohistorique.* Paris.

Robert H. Dyson, Jr.

ʿIRAQ EL-EMIR (M.R. 221147). A little village, 20 km W of Amman. In this area, the well-watered and green valley of the Wadi es-Sir takes a last turn before falling into the Wadi Kefrein, which was in antiquity one of the roads leading to Jericho. A towering cliff to the N, steep heights to the W, and on the E, a sheer descent to the wadi bound a large piece of land descending in terraces to the S. In this area are remains of an enclosure which delimits an estate of about 150 acres, within which are several ruins: two stories of caves carved out of the cliff, various remains on a nearby mound (where the modern village rests), and, 600 m to the S, the stately ruins of the Qasr el-ʿAbd near a mighty dam.

A. Identification and History

The first European visitors were C. L. Irby, J. Mangles, and their companion Bankes (in 1817), who identified the site with the Tyros described by Josephus (*Ant* 12.4.1 §229–35). Josephus narrated that the Tobiad Hyrcanus built in the vicinity of Amman a castle or palace, decorated with large animal figures and surrounded by an artificial lake. It is fairly certain that the Qasr, with its lion friezes and its dam, was the area described by Josephus as Hyrcanus' last place of refuge.

The historian credits Hyrcanus with all the installations in ʿIraq el-Emir; but the first-known Tobiah is mentioned by Ezra (2:60) and Nehemiah (2:10ff.) in the 5th century B.C. as the "Ammonite servant," i.e., servant of the Great King of Persia, which means he was the governor of the land of Ammon. According to the Zenon papyri, another Tobiah was still in Ammon in the 3d century, at that time in the service of the Lagid kings of Egypt. Moreover, it has been argued that ʿIraq el-Emir is mentioned in those papyri (cf. Mittmann 1970). The name Tobiah has been found carved twice in Aramaic letters, each time next to the doorway of a cave; these are dated to the 4th or 5th century B.C. Finally, the name Tyros, which survives in Wadi es-Sir, is the Greek transliteration of the Aramaic *ṣour,* meaning "rock," a word by which the site may have been known long before Hyrcanus.

Thus, we may reasonably assume that by the 5th century, ʿIraq el-Emir was one of the estates of the Tobiads, a Jewish family that settled in the land of Ammon and became locally powerful. The livelihood of the estate was derived from farming on a large scale, which relied on the diverted waters of the wadi for irrigation.

However, quarrels with his brothers, his Arab (= Nabatean) neighbors, and the Seleucid kings who had been masters of Syria and Palestine since 200 B.C., prompted Hyrcanus to take refuge in ʿIraq el-Emir, where he intended to erect a residence of princely standing.

Excavations in the village (which is not mentioned by Josephus) have revealed remains from the time of Hyrcanus—a beautiful house with painted stuccos (the "plaster building" of P. W. Lapp 1976), and columns, capitals, and entablature which are very similar to those retrieved in the Qasr. A segment of a fortification wall in which is set a doorway dates at least to Persian times, but, after several modifications, the wall fell into disuse in the 1st century A.D. The village was permanently inhabited and was the center of the site from very ancient times. Indeed, the site has yielded archaeological material from the EB through the Ummayads.

Hyrcanus was compelled by Antiochus IV (175–164 B.C.) to take his own life, after which the estate was confiscated. The Qasr was unfinished at that time and stood vacant for five centuries. In the first half of the 4th century A.D., it was remodeled and occupied. Although seriously damaged by a violent earthquake (probably in 365), it remained inhabited. The lions of the friezes were eventually, with one exception, savagely mutilated, probably the result of the iconoclastic edict in 723 by the Sultan Al Yazid.

B. Exploration

The site was first explored by M. de Vogüe and F. de Saulcy in 1863 and 1864; both were primarily interested in the Qasr. The same is true of the American, H. C. Butler, who visited the Qasr for six days in 1906. In 1962 and 1963, P. W. Lapp carried out the first systematic excavations in the "plaster building" of the village, in the "square building" (a water-supply regulator) outside the village, and in the Qasr itself. From 1977 to 1987, a team directed by E. Will cleared the entire Qasr, which has permitted a partial reconstruction. In 1977, the monumental gateway to the estate, near the Qasr, was studied by J. M. Dentzer and F. Villeneuve; the latter also conducted soundings in the village and in the caves in 1980 and 1981.

1. The Qasr el-ʿAbd. The Qasr has been the subject of a long dispute, since most scholars are inclined to identify it as a temple. However, since the owner of the building was a Jew, these scholars must assume that this owner violated Jewish orthodoxy, since there was no legitimate temple outside Jerusalem; if this were a temple, it would therefore be a "rival sanctuary." An event of such significance hardly would have been ignored by Josephus, who otherwise mentions the existence of a schismatic temple in Leontopolis in Egypt, which was built by the discharged high priest, Onias IV. The recent French excavations, however, have completely vindicated Josephus' descriptions: the Qasr was indeed a castle or palace—the *baris* of Hyrcanus.

The building, a rectangular block of 18.5 m × 37 m, stood with two stories to a height of 14 m. The N and S facades each had a broad, two-columned porch leading into an entrance hall flanked by two square rooms. A staircase still occupies the NE corner; another staircase was intended for the SE corner, but it was never built. The N hall leads through a monumental doorway to a second broad room flanked by two cisterns. The central part of the building, obviously altered in Byzantine times, is unfortunately in very bad condition and only the ground floor is partially preserved. A U-shaped corridor, lit on the E and W sides by seven large windows, surrounds a complex of four identical rooms. In the upper story, a two-columned, but unroofed, loggia rose above the N entrance hall. The S loggia looked out on the valley through seven bays framed by Corinthian half-columns. Various architectural blocks, bases, capitals, and half-columns point to the existence of several decorated rooms, one of which was probably a large reception room.

A two-storied building, with each story divided into a number of rooms and corridors, should not be identified as a temple, since no such temple is known elsewhere in the Near East. This was clearly a palatial dwelling and, according to an ancient and still extant Oriental custom, the ground floor was used for practical purposes (servants' quarters, storerooms, etc.), and the upper story was reserved for residence and reception areas.

The outer walls are made of huge slabs set on edge, according to traditional Phoenician and Syrian construction techniques which continued into Hellenistic and Roman times. The architectural ornamentation, however, is Hellenistic, in particular the combination of Corinthian columns and capitals with Doric entablatures. Both the N and the S facades have counterparts in the Greece and Macedonia of the 4th and 3d centuries B.C.

Greek-style sculptures also graced the building: the two panthers at the base of the E and W walls (which served as outlets for the internal cisterns), the lions and the lionesses with their cubs (from the lower course of the upper story), and the eagles whose wings partly concealed the Corinthian corner capitals at the top of the building. Clearly a Greek-schooled architect used an Oriental prototype in a new spirit and was assisted by a Greek-schooled sculptor. The exact origin of these masters cannot be determined, but some of the evidence points to ties with Alexandria.

Josephus called the Qasr a *baris,* a term of unknown origin used to refer to fortified residences in towns, as well as to large estates in the Hellenistic world. Qasr el-ᶜAbd, cut off from the village and the caves, surrounded by its lake, and superbly decorated, is indeed a princely residence. The eagles and the lions, in addition to their possible magical protection, could have a political significance: they are symbols of royal power. Perhaps Hyrcanus dreamed of gaining some form of independence from the Seleucid king—a dream expressed in the Qasr. In any case, the Qasr stands as the only known, though much less splendid, preview of Herod's extravagant palaces.

Bibliography

Lapp, N. 1983. *The Excavations of Araq el Emir, Vol. 1.* AASOR 47. Cambridge, MA.

Lapp, P. W. 1976. Iraq el Emir. *EAEHL* 2: 527–31.

Mazar, B. 1957. The Tobiads. *IEJ* 7: 137–45; 229–38.

Mittmann, S. 1970. Zenon im Ostjordanland. Pp. 199–210 in *Archäologie und Altes Testament,* ed. A. Kuschke and E. Kutsch. Tübingen.

Momigliano, A. 1932. I Tobiadi nella preistoria del moto maccabaico. *Atti della Reale Accademia di Torino* 67: 165–97.

Villeneuve, F. 1986. Recherches en cours sur les systèmes défensifs d'un petit site d'époque hellénistique en Transjordanie: ᶜIraq al Amir. Pp. 157–66 in *La fortification dans l'histoire du monde grec,* ed. P. Leriche and H. Tréziny. Paris.

Will, E. 1979. Recherches au Qasr el Abd à ᶜIraq al Amir. *ADAJ* 23: 139–49.

———. 1982. Un monument hellénistique de Jordanie: Le Qasr el Abd d'Iraq al Amir. Vol. 1. Pp. 197–200 in *Studies in the History and Archaeology of Jordan,* ed. A. Hadidi. Amman.

ERNEST WILL

IRBID, TELL

IRBID, TELL (M.R. 229218). A site in Jordan, perhaps to be identified with BETH-ARBEL (Hos 10:14).

A. Name and Identification

Mostly hidden from the S by the buildings of modern Irbid, the tell is one of the largest in the region, approximately 350 m × 400 m. Recent economic development has removed portions of the site. Tell Irbid (597 m above sea level) dominates the surrounding plateau, which is one of the most fertile in Jordan. There is one spring in the vicinity of the tell, located in the modern city.

The name "Irbid" is attested since the 14th century A.D. In the 8th century A.D., the town was known as "Arbad," which might be a hypercorrection and presuppose the present name of the site. Irbid was the site of the Roman town or village of Arbela, mentioned by Eusebius of Caesarea in the early 4th century A.D. The east bank Irbid was not the only Arbela that changed to Irbid via Irbil (Knauf and Lenzen fc.). It is likely that Irbid/Arbela is identical with the Beth-arbel mentioned in Hos 10:14. This reference is enigmatic and does not allow clear conclusions concerning the history of the site in the Iron Age, except to provide its name for this period. The name of the site in the LB was possibly *gintôt,* "the place of winepresses," mentioned by Thutmose III and in the Amarna letters (Lenzen and Knauf 1987).

B. History of Research

Early travelers and explorers noted mainly the remnants of classical antiquity in the vicinity of the modern city and of Bârha, W of the city (Seetzen 1854: 360–61; Burckhardt 1822: 268–69; Buckingham 1827: 350–52; Merrill 1881: 293–96; Oliphant 1880: 103–14; Schumacher 1890: 149–54). The significance of the tell was first noted by Albright (1929: 10) and Glueck (1951: 153–54), who associated the tell with the LB. Salvage excavations have been conducted at the site since the 1960s, and research excavations have been conducted since 1984 (Lenzen 1986; Lenzen, Gordon, and McQuitty 1985; Lenzen and Gordon fc.).

C. History of Settlement

Stratified occupational deposits have been dated from ca. 3500 B.C. to ca. 800 B.C. During the MB, the tell was enclosed by a city wall built of basalt boulders, many of which measured well over 4 m × 4 m. These boulders were indigenous to the region, probably having been scattered throughout the Irbid plateau from the E during the Late Pleistocene period. The LB II city incorporated the earlier city wall, while at the same time expanding the interior of the city by building a wall outside the first. An excavated architectural complex—consisting of an outside perimeter wall, four to five separate rooms, a tower, and a sanctuary—has provided cultic objects and ceramics which date to the LB/Iron Age transition. Above the structures were 4 m of destruction debris which extended to the SW for over 100 m. Since only two arrowheads were found in the destruction debris, a military destruction seems unlikely. Occupation of the area resumed following the destruction of the public buildings, but the nature of the occupation changed from a public sector to one of domestic and light industrial use. The top of the tell has been completely obliterated by the construction of modern buildings; hence, essentially no archaeological data exist for the site after ca. 800 B.C. Later occupational periods, however, are represented in wash. Although it is likely that the tell was always occupied to some degree, probably in the 1st century A.D. the main settlement shifted from the summit to its immediate surroundings.

The later history of Irbid is derived primarily from textual sources. Prior to the establishment of the DECAPOLIS city of Capitolias (BEIT RAS, 5 km N of Irbid), Arbela belonged to the territory of Pella. According to a Greek inscription from the town, Arbela belonged to Provincia Arabia in 239 A.D. (assuming this inscription was not imported from elsewhere).

Bibliography

Albright, W. F. 1929. New Israelite and Pre-Israelite Sites: The Spring Trip of 1929. *BASOR* 35: 12–14.

Buckingham, J. S. 1827. *Reisen durch Syrien und Palestina.* Weimar.

Burckhardt, J. L. 1822. *Travels in Syria and the Holy Land.* London.

Glueck, N. 1951. *Explorations in Eastern Palestine, IV.* AASOR 25–28. New Haven.

Knauf, E. A., and Lenzen, C. J. fc. Arbela-Irbil-Irbid: The Transmission of a Name. *BN.*

Lenzen, C. J. 1986. Tell Irbid and Beit Ras. *AfO* 33: 164–66.

Lenzen, C. J., and Gordon, R. L. fc. Tell Irbid 1986. *ADAJ.*

Lenzen, C. J.; Gordon, R. L.; and McQuitty, A. M. 1985. Excavations at Tell Irbid and Beit Ras, 1985. *ADAJ* 29: 151–59.

Lenzen, C. J., and Knauf, E. A. 1987. *Notes on Syrian Place Names in Egyptian Sources.* Göttingen.

———. 1988. Irbid (Jordanie). *RB* 95: 239–47.

Lenzen, C. J., and McQuitty, A. M. 1983. A Preliminary Survey of the Irbid—Beit Ras Region, North-Western Jordan. *ADAJ* 27: 656.

———. 1984. Tell Irbid. *ADAJ* 28: 297.

Merrill, S. 1881. *East of the Jordan.* London.

Oliphant, L. 1880. *The Land of Gilead with Excursions in the Lebanon.* London.

Schumacher, G. 1890. *Northern ʿAjlun "Within the Decapolis."* London.

Seetzen, U. J. 1854. *Ulrich Jasper Seetzen's Reisen durch Syrien, Palaestina, Phoenicien, die Transjordan-Laender, Arabia Petraea und Unter-Aegypten,* vol. 1, ed. F. Kruse. Berlin.

C. J. LENZEN

IRENAEUS. Irenaeus (ca. 140–ca. 202) was bishop of Lyons in Gaul in the late 2d century. His exposition of Christian theology developed out of his critique of the gnostic systems. He is considered by many to be the first systematic theologian.

A. The Man and His Work
B. Irenaeus and the Gnostics
C. Unity of *Adversus Haereses* and Biblical Methodology
D. Irenaeus and Canon
E. Irenaeus' Exegesis
F. Summary of Argument of *Haer.* 3–5

A. The Man and His Work

As is the case with most ancient writers, Irenaeus is known from his work and, indirectly, from the personality revealed in that work rather than from an abundance of biographical detail. Irenaeus does tell of spending his early years in Smyrna, during the bishopric of Polycarp, his teacher (Iren. *Haer.* 3.3.4; Eus. *Hist. Eccl.* 5.20.4–8). The date of Polycarp's martyrdom, between A.D. 161 and 168, helps fix the date of Irenaeus' birth at ca. A.D. 140. The few other known details depend on Eusebius, who compiled his Church history in the first decades of the 4th century. It is certain that Irenaeus, having become a presbyter, was the emissary of the church of Lyons to the bishop of Rome in 177 (Eus. *Hist. Eccl.* 5.4.1–2). When Pothinus, bishop of Lyons, died in prison that same year, Irenaeus succeeded him (Eus. *Hist. Eccl.* 5.5.8). Irenaeus' activity as bishop continued through the Paschal controversy of the late 2d century. His intervention took the form of a letter to Victor, bishop of Rome, ca. 188 to ca. 198, urging that Victor tolerate diversity of practice in fixing the date of Easter and in keeping the pre-Easter fast (Eus. *Hist. Eccl.* 5.24.11–18). The date of Irenaeus' death is unknown, although convention places it ca. 202 to correspond with the renewed persecution under Septimus Severus. However, the texts which mention Irenaeus' martyrdom are late and uncertain: Jerome, writing ca. 397 (*Commentary on Is,* 64 [*PL* 24, 623 A]); Theodoret(?), writing between 430 and 450 (*Quaestiones et responsiones* [*PG* 6, 1363]); Gregory of Tours, writing ca. 575 (*Historia Francorum 1,* 27 [*PL* 71, 174 C–175 A]) and again in 590 (*De gloria martyrum* 50 [*PL* 71, 752 A]).

Irenaeus' major extant writing is the *Adversus Haereses* (the full title of which is the *Refutation and Overthrow of Knowledge falsely so-called*). Its composition is dated ca. 180 from the succession lists in which the author names Eleutherus (ca.174–ca.189) as current bishop of Rome (*Haer.* 3.3.3), although it seems from remarks Irenaeus makes in the prefaces to *Haer.* 3 and 4 that he followed the practice of sending on the separate books of the work as they were completed. The other complete extant work is the *Demonstration [or Proof] of the Apostolic Preaching.* It was written after at least the earlier books of *Adversus Haereses,* to which reference is made in chap. 99. An Armenian version of this long-lost work was discovered in 1904, and Smith (1952: 4–11) discusses its textual history. Eusebius (ca. 263–ca. 339) is the principal source for our knowledge of the lost works of Irenaeus. These include at least the treatises "On the Ogdoad" and "Concerning Knowledge" and letters "On Schism" and "On the Monarchy [of God]" (Eus. *Hist. Eccl.* 5.20.1), as well as the full text of the letter to Victor already mentioned.

Irenaeus wrote in Greek, but his Greek text has survived only in material quoted by others. For both the *Demonstration* and *Adversus Haereses,* our direct knowledge of Irenaeus' text depends on translations. *Adversus Haereses* survived in a Latin version made before A.D. 422, when Augustine cites it in the *Contra Julianum* (*PL* 44, 644). In addition, a 6th-century Armenian version of Books 4 and 5 was discovered with the *Demonstration* in 1904, and fragments exist in Armenian and Syriac as well as in Greek. Full discussion of the manuscript tradition of the Latin version with its editions, as well as of the Armenian version and of the fragments, appears in the critical edition completed under the direction of Rousseau in 1982, and published by Sources chrétiennes between 1965 and 1982. This edition includes a partial Greek retroversion as well as a French translation. The only English translation remains that in ANF vol. 1 (1885: 9–567), although the editors of ACW have announced the forthcoming publication of Unger's new English translation (Burghardt 1984: 293).

B. Irenaeus and the Gnostics

A major context of Irenaeus' contribution is his response to the threat of Gnosticism. In the last quarter of the 2d century, Valentinian Gnosticism posed a serious challenge to mainline Christianity in the Rhone valley. Anti-gnostic polemic shapes both *Adversus Haereses* and the *Demonstration.* The latter is concerned with demonstrating that the preaching received from the apostles is true; its emphasis throughout is soundness of doctrine. The former, larger work derives form, method, and content from the purpose, set forth in its title, that was "the refutation and overthrow of so-called gnosis" (Eus. *Hist. Eccl.* 5.7).

In a body of work so keyed to polemical response, the question of the writer's reliability as a witness to his opponents' positions must be raised. The question is all the more acute because Irenaeus has long been a principal source for knowledge of Gnosticism. Nineteenth-century historical-critical scholarship recognized the polemical character of heresiological reports of opponents and so treated this material, including that of Irenaeus, as suspect. Schmidt (1907) and DeFaye (1925) recognized the corroborative value of gnostic material like that in the then newly discovered Codex Berolinensis 8502. Sagnard (1947: 100) was cautious about all but firsthand accounts; in his view Irenaeus can be trusted when writing about those of whom he has personal knowledge. What remained problematic was the use of secondary sources by Irenaeus as well as by others.

Discovery of the Nag Hammadi library changed the situation. Wisse (1971: 205–23) has compared the writings of the heresiologists with the Nag Hammadi library. He finds two major discrepancies that must be accounted for. The first is lack of significant overlapping in material and detail. One might expect in so large a collection to find some of the sources used by the heresiologists. In fact, there are only five cases of clear agreement. Of these, three certainly and one possibly are with Irenaeus (Wisse 1971: 217–18). A second discrepancy is that the heresiologists name various sects, describing them in terms of characteristic traits and teachings as if each had developed its own distinct doctrines. The collection as a whole, as well as individual writings within it, contains ideas that according to the heresiologists are appropriate to different sects. This raises the question whether the sects were indeed as differentiated by doctrine as the ancient Church writers indicated.

In Wisse's own view, the sections in which Irenaeus discusses Ptolemy (*Haer.* 1.1–8) and the Marcosians (*Haer.* 1.13–21), as well as *Haer.* 1.9–10 and 1.31.3–4, are of the bishop's own composition and draw on his direct knowledge of the disciples of Ptolemy and Marcus. Wisse thinks the remaining passages describing gnostic sects derive from an earlier catalogue of heresies (1971: 212–15). To such a source Wisse attaches the blame for describing gnostics as "pathological systems builders" comprising numerous sects; this differs from what we read in the Nag Hammadi library (1971: 218–19).

Perkins (1976: 193–200) attacks Wisse's position, maintaining that considerations of style and literary genre raise problems. Drawing on studies by Schoedel (1959: 22–32) and Grant (1949: 41–51), she recalls that oral and rhetorical models greatly influenced ancient writers and shows how, in *Haer.* 1, Irenaeus follows the model of a rhetorical refutation. (In 1981, Vallée developed this insight but without giving attention to the reliability of Irenaeus' presentation of gnostic thought.) What of Wisse's theory of an earlier heresiological source? In Perkins' judgment, *Haer.* 1.11 and 12 are rightly ascribed to Irenaeus since each contains elements proper to the refutation. *Haer.* 1.29 and 30 are also ascribed to Irenaeus, in this case as a result of comparison of style and method between clear Irenaean materials and clear source material.

Pagels (1974: 35–53) has challenged the dependability of Irenaeus' accounts of gnostic teaching in another passage, contending that in *Haer.* 1.7.1 Irenaeus distorts the correct account preserved in Clement of Alexandria. In a review of Pagels' publications through 1977, Grant (1977: 30–34) finds minimal differences between the texts. He notes that this aspect of Pagels' position has been questioned by Schoedel and rejected by Mühlenberg. McCue (1980) also questions the attack on Irenaeus' reliability. The issue remains controversial.

Study of this Irenaean material in the context of available gnostic writings is now expedited by Layton (1987), who translates the Valentinian material from Irenaeus together with the Valentinian fragments, and performs a similar service for the other types of gnostic sources.

C. Unity of *Adversus Haereses* and Biblical Methodology

Study of the unity of *Adversus Haereses* is directly connected with study of its author's role as a biblical theologian. This role has long been recognized, notably by Lawson (1948) and Wingren (1959). Equally, Irenaeus has long been criticized for an incoherent, rambling, and unsystematic style. Both the formal and theological unity of *Adversus Haereses* were severely attacked by source critics beginning with Harnack (1907: 1–38), followed by Bousset (1915) and Loofs (1930), and more recently by the scholars Widmann (1957: 156–73) and Benoit (1960). However, Bacq's careful study (1978) of Irenaeus' biblical methodology has uncovered the tightly structured unity of *Haer.* 4, a unity at once theological and literary. The basic unit of structure is a "word of the Lord" or scriptural text announced, cited, and commented upon, with various allusions to that word linking one structural unit to another. Understanding and application of this principle of organization may well permit the unity of the entire work to be uncovered.

D. Irenaeus and Canon

Because the last three books of *Adversus Haereses* offer proof from the Scriptures, it is particularly important to know what Irenaeus considers to be the Scriptures. As Schneemelcher (*NTApocr* 1: 28–59) indicates, Irenaeus affirmed the number of Gospels to be fixed at four (*Haer.* 3.11.8); in addition, Acts and twelve epistles of Paul belong to the canon, and 1 Peter and 1 and 2 John are on a par with Paul (Schneemelcher *NTApocr* 1: 34). In 1960, Benoit pointed out that Irenaeus reserves the phrases *ait Scriptura* ("Scripture has") and *dicit Scriptura* ("Scripture says") for OT citations. At the same time, phrases such as *scriptum est* ("it is written") and *quod scriptum est* ("which is written") are used to introduce both NT and OT passages (Benoit 1960:

76). More recently, Sesboüë (1981) has reviewed the meanings of *scriptura* and *scripturae* in Irenaeus. He concludes that undoubtedly Irenaeus did treat the NT as Scripture. But in Irenaeus' day a current usage, held over from the NT identified Scripture with the OT; Irenaeus also continued to share in that perspective. Specifically, his proof from the Scriptures involved proof from the prophets and consisted of the systematic elaboration of the agreements between the two testaments. In proceeding thus, he simply developed the pattern set by the NT writers. But Sesboüë has shown that Irenaeus adds a dimension to the argument. Against his opponents, he wants to show that both Testaments are the work of the one God. So for the bishop, not only is prophecy a proof of the event but the event in turn is also a proof of prophecy.

Peretto, in his investigation (1971) of Romans 1–8 in *Adversus Haereses,* finds Irenaeus reluctant to apply the term "Scripture" to the Pauline letters. Unlike Sesboüë, Peretto does not discuss Irenaeus' use of the term as applied to the whole complex of the OT and the NT, but he does enter the ongoing discussion of the relation of the Latin version of *Adversus Haereses* to the Latin version of the NT. Specifically, he demonstrates that the text of Roman 1–8 in the Latin *Adversus Haereses* is simply the translation of the Greek text; it does not enter into the line of development of the VL. In his section on the Irenaean use of the Romans material, Peretto finds selection and interpretation clearly adapted to the polemical situation. He holds that Irenaeus does respect the literal meaning of the texts. Finally, his work includes a complete and helpful review of the study of Irenaeus and Sacred Scripture (1971: 41–45).

E. Irenaeus' Exegesis

Herrera (1920) studied Irenaeus as exegete. He indicated that Irenaeus employs both the literal and the spiritual sense, although Herrera judged his use of the literal sense to be sometimes less happy than one might desire (1920: 98–118). According to Herrera, Irenaeus adopts four rules of exegesis: (1) By the rule of clarity, the obscure should be explained by the clear (1920: 120–23). (2) According to the rule of truth, a text should be read within the context of the creed delivered at baptism, and within the context of the whole of the Scriptures (1920: 124–26). (3) Holding to the rule of tradition, a text should be read within the context of the truth handed on by the living tradition through the succession (1920: 127–39). (4) According to the rule of mystery, the student of the Scriptures should admit that the Scriptures contain mysteries beyond human understanding (1920: 139–46). Later developments in Scripture studies are reflected in Bacq's 1978 work (*C* above), which adds considerable sophistication to the understanding of Irenaeus' exegetical method.

Orbe (1981) focuses on *Haer.* 5.23.1–2, where Irenaeus, in typical 2d-century style, offers five exegeses of Gen 2:17b. Marcion and the gnostics made capital of the apparently unfulfilled divine threat of death to be inflicted "in the day that you eat." Orbe's service here is, first, to point out Irenaeus' great concern for the literal meaning of the passage (a concern Peretto also notes). Second, Orbe makes clear the bishop's familiarity with a variety of interpretations, ranging from that of Philo through the *Book of Jubilees* and Justin's. Third, Orbe analyzes the various interpretations Irenaeus offers, in light of the rest of his teaching, in order to suggest which of the five are most likely to have been Irenaeus' own.

This familiarity with a broad spectrum of relevant material is apparent in Orbe's comprehensive work (1972) on the gospel parables in Irenaeus. There, he treats one by one the parables to which Irenaeus refers, and for each he examines all occurrences in the literature, both heterodox and orthodox, prior and immediately posterior to Irenaeus. Parables that receive only marginal mention in Irenaeus are also noted and located in the literature. The consequence of this immense labor is to place Irenaeus solidly within the literary milieu to which his work belongs. A particularly helpful result is Orbe's clarification of the distinction between Valentinian exegesis, Alexandrian exegesis, and Irenaeus' Asiatic exegesis. The diagram illustrates his comparison of the three exegeses of the parable of the Good Samaritan.

	VALENTINIAN	ALEXANDRIAN	ASIATIC
WOUNDED MAN	Spiritual man,	*Homo (nous)*	Man of clay, the human race,
	lost on earth,	descended from noetic world,	
	because of fall of Sophia.	because of sin.	transgressor in Adam.
SAMARITAN	Gnostic Savior made man "in his own way."	Savior made man, even flesh.	Son of God incarnate, dead and risen.
HELPER	For soteriological efficacy needs help of angels		Efficacy is in His glorified flesh;
	= gnostic leaders.	= apostles.	uses Holy Spirit to cure the man during interval between 2 comings.

(Adapted from A. Orbe [1972: 2.488]. First published Donovan [1984: 229].)

All three approaches respect the letter of the parable. All follow the pattern: the situation of the human person in a state of mortal danger from which the Son of Man redeems him, assisted by another (or others). As Orbe points out, we have here a generic synthesis of the *historia salutis*. Further, he reminds us that in these models, originating fairly close to one another in time and place, there already appear three distinct thought patterns, each of which constitutes a tradition.

The Irenaean interpretation of parables is key to Schoedel's exploration of the theological method in *Haer.* 2.25–28 (1984: 31–49). Schoedel identifies the methodological point made by Irenaeus at the theological climax of *Haer.* 2.25–28, where he distinguishes between "knowing *that*" and "knowing *how.*" Scriptures often teach us *that* God has done thus and so without explaining *how* or *why*. This must be so as God transcends ordinary ways of thought. Gnostics err by not recognizing this aspect of transcendence and proffering explanations of the humanly inexplicable. Schoedel points out that Irenaeus is especially concerned about the way in which gnostics were using the NT parables. Irenaeus' distinction is not simply between difficult and easy problems either in the study of nature or in

Scriptural exegesis; rather, it is in the study of nature that we know *that* natural things are; knowledge of *how* they come to exist is left to God. With respect to things in Scripture, the contrast is between the assertions (as, There is one God who created matter) and *speculation* about such assertions (as, when or how God created matter). As Schoedel remarks: "The important point, then, is that when Irenaeus worries about the gnostic interpretation of parables, it is because such exegesis reflects dissatisfaction with knowing 'that' and an unhealthy desire to know 'why' " (1984: 35). The parables must be read in harmony with the rest of Scriptures.

Schoedel locates parallels to the distinction between "knowing *that*" and "knowing *how*" in Empiric medical writings and in philosophical Skepticism. As Irenaeus' sound "art of discovery" rests on interpretation of the parables in light of the clarity of the prophets and Gospels, so Schoedel notes the Empiricists' "way of discovery" took as point of departure things that were certain. Irenaeus uses the question of what God was doing before creation of the world as an illustration of the futility of speculation on questions beyond our capacity to know. Schoedel situates this question in the debates of the philosophy of Irenaeus' day, showing that "in both Empirical and Skeptical circles Irenaeus could find a measure of sympathy for his view that it was enough to affirm divine providence without attempting to solve the metaphysical issues involved" (1984: 44).

While Irenaeus' adherence to what is obvious may have some connection with popular distrust of philosophy, Schoedel says that distrust "has been focused more precisely under the influence of more highly developed intellectual tools" (1984: 48). Thus, Schoedel concludes that the very use Irenaeus makes of such tools shows (contrary to van Unnik 1979: 33–43) that it is possible to read Irenaeus in the light of Skepticism without reducing him to a precursor of "God of the gaps" theology. Rather, Irenaeus' very debt to Empiric method and Skepticism in challenging speculation betrays his impressive achievement in the development of sound theological method.

F. Summary of Argument of *Haer.* 3–5

After the discussion of method which concludes *Haer.* 2, Irenaeus devotes the next three books to presenting the true gnosis of Christ's teachings. By way of prologue he develops an understanding of true doctrine, tradition, and succession destined to be extremely influential in the Western Church (*Haer.* 3, pref.–5). He agrees with the gnostics that Jesus gave true teaching (which he calls the "rule of truth") to his apostles, directing them to pass it on to their successors. Thus, in both the gnostic and Irenaean versions, the truth is given into the keeping of the succession of teachers in the Church. It is their task to "pass it on," i.e., to perform the work of tradition. However, Irenaeus introduces one sharp and major difference. In his view, there is no secret succession or tradition; the tradition is guarded by a public, known succession to the apostles: hence, the importance he attaches to the episcopal succession lists.

Equally in response to gnostic positions, Irenaeus stresses the unity of God who made all through his hands the Word and Wisdom, and the oneness of being of Jesus Christ who is only-begotten son, savior, word, truly divine, and truly human (*Haer.* 3.5–25). Here, as elsewhere in the Irenaean corpus, the God who is one—yet is Father, Son, and Spirit—is known as such through the divine economy or plan of salvation. Thus, Irenaeus' position is a form of economic trinitarianism.

The theme of *Haer.* 4 is the unity of the old and new covenants summed up in the person of Jesus Christ, who recapitulates all of salvation history in his person and through his life, death, and resurrection in order to join the end to the beginning, so humankind to God. "Recapitulation" is an important subtheme in Irenaeus, a development of Pauline theology (Romans 5 and 6; Col 1:15–20; Eph 1:9–10). In Irenaeus' view, the entire life and work of the Son was both a fulfillment of prophecy (see *Dem.* 53–85) and a recapitulation or summing up of all that has been since Adam (see *Haer.* 3.22.3; *Dem.* 37). This summing up pertains to the circumstances of his birth by Mary (*Haer.* 3.21.10 and 22.1–2) and even to the ages he passed through (*Haer.* 2.22.4). It includes his passion-resurrection and the saving significance of his life (see *Haer.* 5.19.1; 5.21.1–2; 5.18.1–3; 3.16.6; 3.18.7).

In *Haer.* 5, Irenaeus emphasizes the reality of Jesus' body, before and after the resurrection. Repeatedly in these last three books, Irenaeus stresses the value in God's eyes of human physicality, and the importance of free human choice in the working out of salvation by permitting the Spirit to penetrate one's life, so that ultimately one might enter into the glory-filled vision of God. The Irenaean picture of the human person adopts the biblical notion of a threefold organization of flesh, soul, and spirit (1 Thess 5:23). The image imprinted from creation is in the flesh (*Haer.* 5.6.1), the dynamism leading toward holiness involves a distinction between image and likeness (Fantino 1986), and growth in the likeness is through the work of the Holy Spirit, freely welcomed by the individual (see especially *Haer.* 4.37–9). The result will be progress toward the life-giving vision of God as expressed in the often-quoted Irenaean text: "The glory of God is a human person fully alive, and the life of the human person is the vision of God" (*Haer.* 4.20.7).

Bibliography

Bacq, P. 1978. *De l'ancienne à la nouvelle alliance selon S. Irénée: Unité du livre IV de l'*Adversus Haereses. Paris.

Benoit, A. 1960. *Saint Irénée: Introduction à l'étude de sa théologie.* Études d'histoire et de philosophie religieuses 52. Paris.

Berthouzoz, R. 1980. *Liberté et grâce suivant la théologie d'Irénée de Lyon.* Études d'ethique chrétienne 8. Paris.

Bousset, W. 1915. *Judisch-Christlicher Schulbetrieb in Alexandria und Rom.* FRLANT, n.s. Göttingen.

Brox, N. 1966. *Offenbarung, Gnosis und gnostischer Mythos bei Irenäus von Lyon.* Salzburger Patristische Studien 1. Salzburg.

———. 1975. Rom und 'jede Kirche' im 2. Jahrhundert: Zu Irenäus, *adv. haer.* III,3,2. *Annuarium historiae Conciliorum* 7: 42–78.

Burghardt, W. J. 1984. Current Theology: Literature of Christian Antiquity, 1979–83. *TS* 45: 275–306.

De Andia, Y. 1986. *Homo Vivens: Incorruptibilité et divinisation de l'homme selon Irénée de Lyon.* Études Augustiniennes. Paris.

DeFaye, E. 1925. *Gnostiques et gnosticisme.* 2d ed. Paris.

Donovan, M. A. 1984. Irenaeus in Recent Scholarship. *SecondCent* 4: 219–41.
———. 1988. Alive to the Glory of God: A Key Insight in St. Irenaeus. *TS* 49: 283–97.
Fantino, J. 1986. *L'Homme Image de Dieu chez saint Irénée de Lyon.* Paris.
Faus, J. I. G. 1970. *Carne de Dios: Significado salvador de la encarnación en la teología de San Ireneo.* Barcelona.
Grant, R. M. 1949. Irenaeus and Hellenistic Culture. *HTR* 43: 41–51.
———. 1977. Review of *The Johannine Gospel in Gnostic Exegesis* and *The Gnostic Paul,* by Elaine Hiesey Pagels. *RelSRev* 3: 30–34.
Harnack, A. 1907. Der Presbyter-Prediger des Irenaeus (IV,27,1–32,1). Pp. 1–38 in *Philotesia zu Paul Kleinert zum LXX. Geburtstage dargebracht.* Berlin.
Herrera, S. 1920. *Saint Irénée de Lyon exégète.* Paris.
Houssiau, A. 1955. *La christologie de saint Irénée.* Louvain.
Jaschke, H.-J. 1976. *Der Heilige Geist im Bekenntnis der Kirche.* Münster.
Javierre, A. M. 1972. 'In Ecclesia': Ireneo, *Adv. Haer.* 3,3,2. *Communio* 12: 221–317.
Lanne, E. 1976. L'Église de Rome: 'a gloriosissimis duobus apostolis Petro et Paulo Romae fundatae et constitutae ecclesiae' (*Adv. Haer.* III,3,2). *Irenikon* 49: 275–322.
Lassiat, H. 1974. *Promotion de l'homme en Jésus-Christ d'après Irénée de Lyon, témoin de la Tradition des Apôtres.* Paris.
———. 1976. *Dieu veut-il des hommes libres? La catéchèse de l'Église des martyres d'après Irénée de Lyon.* Paris.
———. 1978. L'anthropologie d'Irénée. *NRT* 100: 399–417.
Lawson, J. 1948. *The Biblical Theology of St. Irenaeus.* London.
Layton, B. trans. 1987. *The Gnostic Scriptures.* Garden City, NY.
Loofs, F. 1930. *Theophilus von Antiochien Adversus Marcionem und die anderen theologischen Quellen bei Irenäus,* TU 46/2. Leipzig.
McCue, J. F. 1980. Conflicting Versions of Valentinianism? Irenaeus and the *Excerpta ex Theodoto.* Pp. 404–16 in *The Rediscovery of Gnosticism,* ed. B. Layton. Leiden.
Mühlenberg, E. 1975. Weiviel Erlösungen kennt der Gnostiker Herakleon? *ZNW* 66: 170–93.
Orbe, A. 1967. La definición del hombre en la teología del s. II. *Greg* 48: 522–76.
———. 1969. *Antropología de San Ireneo.* Madrid.
———. 1972. *Parabolas evangelicas in San Ireneo,* 2 vols. Madrid.
———. 1978. San Ireneo y la creación de la materia. *Greg* 59: 71–127.
———. 1979. Adversarios anónimos de la *Salus carnis* (Iren. *adv. haer.* V,2,2s). *Greg* 60: 9–53.
———. 1980. S. Ireneo y la doctrina de la reconciliación. *Greg* 61: 5–50.
———. 1981. Cinco exegesis ireneanas de Gen. 2, 17b *adv. haer.* V,23,1–2. *Greg* 62: 75–113.
———. 1984. San Ireneo adopciónista? En torna a *adv. haer.* III.19.1. *Greg* 65: 5–52.
Pagels, E. H. 1974. Conflicting Versions of Valentinian Eschatology: Irenaeus' Treatise vs. the Excerpts from Theodotus. *HTR* 67: 35–53.
Peretto, E. 1971. *La lettera ai Romani, cc.1–8, nell'* "Adversus Haereses" *d'Ireneo.* Bari.
Perkins, P. 1976. Irenaeus and the Gnostics: Rhetoric and Composition in *Adversus Haereses* book one. *VC* 30: 193–200.
Reynders, B. 1954. *Lexique comparé du texts grec et des versions latine, arménienne et syriaque de l'*"Adversus Haereses" *de saint Irénée.* CSCO 141. Subsidia 5–6. Louvain.
Roberts, A., and Donaldson, J., eds. 1973. Irenaeus, *Adversus Haereses. ANF* 1: 309–567, 568–78.
Rousseau, A. 1977. L'éternité des peines de l'enfer et l'immortalité naturelle de l'âme selon saint Irénée. *NRT* 100: 399–417.
Rousseau, A., et al., eds. 1965–82. *Contre les Hérésies 1–5.* SC 100, 152–53, 210–11, 263–64, 293–94. Paris.
Sagnard, F. 1947. *La gnose valentinienne et le témoignage de saint Irénée.* Paris.
Schmidt, C. 1907. Irenaus und seine Quelle in *Adversus Haereses* I, 29. Pp. 315–36 in *Philotesia zu Paul Kleinert zum LXX. Geburtstage dargebracht.* Berlin.
Schoedel, W. R. 1959. Philosophy and Rhetoric in the *Adversus Haereses* of Irenaeus. *VC* 13: 22–32.
———. 1974. Review of *The Johannine Gospel in Gnostic Exegesis: Heracleon's Commentary on John,* by E. H. Pagels. *JBL* 93: 115–16.
———. 1984. Theological Method in Irenaeus. *JTS* n.s. 35: 31–49.
Sesboüé, B. 1981. La preuve par les Écritures chez S. Irénée; à propos d'une texte difficile du Livre III de l'*Adversus Haereses. NRT* 103: 872–87.
Smith, J. P., trans. and annot. 1952. *St. Irenaeus: Proof of the Apostolic Preaching.* ACW 16. New York.
Unnik, W. C. van. 1979. Theological Speculation and Its Limits. Pp. 33–43 in *Early Christian Literature and the Classical Tradition, In Honorem Robert M. Grant,* ed. W. R. Schoedel and R. L. Wilken. ThH 53. Paris.
Vallée, G. 1981. *A Study in Anti-Gnostic Polemics.* Waterloo, Ontario.
Widmann, M. 1957. Irenäus und seine theologischen Väter. *ZTK* 54: 156–73.
Wingren, G. 1959. *Man and the Incarnation: A Study in the Biblical Theology of Irenaeus,* trans. R. MacKenzie. Philadelphia.
Wisse, F. 1971. The Nag Hammadi Library and the Heresiologists. *VC* 25: 205–23.

MARY ANN DONOVAN

IRI (PERSON) [Heb *ʿîrî*]. A descendant of Benjamin who appears in a curious Benjaminite genealogy in 1 Chr 7:6–12a. The name means something like "my city" or "my town." This is the only appearance of the name in the MT, and it does not appear in the Apocrypha or the deuterocanonical literature. Iri is mentioned as one of the five sons of Bela, along with Ezbon, Uzzi, Uzziel, and Jerimoth. The tradition is strong at this point, since Bela is the only one of the three sons of Benjamin mentioned in 1 Chr 7:6 who appears in all genealogical lists of the tribe of Benjamin (Coggins *Chronicles* CBC, 50). This genealogy represents the simplest form, numberwise, of any genealogical listing, with only three sons of Benjamin named (*1 Chronicles* WBC, 108). The five sons of Bela are called *roʾšê hāʾābôt,* or "heads of families." There may be some reflection of political and social organization in this designation, as well as military status. Harmon (1983: 150) has suggested that perhaps the head man of a *bēt ʾāb* functioned along the lines of the "big men" of anthropological terminology. Orme (1981: 139) points out that big men are successful, involved in community affairs, associated with feasts, and involved in arbitration in local disputes.

Bibliography

Harmon, G. E. 1983. *Floor Area and Population Determination.* Diss. Southern Baptist Theological Seminary.
Orme, B. 1981. *Anthropology for Archaeologists.* Ithaca, NY.

G. EDWIN HARMON

IRIJAH (PERSON) [Heb *yirʾîyāh*]. The sentry at the Benjamin Gate who arrested Jeremiah and accused him of deserting to the Chaldeans (Jer 37:13–14). Certainly, Irijah had cause to suspect Jeremiah of desertion since Jeremiah had urged others to do so (Jer 21:9). Jeremiah denies the charge of Irijah, but the text indicates that "Irijah would not listen to him, and seized Jeremiah, and brought him to the princes" (Jer 37:14). It was the failure of Judah and its leaders to listen to the prophet that the Jeremiah tradition believes is responsible for the Exile. This theme is expressed twice (Jer 36:21 and Jer 37:2), immediately preceding the account of Jeremiah's arrest by Irijah in Jer 37:13–14. Thus, in the context of the book of Jeremiah, Irijah typifies the problem that leads to God's judgment of Judah and Jerusalem. The LXX has a different account of Jeremiah's arrest that does not mention Irijah, but a "Sauria with whom Jeremiah dwelt." The Syr gives the name as *nērîyāh*. Irijah is identified as the son of Shelemiah and the grandson of Hananiah. Shelemiah, son of Hananiah, is apparently a different person from Shelemiah, son of Cushi (Jer 36:14), or Shelemiah, son of Abdeel (Jer 36:26). It is not possible to determine if Irijah's grandfather, Hananiah, is the same person identified as the father of one of the princes mentioned in Jer 36:12. Irijah means "Yahweh sees" (*TPNAH* 102), though this meaning plays no evident role in Jeremiah 37.

John M. Bracke

IRNAHASH (PLACE) [Heb *ʿîr nāḥāš*]. A city in Judah of unknown location (1 Chr 4:12). The name is found listed in the genealogy of the sons of Caleb as "Tehinnah the father of Irnahash." Although it is found in a genealogical list, references in the same passage to other place names and their founders, such as "Ephrathah, the father of Bethlehem" (1 Chr 4:4) and "Joab the father of Geharashim" (Valley of the Craftsmen; 1 Chr 4:14), make a place identification probable. Noth suggested and Aharoni concurred that many of the clansmen are listed in the genealogies as the "father" of the settlement they either founded or adopted as their own (*LBHG*, 245–48). The LXX supports this view, translating Irnahash as the "City of Naas" (Gk *poleōs naas*) rather than as the name of an individual.

Three possible locations have been suggested. The two with modern place names are Deir Nakhkhas (M.R. 142113) near Beit Gibrin, following Abel (*GP* 2: 351), and Kh. en-Nahas (M.R. 191010) located S of the Dead Sea in the Arabah near Punan, preferred by Glueck (1959: 156) and Kallai (*HGB*, 117). The nearby mining areas make the latter suggestion attractive since Heb *nāḥāš*, "serpent," is cognate with *nĕḥōšet*, "copper," and since Glueck suggested that the name Ge-harashim was used interchangeably in biblical times for Arabah (1959: 156). Aharoni (*LBHG*, 282 n. 164) connected Ir-Nahash with the Kenites of the "house of Rechab," following LXX "Rechab" instead of MT "Recah" in 1 Chr 4:12. Since the Kenites were associated with the Arabah, this would support the location of Kh. en-Nahas. At the same time, Aharoni (*LBHG*, 248) proposed a third location in the hill country between Bethlehem and Hebron somewhere in the area of Tekoa, basing this on a reconstruction of the clansmen and their settlements in 1 Chronicles 4.

Bibliography

Glueck, N. 1959. *Rivers in the Desert.* New York.

Jo Ann H. Seely

IRPEEL (PLACE) [Heb *yirpĕʾēl*]. A town located in the tribal territory of Benjamin (Josh 18:27). It is listed with other towns mostly N and W of Jerusalem, and it has been suggested (*IDB* 2: 728) that Kh. Rafat (M.R. 170142), about 1.5 miles E of the Jerusalem airport, might be associated with Irpeel, although others prefer to identify Kh. Rafat with biblical Ataroth.

Gary A. Herion

IRU (PERSON) [Heb *ʿîrû*]. A son of Caleb ben Jephunneh, listed in the genealogy of the tribe of Judah (1 Chr 4:15). His brothers were Elah and Naam. Iru is named first, probably because he was the eldest brother. Possibly the name should be read Ir *[ʿîr]*, with the final *û* actually being the conjunction "and," connected to the next name, i.e., "Ir and Elah" (cf. KB 702; Vg and LXX). If Myers' suggestion (*1 Chronicles* AB, 26) that "Elah" and "sons" are transposed is correct, Iru would also be described at the end of the list as one of the sons of Kenaz (*ʾēlleh* as demonstrative pronoun "these" and not the proper name "Elah" *[ʾēlâ]*: "and these were the sons of Kenaz;" cf. Rudolph *Chronikbücher* HAT, 32). The Syr codex Ambrosianus completely eliminates Iru from the list, beginning the list "the name of his first-born Elah. . . ." *(šēm bĕkōrô)*.

Iru has been linked with the word *ʿîr*, meaning "ass's foal" (*HALAT* 3: 777–78). Note also the names found in the list for the tribe of Benjamin: IRI (1 Chr 7:7) and IR (1 Chr 7:12).

Kenneth H. Cuffey

ISAAC (PERSON) [Heb *yiṣḥāq*]. The second of the patriarchs in whom Israel recognized a father figure; he is traditionally associated with Abraham and Jacob. Genesis presents him as the son of Abraham (17:18; 21:3) and the father of Jacob (25:26). Isaac is mentioned by name more than seventy times in the book of Genesis. Outside Genesis, Isaac finds limited mention in the canonical text of the OT: only thirty-three mentions, and in four of these instances (Jer 33:26; Amos 7:9, 16; Ps 105:9) in the orthographic variant *yiśḥaq*. Generally, except where the context demands otherwise, he is part of the "patriarchal triad" of Abraham, Isaac, and Jacob. One can note the importance of this phraseology for Deut (1:8; 6:10; 9:5, 27; 29:12; 30:20; 34:4), and also of the expression "the God of Abraham, Isaac, and Jacob (Israel)" (Exod 3:16; 1 Kgs 18:36) and that of "the God of Abraham, the God of Isaac, the God of Jacob" (Exod 3:6, 15; 4:5 [for specific details, see Diebner 1974: 38–50; Gispen 1982: 123–29]).

It seems that Isaac plays a role of little importance in the OT tradition; even in Genesis he appears as a secondary personality alongside Abraham and Jacob. The majority of commentators, accordingly, speak of an Abraham cycle and one of Jacob, which together share the bulk of Genesis 12–36. They seem to pass over unawares an "Isaac cycle" that is limited to chap. 26.

It is no less true, however, that the patriarch Isaac is, in the biblical narrative, the indispensable link that connects the history of Abraham to that of Jacob, the father of the tribes of Israel. This is the function that gives him his primary significance, independently of the Jewish and Christian traditions about his presence on Mt. Moriah (Genesis 22).

A. The Name Isaac
  1. Etymology
  2. Significance
B. Biography of Isaac
C. A Secondary Character
D. Literary Problems
E. Historical Approaches
F. Religious Problems
G. Jewish and Christian Traditions

A. The Name Isaac

1. Etymology. The second patriarch's name, Isaac (Heb *yiṣḥāq*), derives from the common Semitic root *ṣḥq;* it implies laughter, a smile, benevolence, gaiety, pleasantness, scoffing, fondling, cajolery (*HALAT,* 955). The Hebrew form of the name Isaac, *yiṣḥāq,* is an imperfect, meaning either "he laughs" or "he is favorable." Speiser (*Genesis* AB, 125) refers the subject of the verb to the father who smiles at his new-born son and receives him with joy. A symbolic gesture such as this could be the origin of the name Isaac. Others have argued that the name evokes the baby's first smile or expresses the good wishes that his parents express in his regard.

Generally, scholars accept another explanation, presented by M. Noth (*IPN,* 210–12) and vigorously defended by J. J. Stamm (1950; one finds it also handed on by R. de Vaux [*EHI,* 198–99], as well as by C. Westermann [1985: 269; cf. *HALAT,* 408]).

Isaac is an abbreviated form of a name composed of a prefixing verb and a divine name—in technical terms, a hypocoristic name (see NAMES, HYPOCORISTIC)—as is the case with the name Jacob. Isaac would then be a short form of **yiṣḥāq-ʾēl,* (or an equivalent form with some other divine name), analogous to the name Ishmael (*yišmaʿ-ʾēl,* that is, "El hears" or "may El hear"; note Gen 16:11). The subject of the verb *ṣḥq* is the deity, not some human being (the father or the child); thus, Isaac(el) would mean "El smiles" or "El is favorable" (or "may El smile/be favorable"). This explanation perhaps finds support from Ugaritic mythological texts, in which are several examples where the god El is said to smile in expressing his satisfaction or favor (Stamm 1950: 35). Unlike the names of the other patriarchs, the name Isaac has thus far not been found attested as a NW Semitic proper name.

2. Significance. Genesis highlights the joyful or amused aura that surrounds Isaac from before his birth and then explains his name in a more or less allusive way through the several episodes in which the son of Abraham and Sarah is featured. According to the present order of the biblical narrative, Gen 17:7 tells of the probably wonderstruck laughter *(wayyiṣḥāq)* of Abraham when he heard the unbelievable news that to him, a hundred-year-old man whose wife was in her nineties, would be born a son. According to Gen 18:12–15, Sarah, when she heard the divine promise, expressed particularly by her laughter (Heb *wattiṣḥaq* [Gen 18:12]) a doubt that she vainly tried to deny (18:15). In another reference to Isaac's name (21:6), his mother seems to be torn between joy *(ṣĕḥōq)* and a fear of being the object of mocking remarks from her attendants *(yiṣḥaq).* Other allusions to laughter coupled with the name of Isaac are found as well in 21:9 and 26:8, but there we find them depicted in a different perspective. In the first case, the attitude of Ishmael who is amusing himself (Heb *mĕṣaḥēq* [*Piʿel;* 21:9]) with Isaac seems suspicious to Sarah (cf. Gen 39:14, 17), and this provokes the expulsion of Hagar and her son; in the second case, Isaac, who had passed off his wife Rebekah as his sister, is given away by his conniving about her, for Abimelech guesses the truth of the matter when he sees him fondling *(mĕṣaḥēq)* his wife. The biblical account thus plays on what is suggested by the name of the child of Abraham and Sarah.

B. Biography of Isaac

Genesis offers a certain amount of information on the patriarch that allows us to reconstruct a "life of Isaac" (cf. *EncJud* 9:1–7). According to Gen 12:5, Abram left his native land by divine command at the age of seventy-five; afterwards, when he was ninety-nine, the Lord appeared to him and promised him a son that he would have by Sarai (17:1–22). Thus, Isaac would be born of a hundred-year-old father (Abram is called Abraham from now on) and of a ninety-year-old mother (Sarai becomes Sarah; Gen 17:15–21). According to 21:3–5, Isaac was circumcised in conformity with the divine ordinance eight days after his birth; at the time of his being weaned from his mother, his father gave a banquet (21:8), and the child grew up among his kinfolk, playing with his half-brother Ishmael up to the very day that Sarah drove this latter out of the family unit along with his mother Hagar (21:9–21).

We reencounter Isaac in Genesis 22, in the episode that took place on Mt. Moriah, an event often designated—though this designation may be contested—"the sacrifice of Isaac," when it really deals with the "testing of Abraham"; with better reason, Jewish tradition calls this the *Aqedah* of Isaac; that is, "the binding of Isaac" (Gen 22:9). Spared at the last possible moment, Isaac next appears with his father at Beer-sheba (22:19).

Abraham then decides to marry off his son and asks his servant to find him a wife among his relations in the home country (Gen 24:1–61). Abraham's plan has a positive outcome; his envoy comes back with Rebekah, who meets her future husband at Beer-lahai-roi. Then, Rebekah consoles Isaac after the death of his mother (24:62–67).

Isaac was forty years old at the time of his marriage and his wife would long remain barren (Gen 25:19–20), for it would only be twenty years later—once Isaac had inherited his father's goods after he and Ishmael had buried their father in the cave of Machpelah, and Isaac had settled near Beer-lahai-roi (?) (25:5–11)—that Rebekah would present him with two sons at once (25:21–28), Esau and Jacob; by trickery, the latter would come to obtain Isaac's paternal blessing (according to 27:1–29).

Chapter 26, sometimes called, with some exaggeration,

the "Isaac cycle," recounts several episodes from Isaac's life. A famine obliges the patriarch, with the blessing of his God, to move on to Gerar, where he has dealings with Abimelech, designated "king of the Philistines" (Gen 26:1–5). Then takes place the incident of Rebekah's seizure, which recalls similar scenes recounted about Abraham and Sarah (12:10–20; 20:1–18): Isaac passes off Rebekah as his sister, but his deceit is discovered by the king; afterwards, everything gets settled between Abimelech and Isaac, whose prosperity, due to divine protection, comes to surpass every measure (26:6–13). There is no mention of the reaction of the Philistines; however, they launch a kind of "war of the wells," which leads the patriarch to go up again to Beer-sheba, where Isaac receives confirmation of the promise made to his father (26:19–25). Abimelech, understanding that Isaac enjoys the favor of his God, concludes a nonaggression pact with him (26:26–33).

Esau, Isaac's favorite (Gen 25:28), later on enters into a marriage that displeases his parents (26:34–35); he sees himself dispossessed of his father's blessing through a heinous stratagem, concocted by Rebekah and carried out by Jacob (27:1–40). Out of fear of Esau's wrath, Jacob goes into exile (27:41–45). Isaac (later on) sends him to look, in his turn, for a wife in the household at Bethuel, in the territory where the paternal clan originated; he gives him the blessing he had received from his father (27:46–28:9). According to Genesis, this is the last intervention by Isaac.

Following a long absence, Jacob, with his wives, his servants, and his children, returns to his country to be present at the death of his father—who is now situated at Mamre, near Hebron—and, with Esau, to oversee the burial of Isaac in the family burial place. At the time of his death, the patriarch was 180 years old (Gen 35:27–29).

C. A Secondary Character

In relation to the rather extensive information furnished by Genesis about Abraham and Jacob, we know very few things about the second patriarch, Isaac. We find, scattered through chaps. 17 to 35, several bits of very precise but succinct information: his birth is foretold (chap. 17) and takes place; his childhood (Genesis 21); his marriage to Rebekah when he was forty years old (Genesis 24); the arrival in the world of his sons, Esau and Jacob, twenty years later (Genesis 25); and his death 120 years after that (Genesis 35). Most of these facts were borrowed from the P source, whose date scholars consider to be late and whose preoccupations reflect a priestly milieu. See PRIESTLY ("P") SOURCE. The principal concern of this version is that of giving outline and shape to the patriarch's life.

The other elements of the history of Isaac pick up again—prescinding, for the moment, from chap. 26—the cycles of Abraham and Jacob. All that has to do with his birth, both its promise and its final accomplishment, belongs to the story of the first of the patriarchs: he is born a son of Abraham, and on him will come to rest the blessing granted to his father. The story of the "testing of Abraham" makes up part of the narratives dedicated to the latter; Isaac, moreover, plays, in Genesis 22, an astonishingly passive role, which Jewish tradition would afterwards seek to amplify. According to the biblical account, he was content to walk along in silence at his father's side; the only time he spoke gave Abraham an opportunity to utter an ambiguous response (an expression of faith that, in another context, the apostle Paul would write, "hoped against hope" [Rom 4:18]). At the time of his marriage, it was again the father who intervened in order to secure a legitimate offspring for his family; Isaac restricted himself to welcoming the woman that was sought out for him (Genesis 24).

Once Abraham died, Isaac inherited his possessions (chap. 25) and, in particular, the promise made to his father (chap. 26), but, for all that, he did not take any noteworthy initiatives—if we exclude chap. 26 from consideration. The biblical narrative shows him grown old, infirm and the victim of intrigue devised by his wife and one of his sons. He passes on to the latter, without really wanting to, one of the most precious things he had inherited, the divine blessing (Genesis 27). Once Abraham has disappeared from the scene, Isaac, in effect, belongs to the Jacob cycle; above all, his role consists in his transmitting to his son a benefit that had come to him from his father: "the promise" made to Abraham and which accompanied the first patriarch his whole life long.

Even Genesis 26, though it is consecrated entirely to him, does not correct, except moderately, the conclusion to which our reading of Genesis has brought us. The various episodes of this chapter are not, properly speaking, original; they almost all have parallels in the lot of the first of the patriarchs. When Isaac is threatened with famine, he goes into exile as Abraham had done before him (according to Gen 12:10–20) and as, later on, the sons of Jacob would do (Genesis 42). Abraham had dealings with Abimelech, "king of Gerar," in the Ṇegeb (Genesis 20), as would his son (according to chap. 26). The history of the seizure of the patriarch's wife is attested three times in Genesis (chaps. 12; 20; 26); in two of these episodes Abraham is the protagonist. Abraham concluded a peace treaty with Abimelech, as his son would do after him (chaps. 21 and 26).

Following these observations, we might ask ourselves how we should characterize Genesis 26. This chapter, far from exposing—even if to a very limited extent—an "Isaac cycle," might not be anything more than a composite—or better, a redactional—work reporting, in summary fashion, several samples taken from a life of Isaac, conceived on the model of those stories narrated about Jacob and, above all, about Abraham. (For a contrary view, see Lutz 1969.)

Finally, a careful reading of Genesis sets in relief the slender nature of the information we have on the destiny of Isaac and the reduced importance of the biblical tradition devoted to him. Nonetheless, this somewhat shadowy figure, who is more or less the plaything of others' interests, by handing on the blessing of the God of Abraham to Jacob in conformity with the divine plan fulfills in this a decisive action and completes the mission that had devolved upon him.

D. Literary Problems

An examination of the literary data about Isaac confirms the impression formed about him from a first reading of Genesis (chaps. 17–35); it also contributes to making even more tenuous the information that the biblical texts communicate about the second patriarch.

Since the time of J. Wellhausen (1844–1918), scholars have reckoned that the Pentateuch is the result of a slow process carried out over several centuries, and thus is a composite work. See TORAH (PENTATEUCH). According to the generally accepted view, there are four principal "layers" of different eras, styles, and perspectives: two of these, called the Yahwist (J) and the Elohist (E), are preexilic; the third shares Deuteronomistic (D) concerns; and the last (P) belongs to the postexilic era. This way of envisaging the Pentateuch's history as the successive combination of literary sources, while long accepted—though with qualifications—by the majority of critics, has been seriously called into question today, and the problem of the composition of the "Five Books of Moses" seems to be more tangled than ever.

Currently, researchers tend to substitute for the synthetic views of the formation of the Pentateuch (such as those found, for example, in the writings of G. von Rad) rather detailed analyses—often voluntarily restricted ones—which recall the so-called "fragment" hypothesis that was defended some time ago. According to these analyses, the Pentateuch would be made up of many pieces more or less successfully joined together at the end of a complex redactional process. Even the existence of the Yahwistic (J) framework as a unity—the basis of the whole reconstruction process—would be contested today.

Moreover, modern-day studies of the OT often insist on the *late* elaboration and completion of biblical texts. If one were to believe some scholars, the essential aspect of Israel's literary productivity took place in the 7th, 6th, and 5th centuries B.C., with and around the time of Deuteronomy. Some claim to be able to recover almost everywhere, including in the Pentateuch, traces of a "Deuteronomistic School," which appeared at the end of the Kingdom of Judah and whose influence extended well beyond the Exile; OT witnesses from the preexilic period would be, as a consequence, few in number and of secondary importance.

As a result of this, the documents relating to the patriarchs today are considered not as the constituent parts of the three or four large "sources" which branch throughout the Pentateuch and sometimes extend even as far as into the book of Joshua, but rather as more or less disparate collections, worked over by redactors, whose role was preponderant during the particularly troubled time that saw the end of the Judean state, the destruction of the Jerusalem temple, and the reconstitution of a Yahwistic community around the reconstructed sanctuary. Hence, the biblical narratives concerning the patriarchs appear to be rather more recent than the ancient events they are thought to report.

Specialists in earlier days were generally in agreement in assigning Genesis 17–35 to the various sources (J, E, D, P) of the biblical narrative found in the Pentateuch; in many cases, scholars were in agreement on the essential points of this source analysis and differed with one another only on specific details.

According to J. Skinner (*Genesis* ICC [1910]), Genesis 17 points to the concerns of P, as its vocabulary, expressions, and aim testify; while the account in Gen 18:1–16, from its style and content, belongs to the J source. Gen 21:1–7 is a composite piece, shared by J (vv 1a, 2a, 7, 6b), E (only v 6a, but this source is rejoined with vv 8 and following), and P (vv 1b, 2b–5).

In Genesis 22, the narrative of the "sacrifice of Isaac" has the characteristic traits of E in vv 1–14 and v 19; vv 15–18 constitute a complementary note by a redactor (R) who has combined the conceptions of E with a Yahwistic phraseology (R^{JE}). With regard to chap. 24, devoted to the steps taken for Isaac's marriage, this is Yahwistic (J); the presence of several doublets or contradictions (such as vv 29–30; 23b, 28; 50, 53, 55; 59, 61; etc.) may be explained by the presence of an Elohist version.

The pericope in Gen 25:7–11a continues the thought of 23:20 and belongs to P, while v 11b is Yahwistic, as is 25:5, whose original location must have been chap. 24, and which the final redactor of the Pentateuch (R^{JEP}) has displaced. From P we also have vv 19, 20, and 26b, while the text on the birth of the twins (25:21–26a and 27, 28) is mainly from J, with Elohistic traits in vv 25, 27.

Chap. 26 is reserved to Isaac, but the bulk of the episodes recounted there—with the exception of vv 12–16—have their parallels in the Abraham cycle: thus, Gen 26:1–6 recalls 20:1–2; 26:7–11 corresponds to 12:10–20 and to 20:2–18; 26:17–22 evokes 21:25–26; and 26:23–33 evokes 21:22–34 (26:34–35, a notice which concerns Esau, is from P). For Skinner, the tradition in Genesis 26 is Yahwistic (J); it derives from an account connected with Hebron—more recent than another, which was connected with the Negeb. The ensemble of the chapter constitutes a specific unit, which breaks the narrative thread between the end of chap. 25 and the beginning of chap. 27.

In Genesis 27, the presence of repetitions testifies in favor of a double association, that of J and E (cf., for example, vv 33, 34, and 35–38; 21–23 and 24–27a; 11–13 and 16); it is sometimes difficult to establish in detail divisions between the Yahwist, whose terminology predominates, and the Elohist. Gen 35:27–29 (the death of Isaac) belongs to P.

For O. Eissfeldt (1922; 1965), the division of the sources of Genesis with regard to what concerns Isaac is apparently the same, except that he admits the existence of a version prior to J, containing ancient materials, which he designates as L (*Laienquelle* or "Lay source"). This leads him to the following conclusions:

L Source: Gen 18:1–9 (the essential aspects of the pericope, completed with several amplifications of J: the most ancient account foretold the birth of Isaac); Gen 25: 11b (the notice of Isaac's settlement at Beer-lahai-roi) and vv 21–26a (the birth of the twins, Esau and Jacob); Gen 26:1–2a, 3a, 6–23, 25b–33 (Isaac goes to Gerar, the seizure of Rebekah, the covenant with Abimelech at Beer-sheba). One should note that, for Eissfeldt, the key chapter on Isaac, chap. 26, goes back to the old layer L.

J Source: Gen 18: 1a, 3, 10–15 (details complementary to the foretelling of Isaac's birth and his being placed under Yahweh's "patronage"; allusions to the name Isaac); Gen 21: 1a, 2a, 7 (the birth of Sarah's son); Gen 24:1–67 (the essential core of the chapter is Yahwistic, with some Elohistic fragments); Gen 25; 27–28 (the introduction to chap. 27); Gen 26:2b, 3b, 24, 25 (the transfer of Abraham's blessing onto Isaac, according to J); Gen 27:1–46 (the essential core of the chapter belongs to J, with several elements from E, especially from vv 37–39 and 41–45). One might draw attention to the fact that the two large narratives in chaps. 24 and 27 are considered Yahwistic; according to J, moreover, Yahweh promises Abraham a son and keeps his word (chaps. 18 and 21).

E Source: Gen 21:1b, 6, 8–13 (allusions to the name of Isaac at his birth, the sending away of Hagar); Gen 22:1–19 (the essential aspects of the Aqedah of Isaac, reworked here and there); Genesis 24 (the elements of an Elohistic version, such as vv 5, 6, 8, 10b, 11b, 22b, 23b, 25, 29a, 30, etc.); Gen 25:11a (Isaac blessed by God); Gen 26:3c, 4, 5 (the transfer of the blessing of Abraham to Isaac, according to E); Genesis 27 (Elohistic complements to the narrative of the deception of Isaac by Jacob, as well as vv 1b, 15, 18b, 24–28, 29b, etc., and, notably, vv 41a, 42–44, 45b, on Jacob's flight after his heinous crime). One should note that Eissfeldt finds traces of an Elohistic version in the bulk of chaps. 20–22 and attributes to E the account of the testing of Abraham (chap. 22).

P Source: Gen 17:1–27 (the chapter in its entirety: the announcement of a posterity for Abraham; circumcision, the sign of the covenant; reference to the name of Isaac); Gen 21:2b–5 (the birth and circumcision of Isaac; Abraham's age); Gen 25:7–10 (Abraham's death, his burial by his sons) and vv 19, 20, 26b (Isaac's posterity; Isaac's age at his marriage and the birth of his sons); Gen 26:34, 35 (notice of Esau's marriages) followed by Gen 27:46–28:5 (Jacob's departure blessed by his father); Gen 35:27–29 (Isaac's death at Hebron at the age of 180). Apart from the great "theological" chapter (Genesis 17), P is content with very brief notices which mark out the stages in the life of the second patriarch.

H. Cazelles states that "the Isaac cycle belongs to the Yahwistic tradition (for the most part) and to the priestly tradition, in the case of the latter beginning with the birth of Isaac (21:1–7)" (*DBSup* 7: 130). He notes, as well, the presence of an Elohistic tradition. Thus, he attributes to the J source Gen 18:1ff.; Gen 21:1, 2a, 7, 8; Gen 22:15–18 (the residue of a Yahwistic narrative that "has even contaminated v 11" [*DBSup* 7: 773]); Genesis 24; Gen 25:5 (which derives from the source used by J in Genesis 24); 11b, 18, 21–26a (the settlement at Beer-lahai-roi, where Isaac was born); Genesis 27 (according to Cazelles, the difficulties in the narrative come, as in chap. 24, from J's use of an earlier source and not from an Elohistic version). With regard to Genesis 26, devoted to Isaac, which everyone says is Yahwistic, we should note in it an ancient substratum that has been reworked by J; v 5 would be not a "Deuteronomism" but a trace of P (*DBSup* 7: 744). E finds little place in the narratives given over to Isaac, except for chap. 22 (vv 1–13, 19, with the reworkings in vv 11–12), perhaps Gen 21:1, 2a, 6b–8 (doubtful), and 9–21 (Isaac's birth; the expulsion of Hagar). In Gen 25 we may uncover "an Elohistic base . . . perhaps vv 25–26a, 27a . . . and 29–34" (*DBSup* 7: 804). With regard to the "Sacerdotal History," according to P, it connects Isaac with the second covenant, whose sign is circumcision, between God (El Shaddai) and Abram (chap. 17). "Isaac constitutes precisely the first fruits of it" (Gen 21:2b–6 [*DBSup* 7: 831]); along with Ishmael, he buries his father in the cave of Machpelah (Gen 25:7–10). Then, Isaac is associated with the destiny of his son (cf. his posterity, Gen 25:19, 20, 26b; the text is incomplete); the marriages of Esau and Jacob (Gen 26:34–35; 27:46; 28:1–9); Isaac's death and burial (Gen 35:27–29). Henceforth, Jacob is the principal personality of the patriarchal tradition and "does not participate in Abraham's blessing except by avoiding marriages with the Canaanites" (*DBSup* 7: 831).

Here we could terminate our quick survey of the works of previous generations concerning the composition of the Pentateuch; for in continuing this line of inquiry, we would, in general, come up with the essential data of theses issuing from the school of Wellhausen.

C. Westermann, in his massive commentary on Genesis, while admitting the existence of the Yahwistic (J) and Priestly (P) strata in chaps. 12–36, contests the presence of an Elohistic source parallel to J in these chapters (see his conclusion [1985: 571–741]). Westermann, with other specialists, insists on the role of oral tradition in the history of the Pentateuch, and on the fact that the Yahwist presents a narrative that is not uniform but rich and varied, issuing from what had been put together in the course of time out of many elements. Westermann nonetheless stresses the redactional activity that is at the origin of the actual biblical text. It is a redactor (R), in fact, that undertook the joining together of the J and P sources and the quasi-definitive deposition of the traditions relative to the patriarchs. For example, R is responsible, in the Abraham cycle (chaps. 12–25), for the introduction (Gen 11:27–32, with the notice of Sarai's barrenness), the conclusion (Gen 21:1–7, with its mention of Isaac's birth) that matches it, and, in the Jacob cycle, for Gen 25:19–28, which inaugurates the story of Jacob and Esau (with its account of the twins' rivalry), as well as for Gen 35:1–29, which brings it to an end (the newly reunited Esau and Jacob bury their father). This redactional activity would get followed up on after R; as witness he cites the addition of several units or even chapters (e.g., chap. 26) which break the link between Genesis 25 and 27. This does not consist of the mere juxtaposition of different versions but rather of the elaboration of pericopes constructed with care to give direction to an understanding of the patriarchal traditions.

In the case of the texts where Isaac is the topic, Westermann admires the artistry with which Genesis 17 (P) has been composed, even to its most minute details; he thinks that in Gen 18:1–16a, currently situated within the totality of chaps. 18–19, two themes are mixed together that originally were independent of one another (the visit of the divine beings, the announcement of the birth). In his commentary, there is no explicit statement that this pericope derives from the Yahwistic (J) stratum.

Regarding Gen 21:1–17 (Isaac's birth), far from seeing in it an amalgam of J, E, and P, as many critics before him did, Westermann discovers in it the work of a redactor (R), who recounts the sequence of events within a passage that matches the introductory piece (Gen 11:27–32). In place of sources more or less carefully joined together, these verses thus testify to a reflective redactional exercise.

Genesis 22, a theological narrative in which Abraham is put to the test, must belong to a more recent period (the end of the kingdom of Judah), but it may reuse an earlier and different version. Westermann does not make any special mention of E here, for he considers its foundation to be almost negligible (1985: 353–57). Genesis 24 goes back to an ancient family tradition, but its redaction within Genesis is later than J (if this source is to be dated in the 10th or the 9th century (1985: 383–84).

According to Westermann, with Gen 25:7–18 (P), the history of Abraham reaches its conclusion; consequently, 25:1–6 derives neither from J nor P and appears to be a late addition. Gen 25:19–28 is a redactional work that introduces the history of Jacob and Esau and makes use of elements from both J and P; its continuation is found in chap. 27, after the paragraph (25:29–34) placed there by R (1985: 406–9). Genesis 27 itself presupposes a long development from the oral stage, and may date from the patriarchal era in its Yahwistic redaction, but it is without an Elohistic parallel, despite the presence of doublets (such as 33–34 and 35–38) and the late addition of blessings (27b–29; 39–40).

Genesis 26, totally devoted to Isaac, does not appear to be a mosaic of units relating to the second patriarch (combined at a late date into a more or less homogenous whole), as G. von Rad, among others, thinks, but a composition cleverly constructed to treat, above all else, the relationships between Isaac and Abimelech (vv 12–17 [not counting v 15] and 26–31). The narrative, which presupposes Gen 21:22–34, is associated with a series of notices concerning wells (26:15, 18, 19–25, 32–33; an ancient element) and a fragment concerning an itinerary (26:17, 22a, 23, 25b; equally ancient), and introduced by vv 1–11 (taken up again in vv 12 and 20). The author of the chapter intends to show how Isaac, behind whom Israel itself is profiled, entered into contact with the Philistines: Isaac appears as the heir of the promise made to Abraham (26:2a, 3a, 24; 2b, 3b, and 4–5 form a complementary addition), which became notably manifest in an abundance of harvests (26:12–14) and in the successful outcome of his negotiations with the Philistine king (26:26–31; there is a double use of *šālōm* in vv 29, 31). The chapter is located after a break in the narrative about the two brothers, Esau and Jacob: Gen 25:19–28 (29–34 is an addition), followed by Gen 27:4; it cannot go back to J. Thus, the principal witness to an "Isaac cycle," according to Westermann's analysis, is a redactional work, elaborated at a late date and associated with the unit formed out of J and P.

Here again, the commentary of Westermann insists not on Genesis' division into classical Pentateuchal sources but on the presence, within the patriarchal texts, of skillful constructions which addressed a thought-out theological and historical purpose; where other exegetes saw only disorder, one may uncover a carefully constructed whole.

The work of E. Blum, dedicated to the composition of the patriarchal history (1984), is typical of the tendencies that today dominate some of the research activity into the origin and development of the Pentateuch. As R. Rendtorff has argued in a volume dealing with a study of this same ensemble (1976), the principle task is not grappling with the classical hypothesis of the sources J, E, D, and P, but instead examining the "large units" out of which the Pentateuch is built (the history of the fathers; the narratives about Moses; the Sinai pericope, etc.) that have their own proper theological meanings, were bound together only at a quite late date, and afterwards were completed and corrected within a point of view that is close to that of Deuteronomy (here people sometimes speak of a Deuteronomistic or a pre- or proto-Deuteronomistic edition), and, much later still, by P, whom strictly speaking, one must think of more as a reviser than an author.

So it is that for Blum, one of the important units of the Pentateuch, Genesis 12–50, is the result of a succession of redactions at relatively late dates. In these redactions, a Deuteronomistic current is especially in evidence, rather than an assemblage of the J, E, and P sources, whose very existence seems more or less problematical.

According to Blum, we should note the following with regard to the notices in Genesis about Isaac: Gen 18:1ff., which recount the extraordinary continuity of the Abrahamic lineage, are a kind of etiology of Israel (1984: 279); Genesis 22, which highlights the testing of Abraham's obedience, must date—at the earliest—from the late royal period (328ff.); Genesis 24 belongs to a Deuteronomistic perspective of the postexilic period when there was a great deal of questioning about marriages with foreigners, as the interventions of Ezra and Nehemiah testify (383ff.). As regards chap. 26, it constitutes, with the exception of vv 2–5—or, more exactly, of vv 3b–5 (D; 362ff.), which develop v 24—a remarkable unity, despite the various elements out of which it is composed; it supposes a period that is neither prior to the formation of the kingdom of Israel nor later than 587, and reflects a relatively balanced political situation between the state of Judah and her Philistine neighbors (301ff.). Moreover, Genesis 26 was reworked and completed at the time of the Exile from the Deuteronomistic perspective (cf. particularly, the promises in Gen 26:2b–5). The calling into question of the hypothesis concerning literary sources—particularly those of the preexilic strata (J, E)—and the tendency to date texts relating to the patriarchs to generally later periods lead to a still greater reduction of the strength of OT testimony regarding the second of the patriarchs: Isaac appears as a secondary character, whose mention appears in passages that are secondary, often marginal and edited late.

It may well be, however, that the Isaac cycle is more ancient and more important than is generally imagined. A. de Pury (1975: 1.189–201) thinks he has uncovered in the "promises" made to the patriarchs, more precisely in 26:2b, 3a; 26:24 (and 46:3, 4), a tradition that is common to these passages and independent of their present context: according to this tradition, Isaac would have been constrained by the threat of a famine to go down into Egypt. Before his departure he would have received an oracle of salvation guaranteeing him the protection of his God and his return to the region of Beer-sheba, where he could then settle. Of this narrative, there remain today but a few fragments more or less connected to a theophany seemingly situated at Beer-sheba, but, in its original form—as reconstructed by de Pury—it presents a startling, even if original, resemblance to the cycle of Jacob, relative to the latter and to his group's seasonal migration pattern. Thus, Genesis would indirectly furnish more numerous data on Isaac than would be supposed from a first reading of the passages concerning him, the antiquity of which would be undeniable, no matter what certain recent commentators of the patriarchal texts would say about them.

A position further removed from the above was defended by D. A. Lutz (1969). He maintains that a careful reading of Gen 26:1–33, many elements of which are found again in the Abrahamic tradition, permits us to affirm that the figure of Isaac was originally more important than Genesis suggests today. The traditions about Isaac would be earlier than those about Abraham, but were eclipsed by the Abraham traditions, probably because the latter's clan, with its cultic center at Hebron, assumed the preponderant place at the heart of the "southern" confederation. But Isaac, Lutz reckons, played a sufficiently important role that he did not completely disappear from the tradition reported in Genesis.

While this hypothesis is interesting (note also Diebner 1974), it remains true, finally, that exegetes are dealing with a biblical text that leaves little room to the second of the patriarchs.

E. Historical Approaches

The problem of the "historicity" of Isaac, or rather of the relationship between history and the traditions concerning him, is evidently the same issue that is posed with regard to Abraham or to Jacob, even though the information regarding these two is clearly more amply supplied than the indications from Genesis on Abraham's son. See also ABRAHAM (PERSON); JACOB NARRATIVE.

Here, we limit ourselves to making two final observations. First, archaeological evidence ought not to be accorded too much nor too little importance. See ARCHAEOLOGY, SYRO-PALESTINIAN. Two diametrically opposite attitudes are often manifest among scholars. Some base themselves on archaeology in order to insist on the exactitude of the biblical facts concerning Israel's origins—that is to prove the truthfulness of the patriarchal tradition—while neglecting the fact, on the one hand, that the "bare facts" brought to light by archaeologists are necessarily the object of an interpretation which remains always subject to revision and, on the other hand, that the biblical documents have come down to us by means of a historical process whose complexity appears ever greater—a situation that invites us, here as well, to exercise prudence in our reconstruction of the facts. Others commit themselves precisely to unraveling the many threads of the traditions that form the Pentateuch in general and Genesis in particular; they never stop inquiring about the importance—that is, about the existence—of the very sources which might lie at the base of the first biblical books. These waver between contradictory theses without ever arriving at solutions satisfactory for the whole gamut of researchers; often beclouded by the examination of the variants, doublets, and hiatuses which they establish and sometimes exaggeratedly highlight, they forget that information on the world to which the authors of Genesis belonged does not stop expanding, with the result that every step forward in its regard enriches a reading of the patriarchal texts, adds greater clarity to the milieu from which they derived, and eventually verifies or completes any given fact about one or another of the Fathers of Israel. Although it is not possible for us to write a "historical biography" about each (so also maintained R. de Vaux, who devoted many years of his life to writing a history of early Israel *[EHI]*), knowledge of Israel's remotest past, acquired through a study of the texts and the contribution of archaeological documentation, is not without consequence.

Our second remark concerns the tradition about Isaac, whose antiquity is hard to estimate, since it seemingly goes back to the oral traditions, of which there remain only snippets, but which may be more easily situated on the geographical level. In fact, the texts of Genesis associate the second patriarch with the reign of S Palestine, principally mentioning three places: Beer-lahai-roi (Gen 24:62; 25:11), Gerar (Gen 26:1, 6, 17, 20, 26), and Beer-sheba (Gen 22:19; 26:25 [21:33; 46:1]; 26:26–31; 26:32–33). Beer-sheba was without doubt the most important place and constituted, according to de Pury (1975: 189–91), the cultic center (the "point of attachment") of the "Isaacite" tradition.

It seems that this tradition was also known in the N of Israel. In the time of Amos, the sanctuary of Beer-sheba was visited—with the same status as Bethel and Gilgal—by pilgrims who had come from that region (Amos 5:5–6; 8:14). Amos denounced the "high places of Isaac" (among which Beer-sheba might have been reckoned, 7:9) and went so far as to qualify Israel as the "house of Isaac" (7:16). For Diebner (1974), Isaac would here be the personification of the kingdom of the S, and Israel would have represented the kingdom of the N. (Note that in these last two texts, the orthography of Isaac differs from its usual form: as in Jer 33:26 and Ps 105:9, the *śin* replaces a *ṣādê;* this is generally considered to be a dialectical variation.)

This reference to Isaac has led certain exegetes to suppose that a displacement of the Isaac clan (the tribe of Simeon?) took place toward the N (Zimmerli 1932) or that it settled in the territory of Penuel-Mahanaim in Transjordan (van Selms 1966) or that there was some contact between the "Moses group" (the origin of the Joseph tribe) and that of "Isaac" (Seebass 1966; cf. de Pury 1975: 191ff.). This could have been intentional, with Amos, a person from the S, recalling to the people of the N the ties that united them to his country and, at the same time, of the right they had to call upon them. In any case, the geographic area where Isaac wandered, according to the explicit tradition of Genesis, was relatively well restricted.

F. Religious Problems

The question about the nature of the religion of the patriarchs is particularly complex; to verify this, one need only consult the numerous works of the specialists (*IJH,* 135–37; *BHI,* 96–103; bibliography in Westermann 1985: 114–16). The patriarchs, including Isaac, are often located in relationship to a divinity called "the god of the father" (or "God of my/your/his/father"), an expression to which A. Alt drew attention some time ago in an article that was greatly appreciated and discussed (1966; cf., for example, Gen 31:5, 29 [according to the Greek text], 42, 53; or, in addition, Gen 43:23; 46:1, 3, etc.). "The god of the father" (whether this latter remains anonymous or not) appears as the protector of the family or clan, which appeals to its ancestor.

Genesis at times gives a specific name to this deity; in two instances, the term is *paḥad yiṣḥāq,* whom Jacob acknowledges or whose presence he invokes (Gen 31:42, 53), a formula that for a long time has been translated, following the lead of the ancients, as the "Terror of Isaac" (see FEAR OF ISAAC).

There is another meaning of Heb *pḥd* attested in Job

40:17, where the noun is dual, designating the "thighs" of the hippopotamus (a euphemism for its testicles); the word *paḥad* could evoke, in addition to its primitive signification, the *clan, lineage,* or *descent.* Several authors explain *paḥad yiṣḥāq* from this second root (see FEAR OF ISAAC on this and additional interpretations).

Discussion of the precise meaning of the phrase *paḥad yiṣḥāq* is certainly not finished, but it seems that this second meaning, which associates it with divine power, the life force that is connected with sexuality and the fate of human grouping, is preferable to one that has recourse to the holy "tremendum" to elucidate the mysterious expression used in Genesis 31 (*HALAT,* 872). The *paḥad yiṣḥāq,* from which all ambiguity had not yet been removed, appears as the specific contribution of the second of the patriarchs to the religion of the Fathers.

G. Jewish and Christian Traditions

If Genesis in particular and the OT in general reserve a somewhat limited place for Isaac, later tradition attributed to him a much more important role, notably in the scene located on Mt. Moriah, in which the passive child of chap. 22 has become a responsible adult who voluntarily takes an active part in his "sacrifice." For Judaism and the Church, Isaac is in the fullest sense one of the three patriarchs of Israel.

The deuterocanonical texts restrict themselves to briefly taking up again the indications of the Hebrew Bible concerning Isaac: Sir 44:22; Dan (LXX) 3:35; Jdt 8:26. In contrast, the rabbinical texts which comment on Scripture abound in details concerning his destiny and recognize the decisive significance that he had for his descendants. Thus it is that a midrash situates his birth on first day of the feast of Passover and recounts that it was accompanied by numerous miracles, so much so that Isaac's coming into the world bears messianic traits. His naming is related to the gift of the Law ("the coming out of the commandment"), a pledge of liberty, and each of the letters making up his name leaves room for speculations relating generally to the patriarch. The marriage of the son of Abraham to Rebekah unfolded in a marvelous manner, and the contacts of Abraham and Isaac with the Philistines allowed the rabbis scope to insist on the identical lot of the two patriarchs. If the happiness that Isaac knew here below was due to the merits of his father, his own proper merits will assure him of a recompense in the hereafter, and his descendants will be the beneficiaries. Isaac will, in fact, plead for them and will snatch them away from Gehenna; also, he will be greeted by his sons and daughters with this exclamation, "This man is truly our father. . . !"

It is particularly with regard to the Aqedah that, in the Jewish texts, the role of Isaac and his "virtues" are shown to advantage. Josephus (*Ant* 1.13.1–4 §222–36) gives Isaac's age as 25 when he ascended Mt. Moriah; he describes him as throwing himself joyfully toward the altar, even though he escaped the fate awaiting him. Isaac conducted himself there as the worthy son of Abraham, and the Aqedah was as much his affair as it was his father's.

Philo of Alexandria, in his treatise on Abraham (the one on Isaac has been lost), devoted several paragraphs to Isaac (*Abr* 32–36, §167–207). He insisted on the perfect accord between the father and the son who journeyed to the place of sacrifice, and he retained of the traditions concerning the name of Isaac only the note of laughter, which he mentioned to designate his joy (and that he had to learn to sacrifice in favor of a higher joy). Also, he considered the Aqedah as a veritable sacrifice, even though Abraham did not have to carry out the deed to its end.

Already in the first century prior to the Christian era, the Jewish book of *Jubilees* related the "binding" of Isaac to the paschal sacrifice (17:15): Isaac was to have been immolated at the very hour that the ritual of the feast foresaw for the putting to death of the lamb (49:1) and on the very spot where the temple would be erected, that is on Mt. Zion (18:7–13). A later text, the *Biblical Antiquities* (of Pseudo-Philo, 1st century C.E.), equally considered that the sacrifice of Isaac had been accomplished and saw in this the reason for the election of the Israelites (18:5): the blood of Isaac thus sealed God's covenant with his people (*L. A. B.* 18:5; cf. 32:1–4; 40:2).

The sacrificial character of Abraham's gesture is found as well in various Targums (the Aramaic translations of the Pentateuch), which call attention to the benefits that Israel ought to draw from the Aqedah. Codex Neofiti, identified in 1956, in its expansion of Lev 22:27, associates Isaac with the lamb bound as a holocaust and foretells the day on which the Israelites will say, "Recall in our favor the Aqedah of Isaac, our father." The same manuscript, in the "poem of the four nights" at Exod 12:42, relates the celestial vision of Isaac (which explains his quasi-blindness; cf. chap. 27) to the moment of his immolation and, in Gen 22:10, evokes Isaac's prayer to his father on the occasion of the Aqedah in this way: "My father, bind me well so that I do not kick you in a way that your offering might be invalid" (following the translation of R. Le Déaut 1978). Among other elements, the Targum mentions the intercession of Abraham at the hour of sacrifice in favor of generations to come: "And now, when his sons find themselves in a time of distress, remember the Aqedah of their father Isaac and hear the voice of their supplication. Hear and answer them and deliver them from all tribulation" (*T. Neof.* Gen 22:14).

Other targumic traditions imply that Israel's lot has repeatedly been determined by the "binding" of Isaac: thus, thanks to the merits of the Aqedah, the sin of the golden calf was pardoned (*Tg. Cant.* 1:13), the Jordan was crossed (*Tg. Cant.* 3:6), Jerusalem was delivered (*Tg. 1 Chr.* 21:15). According to another *midrash,* the (expiatory?) sacrifice of the son of Abraham was associated with the *tāmîd* (perpetual sacrifice; *Lev. Rab.* on 1:5) as it also was with the ritual of the New Year (*Lev. Rab.* on 23:24). Theologians have even found in texts dealing with the Aqedah a theology of redemption antedating the Pauline doctrine of salvation in Christ.

This issue remains a controverted one, especially since specialists in the NT are far from being in agreement on the place that Isaac and notably his "sacrifice" occupy in the NT writings. At first sight, references to Genesis 22 appear rarely, except for explicit mentions such as those in Heb 11:17–19 and in Jas 2:21–24. The following texts are generally cited: Rom 8:32; John 1:29 (?); John 3:16 (?); Mark 1:11 and parallels. For G. Vermes (1973), for example, the theme of the Aqedah points to one of the oldest strata of the Christian kerygma; by contrast, P. R. Davies and B. D. Chilton (1978) think the Gospel proclamation has influenced Jewish interpretation of Genesis 22, obliging the rabbis to make of the "binding" of Isaac a vicarious expiatory sacrifice. The problem remains as it has been articulated; it has not yet been freed of apologetical, ulterior motive, and its resolution depends in part on the dating of the texts that are called on to support one thesis or another. It is probable that, over time, the Aqedah underwent a change in signification, and one cannot exclude the possibility that it had acquired a redemptive import prior to the Christian era.

For patristic theology, Isaac was not only an example of the perfect sacrifice (*Ep. Barn.* 7:3), but he was also one of the anticipatory figures of the crucified Christ. For Melito of Sardis (in a 2d-century work, *On the Passover*) Isaac, who did not suffer death, was a "type" of the coming suffering of Christ, who was bound (like Isaac) to unbind us and was put to death (like the ram) to redeem us (so Gribomont 1971: 1993). Irenaeus of Lyons also refers back to Genesis 22 when he writes, "We, too, holding to the same faith as Abraham, carrying our cross as Isaac the wood, we follow behind him. . . . Abraham followed the Commandment of the Word of God, delivering up with a great heart his only and beloved Son as a sacrifice . . . for our redemption" (*Haer.* 4.5.4; [according to Gribomont 1971: 1993]). One can find a typological interpretation in the writings of the majority of the Fathers of the Church, as for example in Tertullian, for whom the death of Christ on the cross was at once prefigured in Genesis 22 by Isaac, brought to the place of sacrifice by his father and bearing himself the wood, and by the ram who redeems him while hung by his horns, as Christ was hung on the "horns" of the cross and was crowned with thorns (*Adv. Marcionem* 3.18; *Adv. Jud.* 10.5–6; 13.20–21; Gribomont 1971: 1994). These themes would get taken up and developed in the tradition of the Church.

Genesis 22 has never ceased to inspire not only the commentaries of the theologians but also the works of poets, artists, and playwrights; from the mystery plays of the Middle Ages to the words of Elie Wiesel after Auschwitz; from Theodore of Beza, author of "Abraham Sacrificing" (1549), to the song writer Leonard Cohen (1970); from Rembrandt (in 1635) to Marc Chagall (in the 20th century), and from Kierkegaard in *Fear and Trembling* (1843) to George Steiner in *A Conversation Piece* (1985). The immolation of the son of Abraham—which is, let us recall, the origin of the Feast of the Sheep in Muslim tradition, in which the victim is Ishmael, not Isaac (but, cf. *Quran* Sura 37.97ff.)—continues to summon all readers of Genesis to give an account of themselves by sending them back to a child whose name means "laughter" and to the cruelest story of human destinies.

Bibliography

Alt, A. 1966. The Gods of the Fathers. Pp. 1–77 in *Essays on Old Testament History and Religion.* Oxford.

Berge, K. 1990. *Die Zeit des Jahwisten.* BZAW 186. Berlin.

Blum, E. 1984. *Die Komposition der Vätergeschichte.* WMANT 57. Neukirchen-Vluyn.

Coats, G. W. 1983. *Genesis.* FOTL 1. Grand Rapids.

Couffignal, R. 1976. *L'épreuve d'Abraham.* Publications de l'Université de Toulouse–Le Mirail A30. Toulouse.

Davies, P. R., and Chilton, B. D. 1978. The Aqedah: A Revised Tradition-History. *CBQ* 40: 514–46.

Diebner, B. 1974. "Isaak" und "Abraham" in der alttestamentlichen Literatur ausserhalb Gen. 12–50. *DBAT* 7: 38–50.

Eissfeldt, O. 1922. *Hexateuch-Synopse.* Leipzig. Repr. Darmstadt, 1962.

———. 1965. *The Old Testament: An Introduction.* Trans. P. R. Ackroyd. Oxford and New York.

Ginsberg, L. 1909–47. *The Legends of the Jews.* 5 vols. Trans. H. Szold. Philadelphia.

Gispen, W. H. 1982. A Blessed Son for Abraham. Pp. 123–29 in *Von Kanaan bis Kerala: Festshrift für J. P. M. van der Ploeg, O. P.* AOAT 211. Neukirchen-Vluyn.

Gribomont, J. 1971. Isaac de patriarche. *Dictionnaire de spiritualité* 7: 1987–2005.

Hillers, D. R. 1972. *Paḥad Yiṣḥāq. JBL* 91: 90–92.

Koch, K. 1980. *pāḥād jiṣḥaq*—eine Gottesbezeichnung? Pp. 107–15 in *Werden und Wirken des Alten Testaments: Festschrift für Claus Westermann zum 70. Geburtstag,* ed. R. Albertz, H. P. Müller, H. W. Wolff, and W. Zimmerli. Göttingen.

Le Déaut, R. 1963. *La nuit pascale.* AnBib 22. Rome.

———. 1978. *Targum du Pentateuque (Genèse).* SC 245/1. Paris.

Lemaire, A. 1978. Les *Benê Jacob:* Essai d'interprétation historique d'une tradition patriarchale. *RB* 85: 321–37.

Lerch, D. 1950. *Isaaks Opferung christlich gedeutet.* BHT 12. Tübingen.

Lutz, D. A. 1969. *The Isaac Tradition in the Book of Genesis.* Diss. Drew University.

Malul, M. 1985. More on *Paḥad Yiṣḥāq* (Genesis XXXI: 42, 53) and the Oath by the Thigh. *VT* 35: 192–200.

Martin-Achard, R. 1982. La figure d'Isaac dans l'Ancien Testament et dans la tradition juive. *Bulletin des facultés catholiques de Lyon* 106 no. 66: 5–10.

Puech, E. 1984. "La crainte d' Isaac" en Genèse XXXI: 42 et 53. *VT* 34: 356–61.

Pury, A. de. 1975. *Promesse divine et légende cultuelle dans le cycle de Jacob, Genèse 28 et les traditions patriarchales.* 2 vols. Paris.

Pury, A. de, ed. 1989. *La Pentateuque en question.* Geneva.

Rendtorff, R. 1976. *Das überlieferungsgeschichtliche Problem des Pentateuch.* BZAW 147. Berlin.

Seebass, H. 1966. *Der Erzvater Israel und der Einführung der Jahweverehrung in Israel.* BZAW 98. Berlin.

Selms, A. van. 1966. *Studies on the Books of Hosea and Amos.* Ou testamentiese werkgemeenskap in Suid-Afrika. Pretoria.

Stamm, J. J. 1950. Der Name Isaak. Pp. 33–38 in *Festschrift für A. Schädelin.* Repr. pp. 9–14 in *Beiträge zur hebräischen und altorientalischen Namenkunde,* ed. E. Jenni and M. A. Klopfenstein. OBO 30. Freiburg and Göttingen, 1980.

Swetnam, J. 1981. *Jesus and Isaac.* AnBib 94. Rome.

Vermes, G. 1973. *Scripture and Tradition in Judaism.* 2d ed. SPB 4. Leiden.

Weidmann, H. 1968. *Die Patriarchen und ihre Religion im Licht der Forschung seit Julius Wellhausen.* FRLANT 94. Göttingen.

Westermann, C. 1985. *Genesis 12–36.* Trans. J. Scullion. Minneapolis.

Zimmerli, W. 1932. *Geschichte und Tradition von Beerseba im Alten Testaments.* Diss. Göttingen.

ROBERT MARTIN-ACHARD
Trans. Terrence Prendergast

ISAIAH SCROLL, THE (1QIsa[a]). Nineteen copies of the book of Isaiah have been found among the Qumran biblical mss. Most of these are very fragmentary. The most important among them are two scrolls coming from cave 1, in particular the scroll 1QIsa[a]. The second, 1QIsa[b], only preserves a part of the text of Isaiah, because the scroll has been badly damaged.

1QIsa[a] was among the first mss first discovered by the bedouin at the end of 1946 or the beginning of 1947. It was also the first to be identified. Physically, the scroll is made up of seventeen sheepskin sheets, sewn together by a linen thread. Its average height is 26.2 cm, and it is 7.34 m long. Apart from some minor lacunae at the beginning and in the lower part of the scroll, 1QIsa[a] contains the complete text of the book of Isaiah, arranged in 54 columns. A facsimile of this scroll is now in the Shrine of the Book at Jerusalem.

1QIsa[a] was written by a single hand in the latter half of the 2d century B.C., probably between 125 and 100. Omissions were filled in and corrections were made for about a century afterwards. 1QIsa[a], like the other Isaiah manuscripts found at Qumran, precedes by about a thousand years the most ancient manuscripts of the book of Isaiah previously known.

Although 1QIsa[a] and the consonantal basis of the MT are basically identical, there are a few hundred textual variants. Drawing his conclusions from an analysis of the spelling, pronunciation, morphology, vocabulary, and syntax, Kutscher (1974) has shown that 1QIsa[a] presents an example of the Hebrew of the Second Temple period. This is distinct from classical Hebrew and is representative of a more recent stage of the language than that attested by the MT. A great number of the textual variants between 1QIsa[a] and the MT are purely linguistic. These are due to the influence of late 2d-century B.C. Hebrew on the text of the book of Isaiah. More precisely, 1QIsa[a] contains a deliberate linguistic updating of the text, carried out at a time when Aramaic and Greek were spoken alongside Hebrew in Palestine. This updating is most strikingly obvious in the modernization of the spelling; full forms are found consistently in chaps. 34–66 and somewhat less so in chaps. 1–33. Every instance of the vowels *o* and *u*, whether long or short, is rendered by *waw;* the pronominal suffixes and the verbal endings are followed by *he*. *ʾAlep* follows the endings of words normally ending in *-î*, *-ô*, or *-û*. The act of reading is thus made easier for people whose first language is Hebrew, but who are not very literate, as well as for those for whom Aramaic was the first language. In fact, the fuller forms are intended in some cases to distinguish the Hebrew pronunciation from that of Aramaic.

The updating of the language is shown equally in the replacement of certain terms which had fallen into disuse or become rare at the end of the 2d century B.C. by others in more common use. For example, in 13:10 1QIsa[a] uses the synonym *yʾyrw,* very common in the Bible and in rabbinic Hebrew, to replace the verb *yhlw* ("cause to shine"), rare in the Bible in this sense (Isa 13:10; Job 29:3; 31:26; 41:10) and not found in rabbinic Hebrew. Likewise in 33:7; 42:2; 46:7, 1QIsa[a] replaces *ṣʿq* ("to cry out") with its synonym *zʿq,* which was more common after the Exile.

In most instances where variants are not simply linguistic, the 1QIsa[a] readings are secondary, and show characteristics similar to those of the ancient versions. Thus 1QIsa[a] often changes terms and expressions under the influence of either the immediate context, a more remote parallel passage in Isaiah, or another biblical book. For example, in 43:19, instead of the word *nhrwt* ("rivers"), 1QIsa[a] has *ntybwt* ("tracks"), a term probably suggested by the context. This term is found in the singular in 43:16, where it is likewise associated with *drk* ("path"), for which it provides a better parallel. In 51:2, 1QIsa[a] replaces *wʾbrkhw wʾrbhw* ("I have blessed him and made him multiply") with *wʾprhw wʾrbhw* ("I have made him fruitful and made him multiply") because of the frequency with which the latter pair of verbs is found, especially in Genesis (Gen 1:22, 28; 8:17; 9:1, 7; 17:20; 28:3; 35:11; 47:27; 48:4; Lev 26:9; Jer 3:16; 23:3; Ezek 36:11). Sometimes 1QIsa[a] amplifies the text. For example, in 30:6a it inserts the word *wṣyh* ("and aridity") between the terms *ṣrh wṣwqh* ("anguish and distress"). The term added is probably taken from 35:1, 41:18, and 53:2.

Finally, one may mention a particularly interesting category of textual variant resulting from exegesis. Occasionally the author of 1QIsa[a] has altered the text, normally very slightly, in such a way as to make it conform to his interpretation. One may cite 8:11 as a simple but significant example. In place of the word *wysrny,* 1QIsa[a] has *ysyrnw/y* (the final letter is uncertain). So, whereas the Masoretes derive the verb from the root *ysr* ("*he corrected me* so that I would not follow the path of this people . . ."), 1QIsa[a] sees there the *Hipʿil* of the root *swr* ("*he turned me away* from following the path of this people . . ."). This text is applied in 4QFlor 1,14–15 to the community of Qumran, seen as the community of those whom God has separated from the remainder of the people. So this explains the variant of 1QIsa[a]: it is the fruit of the updating process, which sees in the community of Qumran the accomplishment of the oracle of the prophet.

In conclusion, one can say that the specific contribution of 1QIsa[a], as of the other Isaian mss from Qumran, is related to the history of the textual tradition of the book of Isaiah. When one adds to that the witness of the LXX, the mss of Qumran have confirmed that, unlike other biblical books, there was only one text of the book of Isaiah from the 3d century B.C.

That being said, the mss from Qumran show at the same time a considerable fluidity of this text. 1QIsa[a] represents, in a general way, a secondary text with reference to the MT. It is to some extent a revised updated edition of the book of Isaiah. It occasionally comes close to a commentary *(Pesher).* The author of 1QIsa[a] modernizes the language of the book and introduces different kinds of harmonizations and expansions. On occasion, influenced by his exegesis, the author does not hesitate to change the text. He exhibits a fairly broad liberty with regard to the text, a liberty he shares with the Gk translators, who were roughly his contemporaries. It is this liberty that is perhaps the most important common trait between 1QIsa[a] and the LXX of Isaiah, two texts which have often been compared. This innovative approach did not serve as a precedent in the Hebrew textual tradition of the bock of Isaiah.

The Qumran mss also witness to a conservative tradition in regard to the book of Isaiah. This conservatism is represented by 1QIsa[a] and by the majority of the other examples of the text of Isaiah found at Qumran, all of which are closer to the MT than is 1QIsa[a]. This tendency will be accentuated and strengthened. In the end, it will dominate and will have as its consequence the definitive stabilization of the text of Isaiah.

Bibliography

Barthélemy, D., and Milik, J. T. 1955. *Discoveries in the Judaean Desert. I. Qumran Cave I.* Oxford.

Burrows, M.; Trever, J. C.; and Brownlee, W., eds. 1950. *The Dead Sea Scrolls of St. Mark's Monastery.* Vol. I, *The Isaiah Manuscript and the Habakkuk Commentary.* New Haven.

Evans, C. A. 1984. 1QIsaiah[a] and the absence of Prophetic critique at Qumran. *RevQ* 11: 537–42.

Hoegenhaven, J. 1984. The First Isaiah Scroll from Qumran (1QIsa) and the Massoretic Text. *JSOT* 28: 17–35.

Koenig, J. 1982. *L'herméneutique analogique du Judaïsme antique d'après les témoins textuels d'Isaïe.* VTSup 33. Leiden.

Kooij, A. van der. 1981. *Die alten Textzeugen des Jesajabuches.* OBO 35. Freiburg.

Kutscher, E. Y. 1974. *The Language and Linguistic Background of the Isaiah Scroll (1QIsa[a]).* STDJ 6. Leiden.

Qimron, E. 1979. *E. Y. Kutscher, The Language and Linguistic Background of the Isaiah Scroll* (1QIsa[a]). *Indices and Corrections.* STDJ 6a. Leiden.

Rosenbloom, J. R. 1970. *The Dead Sea Isaiah Scroll.* Grand Rapids.

Talmon, S. 1962. DSIa as a witness to the Ancient Exegesis of the Book of Isaiah. *ASTI* 1: 62–72.

Ziegler, J. 1959. Die Vorlage der Isaias-Septuaginta (LXX) und die erste Isaias-Rolle von Qumran (IQIs[a]). *JBL* 78: 34–59.

FRANCOLINO J. GONÇALVES

ISAIAH, BOOK OF.

The sixty-six chapters of the book of Isaiah form a whole in the canon of the Hebrew Bible and in all of the versions, but internal indications of diversity have led critical scholarship to distinguish three major works of literature in the book. First Isaiah (chaps. 1–39), Second Isaiah (chaps. 40–55), and Third Isaiah (chaps. 56–66) are now generally treated as separate writings or collections with distinct authors. The "Little Apocalypse" (chaps. 24–27) is also viewed by many as a separate work within the larger unit called First Isaiah. In view of the current critical consensus, the works composing the biblical book associated with the prophet Isaiah are treated separately in individual articles in the order First Isaiah, The Little Apocalypse, Second Isaiah, Third Isaiah.

FIRST ISAIAH

The widest possible range of positions is represented in the scholarly literature concerning First Isaiah. First Isaiah is viewed by some as a rhetorical unity accurately depicting historical and political events during the lifetime and from the perspective of the 8th-century prophet Isaiah. Others view only sections of chaps. 1–39 as emerging from the context of 8th-century Judah and understand the present form of First Isaiah to be under major redactional influence. Still others reject the view altogether that First Isaiah is about the prophet Isaiah and events in his day, preferring to see chaps. 1–39 as a pseudepigraphical magnet attracting various postexilic concerns and aspirations.

As a consequence of this radical divergence of views, an accounting of the present state of the inquiry—its history, limitations, and future—will open the treatment. This will be followed by a general introduction to First Isaiah sensitive to its many literary, historical, and theological complexities, yet receptive to the possibility of significant efforts at coherence in all three areas in the final form of the Isaiah presentation. In this manner we hope successfully to introduce Isaiah 1–39 without minimizing the many exegetical complexities which confront even the general reader of this rich prophetic collection.

A. Critical Orientation: The Literary Composition of Isaiah 1–39
  1. First Isaiah: Terminological Background
  2. First Isaiah in the 20th Century
B. Isaiah and History: Preliminary Considerations
C. The Canonical Presentation of the Book of Isaiah
  1. Isaiah and the Emergence of Assyria
  2. The Syro-Ephraimite Debacle and Isaiah 1–12
  3. The 701 Assault: Isaiah 36–39 and Kings Presentations
  4. The 701 Assault: General ANE Perspective
  5. Isaiah 28–33
  6. Isaiah 34–35
  7. Isaiah 13–23 and 24–27
D. Conclusions

A. Critical Orientation: The Literary Composition of Isaiah 1–39

A general introduction to First Isaiah can be given in part through a discussion of terminology. What exactly is meant by the term "First Isaiah"? Is this a literary, sociological, or historical classification—or some admixture of all three? A discussion of this issue also serves as an introduction to the background of modern critical exegesis of the book of Isaiah. The section concludes with an examination of the variety of methods used to interpret the literary composition of Isaiah 1–39.

1. First Isaiah: Terminological Background. Early critical treatments of the prophets stressed their poetic and creative capacities. Bishop Robert Lowth's 18th-century study of Hebrew poetry (*De sacra poesi Hebraeorum,* 1753) and his translation of and notes on the book of Isaiah are cases in point (Lowth 1778; 10th ed. 1834). What in Lowth's hands were essentially aesthetic and appreciative observations about the genius of the prophetic consciousness quickly became a warrant for seeing the prophets as men of like nature with ourselves, in virtually all respects. Only their higher moral and natural sensibility set them apart.

Lowth was still able to stretch this sensibility to its limit in the case of Isaiah, a book which would prove an unusually demanding arena in which to fight for enlightened approaches while at the same time defending so-called traditional views of prophecy. In Isaiah's case the problem was one of strained temporal reference, most specifically concerning the ability of an 8th-century Isaiah to speak of 6th-century events, nations, and rulers (e.g., Cyrus), with at times remarkable attention to detail, especially in chaps. 40–66. To applaud prophetic genius in respect of ethical insight was one thing; but to claim for this same genius the ability to foresee events centuries in advance went beyond enlightened logic. Here the book of Isaiah presented a set of challenges for the early critical reader without real analogy in Jeremiah or Ezekiel, although an even tougher problem was admitted to exist in the case of Daniel. Lowth's position that Isaiah delivered the prophecies of chaps. 40–66 "in the latter part of the reign of Hezekiah" (Lowth 1834: 309) is a good example of an alliance between traditional and enlightened views which would very soon collapse. *Fore*teller and *forth*-teller would begin to look like incompatible conceptions of Isaiah the prophet.

In an interesting bit of intellectual history, the German edition of Lowth's Isaiah commentary included marginal additions and amplifications by the Göttingen professor and chief translator J. B. Koppe, who suggested that chap. 50 was written by Ezekiel or "another prophet living in Babylon" (Koppe 1780: 43). Eventually, "Pseudo-Isaiah" or "Deutero-Isaiah" would emerge as appropriate terms of reference for chaps. 40–66 in their entirety, on analogy with such usage in classics (Pseudo-Philo) or NT studies (Deutero-Pauline). The book of the prophet Isaiah was thus viewed as including an appendix, "Deutero-Isaiah," comprising twenty-seven chapters.

Many attribute the proposal for a Deutero-Isaiah comprising chaps. 40–66 to J. C. Döderlein (1775), or even to the Jewish scholars Moses ben Samuel Gikatilla and Ibn Ezra (Friedlander 1873) long before him (the former active in the 11th century). There is some debate about the correct evaluation of Ibn Ezra, whose translation notes are often cryptic and open to interpretation; it is never entirely clear if his allusions to "the prophet" in chaps. 40–66 refer to an incipient "Deutero-Isaiah" or to a figure spoken about by the original Isaiah. His frequent counsel to the wise interpreter to exercise restraint may imply he is aware of difficulties which would arise from an overly historicist reading; chaps. 40–66 refer for Ibn Ezra to his own day! In a somewhat similar vein, traditional Christian interpretation of chaps. 40–66 was not concerned so much with linking these chapters back in history to an 8th-century prophet as with linking them forward in time to Christ, a reading urged by the NT. In this spirit, the Church Fathers refer to Isaiah not just as the greatest prophet but also as apostle and evangelist (e.g., Eusebius, Theodoret, Jerome, Augustine). Much of the appeal for single Isaiah authorship against emerging critical positions looks in retrospect like defense of a view of Isaiah that never really functioned with primary exegetical or theological significance in the precritical period (see Levenson's remarks on Mosaic authorship of the Pentateuch, 1988: 205–13). Oddly enough, the Talmudic reference used as a source for traditional positions attributes Isaiah's authorship to the "assembly of Hezekiah" (*B. Bat.* 15a).

Eichhorn's analysis of Isaiah in his *Einleitung* (1803), originally published in 1783, foreshadowed the method of procedure and many of the critical conclusions which were to emerge in Isaiah scholarship in the following two centuries. Eichhorn begins to use language like "inauthentic" and "secondary" in his analysis of Isaiah oracles, in a manner which logically proceeds from prior assumptions regarding "authenticity" and "primacy" (Eichhorn 1803: 50–55). Authentic oracles can be traced with confidence to the historical prophet Isaiah. It is Eichhorn who inaugurates the modern critical subsection "Life of Isaiah" (*Jesaias Leben* §523), where he tells the reader who Isaiah really is and when he was active, having successfully extracted him from the literature's own construal.

Significantly, Eichhorn does not use the term "Second Isaiah" in reference to chaps. 40–66; neither does the term "First Isaiah" have relevance for him. "Isaiah" refers to the historical man critically reconstructed. But the book of Isaiah itself, in literary terms, is an anthology from many diverse periods. Secondary additions are made in chaps. 40–52 in a sustained manner; but similar additions can be found in chaps. 1–39, including many brief glosses, as well as the oracle against Moab (chap. 17), chaps. 24–27, and chap. 21 (where reference to "riders on camels" at v 7 sends Eichhorn to Xenophon's reports of later, Persian warfare). In an intriguing conclusion, Eichhorn argues that the order of the major prophets given in the Talmud (*B. Bat.* 14a) is correct, with Isaiah following Jeremiah and Ezekiel. He reasons that Jeremiah and Ezekiel stand first because there is an assumed identity between author and book. Isaiah, by distinction, contains many different prophecies from many different authors and periods and so is an anthology like the Book of the Twelve, which it resembles and next to which it has been placed (Eichhorn 1803: 101–4).

Eichhorn's theory, as peculiar as it may sound, reveals important problems of dating in Isaiah that frustrate easy adoption of the terms "First," "Second," and "Third" Isaiah as referring to simple, historically evolving additions to an original Isaiah core. As for actual historical "authors" of the material, Eichhorn treats only "Isaiah" as a prophetic figure, alongside the many other anonymous contributors. Not until the later chapters (40–66) take on sharper literary and historical definition does the profile of a prophet ("Second Isaiah") emerge, with a fixed sociological and historical provenance to be contrasted with that of an Isaiah located in "First Isaiah" chapters.

The beginning of this process can be detected in Gesenius' Isaiah commentary of 1821. Gesenius expands the list of texts in chaps. 1–39 from later periods to include chaps. 13, 14, 34, and 35. He then speaks of a distinct author *(Verfasser)* of 40–66, whom he calls "Pseudo-Isaiah" (Gesenius 1821: 17). But above all, the decision to treat chaps. 40–66 in a formally separate volume, with its own introduction, helped drive home the independent nature of "Second Isaiah"—to be contrasted not only with authentic Isaiah oracles but also with the other editorial additions to the Isaiah anthology (as he continued to call it). Gradually "Second Isaiah" became more than a literary designation. As these final chapters took on their own theological profile, a prophetic individual began to emerge from behind their cover.

Gesenius also initiated a form of inquiry that had not been of much interest to Eichhorn. Despite the anthological nature chaps. 1–39 shared with the book as a whole, Gesenius was convinced that significant internal organization and structure could be detected in these chapters. Anticipating modern internal divisions in First Isaiah, he spoke of three books within these chapters: 1–12, 13–23, and 24–35. A collector was responsible for their shaping and (often curious) internal organization (the call of the prophet should be at the beginning, not in chap. 6). A fourth book was Pseudo-Isaiah (40–66). Isaiah chaps. 36–

39 were drafted from 2 Kings 18–20 to serve as a conclusion for the originally separate book of Isaiah, on analogy with Jeremiah 52's function as historical appendix to the book of Jeremiah (cf. 2 Kings 25). Since the original book of Isaiah reached a logical conclusion thereby, explanations were required for the addition of the fourth book ("Second Isaiah"), and these ranged from the accidental, to the expedient (scroll size), to the coincidence of name (both prophets had the name Isaiah), to the pseudepigraphic (anonymous oracles required the imprimatur of a former, recognized prophet). Gesenius inclines toward the later view (Gesenius 1821: 17–18).

It was the inquiry into internal organization that led Gesenius to conclude that Isaiah once had a concluded form, assisted by chaps. 36–39, which was independent of Pseudo-Isaiah and yet prior to the final anthological arrangement of the whole sixty-six-chapter book of Isaiah. In many respects, this important observation would begin to allow a certain logic to obtain in the use of what are now practically conventional terms: "First Isaiah" and "Second Isaiah." "First Isaiah" would eventually refer to the literary corpus found in chaps. 1–39, regardless of whether its individual sections were historically anterior. "Second Isaiah" would come to refer to chaps. 40–66. Gesenius' work anticipates the mature theory that behind both literary complexes stand prophetic figures, for whom these names also apply. In sum, use of the term "First Isaiah" would emerge as the consequence of (1) a growing recognition of the literary integrity and independence of "Second Isaiah" and (2) arguments for the structural logic and "closing off" of the Isaiah book with chaps. 36–39. That much of "First Isaiah" was historically contemporaneous with or later than "Second Isaiah" was a paradox the terminology would have to bear.

Bernhard Duhm's influential commentary on Isaiah drives this point home. Duhm maintained that the four-book theory of Gesenius, in somewhat modified form, was a helpful explanation for clear internal collections within Isaiah. Duhm is quite clear, however, that the final collecting and arranging of books in Isaiah takes us practically into the Common Era. And much of the material in Isaiah 1–39 postdates Isaiah 40–66; the *Buchlein* "little book" of chaps. 24–27, for example, Duhm dates to ca. 128 B.C.E. (Duhm *Jesaia* HKAT, xii). Although much in chaps. 1–39 postdates Second Isaiah, Duhm is convinced that these chapters developed internally independent of chaps. 40–66. Consequently, there is a certain propriety in treating Isaiah 1–39 on their own. Like Gesenius, Duhm prefers to talk about Isaiah and the Isaiah Book *(Jesajabuch)*, rather than "First Isaiah" in distinction from "Second Isaiah." Duhm also introduces "Third Isaiah" as the prophetic figure responsible for chaps. 56–66. It would be fair to say that once "Second Isaiah" took on sharper profile as an exilic prophet (cf. Eichhorn's "Pseudo-Isaiah"), a new prophet was demanded for chaps. 56–66, given their distinct tone and seemingly different historical backdrop. In summary, with Duhm's Isaiah commentary three prophetic personalities emerge: Isaiah, Deutero-Isaiah, and Trito-Isaiah. Ironically, greater identity is presumed to exist between prophet and literature in the latter sections (chaps. 40–55 and 56–66) than in the *Jesajabuch* itself (chaps. 1–39).

From a very different angle, this fact has led one recent scholar to conclude that the middle section (chaps. 40–55) is indeed the most stable and has in fact given rise to the other two (Rendtorff 1984). Though overstated, Rendtorff's position has at least pointed out problems inherent in the terms "First Isaiah" and "Second Isaiah." Not all of First Isaiah is historically prior to Second Isaiah; the author of Second Isaiah is more responsible for chaps. 40–55 than Isaiah for 1–39; First Isaiah is a far more complex redactional product, with far greater historical range, than either Second or Third Isaiah. Such was the recognition of Isaiah scholarship by the end of the 19th century. A century later, the situation has changed little.

In conclusion, the term "First Isaiah" is helpful as a literary classification for chaps. 1–39 because they appear first in the book of Isaiah. As a historical or sociological term, however, it must be used with caution, lest one presume an identity of author and literature, with both historically prior to Second and Third Isaiah.

2. First Isaiah in the 20th Century. Even if resistance to Duhm's three-Isaiah model was quickly registered, this century has seen widespread acceptance of his basic critical presuppositions. Conservative exegetes continued to produce commentaries on the whole book and inveigh against a model which impugned the prophet's inspirational capacities, especially in the realm of historical foresight. But Gesenius' treatment of Isaiah in two separate volumes was clearly a harbinger of the future. Considerations of historical reference proved more weighty than those respecting the book's present literary unity—however one accounted for it. Second Isaiah emerged into the full light of day, breathing promise and good will, in literature both coherent and historically uniform. First Isaiah, by ironic contrast, required critical extraction from a literature mixed in form, diverse in historical background, and unparalleled in redactional and organizational complexity. In no small measure, Second Isaiah's gain in critical stature was First Isaiah's loss.

One basic problem confronting interpreters of First Isaiah is its baffling internal movement and structure. Luther probably had First Isaiah in mind when he spoke of the prophets' "queer way of talking, like people who, instead of proceeding in an orderly manner, ramble off from one thing to the next, so that you cannot make head or tail of them or see what they are getting at" (*ROTT*, 33). Here, precritical and modern interpreters are in agreement.

Jerome, Michaelis, and Rosenmüller had argued the arrangement was chronological (1–6: Uzziah to Jotham; 7–14: Ahaz; 15ff.: Hezekiah), though on this score Isaiah offers far fewer clues than the explicitly dated Jeremiah and Ezekiel. A similar position was taken by the conservative Hengstenberg in the 19th century, who spoke of a special "prophetic gift" conferred upon the prophet in the reign of Hezekiah (36–39) which enabled him to see chaps. 40–66; the "vision" presumably had its own internal chronological movement as well (Hengstenberg 1872: 2.2–3). Rationalist attempts to use Assyrian history as a clue to the chronology of Isaiah were popular in the late 19th century; a revised version of this sort of inquiry can be seen in the recent study by Hayes and Irvine (1987). On this logic, the movement of the literature—even through sections of text formally quite diverse (compare chaps. 6–8 with chaps. 9–11)—reflects the temporally unfolding activity of Isaiah as his preaching addresses peoples, nations, and events in chronological order. Chronological order is not editorially imposed, but is the direct consequence of the prophet's own historical activity.

Others, with Vitringae, Jahn, and Bauer among the early critical proponents, have argued that the internal organization is thematic. Modern interpreters have spoken about a general tripartite scheme in the major prophetic collections, with indigenous judgment oracles followed by oracles against nations, themselves followed by oracles of promise and salvation (Kaiser 1984: 232). The scheme may work best in Ezekiel; it could only work with LXX Jeremiah; it would work better in Isaiah if chaps. 28–39 did not intervene before oracles of salvation (40–66). In the final analysis, the scheme is artificial and creates more problems than it solves: clear elements of promise are found in 1–12 and 13–27; chaps. 40–66 contain much sharp judgment material (50:10–11; 57:1–13; 58:1–7; 59:1–8; 65:1–16; 66:17, 24).

Introduction of a category like "thematic" moves one's conception of the literature in a different direction than chronological explanations advocate, since "thematic" arrangement requires some form of conscious reflection on the shape the literature will take, whether by the prophet himself or, more likely, by others (editors, disciples, arrangers). Direct access to the historical prophet is more complicated in this model. In many respects, thematic explanations foreshadow more mature critical views, which require editorial decisions and the shaping of Isaiah's once-oral speech into literary presentation. One cannot so easily follow Isaiah as he chronologically addresses events of his day.

Just what the thematic structure of Isaiah is, is quite another question—as is the extent and nature of editorial intervention. Both Gesenius and Duhm argued for internal collections in First Isaiah, seen in most recent treatments as consisting of 1–12; 13–23; 24–27; 28–32(33); 34–35; and 36–39. Whether this structure is thematically significant is another question altogether. It is probably safer to say that the position of these 19th-century interpreters foreshadows recent redactional arguments for structural organization in First Isaiah. On this view, the consecution of Isaiah oracles may be incomprehensible as it stands, but it is capable of explanation as due to editorial factors and the addition of new levels of text from later periods, quite randomly and without regard for overall literary organization. The roughness of the final form of the text is the result of secondary filling in and elaboration, without regard for literary coherence as a final *desideratum.* From time to time, major structural seams can be detected, as in the collections noted above; but the internal movement within these collections is haphazard, diachronically erratic, and explicable only through complex redactional theories. Here we have a view of the literature and its genesis diametrically opposed to the chronological model, where temporal logic is grounded in the historical activity of the man Isaiah. More recent forms of redactional argumentation may urge far greater appreciation of the present structure of the text, even as chronologically significant (Ackroyd 1974: 330–32; Seitz 1988: 112–16; Smelik 1986: 74–76). But this chronology is by no means connected to the actions in time of the man Isaiah; rather, it is the consequence of editorial decisions concerning the presentation of Isaiah's activity in the literature—an activity whose chronology forms only one part of a larger view of time and the movement of the Word of God in history, as understood by final shapers of the text. (More on "redactional chronology" is presented below.)

Approaches to First Isaiah in this century can be grouped in three categories: (a) direct referential; (b) form and tradition-critical; (c) redactional.

a. Direct Referential. The direct referential approach tends to maximize the extent of the present literature attributable to the prophet Isaiah on a variety of grounds (historical, biographical, rhetorical). The text refers directly to events in the lifetime of Isaiah and also reveals much about the prophet's internal state. A good example of this approach is George Adam Smith's study on Isaiah, written at the turn of the century (Smith *Isaiah* ExB). Smith sees the book unfolding chronologically, so that a sequential reading of chaps. 1–39 traces events in Israelite history from 740 to just after 701. Some sections cannot be dated with certainty (e.g., Oracle against Tyre—chap. 23; Hezekiah on his sick-bed—chap. 38); certain prophecies are not related to Isaiah's time (chaps. 13, 24–27). Smith acknowledges some dislocations (chap. 1; chap. 6), but he usually explains these as due to psychological factors (Isaiah's "call" in chap. 6 is also his reflection back on a difficult career) or matters of priority involving the prophet's own editorial principles.

Hayes and Irvine offer a recent version of this approach, based on a more sophisticated historical investigation and a more rigid commitment to the principle of chronological order. The judgment presupposed in chap. 1 involves the great earthquake reported at Amos 1:1 and Zech 14:5, making the oracle Isaiah's earliest (Hayes and Irvine 1987: 70). Chap. 13 belongs to the period of Tiglath-pileser's efforts to subdue rebellion in the city of Babylon, thus firmly placed in the lifetime of Isaiah and next in order of delivery after chap. 12 and before chap. 14 (Hayes and Irvine 1987: 222). Not even Smith held to his chronological approach in chap. 13, dated by most after 587, presupposing later Neo-Babylonian resurgence under Nebuchadnezzar (Clements *Isaiah 1–39* NCBC, 132), if not the rise of Persia under Cyrus (Wildberger *Jesaja* BKAT, 511). The view of Isaiah that emerges from this portrayal is, not surprisingly, one of a shrewd political observer. Isaiah's interest in world events, particularly in the Nation Oracles section (chaps. 13–23), make him the theological equivalent of modern global-political analysts.

b. Form and Tradition Criticism. Form and tradition criticism disagree in the first instance with the literary presuppositions of direct referential approaches. The book of Isaiah is composed of a wide variety of material, whose principle agenda is not direct cameralike access to political events in the days of Isaiah, nor biographical revelations of the prophet's inner life. Rather, much of the present book began as oral speech of the prophet, delivered on different occasions and for different purposes, the present arrangement of which is a matter for separate inquiry. Moreover, much of the speech of Isaiah already conforms to typical forms of expression, whose history and social location are themselves a helpful index of the theology of the prophet. In Gerhard von Rad's treatment of Isaiah (*ROTT,* 147–75), it was important to place Isaiah within Israel's traditional theological confessions if one was to understand his "genius"—a view which cut against overly individualistic readings of Isaiah as rhapsodic poet, ethical loner, political pundit, or unparalleled *homo religio.* Isaiah's genius lay in his powerful transformation of Israel's traditions.

Von Rad's best example is Isaiah's use of Zion traditions. Von Rad sketches out a coherent Zion theology at home in certain psalms (46, 48, 76), rooted in Israel's historical memory, distinct from Exodus and Conquest traditions. This Zion theology describes Yahweh's choice of Zion for a dwelling place, and his protection of Zion against all foes, frequently spoken of in mythological language. Von Rad notes that this traditional complex of ideas, with its attendant language and forms, is to be seen at numerous points in Isaiah (see esp. chaps. 28–32), together with royal traditions (chaps. 7, 9, 11) ultimately from a similar background. Isaiah uses Zion traditions, however, in a modified form as follows: (1) to express the possibility of God's turning the judgment for the nations back against Israel (29:1–8); (2) therefore demanding a stance of faith (7:1–9), in that sense reflecting a merger of Zion motifs with those of Holy War, where belief was a prerequisite for deliverance (Judges 7); and (3) this modification finally giving way to trust in the mysterious plan of Yahweh (5:12, 19; 14:24–27; 28:21), revealed in an act of grace shown to the prophet. The final transformation strained Zion tradition to its limit and is therefore seen by von Rad as Isaiah's own unique contribution, permitted only when the original Zion form had been faithfully applied and finally found wanting, due to the loss of faith of those around the prophet. Only then does von Rad believe access is granted to the inner life of Isaiah (*ROTT,* 160–66).

The tradition-critical approach of von Rad operates with broader form-critical assumptions about the role of the prophet vis à vis the literature. Isaiah's adaptations of Israel's tradition come in the form of public address, akin to preaching. First Isaiah (1–39) contains this preaching, but it cannot everywhere be simply identified with this preaching, either in neat chronological order, or thematic presentation, or even haphazard arrangement. Von Rad does see some rough chronological movement in the present book, and one might well assume that early chapters are related to events in the days of Ahaz (5–12), later chapters to the days of Hezekiah (28–39). Still, critical judgments are required about the historical events of Isaiah's day, and canons of literary analysis help to determine consistent patterns in Isaiah's own speech. What falls outside either of these areas is clearly secondary and editorially supplied. It would be fair to conclude that von Rad's primary area of interest lay in interpreting the theological significance of those portions of First Isaiah which could reasonably be traced to the historical prophet, using the methods of form- and tradition-criticism. Von Rad remained vitally interested in the prophet Isaiah, as a man of history theologically actualizing Israel's traditions. But this Isaiah could not be simply read off the top of the text; it required highly sophisticated literary and historical tools to lay him bare.

c. Redactional Approaches. Much recent work on Isaiah has a primary redactional interest (Kaiser 1983; Vermeylen 1977–78; Clements *Isaiah 1–39* NCBC; Sweeney 1988b). With increased awareness of the major role editorial and supplemental material plays in the present book of Isaiah, the focus on the man Isaiah has moved to the background, thus inverting the task of interpretation as understood by both referential and form-critical readings. To the foreground has moved concern for (1) separating out by literary means various redactional levels, (2) locating them with historical and sociological analysis, and (3) describing their theological burden or *tendenz.* Once the levels are repristinated apart from their present literary context, there may follow an attempt to reintegrate them and describe their present function in the final form of the text (Ackroyd 1974; 1978; 1982; Anderson 1988). But generally the process is reversed (Sweeney 1988b) or the integrative function of redactional additions is not a source of interest.

One can see the shift of critical focus in the work of Kaiser. The first editions of his (First) Isaiah commentary retained the form-critical emphasis of von Rad, with attendant concern for theological reflection on the preaching of the man Isaiah. The recent fifth edition (German 1981; English 1983) has been completely rewritten, and now what with confidence can be traced back to Isaiah is to be found in a scattering of verses in chaps. 1, 28–31 (Kaiser 1983: 1–2). The book largely reflects the theological concerns of historicizing, eschatologizing, and deuteronomizing forces in the postexilic period. This is a return to Duhm with subtle vengeance. The net effect is a curious open literature which serves as a collecting tank for various forms of theological reflection from later periods, presumably requiring the pseudepigraphical imprimatur of an Isaiah who has in the meantime vanished from view. The kind of subtle balance, effected by von Rad between form-critical circumspection regarding the nature of the literature on the one side and the claims of the historical Isaiah on the other, is gone. It is probably the case that von Rad's reading was too selective and did not take into sufficient account the extent of redactional *relecture* in the final form of the book. Redactional analysis has recognized just how complex is the First Isaiah material before us, having given rise to such extensive reinterpretation of the prophetic word that the original preaching of the man Isaiah does at times recede from view.

To its credit, redactional analysis is more than the reading of erasures and the arbitrary assigning of verses to obscure groups of later interpreters. In the case of Isaiah, there has come the honest recognition that the original proclamation of the prophet has undergone major reinterpretation in the light of subsequent historical events. The final literary movement of the book is difficult to follow, as Luther recognized, in no small part because of redactional influence. To isolate the preaching of the man Isaiah, even in the compelling manner of von Rad, is to ignore a significant portion of the literature and lose the theological force of the final form of the text, extending even beyond chaps. 1–39.

Redactional analysis has given rise to a form of observation about First Isaiah that strikes to the heart of the critical consensus regarding division of the whole book into three independent collections (1–39; 40–55; 56–66). By recognizing the later reappropriation of First Isaiah traditions and the literary effect this has had on chaps. 1–39, features of literary, theological, and thematic commonality have been spotted that span critical divisions of the book going back to Gesenius. Much of chaps. 1–39 appears to reflect a conscious post-587 B.C.E. redactional shaping meant to foreshadow themes which emerge in full force in chaps. 40–55 and 56–66 (Clements 1980; Sweeney 1988b). The Assyrian foe of Isaiah's day (10:5–11) is viewed as a type for which the later Babylonian destroyer serves as antitype (23:13). The assault of 701 B.C.E. (1:1–9) foreshadows the destruction of 587 B.C.E. (6:13), just as the return of the destroyed N kingdom (721 B.C.E.) anticipates the full restoration of Israel following the Exile (11:10–16).

Some of these linkages are redactionally reinforced, while others trade on a reader competence "outside" the text—but in both cases an intentionality is assumed regarding the present "merger" of First, Second, and Third Isaiah (or Isaiah and Pseudo-Isaiah, to use the older terminology). The reader of the first half of the book knows about the fuller effect of Isaiah's word, beyond the days of Assyrian threat to those of Babylonian destruction and longed-for restoration. On occasions, the linkages are explicit: chap. 39 speaks of the coming days of Babylonian assault; chaps. 13–14 "merge" the Babylonian and the Assyrian foe and then describe restoration to come following Babylon's fall (14:1–3); the "death" of king and city is postponed by Hezekiah's piety (chap. 38), only to have later effect. At other points, the events of 701 B.C.E. are simply allowed to resonate for a reader cognizant of later, more serious judgment: "The daughter of Zion is left like a booth in a vineyard . . . if the Lord had not left us a few survivors, we should have been like Sodom" (1:8–9). Seen in the light of 587 B.C.E., these words have a decided penitential effect.

The direction of influence runs backward as well as foward. The frequent reference to the "former things" in Second Isaiah (esp. chaps. 40–48) is cued to the preaching of First Isaiah, as this has taken a certain redactional form in chaps. 1–39 (*IOTS*, 328–30). The "former things" consist of God's word of judgment spoken through Isaiah (viz. 6:9–10), which was to culminate in destruction and exile (6:11–13). Second Isaiah chapters look back on this word as fulfilled in the Babylonian assault of 587 B.C.E. (43:18). The former things are divinely linked, however, to new, latter things, involving restoration and new creation following destruction (43:18). Much of chaps. 1–39 looks forward to this day as well (2:1–5; 12:1–6), ultimately fulfilled in Second Isaiah (55:1–13). The reciprocal relationships between First and Second Isaiah are on occasion redactionally assisted in 40–55, just as in 1–39 (Clements 1985). At other times the simple juxtaposition of "First" and "Second" Isaiah is the major force encouraging coordinated reading. Indeed, recent redactional examinations of the book of Isaiah call into question the propriety of the terminology now employed (viz. First, Second, and Third Isaiah), especially when an emphasis on the independence of these "three Isaiahs" is the consequence. The day may come when commentaries and dictionary articles treat the book of Isaiah in two major sections under the rubrics "Former Things" (1–39) and "New Things" (40–66). From a certain redaction-critical perspective, this shift in terminology would more accurately reflect editorial efforts at unity within the larger book of Isaiah, while at the same time recognizing an important historical, literary, and theological break at chaps. 39 and 40.

d. Summary and Prospective. The strength of certain referential and form-critical readings was the ability to keep Isaiah the prophet historically and theologically vibrant. The shift toward redactional analysis has made this perspective more difficult to unlock, as the book's message overshadows the one-time proclamation of an 8th-century prophet. Moreover, a host of questions now hovers over the nature of prophetic activity, when it is acknowledged that the word of Isaiah does not stand alone as a prophetic word in the final form of the book.

These questions are literary, historical, sociological, and theological. What was the literary form and scope of the Isaiah tradition available to later interpreters? In what historical period did it first take shape and then subsequently develop? What sociological forces were at work in its formation, along with and apart from the prophet Isaiah? On what theological basis are redactional additions made to the original word of Isaiah? Are additions made only to respond to later existential needs, or are they the consequence of the ongoing effect of the word of God, somewhat independent of the prophet Isaiah (Meade 1986: 22–26)? Does the book take a final literary shape that is coherent and theologically normative, itself relativizing the theological force of earlier redactional levels?

As redactional analysis brings important hermeneutical issues to the fore, a reasonable accounting of basic historical and sociological factors will still have to be made. To take one example, a sizable historical gap separates the man Isaiah and his preaching from a Babylonian redaction and the proclamation of chaps. 40–66. Why was that gap overcome and the message of Isaiah extended into later periods—a fact without real analogy in other prophetic books? Ultimately, the answer to that question is dependent upon one's prior view of "First Isaiah." For important heuristic reasons, interpretation of the "Former Things" in the book of Isaiah cannot proceed without a clear sense of "First Isaiah," man and literature. Future work on the composition of Isaiah 1–39 will have to continue to address fundamental historical, sociological, and literary problems if the theological message of the book of Isaiah is to be heard.

B. Isaiah and History: Preliminary Considerations

The previous section focused on the history of research and the problems of method regarding the literary composition of the book of Isaiah. The book of Isaiah undeniably goes back to the oral proclamation of the man Isaiah, however one reconstructs the development of the literature. Isaiah was a prophet whose message had primary relevance for Judah and Jerusalem (1:1; 2:1), a fact verified by the two large narrative sections of the book which depict the prophet as close to, and with remarkable authority vis à vis, the royal house and affairs of state in the capital (6:1–8:23 and 36:1–39:8). As the tradition has remembered him, Isaiah plays a role in political affairs without real analogy for contemporaries Amos, Hosea,

Micah, and Zephaniah. Isaiah's closest counterpart is probably the prophet Nathan, who likewise had access to the royal house, wielding direct authority over the Davidic line (2 Sam 7; 12:1–15).

As von Rad rightly saw, Isaiah also operates out of a distinct theological framework involving God's establishment of Zion (chaps. 28–32; 37:35). Zion, Judah/Jerusalem, and the Davidic house together form the center of attention for both prophet and book; this fact likewise distinguishes Isaiah from prophetic contemporaries. The fate of all three (Zion/Judah/David) is inextricably bound up with the movements of history, involving affairs in the immediate N kingdom (7:1–17b; 8:1–13; 9:8–21; 11:12–16; 17:1–14; 28:1–6), in the more distant Syria (7:1–9; 8:5–8; 17:1–14), and especially in the Assyrian empire (5:26–30; 7:17c–25; 8:1–4; 10:5–11, 13:19, 27c–34; 14:24–27). Even the Babylon of Marduk-apla-iddinna (ca. 721/20–700 B.C.E.) puts in a brief and ominous appearance (39:1–8). Isaiah's distinctive Judah/Jerusalem perspective functions within a broader conception of God's sovereignty over Israel and the nations.

With Isaiah we stand firmly in the 8th century, at the period in history which witnessed the full emergence of the Assyrian empire as a force to reckon with in Israel (2 Kgs 15:19, 29). It can be no accident that classical prophecy also emerged at this period, taking on a certain distinctive profile but sharing a belief that the God of Israel was also the God of the nations and the cosmos (Amos 1–2; Hosea 11–13; Micah 7; Zeph 2:5–15).

Given the significant roles exercised by Assyria and the nations within God's sovereignty over Israel, it is important to reconstruct events of the day in as clear a manner as possible. Put in another way, the actual historical sharpness of descriptions of the nations has not yet been blurred or relativized, such as we see in apocalyptic and later literature, where the nations are ciphers that can be used almost interchangeably and indiscriminantly to represent forces of general evil. Even where Babylon and Assyria seem to function as "types" of destructive arrogance (chaps. 13–14), the literature also keeps them functionally distinct (e.g., 23:13) and registers as significant specific historical events from distinct periods (compare Isa 7:1–9 [Syria-Ephraim], 36–37 [Assyria], 13:1–16 [Babylon], and 13:17–22 [Persia]). The final shaping of the book of Isaiah works with certain incipient apocalyptic literary techniques, especially in its appraisal of history in broad scope. But the original sharpness of historical events and figures from the 8th century remains. For this reason it is important to gain as clear a focus on events as possible and to pursue questions regarding the historical Isaiah. But the task of historical analysis cannot be considered successfully completed until one is able to see how these events and this man have been construed in the final textualization of the tradition.

That this line of historical inquiry is distinct from the direct referential reading should be briefly illustrated. We possess substantial records regarding ANE history during the 8th century, from Assyrian and Babylonian annals, to material finds, scattered papyri and correspondence, and the various biblical sources themselves (esp. Isaiah, Kings, and Chronicles). These various sources of information are frequently thought to reflect one systematic temporal network, internally consistent and capable of rational reconstruction. The task of the historian is to reconstruct this interlocking network of "meaning" with the help of the various literary and material sources, and then interpret the book of Isaiah in light of it. Even more radical redactional approaches, with skepticism about the 8th-century setting of Isaiah, simply substitute a later period (postexilic Israel), which also functions as the appropriate control and guide for exegesis.

An optimism about historical analysis animates the quest of direct referential readings, namely, that all records, regardless of their form and intention, are ultimately reflections of one overarching temporal reality which *is itself* the final arbiter of interpretation. Contradictions which arise in the sources are therefore thought to be departures from this canonical reality, demanding rejection or decoding and reintegration. Classic examples of the latter are the various clever reconstructions of chronology in Israel which attempt to square the divergent sources through recourse to plausible but abstruse theories of coregencies, different calendrics, accession-year adjustments, and the like (see esp. Thiele 1965; Hayes and Hooker 1988). The assumptions are that (1) the sources are indeed capable of such coordination, and (2) coordination must be carried out as the necessary prerequisite for proper interpretation of the book of Isaiah.

Another interpretation of Isaiah and history is possible and will be adopted in the historical treatment to follow. We assume that ancient historical writing is self-consciously interpretive and always stands at one remove from the *bruta facta* themselves or schemes for their temporal coordination—including even theoretically "objective" records (annals citations and the like). Tied to this is the view that chronological logic and consistency in ancient "historiography" is frequently overshadowed by other subjective and interpretive considerations. We are able to set forth major movements in Assyrian and Babylonian history, often with a precision that would have baffled those who experienced them directly. But what the prophet Isaiah made of these same events, and what the later shapers of the book of Isaiah perceived of their significance—whether they or he were informed about them in the way we are millennia hence—are far more relevant questions for modern historical analysis. On occasion the various sources operate from such radically different perspectives that their reciprocal coordination would result in a highly artificial presentation. Moreover, the final structure of the book of Isaiah presents views of history which are frequently illogical, given modern historiographical data and assumptions regarding events in linear time consecution. What is most important in reconstructing movements in ANE history is not to coordinate Isaiah with them and then translate them both into some network of external temporal reference, but to discover the temporal logic appropriate to each. In this fashion, the modern fiction of independent "history" will not emerge as the interpretive arbiter of the book of Isaiah; the reverse will be true.

In sum, the book of Isaiah is like history in its presentation (Frei 1974) and for this reason demands an assessment of its field of historical referentiality. But the two should be kept distinct, and the latter should not be allowed to eclipse the former. The book of Isaiah is more than a set of clues from which to reconstruct a network of "real" historical meaning. Isaiah draws from the world of external reference in order to produce its own chronological "scale" and internal perspective.

C. The Canonical Presentation of the Book of Isaiah

In what follows, the content of the book of Isaiah will be surveyed with particular attention to the literary presentation of chaps. 1–39 in their present form. This presentation is the work of redactional hands concerned with setting forth the man Isaiah, his message in the 8th century, and the deeper significance of that message for God's dealings with Israel up to and through the exilic crisis of 587 B.C.E. (All subsequent dates are B.C.E. unless noted.)

1. Isaiah and the Emergence of Assyria. By the most generous estimate, Isaiah's prophetic activity extended from the latter years of King Uzziah (1:1; 6:1) to the 14th year of King Hezekiah (36:1) and the aftermath of Sennacherib's invasion (701). Even allowing for problems of chronology (see below), this would plausibly grant to Isaiah a career of approximately forty years (742–700), analogous to that assumed by the book of Jeremiah (1:1–3) for the prophet Jeremiah (627–587). A forty-year career for two of Israel's major prophets is consistent with the status they are eventually accorded in the canon (Seitz 1989).

Problems exist at either end of this reckoning, making assignment of exact dates for Isaiah's career difficult. On the one hand, Isaiah shares with other canonical literature a general confusion over chronology. The broader problem lies outside of this treatment, involving regnal year accounting in the books of Kings and Chronicles. The following table illustrates the latitude that is possible in reckoning, depending upon one's assessment of coregencies, accession-year tally, synchronisms, and competing calendric systems—not to mention coordination with ANE records (see *IJH,* 683; Hayes and Hooker 1988).

	Begrich/Jepsen	Albright	Hayes/Hooker
Uzziah	787–736	783–742	785–734
Jotham	756–741	750–735	759–744
Ahaz	741–725	735–715	743–728
Hezekiah	725–697	715–687	727–699

For the purpose of this treatment, we adopt the Albright reckoning and assume a career for Isaiah from roughly 742 to 700; that is, from the final years of Uzziah until the aftermath of the Assyrian invasion reported in chaps. 36–37, in the 14th year of King Hezekiah (701). We take seriously the intent of the superscription of the book (1:1) to locate the beginning of Isaiah's career in the reign of Uzziah.

Many have contested the possibility of Uzziah-period preaching for Isaiah. The chief objection is said to exist in chap. 6, which is taken as a call narrative of the prophet (Clements *Isaiah 1–39* NCBC, 8–9). Following this logic, Isaiah's "call" came in "the year that King Uzziah died" (6:1); there can be no preaching before this period, therefore, and chaps. 1–5 must postdate chap. 6. Various explanations are given for the placement of a call narrative six chapters into the book (cf. Jeremiah and Ezekiel). On purely historical and literary-critical grounds, others deny the possibility of Uzziah-period preaching.

The problem remains why redactors would have invented a Uzziah reference in the superscription if this was so clearly at odds with the "call narrative" interpretation of chap. 6. Chap. 6 also presents a thorny theological problem felt by interpreters from early on. Isaiah is "called" to "make hearts fat" (6:10), thus making impossible acceptance of the divine word from the very beginning. Again, there is also the question of why a "call narrative" inaugurating Isaiah should appear six chapters into the book.

It appears that the redactors of the book wish chap. 6 to be interpreted along different lines, and herein lies the solution to the chronological problem and the curious literary arrangement of the opening chapters. Chap. 6 is not an inaugural call, but a commission for a specific task from the heavenly council, given in the year King Uzziah died (6:1; see also Hayes and Irvine 1987: 108–13). The woes of the preceding chapter (5:8, 11, 18, 21–22) potentially implicate Isaiah as well, so he cries: "Woe is me—I am lost" (6:5). Isaiah is truly a man of unclean lips dwelling in the midst of a people of unclean lips (6:5). In the final shape of the tradition, Isaiah is presented as having preached warning and exhortation prior to the death of King Uzziah, and prior to his commission to "make hearts fat" (6:10)—a decree rendered in the heavenly council and shared with an Isaiah who must still go forth and preach repentance (see chap. 7), not smug announcements of sure doom. The main function of chap. 6 is to set the prophet apart from the people in clear fashion (6:7) and reveal to the reader the content of his commission, in all its historical breadth and theological force (6:11–13). Isaiah's inaugural "call" is not registered as significant in the final form of the book; from the divine perspective it reaches back before his consciousness of it, like Jeremiah's "call" before he was formed in his mother's womb (Jer 1:5). The precise end of the prophet's career is likewise not a matter for attention; Isaiah disappears with the same mystery as when he began his preaching "in the days of Uzziah" (1:1).

There is another dimension to the chronological presentation of Isaiah which locates his initial activity in the reign of Uzziah. This feature Isaiah shares with the prophets Amos and Hosea, who likewise are seen as preaching during the reign of Uzziah (Amos 1:1; Hos 1:1). It appears that these prophetic books, apart from their claim to actual historical memory of Uzziah-period preaching, are coordinated with a temporal perspective operative in 2 Kings, which places the emergence of the Assyrian threat as far back as the reign of Uzziah (2 Kgs 15:17–19). The superscriptions of these three prophetic books do not specify the precise year of the respective prophet's inauguration; a general reference to Uzziah suffices. Far too great an emphasis has been placed upon the psychologically alluring notion of a specific "call," to the exclusion of other important considerations at work in the final presentation of the book. Among these is the signal awareness that with the rise of the Assyrian empire, God was beginning a strange work in Israel—something the prophet Isaiah saw and proclaimed. Tiglath-pileser (Pul) is thus depicted as the king of Assyria who "came against the land" as far back as the reign of Menachem (2 Kgs 15:19), who began to reign in the 39th year of his Judahite counterpart

Uzziah (2 Kgs 15:17). From a modern historiographic perspective, the reigns of Uzziah and Tiglath-pileser can be roughly coordinated. This conforms with the literature's general reference to Isaiah's preaching "in the days of Uzziah" at 1:1, and the equally general reference to the "king of Assyria" at 2 Kgs 15:19. Here is an instance where more precise chronological synthesis might overlook the very general explanations at work in the literature, which have a significance all their own.

The following table indicates important dates in ANE history that are relevant for the book of Isaiah.

Tiglath-pileser	744–727
Syro-Ephraimite Debacle	734–732
Shalmaneser V	726–722
Sargon II	721–705
Fall of Northern Kingdom	721
Sennacherib	704–681
Assault on Judah	701

It should prove no surprise that the final shapers of the prophetic canon came to associate the rise of Assyria, instrument of Yahweh (Isa 10:5), with the final days of Uzziah.

Here we also find an explanation for the seemingly broken cycle of woes (5:8–23 and 10:1–4) and "outstretched hand" passages (5:25–30 and 9:8–10:4), now separated by the narrative "memoir" section of 6:1–8:22 and the messianic oracle at 9:1–7 (see recently Anderson 1988: 230–40; Clements *Isaiah 1–39* NCBC, 60–70; Sheppard 1985: 195–8). Warning and woe precede the stark commissioning of Isaiah in 6:9–13. Utilizing its own temporal logic, the book of Isaiah also depicts God's hand stretched out against Israel through the agency of the "nation afar off" (5:26) even before the death of Uzziah (6:1), consistent with the portrayal of 2 Kings and general staging in ANE history at large. God's hand "remains stretched out still" after the death of Uzziah, beyond the reign of Jotham to that of Ahaz (7:1), in the events of the Syro-Ephraimite debacle (734–732), and beyond to the fall of Samaria/Ephraim itself in 721 (9:8–10, 13–14; 10:3–4). Repetition of the motif "his anger is not turned away" (9:12, 17, 21; 10:4) serves to drive home the incremental and yet relentless way in which God's judgment is effected through the agency of Assyria, "the rod of my anger, the staff of my fury" (10:5). The rhetorical piece, the Song of the Vineyard, opens this temporal depiction by predicting the gradual but sure assault on "the vineyard of the Lord of Hosts" (5:7). God has removed its hedge and broken down its wall (5:5); it is left to be devoured and trampled, becoming a waste, full of briers and thorns (5:5–6). In what follows, all this gradually comes about (see especially the briers/thorns motif [5:6; 7:23–25; 9:18]) until Assyria is herself judged, turning "the glory of his forest" into "thorns and briers in one day" (10:17).

These key chapters (5–11), representing a variety of historical preaching and secondary redaction, have been editorially shaped to underscore (1) the widespread and chronic sinfulness of Judah/Jerusalem; (2) the commissioning of Assyria as God's instrument of purging judgment; (3) the commissioning of Isaiah as proclaimer of God's word of judgment; (4) the assault, in stages, on God's vineyard; and (5) the final judgment of Assyria for arrogance. Within this major movement of the Isaiah presentation, one sees other themes emerging as well. These include (1) the Syro-Ephraimite debacle (chaps. 7–8); (2) royal disobedience contrasted with future promise (9:1–7 and 11:1–9); and (3) a vision of future restoration (11:10–16). The beginning of Isaiah's career is set in the "days of Uzziah," when the Assyrian threat began to take form. Judah's unwillingness to be the pleasant planting and choice vine God intends (5:2, 7) means death and destruction for the vineyard (Israel). The special responsibility of Judah/Jerusalem in God's vineyard (1:8; 2:1; 3:14; 5:7) is balanced by interest in the royal house, which has also been set apart for special service (Yee 1981: 37–40). At the center of the Isaiah memoir (6–8) stands a prose narrative focusing on God's word to the royal house, in the person of Ahaz, at a key moment in history.

2. The Syro-Ephraimite Debacle and Isaiah 1–12. The depiction of the gradual assault by the Assyrian instrument of judgment now frames a special episode in Israel's history (referred to as the Syro-Ephraimite War), described in the literarily complex chaps. 7–8. With the gradual ascendency of Assyria in the ANE, neighboring and more distant nations were taxed and placed under state control, with various degrees of severity (*IJH*, 415–21). Revolts were frequent, and if successfully put down, the consequences could be (1) renewed vassalage; (2) puppet rule; or (3) population deportation and exchange.

In an act of defiance most date to the year 734, presumably calculated for some strategic advantage, Israel and her northern neighbor Syria decided to revolt against Assyrian rule. This seems the most likely explanation for the notice of Isa 7:1, which says without elaboration that "in the days of Ahaz," Rezin and Pekah, kings of Syria and Israel, respectively, "came up to Jerusalem to wage war against it." Interestingly, the action is described as though it were a purely hostile, almost wanton act of violence: "Let us go up against Judah and terrify it" (7:6a). Most assume that Syria and Israel, in league together (7:2), sought to gain Judah's support in alliance against Assyria—hence the specific reference to the deposing of Ahaz and his replacement with one "son of Tabeel" (7:6b).

Isaiah's response to all this is quite direct. His words are addressed to the Davidic house, and he stands firm on traditions which speak of God's choice of David and his line (2 Sam 7; Ps 2; see Mays 1988: 39–48). Ahaz is to "take heed, be quiet, fear not" (7:4). God will see to the eventual fall of the alliance against Judah, the implication being that God stands at Judah's head, while Ephraim and Syria are ruled by men alone (7:7–9).

Together with the word of God, Ahaz is confronted by three sign-children, whose names are significant carriers of God's message. All three names are unambiguously positive for Judah: Remnant Restored (Shear-jashub), God with Us (Immanuel), and Spoil Speeds, Prey Hastes (Maher-shalal-hash-baz). The positive force of the names is driven home by the language which immediately follows in each instance (7:4; 7:15–16; 8:4). The first child is already born. The second and third are about to be born, and the message of deliverance is keyed to certain temporal indicators associated with their maturation. Clearly, the period of weal is just around the corner, no matter what the circumstances look like to Ahaz (8:4). At their earliest literary stage, chaps. 7–8 are frequently termed a Book of Signs because of the motif of the sign-children (all three Isaiah's) that unifies them (Gottwald 1958; Roberts 1985).

But the original literary tradition has clearly been expanded (Clements *Isaiah 1–39* NCBC, 78–103). The motif of conditionality integral to the original tradition (7:9b) has opened up one dimension of so-called Zion and Royal Theology. God provides concrete and repeated signs of his special care for Zion and David, in spite of the pious intransigence of Ahaz (cf. Hezekiah in 36–38). But lack of belief can turn God's protection to nought. Those who shaped these chapters clearly look back on King Ahaz as the one who refused to believe and was therefore not established. The juxtaposition of the oracle at 9:1–7, which speaks of a glorious new king, helps drive this home. Ahaz' lack of belief has caused certain distinct editorial moves within chaps. 7–8 as well.

On the one hand, a new level of tradition has been introduced which speaks of the coming assault—not of the Syro-Ephraimite coalition (their future is decidedly inauspicious)—but of Assyria (7:17c–25). Syro-Ephraim is replaced by a divinely appointed Assyria, who will judge the unfaithful royal house and Judah "in that day" (7:18, 20–21, 23). As a consequence of Ahaz' unbelief, the positive signs become more restrictedly positive, if not negative, reminders of lack of faith. "God is with us"—as a judged remnant confident God will halt the future Assyrian assault (8:10), but only after much destruction ("even to the neck," 8:8). "Spoil speeds"—not just against the Syro-Ephraimite coalition (8:4), but ultimately against Judah as well (8:6–7). "Remnant restored"—not Judah vis à vis Israel in the Syro-Ephraimite debacle, but as a later purged remnant vis à vis the unfaithful generation of Ahaz, who rightly perceive the judgment of God and the promise of a righteous future in the teaching of Isaiah (8:16–20).

As von Rad correctly noted, Zion theology is transformed in the book of Isaiah, as God himself through the agency of Assyria turns against his own people in order to purge them and set apart a righteous remnant. But the nations cannot rage (Ps 2:1) without restraint (so Isa 8:9–10). God remains with Zion to cleanse her for a new future. What von Rad wished to locate in the prophetic consciousness, one can see at work at the editorial level, as witnessed in the final redaction of the Book of Signs. This same theological perspective is exhibited at other points in the tradition as well. The form-critical insight of von Rad, especially focused on chaps. 28–31 and the prophet Isaiah's own consciousness, has broader relevance for a distinct editorial perspective operative throughout the First Isaiah chapters.

In the complex tapestry of the Book of Signs, positive signs were to function positively in the events of the Syro-Ephraimite debacle of 734; but they also stand in judgment over lack of faith in the royal house and point to a new day. It can be no coincidence that immediately juxtaposed with this Book of Signs is an oracle describing a just and faithful ruler (8:23b–9:6 = Eng. 9:1–7). Whether this is a typical figure supplied by accession liturgy of preexilic Israel (von Rad *PHOE,* 222–31; Becker 1980: 45–47), or an eschatological (messianic) figure from the postexilic period (Kaiser (1983: 203–18), or Isaiah's (private) hope for a king at the time of Sennacherib (Duhm *Jesaia* HKAT, 66–69), or Ahaz's actual successor Hezekiah (Alt *KlSchr* 2: 206–25; Clements *Isaiah 1–39* NCBC, 103–9) is not made explicit in the text (and therefore occasions much debate). The latter interpretation is highly suggestive, though much of the reference to Assyrian assault in the final form of chaps. 7–8 seems geared to events of 701, thus postdating Hezekiah's accession. For this reason, Josiah has also been considered a likely candidate (Vermeylen 1977–78: 231–49; Barth 1977: 176–77). It cannot be ruled out that a certain obscurity has been intended in the final redaction of this oracle, as well as in its more idealized counterpart at 11:1–9. What is clear is that a new ruler will emerge in a new day and stand in utter contrast to the faithless Ahaz, a depiction consistent with the force of chaps. 36–38, where Hezekiah forms a distinct counterpoint to Ahaz (Ackroyd 1974: 350–2; 1981: 219–22).

In the Book of Signs and in the broader literary context surrounding it (esp. chaps. 5–11), historical events with significance in the days of Uzziah and Ahaz have taken on new meaning. The Syro-Ephraimite assault fails in 734, only to foreshadow later Assyrian success as the instrument of Yahweh. Faithless Ahaz is replaced by a new king. The Assyrian assault, hinted at in Isaiah's early days (5:26–30), seems especially related to events in 701, during the reign of Hezekiah, at which time Judah was completely overrun by Sennacherib's forces (36:1), and Jerusalem was left "like a booth in a vineyard" (1:8). The imagery of near-total destruction persists throughout these chapters (6:13; 8:8; 10:32), with the clear suggestion that only Jerusalem will be spared ("he will shake his fist at the mount of the daughter of Zion"). At this key moment, a new act will begin, whereby Assyria will be judged for arrogance and the overstepping of her divine commission; this theme likewise finds persistent articulation in chaps. 5–11 (see 8:9–10; 10:12–19; 10:33–34). Apart from sporadic and incidental editorial work focused on even later events (esp. 587; Clements 1980), the major redactional work on these chapters is keyed toward the events of 701 and their aftermath. This is consistent with the way the Assyrian assault is depicted in chaps. 5–11, namely, as involving widespread assault on Judah and the near destruction of Jerusalem, which in turn gave rise to sober hopes for restoration following this cleansing.

Chaps. 2–4 contain a diverse assortment of material, some of it pre-Ahaz and consistent with the depiction of chap. 5 in seeing Judah/Jerusalem as chronically sinful. Other material in these chapters reflects the post-701 concern with future restoration. Still other sections appear to see the assault of 701 as but a foreshadowing of a yet future judgment in 587, resulting in the fall of Jerusalem. It is extremely difficult to sort out the various redactional strata (Sweeney 1988b), due to a lack of explicit literary and historical indexing at work in the literature. Whatever one concedes about a Babylonian period redaction (Clements 1980), the final presentation of chaps. 1–12 has not lifted the events of 587 and their theological significance into such prominence that original 8th-century rooting has been completely loosened. In fact, strong arguments can be mounted in defense of a general 701 backdrop for all of chap. 1, on literary, historical, and redactional grounds. The opening superscription interprets chap. 1 as a summary vision from the prophet, presenting major themes of the prophet's message culminating in the reign of Hezekiah (Fohrer 1967: 148–66). The deliverance in 701 (see 1:8) is not taken as a matter of rejoicing nor as the validation of a Zion theology requiring no faith, but rather as a matter for penitence and exhortation (1:10–20). Afterwards, Zion can be reclaimed by God (1:24–31). This in turn gives way to a new vision of the future, not yet realized in time (see 2:1–4 and 12:1–6).

Ackroyd (1978) and others have correctly noted the existence of a major subsection in Isaiah 1–12. Here, something of the whole history of God with his people during the career of Isaiah is set forth, from the days of Uzziah to the days of Hezekiah and the deliverance of 701. The actual account of the 701 deliverance is found in a narrative section not unlike the Book of Signs, in terms of form and thematic shape, at the end of the First Isaiah material (chaps. 36–37). In chaps. 1–12 Isaiah is presented as a prophet of judgment for whom Zion theology took on transformed significance. Within the cleansing judgments of 734 and 701 lie the seeds for future hope and restoration. Against the faithlessness of Ahaz and his generation is to be viewed the trust of a righteous king and a faithful remnant. The final doxology rounds off this section as a new day is envisioned (12:1–6).

That these events from the days of Isaiah were capable of occasioning yet further reflection after 587, when Jerusalem became a new kind of booth in the vineyard of God, is testimony to the power of the prophetic word (Meade 1986: 17–26). But evidence for widespread literary supplementation keyed to this later episode demands greater precision than redactional analysis has yet put forward (cf. Clements *Isaiah 1–39* NCBC; Sweeney 1988b; Kaiser 1983). At most one sees only occasional glossing (e.g., 4:2–6) keyed to the events of 587 and their aftermath, expanding the depiction of judgment as well as the vision of restoration. The post-701 redaction of chaps. 1–12 was capable of reappropriation in light of events in 587, with very little need of explicit literary intervention. There was a "fit" to the word of God already structured into the final shape of the material that made it an appropriate lens through which to understand the later events of 587 and the fall of Jerusalem.

The editorial decision to present the fuller implications of Isaiah's message from the days of Uzziah to those of Hezekiah in a major opening section (chaps. 1–12), ending with a hymn of praise, has meant that kindred material has now been set into different literary contexts. More specifically, it is clear that much of the focus on Assyria and her ultimate judgment carries over into the next major section of the book (chaps. 13–27), where Assyria becomes just one of many nations who rage against Jerusalem. Barth (1977: 103–18) is probably correct to speak of a uniform Assyrian redaction that includes 14:24–27. However, that this redaction is related to the figure of Josiah seems unlikely in view of the absolute silence of the text regarding this later 7th-century king. A recension of Hezekiah composed after the deliverance of 701 is far more likely and is consistent with the references to reapplication and future interpretation of the prophetic word suggested by 8:16–20 and 30:8 (cf. 29:11–12). Such a recension would have been composed by Isaiah's disciples after his death, focusing on Isaiah's past message and its implications for future deliverance. Support for this thesis requires correct interpretation of chaps. 36–39 and the events of 701 (see the following section).

Gesenius and Duhm were correct to point out major internal divisions within First Isaiah. A set of superscriptions (13:1; 15:1; 17:1; 19:1; 21:1; 22:1; 23:1) indicates an independent collection within chaps. 13–23 focused on the nations and culminating in God's judgment on the cosmos itself (24–27). From beginning to end, this section evidences significant redactional coordination in light of the events of 587 ("Behold the land of the Chaldeans! This is the people; it was not Assyria," 23:13). Original oracles against nations from Isaiah's day (14:24–27; 14:28–32; 17:1–14; 18:1–7; 19:1–15) have been filled out to depict a massive assault against Jerusalem from all quarters, on form-critical analogy with the depiction of the nations' assembling in the Psalms of Zion.

As with 1–12, these chapters have developed with their own internal logic, independently of surrounding collections. The Nation Oracle section (13–27) is formally analogous to nation sections in Jeremiah and Ezekiel, though its function in Isaiah is differently conceived. The historical judgment of the Assyrians against Judah and Jerusalem in the 8th century (1–12) is seen to foreshadow a far more decisive, global assault (13–27). In order to develop this depiction fully; keyed to the historical events of 587, chaps. 13–27 speak of events well beyond the lifetime of the prophet Isaiah (noted by interpreters since Eichhorn). A series of six longer poetic compositions, introduced with the Heb interjection *hôy*, then follow in 28–33 (cf. 32:1, Heb *hēn*). A small final collection (34–35) reiterating the themes of 24–27 rounds off the First Isaiah material. In their final presentation, chaps. 1–39 reflect a complex interweaving of Assyrian period (post-701) and Babylonian period (post-587) redaction (1–12 + 13–27 + 28–33 + 34–35). A fuller discussion of these sections will follow after an analysis of the next key historical event in the book of Isaiah: the 701 invasion.

3. The 701 Assault: Isaiah 36–39 and Kings Presentations. In formal terms, chaps. 36–37 are quite similar to chaps. 7–8. They both focus on the encounter between prophet and king, utilizing narrative and poetic forms of expression. Moreover, the depiction of King Hezekiah appears to have been shaped as a direct counterpoise to that of Ahaz during the Syro-Ephraimite debacle. Hezekiah is the man of faith par excellence: he is the famous reformer whose deeds of faith are thrown into his teeth by foreigners (36:4–10). He rends his garments and asks for the prophet Isaiah's prayer (37:1–2); he offers his own prayer, which turns God's verdict against Sennacherib (37:21); signs are provided and not scorned (37:30–32). That a common editorial hand and purpose is at work in these two narrative sections seems beyond doubt. At these two key moments in history, the faith of the royal house was put to the test. While Ahaz failed, Hezekiah emerged as the paradigmatic king—described in 2 Kgs 18:5 as without peer: "He trusted in the Lord the God of Israel; so that there was none like him among all the kings of Judah after him, nor among those who were before him."

Because of their close relationship with 2 Kgs 18:13–20:21, chaps. 36–39 present a literary problem without analogy in chaps. 7–8. Going back to Gesenius (1821: 932–36), most assume that the synoptic relationship is to be explained by seeing the book of Kings report as having priority over that of Isaiah (Wildberger 1979: 35–47). It is argued that the Kings account has been brought over into the Isaiah corpus on analogy with the function of 2 Kings 25 (= Jeremiah 52) in the book of Jeremiah, namely, as bringing to a close the First Isaiah material (Gesenius 1821: 22). But problems with this theory are obvious: (1) the independence of First Isaiah chapters as a distinct collection is overstated (Seitz 1988: 109–16); (2) one can explain the chronological disorder in the movement from 36–37 to 38 and 39 in the book of Isaiah is due to editorial factors, whereby the chronologically earlier Merodach-Baladan episode is placed last to evoke the Babylonian setting and judgment presupposed in 40–66 (Ackroyd 1974), but the temporal illogic makes no sense in Kings, where the next chapter (2 Kings 21) continues with the reign of Manasseh (Smelik 1986: 73–74); (3) problems of a literary and historical nature have been introduced into the Kings narrative because of broader concerns that can be detected in the Deuteronomistic History, especially involving the relative evaluations of Judah's monarchs, but the absence of these problems in Isaiah suggests an earlier consistency of presentation in Isaiah.

Most pointed in this regard is the brief insert regarding Hezekiah's capitulation to the Assyrians (2 Kgs 18:14–16), frequently termed Account A and regarded as historically objective, in contrast to the surrounding narrative (see Childs 1967: 69–103). Historians have tended to grant a degree of reliability to this three-verse account that is denied to the longer "legendary" report, itself an interweaving of two separate episodes in history (Account B1 and B2). Yet, clearly, this unit interrupts the flow of logic from v 13 to v 17, forcing scholars to wonder why, if Hezekiah in fact capitulated (18:14), the Assyrians went on a siege campaign against Judah (18:17). The answer to this question is given by speculation about hidden material regarding gaps in time, more than one campaign, changes in foreign policy by Hezekiah, and the like—all matters about which the biblical text is silent (see Smelik 1986: 76–85).

The simplest explanation is that—the boasting tone of the Assyrian annals notwithstanding—Hezekiah did not capitulate to any major degree. At a minimum, it must be conceded that this is the perspective of the Isaiah presentation, which knows nothing of Hezekiah's disobedience and in fact underscores the piety of this king in contrast to his predecessor Ahaz. One wonders if the whole point of the account in chap. 38 of Hezekiah's sickness is to stress the ability of the royal house to divert a merited sentence of judgment. Hezekiah's sickness mirrors Jerusalem's sickness—his faithful prayer postpones a sentence of judgment spoken by the prophet Isaiah (38:1). The key verse in this regard (38:6) links Hezekiah's recovery to the recovery of the city, even though this upsets the narrative depiction of chaps. 36–37, where the deliverance of the city had already been concluded (37:36–38).

Ambiguity regarding Hezekiah's demeanor exists only in the book of Kings narrative, where the insert at 18:14–16 frustrates the logic of the depiction. Why has Kings supplied this admittedly intrusive note? The answer involves the larger scheme of royal evaluation in Kings, whereby Hezekiah's unparalleled role (2 Kgs 18:5) was revised in light of Josiah's subsequent career and the later judgment that he was Judah's finest king (2 Kgs 23:25). Failure to accomplish absolute deliverance in 701 was traced by the Dtr Historian to the sin of Hezekiah in Assyrian capitulation, while Josiah became a reformer whose zeal outstripped all before him, the notice of 2 Kgs 18:5 notwithstanding.

A far more subtle version of this is to be seen in Isaiah 39 (2 Kgs 20:12–19), where the coming destruction of the Babylonians is somehow vaguely related to Hezekiah's action in showing the Babylonian envoy treasures in the capital (which, if 2 Kgs 18:15 were taken literally, had already been given to the Assyrians). But this is far from the direct (and literarily intrusive) charge of 2 Kgs 18:14–16. Moreover, the near testimony of Chronicles has chosen to view Hezekiah's action vis à vis the Merodach-Baladan envoy *positively* (Ackroyd 1974: 337–38; 1982: 222–25); he was tested and found worthy (2 Chr 32:31), presumably because he avoided the greater sin of paying tribute to foreigners and depleting the temple treasury, only *showing* the emissaries his riches (Isa 39:2). The final remark of Hezekiah (39:8), as noted by Ackroyd (1974: 335–36), is not to be taken as a private *"après moi le déluge,"* but as an acknowledgment from a pious king that God had postponed a massive judgment and so provided "peace and security" in his day. A similar technique is employed with Josiah in 2 Kgs 22:20, where the prophetic word from Huldah is linked to days ahead, after Josiah will have been gathered to his grave in peace. In sum, this final narrative account (chap. 39) does not focus on the disobedience, even inadvertent, of King Hezekiah; it simply explains that the Babylonians will eventually replace the Assyrians (39:7), without assigning blame to the royal house. Only in this way can one understand the positive face Hezekiah is able to put on the dark words of Isaiah. In allowing the Babylonians access to the capital, without paying them tribute, Hezekiah could even be viewed as doing the will of God. In the final perspective of the Isaiah presentation, the Babylonians are the consecrated ones designated by God for judgment (13:3; Clements *Isaiah 1–39* NCBC, 132–36). Hezekiah did not turn them away; neither did he seek to make agreements with them—not the Babylonians of Merodach-Baladan's day (8th century), but of a later day (6th century) accomplish the massive judgment depicted in chap. 13.

There is every reason to believe that the Isaiah narrative in 36–37 has priority over the Kings account. At a minimum, it can be said that the Hezekiah depiction in Isaiah is finally independent of that which develops in Kings (Ackroyd 1982: 15). The book of Isaiah understands Hezekiah as the obedient counterpart to his predecessor Ahaz; but ultimately, even this royal paradigm could only postpone God's judgment and present a model of obedient trust for future generations under siege. Deeds of disobedience and mistrust from the days of Uzziah and Ahaz had set into motion a process of cleansing that would not be completed until after Hezekiah's lifetime.

4. The 701 Assault: General ANE Perspective. The picture of Hezekiah's paradigmatic obedience developed in Isaiah 36–39 finds confirmation at other points in the biblical and extrabiblical records. The books of Kings and, especially, Chronicles, present Hezekiah as a bold reformer who purified the cult of pagan practices (2 Chronicles 29–31; see also Isa 36:7). Hezekiah is also remembered as one who accomplished significant Judean expansion into the region of Philistia (2 Kgs 18:8). The memory of Hezekiah as one who attempted to restore the kingdom of David to its former glory, shortly after the fall of Samaria, is not lost on the biblical record; neither was it lost on his Assyrian overlords.

Sargon died on the battlefield in 705 and was replaced by Sennacherib. But upheavals were registered across the ANE: (1) the Egyptians recovered strength under the 25th Nubian dynasty; (2) the Chaldean Merodach-Baladan came out of hiding and gathered support from Elamite and Arab tribes; and (3) Luli, king of Tyre and Sidon, revolted. Hezekiah's aggressive activity is probably to be measured against this broader maneuvering within the Assyrian empire (*IJH*, 446–48).

Reaction from Sennacherib was not long in coming. In 701 he succeeded in putting down the Tyrian revolt, and Luli was replaced by a puppet king. Similar action was taken against the Philistine city-states, and Egyptian military assistance in support of Ekron was sent packing. Sennacherib then turned his attention to Judah/Jerusalem.

The Assyrian annals acknowledge the nonsubmission of Hezekiah. They report that Sennacherib then laid siege to 46 strong cities in Judah and "counted and considered as booty" 200,150 of her citizenry. Doubtless only a certain percentage of these were actually deported (Stohlmann 1983: 147–75). A massive formal siege of Jerusalem is not described, though the Assyrian king boasts of reducing Hezekiah to a virtual prisoner "like a bird in a cage" and of setting up earthwork "in order to molest those who were leaving the city" (*ANET,* 288). But there is no mention of actual victory in the "siege." The annals proudly note that Sennacherib "reduced his country" and increased the annual tribute, but it must be admitted that all this is fairly light treatment when compared with actions taken against Tyre, Ashkelon, and Ekron.

Where the biblical and Assyrian records agree is over the assault of Judah. Isaiah reports as bluntly as possible that in 701 Sennacherib "came up against all the fortified cities of Judah and took them" (36:1; 2 Kgs 18:13). It is no surprise that the records disagree over the interpretation of 701 events more narrowly involving Jerusalem. The annals emphasize the restriction of Hezekiah to the capital and conclude with a notice about the broader success of the campaign against Judah at large. The biblical record, in stark contrast, emphasizes the utter failure of Assyrian attempts to take Jerusalem (Isa 37:36–38), being particularly mindful of the boastful arrogance of siege troops in the region (36:4–20). Not surprisingly, it attributes the defeat to divine intervention, occasioned by the prayer of Jerusalem's faithful king (37:15–20). Especially in view of the treatment of Judah and of neighboring nations, the failure of Sennacherib to take Jerusalem was a matter of no small theological significance. But the biblical sources do not relate the Assyrian "defeat" to some iron-clad commitment on God's part to Zion—in many respects, just the opposite is true. The cleansing judgment was accomplished by God himself, as spoken beforehand by his prophet Isaiah (chaps. 28–32). Isaiah spoke of a "decree of destruction from the Lord of hosts upon the whole land" (28:22) and upon the city and its rulers (29:1–10). Deliverance is solely the consequence of the grace of God and the prayerful obedience of his servant Hezekiah: "I will defend this city for my own sake and for the sake of my servant David" (37:35). Measured against the widespread assault on Judah and her citizenry, the deliverance is held up as a graceful warning against the very citizenry that is spared: this note is particularly sounded in the opening chapter of Isaiah (1:2–31). The deliverance becomes an occasion for exhortation and penitence. Seen from the perspective of 587 and the fall of Jerusalem, the warning was not heeded. Hezekiah could only postpone a yet greater judgment. On this note, the First Isaiah chapters conclude (39:5–7).

Attempts to precisely coordinate the Isaiah, Kings, and Assyrian accounts will fail, if by coordination it is meant that there is synthesis and final agreement among the various sources. Isaiah focuses on the exemplary action of Hezekiah vis à vis Ahaz and other arrogant leaders in Judah/Jerusalem (28:7, 14; 29:20; 30:1, 8; 31:1—cf. 32:1–20) and the deliverance of the capital vis à vis the countryside. Kings adjusts this picture in light of other theological and interpretive concerns within the broader Dtr History, tugging the depiction of Hezekiah in the direction of the Assyrian reports by (awkwardly) mentioning his capitulation. Not surprisingly, the Assyrian annals emphasize the successes that were achieved in the 701 campaign against Judah/Jerusalem: a massive assault against Judah's cities and citizenry, increased tribute, and the shutting up of Hezekiah in the capital. Why Assyrian forces were forced to withdraw and give up the siege against Jerusalem (cf. Askelon, Ekron) is not clear; nor is it possible to trust the Greek historian Herodotus' report (learned in Egypt), which speaks of a signal defeat of Assyrian forces, whose weapons were devoured by a horde of field mice. Whatever the rational explanation, the Isaiah (and Kings) account sees the ultimate cause as divine intervention. Not only were the forces of Sennacherib done in, but the Assyrian king was slain by his own sons (37:38) while worshipping "Nisroch his god." On this note, the report clearly concludes that there is a limit to which the God of Israel can be mocked: "A blasphemer is nowhere safe from the power of the omnipotent God" (Smelik 1986: 84).

5. Isaiah 28–33. We have had occasion to note already that these chapters are formally linked by repetition of the Hebrew interjection *hôy* (28:1; 29:1; 30:1; 31:1; 33:1). They focus on the arrogance and misplaced trust of the people, from all quarters (Judah, Ephraim, Ariel) and from every area of society (priest and prophet, rulers in Jerusalem, military forces), in their blind disregard for the coming judgment of Yahweh. They trust wrongly in military alliances with Egypt (30:1–14; 31:1–5), in covenants with death (28:15), and in perversions of Zion theology whereby God blindly protects Jerusalem regardless of the faith of her people. To counter this false trust, the prophet speaks of a Zion theology in which God fights against his own people (29:1–8) and engages in strange action against Judah/Jerusalem (28:21). In the fighting of the nations against Zion, God is himself active (29:3). But paradoxically, God will also fight upon Mt. Zion to "protect and deliver it, spare and rescue it" (31:5). There is a dimension of his work that is simply described as "marvelous" (29:14), whereby the "wisdom of their wise shall perish" (29:14) while the deaf shall hear, the blind see, and the meek obtain fresh joy (29:18). Zion theology is a defense only for those who place their trust in Yahweh, as he comes to judge his own people; for others, he will prove to be a "stone of offense" and a "rock of stumbling" (8:14), not a "cornerstone valuable for a foundation" (28:16; Roberts 1987: 37). In the cleansing action of God's judgment, the goal is not obliteration but transformation, as the message of the prophet is truly perceived and finally vindicated as the word of God (29:24; 30:8). The Assyrian will ultimately be judged for arrogance (31:8), in similar fashion as in chaps. 1–12.

There is an attitude of faith and trust that will sustain those during the coming crisis (28:16; 30:15), relinquished only at one's peril. It is precisely this attitude that is exhibited by Hezekiah during the Assyrian assault. Not surprisingly, chap. 32 speaks of the king who reigns in righteousness (32:1), as an age of peace and security is envisioned (32:14–20). The final liturgy (chap. 33) looks ahead to the vindication of God against the Assyrians and against the sinners within Israel, as all eyes turn toward a just king and a forgiven people (33:17, 24).

It cannot be determined precisely if this material is keyed toward the narrative denouement of chaps. 36–37 and the specific figure of Hezekiah, toward his successor, or toward an eschatological figure from the postexilic period. Clearly, Hezekiah acts with a righteousness and faith in the events of 701 in such a way as to embody the Davidic ideal, and the hopes of chaps. 32–33 may be modeled on him. It is beguiling to consider that significant hopes may have been attached to Hezekiah's successor Manasseh, whose very name seems to signal hopes for the reunification of Israel (note the contrast between 9:21 and 11:13). Did the redactors of First Isaiah at one point believe that following the Assyrian defeat in 701 and the death of Sennacherib there would be a period of peace and prosperity and a restoration of Israel (11:12–16) and the Davidic house (11:1–9; 32:1–8)? If so, that hope has now been shifted to the future and to the expectation of restoration following not the Assyrian destruction but the Babylonian one of 587.

6. Isaiah 34–35. A similar question can be raised about chaps. 34–35, both with regard to setting, date, and general purpose within the Isaiah corpus. Chap. 34 describes a massive scene of destruction. Throughout the chapter, the language and imagery employed resemble that found in 24–27, leading some to refer to 34–35 as a "little apocalypse" depicting a great cosmic judgment. Like the "great apocalypse," it is dated to the late postexilic period and broader apocalyptic thought (Vermeylen 1977: 440–46). The specific reference to Edom (vv 8–12) is taken as a symbol for God's enemies in general.

In 1928, C. C. Torrey argued that chaps. 34 and 35 were a unity ("two sides of one coin"), depicting the doom of the wicked on the one hand and the blessing of the righteous on the other (Torrey 1928: 279). Noting the similarity with chap. 63, Torrey argued that these chapters were of a piece with Second Isaiah and should be interpreted as such. Torrey placed this Second Isaiah in Judah in the late postexilic period. Modifications of his position would view chaps. 34–35 as based upon the prophecies of 40–55 and dated at the same period as 56–66, the so-called Third Isaiah (Clements *Isaiah 1–39* NCBC, 271–72).

In a recent monograph (1985), Steck argues that chaps. 34–35 were composed precisely to serve the function of providing a bridge *(eine redaktionelle Brücke)* between relatively closed First and Second Isaiah sections, thus representing the latest stratum of the book. Admittedly, the language of chap. 35 in particular resembles that found in chaps. 40–55, as a highway of return is depicted (35:8–10) and nature is rejuvenated (35:1–7). Steck reasons that these chapters were composed to anticipate 40–62 and ease the transition from First to Second Isaiah. However, their primary purpose is not to provide literary integration but to offer an isolated redactional word regarding Israel's restoration and purification beyond what existed in other sections of the developing Isaiah corpus (a *Sinnveränderung* of other Isaiah tradition; Steck 1985: 94–96). God would work more subtly and indirectly to effect the final eschatological conclusion of his work with Israel and Zion, with a different understanding of the role of the nations and the return of Diaspora Israel.

At a minimum, it appears that the function of these two chapters is to describe a future world judgment over nations and nature, and then to report the transformation of creation and the return of the dispersed. Steck overstates the unique and isolated nature of these themes. In the present form of the book, the chapters do not bridge First and Second Isaiah as closed literary collections; rather, they amplify and extend the message of the preceding chapters (32–33) regarding the future judgment and the ensuing reign of peace and forgiveness, at the same time reminding the reader of 36–39 that the deliverance of 701 is temporary and that the cleansing judgment will continue beyond Hezekiah's day. In so doing, they ease the transition (temporal and literary) between the former and the latter things—or between the judgments of the Assyrian period and of the Babylonian period and the dawn of a new day in God's dealings with Israel, such as this takes form in Isaiah 40–66.

7. Isaiah 13–23 and 24–27. Similar redactional and compositional concerns can be detected in the major sections running from chap. 13 through chap. 27. Material arguably Isaianic, reflecting 8th-century proclamations against Assyria (14:24–27), Philistia (14:28–31), Syro-Ephraim (17:1–14), Egypt (chaps. 18–19), and Judah (chap. 22) has been filled out to present a massive Nation Oracle section involving Babylon (13:1–16; 14:3–23; chap. 21), Persia (13:17–22), Moab (chaps. 15–16), and Tyre (chap. 23) as well. The section culminates in a scene of cosmic judgment (chaps. 24–27).

Though this latter judgment has often been dated to the latest period of postexilic Israel (Duhm *Jesaia* HKAT, xii), a more recent interpretation that focuses on the events of 587 and the destruction of Jerusalem has been put forward (Johnson 1988). This is certainly consistent with the broader parameters of a Babylonian redaction notable elsewhere in the book, and one with the general historical range of 13–23 in its present form (namely, the focus on Babylon, Persia, Moab, and Tyre as 6th-century entities). The description of judgment found in chaps. 24–27 is correlated with the commissioning of Babylon at the opening of the Nation Oracle section (13:1–16; Clements *Isaiah 1–39* NCBC, 132–36). Through the agency of the Babylonians, Yahweh determines to "lay waste the whole earth" (13:5–24:1), returning it to a state of near chaos, as it was at the time of Noah (note the reference to "the everlasting covenant" at 24:5). All this comes about as a consequence not just of Israel's disobedience (as reported in 1–12), but because of the massive bloodletting of the nations as a whole (13–23), so that the earth "lies polluted" (24:5) and threatens to fall back into chaos and total disorder. This is clearly reminiscent of God's decision to "make an end of all flesh" because "God saw the earth, and behold, it was corrupt, for all flesh had corrupted their way upon earth" in the days of Noah (Gen 6:12–13; cf. Isa 24:20). The "everlasting covenant" has been broken. Just as in the days of Noah, "the windows of heaven are opened, and the foundations of the earth tremble" (Isa 24:18; cf. Gen 7:11: ". . . all the fountains of the great deep burst forth, and the windows of heaven were opened"). It is as though God has demanded a reckoning for the lifeblood of humans and animals, as he had warned Noah (Gen 9:5).

Readings of Duhm and others (Plöger 1968: 53–78; Hanson 1975), which seek to interpret 24–27 as a late apocalyptic insert, fail to deal with the integrative function of these chapters viewed with an eye toward their surrounding literary context. There is significant evidence of a form of inner-biblical exegesis at work in these chapters (Sweeney 1988a), suggesting far greater integration in the final level of composition than is recognized when the independence of 24–27 is stressed. Moreover, the eschatological time frame of the chapters has been overstated and depends on certain views of evolution in Hebrew thought and cognate movements in other so-called apocalyptic literature (Daniel, Joel, Zechariah 12–14) whose relationship to Isaiah 24–27 is highly speculative. Interestingly, the future references within these chapters are *not* keyed toward global judgment but toward final restoration (25:6–12; 26:1–6; 27:2–6; 27:12–13). The depiction of judgment is not conceived of as an end-time event but as a near-future or imminent affair. The frequent general references to the "city" and the "earth" suggest an all-encompassing judgment, not one simply focused on Judah/Jerusalem, though Zion is the ultimate pivot in God's dealings with the cosmos (24:23).

In the final form of the Isaiah presentation, this judgment comes about in the Babylonian assault of 587, creating utter desolation of nature and the whole earth. In fact, chaps. 24–27 form the only real account of the destruction of 587 in the whole book, there being no explicit report of this otherwise central historical episode in the Isaiah presentation beyond the cryptic note at 39:5–8 (cf. Jer 39:1–10; 52:4–30). The crucial event of 587 is handled in Isaiah in poetic and near-mythical terms, as the language of creation and chaos—familiar from the Songs of Zion—is evoked (Psalm 29; 46; 47; 93; 99); but the historical moorings of this language have not been completely severed, just as the threat of the nations is never fully detached from history in the Zion hymns.

When Second Isaiah chapters speak of nature's restoration, they speak from the other side of a judgment envisioned in chaps. 13–27. Not until the Persians are sent forth (14:17–22) to bring down the Babylonian instrument of destruction (on analogy with Assyria's demise in 1–12) can the reign of peace be ushered in; this is the same "bird of prey" commissioned for God's purpose in 18:6 which carries out the commission in Second Isaiah (46:11). It is clear that the Nation Oracle section, with its culmination in 24–27, has been redactionally shaped to anticipate Second Isaiah material, especially the frequent reference to the assembling of the nations for trial (esp. 40–48). There, the reader learns that all this was planned by God long ago (40:21; 41:4, 21–29; 42:9; 43:9; 44:7). The nations did not act on their own and therefore are not in a position to have known what the outcome would be (41:26; 43:9; 44:7). God was at work through them to effect not only Israel's judgment but also her restoration. He has called Cyrus to begin this work of restoration (41:25), just as was promised long ago also (13:17–22; 18:3–6).

The explicit mention of the rise of Persia belongs to a redactional stage of development within the book of Isaiah that is meant to draw out the significance of God's actions in history spanning the age of Isaiah and events centuries later. Redactors working seriously with the word of God, as it was preserved from the prophet Isaiah, saw in his message a significance that transcended its own narrower field of historical reference. Analogies were seen to be apposite. Assyria would ultimately be judged by God for arrogance, after she had fulfilled God's bidding vis à vis Israel and Judah/Jerusalem. This was a prominent theme in the 1–12 collection. Chaps. 13–14, which open the Nation Section, clearly indicate that Babylon is then to be likewise consecrated for service (13:2–5). It is quite likely that the seeds for this redactional perspective were to be found in the report of chap. 39, or in its broader frame of reference, whereby the 8th-century Babylonians were seen as embodying a significance in God's plan of judgment that they themselves did not comprehend. By placing 14:24–27, an oracle of judgment against Assyria similar to material in 1–12 (e.g., 10:5–19), in the context of chaps. 13–14, the "breaking of Assyria" (14:25) is to be understood as part of God's broader work with Israel and the nations, now including Babylon and Persia (13:17–22). Assyria's breakdown is analogous to Babylon's centuries later, after both serve their respective purpose in God's larger work with Israel.

Secondary redactional interpretation has drawn out the deeper significance of Isaiah's proclamation regarding the role of Assyria, by seeing Babylon as functionally analogous at a later period in time. Moreover, hopes associated with the fall of Assyria for the restoration of Israel, perhaps from the reign of Hezekiah or Manasseh (9:1–7; 11:1–9; 11:12–16; 32:1–20), are now fully interwoven with a vision of restoration which follows a much more pervasive, cleansing judgment (14:1–2; 19:16–24; 25:6–12; 26:1–19; 27:2–6; 27:12–13; 35:1–10). The faithful remnant headed by Hezekiah in 701 gives way to a yet smaller remnant in 587—"a tenth burned again," to use the language of 6:13. This purged remnant will experience the new Jerusalem and a fully restored Zion in a transformed creation. Here, the reciprocal relationships between First Isaiah and Second Isaiah could not be clearer, as both sections of the present book of Isaiah are shaped to span several centuries in time, in order that the abiding and persistent hand of God at work with Zion and his people might be laid bare. Second Isaiah chapters address a remnant spoken of as far back as Isaiah's commission in the year that King Uzziah died (6:13). The comfort spoken to Zion/Jerusalem (40:2) is comfort for a people whose warfare is at last ended, whose iniquity is finally pardoned. At this point in the Isaiah presentation, it is clear that the vision of restoration prepared for in Isaiah's day is about to take shape. The hymn praising God's comforting of Zion (12:1–6) is now to be sung.

Sections of the book under major Assyrian-period (1–12; 28–33; 36–37) and Babylonian-period (13–27; 34–35; 38–39) redactional influence have been fused and coordinated precisely so that First Isaiah might function as a coherent prelude to Second Isaiah, and so that Second Isaiah might look back on First Isaiah for its own literary, historical, and theological bearings. In this way, the former things of Isaiah are coordinated with the latter things, as the age of judgment is brought to a close and a new day of transformation begins to dawn.

In the final presentation of First Isaiah, the vision of restoration remains a vision without complete fulfillment. Second Isaiah attests to the close of an old age and the beginning of the fulfillment of an earlier vision and hope, rooted in the period of Hezekiah and the final days of the historical Isaiah. As the vision is filled out and enriched in First Isaiah, in light of the events of 587, it nevertheless remains a vision lacking complete fulfillment in the final form of the completed book of Isaiah. As the rabbis once remarked, the book of Isaiah is a vision of future promise ("all consolation," *b. Bat.* 14b), following a book full of doom (Jeremiah) and one of doom and promise mixed (Ezekiel). In the confession of the Christian Church over the ages, the Church's messianic hope has been "filled full" in Jesus of Nazareth. The King of Peace has, however, only inaugurated the age of weal proclaimed by this great prophet. The final fulfillment of God's word proclaimed in the vision of Isaiah forms the centerpiece of Jewish and Christian hope for the future and God's ultimate reign on earth. In a very real sense, the book of Isaiah presents a prophet who is both forth-teller and fore-teller, and it would be wrong to focus on one dimension of that portrayal to the exclusion of the other. The historical dimension gives rise to the eschatological, and they must be allowed to illuminate and enrich one another.

D. Conclusions

First Isaiah is a rich and complex tapestry of prophetic proclamation and secondary interpretation. Form criticism is right to locate the origin of that proclamation in the oral speech of the man Isaiah addressing events in his day. Direct referential readings appropriately search for signs of larger structure and purpose in the present literary organization of these chapters. However, the logic of that structure is not to be sought in the chronological movements of the historical Isaiah but in certain understandings of how Isaiah, time, and God's work with Israel will operate for generations of new interpreters.

Against more radical redactional approaches, the final structure of First Isaiah is not thoroughly haphazard, resulting from the sporadic accretion of modifying interpretations from hands uninterested in mutual coordination. Redactors of chapters 1–39 have worked with certain recognizable principles which honor the original proclamation of the man Isaiah on the one hand, but also seek to hear in his word something of God's larger purpose for Israel, the nations, and the cosmos on the other. The result is more than an erratic literary potpourri, demanding complex reshuffling and explanation; rather, redaction has been carried out *synthetically,* in such a way that new levels of interpretation are allowed to function integrally with sections of text that gave rise to them. That the process is not everywhere uniform and without seam is testimony to the fact that the book of Isaiah is more than the prophet's personal diary or memoir. Here, redactional analysis has simply pointed out a truth about prophetic literature difficult for direct referential readings to parry. In its zeal for spotting disjuncture and modification, though, redactional analysis frequently stops too short, failing to recognize attempts at synthesis and coordination in the final form of the literature.

Larger structural principles can be detected in First Isaiah. As in Second Isaiah (see below), one can speak of these as polarities. The two major prose sections of Isaiah are cases in point (6–8 and 36–39). These offer a studied contrast between proper and improper patterns of behavior and response to God's word under pressure, especially true for the royal house but by no means restricted to Israel's kings Ahaz and Hezekiah. In First Isaiah, Hezekiah presents a model for obedience and prayerful trust in stark contrast to his predecessor Ahaz.

Related to this, First Isaiah holds up two key moments in history as particularly illustrative of God's work with Judah/Jerusalem and Israel: the Syro-Ephraimite threat of 734 B.C.E. and the 701 Assyrian assault. Within a much broader range of historical events, involving Babylon and Persia and a host of nations (13–27), these two events are especially noteworthy. Lack of trust in the royal house and in Judah at large, before, during, and after this first crisis, sets in motion a much broader series of events in Israel's history, involving the fall of Samaria, increased Assyrian hostility, and finally the 701 invasion itself. Hezekiah's proper response in the crisis retards an even larger design for cleansing judgment revealed in chaps. 13–27/34–35 and repeals the immediate word of judgment of chaps. 28–33. But the final word of First Isaiah chapters indicates that very shortly the Babylonians will arise to replace the Assyrians thwarted by Israel's faithful king and God. Here, a third polarity, or pairing, is to be seen as Assyria and Babylon function as successive instruments of judgment in God's dealing with Israel and the cosmos.

Finally, one must also speak of the polarity of judgment and promise woven into these chapters. Judgment comes at numerous points, and for countless reasons, in the relentless "here a little, there a little" (28:13) of God's dealings with an unjust people, through events of ANE history, and through events more mundane. For First Isaiah, the judgment is always a cleansing one with a broader goal and final purpose. This has everything to do with the prophet's conception of Zion and what Zion means from God's standpoint. Zion is not an inviolable fortress offering sure defense against all foes. Zion is God's own abode, and the nations frequently do God's explicit bidding. This combination means that God fights both for and against Zion, depending on its internal state and the state of its king and people. Lack of faith and justice within Zion means inevitable judgment.

First Isaiah is not willing to let this be the final word, for God's ultimate purpose revealed to the prophet indicates a day of proper rule, peace among nations who worship Israel's one Lord at Zion, and the full restoration of a creation wracked by bloodshed and the forces of chaos themselves. This day may live beyond the horizon of Isaiah's own time, but sufficient is the vision and clear are the signs of near fulfillment granted to him.

Ahaz and Hezekiah, the Syro-Ephraimite and Assyrian assaults, Assyria and Babylon, and judgment and promise represent four pairings in the final structure of First Isaiah. These pairings function within a temporal design spanning several centuries, set forth not by means of linear consecution, beginning with chapter 1 and concluding in chapter 39. Nevertheless, the temporal scheme is recognizable and functions clearly in the final literary presentation of First Isaiah chapters.

Bibliography

Ackroyd, P. R. 1974. An Interpretation of the Babylonian Exile: A Study of 2 Kings 20, Isaiah 38–39. *SJT* 27: 329–52.

———. 1978. Isaiah I–XII: The Presentation of a Prophet. *VTS* 29: 16–48.

———. 1981. The Death of Hezekiah—A Pointer to the Future? *De la Tôrah au Messie*, ed. M. Carrez. Paris.

———. 1982. Isaiah 36–39: Structure and Function. *Von Kanaan bis Kerala*, ed. W. Delsman et al. AOAT 211. Neukirchen-Vluyn.

Anderson, B. W. 1988. "God with Us"—In Judgment and in Mercy: The Editorial Structure of Isaiah 5–10 (11). Pp. 230–45 in *Canon, Theology, and Old Testament Interpretation*, ed. G. M. Tucker, D. L. Petersen, and R. R. Wilson. Philadelphia.

Barth, H. 1977. *Die Jesaja-Worte in der Josiazeit.* WMANT 48. Neukirchen-Vluyn.

Becker, J. 1980. *Messianic Expectation in the Old Testament.* Philadelphia.

Childs, B. S. 1967. *Isaiah and the Assyrian Crisis.* SBT 3. London.

Clements, R. E. 1980. The Prophecies of Isaiah and the Fall of Jerusalem in 587 B.C. *VT* 30: 421–36.

———. 1985. Beyond Tradition History: Deutero-Isaianic Development of First Isaiah's Themes. *JSOT* 31: 95–113.

Eichhorn, J. G. 1803. *Einleitung in das Alte Testament.* Vol. 3. 3d rev. and expanded ed. Leipzig.

Fohrer, G. 1967. Jesaja 1 als Zusammenfassung der Verkündigung Jesajas. *BZAW* 99: 148–66.

Frei, H. 1974. *The Eclipse of Biblical Narrative.* New Haven.

Friedlander, M., ed. 1873. *The Commentary of Ibn Ezra on Isaiah.* London.

Gesenius, W. 1821. *Philologisch-kritischer und historischer Commentar über den Jesaia.* 3 Vols. Leipzig.

Gottwald, N. K. 1958. Immanuel as the Prophet's Son. *VT* 8: 36–47.

Hanson, P. D. 1975. *The Dawn of Apocalyptic.* Philadelphia.

Hayes, J. R., and Hooker, P. K. 1988. *A New Chronology for the Kings of Israel and Judah, and Its Implications for Biblical History and Literature.* Atlanta.

Hayes, J. R., and Irvine, S. A. 1987. *Isaiah. The Eighth-Century Prophet.* Nashville.

Hengstenberg, E. W. 1872. *Christology of the Old Testament.* 2 vols. Edinburgh.

Johnson, D. 1988. *From Chaos to Restoration: An Integrative Reading of Isaiah 24–27.* JSOTSup 61. Sheffield.

Kaiser, O. 1983. *Isaiah 1–12. A Commentary.* 2d ed. completely rewritten. Philadelphia.

———. 1984. *Einleitung in das Alte Testament.* 5th rev. ed. Gütersloh.

Koppe, J. B. 1780. *Robert Lowth's Jesaias: Neu übersetzt nebst einer Einleitung und critischen philologischen und erläuternden Anmerkungen.* Vol. 2. Leipzig.

Levenson, J. D. 1988. The Eighth Principle of Judaism and the Literary Simultaneity of Scripture. *JR* 68: 205–25.

Lowth, R. 1753. *De sacra poesi Hebraeorum.* Oxford.

———. 1834. *Isaiah: A New Translation.* 10th Eng. ed. Boston.

Mays, J. L. 1988. Isaiah's Royal Theology and the Messiah. Pp. 39–51 in *Reading and Preaching the Book of Isaiah*, ed. C. R. Seitz. Philadelphia.

Meade, D. 1986. *Pseudonymity and Canon.* WUNT 39. Tübingen.

Plöger, O. 1968. *Theocracy and Eschatology.* Richmond.

Rendtorff, R. 1984. Zur Komposition des Buches Jesajas. *VT* 34: 295–320.

Roberts, J. J. M. 1985. Isaiah and His Children. Pp. 193–203 in *Biblical and Related Studies Presented to Samuel Iwry*, ed. A. Kort and S. Morschauser. Winona Lake, IN.

———. 1987. Yahweh's Foundation in Zion (Isa 28:16). *JBL* 106: 27–45.

Seitz, C. R., ed. 1988. *Reading and Preaching the Book of Isaiah.* Philadelphia.

———. 1989. The Prophet Moses and the Canonical Shape of Jeremiah. *ZAW* 101: 3–27.

Sheppard, G. T. 1985. The Anti-Assyrian Redaction and the Canonical Context of Isaiah 1–39. *JBL* 104: 193–216.

Smelik, K. A. D. 1986. Distortion of Old Testament Prophecy: The Purpose of Isaiah xxxvi and xxxvii. *OTS* 24: 70–93.

Steck, O. H. 1985. *Bereitete Heimkehr: Jesaja 35 als redaktionelle Brücke zwischen dem Ersten und dem Zweiten Jesaja.* SBS 121. Stuttgart.

Stohlmann, S. 1983. The Judaean Exile after 701 B.C.E. Pp. 147–75 in *Scripture in Context II: More Essays on the Comparative Method*, ed. W. W. Hallo, J. C. Moyer, and L. G. Perdue. Winona Lake, IN.

Sweeney, M. 1988a. Textual Citations in Isaiah 24–27. *JBL* 107: 39–52.

———. 1988b. *Isaiah 1–4 and the Post-Exilic Understanding of the Isaianic Tradition.* BZAW 171. Berlin.

Thiele, E. R. 1965. *The Mysterious Numbers of the Hebrew Kings.* 2d ed. Grand Rapids and Exeter.

Torrey, C. C. 1928. *The Second Isaiah.* New York.

Vermeylen, J. 1977–78. *Du prophète Isaïe à l'apocalyptique.* 2 vols. Paris.

Wildberger, H. 1979. Die Rede des Rabsake vor Jerusalem. *TZ* 35: 35–47.

Yee, G. A. 1981. A Form-Critical Study of Isaiah 5:1–7 as a Song and a Juridical Parable. *CBQ* 43: 30–40.

CHRISTOPHER R. SEITZ

ISAIAH 24–27 (LITTLE APOCALYPSE)

At one extreme, Isaiah 24–27 has been identified as a late postexilic apocalyptic work (Duhm *Jesaja* HKAT, 172–94). At another, it has been read as preexilic prophetic judgment literature thoroughly at home in the work of First Isaiah (Kissane 1941: 276, 303). Between these positions, it has been understood as prophetic eschatology (Lindblom 1938) or early apocalyptic (Hanson 1979: 313–14). Isaiah chaps. 24–27 are important 6th-century passages that offer insights into the origins of apocalyptic; hence our label, proto-apocalyptic.

If we assume that First Isaiah was the founder of a school of prophecy, perhaps with royal support, given First Isaiah's easy access to kings Ahaz and Hezekiah and Isaiah's belief that Zion would not fall to the Assyrian threat (37:34–35), and if we assume that chaps. 24–27 owe their current location in the canon of Isaiah to the reference to Moab (25:10) so that these chapters were editorially grouped with other oracles against foreign nations, it becomes possible to reconstruct a context for the interpretation of these chapters. Given their belief in the inviolability of Zion, Jerusalem's fall would have presented the members of the school of Isaiah with a major theological problem demanding a solution. Our suggestion is that the writer of Isaiah chaps. 24–27 was a member of the school of Isaiah who used material from an older oracle against Moab, inspired by but moving beyond Second Isaiah, to seek a solution to the destruction of Jerusalem, our identification of the destroyed city. Note a similar use of an oracle against Edom in chap. 34, producing what can be labeled proto-apocalyptic writing.

The secondary literature interpreting Isaiah 24–27 has centered on three interrelated issues: (1) the problems presented by the text and its structure; (2) the problem of literary genre; and (3) the difficulty in establishing the historical setting. Using the relatively objective controls of prosodic and thematic analyses of the text, it is possible to offer the following interpretation of these chapters.

A. Text and Structure

There is a stratum of poetry in Isaiah 24–27 that can be compared with the best in Second Isaiah. These poetic units are Isaiah 24:1–16a, 24:16b–25:9, and 26:1–8 (Millar 1976: 23–49). The most common prosodic pattern in these units is the alternation between bicola and tricola. Within a tight syllabic symmetry are couched many examples of paronomasia, alliteration, assonance, chiasm, *inclusio,* and climactic and repetitive parallelism. We would argue on the basis of the similarities in prosodic style to Second Isaiah that these units form the earliest material of Isaiah 24–27 and can be dated close to the time of Second Isaiah.

Typologically, the prosodic style of Isaiah 26:11–27:6 is different (Millar 1976: 49–58). The meter is mixed. The poetry is not as good as that encountered in the former units. We would conclude on prosodic grounds that the passages of 26:11–27:6 were composed later.

The prose of 27:12–13 would appear to be later still (Millar 1976: 58–59). We have deleted 24:5, 24:20b, and 26:9d–10 as editorial expansion. In each case they interpret what can be read as an earlier text. As yet, Isaiah 27:9–11 does not yield to our prosodic analysis, so it is not included in this summary.

Regarding structure, our study of the themes of Isaiah 24–27 (Millar 1976: 65–70) has revealed the frequent use of portions or all of the following thematic pattern: threat, war, victory, and feast (a Divine Warrior hymn). In what we have identified on prosodic grounds as the earliest layer—24:1–16a, 24:16b–25:9, and 26:1–8—this thematic pattern conforms to the poem's own content; that is, the poems themselves seem to have been created with these themes in mind. This, again, would place them typologically prior to what we find in 26:11–27:6.

In Isaiah 26:11–27:6, the forms are more mixed. There appear to be traces of a lament of the people (26:16–20), a salvation oracle (26:21), an ancient Divine Warrior hymn (27:1), and a modified Song of the Vineyard (27:2–6). They have been arranged, however, according to the basic thematic pattern we have discerned in the earlier material. We suggest, then, that the author or editor was readapting other relevant materials he had, according to the pattern suggested above. These materials probably circulated independently prior to their current use in Isaiah 24–27.

The prose passage of Isaiah 27:12–13 and editorial expansions at 24:5, 24:20b, and 26:9d–10 could have been added at that time when Isaiah 24–27 was joined to the collection of oracles against the nations found in the larger context of Isaiah.

B. Genre and Date

The prosodic style of Isaiah chaps. 24–27 and their themes, both separately and in pattern, do establish a literary context for us to understand these chapters. The author emerges as one very much influenced by the work of Second Isaiah; one who shared in Second Isaiah's visions for the reconstruction of Israel. For that reason, we label the genre of Isaiah 24–27 proto-apocalyptic. A 6th-century date is not unreasonable. We would place the earlier portions of the chapters closer to 587 B.C.E., the fall of Jerusalem, than to 520 B.C.E., the temple controversy.

C. Historical Setting

Identification of the destroyed city as Jerusalem would make sense with the textual and thematic data gathered above. The fall of Jerusalem touched off a profound search for meaning and explanation. Why would Yahweh allow his own city to be destroyed? The language appropriate to such a search for meaning was myth. One witnesses in the literature of the period a ground swell in the use of mythic patterns and images to interpret the tragic events of the day. Second Isaiah was particularly instrumental in reusing mythic materials to interpret God's action in the events.

The pattern of the Divine Warrior hymn reemerged with its full power. It provided an explanation for the destruction. Chaos was reasserting its destructive power. The fall of Jerusalem was part of the collapse of creation and return to chaos (24:10). The Divine Warrior hymn also provided hope in that one day Yahweh, the Warrior Deity, would reaffirm his position as king on his mount (24:23); hence, shouts of victory and hymns of praise (25:1–4c). Hope for victory was held even within a description of the devastated city of Jerusalem and a shuddering earth. From his mountain, Yahweh would prepare a feast for all peoples, a feast at which the power of death and chaos would be consumed forever (25:6–8).

Isaiah 24:1–16a, 24:16b–25:9, and 26:1–8 shared the visions of a restored Israel with Second Isaiah, though the author did move beyond the vision of the events taking place within plain history. The power of myth to see beyond the limits imposed by historical events was beginning to take hold. Yahweh was preparing his feast for *all* people. *All* the kings of the earth were being caught up in this return to chaos that was to be a prelude to a new creation (24:21).

Isaiah 26:11–27:6 was added to the earlier materials as the delay of Yahweh's victory became apparent to some of Isaiah's disciples. The reference to the destroyed city trampled by the faithful (26:6) could have been introduced into the earlier poems as the tensions between the contending parties in postexilic Israel increased (see Hanson 1979). For the Isaianic visionaries, the Jerusalem of reality and the Zion of faith remained separate. As Jerusalem was defiled by oppressive leaders (possibly Aaronid Zadokites), Mushite Levites pushed to peripheral status may have believed that the city deserved Yahweh's continued wrath. The hope was strong, however, that one day Israel would truly be restored along the lines envisioned in Isaiah 60–61.

It was in the years of exile and shortly thereafter that the apocalyptic movement was born. Isaiah chaps. 24–27 constitute one of those important passages that offers us insight into the dynamics of that birth.

Bibliography

Hanson, P. D. 1979. *The Dawn of Apocalyptic.* Rev. ed. Philadelphia.
Kissane, E. 1941. *The Book of Isaiah.* Dublin.
Lindblom, J. 1938. *Die Jesaia-Apocalypse, Jes. 24–27.* LUÅ N.F. 1/34/3. Lund.
Millar, W. 1976. *Isaiah 24–27 and the Origin of Apocalyptic.* HSM 11. Missoula, MT.

William R. Millar

SECOND ISAIAH

The designation Second Isaiah for chaps. 40–55 of the book of Isaiah has gained currency in the last century. The conclusion that these chapters form a unit of separate origin from the preceding thirty-nine chapters is compelled by their language and by numerous details of their content.

A. Designation, Contents, and Text
  1. Designation
  2. Contents
  3. Text
B. Second Isaiah and His Times
  1. The Prophet in Chaps. 40–55
  2. History of the Period
C. The Prophetic Tradition
  1. The Literary Tradition
  2. The Social Role of the Prophet
D. Rhetoric and Genres
  1. Parallelism
  2. Genres
E. The Message of Second Isaiah
  1. Overview
  2. The Five Polarities
  3. The Servant
  4. Creation

A. Designation, Contents, and Text

1. Designation. Chaps. 40–55 are a distinct segment within the sixty-six chapters of the scroll, or book, of Isaiah. Chaps. 36–39 (except for 38:9–20) were taken from 2 Kgs 18:13–20:19 at one stage in the compilation of the scroll in order to serve as an appendix to the works and writings of Isaiah of Jerusalem, who lived from the mid-8th to the early-7th centuries B.C. To be sure, not all of chaps. 1–35 are from Isaiah, yet the appendix closes off that part of the work.

The historical context of chaps. 40–55 differs entirely from that of chaps. 1–39. The enemy of Israel is the Neo-Babylonian Empire (626–539 B.C.; cf. chaps. 46; 47; 48:20–21), not the Neo-Assyrian Empire of Isaiah (935–612 B.C.; cf. chaps. 10; 14:24–27), which collapsed with the destruction of Nineveh in 612 B.C. The gentile king in chaps. 40–55 is Cyrus of Persia (fl. 560–530 B.C.; cf. 41:2–3, 25; 44:24–45:13; 48:14), not the Assyrian king of Isaiah (10:5–19). The people are in Babylon, not in Isaiah's 8th-century Jerusalem; the message is to leave Babylon, cross the desert, and return to Zion.

The difference in locale and themes must have been apparent to careful readers of the book in every age; indeed, the medieval Jewish scholar Ibn Ezra constantly noted them in his 12th-century commentary. He subtly raised the question of non-Isaian authorship for the chapters. However, such observations had little effect. A major reason that the unity of Isaiah went unchallenged for so long was a centuries-old unexamined theory of verbal inspiration: the sacred author wrote at the dictation of God or the Holy Spirit. This theory allowed readers to assume unity of authorship despite obviously different historical contexts; events later than Isaiah were considered to have been shown to him in vision. Inevitably, post-Renaissance critical scrutiny of ancient documents, rising historical awareness, and the skepticism of the Enlightenment challenged the unexamined tradition that Isaiah of Jerusalem wrote all sixty-six chapters in the 8th century.

Challenges to the unity of authorship are recorded as early as 1775, when J. C. Doderlein used the name Deutero-Isaiah for chaps. 40–66 in his *Esaias. Ex recensione textus Hebraei.* In 1780, J. B. Koppe, a Göttingen professor, argued in his preface to the German edition of Robert Lowth's translation of Isaiah that chaps. 40–66 had been written in the Babylonian Exile. In the 1793, E. F. K. Rosenmüller (anticipating Duhm a hundred years later) suggested in his *Scholia* that 42:1–7; 49:1–5; 50:4–10, and 52:13–53:12 were added to the book, and that 53:2–12 were the work of a postexilic poet (Rogerson 1984: 23). J. G. Eichhorn (1752–1827) in his widely used *Einleitung in das alte Testament* (1st ed. 1780–83) energetically championed the view that the book was not written by one person, but was rather an anthology of material from the 8th century to postexilic times. Of chaps. 40–52 he wrote: "In the series of oracles just mentioned the Babylonian exile is the general setting; the poet speaks as if he lived in exile, as if he spoke to the exiles who, in the delay of their return to the homeland, doubt whether the promise of their old prophets will be fulfilled. Must not the author of the consoling tradition contained in them have lived in the exile?" (Eichhorn 1803: 69). Nearly a century later, Bernhard Duhm's influential commentary on Isaiah (HKAT,

1892), succeeded in persuading most critical scholars that chaps. 56–66 were from a postexilic Third Isaiah. In contrast to Second Isaiah, he noted, the Jewish community is founded, Jerusalem is inhabited, and the temple is rebuilt. The people are unhappy, the rulers are ineffective, the rich oppress the poor; Yahweh has no instrument like Cyrus but promises to act alone to uphold the righteous, rebuild the city, and bring back the remaining exiles (*Jesaia* HKAT, 418).

That a 6th-century author, name unknown, wrote chaps. 40–55, and another author or authors, also anonymous, wrote chaps. 56–66, is now accepted by all but a scholarly minority, who hold out for the unity of Isaiah. Some scholars believe that chaps. 34–35 and 60–62 are also from Second Isaiah because of their themes and elevated style. In any case, two or more prophets who stood in the tradition of Isaiah of Jerusalem addressed Israel in the 6th century. Their speeches were added to the Isaiah collection some time between the 540s (the date of Second Isaiah) and the 3d or 2d century B.C., when the Greek translation (LXX), which witnesses to the present order of chaps. 1–66, was made. It is usually assumed that chaps. 40–55 were appended very early in that time span.

2. Contents. Second Isaiah urges his fellow exiles to regard Babylon as their ancestors had regarded Egypt and to depart with him on a new Exodus and entry into Zion, by which acts they will become Israel once again. His program is clear and pervades all the speeches. The speeches, by their nature occasional and responsive to audience moods and changing circumstances of which we are not well informed, do not appear to be arranged according to an overarching design. There is, however, some indication of arrangement. The opening commission of the prophet to announce God's new act of restoring Israel to Zion (40:1–11) is echoed by the last scene, the invitation to banquet in Zion. Cyrus, the instrument of return, is mentioned only in chaps. 41–48; Zion is in the forefront from the speech of 44:24–45:13 to the climactic chap. 55. The first trial scenes about the nations in 41:1–42:9 are described in detail; later trial scenes (43:9–44:5; 44:6–23; 45:20–25) seem to presuppose that the reader is familiar with the first detailed scene. Passage 48:20–21, the short, urgent call to leave Babylon, seems to close off chaps. 40–48, the first section. The other striking exhortation to depart, 52:11–12, may end another section; at any rate the immediately following section (52:13–53:13) abruptly rises to a new level.

Descriptions of the contents of Second Isaiah will differ according to whether scholars assume there were originally a few speeches of extended length, or originally dozens of brief, even fragmentary, pieces. Some commentators who posit originally short units for the prophets grant that redactors made kerygmatic units from the original short utterances (Melugin 1976). The description of the contents below describes the larger units, leaving open the question of whether the units are the work of Second Isaiah or later redactors.

The prophet is commissioned in 40:1–11 in a heavenly ceremony, reminiscent of Isaiah's commission (chap. 6). The major difference between the two commissions is that in chap. 40 God announces not destruction but salvation: a new Exodus-Conquest, a triumphant procession through the wilderness interposing itself between Babylon and Zion, the true homeland. The book then attacks the causes of the popular discouragement preventing the new Exodus (40:12–31) in a disputation, a series of Joban questions (cf. Job 38–41) designed to show that nothing can hinder Yahweh's saving purpose; neither the nations (vv 12–17), nor the gods represented by statues and kings (vv 18–24), nor any member of the heavenly court (vv 25–31). A great trial between Yahweh and the gods, Israel and the nations, takes place in 41:1–42:9; Yahweh, in two parallel scenes (41:1–20 = 41:21–42:9) judges the nations and their gods (in their cultic images) to be in the wrong, and upholds Israel as his image and servant. Chaps. 42:10–43:8, though usually subdivided into small units on the basis of diverse genres, form a single celebration of Yahweh's victory over chaotic waters and primordial night (vv 10–16); Israel, blind because of that night, will have light for the journey (vv 18–20). Israel's punishment is deserved, as inflicted by Yahweh (vv 21–25). Now, however, the people are to return to Zion (43:1–8).

The next major section, 43:9–44:5, reminds Israel it is to be God's witness to the nations of Yahweh's supremacy by its reenactment of the Exodus-Conquest; up to now it has refused to live up to its vocation. In 44:6–23, Israel is called to be a living witness to the living and victorious Yahweh, in contrast to the inert witnesses, the manufactured statues of the gods that represent powerless deities. In the poem, 44:24–45:13, Cyrus is central. Though he has been referred to in 41:2–3, 25, as Yahweh's instrument, he is mentioned by name for the first time in 45:1 and is given the task befitting the anointed (messiah) of the victorious deity. He is the king appointed by Yahweh to carry out his plan for Israel, as the Assyrian king had carried out the divine will regarding Israel in the days of Isaiah. The next large unit, 45:14–25, is closely connected to Cyrus' commission from the preceding section; in the ANE, rebuilding the temple city was the task of the regent of the victorious deity. Zion, the goal of the return, will not be left in ruins in the new event.

Chaps. 46 and 47 contrast dramatically with the two preceding sections. The holy city of Babylon will be destroyed as its inhabitants carry out the statues of its powerless gods; Yahweh always carries Israel (chap. 46). Dame Babylon's disgrace is the polar opposite of Dame Zion's: reunion with her husband and children. Chap. 48 powerfully urges the people to be ready to act in the new creative event. The past creative event was accompanied by a word, which both interpreted it and invited the people to take part. Second Isaiah's word now interprets Cyrus as the agent of the new event and invites the people to leave Babylon in a new Exodus. Chapters 40–48 form a section, discernible in its focus on Cyrus as Yahweh's agent.

In the second great section, chaps. 49–55, Zion, Babylon's counterpart, exerts an increasingly powerful hold on the prophet's imagination. In chap. 49, the servant is gently persuaded, as Moses was, to lead the people in a new Exodus-Conquest; correspondingly, Zion is gently persuaded to believe her children will return. Chaps. 50:1–51:8, again often subdivided into several discrete units, explain how God was present to authentic believers in the night of Exile and will be even more present in restored Zion. Chaps. 51:9–52:12 adapt the elements of a national lament to pray that Yahweh defeat the foe and bring the people to Zion. As Yahweh once defeated the sea to bring his people to Zion, so may he again defeat the historic and suprahistoric oppressors of Zion. The fourth servant song in 52:13–53:12, unparalleled in the OT, vindicates the servant who risked everything to obey God's word. The people are amazed to see the despised servant bearing their sins and receiving his reward. Chap. 54 extols Zion, the goal of the Exile, now restored with husband, children, and buildings. Chap. 55 invites all to come to Zion to the banquet, and from that holy shrine, to witness to Yahweh's victory that brought them there.

3. Text. The Hebrew text of Isaiah is comparatively well preserved. The modern printed Hebrew text is based upon relatively late manuscripts, of the 10th and 11th centuries A.D., products of the Masoretic copying and vocalizing of the several preceding centuries. The essential reliability of the printed text is amply demonstrated by the Qumran scrolls of a millennium earlier, the oldest extant Hebrew manuscripts of Isaiah; the most important are the virtually complete 1QIsa^a, written about 140 B.C., a vulgar text, with plene spelling, and 1QIsa^b, of a century and a half later, with sparer vocalization. The latter, preserving portions of chaps. 7–66, stands somewhat outside the other seventeen Qumran manuscripts and fragments of Isaiah, which show that the book's textual tradition was already standardized by the 2d century B.C. 1QIsa^b is variously assessed, but its readings seem secondary to the MT in most instances where the two diverge, and it has no real kinship to the Hebrew prototype of LXX Isaiah. The Qumran manuscripts of Isaiah, therefore, witness to a full, even expansionistic, textual tradition. The same tradition, sometimes called "proto-rabbinic," will show up in the standardized MT of several centuries later. There is no evidence of variant textual families for Isaiah, in contrast, say, to the textual tradition of Jeremiah.

The Old Greek translation (OG) was made some time between the late 3d and mid-2d centuries B.C. The best witness to OG is the group of manuscripts represented chiefly by the uncials A and Q, frequently S and S^c, with important confirmation from the fragmentary Chester Beatty papyrus 965. This is J. Ziegler's Alexandrian group. Ziegler's second recensional group, the Hexaplaric, is theoretically the result of Origen's editorial activity of the second quarter of the 3d century A.D. and is of less value in reconstructing the OG; chief witnesses are the Hexaplaric uncials BV, with the minuscule 88, and the Syrohexapla. The OG for Isaiah is free, bordering on paraphrastic, rendering meaning for meaning, not word for word; it frequently misunderstands the Hebrew and smooths over difficult passages.

The Syriac, as frequently, is very close to the Hebrew. So also is the Aramaic Targum, which was given its final form in Babylonia in the 5th century C.E., though it was preceded by earlier Targums.

The evidence from the extant witnesses, therefore, is that the text of Isaiah was clearly established at least by the 2d century B.C.

B. Second Isaiah and His Times

1. The Prophet in Chaps. 40–55. Unlike other prophetic books, Isaiah chaps. 40–55 have no introductory heading like "The vision of Isaiah the son of Amoz, which he saw concerning Judah and Jerusalem in the time of Uzziah, Jotham, Ahaz, and Hezekiah, kings of Judah" (Isa 1:1); nor are there narratives of his life and ministry, like Isaiah 6–3; 20; 21:15–25; 36–39 and the biographical sections of Jeremiah and Ezekiel. We have only the speeches.

Though they provide little biographical information, the speeches do permit fairly precise dating. They assume that the readers or hearers know that Cyrus, king of Persia, will soon conquer the Babylonian Empire. Such an assumption was only possible after Cyrus deposed his sovereign Astyages in 550 B.C., incorporating Media into the Persian Empire, and conquered Lydia in 546 B.C. That conquest, along with the palpable decline of the Babylonian Empire, signaled one of those great changes of fortune that every so often reshaped the ancient Near East. The speeches do not mention the entry of Cyrus' army into Babylon in 539 B.C. The speeches were therefore given in the 540s B.C.

It is reasonably assumed, because of the immediacy of his preaching, that the prophet lived in Babylon, in one of several exiled Jewish communities of the time. His message consistently is addressed to the Babylonian community (cf. esp. 48:20; 52:11–12; chaps. 46; 47), inviting them to join him in a new Exodus-Conquest (esp. 49:1–12).

The prophet's references to himself are few and in conventional terms, making it difficult to reconstruct even a biographical sketch. He announces that his divine commission (customary in prophetic books to establish the prophet's authority) took place as he attended a session of the heavenly court. There he overheard Yahweh announce that the time of salvation was replacing the time of punishment (40:1–11). The prophet's report of attending the divine assembly and hearing its decrees is a traditional component, attested for the 9th-century prophet Micaiah ben Imlah (1 Kgs 22:19–23) and for Isaiah in the 8th century (chap. 6). In 40:6, the prophet is told: "Announce!" He immediately asks how he can do so, since the people whom he represents are like withered grass. His lament for the people, (like Isaiah's of 6:11) is part of the process that makes him into the extraordinarily confident proclaimer of Yahweh's saving plan. No other prophet speaks from such a coherent and grand vision.

Other references to the prophet are in the "servant songs" (Duhm's term): 42:1–4; 49:1–6; 50:4–6; 52:13–53:12, already noted by E. F. K. Rosenmüller in his *Scholia* of 1793 as witnessing to the prophet and his office (Rogerson 1984: 23). Again, it is difficult to ferret out biographical details because the passages are conventional and because the people's vocation is intertwined with the prophet's. Moreover, many scholars, following Duhm, regard the passages as later insertions either from Second Isaiah or from another hand. In 49:1–7, the prophet's call is narrated in imitation of the calls of Moses (Exodus 3–4) and of Jeremiah (Jer 1:4–10). Chap. 50:4–6 suggests that the prophet saw his own exilic suffering as part of the divine plan of punishment, and faithfully submitted to it, like the author of Lamentations 3. If, as seems likely, chaps. 52:13–53:12 are to be attributed to Second Isaiah, the prophet was rejected by his fellow Israelites, undergoing even a deathlike experience, if not death, before being given the great prize, a share in the holy land. A single verse, 48:16, states that "now the Lord Yahweh has sent me, endowed with his spirit." The prophet here sees himself as the one who provides the interpretive word accompanying the new creation and new Exodus-Conquest.

The very position of chaps. 40–55 after chaps. 1–39, and the anonymity of the author, argue that the prophet, or the disciple who appended the passage, understood his preaching to be continuous with Isaiah, perhaps even revealing the contents of the scroll of 8:16–20 and 30:8 and of the secret of the darkness-light sequence of 8:22–9:1. Quite possibly, the absence of biographical detail was deliberate, to show that the speeches actualize the ancient Isaian tradition for the exiles (Childs *IOTS*, 325–33).

2. History of the Period. That chaps. 40–55 were written in Babylon in the 540s B.C. is the position of the vast majority of scholars today. Chaps. 56–66 are apparently addressed to a community that has returned to Jerusalem to rebuild the community and the temple; allusions to Second Isaiah show that the speeches of that prophet were still alive in the period from 538 to 515 B.C., the time of the rebuilding of the community and the temple.

The exile of segments of the population of Judah to Babylon, Nippur, and other areas of Mesopotamia has its beginnings in the last two decades of the preceding century. The Josianic renaissance and attempted restoration of the boundaries of the old Davidic empire beginning in 621, permitted by the decline of the Neo-Assyrian Empire (935–612), collapsed with Josiah's death in battle in 609. The Neo-Babylonian Empire (626–539) quickly took over Assyria's rule of the Levant.

Babylonia, or S Mesopotamia, had become dominantly Chaldean during the last years of the Neo-Assyrian Empire. A Chaldean sheikh, Nabopolassar (fl. 626–605), organized this power politically into a dynasty. In 605, his son Nebuchadnezzar led the victory at Carchemish and in the same year inherited Assyria's western empire. Governing the W states from Babylonia was no easy matter. Egypt consistently enticed the states to rebel but retreated whenever the Babylonians came west to retaliate, leaving her allies to bear the brunt of punishment and taxation. Josiah's successor, Jehoahaz, reigned but three months in 609 before the Egyptians replaced him with Jehoiakim (609–598). At first pro-Egypt, Jehoiakim shifted to Babylon after the victory at Carchemish, then shifted back to Egypt in 601. In 598 he died, leaving his son Jehoiachin to face the avenging Babylonian army. After three months, Jehoiachin and many other Judahites were deported to Babylon (2 Kgs 24:15–16), the first of three such deportations recorded in the Bible, the others taking place in 586 (2 Kgs 25:11) and 582 (Jer 52:30). Jehoiachin was replaced by Zedekiah (597–587), who again wavered between Babylon and Egypt, provoking Nebuchadnezzar's destruction of Jerusalem in 586.

With the deportations, the creative center of Jewish life shifted from Jerusalem to Babylon. Judah and Jerusalem were left desolate; we are not well informed about life there. The most important historical sources for Jewish life in the Exile are the 650 cuneiform tablets from the business house of Murashu in Nippur, written between 445 and 403 B.C., over a hundred years after Second Isaiah. Jewish names occur in about 8 percent of the published documents; in the absence of ethnic designations, scholars must rely on the Yahwistic elements in the names, an uncertain guide. From the names, Jews appear to inhabit 28 of the approximately 200 settlements in the whole region of Nippur. There seems to have been no exclusively Jewish corporations (*ḫatru);* individual Jews belong to various organized groups, e.g., carpenters, settlers on certain lands. Some held military fiefs, being liable for conscription in time of war. They appear to have been integrated into the agricultural system; men with Jewish names work side by side with native Babylonians. It is probable, however, that Jews were able to maintain their own institutions alongside civil institutions, like the separate groups, Gk *politeumata,* which in Hellenistic times coexisted with the civic body within the same city. Fathers with Yahwistic names have sons named after Babylonian gods, and sons of fathers with Babylonian names bear Yahwistic names. Such naming indicates the willingness of many to follow the syncretistic custom of the ANE: to worship the local gods along with their ancestral god (*CHJ* 1: 342–58). In spite of pressures to conform, the Jewish community in Babylonia managed to maintain its identity and, among other achievements, produced literature such as the prophecies of Ezekiel and Second Isaiah and edited the Pentateuch and the Deuteronomistic History.

The literature produced in the Exile pointed toward the holy land as the people's rightful place. The Pentateuch ended with Israel in the plains of Moab, poised for entry, listening to the words of Moses—ready, it seems, to enter the land. Second Isaiah's preaching was similarly addressed to the immediate situation and points to Zion as the people's true home; Cyrus' defeat of Babylon was the sign to return, the "appointed time of favor" (49:8). The people must "go forth from Babylon, flee from Chaldea" (48:20).

Second Isaiah's interpretation of 6th-century national and international events draws heavily on First Isaiah's interpretation of the nation and the great empires. An understanding of the 8th century and of First Isaiah's interpretation is therefore essential. When Isaiah was a young man, the Neo-Assyrian Empire began to intrude into the territory of Israel and Judah. Tiglath-pileser III (745–728) made his first great western campaign in 743–738. A coalition of W states under Uzziah of Judah was defeated, leading to the payment of tribute. A second campaign in 734–732 resulted in Gilead, Galilee, and Damascus becoming Assyrian provinces. Pro- and anti-Assyrian parties thereafter entangled the politics of Israel. Menahem of Israel paid tribute to Tiglath-pileser in 738. The anti-Assyrian Pekah (736–732) assassinated Pekahiah and then, in 734, joined with Rezin, king of Aram, in an unsuccessful attempt to force neutral Judah to join their anti-Assyrian coalition. Consequently, Hosea (732–723) was appointed king of Samaria by the Assyrians. Relying on Egyptian aid, he rebelled in 725, which precipitated the destruction of Samaria in 722 by Sargon II, and the deportation of 27,290 Israelites (*ANET,* 284). In the south, Judah managed to carry out a religious reform under the strong Hezekiah. Like the renaissance under Josiah a century later, it sought a revival of national life and a restoration of the boundaries of the ancient Davidic empire. Hezekiah's own coalition against Assyria, however, did not prove long-lasting. In 701, he found himself besieged in Jerusalem, "like a bird in a cage," according to Assyrian annals (*ANET,* 288). Though Jerusalem was not destroyed, Hezekiah had to capitulate, his heavy tribute ending dreams of a return to the glorious days of old.

First Isaiah's interpretation of 8th-century events, the role of the Assyrian king as Yahweh's instrument in punishing, Zion as the privileged site of a renewed people, and the ultimate punishment of the nations for exceeding their mandate to punish Judah, all deeply influenced Second Isaiah's interpretation of the Babylonian Empire, of Cyrus the Persian, and of the renewal of the people.

First Isaiah's interpretive framework for 8th-century history proved useful for Second Isaiah's interpretation of mid–6th-century national and international history. The masterful Nebuchadnezzar died in 562 and was replaced by his son Amel-Marduk (biblical Evil-merodach), who released the long-imprisoned Davidic scion, Jehoiachin (2 Kgs 25:27–30; Jer 52:31–34). The release of the king did not apparently stir messianic hopes in Second Isaiah as it did in other exiles; his vision has no place for a Davidic messiah.

Nergal-sharezer (biblical Neriglissar; 539–536) was succeeded by Labashi-Marduk, after whose brief reign Nabonidus (555–539) came to the Babylonian throne; he was to preside over the decline of the empire. Nabonidus' administrative and religious reforms were unpopular in Babylonia; chief among the latter were his championing of the cult of the moon god Sin at the temple he rebuilt in Harran. Not yet satisfactorily explained is his ten-year stay at the desert oasis of Teima in NW Arabia; during that time his son Belshazzar ruled in Babylon. In the king's absence, the new year festival could not be held, increasing the king's unpopularity.

As Babylon declined, a new figure came to the fore, Cyrus the Persian. The Persians were an Indo-European tribe who settled in the ancient territory of Elam. Their name is derived from Persua (modern Fars), one of their first strongholds. The Persian prince Cambyses had married the daughter of the Median king Astyages, from which union Cyrus was born. The Median army revolted against Astyages and handed him over to Cyrus around 550 B.C. Having consolidated his position in the east, Cyrus then led a campaign into Asia Minor against Croesus of Lydia, taking Sardis and making Lydia a Persian province in 546. His propaganda made him out to be liberal toward those whom he defeated. He treated Croesus well and won over the Greek colonies in Asia Minor. Nabonidus' unpopularity contrasted with Cyrus' popularity. Nabonidus' return to Babylon in 539 made possible the celebration of the New Year Festival, apparently for the first time since he had left for Teima ten years before, but the king's sacrilegious behavior in the ceremonies alienated the priests. The famous "Cyrus Cylinder" shows how their allegiance had shifted to Cyrus. In language akin to Second Isaiah's about Cyrus (cf. 41:2–4, 25; 44:24–45:13), it declares, "[Marduk] pronounced the name Cyrus, king of Anshan, declared him [lit. pronounced (his) name] to be (come) the ruler of the world. . . . Marduk beheld with pleasure his good deeds and upright mind (lit. heart) (and therefore) ordered him to march against his city Babylon" (*ANET,* 315–16). Second Isaiah shared this view of Cyrus as liberator and respecter of native religions, declaring him to be the anointed of Yahweh (45:1). In the fall of 539, Nabonidus fled and Cyrus' army entered Babylon without a battle. Cyrus himself later entered, forbade looting, and appointed a Persian governor, leaving native institutions and traditions undisturbed.

Soon after, Cyrus issued a decree, preserved in Ezra 6:3–5, allowing the temple of Jerusalem to be rebuilt, the cost to be paid from the royal treasury. Judah became the province of Abr Nahara in the Persian Empire, under a Persian satrap, or governor.

We are not well informed as to how many of the Babylonian Jews, by now seemingly well established in their new land, elected to return to their devastated homeland, where preexilic claims on the land were likely to be contested by new inhabitants. Some did, however, and most scholars are persuaded that chaps. 56–66 were delivered to those returnees, who struggled to rebuild their temple and community in the spirit of Second Isaiah's grandiose prophecies.

C. The Prophetic Tradition

1. The Literary Tradition. When Second Isaiah wrote, the prophetic tradition from which he spoke was already half a millennium old. According to 1 Sam 9:9, the designation "prophet" was first applied to Samuel of the late 11th century. The Deuteronomistic History (DH) saw Samuel as the last of the judges and the first of the prophets. In the account of the rise of kingship in 1 Samuel 1–15, Samuel speaks and acts as the first of a line of prophets; in the biblical conception, the first person in a line often exercised on a grand scale the office later exercised by successors. Samuel does three major tasks in 1 Samuel: he anoints kings and rejects them, thereby foreshadowing later prophets' authority vis à vis the king; he declares holy war, thereby foreshadowing later oracles regarding the nations and their relation to Yahweh; and he interprets the ancient Mosaic tradition for a new situation (kingship), thereby foreshadowing prophets' preaching of the law and of their reinterpretation of tradition. The last task, the prophetic right to interpret the tradition, has sometimes been neglected through scholarly overemphasis on the prophets as sent by God to speak the law in all its denunciatory force to a disobedient Israel. In 1 Samuel 12, however, Samuel is presented as carefully reinterpreting the new institution of monarchy within the Mosaic covenant; a similar interpretive task is done by later prophets.

Prophets subsequently included in the DH carry out routinely the prophetic tasks of the heroic original, Samuel. Nathan legitimates David and his project of building a temple (2 Samuel 7); he rebukes David (2 Samuel 12) and takes part in the anointing of Solomon (1 Kgs 1:38–40, 45). In the "writing prophets," the same general assignment of prophetic functions holds true, though with nuance for each.

The new emphasis in the 8th-century prophets is the conviction that Yahweh has found his people guilty of fundamental disloyalty and will punish them; the people have broken the covenant by worshiping other deities and by oppressing the poor. The task of each prophet is to announce the punishment and to ready the people for it. Later, prophets—Jeremiah, Ezekiel, and Second Isaiah—

who live through the destruction of the Jerusalem temple in 586 and the several deportations of thousands of its citizens consider that destruction and the deportations to be the long-awaited punishment of God. These prophets begin to ready the exiles to prepare for a return. From the prophets of the 8th to the 6th centuries, a three-stage scenario of Yahweh's dealing with the people can therefore be abstracted: the period of Israel's sins, the punishment, and the restoration. Though the emphases differ, and for some prophets the period of restoration is but dimly seen (e.g., as in Amos' "maybe" in 5:15), there is nonetheless a common outline to their preaching.

Second Isaiah's mentor, First Isaiah, and to some extent Micah, call upon a different tradition than the other writing prophets. The other prophets generally allude to the Exodus-Conquest and the traditions that surround it as the great act of Yahweh on behalf of the people. Isaiah draws on the Zion and Davidic traditions. According to the Zion tradition, Yahweh's domain is a holy mountain, towering over all else, impregnable to enemies, the residence of Yahweh and his client people. Outside of Isaiah, the tradition appears in the "Zion Songs" of the Psalter (e.g., Psalms 46, 48, 76). First Isaiah turns the tradition into preaching; Yahweh, not the enemy kings, will attack the city to purify it of sinners and vindicate the just within its walls (1:21–28). The tradition occurs frequently, e.g., 2:1–5; 4:2–6; 8:5–8; 14:24–27; 29:1–8; 30:15–26; chap. 33; 37:21–35. The Davidic tradition that Yahweh has placed his son on the throne to be a conduit of blessings for the people is also prominent in Isaiah (chap. 7; 9:1–7; 11:1–10; 29:1–8; 32:1–8). Scholars sometimes separate the Davidic tradition from the Zion tradition, but king and mountain are closely connected; Psalm 2 places "my king on Zion, my holy mountain" (v 6), and Psalm 89 speaks of the procession to the shrine (vv 13–18) where the installation of David takes place (vv 19–37).

By Second Isaiah's time, the prophetic literary tradition was well established. The prophetic corpus may even have been edited by his time. Previous prophets had reinterpreted the old Exodus-Conquest tradition according to which Israel had been installed in the land, and the Isaian tradition that Israel dwelt securely in Zion under a Davidic king. Instead of being secure in the land, the sinful people had to encounter God anew in a punishing act, after which there was to be a restoration.

2. The Social Role of the Prophet. The role of the prophets in Israelite society must be distinguished from the literary tradition of the prophetic scrolls. In the Deuteronomistic Historian's portrait of Samuel, the first prophet, Samuel's role is defined in relation to the king's traditional roles. The story of David, and of subsequent kings, describes the prophets similarly in relation to the royal office and also in relation to the priesthood and to other prophets. The prophetic books of the 8th to the 6th centuries show the prophet within the same configuration. Jer 18:18 associates Torah with priests, counsel with the wise, and the word with prophets. The verse shows a variety of related figures in the authority structure of Israelite society, in addition to the omnipresent royal authority.

As a group, prophets had a recognized role in society, which can be described as an "office." The role need not have been precisely defined nor official (even though some prophets seem to have been employed by royally sponsored shrines). The writing prophets' emphasis upon their commission by Yahweh, in the face of opposition, suggests they were outside the circle of cult prophets, whose authority was established by their sanctuary position.

If the social fabric of preexilic Israel included the prophet, cultic or otherwise, what happened to the prophet after the exilic destruction of kingship, temple, and priesthood, the institutions that "defined" the prophetic "office"? Paucity of sources makes a clear answer impossible. Ezekiel occasionally teaches the elders (14:1), and Jeremiah deals with kings and important officials. But the old configuration of authority—royal, priestly, prophetic—disappeared with the Exile, or at least was seriously eroded; and it is not clear how a prophet like Second Isaiah made his appeal. It is noteworthy that his preaching is treatiselike, as if its authority lay, not in its author's role, but in the speeches' power to persuade. In other words, since the prophet's role in the exilic social fabric was no longer clear, prophetic authority was transferred to the persuasive power of written speech.

D. Rhetoric and Genres

Second Isaiah is a skilled rhetorician, who presents his argument effectively. Limited space allows examination of only one element of his rhetoric: large-scale parallelism. For other techniques of exposition—chiasm, wordplay, rhyme, alliteration, and assonance—see *IB* 5:381–773.

Rhetoric organizes the tradition to persuade. The tradition that Second Isaiah uses is couched in the language and patterns of his people's daily life.

1. Parallelism. The speeches are poems, part of a rich and sophisticated tradition of poetry that predated the Israelites. The tradition made only slight use of rhyme, relying instead on alliteration, assonance, wordplays on triliteral roots, and especially parallelism of two (bicola), three (tricola), or more lines. Parallelism is the development of an idea by its repetition. Second Isaiah utilizes this virtually universal technique in Hebrew poetry in striking ways. Not only lines, but actors, scenes, and whole passages are repeated for emphasis or contrast.

Large-scale parallelism is not unique to Second Isaiah. In Exodus 7–12, Yahweh and his servants Moses and Aaron are deliberately paralleled with Pharaoh and his servants, the magicians. In Proverbs 9, Dame Wisdom and Dame Folly are artfully paralleled. In the ancient poem in Exodus 15, vv 1–12 and vv 13–18 form two matching panels. Second Isaiah, however, makes special use of the technique. Several of his speeches can be divided into two parts, the second part repeating with variations the first. The part 41:21–42:9 repeats with variations the pattern of 41:1–20, the sequence of summons to trial (41:1, 5–7 = 21–22b), legal questioning of the nations/their gods (41:2–4 = 22c–24), and the divine verdict on the nations and Israel (41:8–20 = 42:1–9). Chap. 48 can be divided into vv 1–11 (38 cola) and vv 12–21 (37 cola); in the first section, the Hebrew root *qrʾ*, "to call," is used three times in mentions of humans calling or naming themselves, and in the second section, three times of Yahweh calling Israel. Chap. 49 divides into vv 1–13 (55 cola) and vv 14–26 (52 cola), the former concerned with readying the servant for a new Exodus-Entry into Zion, and the latter, with readying Lady Zion for her children's return. Verses 1–5 and 6–11 of chap. 55 are parallel exhortations to put aside profane conduct and enter the sanctuary for life-giving divine sustenance.

The five great polarities that structure Second Isaiah's message (discussed in E.2 below) are instances of large-scale antithetic parallelism. Zion, the residence of the true God, is portrayed with an eye to Babylon, the residence of false gods; the one is built up for her numerous children (40:9–11; 45; 49:14–26; 54; 55); the other is destroyed while her divine husband and children flee (chaps. 46 and 47). Yahweh is contrasted with the gods, Israel with the nations, the servant with the people, all in service of one overarching parallel: the first Exodus-Conquest/cosmogony and the new Exodus-Conquest/cosmogony.

Parallelism is particularly important for the prophet-orator's plan of action: leave Babylon and return to Zion (48:20–21; 52:11–12). It provides the redundancy necessary for effective oratory. Good oratory generally has a limited fund of ideas but develops them in a great variety of ways; parallelism of scenes, actors, and ideas make possible repetition without boredom.

2. Genres. The prophetic tradition was expressed by individual prophets in a variety of genres or forms. The ANE speaker or writer stood consciously within an ancestral tradition, defined in content and expression. Hermann Gunkel (1862–1932), from his work on Psalms and Genesis, correctly affirmed "that types in the literature of an ancient people play a much greater role than today and that the individual personalities of authors, which in modern literature are, or appear to be, everything, in antiquity step back in a manner quite bewildering to us" (*apud* Kraus 1982: 361). Prior to form criticism, Bernhard Duhm's watershed commentary had applied to the chapters the then-dominant *Literaturkritik* (derived from analysis of the Pentateuch) with important results. Among his literary-critical decisions was the separation of his "servant songs" (42:1–4; 49:1–6; 50:4–9; 52:13–53:12) and the idol passages (41:5–7; 46:6–8; 44:9–20), attributing them to distinct "sources." Duhm often appealed to the logic of the passages to reach his decisions about the extent of the individual speeches, and he aggressively emended and transposed verses.

Duhm's reliance on literary criticism and Western ideas of oriental logic did not suffice for analyzing the speeches; new criteria were needed. The criteria were partly supplied by a method developed shortly after Duhm's commentary appeared: form criticism, brilliantly worked out by Gunkel in his commentary on Genesis (*Genesis* HKAT) and later in his work on Psalms. Gunkel placed the study of Genesis on new and solid ground with his recognition of the traditional and even folkloric origin and transmission of the stories in Genesis. Analysis of genres such as *Sagen,* genealogies, and lists of peoples yielded a rich interpretive harvest in Genesis. In 1914, Hugo Gressmann applied the approach to Second Isaiah in an important article (1914). Ludwig Kohler borrowed some of the concerns of form criticism in his *Deuterojesaja stilkritisch untersucht* (1923). Most influential upon the modern generation was Joachim Begrich's concise and well-argued *Studien* (1938). Begrich advanced the form critical analysis, especially regarding the oracle of salvation. His synthesis has influenced modern interpreters, among them Claus Westermann, author of the most widely used modern commentary (*Isaiah 40–66* OTL).

Form criticism was applied to Second Isaiah at a time when the question of unit length was very much in need of a solution and when methods for analyzing the formal rhetoric of the speeches had not been clearly worked out. In the absence of the ordinary criteria for judging unit length in the prophets—superscriptions, third-person accounts, episodes—scholars tended to rely heavily on genre to provide clues to the length of passages. They sometimes failed to realize that an original author like Second Isaiah might incorporate several genres within one speech. Form criticism, nonetheless, has proved to be an indispensable tool in understanding the world of Second Isaiah, particularly in showing how innovative the prophet was regarding the tradition. Apart from isolated voices, the method remained dominant until James Muilenburg's 1956 commentary (*IB* 5: 381–773) introduced rhetorical criticism as a consistent approach. Even now it is the most common approach. Muilenburg successfully showed in general, if not in every case convincingly, that the prophet used several forms in one speech as he used several meters, and that to assume the extent of the form is the extent of the unit is faulty methodology.

The chief source of Second Isaiah's genres was the liturgical poetry of Israel: laments and the attendant oracles of salvation, thanksgivings, hymns, Zion, and victory songs.

Individual laments are the most frequent of the Psalter genres. They typically portray a drama with three actors. The speaker, oppressed by the "workers of evil," cries out to God for redress of the situation. In communal laments, the speaker recites before Yahweh the event that founded Israel in order to persuade Yahweh not to let the original event be annulled; the version of the event varies according to the nature of the event. In 51:9–52:12 Second Isaiah adapts the communal lament in preaching to lead the community to pray for the restoration.

Second Isaiah made extensive use of one element of the psalmic lament, the *Heilsorakel,* or assurance of salvation, delivered to the individual or community during the lament liturgy. Good evidence exists that laments were answered by a cultic official promising that God had heard the appeal and would help. This hypothesis explains the sudden change of mood in laments, e.g., "I will give thanks to Yahweh according to his vindication. I will sing of the name of the Most High," in Ps 7:18. Some laments seem to contain the actual oracle, e.g., " 'Because the poor are despoiled, because the needy groan, now I will arise,' says Yahweh" (Ps 12:5, an individual lament; cf. Ps 60:6–8 for an oracle of salvation to a group lament). Usually, however, the Psalter does not transmit the assuring responses, since it was the priest's part. Several extrapsalmic passages also suggest official responses to laments, e.g., 1 Sam 1:17, the priest Eli to the weeping Hannah; Judg 20:23, 27; Josh 7:7–15; 2 Chr 20:3–17.

Begrich synthesized earlier suggestions in his *Studien* of 1938, in which he found twenty-four such oracles in Second Isaiah, prophetic imitations of priestly oracles. To the prophet, Yahweh was formally answering the exile's laments. An ideal structure can be abstracted: (1) the assurance of Yahweh's intervention (usually the subject is Yahweh and the verb is perfect); (2) clauses expressing the consequences of divine intervention and the reversal of the situation; and (3) the aim (the glory or acknowledgment of Yahweh). Westermann modified Begrich's conclusions, suggesting a distinction between oracles of salvation, given in response to individual laments, and proclamations of salvation, given in response to communal laments (*Isaiah 40–66* OTL, 13–15). Westermann proposed an ideal structure for his proclamation of salvation: (1) an allusion to the collective lament (e.g., "the poor and the needy are seeking water, there is none" [42:17]); (2) the proclamation of salvation: (a) God turns toward Israel; (b) God's intervention (specific, not general); and (3) the final goal. For Westermann, the proclamation of salvation is found only in Second Isaiah; unlike the oracle of salvation, which had a concrete *Sitz im Leben,* it is Second Isaiah's creation, born of his conviction that now God was responding to the communal lament of Israel. Antoon Schoors, who accepts the refinement of Westermann, proposes the following oracles of salvation: 42:8–13, 14–16; 43:1–4, 5–7; 44:1–5; 54:4–6, and the following proclamations of salvation: 41:17–20; 42:14–17; 43:16–21; 46:12–13; 49:7–12, 14:26; 53:1–6, 7–8, 9–14, 17–23; 54:7–10, 11–17; 55:1–5 (Schoors 1973: 38–45, 167–71). H. E. von Waldow's suggestion that the Deutero-Isaiah salvation oracles are real cultic oracles and not prophetic imitations of such oracles has not been widely accepted.

That Second Isaiah saw his prophecy responding to exilic laments is an extremely valuable insight, as is the noting of salvation and its goal. To many scholars, however, Westermann's distinction is too refined, and may grant the status of form to simple variations within a genre. Isa 55:1–5, for example, is not a proclamation of salvation but an invitation to a banquet, an amply attested genre in Ugaritic and in the Bible.

Moreover, the citation of Neo-Assyrian oracles to support the distinction between oracle and proclamation of salvation is perilous. Previous comparisons of Neo-Assyrian oracles have been excessively dependent on questionable translations of fragmentary and difficult texts; they cannot be used to provide OT parallels. In addition, prophecy is not attested in Babylonia. Extant texts are all northern, the products of the Neo-Assyrian religious world, which was quite different from the Neo-Babylonian world.

Other psalmic genres utilized by the prophet are less problematic. The thanksgiving, essentially a report of divine rescue, has been adapted in the fourth servant song (52:13–53:12). In the Psalms, the rescued and vindicated person tells the assembly, "the many," what God has done for him, in order that they too might praise God's mercy. In the song, "the many" speak of the rescue, whereas the rescued and vindicated person is silent. Hymns are also used by Second Isaiah. In 42:10–43:8 is an adapted song of victory, comparable to Psalms 93, 96, 97, 98, and 99; Psalms 96 and 98 are especially relevant, because of the nearly identical invitatory, of the role of Israel as witness, and of the call to the world, animate and inanimate, to ascribe the glory of victory to Yahweh alone. The victory is narrated by Yahweh in Second Isaiah. The most striking evidence of the genre in Second Isaiah is the hymnic participles, e.g., 42:5; 44:23, 28; 45:18–19; 46:10–11. Another category of Psalms drawn on in chaps. 40–55 is the Zion songs, e.g., Psalms 46, 48, and 76, which hail Zion as the impregnable divine dwelling, the site of Yahweh's self-disclosure, and the only proper gathering place of Israel. Zion songs are distinguished by their subject matter rather than their formal structure; their themes appear in 45:14–25; 49:14–26; 51:1–8; 51:9–52:12; 54; and 55.

A major genre in Second Isaiah from the secular world is the trial speech: 41:1–42:9; 43:9–44:5; 44:6–23; 45:21. Rebukes against Israel are sometimes included in the concept of the trial scene (*Isaiah 40–66* OTL, 15–17; Schoors 1973: 197–203), but such rebukes are without the specific call to judicial assembly. 41:1–42:9 is the most detailed account of the trial.

	A. 41:1–20	B. 41:21–42:9
Summons to trial	41:1, 5–7	41:21–22b
Legal questions to the nations/their gods	41:2–4	41:22c–29
Verdict on the nations and Israel	41:8–20	42:1–9

The whole world is summoned to a judicial proceeding, in which Yahweh is both judge and questioner. The Deutero-Isaiah polarities, Yahweh and the gods, Israel and the nations, are central. To the question of which deities are powering Cyrus' changing of the course of history, the other deities (in the person of their images carried by the nations) are silent. In contrast to the nations and the gods who rule them stands Israel and its God Yahweh. Israel is the witness to Yahweh's sole sovereignty by its reemergence as a people through its return to its homeland Zion.

The origin of the trial scene is not clear. Is it based upon the actual practice of "justice in the gate," i.e., daily legal practice, or is it a purely literary creation to give a cosmic dimension to the trial? The question cannot be answered with certainty. The genre may be an elaboration of a judgment such as that in Psalm 7, where the appeal of the afflicted one (the king?) includes the wish that the peoples assemble to see the vindication of God's favorite.

Second Isaiah often takes issue with opponents whose ideas are refuted point by point. These disputations are in 40:12–31; 45:9–13; 46:5–11; 48; and 49:14–26, among other places. Isaiah 40:12–31, a series of questions about who has created and now maintains the world, has its nearest parallel in Job 38–41. In Job, the questions are designed to sweep Job from his self-confidence and make him bow before the divine freedom and power. Second Isaiah has a number of affinities with Job; 40:12–31 is especially Joban.

There are other genres in Second Isaiah: a taunt song (chap. 47), an invitation to a holy place (chap. 55; cf. Psalms 15 and 24), the prophetic commission (40:1–11; cf. 1 Kgs 22:19–22; Isaiah 6). Chaps. 40–55, for all their originality, are grounded in the ancestral traditions.

E. The Message of Second Isaiah

1. Overview. Second Isaiah intends to persuade his fellow exiles that the time has come to leave Babylon and return to Jerusalem (Zion). His is a program, not a theology; ideas are arranged to persuade, not to make a system.

As an orator he gives his audience reasons to change their attitudes and to act. He must show that the ancestral traditions, to which all prophets appealed, contain an imperative for his day. For him, the tradition tells the people that Babylon with its false gods is doomed and Zion is about to be rebuilt and repopulated. Israel's journey to Zion will be a new Exodus-Conquest, a new participation in the defeat of chaos (= cosmogony).

Two problems make synthesizing his message difficult: the lack of scholarly consensus on the boundaries of Second Isaiah's speeches, and the vary nature of oratory. Scholars relying on form criticism usually find between 45 and 70 discrete units; the resultant units are generally too short to develop serious ideas. Moreover, form criticism as a method is disposed to concentrate on the typical and the recurrent rather than on the new and creative, and thus may underrate new syntheses. Rhetorical criticism, with its focus on texture and rhetorical development, is disposed to discern units of sufficient length for the development of ideas. J. Muilenburg, for example, isolates 21 lengthy compositions (*IB* 5: 381–773).

Beside the lack of scholarly consensus regarding the boundaries of the speeches, the nature of oratory itself, occasional and nonsystematic, makes it difficult to synthesize the prophet's message by simply summarizing each speech.

The prophet's own oratorical method offers the best way of systematizing his thought. It makes use of five major contrasts, or polarities, which are so pervasive that they can serve as a sketch of his message. They are: the two related polarities, the first and the last things, and Babylon and Zion; the two related polarities, Yahweh and the gods, and Israel and the nations; and finally, the servant and Israel. They are at once the substance of much of the oratory and the chief mode of development. They bear on both form and content. Using them as a guide to Second Isaiah's thought overcomes to some extent the divorce between content and expression.

2. The Five Polarities. a. First and Last Things. The polarity "first" and "last" has more than one meaning in Second Isaiah; it is a merism for eternity ("I, Yahweh, the first, with the last, I am he," 41:4); it can also be the words that predict the subsequent divine deed (41:22–23; 42:9; 43:9–13; 44:6–8; 45:21; chap. 48). A third meaning, "the first (deeds)," "the last (deeds)," expresses succinctly the central analogy of Second Isaiah: the first and the second Exodus-Conquest, the old and the new cosmogony. The clearest statement of the analogy is 43:16–21:

> 16Thus says Yahweh,
> the one who makes a way in Sea
> a path in the Mighty Waters.
> 17the One who musters chariot and horse,
> all the mighty army.
> They lie prostrate, no more to rise,
> they are extinguished, quenched like a wick.
> 18Recall no more the former things,
> the ancient events bring no longer to mind.
> 19I am now doing something new,
> now it springs forth, do you not recognize it?
> I am making a way in the wilderness,
> paths (*ntybwt* with 1QIsa[a]) in the desert.
> 20The wild beasts will honor me,
> jackals and ostriches.
> For I have placed waters in the wilderness,
> rivers in the desert,
> to give drink to my chosen people,
> 21The people whom I have formed for myself,
> to narrate my praiseworthy deeds.

Two statements are made: (1) historical events (the defeat of pharaoh, crossing the wilderness) are paralleled with suprahistoric, or mythic, events (making a path through the Waters by defeating the Sea, v 16; making a path through the desert by defeating sterility, vv 19–20); (2) the crossing of the desert replaces the crossing of the Red Sea and the defeat of pharaoh as the national story.

Though clearest in this text, the same historical analogy pervades Second Isaiah. In chap. 46, Yahweh is the one who carries Israel (the word "carry" echoes old texts like Exod 19:4 and Deut 32:11) of old from Egypt and now from Babylon. Isa 41:14–20 and 42:13–16 similarly allude to the old and the new Exodus. The passages 48:20–21 and 52:11–12 explicitly call upon Jews to leave Babylon, as their ancestors left Egypt. Chapter 49 puts the commission of the servant in the categories of Moses, imitating in vv 1–7 Moses' commission in Exodus 3–4, and in vv 8–12 Moses' leading the people and apportioning their land. The communal lament beginning in 51:9 recites the defeat of Rahab and the crossing of the sea (mixing historic and suprahistoric language) to persuade God to renew that founding event of defeating chaos and leading the Exodus. Isa 55:12–13 equates the trees that line the road through the wilderness with the twelve stones of the path through the Jordan in Josh 4:6–7; both commemorate Israel's crossing of territories belonging to hostile powers.

The analogy between the event that brought Israel into existence in days of old and the event that brings them into existence now is the central idea in Second Isaiah. It accounts for much of the drama in the chapters.

b. Babylon and Zion. Related to the great analogy between old and new founding events is the contrast between Babylon and Zion and Egypt and Canaan in the old tradition. Isa 48:20–21 and 52:11–12 exhort the Jews to leave Babylon in the words of the first Exodus, "Go forth from Babylon. . . . Water from the rock he made flow for them"; "Go out from her midst. . . . Do not go forth in haste" (reversing Exod 12:11). The seemingly odd picture of Zion rising in 40:9 makes sense as the antithesis of Babylon's descent in 47:1: "Get down, sit in the dust, Fair Maiden Babylon." From 44:24 to chap. 55, Zion is in the foreground; Babylon as mirror image provides depth to the portrait of Zion. Isa 45:14–25 speaks of the rebuilding of Zion, in contrast to the ruin of Babylon in chap. 47. In chap. 46 the gods are carried away from a doomed Babylon, whereas Yahweh carries Israel to safety. Zion receives back her husband Yahweh and her children in 49:14–26 and in 50:1–3; Babylon loses both in chap. 47. The concluding chaps. 54 and 55 are exclusively about Zion, a reminder of the centrality of place in the worship of Yahweh. Dominion is conceived spatially; Babylon is the land of servitude to non-gods, and Zion is the land of servitude to Yahweh. Israel must therefore leave Babylon and go to Zion. The polarity is designed to support Second Isaiah's program of action—leave doomed Babylon and go to renewed Zion.

c. Yahweh and the Gods. Like the previous two polarities, first event/last event and Babylon/Zion, the next two are closely related: Yahweh and the gods, and Israel and the nations. The contest between Yahweh and the gods occurs chiefly in the trial scenes, contained in the following sections: 41:1–42:9; 43:9–44:5; 44:6–23; 45:20–25. Also relevant are 40:12–31 and chap. 48. To be decided in the trial is not the mere existence of deities, but the question about which deity is the true patron of Cyrus, the Persian king, enabling him to change the shape of the world. Yahweh presides at the trial; he questions and renders the verdict.

The proof that Yahweh, not the other gods, empowers Cyrus is not simply that he predicts events before they happen, but that his word alone overcomes the chaotic forces threatening the populated world, enabling Cyrus to triumph. Such was the understanding of creation in Second Isaiah's world. Yahweh is the sole deity because he alone creates, he alone leads the Exodus.

Cyrus, the instrument of Yahweh's creation, is always mentioned in connection with cosmogony. He embodies the storm wind of Yahweh, "He makes [kings] like dust with his sword, like driven chaff with his bow. He chases them, he blows on unscathed, by road on foot he does not go" (41:3). He does the work of the divine molder, "he has trampled rulers like clay, like a potter kneading clay" (41:25). He builds the temple that celebrates creation (44:28) and is appointed as regent of the new order (45: 1–6).

Yahweh's unhindered word alone has effected all this; the other gods are silent (41:21–23, 25–26; 44:7). "Whatever Yahweh pleases, he does, in the heavens and on the earth, in the waters and on the deeps" (Ps 135:6).

d. Israel and the Nations. In the ANE, the ordinary means through which the god became present to human worshipers were images. The image represented the god on earth. Israelite law forbade statues as a means of encounter (e.g., Exod 20:4), a prohibition echoed in Second Isaiah, "I am Yahweh, that is my name; my glory I shall not give to another, my renown to carved images" (42:8). Unlike Israel, the nations ordinarily use images to represent their patron deities. In the two parallel trial scenes of 41:1–20 = 41:21–42:9, the statues that the nations bring to the trial represent their patron deities (41:5–7, 21–29). To Second Isaiah, the immobile and mute statues in fact represent the powerless deities only too well; the workers who made and carry them move and speak, but their deities/statues do not. In striking contrast to the mute deities and their frenetic worshipers is silent Israel and its active deity, Yahweh. In both scenes, Yahweh addresses Israel after questioning the nations (41:8–20 and 42:1–9) and commissions Israel to a new Exodus-Conquest. Israel by its action will embody Yahweh's glory. In both addresses the nations view Yahweh's action (41:20; 42:1, 4, 6).

The conception of Israel as the icon of God is most succinctly expressed in the term witness (Heb *ʿēd*), which is used three times of Israel witnessing to Yahweh's supreme power. In 43:9, the nations are challenged to bring forth witnesses to prove that they and their gods predicted the success of Cyrus, i.e., brought about his epochal victories by their word. "You are my witnesses," says Yahweh in vv 10 and 12; only Yahweh speaks words that effect action. The same scene is repeated in 44:6–9 and in 55:4–5. The preexilic kings' task of demonstrating Yahweh's power to the nations (cf. Pss 18:43–44; 89:9–27) is here assigned to all the people.

Israel is to witness by its act of participating in the Exodus-Conquest, the defeat of the desert. By its coming to life in the act, it will demonstrate to the nations that its God, Yahweh, lives and triumphs.

e. The Servant and Israel. The polarity between Israel and the servant is traditional in the OT; Second Isaiah exploits a familiar theme. The servants whom Yahweh chose often exemplified in their own lives the divine intent for all the people. Abraham and Jacob anticipated the people's adventures in the land; Jacob is even called Israel. Moses' flight from pharaoh and his encounter with Yahweh at Sinai anticipate the people's flight and divine encounter. Jeremiah in his "confessions" experienced in advance the divine punishment that was later to engulf the people. Isaiah and Ezekiel mimed the punishment that was to overtake the people. These servants represented what all Israel was called to be and do. All Israel becomes a servant when it embraces the divine will and plan as shown by the individual servants. When the people do not obey God's word, then the servant stands over against the people as a rebuke and as an invitation to conversion.

The servant in Second Isaiah is therefore at once a chosen individual and what all Israel is called to be and do. It is significant that Mosaic traits characterize the servant in 49:1–21; like Moses he is reluctant to accept the call, and he leads the people through the desert and apportions the land. Most scholars, following Duhm, distinguish the servant in the four servant songs from the servant in the rest of Second Isaiah; the servant in the songs is an individual, not Israel (though elsewhere the servant is Israel). Such a disjunction, in the light of the traditional relation of servant and people, sketched above, is questionable. The Duhm analysis nonetheless remains influential today.

3. The Servant. The word servant occurs twenty times in chaps. 40–55 (once in the plural). There is agreement that thirteen of the occurrences refer to Israel as the servant. The remaining seven occur in 42:1–4; 49:1–6; 50:4–9; 52:13–53:12, and the verses connected to them (45:5–7; 50:10, 11), the "servant songs" of B. Duhm. In these passages, according to Duhm, the servant is an individual, not Israel: "On the contrary, the hero of these poems is set over against the people, is innocent, Yahweh's disciple clearly enlightened by him, called to a mission to the people and to the gentiles and attending to his call in complete calm." The poems are probably from an author different from Second Isaiah and were inserted awkwardly in their present context (Duhm *Jesaia* HKAT, 311).

Scholars who see the servant of the songs as an individual distinct from Israel are not agreed on his or her identity. Virtually every important figure in the Bible—Moses, one of the prophets, or the kings, even Cyrus, or Second Isaiah himself—has been identified as the servant

(*IDB* 4: 292–94 and C. G. Kruse 1978: 3–27). For scholars who judge the poems to be integral to their contexts, the servant is the servant-prophet and Israel.

The servant exercises a role like that of the preexilic kings and especially prophets; royal and prophetic language is used of him. The role of the servant of Yahweh in the OT is a religio-political office; the servant is privy to the divine plan which he carries out and persuades the people to obey. The call of the servant in 49:1–6 imitates the call of Moses (Exodus 3–4 and Jer 1:4–10, itself modeled on Moses' call) and the related vv 8–12 describe the servant's Moses-like task of leading the people in the wilderness and apportioning to them the land. The reference to the servant as Moses is not surprising in view of the prominence of the new Exodus in chaps. 40–55. Servants, such as Moses, Joshua, the king of the Deuteronomic ideal (Deut 17:14–20), and the preexilic prophets, are models of obedience for Israel. In this sense, the servant can be at the same time an obedient friend of Yahweh and the nation. The obedient servant is what Israel is called to be. The servant can therefore be the witness to Yahweh's supremacy (42:1–4), called like Moses to embark on a new Exodus-Conquest (49:1–6), and submissive to the exilic punishment (50:4–11). In this view, the servant is the prophet himself and those who join him in his task. The question however is not settled.

Isa 52:13–53:12, the fourth servant song, remains especially controverted. Who is the servant, ideal Israel or a historical individual? Whose sins has he borne—the nations' or Israel's? What is meant by is vicarious suffering, otherwise unattested in the OT? The boundaries of the poem, and the genres that have influenced it—thanksgiving and confession—are generally agreed on, but consensus regarding the other questions has not been achieved.

Some observations can be made regarding the passage. Elsewhere in Second Isaiah, the nations are onlookers, the chorus rather than the protagonist. Hence, those whose sins are borne are likely the Israelites, not the nations. Secondly, the sins the servant has borne are not only the sinful acts of others but their consequences; Hebrew words for sin can designate both the act and its unhappy consequences. The ancestors have sinned, and the exiles are bearing the consequences. Now, however, Israel is invited back into existence through the new Exodus from Babylon to Zion. Many exiles were unwilling to undertake the journey. But as long as some of the people make the journey, the servant (and those allied with him), Israel comes into existence. "The many" who did not make the journey exist as Israel once more because of the servant's obedient act. When they see what the servant has done for them, they cry out that he has borne their sins, i.e., taken away the evil consequences of their refusal to go in the new Exodus. It is noteworthy that the servant's reward is life in the holy land (53:11–12; cf. 9:3). As long as the servant does the act, the whole people live again. The above interpretation is tentative, but it does have the merit of staying within OT categories.

Daniel 11:33–12:10 has been called the earliest interpretation of the fourth servant song. It interprets the Jewish loyalists of the Antiochene period in the 2d century B.C. as the servant of 52:13–53:12 (Ginsberg 1953: 100–4). The NT interpreted Jesus Christ as the Isaianic servant.

4. Creation. Second Isaiah differs from other prophets in his use of creation terminology. Verbs of creation abound: *baraʾ*, "to create" (16x); *yāṣar,* "to mold, shape" (14x); *ʿāśâ,* "to make" (24x); *pāʿal,* "to make" (5x); *nāṭâ šāmayim,* "stretch out the heavens" (6x); *rāqaʿ hāʾāreṣ,* "to spread out the earth" (2x); *kûn,* "to found" (1x); and *yāsad,* "to found" (1x). The objects of the verbs of creation are, variously: Israel, the physical world, the servant of Yahweh, "the new things," Cyrus, and Zion.

Scholarly interpretation of the meaning of creation in Second Isaiah varies according to scholars' definitions of creation and its relation to redemption (primarily the Exodus). All recent discussion has been influenced by Gerhard von Rad's 1936 article insisting that creation in the OT is joined closely to historical redemption and is subordinated to it. Consequently, the Exodus tradition can be enriched by references to Yahweh's creation of the world, but the two concepts are not on the same level; creation is subordinate to redemption. Westermann insists that the two are closely connected but do not merge; the polarity between the two is used to show that God's saving of his people "was, as it were, an island within the mighty universe of God's work as creator" (*Isaiah 40–66* OTL, 25). Other scholars distinguish in Second Isaiah creation of the world from creation of humans, finding the former in disputations (40:12–31; 45:18–19) and the self-prediction of 48:12–16, and the latter in the adapted oracles of salvation in 43:1–7, 14–15, 16–21; 44:1–5; 54:4–6, and in the warning in 44:21–22. The two themes are combined in several passages: 44:24–28; 45:9–13; 51:12–16 (Haag 1976: 193–203; Albertz 1974: 173–75).

To understand creation in Second Isaiah, one must recognize the important differences between ancient Near Eastern and modern Western conceptions of creation, or cosmogony. There are at least four important differences: the process, the product, the description, and the criteria for truth.

Ancient Near Eastern cosmogonies often involved personal wills in conflict. Typically, creation is portrayed as a series of acts in a drama: chaos or the threat of it, a battle between the gods and the forces of chaos resulting in the gods' victory, and celebration of the victory with kingship and temple. Both in the Ugaritic texts of late 2d-millennium Syria and in the Bible, the storm god (or Yahweh) tames the destructive power of sea or death-dealing desert. In contrast, moderns see creation as impersonal, evolutionary, and proceeding according to physical "laws."

A second major difference is the product, or emergent. For the modern, it is the physical world, usually the earth in the planetary system. Living organisms, if they figure in creation at all, are usually the most primitive forms of life; human culture is outside the purview of modern creation theories. In the ANE, on the other hand, what was produced was a *peopled* universe. The 2d-millennium Akkadian text *Enuma eliš,* often cited as the standard ANE cosmogony, is essentially the exaltation of Marduk, the founder of Babylonian society. Marduk defeats Tiamat and establishes his temple Esagila in Babylon so that he might receive the praise of his people. Another Akkadian account, *Atraḫasis,* tells of the balances that make human society possible. Genesis 1 tells how man and woman

(= society) are constituted by God's command to fill the earth and propagate their kind. Isa 42:5 puts it nicely:

Thus says the God Yahweh,
(who) creates the heavens and stretches them out,
who spreads out the earth and what it brings forth;
(who) gives breath to the people upon it,
spirit to those who walk upon it.

In the light of the above remarks, the scholarly distinction between creation of the world and the creation of man is artificial. The ancients were interested in the creation of the physical world primarily as an explanation for the human race or a particular people.

A third difference is a corollary of the first: cosmogony, being a conflict of wills, is naturally told as a drama. Modern creation accounts are impersonal and scientific.

Lastly, the criterion of truth differs according to the account used. For ancients, it is the dramatic plausibility of the story; the ancients had a tolerance for various versions of the same event. In Akkadian, different deities create, though it is usually Anu and Ea, occasionally Anu, Enlil, and Ea. In the Ugaritic texts, Baal or his consort Anat, combat Sea or Death. In the Psalms and in Second Isaiah, Yahweh's combat with Sea is told with varying details (cf. Pss 77:11–20; 89:9–14; 93; Isa 42:13–16; 50:23; 51:9–11). Modern accounts, being scientific, are subject as far as possible to verification and must be consistent and compatible with other likely hypotheses (Clifford 1985).

Ancient Near Eastern creation accounts tell how a structured society arose; biblical writers use them to describe the making or remaking of Israel. In Isa 43:16–21 is the clearest instance of a Deutero-Isaiah account of the creation of Israel. According to the passage, in the "former event," Yahweh defeated pharaoh's armies and Sea, which prevented Israel from coming into its divinely appointed territory. In the "something new," Yahweh destroys Desert's power to keep the people from Zion by making roads through it and by overturning its infertility. The new creation is the people, "the people whom I have formed for myself," enabled to give praise (vv 20–21). Creation and redemption language describe the same event—the movement from Babylon to Zion. The same mix of redemption and creation language is found in 51:9–11: "Was it not you who hacked Rahab [the primordial sea monster] in pieces . . . that the redeemed might cross?" Isa 41:14–20 commissions Israel itself to destroy the desert's obstructive power by crushing the mountains to powder, so that the divine wind may blow it away (vv 14–16); Yahweh then changes the desert's sterility to fertility that supports human life (vv 17–20).

The king's building of the temple to celebrate the god's world-creating victory is a theme in *Enuma elish* and in the Ugaritic texts. It is also prominent in Second Isaiah. Zion is to be rebuilt by Cyrus (44:24–45:13) and is to be a place of the festive banquet (chap. 55).

The word of God that predicts these things is a proof of divinity, not simply because it predicts the future accurately but because it is unhindered and effective; there are no deities to oppose it. It not only predicts but also invites participation (chap. 48). By participating in the cosmogony, Israel vanquishes the desert's sterility, proclaiming to the nations Yahweh's sole divinity.

Second Isaiah, therefore, does not refer to the "first creation" in Genesis as an argument that God can do today what he did then. He formulates creation differently. For him, it is one way of describing the act of remaking the people, the other being the redemption. Redemption, the Exodus-Entry into the land, and creation, the participation in the defeat of the desert and the rebuilding of the temple, are simply two modes of expressing the same event, the one suprahistoric (or mythic), the other historic.

Bibliography

Albertz, R. 1974. *Weltschopfung und Menschenschopfung untersucht bei Deuterojesaja, Hiob und in den Psalmen.* Stuttgart.

Begrich, J. 1938. *Studien zu Deuterojesaja.* BWANT 77. Stuttgart.

Bonnard, P.-E. 1972. *Le Second Isaïe: Son disciple et leurs editeurs Isaïe 40–66.* EBib. Paris.

Clifford, R. J. 1984. *Fair Spoken and Persuading: An Interpretation of Second Isaiah.* New York.

———. 1985. The Hebrew Scriptures and the Theology of Creation. *TS* 46: 507–23.

Eichhorn, J. G. 1803. *Einleitung in das alte Testament.* Vol. 3. Leipzig.

Friedlander, M., ed. 1873. *A Commentary of Ibn Ezra on Isaiah.* New York.

Ginsberg, H. L. 1953. The Oldest Interpretation of the Suffering Servant. *VT* 3: 400–404.

———. 1973. *The Book of Isaiah: A New Translation.* Philadelphia.

Gressmann, H. 1914. Die literarische Analyse Deuterojesajas (Kp. 40–55). *ZAW* 34: 254–97.

Haag, E. 1976. Gott as Schopfer und Erloser in der Prophetie des Deuterojesaja. *TTZ* 85: 193–213.

Kohler, L. 1923. *Deuterojesaja stilkritisch untersucht.* BZAW 37. Berlin.

Kooij, A. van der. 1981. *Die alten Textzeugen Jesajabuches.* OBO 35. Göttingen.

Kraus, H. J. 1982. *Geschichte der historisch-kritischen Erforschung des Alten Testaments.* 3d ed. Neukirchen-Vluyn.

Kruse, C. C. 1978. The Servant Songs: Interpretive Trends since C. R. North. *StudBT* 8: 3–27.

Melugin, R. 1976. *The Formation of Isaiah 40–55.* BZAW 141. Berlin.

Rogerson, J. 1984. *Old Testament Criticism in the Nineteenth Century: England and Germany.* Philadelphia.

Schoors, A. 1973. *I Am God Your Saviour: A Form-critical Study of the Main Genres in Is. XL–LV.* VTSup 24. Leiden.

Smith, S. 1944. *Isaiah Chapters XL–LV: Literary Criticism and History.* London.

RICHARD J. CLIFFORD

THIRD ISAIAH

Third Isaiah (TI) is the name given by scholars to the last eleven chapters of the book of Isaiah (56–66). The term is therefore primarily a literary one, analogous to the use of First Isaiah and Second Isaiah to designate chaps. 1–39 and 40–55, respectively. For those who argue that an essential unity exists within this final section of the book of Isaiah (Duhm *Jesaia* HKAT; Elliger 1928; Kessler 1960), Third Isaiah also refers to the prophet who authored the dozen or so separate pericopes within chaps. 56–66. A very rough consensus exists over the delimitation of these pericopes, going back to Duhm and Elliger; it is also shared in broad view by those who are unconvinced of the unity of Third Isaiah (Westermann *Isaiah 40–66* OTL; Pauritsch 1971; Hanson 1975; Sekine 1989): (1) 56:1–8; (2) 56:9–57:13; (3) 57:14–21; (4) 58:1–14; (5) 59:1–21; (6) 60:1–22; (7) 61:1–11; (8) 62:1–12; (9) 63:1–6; (10) 63:7–64:11; (11) 65:1–25; (12) 66:1–4; (13) 66:5–16.

A. Third Isaiah in Modern Scholarship
B. Historical Location
C. Social Location
D. Literary Analysis
E. The Future of Third Isaiah

A. Third Isaiah in Modern Scholarship

Karl Elliger, the early and by recent judgment methodologically sound proponent of the unity of TI (Sekine 1989: 8), used a careful literary and stylistic investigation to isolate these 13 pericopes and demonstrate TI's essential uniqueness vis à vis Second Isaiah. The latter argument was advanced by Elliger against those who wished to see no special break between Second and Third Isaiah chapters (all pre-Duhm interpreters; Sellin 1901; Cobb 1908), and it depended upon (by his own admission) a tedious isolation of linguistic terms and phrases reputed to be unique to TI (Elliger 1928: 57). The argument for unity was advanced against those who viewed 56–66 as coming from diverse prophetic hands and widely divergent periods, a much more broadly represented position at the time (Cheyne 1895; Cramer 1905; Kennet 1910; Budde *Jesaia* HSAT; Abramowski 1925). Elliger allowed a secondary hand in TI only at isolated intervals (56:3–8; 57:13c, 20; 58:13; 59:5–8, 21; 60:12, 17b; 65:20b; 66:17, 18–22, 23).

Partly because Third Isaiah is so bereft of concrete historical indicators, it has given rise to wide-ranging and speculative proposals as to historical and social location, from the preexilic period (for 56:9–57:13) to the late Hellenistic period (for 65; 66:3–24*), as being representative of theocratic ideals (Duhm), to their opponent in the name of inclusivity and apocalyptic fervor (Pauritsch 1971; Wallis 1971; Hanson 1975). Volz's 1932 commentary (*Jesaja* KAT) is a good example of the chronological approach at full throttle (oracles dated from the 7th to 3d centuries B.C.E.), though less extreme vestiges of the diachronic inquiry are to be seen in virtually all modern studies, which tend to place the bulk of TI in the late 6th or early 5th century. Westermann and Hanson are good popular representatives of the diachronic approach, despite their insistence that literary observations have fundamental priority over historical considerations.

Cobb pointed out quite early that the problems of specifically dating oracles in TI, where so little indication is provided of temporal location at the level of plain literary expression (Cobb 1908: 48–52). Beyond this, one wonders if a diachronic approach misunderstands its limits in TI when the literature does not emphasize new or radically altered historical circumstances, as is held to be the case when one moves from chaps. 40–55 to 56–66. Put in another way, the book of Isaiah consciously reacts to the temporal move accomplished when Assyrian period proclamation from Isaiah is stretched into a new Babylonian, post–587 B.C.E. framework, so that a formal break at chap. 40 can be seen in the literature's own portrayal (see article on "First Isaiah" above). It is difficult to note the same conscious move at work in the transition from 40–55 to 56–66. Factors other than altered temporal reference probably account for the changes encountered in these final eleven chapters, which make them distinctive from the preceding material in chaps. 40–55.

Elliger's 1928 monograph paid more meticulous attention to the literary side of the heavily religio-historical approach of Duhm, the creator of Third Isaiah. Duhm's TI functioned within his own special reconstruction of the postexilic period, as a figure absolutely distinct (*Jesaia* HKAT, 390) from Second Isaiah (SI), the theocratic forerunner of Ezra, for whom "sacrifice, the law, the sabbath, etc., were of highest concern" (*Jesaia* HKAT, 390). Compared with the poetry of SI, TI's proclamation has sunk into "versified prose." The popular modern view, which sees the TI chapters as attempting to extend the visionary message of a Babylonian Second Isaiah against theocratic opposition into the postexilic period (Hanson 1975; Pauritsch 1971), was not shared by Duhm. For Duhm (and the scholars of his day, including Ewald, Bunsen, Mowinckel, Hölscher, Marty, and Torrey), Second Isaiah was not active in Babylon; TI was, moreover, temporally quite distant from SI, working at a period long after the return from Exile.

Challenging Duhm on this latter front, Elliger moved TI to the period just before and after the restoration of the temple (ca. 515 B.C.E.), thereby allowing for a more intimate relationship to develop between TI and SI (1928: 111). A disciple or school relationship is reputed by many to exist between these two anonymous figures (Elliger 1933; Zimmerli 1950; Westermann *Isaiah 40–66* OTL). This is, by and large, the modern consensus, even when allowances are made for the internal inconsistencies found within chaps. 56–66 (especially over the treatment of foreigners, compare 56:3 and 60:10; 61:5–6). Passages which extend the message of SI are thought to be from the individual TI (Westermann *Isaiah 40–66* OTL); passages inconsistent with SI's thinking are the consequence of developments within the postexilic community toward a more apocalyptic orientation (Hanson 1975).

Hanson summarily rejects the search for authorship, opting for what he terms a contextual-typological approach, which plots increasing oppression and aligns portions of the text accordingly (1975: 41–46). Basic sociological questions remain. How "communities" compose texts, and in what conrete (i.e., other than ideological) setting, is not clarified. Moreover, the evolution from "classic prophecy" toward apocalyptic is not structured into the text, in its present form; rather, Hanson imposes the theory from outside the text's final arrangement and then extracts oracles and places them in their proper ideological and diachronic alignment. Why TI exhibits a certain final literary organization is not of particular importance to Hanson, since the final arrangement of the material nowhere supports his ideological theory.

B. Historical Location

The difficulty of dating oracles in TI has already been mentioned and is usually admitted by scholars at the start of their labors. Almost all feel that chaps. 56–66 are, in their entirety, later than 40–55. The exceptions are those who challenge the distinction between SI and TI altogether (Torrey 1928; Smart 1965); one scholar dated 56–66 earlier than 40–55 (McCollough 1948); Haran (1963) argued that chaps. 40–48 were composed by a prophet in Babylon and that chaps. 49–66 were composed by the same prophet upon his return to Palestine; Glahn's view (1934) is similar, but he maintains the traditional break at 40–55 and 56–66, while viewing both sections as oracles from the same prophet in different geographic settings. For those who regard unity within 56–66 as a fiction, the oracles are free to be placed at various points in the preexilic and postexilic periods, depending on one's view of postexilic ideology and poetic typology (Hanson), form- and tradition-critical development (Westermann), or larger thematic patterns within the book of Isaiah as a whole (Vermeylen 1978).

A forceful challenger of the TI hypothesis, Fritz Maass (1967), pointed to two chief facts in defense of TI's existence: the sense of extreme break one has immediately, in chap. 56 (and not nearly so extreme elsewhere), and the references to the temple, which pop up from time to time. Smart had already noted that 56:1–6 "is as alien in content to the author of 56:8 to 66 as to the author of 55–66" (Smart 1965: 230). In addition, it is difficult to know how to use the obscure references to the temple to date TI more specifically (compare 56:7; 60:13; 62:7; 63:18; 64:11). Westermann (p. 296) uses the reference at 60:13 to argue that the temple has not yet been built (see also his treatment of 63:15–64:11). Others see the argument over inclusion in chap. 56 as evidence that the temple is already standing and community life well under way, a view that is made possible in Westermann's model by his theory of levels of text development, ultimately carrying us into the period of the reforms of Ezra and Nehemiah (455 B.C.E.).

References to a completed temple, however, cannot resolve the problem of more specific dating in the postexilic community, as the disagreement between Duhm and Elliger, for example, highlights. Are we in the 5th-century world of Ezra-Nehemiah (Duhm), or the 6th-century world of Haggai-Zechariah (Elliger), or both (Westermann)? In every case, recourse must be made to a larger reconstruction of postexilic life, utilizing the internally contradictory and by no means perspicuous historical sources of Chronicles, Ezra-Nehemiah, Malachi, Haggai, and Zechariah. Ezra gives the closest thing to a straightforward account of the restoration of the temple; nonetheless, the difficulty of its use as a historical source is everywhere admitted. Malachi provides, at best, oblique assistance in reconstructing postexilic life. The date provided by Haggai and Zechariah for the consecration of the temple (2d year of Darius) is not consistent with that given by Ezra (Darius' 6th year, Ezra 6:15); nor is there a complete and consistent depiction in our sources of the return of exiles from Babylon.

Perhaps the most obscure area of knowledge concerns life within the Israelite community not deported—surely the largest population group, and one we know to have existed as a worshipping community during the exilic period from various incidental references (Zech 7:5; Jer 41:5; book of Lamentations). It is one of the ironies of historical analysis in biblical studies that while skepticism over historical veracity rules in one part of the canon, other literary witnesses are accorded absolute historical reliability; the nature and dosage of selectivity is what produces different results. Barstad (1982) has recently reminded us just how fragile is the picture of massive deportation to Babylon and total evacuation from Palestine—a picture given us by Chronicles and Ezra-Nehemiah and one which is absolutely necessary for most Second Isaiah in Babylon and Third Isaiah in Palestine theories.

It must be determined whether the theory of TI turns exclusively on too tidy a view of the destruction of the temple and its subsequent restoration. In this light it should be remembered that if chaps. 56–66 are read more narrowly in the context of the book of Isaiah, as against their putative diachronic neighbors Haggai, Zechariah, Malachi, and Ezra-Nehemiah, a very different picture of the role of the temple emerges; for nowhere in Isaiah is the destruction of the temple explicitly related. Rather, what we have is a depiction of God's judgment over the cosmos and the nations (Isaiah 13–27), and the proclamation of a thorough cleansing of Zion, resulting in a completely new state of affairs (2:1–5; 12:1–6; cf. 65:17–25). In other words, the fall of the temple and its restoration, as such, are not meaningful literary, historical, or theological indexes in Isaiah.

What is important is God's cleansing of Zion and its reestablishment (1:24–31; 2:1–5; 11:6–9; 27:12–13; 35:1–10)—matters that are depicted independently of the fate of the temple, which was more narrowly conceived (receiving virtually no discussion in chaps. 1–39). Along this axis, the decisive break in the book of Isaiah is located at chap. 40—not at chap. 56—following the clear hint in chap. 39 that the Babylonians are God's agents of cleansing judgment. The full restoration of Zion is nowhere identified in Isaiah—in any of its sections—with the literal restoration of the temple. Consequently, one wonders if undue stress has been laid upon the restoration of the temple as an important historical datum in differentiating Second from Third Isaiah. It is quite possible that chaps. 40–55 treat different *aspects* of the restoration of Zion than do chaps. 56–66, which demonstrate special interest in the requirements for membership in God's Zion. But then the sharp distinction drawn between these sections on historical grounds falls away. The distinction becomes thematic and theological, and it does not necessitate separation along Babylonian/Palestinian, exilic/postexilic, or visionary prophet/disillusioned community lines (Hanson 1986: 153–59). If one adds to these considerations the possibility that SI was not a Babylonian prophet (Barstad 1982; Duhm; Torrey 1928; Smart 1965), then any significant break at chap. 56 is completely unwarranted.

That this type of objection has not been registered is witness to the hegemony of a fixed form of diachronic analysis which refuses to take the literary context of the book of Isaiah as a meaningful guide to exegesis, preferring instead to line up these (historically) obscure chapters with equally obscure references in other biblical literature judged to be contemporaneous. That disagreement continues to exist among scholars over key features in the historical background of TI is testimony to the level of speculation required when historical analysis is forced to work in such shallow waters. The plausibility that the biblical sources are in fact capable of integration for thorough historical reconstruction is also never challenged.

What if the books of Isaiah and Ezra-Nehemiah present different, even historically incompatible, pictures of restoration? On the other hand, what if the differences are aspectual and not substantive, resulting from different emphases within the literary presentation of each given witness, to be read independently of each other? In scholars' zeal for reconstructing historical circumstances as the necessary prerequisite for proper exegesis, these sorts of considerations have not been popular.

In sum, the possibility exists that factors other than changed historical circumstances may account for the different literary and theological emphases at work in TI, compared with SI. This would also raise questions about the propriety of language comparisons and theories of master (SI) and disciple (TI) which attempt to explain the balance of distinctiveness and borrowing often noted in chaps. 56–66 (Zimmerli 1950). If the differences in language are the consequence of differences in content and the subject matter handled, then a sharp break at chap. 56, on grounds of a new prophetic voice or clearly changed historical circumstances, is unfounded.

C. Social Location

Most have seen behind at least a portion of the chapters of TI an actual prophet at work, analogous to SI and, like him, also anonymous. Form and tradition critics have tended to draw a picture of the prophet as oral speaker, and the prophet TI generally is accepted into this category. Duhm, adamant in his insistence that Israel's prophets were primarily speakers, not writers (1875: 203–4), spoke of TI as a *Schriftsteller* whose proclamation was best described as "versified prose" (HKAT, 390–91). Duhm felt that prophecy underwent certain fundamental changes (not improperly categorized as decadent) in the later years of the postexilic period. TI was a representative of these changes.

Duhm was not more specific about the social location of TI's activities. A similar vagueness marks most form- and tradition-critical investigations. If the prophet is considered an oral speaker, then he presumably exercises the same freedom of movement as did his preexilic forebears, and no further social location is stipulated. Westermann has rightly noted the existence in chaps. 56–66 of fixed tradition, utilized at a redactional stage in the final literary development of TI chapters, thus holding in appropriate tension form- and redactional-critical observations. So, for example, chaps. 59 and 63, which surround the core TI proclamation (chaps. 60–62), are for Westermann "genuine community laments," not compositions of TI, and "their birth-place was Israel's worship" (OTL, 300). Similarly, the long unit 56:9–57:13 is comprised of three oracles of judgment, borrowed from the preexilic period, drafted to serve a redactional purpose in TI.

Westermann's TI is a prophet analogous to the classical prophets of the preexilic period; TI as a literary product, however, includes fixed forms of literature from a variety of social contexts, most notable among them being contexts of worship. This accords well with the generally accepted view that another piece of literature of the period, the book of Lamentations, finds its home as well in the worship life of the exilic period. It would be no surprise if TI as prophetic figure was to be sought within the cultic life of the exilic or immediate postexilic period. As we have noted, there are several references to the worship life of Israel during the exilic period in the biblical sources; prophets are increasingly active within Israel's cult in the postexilic period (Petersen 1977); cult prophecy would explain the use of traditional material within TI. Prophecy in such a social context would involve both exegesis of existing prophetic material and independent prophetic proclamation modeled on Israel's early prophets Amos, Hosea, Jeremiah, or Isaiah, all set within the context of Israel's worship life. This would explain (1) the present inclusion of TI material within the larger book of Isaiah, (2) the rightly noted presence in TI of themes and language not just from SI (Zimmerli 1950) but from First Isaiah as well (Vermeylen 1978: 504–5), and (3) the clear similarity between SI and TI chapters and the Psalter. It is by no means clear that SI (and TI) ought to be sought, apart from the cultic proclamation of the exilic period, in Judah proper; if this (minority) view proved true, then the separation of SI from TI on other than thematic grounds would be even less warranted.

Hanson has not sought a more specific social location for a prophet TI, since the authorship/individual prophet question is set to the side in his reconstruction. The oracles are seen simply as representative of ideological positions becoming increasingly apocalyptic. This ideational emphasis gives the TI material a certain weightlessness, in terms of precise social location.

The work of Pauritsch (1971) should be mentioned at this juncture, since the classic search for *Sitz im Leben* is one of his chief concerns. He develops the intriguing theory that TI is a collection of traditions originating in the immediate postexilic period. In its present (redacted) form, it was meant to serve as a response to the question of a delegation from Babylon, put to community leaders in Judah, as to whether eunuchs and foreigners should be included in the congregation (56:3–8). Using the oracles of TI, and new tradition, the prophetic redactor answers affirmatively and emphasizes that God is on the side of the poor and those who tremble at his word (66:2). The passage in Isa 56:1–6 serves as a kind of motto for the whole collection and is its interpretive key; the final chapter (66) reiterates the main themes of the opening unit in such a way that chaps. 56 and 66 act as bookends, now enclosing two sections with roughly the same number of verses (56–60; 62–66) and a central core (chap. 61). Pauritsch finds diverse elements of tradition, from various backgrounds (wisdom, cultic, prophetic) in TI, and therefore rejects a single *Sitz im Leben* and a single prophetic voice; nevertheless, in Pauritsch's reading there is one fairly consistent message from TI in its present literary form. A refinement of his position, with similar emphasis on TI as anti-cult, can be seen in the work of Wallis (1971).

Several objections come to mind with this type of analysis. First, the specification of the occasion and the use to which TI is put weigh against the theory as too speculative and overdrawn. Second, the presence of wisdom elements in TI should not seriously call into question a possible cultic setting for the material in its entirety (cf. wisdom psalms, priestly instruction). Third, the complexity of TI's overall message is flattened by too tightly linking it to a program for inclusion that theoretically is aimed at setting aside the legislation of Deut 23:2–9 (the same criticism applies to Westermann, *Isaiah 40–66* OTL, 311–16; Sekine 1989: 31–42). To be sure, TI does envision new participants in the assembly, but this is in full accord with statements found elsewhere in the book of Isaiah; it is not aimed exclusively at countermanding the Deuteronomic legislation. Note (1) the different terminology used in TI (Heb *ben-hannēkār; hassārîs*) and Deuteronomy (Heb *pĕṣûaᶜ-dakkāʾ ûkĕrût šopkâ;* "the Ammonite and Moabite"), (2) the complexities within the respective contexts (Deuteronomy's favorable inclusion of the Edomite [23:6] and TI's use of Edom as paradigm for Yahweh's foes [63:1–6]), and (3) the heavy emphasis on allegiance to Yahweh found in TI ("the foreigner *who joins himself to the Lord*"; "the eunuchs *who keep my sabbaths, choose what delights me, and hold fast my covenant*"). All this suggests something less than the attempt to cancel previously binding legal injunctions as the chief agenda of TI. The differences between TI and Deuteronomy over this issue are contextual and are not as substantive as those zealous for spotting tension would have us believe (Donner 1983).

Moreover, foreigners continue to exercise a role, developed in both First (2:3; 18:7; 19:19–22; 23:17–18) and Second Isaiah (45:14–17, 20–25; 49:22–26), that involves the vindication of Israel and the nations' acknowledgment of the authority of Yahweh as the one God (60:3–14; 61:5–6; 62:2–3; 63:6; 64:2; 66:18–21), if not their humiliation and debasement. The consistent interest in proper attention to cultic requirements and the sanctuary, or punishment for their abrogation, lack of care for Zion, uncleanness, iniquity, and idolotry, spans all chapters (56:2, 4, 7; 57:3–10; 58:13; 59:2; 60:7, 13; 61:6; 62:9; 63:18; 64:6, 11; 65:2–7; 66:3–4, 24) and suggests that attempts to interpret TI as a universalist or fierce inclusion advocate against cultic leaders (Hanson; Pauritsch; Wallis) overstate the literary evidence. In this instance, the picture of TI's originator, B. Duhm, seems more accurate, whereby TI is one concerned with cultic purity, the proper restoration of Zion, the Sabbath, and proper sacrifice. For these reasons, it would be more appropriate to locate TI in a cultic setting, exegetically extending the vision of First and Second Isaiah regarding the nations, while at the same time defending the holiness of Zion and the requirements of proper worship, first for Israel and then by extension for the nations who come to worship Yahweh (see also Sekine 1989: 236–37).

D. Literary Analysis

We have had occasion to note above the various literary methods that have been used to analyze TI chapters. Following Duhm's initial efforts, which are best characterized as a combination of literary-poetical, historical, and crude sociological investigation, scholars developed either the historical (Budde, Kennett, Volz) or the literary (Elliger) sides of his project. Even in a primarily literary and stylistic work like that of Elliger, questions of social and temporal location were not forgotten. It was the order of inquiry that determined the priorities of the interpreter.

Form-critical work occupied itself with the proper delimitation of oral units in TI. Alongside this went the determination of secondary and later glosses and the plotting of levels of the text as they found their place in TI. Westermann's study is a model of form and tradition-critical analysis. A TI nucleus is to be found in chaps. 60–62, set in the framework of two community laments located in chaps. 59 and 63. Other material original to TI is to be found in 57:14–20; 65:15b–25; and 66:1–16. The message of TI is "salvation and nothing but salvation" (*Isaiah 40–66* OTL, 296), in Westermann's view, thus linking him closely with a SI for whom such proclamation was standard fare. The prophet TI reveals something of himself in chaps. 61 and 62, in first-person speech reminiscent of 49:1–6 and 50:4–9.

Editorial work is most evident in the beginning and ending units (56:1–8 and 66:18–24). Independent utterances and additions are made at various points, emphasizing the "cleavage between the devout and the faithful" (*Isaiah 40–66* OTL, 307). Westermann claims that TI's altogether friendly attitude toward foreign nations has been altered by judgment additions in 60:12; 63:1–6; 66:6, 15–20*. Apocalyptic material has also been added to the salvation oracles in 60–66.

Though Hanson's analysis differs over details and larger conceptual perspective, a similar view of levels within the literature, moving toward the apocalyptic away from the visions of SI, is to be found in Hanson's work. To his credit, Westermann still operates within a traditional picture of prophecy in which questions of authorship, redaction, and situation-in-life are handled systematically. Moreover, in Westermann's work one begins to see an attempt to come to grips with the text in its present literary organization, as he wrestles with trying to explain why TI chapters are arranged as they are. Nothing of this kind of literary inquiry animates the work of Hanson. In this sense, it is fair to say that Westermann's form-critical analysis clearly anticipates redactional and rhetorical studies produced in the last two decades (Pauritsch 1971; Sehmsdorf 1972; Polan 1986; Sekine 1989).

The most recent redaction-critical investigation is that of Sekine (1989), who seeks to challenge Elliger's argument for literary and authorial unity in TI, a position Sekine respects and feels has never been sufficiently set aside on primarily literary grounds. Sekine establishes through minute analysis a clear redactional hand at work in TI, particularly in opening and closing chapters. He avoids the tendency to reduce the complexity of TI by seeing the message of the book as predominantly anticultic, though in individual sections this is the reading he isolates for the final redactional hand. While Sekine's primary interest is in separating out redactional layers and establishing their distinctive theological viewpoints, he concludes his labors with an analysis of TI in its present literary organization (1989: 228–33). In so doing, he puts forth the implicit argument that the final form of the material presents a message that, while redactionally complex, is nevertheless coherent on literary and theological grounds.

E. The Future of Third Isaiah

Sekine's modest efforts in the direction of post-redactional synthesis may represent the future of TI analysis. Rhetorical studies (Polan 1986) likewise seek to identify indications of final structure and larger literary shape, though frequently without prior inquiry into the text's depth-dimension, redactional analysis, or a serious probe into the historical and social worlds that spawned the material.

The remarks above have been sufficient to indicate that one fruitful area of future TI research will include an analysis of the exegetical relationship between chaps. 56–66 and First and Second Isaiah sections, as well as a determination of the role TI plays in the final redactional shape of the book of Isaiah as a whole. Have the indications of historical, literary, and sociological cleavage between chapters 40–55 and 56–66 been overplayed in the interest of pursuing one type of diachronic analysis? Are the differences between Isaiah 40–55 and 56–66 explicable on other grounds? Are there indications of clear linkage between these two sections which do not depend upon a Babylonian prophet and Palestinian disciple model of interpretation but are rather the consequence of a far greater common purpose in authorial, redactional, and theological intention?

To take one example, to what extent is the first-person (nondivine) voice in SI distinct from that found in TI, and what would prevent one from seeing essentially the same prophetic voice at work in both sections (e.g., 48:16c; 49:1–6; 50:4–9; 61:1–4)? Second, Westermann has overplayed the notion that SI and nuclear TI sections are predominantly salvation oracles. SI contains material that reflects internal community debate (42:18–20; 43:22–24; 44:25; 45:9–13; 46:12–13; 48:22; 50:10–11; 54:15–17), especially when one includes the persistent exhortation that marks SI; it is difficult to see how distinct the TI material is on this score. Israel's flirting with idolotry is condemned in both sections, (see 41:5–7; 44:9–20; 45:20; 48:3–5), although the tendency has been to see that most of the idolotry condemned in SI is that of Babylon or foreign nations.

Finally, and most importantly, it is by no means clear that SI should be distinguished from TI on the basis of the state of the temple. Trying to link references to the walls of Jerusalem in TI to similar references in Ezra-Nehemiah for historical purposes is a highly speculative enterprise, especially when the historical value of biblical sources from this period is itself a thorny problem (see the most recent attempts of Sekine [1989] to fix the *Wirkungszeit* of individual passages in TI). The same is true of references to the temple, which at times seem to suggest a finished structure (56:7) but at other points clearly state that something is yet unfinished (61:4) and that the condition of the temple is quite desperate (64:10–11). The issue is complicated because we do not know the exact state of the temple in the exilic period, whether that state prevented its usage, or whether such matters are specifically of concern to TI. What we do know is that both SI and TI see the restoration of Zion as involving God's full presence, and that the community stands just before the full enactment of that event. In that sense, it is wrong to think of the full restoration of the temple as some clear and significant past event in the background of TI.

The burning question for TI, and one which the final chapter continues to pose, is whether the community and the nations that join them are worthy to stand when God appears and Zion is restored. Can Zion be fully restored, as earlier chapters in Isaiah had promised, given the state in which Israel as a community stands? Can Israel's people be fully the servants of God? The answer the final chapter gives is, *Yes* (66:12–14). At the same time it refuses to relax the judgment that accompanies God's holy presence (66:15–16). The final warning of 66:24 indicates the seriousness with which God punishes rebellion, and on that note the Isaiah collection is drawn to a close. Now the nations are to share with Israel the mercy—and the holy judgment—that comes with the knowledge and presence of Israel's God.

Bibliography

Abramowski, R. 1925. Zum literarischen Problem des Tritojesaja. *TSK* 96–97: 90–143.

Barstad, H. 1982. Lebte Deuterojesaja in Judäa? *NorTT* 83: 77–87.

Cheyne, T. K. 1895. *Introduction to the Book of Isaiah.* London.

Cobb, H. W. 1908. Where was Isaiah XL–LXVI Written? *JBL* 27: 48–64.

Cramer, K. 1905. *Der geschichtliche Hintergrund der c. 56–66 im Buche Jesaja.* Dorpat.

Donner, H. 1983. Jes 56, 1–7: Ein Abrogationsfall innerhalb des Kanons—Implikationen und Konsequenzen. *VTSup* 36: 81–95.

Duhm, B. 1875. *Die Theologie der Propheten als Grundlage für die innere Entwicklungsgeschichte der israelitischen Religion.* Bonn.

Elliger, K. 1928. *Die Einheit des Tritojesaia (Jesaia 56–66).* Stuttgart.

———. 1933. *Deuterojesaja in seinem Verhältnis zu Tritojesaja.* Stuttgart.

Glahn, L. 1934. *Der Prophet der Heimkehr.* Giessen.

Hanson, P. D. 1975. *The Dawn of Apocalyptic.* Philadelphia.

———. 1986. *The People Called: The Growth of Community in the Bible.* San Francisco.

Haran, M. 1963. The Literary Structure and Chronological Framework of the Prophecies in Is. XL–XLVIII. *VTSup* 9: 127–55.

Kennett, R. H. 1910. *The Composition of the Book of Isaiah in the Light of History and Archaeology.* Schweich Lectures 1909. London.

Kessler, W. 1960. *Gott geht es um das Ganze. Jesaja 56–66 und Jesaja 24–27 übersetzt und ausgelegt.* BAT 19. Stuttgart.

Maass, F. 1967. "Tritojesaja"? Pp. 153–63 in *Das Ferne und Nahe Wort.* BZAW 105. Berlin.

McCullough, W. S. 1948. A Re-examination of Isaiah 56–66. *JBL* 67: 27–36.

Pauritsch, K. 1971. *Die neue Gemeinde: Gott sammelt Ausgestossene und Arme (Jesaia 56–66).* AnBib 47. Rome.

Petersen, D. 1977. *Late Israelite Prophecy.* SBLMS 23. Missoula, MT.

Polan, G. J. 1986. *In the Ways of Justice Toward Salvation: A Rhetorical Analysis of Isaiah 56–59.* American University Studies 7/13. Frankfurt.

Sehmsdorf, E. 1972. Studien zur Redaktionsgeschichte von Jesaja 56–66. *ZAW* 84: 517–76.

Sekine, S. 1989. *Die Tritojesajanische Sammlung (Jes 56–66) redaktionsgeschichtlich untersucht.* BZAW 175. Berlin.

Sellin, E. 1901. *Studien zur Entstehungsgeschichte der jüdischen Gemeinde nach dem babylonischen Exil.* Leipzig.

———. 1930. Tritosjesaja, Deuterojesaja und das Gottesknechtsproblem. *NKZ* 41: 73–93, 141–73.

Smart, J. D. 1965. *History and Theology in Second Isaiah.* Philadelphia.

Torrey, C. C. 1928. *The Second Isaiah.* New York.

Vermeylen, J. 1978. *Du prophète Isaïe à l'apocalyptique.* Vol. 2. Paris.

Wallis, G. 1971. Gott und seine Gemeinde. Eine Betrachtung zum Tritojesaja-Buch. *TZ* 27: 182–200.

Zimmerli, W. 1950. Zur Sprache Tritojesajas. *Schweizerische Theologische Umschau* 20: 110–22. Repr., pp. 217–33 in *Gottes Offenborung*. Munich, 1963.

CHRISTOPHER R. SEITZ

ISAIAH, MARTYRDOM AND ASCENSION OF. A pseudepigraphic work containing both Jewish and Christian elements. It divides naturally into two sections: chaps. 1–5, generally called the *Martyrdom of Isaiah,* and chaps. 6–11, known as the *Vision of Isaiah.* The *Mart. Is.* contains further a distinct unit, 3:13–4:22, which is often called the *Testament of Hezekiah.*

The work is extant in its entirety only in Ethiopic. There exist also Greek and Latin fragments of the textual tradition represented by the Ethiopic version. A second textual tradition, containing only chaps. 6–11, is represented by a second Latin translation and a Slavonic version. There are also Coptic fragments, as well as a Greek legend, which is based on a Greek text of the first type, but in which the story has been rewritten significantly. Most scholars agree that the *Martyrdom* was composed in Hebrew. It was then translated into Greek, which served as the basis for the extant versions. The Christian sections (*Vis. Is.* and *T. Hez.*) were probably composed in Greek.

Most scholars agree that the *Mart. Is.* was composed by a Jew in Palestine no later than the 1st century C.E. The legend behind the book, if not the book itself, may be considerably older.

The composite nature of the work is confirmed both on internal and external grounds. First, chaps. 1–5 and 6–11 are each a self-contained unit. Chaps. 1–5 provide a legendary account of Isaiah's martyrdom at the hands of Manasseh. Chaps. 6–11 describe a visionary journey of Isaiah during the reign of Hezekiah. Not only are the sections out of chronological order, but, as noted above, one major textual tradition contains only chaps. 6–11. Furthermore, chaps. 1–5 are strongly Jewish, and chaps. 6–11 are clearly Christian. Second, 3:13–4:22 also seems to be a self-contained unit. It disrupts the narrative with a Christian section which seems out of character with the rest of the story. Debate on this section has centered on the question of whether it existed at one time independently, and specifically whether it was part of a now-lost *Testament of Hezekiah.* Although the issue has not been settled, the "Testament of Hezekiah" has become a convenient title for this section. The presence of smaller Christian interpolations in chaps. 1–5 indicates that although the composite character of the *Martyrdom and Ascension of Isaiah* can be seen in a broad sense, the precise nature of the final Christian redaction is not clear. A few scholars have even suggested that the entire work is, in fact, a unified Christian composition, but their arguments have not been persuasive.

The *Martyrdom* begins with King Hezekiah summoning his son Manasseh in the presence of the prophet Isaiah and Josab the son of Isaiah. As Hezekiah instructs his son, Isaiah predicts Manasseh's apostasy and his own death at Manasseh's hands. When Manasseh becomes king, Isaiah's prophecy begins to be fulfilled. Isaiah withdraws to a mountain in the company of some other prophets. The false prophet Belkira learns of this and accuses Isaiah before Manasseh, who arrests Isaiah and has him sawn in half. The narrative, based loosely on several OT books, is striking in its affirmation that Isaiah was martyred by being sawn asunder. This tradition is not found in the OT, but it is recorded (with different details) in the Babylonian and the Jerusalem Talmuds. It is also reflected in the *Lives of the Prophets* (1st century C.E.) and in several patristic writers, and apparently stands behind Heb 11:37.

Also noteworthy is the demonology of the *Mart. Is.* The leader of the evil host is given several different names, most frequently Sammael, Beliar, and Satan. The strong dualism of this section has suggested to some scholars that the *Mart. Is.* is a product of the Qumran community, which shared a dualistic outlook (Flusser 1953, Philonenko 1967). Indeed, a few have even argued that the narrative reflects the early history of the community and its founder, the Teacher of Righteousness. But such arguments are highly speculative, and it should be noted that not only are the distinctive theological emphases of the Qumran community absent from the *Mart. Is.,* but there have been no fragments of the Martyrdom found among the Qumran scrolls.

Between Isaiah's arrest and martyrdom comes the *Testament of Hezekiah* (3:13–4:22). This section describes a previous vision of Isaiah, which consists of four parts. The first part concerns the coming of the Beloved and the establishment of the church. Although some of the details are similar to the NT gospel accounts, especially Matthew, others—e.g., the Beloved's descent from/ascent to the seventh heaven (cf. *Ap. Jas.* 8–9); his transformation into the form of a man; the descent of the angel of the church; the role of the Holy Spirit and Michael in the resurrection, hoisting the Beloved onto their shoulders (cf. *Gos. Pet.* 10); the call to believe in the cross (cf. *Ap. Jas.* 6)—are different.

The second part of the *T. Hez.* describes the corruption of the church at the end of time. The key focus here is on the leaders of the church, the "elders" and the "shepherds," who are castigated for their worldliness and contentiousness and who will become so influential as to render ineffective the few remaining prophets.

The third part of the *T. Hez.* deals with the end-time reign of Beliar. He bears a strong resemblance to the Beast of Revelation 13, but the Neronic characterization is made more explicit here. Beliar's royal and miracle-working roles are emphasized, as well as his claim to deity. He will rule for 1335 days (cf. Dan 12:12), during which time he will persecute the "plant" (i.e., church). The few who remain faithful will flee as they await the coming of Jesus.

The final part of the *T. Hez.* depicts the coming of the Lord and the Final Judgment. Although there are strong parallels to Revelation 19–20, again there are significant differences. The most striking is the description of what happens to the saints. Those saints who have been reclothed with robes from the seventh heaven (i.e., those who have died) will descend with the Lord to strengthen those who are still alive and to serve in the world for an indefinite time. Afterwards, the rest of the saints will receive robes from above and will leave their bodies in this world. The *T. Hez.* concludes with a relatively lengthy section (added by the final redactor?) linking this vision with the canonical book of Isaiah, the OT Psalms and Proverbs, the Minor

Prophets, Daniel, and, apparently, the Jewish pseudepigraphon known as the *Prayer of Joseph*.

The Christian perspective behind the *Testament of Hezekiah* is a fascinating blend of traditions both "canonical" (especially Matthew and Revelation) and "extracanonical" (e.g., *Gospel of Peter, Apocryphon of James*). The freedom with which the traditions are handled and mixed, coupled with matters such as the relatively primitive portrait of the church hierarchy and the strong Nero *redivivus* emphasis, suggest a late 1st century or early 2d century C.E. date. The distinctive Christology, along with the strong criticism of ecclesiastical leaders, might point to a "heterodox" community as that which produced the Testament.

The *Vision of Isaiah* narrates Isaiah's ascent through the seven heavens (cf., e.g., *Testament of Levi, 2 Enoch, 3 Baruch*). Like the *Mart. Is.*, the *Vis. Is.* begins with Isaiah and his son Josab in the presence of King Hezekiah. Many other dignitaries are present, along with a number of prophets. In the midst of this assembly, Isaiah receives a vision, which he then recounts to Hezekiah, Josab, and the prophets. First, an angel appears to Isaiah in order to take him on a journey. As he ascends, Isaiah views the struggle, led by Sammael, on earth. As he passes through the first five heavens, he sees and hears angels singing praises to the One who sits in the seventh heaven, with the glory increasing at each level. For the last two heavens, Isaiah is first taken into the "air" of the heaven before entering the heaven itself. In the air of the sixth heaven, the angel prepares him for his final ascent and what he is about to see. In the sixth heaven, which is significantly more glorious than the first five, Isaiah and his guide join the angels in praising the Father, his Beloved, and the Holy Spirit. In the air of the seventh heaven, the head angel of the sixth heaven attempts to prevent Isaiah from ascending any higher, but the voice of Christ permits him to proceed.

Isaiah then ascends to the seventh heaven, where he sees a wonderful light, innumerable angels, and all the righteous from Adam onwards, stripped of their flesh and clothed in robes from above. The angel predicts for Isaiah the descent of the Beloved into the world, his crucifixion and resurrection, and his remaining in the world for 545 days before his ascent back to the seventh heaven. Central to the prediction is the emphasis that the Beloved's true identity is concealed even from "the god of that world" who puts him to death (cf. Ign. *Eph.* 19). Isaiah next sees the books which record the deeds of the children of Israel, and many robes, thrones, and crowns, which are reserved for those who will believe in the words of the Beloved and in his cross. Isaiah then sees and worships the Lord (i.e., Christ), the Holy Spirit, and the Great Glory (i.e., the Father). After hearing the Father commission Christ to descend *incognito* into the world, there to destroy "the princes and the angels and gods of that world" and to ascend again to his rightful place, Isaiah observes the descent and transformation of the Lord, his Virgin Birth, his crucifixion and resurrection, his commissioning of the twelve disciples, and his ascension. Again the concealment of his identity is emphasized, at least until his ascension, when he is recognized by all, much to their surprise. Also noteworthy is the Virgin Birth account, which is an amalgam of traditions, including some found in Matthew and others found in the *Protevangelium of James*. At this point Isaiah's vision ends. He tells Hezekiah to tell no one about the vision. A concluding postscript explains that it is because of these visions and prophecies that Sammael had Isaiah sawn in half by Manasseh.

The *Vision of Isaiah* contains some striking parallels to certain strands of Gnosticism, especially the Ophites, who, according to Irenaeus (*Haer.* 1.30), affirmed Christ's descent through the seven heavens and his stay in the world for 545 days after his resurrection (cf. *Ap. Jas.* 2). As a result, some scholars have viewed the *Vis. Is.* as gnostic (Helmbold 1972). But there is no full-blown gnostic myth, Ophite or otherwise, in the *Vis. Is.* Thus, the precise relationship between the Vision and Gnosticism, or perhaps some primitive form of it, remains unclear.

In addition to its descent/transformation Christology, two theological motifs in the *Vis. Is.* stand out. First, there is a strong emphasis on the miraculous nature of Jesus' birth, almost to the point of denying the actual birth process altogether (cf. *Odes Sol.* 19). Second, there is a distinctive Trinitarian concern. On the one hand, worship in the seventh heaven is directed toward "the Lord" (i.e., Christ), the Holy Spirit (frequently called an "angel"), and the Father. On the other hand, both "the Lord" and the Holy Spirit worship and praise the Father, giving him a superior status.

The apparent quotation of 11:14 in the *Acts of Peter* 24 (ca. 190 C.E.) fixes the date of the Vision prior to the end of the 2d century C.E. Parallels with Ignatius (ca. 115 C.E.) and the *Protevangelium of James* (ca. 150 C.E.) might suggest a date in the first half of the 2d century. The clear reference to the *Vis. Is.* in 3:13 might even indicate that it was composed prior to the *T. Hez.*, thus pushing its date back to the end of the 1st century. But it is also possible that the *T. Hez.* was composed first, and that 3:13 was part of the final redaction, being an attempt to link the three strata together. A third possibility, given other parallels between the *T. Hez.* and the *Vis. Is.* (e.g., the descent of Christ from the seventh heaven, the appellation "the Beloved," the angel of the Holy Spirit, belief in the cross), is that the *T. Hez.* and the *Vis. Is.* were composed together and jointly redacted into the *Mart. Is.* In any event, the *Vis. Is.*, like the *T. Hez.*, is an intriguing blend of "canonical" and "extracanonical" traditions and was probably composed within a "heterodox" community.

The dating of the Coptic fragments to the mid-4th century C.E., points to a final redaction of the composite document prior to ca. 350, and probably considerably earlier. The final editor apparently added several other passages (e.g., 1:2b–6a, 7, 13; 2:9; 5:15–16) as well.

The *Martyrdom and Ascension of Isaiah*, then, is an important document both as a witness to an ancient Jewish legend concerning Isaiah's martyrdom and as evidence for an early form of Christianity which set forth its distinctive understanding of its faith at a time before there was a fixed NT canon and before "orthodoxy" was clearly defined. For text see *APOT* 2: 155–62, *NTApocr* 2: 454–68, and *OTP* 2: 143–55.

Bibliography

Barton, J. M. T., 1984. The Ascension of Isaiah. Pp. 775–812 in *The Apocryphal Old Testament*, ed. H. F. D. Sparks. Oxford.

Box, G. H. and Charles, R. H. 1919. *The Ascension of Isaiah.* London.
Burch, V. 1919. The Literary Unity of the Ascensio Isaiae. *JTS* 20: 17–23.
———. 1920. Material for the Interpretation of the Ascension Isaiae. *JTS* 21: 249–65.
Burkitt, F. C. 1914. *Jewish and Christian Apocalypses.* London.
Caquot, A. 1973. Bref commentaire du "Martyre d'Isaïe." *Sem* 23: 65–93.
Charles, R. H. 1900. *The Ascension of Isaiah.* London.
Charlesworth, J. H. 1976. *The Pseudepigrapha and Modern Research.* SBLSCS 7. Missoula, MT.
Flusser, D. 1953. The Apocryphal Book of *Ascensio Isiae* and the Dead Sea Sect. *IEJ* 3: 34–47.
Hammershaimb, E. 1974. Das Martyrium Jesajas. JSHRZ 2: 15–34.
Helmbold, A. K. 1972. Gnostic Elements in the "Ascension of Isaiah." *NTS* 18: 222–27.
Philonenko, M. 1967. Le *Martyre d'Ésaïe* et l'histoire de la secte de Qoumrân. Pp. 1–10 in *Pseudépigraphes de l'Ancien Testament et manuscrits de la mer Morte.* Paris.
Tisserant, E. 1909. *Ascension d'Isaïe.* Paris.
Turdeanu, E. 1974. *Apocryphes slaves et roumains de l'Ancien Testament.* SVTP 5:1–74, 145–72.
Vaillant, A. 1963. Un Apocryphe pseudo-bogomile: La Vision d'Isaïe. *Revue des études slaves* 42: 109–21.

JOSEPH L. TRAFTON

ISCAH (PERSON) [Heb *yiskâ*]. Daughter of Haran and sister of Milcah (Gen 11:29). Later associations of Iscah with Sarah are not based on any clear evidence in the biblical text. The name itself appears to be a prefixed form of a weak verb, either *nsk,* "to pour" (referring to perfume; cf. Cassuto 1964: 277), or *skh,* "to see" (referring to divine favor at the birth of the child; cf. *EncMiqr* 3: 707). The former suggestion does not have onomastic parallels in Semitic personal names; the latter option does have such parallels, although the root *skh* is not attested in biblical Hebrew.

Bibliography

Cassuto, U. 1964. *A Commentary on the Book of Genesis.* Pt 2, *From Noah to Abraham.* Trans. I. Abrahams. Jerusalem.

RICHARD S. HESS

ISCARIOT. See JUDAS ISCARIOT.

ISH-BOSHETH (PERSON) [Heb *ʾîš bōšet*]. An alternative, perhaps artificially created name for Saul's youngest son by Ahinoam bat Ahimaaz, Eshbaal. The present form is found consistently in the MT text of 2 Samuel and is reflected in LXX's *Iebosthe* (cf. *Memphibosthe,* 3:8; 2:8, 10, 12, 15; 3:8, 14, 15; 4:5, 8, 12), while the form Eshbaal is found exclusively in both textual traditions of the Saulide genealogy quoted in 1 Chr 8:33 (LXX *Asabal*); 9:39 (LXX *Isbaal*). It is generally thought that the form of the name in Chronicles with *baʿal* "master, possessor" is authentic, and that the term *bōšet,* "shame," was later substituted for the former divine epithet *baʿal* when it became commonly associated with the fertility god Baal (Geiger 1857: 301; Gray 1896: 121; *IPN* 118–19). "Baal" appears to have been an accepted epithet for Yahweh until the early monarchic period, but after this time, it seems to have become restricted to use for Yahweh's main rival, the Canaanite storm god.

Other examples commonly cited to illustrate the substitution of *bōšet* for *baʿal* in personal names all derive from 2 Samuel: Saul's grandson Meribaal/Mephibosheth (1 Chr 8:34; 2 Sam 4:4); Jerubbaal/Jerubbesheth (Judg 6:32; 1 Sam 12:11; 2 Sam 11:21); and Josheb-basshebeth (2 Sam 23:8), which is thought to be a corruption of Ishbosheth, and presumably derived from an original Ishbaal, although the form Jashobeam occurs in 1 Chr 11:11 (Geiger 1857: 301; Tsevat 1975: 80–85). None of the three examples is airtight; the first involves a change in the first element of the name as well as the second; the second one was not vocalized by the Massoretes as *bōšet,* and may not have represented this element historically; and the third name never appears with the *baʿal* element. On the other hand, there are additional textual examples, (e.g., 1 Kgs 18:9, 25; Hos 9:10; Jer 11:13) where the title *baʿal* has been interchanged with the term *bōšet* in the LXX text (Dillmann 1881: 614–15; McCarter *II Samuel* AB, 86).

Additional names containing the element *baʿal* occur very infrequently in the Bible (Baal-hanan, Beeliada, Baanah, and Baasha), perhaps confirming the developing aversion to the term. In the case of Beeliada, an alternate form Eliada is found, possibly providing a variant solution to the elimination of the offensive *baʿal* element (Noth *IPN,* 119).

A small minority has suggested that the name form be accepted as genuine, arguing that the "bosheth" element represents the divine feature "dignity, pride," which became a divine epithet and type of guardian angel. It is attested in this sense in extrabiblical texts. According to this view, Ish-bohseth would have been either the person's original name, or possibly an additional throne name given to him when he succeeded Saul as king over Israel (Tsevat 1975).

Some have argued that a third form of the name of the same individual, Ishvi, occurs in 1 Sam 14:49 in the list of Saul's family members (e.g., *NHT* 92; Gray 1896: 121). The Lucianic LXX reading *Iessou* could preserve an original Hebrew reading **ʾîšyô,* "man of Yahweh." However, the appearance of Ishvi as the second-born son in this list, together with the absence of Abinadab and Eshbaal, who are named in the Chronicles genealogy as the two youngest sons of Ahinoam, tend to suggest that he is not identical with Eshbaal. He would seem to be an older son who died in his childhood (see AHINOAM; for the career of Ishbosheth, see ESHBAAL).

Bibliography

Dillmann, A. 1881. "Über Baal mit dem weiblichen Artikel *(hē Baal). Monatsbericht der königlich preussischen Akademie der Wissenschaften zu Berlin* June 16: 601–20.
Geiger, A. 1857. *Urschrift und Übersetzungen der Bibel in ihrer Abhängigkeit von der inneren Entwicklung des Judenthums.* Breslau.
Gray, G. B. 1896. *Studies in Hebrew Proper Names.* London.
Soggin, J. A. 1975. *Old Testament and Oriental Studies.* BibOr 29. Rome.

Tsevat, M. 1975. Ishbosheth and Congeners: The Names and Their Study. *HUCA* 46: 71–88.

DIANA V. EDELMAN

ISH-HAI (PERSON) [Heb *ʾîš-ḥayi*]. According to the *Kĕtib,* Ish-hai is the father of Jehoiada, the father of Benaiah, but the *Qĕrēʾ*, "Benaiah, the son of Jehoiada, was a valiant man" is the more commonly accepted reading (2 Sam 23:20). The *Qĕrēʾ*, which substitutes *ḥayil* for *ḥayi,* causes less problems grammatically and is found in the parallel text in 1 Chr 11:22.

PAULINE A. VIVIANO

ISHBAH (PERSON) [Heb *yišbāḥ*]. The father of Eshtemoa, mentioned in the genealogical list of the tribe of Judah (1 Chr 4:17). His siblings included Miriam and Shammai. Though there are problems with the Heb text, it appears that Ishbah is the son of Mered and Bithiah, the daughter of pharaoh. Bithiah is not mentioned until v 18 in the Heb, after the children of a Judean wife of Mered are listed. RSV placed the clause that refers to Bithiah in v 17 to clarify the apparent connection of Bithiah with the list (in v 17b) preceding that of the Judean wife's children (v 18a). As this seems the best way to make sense of the text, Ishbah then would not have been a pure-blooded Judahite. Note that there is no attempt in the text to exclude the descendants of foreign marriages (cf. Ackroyd *Chronicles Ezra Nehemiah* TBC, 36; and Myers *1 Chronicles* AB, 29, who believes that this list is preexilic).

In discussing a class of Heb personal names that have to do with guilt and petitioning for forgiveness, Noth (*IPN* 211; cf. *IDB* 2: 746) links the name with the Heb root *šbḥ* to mean "may [God's wrath] subside."

KENNETH H. CUFFEY

ISHBAK (PERSON) [Heb *yišbāq*]. The fifth son of Abraham and Keturah (Gen 25:2; 1 Chr 1:32). Abraham, in order to remove rivals to Isaac's claim to his inheritance, provided gifts to Ishbak and his brothers and sent them to eastern areas (Gen 25:6). No descendants of Ishbak are mentioned in either list of Abraham and Keturah's offspring, making it impossible to trace his genealogical relationship to other groups (in contrast to Jokshan and Midian whose lines are traced through further generations).

RICHARD W. NYSSE

ISHBI-BENOB (PERSON) [Heb *yišbî bĕnōb*]. A Philistine champion descended from, or a votary of (McCarter *II Samuel* AB, 449–50) Raphah. Ishbi-Benob sought to kill David (2 Sam 21:16), but he was himself killed by Abishai, one of David's heroes (v 17). This episode appears as the first in a series of four episodes recounting the defeat of Philistine champions by David's warriors (2 Sam 21:15–22). Although variant versions of the latter three episodes are to be found in 1 Chr 20:4–8, Ishbi-Benob's threat to David's life, which took place at a time of the latter's weariness (2 Sam 21:15) and led to David's being barred by his troops from further battles (v 17), is not recounted in Chronicles (about which see Curtis and Madsen *Chronicles* ICC, 243; Myers *I Chronicles* AB, 142). The first element of the name Ishbi-Benob is derived from the marginal MT *Qere* to 2 Sam 21:16, *wyšby*. The consonantal text, however, reads *wyšbw*. Most modern scholars have followed the *Kethib* and read the putative name as *wayyēšĕbû bĕgōb* "and they dwelt at Gob." This is achieved through the vocalization of the MT *Kethib* and the emendation of Nob to Gob on the basis of vv 18 and 19 (*NHT* 270–71; but see Ehrlich 1910: 331). Recently McCarter (p. 448) has restored the text of vv 15 and 16 on the basis of an originally marginal note which has crept into the LXX traditions in the vicinity of v 11, and on the basis of the Lucianic tradition in which the name Dadou son of Ioas appears in place of Ishbi-Benob. McCarter's suggestion is to restore the beginning of v 16 from the MT *wyšbw bnbʾšr* "and Jishbo of Nob, who" to *wyšbw (wayyišbēw) ddw bn ywʾš* "and Dodo son of Joash captured him [David]." The conjectured corruption of the MT would have been occasioned by the dropping of *ddw* by homoioteleuton and the change of *bn ywʾš* to *bnb ʾšr* under the influence of *bgwb* "in Gob" in vv 18 and 19, for which some manuscripts read *bnwb* "in Nob."

Bibliography

Ehrlich, A. B. 1910. *Randglossen zur hebräischen Bibel* Vol. 3. Leipzig.

CARL S. EHRLICH

ISHHOD (PERSON) [Heb *ʾîšhôd*]. Manassite son of Hammolecheth (1 Chr 7:18). His name, suggesting (parental wishes for his) physical strength, probably meant "man of vitality" (*ʾîš* + *hôd*) (Noth IPN, 225). His brothers were Abiezer and Mahlah, although the latter name may be feminine in form and so designate a sister (cf. Josh 17:3). In addition, Curtis and Madsen (*Chronicles* ICC, 152) have proposed that Shemida (1 Chr 7:19), whose relation to the rest of the tribe of Manasseh in the chapter is uncertain, was Hammolecheth's fourth son. Few interpreters, however, have found this suggestion convincing. See SHEMIDA.

Although it is clear that Ishhod's mother was Hammolecheth, his father is not identified, and it is unclear why the name of his mother, rather than that of his father, is given in the genealogy. In addition, the relationship of Hammolecheth (and so Ishhod) to the rest of Manasseh is unclear. It seems most likely that she was the sister of Gilead (vv 17–18), although this is by no means certain. In this case, Ishhod's grandfather and great-grandfather would have been Gilead and Machir, respectively. See HAMMOLECHETH.

M. PATRICK GRAHAM

ISHI (DEITY) [Heb *ʾîšî*]. KJV rendering (actually, transliteration) of Heb *ʾîšî* in Hos 2:18—Eng 2:16. Most versions now translate *ʾîšî* as "my husband" (lit. "my man"). The context of the verse, Hosea 2 (in a broader sense, Hosea 1–3), likens the covenant relationship of God (Yahweh) with Israel (here, specifically, the N kingdom) to a marriage, in which Yahweh is the husband and Israel the wife. Israel at present (during the reign of Jeroboam II), according to Hos 2:4–15—Eng 2:2–13, is the unfaithful spouse, but, as vv 16–25—Eng 14–23 announce, she will be led to repentance and a return to Yahweh. In that future day of renewed, restored fellowship with Yahweh, Israel (according to the imagery of the marriage metaphor) will call Yahweh *ʾîšî,* "my husband" (cf. v 4—Eng 2), no longer calling him *baʿlî,* "my lord" (v 18—Eng 16). This change in terms of address for Yahweh signifies the change that will take place in the nation. The old term, *baʿal,* which can also be translated "husband," comes from a verbal root meaning "to rule over," "to possess." When *baʿal* is used in the sense of "husband," there often is an implied emphasis on the formal, contractual relationship between the man and woman, on the legal rights of the man as husband ("lord") of the woman (Gen 20:3; Exod 21:3, 22; Deut 22:22; 24:4; cf. 2 Sam 11:26). On the other hand, *ʾîš* ("man"), used in the sense of "husband," can carry connotations of the man as counterpart, companion of the woman, of his being in a close relationship with the woman (Gen 2:23–24; 3:6; cf. Gen 3:16; 29:32, 34; 30:15, 20; 2 Sam 14:5; 2 Kgs 4:1). In the context of Hosea 2, *ʾîšî* is a more personal, intimate term than *baʿlî.* When Israel at some future date is brought to repentance and renewal, she will no longer call Yahweh her "lord," someone she grudgingly has to acknowledge as her husband simply because she is bound to him by legal contract. Rather, she will sincerely, affectionately call Yahweh *ʾîšî,* "my man," "my husband," genuinely loving him and willingly remaining faithful to him.

However, Hos 2:18—Eng 2:16 has further meaning. Because the word translated "(my) lord" is also the name of the great Canaanite deity Baal, *baʿal,* and because of the context (see 2:10, 15, and especially 19—Eng 2:8, 13, 17), this verse should also be seen as a polemic against Baal worship. Such an understanding assumes that the Israelites referred to Yahweh as *baʿal,* "lord," which, according to onomastic data, was the case. In some instances, at least during earlier times, this was done apparently in an innocent, uncompromising fashion. By the 8th century, though, any use of *baʿal* in a religious connection would be dangerous. If mentioned in reference to Yahweh, *baʿal* could still have the generic sense "lord," yet nevertheless would be suggestive of the Canaanite deity; worse, it could indicate a syncretism, in which Yahweh was venerated as Baal. Thus, according to the marriage metaphor of Hosea 2, when Israel in the future will no longer call Yahweh *baʿlî,* "my lord," but *ʾîšî,* "my husband," the underlying message is twofold. Israel will be lovingly devoted to Yahweh and—what goes hand in hand with this—there will be no problem with, not even any reminder of, Baal worship. There will only be pure worship of Yahweh.

WALTER A. MAIER III

ISHI (PERSON) [Heb *yišʿî*]. **1.** The son of Appaim and descendant of Jerahmeel (1 Chr 2:31). He was the father of Sheshan. This verse occurs as part of a general chiastic structure within the genealogy of Judah, with the descendants of Jerahmeel forming the central unit of the chiasm (Williamson 1979). LXX^{B} reads *Isemiēl* for the MT *yišʿî.* The MT of 1 Chr 2:31 is puzzling since it introduces Ishi as the son of Appaim and Sheshan as the son of Ishi with the plural, *bĕnê,* even though only one son is mentioned each time. It may be that this is simply a scribal error since the plural is regularly used throughout 1 Chronicles 2 for the introduction of groups of sons. However, the possibility exists that such a genealogical list does not refer to individuals but to families or clans designated by their ancestor. It is well known that such lists often reflect important social and political relationships between different groups at the time of their composition (Wilson 1980). Although it is impossible to date this list, the importance of Judah in the work of the Chronicler meant that groups attached to this genealogy were accorded a privileged position. It might well be that the purpose was to legitimate the position of various clans or groups during the time of the Chronicler (Braun *1 Chronicles* WBC, 38–47).

2. The father of Zoheth and Betzoheth of the tribe of Judah (1 Chr 4:20). The name occurs in what appears to be a disconnected list of the members of the tribe of Judah (Braun *1 Chronicles* WBC, 57). The connection of Ishi to the tribe of Judah means that it attains a privileged position in the work and time of the Chronicler. Williamson (1979) understands vv 20–23 as the conclusion of the intricate chiasm which comprises the genealogy of Judah.

3. A Simeonite whose sons are said to have destroyed the remnant of the Amalekites at Mount Seir and to have settled in the area (1 Chr 4:42). The Syriac reads "these four men sons of Ishi came" for MT "sons of Ishi." 1 Chr 4:34–43 contains traditions of the movements of various groups and their acquisition of territory. This information is peculiar to the Chronicler which makes it difficult to assess its historical value. It is reported that four sons of Ishi led five hundred Simeonites to Mount Seir where they destroyed "the remnant of the Amalekites" and occupied their territory. It is not known if the phrase "the remnant of the Amalekites" refers to those who escaped David's pursuit and massacre of the Amalekites following their looting of Ziklag (1 Sam 30:17). This tradition seems to reflect a claim to land but it is difficult to date or to be precise about its social location.

4. A member of the tribe of Manasseh and head of a clan (1 Chr 5:24). Ishi is mentioned with six others as a warrior and famous man. Braun (*1 Chronicles* WBC, 78) believes that these phrases, which are common in Chronicles, have military associations and may indicate that the information is derived from an old military source. The explanation that their exile was due to apostasy reflects one of the major themes of the Deuteronomistic History (1 Chr 5:25–26; cf. 2 Kgs 17:7–23). However, it is not entirely clear whether 5:25–26 applies to all the groups mentioned throughout the chapter or simply the seven clans referred to in 5:24.

Bibliography

Williamson, H. G. 1979. Sources and Redaction in the Chronicler's Genealogy of Judah. *JBL* 98: 351–59.

Wilson, R. R. 1980. *Genealogy and History in the Biblical World.* Yale.

KEITH W. WHITELAM

ISHMA (PERSON) [Heb *yišmāʾ*]. A Judahite, the brother of Jezreel, Idbash, and Hazzelelponi (1 Chr 4:3). LXX identifies Ishma (Gk *ragma*) as a son of Etam (RSV adopts this reading), while MT refers to him as a father of Etam. In the latter case, Etam would probably denote a group of people at a particular location (the Etam near Bethlehem, modern Kh. el-Khokh?; *LBHG* 272, 434). Or possibly something has dropped out of the text "and these were the father of Etam" *(wĕʾēlleh ʾăbî ʿêṭām)* between "these" and "father." See discussion of the text at HAZZELEL-PONI. The name Ishma is a shortened form of Ishmael *(yišmāʿēʾl,* "God hears," Gen 16:11; HALAT 2, 426; cf. *IPN,* 28, 39, 198).

KENNETH H. CUFFEY

ISHMAEL (PERSON) [Heb *yišmāʿēʾl*]. The name of six persons in the OT.

1. The son of Hagar and Abraham (Gen 16; 17:18–26; 21:8–21; 25:9, 12–17; 28:9; 36:3; 1 Chr 1:28–31) and the eponymous ancestor of the Ishmaelites. See ISHMAEL-ITES; HAGAR.

2. Son of Nethaniah. One of the Judean troop commanders who, following the destruction of Jerusalem in 587/586 B.C.E., chose to join Gedaliah, the ruler of Judah, at his administrative center at Mizpah (Jer 40:7–8; 2 Kgs 25:23). Ishmael was a member of the royal house (Jer 41:11; 2 Kgs 25:25) and "one of the chief officers of the king" (Jer 41:1).

Apparently incited by Baalis (an Ammonite seal impression discovered in 1984 reveals that the correct spelling of this name is *Baʿalyišʿa*), king of the Ammonites (cf. Jer 40:14), Ishmael and ten of his men assassinated Gedaliah during a meal shared with Gedaliah on their arrival in Mizpah. (According to Jer 40:13–16, Gedaliah did not believe a warning issued by Johanan, and rejected Johanan's offer to kill Ishmael secretly.) Ishmael also murdered some of Gedaliah's supporters and a number of Babylonians, possibly men attached to a Babylonian garrison stationed at Mizpah (Jer 41:1–3; 2 Kgs 25:25). Although the Hebrew Bible does not give the year of the assassination, the fact that the text states only that it took place "in the seventh month" (Jer 41:1; 2 Kgs 25:25) implies that the assassination occurred in the same year as the fall of Jerusalem ("in the fourth month," Jer 39:2). But it is also possible that Gedaliah remained in power for a few years, and that it was his assassination which led to the deportation which, according to Jer 52:30 (cf. Josephus, *Ant* 10.9.7), took place in Nebuchadnezzar's 23d year (582/581 B.C.E.).

On the day following Gedaliah's assassination, Ishmael treacherously slaughtered a number of pilgrims en route from N Israel to Jerusalem. Their bodies were cast into a cistern built by King Asa of Judah (Jer 41:4–9). Ishmael then set out for Ammon, taking as hostages the daughters of the king who had been entrusted to Gedaliah, and "the rest of the people who were in Mizpah" (Jer 41:10). Ishmael's plans were foiled when he and his band were intercepted at Gibeon by Johanan and other troop commanders and their men. With only eight of his supporters, Ishmael was able to escape to Ammon (Jer 41:15). Fearing Babylonian reprisals for the assassination of Gedaliah (Jer 41:18; 2 Kgs 25:26), Johanan and "all the remnant of Judah" rejected Yahweh's word as spoken by the prophet Jeremiah and fled to Egypt (Jer 41:16–43:7). These events are related in some detail in Jer 40:7–43:7. 2 Kgs 25:22–26 contains only a brief account of the appointment and assassination of Gedaliah, and the flight to Egypt. There is no reference to this material in either Chronicles or Jeremiah 52.

The Hebrew Bible does not say what motivated Ishmael to assassinate Gedaliah. It can be assumed, however, that Ishmael was a staunch nationalist who would have viewed Gedaliah not only as a traitor who had collaborated with the Babylonians but also as the usurper of a role which rightfully belonged to the house of David. (No title is given for the office to which Gedaliah, a member of the prominent family of Shaphan, was appointed by the Babylonians; while it is usually assumed that Gedaliah's appointment was to the office of "governor," one must also reckon with the possibility that he was appointed "king" [see *IJH,* 421–23].) Although Ishmael may have been motivated by nothing more than an intense hatred for both Gedaliah and the Babylonians, it is also possible that as a member of the house of David he also entertained the hope of laying claim to the throne of Judah (cf. Josephus, *Ant* 10.9.3), perhaps with the support of the Ammonites (cf. Jer 40:14).

Ishmael's assassination of Gedaliah is of pivotal importance in the chain of events leading from Gedaliah's appointment to the flight to Egypt. Both Jer 40:7–43:7 and 2 Kgs 25:22–26 underscore the view that hope for the future lies not with those who remained in the land (and who later left for Egypt), but rather with the exiles in Babylon.

Bibliography

Ackroyd, P. R. 1982. Archaeology, Politics and Religion: The Persian Period. *Iliff Review* 39: 5–23.

Baltzer, K. 1961. Das Ende des Staates Juda und die Messias-Frage. Pp. 33–43 in *Studien zur Theologie der alttestamentlichen Überlieferungen,* eds. R. Rendtorff and K. Koch. Neukirchen-Vluyn.

Herr, L. G. 1985. The Servant of Baalis. *BA* 48: 169–72.

Lohfink, N. 1978. Die Gattung der "Historischen Kurzgeschichte" in den letzten Jahren von Juda und in der Zeit des Babylonischen Exils. *ZAW* 90: 319–47.

Seitz, C. R. 1985. The Crisis of Interpretation over the Meaning and Purpose of the Exile. *VT* 25: 78–97.

JOHN M. BERRIDGE

3. A Benjaminite, and descendant of Saul in the thirteenth generation (1 Chr 8:38; 9:44). Accordingly, he should have lived in the 7th century B.C.

4. The father of Zebadiah, "chief" (Heb *nāgîd*) of Judah at the time of Jehoshaphat (2 Chr 19:11). The historicity of Jehoshaphat's juridical reform (2 Chr 19:4–11) is difficult to defend (Welten 1973: 142, 184–85); so is the assumption of a Judean "chief" in the preexilic period; the constellation king—high priest—secular leader of Judah recalls the political structure of the Persian province Yehud.

5. A captain (literally "officer of hundred") operative in the revolt against Athaliah in the version of the Chronicler, 2 Chr 23:1. The officers are nameless in the Chronicler's source, 2 Kgs 11:4; calling them by names follows the same line as the other "improvements" introduced by the Chronicler into the account of 2 Kings 11.

6. A priest found guilty of marrying a foreign woman, and who subsequently agreed to divorce her (Esra 10:22).

The name Ishmael means "God listened (namely, to the parents' prayer)" and is attested throughout W Semitic, from Amorite to Safaitic (Knauf 1989: 38, n. 170). In Hebrew, it was a very popular name in the 7th (#3) and 6th (#2) centuries, and in the postexilic period (#4–6). Epigraphical attestations of the name show the same distribution; there may be up to nine Ishmaels in Avigad's bullae from the time of Jeremiah (1986).

Bibliography

Avigad, N. 1986. *Hebrew Bullae from the Time of Jeremiah.* Jerusalem.

Knauf, E. A. 1989. *Ishmael.* 2d ed. ADPV. Wiesbaden.

Welten, P. 1973. *Geschichte und Geschichtsdarstellung in den Chronikbüchern.* WMANT 42. Neukirchen-Vluyn.

ERNST AXEL KNAUF

ISHMAEL, RABBI. Leading rabbinic authority of the first third of the 2d century B.C.E. (contemporary with but in the long run overshadowed by Akiba ben Joseph); Ishmael's father was named Elisha, but in recognition of his importance he is often named in ancient sources without his patronymic. It has long been taken as established that Ishmael and Akiba were the founders of two rival schools of exegesis, of which Ishmael's was characterized by a tendency to treat biblical language as ordinary language while Akiba treated it as a special discourse in which every particle and every letter had specific meaning (so, e.g., Heschel 1962–65), but recent scholarship has cast doubt on the idea that two so clearly distinct hermeneutical systems can be isolated from the extant texts (see Porton 1976–82 4: 159–211). In any event, several of the most important early midrashic elaborations of the Pentateuch (chiefly *Mek. de-Rabbi Ishmael* and *Sipre Num.*) are widely attributed to his school, as the traditional title of the first clearly indicates; elsewhere in rabbinic literature many additional exegetical traditions are ascribed to those of the house/school of *R. Ishmael.* The introductory section of *Sipra* contains a list of thirteen rules for the proper exegesis of the Torah which also is attributed to Ishmael, even though *Sipra* as a whole is usually assigned to the school of Akiba; this list was eventually incorporated into the daily prayer book.

The nature of rabbinic literature makes it difficult to reach secure conclusions about the details of Ishmael's life or teachings, but it can be noted that numerous sources (e.g., *b. Ketub.* 105b; *Ḥul.* 49a; *t. Ḥal.* 1:10) assign him a priestly ancestry, and that he seems at some point to have taken up residence in the southern portion of the Land of Israel (*Ketub.* 5:8). A widespread tradition includes among the martyrs of the Hadrianic persecution a teacher named Ishmael (see, e.g., *Mek. Neziqin* 18), but aside from Finkelstein (1938) and Porton (1976–82: 2.129–33) most modern authorities agree that the reference, if at all historical, must have been to some other individual (see Lieberman 1973: 737–38, Safrai *EncJud* 9:83–86).

In the mystical literature of the *hêkālôt* ("heavenly palaces"), Ishmael's name appears very frequently; in fact he and Akiba are the main teachers in whose names these traditions are reported. No satisfactory explanation of this connection has been proposed. Talmudic tradition reports that Akiba was also connected to the *merkābâ* movement (chariot-throne mysticism), but asserts no such link for Ishmael. Perhaps Ishmael's name was attached to these materials through his well-known association with Akiba.

J. Neusner (1969) has observed that the names of Ishmael's closest disciples are generally absent from the Mishnah, and has hypothesized that Ishmael's followers fled to Babylonia during the Bar Kokhba war and the Hadrianic persecution and did not all return to Israel when it later became possible to do so; this would imply a very important role for Ishmael's students in the transfer of rabbinic Judaism to Babylonia during the middle and late 2d century C.E.

Bibliography

Finkelstein, L. 1938. The Ten Martyrs. Pp. 29–55 in *Essays and Studies in Memory of Linda R. Miller.* New York.

Heschel, A. J. 1962–65. *Torah min ha-Shamayim ba-Aspaklaria shel ha-Dorot* (Theology of Ancient Judaism). 2 vols. New York (in Hebrew).

Lieberman, S. 1973. *Tosefta Ki-Fshutah.* Pt. 8. New York (in Hebrew).

Neusner, J. 1969. *A History of the Jews in Babylonia.* Vol. 1. Rev. ed. Leiden.

Porton, G. 1976–82. *The Traditions of Rabbi Ishmael.* 4 vols. Leiden.

ROBERT GOLDENBERG

ISHMAELITES [Heb *yišmĕʿēʾlîm*]. In the OT there are five contexts in which this group of people is mentioned. In the Joseph story, it is variously the Ishmaelites or the Midianites (or both together) who transport and sell Joseph to Egypt (Gen 27:25, 27ff.; 39:1). In Judg 8:24 the Midianites are (again) called Ishmaelites. The Ishmaelites are listed in Ps 83:7 among a number of peoples hostile to Israel (Edomites, Moabites, Hagarites, and Amalekites). 1 Chr 2:17 identifies one of David's officials as an Ishmaelite, who is identified as an "Israelite" in 2 Sam 17:25. According to 1 Chr 27:30 an Ishmaelite was in charge of David's camels.

A. Name and Identification
   1. Ishmael
   2. Sons of Ishmael
B. History of Research
C. The Rise and Decline of the Ishmaelites
   1. The 8th Century B.C.
   2. The 7th Century B.C.
   3. The 6th and 5th Centuries B.C.

A. Name and Identification

1. Ishmael. Ishmael, the eponymous ancestor of the Ishmaelites, and his mother Hagar are the subject of two biblical narratives. According to Genesis 16, Abram fathered Ishmael, but the jealous Sarai drove the still-pregnant Hagar into the desert (vv 3–6). There an angel revealed to Hagar the eventual destiny of the child she would soon bear. However, in v 15 (usually assigned to P, but see Thompson 1987: 89–91) Abram is portrayed as being present for the birth of his son, and indeed it is he who gives the child the name "Ishmael."

In Gen 21:1–21, Sarah, after giving birth to Isaac,

(again) incites Abraham to expel Hagar and Ishmael, who at this time is at least 15 or 16 years old (cf. 16:16 with 21:5, 8). In a passage that has long baffled commentators, the outcast Hagar carries her (approximately 15-year-old) son into the wilderness, where she abandons the crying child (Heb *yeled,* usually reserved for sub-teenagers!) under a bush (vv 14–16). At this point, an angel intervenes and (again) reveals the destiny of the child.

It is evident from the repeated emphasis on Ishmael's destiny that these two similar stories serve an ethnographic purpose: "He will be a wild ass of a man, his fist against all, and everyone's fist against him" (16:12). This verse describes not an individual person, but the bedouin lifestyle. The same holds true for Gen 21:20–21 (Knauf 1989: 22–24). However, this does not mean that the intention behind the two narratives is solely ethnographic (cf. Trible 1984: 9–35; Görg 1986).

In the P source (or redactional layer), the basic content of the two narratives, Genesis 16 and 21:1–21, is condensed into four sentences and a short dialogue. Gen 16:3 and 16:15–16 state the relationship between Abram, Hagar, and Ishmael baldly. When Abram fails to believe God's promise of another son and wishes to designate Ishmael as heir of the covenant, Yahweh rejects this (Gen 17:15–19). Abram is reassured, however, that Ishmael shall also become the father of a large people (v 20). The fulfillment of this promise is described in Gen 25:12–17, where the twelve sons of Ishmael, all well-known and powerful Arab tribes, are listed.

Yišmaᶜ(ʾ)el is a typical W Semitic personal name, a sentence name of the type imperfect (preterite) plus subject (theophorous element). The type is attested from the earliest W Semitic texts (second half of the 3d millennium B.C.) to Pre-Islamic Arabic (first half of the 1st millennium A.D.; Knauf 1989: 38, n. 170). Even without the stories about Ishmael in Genesis 16 and 21, and the list of the sons of Ishmael in Gen 25:12–17, it could still be concluded from the generic term *yišmēᶜ(ʾ)ēlîm* that this group of tribes derived itself from an eponymous ancestor named *yišmaᶜēl.*

2. Sons of Ishmael. It is a subject of scholarly dispute whether the "Ishmaelites" of the biblical sources outside the P source have anything to do with the "Sons of Ishmael" listed in Genesis 25; and, whether there are extrabiblical references to "Ishmael" as an ethnonym, particularly with reference to the Arabian tribal entity *Su-mu-(ʾ-)*AN, mentioned by Sennacherib and Ashurbanipal (see B below). The "Sons of Ishmael," in any case, are well attested both inside and outside the OT.

NEBAIOTH (ancient Arabic **Nabayāt*) is called the "firstborn of Ishmael," and listed first in Gen 25:13. This may reflect a specific Palestinian point of view (Knauf 1989: 108–9). His sister is married to Esau/Edom in Gen 28:9 and Gen 36:3 (with two different names, cf. Knauf 1989: 93, n. 509). For Isa 60:7, they are breeders of small stock *par excellence.* Ashurbanipal seems to have been the first Assyrian ruler who established contacts with this Arabian tribe (Ephʾal 1982: 221f.; Knauf 1989: 93–95). According to the Thamudic inscriptions from Jebel Ghuneim near Taymâʾ, the people of Taymâʾ had to fight at least one war against the *nbyt* (**Nabayāt;* Winnett and Reed 1970: 90–92). These inscriptions are dated to the 6th century B.C. by Winnett (1980), and to ca. 400 B.C. by Roschinski (1980) and Knauf (1989: 76–77). Linguistically, it is impossible to connect the later Nabataeans with the Nebaioth; historically, it can be argued that the Nabataeans derived from the Qedarites (Knauf 1989: 92–111).

KEDAR (more properly, Qedar) is listed second in Gen 25:13, but was undoubtedly the most numerous and the most powerful tribe among the "Sons of Ishmael." Queens, and later kings, of the Qedarites are attested in the Assyrian inscriptions from 738 B.C. until the reign of Ashurbanipal (see C below; Ephʾal 1982: 223–227; Knauf 1989: 2–5, 66, 96–108). In 599/98 B.C., the Neo-Babylonian king Nebuchadnezzar led a campaign against this tribe. The Babylonian offensive is reflected in Jer 49:28–33 (Dumbrell 1972; Knauf 1989: 103). For Jeremiah (2:10), and for Deutero- and Trito-Isaiah (42:10 and 60:5–9), these represent in general the inhabitants of the desert E of Palestine. The latest texts that refer to them are Ezek 27:21; Isa 21:16f.; Cant 1:5; and Pliny, *HN* V.11.(12).65.

ADBEEL, probably identical with Nodab (1 Chr 5:19; Albright 1956: 13; Knauf 1989: 67–68), is attested in the inscriptions of Tiglath-pileser III (Ephʾal 1982: 215f.; Knauf 1989: 66–67).

MIBSAM and MISHMA occur together in 1 Chr 4:25 in the genealogy of Simeon. This may reflect the presence of members of these two tribes in S Palestine in the Persian period (Knauf 1989: 68). Mishma may be mentioned by Ashurbanipal under the name of Išammeʾ, which can represent Arabic **Yus₁āmiᶜ*, an imperfect of the III stem with the meaning "(The ones) who joined Ishmael–*S₁amaᶜʾil*" (Weippert, *RLA* 5: 172–73; Knauf 1989: 9, n. 40).

DUMAH, in classical Arabic Dūmat al-Jandal, now al-Jawf at the lower end of the Wādī Sirḥān, was the political and cultic center of the Qedarites during the reigns of Sennacherib and Esarhaddon (Knauf 1989: 69, 81–88). Whether Isa 21:11–12 relates to this central N Arabian town is unclear.

MASSA is mentioned in Assyrian texts from the 8th and 7th centuries B.C. (Albright 1956; Ephʾal 1982: 218; Knauf 1983b) and in 4th century B.C. Thamudic inscriptions from Jebel Ghuneim near Taymâʾ (Winnett and Reed 1970: 101–2). "Massaʾ" is usually restored in Ps 120:5 (Müller, *TRE* 3: 573, but cf. Knauf 1989: 72, with n. 363) and in Prov 30:1. The admonitions of Prov 31:1–9 are attributed to the mother of a "king of Massaʾ."

HADAD may be attested as a clan in the Jebel Ghuneim inscriptions (Knauf 1989: 73–74). This would place the tribe in the vicinity of Taymâʾ.

TEMA (or Taymâʾ) was a major trade center in N Arabia, as is attested by Jer 25:23–24; Isa 21:13–15; Job 6:19. The town paid tribute to Tiglath-pileser III in 734 B.C. For ten years (between 553 and 543 B.C.) it was the residence of the Neo-Babylonian king Nabonidus. When the Minaeans gained the supremacy over the incense route from the Sabaeans (cf. Job 6:19!) ca. 400 B.C., Taymâʾs role in the trans-Arabian trade seems to have declined to the favor of Dedan/el-ᶜUlā, where the Minaeans established a colony (Knauf 1989: 74–80). How much of the archaeological and epigraphical heritage of Taymâʾ derives from the time of Nabonidus (Bawden et al. 1980; Bawden 1981; 1983; Winnett 1980; Abu-Duruk 1986) or rather from the Persian period (Roschinski 1980; Knauf 1983c: 37–41), is disputed. Recent archaeological work has enhanced our understanding of this heritage considerably (Livingstone et al. 1983; Aggoula 1985; Cross 1986).

JETUR is apparently located in N Transjordan according to 1 Chr 5:19 (a tradition most probably stemming from the Persian period). The tribe, better known under its Greek/Latin name "Ituraeans," moved into the Biqaʿ valley of Lebanon in the 2d century B.C. and became famous—or infamous—for its fierce raids (Marfoe 1979: 23–25; Knauf 1984: 19–21). The Roman imperial army recruited from them a number of elite units of archers. The Ituraeans are attested in Safaitic inscriptions as well as in the Greek and Latin literary record (Knauf 1983c: 41–47; 1989: 80f).

NAPHISH is associated with Jetur in 1 Chr 5:19, but with Massaʾ in a recently published cuneiform letter to the Assyrian king Ashurbanipal (K 5580 = CT 53, 289; Knauf 1983b: 34–36).

KEDEMAH (or Qedmah) is the only "son of Ishmael" not attested in any extrabiblical source, giving rise to the assumption that this "tribe" is nothing but a transformation of the *"bene qedem"* (the "People of the East") into a tribe in order to make the number of Ishmael's sons the requisite twelve.

B. History of Research

The basic outlines of a history of the Ishmaelites that became the accepted view for over a century were drawn by T. Nöldeke in 1864 (pp. 3–6). According to this view, the Ishmaelites were part of the early history, or even prehistory, of Israel, not attested after ca. 1000 B.C. With the *formgeschichte* school of thought, the assumption of a J source and an E source in the Pentateuch, and the widely shared acceptance of an early date for both, it became possible to see in the Ishmaelites only a minor tribe in the Negeb desert of S Palestine, somehow bordering upon the "Isaac-People" around Beersheba. This view was based upon Genesis 16; 21:1–21; 37:25; 27f.; 39:1; 1 Chr 2:17; 27:30; and Judg 8:24, but had to ignore the Assyrian evidence which was not yet known to Nöldeke. However, this evidence was known to Meyer (1906: 322–26) and Noth (*RGG* 3: 935–36), who nonetheless reconstructed their histories of the Ishmaelites along similar lines.

Full justice was done to the Assyrian evidence by Dumbrell (1970: 184–246). According to him, the Ishmaelites were a major tribal confederacy extending all over N Arabia. They took over from the Midianites ca. 1100 B.C., and were succeeded, in turn, by the Qedarites in the 8th century B.C., who in turn fell victim to the Nabataeans. Knauf (1989) agrees with Dumbrell's geographical and political concept of the Ishmaelites, but not with his dating. The Midianites, according to his view, do not belong in this series of N Arabian desert supremacies (Knauf 1983a; 1988), nor were the relationships between the Ishmaelites and the Qedarites, or between the Qedarites and the Nabataeans, as antagonistic as Dumbrell assumes, if for no other reason than because the latter (in each case) were originally a tribe (or a clan) of the former.

Ephʾal (1982), who most completely collated the cuneiform evidence for Arab tribes of the first half of the 1st millennium B.C., returned to the view that the Ishmaelites, a S Palestinian tribe not of Arab extraction and not attested later than 1000 B.C., had nothing to do with the various "sons of Ishmael" subsequently listed by the P source of the Pentateuch and attested in the Assyrian, Aramaic, and ancient N Arabian inscriptions (Ephʾal 1982: 233–240). Knauf (1989), on the contrary, assumes that Genesis 16; 21:1–21; 25:12–17, and the Assyrian texts of the 8th–7th centuries B.C. all testify to the same ethnic and political entity: an Ishmaelite tribal confederacy extending over the whole of N Arabia from the time of Tiglath-pileser III to the time of Ashurbanipal.

The issues underlying these different views are the date and the reliability of the OT references to Ishmael, and the question whether biblical Ishmael is identical with the ethnic group *Su-mu-(ʾ)-il* mentioned by Sennacherib and Ashurbanipal. The answer to the first question depends on one's position with respect to recent discussions of the Pentateuchal sources. According to Ephʾal, who wrote the bulk of his work before this discussion was renewed in the 1980s, all biblical references to Ishmael antedate the end of the 10th century B.C. It is only the list in Gen 25:12–17 that must be later, according to the epigraphic evidence for the tribes listed therein. Ephʾal assumes that the author of this list sought a common ancestor for the individual Arab tribes of his day, and that he found the traditional (but by his time meaningless) name of Ishmael suitable for this purpose (Ephʾal 1976; 1982: 233–240). For Knauf, the oldest traditions in Genesis 16; 25:13–15; 37:25, 27f.; and 39:1 are more or less contemporary (early to mid-7th century B.C.; see Knauf 1989: 35–45, 61–65). In his view, Gen 21:1–21 is later than the P account (which consists of Genesis 17; 25:12–17; Knauf 1989: 16–25). Also 1 Chr 2:17; 27:30; Ps 83:7 are assumed to be without historical value for the preexilic period (Knauf 1989: 10–14), as is Judg 8:24, which is a gloss from the exilic period.

As for the identity of *Yišmaʿʾel* and *Šumuʾil* (*Su-mu-*[ʾ-]AN), Ephʾal denies any possibility of the equation (1976: 230; 1982: 167, 230). He does not realize, however, that Assyrian *s* consistently represents W Semitic *š* in proper names, and that Assyrian *u* occurs in a number of Arabian names in Assyrian transcriptions instead of Semitic *a* (probably due to a pronunciation in ancient Arabic that resembled the *tafkhīm* of contemporary Arabic). Assyrian Šumuʾil therefore renders, in all likelihood, an ancient N Arabian tribal name *S_1amaʿ(ʾ)il,* which had the same meaning as *Yišmaʿ(ʾ)il.* Both historically and linguistically, the identity of Ishmael/*Yišmaʿʾil* with Šumuʾil/*S_1amaʿ(ʾ)il* is highly probable (Knauf 1989: 5–9, 45).

Minor points at issue are the identity of Beer-Lahai-Roi (Gen 16:13f.) and that of the mother of Ishmael, Hagar. According to the *formgeschichte* method, the enigmatic passage Gen 16:13f. is the core of the "tradition," originating in connection with a place of unknown location, Beer-Lahai-Roi, which was the Ishmaelites' cultic center where they worshipped a certain El-Roi (Noth, *RGG* 3: 935–36, and many others). According to Knauf (1989: 45–49), Gen 16:13f. is a postexilic learned addition to Gen 16:1–12, a short story of high literary quality. Lahai-Roi *(lḥyrʾy)* is structurally possible as an ancient N Arabian personal or tribal name. A tribe or a clan of this name may have given its name to a well within its area of pasturage. There is no hard evidence that a god "El Roi" ever existed. The cultic

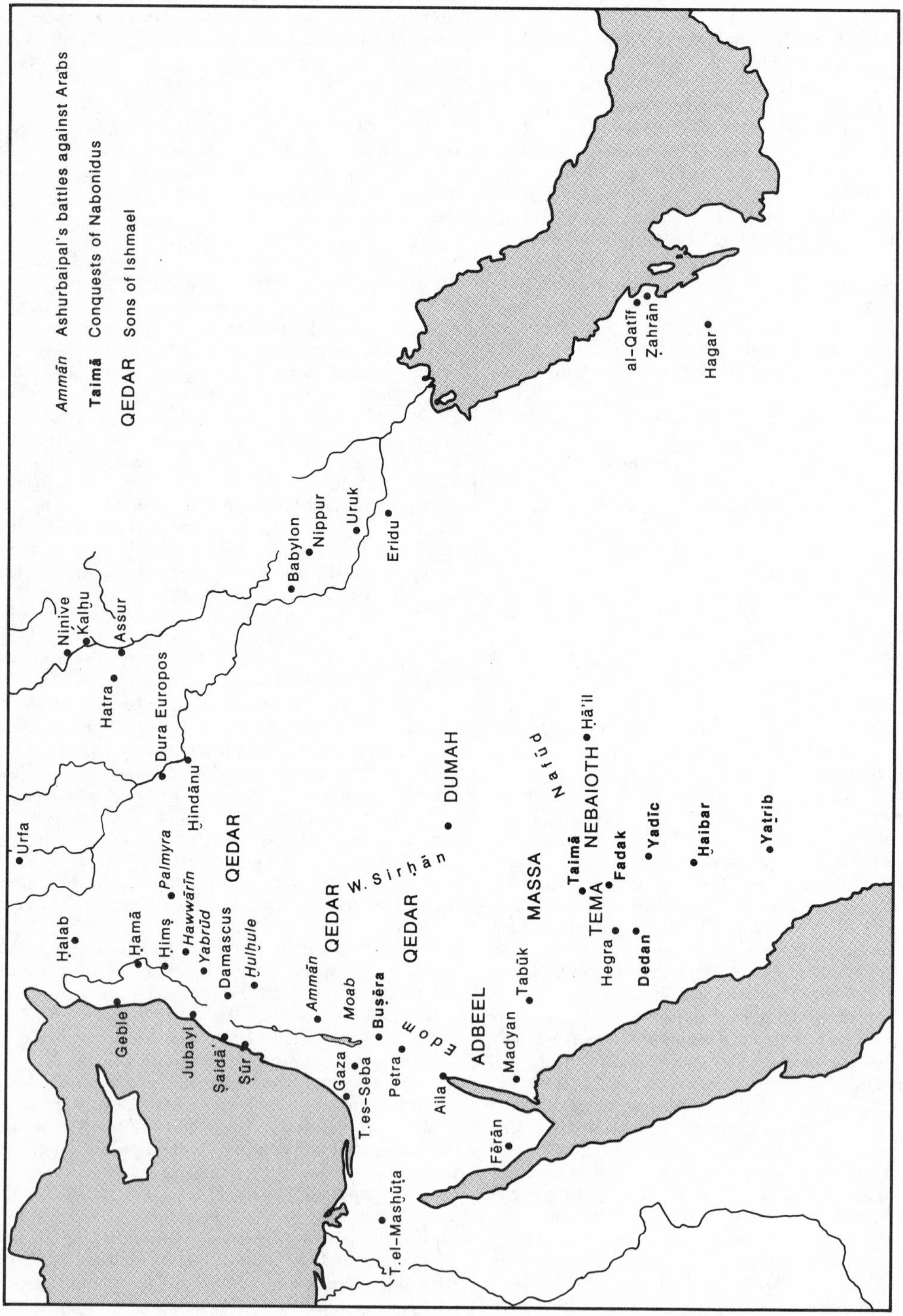

ISH.01. Ishmaelites in the ANE.

center of the Ishmaelites was Duma, and their deities were ʿAttaršamayn, Daʾa(y), Nuha(y), Ruḍā, Ab(b)irīlu, and ʿAttar-Qurumâ (Knauf 1989: 81–88).

Hagar has been connected with the Hagarites, an Arab tribe of N Transjordan and central Arabia in the Persian and early Hellenistic periods. The problem, however, arises from the fact that the Hagarites are attested later than the Ishmaelites (Meyer 1906: 328; Knauf 1989: 49–52). The most prominent "Hagar" of the ANE was a trading metropolis in E Arabia, the Gerrha of the Greek sources (see HAGAR). It is possible that the Hagar-Ishmael relationship depicted in the OT actually indicates some sort of political relationship between the central N Arabian Ishmaelites and E Arabia in the 1st millennium B.C. For the time being, however, nothing can be said positively due to the lack of sufficient archaeological and epigraphical data on E Arabia for the period 1500–500 B.C. (Potts 1983; Knauf 1989: 53–55; but cf. also Potts 1984 and 1985).

The contributions of Musil to the history of N Arabia in the 1st millennium B.C. remained outside the mainstream of scholarly discussion. This explorer discussed most of the tribes, and the sources that were available in his day, in the appendices of his travelogues (Musil 1926; 1927). However, he completely disregarded the secondary literature and was in turn disregarded in subsequent research. It is his original observations on Arab tribal life at the beginning of the 20th century, more than his attempts in historical reconstruction, that make his books a necessity for anyone who wants to study the ancient Arabs.

C. The Rise and Decline of the Ishmaelites

The Ishmaelites were the first central N Arabian desert power to appear in history. The Midianites (end of the 2d millennium B.C.) had been geographically a rather restricted group of sedentary and semisedentary agriculturalists, pastoralists, craftsmen, and traders; they never exerted political power beyond their small homeland (Knauf 1983a; 1988). The participation of the Arab Gindibu with 1000 camels in the battle of Qarqar in 853 B.C. (Ephʾal 1982: 75–77) remained an isolated episode not to be repeated for the next hundred years. The Ishmaelite tribal confederacy that reached its zenith during the heyday of the Assyrian empire comprised camel-breeding bedouin tribes and oasis towns. Tribes and towns together were able to organize and control long-distance trade through the deserts of Arabia. The Assyrian references to Ishmael/Šumuʾil all belong to the 7th century B.C. Some of the tribes of Ishmael, however, are attested as early as the end of the 8th century B.C.; attestations continue through the 3d century B.C. (Qedar) and even later (Yetur). The rise and decline of the Ishmaelite tribal confederacy can be traced as follows:

1. The 8th Century B.C. The first reference to a tribe of the *Yišmaʿʾel/Šumuʾil/S₁amaʿʾil* confederacy comes from the year 738 B.C., when Tiglath-pileser III campaigned in N and central Syria and received a tribute of male and female camels from Zabībê, queen of the Qedarites (Weippert 1973; Ephʾal 1982: 82f.; Knauf 1989: 4f.; see *ANET,* 283). While this Assyrian king laid siege to Damascus in 733 B.C., he conducted a campaign against another queen of the "Arabs," Shamshî, whom he regarded as successor to Zabībê, charging Shamshî with having broken Zabibe's oath of fealty. His booty consisted of camels, incense, and spices (Ephʾal 1982: 83–87; Knauf 1989: 3f.; see *ANET,* 283). The same Shamshî paid tribute to Sargon II in 716 B.C., together with the Pharaoh of Egypt and Yithaʿʾamar (i.e., Yathaʿʾamar Bayyin bin Sumuhūʿalīy) of Sabaʾ (Knauf 1989: 2f.; see *ANET,* 286). This tribute was due, in all probability, to the Assyrian seizure of Gaza, the Mediterranean port of the incense route. In a similar situation a number of tribes and towns of Ishmael had already paid tribute to the Assyrians in 734 B.C. These were Massaʾ, Taymâʾ, and Adbeʾel, who acted together with the Midianite tribe of ʿEpha, two other tribes, and the Sabaeans (see *ANET,* 284). This list of Arabian tribes, towns, and states, all of which can be aligned along the incense route through W Arabia, are the first attestation of this route and its trade (Weippert 1982: 25, 51; Knauf 1989: 2, n. 10; 3, n. 16).

The picture that emerges is quite clear: at the end of the 8th century B.C., the tribes of Ishmael, or at least some of them, dwelt along the incense route and controlled the incense trade. One of them, the Qedarites, held a territory that spread from the central Syrian desert through S Syria to S Palestine. See Fig. ISH.01. The extent of the tribal territory implies that it was a camel-breeding tribe; an implication supported by the listing of camels among the tributes paid. It is not known whether or not the tribes of Ishmael, or some of them, formed a confederacy as early as the end of the 8th century.

A cylinder seal, bought at the Syrian port city of Jeble, once belonged to *Baraq ʿabd ʿAttaršamayn.* ʿAttarsamayn (a goddess) was the chief deity of the Ishmaelites. It is possible, therefore, that the seal belonged to an official (e.g., a priest with political functions) of the confederacy who had it inscribed with his name. The inscription dates to the 8th (Knauf 1989: 82, n. 445) not the 9th century B.C. (Herr 1978: 40) and may be the first, albeit indirect, attestation of the Ishmaelite confederacy. This remains uncertain, since other people and tribes worshipped this goddess as well.

Obviously, it was not until the establishment of the "incense route" and the Assyrian take-over of the political power and the economic organization of the Near East that larger political entities—powerful tribes and tribal confederacies—emerged in N Arabia. The economic upsurge of the Near East, and the growing demand for incense from the 8th century B.C. onward, brought increasing political and economic power to those who controlled the Arabian deserts. This may have prompted the camel-breeders of Arabia to organize themselves into larger, politically more powerful tribes. On the basis of their riding technique, it is appropriate to call the desert tribes of the 9th to 6th centuries B.C. "proto-bedouin" (Dostal 1959; 1979; Knauf 1983a; 1983d: 30; 1986: 22–24). Their saddle technique did not allow them to use a spear, a lance, or a sword while seated on camelback. Therefore, they had to dismount for battle and were at a severe disadvantage against, e.g., the Assyrians. Assyrian reliefs give ample illustration of this (Knauf 1989: 22f., with n. 95).

The first rulers of the "Arabs" (referring here only to N Arabians) were, to a large extent, women. Seventh century B.C. Assyrian references describe the functions of these Arab queens as partially cultic in nature (Abbott 1941;

Knauf 1989: 2–6, 24, with n. 105; 1986: 25, with n. 20). Queen Shamshi may be depicted on an Assyrian relief, now in the British Museum (Knauf 1989: 3; *ANEP,* 58: 187).

2. The 7th Century B.C. The tribal confederacy of Šumuʾil/*S₁amaʿʾil*/Ishmael is clearly attested for the first time in texts from this century. The confederacy is lead by the tribe of Qedar, specifically by this tribe's ruling family. The political and cultic center of this family and, presumably, the whole tribe was Duma at the lower end of the Wādī Sirḥān (Knauf 1989: 1–5, 81–91). The individual tribal leaders fought each other constantly, allied themselves to the Assyrians, and fought the Assyrians when they were allies of Assyria's enemies. Assyrian attempts to establish a vassal kingdom in Arabia failed. This, and growing pressure exerted by the proto-bedouin on the decaying Assyrian empire (an empire weakened by epidemics and ruled by kings whose attitudes towards daily affairs were governed less by rational decisions than by irrational fears; Spieckermann 1982), may have led to a final campaign against the Arabs, probably fought ca. 644 B.C.—a campaign that was cruel even according to Assyrian standards (Knauf 1989: 96–103).

The growing importance that the Assyrians attributed to the Arabs is reflected, at the same time, by the increasing references to Arabian affairs in the various editions of Ashurbanipal's annals (*ANET,* 297–301). These annals give a vivid account of the fear and hostility that the Assyrians felt towards the Arabs. They cannot, however, be taken at face value as factual accounts; they owe their narrative sequence mostly to literary composition and redactional compilation (Weippert 1973–74; Ephʾal 1982; Knauf 1989; these three authors agree in their redaction-critical approach to Assyrian literature more than in their assessment of how much reliable factual evidence this literature contains).

The following political events can be stated with certainty. Between 691 and 689 B.C. Sennacherib conquered Duma, took queen Teʾelḫunu captive, and deported her gods. He installed Ḥazāʾil, a tribal leader who had previously supported Teʾelḫunu, as vassal king of the Arabs (Ephʾal 1982: 118–23; Knauf 1989: 4f.; 81f.). Preceding the conquest of Duma, Sennacherib mentioned "gifts" from Taymâʾ and Šumuʾil (Ephʾal 1982: 124f.). Ḥazāʾil was succeeded by his son Yauthaʿ.

Between 676 and 673 B.C., another tribal leader, named Wahb, "rebelled" against Yauthaʿ and was defeated by Assyrian support (Ephʾal 1982: 125–30; Knauf 1989: 99). According to Ephʾal, Yauthaʿ rebelled against Esarhaddon between 673 and 669 B.C., but according to Knauf (1989: 98–100) the texts refer only to one "rebellion" of Yauthaʿ, and this was directed against Ashurbanipal who defeated him sometime before 649 B.C. Yauthaʿ disappears after his defeat, and another "king" of Qedar, Abyathaʿ bin Śahrî, was appointed "king of the Arabs" by the Assyrians. ʿAmmuladdin, yet another king of Qedar, pillaged Syria before, during, or after the "rebellion" of Yauthaʿ, and was defeated by the king of Moab, Kamosh-ʿaśā.

Sometime before 649 B.C. the Assyrians established trade contacts with the Nebaioth; one of their caravans heading for Assyria was plundered by a shaykh from the tribe of Massaʾ (Knauf 1989: 93f.). After 649 B.C., another Qedarite shaykh, Yuhaythiʿ bin Birdād (who may have been a relative of the family of Ḥazāʾil), united most of N Arabia under his rule. About 644 B.C., the Assyrians conducted two major campaigns against him and his followers. The Assyrians crossed the Syrian desert, passed the vicinity of Palmyra, and ended their pursuit of the Arabs S of Damascus. Both Nebaioth and Abyathaʿ bin Śahrî fought alongside of Yuhaythiʿ despite what allegiance they may have previously sworn to the Assyrians. Ashurbanipal captured some tribal leaders in the course of this campaign, but not Yuhaythiʿ, who was the first and last ruler ever to be called "king of Šumuʾil" in the sources (Knauf 1989: 99–103). The Assyrian literary accounts of these Arabian wars are supplemented by a series of palace reliefs that show defeated camel riders (*ANEP,* 20: 63).

The tribes that are mentioned in the 7th century B.C. Assyrian texts as fighting side-by-side are Qedar, Nebaioth, Massaʾ, Naphish, and probably Mishmaʿ (Isammeʾ). Adbeel is no longer mentioned in the 7th century records. Duma is clearly attested as the political center of the tribe of Qedar and as the seat of the six deities of the "kings of the Arabs." Among these were ʿAttarsamayn, Ruḍā, and Nuhay, who are frequently attested in the Thamudic inscriptions of Nejd. These three deities are invoked together in one inscription from the vicinity of Duma which may well date back to the 7th or 6th century B.C. (Winnett and Reed 1970: 80; Knauf 1989: 81–88). After Duma was conquered by Sennacherib, it is not mentioned in any source for another five hundred years.

Although Sennacherib mentions Taymâʾ alongside of Šumuʾil, it is rather unlikely that this city formed part of the Ishmaelite confederacy. The pantheon of Duma, the Ishmaelites' capital, and that of Taymâʾ are quite different in their structures, and comprise different gods. The chief deity of the Ishmaelites and of Duma was a goddess, while the chief deity of Taymâʾ was a god. This difference would likely preclude any significant political unity among these two cities, given the political nature of religion in the ANE (Knauf 1989: 81–91).

It is quite clear, then, that not all of the (twelve!) "sons of Ishmael" listed in Gen 25:13–15 were actually part of the Ishmaelite confederacy. The rather fluid and unstable nature of bedouin tribal confederacies may mean, in the case of the Ishmaelites, that tribes who joined the leaders of the confederacy on one occasion did not join on the next. Clearly, membership in a common political superstructure did not mean for the N Arabian tribes that they were no longer able to fight among one another, nor did the actions of one shaykh of the large tribe of Qedar necessarily determine the actions of other parts of this tribe, or reflect the others' attitudes. It is as difficult for the modern historian to describe this type of political entity and its history as it was for the Assyrians to deal with it politically and militarily.

Arguing from the structure of the list in Gen 25:13–15, Knauf (1989: 89) suggests that only the first seven of the twelve tribes/cities actually formed part of the Ishmaelite confederacy in the 7th century B.C. (Qedar, Nebaioth, Adbeel, Massaʾ, Duma, Mishmaʿ). However this reconstruction has been complicated by the publication of an Assyrian letter that clearly derives from the context of the major Assyrian–Arab wars of the mid-7th century B.C. (Knauf

1983b) and mentions the tribe Naphish (which, according to Knauf, belongs to the latest additions to the Gen 25:13–15 list).

3. The 6th and 5th Centuries B.C. Since it is unknown how much of the Assyrian accounts of their victories over the Arabs of the mid-7th century B.C. are fictional, the disappearance of the term "Ishmaelites" (Šumuʾil) from the documentary sources after the collapse of the Assyrian empire need not necessarily be attributed to the success of the Assyrian campaigns. Presumably the nonurban population of the ANE, including the bedouin, was less affected by the turmoil, wars, epidemics, and chaos of the late 7th and early 6th centuries that marked the transitions from the Assyrian and Neo-Babylonian empires to that of the Persians. When the Persians started to reorganize the W part of their inherited empire, they had to reckon with only two politically noteworthy ethnic groups in Syria-Palestine: the kings of the Phoenician coastal cities, and the "kings that lived in tents" (Knauf 1989: 63, n. 300). Arabs had gained power in the territories of Ammon, Moab, Edom, and S Palestine and, from then on, formed a considerable part of the population of these areas (cf. Ezek 25:1–14). It was this territorial and political extension of their realm, resulting in decreased contacts between the disparate tribes and clans, not military defeat by one of the empires, that brought the Ishmaelite confederacy to an end.

The Qedarites remained in power between the Euphrates and the Gulf of Aqaba well into the 5th century B.C. In 599/598 B.C., Nebuchadnezzar campaigned against them in the Syrian desert. In the middle of the 5th century, a shaykh of Qedar, Guśam bin Śahr (the biblical Geshem) ruled over S Palestine, the Sinai to the borders of Egypt, Transjordan and NW Arabia, all areas under Persian control. This fact demonstrates clearly the rise in prominence of the Arabs among the ethnic and political groups of the ANE between the 7th and the 5th centuries B.C. Aramaic dedicatory inscriptions left by Geshem's son at Tell el-Maskhūṭa (ancient Patoumos) in the E delta of Egypt ca. 400 B.C. prove that Geshem was a Qedarite (Dumbrell 1971). A Lihyanite inscription testifies that the influence of "Geshem the Arab" (Neh 2:16) extended well into the Ḥijâz. On the basis of an inscription from Taymâʾ, the Lihyanite reference can now be confidently dated to the middle of the 5th century B.C. (Aggoula 1985: 66; Cross 1986); the dating of the Lihyanite kingdom and the Lihyanite inscriptions had previously been the subject of controversy (Roschinski 1980; Knauf 1989: 104–106).

The sphere of influence of Geshem the Qedarite was actually contiguous with the region that later became the Nabatean empire. Knauf assumes that the Nabateans were a Qedarite clan which moved into S Jordan in the course of the 6th century B.C. The "Nebaioth" of Isa 60:7; Gen 28:9; 36:3 may actually refer to the Qedarite clan **Nabaṭ* and not to the more distant Nabayat of the Taymâʾ area (Winnett and Reed 1970: 100; Knauf 1989: 108f.). Most likely, the "tents of Qedar" mentioned in Cant 1:5 (probably from the 3d century B.C.) refer to the Nabatean bedouin camping between Palestine and the Šalamaeans in the N Hijaz (Knauf 1989: 106–107). See also SHALMA. Around 400 B.C. the Persians lost control over Egypt, Arabia, and probably S Jordan. With the disappearance of the power that supported them, the supremacy of the family of Guśam bin Śahr of the tribe of Qedar came to an end. This opened the path to wealth, fame and glory to those tribes and clans formerly under their control that were now either active enough to seize their chance, or enjoyed a favorable enough strategic position along the international trade routes. The Nabataeans, as is well known, had already accumulated a considerable fortune when they first appear in the literary record under their own name in 312 B.C.

Bibliography

Abbott, N. 1941. Pre-Islamic Arabic Queens. *AJSL* 58: 1–22.

Abu-Duruk, H. 1986. *A Critical and Comparative Discussion of Certain Ancient Monuments . . . in the N Arabian City of Taymâʾ*. Riyadh.

Aggoula, B. 1985. Studia Aramaica II. *Syria* 62: 61–76.

Albright, W. F. 1956. The Biblical Tribe of Massaʾ and Some Congeners. Vol. 1, pp. 1–14 in *Studi orientalistici in onore di Giorgi Levi della Vida*. Rome.

Bawden, G. 1981. Recent Radiocarbon Dates from Tayma. *Atlal* 5: 149–53.

———. 1983. Painted Pottery from Tayma and Problems of Cultural Chronology in NW Arabia. Pp. 37–52 in *Midian, Moab and Edom,* ed. J. F. A. Sawyers and D. J. A. Clines. Sheffield.

Bawden, G., Edens, C., and Miller, R. 1980. Preliminary Archaeological Investigations at Tayma. *Atlal* 4: 69–106.

Cross, F. M. 1986. A New Aramaic Stele from Taymâʾ. *CBQ* 48: 387–94.

Dostal, W. 1959. The Evolution of Bedouin Life. Pp. 11–34 in *L'Antica società beduina*, ed. S. Moscati and F. Gabrieli. Rome.

———. 1979. The Development of Bedouin Life in Arabia Seen from Archaeological Material. Vol. 1, pp. 125–44 in *Studies in the History of Arabia.* Ed. A. H. Masri. Riyadh.

Dumbrell, W. I. 1970. *The Midianites and their Transjordanian Successors.* Diss., Harvard.

———. 1971. The Tell el-Maskhûta Bowls and the "Kingdom" of Qedar in the Persian Period. *BASOR* 203: 33–44.

———. 1972. Jeremiah 49:29–33. An Oracle Against a Proud Desert Power. *AJBA* 1/5: 99–109.

Ephʾal, I. 1976. "Ishmael" and "Arab(s)": A Transformation of Ethnological Terms. *JNES* 35: 225–35.

———. 1982. *The Ancient Arabs.* Jerusalem.

Görg, M. 1986. Hagar die Ägypterin. *BN* 33: 17–20.

Herr, L. G. 1978. *The Scripts of Ancient NW Semitic Seals.* Missoula, MT.

Knauf, E. A. 1983a. Midianites and Ishmaelites. Pp. 147–62 in *Midian, Moab and Edom,* ed. J. F. A. Sawyer and D. J. A. Clines. Sheffield.

———. 1983b. Supplementa Ismaelitica. *BN* 20: 34–36.

———. 1983c. Supplementa Ismaelitica. *BN* 21: 37–47.

———. 1983d. Supplementa Ismaelitica. *BN* 22: 25–33.

———. 1984. Supplementa Ismaelitica. *BN* 25: 19–26.

———. 1986. Supplementa Ismaelitica. *BN* 30: 19–28.

———. 1988. *Midian.* ADPV. Wiesbaden.

———. 1989. *Ismael.* 2d ed. ADPV. Wiesbaden.

Livingstone, A., et al. 1983. Taimaʾ: Recent Soundings and New Inscribed Material. *Atlal* 7: 102–16.

Marfoe, L. 1979. The Integrative Transformation: Patterns of Sociopolitical Organization in Southern Syria. *BASOR* 234: 1–42.

Meyer, E. 1906. *Die Israeliten und ihre Nachbarstämme.* Halle.

Musil, A. 1926. *The Northern Hegâz.* New York.

———. 1927. *Arabia Deserta.* New York.
Nöldeke, T. 1864. *Über die Amalekiter und einige andere Nachbarvölker der Israeliten.* Göttingen.
Potts, D. T., ed. 1983. *Dilmun: New Studies in the Archaeology and Early History of Bahrain.* Berlin.
Potts, D. T. 1984. Thaj and the Location of Gerrha. *Proceedings of the Seminar for Arabian Studies* 14: 87–91.
———. 1985. From Qadê to Mazûn: Four Notes on Oman, ca. 700 B.C. to 700 A.D. *Journal of Oman Studies* 8: 81–95.
Roschinski, H. P. 1980. Sprachen, Schriften und Inschriften in Nordwestarabien. *Bonner Jahrbücher* 180: 155–88.
Spieckermann, H. 1982. *Juda unter Assur in der Sargonidenzeit.* Göttingen.
Thompson, T. L. 1987. *The Origin Traditions of Ancient Israel.* Vol. 1. JSOTSup 55. Sheffield.
Trible, P. 1984. *Texts of Terror.* Philadelphia.
Weippert, M. 1973. Menahem von Israel und seine Zeitgenossen in einer Steleninschrift des assyrischen Königs Tiglatpileser III aus dem Iran. *ZDPV* 89: 26–53.
———. 1973–74. Die Kämpfe des assyrischen Königs Assurbanipal gegen die Araber. *WO* 7: 39–85.
———. 1982. Zur Syrienpolitik Tiglatpilesers III. Vol. 2, pp. 395–408 in *Mesoptamien und seine Nachbarn,* Ed. H. J. Nissen and J. Renger. Berlin.
Winnett, F. V. 1980. A Reconstruction of Some Inscriptions from the Tayma Area. *Proceedings of the Seminar for Arabian Studies* 10: 133–40.
Winnett, F. V., and Reed, W. L. 1970. *Ancient Records from North Arabia.* Toronto.

ERNST AXEL KNAUF

ISHMAIAH (PERSON) [Heb *yišmaʿyāh*]. **1.** A Benjaminite warrior from Gibeon who joined David's band at Ziklag (1 Chr 12:4; cf. 1 Sam 27:6). Ishmaiah is noted as "a mighty man among the thirty and a leader over the thirty." What exactly "the thirty" refers to is not clear. It is possibly a technical term for the king's bodyguard. This group therefore could have consisted of a varying number of men at different times (Elliger 1935). This possibly explains why Joab can be said to be "over the thirty" in 11:20 and Amisai as "chief of the thirty" in 12:19—Eng 12:18 (Myers *1 Chronicles* AB). Perhaps this also explains why Ishmaiah does not appear as one the thirty in 2 Sam 23:24–39. The allusion in 1 Chr 12:1 to events at Ziklag, which occurred before David became king, participates in the Chronicler's "all Israel" theme by portraying northerners as coming to David's side even before the death of Saul, a Benjaminite himself.

2. A member of the tribe of Zebulun and father of Obadiah (1 Chr 27:19). 1 Chr 27:16–24 lists the leaders of the tribes during the reign of David; Ishmaiah is noted as the leader of the tribe of Zebulun. The tribal list varies from that given in Numbers 1. Here the tribes of Asher and Gad are not included and Aaron and Levi are listed as two separate groups. The specific bureaucratic task of the tribal leaders is not clear but vv 23 and 24 suggest that they were responsible in some way for assisting in a census.

Bibliography

Elliger, K. 1935. Die dreissig Helden Davids. *PJ* 31: 29–75.

JAMES M. KENNEDY

ISHMERAI (PERSON) [Heb *yišmĕray*]. Son of Elpaal, a Benjaminite (1 Chr 8:18) appearing in an extended Benjaminite genealogy (1 Chr 8:1–40). The name occurs nowhere else in this form in the MT, the Apocrypha, or the deuterocanonical literature. The name itself comes from the verbal form *šāmar* meaning "keep" or "preserve," and may be a somewhat abbreviated form which means "may [Yahweh] preserve." The family of Ishmerai, according to 1 Chr 8:12 is associated with Ono and Lod. Ezra 2:33, Neh 7:37, and 11:35 bear witness to this association. However, the fact that these cities and their satellite villages are located in the maritime plain in what is traditionally Danite territory (Adams and Callaway 1965: 55) poses an interesting problem. Myers (*1 Chronicles* AB, 60) has suggested that Benjaminites may have settled this region during the reign of Rehoboam. There is little mention of Dan in 1 Chronicles (2:2; 27:22) which may reflect that this inheritance had been absorbed by Ephraimite and Judahite groups. Ishmerai is called a "chief living in Jerusalem" (1 Chr 8:28). Besides implications of social organizations, this designation may reflect a mixing of the tribal groups of Judah and Benjamin at various points from the time of the kingdom's schism. Coggins (*Chronicles* CBC, 54) has indicated that tribal mixing resulted in certain areas never being absorbed into definite tribal holdings, with Jerusalem being a prime example. Judges 1:8, 21 show Judahite and Benjaminite groups struggling to control Jerusalem.

Bibliography

Adams, J. M., and Callaway, J. A. 1965. *Biblical Backgrounds.* Nashville, TN.

G. EDWIN HARMON

ISHPAH (PERSON) [Heb *yišpâ*]. Son of Beriah (1 Chr 8:16) appearing in an extended Benjaminite genealogy (1 Chr 8:1–40). The name means "smooth" or "swept bare." This is the only appearance of the name in the MT, and it does not occur in the Apocrypha or the deuterocanonical literature. Ishpah and his relatives are associated with the city of Aijalon (1 Chr 8:13). Ishpah is called a *roʾšê hāʾābôt* of those who settled in Aijalon and drove out the residents of Gath. Myers (*1 Chronicles* AB, 60) has indicated that this reference is an indication of tribal mixings that occurred throughout Israelite history. Rudolph (*Chronikbücher* HAT, 77) has emphasized the geographical breaks in this genealogy which show parallel lists of Benjaminite families and their dwelling locations at a particular time, probably either during the reign of Josiah or the postexilic period. Williamson (*Chronicles* NCBC, 82), however, suggests that there is no apparent structure to this genealogy. As strange as it seems both scholars may be correct. With the mixing of tribal groupings, traditions emphasizing one tribal group over another and vice versa would have held sway at different periods of time depending upon which group was in control at a given time. 2 Chr 11:10 indicates that Aijalon, among others, belonged to Judah and/or Benjamin, however, 28:18 clearly states that it belongs to Judah. According to 1 Chr 6:6 Ephraim took Aijalon over from Dan. Because of its strategic location, this kind of transfer from tribal grouping to tribal grouping would not be unusual (Adams and Callaway 1965: 61).

Bibliography

Adams, J. M., and Callaway, J. A. 1965. *Biblical Backgrounds.* Nashville.

G. Edwin Harmon

ISHPAN (PERSON) [Heb *yišpān*]. One of the eleven sons of Shashak, the Benjaminite (1 Chr 8:22) appearing in an extended Benjaminite genealogy (1 Chr 8:40). The meaning is somewhat difficult, but could be translated "he will hide" or a "strong one." This is the only occurrence of the name in the MT, and it does not appear in the Apocrypha or the deuterocanonical literature. Both Braun (*1 Chronicles* WBC 124) and Coggins (*Chronicles* CBC, 54) point to the scarcity of material associated with the names found in 1 Chr 8:6–27. However, the text states that Ishpan was a *roʾšê ʾābôt,* and one of the *tōlĕdôtām roʾšîm* living in Jerusalem. This points to probable mixing of tribal groups which intensified after the monarchical schism. One might infer a high status for Ishpan in political, social, and military circles, because of his designation as a head of a family and a genealogy. In early Israel (Harmon 1983: 153) the *bēt ʾāb* would have been the primary social unit which further comprised the *mišpāḥā,* the clan or protective association of families (Gottwald 1979: 258), and then the *maṭṭeh/šēbeṭ,* or tribe. The head of the family may have functioned much like the bigmen of anthropological terminology. Though tribes eventually became more of a geographical designation than an organizational one (Anderson 1969: 34; de Geus 1976: 133), the social pattern would have held without great change to the time of Ishpan.

Bibliography

Anderson, F. J. 1969. Israelite Kinship Terminology and Social Structure. *The Bible Translator* 20: 29–39.

Geus, C. H. J. de. 1976. *The Tribes of Israel.* Amsterdam.

Gottwald, N. K. 1979. *The Tribes of Yahweh.* Maryknoll, NY.

Harmon, G. E. 1983. *Floor Area and Population Determination.* Diss. Southern Baptist Theological Seminary.

G. Edwin Harmon

ISHTAR (DEITY). The principal goddess of ancient Mesopotamia (See Wilcke, *RLA* 5: 74–87). Comparative evidence suggests that the Akkadian (Assyro-Babylonian) deity was perhaps masculine (Heimpel 1982: 13–15), but when the Akkadians assimilated Sumerian culture, Ishtar was adjusted to correspond to the feminine Sum goddess Inanna; both Ishtar and Inanna were personifications of the planet Venus. The extraordinarily diverse characterizations of Inanna-Ishtar in the subsequent literature, together with traditions from a multiplicity of shrine sites, would indicate that other goddesses were also gradually subsumed into the Inanna-Ishtar complex.

Astarte was the W Semitic counterpart of Ishtar, but it should be emphasized that Ishtar and Astarte are not simply to be identified (see Fulco *EncRel* 1: 471). In later Greek and Roman mythology Aphrodite and Venus undoubtedly had absorbed some Ishtar and Astarte traditions from the East (Astour 1967: 267, n.2).

The principal image of Ishtar that emerges from the extant hymns and myths is a goddess of love and sexuality, and it is here that she is closely associated with the shepherd-king Tammuz (or Sum Dumuzi) in a large complex of stories. Most notable are the parallel Sum *Inanna's Descent to the Nether World* (*ANET,* 52–57) and Akk *Descent of Ishtar* (*ANET,* 106–9). After a passionate courtship with Dumuzi, Inanna (or Ishtar) visits the netherworld to contend there with her sister Ereshkigal. Ereshkigal has her killed, but Inanna's servants revivify her and bring her back to earth. Here, although there are different and even contradictory traditions, she evidently finds Dumuzi at best indifferent about her apparent death. She sets demons after him and they drag him down to the underworld. Eventually it is arranged that he dwell there half a year, on earth the other half.

The relationship between Inanna-Ishtar and Dumuzi-Tammuz was ritualized in Mesopotamian cult with the sacred marriage: the mating of the king with a sacred temple prostitute renewed the generative forces in nature. The seasonal cycle was seen as a mirror of Dumuzi's yearly descent into and ascent from the underworld, a religious element that wends its way even to the temple courtyard in Jerusalem (see Ezek 8:14). Some (e.g., Pope *Song of Songs* AB) hear strong echos of the Ishtar-Tammuz tales throughout the Song of Songs.

A rather petulant Ishtar appears in the epic of *Gilgamešh.* She tries to seduce the hero, but he points out to her the less than gracious treatment she has meted out to her other lovers, especially Tammuz.

Among the many hymns to Inanna-Ishtar, the work entitled *Nin-me-šár-ra* (Hallo and van Dijk 1968) is the richest in epithets for Ishtar: "Queen of the divine decrees, resplendent light, righteous woman clothed in radiance, beloved of Heaven and Earth." It is widely thought that the "queen of heaven" in Jer 7:18; 44:17–19, 25, is actually Ishtar. The women of Jerusalem and subsequently the women of the Egyptian diaspora burn incense and pour our libations to the goddess and make cakes with her image. They complain (Jer 44:18) that not doing so brings disaster. Porten (1968: 165, 176–78) argues that this may be Anat rather than Ishtar. He cites the position of Anat in the Jewish texts from Elephantine in Egypt. Other Egyptian evidence (see Fulco 1976: 23–28) suggests Asherah-Qudšu as a candidate.

Bibliography

Astour, M. C. 1967. *Hellenosemitica.* Leiden.

Dahood, M. J. 1960. La Regina del Cielo in Geremia. *RBI* 8: 166–68.

Fulco, W. J. 1976. *The Canaanite God Rešep.* New Haven.

Hallo, W. W. and Dijk, J. van. 1968. *The Exaltation of Inanna.* New Haven.

Heimpel, W. 1982. A Catalog of Near Eastern Venus Deities. Pp. 9–22 in *SMS* 4.

Jacobsen, T. 1976. *The Treasures of Darkness.* New Haven.

Kramer, S. N. 1963. *The Sumerians.* Chicago.

———. 1969. *The Sacred Marriage Rite.* Bloomington.

Porten, B. 1968. *Archives from Elephantine.* Berkeley.
Wolkstein, D., and Kramer, S. N. 1984. *Inanna, Queen of Heaven and Earth.* London.

WILLIAM J. FULCO

ISHVAH (PERSON) [Heb *yišwâ*]. Second son of Asher. In the genealogical list of Jacob's family (Gen 46:8–27), his children are listed by families, according to their mothers. Ishvah is a grandson of Jacob and Leah by her maid Zilpah (Gen 46:17; 1 Chr 7:30). The name Ishvah does not appear in the list of the clans of Asher (Num 26:44–47). The absence of Ishvah among the clans of Asher has been explained differently by scholars. Some say that Ishvah is a variant name of ISHVI, but according to Gen 46:17 and 1 Chr 7:30 Ishvi is listed as the third son of Asher. Others say that the two names represent the same clan, that the Chronicler copied the dittography of Genesis (Curtis *Chronicles* ICC, 153). It is possible that only the name of the family of Ishvi is given because Ishvah died childless. Wieder (1965: 161) has demonstrated that the Hebrew names Ishvah and Ishvi probably were abbreviated theophoric names derived from an Ugaritic word meaning "to rule."

Bibliography

Wieder, A. A. 1965. Ugaritic-Hebrew Lexicographical Notes. *JBL* 84: 160–64.

CLAUDE F. MARIOTTINI

ISHVI (PERSON) [Heb *yišwî*]. **1.** The son of Saul ben Kish and Ahinoam, the daughter of Ahimaaz (1 Sam 14:49). The MT vocalization would seem to relate the name to the Hebrew root *šwh,* "to resemble, to be like; to be smooth, even." The name would represent an imperfect verbal form "he will smooth" or "he will requite." As such, it could be a hypocoristicon of a common category of name composed of a verbal element followed by a deity name. Alternatively, the consonantal Hebrew text *yšwy* is perhaps to be understood as a passive *Qal* participle meaning "with a damaged hand" (so IPN 227, n. 17). G^L (LXX) reads Iessiou, which would seem to presume an underlying Hebrew text of *yšyw* or *yšyhw* (for the latter, see Driver 1890: 92), while G^B reads *Iessioul,* presuming a Hebrew original *yšywl.* On the basis of G^L's presumed *yšyw,* it might be possible to suggest that the MT consonantal text *yšwy* arose accidentally through metathesis of the final two letters (i.e., Klein *1 Samuel* WBC, 142).

It is common practice to suggest that the LXX reading *Iessiou* reflects an underlying Hebrew form *ʾîšyô* or *ʾîšyahû,* "man of Yahweh," and that the name is a variant form of ESHBAAL, the name of one of Saul's sons in 1 Chr 8:33 and 9:39, which appears as ISH-BOSHETH in 2 Sam 2:8, 10, 12, 15; 3:8, 14, 15; 4:5, 8, 12 (so i.e. Driver 1890: 92; Gray 1896: 121; Budde *Samuel* KHC, 106; Dhorme 1910: 127; Stoebe *Erste Buch Samuels* KAT, 276; Soggin 1975: 32, n. 1). The presumption is that Eshbaal was the original form of the name, and that with the passage of time, the epithet *baʿal,* "lord," which had originally been applied to Yahweh, came to be equated with the storm deity Baal and fell from favor. This is to have led to the substitution of the term *bōšet,* "shame," on the one hand, and in the case of 1 Sam 14:49, of *Yo*/*Yahu,* the original deity to whom the epithet "lord" was intended to be related. All forms of the name in the LXX presume an initial *yod,* however, not an initial *alep,* and there is no textual evidence that would support the proposed emendation.

A minority favor viewing Ishvi as an additional son of Saul's, separate from the individual Eshbaal/Ishbosheth (i.e. *IPN* 228, n. 17; McCarter *1 Samuel* AB, 254). Even if one were to equate Ishvi with Eshbaal, the list of Saulide family members in 1 Sam 14:49 would still be missing Abinadab. It is not possible to argue that the list in 14:49 is a specious genealogy intended only to introduce family members who will figure in the subsequent narrative segment devoted to Saul, 1 Samuel 15–2 Samuel 1 (indirectly, Miscall 1986: 97). Abinadab appears alongside his father and brothers Malchishua and Jonathan at the battle of Gilboa in 1 Samuel 31, and so logically should have been included in the list in 14:49. A plausible explanation for the differences between the two lists of royal offspring found in 1 Sam 14:49 and 1 Chr 8:33 (= 1 Chr 9:39) would be that the list in Samuel was derived from an early source that reflected the birth order of the royal family before the arrival of the two youngest children, Abinadab and Eshbaal, while the list in Chronicles reflects a later stage, after the death of the second-born son, Ishvi, and the subsequent birth of two additional sons, Abinadab and Eshbaal.

2. A son of Asher, the eponymous son of Jacob and founder of the tribe bearing his name (Gen 46:17; Num 26:44; 1 Chr 7:30). In biblical historiographic tradition, Ishvi is to have been among the descendants of Israel who went to Egypt to join Jacob during the prolonged famine (Gen 46:17). Similarly, his *mišpāḥâ,* "maximal lineage or clan" (Lemche 1985: 260–72) is reported to have been among those who were part of the census taken during the wilderness wandering period, after the Baal of Peor incident (Num 26:44).

The occurrence of the name in 1 Chr 7:30 reflects the Chronicler's use of the same genealogical tradition as the one in Gen 46:17. The identical set of names appears in the same sequence, including what appears to be variant readings of the name in question side by side: Ishvah and Ishvi. It should be noted that various manuscripts read "Ishvah" instead of "Ishvi" as the name of Jacob's son in Num 26:44, but are unanimous in their use of Ishvi to designate his family group. This may suggest that Ishvi is a gentilic form and that the correct spelling of the nominative absolute form of the Asherite name in question should be Ishvah.

Bibliography

Dhorme, P. 1910. *Les livres de Samuel.* EB. Paris.
Driver, S. R. 1890. *Notes on the Hebrew Text of the Books of Samuel.* Oxford.
Gray, G. B. 1896. *Studies in Hebrew Proper Names.* London.
Lemche, N. P. 1985. *Early Israel.* VTSup 37. Leiden.
Miscall, P. 1986. *1 Samuel: A Literary Reading.* Indiana Studies in Biblical Literature. Bloomington, IN.
Soggin, J. A. 1975. The Reign of ʾEšbaʿal, Son of Saul. Pp. 31–49 in *Old Testament and Oriental Studies,* ed. J. A. Soggin. BibOr 29. Rome.

DIANA V. EDELMAN

ISKANDER, KHIRBET (M.R. 223107). An EB IV site in Jordan which has provided unequivocal evidence of a sedentary character for this period which had earlier been characterized as nomadic.

A. Identification of the Site
B. Location and Topographical Description
C. Exploration of the Site
D. History of the Settlement
E. Early Bronze I
F. Early Bronze IV
G. Cemeteries
H. Sociocultural Considerations

A. Identification of the Site

The ancient name of the site is unknown. The name Iskander appears to derive from the nearby Roman site of Iskander and the adjacent modern village of the same name, both of which are located ca. 2 km to the W of the EB Age site. Although an attempt has been made (Bernhardt 1960) to identify the latter with the biblical site of Jahaz (Num 21:23; Deut 2:23; Judg 11:20), the fact that Kh. Iskander's periods of occupation are the Late Chalcolithic through EB IV periods renders this correlation untenable. Recently, based on Glueck's and the recent expedition's survey work, the site of Kh. Medeinyeh with its Iron Age occupation has been suggested as the biblical site of Jahaz (Dearman 1984).

B. Location and Topographical Description

Kh. Iskander lies approximately 24.0 km S of Madaba and some 400 m W of the bridge where the Madaba-Dhiban road crosses the perennial Wâdī el-Wâlā. This region is called the Mishôr in the biblical text (e.g., Deut 3:10; 4:43) and is perhaps best described as a mountain tableland. The site rises ca. 20 m above the landscape and covers ca. 7.5 acres; its S boundary is steeply cut by the bank of the Wâlā. The Iskander settlement is strategically situated at a major crossing of the ancient Roman road, undoubtedly the same route as the biblical "King's Highway." Today the area in the immediate vicinity of Iskander supports intensive agriculture: orchards and fields with grape vineyards, olive groves, and deep plowing for field crops. The character of the occupational history of the area indicates that the valley has historically been agriculturally productive.

C. Exploration of the Site

While the site has been known for some time (Schick 1879; Brünnow and von Domaszewski 1904; Musil 1907), Glueck (1939: 127–29) was the first systematically to survey and record its architectural features and to date the site to the EB IV. He observed extensive domestic occupation within the walls of a thick perimeter fortification that included square towers. Based on large standing and fallen *menhirs, menhir*-circles, and platform foundations, he concluded that a large cemetery lay E of the site. It was not until soundings by P. Parr (1960), however, that definitive evidence for important EB IV sedentary occupation at the site became known. In his two trenches on the E ridge, Parr identified multiphased EB IV occupation, as well as Late Chalcolithic/EB I materials. His walled, cobblestoned courtyard and earlier massive fortifications in Trench I appear to correlate with discoveries of the present expedition (below). S. Richard became director of the current excavations which conducted its pilot season of survey and soundings in 1981 (Richard 1982), followed by three major seasons of excavation in 1982 (Richard 1983; Richard and Boraas 1984), 1984 (Richard 1986; Richard and Boraas 1988), and 1987 (Richard 1989). Work has concentrated primarily in three areas: Area A at the SW corner; Area B at the NW corner; Area C at the SE corner; and in cemeteries D, E, and J (to the S, E, and W of the site respectively). The seven phases uncovered thus far (in Area B) include one (phase G) from the EB I, and six (F-A) in the EB IV.

D. History of the Settlement

The current excavations have confirmed Parr's earlier findings of two periods of occupation—the Late Chalcolithic/EB I and the EB IV. The current expedition has concentrated on the EB IV strata on the mound, specifically to examine sedentary adaptations in a way that should offer suggestions about the nature of this enigmatic culture and its relationship to the preceding (EB III) urban city-state system. The EB IV (formerly MB I or Intermediate EB-MB) period has traditionally been considered a "nomadic interlude" between the urban EB and MB Ages (Richard 1987a). Although Kathleen Kenyon disassociated EB IV culture from the EB Age proper (*CAH*[3] 1/2: 532–94), a growing body of evidence from Transjordan and, in particular Kh. Iskander, demonstrates strong continuities with EB III traditions, including urban traditions. Kh. Iskander is the first-known fortified site in the EB IV period, although surveys in Jordan have identified at least a half dozen other walled sites at that time. It is increasingly evident from excavations in Jordan over the past 15 years that the EB IV was a period of urban regression, not a nomadic interlude (Richard 1980; 1987a, b). Given this new view from Transjordan, it is now evident that the model of pastoral-nomadism, as suggested by Dever (1980), has important regional applications, but is not comprehensive enough to characterize the totality of EB IV remains.

E. Early Bronze I

The lowest level reached thus far is Phase G in the Area B probe. It consists of a partial structure associated with EB I pottery (e.g., a red-slipped omphalos base and several sherds of line-group painted wares). The probe is on the N edge of the site and has yielded no evidence of a fortification system, from which it appears that the site was an unwalled village. Parr's earlier work, the results of our sherd survey, and the discovery of an EB I tomb (see below) suggest, however, that the site sustained a rather significant occupation during the EB I.

F. Early Bronze IV

1. Area B. The EB IV is characterized on the tell by three stages of occupation, which encompass six phases: prefortified (Phase F), fortified (Phases E–B), and postfortified (Phase A). This profile is derived primarily on discoveries at the NW corner in the Area B domestic complex.

The earliest phase (F) is thus far evident only by the corner of a domestic structure lying immediately below the NW corner fortifications and above the EB I layer. The data suggest that it was a transitional open settlement in the EB IV prior to the erection of the fortifications.

There are two wall systems, the earlier inner wall founded in Phase E and the later outer wall founded in Phase D. The Phase E system is composed of a base of massive stones and a superstructure of mudbrick faced with large cobbles. This wall and superstructure slope at an angle of ca. 30°, perhaps indicating destruction by earthquake. Apparently the site was immediately rebuilt and strengthened, and involved buttressing the fortifications, building an outer wall and towers, and filling the interior with rubble (Phase D).

The Phase D settlement consists of an eleven-stone course, 3 m high, and 2.5 m wide defensive perimeter wall on the N edge of the site. A 20 m stretch of this wall has been exposed (B4, B3, B8, B12). A foundation trench containing an EB IV holemouth and the rim of an imported caliciform cup from Syria of the "white on black" variety provided the date for the erection of this later defensive line. Steps uncovered in 1987 make it clear that the corner structure was a tower. Excavations on the interior of the wall have not reached the founding domestic occupational level.

The earliest evidence for occupation within the fortifications is the Phase C (may equal Phase D) "lower storeroom" in B8. This level lies immediately below the "benchroom" of Phase B. The pottery, EB IV whole and restorable vessels along with extraordinary quantities of sherds, was found in a matrix of mudbrick debris and rubble, clear evidence of the destruction of Phase C. The E wall of this room bonded into the outer fortifications and provides additional evidence for the EB IV date of the fortifications.

The Phase B remains provide a partial architectural plan of the domestic area within the fortifications. The excavated area comprised two rooms of a large building whose total dimensions are not yet known. B8-B7, a bench-lined "upper storeroom," contained quantities of whole and restorable EB IV pottery. Storejars containing carbonized grain lay on the bench. Alongside the bench, resting on a pavement was a pithos with rope molding.

In an adjoining room, excavation uncovered a perfectly preserved stone-lined bin constructed of eight upright slabs (ca. 1 m high), with a well-hewn circular stone (ca. 0.80 m in diameter) at the bottom. The area around the bin was plastered. The nature of the material culture associated with this bin, including the unusual quantity (large storejars in particular) and quality of the pottery, indicates that the building complex functioned as a public facility—the evidence suggests a cultic use. The bin contained a variety of botanical remains (indicating perhaps a *favissa*), and nearby were both a hearth and ash pit as well as miniature vessels. On the surface nearby were two goat horns and a beautifully painted bowl (perhaps an offering dish) containing a bovine hoof. Finally the Iskander bin closely parallels the *favissa* found at Arad in association with the *bamah* and the twin-temples.

Phase A represents the latest EB IV occupation on the mound. Extensive domestic occupation in broad- and long-room houses with common walls were located about 4 m S of the outer fortifications, which were certainly not in use in this phase. The nature of the evidence in Phase A contrasts with that of Phase B where, as noted above, the material remains suggest a different set of activities.

One large room, 8.5 m × 3.5 m, accommodated cooking activities as attested by its two-phased ṭabûn, several large firepits or hearths nearby, and its ash-covered surface. An adjacent courtyard contained a number of pounding stones and a ṭabûn built at the junction of two walls. Large saddle querns and grinding stones were numerous in this phase. Located just beyond the housing area were a series of small work areas or pens at the edge of the mound. In 1987, we uncovered an interesting house structure inside of which were a large stone mortar, a square stone table with a center depression, a round stone worktable, and an unusual stone platform with a shelf. Notably, two of the Phase A buildings proved to be "pillar" buildings, once the later phased blockages were removed.

On the basis of the plans we now have for area B, we may observe that town planning at Kh. Iskander is not inconsistent with the settlement plans for EB II–III urban sites such as Arad, Bâb edh-Dhrâᶜ, and Numeira. Series of interconnected broad- and long-room houses of various sizes are arranged around courtyard areas. The pottery storeroom with its grain containers, the cooking installations, food preparation accoutrements, etc. underscore the sedentary and agricultural basis of this community. As at Arad, the habitation arrangement probably implies an extended family social organization.

2. Area C. At the SE corner of the mound, excavation has revealed a complex of buildings, some of which are monumental in character. Three phases have been excavated: Phase C (bottom) was a domestic level with rectangular houses; Phase B was a domestic level whose distinguishing feature was its interconnected broad-room houses with well-made walls still preserved to a height of ca. 1.25 m; and Phase A (1–2), a level whose public function is seen in the discovery of a gateway.

A considerable horizontal exposure in Phase B showed what appeared to be a string of workshops. The best evidence came from Square C6, where a number of stone slab constructions/platforms were found in a context with hammerstones and quantities of flint debitage, implying specialized activities connected with a flint-knapping workshop.

In Phase A, a profound alteration in the architectural plan and function of Area C is evident with the construction of what appears to have been a gateway: it is a complex that comprises two chambers ("guardrooms") which flank a gypsum-coated passageway lined with benches on either side. At the N end, a stepped platform forms the boundary of the passageway, although it extends beyond the line of the building complex. These steps lead to a cobbled courtyard and beyond to the "upper town." At the S, where steps give access to the passageway, this complex adjoins an E-W wall line, the one that Glueck had earlier noticed. The gate complex is not entirely symmetrical. The W structure is better preserved, better constructed, and included a fully intact stone pavement; no corresponding pavement was uncovered in the E chamber, which is further differentiated by a partition wall. Bin-like features adjoin this structure on the E. The 1987 season's investigation of the W perimeter of the gate complex revealed the largest (ca. 11.0 m long), most massively constructed building on the tell, against whose walls abutted the W flank of the gateway.

Parr made similar discoveries in his Trench 1 (apparently just E of our Area C). His cobbled room, enclosed on the N by a 0.75 m × 1.25 m wall, bears a certain resemblance to the Area C western chamber.

3. Area A. Although excavation has not been extensive in Area A (the SW corner of the mound), the wall from Area C continues to form the N boundary of domestic structures. The "Glueck" wall appears to cross Area A on the S. This continuous wall appears to characterize the latest phase, and may represent a type of perimeter fortification of a diminished settlement after the monumental outer fortifications went out of use.

G. Cemeteries

The expedition explored two cemeteries, Area D on the ridge S of the site across the wadi, and Area E immediately E of the site. In the latter, several chamber tombs have disclosed the typical EB IV disarticulated burials. E3, a very small chamber tomb, contained two skulls—one of a child—disposed on either side of a central bonepile. Four vessels had been set at the entrance. Shaft tombs also appear to exist in this cemetery. Cemetery D comprises a hillside cemetery of numerous shaft tombs. Excavation of four of these tombs shows them to be of the round shaft, single chamber variety. Disarticulated multiple burials and typical EB IV grave goods characterized the group. Notably, one tomb included close to 100 vessels, mostly red-slipped and burnished.

In 1987, the expedition discovered its first pre-EB IV usage of the cemeteries in Area J, west of the tell. It was an unusual structure cut into the bedrock. This was divided by a rough stone wall, and was used as a collective burial place during EB I. West of the wall were disarticulated interments including at least 15 skulls, many of which were found totally fragmented or smashed below rocks. East of the wall, an antechamber yielded only pottery goods. A similar construction exists at Jericho in tombs K2 and A13. An EB IV tomb also came to light in Cemetery J.

H. Sociocultural Considerations

The results of four seasons of excavation at Kh. Iskander demonstrate clearly that sedentary strategies, in this case, a small town or regional center, were important socioeconomic components of the EB IV culture. The growing list of EB IV settlement sites from Transjordan corroborates this view. Moreover, irrespective of an almost universal stratigraphic break throughout Palestine-Transjordan ca. 2350 B.C., recent discoveries have shown many continuities with the EB tradition: (1) red-slipped and burnished pottery; (2) multiple burials; (3) shaft tombs; (4) similar metal types; (5) bench-lined broad- and long-room houses; (6) massive fortifications; (7) public complexes; (8) permanent storage facilities; (9) similar lithics; (10) significant pottery production; (11) multiphased sedentary occupation; (12) evidence for sociopolitical stratification; (13) sanctuaries; (14) significant amounts of food production equipment; and (15) town planning. Almost all the reasons Kenyon cited for designating the period a seminomadic one are now untenable (*CAH*[3] 1/2: 567–68).

In light of the strong continuities with EB Age tradition, it is difficult to support any view (including the terminology) of this period as "intermediate." The most important obstruction to a view of the EB IV peoples as indigenous has been the misconception that the shift from EB III to EB IV was from sedentarism to nomadism; in reality the shift was from urban to nonurban i.e., to village/town and pastoral adaptive strategies. Indeed the only conceivable means to understand the level of sedentarism in EB IV and the continuation of EB III urban traditions is to posit a model of cultural change, especially for Transjordan, which is less abrupt than hitherto believed (Richard 1980; 1987a).

Sociocultural change at the EB III/IV horizon (in this case greater pastoralism and village/town life as opposed to urban settlement) is better understood as a change in emphasis of production and organization in response to irreversible stresses on the urban system, than as an abrupt shift to a new sociocultural phenomenon (see Salzman 1978). Newer views on sociocultural change suggest a greater fluidity in subsistence strategies (cultural adaptation) along the urban/nonurban continuum. It is this fluidity that provides the mechanism for change. Thus, depending on circumstances (e.g., political stability) there will be a greater or lesser stress on a range of adaptive strategies that are institutionalized with the culture (see Salzman 1978; 1980). As the new data for sedentism mount, the explanatory value of these new views of cultural change are manifest.

Having recovered the "missing" sedentary component of EB IV society, we must now look for newer hypotheses to explain the variation in adaptive strategies. Such hypotheses should be broad enough to explain also the transition to mixed subsistence strategies and concomitant decentralization of political control and the abatement of urban complexity at the EB III/EB IV transition. Such a model should explain both continuity and change at the EB III/EB IV transition. It has recently been suggested that the model of specialization/despecialization is a conceptual construct that is applicable to the organizational shift from specialized modes of production to the despecialized nonurban economies that appeared at the end of the third millennium B.C. (Richard and Long fc.). This model allows for a more process-oriented view that explains culture change at the EB III/EB IV transition as well as the variation in adaptation in EB IV.

Thus, the research at Kh. Iskander forces a reassessment of this period. In light of new data and current scholarly trends, there is no compelling evidence to suggest that there was an invasion; that Amorite nomads from Syria overran the country; or that town/village life was completely eradicated at the end of EB III. Indeed, the growing evidence for cultural continuity between EB III and IV supports our contention that the collapse of the city-state system and the subsequent adaptation to nonurban and pastoral subsistence strategies were a result of gradual internal processes (for an opposing view see Amiran and Kochavi 1985). Such a view of the EB III/EB IV transition is totally in concert with the perspective that a cultural continuum can be traced throughout the EB Age (ca. 3400–2000 B.C.), notwithstanding great peaks of adaptation and change in the process from preurban and finally to nonurban social systems (Richard 1987a).

Bibliography

Amiran, R., and Kochavi, M. 1985. Canaan at the Close of the Third Millennium B.C.E.—An Independent Culture or the Final Phase of the Early Bronze Age? *EI* 18: 361–65 (in Hebrew).

Bernhardt, K. H. 1960. Beobachtungen zur Identifizierung moabitischer Ortslagen. *ZDPV* 76: 136–58.

Brünnow, R., and von Domaszewski, A. 1904. *Die Provincia Arabia,* vol. 1. Strassbourg.

Dearman, J. A. 1984. The Location of Jahaz. *ZDPV* 100: 122–25.

Dever, W. G. 1980. New Vistas on the EB IV ("MB I") Horizon in Syria-Palestine. *BASOR*.

Glueck, N. 1939. *Explorations in Eastern Palestine.* AASOR 18–19. New Haven.

Musil, A. 1907. *Arabia Petraea* I. Vienna.

Parr, P. J. 1960. Excavations at Khirbet Iskander. *ADAJ* 4–6: 128–33.

Richard, S. 1980. Toward a Consensus of Opinion on the End of the Early Bronze Age in Palestine-Transjordan. *BASOR* 237: 5–34.

———. 1982. Report on the 1981 Season of Soundings and Survey at Khirbet Iskander. *ADAJ* 16: 289–99.

———. 1983. Report on the 1982 Season of Soundings and Survey at Khirbet Iskander. *ADAJ* 28: 45–53.

———. 1986. Excavations at Khirbet Iskander, Jordan: A Glimpse at Settled Life During the "Dark Age" in Palestinian Archaeology. *Expedition* 28: 3–12.

———. 1987a. The Early Bronze Age: The Rise and Collapse of Urbanism. *BA* 50: 22–43.

———. 1987b. Questions of Nomadic Incursions at the end of the 3d Millennium, B.C. Pp. 323–30 in *Studies in the History and Archaeology of Jordan* III, ed. A. Hadidi. Amman.

———. 1989. The 1987 Expedition to Khirbet Iskander and Its Vicinity: Fourth Preliminary Report. *BASORSup* 26: 33–58.

Richard, S., and Boraas, R. S. 1984. Preliminary Report of the 1981–82 Seasons of the Expedition to Khirbet Iskander and Its Vicinity. *BASOR* 254: 63–87.

———. 1988. The Early Bronze IV Fortified Site of Khirbet Iskander, Jordan: Third Preliminary Report, 1984 Season. *BASORSup* 25: 107–30.

Richard, S., and Long, J. C., Jr. fc. Specialization/Despecialization: A Model to Explain Culture Change and Continuity at the End of the Third Millennium, B.C., ca. 2350–2000 B.C. *BASOR*.

Salzman, P. C. 1978. Ideology and Change in Middle Eastern Tribal Societies. *Man* 13: 618–37.

———. 1980. Introduction: Processes of Sedentarization as Adaptation and Response. Pp. 1–19 in *When Nomads Settle,* ed. P. C. Salzman. New York.

Schick, C. 1879. Journey into Moab. *PEFQS,* 187–92.

SUZANNE RICHARD

ISMACHIAH (PERSON) [Heb *yismakyāhû*]. One of ten overseers *(pĕqîdîm)* responsible for gifts brought into the temple during the reign of Hezekiah (2 Chr 31:13). King Hezekiah and Azariah the chief officer of the temple appointed Ismachiah and the other nine. Their role was to assist Conaniah and his brother Shimei in managing "the contributions, the tithes and the dedicated things" that were brought into and stored in the temple (2 Chr 31:12–13). The name means "Yahweh supports/sustains" (*HALAT* 2: 399; cf. *IPN* 28, 196; LXX *samachia*).

KENNETH H. CUFFEY

ISRAEL COURT. See TEMPLE, JERUSALEM.

ISRAEL, HISTORY OF. This entry consists of four articles that survey various periods of the history of ancient Israel and the critical issues associated with reconstructing that history. The first article focuses on the premonarchic period (ca. 1200–1000 B.C.), dealing especially with the question of the Israelite "conquest" of Canaan and the subsequent rise of the Israelite monarchy. The second article provides a comprehensive treatment about how archaeological evidence associated with the LB-early Iron Age transition bears upon the question of the Israelite "conquest." The third article sketches broadly the political history of the monarchy up to the Babylonian exile (ca. 1000–586 B.C.). The fourth article addresses the problems of method arising from the nature of biblical books dealing with the period after the Babylonian exile (ca. 538–330 B.C.), and offers a tentative historical reconstruction with attention to the ideological tendencies of the sources. In addition to these articles, other entries discuss particular individuals and places, neighboring peoples and nations, biblical books, and critical methodologies. Note also the following entries: CHRONOLOGY (HEBREW BIBLE); COURT NARRATIVE; COVENANT; EPHRAIM; EXODUS, THE; GALILEE; KING AND KINGSHIP; MESHA STELE; NEGEB; PALESTINE, ADMINISTRATION OF; PALESTINE, ARCHAEOLOGY OF; SYRO-EPHRAIMITE WAR. For the later periods, see also MACCABEAN REVOLT; JEWISH WAR; BAR KOKHBA REVOLT.

PREMONARCHIC PERIOD

A. Merneptah's "Israel" and the Earliest Israel
B. Sources for the Earliest Israel
  1. The OT as a Historical Source
  2. The Value of Palestinian Archaeology as a Historical Source
C. The Historical Investigation of the Earliest Israel
  1. The Traditional Historical Approach
  2. The Modern Study of Israel's Earliest History
D. Sociology and the Study of Israel's Earliest History
E. Israelite History in the Pre-national Period
  1. The OT Narrative and "External Evidence"
  2. Early Israelite History
    a. Choice of Method—Delimiting the Object of Study
    b. Palestine in the LB Age
    c. Palestine in the Early Iron Age
    d. Formation of the Israelite State

A. Merneptah's "Israel" and the Earliest Israel

According to the Egyptian inscription of Merneptah, some sort of ethnic entity called "Israel" must have existed in Israel shortly before 1200 B.C. However, the question that concerns us is the nature of the relationship between the "Israel" in the inscription and the historical Israel which we encounter in the OT. The OT describes this Israel in the pre-national period as a tribal society consisting of twelve tribes, unified by a common historical past and by a common monotheistic religion (the worship of Yahweh). The relevant passage in the Egyptian text informs us that "Israel is laid waste, his seed is not" (*ANET,* 378).

For quite some time, scholars preferred to believe that this passage referred to a unified Israelite society of twelve tribes, but they had a variety of reasons for claiming this. On the one side were scholars who attempted to retain, in one form or another, the OT description of Israel's conquest of Canaan, and who accordingly regarded Merneptah's reference to Israel as the final proof that the Israelite conquest had already taken place by this time (cf., e.g., Kaufmann 1953; Albright 1963: 24–34; *BHI*[1], 97–127). On the other side were a number of (mainly German) scholars who abandoned the attempt to reconcile the biblical account of the conquest with the actual historical development which eventually led to the emergence of Israel (see Alt, *KlSchr* 1: 89–175; Noth 1950: 67–82). But the latter group also reckoned with an ethnic Israelite entity which was held together in the premonarchic period by the presence of an Israelite amphictyony, that is, a tribal league of twelve tribes (Noth 1930). They felt that Merneptah's inscription could be related to this entity in some fashion. See AMPHICTYONY.

However, a critical reevaluation of the OT sources and the social situation which existed in pre-national Israel has forced scholars to surrender the notion that Israel was organized in an amphictyony in the pre-national period (Mayes 1974; de Geus 1976; Lemche 1984a). Moreover, recent studies of Israel's origin have been forced to reject the OT claim that Israel, understood as a nation, could have arisen outside of the borders of Palestine (Mendenhall 1962; Gottwald 1979; Lemche 1985; Ahlström 1986). The process which led to the emergence of the historical Israel, understood as that state which dominated the whole of Palestine as well as some of the surrounding lands under the kings David and Solomon, was much more complicated than the biblical account allows; moreover, this development can hardly have been concluded before the 10th century or shortly before.

This is to say that we are left with a historically certain reference to an "Israel" in Palestine around 1200 B.C.; by the same token, however, we encounter a complicated course of events which is only marginally reflected in the OT accounts of Israel's past. This also means that although Merneptah's "Israel" is situated at the beginning of the long development which led to the emergence of the historical Israel, it is far from certain that the Egyptian inscription refers to any extensive ethnic group in then-contemporary Palestine. On the contrary, there is reason to believe that the Israel in question comprised at most the nucleus of the later Israelite state. However, it is very difficult to be more precise about the extent and nature of this Israel, apart from the fact that Merneptah's Israel seems to be associated with the mountainous region of central Palestine (see Ahlström 1986: 37–43).

B. Sources for the Earliest Israel

Two types of sources are at least theoretically relevant to the study of pre-national Israel: the OT historical narratives about Israel in the time prior to David and Solomon (so-called internal evidence), and the information which derives from sources other than the OT (so-called external evidence). The latter type of evidence consists mainly of materials which have emerged through archaeological excavations in Palestine and the surrounding regions. These archaeological materials consist mainly of mute material remains, which is to say that they are not connected with any written evidence which might explain them to us. However, some individual inscriptions have also come to light, and these sometimes shed sporadic light on events transpiring in Palestine in this period. In addition to these finds, there are some of a more or less accidental nature, such as the discovery of the Amarna correspondence in Egypt in 1888, which nevertheless may be of importance for the description of the historical course of events in Palestine in the last part of the 2d millennium B.C.

The fundamental problem facing any scholar who concerns himself with the history of Israel is that it is difficult to correlate the two types of evidence so as to unify them into a connected picture of the historical course of events. It would be more correct to say that it is only occasionally that we seem able to establish some agreement between an OT source and the extrabiblical materials, at least as far as the period before 1000 B.C. is concerned (some students of the history of the united monarchy in the 10th century B.C. would even go further to include the period 1000–900 B.C. in the so-called dark age preceding Israel's really "historical" periods [cf. Garbini 1988: 21–32]).

1. The OT as a Historical Source. The OT contains a collected description of Israel's pre-national history; this account is related in the Pentateuch plus the books from Joshua to the first or second book of Samuel (depending on whether one includes the episode of Saul's kingship within the history of the monarchy or of the pre-national period).

However, no part of this OT narrative is contemporaneous with the events it depicts and which, according to the biblical chronology (translated into modern terms), are supposed to have taken place in the period between 2300 B.C. (the traditional date of Abraham's departure from Mesopotamia) and 1000 B.C. (the accession of David to the throne). The temporal distance is possibly closest in the case of the description of a battle that took place between an alliance of Canaanite kings and an Israelite coalition of tribes which is related in Judges 5 ("the Song of Deborah"). This text has often been held ultimately to derive from pre-national times, although there is no agreement as far as a precise date is concerned (see, among others, Mayes 1969; 1974: 84–105; contradicted by Ahlström 1977; 1986: 54). But even in this case individual scholars have dated the text to a period subsequent to the introduction of the monarchy into Israel (cf. Garbini 1978).

In any case, we are forced to assume that literally every source relative to Israel's pre-national history was first written down after the formation of the Israelite state around 1000 B.C., that is, some or even many generations after the events mentioned in the sources in question. On the other hand, there is today no consensus among scholars as to just when the earliest portions of the historical literature were written down; the suggested dates have fluctuated between the 10th century B.C. for the "Yahwist" or "J" source (cf. von Rad 1944; Noth 1948) and the 7th century, or even down to the 6th or 5th centuries (see, among others, Schmid 1977; Van Seters 1975; 1983; and the survey of research by Whybray 1987). However, no one disagrees that the *conclusion* of the composition of the historical literature of the OT cannot have taken place before the end of the early postexilic period.

The question as to whether the authors of the historical literature in the OT have described the events of the pre-national period in a historically correct way depends on the date one assigns to the earliest part of this literature. It is naturally not unimportant whether the Yahwist lived during Solomon's reign or shortly after, or under that of Josiah, or perhaps that of Xerxes or some other ruler of the Persian period. If the earliest parts of the historical literature are in fact removed from the pre-national period by more than half a millennium, this would automatically dictate that we regard the historical contents of this literature with appropriate scepticism. However, there might be some reason to suppose that one or another historical event managed to survive in traditional transmission and hence was more or less correctly described back in the 10th century. The latter point of view, which has been dominant in OT scholarship up to the present, has sometimes been challenged on the grounds that it is reasonable to ask whether the biblical historians intended to write history in any sense (cf. Halpern 1988, who claims that a historical interest underlies OT narratives), and even whether, in the event, they were actually able to (cf. Coote, who defends an early date for the Yahwist in Coote and Ord 1989, but who, in Coote and Whitelam 1987, completely ignores the OT account in his attempt to explain the historical developments connected with the emergence of Israel).

The various attempts which have been made to argue for the historicity of at least the nucleus of the OT narrative on the basis of an earlier oral tradition which is thought to have preceded the written stage (see *FSAC,* 64–76; cf. also *CMHE,* and, recently, Hendel 1987; expressly negative toward this approach is Van Seters 1975) have been unsuccessful. Even if the biblical historical narratives may derive to a greater or lesser degree from orally transmitted stories which are susceptible to comparison in terms of narrative technique with other poetic literature from the ANE (particularly the Ugaritic epic literature has been employed as the narrative model for the OT narratives), the question of their historicity cannot be determined in this fashion, because such oral traditions are, in the nature of things, incapable of objective control (further on this see Lemche 1985: 377–85, and the survey of literature on the subject in Kirkpatrick 1988). It is even conceivable that, if it were shown that parts of the Israelite traditions concerning the earliest periods hold a variety of characteristics in common with the epic literatures from other parts of the Near East, we should then be forced to conclude that the Israelite traditions are ahistorical, like the vast majority of the stories with which they have been compared.

In itself, the composition of the OT historical narrative furnishes us with reason to wonder whether its author(s) was/were actually able to write history. Although the "author" (sing., for convenience' sake) of the historical books does not call attention to the phenomenon, the work contains a wide variety of different genres, all pieced together: myths, sagas, fairy tales, genealogical lists, lists of officeholders, laws of various types (religious as well as secular), and so forth; he never signifies when he shifts from one type of information to another, or indicates that one tradition is more reliable in a historical sense than another.

Some scholars have attempted to explain the failure of OT history writers to write history in a technical sense by pointing to the possibility that the authors in question lived in a different epistemological "space" than their modern colleagues. To this end they have characterized Israelite history writing as *prelogical* or *mythical* (see Lemche 1984b; on history writing in antiquity, see Liverani 1973a, with examples in Liverani 1972; 1973b; 1974; 1977); that is, they have held it to have been dictated by other than strictly scientific interests. This even applies to sizable narratives like, for example, the story of David's rise to power (roughly 1 Samuel 16 to 2 Samuel 6, although the delimitation of this narrative is uncertain both as far as its beginning and its conclusion are concerned; see Grønbaek 1971), which displays considerable structural similarities with a N Syrian royal inscription from the 15th century B.C. relating how King IDRIMI of Alalakh acceded to his throne (*ANET,* 557–58; and see Buccellati 1962). The narratives about David and Idrimi follow a common scheme which was borrowed from the fairy tale genre, and which seems to have been used to defend successful pretenders against the imputation of usurpation (cf. Liverani 1972).

In this connection, however, it is not unimportant that biblical narrative art is guided by a certain *diachronic interest,* which is to say that the individual events in the course of a story are related according to a chronological scheme which structures the entire narrative. But it should be pointed out that the concern with chronology in OT narratives can be advanced as an argument in favor of the view that Israelite history writing did not predate the earliest Greek history writing, which implies that it is to be dated to the exilic period or even later (Van Seters 1983).

We should note that the study of OT historical literature as a source for Israel's earliest history is inhibited by the fact that no event which is related in the OT historical books is touched on by other ANE written sources: it is only in the Omride dynasty in the 9th century B.C. that Mesopotamian sources begin to mention historical figures of Israelite origin who also appear in the OT.

Accordingly, whoever attempts to derive historical information from the OT sources is necessarily forced to attempt his own analyses of the OT traditions in order to argue for the possibility that these sources contain historical information. In other words, one is in reality left to one's own devices to determine the question of historicity. From the point of view of scientific method this is very much a problematical procedure, because its results often have the character of postulates which can be neither confirmed nor disconfirmed.

There seem to be only two ways out of this dilemma, which consists in the facts that we cannot control the information contained in the witness of the OT and that other ancient written evidence provides no help. The scholar can either choose to ignore the OT information, as is the case in a number of recent reconstructions of Israel's pre-national history (see Frick 1985; Coote and Whitelam 1987), or he can attempt to confront the information in the OT with the results of archaeological excavations in Palestine and surrounding regions.

2. The Value of Palestinian Archaeology as a Historical Source. Since the close of the 19th century, no region in the Near East has been so intensely explored as Palestine. However, it has been the case that the archaeology of Palestine has been, for most of its history, narrowly connected to OT scholarship in general. In the early phase of this study, archaeological activity was dominated by biblical scholars, with the result that there have been jurisdictional disputes between the biblical scholar and the archaeologist, who in many cases was one and the same person. See ARCHAEOLOGY, SYRO-PALESTINIAN.

The question as to who was eventually to win this struggle was virtually a foregone conclusion. It would have been extremely difficult, if not actually impossible, for the archaeologist to justify his activity in the region if his conclusions were not in some way capable of correlation with the information contained in the OT or NT. Archaeological excavations in Palestine have practically never been able to produce the spectacular sorts of results which have characterized many excavations in both Egypt and Mesopotamia, or which the archaeologists active in Asia Minor or N Syria are justifiably proud. Admittedly, there have been a great many finds, but these have been modest in kind; particularly the epigraphical materials have been extraordinarily limited, although we must not forget that many important small texts have been found.

One's immediate impression upon studying the results of Palestinian archaeology is that, at least in pre-Hellenistic times, the material culture of Palestine was extremely poor. Nowhere do we find temple complexes such as those for which Mesopotamia and Egypt are famed. Nor has a palatial complex been unearthed anywhere in Palestine which could measure itself even approximately with the royal dwelling in N Syrian Ugarit. The great golden treasures which have above all been found in excavations of Egyptian tombs or in ancient Ur, in S Iraq, are entirely lacking in Palestine. And the closest thing we have to a palace archive in Palestine is the collection of bullae which were perhaps attached to documents in the Jerusalem archives towards the close of the period of the monarchy (cf. Avigad 1986), although the documents themselves are lost forever.

It was only by virtue of their usefulness for allowing us to confirm or disconfirm the accuracy of certain biblical information that the individual results of excavations have been able to distinguish themselves and legitimate so much archaeological activity. It is therefore obvious that the archaeology of Palestine had to develop into a *biblical archaeology*, the primary goal of which was to correlate its results with OT information. Thus the sites which were chosen for excavation corresponded to this underlying intention; scholars concentrated their efforts to a high degree on the best-known sites mentioned in the OT (with the exception of Jerusalem, which, because of modern construction only allowed itself to be explored to a limited extent). Such sites included especially the towns of Jericho and Shechem.

Finally, the biblicistic element in earlier Palestinian archaeology was also expressed in the rather over-simplifying interpretations of the OT materials which were sometimes proposed even by such superb American archaeologists as W. F. Albright and G. E. Wright, or, in fact, even by their diametrical opposite, the English archaeologist K. M. Kenyon (Kenyon 1960). Kenyon's work contains numerous examples of historical interpretations which are not on the same level as the then-contemporary historical research which was being conducted into the OT texts.

As far as the sometimes problematical character of Palestinian archaeology is concerned, the discussion of Israel's conquest of Canaan may serve as a model, since the point of departure of countless archaeological investigations seems to have been the concern to find evidence of the Israelite occupation of the country shortly before 1200 B.C. A number of destructions of well-known Palestinian towns which must have taken place during the transition from the Late Bronze to the Early Iron Age were thus understood as direct evidence of the Israelite conquest (cf., e.g., the sections dealing with traces of the Israelite settlement in the chapters on the LB and Early Iron Ages in *ArchPal* 1960: 80–109, 110–45).

However, as matters developed archaeology began to create so many problems for the presumed historical accuracy of the OT account of the conquest of Canaan that it eventually became increasingly difficult to retain the conviction of historicity underlying the OT narrative. The best-known of these many difficulties are those accruing around the date to be assigned to the destruction of Bronze Age Jericho, which had to be pushed back for archaeological reasons to the 16th century B.C. (cf. Kenyon's date of 1580 B.C. [1960: 316] with her defense of the historicity of Joshua 5–6 [*EAEHL* 2: 563–564]). Even more clear is the evidence from the excavation of Ai, which is also supposed to have been destroyed in the course of the Israelite invasion under Joshua, since it was demonstrated already by J. Marquet-Krause, the early French excavator of the town, that Ai was not immediately resettled after its destruction at the end of the EB Age (around 2300 B.C.). Marquet-Krause's conclusions have been confirmed by later American excavations undertaken since World War II, although it is now apparent that Ai was resettled in the early Iron Age. See AI (PLACE).

These clear conclusions, which so evidently annihilate the historical value of the OT account, had to have consequences sooner or later for the historical discussion of the Israelite settlement, just as they also led to warnings about the use and misuse of archaeology in the study of the OT (see, e.g., Noth 1971: 34–51; de Vaux 1970). Ultimately, this situation has led to the demand that the archaeological work be conducted for its own sake, and that its conclusions be drawn before one proceeds to involve the OT texts in the discussion of the interpretation of the archaeological materials (see Lemche 1985: 391).

As it happens, when we separate archaeology from the study of the OT texts we discover that the archaeological evidence has a decisive statement to make in connection with the reconstruction of the course of events in Palestine in the second half of the 2d millennium B.C. Admittedly, it has become more and more difficult to retain the biblical account of this course of events, but archaeology has, for one thing, produced material which allows the historians scope for further work. Furthermore, by increasing the distance between its results and the OT sources it has brought about a reevaluation of the character of the OT sources themselves. Archaeology can show us concretely that the OT narratives of the conquest cannot be taken at face value in a historical sense; rather, we see that in the OT we have reflections formulated at a late date about the question of Israel's origin. We find narratives which, admittedly, contain such things as etiological legends which associate particular localities with particular events in the historical narratives.

C. The Historical Investigation of the Earliest Israel

Confronted with the previously described source materials (OT texts composed long after Israel had begun to be governed by kings, and archaeological finds), the historian who intends to describe Israel's history in the premonarchic period is forced to make a number of choices. These choices have, above all, to do with securing appropriate methods for deriving historical information from the written sources. However, as far as the OT is concerned, even before the choice of method is made a decision has to be arrived at as to whether the OT may be used to provide any historical information whatsoever about the past.

There is somewhat of a consensus among scholars as to the understanding of the OT sources: only a handful are prepared to ignore the OT information entirely (cf. perhaps most prominently Frick 1985; Coote and Whitelam 1987). Moreover, an important question is whether OT scholars' choices in this regard have been made solely on the basis of the sources present in the OT, correlated with archaeological data, or whether other features have played a role, most notably the OT's character as sacred scripture for two religions. Ultimately, the historian's method is determined by his or her *understanding of the Bible.*

1. The Traditional Historical Approach. The traditional historical study of the OT has been characterized by a number of special features (cf. Lemche 1987–88; cf. also Sasson 1981; Coote and Whitelam 1987: 11–16). First, the various accounts of Israel's history have usually been very detailed. In this connection, the analysis of premonarchical Israel's history has generally received the lion's share of attention (this is every bit as striking in such early accounts as that of Kittel 1932 as in more recent ones, such as Donner 1984–86, where this analysis fills in reality half the work). These accounts have usually been founded on very extensive analyses of the OT texts, which have been searched in order to derive historical information.

Second, only a few histories of Israel contain cohesive sections dedicated to the epistemological questions which, because of Israel's practically unique history, must be posed.

Third, the lack of methodological reflection has invariably entailed that modern histories of Israel have been written along the premises laid down by the Israelite history writers themselves; it is the authors of the historical books of the OT who have established the *agenda* for the historical reconstructions of later times. This applies to the subdivision of the history of Israel into a series of discrete historical epochs, a "patriarchal period," a "sojourn in Egypt," a "conquest," a "period of the judges," and a "period of the monarchy." But it also applies to scholars' descriptions of the individual periods, which not uncommonly seem like attempts to "translate" the OT accounts into historical reports. There is extensive use of the renarration of OT history or even of "rationalistic paraphrases" of it (a notable recent example of this is *HAIJ*). In this process, OT narratives are usually "cleansed" of all mythical, not to mention "miraculous" features, so as to appear as secular rather than sacred history.

Fourth, the concern to develop methods suitable for studying OT texts for their historical content was determined by historical preoccupations; but this entailed that other concerns, such as the literary qualities of OT literature, were neglected. For example, when scholars chose to incorporate the study of legends and sagas into historical research on the earliest Israel, they emphasized those aspects of such studies which sought to find "historical nuclei" in folkloristic materials. At the same time, other competing views of folklore scholars (which were highly skeptical of the question of historicity or which did not regard this aspect as important in the creation of sagas and legends) were neglected.

Fifth, by the same token the lack of historical consciousness in much recent scholarship on Israel's history has meant that the gaps in that history have often been closed by the imagination (frequently characterized as "common sense") of the individual scholars, since they have attempted to produce cohesive accounts of the historical sequence on the basis of the OT narratives. This has entailed that such accounts lack any comprehensive historico-methodological foundation.

Sixth, the treatment of "external evidence" (see above) in the various histories of Israel has often been eclectic, in the sense that they have either been used to confirm OT statements or else they have been distorted slightly so as not to collide with those statements. This tendency has been especially notable in connection with the study of the Israelite patriarchs (on this method, see esp. Thompson 1974). An expression of this tendency is the enthusiasm which has greeted new discoveries from the ANE, such as, e.g., the Mari texts (ca. 18th century B.C.) or those from Ugarit (14th/13th century B.C.).

If one reads through any number of descriptions of the earliest history of Israel dating from the end of the 19th century (i.e., from Stade 1887 up to de Vaux 1971–73) one sees the features mentioned above recurring time and again. Particularly striking is the extent to which this historiography has concentrated on the discussion of questions concerned with the historical identity of the figures who feature in this early phase of Israel's history, from Abraham to Moses and Joshua, to the judges, who are supposed to have exercised some type of leadership in Israel before the introduction of the monarchy. Research has to a large extent been concentrated on isolated individuals and events, whereas the broad outline has usually been drawn in such a way as to connect one important figure from Israel's past with yet another.

Naturally, there are exceptions to this picture, as, for example, in several sections of Noth's important history of Israel which appeared shortly after World War II (Noth 1950). Noth's study was in turn based on a number of publications by the important German scholar A. Alt, in which the latter used a broader brush in his attempts to depict the outline of early Israelite history (cf., e.g., Alt, *KlSchr* 1: 89–175; 2: 1–65). Nevertheless, it would not be wrong to claim that the various descriptions of Israelite history before the monarchy have often looked more like historical analyses of OT texts than synthetic surveys of Israel's history.

2. The Modern Study of Israel's Earliest History. The historical studies since the early 1970's have, to some extent, pointed to new directions, not least because of the stimulus provided by a number of individual studies which have cast doubt on the historical contents of the OT narratives.

The historicity of the patriarchs came into focus when T. L. Thompson and J. Van Seters more or less simultaneously and with complementary arguments posed a number of well-chosen questions to the traditional understanding of the patriarchal period as a historical phase in Israelite history (Thompson 1974; Van Seters 1975). Several studies have since appeared which have advocated the view that Abraham, Isaac, and Jacob once did live, perhaps in the early 2d millennium, and that their memory is preserved in OT narratives. See ABRAHAM. It would nonetheless be correct to assert that these efforts, too, must take their point of departure in the researches of Thompson and Van Seters. Moreover, a number of OT scholars have now abandoned the idea that the patriarchal period was ever a historical epoch (cf. Soggin 1984: 89–108; Lemche 1988: 114–16; cf. already Noth 1950: 114–20).

The account of Israel's sojourn in Egypt, the exodus, and the wilderness wanderings under Moses' leadership were previously defended fiercely in most studies (cf., e.g., *FSAC*, 249–72; *BHI*[1], 110–20); current research now regards them with extreme skepticism. Thus, today the story of Joseph and his brothers seems to be a historical "novel" which was written in the 1st millennium (Redford 1970; *IJH*, 167–203) rather than an ancient historical record. Correspondingly, the other parts of the narrative complex stretching from Exodus to Numbers can hardly be other than late "recollections" of the historical past of the nation which were current in the 1st millennium B.C.

The OT narrative of Israel's conquest of Canaan has been efficiently neutralized by modern scholarship and may no longer be assigned historical worth as a source for the events which led to the formation of the Israelite people. A number of alternative conceptions of Israel's origins have now taken its place. On the other hand, the OT account of the period of the judges has been slightly rehabilitated, not so much because the narratives in the book of Judges deserve historical credence, but rather because the framework for the history of the period of the judges—the "amphictyony" which numerous scholars in Noth's train alleged for the pre-national period—no longer exists. In 1930 Noth presented the hypothesis that pre-national Israel was organized as an amphictyony along Greek lines, which is to say, he held that it was a union consisting of twelve tribes (Noth 1930). Noth's position, however, came under heavy fire, particularly in the 1970s (cf. esp. Mayes 1974; *IJH*, 285–331; de Geus 1976), and has today been abandoned by the majority of OT scholars (Lemche 1984a).

Taken together, these developments require us to surrender the idea that the OT historical accounts comprise a coherent narrative capable of forming the foundation for a reconstruction of pre-national Israelite history. Historians have accordingly seen themselves to be forced to employ other methods to depict the historical development of Palestine prior to the year 1000 B.C. These methods have to be based on the archaeological materials and not on the OT stories. By the same token, however, new methods are also required for the evaluation of the archaeological data, and primary among these methods are sociology and social anthropology.

It is likewise also necessary to incorporate insights deriving from modern historical study into the investigation of Israel's history. It is characteristic of recent historical research that there is still a powerful interest in the detailed description of the past, to the extent that such description is at all possible; at the same time, however, such research attempts to focus on the relationship of the individual historical events to a greater historical perspective. The terminology employed here is that of the *Annales*-school of French historians, namely *la longue durée.* The ruling concept is that a historical event cannot be studied in isolation; rather, it is inevitably part of some greater context or chain of events which, taken together, form the pattern of development which can be described and reconstructed by historians (on this and the study of Israel's history, see Whitelam 1986: 55–62; Coote and Whitelam 1987: 17–25).

D. Sociology and the Study of Israel's Earliest History

In the last couple of decades a third path toward the exploration of the earliest history of Israel has been increasingly attempted by a growing number of scholars. Through the study of population groups in preindustrial societies, such researchers have argued that "our contemporary ancestor" can help provide information which is also relevant to the evaluation of ancient Israel. By studying people who live in a society which (in terms of means of production) is still undeveloped, it may be possible to isolate characteristic features capable of generalization as "rules," and so to explain phenomena which we either know from the OT narratives about Israel in the pre-national period, or which we have deduced from the archaeological materials. See also ANTHROPOLOGY AND THE OT; SOCIOLOGY (ANCIENT ISRAEL).

The last two centuries of OT scholarship have seen many attempts to employ viewpoints, just as we have also seen a number of treatments of Israelite society (the best known is probably de Vaux 1961; but see also Pedersen 1926–40). Characteristic of these early efforts was, on the one hand, the lack of a coherent sociological theory and, on the other, a very limited sociological background material.

The lack of adequate theory underlying the attempts by OT scholars to describe Israelite society is probably owing to the inadequate sociological background of such scholars, which they have on occasion defended by their conviction that such an education is not necessary (cf. also Gottwald 1979: 5–7). Instead, one frequently encounters so-called common sense observations in conjunction with social phenomena which, in the eyes of a skilled sociologist, can only seem to be arbitrary or even directly misleading.

As far as the lack of materials is concerned, already prior to World War II there existed a limited number of social anthropological studies of Near Eastern social phenomena. However, the social-anthropological exploration of the Near East was deficient both with respect to quality and to extent, in comparison with other social anthropological fields of interest, such as sub-Saharan Africa, Melanesia, and so on. It was first in the time after World War II that a properly scientific study of the Near East began, which is to say, that it was also first at this time that it became possible to incorporate sociological methods into the study of social conditions in ancient Israel.

In general, sociology/social anthropology has been used in two ways by OT scholars. (1) The most ambitious method leads to the presentation of "model solutions" on the basis of the available sociological data, following which the models in question are used as heuristic tools in the study of ancient Israel. (2) A second path is less ambitious as far as what it expects to be able to derive from sociology/social anthropology; it balks at the use of models, on the assumption that such models do not sufficiently take account of the mutability of human nature, that is, of man's ability in a given situation to choose between numerous alternatives.

The first-mentioned approach has been preferred above all by a considerable number of American OT scholars. In America its development has gone hand in hand with the emergence of new archaeological methods (the "New Archaeology") which have been developed specifically to describe the historical development of peoples who have not left written records behind them. In studying a number of traditional ethnic groups, social anthropologists who pursue this course seek to isolate a limited number of individual phenomena or variables which they regard as characteristic of certain types of social organization. Thus, by assigning the numerous variables to such types of social organization as "band societies," "tribal societies," "chiefdoms," and "states," they believe it is possible to work out "heuristic models" for each type of society. It is further thought that such models are useful for the investigation of the social and political systems of other ethnic groups of which scholars are only sporadically informed. This social anthropological method or approach may be called *cultural evolutionism*.

For example, evolutionistic scholars would think it sensible that, if we possess limited information showing that a small number of all the variables which are normally associated with a "chieftainship" were present in a given society, then they are entitled to supplement the available information with other variables which belong to the same organizational level, and so ultimately to term the society in question a "chieftainship." Thus, if only a limited number of the variables which figure in the model of the chieftainship are present in the OT witness about Israel in the pre-national period, evolutionistic scholars would accordingly deduce that Israel in the period of the judges was a chieftainship (cf., e.g., Flanagan 1981), and, necessarily, that the other variables must also have been present.

Moreover, if the source materials permit a chronological distinction between the variables attested, so that some may be assigned to a relatively primitive socio-political stage of organization (tribal society) while others may be assigned to a higher stage (kingship), such evolutionistic studies enable the historic analysis of periods which had previously been held to be prehistoric.

Among the OT scholars who have chosen this approach in one form or another, we find primarily those who have advocated the notion that Israel arose in consequence of a revolutionary movement in Palestine during the transition between the Bronze and Iron Ages (Mendenhall 1962; 1973; Gottwald 1979; cf. among others also Chaney 1983). Disregarding their respective differences, what Mendenhall and Gottwald have in common is that their use of cultural evolutionistic views has been idiosyncratic and at least to some extent not anchored in their respective social anthropological foundations (in Mendenhall's case, Service 1962; for Gottwald's, Fried 1967). In particular, both have introduced a variable pertaining to ideology and religion which is not to be found in the works of their "originals" (cf. Lemche 1985: 209–16).

Other scholars have directed their investigations either within the framework of the same social-anthropological school, or else on its periphery; they have thus introduced into the study of ancient Israelite history a number of heuristic models which both complement one another and compete with one another internally (e.g., Frick 1985; Coote and Whitelam 1987). It is further characteristic that, as the social anthropological models scholars have used in recent decades have become increasingly complicated because ever more variables have been included within them (a fact which has opened the possibility of variation on the basic model), the various models of pre-national Israelite society have become correspondingly sophisticated, but at the same time also less immediately intelligible (see in this respect Flanagan 1988).

The strength in this approach is the relatively clear results it produces, since in practice it has been possible to offer well-founded descriptions of the structure and history of pre-national Israelite society, in the process also characterizing the various social processes which led Israel from the status of a tribal society to that of a state ruled by kings.

However, this method also has its obvious weaknesses, because it rests on a number of assumptions which are not self-evident (Lemche 1985: 216–19). A fundamental assumption of the method is, for example, that human societies generally follow the same developmental course and are determined by the same forces. In other words, it is presupposed that there is only a relatively limited number of variables present in the sources bearing on a given society, and also that it is possible to interpret these variables in such a way that they can be seen to be determinative for the reconstruction of the social development. If the number of variables grows too large, the model becomes impenetrable and hence useless as a heuristic tool. If one further introduces an element of uncertainty, by noting that a given variable figures on several different sociopolitical levels (e.g., if one observes that segmentary social systems exist in tribal societies, chieftainships, and states), then it becomes necessary to pose serious questions as to the ultimate usefulness of the entire method. Finally, there is a variable for which it is virtually impossible to provide scientific controls: namely, the multiplicity of human nature, which includes man's ability to distinguish between different possibilities.

To describe Israelite social development in the pre-national period by means of heuristic models of the sort mentioned above it would have to be the case that peoples on the same level of development always choose either the same or analogous solutions to the problems which necessitate even basic changes in their respective societies.

In order for pre-national Israel to develop into a state, it was essential that, at particular times in their history, the pre-national Israelites should choose solutions to the political, economic, social, and ecological problems which arose and which required a restructuring of the society, if the effects of such problems were to be absorbed so that the society might survive. Such problems were no doubt present in the earliest Israelite society, and some of them may conceivably be demonstrable on the basis of the available source materials. However, it is far from certain that the solutions which the early Israelites chose were invariably such predictable ones that they can be fitted into a heuristic model of the development of societies at the same socio-political stage as early Israel.

There is therefore a latent danger that the use of heuristic models borrowed from cultural-evolutionistic social anthropology can provide only very superficial answers to historical questions. This in turn means that we do not really know what happened in early Israel. We possess what are in fact only very general and quite banal conceptions as to the social development of Israel prior to the introduction of the monarchy, namely the assumption that Israel developed from a tribal society into a monarchy. What determined this course of development are factors of which we are still painfully ignorant.

It is therefore necessary to supplement or replace the heuristic method with alternative procedures which pave the way to a greater degree for the acknowledgment of the endless richness of variation of human societies.

One such procedure would entail the inclusion of as much social anthropological material as possible in one's analysis of pre-national Israel. It is essential that we include in our evaluation socio-anthropological accounts of as many traditional societies as possible which are at an evolutionary stage comparable to that of pre-national Israel. Of course, the ideal solution would entail that the OT scholar in question himself participated in the examination and description of such traditional societies, but, apart from rare exceptions, this possibility is generally excluded. In place of such experience, the OT scholar must study ethnographic reports of fieldwork studies conducted in traditional societies with a view to determining for himself the sorts of social, political, and religious forces which obtain in such societies (e.g., Lemche 1985: 84–244). It is only in this manner that the concerned scholar can hope to avoid the impression of superimposing a mold upon his study of ancient Israel, as all too easily occurs if his work is based on heuristic models alone whose basis is a quite limited number of variables.

In this way it should be possible to arrive at a fruitful interplay between heuristic models and actual societies, so that the scholar in question will be better able to evaluate his source materials, not only with respect to his efforts to describe the historical course of events, but also with respect to recognizing how limited are his possibilities to describe this course of events. No matter what sociological method should happen to be chosen, the goal remains to arrive at a characterization of prenational Israelite history. Cultural evolutionism seemingly produces the most spectacular results. However, scientific controls on this approach, which are provided by the application of the alternative sociological method, reveal that evolutionistic models are based on a much less solid foundation than is immediately apparent when we consider the historical reconstructions which have been presented by adherents of the cultural evolutionistic method.

E. Israelite History in the Pre-national Period

1. The OT Narrative and "External Evidence." a. The OT Narrative. According to the OT, the history of Israel begins when Yahweh, the God of Israel, chooses a man named Abram and dispatches him on a journey from Mesopotamia to the land of Canaan, the promised land, where he is intended to become the ancestral father of Yahweh's peculiar people, Israel. Abram/Abraham travels to this land and becomes the father of a son, Isaac, who in turn sires two sons, Jacob and Esau. The former eventually receives the name "Israel" and becomes the tribal ancestor of the Israelite people.

Neither Abraham, Isaac, nor Jacob succeeds in becoming fully sedentary in the land of Canaan, and indeed Jacob is ultimately forced to abandon Canaan with his twelve sons, the tribal ancestors of the later Israelite tribes, and to take up residence in Egypt. In Egypt, Jacob's line in the course of 400 years develops into a nation. With Yahweh's aid and the leadership of Moses they manage to depart from Egypt and return to the land of Canaan. The return journey across Sinai and up through the region E of the Jordan takes 40 years, but Yahweh has revealed himself during this period as Israel's true and only God; he has also bound the Israelite people to himself in a covenantal relationship.

Under the leadership of Joshua and in a massive wave of conquest Israel moves into the land of Canaan and, following Yahweh's explicit orders (and admitting only a few individual exceptions), eradicates large portions of the Canaanite population. After the conclusion of the conquest, the depopulated Canaanite territory is redistributed among the Israelite tribes, Joshua himself presiding over a ceremony in which the covenant between Yahweh and Israel is confirmed.

After the death of Joshua there follows a period in which the Israelites forget who their God is, so that they begin to worship the gods of the Canaanites. Yahweh punishes Israel's apostasy by allowing foreign enemies to assail and plunder the country. However, he also saves it as soon as the Israelites return to Yahweh and pray for help. The saviors who are sent by Yahweh are the "Judges" of Israel who govern Israel in peace and ensure the maintenance of the right religion as long as they live. However, whenever any Judge happens to die, Israel relapses to her old ways, so that history repeats itself.

Ultimately the problems confronting the Israelite tribes become so serious that divine assistance is not felt to be sufficient: the Israelites demand a king. At the request of the Israelite people, the last Judge, Samuel, is forced to find a successor, a king, a man able to free Israel from her dire situation. At the same time, however, it is proclaimed to the Israelites that the introduction of the monarchy must be seen as the final treachery against Yahweh, who is Israel's real king. Furthermore, it is predicted (although one has to "read between the lines" to appreciate this) that this treason will have weighty consequences at some future time.

b. The "External Evidence." First of all, it is important to note the simple fact that the ANE sources from the 3d and 2d millennia B.C. do not contain a single direct reference to any of the features mentioned in the OT narrative. There is not a single reference to Abraham the patriarch, or to Joseph and his brothers in Egypt, or to Moses and the Exodus, or to the conquest of Canaan, or even to a single one of the Judges. Furthermore, when we turn to the period during which the Israelite monarchy developed, we discover that the ANE sources are completely silent on the subject of Israelite kings until we come to Omri in the 9th century B.C.

In other words, the use of ANE evidence to illuminate the biblical historical account is always a matter of indirect references and information, never of direct mention. In order to exemplify the nature of such "external evidence" it will be necessary briefly to present some examples of the sorts of information in question, and to point to the types of problems associated with them.

In the case of Abraham, the narrative about the biblical patriarch mentions a number of localities which must be acknowledged to be historical, namely Ur in Chaldea and Haran in upper Mesopotamia, in addition to numerous sites in Palestine which are mentioned by name (Shechem, Bethel, Ai, Hebron, etc.). The connection with upper Mesopotamia is additionally strengthened by the fact that some of the proper names connected with the members of Abraham's family who continued to dwell in Mesopotamia are also place names in the vicinity of Haran. Taken in isolation, this sort of "external evidence" implies only that the biblical narrators made use of place names and localities which were known in their own time either as existing localities or as names preserved by tradition. Thus the references to such names tells us nothing about the historical contents of the narrative.

On the other hand, the way some of the names are mentioned shows that the Abraham narratives cannot have been concluded before a very late point in time. Thus, for example, Ur is said to be situated in Chaldea, which only became the case after the Chaldeans settled in the S part of Mesopotamia, that is, not earlier than the 9th–8th centuries B.C.—long after the time when, according to the biblical chronology, Abraham is supposed to have lived (towards the close of the 3d millennium B.C.). These sorts of "errors" have often been explained as anachronisms (on the debate concerning anachronisms in the patriarchal narratives see Westermann *Genesis 2* BKAT, 62–64; Thompson 1974: 298–308), a possibility which must be taken seriously. On the other hand, such "anachronisms" correspond to the finds the archaeologist uncovers during excavation which make possible a precise date for the concluding phase of a given archaeological stratum. The patriarchal narratives could not have received their final form before the latest "anachronistic" datum in them was worked into the story. But this does not rule out the possibility that there could be older components in the story.

Concrete information from Israel's environment of a similar nature also recurs in connection with the other epochs in the OT account of Israel's earliest history. The Egyptian sources never directly refer to the presence of the Israelites in Egypt, although analogous phenomena are described in some documents which, among other things, describe the entry of Semitic nomads into Egypt (*ANET,* 259), just as they also mention the presence of *ʿapr.w* (*ḫab/piru,* possibly "Hebrews") in Egypt (Greenberg 1955: 55–57; Bottéro 1954: 165–75). The description in Exodus of the forced labor of the Israelites in the construction of Pharaoh's garrison cities, Pithom and Rameses (Exod 1:11), is often seen by scholars in relation to conditions which obtained under the 19th or 20th Dynasty, when Egypt was ruled by a number of pharaohs called Rameses.

While this sort of "external" information shows that the Israelites, or their ancestors, *could* have been present in Egypt in the time of the New Kingdom, it does not *prove* that this was the case. In the first place, it is entirely possible that the Israelites were originally *ḫab/piru.* See HABIRU, HAPIRU; HEBREW. However, this particular sociological phenomenon appeared everywhere in the ANE in the 2d millennium B.C., from the Zagros mountains in the NE to Egypt in the SW, and from the Persian Gulf in the SE to Asia Minor in the NW. The term accordingly designates a population of heterogeneous ethnic origins which was so far-flung that they cannot possibly be identified with the early Israelite population. In short, even though the earliest Israelites may have been part of the LB *ḫab/piru*-movement, this does not prove that the Israelites were ever in Egypt simply because *ḫab/piru*-peoples were also present there.

Furthermore, not even the information pertaining to Pharaoh's garrison cities, Pithom and Rameses, can decide the issue and prove that the Israelites were in Egypt, since archaeological and topographical research leaves open the question as to which sites are actually designated, when they were founded, and where they were situated (Redford 1987; cf. Bietak 1987).

Other types of "external evidence" include such things as proper names, usages and customs, relationships to particular sociological phenomena (were the patriarchs or Israelites nomads or *ḫab/piru,* or was Abraham a wandering merchant [Albright 1961]?) or ethnic groups (were the Israelites Amorites or Aramaeans?). But we shall have no certainty in this area as long as Israel's environment continues to deny us information about particular individuals whom we otherwise know from the OT account of the prenational period, and also because it is not possible to reestablish a socio-historical framework which is so exclusive that, for example, the patriarchs must necessarily belong within it—a procedure which would entail assigning the patriarchs to the period to which such a framework could be dated.

Admittedly, most, but not all, information of a historical, sociological, or economic nature pertaining to the patriarchs may be compared with "external evidence" from the 2d millennium B.C. However, such comparisons require the use of materials which extend, in terms of time, over most of a millennium, and, in terms of space, run from the NE part of Mesopotamia to the Persian Gulf and to the Mediterranean and Egypt to the W and SW. Finally, the year 1000 B.C. is by no means some kind of *magical* barrier. Most or even all of the individual details in the patriarchal narratives (or, for that matter, in the account of the Israelite sojourn in Egypt) can be seen against a Near Eastern background which locates the patriarchs in the 1st millennium B.C.

"External evidence" is important to the extent that it is able to show that certain components in the OT narratives about Israel's earliest history were not free inventions. Rather, it helps us to see that in writing their stories about the ancestors of Israel the "historians" (so to speak) created a socio-cultural framework for their heroes and heroines, a framework whose authenticity is confirmed by other ANE sources. On the other hand, "external evidence" cannot be used to show that the patriarchs ever existed, or that Israel was ever in Egypt.

Against this, it has been argued that the OT account of Israel's earliest history cannot be *disconfirmed,* and that scholars cannot therefore allow themselves to claim that Israel was *not* in Egypt. Of course, this is correct, but this counterargument accords the OT narratives the status of postulates which are not subject to scholarly criticism as to their historical contents. On the one hand, it is conceivable that what we find in the narratives is true; on the other hand, scholars can neither prove nor disprove this. This means that the narratives in question have no role to play in a scientific analysis of Israel's past, since the only argument which can be advanced for their inclusion is that we *think,* that is, "believe," that there are historical elements in them. In this connection it might be argued, as in the question of Moses' historicity, for example, that Moses is a necessary presupposition for the understanding of the earliest history and prehistory of Israel, and, further, that if he had not lived it would have been necessary to invent him (the expression is supposed to derive from N. Soederblom; cf. de Vaux 1971–73, 1: 311 n. 33); it is then possible to reply, with Liverani (1976: 153), "That's what they did!"

2. Early Israelite History. a. Choice of Method—Delimiting the Object of Study. Ultimately, the history of pre-national Israel must be written without the aid of the OT narratives. The time prior to the formation of the state (and perhaps also somewhat later in the monarchical period than is usually assumed) is, from a scholarly point of view, *prehistory* (i.e., in technical terms, "the time without history"), since there are no contemporary written sources which inform us as to events in Israel before the introduction of the monarchy.

Of course, it is true that some scholars have argued in favor of a distinction between this history-less prehistory and early history *("Frühgeschichte/protohistory"),* where the latter is held to reside in the dusky terminator separating the history-less past and historical time proper. They thus hold that it should be possible to glimpse the contours of this early history in the sources which date from the historical time (Malamat 1983). This view is problematical in that it presupposes as given that the late sources may possess historical information about the past, and also because it assumes that we are able to cross-examine the information contained in the late sources in such a way that it is possible to distinguish between historical information and ahistorical story (Lemche 1984b).

This means that in our efforts to reconstruct Israel's earliest history we must renounce the possibility of reconstructing that history prior to Israel's emergence in Palestine. We must stop attempting to describe the history of the patriarchal age, or Israel's situation in Egypt, or in the desert. Even though we have to deal in certain cases with periods of Israel's prehistory, as the OT itself asserts, we are unable to check the OT information in such a way as to permit us to write a coherent historical account. Accordingly, our narrative about Israel has to start at a point in time at which it is possible, in however rudimentary fashion, to shape for ourselves a picture of Israel's early existence.

Instead of "retelling" yet again the OT narrative of Israel's earliest history, the historian's primary task now is to concentrate on the *scene* against which Israelite history unrolled, which is to say that the historian must attempt to account for the development in the area in which Israel arose and existed. Moreover, the historian must do this on the basis of sources which derive from the period, a period which may be termed "Israel's formative time."

This method is not new. The most famous example of a similar approach in OT studies is Alt's use of *territorial history ("Territorialgeschichte")* in his pathfinding study of Israel's emergence (Alt, *KlSchr* 1: 89–125). By studying the socio-political features which obtained before Israel settled in Palestine and again after the completion of the process of settlement, Alt thought it possible to determine the character of Israelite settlement, and thus to render an account of Israel's origin and earliest history in Palestine.

Alt's reconstruction of the developmental history of Israel must be regarded today as outdated (although one should not forget the fact that it still has many adherents among OT scholars). The reason for this does not have to do with the method which Alt employed, but rather with the sources which formed the basis of his theories. In part, the source materials have grown considerably thanks to the addition of extra information; moreover, we have studied the sources for almost three-quarters of a century, with the result that we are now better able to evaluate the information contained in those sources which were already available to Alt. Thus we are better off than Alt was on three decisive points.

First, today we are much better informed about the ANE civilizations of the LB Age, a remark which also applies to the situation in Palestine. Admittedly, the source materials available to Alt consisted mainly of the Amarna correspondence; these have been only slightly supplemented by the addition of individual documents from Palestine itself. But if we move beyond the narrow borders of Palestine, we discover that it is now possible to form a much better impression as to the history, culture, and political and social system of the region by studying a number of archives which have been found since 1925, or which only since that time have made an impression on the scientific community. In particular there are the archives from Ugarit and Alalakh, but additional information is also derivable from the archives of the old Hittite capital of Hattusas (modern Bogazköy in Turkey). It is now possible to draw the broad outline of the history of Syria in the LB Age (for surveys extending up to ca. 1970, see Klengel 1965–70). It is likewise possible to reconstruct in some detail the social life of the Near Eastern states in this period (on Ugarit, see Rainey 1962; Heltzer 1976; 1982; cf. also Buccellati 1967).

Second, archaeological work both within and outside of Palestine has not merely provided researchers with much more extensive materials than those which were available to Alt. Rather, the changed archaeological methods since 1970, including above all the modern archaeological concern to study entire areas instead of concentrating on the excavation of the great tells, has enabled scholars to stratify the archaeological history of sizable parts of the later Israelite region (cf. esp. *AIS*).

Third, the appearance of a truly scientific socio-anthropological study of Near Eastern societies in the decades following World War II, including particularly studies of nomadic societies and their relations to other types of societies in the region, has entailed that the sociological observations which also figured in Alt's reconstructions have either had to be extensively modified or exchanged for other sociological theories.

Taken together, these facts mean that the scientific description of the history of Israel before the emergence of the monarchy has had to be rewritten (strikingly expressed by Gottwald 1975 in the form of a number of demands which would have to be met by any renewed discussion of Israelite history). At this time, however, it is too early to claim that the modern reconstruction of Israelite history has been fully established, although a number of possibilities now present themselves for the consideration of the scholar. Thus every historical reconstruction offered at present necessarily has a hypothetical character, even if the main lines of such reconstructions are by now relatively well drawn.

b. Palestine in the LB Age. Considering the modest size of the region (ca. 28,000 sq. km), it is remarkable that Palestine seems to have been subdivided into a number of mini-states throughout the entire Bronze Age, each with a more or less sizable town as its center, and each governed by a king. This political structure, which we can barely make out, at least as far as the EB Age (3d millennium B.C.) is concerned, became sharply defined in the MB Age (the first half of the 2d millennium B.C.), as we can deduce from the Egyptian EXECRATION TEXTS.

This political structure survived the Egyptian conquest of the country in the 16th century B.C. Indeed, it would even be possible to assert that the political fragmentation of the country made the task of its occupiers easier; they tended to leave the political structure untouched, with the exception of appointing their own political governor for the region. On the other hand, the Egyptians were able to play the various mini-states off against one another in a sort of "divide and conquer" policy which prevented the emergence of any effective opposition to the Egyptian dominance. Thus the Egyptian occupation did not lead to peace in Palestine; rather, it augmented the tendencies to political divisiveness and the internal rivalries of the various states which were already latent in the area. In this connection, two factors were especially important:

(1) On the economic level, the Egyptian occupation represented a burden on the resources of the region because of the taxes which the Egyptian provinces were obliged to pay. Admittedly, we do not know the precise dimensions of this taxation, but its consequence seems to have been a gradual but nevertheless noticeable decline in the material culture of the region in the LB Age. This development seems to have accelerated in the 14th century B.C. (Kenyon 1979: 206), possibly as a result of difficulties presented to the trade exchanges caused by the establishment of the Hittite Empire around 1400 B.C. Also, the Palestinian states had perforce to bear the consequences of the later conflicts between the Egyptian armies, which utilized Palestine as a staging-ground, and the Hittite troops. Palestine was, however, outside of the immediate combat zone, which was located further to the N in Syria.

(2) On the ideological plane, the Egyptian dominance also created problems by utilizing a political ideology which was foreign to the local Palestinian kings, since the Egyptian political ideology could not guarantee the security of these kings. A consequence of the Egyptian attitude towards their subject-kings was that the latter were forced to fend for themselves. The Egyptians apparently only intervened in conflicts between the various kings in the event the Egyptian sovereignty was directly threatened by particularly ambitious vassals (Liverani 1983).

We do not know the details of the socio-political structure of the Palestinian mini-states. However, it would be reasonable to assume that the local societies were reminiscent of those situated in the larger states to the N, Ugarit and Alalakh, from which we possess a wealth of information. Briefly, the structure in question may be characterized as a *palatine system* in which the palace was the all-dominating center of the state, and in which the king, enthroned in his palace, was regarded as the ideological (religious), political, and economic center. The king had at his disposal a corps of both civilian and military functionaries who controlled the various social sectors. Everything suggests that economic life and the production of manufactured goods was also directed from the palace. The ordinary population consisted in part of artisans who, at least in the case of N Syria, were subject to the palatial administration; and of peasants, who made up the largest social group in the society. The slaves were located at the bottom of society, but we have no idea how extensive the practice of slavery was in the Palestinian states.

It was characteristic of the Palestinian area, in contradistinction to the larger Syrian states, that there was little village structure outside of the urban centers, since one of the notable features of the LB Age was a clearly-defined decline in the number of villages in the country (Thompson 1978: 32; 1979: 66). To a large extent, the peasant population must have dwelt in the towns where they could be protected by the defensive walls and by the local military. In consideration of the very limited territorial extension of the individual states, this did not rule out agriculture around the towns, although the marginal areas must have been neglected. Considerable transition of the peasant population to other occupations, including nomadism, is likewise probable.

The reasons for the decline of village culture are not difficult to describe. Throughout the history of the ANE the peasant populations were exposed groups (see extensively on this Lemche 1985: 164–201). In the first place, they had to bear the tax burdens of the state more than any other group in society, since agricultural products are immediately convertible in any economy based on barter. In the second place, to the extent that the peasant populations lived in villages they were practically unprotected. When peace obtained in the country, the peasants had no need of protection. Maintaining order was ordinarily the job of the state authorities, and during more hostile times the struggle between the states was much concerned with the control of the villages and their ability to pay taxes. Palestinian peasants accordingly had only two possibilities open to them: they could seek the protection of the walled towns—and in this connection we note that, particularly in the earlier part of the LB Age, a sizable increase in the population of the towns seems to have taken place (Kenyon 1979: 189–92)—or they could abandon their occupation and land in order to flee and try to find security elsewhere.

In the latter event, a number of escape routes were possible. The peasants could either become nomads, a process which was made all the easier by the fact that most of the peasant societies in question also to some extent practiced *transhumant* pastoralism; or they had the possibility to become *ḫap/piru,* that is, refugees who survived either by fleeing to other states or by becoming outlaws in the impassible mountainous regions in Palestine. We do not know how sizable a percentage of the peasant population chose to survive as nomads on the margins of the existing states. However, if we compare the developments in the LB Age with other and similar situations in Palestine's history—occasions when village culture declined sharply (see the survey in Coote and Whitelam 1987: 27–80)—then we must assume that the desedentarization of the peasants was in fact considerable.

Furthermore, it is clearly implied by the written sources from this period that the refugee problem eventually reached such dimensions that the Egyptian suzerains were compelled to intervene, although it does not look as if the problem was ever solved. At all events, the refugees *(ḫap/piru)* figure in the sources all the way from the days of Amenophis II (ca. 1450 B.C.; cf. Greenberg 1955: 56, no. 159; Bottéro 1954: 167, no. 183) to those of Sethi I (ca. 1310 B.C.; Greenberg 1955: 56, no. 160; Bottéro 1954: 168, no. 184; Albright 1952). The main part of the evidence derives from the Amarna correspondence from the first half of the 14th century B.C. (Greenberg 1955: 32–50; Bottéro 1954: 85–118). The Amarna letters also show that the phenomenon gave cause for alarm in the small Palestinian states, especially because it was possible to designate anyone in opposition to those in power as an *ḫap/piru,* i.e., an enemy of the Egyptians (cf. Mendenhall 1973: 122–41; Liverani 1979a).

But whether the peasants chose an existence as nomads or instead decided to flee entirely and try their luck as *ḫap/piru,* the consequences for the Palestinian states remained considerable. On the one hand, the reduction in the number of peasants—with the attendant probable reduction of land under cultivation—meant a painful decline in the base of taxation. Moreover, this must have taken place at a time when the Egyptian overlords felt the need to levy even greater imposts on their provinces. On the other hand, the increase in population which was no longer subject to control by the states (nomads and outlaws) constituted a threat to trade relations, including the international trade between the Egyptian region and the Syro-Mesopotamian sphere, since the caravans must have made tempting targets for bandits and for the raids of the nomads. Thus the socio-political development towards the close of the LB Age contributed to the collapse of what had been, in economic terms, an "internationalist" phase based on the exchange of trade goods; and this collapse no doubt in turn accelerated the political disintegration of the area. We cannot claim that the city-state system in Syro-Palestine completely succumbed during the transition from the LB Age to the early Iron Age (the period from the 13th to the 11th centuries B.C.), as a considerable number of towns survived the economic and political turbulence of the period. It remains nevertheless true that the power relationships in the country changed significantly during the early Iron Age. Not the least important reason for this was the beginning of a new socio-political process which led to the emergence of wholly new centers of power in the Iron Age, and which culminated in the appearance of the state(s) of Israel.

c. Palestine in the Early Iron Age. The most important change in the evolution of Palestine in the early Iron Age (the period between 1200 B.C. and the beginning of the 1st millennium B.C.) was the reflowering of village culture in the entire country. This development already seems to have started prior to the close of the 13th century B.C., but it accelerated in the subsequent couple of centuries (fundamentally on this development, see *AIS*).

As we have seen, this flowering of village culture did not mean that the towns disappeared at the same time, even though the archaeological picture of the urban societies in this period points to a serious crisis which affected a number of the larger towns. Admittedly, certain towns were in fact destroyed in the course of this period, particularly towards the end of the 13th century or the beginning of the 12th century B.C. Others, however, lived on and show no signs of destruction; indeed, some of them continued down into the 10th century (the time of the Israelite monarchy).

There is no simple answer as to why things took this course, such as, for example, suggesting that the destruction in this period of several urban societies was a facet of the Israelite invasion and conquest of the country, as scholars previously assumed. There seem to be no correlation between the distribution of destruction and the OT account of Israel's invasion of the land of Canaan.

On the other hand, the results of the archaeological excavations and surveys do suggest a completely different explanation of the socio-political development than the one which appears in the OT. Most notably, it has proven to be practically impossible to distinguish between the material culture of the early Iron Age village societies and that which prevailed in the urban societies, except, of course, for the fact that the material culture in the villages was never as rich as it was in the towns. Moreover, with the sole exception of the Philistines, it has proven to be extraordinarily difficult to point to so-called index fossils which might imply the presence of foreign immigrants, since such a presence literally always manifests itself in the form of a pottery tradition which differed radically from that which obtained in the rest of the country. In general, it would be correct to characterize the material culture in both the villages and the towns as a continuation of the material culture of the LB Age, even if the level of this culture depreciated considerably.

This does not mean that there are no archaeological "novelties" associated with the Iron Age, when compared with the previous period; there was in fact a new house type which appears in a number of villages (the so-called four-room house). However, the distribution of these structures was not confined to Israelite territory, since it also appeared in the Philistine region and elsewhere. Furthermore, this type of house does not seem to have appeared before the development of the Iron Age villages; rather, its appearance went hand in hand with the general development of the material culture in the Iron Age (*AIS,* 254–59). See also HOUSE, ISRAELITE. Other, supposedly "new" elements might be mentioned in this connection, such as the so-called collared-rim jar, which Albright in particular (*ArchPal,* 118–19) associated with the arrival of the Israelites in the country. However, here also we are dealing with a cultural feature whose roots lay in the LB Age and which, incidentally, was not confined to the later Israelite territory (*AIS,* 275–85).

In short, there are no indications that Palestine was struck by any sizable wave of immigration from the surrounding regions in the period between ca. 1300 and 1000 B.C., with the exception, of course, of the Philistine settlements along the coast, which have their own history. See PHILISTINES. This means in turn that an explanation of the origin and early history of Israel is to be sought in the context of a more general evaluation of the socio-political development of the region, which is reflected in the emergence of an extensive village culture in the early Iron Age. It is furthermore essential that any reconstruction of this history be based on conditions in Palestine itself, and not, for example, be grounded in the information in late literary sources about foreign peoples and conquerors—a process which has, in the scholarly discussion of the problem, allowed these foreign *ethnoi* to serve as some sort of *dei ex machina,* that is, as simplistic explanations for developments which can in reality be explained without recourse to such "models" (on this sort of explanation in scientific literature, see Adams 1968; Tritsch 1974).

An especially interesting characteristic of the revived village culture of the Iron Age was the fact that it was largely concentrated in areas which either had not previously been under cultivation, or which had been unexploited marginal areas during the LB Age. This applies especially to the Galilean highlands to the N and the mountainous region of central Palestine; but it also applies to the Negeb desert and the hill country to the S. Scholars have previously pointed to at least three technical innovations as factors which enabled this change in the settlement pattern: (1) the introduction of iron tools, (2) the introduction of cement-lined cisterns for collecting rainwater, and (3) the introduction of the technique of terracing the mountain slopes to retain the soil after clearance of the natural mountain vegetation (*ArchPal,* 110–13; de Geus 1975; Gottwald 1979: 658–59; and, as far as points 2 and 3 are concerned, Lemche 1988: 90). However, all three claims now seem to be untenable (*AIS,* 202). As far as iron is concerned, there was no decisive breakthrough before the 10th century B.C. when steel technology was developed (Waldbaum 1978: 24–27); until then the material had been useless for the production of durable tools. As far as the cisterns and terraces are concerned, the techniques in question already existed at an earlier date; thus it was more a matter of more extensive use of known technology than of the discovery of new technology (Hopkins 1985: 265–69; on terracing, see also Borowski 1987: 15–18). The fact that both cisterns and terracing were in greater use after 1200 B.C. than earlier is best explained by the nature of the newly-cultivated territories, and by the political factors which necessitated the cultivation of the areas in question. The technologies in question, like other corresponding ones—such as the extensive use of storage pits in Iron Age complexes (Hopkins 1985: 149–51)—were the basic presuppositions which made the settlements in the mountainous regions and on the borders of the desert at all possible. Therefore they must have been known *before* the settlements; they could not have been introduced after the settlements were established.

This fact further implies that the concept of the Israelites as nomads wandering in from the deserts and steppe areas E and SE of the cultivable lands in Palestine and Transjordan can scarcely be maintained. The new settlements must have been established by people who had lived in contact with the pastoral culture of Palestine. Naturally, the identification of such groups is debatable. Parallels from later periods in the history of the region suggest that nomads must have had some share in the process of settlement, but in the event these would have been nomads who had been in contact with the sedentary population for a long time in a variety of forms of symbiotic coexistence.

However, there are a number of factors which suggest that we cannot reckon with an automatic sedentarization of nomads; the process must have been coerced by other circumstances. In the first place, only some parts of the regions which became subjected to cultivation in the Iron Age were actually suited for flocks and herds. As long as the mountains were covered with forest (as they were to a large extent in the Palestinian highlands until the LB Age; cf. Rowton 1967), they were unsuited to raising flocks and herds to any significant extent. It was only in the valleys and in the northern Negeb that it was possible to herd sheep, goats, and cattle on a large scale. In the second place, it is a fact that Near Eastern nomads do not voluntarily submit to sedentarization. The primary reason for this is economic, since, at least in theory, the nomadic way of life contains more possibilities for economic expansion, and thus for population expansion, than does agriculture (ecological factors profoundly circumscribe the growth of agriculture in the Near East). Ethnographic studies of the sedentarization of nomads have shown that nomads continue to resist sedentarization even when political organizations beyond the control of the nomads themselves (i.e., centralized states) force them to do so. Such resistance is not always successful. However, some nomads may voluntarily "sedentarize" if the already-existing peasant society contains population elements which are *ethnically* related to the nomads (on nomadism in the Near East, see Lemche 1985: 84–163; on the process of sedentarization, see esp. pp. 136–47).

Thus any theory which seeks to explain the emergence of the villages, and which at the same time allows for the possibility of nomadic participation in this process, will necessarily assert that the mountain settlements were introduced by people who could not have been nomads per se. Rather, they were people who attempted to perpetuate a way of life which they had known previously in other regions of the country. The nomadic elements which subsequently participated in these settlements must have understood themselves to be so closely related to this peasant population that this relationship encouraged their sedentarization. On the other hand, there is no reason to imagine that the city states in any way participated in the settlement process, or that they forced the nomadic elements of the hill-country to give up that way of life. Neither these city-states nor the Egyptian empire (which still nominally ruled the area) possessed the strength necessary to influence and control developments in the highlands.

Thus our materials suggest that the process of settlement in the mountains was begun by peasants who came from parts of Palestine which had already known agriculture (i.e., from the territories of the city-states in the lowlands along the coast and in the valleys in the N part of the country). In this connection it is relevant to include the refugee problem which was so characteristic of the LB Age, and which is connected with the *ḫab/piru* movement. It was already pointed out above that the main body of these refugees consisted of peasants who, under insupportable economic and political pressures, were forced to abandon their lands and seek their survival outside of the sphere of influence of the city-states and the authority of the Egyptian empire. In the course of time, it became possible for this "outlaw" population group to consolidate their toehold in the highlands and, through socio-political integration, to achieve such a degree of independence that they were able, as tribes, to administer their own territories, settle in them, clear new land for a growing population, and defend them against outside interference. In the course of all this, their successes became so appealing to their nomadic cousins (who, in most cases, must have had the same origins) that parts of the Palestinian nomadic population also settled in these new villages. Moreover, at least in the N Negeb these elements must have comprised the most important segment of the population of the newly-established settlements (on Tel Masos, see Fritz 1980).

This process is explicable in sociological terms, since the social structure of this mixed peasant and nomadic population underwent only slight changes. The main lines of the fundamental social structure of the new societies were preserved; only a single new element was added: the tribal society. This is to be explained on the basis of the fact that the fundamental social structure of preindustrial Near Eastern societies has survived unchanged for thousands of years. It does not mean that major changes did not occur on the local level, or that relationships were identical from site to site and through all time. Rather, it means that all of these societies were fundamentally constituted as kinship structures, either real or false. The lowest level of these societies consisted of *nuclear families* (in individual cases "extended families" consisting of several nuclear families). The ascending stages thereafter consisted of *minimal lineages, lineages, maximal lineages* and *clans.* All or most of these levels will have been present no matter how the political structure of the society as a whole was organized—i.e., they were independent of whether or not there were centralized states.

Only the highest level of the socio-political structure, the tribe, appears to have clashed on occasion with the forces of the state, since the tribe as a form of political organization competed with the state administrative organs. To put it another way, the state performed the same functions as the tribal organization, that is, the state's primary function was to protect the interests of its citizens. The tribes had themselves arisen out of what were previous nontribal societies to meet a common need perceived by its members, thus forming a type of organization capable of offering protections to the individual family, lineage, or clan which they could not provide for themselves. Just as the state provided a *forum* for the life and well-being of its citizens, the tribe designated the extreme horizon for the existence of its members. If one was not a citizen of a state, one was automatically regarded as a foreigner; if one did not belong to a tribe, one was not embraced by the reciprocal protective system which the tribe represented. There was, however, a single decisive difference between state and tribe, namely that the state controlled its citizens by the exercise of *political force;* to this end it possessed mechanisms for getting its way with the citizens. By contrast, the members of the tribe were united by ties of *social solidarity* based on the fact that they were, at least on the ideological plane, related by kinship ties (on the transformations of Near Eastern state-citizens into tribal members and vice versa, see Salzmann 1978).

No written source deriving from the early Iron Age tells us what names the tribal organizations in question actually used. Probably part, if not all, of the twelve "official" Israelite tribes came into being in conjunction with these new developments in the highlands and the N Negeb during the LB-early Iron Age transition. On the other hand, there is no reason to believe that it was only the twelve Israelite tribes attested in the OT which took part in this process. An Egyptian inscription from ca. 1310 B.C. mentions some groups which might well have been tribes active in the region around Beth-shan (*ANET,* 255; Albright 1952). None of the tribes in question is mentioned in the OT although it has been supposed that the patriarch Abraham might have been the apical ancestor of one of them, namely the tribe *Rhm* (cf. Liverani 1979b). Another of the names, *Yrmt,* is familiar to us as a toponym which, in the geographical lists in the book of Joshua (21:29), appears as Jarmuth, in the tribal territory of Issachar. On the other hand, the third name mentioned in the inscription, *Tyr,* is not attested elsewhere.

Correspondingly, the Song of Deborah (Judges; which is probably the oldest source in the OT regardless of whether or not it derives from the premonarchic period) informs us of the existence of tribal units which did not receive placings in the official lists of Israel's twelve tribes. These are Machir and Gilead; in the OT the former figures as a toponym, while the latter is a clan within the tribe of Manasseh.

Such indications show that the course of the socio-political process in the early Iron Age was much more complicated than is suggested by the much later OT sources. At the same time, it shows that the OT information about the twelve tribes and their tribal territories cannot be regarded as information deriving from pre-national times. Rather, in the OT we are dealing with a systematic reconstruction of early Israelite history which was undertaken at a much later date. Similarly, the tribal boundaries mentioned in the book of Joshua must be seen to reflect the district subdivisions of the later Israel, whether or not the description of the tribal territories in Joshua 13–21 derive from early monarchical times or were first composed in the reign of king Josiah, or even later (see the summary by Miller in *IJH,* 235–36).

The connection between the process of retribalization adumbrated here and the social movements which were already so prominent in the LB Age is possibly also supported by the use of the term "Hebrew" in the OT. In the Bible the term appears in certain contexts as a designation for the early Israelites. The most remarkable such usage probably occurs in the books of Samuel, where it is always the Philistines who employ the term of the Israelites (1 Sam 4:6, 9; 13:3, 19; 14:11, 21; 29:3). Although the contexts in question do not necessarily harken back to Israel's pre-national time, they do nevertheless imply, like other OT references to the Israelites as Hebrews (esp. in Exodus 1–15) that, in the eyes of the city-states, the tribal societies in the highlands were regarded as "Hebrew" societies, which probably means *ḫab/piru* (Lemche 1979; and, partially, Na'aman 1986). See HEBREW. This does not necessarily mean that there was a direct line connecting Israel's origin to, for example, the *ḫab/piru* movements of the Amarna period; but it might be taken to suggest that the authorities in the early Iron Age (and perhaps even later) city-states linked the developments in the highlands with the *ḫab/piru* phenomenon. Admittedly, with the single exception of the very late text of Jonah 1:9, there is no evidence to suggest that the Israelites ever called themselves "Hebrews." This fact need not mean very much, however, since there are also no ANE sources which show that the *ḫab/piru*-peoples ever applied the term to themselves. Rather, *ḫab/piru* was a social designation which was employed by the official authorities to refer to a special group of needy people; it had no ethnic connotations. Such ethnic connotations probably emerged only later in Israel when the "Hebrews" mentioned in the OT were also regarded as Israelites.

One particular problem adheres to the question of the motives underlying the process of retribalization in the mountain regions and in the Negeb in the early Iron Age. As the development has been sketched out here, it has been explained in terms of political, economic, and social relationships. However, there is some question as to whether some *ideological motivation* also lies behind the origin of earliest Israel. George Mendenhall, the first scholar to suggest that Israel's emergence was the result of a social process taking place in the Palestinian highlands rather than the result of the immigration of foreign peoples from other parts of the Near East, especially characterized the process as an expression of a conscious, ideologically-motivated reaction to the city-state system. As he saw it, the peasants had suffered such intolerable conditions that they were forced to rebel against that system (Mendenhall 1962). Thus the proponents of this theory have chosen to see Israel as the result of a *peasants' revolt* against the feudal Canaanite political "establishment," a revolt which was, additionally, influenced by the introduction of a new religion into Palestinian society. Mendenhall accordingly gives the honor for the arrival of the god Yahweh, which in reality means the arrival of the group of people who had encountered Yahweh in "the desert," to the early "Yahwists." It was they, he holds, who created an ideology which was able to serve as a focus of centralization for the dissatisfied forces in the country. This also meant that when the new society constituted itself as a tribal league (Mendenhall originally retained much of Noth's conception of an Israelite amphictyony), the statutes of the Yahwistic religion—i.e., the covenant between Yahweh and Israel—served as the constitution of the new Israelite society. Mendenhall sees this society as essentially an *egalitarian* one, that is, a society in which all Israelites, at least in theory, were on the same footing.

However, this thesis, which has been revised and developed by N. K. Gottwald (1979), has a number of serious weaknesses, a situation which above all relates to the fact that it is impossible to check in a scholarly manner. Since these early Israelites have not bequeathed to us so much as a single document, it is impossible to say what conceptions they entertained as to their situation or to the divine. The "revolutionary hypothesis," as Mendenhall's reconstruction of Israel's origin is usually called, stands or falls on the question of whether the OT description of the origin of Israelite religion can bear religio-historical analysis. In this connection it is correct to assert that there is no indication that the OT sources pertaining to the earliest Israelite *religion* differ qualitatively from the OT information about early Israelite *history.* This means that scholars intending to reconstruct the religious history are obliged to renounce the use of the OT narratives for this purpose, just as they cannot use them for their reconstructions of the historical course of development. It is therefore possible that early Yahwism had a completely different content than the OT narratives suggest. It is probable that early Israelite religious life differed significantly from the idealized conception in the OT account which, in its present form, derives from the early Judaism of the postexilic period.

Concrete criticism of this hypothesis may be directed against the following individual issues. First, according to Mendenhall and others, Yahweh's rule in ancient Israel was founded on the Sinai covenant as Israel's earliest constitution. However, analyses of the Sinai narratives in Exodus–Numbers reveal that they may possibly have been written in a period separated by half a millennium from the events depicted in the Sinai stories. As far as the idea of the covenant is concerned, particularly the German scholar L. Perlitt (1969) has argued that there could not possibly have been an Israelite covenantal theology prior to the Deuteronomistic movement around the middle of the 1st millennium B.C. Moreover, Mendenhall had claimed that Hittite treaties in the 2d millennium B.C. offer the best parallels to the Sinai covenant and the OT covenantal theology. However, later investigations have shown that comparative materials from the 1st millennium B.C., above all the Assyrian treaties from the 8th–7th century, contain parallels which are at least as appropriate (McCarthy 1963; the texts have been collected in Parpola 1988). But see also COVENANT.

Second, the concept of a peasant revolt (particularly as it is developed by Gottwald) is an over-simplification in that it presupposes that the process followed a coordinated plan whose goal was the establishment of an alternative government and state in Palestine which would be able to compete with the city-states. This concept of peasants deliberately and militantly revolting is romantic, since sociological studies of historical peasant revolts have shown that they are usually uncoordinated, spontaneous, and lack any clear goal. Alternatively, they have been led by members of the intellectual or political elite in the societies in question.

Finally—and this applies particularly to Gottwald's discussion of "egalitarian" Israel—the theories about revolutionary Israel confuse two different logical categories with one another. In Gottwald's terms, early Israel was an egalitarian society because it was a *segmentary* society. However, all ANE societies were segmentary, whether they were organized in tribes or in states. Segmentation has to do with a socio-political mode of organization. By way of contrast, egalitarianism is an *ideological* category. There is no necessary correlation between segmentary society and egalitarian ideology. Moreover, a segmentary society can possess an egalitarian ideology without in fact being organized as an egalitarian society. Indeed, there exist clear examples of segmentary societies which are ideologically egalitarian, but which have to be regarded as hierarchically, that is, rank-organized. There are also societies in which the egalitarian ideology, which primarily serves to strengthen the ties of solidarity among its members, is also used to oppress less wealthy members of the tribes (see, comprehensively, Lemche 1985: 202–44).

The revolutionary hypothesis may therefore be left out of account in the study of the process which led to the emergence of early Israel. The nature of the OT source materials do not permit us either to confirm or disconfirm the hypothesis, for which reason it remains a mere postulate. By the same token, it has the feel of a modern theory whose basis is modern European conceptions of traditional societies; but it is one which has no foundation in scholarly social anthropological studies of traditional societies. The theory has, however, one advantage, namely that it may serve as a point of departure for scholarly reconstructions of the history of emergent Israel in the early Iron Age. It describes this process as one which took place within the borders of Palestine, since it renders superfluous the notion of the immigration of foreign peoples to explain this development. Moreover, in so doing it does not assign to the OT narratives a value as historical sources which (because they derive from a much later time) they cannot bear.

At the same time, along with other theories which go beyond it and which are based on a more realistic foundation, the revolutionary hypothesis opens the possibility for studying the on-going development of early Israel up to the formation of the state as a continuous process. By way of contrast, the OT account of Israel in the period of the judges actually describes this phase of Israelite history as essentially unchanging, a variety of homoiostasis, as if the process of becoming had already ceased with the establishment of the tribal society back in the pre-national period, a situation which first became unbalanced when new circumstances demanded a new form of government.

d. Formation of the Israelite State. There is a tradition in OT research which insists that we separate the study of the formation of the state from the descriptions of the process of Israelite settlement and of the situation of the tribes of Israel in the period of the judges. Thus the formation of the state seems to constitute a special period in early Israelite history.

In terms of chronology, it is correct that the formation of the Israelite state, which the OT connects with the figure of Saul, took place a couple of centuries after the close of the LB Age. Thus it might seem superficially to be the case that this distinction between the settlement process and the formation of the state is valid from an academic point of view. However, the introduction of improved methods of historical analysis, including above all the concept of *la longue durée* under the influence of the French *Annales* school, suggests that the OT tripartition into a "settlement period," a "period of the judges," and a "monarchical period" disrupts the actual historical process. It distorts this process in an unfortunate way, in that it severs the connections between the various phases in early Israelite history. It would therefore be more correct to regard the formation of the state as the final consequence of the formation of the Israelite tribal societies at the beginning of the Iron Age. In short, we should study the establishment of the Israelite state against the background of the previously-adumbrated socio-political process and as an expression of the continued dynamic thrust of that process.

At the same time, such an approach demands that our historical analysis ignore the tendency to write personality-centered history which has characterized most of the descriptions of state-formation in ancient Israel. No doubt remarkable figures did take part in the process which led to the Israelite monarchy; such names as Samuel, Saul, and David announce themselves automatically. However, such individuals should rather be seen as the results of a social development which followed its own imperatives rather than as agents directing the process which resulted in the state. Any study of the great personalities involved in this phase of Israelite history would necessarily be confined to points on a line, rather than to the line itself; it would concentrate on isolated individuals, break the continuity of the process, and thereby sunder the historical course of development. It is, incidentally, remarkable that such emphasis on the continuity of the process does not entirely conflict with the OT account, since also that narrative recalls that there were tendencies within Israelite tribal society towards the emergence of chieftainships or even kingships. The well-known examples are from the territory of Manasseh, where the judge Gideon is said to have been offered the monarchy by grateful kinsmen (Judg 8:22–23), and where Abimelech subsequently made himself king of a city-state whose center was at Shechem (Judges 9).

The formation of the state has been only brusquely treated at best in recent OT research, in the sense that only a few *synthetic* surveys have appeared; of these, by far the most important is Alt's old study which appeared between the two World Wars (*KlSchr* 2: 1–65). It is only very recently that new investigations have appeared which employ sociological background insights to create organic perspective on the course of the evolution of the state and its presuppositions (cf. esp. Gottwald ed. 1986; see also Frick 1985, as well as the reconstruction of the establishment of the monarchy in Lemche 1988: 102–4, 130–41).

In the following, we shall disregard the attempts to write history from a personality-centered point of view. Instead, an effort will be made to depict the establishment of the monarchy as the consequence of the emergence of Israelite tribal society, assuming that the reasons for the development of the monarchy should be sought in circumstances internal to Israelite society, rather than outside of it.

Although it is somewhat crude and simplistic, the presuppositions which required the tribal societies to be replaced by one or more states may be subdivided into economic and political spheres where each sphere contains numerous factors. Therefore, the following listing can make no claim to being exhaustive:

(1) Economic Reasons for the Changes in the Tribal Society. The Israelite tribes dwelt in a region which may best be described as a marginal territory, that is, the highlands of Palestine and the territory E of the Jordan, as well as the steppes which especially border along the N part of the Negeb. In terms of area the territory is fairly limited. Even in the most favorable conditions, in which the precipitation is higher than normal, the region could only feed a small population. As far as the Palestinian highlands are concerned, this means that once they had been deforested and cleared of their natural growth to make room for cultivation, there were no further possibilities either for economic expansion or for population increase. The steppes, too, must have had only limited flexibility for an agriculture which was dependent from year to year on shifting quantities of rain. Here it was only possible to compensate for the regular cycles of drought by raising sheep and goats.

The development of village culture which is now archaeologically demonstrable in early Iron Age Palestine enables us to assert that this ecological factor was decisive. The continual growth of settlements throughout the period points to a considerable population increase, which in turn means that there was increased pressure on the natural resources of the country. All factors suggest that this led to a stressful situation which must have had an impact on Israelite tribal society. The ideal solution for such a dilemma would be expansion of the territory controlled by the Israelite tribes. However, such expansion could only have taken place if it included absorbing the cultivated areas belonging to other political entities, meaning, above all, the city-states in the coastal plain to the W and in Jezreel to the N. It is likely that such a compulsion to expand may be read directly from the course of events well into the monarchical period. The early Israelite monarchy dealt decisively with these ancient city-states, while at the same time it competed with the Philistine pentapolis in the S part of the coastal plain for control over the fertile marginal highland known as the *Shephelah*.

A second consequence of economic stress within the Israelite tribal societies may have consisted in the weakening of the "egalitarian ideology" (i.e., the feelings of solidarity within and among the tribal societies). At all events, a growing degree of inequality between individual Israelite family groups has been suggested by modern researchers as having contributed to the collapse of tribal society (Chaney 1986; Gottwald 1986; Coote and Whitelam 1986). Such a state of affairs cannot be proven on the basis of the sources presently available to us. However, it is not unknown in the history of the Near East, including up to the present. Its consequence would have been that the more fortunate Israelites were in a position to bind their poorer kinsmen to them by means of contracts which transformed what were originally independent peasants into indentured peasants in the service of their fellow countrymen. Over the course of time the latter took on the character of local petty nobles or wealthy farmers.

(2) Political Reasons for the Collapse of Tribal Society. Connected with the above situation in which inequality grew in the tribal society while the society itself was exposed to ecological pressure, was the increasing tendency toward centralized government. The egalitarian ideology which, as mentioned above, contained the possibility for exploitation, was capable of developing into a tyrannical system (cf. Black 1972) in which solidarity is employed as an argument which serves to keep the poorer part of the population down. Since, according to the ideology, all members of the society are "brothers," i.e., members of the same family, protests against the behavior of local "big men" are tantamount to objections to familial solidarity, and therefore constitute a threat to the survival of the society.

One consequence of such a situation would be the bifurcation of the society into wealthy patrons and bonded peasants, each class with its own peculiar interests. The wealthy patrons would naturally tend to support the establishment of a type of government capable of protecting their interests, creating in the process a power apparatus which would be able to repress the less fortunately situated part of the population. In the first instance, the solution to this political problem would probably have consisted in the election of chieftains who, following the notional tribal ideology, would still count as everyone's kinsmen. Thus the wealthy would have found their *primus inter pares*, which would have allowed them to continue to believe that they controlled the chief. On the other hand, the peasants would have been able to regard the chief as their "big brother," that is, their protector. Furthermore, the emergence of such a chieftainship would have been a politically unifying factor, in that it better enabled the tribal society in question to compete with other societies for control of the resources of the country.

The risk involved with their new system was that, sooner or later, the chieftain might conceive interests, such as dynastic ones, which no longer agreed with the wishes of those who had elected him. As a rule, this sort of situation could take one of two possible outcomes: either the chieftainship, and thereby the tribe, dissolved through internal faction and conflict, or the chief's interests won the day, so that he was able to figure as the sole ruler, that is, as a *king* endowed with the potential to build a centralized power apparatus as an adjunct to the perquisites of royal office. In such a course of development, both wealthy patrons and bonded peasants are the losers, since none of them are in any position to control the king's actions. One might say that, while a tribal society hires its chief, the king hires his people so that they may serve his interests. In the latter situation the tribal ideology and feelings of solidarity no longer play any kind of role. Accordingly, we note that centralized authority and the tribal system have to collide sooner or later, and in such a way that one or the other must disappear.

Yet another political possibility is that a tribal society may become encapsulated by superior political units. This may happen at any time in the history of the tribe, and it invariably leads to changes in the structure of the tribe. "Encapsulation" means that political formations arise on the borders of the tribe in question which are on a more centrally structured level than the tribe itself. For example, if a tribe which has not yet made the transition into a chieftainship comes into contact with other tribes which have made this transition, there is a considerable possibility that the tribe in question will experience difficulties in asserting its independence, and it may instead ultimately have to pay tribute to the "foreign" chieftainship.

A contributory cause of the relatively weak political position of the tribe is the status of the members of the tribe, which in this sort of society can best be characterized as individualistic and autonomous. The individual members of the tribe are autonomous as far as their economic strategies and their alliances with other members of the tribe are concerned. There are countless ethnographic records which show that even in wartime, and even if several tribes are involved, this does not interfere with the autonomy of the individual. Rather, he is invariably left to himself to decide whether he wants to go off to war with his kin or whether he prefers to stay home.

The individualism which manifests itself within the individual tribe is also able to affect behavior at higher levels, for example, if a tribe is a member of a coalition of tribes. In this event, it would be up to the individual tribe to decide for itself whether it chooses to participate in the greater fellowship, even in time of war. It is not difficult to point to a parallel example of this phenomenon on the basis of the OT materials. In Judges 5 we note that the list of tribes constituting the Israelite army clearly indicates that most of the tribal units which the poet thought *should* have lent their contingents to the common defense in fact did not take part.

Incidentally, this point is one of the important reasons why the notion of an Israelite twelve-tribe league in 1200 or 1000 B.C. is unrealistic, when seen from a sociological point of view. At this level, too, the various members of the coalition would have been characterized by individualism and guided by autonomous interests to such an extent that such a league, understood as a stable political organization, is illusory.

If a tribal society were to be confronted with a centralized state, the sort of politically atomized and individualistic structure depicted above would exercise a decisively negative influence on the society's ability to survive. The probable upshot would be that if drastic changes did not occur in the political structure of the tribe in question, it would dissolve and be integrated into the state which had challenged the tribal society. Another possible consequence is that the tribe might make the transition from tribal society to an organized state led by a king. This might happen in the course of an extremely short period of time, and the development could well permit the society to survive.

It is impossible to say just how many of the factors mentioned here were responsible for the transformation of the Israelite tribal society into a centralized state with its own kings. However, there are indications among the archaeological materials and in the OT sources which suggest that all of these factors, and presumably more besides, played contributory roles. The OT itself regards the decisive factor as the collision with foreign states. In the face of the confrontation with the Philistine city-states in the coastal plain, the Israelite tribal organization had to give way and, in order to survive, it transformed itself into a state. The Philistines were at the time in the process of occupying Israelite territory in central Palestine. Seeking a way out, the Israelites first chose for themselves a chieftain, Saul (we should not be confused by the fact that the OT uses Heb *melek* for both chieftains and kings; in organizational terms, Saul's monarchy was actually more of a chieftainship than a monarchy, although it contained in it the seed of the later development). However, the Philistine challenge was so grave that the Saulide chieftainship was not equal to the task. Only the self-made king David, who could permit himself to ignore narrow tribal interests, was able to transform the Israelite tribes from a defensive to an offensive force, one which proved able to unite almost the whole of Palestine under a single prince in the course of a very short span of years.

If we disregard the descriptions of the individuals, the OT account of the introduction of the monarchy appears to contain sufficient information to enable us to write the history of this epoch. A foreign entity, namely the union of the five Philistine coastal cities, would all by itself have been able to assemble more resources than the ordinary Canaanite city-states could have done. Thus it would have represented a power factor with which a noncentralized Israelite tribal system could not have dealt merely by assembling its own traditional resources. Thus the chieftainship arose as a direct answer to the foreign political challenge; it was subsequently replaced by the monarchy in order to complete the task of defending the independence of the members of the Israelite tribes.

At this point, however, it must be permissible to ask whether the actual historical development was so simple as is recounted in the book of Samuel. For example, it has been suggested that Saul's battles with the Philistines in reality represented not merely an Israelite war of liberation, but rather are to be seen as an expression of an Israelite tendency to expansion which was specially directed towards the N regions (Ahlström 1986: 90–92). In the event, the actual course might suggest that parts of what later became Israel had already organized themselves as a chieftainship by around 1000 B.C. Thus the warlike altercations in the period were not merely a question of defense against external enemies; they had perhaps just as much to do with gaining control over the rich Galilean territories and the traditional trade routes to Syria in the N.

If this was the case then David's foreign policy may have followed a course already mapped out by the chieftain, Saul. The difference was that David was able to dispose over much greater resources than Saul had done, and in particular was able to utilize as his base of operations the entire central Palestinian area. At the same time, he created what was, admittedly, at first only a limited centralized state apparatus, and so he became the founder of the real Israelite monarchy as such.

This was the beginning of the end for the Israelite tribes since, although the days of foreign encirclement soon seemed to have come to an end, the independence of the tribes also speedily ended. There is relatively little information in the OT about the developments which led to the disappearance of the tribal society. However, it is noteworthy that persons who appear at the beginning of the time of the monarchy are occasionally mentioned as belonging to one or another tribe (e.g., Jeroboam the son of Nebat was an Ephraimite, just as Baʿasha the son of Ahijah came from the tribe of Issachar); such references to tribal affiliation disappear already in the course of the 9th century B.C. Such relationships were apparently no longer relevant, because Israelite society was now organized into centralized kingships in a way that did not depart significantly from the political system of the LB Age. As far as their policies are concerned, the Israelite kings do not seem to have been guided by narrow Israelite interests. Rather, they followed their own political and economic goals irrespective of the possible consequences for the Israelite populace. Seen in this way, there is a certain degree of irony present in the history of the Israelite tribes from the close of the LB Age down to the early part of the monarchical period. When this phase of Israelite history had come to an end, the ordinary Israelite was in reality in a situation which was not significantly different from the one his ancestors had experienced several centuries earlier under the kings of the Canaanite city-states.

Bibliography

Adams, W. Y. 1968. Invasion, Diffusion, Evolution? *Antiquity* 42: 194–215.

Ahlström, G. W. 1977. Judges 5:20f. and History. *JNES* 36: 287–88.

———. 1986. *Who Were the Israelites?* Winona Lake, IN.

Albright, W. F. 1952. The Smaller Beth-Shan Stele of Sethos I (1309–1290 B.C.). *BASOR* 125: 24–32.

———. 1961. Abram the Hebrew, a New Archaeological Interpretation. *BASOR* 163: 36–54.

———. 1963. *The Biblical Period from Abraham to Ezra.* New York.

Avigad, N. 1986. *Hebrew Bullae from the Time of Jeremiah.* Jerusalem.

Bietak, M. 1987. Comments on the "Exodus." Pp. 163–71 in Rainey 1987.

Black, J. 1972. Tyranny as a Strategy for Survival in an "egalitarian" Society: Luri Facts Versus an Anthropological Mystique. *Man* n.s. 7: 614–634.

Borowski, O. 1987. *Agriculture in Iron Age Palestine.* Winona Lake, IN.

Bottéro, J. 1954. *Le problème des habiru à la 4e rencontre assyriologique internationale.* Cahiers de la Société asiatique XII. Paris.

Buccellati, G. 1962. La 'carriera' di David e quella di Idrimi, re di Alalac. *BeO* 4: 95–99.

———. 1967. *Cities and Nations of Ancient Syria.* Studi Semitici 26. Rome.

Chaney, M. L. 1983. Ancient Palestinian Peasant Movements and the Formation of Premonarchic Israel. Pp. 39–94 in *Palestine in Transition.* Ed. D. N. Freedman and D. F. Graf. The Social World of Biblical Antiquity 2. Sheffield.

———. 1986. Systemic Study of the Israelite Monarchy. Pp. 53–76 in Gottwald ed. 1986.

Coote, R. B., and Ord, D. R. 1989. *The Bible's First History.* Philadelphia.

Coote, R. B., and Whitelam, K. W. 1986. The Emergence of Israel: Social Transformation and State Formation Following the Decline in Late Bronze Age Trade. Pp. 107–46 in Gottwald ed. 1986.

———. 1987. *The Emergence of Early Israel in Historical Perspective.* The Social World of Biblical Antiquity 5. Sheffield.

Donner, H. 1984–86. *Geschichte des Volkes Israel und seiner Nachbarn in Grundzügen.* 2 vols. Altes Testament Deutsch Ergänzungsreihe 4/1. Göttingen.

Flanagan, J. W. 1981. Chiefs in Israel. *JSOT* 20: 47–73.

———. 1988. *David's Social Drama.* The Social World of Biblical Antiquity Series 7/JSOTSup 73. Sheffield.

Frick, F. S. 1985. *The Formation of the State in Ancient Israel.* The Social World of Biblical Antiquities Series 4. Sheffield.

Fried, M. H. 1967. *The Evolution of Political Society.* New York.

Fritz, V. 1980. Die kulturgeschichtliche Bedeutung des früheisenzeitlichen Siedlung auf der *ḫirbet el-Mšāš. ZDPV* 96: 121–35.

Garbini, G. 1978. Il Cantico di Debora. *La Parola del Passato* 33: 5–31.

———. 1988. *History and Ideology in Ancient Israel.* London.

Geus, C. H. J. de. 1975. The Importance of Archaeological Research into the Palestinian Agricultural Terraces, with an Excursus on the Hebrew Word *gbī. PEQ* 107: 65–74.

———. 1976. *The Tribes of Israel.* Studia Theologica Neerlandica 18. Assen/Amsterdam.

Gottwald, N. K. 1975. Domain Assumptions and Societal Models in the Study of Pre-Monarchic Israel. VTSup 28: 89–100.

———. 1979. *The Tribes of Yahweh.* Maryknoll, NY.

———. 1986. The Participation of Free Agrarians in the Introduction of Monarchy to Ancient Israel. Pp. 77–106 in Gottwald ed. 1986.

Gottwald, N. K., ed. 1986. *Social Scientific Criticism of the Hebrew Bible and Its Social World: The Israelite Monarchy.* Semeia 37. Chico, CA.

Greenberg, M. 1955. *The Ḫab/piru.* AOS 39. New Haven, CT.

Grønbaek, J. H. 1971. *Die Geschichte vom Aufstieg Davids (1 Sam 15–2 Sam 5).* ATDan 10. Copenhagen.

Halpern, B. 1988. *The First Historians.* San Francisco.

Heltzer, M. 1976. *The Rural Community in Ancient Ugarit.* Wiesbaden.

———. 1982. *The Internal Organization of the Kingdom of Ugarit.* Wiesbaden.

Hendel, R. S. 1987. *The Epic of the Patriarch.* HSM 42. Atlanta, GA.

Hopkins, D. C. 1985. *The Highlands of Canaan.* The Social World of Biblical Antiquity Series 3. Sheffield.

Kaufmann, Y. 1953. *The Biblical Account of the Conquest of Palestine.* Jerusalem.

Kenyon, K. M. 1960. *Archaeology in the Holy Land.* London. 4th ed. 1979.

Kirkpatrick, P. G. 1988. *The Old Testament and Folklore Study.* JSOT Monograph Series 62. Sheffield.

Kittel, R. 1932. *Geschichte des Volkes Israel.* Vol. 1. 7th ed. Stuttgart.

Klengel, H. 1965–70. *Geschichte Syriens im 2. Jahrtausend v. u. Z.* 3 vols. Deutsche Akademie der Wissenschaften zu Berlin. Institut für Orientforschung Veröffentlichung 40. Berlin.

Lemche, N. P. 1979. 'Hebrew' as a National Name for Israel. *ST* 33: 1–23.

———. 1984a. "Israel in the Period of the Judges"—The Tribal League in Recent Research. *ST* 38: 1–28.

———. 1984b. On the Problem of Studying Early Israelite History. Apropos Abraham Malamat's View of Historical Research. *BN* 24: 94–124.

———. 1985. *Early Israel. Anthropological and Sociological Studies on the Israelite Society Before the Monarchy.* VTSup 37. Leiden.

———. 1987–88. Rachel and Lea. Or: On the Survival of Outdated Paradigmas in the Study of the Origin of Israel, 1–2. *Scandinavian Journal of the Old Testament* 2/1987: 127–153; 1/1988: 39–65.

———. 1988. *Ancient Israel: A New History of Israelite Society.* Sheffield.

Liverani, M. 1972. Partire sul carro, per il deserto. *AION* N.S. 22: 403–15.

———. 1973a. Memorandum on the Approach to Historiographic Texts. *Or* N.S. 42: 178–94.

———. 1973b. Storiografia politica hittita—I: Šunāšura, ovvero: Della Reciprocità. *OrAnt* 12: 267–97.

———. 1974. Rib-Adda, giusto sofferente. *Altorientalische Forschungen* 1: 175–205.

———. 1976. Review of R. de Vaux, *Histoire ancienne d'Israël* I-11. *OrAnt* 15: 145–59.

———. 1977. Storiografia politica hittita—II: Telipino, ovvero: Della Solidarietà. *OrAnt* 16: 105–31.

———. 1979a. Farsi Ḫabiru. *Vicino Oriente* 2: 65–77.

———. 1979b. Un'ipotesa sul nome di Abram. *Henoch* 1: 9–18.

———. 1983. Political Lexicon and Political Ideologies in the Amarna Letters. *Berytus* 31: 41–56.

Malamat, A. 1983. Die Frühgeschichte Israels—eine methodologische Studie. *TZ* 38: 1–16.

Mayes, A. D. H. 1969. The Historical Context of the Battle Against Sisera. *VT* 19: 353–60.

———. 1974. *Israel in the Period of the Judges.* SBT 2/29. London.

McCarthy, D. J. 1963. *Treaty and Covenant.* AnBib 21. Rome.

Mendenhall, G. E. 1962. The Hebrew Conquest of Palestine. *BA* 25: 66–87. Repr. *BAR* 3: 100–120.

———. 1973. *The Tenth Generation: The Origins of the Biblical Tradition.* Baltimore.

Na'aman, N. 1986. Ḫabiru and Hebrews: The Transfer of a Social Term to the Literary Sphere. *JNES* 45: 271–88.

Noth, M. 1930. *Das System der zwölf Stämme Israels.* BWANT 4/1. Stuttgart.

———. 1948. *Überlieferungsgeschichte des Pentateuch.* Stuttgart.

———. 1950. *Geschichte Israels.* Göttingen. ET = *NHI.*

———. 1971. *Aufsätze zur biblischen Landes- und Altertumskunde.* I–II. Neukirchen.

Parpola, S., and Watanabe, K. 1988. *Neo-Assyrian Treaties and Loyalty Oaths.* State Archives of Assyria II. Helsinki.

Pedersen, J. 1926–40. *Israel. Its Life and Culture.* Vols. 1–2. Oxford.

Perlitt, L. 1969. *Bundestheologie im Alten Testament.* WMANT 36. Neukirchen.

Rad, G. von. 1944. Der Anfang der Geschichtschreibung im alten Israel. Repr. *Gesammelte Studien zum Alten Testament.* Theologische Bücherei 8. Munich.

Rainey, A. F. 1962. *The Social Stratification of Ugarit.* Ann Arbor.

Rainey, A. F., ed. 1987. *Egypt, Israel, Sinai.* Tel Aviv.

Redford, D. B. 1970. *A Study of the Biblical Story of Joseph (Genesis 37–50).* VTSup 20. Leiden.

———. 1987. An Egyptological Perspective on the Exodus Narrative. Pp. 137–61 in Rainey 1987.

Rowton, M. B. 1967. The Woodlands of Ancient Western Asia. *JNES* 26: 261–77.

Salzman, F. C. 1978. Ideology and Change in Middle Eastern Tribal Societies. *Man* N.S. 13: 618–37.

Sasson, J. 1981. On Choosing Models for Recreating Israelite Pre-Monarchic History. *JSOT* 21: 3–24.

Schmid, H. H. 1977. *Der sogenannte Jahwist.* Zurich.

Service, E. R. 1962. *Primitive Social Organization.* New York.

Soggin, J. A. 1984. *A History of Israel: From the Beginnings to the Bar Kochba Revolt, AD 135.* London.

Stade, B. 1887. *Geschichte des Volkes Israel.* Berlin.

Thompson, T. L. 1974. *The Historicity of the Patriarchal Narratives.* BZAW 133. Berlin.

———. 1978. The Background of the Patriarchs: A Reply to William Dever and Malcolm Clark. *JSOT* 9: 2–43.

———. 1979. *The Settlement of Palestine in the Bronze Age.* BTAVO B 34. Wiesbaden.

Tritsch, F. J. 1974. The "Sackers of Cities" and the "Movement of Populations." Pp. 233–38 in *Bronze Age Migrations in the Aegean,* ed. R. A. Crossland and A. Birchall. Sheffield.

Van Seters, J. 1975. *Abraham in History and Tradition.* New Haven.

———. 1983. *In Search of History.* New Haven.

Vaux, R. de. 1961. *Les institutions de l'Ancien Testament.* 2 vols. Paris.

———. 1970. On Right and Wrong Use of Archaeology. In *Near Eastern Archaeology in the Twentieth Century,* ed. J. Sanders. New York.

———. 1971–73. *Histoire ancienne d'Israël.* 2 vols. Paris. ET = *EHI.*

Waldbaum, J. C. 1978. *From Bronze to Iron.* Studies in Mediterranean Archaeology 54. Göteborg.

Whitelam, K. W. 1986. Recreating the History of Israel. *JSOT* 35: 45–70.

Whybray, R. N. 1987. *The Making of the Pentateuch.* JSOTSup 53. Sheffield.

NIELS PETER LEMCHE
Trans. Frederick Cryer

ARCHAEOLOGY AND THE ISRAELITE "CONQUEST"

The purpose of this article is (1) to summarize and evaluate recent archaeological data that bear on the early Israelite settlement in Canaan in the 13th–11th centuries B.C.; (2) to critique current explanatory models of Israelite origins in the light of this newer data; and (3) to suggest ways of harmonizing the archaeological and textual evidence that may eventually lead to better syntheses. The approach throughout is heuristic, rather than definitive in attempting solutions.

A. Issues in the Discussion
B. An Archaeological Critique of the Conquest Model
  1. Israel in Egypt
  2. The Sinai Tradition

A. Issues in the Discussion

The problem, although exceedingly complex, may be stated rather simply by focusing on the several levels at which the majority of scholars encounter difficulties. There is first the *historical* problem, which faces the task of ascertaining, if possible, what really happened in the Israelite settlement of Canaan, that is, of getting at the "history behind the history." It is now recognized by nearly all that the biblical tradition concerning Israel's emergence in Canaan, while our only direct literary source, is limited by its nature as theocratic literature—particularly the "conquest" version in Joshua. But is it possible to write a "secular history" of Palestine in this period that will elucidate Israelite origins better by placing them in a larger context, based chiefly on archaeological evidence?

This leads to a *methodological* problem. What are the possibilities and limitations of each of the two basic types of data from which history may be reconstructed? In short, how are the two histories related, if at all? Are they parallel, or does one take *precedence?*

Finally, there is what appears to be, at least, a *theological* problem. In Israel's recitation of the "mighty acts of God," the central events are Yahweh's redemption of the Israelites from Egyptian bondage, his subsequent granting of miraculous victory over the Canaanites to the Twelve Tribe League, and finally his deliverance of the promised land to the settlers as the sign and seal of his covenant with them. These are the formative events that constitute Israel's existence, the very heart of her Credo. But if these events have no basis in the actualities of history, is not Israel's faith, and ours, without foundation? As one noted biblical archaeologist and theologian, G. E. Wright, put it in his classic *God Who Acts: Biblical Theology as Recital:* "In Biblical faith, everything depends upon whether the central events [i.e., Exodus-Conquest-Settlement] actually occurred" (1952: 126). But what if they did *not* occur?

B. An Archaeological Critique of the Conquest Model

The regnant theories that attempt to explain the emergence of Israel in Canaan are too well known to need documentation here. They are: (1) the "conquest" model, espoused chiefly by Albright and his followers in America, as well as by Yadin and several Israeli scholars; (2) the "peaceful infiltration" model, first proposed by Alt and the German school in the 1920s, but still widely influential; and (3) the "peasants' revolt" model, introduced originally by Mendenhall in the 1960s and recently elaborated by Gottwald. All of these models make some use of the archaeological data, but only the first is heavily dependent upon such evidence. Yet because these are models developed and employed mainly by *biblical* historians, the pertinent archaeological data have not always been adequately evaluated. As Syro-Palestinian archaeology and biblical studies have increasingly diverged (see ARCHAEOLOGY, SYRO-PALESTINIAN AND BIBLICAL), such a critique becomes a task for specialists. Let us look first at the "conquest" model. This model presupposes several sequential phases, each of which, however, presents archaeological difficulties.

1. Israel in Egypt. As is often observed, there is no direct archaeological evidence that any constituents of later Israel were ever in Egypt. The only Egyptian textual reference, the well known "Victory Stela" of Merneptah (now dated ca. 1207 B.C.; see further Stager 1985b) mentions "Israel" as a "people," probably an ethnic element, not in Egypt but in Canaan, with no apparent knowledge of any Egyptian derivation. Nor is there anything in the material culture of the early Israelite settlements in Palestine that points to an Egyptian origin for that culture. The few Egyptian scarabs and possible house-types (as at Tel Masos; Fritz and Kempinski 1983) can easily be explained by the continuity of Egyptian elements from the local LB Canaanite culture into the early Iron Age.

Among the scant references in the Hebrew Bible to specific details of an Egyptian sojourn that might be identified archaeologically is the reference to the Israelites being in servitude in the Delta cities of Pithom and Rameses (Exod 1:11). Pithom is possibly to be identified with Tell el-Maskhuta, or with Tell el-Reṭabe (Holladay 1982: 3–6); and Rameses has now almost certainly been located at Tell ed-Dabʿa near Qantir by the recent excavations of Manfred Bietak (1979). The significance of the new data is considerable. First, all three sites are among the few Delta sites that are now known from recent excavations to have been Canaanite colonies in Egypt in the Middle Kingdom (Dynasties 12–17, ca. 1991–1540 B.C.). Tell ed-Dabʿa was, in fact, the Hyksos capitol of Avaris, destroyed ca. 1540 B.C. with the expulsion of the Hyksos at the beginning of the 18th Dynasty. Second, these sites also have Ramesside levels of the 13th or 12th centuries B.C. Thus Tell ed-Dabʿa, although deserted throughout the New Kingdom after its destruction, was *re*occupied precisely in the time of Rameses II, in the early–mid-13th century B.C. (Rameses II = 1304–1237 B.C.). (Cf. Bietak 1979; but see Dever 1985a for the raising of dates for the earlier levels.) Tell el-Maskhuta has no known Ramesside occupation, but Tell el-Reṭabe, like Tell ed-Dabʿa, was occupied in the Middle Kingdom, abandoned in the New Kingdom, then reoccupied in the 20th Dynasty and onward (ca. 1200 B.C. onward).

Is it merely fortuitous that these Delta sites, known to the biblical writers, *did* have a substantial Canaanite presence in the so-called Patriarchal period, and then were rebuilt under Egyptian aegis in Ramesside times, which is when an Israelite sojourn in Egypt would have to be placed archaeologically? The new evidence is not conclusive, of course (i.e., there are questions regarding the exact location and date of Pithom), but it may lend support to the long-held view of some biblical scholars that at least *some* constituent elements of later Israel had actually stemmed from Egypt, i.e., the "House of Joseph." Only one thing is certain, and that is that the scant Egyptian evidence at least points unanimously to a 13th century B.C. *date* for an Israelite "exodus," if any. (See Hermann 1973: 19–50; Miller *IJH,* 246–52; contra Bimson 1981.)

2. The Sinai Tradition. The "crossing of the Red (Reed) Sea" is obviously a miraculous tale that can in no way be validated or even illuminated by archaeological investigation. Furthermore, of the subsequent "wandering in the wilderness" theme (Num 33:1–49), little can be said archaeologically. If indeed the Israelites are to be pictured as a band of wanderers, or even as semi-sedentary pastoralists, we would still probably find no remains of their ephemeral camps in the desert. Thus all attempts to trace the "route of the Sinai crossing" have been doomed to failure, reduced as they are to inconclusive efforts to identify hazy topographical references in the Bible with modern Arab place names that usually have no clear historical associations. E. Anati has recently claimed (1986) that he has located biblical Mt. Sinai at Har Karkom, in the W Negeb near the present Egyptian border, but few will find the petroglyphs and other data convincing evidence that this is anything more than another of the "holy mountains" frequented from time immemorial by the nomads of the desert.

The only 2d millennium B.C. Sinai route that is attested archaeologically is the N route along the coastal dunes, which recent archaeological investigation has indeed illuminated, precisely in Egyptian New Kingdom times (Oren 1984 and references there). But this is precisely the route that was bypassed according to the biblical tradition, because of Egyptian control. All we can say is that recent, extensive exploration of the entire Sinai by Israeli archaeologists, geologists, and others has turned up virtually no MB-LB presence in the central or S Sinai. Our current detailed knowledge of this remote and hostile area calls into question the biblical tradition of a million-and-a-half or more people migrating there (Num 11:21) for some forty years (Deut 2:7). The barren terrain and sparse oases might have supported a few straggling nomads, but no more than that.

The description of a thirty-eight-year encampment at Kadesh-barnea (Deut 1:19–2:15), which is prominent in the biblical tradition and gave rise to an important pilgrimage-festival in the time of the Monarchy, has long intrigued biblical scholars and archaeologists. Following the topographical indications in the Bible, Kadesh-barnea has been quite plausibly identified since the 19th century with the well-known oasis at ʿAin el-Qudeirat, near Quseima on the modern Israel–Egypt border. The small *tell* near the spring was sounded in 1956 by Moshe Dothan and was then extensively excavated to virgin soil in 1976–1982 by Rudolph Cohen. The latter has shown conclusively that these remains consist of three successive Israelite forts (Levels I–III) of the 10th–7th/6th centuries B.C., with nothing whatsoever of earlier occupation, not even scattered sherds (Cohen 1983). Thus the Kadesh-barnea episode, on present evidence, has little historical basis and appears to have become significant only in the united monarchy, when the Exodus tradition was crystallizing.

3. The Transjordanian Campaigns. The first phase of the conquest of Canaan, according to biblical accounts, focused on central and S Transjordan, which the tribes of Gad, Reuben, and half-Manasseh are said to have occupied (Numbers 21). The incoming Israelites are portrayed as encountering a settled population in Ammon, Moab, and Edom. Among specific cities mentioned as taken (and by implication destroyed) are Heshbon and Dibon; transparently identifed with the large *tells* of *Hesbân* and *Dhibân,* respectively. Yet the extensive excavation of both has revealed that neither had any LB occupation. Hesbân had scant 12th–11th century material, with Iron Age occupation beginning principally in the 10th century B.C. (Geraty 1983). Dhibân may have had some Iron I material, but nothing earlier, and most of the Iron Age remains were 8th–7th century B.C. (Dornemann 1983: 45, 63; Sauer 1986: 8–18). Thus neither site can have been destroyed by the Israelites under Joshua in the mid-13th century as required by Num 21:21–30. The same is probably true of Madeba (Num 21:30), which has produced thus far only a 12th century tomb for this horizon (Dornemann 1983: 34, 35).

Elsewhere in Transjordan, the general picture of LB and early Iron I occupation is complex, but it is clear that there is relatively little sedentary occupation of *southern* Transjordan in LB. N. Glueck's surveys in the 1930s–1940s already suggested this (although he interpreted the evidence as *supporting* the biblical tradition of early Israelite settlement). Subsequent correction and expansion of Glueck's site maps, including the discovery of a few more LB Age sites farther N in the Jordan valley and up on the plateau, has not substantially changed this view. Newer excavated evidence from Amman, the Beqaʿ valley, Sahab, Irbid, Tell es-Saʿidiyeh, Deir ʿAlla, Kataret es-Samra, and a few other sites, as well as surveys from N Jordan, the Jordan valley, and Edom, all yield the same picture. Moab and Edom were not yet established, fortified kingdoms that would have posed any threat to Israelite tribes moving through the area, and even Ammon was rather sparsely occupied and defended. (For the most authoritative review, see Sauer 1986: 6–14; and cf. Dornemann 1983: 20–24). Thus throughout most of S Transjordan in LB-Iron I, outside the few settled towns, pastoralists and nomads must have dominated the countryside, like the "Shasu" tribes well known from Egyptian New Kingdom texts (Giveon 1971). In Moab, Heshbon and Dibon did not become significant urban centers until the 9th–8th centuries B.C. (Dornemann 1983: 63; Sauer 1986: 10, 15, 16). Ongoing excavations of the Iron Age sites in Edom indicates that the majority of these, including ʿArôʿer, Buseirah (Bozra), Tawilan, and Umm el-Biyarah, were first settled only in the 8th or 7th centuries B.C. (Dornemann 1983: 47–63; Sauer 1986: 14–19). Thus the notion of large-scale 13th–12th century B.C. Israelite military campaigns in S Transjordan, or even of peaceful settlement there, is no longer tenable; the occupational history of the region simply does not fit (contra Boling and Wright *Joshua* AB). As for destructions, the only known LB II destructions are farther N—at Deir ʿAllā, Tell es-Saʿidiyeh, and Irbid—in Gilead; and in all cases, both the biblical identification and the agents of destruction remain unclear.

4. The Conquest of Canaan. The biblical tradition of the main phases of the occupation of the land of Canaan

W of the Jordan is too well known to need summarizing here (cf. the principal accounts in Joshua, plus Num 21:1–3 and Judges 1). Since the infancy of modern topographical research and archaeology more than a century ago, biblical scholars and archaeologists have sought to locate the numerous cities said to have been taken and to identify 13th–12th century "destruction layers" that might be attributed to incoming Israelites. Indeed, confirming the Israelite conquest of Canaan archaeologically became one of the major priorities on the agenda of the "biblical archaeology" movement led by Albright and his followers from ca. 1925–1970, which adopted almost exclusively the "conquest" model presented in the book of Joshua (see also Lapp 1967). This approach was also taken up by several prominent members of the "Israeli school," notably Yadin (1979; but cf. Aharoni *WHJP* 3: 94–128). And the effort still continues among a few conservative biblical scholars, some of whom, however, opt for the now totally discredited "high date of the Exodus" (thus Bimson 1981). Rather than reviewing the vast bibliography (see Miller *IJH,* 213–84), the latest and best archaeological data can be summarized in chart form (see table; and see further the latest syntheses in Callaway 1988, and especially Finkelstein *AIS*).

Canaanite Sites Claimed to Have Been Taken by the Israelites.

SITE	REFERENCES	BIBLICAL DESCRIPTION; REMARKS	ARCHAEOLOGICAL EVIDENCE
1. Zephath/ Hormah	Num 21:1–3; Judg 1:17	"Destroyed."	If Tel Masos, no LB occupation there.
2. Jericho	Judg 6:1–21	"Destroyed."	No LB II occupation.
3. ᶜAi	Josh 8:24	"Destroyed."	No LB II occupation.
4. Bethel	Josh 8:17; Judg 1:22–28	"Destroyed."	Destruction at end of LB II.
5. Jerusalem	Josh 10:1–27; Judg 1:8, 21	Texts contradictory.	LB II occupation, but no evidence of destruction.
6. Libnah	Josh 10:29, 31	"Destroyed."	Tell es-Sâfi? Occupation?
7. Lachish	Josh 10:31, 32	"Destroyed."	Level VI destroyed ca. 1150 B.C.
8. Hebron	Josh 14:13–15; 15:13, 14; Judg 1:10	Texts imply capture but no destruction described.	No evidence.
9. Debir	Josh 10:38, 39; 15: 15–17; Judg 1:11–13.	"Destroyed."	If Tell Beit Mirsim C, yes; if Tell Rabûd, no.
10. Makkedah	Josh 10:28	"Destroyed."	If Kh. el-Qôm, no LB II.
11. Eglon	Josh 10:34, 35	"Destroyed."	Tell el-Ḥesi IV?; no destruction.
12. Hazor	Josh 11:10–13	"Destroyed," but described as still existing later.	Lower City, Gnl. Str. XIII, violently destroyed ca. 1200.
13. Dan	Judg 18:11–28	"Destroyed."	LB II occupation, whether destruction at end unclear.
14. Gaza	Judg 1:18	"Taken."	No evidence.
15. Ashkelon	Judg 1:18	"Taken."	No evidence.
16. Ekron	Judg 1:18	"Taken."	No evidence.
17. Heshbon	Num 21:25–30	"Destroyed."	No LB II occupation.
18. Dibon	Num 21:30	Destruction implied.	No LB II occupation.
19. Medeba	Num 21:30	Destruction implied.	No evidence.

It is obvious that of the nearly 20 identifiable LB/Iron I sites that the biblical writers claim were forcibly taken by the Israelites under Joshua or his immediate successors, only Bethel and Hazor have any *archaeological* claims to destructions, i.e., historical claims supported by extrabiblical evidence. And even here, there is no conclusive data to support the notion that Israelites were the agents of destruction. (The new evidence dating the destruction of Lachish VI to Rameses III or later, ca. 1150 B.C., is much too late; cf. Ussishkin 1985). Thus the "conquest" model derived principally from the book of Joshua, so promising in the beginning, is now seen to have fared rather badly in more recent research. We must conclude that as an overall model for understanding the origins of Israel, the whole notion of a literal "Exodus-wilderness wanderings-Conquest" episode is now unproductive and indeed detrimental, since it is challenged by current archaeological and historical research. The possible experience of some tribal elements in Egypt and Transjordan, or the scattered violence accompanying early phases of the settlement in Canaan, were undoubtedly minor factors. The emergence of Israel must be seen rather as part of a larger, enormously complex, long drawn-out process of socio-economic change on the LB/Iron I horizon in Palestine with many regional variations. Newer and more sophisticated models, as well as a "secular history" of Palestine (particularly settlement history) are required if we are to understand Israel's origins adequately. Furthermore, it may be the continuity with Canaanite culture, *not* the changes, that in the long run turns out to be the most significant factor.

C. New Data, New Models

Today there are considerable data to support "non-invasion" models of the Israelite settlement in Canaan. Although these data are recent and scarcely published, and thus remain largely unknown to most biblical scholars, archaeological excavations and surveys in the past fifteen years have brought to light hundreds of small, Iron I sites of the late 13th–11th centuries B.C. These are located primarily in the central hills, but are also found as far N as Galilee and southward into the N Negeb. Nearly all are very small, unwalled sites, many founded *de novo* in the late 13th or 12th century, and most abandoned by the 11th century. If we could identify these Iron I sites as "early Israelite" villages, they would yield the *first* such *external* evidence we have found of this phase of the Israelite settlement of Canaan. Yet we must defer that question for the moment.

1. Survey and Excavation. The evidence can only be summarized very briefly here. Most of the new Iron Age sites noted above have been discovered through Israeli surface surveys, still largely unpublished: those of I. Finkelstein in Ephraim; of A. Zertal in N Ephraim and Manasseh; of several Tel Aviv University archaeologists in the Shephelah and along the Sharon Plain; and of Zvi Gal in Lower Galilee (see references in Finkelstein 1986; *AIS;* Gal 1989; Stager 1985a; Dever 1987; Dever fc.b.; Zertal 1987). Finkelstein, for instance, has discovered no fewer than 409 Iron Age I sites E of Aphek up into the Jerusalem hills, of which more than 75 were first founded in Iron I. In the central hills area, L. Stager (1985a) has shown that the number and density of settlements increased dramatically just after 1200 B.C.—from 23 LB sites, to 114 Iron I sites, 97 of them first founded in Iron I. Although the individual LB sites were larger urban Canaanite sites (median size = 12–13 acres) and the individual Iron I sites were smaller villages (median size = 2–3 acres), the total occupied area in the central hills region surveyed by Stager rose dramatically from ca. 175 acres in LB to ca. 475 acres in Iron I. Demographers would hardly attribute this sharp increase to natural growth alone. Clearly there has been an influx of new settlers; but who *were* they, and where did they *come* from?

Actual excavations have been undertaken on relatively few of these Iron Age I villages, notably by J. A. Callaway and R. Cooley at ʿAi and Radannah (the latter possibly biblical Beeroth), N of Jerusalem (Callaway 1985; 1988); by A. Mazar (1981) at Giloh, on the S outskirts of Jerusalem; by M. Kochavi, I. Finkelstein, and others at ʿIzbet Ṣarṭeh, near Aphek (probably biblical Ebenezer; Finkelstein 1986); and by A. Kempinski and V. Fritz (1983) at Tel Masos, in the N Negeb (possibly biblical Hormah; on all the above, see further, with bibliography, Dever 1987; Stager 1985a).

ʿIzbet Ṣarṭeh is particularly significant, since it can probably be identified with a known Israelite site; it has only three levels, all belonging to the 12th–10th centuries B.C., all relatively well exposed in excavation (up to 35 percent); and the material has now appeared in a definitive final publication (Finkelstein 1986). Stratum III, of the late 13th–early 11th centuries, consists of a simple "oval courtyard settlement" that may reflect a herdsmen's encampment (contra Finkelstein's settlement of "recently sedentarized desert nomads"; 1986: 108). After abandonment and a gap in occupation, it was succeeded by stratum II, a substantial village of perhaps 100 or so, with several four-room courtyard houses and many stone-lined silos, dating to the late 11th century B.C. Stratum I represents a decline, but continues into the early 10th century, after which the site was permanently abandoned. It is noteworthy that ʿIzbet Ṣarṭeh was peacefully established, and although it was abandoned at the end of each phase, there were no restrictions. The economy, especially that of strata III–II, was based on agriculture and animal husbandry. The pottery is in *strong* continuity with the LB Age Canaanite repertoire, most closely paralleled by the Iron I N Shephelah and hill country sites (Gezer, Beth-shemesh, Giloh, Shiloh, etc.), but it also has lesser affinities with coastal Canaanite or Philistine sites (Aphek, Tell Qasile; on the above, see especially Finkelstein 1986; and cf. the greater stress on ceramic continuity in *AIS*, confirmed by Dever fc.a.).

Only preliminary reports are available for some of these sites, but already we may draw at least a *provisional* picture of the material culture—and possibly of the social structure and even of the ethnic identity—of these villagers.

(1) We can see a significant shift in *settlement patterns* from the LB to Iron Age I. The typical Iron I sites known thus far are located mostly in the central regions of Canaan, especially the hill country, not on destroyed LB *tells* (where they had been sought). They are founded *de novo* and peacefully, in the late 13th–early 12th century B.C., in a decentralized or nonnucleated pattern of settlement. This growth of new settlements resulted in a sharp rise in population in the central hills in early Iron I.

(2) We have a shift in *settlement type* as well, from large, walled urban to nonurban sites. Most of the Iron I sites are small, unwalled hilltop villages, with a population of from several dozen to as many as 300 or so. All these villages are characterized by a distinctive and homogeneous style of "four-room" courtyard house (often misleadingly called the "Israelite" type-house), which usually features rock-hewn cisterns and subterranean silos. Such self-contained courtyard houses—really "peasant farmhouses"—are ideally suited to an agrarian economy; and, indeed, similar houses are found widely throughout rural areas of the E Mediterranean, from ancient to modern times. See also HOUSE, ISRAELITE.

(3) The *economy* of these Iron I villages was largely self-sufficient, based mainly on small-scale but intensive terrace farming, with some admixture of livestock herding and primitive "cottage industry." A few trade items, however, principally ceramics, indicate that these villages were not totally isolated, but had limited contact with the Canaanite urban centers some distance away.

(4) A changed *technology* is now in evidence, marked particularly by the mastery and extension of terrace agriculture to exploit the cleared hillsides, aided perhaps by the utilization of iron implements, now gradually coming into use in Palestine. Lime-plastered cisterns, while known long before, were now more widely adopted to solve the perennial problem of summer water shortage in the hill country. Ceramic production generally followed that of the LB Canaanite culture, with the introduction of a few new forms (including the popularization of the "collar-rim" storejar), generally inferior in manufacture.

(5) The *social structure* of these small Iron I villages appears to be much less "stratified" than that of the urban LB Age, with no indications of a hierarchically-ranked social order, no "elite" residences or palaces, and no public or adminstrative structures, not even sanctuaries or temples. The rather stereotypical house-plans show little variation and are clustered closely together; their type and arrangement do not even differ significantly from village to village. The general picture to be derived from the new archaeological data for Iron I is that of a simple, agrarian, cohesive society, probably kin-based. The villages are in relatively close proximity; they are apparently organized for internal occupation, but have little need for defense against external pressures. Although the simpler Iron I social and political structures mark a retrogression from the "state-level" organization of the LB to a "tribal level," some sophistication is nevertheless still seen in a few epigraphic remains, including an abecedary from ʿIzbet Ṣarṭeh that may suggest fairly widespread literacy.

(6) In terms of *provenance,* it must be stressed that there is no evidence whatsoever in the material culture that would indicate that these Iron I villagers originated outside Palestine, not even in Transjordan, much less in Egypt or the Sinai. There is nothing in the material remains to suggest that these are "pastoral nomads settling down"—on the contrary, they appear to be skilled and well-adapted

peasant farmers, long familiar with local conditions in Canaan. What is "new" is simply the *combination* and adaptation of existing cultural elements—such as the courtyard houses, silos, and terrace agriculture—with a few novel elements. This distinctive "hybrid" material culture served as the basis for the agricultural settlement of the hill country and the emergence of a distinctive new social order, as well as, in all probability, a new ethnic identity and solidarity. Nevertheless, the overall cultural traditions of these Iron I villages show rather strong continuity with LB Age Canaan, especially in the pottery.

(7) Finally, in terms of *duration*, nearly all of these Iron I villages were abandoned by the late 11th or early 10th century B.C., with the growth of a more concentrated urban culture at the beginning of the united monarchy and the emergence and full development of the true "Iron Age" or "Israelite" culture.

2. Early "Israelite" Villages? On the basis of the foregoing cultural traits, it would be tempting to conclude that these new Iron I sites represent the first definitive *archaeological* evidence we have had of the formative phase of the Israelite settlement in Palestine. These would then be the very early Israelite villages described typically in the book of Judges (thus A. Mazar 1981; Stager 1985a; Callaway 1985; 1988; Fritz 1987; Finkelstein 1986; *AIS*). If that proposition should be sustained by further data, these discoveries would constitute the most significant correlation yet between archaeology and biblical history.

Before we can be quite so sanguine, however, we must address several neglected, yet crucial, questions in the interpretation of the archaeological data—particularly as these data relate to textual analysis and historical reconstruction (see further Dever fc.a.).

a. Social and Economic Structure. Skeptics have often observed that "archaeologists do not dig up social systems." Perhaps not; but they do uncover traces of social systems, since modern archaeology concentrates on recovering the "material correlates" of both individual and collective human behavior. See ARCHAEOLOGY. What do recent data reveal about the social and economic structure of the Iron I villages?

(1) Social Structure. As Stager has shown (1985a), the typical four-room courtyard houses, their clustering into larger units, and the overall village plan, all appear to be a direct reflection of the social structure embodied in the terminology of the Hebrew Bible, especially in Judges. Thus, in ascending levels of complexity, we can recognize: (1) in the individual house, Heb *geber,* which really designates the conjugal or *"nuclear family"* of 4–5 people; (2) in the compound, or cluster of 2–3 such houses, Heb *bêt ʾāb,* "house of the father," meaning "lineage," or in sociological terms an "extended or multi-generational" family, of up to 20 persons; (3) in the whole village plan, with several family compounds, Heb *mišpāḥâ,* "family" in the larger sense of "clan," with anywhere from several dozen to several hundred related persons; (4) in the grouping of many such villages, Heb *šēbeṭ* or *maṭṭeh,* "tribe"; and (5) in the overall distribution of settlements, Heb *ʿam yiśrāʾel* or *bĕnê yiśrāʾel,* or "tribal confederation," "nation" (the latter two *not* separated by Stager). If this analysis, probably the best example yet of the newer style of "biblical archaeology," is correct, then the archaeological remains corroborate the textual evidence decisively. Early Israel was a kin-based (or "segmentary") society, strongly egalitarian. Archaeology shows that the characteristic settlement type and distribution of the Iron I highland villages reflect the essential social structure of early Israel—almost precisely as the book of Judges (Joshua much less so) has faithfully preserved it in the written record.

(2) Economy. The subsistence system of the Iron I villages is equally clear. The economy is based primarily on small-scale but intensive agriculture, with some admixture of specialized stockbreeding. This is indicated by the relatively isolated location of the villages away from river valleys and major trade routes, but in areas still suitable for hillside farming and herding. Furthermore, the efficient size and compact layout of the villages, as well as the family-based social structure, are well suited to such an agrarian economy. The typical four-room courtyard house is an ideal "peasant farmhouse," with provisions for the number of people, animals, and installations typically needed for an individual household production unit (Stager 1985a: 11–17). Finally, the new technology reflects a successful adaptation to hill country agriculture, particularly the near perfection of the art of terracing hillsides, excavating waterproof cisterns in the bedrock, and constructing stone-lined storage silos.

(3) The "Domestic Mode of Production." The socioeconomic structure that we confront in these Iron I villages is thus obviously simple and agrarian. On a cultural-evolutionary scale of development we could regard it as being at a "pre-State" level, either "tribal" or "chiefdom" (Service 1962). This is also suggested by the biblical sources, especially Judges-Samuel, in their vivid and often detailed description of conditions in the premonarchical periods (Frick 1985). Unfortunately, because of the "idealist" bias of most biblical historians (and even the biblical writers themselves) little research has been done either on the material and technological basis of early Israelite culture, or on its social consequences.

Recently, however, there has been growing interest in early Iron Age agriculture (cf. de Geus 1976; Stager 1985a and references there; and especially Hopkins 1985; Borowski 1987). Certainly Gottwald (1979) has gone furthest in his determined "program of historical cultural-material research into early Israel" (1979: 650–63). Many regard this, of course, as economic determinism, others as simply 20th century Marxism projected back upon early Israel. But the archaeologist, who specializes in material culture, can only applaud Gottwald when he declares: "Only as the full *materiality* of ancient Israel is more securely grasped will we be able to make proper sense of its *spirituality*" (1979: xxv). Thus Gottwald's *Tribes of Yahweh expands* upon the sociological and anthropological approach of Mendenhall's "peasants' revolt" model by looking not only at ideological factors like "Yahwism" as the driving force behind Israelite social structure and solidarity, but also at the agrarian economy and technology of the supposed peasants. Gottwald makes admirable use of what little the "new archaeology" could offer in the mid-1970s, sensing correctly that its research objectives are complementary to his own, but there were few data available then (see also Chaney 1983). In our view, Gottwald's materialist perspective on early Israel seems more promising than most later treatments of a more conventional sort, based as they are almost solely on the biblical texts (thus Halpern 1983) which are clearly limited in their usefulness.

It is not merely early Israelite agriculture and technology at which we must look, however, but rather at the *total* subsistence system and its related social system. This is what Marx and Engels (unlike some later Marxist theorists) meant by "mode of production," which delineated not simply an economic system, but a *social-evolutionary stage*. The "mode of production" included a society's adaptation to its environment, technology, class structure, political organization, conceptual systems, and even religion.

Marshall Sahlins' *Stone Age Economics* (1972) elaborates further on the "Domestic Mode of Production" (DMP) that often characterizes peasant or pre-State societies. At this level of social evolution, the individual self-sufficient household is the basic unit of production, and production is for consumption rather than for exchange, hence family labor and cumulative skills are more significant than technology. The DMP, according to Sahlins, tends to be "anti-autocratic" by nature, but it nevertheless obliges household groups to form voluntary social compacts, i.e., to pool labor and resources. Sahlins observes: "As the domestic economy is in effect the tribal economy in miniature, so politically it underwrites the condition of primitive society—society without a Sovereign" (1972: 95). This would be an astonishingly accurate portrait of early Israel, whose only sovereign was Yahweh. A unique "theology" was organically related in part to a distinctive technology, economy, and social order. While archaeology can get at the former only partially and with some difficulty (i.e., evidence of possible cult *practice*), it is superbly equipped for investigating the latter, even though this task has been neglected until recently. A beginning *has* been made, but much more must be done on peasant economy and society if we are to comprehend Israel's origins in Canaan—especially if we are increasingly to employ the "peasants' revolt" model.

b. Continuity and Coexistence. In asking what is new *archaeologically,* and thus culturally, in the Iron I villages, we must remember that Palestinian archaeology has long been dominated by a certain biblical notion of "political history" and has thus sought unicausal explanations of cultural change in general. Furthermore, in this case of the Israelite settlement, the almost-exclusive adoption of the "conquest model" by those of the Albright school has meant that stress was placed upon the *discontinuity* between the LB/Canaanite and Iron I/Israelite cultures. The result was twofold: (1) a reductionist view of the emergence of Israel, as due to a relatively abrupt, violent, and complete triumph of newcomers who overwhelmed Canaan ca. 1250–1200 B.C.; and (2) an overemphasis on the supposed cultural discontinuities throughout the transitional LB-Iron I horizon in the 13th–11th centuries B.C.

Recently, however, newly accumulating archaeological evidence has shown that the abruptness of the break has been greatly exaggerated (cf. Kempinski 1985). We now know that many LB II sites were not destroyed at all, by either Israelites or Sea Peoples. Also, Egyptian New Kingdom influence did not cease with the 19th (First Ramesside) Dynasty ca. 1200 B.C., but extended perhaps as late as the time of Rameses VI, ca. 1140 B.C. (especially at sites like Megiddo, Beth-shan, and Lachish; cf. Tadmor 1979; Weinstein 1981; Ussishkin 1985; A. Mazar 1985). And Canaanite material culture flourished well into the 12th and even 11th centuries B.C. in some areas, particularly in ceramics, where, apart from imports or Philistine Bichrome ware, it is often difficult to distinguish 13th from 12th century pottery (A. Mazar 1981; Wood 1985; Dever 1987). Finally, not even the appearance of iron provides a firm criterion for the beginning of the "Iron" Age, since iron begins as early as the 14th century B.C. but comes into common use only in the 11th–10th centuries B.C. Furthermore, its connection with the new technology and culture is more debated than ever in recent research (cf. Stager 1985a: 10–11).

The logical conclusion to be drawn is that the "invasion hypotheses" of which earlier archaeologists were inordinately fond are almost never useful models, certainly not for the LB/Iron I transition. We must look rather at the largely *indigenous* factors in socio-cultural change. For example, we need posit no hypothetical external forces whatsoever to account for the actual changes that we observe in the material culture of Palestine on the LB/Iron I horizon (except for the impact of the Sea Peoples, who were indeed newcomers). It cannot be stated too categorically: the emergence of Israel in Canaan was not an isolated, "unique" event, but rather an integral (albeit small) part of a gradual, exceedingly complex set of socio-economic, cultural, and political changes on the LB-Iron I horizon in the Levant, with many regional variations. It was but one episode in the long settlement history of Palestine and cannot be understood apart from the larger context of that history (see especially Coote and Whitelam 1987). The early Israelites, who first appear in our textual sources at this time, may have come to constitute a distinct *ethnic group* by the late 13th–early 12th centuries B.C., but there is no archaeological evidence whatsoever that they were recent arrivals in Canaan, much less an invading military horde. And the ensuing struggle between Israelite and Canaanite culture continued for centuries, even to the end of the Monarchy (Dever 1984; see also Fritz 1987 and his "symbiosis hypothesis").

Having enunciated a general interpretative principle, however, we need to be as specific as possible on the elements of continuity/discontinuity, since so much hangs on this question, and yet previous discussions seem inconclusive.

(1) Continuity. Of the diagnostic feature enumerated above for the Iron I villages, the pottery, in particular, shows strong continuity with the 13th century LB Age repertoire. For instance, the pottery of ʿIzbet Ṣarṭeh, which is no doubt Israelite, is virtually *identical* to that of the 13th–12th centuries B.C. at nearby Gezer, which both archaeology and the biblical tradition agree is non-Israelite (i.e., LB Canaanite, with some new Iron I Philistine elements). The *only* significant difference is that ʿIzbet Ṣarṭeh has "collar rim" storejars, while Gezer does not; and Gezer has much more Philistine pottery. This is precisely what we should expect. It is interesting that Finkelstein had argued in his Hebrew dissertation (1983) that the ʿIzbet Ṣarṭeh pottery reflected a "Transjordanian pastoral-nomadic" origin, but in the full publication of the site (1986) he quite correctly makes no mention of such a possibility.

(See SETTLEMENT OF CANAAN, which also posits a Transjordanian background for early Israelite culture, but cites no *archaeological* evidence; Boling 1988 adduces some data but none that is decisive). It needs to be emphasized that not only is the Iron I village pottery in direct continuity with the typical local LB ceramic repertoire, but its further development in the 12th–early 11th centuries B.C. cannot be explained *otherwise*. This is seen in all the principal forms: storejars, kraters, bowls, cooking pots, even juglets, chalices, and lamps (cf. A. Mazar 1981; Finkelstein 1986: 38–92; Dever fc.a). The principal continuity between the LB Canaanite material culture and the early Iron I "Israelite" material culture is seen in the pottery. Yet it must always be remembered that among archaeologists and anthropologists pottery is regarded as our most sensitive medium for perceiving cultural contact and cultural change.

(2) Discontinuity. On the other hand, several diagnostic features of the Iron I villages are clearly innovative, specifically settlement type and distribution; and an almost total shift to a nonurban, agrarian economy and social structure (see above).

(3) Continuity, Discontinuity, and Adaptation. Still other features show a mixture of continuity and discontinuity and must therefore be evaluated most judiciously. For instance, hillside terraces, rock-hewn cisterns, and stone-lined silos now appear in relatively greater proportions, and they do indeed seem to characterize the technology of our early "Israelite" villages. But it is only the *combination* and *intensified* use that are new. All these elements have clear antecedents in the MB-LB Age, and even earlier (Stager 1985a: 5–10 and references there).

The case of the four-room courtyard house, or "Israelite type-house" (Shiloh 1970), is even more instructive. It is true that only in the Iron Age, and most often in the Iron I villages in question, does this distinctive house style become ubiquitous. But a few prototypes do appear in the LB; and a growing number of fully developed houses of this style are now known from obviously *non*-Israelite Iron I sites both in Palestine and in Transjordan (cf. A. Mazar 1981: 10, 11; Stager 1985a: 5–10; Finkelstein 1986: 121–24). Thus the four-room courtyard house was not so much an "Israelite invention" (and therefore a reliable diagnostic trait) as it was a successful adoption and modification of a common Iron I style of peasant farmhouse, one which was peculiarly suitable to early Israel's agrarian economy and social order. See also HOUSE, ISRAELITE.

Finally, we note the problem of the "collar rim" storejar, which Albright, Aharoni, and others had thought another "Israelite type-fossil." These pithoi are simply large variants of the LB-Iron I storejar, with a reenforcing band around the neck. They are particularly suitable for storage of liquids and foodstuffs, and it is probably for that reason that they are especially common in the Iron I villages we have discussed. But they are now known from LB contexts, as well as from non-Israelite sites in both Palestine and Transjordan (Ibrahim 1978; A. Mazar 1981: 27–31; Finkelstein 1986: 76–84).

All the above elements do indeed *become* "Israelite"; but they are not exclusively so, they are not necessarily innovations, and the individual elements in themselves cannot define "Israelite ethnicity."

c. Ultimate Origins. Another, larger aspect of LB-Iron I continuity must now be examined, namely the question of early Israel's *ultimate* origins. Is the demonstrable continuity with local LB Canaanite culture compatible with the customary models for the Israelite settlement; and, if so, is the archaeological evidence decisive for any *one* of them?

(1) "Conquest." Clearly, from our discussion the conquest model is ruled out. The founders of the Iron I villagers do not appear to have been newcomers to Palestine, much less settlers displacing Canaanites in the urban centers by military force. The few sites actually destroyed ca. 1200 B.C. were destroyed either by the Philistines, or by unknown agents; and none is resettled within a reasonable time by people who could be implicated in the destruction, or could otherwise be identified as "Israelites."

(2) "Peaceful Infiltration." The "peaceful infiltration" model has fared somewhat better, in that it always eschewed sudden conquest in favor of a process that envisions the Israelites emerging in Canaan gradually and largely without armed conflict. That may not have squared very well with the archaeological picture as viewed a generation ago when Alt and others advanced the "peaceful infiltration" model in the face of the dominant Albrightian interpretation, but the newer data surveyed above tend to confirm it in general. In certain *specifics*, however, this model, although relatively sophisticated, is not broad enough to accommodate some of the newer data (contra SETTLEMENT OF CANAAN). In its classic form, it assumed that the Iron I hill country settlers were pastoral nomads immigrating from Transjordan at first seasonally and then gradually becoming fully sedentarized (see Weippert 1971; 1979). More recently, however, this notion of *Siedlungsgeschichte*, or the sedentarization of nomads, has come under criticism from better informed ethnographic studies of pastoralists. (In addition, the "nomadic ideal" posited by some scholars as basic to the biblical writers has been shown to be largely a modern fiction). Furthermore, nearly all the archaeological data we have seen in the material culture of the Iron I sites, now that they are finally being investigated, contradicts *both* these notions of Transjordanian and pastoralist backgrounds. The Iron I pottery derives directly from LB traditions, which *must* be local to W Palestine, since there is no appreciable LB occupation in S Transjordan (contra both this model and the biblical tradition).

As for "pastoral origins," relatively few of the new Iron I villages suggest nomads gradually becoming farmers. Only Giloh and ʿIzbet Ṣarṭeh III appear to be "fortified herdsman's encampments," and even so there is no evidence that the occupants are either newcomers or former nomads. The houses at Tel Masos have been interpreted as modeled upon bedouin-like tents (Fritz 1981), but this is generally disputed (Stager 1985a: 17). Furthermore, the evidence of cattle breeding and of sophisticated ceramics at Tel Masos suggests anything but pastoralists settling down. Elsewhere, the Iron I hill-country sites exhibit a very advanced, multifaceted agricultural technology, one that was labor-intensive but nevertheless almost ideally adapted to high-risk agriculture under difficult conditions in this former marginal zone (see Hopkins 1985; Stager 1985a: 5–9; Borowski 1987). These are hardy first-generation farmers, i.e., refugees from the cities, much less recently sedentarized pastoralists (or "urban peasants"). They appear rather to be farmers who already had a thorough knowledge of local agricultural conditions in Canaan and needed only to adapt their experience to the hill country. The fact that the new technology is really a *combination* of strategies already utilized in the MB-LB Age, and thus well-proven, is further evidence of the Iron I villagers' local Canaanite derivation. It could be argued on the other hand that they merely borrowed this technology. But if they were really recently sedentarized Transjordanian pastoralists, they would have had little access to the source, isolated as they were in the hill country far from the centers of Canaanite culture.

All things considered, both the ethnographic and archaeological evidence militate against the "peaceful infiltration" model for the emergence of Israel, despite the fact that its notion of Transjordanian origins is consonant with some strands of the biblical tradition.

3. "Peasants' Revolt." The "peasants' revolt" (or "internal conquest") model seems more compatible with current archaeological data and theory than any other—especially in the modified form advanced by Gottwald (1979), with its emphasis on the role of technology and economy in social change. This model presumes that the early Israelite movement was made up of various dissident elements of LB Age Canaanite society, mostly dispossessed peasant farmers, who colonized new areas in the hinterland and there adopted a less stratified social order better suited to an agrarian economy. That appears very similar to the picture derived from the newer archaeology, except that Gottwald's "revolutionary, egalitarian" social (and religious) force presumed to be behind this movement is not susceptible to direct archaeological illumination. Of course, these former Canaanite "peasants" were already "liberated" (to use Gottwald's phrase) by the time we encounter them in the Iron I hill-country villages, so that they are now freeholders and self-sufficient homesteaders. But their *background* as peasant farmers is still clear in the archaeological record, as is the distinctiveness of their emerging social structure *vis à vis* old Canaan. Thus at least some aspects of the "peasants' revolt" formulation are now well attested archaeologically—a measure of support (if not confirmation) that no other model can boast. The nucleus of later Israel appears to have derived from the local LB culture of Canaan through relatively normal social processes of peasant withdrawal and what has been termed "retribalization," rather than originating outside Canaan and then either being superimposed on the local population or displacing them entirely in the early Iron I period. (For the possibility of *some* extra-Palestinian elements, however, see below.)

D. Archaeological Identification of "Israelite" Ethnicity

If the point has been made that the early Israelites in Canaan were largely of local derivation, we still have not answered the question of who they *were*. That is, how did they differ from Canaanites, how and when did they come to identify themselves as "Israelites," and what did that self-consciousness mean culturally? These, of course, have always been recognized as the fundamental questions, all attempting to ascertain: What was *"unique"* about ancient Israel, and *when* did it emerge as such? (cf. Lemche 1985; Thompson 1987). But until recently both biblical theologians and historians have sought the answers almost exclusively through the analysis of *texts*. That may be methodologically sound, as far as it goes, for "ethnicity" is usually defined mainly in terms of self-image; a social group may constitute a separate ethnic group if the majority of its members feel themselves to be a distinct "people." And certainly some biblical texts do posit a strong sense of "Israelite" ethnicity as though it characterized the tradition from beginning to end. Yet it is increasingly recognized that the biblical texts are often late, elitist, and propagandistic. And because the Bible is theocratic history, Israel is often portrayed in such radically disjunctive terms with respect to neighboring peoples that the result is more caricature than characterization. (To be fair, many other biblical texts do portray Israel in a less flattering—and thus more realistic—light.)

What was it that really constituted the distinctiveness of Israelite culture, spiritually *and* materially? It is suggested here that the biblical texts alone cannot and should not be expected adequately to illuminate "ethnicity," and, moreover, that it is only through the contribution of archaeology that we can achieve a more balanced picture, both by putting the biblical texts into larger context, as well as by supplying some of the missing information. It may be objected, of course, that even the "new archaeology," with its incomparably more sophisticated techniques, is ultimately limited, too, in its ability to discern thought processes *behind* material culture remains, and thus is powerless to illuminate such matters as self-consciousness or "ethnicity." It must be admitted that without the Merneptah reference to "Israel" ca. 1210 B.C. and the later biblical texts, we would not be sure that our Iron I villages are indeed "Israelite." That is, we could recognize the emergence of a distinctive new culture ca. 1200 B.C. in Canaan, but it would remain anonymous, we would not be able to affix a specific *ethnic label* to it. But even so, the mere name, however valuable, does not define, much less "explain," the nature and origin of this new culture. Only the *combination* of the textual and artifactual data—of history and archaeology—can aid in this inquiry.

Archeology can certainly contribute more than it has thus far to the identification of "Israelite ethnicity." It can do so first because the "new archaeology" is multidisciplinary in nature and therefore attempts to elucidate culture in *all* its aspects, not merely to describe "ceramic culture" and then proceed immediately to the writing of "political history" (as the older-style "biblical archaeology" really did). Surely ancient Israelite culture had its secular components, no less formative than its religious components, and it is these that archaeology can often illuminate uniquely and brilliantly. And *both* aspects of a culture must be so illuminated if it is to be comprehended in its own terms, rather than in some "idealistic" scheme that robs it of its variety and vitality.

Second, archaeology today is strongly behavioral. It focuses not merely on artifacts in themselves, but on the archaeological record as a whole, which is seen to reflect the "material correlates of human behavior." Archaeologists may not be very well equipped to be "paleo-psychologists" (as Binford reminds us); but if they cannot get at ideology, they nevertheless have an unparalleled opportunity to analyze the material *consequences* of human behavior, insofar as they reflect upon the thoughts and actions that produced the artifacts they study. Surely these "material correlates" of behavior, if anything, are clues to ethnicity.

Here we are clearly advocating a structural-functional model, at least at the fundamental level of analysis—without, however, denying the validity, and indeed the necessity, of a historical-cultural model at the higher level of synthesis (much as Gottwald 1979: 622–49; also 1985: 230–38). Thus the attempt at an archaeological identification of "ethnicity" need not be susceptible to the charge of reductionism, or material determinism. Nor is such an attempt necessarily confined to the old-fashioned "trait-list" approach that most archaeologists today would find unproductive.

Whatever model we may adopt in assessing the archaeological evidence for "Israelite ethnicity," we must begin by assuming that no matter what *else* early Israel was (or later thought itself to be), it was *also* a minority ethnic group in a multi-ethnic society in Iron I Canaan. By "ethnic group" we mean, at minimum, a social group that: (1) is biologically self-perpetuating; (2) shares a fundamental, uniform set of cultural values, including language; (3) constitutes a partly independent "interaction sphere"; (4) has a membership that defines itself, as well as being defined by others, as a category distinct from other categories of the same order; and (5) perpetuates its sense of separate identity both by developing rules for maintaining "ethnic boundaries," as well as for participating in inter-ethnic social encounters. (See further Barth 1969: 9–38.) It is especially important to note certain ways in which ethnic groups typically originate, maintain themselves, and assimilate or otherwise change. The *origins* of ethnic groups, in particular, are difficult, often impossible to ascertain (cf. Barth 1969: 17, 18), even where we have historical documentation; but we can point to some *reasons* for both the existence and the persistence of such groups.

It would seem that early Israel clearly qualifies as an ethnic group in the above definition, although that does not imply the unity that later biblical writers presupposed. The question here is simply to what degree *any* of this ethnic identity may be reflected in the archaeological remains, particularly of the early Iron Age village culture surveyed above. And would a positive identification of these villages as "Israelite" help one to choose between the various models proposed for understanding Israelite origins (whether by confirming, contradicting, or modifying biblical tradition)?

The results of our inquiry, even at best, may seem meager, for the question of archaeological identification of ethnicity is one of the most vexed interpretive issues in current archaeology. (For orientation, see Kamp and Yoffee 1980, with programmatic suggestions that the authors evidently regard positively but that are actually unachievable.) The usual "ethnic markers" would consist of such features as language (including "body language"), physical type, dress, food preferences, kinship patterns, general cultural and social values, religion, and the always-nebulous "self-identity." It is obvious that *none* of these traits will be very well represented, if at all, in the archaeological record—even if we regarded a "trait-list" approach as adequate. And their origins will remain even more obscure. But *collective behavior* will often be reflected archaeologically, i.e., the economy in settlement types and distribution; technology and subsistence practices in both artifacts and "ecofacts"; social structure in house form and function; social stratification in elite goods in tombs and elsewhere; ideology in expressions in art; and even religious practices in cultic remains.

We have already treated the archaeological data on settlement patterns, technology, subsistence, and social structure. We concluded that *all* the newer data are consonant with some strands of the biblical tradition, especially in Judges-Samuel. Thus we regard Stager's seminal work on the "archaeology of the family" in early Israel (1985a) as an almost ideal model of the proper dialogue between the "new archaeology" and biblical history, indeed a point of departure for all future studies. Yet even Stager begs the question. He *assumes* that the Iron I hill-country villages are "Israelite," and his own research goes further than anyone else to date in demonstrating that, but nowhere does he explicitly state his conclusion (or, for that matter address the radical implication for biblical history and scholarship).

Can we do better? Perhaps; but not without vastly improved research designs and much more survey and excavation focused *specifically* on this problem. For instance, we have very few Iron I cemeteries, which potentially would be most revealing; and even fewer cultic installations (on the latter, see Dever 1987). We may even hope, in time, for definitive epigraphic discoveries. Meanwhile, we need many more excavation and research projects that are conducive to *cross-cultural* comparisons. In practice, this would entail excavating, with identical research designs and preferably simultaneously, several small one-period Iron I sites in various areas of Israel and Transjordan that could be presumed on independent (textual) witness to be: (1) Canaanite; (2) Philistine; (3) Israelite; and (4) Ammonite-Moabite-Edomite. The excavations would concentrate on total, systemic retrieval of all cultural deposits, which methods already introduced by the "newer archaeology"; then on exhaustive intersite comparisons. The results of such a deliberate archaeological research program—carried out over a ten-year period or so, and properly integrated with ethnographic, textual, and other studies—might well prove decisive. The question "Who were the early Israelites *archaeologically?*" is now theoretically answerable. And when we do answer it, one suspects that the "peasants' revolt" or "indigenous peasant" model—already the most fruitful for research—will be further enhanced. (The most explicit attempt thus far at resolving the problem *archaeologically,* based on new data, is Finkelstein, although he adopts a modified "peaceful infiltration" model and at first scarcely refers to Gottwald's work; see Finkelstein 1986: 201–13; and further *AIS;* for a critique of Finkelstein, see Dever 1989).

E. Toward a New Synthesis of Archaeology and Biblical History

The problem with which we began this survey has not yet been resolved, either on the basis of textual or archaeological evidence.

1. Facing the Dilemma. The dilemma is simply that in ancient Israel's Credo and epic literature—indeed in her cult and tradition as a whole—the Exodus-Sinai-Conquest themes are absolutely fundamental. It is the "conquest of Canaan" that is the fulfillment of Yahweh's promise, the constitutive event that brings his Israelite people into existence. Yet if there is little *real* history in Israel's proclamation of her "salvation-history," is the tradition any more than a pious fraud? (For the latest, most radical view, see Lemche 1985.)

All critical scholars recognize that the biblical sources in the Pentateuch and Deuteronomistic History are relatively late, composite works that simply cannot be read at face value as history. Even the *earliest* written materials, the several archaic poems such as Exodus 15, are probably not eyewitness accounts. Thus concerning Exodus 15, dealing with the "crossing of the Red Sea"—which Cross dates to just after 1200 and regards as "a primary source for the central event in Israel's history" (*CMHE,* 123)—we must ask: "*What* event?" Are there any external data that would confirm that we are dealing here with history, and not myth?

Today, skeptical voices dominate the scene. As G. E. Wright himself acknowledged in his Introduction to the Anchor Bible *Joshua:* "In this book ancient Israel recorded her belief as to how the nation came to live in ancient Palestine. Yet during the last century a majority of those attempting to apply the methods of modern historiography to Hebrew tradition have said the book is wrong; it never happened that way at all" (page 4). And now, as we have seen, the cumulative results of a century of *archaeological* investigation powerfully buttress the negative view of the conquest, much to the consternation of those who expected the "archaeological revolution" to confirm the tradition. Where does that leave us?

2. Methodological Considerations. Assuming that we cannot simply dismiss either the textual or the artificial evidence, there are nevertheless some methodological approaches that may lead at least to partial solutions.

a. Two Traditions. First, we need to recall that there are *two* strands to the tradition as elaborated by the Deuteronomistic History: that preserved in Joshua, and that in Judges. While modern archaeology may call into question the historicity of Joshua, it provides rather dramatic corroboration of the account in Judges, even in obscure details. In the view advocated here, it is futile, indeed unnecessary, to attempt to reconcile these two conflicting versions (as Wright 1946). Instead of trying to "salvage" Joshua archaeologically, future research into Israelite origins should concentrate on Judges, as by far the most realistic and reliable source. There, the results will likely *not* be so negative.

b. Reconciling Joshua and Judges? If one asks, however, *why* the Israelite historiographers preserved two diametrically opposed versions of their own history, we can at least offer new critical approaches that may prove constructive. Recent structuralist analyses, such as those of Polzin (1980), Gottwald (1985), and others, have suggested that the redactors of the DH were fully aware of the radically divergent nature of the Joshua and the Judges materials they incorporated, but they left them in tension in a deliberately dialectic manner. As Gottwald (1985: 258) puts it: "By counterposing speech about how the Canaanites *must be* and *were* destroyed against speech about how Canaanites *remained* in the land and were even *accepted* into Israel, DH [the Deuteronomistic history] weaves an ironic exposition on the problematic of carrying out God's commands."

Another explanation for why the tradition has deliberately obscured much of its own origins is offered by Coote and Whitelam (1987). They suggest that the story of Israel's humble origins in social conflict did not suit the propagandistic purposes of the elite "House of David" in its rise to power and were thus downplayed, a point that Mendenhall had made earlier.

Finally, of the Joshua tradition, however folkloristic it may be, it must nevertheless be acknowledged that these materials may contain some raw source-data for the historian: (1) Archaeologically, we should observe that the evidence does not rule out the possibility that *some* constituents of the later Israelite tribal confederation may have derived from Egypt. In this connection, it is worth remembering that many biblical scholars have long held that only the "House of Joseph" (or elements of the later tribes of Benjamin and Judah—which have so obviously shaped the tradition) was ever in Egypt. The fact that most of the numerous Iron I villages we now have are precisely in the area of the Benjamin–Judah tribal territories may seem to lend credence to that suggestion. However, even if this area is the chief locus of early Israelite occupation, there is no direct *archaeological* evidence of Egyptian origins for the settlers, as we have seen, so the question must remain open.

(2) Even the minimalist "peasants' revolt," or "internal conquest," model would allow for *some* of the military actions against the Canaanites described in the book of Joshua. Thus armed conflict may have been a contributing factor in the cultural struggle, even if not the principle cause.

3. Toward a Synthesis? Is it possible to move further, however, in reconciling what may seem to be conflicting approaches to archaeological and textual reconstructions of Israelite origins? There would seem to be two primary possibilities for a synthesis, at least of method, if not of results. (See further Dever fc.b., for a symposium on this problem.)

a. Parallel Histories. The notion of producing two *alternate* versions of early Israelite history has recently become an option for the first time, due to the growing sophistication and maturity of the newer archaeology. At the "descriptive" level, the first approach would assay a history of ancient *Israel,* based on the biblical texts and focusing mainly on political and religious history. The second, or "secular," approach would utilize archaeological remains and extrabiblical texts to outline a socio-economic history of *Palestine,* primarily in the Bronze–Iron Ages in this connection (but extending, of course, from earliest to relatively modern times). As the "normative" level, the first approach might result in a history of the religion of Israel (or at least a history of the literature *about* that religion), and possibly even in an OT theology. The "secular" approach, however, would necessarily be confined to the illumination of Israelite cultic practice in its larger ANE context, without reference to theology, i.e., its significance for the modern religious community, Jewish or Christian. (See the provisional efforts of Lemche 1985; Thompson 1987).

Each of these separate histories would concentrate on one class of data, and each would be pursued by competent specialists. Needless to say, these two disciplines would both be devoted to legitimate, truly historical tasks. Yet however ideal such a division of labor might seem in theory, in actual practice these two histories would tend to remain *parallel.* They might be complementary, but they would never converge; each would present but a partial view of the total reality we seek to comprehend, the phenomenon of ancient Israel in all its richness and diversity.

b. Converging Histories. Far more preferable, it would seem, would be a *combination* of the two approaches, "sacred" and "secular"—or at least a dialogue between the two, which would point toward a truly multidisciplinary synthesis. And today there are indeed signs of such a development, bringing together the insights of the discipline of Palestinian archaeology in its newer guise, coupled with the newer sociological and anthropological approaches to the early history of Israel.

We have already outlined the nature and contribution of archaeology in this cooperative task, both here and elsewhere. See ARCHAEOLOGY. In biblical studies, the most promising trends are seen in the early analysis of Gottwald in his *Tribes of Yahweh* (1979), together with de Geus' *Tribes of Israel* (1976). More recently, the work of Marvin Chaney (1983) points in the same direction, as does Gottwald's *The Hebrew Bible—A Socio-Literary Introduction* (1985) and N. P. Lemche's *Early Israel* (1985). We have also called attention to two recent, specialized treatments of early Israelite agriculture, one by a biblical scholar (Hopkins 1985) and one by an archaeologist (Borowski 1987). Perhaps the most ambitious interdisciplinary synthesis yet may be the work of R. B. Coote and K. W. Whitelam, *The Emergence of Israel in Historical Perspective* (1987), based on a comprehensive settlement-history of Palestine from earliest to modern times. Finally, although it deals with a slightly later horizon, Frick's *The Formation of the State in Ancient Israel: A Survey of Models and Theories* (1985; see also Frick 1979) also rests upon the newer methodology and approach. All these recent analyses embody socio-anthropological models, as well as the newer archaeology.

Despite the recent proliferation of works on early Israel, however, many remain more traditional, based almost exclusively on the biblical texts, such as Halpern's *The Emergence of Israel in Canaan* (1983); Åhlström's *Who Were the Israelites?* (1986); and Miller and Hayes' *A History of Ancient Israel and Judah* (1986). These and other attempts at synthesis may be faulted for making little or inept use of the abundant archaeological data now available. Even B. Mazar's *The Early Biblical Period: Historical Essays* (1986; see also Mazar 1981), while masterly, is almost totally out of touch with both the methods and results of modern archaeology. It is regrettable that most biblical scholars still cling to the notion that artifacts without texts are "mute"; that archaeological evidence can only serve to "clarify matters of historical detail," or is useful "only when correlated with specific items in biblical history" (thus *HAIJ* 102, 189; cf. also Miller 1976: 5, 40–48; 1982; *idem* in Knight and Tucker 1985: 1–30). On the contrary, given the skepticism of most biblical historians on the value of the biblical tradition for the premonarchic history of Israel, archaeology is rapidly becoming our *primary* datum (see also Callaway 1985; 1988; Lemche 1985: 385).

Clearly we are implying that a *multi*disciplinary approach to reconstructing early Israelite origins is preferable, indeed infinitely superior. Why do we assume that? In the first place, this approach helps to break the circular reasoning inevitably involved when the biblical texts alone are utilized to write the early history of Israel. One has only to browse through the various essays in the recent handbook *The Hebrew Bible and Its Modern Interpreters* (Knight and Tucker 1985) to see how inconclusive—indeed how devoid of much *real* history in the usual sense—most of current biblical criticism is when largely text-based and confined to the biblical tradition. This is true whether the methods are those of literary, form, traditional, canonical, or structuralist criticism (see especially the essays of Ackroyd, Knierim, and Knight). The result tends to be simply a history of the *literature* concerning the religion of Israel and her self-understanding of her experience in Canaan. Only new data from other sources, and perhaps new models from other disciplines, can break that impasse.

Albright's original intuition—that nothing except the "external" evidence from archaeology could throw *new* light on the tradition as received—was sound; he erred only in assuming that archaeology would always confirm, never challenge, the "historical" reconstruction presented in the Hebrew Bible. Archaeology, in particular, allows us to get at the "history *behind* the history." At the same time, it broadens the picture by supplementing political history with socio-economic and cultural history.

Second, the multidisciplinary approach, particularly in the new "secular" archaeology, allows us to focus on factors in cultural change in addition to primarily *ideological ones,* especially on the role of ecological adaptation, subsistence and economy, technology, and social structure. These *material* factors are obviously powerful agents in shaping history, yet concerning them the Bible is largely silent.

Finally, the multidisciplinary approach to history-writing—like archaeology today—is more systemic, more processual, and is thus more truly "explanatory" than the traditional, purely descriptive approach. We may be able to learn not only *what* happened in the past, but *why* (i.e., apart from "theological explanations").

c. Faith and History. A final issue must be addressed, if only to acknowledge its fundamental importance to the current discussion of Israelite origins. The issue is simply this: if archaeological data are now as "primary" as those in the biblical texts, they may force a radical rewriting of the early history of Israel, one at variance with the tradition at crucial points. But does that not *undermine* the religious significance of the tradition? To put it another way, how shall those who espouse biblical faith remain *historians,* and not take flight into the realm of "suprahistory"? (Cf. further Porteous 1970–71.) It may be a matter of balance. That is, while the fallacy of historicism has by now been well exposed, how shall we avoid the other extreme, that of existentialism? It was precisely this issue, never resolved, that vexed the earlier "biblical archaeology" movement, aligned as it was with Neo-orthodox-style "biblical theology" in the 1950s–1960s (cf. Dever

1980; 1985b). The new "secular" archaeology might simply declare this a "non-issue," but in doing so it would forfeit any possibility for the dialogue that we regard as essential to *both* disciplines (specifically on the issue of the Israelite settlement, see Dever fc.a., Dever fc.b.).

The "faith and history" issue has generated a literature much too vast to be surveyed here. What we *can* do is to point to two methodological principles that should govern the input of archaeology. First, insofar as we are historians, it really *is* important to ascertain "what happened in history," as nearly as possible. Obviously, this historical inquiry must proceed independent of any theological presuppositions or biases, but the inquiry is not thereby *irrelevant* to questions of belief, as several current schools of biblical interpretation seem to imply. History cannot be allowed to become merely hermeneutics. (See further Knierim's enlightening analysis of the current situation in biblical criticism in Knight and Tucker 1985: 123–65.) Second, whatever the results of our historical investigation, the outcome should not be considered determinative in matters of religious belief, one way or another. Stendahl's prescient exposé of the weaknesses of the "biblical theology" movement criticized G. E. Wright's notion that religious *meaning* for us consists of our affirming the Bible's claims concerning "God's saving acts in history." Stendahl (*IDB* 1: 424) reminded us that "History does not answer such questions: it only poses them." And *archaeology* cannot answer these questions of faith, either. Archaeology can illumine historical events, but it cannot confirm the theological inferences drawn from those events, past or present.

F. Conclusion

Ancient Israel's problem in comprehending her own history was the same as ours: how to account for the unique *reality* of the people of Israel. The biblical writers fell back on the only analogy they had, historical experience, which for them was their own first-hand knowledge of the power of Yahweh over their pagan neighbors, and his ability to save and shape them as his people—despite their obscure origins, their lack of merit, and their disobedience. In the end, the biblical writers concluded that Israel's election was nothing less than a "miracle"; and who are we, their spiritual heirs, to disagree?

Although archaeology may be successful in recognizing in the material remains certain elements of human behavior and social organization, it reaches its limitations when it comes to ideology. Archaeology does not yet, and probably cannot, comment on the complex, diverse, tangled, and on occasion conflicting political or religious motivations behind the emergence of ancient Israel. We may tend to agree that "Yahwism," whether a revolutionary social movement or not, was probably the driving force. But we cannot define "Yahwism" archaeologically beyond describing religious *practice*. We can only suppose that in the cultural vacuum following the collapse of Canaanite society in the 12th century B.C., there arose in central Palestine a new ethnic consciousness and solidarity, a new polity, a new social order. The emergence of this ethnicity need not have been accompanied by a "revolt" at all; it may be viewed rather as simply a normal and even predictable historical development in the evolution of complex society. Archaeology may provide an "ecology" in which socio-economic change becomes explicable, but it cannot explain the ultimate *derivation* of that change. Insofar, however, as the ideology of the Israelite movement found concrete expression in new economic, social, and religious *forms*, we can hope to trace these forms in the archeological record, since this comprises the "material correlates" of human behavior.

Bibliography

Åhlström, G. 1986. *Who Were the Israelites?* Winona Lake, IN.
Anati, E. 1986. *The Mountain of God: Har Karkom.* New York.
Barth, F. 1969. *Ethnic Groups and Boundaries.* Bergen.
Bietak, M. 1979. *Avaris and Piramesse.* London.
Bimson, J. J. 1981. *Redating the Exodus and Conquest.* 2d ed. Sheffield.
Boling, R. G. 1988. *The Early Biblical Community in Transjordan.* Sheffield.
Borowski, O. 1987. *Agriculture in Iron Age Israel.* Winona Lake, IN.
Callaway, J. A. 1985. A New Perspective on the Hill Country Settlement of Canaan in Iron Age I. Pp. 31–49 in Tubb 1985.
———. 1988. The Settlement in Canaan. The Period of the Judges. Pp. 53–84 in *A Short History from Abraham to the Roman Destruction of the Temple,* ed. H. Shanks. Washington.
Chaney, M. L. 1983. Ancient Palestinian Peasant Movements and the Formation of Premonarchic Israel. Pp. 39–90 in Freedman and Graf 1983.
Cohen, R. 1983. *Kadesh-barnea.* Jerusalem.
Coote, R. B., and Whitelam, K. W. 1987. *The Emergence of Israel in Historical Perspective.* Sheffield.
Cross, F. M., ed. 1979. *Symposia Celebrating the Seventy-fifth Anniversary of the American Schools of Oriental Research (1900–1975).* Cambridge, MA.
Dever, W. G. 1980. Biblical Theology and Biblical Archaeology: An Appreciation of G. Ernest Wright. *HTR* 73: 1–15.
———. 1984. Asherah, Consort of Yahweh? New Evidence from Kuntillet ʿAjrûd. *BASOR* 255: 29–37.
———. 1985a. Relations Between Syria-Palestine and Egypt in the "Hyksos Period." Pp. 69–87 in Tubb 1985.
———. 1985b. Syro-Palestinian and Biblical Archaeology. Pp. 31–74 in Knight and Tucker 1985.
———. 1987. The Archaeological Background of Canaanite and Israelite Religion. Pp. 209–247 in *AIR.*
———. 1989. Yigael Yadin: Proto-typical Israeli "Biblical Archaeologist." *EI* 20: 44–51.
———. fc.a. Archaeology and Israelite Origins: A Review Article. *BASOR.*
———. ed. fc.b. *New Vistas on the Israelite Settlement in Canaan.* Atlanta.
Dever, W. G., et al. 1987. *Gezer IV.* Jerusalem.
Dornemann, R. H. 1983. *The Archaeology of the Transjordan in the Bronze and Iron Ages.* Milwaukee.
Finkelstein, I. 1985. Where Did the Israelites Live? Pp. 80–82 in *BibAT.*
———. 1986. *ʿIzbet Ṣarṭah.* Oxford.
Freedman, D. N., and Graf, D. F., eds. 1983. *Palestine in Transition.* Sheffield.
Frick, F. 1979. Regional and Sociopolitical Structure in Early Israel: An Ethno-Archaeological Approach. *SBLSP* 17: 233–53.
———. 1985. *The Formation of the State in Ancient Israel.* Sheffield.
Fritz, V. 1981. The Israelite "Conquest" in the Light of Recent Excavations of Khirbet el-Meshâsh. *BASOR* 241: 61–73.

———. 1987. Conquest or Settlement? The Early Iron Age in Palestine. *BA* 50: 84–100.
Fritz, V., and Kempinski, A. 1983. *Ergebnisse der Aussgrabungen auf der Hirbet el-Mšāš (Tel Māśōś).* Wiesbaden.
Gal, Z. 1989. *The Lower Galilee in the Iron Age.* Baltimore.
Geraty, L. T. 1983. Heshbon: The First Casualty in the Israelite Quest for the Kingdom of God. Pp. 239–48 in *The Quest for the Kingdom of God,* ed. H. B. Huffmon, F. A. Spina, and A. R. W. Green. Winona Lake, IN.
Geus, C. H. J. de. 1976. *The Tribes of Israel.* Assen.
Giveon, R. 1971. *Les bédouins Shosou des documents égyptiens.* Leiden.
Gottwald, N. K. 1979. *The Tribes of Yahweh.* Maryknoll, NY.
———. 1985. *The Hebrew Bible.* Philadelphia.
Halpern, B. 1983. *The Emergence of Israel in Canaan.* SBLMS 29. Chico, CA.
Hermann, S. 1973. *Israel in Egypt.* SBT, 2d series, 27. London.
Holladay, J. S., et al. 1982. *Cities of the Delta, Part III. Tell el-Maskhuta.* Malibu, CA.
Hopkins, D. L. 1985. *The Highlands of Canaan.* Sheffield.
Ibrahim, M. 1978. The Collared-Rim Jar of the Early Iron Age. Pp. 117–26 in *Archaeology in the Levant,* ed. P. R. S. Moorey and P. J. Parr. Warminster.
Kamp, K. A., and N. Yoffee. 1960. Ethnicity in Ancient Western Asia During the Early Second Millennium B.C. *BASOR* 237: 85–104.
Kempinski, A. 1985. The Overlap of Cultures at the End of the Late Bronze and the Beginning of the Iron Age. *EI* 18: 399–407 (in Hebrew).
Knight, D. A., and Tucker, G. M., eds. 1985. *The Hebrew Bible and Its Modern Interpreters.* Philadelphia.
Lapp, P. W. 1967. The Conquest of Palestine in the Light of Archaeology. *CTM* 38: 282–300.
Lemche, N. P. 1985. *Early Israel: Anthropological and Historical Studies on the Israelite Society Before the Monarchy.* VTSup 37. Leiden.
Mattingly, G. L. 1983. The Exodus-Conquest and the Archaeology of Transjordan: New Light on an Old Problem. *GTJ* 4: 245–62.
Mazar, A. 1981. Giloh: An Early Israelite Settlement Site near Jerusalem. *IEJ* 31: 1–36.
———. 1985. The Emergence of the Philistine Material Culture. *IEJ* 35: 95–107.
Mazar, B. 1981. The Early Israelite Settlement in the Hill Country. *BASOR* 241: 75–85.
———. 1986. *The Early Biblical Period: Historical Essays.* Jerusalem.
Miller, J. M. 1976. *The Old Testament and the Historian.* Philadelphia.
———. 1977. The Israelite Occupation of Canaan. Pp. 213–284 in *IJH.*
———. 1982. Approaches to the Bible Through History and Archaeology: Biblical History as a Discipline. *BA* 45: 211–23.
———. 1985. Israelite History. Pp. 1–30 in Knight and Tucker 1985.
Miller, J. M., and Hayes, J. H. 1986. *A History of Ancient Israel and Judah.* Philadelphia.
Oren, E. D. 1984. Migdal: A New Fortress on the Edge of the Eastern Nile Delta. *BASOR* 256: 7–44.
Polzin, R. 1980. *Moses and the Deuteronomist.* New York.
Porteous, N. 1970–71. Old Testament and History. *ASTI* 8: 21–77.
Sahlins, M. 1972. *Stone Age Economics.* London.
Sasson, J. M. 1981. On Choosing Models for Recreating Israelite Premonarchic History. *JSOT* 21: 3–24.
Sauer, J. A. 1986. Transjordan in the Bronze and Iron Ages: A Critique of Glueck's Synthesis. *BASOR* 263: 1–26.
Service, E. R. 1962. *Primitive Social Organization.* New York.
Shiloh, Y. 1970. The Four-Room House: Its Situation and Function in the Israelite City. *IEJ* 20: 180–90.
Stager, L. E. 1985a. The Archaeology of the Family in Early Israel. *BASOR* 260: 1–35.
———. 1985b. Merneptah, Israel and Sea Peoples: New Light on an Old Relief. *EI* 18: 56–64.
Tadmor, H. 1979. The Decline of Empires ca. 1200 B.C.E. Pp. 1–14 in Cross 1979.
Thompson, T. L. 1987. *The Origin Tradition of Ancient Israel.* Sheffield.
Tubb, J. N., ed. 1985. *Palestine in the Bronze and Iron Ages.* London.
Ussishkin, D. 1985. Lachish VII and VI and the End of the Late Bronze Age in Canaan. Pp. 213–28 in Tubb 1985.
Weinstein, J. M. 1981. The Egyptian Empire in Palestine: A Reassessment. *BASOR* 241: 1–28.
Weippert, M. 1971. *The Settlement of the Israelite Tribes in Palestine.* SBT, 2d Series 21. London.
———. 1979. The Israelite "Conquest" and the Evidence from Transjordan. Pp. 15–34 in Cross 1979.
Wood, B. G. 1985. *Palestinian Pottery of the Late Bronze Age.* Ph.D. diss., University of Toronto.
Wright, G. E. 1946. The Literary and Historical Problem of Joshua 10 and Judges 1. *JNES* 5/2: 105–14.
———. 1952. *God Who Acts.* SBT 8. London.
Yadin, Y. 1979. The Transition from a Semi-Nomadic to a Sedentary Society. Pp. 57–68 in Cross 1979.
Zertal, A. 1987. The Settlement of the Tribes of Israel in the Manasseh Region. Ph.D. diss., Tel Aviv University (in Hebrew).

WILLIAM G. DEVER

MONARCHIC PERIOD

A. Sources
  1. Biblical
  2. Epigraphic
  3. Archaeological
B. Origins of the Israelite Monarchy and National State
  1. Settlement of the Tribes in Canaan
  2. Early Attempts at Monarchy
C. Davidic–Solomonic Empire
  1. Sources
  2. David
  3. Solomon
D. Kingdoms of Israel and Judah
  1. Collapse of the Davidic–Solomonic Kingdom
  2. Politics of the Two Kingdoms
  3. Economy of the Two Kingdoms
E. Israel and Judah: Jeroboam I—Fall of Israel
  1. Period of Conflict
  2. Period of Cooperation
  3. Revolution and Its Aftermath
  4. Period of Prosperity
  5. Fall of Israel
F. Final Years of Judah
  1. Judah and the Neo-Assyrian Empire
  2. Reign of Josiah
  3. Judah and the Neo-Babylonian Empire

A. Sources

There are three types of sources that the historian can use in reconstructing the history of the monarchy in ancient Israel: the Bible, epigraphical material, and archaeological data. While these sources make the monarchic period the best documented era in the life of ancient Israel, still significant problems remain. The most obvious of these is the chronology of the Israelite monarchy. No universally accepted dating system existed in the ANE. Compounding this problem is the apparent artificial scheme that the Deuteronomistic Historian used in determining various time periods—for example 40 years for the reigns of David (2 Sam 5:40) and Solomon (1 Kgs 11:42) and 480 years from the Exodus to the building of the temple (1 Kgs 6:1).

The first securely dated event in the history of the two kingdoms is the surrender of Jerusalem to Nebuchadnezzar on March 15–16, 597 B.C.E. The Babylonian Chronicles (*ANET,* 564) supply the exact date. All other dates in the chronology of the two kingdoms are approximate within a range of ten to two years. The closer one gets to the fall of Jerusalem, the more precise dating becomes. Theoretically, with the date of Jerusalem's fall in hand, it should be possible to date the other events in the history of the two kingdoms by using the relative chronology provided by the Bible. That is not possible since the Bible's chronology does not allow for precise calculation. It may reflect a schematic rather than an exact presentation of the chronology of the monarchic period. Second there are serious discrepancies between the MT and the LXX that make it difficult to use the Bible to reconstruct this chronology. Any such chronology should be considered approximate (Miller 1967a; Thiele 1984; Wifall 1968). See also CHRONOLOGY (HEBREW BIBLE).

1. Biblical. There are two major blocks of biblical material that purport to tell the story of the Israelite monarchy. The first is part of what M. Noth *(NDH)* has called the Deuteronomistic History of Israel that includes Joshua to 2 Kings with Deuteronomy as its theological preface. The portion dealing with the monarchic period includes 1 Samuel to 2 Kings. Though the Deuteronomistic History (DH) tells the story of ancient Israel's monarchy, its purpose was to explain the fall of both Israel and Judah as the result of infidelity to Yahweh (2 Kgs 17:7–23; 21:10–15). Whatever details the modern historian can distill from the books of Samuel and Kings to reconstruct the history of monarchic period are secondary for the ancient writer who wished to assign the blame for the fall of the ancient Israelite states on those who ruled it.

The books of Chronicles also tell the story of the monarchic period but from a perspective that differs from that of the DH. At the center of the Chronicler's concern is the temple of Jerusalem. The stories about David and Solomon deal with the building of the temple. Interest in later kings depends on their loyalty to the temple. That is why the Chronicler all but ignores the rulers of the N Kingdom. In matters that pertain to the history of the monarchy, the books of Chronicles rarely differ from parallel texts in Samuel and Kings.

The Latter Prophets also provide some material for historical reconstruction. Prophets such as Amos, Isaiah, and Jeremiah found themselves directly involved with the king or his ministers (Amos 7:10–13; Isaiah 7; Jeremiah 21). Other prophets, such as Hosea and Micah, describe the social, economic, and religious realities created by the monarchy.

2. Epigraphic. A second category of materials for reconstructing the history of the monarchy is epigraphic materials: inscriptions and other texts from throughout the ANE. These are particularly helpful because they are usually contemporary with the events they describe. Little epigraphic material has survived from ancient Israel. Some inscriptions, ostraca, seals, and seal impressions have surfaced and provide important information. The most famous of these is the 8th century inscription from the Siloam tunnel (*ANET,* 321). Ostraca (8th century) from Samaria (*ANET,* 321) are administrative texts while those from Lachish (6th century) are military communiqués (*ANET,* 321–22). Several seals, seal impressions and bullae from 6th century Jerusalem bear names of people who may be associated with persons known from the Bible (Shiloh 1986).

More significant have been the recovery and deciphering of ANE texts that relate to the history of ancient Israel. The first of these to mention events in Israel's monarchic period date from the 10th century and are Pharaoh Shishak's pylon at the temple of Aton at Karnak and his stele found at Megiddo (*ANET,* 263–64). The first inscription to mention an Israelite king is the stele of Mesha of Moab (9th century) that refers to "the house of Omri" (*ANET,* 320). The Black Obelisk of Shalmaneser III (9th century) has the only contemporary portrait of an Israelite king. It shows Jehu kneeling in tribute before the Assyrian emperor (*ANEP,* 100a). There are other Assyrian and Babylonian texts that make direct references to Israelite and Judahite kings (The Black Obelisk, *ANET,* p. 281, and the Annals of Sennacherib [7th century], *ANET,* 287–88).

3. Archaeological. Besides the literary sources, there are significant nonliterary data that can help the historian have a more complete picture of the monarchic period. The archaeological record clearly marks the 9th century as the apex of ancient Israel's security and prosperity. Remains from the 8th to the 6th centuries suggest economic decline and military weakness with significant destruction of cities.

Unfortunately the archaeological record of the monarchic period is silent for the most part. Only rarely do epigraphic data emerge with the nonliterary material. This makes the interpretation of the archaeological remains difficult. It is not always possible to correlate the archaeological record with the biblical text. Archaeology is useful in helping the historian understand the physical conditions and everyday life of the monarchic period. But with careful use of the more recent technological advancements and cross-disciplinary insights, archaeological evidence may—though with difficulty—clarify matters of historical detail. Archaeology is most useful in illuminating the state of the general material culture.

B. Origins of the Israelite Monarchy and National State

1. Settlement of the Tribes in Canaan. The Late Bronze Age (1550–1200) was a period of great empires in the ANE. The land of Canaan was between two rival imperial powers. To the S was Egypt and to the N was Mitanni and the Hittites. They sought to control Canaan because of the lucrative trade routes that passed through the region.

The end of the LB Age witnessed the disintegration of these imperial powers. The kingdom of Mitanni was in decline. The Hittite Empire took its place. The Hittites and Egyptians wore themselves out in the contest for hegemony over Canaan. This created a vacuum of power that smaller political entities began to fill. This was the period when tribal groupings, city-states, and small kingdoms emerged in Canaan. This was when the Israelite tribes made their appearance in the sparsely inhabited central highlands of the Cis- and Transjordan regions of Canaan. The Amarna Letters (*ANET,* 483–90) describe the unsettled conditions in Canaan in the 14th century with the breakdown of Egyptian hegemony.

It is not certain exactly when the Israelite tribes came into distinct existence in Canaan. Outside of the Bible, the only mention of the name, Israel, occurs in the Merneptah stele (*ANET,* 376–78) from the late 13th century. It is not certain whether the term, Israel, refers to a place or a people. It can only be said that Egypt probably encountered some kind of entity called Israel. Due to this lack of clarity in information, historians of ancient Israel have developed several hypothetical models to describe the settlement period. The nomadic infiltration model claims that before the founding of the monarchy the Israelite tribes were nomads who began to settle in the highlands of central Canaan. A second model uses the archaeological record to suggest that the biblical narratives of Joshua are historically accurate as they describe ancient Israel's entrance into the land as the result of a military conquest. G. Mendenhall (1962) saw the Israelite settlement of Canaan as the result of a socio-political process that he described as a "peasants' revolt." N. K. Gottwald (1979) used a sociological model based on Marxian categories in his massive elaboration of Mendenhall's hypothesis.

2. Early Attempts at Monarchy. When the Israelites entered Canaan in the middle of the 13th century, they claimed their land without the benefit of a highly centralized political or military establishment. They continued to live without a monarchy or other forms of strong centralized authority for 200 years. The Israelite tribes prized their autonomy. When faced with military threats from Canaanite city-states such as Hazor (Judges 4–5) or from bedouin raiders such as the Midianites (Judges 6–8), the Israelite tribes depended on military leaders who emerged in response to specific crises. It was in the aftermath of such a crisis (1 Samuel 8–10) that the first attempts at establishing a permanent form of leadership took place (Halpern 1981).

The first bid at establishing a monarchy in Israel took place after Gideon's victory over the Midianites. The Israelites offered to accept Gideon and his heirs as their permanent rulers but Gideon declined their offer (Judg 8:22–23). Abimelech, Gideon's son, supported by the non-Israelite population of Shechem, led a brief and tragic experiment with a monarchic form of government (Judges 9). A more successful effort at establishing the monarchy took place in the mid-11th century when the Israelite tribes began expanding beyond their enclaves in the central highlands of Canaan. In doing so they met resistance from the Philistines with whom they had to contend for supremacy in Canaan. Saul had shown himself capable in dealing with a threat from the Ammonites (1 Samuel 11). He led the Israelite armies against the Philistines as well (1 Samuel 13–14). His initial success led to his election as king of the Israelite tribes. Saul's death and the devastation of the Israelite army during a conflict with the Philistines (1 Samuel 31) did not end the Israelite experiment with the monarchy because of the achievements of David who was the founder of the Israelite national state and its monarchy.

Near the end of the 11th century the Israelite tribes united under David to form a small national state. The state David founded bifurcated into the Kingdom of Israel and the Kingdom of Judah following the death of Solomon. In the 8th century B.C. the rise of the Neo-Assyrian Empire signaled a new age of imperial power in the ANE and the end of small national states such as Israel and Judah. The Israelite kingdoms were able to rise and flourish when the absence of imperial powers made this possible. The succession of imperial powers beginning with Assyria made it difficult for small national states to survive in the region.

There is no consensus on attitude of the DH toward the establishment of the monarchy since the composition history of 1 Samuel 7–15 is unclear (Birch 1976). Noth *(NDH)* held that the Deuteronomist opposed the monarchy. Sociological analysis sees a royal versus an egalitarian dialectic in these texts. There is no need to conclude that the Deuteronomistic tradition had a negative view of the monarchy (Campbell 1986). The text reflects mixed attitudes. There is rejection when the institution of the kingship led Israel to cease trusting in God. There is approval when the king acts responsibly toward the law (Gerbrandt 1986).

C. Davidic–Solomonic Empire

1. Sources. Though the Bible contains much material about David, the modern historian cannot use it all uncritically to reconstruct the history of the ancient Israelite monarchy. The Chronicler is dependent upon the presentation in Samuel and Kings. The Chronicler's use of this material shows that historical considerations are secondary. The principal concern of the Chronicler is the presentation of David as the great Israelite hero who organized the worship of the Jerusalem temple. The Chronicler ignores all problems of David's reign to avoid detracting from the image of David as a pious king wholly devoted to Yahweh.

The portrait of David in the books of Samuel comes from pro-David circles and is dependent in part on legendary material. Despite this, it is the judgment of most historians that there are historical persons and events behind these traditions (*HAIJ,* 159–60). Unfortunately there are no ANE texts other than the Bible that mention David, and the archaeological data presently yields little that is useful for clarifying matters of historical detail (*IJH,* 340–43). What follows is dependent upon the narratives in Samuel and Kings with the recognition that determining what from these narratives belongs to the historical and what belongs to the legendary is subjective to some extent (Carlson 1964).

2. David (ca. 1000–961). Following the death of Saul, the Philistines asserted their control over the central highlands. Abner, Saul's general, survived the Israelite defeat and sought to prevent the monarchy from dying with Saul. He crowned Ishbaal (Ish-bosheth), one of Saul's surviving sons, as king of Israel at Mahanaim (2 Sam 2:8). David persuaded the elders of Judah, his own tribe, to anoint him as their king. They did so and he ruled over Judah at Hebron for seven years (2 Sam 2:1–4, 11).

The Philistines probably considered the division of Saul's kingdom with Ishbaal at Mahanaim and David at Hebron as convenient for their purposes. They believed that Saul's kingdom was no more. In its place were two small rival kingdoms. David strove to forge a new and powerful Israelite kingdom.

David's rise to power over Israel became easier because of the death of Abner (2 Sam 3:26–27). Without Abner's support Ishbaal's position became untenable and the king's own officers assassinated him (2 Sam 4:1–7). The way was now clear for David to take the throne of all Israel, which the elders of Israel offered to him voluntarily so that military force or political maneuvering on David's part became unnecessary (2 Sam 5:1–5). This was the end of the first Israelite dynasty and the beginning of a new age for the monarchy under David whom later generations would remember as the paradigm of the Israelite king (Weiser 1966).

David's first act in consolidating his position was to take Jerusalem, which had remained a Jebusite enclave between the territories of Judah and Benjamin. David made the city his capital (2 Sam 5:6–12). Since Jerusalem was not under the control of any tribe, David's choice had the appearance of not favoring any single faction of the Israelite coalition. David also brought the ark of the covenant to Jerusalem and place it in a special tent (2 Sam 6:17). This move had the double effect of presenting David as the protector of Israel's ancient religious traditions and of making Jerusalem the new religious center of Israel. The presence of the ark in Jerusalem marks a new moment in Israel's life, but it also emphasizes continuity with ancient traditions (Campbell 1975; Timm 1966).

The conquest of Jerusalem was the first step David took to expand his kingdom beyond the territories of the Israelite tribes. This brought him into direct conflict with the Philistines who took immediate action by sending two military forces against David. He defeated both armies (2 Sam 5:17–25). After his victories over the Philistines, David moved against the Transjordanian kingdoms. His victories there brought the King's Highway under Israel's control (2 Sam 8:2; 9:6–14). David then subjugated the Arameans and by that extended Israel's frontier to the Euphrates (2 Sam 10:15–19). His victory over Edom (2 Sam 8:12) gave him a port on the Red Sea.

Despite David's spectacular rise to power, his military victories, and his religious gestures, there was still some Israelite support for the dynasty of Saul. David tried to eliminate any possible rivals from Saul's family (2 Sam 21:1–4). Out of respect for the memory of his friend Jonathan, he spared Mephibosheth, Jonathan's crippled son. David gave him what remained of Saul's estates, but required him to live in Jerusalem (2 Samuel 9).

While David showed that he was a political and military genius, his personal life was a shambles. His desire for Bathsheba, the wife of a Hittite mercenary, led David to acts of adultery and murder (2 Samuel 11). Second while David was able to manage a small empire, he had little control over his own family (2 Sam 14:28–33). Ultimately this lack of control laid the foundation for the first revolt against David, a revolt led by his son Absalom, who took advantage of popular grievances against his father and had himself proclaimed king at Hebron. Joab killed Absalom bringing his revolt to an end. Led by the elders of Judah, the people reinstated David to the throne (2 Samuel 15–19). Despite this reinstatement, support for David was still not unanimous. A second revolt broke out. Sheba ben Bichri from Saul's tribe of Benjamin led this new threat to David's rule. David moved quickly to crush this rebellion (2 Samuel 20).

Without question it was David who transformed the loose coalition of Israelite tribes into a national state with himself as king and founder of a dynasty. There is no single explanation for David's success. He was a master of both military and political affairs, but it was only the absence of a foreign imperial power in Canaan that allowed these qualities to emerge in an Israelite of the 10th century. The Philistine menace that Saul was unable to keep in check led the fiercely independent Israelite tribes to submit to David's rule since David eliminated that menace. David had to face serious internal problems despite his military and political successes. He had to put down two revolutions one of which his son Absalom led. Despite these problems David survived and his dynasty ruled for more than four hundred years. His most lasting achievement was his decision to make Jerusalem the center of the nation's national life.

3. Solomon (961–922). One measure of the difficulties that David faced was the struggle for the succession to the throne. The narrative of the succession takes up 2 Samuel 9–20 and 1 Kings 1–2. Estimates of the historical value of these chapters range from L. Rost's view (1982) that they were work of an eyewitness to the events described to the J. A. Soggin's assertion (*IJH*, 338) that these chapters are a "novel." Even if one agrees with Soggin that the story of Solomon's succession was the product of a storyteller's imagination, it is still possible to draw some historical conclusions from the narrative. Solomon was not the heir apparent to David but gained the throne following court intrigues. These took place in David's dotage when he was no longer effectively in control as king. Though Solomon replaced his senile father on the throne, the narratives make it appear as if Solomon displaced Adonijah who had begun functioning as king (1 Kgs 1:5–8).

The story of Solomon's succession may not be an objective record, but it is not the pro-Solomon propagandistic document that Miller and Hayes believe it to be (*HAIJ*, 200). It is as searing an indictment of the monarchy as one finds in the Bible. To be sure the critique is indirect, but the reader cannot but be appalled by the spectacle created by David and his family. There is adultery, murder, rape, fratricide, rebellion, and intrigue—all perpetrated by those who present themselves as leaders of Israel.

Despite this veiled voice of protest, Solomon ruled a people who had become accustomed to the centralized administration of a king. He sought to consolidate the gains that his father David made. Though Solomon met some internal opposition to his accession to the throne, politically inspired marriages and negotiated alliances secured international recognition for David's successor. He protected the borders of his kingdom by peaceful relations with neighboring kings (1 Kgs 3:1; 5:1–6; 11:1–3).

David's foreign policy was so successful and his military victories so complete that Solomon's reign was peaceful for the most part. This enabled Solomon to take advantage of Israel's unique geographical position as the commercial crossroads in the ANE. Israel controlled the two main and several secondary commercial roads in the region. Solomon also had ports on the Mediterranean and Red Seas (*IJH,* 373–76).

Solomon's commercial success led to great building projects that served to showcase his wealth and power for his subjects and potential rivals. David's Jerusalem was confined to the Ophel hill. Solomon enlarged the city by building his palace to the N. The temple that Solomon built was one component of his palace, but it was the temple that received the most attention in the Bible, which sees the temple as Solomon's greatest single achievement (Busink 1970; Parrot 1957). Solomon also built outside of Jerusalem. He fortified Megiddo, Gezer, and Hazor (1 Kgs 9:15–19). The archaeological record of these cities points to much activity in Solomon's day though archaeologists debate what can be attributed to Solomon and what was built because of local initiative (Kenyon 1971).

Solomon surrounded himself with able administrators to ensure that his projects ran smoothly and were adequately financed (1 Kgs 4:1–6; Mettinger 1971). Unfortunately these building projects emptied Solomon's treasury faster than he could fill it so that he had to tax his people to make up the balance. In addition, able-bodied people had to present themselves for unpaid labor on these projects. Solomon's financial problems moved him beyond centralization to despotism. His policies of taxation and forced labor were a source of discontent and contributed to the undoing of his empire following his death (Redford 1972; Mendelsohn 1962).

The income from commerce and taxation was still insufficient to support all Solomon's building projects so he ceded twenty cities in Galilee to Tyre to ease his financial problems (1 Kgs 9:10–13). There were other signs that his empire was in trouble. Both Edom and Aram successfully rebelled against Israelite rule (1 Kgs 11:14–25). The most serious threat to Solomon's rule came not from outside but from within Israel. Encouraged by the prophet Ahijah, Jeroboam became the leader of those Israelites who opposed Solomon's rule. Ironically Jeroboam had been Solomon's administrator of forced labor (1 Kgs 11:26–40).

What helped prevent Solomon's empire from disintegrating during his lifetime was the theological support that propped up his rule. Like all ANE monarchies, the kingship in Israel needed religious support to maintain its legitimacy. The belief that God had chosen David and his descendants to rule Israel forever (2 Samuel 7) was the theological support for Solomon's rule. Both Saul and David became kings because of arrangements made by the people over whom they ruled. Theirs was a charismatic kingship acknowledged by popular consent. Solomon came to the throne without such popular support. His claim to the throne rested on a dynastic principle in which God became the guarantor of the dynasty. Such a pattern of kingship was no different from that of other nations in the ANE (Kenik 1983; Johnson 1967).

D. Kingdoms of Israel and Judah

1. Collapse of the Davidic–Solomonic Kingdom. The development of a royal ideology that supported the Davidic dynasty was not enough to secure the throne of Solomon for Rehoboam his son. The succession was not an issue in Jerusalem (1 Kgs 11:43b). It was another matter in Shechem where "all Israel" came to confirm Rehoboam as king. The people that the new king went to meet were representatives of the tribes, clans, and settlements of the hill country N of Jerusalem. These people evidently had grievances so serious that they wanted to negotiate with the king. When they asked Rehoboam to modify Solomon's policies of taxation and forced labor, he refused. The assembly then rejected Rehoboam (1 Kgs 12:16). The king fled to the safety of Jerusalem and did not try to compel the loyalty of the northerners.

The assembly at Shechem did not replace the monarchy by reverting to a tribal form of government. Instead it rejected the Davidic dynasty and offered the kingship to Jeroboam, the leader of the anti-Solomonic faction. He established a new state with its capital at Shechem (1 Kgs 12:25).

The book of Kings treats the action of the assembly at Shechem as an act of apostasy though it was sanctioned by the prophet Ahijah (1 Kgs 11:23–39). This interpretation of events following Solomon's death is a reflection of DH's views on the legitimacy of the Davidic dynasty and the centrality of Jerusalem. The Shechem assembly and Jeroboam ignored both (Aberach and Smolar 1969; Klein 1970).

A more balanced evaluation of the circumstances following Solomon's death should conclude that the actions of the Shechem assembly were not surprising given Rehoboam's decision to continue his father's internal policies. The readiness of the northerners to abandon the Davidic dynasty shows that a "united kingdom" never existed. David and Solomon ruled over a "dual monarchy" in which the N and S tribes shared a king in common (2 Sam 3:10; 19:11–15, 43; 24:1–91; 1 Kgs 1:35). Following Solomon's death the dual monarchy collapsed. Replacing it were two small kingdoms that existed alongside each other for about two hundred years. The N kingdom was known as Israel or Ephraim. Its center was the hill country N of Jerusalem though it included the regions of Gilead and Galilee as well. The S kingdom was known as Judah and included the S hill country and the Negeb.

2. Politics of the Two Kingdoms. The S kingdom (Judah) was a sacral and centralized society ruled by what its citizens believed was the divinely chosen Davidic dynasty. It was a slow-moving, conservative, and highly traditional society. Jerusalem and its temple were the focus of Judah's national and religious life. Although the monarchy introduced Judah to foreign cultural perspectives, it absorbed these by modifying gradually its social system and religious traditions without significant social disruptions. Stability was the hallmark of the S kingdom. That is why it retained a single dynasty throughout its existence.

The N kingdom (Israel) did not enjoy the benefits that a stable political structure provided. In its 200 years of existence, it had 19 kings, only 10 of whom succeeded to the throne. Nine came by way of *coups d'état.* Assassination was the fate of seven of Israel's kings. One committed suicide. Theoretically Israel valued the type of leadership that emerges in times of crisis over a hereditary monarchy. In reality, several of Israel's kings were little more than opportunists.

Though religiously, ethnically, and culturally the two kingdoms were parts of one whole, politically they were independent. The N kingdom was the more prosperous and powerful. It had more natural resources, a large population, and a greater military capability. In terms of international relations, Israel and Judah were just two of several minor kingdoms in Canaan (Alt 1966a).

3. Economy of the Two Kingdoms. Though the Davidic–Solomonic kingdom was no more, the economic development and social change that the monarchy brought continued in both kingdoms. Neither Israel nor Judah was a significant political power, however, they enjoyed surprising economic prosperity. The combined population of the two kingdoms was probably one million (800,000 in Israel and 200,000 in Judah) at the height of their prosperity at the end of the 9th century. The population of the two kingdoms was becoming stratified. Just distribution of wealth did not accompany economic growth. The agrarian economy had to support a monarchy, its bureaucracy, and an army. The burden became increasingly more difficult. It led to the injustices that the prophets of the 8th century (Amos, Hosea, Micah, and Isaiah) condemned with so much passion.

Both kingdoms were responsible for maintaining several institutions that had serious economic effects. First there was compulsory military service that provoked great resentment (2 Kgs 25:10). Peasants had to leave their fields and flocks not to defend themselves and their families but to advance the king's political and commercial adventures that were of no concern to them. Second was the burden of forced labor that was the spark that set off the N tribes on a course independent of the Davidic dynasty. Despite this, the hated system continued involving up to one quarter of the population to work on royal building, commercial, and agricultural projects. Taxation took away what little the peasants were able to glean from their work. With the rise of the neo-Assyrian and neo-Babylonian empires, the peasants also had to provide the bulk of the tribute that the two kingdoms had to pay to their imperial masters.

Both the Bible and the archaeological data document the stratification of Israelite society because of the economic developments in the monarchic period. Amos (4:1) in the N and Isaiah (3:14–15) in the S criticize the effects of economic stratification that created poverty in the two kingdoms. The prophets denounced the splendid buildings of the wealthy: Amos 3:15; 5:11; 6:4; Hos 8:14; 12:8; Isa 2:7. Excavations of sites like Tirzah, Shechem, and Hazor show that at one time every family lived like its neighbors, but the 8th century saw these cities divided between the well-built homes of the wealthy and hovels of the poor (Kenyon 1964; 1971). The prophets excoriated the new wealthy class whose prosperity fed off the misery of the poor (Mic 2:1–12; Isa 5:8). Some poor people even had to sell themselves or their children into slavery to pay the debts they owed to the king or to their wealthy neighbors (2 Kgs 4:1–7; Amos 2:6). The political division of the Davidic empire into two rival states had its economic and social parallel in the life of the people who formed two classes: the rich and the poor. Poverty then was the creation of the monarchy and the economic practices it spawned (King 1988).

E. Israel and Judah: Jeroboam I—Fall of Israel (922–721)

1. Period of Conflict (922–876). Jeroboam I (922–901) took steps to establish the N kingdom as religiously independent of Judah. He proposed the old shrines at Dan and Bethel as alternatives to Jerusalem. He changed the date of the pilgrimage festivals and dislodged the Levites who were royal administrators and presumably loyal to the Davidic dynasty (1 Kgs 12:26–32).

The Egyptians welcomed the split of Solomon's kingdom since it fit into their plans to reassert their control over Canaan. Five years after the split, Egypt invaded the territories of the two kingdoms (1 Kgs 14:25–28). Despite its victories, Egypt was unable to maintain a permanent presence in the region (Mazar 1957). Rehoboam built a series of forts to guard his S frontier from Egyptian incursions (2 Chr 11:5–12).

There were continual border hostilities between the two kingdoms throughout the reign of Rehoboam and into that of his successor Abijah (also known as Abijam 915–913). Abijah was able to take the territory of Benjamin and add it to his kingdom. Such reverses at the hand of Judah weakened the prestige of Jeroboam. When he died, Nadab, his son, (901) ruled Israel for just one year. A military *coup* led by Baasha (900–877) deposed Nadab (1 Kgs 15:25–32).

After Asa (913–873) succeeded Abijah in the S, he induced the Arameans to invade the N kingdom. With the army of Israel occupied in the N, Asa had a free hand in the S. He moved Judah's N border to Mizpah where it remained until the fall of the N kingdom.

The continuous ill-fortunes of Israel at the hands of Aram and Judah were a serious problem for Baasha. Though he was able to hold onto the throne, his son Elah (877–876) was not. After a brief reign, Elah was assassinated by Zimri (876). When news of the *coup* reached the Israelite army, the soldiers acclaimed their commander Omri as king. Omri marched to Tirzah where Zimri had already established himself as king. When Zimri saw Omri's army approaching the city, he despaired and committed suicide after a reign of just seven days (1 Kgs 16:15–19).

2. Period of Cooperation (876–842). Omri's seven-year reign (876–869) reversed Israel's fortunes. He ended the Aramean threat to the N kingdom. He revived Israel's commercial fortunes by aligning himself with Phoenicia. He sealed the alliance with the marriage of his son Ahab with Jezebel, the daughter of Ethbaal, king of Sidon. Omri ended 50 years of fruitless conflict with Judah by giving his daughter Athaliah in marriage to Jehoram, the heir to the throne of the S kingdom. Omri retook Moab and this brought the King's Highway under his control. All this brought a new era of peace and prosperity to Israel. Omri was the greatest king to rule over the N though the Bible pays scant attention to him. Knowledge of Omri's achievements comes from extrabiblical sources (Timm 1982; Whiteley 1952).

Ahab (869–850) followed Omri on the throne of Israel. It was the first successful dynastic succession in the N kingdom. From a military, economic, and political perspective, Ahab's reign was remarkably successful. His only defeat was the loss of Moab at the end of his reign. Excavations at several cities in the N show that Ahab's reign was one of economic growth and military strength (Hennessy 1970). Ahab's greatest military achievement took place at the battle of Qarqar, which the Bible ignores. Ahab led a coalition of small states that successfully engaged the Assyrians and prevented them from taking control of the region. Ahab led the largest force in the coalition (*LAR* 1: 595–596, 601, 610–611).

Ahab's most serious problems were internal. His Phoenician wife Jezebel promoted the worship of Baal in the N kingdom. The prophet Elijah forcefully opposed her. The conflict between Elijah and Ahab over Jezebel's activity dominates the portrait of Ahab in the Bible and makes it appear as if he were a weak and ineffective ruler when the opposite was true (1 Kgs 17:1–22:40).

Ahab continued Omri's policy of cooperation with Judah. When the Arameans invaded Israel in 851, Jehosaphat, the king of Judah, joined Ahab in battle. While the Israelite–Judahite coalition prevented Aram from taking more than the N part of Israelite's Transjordanian territories, Ahab fell in battle (1 Kgs 22:34–35).

Jehosaphat's reign (873–849) was a time of peace and prosperity for Judah primarily because of its alliance with Israel. He increased Judah's commercial interests, strengthened its administrative apparatus, established a centralized judicial system, reorganized the army, and fortified many cities (1 Kgs 22:41–51).

In Israel Ahaziah (850–849) succeeded his father Ahab. A deterioration of the good relations that existed with Judah marked his reign. He died childless and his brother Jehoram (also known as Joram 849–842) succeeded him. Jehoram tried to retake Moab. Jehosaphat joined him in this unsuccessful adventure. This failure bred discontent among the army and population.

In Judah Jehosaphat's son Jehoram (849–842) came to the throne amid some internal problems that led Jehoram to have members of his family and court executed (2 Chr 21:4). He also had some external problems. Edom rebelled causing Judah to lose its control of the King's Highway and the income that came with that control (2 Chr 8:20–22). There has been some speculation that the Jehoram of Judah and the Jehoram of Israel were the same person. This means that the two kingdoms would have been one under the rule of the same king (*HAIJ,* 280–84). While this hypothesis has not been proven to be fact, what is certain is that a period of decline began in both kingdoms.

The decline of the last years of Jehoram of Israel had tragic consequences for the dynasty of Omri. The religious conservatives opposed the dynasty because of the willingness of the royal family to promote the worship of Baal. With the rapid economic development fostered by the Omrides, there came discontent because of the social and economic stratification in the kingdom. With wealth and power in the hands of a few, the many were ready for revolution. The revolution that came was another military *coup.*

3. Revolution and Its Aftermath (842–786). The revolution that put Jehu (842–814) on the throne of Israel was the most bloody in the history of the N kingdom. Jehu assassinated Jehoram and executed every other member of the royal family that he could find. In doing so he destroyed the political connections with Tyre and Judah that were the basis of Israel's prosperity (Miller 1967b). This left Jehu to face the Arameans alone. Fortunately for Israel, the neo-Assyrian empire under Shalmaneser III began pressuring the Arameans. When the Assyrians made their appearance in Aram, Jehu rushed to present himself to Shalmaneser to make his obeisance and offer his tribute as a loyal vassal (*ANET,* 281).

Because of Jehu's submission to Assyria, Israel was free from Aramean harassment for a short time, but the Assyrians could not remain in the region for long. This gave Hazael, king of Aram, a free hand to deal with Israel. He seized all Israel's territories in Transjordan. There was no improvement upon the accession of Jehu's son Jehoahaz (815–801). Hazael led a march through the N kingdom on his way to Judah. He thoroughly subjected the Israelite army. Eventually Assyria reasserted its domination of Aram. With the arrival of Adad Nirari III in Damascus in 806 (*ANET,* 281), Israel was free from the Aramean pressure.

Judah too felt the effects of Jehu's revolution. Ahaziah, king of Judah (842), happened to be visiting in Jezreel when Jehu began his purge. He met the same fate as Jehoram (2 Kgs 9:27–28). Athaliah (842–837), Ahaziah's mother, seized power in Judah upon his death. To secure her position she tried to kill the male heirs of the Davidic house. Only one of her grandsons, Joash, managed to escape (1 Kgs 11:1–3). Athaliah was the only ruler of the S kingdom who was not a descendant of David. She aroused opposition from the priests of Jerusalem, and Jehoiada, one of these priests, led a *coup* against her. Athaliah was assassinated and Joash (837–800) came to the throne (2 Kgs 11:4–20).

It is intimated (2 Chronicles 24) that Joash had a falling out with the priests who were his principal supporters. Their opposition may have led to his assassination (2 Kgs 12:20–21). His son Amaziah (800–783) succeeded him. At this time Aram was in a period of decline and this freed Amaziah to retake Edom. Buoyed by his success in the S, he fought the N kingdom for dominance in the region. Israel's new king, Joash (also known as Jehoash 801–876) defeated Amaziah (2 Kgs 14:13–14). This war sealed the separation between Israel and Judah. After the latter's utter defeat, there was no real hope of reuniting the two kingdoms. The defeat also sealed Amaziah's doom. He was assassinated—the third ruler of Judah in succession to die this way (2 Kgs 14:19). Ironically the aftermath of this war ushered in a period of peace and prosperity for both kingdoms.

4. Period of Prosperity (786–746). The rejuvenation of the N kingdom that began with Joash reached its apex during the forty-year reign of Jeroboam II (786–721). Both Joash and Jeroboam were able rulers and their combined 56 years on the throne were a time of territorial expansion and economic success. Israel so dominated the

Arameans that Jeroboam eventually annexed Aram to his kingdom. The Bible features military success of the N kingdom (2 Kgs 13:7, 25; 14:23–29) while excavations at sites such as Samaria and Megiddo reveal its economic prosperity. Amos condemned the darker side of the wealth that the few in Jeroboam's kingdom enjoyed at the expense of the poor. Hosea added his voice to these critiques and put special emphasis on the popularity of Baal worship in the N kingdom. The façade of peace and prosperity did not blind the prophets to the social and religious disintegration that was to be the undoing of the N kingdom.

Though largely ignored by the Deuteronomist, the reign of Uzziah in the S (783–742) was just as successful as that of Jeroboam II in the N. The Chronicler provides a more complete picture of a most prosperous period in Judah's history. Uzziah reorganized Judah's army and led it on several successful campaigns. His victory over the Arabs in the SE (2 Kgs 14:22; 2 Chr 26:2–15) opened the Negeb to intensive agricultural settlement as revealed by archaeology. There is no prophetic commentary on Uzziah's reign, but he did have problems with priests. The Bible attributes Uzziah's leprosy to his attempt to get some priestly prerogatives for himself (2 Chr 26:16–21). Jotham (742–735) acted as regent for his father during his illness and succeeded upon his death. Jotham continued Uzziah's policies and enjoyed similar success.

5. Fall of Israel (746–721). Following the death of Jeroboam II, anarchy reigned in the N kingdom. Zechariah (746–745), Jeroboam's son and the last of Jehu's dynasty, was assassinated after only six months on the throne. Shallum (745) who replaced him ruled for only one month before Menahem (745–738) deposed him. Menahem became a vassal of the Assyrians who required that he pay a heavy tribute to keep his throne (2 Kgs 15:19–20). His son Pekahiah (738–737) continued the policy of submitting to the Assyrians. This led to his assassination by Pekah, one of his military advisors who wanted to rebel against Assyria. After taking the throne of Israel, Pekah put aside old animosities and joined Aram in an anti-Assyrian coalition. They tried to enlist Judah but failed. The coalition collapsed before Assyrian military power. The Assyrians reduced Israel to a rump state ruled by Hoshea (732–724) who assassinated Pekah.

The rulers of Judah handled the Assyrian presence in the region more adroitly than the kings of Israel. Ahaz (735–715) refused to join the anti-Assyrian coalition (Oded 1972). When Pekah tried to depose him, Ahaz sought support from the Assyrians despite Isaiah's advice to the contrary (Isa 7:1–9). Both the Philistines and the Edomites began to exert additional pressure on Judah. Matters go so bad that Ahaz sacrificed his son in an attempt to avoid imminent disaster (2 Kgs 16:3). He also introduced non-Israelite forms of worship in the temple to secure his rule by any means available (2 Kgs 16:10–17).

Unfortunately for Israel, Hoshea did not remain a compliant vassal to Assyria as did Ahaz. Upon hearing of Tiglath-Pileser's death in 724, Hoshea began negotiations with Egypt to secure its support for a revolt against Assyria. When Hoshea made his move, Shalmaneser V, the new Assyrian monarch, easily swept Israel's army aside. After a three year siege, the Assyrians destroyed Samaria, incorporated what remained of the N kingdom into the Assyrian provincial system, and exiled many of Israel's leading citizens (Oded 1970). By 721, the Kingdom of Israel ceased to exist as an independent nation.

The Assyrians rebuilt Samaria and made it the capital of one of their provinces. They absorbed the remnants of the Israelite army into their own. They also repopulated the territory of the former N kingdom with foreigners after deporting a portion of the native population though most of Israel's population remained in their land (Otzen 1979). Because of later conflicts with the people of the Samaria, the Jews of the postexilic period refused to consider the Samaritans as legitimate Israelites because of the intermarriages that took place between the remnants of the native Israelite population and the foreigners introduced by the Assyrians (Coggins 1975).

F. Final Years of Judah (715–687)

1. Judah and the Neo-Assyrian Empire. In view of Israel's fate, the policy of Hezekiah (715–687) toward Assyria seems like folly. He reversed the pro-Assyrian policy of his father Ahaz and began plotting with the Philistines, Egyptians, and Babylonians against Assyria. He prepared for the revolt by strengthening Jerusalem's fortifications and securing its supply of water (2 Kgs 20:20; *ANET,* 321; Broshi 1974). He wrote to the Israelites in the Assyrian provinces of Megiddo and Samaria for support (2 Chr 30:1). Hezekiah signaled his intention to rebel by removing all Assyrian appurtenances from the temple. This led the Deuteronomist to present him as a religious reformer (2 Kgs 20:1–7; Rowley 1962; Ackroyd 1984).

The Assyrians marched through Syria-Palestine in 701. They captured 46 cities in Judah before they began their siege of Jerusalem (*ANET,* 287). At first Isaiah opposed Hezekiah's plans (Isa 31:1–3), but once the siege of Jerusalem was under way the prophet tried to lift the spirits of the city (Isa 10:24–34). Though Jerusalem's fall appeared to be imminent, the Assyrians inexplicably broke off their siege. This led to the belief that Jerusalem was impregnable. Though Jerusalem did not fall to Assyria, Judah had to pay an increased tribute, the kingdom suffered the loss of some territory, and Hezekiah had to swear allegiance to Assyria (2 Kgs 18:14). Isaiah described the outcome of Hezekiah's rebellion as the desolation of Judah (Isa 1:7–9; Cogan 1974).

Judah retained its nominal independence throughout the long reign of Hezekiah's son, Manasseh (687–642). He had little choice but to be a compliant vassal, for Assyria's power was at its height in the early part of the 7th century. The Deuteronomist portrays Manasseh's reign as the darkest in the history of the monarchy because of the non-Israelite cults that flourished in Jerusalem during his reign (2 Kgs 21:1–18; McKay 1973). The Chronicler paints a different picture of Manasseh. Second Chronicles describes a presumed exile of Manasseh to Babylon where purportedly he repented (33:10–13). Attempts have been made to associate this text with an anti-Assyrian rebellion in which Manasseh supposedly participated. It is more likely that the tradition about Manasseh's conversion is legendary. It is unlikely that he ever swayed from his subservience to Assyria (Nielsen 1967).

Manasseh's successors did not enjoy long and peaceful reigns like his. Of the last six Davidic rulers one was assassinated, two died during wartime, and two died in exile. Manasseh's immediate successor, Amon (642–640) died during a *coup* led by anti-Assyrian elements at court. The conspirators were themselves executed by the "people of the land" who placed Amon's eight-year-old son Josiah on the throne (2 Kgs 21:19–26; Malamat 1953; for the role of the "people of the land" see Soggin 1963; Talmon 1967; de Vaux 1964; see also AM HAʾAREZ).

2. Reign of Josiah (640–609). Josiah is the hero of the Deuteronomist who portrays him as a great religious reformer inspired and guided by the "Book of the Law" (2 Kings 22–23). Josiah's program was less a religious reform than a cultural revolution or an effort at national liberation (Lohfink 1977; Weinfeld 1964). The Assyrian empire was disintegrating and Josiah recognized that its hegemony in Syria-Palestine was ending. He had dreams of restoring the old Davidic empire (2 Kgs 23:15–20). His emphasis on the centrality of Jerusalem (2 Kgs 23:21–23) had as its purpose to secure the people's commitment to the dynasty and his political program in the struggle that was ahead.

Josiah's plans ended with his death in 609. He fell at Megiddo while leading the army of Judah against the Egyptians who were trying to prop up a tottering Assyria as a buffer against the emerging Babylonian empire. Josiah saw that it was to his benefit to support Babylon though he should have been content to sit on the sidelines while the great powers settled matters between themselves. With Josiah's death, Judah began an inexorable slide to its destruction as a political entity (Malamat 1955; 1973). In less than 25 years, the Judean state and Davidic dynasty were no more.

Josiah's defeat at Megiddo meant that Judah had to trade masters. It fell under Egyptian hegemony. The pharaoh Neco's first act was to depose Josiah's son Jehoahaz (also known as Shallum, 609) whom the "people of the land" placed on the throne because he wanted to pursue the anti-Egyptian policy of his father. The pharaoh took Jehoahaz prisoner and made his brother Eliakim king with the throne-name Jehoiakim (609–598). Jehoiakim had no choice but to be subservient to Egypt.

3. Judah and the Neo-Babylonian Empire. Judah's destiny passed into Babylonian hands when Nebuchadnezzar defeated Egypt at the battle of Carchemish in 605. Jehoiakim accepted his new master, but four years later he foolishly rebelled (2 Kgs 25:1–2). The Babylonians moved against Jerusalem in 598. Jehoiakim died at the outset of the siege (2 Kgs 25:6). Jeremiah implies that Jehoiakim was assassinated (Jer 22:18–19); but Jer 36:30 and 2 Chr 36:6 assert that he was exiled to Babylon. Jehoiachin (also known as Jeconiah and Coniah 598–597) succeeded his father and surrendered to Nebuchadnezzar after three months. The king, his family, and many leading citizens went to Babylon as prisoners following the surrender of Jerusalem in 597.

Nebuchadnezzar allowed Judah to retain nominal independence. He chose Mattaniah, the third of Josiah's sons to succeed the exiled Jehoiachin as king of Judah. The Babylonians gave him the throne-name Zedekiah (2 Kgs 25:17). Zedekiah (597–587) was unable to deal with the conflicts among his people on how to react to the Babylonian hegemony over Judah. What finally tipped the scales in favor of a second rebellion was the visit of Pharaoh Psammetichus II to Judah in 591. The pharaoh promised to support any rebellion against Babylon. Ezekiel 17 alludes to these negotiations (Greenberg 1957). When Egypt provoked Babylon by invading Phoenicia, Zedekiah withheld his tribute from Nebuchadnezzar.

The Babylonian reaction was swift. Zedekiah soon realized that his rebellion was going to fail so he fled from Jerusalem. The Babylonians captured him near Jericho and led him to exile (2 Kgs 25:5–7). The Babylonians entered Jerusalem, destroyed the temple and palace, and razed a large portion of the city. They executed representatives of the various strata of Judahite society and led the rest of Judah's leadership class into exile (2 Kgs 25:8–21). The Davidic dynasty ended in 587.

Despite this rebellion Nebuchadnezzar did not annex Judah to Babylon nor repopulate it with foreigners as did the Assyrians in Israel. He appointed an administrator named Gedaliah from the local population (2 Kgs 25:22–24). There is some speculation that the Babylonians appointed Gedaliah as king replacing the exiled Zedekiah. The book of Kings does not mention Gedaliah's title (2 Kgs 25:22)—the title "governor" supplied by some English translations is without textual basis. A military officer from the Davidic family assassinated Gedaliah, his family, and his Babylonian guards (2 Kgs 25:25–26; Jer 40:13–41:3). Fearing reprisals, many Judahites fled to Egypt taking with them a reluctant Jeremiah (Jer 41:17–43:7). Gedaliah's murder prompted a third exile in 581. There are no records of what happened in Judah after this. The DH ends with a reference to Jehoiachin's parole in Babylon in 561 (2 Kgs 25:27–30), but without any explicit statement that Judah or its dynasty had any future. The Davidic dynasty would never rise again (Stern 1975).

Imperial powers ruled Judah directly until the victory of the Maccabees in 164. The Hasmonean and Herodian dynasties then ruled in the territories of the former Israelite kingdoms into the Roman period though many Jews considered both dynasties as usurpers of the rights that properly belonged to the Davidic dynasty (see *Psalms of Solomon* 17). Messianism developed in early Judaism as one way to express hope for the eventual restoration of Davidic rule.

Bibliography

Aberach, M., and Smolar, L. 1969. Jeroboam's Rise to Power. *JBL* 88: 69–72.

Ackroyd, P. R. 1984. The Biblical Interpretation of the Reigns of Ahaz and Hezekiah. Pp. 247–59 in *In the Shelter of Elyon,* ed. W. B. Barrick and J. R. Spencer. Sheffield.

Alt, A. 1966a. The Monarchy in the Kingdoms of Israel and Judah. Pp. 239–59 in *Essays on Old Testament History and Religion.* Oxford.

———. 1966b. The Settlement of the Israelites in Palestine. Pp. 135–69 in *Essays on Old Testament History and Religion.* Oxford.

Birch, B. C. 1976. *The Rise of the Israelite Monarchy.* SBLDS 27. Missoula, MT.

Bright, J. 1972. *A History of Israel.* 2d ed. Philadelphia.

Broshi, M. 1974. The Expansion of Jerusalem in the Reigns of Hezekiah and Manasseh. *IEJ* 24: 21–26.

Busink, T. A. 1970. *Der Tempel von Jerusalem.* Leiden.

Campbell, A. F. 1975. *The Ark Narrative.* SBLDS 16. Missoula, MT.
———. 1986. *Of Prophets and Kings.* CBQMS 17. Washington D.C.
Carlson, R. A. 1964. *David, the Chosen King.* Stockholm.
Cogan, M. 1974. *Imperialism and Religion.* Missoula, MT.
Coggins, R. J. 1975. *Samaritans and Jews.* Atlanta.
Freedman, D. N., and Graf, D. F. 1983. *Palestine in Transition.* Sheffield.
Gerbrandt, G. E. 1986. *Kingship According to the Deuteronomistic History.* SBLDS 87. Atlanta.
Gottwald, N. K. 1979. *The Tribes of Yahweh.* Maryknoll, NY.
Greenberg, M. 1957. Ezekiel 17 and the Policy of Psammetichus II. *JBL* 76: 304–9.
Halpern, B. 1981. *The Constitution of the Monarchy in Israel.* HSM 25. Chico, CA.
———. 1983. *The Emergence of Israel in Canaan.* SBLMS 29. Chico, CA.
Hennessy, J. B. 1970. Excavations at Samaria-Sebaste. *Levant* 2: 1–21.
Johnson, A. R. 1967. *Sacral Kingship in Ancient Israel.* 2d ed. Cardiff.
Kenik, H. A. 1983. *Design for Kingship.* SBLDS 69. Chico, CA.
Kenyon, K. 1964. Megiddo, Hazor, Samaria and Chronology. *Bulletin of the Institute of Archaeology* 4: 143–56.
———. 1971. *Royal Cities of the Old Testament.* New York.
King, P. 1988. *Amos, Hosea, Micah.* Philadelphia.
Klein, R. W. 1970. Jeroboam's Rise to Power. *JBL* 89: 217–18.
Lohfink, N. 1977. Culture Shock and Theology. *Biblical Theological Bulletin* 7: 12–21.
Malamat, A. 1953. The Historical Background of the Assassination of Amon King of Judah. *IEJ* 3: 26–29.
———. 1955. The Twilight of Judah: In the Egyptian-Babylonian Maelstrom. *VTSup* 28: 123–45.
———. 1973. Josiah's Bid for Armageddon. *JANES* 5: 267–78.
Mazar, B. 1957. The Campaign of Pharaoh Shishak to Palestine. *VTSup* 4: 57–66.
McKay, J. 1973. *Religion in Judah Under the Assyrians.* London.
Mendelsohn, I. 1962. On Corvée Labor in Ancient Canaan and Israel. *BASOR* 167: 31–35.
Mendenhall, G. E. 1962. The Hebrew Conquest of Palestine. *BAR* 2: 100–20.
Mettinger, T. N. D. 1971. *Solomonic State Officials.* Lund.
Miller, J. M. 1967a. Another Look at the Chronology of the Early Divided Monarchy. *JBL* 86: 276–88.
———. 1967b. The Fall of the House of Arab. *VT* 17: 307–24.
Nielsen, E. 1967. Political Conditions and Cultural Developments in Israel and Judah During the Reign of Manasseh. *PWCJS* 1: 103–6.
Oded, B. 1970. *Mass Deportations and Deportees in the Neo-Assyrian Empire.* Wiesbaden.
———. 1972. The Historical Background of the Syro-Ephraimite War Reconsidered. *CBQ* 34: 153–65.
Otzen, B. 1979. Israel Under the Assyrians. Pp. 251–61 in *Power and Propaganda,* ed. M. T. Larsen. Copenhagen.
Parrot, A. 1957. *The Temple of Jerusalem.* London.
Redford, D. B. 1972. Studies in Relations Between Palestine and Egypt During the First Millennium B.C.: I The Taxation System of Solomon. Pp. 141–56 in *Studies on the Ancient Palestinian World,* ed. D. B. Redford and J. W. Wevers. Toronto.
Rost, L. 1982. *The Succession to the Throne of David.* Sheffield.
Rowley, H. H. 1962. Hezekiah's Reform and Rebellion. *BJRL* 44: 395–431.
Shiloh, Y. 1986. A Group of Hebrew Bullae from the City of David. *IEJ* 36: 16–38.
Soggin, J. A. 1963. Der judäische ʿam-ha-ʾares und das Köningtum in Juda. *VT* 13: 187–96.
Stern, E. 1975. Israel at the Close of the Monarchy. *BA* 38: 26–54.
Talmon, S. 1967. The Judean ʿam-haʾares in Historical Perspective. *PWCJS* 1: 71–76.
Thiele, E. 1984. *The Mysterious Numbers of the Hebrew Kings.* Rev. ed. Grand Rapids, MI.
Timm, H. 1966. Die Ladeerzählung (1 Sam 4–6; 2 Sam 6) und das Kerygma des deuteronomistischen Geschichtswerk. *EvT* 29: 509–26.
———. 1982. *Die Dynastie Omri.* Göttingen.
Vaux, R., de. 1964. Les sens de L'expression 'peuple du pays' dans l'Ancien Testament et le role politique du peuple en Israël. *RA* 63: 167–72.
Weinfeld, M. 1964. Cult Centralization in Israel in the Light of a Neo-Babylonian Analogy. *JNES* 23: 202–12.
Weippert, M. 1971. *The Settlement of the Israelite Tribes in Palestine.* SBT n.s. 21. London.
Weiser, A. 1966. Die Legitimation des Königs David. *VT* 16: 325–54.
Whiteley, C. F. 1952. The Deuteronomic Presentation of the House of Omri. *VT* 2: 137–52.
Wifall, W. R. 1968. The Chronology of the Divided Monarchy of Israel. *ZAW* 80: 319–37.

LESLIE J. HOPPE

POST-MONARCHIC PERIOD

Coming out of what historians call the ages of confusion in the ANE (see Roberts 1980: 118–30) the story of ancient Israel is an obscure one. Little reliable historical data is available for historians to utilize with confidence. Apart from retellings of biblical stories—so-called histories of Israel—and hints gleaned from imperial annals, little may be asserted with any certitude about the relation of the Hebrew Bible to history. This state of affairs is especially true of the period between Cyrus of Pasargadae and Alexander of Macedon when Indo-European hegemony dominated the Near East (ca. 500–332 B.C.E.). The Persian period, as it may be called, was the first stage in the seven-centuries-long gestation period of what may now be regarded as the roots and origins of (orthodox) Judaism. Between the Babylonian destruction of the first Jerusalem temple (587/6 B.C.E.) and the Roman destruction of the second Jerusalem temple (70 C.E.) were created the formative elements of Judaism as a major religious system. These two demolitions focus attention on the centrality of the Jerusalem temple for the period and emphasize the importance of outside imperial powers in determining the shape of Jewish religion. Transformed by Babylonian and Persian influences, the fragments of Israelite religion which survived the devastations of land and culture were transfigured into a series of sectarian and diffused religious communities which dominated the period and provide what little we know about the early stages of the Second Temple era.

A. Interpretive Ground Rules
   1. Ideological Control
   2. Obscurity of Data
   3. Tentativeness of Scholarly Opinion

A. Interpretive Ground Rules

1. Ideological Control. The problems of data and interpretation for the Persian period are such that it is necessary to delineate the limited terms of reference for handling the available biblical sources. Throughout the Hebrew Bible there is a tendency, which is virtually a principle, for the writers to retroject their material into the distant past. This is obvious in the Pentateuch and the Deuteronomistic History; but it is hardly less obvious in the collection of the prophetic texts which are prefaced by colophons placing them in a past determined by the DH (e.g., Isa 1:1; Jer 1:1–3; Amos 1:1; Hos 1:1). Setting the books in the past helps to conceal period and place of authorship as well as authorship itself. Attention is directed toward the text and not to the conditions or context of its production. If this artifice of concealment is also to be found in the writings set in the early Second Temple period, then it would be wise to read the literature traditionally assigned to that period as coming perhaps from a somewhat later time. This would help to explain the confusion of data and detail which abound in the books of Haggai, Zechariah, Isaiah 40–66, Ezra-Nehemiah, and Chronicles. It would acknowledge an ideology of concealment in the Second Temple period and alert the historian to the need to explain such constructions. James Joyce's character Stephen Dedalus talked about "silence, exile, and cunning," and an exploration of the literature of the Second Temple period, especially during the Persian era, would do well to keep those three elements of silence, exile, and cunning to the fore in analyzing this obscure period of the production of biblical texts. In the absence of reliable evidence for reconstructing the history of the period, the literature set in this period may not be the most reliable guide for a historical analysis; historical accuracy cannot be assumed in the absence of data to the contrary. Subtler forms of literary and ideological investigation are required to provide a properly historical account of the matter. Even then, hypothetical reconstructions of scholars will not necessarily bear much resemblance to actual events in the past. This acknowledgment of ignorance and, more importantly, of the consequences of such ignorance must be a fundamental ground rule for investigating the Persian period.

2. Obscurity of Data. If the ideological control of literature is an important datum of this period, the obscurity of the available data should also be recognized. Information is eclipsed by ignorance and obscurity, which makes every historical account of the period open to serious debate. It is easy enough to amalgamate a number of elements drawn from each literary source and so to form an idealized picture of the Jewish community in and around the Jerusalem of the 5th and 4th centuries. However, the sources really do not permit such a selective production. They are confused ideological constructs which often telescope characters and events (see Blenkinsopp *Ezra* OTL, 41–47) and which to some extent must be regarded as sectarian documents attempting to present a particular picture of the "past" as a legitimation of the present (i.e., the present of the writer). The interpretation of documents is far from straightforward and the nature of the documents is not easily determined. In the case of the Ezra-Nehemiah, Chronicles corpus (whether all from one or multiple authors) the very textuality of Ezra-Nehemiah (what Eskenazi happily called "the perpetuation of documents" [1988: 87]) puts the historian in a quandary about what textuality may indicate regarding the production of that strange work (there really is nothing else like Ezra-Nehemiah in the Hebrew Bible). Thus, the amalgamation approach is unacceptable because it only results in a form of "rationalizing paraphrase" of texts long recognized to be themselves partisan constructs of ideological groups in conflict with other groups.

While the texts presented as reflecting the Persian period may well be indispensable sources for our knowledge of the period (see Blenkinsopp *Ezra* OTL, 38 with reference to Ezra-Nehemiah), it is a compromised indispensability which they possess and one which undermines their reliability as historical resources. The precise amount of weight the historian should allow to this evidence is difficult to judge, but to ignore these inherent difficulties is to participate in the ideological distortion of the material rather than to practice historical reconstruction.

3. Tentativeness of Conclusions. Having acknowledged the difficulties of reconstructing the history of the Jewish communities in the Persian period, it becomes necessary to recognize that all accounts of the period and each scholar's account of it are open to question. It is also very important to avoid the tendency in biblical scholarship to equate textual exegesis with history. Repeating what is to be found in texts is not history writing. We lack the necessary extra-textual information to move from exegesis to historiography. Material remains of the period (as analyzed in Stern 1982) are remarkably uninformative in relation to biblical texts. Furthermore, archaeological data require interpretation and contextualization, so they cannot simply be assumed to bear on a specific text (just because the writer brings the two into conjunction). The many technical and substantive issues involved here cannot as yet be handled within biblical scholarship, which lacks a sound methodology for dealing with these matters. A properly theoretical account of how best to read the literature of the Second Temple period remains to be developed. In the absence of such important requirements, any attempt at delineating the history of the period is more likely to become an outline of the contents of the various pieces of literature associated with the period. There are too many serious gaps in our knowledge and the textual sources are too obscure, as well as ideologically compromised, adequately to write the history of the Persian period. See also PERSIAN EMPIRE. Therefore, this discussion must be regarded as a mere sketch of the main features of the period, which indicates areas where scholars struggle with the method and data available to write a history of the Persian era in relation to the different Jewish communities which developed then.

B. The Period

1. Major Influences. The facts and relevant data have been rehearsed many times in the standard "History of Israel" volumes, which may be referred to for details and discussions of the most important issues (see especially *CHJ* 1; Widengren *IHJ* 489–538; *HAIJ,* 438–75; and particularly cognizant of the difficulties of writing the history of this period is Lemche 1988: 173–96). See also PALESTINE, PERSIAN ADMINISTRATION; EZRA-NEHEMIAH, BOOKS OF; and CHRONICLES, BOOK OF 1–2. The hegemony of the neo-Babylonian empire under the leadership of Nebuchadnezzar and his family, a relatively short-lived empire (ca. 605–539), was brought to an end by the emergent Persian imperium under the leadership of Cyrus II of Pasargadae. In the space of a decade, Cyrus had conquered Media, Lydia, and Babylonia, and in 539 the city of Babylon fell to Gobryas "without a battle" (see the pro-Persian report cited in *HAIJ,* 439). Under neo-Babylonian domination the city of Jerusalem and the state of Judah had been devastated, the temple of the god Yahweh demolished, and some leading citizens deported to Babylonia (others had fled to Egypt). In an ideologically constructed account 2 Kings 17 posits a similar fate for the state of Israel in the 8th century at the hands of the Assyrians. With the Babylonian deportation of powerful families and the collapse of what remained of the Judean state (already a puppet state of the Egyptians until the emergence of the Babylonian power), the roots of what later became Jewish and Christian communities began to grow. For more than the next two-and-a-half millennia the Jewish communities would flourish more outside the region of Palestine than they would inside it. This diasporic nature of the community would be one of its most enduring qualities and must be traced to the 6th century and afterwards.

Babylonian and Persian (Iranian) influences would shape these communities and provide a cross-fertilization of religious, ideological, and social structures which would determine the matrix out of which came Jewish sectarian religion. A third major influence would be Egypt where refugee groups of Jews spread throughout the land after fleeing from the invading imperial powers. The two great areas of influence, Babylonia and Egypt, were embodied in the foundational myths of the communities as stories about Abraham (Babylonia) and Moses (Egypt).

The Jews of Egypt and the Jews of Babylon told different stories but both stories have been incorporated into the Hebrew Bible in terms of the story of the Jews of Jerusalem (see Garbini 1988: 133–50). From the province of Judah/Judaea comes the epithet "Jew" (Heb *yĕhûd*) which describes the people who lived there and gave their allegiance to Jerusalem; yet the term is used indiscriminately of communities in Babylonia, Persia, and Egypt. A careful scrutiny must, therefore, be made of all the literature in order to allow for the ideological nature of the terms of reference which reflect the Jerusalem/Judaea center of influence. At the same time, note that the term "Jew" in this period was on the way to becoming a marker of religious ideology and practice, i.e., identity, and not simply an indicator of geophysical origin. In the Second Temple period groups in Egypt, Babylonia, Persia, and Palestine ("the holy land" as it came to be called in the literature of this period) developed many different strategies of religious affiliation which have tended to be lumped together by subsequent writers as if there had been a uniformity of ideology, praxis, and identity throughout the period. The extant literature of the period, including Qumran, the apocalypses, and early Christian literature, reveals a wide diversity of beliefs and practices. Terms derived from conciliar Christianity and the period of the Talmuds attempted to impose a false uniformity on what were many and diverse groups.

According to Stern (1982: 229), the Babylonian destruction of Jerusalem had little effect on the culture of the Israelite period. Life continued as before and changes only began to appear with the emergence of the Persian hegemony. From a regional perspective, the collapse of the Jerusalem economy and the concomitant defeat of whatever state apparatus Judah possessed were not major features of the 6th century. Yet from the perspective of the Hebrew Bible the destruction of Jerusalem was a people-endangering catastrophe and the subsequent deportation of the leading citizens to Babylonia was a veritable emptying of the land. The contrast between the story of the material remains of the larger geophysical area and the ideological writings of a certain social stratum of the smaller territory is striking. In much of these writings the deportees are represented as superior to the people of the land who were not deported to Babylonia (e.g., Jer 24:29), and a good deal of the writing appears to support an ideology of control over the land on behalf of the deported group. The phrases "people of the land" (Heb *ʿam hāʾāreṣ*) and "people of the exile" (Heb *ʿam haggôlâ;* sometimes *bĕnê haggôlâ*) in the literature related to the period would appear to reflect an ideology of conflict, with special claims to status and land being made on behalf of the deported party. This claim to the land is one of the most fundamental features of the Second Temple period and is the basis of many of the foundational stories in Genesis 12–50 and the Tetrateuch (or the Pentateuch and the Deuteronomistic History as some classifiers would label what is traditionally known as the Torah and the Former Prophets). Temple and land are the key concepts in the development of the Persian period and tend to subsume most of the literature of that time (including such books as Isaiah, Jeremiah, and Ezekiel which may owe their present form to the Greek period). That means the literature must be read primarily in ideological terms rather than in modern historical terms, though historical elements in the texts are not ruled out by this judgment. The myth of "the empty land" (2 Chr 36:21) is a good example of the difference between reading literature as ideology and reading it as history. At this juncture in history the land lost some people; very much a minority of people, even important people of status were deported. Most people lived on in the land as if nothing, except the burning of Jerusalem, had happened. But from an ideological point of view, the few who were deported were the cream of society and the nucleus of the future. The Persian party represented in the literature of Ezra-Nehemiah as the exiles (or the descendants of the original deportees) returned from Babylonia in order to occupy the "empty land" and to claim it as their divinely appointed territory.

Much of what constitutes the Hebrew Bible is the myth of this claim—how much is a matter for debate.

Where ideology is concerned history has a habit of being subverted. The Babylonian control of the Judaean territory by the deportation of some of its leading citizens and powerful interests became the legitimation of a party takeover bid in the Persian period. Denunciations of the Jerusalem elite which appear in Jeremiah and Ezekiel have become, with time, justifications of a later foreign group's claim to control the Jerusalem economy and cult. The biblical literature primarily must be read from an ideological viewpoint and only secondarily from a historical perspective. The two are to some extent mingled (rather like a double helix) but the ideological predominates and determines how the history is read. Thus conventional biblical scholarship generally treats the Persian period under the terms "exile" and "restoration" (e.g., Ackroyd 1968; *BHI*); hence the traditional markers pre- and postexilic. The ideological perspective of the texts colors the attempt of modern scholarship to be historical. See, for example, Jer 24:29 where the deported citizens are treated as noble and good in contrast to the rubbish which inhabits Jerusalem (cf. Ezek 11:14–21). Similar attitudes may be found in the Ezra-Nehemiah corpus where the incoming foreigners impose their values and ideology on the people of Jerusalem. These key factors of ideology, conflict, and partisanship constitute the essence of the sectarianism which dominates the literature of the period. Thus sectarianism is the ideological key to understanding the whole period of the Second Temple and it must be regarded as having had its origins in the Persian period.

According to Haggai, Zechariah, and Ezra-Nehemiah the (re)building of the temple in Jerusalem was the primary activity of the period immediately following the defeat of the Babylonians. Sheshbazzar and Zerubbabel are variously credited with the operation of rebuilding the temple and scholars differ in their attempts to reconcile the problems caused by this information (cf. Ackroyd *CHJ* 1: 136–43). Rationalization of awkward data is a standard procedure in biblical scholarship and tends to reflect particular ideological commitments within the guild. Whatever the facts may have been in the matter of the temple, it is clear from the biblical literature that claims about reestablishing the temple cult were an important aspect of constructing the story of the Persian period. The temple was the center of economic, ideological, and religious control in the community and control of it gave immense power in the province to the party which could acquire and maintain that control. It is impossible to determine whether the rebuilding of the temple actually took place between 539 and 516 (the dates deduced from the biblical literature) or whether these dates reflect an ideological presentation of the rebuilt temple coinciding with the new (Persian) era to legitimate the party in control of the temple whenever the documents were written. In spite of the tendency of scholars to accept the text at face value it should be noted that it is characteristic of the biblical literature to retroject "facts" into the past.

2. Spheres of Activity. The fortunes of the various communities in Babylonia, Egypt, and Palestine are not easy to reconstruct for the Persian period. Material remains give little particular information and the general picture they afford of social life in the era is sketchy in the extreme. Aramaic papyri, parchments and ostraca from Egypt, especially from the border posts of Syene and its adjacent island of Elephantine, give some idea of life in a Jewish colony during the 5th century B.C.E. (see *ArchEleph; CHJ* 1: 376–400). The colony was a socio-military one under the command of Persians and the documentation from there reflects legal and contractual features of life in a Persian outpost. The presence of a temple of the god *YWH* there has surprised many biblical and Jewish scholars, but only because the Hebrew scriptures espouse the centrality of Yahwism in Jerusalem. Elephantine indicates that other shrines to the god Yahweh flourished and it may well be the case that Deuteronomistic ideology was only enforceable among the Jews of Jerusalem in the Second Temple period. So little is known about the social circumstances of the diasporic communities outside Palestine that, as with the perception of the Babylonian depopulation of the land, it is difficult to state what was normative and what otherwise. The religion of the cult in Elephantine suggests that the god Yahweh had a female consort (Anath), which reflects the normal type of Semitic religion in the ANE as opposed to the special ideology of Yahweh-alone religion constructed by the deuteronomists for the Jerusalem cult (see Smith 1971). Opposition to the Jewish communities in Egypt from Palestinian Jews (Jeremiah 44) may indicate social and political conflicts as well as ideological differences which developed in the Persian era. However, too much hard data should not be extrapolated from rare and isolated sources which are themselves open to various and disputed interpretations.

We know from much later periods that Jewish communities in Egypt (Alexandria) and Babylonia were important centers of Jewish religion and it is a reasonable assumption that the roots of these communities were put down in the Persian period. But documents which purport to be about that period only obscurely convey the information: e.g., in Jer 29:4–7, a letter attributed to the prophet Jeremiah, the image is presented of a free society in which Jews own land and may flourish as a community. This may well be an accurate depiction of the Jews of Babylon—but of what century? Can the letter really be dated to the period *immediately* after the deportation of 597? The chapter in Jeremiah where it appears is a complex and highly edited piece of writing which reflects ideological conflicts between the Jews of Babylon and the Jews of Jerusalem. What do they represent and what period do they reflect? The scholarly tendency to read the chapter at face value is bad exegesis and leads inevitably to misprisions of the text. But without controls on the text or extra-textual information the historian is forced back on exegesis and ceases to be a historian (the central problems of the literature of the period will be dealt with in the next section).

The exceptional wealth of written source material for the Persian period in Babylonian history affords much information on administrative, legal, and domestic affairs in the province (Dandamayev *CHJ* 1: 330–42). Because Babylonia was one of the richest satrapies of the Persian empire it may be assumed that communities living there had ample opportunities for material development and the Jews there must have shared in this affluence. This is a reasonable assumption made in the absence of concrete evidence.

Jewish names appear in the documents (cuneiform tablets) from the archives of the business houses of Murashu found at Nippur and dated to the second half of the 5th century (Bickerman *CJH* 1: 344–48). The house of Murashu managed land property and acted as agents for the maintenance of the crown land by controlling tenure and collecting rents and taxes. Jews in the region of Nippur held land or military fiefs and could mortgage their land to the house of Murashu, renting it back under yearly terms. These Murashu archives depict a range of activities which included Jewish participants and thus a sketchy picture of Jewish life in Babylonia emerges from a careful scrutiny of the documents. Jews could become agents of the Persian government or could manage the canals which were the center of the great Babylonian irrigation economy. Some Jews named their sons *Shulum-babili* "welfare of Babylon" (a phrase which has echoes in Jer 29:7). There is some evidence that the banking family Egibi was Jewish and this would further indicate an integration of the Babylonian Jews into the structures of the administration of the Persian satrapy of Babylonia (Baron 1952: 109; Garbini 1988: 92, 192–93). Fictional aspects of this interpretation may be found in the books of Daniel, Esther, and Tobit. At the other end of the social spectrum the Murashu documents refer to a small number of Jewish slaves.

According to Ezra-Nehemiah the reconstruction of Jerusalem in the 5th century was undertaken by agents of the Persian authorities who came from the imperial city of Susa (Nehemiah) and from Babylonia (Ezra), and who imposed on the Palestinian community Persian structures. There are enormous difficulties of doing history from this ideological biblical material. In addressing the issue of Ezra's existence, the majority of scholars tend to affirm that he did, while an important minority of scholars says "no" (Blenkinsopp *Ezra* OTL does not debate the question; see also Garbini 1988 and Smith 1971). Commentators on the Ezra-Nehemiah corpus readily recognize the difficulties of the literature and its tendency to stitch events and persons together in a curiously fictional mode and yet without Ezra-Nehemiah there is no account of the reconstruction of Jerusalem. Once more "silence, exile, and cunning" best determine the matter.

Ezra-Nehemiah traces the founding of the Second Temple to the decree of Cyrus which permitted the repatriation of the Jews of Babylonia and the return of some fifty thousand Jews to Jerusalem led by Sheshbazzar with the ancient vessels of the previous Jerusalem temple. The foundations of the temple were subsequently laid in a context of the correct liturgical observances. Throughout the reigns of Darius I, Xerxes, and Artaxerxes, sustained local opposition disrupted the community, though the temple was completed by 516 in the reign of Darius under Zerubbabel and Joshua (see Haggai; Zechariah 1–8). In the time of Artaxerxes (I or II—which is not certain), Ezra the scribe arrived with further repatriates and imposed on the Jerusalem community a Persian injunction to follow traditional laws. Confiscation of land and the breaking up of marriages contracted with the local Palestinian people followed the imposition of Ezra's law with the support of prominent pietistic laymen in the community. At least that is what appears to have happened, but the Ezra text breaks off in mid-sentence and is continued by the story of Nehemiah. By order of the Persian king, Nehemiah made two delegated visits to Jerusalem, assisted in the rebuilding of the wall of Jerusalem, opposed Palestinian involvement in the project, and broke up various marriages of the kind which Ezra had previously broken up. He also imposed strict Sabbath regulations on the work economy of the city (Neh 13:15–22; cf. Jer 17:19–27). There are sufficient similarities between the functions of Ezra and Nehemiah to make the competent reader of the biblical text wonder to what extent they represent the same story told with variations, and to what extent the stories are a patchwork quilt of social and ideological movements of the Second Temple period reflecting dimly discerned historical events. Every writer on the subject offers a different opinion and one of the most dominant views in 20th century biblical scholarship insists on treating Nehemiah's visit to Jerusalem as occurring *before* that of Ezra's. Placing Ezra's visit in 458 (traditional view) or 399 (revised view), with Nehemiah's visit assigned to 445 (with a second visit some years later), avoids having the two working together as appears to be the case in Nehemiah 8, but it must be freely admitted that the corpus abounds in problems which are not easily rationalized.

There are glimpses of a struggling community in and around Jerusalem in parts of Nehemiah which would fit with what little we know about the period from the Murashu documents. Neh 5:1–5 provides a good example of people having mortgaged their land to pay their taxes and complaining about the enslavement of their children and the loss of their property. As Blenkinsopp says of this section, "The traditional agrarian economy was thereby slowly undermined, holdings which had stayed in the same family for generations were enclosed, and we begin to see the emergence of the great estates which flourished during the Hellenistic period" (*Ezra* OTL, 67). This creation of latifundia in the Second Temple period can be found reflected in a number of texts which have been assigned conventionally by biblical scholarship to the wrong period. Thus 1 Kings 21 in its treatment of Naboth's vineyard (cf. what may be the older story of the Naboth murder in 2 Kgs 9:21–26) is more likely a reflection of the 5th–4th centuries than of the 9th–8th centuries (see Rofé 1988b). Also, the standard references to similar practices in Isa 5:8–10 and the so-called 8th century prophets (Isaiah, Micah, Amos, Hosea) should be treated as observations on developments in the Persian and Greek periods. While this view of the matter runs counter to most commentators on these prophets, it seems to be a better account of property relations, especially in the light of Leviticus 25–27, in biblical times than is posited otherwise. It is also a good example of that misdirection in texts which leads to their misprisions. The acquisition and exchange of land in biblical times remains a topic on which little definitive knowledge is as yet available. If the Ezra-Nehemiah corpus contains reliable historical information, then the material in Nehemiah 9 suggests that land was one of the most fundamental issues in the Persian period.

3. From Ezra-Nehemiah to Alexander of Macedon. Practically nothing is known about the period between

Ezra-Nehemiah and the conquest of the Persian empire by Alexander of Macedon as far as the Jewish communities are concerned. The protracted Persian-Egyptian wars, the Tennes rebellion, and other events of the period appear to have left no identifiable impression on any surviving literature. At this point historians often have recourse to Josephus (*Ant* 11) or to Diodorus Siculus (Dio. 16) for incidents in the reign of Artaxerxes III which may have had some bearing on the life of the Jerusalem community (see *IHJ*, 474–75). With the transition of power from Persian authority to the Greeks little changed for the Jewish communities throughout the empire. Time would eventually bring about the Hellenization of some of the communities and this transformation in turn would contribute greatly to the eventual development of later Jerusalem.

C. The Literature

In a very real sense any history of the Persian period must also be a treatment of the Jewish literature of the period because the material remains do not afford sufficient data to construct a proper history. Yet the literary aspects of the Jewish communities in this period are fraught with interpretative difficulties as well as the general principle of misdirected periodization. In conventional biblical scholarship a good deal of the Hebrew Bible is assigned to a production period before the fall of Jerusalem to the Babylonians (e.g., the Yahwist or J writer, the bulk of the DH, the original material in the 8th century prophets) and only the lesser material is thought of as having come from the Persian period. One consequence of this judgment is that the pre-catastrophe period is regarded as the great age of Hebrew literature and religion and the so-called postexilic era as a period of degeneration and poor literary production. This approach to the Hebrew Bible needs a radical rethinking and a complete transformation in the evaluation of literary and religious matters. There are clear signs of such a transformation in current biblical scholarship.

The Hebrew Bible was the product of the Second Temple period, though how much of it was produced in the Persian era cannot be determined. If this literature is to be taken seriously, then its production reflects on the creativity and importance of the Second Temple period as the foundational matrix of the roots of Judaism—matched only, perhaps, by the post-70 C.E. rabbinic period which produced the Talmuds. Elements of the Hebrew Bible may have been produced in writing before the Persian era, but there is no concrete evidence for this presupposition nor is it possible to say which parts existed in writing before the destruction of the temple. It is logical to locate the framing of the various scrolls and the production of the bulk of the biblical books in the period of the Second Temple because one of the most dominant traits of that period is the production of writings which later became scripture for many religious communities. Temple and texts are therefore two of the key elements in the understanding of the period. This period has traditionally taken back seat to the so-called classical ages of religious thought and the great "writing" prophets, which has resulted in little valuable investigation that can help us understand the era. This consistent underevaluation of the Persian and Greek periods skews the whole history of the roots of Judaism and renders much scholarly work irrelevant as an assessment of the productions of the period. A thorough revision of theories about the origins and significant processes of the creation of the Hebrew Bible is urgently required in biblical scholarship, after which it should be possible to reevaluate the true importance of the Second Temple period.

Here it is only possible to note the productions of Genesis and the primary narrative about Israel's origins, the DH and the various writings incorporating anthologies of prophetic material, wisdom sayings and discourses, and the Psalms. What became the Torah (Genesis-Deuteronomy) ends with the death of the greatest of all prophets, Moses, and the DH ends with the death of the last Judean king. An eschatologizing hermeneutic can be detected in the production of Isaiah, Jeremiah (only to a very limited extent), Ezekiel, and the book of the Twelve (prophets). This is especially apparent in the book of the Twelve, in particular in the appendices to Zechariah 1–8 (Zech 9–14; Malachi). No specific date can be given to these productions but the period of the 4th–3d centuries would make sense for the prophetic collections (along with Chronicles, Ezra-Nehemiah, and possibly a good deal of the DH and elements of Torah). Conventional scholarship favors an earlier dating for Torah but mainly because it insists on viewing Ezra's lawbook as some form of the Pentateuch. There is little or no hard evidence for this claim and its only force is as a commonplace of traditional scholarship. Our ignorance of these matters is almost total, and it is part of the problem of reconstructing the history of the Second Temple period that we know next to nothing about how, when, or why these writings were produced. That they were produced is self-evident, but no *reliable* information is available which would take the matter beyond the level of scholarly hypotheses. From Ezra-Nehemiah to the Qumran scrolls we have a family resemblance of the production of scrolls imposing regulations of purity on the community and differentiating between various groups in a fundamentally sectarian way. A key to understanding this phenomenon is the (lay) interpretation of texts, and reflections of this practice are to be found in many of the writings of the period (e.g., Isa 29:9–14; 30:8–14; Jer 36; Dan 9:2).

A brief treatment of the Persian period cannot become an investigation of the production of the Hebrew Bible and the periodization of the Second Temple era into Persian, Greek, and Roman is at best a convention rather than a reflection of substantive differences in the development of the various Jewish communities in the empires. Yet the student of the period ought to be aware of the fact that the biblical books were put together in the Second Temple period and that this process was part of the structural developments which constituted the communities of the time. This makes the presentation of Ezra with his imposition of a document (possibly Iranian) on the Jerusalem community regulating its identity and behavior a very important reflection of the period. And this remains the case whether Ezra is regarded as a historical or a fictional character and whether he is assigned a date in the 5th or 2nd century (see Garbini 1988: 151–69 for this second option). The Temple Scroll of Qumran, the Priestly Writing incorporated into the Pentateuch, Ezekiel 40–48, and other ritual texts indicate various moves to impose regulatory ritual character on the communities of Jews living in the Second Temple period and allow us to characterize the period in terms of its emphasis on ritual purity and identity. Elements of this character are also to be found in the NT Gospels and some of the writings of Paul, thus indicating a continuity of concern with halakic interpretation and ritual prescription throughout the whole period of the Second Temple.

The book of Ezekiel apart, most of the writings which later formed the prophetic collection appear to be less concerned with ritual purity (Haggai and Malachi belong more with the halakic mode) than with ethics and expectations. However, the colophons introducing many of these scrolls suggest that a final stage of the editing made them supplementary to the DH (i.e., to be read in the light of that collection as a kind of *Ergänzungstext*). Later rabbinic understanding of these texts read them as commentary on Torah, but in the Second Temple period it is unknown how they functioned or what relationship they may have had to whatever constituted Torah. Here our ignorance of the period is part of the problem for historical reconstruction. The Qumran texts' use of the prophetic texts (Dan 9:24–27) may represent a common understanding of them in the 2d century which maintained earlier uses of them, but we do not know what was normative and what innovative in the communities of the period. The collections of prophetic texts may have functioned as revitalization movements throughout the period or may have supported oppositional groups in conflict with the urban centers or may even have opposed the cult centers in the name of inspired individuals (see Blenkinsopp 1977 for a very good treatment of the opposition between prophecy and Torah). What is urgently needed in (professional) biblical scholarship is a good theoretical treatment of the prophetic literature which would contextualize it in the period of its production as writing rather than the usual historicist treatment which reads it as the expositions of its colophons.

The production of the literature of the past (which is how most of the biblical literature is presented, cf. the introductions to Proverbs, Qoheleth, Jonah, and especially Ben Sira) in the Second Temple period may reflect a movement to differentiate between past and present in terms of warranting authorities, as well as a concealment of ideological controls on the receiving communities. At the same time such literature facilitated the role of the authoritative (and authorized) interpreter who could lead the community in the correct interpretation of the texts. Nehemiah might be regarded as the classical example of this activity which seems to have bypassed priestly authority on issues of purity and temple regulation (see Smith 1971: 101–2); the "correct/legitimate teacher" of Qumran may be seen as an equivalent interpreter of texts. Here then are to be found the roots of the scriptural interpreter figure so important in the development of post-Second Temple Judaism, one element of which was Christianity.

The problematics of the literature of the Second Temple period are formidable. The Ezra-Nehemiah corpus is complicated by its association with Chronicles. Some scholars identify the Chronicler as the producer of the two works, while a small group of scholars insists that the Chronicler is *not* the author of Ezra-Nehemiah (e.g., Eskenazi 1988; Williamson *Ezra* WBC; Blenkinsopp *Ezra* OTL 47–53, opposes this latter view). The difficulty of determining such issues directly relates to the diversity of evidence deemed relevant to it. Individual scholars must decide questions like the historicity of Ezra by relying on the weight they give to extratextual considerations.

Some biblical literature, such as Job or Lamentations, may have been produced in the Persian period, other pieces, such as Esther, Tobit, Judith, and Susanna, while set in the Assyrian-Babylonian-Persian periods were most probably produced in the Greek period. These variations of presentation and production illustrate further difficulties in dealing with Jewish literature of the Second Temple period. The tendency to set a story in the (distant) past is so prevalent that it must indicate some ideological value reflecting the past as authoritative. It certainly conceals the period of (and reason for) production and misdirects the attention of the historian who may be tempted to use the work for historical reconstruction. Beautiful women of immense power flourish in these novellas (e.g., Esther, Judith, Susanna), Jewish figures run the empire and guide the thoughts of the pagan emperor (e.g., Mordecai and Daniel), and various shrewd stratagems save the Jewish people from annihilation (see the books of Esther and Judith). While the books have a certain lyrical and romantic charm, it is difficult to credit them with any historical or social value which would illuminate either the Persian or the Greek period. They may be used to construct a sense of fantasy or aspiration among various Jewish groups of the period, or be thought of as reflecting teaching aids inculcating loyalty to group identity and religious affiliation (cf. the Maccabean literature of the Greek period). In many cases they illustrate in story form the (moral) principles behind Torah and as such may be seen as typifying the piety of various Jewish communities in the Second Temple period. At the same time, it cannot be ruled out that the tales of Jewish pietists flourishing in the corridors of power (Babylonian, Persian, Greek) may reflect the political and social integration of Jews (individual or in groups) in the structures of power or may represent the internalization of imperial values as a result of being a low-status group among the communities of the empire (cf. the story of Joseph in Egypt).

D. The Roots of Sectarian Judaism

It would be difficult to exaggerate the importance of Babylonian, Egyptian, and Persian influences on the development of Judaism in the Second Temple period. It may be rather difficult to itemize them or to separate them into coherent strands, but the foreign context of much of the ideological influence on the Jerusalem community cannot be denied. Whatever the historical truth behind the stories in the literature of the period (especially Jeremiah, Ezra-Nehemiah), it is hard to avoid the conclusion that a Persian instrument of control was used to construct in Jerusalem an ideologically defined elite group commanding the regulation of temple purity and religious identity. The subsequent production of apocalypses also points in the direction of Persian influences, especially the Gathic teachings about fate after death in Zoroastrianism (see Boyce *CHJ* 1: 298–301). If an elite from the Persian satrapy of Babylonia did travel to Jerusalem in order to restructure temple and community in ways quite contrary to what previously had obtained there, then it must be admitted that a Persian shaping of Jewish thought was one of the most fundamentally creative forces in determining the roots of Second Temple Judaism. Behind the complex textuality of Ezra-Nehemiah may be discerned the creation of a sect distinct from the general populace of Jerusalem and its environs. The later community of Qumran may afford perfect parallels to this emergent sectarianism in 5th–4th century Jerusalem. In fact, it might be a sound methodological principle to treat the whole period of the Second Temple as a single period dominated by sectarian ideology and struggles and to read *all* the literature as bearing on different aspects of these ideological struggles (including a good deal of the Gospels and Paul in the NT).

A history of the different Jewish communities in Babylonia, Egypt, and Palestine cannot be written because of a lack of data, so the argument here must be based on an attempt to read what data there are in the light of how the communities developed in the Roman period. A reading of the book of Isaiah will show some evidence of sectarian pressures in the Second Temple period (small wonder that the Isaiah scroll should feature so much at Qumran). Conflict over the temple is obvious in Isa 65:1–7; 66:1–6, and the closing chapters of Isaiah sharply differentiate between the servants of Yahweh and their opposers (65:13–16). Reference to those "who tremble at his word" (66:5; cf. Ezra 9:4; 10:3) in contrast to an unnamed group which shares certain Yahwistic beliefs in common indicates some inner-community conflict which is best described as sectarian (see Blenkinsopp *Ezra* OTL for a good analysis of the sectarian tendencies of the Second Temple period; see also Rofé 1988a). Conflicts of interpretation have always been a major feature of sectarian readings of texts and the use of controlling documents in Ezra-Nehemiah to enforce purity and identity points to sectarian aspects at the root of the developing Jewish community in Jerusalem. The long history of argument about texts and their meanings which has characterized Jewish and Christian communities (so quintessentially sectarian are these religions) has its beginnings in the Second Temple period when documents and texts were produced in order to shape, regulate, and control religious parties in contradistinction to the larger populace occupying the territory.

The precondition of this sectarian development was the destruction of the temple by the Babylonians and the isolation of a deported elite in different cultural surroundings. The Babylonian deportation provided a radicalizing enculturation of Judean elements which helped to create the impetus toward change in a later period. Some of the impact of Babylonian culture on Judean religious thought may be seen in the polemic against idols in Isaiah (40–48) and in Isaiah's use of the hymns to Marduk as models for a Yahwistic rhetoric. Elements of Babylonian cosmogony also helped to transform the Canaanite mythology of pre-catastrophe Israelite thought in the direction of the myth of Yahweh the creator (here Isaiah 40–66 and Genesis 1 are rather different examples of Babylonian influence). While the general outlines of Babylonian and Persian influences on Jewish thought may be straightforward, it is far from clear how the dynamics of these transformations worked. In superficial terms what went into the Babylonian deportation were elements of polytheistic Yahwism and what, some centuries later, came back from Babylonia was a transformed Yahwism capable of reshaping Palestinian culture effectively. The controlling ideological myth of the Hebrew Bible produced in the Second Temple period (i.e., that Yahwism was as old as Abraham) needs to be read as a direct indication of the fact that Yahwism came from Mesopotamia, but not in the distant past of the Bronze age. Rather, it came out of Babylonia as a direct consequence of an elite's experiences arising out of the deportation. Only the Jerusalem territory in Palestine, however, afforded the Persian group the opportunity to impose their ideology on whatever factions would support them.

This account of what may have taken place during the Persian period would account for the priority of Genesis over Exodus in the Hebrew Bible (see Garbini 1988). The Egyptian Jewish communities had a rather different myth which made Egypt the source of the nation and Moses the revealer of Yahwism and creator of the community. Much of the Hebrew Bible (especially the deuteronomistically influenced sections) is very hostile to Egypt and all things Egyptian and yet the story of Moses and the people in Egypt remains the central feature of the Bible. The denunciations of the Egyptian Jews in Jeremiah 44 are typical of such sectarian fervor and the DH is extremely hostile to most Israelite involvements with Egypt. Yet the basic myth of the Exodus is required to give legitimation to the Jews of Egypt and is only put into perspective from a Babylonian point of view by having Abraham precede the period of the Exodus and function as the "father" of the nation. Second Isaiah is an important reflection of the emergence of Abraham as a founding feature of the nation's history (Isa 41:8; 51:1–2), but the traditional dating of this part of Isaiah by scholars to the 6th century is undoubtedly rather early (see Torrey 1928 for a late 5th century date; see ISAIAH, BOOK OF).

The Babylonian ideology which shaped parts of the Bible has deformed the record in a number of ways by creating the myth of an "exile and return." This may be seen in the Ezra-Nehemiah volume, also in part of Chronicles, Isaiah, Jeremiah, and Ezekiel (cf. Zech 1). From this perspective (i.e., the production of the *ʿam haggôlâ* party) the Babylonian deportation was a *temporary* taking into exile of a favored group of people (see Jer 24; 29: 10–14) which eventually returned in triumph to Jerusalem after seventy years (or at least their descendants returned some generations later). From the Babylonian perspective, those who had remained behind and who had survived the Babylonian depradations of Jerusalem counted for nothing (note how this reverses the ideological force of 2 Kings 17). In fact, the myth of the "empty land" (2 Chronicles 36; Leviticus 26) simply wrote these survivors out of existence. Thus the triumphal procession which went back from Babylonia to Jerusalem (Ezra 1) took over an empty land, rebuilt the temple, and constituted the official inheritors of all the sacred traditions. This is the Babylonian myth enabling a sectarian takeover of Jerusalem by an elite which determined identity and purity in accordance with its ideological regulations. A squalid deportation of disruptive elements has been thereby transformed into a significant exile of leadership elements awaiting the work of Yahweh in restoration. As an enabling myth it has certain charms and a good deal of power. Unfortunately it has misled generations of biblical scholars into taking it seriously as if it were a historical account without ideological factors. Jewish history is dated by reference to it, (e.g., preexilic, postexilic, etc.). But there are very important contrary elements in the Hebrew Bible which need to be taken into account to provide a balance to this myth.

These other elements also probably represent sectarian movements in the Second Temple period and therefore should be noted as evidence for the complexity of sectarian Judaism in that period. Jeremiah 42 indicated a different and distinctive Palestinian perspective on the period after the fall of Jerusalem. The flourishing of Jewish communities in Egypt throughout the period points to an alternative account of things. Diasporic communities in the empires of Persia, Greece, and Rome also indicate a nonrecognition (or acceptance) of the myth of exile and return in the specific terms of the Jerusalem sectarian elite. In fact, the diffused diasporic communities are evidence for rather different perspectives on the deportations of the Babylonian period. Jer 29:4–7 counsels permanent residence in Babylonia (the supplementation of the text by 29:10–14 attempts to deconstruct the sound counsel of permanence). That some Jewish communities regard themselves in exile and looked forward to an eventual return to Palestine need not be denied, but whether this view was normative for *all* Jewish communities cannot be determined. The myth of a return belongs to a particular set of sectarian beliefs and values which was probably not shared by all (perhaps not even many) Jewish communities.

A more important distinction should be made with reference to the motif of "exile and return." Much of the literature of the Second Temple period recognizes a category of exile after the destruction of Jerusalem in 587/86, but it does not recognize any return in subsequent centuries. This literature (usefully surveyed by Knibb 1976) represents Israel as being in exile for centuries; virtually in permanent exile. (See the interpretation of the seventy *weeks* of years in Dan 9:24 which replaces the seventy years of other texts.) Exile becomes a symbol in this literature; a symbol for the alienation of the group (or sect) from power in Jerusalem, or one related to messianic expectations which alone would restore the people to their land. Here the Qumran literature has a rather different understanding of exile from that represented by Ezra-Nehemiah and one wonders if these differences do not indicate a clash of ideological and sectarian holdings. If the origins of Qumran were to be traced to Babylonian reform groups which only arrived in Palestine during the Maccabean period, this would account for its nonrecognition and for its belief that the exile as punishment of Israel's sins had continued unbroken to its own time (see CD 3:10–14, and the discussion in Davies 1983: 119–25). Whatever the origins of Qumran may have been, the community clearly believed in exile as a continuing experience, even though it might be regarded as living in its own land. The books of *1–3 Enoch*, Baruch, *4 Ezra*, *2 Baruch*, the Qumran *Damascus Document*, and the *Testament of the Twelve Patriarchs* all represent exile as a permanent state of the community and recognize no restoration or return from exile. All this literature may be no earlier than the 2d century B.C.E. but it puts the biblical material which focuses on "exile and return" into perspective by suggesting that there is a preponderance of one type of literature on the subject included in the Hebrew Bible. If this is a correct judgment, then we must recognize the sectarian nature of the biblical material as being one-sided in its emphasis. The claim that the exile had ended with a restoration to Jerusalem would inevitably empower those running the cult center in Jerusalem. Other voices can be heard in different texts, and a much greater divergency of opinion has to be allowed for in the Second Temple period. It is important that developments in the Persian period should not be narrowed down to an uncritical acceptance of the ideology behind Ezra-Nehemiah.

Other factors which contributed to the sectarian developments of Jewish communities in the Persian period included the transformation of circumcision into a symbol of group identity in religious (rather than tribal) terms. This was facilitated by the deportation of Judeans to Babylon where a normal cultural trait became something special by virtue of a new social context. Many scholars also see in the disruptions caused by the Babylonian deportations the acceleration of institutions such as the sabbath into significant religious occasions. So little historical information is known about the sabbath (outside the ideological texts contained in the Pentateuch which have little intrinsic historical value, there is not much in the Hebrew Bible which is informative about it) that it would be unwise to turn the 6th century into a "pandora's box" of cultural creations. Indeed, a reliable historical account of the sabbath has yet to be written and until one is produced it would be better to recognize the sabbath as a sectarian element in the Second Temple period reflecting the sectarian literature generated by the ideological movements of that period. Scholarly speculation also claims to find in the deported communities in Babylon the beginnings of the creation of the synagogue. No evidence exists for this claim and the lack of data for life in Babylonia is such that we do not know how the deportees constructed the institutional aspects of their religious life. Sabbath and synagogue may have come out of Babylonia in the Greek period but we know nothing of a definitive nature about either institution.

What the Persian period may have given to the Palestinian Jews was the beginnings of a temple sectarian party. A temple community was created in Jerusalem which was to determine the shape of nondiasporic Jewish communities for centuries and, in many cases, to create the terminology with which Jewish history has been written ever since. Comparative work on temple communities (what Weinberg 1976 terms *Bürger-Tempel-Gemeinde;* cf. Blenkinsopp *Ezra* OTL, 69) suggests a model for describing the Jerusalem community as a cult with high social and economic status in the land. Control of the temple is a wealth-creating operation which endows the party in charge with powerful opportunities for shaping and controlling the community. Temple taxes, maintenance of the expiatory rites, control of the temple lands and herds, collection and disbursement of funds, enforcement of sabbath prescriptions, regulation of trade and merchandising, and the oversight of purity rules and membership of the cult would afford enormous power to those in charge of the temple. As the economic center of ancient cities, the temple afforded virtually unlimited power to the families controlling it. The history of the Second Temple period is very much one of control of the temple and conflict between sectarian parties vying for that control, with a variety of regulatory documents and visionary programs relating to the cult center constituting a dominant element of what eventually became the Jewish scriptures of a later period.

E. Conclusion

According to Ezra 9:1–4, the "holy race" (i.e., the deportees who had returned from Babylonia) had corrupted itself by mixing with the peoples of the lands and a great divorcing ceremony was imposed on all those who wished to purify themselves from such assimilation with the godless of Palestine. Whether historical or ideological (conceivably both) the material in Ezra 9–10 epitomizes the sectarian spirit of the Second Temple period with its drive to create a sacred enclave of "pure" returned deportees (and their descendants). Purity of people, of priesthood, of temple and correct interpretation of texts became the guiding principles of the period, though it is arguable that the Chronicler had a broader view of things. The paucity of data and the complexity of interpreting what data exist do not make the historian's task an easy one. The material is capable of being interpreted in a number of ways and the reading of it followed in this article is very much informed by how the Jewish communities developed in the post-Persian period (hindsight is inevitable given the obscurity of the period and the indeterminacy of the documents). The appearance of Cyrus in Isa 44:28; 45:1 (whether as gloss or genuine element in the text is disputable and immaterial to the point being made here) indicates an interpretation of the period which wished to make the Persian emperor the key to understanding the reconstruction of Jerusalem. It is a historicizing of the text which makes the foundational element in the community's existence an event in the (distant) past and has the same ideological profile as the statement in Ezra 6:14, "They finished their building by command of the God of Israel and by decree of Cyrus and Darius and Artaxerxes king of Persia." Such imperial authorities gave the temple a pedigree which was unimpeachable in the community.

The Persian imperial power gave way to the irresistible conquests of Alexander of Macedon in the late 4th century, though biblical literature hardly reflects anything of the transition from one empire to the other. A summary of the transition appears in 1 Macc 1:1–9 as the background to the Maccabean struggle in the mid-2d century. This literature only appears in the Greek Alexandrian canon of the Bible (LXX), it is therefore obvious that the Hebrew canon maintains the principle of using only literature which directs the attention to the pre-Hellenistic period. Much of the literature usually associated with the Persian era most likely comes from the Greek period, but scholars have a great tendency to date biblical books according to the period in which they are set (Daniel being a notable exception here). More important than this academic tendency is the need to recognize the ideology of concealment behind the presentation of so much material as taking place in the Persian era. Portraying events in the distant past, the documents took on a legitimation of antiquity and shaped influence from past authorities. While biblical scholarship has tended to play down the importance of the Second Temple period, treating it as an age of decline in contrast to the period before the fall of Jerusalem, it is important to see that the real significance of the period is determined by the fact that it produced the Hebrew Bible and that therefore all our evaluations of different periods need to be modified by a serious reassessment of the period. Whether the Persian period was more significant than the Greek period must be left open to debate, because periodization is a category imposed by historians on the data which awkwardly maps the contours of an age without adequately representing them. Different accounts may be given of the period (see Cross 1975), but the reading which I have followed is intended to emphasize the fact that "the day of small things" (Zech 4:10) is not something to be despised.

Bibliography

Ackroyd, P. R. 1968. *Exile and Restoration.* Philadelphia.

Baron, S. W. 1952. *A Social and Religious History of the Jews.* Vol. 1. 2d ed., rev. and enl. New York.

Blenkinsopp, J. 1977. *Prophecy and Canon.* Notre Dame, IN.

———. 1981. Interpretation and the Tendency to Sectarianism: An Aspect of Second Temple History. Vol. 2, pp. 1026 in *Jewish and Christian Self-Definition,* ed. E. P. Sanders. Philadelphia.

Cross, F. M. 1975. A Reconstruction of the Judean Restoration. *JBL* 94: 4–18.

Davies, P. R. 1983. *The Damascus Covenant: An Interpretation of the "Damascus Document."* JSOTSup 25. Sheffield.

Eskenazi, T. C. 1988. *In An Age of Prose: A Literary Approach of Ezra-Nehemiah.* SBLMS 36. Atlanta.

Garbini, G. 1988. *History and Ideology in Ancient Israel.* Trans. John Bowden. New York.

Joyce, J. 1982. *Portrait of the Artist as a Young Man.* New York.

Knibb, M. A. 1976. The Exile in the Literature of the Intertestamental Period. *HeyJ* 17: 253–72.

Lemche, N. P. 1988. *Ancient Israel: A New History of Israelite Society.* Sheffield.

Roberts, J. M. 1980. *History of the World.* Rev. ed. New York.

Rofé, A. 1988a. The Onset of Sects in Postexilic Judaism: Neglected Evidence from the Septuagint, Trito-Isaiah, Ben Sira, and Malachi. Pp. 39–49 in *The Social World of Formative Christianity and Judaism,* ed. J. Neusner et al. Philadelphia.

———. 1988b. The Vineyard of Naboth: The Origin and Message of the Story. *VT* 38: 89–104.

Smith, M. 1971. *Palestinian Parties and Politics that Shaped the Old Testament.* New York. Repr. 1987.

Stern, E. 1982. *Material Culture of the Land of the Bible in the Persian Period 538–332 B.C.* Warminster, England and Jerusalem.

Torrey, C. C. 1928. *The Second Isaiah: A New Interpretation.* New York.

Weinberg, J. 1976. Die Agrarverhältnisse in der Bürger-Tempel-Gemeinde der Achämenidenzeit. Pp. 473–86 in *Wirtschaft und Gesellschaft im alten Vorderasien,* ed. J. Harmatta and G. Komoróczy. Budapest.

ROBERT P. CARROLL

ISRAEL, SOCIOLOGY OF ANCIENT. See SOCIOLOGY (ANCIENT ISRAEL).

ISSACHAR (PERSON) [Heb *yiśśākār* (Q); *yiśśāśkār* (K)]. **1.** The eponymous ancestor of the Israelite tribe of Issachar, and the fifth son that Leah bore to Israel's eponymous ancestor Jacob (Gen 30:17–18). The etymology of the name is problematic, and any attempt to understand it must begin with a brief review of the narrative that culminates in the birth of Issachar.

Leah's ability to bear children seemingly came to an end after the birth of Judah, Jacob's fourth son. Leah's envious but barren sister Rachel then arranged to have her handmaid Bilhah bear children for Jacob on her behalf (Gen 30:1–8), a stratagem that the now-barren Leah also utilized with her handmaid Zilpah (vv 9–13). Each handmaid bore two sons to Jacob. When Reuben, Leah's oldest son, discovered some mandrakes (believed to have aphrodisiac properties), and when Rachel expressed an interest in acquiring them (v 14), the stage seems to have been set for Rachel herself to begin bearing sons for Jacob. But Leah gave Rachel the mandrakes on one condition: that she agree to let Leah sleep with Jacob that night. Indeed, that night Leah conceived Issachar (Jacob's ninth son; vv 15–17).

This story itself contains two folk etymologies for the name Issachar, both based on wordplay involving the root *śkr,* "to hire, pay wages, recompense." In v 16, when Leah first informs Jacob that he is to sleep with her, she says "I have surely hired you *(śākōr śĕkartîkā)* with my son's mandrakes." Then, after Issachar's birth, Leah notes that the child is "my compensation *(śĕkārî)* for me having to give my handmaid to my husband" (v 18). Attempts to attribute these two popular etymologies respectively to J and E (Speiser *Genesis* AB, 232) underestimate the literary art of the writer, who was trying to create some memorable way by which the name of an eponymous ancestor would become especially meaningful.

The only thing that seems relatively certain is that the name indeed seems to be linked to the root *śkr*. The Ketib seems to suggest an original *yēš śākār,* "there is recompense" (cf. Jer 31:16; 2 Chr 15:7), but this yields a very unusual linguistic construction for a personal name. For the same reason, it is equally problematic to view the name straightforwardly on the basis of the Qere, which appears to be a *Nipᶜal* imperfect ("he hires himself out"). Wellhausen (1871: 95) suggested that a more typical personal name construction would be *ʾîš* + divine name (in this case, the Egyptian god Sokar); the name would hence mean "devotee of Sokar." The name for many Israelites seems to have contained echoes of **ʾîš śākār,* "man of hire, hired workman" (GesB, 322; *KB,* 408). Although such wordplay is not attested textually, these echoes surface in Gen 49:15, where Jacob "blesses" Issachar by noting that his territorial land was so appealing that, to obtain it, he "became a slave at forced labor" (Heb *lĕmas-ᶜōbēd*).

The tribal territory of Issachar is described in Josh 19:17–23, and enough place names there have been identified to confirm that it consisted of the E section of the fertile Jezreel valley and the low hills SE of Mt. Tabor. See GALILEE (PRE-HELLENISTIC) C.3.a. Deut 33:18–19 suggests that the tribe of Issachar shared a common mountain sanctuary with Zebulun. See TABOR, MOUNT. The two also shared a common boundary (Saarisalo 1927). Issachar is often listed along with Zebulun, his "younger brother" whom Leah subsequently bore to Jacob. Interestingly, the younger Zebulun is often given priority in these lists (*IDB* 2: 770–71).

LB sources indicate that in the 14th century the E Jezreel area was worked by Canaanite kings using forced labor (EA 365), and from this Alt (*KlSchr* 3: 169–74) suggested that this was evidence of the tribe's early settlement and status among the Canaanites, a claim that has been widely followed (see *NHI,* 78–79; *LBHG,* 175). He furthermore claimed that since there is no S border for Issachar in Joshua 19 its N border actually constituted part of the original description of Manasseh's territory; thus, the tribe no longer existed as a functioning entity when the Joshua 19 list was compiled in the time of the Judges, and thus Issachar is conspicuously absent in the Gideon story (set in the E Jezreel valley). Indeed, there is some evidence of close ties between Issachar and Manasseh: Tola, a man of Issachar, dwelt in Mt. Ephraim (Judg 10:1); Shimron the son of Issachar may apparently be associated with Mt. Shomron, Samaria (Gen 46:13; 1 Kgs 16:24); and Jashub, another son of Issachar (1 Chr 7:1), may be connected to the place Jashub mentioned in the Samaria ostraca (*LBHG,* 223, 325).

Gottwald (1979: 216), on the other hand, contends that the tribe of Issachar coalesced around Canaanite serfs in the Jezreel who, aided by already-free Israelite tribes in the highlands of Galilee and Samaria, rejected their underclass service to their masters in nearby city-states (Megiddo, Taanach, Beth-shean). Thus, he suggests that the tribe, as a functioning unit, appeared late rather than disappeared early. Indeed, one of the judges, Tola, is said to have been from the tribe of Issachar (Judg 10:1), and Issachar is listed as the 10th of Solomon's administrative districts (1 Kgs 4:17).

Bibliography

Gottwald, N. 1979. *The Tribes of Yahweh.* Maryknoll, NY.

Saarisalo, A. 1927. *The Boundary Between Issachar and Naphtali.* Helsinki.

Wellhausen, J. 1871. *Text der Bücher Samuelis untersucht.* Göttingen.

GARY A. HERION

2. A levitical gatekeeper, the seventh of Obed-edom's eight sons, and namesake of the patriarchal/tribal ancestor (Gen 30:15–18; 49:14–15); mentioned once in the OT (1 Chr 26:4–5). Issachar served with his family (the Obed-edom clan) at the S gate of the temple precinct and the storehouses related to it (26:15). By bracketing their list (26:4–8) with the Korahite family of Meshelemiah (26:2–3, 9), the Chronicler presents Issachar and the Obed-edom clan as descendants of Levi through Korah (1 Chr 26:1, 19; 9:17–20). If the Chronicler intends all four persons named Obed-edom in his Davidic narrative to refer to the same individual (the Gittite, 1 Chr 13:13–14; 15:25; gatekeeper-musician, 15:18; gatekeeper, son of Jeduthun, 16:38; gatekeeper, son of Korah 26:4, 15), he has left clues that Issachar's ancestry and therefore his clan's professional credentialing was at best complex (Williamson 1979: 253–54). The size (26:8; cf. 16:38) and fitness (26:6, 8) of the family for temple service are stressed, perhaps giving further indication of debate over their place in the levitical divisions in the time of the Second Temple whose architecture 1 Chronicles 26 seems to assume.

Bibliography

Japhet, S. 1985. The Historical Reliability of Chronicles: The History of the Problem and its Place in Biblical Research. *JSOT* 33: 83–107.

Williamson, H. G. M. 1979. The Origins of the Twenty-Four Priestly Courses. *VTSup* 30: 250–68.

DAVID L. THOMPSON

ISSHIAH (PERSON) [Heb *yiššîyāh*]. Var. ISSHIJAH. The name of three different persons mentioned in the OT.

1. The son of Izrahiah and, according to 1 Chronicles, a military leader from the tribe of Issachar during the reign of David (1 Chr 7:3). While it is possible that the Chronicler found Isshiah in source material from an earlier military census (Williamson *1 and 2 Chronicles* NCBC, 46, 76), the stylistic characteristics of 1 Chr 7:1–5 suggest that the unit was composed by the Chronicler himself. Isshiah may represent a postexilic name that the Chronicler retrojected into the time of David in order to establish impressive military support for David's rule.

2. The son of Rehabiah and one of the "remaining Levites" who, according to the Chronicler, casts lots before David, Zadok, and Ahimelek in order to receive his place among the levitical household leaders (1 Chr 24:21). Although Liver (1968: 8. 29–32) believes that this list may have originated from an authentic source composed during the reign of David or Solomon, most commentators have attributed the list in which Isshiah appears to a time later than the main composition of Chronicles, either to the late Persian period (Williamson 1979: 259–60, 265–68) or, more commonly, to the Maccabean era (Rudolph *Chronikbücher* HAT, 163–65). The style of the list, however, corresponds closely with the compositional techniques of the Chronicler. The Chronicler may have borrowed the name from a postexilic individual in order to complete a suitable list of levitical names for the reign of David.

3. A member of the family of Harim who lived in the Persian province of Judah during the mission of Ezra (Ezra 10:31). Ishijah married a non-Judean wife. He consented to divorce her during the reforms of Ezra under the threat of complete ostracism from the Jerusalem temple-state. Though the list of Ishijah's peers may be abbreviated (Rudolph *Ezra und Nehemiah* HAT, 97–99), it is generally agreed that the names in the list of Ezra 10:18–43 authentically represent individuals from the Persian province of Judah during the mission of Ezra.

Bibliography

Liver, J. 1968. *Chapters in the History of Priests and Levites*. Jerusalem (in Hebrew).

Williamson, H. G. M. 1979. The Origins of the Twenty-Four Priestly Courses, A Study of 1 Chronicles xxiii–xxvii. Pp. 251–68 in *Studies in the Historical Books of the Old Testament*, ed. J. A. Emerton. VTSup 30. Leiden.

JOHN W. WRIGHT

ISSHIJAH (PERSON) [Heb *yiššîyāh*]. Var. ASAIAS. A descendant of Harim and one of the returned exiles who was required by Ezra to divorce his foreign wife (Ezra 10:31). According to Noth, the name Isshijah is derived from the root *nšh* and may mean "Yahweh will forget"; but we are left wondering who or what Yahweh will forget. Alternatively, Noth suggests the meaning "Yahweh will cause to forget"—perhaps an older child who died or a previous barrenness (*IPN,* 211; cf. also Manasseh). In the parallel text of 1 Esdr 9:32, the name Asaias appears in the position Isshijah holds in Ezra 10:31. Isshijah was a member of a family from which a group of exiles returned with Zerubbabel (Ezra 2:32; Neh 7:35). For further discussion, see BEDEIAH.

JEFFREY A. FAGER

ISTALCURUS (PERSON) [Gk *Istalkouros*]. A descendant of Bigvai whose son Uthai returned with Ezra to Jerusalem from Babylon (1 Esdr 8:40). In Ezra 8:14, ZACCUR occurs in the place of Istalcurus, and both Uthai and Zaccur are listed as brothers. Swaim (*IDB* 2: 771) suggests that "Uthai the son of Istalcurus" in 1 Esdras is a "corruption of 'Uthai and Zaccur' in the parallel Ezra 8:14." Swaim's conclusion can be supported by a portion of the manuscript tradition, but Hanhart (1974) still preferred "Istalcurus" in his critical edition of 1 Esdras. The Vg adds to the complexity of this problem in identification by listing Uthai as a son of Zaccur (Lat *filius zaccuri*).

Bibliography

Hanhart, R. 1974. *Esdrae liber I.* Vol. 8/1 in *Septuaginta: Vetus Testamentum Graecum.* Göttingen.

MICHAEL DAVID MCGEHEE

ITALIAN COHORT [Gk *speira Italikē*]. An auxiliary unit in the Roman army, one of whose centurions became the first reported Gentile to receive the gift of the Holy Spirit and to be baptized in the name of Jesus (Acts 10). CORNELIUS, the centurion, sent one of his devout soldiers along with two servants to bring Peter back to Caesarea; there, upon hearing Peter, Cornelius and several others were converted.

The Italian Cohort was probably an infantry unit with a paper strength of 500 or 1,000 troops, roughly the size of a modern army battalion. Inscriptional evidence suggests that this unit was the *Cohors II Italica Civium Romanorum* or "Second Italian Cohort of Roman Citizens" (*ILS* 3/2: 9168). Originally the unit was composed of men from Italy; Cheesman hypothesizes that they may have been freedmen enrolled by Tiberius and transferred E to the area around Caesarea (1914: 66). Once in the East the cohort would have drawn replacement recruits from the local area, including many Syrians. Inscriptional evidence shows that Proculous, a Syrian officer, was transferred with this same unit from the province of Syria in 69 C.E. to aid the accession of Vespasian to the throne. The cohort was shortly moved back to Syria and remained their until at least 157 C.E. (Broughton 1933: 441–42).

Because there is no evidence that the Italian Cohort was stationed near Caesarea before the 60s, Haenchen doubts the accuracy of Acts 10:1 and suggests that Luke's mention of the unit is anachronistic. He further notes that Roman troops cannot have been stationed in Caesarea during the years 41–44 when Herod Agrippa ruled the area as a semiautonomous kingdom (*Acts* MeyerK, 346, n. 2). However, Acts only places Cornelius and his cohort in Caesarea between the time of Paul's conversion ca. 35 C.E. (9:26) and the death of James in 44 C.E. (12:1–2); Roman troops would have been stationed in Caesarea from 35 to 41 C.E. Furthermore, there is no evidence that the Italian Cohort was stationed anywhere else during this period. Therefore, Luke's account in Acts 10:1 may have been accurate. See also PW 4/1: 231–356.

Bibliography

Broughton, T. R. S. 1933. The Roman Army. Vol. 5, pp. 427–45 in *The Beginnings of Christianity, Part I: The Acts of the Apostles,* ed. F. J. Foakes Jackson and K. Lake. London.

Cheesman, G. L. 1914. *The Auxilia of the Roman Imperial Army.* Oxford.

MARK J. OLSON

ITALY (PLACE) [Gk *Italia*]. The word "Italy" appears four times in the NT. Rome was the capital of Italy and of the Roman Empire, which ruled most of the NT world. Sometimes Rome is used synonymously with Italy. See ROME.

The first account of Jews visiting Italy is found in 1 Maccabees 8, where the account of a Jewish delegation was sent to Rome by Judas Maccabeus to sign a treaty with the Romans (ca. 160 B.C.). Later delegations were sent by his brother, Jonathan, and then by Simon to renew the alliance (1 Macc 12:1–4; 14:16–19, 24). Jews first received importance in Italy after Pompey conquered Palestine for Rome in 63 B.C. They increased in number under the protection of Julius Caesar. Christianity was probably introduced to Italy at an early date when the "visitors from Rome" returned to their country after Pentecost (Acts 2:10). Paul's letter to the Romans was written about 58 A.D., and it recognized many Christians who were both Jewish and Gentile (Rom 1:13).

The first NT reference to Italy pertains to Aquila and Priscilla who moved to Corinth from Italy because of the expulsion of Jews from Rome by Claudius in 49 A.D. (Acts 18:2). In Corinth they met Paul and aided in his ministry. The second reference is to the decision of Paul to claim his right as a Roman citizen to stand trial before Caesar (Acts 27:1). On his journey, Paul sailed along the coast of Italy, where he met Christians who offered their hospitality and who welcomed him to Rome (Acts 28:13–16). The third reference is a salutation in the letter to the Hebrews from those who "come from Italy" (Heb 13:24), which may help to determine the community from which the letter arose.

The adjectival form "Italian" occurs in Acts 10:1, to refer to an Italian cohort (band, military unit). Cornelius was the Roman centurion in charge, whom some consider the first gentile convert to Christianity.

DONALD A. D. THORSEN

ITCH. See SICKNESS AND DISEASE.

ITHAI (PERSON) [Heb *ʾîtay*]. One of David's champions, the son of Ribai from Gibeah of Benjamin, Saul's stronghold (1 Chr 11:31 [Gk *Aithi*]). 2 Sam 23:29b names one Ittai (Heb *ʾittay;* Gk *eththi*) in the parallel list. Since Ittai is designated as "the son of Ribai of Gibeah of the Benjaminites," the same person is meant.

D. G. SCHLEY

ITHAMAR (PERSON) [Heb *ʾîtāmār*]. The fourth son of Aaron and Elisheba. Unlike his brothers Nadab, Abihu, and Eleazar, Ithamar has a name of uncertain derivation. The etymology most often given, "isle of palm trees" (e.g., BDB, 16), hardly commends itself for a personal name. A more promising etymology is suggested by the various early NW Semitic names from Mari (ca. 18th century B.C.E.) seemingly containing *t*-infixed forms of the root *ʾmr,* which in some Semitic languages means "say, command" (Hebrew, Phoenician, Aramaic, Arabic) and in others "see" (Ugaritic, Akkadian). The form *ʾîtāmār* most closely resembles the Arabic eighth form (Gt) of the root *ʾmr, ʾītamara* ("he obeyed"); the loss of the final short vowel is expected in Hebrew. A NW Semitic dialect might also have contained a form **ʾītamara* < **ʾiʾtamara,* for in Ugaritic, in this very word, the root *ʾalep* quiesces; note the coexistent spellings *yʾitmr* (*CTA* 2.1.32) and *ytmr* (*CTA* 3.1.22). There may be cognate personal names attested in Mari: *Taʾtamar, Atamra,* and *Atamri-ilu;* we may even have a parallel name from Canaan proper in the slightly older Execration Texts from Egypt (*APNM,* 168). If such is the etymology of Ithamar, the name means either "He appeared" or "He obeyed."

In the Elohistic (E) source Aaron appears besides two men named Nadab and Abihu (Exod 24:1, 9), but their relation to him and to each other is unspecified. Since in the Priestly (P) source Aaron has four sons who are priests—Nadab, Abihu, Eleazar, and Ithamar (Exod 6:23; 28:1; etc.)—it is reasonable to suppose that likewise in E Aaron is the father of priests named Nadab and Abihu. What induced the priestly author, or his sources, to add the names Eleazar and Ithamar to the list?

The answer is that the author of P was a Zadokite priest claiming descent from Eleazar (Ezra 7:2–5; 1 Chr 5:30–33; 6:35–38). Although in P Eleazar is Aaron's third son, he inherits his father's office due to the mishap recorded in Leviticus 9–10 at the inauguration of the Tabernacle, where Nadab and Abihu die and Aaron is left, as in E, with only two sons. Much is obscure in these chapters, but the following interpretation is tentatively offered.

In Lev 9:2, 7–11 the priests sacrifice a calf as their own purification offering (usually rendered "sin offering," but see Milgrom 1971) and then a goat as the people's (Lev 9:3, 15). Instead of eating the goat as commanded in Lev 6:17–23—Eng 6:24–30), however, Aaron's sons burn it (Lev 9:15, 10:16), which is the correct practice only in the case of a priest's purification offering (Lev 6:23, cf. 4:8–10; 9:2, 7–11). Perhaps the priests fear to bear the sin of the community. To conclude the ceremony, a miraculous fire comes forth from Yahweh and ignites the offerings

(Lev 9:24). Then Nadab and Abihu kindle "strange fire" (i.e., fire not sent down by Yahweh) in their censers and are killed by another emission of divine fire (Lev 10:1–7). Perhaps the deity is displeased, too, by their failure to eat the people's purification offering. After this disaster, part of the ceremony is reenacted (Lev 10:12–15; cf. 9:17, 21), and only then does Moses discover that the priests had not followed proper procedure the first time (Lev 10:16). Although Moses addresses Eleazar and Ithamar, Aaron responds: "They [my four sons] have sacrificed today their purification offering and their holocaust before Yahweh and [nevertheless] such a thing [the death of two sons] has happened to me. Would it be right in Yahweh's opinion for me to eat the purification offering today?" (Lev 10:19). Moses accepts this argument. It seems that, because of the ritual pollution caused by the deaths of Nadab and Abihu (and perhaps by their crime as well), Aaron, Eleazar, and Ithamar are temporarily unfit to consume the people's offering. The story's most important outcome, for our purposes, is that Eleazar and Ithamar are left as sole priests of Yahweh, with the former the chief priest (Lev 10:12–15; Num 3:4).

Whence such a strange story about the Aaronic succession? It is widely believed that this is one of several biblical traditions originating in rivalries between priestly families; the best parallel is the rebellion of Korah in Numbers 16–17. In other words, some priests boasts Aaronic descent through Nadab and Abihu, but the Zadokites, of the clan of Eleazar, rejected their claims by telling a story of the crime and premature deaths of their adversaries' ancestors. Who these rivals were is a mystery, but below a possible solution is given. At any rate, if Nadab, Abihu, and Eleazar are ancestors of clans, this is presumably true of Ithamar as well.

Unfortunately, the priestly author gives no indication of who among his contemporaries claimed descent from Ithamar. We only know that they were in charge of the Levites, in particular of the lesser clans of Gershon and Merari (Exod 38:21; Num 4:28, 33; 7:8). We thus infer that there was in Jerusalem a minor priestly clan descended from Ithamar.

The Chronicler, however, gives Ithamar and his descendants greater stature. According to 1 Chr 24:3, 6, 31, David's two priests were Zadok the son of Ahitub (cf. 1 Chr 5:34; 6:37–38; Ezra 7:2) from the house of Eleazar, and Ahimelek (1 Chr 18:16 has "Abimelek," which is widely attested in ancient textual witnesses; see *CMHE,* 212, n. 66) the son of Abiathar from the house of Ithamar. In all, eight Ithamarite clans and sixteen Eleazarite clans ministered in David's day (1 Chr 24:3–19). Abiathar was the scion of the house of Eli, which had served in the important shrine at Shiloh. In other words, the Chronicler ascribed the Shilonite priesthood to the line of Ithamar.

The Chronicler's record of David's priests is related to 2 Sam 8:17, "Zadok the son of Ahitub and Ahimelek the son of Abiathar were priests." This reading is regarded as the result of textual error by almost all commentators, who either assume that Ahitub is Abiathar's grandfather or Ahimelek his father (*CMHE,* 212–14), since Zadok and Abiathar are elsewhere David's priests (e.g., 2 Sam 17:15). The simplest explanation is that Zadok did have a father named Ahitub and Abiathar did have a son Ahimelek named for his murdered grandfather (1 Sam 22:18–19) who shared his father's duties towards the end of David's reign. By this interpretation 2 Sam 8:17 is textually intact but chronologically misplaced. It is true that elsewhere Abiathar's son is called Jonathan (2 Sam 15:27, 36; 17:17, 20; 1 Kgs 1:42–43), but he was famous as a runner, not as a priest, and may have had an older brother. But even if 2 Sam 8:17 is corrupt, we cannot attribute the error to a careless scribe whom the Chronicler blindly followed. Ezra 7:5 and 1 Chr 6:37–38—Eng vv 11–12—record that during the monarchy there was a later Zadok the son of Ahitub. If the Chronicler's patronymic of the original Zadok is erroneous, it must be consciously derived from subsequent priestly genealogy.

The author of Chronicles, however, was not free to fabricate traditions about Ithamar, nor can he have been totally ignorant of the clan's history, because Ithamarites were prominent in the postexilic restoration; according to Ezra 8:2, their head was Daniel (cf. Neh 10:7), while 1 Esdr 8:29 refers to a Gamael (possibly the Gamul mentioned in 1 Chr 24:17). Moreover, 1 Chr 23:15–18 lists Ithamarite families, and the last, Maaziah, is also the name of a priest contemporary with Nehemiah (Neh 10:9). Therefore, the Chronicler had to reckon with living tradition. If 2 Sam 8:17 is corrupt, it must have been willfully altered at the same time that the Chronicler was assigning to the Ithamarites an important role in his reconstruction of the Davidic cult (1 Chr 24:3–19). If the figure of Ahimelek the son of Abiathar is a fiction created in this period, he likely comes from the Ithamarites' own tradition.

In short, after the exile Ithamarite priests purported to be the heirs of the house of Eli. If their claim was valid, the house of Ithamar looms larger in Israelite history. Was it a ploy for greater prestige, or did the claim reflect preexilic history? This question cannot be answered definitively, for other evidence of the affiliation of the Shilonite priesthood is ambiguous. 1 Sam 2:27–36 speaks of the rejection of the house of Eli and its replacement by a "faithful priest who will perpetually serve [lit., 'walk before'] my anointed," i.e., Zadok (v 25). The crux is vv 27–28, which, partly emended to the Old Greek, reads: "I revealed myself to your clan [lit., 'father's house'] when they were slaves ['slaves' not in MT] to Pharoah's household, and I chose it from all the tribes of Israel to be my priest to ascend to [alternatively, 'to sacrifice upon'] my altar and to burn incense and to bear the ephod before me, and I gave your clan all the offerings of Israel." Some have regarded the reference to revelation as evidence that the Shilonite priests claimed descent from Moses (e.g., *CMHE,* 195–215), but Moses and his descendants were never slaves in Egypt. There may have been a Mushite (from *mōšeh,* Moses?) priesthood descended from Moses (*CMHE,* 195–215), but it is unlikely that it claimed sole legitimacy, as implied here. To our knowledge, only three groups in Israel ever claimed the exclusive right to be Yahweh's priests—the tribe of Levi (in Deuteronomy-Kings, Jeremiah, and Malachi), the house of Aaron (in P and Chronicles) and the family of Zadok (Ezekiel). The Shilonite priests were obviously not Zadokite, but might have been Aaronic or Levitic.

Our only direct evidence on the matter suggests that the

house of Eli was Aaronic. In the time of Solomon Abiathar possessed an estate in Anathoth (1 Kgs 2:26), and the 8th-century (Peterson 1977; Boling *Joshua* AB, 492–97) list of levitical cities assigns Anathoth to the Aaronids (Josh 21:18; 1 Chr 6:45—Eng v 60). The Zadokites were of the clan of Eleazar. If the Shilonites were Aaronid, they probably claimed descent from Ithamar, Nadab, or Abihu. In favor of the identification with Ithamar, perhaps, is 1 Sam 2:33, which says that there will always be an Elid by Yahweh's altar, reminiscent of Ithamar's role as minor clergy. But the same could have been true, in some period, of Nadab and Abihu. Despite postexilic claims, it seems unlikely that the Priestly writer considered Ithamar the ancestor of Eli, for Ithamar is a neutral figure in P, while other rival priests (Nadab, Abihu, Korah, and the Levites) are excoriated. The only Aaronids condemned in P are Nadab and Abihu, who also figure in the old, N E source, and hence they are prime suspects as the ancestors of the priests of Shiloh. Admittedly, the Chronicler denies that Nadab and Abihu had descendants (1 Chr 24:2), but this merely means that by his time there were no longer clans with that name; after the codification of the Torah, no one would claim such ancestry. Note that like Eli, Aaron loses two sons who die for cultic offenses.

On the other hand, "I chose him *from all the tribes of Israel*" (1 Sam 2:28; cf. Deut 18:5) might indicate that the clan in question is the entire tribe of Levi. The text then corroborates such passages as Deuteronomy 18, which seems to maintain that all the tribe of Levi are potential priests (cf. Deut 10:8; Jer 33:21–22; Mal 2:4–9). In particular, our passage recalls the blessing of Levi in Deut 33:8–11, which must be reconstructed with the help of the LXX and Dead Sea Scrolls (*CMHE,* 197). Both 1 Sam 2:28 and Deut 33:8, 10 entrust the priesthood with sacrifice and censing, and both allude to oracles, though Deut 33:8 mentions the Urim and Thummim, while 1 Sam 2:28 refers to the Ephod, a garment or a pouch associated with oracles in general (1 Sam 14:3, 18–19 [OG]; 23:9–12; 30:7–8) and with the Urim and Thummim in particular (1 Sam 14:41 [OG] cf. 28:6). Later, the P document arrogated the use of the Urim and Thummim to the descendants of Eleazar (Num 27:21), and though they were kept in a pouch called the *ḥōšen,* they still were part of the Ephod assemblage (Exod 28:25–28). If the Shilonite priesthood was Levitic, its rejection here accords with other texts that exclude the Levites from the priesthood in favor of the Zadokite clergy (cf. Num 16:8–10; Ezek 44:10–16; 48:11). Of course, the Zadokites were themselves Levites, but note that the brunt of the curse falls upon "your house" (vv 31–33, 36), i.e., the descendants of Eli. In any case, the Zadokites were wont to use the term "Levite" ambiguously—sometimes it included them but at other times it referred to the other Levites, their servants. But the theory of the Levitic (as opposed to Aaronic) ancestry of Eli rests primarily on the phrase "I chose it from all the tribes of Israel," and Deut 12:5, 14; 1 Kgs 11:32; 14:21 (= 2 Chr 12:13); 2 Kgs 21:7 (= 2 Chr 33:7), its closest parallels, refer not to a tribe, but to a shrine or to the city Jerusalem. We might also compare Deut 29:30, which speaks of punishing an *individual* (but cf. v 17) "from all the tribes of Israel." On the whole, it is more probable that the house of Eli was Aaronic.

In short, it is possible, but not demonstrable, that the Shiloh priesthood was of the clan of Ithamar. Before the exile, the house of Eli was anathema to the Zadokites, but after the exile, the issue was dead. Perhaps at that time, in order to enhance the prestige and antiquity of their lineage, the postexilic Ithamarites, hithertofore a minor Aaronic order subservient to the Zadokites, claimed descent from Eli, chief priest of Israel before Samuel.

Bibliography

Cody, A. 1969. *A History of the Old Testament Priesthood.* AnBib 35 Rome.

Gunneweg, A. H. J. 1965. *Leviten und Priester.* Göttingen.

Milgrom, J. 1971. Sin-offering or Purification Offering. *VT* 21: 237–39.

Möhlenbrink, K. 1923. Die levitischen überlieferungen. *ZAW* 52: 184–231.

Peterson, J. L. 1977. *A Topographical Surface Survey of the Levitical "Cities" of Joshua 21 and 1 Chronicles 6.* Th.D. Diss. Seabury-Western Theological Seminary.

William H. Propp

ITHIEL (PERSON) [Heb *ʾîtîʾēl*]. **1.** An ancestor of Sallu, a Benjaminite and provincial leader who agreed to settle in Jerusalem (Neh 11:7). Although Sallu's line is referred to in both the list in Nehemiah 11 and 1 Chronicles 9 (cf. v 7), Ithiel is not mentioned. This, like other differences in the two lists, suggests that there is no direct literary relationship between the two lists (contra Kellermann 1966: 208–27 and Mowinckel 1964: 146–47). Some, however, have conjectured that both writers were dependent upon common archival materials (Brockington *Ezra, Nehemiah and Esther* NCBC, 187; cf. Myers *Ezra, Nehemiah* AB, 185). In any event, the presence of Ithiel in the list provides no further evidence of use in resolving the problem. Apart from the probable significance of the name itself ("With me is God"), nothing is known about this Benjaminite patriarch (Brockington, 189).

2. Perhaps one of two sages to whom the words of Agur are addressed (Prov 30:1). Along with the other addressee (Ucal), their names may have symbolic significance. So understood, Ithiel may mean a number of things: "signs or precepts of God," "with me is God," or perhaps, "there is a God" (Toy *Proverbs* ICC, 519). However, the names are missing from the LXX and the Hebrew of the verse is corrupt (Whybray *Proverbs* CBC, 172). Accordingly, a number of translators and commentators treat this opening line as an introductory confession, reconstructing the original in a variety of ways (McKane *Proverbs* OTL, 644–46).

Bibliography

Kellermann, U. 1966. "Die Listen in Nehemia 11 eine Dokummentation aus den letzten Jahren des Reiches Juda?" *ZDPV* 82: 209–27.

Mowinckel, S. 1964. *Studien zu dem Buche Ezra-Nehemia I: Die nachchronistische Redaktion des Buches. Des Listen.* Skrifter utgitt av Det Norske Videnskaps-Akademii Oslo. Oslo.

Frederick W. Schmidt

ITHLAH (PLACE) [Heb *yitlâ*]. A town listed in the tribal territory of Dan, before the tribe migrated N of the Sea of Galilee (Josh 19:42). The town is unidentified, but the context suggests that it was probably located somewhere between Nahal Ayyalon and Nahal Sorek.

GARY A. HERION

ITHMAH (PERSON) [Heb *yitmâ*]. One of David's champions, a select class of warriors directly attached to the king for special assignments, named in the list of 1 Chr 11:10–47 (v 46), a list which, up to v 41a, parallels that of 2 Sam 23:8–39. Ithmah, a Moabite, is found among the 16 persons mentioned in portion of the list which is unique to Chronicles (vv 41b–47). Characteristic of this portion is the fact that all of the identifiable places from which these champions came are in the area of Transjordan (Williamson *Chronicles* NCBC, 104).

RODNEY K. DUKE

ITHNAN (PLACE) [Heb *yitnān*]. A settlement of the tribe of Judah. Ithnan is only mentioned once in Josh 15:23, where it is listed among the settlements occupied by Judah in the aftermath of the conquest. Though the present literary context of the Judean town list is set in the period of Joshua, its original setting was as part of a post-Solomonic administrative division of the S kingdom. The date for the establishment of this system is debated, with suggestions ranging from the early 9th to the late 7th centuries B.C. Ithnan is in the southernmost district of Judah, the Negeb. An Ethnan is mentioned as one of the descendants of Judah in 1 Chr 4:7, but no certain connection can be made between these two.

The location of Ithnan is problematic. In the list it is placed between Hazor and Ziph, in a context which would place it in the E Negeb. Some would combine Ithnan and Hazor on the basis of the LXX reading, Asorionain, and read Hazor-Ithnan. Some have identified it with el-Jebaryiah on the Wadi Umm Ethnan (WHAB, 124), but this is too far S. Abel suggested it might be found in the vicinity of Imitnan 21.5 km S of Beer-sheba (*GP,* 351; M.R. 132050), but this too seems too far S.

Bibliography

Cross, F. M., and Wright, G. E. 1956. The Boundary and Province Lists of the Kingdom of Judah. *JBL* 75: 202–26.

JEFFREY R. ZORN

ITHRA (PERSON) [Heb *yitrāʾ*]. Father of Amasah, commander of the Israelite army under Absalom during the revolt against David (2 Sam 17:25 [Heb *yitrāʾ*]; 1 Kgs 2:5, 32, 1 Chr 2:17 [Heb *yeter* is a variant]) and who was later assassinated by Joab (2 Sam 20:5–10). Although it is stated that Ithra was an "Israelite" in 2 Sam 17:25, this is probably a textual error for "Ishmaelite" since the former description would be superfluous. The correct reading, "Ishmaelite," is preserved in 1 Chr 2:17.

Ithra was probably not legally married (in the traditional sense) to Amasah's mother, Abigail, who was also the sister of David (1 Chr 2:15–17). The language of the text in 2 Sam 17:25 suggests he may have had a casual encounter with Abigail ("he went into her" [Heb *bāʾ ʾel*]). Scholars suggest that the relationship was a *ṣadiqa* marriage, one in which the wife and children remained with her parents, with the husband having visiting privileges (Hertzberg *I and II Samuel* OTL, 357; McCarter *II Samuel* AB, 393).

The provocative theory that Ithra was in fact Nabal (1 Samuel 25) and had married Abigail (David's sister!) for political advantage is extremely speculative (Levenson and Halpern 1980). Such a view postulates that David married his own sister after the death of Ithra/Nabal for a similar political benefit. But such an act would have been politically fatal for David. Moreover, the theory abounds with tenuous assumptions, an example being the unlikelihood of David having both a sister and wife with the name Abigail, when these are the only persons with this name in the Hebrew Bible.

Bibliography

Levenson, J. D., and Halpern, B. 1980. The Political Import of David's Marriages. *JBL* 99: 507–18.

STEPHEN G. DEMPSTER

ITHRAN (PERSON) [Heb *yitrān*]. **1.** A clan name in the genealogy of Seir the Horite in Gen 36:26. Ithran is listed as the third of four sons of Dishon and thus he is a grandson of Seir. The name also appears in the parallel genealogical clan list in 1 Chr 1:41. These clans, not to be confused with the Hurrians of Mesopotamia, inhabited the region of Edom prior to the coming of the Esau clans and are said to have been subsequently dispossessed by these more aggressive peoples (Deut 2:12–22). Their designation as "cave dwellers" may be a reflection of their true condition or a disparaging remark by their conquerors.

2. A clan name in the genealogy of Asher in 1 Chr 7:37. Ithran is listed as the tenth of eleven sons of Zophah in the sixth generation after Asher. This genealogy has no tie to a historical narrative as in Gen 36. The only relevant information associated with the listing is a summary of the number of fighting men provided by these clans as well as a certification of the clan chiefs as proven leaders of the people (1 Chr 7:40). The Gk codex Alexandrinus has *yetren.*

VICTOR H. MATTHEWS

ITHREAM (PERSON) [Heb *yitrĕʿām*]. The sixth and youngest son of David born at Hebron, during David's seven-year reign as king there (2 Sam 3:5; 1 Chr 3:3). The rest of his sons were born in Jerusalem. The name of Ithream's mother was Eglah. Of David's six wives at Hebron, Eglah is the only one specifically called "David's wife." This could indicate some special stature or significance accorded her. See also DAVID, SONS OF.

DAVID M. HOWARD, JR.

ITHRITE [Heb *hayyitrî*]. A gentilic adjective describing the clan or tribe of two of David's distinguished warriors (2 Sam 23:38 = 1 Chr 11:40). The names of the soldiers were Ira and Gareb. The Ithrite clan, located near Kiriath-

Jearim, was associated with the lineage of Caleb (1 Chr 2:53). It was probably an indigenous clan of Canaan, incorporated into the Caleb tribe during the Israelite settlement of the land (cf. Josh 9:17, Mazar 1963: 318–19). The placement of Ira and Gareb at the end of the list in 2 Samuel argues for their non-Israelite origin, since this position seems to be reserved for such persons (Mazar 1963: 318–19).

There is some evidence that Ithrite in the above lists should be read Jattirite (Heb **hayyattīrî*). This would then be an adjective describing the location from which the two warriors came, i.e., the town of Jattir (M.R. 151084) in the hill country of Debir (Josh 15:48; 21:14; 1 Chr 6:42—Eng 6:57). The evidence of the LXX, particularly in 2 Samuel, suggests this reading. For Gareb's name, B reads the gentilic as *eththenaios* (cf. A: *tethriteis*). In Chronicles, B reads consistently a long vowel after the Heb *t: eitheiri, iotheiri* (cf. also the Syriac). However, this evidence remains inconclusive. The simplest solution is to follow the MT.

Bibliography

Mazar, B. 1963. The Military Elite of King David. *VT* 13: 210–20.

Stephen G. Dempster

ITTAI (PERSON) [Heb *ʾittay*]. **1.** Leader of a mercenary troop from Philistine Gath, he evidenced great loyalty to David at the time of the latter's flight from Absalom (2 Sam 15:19, 21, 22). The Bible narrates a number of encounters that David had on his flight from Jerusalem at the time of Absalom's revolt (2 Sam 15:13–16:14). Upon exiting from the city, David reviewed the troops accompanying him. Following the Cherethites and the Pelethites was a contingent of six hundred men from Gath (2 Sam 15:18; but see McCarter [*II Samuel* AB, 364] who excises the number 600; many commentators [e.g. Driver *NHT* 242] restore the name Ittai in this verse). David turned to Ittai, their leader, and pleaded with him to turn back and serve the new king. After all, Ittai was a foreigner and an exile, why should he take upon himself David's additional burden (vv 19–20)? Ittai, however, refused to abandon David and swore to share his fate, whether good or bad (v 21). Presumably impressed with his loyalty and devotion, David tersely assented (v 22). Two aspects in particular of this story have struck commentators. First is David's selfless concern for those serving him, even in a time of great personal stress (Smith *Samuel* ICC, 343). Second is the great loyalty, indeed love, which David commanded from his followers (Hertzberg *I and II Samuel* OTL, 342). David rewarded Ittai's devotion in what Hertzberg (342) terms "the way in which a king expresses his thanks" by appointing him, along with Joab and Abishai, to the command of one third of his troops each in the war against Absalom (2 Sam 18:2). Although there is a play on words on the name Ittai in the Hebrew of the MT, in which David asks Ittai (*ʾittay*) why he is "with us" (*ʾittānû*, 2 Sam 15:19), the etymology of the name, whether Hurrian, Hittite, general Semitic, or specifically Yahwistic, is unclear (see the discussions in Delcor 1978: 411–13, and McCarter, 370).

2. One of David's mighty men, called the "thirty" (2 Sam 23:29; but see Naʾaman 1988 for an argument that the Hebrew consonantal *šlšym* should be pointed *šālīšîm* "officers" and not as in the MT *šĕlōšîm* "thirty"). He was the son of Ribai from Benjaminite Gibeah, the home also of Saul. In the parallel passage in 1 Chr 11:31, he is named Ithai (*ʾîtay*). See also DAVID'S CHAMPIONS.

Bibliography

Delcor, M. 1978. Les Kéréthim et les Cretois. *VT* 28: 409–22.
Naʾaman, N. 1988. The List of David's Officers (*šālīšîm*). *VT* 38: 71–79.

Carl S. Ehrlich

ITURAEA (PLACE) [Gk *Itouraía*]. ITURAEANS. A short-lived principality located in the Biqâʿ valley of Lebanon, founded by an Arab tribe of N Transjordan, who migrated into the Biqâʿ valley in the course of the 2d century B.C. Ituraea became a Roman vassal state in 63 B.C. and was split up in various petty principalities in 36 B.C. One of these was "the Ituraean country and Trachonitis" (Luke 3:1), ruled by Philippus, son of Herodes the Great (4 B.C.–A.D. 34).

The Ituraeans tribe is listed among the "sons of Ishmael" (7th century B.C.) in Gen 25:15 and 1 Chr 1:31 (Heb *yĕtûr*); in this list, they form, however, a redactional addition, probably from the 5th century B.C. See ISHMAELITES.

Thus, the origin of the Ituraeans cannot be traced beyond N Transjordan in the late Persian or early Hellenistic periods. 1 Chr 5:18–22 reports a war waged by Reuben, Gad, and half of Manasseh against "the Hagrites, Jetur, Naphish, and Nodab" (5:19), which is dated by 1 Chr 5:10 to the reign of Saul. See also HAGAR; HAGRITES; NAPHISH; NODAB. Because orthographically the name "Jetur" cannot have entered the biblical tradition before the 7th century B.C. (see JETUR), this dating must be incorrect. Most probably, the Chronicler (or one of his redactors, Knauf 1989: 49–52) had in mind contemporary Arab tribes from N Transjordan (and a conflict between them and Judean settlers?) when he wrote his account, which then dates to the 4th–3d centuries B.C.

Whereas the LXX transcribes Heb Jetur in Gen 25:15 (*Ietoúr*), it renders the tribe's name by *Itouraîoi* in 1 Chr 5:19. Under the Greek form of its name (and the corresponding Latin, *Ituraei*), the tribe became widely known in antiquity, and was infamous for its ferocity (cf., e.g., Cic. *Phil.* II, 8 [19]; 44 [112]; XIII, 8 [18]).

In the first half of the 2d century B.C., the tribe was still living in N Transjordan (Eupolemos Frg. 2 = Eus. *Praep. evang.* IX 30,3). By this time, the Ituraeans may have started to infiltrate Galilee. In 104/103 B.C., the Hasmonean Aristobulos conquered the Ituraean territory in Galilee and Transjordan, and forcefully converted the inhabitants to Judaism (*Ant* 13.11.3 §318). The Ituraeans, however, kept the area of Lake Huleh and Paneas (Caesarea Philippi; Schottroff 1982: 134). Most of the tribe may have migrated into the Biqâʿ valley at this time in order to escape Aristobulos. A migration of the Ituraeans is mentioned in the Safaitic inscription CIS V 4677; another Safaitic inscription, CIS V 2209, is dated to "the year of the Ituraean war," which is not a very precise date, given the belligerent character of this early bedouin tribe. Three Safaitic inscriptions (CIS V 784, 2209 and Ox 58) were written by Ituraeans (in Safaitic, ʾl yzr; Winnett in Winnett and Harding 1978 *ad* WH 3735; Knauf 1989: 81). These inscriptions do not necessarily antedate 103 B.C., since Ituraeans may have pastured in the Haurân area well after this date (cf. Luke 3:1, and the alleged cooperation of the Ituraean Zenodorus with the "robbers" of Trachonitis, i.e., the Safaites, before 24 B.C.; see below). The Safaitic inscriptions found in the Biqâᶜ (Ghadbân 1971; Harding 1975) cannot be attributed to Ituraean authors with any certainty. As early as in the time of Tiglath-pileser III, the Biqâᶜ was frequently visited by Arab nomads (Eph'al 1982: 95–97; Knauf 1984).

In the Biqâᶜ, the Ituraean tribal leader Ptolemaios (85–40 B.C.) founded a principality with its capital at Chalcis (ᶜAnjar; but see Will 1983); he minted coins and acted as supreme priest at the central sanctuary of Baᶜlbak-Heliopolis (Schottroff 1982: 138f.). In 85 B.C., he tried in vain to gain possession of Damascus; however, the people of Damascus preferred the rule of a more distant Arab, the Nabatean Aretas (*Ant* 13.15.1–2 §387–393; *JW* 1.4.7–8 §99–103). In 64/63, Pompey conquered the fortresses of Ptolemaios and imposed a tribute of 1000 talents upon him (*Ant* 14.3.2 §39). Ptolemaios' son Lysanias (40–36 B.C.) allied himself with the Parthians who occupied Palestine in 40 B.C.; he was subsequently beheaded when Rome regained its oriental realm (*JW* 1.13.1 §248–49; 1.22.3 §440; *Ant* 15.4.1 §91–92). Marc Anthony gave the Ituraean principality (together with other areas) to Cleopatra as a gift. Octavian/Augustus reversed this decision in 30 B.C. and invested Zenodoros, the son of Lysanias, with the S part of the previous Ituraean realm: the Huleh Area, Paneas, and the Trachonitis. Because Zenodoros could not, or would not, pacify the predatory bedouin in these areas (the same people who left the majority of the Safaitic inscriptions), Trachonitis was transferred to Herod the Great in 24/23 B.C. (*Ant* 15.10.1–2 §342–353; *JW* 1.20.4 §398–99). When Zenodorus died in 20 B.C., Herod "inherited" what had remained in the former's possession (*Ant* 15.10.3 §354–55; *JW* 1.20.4 §400). After Herod's death in 4 B.C., this area became the tetrarchy of his son Philippus (4 B.C.–A.D. 34; Luke 3:1), who refounded Paneas as Caesarea Philippi. In 20 B.C., the Ituraean principality of Chalcis in Lebanon had ceased to exist; whatever Chalcis is mentioned in later references must be sought in N Syria (Schmitt 1982). In 15 B.C., Baᶜlbak became a Roman colony.

Although the Ituraeans adopted the paraphernalia of statehood in the course of the 1st century B.C., including Greek names for their tribal leaders, they basically remained a bedouin tribe, pasturing in the mountains, extorting taxes from the peasants within their reach, and conducting raids into neighboring territories. For the sake of raiding, they constructed fortresses, fortified camps, or used natural strongholds for gathering (Strabo 16.2.18; Marfoe 1979). Knauf (1989) interprets Tell Ḥîra (Kuschke et al 1976: 32–34) as such a fortified camp of the Ituraeans. Although this peculiar type of military architecture can be linked to the Ituraeans, this does not imply that they became sedentarized. Even after the dismissal of Zenodorus, the last Ituraean ruler, Aemilius Palatinus, a subordinate of the Syrian governor Quirinius (Luke 2:2), had to fight against the Ituraeans in Lebanon; he conquered one of their "castles" (CIL III 6687; Schottroff 1982: 133, n. 33).

The Romans finally pacified the Ituraeans by exploiting their belligerent habits to the benefit of the empire: they recruited eight cohorts and one *ala* from the Ituraeans (Holder 1980; Schottroff 1982: 148–152; Dabrova 1986), especially archers. The paradoxical fact that more "Ituraeans" became Roman soldiers than probably ever really existed can be explained by the high reputation which the Ituraean archers had achieved in the course of the civil war (Lukan *Bell. Civ.* 7.230, 514) and subsequent military encounters. Consequently, these fierce elite units of "Ituraean archers" were being replenished with any recruits who happened to have expertise as archers, regardless of whether or not they were actually of Ituraean descent. Thus, as part of the Roman army, these "Ituraean" cohorts preserved the tribe's name long after the dispersion of the tribe itself (*Hist. Aug. Aurelian* 11.3).

Bibliography

Dabrova, F. 1986. Cohortes Ituraeorum. *ZPE* 63: 221–31.

Eph'al, I. 1982. *The Ancient Arabs.* Jerusalem.

Ghadbân, C. 1971. Un site safaitique dans l'Antiliban. *ADAJ* 16: 77–82.

Harding, G. L. 1975. Further Safaitic Texts from Lebanon. *ADAJ* 20: 99–102.

Holder, P. A. 1980. *Studies in the Auxilia of the Roman Army from Augustus to Trajan.* Oxford.

Knauf, E. A. 1984. Zum Vordringen des Arabischen im Libanon vor dem Islam. *WO* 15: 119–22.

———. 1989. *Ismael.* 2d ed. ADPV. Wiesbaden.

Kuschke, A.; Mittmann, S.; and Müller, U. 1976. *Archäologischer Survey in der nördlichen Biqaᶜ, Herbst 1972.* Tübinger Atlas des Vorderen Orients B 11. Wiesbaden.

Marfoe, L. 1979. The Integrative Transformation: Patterns of Sociopolitical Organization in Southern Syria. *BASOR* 234: 1–42.

Schmitt, G. 1982. Zum Königreich Chalkis. *ZDPV* 98: 110–24.

Schottroff, W. 1982. Die Ituräer. *ZDPV* 98: 125–52.

Will, E. 1983. Un vieux problème de la topographie de la Beqaᶜ antique: Chalcis du Liban. *ZDPV* 99: 141–46.

Winnett, F. V., and Harding, G. L. 1978. *Inscriptions from Fifty Safaitic Cairns.* Toronto.

Ernst Axel Knauf

IVORY. Ivory was used in the ANE primarily as a medium for sculpture from Chalcolithic times until the close of the biblical period. Since this study was prepared for a biblical dictionary, it is not intended as a comprehensive treatment of ivory-working in the ancient world, but rather as a discussion of the uses of ivory in the Levant. While this article is devoted primarily to ivory, representative types of objects fashioned in bone will be cited as ancillary products, since several fine objects (not discussed elsewhere in this volume) were also fashioned from bone.

There were four key periods of ivory-working: the Chalcolithic period, the Late Bronze Age, the Iron Age, and the Greco-Roman/Byzantine period. While the repertoire, style, and techniques of production changed radically during the periods under consideration, two facets of ivory use have remained constant: the use of ivory for small-scale carving of the human figure, which began as early as the Chalcolithic period, and the use of plaques for relief-carving and incision, which began in the LB Age.

A. Production

1. Material. Recent technical studies have focused attention on the differing types of ivory available (Caubet and Poplin 1987: 273–306; Reese 1985) and have thereby added a significant dimension to the study of ivory-working. While the tusks of the Indian and African elephants were primarily utilized, hippopotamus ivory was also used. However, it may be premature to determine the preference of one kind of material for one type of object vis à vis another type, or changes in popularity of material from period to period.

2. Technique. The ivory worker would carve, incise, bore holes, or combine any of these techniques. In the Chalcolithic period, incision was rarely used, and the utilization of ivory as a flat plaque—as a miniature wall surface—did not begin until the LB. The technique of openwork was also introduced into the repertoire of Palestinian ivory-working during the LB Age, probably no earlier than ca. 1400 B.C.

3. Workshops and Sources of Raw Material. Few workshops have been found. Barnett concurs with the excavator that a Chalcolithic workshop was discovered in the excavations of Bir Safadi, near Beer-sheba, where "a work bench, an elephant tusk, three awls with bone handles, and probably a bow-drill" were found (Barnett 1982: 23), yet he does express reservations (Barnett 1982: 76, n. 26). Nevertheless, the discovery of elephant tusks at a site suggests the existence of a workshop, or a way station in the transportation of tusks to a workshop. Elephant tusks have been found in subsequent periods in Syria at sites such as Ras Shamra, Chagar Bazar, and Alalakh, suggesting the existence of workshops at these sites.

While the elephant tusks apparently came from herds which roamed in Syria until the Iron Age (Barnett 1982: 23), hippopotamus tusks would have come from Africa where until recent times, hippopotami were common.

4. Society. Ivory objects were undoubtedly expensive and constituted a class of luxury items produced for the upper class—or in some instances, for a clerical group—and represented community wealth. We know little about the craftsmen who produced the items, but it is likely that sociologically they were part of the general class of craftsmen who, by analogy from Egyptian Middle Kingdom (Erman 1971: 446) and New Kingdom sources, were viewed as common laborers (Montet 1981: 157), though the craftsmen themselves recognized their own talent, as demonstrated in one Middle Kingdom text (Montet 1981: 158). Though we lack information from the Bible and other sources about the status of craftsmen in general, and the ivory worker in particular, it is unlikely that in the Iron Age their status differed substantially from that of Egyptian craftsmen.

B. The Periods

1. The Chalcolithic Period. A great age of ivory-carving dawned in the Levant in the Chalcolithic period. The phenomenon had no known local antecedents—it emerged as a fully developed style. It appears, however, to have been a regional phenomenon that was limited to the area around Beer-sheba (Bir es-Safadi and Tell Abu Matar). On the basis of the associated ceramic assemblages and C_{14} tests of material from the ivory workshop at Safadi, the ivories date to ca. 3320 B.C. ±300. The repertoire consists primarily of stylized, standing human figurines. These figures have prominent noses; circular eyes consisting of perforations in the ivory which were filled with another substance, or, as in the case of one example, with a rondel, which probably housed another substance for a pupil (Perrot 1957: Pl. III.1); circular, knob-like ears; oftentime short necks; narrow, angular shoulders; thin, spindly arms which descend vertically from the shoulders; hands bent at a 90° angle at the wrists and resting on their waists; and elongated legs. Both male and female figurines are found, though not in pairs. The head of an almost complete male figure found in a subterranean house has two rows of holes bored around the contour of the face for the application of a beard, and the top of his head is hollow. Though one is tempted to think that all the heads hollowed out at the top are males, one such head (found without a body) has no holes surrounding the face. The statue of this male figure is more rigid and somewhat less three-dimensional than the females, who have large breasts, thickened calves, and slightly flexed legs. Assuming that only the figures with holes bored along the outer contours of the face are male, the female figurines outnumber the males, but the sample is too small to permit the positing of definite ratios. The figurines are relatively large. The nearly complete male figure, whose left foot is missing, measures 33 cm tall. An example of a female figurine purchased on the antiquities market, whose feet are missing, measures 29 cm.

Though human figures in ivory are known from Egypt in late Pre-Dynastic times (a period generally corresponding with the Palestinian Late Chalcolithic), the Egyptian figures differ significantly from the Palestinian examples and were not prototypes for the Palestinian examples. Indeed, the single Egyptian example from a Badarian grave, a figurine of the Beer-sheba culture which resembles a 12 cm headless pregnant woman, was in all likelihood an import from Palestine (Liebowitz 1978: 28–29 n. 13).

Though the tusks used by the Palestinian Chalcolithic ivory carvers may have come from elephant herds which are presumed to have existed at that time in Syria (Barnett 1982: 23), no examples of ivory statuettes, or for that matter, significant ivories of any kind, are known from Chalcolithic Syria. Indeed, the suggestion that the Beer-sheba tradition "derives from the north or northeast and descends via the Jordan valley," and that "it is in the north that it may have continued, after the trail is lost in the south" (Barnett 1982: 24), has no basis from evidence. The homogeneity of the Palestinian ivories, the existence of a workshop in Safadi, and a stylistic link with Egypt, all suggest that the impetus for ivory-carving and the raw material as well, may have come from Egypt rather than the N. Yet the distinctive quality of the Palestinian ivories indicates that they were locally made, and that they represent a native tradition. The link with Egypt in the Chalcolithic period is not an isolated phenomenon. Other indications of links with Egypt include the discovery of shells and fish from the Nile at several Chalcolithic sites (Reese, Miemis, and Woodward 1986: 79–80) and an Egyptian building found at ʾEn-Besor.

The only other ivory objects found in this phase include a small carving of a pin handle (or possibly the headdress of a figurine) in the shape of a bird (identified as bone), a bell-shaped pendant, a fragment of what may be a hippopotamus head, and a fragment of an arc-shaped plaque with two concentric rows of punctuate dots. A 3.5-cm horned head purchased on the antiquities market is an isolated example, yet stylistically accords with the Beer-sheba ivory assemblage (Tadmor 1985). The human figure was clearly dominant and of greatest interest to the sculptor and the society for which the objects were crafted. Nevertheless, the purpose and meaning of the objects are indeterminant.

The use of bone was fairly widespread and was used for utilitarian objects such as awls fashioned from long bones, and polished flat-bone tools, fashioned from ribs tapered to a point at one end and pierced at the other.

2. The Late Bronze Age. Following a virtual halt in ivory production in the EB and MB periods, it resumed in the LB. However, the resurgence was gradual, and few objects dating to the LB I period are known. The great age ivory-carving in the LB-Levant, as in the Mycenaean world, was in the LB II period. During the LB, there was an expansion both in the repertoire and the technique of ivorywork. A genre from this period which exhibits the most complex compositions in ivory in the Levant, consists of a series of plaques depicting feasts and military scenes. Examples are found at Megiddo and at Tel Faraʾ (S). While the example from Tel Faraʾ (S) and one of the examples from Megiddo are incised, the series of four plaques from Megiddo are carved in relatively bold relief. Though these feast and military scenes show different degrees of Egyptianizing tendencies, they clearly betray a non-Egyptian origin. It may also be argued that these plaques were locally made, and were not imported from sites in Syria, since no objects of the type have been found in Syria.

Fragments of openwork plaques depicting females dressed in long robes have been found at Megiddo, and represent another tradition of ivory-carving. Another series of openwork plaques featuring Anubis, Bes, and winged female sphinx figures was also found at Megiddo, and apparently came from the same workshop. Again since evidence of this technique was unknown in Syria, it seems that the Megiddo examples of this technique also represent a local Palestinian tradition (Liebowitz 1987). Though the proposed idea of a local, Palestinian school of ivory-working contrasts with prevailing opinion, the discovery of ivory tusks at Megiddo (Barnett 1957: 165, no. 3) further supports the idea.

Ivory sculpture in the round constitutes another important genre. An excellently carved figurine of a nude female wearing a polos cap decorated with alternating lotus blossoms and buds, and the small, frequently overlooked statuette of a seated king, whose throne resembles that on the incised ivory plaque depicting a feast and military scene at Megiddo, are minor masterpieces of ivory-carving. Objects such as hands (e.g., the 13.5 cm example restored from fist to mid-forearm found at Lachish VI; Ussishkin 1983: 115, Pl. 26: 2), represent an example of the use of ivory for approximately half-life-sized statues. In these cases ivory would have been used to represent fleshy parts of the statue only; the clothed part of the statue would have been made of another material.

Ivory was also used in this period to produce a variety of objects associated with perfumes and cosmetics. A class of objects in the shape of naked slave girls holding before them lidded bowls, was found at several sites in Israel, including Megiddo, Beth-shan, and Tell es-Saʿidiyeh. While the type originated in Egypt, where it was usually made out of wood or stone; examples found at sites in Canaan are normally made of ivory and are rendered in less detail than those from Egypt.

Additional toilet objects made from ivory include a series of duck-shaped cosmetic vessels, the lids of which consisted of the wings of the duck, which swiveled open and closed. The necks and heads of these ducks were made of separate pieces attached to the cosmetic bowl. Examples of this type were found at many sites including Megiddo, Lachish, a tomb near Shechem, Tel Dan, and most recently at Acco. Though an example from Megiddo was said by the excavator to date to the LB I period, the tomb also had LB II material, and it is likely that the Megiddo example is out of context and that objects of this type did not appear until the LB II period.

Ivory working continued in the Levant into the middle of the 12th century and part of the Megiddo VIIA hoard may date to that period as evidenced by discovery of a model pen case inscribed with the cartouche of Rameses III.

Following the LB, there is only sporadic use of ivory in Palestine until the Iron II period.

Bone work in the LB is essentially limited to awls, pins, and spindle whorls. It was exceptional to find the Hathor sistrum handle from Bethel made from bone, since it was customary to make such sophisticated items in ivory.

3. The Iron Age. Few ivory objects have been found which date to the Iron Age I. A 3 cm long, well-carved lion's head from an Iron I context was found at Tel Masos—though it is presumed to be a Phoenician import (Crüsemann 1983: 99). However, as noted above, the true resurgence of ivory-working did not occur until the 9th and 8th centuries B.C. While an overwhelming mass of Iron Age ivories was found at Nimrud, other important collections were found at Khorsabad; Arslan Tash in Syria; at Samaria, the former capital of the N kingdom; and some small objects at Zincirli and Carchemish.

The ivories at Samaria, which apparently came from furniture (and possibly from inlaid walls), were found in one or more of the rooms of the Omride palace complex. These shed light on the reference to an ivory house built at Ahab (1 Kgs 22:34) and indirectly on the reference in Amos (6:4) in which he describes the people of Samaria as those "that lie upon couches of ivory." While none of the Iron Age ivories displays the complex compositions which characterized the LB, several LB motifs—such as cherubs and palm fronds—are repeated in variation. The Iron Age cherubs differ from the LB cherubs at Megiddo in that they are placed in Nilotic settings and usually wear a distorted type of Egyptian double crown. The prominent Iron Age palms have long, drooping fronds. On the other hand, many new motifs and radical changes in technique appear. The repertoire of Egyptianizing motifs (such as the infant Horus on a lotus blossom and a plaque featuring Isis and Nepthys) is expanded, and new non-Egyptianizing motifs (such as the woman at the window, and standing, winged human figures) are introduced. Barnett, in his pioneering work in 1939, had already distinguished between the Phoenician style with its Egyptianizing tendency and the Syrian style (i.e., N Syrian).

The change in repertoire in the Iron Age is seen also in that ivory was not used for cosmetic items, which are not even well documented in the archaeological record for this period. However, stone vessels with round, relatively small central depressions and dotted circles and other geometric patterns incised on the flat, encircling rims have been found at numerous sites both in the N and S of the country.

The techniques of ivory-working in the Iron Age were similar to those of the LB, with the added decoration, however, of glass paste and semiprecious stones.

Only random objects of ivory were found at other sites either in the N or S kingdoms. However, the annals of Sennacherib list furniture with ivory inlay among the spoils following the campaign in 701 (*ANET,* 288).

The question remains unresolved if any ivories were produced in Palestine—either in the N or S kingdoms—or if all were produced in N Syria, or, as Winter argued, possibly in a S Syrian school with its center of production at Damascus (Winter 1981).

While use of bone is even more limited in the Iron I period than in the LB, in the Iron II, there is a resurgence of bone work for luxury items, and elongated pendants decorated with incised dots and circles, or by horizontal grooving are found at many N and S sites dating from the 10th to the 7th or 6th centuries. The bone assemblage of the Iron II period is also characterized by bone spatulae (rounded at one end and pointed at the other, and which were apparently used in weaving), spindle whorls, pendants, tubes (possible serving as handles), and flutes.

4. Greco-Roman/Byzantine Period. In this era, corresponding with the Second Temple, Rabbinic, and Early Christian periods, ivory-working was less prevalent in Palestine and few objects of ivory have been found. While the Hellenistic period witnessed a wide repertoire of small-scale ivories, at places such as Bactria, Mysa, and Begram (Barnett 1982: 65–68), practically nothing of ivory is known from Palestine.

In the Roman period, bone replaced ivory even in Rome itself (Barnett 1982: 69); only isolated fragments and small simple objects of ivory have been found in Palestine. Bits of ivories were found in the apse of the synagogue at Maʾon, and a pin, identified as ivory by the excavators, was found at Khirbet Shema. Interestingly, no references to ivory are found either in the Mishnah or the Babylonian Talmud. The use of bone, however, was more prevalent. Bone was used for combs, spoons (cosmetic?), pins, and needles. However, it must be pointed out that the identification of the material of small objects is often neither clearly specified nor scientifically identified, and in some published reports, plates illustrate small objects that are often labeled "ivory and bone objects." Nevertheless, the apparent dearth of ivories in Palestine accords well with the written report and with the situation in Rome, as attested to by both the archaeological record and the literary evidence.

Bibliography

Barnett, R. D. 1939. Phoenician and Syrian Ivory Carving. *PEQ,* 4–19.

———. 1957. *A Catalogue of the Nimrud Ivories with other Examples of Ancient Near Eastern Ivories in the British Museum.* London.

———. 1982. *Ancient Ivories in the Middle East.* Qedem 14. Jerusalem.

Caubet, A., and Poplin, F. 1987. Les objects de matière dure animale: étude du materiau. *Ras Shamra-Ougarit* III. Paris.

Crüsemann, F. 1983. Die Kleinfunde. Pp 91–101 in *Ergebnisse der Ausgrabungen auf der hirbet el-Msas (Tel Masos),* ed. V. Frtiz and A. Kempinski. Wiesbaden.

Erman, E. 1971. *Life in Ancient Egypt.* Trans. H. M. Tirad. New York.

Kantor, H. 1956. Syro-Palestinian Ivories. *JNES* 15/3: 153–74.

Liebowitz, H. 1978. The Impact of the Art of Egypt on the Art of Syria and Palestine. Pp. 27–36 in *Immortal Egypt,* ed. D. Besserat. Malibu, CA.

———. 1987. Late Bronze II Ivory Work in Palestine: Evidence of a Cultural Highpoint. *BASOR* 265: 3–24.

Montet, P. 1981. *Everyday Life in Egypt: In the Days of Ramesses the Great.* Trans. A. Maxwell-Hyslop and M. Drower; with new introduction by D. O'Connor. Philadelphia.

Perrot, J. 1957. Les touelles d'Abou matar prés de Béersheba. *Syria* 34: 1–38.

———. 1959. Statuettes en Ivoire et autres objets en ivoire et en os provenant des quiesments prehistoriques de la région de Béersheba. *Syria* 36: 8–19.

Reese, D. 1985. Hippopotamus and Elephant Teeth from Kition: Appendix VIII (D). Pp. 391–409 in *Excavations at Kition V,* Pt 2, ed. V. Karageorghis. Nicosia.

Reese, D.; Minenis, H.; and Woodward, F. 1986. On the Trade of Shells and Fish from the Nile River. *BASOR* 264: 79–84.

Tadmor, M. 1985. Two Chalcolithic Ivory Figurines—Technique and Iconography. *EI* 18: 428–34.

Ussishkin, D. 1983. Excavations at Tel Lachish 1978–1983: Second Preliminary Report. *TA* 10: 97–175.

Winter, I. 1981. Is There a South Syrian Style of Ivory Carving in the Early First Millennium B.C.? *Iraq* 43: 101–30.

HAROLD A. LIEBOWITZ

IVVAH (PLACE) [Heb *ʿiwwâ*]. An unidentified place which served as one of the many examples of towns which could not survive the Assyrian onslaught in 2 Kings 18:34 (= Isa 36:19) and 2 Kgs 19:13 (= Isa 37:13). Though the occurrence of Ivvah alongside Hena and Sepharvaim in 2 Kgs 19:13 seems textually sound, Isa 36:19 and the LXX, however, omit the phrase *hēnaʿ wĕʿiwwâ* which suggests a textual problem in 2 Kgs 18:34. The Targum interprets the words *hnʿ wʿwh* in 2 Kgs 18:34 as verbs ("transported and carried off"). Perhaps *ʿiwwâ* is a variant of the place called *ʿawwâ* in 2 Kgs 17:24 whose location is also uncertain. M. C. Astour (*IDBSup,* 807) regards *ʿiwwâ* as the result of a dittography of an original *ʾyh mlk sprdym hnʿwh* (= "Where is the perverse King of the Sapardians?"). This otherwise attractive proposal is unsatisfactory because such an adjectival use of the *Nipʿal* participle of *ʿwh* after a noun is as unattested in the Hebrew Bible as the places he attempts to explain are in the ANE. Moreover, even if such a construction were allowed, the supposed dittography would yield *ʿiwwâ* only after additional emendations to the text. For the moment, one must concur with Cogan and Tadmor (*2 Kings* AB, 233) that Ivvah remains as enigmatic as ever.

HECTOR AVALOS

IYE-ABARIM (PLACE) [Heb *ʿîyê hāʿăbārîm*]. Var. IYIM. Hebrew for "ruins of Abarim," a place visited by the Israelites in their passage from the wilderness to the plains of Moab. Although no site has been linked to Iye-abarim with certainty, Num 21:11–12 points to a location between Oboth and Wadi Zered, and at least two sites in this area have been proposed: (1) Muhai, located ca. 11 miles SE of Mazar, is on the wilderness side of Moab, but it is N of the Zered; and (2) Medeiyineh (M.R. 223041) is on a hilltop that rises out of the Zered canyon and would therefore be more like the place of encampment that followed Iye-abarim. Num 33:44–45 seems to indicate that this site was in Moabite territory and that its shorter name was Iyim.

GERALD L. MATTINGLY

IYYAR [Heb *ʾîyāyr; ʾîyār*]. The second month of the Hebrew calendar, roughly corresponding to April and May. See CALENDARS (ANCIENT ISRAELITE).

ʿIZBET ṢARṬAH (M.R. 146167). A site situated on a moderate hill NE of Rosh Haʿayin and SW of Kafr Qasem, next to a place known as ʿIzbet Ṣarṭah, which has seen seasonal agricultural activity over the past few generations by the inhabitants of the village of Sarta. The hill is at the W end of a spur overlooking the coastal plain. Three km to the W, on the other side of the strategic Aphek pass and on the sources of the Yarkon River, lies Tel Aphek. Quarrying which took place on the periphery of the hill during the British Mandate has altered its natural shape. Rock cut cisterns scattered down the slopes supplied water to the inhabitants.

The site was discovered in 1973 by an archaeological survey team from Tel Aviv University directed by M. Kochavi, and four seasons of excavations were conducted between 1976–1978 under the direction of M. Kochavi and supervised in the field by I. Finkelstein.

Three strata were uncovered at ʿIzbet Ṣarṭah. The earliest two are from the Iron Age I and the last is from the beginning of the Iron Age II. Six more Iron Age I sites were discovered in the vicinity during the survey; these were situated in similar locations on the border between the foothills and the coastal plain. Various considerations, which include the general pattern of settlement of the region, the architectural features of the site in each level, and the pottery finds, all lead to the conclusion that the inhabitants of the site belonged to the Israelite population of the hill country.

The earliest level, Stratum III, was established at the end of the 13th century or at the beginning of the 12th century and was abandoned at the beginning of the 11th century B.C.E. The settlement of this period had an elliptical layout and covered an area of some 2.2 dunams. In the center of the site was a large oval courtyard surrounded by a wall on the outside of which were attached rooms in a row, similar to "casemates." The only entrance into the rooms was from the courtyard with no openings between the adjoining rooms. The width of the rooms is not uniform and in contrast to the inner wall, the outer wall of the site does not form a single line. The walls were constructed of large stones, of which only a single course has survived, with the natural rock usually forming the floors of the rooms. The entrance to the settlement was on the NE side of the site—a narrow opening between two monolithic posts leading into an area paved with stone slabs. Within the courtyard were several stone-lined storage pits. A very light colored brick material was found in every place where excavation of this stratum took place; this had been leveled at a later period, to serve as foundations for the structures of Stratum II. The settlement of Stratum III seems to have been peacefully abandoned, thereby leaving behind only a few complete vessels, among which were three collared rim jars. Since this was the first occupation on the hill, the pottery sherds apparently reflect the accumulation during the whole period of activity. Among the earliest finds were a small sherd of a stirrup jar of the Late Mycenaean III type, part of a krater decorated with the "gazelle and palm" motif, the sherd of a krater with a "palm" motif in applied relief, bases of "Canaanite" jars, cooking pots with rims, and various bowls in the LB tradition. Several rims of rounded bowls with red slip and sherds of jars with unmolded straight rims provide a date for the end of activity in Stratum III. The ceramic repertoire attests the close contacts of the inhabitants with the nearby coastal plain. Since the site is situated on the border between the hill country and the coastal plain, its history reflects the political changes in this sensitive area. The Israelite expansion from the center of the hill country to its W fringes can probably be attributed to the period immediately following the destruction of Canaanite/Egyptian Aphek and prior to the Philistines establishing themselves there (or, for mutual economic reasons, to the period prior to the destruction of Aphek). The site was probably abandoned as a result of the increasing tension between the Israelites and Philistines in the region at the beginning of the 11th century, a tension which led to the decisive battle at EBENEZER a short time later (some have identified ʿIzbet Ṣarṭah as Ebenezer; Kochavi 1977; Kochavi and Demsky 1978; Cross 1980).

Following a gap in occupation, settlement was reestablished towards the end of the 11th century B.C.E., once conditions were suitable for a renewed Israelite westward expansion from the hill country, possibly during the reign of Saul. Stratum II is completely different from Stratum III in its layout, with a certain degree of planning evident. In the center of the settlement, which covered an area of some 4 dunams, a large four-room house was erected. This was surrounded by dozens of storage pits, densely excavated into the light mudbrick material and into the structures of the previous level. On the edge of the settlement a belt of small houses were built. The central house measured 12 x 16 m. The outer walls, 1.4 m thick, were built of large fieldstones; only 2–3 courses have survived. Parts of the walls were robbed of their stones in later periods for secondary use. Two rows of pillars made of flat stones divide the three longitudinal units. The side units were paved with stone slabs, with the natural rock together with compacted earth forming the floor in the courtyard. A small room was attached onto the building from the outside. The average volume of a storage pit at ᶜIzbet Ṣarṭah is about 1.3 m³. Their floors were composed of the natural rock or of small stones, with the lining made with small- and medium-sized stones. Several storage pits lean against the walls of the central building and at times the pits touch one another. A total of 43 silos of Stratum II were excavated. In various places between the pits a compacted earth floor was unearthed. In one of the silos (No. 605) the ᶜIzbet Ṣarṭah ostracon was found (see Kochavi 1977; Demsky 1977; Naveh 1978). It is worth noting that at least two of the smaller houses built on the edge of the settlement were also constructed in the four-room plan. The peripheral houses do not join one another, hence the settlement had no defense system. Stratum II existed for a short time only—a decade or two at the most—and its abandonment is attributed to the increase of the Philistines' power in their struggle against Saul.

A short time later, at the beginning of the 10th century B.C.E., occupation of the site was renewed, once again for a very brief period (Stratum I). The settlement was much smaller; the four-room house was restored and several new silos were dug to replace the old ones that had gone out of use. The peripheral buildings of Stratum II were not reused. The central four-room house underwent certain changes: partitions were built between the pillars; two rooms were added on its N side and various installations were constructed within its rooms. The ceramic repertoire of Stratum I is similar to that of Stratum II, and only a quantitative study of the different types made it possible to distinguish between them. The renewed activity at the site can be attributed to the resumption of the westward expansion of the Israelites during the reign of David. A short time later, once the fertile plain of the Yarkon basin opened up to Israelite settlement, ᶜIzbet Ṣarṭah was abandoned once and for all.

During the Byzantine period some agricultural activity occurred. A terrace wall made of large stones which appear to have been taken from the older structures was erected on the edge of the top of the hill, and other walls were constructed to enclose heaps of stones gathered from field clearing.

The excavations of ᶜIzbet Ṣarṭah shed light on several issues which lie at the heart of research into the settlement processes and the material culture of the Israelite population during Iron Age I. The history of the site represents the ethno-demographic developments in a sensitive region which lay on the W periphery of the Israelite settlement. The occupation of the site reflects periods of expansion from the heart of the hill country towards the edge of the coastal plain, while the two gaps of occupation reflect periods of retreat from the foothills. As for the material culture, the fact that a large part of the site was excavated, allow a nearly complete reconstruction of its layout within the different levels, contributing to the study of the early Israelite architecture and its relationship to the socio-economic system of the inhabitants. The ceramic repertoire shows two different tendencies: the influence of the hill country culture on the one hand and of the coastal plain traditions on the other.

Bibliography

Cross, F. M. 1980. Newly Found Inscriptions in Old Canaanite and Early Phoenician Scripts. *BASOR* 238: 1–20.

Demsky, A. 1977. A Proto-Canaanite Abecedary (ᶜIzbet Ṣarṭah). *TA* 4: 14–27.

Finkelstein, I. 1986. *ᶜIzbet Ṣarṭah: an Early Iron Age Site Near Rosh Haᶜayin, Israel.* British Archaeological Reports International Series 299. Oxford.

Kochavi, M. 1977. An Ostracon of the Period of Judges from ᶜIzbet Ṣarṭah. *TA* 4: 1–13.

Kochavi, M., and Demsky, A. 1978. An Israelite Village from the Days of the Judges. *BARev* 4/3: 19–21.

Naveh, J. 1978. Some Considerations on the Ostracon from ᶜIzbet Ṣarṭah. *IEJ* 28: 31–35.

Israel Finkelstein

IZHAR (PERSON) [Heb *yiṣhār*]. IZHARITE.

1. A son of Kohath [Heb *qĕhāt*] and grandson of Levi (Exod 6:18; Num 3:19 [KJV Izehar]; 1 Chr 5:27–28—Eng 6:1–2; 1 Chr 6:1, 3—Eng 6:16, 18; 23:12). See KOHATH. Izhar was the brother of Amram, Hebron, and Uzziel and the uncle of Moses, Aaron, and Miriam (1 Chr 5:28–29—Eng 6:2–3). Less fortunately, he was also the father of Korah, Nepheg, and Zichri (Exod 6:21; 1 Chr 6:22–23—Eng 6:37–38), as Korah was the prominent ringleader of the infamous rebellion in the wilderness (Num 16:1). See KORAH. While Amminadab is said to have been the father of Korah in one text (1 Chr 6:7—Eng 6:22), "Izhar" is most likely to be read there instead of the name "Amminadab," as in LXX A and L (Gk *issaar*). This would be in line with the observation that while every other list of Kohath's children always includes Izhar, no other levitical list ever mentions Amminadab (*IDB* 1: 108). See AMMINADAB. In the wilderness period, as one of the four important Kohathite families their place of encampment was reportedly on the S side of the tabernacle and their assigned charge was the care of the ark, table, lampstand, altar, and vessels of the sanctuary (Num 3:27 [KJV here Izeharites], 29, 31). In 1 Chr 6:18–23—Eng 6:33–38 Izhar's name is cited as proof of the strong levitical pedigree of Heman, David's chief levitical singer. Izhar is also said to count among his descendants Shelomith/Shelomoth and his son Jahath (1 Chr 23:18; 24:22). Other known Izharites include Chenaniah and his sons who were asked to serve as officials and judges outside the temple (1 Chr 26:29).

2. A Judahite, the son of Ashhur by his wife Helah (1 Chr 4:5, 7). Instead of Izhar, the name of this person should more probably be read as "Zohar" (see MT's Q "and Zohar" = Heb *wĕṣōhar* [LXX *kai saar;* LXX L *eisar*] instead of MT's K *yiṣhār*). His father Asshur is said to be the son of Caleb and is apparently credited with the founding of the village of Tekoa (1 Chr 2:24). See ASSHUR; TEKOA. The name Izhar/Zohar occurs as part of a larger genealogical delineation by the Chronicler of Hezron ben Perez ben Judah's supposed two sons, Jerahmeel (1 Chr 2:25–41) and Caleb (1 Chr 2:18–24, 42–55; 4:1–7). These fragmentary lists suggest additions to the tribe of Judah not by birth, but by adoption and territorial absorption over time.

Bibliography

Williamson, H. G. M. 1979. Sources and Redaction in the Chronicler's Genealogy of Judah. *JBL* 98: 351–59.

Roger W. Uitti

IZLIAH (PERSON) [Heb *yizlîʾâ*]. Descendant of Benjamin (1 Chr 8:18) appearing in an extended genealogy (1 Chr 8:1–40). The name occurs nowhere else in this form in the MT, the Apocrypha, or the deuterocanonical literature. Izliah is a son of Elpaal. The meaning of the name is uncertain (cf. Noth *IP*, 248). According to 1 Chr 8:12, the family of Elpaal, and thus Izliah, is associated with the sites of Ono and Lod. This association is further referred to in Ezra 2:33, Neh 7:37, and 11:35. Ono and Lod are located in traditional Danite territory in the maritime plain (Adams and Callaway 1965: 55). A settlement by Benjamin of this area during the reign of Rehoboam is proposed by Myers (*1 Chronicles* AB, 60). The relative scarcity of Danite material in Chronicles suggests a possible absorption of tribal inheritance by Judahite and Ephraimite tribes. The fact that Izliah and others associated with Lod and Ono are called *roʾšê ʾābôt,* or heads of families, and "chiefs living in Jerusalem" (v 28), may reflect some tribal mixing of Judah and Benjamin at various points after the monarchical schism. This designation also holds implications for social organization. Coggins (*Chronicles* CBC, 54) has shown that tribal mixing caused certain areas, like Jerusalem itself, to be never fully absorbed into any one tribal holding. Judahite and Benjaminite groups are seen struggling for control of Jerusalem in Judg 1:8, 21.

Bibliography

Adams, J. M., and Callaway, J. A. 1965. *Biblical Backgrounds.* Nashville.

G. Edwin Harmon

IZRAHIAH (PERSON) [Heb *yizraḥyāh*]. A descendant of Issachar (1 Chr 7:3). His name means "May Yahweh shine forth." Izrahiah is listed as a great grandson of Issachar but in what time period the Chronicler might have viewed him as having lived is not clear. If, along generational lines, one compares Izrahiah's descent from Issachar with Moses's descent from Levi in 1 Chr 6:1–3, it appears that the Chronicler views him as contemporary with Moses. In 1 Chronicles 7 the list of descendants from Issachar and other N tribes serves to emphasize the Chronicler's "all Israel" theme.

James M. Kennedy

IZRAHITE [Heb *yizrāḥ*]. A descriptive adjective of Shamhuth, one of twelve commanders supervising monthly courses of men in the armed service of the king (1 Chr 27:1–15; v 8). The term (lit. "Izrah") is probably intended to be a gentilic designation for one from the otherwise unknown place Izrah (therefore RSV, "Izrahite"), although the term is missing the usual gentilic indicator (*î*). Variants of this designation occur in other lists which apparently refer to the same person, who is one of David's champions, although in these lists his name is spelled differently: Shammah of Harod (lit. "the Harodite," 2 Sam 23:8–39, v 25) = Shammoth of Harod (lit. "the Harorite," 1 Chr 11:10–47, v 27). "Harorite" in the Chronicler's text might be explained as a scribal error for "Harodite," arising through the confusion of similar letters (*ḥ* for *ḥ* and *r* for *d*). Alternatively, it might be suggested that some transmitter of the text, recognizing a corruption, borrowed the designation from a different Shammah, Shammah the Hararite of 2 Sam 23:33 (= Shagee the Hararite of 1 Chr 11:34). The widely divergent "Izrah" in 1 Chr 27:8 suggests again that the designation of Shamhuth was recognized by some transmitter as missing or corrupt; and, perhaps, in seeking to restore it the transmitter drew on a recognized gentilic adjective occurring elsewhere in the same list, "Zerahite" (vv 11, 13; Heb *zrḥ;* see BDB; Curtis *Chronicles* ICC, 192).

Rodney K. Duke

IZRI (PERSON) [Heb *yiṣrî*]. Person who receives the fourth lot cast (1 Chr 25:11) to determine the duties of the sons of Asaph, Heman, and Jeduthun listed in 1 Chr 25:2–4. The problem is that Izri does not appear in 1 Chr 25:2–4 as one would expect; however, the name Zeri appears in 1 Chr 25:3 in precisely the spot where Izri would be expected, since the sons of Jeduthun receive all but one of the even-numbered lots cast up to fourteen in 1 Chr 25:9–31. This fact, plus the similarity of the two names, suggest that Izri and Zeri are variant names for the same person.

Most scholars suggest that the list in 1 Chr 25:9–31 is literarily dependent upon the list in 25:2–4 (Williamson 1979: 255–57). Thus, Izri would be an expansion of an original Zeri, which is identical to a word which means "balsam" (RSV "balm," Jer 8:22, 46:11, 51:8). In contrast, Petersen contends that 1 Chr 25:9–31 contains the more original forms of the variant names (1977: 68, 92). He suggests that Zeri *(ṣĕrî)* is a shortened form of Izri *(yiṣrî),* which in turn should be understood as an abbreviated form of *yṣryhw,* "God created *[yṣr].*"

Bibliography

Petersen, D. L. 1977. *Late Israelite Prophecy: Studies in Deutero-Prophetic Literature and in Chronicles.* SBLMS 23. Missoula, MT.

Williamson, H. G. M. 1979. The Origin of the Twenty-Four Priestly Courses, A Study of 1 Chronicles xxiii–xxvii. Pp. 251–68 in *Studies in the Historical Books of the Old Testament,* ed. J. A. Emerton. VTSup 30. Leiden.

J. Clinton McCann, Jr.

IZZIAH (PERSON) [Heb *yizzîyāh*]. A descendant of Parosh and one of the returned exiles who was required by Ezra to divorce his foreign wife (Ezra 10:25 = 1 Esdr 9:26). According to Noth, the name "Izziah" is derived from the root *nzh* and may mean "Yahweh will sprinkle," referring to a cultic purification or absolution (*IPN*, 245). A slight variation occurs in the parallel text of 1 Esdr 9:26 where the LXX renders the name *iezias,* while the form in Ezra 10:25 is *iazia.* Izziah was a member of a family group which returned from exile with Zerubbabel (Ezra 2:3; Neh 7:8). For further discussion, see BEDEIAH.

Jeffrey A. Fager

J

J. The abbreviation (of German "Jahvist") used by scholars to designate the Yahwist source in Pentateuchal source criticism. See YAHWIST ("J") SOURCE.

JAAKAN (PERSON) [Heb *yaʿăqān*]. A clan name in the genealogy of Seir the Horite in 1 Chr 1:42. Jaakan is listed as the third son of Ezer and he is thus a grandson of Seir. The Horites are not to be confused with the Hurrians of Mesopotamia. They are described as the original "inhabitants of the land" in Gen 36:20. They occupied the region of Edom until the incursions of the Esau clans drove them out. This conquest is paired in the text with the conquest of Canaan by the tribes of Israel. The designation of the Horites as "cave dwellers" may be a reflection of their use of these natural shelters for themselves and their animals or it may be a disparaging remark by their conquerors to demonstrate how "uncivilized" they were. The name Jaakan appears in this form only in 1 Chr 1:42 (Jakan in KJV). In some Gk mss and in the parallel genealogical clan list in Gen 36:27 it appears as Akan.

Jaakan's name apparently became associated with two places in the region of Edom, Bene-Jaakan (Num 33:31–32) and Beeroth Bene-Jaakan (Deut 10:6). This probably reflects the usage of water resources at these sites by the Horite clans and perhaps the control over water rights by the clan of Jaakan. Matthews (1986: 123) discusses a similar example of the regular use and proprietorship over wells and springs in Genesis 26 by Isaac and his herdsmen. Names were often given to clan wells and eventually these names were expanded or modified to include the name of the principal clan in the area.

Bibliography

Matthews, V. H. 1986. The Wells of Gerar. *BA* 49: 118–26.

VICTOR H. MATTHEWS

JAAKOBAH (PERSON) [Heb *yaʿăqōbâ*]. Simeonite family leader (1 Chr 4:36). Jaakobah is included in a list of Simeonites who migrated to "the entrance of Gedor" (v 39, the RSV follows the MT; however, the LXX reading "Gerar" is usually favored) in search of suitable grazing for their flocks. The Chronicler attributes this movement to the time of King Hezekiah of Judah (715–687/86). According to Noth (*IPN,* 177–78, 197) the name means "may (the deity) protect."

DANA M. PIKE

JAALA (PERSON) [Heb *yaʿălāʾ*]. Var. JAALAH. A servant of Solomon who was the progenitor of a family which returned from Babylon with Zerubbabel (Neh 7:58). The variant Jaalah occurs in the parallel passage Ezra 2:56 (Heb *yaʿălâ*) and 1 Esdr 5:33 (Gk *ieēli*).

MICHAEL DAVID MCGEHEE

JAAR (PLACE) [Heb *yaʿar*]. A poetic reference to KIRIATH-JEARIM [Eng "city of forests"], or its environs, in Psalms 132:6. The noun is the Hebrew word for "forest," and the precise phrase is *biśdê-yaʿar,* literally, "in fields of [other ancient texts read 'a field of,' see *BHS* and BDB: 961] a forest" (cf. LXX); but parallelism with Ephrathah and consistent allusion throughout the Psalm to the resting place of the ark of the covenant make it likely that *yaʿar* is better translated as a *nomen proprium loci,* hence, "the fields of Jaar." The reference may be to Kiriath-jearim (on the border between Benjamin and Judah) itself, or to the open areas around it. This literary-critical decision squares well with the history of traditions. The ark was returned, via Beth-shemesh, to Kiriath-jearim, where it remained for some 20 years, whence David brought it with pomp and circumstance to Jerusalem (1 Sam 6:20–7:2; 2 Sam 6:1–15; 1 Chr 13:5–8). Psalm 132 is a preexilic festival liturgy uniting the traditions of the ark, the clan of David, and the election of Zion (cf. 2 Samuel 7 and Ps 78:68–71). The song celebrates the movement of the ark from the fields of Jaar, on the N edge of David's Ephrathite clan territory, to Zion, which David chose as the seat of his dynasty. It is not surprising, therefore, that 2 Chr 6:41–42 quotes Ps 132:8–10 to conclude Solomon's prayer at the dedication of the temple where the ark eventually came to rest. This allows also a better understanding of Micah's reversal of the traditions: the God who came from Jaar of Ephrathah to settle in Zion will abandon the capital for older roots in Bethlehem of Ephrathah (4:14–5:1—Eng 5:1–2).

Bibliography

Anderson, A. A. 1981. *Book of Psalms.* Vol. 2. Grand Rapids.

LAMONTTE M. LUKER

JAARESHIAH (PERSON) [Heb *yaʿărešyāh*]. Benjaminite family leader (1 Chr 8:27). Jaareshiah is listed with other Benjaminites as a resident of Jerusalem. This situation illustrates a certain mixing between neighboring tribes, a trend facilitated in this case by the location and status of the city of Jerusalem. Although this list of names appears to reflect a certain period, no time indicators have been included by the Chronicler. On the basis of Ar *ǵarasa* and Akk *erēšu,* the name probably means "may Yahweh plant" (Fowler *TPNAH,* 110).

DANA M. PIKE

JAASIEL (PERSON) [Heb *yaᶜăśîʾēl*]. The name of two different persons mentioned in the OT.

1. The son of Abner, Saul's cousin, who is reported to have been made the official in charge of the tribe of Benjamin during David's administration (1 Chr 27:21). The nature of his office is not clear. The list enumerating the leaders of the tribes is not found in the books of Samuel or Kings. It seems to be associated with David's census (1 Chr 27:22), and might preserve the names of individuals within various areas and groups who were made responsible for overseeing the registration of the local citizens during the census. None of the names of the officials appear elsewhere in biblical tradition, so the historical reliability of the list cannot be ascertained. Jaasiel's appointment to oversee Benjamin in such a capacity is plausible in light of his father's negotiations with David to remove Eshbaal from the throne of Israel. See ABNER. His appointment may have been made in the wake of Abner's murder, as a gesture of goodwill by David, to demonstrate his innocence in Abner's death. Jaasiel would have been a Benjaminite by birth, perhaps a member of the clan of Matri like Saul, and would have been a logical candidate to oversee a census among his fellow Benjaminites.

2. The "Mezobahite," perhaps a conflation of "the Zobahite" and "from Zobah," named as one of David's elite corps of warriors in 1 Chr 11:47. He is the last of 16 names added to the list of "the thirty" by the Chronicler, none of which are found in the parallel list in 2 Sam 23:18–39. Most of the additional names are associated with places of origin in Transjordan (Klein 1940). The epithet "Zobahite" could be equated either with Aram-Zobah, which would be consistent with the geography of the other additional names (Rudolph *Chronikbücher* HAT, 103), or with Benjaminite Zoba W of Jerusalem (modern Ṣuba), the probable home of another hero, Igal ben Nathan (2 Sam 23:36) (Klein 1940: 101). In the latter case, it might be possible to identify the two Jaasiels.

Bibliography

Klein, S. 1940. The Warriors of David. *Yediot* 7: 95–106 (in Hebrew).

DIANA V. EDELMAN

JAASU (PERSON) [Heb *yaᶜăśû*]. Israelite, descended from Bani (Ezra 10:37), who gave up his foreign wife because of Ezra's influence in the postexilic community. Jaasu is included in a list of about 110 men, subdivided into priests, Levites, singers, gatekeepers, and Israelites (the most numerous), who participated in this action. The MT consonantal form of the name, ending in *-w* (K *yᶜśw*), is represented in the English form Jaasu, although the traditional Hebrew vocalization ends in *-ay* (Q *yᶜśy*). The LXX renders Jaasu not as a personal name, but as a verb, *epoiēsan* "they produced." Jaasu is not included in the 1 Esdras 9 parallel to this list. Noth designates this as a "wish" name meaning "(the deity) should treat well" (*IPN,* 206).

DANA M. PIKE

JAAZANIAH (PERSON) [Heb *yaʾăzanyāh, yaʾăzanyāhû*]. Var. JEZANIAH. **1.** One of the troop commanders, who, following the destruction of Jerusalem in 587/6, chose to join Gedaliah, the ruler of Judah, at his administrative center at Mizpah (2 Kgs 25:23; "Jezaniah" in Jer 40:8). He is identified as "the son of the Maacathite." Although this could signify that Jaazaniah was from the clan of Maacah (cf. 1 Chr 2:48) and thus a native Judahite, it is also possible that he was from either the settlement of Abel Beth Maacah in N Galilee (cf. 2 Sam 20:14) or the small Aramean kingdom of Maacah (cf. Josh 13:11, 13). Presumably Jaazaniah and his men were among those who, fearing Babylonian reprisals for the assassination of Gedaliah (Jer 41:18; 2 Kgs 25:26), fled to Egypt (Jer 43:5–7). An onyx seal discovered in a tomb at Tell en-Naṣbeh (usually identified with biblical Mizpah), and which probably dates from the 6th century B.C.E., is inscribed *lyʾznyhw ᶜbd hmlk* ("[belonging] to Jaazaniah, servant of the king"). Beneath the inscription is the figure of a fighting cock. While certainty is impossible, it may be that the Jaazaniah of the seal is to be identified with the Jaazaniah of 2 Kgs 25:23. Each of the following suggests that the owner of the seal was a high-ranking official: the title *ᶜbd hmlk* ("servant of the king"), the representation of the fighting cock, and the fine quality of the seal itself. The name Jaazaniah also appears in a list of names contained in another contemporary document, one of the ostraca (Ostracon I) found at Lachish ("Yaazanyahu son of Tobshillem" and "Hagab son of Yaazanyahu" [*DOTT,* 213]).

2. Son of Jeremiah (not the prophet), and presumably a chief of the Rechabite community which had taken refuge in Jerusalem at the close of Jehoiakim's reign (Jer 35:3). Tested by the prophet Jeremiah, the Rechabites demonstrated that they had remained faithful to the command of their ancestor Jonadab.

3. Son of Shaphan and one of the 70 idolatrous elders seen by Ezekiel in a vision (Ezek 8:11). The fact that Jaazaniah is the only elder mentioned by name suggests that he was a prominent member of this group. There is good reason to believe, however, that the words "and Jaazaniah son of Shaphan standing in their midst" are a later gloss.

4. Son of Azzur and one of the 25 men seen by Ezekiel in a vision and against whom he was commanded to prophesy (Ezek 11:1). Jaazaniah and Pelatiah, the only men whose names are provided, are identified as "princes *(śārîm)* of the people." That is, they were leading officials (cf. e.g., "the princes of Judah" in Jer 26:10). Whereas the death of Pelatiah is mentioned in Ezek 11:13, nothing is said of the fate of Jaazaniah.

Bibliography

Diringer, D. 1967. Mizpah. Pp. 329–42 in *Archaeology and Old Testament Study,* ed. D. W. Thomas. Oxford.

Hestrin, R. 1983. Hebrew Seals of Officials. Pp. 50–54 in *Ancient Seals and the Bible,* ed. L. Gorelick and E. Williams-Forte. Malibu.

McCown, C. C. 1947. *Tell en-Naṣbeh.* Vol. 1. Berkeley and New Haven.

JOHN M. BERRIDGE

JAAZIAH (PERSON) [Heb *yaʿăzîyāhu*]. Son of Merari the Levite (1 Chr 24:26, 27). He is mentioned in a list of levitical families which received assignments from King David for service in the temple, soon to be built. That the Chronicler considered Jaaziah to be a literal son of Merari, even though he is never mentioned in the Pentateuch or 1 Chr 23:31 with Merari's other sons Mahli and Mushi, is evident from the structure of vv 27–30, in which descendants of Merari's three "sons" mentioned in v 26 are listed. Jaaziah and his descendants are placed even before Mahli and Mushi, while Kish (v 29), a son of Mahli (1 Chr 23:21), is listed after his father. For the name Jaaziah, the LXX reads *ozia,* Uzziah, in both verses. The name probably means "may Yahweh nourish" (Fowler *TPNAH,* 100).

DANA M. PIKE

JAAZIEL (PERSON) [Heb *yaʿăzîʾēl*]. Var. AZIEL. Levite musician (1 Chr 15:18). Jaaziel participated in the ceremony which accompanied the transfer of the ark of the covenant from Obed-edom's house to Jerusalem during the reign of King David. The musician Aziel (Heb *ʿăzîʾēl*) in v 20 must be considered the same individual. The LXX preserves *oziēl,* Uzziel, in both vv 18 and 20. It is also possible that the first Jeiel mentioned in 1 Chr 16:5 (Heb *yĕʿîʾēl,* Gk *Iiēl*) is this same Levite musician. The name probably means "may El nourish" (*TPNAH,* 100).

DANA M. PIKE

JABAL (PERSON) [Heb *yābāl*]. Son of Lamech and Adah, and the brother of Jubal, a descendant of Cain (Gen 4:20). Jabal is described as the father of tent dwellers and herds (Heb *miqneh;* for the more general meaning, "possessions," cf. below). It is not clear from the sentence construction (4:20) whether Jabal is said to have originated the practice of herding animals or whether he was the first to travel with his herds by living in tents (*GHBW,* 142 n. 10; Wenham *Genesis 1–15* WBC, 95 n. 20). These two concerns have been compared with the labors of Amynos and Magos, who were connected by Philo of Byblos with the origin of villages and sheep herding (Cassuto 1961: 235; Attridge and Oden 1981: 45).

Wordplay is apparently found in the word *miqneh,* which shares consonants with the name of Jabal's ancestor, Cain (Heb *qyn*). Paronomasia also seems to occur in the name, Jabal, whose root, *ybl,* is the same as that of his brother, Jubal, and suggests the first caretaker of livestock, Abel *(hbl).* (Cf. also the roots of the name of the half-brother, Tubal-Cain, *tbl* and *qyn.*)

The comparison with Abel suggests the development from sheep herding to the raising of livestock in general, perhaps either as part of an urban economy (if Cain's descendants are to be associated with urban culture; cf. Wallis 1966: 134–35) or as part of a nomadic lifestyle (if Cain's descendants are to be associated with the Kenites; cf. Miller 1974: 168). This latter interpretation is also likely if *miqneh* is understood in its more general sense of "possessions"; and thus describes Jabal's occupation as that of a "tent-dwelling trader" (Sawyer 1986: 160). The root *ybl,* common to many ancient Semitic languages, conveys the meaning, "to bring"; if compounded with a theophoric element, Jabal could mean, "(divine name) leads (in procession)" (North 1964: 380). The proposal to take the name as a noun, "wanderer (nomad)" (Gabriel 1959: 417), is less likely.

Bibliography

Attridge, H. W., and Oden, R. A., Jr., eds. 1981. *Philo of Byblos The Phoenician History. Introduction, Critical Text, Translation, Notes.* CBQMS 9. Washington, D.C.

Cassuto, U. 1961. *A Commentary on the Book of Genesis. Pt 1, From Adam to Noah.* Trans. I Abrahams. Jerusalem.

Gabriel, J. 1959. Die Kainitengenealogie. Gn 4, 17–24. *Bib* 40: 409–27.

Miller, J. M. 1974. The Descendants of Cain: Notes on Genesis 4. *ZAW* 86: 164–74.

North, R. 1964. The Cain Music. *JBL* 83: 373–89.

Sawyer, J. F. A. 1986. Cain and Hephaestus. Possible Relics of Metalworking Traditions in Genesis 4. *AbrN* 24: 155–66.

Wallis, G. 1966. Die Stadt in den Überlieferungen der Genesis. ZAW 78: 133–48.

RICHARD S. HESS

JABBOK (PLACE) [Heb *yabbōq*]. One of the four major streams of Transjordan, now known as the Wadi Zerqa or the *Nahr ez-Zerqa,* "the blue river." Its sources are near Amman, the biblical Rabbath-ammon. Its upper courses flow in a NE direction to modern Zerqa. From there the stream curves to the W where the lower courses rapidly descend into the Great Rift valley, a drop that begins at ca. 820 m above sea level to ca. 300 m below. It joins the Jordan river just N of Adam, ca. 37 km N of the Dead Sea. Its total length is about 100 km.

Gen 32:22 locates Jacob's struggle with his divine adversary at the ford of the Jabbok near Penuel. Several scholars have noted that the Hebrew text of this passage suggests a wordplay: Jacob (Heb *yaʿăqōb*) wrestled *(wayyēʾābēq)* at the Jabbok *(yabbōq).* It has also been suggested there may have been an older form of the story in which the adversary was a river demon.

According to Num 21:24; Josh 12:2; and Judg 11:13, 22, the Jabbok served as the border of Sihon's kingdom; the upper course separated it from the Ammonites to the E and the lower course from Og of Bashan's kingdom to the N. After Israel moved into the region, the lower course served as a boundary dividing the half tribe of Manasseh on the N from Gad and Reuben on the S (Deut 3:12, 16; Josh 12:2–6). Noth and Bartlett have argued, however, that this division of the land is the result of a Deuteronomist compiler who, in an attempt to portray the kingdoms of Sihon and Og as contemporary, reorganized the traditional threefold division of this region—the plain, Gilead, and Bashan—into a twofold division with the middle area of Gilead (through which the Jabbok flows) being divided between the two kings. Thus, instead of seeing the Jabbok as dividing areas, the river was originally viewed as the central feature of the one mountain range of Gilead.

Eusebius indicates that in later times the E-W stretch of the Jabbok did serve as a border, separating the territories of Gerasa and Philadelphia (*Onomast.* 102.19, 21).

The valley in which the Jabbok flowed served as a major highway between the Jordan valley and the Transjordanian plateau. It was along this route that Gideon pursued the Midianites (Judg 8:4–9); this route was also used by Shishak in his conquest of Palestine. Sites along the route included Adam, Succoth, Penuel, and Mahanaim.

Bibliography

Bartlett, J. R. 1970. Sihon and Og, Kings of the Amorites. *VT* 20: 257–77.

Noth, M. 1941. Das Land Gilead als Siedlungsgebiet israelitischer Sippen. *PJ* 37: 50–101.

Randall W. Younker

JABESH (PERSON) [Heb *yābēš*]. The father of Shallum, king of Israel (2 Kgs 15:10, 13–14). Jabesh, however, may be a place name, rather than a personal name. If such is the case, the phrase "son of Jabesh" would refer to Shallum's place of origin, "a person from Jabesh," and not patronymic. This would suggest that opposition to Jehu's dynasty came from the region of Jabesh-Gilead. In Assyrian records Shallum is referred to as a "son of a nobody."

Pauline A. Viviano

JABESH-GILEAD (PLACE) [Heb *yābēš gilʿād*]. Var. JABESH. An ancient city in Transjordan, which became part of the Israelite state during the early Monarchy, probably under David.

A. Location

The ancient name, which means "well-draining soil of Gilead," is preserved in Wadi el-Yabis, one of the main E-W tributaries that cuts through the N Gileadite hill country and empties into the Jordan. A site somewhere along the wadi is probable. Proposed locations include ed-Deir/Deir el-Halawe (Abel, *GP* 2, 352); Miryamim (Merrill 1881: 325; Oliphant 1881: 160–61); Meqbereh–Tell abu Kharaz (Glueck 1943); and Tell Maqlub (Merrill 1881: 440; Naor 1947; Noth 1953: 28–30; Simons *GTTOT,* 315; Aharoni *LBHG,* 379; Ottosson 1969: 195–96). Two factors are pertinent for locating the site. According to 1 Sam 31:11–13, men from Jabesh were able to reach Beth-shan on the W side of the Jordan in the Jezreel valley to retrieve the bodies of Saul and his sons from the city walls by traveling all night from their city. The text does not specify whether the men departed in the morning and traveled all day and night to arrive in the early morning hours of the following day, but still under cover of darkness, or whether they left only in the evening and traveled overnight. Accordingly, any site along the Yabis that lies somewhere between eight and twenty hours travel time from Beth-shan, with evidence of Iron I occupation (1200–1000 B.C.), is a possible candidate.

According to Eusebius, Jabesh-gilead lay in the vicinity of the sixth Roman milestone on the road from Pella to Gerasa (*Onomast.* 110.11–13). No milestone #6 has been uncovered, but a #5 milestone has been found at Kufr Abil (Thomsen 1917: 66–67). Assuming Eusebius' identification is accurate, Tell Maqlub (M.R. 214201) is the only possible candidate for Jabesh. It lies within the range of travel time described in 1 Sam 31:11–13, and has yielded evidence of Iron I occupation in surface survey (Glueck 1951: 214). The site lies on the N edge of a fertile bend in the Yabis River, at the point where the Roman road crosses the wadi. A modern road also crosses the wadi at this point, and it is likely that the pre-Roman road through the N hill country similarly forded the wadi here. Ancient Jabesh apparently was strategically located to control the flow of traffic crossing the wadi below it.

B. History

Jabesh is depicted as an Israelite city as early as the premonarchic period in Judges 21 and 1 Samuel 11. Nevertheless, 2 Sam 2:4–7 indicates that the city stood in a treaty relationship with Saul during his reign, and that David tried to persuade the city to switch its allegiance from the Saulide house at Saul's death and become allies of the newly-founded Davidic state of Judah, centered in Hebron. The phrase "do good" in v 6 is ancient technical treaty language (Moran 1963: 173–76; Edelman 1984: 202–3). Since Jabesh apparently was not incorporated into the Israelite state until sometime after the reign of Saul, the two depictions of the city as "Israelite" in the premonarchic period should be understood as literary fictionalizations. They probably are to be associated with the later idealization of premonarchic Israel as a union of twelve tribes, which were comprised of groups whose territory eventually became included within the borders of the Davidic-Solomonic state.

The Jabesh-gileadite practice of cremation and subsequent interment of the remaining bones (1 Sam 31:11–13) points to their non-Semitic background. No evidence yet exists that links any Semitic group with cremation as an accepted form of burial. On the other hand, both textual and archaeological material indicates that it was an accepted custom among groups of both Greek and Anatolian backgrounds, and that on the Greek mainland, it became the dominant form of adult burial during the 11th–10th centuries B.C. (Kurtz and Boardman 1971: 26, 33, 37). An excellent description of the Greek rite is found in the Odyssey (24.11.60–80). In Anatolia, it was the regular form of burial for kings (Bittel 1940; Otten 1940: 3–5). The cremations known from Hamath (Riis 1948: 47, 210–12) and the Amman airport "temple" crematorium (Herr 1983) both are associated with local Semitic pottery traditions, but in each case, have non-Semitic features. At Hamath, the pottery has Cypriot and Mycenaean decorative motifs and inscriptions written in Hittite and Phrygian, while at the Amman structure, a significant amount of imported Mycenaean ware, together with lesser amounts of imported Cretan, Cypriot, and Egyptian objects are found alongside the local ware in the burials. In both cases, it appears that the cremations should be associated with non-Semitic groups who had recently arrived in the two regions.

Saul's rescue of Jabesh-gilead from Ammonite oppression (1 Sam 11:1–11) is reported to have been the military deed that led to his elevation to kingship over Israel. As mentioned above, the story's depiction of Jabesh-gileadites as Israelites who appeal to their brethren for help cannot be historically accurate. The setting of the battle at the beginning of Saul's career, before he had built up a professional army and had the military support of his state's citizenry, is also impossible. The battle presumes that Saul was known to have been an established power in Transjordan, which would have had to be the case for them to take on the national Ammonite army with any chance for success. See SAUL (PERSON).

1 Sam 14:47 indicates that Saul waged successful war against the Ammonites, and there is no reason to doubt that at least some of the details found in the present account in 1 Samuel 11 have been derived from an account of one of those battles—one that involved Nahash's siege of Jabesh-gilead, and Saul's successful lifting of the siege by surprise attack. What is not certain is whether Jabesh would already have established the treaty with Saul prior to the battle, so that he became involved out of treaty obligations, or whether the treaty was arranged in the wake of the battle, after Saul voluntarily aided the city, perhaps as a result of overtures that promised the treaty in exchange for assistance in the existing crisis. In either case, the battle could not have been the historical event that triggered Saul's initial coronation as king. The story's use is part of the tripartite kingship ritual pattern (designation of the candidate, testing, coronation) to structure the current account of the introduction of the kingship in 1 Samuel 9–11, which required the military testing of the king-designate before his final coronation (Edelman 1984).

Bibliography

Bittel, K. 1940. Hethitische Bestattungsbräuche. *MDOG* 78: 12–28.

Edelman, D. 1984. Saul's Rescue of Jabesh-Gilead (1 Sam 11:1–11): Sorting Story from History. *ZAW* 96: 195–209.

Glueck, N. 1943. Jabesh-Gilead. *BASOR* 89: 2–6.

———. 1951. *Explorations in Eastern Palestine IV*, Pt. 1. AASOR 25–28. New Haven.

Herr, L. 1983. The Amman Airport Structure and the Geopolitics of Ancient Transjordan. *BA* 46: 223–39.

Kurtz, D., and Boardman, J. 1971. *Greek Burial Customs*. Ithaca.

Merrill, S. 1881. *East of Jordan*. London.

Moran, W. L. 1963. A Note on Some Treaty Terminology of the Sefire Stelas. *JNES* 22: 173–76.

Naor, M. 1947. Jabesh-Gilead, Abel Mehola, and Zarethan. *BIES* 13: 90–93 (in Hebrew).

Noth, M. 1953. Jabesh-Gilead. Ein Beitrag zur Methode alttestamentlicher Topogrphie. *ZDPV* 69: 28–41.

Oliphant, L. 1881. *The Land of Gilead*. New York.

Otten, H. 1940. Ein Totenritual hethitischer Könige. *MDOG* 78: 3–11.

Ottosson, M. 1969. *Gilead*. Trans. J. Gray. Lund.

Riis, P. J. 1948. *Hama, fouilles et recherches 1931–1938* 2/3. Nationalmuseets Skrifter 1. Copenhagen.

Thomsen, P. 1917. Die römischen Meilensteinen der Provinzen Syria, Arabia, und Palaestina. *ZDPV* 40: 1–103.

DIANA V. EDELMAN

JABEZ (PERSON) [Heb *yaʿbēṣ*]. A person introduced abruptly into the genealogy of Judah (1 Chr 4:9–10). No other detail regarding him except the content of his prayer is given. There appears to be a play on the name in the text in that the name Jabez is related to "pain" (Heb *ʿoṣeb*) in v 9 on the one hand and to "hurt" (Heb *ʿoṣbî*) in v 10 on the other. Curtis (*Chronicles* ICC, 107), assuming that he was the founder of Jabez the town (cf. 1 Chr 2:55), suggested that Jabez may be a Calebite scribe belonging to the family of Hur. Williamson (*Chronicles* NCBC, 59), on the other hand, sees no substantial evidence to suggest a connection between the two names.

H. C. LO

JABEZ (PLACE) [Heb *yaʿbēṣ*]. A city of Judah, apparently near Bethlehem, but not yet identified. It is only mentioned as the city of the Kenite families of scribes who descended from Hammath where the Tirathites, the Shimeathites, and the Sucathites resided (1 Chr 2:55). The meaning of this name is etymologically explained in 1 Chr 4:9. There a man was called Jabez by his mother's words "I bore him with pain (*ʿṣb*)." Here the Hebrew verb *ʿṣb* is apparently understood as the transposition of the other verb *ʿbṣ* which is neither used in Hebrew nor in Aramaic, but probably an Amorite verb which corresponds to the Hebrew verb *ʿṣb*. People commonly understood that Jabez meant "He (=God) causes pain" suggested from the word "in pain." However, because of dual meanings of the Hebrew verb *ʿṣb*, it may be also possible to see another meaning "He (=God) fashions (=makes)" suggested from his mother's word "I bore." Then the latter meaning of this name is quite suitable as a city name like Yabneh, "He builds," which may be taken as an Amorite noncausative *Yaqtel* verbal pattern like Yahweh.

YOSHITAKA KOBAYASHI

JABIN (PERSON) [Heb *yābîn*]. **1.** The King of Hazor who, along with his allies fought Joshua and Israel (Josh 11:1–14). That Jabin held a position of preeminence is made clear by the initiative that he had taken to summon the kings and groups of people in N Canaan when the region was under threat. The powerful alliance brought together by Jabin was defeated by Israel. Jabin was finally killed and Hazor put to the torch.

2. The King of Canaan, who reigned in Hazor, when Deborah was judging Israel (Judges 4). Sisera was the commander of Jabin's army. Deborah instructed Barak to engage Sisera in a battle and Sisera's army suffered a crushing defeat. Eventually, both Sisera and Jabin were killed.

The discussions concerning the Jabin in the two episodes have not reached unanimity in details and conclusion. One opinion holds that "Jabin" is a dynastic name of the kings of Hazor. It is noteworthy that the Mari texts of the 18th century B.C. as well as the Amarna Letters of the 14th century B.C. make reference to the city-state of Hazor. These indicate some measure of continuity. Another opinion holds that both episodes are in fact two varying traditions of the same event; they belong together. A third opinion points out that in Judges 4, Sisera is central to the story while chap. 5 does not mention Jabin at all. Therefore, the account in Judges may actually be about Sisera, who governed in Harosheth-ha-goiim, meaning the forested region of the gentiles as indicated by the LXX reading. It is possible that the battle of Merom (Joshua 11) took place subsequent to the battle of Deborah (Judges 4–5). Archaeology in this region supports an initial penetration by the Israelites and battles being fought much later. One such battle may have been given a national orientation and become a part of the conquest stories in the book of Joshua. The Deuteronomistic History has made use of the two episodes to contrast the strength of the enemies and the victory that is possible when the leaders are obedient to the Lord.

PAUL BENJAMIN

JABNEEL (PLACE) [Heb *yabnĕʾēl*]. Var. JABNEH. **1.** A town along the N border of the tribe of Judah (Josh 15:11), which is probably the same Philistine town (Heb *yabnēh*) conquered by Uzziah, king of Judah (2 Chr 26:6). Two essentially unexcavated sites named "Jabneh" are attested in the region: Yavneh-Yam (M.R. 121147), a large site situated along the Mediterranean Sea S of Kibbutz Palmahim; and an inland site associated with the Arab village of Yibna (M.R. 126141) situated on the coastal plain between Lod and Ashdod, S of Nahal Sorek. The biblical site is identified with the latter, which contains Iron Age, Hellenistic, and Byzantine remains. In the Hellenistic period the town was called Jamnia/Iamnia (the name having gone from Jabneel to Jabneh to Jamnia).

Judah Maccabeus—or, according to Josephus (*Ant* 13.6.7), Simon—captured and burned the city (2 Macc 12:8–9). In Hellenistic times, Jamnia had a Jewish population, and by the time of Alexander Janneaus it was listed among the cities under his control, and had a totally Jewish population. From the fall of Jerusalem in 70 C.E. until some time around the Bar Kokhba revolt (132–135 C.E.), the reconstituted Sanhedrin met at Jamnia, which then became a great spiritual and intellectual center of Jewish learning. See JAMNIA (JABNEH), COUNCIL OF.

In rabbinic texts the vicinity of Jabneh was part of a significant district region referred to as "the South" (as opposed to Galilee, known as "the North"). Following the Bar Kokhba revolt, much of the city was Samaritan, and a Christian population predominated by the 5th century. While Jamnia of the post-Temple period is tentatively identified with the Yibna site, no regular excavations have been conducted there and there is no evidence to substantiate this identification. A 1988 salvage excavation on the NE slope of the tell yielded only an assemblage of 6th century Byzantine pottery. Three sondages cut on the NE and NW sides of the tell to determine the N extent of the Byzantine occupation yielded traces of architecture, and possibly Hellenistic and additional 6th century Byzantine pottery. Thus far, no 1st century C.E. pottery has been identified to warrant identifying this site with the post-Temple Jamnia. However, tombs excavated about 1.5 miles S of the tell contain pottery from the end of the Hellenistic period, Herodian lamps, a coin of Emperor Tiberius, as well as later finds dating to the Byzantine period; this suggests that these tombs, as well as those located on a hill about 1.5 km N of the tell containing complete 2d century C.E. lamps, served as the necropolis for the tell, which was probably occupied during the early rabbinic period (1st–2d century C.E.).

2. A town along the S border of the tribe of Naphtali (Josh 19:33) in E lower Galilee, identified in the Jerusalem Talmud (*Meg.* 1:1, 70a) with Kfar Yamma (Khirbet Yamma; M.R. 198233), a large, unexcavated site on the grounds of Moshava Jabneel. However, the paucity of LB and Iron Age sherds at Kh. Yamma, in contrast to the plethora of archaeological remains of those periods at Tel Yinʿam (M.R. 198235) suggests that biblical Jabneel should be identified with the latter, which is located 1.5 km NE of modern Moshava Jabneel. For a summary of the results of excavations, see YINʿAM, TEL.

While the LB town that existed on the tell has been identified with Yenoam of Egyptian New Kingdom texts, that identification is no longer considered reliable, although the plethora of LB finds and evidence for fiery destruction levels accord with the Egyptian texts. The consensus of opinion is that Tel Yinʿam is identifiable with Jabneel. Like the Judean Jabneel further S, the name underwent a change from Jabneel to Jabneh to Jamnia, and ultimately to Yinʿam.

HAROLD A. LIEBOWITZ

JABNEH (PLACE) [Heb *yabneh*]. See JABNEEL (PLACE); JAMNIA (JABNEH), COUNCIL OF.

JACAN (PERSON) [Heb *yaʿkān*]. A Gadite, who was a son of Abihail and one of seven kinsmen, who are named alongside four (or three; see SHAPHAT) tribal leaders (1 Chr 5:13). According to 1 Chronicles 5, Jacan and his kinsmen lived opposite the Reubenites in "Bashan as far as Salecah" (v 11) and "in Gilead, in Bashan . . . and in all the pasture lands of Sharon to their limits" (v 17). Although Num 13:24–28 assigns Gilead to Gad, neither Bashan, which is too far N, nor Sharon, which is too far W, is mentioned. It may be that the reference in 1 Chronicles 5 to Bashan reflects confusion about the N boundary of the tribe or about the extent of Bashan (cf. Deut 3:10). The inclusion of Sharon within Gad's allotment coincides with a reference in the Mesha Inscription (line 13; *ANET,* 320) to an otherwise unknown city or region by that name in Transjordania.

The claim that Jacan and the other sons of Abihail were enrolled "in the days of Jotham . . . and . . . Jeroboam" (1 Chr 5:17) is problematic, since several years separated their reigns (unless Jotham's co-regency with his father Azariah/Uzziah is counted). Neither Jacan nor the others named in the Chronicler's genealogy for Gad (1 Chr 5:11–

17) appear in other lists of Gadites (Gen 46:16; Num 26:15–18; 1 Chr 12:9–16—Eng 12:8–15).

M. PATRICK GRAHAM

JACHIN (PERSON) [Heb *yākîn*]. JACHINITES. Three individuals mentioned in the OT bear this name.

1. A son of Simeon, the second son of Jacob and Leah. His name is included in the genealogy of Jacob's family at the time they migrated to Egypt to see Joseph. The genealogy of Simeon is presented in four different places in the Hebrew Bible. In the identical genealogies of Gen 46:10 and Exod 6:15, Jachin is the fourth of six sons of Simeon. In the genealogy of 1 Chr 4:2–25 and in the list of Simeon's clans in Num 26:12–14, Jachin is the third of five sons, the name of Ohab being omitted. He is probably identified with Jarib, who appears in the parallel list of Simeon's sons in 1 Chr 4:24. Jachin was the ancestral head of the Jachinites, a clan of the tribe of Simeon (Num 26:12).

2. A priest who was the 21st chosen by lot at the time when David organized the priests for service in the temple (1 Chr 24:17). He was one of the outstanding men from among the sons of Eleazar and Ithamar who were selected to form the 24 priestly courses in Israel (Williamson 1979).

3. One of the priests who came from Babylon and who lived in Jerusalem (1 Chr 9:10; Neh 11:10). His name is included among those who were chosen by lots to live in Jerusalem (Neh 11:1–2, 10). The appearance of Jachin among the priestly list and his association with two other priests, Jedaiah and Jehoiarib, has been debated. Bartlett (1968: 4, n. 1) has suggested that since Jachin's name is replaced by Jarib in 1 Chr 4:25 and since he appears without pedigree, his name was entered on the list because of his association with Jehoiarib. Williamson regards the name of Jachin in the book of Nehemiah as a gloss which later redactors thought to be a correction to the text (Williamson, *Ezra, Nehemiah* NCBC, 343).

Bibliography

Bartlett, J. R. 1968. Zadok and His Successors at Jerusalem. *JTS* 19: 1–18.

Williamson, H. G. M. 1979. The Origin of the Twenty-Four Priestly Courses: A Study of I Chronicles xxiii–xxvii. *VTSup* 30: 251–58.

CLAUDE F. MARIOTTINI

JACHIN AND BOAZ [Heb *yākîn, bōᶜaz*]. The names given to two pillars that flanked the entrance to the Jerusalem temple. They are described in 1 Kgs 7:15–22, 41–42 and are also mentioned in 2 Chr 3:15–17, which parallels the Kings source. In 2 Kgs 25:16–17 and Jer 52:17, 20–23, the pillars are again described in the context of the report of the Babylonian sack of the temple in 587 B.C.E.

The temple texts that present Jachin and Boaz contain detailed information, but the exact appearance and function of the pillars remains difficult to reconstruct. The biblical verses describing them are replete with textual problems and obscure technical words. Furthermore, there are discrepancies between the information in the core text of 1 Kings 7 and the other places that mention these pillars. Both of these problems are to be expected. Textual difficulties are often present when specific technological language is involved. Inconsistency in details arises when the structure presented in one set of texts is hundreds of years older than that in another set. In the case of the temple, alterations and refurbishings over the centuries surely took place (Meyers 1982).

Despite these difficulties, the information in the Bible provides a good idea of the physical appearance of the pillars. According to the Kings account, each stood 18 cubits high (ca. 26.5 ft.) and was 12 cubits (ca. 17.5 ft.) in circumference. The pillars were made of cast bronze and were hollow, with the metal being four fingers (ca. 3 inches) thick. Each pillar was surmounted by a bowl-shaped capital (or double capital, so Yeivin 1959) five cubits (ca. 7.5 ft.) in height, giving the pillars a total height of 23 cubits (ca. 34 ft.).

The capitals were elaborately decorated, with "nets of checker work," "wreaths of chain work," and "two rows of pomegranates." Although these features cannot be exactly understood, the text (1 Kgs 7:19) apparently summarizes them as "lily-work," a designation that relates the capitals of Jachin and Boaz to the complex floral capitals that were characteristic of monumental architecture in the ANE. Egyptian architecture in particular is notable for its use of plant forms in structural elements, and the Phoenician workmanship responsible for the Jerusalem temple no doubt meant the use of many of the Egyptianizing forms that characterized Phoenician and W Syrian art.

Once fabricated by Hiram of Tyre, the pillars were erected at the entrance to the temple, the one on the S being called Jachin, perhaps meaning "the establisher," and the one on the N named Boaz, which is also the name of the great-grandfather of David. See BOAZ (PERSON). Their enigmatic names, their great size, the use of a term *(gullâ)* meaning "bowl" for part of their capitals, and ambiguity about whether they were freestanding or structural elements has led to much speculation about the role of these prominent elements of the Jerusalem temple. They have been called cressets (Albright 1942, following W. R. Smith; cf. Myres 1948); and they have been identified as fire altars, obelisks, phalli, twin mountains, sacred stones, pillars of heaven, and trees of life (see, e.g., Scott 1939; *IDB* 4: 534–60; Wright 1941; and the summary of the literature in Busink 1970). The variety of suggestions indicates a strong measure of conjecture.

All of these suggestions focus upon the symbolic nature of the pillar and upon an understanding of them as freestanding. However, analyzing the Jerusalem temple in relation to contemporary Syrian architecture has led to the supposition (Ouellette 1976) that the pillars were functional, just as were the pillars in an analogous building at Tell Tainat.

The symbolic nature of Jachin and Boaz deserves the attention that it has received. That they are fundamentally decorative (and therefore symbolic) rather than structural (and therefore functional) can best be demonstrated not by any analysis of their form but rather by noting their place in the biblical presentation of the temple and its furbishings. The description of Jachin and Boaz comes at the beginnings of the description of the series of bronze vessels that were fashioned for use in the rituals of the temple courtyard. The pillars are thus categorized by the text itself as temple appurtenances, all of which have strong symbolic value. Yet, as first in that series, they follow immediately upon the description of the construction of the temple itself and of the royal palace complex. That description is summarized (in 1 Kgs 7:9–12) by reference to the stonework of all these structures, in particular the masonry of two courts ("the great court" and the "inner court of the house of Yahweh") and the ʾ*ûlām* (RSV "vestibule"), which may itself be a court since it appears in this short list of courts. The position of the pillars in the Kings account is thus transitional: from the buildings, notably the courtyards, to the appurtenances. While the second category may dominate, the participation of the pillar in the first category—courtyard architecture—also is present. If this be the case, a structural role that is compatible with their being freestanding is indeed possible.

Greater understanding of the symbolic and structural significance of the columns comes from considering their architectural location. They flank the entry to the ʾ*ûlām,* a word translated by so many different words in the English versions as to reveal the uncertainty about its identity as part of the temple. Close analysis of the ʾ*ûlām* (Meyers 1983a) and the details of its construction indicates that it belongs, architecturally and conceptually, to the world of courtyards as they functioned within Near Eastern buildings. The temple precincts as a whole contained courts; but the temple itself, as an essentially private dwelling for Yahweh, had its own indispensable courtyard. Jachin and Boaz thus belong to the structural category of pillars as gateposts rather than as load-bearing elements.

As gateposts, Jachin and Boaz were extraordinarily elaborate and large. With their ornate capitals, their shiny bronze surfaces, and their great height, they stood out against the rather flat and relatively unbroken exterior that the fortress-like temple would have presented to the viewer. Since the grandeur of the temple construction and decoration was largely contained inside the building itself, and since the interior was not public space (that is, it was off-limits to laity and to the general clergy), the imposing pillars at the entrance represented to the world at large that which existed unseen within the building.

The symbolic value of the pillars is contained in their position as gateposts. Archaeologically retrieved parallels and representations of entry pillars in ancient artistic sources indicate that the doorposts or gateposts of a temple convey to the viewer the notion of passage: that the god meant to inhabit the earthly dwelling (the temple) has indeed traversed the threshold of the building, entered the sanctuary built for the deity, is accessible to the human community, and legitimizes the political unit that has constructed the temple.

In the case of the Solomonic temple, the entry pillars proclaimed that Yahweh had entered his abode in Israel. Furthermore, since Jerusalem under David and Solomon had become the capital of an empire, a unique situation in the political history of the Near East, the monumental palace-temple complex signified both for the inhabitants of Israel and for the representatives of vassal and foreign states (including Solomon's wives and their entourages) that came to Jerusalem, the authority of the imperial rule of the house of David. Within the ancient religious-political conceptualization, the presence of the nation's God, Yahweh, in the temple adjoining the palace helped to legitimize Solomon's reign (Meyers 1983b).

Neither foreigners nor most Israelites had access to the temple, or to the holy ark that signified Yahweh's unseen presence. Yet they all could see Jachin and Boaz, which communicated visually the entrance of God to this abode. The very size of the pillars in relation to temple entry column bases excavated at analogous buildings in the Levant is significant. The pillars flanking the Jerusalem temple's entry were considerably larger according to the dimensions in 1 Kings. This magnitude was appropriate to the religious and political role of Jerusalem and its state buildings as the seat of an empire.

Bibliography

Albright, W. F. 1942. Two Cressets from Marissa and the Pillars of Jachin and Boaz. *BASOR* 85: 18–27.

Busink, T. A. 1970. *Der Tempel von Jerusalem.* Vol. 1. Leiden.

Meyers, C. 1982. The Elusive Temple. *BA* 45: 33–41.

———. 1983a. Jachin and Boaz in Religious and Political Perspective. *CBQ* 45: 167–78.

———. 1983b. The Israelite Empire: In Defense of King Solomon. *Michigan Quarterly Review* 22: 412–28.

Myres, J. L. 1948. King Solomon's Temple and Other Buildings and Works of Art. *PEQ* 80: 14–41.

Ouellette, J. 1976. The Basic Structure of Solomon's Temple and Archaeological Research. Pp. 1–20 in *The Temple of Solomon,* ed. J. Gutmann. Missoula, MT.

Scott, R. B. Y. 1939. The Pillars of Jachin and Boaz. *JBL* 58: 143–49.

Wright, G. E. 1941. Solomon's Temple Resurrected. *BA* 4: 17–31.

Yeivin, S. 1959. Jachin and Boaz. *PEQ* 91: 1–15.

CAROL MEYERS

JACKAL. See ZOOLOGY.

JACKAL'S WELL (PLACE) [Heb ʿ*ên hattanîn*]. A place located outside the ruined walls of Jerusalem, apparently between the Valley Gate and the Dung Gate (Neh 2:13). The Heb name can also be translated "Spring of the Dragon" or even "Eye of the Dragon" (in which case it would not necessarily even allude to a source of water). The LXX instead reads *pēgē tōn sykōn,* "fountain of the figs." The Dung Gate is undoubtedly located near the juncture of the Hinnom and Kidron valleys, but the location of the Valley Gate is problematic. See VALLEY GATE (PLACE). If it provided exit from the City of David to the Tyropoeon valley, then Jackal's Well should be located in the Tyropoeon valley N of the Dung Gate, outside the 10th century W wall of the City of David, but inside the W wall that was built when Hezekiah enlarged the city in the late 6th/early 7th century B.C. However, if the Valley Gate provided exit from Hezekiah's larger Jerusalem to the Hinnom valley, then Jackal's Well would be located in that valley W of the Dung Gate. No known source of water exists in either the Tyropoeon or Hinnom valleys, and hence most scholars simply equate Jackal's Well with En-rogel outside the Dung Gate at the juncture of the Hinnom and Kidron valleys.

GARY A. HERION

JACOB (PERSON) [Heb *yaʿăqob*]. Var. ISRAEL. **1.** The biblical patriarch and eponymous ancestor of the twelve tribes of Israel. See JACOB NARRATIVE.

2. The son of Matthan and father of Joseph, the husband of Mary, according to Matthew's genealogy tying Joseph to the house of David and Solomon (Matt 1:15, 16). The name Jacob was apparently a common one in several periods of Jewish history. Jacob the son of Isaac is known elsewhere in this same genealogy (1:12) as Jesus' ancestor, and according to Albright and Mann (*Matthew* AB, 4–5) Jacob was a characteristic name of the last two centuries B.C. The major point of discussion about Jacob as the son of Matthan in 1:15 and 16, who does not appear elsewhere in any other genealogy or list of Jesus' ancestors, is his relation to Heli as the son of Matthat in Luke 3:23. See MATTHAT (PERSON) for discussion of the major proposals, although Gundry (1982: 18) posits simply that Jacob was put in place of Heli by Matthew "to conform to the fathering of the patriarch Joseph by the patriarch Jacob." The solution is probably more complex than this. A few late mss include "of Jacob" after Joseph and before "of Heli" in Luke 3:23.

Bibliography

Gundry, R. H. 1982. *Matthew: A Commentary on his Literary and Theological Art.* Grand Rapids.

STANLEY E. PORTER

JACOB NARRATIVE. Jacob was the younger son of Isaac and Rebekah, twin brother of Esau, and father of the 12 sons after whom were named the 12 tribes of Israel. He is the central figure in the cycle of stories in Gen 25:19–35:29 and reappears as a lesser figure in the Joseph stories (Genesis 37–50). In separate popular etymologies, the Heb name *yaʿăqōb* is connected with Heb *ʿāqēb,* "heel," because Jacob was born clutching the heel of his brother Esau (Gen 25:26), and with the verb *ʿāqab,* "cheat," because Esau said that Jacob had cheated him twice (27:36). The name may be a shortened form of Heb *yʿqb-ʾl,* "God protects," a name known from extrabiblical sources (Noth 1953). Jacob later received the name "Israel" as a mark of his struggle (32:29) and piety (35:10), and his descendants were later identified by this name ("children of Israel").

Biblical Jacob is unknown outside the Bible, although the general congruence of the patriarchal narratives with customs and artifacts known from archaeology to belong to the 2d millennium (especially the material from Nuzi and Mari) has sometimes been used to support his historicity. Later scrutiny called much of that argument into question (Van Seters 1975; Thompson 1974) on the grounds that the alleged parallels were inexact or unrepresentative, or had been misunderstood. For example, the claim that possession of household idols (Gen 31:19) helped constitute the family of Jacob as a legitimate clan has been given up (Selman 1980: 110). Some writers have refused even to attempt historical reconstructions (*HAIJ,* 79). Where historical questions remain open, Jacob has been dated to the 1900s B.C.E. (Bimson 1980: 84), and a number of extrabiblical customs are seen to retain their pertinence (Selman 1980: 125–229; see also Morrison 1983).

Until recently, critical scholarship assumed that the documentary hypothesis was a key to understanding the Jacob material, namely, strands of J and E with later additions or redaction by P (Van Seters 1975 dates J to the Exile rather than to the time of Solomon; *CMHE,* 293–325, and Hendel 1987 hold to the early oral-epic origin of JE, enlarged and ordered by P late in the Exile). Noth had postulated an East-Jordan Jacob and a West-Jordan Jacob, the latter stories being secondary and less interesting (*HPT,* 89ff.). Farmer (1978) approaches the story as folklore, focusing on how trickster figures such as Jacob and Samson, operating from a position of weakness, trick others or are themselves tricked. Oden (1983) employs data from the field of anthropology.

Meanwhile a plethora of holistic literary treatments have appeared, based on a reassessment of the form and style of "narrative" (Frei 1974; Alter 1981) and reflecting a fundamental hermeneutic shift. In general, this approach does not deny the composite character of the Jacob material, but downplays the cycle's prehistory in favor of questions of meaning, and it sets aside historical questions as inappropriate to the material (Fokkelman 1975; Clines 1978; Buss 1979; Thompson 1987). Such is the general perspective of the present article, which is more about the Jacob cycle than about Jacob and is literary rather than biographical in method.

A. Structure of the Jacob Cycle
B. The Cycle's Stories
C. Meaning

A. Structure of the Jacob Cycle

The stories of the Jacob cycle have been artfully arranged to gather around Jacob's return to the land of his birth, Canaan, after a hasty flight and long residence abroad to avoid his brother's revenge. They are thus informed by a dual tension: (1) How can the duplicitous Jacob become the father of God's people? and (2) How can he inherit the promise made to Abraham and Isaac if he leaves the land which God has given to them? The fundamental theme of the cycle has to do with the life and character of "Israel," that is, the people of God. The Jacob stories are about the essence and meaning of a people (Thompson 1987: 39–40). The biblical text presents the Jacob stories in a concentric pattern which has been independently observed by several scholars (Fishbane 1975; see also Fokkelman 1975: 240; Gammie 1979; otherwise Hendel 1987: 144, n. 20) and which is signalled both by cross-references in vocabulary and by thematic similarities. The cycle breaks into 2 equal halves at Gen 30:24–25, each having 7 matching segments, presented thematically in exact reverse order. The entire cycle is bracketed at beginning and end by genealogies of the 2 sons who stand outside the line of promise, Ishmael (25:12–18) and Esau (chap. 36), so that Jacob's role as the bearer of the promise is unmistakable.

The Unchosen Son (Ishmael) (25:12–18)
- **A.** Beginnings. Birth, prediction, early conflict between Jacob and Esau (25:19–34)
  - **B.** Relations with indigenous population (26:1–22)
    - **C.** Blessing obtained ["He took away (*lāqaḥ*) my *bĕrākâ*" (27:35–36)] (27:1–40)
      - **D.** Jacob's flight from Esau (27:41–28:5)
        - **E.** Encounter with God's agents (28:10–22)
          - **F.** Arrival in Haran: Rachel, Laban (29:1–30)
            - **G.** Children: Jacob acquires a family (30:1–24)
              - *Jacob's return to Canaan begins as soon as Joseph is born*
            - **G′** Flocks: Jacob acquires wealth (30:25–43)
          - **F′** Departure from Haran: Rachel, Laban (31:1–32:1—Eng 31:1–55)
        - **E′** Encounter with God's agent (32:2–3—Eng 32:1–2)
      - **D′** Jacob's approach to Esau (32:4–33—Eng 32:3–32)
    - **C′** Blessing returned ["Accept (*lāqaḥ*) my *bĕrākâ*" (33:11)] (33:1–20)
  - **B′** Relations with indigenous population (chap. 34)
- **A′** Endings. Death, fulfillment, Jacob and Esau together (chap. 35)

The Unchosen Son (Esau) (chap. 36)

The 2 segments on Esau's wives which frame segment C (26:34–35; 28:6–9) seem to stand outside the above topical descriptions.

Some of the thematic correspondences are especially clear. For example, segments B/B′ both deal with relations between the people of the promise and the indigenous residents of Canaan, in sharply contrasting modes. In terms of narrative sequence, however, B is out of order (since the twins have not yet been born, 26:11), and belongs to the 20-year period of Rebekah's barrenness (25:20, 26); its chronological dislocation was necessary for it to function topically in the cycle. *Placement and juxtaposition are among the writer's major techniques.*

This topical match between the segments in each of the halves is confirmed by several striking cross-references in writing. The numinous experiences in E/E′ each feature God's "agents" (or "angels"), an expression recurring nowhere else in the Bible. The same 2 sections also use the Hebrew verb *pāgaʿ*, "encounter," which occurs nowhere else in the sense of "reach a place," suggesting that the writer chose the unusual verb at 28:10 in order to effect the linkage with E′. Again, the occurrence of *bĕrākâ* "blessing" in the antonymic expressions "he took away your/my blessing" and "accept my blessing," both with the verb *lāqaḥ*, "take," is the thread connecting segments C/C′.

Thus the cycle is not only a narrative sequence with its own inner movement, but an artful arrangement which invites the reader to compare each segment with its complement later (or earlier) in the sequence.

To illustrate: segments A/A′ clearly open and close the cycle. Certain information is repeated from earlier in Genesis in order to give the cycle a proper beginning: Isaac's birth (21:1–5), marriage (24:67), and Rebekah's family (24:15, 29), adding the characterization "Aramean." An oracle predicts that Rebekah's children will become two "nations," one submissive to the other. The twins are born, and both their prenatal struggle (v 22) and Jacob's manipulation of Esau (vv 27–34) prefigure Jacob's character as a loner who lives by his wits at the expense of other people, as well as the bad blood between the twins (chap. 27) and the later hostility between Israel and Edom (36:1, 8–9, 19; cf. Ps 137:7; Ezekiel 35).

A′ echoes the theme of A in conclusion: the deaths of Isaac, Jacob's wife Rachel, and Rebekah's nurse Deborah; Jacob's 12 sons are listed by name and mother, a "nation"; the twins, having come together (chap. 33), stand at their father's grave; and Jacob appears as a religious reformer (vv 1–7) and recipient of the full divine promise (vv 9–25).

B. The Cycle's Stories

Segment A (25:19–34). Jacob and Esau were born as a result of Isaac's intercession with God, because Rebekah (like Sarah before her and Rachel after her) was barren; offspring are the gift of God. Among the Bible's several husbands of barren wives, only Isaac prayed for a change (contrast Jacob in Gen 30:2), marking him as a man of piety and intimating a synergism which runs throughout the whole cycle.

Rebekah's only words in this section arise out of the prenatal jostling of the twins, but the Hebrew sentence is incomplete: "If so, why am I . . . ?" The text leaves Rebekah musing uncertainly about the events which her pregnancy portends; hers is an unfinished question, a verbless and ambiguous reflection which prefigures her incomplete and partial role in the cycle as a whole, just as the jostling forecasts enmity between the twins.

The oracle which she sought disclosed that her children would become separate peoples of unequal power, and that the nation springing from the older would be submissive to the younger. By identifying the sons with the peoples who sprang from them, the oracle at once implies a collective as well as an individual reading of the stories that follow: They recount the outward and inner movements of Jacob, the son of Isaac and Rebekah; but they refer also to the movements, the calling, and the character of the people named "Israel" after him. A collective reference is also suggested by the allusions associated with the naming of Esau: His hirsute appearance at birth (Heb *śēʿār*, 25:25; 27:11) alludes to his country Seir (33:16), while his ruddy color (Heb *ʾadmônî*, v 25) and preference for red stew (Heb *hāʾādōm*, v 30) refer to his region Edom. By contrast, the name Jacob is explained with reference to personal behavior, since the collective reference belongs especially to his second name, Israel.

The narrative moves from the birth of the twins directly to an event showing that their relationships as adults realized the conflict portended by prenatal and birth events. Jacob took advantage of Esau's fatigue and hunger by requiring him to trade his birthright for some food. The cycle has thus barely opened when Esau has ceded to Jacob the *bĕkōrâ*, his inheritance rights as firstborn. In a rare show of appraisal, the text says that Esau "spurned" his birthright. Yet, Jacob's behavior was hardly exemplary: His hand was clearly on Esau's heel, and the pairing of this episode with the birth story types Jacob's character as the grasping and manipulative.

This falls short of expectations, as compared with Abraham and Isaac and in view of Jacob's subsequent role as the father of the Israelite people. The dissonance is even in the text, for in the parallel description of the twins' way of life (25:27), opposite the assessment "Esau was a skillful hunter," we read, "Jacob was a blameless man" (Heb *ʾîš tām*, exactly as Job 1:8; 2:3). Translations use attenuated words ("plain" KJV, "quiet" RSV, "mild" JPS), but *tām* clearly implies moral excellence. This, then—moral excellence—is to be Israel's vocation; and the same story which asserts it so boldly goes on to show Jacob as something other than blameless. The disparity introduces a tension at the beginning of the cycle which is not fully relaxed until the end.

Segment B (26:1–33). This story belongs chronologically to the time before the twins were born, but its placement within the cycle gives it pertinence to him. It opens with a direct reference to Abraham's behavior in an earlier famine (v 1: the reference is thematic, not chronological, since a minimum of 64 years in narrative time separates the 2 [10 years 16:3; 14 years 16:16 and 21:5; 40 years 26:20]). As Abraham had done, Isaac started out for Egypt, but in the "Philistine" city of Gerar, God appeared to warn against leaving the land and to reiterate to Isaac the Abrahamic promise of land and progeny (vv 2–5).

Isaac's anxiety over their safety in Gerar proved to be unfounded (vv 6–11), and the juxtaposition of this episode to v 5's prolix "my charge, my commandments, my laws, my teachings," suggests that residence in the land also required obedience to the divine pattern for life. To "remain in the land" is synonymous with obedience to Torah (Ps 37:3).

The use of "Philistine" suggests the story's rise at a time when relations with the Philistines were a problem to Israel. In the cycle, however, they typify the land's indigenous residents, because Isaac visits them as a stranger and is subject to pressure from them.

Isaac's prosperity under divine blessing led to envy and to contention over water rights; he had to move several times, thereby surrendering valuable excavated wells in the process, before finding "space" (vv 12–22; "Rehoboth" is symbolic). Following this sacrificial determination to occupy the land amicably, another divine appearance (at the pilgrim site of Beer-sheba) reiterated the promise of progeny, and added the promise of God's presence (v 24, unique to the Jacob cycle, see also 28:15, 20; 35:3).

A final threatening approach of the Philistines resulted in a treaty (Heb *bĕrît* "covenant") between the 2 groups, sealed with a feast and the exchange of oaths (vv 23–33). The treaty episode interrupts the account of digging one more well (vv 25b, 32), so that the servant's report, "We have found water," takes on symbolic importance: Water is life, especially in the arid Negeb where Beer-sheba is located, and so also is the treaty life. Isaac has shown that it is possible to occupy the land of promise, to observe Torah, to prosper, and to maintain good relations with the other residents. He has found life. The other treaty, between God and Abraham, is also in the background: Although the word *bĕrît* is not used in the promise reports of chap. 26, it has been used in the earlier promises which are now being extended to Isaac (15:8; chap. 17); it, too, is life.

This segment on indigenous relations stands between 2 sections (A and C) on relations between Jacob and Esau, which are marked as a pair by common themes (e.g., Jacob outwits Esau to his own advantage) and by similar key words, such as *bĕkōrâ* and *bĕrākâ* ("birthright" and "blessing"). These words not only sound alike but are visually similar on the written page—*bkrh* and *brkh*—being distinguished only by the transposition of the middle 2 consonants.

This placement both links Isaac's example with the subsequent B′, a different mode of engagement with the people of the land, and unmistakably juxtaposes Isaac's style of relationship to Jacob's. The juxtaposition announces, "Jacob may be living by strife and deceit, but if you want to see life under the promise, in the middle of all the ambiguity of threatening sociopolitical relationships, take a look at Isaac." The story also stresses the need for the recipients of the promise to maintain residence in the land, something which will add additional tension in segment C.

Segment C (27:1–40). In the second of the paired stories of dealings between Jacob and Esau, Rebekah led Jacob to deceive his father into bestowing the patriarchal blessing—*bĕrākâ*—on him instead of on Esau the firstborn. Jacob disguised himself as Esau, and, although the blind Isaac was never free from suspicion, the ruse worked: The father ate his favorite dish and conferred on Jacob a promise of agricultural prosperity and hegemony over other people, including his brother (vv 28–29). Only when Esau actually showed up to receive the blessing did Isaac discover the trick; the blessing was already Jacob's, but Isaac gave Esau a similar promise of bounty along with the promise that he should eventually free himself from Jacob's yoke (vv 39–40).

This detailed and extended story—7 times as long as the *bĕkōrâ*—shows Jacob firmly in the legal and financial position of the firstborn. Both stories involve manipulation, and both involve meals, to which Isaac's amicable covenant meal with Abimelech is a pointed contrast. They offer complementary explanations of Jacob's priority, the shorter being more favorable to Jacob (there is no outright deception, and Esau "spurns" his birthright), the latter being marked by a deliberate and callous duplicity involving Rebekah as prime mover (the verbs in vv 14–17 have Rebekah, not Jacob, as their subject). Jacob's impersonation of Esau symbolizes his priority: He dresses in Esau's clothes and simulates Esau's tomentose appearance (vv 15–16); he smells of the outdoors (v 27); he twice says, "I am your firstborn" (vv 19, 24). He has taken Esau's place.

The Masoretic editors of the Hebrew text have signalled this in another way in Isaac's reply to Jacob's address in v 18. Isaac says "Yes?" (Heb *hinnennî*), a common locution normally spelled *hinnēnî*, but with 2 doubled "n"s only here and in Gen 22:7 where Isaac's address to Abraham and the father's reply are in the identical words. In both stories the father replies to the younger but favored son.

This linkage also highlights the tension which the second episode of cheating introduces into the cycle. In Gen 22:7 Isaac was the obedient and compliant son, enquiring about sacrificial procedures; but in Gen 27:18 Jacob—equally born by divine intervention—says, "I am Esau, your firstborn." How can such mendacity inherit and bear the promise? And indeed, the fathers' replies in each case signal this, for Abraham said to Isaac, "Yes, my son," but Isaac said to Jacob, "Yes, *who are you,* my son?" Thus, one of the central themes of the whole cycle of stories comes to expression—the unclear identity of Jacob.

The story expresses this ambiguity in other ways. In talking to Rebekah about the deception, Jacob offered descriptions of both himself and Esau (v 11), in which there are wordplays pointing beyond the immediate situation. Esau, said Jacob, is a hairy man (Heb *ʾîš śāʿir*). The adjective is a homophone of *śāʿîr* "he-goat, buck," and thus alludes playfully to Esau's outdoor life and to the skins of kids with which Jacob disguised himself (v 16). I, said Jacob, am a smooth man (Heb *ʾîš ḥālāq*). The same adjective occurs elsewhere of deceptive speech (Prov 5:3; 26:28). Who are you, Jacob? By his own mouth, he is not a "blameless man" (25:27), but a "slippery man."

Although Isaac could give the patriarchal blessing to only one of his sons, he also gave Esau a promise very similar in that it predicted the same agricultural boons—the fat of the land and the dew of heaven (in reverse order, vv 28 and 39). Translations usually obscure this similarity, since the preposition *min* can mean both "have a share in" and "be far from," but the reader of the story in Hebrew may wonder if there is still a chance for Esau to recoup his position, especially since Isaac told him he would throw off Jacob's yoke.

Segment D (27:41–28:5). Esau's anger at a second supplanting (v 36) made it necessary for Jacob to flee, and his mother arranged his departure for her own country where he could stay with her brother Laban (vv 41–45), representing the trip to Isaac as required so that Jacob should not marry a local woman (27:46–28:5). Classical literary criticism has seen these two sets of arrangements as duplicate accounts from different sources: The former, which calls Rebekah's homeland "Haran," from JE, and the latter, using "Paddan-aram" from P. But each paragraph plays its own role in the movement of the narrative.

This sly provision for Jacob's sudden need to leave home is the cycle's final glimpse of Rebekah. Her last words follow the "if . . . then . . ." pattern of her first (25:22), but here the sentence is complete: *lāmmâ lî ḥayyîm* "What good will life be to me?" (v 46). These 2 sentences—freighted with import by their position—show Rebekah preoccupied with her own feelings and well-being. Her single significant action has been to engineer the deception by which her second-born son Jacob, instead of Esau her firstborn, received Isaac's blessing. Her way of life has affinities with that of her brother Laban (29:15–30; 31:6–7, 14–15, 41–42), and Jacob's own slippery character displays a family resemblance.

This way of life is new in the Genesis narratives. Apart from their lies about their wives (chaps. 12, 20, 26), both Abraham and Isaac are exemplary persons, and in chap. 26 Isaac is conscientious and sacrificial in his relations with the herdsmen of Gerar. The term "Aramean," found first in Rebekah's genealogy (25:20; 28:5) and elsewhere applied to Laban alone (31:20, 24), while obviously denoting the N Syrian region of their origin as "Aram," seems also to connote this behavioral pattern in the Haran side of the family; "Aramean" is new in the Jacob cycle, even though all the other genealogical information of 25:20 is already found in 24:15, 28.

It is thus a central tension within the cycle whether Jacob will actually become the chosen leader which later Israelites knew him to be. His departure from Canaan raises the possibility that he has abandoned the land promised to Abraham and which Isaac has resolutely occupied at great cost (chap. 26), and has adopted another way of life altogether. Deut 26:5 describes him as "an Aramean given up for lost."

Before Jacob left, Isaac gave another blessing, this one clearly linked to earlier traditions in Genesis by the words "fertile and numerous" (28:3), alluding to Gen 1:28 and 9:1: Like Adam and Noah, Jacob is to be the start of something new and big, becoming "an assembly of peoples." Isaac went on (28:4) to link Jacob with the Abrahamic promise and possession of the land, something new in the narrative and especially incongruous in view of his imminent departure. Unlikely as it seems, Jacob has been marked as the bearer of the promise.

At this point, Esau does not look as bad as later tradition painted him (especially Heb 12:16, which called him "irreligious"), since he has been victimized in both stories of rivalry with Jacob. His rehabilitation is further suggested by the 2 snippets of information about his wives which frame the deception story (26:34–35 and 28:6–9). The first reports that his Hittite wives "were a source of bitterness" to his parents; the second notes that he married Mahalath, the daughter of Ishmael, Isaac's half-brother. Moreover, Esau remains in Canaan, and the promise concerns the land (28:4).

This, then, is the situation: Jacob has spurned the Abrahamic promise and has decamped the land which the promise conveyed to Abraham's offspring; Esau has received a patriarchal promise only slightly less complete than Jacob's, and has married within the Abrahamic family in order to please his parents; he is on the land. The narrative retains Esau more as a peer than as a subordinate, and everything points toward his regaining his lost privileged position. Naturally, the informed reader knows that this did not happen, but the story's willingness to let this prospect arise heightens the tension which Jacob's moral deficiencies and his flight have already raised.

Segment E (28:10–22). In a brief but pivotal episode—the only event from his journey to the north—Jacob dreamed of a stairway between earth and heaven, with God's agents going up and down on it. The Lord stood beside him and promised him the land, innumerable offspring, and the divine presence to protect and return him to the land (vv 13–15). Jacob awoke, recognizing the numinous character of both the place and his experience, and responded by setting up a stone pillar and naming the site Bethel, "God's House" (vv 16–19). He reciprocated the promise by a conditional vow, "the Lord shall be my God" (v 21).

The stairway (traditionally "ladder"; the word does not occur elsewhere in the Bible) is a symbol of the accessibility of God's help and presence, a theme distinctive to the Jacob stories. It is not a means for human ascent; God's agents go up and come down. The stairway is like a fireman's pole: when people are in need, helpers come down to render it. Their place is not in heaven, but on earth, where the divine presence is required.

In Jacob's life, this event is epochal because (a) it is the first time that the divine promise which had come to both Abraham and Isaac now comes to Jacob, directly from God (earlier only from Isaac in Gen 28:3–4), and because (b) it is the first time that Jacob shows any interest whatsoever in the religious side of his family tradition (previously only focusing on priority over Esau). The divine initiative arrested him as he was in flight from his land and his people, and Jacob was sufficiently moved to acknowledge God's presence and to perform religious acts.

The sections 28:6–9 and 10–22 interrupt what would otherwise be a summary account of Jacob's trip to Haran (28:5 plus 29:1; 28:10 duplicates 28:5), suggesting that each element had an earlier and different context. The genealogical interests of vv 6–9 have led many scholars to associate it with P, and the use of "Elohim" in segment E′ connects it with E. The Bethel story certainly functions as an etiology of a sacred place and location of a sanctuary where the faithful later came to worship and pay tithes (v 22). But its incorporation into the Jacob cycle has enlarged its function and meaning. Particularly the use of "YHWH" (vv 13, 16, 21) shows the story's links with Israel's distinctive religion, and gives to Jacob's words in v 21 a confessional character which marks the event as a kind of conversion, occurring just as he seems firmly to have closed the door on becoming what later generations knew he became: the ancestor of Israel, God's people.

At the same time, Jacob's vow falls short of hearty embrace of the promise. Its conditionality ("If . . ." v 20) is confirmed by its content. In reiterating it (vv 20–21a), Jacob omits all references to the land, progeny, expansion, and the families of the earth—essential to the patriarchal promise (vv 12–14); he is preoccupied with personal well-being (he adds food and clothes), and he alters (v 21) the promise of v 15 in subtle ways (e.g., "I [the Lord] will bring you back" becomes "if I [Jacob] return," and "this land" becomes "my father's house"), all of which shows that Jacob wishes to retain the initiative and is more interested in the family estate than the land. In short, although the Bethel event marks Jacob's awakening to God and to the promise, he is still a "smooth man," and his vows appear to be as much a bargain as a commitment.

Segment F (29:1–30). Jacob's 20-year residence in Haran (31:38, 41) is recounted in the stories of Segments F–G and G′–F′. He married, serving his mother's brother 14 years as a bride price; 11 sons and a daughter were born to him by 4 women; and he eventually became wealthy in livestock and servants. His relationships with Laban (in whom Jacob almost met his match in craftiness) dominate these sections. The initial encounter was apparently cordial (vv 13–14), and the final scene is of a covenant meal between them (31:51–54), but in between the 2 men circle warily, each looking to his own advantage.

Jacob's first contact with his mother's people was at a well where shepherds were gathered with their flocks. As they spoke, Laban's daughter Rachel arrived with his flock. The well (v 2) introduces a double entendre (Prov 5:15; Cant 4:15): The large stone on the mouth of the well intimates that Rachel will be hard to get; when Jacob, singlehanded, rolls the stone from the mouth, we have not only a show of masculine strength, but also an intimation that Jacob will marry her. There is no other example in the Bible of a man kissing a woman (v 11).

Jacob stayed with Laban, and after a month proposed to work 7 years in order to marry Rachel. Laban agreed, but when the time was up he substituted his older and less-attractive daughter Leah, a deception Jacob did not discover until the next morning. When Jacob protested, Laban pled local custom, and offered to give him Rachel at the same time, in exchange for another 7 years of work. Thus Jacob came to have 2 wives, each of whom had a maid.

There is an ironic fitness in Laban's deception. Jacob's reach for the rights of the firstborn son (Esau, Heb *běkōr* 27:32) got him the firstborn daughter (Heb *běkîrâ* 29:26), as well. He, eschewing the place of the younger son (*ṣāʿîr* 25:23) was at first denied the younger daughter (*ṣeʿîrâ* 29:26). The man who imposed this sentence was the brother of the woman who led Jacob to deceive Isaac. Jacob's befuddlement is so complete that he did not discover the substitution even in intercourse.

Jacob and Rachel initially have a romantic and tender relationship. She was shapely and beautiful (v 17), and Jacob's first 7 years' work seemed like only a few days because of his love for her (v 20). To fall in love is to become vulnerable, and in this relationship the loner began to emerge from his private world of wit and manipulation. As the stairway dream signalled a new direction in Jacob's relation to God and the promise, so does his love for Rachel in his relationships with other people.

His relationship with Laban was more complex. The uncle embraced and kissed the nephew (v 13), as Jacob and Esau were to do later (33:4), and regarded Jacob as an insider who might suitably marry his daughter (v 19). But Laban's exclamation, "You are truly my bone and my flesh" (v 14) has as much to do with Jacob's duplicity as it does with blood, since Laban said this after Jacob had told him all that had happened (v 13), presumably including the reason for his flight from home. The young Laban had been remarked for his cupidity (Gen 24:22, 30–31); the fact that Jacob brought no rich gifts with him did not save him from the mature Laban's canny eye. Fourteen years' work would buy many gold bracelets.

Segment G (29:31–30:24). The narrative next turns to the building up of Jacob's family through the birth of 12 children (including his daughter Dinah). The names of the 11 sons have popular etymologies attached to them which, for the most part, have to do with the wives' standing with one another or with Jacob. The sense of rivalry and even hostility is very strong (Levi 29:34, Naphtali 30:8, Joseph 30:23), reflecting the reality of a polygamous household and perhaps also of tribal rivalries in later years. None of the names is distinctly theophoric, but God/the Lord is mentioned in most of the explanations.

The Lord favored Leah because she was unloved, and consequently she bore 4 sons. Rachel became envious and burst out at Jacob, "Give me children, or I shall die," a peremptory demand which recalls Rebekah's brusque rhetoric (25:22; 27:46). Jacob's response (v 2) was in kind, and Rachel then offered him her maid Bilhah, using identical words to Sarai's (Gen 16:2), "that I also may acquire a family through her" (v 3). The story thus compares her not only with Leah but tacitly with her husband's grandmother, Israel's primal progenitress, as well. Two sons were born to Jacob through Bilhah, and 2 more through Leah's maid Zilpah. Rachel sought fecundity with an aphrodisiac (v 14), the only result of which was that Jacob returned to Leah, who bore him 2 more sons (vv 15–20).

Rachel thus remained childless, although Jacob had 10 sons by the other 3 women of the household. The birth of her son Joseph marks the midpoint of the Jacob cycle, and came about because "God remembered Rachel" (v 22). The expression is rich in associations (Noah, at the height of the flood [Gen 8:1], or the subsequent birth of the prophet Samuel in answer to Hannah's prayer [1 Sam 1:19]), and implies God's redemptive attention to people's needs, especially in connection with the covenant (Exod 2:24). With 12 children, Jacob has grown into a complete family. (Dinah is the 12th; the 12th son, Benjamin, was born later on Canaanite soil [35:16–19] although the concluding summary of the cycle lists him as one of the 12 sons born in Paddan-Aram [35:22b–26]). Jacob can now return home.

Segment G′ (30:25–43). But before Jacob was actually to go back, his growth as a family must be matched by his wealth. This and the preceding section—the 2 innermost sections of the cycle—match each other well: The competitiveness and trickery (30:15) of the wives is matched by Laban's new tricks; the growth of both groups does not come without difficulty, but in the end is ample. Since the Israelite people were later often known as a "flock" under God's care (e.g., Ezekiel 34; Pss 77:21; 78:20–22; 79:13; 96:6–7; 100:3), the collocation is especially apt; *figurally the 2 groups are the same.*

Jacob asked Laban's permission to go back to his homeland: The required time had been more than served (v 26). But when Laban urged him to stay in his service and to name his wages, Jacob proposed to take all the irregularly colored animals out of Laban's flocks as a nuclear flock of his own. The wily uncle agreed, but at once culled and moved those animals, so that Jacob still had nothing. Jacob responded with certain obscure procedures by which Laban's good flocks bred miscolored offspring; these then became Jacob's, in accordance with the agreement. In the end, his large family was equalled by his enormous holdings of servants and livestock (v 43).

Segment F′ (31:1–32:1—Eng 31:1–55). Jacob once more decided to return home. Although his mother had told him that she would send for him, the story is silent about her. There were 3 reasons for his decision: hostility from Laban's sons (v 1), a change in Laban's attitude toward him (v 2), and instructions from the Lord to do so (v 3). The synergism of human motives and divine direction is striking. He discussed it secretly (v 4) with Rachel and Leah, referring to Laban's guile, crediting God with his wealth, and reporting a dream in which "God's agent" had directed him to return home (vv 7–13). The wives supported Jacob's decision, describing themselves as "outsiders" in their own clan, since Laban had "sold us and used up our purchase price" (v 15).

It was not only Jacob who credited God with his wealth; the angel said the same thing (v 12), and the wives also, adding that the wealth was justly theirs (v 16). The story thus responds to the brothers' charge that Jacob had grown rich at Laban's expense.

Both here and in his earlier wish to return, Jacob spoke of his "land" (30:25; 31:3, 13), as does the summary of his departure (v 18). This language goes beyond that of his previous vow, which spoke only of returning to his "father's house" (28:21); Jacob will now do more than possess the estate; he will occupy the land. (Laban speaks only of "your father's house" [v 30], since he knows nothing of the promise.) Moreover, although Jacob was Rebekah's favorite, he left "to go to his father Isaac" (v 18). Where is Rebekah?

This time Jacob did not ask permission, but left while Laban was away shearing sheep. Unknown to Jacob, Rachel stole the household idols (v 19), perhaps for their religious and financial value. When Laban learned what had happened, he pursued, overtaking them near Canaan. Warned by God not to mistreat them, Laban nevertheless berated Jacob and accused him of stealing the household idols. Swearing death to anyone having the idols, Jacob invited Laban to find them. He searched all the tents, finally coming to Rachel's. She had hidden them, and, by a ruse, prevented Laban from finding them.

It was Jacob's turn to berate Laban, and he did so, more harshly than Laban deserved under the immediate circumstances, but not more so, considering the past 20 years. In a speech (vv 38–42) summarizing their relations during that time, Jacob accused his shifty uncle and cited his own conscientious service and God's protection. In exile, the "slippery man" of Canaan was learning to be a "blameless man."

Laban proposed a treaty (Heb *bĕrît,* "covenant"), marking the boundary between them by a heap of stones; each swore by his own deity (v 53), and sealed the agreement with a sacrifice and a meal. Within the story, it is the first meal that Jacob has ever eaten with anyone, and a distinct contrast to the 2 meals which he had arranged and used to get the better of Esau. The narrative thus does not allow Jacob to leave Haran without a reconciliation with Laban—unsought by Jacob—which put an end to 2 decades of mistrust.

Segment E′ (32:3–3—Eng 32:1–2). Parting amicably from Laban, Jacob continued his journey to face a similar encounter with Esau in which he has no blamelessness to plead. In a matching spiritual event to the stairway dream, God's agents encountered him. Jacob said, "This is God's camp," and named that site Mahanaim, "Doublecamp." The name is or resembles a Hebrew noun (dual number), a form used for objects which occur naturally in pairs, such as hands and ears. His own entourage is one camp (cf. 32:8—Eng 32:7), and God's agents form the other—a natural pair. He can go on to meet Esau in tandem with the same divine company that he met at Bethel and that have been with him ever since (see 31:11).

Segment D′ (32:4–33—Eng 32:3–32). The cycle returns to Esau, who has not appeared since the end of segment D, and who is now mentioned together with the two geographical names to which the cycle early made allusion (segment A). Expecting Esau to attack, Jacob broke his retinue into 2 camps so that at least half might escape. (He is now a "people" [v 7], a term never applied to Abraham or Isaac.)

He then prayed for help, another first (vv 9–12). First, his *address* to God reaches back in time by speaking of the "God of Abraham and Isaac," and forward by using "Yahweh," the distinctive name of Israel's deity. Second, as *grounds* he quotes the divine directive (from 31:3) pursuing which he had come to the present hazardous moment, substituting "deal bountifully with" for "be with." His return to the promise at the end of the prayer uses words ("offspring as the sands of the sea") which have not appeared in the cycle applied to Jacob (28:14 spoke of the "dust of the earth"); the narrative telescopes the promises here, drawing this line from Gen 22:17—the promise to Abraham—and identifying Jacob with the promise in its historical depth. Third, he *acknowledges* God's gifts. He had left Canaan in naked flight, and was now two camps. His words "I am unworthy" (v 10), literally, "I am too small" (Heb *qāṭōntî*), express more than unworthiness; they also allude to Jacob's being the younger (*qāṭōn* 29:15, 42) and to the reversal of primogeniture (Brueggemann 1982). Fourth, the *petition* beseeches rescue from Esau, specifically mentioning the mothers and children; the language is that of the biblical psalms (e.g., 31:16; 59:2–3; 142:7; 143:9). The absence of any acknowledgement of wrongdoing is noteworthy.

"A man wrestled with him until dawn" (v 24). This best-known of the Jacob stories remains mysterious. In their southward march they had reached the river Jabbok and were camped on its N bank. During the night after Jacob had dispatched the gifts to Esau, he got up and took his family over to the S bank; he did the same with his possessions—no motive for this is given. Jacob remained alone in the camp. There is no "angel" in this story (an interpretation found in Hos 12:4), and the introduction of an adversary is abrupt and unexpected. Is it Esau, taking revenge in kind by a sneak attack in the dark? The match was even, but the adversary managed to wrench Jacob's hip at its socket before asking for release as the dawn broke. Jacob refused, "unless you bless me." The adversary required him to say his name—"Jacob"—and then changed it to "Israel," giving a popular etymology by which it means "he strives with God." When Jacob asked his adversary's name, he was told, "You must not ask my name," and they parted (see Gen 35:9–15). Jacob named the place "God's Face," and went his way, limping, as the sun rose. A dietary etiology concludes the story.

In its present form and position, the story concerns struggle with people and with God (see also Kodell 1980). The unnamed "man" symbolizes every person with whom Jacob struggled—Esau, Isaac, Laban—and yet, the "man" at the beginning of the story is certainly God at the end, for who else is it whose name cannot be spoken? When else did Jacob strive with God? The story, therefore, in an overt polyvalence, blends Jacob's conflict with people and with God into one event. The larger narrative also suggests this identification. First, Jacob prayed, "Rescue me (Heb *haṣṣîlēnî*) from my brother" (v 11), then he named the wrestling-site "God's Face," saying, "My life has been rescued" (Heb *wattinnāṣēl*, v 30). Second, after wrestling, he said, "I have seen God face to face" (v 30), and when he met Esau, he said, "To see your face is like seeing God's face" (33:10).

To utter his name was to speak his character—"cheat"—making good the lack of any confession in the prayer, and acknowledging that his alienation from Esau was not an episode but a way of life. The story is thus made psychologically and theologically profound by superimposing on one another Jacob's need to face his own character, his relations with people, and his relation with God.

The limp suggests the costliness of the lonely struggle. It also shows Jacob advancing to meet Esau in a painful vulnerability; whatever he might have thought previously of victory in struggle or of escape (v 8) is now quite impossible. He limps. But the sun is rising, and he is on his way to becoming a new man, a process begun as the sun was setting (28:11).

Segment C′ (33:1–20). The story moves immediately to the encounter between the 2 brothers. Jacob now leads his entourage, having previously followed it from behind. His elaborate obeisance before Esau (v 3) is without parallel in the Bible. But Esau does not want a fight: they embrace, kiss, and weep.

In the next segment (B′) the text plays on two Hebrew words similar in appearance and sound: *maḥăneh* "company" (32:3, 8–9, 11, 22 [—Eng 32:2, 7–8, 10, 21]), and *minḥâ* "gift" (32:14, 19, 21–22 [—Eng 13, 18, 20–21]; cf. *bĕrākâ* and *bĕkōrâ* in segments A and C). Now in 33:8, 10, the *maḥăneh* has become the *minḥâ*; Jacob urges Esau to accept the company/gift as a sign of the acceptance of his person. Then comes the jolt (Fishbane 1975), "Please take," Jacob urged, "my blessing *(bĕrākâ)*" (v 11). Dropping *minḥâ,* he utilizes the same noun and verb used by Esau and Isaac when Jacob took the blessing which was not his (27:35–36). The pairing of *minḥâ* with *maḥăneh* throughout these 2 sections makes the use of *bĕrākâ* particularly obtrusive, and the reference to segment C is very clear.

Yet, this is as far as the narrative can go in describing the reconciliation, for Jacob did not actually return the right of primogeniture, and historically Israel never conceded Edom's priority. Dramatically and symbolically, Jacob's acceptance by Esau could have been marked by a meal; its absence suggests that the reconciliation fell short of the solidity which Israel felt with the Syrian homeland of Rebekah and Rachel, and the narrative expresses this overtly by Jacob's wariness of Esau's two offers of company and assistance (vv 12–16).

They went their separate ways, Esau to Seir and Jacob to Canaan. His first act there was to buy land and set up an altar; by naming it "El, the God of Israel," he identified himself with the land and with the God who wrestled with him and gave him the name which became that of the people of God. Apart from the etiology of 32:33 it is the cycle's first use of the name "Israel" since it was given.

Segment B′ (34:1–31). Jacob's family settled on land that Jacob bought near Shechem. Dinah, his daughter by Leah, was raped by Shechem (his name is the same as the city's), son of the city's chief, Hamor. Jacob's involvement in the episode which followed is minimal, being restricted to the notice that he was silent about the rape until his sons came in from the field (v 5), and to his protest against his sons' subsequent actions (v 30).

Shechem wished to marry Dinah. His father's negotiations were entirely with Jacob's sons; Hamor even referred to their sister as "your [plural] daughter" (v 8). He proposed intermarriage between the family of Jacob and the Shechemites, to include full and free rights in the land. The brothers agreed, provided the Shechemite men accepted circumcision (already a mark of the Abrahamic tradition, Genesis 17). Then the newcomers would mingle and become "one people" with them (vv 16, 22). The Shechemites agreed. But on the third day, Dinah's uterine brothers Simeon and Levi attacked the city by surprise, killing all its men, including Hamor and Shechem, and taking Dinah away. The other brothers followed and pillaged the town, taking the women and children and all its wealth. The story closes with Jacob's effete protest that Simeon and Levi have made him "odious" in the land; he fears an attack which his small forces could not resist. The sons say only, "Should he treat our sister like a whore?"

The violence and duplicity of this story surpass anything ever done by Jacob, Rebekah, or Laban. Jacob's protest—feeble and motivated by fear of revenge rather than by moral outrage—and his silence at the outset raise the question whether we have here the new or the old Jacob; indeed, the new name is not used at all in the story (except in the anachronistic national sense in v 7).

To be sure, the threat was great and the accommodation proposed by Hamor ("one people," vv 16, 22) went far beyond the treaty designed by Abimelech (Gen 26:29 [segment B]); to "intermarry" *(hitḥattēn)* was forbidden (Deut 7:2–3; Josh 23:12; Ezra 9:14); and the Shechemites were clearly seeking their own advantage at Jacob's expense: "Their cattle and substance and all their beasts will be ours." The story is a justly sharp warning against sexual irregularity and against assimilation. But the circumcision proposal was a ruse from the beginning; the brokers spoke "with guile" (Heb *bĕmirmâ*, v 13) and never intended intermarriage.

The cycle, therefore, presents 2 paradigms for relationships with the residents of the land: First, a sacrificial self-giving which leads to "space" and to mutual acceptance and respect; second, a murderous and vindictive exclusivism. In segment B (Gen 26:1–33), Isaac's way resulted in God's blessing and agricultural prosperity: He found water. There is but one word of evaluation in B′: "guile" *(mirmâ)*. But, given the larger Israelite religious context, that is quite enough. It is the same word already used of Jacob's deceit of Isaac (27:35), and otherwise occurs 37 times, always negatively, exclusively in the Prophets and Wisdom literature (except 2 Kgs 9:23). Jer 9:5 (—Eng 9:6) uses *mirmâ* twice, and also alludes to Jacob by using the verb *ʿāqab* (also twice, in 9:3—Eng 9:4). The word *mirmâ* is almost a code word for social evil, and particular condemnation falls on guileful speech (Ps 52:6; Dan 8:25; 11:23). Note its use in Hos 12:1, 8, enclosing a passage which refers to Jacob.

Thus Jacob found that it was not easy to shed a whole way of life; more was yet needed before the promise (segment A) can be realized.

This chapter has long been a textbook example for source critics, who see in some of its internal confusions evidence that 2 versions have been combined—one from J (Hamor speaks) and one from P (Shechem speaks).

Segment A′ (35:1–29). The last chapter of a cycle of stories should be highly important, especially in an "anatomy," where the ideas are as important as the stories. Chap. 35 has generally puzzled scholars because it comprises discrete and diverse fragments, a feature which may find a parallel in early Arabic biographies (Delitzsch), and because parts of it duplicate earlier material (Jacob becomes Israel, he names Bethel). But everything here plays a role, either in bringing some of the cycle's themes to a conclusion or in echoing something in segment A. There are 7 fragments to consider.

1. Vv 1–7. Responding to God's direction, Jacob led a pilgrimage to Bethel, preceded by religious reforms involving his own household and (in the context of chap. 34) the Shechemite captives. The language of Jacob's appeal to the people, especially "Rid yourselves of the alien gods in your midst" (v 2), makes him the prototype of later reformers who called on God's people to repent: Joshua (Josh 24:23) and Samuel (1 Sam 7:3). Who are you, Jacob? The sly loner of segment A has become the zealous religious leader of a people (vv 2, 6).

2. Vv 9–15. God appeared, not only to bless Jacob, but also to change his name to "Israel," and to reiterate the twofold promise of progeny and land previously given to Abraham and Isaac. The cycle knows 2 traditions of Jacob's name-change, one associated with the wrestling in Transjordan (segment D′) and one here with Bethel in Canaan. The former is a personal episode in which Jacob struggled to lay aside his fractious and estranging way of life; the latter follows his engagement in the religious life of his people, showing that the story of Jacob as person was also read and told of Jacob as national progenitor. Accordingly, the Heb *wayĕbārek ʾōtô* (v 9) should be translated "he blessed him" but at 32:30 "he took leave of him" (so JPSV), since the blessing and promise come only after Jacob shows this collective concern. The story can now call him "Israel" (v 21), which it has not done previously.

The promise uses the words "be fertile and increase," which Isaac had also used (28:3, see segment D). The hint there of Jacob as the first man—who, like Adam and Noah, initiates something new and big and who can justly inherit the promise of the land—can now be seen enfleshed in the chastened and returned Jacob. Now the new beginning can occur, because Jacob cares about his people.

The cycle also knows two traditions of the naming of Bethel, one on Jacob's flight (segment E), and one here upon his return. The pair of duplicate name-givings in A′, therefore, link it specifically with the 2 previous epochal religious experiences of Jacob's life: when God arrested his attention and obtained a preliminary if wary response (28:10–22), and when God brought Jacob to face himself and his wider relationships with both people and the divine (32:22–32). It forms itself a third, in which Jacob's development comes to the necessary stage of religious leadership in a distinctly Israelite context. The placement of vv 9–15 at the close of the cycle is necessary in view of the process through which Jacob passed, but it also nicely balances segment A's giving of the name "Jacob" with the giving of the new name "Israel."

3. V 8. Verses 1–15 form a unity enclosed by references to Bethel at beginning and end. Verse 8 is geographically appropriate, but intrusive in every other way. It may be understood in connection with segment A's hint that Rebekah's role in the cycle will be incomplete. When A′ reports 3 deaths—two of them expected through the passage of time—the absence of any word about Rebekah becomes noticeable. What *has* happened to her?

Rebekah's unfinished question (25:22) finds its complement here in 35:8, which is not so much the notice of Deborah's death as a non-notice of Rebekah's. As far as the cycle goes, Rebekah's life is an unfinished story. After her complaint, "What good will life be to me?" (27:46) we never hear of her again. She had told Jacob, "When your brother's anger subsides, I will bring you back from Haran" (27:44–45), but Jacob's return has its own motives (31:1–3). Rebekah disappears from the story without a trace. The necrology of v 8 is positioned anomalously between 2 paragraphs showing the new Jacob at his best: He leads a religious reform, and he receives a new name and the divine promise. Its obtrusive position is hermeneutic: The Aramean way of life is gone; Israel—both person and people—will put away alien gods and will occupy the land of promise.

4. Vv 16–21. As they travelled from Bethel, Rachel died giving birth to Benjamin. Jacob's sons now number 12, and the death of the beloved wife signals that the cycle is drawing to a close. But it closes on a note of hope: Rachel's name for the infant—Ben-oni "Son of my suffering"—looks backward, to her untimely death and to the rivalries and disappointments of the years in Haran; but Jacob's alternate name "Son of the right hand," looks forward by suggesting his own favor and by evoking the right hand of God which saves (Isa 41:10; Pss 20:7; 118:15–16).

5. V 22a. The brusque notice that Reuben slept with Bilhah, who is called Israel's concubine rather than Rachel's maid, also suggests the passing of the old order. Reuben was Jacob's firstborn; to sleep with a man's women is to lay claim to his position.

6. Vv 22b–26. Segment A had said that 2 peoples would issue from Rebekah. The list of the 12 sons, grouped by mother, matches this prediction, in that one of these peoples (the 12 tribes of Israel) sprang from one of Rebekah's sons.

7. Vv 27–29. Finally Jacob reaches his father Isaac, at the ancestral residence of Abraham and Isaac (Gen 13:18; 23:2; 25:9). There Isaac died, and the story which began with prenatal jostling closes with the brothers Jacob and Esau joined in burying the father who prayed for their birth.

The divine plan for Jacob has been achieved, against human custom (primogeniture) and against human suitability (Jacob is the one who seeks his own advantage at others' expense, in flight from intimacy). Yet it has come about without any divine overriding of Jacob's "free will"; all human actions have adequate human motivation, including the pivotal decision to return to Canaan. In and through these actions, the sovereign will guides human thought and choice in a gracious interplay both reasonable and mysterious.

C. Meaning

The cycle's internal indications that "Jacob" is a collective reference for Israel find their parallel in the Bible's frequent use of "Jacob," either alone or in parallelism with "Israel," to denote the nation and/or the religious community (e.g., Deut 32:9; Jer 10:25; 30:7; Isa 10:21; 17:4; Ps 44:5; see BDB, 785). Note Isa 29:22–23, which expressly equates "Jacob" with "his children": "For when he [Jacob]—that is, his children—behold what my hands have wrought in their midst, they will hallow My name." The same equivalence is frequent in Second Isaiah where the Lord (a) addresses "Jacob/Israel" directly (40:27; 41:8, 14; 43:1, 22; 44:1, 2, 21, 23; 44:4; 48:12, 21; 49:5), (b) speaks of having given "Jacob" over to disaster (42:4; 43:28), and (c) speaks hopefully of "Jacob's" return to the Lord (49:5–6; 59:20). Some of these refer to the "servant," a figure whose identity is ambiguous, but others refer unmistakably to the prophet's audience and readers. The presumed exilic setting of Second Isaiah suggests a particular linking of the narrative's out-and-back axis with the experience of exile and (hope for) return; the exilic or early postexilic period would be a time in which this particular figural reading of the Jacob stories might have developed (Cross has noted similarities between P and Second Isaiah, *CMHE,* 322–23). One could also compare Second Isaiah's assertion of the Lord's presence with the people (Isa 41:10; 43:2, 5) with God's promise to be with Jacob and not leave him, a motif that is distinctive to the Jacob stories and is especially enshrined in the two theophanic passages about the Lord's agents (explicitly in Gen 28:10–22; implicitly in 32:2–3—Eng 32:1–2).

The tradents and users understood themselves as "Israel," automatically giving the stories a referred meaning in which they are also about the people of the covenant, whose existence and survival were often against both convention and suitability. The narratives are "typical and representational rather than realistic" (Blenkinsopp 1981: 41). When prominence is given to political relationships, especially under the influence of the documentary hypothesis, the cycle has to do with Israel's hegemony over her enemies and her occupation of the land (de Pury 1975; *CMHE,* 263–64), both in the time of Solomon (the Yahwist) and later after the Exile (P, see McKenzie 1980: 230–31). But in the present biblical context, religious interests come to the fore. Jacob's vocation is to be an *ʾîš tām,* a "moral person" (Gen 25:27). Note how many of the Isaiah passages stress repentence, redemption, and obedience to Torah (14:1; 27:9; 29:22–24; 41:14; 43:1, 22–28; 44:21–22; 48:21; 49:5–6; 59:20). The question of Israel's origins is a question of "the essence and meaning of a people. It is ideological rather than historiographical"; the existence of Israel as a people does not depend on a physical or political context but on their observance of the Lord's commands and statutes (Thompson 1987: 40, 194). Jacob's return to the land means not just Israel's return to the land from exile (McKay 1987) but also Israel's return to God. The cycle was paradigmatic for their own character and vocation, and in turn for the people of God in every time and place.

There are other inner-biblical indicators of the Jacob cycle's religious use. In Hosea 12, "Jacob" denotes what was left of the N kingdom and is the object of the prophet's preaching; note especially the "Jacob"/"us" equivalence ("[Jacob] would find Him at Bethel, and there He speaks with us," Hos 12:5—Eng 12:4) and the return (Heb *šûb*) motif in Hos 12:7—Eng 12:6. In Isa 49:5–6, the statement that the Lord "will bring back (Heb *šôbēb*) Jacob to Himself" suggests a figural reading of Jacob's return; furthermore, Israel as a "light to the nations" expresses the idea of service and mission intimated in Gen 30:30 (one of Jacob's 4 anomalous uses of YHWH). Brodie (1981) argues that the Jabbok story has been constructed to reflect the oracle in Jer 30:1–13; the cycle has been shaped by a sermon. Jer 9:3 warns against trusting even a brother, "for every brother takes advantage" (Heb *ʿāqôb yaʿqōb* [the form differs from the name "Jacob" only by a single *šĕwa*]), and v 5 adds, "You dwell in the midst of deceit *(mirmâ),* in their deceit they refuse to heed me, declares the Lord" (v 5); in v 3's resonance with "Jacob" and v 5's use of *mirmâ* we see a figural application of the Jacob material to Israel's moral life.

The cycle, therefore, is not historical; it is homiletic, and bears the marks of shaping to that end. The individual "Jacob" and the collective "Israel" overlap—even coalesce—at the artistically most significant points in the cycle: the beginning, the ending, and the middle. At the beginning, this overlap is accomplished by identifying the twins with nations (Gen 25:23) and by allusions associated with Esau's name; at the ending, by Jacob's receiving the name "Israel" (35:10) and by his engagement in the religious life of his people (vv 1–7); and at the middle by the collocation of the sections on children and flocks (Gen 29:31–30:43). It is a cycle about the people of God.

Bibliography

Alter, R. 1981. *The Art of Biblical Narrative.* New York.

Bimson, J. J. 1980. Archaeological Data and the Dating of the Patriarchs. Pp. 59–92 in *Essays on the Patriarchal Narrative,* ed. A. Millard and D. Wiseman. Leicester.

Blenkinsopp, J. 1981. Biographical Patterns in Biblical Narrative. *JSOT* 20: 27–46.

Brodie, L. T. 1981. Jacob's Travail (Jer 30:1–13) and Jacob's Struggle (Gen 32:22–32). *JSOT* 19: 31–60.

Brueggemann, W. 1982. *Genesis.* Atlanta.

Buss, M. J. 1979. Understanding Communication. Pp. 3–44 in *Encounter With the Text,* ed. M. J. Buss. Philadelphia.

Clines, D. 1978. *The Theme of the Pentateuch.* JSOTSup 10. Sheffield.

Coats, G. W. 1980. Strife Without Reconciliation. Pp. 82–106 in *Werden und Wirken des Alten Testaments,* ed. R. Albertz et al. Göttingen and Neukirchen-Vluyn.

Farmer, A. K. 1978. The Trickster Genre in the OT. Diss. Southern Methodist University.

Fishbane, M. 1975. Composition and Structure in the Jacob Cycle. *JJS* 27: 15–38. Repr. 1979, pp. 40–62 in *Text and Texture: Close Reading of Selected Biblical Texts.* New York.

Fokkelman, J. P. 1975. *Narrative Art in Genesis.* SN 17. Assen.

Frei, H. W. 1974. *The Eclipse of Biblical Narrative.* New Haven.

Friedman, R. E. 1986. Deception for Deception. *BibRev* 2: 22–31.

Gammie, J. G. 1979. Theological Interpretation by Way of Literary and Tradition Analysis: Genesis 25–36. Pp. 117–34 in *Encounter With the Text,* ed. M. J. Buss. Philadelphia.

Hendel, R. S. 1987. *The Epic of the Patriarch.* HSM 42. Atlanta.

Kodell, J. 1980. Jacob Wrestles with Esau. *BibTB* 10: 65–70.

McKay, H. A. 1987. Jacob Makes it Across the Jabbok. *JSOT* 38: 3–13.

McKenzie, S. 1980. "You Have Prevailed": The Function of Jacob's Encounter at Peniel in the Jacob Cycle. *ResQ* 23: 225–32.

Morrison, M. A. 1983. The Jacob and Laban Narrative in Light of Near Eastern Sources. *BA* 46: 155–64.

Noth, M. 1953. Mari und Israel: Eine Personnennamestudie. In *Geschichte und Altes Testament,* ed. G. Ebeling. Tübingen. Repr. Vol. 2, pp. 213–33 in *Gesammelte Aufsätze* (1971).

Oden, R. A., Jr. 1983. Jacob as Father, Husband, and Nephew. *JBL* 102: 189–205.

Pury, A. de. 1975. *Promesse divine et legende cultuelle dans le cycle de Jacob.* Paris.

Selman, M. J. 1980. Comparative Customs and the Patriarchal Age. Pp. 93–138 in *Essays on the Patriarchal Narratives,* ed. A. R. Millard and D. J. Wiseman. Leicester, England.

Thompson, T. L. 1974. *The Historicity of the Patriarchal Narratives.* BZAW 133. Berlin.

———. 1979. Conflict Themes in the Jacob Narratives. *Semeia* 15: 5–26.

———. 1987. *The Origin Tradition of Ancient Israel.* JSOTSup 55. Sheffield.

Van Seters, J. 1975. *Abraham in History and Tradition.* New Haven.

Westermann, C. 1985. *Genesis 12–26.* Minneapolis.

STANLEY D. WALTERS

JACOB'S WELL (PLACE) [Gk *Pēgē tou Iakōb*]. The only well which is specifically mentioned in the NT, and the place where Jesus talked with the Samaritan woman (John 4:6). It is not mentioned by that name in the OT, even though Jacob's dwelling is reported to be in that region.

The text in John connects the well with the city of Sychar (John 4:5), but opinions on the identification of this town are divided between those who see in the place-name the modern town of Askar located N of this well and others who associate Sychar with Shechem. See SHECHEM; SYCHAR. The former position favoring Sychar was held by the Old Syriac Bible, Jerome, and more recently Albright. Two of the most-frequently used arguments are the alleged corruption of Sychar to Shechem, and the text of Genesis 33:18 which mentions Jacob as having dwelt before the city, i.e., to the E of it. This identification has been shaken by recent archaeological evidence according to which Shechem ceased to exist by the 1st century B.C. Thus, nearby Askar receives more attention today despite the fact that the town is not as close to the traditional well as the proponents of this thesis would wish; in addition to this, Askar has its own well whose water is not as good as the one of the well in question.

Yet in spite of the difficulties connected with the identification of the city of Sychar, the well has been confidently identified with *Bir Yaʿaqub* (M.R. 177179) in the proximity of Tell Balatah. This well is located at the entrance to the ravine which separates Mt. Ebal from Mt. Gerizim in a Greek Orthodox church that has been under construction since 1903. This location is plausible since it agrees with the evidence from the narrative, namely that the well is found at the foot of Mt. Gerizim (John 4:20) and about 1 mile SE of Nablus. It is near the fork of a road which comes from Jerusalem and branches to Samaria and Tirzah respectively.

The authenticity of this well is not only based on the details from the story, which agree with its identification, but also upon the fact that all traditions—Jewish, Samaritan, Christian, and Muslim—support it. This led A. Parrot to declare that this site is the most authentic of all the Holy Places in Palestine. The earliest evidence comes from A.D. 333 when Pilgrim of Bordeaux mentions a pool or a bath filled with water from this well. Also, Eusebius in the 4th century speaks of the well in his *Onomasticon.*

According to Jerome there was a church in this place toward the end of the 4th century, a fact confirmed by the story of Arculf's pilgrimage in A.D. 670, which states that the church was built in the shape of a cruciform. Archaeological excavations of the site have unearthed the ruins of an old crusader's church which dates to the 11th century. In 1881 a stone was discovered nearby which is believed to have been a cover of the well.

The well itself is ca. 100 feet deep, a fact reminiscent of the woman's words in John 4:11. The water is clear and cool and visitors today are still offered a cup of this refreshment. The upper part of the well is built in masonry, while the lower is cut through rock. The words from John 4:6 can be translated as "on the well" which suggests that the well was covered by stone blocks. The well is supplied in 2 ways, by underground sources and also by surface water—like rainwater. Based on the use of the Gk word *phrear* (4:11) some are inclined to call the source a draw-well. The water source was certainly not a cistern, nor is it today but rather a rich supply of water at a great depth.

Some of the important parallels between the report of John and the actual description of the place demonstrate the author's good knowledge of the geographical data of this Palestinian region.

Bibliography

Albright, W. F. 1956. *Background of the New Testament and Its Eschatology.* Cambridge.

Parrot, A. 1968. *Land of Christ.* Philadelphia.

ZDRAVKO STEFANOVIC

JACOB, LADDER OF. This pseudepigraphon is a haggadic exegetical expansion of Jacob's vision (Gen 28:11–22) with apocalyptic elements. Seven chapters describe the ladder stretching into heaven; the first 6 are probably Jewish, and the final one is an expansion by a Christian, who prophesies regarding the birth and crucifixion of Christ. The document is preserved only in 2 Slavonic recensions. Since these texts are part of the Explanatory Palaia (*Tolkovaja paleja*), which is a medieval Slavic reworking of OT stories, there is not sufficient data to discern how much of each text, if any, antedates 200 C.E. Critical work and discussion of this document is just beginning. Nothing certain can be reported regarding the original language, provenience, date, or character of the *Ladder of Jacob.*

The original language of chap. 1–6 may be Gk (Lunt, *OTP* 2: 403). They seem to be written by a Jew—perhaps late in the 1st century C.E. or sometime in the 2d century C.E.—who wrote for readers ignorant of Hebrew. The choice of the base text (esp. Gen 28:13–15) and the emphasis on the land (1:9) may indicate a Palestinian provenience.

Monotheism is stressed in the document. Angels, which in most Jewish pseudepigraphical works descend from heaven to earth and then ascend back into heaven, are described instead as first ascending and then descending. The source for this imagery is Gen 28:12b (cf. John 1:51). The angel sent to Jacob "to understand the meaning of the dream" (3:2) is Sariel, who is "in charge of dreams" (3:2). The Voice in this document is a hypostatic creature, as in the *Apocalypse of Abraham,* the *Apocalypse of Sedrach,* and other documents (Charlesworth 1985: 19–41). The work is anti-astrological, in contrast to the *Treatise of Shem.* Apocalyptic emphases permeate the work, with predictions of exile, slavery, and persecution, but angels, and even God, will fight for Jacob's descendants (as in 1QM), and the eschaton will be blessed: "And through your seed all the earth and those living on it in the last times of the years of completion shall be blessed" (1:11; Lunt *OTP* 2: 407).

Bibliography

Charlesworth, J. H. 1985. The Jewish Roots of Christology: The Discovery of the Hypostatic Voice. *SJT* 39: 19–41.

James, M. R. 1920. Ladder of Jacob. Pp. 96–103 in *The Lost Apocrypha of the Old Testament.* London.

Pennington, A. 1984. The Ladder of Jacob. Pp. 453–63 in *The Apocryphal Old Testament,* ed. H. F. D. Sparks. Oxford.

Vassiliev, A. 1893. *Anecdota Graeco-Byzantina.* Moscow.

JAMES H. CHARLESWORTH

JACOB, PRAYER OF. A document preserved in only one 4th-century Gk papyrus. Greek is probably the original language. The work must antedate the 4th century, and parallels with other similar works indicate that the prayer was composed in the 2d or even late 1st century C.E. The provenience seems to be Egyptian because of the veneration of Sinai and links with other Egyptian documents. The author is thought to be a Jew; he refers to himself as "[fro]m the rac[e] of Israel" (line 14), prays to the "Lord God of the Hebrews" (line 13), and is influenced by Jewish magic.

Interesting features include the claim that God sits "upon (the) mountain of h[oly] [S]inaios" (line 8) and that the author is immortal, indeed an angel: "an ear[th]ly angel,/ as [hav]ing become immortal" (line 19). E. R. Goodenough (1953: 161–207) rightly saw that the author is an angel on the earth; but how and when the author became an angel, presumably through some magical means, is unclear. See also *OTP* 2: 715–23, and *PGM,* 148–49.

Bibliography

Goodenough, E. R. 1953. Charms in Judaism. Vol. 2, pp. 161–207 in *Jewish Symbols in the Greco-Roman Period.* Bollingen Series 37. New York.

JAMES H. CHARLESWORTH

JADA (PERSON) [Heb *yādāᶜ*]. Younger son of Onam and grandson of an important leader in the tribe of Judah, Jerahmeel, by his wife Atarah; mentioned twice in the genealogies of 1 Chronicles (1 Chr 2:28, 32). Jada is the brother of Shammai (whose descendants are enumerated for 18 generations in 1 Chronicles 2) and father of Jether and Jonathan. Jether died without issue (v 32) and Jonathan's 2 sons, Peleth and Zaza, complete Jada's genealogy. Variant spellings of Jada appear in the LXX, although many scholars consider those genealogies corrupt (especially Codex Vaticanus); however, the genealogies of Jerahmeel in the MT are viewed by most contemporary scholars as being in good order. Williamson (1979: 352) summarizes recent source critical scholarship of the genealogies in 1 Chronicles 1–9 concluding that 2:25–33 (of which Jada is a part) and 42–50a form a related unit. This independent source was used by the Chronicler and probably already contained the distinctive parallel opening and closing formulae.

Although little is known of the clan of Jerahmeel, current scholarship concludes a preexilic origin and historical nature to the Jerahmeelite genealogy (Jerahmeelites do not appear in discussions of the restoration). This clan is mentioned in 1 Sam 27:10 and 30:29, in connection with the Kenites, as inhabiting the S portion of Judah at the time of David. Some scholars identify them with foreign elements in Israel (Gen 15:19) and the shift of Edomites from S Judah northward following the destruction of Jerusalem (Braun *1 Chronicles* WBC, 45; Myers *1 Chronicles* AB, 15). Elmslie (*Chronicles* CBC, 15) suggests that names of Jerahmeelite ancestry may not reflect either specific individuals or places but rather preserves the idea that these formerly nomadic families now enjoyed a more settled life. More recent scholarship favors viewing all of the names listed as personal (Braun *1 Chronicles* WBC, 45). Specific dating of Jada is impossible at this time and suggestions range from before the Exodus (Keil 1872: 67) to a time closer to the period of restoration. See Braun (*1 Chronicles* WBC, 46) for discussion and evaluation. The name Jada is derived from the verb meaning "know" and some of the many suggestions offered for the meaning of this name are "the caring one," "(God) has cared," "known," "skillful," and "shrewd one."

Bibliography

Keil, C. F. 1872. *The Books of Chronicles.* Vol. 3 in *Commentary on the Old Testament.* Grand Rapids. Repr. 1978.

Williamson, H. G. M. 1979. Sources and Redaction in the Chronicler's Genealogy of Judah. *JBL* 98: 351–59.

W. P. Steeger

JADDAI (PERSON) [Heb *yadday*]. See IDDO.

JADDUA (PERSON) [Heb *yaddûaᶜ*]. The name of 2 different persons mentioned in the OT.

1. A leader of the people and a signatory to the covenant established by Ezra (Neh 10:21). Some scholars conjecture that the name is a shortened form of either the name, Jolada (Neh 3:6) or Jedalah (Ezra 2:36). If so, the name, Jaddua, means "Yahweh has known or cares for" (Brockington *Ezra, Nehemiah and Esther* NCBC, 182; cf. *TPNAH* 168).

2. A high priest during the postexilic period (Neh 12:11, 22). According to v 11 he was the son of Jonathan. Although this may be (Brockington, 200), it is more likely that an error has been made in copying the text and that, as v 22 would seem to suggest, he was the son of Johanan (Brockington, 199–200; Ward *IDB* 2: 787; Myers *Ezra, Nehemiah* AB, 195). According to Josephus, he "shared" the office of high priest with Manasses early in the reign of Alexander the Great (*Ant* 11.8.2). Precisely what Josephus means is unclear, unless Manasses served as Jaddua's assistant or *sāgān.* Beyond what we know about Jaddua, no further information about the order of succession to the high priesthood is again available until the Hellenistic period (Albright 1949: 54, 55). More significant is the clue that his name may provide to a date for the final compilation of Ezra-Nehemiah (Brockington, 200). However, any conjectures ventured on this basis must be tempered by the possibility that Jaddua's name has been added to the manuscript (Ward *IDB* 2: 787; Myers, 198).

Bibliography

Albright, W. F. 1949. The Biblical Period. Vol. 1, pp. 3–69 in *The Jews: Their History, Culture, and Religion,* ed. L. Finkelstein. New York.

Frederick W. Schmidt

JADDUS (PERSON) [Gk *Ioddous*]. The progenitor of a family of priests which returned from Babylon with Zerubbabel (1 Esdr 5:38). When the family was unable to establish its priestly lineage by genealogical records, the men were excluded from serving as priests (1 Esdr 5:38–40 = Ezra 2:61–63 = Neh 7:63–65). Neither Ezra nor Nehemiah record the name "Jaddus," using in its place "Barzillai" (Ezra 2:61; Neh 7:63). There are, however, a number of manuscripts in which 1 Esdras states that Jaddus took the name of his father-in-law Barzillai when he married Agia.

Michael David McGehee

JADON (PERSON) [Heb *yādôn*]. One of those who repaired the wall of Jerusalem following the return from Babylonian exile (Neh 3:7). Newman (*IDB* 2: 787) offers 2 possible derivations for the name: (1) from an Arabic word meaning "frail" or (2) a shortened form of *ydnyh,* which occurs in the Elephantine Papyri and means "Yahweh rules." Jadon is identified as a "Meronothite." This appellation occurs elsewhere only in 1 Chr 27:30. Meronoth has been identified with Beit Unia, which lies about 3 miles NW of Gibeon (*IDB* 2: 787). Since the entire identifying clause reads "Melatiah the Gibeonite and Jadon the Meronothite, the men of Gibeon and of Mizpah," it stands to reason that Meronoth should be connected with Mizpah. This Mizpah would be the "Mizpah of Benjamin," which has been identified with Tell en-Nasbeh (*IDB* 3: 407–8). In fact, Batten (*Ezra and Nehemiah* ICC, 210) suggests reading "Mispite" for "Meronothite." Brockington (*Ezra, Nehemiah, and Esther* NCBC, 136–37) offers the more-balanced suggestion that Meronoth must be in some way identified with Mizpah. Therefore, Jadon was from Meronoth, which probably lay in the vicinity of Mizpah of Benjamin.

Michael L. Ruffin

JAEL (PERSON) [Heb *yāᶜēl*]. The wife of Heber the Kenite (Judg 4:17) who gave shelter and then murdered Sisera, commander of the Canaanite coalition armies of Jabin, king of Hazor. He had been defeated by the combined armies of Israel under the leadership of Barak and Deborah (Judg 4:16). What motive did she have for her act? She was a member of a splinter group of the generally pro-Israelite Kenites (Judg 4:11; cf. Fensham 1964), who originated in the N of Sinai and evidently were metalworkers who had peaceful relations with Hazor (Judg 11:16; *YGC,* 38–42). Sisera naturally would expect sanctuary since this small seminomadic clan would be dependent upon good relations with its neighbors for trade and for land to live on (Soggin *Judges* OTL, 77). Caught in a dilemma of conflicting loyalties, she evidently made a political choice, since the text makes no mention of a personal motive. The story of Jael and Sisera is told twice: once in prose form (Judg 4:17–22) and a second time as part of the ancient poem, the Song of Deborah (Judg 5:24–27). Because of differences in reconstructing the chronology of the period of the Judges, the mention of Jael as a contemporary of Shamgar (Judg 5:6) has been variously understood as a textual problem or a historical one (cf. Soggin *Judges* OTL, 85–86). Others see no problem with the reference at all (Boling *Judges* AB, 109). The phrase "wife of Heber the Kenite" (Judg 5:24) is often interpreted as an interpolation from Judg 4:16 on metrical grounds, although Boling (*Judges* AB, 114) retains the phrase, also appealing to the metrics of the poem. Jael means "ibex" or "wild goat" (United Bible Societies 1972: 46), and is a member of a broad class of nontheological personal names in the Semitic world using the names of animals for women (Stamm 1967: 329).

Bibliography

Fensham, F. C. 1964. Did a Treaty between the Israelites and the Kenites Exist? *BASOR* 175: 51–54.

Stamm, J. J. 1967. Hebräisches Frauennamen. Pp. 301–39 in *Hebräische Wortforschung*, ed. B. Hartman et al. VTSup 16. Leiden.

United Bible Societies. 1972. *Fauna and Flora of the Bible*. Helps for Translators 9. New York.

Kirk E. Lowery

JAGUR (PLACE) [Heb *yāgûr*]. A settlement of the tribe of Judah (Josh 15:21). Jagur is only mentioned once, in Josh 15:21, where it is listed among the settlements occupied by Judah in the aftermath of the conquest. Though the present literary context of the Judean town list is set in the period of Joshua, its original setting was as part of a post-Solomonic administrative division of the S kingdom. The date for the establishment of this system is debated, with suggestions ranging from the early 9th to the late 7th centuries B.C. Jagur is in the southernmost district of Judah, the Negeb.

The location of Jagur is problematic. It is mentioned 3rd in the list of Negeb towns, and it may be that the explanatory clause which begins the list, "toward the boundary of Edom," does point to an area in the E Negeb. It is placed between Eder (probably a mistake for Arad) and Kinah (probably to the N of Arad, somewhere along the Wadi el Qeini). Arad inscription 42 mentions Jagur in a very fragmentary context (*AI*, 76). Its probable mention in Josh 15:21 near Arad, and the occurrence of Jagur on an ostracon from Arad, suggest a location in its vicinity. Both Abel (*GP*, 353) and Simons (*GTTOT*, 142) place it at Khirbet el-Gharrah, 18 km E of Beer-sheba (M.R. 148071).

Bibliography

Cross, F. M., and Wright, G. E. 1956. The Boundary and Province Lists of the Kingdom of Judah. *JBL* 75: 202–26.

Jeffrey R. Zorn

JAH/JAHVEH/JAHWEH. See YAHWEH.

JAHATH (PERSON) [Heb *yaḥat*]. **1.** A Judahite, the son of Reaiah and the father of Ahumai and Lahad (1 Chr 4:2). Williamson (1979a: 351–59) has argued that the Judahite genealogy of 1 Chr 4:2–4 reflects a preexilic source, whose beginnings may be detected in 1 Chr 2:50b–52. It should be noted, however, that Reaiah represents a family name of a group that returned from exile with Zerubbabel (Ezra 2:47 [= Neh 7:56]) and that an explicit relationship is drawn between Jahath and his kin and Zorah, a town inhabited by Judahites in the Persian period (Neh 11:29). These facts suggest that Jakim and kin represent individuals from the postexilic period that the Chronicler has transposed back before the reign of David in order to construct a genealogy that reflects the social realia of the Chronicler's own day.

2. The name of several Gershomites who appear with slightly divergent lineages in different genealogical lists within 1 Chronicles (1 Chr 6:5, 28—Eng 6:20, 43 and 1 Chr 23:10–11). Jahath first appears in 1 Chr 6:5 (—Eng 6:20) as the grandson of Gershom through Libni and as the father of Zimmah. He appears soon after in 1 Chr 6:28 (—Eng 6:43) within the genealogy of Asaph. This text portrays him directly as the son of Gershom and the father of Shimei. Zimmah becomes one generation removed as Jahath's grandson, rather than his son. In 1 Chr 23:10–11 Jahath represents a Gershomite whom David assigns to the maintenance of the Temple and its cult. Here Jahath is portrayed as the son, rather than the father, of Shimei. The relationship between these 3 instances of "Jahath the Gershomite" may be interpreted in several ways. Most commonly, modern interpreters have regarded the variance in these Levitical genealogies as an indication of later additions to 1 Chronicles that reflect the changing status of Levitical families in the Second Temple period (Rudolph *Chronikbücher* HAT, 57–59, 155). Curtis and Madsen (*Books of Chronicles* ICC, 130–35) attempted to emend the texts in order to remove inconsistencies. Yet the stylistic commonalities of the narrative frameworks where Jahath appears suggest that the Chronicler himself consciously altered the arrangement of the lists in order to generate different Levitical lists for distinct purposes and historical eras. The Chronicler, therefore, may have borrowed the name "Jahath" from a Benjaminite family of his day and utilized it to construct artificial genealogical lists.

3. The son of Rehabiah and one of the "remaining Levites" who, according to the Chronicler, casts lots before David, Zadok, and Ahimelek in order to receive his place among the Levitical household leaders (1 Chr 24:22). Liver (1968: 8.29–32) believes that this list may have originated from an authentic source composed during the reign of David or Solomon; most commentators, however, have attributed the list, in which Isshiah appears, to a time later than the main composition of Chronicles—either to the late Persian period (Williamson 1979b: 259–60, 265–68) or, more commonly, to the Maccabean era (Rudolph, 163–65). The style of the list, however, corresponds closely with the compositional techniques of the Chronicler. The Chronicler may have borrowed the name from a postexilic individual in order to complete a suitable list of Levitical names for the reign of David.

4. A Levite from the family of Merari, who, according to the Chronicler, supervised the renovation of the Temple during the reign of Josiah (2 Chr 34:12). Curtis and Madsen (p. 506) describe 2 Chr 34:12 as "a characteristic addition of the Chronicler." The Chronicler seems to have borrowed the names of Jahath and the other Levitical foremen from prominent Levitical names elsewhere in his work. Jahath's appearance within the reign of Josiah provides an important illustration of the Chronicler's use and reuse of Levitical names in his attempt to legitimize his version of the history of Judah.

Bibliography

Liver, J. 1968. *Chapters in the History of Priests and Levites.* Jerusalem (in Hebrew).

Williamson, H. G. M. 1979a. The Origins of the Twenty-Four Priestly Courses, A Study of 1 Chronicles xxiii–xxvii. Pp. 251–68 in *Studies in the Historical Books of the Old Testament,* ed. J. A. Emerton. VTSup 30. Leiden.

———. 1979b. Sources and Redaction in the Chronicler's Genealogy of Judah. *JBL* 98: 351–59.

JOHN W. WRIGHT

JAHAZ (PLACE) [Heb *yahaṣ*]. Var. JAHZAH. A settlement in Transjordan known from the OT and the Mesha Inscription. The present state of scholarship does not allow for a conclusive identification of Jahaz although there are several viable proposals (below).

According to various accounts, the Amorite king, Sihon, whose capital was located as Heshbon (Tell Hesban), came to Jahaz to oppose the Israelite tribes as they passed through Transjordan (Num 21:23; Deut 2:32; Judg 11:20). The geographical details are vague, but imply that Jahaz was located S of Heshbon, perhaps along the E border of the settled plateau as it stretched out to the desert. This possibility is complicated by the difficult issues regarding the wilderness itineraries and by the question of how to depict Israel: as passing around Edom and Moab to the E, or rather passing through their territories.

Jahaz is included in Reuben's tribal inheritance (Josh 13:18) and is made a levitical city (Josh 21:36). Prophetic oracles of a later period presuppose Jahaz is a Moabite town (Isa 15:4; Jeremiah 48:21, 34 [v 21 reads "Jahzah" as does 1 Chr 6:78]). Precisely this kind of conflict is presupposed in the Mesha Inscription (lines 18–21) from the 9th century B.C.E. which narrates that Moab regained Jahaz from an Israelite king who had fortified the town. Mesha notes that he "annexed" Jahaz to Dibon (Tell Dhiban), almost certainly as part of his efforts to regain control of the plateau between Madeba and Dibon.

The Mesha Inscription states that Israel had fortified 2 towns, Ataroth and Jahaz. Ataroth (*Kh. 'Atarus*) is located ca. 14 km NW of Dibon on the edge of the W slopes of the plateau. Since Dibon was Mesha's administrative center, somewhere between it and Ataroth was the effective border between Israel and Moab. The obvious candidate for such a demarcation is the N tributary of the Wadi Mujib (the biblical Arnon), which cuts through the plateau in a SW direction from its beginnings near the E edge of the settled plateau. This wadi is known by various modern names as one climbs W–E: Wadi Heidan, Wadi Wala, Wadi Remeil, and Wadi et Themed. Jahaz, therefore, should be located along or just N of this wadi system and E of Ataroth.

Among the likely possibilities are the following:

1. Khirbet Libb (M.R. 222112), ca. 11 km N of Dibon on the King's Highway, is now the site of a modern village which obscures the Iron Age ruins. This location would fit the comment of Eusebius that Jahaz was between Madeba and Dibon (*Onomast.* 104.9).
2. Khirbet Iskander (M.R. 223107), a site just W of the modern King's Highway as it crosses the Wadi Wala, and ca. 6 km N of Dibon. Limited excavations suggest the site is primarily EB IV; no architectural remains as yet have been found from the Iron Age.
3. Khirbet Remeil (M.R. 228114), an Iron Age fort ca. 5 km NE of Iskander set on an isolated hill. The exposed ruins provide evidence of a walled enclosure and tower/fortress complex. An unresolved question is whether Remeil is large enough to be known independently or whether the fort was used in the service of a larger settlement nearby such as Kh. Medeiniyeh.
4. Khirbet Medeiniyeh on the Themed (M.R. 236110), ca. 2.5 km NE of Kh. Remeil. This tell projects substantial wall lines and a possible moat that Nelson Glueck likened to Maiden Castle in England. The site's size and surface pottery suggest it is the largest predominately Iron Age settlement along the E edge of the settled plateau.
5. Khirbet Qureiyet 'Aleiyan (M.R. 233104), ca. 8 km NE of Dibon, is a series of Iron Age ruins.
6. Jalul (M.R. 231125), located ca. 5 km E of Madeba, this is the largest tell in the area with surface remains indicating Iron Age occupation. It is located too far N to meet the criterion of placement between Madeba and Dibon. It is, however, located SE of Hesban nearer the edge of the desert.

Among these options, Khirbet Medeiniyeh is the best possibility as the site of Jahaz. It is the largest site in the immediate vicinity, just as Ataroth is for the W section of the plateau, and it is located along the proposed border between Israelite-controlled territory and Moab as deduced from the Mesha Inscription. If the presence of pottery figurines among surface pottery is any indication, it was also a cultic center. If a site on or near the King's Highway is sought, then either Khirbet Libb or perhaps Khirbet Iskander are likely choices.

Bibliography

Dearman, J. A. 1984. The Location of Jahaz. *ZDPV* 100: 122–26.

Wüst, M. 1975. *Untersuchungen zu den Siedlungsgeographischen Texten des Alten Testaments.* Wiesbaden.

J. ANDREW DEARMAN

JAHAZIEL (PERSON) [Heb *yaḥăzîʾēl*]. A personal name which combines an imperfect form of the verb *ḥzh* "see" with the substantive *ʾēl* "God" and may be understood as expressing a request for help (*IPN*, 27, 198): "may God see," or as a simple statement, "God sees." Bauer (1930: 74) allows that it might reflect an older perfect meaning: "God has seen." Five individuals are so named.

1. A Benjaminite relative of Saul listed among those

who came to David at Ziklag (1 Chr 12:5—Eng 12:4). These 23 are described (v 1) as "mighty men" (Heb *gibbôrîm*) and as "warriors" (Heb *ʿōzre hammilḥāmāh*; Gordon 1955: 88, Gray 1965: 42, 263). They were "equipped with bow" and were ambidextrous in shooting arrows and slinging stones (v 2). Curtis and Madsen (*Chronicles* ICC, 196) believed those listed were Judeans.

2. One of the priests (1 Chr 16:6) appointed during the reign of David to sound "with trumpets" (Heb *ḥăṣōṣrôt*) continually before the ark of the covenant of God. His name is omitted from the original reading of Codex Sinaiticus and from the list of priests in 1 Chr 15:5. In the LXX his name is rendered *oziēl* (cf. 15:18, 20).

3. A Levite, the 3d son of Hebron who was a son of Kohath (1 Chr 23:19; 24:23), one of the familial divisions of the Levitical organizational structure attributed to David.

4. A Levite, son of Zechariah, whose lineage was traced to Asaph (2 Chr 20:14). As a son of Asaph he was a member of that guild of temple musicians, instrumentalists, and singers (1 Chr 25:1–2; 2 Chr 35:15) whose musical function was also described as prophesying (Heb *nibbĕʾîm*, 1 Chr 25:1, cf. 2b). Speaking "in the midst of the assembly" (2 Chr 20:14) in true prophetic fashion, he delivered a salvation oracle (Shearer 1986: 194, 241) in response to the king's lament. "All Judah and inhabitants of Jerusalem and King Jehoshaphat" (v 15) were assured the Lord would engage and be victorious (vv 15b, 17) over a threatening coalition of enemy forces from the E and SE.

5. According to the MT of Ezra 8:5 the father of an unnamed member of the sons of Shecaniah who, along with 300 males of the extended family (Blenkinsopp *Ezra-Nehemiah* OTL, 161; *IB* 3) returned with Ezra to Judah from Babylonian exile during the reign of the Persian King Artaxerxes. The LXX (Codex Alexandrinus) and 1 Esdr 8:32 name *Zathoēs* (RSV Zattu) as the eponymous ancestor with Jahaziel as the father of Shecaniah who is the living head of the returning group.

Bibliography

Bauer, H. 1930. Die hebräischen Eigennamen als sprachliche Erkenntnisquelle. *ZAW* 48: 73–80.

Gordon, C. H. 1955. North Israelite Influence on Post Exilic Hebrew. *IEJ* 5: 85–88.

Gray, J. 1965. *The Legacy of Canaan: The Ras Shamra Texts and Their Relevance To The Old Testament.* VTSup 5. Leiden.

Shearer, R. H. 1986. A Contextual Analysis of the Phrase *ʾal-tîrāʾ* As It Occurs in The Hebrew Bible and in Selected Related Literature. Diss. Drew University.

RODNEY H. SHEARER

JAHDAI (PERSON) [Heb *yahday*]. Descendant of Caleb and father (or mother) of 6 sons (1 Chr 2:47). Whether this person is a man or a concubine (of Caleb's) is not certain (cf. 2 Chr 2:48); nor is it certain that this portion of the genealogy is in its original position. On the difficulties of the genealogy in 1 Chr 2:42–50a see Williamson (*Chronicles* NCBC, 54–55) and Braun (*1 Chronicles* WBC, 40–41). This name, meaning "directed of the Lord," occurs nowhere else in biblical literature.

CRAIG A. EVANS

JAHDIEL (PERSON) [Heb *yaḥdîʾēl*]. Manassite tribal leader in Transjordania. The name means "May God rejoice" (*ḥādâ* + *ēl*). He is described as a mighty warrior and included in the part of the tribe of Manasseh that occupied the area from Bashan to Mount Hermon (1 Chr 5:24). According to 1 Chr 5:26, these Manassites, along with the Gadites and Reubenites in Transjordania, were exiled by the Assyrians under Tiglath-pileser III. This note finds support in other texts (e.g., 2 Kgs 15:29) that mention the Assyrian campaign in Galilee and Gilead during the Syro-Ephraimitic War (ca. 733 B.C.E.).

The list of 7 "mighty warriors, famous men, heads of their fathers' houses" in 1 Chr 5:24, which includes Jahdiel, is not part of a larger sequence, but is a genealogical fragment. It makes no attempt to relate any of the 7 men to Manassite clans, and in none of the other genealogies for the tribe (Num 26:29–34; Josh 17:1–2) is one of the 7 mentioned (unless Epher is the corrupted form of Hepher, who appears in the other lists). This has led some to question the source and accuracy of 1 Chr 5:24 (Williamson *Chronicles* NCBC, 66–67). In addition, the verse itself shows evidence of textual corruption. Although Jahdiel's name occupies the prominent 7th position in the present form of the Heb text, there is a *waw* (a conjunctive particle) that precedes the 1st name on the list, and this may indicate that the name (or names), which originally began the sequence, have been lost.

Finally, it is surprising to find Manasseh treated at all in 1 Chronicles 5, since the tribe is the subject of a much more extensive genealogy in 1 Chr 7:14–19. It may be that the author or a later editor was motivated to treat Manasseh with the other Transjordanian tribes in chap. 5, since Manasseh itself was divided into 2 segments—one in Transjordania (1 Chr 5:24) and one in W Palestine (1 Chr 7:14–19; Williamson NCBC, 66–67).

M. PATRICK GRAHAM

JAHDO (PERSON) [Heb *yaḥdô*]. A Gadite who is mentioned only in 1 Chr 5:14. The suggestions that his name should be spelled *yaḥday* or *yaḥdōy* are supported (but by no means established) by the Gk mss that conclude the name with an *iota*. It may be that the name was derived from the imperfect form of the Heb verb *ḥādâ* "rejoice" and expresses the desire that deity rejoice over the one named (Noth *IP*, 28, 210). Usually, however, the name has been associated with *yāḥad* "to be united" and given no particular meaning aside from its significance as a personal name.

M. PATRICK GRAHAM

JAHLEEL (PERSON) [Heb *yaḥlĕʾēl*]. JAHLEELITES. Third of the 3 sons of Zebulun mentioned in the genealogy of Jacob (Gen 46:14). Jahleel was the grandson of Jacob and Leah by their 6th and youngest son Zebulun (Gen 30:20). His name is included among the 33 sons and grandsons of Jacob and Leah (Gen 46:15) who descended with their families to join Joseph in Egypt, after Jacob heard that his son was alive. Jahleel became the clan leader of the Jahleelites, one of the clans of Zebulun (Num 26:26); however, nothing else is known about Jahleel and his family outside these two genealogical lists. His name does not appear in the Chronicler's list because in the genealogies of the sons of Jacob (1 Chronicles 4–7) the name of Zebulun is not included among the genealogies of the other tribes.

CLAUDE F. MARIOTTINI

JAHMAI (PERSON) [Heb *yaḥmay*]. Descendant, perhaps grandson, of Issachar according to the genealogy of 1 Chr 7:1–5. See IBSAM.

M. STEPHEN DAVIS

JAHZAH (PLACE) [Heb *yahṣâ*]. See JAHAZ.

JAHZEEL (PERSON) [Heb *yaḥṣĕʾēl*]. Var. JAHZIEL. JAHZEELITES. The 1st of the 4 sons of Naphtali (Gen 46:24). Jahzeel was also the grandson of Jacob and Bilhah (Gen 30:7–8), the maid whom Laban gave to his daughter Rachel at the occasion of Jacob's marriage to Rachel (Gen 29:29). He is included in the genealogy of the family of Jacob at the time the patriarch sojourned to Egypt to visit his son Joseph. Nothing is known about Jahzeel. According to the list of the clans and tribes of Israel in the book of Numbers, Jahzeel became the ancestral leader of the clan of the Jahzeelites, one of the clans of Naphtali (Num 26:48). In the genealogy of Naphtali in 1 Chr 7:13, Jahzeel's name is spelled Jahziel (Heb *yaḥṣîʾēl*).

CLAUDE F. MARIOTTINI

JAHZEIAH (PERSON) [Heb *yaḥzĕyāh*]. An opponent of Ezra's investigation of the men who had married foreign women (Ezra 10:15 = 1 Esdr 9:14). Noth categorized the name Jahzeiah as a "wish name" meaning "may Yahweh see" (*IPN*, 198). The Hebrew text reads literally that Jonathan and Jahzeiah "stood 'against' (*ʿal*) this," and most scholars take this to mean that they were opposed to the plan to have officials investigate the alleged marriages between Israelite men and foreign women on a case by case basis (so the RSV). It is possible to translate *ʿal* as "beside," implying their support for this program. In addition, the LXX reads "were with me on this," a reading apparently based on a slight emendation of the Hebrew text (from *ʿāmĕdû* to *ʿimmādî*). This may receive further support from the parallel text in 1 Esdr 9:14–15 which states that Jonathan and Jahzeiah "undertook the matter on these terms, and Meshullam and Levi and Shabbethai served with them as judges." On the other hand, the context in Ezra 10 implies that the majority of the people supported the plan and only these two opposed it. However, they may well have favored the forced divorces and were opposed only to the delay in implementing Ezra's policy. Regarding the two who "helped" Jonathan and Jahzeiah in their opposition, Meshullam was a companion of Ezra (8:16) and Shabbathai was a Levite whose name suggests he was from a family of strict observers (Clines *Ezra, Nehemiah, Esther* NCBC, 130). Thus, Jahzeiah probably sought even swifter and harsher treatment of the offenders (Williamson *Ezra, Nehemiah* WBC, 156).

JEFFREY A. FAGER

JAHZERAH (PERSON) [Heb *yaḥzērâ*]. A member of the priestly brotherhood of Immer and the grandfather of Maasai. In 1 Chr 9:12 he is listed in the genealogy of Maasai, who was one of the priests to settle in Jerusalem following the return from exile. A similar list in Neh 11:13 records the name as Ahzai, and gives his grandson's name as Amashsai. The genealogies presented in these 2 texts are as follows:

1 Chr 9:12
Immer → Meshillemith → Meshullam → Jahzerah → Adiel → Maasai

Neh 11:13
Immer → Meshillemoth → → Ahzai → Azarel → Amashsai

Scholars generally assume that the list in 1 Chronicles is dependent in some way upon that in Nehemiah, and the former appears to be a later updated version which reflects continuing developments and interests in the postexilic community. The priority of the list in Nehemiah is supported by the fact that the names in v 13 are better attested than are those in 1 Chr 9:12. Thus Maasai, though attested elsewhere, is likely a scribal error for Amasai or its variant Amaśai, both of which are reflected in the conflated reading Amashsai found in Neh 11:13.

The preferable reading of the name Jahzerah, therefore, is Ahzai. While the name Jahzerah is dubious in meaning, the name Ahzai is well attested in such forms as Ahaz and Ahaziah ("The Lord has seized"). The name Jahzerah perhaps found its way into the list in 1 Chr 9:12 because of the association of the name Hezir (from the same root as Jahzerah) with the eponym Immer in 1 Chr 24:14–15 where they are listed together as the 16th and 17th courses of priests established by David. In addition, Neh 10:20 juxtaposes the names Meshullam and Hezir. It seems possible, then, that the name Ahzai was changed in the development of the tradition to Yahzerah under the influence of the association of the names Immer and Meshullam with Hezir. For further discussion see *1 Chronicles* WBC and *Ezra Nehemiah* NICOT.

RODNEY R. HUTTON

JAHZIEL (PERSON) [Heb *yaḥăṣîʾēl*]. See JAHZEEL.

JAILOR, PHILIPPIAN. See PHILIPPIAN JAILOR.

JAIR (PERSON) [Heb *yāʾîr; yaʿîr* Q/*yaʿûr* K]. The English spelling represents 2 Hebrew personal names with different spellings. Spelled with *ʾalep*, 3 persons mentioned in the OT bear this name ("Let [God] enlighten"). A fourth, spelled with *ʿayin*, is named in 1 Chr 20:5 ("Let [God] arouse").

1. An eponymous son of Manasseh in Num 32:41; Deut 3:14; 1 Kgs 4:13 (cf. Josh 13:30). For the related gentilic

JAIRITE, see 2 Sam 20:26. Jair acquired control of a number of villages in Gilead, more specifically in the region of ARGOB (Num 32:41), which is equated with Bashan in Deut 3:14. The group came to be known as Jair's Villages (see also HAVVOTH-JAIR). In 1 Chr 2:22, theology may have crept into genealogy (Myers *1 Chronicles* AB, 14). There Jair's father is Segub of Judah and his mother a daughter of Machir, which may also stand for Manasseh.

2. One of the leaders of Israel in the pre-monarchy era (Judg 10:3–5), about whom very little information survives. The designation "minor judge" should be taken as a merely quantitative description of narrative scope, not suggestive of an office different from that of the so-called deliverer-judge (Mullen 1982). Jair was a Gileadite whose leadership lasted for 22 years. He had 30 sons and controlled 30 towns. His tomb was at Kamon, usually identified with modern Qamm, on the Jordan-Irbid road, a location considerably S of Argob-Bashan. Yet there is surely some relation to 1. above.

3. A Benjaminite, with no indication of relationship to the above. Jair is the (immediate?) ancestor of Mordechai, Esther's guardian (Esth 2:5).

4. The father of Elhanan who killed Lahmi the brother of Goliath, according to 1 Chr 20:5. But according to 2 Sam 21:19, the one who slew Goliath was Elhanan son of Jaareoregim. The latter may be corrected on the basis of LXX LMN and 1 Chr 20:5, to read "a Jearite." Elhanan's home Bethlehem is closely associated with Kiriath-jearim, "village of the Jearites" (McCarter *2 Samuel* AB, 449).

Bibliography

Mullen, E. T., Jr. 1982. The "Minor Judges": Some Literary and Historical Considerations. *CBQ* 44: 185–201.

ROBERT G. BOLING

JAIRITE [Heb *yāʾīrî*]. An adjective used to describe Ira, one of David's personal priests (2 Sam 20:26). The adjective refers to clan origin, Jair having been the head of a clan in the tribe of Manasseh (Num 32:41; Deut 3:14; 1 Kgs 4:13; 1 Chr 2:22, 23). The obvious problem that arises from this data is that Ira is a non-levitical priest. Some scholars propose the reading "Yattirite" instead of "Jairite" since Yattir was a priestly city in the hill country of Judah (cf. LXX [Codex Coislinias, Basiliano-Vaticanus] and the Peshitta). Ira would then probably have been a Levite. This expedient, however, is unnecessary since it is clear in the early monarchy that a special class of priests served the king (Armerding 1975; McCarter *2 Samuel* AB, 256–57).

Bibliography

Armerding, C. E. 1975. Were David's Sons Really Priests? Pp. 75–86 in *Current Issues in Biblical and Patristic Interpretation: Studies in Honor of Merill C. Tenney,* ed. G. F. Hawthorne. Grand Rapids, MI.

STEPHEN G. DEMPSTER

JAIRUS (PERSON) [Gk *Iairos*]. A Greek form of the Hebrew proper name, *Yāʾîr,* "he enlightens" (Num 32:41; Deut 3:14; Josh 13:30; Judg 10:3; Esth 2:5). Jairus is identified as a "ruler of the synagogue," (*archisynagōgos*), a title associated with a broad range of duties within the ancient synagogue. He comes to Jesus and asks him to heal his dying daughter (Mark 5:21–24, 35–43; Luke 8:40–42, 49–56; cf. Matt 9:18–19, 23–26 where Jairus is not mentioned by name). In the interval between Jairus' request and the arrival at his house, the girl is reported dead; Jesus insists she is merely sleeping and raises her up. Mark transmits his command in Aramaic, *"Talitha, koum,"* "Little girl, arise"; while Luke has only the Greek, "Child, arise." Matthew does not report a command.

Scholars disagree as to whether Jesus' reference to the child's sleep is meant literally, figuratively (1 Thess 5:6) or as a synonym for death (1 Thess 5:10). In any case, the 3 evangelists clearly mean to report a miracle of Jesus and not a mere misunderstanding of the girl's state.

In all 3 synoptic accounts, the story of the raising of Jairus' daughter is interrupted by the story of Jesus' healing the woman with a hemorrhage. Scholars disagree as to whether the 2 stories were joined by Mark and the arrangement retained by Matthew and Luke, or if they were joined in an earlier, pre-Marcan cycle of miracle stories.

Since the name "Jairus" is missing in Matthew's account and in MS D of Mark, some scholars question whether it was original to Mark's version or was added by a later scribe. Luke may have supplied a name for an anonymous figure as later writers were known to do, and a scribe may have then added it to Mark in light of Luke's account. However, more recent opinion generally favors the view that the occurrence of Jairus's name is at least as old as the traditions of his daughter's resuscitation.

Bibliography

Bultmann, R. 1963. *The History of the Synoptic Tradition.* Oxford.
Kertelge, K. 1970. *Die Wunder Jesu im Markusevangelium.* Munich.
Pesch, R. 1970. Jaïrus (Mk 5,22/Lk 8,41). *BZ* 14: 252–56.
Van der Loos, H. 1965. *The Miracles of Jesus.* Leiden.

CLAUDIA J. SETZER

JAKEH (PERSON) [Heb *yāqeh*]. The father of Agur according to Prov 30:1. Beyond this reference nothing is known of Jakeh, and the LXX does not even recognize *yāqeh* as a proper name. As the verse is translated in the RSV, he was from a place known as Massa, but even this is questionable. See discussion in AGUR; LEMUEL. Traditionally, the name Jakeh was associated with David, while Agur was identified as Solomon. The name is derived from various Hebrew stems by modern authors. It is most often traced to an Arabic word with the meaning "to preserve." Another possible Hebrew stem is identical to the one given above except for a *mappiq* in the final *he.* This stem basically means, "to be obedient" (*BDB,* 429). It is possible that either of these stems was attached to a divine name (Gemser *Sprüche Salomos* HAT 16, 103). The resulting form would be *yākehyāh* ("Yahweh preserves" or "one obedient to Yahweh"). The stems mentioned do not occur often enough to provide a certain etymology.

DONALD K. BERRY

JAKIM (PERSON) [Heb *yāqîm*]. **1.** A Benjaminite, the son of Shimei and inhabitant of Jerusalem (1 Chr 8:19). Geography seems to provide the organizing principle of the genealogical list in which Jakim appears. He thereby provides important demographic evidence for the population of Jerusalem at some point in its history. Rudolph (*Chronikbücher* HAT, 77) has argued that either Josiah's reign or Nehemiah's governorship provides a suitable background for the appearance of Benjaminites in Jerusalem. The commonality of the names of the 9 sons of Shimei with names recorded elsewhere in Chronicles or in Ezra and Nehemiah (Curtis and Masden *The Books of Chronicles* ICC, 162) suggests that Jakim represents a segment of the postexilic, rather than the preexilic, population of Jerusalem.

2. A priest who received the 12th position in the priestly order of the temple during David's reign (1 Chr 24:12). An evaluation of the historical reliability of his appearance depends basically upon the literary context of 1 Chr 24:1–19. Though generally agreed that this list of priests originated after the Exile, its exact date remains debated. Liver (1968: 9.33–52) associates the 24-course priestly organization to the reforms of Nehemiah, while Williamson (1979: 262–68) assigns it to the late Persian period. Due to genealogical connections between 1 Chr 24: 7–18 and the Hasmonean priestly claims, Dequecker (1986: 94–106) dates the list to the Hasmonean era. The stylistic characteristics of the list, however, seem to link the list to the time of the composition of Chronicles. The Chronicler may have retrojected the name "Jakim" into the reign of David from an individual from Jerusalem in his day.

Bibliography

Dequecker, L. 1986. 1 Chron xxiv and the Royal Priesthood of the Hasmoneans. *OTS* 24: 94–106.

Liver, J. 1968. *Chapters in the History of Priests and Levites.* Jerusalem (in Hebrew).

Williamson, H. G. M. 1979. The Origins of the Twenty-Four Priestly Courses, A Study of 1 Chronicles xxiii–xxvii. Pp. 251–68 in *Studies in the Historical Books of the Old Testament,* ed. J. A. Emerton. VTSup 30. Leiden.

JOHN W. WRIGHT

JALAM (PERSON) [Heb *yaʿlām*]. The 2d son of Esau and Oholibamah (Gen 36:5, 14; 1 Chr 1:35). He is counted among the Edomite "tribal chiefs" (Heb *ʾallûpîm*) in Gen 36:18, and as such was likely considered to be one of the Edomite clans (or tribes?). The name could be interpreted as an animal name **w/yʿl,* "ibex," or perhaps it could be derived from **ʿlm,* "to be strong (?)". Psalm 55:20 [—Eng 55:19], which read *yšmʿ ʾl wyʿnm wyšb qdm,* could be emended to read *yšmʿʾl wyʿlm wyšb qdm,* "Ishmael, Jalam, and the inhabitants of the east."

ULRICH HÜBNER

JALON (PERSON) [Heb *yālôn*]. One of the sons of Ezrah (1 Chr 4:17). Nothing is otherwise known of him.

H. C. LO

JAMB [Heb *ʾayil*]. An architectural term. The Heb word is found in the description of Solomon's Temple, where it refers to the "doorposts" (RSV) of the entrance to the inner sanctuary (*dĕbîr*). The RSV uses the word "jamb" to translate the 18 occurrences of *ʾayil* in Ezekiel's temple description (between Ezek 40:9 and 41:3). Although the exact nature of these architectural elements is difficult to determine, a prominent feature of the jambs that were part of the courtyard gateways was that they were decorated with palm trees. This detail is omitted for the jambs of the doorways of the temple building itself.

CAROL MEYERS

JAMBRES (PERSON). See JANNES AND JAMBRES.

JAMBRI (PERSON) [Gk *Iambri*]. The sons of Jambri from Medeba waylaid and killed John, brother of Jonathan the Hasmonean, on his way to parley with the Nabateans (1 Macc 9:36). Jonathan and Simon proceeded to exact revenge for the murder of their brother by attacking the Jambrites at a wedding celebration (9:37–42). The Gk *iambri* would appear to be derived from the Heb *bĕnê yăʿamrî.* The personal name *yʿmry* was found on a Nabatean inscription dated from ca. 39 C.E. (*CIS* 2/1/2: 195; Clermont-Ganneau 1888: 185). It is thus plausible that the Jambrites were themselves a Nabatean clan; however, the text in 1 Maccabees does not so indicate. Josephus refers to the Jambrites as "sons of Amaraios (*amaraious*)" (*Ant* 13.1.2 and 4 §§11, 18–21). Older scholarship contended that Josephus reflected the original Heb behind the LXX which was Jambri was "Amorite" in that Num 21:29–31 identifies Medeba as an Amorite city (Marcus 1933: 233, n.d). Goldstein (*1 Maccabees* AB, 384) posits that Josephus' use of Amaraios suggests the Semitic *ʿmry* which, through slurring, doubling *yod,* or scribal corruption, resulted in *amaraious.*

Bibliography

Clermont-Ganneau, C. 1888. *Recueil d'archéologie orientale.* Vol. 2. Paris.

Marcus, R. 1933. *Jewish Antiquities, Books XII–XIV.* Vol. 7 of *Josephus.* LCL. Cambridge, MA.

MICHAEL E. HARDWICK

JAMES (PERSON) [Gk *Iakōbos*]. It is unclear how many different persons bear this name in the NT, where it occurs 42 times (the majority of these are in Mark; the name never occurs in John). The name was evidently quite popular in the 1st century. Three persons bearing the name James are relatively familiar to us from the NT. Fully half of the occurrences refer unquestionably to James the son of Zebedee, one of the twelve disciples chosen by Jesus. Next most frequently referred to, in about a quarter of the occurrences, is James the brother of Jesus, who was to assume the leadership of the early Jerusalem church. See JAMES, BROTHER OF JESUS. A second disciple named James is mentioned in all four lists of the Twelve, being specified as the son of Alphaeus. Beyond the clear references to these three, we know of probably at least two others named James: one a son of a certain Mary (unless this James is to be regarded as the "brother" of Jesus mentioned above, and thus in reality his cousin, or unless he is to be identified with James the son of Alphaeus); the other the father of the Judas who is listed as one of the Twelve in the Lukan lists. The identity of two other persons named James remains unclear: the author of the book of James (Jas 1:1) and the brother of the author of the book of Jude (Jude 1). These probably refer to the brother of Jesus, at least pseudonymously, but it is still possible that one or two other persons could be in view. If so, and if these two are not the same and not to be identified with any of the other persons named James mentioned above, we could have up to as many as seven individuals bearing the name James in the NT.

1. James the son of Zebedee. Among the first of the twelve disciples called by Jesus were James and his younger brother John, "the sons of Zebedee" (by which expression they are sometimes referred to without the mention of their specific names, as in Matt 20:20; 26:37; 27:56; John 21:2). According to Matt 27:56, the third of the three women watching the crucifixion at a distance was "the mother of the sons of Zebedee." Matthew's source (Mark 15:40) refers to this third woman as Salome. If, as seems probable, Matthew is identifying Salome for his readers, rather than substituting another woman, then the wife of Zebedee and the mother of James and John was Salome. The further speculation that this Salome was a sister of Mary, the mother of Jesus, and that therefore James and John were cousins of Jesus, rests on a very precarious identification of the unnamed "sister of his mother" among those standing beside the cross, mentioned in John 19:25 (cf. the reference to "many other women" at the crucifixion in Mark 15:41).

Because Zebedee has "hired servants" (*misthōtoi,* Mark 1:20) and Salome seems to have materially supported Jesus during his Galilean ministry (Mark 15:40–41; Matt 27:55–56; cf. Luke 8:2–3), it is arguable that James and John grew up in a relatively prosperous home. Like their father, they were fishermen and had become partners with Simon Peter in a fishing business (Luke 5:10) in Bethsaida on the Sea of Galilee, presumably near their home.

James the son of Zebedee is never mentioned in the NT apart from reference also to his brother John. Since he is almost consistently named first (except in Luke 8:51; 9:28; and in the list of the eleven in Acts 1:13), and John is repeatedly designated "the brother of James" (while the reverse never happens, except in Acts 12:2, where it is necessary to indicate which James was martyred), he was probably the elder of the two. He has also sometimes been called "the greater," in order to distinguish him from others named James in the NT (cf. James "the less" in Mark 15:40).

In the lists of the Twelve, his name is the third (Matt 10:2; Luke 6:14; Acts 1:13), except in Mark 3:17, where it is the second, probably in order to group the names of the three—Peter, James, and John—who formed the inner, privileged circle of disciples. These three alone were allowed to accompany Jesus to witness the raising of the little daughter of Jairus (Mark 5:37 = Luke 8:51), to witness the transfiguration of Jesus (Mark 9:2 = Matt 17:1; Luke 9:28), and to accompany Jesus in the garden of Gethsemane (Mark 14:33; cf. Matt 26:37). The three are joined by Andrew in the private questioning of Jesus that leads to the Markan eschatological discourse (Mark 13:3; cf. too the presence of these four at the healing of Peter's mother-in-law, Mark 1:29).

The immediate response of James and John to the call of Jesus, even to the point of leaving their father with the servants in the boat (Mark 1:19–20 = Matt 4:21–22), suggests the possibility of some previous contact. If, on the other hand, Peter and Andrew had learned of Jesus as disciples of John the Baptist (John 1:35–42), James and John would undoubtedly have heard the good news from them.

According to Mark 3:17, Jesus gave the appellation "Boanerges" to James and John, an Aramaic name meaning probably "sons of thunder" or "sons of trembling." This has been taken to indicate the volatile temperament of the brothers as revealed, for example, in their suggestion that the unreceptive Samaritans be consumed by fire called down from heaven (Luke 9:54; cf. Mark 9:38). Further evidence of a certain impetuosity on the part of the brothers may be seen in their extraordinary request to sit at the positions of honor on either side of Jesus when he came into his glory (Mark 10:35–37; the request is made by their mother, according to Matt 20:20–21).

In his response to their improper request, Jesus tells the brothers that they must be prepared to "drink the cup" that he is to drink and to be "baptized with the baptism" that he must accept, i.e., to be killed (Mark 10:38 = Matt 20:22). Their easy acceptance of this eventuality is followed by the ominous prophecy of Jesus that it would indeed be so. This came true for James who, so far as can be known, was the first of the Twelve to suffer martyrdom (Acts 12:1–2), and the only one of the Twelve whose martyrdom the NT records. Probably in A.D. 44, but not later, Herod Agrippa I killed James in a campaign against the Church designed apparently to gain the favor of his Jewish subjects. Given the importance of James in the synoptic tradition, it is remarkable that this reference to the martyrdom of James is the only mention of him in the book of Acts after the list of the eleven in Acts 1:13. Book IV of the *Apostolic History* of Abdias attempts, in the fashion of the NT apocrypha, to fill in this gap by recounting some of the (fictional) deeds of James.

Eusebius records a tradition from Clement of Alexandria's *Hypotyposes* that the guard (or possibly accuser) who brought James to the court was so deeply affected by his witness that he became a believer on the spot and then went with James to be beheaded with him, after having first received forgiveness from him (*Hist. Eccl.* 2.9.2–3). Much later tradition (6th or 7th century) alleges that James preached the gospel in Spain and accounts for the fact that James (St. Iago) was to become the patron saint of Spain. Further romantic tradition maintained that the body of James was placed in a ship which was guided by angels to Iria in NW Spain, and was ultimately brought to Santiago de Compostela, where the shrine of St. Iago remains the goal of pilgrimages to this day.

2. James the son of Alphaeus. One of the twelve apostles about whom nothing is known. He is referred to only four times in the NT, namely in the four lists (Matt 10:3; Mark 3:18; Luke 6:15; and Acts 1:13). Here he is always called

James the son of Alphaeus and his name is firmly fixed in the ninth position, at the head of the third group of four names. He is known in church tradition as James "the Less" in contrast to the son of Zebedee, who is known as "the Great." This does not, however, require identifying him with the James, the son of Mary, referred to in Mark 15:40, who is designated *ho mikros* ("the small" or "the younger," so RSV). On this possible but unnecessary identification, see below.

In the only other occurrence of the name Alphaeus in the NT, Levi is described as "the son of Alphaeus" (Mark 2:14; Levi is probably another name given to Matthew, cf. Matt 9:9 and Luke 5:27). This has naturally given rise to the speculation that Levi (Matthew) and James were brothers. But since the evangelists seem eager to point out pairs of brothers among the Twelve (as in Peter and Andrew, and James and John) but never refer to Matthew and James as brothers, this conclusion seems very improbable.

The only further question that calls for discussion is whether this James is possibly referred to in any of the other occurrences of the name in the NT, although this may initially seem unlikely since he is so consistently referred to as "the son of Alphaeus." Several possibilities have nevertheless been argued.

a. Jerome (*adv. Helvid.*), who was followed by Augustine, in fact identified this James with the James who is elsewhere called "the brother" of Jesus. He and his brother Joses (= Joseph) are then understood as the sons of the Mary mentioned in Mark 15:40 (= Matt 27:56; cf. Mark 6:3), who in turn is identified as the Mary who is the husband of Clopas and the sister of the mother of Jesus according to John 19:25. The fact that James is the son of Alphaeus, however, necessitates the further speculation that Clopas and Alphaeus are names of the same person. The acceptance of such an implausible conclusion (despite the later argument that the two names trace back to the same Aramaic name, *ḥlpy*) is to be explained by Jerome's desire to defend the perpetual virginity of Mary, and so to understand the "brothers" of Jesus as in reality cousins (with the added advantage that James "the brother of Jesus" who assumes so important a position in the early Church becomes one of the Twelve).

b. James the son of Alphaeus has also been identified as the James referred to in the Lukan lists (Luke 6:16; Acts 1:13) in the phrase "Judas of James," by understanding this as "Judas the brother of James" (so KJV). This view is taken up by proponents of the preceding view to identify this Judas with the "brother" (in their view "cousin") of Jesus mentioned in Mark 6:3 (= Matt 13:55). In these two lists, however, nowhere is the relationship of brothers indicated by the simple genitive (in Luke 6:14 Andrew is very specifically "the brother" [*ton adelphon*] of Simon Peter) and Luke regularly inserts *adelphos* when it is called for (cf. Luke 3:1; 6:14; Acts 12:2). The most natural understanding of the simple genitive is "the son of," as in the case of "James of Alphaeus," which is universally understood as "the son of Alphaeus."

c. It remains a possibility, although an extremely remote one, that James the son of Alphaeus is the author, or pseudonymous author, of the book of James (Jas 1:1), and further that he is the brother of Jude who is referred to in Jude 1. James the son of Alphaeus is so consistently known as such in the lists of the Twelve, in order to distinguish him from others bearing the same name, that it is most improbable that he is in view here, where the name occurs without the similar designation. There is furthermore reason to believe that the James in view in these two instances is meant to be James the brother of Jesus.

Late tradition relates the legend that James the son of Alphaeus labored in SW Palestine and Egypt and that he was martyred by crucifixion in Ostrakine, in lower Egypt (Nicephorus, 2.40; but in Persia according to Martyrologium Hieronymi [*Patrol.* 30.478]).

3. James the son of Mary. If the arguments presented above are sound, then this James is yet another James, and again one of whom we know next to nothing. He is probably referred to four times in the NT, in each instance as the son of Mary. He is mentioned alone in Mark 16:1 and Luke 24:10 (where his mother is mentioned as a witness of the empty tomb), while in a second pair of passages he is mentioned with his brother Joseph (Matt 27:56), who is also called Joses, a Grecized form of Joseph (Mark 15:40; cf. 15:47). The way the mother of these brothers is named, not to mention that she is named after Mary Magdalene among the women at the crucifixion of Jesus, makes it virtually impossible that she is the same Mary as the mother of Jesus. We have, therefore, to reckon with a second Mary who had sons named James and Joses (cf. Mark 6:3, where two additional brothers of Jesus, Judas and Simon, are also named). If this Mary can be identified with the Mary the wife of Clopas, the sister of Mary the mother of Jesus, in John 19:25—at best a matter of speculation—then this James would be a cousin of Jesus.

In Mark 15:40 this James is called *ho mikros,* obviously to distinguish him from others named James. This epithet probably refers to the small stature of this James (cf. Luke 19:3) or possibly to his youth, but less likely is the view that it is used metaphorically to suggest his relative unimportance. The later custom of referring to the apostle James the son of Alphaeus as "the Less," in comparison with James the son of Zebedee as "the Great," probably depends (and perhaps mistakenly) on this passage, although there is little else that supports the view that this James is the same person as James the son of Alphaeus.

4. James the father of Judas. This James is mentioned only in the Lukan lists of the apostles (Luke 6:16; Acts 1:13), as the father of the apostle Judas, who is listed in the eleventh position but whose name does not occur in the other two lists (the same as the Judas in John 14:22?). It is very unlikely that the simple genitive *iakōbou* is to be understood as "the brother of James" (see above). The name of the father is apparently used to distinguish his son from the other, the infamous, Judas among the Twelve. There is no reason to identify this otherwise unknown James with any of the persons of the same name discussed above.

Bibliography

Lightfoot, J. B. 1865. *The Epistle of St. Paul to the Galatians.* London.

Mayor, J. B. 1913. *The Epistle of St. James.* 3d ed. London.

Sieffert, F. 1910. James. Pp. 89–94 in vol. 6 of *New Schaff-Herzog Encyclopedia of Religious Knowledge,* ed. S. M. Jackson. New York.

Donald A. Hagner

JAMES, THE APOCRYPHON OF (NHC I,*2*). A Coptic translation of an originally Greek document that gives an account of the teachings of Jesus in the form of a postresurrection discourse of the Lord and dialogue with two of his disciples, James and Peter. Since the document is untitled in the original, scholars have assigned its title on the basis of the text's own reference to itself as a "secret book" (Gk: *apokryphon*) that allegedly was revealed by Jesus to his brother, James the Just. It survives as the second of five tractates of Codex I of the Coptic Gnostic Library from Nag Hammadi, which was buried in the 4th century and discovered in Egypt in 1945. The Coptic (Subachmimic) text, which is well preserved, is conserved in the Coptic Museum of Old Cairo. When first published in 1968, the document was referred to as the "Apocryphal Letter of James" (*Epistula Iacobi Apocrypha*). Today it is customarily cited with the abbreviation *Ap. Jas.*

Although *Ap. Jas.* has the external appearance of a letter (prescript: 1.1–8; proem: 1.8–2.7; postscript: 16.12–30) and narrates accounts of Jesus' postresurrection appearance (2.7–39) and ascension (15.5–16.11), the body of the text (2.39–15.5) has no narrative structure. Instead, it is composed largely of sayings: parables, prophecies, wisdom sayings, rules for the community, and creedal formulas make up the bulk of the traditions presented as instructions of the risen Lord. The letter frame is a secondary addition by the editor of *Ap. Jas.*, designed to preface the revelatory discourse and dialogue that constitute three-fourths of the text, and constructed to give that revelation the authority of a "secret book" which only the elect were privileged to receive.

Since *Ap. Jas.* apparently has not been quoted or referred to in other early Christian literature, and is extant solely in translation in a 4th-century Coptic manuscript, the identification of the sources of its traditions and of the date and nature of its composition has been a matter of considerable debate. However, a clue is provided in the opening scene of the text (2.7–16), which purports to describe the disciples' scribal activity as "remembering what the Savior had said" and "setting it down in books." This scene portrays a situation in which the literary production of sayings of Jesus was still being vigorously pursued; it reflects a time in which written texts with scriptural authority were not yet normative. The reference to "remembering" provides the critical clue to the date and character of this activity, since this term was employed technically in the early Church to describe the process of creating, collecting, and transmitting sayings of Jesus (*1 Clem.* 13.1–2; 46.7–8; Papias's "Exegesis of the Sayings of the Lord," in Eus. *Hist. Eccl.* 3.39.3–4, 15–16; Polyc. *ep.* 2.3; Jude 17; Acts 20:35; John 2:17, 22; 15:20). The widespread use of the formula of "remembering" to introduce collections of sayings, both oral and written, and to refer to their composition in written documents, was a practice which began with the relatively free production of sayings traditions and which continued, despite the existence of written gospels, without restriction to the Gospels of the NT. The fact that every such reference to "remembering" is attested in documents that date from the end of the 1st to the middle of the 2d century C.E. strongly suggests that *Ap. Jas.* was also composed during this period. By identifying its discourse and dialogue as the "remembered" words which the risen Lord revealed privately to James and Peter, *Ap. Jas.* indicates that the text is to be understood principally and programmatically as a collection of "secret sayings" of Jesus.

Examples of early and independent sayings embedded in *Ap. Jas.* include the following: "I shall go to the place from which I have come" (2.24–25); "Truly I say to you, no one ever will enter the kingdom of heaven ⟨unless⟩ I bid him" (2.29–32); "For it (the kingdom) is like a date palm ⟨shoot⟩ whose fruits dropped down around it. They caused the productivity (of the date palm) to dry up" (7.24–26, 28); "For the kingdom of heaven is like an ear of grain which sprouted in a field. And when it ripened, it scattered its fruit and, in turn, filled the field with ears of grain for another year" (12.22–27). Some of *Ap. Jas.*'s sayings are also found in the canonical Gospels. The beatitude, "Blessed are those who have not seen [but] have [had faith]," that is preserved in *Ap. Jas.* 12.40–13.1 = John 20:29 is the closest parallel with any saying in the NT.

Careful examination of this and other parallels provides no evidence that *Ap. Jas.* is literarily dependent on the NT as a source for its traditions. In a few instances, sayings that are transmitted as words of Jesus in the Synoptic Gospels are, in *Ap. Jas.*, preserved as questions or comments of the disciples. This use of originally discrete sayings to compose discourses and dialogues marks an important stage in the development of the tradition leading from the simple collection of sayings to the creation of longer revelation discourses and dialogues. As a wisdom book based on an independent sayings collection that was contemporary with other early Christian writings which presented sayings of Jesus, *Ap. Jas.* is to be acknowledged as a primary source of, as well as witness to, the Jesus tradition.

Bibliography

Attridge, H. W., and Williams, F. E. 1985. The Apocryphon of James: I,*2*:1.1–16.30. Vol. 1, pp. 13–53 and vol. 2, pp. 7–37 in *Nag Hammadi Codex I (The Jung Codex)*, ed. H. W. Attridge. NHS 22–23. Leiden.

Cameron, R. 1982. The Apocryphon of James. Pp. 55–64 in *The Other Gospels: Non-Canonical Gospel Texts*, ed. R. Cameron. Philadelphia = Apocryphon of James. Vol. 2, pp. 218–31 in *New Gospel Parallels*, ed. R. W. Funk. Philadelphia, 1985.

———. 1984. *Sayings Traditions in the Apocryphon of James*. HTS 34. Philadelphia.

Dehandschutter, B. 1988. L'Epistula Jacobi apocrypha de Nag Hammadi (CG I,2) comme apocryphe néotestamentaire. *ANRW* 2/25/6: 4529–50.

Department of Antiquities of the Arab Republic of Egypt. 1977. *The Facsimile Edition of the Nag Hammadi Codices: Codex I.* Leiden.

Kipgen, K. 1975. Gnosticism in Early Christianity: A Study of the Epistula Jacobi Apocrypha with Particular Reference to Salvation. Diss. Oxford.

Kirchner, D. 1977. Epistula Jacobi Apocrypha: Die erste Schrift aus Nag-Hammadi-Codex I (Codex Jung). Diss. Humboldt University of Berlin.

———. 1987. Brief des Jakobus. Vol. 1, pp. 234–44 in *Neutestamentliche Apokryphen in deutscher Übersetzung*, ed. W. Schneemelcher. 5th ed. Tübingen.

Malinine, M. et al. 1968. *Epistula Iacobi Apocrypha*. Zurich.

Meyer, M. W. 1984. The Secret Book of James. Pp. 1–15 and 91–

97 in *The Secret Teachings of Jesus: Four Gnostic Gospels*, ed. M. W. Meyer. New York.

Perkins, P. 1982. Johannine Traditions in *Ap. Jas.* (NHC I,2). *JBL* 101: 403–14.

Williams, F. E. 1988. The Apocryphon of James (I,2). *NHL*, 29–37.

RON CAMERON

JAMES, BROTHER OF JESUS. One of the various Christians named James in the NT is the James who is identified as "the Lord's brother" (Gal 1:19), a "pillar" of the Jerusalem Church (Gal 2:9), a participant in the conference(s) at Jerusalem (Gal 2:1–10; Acts 15:1–20), and as one who experienced the risen Lord (1 Cor 15:7). It is generally agreed that this person, mentioned by Paul in 1 Cor 15:7; Gal 1:19; 2:9, 12 is the same man referred to by Acts 12:17; 15:13; 21:18. As "the Lord's brother," this person is also equated with the James of Mark 6:3 (= Matt 13:55); Jas 1:1 and Jude 1.

The degree of blood relationship between James and Jesus has been debated at length. See JESUS, BROTHERS AND SISTERS OF. Explanations fall into 3 categories. (1) Some hold, following the most normal interpretation of the NT language, that James was a son of Joseph and Mary, evidently born after Jesus. (2) Others, with reference to various apocryphal sources, maintain that James was an older foster brother of Jesus, i.e., a son of Joseph by a previous marriage. This view has been held by many Protestants and is favored by the Greek Orthodox and other Eastern churches. (3) A third interpretation theorizes that James and Jesus as brothers were, according to Semitic idiom, cousins. This third approach concludes that since James is called an apostle (Gal 1:19), he was in fact James the son of Alphaeus (Mark 3:18), also known as James "the Younger" (Mark 15:40), the brother of Joses. The mother of James and Joses, named Mary in Mark 15:40 and Matt 27:56, is taken to be identical with Mary the wife of Clopas (equated with Alphaeus), the sister of Jesus' mother, referred to in John 19:25. By this reasoning Jesus and James would have been first cousins. While this has been the preferred Roman Catholic explanation, the German Catholic exegete Pesch (*Markusevangelium I* HTKNT, 322–24) has affirmed the validity of the first approach, thus stimulating renewed debate among Catholics (see Rahner 1983: 218–31).

The identification of James the brother of the Lord with James the son of Alphaeus has caused him to be known in Christian tradition as "James the Less" (from Mark 15:40 KJV) in contrast to "James the Great," the son of Zebedee. (There is no doubt that James the brother of the Lord is to be distinguished from the son of Zebedee since the latter James was martyred about 44 C.E. and therefore could not be the James referred to by Paul and Acts.)

Whatever the blood tie between James and Jesus (see the critical evaluation of the three views by Filson, *IDB* 1: 471–72), it is evident from references to James in Paul's letters and Acts that this man played a significant leadership role in the Jerusalem church. In a much discussed statement in Gal 1:19 (see e.g. Trudinger 1975; Howard 1977), Paul appears to accord to James the status of apostle, although not necessarily implying that he was one of the Twelve. Rather, like himself, Paul includes James among all those apostles to whom the risen Christ had appeared (1 Cor 15:7). Since James is not known to have been one of the followers of Jesus before his death, it is possible that it was this postresurrection appearance of the Lord which produced in James a conversion to discipleship comparable to that which Paul himself later experienced (Bruce 1977: 87).

James is also referred to by Paul, along with Cephas and John, as reputed to be one of the "pillars" *(stuloi)* of the Jerusalem church (Gal 2:9). The metaphor could be an eschatological one which originated not with Paul but with the Jerusalem Christians. Paul was apparently aware that they spoke of their leading apostles as "pillars" because of the positions of importance they believed Paul, James, and John would occupy in the eschatological temple in the age to come (Barrett 1953: 12–13). Paul evidently regarded the views of the pillar apostles as important, yet he was also concerned to preserve the independence of his own apostleship. Hence, he reports that James and the others, having "perceived the grace" given to Paul, extended "the right hand of fellowship," i.e., approved the mission of Paul and Barnabas to the gentiles (Gal 2:9). At the same time the pillar apostles affirmed that their own mission was to the circumcised. The only restriction attached to their approval was that Paul and Barnabas should "remember the poor" (2:10), probably meaning the believers in Jerusalem.

Paul's description of James as a pillar occurs in the context of a discussion in Gal 2:1–10 about a conference in Jerusalem. James figures prominently also in the conference concerning Paul's work detailed in Acts 15:1–29. The two accounts are difficult to harmonize and discussion continues as to whether Galatians and Acts refer to the same meeting (see e.g. Catchpole 1976–77: 432–38). According to the latter account, James proposed certain minimum requirements for gentile converts to Christianity, the so-called apostolic decree. He recommended that a letter should be sent to gentile converts telling them "to abstain from the pollutions of idols and unchastity and from what is strangled and from blood" (Acts 15:20). Problems arise concerning the promulgation of this decree, however, since Paul never refers to it and Acts itself has James informing Paul about it only late in his missionary career (cf. 21:25) (see Schmithals, 1965: 97–102). In any case, the position taken by James at the Acts 15 conference depicts him in a mediating role, falling between those who would not impose the Jewish law on gentile Christians and those who would (see Brown, 1983: 77). At the same time, James's support was claimed by some who required full observance of Jewish dietary laws by Jewish Christians and thereby caused a dispute between Cephas and Paul in Antioch during table fellowship (cf. Gal 2:11–14). According to Paul, before "certain men came from James" (2:12) Cephas ate with gentiles. Their arrival, however, caused Cephas, Barnabas, and other Jewish Christians in fear of "the circumcision party" (2:12) to separate themselves from the gentiles. See BARNABAS.

Thus, while the Acts 15 conference reflects a minimal imposition of the Jewish law on the gentile Christians by James, his authority as felt in the Antiochian dispute conveys a strictness on his part concerning Jewish Christian observance of the law. That adherence to the law by James is seen also in Acts' portrayal of his meeting with Paul at the end of the latter's third journey. Upon Paul's arrival in Jerusalem, James and the elders advise him to prove his respect for the law by taking part in a temple vow ceremony (Acts 21:18–24).

James's devotion to the law was underscored in later tradition. For example, according to Hegesippus (writing ca. 180 and as quoted by Eusebius, *Hist. Eccl.* II.23.4–18), "from his excessive righteousness he [James] was called the Just and *Oblias*, that is in Greek, 'Rampart of the people and righteousness,' as the prophets declare concerning him." While the precise meaning of the attribution *"Oblias"* remains obscure (see Barrett 1953:15), it appears to witness to James's role as a support, i.e. a pillar, among his people. Hegesippus also reports that James constantly prayed in the temple where he spent so much time on his knees that they became hard like a camel's.

According to this same source, James was martyred at the hands of Scribes and Pharisees in Jerusalem by being cast down from a pinnacle of the temple and then stoned and clubbed to death. Josephus (*Ant* 20.200) had earlier and in less detail reported a similar tradition according to which the high priest Ananus accused James and "certain others" of having "transgressed the law" and delivered them up to be stoned. Both of these traditions place the death of James shortly before the destruction of Jerusalem in 70 C.E. The Hegesippus narrative says James was buried on the spot by the temple where he was killed.

The source of Hegesippus's report was apparently an Ebionite *Acts of the Apostles.* This work is not preserved in its original form but is mostly incorporated into the pseudo-Clementine literature (i.e. the Clementine *Recognitions* and *Homilies*). The Ebionites' veneration of their patron James the Just is also reflected in the *Gospel of Thomas,* an Egyptian compilation evidently dependent in part on a Jewish-Christian, probably Ebionite, source (Bruce 1977:119). According to Saying 12: "The disciples said to Jesus, 'We know that you are going to leave us: Who will be chief over us?' Jesus said to them, 'In the place to which you go, betake yourselves to James the Just, on whose behalf heaven and earth alike were made'."

The patronage of James was also claimed in some gnostic writings, and the gnostic apocryphal Epistle of James was ascribed to him. In addition, James was accepted as having been the author of the apocryphal gospel, the *Book of James,* as well as the canonical Epistle of James. Concerning his reputed authorship of the latter, see JAMES, EPISTLE OF.

Bibliography

Barrett, C. K. 1953. Paul and the 'Pillar' Apostles. Pp. 1–19. *Studia Paulina. In Honorem Johannis De Zwaan Septuagenarii,* ed. J. N. Sevenster and W. C. van Unnik. Haarlem.

Brown, R. E. 1983. Not Jewish Christianity and Gentile Christianity, but Types of Jewish/Gentile Christianity. *CBQ* 45: 74–79.

Bruce, F. F. 1977. James and the Church of Jerusalem. Pp. 86–119. *Men and Movements in the Primitive Church.* Exeter.

Catchpole, D. R. 1976–77. Paul, James and the Apostolic Decree. *NTS* 23: 428–44.

Howard, G. 1977. Was James an Apostle? A Reflection on a New Proposal for Gal i.19. *NovT* 19: 63–64.

Rahner, K. 1983. Mary's Virginity. *Theological Investigations XIX. Faith and Ministry.* Trans. by E. Quinn. New York.

Schmithals, W. 1965. *Paul and James.* Trans. D. M. Barton. SBT 46. Naperville, IN.

Scott, J. J. 1982. James the Relative of Jesus and the Expectation of an Eschatological Priest. *JETS* 25: 323–32.

Trudinger, L. P. 1975. *Heteron de ton apostolon ouk eidon, ei mē Iakōbon . . .* : A Note on Galatians i.19. *NovT* 17: 200–2.

FLORENCE MORGAN GILLMAN

JAMES, EPISTLE OF. The epistle of James stands in the canon of the NT as the first of the "catholic" or "general" epistles: that is, letters addressed not to a specific church or person, but to a widely defined audience.

A. Canon History
B. Author, Date, and Place of Composition
C. Situation of Author and Readers
D. Christianity of the Epistle
  1. James and Jesus
  2. James and Paul
E. Content and Distinctive Ideas
  1. Faith and Action
  2. Consistency in Action
  3. Mutual Concern
F. Language and Text

A. Canon History

The epistle appears fairly late in the history of the NT canon. It is first quoted with attribution by Origen of Alexandria (ca. 185–254 C.E.). The claims of Eusebius (*Hist. Eccl.* 6.14.1) and Cassiodorus (*Inst.* 8) that it had been earlier commented on by Clement of Alexandria are not substantiated by any reference to the epistle in Clement's surviving writings. It is probable that Origen came to know the epistle not from its use in his native Alexandria but in Palestine where he later settled, since it is quoted, though without attribution, in the pseudo-Clementine *Epistles to Virgins,* which are thought to be of 3d-century Palestinian provenance, and since the church of Jerusalem took a pride in preserving links with James, its traditional founder. After Origen the epistle came into use in the church of Alexandria: Eusebius classes it among the "disputed" books of the NT, that is those not in universal use in the Church (*Hist. Eccl.* 3.25.3, 2.23.24–25), but its place is unqualified by Athanasius in the canon list of his 39th Festal Letter of 367 C.E. It is not until the latter part of the 4th century that it begins to be similarly known and quoted in the Western church. It is absent both from the Muratorian Canon, thought to represent the scriptures of the church of Rome ca. 200, and from the Cheltenham List, similarly thought to represent the church in Africa ca. 359; but its place in the West is established through its use by Hilary of Poitiers, Augustine, and Jerome, and it appears in the lists affirmed by the Councils of Hippo in 393 and Carthage in 397. It is probable that the Western church came to know the epistle through leaders who had contact with the churches of Egypt and Palestine, though the Eastern church of Syria continued to be ignorant of it, or to ignore it. James appears in the "authorized" Syriac translation, the Peshitta, ca. 412 C.E., but contemporary writers Theodore of Mopsuestia and Theodoret make no reference to it.

Once generally established in the canon, however belatedly, the epistle's place remained secure until Luther's celebrated attack on it as "an epistle of straw" in his 1522 Preface to the NT. Because of what he saw to be James's rejection of the Pauline doctrine of justification by faith, Luther denied that the epistle had apostolic authority; and in his translation of the NT he relegated it from its canonical position to the end, together with his equally disliked Hebrews, Jude, and Revelation. Despite Luther, however, James has maintained its position in the Protestant, as well as the Catholic, Bible.

B. Author, Date, and Place of Composition

Origen refers to the author simply as "James" or "James the apostle" (fr. 126 in *Jo.*). Eusebius assumes that this James is the one referred to in the NT as "the Lord's brother" (Gal 1:19), the leader of the church in Jerusalem (Acts 15:13, 21:18), and there is no reason to suppose that Origen thought otherwise, although reference to James as "the brother of the Lord" comes only in Rufinus's Latin translation of his *Commentary on Romans,* 4.8. There is no other serious contender among the Jameses of the NT. Jerome, who agonized about the degree of relationship between James and Jesus, identified James of Jerusalem with James the son of Alphaeus (Mark 3:18), whom he also argued was Jesus' cousin, and this has been widely accepted in Catholic tradition. The question is whether the "James" of the epistle's address is genuinely James of Jerusalem, or whether his name is being used as a pseudonym by an unknown author to give his writing authority.

Arguments in favor of the traditional authorship include (a) the simplicity of the introduction of "James, a servant of God and of the Lord Jesus Christ" (1:1), which a pseudonymous author might have been expected to embellish; (b) the author's reverence for "the perfect law, the law of liberty" (1:25, cf. 2:8–12), which is consistent with the tradition of James's loyalty to the Jewish Torah and concern for its observance (Acts 15:13–21, 21:18–24; Euseb. *Hist. Eccl.* 2.23.4–7, quoting Hegesippus); (c) some linguistic similarities between the epistle and the speech and letter of James in Acts 15; (d) reference to "the early and the late rain" (5:7), a phenomenon of the Palestinian climate.

Against the traditional authorship are (a) the quality of the written Greek of the epistle, which is higher than might have been expected of the family of a Galilean artisan, even though they would most probably have spoken the language; (b) the paucity of reference to Jesus himself which would be surprising for one who was so closely associated with him in his lifetime, even though the Gospels are unanimous that Jesus' brothers were unsympathetic to his ministry (Mark 3:21, 31–35 and par.; John 7:3–9), and who was also a witness of his resurrection (1 Cor 15:7); (c) the discussion of faith and works without reference specifically to "works of the law" (2:14–26).

The arguments on each side are of varying weight, and some may be readily countered: As, for instance, the supposed Palestinian reference may derive from a knowledge of the OT (e.g. Deut 11:14; Joel 2:23) rather than from actual experience; while the literary quality of the epistle's Greek might be due to James's using a secretary, or to a two-stage process of composition whereby some original sermons of James have been edited by another author. The last argument is, however, the most telling against the traditional authorship. The claim that "a man is justified by works and not by faith alone" (2:24) unmistakably recalls the terms of the Pauline debate about the role of the law in salvation (as in Rom 2:9–5:1; Gal 2:15–3:24), and James of Jerusalem—who knew Paul personally and was himself so loyal to the Jewish law—must have appreciated the content and terms of that debate.

If the traditional authorship is maintained, then the epistle must be dated before James's death, which is variously reported as in 62 C.E. during the interregnum between Festus and Albinus as procurators of Judea (Joseph. *JW* 20.200) or as in 67 C.E. immediately before Vespasian's invasion of Palestine (Hegesippus, in Euseb. *Hist. Eccl.* 2.23.18). It would remain to be decided whether the epistle belongs to the early period of James's leadership of the church in Jerusalem, in the 40s or early 50s, or to the later troubled times preceding the Jewish revolt.

If the authorship is pseudonymous, then the question is wide open, for the epistle contains no reference to external events by which it might be dated. Some have found internal indications of an early date in supposedly "primitive" features such as the simple, undeveloped Christology; allusions to the words of Jesus independent of their fixed form in the written gospels; the absence of developed forms of church leadership and organization, leaders being described simply as "elders" (5:14) and a meeting either taking place in or being described as *synagōgē* (2:2). On the other hand, a later date, into the second generation or even 2d century of Christianity, has been argued from some of the same material: from what is seen as growing institutionalization, in which charismatic gifts are vested in church officials (5:14–15, the elders who heal; cf. 3:1 where to teach is to choose to take on that role, not to exercise a spiritual gift); from indications of a settled community, conforming to the values of the surrounding society in welcoming a rich visitor to its meeting (2:2–4); and also from a waning of eschatological expectation seen in the translation of the idea of a "trial" to be endured from apocalyptic tribulation to psychological experience (1:12–15, cf. 1:2–4) or to everyday afflictions (1:27, 5:10–11). All of these considerations are not only speculative in themselves, but unreliable for dating purposes, since matters such as the development of institutions and the survival of oral tradition may be dictated by quite other considerations than merely the passage of time: for example, the cultural inheritance and environment of the community.

External evidence provides a more reliable guide to the document's date. If the author has adopted the pseudonym of James of Jerusalem, he is not likely to have done so in James's lifetime, but when he had become a revered figure of the past. In that case, the death of James would provide the *terminus a quo* for the epistle, and its quotation by Origen the *terminus ad quem.* It may be possible to narrow this bracket. Although Origen is the first to quote the epistle *verbatim* and with acknowledgment, there are considerable parallels in language and ideas between James and the *Shepherd of Hermas,* concentrated in certain sections of that lengthy work (Mandates 5, 9 and 12), and these have led some scholars to conclude that the author of the *Shepherd* was also familiar with the epistle. The date of the *Shepherd* is itself debatable, since Hermas is presented in the book as a contemporary of Clement of Rome, ca. 96 C.E. (Vis. 2.4.3), but the author is identified by the Muratorian Canon as the brother of Pius, bishop of Rome from 139–54 C.E. A date in the early decades of the 2d century is usually preferred. See HERMAS' THE SHEPHERD. So far as dating James is concerned, then, we cannot confidently suggest anything more precise than the last three decades of the 1st century or the beginning of the 2d.

The address of James "to the twelve tribes in the Dispersion" (1:1) is impossibly wide for a real destination in geographical terms. It might serve to identify the readers racially or religously as Jewish Christians, or it may be an idealized description of them as the "new Israel." This epistle is not a letter sent from one place to another like the letters of Paul; rather the author has adopted the letter form as a literary convention, to address the community to which he belonged. He and his readers are to be located together. If James of Jerusalem is the author, then the place of origin is of course Palestine. If pseudonymous authorship is adopted, Palestine may still be claimed on such arguments as (a) the memory of James was most potent there, so that the choice of precisely that pseudonym is readily understandable; (b) contact with the oral tradition of the teaching of Jesus would be more readily available in the place of his actual ministry; (c) James emphasizes God's choice of and rewards for the poor and his retribution on the rich (1:9–11, 2:2–7, 5:1–6), which would be relevant to the church of Palestine whose real poverty occasioned Paul's charitable collection from his gentile churches and is likely to have been exacerbated by the Jewish revolt (Gal 2:10; 1 Cor 9:1–15; Rom 15:25–27); (d) it is likely that Origen came to know the epistle after his move to Palestine, and it may well have been preserved in its place of origin while remaining unknown elsewhere; (e) the allusion to the Palestinian climate already referred to (5:7). "The early and the late rain" is also experienced in Syria, which is another frequently suggested place of origin, and support for this is also found in similarities between James and the gospel of Matthew (e.g. James 5:12, cf. Matt 5:33–37), which is widely thought to have originated in Antioch. This argument, however, proceeds from an unknown to an unknown, and the continued neglect of the epistle by the church in Syria after it had been recognized in all other areas of the Church must militate against it.

If the evidence that James was known to the author of the *Shepherd of Hermas* is accepted, then Rome becomes a probable place of origin, since it is certainly there that the *Shepherd* was written, and this would be consistent with similarities between James and other Roman documents, 1 Peter and *1 Clement.* The subsequent disuse of the epistle in the Western church and its reappearance in Palestine would be explained by the general nature of the document's contents, which might only have a lasting appeal to those concerned to preserve links with the authority of James of Jerusalem.

C. Situation of Author and Readers

If the date and place of origin of the epistle cannot be conclusively identified, much more can be said about the general situation and environment of author and readers. The epistle envisages an established, settled community which holds meetings (2:2); has as leaders its own "elders" (5:14); and also recognizes individuals as "teachers" (3:1), a category in which the author appears to include himself. (Teachers might, of course, be included among the elders rather than having a separate ministry, cf. 1 Tim 5:17). The members of the community would no doubt regard themselves as among "the poor," but they are assumed to have the means to relieve each other's needs (2:15–16), and resentment of the rich does not prevent them welcoming a rich visitor to their meetings; indeed the vehemence of the author's attack on the rich in 2:6–7 and 5:1–3 may indicate that they were rather too ready to do so. They are not subject to persecution: the oppression and abuse referred to in 2:6–7 is more likely to reflect the legal and economic pressures that can be put on the disadvantaged by those more powerful in their society than an attack launched on the faith per se. The assumption that their meetings are open to visitors means that they have not been forced into a ghetto nor have they created a closed community as a defensive reaction. Not subject to external attack, they are also untroubled by internal divisions either on doctrinal and ideological or on economic and social grounds (contrast the church in Corinth which experienced all these). Tensions are those of personal relationships in a small society: anger (1:19–20), jealousy (4:1–2), slander and criticism (4:11–12). They need to be roused from inactivity to positive action (1:22–27, 2:14–17, 3:13–18) rather than deterred from any misguided enthusiasm.

This community is variously located in the country and the town: there is reference to agricultural conditions in 5:4, 7, and to trading activity in 4:13–15. The former may, however, be understood in terms of biblical allusion rather than of actual experience. An urban environment is more probable in general because Christianity first established itself in cities and towns, only gradually spreading into the countryside; and in particular because James clearly belongs to the multicultural environment of the Hellenistic cities. The author employs catchphrases from popular philosophy (1:21, "the implanted word"; 3:6, "the cycle of nature"); metaphors with little biblical background but common in Greek and Latin literature (3:3–4, horses and ships; 3:7, the four orders of nature; 4:14, the mist); the technical vocabulary, if somewhat inaccurately used, of astronomy (1:17); and the language of popular pious superstition (4:15, "If the Lord wills . . .") and magic (2:19, 4:7, the shuddering and flight of demons are known in the magical papyri).

Judaism, which took its place in this world, is also obviously part of his cultural heritage. He affirms the central Jewish proposition "that God is one," in the terms of its central prayer (2:19, cf. Deut 6:4, part of the *Shema*), and warns of Gehenna, the place of punishment (3:6). He draws freely on the OT for quotation (2:8, 2:11, 2:23, 4:6), for example (2:21, 2:25, 5:10–11, 5:17–18), and in the telling allusions that an author can make in the confidence that his readers will catch them (1:10, "the flower of grass," from Isa 40:6 LXX; 3:9, "men . . . made in the likeness of

God," from Gen 1:26; 5:4, "the ears of the Lord of hosts," *Sabaōth,* from Isa 5:9 LXX).

The epistle is often characterized as a document of "Jewish Christianity," but it is not clear from its contents that the author and readers were themselves Jews. Despite the puzzle of the unidentified quotation of 4:5, the appeal to the OT is straightforwardly to the text, without requiring any explanation from Jewish exegetical tradition. James's praise of "the perfect law, the law of liberty" (1:25, cf. 2:12), and his insistence that it be kept in full (2:10) may readily be paralleled in Jewish literature, but his appeal to actual tenets of the law is confined to the decalogue (2:11), and to Lev 19:18, singled out as "the royal law" most probably on the authority of Jesus (2:8). This may be contrasted with the implications drawn from the principle of the wholeness of the Law by Paul (Gal 5:3) and Matthew (5:18–19, 22:40). James shows no interest in the cultic observances that served to affirm Jewish identity in the Hellenistic world: the observance of the sabbath and the food laws, and the practice of circumcision which was a key issue in Paul's debate with Judaizing Christianity. It could be argued that, as a Jew, the author of James took these matters for granted; but against this has to be set his failure, already noted, to appreciate that the faith-works controversy had any implications for the Jewish law. His use of *synagōgē* in 2:2 is sometimes appealed to as indicating that James's community met in a Jewish synagogue, or, as Jewish Christians, had constructed their own "synagogue" after the model with which they were familiar; but, leaving aside the question of whether any Christian community could have had its own building at this time, the word is widely used in the general sense of "an assembly of persons," or "a meeting" as the occasion of an assembly, either of which would make sense in this context.

Even the adoption of James of Jerusalem as his pseudonymous authority does not mark the author out as a Jewish Christian, for although James was the leader of Jewish Christianity, and documents like the pseudo-Clementine *Homilies* and *Recognitions* show that he was revered by later heterodox Jewish Christians as their founding father, he is similarly revered in gnostic literature not obviously influenced by Judaism (*Gos. Thom.* 12; *Ap. Jas.* and *1 and 2 Apoc. Jas.*, NHC 1.2, 5.3,4), and his leadership is remembered and commemorated in the mainstream of Christian tradition (Clem. Alex. in Eusebius, *Hist. Eccl.* 2.1.3, 23.1; Epiphanius, *Haer.* 78.7). "James" is a pseudonym which might be adopted by a Christian author of any background who desired to address his specific community in terms, and with an authority, appropriate to the Church at large. The "twelve tribes in the Dispersion," too, could never be a literal address to Diaspora Jewry, since the reconstitution of the twelve tribes had long been part of eschatological hope only (e.g. Isa 11:11–16; Zech 10:6–12; 2 Esdr 13:39–47), but is most readily understandable as an ideal description of the Church in its role as the new, or true, Israel in the world (cf. Gal 6:16; Heb 4:9; 1 Pet 2:9–10; and for gentile Christian churches as the "dispersion," cf. 1 Pet 1:1 and the addresses of *1 Clement*, the *Epistle of Polycarp*, and the *Martyrdom of Polycarp*.)

James shows, then, something of the ethos of Judaism: its monotheism, its appeal to the holy book, and its broad moral concern, without the clear marks of belonging to the Jewish community. It is probable that the background of author and readers is to be found among the "god-fearers": those non-Jews who were attracted to what they saw as the Jewish philosophy; who stood on the fringe of the synagogues of the Diaspora, though possibly also of Palestine as well (cf. Luke 7:2–5), without being full proselytes; and who formed, it seems, a ready audience for Christian preaching (Acts 10:2, 22, 13:16, 26, 16:14, 17:4, 17, 18:7). They would bring that ethos into their Christianity, together with forms of organization with which they had been familiar in the synagogues, but without any concern to be involved in debates touching on Jewish identity, to which they had never committed themselves.

D. Christianity of the Epistle

The Jewish characteristics of James are thrown into prominence by its lack of a strong Christian coloring. "Jesus Christ" is referred to only twice, in 1:1 and 2:1, which some older scholars even suggested excising as glosses to reveal an originally Jewish tract. This expedient, which has no justification from textual evidence, is not to be adopted, since the evidence of Christian character is considerably more extensive than those two explicit references. In both of them, Jesus is identified as "the Lord" or "our Lord," using the title by which Christians acclaimed the risen Jesus (Acts 2:36; Rom 10:9; Phil 2:8–11). In 2:1 he is further described as "the Lord of glory" in a syntactically difficult phrase which might also be translated as "the glorious Lord" or "the Lord, the glory"; the association of Jesus with glory may relate either to his role as the revealer of the glory of God (cf. John 1:14; 2 Cor 4:6; Heb 1:3), or to his coming in glory at the last judgment (Matt 25:31; 2 Thess 1:7–10). In 5:7–8 "the coming of the Lord" certainly refers to the return of Jesus, since the word used, *parousia,* "coming," is a technical term for that event in early Christian literature (e.g. 1 Thess 2:19; 1 Cor 15:23; Matt 24:3; 1 John 2:28; 2 Pet 1:16). James's community is termed "the church," *ekklēsia,* (5:14), in the characteristic self-designation of the Christian community, considered both as a local group and an (at least potentially) universal phenomenon (Matt 16:18, 18:17; 1 Cor 1:2, 12:28; Phlm 2, Col 1:18); and its elders anoint "in the name of the Lord" as other Christian healers acted in the name of Jesus (Acts 3:6, 4:30, 16:18; Mark 16:17). The allusion in 1:18 to God's having "brought us forth by the word of truth" is probably to be understood as James's echoing the language of rebirth in which other Christians expressed their understanding of the experience of conversion and baptism (John 3:3–8; Titus 3:5; 1 Pet 1:3, 23; baptismal ideas and language may also be found in Jas 1:21 and 2:7); and parallels between James and 1 Peter have been taken to show their sharing in a common pattern of Christian catechetical teaching (1:2–4 and 1 Pet 1:6–7; 1:18, 21 and 1 Pet 1:23–2:2; 4:6–8 and 1 Pet 5:5–9). The two most interesting areas of discussion in assessing the Christianity of James are, however, his use of the teaching of Jesus and his involvement in controversy with Paul.

1. James and Jesus. James nowhere cites the teaching of Jesus as such, but his prohibition of oaths in 5:12 unmistakably recalls Jesus' prohibition in Matt 5:33–37. Although reticence in the use of oaths was counseled both by Jewish teachers and Greek philosophers, there is no certain evidence of a comparable absolute ban on their use, which would seem therefore to be unique to Jesus. If James may confidently be seen to draw on the teaching of Jesus here, then he may arguably do so in contexts where the similarity of language and distinctiveness of content are not so marked. Thus in 2:8 he identifies Lev 19:18 as "the royal law" to be fulfilled, as Jesus also singled it out in Mark 12:31 (with parallels in Matt 22:39 and Luke 10:27). R. Akiba (ca. 50–132 C.E.) also singled out Lev 19:18 as the most comprehensive principle of the law, so Jesus may not have been unique in doing so in his day, but James's description of the commandment may indicate that he regarded it as the law of "the kingdom of God" which Jesus preached. His encouragement to "ask . . . and it will be given (1:5) recalls Jesus' instruction to do so in Matt 5:7–11 and Luke 11:9–13; and his reminder that God has "chosen those who are poor in the world to be . . . heirs of the kingdom" (2:5) echoes Jesus' beatitude on the poor, who are promised the kingdom in Matt 5:3 and Luke 6:20.

Because the closest parallel between James and the teaching of Jesus occurs in material peculiar to Matthew's gospel, while all the others are with material present in Matthew as well as other gospels, it is often argued that James has a special connection with Matthew, either in terms of a literary knowledge of and dependence on that gospel or of belonging to the community or tradition from which the gospel also came. This is unlikely. Even in the closest parallel there are significant differences in wording between Jas 5:12 and Matt 5:33–37, while in the other parallels James is not markedly closer to Matthew's version than to the other gospels (in the beatitude on the poor he is closer to Luke's simple blessing of "the poor" than to Matthew's spiritualized "poor in spirit"). More generally, Matthew is clearly engaged in debate about the relation between Judaism and Christianity, hostile to the Jewish leadership yet concerned to maintain the integrity of the law; thus the prohibition of oaths is given a polemical edge in an attack on Jewish casuistry, and the great commandment is seen to involve "all the law and the prophets" (Matt 22:40). These concerns do not color James's teaching, and he and his community would not therefore seem to be in the same situation as Matthew's.

James's contact with the teaching of Jesus is more likely to have been with a continuing oral tradition than through dependence on any of the written gospels, since the various similarities, though striking, do not amount to exact verbal correspondence. If so, there are three points of particular interest. (a) His contact is with material across the range of what are usually identified as the sources of the Synoptic Gospels. The singling out of Lev 19:18 belongs to the Markan tradition; the encouragement to ask and receive, and the beatitude on the poor, to that common to Matthew and Luke ("Q"); the prohibition of oaths to Matthew alone. This might indicate that the gospel material was more widely transmitted, and sources less insulated from each other, than their separate identification sometimes seems to imply. (b) While James's material may be independent of gospel fixity and derived from oral tradition, it is not therefore necessarily the more-original form, for he has related it to his own interests. Thus he identifies the gift to be asked of God as specifically the gift of "wisdom" (1:5—contrast Luke's "Holy Spirit," 11:13, and Matthew's "good gifts," 5:11, but compare James's interest in wisdom in 3:13–18)—and raises the possibility of the request that is not answered (1:6–8, cf. the same concern in 4:3–4). (c) The comparisons between James and the Gospels show two ways in which the teaching of Jesus might be used. In the context of the Gospels, the teaching is obviously attributed to Jesus and carries his authority, whether or not it was uniquely (or even authentically) his. There is no such attribution of the teaching in James. Although he is most probably aware, especially in 2:8, that he is drawing on Jesus' words, it is not important to him to single them out as having a distinctive authority; rather they contribute to the general stock of Christian ethical instruction along with material from other sources and the author's own insights. We may compare the practice of Paul, for whom it was sometimes important to invoke a "word of the Lord" as such (1 Cor 7:10), but who would also draw the teaching of Jesus without discrimination into the course of his own argument (Rom 13:7; cf. Mark 12:17; Rom 13:9; cf. Mark 12:31).

2. James and Paul. James does not refer directly to Paul any more than he does to Jesus, but when, in the course of his discussion of the necessary association of faith and works (2:14–26), he conducts that discussion in terms of "justification" and of the example of Abraham (2:21–25), his argument inevitably recalls that of Paul in Romans 3–4 and Galatians 2–3. The differences between the two may be seen polarized in Paul's conclusion that "we hold that a man is justified by faith and not by works" (Rom 3:28, cf. Gal 2:15) and James's that "a man is justified by works and not by faith alone" (2:24). It is sometimes suggested that James's argument is prior to Paul's and that Paul wrote in part to answer it, but while Paul's argument on justification does not require James's to explain it, the strongly polemical tone of James's language indicates that he knows a position which he is concerned to refute: "and not by faith alone".

It is, however, unlikely that James was familiar with Paul's argument as Paul himself presented it, for he ignores a number of important points. (a) Paul talks specifically about works done in obedience to and fulfilment of the Jewish law, while James makes no such reference to the law, but thinks of works of charity in general. (b) Paul attacks such works when done with a view to gaining justification from God, which he deems to be impossible; James commends works as part of the response of faith in God. (c) Although both appeal to the example of Abraham and the statement of his justification in Gen 15:6, Paul relates Abraham's justifying faith to his acceptance of the promises of Gen 15:5; James relates it to Abraham's willingness to sacrifice his son in Genesis 22, thus missing Paul's carefully made point that Abraham's justification preceded, and had nothing to do with, his circumcision and implicit acceptance of the law in Gen 17:9–27 (Rom 4:10–11). (d) James does not deal with Paul's other major proof-text, Hab 2:4 (Rom 1:17; Gal 3:11); and conversely James's other example, Rahab (2:25), is not derived from Paul. In spite of the apparent similarity of their language, James does not seem to know what Paul's argument was really about, and it is highly improbable that he had either read Paul's letters or heard Paul's own exposition of his views.

Whether he thinks that the position he is himself concerned to refute has Pauline authority is another matter. The absolute detachment of faith from works in relation to justification seems to have been an original insight of Paul's, and justification as the language of salvation is as associated with him in the NT as it has been by later generations. The term appears in Acts only in Luke's record of Paul's speech in the synagogue at Pisidian Antioch (Acts 13:38–39); and in the Pastoral Epistles, written under the pseudonym of Paul, in a summary statement of salvation, perhaps in an attempt to "Paulinize" an existing credal formula (Titus 3:7). This latter passage shows that Paul's rejection of justification by works could be reinterpreted outside the context of the Judaizing argument to relate to righteous works in general which might be thought to earn salvation, and this reapplication is also found in *1 Clem.* 32:4, whose author is clearly familiar with Paul's argument in Romans. James has heard the language used even more generally, to support a religious attitude which emphasized the pious expression of trust in God and regarded works of active charity as of little importance, if not indeed to be actually discouraged. It is probable that those who thus appealed to "justification by faith" as their slogan did so on what they saw to be Paul's authority, and that James knew this; if so, the debate must have been conducted in an area of the Church where Paul was remembered and revered (as, for instance, Clement shows that he was in Rome a generation after his death).

James's Christianity, then, is characterized by a strong ethical concern, reinforced by the certainty of having entered a new life, and also by the certainty of eschatological rewards and punishment. The authority of Jesus as risen Lord is acknowledged, and his teaching drawn upon. There is room for ideological dispute in his community, over the relative importance of charity in the life of faith, but no evidence of any speculative interest in doctrinal matters. This is not a Christianity likely to produce either heresy or creative theology, but was no doubt congenial to those who had been attracted to a similar concern in Judaism, but were now offered a community centered on its own Lord and of which they could more fully and readily become part.

E. Content and Distinctive Ideas

Analyses of the structure of the epistle range between the detection of an underlying plan or pattern into which each section may be seen to fit, and regarding it as a collection of disparate material assembled from oral sources and linked together only by "stitch-words" or verbal echoes. The first suffers from the very general nature of much of James's material which seems artificially forced into too tight and comprehensive a scheme; the second ignores the presence of themes which run through the five chapters. It is better to see the author as developing some leading ideas in a variety of expressions and connections. His main concern is with Christian behavior, its consistency, and its community context. There should be consistency between faith and action; consistency in different activities; a common concern for each other. (There does not appear to be any impulse to mission outside the community.)

1. Faith and Action. The testing of faith produces wholeness of character (1:2–4). Since God tempts no one, the overcoming of temptation is the subduing of one's own destructive desires (1:12–15). To appropriate the baptismal word of salvation is to renounce evil deeds (1:21). To hold the faith of the Lord Jesus Christ is to exclude partiality (2:1). Faith must issue in works to be a living faith (2:14–26). God-given wisdom reveals itself in characteristic action (3:13–18, cf. 1:5). To follow one's own passions is to seek the friendship of the world and thus to be at enmity with God (4:1–4); the remedy being a wholehearted repentance and return to him (4:6–10). Plans for the future should be made subject to divine permission (4:13–15), and endurance of the present is rendered possible by the hope of the coming of the Lord (5:7–8), and by the example of former men of faith (5:10–11).

James returns frequently to the subject of prayer. As action should be consistent with faith, so prayer, as the expression of faith, should be wholehearted and related to action. God is one: an article of faith to which the demons rightly respond with terror (2:19), and as the one God he is the only giver of good gifts (1:17), giving generously and unreservedly (1:5). Requests to him should therefore be made wholeheartedly, with no doubt about his ability or willingness to give (1:5–8); and should be for objects consistent with his character (4:2–4). James sees no problem in unanswered prayer; it is to be explained by the inadequacy of the prayer, either untrusting or misdirected. He applies to the man whose prayer thus fails his most characteristic pejorative adjective "double-minded," *dipsychos* (1:8, cf. 4:8; a term unparalleled in the LXX or the NT, though found in other early Christian literature, notably the *Shepherd of Hermas,* Mandate 9, and perhaps related to the Jewish analysis of man as having "two impulses"). Even where prayer expresses a proper confidence in God, it should be accompanied by action if it is to be worth anything (2:15–16). True and fervent prayer is, however, powerfully effective, as in the example of Elijah (5:17–18). Prayer and praise are the proper response of the individual to suffering or joy (5:13), and James encourages prayer within the community for its members, both in the specific case of sickness (5:14–15) and in general as a remedy for sins (5:16).

2. Consistency in Action. As Christian behavior should be consistent with Christian faith, so it should be consistent in itself. Those who hear the word should also be doers of it (1:22–25). The law (whatever its contents in practice) should be kept in full, with each commandment given weight; and all persons should be treated alike under it (2:8–11). It is intolerable to bless God and curse men made in his image (3:9–11). James is especially concerned with "sins of speech," where he sees inconsistency as most blatant; this relates of course to his concern with prayer, but he expresses his concern at large. It is best to be swift to hear but slow to speak (1:19). True religion involves bridling the tongue (1:26, cf. 3:2–4). Teachers, who deal in words, are at greatest risk, and few should assume this responsibility (3:1). Speaking evil of each other in the community, whether in slander or criticism, is to be condemned (4:11–12). Speech should be a straightforward and truthful matter, where "yes" means yes and "no" no, without need of the dangerous reinforcement of oaths (5:12). James gives vent to his conviction of the seriousness of sins of speech in a highly rhetorical description of the tongue, smallest but most powerful member of the body: It is "a fire"; "a world of wickedness"; untamable, polluting, poisonous, inflamed by hell (3:5–8).

3. Mutual Concern. The pursuit of consistency and integrity is not, however, a quest for personal and individual purity: James's concern is for Christian behavior in the community. As prayer for God to relieve hardship should be accompanied by efforts to do so oneself (2:15–16), so "true religion" involves both the care of widows and orphans and keeping oneself uncorrupted by the world (1:27). The epistle closes with the vision of a mutually supportive community, confessing sins to one another and praying for one another, each watchful for anyone who goes astray, since to reclaim him is for the benefit of both (5:16, 19–20).

Rich and poor are among the most basic of social divisions, and James's concern for the poor and hostility to the rich may relate to his desire to encourage the ideal of Christian community as much as to the empirical experience of his own group. He regards the rich as almost by definition excluded from the Church. The lowly brother may be confident of his future exaltation, but the rich man (surely not a "brother") can only look forward to humiliation and ultimate annihilation (1:9–11). Although the rich visitor is not to be excluded from the Christian meeting, those who are tempted to welcome him over-enthusiastically are reminded of the usual role of the rich as their oppressors (2:1–7). Prosperous traders are reminded of their essential impermanence (4:13–16); and, in a passage of dramatic invective like his tirade against the tongue, James calls upon the rich to "weep and howl," to recognize the corruption of their treasure, and to await their inevitable fate in "the last days" or "the day of slaughter" (5:1–5). In his equation of the rich as wicked and the poor as God's chosen, James is following a long-standing convention running from the OT (e.g. Psalms 10, 49, 140) into the self-understanding of the Qumran community and some early Christian groups. It should be noted though that he does not idealize poverty per se, but indicates that it is the poor who are in fact righteous, who are the object of God's favor. Thus it is the poor brother who will be exalted, not simply the poor man (1:9); the poor are chosen to be "rich in faith" and to inherit the kingdom (2:5); the oppression of the poor by the rich which calls for vindication is epitomized in the death of the unresisting "righteous man" (5:6). Here as elsewhere James is an interpreter and not merely an inheritor of tradition, and through his varied material runs his conviction of the need for the Christian man to be whole in word and deed, singleheartedly serving both the one God and his brethren.

F. Language and Text

The author uses the Greek language with fluency and a certain sense of style. Although not of the quality of classical literature, his writing shows grammatical ability and is virtually free of solecisms and colloquialisms. He opens with "Greeting", using the infinitive *chairein* as is usual in a Hellenistic letter (1:1, cf. 1 Macc 10:18, 25, 12:6; Acts 23:26); uses the rhetorical *age nun* (4:13, 5:1); and gives the correct oath form of the accusative of the thing sworn by (5:12), by contrast with Matthew's semitic idiom of *en* plus the dative. He has a wide vocabulary, including some words not found elsewhere in the NT or the LXX (e.g. "sea creature," *enalios,* 3:7; "daily," *ephēmeros,* 2:15; "dejection," *katēpheia,* 4:9). His style shows a fondness for alliteration, as in *peirasmois peripesēte poikilois* (1:2, "you meet various trials") and *mikron melos estin kai megala auchei* (3:5, the tongue "is a little member and boasts of great things"); and for the cadence of words with similar endings, as in *exelkomenos kai deleazomenos* (1:14, "lured and enticed") and *anemizomeno kai ripizomeno* (1:6, "driven and tossed by the wind"—the former word even may have been coined by James for this effect, as he may also have coined the evocative *chrysodaktylios,* "gold-ringed," 2:2). Alliteration and cadence are both found in James's admittedly imperfect hexameter: *pasa dosis agathē kai pan dōrēma teleion* (1:17, "every good endowment and every perfect gift").

This sensitivity to, and ability to make effective use of, the sound of the Gk language tells against any theory that the epistle has been translated from an Aramaic or Hebrew original. We have already illustrated his use of biblical quotation and allusion, and his familiarity with the LXX has influenced his language more generally. Most "semitic" idioms are to be explained by the author's knowledge of the LXX. Thus he uses the compounds *prosōpolēmpsia* and *prosōpolēmpteo* (2:1, 9, "partiality" and "to show partiality," derived from the LXX *prosōpon lambanein*), and compound phrases like *poiein eleos* (2:13, "to show mercy"); *poiētēs logou* (1:22, "a doer of the word," cf. 4:11, *poiētēs nomou,* "a doer of the law"); *prosōpon tēs geneseōs* (1:23, "natural face"); and *en pasais tais hodois autou* (1:8, "in all his ways," cf. 1:11). As he can draw on vivid Hellenistic imagery in his rhetorical attack on the tongue (3:2–8), so he can adopt an archaic or biblical style in his "prophetic" denunciation of the rich (5:1–6). There is no need to resort to theories of multiple authorship or different editors to explain this variety of style: It simply requires an author who is sufficiently at ease with his language. (Luke can similarly adapt his style to include the poetic and archaic birth-narratives of Luke 1–2 and the almost classically heroic account of Paul's shipwreck in Acts 27.)

The textual history of the epistle reflects its canon history. It was in the church of Alexandria that James first came into regular use, and it has early and strong support in mss of the Egyptian text-type: Among the papyri the fragmentary 3d-century papyri 20 and 23 and 5th-century papyrus 54 contain some verses each of the epistle, while the 6th or 7th-century papyrus 74 has a substantial part of the whole; the major 4th and 5th-century uncials Sinaiticus, Vaticanus (B), Alexandrinus (A), and Ephraem (C) all have it, Vaticanus being generally regarded as the best witness to the text. From Origen onwards quotations by Alexandrian authorities are also available to the textual critic, as also the Sahidic and later the Bohairic Coptic versions. Conversely, the long disuse of the epistle in the Western Church is apparent in its lack of representation in Gk mss of the Western text, and there is, of course, no quotation by the early Western fathers, whether in Greek or Latin. The Old Latin version is found in the 9th-century Codex Corbeiensis (ff) and *Speculum Pseudo-Augustini* (m), and peculiarities there indicate that James was translated separately from, and probably later than, the other catholic epistles which earlier achieved popularity in the West. Augustine was to complain of the unusual badness of the Latin translation available to him (*Retractationes* 2.32), but the epistle came firmly into Latin textual history with the Vulgate, under the authority of Jerome. In Syria, canon history begins with the Peshitta, and so also the history of the Syriac text; the 9th-century mss K and L of the Koine or Lucianic text-type present James as it would have come to be read in the Greek-speaking church of Syria, and on into the Byzantine text of the Middle Ages.

The long neglect of the epistle may have served to insulate its text against copying error and emendation, for major textual variants are few. (It is always possible, of course, that errors could have been made at an early stage, left uncorrected, and so become entrenched with no textual variance to indicate them.) Some occur where James's language is obviously obscure or unfamiliar and scribes have tried to make the best of it: at 1:17, with the somewhat pretentious astronomical language; and at 5:8, where the "early and late" have been variously specified as "rain" or "fruit" by copyists more or less familiar with climatic conditions or biblical idiom. At 2:19 some have failed to catch the echo of the *Shema*, Deut 4:6, "God is one," and found instead a simple statement of monotheism, "there is one God." At 2:3 the poor man is offered a whole range of options as to where to place himself inconspicuously; at 4:4 "adulterers" have been pedantically added to "adulteresses"; and at 5:20 the epistle's seemingly abrupt ending has been rounded off with a final "Amen." Although not always easily soluble, none of these textual questions seriously affects the author's essential meaning.

Bibliography

Cantinat, J. 1973. *Les Épîtres de Saint Jacques et de Saint Jude*. SB. Paris.

Chaine, J. 1927. *L'épître de Saint Jacques*. EBib. Paris.

Marty, J. 1935. *L'épître de Jacques: Étude critique*. Paris.

Mayor, J. B. 1910. *The Epistle of St. James*. 3d ed. London.

SOPHIE LAWS

JAMES, FIRST APOCALYPSE OF (NHC V,*3*).

The first of two apocalypses attributed to James, the brother of the Lord, in the collection of materials from Nag Hammadi. These two apocalypses and the *Apocryphon of James* (NHC 1,*2*) constitute the literature attributed to the brother of Jesus in the Nag Hammadi collection. The first apocalypse is a particularly clear example of what many now call a "revelation dialogue" (Perkins 1980: 25–73). Here the Lord responds to the anxious inquiries of James within the framework of a narrative setting connected with the death and resurrection of Jesus. Very little is said about the events themselves, however, and it is clear that the narrative is relatively unimportant. A curious literary feature of the apocalypse is the fact that the Lord addresses James in the first person in 3 passages at or near the beginning of the writing (24,11; 25,12; 27,18) and everywhere else in the third person. Also curious is the fact that a question of James is referred to near the beginning of the writing (24,26–27) that has not actually been asked. Such difficulties point to dislocations, the use of sources, or imperfect control of materials.

In the first part of the writing (24,10–30,11) the Lord answers questions of James that for the most part reflect his fearfulness at the prospect of the suffering in store both for the Lord and for himself. The various doctrines expounded by the Lord in this connection (concerning the One-Who-Is, the structure of the cosmos, the kinship between James and the One-Who-Is, and much else) are intended to encourage the anxious enquirer.

After he had promised to reveal the way of redemption to James, "the Lord said farewell to him and fulfilled what was fitting" (30,12–13). The brevity of this reference to the crucifixion is noteworthy.

"After several days" the Lord again appeared to James who was walking with his disciples on a mountain called "Gaugelan"—probably a variant of Golgotha (30,17–18). In the exchanges that follow, Jesus first indicates that he had never suffered in any way at the hands of his tormenters. He then comforts James at the prospect of his own suffering and provides him with a set of formulae to be used after his martyrdom in response to the challenges of the hostile powers (including three heavenly "toll collectors") who will attempt to block his ascent to "the Preexistent One."

The text of the apocalypse becomes more and more fragmentary as it concludes. The following points stand out. (a) We are told (36,13–38,11) that the secret tradition is to be entrusted by James to a succession of figures that will include Addai (= Thaddaeus), a certain Levi, a woman of Jerusalem, and 2 sons (the younger of whom will proclaim these things). (b) The value of women as disciples of the Lord (on condition, it seems, that "the female element" should "attain to this male element") is upheld in the face of James' perplexity on the point (38,15–41,18). (c) James is presented as rebuking the 12 disciples (42,20–24) who earlier are said to correspond to "12 pairs" associated with Achamoth, the lesser Sophia (36,1–6). (d) James' martyrdom (probably viewed as the prelude to the fall of Jerusalem announced earlier) is described in some detail (though the text is badly damaged).

Some features of the first *Apocalypse of James* suggest that it had roots in Jewish Christianity. Chief of these is the choice of James himself as the bearer of revelation and particularly the reference to him as James the Just (32,2–3). For this title is attested especially in Jewish-Christian tradition (Hegesippus in Euseb. *Hist. Eccl.* 2.23.4,7; *Gos. Heb.* in Jerome, *De viris inl.* 2; cf. *Gos. Thom.* log. 12). Yet Clement of Alexandria also mentions James the Just as one who (along with John and Peter) received a special *gnosis* from the Lord (Euseb. *Hist Eccl.* 2.1.3–5). And the Naassene Gnostics (never credited with Jewish-Christian connections) made special appeal to the authority of James the Lord's brother (Hippolytus, *Haer.* 5.7.1). To be sure, the surprising link forged between James and Addai probably points to a Syrian milieu for the apocalypse (cf. Euseb. *Hist. Eccl.* 1.13) and thereby possibly also to a semitically colored form of Christianity. But there is little in the doctrine of the apocalypse that is reminiscent of Jewish Christianity. The points listed by Böhlig (1968: 103–7) to indicate such a background are not sufficiently distinctive to prove any connection.

What is clear is that the formulae revealed to James to

assist him in his ascent to the Pre-existent One represent a dramatized version of texts that appear elsewhere as cultic expressions in the context of Valentinian Gnosticism (Iren. *Haer.* 1.21.5; Epiph. *Pan.* 36.3.1–6). And there are other elements in the apocalypse that have at least a Valentinian flavor (Tröger 1973: 44–45). It is interesting to note, however, that at least one characteristic line found in the formulae transmitted to James for recitation during his ascent ("I am an alien, a son of the Father's race") was more widely dispersed and appears in the *Corpus Hermeticum* 13.3.

Finally, esoteric Jewish doctrine may have something to do with the 72 heavens (i.e., 12 × 7 heavens) of the revised cosmology presented by the apocalypse (26,2–23; Schoedel 1970; Séd 1979). The selection of the number, however, was probably prompted by the number of apostles; and if this is so, a devaluation of the Twelve is again implied.

One striking feature of the apocalypse is a positive evaluation of martyrdom unusual in Gnosticism. Such a positive evaluation is in fact found in all three of the writings attributed to James at Nag Hammadi. Yet whereas the *Apocryphon of James* calls for imitating the suffering of Jesus and seeking martyrdom, the first apocalypse builds on docetic ideas and denies that Christ (or more precisely, he who was "within" Christ) suffered in any way (31,15–22). Closely connected with this is a more or less docetic treatment of history: The Jewish people are considered counterparts of the archons (31,23–26), and their destruction is apparently symbolic of the defeat of the cosmic powers that threaten James. For Jerusalem, which James is to leave behind (25,16–18), "is a dwelling place of a great number of archons" (25,18–19). Thus James' own martyrdom at the hands of his countrymen can affect only his "flesh" and loses its fearfulness (32,17–22).

The selection of James (and other "non-apostles" elsewhere) as the recipient of revelation has been persuasively interpreted as a final step taken by writers of "Gnostic revelation dialogues" to provide an alternative to the apostolic authority claimed by a steadily advancing catholic form of Christianity (Perkins 1980: 131–56). The Twelve, as we have seen, are rebuked by James and associated with Achamoth. Thus, although they are apparently pictured as no longer under the power of the archons like the Jewish people, they have not yet attained the highest gnosis. The "brother" of the Lord—although not the Lord's brother "materially" (24,15–16)—obviously will have a more intimate relation with the revealer than his disciples. That the revelation to James takes place both before and after the reappearance of the crucified Lord suggests that a response is being made to the emphasis in the catholic community on what was said and done by Jesus during his ministry. Moreover, although the apocalypse has evidently accepted the historical argument of catholic Christianity that gnostic doctrine appeared after the age of the apostles, it deals with the point by having the higher gnosis handed on secretly through an obscure succession of figures until some time after the fall of Jerusalem. This event is apparently singled out because it symbolizes the defeat of the archons and because it was itself occasioned, according to the tradition on which our apocalypse depends, by the martyrdom of James (36,16–19).

Thus the selection of James as the recipient of revelation makes sense of the history of 1st-century Christianity by providing a reason for the failure of the fall of Jerusalem to follow immediately on the crucifixion of Jesus (Origen, *Cels.* 1.47) and consequently also for the failure of gnostic truth to make itself known earlier. The crucifixion of Jesus and the martyrdom of James are seen as complementary events, both of which are required for the full exemplification of the possibility of the Gnostic's victory over the terrors of this world. Finally, it should be observed that the relative openness to women as disciples of the Lord in this writing reinforces the emphasis on the value of non-apostolic (non-catholic) versions of the meaning of the Christian tradition.

Bibliography

Böhlig, A., and Labib, P., eds. 1963. *Koptisch-gnostische Apokalypsen aus Codex V von Nag Hammadi im Koptischen Museum zu Alt-Kairo.* Sonderband, Wissenschaftliche Zeitschrift der Martin Luther-Universität. Halle.

Böhlig, A. 1968. *Mysterion und Wahrheit: Gesammelte Beiträge zur spätantiken Religionsgeschichte.* AGJU 6. Leiden.

Brown, S. K. 1972. *James: A Religio-Historical Study of the Relations between Jewish, Gnostic and Catholic Christianity in the Early Period through an Investigation of the Traditions about James, the Lord's Brother.* Diss. Brown University.

Gianotto, C. 1983. La letteratura apocrifa attribuita a Giacomo a Nag Hammadi (NHC 1,2; V,3; V,4). *Aug* 23: 111–21.

Kasser, R. 1965. Textes gnostiques: Remarques à propos des éditions récentes du Livre secret de Jean et des Apocalypses de Paul, Jacques et Adam. *Mus* 78: 71–98.

———. 1965. Textes gnostiques: Nouvelles remarques à propos des Apocalypses de Paul, Jacques et Adam. *Mus* 78: 299–306.

Perkins, P. 1980. *The Gnostic Dialogue.* New York.

Schenke, H.-M. 1966. Review of *Koptisch-gnostische Apocalypsen,* by Böhlig-Labib. *OLZ* 61: 23–34.

Schoedel, W. R. 1970. Scripture and the Seventy-two Heavens of the First Apocalypse of James. *NovT* 12: 118–29.

Schoedel, W. R., ed. 1979. The (First) Apocalypse of James. Pp. 67–103 in *Nag Hammadi Codices V,2–5 and VI with Papyrus Berolinensis 8502, 1 and 4,* ed. Douglas M. Parrott. NHS 11. Leiden.

Séd, N. 1979. Les douze hebdomades, le char de Sabaoth et les soixante-douze langues. *NovT* 21: 156–84.

Tröger, K.-W. ed. 1973. *Gnosis und Neues Testament.* Berlin.

WILLIAM R. SCHOEDEL

JAMES, PROTEVANGELIUM OF. In the NT little information is given about the birth and childhood of Jesus. Except for the infancy stories in the Gospels according to Matthew and Luke, no other NT writings deal directly with that part of the life of Jesus. This gave rise to the origin of a number of so-called apocryphal infancy gospels, in which themes that were lacking in the canonical gospels were developed. The *Protevangelium of James (Prot. Jas.)* is usually classified as one of these apocryphal gospels of the early church.

A. Authorship, Place, and Date of Writing
B. Contents
C. Sources and Language

D. Purpose
E. Title and Transmission of the Text
F. Impact on the Church

A. Authorship, Place, and Date of Writing

Little is known about the author of *Prot. Jas.*, or the place and time of its writing. The James referred to in the postscript is presumably the brother of Jesus, who here recounts the life story of Mary. Because of the author's seeming ignorance about the geography of Palestine and religious practices there, we can safely assume that James is pseudonymous and that Palestine was not the place of origin. Egypt and Syria have been proposed as places of origin (de Strycker 1961: 412–23; Smid 1965: 20–22). There seems to be no decisive reason why Syria should be preferred to Egypt except perhaps for the fact that most of the virgin birth material probably originated in Syria (von Campenhausen 1962: 13). The book is normally dated in the 2d century. It was already known by Clement of Alexandria (*Str.* 7.16.93) and Origen (*Comm. in Mt.* 10:17), which necessitates a date before 200. It is sometimes argued that the author made use of material from Justin's *Apologia,* which means that it could not have been written before 160 (de Strycker 1961: 412–19; van Stempvoort 1964: 420–25).

B. Contents

In the *Prot. Jas.* the theme of the birth of Jesus is developed and retold from the perspective of the virgin Mary. It relates the life story of Mary, the daughter of a rich man Joachim and his wife Anne (Anna). Her birth is based on the OT story of Hannah in 1 Samuel 1–2 (*Prot. Jas.* chaps. 1–5). Chaps. 6–8 deal with her childhood in the temple. Then her "marriage" (cf. chap. 19) to a widower and building contractor, Joseph, who already had children, is recounted. The annunciation of the birth of Jesus in Jerusalem is told in chap. 11. This is followed by Mary's visit to Elizabeth (chap. 12); Joseph's doubt and comfort by an angel (chaps. 13–14); the vindication of Mary before the High Priest (chaps. 15–16); the birth of Jesus in a cave outside Bethlehem (chaps. 17–18); the vision of Joseph (chap. 18); Salome's unbelief about a miraculous virgin birth (chaps. 19–20) and the adoration of the Magi (chap. 21). The story ends with Herod's infanticide; the murder of Zechariah, the father of John the Baptist, in the temple (chaps. 22–24); and a postscript. In the postscript it is asserted that the story was written by James, who withdrew to the desert when a tumult arose in Jerusalem on the death of Herod. Then the title of the story follows: *Birth of Mary. Revelation. James.* Although a large part of *Prot. Jas.* deals with Mary, her background and childhood, the focus of the story is on the development of the theme of the miraculous birth of Jesus as is clearly indicated by the words in 20:1: "The controversy about you is not small."

The story consists of various episodes, mostly told from the third-person omniscient, narrative point of view. Only the vision of Joseph (18:2) and the postscript are narrated in the first person. The time covered in the narrative includes the period of Mary's parents, through her birth and childhood, the birth of Jesus to the massacre of the children by Herod and the death of Zechariah. The story takes place in Palestine and in particular Jerusalem. Prominent locations are the temple, the house of the parents, the house of Joseph and Mary, the road to Bethlehem, and the cave where Jesus was born. The main characters include Joachim and Anne, Mary, Joseph, the Jewish religious leaders, and minor helpers like Elizabeth, Zechariah, the midwives, Simeon, the Magi, and angels. Euthine, the servant of Mary's parents, Herod, and the Romans all act as opponents in the development of the story.

Despite similarities, the characterization of the main characters is in many aspects different from their characterization in the NT. Mary is the central character: It is she who is the long-expected child and whose childhood is based on OT examples. It is her name that is hailed by the entire nation because it will be remembered by all generations (*Prot. Jas.* 6:2; 7:2; 12:2); it is she who is raised for the service of the Lord and kept holy (6:3), beloved of the whole of Israel (7:3); and it is she who is fed like a dove by an angel (8:1). She is a *Davidid,* an undefiled, pure virgin (10:1). Put into the care of a widower at the age of 12 (9:1), she remains a willing servant of the Lord (11:3) who works in his temple. She is visited by angels (11 *passim*) and becomes bearer of a child conceived in an atypical way (11); she is the mother of the Lord (12:2) and is a chaste adherent to the moral strictures of Israel (12:3). Similar to her predecessor Eve (13:1), she is accused but later vindicated (16:3). She is a virgin who abstains from intercourse with her betrothed, and husband, Joseph (13:3; 15:3, 19); she is betrothed to Joseph (19:1); and she is a mother who cares for her child (17:2; 19:2; 22:2).

Joseph is portrayed as a widower with children, elected to take care of Mary (9:1). He is a builder (9:3), a man given to emotions of fear (9:3; 14:1; 17:3), reproach, doubt, suspicion (9:3; 13:1–2), and joy (13:2). He is also a "father" who cares for the girl Mary and her child (17:3; 22:2). Jesus is the child conceived in an unusual way (9:2) and whose name shall be Jesus because he will save his people from their sins (11:3; 14:2; 19:2). He is presented as conceived of the Holy Spirit (14:2; 19:1). He is the Christ (21:2, 4) and the Christ of the Lord (21:4), the king to be born for Israel (20:2, 21:2). Soon after his birth he is able to take his mother's breast and also to be a great salvation to Salome (20:3). He is a king to be worshipped (21:2, 3) and is cared for as a baby (22:2).

Unlike the canonical gospels where the Jewish religious leaders are presented negatively, in *Prot. Jas.* they are characterized in a positive manner: They perform religious rites (6:2, 8:2–3, 24 *passim*); bless (17:3 *passim*); pray (8:3 *passim*); take care of the temple and establish norms and beliefs (10:1; 15:3) by seeking the will of God and revealing it (8:3–10:1). In accordance with the narrative world of *Prot. Jas.* they are the helpers of, and not the opponents of Mary and her son. Israel is pictured positively in *Prot. Jas.* (1:2; 7:2 *passim*). In fact, the characterization of the Jewish religious leaders and Israel is such that the impression is given that the story is told on their behalf.

C. Sources and Language

It is commonly accepted that the author of *Prot. Jas.* used "biblical" material to create his story. At the end of the 19th century, it was argued that the infancy stories of Matthew and Luke as well as *Prot. Jas.* originated from a common Hebrew source, or that Matthew's and Luke's versions of the birth of Jesus were based on *Prot. Jas.* (cf. Smid 1965: 193). Another view is that 3 independent sources, namely, *The Birth of Mary, The Apocryphon of Joseph,* and *The Apocryphon of Zechariah,* were used to produce this story (Cothenet *ANRW* 25/6: 4252–69). This was replaced by the idea that *Prot. Jas.* is a Christian midrash of the birth stories of Jesus told by Matthew and Luke, in which biblical models, phrases, themes, and words, along with other existing stories and traditions such as the martyrdom of Zechariah, were used (cf. van Stempvoort 1964: 410–26 and Smid 1965: 8; 178–80). The author used his imagination to create legendary material about the life of Mary and the birth of her child.

There is little doubt that the author of *Prot. Jas.* used existing material, free quotations, and allusions from a variety of texts. The remarkable thing, however, is that he integrated these "sources" into a new story. Even in passages such as chapter 11 (the annunciation of the birth of Jesus), where the narrative comes very close to the canonical gospel stories, the author has retold the story in such a manner that the canonical sources became integrated into the text. The episodic nature of *Prot. Jas.* accounts for various texts such as 1 Samuel 1 and 2, Num 5:1–11, Mark 1:9, Matthew 1–2, Luke 1–2, John 20:25, and others, being used in the composition of the story. On the whole it is the Lukan version of the infancy story of Jesus which seems to have served as basis for *Prot. Jas.* This becomes apparent from the many allusions to the Gospel of Luke (Vorster 1988: 266, n. 15).

The story was originally written in Greek. The style is simple and vivid. Sentences are mainly joined by "and" (parataxis) and not by participles as is often the case in Greek. It resembles "biblical" Greek. The language used in *Prot. Jas.* indicates the author's familiarity with the LXX and the NT. Although the major part is written in prose, the lamentations of Anne (chap. 3), her hymn of praise (6:3) and the vision of Joseph (chap. 18) are presented in poetic style.

D. Purpose

The purpose of *Prot. Jas.* is often said to be the glorification of Mary (Smid 1965: 14–20), since so much of the narrative focuses upon the virginal conception, virgin birth, and enduring virginity of Mary (20:1). However, one should be prepared to qualify this: The author of *Prot. Jas.* used the annunciation stories of the NT to convince his readers of the extraordinary birth of Jesus. The story was written with an apologetic interest to defend the virgin birth and origin of Jesus, and to refute accusations that he was an illegitimate child. At the end of the 2d century (when *Prot. Jas.* was probably written), Christians had to defend and explain the origin and birth of Jesus (as well as the reputation of Mary), as both Justin (*Dial.* 48) and Origen (*Cels.* 1.32) clearly show. The presentation of Mary as the child of rich parents and a virgin who was dedicated to the Lord is used in *Prot. Jas.* as a refutation of accusations about her background and conduct. The purpose of the book is not biographical, and therefore it has limited value as an additional source concerning the "Mary of history." On the other hand it is an important witness for the development of early Christian apologetic. That the story was later used to glorify Mary and that it was regarded as a plea for asceticism is clear, however, from its reception in the history of the church (de Strycker 1968).

E. Title and Transmission of the Text

The different titles attributed to the book demonstrate the different ways in which the *Prot. Jas.* was received by Christian readers. The designation "Protevangelium of James," commonly used in the West since the 16th century, indicates that the book contains information chronologically preceding (*proto-*) that given in the canonical gospels (*evangelium*). The French humanist Guillaume Postel discovered a Greek manuscript of the book on a trip to the East, and in 1552 published his Latin version of this book under a long title which started with the words "Protevangelium, or concerning the birth of Jesus Christ and his mother, the virgin Mary: A historical discussion of the divine James . . ." Since then the story has become known in the West as the *Protevangelium of James* (de Strycker 1968: 5). However, in the East, *Prot. Jas.* continued to be referred to by the title *Birth of Mary,* to which was sometimes added *Revelation of James* (as in the case of the 3d century Greek manuscript Papyrus Bodmer V, which is the oldest Greek manuscript of *Prot. Jas.* we have). In his commentary on Matthew 10:17, Origen (*Comm. in Mt.*) refers to it as the *Book of James.*

These different titles indicate the contents as well as the reception of the text. The reference to James in the postscript, as well as the addition of "revelation" which is probably not original, obviously served to authenticate the contents of the story. It was intended for the reader who had to relate it to James, the brother of Jesus. On the other hand, the title *Birth of Mary* prompted readers in the East to interpret the text as a story about the birth of Mary (de Strycker 1968: 5).

Due to the collection of manuscripts since the 16th century and the critical editions which followed, the history of the transmission of the text as well as the history of the Greek text of *Prot. Jas.* have been studied thoroughly (by de Strycker 1968). There are more than 147 complete manuscripts or fragments of manuscripts of *Prot. Jas* available, of which only a few are early uncials. The 3 oldest manuscripts were discovered in Egypt, the oldest being Papyrus Bodmer V. All 3 of these manuscripts were intended for private reading. Because of its use in Byzantine liturgy, especially on the 8th of September when the birth of Mary is celebrated, a large number of minuscules are extant. In addition to the Latin version, there are also Armenian, Ethiopic, Georgian, Sahidic, and Syriac versions, as well as many modern versions (cf. Culmann, *NTApocr* 1: 374–88 for an English translation based mainly on Papyrus Bodmer V).

F. Impact on the Church

The history of the transmission of the text of the *Prot. Jas.* (de Strycker 1968) clearly demonstrates its popularity, especially in the East, since it was written. It was used through the ages as an important witness to the miraculous birth of Jesus and the life of Mary, and was transmitted in various translations. However, *Prot. Jas.* was not accepted as an authoritative document of the Western church. Nevertheless, despite rejection by the Gelasian Decree (ca. 500 C.E.), where it is listed as an apocryphon not received by the catholic and apostolic Roman Church, it has had a significant influence on the evolution of mariological tradition and dogma. This is confirmed by catholic piety, in eastern and western art, and also in the evolution of Mariology. The infancy gospels, and in particular *Prot. Jas.*, had a tremendous impact in the early church, and especially on the literature and art of the Middle Ages and the Renaissance.

Bibliography

Brown, R. E. et al., eds. 1978. *Mary in the New Testament.* Philadelphia.

Campenhausen, H. von. 1962. *Die Jungfrauengeburt in der Theologie der Alten Kirche.* Heidelberg.

Charlesworth, J. H. 1987. James, Protevangelium of. Pp. 218–34 in *The New Testament Apocrypha and Pseudepigrapha: A Guide to Publications, with Excurses on Apocalypses.* Metuchen, NJ.

Delius, W. 1973. *Texte zur Geschichte der marienverehrung und Marienverkündigung in der Alten Kirche.* 2d ed. Berlin.

Santos Otero, A. de. 1975. *Los evangelios apocrifos.* 3d ed. Madrid.

Smid, H. R. 1965. *Protevangelium Jacobi: A Commentary.* Assen.

Stempvoort, P. A. van. 1964. The Protevangelium Jacobi: The Sources of Its Theme and Style and Their Bearing on Its Date. *SE* 3: 410–26.

Strycker, E. de. 1961. *La forme la plus ancienne du Protevangile de Jacques.* Brussels.

———. 1968. *De Griekse Handschrifte van het Protevangelie van Jacobus.* Brussels.

Testuz, M., ed. 1958. *Papyrus Bodmer V: Nativite de Marie.* Geneva.

Vorster, W. S. 1986. The Annunciation of the Birth of Jesus in the Protevangelium of James. Pp. 34–53 in *A South African Perspective on the New Testament,* ed. J. H. Petzer and P. J. Hartin. Leiden.

———. 1988. The Protevangelium of James and Intertextuality. Pp. 262–75 in *Text and Testimony,* ed. T. Baarda, A. Hilhorst, G. P. Luttinkhuizen, and A. S. van der Woude. Kampen.

WILLEM S. VORSTER

JAMES, SECOND APOCALYPSE OF (NHC V,*4*).

A Jewish-Christian gnostic text found in the Nag Hammadi Library, a collection of manuscripts discovered in Upper Egypt in 1946. It contains speeches by James "the Just" and Jesus, as well as an account of the death of James by stoning. It is the fourth tractate in Nag Hammadi Codex V, and has been given the modern title the *(Second) Apocalypse of James* in order to distinguish it from tractate three, since both documents have the same ancient prescript title (24,10; 44,11–12): the *Apocalypse of James.* The last 4 of the 5 tractates in NHC V bear the title "apocalypse." The inclusion of 4 apocalypses in one book is unusual in the Nag Hammadi Library and does seem to be the result of deliberate scribal collection.

A. Setting

The order of the two apocalypses of James in codex V appears to be the result of deliberate scribal interpretation. The two documents stress different aspects of the James tradition and in their present position complement one another. In both tractates it is James, the brother of Jesus, who receives the revelation (24,12–14; 50,1–23). In the *(First) Apocalypse of James* James is warned about future sufferings (25,12–14; 30,13–15) at the hands of an angry mob (33,2–5) whom James agitates (32,9–11). Although there is an allusion to James' suffering in the fragmentary conclusion to *1 Apoc.Jas.* (43,17–21), this document contains no account of the predicted suffering. See JAMES, FIRST APOCALYPSE OF.

On the other hand, the *2 Apoc.Jas.* gives a detailed account of James' stoning and death at the hands of a mob stirred to anger by James' preaching. In short, *2 Apoc.Jas.* fulfills the predictions of *1 Apoc.Jas.* and in that sense "completes" the narrative that *1 Apoc.Jas.* began.

B. Text

The manuscript is preserved in the Coptic Museum in Old Cairo (codex inventory number 10548). The 20 pages of text (44–63) are preserved in fragmentary condition. With 2 exceptions (53/54, 63) the bottoms of the pages are lost and the tops of pages 44–52 are also lacking except for a small strip of papyrus that preserves part of the first line. Pages 53–63 are all missing text in varying degrees.

As to date and provenence little can be said with certainty. It was probably originally written in Greek and then translated into Coptic (Sahidic dialect) sometime before the middle of the 4th century C.E., when the books of the Nag Hammadi Library were manufactured. Lack of allusions to the NT and the developed gnostic systems of the 2d century C.E. suggest an early date for the origin of the document, perhaps as early as the first half of the 2d century C.E.

C. Character and Contents

The document takes the form of a two-part report made to Theuda, or perhaps Theuda(s), the father of James, by a priest who apparently was present at the ritual stoning of James. The title, however, designates it as an apocalypse (perhaps to characterize the text as secret teaching) while the incipit (44,13–15) describes it as the "discourse that James the Just spoke in Jerusalem."

The first part of the priest's report contains several separate discourses in the form of a dialogue between James and Jesus; the second part is a description of the death of James. Because of the fragmentary character of the text it is not always clear when the speakers change. The following outline will help to make clear the shift between speakers:

A. Prologue: 44,11–20.
B. The report of Mareim: 44,21–63,32.
  1. Mareim comes to Theuda with the report: 44,21–45,30(?).
  2. The discourses of James: 46,1(?)–60,29(?).
    a. James claims to be the revelation bearer: 46,1(?)–47,30(?).
    b. The first discourse of Jesus reported by James: 48,1(?)–49,30(?).
    c. The report of James on the appearance of Jesus: 50,1(?)–30(?).
    d. The second discourse of Jesus reported by James: 51,1(?)–57,11.
    e. The reaction of James to the appearance of Jesus: 57,12–19.
    f. The final exhortation of James: 57,20–60,29(?).

3. The death of James: 61,1(?)–63,32.
   a. The setting: 61,1(?)–14.
   b. The account of the stoning: 61,15–62,12.
   c. The prayer of James: 62,12–63,29.
   d. Conclusion: 63,30–32.

At least four of these sections are written in a balanced and stylized prose that may possibly originally have been used liturgically. Three of these may be classified as aretalogies: 49,5–15 is a series of self-assertions by Jesus in the *ego eimi* style; a second (58,2–20) is a series of statements about the resurrected Jesus made by James in the third person *(autos estin)*; in the third (55,15–56,13) the resurrected Jesus describes James' special role as an illuminator figure in the second person *(sy ei)*. This third unit is remarkable in its lofty regard for James: He is called "illuminator" (55,17) and "redeemer" (55,18). He will astonish people by his "powerful deeds" (55,22–23). He is the one whom "the heavens will bless" (55,24–25), and because of him people "will reign and become kings" (56,4–5). The fourth unit (62,16–63,29) is an originally independent piece of liturgical tradition cast as the martyr's prayer James prays shortly before his death.

There is a noticeable difference in both style and perspective between the first part of the tractate (44–60) and the description of the death of James in the second part (61–63). It has been argued that the two parts were originally two separate documents brought together at the expense of the conclusion of the former and the beginning of the latter (Funk).

The overall tone of the document is clearly gnostic; yet its use of usual gnostic themes is remarkably superficial. Aeons (53,8) and Archons (56,19), common in the more speculative gnostic texts, are each mentioned only once. It does describe salvation through knowledge (57,4–8) and makes a contrast between the arrogant boastful creator (56,20–57,3), responsible for human imprisonment in the world (54,10–15), and the unknown gracious father who exists without the creator's knowledge (58,2–6). These motifs, however, are too general to be associated with any one particular group in antiquity.

The text draws extensively on Jewish-Christian traditions. James the Just, who held a position of special prominence in early Jewish-Christian circles is presented as the possessor of a special revelation from Jesus and assigned a role that rivals, and perhaps exceeds, that of Peter in canonical tradition. James is the revealer who escorts the "illuminated" ones through the door of the heavenly kingdom and rewards them (55,6–14; 55,15–56,13). The description is similar to Peter's charge as the keeper of the keys of heaven (Matt 16:19). The report on the story of James has certain verbal parallels with the report of Hegesippus in Eusebius (*Hist. Eccl.* 2.23), and follows exactly the Jewish regulations for ritual stoning in the Mishnah (*m. Sanh.* 6.6).

D. Significance

The text documents the elevation of James, an ideal leader in a Jewish-Christian gnostic community that looked to him as guarantor of their traditions, as fulfilling the role of a redeemer-illuminator figure rivaling and perhaps exceeding that of Peter in the canonical tradition. The text will help to clarify the processes by which authority evolved in early Christianity. But what is more important, it may help to unravel the processes by which cult leaders become redeemer figures, a shift that has occurred, for example, in Christianity and Manichaeism. In any case this text clearly attests one such shift in a Jewish-gnostic community.

Bibliography

Böhlig, A., and Labib, P., eds. 1963. *Koptisch-gnostische Apokalypsen aus Codex V von Nag Hammadi im Koptischen Museum zu Alt-Kairo.* Wissenschaftliche Zeitschrift der Martin-Luther-Universität. Halle-Wittenberg.

Böhlig, A. 1968. Der Judenchristliche Hintergrund in gnostischen Schriften von Nag Hammadi: Zum Martyrium des Jakobus. Pp. 102–18 in *Mysterion und Wahrheit: Gessamelte Beiträge zur spätantiken Religionsgeschichte.* AGJU 6. Leiden.

Brown, S. K. 1972. James. Diss. Brown University.

———. 1975. Jewish and Gnostic Elements in the Second Apocalypse of James (CG V,*4*). *NovT* 225–37.

Funk, W.-P. 1976. *Die zweite Apokalypse des Jakobus aus Nag Hammadi-Codex V.* TU 119. Berlin.

Hedrick, C. W. 1979. The (Second) Apocalypse of James. Pp. 105–49 in *Nag Hammadi Codices V,2–5 and VI with Papyrus Berolinensis 8502,1 and 4,* ed. D. Parrott. Leiden.

Kasser, R. 1968. Bibliothèque gnostique VI: Les Deux Apocalypses de Jacques. *RTP* 18: 163–86.

Little, D. H. 1971. The Death of James the Brother of Jesus. Diss. Rice University.

Robinson, J. M., ed. 1975. *The Facsimile Edition of the Nag Hammadi Codices: Codex V.* Leiden.

Schenke, H. M. 1966. Review of Böhlig and Labib 1963. *OLZ* 61: 24–34.

———. 1968. Exegetische Probleme der zweiten Jakobus-Apokalypse in Nag-Hammadi-Codex V. Pp. 109–14 in *Probleme der koptischen Literature,* ed. P. Nagel. Wissenschaftliche Beiträge der Martin-Luther-Universität. Halle-Wittenberg.

Tröger, K.-W., ed. 1972. *Gnosis und Neues Testament.* Berlin.

Charles W. Hedrick

JAMIN (PERSON) [Heb *yāmîn*]. JAMINITES. Three persons bear this name in the OT.

1. The second of the 6 sons of Simeon (Gen 46:10; Exod 6:15) who descended to Egypt with Jacob's family after Jacob had demonstrated his desire to see his long-lost son Joseph. Simeon's genealogy is given in four places in the OT. The genealogy in Gen 46:10 agrees with the one in Exod 6:15 and says that Simeon had 6 sons and that Jamin was his second son. However, the genealogy given in Num 26:12 agrees, with some variations, with the genealogy in 1 Chr 4:24. This genealogy declares that Simeon had 5 sons and omits the name of Ohad, one of Jamin's brothers. According to Num 26:12, Jamin was the clan leader of the Jaminites, one of the clans of Simeon.

2. A man from Judah who was the second son of Ram, the son of Jerahmeel, of the family of Hezron, an important clan of Judah (1 Chr 2:27).

3. A Levite who assisted Ezra in the reading and in the interpretation of the book of the Law of Moses (Neh 8:7). He is called Jadinus (Gk *Iadinos*) in the Gk text of 1 Esdr 9:48. According to the record in the book of Nehemiah,

Ezra read the law, probably in Hebrew, while the Levites helped the people to understand the reading by translating and interpreting it into Aramaic, the language the people spoke when they returned from Babylon. The name of Jamin and several other Levites who helped Ezra are omitted in the LXX.

CLAUDE F. MARIOTTINI

JAMLECH (PERSON) [Heb *yamlēk*]. A descendant of Simeon (1 Chr 4:34), described as one of the "princes in their families" (1 Chr 4:38). The name probably means "(Yahweh) reigns." (Indeed, Lucian translates, "he reigns.") In the LXX the name appears as *Iemoloch.* See Williamson *Chronicles* NCBC, 62.

CRAIG A. EVANS

JAMNIA (JABNEH), COUNCIL OF. The concept of the Council of Jamnia is an hypothesis to explain the canonization of the Writings (the third division of the Hebrew Bible) resulting in the closing of the Hebrew canon.

A. Theory of Jamnia and the Canon
B. The City
C. Jamnia Gatherings
D. Study of Jamnia and the Canon

A. Theory of Jamnia and the Canon

H. Graetz first cautiously proposed and defended the theory in his Excursus to Qoheleth (1871:155–56), a theory later stated positively by F. Buhl, H. E. Ryle, Robert Pfeiffer, O. Eissfeldt, and others. By the hypothesis, based on an interpretation of *m. Yad.* 3:5, the OT canon was closed for all time by the specific religious authority of 72 elders when R. Eleazar ben Azariah became head of the Academy at Yavneh about A.D. 90. The hypothesis rendered yeoman service in turning scholars from earlier positions that the canon was fixed either by Ezra or by the Great Synagogue.

Despite the absence of significant support in ancient Jewish, Christian, or classical texts, the hypothesis enjoyed vogue in the 20th century by repetition rather than by proof. Various degrees of dogmatism are encountered in assertions about actions of the council such as the closing of the canon with one stroke and the exclusion of the Apocrypha.

After the concept that the council closed the canon was accepted, some scholars projected that the standardization of the OT text also took place in formal action at Jamnia (also called Jabneh or Yavneh). According to S. Talmon (1970: 174–79), the 19th century began with Rosenmueller's contention that the MT went back to one recension. De Lagarde then projected that all texts depended on one exemplar considered to have been developed after the rise of Jewish-Christian controversy. The standardization then became attached to Jamnia and R. Akiba's exegetical method. Olshausen argued for a deliberate choice made by some official Jewish body, while Noeldeke argued for the use of a readily available manuscript as the basis of the standard text. An investigation of rabbinic citations revealed more text variety than earlier scholars had been aware of. P. Kahle, after studying manuscripts of the Cairo Geniza, postulated vulgar text-types existing beside the standard text; the latter he conceived of as being formed by rabbinic activity at Jamnia. Following the Qumran discoveries, the Jamnia portion of the hypothesis has found new advocates and is often stated as an established fact.

S. Krauss (1893) proposed that the *birkat hammînîm* (a prayer against sects) in the 18 benedictions must originally have had within it the term *nôṣrîm* (Jewish Christians). The theory, considered to be supported by the occurrence of "*mînîm*" and "*nôṣrîm*" in a Geniza text of the benediction, was popularized by I. Elbogen (1931: 36) and then accepted by many Christian theologians. In Johannine studies, when considering "casting out of the synagogue" (*aposynagogos*; John 9:22; 12:42; 16:2), the council is credited with accomplishing the breech between Judaism and Christianity. It is considered that the *birkat hammînîm,* composed by Samuel the Younger in the time of Gamaliel II (*b. Ber.* 28b–29a), was introduced into the 18 benedictions to expose and expel Jewish Christians despite the fact that the tradition is not attested in either the *Mishna* or *Tosephta.* Some Johannine scholars have hypothesized the Fourth Gospel to be a Christian response to Jamnia.

In short, the Council of Jamnia and its alleged date of about A.D. 90 is, in the absence of attestation in specific texts, used in scholarship as a convenient symbol for the culmination of long processes in early Judaism. Sometimes used for any development between A.D. 70 and 135, the terminology has the disadvantage of inviting the uninformed to assume official action taken at specific meetings on specific dates.

B. The City

Yavneh (LXX: *Iabne;* Vg: *Iabniae*), a Philistine city whose walls Uzziah demolished, is mentioned between Gath and Ashdod (2 Chr 26:6) and is conjectured to be identical with Jabneel (LXX: *Iabnel;* Vg *Iebnehel:* Josh 15:11; cf. Josephus *Ant* 5.1.22 [87] who describes it as a city of Dan) earlier mentioned in the border list of Judah. The town does not again appear in Judah town lists until the Maccabean period, but may be *Jemnaan* of the book of Judith (2:28) listed among coastal cities whose people feared Holofernes.

That Josephus at times mentions Jamnia as a coastal city (*Ant* 13.15.4 [395]) and at times as an inland one (*Ant* 14.4.5 [75]; *JW* 1.7.7 [156]) suggests that the inland city also had a harbor. Both Pliny (*N.H.* 5.13.68) and Ptolemy (5.16.2) suggest that there are 2 towns. Strabo (16.759) describes Jamnia as so populus that with its surrounding villages it could supply an army of 40,000 able soldiers. See also JABNEEL; YAVNEH-YAM.

Eusebius (Klostermann ed., 106) places Jamnia between Diospolis (Lydda) and Azotos (Ashdod). Bishops of the church in Jamnia participated in councils at Nicea, Chalcedon, and Jerusalem. Benjamin of Tudela, identifying Ibelin or Jabneh as the seat of the Academy, places it 5 parasangs from Jaffa, but commented that there were no Jews there in his day (Adler 1907: 27). E. Robinson (1841–57: 2.420), mentioning Jamnia in discussing the location of Gath, remarks that "Yebna is situated on a small eminence on the W side of the Wadi Rubin, an hour or more distance from the sea." Robinson also notices "The crusaders built here the fortress Ibelin" (3.22, 23, n. 2).

Jamnia experienced varying vicissitudes during its later history. In the Maccabean period, Judas, having learned that the inhabitants of Jamnia intended to murder the Jewish inhabitants (as those of Joppa had earlier murdered its Jewish inhabitants), attacked the city at night and burned the harbor and fleet so that the glare of the fire was seen in Jerusalem 240 stades away (2 Macc 13:8, 9). Georgias, commander of Jamnia, routed the troops of Joseph and Azarias, whom Judas had left in command while he was in Galaaditis (Josephus *Ant* 12.8.6 [350–51]). Following Judas' routing of the troops of Georgias, Judas went to Adullam. After the Sabbath, his men went to recover the bodies of the slain for burial only to discover that under the shirt of each were consecrated objects of the idols of Jamnia (2 Macc 12:40), a fact the author of 2 Maccabees considers the cause of their deaths.

Later Simon (142–135 B.C.) captured Jamnia (Josephus *JW* 1.2.2 [50]; *Ant* 13.6.7 [215]) from the Syrians; and in the time of Alexander Jannaeus, Jews held it as well as other coastal cities (Joseph. *Ant* 13.15.4 [395]).

Jamnia was included in the cities Pompey liberated from Jewish rule, restoring it to its Syrian inhabitants and annexing it to the province of Syria under the administration of Scarus (*JW* 1.7.7 [156]; *Ant* 14.4.4 [75, 76]). Then Gabinus (57–55 B.C.), after defeating Alexander Jannai, rebuilt cities which he found in ruins (including Jamnia), and repeopled them with colonists (*Ant* 14.5.3 [88]; *JW* 1.8.1 [166]).

While it is conjectured that Jamnia must have been given by Augustus to Herod about 40 B.C. (Avi-Yonah 1977: 87), no actual record survives. It was a Judean toparchy (Avi-Yonah 1977: 96). Herod in 4 B.C. left the toparchy of Jamnia, Azotus, and Phasaelis in his will to his sister Salome (*Ant* 17.8.1 [189], 11.5 [321]; *JW* 2.6.3 [98]). When Salome died (ca. A.D. 9–12), she bequeathed the city and its territory to Julia (Livia) the wife of Augustus (Joseph. *Ant* 18.2.2 [31]; *JW* 2.9.1 [167]). At her death it became the property of Tiberius who entrusted a special procurator (apparently residing in Jamnia) with its administration as an inscription found at Jamnia (Avi-Yonah 1946: 84f, no. 1) and Josephus (*Ant* 18.6.3 [158]) attest. Jamnia is described by Philo as being one of the most populous cities in Judea with the majority being Jewish but also having others of alien races (*Gaium* 30 [200]).

In the time of King Agrippa, Cestius sent the tribune Neopolitanus to investigate charges against the Jews. Neopolitanus joined King Agrippa (who was returning from Egypt) at Jamnia. The chief priests of the Jews and the leading citizens of the council also came to Jamnia to welcome the king (Joseph. *JW* 2.16.1–2 [33–37]).

Upon Caligula's assertion of his divinity, the new settlers in Jamnia made themselves despicable to the indigenous inhabitants by making an altar of bricks which the Jews promptly pulled down. The non-Jews complained to Herennius Capito, the imperial procurator of Jamnia, who was in direct contact with the court at Rome (*Ant* 18.6.4 [163]), and he sent a report to the emperor. Capito, fearing an inquiry into his finances, wished to blacken the Jews in the emperor's eyes (Philo *Gaium* 199). Gaius (Caligula) then ordered the erection of a statue of gold of himself set up in the temple in Jerusalem (Philo *Gaium* 30 [200–3]); but the assassination of Caligula in Rome (Jan. 24, A.D. 41) terminated the crisis (Tacitus *Histories* 5.92) before the order was carried out.

During the Jewish revolt, Vespasian first subdued Jamnia following the fall of Gamla (*JW* 4.3.2 [130]. Then, while waiting for Jerusalem to destroy itself (A.D. 68–69), he set out from Caesarea, occupied Antipatris, captured Lydda and Jamnia, quartering on them an adequate number of residents from other places that had surrendered, and posted the 5th legion outside Emmaus (*JW* 4.8.1 [443]).

After the war, Jamnia was among the cities which Vespasian made autonomous as is attested by coins struck under the later empire (G. Hill 1914; Avi-Yonah 1977: 111).

C. Jamnia Gatherings

In the absence of any contemporary documents on the Yavneh (Jamnia) period, an account of actions of Yavneh must be drawn from sources redacted at a later period without any objective way to know how much the information has been distorted in the process of transmission. Legend was developing, and one is never certain what is legend and what is fact. The extant materials do not permit writing biographies of any of the participants of the gatherings. The sources are at variance on details with each other. The nature of the sources makes it impossible to be specific about the nature of the Yavneh gatherings as well as specific about their enactments, especially in the 3 areas discussed above—canon, text, and the exclusion of Christians.

In the tradition, R. Yohanan ben Zakkai, already an aged man of possibly 70 years, was brought out of besieged Jerusalem as a dead man by his 2 students Eliezer and Joshua. Yohanan asked Vespasian for Yavneh and its scholars. Qualified for leadership only by his knowledge and his teaching, Yohanan and his associates in Yavneh began the reconstruction of Judaism apart from the temple. The good life as he saw it was the life of study, and the good society was the academy. He removed from the priests the monopoly on the sacred calendar, festivals, and rites, making the priest subject to the rabbi. Temple practices were taken over "as a memorial." Enactments were established by precedent rather than by group vote or agreement. A late source has Yohanan state that good works take the place of sacrifice. There is no evidence of Yohanan's exercising civil authority and making civil enactments.

After a period of leadership of undefined length, Yohanan retired to Beror Hayil where he had a school and court, and leadership in Yavneh passed to Gamaliel II. With Gamaliel as *nasî* (prince), political institutions began to develop which flourished after the Bar Kokhba war. Gamaliel was confirmed by the governor of Syria, and his leadership was recognized by Rome which he visited in company with other prominent scholars. More important, his leadership was accepted by the Jewish communities which looked to Yavneh and its scholars for decisions on various ritual questions.

Gamaliel is depicted as being moody, domineering, and arbitrary. He forced R. Joshua ben Hananiah to yield to his calendar even when the testimony on which his decision rested was in error. After he had humiliated R. Joshua over the question of the obligation of the evening prayer, the academy (*bêt hammidrāš*) rose in revolt, displaced Gamaliel as its head, and seated young R. Eleazar ben Azariah as head of the group. The doors were opened, and students previously denied admission were seated.

In the Mishna, the narrative of the seating of R. Eleazar is followed by a series of enactments introduced by the phrase *bô bayyôm* ("in that day"; *m. Yad.* 4:1–4; *m. Zeb.* 1:3) which suggested to scholars actions of one session and the concept, in part, of the Council/Synod of Jamnia. In later tradition (*b. Ber.* 28a) it is said that every *bô bayyôm* refers to this same occasion and that no legal question pending before the group was left undecided that day.

Gamaliel continued in attendance without missing an hour, ultimately apologized to Joshua, and was restored to leadership. In the compromise, he taught three sabbaths a month and Eleazar one. While Gamaliel was *nāśî* (Prince), the sources differ over whether Eleazar was *rēš mětîbtā*ʾ (head of the academy) or ʾ*ab bêt dîn* (head of the court). Gamaliel lived on to about A.D. 117. Following his death, a new *nāśî* was not immediately appointed; but R. Joshua, R. Tarfon, and R. Akiba exercised great influence. Ultimately the Sanhedrin moved to Usha (in one tradition back to Yavneh and then back to Usha). With the Bar Kokhba war (135 A.D.) the Yavnehian period was at an end.

In the sources the gatherings in Yavneh are spoken of as *bêt hammîdrāš* (house of study), *yěšîbâ*/*mětîbtā*ʾ (academy), *bêt dîn* (court), *bêt wa*ᶜ*ad* (meeting place), the vineyard in Yavneh, the ᶜ*ălîyâ* (upper room), and the ʾ*ôṣār* (treasury). Whether the meetings were actually in a vineyard or the term is to be understood figuratively because the disciples sat in rows like vines is disputed. One Tosefta passage speaks of the Sanhedrin.

The participants are called *zěqēnîm* (elders), rabbis, or *ḥăkāmîm* (scholars). They are described as sitting in a half circle like a threshing floor so that each elder could see the other. The *nāśî* sat in the middle with elders on each side. The disciples were arranged by rank in 3 rows.

There was not a fixed plenary session in Yavneh. The sessions were not continuous, nor was there a full complement of scholars for each meeting. Over about a 60 year period, scholars, rich and poor, lay and priestly, rural and urban—some of whom lived in other towns and had their own courts and schools—came to Yavneh for meetings. The sources report continuous differences of opinion. While differing, however, the scholars did not divide into sects (Cohen 1986). Sometimes a consensus was reached without a formal vote. The majority opinion prevailed.

Catholic Christianity from the 2d century solved its problems by councils; Judaism did not. In the light of the concept of 21 ecumenical councils, as well as of modern meetings where delegates meet and vote on making binding decisions, use of the terminology "council" or "synod" invites a misconception when used for the Yavneh meetings. School, academy, or court is nearer the nature of the meetings (Lewis 1964).

D. Study of Jamnia and the Canon

Recent studies of legal traditions in the Mishna and Tosefta concerning prominent Yavneans such as R. Yohanan (J. Neusner 1970, 1973), Joshua ben Hananiah (W. S. Green 1981), Gamaliel II (Shamai Kanter 1980), Eliezer ben Hyrcanus (J. Neusner 1973), Eleazar ben Azariah (T. Zahavy 1977), R. Tarfon (J. Gereboff 1979), R. Yose (J. N. Lightstone 1979), R. Ishmael (Gary G. Porton 1982), R. Sadoq (J. N. Lightstone 1977), and R. Akiba (L. Finkelstein 1964) reveal concerns about the religious calendar, prayer obligations, sabbath, festivals, cleanness, family laws, release from vows, rules of testimony, and other questions of hypothetical and practical concern to Judaism of the period. However, there is only minor attention to the area of canon, possibly some to separation from Christians, but none to standardization of text.

As Lewis (1964) and Leiman (1976) pointed out, *m. Yad.* 3:5 speaks only of a discussion of the Song of Songs and of Ecclesiastes which discussion is continued after Yavneh times, furnishing no basis for the assertion that the canon was closed at Yavneh. To the contrary, the sources report later debate about these and also other books. No text speaks of the discussion and exclusion of apocryphal books at Yavneh.

Rabbinic scholars now point out that *bô bayyôm* may refer to the occasion of the preceding statement in the source (e.g., *m. Šabb.* 1:4) and not to the day of R. Eleazar's appointment. The questions said to have been discussed "on that day" are questions of distinctly Jewish interest; e.g., the gathering ruled that any animal offerings which must be consumed remain valid although slaughtered under some other name (*m. Yad.* 4:2; *m. Zeb.* 1:3). The scholars dealt with a footbath that is cracked (*m. Yad.* 4:1) and whether Ammon and Moab must give the poor man's tithe in the 7th year (*m. Yad.* 4:3). R. Joshua argued that Sennacherib had so mixed the races that the prohibition of an Ammonite or Moabite entering the Assembly no longer applied. An Ammonite proselyte was accepted (*m. Yad.* 4:4).

Talmud texts (*b. Ber.* 28b–29a; *b. Meg.* 17b; *Num. Rab.* 18:210) speak of the composition of the *birkat hammînîm* by Samuel the Little during Gamaliel's leadership of the academy, but not on the day of R. Eleazar's elevation. The debate continues among current scholars over the meaning of the term *mînîm* in rabbinic texts. Kimelman (1981) insists that there is a lack of evidence that the *birkat hammînîm* reflects a watershed in the history of the relations between Jews and Christians in the 1st centuries of our era. Horbury (1983) replies that patristic evidence supports the contention that Christians were cursed in the synagogues.

While a late tradition (*y. Ta*ᶜ*an* 4:2; *Sof.* 6:4; *Sifre* 2:356; *Abot R. Nat.* B. 46) speaks of the selecting of a text from 3 manuscripts in the temple, no specific text discusses standardization of the Hebrew text at a Council of Yavneh. Rabbinic literature does not discuss divergencies of opinion about Bible readings. The opinion that the text was standardized at Jamnia is an extrapolation from the types of texts attested in the Qumran materials, as compared with the texts from Wadi Murabbaᶜat, and from the supposition that the type of exegesis connected with Akiba's name requires a fixed text. Further evidence is claimed from the type of translation produced by Aquila. However, seeing text stabilization as a long continued process, Segal (1974) tried to place the beginning as early as immediately after the restoration of the temple service in 164 B.C., but culminating near the mid-1st century A.D. Greenberg

(1974) pointed out that Akiba's method of hermeneutics went back to Nahum of Gimzu and that Hillel the elder already was using hermeneutical methods which presuppose a text verbally stable. Albrektson (1978) challenged the common conception that the text was standardized by deliberate text-critical activity. He showed that rabbinic exegesis sometimes relies on a spelling which deviates from the MT. Emphasis on carefulness in copying (*y. Sanh.* 2:6; *b. Meg.* 18b) is to be distinguished from standardization. Albrektson, admitting that we have little demonstrable evidence, suggested that rather than official activity, a group of scholars who became dominant may have preserved and transmitted their preferable type of text.

These ongoing debates suggest the paucity of evidence on which the hypothesis of the Council of Jamnia rests and raise the question whether it has not served its usefulness and should be relegated to the limbo of unestablished hypotheses. It should not be allowed to be considered a consensus established by mere repetition of assertion.

Bibliography

Adler, M. N. 1907. *The Itinerary of Benjamin of Tudela.* London.
Albrektson, B. 1978. Reflections on the Emergence of a Standard Text of the Hebrew Bible. *Congress Volume Götingen 1977.* VTSup 29: 45–65. Leiden.
Avi-Yonah, M. 1946. Newly Discovered Latin and Greek Inscriptions. *QDAP* 12: 84–102.
———. 1977. *The Holy Land, From the Persian to the Arab Conquest.* Rev. ed. Grand Rapids.
Bokser, B. Z. 1935. *Pharisaic Judaism in Transition.* New York.
Christie, W. M. 1925. The Jamnia Period in Jewish History. *JTS* 26: 347–61.
Cohen, S. J. D. 1986. The Significance of Yavneh, Pharisees, Rabbis, and the End of Jewish Sectarianism. *HUCA* 55: 17–53.
Elbogen, I. 1931. *Der judische Gottesdinst in seiner geschichtlichen Entwicklung.* 3d ed. Repr. Hildelsheim, 1967.
Finkelstein, L. 1964. *Akiba: Scholar, Saint and Martyr.* New York.
Gereboff, J. 1979. *Rabbi Tarfon: The Tradition, the Man, and Early Rabbinic Judaism.* Brown Judaic Studies 7. Missoula, MT.
Goldenberg, R. 1972. The Deposition of Rabban Gamaliel II: An Examination of the Sources. *JJS* 22: 167–90.
Graetz, H. 1871. *Kohelet oder des Somonische Prediger.* Leipzig.
Green, W. S. 1981. *The Traditions of Joshua ben Hananiah.* Pt. 1. Leiden.
Greenberg, M. 1974. The Stabilization of the Text of the Hebrew Bible, Reviewed in the Light of Biblical Materials from the Judean Desert. Pp. 298–326 in *The Canon and Masora of the Hebrew Bible,* ed. S. Z. Leiman. New York.
Hill, G. F. 1914. *BMC, Palestine.* London.
Hoenig, S. B. 1953. *The Great Sanhedrin.* Philadelphia.
Horbury, W. 1983. The Benediction of the Minim and early Christian Controversy. *JTS* 33: 19–61.
Kanter, S. 1980. *Rabban Gamaliel II: The Legal Traditions.* Brown Judaic Studies 8. Chico, CA.
Kimelman, R. 1981. Birkat Ha-Minim and the Lack of Evidence for an Anti-Christian Jewish Prayer in late Antiquity. Pp. 228–30 in *Jewish and Christian Self Definition. Vol. 2, Aspects of Judaism in the Graeco-Roman Period,* ed. E. P. Sanders et al. Philadelphia.
Krauss, S. 1893. The Jews in the Works of the Church Fathers. *JQR* 5: 122–57.
Leiman, S. Z. 1976. *The Canonization of the Hebrew Scriptures.* Transactions of the Connecticut Academy of Arts and Sciences 47. Hamden, CT
Lewis, J. P. 1964. What Do We Mean by Jabneh? *JBR* 32: 125–32.
Lightstone, J. N. 1977. Sadoq the Yavnean. Pp. 48–147 in *Persons and Institutions in Early Judaism,* ed. W. S. Green, Missoula, MT.
———. 1979. *Jose the Galilean.* Leiden.
Manns, F. 1980–82. L'evangile de Jean, Response chretienne aus decisions de Jabne. *LASBF* 30: 47–92; 32: 85–108.
Mantel, H. 1961. *Studies in the History of the Sanhedrin.* Cambridge.
Martyn, J. L. 1968. *History and Theology in the Fourth Gospel.* Nashville.
Neusner, J. 1970a. *The Life of Rabban Yohanan Ben Zakkai.* 2d ed. Leiden.
———. 1970b. *Development of a Legend.* Leiden.
———. 1970c. Studies in the TAQQANOT of Yavneh. *HTR* 63: 183–98.
———. 1973. *Eliezer ben Hyrcanus: The Traditions and the Man.* 2 vols. Leiden.
———. 1979. The Formation of Rabbinic Judaism: Yavneh (Jamnia) from A.D. 70–100. *ANRW* 2/19/2: 3–42.
Newman, R. C. 1978. The Council of Jamnia and the Old Testament Canon. *WTS* 38: 319–49.
Podro, J. 1959. *The Last Pharisee.* London.
Porton, G. G. 1982. *The Traditions of Rabbi Ishmael.* Leiden.
Rengstorf, K. H. 1968. Der Glanz von Jabne. Pp. 232–44 in *Festschrift Werner Caskel,* ed. E. Gräf. Leiden.
Robinson, E. 1841–57. *Biblical Researches in Palestine, Mount Sinai and Arabia Petraea.* 3 vols. London.
Saldarini, A. J. 1975. Johanan ben Zakkai's Escape from Jerusalem. Origin and Development of a Rabbinic Story. *JSJ* 6: 189–204.
Schäfer, P. 1975. Die Sogenannte Synode von Jabne: Zur Trennung von Juden und Christen im ersten/zweiten Jh. n. Chr. *Judaica* 31: 54–124.
———. 1979. Die Flucht Johanan b. Zakkais aus Jerusalem und die Grundung des 'Lehrhauses' in Jabne. *ANRW* 2/19/2: 43–101.
Segal, M. H. 1974. The Promulgation of the Authoritative Text of the Hebrew Bible. Pp. 285–97 in *The Canon and Masora of the Hebrew Bible,* ed. S. Z. Leiman. New York.
Talmon, S. 1970. The Old Testament Text. *CHB* 1: 159–99.
Zahavy, T. 1977. *The Traditions of Eleazar ben Azariah.* Brown Judaic Studies 2. Missoula, MT.
Zeitlin, S. 1978. *The Rise and Fall of the Judean State.* Philadelphia.

JACK P. LEWIS

JANAI (PERSON) [Heb *yaʿnay*]. A Gadite who was the son of Abihail and the third tribal leader named in the genealogy (1 Chr 5:12). It may be that "Shaphat," the fourth name in the list, should not be rendered as a personal name but as the noun "judge." In this case, Joel was the head of the tribe, Shapham the second in authority, and Janai a judge in Bashan (Rudolph *Chronikbücher* HAT, 47). This interpretation is supported by the Targum and LXX. Although Janai's name has been related to *yaʿanâ* ("ostrich"), others regard it as a derivative of the imperfect form of the verb *ʿānâ* ("answer") and interpret it as expressing the wish that deity answer the prayer of the name-giver (e.g., for health or strength; Noth *IPN,* 28, 198).

According to 1 Chronicles 5, Janai and the other Gadites lived opposite the Reubenites in "Bashan as far as Salecah" (v 11) and "in Gilead, in Bashan . . . and in all the pasture lands of Sharon to their limits" (v 17). The tribe of Gad receives Gilead (Num 13:24–28), but Bashan and Sharon are not mentioned, since the first is too far N and the second too far W. The reference in 1 Chronicles 5 to Bashan may be the result of confusion in a later day about the N boundary of Gad or about the limits of Bashan (cf. Deut 3:10). Evidence of a city or region in Transjordania named Sharon is also found in the Mesha Inscription (line 13; *ANET* 320). Neither Janai nor the others named in the Chronicler's genealogy for Gad (1 Chr 5:11–17) appear in other lists of Gadites (Gen 46:16; Num 26:15–18; 1 Chr 12:9–16—Eng 12:8–15).

M. PATRICK GRAHAM

JANIM (PLACE) [Heb *yānîm*]. A village in the hill country of Judah alloted by Joshua to that tribe (Josh 15:53). The exact location is unknown, though it may possibly be identified with Beni Naʿim about 4 miles E of Hebron.

ELMER H. DYCK

JANNAI (PERSON) [Gk *Iannai*]. The father of Melchi and son of Joseph (an earlier ancestor of Jesus), according to Luke's genealogy tying Joseph, the "supposed father" of Jesus, to descent from Adam and God (Luke 3:24). D omits Jannai, substituting a genealogy adapted from Matt 1:6–15 for Luke 3:23–31, while some manuscripts and versions read *ianna*. The name Jannai occurs nowhere else in the biblical documents, including Matthew's genealogy, and falls within a list of 18 otherwise unknown descendents of David's son Nathan (Fitzmyer *Luke 1–9* AB, 500). Kuhn (1923: 208–9) argues that two seemingly parallel lists of names—Luke 3:23–26 (Jesus to Mattathias) and 3:29–31 (Joshua/Jesus to Mattatha)—were originally identical, the first perhaps reflecting a Hebrew context and the second an Aramaic context, tracing Mary's line of descent (since it does not mention Joseph as Jesus' father). Jannai in the first list corresponds to Juda in the second list. With no textual variants for either name to support confusion of the two, Kuhn's theory has little plausibility.

Bibliography

Kuhn, G. 1923. Die Gaschlechtsregister Jesu bei Lukas und Matthäus, nach ihrer Herkunft untersucht. *ZNW* 22: 206–28.

STANLEY E. PORTER

JANNES AND JAMBRES (PERSONS) [Gk *Iannēs, Iambrēs*]. The names traditionally assigned to the magicians who, according to Exod 7:11–12, 22, opposed Moses and Aaron before Pharaoh on the occasion of Israel's exodus from Egypt. Tradition characterizes them as willful and persistent opponents to God and Moses (2 Tim 3:8–9). There was also a pseudepigraphic book entitled *Jannes and Jambres.*

A. The Traditions

Though not named in the OT and only once in the NT, the two brother magicians appear frequently in Jewish, Christian, and pagan sources extant in Arabic, Aramaic, Greek, Hebrew, Latin, Old and Middle English, and Syriac. Hebrew and Aramaic literature gives the names as *y(w)hny/ʾ* and *mmrʾ* as well as in more Hellenized guise with final *samek: ynys* and *ym(b)rys.* In Gk sources the usual forms are *Iannēs* and (through analogical development) *Iambrēs,* though the former occasionally appears in its typologically earlier form *Iōannēs.* (Syriac follows the Gk spelling.) Latin tradition features *Iamnes/Iannes* (and rarely *Iohannes*), but virtually uniformly gives the second name as *mambres,* a form to be traced via the VL (apparently corrected to *Iambrēs* by Jerome in conformity with the Gk of 2 Tim 3:8) to the early Jewish Church. That the first name is Semitic is no longer in doubt, but it is significant that Moses' chief opponent should have been assigned a popular Yahwistic name. The second name presents more of a problem. A derivation from the Heb root *mrh,* "be contentious, refractory, rebellious," has found widespread favor.

An early reference to two brothers as opponents of Moses and Aaron occurs in the *Damascus Document* (CD) 5, 17b–19: "For in earlier times Moses and Aaron arose with the help of the Prince of Lights, while Belial raised up Yoḥanah *(yḥnh)* and his brother." Though the Cairo Genizah mss of CD are medieval in date, the passage in question has also been identified among the finds in the Judean desert (6Q15 3; 1st century C.E.), but its date of composition is wrapped in the controversial literary history of CD. Beginning with S. Schechter's 1910 edition of CD, Yoḥanah and his brother have been equated, without qualification, with the Jannes and Jambres of later literature. Such an interpretation is, however, open to serious doubt, since in CD, as opponents of Moses and Aaron, they are portrayed as *Israelite* leaders of apostate Israel in Egypt (see CD 3, 5–6, Ezek 20:7–8; 23:3, Josh 24:14). Their role is typological for contemporary (non-Essene) Jewish leadership, reflecting, therefore, socioreligious conflict within Palestinian Jewry. A number of historical identifications have thus far been proposed.

Subsequent tradition identified Yoḥanah and his brother as pharaoh's magicians (Exod 7:11). By the 1st century C.E., the pagan writer Pliny the Elder mentions Moses, Jannes, and Lotapes (= Jambres?) as magicians among the Jews "many thousands of years after Zoroaster" (*HN* 30.2.11), and in similar vein Lucius Apuleius (2d century C.E.) includes Moses and Johannes (Jannes) in a list of renowned magicians (*Apol.* 2.90). However, the most interesting reference in pagan authors is the note preserved in Eusebius' *Praeparatio Evangelica* (9.8) from the Neoplatonist Numenius of Apamea (2d century C.E.) that Jannes and Jambres were able to undo even the greatest of the disasters which Moses brought against Egypt—a claim which contradicts the biblical account (cf. Exod 8:18). A statement by Origen (*Cels.* 4.51) that Numenius had recounted the story of Moses and the two magicians suggests that Origen must have been acquainted with extensive traditions about the magicians and may well have known the book entitled *Jannes and Jambres* (see B. below).

Because of their mention in 2 Tim 3:8–9, Jannes and Jambres frequently appear in later Christian sources which merely echo the NT reference or give more details of their wicked behavior. The story was clearly well-known since most references presuppose an acquaintance with it. Unfortunately, only snippets of the tale have survived. The two brothers are said to have been magicians at the court of Pharaoh Ahmoses (John of Nikiu) or Pharaoh Chencheres, who was the pharaoh that drowned with his army in the Arabian Gulf (Ps-Dionysius of Telmaḥre). Pharaoh's daughter reputedly entrusted Moses to Jannes and Jambres for instruction in wisdom (e.g., Bar Hebraeus). They were regarded as gods by the Egyptians (*Acts Pil.*), and Satan counted them his brothers *(Ques. Bart.)*. Moreover, Abezethibou, the demon from the Red Sea, claimed to have come to their aid *(T. Sol.)*; it was they who were responsible for leading pharaoh astray until the king and his host met their death in the sea *(Mart. Pet. Paul; Pal. hist.)*. Moses, in the course of their altercations with him, afflicted their adherents with sores and sent the mother of one of them (sic) to their death (Philostorgius). The two brothers tried to withstand God's mighty acts by means of fake magic; but when bested by Moses they confessed in pain from their sores that God was active in Moses (Ambrosiaster). They practised necromancy, *(A.Cath.)* and as a result of their wickedness they perished (Abdias). In spite of their having acknowledged "the finger of God," they received no divine forgiveness *(Pen. Cyp.)*. Their garden tomb, a monument to their former power and wealth, was visited by Macarius of Alexandria, who found it inhabited by 70 demons (Palladius).

In Jewish literature of the common era Jannes and Jambres are especially prominent in legends connected with the birth and early years of Moses, but the time and circumstances of their demise vary in the sources. According to some traditions *(Tg. Ps.-J.; Yal. Reu.)* they were assistants of Balaam (cf. Num 22:22), Israel's staunch opponent at the pharaonic court. Commonly, however, they are called his sons, a tradition which may be as old as the 3d century C.E. A dream of pharaoh was interpreted by them to augur destruction for Egypt at the hands of an Israelite about to be born *(Tg. Ps.-J)*. At a royal banquet, when Moses was two, he placed pharaoh's crown on his own head. Balaam, who was in attendance with his sons, reminded the king of his earlier dream and counseled Moses' death. Pharaoh, however, heeded contrary advice and decided to put Moses to the test. When the child was directed to choose between a glowing ember and a gem, under angelic prompting he picked the former, stuck it in his mouth, and thus contracted his speech impediment (cf. Exod 4:10). Balaam and his sons fled to Ethiopia where they usurped the throne during the king's absence. But when their city subsequently fell to a strategem of Moses, who had succeeded the king of Ethiopia, they returned to pharaoh's court. In due time Moses and Aaron presented themselves at pharaoh's palace, where they gained entrance by casting a spell on the two lions that barred their way. The king, frightened by their divine appearance, delayed answering until the following day their demand for the release of the Israelites. Meanwhile he summoned Balaam and his two sons who counseled him to put their authenticity to the test (*ShY* cf. *Yal. Sim., ChronJ, ChronM, Exod. Rab.*). Jannes and Jambres cheated at magic by exchanging their staffs for snakes. Though they managed to check the majority of the angels, they could not prevail against the angel of the (divine) presence *(mlʾk pnyw)* who sided with Moses.

Outdone by Moses, they came to him to become proselytes and, against God's explicit directive, were accepted. Thus a "mixed multitude" (Exod 12:38) with Jannes and Jambres at the head accompanied Israel out of Egypt. It was they who were the real culprits in Israel's idolatrous debacle at Sinai and consequently were killed by the Levites (*Yal. Reu.*; cf. *Midr. Tanh.*). Alternatively in Jewish tradition, Jannes and Jambres, flying above the Red Sea on self-made wings, were destroyed by an angel dispatched by God (*Yal. Sim.*; cf. *Yal. Reu.*; *ChronJ* 54). A minor tradition as them executed together with Balaam and the princes of Midian in accordance with Num 31:8 (*ChronJ* 48, Zohar).

B. The Book

The earliest reference to a book entitled *Jannes and Jambres* is in the Latin translation of Origen's commentary on the gospel of Matthew (*comm. in Matt.* (GCS 11,250). This book was thought by Origen to have been the source for Paul the presumed author of 2 Timothy. Later references are found in the Ambrosiaster, the *Decretum Gelasianum*, and some Syriac and Middle English sources. Fragments of the book in Greek are extant in a Vienna papyrus (P. Vindob G 29456 + 29828 verso; 3d century C.E.), Papyrus Chester Beatty XVI (3d/4th century C.E.), and in a Michigan papyrus fragment (3d century C.E.). A fragment of a translation into Latin has been preserved in a manuscript of the British Library (Cotton Tiberius B.V fol. 87; 11th century C.E.). All texts are fragmentary, but they add a wealth of detail to our knowledge of the story.

The remnants of the book commence with the magicians' genealogy and then move through various phases of Jannes' opposition to Moses. Summoned to the palace, he matches Moses and Aaron's feats but is laid low by disease. In the course of events, clear omens of impending doom are sent his way; yet, his fight continues unabated. Ill and near death he takes leave of mother and friends, and, in Memphis, entrusts his brother with the book of magic. After receiving news of the disaster at the Red Sea, Jannes meets his own end. He is lamented by his mother who subsequently dies a violent death and is buried by her surviving son near the tomb of Jannes. Brought up from Hades by Jambres, the shade of Jannes launches into a lengthy admission of wrongdoing. We do not know the response of Jambres and his final end.

In at least its final literary form the book quite clearly is a confession, hence underscoring the title given it in the *Decretum Gelasianum: The Confession (Penitence) of Jannes and Jambres*. The essence of the tale is the magicians' deliberate and determined opposition to Moses (God) in the face of repeated divine warnings. Their obdurate behavior precluded forgiveness forever. It is this aspect of the plot that suggests *Jannes and Jambres* as one of the precursors of the Faust legend. The end of Jannes (and Jambres?) was no doubt intended to serve as a warning to the believing community.

Though the Jannes and Jambres *tradition* probably arose on Palestinian soil and in a Semitic-speaking environment, there is no indication that the original language of the *book* was other than Greek. The date of origin of the tradition can hardly be much later than the 2d century B.C.E., while the book was written probably at least as early as the 2d century C.E. For further discussion, see *OTP* 2: 427–42; *HJP*² 3/2: 781–83; Str-B 3: 660–64.

Bibliography

Baillet, M.; Milik, J. T.; and de Vaux, R. 1962. *Les 'petites grottes' de Qumran.* DJD 3/15/3. Oxford.

Förster, M. 1902. Das lateinisch-altenglische Fragment der Apocryphe von Jamnes und Mambres. *Archiv für das Studium der neueren Sprachen und Literaturen* 108: 15–28.

Maraval, P. 1977. Fragments grecs du livre de Jannès et Jambré Pap. Vindob. 29456 et 29828 (verso). *Zeitschrift für Papyrologie und Epigraphik* 25: 199–207.

ALBERT PIETERSMA

JANNEUS (PERSON). A Hasmonean king and high priest of Judea (103–76 B.C.E.). After Aristobulus died, his widow, Salome Alexandra, set free three of his brothers, one of whom, Janneus, she subsequently married. Janneus is known by the Gk form of his name to which he added Alexander. Alexander Janneus succeeded his brother as high priest and officially claimed the title of "king," which he inscribed on his coins.

Janneus was a ruthless ruler and profligate in character. Early in his career he arranged for the murder of one of his two surviving brothers. He was primarily a man of war. He instigated an aggressive plan of expansion, enlarging by conquest and proselyzation his kingdom to the size of the ancient kingdom under David and Solomon (Josephus *Ant* 13.15.4). Janneus attacked Greek cities which posed an economic threat to the survival of the Jewish state, particularly along the coast, and he forcibly converted the inhabitants to Judaism. After conquering the coastal cities from Carmel to Gaza, with the exception of Ascalon, Janneus successfully established his power in the Transjordan. Moving to the S, Janneus was severely defeated by King Obedas of the Nabateans (*Ant* 13.15.2) and later by King Aretas (*Ant* 13.15.2). As a result of his excessive drinking, Janneus contracted a disease and died, leaving control to his widow.

The orthodox Jews and the Pharisees resisted Janneus because they felt that his reprobate behavior and willful neglect of his spiritual duties disqualified him from the office of high priest. The controversy was heightened by Janneus' sympathetic support of Sadducaean families. The Pharisaic opposition was led by Simeon ben Shetah, who may have actually been the queen's brother. Rabbinical legends depict him as a fearless, hot-tempered opponent of the king's.

Janneus and the Pharisees were on a collision course. Unrest gave place to rebellion as Janneus was officiating one day as high priest at the altar during the Feast of Tabernacles. According to the Talmud, the riot was caused by Janneus' insolence when he deliberately poured a libation over his own feet rather than on the altar, as dictated by Pharisaic tradition. The crowds hurled citrons at him and declared that he was unfit to hold the office. According to Josephus, Janneus retaliated and 6,000 people were massacred by his foreign mercenaries. The Jews, incited by the Pharisees, rebelled in 94 B.C.E. A civil war broke out which lasted 6 years, during which time Janneus killed over 50,000 Jews with his mercenaries (*Ant* 13.13.5).

The Pharisees called for the assistance of the Seleucid, Demetrius III (Eukairos), who defeated Janneus at Shechem. This incident may be referred to in the commentary on Nahum found at Qumran which relates that "Demetrius sought to enter Jerusalem on the counsel of those who seek smooth things." If this passage is indeed referring to the Pharisees and to Demetrius the Seleucid, it may shed light on the turn of events which took place afterwards. While in hiding, Janneus was joined by 6,000 Jews who thought life under Janneus was preferable to Seleucid domination. With their aid, Janneus drove Demetrius out, reestablished his authority, and poured vengeance on the Pharisees. While Janneus banqueted and caroused with his concubines, he had 800 of his enemies crucified while their wives and children were slain before their eyes (*Ant* 13.14.1–2; *JW* 1.4.5–6). This incident is also related in the Nahum Commentary which states, "He hanged living men on wood . . . which was not formerly done in Israel."

According to Josephus, 8,000 of his enemies escaped from Jerusalem by night and remained in hiding until Janneus died, harboring a hatred for their king and the Sadducees. A number of scholars identify the flight of Janneus' enemies with the founding of the Qumran community. Janneus is identified as the Wicked Priest and persecutor of the Teacher of Righteousness, both appearing frequently in the Dead Sea Scrolls. Clearly, the Qumran Essenes were not Pharisees. It is argued, however, that the opposition to Janneus should not be confined strictly to the Pharisees and that among those who fled from Jerusalem were the Teacher of Righteousness and his disciples. Archaeological evidence indicates that Qumran was expanded at this same time.

According to tradition, before Janneus died he counseled his wife not to imitate his course of action with the Pharisees. He suggested to take the Pharisees into her confidence and to elevate them to positions of authority and thereby win the allegiance of the masses, which she did (*Ant* 13.15.5).

SCOTT T. CARROLL

JANOAH (PLACE) [Heb *yānôḥâ; yānôaḥ*]. The name of 2 Israelite towns.

1. A town listed after Taanath-Shiloh in the description of the E border of the territory of Ephraim (Josh 16:6–7). Since the name appears twice in the same form (Heb *ynwḥh*), the final *he* is apparently part of the name and not a *he* of direction. Eusebius identifies it with "Ianō in Acrabattene at the twelfth mile from Neas Polis eastwards" (Klosterman 1904: 108, line 20). Biblical Janoah and Ianō of Eusebius are identified with Yanun (M.R. 183172), 11 km SE of Nablus and 2 km NE of Aqraba, or with Kh. Yānūn (M.R. 184173), 1.5 km NE of Yanun. There is evidence of Iron Age occupation at both sites (*HGB*, 159). Textually it is not clear whether Janoah or Taanath-Shiloh is being referred to by the phrase "and passes along beyond it on the E" (Josh 16:6). The topography however leads to the conclusion that the territory of Ephraim included the hills to the E of both sites.

2. A city in Galilee captured by Tiglath-Pileser III in 732 B.C.E. (2 Kgs 15:29). It is mentioned in the Bible only once (MT *ynwḥ*) as the third of the 5 cities captured in that campaign: "Ijon and Abel-Beth-Maachah and Janoah and Kadesh and Hazor." The other 4 cities are all clearly identified and appear in the text in geographically logical order from N to S. They are situated near the N border of the kingdom of Israel, 3 in the Jordan valley and 1 (Kadesh) in the mountains of upper Galilee to the W. Some have proposed identifying Janoah with Kh. en-Na'imeh (M.R. 205286), a site in the Jordan valley between Abel-Beth-Maachah (M.R. 204296) and Hazor (M.R. 203269; Vincent 1926: 470). Others have identified it with Giv'at ha-Shoqet (M.R. 203293; Kaplan 1978: 159–60). However, there exist 2 villages by the name of Yanuḥ: one in Upper Galilee (M.R. 173265) 18 km NE of Acco and the other in Lebanon 10 km E of Tyre. Klein (*EJ* 8:875) proposed identifying Janoah with the former, as did Aharoni (1957: 131), who suggested that an ancient route from Acre to Lebanon passed by this site. Conder, on the other hand, identified Janoah with the Lebanese Yanuḥ (*SWP* 1: 96), and Rainey (1981: 147–49) supported this identification by suggesting that the Assyrian army advanced from Abel-Beth-Maacah not only S but also W along the Tyre-Dan road to the Lebanese Yanuḥ and then S again to Kadesh. At the same time he identified the Tyre-Dan road with "the way of the sea" referred to in Isa 8:23 (—Eng 9:1).

Bibliography

Aharoni, Y. 1957. *The Settlements of the Israelite Tribes in Upper Galilee.* Jerusalem (in Hebrew).
Kaplan, J. 1978. The identification of Abel-Beth-Maachah and Janoah. *IEJ* 28: 157–69.
Klosterman, E., ed. 1904. *Eusbius Das Onomastikon der Biblischen Ortsnamen.* Leipzig. Repr. 1966.
Rainey, A. F. 1981. Toponymic Problems (cont.). *TA* 8: 146–51.
Vincent, L. H. 1926. Bulletin. *RB* 35: 439–71.

RAFAEL FRANKEL

JAOEL (ANGEL). The name of an archangel (Gk *Iaoēl*) also called Jael in pseudepigraphic writings. In the *Apocalypse of Abraham* (from the late 1st or early 2d century C.E.) Jaoel serves as Abraham's heavenly guide and also strengthens and protects him (10:3). The name Jaoel is one of the indications that the work was originally composed in Hebrew. The reference to the archangel should probably be distinguished from the use of Jaoel in *Apoc. Ab.* 17:13, where it refers to God. However, Box (1918: xxv–xxvi) understood these two uses of Jaoel to be complementary. He described Jaoel as the supreme figure in Jewish angelology, God's vicegerent, and in fact a substitute for Yahweh.

The occurrences of the name Jael in the *Apocalypse of Moses* are very similar to those of Jaoel in the *Apocalypse of Abraham.* Again, the name Jael is one indication that the *Apocalypse of Moses* was originally written in Hebrew, probably in the 2d century C.E. "Jael" is found twice in the work (29:4; 33:5), both times as an epithet for God combining the Hebrew names Yahweh and Elohim. However, in the Slavonic *Life of Adam and Eve* (an important witness to the Greek version of the *Apocalypse of Moses*) the archangel Jael plays an important role. There are several references to Jael as a heavenly envoy (*L.A.E.* 31:1–2; 32:1–2; 43:4; and the doxology appended to chapter 43).

Bibliography

Box, G. H. 1918. *The Apocalypse of Abraham.* New York.
Johnson, M. D. 1985. Life of Adam and Eve. *OTP* 2: 249–95.
Rabinkiewicz, R. 1983. Apocalypse of Abraham. *OTP* 1: 681–719.
Wells, L. S. A. 1913. The Books of Adam and Eve. *OTP* 2: 123–54.

STEVEN L. MCKENZIE

JAPANESE BIBLICAL SCHOLARSHIP. See BIBLICAL SCHOLARSHIP, JAPANESE.

JAPHETH (PERSON) [Heb *yepet*]. The name of the third son of Noah. Japheth appears in the Hebrew Bible 11 times, in the primeval history and the Chronicler's history (Gen 5:32; 6:10; 7:13; 9:18, 23, 27; 10:1, 2, 21; 1 Chr 1:4, 5).

A. The Name

The etymological origin and meaning of the name Japheth is uncertain. Some modern interpreters, following Saadia Gaon (9th century C.E.), take it to mean "fair, beautiful," from *yph* "to be fair, beautiful." According to some earlier Talmudic sages the beauty refers to the Greek language. However, this etymology was already correctly rejected by Abraham Ibn Ezra (12th century). Others suggest that the name is related to the Egyptian Keftiu (Crete) or to the name of the Greek mythological Titan Iapetos, father of Atlas, Prometheus, and Epimetheus. A possible meaning of Japheth is hinted at in the Hebrew pun *yapt ʾĕlōhîm lĕyepet,* "May God make wide for Japheth" (Gen 9:27). Thus the name may mean "spacious," an allusion, at least in Genesis, to an expanded inheritance of land by Japheth. This possible interpretation is based in the name's derivation from the root *pty,* "to be wide, spacious."

B. Biblical Data

Japheth is the youngest of Noah's 3 sons, the brother of Shem and Ham (Gen 5:32; 6:10). According to the genealogical table, Japheth comes first (10:1–5). Therefore, some modern scholars (as some Talmudic sages) consider him the eldest; but this is merely conjectural. Japheth, together with his brothers Shem and Ham and their wives, joined Noah in the Ark and escaped the Flood (6:9; 7:13–15; 9:1–18). He also shares together with his brothers the divine blessing and covenant (9:1, 17). Children were born to him, as to his other brothers, after the flood (10:1). In the story of Noah's drunkenness (Gen 9:20–27), Japheth, after receiving the report of his father's nakedness from his brother Ham, discreetly walked backward, together with his other brother Shem, and covered his father. As a result, he became the beneficiary of his father's blessing. See also HAM.

Japheth had 7 sons (Gomer, Magog, Madai, Javan, Tubal, Meshech, and Tiras) and 7 descendants (Gen 10:2–5; 1 Chr 1:5–7). Unlike the sons and descendants of Shem and Ham, who are mentioned in numerous places throughout the Hebrew Bible, the sons and descendants of Japheth are conspicuous by their absence from most of the biblical books. Outside the genealogical tables in Genesis and Chronicles, four of Japheth's sons—Gomer, Javan, Tubal, and Meshech—are mentioned chiefly in two books: Isa 66:19 (Javan, Tubal, and Meshech) and Ezek 27:13; 32:26; 38:2, 3, 6; 39:1, 6 (Gomer and Tubal). Of Japheth's descendants, the best known are two of Javan's sons: Tarshish (mentioned about 29 times in the Hebrew Bible) and Kittim (mentioned 5 times). According to ethnographic conceptions informing the primeval history, Japheth is the ancestor of the peoples who inhabit the lands N of Canaan. According to later Jewish tradition he also occupies the far east (cf. Jdt 2:25, "east of Gog"; *Jub.* 8:29, "east . . . as far as the region of the waters"; cf. 9:7–13).

C. Jewish Tradition

Hardly any references are made to Japheth in the Apocrypha or Pseudepigrapha outside of the genealogical references to Noah's family (*2 En.* 73:5; *Apoc. Adam* 4:1; *T. Sim.* 6:5; *T. Isaac* 3:15; *L.A.B.* 1:22; 4:1ff.). The most-extensive such reference to Japheth is in *Jubilees:* his birth (4:33), his role in the Noah story (7:9, 12), and his inheritance in the divine land distribution (8:10, 12, 25, 29; 9:7–13; 10:35, 36). *Jubilees* also gives the most detailed information about Japheth's land portion, "The third part [of the earth] was assigned to Japheth, the land beyond the Tina river to the north of its mouth . . . the direction of the northeast, all the area of Gog and all the land east of it, all the way to the farthest north . . . towards the mountains of Qelt . . . towards the Ma'uk Sea . . . east of Gadir . . . west of Fereg . . . towards the Me'at Sea . . . toward Mount Rafa . . . five big islands and a huge land in the north . . ." (8:25–30). "The land given to Ham is hot, to Japheth cold, to Shem neither cold or hot" *(ibid.).* Josephus says that Phrygia belongs to Japheth. See Fig. GEO.05.

An interesting detail given in *Jubilees* about Japheth is that he became jealous of Ham and built a city named Adataneses (Athens?) after his wife (7:15). His granddaughter Melka, daughter of Madai (8:5), married Arphaxad, Shem's son. In the quasi-Jewish *Sibylline Oracles*—in which the sons of Noah are given the names of Greek gods—Shem is identified with Cronos, Ham with Titan, and Japheth as Iapetus (3:110–15). Sethian Gnostic tractate *Apocalypse of Adam* (V,5 72:17; 73:14, 25; 74:11; 76:13–14) deals with the division of the world and empires among the sons of Noah.

Tannaitic and Amoraitic teachers considered Japheth the eldest of Noah's sons. They held Shem to be Noah's youngest son, and said that in the Bible he is mentioned first among the members of his family because he was the most righteous, wisest, and most-important son, not because he was the oldest (*Sanh.* 69b; *Gen. Rab.* 26:3; 37:7). Japheth assisted Shem in covering Noah's nakedness and was blessed with a burial place for his sons Gog [Gomer?] (cf. Ezek 39:1) and Magog (*Gen. Rab.* 36; cf. Ezek 39:11). The sages propounded Gen 9:27 (see above) as referring to the rebuilding of the Temple by Cyrus, King of Persia, a descendant of Japheth (*Yoma* 10a). Another rabbi argued that Gen 9:27 refers to the teaching of the Law in the Greek language (*Gen. Rab.* 36: *Deut. Rab.* 1).

D. Christian and Islamic Literature

In the NT Japheth is mentioned, but his descendants Gog (see above) and Magog figure in the major international war of Revelation (20:8). In the early Christian literature, particularly in Irenaeus of Lyon, Lactantius, Hyppolytus of Rome, Clement, Origen, Epiphanius, and Eusebius, the sons of Noah and their generations are often alluded to but without much elaboration.

EPHRAIM ISAAC

JAPHETH (PLACE) [Gk *Iapheth*]. A region mentioned only in the book of Judith, Japheth is described as having S borders "fronting toward Arabia" and constitutes a landmark in the southward advances made by Holofernes (2:25). As Zimmerman suggests, this description may mean that the S borders of Japheth were on the same latitude as the Syrian desert (Zimmerman 1972: 73; cf. Moore *Judith* AB, 139). However, the book's geography is confused here, as well as elsewhere (Pfeiffer 1949: 296–97; Metzger 1957: 50), and the meaning of the phrase remains obscure (Cowley *APOT* 1: 250). The text of v 25 suggests that the author has Philistia in mind, but then in v 27, Holofernes is described as moving "down into the plain of Damascus," which suggests that the latter was still in Cilicia (Zimmermann 1972: 73).

Bibliography

Metzger, B. 1957. *An Introduction to the Bible.* New York.

Pfeiffer, R. 1949. *History of New Testament Times, with an Introduction to the Apocrypha.* New York.

Zimmermann, F. 1972. *Book of Tobit.* Jewish Apocryphal Literature. New York.

FREDERICK W. SCHMIDT

JAPHIA (PERSON) [Heb *yāpîaᶜ*]. **1.** King of Lachish (Josh 10:3). He was one of 5 Canaanite kings from cities SW of Jerusalem that came together at the instigation of Adonizedek, king of Jerusalem, to oppose the Gibeonites, who had just concluded a treaty with Israel (Josh 10:1–5). This challenge was born out of fear of the Israelites, in response to their conquests of Jericho and Ai, and their treaty with the powerful city of Gibeon. Japhia was executed by Joshua, along with the other kings, after Israel routed their armies with YHWH's help. Their bodies—like the king of Ai's had been (8:29)—were hung on 5 trees until sundown; ironically, they were then thrown into the very cave in which they had attempted to hide from Joshua earlier. The first time, Joshua had sealed them in with large stones in order to capture them; he now sealed them in permanently (Josh 10:6–27).

2. One of 13 sons of David listed as having been born to David's wives in Jerusalem (2 Sam 5:15; 1 Chr 3:7; 14:6), in addition to his 6 sons born at Hebron. His mother's name is unknown: 4 of the 13 sons born in Jerusalem were Bathsheba's sons; the remainder were born to unnamed wives. Besides these 13, David had numerous (unnamed) sons born to his concubines, according to 1 Chr 3:9. See also DAVID, SONS OF.

DAVID M. HOWARD, JR.

JAPHIA (PLACE) [Heb *yāpîaᶜ*]. A town along the E portion of the S border of Zebulun, mentioned only once in the Bible (Josh 19:12). The location of the late Roman-Byzantine site of Japhia is clearly at modern-day Yafa, ca. 1.5 miles SW of Nazareth (M.R. 176232). The Bronze Age and Iron Age site location is uncertain (Barag in *EAEHL* 2: 541–43); a case has been made for the early site being NE of Nazareth (Boling *Joshua* AB, 445). In a citation roughly contemporary with the events in the book of Joshua (LB), it appears in the Amarna Letters as "the town of Yapu" (*ANET,* 485). It was one of several cities that supplied corveé labor for Egypt. Japhia still stood in Josephus' day, as it was one of the cities he fortified during the great war with Rome in 66–70 C.E. (*JW* 2.20.6). Josephus described it as the largest village in Galilee, with strong walls, and he stayed there on occasion (*Life* 45, 52).

DAVID M. HOWARD, JR.

JAPHLET (PERSON) [Heb *yaplēṭ*]. An Asherite, son of Heber (1 Chr 7:32–33). Heber is listed as a son of Beriah in Gen 46:17 and Num 26:45, but 1 Chronicles 7 is the only place in the OT which lists the sons of Heber. Japhlet is possibly connected to the JAPHLETITES mentioned in Josh 16:3. The Chronicler also uses the similar name Pelet (1 Chr 2:47; 12:3).

TOM WAYNE WILLETT

JAPHLETITES [Heb *yaplēṭî*]. A group of people whose territory helped identify the border between Ephraim and Benjamin (Josh 16:3). Their territory was located somewhere between Bethel and Lower Beth-horon. In order to explain why the term Japhletites is found in Josh 16:1–3 but not in other descriptions of the border of Benjamin (Josh 16:5; 18:11–13), Aharoni (*LBHG,* 256) suggests that "these three parallel passages represent three shortened versions of the same list." The size, nature, and origin of this group of people is not known. It may have been a clan, family, village, or ethnic group. An Asherite named JAPHLET is mentioned in 1 Chr 7:32–33. See also *HGB* and Joshua AB.

STEPHEN A. REED

JAR HANDLE STAMPS, ROYAL. See STAMPS, ROYAL JAR HANDLE.

JARAH (PERSON) [Heb *yaʿrâ*]. Son of Ahaz, a descendant of King Saul of the tribe of Benjamin according to the genealogy in 1 Chr 9:42. However, the textual attestation of this name is problematic; in the parallel genealogy in 1 Chr 8:36, this person is named Jehoaddah *[yĕhôʿaddâ]*, and the more important LXX manuscripts to 1 Chr 9:42 read *Iada.* Finally, the etymology of MT's Jarah, somehow connected to *yʿr* "forest," is problematic; *yʿr* is not used in other Hebrew personal names, though it is known from NW Semitic names (Benz 1972: 324). Thus many scholars, accepting the LXX, have emended the name to Jadah (Heb *yaʿdâ*) (Noth *IPN,* 246; Rudolph *Chronikbücher* HAT, 90; *HALAT,* 404), which is etymologically related to "ornaments," and incorporates the element *ʿdh* typically used in Israelite names (Fowler *TPNAH,* 353–54). This emendation assumes confusion between the letters *dalet* and *reš,* which were graphically similar in both the old and new scripts. Many clear cases of *d-r* interchange are attested to (Delitzsch 1920: 105–7). The name Jenoaddah in the MT of the parallel genealogy would then be seen as an expansionistic form of an original Jadah. Alternatively, Demsky (1971: 19) has shown that this section of the Benjaminite genealogy relates various Benjaminite clans through geographical locations; he thus suggests that Jarah be connected to Kiriath-Jearim. If this is correct, the readings in the LXX and in 1 Chr 9:42 are scribal errors or are secondary attempts to understand the unusual personal name Jarah.

Bibliography

Benz, F. L. 1972. *Personal Names in the Phoenician and Punic Inscriptions.* Studia Pohl 18. Rome.

Delitzsch, F. 1920. *Die Lese- und Schreibfehler im Alten Testament.* Berlin.

Demsky, A. 1971. The Genealogy of Gibeon (1 Chronicles 9:35–44): Biblical and Epigraphic Considerations. *BASOR* 202: 16–23.

MARC Z. BRETTLER

JARBA, ʿEIN EL- (M.R. 162227). A site located in the SW part of the Plain of Esdraelon about 100 m N of the Jokneam–Megiddo road, an area rich in springs and containing many prehistoric sites. In 1955, during the digging of a nearby drainage channel, fragments of pottery (including a hole-mouth jar decorated with reliefs of dancing people masked like rams), stone vessels, and flints were brought to the surface, all belonging to the Wadi Rabah culture. See RABAH, WADI.

In excavations in the drainage channel during July 1967, 4 strata of settlement (all belonging to the Wadi Rabah culture) were identified. In stratum I, close to the surface, only scattered stones but no buildings had survived, although parts of structures were uncovered in strata II–III. These consisted of a rectangular room with an enclosed courtyard adjacent. In stratum IV (on virgin soil) were discovered two sections of thin walls. Near one wall was a secondary burial, containing parts of 5 human skulls and fragments of a large jar, which probably served as a funerary offering. The decorated hole-mouth jar mentioned above, whose base was found in situ, apparently had also been deposited as one of the grave goods. A hearth and 7 shallow pits dug into the virgin soil were also discovered. Elliptical-shaped plastered floors were uncovered in all 4 strata, suggesting that these all existed close in time.

The pottery finds included all types of vessels and decorations already known from the excavations at Wadi Rabah and other sites attesting that culture. It also included hitherto unattested types of vessels and decoration (e.g., the hole-mouth jar with dancing figures, and the large jar of stratum IV). Carbon 14 tests from level IV indicate a date of 3740 B.C. ± 140 years. Even assuming that ʿEin el-Jarba is not the oldest Wadi Rabah settlement, it is hard to conceive that other sites of this culture will be attested earlier than 4000 B.C. The excavations at ʿEin el-Jarba have therefore added to our knowledge of the Wadi Rabah culture and of the Chalcolithic period in Palestine in general.

Bibliography

Kaplan, J. 1969. ᶜEin el-Jarba. *BASOR* 194: 2–39.

JACOB KAPLAN

JARED (PERSON) [Heb *yered; yāred*]. Son of Mahalalel, born when Mahalalel was 65 years old (Gen 5:15–20). At 162 years of age, Jared sired Enoch. Jared lived a total of 962 years. Comparison with the genealogy of Cain in Genesis 4 has suggested a correspondence between Jared and Irad (Gabriel 1959: 417; *GHBW,* 161; Sasson 1978: 174). However, the initial consonants of the two names differ (*ᶜayin* vs. *yod*) to such an extent as to render explanations of parallel development from a common source unlikely. Explanations for the name Jared include: the Hebrew word for "rose" (Noth *IPN,* 231); the Akkadian word for "servant," *(w)ardu* (*HALAT* 2: 416); the Arabic word for "courageous"; the Hebrew root, *yrd,* "to descend." Noth's analysis is possible, but it lacks parallels. While the use of the Akkadian *(w)ardu* in personal names is extremely common, the word does not appear in W Semitic. There it is replaced by the root *ᶜbd,* which is rendered *abdu* in cuneiform. The suggestion of an Arabic cognate also reaches outside of the W Semitic world for a comparison. On the other hand, the Hebrew root, *yrd,* "to descend," does appear in W Semitic personal names.

Bibliography

Gabriel, J. 1959. Die Kainitengenealogie. Gn 4, 17–24. *Bib* 40: 409–27.

Sasson, J. M. 1978. A Genealogical "Convention" in Biblical Chronography? *ZAW* 90: 171–85.

RICHARD S. HESS

JARHA (PERSON) [Heb *yarḥāᶜ*]. An Egyptian slave of Sheshan, who married his master's daughter (Ahlai?) and became the founder of a house of the Jerahmeelites (1 Chr 2:34, 35) cf v 31. No additional information is provided for this Egyptian. His 13 descendants can not be identified with any degree of certainty with names occurring elsewhere in the OT. The identity of Jarha's wife is a complex and unsolved problem centering on the name Ahlai. The masculine form of this name (however see Keil 1872: 67) and its appearance in the list of David's mighty men (1 Chr 11:41) presents some problem to this conclusion. Consequently, some suggest that Ahlai of v 31 should be read Attai as in v 36; or that Ahlai (if modified to mean "a brother to me") was a name given to Jarha at the time of his adoption into the family of Sheshan; or that Ahlai, though a son of Sheshan, was born after the marriage of his daughter (however note v 34); or that different sources are reflected in this genealogy. See Williamson (1979: 352) for a recent discussion of sources in this genealogy and the conclusion that 2:25–33 and 42–50a stand as a related unit, but that v 34 reflects a different source. See also Curtis (*Chronicles* ICC, 83) for an analysis of older, but still-debated, theories of genealogical sources. The wording of v 35 "So Sheshan gave his daughter in marriage to Jarha his slave . . ." is considered by some commentators as equivalent to making his servant his heir (Elmslie *Chronicles* CBC, 19), similar to Eliezer's relationship to Abraham (Gen 15:2–3). See NUZI for discussions of patriarchal customs possibly reflecting similar arrangements. From such records, a few scholars consider Jarha a proselyte and date this incident to the period of sojourn in Egypt; others, however, consider it difficult to understand how an Egyptian could be a slave to an Israelite at that time. Still others regard Jarha as an eponym of Jerahmeel and proceed to identify Sheshan with Sheshai of Hebron, concluding that the genealogy presents a northward movement of this tribe to the area around Hebron. Locating Jarha in time is difficult, and suggestions range from shortly before the Exodus (Keil 1872: 67) to the days of Eli, or even to some date nearer to the Chronicler's own time (see Braun, *Chronicles* WBC, 46). Lacking sufficient evidence the question must remain open.

Bibliography

Keil, C. F. 1872. *The Books of Chronicles.* Vol. 3 in *Commentary on the Old Testament.* Grand Rapids. Repr. 1978.

Williamson, H. G. M. 1979. Sources and Redaction in the Chronicler's Genealogy of Judah. *JBL* 98: 351–59.

W. P. STEEGER

JARIB (PERSON) [Heb *yārîb*]. A personal name utilizing an imperfect form of the verb *ryb* ("strive," "contend") and translated "he contends" in the sense of conducting a legal case or suit on behalf of someone. It may also mean "may he (i.e. Yahweh) contend" thus suggesting the possibility that it is a shortened form of *yĕ(h)ôyārîb* (*IPN,* 201, 245). See JOIARIB. Three individuals are so named.

1. The third of 5 sons of Simeon as recorded only by the Chronicler (1 Chr 4:24). In the other Simeonite lists (Gen 46:10, Exod 6:15—both of which name 6 sons; Num 26:12) the name *yākin* appears. See JACHIN.

2. One of 11 (Ezra 8:16) or 10 (1 Esdr 8:43—Eng 8:44) men who were sent by Ezra to Iddo at "Casiphia the place" with a request for "ministers for the house of our God" (Ezra 8:17) or "men to serve as priests in the house of our Lord" (1 Esdr 8:45—Eng 8:46). In Ezra he is listed among 9 "heads," understood by Blenkinsopp (*Ezra-Nehemiah* OTL, 164) as "heads of ancestral houses" with the 2 remaining individuals described as possessing understanding. When these 2 last-mentioned individuals—Joiarib (maybe a longer form of Jarib) and Elnathan (mentioned twice previously)—are deleted as a misplaced marginal gloss (Rudolph *Esra und Nehemia* HAT, 80; Williamson *Ezra-Nehemiah* WBC, 113), both designations ("head" and "understanding") apply to Jarib's group. In 1 Esdr he (Gk *Iōribos*) is included among 10 who are described as "leaders" and "wise" (8:43—Eng 8:44).

3. A priest of the house of Jeshua, son of Jozadak, who had married a foreign woman and pledged to put her away and offer a ram as a guilt offering (Ezra 10:18; 1 Esdr 9:19).

RODNEY H. SHEARER

JARMUTH (PLACE) [Heb *yarmût*]. The name of 2 towns in ancient Israel.

1. A town of Issachar which was allotted to the Gershonite family of the Levites as part of their inheritance (Josh

21:29). In a parallel list of the Levitical cities (1 Chr 6:57–58—Eng 6:72–73) the order of the towns appears to be the same, but Jarmuth is called Ramoth (Heb *raʾmôt;* in which the *ʾalep* appears to function as a vowel letter [cf. GKC 7]). Ramoth, in turn, is probably a variation of the name Remeth (Josh 19:21; Heb *remet*). Each of these renderings preserve the same essential consonantal arrangements. The LXX refers to the town by various names: *Rhemmath* or *Iermōth* (Josh 21:29), and *Rhemmas* or *Rhamath* (Josh 19:21, B and A respectively).

Some earlier scholarship sought to identify the site with a village, *er-Rameh,* approximately 11 miles SW of Jenin (*ISBE* 4: 2557). While this site preserves the consonantal tradition, it lay outside Issachar's borders and hence is not likely the location of Remeth (or of Jarmuth).

In 1921, C. S. Fisher discovered a basalt stele at the site of Bethshan. While the stele was found in secondary use in Byzantine levels, it contained a hieroglyphic inscription of Seti I (ca. 1300 B.C.; Rowe 1930: 29–30). The inscription refers to some disturbances involving the *ʿapiru* of Mount Yarmuta and a group called "Teyer . . ." (so *ANET,* 255; but cf. Albright 1952) who were attacking Asiatics. Seti dispatched a contingent of infantry and chariotry who purportedly suppressed the rebellion and returned in 2 days.

While the plain of Issachar is not particularly mountainous or hilly, the most impressive site is the location of the Crusader castle of Belvoir (M.R. 199222), which Aharoni suggests as the possible site of Jarmuth (*LBHG,* 28). While only 312 m above sea level, it appears more dramatically high as it stands 550 m above the Jordan Valley providing a panoramic view of the valley into Gilead (*EAEHL* 1: 179). If the names of the site—*yarmût, raʾmôt,* and *remet*—are all derived from the Heb root *rûm* ("be high, rise"; cf. BDB, 926–28), then several elements converge to lend credence to the identification of Belvoir with Jarmuth: (1) the correlation of the linguistic evidence with the geographic prominence of the site; (2) the inscriptional evidence of Seti I and its reference to a "Mount Yarmuta"; (3) its location within the recognized borders of Issachar; and (4) its proximity to Beth-shan (ca. 10 km N) which puts it within range of a two-day long military mission.

However, a significant and serious detraction from this identification is that essentially no Iron Age materials are known from the site. It is possible that either Crusader construction techniques have obliterated underlying ruins (which sometimes is the case), or the identification of Jarmuth with Belvoir is erroneous. Obviously, further investigation is necessary.

Bibliography

Albright, W. F. 1952. The Smaller Beth-shan Stele of Sethos I (1309–1290 B.C.). *BASOR* 125: 24–32.

Rowe, A. 1930. *The Topography and History of Beth-shan.* Philadelphia.

DALE W. MANOR

2. A town which joined the S Canaanite coalition (Jerusalem, Hebron, Jarmuth, Lachish, and Eglon) against Joshua (Josh 10:3, 5), whose king Joshua temporarily imprisoned in a cave before executing him (Josh 10:23; 12:11). The town was allotted to Judah (Josh 15:35) and was reoccupied following the return from Exile (Neh 11:29).

The biblical site is identified with a Byzantine village by the name of *Iermochos,* which is about 10 miles from Beth Govrin (Eleutheropolis) on the road to Jerusalem. Eusebius (*Onomast.* 106.24) identified this site with the LXX *Iermous.* This identification is now generally accepted, although archaeological evidence has neither confirmed nor dismissed its biblical connection. It is located (M.R. 147124) ca. 25 km SW of Jerusalem in the central Shephelah between the Sorek and Elah valleys. The site covers ca. 40 acres (640 × 420 m) including a small acropolis (ca. 3 acres).

First described by V. Guérin, who visited it in 1854 and suggested its biblical identification, the site was tested in 1970 by A. Ben-Tor and has been excavated since 1980 by P. de Miroschedji. Both the acropolis and the lower city were first settled during the 2d half of the 4th millennium B.C. (EB I) and was continuously occupied until the end of the EB III, ca. 2300, when the entire settlement was abandoned. Reoccupation took place in the LB, but only on the acropolis and its immediate vicinity. This restricted area remained inhabited more or less continuously until the 4th century A.D., when some sectors of the lower city were settled again for a brief period.

The EB II–III city was protected by a fortification system of exceptional size and complexity. Built in the early EB II, ca. 2900 B.C., the first rampart consisted of a stone wall 5–6 m thick with large buttresses placed at regular intervals and a massive stone bastion (30 × 15 m) in the corner. This rampart was later reinforced with a glacis, part stone and part earth. A second wall 3 m thick with cyclopean masonry was erected at the end of the EB II, bringing the total thickness of the fortification system to nearly 40 m. The area between the 2 walls was later subjected to a vast terracing operation. Finally, 6 monumental platforms, 30–40 × 10–12 m, were built in this intermediate space along the corner of the city in the EB III.

Access to this part of the city was through a monumental gate established in the outer wall. During the EB III period, it underwent several changes and rebuildings. It was approached from the outside by means of a plastered ramp limited on both sides by retaining walls. Rebuilt and raised 3 times, the ramp climbed in its final stage to nearly 8 m above bedrock.

A prominent feature of the topography of Tell Jarmuth is the existence over the slopes of the entire lower city of a terrace system with retaining walls up to 6 m high. The excavations suggest that these were artificial terraces built with a fill of stone with inner partition walls. Each supported a series of constructions which, once destroyed and levelled, served as foundations for new buildings.

The EB III strata have been extensively cleared in 3 areas in the lower city. Large buildings of a public character were identified in area C. The most interesting is the so-called "White Building," probably a sanctuary. It is a rectangular hall of the broadroom type (13.5 × 6.75 m) with a central row of 4 pillars resting on large stone bases. The main entrance was through a door in the middle of the S facade. This building was part of an architectural complex including a chamber built around its SE corner, a courtyard established in front, and 2 adjacent rooms to the S. That this was a sanctuary is suggested by the typical features of its plan, its careful construction, and comparisons with similar buildings of a cultic nature, i.e., the temples at En-gedi (Chalcolithic), at Megiddo XIX (EB I), at ʿAi and Arad (EB II), and at Megiddo XV and Bâb edh-Dhrâʿ (EB III).

EB III private houses grouped in an *insula* surrounded by a street were also excavated (area G). The *insula* resulted from the progressive agglutination of several dwelling units which were modified, enlarged, and finally linked together. The typical dwelling was composed of 1 or 2 rooms and a courtyard with several domestic installations. On the other side of the lower city, an area of specialized activities, probably "industrial," has been identified (area H). A row of 6 small rooms and courtyards was cleared; they contained only coarse pottery, large mortars, and several enigmatic installations, including two kiln-like structures.

Given its size and the density of its construction, the EB III city of Jarmuth may have had a population of ca. 3,000, engaged mainly in agriculture (cereals, vegetables, grapes, and especially olives) and animal husbandry (mostly sheep and goats, cattle and donkeys being used for traction and transport). Finds indicate that the city had trade connections with the Golan in the N, the Dead Sea in the E, and the Negeb, and that it was in contact with Egypt. Tell Jarmuth is a type site for EB III pottery, where almost every known pottery shape is represented. An interesting corpus of EB III human and animal figurines was also discovered.

Soundings on the acropolis have revealed traces of more or less continuous occupation from the LB to the early Byzantine periods. Noteworthy is an Iron Age I destruction level dated to the mid-11th century with pottery similar to Tell Qasile XI–X. Surface finds include a Hellenistic cooking-pot handle bearing a stamp of a 5-pointed star and the letters *yršlm,* and a coin of Herod the Great. The early Byzantine remains (ca. 4th century A.D.) are represented on the acropolis by the ruins of a small village, to be identified with Eusebius' *Iermochos* and in the lower city by the remains of a large building, possibly square in plan and measuring ca. 75 m on each side. This complex was apparently unfinished and may have been intended as a large farm or a caravanserai.

Bibliography

Ben-Tor, A. 1975. The First Season of Excavations at Tell-Yarmuth: August 1970. *Qedem* 1: 55–87.

Miroschedji, P. de. 1985. Khirbet el-Yarmûk (Tell Yarmouth) 1984. *IEJ* 35: 71–73.

———. 1988. Khirbet el-Yarmûk (Tell Yarmouth) 1986–87. *RB* 95: 217–25.

Miroschedji, P. de et al. 1988. *Yarmouth 1.* Paris.

PIERRE DE MIROSCHEDJI

JAROAH

JAROAH (PERSON) [Heb *yārôaḥ*]. A Gadite, who was the grandfather of Abihail (1 Chr 5:14), the father of the 11 (or 10; see SHAPHAT) sons listed in 1 Chr 5:12–13. His name may be cognate with an Arabic term *(wariḥa)* that means "soft" or "delicate" (Noth *IPN,* 226). The several textual variants in 1 Chr 5:14 that concern the spelling of the Gadite's name probably arose from scribes confusing Hebrew letters that sounded or were written similarly (e.g., *ḥet* with *ʿayin* or *he,* and *reš* with *dalet*). Neither Jaroah nor the others named in the Chronicler's genealogy for Gad (1 Chr 5:11–17) appear in other lists of Gadites (Gen 46:16; Num 26:15–18; 1 Chr 12:9–16—Eng 12:8–15).

M. PATRICK GRAHAM

JASHAR, BOOK OF

JASHAR, BOOK OF [Heb *sēper hayyāšar*]. A lost source book of early Israelite poetry, quoted in Josh 10:12b–13a (Joshua's command to the sun and moon) and 2 Sam 1:19–27 (David's lament for Saul and Jonathan). A third probable excerpt appears in 1 Kgs 8:12–13, a couplet imbedded in Solomon's prayer at the dedication of the Temple, which survives in fullest form in the LXX where it appears at the end of the prayer, directing the reader to the "Book of the Song" (Gk *biblio tēs ōdēs*). It has been suggested that this reference stems from an accidental metathesis of letters in the Hebrew text *(šyr* for *yšr),* though the reverse is also possible.

The term "Jashar" is a common Hebrew word meaning "one who [or that which] is straight, honest, just, righteous, upright." Thus, it is commonly assumed that the title refers either to the heroic individuals who are the subjects of its contents or perhaps to all Israel as the upright people. If the latter is the case, the title may be related to the term Jeshurun, a variant form of the name Israel (cf. Deut 32:15 and 33:5, 26).

The 3 quotations from the Book of Jashar are all archaic poetry, which is sometimes designated "song" *(šyr)* elsewhere when inserted in prose contexts (cf. Exod 15:1; Num 21:17; Deut 31:30). Because of this fact, and because the term "Jashar" in the title has not been satisfactorily explained and is obviously similar to various forms of the verbal root *(šyr),* "to sing," some scholars have argued that the LXX rendering, "Book of Song," is the correct title. If so, there is some doubt whether the book ever existed in written form as such. The reference in each case may be to the familiar oral repertoire of professional singers in ancient Israel who preserved Israel's epic and lyric traditions within various worship settings, particularly in conjunction with the major festivals. In this regard it is interesting to note that the masculine noun *šîr* eventually becomes a specific term for Temple music on the part of Levitical choirs, with instrumental accompaniment (cf. 1 Chr 25:6–7).

The nature of the book may be inferred from its 3 citations. It seems to have been a collection of ancient national songs, the antiquity of which is suggested by the relatively poor state of preservation of the Hebrew text in each case. The book must have contained a variety of songs, for each of the 3 citations is quite different. The first (Josh 10:12b–13a) is apparently an ancient incantation addressed to the heavenly bodies to prolong daylight, or perhaps to lengthen predawn darkness—until Israel has time to complete its victory in battle against the Amorites (van den Bussche 1951; Eisler 1926; Holladay 1968). It has been rendered as follows:

Sun, stand still in Gibeon!
Moon, (stand still) in the valley of Aijalon!
The Sun stood still, the Moon stayed;
Until He had taken vengeance upon the nations of His enemies.

The second (2 Sam 1:19–27) is the well-known lament over Saul and Jonathan, which is a remarkable witness to David's poetic skill and to his personal friendship with the tragic heroes involved. The third (1 Kgs 8:12–13) appears to be a couplet taken from an ancient song establishing God's supremacy over nature and ritual, reminiscent of Ugaritic parallels (Loretz 1974; cf. also van den Born 1965); which has been translated:

A sun Yahweh established in the heavens,
but He hath purposed to dwell in thick darkness;
I have surely built a noble house for Thee,
a residence where Thou shalt dwell perpetually.

The content, structure, and origin of the Book of Jashar are all uncertain. In a detailed study of LXX traditions, Thackeray (1910) argued that the book included minor collections, like the Psalter, two of which are known: "Of the Children of Judah" and "Of the Children of Israel." He compared these names to both the J and E sources of Pentateuchal criticism and to the title "Of the children of Korah" in the Psalter, which apparently derived its title from a guild of temple singers in a later period. Some think the book was a written collection begun in premonarchic Israel and expanded from time to time. Others consider it a compilation of oral traditions, not earlier than the days of Solomon and perhaps much later. It's nearest parallel is the "Book of the Wars of the Lord" (Num 21:14). In fact, some scholars have identified these two books as one. There has been speculation as to whether such archaic works as the "Song of the Sea" (Exod 15:1–18), the Song of Miriam (Exod 15:21), the Song of Moses (Deut 32), the Song of Deborah (Judges 5), and the Song of Hannah (1 Sam 2:1–10) were included in these ancient anthologies of Israel's heroic past. If these collections are understood to be the oral repertoire of Israel's professional singers, there is little difficulty including such works in the so-called Book of Jashar (see Mowinckel 1935; Nielsen 1954: 39–62).

The mysterious nature of the Book of Jashar has given rise to false identifications and imitations of the book. The Talmud (*ᶜAbod. Zar.* 25a) homiletically identifies the Book of Jashar with the "book of Abraham, Isaac, and Jacob" (i.e. Genesis), who were "upright." Certain ancient Jewish commentators considered the title to be a reference to the Torah. A medieval Book of Jashar paralleled, in part, the pseudepigraphic *Testament of Judah.* Still other medieval rabbinical works with this title appeared. An interesting example of a more recent forgery from Christian circles is associated with Alcuin, Bishop of Canterbury (d. A.D. 804), who is said to have discovered it in the city of Gazna on a "Pilgrimage into the Holy Land, and Persia." First published in 1829, it is reputed to have been the words of "Jashar, the son of Caleb" rediscovered in England in 1721. The Rosicrucian Order published a 5th edition of this particular text in 1953.

Bibliography

Born, A. von den. 1965. Zum Tempelweihespruch (1 Kgs 8:12f). *OTS* 14: 235–44.
Bussche, H. van den. 1951. Het zogennaamd sonnewonder in Jos. 10:12–15. *Collationes Gandavenses* 1: 48–53.
Eisler, R. 1926. Joshua and the Sun. *AJSL* 42: 73–85.
Holladay, J. S. 1968. The Day(s) the Moon Stood Still. *JBL* 87: 166–78.
Loretz, O. 1974. Der Torso eines kanaanaisch-israelitischen Tempelweihespruches in 1 Kon 8:12–13. *UF* 6: 478–80.
Mowinckel, S. 1935. Hat es ein israelitisches Nationalepos gegeben? *ZAW* N.F. 12: 130–52.
Nielsen, E. 1954. *Oral Tradition.* Chicago.
Thackeray, H. St. J. 1910. New Light on the Book of Jashar (A Study of 3 Regn. VIII 53b LXX). *JTS* 11: 518–32.

DUANE L. CHRISTENSEN

JASHEN (PERSON) [Heb *yāšēn*]. One of the members of the "the Thirty," the elite class of David's warriors (2 Sam 23:32 = 1 Chr 11:34). He was known as "the Gizonite," probably a description of the location of his origin. Both the personal name, Jashen, and the qualifying adjective, Gizonite, are uncertain due to the corrupt condition of the text in 2 Sam 23:32 (cf. 1 Chr 11:34) but are regarded by scholars as highly probable readings. The evidence and argument for them follows.

(1) The Hebrew orthography of 2 Sam 23:24 reads: *ʾlyḥbʾ hšᶜlbny bny yšn yhwntn* ("Eliahba the Shaalbonite, the sons of Yashen, Jonathan"). The referent for *bny yšn* (sons of Jashen) is missing in the text. The expression has become *bny hšm* ("sons of fame") in 1 Chronicles as an attempt to make sense of it, but the referent is still lacking. (2) The word *bny* can be explained as dittography, the last 3 letters of the previous word *(hšᶜlbny)* being the same (Luc does not translate *bny*). (3) The name, Jashen, does not have a qualifying adjective in 2 Samuel. This would be anomalous in the list of the warriors there, since every name is qualified by either a patronymic or a gentilic (accepting with LXX a patronymic for Jonathan). The missing description is preserved in 1 Chronicles as "the Gizonite."

A problem, however, remains. The term "Gizonite" is unique in MT and there is no evidence of a proper noun "Gizon." Two solutions have been proposed: (1) The LXX reads *Gōuni* (A), "the Gunite," a reference to a man who was the head of a clan in the tribe of Napthali (Num 26:48). This reading has arisen as a result of confusing the Heb *zayin* for *waw.* (2) The reading is a textual corruption of "Gimzoni," and thus a reference to the town, Gimzo, in S Judah (Elliger 1966: 73 n. 4, 96–97).

Bibliography

Elliger, K. 1966. Die dreissig Helden Davids. *KlSchr,* 72–118.

STEPHEN G. DEMPSTER

JASHOBEAM (PERSON) [Heb *yāšābĕᶜām*]. Var. JOSHEB-BASSHEBETH. **1.** One of David's champions, a select class of warriors directly attached to the king for special assignments (1 Chr 11:10–47, v 11; = 2 Sam 23:8–39, v 8 in which the variant Josheb-Basshebeth occurs).

Jashobeam is identified as "a son of Hachmoni" (RSV "a Hachmonite"), a designation which means either he is a descendent of the unknown person Hachmoni or is one who came from an unidentified people or place named "Hachmon" (see, also, the variant in 2 Sam 23:8, "Tahchemonite"). Jashobeam stands exalted as foremost among David's champions, identified as the chief of a military unit of some sort, which due to the ambiguity of the term has been understood variously as: "the thirty," according to the consonantal text of the MT; "the officers," a conjectured meaning in accord with the vowel pointing of the MT; or "the three/s." As an example of his prowess, he is said to have killed 300 men with his spear in one encounter. The higher number of 800 in the parallel text (2 Sam 23:8) is to be preferred, since his exploits presumably surpassed that of Abishai (1 Chr 11:30–31 = 2 Sam 23:18–19; Williamson *Chronicles* NCBC, 102).

In certain Gk mss, both at 1 Chr 11:11 and 2 Sam 23:8, one finds a variant name *Iesbaal,* which would be the equivalent of the Heb *yišbaʿal* (possibly meaning, "man of Baal" [BDB, 36; for a review of contrary opinions see Tsevat 1975: 77–79; *TPNAH,* 57]). Generally, this name has been recognized as the original name. If this is the case, the form "Jashobeam" might have arisen through a confusion of the final letters, an *m* in the place of the *l.* The form of this name found in 2 Samuel is generally explained as having arisen in two steps. First, the element *bōšet,* "shame," was deliberately substituted for "baal," a term which could mean "lord" and refer to Yahweh, but which also was a title for a Canaanite god and, therefore, presented the possibility of theological offense (postulated first by Geiger, followed by Wellhausen and others; see *NHT,* 253–55, 363–64). (A tendency to transform names compounded with the element "baal" does not occur in Chronicles.) Secondly, an accidental repetition of the letter *b* occurred. Contrary to the above thesis, it has been pointed out that the element *baštu* occurs in Akkadian names in which it means "dignity, pride, vigor" or possibly "guardian angel, patron saint"; several characters in the OT were known by more than one name, and the postulated principle of substitution meets with various inconsistencies (Tsevat 1975: 75, 84–86).

Apparently the same Jashobeam is mentioned in a list of commanders found in 1 Chr 27:1–15 (v 2), since this list mentions 11 other mighty men found in 1 Chr 11:10–47. Here he is designated as the "son of Zabdiel" (v 2) and a "descendant of Perez" (v 3) of the tribe of Judah, a designation which differs from that of 1 Chr 11:11. Differences between the two lists in 1 Chronicles suggest that the composition of neither was dependent upon the other (Williamson *Chronicles* NCBC, 174). These commanders were each in charge of a monthly course of 24,000 men (or possibly 24 "units," rather than "thousands," Myers *Chronicles* AB, 183, 53, 98) in the armed service of the king; Jashobeam was in charge of the first month. This list of commanders and their functions is possibly a construct of its composer, since (a) no such monthly, conscripted, civilian army is mentioned elsewhere during David's reign; (b) the large number of 288,000 men, if the term is understood correctly, is improbable; and (c) one of the commanders, Asahel (v 7) was dead before David had rule over all Israel (Williamson *Chronicles* NCBC, 174–75). However, the author/redactor's thesis—that David made preparations for the proper ongoing cultic and national life of Israel (as illustrated throughout chapters 23–27)—draws on the fact that David took a census (vv 23–24; chap 21) which could have been utilized for designing a monthly plan of conscription; such a plan would have been analogous to Solomon's monthly courses for his provision (1 Kgs 4:7–19).

2. One of a group of Benjaminite warriors who defected from Saul, also a Benjaminite, and who gave their allegiance to David at Ziklag during the period in which David was banned from Saul's court (1 Chr 12:1–7). These men were noted for their ambidextrous fighting skills as bowmen and stone slingers (Judg 20:16). This Jashobeam is designated a "Korahite," and would, therefore, appear to be a different individual from the Jashobeam of 1 Chr 11:11 and 27:2. If the designation "Korahite" is a reference to the Levitical family of Korah, then Jashobeam was a Levite would had resided in Benjaminite territory. Otherwise, he originated from an unknown place named "Korah" (Rudolph *Chronikbücher* HAT, 104); or, as Miller (1970: 66–67) has suggested, there is some confusion in the list, and Jashobeam was really a non-Benjaminite who came from a group of Korahites located in S Judah.

Bibliography

Miller, J. M. 1970. The Korahites of Southern Judah. *CBQ* 32: 58–68.

Tsevat, M. 1975. Ishbosheth and Congeners: The Names and Their Study. *HUCA* 46: 71–87.

RODNEY K. DUKE

JASHUB (PERSON) [Heb *yāšûb*]. The name of 2 individuals in the Hebrew Bible. Noth categorized "Jasub" as a "wish name" which means "may be (Yaweh) turn (to us again)" (*IPN*, 199).

1. One of the 4 sons of Issachar (Num 26:24; 1 Chr 7:1 [K *yšyb,* Q *yāšûb*]). Noth also stated that the section concerning Issachar in Num 26:23–27 appears in its "original form without additions" (*Numbers* OTL, 206). But Meyers argued that the final editor of the genealogy in 1 Chronicles probably drew from several census lists whose significance was lost (*1 Chronicles* AB, 53), while Williamson detected a military census put in genealogical form (*Chronicles* NCBC, 76). The 2 lists agree substantially, with only a slight variation in the spelling of one of the sons (Puvah [Num 26:23] and Puah [1 Chr 7:1]). The genealogy of Gen 46:8–27 names Iob (Heb *yôb*) instead of Jashub (v 13—LXX v 20). The LXX and the Samaritan Pentateuch list Jashub here, but these are probably corrections based on the texts in Numbers and 1 Chronicles. Even so, Jashub may be taken as part of the most ancient census tradition.

2. A descendent of Bani and one of the returned exiles who was required by Ezra to divorce his foreign wife (Ezra 10:29 = 1 Esdr 9:30). Jashub was a member of a family from which a group of exiles returned with Zerubbabel (Ezra 2:10; cf. Neh 7:8 which lists the family of Binnui). For further discussion, see BEDEIAH.

JEFFREY A. FAGER

JASON (PERSON) [Gk *Iasōn*]. **1.** A Christian in Thessalonica (Acts 17:5–9). Because his Greek name was often used in the Diaspora for such Hebrew names as Joshua or Jeshua, it may be assumed he was a Hellenistic Jew, and probably one of those converted during Paul's preaching in the Thessalonian synagogue (17:2–4). Jason became host to Paul and Silas (17:7), and it was therefore his house which was attacked by those in opposition to the missionaries. When the mob could not find Paul and Silas, they dragged Jason and other brethren to the city authorities. Jason was accused of welcoming people who had "turned the world upside down" (17:6). He and his guests were said to be "acting against the decrees of Caesar, saying that there is another king, Jesus" (17:7). Only when Jason and the others posted bond were they let go (17:9).

Jason may have been prosperous since he could offer hospitality to Paul and Silas and apparently host as well the housechurch they had begun. Once the missionaries had left Thessalonica, Jason probably was locally recognized as the leader of the church. It has generally been assumed that he and the brethren were arrested in Paul's stead and that the security they supplied functioned as a promise to the authorities to keep Paul from returning. Yet it is quite probable that Jason was in trouble not merely by default, but in his own right. Evidence for this is that the bond he posted seems related not directly to Paul's activities but rather to actions by the church members themselves (Jewett 1986: 117; cf. Gillman fc.). Whatever these actions were, they resulted in ongoing suffering for the Thessalonian Christians at the hands of their "countrymen" after Paul had left (1 Thess 2:14). A further argument that Jason's bond did not relate to Paul is the latter's remark in 1 Thess 2:18 that he had attempted to return to Thessalonica "again and again—but Satan hindered us." Paul attributes his inability to return not to a bond, but to Satan (Whitely 1969: 49–50). In sum, these observations suggest another perspective than the traditional view that Jason was a person who ended up in trouble with the authorities primarily because Paul could not be found. Jason and his brethren evidently posted bond for their own independent actions.

2. A person who along with two others, Lucius and Sosipater, is identified as one of Paul's kinsmen; thus a fellow Jewish Christian (Rom 16:21). Paul conveys greetings from these 3 to the recipients of Romans. This indicates that a person named Jason was present with Paul in Corinth as he wrote Romans, presumably ca. 58 C.E.

Although the commonality of the name argues against too readily equating this Jason in Corinth with Jason of Thessalonica, in fact it is probable that the two were the same person (Cranfield *Romans* ICC, 805–6). The association of Jason with Sosipater in Rom 16:21 when read in conjunction with Acts 20:4 suggests the link. Among those who travel with Paul after he leaves Corinth according to 20:4 are said to be Sopater of Beroea and various Thessalonians (Jason is not one of those named, however). Since Sopater's name is a shortened form of Sosipater and his town, Beroea, was located near Thessalonica, it seems that Sosipater and Jason of Rom 16:21 were in fact companions from Beroea and Thessalonica respectively. On this supposition, Rom 16:21 adds to what can be known of Jason of Thessalonica from Acts 17:5–9 that he was definitely a Jew and that at some point in the years following the Thessalonian church's founding, he apparently left to travel or move with Paul to Corinth.

Bibliography

Gillman, F. M. fc. Jason of Thessalonica. In *BETL*.

Jewett, R. 1986. *The Thessalonian Correspondence: Pauline Rhetoric and Millenarian Piety*. Philadelphia.

Manus, C. fc. In *BETL*.

Whitely, D. E. H. 1969. *Thessalonians*. Oxford.

FLORENCE MORGAN GILLMAN

JATHAN (PERSON) [Gk *Iathan*]. A son of Shemaiah and a possible kinsman of Tobit (Tob 5:14—Eng 5:13). The archangel Raphael (sent by God to help cure Tobit's blindness) identified himself as Azarias, the son of Ananias, a relative of Tobit. Tobit, in turn, mentioned the brothers Ananias and Jathan as persons with whom he used to travel to Jerusalem to pay his tithes. One might infer that Jathan was a kinsman of Tobit, though the text does not say so explicitly, and that Tobit might have been related to Ananias through marriage, and not to Jathan at all. While Codices Alexandrinus and Vaticanus read the name as "Jathan," Sinaiticus reads it as "Nathan." The second reading suggests a play on names. The name "Ananias" means "God favors," and the name "Nathan" means "he gives." Zimmermann (1958: 75) argues that the previous verse (5:13—Eng 5:12) exhibits word plays on the names Azariah (God helps) and Ananias (God favors). (Cf. 6:6 for another word play on Azariah.) Given the proclivity for word plays on names in the book of Tobit and its fictional character, the author of Tobit and/or the translator of Sinaiticus may have intended to delight the reader with the names "God favors" and "he gives" as those persons with whom Tobit worshipped in Jersualem.

Bibliography

Zimmermann, F. 1958. *The Book of Tobit*. New York.

PAUL L. REDDITT

JATHNIEL (PERSON) [Heb *yatnîʾēl*]. A Levitical gatekeeper from the Korahite family of Meshelemiah. The fourth son of this family, he is named only in 1 Chr 26:2, in the Chronicler's (Williamson *Chronicles* NCBC, 169) or perhaps a later (Rudolph *Chronikbücher* HAT, 173) organization of the gatekeepers in the temple at Jerusalem. The Lucianic recension renders this etymologically obscure (*IPN*, 248) name *Nathanaēl* (compare the Syriac, *ntnʾjl*).

J. S. ROGERS

JATTIR (PLACE) [Heb *yattîr*]. The third Levitical city in the Judah/Simeon list. There are no Hebrew variations in either the Joshua (21:14) or 1 Chronicles (6:42—Eng 6:57) account. Besides being mentioned in the 2 Levitical city lists, Jattir appears in the allotment to Judah (Josh 15:48). Here Jattir is described as being in the hill country. Jattir also appears in one of the stories about David and the Amalekites. When David arrived at Ziklag and saw the city burned by the Amalekites he inquired of the Lord what he should do. He was instructed to pursue and overtake the Amalekites and did so. The victory was great, only 400 young men and camels escaped. David's spoil was large; he recovered everything the Amalekites had taken from Ziklag, all of the flocks and herds, "nothing was missing, whether small or great, sons and daughters" (1 Sam 30:19). Then David divided the spoils, sending them to the elders of Judah. One of the recipients was the elder in Jattir (1 Sam 30:27).

Biblical Jattir has been identified with Khirbet ʿAttir (M.R. 151084). Khirbet ʿAttir is in the rolling hill and mountainous country NE of Beer-sheba, lying at one of the S outreaches of mountains stretching into the Negeb flatlands. The site is located 21 km SW of Hebron, 7 km SW of es-Samûʿ and 15 km SE of Tell Beit Mirsim. It is a difficult site to reach because of the rugged terrain.

Eusebius (*Onomast.* 108) was the first geographer to mention Jattir, but it was Robinson (1841: 194) who made the association between Jattir and Khirbet ʿAttir. The identification of Jattir with Khirbet ʿAttir has been accepted by Guérin (1869: 199), Conder and Kitchener (1881: 408), Alt (1932: 15), Noth (*Josua* HAT, 97), and Boling (*Joshua* AB, 493).

There have been numerous surveys conducted at Khirbet ʿAttir, but very few identifying the historical occupation of the site. Although the Archaeological Survey of Israel in 1967–68 examined many tells in the region S of Hebron, Khirbet ʿAttir was not one of them. In 1971 the Levitical City Survey found that the earliest occupation at Khirbet ʿAttir was late Iron II. There was also pottery from the Hellenistic, Roman, Islamic, and Arabic periods. Most of the Iron II pottery comes from the 7th/6th centuries; the 8th century was also represented. The identification of Khirbet ʿAttir with biblical Jattir stands. Although the archaeological evidence does not support an occupation of the site during the conquests of King David, it was occupied during the writing of the Deuteronomistic history.

Bibliography

Albright, W. F. 1945. The List of Levitic Cities. Pp. 49–73 in *Louis Ginzberg Jubilee Volume.* New York.

Alt, A. 1932. Das Institut im Jahre 1931. *PJB* 28: 5–47.

Conder, C. R., and Kitchener, H. H. 1881. *The Survey of Western Palestine.* Vol. 1. London.

Guérin, M. V. 1869. *Description Géographie, historique et archaéologique de la Palestine.* Vol. 3, *Judee.* Paris.

Peterson, J. L. 1977. *A Topographical Surface Survey of the Levitical "Cities" of Joshua 21 and I Chronicles 6.* Diss. Seabury-Western Theological Seminary.

Robinson, E. 1841. *Biblical Researches in Palestine.* Vol. 2. Boston.

JOHN L. PETERSON

JAVAN (PERSON) [Heb *yāwān*]. One of 7 sons of Japheth and a grandson of Noah according to the Table of Nations (Gen 10:2) and the parallel genealogy in 1 Chr 1:5. The former text presents him as the ancestor of maritime peoples ("islands of the nations," Gen 10:5). This refers to the area of the Aegean and E Mediterranean seas, as is shown by the inclusion of Elishah (Alashiya, Crete) and Kittim (Cyprus; Gen 10:4; 1 Chr 1:7) in the list. Maritime trade of Javan is highlighted in Ezek 27:13, 19, while their distance from Palestine is the point of Isa 66:19. This distance explains the severity of the wrong inflicted on the Judeans by the Tyrians and Sidonians, who sold them into captivity even as far away as Javan (Joel 3:6).

Javan is to be identified with Ionia, an area of Greek settlement in SW Asia Minor from at least the 1st millennium B.C., and possibly several centuries earlier. Cities in the area included Smyrna and Ephesus (cf. Rev 2:1–11). Contact between the Greeks and the Assyrians as early as the reign of Sargon II (8th century B.C.) is shown from Akkadian records, which call the area Jawan or Jaman (Parpola 1970: 186–87). Under Cyrus (late 6th century B.C.), this coastal area of Asia Minor became the satrapy of Ionia. Later the name was expanded to describe the entire Greek population on both sides of the Aegean—an example of the whole being identified by one of its parts, as in our use of the name Russia. Because of the territorial expansion of the Greeks under Alexander the Great (4th century B.C.), the related term Javana is known even in the Sanskrit of India.

The extended usage of the name is evident in the book of Daniel. Here the empire of the Persians will be replaced by that of Javan and its king, referring to Alexander (Dan 8:21; 10:20; 11:2). This, yet another foreign domination, will not satisfy Israel. Rather they will rise against their Greek overlords (Zech 9:13), possibly a prophetic allusion to the period of the Maccabees (mid-2d century B.C.).

A second identification of a more limited use of the name Javan associates it with Gaza (Berger). Some have proposed this based on the collocation of Javan with the Danites (Ezek 27:19), a tribe which has early S ties. The LXX and several other Greek and Persian texts also support this identification. This interpretation cannot be valid for most of the uses of Javan, however, because of its much more northerly association in most texts.

Bibliography

Berger, P.-R. 1982. Ellasar, Tarschisch und Jawan, Gn 14 und 10. *WO* 13: 68–73.

Parpola, S. 1970. *Neo-Assyrian Toponyms.* AOAT 6. Neukirchen-Vluyn.

DAVID W. BAKER

JAVELIN. See WEAPONS AND IMPLEMENTS OF WARFARE.

JAZER (PLACE) [Heb *yaʿzēr*]. The fourth Levitical city allotted to the tribe of Gad is Jazer (Josh 21:39, 1 Chr 6:66—Eng 6:81). This city is mentioned many times in the OT, but its location is obscure. Jazer is first cited in the conquest narratives in Numbers and in an inheritance account in Joshua. When the Israelites arrived in the land of the Amorites, Moses sent messengers to Sihon to request permission to pass through the land; but Sihon refused. As a result Sihon came to Jahaz and fought against Israel. The forces of Israel were victorious "and took possession of his land from the Arnon to the Jabbok, as far as to the Ammonites: for Jazer was the boundary of the Ammonites" (Num 21:24). Israel therefore dwelt in the land of the Amorites and "Moses sent to spy out Jazer; and they took its villages, and dispossessed the Amorites that were there" (Num 21:31). Jazer is to be understood not only as a city, but also as the name of a region. In Num 32:1 the land of Jazer is described as a place for grazing cattle. Moses gave Jazer, a fortified city with folds for sheep (Num 32:35; Josh 13:25), to God. The next reference to Jazer occurs in the reign of David when the city was part of a census list (2 Sam 24:5). Jazer is referred to in a "footnote" in 1 Chr 26:31 as the city garrisoned by Judah from Hebron. There are two references to Jazer in the prophets—one in Isa 16:8 in an oracle against Moab, and a parallel text in Jer 48:32 where Jazer weeps for the vines of Sibmah.

Jazer is mentioned in the early campaign of Judas Maccabeus. At that time the city was under the rule of the Amorites; but Judas "crossed over to the Amorites, and came upon a strong and numerous force under the command of a certain Timotheus. He fought many battles with them, and they broke before him and were crushed. After capturing Jazer and its dependent villages, he returned to Judaea" (1 Macc 5:6–8, NEB). Outside of the OT and Apocrypha, Jazer appears in Josephus' *Antiquities* (12.329–30) and in Eusebius' *Onomasticon* (12.1–4) where he describes the city as being 10 Roman miles W of Philadelphia, situated at the source of a large stream which flows into the Jordan, and 15 from Heshbon.

The location of biblical Jazer has been of considerable dispute since the early part of the 19th century. Four sites have been associated with this biblical city: Kh. Sar, Yajuz, Kh. es-Sireh, and Kh. Jazzir.

Seetzen and later Merrill (1883: 484) have identified Jazer with Kh. Sar. The first major survey of Khirbet Sar (M.R. 228150) was done by Conder (1899: 154) in October, 1881, but Conder did not accept Seetzen's identification because Sar had no etymological connection with the name Jazer. The tell is located 9 km W of Amman and 1.5 km SE of Ain es-Sir. It is located in a rolling, fertile expanse between Naᶜur on the S and Suweileh on the N. The fields around the site are terraced. From Kh. Sar, a portion of the Dead Sea is visible and the Wadi esh-Shita descends to the S. The remains at Kh. Sar are extensive. The most extensive survey work has been conducted by N. Glueck (1937: 153–57), who found extensive Roman, Iron I, and Iron II.

There are 2 sites by the name of Yajuz that have been associated with biblical Jazer, one called Kom Yajuz, the other Yajuz. Oliphant (1880: 223–35) proposed identifying Yajuz (M.R. 237159) with Jazer and T. K. Cheyne (*EncBib* 2: 2340–41) has been the strongest defender of this association. Yajuz is located 7 Roman miles N of Philadelphia (Amman) and 33 S of Gerasa. During the Roman occupation Yajuz was on the road that ran from Philadelphia and Petra S to Arabia. When Glueck (1939: 177) visited Yajuz he found only Roman and Byzantine remains.

Cohen (*IDB* 2: 805–06) has suggested that Kom Yajuz (M.R. 238160) is biblical Jazer, but gives no reasons other than it is the site that best suits this location. Kom Yajuz is located less than 1.5 km E-NE of Yajuz situated between the Wadi Kom and the Wadi Yajuz. Glueck found pottery that was associated with EB IV, Iron I, and Iron II. On later surveys, 7th–6th century pottery was found.

In 1956, G. Landes (1956: 30–37) proposed that Jazer be identified with Kh. es-Sireh. Although Landes did not have any ceramic evidence for his identification, he argued for this "tentative" location on the basis of Eusebius and the prophetic passages in Isaiah and Jeremiah referring to the "spring." Landes pointed out that Eusebius located Jazer 8–10 Roman miles W of Philadelphia, 15 Roman miles from Heshbon, also that a large river flowed from the town emptying into the Jordan. Kh. es-Sireh is located 2 km NE of Kh. Sar, making Sireh 12.5 km or 8.5 Roman miles from Amman, and 18.7 km or 12 Roman miles from Heshbon. The Amman-Sireh mileage fits well with Eusebius' figures; however, that between Heshbon-Sireh is short. The major argument of Landes was a reconstruction of the Isa 16:9 and Jer 48:32 texts. Landes suggested that *bkh* in these 2 prophetic texts should be translated "water source, fountain, well." Because Eusebius commented that at Jazer there was a large river which emptied into the Jordan, Landes observed that the source of this river must have been the "fountain" at Jazer. However, there is no archaeological evidence to support this identification and furthermore, Landes' elaborate discussion on *bkh* really does not support the identification of Kh. es-Sireh any more than it would numerous other sites along the Wadi Sir and Wadi Kefren.

The most attractive identification for the location of Jazer has been made by Abel (*GP* 2: 69) and R. de Vaux (1941: 25–27), who propose that the ancient city was at Kh. Jazzir (M.R. 219156). Not only does it correspond to most of the location details of Eusebius, but the names do not present any difficulties, and de Vaux also found good ceramic evidence there. Kh. Jazzir is located 4 km S of es-Salt. Jazzir is at the head of the Wadi Šuᶜeib which flows into the Jordan. Less than a km from Jazzir is ᶜAin Hazer. On his survey de Vaux identified pottery from the Iron and Hellenistic periods. He suggested that the site was abandoned at the end of the Iron Age and was not reoccupied until the Hellenistic. Because de Vaux speaks only of the Iron Age it is impossible to date this city any more precisely. However, little doubt remains that the Levitical city Jazer is Kh. Jazzir.

Bibliography

Conder, C. R. 1899. *Survey of Eastern Palestine,* vol. 1. London.

Glueck, N. 1937. Explorations in the Land of Ammon. *BASOR* 68: 13–21.

———. 1939. *Explorations in Eastern Palestine,* III. AASOR 18–19. New Haven.

Landes, G. 1956. The Foundation at Jazer. *BASOR* 144: 30–37.

Merrill, S. 1883. *East of the Jordan.* New York.

Oliphant, L. 1880. *Land of Gilead, with Excursions in the Lebanon.* New York.

Vaux, R. de. 1941. Notes d'Histoire et de Topographie Transjordaniennes. *Vivre et Penser* 1: 16–47.

John L. Peterson

JAZIZ (PERSON) [Heb *yāzîz*]. A state official; a Hagrite. The majority of the LXX mss by reading *iōaz* do not reflect the first *zayin* in his name. One of 12 stewards of royal property appointed by David, his specific charge was to oversee the flocks (1 Chr 27:31). Of the 12 he is one of 7 identified with a gentilic rather than by paternity. Perhaps he was from a conquered group, making his nationality or ethnic origin more important than his particular genealogy. Although most of the 7 gentilics are not otherwise known, 1 Chr 5:10, 18–22 indicates that the Hagrites were conquered by the Reubenites, Gadites, and half of the tribe of Manasseh during the reign of Saul. In Ps 83:7ff (—Eng 83:6ff) they are mentioned as allied with the Ishmaelites (note Obil, the Ishmaelite, steward of the camels [1 Chr 27:30]), Moab, Edom, and other traditional enemies.

RICHARD W. NYSSE

JEARIM, MOUNT (PLACE) [Heb *har-yĕʿārîm*]. A mountain peak on the N boundary of the territory of Judah about halfway between Kiriath-Jearim and Beth-Shemesh (Josh 15:10). This is the only reference to the peak. Mt. Jearim, which probably means "mountain of forests" or "wooded mountain," is located at Chesalon, modern Kesla (M.R. 154132) approximately 17 km W of Jersualem. It forms part of a range referred to as the Jerusalem Hills. Because of the similarities between Jearim, "forest," and Seir, "shaggy," it has been suggested that the two peaks of Josh 15:10, Seir and Mt. Jearim, may be identical (see Boling, *Joshua* AB, 369–70). If so, this place also marks the farthest penetration of the abortive attempt by the Israelites to conquer Canaan after initially accepting the prejudiced report of 10 of the 12 spies (cf. Numbers 14 and Deut 1:44).

WANN M. FANWAR

JEATHERAI (PERSON) [Heb *yĕʾātĕray*]. A Levite of the exilic period, a descendant of Gershom (1 Chr 6:6—Eng 6:21). The origin of the name is unknown, perhaps resulting from a scribal error. Rudolph (*Chronikbücher* HAT, 54) suggested that it should be read as either Ethni (*ʾetnî*) as in 1 Chr 6:26—Eng 6:41 or Joel (*yôʾēl*) as in 1 Chr 15:7.

TOM WAYNE WILLETT

JEBEL. Geographic names containing the term "jebel," meaning "mountain," are found alphabetized under the second term of the name. For example, the Jebel Qa'aqir entry can be found under QA'AQIR, JEBEL.

JEBERECHIAH (PERSON) [Heb *yĕberekyāhû*]. The father of Zechariah, whom Isaiah summoned to witness a prophetic document announcing the impending overthrow of Israel and Syria by the Assyrians (Isa 8:2). Near the time of the Syro-Ephraimite War, Isaiah called on two witnesses to verify his prophetic announcement: Uriah the priest and Zechariah the son of Jeberechiah. Uriah is apparently the high priest (2 Kgs 16:10–16). Wildberger (*Isaiah 1–12* BKAT, 316) has suggested that the Zechariah in question is the father of Abi who was the wife of King Ahaz and mother of King Hezekiah (cf. 2 Kgs 18:2). In any case, since Uriah and Zechariah appear to be leading citizens, the same must also be true for Zechariah's father, Jeberechiah. All the names mentioned in Isa 8:2 belong to the world of cult piety which is best known to us from the Psalms (Wildberger *Isaiah 1–12* BKAT, 317; *IPN* 195). The name Jeberechiah means "May YHWH bless." This type of name (formed with an imperfect verb) occurs occasionally in texts dealing with ancient Israel down to the time of David, but then falls into general disuse until shortly before the Exile (*IPN* 28). This fact has led some to suggest that the name should actually be Berechiah (cf. LXX). It is interesting to note that the father of the postexilic prophet Zechariah is Berechiah (Zech 1:1, 7). See BERECHIAH.

JOHN H. HULL, JR.

JEBUS (PLACE) [Heb *yĕbûs*]. JEBUSITE. The name of the city where the Jebusites lived, which is used as the pre-Israelite name for Jerusalem.

A. Relationship and Use of Terms
B. Use in Lists of Nations
C. Ethnic Origin
D. Geographic Location
E. Historical Data

A. Relationship and Use of Terms

Boling and Wright (*Joshua* AB, 167) argue that Jebus was a clan name and that "linguistically, the name correlates with Amorite *yabusum* and the name of a town in Transjordan, Jabesh (-Gilead)." The term Jebusite may have been a gentilic adjective derived from the name Jebus, or Jebus may have received its name from its inhabitants (Simons *GTTOT,* 47). Since Jebus occurs only 4 times in the Hebrew Bible and is otherwise unknown, while Jebusite occurs 41 times, the latter possibility is more likely. While the term Jebusite can be used as a descriptive adjective with the name of an individual such as Araunah (2 Sam 24:16, 18), it is most often used with the article as a collective name for Jebusites.

B. Use in Lists of Nations

The term Jebusite is found in 22 of the 27 lists of pre-Israelite nations. In the most common 6-name lists, the Jebusites occur in the latter half of the lists among other little known nations, including the Perizzites and the Hivites (Exod 3:8; 33:2). The Jebusites usually occur last in the lists possibly because they were the last group to be conquered by the Israelites (Ishida 1979: 461–65).

C. Ethnic Origin

The Jebusites are listed in the Table of Nations as descendents of Canaan (Gen 10:16). Since the table seems to be organized by different criteria—ethnopolitical, linguistic, geographic, genealogical, socioeconomic, and sociocultural (Gen 10:5, 20, 31; Oded 1986: 14–17)—the precise meaning of the Jebusites in this list is debatable. They are probably listed as descendents of Canaan because they lived in the land of Canaan (Speiser *IDB* 3: 235–42).

Little is known about the origin of the Jebusites. Scholars have suggested that they may be related to the Hurrians (Hoffner *POTT,* 225) or to the Hittites—although this last possibility is unlikely. Ishida contends that the Jebusites were a subdivision of the Perizzites (1979: 479–80). Most agree that the Jebusites were a non-Semitic people.

D. Geographic Location

The Jebusites were located in the hill country of Canaan (Num 13:29; Josh 11:3). The phrase "shoulder of the Jebusite" was a landmark for the S border of Benjamin (Josh 15:8; 18:16). While some have maintained that the "shoulder of the Jebusite" refers to the "western hill of the present-day Old City or perhaps to both of the hills," Kallai maintains that it refers to the E hill or the inhabited city of Jebus/Jerusalem of earliest times (*HGB,* 136–37). Jebus is usually located in Benjaminite territory except for one text in which it may be located in Judah (Josh 15:63). The confusion may be because Jebus was on the border of the 2 tribal regions or because of shifting boundaries over time (Aharoni *LBHG,* 251, 254, 315; Kallai *HGB,* 396–97).

The Jebusites are said to have been inhabitants of Jerusalem in Josh 15:63 and 2 Sam 5:6. In Judg 19:10, Jebus is mentioned with the explanatory note that it was Jerusalem (see also Josh 18:28). 1 Chr 11:4 mentions Jerusalem with the explanatory note that it was Jebus.

Some scholars have been troubled by this identification of Jebus and Jerusalem for several reasons. First, this identification is found in each case in a parenthetical note which could be a later redactional or scribal addition to the text. Second, while the name Jerusalem occurs in the 14th century Tell el-Amarna texts and in the 19th–18th century Egyptian Execration texts, no reference is made to Jebus (Soggin, *Judges,* ET, OTL, 1981: 286). Third, Jerusalem seems to be too far S to be located on the S border of Benjamin (Miller and Tucker, 121).

While the Jebusites inhabited and controlled Jerusalem, this does not necessarily mean that Jebus was Jerusalem. Miller contends that later scribes misidentified Jebus with Jerusalem on the basis of the Jebusite control of Jerusalem and suggests that Jebus should actually be located at present-day Shaʿfât (Miller 1975: 154; see map in Miller and Tucker *Joshua* CBC, 130). If Jebus was actually used as a name for Jerusalem, it must have been a temporary name and must have existed alongside the older name Jerusalem (Simons *GTTOT,* 47; see Josh 10:5 where the name Jerusalem is used by itself). D. R. Ap-Thomas (1967: 286) argues that the identification of Jebus with Jerusalem was useful "to distinguish in the story between pre-Israelite and Israelite occupation—especially where the inhabitants are guilty of 'Canaanite crimes.' "

E. Historical Data

While the land of the Jebusites was promised to Abraham and his descendents (Gen 15:21), the Israelites found it difficult to defeat these people, who remained in power during the period of the judges until the time of David (Judg 3:5). Neither the Judahites (Josh 15:63) nor the Benjaminites could drive the Jebusites out of Jerusalem (Judg 1:21). The puzzling mention of the Judahites' destruction of the city of Jerusalem in Judg 1:8 has been variously understood as only a partial conquest of the city or a temporary and indecisive victory (Boling *Judges* AB, 55–56). In Judg 19:10–12 the traveling Levite avoids spending the night at Jebus/Jerusalem because it is a city of foreigners. The reference to David bringing the head of Goliath to Jerusalem—still occupied by Jebusites—in 1 Sam 17:54 may have been an anachronism reflecting a tradition that the skull was later kept at Jerusalem as a trophy (see also 1 Sam 17:57; Klein *1 Samuel* WBC, 181).

David finally succeeds in capturing Jerusalem from the Jebusites (2 Sam 5:6–9; 1 Chr 11:4–9). The precise details of the event are difficult to reconstruct because of the complicated textual and redactional history of these two accounts (McCarter *2 Samuel* AB, 135–43). Assumedly, even though the city was taken, not all of the Jebusites were annihilated, because David later bought the threshing floor of Araunah the Jebusite (2 Sam 24:18–24). The descendents of the pre-Israelite nations who still lived in the land were reportedly reduced to slavery by Solomon (1 Kgs 9:20–21). Except for the Jebusites' place in the traditional lists of pre-Israelite inhabitants of Canaan (Ezra 9:1; Neh 9:8; Jdt 5:16; 1 Esdr 8:69) nothing more is said about these people.

Bibliography

Ap-Thomas, D. R. 1967. Jerusalem. Pp. 277–95 in *Archaeology and Old Testament Study,* ed. D. W. Thomas. Oxford.

Ishida, T. 1979. The Structure and Historical Implications of the Lists of Pre-Israelite Nations. *Bib* 60: 461–90.

Miller, J. M. 1974. Jebus and Jerusalem: A Case of Mistaken Identity. *ZDPV* 90: 115–27.

———. 1975. Geba/Gibeah of Benjamin. *VT* 25: 145–66.

Oded, B. 1986. The Table of Nations (Genesis 10)—A Socio-Cultural Approach. *ZAW* 98: 14–31.

Stephen A. Reed

JECOLIAH

JECOLIAH (PERSON) [Heb *yĕkolyāh*]. Mother of Azariah, King of Judah (2 Kgs 15:2 = 2 Chr 26:3). Her name means "YHWH is able/has the power" (Stamm 1967: 311). Jecoliah was one of 3 queen mothers from Jerusalem (the others being Jehoaddan and Nehushta). Her father's name is unknown. The form Jecoliah reflects the *Qere* of 2 Chr 26:3. The spelling found in 2 Kgs 15:2 has a final *û* and reads *yĕkolyāhû.* See also AZARIAH; QUEEN.

Bibliography

Stamm, J. J. 1967. Hebräische Frauennamen. *VTSup* 16: 311.

Linda S. Schearing

JECONIAH

JECONIAH (PERSON) [Heb *yĕkonyāh; yĕkonyāhû*]. A variant form for 3 names in the Hebrew Bible and the deuterocanonical texts.

1. An alternate form of the name JEHOIACHIN king of Judah, the son and successor of Jehoiakim (1 Chr 3:16, 17). He was taken into exile by Nebuchadnezzar king of Babylon (Esth 2:6; Jer 24:1; 27:20; 28:4; 29:2; Bar 1:3, 9).

2. Occurs in 1 Esdr 1:9 as an alternate form of the name CONANIAH.

3. An alternate form of the name JEHOAHAZ, king of Judah, the son and successor of Josiah (1 Esdr 1:34).

JEDAIAH

JEDAIAH (PERSON) [Heb *yĕdaʿyāh; yĕdāyāh*]. There are 2 forms of the name Jedaiah, the first *(yĕdaʿyāh)* meaning "Yahweh knows" and the second *(yĕdāyāh)* meaning "Yahweh has favored." The first is represented by #1–#3 below, the second by #4–#5.

1. One of the major priestly houses of Judah which is regularly mentioned among those priests who returned from exile with Zerubbabel. The earliest tradition, likely reflected in Ezra 2:36 and Neh 7:39, lists Jedaiah as one of 4 priestly families which returned, and further identifies him as being "of the house of Jeshua," that is Joshua the high priest. In this early tradition Joshua rather than Jedaiah is the major eponym of the family.

In a secondary tradition, reflected in Neh 11:10, Jedaiah is listed alongside a number of other priests as among those living in Jerusalem after the return. Vv 10–11 seem badly damaged, however, and many scholars reconstruct the text in various ways. It may originally have listed the genealogies for only 3 such priests: Jedaiah, Jachin, and Seraiah. If correct, the effect would be to provide Jedaiah with the title "the ruler of the house of God" and with a linear genealogy reaching back 7 (or 8) generations through Zadok to Ahitub, thus legitimating his status in the postexilic community. This reconstruction would also bring vv 10–11 into line with the rest of the passage.

The lists in Neh 12:1–7 and 12–21 have also been disturbed, as is evidenced by the variance in names. They list Jedaiah as among the 22 (var. 21) priests who returned with Zerubbabel, but now only in 18th (var. 17th) position. Whereas in Neh 11:10 Jedaiah was listed as the son of Joiarib, here he is listed as a colleague. The same relationship may be inferred, however, in that Joiarib is the 17th (var. 16th) listed, that is one above Jedaiah.

The importance of Jedaiah as suggested by even the earlier texts is finally "codified" for the postexilic community by the Chronicler who gives to Jedaiah priority in the Davidic temple. In 1 Chr 24:7 Jedaiah is given the second lot in the Davidic establishment of the 24 priestly courses, still behind J(eh)oiarib. But in 1 Chr 9:10 Jedaiah finally has priority over his rival.

Rather than being considered individual persons, these names should be taken as family designations and as indications of fluctuating political dynamics in the Second Temple period.

2. In addition to this Jedaiah, there is also a minor priestly figure by the same name who is mentioned in the lists in Neh 12:7 and 21. That he is listed in last position, however, suggests that his place in tradition was slight. The LXX distinguishes between this person and the Jedaiah in v 19 by assigning different names. In v 19 the name is Idia, but in v 21 Iedeiou, Ideiou or Odouia, depending upon the manuscript.

3. One of 3 returned exiles who, according to Zech 6:10, 14, provided gold and silver to Zechariah so that a crown could be made for Joshua the priest. A major question concerns how many crowns were made and for whom. The Heb text suggests that 2 were made, and vv 12–13 certainly suggest that Zerubbabel, who would bear royal honor and would rule upon his throne, was the recipient of one. This question is connected to the issue of whether or not a diarchic messianism developed in the postexilic period.

The mention of the 3 "benefactors" also is problematic. First, the names Heldai, Tobijah, and Jedaiah are understood by the LXX not as individuals but as groups of people: "the leaders, those who are useful among it, and those who recognize it." The Heb *yĕdaʿyāh* was, like the others, understood as an appellative (Gk *epegnokotos*) rather than as a proper noun.

Assuming that they are personal names, however, the question is why these 4 men (including Josiah) should have been singled out for the giving of such "gifts" of silver and gold. Petersen (*Haggai Zechariah 1–8* OTL, 274) suggests that they were exemplary men who were chosen for their orthodoxy and faithfulness, symbolized by the fact that 3 of the 4 have theophoric "Yahweh" names. It seems more likely, however, that something more polemical is at work. In v 14 it is said that the crowns are to serve as "a reminder" to these four. A reminder of what? Often times a "reminder" is left in the midst of the people to fix their attention upon the broken apostasy of the past and as a warning for the future. Such a situation is suggested by Exod 30:16 and Num 10:9–10, cited by Petersen himself. The warning function of such a "remembrance" is particularly clear in Num 17:5 (—Eng 16:40), where the censers of "Korah and his company" are pounded out into a sheet for an alter covering as a "reminder" of the sin of the past and a warning for the future, "so that no one who is not a priest should draw near . . . lest he become as Korah and his company." If the crowns in Zech 6:14 are to function as such a "reminder," then Jedaiah appears to have been singled out with the others not for exemplary faithfulness but for some unstated act of resistance to the royal aspirations of Zerubbabel and Joshua.

4. A Simeonite who, according to 1 Chr 4:37, appears in the genealogical listing of 13 "princes" of Simeon. During the reign of Hezekiah these princes migrated to Gedor (Gerar?). Of the 13 princes named, 3 are attributed linear genealogies: Joshah (1 generation), Jehu (3 generations), and Ziza (5 generations). Jedaiah appears as the third in this last list of five.

The major critical question concerning this genealogy has been its connection to the prior list in vv 24–27. Most take the material concerning Simeon to be a combination of genealogical information, geographical notes, and miscellaneous scraps. As such, the list in vv 34–37 is taken to be totally unconnected to the earlier list, and may have found its way into the present context due to its traditional linkage with the historical note concerning the expansion of Simeon in vv 39–41.

In the present context, however, the genealogy of the princes of Simeon in vv 34–37 has the function of filling out the earlier genealogy, ending as it does with the expectant note that "Shimei had 16 sons and 6 daughters" (v 27). Some have taken the reference to Shemaiah in v 37 to be a scribal error for this same Shimei, thereby attributing to the genealogies a close connection. The LXX likewise tried to connect the 2 genealogies by reading the name Shemaiah in v 37 as Simeon. Though undoubtedly misinterpretations of the text, these efforts nonetheless demonstrate the purpose of the text in its final form.

5. In Neh 3:10 Jedaiah is listed as one of those who repaired a portion of the defensive wall on the W side of Jerusalem "opposite his house" during the days of Nehemiah. This note about the location of the wall "opposite his house" is peculiar, since otherwise this note is used only with regard to the building of the wall on the E side. It could, therefore, be a misplaced note. More likely, however, it represents an intentional point made by the Chronicler. Modern commentators generally argue that, unlike the W wall, the E wall was totally rebuilt on a new line because of the extensive destruction involved (*Ezra Nehemiah* WBC, 200, 209). If so, then the frequent reference to "opposite his house" in relation to the E wall might suggest that this new defensive line was built into the existing walls of the houses on that side of the city. In this case, the note concerning Jedaiah rebuilding the wall "opposite his house" might mean that, in this particular place on the W wall, the wall had to be rebuilt on a new line and was built into the existing wall of Jedaiah's house.

RODNEY R. HUTTON

JEDIAEL (PERSON) [Heb *yĕdîʿăʾēl*]. Four persons in the OT bear this name which means "Known of God." In addition, it also appears in Neo-Babylonian texts as *Ia-di-iḫ-ilî*/*Ia-a-di-ḫu-ilî* (Coogan 1976: 27, 75) and *Ia-di-ʾ-ilu* (Tallqvist 1905: 68). For similarly constructed names with the divine element *yh(w)*, see biblical JEDAIAH and Coogan 1976: 27, 75.

1. The third and smallest of 3 Benjaminite families named in 1 Chr 7:6–12, a postexilic list (Rudolph *Chronikbücher* HAT 67; Williamson *Chronicles* NCBC, 78) on the order of a military census which appears to be independent of the genealogies of the tribe of Benjamin given in Gen 46:21 and Num 26:38–41, where Jediael is not named. The proposal that this list is a corrupted form of the genealogy of Zebulun which is otherwise omitted in this context (Curtis and Madsen *Chronicles* ICC, 145–49) has lost favor (see Rudolph *Chronikbücher* HAT, 65; Williamson *Chronicles* NCBC, 77). The Syriac and Vulgate replace Jediael in 1 Chr 7:6 with the names following Becher in Gen 46:21 (see also the Syriac in 1 Chr 7:10, 11) in an attempt to harmonize the lists.

2. Jediael the son of Shimri is mentioned as one of David's mighty men in 1 Chr 11:45, in a list of 16 names which the Chronicler has appended to those given in 2 Sam 23:8–39. Noth's proposal that this list is a postexilic fiction (*ÜgS*, 136, n. 8), by which certain families attempted to establish their early association with David, has been rebutted (Rudolph *Chronikbücher* HAT, 101).

3. One of 7 Manassites of substantial status (the title "chief of thousands" refers to his leadership of a tribal sub-group, not a number of men—Mendenhall 1958) who deserted to David at Ziklag (1 Chr 12:21—Eng 12:20).

4. A Levitical gatekeeper of the Korahite family of Meshelemiah. The second son of this family, he is named only in 1 Chr 26:2, in the Chronicler's (Williamson *Chronicles* NCBC, 169) or perhaps a later (Rudolph *Chronikbücher* HAT, 173) organization of the gatekeepers in the temple at Jerusalem.

Bibliography

Coogan, M. D. 1976. *West Semitic Personal Names in the Murašû Documents.* HSM 7. Missoula, MT.

Diringer, D. 1934. *Le iscrizioni antico-ebraiche palestinesi.* Florence.

Mendenhall, G. 1958. The Census Lists of Numbers 1 and 26. *JBL* 77: 52–66.

Tallqvist, K. L. 1905. *Neubabylonisches Namenbuch zu den Geschaeftsurkunden aus der Zeit des Šamaššumukin bis Xerxes.* Acta Societatis Scientarum Fennicae 32/2. Leipzig.

J. S. ROGERS

JEDIDAH (PERSON) [Heb *yĕdîdâ*]. The daughter of Adaiah of Bozkath and mother of King Josiah (2 Kgs 22:1). Bozkath is a place between Lachish and Elgon according to Josh 15:39, to the SE of Lachish (Gray *1 and 2 Kings* OTL, 721). The name of this individual means "Beloved [of Yahweh]" (*IPN*, 149, 223; cf. the name JEDIDIAH). In the Ugaritic texts, *ydd*, "Beloved [of El]," is an epithet of the god Mot (*UT*, p. 409 s.v. # 1074).

ROBERT ALTHANN

JEDIDIAH (PERSON) [Heb *yĕdîdĕyāh*]. The name given to Solomon by Nathan in 2 Sam 12:25. The name and its occurrence are unusual for several reasons. First, the Hebrew orthography, *ydydyh*, is similar to that for David, *dwd*. Second, since the child had already been named by his parents, as was the custom, one does not expect to read about another naming by the deity. Third, the name is unusual since its meaning, "beloved of Yahweh," does not fit the etymology suggested by the succeeding phrase, "for the sake of Yahweh," *bbr yhwh*.

It has thus been argued that Jedidiah was the child's private name and that Solomon was the throne name (Honeyman 1948). Others have argued that this was really the name of the first-born child of David and Bathsheba whose death is recorded in 2 Sam 12:18 (Klostermann 1887). Others have speculated that the closeness to the name of David suggests that the name is a sign to David of divine grace after the death of Uriah, marriage to Bathsheba, and death of the firstborn child (Caspari *Samuelbücher* KAT) and that the etymology be understood to mean "by the grace of Yahweh" (de Boer 1966). In this way the narrator signals that David's penance (2 Sam 12:17), though ineffective in averting the death of the first child, did exonerate him for future actions and that once again he could claim to be one "after Yahweh's own heart."

Bibliography

Boer, P. A. H. de. 1966. 2 Sam 12,25. In *Studia Biblica et Semitica.* Wageningen.

Honeyman, A. M. 1948. The Evidence for Regnal Names Among the Hebrews. *JBL* 67: 13–25.

Klostermann, A. 1887. *Die Bücher Samuelis und der Könige.* Nördingen.

RANDALL C. BAILEY

JEDUTHUN (PERSON) [Heb *yĕdûtûn*]. A levitical singer in the time of David, said in some texts to be a founder (along with Asaph and Heman) of a family of musical singers (see 1 Chr 25:1–6; and cf. 2 Chr 5:12; 29:14; 35:15). Elsewhere, however, the name Ethan, rather than Jeduthun, is associated with Asaph and Heman (1 Chr 15:17, 19), leading some to suggest that they are 2 different names for the same person (Corney *IDB* 2: 809; but see below for a different reconstruction). In the list of

1 Esdras 1, the name Eddinus seems to occupy the position held by Jeduthun (v 15). To complicate matters even further, in 1 Chr 16:38, 42b, Jeduthun is said to be the father of some of the levitical gatekeepers, also in the time of David. The most noteworthy of these is one Obed-edom, who, however, is elsewhere said to be a singer (1 Chr 16:5; but note that in the list of singers in the previous chap. [see vv 16–24] where he is mentioned 3 times [vv 18, 21, 24], twice he is described as a gatekeeper [vv 18, 24]). Inasmuch as the more comprehensive lists of Davidic singers and gatekeepers found in 1 Chronicles 25–26 unequivocally place Jeduthun in the former category and Obed-edom in the latter, divergent levels of tradition seem to be attested side by side in the Chronicler's work.

Williamson, following Gese, has pointed to some 4 levels of tradition concerning the genealogies of the various families of singers as attested in 1–2 Chronicles, Ezra, and Nehemiah (1979: 263). Simply put, in the 1st stage, all the singers are reckoned as "sons of Asaph" (Ezra 2:41; Neh 7:44); in the 2d stage, the singers are designated sons of Asaph and sons of Jeduthun (Neh 11:3–19; 1 Chr 9:1–18; but see below); the 3d stage includes the 3 familiar groups, Asaph, Heman, and Jeduthun (references already cited); and finally, the 4th stage replaces Jeduthun by Ethan, and Heman is now more prominent than Asaph (1 Chr 15:16–22; cf. 1 Chr 6:16–32—Eng 6:31–47). Certainly, some reconstruction such as this is probably necessary to reconcile all the disparate genealogical data concerning these musical families (a similar situation obtains for the gatekeepers, as well).

As noted above, later references to Jeduthun and his descendants are found in 2 Chr 5:12 (Solomon's dedication of the First Temple), 29:14 (Hezekiah's cleansing of the Temple), and 35:15 (Josiah's famous Passover). Although all 3 of these references continue to link the family of Jeduthun with Asaph and Heman, the last reference uniquely describes Jeduthun as "the king's seer" (*ḥôzê hammelek*). Such an appellation for Jeduthun accords with that given to Heman in 1 Chr 25:5, and, to a lesser degree, Asaph in 2 Chr 29:30; and it confirms the significant link between prophecy and musicianship attested elsewhere in the Hebrew Bible (e.g., 1 Sam 10:5, where a band of prophets is described as "prophesying" with harp, tambourine, flute, and lyre; 2 Kgs 3:15, where Elisha the prophet requests a minstrel to help him prophesy; and, not least, 1 Chr 25:1, where the sons of Asaph, Heman, and Jeduthun are commissioned to "prophesy" with lyres, harps, and cymbals [Williamson *1 and 2 Chronicles* NCBC, 166]).

Yet another reference to Jeduthun is to be found in Neh 11:17 MT (along with its parallel in 1 Chr 9:16), where a certain Abda (or "Obadiah," in the Chronicles text), descendant of Jeduthun, is listed as a temple musician in the days of Nehemiah (concerning the authenticity of this list and the likelihood that it originally represented a list of all those who lived in Jerusalem, see Williamson *Ezra, Nehemiah* WBC, 344–50). It should be noted that the earliest LXX mss of Neh 11:17 lack the name Jeduthun along with a number of other names (including Asaph) found in the MT; Tov (1981: 301) argues that the shorter LXX list of priests and Levites in Nehemiah 11 (and 12) is probably more original. Hence, the reference to Jeduthun in 11:17 MT may well represent a later addition (also cf. Batten *Ezra and Nehemiah* ICC, 271; Myers *Ezra-Nehemiah* AB, lxvi), and, if one assumes that the parallel list of priests and Levites in 1 Chronicles 9 is dependent upon the Nehemiah 11 list (cf. the arguments for this view cited in Williamson *1 and 2 Chronicles* NCBC, 87–88), one may query the likelihood of the existence of the hypothetical second stage of Gese and Williamson mentioned above.

Finally, there appear to be 3 references to the name Jeduthun in the titles to Psalms 39, 62, and 77. Mowinckel, however, has suggested that the term should be interpreted as a common noun derived from the root *ydh*, and translated as "confession" or the like, these Psalms being employed in some liturgical context of penance (1962: 213). As he pointed out, all 3 of these Psalms fit quite well into such a context. Nonetheless, it seems more likely that the term should be read as a personal name (cf. RSV), presumably a reference to the same Jeduthun which the Chronicler has reckoned as a musical leader in the time of David. As Craigie (*Psalms 1–50* WBC, 308) has pointed out, the names of the other 2 Davidic musical leaders, Asaph and Heman, are also found in Psalm titles (it should also be noted that there is a reference to "Ethan the Ezrahite" in the title of Psalm 89). Alternatively, the term may have come to refer to the name of a tune or musical setting which later tradition attributed to the Davidic musician (especially note the use of the preposition *ʿal*, "on, upon, after the manner of," in the titles of Psalms 62 and 77; see Craigie *Psalms 1–50* WBC, 308; cf. Corney *IDB* 2: 809).

Bibliography

Mowinckel, S. 1962. *The Psalms in Israel's Worship.* Vol. 2. Trans. D. R. Ap-Thomas. New York.

Tov, E. 1981. *The Text-Critical Use of the Septuagint in Biblical Research.* Jerusalem.

Williamson, H. G. M. 1979. The Origins of the Twenty-Four Priestly Courses, A Study of 1 Chronicles xxiii–xxvii. Pp. 251–68 in *Studies in the Historical Books of the Old Testament,* ed. J. A. Emerton. VTSup 30. Leiden.

William H. Barnes

JEGAR-SAHADUTHA (PLACE) [Aram *yĕgar-śāhădûtāʾ*]. The Aramaic name given by Laban to the pile of stones heaped up by his and Jacob's households apparently near the stone pillar set up by Jacob and Laban in the mountain of Gilead (Gen 31:24, 45–47). Gilead was then a sparsely populated area, and the place was identified with Mizpah of Gilead (31:49) which later became Jephthah's hometown (Judg 10:17). The location is not identified yet. See MIZPAH. "They ate there on the heap" (Gen 31:46), but actually they might have eaten food set on top of the heap which functioned as an oversized table. The meaning of Jegar-sahadutha is "(Stone-)heap of testimony" which corresponds to Jacob's word *Galʿēd* "heap of witness." LXX translates Laban's Aramaic words "heap of testimony," and Jacob's word "witness heap." Laban's words are the oldest attestation of the Aramaic language in the historical books of the Bible. It suggests that Abraham's kinsmen spoke Aramaic at Haran and he came to know Hebrew in Canaan. See MBA, map no. 27.

Yoshitaka Kobayashi

JEHALLELEL (PERSON) [Heb *yĕhallelʾēl*]. Name of 2 individuals in Chronicles. The etymology of the name is difficult to ascertain. Its verbal element *(yĕhallel)* is a *Piʿel,* and would seem to be derived from the *Piʿel* verb, *hillel,* "to praise," which is common in the Hebrew Bible. But as a Semitic name, the divine element, *ʾel,* must be the subject of this verb and not its object. Some scholars, therefore, have related the verbal element to a different root, *hll,* meaning "to shine," suggesting the meanings, "may God shine forth" from the Qal (*IDB* 2: 809) or "may God cause to shine" from the *Hipʿil* (Noth *IPN,* 205). Another suggestion is that the *Piʿel* be retained and the name be understood as meaning "may God praise (the child)" (Fowler *TPNAH,* 136).

1. Descendent of Judah (1 Chr 4:16). The list of Jehallelel's descendants bears no obvious relationship either to the lists that precede it or to those that follow it. The only one whose name is otherwise attested is Ziph (Ziphah may be a dittography), a village S of Hebron (1 Sam 23:14–15). This suggests that the list is eponymic. Jehallelel and his "descendants" were probably Judahite or Calebite clans or villages.

2. A Levite, descended from Merari, whose son, Azariah, is listed among the Levites who cleansed the temple under Hezekiah (2 Chr 29:12).

STEVEN L. MCKENZIE

JEHDEIAH (PERSON) [Heb *yeḥdĕyāhû*]. **1.** A state official; a Meronothite. One of 12 stewards of royal property appointed by David, his specific charge was to oversee the donkeys (1 Chr 27:30). Of the 12, he is one of 7 identified with a gentilic rather than by paternity, indicating perhaps that he was from outside the tribal structure. The only other person identified as a Meronothite is Jadon, who worked on the reconstruction of the walls of Jerusalem during the time of Nehemiah (Neh 3:7). See MERONOTHITE.

2. A Levite of the clan of Shubael (1 Chr 24:20). 1 Chronicles 23–27 reports David's organization of the Levites in the light of the coming transition from tabernacle to temple worship. The list of Levitical officials in 1 Chr 24:20–31 in which Jehdeiah is mentioned extends by 1 generation the list in 1 Chr 23:6–23. The purpose of the 2 lists is to sharply differentiate the priests (sons of Aaron) from the Levites. Jehdeiah, a son of Shubael, is part of the Kohathite branch of the Levites; his lineage is traced from Kohath to Amran to Moses to Gershom to Shubael (1 Chr 24:12–16 [read Shubael for Shebuel in v 16]). See SHEBUEL.

RICHARD W. NYSSE

JEHEZKEL (PERSON) [Heb *yĕḥezqēʾl*]. Priest who received the 20th position in the priestly order of the Temple during the reign of David (1 Chr 24:16). 1 Chronicles 24 is the only place where Jehezkel appears in the OT. The name, however, represents a very slight modification from the name of the priest-prophet, Ezekiel, a variation that is preserved as early as the LXX (cf. 1 Chr 24:16 with Ezek 1:3 [LXX]). An evaluation of the historical reliability of the existence of Jehezkel in the time of David rests largely upon the literary context of 1 Chr 24:1–19 (see GAMUL), although the relationship between the name and the prophet Ezekiel may suggest an exilic or postexilic setting for the name Jehezkel. The stylistic characteristics of 1 Chr 24:1–19 seem to link the list to the time of the composition of Chronicles. Jehezkel may represent the Chronicler's use of the prophet Ezekiel's priestly lineage to complete an artificial 24-course arrangement of priests for the time of David.

JOHN W. WRIGHT

JEHIAH (PERSON) [Heb *yĕḥîyāh*]. A Levite who was appointed by David to serve with Obed-edom as a gatekeeper when the ark was moved to Jerusalem (1 Chr 15:24). Obed-edom and one Jeiel are named as gatekeepers in 1 Chr 15:18, but in 15:21 and 16:5, they are named among the musicians. The similarity of the names Jeiel and Jehiah has prompted many to suggest these are in fact the same individual, and that a reviser may have described the status of Obed-edom and Jehiah/Jeiel in his own day as it differed from the situation described at the time of the Chronicler. Many commentators identify various portions of the lists in 1 Chr 15–16 as later additions to the Chronicler's work, though differing on the specifics. Gese (1974) used the various lists of Levitical musicians in an effort to trace the postexilic development of the musical guilds; he assigned 15:16–24 to his stage IIIB, a stage reflecting later accretions to the work of the Chronicler (at stage IIIA). Others have accepted the disputed passages as essentially original material, though allowing for minor corrections and additions (Williamson *Chronicles* NCBC).

Bibliography

Gese, H. 1974. Zur Geschichte der Kultsänger am zweiten Tempel. Pp. 147–58 in *Von Sinai zum Zion: alttestamentliche Beiträge zur biblische Theologie.* Munich.

RAYMOND B. DILLARD

JEHIEL (PERSON) [Heb *yĕhîʾēl*]. Var. JEHIELI. Nine persons in the Hebrew Bible, along with the parallel references in 1 Esdras, bear this name.

1. A Levite musician appointed at the time of David. At the command of David, the levitical leaders selected musicians; Jehiel was among those of 2d rank (1 Chr 15:18). The list is repeated in the subsequent verses where Jehiel is listed as one of 8 harpists, the rest being either cymbalists or lyrists (1 Chr 15:19ff.). In 1 Chr 16:5–6 most of the names are repeated (including that of Jehiel) but without distinction by instrument. Despite variation among the three lists, Jehiel is consistently listed fourth among those of 2d rank.

2. A levitical official, descendant of Gershon. When David divided the Levites into groups according to the sons of Levi, the Gershonites were subdivided between Ladan and Shimei. Jehiel was the first of the sons of Ladan (1 Chr 23:7–11). In 1 Chr 26:21–22 Jehieli [Heb *yĕhîʾēlî*] (= Jehiel) and his sons Zetham and Joel are described as the ones in charge of the treasuries of the temple of the Lord; they are levitical heads of families belonging to Ladan the Gershonite. 1 Chr 29:8 later notes that, when the gifts for the building of the temple were collected, the (precious) stones brought to the treasury of the temple were placed in the care of Jehiel, the Gershonite.

3. The son of Hachmoni. In 1 Chr 27:32–34 Jehiel is listed among several close associates of David; he attended the king's sons. He is not otherwise known, but one of David's warriors is also described as a son of Hachmoni (1 Chr 11:11).

4. Son of Jehoshaphat, brother of Jehoram. Among the 6 brothers of Jehoram, Jehiel is the second named in 2 Chr 21:2. The 6 brothers each received a lavish inheritance including fortified cities from Jehoshaphat, seemingly to provide them with a power base to offset the strength Jehoram would have as successor. Jehoshaphat's reticence about Jehoram, his firstborn, was borne out, for Jehoram killed these 6 as well as other princes when he assumed the throne (1 Chr 21:3–4). A subsequent letter from Elijah announced Jehoram's death and, in an aside, described the brothers as better than Jehoram (1 Chr 21:12–15).

5. A levitical temple official during the reign of Hezekiah (2 Chr 29:14, written as Jehuel, but read as Jehiel [so also the versions]). Jehiel and his brother Shimei, descendants of Heman (a family of levitical singers) are listed among the levitical families that responded to Hezekiah's call for temple cleansing after the desecrations of Ahaz (2 Chr 29:3–19). In 2 Chr 31:13 Jehiel is listed among 10 temple overseers who served under Conaniah, identified as a Levite, and his brother Shimei, who was second in command. These 12 were appointed by Hezekiah and Azariah, the chief officer of the temple, to oversee the storerooms for the contributions of the people. Since Jehiel is not connected explicitly to Shimei in both lists and it is a common levitical and priestly name, one cannot be certain that the references are to the same person.

6. A priestly official during the reign of Josiah. Jehiel was one of 3 administrators of the temple who contributed animals for the Passover offering in behalf of the other priests (2 Chr 35:8; 1 Esdr 1:8).

7. Father of Obadiah, of the family of Joab. Jehiel's son Obadiah headed the second largest family (218 men) to accompany Ezra on his departure from Babylon (Ezra 8:9; cf. 1 Esdr 8:35).

8. A priest during the time of Ezra, father of Shecaniah. Jehiel was one of 6 priests from the family of Elam found to have married foreign women (Ezra 10:26; cf. 1 Esdr 9:27). The family of Elam was among both the first returnees from the Babylonian exile (Ezra 2:7) and those who returned later with Ezra (Ezra 8:7). He is presumably the same as Jehiel, father of Shecaniah, also from the family of Elam (Ezra 10:2; cf. 1 Esdr 8:92). Shecaniah was the spokesman for those who confessed unfaithfulness to God because of marriage to foreign women. He suggested a pact to send them away, and expressed support and encouragement for Ezra (Ezra 10:2–4). As the son of one of the unfaithful, his own position was somewhat ambiguous (see Williamson *Ezra, Nehemiah* WBC, 149–50).

9. A priest during the time of Ezra. Jehiel was one of 5 priests from the family of Harim found to have married foreign women (Ezra 10:21; cf. 1 Esdr 9:21). The family of Harim was among the first returnees from the Babylonian exile (Ezra 2:39).

RICHARD W. NYSSE

JEHIZKIAH (PERSON) [Heb *yĕḥizqîyāhû*].

Jehizkiah, the son of Shallum, was one of the 4 leaders of the tribe of Ephraim during the time of Pekah, ruler of the N kingdom of Israel (2 Chr 28:12). He, with the others, urged the release of the Judean prisoners taken during a battle between Pekah and Ahaz, king of Judah. His name belongs to a class of names which is a phrase or sentence and means either "Yahweh is my strength" (interpreting the *-î-* as a 1st person sing. poss. suffix and *yeḥizqî-* as a noun) or "Yahweh strengthens me" (*yeḥizqî-* is understood as a verb with a 1st person sing. suffix as the object of the verb). Yet another way to translate the name is "the strength of Yahweh," the *î* being an archaic genitive ending as found in the name Melchizedek, "king of righteousness" (Heb *malkî-ṣedek,* Gen 14:18). Koehler (*HALET,* 388) along with Noth (*IPN,* 246) believe Jehizkiah to be a "contaminated" variant of the name Hezekiah (Heb *ḥizqîyâ*), in which case the third interpretation of the name's meaning would be most likely. Otherwise, the *yod* prefix marks a verb, the translation of the name being "Yahweh strengthens me."

KIRK E. LOWERY

JEHOADDAH (PERSON) [Heb *yĕhôʿaddâ*].

Son of Ahaz, a descendant of King Saul of the tribe of Benjamin according to the genealogy in 1 Chr 8:36. However, the textual attestation of this name is problematic; in the parallel genealogy in 1 Chr 9:42, this person is named Jarah [Heb *yaʿrâ*]. Furthermore, the Vaticanus LXX manuscript reads the name as *Iada,* equivalent to the LXX reading for MT's Jarah at 9:42, while other mss read *Ioiada,* implying the Heb *yĕhôyādāʿ*, Jehoiada. Thus, many scholars have reconciled the differences between the 2 genealogies in the MT and the LXX by accepting Jadah *[yaʿdâ]* as the original name (Noth *IPN,* 246; Baumgartner *HALAT,* 404), which is etymologically related to "ornaments," and incorporates the element *ʿdh* which is typically used in Israelite names (Fowler *TPNAH,* 353–54). Alternatively, the name may have *ʿdd,* "to count" as its root (*TPNAH,* 144); however, this root is not elsewhere used in names. The forms Jehoaddah in the MT and Jadah would then be seen as variant long and short forms of the same name (Rudolph *Chronikbücher* HAT, 80). Alternatively, Demsky (1971: 19) has shown that this section of the Benjaminite genealogy is relating various Benjaminite clans through geographical locations; he thus has suggested that Jarah of 9:42 is correct and should be connected to the town Kiriath-jearim. If this is correct, the reading in 1 Chr 9:42 is a scribal error or a secondary attempt to understand the unusual personal name Jarah.

Bibliography

Demsky, A. 1971. The Genealogy of Gibeon (1 Chronicles 9:35–44): Biblical and Epigraphic Considerations. *BASOR* 202: 16–23.

MARC Z. BRETTLER

JEHOADDIN (PERSON) [Heb *yĕhōʿaddîn*].

Var. JEHOADDAN. Mother of Amaziah, king of Judah (2 Kgs 14:2

= 2 Chr 25:1). She is one of the three queen mothers from Jerusalem (the others being Jecoliah and Nehushta). Her father's name is unknown.

LINDA S. SCHEARING

JEHOAHAZ (PERSON) [Heb *yehô*ʾ*āḥāz*]. Var. AHAZIAH; SHALLUM. **1.** The name once given (2 Chr 21:17) to Ahaziah, king of Judah, son of Jehoram and Athaliah. The idea that the Chronicler was using different sources (Maclean *IDB* 1: 66) is unsound. Such transfer of the elements of a name using the divine epithet is also seen in Jer 22:24, 28. In whichever form, the name is a longer version of Ahaz, and is a combination of the divine name and the verb ʾ*āḥāz,* "to grasp." See also AHAZ. The full name is rare in extrabiblical inscriptions (see Avigad 1969). Hayes and Hooker (1988: 33–35) suggest that Jehoram of Judah and Jehoram of Israel were one and the same person and the father of Ahaziah/Jehoahaz (see also Strange 1975). The advantages of this proposal are many: (1) It would forge a stronger link between the house of Omri and the S throne, which would help explain Athaliah's accession to the Jerusalem throne after the death of Jehoram (her husband) and Ahaziah (her son). (2) A difference of one year in the accession dates of Jehoram to the thrones of Jerusalem and Samaria (852 and 851 B.C.E. respectively) would explain the variant figures for the accession of Ahaziah to the Jerusalem throne in 2 Kgs 8:25 (the 12th year) and 2 Kgs 9:29 (the 11th year), this latter being dated from his father's accession in Samaria. (3) It would explain the strong alliance between N and S against Aram-Damascus at this time, and the visit of Ahaziah to Jezreel to see his ailing father. It might also explain the role of the "inhabitants of Jerusalem" in the ascent to the throne of the youngest of Jehoram's sons (2 Chr 22:1). There is evidence to suggest that the "inhabitants of Jerusalem" were more than city-dwellers (note the associations they have in 2 Kgs 23:2; Jer 2:1; 8:1; 13:13; 17:20). The suggestion to identify the 2 Jehorams as one is attractive, but still quite speculative.

2. The son and successor of Jehu (2 Kgs 10:35; 13:1–9). Like all N kings he is judged as apostate by the Deuteronomist. The account of his reign in 2 Kgs 13:1–9 (there is no parallel account in Chronicles) begins with the typical introductory formula for N kings (13:1), and an evaluation (13:2). The conclusion of his reign (13:8–9) is also typical and formulaic. A number of commentators see secondary, albeit deuteronomistic material, in 13:3–7, and especially 13:4–6 (Gray *1 and 2 Kings* OTL, 591–93). Others (McCarthy 1973: 409–10) believe that 13:3 also betrays signs of a secondary character because of a parallel with the style of the Moabite Stone, line 5 (*ANET,* 320). (For an alternative view on these divisions see Hobbs *2 Kings* WBC, 163.)

Jehoahaz is normally given the dates 815–802 B.C.E. (adjusting the figure "17" of 2 Kgs 13:1 to "15"), but recently Hayes and Hooker (1988: 38–49) have suggested 821–805 B.C.E. Jehoahaz inherited from his father Jehu subservience to Assyria—the evidence of which is found in Shalmaneser III's "black obelisk" (*ANET,* 281)—and presumably the burden of annual tribute. He also inherited a kingdom severely truncated because of repeated wars with Aram-Damascus. These wars resulted in the final loss of the territories on the E side of the Jordan (2 Kgs 10:32–33).

The background to these conflicts was the intense pressure which had been exerted by Shalmaneser III (858–824 B.C.E.) on Aram-Damascus in the decades following the battle of Qarqar in 853 B.C.E. In response to the pressure from the NE, Hazael developed a strategy of strengthening his control of the states to the W (2 Kgs 12:17). Opportunity to do this would have increased in the confusion following the death of Shalmaneser III in 824 B.C.E., and during the reign of his successor, Šamši-Adad (824–810 B.C.E.). It is in this context that the comment in 2 Kgs 13:3 should be understood. During the reign of Adad-nirari III (810–783 B.C.E.) Syria suffered badly, and Hazael died. Adad-nirari's own records tell of the sacking of Damascus (*ANET,* 281–82) in the year 805 B.C.E. Damascus' fall undoubtedly would have relieved the Aramean pressure on Samaria. However, Adad-Nirari also claims to have conquered the coastal states from Tyre in the N to the Philistine territory in the S (*ANET,* 281).

As a result of the constant wars between Israel and Aram-Damascus during the reign of Jehoahaz, the army was greatly reduced until it consisted of 50 cavalry, 10 chariots and 10,000 infantrymen (2 Kgs 13:7). It is not necessary to adjust the figures to larger amounts (so Cogan and Tadmor *2 Kings* AB, 143). These figures as they stand tell a tale. Cavalry and chariotry were campaign units of the army, and would have been used in attacks on Aramean territory, as is seen in the case of the siege of Ramoth-gilead, at which Jehu was anointed king (2 Kings 9). A normal ratio of chariotry to infantry on such campaigns was from 1:30 to 1:50. Ahab fielded a force of 10,000 infantry and 2,000 chariotry at Qarqar. It was also a deliberate policy of Jehu to cultivate the chariot brigade of the army (2 Kgs 10:15–17), and one can imagine that this was a strong element of his forces. However repeated struggles to maintain the E side of the Jordan had taken their toll and the chariot brigade had been severely reduced, many of them no doubt captured as prizes of war with the loss of their skilled crews. The 10,000 infantry remaining might well have constituted a home-based force, but in an age of increasing tactical sophistication on the battlefield, infantry without chariot and cavalry support would have been very vulnerable.

From this situation of reduced territory, external pressure by Syria and the lack of adequate means of defense Israel was rescued by a "savior" (Heb *môšîa*ʿ; (2 Kgs 13:5). This term has been the cause of much discussion among interpreters. Set against this political and military background, it seems reasonable that the "savior" should have been a political or military figure, and a number of scholars suggest that the relief brought by Adad-Nirari's campaign in 805 B.C.E. against Damascus qualifies the Assyrian for the title (Haran 1967; Hallo 1962; Cogan and Tadmor *2 Kings* AB, 143). Herrmann argued for Zakir of Hamath (*HHI*), but the dates are wrong. Other candidates have been Jeroboam II and Joash. A major alternative to these identifications is the prophet Elisha, who now returns to the scene of Israelite history after a gap of almost 50 years (so Hobbs *2 Kings* WBC; Gray *1 and 2 Kings* OTL; *UgS*). The description of Jehoahaz's reign and its misfortunes reflects the depiction of the theological significance of the

Exodus in Deut 26:7–9, and the activity of Elisha narrated in 2 Kgs 13:14–20 ensures further respite from the attacks of the Arameans, a fact not missed by the Deuteronomist (2 Kgs 13:23), and echoed later in the activity of Isaiah of Jerusalem in his dealings with Hezekiah (2 Kgs 20:1–11).

Bibliography

Avigad, N. 1969. A Group of Hebrew Seals. *EI* 9:1–9.

Hallo, W. 1962. From Qarqar to Carchemish. *BA* 23: 34–61.

Haran, M. 1967. The Empire of Jeroboam ben Joash. *VT* 17: 267–97.

Hayes, J. H. and Hooker, P. K. 1988. *A New Chronology for the Kings of Israel and Judah.* Atlanta.

Malamat, A. 1973. The Aramaeans. Pp. 134–55 in POTT.

Mazar, B. 1986. The Aramaean Empire and Its Relations with Israel. Pp. 151–72 in *The Early Biblical Period. Historical Essays.* Jerusalem.

McCarthy, D. J. 1973. 2 Kings 13:4–6. *Bib* 54: 409-10.

Stillman, N., and Tallis, N. 1984. *Armies of the Ancient Near East, 3000 BC to 539 BC.* London.

Strange, J. 1975. Joram, King of Israel and Judah. *VT* 15: 191–201.

T. R. Hobbs

3. King of Judah for 3 months in 609 B.C.; fourth son and successor of Josiah; exiled to Egypt by Pharaoh Neco II. This king is called by two names: Jehoahaz and Shallum (1 Chr 3:15; Jer 22:11; see SHALLUM). It seems likely that Shallum was his personal name and that he assumed a throne name, Jehoahaz ("Yahweh has seized"), when he became king, emphasizing that he was the legitimate ruler. In similar fashion his successor Eliakim became Jehoiakim (2 Kgs 23:34), Jeconiah (Coniah) became Jehoiachin (Joiachin; 2 Kgs 24:6; Jer 22:24; 24:1; Ezek 1:2), and Mattaniah became Zedekiah (2 Kgs 24:17). See Honeyman 1948: 13–25. In 1 Esdr 1:34, Jeconiah occurs as an alternate form for Jehoahaz (though not to be confused with Jehoiachin; see JECONIAH).

Jehoahaz succeeded at the age of 23 and reigned for 3 months in Jerusalem. His mother was Hamutal (or Hamital), the daughter of Jeremiah of Libnah (2 Kgs 23:31; 2 Chr 36:2). According to the family tree in 1 Chr 3:15 Shallum was the youngest of Josiah's four sons, and yet the "people of the land" chose him as king after Pharaoh Neco had killed his father at Megiddo (2 Kgs 23:30). The anti-Egyptian sentiments of the group would have influenced this choice which the prevailing mood of the people may have supported (Malamat 1975: 126).

The brief reign of Jehoahaz coincides with Neco's expedition to Haran, where he tried to establish Ashur-uballit on the throne between June/July and August/September 609 B.C. (Wiseman 1956: 62–64). The Babylonians were, however, able to retain Haran which they had captured from the Assyrians the previous year. The pharaoh then proceeded to consolidate his possession of Syria and Palestine, territories that had belonged to the Assyrian empire. Jehoahaz was summoned to Neco's strategically placed headquarters at Riblah on the Orontes in central Syria and put in bonds "so that he should not reign in Jerusalem" (2 Kgs 23:33; see Dahood 1978: 92 n. 6). A fine of 100 talents of silver and a talent of gold was also levied. This is small when compared with the indemnity required of Hezekiah by Sennacherib 100 years earlier (2 Kgs 18:14: 300 talents of silver and 10 of gold), but the offense of Josiah was smaller. In fact he may have been victim rather than aggressor (Nelson 1983: 188). The pharaoh perhaps also wished to be conciliatory in view of his unresolved conflict with Babylon (Gray *1 and 2 Kings* OTL, 750–51). He therefore deposed Jehoahaz, who was allied with anti-Egyptian interests, and made his elder half-brother Eliakim king, giving him the throne name Jehoiakim. Jehoahaz was sent to Egypt where he died (2 Kgs 23:34; 2 Chr 36:4).

The Deuteronomistic judgment on his reign is that "he did evil in the sight of Yahweh according to all that his fathers had done" (2 Kgs 23:32), a standard formula which is hardly very meaningful in relation to the 3-month reign of Jehoahaz (Jones *1 and 2 Kings* NCBC, 631). It might simply be an inference from his fate, or he may have been too ready to go to Neco at Riblah, perhaps with a view to being confirmed in office (Gray *1 and 2 Kings* OTL, 749–50).

The prophet Jeremiah alludes to the exile of Jehoahaz in a dirge (22:10–12). People are not to weep for Josiah, who is dead, but for Shallum, who will never return from exile. Scharbert (1981: 47–48) considers that the prophet is not revealing any personal pity for either of them. The dirge is followed by a strong condemnation of Shallum's successor Jehoiakim (vv 13–19); no doubt the rampant injustice of this king furnished an important motive for regretting his predecessor.

The exile of Jehoahaz marked the end of Judah's independence, which had lasted about 20 years. Subsequent kings were reluctant to accept their dependent status, especially after Nebuchadnezzar's victories over the Egyptians in 605 B.C. resulted in Judah becoming subject to Babylon. Attempts to throw off the Babylonian yoke led to Jehoiachin being exiled in 597 B.C. and Zedekiah in 587 B.C. Both rulers were accompanied by many of their subjects. And so the fate of Jehoahaz foreshadowed that of the people in the Babylonian captivity.

Bibliography

Dahood, M. 1978. "Weaker than Water": Comparative *beth* in Isaiah 1,22. *Bib* 59: 91–92.

Honeyman, A. M. 1948. The Evidence for Regnal Names among the Hebrews. *JBL* 67: 13–25.

Malamat, A. 1975. The Twilight of Judah: in the Egyptian-Mesopotamian Maelstrom. *VTSup* 28: 123–45.

Nelson, R. D. 1983. *Realpolitik* in Judah (687–609 B.C.E.). Pp. 177–89 in *Scripture in Context II,* ed. W. W. Hallo, J. C. Moyer, and L. C. Perdue. Winona Lake, IN.

Scharbert, J. 1981. Jeremia und die Reform des Joschija. Pp. 40–57 in *Le Livre de Jérémie,* ed. P.-M. Bogaert. BETL 54. Leuven.

Wiseman, D. J. 1956. *Chronicles of Chaldaean Kings (626–556 B.C.) in the British Museum.* London.

Robert Althann

JEHOHANAN (PERSON) [Heb *yĕhôḥānān*]. Eight persons in the OT bear this name, which means "Yahweh has been gracious." It also appears in the Elephantine papyri in *CAP* 30.18 and 31.17 (see 4. below). It is normally rendered in Gk *Iōanan,* although 1 Esdr 9:29 see #5 below) reads *Iōannēs.*

1. A Levitical gatekeeper of the Korahite family of Meshelemiah. He is named as the 6th son of this family in 1 Chr 26:3, in the Chronicler's (Williamson *Chronicles* NCBC, 169) or perhaps a later (Rudolph *Chronikbücher* HAT, 173) organization of the gatekeepers in the temple at Jerusalem.

2. The second of 3 military "commanders of thousands" from Judah under Jehoshaphat named in 2 Chr 17:14–16. In the present setting, framed by vv 13b and 19, Jehohanan and the others named appear to have been officers over troops in the standing army. However, since within that framework they were mustered according to "their fathers' houses" (v 14) and organized by tribal divisions (vv 14, 17), Jehohanan may more likely have been a commander of the militia or conscript forces (Williamson *Chronicles* NCBC, 284).

3. The father of Ishmael, one of the leading officers named by the Chronicler as having supported Jehoiada in his revolt against Athaliah. However, the names of these men (with only one exception, including their fathers) are all priestly or levitical and are probably a tendentious replacement of "the captains of the Carites and of the guards" in the account of the conspiracy in 1 Kgs 11:4, since such would have been excluded from entering the Chronicler's temple (1 Chr 23:6) (Rudolph *Chronikbücher* HAT, 271).

4. The "chamber of Jehohanan the son of Eliashib" is named as the place to which Ezra withdrew to spend the night (1 Esdr 9:2) in fasting after his great call to the assembly in the temple for an end to mixed marriages (Ezra 10:6 = 1 Esdr 9:1). The identity of this individual is quite problematic.

(a) It has been argued that this designation of the chamber could be simply that by which it was known at the time of the Chronicler, and thus there may not have been a Jehohanan the son of Eliashib who was a contemporary of Ezra (Meyer 1896: 91; Ahlemann 1942/43: 97–98).

(b) The names Jehohanan/Johanan and Eliashib are sufficiently common that this person, even if a contemporary of Ezra, may have been a private individual, not of a priestly family, who was a friend or supporter of Ezra and his attempts at reform (Rudolph *Esra und Nehemia* HAT, 68–69; on temple chambers associated with such individuals see 2 Kgs 23:11; Jer 35:4; 36:10).

(c) If this Jehohanan ben Eliashib is identical to the Johanan who was apparently the grandson of Eliashib named in Neh 12:22 (see also 12:23), then he was the high priest Jehohanan named in the Elephantine papyri *AP* 30–31 (408 B.C.E.). In this case, the contemporaneity of Jehohanan and Ezra would imply that the latter's activity followed rather than preceded Nehemiah, who was a contemporary of the high priest Eliashib (Rowley 1965: 153–59).

(d) More recently, by assuming the practice of papponymy among the high-priestly family in Jerusalem (on the basis of its practice among the Sanballatids of Samaria) it has been proposed that haplography in the high-priestly genealogy has resulted in the loss of an Eliashib I and his son, Johanan I (between Joiakim and Eliashib named in Neh 12:10) (Cross 1975: 9–11). Restoration of these 2 names results in a Jehohanan/Johanan the son of Eliashib who was a high priest; he would have been a contemporary of Ezra according to the traditional dating of Ezra's activity in Jerusalem, and into whose chamber Ezra withdrew.

5. A layman of the family of Bebai named in Ezra 10:28 = 1 Esdr 9:29 in a list of those who were married to foreign wives at the time of Ezra's reforms.

6. A son of Tobiah "the Ammonite," one of Nehemiah's principal opponents in his attempts to rebuild Jerusalem's wall (Neh 6:18). This Jehohanan was married to a Jerusalemite woman, a daughter of Meshullam the son Berechiah who worked on the wall (Neh 3:4).

7. According to Neh 12:13, a certain Jehohanan was the head of the priestly family of Amariah at the time of the high priest Joiakim.

8. One of several Levites (see Clines *Ezra, Nehemiah, Esther* NCBC, 233) who participated in the temple service celebrating the dedication of the rebuilt wall of Jerusalem in the time of Nehemiah (Neh 12:42). The suggestion of Bertheau (1887: 341) that the names are representative of divisions of Levites rather than individuals is still worthy of consideration.

Bibliography

Ahlemann, F. 1942/43. Zur Ezra-Quelle. *ZAW* 59: 77–98.

Bertheau, E. 1887. *Die Buecher Esra, Nechemia und Ester.* 2d ed. Leipzig.

Cross, F. M. 1975. A Reconstruction of the Judean Restoration. *JBL* 94: 4–18.

Meyer, E. 1896. *Die Entstehung des Judentums.* Halle.

Rowley, H. H. 1965. The Chronological Order of Ezra and Nehemiah. Pp. 135–68 in *The Servant of the Lord.* 2d ed. Oxford.

J. S. ROGERS

JEHOIACHIN

JEHOIACHIN (PERSON) [Heb *yĕhôyākîn*]. Var. JOIACHIN; JECONIAH; CONIAH; JECHONIAH. Son of Jehoiakim and king of Judah for 3 months from December 598 (or January 597) to March 597 B.C.E. Jehoiachin (or Joiachin; Heb *yôyākin*) was undoubtedly a throne name, meaning "Yahweh establishes" or "let Yahweh establish." His given name was Jeconiah (Heb *yĕkonyāhû; yĕkonyāh;* Jer 24:1; 27:20; 28:4; 29:2; 1 Chr 3:16–17; Esth 2:6; "Jechoniah" in Matt 1:11–12). A shortened form of this personal name is Coniah (*konyāhû;* Jer 22:24, 28; 37:1).

A. Jehoiachin's Brief Reign

Jehoiachin became king of Judah at the age of 18 (2 Kgs 24:8; the Hebrew text of 2 Chr 36:9 incorrectly states that he was 8 years of age [the LXX reads "eighteen"]), following the death of his father Jehoiakim (2 Kgs 24:6; 2 Chr 36:8; Matt 1:11–17, which fails to include Jehoiakim in the genealogy, presents Jehoiachin as the son of Josiah in v 11). Jehoiachin's mother was Nehushta, the daughter of ELNATHAN of Jerusalem (2 Kgs 24:8). This Elnathan is very possibly to be identified with Elnathan, son of Achbor, a high-ranking government official mentioned in Jer 26:22 and 36:12, 25. If Nehushta was the daughter of this Elnathan, her grandfather was probably Achbor son of Michaiah, an official who plays a prominent role in the account of Josiah's reform (2 Kgs 22:12, 14). The name Elnathan also appears in a contemporary document from Lachish (see Ostracon III in *DOTT,* 214).

With respect to establishing the chronology for Jehoiachin's reign, we are greatly indebted to a section of the Babylonian Chronicle first published in 1956. It is now known that the end of Jehoiachin's reign occurred on the 2d day of the month of Adar in the 7th year of Nebuchadrezzar (BM 21946 verso, line 12; see Wiseman 1956: 73; TCS 5, 102). This date corresponds to either March 15 or March 16 (the Babylonian day extended from sunset to sunset, and thus overlaps 2 days of our calendar), 597 B.C.E.

It may not be possible, however, to assign a precise date to the beginning of Jehoiachin's rule. 2 Kgs 24:8 states that he reigned for 3 months, a figure which is probably a round number. 2 Chr 36:9 assigns 3 months and 10 days to Jehoiachin's rule. Although many scholars favor the Chronicler's reading (which would enable us to date Jehoiachin's accession to December 9/10, 598 B.C.E.), it is possible that this more precise reading rests on a scribal error. After having served as vassal to Babylonia for 3 years, Jehoiachin's predecessor Jehoiakim rebelled in 601 or 600 B.C.E. (2 Kgs 24:1), provoking Nebuchadrezzar to take retaliatory measures. Babylonian reprisals (cf. 2 Kgs 24:2) culminated in the siege of Jerusalem (2 Kgs 24:10–17). According to the Babylonian Chronicle, it was during the month of Kislev in Nebuchadrezzar's 7th year (December 18, 598–January 15, 597 B.C.E.) that the Babylonian king and his troops left Babylon on an expedition directed against Judah (BM 21946 verso, line 11). It would appear that Jehoiakim died (possibly he was assassinated; cf. Jer 22:18–19; 36:30) during (or perhaps just before) the early part of the siege, prior to Nebuchadrezzar's arrival in Jerusalem (cf. 2 Kgs 24:10–11). See JEHOIAKIM.

Thus it was the young king Jehoiachin who found himself in the unfortunate position of having to confront Nebuchadrezzar in Jerusalem. Jehoiachin chose to surrender (2 Kgs 24:12), undoubtedly thereby hoping that the Babylonians would withdraw. The siege was indeed lifted, but Jehoiachin himself was deposed by Nebuchadrezzar and deported to Babylon. The Babylonian Chronicle states that Nebuchadrezzar "seized the city and captured the king. He appointed there a king of his own choice (lit. heart), received its heavy tribute and sent (them) to Babylon" (BM 21946 verso, lines 12–13 in Wiseman 1956: 73; TCS 5, 102). Although the Babylonian document does not provide the names of the two kings, it is clear that the deposed king was Jehoiachin (cf. 2 Kgs 24:12, 15; 2 Chr 36:10). The king of Nebuchadrezzar's choice was Mattaniah, Jehoiachin's uncle, who was then given the name Zedekiah (2 Kgs 24:17). According to the MT of 2 Chr 36:10, Zedekiah was Jehoiachin's brother; the LXX and other versions, however, read "father's brother" (cf. 1 Chr 3:15).

Also deported, in addition to the king, the queen mother, and other members of the royal family, were various court officials, leading citizens, military figures, craftsmen, artisans, prophets, and priests (cf. 2 Kgs 24:12, 14–16; Jer 24:1; 27:20; 29:1–2; most commentators believe that the passage Jer 13:18–19 relates to Jehoiachin and his mother Nehushta). Treasure from both the temple and the royal palace was taken as tribute (2 Kgs 24:13; 2 Chr 36:10; Jer 27:16–22; 28:3, 6).

B. Jehoiachin in Exile

Cuneiform tablets found at Babylon shed some light on Jehoiachin's fate in exile (Albright 1942). The tablets, which date from the 10th to the 35th year of Nebuchadrezzar (595/594–570/569 B.C.E.), list the rations distributed by the Babylonians to various captives and skilled workmen. A number of Judeans are among the foreigners named in these documents. The tablets include the monthly rations of oil for *Yaʾu-kīnu* (alternately *Yakū-kinu*), "king of the land of *Yahudu*" (= Judah; alternately *Yaudu, Yakudu*) and his 5 sons (*DOTT*, 86; Weidner 1939: 925–26). One of the four texts which speaks of Jehoiachin and his sons is dated to Nebuchadrezzar's 13th year (592/591 B.C.E.). Since Jehoiachin was only 24 years of age at this time, some believe that the documents must be referring to Jehoiachin's brothers. However, it is most probable that the references are to Jehoiachin's young sons. That the 5 are infants is indicated by the mention made of the boys' attendant. Further, it should be noted that Jehoiachin apparently had more than one wife (2 Kgs 24:15). 2 Kgs 25:27–30 (a close parallel is found in Jer 52:31–34) implies that at least in the year 561/560 B.C.E., Jehoiachin was imprisoned.

Yet the Babylonian documents just cited give the impression that Jehoiachin and his family enjoyed relative freedom in exile and were treated very favorably. It is probable that Jehoiachin and his family, and perhaps some of the nobles, were placed under house arrest in the South Citadel in Babylon. The large quantity of oil allocated to Jehoiachin (he received approximately 5 liters of oil, this being 12 times the amount received by each of his sons) suggests that Jehoiachin was responsible for supporting his own household. Many scholars are of the opinion that the Babylonians continued to regard the exiled Jehoiachin as the legitimate king of Judah, and in these documents Jehoiachin is referred to as "king of Judah." It is doubtful, however, that such a use of Jehoiachin's title in these Babylonian documents supports this hypothesis. Nevertheless, the fact that Jehoiachin was well treated in captivity could indicate that the Babylonians were prepared to reinstate Jehoiachin should problems arise with Zedekiah's leadership in Jerusalem.

It is apparent that both in Babylonia and in Judah, there were circles which viewed Jehoiachin as the legitimate ruler of Judah, with Zedekiah being regarded as Jehoiachin's regent. The fact that the book of Ezekiel favors a dating system based on the year of Jehoiachin's deportation (e.g., Ezek 1:2) may reflect this view. In Judah, storage jar handles have been discovered at the sites of Tell Beit Mirsim, Beth-shemesh, and Ramat Raḥel, which bear the stamp *lʾlyqm nʿr ywkn* ("to Eliakim, steward of Yaukin"). Most scholars accept the identification of the Yaukin of this seal impression with Jehoiachin. It is assumed that although in exile, Jehoiachin continued to hold crown property in Judah, property which was administered by the Eliakim of the stamp. Some scholars, however, have argued that the evidence antedates Jehoiachin's reign, and thus cannot relate to Jehoiachin. It has also been hypothesized that in addition to the Eliakim seal impressions, 2 contemporary seals (inscribed "to Jaazaniah, servant of the king" and "to Gedaliah, who is over the house") may constitute further evidence that both the people of Judah and the

Babylonians continued to regard the exiled Jehoiachin as king, with Gedaliah acting as regent (following the supposed regency of Zedekiah) for Jehoiachin (see May 1939).

The political divisions which characterized this period were shared by Judah's prophets. Hannaniah prophesied (in either the 1st or 4th year of Zedekiah's reign) that Jehoiachin would return to Judah within 2 years, together with those taken captive and the temple vessels carried off as tribute (Jer 28:2–4). The prophet Jeremiah, who maintained a pro-Babylonian position throughout his ministry, strongly opposed such a view. He announced that Jehoiachin would never return to the land of Judah (Jer 22:27; cf. the lamentation Ezek 19:1–9, where many commentators believe that the king of vv 5–9 is Jehoiachin). Moreover, according to Jeremiah, none of Jehoiachin's offspring would sit on the throne of David (Jer 22:30; see Hermisson 1980). In a letter written to the exiles, Jeremiah enjoined them to prepare for a lengthy stay of 70 years (Jer 29:10). He cautioned against paying heed to prophets (addressing them in exile, Jer 29:8–9) who shared the political ideology of a figure like Hananiah. Whereas Jeremiah rejected any element of hope centered in Jehoiachin and his children, the messianic promise contained in Ezek 17:22–24 may refer to the descendants of Jehoiachin. Such hope is not expressed, however, in Ezek 19:10–14, a dirge which laments the full end of the monarchy in Judah.

The Deuteronomistic History closes with 2 Kgs 25:27–30 (cf. the close parallel in Jer 52:31–34), a passage which contains an account of the release of Jehoiachin by the Babylonian king Amel-Marduk (called Evil-Merodach in the Hebrew Bible; see Levenson 1984). This occurred in the 37th year of Jehoiachin's captivity (561/560 B.C.E.), and was possibly part of an amnesty marking Amel-Marduk's enthronement (cf. 2 Kgs 25:27; Jer 52:31). Jehoiachin put off his prison garments, and was given a seat above the other exiled kings. He dined regularly at the royal table, and was provided with an allowance for the remainder of his life (cf. especially Jer 52:34, which adds "until the day of his death"). As is indicated in particular by the words *waydabbēr ʾittô ṭōbôt* (usually translated "and he spoke kindly to him") in 2 Kgs 25:28 (Jer 52:32), it is possible that 2 Kgs 25:27–30 (cf. Jer 52:31–34) reflects the establishment of a treaty between the Babylonian king and Jehoiachin. Amel-Marduk may have intended to restore Jehoiachin or one of his sons to the throne as a vassal king; however, Amel-Marduk died in 560 B.C.E., shortly after Jehoiachin's release.

Jehoiachin's 7 sons are listed in 1 Chr 3:17–18. His son Shenazzar is very possibly to be identified with Sheshbazzar, the first governor of Judah during the Persian period (e.g. Ezra 5:14). Sheshbazzar is referred to by the title "the prince of Judah" in Ezra 1:8. He was succeeded in this office by Zerubbabel, the son of Jehoiachin's son Shealtiel (e.g. Ezra 3:2; Hag 1:1; 1 Chr 3:19 in the LXX; in the MT, 1 Chr 3:19 states that Zerubbabel's father was Pedaiah, another son of Jehoiachin).

Bibliography

Albright, W. F. 1942. King Joiachin in Exile. *BA* 5: 49–55.

Hermisson, H. J. 1980. Jeremias Wort über Jojachin. Pp. 252–70 in *Werden und Wirken des Alten Testaments,* ed. R. Albertz et al. Göttingen.

Levenson, J. D. 1984. The Last Four Verses in Kings. *JBL* 103: 353–61.

Malamat, A. 1975. The Twilight of Judah: In the Egyptian-Babylonian Maelstrom. *VTSup* 28: 123–45.

May, H. G. 1939. Three Hebrew Seals and the Status of Exiled Jehoiachin. *AJSL* 61: 146–48.

Ussishkin, D. 1976. Royal Judean Storage Jars and Private Seal Impressions. *BASOR* 223: 1–13.

Weidner, E. F. 1939. Jojachin, König von Juda, in Babylonischen Keilschrifttexten. Vol. 2, pp. 923–35 in *Mélanges syriens offerts à M. René Dussaud.* Paris.

Wiseman, D. J. 1956. *Chronicles of Chaldaean Kings (626–556 B.C.) in the British Museum.* London. Repr. 1961.

JOHN M. BERRIDGE

JEHOIADA (PERSON) [Heb *yĕhôyādāᶜ*]. **1.** The father of Benaiah who was commander of the personal bodyguard of King David (2 Sam 8:18). It is perhaps this same Jehoiada who joined David at Hebron (1 Chr 12:28—Eng 12:27). There Jehoiada is called a prince and is from the house of Aaron. The Chronicler appears to be emphasizing this Aaronic connection when he refers to Jehoiada as a priest (1 Chr 27:5).

2. The son of Benaiah (1 Chr 27:34). He was counselor to David after Ahithophel committed suicide during the revolt of Absalom. It is possible that the genealogical reference has been reversed here and that this should be "Benaiah son of Jehoiada" (*HAIJ,* 188). In this case, this individual would be the same as #1 above.

3. The priest in Jerusalem who organized the overthrow of Queen Athaliah and placed Joash son of Ahaziah on the throne as the rightful heir of the Davidic family (2 Kgs 11:4–20). Athaliah, the mother of Ahaziah, had seized control when her son was killed in battle. In order to secure her hold on the throne, she ordered all other members of the royal family executed. Joash, the infant son of Ahaziah, was hidden by his aunt Jehosheba and protected for 6 years. Jehoiada then enlisted the help of the palace guard and publicly revealed the existence of the young Joash. Queen Athaliah was taken from the palace and executed and the 7-year-old Joash was proclaimed king of Judah (2 Kgs 12:1—Eng 11:21). Jehoiada also renewed the covenant between the Lord and the king and the people (2 Kgs 11:17). In connection with this covenant renewal, the house of Baal was torn down and the priest of Baal was executed. The Baal worship probably had been supported by Athaliah who was the granddaughter of Omri king of Israel.

Jehoiada served as counselor and advisor to the young king Joash who is reported to have done "what is right in the eyes of the Lord" (2 Kgs 12:3—Eng 12:2). Joash, also called Jehoash, initiated repairs on the house of the Lord, but there was little progress. In the 23d year of his reign, he called Jehoiada the priest to account for this failure to complete the temple repairs. Jehoiada then placed a collection box and armed guards at the entrance of the temple in order to ensure that all money contributed would be used for the intended repairs. The work was carried out in stages as the money was collected (2 Kgs 12:10).

In the parallel account in 2 Chr 22:11, Jehosheba, the

aunt who hid the young king, was also the wife of Jehoiada. This would make Jehoiada the uncle of king Joash.

4. A priest in the time of Jeremiah who was replaced by Zephaniah (Jer 29:26).

PHILLIP E. MCMILLION

JEHOIAKIM (PERSON) [Heb *yĕhôyāqîm*]. King of Judah who reigned 609/8–598/7 B.C.E. Jehoiakim, whose given name was Eliakim (meaning "God raises up"), was the son of Josiah. His mother was Zebidah, daughter of Pedaiah of Rumah (2 Kgs 23:36) in Galilee.

A. Jehoiakim's Reign

Following the death of Josiah at Megiddo (2 Kgs 23:29) in 609, the "people of the land" (*ʿam-hāʾāreṣ*) anointed Josiah's son Jehoahaz king of Judah (2 Kgs 23:30; 2 Chr 36:1). It was undoubtedly because the "people of the land" expected Jehoahaz to continue the anti-Egyptian policy of his father that they chose Jehoahaz over Eliakim, his elder brother (cf. 2 Kgs 23:31 and 36; also 1 Chr 3:15 [Jehoahaz is here called by his personal name Shallum]).

1. Jehoiakim as Egyptian Vassal. Under Neco II (610–595), the Egyptians gained control of Syria and Palestine in 609. The brief reign of Jehoahaz came to an end when he was deposed by Neco at the Egyptian headquarters at Riblah on the Orontes. Neco then placed his half-brother Eliakim on the throne, giving him the Yahwistic throne-name Jehoiakim (2 Kgs 23:33–34; 2 Chr 36:3–4). Jehoahaz was deported to Egypt, where he died (2 Kgs 23:34; cf. Jer 22:10–12; Ezek 19:1–4).

Jehoiakim was installed as king of Judah following an Egyptian campaign in N Syria, where Neco was unsuccessful in his attempt to wrest Haran from the Babylonians. The Babylonian Chronicle (see the translations in TCS 5 and Wiseman 1956) informs us that this campaign lasted until the month Elul (August/September). Thus it is probable that Jehoiakim was placed on the throne late in 609. He reigned over Judah for 11 years (2 Kgs 23:36; 2 Chr 36:5). Jehoiakim's 1st regnal year was 608/607, his 11th and last 598/597. He was 25 years of age when he began his reign (2 Kgs 23:36; 2 Chr 36:5). He died shortly before the Babylonians captured the city of Jerusalem on the 2d day of the month Adar in Nebuchadrezzar's 7th year (March 15/16, 597). Jehoiakim was succeeded by his son Jehoiachin (Matthew 1 does not include Jehoiakim in the genealogy, and lists Jehoiachin (called by his personal name Jechoniah) as the son of Josiah in Matt 1:11) and by his half brother Mattaniah (renamed Zedekiah), the last two kings of Judah (2 Kgs 24:6, 17).

Judah's vassal status is clearly indicated by the fact that it was Neco who determined who would sit on the throne of Judah and who gave this king his throne name (2 Kgs 23:34). The Egyptians exacted a heavy tribute from Jehoiakim. According to the Hebrew text, Neco demanded a tribute of 100 talents of silver and a talent of gold (2 Kgs 23:33 [2 Chr 36:3]; the LXX, however, reads "a hundred talents of gold"; the Lucianic recensions of the Greek and the Peshitta read "ten talents of gold"). Jehoiakim met this demand by taxing those who had earlier anointed Jehoahaz king, the "people of the land" (2 Kgs 23:35).

Jehoiakim remained Egypt's vassal until 605. In that year the Babylonian crown prince Nebuchadrezzar led the Babylonian forces to a decisive victory over the Egyptians at Carchemish (cf. Jer 46:2–12), followed by another at Hamath (cf. TCS 5, 99; Wiseman 1956: 67, 69), thereby paving the way for Babylonian domination over Syria and Palestine. 2 Kgs 24:7 correctly notes that "the king of Egypt did not come again out of his land, for the king of Babylon had taken all that belonged to the king of Egypt from the Brook of Egypt to the river Euphrates."

2. Jehoiakim as Babylonian Vassal. The Babylonian Chronicle reports that Nebuchadrezzar interrupted his advance to the S when he learned of the death of his father Nabopolassar. He returned to Babylon immediately, and ascended the throne on the 1st day of the month Elul (September 6/7, 605). Nebuchadrezzar did, however, return to the W later in the same year (his "accession year"), following his coronation. He also campaigned in Syria-Palestine ("Hattu" ["the land of Hatti"] in the Babylonian Chronicle) during each of his first 4 regnal years (although we cannot be certain that he campaigned in the W during his second year, it is probable that he did so). It was in connection with one of these campaigns that Jehoiakim became Nebuchadrezzar's vassal. Most scholars believe that this probably occurred during the lengthy campaign conducted during Nebuchadrezzar's first regnal year (604/3). The Babylonian Chronicle states that "in the month Sivan he mustered his army and marched to Hattu. Until the month Kislev he marched about victoriously in Hattu. All the kings of Hattu came into his presence and he received their vast tribute (TCS 5, 100; cf. Wiseman 1956: 69).

The closing lines of this section of the Babylonian Chronicle focus on Nebuchadrezzar's destruction of a particular city. Although the reading here is uncertain, it is probable that the Chronicle is speaking of the city of Ashkelon, located on the Philistine Plain. This event occurred in the month Kislev (December 604). A public fast which was observed in Jerusalem in the same month (cf. Jer 36:9, which states that this fast was held in the 9th month of Jehoiakim's 5th year), may have been called in response to the Babylonian conquest of Ashkelon. It is possible that Jehoiakim submitted to the Babylonians shortly after the fall of Ashkelon.

2 Kgs 24:1 observes that "in his days, Nebuchadnezzar king of Babylon came up, and Jehoiakim became his servant three years; then he turned and rebelled against him." It is probable that Jehoiakim paid tribute to Nebuchadrezzar in the years 603, 602, and 601. Jehoiakim's decision to revolt was undoubtedly influenced by a serious military setback experienced by the Babylonians during Nebuchadrezzar's 4th year (601/600). In the month Kislev, Nebuchadrezzar led his army from Syria-Palestine to Egypt, where they were met by Neco's forces. The Chronicle reports that "they fought one another in the battlefield and both sides suffered severe losses (lit. they inflicted a major defeat upon one another). The king of Akkad and his army turned and (went back) to Babylon" (TCS 5, 101; cf. Wiseman 1956: 71). While it is very possible that the Egyptians encouraged Jehoiakim to revolt, it is unlikely that he would have rebelled before witnessing this clear demonstration of Babylonian weakness. (It would appear that Egypt was able to take Gaza at this time [cf. Jer 47:1].) Thus it is probable that Jehoiakim withheld tribute in

Nisan of the year 600, at the beginning of Nebuchadrezzar's 5th regnal year (see Katzenstein 1983).

It was some time before Nebuchadrezzar took direct punitive action against Jehoiakim. The Babylonian Chronicle notes that in his 5th year (600/599), Nebuchadrezzar "stayed home (and) refitted his numerous horses and chariotry" (TCS 5, 101; cf. Wiseman 1956: 71). And, although Nebuchadrezzar returned to the W during the following year (599/8), on this occasion he "despatched his army from Hattu and they went off to the desert. They plundered extensively the possessions, animals, and gods of the numerous Arabs" (TCS 5, 101; cf. Wiseman 1956: 71). We learn from 2 Kgs 24:2, however, that Nebuchadrezzar did respond to Jehoiakim's rebellion by dispatching Babylonian units already stationed in Syria-Palestine, together with bands of Syrians (it is unnecessary to amend the text to read "Edomites" [cf. Jer 35:11]), Moabites, and Ammonites. Nothing is known of the outcome of this attack on Judah.

In the Babylonian Chronicle, the entry for the 7th year of Nebuchadrezzar's reign (598/7) relates solely to the capture of Jerusalem: "In the month Kislev the king of Akkad mustered his army and marched to Hattu. He encamped against the city of Judah and on the second day of the month Adar he captured the city (and) seized (its) king. A king of his own choice he appointed in the city (and) taking the vast tribute he brought it into Babylon" (TCS 5, 102; cf. Wiseman 1956: 73). Thus, following a short siege, Jerusalem was taken (cf. 2 Kgs 24:10–17) on March 15/16, 597 (the Babylonian day extended from sunset to sunset, and thus overlaps 2 days of our calendar). Jehoiakim died some time before the fall of the city, either before or during the siege (but before Nebuchadrezzar himself arrived in Jerusalem [cf. 2 Kgs 24:11]). The king seized by Nebuchadrezzar was Jehoiakim's successor, his son Jehoiachin (2 Kgs 24:12, 15). The "king of his own choice" was Mattaniah, to whom Nebuchadrezzar gave the name Zedekiah (2 Kgs 24:17).

3. Jehoiakim's Death. There are conflicting traditions relating to the death of Jehoiakim (see Green 1982). 2 Kgs 24:6, which states that Jehoiakim "slept with his fathers," implies that Jehoiakim died a natural and peaceful death. The Lucianic recension of 2 Kgs 24:6 (cf. also 2 Chr 36:8 in the LXX) adds that Jehoiakim "was buried with his fathers in the Garden of Uzzah" (cf. 2 Kgs 21:18, 26, where this garden is reported to be the burial place of both Manasseh and Amon). The Chronicler says nothing of Jehoiakim's death. Instead, there is the suggestion in 2 Chr 36:6 that Jehoiakim (like Jehoiachin) was deported by Nebuchadrezzar (e.g., NEB: "put him in fetters and took him to Babylon"). However, although this reading is supported by the LXX (cf. 1 Esdr 1:38 [40]; also Dan 1:1–2), and although 2 Chr 36:7 states that treasure from the temple was taken to Babylon at this time, 2 Chr 36:6 probably states only that Nebuchadrezzar "bound him in fetters to take him to Babylon" (RSV).

Josephus reports that Jehoiakim was killed in Jerusalem at the command of Nebuchadrezzar, his body "to be thrown before the walls, without any burial" (*Ant* 10.6.3). This account probably reflects 2 oracles contained in the book of Jeremiah. In Jer 36:30 it is announced that Jehoiakim's "dead body shall be cast out to the heat by day and the frost by night." Similarly, Jer 22:13–19 closes with the prediction that Jehoiakim's death will not be lamented in the usual manner. Instead, he will receive "the burial of an ass" (that is, his body will remain unburied), and his body will be "dragged and cast forth beyond the gates of Jerusalem" (vv 18–19). Although some scholars believe that Jehoiakim may have been assassinated by members of the pro-Babylonian minority in Judah, there is no evidence that this occurred. Further, there is no evidence to support the view that upon his arrival in Jerusalem, Nebuchadrezzar disinterred Jehoiakim's body. It is most probable that Jehoiakim died a natural death (in December 598, or possibly in January 597), and that the predictions of Jer 22:18–19 and 36:30 were thus unfulfilled.

B. Prophetic Opposition to Jehoiakim

It is clear that under Jehoiakim, the reform instituted by Josiah lapsed. The prophet Jeremiah was an outspoken critic of the socioreligious conditions which prevailed in Judah during Jehoiakim's reign. His "Temple Sermon" (Jer 7:1–15) suggests that part of Jehoiakim's policy was an affirmation of the inviolability of the temple (see Wilcoxen 1977). However, although this oracle is indeed critical of blind trust placed in the temple, its focal point is a denunciation of the people for their failure to be obedient to the Torah (see Holt 1986). It is known, for example, that during Jehoiakim's reign, foreign cults again made their appearance (cf. Jer 7:9, 18, 31; 11:9–13). Further, the pro-Egyptian foreign policy pursued by Jehoiakim stood opposed to the pro-Babylonian position consistently advocated by Jeremiah. That Jeremiah was not alone in his opposition to Jehoiakim and his policies is indicated by Jer 26:20–23.

In the book of Jeremiah, Jehoiakim is depicted as a petty tyrant whose rule was characterized by social injustice. His rule is contrasted with that of his father Josiah. Whereas Josiah "did justice and righteousness," Jehoiakim is accused of having "eyes and heart only for dishonest gain, for shedding innocent blood, and for practising oppression and violence" (Jer 22:15–17 [RSV]; cf. 2 Kgs 24:4). The oracle Jer 22:13–19 provides a concrete example of Jehoiakim's avarice, arrogance, and oppressive rule (see Wessels 1984). Probably at the beginning of his reign, at a time when the country was already under a heavy financial strain, Jehoiakim either renovated the existing palace in Jerusalem, or perhaps built a new palace (very possibly to be identified with the remains of a palace discovered at Ramat Raḥel). In addition to castigating Jehoiakim for the size and opulence of this project, the king is accused of having used forced labor to carry out this work (Jer 22:13–15).

A contrast between Jehoiakim and Josiah is also intended in Jeremiah 36, a narrative which probably has been patterned after 2 Kgs 22:3–23:24 (see Isbell 1978). Jehoiakim's rejection of Yahweh's written word (Jer 36:21–26) stands in marked contrast to the obedience shown by Josiah when the book of the law was read to him. Similarly, although Jehoiakim is not mentioned in Jer 26:7–19, it is clearly the intention of the narrator to demonstrate that it is the king himself who is responsible for the rejection of Yahweh's word (note the implied contrast with the "good" king Hezekiah in verses 18–19, and the brief narrative relating to the prophet Uriah [vv 20–23], who was executed by Jehoiakim for having preached a message similar to that of Jeremiah).

Together with the other 3 men who served as the last kings of Judah (Jehoahaz, Jehoiachin, and Zedekiah), Jehoiakim is given a negative evaluation in the Deuteronomistic History (2 Kgs 23:37 [cf. 2 Chr 36:5]). The evaluation of these 4 kings follows a similar pattern. Whereas the first element also occurs in the evaluation of earlier kings ("he did what was evil in the sight of Yahweh"), the second element is distinctive to the evaluation of these last kings of Judah. Of each it is stated that he did what was evil "according to all that his father(s) had done"; a variation occurs in 2 Kgs 24:19, where Zedekiah is said to have done evil "according to all that Jehoiakim had done" (see Weippert 1972: 333–34).

Bibliography

Freedman, D. N. 1956. The Babylonian Chronicle. *BA* 19: 50–60.

Green, A. R. 1982. The Fate of Jehoiakim. *AUSS* 20: 103–9.

Holt, E. K. 1986. Jeremiah's Temple Sermon and the Deuteronomists: An Investigation of the Redactional Relationship Between Jeremiah 7 and 26. *JSOT* 36: 73–87.

Isbell, C. D. 1978. 2 Kings 22:3–23:24 and Jeremiah 36: A Stylistic Comparison. *JSOT* 8: 33–45.

Katzenstein, H. J. 1983. 'Before Pharaoh Conquered Gaza' (Jeremiah XLVII 1). *VT* 33: 249–50.

Weippert, H. 1972. Die 'deuteronomistischen' Beurteilungen der Könige von Israel und Juda und das Problem der Redaktion der Königsbücher. *Bib* 53: 301–39.

Wessels, W. J. 1984. Towards a Historical-Ideological Understanding of Jeremiah 22:13–19. *OTE* 2: 61–80.

Wilcoxen, J. A. 1977. The Political Background of Jeremiah's Temple Sermon. Pp. 151–66 in *Scripture in History and Theology: Essays in Honour of J. Coert Rylaarsdam*, ed. A. L. Merrill and T. W. Overholt. PTMS 17. Pittsburgh.

Wiseman, D. J. 1956. *Chronicles of Chaldaean Kings (626–556 B.C.) in the British Museum*. London. Repr. 1961.

John M. Berridge

JEHOIARIB (PERSON) [Heb *yĕhôyārîb*]. Var. JOIARIB. A priestly family, descended from Aaron, whose name means "May Yahweh contend (for me)" (*IPN*, 28, 201; cf. Jerubbaal, "May Baal contend").

1. According to 1 Chr 24:4, 7, Jehoiarib was an eponymous head of a family and the one to whom the first lot fell in David's establishment of 24 priestly courses. In the list provided in 1 Chr 24:7–18, Jedaiah is the 2d family chosen by lot.

2. A priestly family, most likely descended from #1, which returned from exile in Babylon. 1 Chr 9:10 lists Jehoiarib, along with Jedaiah, Jachin, Azariah, Adaiah, and Maasai, as the 6 priestly heads of family who were the first to return to Jerusalem. The list in Neh 11:10–14, parallel but not identical to 1 Chr 9:10–13, identifies Joiarib (v 10) as an ancestor of Jedaiah, who was among the 5 priestly families who returned to Jerusalem following the exile. Similarly, in Neh 12:6 and 19, Joiarib, again listed alongside Jedaiah, is recorded among the 22 priestly families who returned from exile under Zerubbabel. It therefore seems certain that Joiarib in Nehemiah 11 and 12 is identical to the Jehoiarib in 1 Chr 9:10, because of (1) the similarity of the lists of the first returnees recorded in 1 Chronicles 9 and Nehemiah 11; and (2) the association of J(eh)oiarib with Jedaiah in all cases (including 1 Chr 24:7).

The significance of J(eh)oiarib in these lists has been questioned by recent commentators. The earliest tradition, reflected in Ezra 2, speaks of 4 priestly houses. The expansion to 5, 6, 22, and finally to 24 priestly courses suggests a growth process which was not fixed until at least the mid-5th century.

Part of this growth process involved the addition of certain families to earlier lists, including that of J(eh)oiarib. His appearance in the lists of Nehemiah 12, together with that of the following 5 names, appears to be secondary for 2 reasons. First, they are set off from the list syntactically by a conjunction. Second, it is precisely these 6 names which are omitted from the list of those priests who signed the covenant in Neh 10:1–8. There are also problems with the occurrence of the name in the listing of Neh 11:10.

It has often been assumed that J(eh)oiarib was added to the list of priestly families at a relatively late date because it was from this family that the Hasmoneans descended. However, the name was probably already fixed in the listing of priestly families by the early 4th century. (For further discussion, see Williamson *Ezra, Nehemiah* WBC; Braun *1 Chronicles* WBC.)

Rodney R. Hutton

JEHONATHAN (PERSON) [Heb *yĕhônātān*]. A name meaning "Yahu has given." This name is frequently rendered from Hebrew into English in the contracted form Jonathan. There are several instances where the name has been transliterated into English in complete form.

1. One of a group of Levites (2 Chr 17:8) who was called by Jehoshaphat to go with other princes and priests to teach the Torah in the cities of Judah. They travelled through Judah and taught among the people.

2. A priest who is listed as the head of a postexilic family of Shemaiah (Neh 12:18). Shemaiah was a contemporary of Nehemiah (Neh 10:8; 12:6). Jehonathan, as the head of this family, is identified in the list as a 2d generation priest under the high priest Eliashib.

3. A treasurer during the time of Uzziah.

Gary C. Augustin

JEHORAM (PERSON) [Heb *yĕhôrām*]. An alternate form of JORAM.

JEHOSHABEATH (PERSON) [Heb *yĕhôšabᶜat*]. An alternate form of JEHOSHEBA.

JEHOSHAPHAT (PERSON) [Heb *yĕhôšāpāṭ*]. **1.** The son of Ahilud and recorder (*mazkîr*) in the administration of David (2 Sam 8:16; 20:24; 1 Chr 18:15) and Solomon (1 Kgs 4:3). Drawing on the use of the root *zkr* in Isa 62:6, Driver (*NHT* 283) argued that the noun should be rendered "remembrancer" rather than "recorder." Thus Jehoshaphat's task centered not on maintaining archives, but on focusing the king's attention on important matters of state and offering advice. The office of *mazkîr* was not unlike that of secretary of state. Hertzberg (*1 and 2 Samuel* OTL, 293) considers the *mazkîr* to be the chief domestic officer in the Davidic bureaucracy: "he is the spokesman who has to keep the king continually informed and to transmit his decisions." Influenced by the research of Reventlow (1959: 161–75) and Boecker (1961: 212–16), DeVries (*1 Kings* WBC, 63, 69–70) translates the Heb noun "herald" which accords well with the assertion of Gray (*1 and 2 Kings* OTL, 132) that the *mazkîr* "makes the king's mind known to the people." De Vaux (*AncIsr,* 132) observes that a precisely equivalent title in ancient Egyptian bureaucracy was given to one who regulated palace ceremonies, prepared the pharaoh's journeys, and served as his official spokesperson.

2. The son of Paruah and one of Solomon's 12 administrative officers (*niṣṣābîm,* 1 Kgs 4:7) who were appointed to the task of fiscally sustaining the royal household. Exercising supervision over the district of Issachar (4:17), Jehoshaphat monitored the shipment of a month's supply of food rations for the Solomonic court each year (4:7) and kept the horses of the king's chariotry supplied with barley and straw (4:28).

3. A king of Judah (ca. 873–849 B.C.E), the son and successor of Asa, and a contemporary of Ahab, Ahaziah, and perhaps Jehoram, kings of Israel. At the age of 35, Jehoshaphat mounted the throne in Jerusalem to begin a 25-year reign. His mother was Azubah, daughter of Shilhi (1 Kgs 22:42; 2 Chr 20:31). The political climate surrounding Jehoshaphat's rule, his portrayal in the Deuteronomistic history (notably 1 Kings 22), and his portrayal in the work of the Chronicler (notably 2 Chronicles 17–20) are the categories under which various particulars about his Judean rule are gathered.

a. Political Climate. Though the independent states of Israel and Judah were often locked in sectional warfare during the first half-century following the rupture of the united monarchy in ca. 922 B.C.E., when Omri seized the throne of Israel in ca. 876 B.C.E. both kingdoms were on the verge of experiencing at least 4 decades of needful resurgence. Thanks to Omri's initiative, Israel and Judah embarked on an alliance that was confirmed within a few years by the marriage of Ahab's sister (or daughter) Athaliah to Jehoram, the son and successor of Jehoshaphat (2 Kgs 8:18, 27; 2 Chr 18:1). Given the military and commercial advantages that such an alliance fostered, Ahab of Israel (ca. 869–850 B.C.E.) and Jehoshaphat of Judah governed their people under politically favorable conditions. Israel may have been the stronger of the 2 kingdoms, but the close links that now developed were beneficial to both. Morover, archaeologist Aharoni (1982: 243–49) points to restorations at Mizpah and Beer-sheba as well as to new fortresses at Arad and Ezion-geber in the Negeb that were sponsored by Jehoshaphat and/or his father Asa. In sum, Jehoshaphat governed Judah during a relatively prosperous period.

b. Jehoshaphat in the Deuteronomistic History. Presumably drawing upon the annals of the Kingdom of Judah, the Deuteronomistic historian briefly summarizes Jehoshaphat's reign in 1 Kgs 22:41–51—Eng 22:41–50. In this basically positive statement, the spotlight falls on the king's religious policy, peaceful relations with the king of Israel, influence in Edom, and unsuccessful maritime expedition on the Red Sea.

In "doing what was right in the sight of the Lord" (22:43), Jehoshaphat is favorably compared with his father (see 1 Kgs 15:11). Thus he is credited with completing the task begun by Asa (15:12) of eliminating "the male cult-prostitutes" (*qādēš,* 22:47—Eng 22:46). Even so, the approval is qualified by the notation that the king did not dismantle the country shrines ("high places" [*bāmôt*], 22:44—Eng 22:43). The statement that Edom was governed by a deputy rather than by a king (22:48—Eng 22:47) is cryptic. One is led to assume that whereas Solomon had lost control over Edom (1 Kgs 11:14–25), one of his successors regained it. Although Judah's influence in Edom may have augmented during Jehoshaphat's quarter century of rule, it may not have ranged much beyond maintaining open access to the Gulf of Aqabah where the port of Ezion-geber (22:49—Eng 22:48) was situated.

A definitive understanding of the laconic mention of Jehoshaphat's maritime operations in this summary (22:49–50—Eng 22:48–49) lies beyond our reach. At first blush, the text suggests that toward the end of his reign, Jehoshaphat sought to resume a lucrative trade program on the Red Sea that had been suspended since the period of Solomon. Jehoshaphat's use of inexperienced sailors might explain why the king's ships were wrecked while docked at Ezion-geber. When Israel's new king Ahaziah proposed that Judah and Israel might pursue a joint maritime expedition, Jehoshaphat refused. Miller and Hayes (*HAIJ,* 279–80) argue that since the allied nations of Phoenicia, Israel, and Judah surely would have taken control of the Gulf of Aqabah "earlier in the Omride period," it is unlikely that Jehoshaphat was initiating a new maritime venture. Rather, he may have been seeking to win this opportunity for Judah alone. If so, his rejection of Ahaziah's offer was an attempt to establish "Judah's claim of independence from Omride domination." On balance, this Deuteronomistic summary presents Jehoshaphat as a reasonably pious Yahwist whose deeds were less than spectacular.

Two episodes in the Deuteronomistic history depict Jehoshaphat as living in the shadow of the N kingdom. The first (1 Kgs 22:1–38) focuses on Ahab's ill-fated attempt to reclaim the Transjordanian fortress of Ramoth-gilead for Israel. Momentarily a visitor in Ahab's court, Jehoshaphat is persuaded to join forces with the king of Israel. Though Jehoshaphat's name appears 13 times in the story, Ahab's name appears but once (22:20). The prevailing designation is simply "the king of Israel." It is commonly held that when this tale originated, the kings of Israel and Judah were anonymous. Whitley (1952: 148–49) and Miller (1966: 445) submit that this campaign against Aram unfolded a generation later during the dynasty of Jehu. Though their arguments are persuasive, the Deuteronomistic history unmistakably seats the event in Ahab's reign. Indeed, the verse that immediately follows this narrative begins, "Now the rest of the acts of Ahab . . ." (22:39).

Three elements in the story invite consideration here. First, though offered a choice as the lesser partner of the

Israelite-Judean alliance rather than ordered as a vassal to comply with the command of an overlord, Jehoshaphat seems most willing to support Ahab in his move against Aram. His response to the Israelite king's invitation is: "I am as you are, my people as your people, my horses as your horses" (22:4). That the victory is only immediately crucial to the N kingdom seems not to matter. Second, manifesting an exacting piety, Jehoshaphat addresses his colleague with this imperative: "Inquire first for the word of the Lord" (22:5). Then wary about the unison voice of Ahab's 400 prophets who forecast the success of this venture, Jehoshaphat asks whether all of Ahab's prophets have been heard (22:7). Jehoshaphat is zealous in his desire to ascertain the divine will. Third, despite his disguise during the combat, Ahab is mortally wounded by a randomly shot arrow, yet Jehoshaphat, who is instructed by Ahab to wear his robes (following the LXX), remains unharmed (22:30–34). Did the complying king of Judah subscribe to the view that man proposes, but God disposes? Though the narrative is silent, with the campaign now aborted, Jehoshaphat likely withdrew to Jerusalem.

The second narrative (2 Kgs 3:4–27) reports a retaliatory campaign that Israel and its allies Judah and Edom waged against a recently rebellious Moab. Striking affinities with the preceding text detract from its historical credibility. Anonymous mention of the kings of Israel, Judah, and Edom (3:9) triggers the inference that Jehoshaphat's name may be an accretion. Jehoshaphat's willing response to the invitation to join Israel in this military expedition replicates 1 Kgs 22:4, and his scrupulous piety is again manifested in his desire to seek a prophetic disclosure of the divine will prior to actual combat (2 Kgs 3:11; cf. 1 Kgs 22:5). Once more, the victory primarily matters to Israel, not Judah. Jehoshaphat is now the regal colleague of Ahab's son Jehoram (ca. 849–842 B.C.E.), whose triumph over Moab's king Mesha is temporary (see The Moabite Stone, *ANET,* 320–21). Elisha's generous commendation of Jehoshaphat (2 Kgs 3:14) is further evidence that the Deuteronomistic history assigns this Judean king high marks.

c. Jehoshaphat in Chronicles. At the outset of his lengthy portrayal (2 Chr 17:1–20:37), the Chronicler emphasizes Jehoshaphat's uncompromising piety. Shunning the Baalim and seeking the God of his ancestral faith, Jehoshaphat "walked in the earlier ways of his father" (17:3). In the Chronicler's perspective, it naturally followed that Jehoshaphat was a richly blessed monarch around whom swarmed signs of grandeur. Respectful Philistines and Arabs honored Jehoshaphat with tribute (17:11); he constructed fortresses and store cities (17:12); and not counting those soldiers who were stationed in the fortified cities throughout Judah, his army numbered 1,160,000 men (17:14–19). As reported in 2 Chr 20:1–30, when a "great multitude" of Moabites, Ammonites, and men from Mount Seir marched on Jerusalem, fasting and prayer sufficed to ensure a Judean victory. Jehoshaphat's forces had no need to engage in combat since the deity set an ambush against the enemy coalition. These invaders so thoroughly fought among themselves that none was spared. Such disclosures obviously mask the Jehoshaphat of history.

Moreover, traditions about Jehoshaphat that were earlier reported in 1–2 Kings are appreciably refracted in the Chronicler's own work. Whereas his account of the Israelite-Judean expedition to seize Ramoth-gilead from Aram is drawn almost verbatim from 1 Kgs 22:1–35a, the Chronicler accords Jehoshaphat a more honorific status at the outset of the story (2 Chr 18:1–2) and appends a word of censure from the prophet Jehu against Jehoshaphat for having allied himself with the wicked Ahab (19:2–3). Moreover, the Chronicler's account of Jehoshaphat's abortive maritime enterprise (2 Chr 20:35–37) boldly departs from the rendering in 1 Kgs 22:49–50—Eng 22:48–49. Jehoshaphat now *permits* Ahaziah's partnership in this effort which incurs condemnation from Eliezer to the effect that the imminent destruction of the Ezion-geber fleet is Yahweh's judgment against Jehoshaphat's unseemly association with Ahaziah of Israel.

Though the Chronicler may be faulted for his enormous claims about Jehoshaphat and even for inconsistent coverage (in 2 Chr 17:6 the king is praised for having eliminated the "high places" [*bāmôt*], but in 20:33 condemned for having failed to do so!), his recognition of Jehoshaphat's commitment to military preparedness and judicial reform is entirely justified. Jehoshaphat's normalization of judicial procedures in Judah is spelled out in 2 Chr 19:5–11, a text accepted by Albright (1950: 82) as "a substantially correct account." During Jehoshaphat's tenure, local Levites, priests, and prominent laymen were called to Jerusalem as royally appointed judges. This early a date for the transformation of the judicial system is not improbable.

4. The son of Nimshi and father of Jehu, who exterminated the dynasty of Omri and established one of his own (2 Kgs 9:2, 14).

Bibliography

Aharoni, Y. 1982. *The Archaeology of the Land of Israel.* Trans. A. F. Rainey. Philadelphia.

Albright, W. F. 1950. The Judicial Reform of Jehoshaphat. Pp. 61–82 in *Alexander Marx Jubilee Volume,* ed. S. Lieberman. New York.

Boecker, H. J. 1961. Erwägungen zum Amt des Mazkir. *TZ* 17: 212–16.

Miller, J. M. 1966. The Elisha Cycle and the Accounts of the Omride Wars. *JBL* 85: 441–54.

Reventlow, H. Graf. 1959. Das Amt des Mazkir. *TZ* 15: 161–75.

Whitley, C. F. 1952. The Deuteronomic Presentation of the House of Omri. *VT* 2: 137–52.

J. KENNETH KUNTZ

JEHOSHAPHAT, VALLEY OF (PLACE) [Heb *ʿēmeq yehôšāpāṭ*]. "The Valley of the Lord will Judge"; the *place* where the Lord will gather together and judge the nations (Joel 4:2, 12—Eng 3:2, 12; cf. Joel 4:14, Valley of Decision—Eng 3:14). The exact location of the valley is uncertain, but since Joel 4:1 (—Eng 3:1) speaks of restoring the fortunes of Judah—and of Jerusalem in particular—it may be assumed that the location is somewhere near Jerusalem. The King's Valley mentioned in 2 Sam 18:18, where Absalom erected his commemorative pillar (not to be confused with the much later Absalom's Tomb), may also be another earlier name for the valley.

Traditionally, the Valley of Jehoshaphat has been associated with the last judgment and has been identified by Jews, Christians, and Muslims with that part of the Kidron Valley just E of Jerusalem, including the valley slopes. In line with these beliefs a great many tombs are to be found on the Kidron slopes, the Muslim cemetery on the W and the Jewish on the E. In Jewish tradition, *1 Enoch* 53:1 speaks of final judgment in a deep valley where all people come to be judged, a place which many equate with the Valley of Jehoshaphat. Some rabbinic scholars taught that to have a part in the resurrection it was necessary to be born in Palestine, and the bodies of those who were buried elsewhere would roll underground "like bottles" until they reached Palestine (*Ketub.* 12.3). According to Muslim belief, on the Day of Judgment the Angel Israfel will blow his trumpet as he stands on the sacred rock, es-Sakhra (housed in the present Dome of the Rock), and Mohammad will lead the believers from Jerusalem across a bridge over the gulf of Jahannum (a word, no doubt, derived from "gehenna"). Early Christian belief also places emphasis on the Valley of Jehoshaphat as a place of judgment. Although Eusebius (ca. A.D. 263–339; *Onomast.* 70) locates the Valley of Jehoshaphat in the Hinnom Valley—possibly because he remembered that in the Hinnom Valley (the scene of child sacrifice by Ahaz and Manasseh, 2 Kgs 16:2–3; 21:6)—the Lord had promised to deal out death in the "Valley of Slaughter" (Jer 7:31–32; 19:5–6). Jerome, however, in his revision of the *Onomasticon* places the Valley of Jehoshaphat in the Kidron Valley and cites the prophecy of Joel 4:2, 12 (—Eng 3:2, 12). The Bordeaux Pilgrim (A.D. 333) identifies the Valley of "Iosafath" at the Mount of Olives (*CChr Series Latina* [= CCSL].175.17); Theodosius (A.D. 530) knows of the Valley of "Iosaphat" and the Church of St. Mary the mother of the Lord (CCSL 175.119), as does Arculf (A.D. 670) who also speaks of a Church of St. Mary in the Valley of "Iosaphat" (CCSL 175.195).

This church was no doubt in existence as early as the 5th century A.D., and later was rebuilt by the Crusaders who also constructed next to it a large monastery, the Abbey of St. Mary of the Valley of Jehoshaphat (Finegan 1969: 106–7). Other features in the Valley of Jehoshaphat were also associated with the theme of judgment. The gate now known as St. Stephen's Gate, or the Lion Gate, on the E wall of the city was once known as the Gate of the Valley of Jehoshaphat (Simons 1952: 10), and in the Vulgate the translation for the Inspection Gate (Neh 3:31) is Porto Judicialis, "Gate of Judgment." According to Muslim folklore the last judgment in the Valley of Jehoshaphat is associated with the Golden Gate with its two doors: the Gate of Mercy and the Gate of Contrition (Simons 1952: 372). Some view the newly formed valley (described in Zech 14:4) at the Mount of Olives, when the Lord brings judgment, as the Valley of Jehoshaphat.

Bibliography

Finegan, J. 1969. *Archeology of the New Testament.* Princeton.
Simons, J. 1952. *Jerusalem in the Old Testament.* Leiden.

W. HAROLD MARE

JEHOSHEBA

JEHOSHEBA (PERSON) [Heb *yĕhôšebaᶜ*]. Var. JEHOSHABEATH. Daughter of Joram and sister of Ahaziah, both Kings of Judah (2 Kgs 11:1–2 = 2 Chr 22:11). According to Chronicles, Jehosheba was the wife of Jehoiada the priest. If this is accurate, it indicates an unusual link by marriage between the royal house and the priesthood.

Upon hearing of Ahaziah's death, Athaliah—the Queen Mother—ordered all the king's sons killed and seized the throne for herself. Unknown to Athaliah, Jehosheba hid an infant son of Ahaziah and the child's nurse in a bedchamber. The infant, Joash, escaped the massacre. Six years later, Joash was brought forth by Jehoiada the priest and anointed king in Athaliah's place.

Jehosheba's actions against Athaliah have prompted speculation concerning her parentage. Josephus (*Ant.* 9.7.1) and Jerome (*Quest. Heb.* on 2 Chr 21:17) argue that Jehosheba was the daughter of Joram but not of Athaliah. This would explain Jehosheba's loyalty to Joash, her half-brother's son. However, if Joram had another wife, she is not mentioned in the text. Moreover, 2 Kgs 11 = 2 Chr 22 contain a number of conflicts, i.e., grandmother vs. grandchildren; priest vs. queen. In this context, a conflict between mother/daughter does not seem unusual.

The account in Chronicles preserves an alternate spelling of Jehosheba: Jehoshabeath (Heb *yĕhôšabᶜat*). See also ATHALIAH, JEHOIADA, JOASH.

LINDA S. SCHEARING

JEHOVAH

JEHOVAH. See YAHWEH.

JEHOZABAD

JEHOZABAD (PERSON) [Heb *yĕhôzābād*]. Three individuals in the OT bear this name. On the form of the name which means "Yahweh has given," compare the biblical Elzabad and the Aramean *Nabû-zabad.*

1. Jehozabad the son of Shomer was a servant of Joash who participated in the assassination of the Judean king (2 Kgs 12:22—Eng 12:21). In 2 Chr 24:26, Jehozabad is said to be the son of a Moabitess named Shimrit, but it appears that the Chronicler has mistaken the name of this conspirator's father for that of his mother (Rudolph *Chronikbücher* HAT, 276, 279). Whether the Moabite connection is based on a source (*Ibid.,* 279) or is the Chronicler's own contribution (Williamson *Chronicles* NCBC, 326) cannot be determined.

2. The second son of Obed-Edom (1 Chr 26:4) in the schematization offered by a reviser of the Chronicler's organization of the gatekeepers in the temple at Jerusalem (Williamson *Chronicles* NCBC, 169; Rudolph *Chronikbücher* HAT, 173).

3. The second of 2 military "commanders of thousands" from Benjamin under Jehoshaphat named in 2 Chr 17:17–18. In the present setting, framed by vv 13b and 19, Jehozabad and the others named appear to have been officers over troops in the standing army. However, since within that framework they were mustered according to "their fathers' houses" (v 14) and organized by tribal divisions (vv 14, 17), Jehozabad may more likely have been a commander of the militia or conscript forces (Williamson *Chronicles* NCBC, 284).

J. S. ROGERS

JEHOZADAK (PERSON) [Heb *yĕhôṣādāq*]. Var. JOZADAK. The father of Joshua, a priest contemporary with Zerubbabel (Hag 1:1, 12, 14; 2:2, 4; Zech 6:11), and the chief priest serving in the First Temple who was taken into exile by Nebuchadnezzar (1 Chr 6:14–15). Jehozadak, along with its shortened form Jozadak, means "Yahweh is righteous." The long form is used for this individual in the texts cited above with his son's name Joshua (*yĕhôšūaᶜ*). In Ezra-Nehemiah, the shortened form is used along with a shortened form for his son, Jeshua (*yēšûaᶜ*). *See* JOZADAK. The textual unit of 1 Chr 6:4–15 lists the names of the chief priests from Eleazar to the fall of Jerusalem. This is clearly a stylized list which may not provide the correct hereditary order (Williamson *Chronicles* WBC, 70–71). A parallel list in Ezra 7:1–5 names Ezra as the Son of Seraiah instead of Jehozadak. However, this is not a complete list, and the intent may merely be to establish Ezra as a direct descendant of Seraiah, not necessarily excluding Jehozadak. As the last chief priest to serve in the First Temple and the father of Joshua, Jehozadak provides a direct link between the preexilic and postexilic priesthoods. This link legitimates Joshua as the proper chief priest to lead worship in the new Temple.

JEFFREY A. FAGER

JEHU (PERSON) [Heb *yēhûʾ*]. The name of 5 individuals in the OT.

1. King of Israel, son of Nimshi, who overthrew the Omride dynasty and founded one of his own. The years of his reign are variously reckoned as 845–818 B.C.E. (Begrich 1929 and Jepsen 1979), 841–814 B.C.E. (Thiele 1965), and 842–815 B.C.E. (Andersen 1969). The most important source for the history of Jehu is 1 Kings 9–10; a very brief summary of his reign is to be found in 2 Chr 22:7–9. Jehu is also mentioned in synchronistic dating lists and truncated genealogies in 2 Kgs 12:2—Eng 12:1; 13:1; 14:8 (= 2 Chr 25:17); 15:12. Quite differing estimations of the impact of Jehu, spoken at greater or lesser remove from the actual time of his reign, are offered in 1 Kgs 19:16–17 and Hos 1:4. The picture of Jehu derived from OT sources is augmented by several Assyrian inscriptions in which Jehu is mentioned by name.

In most cases Jehu is identified as "son of Nimshi" (1 Kgs 19:16; 2 Kgs 9:20; 2 Chr 22:7). In 2 Kgs 9:2 and 14, however, he is called "son of Jehoshaphat, son of Nimshi." On the basis of this latter filiation, it is sometimes suggested that "Nimshi" was the name of Jehu's grandfather, or even the name of the clan to which he belonged. It is more likely, however, that the expression "son of Jehoshaphat" is a later addition to the text, and that the more frequently attested identification of his father is the correct one: Jehu was the son of Nimshi. No other information about the ancestry of Jehu is extant. As he steps onto the stage of history, he is already a high-ranking military figure in the entourage of the Israelite King Joram, an officer or perhaps even the commander of the army.

Jehu emerges at a time when the Israelite army had assembled at Ramoth-gilead (Tell er-Ramith) in order to defend this Transjordanian border town of Israel against attacks by the Syrians. Border clashes between Israel and the Aramean state centered around Damascus had flared up anew following the collapse, in the wake of Hazael's usurpation of the throne in Damascus, of the military alliance of Syrian and Palestinian states which had earlier been established by Hadadezer of Damascus, Irḫuleni of Hamath, and Ahab of Israel in order to check Assyrian expansion. During this conflict in the vicinity of Ramoth-gilead, the Israelite king Joram had been wounded and had been forced to leave his army behind as he returned to his residence in Jezreel (Zerᶜin) to recuperate from his wounds (2 Kgs 8:28–29; 9:14–15). This was the occasion for the coup staged by Jehu. The immediate stimulus for it, however, came from another quarter.

While encamped at Ramoth-gilead, Jehu was sought out by a disciple of the prophet Elisha. Acting on behalf of his master, this disciple anointed Jehu king over Israel and then confirmed the anointing by means of an oracle from Yahweh. The whole proceeding is reminiscent of Samuel's anointing of Saul (1 Sam 9:16; 10:1; 15:1) and David (1 Sam 16:1–13): what takes place occurs in response to divine initiative and confers upon the recipient of the action the status of a *nāgîd* ("designated one"), or even of a king. To be sure, in 2 Kgs 9:1–10 it is not actually the prophet Elisha himself, but only one of his disciples, who does the anointing. Despite that technicality, the other officers around Jehu nonetheless hasten to proclaim him king just as soon as they are informed of the anointing and of the prophetic oracle. However, there is no mention of a general acclamation of Jehu's kingship on the part of the whole army—unlike what apparently happens in the otherwise analogous situation in 1 Kgs 16:16. The revolt of Jehu, therefore, is probably best described as a military coup which originated at the Israelites' Transjordanian encampment. The prophetic anointing gave Jehu's coup its religious legitimation.

During these years a significant undercurrent of resistance to the Omride policies, both foreign and domestic, had obviously arisen. One factor contributing to this groundswell of resentment might well have been the growing influence of the queen mother Jezebel who, after the death of Ahab, played a role in the governing of Israel through her sons Ahaziah and Joram. Along with this the Israelite tribes were experiencing a steady deterioration in their status over against the indigenous Canaanite portion of the population. The cult of Baal, which had been accorded at least equal treatment with that of Yahweh since the beginning of the Omride dynasty, was by now actively being promoted. This development was being protested by loyal Yahwists, who found their spokesmen especially in the prophets Elijah and Elisha, and in the prophetic circles which had gathered around the latter.

It is also possible that the defense program of the Omrides was working economic hardships on the populace. To be sure, the Omride tactic of entering into foreign alliances had evidently brought to Israel a period of peace and prosperity. On the other hand, the necessity of being able to repulse attacks from the N—initially from the Arameans of Damascus and later from the Assyrians—was requiring increased expenditures on armaments. The large contingent of war chariots which Ahab had been able to deploy against the Assyrian king Shalmanezer III in the Battle of Qarqar (853 B.C.E.; cf. *ANET,* 278–79) testifies to the magnitude of the Israelite military buildup, as do the fortresses whose construction the Omrides pushed through. Only a short time after Hazael successfully seized power in Damascus, however, the anti-Assyrian coalition fell apart. Now the former allies, Israel and Aram-Damascus, faced one another with swords drawn. This sudden change in the situation apparently led to considerable dissatisfaction with the basic principles of the Omride foreign policy and stimulated a desire for some sort of change.

All of these factors seem to have contributed, more or less strongly, to the success of Jehu's putsch. Above all else, however, he took advantage of the opportunity for surprise. Jehu commanded his officers to keep silent concerning the proceedings in the military camp at Ramoth-gilead, and he himself then hastened as quickly as possible to Jezreel in order to arrive there before news of his having been proclaimed king in Transjordan could reach the royal residence. The surprise attack was a total success. King Joram, suspecting nothing, went out to meet Jehu in expectation of receiving bad news from the military camp; he was shot by Jehu while still in his war chariot. At this point (2 Kgs 9:25–26) the narrative inserts a comment to the effect that this happened on precisely that parcel of land for the sake of whose possession Ahab had had Naboth of Jezreel and his sons slain (a tradition paralleling that found in 1 Kings 21). The death of Joram at the hand of Jehu thus appears as the fulfilling of an oracle of judgment that was once intended for Ahab. In Jezreel itself Jehu had the queen mother Jezebel thrown down from the palace's appearance-window. With this the city of Jezreel was firmly in the hand of Jehu. Since Jezreel is hardly again mentioned in later texts, one must assume that, under Jehu and his successors, the city lost the function of a secondary royal residence which it had had under the kings of the house of Omri.

As a royal possession founded by the Omride family, Israel's chief city of Samaria (Sebastiya) occupied a special status within the N Kingdom. Jehu respected this special legal position in that he did not immediately set out from Jezreel to Samaria, but rather he initiated a diplomatic exchange of letters with the chiefs of the city. In his first letter Jehu suggested to the recipients that they elevate one of the princes of the Omride family to the kingship and then carry through with this act by defending his claims in battle (2 Kgs 10:1–3). The chiefs of the city immediately recognized the threat contained in Jehu's letter and announced their submission to him (vv 4–5). Next Jehu demanded, as a sign of their obedience, the heads of the princes of the royal house who were in Samaria. Gripped by fear, the representatives of Samaria immediately carried out this command, decapitated the Omride princes, and sent their severed heads to Jehu at Jezreel (vv 6–11). Thus the way was cleared for Jehu to take over the capital city of Samaria.

Before Jehu actually entered Samaria, while he was still on the way there, he encountered Jonadab, the son of Rechab, who assured him of his support. According to Jeremiah 35, Jonadab was leader of the Rechabites, a clan which faithfully adhered to an archaic form of Yahwistic belief. Centuries after the settlement of Israel in Palestine the Rechabites still disdained to lead a sedentary, agrarian style of life. Rather, they continued to pursue a seminomadic type of existence, living in tents rather than in houses, subsisting on stock-farming rather than on tilling the soil, and stoutly refraining from alcoholic beverages. In all likelihood they understood this particular sort of existence in the promised land to be a style of life uniquely suited to Yahwistic faith, especially since they were thereby separated from such religious temptations of the agricultural life as Baal-worship and fertility cult. Since the Rechabites were thus a group particularly responsive to the call of faithfulness to Yahweh, Jehu's immediate course of action is easily understandable: He had Jonadab join him in his chariot in order thereby to demonstrate his own "zeal for Yahweh" (2 Kgs 10:15–16). By having the leader of the Rechabites join him, Jehu was able to demonstrate to the populace his partisanship toward the national Israelite and ancient Yahwistic traditions of Israel, in opposition to the Omride policy of accommodation to Canaanite ways. Keeping the dynamics of these maneuvers in mind, one is also led to conclude that the sequence of events as recounted in 10:15–17 and 10:18–27 does not reflect what actually happened but has somehow gotten reversed.

After his entry into Samaria, Jehu had all the remaining members of the "house of Ahab" slaughtered. In so doing he followed the example of several earlier usurpers of the royal throne in N Israel who had likewise exterminated the families of the toppled monarchs in order to solidify their own hold on the reins of government (1 Kgs 15:29; 16:11). With this bloodbath the Omride dynasty, after not even 40 years in power (from 882 to 845 B.C.E., following the chronology of Jepsen), ceased to exist. With his seizure of the throne, Jehu established yet another dynasty, one that held on to the throne of Israel for nearly a full century (from 845 to 747 B.C.E., again following Jepsen). The royal families of Omri and of Jehu were the only ones during the history of the N Kingdom that succeeded in establishing actual dynasties. In all other cases the duration of rule did not extend beyond that of a king and his son.

A considerable segment of the Judean lineage of David was also destroyed in the overthrow of the Omride dynasty. It so happened that, when the usurper Jehu entered Jezreel in order to seize power and to assassinate the reigning King Joram, the Judean king Ahaziah was also there, visiting Joram. In this way Ahaziah also became entangled in the bloody events of Jehu's putsch (2 Kgs 8:29; 9:16). In company with Joram, the unsuspecting Ahaziah departed the city in order to meet the rapidly approaching Jehu. When Jehu slew Joram with bow and arrow, Ahaziah fled S in the direction of Bethhaggan (En-Gannim), obviously with the intention of escaping toward Jerusalem. Jehu pursued him, however, and ordered that he too be slain. Those in pursuit of Ahaziah caught up with him in the vicinity of Ibleam (Khirbet Belʿameh) and wounded him so severely that he was able to make it only as far as Megiddo (Tell el-Mutesellim), where he died (2 Kgs 9:21–24, 27–28).

In addition to Ahaziah a whole group of people belonging to the Judean royal house ("kinsmen of Ahaziah," 2 Kgs 10:12–14) fell into the hands of Jehu. Clearly having as yet received no news of the bloody events in Jezreel, they were just then journeying through the N Kingdom. Jehu encountered them on the way to Samaria, at Beth-eked (Beit Qad, east of Jenin), and had them all killed. In this way Jehu inflicted such devastation on the Davidic dynasty that the queen mother Athaliah, of the lineage of Omri, was able to seize the throne in Jerusalem (2 Kgs 11:1–3). Just why Jehu so enlarged his circle of murderous activity to include the members of the Judean royal family remains unclear. Perhaps he was intent upon eliminating the possibility of a blood feud with the Davidic lineage, which had become related by marriage with the Omrides. Alternately, Jehu could also simply have intended to liquidate all the allies of the Israelite royal family that he could get his hands on.

Next, in Samaria, Jehu went on the offensive against the Baal cult. Under the pretext of wanting to arrange a large sacrificial feast for Baal, Jehu had the worshipers of Baal, his prophets and priests, gather in the Baal sanctuary in Samaria. He was so thorough in carrying out this deception that he himself presented the sacrifice for Baal. Suddenly, he gave his troops the command to slaughter the Baal worshipers who had gathered in the sanctuary. After this frightful bloodbath the contents of the temple were destroyed and the building itself was torn down. In order to render the site of the sanctuary perpetually unusable for cultic purposes, Jehu then had a public latrine constructed at the same place (2 Kgs 10:18–27). The detailed sources concerning Jehu, which restrict themselves to his seizure of power, end on this note. Despite their restricted focus, however, these sources nonetheless allow one to recognize the broad contours of Jehu's governmental policy.

In both domestic and foreign policy, Jehu made a radical break with the governing principles of the Omride dynasty. In the sociocultural realm, including religion, a definitive end was made of the practice of officially sanctioned equal treatment of the Israelite tribes and the traditionally Canaanite elements of the population. Indeed, through the influence of Jezebel, there had even been a promoting of the Canaanite traditions under the kings Ahaziah and Joram. Through his frightfully bloody assault on the adherents of the Baal cult and the destruction of the Baal temple in Samaria, Jehu established himself as a zealot for Yahwistic faith and as an opponent of Baalism and syncretism. Under Jehu's rule, the Israelite elements of the population doubtlessly were accorded the dominant position in the sociopolitical and religious realm; Canaanite influence was restricted.

In the domain of foreign policy, the system of treaties set up by the Omrides fully collapsed in the wake of Jehu's actions. The slaughtering of Ahaziah and the Judean princes, as well as the extermination of the Omride family from which Athaliah, the queen mother in Jerusalem, herself descended, put an end to Israel's previously good relations with Judah and replaced them with a state of tension. Israel's friendly relations with the Phoenician states likewise came to an end. Under Jehu, Israel suddenly found itself in an isolated position among neighboring states and, without support, was soon handed over to more powerful opponents, specifically Aram-Damascus and Assyria.

In the 18th year of his reign (841 B.C.E.), the Assyrian king Shalmaneser III carried out his 4th campaign against Syria. The anti-Assyrian coalition of Syrian and Palestinian states, which 3 times before had halted his advance, no longer existed. The Assyrian army directed its main assault against Hazael of Damascus. Although Shalmaneser wreaked heavy devastation upon the region of the Syrian state and trapped Hazael in his capital city, he was not able actually to capture Damascus or overthrow Hazael. However, the Assyrian army did manage to reach the highland region of Hauran and there stood on the very boundary of Israel. As Shalmaneser states in a fragmentarily preserved annalistic text (*ANET,* 280), the Phoenician cities of Tyre and Sidon both submitted to him, as did Jehu of Israel. In this Assyrian text Jehu is identified as "son of Omri" (*Iaúa mār Ḫumrî*). This formulation shows not only the ignorance of the Assyrians concerning the change of dynasty that had occurred in Israel, but also the high international esteem enjoyed by the Omrides, whose name increasingly appears in the Assyrian texts as a designator for the whole state of Israel (*Bīt-Ḫumrî*). Apparently Shalmaneser accorded such importance to Jehu's paying of tribute that he had the scene carved as an illustration on the "Black Obelisk" (*ANEP,* 355). Jehu is shown doing homage before the great Assyrian king by prostrating himself upon the ground; other panels of the obelisk depict Israel's tribute, which is described in a superscription.

Although his submission to Shalmaneser meant that Jehu was abandoning the former Israelite policy of resistance to Assyrian expansion, at the same time this was an act of political common sense. With his recognition of Assyrian supremacy, Jehu acquired for himself support against the Arameans, who of course held back for only so long as the Assyrians were able to intervene in the affairs of the Aramean states of Syria. In the 21st year of his reign (838 B.C.E.), Shalmaneser III moved against Damascus for the last time, once again without definitive success. In the ensuing years, due to internal disturbances, the Assyrian empire declined and was unable to find the strength to generate new expansionary expeditions. Hazael of Damascus, seeing himself freed from Assyrian pressure, became in the following years one of the most ruthless and successful enemies of Israel. According to 2 Kgs 10:32–33 he eventually succeeded in conquering the whole of Transjordan between Hauran and the Arnon. Given its summarizing character, it is questionable whether this brief notice is to be taken as referring only to the period of Jehu's rule. It is quite possible that the success which Hazael achieved against Jehu's son Jehoahaz has been collapsed into this report as well. On the other hand, one can probably also infer from this notice that Jehu was successful in forcing the Moabites back to the Arnon and that the region between the N tip of the Dead Sea and the Arnon reverted to Israelite rule.

Despite all the gory details included therein, the textual block encompassing 2 Kgs 9:1–10:27 reports Jehu's seizure of power in a positive light and apparently aims at legitimating his rule. The deeds of Jehu are evaluated in similarly positive fashion in 1 Kgs 19:15–18. This latter text, which one must read as presupposing that the events of the Jehu revolution already lie in the past, speaks of a divine commission laid upon Elijah to anoint, in addition to Elisha and Hazael, also Jehu. Certainly we encounter here no strictly historical statement (cf. the contrasting

2 Kgs 9:1–3). Rather we have the transmittal of a theological evaluation of the deeds of Jehu: Those deeds serve in the struggle against the cult of Baal and therefore stand in continuity with Elijah's battle on behalf of Yahwistic faith.

The prophet Hosea judges the deeds of Jehu in a totally different light (Hos 1:4). According to Hosea, those deeds amounted to a terrible blood guilt which besmirched the whole reign of the Jehu dynasty and so burdened it that God would eventually call the dynasty to account and do away with the whole institution of kingship. On the other hand, the Deuteronomistic redactors of the books of Kings rendered high praise to Jehu for his opposition to the cult of Baal and included in this context a divine promise of dynastic succession. Of course, just as with every other king of the N Kingdom, so also Jehu is reproached for having adhered to the golden calves, which is to say for having continued to support the royal sanctuaries in Bethel and Dan (2 Kgs 10:28–31).

The history of Jehu is briefly summarized in the work of the Chronicler (2 Chr 22:7–9), who paraphrases 2 Kings 9–10 in short strokes (2 Chr 22:7 = 2 Kgs 9:21; 2 Chr 22:8 = 2 Kgs 10:12–14). Only the verse at 2 Chr 22:9 fully deviates from its predecessor at 2 Kgs 9:27–28; it reports that Ahaziah of Judah hid in Samaria but was discovered there and was slain by Jehu. The sparse information concerning Jehu in the work of the Chronicler serves only as historical background for the account of Ahaziah's demise.

2. Prophet in the time of Baasha of Israel, son of Hanani. He delivered to the king a prophetic judgment oracle announcing the king's demise and the downfall of the royal house (1 Kgs 16:1–4). The fulfillment of this pronouncement is reported in 16:7 (proleptically) and in 16:12. The prophetic oracle consists of Deuteronomistic formulations. The historical background of the prophet Jehu remains dark. In the work of the Chronicler he is pictured as confronting the Judean King Jehoshaphat and faulting him for his alliance with the godless Ahab (2 Chr 19:2–3). In 2 Chr 20:34 the Chronicler refers to a collection of "words of Jehu" as one of his sources for the history of Jehoshaphat of Judah. This notice is just as open to historical question as are the other comments about Jehu in the work of the Chronicler.

3. A Judean, son of Obed and father of Azariah, in the family tree of Elishama within the genealogy of Judah (1 Chr 2:38).

4. A Simeonite, son of Joshibiah, within the genealogy of Simeon (1 Chr 4:35).

5. A Benjaminite from Anathoth who, along with other Benjaminites, gave himself over to David at Ziklag in order to serve him as one of his warriors (1 Chr 12:3).

Bibliography

Ahlström, G. W. 1977. King Jehu—A Prophet's Mistake. Pp. 47–69 in *Scripture in History and Theology,* ed. A. L. Merrill and T. W. Overholt. Pittsburgh.

Alt, A. 1954. Der Stadtstaat Samaria. Repr. *KlSchr* 3: 258–302.

Andersen, K. T. 1969. Die Chronologie der Könige von Israel und Juda. *ST* 23: 69–114.

Astour, M. 1971. 841 B.C.: The First Assyrian Invasion of Israel. *JAOS* 91: 383–89.

Begrich, J. 1929. *Die Chronologie der Könige von Israel und Juda.* BHT 3. Tübingen.

Bernhardt, K.-H. 1987. Jehu, König von Israel. *TRE* 16: 553–54.

De Vries, S. J. 1978. Pp. 56, 67–69, 90–91, 119, 122 in *Prophet against Prophet.* Grand Rapids.

Gunkel, H. 1922. Der Aufstand des Jehu. Pp. 67–94, 98–100 in *Geschichten von Elisa.* Berlin.

Jepsen, A., ed. 1979. Pp. 204–18 (chronological table) in *Von Sinuhe bis Nebukadnezar.* 3d ed. Berlin.

Jepsen, A., and Hanhart, R. 1964. Pp. 1–48 in *Untersuchungen zur israelitisch-jüdischen Chronologie.* BZAW 88. Berlin.

Knott, J. B. 1971. *The Jehu Dynasty.* Diss. Emory.

McCarter, P. K. 1974. "Yaw, Son of ʿOmri": A Philological Note on Israelite Chronology. *BASOR* 216: 5–7.

Miller, J. M. 1967. The Fall of the House of Ahab. *VT* 17: 307–24.

Schmitt, H.-C. 1972. Pp. 19–31 in *Elisa.* Gütersloh.

Smith, C. C. 1977. Jehu and the Black Obelisk of Shalmaneser III. Pp. 71–105 in *Scripture in History and Theology: Essays in Honor of J. C. Rylaarsdam,* ed. A. L. Merrill and T. W. Overholt. Pittsburgh.

Thiele, E. R. 1965. *The Mysterious Numbers of the Hebrew Kings.* Rev. ed. Grand Rapids.

———. 1976. An Additional Chronological Note on "Yaw, Son of ʿOmri." *BASOR* 222: 19–23.

Timm, S. 1982. *Die Dynastie Omri.* FRLANT 124. Göttingen.

Trebolle-Barrera, J. C. 1984. *Jehú y Joás: Texto y composición literaria de 2 Reyes 9–11.* Valencia.

Ungnad, A. 1906. Jaua, mâr Ḫumri. *OLZ* 9: 224–26.

Winfried Thiel
Trans. Charles Muenchow

JEHUBBAH (PERSON) [Heb *yĕḥubbâ* K; *wĕḥubbâ* Q]. The grandson of Heber listed in the genealogy of Asher (1 Chr 7:34). While the consonantal Hebrew text spells the name Jehubbah, the Masoretes have vocalized the name to be read "and Hubbah"—a reading supported by various Gk mss. The figure is listed as one of the 3 sons of Shamer, the latter perhaps to be identified with Shomer. The names Jehubbah or Hubbah appear neither in the parallel lists of the Asherite genealogy in Genesis 46 and Numbers 26 nor elsewhere in the Hebrew Bible. Possible roots of these names are *ḥbb,* "to love" (hence, "loved one") and *ḥbh,* "to hide" (hence, "hidden one"). Abel suggests that Hubbah is related to Hobab, a Kenite name (Judges 4:11).

Bibliography

Abel, F.-M. 1937. Une Mention Biblique de Birzeit. *RB* 46: 217–24.

Julia M. O'Brien

JEHUCAL (PERSON) [Heb *yĕhûkal*]. Var. JUCAL. Son of Shelemiah and one of King Zedekiah's (597–586 B.C.E.) court officials (Jer 37:3; 38:1). His high social status is indicated both by his title, "prince" (Heb *śar*; Jer 38:4) and by his presence in a deputation sent by Zedekiah to consult the prophet Jeremiah (37:3). During the siege of Jerusalem, he was one of four (three in the LXX) officials, who, representing the pro-Egyptian faction in Judah, demanded that Zedekiah put Jeremiah to death because of the treasonable nature of his preaching (38:1–4). According to them, Jeremiah's message, which centered on the certain fall of Jerusalem and the necessity of submitting to the Babylonians, was demoralizing the Judean troops (lit. "weakening the hands" of those defending the city of Jerusalem; cf. the use of this expression in one of the ostraca [Ostracon 6] found at Lachish [see *ANET,* 322]).

Bibliography

Migsch, H. 1981. *Gottes Wort über das Ende Jerusalem.* ÖBS 2. Klosterneuberg.

Pohlmann, K.-F. 1978. *Studien zum Jeremiabuch.* FRLANT 118. Göttingen.

John M. Berridge

JEHUD (PLACE) [Heb *yĕhūd*]. A town allotted to the tribe of Dan (Josh 19:45), located in the coastal region which the Danites failed to inherit (Josh 19:47; Judg 1:34). The site of Jehud is identified with el-Yahudiya (modern Yehud; M.R. 139159) where sherds of the MB and Iron Age have been collected.

Raphael Greenberg

JEHUDI (PERSON) [Heb *yĕhûdî*]. An officer at the court of King Jehoiakim (Jer 36:14, 21, 23). It is probable that Jehudi was a scribe. In the prose narrative of Jeremiah 36, the royal officials (*śārîm,* translated "princes" in RSV and NAB) send Jehudi to summon Baruch to appear before them with the scroll dictated by Jeremiah (36:14). Later, Jehoiakim dispatches Jehudi to fetch the scroll from the chamber of Elishama, the state secretary (v 21). Jehudi then reads the scroll to the king and his officials (vv 21, 23).

In Jer 36:14, Jehudi is identified as son of Nethaniah, son of Shelemiah, son of Cushi. It is noteworthy that Jehudi's genealogy is traced back to the 3d generation. Many commentators believe that the text is to be emended slightly to read "then all the royal officials sent Jehudi son of Nethaniah *and* Shelemiah son of Cushi . . ." (see, e.g., the JB's translation). If Jer 36:14 is accepted as it now reads, it is difficult to provide a satisfactory explanation for the extended genealogy, although it is possible that the genealogy is to be viewed in the light of Deut 23:7–8. That text is concerned with the genealogical purity of those who participate in the Israelite cult, and speaks only of the children of the 3d generation born to Edomites and Egyptians. If Jehudi's great-grandfather was indeed a Cushite by birth (this must be questioned, even if one does not emend the text of Jer 36:14), it is very possible that the name "Jehudi" (lit. "Judahite") may indicate that Jehudi was a naturalized Judean.

Bibliography

Mettinger, T. N. D. 1971. *Solomonic State Officials.* ConBOT 5. Lund.

Rice, G. 1975. Two Black Contemporaries of Jeremiah. *JRT* 32: 95–109.

John M. Berridge

JEIEL (PERSON) [Heb *yĕʿîʾēl*]. Name of 11 people in postexilic books of the Hebrew Bible. The form of the name sometimes alternates between Jeiel (*yĕʿîʾēl*) and Jeuel (*yĕʿûʾēl*) either as a *Qere* and *Ketib* or between the MT and some of the versions; this is similar to the variation between the names Peniel and Penuel (*BLe,* 524 h). The etymology of the name is uncertain; perhaps it should be connected to Arabic roots meaning "strong" or "to cure" (*HALAT* 2: 401) in which case the name would mean "God is strong" or "God cures." It has not yet appeared in the extrabiblical epigraphic corpus. There is no obvious reason why Jeiel is mentioned only in postexilic sources.

1. One of the families who returned from the Babylonian exile with Ezra (Ezra 8:13). This list is seen as a generally authentic record (Williamson *Ezra, Nehemiah* WBC, 109–11; Blenkinsopp *Ezra-Nehemiah* OTL, 161). The verse that mentions Jeiel/Jeuel is problematic; it reads "Of the sons of Adonikam, those who came later [*ʾaḥărōnîm*], their names being Eliphelet, Jeiel, and Shemaiah . . ." The meaning of *ʾaḥărōnîm,* which usually means "last ones," is unclear, since additional names follow in v 14. Some have suggested that the families of v 13 were the last to leave Babylon (Williamson WBC, 108; Blenkinsopp OTL, 163), but this is reading too much into the Hebrew of the text. Verse 13 is also exceptional in that no other father's name is followed by more than one child. Most likely, the list of returnees originally ended with v 13, with the list of the family of Adonikam, the "final ones" (*ʾaḥărōnîm*), and his children were listed in full to effect closure. Verse 14, then, is most likely an addition, to bring the total number of lay families to the schematic number 12. RSV's reading Jeuel here is poorly attested in the manuscripts, and Jeiel should be read instead with the vast majority of manuscripts and the LXX.

2. One of the sons of Nebo, who appears in the list of intermarried people in Ezra 10:43. This list is generally seen as authentic (Blenkinsopp OTL, 199–200), though it is unclear if it is complete, and because its concluding v 44 is difficult, it is not known if those enumerated are intermarried, or have divorced their foreign wives (Myers *Ezra Nehemiah* AB, 87–88; Blenkinsopp OTL, 197–98). Cogan (1979) has suggested that Nebo is from the tribe of Reuben, but his evidence from several overlapping names between this verse and the Reubenite genealogy in 1 Chr 5:4–8 is inconclusive (Williamson WBC, 159). The centrality of the prohibition of intermarriage in the postexilic period is seen by the literary placement of this section as the conclusion of the Ezra portion of Ezra-Nehemiah; this prohibition is based on reinterpretation of earlier biblical texts prohibiting intermarriage with the Canaanite population (Fishbane 1985: 114–26).

3. A Reubenite (1 Chr 5:7). The relation of this verse to the previous genealogy, and thus the relationship between this Jeiel and the rest of the Reubenites are unclear. 1 Chr 5:7 MT begins, "And his brothers (*wĕʾeḥāyw*) according to his families. . . ." The immediately preceding referent is Beerah (v 6), who was exiled by Tiglath-Pilesser in the 8th century; however, in v 8, these Reubenites are listed as living in areas which they no longer controlled in the 8th century. Possibly, the participle in v 8, *yôšēb,* "he dwells," describing the descendants of the Reuben, should be understood as a perfect, "who dwealt" (Williamson *Chronicles* NCBC, 64), but this is unlikely. The language of v 7 is unusual; its opening words *wĕʾeḥayw lĕmišpĕḥōtāyw* are unique in the genealogical section of 1 Chronicles and the note that Jeiel is the *rōʾš,* probably "the firstborn," is very unusual. This might suggest that the verse is a fragment of a premonarchical Reubenite genealogy (see v 10, which deals with the period of Saul), which became appended to the main genealogy in vv 1–6. The words *wĕʾḥāyw lĕmišpĕḥōtāyw* "And his brothers according to his families," are thus a clumsy attempt to join the 2 genealogies.

4. One of the families of Judah from the clan of Zerah who settled in Jerusalem at the return from the exile (1 Chr 9:6). According to MT, his name is given as Jeuel (so RSV), while many of the important LXX manuscripts suggest Jeiel. The list in 1 Chronicles 9 is similar to that in Neh 11:3–36, but the exact relationship between the 2 lists and their time of composition remain unclear (Williamson WBC, 344–50). The list in Nehemiah 11 does not include the clan of Zerah, thus Jeiel/Jeuel is not mentioned there.

5. Early Benjaminite, an ancestor of King Saul, and the settler of the Benjaminite city of Gibeon (1 Chr 9:35). This genealogy is probably preexilic (Demsky 1971), though some see the tie of Benjamin to Gibeon rather than Gibeah and the double mention of Ner and Kish in vv 36 and 39 as an indication that this section of the genealogy is artificial (Malamat 1968: 171). Jeiel's name is missing in the parallel genealogy in 8:29, but it appears there in the Lucianic family of the LXX; Rudolph (*Chronikbücher* HAT, 78) and RSV add it to 8:29. Perhaps this Jeiel should be identified with (or emended to) Jediael, *yĕdîʿăʾēl,* the son of Benjamin according to 1 Chr 7:6, who represents one of the major clans of the Benjaminite family. According to 9:35, Jeiel's wife is named Maacah, a name that typifies residents of the Transjordan (Demsky 1971: 18, n. 10). The inclusion of a wife's name is not typical of these genealogies; perhaps this ancestor of Saul was somehow seen as the equivalent of the queen mother, who played an important role in Israelite politics (Andreason 1983).

6. One of David's warriors (Mazar 1963) (1 Chr 11:44). The list of David's warriors in 1 Chr 11:26–47 is derived from various sources: the first section (until the middle of v 41) is derived from 2 Sam 23:24–39 and the second probably reflects an additional preexilic source that was available to the Chronicler (Williamson NCBC, 103–4). If it were a fabrication, it would probably follow the previous section's style more closely. The purpose of 1 Chronicles 11 is to glorify David by showing the extent of the military power that supported him, thus reinforcing the divine legitimation of David (see 1 Chr 11:10); this ideology probably motivated the chapter's editor to go beyond his usual source and to find additional lists of David's warriors. MT gives the warrior's name as Jeuel in the *Kethib* and as Jeiel in the *Qere*; most of the versions support the *Qere.* MT breaks v 44 in half, by inserting a paragraph marker (*sĕtûmâ*) after Jeiel; this suggests that the continuation of the verse, "the sons of Hotham the Aroerite," represents additional (unnamed) warriors who are unrelated to Jeiel. If we ignore this division, then Jeiel's father is Hotham, from the Transjordan city of Aroer.

7. One of the *mĕšōrĕrîm,* "Temple singers" (1 Chr 15:18, 21; 16:5). 1 Chr 15:18 MT lists this Jeiel as one of the *šōʿărîm,* "gatekeepers," but this word should be excised as a gloss (Williamson WBC, 125). According to 1 Chr 15:16, these singers were established by David as part of his preparation for the Temple that Solomon would build; this is consistent with the Chronicler's ideology (Williamson WBC, 30). The list in 1 Chronicles 15 of singers who here are considered to be Levites reflects the realities of the Chronicler's period rather than of David's (Williamson WBC, 122). The list appears twice in chap. 15, once in general terms, and once giving the specific roles of the groups of singers. Verse 16 introduces the list, v 17 lists the three most important singers, Heman, Asaph, and Ethan, and v 18 lists the other singers, who are called *mišnîm,* "of second rank." The word (*wĕ*)*hamešōrĕrîm,* "(and) the Temple singers" should be moved from the beginning of v 19 to replace the incorrect *šōʿărîm,* "gatekeepers" at the end of v 18. Verses 19, 20, and 21 then list groups of singers, assigning to them specific musical roles. Jeiel is among those who play *bĕkinnōrôt ʿal haššĕmînît lĕnaṣṣēaḥ,* which involves some type of lyre (*kinnōr*) music. The meaning of the remaining technical terms is notoriously difficult (Anderson *Psalms* NCBC, 43–50; Kraus 1988: 21–32). Jeiel appears twice in 1 Chr 16:5, in the list of singers accompanying the transport of the ark to Jerusalem, but the first appearance of Jeiel should probably be emended to Jaaziel, following the parallel texts in 1 Chr 15:18 and 20 (Rudolph HAT, 120); the error was caused by the graphic similarity of the names in Heb (*yʿyʾl* and *yʿzyʾl*).

8. Ancestor of Jahaziel, a prophet who encouraged the Judean king Jehoshaphat (2 Chr 20:14). It is likely that this prophet and his lineage are the Chronicler's invention. The name Jahaziel, *yaḥăzîʾēl* is composed from the element *ḥzh,* "to be a seer," and is probably a creation of the Chronicler. The symbolic names Iddo and Jeddo, from *ʿwd,* "to exhort," are similarly used by the Chronicler of prophets that he created. Furthermore, the genealogy of this Jahaziel is highly suspicious. He is supposedly "son of Zechariah, son of Benaiah, son of Jeiel, son of Mattaniah, a Levite of the sons of Asaph." These names are known from the list of *mĕšōrĕrîm,* "Temple singers" in 1 Chr 15:17–21 (Mattaniah = Mattithiah). The creation of a prophet by the Chronicler is in line with the importance that the Chronicler gives to prophecy (Japhet 1977: 154–66); possibly, the Chronicler creates such a long genealogy for Jahaziel to legitimate him by connecting him to the time of David (Williamson WBC, 298).

9. A *sôpēr,* "secretary" during the reign of the Judean king Uzziah (2 Chr 26:11). The exact range of meanings and etymology of *sôpēr* are unclear (Baumgartner *HALAT* 3: 724); in this context, however, he has a military role (cf. 2 Kgs 25:19 = Jer 52:25). The list of officials given here is not found in Kings. Several similar lists are found throughout Chronicles, and they do not show the patterns of fabrications seen in Jeiel #8, above; they are probably authentic preexilic lists which the Chronicler had access to (Williamson WBC, 261–63). The *Ketib* writes the name as Jeuel; but the *Qere* and most versions argue in favor of Jeiel.

10. A descendant of the Elizaphan branch of the Levites, who assisted in the purification of the Temple during the reign of Hezekiah (2 Chr 29:13). The other names in that verse are Shimri, Zechariah, and Mattaniah; these are largely identical with the ancestors of Jahaziel (see #8), who are projections of postexilic Levite clans backward to the preexilic period (see #7). The list is anachronistic, and of no historical value for reconstructing the period of

Hezekiah; it does, however, reflect the importance of the family of Jeiel in the exilic period. The *Ketib* writes the name as Jeuel; but the *Qere* and most versions support Jeiel.

11. One of the Levites who donated animals for the Josiah's Passover (2 Chr 35:9). In the 1 Esdr 1:9 parallel, this name apparently appears as Ochiel. The account of this Passover is largely the creation of the Chronicler (Williamson WBC, 403–5); it is a combination of exegesis of earlier Pentateuchal sources and retrojection of postexilic practices into the preexilic period (Fishbane 1985: 137–38). The list of Levites is therefore of little value for reconstructing preexilic Israel; it is noteworthy, however, that it does not agree with the anachronistic lists discussed in #8 and #10.

Bibliography

Andreasen, N.-E. A. 1983. The Role of the Queen Mother in Israelite Society. *CBQ* 45: 179–94.

Cogan, M. 1979. The Men of Nebo—Repatriated Reubenites. *IEJ* 29: 37–39.

Demsky, A. 1971. The Genealogy of Gibeon (1 Chronicles 9:35–44): Biblical and Epigraphic Considerations. *BASOR* 202: 16–23.

Fishbane, M. 1985. *Biblical Interpretation in Ancient Israel.* Oxford.

Japhet, S. 1977. *The Ideology of the Book of Chronicles and its Place in Biblical Thought.* Jerusalem (in Hebrew).

Kraus, H.-J. 1988. *Psalms 1–59.* Trans. H. C. Oswald. Minneapolis, MN.

Malamat, A. 1968. King Lists in the Old Babylonian Period and Biblical Genealogies. *JAOS* 88: 163–173.

Mazar, B. 1963. The Military Élite of King David. *VT* 13: 310–20.

MARC Z. BRETTLER

JEKABZEEL (PLACE) [Heb *yĕqabṣeʾēl*]. An alternate form of KABZEEL.

JEKAMEAM (PERSON) [Heb *yeqamʿām*]. A Kohathite, the 4th son of Hebron (1 Chr 23:19). Jekameam appears nowhere else in the OT outside of the Levitical lists in 1 Chronicles 23 and 24. The Levitical genealogies of Exodus 6 and Numbers 3 do not include an enumeration of the immediate descendants of Hebron. The source of the Chronicler's use of the name "Jekameam" remains uncertain. Although J. Liver (1968: viii, 29–32) believes that this name, along with the other Levitical names in 1 Chronicles 23, may have originated from an authentic source composed during the reign of David or Solomon, Rudolph (*Chronikbücher* HAT, 152–59, 163–65) argued that Jekameam and the other Levites of 1 Chronicles 23 represent Levitical families after the time of the Chronicler. The style of the list, however, corresponds closely with the compositional techniques of the Chronicler. This suggests that Williamson (*Chronicles* NCBC, 160) may be correct in asserting that "the names of the heads of houses will then be current at the time of the list's composition"—the time of the Chronicler (ca. 385 B.C.E.).

Bibliography

Liver, J. 1968. *Chapters in the History of Priests and Levites.* Jerusalem (in Hebrew).

Williamson, H.G.M. 1979. The Origins of the Twenty-Four Priestly Courses, A Study of 1 Chronicles xxiii–xxvii. Pp. 251–68 in *Studies in the Historical Books of the Old Testament,* ed. J. A. Emerton. VTSup 30. Leiden.

JOHN W. WRIGHT

JEKAMIAH (PERSON) [Heb *yeqamyāh*]. The name held by 2 persons in the Hebrew Bible. This name is also attested in extrabiblical documents (Myers *1 Chronicles* AB, 21). It may mean "may Ya establish" (*IDB* 2: 618).

1. In 1 Chr 2:41 Jekamiah is given as the name of a descendant of Jerahmeel. Verses 34–41 are usually considered to be an addition to this chapter. The descendants of Jerahmeel are given in 1 Chr 2:25–33, which is a genealogy with both vertical and horizontal components. Verses 34–41, however, constitute a vertical genealogy which terminates in Elshama. This section of verses seems to be intended as a pedigree for him (Williamson *Chronicles* NCBC, 54).

2. Jekamiah is also listed in 1 Chr 3:18 as the 5th son of Jeconiah/Jehoiachin, the captive king of Judah.

RUSSELL FULLER

JEKUTHIEL (PERSON) [Heb *yĕqûtîʾēl*]. A descendant of Judah through Mered (1 Chr 4:18).

H. C. LO

JEMIMAH (PERSON) [Heb *yemîmâ*]. The first of Job's daughters born to him after the restoration of his fortunes (42:14). The name may mean "turtledove" if the root has the meaning it carries in Arabic (cf. Dhorme 1967; Cant 2:14). It is noteworthy that Job gave his daughter Jemimah and her 2 sisters an inheritance along with their brothers. According to Num 21:1–8, a daughter would only inherit her father's property if there was no male heir. By including his daughters in the inheritance, Job illustrates a practice of justice that far outstripped the norm in the ancient world (cf. chap. 31). See also KEREN-HAPPUCH; KEZIAH.

Bibliography

Dhorme, E. 1967. *A Commentary on the Book of Job.* Repr. London.

JOHN C. HOLBERT

JEMMEH, TELL (M.R. 097088). An archaeological site in SW Israel. Jemmeh stands on the S bank of Nahal Besor (Wadi Ghazzeh), about 12 km due S of the city of Gaza. It is located in an Asiatic steppe environment, i.e., in a transitional zone, positioned between the wetter Mediterranean climate and the rainless desert climate of the Negeb. Because of marginal rainfall, dry farming was often unreliable, forcing people to migrate N or to Lower Egypt. The soil is loess, rich in calcium carbonate, and when well watered produces abundant harvests. The region lacks good building stone, but the soil makes fine mudbrick, and all structures are built of it.

A. Identification

During the 1920s, Jemmeh was first identified with biblical Gerar by Phythian-Adams (1923: 140) and Petrie (1928: 2). This identification was accepted until 1951, when B. Mazar (1951: 38–41) identified Jemmeh with Yurza, a town mentioned in Egyptian topographical lists and the Tell el-Amarna tablets. Recent evidence of a major Assyrian occupation of the site in the 7th century B.C. strengthens this view, because several Akkadian texts of King Esarhaddon mention the taking of "Arsa (or Arza) near the Brook of Egypt"; linguistically Arza corresponds with Eg Yurza. A Byzantine city, Orda can be identified with remains just S of the mound; Orda is probably the Greek form of Yurza. The name Yurza/Arsa/Arza does not appear in the Bible.

B. Excavations

The first archaeological investigation was undertaken by Phythian-Adams in 1922, when he dug a small step-trench. In 1926–27, Petrie moved his operations from Egypt to Jemmeh. Following a single field season at Jemmeh, he moved to Tell Sharuhen and later to Tell el-Ajjul, other sites along Nahal Besor. At Jemmeh, Petrie excavated 1 acre in the W central portion of the site, repeatedly reducing the area until he reached virgin soil in a small trench in the NW corner of the dig. No further work was undertaken until 1970, when G. Van Beek initiated excavations for the Smithsonian Institution; these continued annually through 1978, and then intermittently for a total of 12 field seasons.

C. The Site

Jemmeh originally occupied a mesa encompassing an area of 4.92 hectares (12.15 acres). It is the most-eroded major site in Israel, the N end having been destroyed by flash floods in Nahal Besor, and the S end by severe erosion. The area on the top of the mound is now reduced to 0.26 hectares (0.64 acres) from an estimated original area of 3.04 hectares (7.51 acres). The site is the highest point in the landscape, reaching a height of 22 m (71 feet) above present ground level. Its upper 15.50 m (50 feet) is occupation debris of successive towns.

D. Chalcolithic

Remains of this period are found only in a small area on the lower E slope of the site. They consist of a series of circular pit structures dug into virgin soil, which may have served as subterranean houses or storage pits. The artifacts are typical of the Beer-sheba Culture. Following this period, Jemmeh had no permanent settlement until the MB. The abandonment of Jemmeh through the EB is characteristic of the region, except for a small Egyptian outpost at En-Besor.

E. Middle Bronze Age

The entire site was resettled in MB II–III, whose remains have been found everywhere on the site to a depth of ca. 2 m. A fortification system, consisting of a rammed earth revetment more than 5 m thick, protected the Canaanite town. A foundation deposit of a small equid was found under one of the lowest walls of this period, and the skull and 2 long bones of another equid were buried in a pit where they too may have served a similar function. An unusual zoomorphic vessel in Tell el-Yehudiyeh ware in the form of a deer or bull head, was discovered on the E slope.

F. Late Bronze Age

During this Canaanite period, lasting about 350 years, 6 m of debris accumulated everywhere on the site testifying to an intensive occupation with many building phases. Below Petrie's excavation, an enormous building complex of the 13th century B.C. was discovered, consisting of (1) a large courtyard, complete with a fine cobblestone floor, mud benches along the wall, a bread oven in one corner enclosed by a low wall or bench forming a quarter circle, and a plastered bathroom, which drained through a wall into a stone built dry well, and (2) a private residence, connected to the courtyard by a series of 3 stone steps, with a private entrance flanked by mud benches, and a series of rooms with an open courtyard complete with a bread oven.

Notable finds of this period include a tankard, uniquely painted in black and red in 3 zones, featuring birds feeding on black fruit on trees; sherds of a Late Helladic III octopus vase; 3 scarabs with the same basic motif: a king, probably Rameses II, worshiping the Eg god, Ptah; and faunal remains including vertebrae of an African ostrich and the horn core of a hartebeest.

G. Iron Age

1. Philistine. This was the lowest continuous stratum excavated by Petrie. This 12th–11th centuries occupation deposited about 2.5 m of debris over the entire site, and is characterized by a new pottery tradition derived from Aegean prototypes and identified with the Philistines.

The most singular structure discovered is a large, technologically advanced ceramic kiln. The kiln, ovoid in ground plan, measuring 3.7 m long by 2 m wide, consisted of a firebox and a baking chamber with a perforated mudbrick floor. This floor was supported by 4 radial mudbrick arches. Between the springing of each arch on both firebox walls was a vertical trough leading upward to a pair of square earthen pipes to distribute heat directly to the upper part of the baking chamber, which was at least 3 m high. Many sherds painted with Philistine running spirals were found in the kiln.

2. Iron II. During the next 300 years, the W half of the site experienced continuous settlement, while the E half was no longer occupied. In the 10th century, a peculiar style of wall construction was used in all buildings excavated to date. Clayey, chocolate-colored brick were set in foundation trenches on a bed of clean, yellow sand and the trench was backfilled with the same sand. During the 10th and 9th centuries, local pottery was finished with a burnished, deep-red slip, somtimes augmented with alternating bands of black and white paint. Indeed, from the 10th century onward, local pottery differs somewhat in form, decoration, and chronological range from that of other regions in Israel, suggesting that the NW Negeb was a cultural microcosm.

The 8th century is represented by 3 building phases, and the earliest casemate fortification system was built at Jemmeh at this time. Noteworthy among the artifacts is a small, solid-bronze bull head, which served as a weight, weighing 14.60 gr.

3. Iron II: Assyrian Occupation. To this period belongs a unique building dating from about 675 B.C. It consisted of a series of 5 basement rooms, although originally there were at least 6 and probably more rooms. All 5 rooms were still partially covered with portions of mudbrick vaults, which had supported an upper floor. The plan of the building consisted of 3 long rooms side-by-side, giving entrance through arched doorways into 3 small rooms on one end, and perhaps also at the now missing other end of the building. The vaults were built using the "pitched brick" technique, but display a considerable technological advance in the use of voussoirs (wedge-shaped bricks, like keystones; Van Beek 1987: 100–2). Room A yielded a large quantity of so-called Assyrian palace ware, commonly found in the palaces and royal storerooms of the Assyrian kings. This pottery and the architecture suggest that Esarhaddon converted Jemmeh into a forward military base for his conquest of Egypt. Two ostraca from this period feature different types of personal names written in a script that varies slightly from Judean and Phoenician scripts (Naveh 1985: 8–21). It seems likely that descendants of the original Philistines continued to dominate this region, at least through the 7th century.

H. Persian Occupation

This period is represented by a massive building excavated by Petrie, which probably served as the fortified residence of an official appointed by the Persian government.

I. Hellenistic Period

With Ptolemaic control of the Levant in the late 4th–3d centuries B.C., the site again ceased to be a normal town. Instead it was occupied by a series of grain silos, making Jemmeh the best example of a grain storage depot in the ANE. The granaries, all built in deep holes cut into earlier debris layers, were round structures built of mudbrick. Petrie excavated 10 silos on the W half of the site; the Smithsonian excavated one and on the E side partially excavated another. More is known about the Smithsonian granary on the W side than the others. It had a flat roof carried by the circular wall and an inner, radially arched, cross wall. There were 2 successive mudbrick floors indicating its long use.

Among the pottery were storage jars of a new type, one of which, made of local ware, bore a painted S Arabic monogram on its shoulder, reading *ʾabum,* a name known in both Sabean and Minean inscriptions. This one, together with a sherd of probable S Arabian ware with an incised S Arabic *m,* established trade between the regions, since camel caravans transported frankincense and myrrh from S Arabia to Gaza, the major Mediterranean incense port.

By about 200 B.C., the occupation of Jemmeh ended, and subsequent settlement in the Late-Roman–Byzantine periods took place in the field S of the tell. During Crusader times, a hoard of 11 silver coins, originally tied in a piece of cloth, was apparently lost on the tell by a pilgrim or traveler. Nine of these coins were minted in the reign of Amaury II (A.D. 1163–74) and bear the inscription *Amairicus Rex De Ierusalem.*

Bibliography

Amiran, R., and Van Beek, G. W. 1976. Tell Jemmeh. *EAEHL* 2: 545–49.

Maisler (Mazar), B. 1952. Yurza: The Identification of Tell Jemmeh. *PEQ* 48: 48–51.

Naveh, J. 1985. Writing and Scripts in Seventh-Century B.C.E. Philistia: The New Evidence from Tell Jemmeh. *IEJ* 35: 8–21.

Petrie, W. M. F. 1928. *Gerar.* London.

Phythian-Adams, W. J. 1923. Report on Soundings at Tell Jemmeh. *PEFQS,* 140–46.

Van Beek, G. W. 1964. Frankincense and Myrrh. Repr. *BAR* 2: 99–126.

———. 1983. Digging Up Tell Jemmeh. *Archaeology* 36: 12–19.

———. 1984. Archeological Investigations at Tell Jemmeh, Israel. *National Geographic Research Reports* 16: 675–96.

———. 1986. Are There Beehive Granaries at Tell Jemmeh? A Rejoinder. *BA* 49: 245–47.

———. 1987. The Arch and the Vault in Ancient Near Eastern Architecture. *Scientific American* 257: 96–103.

Gus W. Van Beek

JEMUEL (PERSON) [Heb *yĕmûʾēl*]. See NEMUEL.

JENIN (M.R. 178207).

A modern Arab town located at the N end of the Wadi Belameh where it empties into the SE edge of the Plain of Jezreel, 100 km N of Jerusalem. In the center of the mouth of the Wadi Belameh lies Tell Jenin, one site among many that was occupied during the British Mandate. Tell Jenin was first identified by P. L. O. Guy in 1926 as the site of an ancient town on top of which was a modern cemetery and a threshing floor. Reports for 1932, 1933, and 1942 describe the vigilant efforts of inspector Makhouly to prevent the dislocation of the rich tell sediments for building houses, dirt for gardens, and the construction of the road to Megiddo. The site is also known as Tell el-Nawar because of annual gypsy encampments on the mount prior to 1948.

Since Kallai (1967: 358) and other historical geographers of the Bible did not seem to know the site, Tsori (1972) assumed that he was the first to locate and identify the tell with biblical En-gannim. The evidence for this judgment was not based on controlled excavation but a few Iron Age sherds gathered from the N section facing the bus station. Precise stratigraphic investigation of the archaeological history of the site and the region of Jenin began in 1977 with salvage excavations at 4 areas on the E and W sides of the remaining S half of the tell. The N half of the tell was removed in 1962 for the construction of the municipal bus station and the Latin Convent. From that work, no records, and only a few artifacts have survived (Rahmani 1980).

Jenin sits astride the junction of 2 major geomorphological features: the down faulted Jezreel Valley to the N, and Eocene chalk blocks to the S. In the N edge of the erosional basin of the Plain of Dothan, the weathered Jenin

Gap was formed creating a passage (the present Wadi Belameh) to the Jezreel. Other wadis E and W of Jenin leading from the high ground to the S are along fault lines. Until the 20th century, the water supply of Jenin was sufficient to make it famed as a garden town (Robinson 1874; *SWP,* 44–45). The average annual rainfall is about 475 mm. In modern times, increased demand on the water supply has lowered the water table so that shallow aquifers have dried up springs that formerly fed wells and perennial streams in and around Jenin. Except during heavy winter rains, today only 'Ain Jenin flows.

Surviving in the Arabic name Jenin is the Hebrew name En-gannim (Josh 19:17, 21; 21:28, 29), possibly also biblical Beth-haggan (2 Kgs 9:27 where the "ascent of Gur" is probably the Wadi Belameh) assigned to the territory of Issachar where it was designated a Gershonite Levitical city. Albright (1926) and Saarisalo (1927) attempted to locate En-gannim at Khirbet Beit Jann near Jabneel in the NE corner of the Jezreel. This identification continues to be upheld (see "En-Gannim," *EncJud* 6: col. 741). Qena, in Amarna Letter 250.17, 21 where Lab'ayu was slain and *kn* in the town lists of Thutmose III also refer to Jenin. However, "Gurra" in the early reading of Taanach Letter 2:6 by Hrozny, must now be abandoned (Glock 1983: 60, n. 27). Josephus places the Samaritan murder of Galilean pilgrim(s) en route to Jerusalem at Ginaea, usually identified with Jenin (*Ant* 20.118; *JW* 2.232; 3.48).

The town was known to the Crusaders as Gerin and was defended by a small fortress. Attacked several times by Salah el-Din in his war on the Crusaders in the late 12th century, Jenin followed Fahma (Umm el Fahm; Hartmann 1916: 489). Jenin is described by at least one Muslim geographer as a "small and beautiful town . . . (with) much water and many springs" (Yaqut, A.D. 1225). In the 17th century Evliya Tschelebi, a pious Muslim pilgrim, describes in detail the Ottoman fortress that guarded the town, which since the Late Byzantine period (6th–7th century), lay on the N slopes of Karem Jenin, ca. 500 m E of the tell.

Recent excavations and surveys of the region indicate that the area of Jenin was continuously occupied from late Neolithic until modern times, not, however, exclusively on the tell, which was periodically inundated. Thus, when the site was abandoned at the end of EB I, a new settlement was established on top of Karem Jenin, about 170 m SE of the tell. As discoveries continue in and around Jenin it is evident that the tell was perhaps only rarely the population center. Two km to the S in the Wadi Belameh is Kh. Belameh (biblical Ibleam), strategically located on an imposing mound adjacent to wadi springs and occupied from EB through the Byzantine periods. Across the wadi to the E is Kh. el-Najjar, settled in the EB, MB, and Byzantine periods. It seems probable that at least until the flowering of the Byzantine period most sites in the region were satellite to Kh. Belameh, which included Tell Jenin.

The present incomplete picture of the stratification of Tell Jenin is based on evidence from the excavation of 4 areas totalling about 250 m^2 or approximately 1.2% of the tell which measures about 200 m N–S and 150 m E–W (actual limits in any period except the last are uncertain). What little has been excavated points to terraced housing after the 13th century B.C. It would seem premature to identify Tell Jenin archaeologically with biblical En-gannim until more of the stratigraphic history of the tell above the street level has been excavated.

Stratum I is assigned to the series of clay sediments laminated with stoney layers which were sorted by repeated flooding. This level is at least 2 m deep over bedrock at the base of the tell and predates cultural activity. The process of accumulation continued after the site was settled. The edges of the tell were annually covered by new layers of eroded wadi sediment, until today in one place the road surface is 5 m above the foundations of the EB I. Stratum II contains the first evidence of cultural activity in the form of eroded plaster surfaces and walls swept clean of artifacts by repeated post-occupation flooding. In the makeup below the floors there were many Neolithic blade and flake tools.

Evidence from stratum III, dated to EB I, is confined to the W side of the tell. Three features stand out: an apsidal house, a "platform" in the SW corner of the tell, and a donkey burial. Covered by the road and a modern building, more than half of the roofed space of the apsidal house was not accessible. See Fig. JEN.01. Preserved were the slab stone doorway and paved courtyard to the E with its gated entrance. This well-built house had 2 clear construction phases. Sixty m S of the house, on what was the SW corner of the tell, a stone platform ca. 1.2 m thick spanned the 10 m E–W width of the excavation and disappeared into the N balk, but was eroded on the S where the floodwater pressure would have been greatest. This structure functioned to break the wadi's flood levels in winter and provided a stable base for domestic architecture above. Protected behind a later (stratum IV) retaining wall was the complete skeleton of a small donkey, 11 or more years old which had suffered from severe arthritis.

After abandonment at the beginning of the 3d millennium B.C., thre is no evidence of occupation in the areas excavated until the 13th–12th centuries (stratum IV). The best preserved evidence comes from a house on the E side of the tell (Glock 1979). On a *mastaba* against the N wall of the house, a typical 12th century assemblage of store jars and jugs was trapped below the collapse of the mudbrick superstructure. The exposure was limited to about 20 square meters, making it impossible to infer anything but local collapse. On the W side of the tell, a well-constructed retaining wall was banked against debris to the N.

Stratum V follows another long abandonment when the SW corner of the tell was occupied in the Late Byzantine period (6th–7th centuries A.D.). The 5 phases of this stratum were severely damaged by extensive pre-archaeological construction digging. Four of these phases represent rebuilding and elaboration of substantial elements of domestic buildings. The unexcavated section 60 m N indicated similarly dated plaster floors and the remains of heavy architecture at a higher level. In the absence of *in situ* evidence of stratum V on the E, it appears that only the W side of the site was occupied by a few well-constructed villas. Stratum VI consists of fragments of plaster floors above the Byzantine buildings on the SW and a heavy stone platform on the NE of the tell dated to Late Ottoman (19th and early 20th centuries). What has been identified as stratum VII dates from the end of Ottoman

JEN.01. Apsidal house wall (center) with courtyard (left) at Tell Jenin—EB I. *(Courtesy of A. Glock)*

rule to the present. The fuller description of these excavated strata will appear in the final report.

Bibliography

Albright, W. F. 1926. The Topography of the Tribe of Issachar. *ZAW* 44: 225–36.

Glock, A. E. 1979. Tell Jenin. *RB* 86: 110–12.

———. 1983. Texts and Archaeology at Tell Ta'annek. *Berytus* 31: 57–66.

Hartmann, R. 1916. Politische Geographie des Mamlukenreichs. *ADMG* 70: 1–40, 477–511.

Kallai, Z. 1967. *The Tribes of Israel.* Jerusalem (in Hebrew).

Le Strange, G. 1980. *Palestine under the Moslems.* Khayats Oriental Reprints 14. Beirut.

Rahmani, L. Y. 1980. Palestinian Incense Burners of the Sixth to Eighth Centuries C.E. *IEJ* 30: 116–22.

Robinson, E., and Smith, E. 1874. *Biblical Researchers in Palestine.* 11th ed. Boston.

Saarisalo, A. 1927. *The Boundary between Issachar and Naphtali.* Helsinki.

Tzori, N. 1972. New Light on en-Ganim. *PEQ* 104: 134–37.

A. E. G.

JEPHTHAH (PERSON) [Heb *yiptāḥ*]. One of the Israelite military leaders in the era of the book of Judges, his career is recounted at considerable length (Judg 10:6–12:7). Jephthah was remembered for mobilizing the resistance, and leading the counter offensive, to defeat the Ammonites in Transjordan (10:6–11:33). He was also remembered for the tragic sequels: the sacrifice of his daughter and only child in fulfillment of a vow (11:34–40), and a slaughter of Ephraimites in inter-Israelite tribal warfare (12:1–6). Jephthah is named among the heroes of faith in the letter to the Hebrews 11:32.

Jephthah's name is the short form of a sentence name, *yiptaḥ ʾēl,* appearing as a place name, located on the boundary between Zebulun and Asher (Josh 19:14, 27). The name means "El (God) opens (the womb?)" or "El (God) frees (the captive?)." The name *yiptāḥ* also occurs as name of a town in Judah (Josh 15:43), probably situated in the Shephelah. See also the related personal name Pethahiah, "Yahweh has opened" (1 Chr 24:16; Ezra 10:23; Neh 9:5; 11:24). Also related is the personal name Japtih-Adda, in the tablets from Tell El-Amarna.

Jephthah's story is framed by brief notices about so-called minor judges (Judg 10:1–5 and 12:8–15), with whom Jephthah is often grouped by scholars, on the theory that he appeared in the same archival source. The intertribal significance of the minor judges remains obscure. There was an older critical notion that the verb *špṭ,* "to judge," as used in these brief units, referred originally to activities of individuals who held a recognized office (local or regional, but rarely intertribal), and was only secondarily applied to the great military leaders; but this notion no longer fares well: The evidence is too scant. Alternatively it is now proposed that the "minor judge" notices do not reflect a difference in office or function but only a difference in literary purpose (Mullen 1982: 201). That is, the brief "minor judge" units have a condensing narrative effect, serving to focus attention on Jephthah, for theological evaluation. The assessment of leadership will be increasingly negative in the remainder of the book of Judges: Samson (chaps. 13–16), Micah and his Levite (chaps. 17–18), the fate of a Levite's concubine, and suppression of the tribe of Benjamin (chaps. 19–21).

The period of Jephthah's activity begins with an expansive introduction (10:6–16) which summarizes the entire preceding period. Seven alien gods have enticed Israelites to worship them, and Yahweh has subjected Israel successively to 7 alien "nations," until they cried out to Yahweh for deliverance. With special attention to Philistines and Ammonites, this is also introduction to all that follows in the book of Judges, "Phase II" (Boling *Judges* AB, 30). This beginning of the second half echoes the introduction to the entire era (2:11–23), but with ironic inversion. To the patterned appeal of Israelites in face of the new threat (10:10), Yahweh's response is, in effect, that he is tired of the pattern. Let the gods they have chosen be the ones to rescue them (10:11–14). The Israelites, however, get serious. They dispose of the gods they have turned to, and Yahweh's compassion is activated once again (10:15–16). The recall of Jephthah (10:17–11:11) would be the solution.

With the stage thus set, the curtain opens on a mustering of Israelites at the Transjordan sanctuary site of Mizpah. The location is uncertain but surely to be sought S of the Jabbok, in the vicinity of Jebel Jelᶜad and Khirbet Jelᶜad. The captains of Gilead need someone to start the fighting against the Ammonites. They promise that the one who does it will be "Head of all inhabitants of Gilead." That the protagonists on Israel's side are regularly called "Gileadites" indicates a period prior to the tribal reorganization which assigned the area to Manasseh (N of the Jabbok) and Gad (S of the Jabbok) (Boling 1988).

Next comes a flashback introducing Jephthah as a "knight," that is, one who is prosperous enough to provide his own armor, but in Jephthah's case lacking pedigree. He was a Gileadite driven from his home because of illegitimate birth and possibly unidentifiable parentage on his father's side, being the child of a prostitute. He could not share in the family inheritance. Thus excluded by his half-brothers, Jephthah had fled and made his home in the region of Tob. The place name is possibly reflected in present-day *et-Tayibeh,* E–SE of Derᶜa, ca. 15 miles E of Ramoth-gilead. There he attracted to himself a band of mercenaries (11:1–3), having become a true Hebrew/Habiru, like David later in flight from Saul.

In the next scene, the Ammonites have pressed their advantage to the point where the elders of Gilead are ready to recall Jephthah and offer him the position of *qāṣîn* (field commander?), a status not mentioned in Judges outside this unit (but see Josh 10:24; Isa 1:10; 3:6, 7; 22:3; Mic 3:1–9; Prov 6:7; 25:15; Dan 11:18). An Arabic cognate means "one who decides judicially." Jephthah holds out, contingent upon his success against the Ammonites, for the more powerful and prestigious title "Head," which the elders had originally proposed for one of their own. The deal was solemnized "before Yahweh" at the Mizpah sanctuary (11:4–11).

The next scene portrays Jephthah as exemplary leader, who seeks first to resolve the crisis through diplomatic channels. There are 2 embassies from Jephthah. The first wants to know why the Ammonites are moving into Israelite territory. The Ammonite king claims that it was in fact his territory, "from the Arnon to the Jabbok and to the Jordan," that early Israel had taken by force. The second embassy, which forms the bulk of this unit, is one long speech by Jephthah, delivered by courier to the Ammonite court. A critical issue arises from the emphasis that this appeal to the *Ammonite* king places on Israel's recognition of *Moabite* sovereignty S of the Arnon. In fact Jephthah mentions Ammonites only in the introductory verses (11:12–15) and conclusion (vv 27–28). These verses form an envelope construction around negotiation which appeals to Moabite and Ammonite history. He argues that Chemosh (god of the Moabites) is the one who gave to Ammon the territory from which it was seeking to expand westward. Two long-standing critical theories are here both inadequate. According to one (Moore *Judges* ICC, 283; Eissfeldt 1925: 76), negotiations were entirely with Moab, not with Ammon. According to the second (Burney 1930: 298–305), the negotiations were in fact with Ammon, with some conflation from another account of a confrontation with Moab. The trouble with both theories is that there are no signs of reflective glossing that generally followed such redactional activity elsewhere; the unit made sense to ancient scribes. Scholars have mostly abandoned the effort to find evidence of sources here, continuous with "J" and "E" in the Hexateuch.

Israel's early involvement in the history of the disputed territory is witnessed in Numbers 21, at which time Ammon, lagging somewhat behind Moab, had only recently emerged as a small territorial state in the upper bend of the Jabbok at the desert fringe, but not extending as far W as the escarpment. Apparently Israel's dismantling of the Amorite kingdoms (Sihon and Og) had only paved the way for Ammonite expansion to the W, while Moab would make repeated incursions N of the recognized border at the Arnon (Boling 1988). Thus the king of Ammon in this later period can only make his claims and charges in the name of Moabite sovereignty, since Israelite claims would antedate his own. Under such circumstances we should not be surprised that Chemosh would be generally recognized for diplomatic purposes. Jephthah's final appeal, "Yahweh, the Judge, will decide . . ." (11:27) is the only occurrence of the noun *šōpēṭ,* "judge," in the book of Judges, a theological key to the Jephthah material, if not the whole book. The reference is to the outcome of the battle pending. As the next unit shows, Jephthah is by no means certain of the outcome. Thus, negotiations having failed, the Gileadites would have to fight.

The warfare story moves quickly to the climax—victory for Israel and subsequent tragedy for Jephthah and his daughter. That Yahweh's spirit came upon Jephthah is offered as explanation for his successful enlistment tour of Gilead and Manasseh (cf. Yahweh's spirit on Othniel, the ideal [3:10]; on Gideon who overreacts [6:34]; and in the initial attack upon Samson's conscience [13:25]). Not at all certain of the outcome, Jephthah will make one more deal—with Yahweh. He vows that in event of victory, he will sacrifice as a burnt offering "anything coming out the doors of my house to meet me . . ." (11:31). Such a vow was not required by either Yahweh or the people. By implication it was an act of unfaithfulness (Trible 1984: 97). Had he really expected that the first to come forth would be a human being? The more or less standard plan of Iron Age houses accommodated livestock as well as family. A promise of human sacrifice would be direct violation of Deuteronomic law (Deut 12:29–31). Human sacrifice was rare, and a desperate last resort, a way of inappropriately seeking divine favor (cf. 2 Kgs 16:3; 17:17; 21:6; Jer 7:31; Mic 6:7). Jephthah could scarcely have been expecting divine intervention, as with Abraham (Genesis 22), where it was necessary *because* Abraham was faithful.

That the vow once made must be kept is the hinge of the story, where it is Jephthah's daughter and only child who shows trusting faith, despite the remarkably one-sided self-pity voiced by her father, who blames the daughter for his loss. It is therefore appropriate that the last word in the scene is about Israelite women's annual mourning for the unnamed daughter, rather than showing overabundant sympathy for the famous father (Trible 1984: 106–7). There are a number of parallels to the tragic sacrifice of the hero's daughter in comparative folklore. That there is no other trace of such practice in ancient Israel suggests that this tale is told for other than an etiological purpose. It heightens the tragic dimension in the story of Jephthah, in many ways an exemplary "Head" of Israel in his day.

Two final episodes briefly told, from the career of Jephthah, are only loosely connected to the preceding (12:1–6). Here Jephthah is represented as dealing with inter-Israelite affairs in much the same way that he had approached the Ammonite threat: diplomacy first.

In the first of these units (12:1–4), the Ephraimites are mustered and cross the Jordan at Zaphon, possibly Tell Mazar (Jordan Valley Survey Site 103; Ibrahim, Sauer, and Yassine 1976). The Ephraimites have taken offense, claiming that they were not invited to take part in the warfare against Ammon. Jephthah replies that he had first tried diplomacy and, that failing, had in fact sent an appeal to Ephraim, with no response. If the text is intact, the battle which ensues, with Gilead's defeat of Ephraim, was apparently triggered by a taunt that remains obscure. The fugitives of Ephraim said, "O Gilead, you are in the midst of Ephraim and Manasseh" (12:4). This is missing from a number of Gk mss and may have originated in a partial dittography of v 5. It is not clear whether this is a direct sequel to the victory over Ammon, or perhaps a separate and private feud between a few individuals, with proportions expanded over years of telling it.

The final unit (12:5–6) is one of the most puzzling. Jephthah is not mentioned. Gileadite sentries disable 42 village contingents (surely not 42,000) of retreating Ephraimites, at the Jordan fords. To be allowed to cross over to Cisjordan, one had to pronounce the word shibboleth to the satisfaction of the Gileadite crossing guards. Ephraimites could only say "sibboleth." There are parallels—ancient and modern—to the use of such a test to distinguish between friend and foe.

The note concerning Jephthah's death, after 6 years of leadership, and burial in "his own city in Gilead," looks like an imitation of the concluding rubrics in the "minor judge" units which follow, and where the places of burial are known and named (12:10, 12, 15). Again, the structure of the "minor judge" framework has a condensing narrative effect, propelling the reader on toward the next focus of attention: Samson.

Bibliography

Boling, R. G. 1988. *The Early Biblical Community in Transjordan.* Decatur, GA.

Burney, C. F. 1930. *The Book of Judges.* 2d ed. London. Repr. New York, 1970.

Eissfeldt, O. 1925. *Die Quellen des Richterbuch.* Leipzig.

Emerton, J. A. 1985. Some comments on the Shibboleth Incident (Judges XII 6). Pp. 149–57 in *Melanges bibliques et orientaux en l'honneur de M. Mathias Delcore,* ed. A. Caquot et al. Neukirchen-Vluyn.

Ibrahim, M.; Sauer, J.; and Yassine, K. 1976. The East Jordan Valley Survey, 1975. *BASOR* 222: 41–66.

Lindars, B. 1979. The Israelite Tribes in Judges. Pp. 95–112 in *Studies in the Historical Books of the Old Testament,* ed. J. A. Emerton. VTSup 30. Leiden.

Mullen, E. T., Jr. 1982. The "Minor Judges": Some Literary and Historical Considerations. *CBQ* 44: 185–201.

Trible, P. 1984. *Texts of Terror.* Philadelphia.

ROBERT G. BOLING

JEPHUNNEH (PERSON) [Heb *yĕpunneh*]. Two persons mentioned in the Hebrew Bible have this name. The meaning of the name is not entirely clear, though several explanations have been proposed. The name Jephunneh can be derived from the root *pnh,* "to turn to," which results in a translation "may (God) turn to (the child)." Another possibility is that Jephunneh is related to the name Peninnah, based on a proposed root *pnn.* A third meaning, also based on the root *pnh,* has the sense of asking God to turn away the obstacles from the life of a child (*EncMiqr* 3: 745).

1. The father of Caleb, one of the spies sent by Moses to reconnoiter the land of Canaan (Num 14:6). This name occurs frequently in Numbers, Deuteronomy, and Joshua in the account of the spies who were sent out to reconnoiter the land of Canaan, but only in the form *ben-yĕpunneh* "son of Jephunneh" (see, e.g., Num 30, 38; 32:12). Therefore, this Jephunneh is only known in relation to Caleb. Jephunneh's tribal affiliation is ambiguously represented in the Pentateuch (Num 13:6; 34:19; cf. Josh 14:6, 14; see also CALEB).

2. The son of Jether, a descendant of Asher (1 Chr

7:37–38). Neither Jephunneh nor his father has a traceable lineage in this series of Israelite tribal genealogies (1 Chronicles 2–8).

RAPHAEL I. PANITZ

JERAH (PERSON) [Heb *yāraḥ,* pausal form of **yeraḥ*]. A son of Joktan (Gen 10:26; 1 Chr 1:20) and hence the name of a S Arabian region or of the tribe residing in it. A place named *wrḫn* occurs in the Old Sabaean inscription RES 3946,2, where it is mentioned as a place on the border of a district which was acquired for the Sabaean state by King Karibʾil Watar, probably in the 7th century B.C. Since it was hitherto impossible to localize the places which are mentioned in the context of the above-cited inscription, it is difficult to say whether the epigraphically attested *wrḫn* should be identified with the later *Warāḫ.* According to al-Hamdānī (1884: 101), *Warāḫ* belongs to the Banū Mūsā of the tribe al-Kalāʿ and lies in the *miḫlāf al-ʿAud,* that is in the region between the present-day Ibb and Qaʿṭaba. *Warāḫ* is also listed among the famous fortresses of Yemen (al-Hamdānī 1884: 125; 1979: 154). Moreover, al-Hamdānī (1979: 153) mentions another fortress named *Yurāḫ,* which was supposed to lie on an inaccessible mountain and which, following his description, was situated SW of the town of Ḏamār.

Montgomery (1969: 40) explained the form of the name *Yeraḥ,* which is identical with the Heb name for "month," as meaning "moon"; inasmuch as the moon was the main deity of the S Arabian pantheon, he considered *Yeraḥ* a tribal name which had been abbreviated to the divine element, as in the case of the Heb tribes Gad and Asher (p. 40, n. 10). Since the personal name *wrḫ* is obviously not attested in epigraphic S Arabic, it occurs, however, as name of an appearance of the moon god, with its sole certain reference in the Qatabanian inscription RES 311,4.5. It should perhaps be considered whether the name *Yeraḥ* in the meaning "new moon" could be the rendering of epigraphic S Arabic *šhr,* "new moon, beginning of the month" (cf. Arabic *šahr*), a noun which likewise occurs as the name of a clan or tribe (e.g. Qatabanian *ḏšhr* [RES 3566,18; RES 3878,15] and *šhr* [AM 368], and Sabaean *bnw/ḏšhr* [YM 349,2] and *bn/šhr* [BR-M.Bayḥān 5,1.11]).

Hommel (1926: 554) assumed that just as the tribes of Israel and the sons of Ismael (Gen 25:13–15) numbered 12, so also the sons of Joktan (Gen 10:26–29) originally numbered 12; thus, *yarēaḥ* (= *yariḥ*) could probably be a gloss on the preceding *ḥăṣarmāwet* (or vice versa) (cf. already Hommel 1901: 316, n. 6). Certainly to be rejected is the proposal of E. Glaser (1890: 425) to combine *yāraḥ* with *hierakōn kōmē,* the "falcon village" in Ptolemaios (*Geog.* 6.7.36), a place which, according to the geographical coordinates given in the text, should be located in E Arabia.

Bibliography

al-Hamdānī. 1884. *Ṣifat Ǧazīrat al-ʿArab.* Ed. D. H. Müller. Leiden.
———. 1979. *al-Iklīl.* Ed. M. al-Akwaʿ. Damascus.
Glaser, E. 1890. *Skizze der Geschichte und Geographie Arabiens.* Vol. 2. Berlin.
Hommel, F. 1901. *Aufsätze und Abhandlungen arabistisch-semitologischen Inhalts.* Vol. 3. Munich.
———. 1926. *Ethnologie und Geographie des Alten Orients.* HAW 3/1/1. Munich.
Montgomery, J. A. 1969. *Arabia and the Bible.* 2d ed. Philadelphia.

W. W. MÜLLER

JERAHMEEL (ANGEL). See JEREMIEL.

JERAHMEEL (PERSON) [Heb *yĕraḥmĕʾēl*]. JERAHMEELITE. **1.** A Judahite, the firstborn son of Hezron the son of Perez the son of Judah by Tamar; the brother of Ram and Chelubai = Caleb ? (1 Chr 2:4–5, 9, 25; 2:18, 42). See HEZRON and CALEB. He is credited with 2 wives, 6 sons (yet cf. the LXX, esp. the Lucian recension, and also the NEB), and numerous progeny through them, including 13 descendants through his distant descendant Sheshan's daughter's marriage to the Egyptian slave Jarha (1 Chr 2:25–26, 27–33, 34–41).

The first historical mention of the Jerahmeelite clan occurs in connection with David's association with Achish, the king of Gath, after David's flight from the court of Saul. David and his men were raiding and killing the Geshurites, the Girzites, and the Amalekites, but when questioned about his military forays by King Achish, David lied, saying that his contingent had raided, as expected, "the Negeb of Judah, the Negeb of the Jerahmeelites, and the Negeb of the Kenites" (1 Sam 27:10). This report, originally intended to convince Achish of David's supposed Philistine loyalty, served to remind later Israelite generations of the great king's unswerving loyalty to his own people. The picture of David whipping the enemies of Israel while his patron envisioned him undermining his own tribe must have elicited a smile, if not outright laughter, in its later retelling. Furthermore, when David came to Ziklag, he is reported to have given the elders of Judah spoil intended for distribution in the towns of the Jerahmeelites, among others (1 Sam 30:26, 29). The probable location of these Jerahmeelite towns was in the area S of Beersheba (*MBA,* 63).

Most scholars today see the Jerahmeelite clan as originally a non-Israelite clan which early came to be absorbed within the tribe of Judah, much like the Kenites/Kenizzites associated with Caleb, who in turn shows linkage with Jerahmeel. The Chronicler, in the postexilic period, is the first to list Jerahmeel as an Israelite clan, within the tribe of Judah. Indeed the Chronicler's mention of Jerahmeel, plus Chelubai (= Caleb ?), as descended from Hezron is without parallel in the rest of the Hebrew Bible. While Williamson (*1 and 2 Chronicles* NCBC, 49) has demonstrated the centrality (2:25–33, 34–41) of the Jerahmeelite clan to the larger genealogical unit on Judah (1 Chr 2:3–4:23), with the Chronicler's prime focus falling on Ram as the progenitor of the house of Jesse and David (1 Chr 2:10–17), his reason for the mention of Jerahmeel and Chelubai (= Caleb ?) is less clear. Quite possibly, the Chronicler sought to legitimate the postexilic pedigree of such clans who had once entered the tribe of Judah by absorption and not by birth. Belonging to Judah, the tribe which had returned to postexilic prominence in the person and work of Zerubbabel, was no doubt a matter of considerable political pride and advantage.

2. A Levite, the son of Kish (1 Chr 24:29), of the clan of Merari (1 Chr 23:21). His name occurs in a list which represents an updating (except for Gershom/Gershon and his sons) of the Levitical families given in 1 Chr 23:7–23. See esp. 1 Chr 23:21–23. As the Levites are said to have been assigned their positions by lot in the presence of David and the larger assembly of priestly and Levitical heads (1 Chr 24:31), it was appropriate to append the names of their courses (1 Chr 24:20–31) to the list of the 24 priestly courses likewise assigned by lot (1 Chr 24:1–19). Because Eleazar, Kish's brother, had no sons, their cousins, "the sons (?) of Kish," married them (1 Chr 23:22; 24:28). Evidently Jerahmeel himself did so as "a son of Kish," even though he is the only son listed! The Kish cited here is obviously not Kish, the father of Saul, who was of the tribe of Benjamin (1 Sam 9:1–3; 1 Chr 8:33).

Roger W. Uitti

3. A royal officer under King Jehoiakim (609–598 B.C.) assigned to police duties (Jer 36:26). He and two others were ordered by Jehoiakim to seize Jeremiah the prophet and Baruch the scribe after the king heard a scroll of Jeremiah's prophecies read and destroyed it in the fireplace. Jerahmeel, despite the title "the king's son," cannot be an actual son of Jehoiakim since Jehoiakim is only about 30 years old at the time (cf. 2 Kgs 23:36; Jer 36:9), too young to have a grown son. The title "the king's son" (Heb *ben-hammelek*) is therefore thought to denote an office of low rank in the royal government, most likely one associated with police duties (de Vaux *AncIsr* 1: 119–20). Joash (1 Kgs 22:26) and Malchiah (Jer 38:6) are both called "the king's son," and are police officers connected with jails. At the same time, an individual so designated could well be from a royal family (Avigad 1978: 54–55). This being so, Jerahmeel would then be the son of a king other than Jehoiakim.

A seal impression has been found which reads, "Belonging to Jerahmeel, the king's son" (Avigad 1978). It was discovered in a horde which also contained a bulla impressed with a seal from Baruch ben Neriah. A late 7th century date for the 2 bullae is therefore virtually assured, and the identification of the owners of the two seals with the individuals mentioned in Jeremiah 36 seems certain. Jerahmeel, then, in carrying out his police duties had occasion to seal legal documents and other official records.

Bibliography

Avigad, N. 1978. Baruch the Scribe and Jerahmeel the King's Son. *IEJ* 28: 52–56. Repr. *BA* 42 (1979): 114–18.

Jack R. Lundbom

JERASH (PLACE). See GERASENES.

JERED (PERSON) [Heb *yered*].

Son of Eshtemoa, brother of Heber and Jekuthiel, and father of Gedor, of the tribe of Judah (1 Chr 4: 18). For the meaning of Jered, see JARED.

Richard S. Hess

JEREMAI (PERSON) [Heb *yĕrēmay*].

A descendant of Hashum and one of the returned exiles who was required by Ezra to divorce his foreign wife (Ezra 10:33). According to Noth, the name Jeremai probably is related to the Arabic root *warima* meaning "fat" or "stout" (*IPN* 226). This individual does not appear in the parallel text of 1 Esdr 9:33. Jeremai is a member of a family from which a group of exiles returned with Zerubbabel (Ezra 2:19; Neh 7:22). For further discussion, see BEDEIAH.

Jeffrey A. Fager

JEREMIAH (PERSON) [Heb *yirmĕyāh; yirmĕyāhû*].

Some 10 individuals bear this name, which may mean "may Yahu raise up" (*IPN,* 201), "Yahu loosens [the womb]" (*BDB,* 941), or "Yahu founded" (*HALAT,* 420). The name *yirmĕyāhû* occurs in an ostracon found at Lachish, which dates to shortly before the destruction of the city by Nebuchadnezzar in 587/6 B.C. (Lachish 1:4; *TSSI* 1:36–37).

1. One of the warriors of the tribe of Benjamin who joined David at Ziklag (1 Chr 12:5—Eng v 4).

2. One of the Gadite warriors who joined David at Ziklag (1 Chr 12:11—Eng v 10).

3. Another Gadite warrior who joined David at Ziklag (1 Chr 12:14—Eng v 13).

4. Head of a family and renowned warrior of the half-tribe of Manasseh which settled in Transjordan (1 Chr 5:24).

5. Of Libnah, the father of Hamutal, wife of Josiah and mother of Jehoahaz (2 Kgs 23:31) and Zedekiah (24:18), kings of Judah.

6. One of Israel's major prophets who was active in 7th to 6th centuries B.C.E. See JEREMIAH (PROPHET).

7. The father of Jaazaniah, a Rechabite, contemporary of Jeremiah the prophet (Jer 35:3).

8. A priest who returned from Babylon with Zerubbabel (Neh 12:1). The name also designates a priestly family in the time of the high priest Joiakim (v 12).

9. One of the priests who signed the covenant of Ezra (Neh 10:3—Eng v 2).

10. A leading man of Judah and member of one of the two large choirs which took part in the feast celebrating the dedication of the Jerusalem wall under Nehemiah (Neh 12:34).

Robert Althann

JEREMIAH (PROPHET).

One of the major prophets in ancient Israel whose dates correspond roughly to the last half-century of Israel's nationhood, i.e., 640–587 B.C. He survived, however, the destruction of Jerusalem in 587 B.C. and lived out the final years of his old age in Egypt where he was taken by refugees who sought exile there. His life and ministry on behalf of Yahweh, God of Israel, are the subject of the OT book bearing his name. See JEREMIAH, BOOK OF.

A. The World of Jeremiah
   1. History of the Period
   2. The Josianic Reform
B. Early Life and Call to Be a Prophet

C. Prophetic Ministry
   1. Early Career (622–605 B.C.)
   2. Late Career (604–586 B.C.)
   3. Sojourn in Egypt (after 586 B.C.)
D. Rhetoric and Preaching
   1. Repetition
   2. Accumulation
   3. Metaphors and Related Tropes
   4. Argumentation
   5. Humor and Irony
   6. Drama
E. Prophetic Symbolism: Act and Being

A. The World of Jeremiah

The late 7th and early 6th centuries B.C. saw Babylon replace Assyria as the major power in Near Eastern affairs. The transition allowed Judah a brief period of independence, which it used with profit to carry out a major religious reform under King Josiah. But the realignment of world power, combined with a repudiation in Judah of the reform program after Josiah's death, resulted in a sorry state of affairs for the once-proud nation called Israel. Its demise came very quickly.

1. History of the Period. Jeremiah was born into this world of tumultuous change. The long reign of Manasseh came to an end in 642 B.C., a reign during which Judah was subservient both politically and religiously to Assyria. Under Manasseh, the reforms of Hezekiah were dismantled and pagan religious practices were allowed to flourish openly. The biblical writers express outrage at what went on during this time, and except for the Chronicler they are unforgiving of Manasseh (2 Kgs 21:1–21; 23:26; 24:3; Jer 15:4; cf. 2 Chronicles 33). Amon sought to continue his father's policies when he became king, but 2 years later he was assassinated by an anti-Assyrian party. The people of the land feared Assyrian reprisal, however, and quickly punished those responsible (2 Kgs 21:23–24). In that same year, i.e., 640 B.C., King Assurbanipal of Assyria regained a measure of control over an empire that for 15 years or more had been in rebellion—since 655 at least when Psammetichus I of Egypt declared his independence. The year 640 was in any case pivotal. In this year Josiah was placed on the Jerusalem throne at 8 years of age. The next 3 decades saw Judah gradually attain political and religious freedom. That national independence came in stages can be seen from the Chronicler's account of the Josianic Reform (2 Chr 34:1–7). We know little about Assurbanipal's activities after 640, except that his years were peaceful enough to enable him to act as a patron of literature and the arts.

At the time of Assurbanipal's death in 627 (Haran Inscription) the once-mighty empire of Assyria was quickly breaking up. Babylon was in open revolt as is known from the Babylonian Chronicle, and in October 626, Nebopolassar defeated the Assyrian army outside the city of Babylon, declaring himself king of Babylon. Assyria was now on the defensive and in less than 20 years would be no more. By 622, when the celebrated Torah of Moses was found in the Jerusalem temple and the reform of Josiah was brought to its grand climax, Judah's subservience to Assyria had ended. We know little about Josiah's latter years. During this time he may have been fortifying major cities N and W of Jerusalem, e.g., Megiddo and Lachish (Aharoni *LBHG*, 403; Rainey 1983: 17). Nineveh fell in 612 to a coalition of Babylonians, Medes, and the Umman-Manda who are perhaps the Scythians (Gadd 1923). Two years later the allies dislodged an Assyrian refugee government from Haran. Egypt went to Assyria's aid in the attempt to retake Haran, in 609, but the mission failed. The Babylonians were now in control of all of Mesopotamia.

The Egyptian-Assyrian defeat was perhaps helped along by Josiah's delay of Pharaoh Neco at Megiddo; but if so, Judah suffered the greater loss, for Josiah was killed in a battle that ensued (2 Chr 35:20–24). Josiah's motives in this adventure are not known. He may have been acting as an ally of Babylon (Malamat 1950: 219; Cross and Freedman 1953). No prophetic voice in any case was heard in Jerusalem. The Chronicler reports belatedly that a word from God came to Josiah via Neco (2 Chr 35:22). When Neco returned from his unsuccessful errand to the N, he took charge of political affairs in Judah. The young Jehoahaz, who had just been made king, was deposed and taken to Egypt. His brother Eliakim, whose regnal became Jehoiakim, was placed on the throne by Neco, and Judah was now an Egyptian vassal. The nation was put under heavy tribute and its "spring of independence" was over.

For the next 4 years, from 609 to 605, Judah was under Egyptian domination. During this time the Egyptian and Babylonian armies were fighting on the N Euphrates, though no decisive battle took place. Then in 605, Nebuchadnezzar, who had taken control of the army from his father, made a surprise attack on the Egyptians at Carchemish and roundly defeated them (Jer 46:2). The Babylonian Chronicle reveals that a second victory followed at Hamath after which Nebuchadnezzar took over the Egyptian base at Riblah (Malamat 1956: 249–50). The Babylonians were now in control of Syria (Malamat 1975: 130). The Babylonian advance was delayed by Nabopolassar's death, but only briefly; for at the end of 604, Nebuchadnezzar and his army were present in the Philistine Plain where they proceeded to destroy Ashkelon (Jeremiah 47). The fast in Jerusalem mentioned in Jer 36:9 was perhaps a response to this threat. Jehoiakim now transferred his allegiance to this new agent in Syro-Palestine affairs and became its unwilling vassal for 3 years (2 Kgs 24:1).

In 601, Nebuchadnezzar was again at war with Egypt—this time on the Egyptian frontier—but both sides suffered heavy losses; Egypt may even have been the victor. Whatever the case, the Babylonian army went home, after which the pro-Egyptian party gained the upper hand in Jerusalem and Jehoiakim declared independence from Babylon (2 Kgs 24:1). This proved to be a fatal step. Babylon responded by sending bands of Syrians, Moabites, and Ammonites, along with some of its own people to ravage Judah (2 Kgs 24:2). The full Babylonian army came shortly after December, 598, the month Jehoiakim died (Freedman 1956). The beaten king was likely assassinated (cf. Jeremiah's predictions of a violent death for him in Jer 22:18–19 and 36:30). Jehoiachin, the 18-year-old son of Jehoiakim, was put on the throne and 3 months later, in March 597, the city surrendered. Jehoiachin, the Queen Mother, high government officials, and most of Jerusalem's skilled workers were deported to Babylon.

The Babylonians put Zedekiah on the throne but little

remained over which to exercise rule. Zedekiah's 10-year reign (597–587) was marked by continual social and political unrest. The die had been cast for Judah's fall. The most capable citizens were gone, and Jehoiachin's preferential treatment in captivity made Zedekiah's position ambiguous; many still considered Jehoiachin the legitimate king (Albright *LBHG,* 102; 1942). A rebellion in Babylon in 594 raised hopes there and at home that Jehoiachin would return (Jeremiah 27–29), but the uprising was put down and the hopes proved illusory. Zedekiah's trip to Babylon in 594/3 (Jer 51:59) may have been to reaffirm his loyalty to Nebuchadnezzar (*BHI,* 329).

By 589, Judah was again rife with unrest and the Babylonian army began another westward march, this time to put down resistance for good. Archaeological evidence, particularly the important Lachish Letters (*ANET,* 321–22), corroborates the biblical account of Judah's last days. The cities of Benjamin, e.g., Ramah and Mizpah, appear to have given up first (Malamat 1950: 226–27). The siege of Jerusalem was broken only briefly when Egypt made an advance, but that came to nothing. In July 587 the wall of Jerusalem was breached and the city was taken. A month later it was burned. Nationhood for Israel had come to an end. Gedaliah, a grandson of Shaphan, was appointed governor over the population that remained, but he was soon assassinated. Jeremiah received preferential treatment by the Babylonians, and Gedaliah, until his assassination, remained with other refugees living at Mizpah. After Gedaliah's death, Jeremiah and Baruch departed with a group for Egypt, where Jeremiah is last heard from. History for a time must now be chronicled in Egypt and Babylon, not Jerusalem.

2. The Josianic Reform. According to 2 Kings 22–23 and 2 Chronicles 34–35, a major reform took place in Judah during Josiah's reign. Each account has its own emphasis in reporting the reform, but of more significance is the way each sequences key events. According to Kings, the entire reform—the purge of syncretistic worship sites, the covenant renewal ceremony, and the celebration of passover—takes place in the 18th year of Josiah, 622, and is the immediate response of the king to the finding of the lawbook in the temple. The Chronicler, however, begins with Josiah's 8th year (632) when he says the young king began to seek Yahweh. The purge of worship sites around Jerusalem and in the Assyrian provinces of Samaria, Gilead, and Galilee, is placed in Josiah's 12th year (628). Then in the king's 18th year (622) the lawbook is found after which covenant renewal ceremony is concluded and passover is celebrated. The Chronicler compresses (also supplements) the Kings account of the purge (both 2 Kgs 23:4–20 and 2 Chr 34:3–7 conclude "Then he returned to Jerusalem"), and states clearly that repair work in the temple, which led to the lawbook's discovery, was begun *after* the purge (2 Chr 34:8).

Critical scholars of an earlier generation preferred the Kings account and reconstructed the beginning of Jeremiah's career against its background. More recently, however, the Chronicler's account has been given preference, one reason being that his scheme of events correlates better with extrabiblical records documenting Assyria's decline (Cross and Freedman 1953). But the Chronicler's scheme renders less likely the widely held view that Deuteronomy 1–28 (or a portion of it) was the lost scroll of 622. If Deuteronomy 1–28 was the catalyst for the purge of idolatrous worship centers as is generally assumed, and the purge took place in 628, then this document cannot have been newly found in 622. Most likely it was not. Judging from a portion of Huldah's oracle which the lawbook seems to have inspired (2 Kgs 22:16–17), the newly found document is best identified with the Song of Moses in Deuteronomy 32 (Lundbom 1976).

The reform lasted only as long as Josiah reigned; when Jehoiakim became king in 609/8 it came to a full stop. Neither Kings nor Chronicles mentions Jeremiah in connection with the reform. The only reference in either to Jeremiah's prophetic activity is 2 Chr 35:25 where it is reported that Jeremiah gave a lament for Josiah at his death.

B. Early Life and Call to Be a Prophet

We know very little about Jeremiah's early life aside from what is mentioned in the superscription to his book (1:1). His father was very glad the day he was born (20:15), and he too was joyful earlier in life (8:18: "My joy is gone"). Jeremiah was born the son of Hilkiah, a priest at Anathoth. Anathoth was a village 2–3 miles north of Jerusalem in the old territory of Benjamin. That village is likely Ras el-Kharrubeh, a half mile or so S of the modern village of ʿAnata. Hilkiah could well be a descendant of Abiathar, a priest of David whom Solomon retired to Anathoth when he became king (1 Kgs 2:26–27). The family possessed land (32:9) and may have been one of some means.

Jeremiah was called to be a prophet in the 13th year of Josiah (1:2, 4). This was 627 B.C., the same year Assurbanipal died. In his account of the call, Jeremiah lays stress on his young age. The Heb *naʿar* (1:6–7) should be translated "boy" (Jerome: *puer*), not "young man," the common rendering of an older generation of scholars who thought Jeremiah's age had to be somewhere between 18 and 25. These scholars assumed that the prophetic ministry began at the same time the call was received. Jeremiah is more like 12 or 13, the approximate age of the "boy" Samuel when he was serving Eli at Shiloh, and the call to be Yahweh's prophet came to him (1 Sam 2:11, 18, 21, 26; 3:1, 8). Jeremiah's birth can be dated then ca. 640 B.C.

Jeremiah's boyhood experience appears to have its closest similarity to that of Samuel which was lived out at the Shiloh sanctuary not far from Anathoth. Traditions about Samuel and Shiloh were doubtless preserved at Anathoth because of the single priestly line linking the 2 sanctuaries. Jeremiah later in his Temple Sermon revives the painful memory of Shiloh's destruction (7:12–14; 26:4–6).

The priestly line extending back through Abiathar and Eli picked up added prestige when it was traced all the way to Moses. We see in Jeremiah's call clear and unmistakable appropriations of traditions about Moses. The vision Jeremiah has before a budding almond tree (1:11–12) recalls Moses' vision at the burning bush (Exod 3:2–6). Jeremiah's protestation about being unable to speak (1:6) has a parallel in the demur Moses made about not being eloquent (Exod 4:10–17). But when Jeremiah reports that Yahweh intends to put his words into Jeremiah's mouth (1:9), repeating a promise made earlier to Moses at the time he was called, we are looking at more than a simple case of role modeling; Jeremiah has understood himself to be the "prophet like Moses" promised in Deut 18:18.

The figures of both Moses and Samuel loom large for Jeremiah (15:1; Holladay 1964; 1966a). Another person exercising an important influence on him is the prophet Hosea (Gross 1931). Traditions of all 3 prophets—in addition to the covenant document of Deuteronomy 1–28 in which Moses is the commanding figure—come out of N Israel, and Anathoth, despite its proximity to Jerusalem, is a N sanctuary. It can be expected, then, that these traditions would be the ones to make a formative impression upon Jeremiah from his earliest years.

Jeremiah gives no indication of accepting Yahweh's call when it comes, despite the impression made upon him that he was chosen for prophetic office before he was born and now on the day of visitation has heard that choice confirmed (1:5, 10). But Yahweh, too, is clear that the call must await a future fulfillment: "I am watching over my word to perform it" (1:12).

C. Prophetic Ministry

Jeremiah's call is to be a prophet to the nations. His life's work is "to pluck up and to break down . . . to build and to plant" (1:10).

1. Early Career (622–605 B.C.). Jeremiah accepts the call in 622 after the temple scroll is found. In a later confession he reflects on the importance of this event to him personally, saying,

> Your words were found, and I ate them
>   and your words became to me a joy
>   and the delight of my heart
> for I am called by your name
>   O Yahweh, God of hosts
> (15:16)

Jeremiah in "eating" words of the temple scroll "eats" words which Yahweh promised earlier would be put into his mouth (1:9). Yahweh's promissory word has thus been fulfilled, and for Jeremiah the eating constitutes an acceptance of the call to be a prophet. If Jeremiah was thirteen, say, when the call came, he would now be 18. No prophetic preaching, in any event, should be dated before the year 622.

Sometime soon after the lawbook's discovery in 622, when the call had been accepted, Jeremiah was given the mandate to begin his career. An account of this is given in 1:13–19. Yahweh's word was conveyed in another vision, this one of a kettle of boiling water tipped away from the N, its contents almost ready to spill out. The vision spoke of a foe who was poised to attack Judah from the N. With this interpretation came also a personal message for Jeremiah to begin his ministry. The people of Jerusalem must be warned, but Jeremiah can expect a battle of his own to contend with for there will be spirited opposition to his message from just about everyone. That ought not dismay him however, for Yahweh promises to him what he will not promise to Jerusalem: protection. Those who fight against Jeremiah will not prevail for Yahweh will be with him and see that his life is spared (1:19).

Precisely what Jeremiah was about between 627 and 622 is unknown. In view of the lifelong bond that existed between him and members of the Shaphan family, it could well be that during these years he was preparing himself for the vocation that awaited him by studying letters and rhetoric at the scribal school in Jerusalem over which Shaphan presided. Judging from his earliest preaching, Jeremiah emerges fully literate and well trained in the rhetoric of his day. At some point early in life, although we do not know precisely when, a move was made from Anathoth to Jerusalem. Here in the capital city was the locus of Jeremiah's prophetic activity from the beginning, and here it continued until the city fell.

The ambiguity characterizing Jeremiah's relationship to religious and political leaders in Jerusalem appears early; in fact we find him isolated and alone when the city is caught up in the celebration of covenant renewal and passover. He says,

> I did not sit in the company of merrymakers
>   nor did I rejoice;
> I sat alone, because your hand was upon me,
>   for you had filled me with indignation.
> (15:17)

Perhaps Jeremiah judged the merriment going on in the city as superficial. He certainly had a different spirit from those more in tune with popular sentiment, one that had been implanted earlier at the time he was called and one akin now to the spirit of Huldah who gave the oracle after the lawbook was found (2 Kgs 22:14–20). There were others who boycotted the Jerusalem celebration, but probably for a different reason (2 Kgs 23:9).

Jeremiah's isolation, however, was never total nor was it continuous in the years after 622. During the Josianic years, he was actively pursuing the vocation of a prophet: preaching Yahweh's word, attending temple worship, and associating with many of the nation's leading citizens (e.g., 19:1). He supported to some extent the national reform program. The persecution which he experienced early from priestly kin at Anathoth (11:18–12:6) is fully understandable if Jeremiah gave support to the reform program of centralized worship at Jerusalem (cf. 3:12–14; 31:2–14), for that would have had the practical effect of closing down the Anathoth sanctuary.

With other reform goals and objectives Jeremiah appears in basic agreement. His earliest preaching against idolatry and religious harlotry in chapters 2–3 is aimed at breaking up the fallow ground of the Manasseh period. But Jeremiah is not a lone voice anticipating an entire reform as many earlier scholars imagined, nor is he acting at the beginning of his career solely on a mandate given him by Yahweh, though he acts on one to be sure. Acting in concert with a host of other people—some of them prophets such as Habakkuk and Zephaniah—he shares the broader hope that Judah will now seize the opportunity it has to renew commitment to the ancient Yahwistic faith. Jeremiah supports a reform already well along, one which has been initiated at the highest levels of state but one which still has to be brought home to the people. His words in 4:1–4 are fully in the spirit of reform. The call for a return to Yahweh and a circumcision of the heart are expressed in Deut 4:30 and 10:16. His preaching on obedience to the covenant (11:1–8) and his call for a more rigorous sabbath observance (17:19–27) also fit well into the period after 622.

Jeremiah reflects nationalistic ideas when he wants Judah divested of its vassalage to Assyria and Egypt (2:18, 36; 13:1–11) and when he calls for a return of the exiles taken away to Assyria in 722 B.C. (3:12–14; 30:31). The same can be said for his support of political union between N and S, a reform idea tied in closely with Josiah's plan for a single sanctuary in Jerusalem.

That early in his ministry Jeremiah faced broad opposition should occasion no surprise when one considers that neither people of high or low status escaped his indictment (2:8; 5:4–5; 8:8). His frustration over a lack of preaching success is expressed in 6:16–17, a passage that also provides a focus on the early career:

> Thus says the Lord:
> "Stand by the roads, and look,
>   and ask for the ancient paths,
> where the good way is; and walk in it,
>   and find rest for your souls.
> But they said, 'We will not walk in it'.
> I set watchmen over you, saying,
>   'Give heed to the sound of the trumpet!'
> But they said, 'We will not give heed.' "

If the sequence here is important, Jeremiah's early career consists of an initial phase during which he called for a return to the Mosaic covenant, i.e., "the ancient paths" and "the good way," and then a later phase during which he preached primarily war and national destruction. A bipartite ministry along these lines is suggested also by the 2 major poetic collections in chapters 2–10 focusing on religious harlotry and the foe from the N. See JEREMIAH, BOOK OF.

When his reform preaching failed to move people to true repentance, Jeremiah turned his attention to the coming foe. Though the identity of Judah's foe is never given, it has to be Babylon. Many earlier scholars who built the early career on a higher chronology identified the foe with the Scythians (Herod. 1.104–6), but this view is now universally abandoned. Jeremiah was first apprised of the foe shortly after 622, at a time when he was still a relatively young man. Yahweh's command that he not marry (16:2) is already predicated on the certainty of war and national destruction.

If the foe poems are correlated with Babylon's rise in Mesopotamia, they begin then ca. 614–612 (Hyatt 1940). Habakkuk announces the rise of this same foe, and the earliest date assigned to his preaching is ca. 615. The laments which conclude the foe cycle follow in due course as prediction gives way to harsh reality. These laments show Jeremiah involved at the deepest level of his own preaching. The dialogues and trialogues contain rapid alternation between divine word, human terror, and the prophet's own expression of personal grief (e.g., 8:13–17, 18–21). Jeremiah is a true divine mediator, which is to say his own personal grief upon receiving the divine word is every bit as intense as his preaching is of that word to others.

The death of Josiah was a national tragedy, and Jeremiah's silence about the Megiddo adventure remains one of the great puzzlements associated with interpreting the early career. He laments this good king (2 Chr 35:25), although soon after he says the greater tragedy for Judah is the permanent departure of young Jehoahaz (Shallum) from the land (22:10). Jeremiah's remembrances of Josiah are positive, particularly when the comparison is made between him and his son Jehoiakim (22:13–17).

The years from 609 to 605 were difficult for the prophet as the earliest dated prose in the book makes all too clear. When Neco installed Jehoiakim, the political climate in Jerusalem changed. That the reform was now over we may conclude from the Temple Sermon which was delivered in Jehoiakim's accession year (26:1). Jeremiah here makes a scathing indictment of the people's shallow religiosity and duplicity before Yahweh (7:1–15). They seem content just to know that the temple sits on Zion and that salvific liturgies are spoken in worship; they care nothing, however, for the weightier matters of executing justice and living in accordance with covenant demands. Jeremiah says the place is rife with every imaginable evil. The real nerve is struck when Jeremiah announces that Yahweh will destroy the temple as he destroyed his first sanctuary at Shiloh. With that the sermon is over and court is called into session at the New Gate in the temple precinct. The priests and the prophets, who were the most offended, demand that Jeremiah be put to death. The princes in attendance are more allied with the defense. In the end they decide the case, acquitting Jeremiah on the strength of his testimony that Yahweh had sent him with this message. Jeremiah has passed the test of a true prophet given in Deut 13:1–5. Some elders in attendance aid the defense by recalling that Micah earlier predicted Jerusalem's destruction, and King Hezekiah did not put him to death. Jeremiah survived the trial then, having received support from both government officials and citizens within the general populace. Still he needed the special protection of Ahikam son of Shaphan (26:24). Another prophet of Yahweh, Uriah of Kiriath-jearim, delivered his judgment on the city and was not so fortunate; Jehoiakim had him killed (26:20–23).

Many of the confessions fit well into the early years of Jehoiakim's reign. These rare glimpses into a prophet's interior life show that bedrock tenets of Jeremiah's faith were being called into question. Why should acceptance of the divine call lead to an intolerable wilderness experience where God is not present (15:15–18)? Preaching the divine word has brought nothing but anguish; it has caused even Jeremiah's close friends to turn on him, which in turn leads the prophet to believe that Yahweh too has betrayed him (20:7–10). In the darkest moment of all he rejects his birth, his call, and early assurances that Yahweh would deliver him from all his enemies (20:14–18; Lundbom 1985). But once the hurt is let out, assurances are renewed (15:19–21) and Jeremiah too is renewed, enough in one case that he is able to sing about Yahweh's deliverance (20:11–13).

Jeremiah is a man of profound religious faith. But his personal piety—also impiety—is balanced by a deep involvement in the religious life of his nation. He cannot be charged with excessively privitizing religion, even though much of a personal nature comes from his lips. He prays for himself but he prays even more for others. Yahweh even has to tell him to stop his prayers of intercession (7:16–20; 11:14–17; 14:11–12; 15:1–4). Persecution comes not because he distances himself from the cult, but because of relentless participation. The punishment received from the chief priest Pashhur comes as the result of an object lesson he gave to senior priests and others in the Valley of Ben-hinnom (19:1–20:6), and his banishment from the temple (36:5) is most likely the result of his Temple Sermon.

The year 605 was pivotal for the nation and for Jeremiah personally. The Battle of Carchemish left Egypt weakened and Babylon the new power in world affairs. Jeremiah addressed the Egyptian defeat with an oracle (46:2–12). Jeremiah also decided in this year to prepare the first written scroll of his oracles, and his doing so signaled the end of his early career. After the scroll was read publicly, Jeremiah and Baruch were forced to go into hiding, for they were now in direct conflict with the king (chap. 36).

2. Late Career (604–586 B.C.). These years are remarkably well documented thanks to the abundance of dated prose in the book from the reign of Zedekiah. Nevertheless there are 2 periods of roughly 7 years each, 604–597, and 594–588, during which we have no definite knowledge of Jeremiah's activities. When Jeremiah and Baruch disappeared from public view in 604, they had most recently been preoccupied with scroll writing. It is possible that in the years following, particularly when the two of them were out of public view, more time was spent in this pursuit. We are told that when the first scroll which had been destroyed was rewritten, it contained added material (36:32). It is unlikely that Jeremiah had any public ministry during Jehoiakim's remaining years. He certainly had nothing good to say about this king. Jehoiakim spent recklessly on luxurious new quarters for himself, and his use of slave labor in this undertaking must have offended others besides Jeremiah. Worst of all, he was violent and dishonest, and cared nothing for justice or for helping the needy (22:13–17). Jeremiah could only predict a shameful end for this king (22:18–19).

When the city surrendered to Nebuchadnezzar in 597, Jeremiah was again active speaking the divine word and articulating as well the expressions of grief which were widespread (10:17–25; 13:15–27). His message to the departing exiles was hopeful yet bittersweet (31:21–22). Jehoiachin, he said, would not return home nor would any of his offspring sit on David's throne (22:24–30).

Nebuchadnezzar put Zedekiah on the throne before departing from Jerusalem, and, with this king, Jeremiah had to endure another round of hard times. It is not that Zedekiah disliked Jeremiah particularly; the problem seems rather to have been Zedekiah's nonprincipled behavior during a time when the city lived continually on the brink of chaos. Zedekiah seems to have been powerless in the midst of this sorry state of affairs. Dated prose in the book indicates that Jeremiah was active during the first 4 years of Zedekiah's reign, 597–594/3, and then again when Jerusalem was under siege for the last time in 588–587. During Zedekiah's middle years we are not sure of Jeremiah's activities. He was perhaps addressing certain foreign nations with oracles (chapters 48–51) in addition to writing more scrolls with Baruch. In 594/3 Jeremiah gave Seraiah, the brother of Baruch, a scroll of oracles written against Babylon (51:59–64).

Jeremiah's final decade of prophetic ministry was controlled by a vision received about good and bad figs (chap. 24). The good figs were the exiles who had gone to Babylon; the bad figs were the people remaining in Jerusalem. This message put Jeremiah at odds with the nation's leaders, who, at the time were talking revolt with their allies (27:3). Certain prophets such as Hananiah lent them support by predicting a speedy return of Jehoiachin and the other exiles (28:1–4). A classic confrontation took place between Jeremiah and Hananiah which brought the question of true and false prophecy into sharp focus (chap. 28). Jeremiah was at first cautious in countering the optimistic claims of Hananiah, but at their second meeting was not and announced Hananiah's death for prophesying lies. This prediction was fulfilled in less than a year showing Jeremiah to be the true prophet according to the test set forth in Deut 18:21–22. Jeremiah sent letters to the exiles in Babylon (chap. 29) in which he gave the same message he had been preaching at home.

We are well informed about Jeremiah's activity just prior to Jerusalem's fall. He had now become the key figure in the tragic drama which was unfolding. Zedekiah continually sought him out, hoping against hope that Yahweh would save the nation as in times past (21:1–2). Jeremiah informed him, however, that Yahweh was fighting against the city. Taking words almost verbatim from Deut 30:15, but giving them a new twist, he told the king: "I set before you (the way) of life and (the way) of death" (21:18). The way of life now was to surrender; to resist was the way of death. But Zedekiah did not listen. He seemed irreversibly bent on plunging himself and the nation into ruinous defeat. Jeremiah told the king there was no way he could escape a face-to-face meeting with Nebuchadnezzar (34:1–7), which is what eventually took place.

When the city was under siege, Zedekiah made a covenant to grant liberty to all Hebrew slaves (34:8–22), something he should have done simply because the law required it (Deut 15:12). But when Egypt marched N and forced the Babylonian army to pull back from Jerusalem, the king reneged on the covenant and took the slaves back. Jeremiah was swift with a word to him and his fellow schemers: "I proclaim to you *liberty* to the sword, to pestilence, and to famine" (34:17). During the lifting of the siege, Jeremiah attempted to leave the city to take care of some personal business at Anathoth, but he was stopped at the Benjamin Gate and accused of deserting to the Babylonians (chap. 37). Jeremiah denied the charge, but to no avail. Royal officials beat him and threw him into prison, where he remained until the king summoned him to his residence—this time secretly—and asked him for another oracle from Yahweh. One came, but there was no change. Jeremiah then pleaded not to be sent back to prison, and Zedekiah granted the request. He was placed instead under house arrest in the court of the guard. There he remained until the city fell, receiving each day one loaf of bread as long as the supply held out (37:21). Jeremiah is also reported during these last days as having been abandoned in a cistern for preaching surrender (chap. 38). There he would have died had not Ebed-melech the Ethiopian rescued him. Zedekiah in this situation is portrayed as powerless over against those who were forcing his hand (38:5).

While Jeremiah was in the court of the guard he received from Yahweh a new word of hope. On the other side of doom would be deliverance and restoration: Exiles would return; the land would be repossessed; Yahweh would replace the broken covenant with a new one. Jeremiah accepted this word, but not without a struggle. He bought a family plot at Anathoth to symbolize Yahweh's promise, but in the long prayer which followed the purchase he admits to having serious questions about what he has just done (32:16–44). The real life ambiguities confronting a prophet—the whole process whereby the divine word is accepted, believed, and acted upon—are nowhere better seen than here. Chapter 32 is certainly an eyewitness account. Virtually no time has elapsed between the event and this report of it. Reports which are written at a much later time telescope the belief process and clarify the ambiguities common to all complex life situations.

Other words of hope—including the important "New Covenant" promise—are likely from this same period when Jeremiah was confined to the court of the guard (23:5–8; 31:23–40; 33:1–13). Despite moments of deep despair, Jeremiah seems not to have lost faith completely in Yahweh's ability to save. During these last days he promises deliverance to Ebed-melech (39:15–18) as he had done earlier to his good friend Baruch (45:5). When the city was taken and large numbers of people were either killed or taken captive, Jeremiah was given his own life "as a prize of war." This fulfilled earlier promises which Yahweh had made to him (1:8, 19; 15:20–21). Nebuzaradan, acting on a direct order from Nebuchadnezzar, freed Jeremiah and allowed him to go wherever he desired (39:11–14; 40:1–6).

With Jerusalem in ruins, the people who remained took up residence at Mizpah under Gedaliah whom Nebuchadnezzar had appointed governor. Jeremiah joined them. The reconstituted community was soon fractured, however, when Gedaliah was murdered along with others in a plot instigated by the king of Ammon (chap. 40–41). Once again the people turned to Jeremiah for a word from Yahweh (chap. 42). Ten days later it came: They should stay in the land, not go to Egypt which is what the current talk was. This word, however, like so many others spoken earlier, was disregarded. In fact the people accused Jeremiah of treasonous collaboration with Baruch (43:2–3). A group consequently left for Egypt, taking Jeremiah and Baruch along, and settled at Tahpanhes (43:7).

3. Sojourn in Egypt (after 586 B.C.). Jeremiah was about 55 when he arrived in Egypt; once there, he reiterated Yahweh's judgment upon that nation (43:8–13). His message to expatriate Jews who were continuing their worship of the Queen of Heaven was essentially what it had been back in Jerusalem some years earlier (chap. 44). These people, however, had a different view of things. They said the destruction of Jerusalem came about because worship of the Queen of Heaven was discontinued. To this Jeremiah could only say ironically: "Go ahead then and confirm your vows!" (44:25). Yahweh, Jeremiah assures, will have the last word. This remnant in Egypt will die though it came there to live.

We hear no more from Jeremiah and the Bible does not mention his death. Later sources contain conflicting reports about martyrdom and a natural death in Egypt (Lipinski *EncJud* 9: 1351).

D. Rhetoric and Preaching

While it is generally agreed that Jeremiah ranks as one of the truly great thinkers in the OT, his language and style have not always won high acclaim. This judgment appears to go back to Jerome who says in his *Prologue to Jeremiah:* "Jeremiah the prophet . . . is seen to be more rustic in language than Isaiah and Hosea and certain other prophets among the Hebrews, but equal in thought . . . Moreover, the simplicity of his speech was the result of his birthplace. For he was a native of Anathoth, which even today is a small village 3 miles distant from Jerusalem" (MPL 28 847). Since Jerome, it has been agreed that Jeremiah suffers when compared to Isaiah, but considerable debate has taken place over his alleged "rusticity in language." Lowth, for example, finds no evidence to support this (1815: 290–91). Driver, who still attributes both poetry and prose to the prophet, agrees with Jerome that Jeremiah's style is not as elevated as his thought, but he evaluates the style somewhat differently. He says Jeremiah's style is "essentially artless," the only adornment being the figures which are found in the poetry. Yet even the poetry, he thinks, sounds much like the repetitive prose of Deuteronomy (1967: 274–75).

Others who separate poetry and prose and isolate the *ipsissima verba* of Jeremiah in the poetry (see JEREMIAH, BOOK OF), come away with a higher estimate of Jeremiah's language and style; some, in fact, rank him as one of the great poets of antiquity (Duhm *Jeremiah* KAC; Skinner 1963: 51; Muilenburg *IDB* 2: 824). This view is corroborated by those who more recently have studied the diction, style, and micro- as well as macro-structures of those compositions judged to be Jeremianic (Holladay 1962; 1966b; *Jeremiah* Hermeneia; Lundbom 1975). Most of these appear in the poetry, but some are found as well in the sermonic prose.

Upon close inspection, Jeremiah is seen to be a skillful poet, someone well trained in the rhetoric of his day and surely perceived, by those who heard him, to be an engaging orator. His poetry is generally well balanced, more so than one finds among the other prophets. There is parallelism; but successive cola embellish an idea (exergasia), show up incongruities, make analogies, and build larger thoughts in yet different ways. One finds both regular (3:3) and Qine (3:2) meter, with other rhythms also being used. Whole poems in some cases contain crescendo and diminution. His syntax and ordering of terms in balanced cola follow both normal and chiastic arrangements. On occasion, whole poems will have chiastic structures made up of key words and/or alternation of speakers. Jeremiah was heir to a rhetorical tradition already ancient, one that had developed in the oldest known cultures of the Near East before it took root in Israel. As an orator, Jeremiah could hold rank with the best Greek and Roman rhetors whose stock in trade one will find in such classical rhetorical handbooks as Aristotle's *Rhetoric,* the *ad Herennium,* and Quintillian's *Institutes.* He anticipates them both in style and modes of argumentation.

1. Repetition. Jeremiah makes effective use of repetition, the most basic element of all in ancient Hebrew rhetoric (Muilenburg 1953). Repetition of words, of word cognates, and of sounds is primarily for emphasis, but it can perform other or in some cases multiple functions. Anaphora, for example, functions for Jeremiah as it does for other poets: to create pathos; when the repeated sounds simulate the sense (onomatopoeia) a bit of drama is added. The inclusio performs in some cases an argumentative function. Here are some of the most common uses of repetition by Jeremiah:

a. Repetition of a word as a paraphrasis for the superlative (GKC 133 1): "peace, peace" in 6:14 (= 8:11).

b. Repetition of a word for emphasis (geminatio): "my bowels, my bowels" in 4:19; "land, land, land" in 22:29; perhaps also "has come, has come" in 46:20. In the prose: "the temple of Yahweh, the temple of Yahweh, the temple of Yahweh" in 7:4.

c. Repetition of a word at the beginning of successive cola, lines, or poetic verses (anaphora). Jeremiah's most powerful illustration is the poem in 51:20–23 where the destroyer of Babylon is addressed. The 9-fold repetition of "with you I break in pieces" emphasizes divine power, and it also simulates the sense by creating the sound of a pounding hammer (onomatopoeia). As a counterbalance to the repetitions, key words in the predication form an expanded chiasmus *(abcded'c'b'a')*:

You are my hammer and weapon of war:

With you I break in pieces *nations* . . . and *kingdoms*
With you I break in pieces *horse* and *its rider*
With you I break in pieces *chariot* and *charioteer*
With you I break in pieces *man* and *woman*
With you I break in pieces *old* and *young*
With you I break in pieces *young man* and *maiden*
With you I break in pieces *shepherd* and *his flock*
With you I break in pieces *farmer* and *his team*
With you I break in pieces *governors* and *commanders*

In 50:35–38 judgment on Babylon is given emphasis by the 5-fold repetition of "sword," again producing onomatopoeia (here the repeated stabbing of the victim). The monotony of repetition is broken at the end with an assonantal wordplay between "sword" and "drought" (*ḥereb* and *ḥōreb*). Earlier, Jeremiah used anaphora to emphasize the might and consuming appetite of Babylon who was poised to attack Israel (5:15–17). There the 4-fold repetition of "they shall eat up" balanced the 4-fold repetition of "nation." The former was again more onomatopoeia (the enemy will eat without stopping). Key words in the predication are chiastically arranged for variation: produce appears at the extremes while in the center are people and animals. In 4:30 the 3-fold repetition of "that" *(kî)* increases the disdain for the harlot daughter of Zion; in 15:5 the 3-fold repetition of "who?" deepens the pity for Jerusalem the rejected. Jeremiah deepens pity for himself in 8:23–9:1—Eng 9:1–2 where successive verses begin "Who can make (me). . . ?" In 20:14–15, successive verses beginning "Cursed" emphasize the prophet's great despair. The repetition of *mipnê* ("before/because") in 4:26b; 23:9c; and 25:38b (MT), in each case giving closure to a passage, leaves the audience astonished—that the entire creation could be destroyed, that Jeremiah should behave like a drunken man, or that the land could be thoroughly devastated before Yahweh or because of what Yahweh will do. In the vision of cosmic destruction the 4-fold "I looked . . . and behold!" creates unusual pathos (4:23–26). Diminution in this poem helps simulate the cessation of activity. But Jeremiah is also able to use anaphora to achieve an opposite effect. In 31:4–5 his 3-fold "again" *(ʿôd)* emphasizes the certainty of Israel's return to Zion, also simulating the renewal of activity which will take place there.

d. Repetition of a word at the end of successive cola, lines, or poetic verses (epiphora). In 4:19 "my heart" ends successive cola; in 8:22–23—Eng 9:1 "daughter of my people" ends successive verses.

e. Repetition of words or word cognates at the end of verses or larger compositions which appeared at the beginning (inclusio). The inclusio commonly functions to effect closure, as it does for example in Deuteronomy, but there it also gives emphasis to the law being preached. Jeremiah uses the inclusio both for closure and for emphasis, but it serves other functions for him as well. He may use it to be ironic, e.g., in 5:21 where he asks a people to hear who cannot hear. More often the inclusio points up some incongruity. In 4:22 "they do not know," which concludes the first and last lines of the verse, emphasizes in the first instance people's ignorance of Yahweh and what constitutes the good; but when the verse is taken as a whole, a basic incongruity is being stressed: namely, that the very same people who show ignorance of Yahweh and the good are knowledgeable when it comes to doing evil. In a similarly constructed verse in 8:4b–5 the inclusio is made with different forms of *šûb* ("return"). Emphasis is again put on a point which is part of a larger incongruity, i.e., that although people who turn away normally return, here we see a people that does not return. In 8:8–9 Jeremiah speaks of people who say they are "wise" but are without "wisdom."

A number of complete poems have inclusio, and in some the repetition gives focus to Jeremiah's argument. In 3:1–5 different forms of the interjection "Behold!" focus the argument that Yahweh does not want rapprochement with Israel, at least not for the time being and not under the present circumstances. In 5:26–28, 30–31 "my people" makes the inclusio. The argument here is ironic in tone: People who are being victimized by criminals somehow want the phenomenon to continue. Repeated key words at beginning and end give focus to other prophetic speeches, e.g., 13:21–27; 20:7–10, 14–18; 51:11–14; etc. (Lundbom 1975: 36–51). The words, "there is none like you" form an inclusio in the doxology of 10:6–7. If this originates with Jeremiah the point he stresses is the incomparability of Yahweh.

f. Inverted repetition of words, word cognates, fixed pairs, and sounds in the bicolon, the verse, and the larger composition (chiasmus). Jeremiah varies the monotony of synonymous parallelism in the bicolon with syntactic chiasmus, where the verbs are commonly placed at the extremes, e.g., 2:9, 19a; 4:5a, 7a, 9c; 5:6a, 12b; 6:21b, 25a; etc. Rarely are the verbs at the center (2:36b; 51:38), and rarely does the syntactic chiasmus form an antithesis (4:22c; and the proverbial 12:13a). In some cases a double-duty subject appears at the center, e.g., 4:2b ("nations") and 4:30c ("lovers"). Jeremiah enjoys making key word chiasmi: "water / cisterns / cisterns / water" in 2:13; "neighbor / brother / brother / neighbor" in 9:3—Eng 9:4; and "man / succeed / succeed / man" in 22:30. Somewhat different is the chiasmus in 14:2: "Judah / gates / [gates] / Jerusalem" (Holladay 1962: 51–52). Here Jeremiah plays on verticality, while at the same time keeping constant the idea of a nation in mourning. The idea is kept constant also in 20:14 where there is another variation of chiasmus: "cursed / I was born / she bore me / blessed".

In the double bicolon we find this chiasmus of sound: *ṣĕʿāqâh / wāšeber / nišbĕrâh / zĕʿāqâh* (48:3–4). Sound and meaning are combined in the chiasmus in 2:7b: *watābōʾû* / my land / my heritage / *lĕtôʿēbâh* (Kselman 1977: 222–23). Here the terms creating the sound balance also form a wordplay.

In poetry, Jeremiah uses words and phraseology to create a variety of larger chiastic structures. In 2:27c–28a, rhetorical form and content come together as Jeremiah turns the people's own words against themselves:

But *in the time of their trouble* they say
'*Arise* and *save* us'
But where are your gods which you made for yourselves?
Let them *arise* if they can *save* you
in your time of trouble

There is a tightly knit chiastic structure in 4:19c–21 where Jeremiah is in conversation with himself. Whole poems in some cases have chiastic structures built with key words, this phenomenon having been first discovered in Lamentations 1–2 by Condamin (1905). Jeremiah will also delimit the same sub-units within the poem by alternating the speaker, and this alternation will be chiastic as well (see 6). Macro-chiastic structures aid in developing the prophetic argument the same way macro-inclusio structures do. Whole poems having key word chiastic structures are: 2:5–9; 5:1–8; 6:1–7, 8–12; 8:13–17; 9:2–5—Eng 9:3–6 (text problems); 51:20–23; 51:34–45; and on a smaller scale (aba'): 2:33–37; and 23:18, 21–22 (Lundbom 1975: 70–96).

g. Double occurrences of a root in succession (multiclinatum), often making paronomasia. In 11:18: "Yahweh made it known to me and I knew"; in 17:14: "Heal me, O Yahweh, and I shall be healed, save me and I shall be saved"; in 20:7: "O Yahweh, you have deceived me and I was deceived"; also 31:4, 18[*bis*]; and the somewhat different constructions in 15:19 and 30:16. These are signatures of Jeremiah (Driver 1967: 276; Holladay 1962: 46).

Jeremiah combines verbs and cognate nouns in succession to great effect, e.g., in 2:5: "they went after worthlessness and became worthless" (paronomasia); in 22:22: "the wind shall shepherd all your shepherds" (paronomasia); and in 51:2: "And I will send to Babylon winnowers and they shall winnow her." In prose see 16:16; 23:4; and 48:12.

h. Repetition of consonants in succession (alliteration). This is a figure of sound, not meaning. Quite often, too, there will be paronomasia (Casanowicz 1893). In 17:12–13a the consonant *k* begins two words, and immediately following are 5 successive words beginning with the *m* consonant (also paronomasia; Casanowicz #176). In 48:15 the combination *bḥ* repeats 3 times (paronomasia; Casanowicz #44); in 49:15 the *b* consonant 3 times; and in 51:44 3 *bl* combinations (paronomasia; Casanowicz #49).

2. Accumulation. The celebrated rhetorical prose which appears in Jeremiah and the Deuteronomic literature is largely accumulation (accumulatio). It is heavy and stereotyped: Nouns heap up in twos, threes, and fours, and longer phrases balance rhythmically in parallelism. The Jeremiah prose contains some of the same noun chains and balanced phrases found in Deuteronomy and 2 Kings; at the same time it has other examples of both which appear nowhere else (Driver *Deuteronomy* ICC, xcii–xciv; Bright 1951: 25–27; *Jeremiah* AB, lxxi–lxxiii). The prose is certainly not the prophet's *ipsissima verba;* nevertheless we might expect that it would approximate his prose utterances and feature also the dominant characteristics of prose spoken by priests, scribes, and others trained in the Deuteronomic school of rhetoric.

Some examples of accumulatio in the prose: "sword, famine, and pestilence" (14:12; 21:9; 24:10; 27:8; etc.); "reproach, byword, taunt, and curse" (24:9); "cities of Judah and streets of Jerusalem" (7:17, 34; 11:6; 33:10; 44:6, 17, 21); "the voice of mirth and the voice of gladness, the voice of the bridegroom and the voice of the bride" (7:34; 16:9; 25:10; 33:11); "their dead bodies shall be food for the birds of the air and for the beasts of the earth" (7:33; 16:4; 19:7; 34:20); "a fortified city, an iron pillar, and bronze walls, against the kings of Judah, its princes, its priests, and the people of the land" (1:18); etc. Some of these phrases together with others have what appear to be prototypes in the poetry (Holladay 1960).

The poetry also contains accumulatio, e.g., 12:7: "I have forsaken my house, I have abandoned my heritage, I have given the beloved of my soul into the hands of her enemies." In the call passage Jeremiah accumulates 6 verbs; the outside 4 are arranged in a chiasmus (1:10).

In both poetry and prose, rapid accumulation of verbs results in asyndeton. In the poetry: "*Blow* the trumpet through the land, *cry aloud* and *say,* '*Assemble,* and *let us go* into the fortified cities' " (4:5); "*Run to and fro* through the streets of Jerusalem, *look* now, and *take note,* and *search* her squares . . ." (5:1); see also 49:8, 30. In the prose: the 6 infinitive absolutes in rapid succession in the Temple Sermon (7:9). Like repetition, accumulatio adds strength to discourse. The classical orators used it when heaping up praise or blame. Here in 7:9 Jeremiah assesses blame. Jeremiah uses accumulatio to press home the message of divine judgment upon the nations in 25:27, and in 31:7b he emphasizes the joy of Israel's future salvation.

3. Metaphors and Related Tropes. Jeremiah, like every good orator, peppers his discourse liberally with tropes. These give added strength to the discourse and also function to kindle the imagination of his audience.

a. Metaphor. Jeremiah uses an array of vivid metaphors. Some are brief, i.e., only a word or two, while others expand into an entire verse of poetry (8:23—Eng 9:1). Jeremiah also employs the simile (see b.), which is a metaphor using "as" or "like" in its comparison (Heb *kĕ*). In poetry, metaphors and similes appear frequently in combination, which can weaken the metaphor. These combinations are weakened still more when a colon before or after contains the other element in the comparison, or else a term of clarification. We find the same thing happening in the prose.

Jeremiah's metaphors describe Yahweh, the false gods, kings, the nation, the enemy, and even Jeremiah himself. They also give lucidity to the enormity of evil within the nation and the destruction which will come as a result of this evil. Yahweh is "the fountain of living waters"; the false gods by contrast are but "broken cisterns" (2:13). Mistaken foreign policies and religious adventurism come under attack when Jeremiah asks why people go to Egypt "to drink the waters of the Nile," and to Assyria "to drink the waters of the Great River?" (2:18). Jeremiah speaks of the fractured covenant relationship when he says to the people, "you broke your yoke and burst your bonds" (2:20). In 2:21 the nation which was once a "choice red vine" is now said to have degenerated into a "wild vine." The nation is also personified as a (shameful) daughter. His metaphors here are "daughter of Zion" (4:31; 6:2, 23); "(virgin) daughter of my people" (4:11; 6:26; 8:19, 21; 14:17 [MT]; etc.); "changeable daughter" (31:22); and "virgin Israel" (18:13; 31:4, 21). The metaphor of the harlot daughter almost becomes an allegory in 4:30–31. The "daughter" metaphor is also used for Egypt (46:11, 24), Ammon (49:4), and Babylon (50:42; 51:33).

The most disparaging metaphors, Jeremiah reserves for his own nation Israel. He calls the nation "a restive young camel interlacing her tracks," or a "wild ass . . . in her heat sniffing the wind" (2:23c–24a); again people are said to be "well-fed lusty stallions" (5:8). Jeremiah attacks the luxurious cedar buildings in Jerusalem, calling them a "forest" (21:14; cf. 1 Kgs 7:2), or else "Lebanon" (22:23). This latter metaphor becomes clarified in the Targums (Vermes 1958: 4). Inhabitants of these buildings are said—with a bit of irony perhaps—to be "nested among the cedars." Jeremiah seeks to evoke repentance from the people with a couple of agricultural metaphors: "Break up your fallow ground, and sow not among thorns" (4:3).

In describing the enemy, Jeremiah uses the common metaphor the "lion." Earlier foes from Assyria were roaring "lions" (2:15); now the foe from the N is another "lion" (4:7; 5:6), or else a "wolf" or a "leopard" (5:6). In 8:17 Babylon is depicted as 2 different varieties of snakes. Other metaphors in 4:11 ("desert wind") and 15:12 ("iron, iron from the north, and bronze") are weakened by clarification, which may mark them as later insertions into the text. In 25:32b the enemy is a "great tempest" (cf. 6:22 which has "great nation"). The foreign kings coming with their armies from the E are "shepherds with their flocks" (6:3). Judah's kings are also "shepherds" (2:8; 22:22; 23:1–4), this metaphor being so common it may not even have been perceived as such. King Jehoiachin, says Jeremiah, has become in defeat a "broken pot" (22:28). As for Jeremiah himself, in order that he may withstand the opposition sure to come from people in Jerusalem, Yahweh promises to make him into "a fortified city, an iron pillar, and bronze walls" (1:18). These metaphors appear in prose, and the narrator expectedly provides words of explanation in the verse following.

b. Simile. This trope is widely used not only in Hebrew but in other ancient Near Eastern languages. People of antiquity had a natural propensity to think analogically. Similes, therefore, are very old, going back all the way to the Sumerians (Kramer 1969). They appear also in Akkadian treaties and in various sapiential writings (*ANET,* 539–41; 598 lines 106–7).

Jeremiah uses the simile extensively, covering with it much of the same ground he covers with the metaphor. The wayward individual is "like a horse plunging headlong into battle" (8:6). Wayward Israel waits on the road (for lovers) "like an Arab in the wilderness" (3:2), yet she cries out rebelliously against Yahweh "like a lion in the forest" (12:8). When judgment comes, however, she will cry "like a woman in labor" (6:24; 13:21; 22:23; etc.). During the drought, wild asses wander on the bare heights where they "pant for air like jackals" (14:6). The besiegers of Jerusalem are "like keepers of a field against her round about" (4:17); their quiver is "like an open tomb" (5:16); and the roar of their coming is "like the sea" (6:23). Yahweh will scatter the people "like the east wind" (18:17), or "like chaff driven by the desert wind" (13:24). His coming will be "like the clouds, his chariots like the whirlwind" (4:13). His wrath goes forth "like fire" (4:4; 21:12). Dead bodies shall fall "like dung upon the open field, like sheaves after the reaper" (9:21—Eng 9:22). Jeremiah questions Yahweh about the grim scenario, "Why should you be like a stranger in the land, like a traveler who turns aside for the night? Why should you be like a man confused, like a mighty man who cannot save?" (14:8–9). Personal enemies treat Jeremiah "like a gentle lamb led to the slaughter" (11:19). But when Jeremiah's faith is renewed, he exclaims, "Yahweh is with me as a dread warrior" (20:11). Similes of this same general sort appear in the foreign nation oracles, e.g., 46:7–8; 51:27c, 34b; etc.

The simile is extended into a comparison (similitudo) when strengthened by the *kĕ . . . kēn* and *ʾākēn . . . kēn* constructions, e.g., in poetry: "*as* a thief is shamed when caught, *so* the house of Israel shall be shamed" (2:26; also 5:27; 6:7; cf. Deut 8:20); "*surely* as a faithless wife leaves her husband, *so* you have been faithless to me, O house of Israel" (3:20); and in prose: "*like* the clay in the potter's hand, *so* are you in my hand, O house of Israel" (18:6; also 24:5, 8).

c. Abusio. One of the harsher tropes is the abusio, which is an implied metaphor. This type of metaphor behaves somewhat extravagantly in that a word is taken from one usage and put to another. Abusios can be made from verbs, e.g., in 5:8: "each man *neighing* for his neighbor's wife"; in 7:28: "truth has *perished,* it is *cut off* from their lips"; in 4:28; 12:4; and 23:10: "the earth *mourns*"; and in 51:44: "the nations shall no longer *flow* to him." Other abusios are created by nouns, e.g., in 4:4: "remove the foreskin of your *hearts*"; and in 18:18: "come, let us smite him with the *tongue.*"

d. Euphemism. On occasion Jeremiah substitutes a more mild term or one with adjunct meaning in order to avoid saying something either too harsh or too explicit. This is euphemism. In 8:14 he says, "Let us go into the fortified cities and *be silent* there, for Yahweh our God *has silenced us.*" "Be silent" (Heb *dmm*) is a euphemism for "die" (RSV: "perish"). The same verb appears in 25:37: "the peaceful folds are *made silent*" (RSV: "devastated"). Other usages of *dmm* in 48:2; 49:26; and 51:6 may also be euphemistic. In 13:22b Jeremiah says, "because of the greatness of your iniquity your *skirts* are uncovered." He really means her *pudenda.* Again in 13:26: "your *shame* will be seen" (BDB 886).

4. Argumentation. To a large extent Jeremiah's rhetoric is a rhetoric of argumentation. It differs in this important respect from the rhetoric of Deuteronomy with which it has other important affinities. Deuteronomy preaches the conditional terms of the covenant warning people what will happen if the covenant is broken. Jeremiah presupposes an entirely different reality: The covenant *has* been broken, and the people now must either repent or be punished. Jeremiah cannot preach this message without encountering argument from others, and it goes without saying that he must also argue in return. It is true, of course, that much of Jeremiah's preaching is like that of the other prophets, i.e., preaching based on authority. His indictments and judgments are stated in unequivocal terms. Jeremiah does not make appeals to ethos as the classical orators do. At the same time a surprising amount of his discourse is dialogical—indeed Jeremiah comes closer to Greek dialectic than any of the other Hebrew prophets. There is a dialectic going on between Yahweh and the people, another between Yahweh and himself, and still another between himself and the people. Certain speeches, e.g., 3:1–5 and 5:1–8, are genuinely open-ended in the sense that the audience is left at the end to draw its own conclusions. This brings the prophet and his audience into partnership; together they must discern the import of Yahweh's word.

a. Protasis—Apodosis. The protasis-apodosis form ("If . . . then . . .") is at home in legal discourse. Deuteronomy, for example, says that if the people obey Yahweh and do his commands, they will be set above the nations and blessings will come upon them; if they do not obey and fail to do Yahweh's commands, then curses will come (Deut 28:1–2, 15). Jeremiah says, however, in one of his early calls for reform, that if Israel returns to Yahweh and clears away the vestiges of false worship, then she can use the oath once again and the Abrahamic covenant will achieve its intended blessing upon the nations of the world (4:1–2; Bright *Jeremiah* AB, 21). Later on after judgment has come Jeremiah uses the form to emphasize Yahweh's ongoing commitment to the Abrahamic covenant (31:36–37).

b. Arguments *a minori ad maius.* The argument *a minori ad maius* (Heb *qal vechomer*) is from the lesser to the greater, and it appears in the OT in legal as well as other parenetic discourse, e.g., Exod 6:12; Deut 31:27. In 3:1 Jeremiah argues that *if* a divorced woman who has remarried cannot return to her former husband (so Deut 24:1–4), *how much more* can Israel—who has had many lovers—not return to Yahweh. In 12:5 Yahweh tells Jeremiah that *if* running on foot has tired him, *how much more* will he not be able to compete with horses; *if* in a safe land he falls down, *how much more* will he likely fall in the jungle of the Jordan. An argument *a minori ad maius* is used against the nations in 25:29.

c. Rhetorical Question. The rhetorical question has an evocative function in discourse, in fact it aims usually at intimidation. Rhetorical questions are posed solely for effect. They call for a response, but none can be made because the answer to the question is either obvious or else one the audience will not want to give. The rhetorical question was widely used in antiquity and appears in various literatures (e.g., *ANET,* 597 lines 36–38).

Jeremiah uses the rhetorical question, sometimes a pair of them, as a foil for some more important statement he wishes to make. Or sometimes his preferred subject is yet another question. In 18:20: "Is evil a recompense for good? Yet they have dug a pit for my life." Jeremiah accumulates rhetorical questions, though not to the extent Amos does in his classic litany in Amos 3:3–8. Jeremiah's questions also differ from those of Amos in that his foils are less mechanical; there is some linkage of thought in almost every case to his preferred subject. Often a common word unites the foil and the preferred subject.

Jeremiah puts the rhetorical question to two specialized uses. In one a single or double question lifts up some paradigmatic behavior, a common happening, or something built into the natural order; what follows is then a portrayal of Israel's behavior, which is scandalous. In 2:11: "Has a nation changed its gods even though they are no gods? But my people have changed their glory for that which does not profit"; in 2:32: "Can a maiden forget her ornaments, or a bride her attire? But my people have forgotten me days without number"; also 5:22a, 23; 18:14–15. Somewhat different is 13:23 where the question foils an ironic comment: "Can the Ethiopian change his skin, or the leopard his spots? Then also you can do good who are accustomed to do evil!"

The other specialized use is the 3-fold question in the form *hă . . . ʾim . . . maddûaʿ* ("If . . . if . . . why then. . . ?"), which appears 8 times in the book and is another signature of Jeremiah (2:14, 31; 8:4–5, 19, 22; 14:19; 22:28; and 49:1). Here the first two questions are a foil for a third which expresses a troubling vexation. This vexation is either about something incongruous which the prophet observes, or else it has to do with the weakened condition of people facing war and imminent defeat. In 2:31: "Have I been a wilderness to Israel? Have I been a land of thick darkness? Why then do my people say, 'We are free, we will come no more to you?' "; in 2:14: "Is Israel a slave? Is he a homeborn servant? Why then has he become a prey?" In 22:28 it is King Jehoiachin who is in a weakened condition. In 30:6 the form is modified to a statement and two questions: "Ask now and see, can a male bear a child? Why then do I see every soldier with his hands on his loins like a woman in labor?" In 8:19 the form works differently because Yahweh interrupts the people to ask the third more pressing question (Holladay 1962: 48–49).

Jeremiah sometimes answers his own rhetorical questions (hypophora), e.g., 6:15 [= 8:12]: "Were they ashamed when they committed abomination? No, they were not at all ashamed; they did not know how to blush." See also 6:20; 30:15; 31:20; 46:7–8. In 12:9 the two rhetorical questions containing a wordplay.

Some climactic rhetorical questions which originally expressed harsh judgment were later converted into affirmations of hope, e.g., "and would you return to me?" in 3:1 becomes "yet return to me"; also "and shall he be saved from it?" in 30:7 becomes "yet from it he shall be saved" (Holladay 1962: 53–4). Numerous rhetorical questions appear also in the prose, e.g., 7:19 (correctio); 23:23–24;

27:17; 37:19; 40:15b; 44:7–9; etc. One finds no rhetorical questions, however, in the oracles against Babylon (chaps. 50–51).

d. The Exaggerated Contrast. In ancient Hebrew as well as in Arabic and some modern languages, two antithetical statements can be juxtaposed solely to emphasize the one appearing second. This has the practical effect of making the second statement more important than the first. The idiom has been called the "exaggerated contrast" (Carleton 1892; Hommel 1899–1900), and good examples are to be found in Deut 5:3 and Amos 7:14. The first statement will negate an idea, but the speaker does not really mean to deny it for the idea is otherwise valid or true. Jeremiah, for example, says that Yahweh did not command the fathers to make burnt offerings and sacrifices when the people left Egypt; he commanded them to obey his voice (7:22–23). Following Josiah's death and the deposition of Jehoahaz, he also says, "Weep not for him who is dead, nor bemoan him, but weep bitterly for him who goes away" (22:10).

e. Surrender. In the trial which followed the Temple Sermon, Jeremiah submits himself to the will of the court. He says, "But as for me, behold, I am in your hands. Do with me as seems good and right to you" (26:14). In classical rhetoric this sort of statement was considered a veiled argument, and it was given the name "surrender" (permissio; *ad Herennium* IV xxix 39).

f. Descriptio. To continue with Jeremiah's remarks to the court, we find him describing the consequences of possible court action. He says, "Only know for certain that if you put me to death, you will bring innocent blood upon yourselves and upon this city and its inhabitants, for in truth Yahweh sent me to you to speak all these words in your ears" (26:15). This too has argumentative value, and classical rhetoricians called such a move descriptio which they said could be used both in prosecution and defense (*ad Herennium* 4.39.51). Here, of course, Jeremiah is arguing his own defense.

5. Humor and Irony. The humorous element in Jeremiah's preaching has not received the attention it deserves, despite the fact that irony in particular is well documented among the ancient Hebrews. Humor is still difficult if not impossible to define precisely, and its identification depends largely upon individual interpretation. There is, in any case, humor in many of Jeremiah's utterances, and one may imagine that the prophet was at times rather playful with his audience. He shares with them sudden flashes of insight, and with his quick wit he creates wordplays, caricatures, and verbal irony for which Hebrew discourse generally has been justly celebrated. His playfulness, however, remains serious when the message is serious (Knox 1963: 329). Wordplays emphasize and threaten; hyperbole becomes his countermeasure for audience resistance; and irony is but another way of telling the truth.

a. Paronomasia. Broadly defined, paronomasia is either a play on multiple meanings of identical or cognate words, or else a play on different words close enough in sound so as to make assonance (near-rhyme) or puns. An extensive list of paronomasia in the OT has been compiled by Casanowicz (1893).

Jeremiah is particularly fond of assonance, which is similar to alliteration (see 1.h.) in that the play is only on sound, although assonance can function to emphasize what is being said (Saydon 1955). Examples of assonance: in 1:10; 18:7; and 31:28, *lintôš wĕlintôṣ* ("to pluck up and to break down"); in 2:12, *šōmû šāmayim* ("Be appalled, O heavens"); in 2:20, *gibʿâ gĕbōhâ* ("high hill"); in 6:11, *mālēʾtî nilʾêtî* ("I am full, I weary myself"); in 9:9—Eng 9:10 and 31:15 (reversed), *bĕkî (wā)nehî* ("weeping and wailing"); in 49:30, *nūsû nūdû* ("flee, wander away"); in 51:44, *bēl bĕbābel* ("Bel in Babylon"); see also 6:1b; 10:25c; 12:13a; 14:6a; 16:19a. Examples of puns: in 1:11–12, *šāqēd* / *šōqēd* ("almond / watching"), which is similar to the pun in Amos 8:1–2; in 17:11, *ʿōśeh ʿōšer* ("he who gets riches"); in 50:37–38, *ḥereb* / *ḥōreb* ("sword / drought"); and 17:6 and 8 where *yirʾeh* / *yiraʾ*(Kt) ("see / fear") balance two verses of poetry. Jeremiah also plays on multiple meanings. In the poetry: on *mʾs* in 6:30 (cf. 1 Sam 15:23); on *ʾsp* in 8:13–14; and on *šûb* in 3:12, 14, 22 (cf. Hos 14:5—Eng 14:4); 8:4–5; and 31:21c–22a. In 6:7 the unusual use of the verb *qrr* in the second colon makes the wordplay: "as a well keeps its water cool, so she keeps cool about her wickedness." In 22:22: "The wind shall shepherd all your shepherds."

There are a number of similar wordplays in the prose. In the second vision of chapter 1 Yahweh says, "Out of the north evil shall *open up* upon all the inhabitants of the land . . . and everyone shall set his throne at the *opening* of the gates of Jerusalem" (vv 14–15). To Jeremiah personally Yahweh says, "Do not *be dismayed* by them, lest *I dismay you* before them" (v 17b). In chap. 19 Yahweh tells Jeremiah to buy a "flask" *(baqbuq)* which, when broken, will dramatize this prophetic word: "And I will make empty *(ûbāqqōtî)* the plans of Judah and Jerusalem . . ." (vv 1, 7). In addressing the false prophets, Jeremiah plays on *maśśāʾ* which can mean either "burden" or "oracle" (23:33 LXX). In 28:15–16 Jeremiah plays on "send" in his judgment upon Hananiah: "Listen, Hananiah, Yahweh has not *sent* you . . . Therefore thus says Yahweh, 'Behold *I will send you* off the face of the earth. . . .' " In 34:15–18 three wordplays appear close together in the judgment upon Zedekiah: the expression *qrʾ dĕrôr* ("proclaim liberty"), double uses of the verb *šûb* ("turn, return, repent"), and the verb *krt* ("cut"). In a couple instances a single word having multiple meanings is played upon. In 5:13 when Jeremiah says the prophets will become *rûaḥ,* he means, of course, "wind" or "hot air," not "spirit." The latter they should possess but do not. In 9:3—Eng 9:4 Jeremiah plays on "Jacob," using its disparaging meaning of "cheater" (cf. Gen 27:35–36).

Like the classical poets, Jeremiah likes to play on names, whether personal names or place names. The name proposed for the future Davidic king is "Yahweh is our righteousness" (23:6), a deliberate play—with reversal—on Zedekiah which means "righteous of Yahweh" or "righteous is Yahweh." The people likewise had fun at the expense of Jeremiah when they dubbed him "Terror on Every Side" (20:10; Bright *Jeremiah* AB, 132–33), which was a favorite expression of his. In 4:15 a play is made on Dan: *maggîd middān;* in 6:1 on Tekoa: *ûbitqôaʾ tiqʿû;* and in 48:2 on Heshbon: *bĕḥešbôn ḥošbû,* and Madmen: *madmēn tiddōmî;* cf. Amos 5:5c; Zeph 2:4a.

b. Hyperbole. Jeremiah very often uses hyperbole, which is deliberate overstatement. Hyperbole is common in impassioned discourse, particularly when there is conflict and the speaker must make his point to an audience that will not listen. Hyperbole is used to lash out against the enormity of evil. Idolatry is Judah's most heinous crime, but another following not far behind is the nation's failure to practice justice and righteousness. Hyperbole appears also in descriptions of the approaching enemy, what destruction that enemy will bring, and the intense grief which all of this will bring to the people, Jeremiah included. But Jeremiah's earliest use of hyperbole comes in a divine affirmation. Yahweh in his call of the prophet is reported as having said, "Before I formed you in the womb I knew you, and before you were born I consecrated you; I appointed you a prophet to the nations" (1:5).

In his earliest preaching Jeremiah resorts to hyperbole in addressing the prevailing fertility worship, e.g., in 2:20: "For upon every high hill and under every green tree you bowed down as a harlot" (cf. 3:6, 13; 17:2); in 2:28 (MT): "For as many as your cities are your gods, O Judah" (cf. 11:13); and in 3:2: "Where have you not been lain with?"

Jeremiah is hyperbolic about the people's inability to listen, exhibit shame, or repent, e.g., in 6:10: "Behold, their ears are uncircumcised, they cannot listen"; in 6:15b [= 8:12b]: "they did not know how to blush"; and in 5:3: "They have made their faces harder than rock, they have refused to repent." Yahweh's command that Jeremiah and his search party run through Jerusalem to find just one righteous man (5:1) is hyperbolic; so also the statement made to King Jehoiakim about being hotly competitive in cedar acquisition for new royal buildings in Jerusalem (22:15). In 22:17 Jeremiah once again caricatures Jehoiakim in saying, "But you have eyes and heart only for your dishonest gain."

Hyperbole comes to the fore in Jeremiah's preaching when he announces the foe coming from the north. In 8:16: "The snorting of their horses is heard from Dan, at the sound of the neighing of their stallions the whole land quakes." Observing the terrified defenders of Jerusalem Jeremiah says, "Why do I see every soldier with his hands on his loins like a woman in labor? Why has every face turned pale?" (30:6). People are told by the prophet to "*roll* in ashes" (6:26). The widows, he says, will be "more in number than the sand of the seas" (15:8). With the fate of Jerusalem sealed, Jeremiah says to those who still harbor illusions of deliverance, "For even if you should defeat the whole army of Chaldeans who are fighting against you, and there remained of them only wounded men, every man in his tent, they would rise up and burn this city with fire" (37:10; cf. 2 Sam 5:6).

Jeremiah uses hyperbole also in the judgments made upon foreign nations, e.g., 25:31, 33; 49:21; 50:46; and 51:9. He is hyperbolic when speaking about his own personal grief, e.g., in 14:17: "Let my eyes run down with tears night and day, and let them not cease." There is hyperbole finally in a passage which speaks about restoration (50:21), but we cannot be certain whether this comes from Jeremiah.

c. Irony. Ancient Hebrew humor is to a large extent irony, and there are few who express irony better than the prophets (Knox 1963: 328–31). Isaiah is the grand master of verbal irony, with Jeremiah a peer certainly and possibly even his equal in certain regards. In verbal irony the underlying meaning is opposite of the surface meaning. Speakers resort to irony when straight talk fails, when they are powerless usually and numbered among the disenfranchised. Ironic language therefore is desperate and at the same time extravagant. It commonly speaks to incongruities, elucidating them with razor sharpness (Good 1965: 24–33).

Jeremiah uses irony to address a variety of incongruities. The greatest of these is Israel's reckless abandonment of Yahweh and the covenant demands, while she at the same time shows enormous devotion to idols and the worship associated with them. Jeremiah observes how adept people are at doing evil, e.g., in 2:33: "How *well* you direct your course to seek lovers"; and 4:22: "They are *skilled* in doing evil." Here and in other examples the ironic statement is followed by a non-ironic statement which gives the former clarification. In 8:5: "They *hold fast* to deceit, they refuse to return"; in 14:10: "They have *loved* to wander thus, they have not restrained their feet." People have, it seems, a commitment to evil; in fact they enjoy being victimized by it: "my people *love* to have it so" (5:31). They are never long away from other attachments (2:24c). Sexual preference as expressed in fertility worship is mocked when Jeremiah deliberately reverses the sexes in 2:27, making the tree masculine and the stone feminine. Idols are helpless, however, when crises develop and deliverance is being sought (2:27b–28; cf. Deut 32:38b). They may be beautiful in appearance, nevertheless because they are without life they can do neither good nor evil (10:2–5, 8–9—if this be from Jeremiah). Jeremiah's urging of the people to increase the number of their abominable sacrifices is an example of epitrope (7:21; see also 44:25b and Hos 4:17). The national character is ironically described in 8:5 where Israel is called a "brilliant apostate" (*mĕšūbâ niṣṣaḥat*), an example of oxymoron.

The personifications "virgin daughter" and "virgin Israel" are also ironic (14:17; 18:13; 31:21; cf. Amos 5:2). Jeremiah is ironic when talking about coming judgment, e.g., "How you will be *favored* when pangs come upon you" (22:23). People when they are in exile "can serve other gods day and night" (16:13). Jeremiah uses epitrope also in 15:2 when he gives the people various options after his own mediation on their behalf has been rejected by Yahweh. The expression, "Nebuchadnezzar, my servant" may be an oxymoron since "my servant," when used by Yahweh, is a term of endearment. The description of exhumed bones which will be set before the astral deities whom the people have loved and served in 8:1–2—if it derives from Jeremiah—is burlesque. Jeremiah uses irony in addressing foreign nations, e.g., 46:11; 48:36; and 51:8. And there is irony in the curses which the prophet hurls at his own birth in 20:14–15. Contrasting terms which frame both of these verses point to a deeply moving incongruity, i.e., the joy and blessedness felt by Jeremiah's parents the day he was born, and the enormous despair which Jeremiah now himself feels (Lundbom 1985).

6. Drama. In the Jeremianic preaching there is more than a little theatrics mixed in. For example, he will now and then turn to address imaginary audiences (apostrophe): the heavens in 2:12; Jerusalem in 4:14; the land in 22:29; and Yahweh's sword in 47:6. He imagines a ready scribe at his side when he says in 22:30, "Write this man down as childless. . . ," referring to the deposed King Jehoiachin. The prophet is engaging in drama also when he alternates speakers in his prophetic speeches. This creates in the speeches an antiphonal quality which Jeremiah may have appropriated from the psalms. In 6:4–5 words spoken by the enemy frame the frightened cry of Jerusalem's besieged ("Woe to us . . ."). In 8:18–21 an entire poem builds on an elaborate speaker chiasmus:

Jeremiah: My joy is gone
grief is upon me
my heart is sick
People: Hark a cry . . .
'Is Yahweh not in Zion?
Is her King not in her?'
Yahweh: Why then have they provoked me to
anger with their images
and with their foreign idols?
People: The harvest is past
the summer is ended
and we are not saved
Jeremiah: For the wound of the daughter of
my people I am wounded
I mourn
dismay has taken hold of me

A similarly constructed poem is found in 17:13–16a. Other Jeremianic poems combine key word structures with alternation of speaker (Lundbom 1975: 36–51, 70–96). Jeremiah's oracles to the foreign nations may also be taken as dramatic presentations since they are spoken to audiences too far distant to hear (cf. Amos 1–2).

E. Prophetic Symbolism: Act and Being

Jeremiah's prophetic message is more than words, although words in the ancient world were believed to be invested with the power to bring about their actualization. Jeremiah like many of his predecessors went a step further and dramatized the spoken word with symbolic action (Robinson 1927). He buried a loin cloth and later recovered it ruined in order to symbolize the spoiled pride awaiting a nation which abandons its covenant with Yahweh (13:1–11). He broke an empty flask at the Potsherd Gate to symbolize Yahweh's determination to make empty the plans of an ambitious people in Judah and Jerusalem (chap. 19). Together with a fringe group of Rechabites, he went to the temple to test their resolve not to drink wine—all for the purpose of giving others an object lesson on obedience (chap. 35). When the Babylonians began asserting rule over Palestine, Jeremiah wore thongs and yoke bars around his neck to symbolize subservience which Judah must now offer to Nebuchadnezzar (chap. 27). Later in Egypt, Jeremiah buried stones in the pavement before Pharaoh's palace at Tahpanhes. These were to symbolize the future erection of Nebuchadnezzar's throne on that site (43:8–13). But when Jerusalem was about to fall, Jeremiah bought property at Anathoth from his cousin Hanamel to point people ahead to the day when Yahweh would restore them to the land (chap. 32).

These actions, like the spoken word in all its fullness, were efficacious in bringing things to pass. Symbolic action, therefore, was a natural extension of prophetic preaching. At the same time it counted for nothing, just as the prophetic word counted for nothing, if Yahweh was not behind it. Jehoiakim's destruction of Jeremiah's scroll (chap. 36) and Hananiah's breaking the yoke bars off Jeremiah's neck (chap. 28) were symbolic acts which came to nothing.

Jeremiah was himself the fullest expression of divine prophecy when his life was perceived to be the symbol (Herder 1833: 48). His celibacy had symbolic meaning (16:1–9), just as Hosea's broken marriage and Ezekiel's loss of his wife did. Jeremiah's suffering, particularly in the days just prior to Judah's collapse, took the focus almost entirely off the prophetic word and the symbolic act and put it on the prophet himself. Jeremiah's entire being had now become the message—a dual message about a suffering nation and a suffering God in whose service the prophet steadfastly remained to the very end. Messages of such a grand scope are repeated in the Suffering Servant of Isaiah 53 and in Job, but they are not seen again until we come to the NT gospels where the divine message is acted out in the life, death, and resurrection of Jesus Christ.

Bibliography

Albright, W. F. 1932. The Seal of Eliakim and the Latest Preëxilic History of Judah. *JBL* 51: 77–106.
———. 1942. King Joiachin in Exile. *BA* 4: 49–55. Repr. *BAR* 1: 106–12.
Bright, J. 1951. The Date of the Prose Sermons of Jeremiah. *JBL* 70: 15–29.
Carleton, J. G. 1892. The Idiom of Exaggerated Contrast. *Expositor* 4/6: 365–72.
Casanowicz, I. M. 1893. Paronomasia in the Old Testament. *JBL* 12: 105–67. Repr. Boston, 1894.
Condamin, A. 1905. Symmetrical Repetitions in *Lamentations* I and II. *JTS* 7: 137–40.
Cross, F. M., Jr., and Freedman, D. N. 1953. Josiah's Revolt against Assyria. *JNES* 12: 56–58.
Driver, S. R. 1967. *An Introduction to the Literature of the Old Testament.* Repr. Cleveland.
Freedman, D. N. 1956. The Babylonian Chronicle. *BA* 19: 50–60.
Gadd, C. J. 1923. *The Fall of Nineveh.* London.
Good, E. M. 1965. *Irony in the Old Testament.* Philadelphia.
Gross, K. 1931. Hoseas Einfluss auf Jeremias Anschauungen. *NKZ* 42: 241–56; 327–43.
Herder, J. G. 1833. *The Spirit of Hebrew Poetry* Vol. 2. Trans. J. Marsh. Burlington, VT.
Holladay, W. L. 1960. Prototypes and Copies: A New Approach to the Poetry-Prose Problem in the Book of Jeremiah. *JBL* 79: 351–67.
———. 1962. Style, Irony and Authenticity in Jeremiah. *JBL* 81: 44–54.
———. 1964. The Background of Jeremiah's Self-Understanding: Moses, Samuel and Psalm 22. *JBL* 83: 153–64.
———. 1966a. Jeremiah and Moses. *JBL* 85: 17–27.
———. 1966b. The Recovery of Poetic Passages of Jeremiah. *JBL* 85: 401–35.
Hommel, F. 1899–1900. A Rhetorical Figure in the Old Testament. *ExpTim* 11: 439–41.
Hyatt, J. P. 1940. The Peril from the North in Jeremiah. *JBL* 59: 499–513.
Knox, I. 1963. The Traditional Roots of Jewish Humor. *Judaism* 12: 327–37.
Kramer, S. N. 1969. Sumerian Similes. *JAOS* 89: 1–10.

Kselman, J. S. 1977. Semantic-Sonant Chiasmus in Biblical Poetry. *Bib* 58: 219–23.
Lowth, R. 1815. *Lectures on the Sacred Poetry of the Hebrews.* Trans. G. Gregory. Boston.
Lundbom, J. R. 1975. *Jeremiah: A Study in Ancient Hebrew Rhetoric.* SBLDS 18. Missoula, MT.
———. 1976. The Lawbook of the Josianic Reform. *CBQ* 38: 293–302.
———. 1985. The Double Curse in Jeremiah 20:14–18. *JBL* 104: 589–600.
Malamat, A. 1950. The Last Wars of the Kingdom of Judah. *JNES* 9: 218–27.
———. 1956. A New Record of Nebuchadrezzar's Palestinian Campaigns. *IEJ* 6: 246–56.
———. 1975. The Twilight of Judah: In the Egyptian-Babylonian Maelstrom. *VTSup* 28: 123–43.
Muilenburg, J. 1953. A Study in Hebrew Rhetoric: Repetition and Style. *VTSup* 1: 97–111.
Rainey, A. F. 1983. The Biblical Shephelah of Judah. *BASOR* 251: 1–22.
Robinson, H. W. 1927. Prophetic Symbolism. Pp. 1–17 in *Old Testament Essays,* ed. D. C. Simpson. London.
Saydon, P. P. 1955. Assonance in Hebrew as a Means of Expressing Emphasis. *Bib* 36: 36–50; 287–304.
Skinner, J. 1963. *Prophecy and Religion: Studies in the Life of Jeremiah.* Cambridge.
Vermes, G. 1958. The Symbolical Interpretation of *Lebanon* in the Targums. *JTS* n.s. 9: 1–12.

JACK R. LUNDBOM

JEREMIAH, ADDITIONS TO. The "Additions to Jeremiah" are those two books in the Septuagint (LXX) which have no counterpart in the canonical text of Jeremiah. These additions consist of two originally separate and independent books: (1) the book of Baruch (Bar 1:1–5:9), consisting of an introduction, prayers, and psalms; and (2) the Epistle of Jeremiah (vv 1–73 [= Baruch 6 in Jerome's Latin Vulgate]), which is a satirical and impassioned harangue against idols and idolatry. These additions are regarded by Jews and Protestants as apocryphal and by Roman Catholics as deuterocanonical.

Just as in antiquity where the book of Baruch and the Epistle of Jeremiah were regarded as separate books (in ancient Greek manuscripts they were usually separated from one another by the canonical book of Lamentations), here also the two additions will be treated separately.

A. The Book of Baruch
  1. The Imputed Author
  2. The Major Sections
  3. The Book as a Whole
  4. Canonical Status
  5. Ancient Versions
B. The Epistle of Jeremiah
  1. Contents
  2. Author
  3. Purpose and Genre
  4. Original Language
  5. Literary Merit
  6. Canonicity
  7. Date
  8. Place of Composition
  9. Ancient Versions

A. The Book of Baruch

The book of Baruch, which is sometimes called 1 Baruch to distinguish it from the *Apocalypse of Baruch* in Syriac and Greek (i.e., *2* and *3 Baruch,* respectively), consists of four major sections: a prose introduction (1:1–14); a prayer of confession (1:15–3:8); a poem in praise of Wisdom (3:9–4:4); and a psalm of encouragement and hope (4:5–5:9). Because each of these sections may have had a different author and date of composition, each must be treated separately.

1. The Imputed Author. The secretary and confidant of the prophet Jeremiah, Baruch son of Neriah was from a very prominent Judean family, his brother Seraiah, for example, being the chief quartermaster of Judah's last king (Jer 51:59), Zedekiah (ca. 597–587 B.C.). It was Baruch who, on two separate occasions, courageously copied and delivered Jeremiah's Oracles of Destruction to King Jehoiakim and who, later on, after being accused by Azariah son of Hoshaiah of being a Babylonian sympathizer, was taken, along with Jeremiah and others, to Egypt (Jer 43:1–7). Inasmuch as the Bible does not say where, when, or how Baruch died, it is not surprising that in this matter quite conflicting traditions abound (see Moore 1977: 268–69). See also BARUCH (PERSON) #1.

This book bearing Baruch's name is best regarded as a pseudepigraphon, its ancient author(s) trying to increase the book's authority by attributing it to the eminent and long-dead scribe. Apart from Kalt (1932), virtually no 20th-century scholar has ascribed Baruchian authorship to the entire book; however, a few scholars, mostly Roman Catholics such as Stoderl (1922: 1–23), Goettsberger (1928), Heinisch (1928), and Penna (1956), have argued for Baruchian authorship of some portion of it, usually Bar 1:1–3:8 (for an extensive survey of scholarly opinion regarding the book's authorship, see Burke 1982: 18–20).

But even though the book of Baruch does indeed contain concepts and phraseology very much reminiscent of Jeremiah (esp. in Bar 1:15–3:8), as well as references to a number of historical personages and events from 597 B.C. to shortly before 539 B.C., there are certain imprecisions and errors of fact in its introduction, certain contradictory moods and attitudes between the various sections as well as certain strikingly different theological positions between them, not to mention Baruch's dependence upon such biblical and extrabiblical books as Job, Daniel, and Sirach—all of which argue against Baruchian authorship for any of the material in Baruch (for details on all these matters, see below; cf. also Burke 1982: 20–23).

As will be argued later, the actual author was probably a Palestinian Jew who, sometime during the early 2d century B.C., compiled several originally independent psalms and then wrote an introduction for them (however, Schürer *HJP*^{2} 3/2: 734–35 would have all of 1:15–3:8 composed by one author). It was sometime after this that someone else interpolated the wisdom poem of 3:9–4:4, which Nickelsburg and Stone (1983: 216) regard as a Greek composition (but see below) dating to the 2d or 1st century B.C.

2. The Major Sections. a. Prose Introduction (1:1–14). The introduction, which serves as a covering letter to Baruch's message, is awkward and imprecise in both style and content (e.g., in the *fifth year* [v 2] of what? Where was the Sud River mentioned in v 4 [Bewer 1942]?). Moreover, the introduction contains serious historical inaccuracies characteristic of later biblical materials; e.g., v 7 has one Jehoiakim (Gk *Ioakim*) serving as high priest (see Myers, *Ezra-Nehemiah* AB, 197–98; Moore 1977: 271); v 8 has Nebuchadnezzar returning the sacred vessels he had taken from the Temple in 597 B.C. (cf. Ezra 1:7–11); and v 11 has Belshazzar rather than Nabonidus as the son of Nebuchadnezzar, an anachronism shared with the book of Daniel (Dan 5:2, 11, 18, 22); however, Stoderl (1922: 22) argues for the correctness of such an assertion.

While Baruch's advice to the Jews to be cooperative and pray for the life of Nebuchadnezzar and his son (v 11) is reminiscent of Jeremiah's advice to the exiles (Jer 27:6–8 and 29:4–7), it nonetheless stands in sharp contrast to Bar 4:15–16, 21, 25–26, 31–35, where a much more hostile attitude prevails.

That the introduction was translated from Hebrew cannot be denied. Not only are there some Hebraisms (e.g., compare the LXX's "the hand was according to each" [v 6] with the LXX of Deut 16:10, 17), but there are two mistranslations that can only be explained from the Hebrew ("prisoners" instead of "craftsmen" in v 9 [the *Hipʿil* participle *masgēr* can mean either]; and "manna" instead of "cereal offerings" [Heb *minḥâ*] in v 10).

The introduction's errors and its awkwardness and imprecision in both content and style heighten for most readers its artificiality and secondary character. Nonetheless, its author was undoubtedly the compiler of most, if not all, of Baruch.

b. Prayer of Confession (1:15–3:8). The prayer consists of two parts: (1) a confession for the Palestinian remnant (1:15–2:5); and (2) a petition for the exiled community (2:6–3:8), expressing both their repentance (2:6–35) and their innocent suffering (3:1–8). Moore (1977: 291–94) argues for there being three separate prayers here, each with a different author (but see Goldstein 1979–80: 180, n. 3 and Nickelsburg 1981: 152, n. 24).

The central theme of the prayer for the Palestinian remnant (1:15–2:5) is well represented by vv 15, 17–18a:

> Righteousness belongs to the Lord our God, but confusion of face, as at this day, to us, the men of Judah, to the inhabitants of Jerusalem . . . because we have sinned before the Lord, and have disobeyed him.

The confession is strongly Jeremianic (cf., for example, "to the men of Judah and the inhabitants of Jerusalem" in v 15 with Jer 4:4; 11:2, 9; 17:25; 32:32; 35:13; the list of the sinners in v 16 with those in Jer 32:32; also 1:21b with Jer 26:4–5). The prayer is also deuteronomistic (cf., for example, v 18 with Deut 4:8; 9:23; v 19 with Deut 9:7, 24; v 21 with Deut 4:30; 9:23; 28:1, 2, 15; and Bar 2:5 with Deut 28:13).

The prayer of the exiled community (2:6–3:8) is even more reminiscent of the book of Jeremiah: distinctive views and phraseology of the prophet are represented in almost every verse. In fact, some of the shared readings are peculiar to either the Hebrew or Greek text of Jeremiah (cf., for example, Bar 2:13, 19, 21, 23, 25, 32 with Jer 30:24; 36:7; 27:11–12; 7:34; 36:30; 43:11, respectively).

That the prayer was translated from Hebrew is suggested, a priori, by the simple fact that it is *a prayer.* But that surmise is confirmed by two mistranslations that can best be explained by presuming a Hebrew *Vorlage,* namely, in 2:23 the Greek translator read Heb *ḥwṣ* ("outside") instead of *ḥṣwt* ("the streets" [Tov 1975: 23, n. i]); and *mēt* ("the dead") for *mĕtê* ("men") in 3:4. In any event, the prayer is appropriate for an exilic community in Babylon, Egypt, or elsewhere.

But even more striking than parallels between the prayer and the book of Jeremiah is the close relationship between the prayer in Baruch and the one in Dan 9:4–19. The two prayers share a number of identical readings (e.g., Bar 1:15b, 21a; 2:1a, 7b, 10a, 17a and Dan 9:7b, 10a, 12a, 13b, 14 [last portion], 18b, respectively) as well as number of parallels which are closer to one another than either is to an older biblical source (e.g., Bar 1:15a, 18; 2:2, 8, 9, 10, 11, 13a, 19 are parallel to Dan 9:71a, 9c–10, 12c–13a, 13c, 14b, 10, 16b, 18, respectively).

Either one prayer is based upon the other, or both are based upon some common source such as a temple or synagogal liturgy. Most scholars, including Wambacq (1959a), Battistone (1968: 48–73), Gilbert (1972), Dancy (1972a: 171, 178–79), Tov (1976a: 27), and Goldstein (1979–80: 196–99), have argued that Baruch's prayer is based on Daniel's. Stoderl (1922) is almost alone in arguing for the reverse scenario. A handful of scholars, including Marshall (*HDB* 1: 251–54), Charles (1929: 227), Hartman and Di Lella (*Daniel* AB, 248–49), Moore (1977: 291–93), and Schürer (*HJP*² 3/2: 736) have maintained that both prayers are based upon a common source.

Those scholars defending the priority of Daniel's prayer rightly observe that Baruch's prayer is the longer (47%) and is more diffused and repetitious, and that in a number of parallel passages the reading in Daniel is closer to the older biblical source than is Baruch's (but proponents for the priority of Baruch's prayer point out other passages where Baruch's readings are closer than Daniel's). In any event, Daniel's prayer, which was probably not originally a part of the "final" form of Daniel but either an inclusion or a later interpolation (Pfeiffer 1949: 774; Moore 1974: 312–17; and Hartman and Di Lella 245–46; but see Jones 1968), is dated by most scholars to anywhere between the 4th century B.C. and ca. 164 B.C.

c. Poem in Praise of Wisdom (3:9–4:4). The poem differs in a variety of ways from what precedes it: it is poetry, not prose; it breathes a different spirit and has a different point of view, relying primarily on Wisdom Literature and virtually ignoring the prophetic perspective—including the book of Jeremiah. In its contents, emphases, and spirit, the sapiential poem is incongruous with the material that precedes and follows it, the only element of commonality among them being the exilic situation.

Whereas the prayer was a mosaic of biblical passages, the poem has the decided character of a logical argument, offering: (1) a statement of the problem, i.e., "Where can Wisdom be found?" (3:9–15); (2) a presentation of the evidence, first in negative terms (3:16–31) and then in positive (3:32–36); and (3) a conclusion, namely, Wisdom is the book of the commandments of God (4:2–4). In terms of both literary form and content, the poem is modeled after Job 28:12–22, 23–27. This identification of Wisdom with the Pentateuch is also found in Sir 24:8–23, esp. v 23:

> All this [i.e., Wisdom] is the book of the covenant of the Most High God, the law which Moses commanded us as an inheritance for the congregations of Jacob.

The Wisdom of Solomon, another intertestamental book, also figures prominently in the poem (cf. Bar 3:29 with Wis 9:4a; Bar 4:4 with Wis 9:18b; and, esp. Bar 3:38 with Wis 9:10, where King Solomon prays for Wisdom, saying: "Send her forth from the holy heavens, and from the throne of thy glory send her, that she may be with me and toil, and that I may learn what is pleasing to thee").

Little is said about Wisdom in 3:9–4:4 that is not also found in the sapiential literature of the biblical and extra-biblical periods. Baruch uses various synonyms for it, each with its own distinctive nuance or emphasis: "wisdom" (Gk *sophia* = Heb *ḥokmâ*); "prudence" (Gk *phronēsis* = Heb *bînâ*); "understanding" (Gk *sunesis* = Heb *tĕbûnâ*). On occasion, each word can represent all the others (e.g., *sophia* in v 23, *phronēsis* in v 28, and *sunesis* in v 23), although *sophia* seems to be the most popular and comprehensive term.

One verse *did* occasion great controversy (for all the Church Fathers involved, see Reusch 1853), especially during and after the Arian Controversy of the 4th century A.D., when Greek and Latin fathers viewed 3:37 ("Afterward she [i.e., Wisdom] appeared upon earth and lived among men") as a prediction of the Incarnation of Jesus Christ (cf. John 1:14). Regarded by 19th-century scholars like Kneucker (1879: 310–12) and Schürer (*HJP*[1] 2/3) as a Christian interpolation, which it may have been, 3:37—at least in its present context—clearly refers to Wisdom (cf. the "her" of v 36 and the "she" of v 37). Such an interpretation is also supported by Sir 24:10–12 and Wis 9:10; cf. also Prov 8:1–4, 31. On the identification of Wisdom with Torah, see G. F. Moore (1927, 1: 263–70), Ringgren (1947: 114–15, 139–41), and Battistone (1968: 189–95).

Although many scholars have maintained that Greek was the original language for Bar 3:9–4:4 (and 4:5–5:9), the majority have concluded that all of Baruch was originally in Hebrew (for a survey of scholarly opinion, see Burke 1982: 23–24). Virtually alone, Marshall (*HDB* 1: 253) argued for the poem having been originally in Aramaic, but Whitehouse (*APOT* 1: 571–72) refuted his argument point for point.

Though not as incontestable or numerous as in Bar 1:1–3:8, Hebraisms in 3:9–4:4 include "beasts of the earth" (3:16), "four-footed creatures" (3:32), and others (Burke 1982: 299–301). Then, too, in 3:18 where the Greek and Latin texts mention "silversmiths," which seems totally inappropriate, the Syriac has "who acquired silver," which suggests that the Hebrew *Vorlage* had *qōnê*, which can be translated either as "worked" or "acquired."

In his retroversion of the LXX of Baruch to Biblical Hebrew, Harwell (1915: 56–58) "found" an almost invariable 3 + 3 meter for the poem. But building upon more recent advances in biblical and intertestamental research, and especially upon our new knowledge growing out of the Dead Sea Scrolls of Qumran, Burke (1982: 65–133, 316–19) has demonstrated that the meter is by no means so rigidly uniform:

> Twenty-one of thirty-one bicola are 3 + 3, and the remainder 3 + 2, 2 + 2, or 4 + 3. There are also ten tricola of which five are 3 + 3 + 3 (other patterns represented are: 2 + 2 + 3, 2 + 2 + 2, 3 + 3 + 2, and 2 + 3 + 3) (Burke 1982: 319).

While one may quarrel with this or that reconstruction of Burke, he has clearly demonstrated that Harwell was guilty of putting Baruch in a Procrustean bed, in this case, an invariable 3 + 3.

Serious efforts to retrovert the entire LXX text of Baruch into Biblical Hebrew were undertaken by Kneucker (1879) and then by Harwell (1915) while, more recently, Bar 1:3–3:8 has been done by Tov (1975; 1976[2]) and 3:9–5:9 by Burke (1982). The Hebrew translation by Kahana (1956) represents just that, a modern translation of the LXX and not an effort to reconstruct the ancient Hebrew text.

The poem's strong affinities with concepts and phrases characteristic of such later Jewish literature as Sirach and the Wisdom of Solomon suggest as the date for its composition either the 2d or 1st century B.C., which is also a time compatible with Bar 3:10–11, where the Diaspora is depicted as being of long-standing duration. (Needless to say, Bar 3:10–11 contradicts the introduction, esp. 1:11–12, where the exile has just begun.) Where the poem was written is unknown, although a presumed Hebrew *Vorlage* argues for a Palestinian provenance. Certainly nothing in the poem's content rules that out.

d. Psalm of Encouragement and Hope (4:5–5:9). The psalm is a dramatic rehearsal of the past and a prediction of the future. Its message, which is addressed first to Jerusalem's exiled children (4:5–29) and then to Mother Jerusalem herself (4:30–5:9), is a mosaic of phrases and images from Deutero-Isaiah (cf. Bar 4:8, 12, 20, 24, 30, 35, 37; 5:1, 2, 5, 7 with Isa 54:1–6; 49:21; 52:1; 60:1–3 of LXX; 62:2, 4; 13:19–21; 43:5; 52:1; 60:10; 51:17 [kai 60:4]; 40:4–5a, respectively).

But even more striking is the similarity of Bar 4:36–5:9 to *Psalms of Solomon* 11, a pseudepigraphic work (dating to ca. 70–45 B.C.) not to be confused with the canonical book of Psalms (Wright, *OTP* 2: 640–41). Often regarded as a work of the Pharisees (so Ryle and James 1891; Schüpphaus 1977), the *Psalms of Solomon* has also been identified as Essene in origin by Eissfeldt (1965: 610–13) and Dupont-Sommer (1962: 296). But Wright (*OTP* 2: 641–42) wisely argues against adopting either label.

The universal God of the wisdom poem is now once more Yahweh, the personal God of Israel who is concerned for his chosen people of the covenant. Yet oddly enough, the psalm never uses Israel's personal name for God, Yahweh (Gk *ho kurios*). Rather, he is referred to as "God" (Gk *theos* [4:7, 12]), "the God" (*ho theos* [passim]), or "the Holy One" (Gk *ho hagios* [4:22, 37; 5:5]). The psalm does, however, have a new name for the Deity, one not used in 1:1–4:4, namely, "the Everlasting" (Gk *ho aiōnios* [4:10, 14, 20, 22, 24, 35; 5:2]). This curious absence of the name "Yahweh," plus the appearance of the new divine appellation, suggests that the Greek translator of the Hebrew poem preferred *ho aiōnios* as his stock poetic translation for the Tetragrammaton, *YHWH* (Burke 1982: 164–66).

That the psalm had a Hebrew *Vorlage* is more hotly contested than is the comparable claim for any other section of Baruch. Marshall (*HDB* 1: 251–54), Whitehouse (*APOT* 1: 569–95), Wambacq (1966: 575), and others have argued that it was originally composed in Greek. But most scholars, including Kneucher, Harwell, Pfeiffer, and Burke, have rightly maintained that all, or at least most (so

Moore 1977: 314–16), of the psalm was originally in Hebrew. Granted, blatant Hebraisms or mistranslations presupposing a Hebrew *Vorlage* are conspicuously absent from this section (for less obvious but probable ones, see Burke 1982: 302–10), thanks to the skills of its Greek translation/revisor (see below). Building upon the work of Harwell (1915: 58–59) who reconstructed a rigidly uniform series of *Qinah,* or Lament Meter (3 + 2 bicola), Burke (1982: 135–297) retroverted a more defensible pattern for the psalm, namely:

> Of a total of forty-eight bicola, approximately a third . . . are 3 + 2, another third . . . are 2 + 2, and yet another third . . . are 3 + 3. The seventeen tricola reveal an even greater variety. The most common patterns are 3 + 3 + 3 (five) and 2 + 2 + 3 (four) (p. 320).

The relative "ease" with which Burke was able to reconstruct numerous semantic, syntactic, and metrical features of biblical Hebrew while still being reasonably faithful to his Greek text also argues for the existence of a Hebrew *Vorlage.*

The number of stanzas in the psalm is much debated by scholars, some arguing for seven (Thackeray 1929: 102–3; Rost 1976: 71), eight (Fitzgerald 1968: 618), or by counting instances of the Isaianic feature of an imperative plus a vocative for beginning a stanza, eleven (Burke 1982: 5).

The striking similarity between Bar 4:36–5:9 and the pseudepigraphical *Ps. Sol.* 11:3–8 cannot be coincidental inasmuch as their parallels even preserve their relative verse sequence (i.e., Bar 5:5, 7, 8 closely correspond to *Ps. Sol.* 11:3, 5, 6–7, respectively). Either Bar 4:36–5:9 is dependent upon *Psalms of Solomon* 11 (so Ryle and James 1891: lxxii–lxxvii, 100–3 and most subsequent scholars, including Goldstein 1979–80: 191–92 and Wright, *OTP* 2: 647–48); or the reverse is true (Pesch 1955; Burke 1982: 30); or the two psalms are dependent upon an unpreserved common source, possibly a synagogal liturgy (Kneucker 1879: 43–44; Charles, *APOT* 1: 573–74 [Editor's Note]; Pfeiffer 1949: 422; Gelin 1959: 286). Schürer (*HJP*² 3/2: 736–37) finds the question of who influenced whom as unclear.

The relationship of Bar 4:36–59 to *Psalms of Solomon* 11 is of crucial importance for establishing not only the upper and lower dates for the composition of the psalm itself (i.e., if the psalm is based on *Psalms of Solomon* 11, then it cannot be older than the *Psalms of Solomon*) but also for the entire book, since many scholars regard Bar 4:5–5:9, along with the introduction (1:1–14), as the most recent section of the entire book.

Unfortunately, little in Bar 4:36–5:9 can be identified with a specific historical event or time. For instance, Kneucker's view that "fire from the Everlasting" (4:35) was an allusion to the eruption of Mount Vesuvius in A.D. 79, in which Pompeii was destroyed, exceeds both the evidence and credibility. And Bar 4:15–16, which ostensibly describes the Babylonians (cf. Deut 28:49–50; Jer 5:15), probably, refers to either the Romans or, more likely, the Seleucids (see below).

3. The Book as a Whole. a. Original Language. Apart from an ancient and puzzling allusion to the use of Baruch in synagogal services (Thackeray 1923: 107–11), there is no external evidence of the book ever having existed in Hebrew. No trace of it has been found yet at Qumran (cf. Tov 1976b: 131, n. 1), albeit the Greek version of the Epistle of Jeremiah has been found there (see below). Neither Origen (185?–?254) nor Jerome (340?–420) knew of an extant Hebrew copy.

Thus, in spite of internal evidence of a Semitic *Vorlage* in each of the four major sections of Baruch, many scholars, past and present, have maintained that at least part, and probably even half, of the book (notably 3:9–5:9) was originally composed in Greek (Schürer, *HJP*² 3/2: 735 would leave open the possibility of a Greek *Vorlage* for 3:9–5:9). Their principal rationale is that: (1) no Hebrew text is extant; (2) there are more Hebraisms in Bar 1:1–3:8 than in 3:9–5:9; and (3) there are some striking differences in translation between the two major parts (Pfeiffer 1949: 412–13).

As for the last point, since 1903 many students of Baruch have subscribed to the views of Thackeray (1903: 245–66), to wit, just as the LXX of Jeremiah had two different Greek translators (Jer *alpha,* who was responsible for translating Jeremiah 1–28; and Jer *beta,* who did Jeremiah 29–51 [Jer *gamma* rendered Jeremiah 52]), so also did Baruch. Moreover, it was Jer *beta* who also translated Bar 1:1–3:8.

Thackeray's theory inevitably raised other questions about Bar 3:9–5:9, namely: Are the pronounced differences in content and style in the two halves of Baruch just a matter of the different skills of their respective translators? Did, perhaps, the second half of Baruch not exist at the time? Or worse, maybe there never was a Semitic text to translate, i.e., maybe Bar 3:9–5:9 had originally been composed in Greek.

Recently, Tov (1976b) has challenged Thackeray's thesis, arguing that both the similarities *and* the differences in the Greek between Jeremiah 1–28 and 29–52 can best be explained by postulating that the Old Greek of Jeremiah and Baruch has survived only in Jeremiah 1–28; and that Jeremiah 29–52 and Bar 1:1–3:8 represent a *revision* (not a translation) of the Old Greek. Uncertain as to exactly why this odd mixture of texts came about (but see pp. 162–63), Tov (1975: 7; 1976b: 126) is even more uncertain whether 3:9–5:9 was composed originally in Hebrew or Greek.

Unconvinced by Tov's findings, Goldstein (1979–80: 188–89) rightly maintains that no test can be devised that can prove whether the Greek translator of Bar 1:1–3:8 was identical to the translator of Jeremiah 29–52 or, rather, skillfully imitated him. Unfortunately, Goldstein's own solution to the differences between the Greek of the two halves of Baruch (1979–80: 188–89) is less persuasive, namely:

> The Greek translator of Baruch noticed how the Hebrew author changed style and content and followed scriptural models, Jeremiah for 1:1–3:8 and Job and Isaiah for 3:9–5:9. In rendering the respective sections, the translator of Baruch then would naturally imitate the existing translations of Jeremiah or of Job and Isaiah.

In sum, while differences in style and content between the major halves of Baruch do indeed pose problems that admit no easy solution, it is probable that all (or nearly all; Moore 1977: 314–15 would omit 5:5–9) of Baruch was originally in Hebrew.

b. Purpose. A composite of the works of several authors, the book consists of originally independent works of uneven quality, bound together only by their having the same assumed historical background, i.e., the exile. Not only does the book have little progression or thread of argument, but several of its sections actually contradict one another (cf. 1:11–12 with 4:15, 21, 33–35; and 1:13c with 4:36–54). Evidently the book's author was not at all concerned with presenting a consistent and accurate chronicle of historical events in the modern sense of the word (after all, his Jewish readers knew full well that the expectations of Jeremiah and Deutero-Isaiah concerning the Ingathering of the Diaspora had not yet taken place). Rather, he was interested in edifying and interpreting past events for the present generation (Burke 1982: 3–4).

Two scholars have constructed very detailed arguments for the book's purpose. Taking as his clue the assertion in the *Constitutions of the Holy Apostles* 5:20 (ca. 380) that the Jews "even now on the tenth day of the month Gorpiaeus, when they assemble together, read the Lamentations of Jeremiah . . . and Baruch in whom it is written, 'This is our God; no other can compare with him . . . appeared on earth and lived among man' " [Bar 3:38, 38], Thackeray (1923: 107–111) constructed an elaborate argument for Baruch's being part of the prescribed synagogal liturgy for the Jewish New Year still observed among 6th-century A.D. Jews in the area of Edessa, Turkey. (For a critical evaluation of Thackeray's argument, see Sundberg 1958: 77).

According to Goldstein (1979–80), the text of Bar 1:1–14, in spite of "minor gaps and corruptions" (pp. 180–81), reflects the situation of Judean Jews under Seleucid rule in the winter or early spring of 163 B.C. More specifically, "Nebuchadnezzar" of vv 9, 11–12 represents the infamous Antiochus IV Epiphanes (175–164 B.C.), who sacked Jerusalem and committed the Abomination of Desolation in 167 B.C.; "Belshazzar" of vv 11–12 stand for Epiphanes' son and successor, Antiochus V (164–162 B.C.); and the high priest "Jehoiakim" of v 7 is really Alcimus. The "fifth year" alluded to in v 2 refers to the 5th year after Antiochus IV had burned and sacked Jerusalem. But now that the Temple of Jerusalem had been purified by Judas Maccabaeus, the author of Baruch was appealing to Judean Jews to acknowledge their past sins (1:15–3:8) and to accept the authority of Antiochus V (1:11–12), meanwhile obeying God's Wisdom, the Law (3:9–4:4), and trusting God in his own good time and way to judge the Seleucids and to bring about the Ingathering (4:5–5:9). Thus, the book of Baruch was propaganda for those pious Jews who were opposed to the continuing military struggles of Judas Maccabaeus.

Goldstein's hypothesis certainly has merit, for it does answer a number of questions. There are problems, however. Difficult though life may have been for Judean Jews ca. 164–163 B.C., they were *not* in exile, although the one unifying thread running throughout the book of Baruch is the exilic experience. Then, too, while the real Nebuchadnezzar (605–562 B.C.) was alive five years after the destruction of Jerusalem, Antiochus IV was not (Nickelsburg 1981: 153, n. 44).

c. Theology of the Book. A mosaic of older biblical passages, Baruch has virtually no new or original religious ideas. Even worse, because of its composite authorship, the book contains almost antithetical attitudes toward the Deity, the poem (3:9–4:4) emphasizing God's transcendence and omnipotence, the other sections his personal and anthropomorphic character. Then, too, there is the striking contrast between the sapiential stance of 3:9–4:4 versus the prophetic one everywhere else. Even as sympathetic a critic as Burke (1982: 33–35) is content simply to describe the book's theology without offering a single word of praise about its doctrine of God, its doctrine of sin and retribution, or its themes of devotion to the Law and hope for national salvation. The simple fact is that the book's religious ideas had already been better expressed elsewhere in the Bible.

d. Date and Place of Composition. The date of the book's final composition, as well as that of each of its four sections (for a survey of scholarly opinion, see Burke 1982: 26–28), is more debated by scholars than is either its authorship or original language, although the latter two items are obviously related to the former.

Dates proposed by scholars for the book's completion range from the period of the exile down until after A.D. 70, with such Baruch scholars as Kneucker, Marshall, Thackeray, and Whitehouse opting for the latest date, in part, because of the relationship between Bar 4:36–5:9 and *Psalms of Solomon* 11.

Nonetheless, the majority of experts have assigned all (or nearly all) of the book to ca. 200–60 B.C. Reasons for this include the following: the book's dependency upon such later biblical works as (Deutero-)Isaiah, Daniel (esp. chap. 9), Job, and Sirach (esp. chap. 24); the close relationship of Bar 4:36–5:9 to *Psalms of Solomon* 11; the "datelessness" of the various sections; the Diaspora is depicted as a situation of long standing (3:10); and the onetime "canonicity" of Bar 1:1–3:8 among Jews (i.e., the translator-recensionist Jer *beta* treated it as being on a par with Jeremiah 29–50). Finally, the docile and conciliatory attitude recommended toward "Nebuchadnezzar" and "Belshazzar" suggests a date between the early Maccabean period and precludes a date after A.D. 70 (for additional reasons in support of the range from 180–100 B.C., see Burke 1982: 28–32).

Albeit an argument from silence, certain "omissions" or absences in the book also argue for the same time span. For example, the concept of Sheol (2:17; 3:11, 19) has yet to be replaced by the concept of resurrection (so Charles 1910: 454, although Oesterley 1914: 499–502 viewed 2:17 as a Sadducee correction of a Pharisee interpolation!). Then, too, messianism, angelology, and eschatology, which are doctrines more common in the later apocryphal and pseudepigraphic works, are also missing.

The *terminus ad quem* for the entire book is A.D. 177, that being when Athenagoras quoted Bar 3:34 in his *Supplications for the Christians* 9. Actually, however, the probability that the translator/recensionist responsible for doing Jeremiah 29–50 also did Bar 1:11–3:8 fixes the date of the latter to that of the former, namely, ca. the 2d century B.C. (Bright, *Jeremiah* AB, cxxii–xxiv).

If the book was composed originally in Hebrew rather than in Greek or Aramaic, then neither the western nor eastern Diaspora, but Palestine was its place of composition (see Schürer *HJP*[2] 3/2: 735).

e. Literary Character. Judging the literary quality of a book known only in translation is admittedly risky. But such judgments are inevitably made. Keerl, as quoted by Gifford (1888a: 248), was perhaps too harsh:

> In comparing the contents of [Baruch's book with those of older prophets], there comes over one a feeling as if some incompetent scribbler had wished to do an exercise in the language and style of the prophets; it reminds one of the rhetorical practice of a feeble schoolboy, who composes an opusculum out of all sorts of passages.

While by no means effusive in his praise, Burke (1982: 7) was probably closer to the truth when he said of the presumed Hebrew *Vorlage* which he had tried to reconstruct:

> It is still not without its own measure of originality and skill. . . . The poetry, while equally derivative, is nonetheless from a technical and stylistic point of view well-conceived and constructed. . . . And, although each poem represents a genre entirely different from the other, the result is in each case a composition that is technically competent.

4. Canonical Status. Well-written or not, Baruch never gained canonical status among the Jews. It was not part of the Palestinian canon as fixed by the Council of Jamnia, ca. A.D. 90. (The decisions of the Pharisaic schools there were "unofficial" and only gradually did their decisions become the accepted positions throughout Judaism.) Perhaps Baruch was denied canonical status by the Jamnian Jews because they recognized its pseudepigraphic character, although some other pseudepigraphic works were ultimately accepted into the Jewish canon after long, hard debate, notably, Esther and Ecclesiastes. More likely, the Jews at Jamnia recognized Baruch's literary and theological inadequacies.

As for the Christians, apart from the so-called "Incarnation" passage (3:36–38), the book was generally ignored. Usually viewed by Church Fathers as simply an adjunct or supplement to Jeremiah rather than a separate book, Baruch was expressly mentioned as being canonical by Athanasius (295–373), Cyril of Jerusalem (d. 386), Epiphanius (315–403), and Nicephorous (758?–829). For details and titles, see Schürer, *HJP*[2] 3/2: 740–41.

In enumerating the canonical books *by name,* none of the Latin fathers mention Baruch, but that may only mean that they thought of it as part of Jeremiah. In any case, the book ultimately found its way into the Vulgate (see below), and at the Council of Trent in 1546 was recognized by the Roman Catholic Church as part of its deuterocanon. Meanwhile, Luther and other Protestants either relegated it, along with the rest of the Apocrypha, to a lesser place (i.e., between or after the OT and NT) or omitted it altogether.

5. Ancient Versions. a. The LXX. The most recent scientific text of Baruch is the one in the Göttingen Septuagint (Ziegler 1976), an eclectic Greek text based upon four uncials (LXX^{ABQV}; unfortunately *Sinaiticus* ends before coming to Baruch) and thirty-four minuscules, plus relevant readings from other ancient versions (see below). Ziegler's reconstructed text most resembles *Vaticanus.* A brief description in English of all the manuscripts used by Ziegler may be found in Burke 1982: 7–17.

b. Syriac Translations. Like other biblical and apocryphal books, Baruch is extant in two Syriac translations: the Syriac Version (or Peshitta) and the Syro-Hexaplar, the latter being a Syriac translation of the fifth column of Origen's Hexaplar made by Paul of Tella in A.D. 616–17. See HEXAPLA OF ORIGEN; SYRO-HEXAPLA; VERSIONS, ANCIENT (SYRIAC).

Whether the Syriac version of Baruch is to be identified with the Peshitta (i.e., a 1st-century Syriac version ordinarily based upon the Hebrew Bible) has been much debated by scholars. Kneucker (1879: 163–73) and Harwell (1915: 10–28), for instance, maintained that the Syriac Baruch was based upon the Greek while Whitehouse (*APOT* 1: 577–79), Pfeiffer (1949: 423), and Burke (1982: 12–14) argued for a Semitic text, albeit one "corrected" by the Greek. In his reconstruction of Baruch, Burke (1982: 13–14, 308–10) depends upon a number of Syriac passages that depart from the LXX tradition and reflect a Hebrew *Vorlage.*

c. Latin Translations. Even though scholars have much debated the origins and relative merits of the Old Latin texts/versions of Baruch, there is little doubt that the *Vetus Latina* (the Old Latin) and the Vulgate are both based upon the Greek (so Harwell 1915: 29–51; Ziegler 1957: 20; and Burke 1982: 14–15). Jerome did not even bother to make a fresh translation of Baruch. In fact, *Amiatinus,* the oldest known manuscript of the Vulgate, contains neither Baruch nor the Epistle of Jeremiah. The most recent scientific edition of the Latin is by Weber (1969).

d. Other Ancient Versions. The other ancient versions of Baruch are all based upon the Greek. According to Ziegler (1957: 41–93), the Coptic and the Ethiopic most resemble LXX^{BS}, while the Arabic is more like LXX^{A}; and the Armenian is part of the Hexaplaric family. Because all of these versions are based upon texts which are either very late, mixed, fragmentary, or unscientific, their readings must be used with great care.

B. The Epistle of Jeremiah

The title is totally misleading, for this short book of seventy-three verses is neither a letter nor was it written by the prophet Jeremiah. On these two points virtually all modern scholars agree. The "epistle" is actually a satire, or harangue, against idols and idolatry. Apart from its "salutation" in vv 2–7, it has none of the features of a letter, not even a closing. (English translations frequently differ in their versification, depending on whether or not they include the superscription.)

1. Contents. The book consists of ten strophes, or stanzas, of unequal length, each one (with the exception of the first and the last) ending with a slight variation of essentially the same refrain, namely:

> Therefore they evidently are not gods; so do not fear them (v 16).

There is no perceptible progression of thought or argument in the poem, all of which creates for the reader the impression of "sameness," along with its lamentable corollary, boredom.

2. Author. To be sure, a number of phrases and images in the epistle do bear a strong resemblance to certain ones in the book of Jeremiah, notably, Jer 10:2–15. Moreover, since the prophet Jeremiah did, in fact, write at least one letter to the Jewish exiles once they were in Babylon (cf. Jer 29:1–23), there is no reason why he could not have written one *before* they left (cf. v 1).

But in its ideas, imagery, and phraseology the epistle depends primarily upon biblical passages which originated long after the prophet Jeremiah, namely, Isa 44:9–20, 46:5–7; Pss 115:3–8; 135:6–7, 15–17; and Deut 4:27–28. Then, too, in terms of literary quality, as well as religious depth and sensitivity, the epistle is, by common consent, decidedly inferior to genuine Jeremianic materials.

3. Purpose and Genre. Ostensibly the epistle was designed to prevent Jews from worshiping false gods in Babylon and, by implication, anywhere else as well (cf. vv 29–30, where the idea of priestesses is especially abhorrent). Pfeiffer's suggestion (1949: 432) that it was also written to reassure Gentiles that Jews were not a godless or god-despising people seems unlikely, even though later on Jews would be so accused by such anti-Semitic writers as Posidonius (130?–50 B.C.) and Apollonius Molon (fl. ca. 70 B.C.).

Given the predominance of Babylonian elements (e.g., the mention of the god Bel [i.e., Marduk] in v 41; the rite of sacred prostitution in v 43; the care and feeding of the idols in vv 11–13, 26–29, 33, 58, 72), the epistle may have been a veiled attack on a Tammuz-type cult (cf. v 32) such as flourished in Jeremiah's day (cf. Ezek 8:14), and presumably, later as well. Used as a *Haftorah* (i.e., a prescribed synagogal reading from the prophets) for the Jewish fast on the 17th of Tammuz (Thackeray 1927: 57–60), the epistle may also have been part of a synagogal pericope for the 9th of Ab and following (Thackeray 1923: 107–11).

In all likelihood, the epistle was inspired by one of the more puzzling phenomena in the book of Jeremiah, namely, its sole Aramaic verse:

> Thus shall you say to them: "The gods who did not make the heavens and the earth shall perish from the earth and from under the heavens" (Jer 10:11).

This Aramaic verse, supported and illuminated by the Hebrew of Jer 10:2–15, inspired the author of the epistle to expand upon it (so Torrey 1945: 64–65). In sum, the epistle is best understood for what it obviously is: an idol parody (on this particular literary genre, see Roth 1975).

4. Original Language. A comparison of the Greek texts of the epistle and the relevant OT passages shows that the author of the epistle was primarily dependent upon the Hebrew Bible rather than upon its Greek translation. For example, v 70 says that idols are "like a scarecrow in a cucumber bed," which is clearly based on Jer 10:5 ("Their idols are like scarecrows in a cucumber field"), a clause not found in the LXX of Jeremiah.

A Hebrew *Vorlage* best explains three egregious mistranslations in the epistle. As Ball long ago noted (*APOT* 1: 601), "food" in v 12 (i.e., idols "cannot save themselves from rust and food") makes no sense; obviously the unpointed Hebrew *Vorlage* had *mʾkl,* which can mean either "food" (so Gen 6:21) or "moth/devourer" (Mal 3:11; Job 13:28). Verse 27 says that "purple and marble rot" upon the idols, which also makes no sense. Obviously the translator had before him the Hebrew word, *šēš,* which can be translated as either "marble" (Esth 1:6; Cant 5:15) or "fine linen" (Exod 25:4): the Greek translator simply chose the wrong meaning. Verse 54 ("for [the idols] have no power; they are like crows between heaven and earth") probably represents a misreading of the Hebrew, inasmuch as the wily crow is anything but helpless. Thus, Ball (APOT 1: 607), taking his clue from the Syriac's "ravens," suggested that the Greek translator erroneously read the Heb *kʿbym* ("like the clouds") as *kʿrbym,* "like the ravens."

That the epistle had an Aramaic *Vorlage* was argued by Torrey (1945: 64–65), who viewed the book as inspired by Jer 10:11, which is in Aramaic. (Jer 10:11 did later inspire the translator of the Targum on Jeremiah to add an Aramaic epistle to it [Thackeray 1927: 591]). Torrey (1945: 66) saw indisputable proof that the epistle was composed in Aramaic by the fact that Aram *ʿl ʾgrʾ* can be read either as "on the roof" (so v 11 of the KJV ["and even give some of it to the harlots on the roof"]) or "for hire." Torrey may be correct, although this was the only "Aramaic" reading he offered in support of his thesis); but the epistle's "on the roof" certainly makes good sense (cf. Herodotus, *Hist.* 1: 181), especially since the Greek word here, *stegos,* means "brothel" in late Greek (LSG, 1636).

5. Literary Merit. Unfortunately, the epistle's literary merit must be judged only on the basis of its Greek translation which, as we have already seen, contains some egregiously bad translation errors. In its general structure, the epistle is not unlike Psalms 42–43 and 107, with their recurring refrains and strophes of varying lengths. Evidently the ordering principle of the epistle's stanzas is that of catchwords (e.g., women in 27/29; deceit 44/47; king 51/53; to deliver 54/57; reproach 72/73) and "catchthoughts" (e.g., to blacken/to wipe off 21/24; blind/dumb 37/41; to do good/to bless 64/66 [Roth 1975:40]). The most persistent argument in the book is a negative one, i.e., what the gods cannot do (Nickelsburg 1981: 36–37).

Apart from a not infrequent uncertainty as to the antecedents of its pronouns, the text is intelligible enough; but its images, analogies, and comparison are rarely new and never memorable. After the first three or four stanzas there is no further development or progression of thought; rather, the same old observations and arguments are rehashed. Nickelsburg (1981: 36) offered a left-handed compliment when he wrote:

> The uniqueness of the Epistle of Jeremiah lies not in the types of arguments presented . . . but in the presistence with which the author pursues his point by means of repetition and rhetorical devices which make that point in a variety of ways.

Dancy (1972b: 199) was perhaps more charitable than accurate when he said:

> But it does not follow that the Letter is haphazard in composition. There is visible in most of it a continuous thread, but it is a thread of images, not of arguments. . . . But this Letter is not so much an argument as a satire, and satire has always relied less on logical structure than on vivid reporting.

Both form and substance contribute to a book's literary stature, and sometimes a weakness in one can be compensated by the greater strength of the other. But in the case of the epistle, both form and substance are lacking. Torrey (1945: 65) may have been a bit harsh when he wrote: "it is a formless composition, rambling and repetitious," but the simple fact is that the epistle was little appreciated by the early church, or at least, it was rarely alluded to by the Church Fathers.

6. Canonicity. Though not a part of the Jewish canon as established by the Council of Jamnia (ca. A.D. 90), the epistle was read earlier by the Dead Sea Community at Qumran; for a tiny fragment of it, consisting of twenty-two Greek letters of v 44, was found there in Cave VII (Baillet, Milik, and de Vaux 1962: 27–30, 43; pl. 13). Its reading appears to agree with that of the LXX^{L} and Syriac, namely, "consider them to be gods or call them gods." More importantly, it attests to the epistle's existence in the 1st century B.C.

Among early Christians, the book was rarely alluded to, although it was used by Aristides of Athens (fl. ca. 130) and was quoted by Tertullian (160?–220), Cyprian of Carthage (d. 258), and Firmicus Maternus (4th cent.). Its canonicity was expressly affirmed by such Eastern fathers as Origen (135?–?254), Athanasius (295–373), Cyril of Jerusalem (d. 386), and Epiphanius (315–403), as well as by the Laodicene Canons (343–381). For details, see Moore 1977: 324–25.

As for Western fathers, while only Hilary (315–367) expressly said the epistle was canonical, other fathers certainly treated it as such, notably, Irenaeus of Lyons (140–?202). So far as we know, Jerome (340?–420) was the first to question the book's canonicity by name, calling it a pseudepigraphon (preface to his *Commentary on Jeremiah*). Jerome, of course, regarded as noncanonical every LXX book which had no parallel in the then-current Hebrew canon.

7. Date. The original version of the epistle must date to sometime between 540 B.C. (i.e., the earliest date for such Deutero-Isaianic passages as Isa 44:9–20 and 46:5–7) and the 1st century B.C., when 2 Macc 2:1–2, 4 alludes to it (see Marshall, *HDB* 2: 579; Goldstein, *1 Maccabees* AB, 36; Schürer, *HJP*² 3/2: 744) and a Greek copy of it dating to that same time existed at Qumran. Albeit an argument from silence, the epistle's failure to utilize the very effective satire and invective against idolatry in Wis 13:10–15:17 suggests that the aforementioned probably antedated the latter.

But even a date in the first third of the 2d century B.C. (which is the period most frequently suggested by scholars) is probably too late; otherwise, how can we explain v 3, where the author of the book predicts that the exiles in Babylon will remain there "up to seven generations" (i.e., ca. 317 B.C. [Moore 1977: 334–35]), after which God will bring them back in peace? Why would the author have given this "future" date if he was already writing at a time long after the predicted events should have occurred *and had not?* (But see *HJP*² 3/2: 744.) Moreover, nothing in the epistle precludes a date as early as the end of the 4th century B.C., a time when its message was especially relevant to the needs of both the eastern and western Diaspora, as well as Palestine itself, where the Hellenization process was making inroads into Judaism.

8. Place of Composition. Confusing the evidence for where the epistle was translated with where it was originally composed, 19th-century scholars like Fritzsche, Schürer (*HJP*¹ 2/3), and Marshall claimed an Egyptian provenance for it. But apart from a very cryptic mention of cats in v 22 (Lee 1968), there is no distinctive Egyptian religious element or practice mentioned in the epistle, not even animal worship, which had becomme so commonplace by the Ptolemaic period (323–30 B.C.). Nor is there any reference to specifically Greek rituals (Dancy 1972b: 198).

On the one hand, virtually everything the epistle says about idols, their priesthood, and their cult is completely compatible with Mesopotamian religion, in general, and with Babylonian in particular (Nauman 1913: 3–31). On the other hand, quintessential Babylonian practices such as divination, astrology, and extispicy go unmentioned, all of which suggests that the author of the epistle was criticizing Mesopotamian religion and its gods *from afar* (but see Artom 1935, who would place its composition in Babylonia ca. 400 B.C.). In sum, there is no reason to reject the claim of v 1 (i.e., that the epistle had a Palestinian provenance), although admittedly much later than the 597 B.C. implied in vv 1–2 (Moore 1977: 334).

9. Ancient Versions. Marshall's statement that "The slightly inflated style of the epistle is thoroughly Alexandrian. The fondness for assonance and for long compound words . . ." (*HDB* 1: 579) is an accurate yet too glowing a characterization. Rightly maintaining that neither the epistle's style nor logic would have appealed to members of the Alexandrine school of Egypt, Nauman (1913: 31–44, 49) has nonetheless established the epistle's *koine* character. A distinction must be made here between the now-lost Hebrew original and its extant Greek translation, the latter rightly characterized by Ball (*APOT* 1: 597) as "a piece so formless, so confused, so utterly destitute of the graces of style."

An excellent scientific edition of the text has been published by Ziegler (1976) in the Göttingen Septuagint, using 134 printed lines for his eclectic text (which is essentially LXX^{B}) and 352 lines for his *apparatus criticus,* where the readings of the various families of Greek manuscripts and the relevant variants of the ancient versions are presented.

The Old Latin, Vulgate, and Syro-Hexaplar are all very literal translations of the LXX, an additional phrase or clause being exceedingly rare (but see v 49 of the OL and Syr; v 52 of the Vg; and v 53 of the Syr). Omissions are also infrequent. The Arabic version is also quite faithful to the LXX, especially to *Alexandrinus.* Only the Syriac is somewhat free, being a bit more expansive and sometimes unintelligible.

Bibliography

Artom, E. 1935. L'origine, la data, et gli scopi dell' epistola di Geremia. *Annuario di Studi Ebraici* 1: 49–74.

Baillet, M., et al. 1962. Lettre de Jérémie (Pl. xxx). P. 143 in *Les 'Petites Grottes' de Qumrân.* DJD 3. Oxford.
Battistone, J. J. 1968. *An Examination of the Literary and Theological Background of the Wisdom Passages of the Book of Baruch.* Diss. Duke.
Bewer, J. A. 1942. The River Sud in the Book of Baruch. *JBL* 43: 226–27.
Burke, D. G. 1982. *The Poetry of Baruch: A Reconstruction and Analysis of the Original Hebrew Text of Baruch 3:9–5:9.* SBLSCS 10. Chico, CA.
Charles, R. H. 1910. Baruch. *EncBrit* (11th ed.) 5: 453–54.
———. 1929. *A Critical and Exegetical Commentary on the Book of Daniel.* Oxford.
Dancy, J. C. 1972a. The Book of Baruch. *The Shorter Books of the Apocrypha.* CBC. Ed. P. R. Ackroyd. Cambridge.
———. 1972b. A Letter of Jeremiah. *The Shorter Books of the Apocrypha.* CBD Ed. P. R. Ackroyd. Cambridge.
Dupont-Sommer, A. 1962. *The Essene Writings from Qumran.* Trans. G. Vermes. New York.
Eissfeldt, O. 1965. *The Old Testament: An Introduction.* Trans. P. R. Ackroyd. New York.
Fitzgerald, A. 1968. Baruch. *JBC* 1: 614–18.
Fritzsche, O. F. 1851a. Das Buch Baruch. *KEHAT* 1: 167–201.
———. 1851b. Der Brief des Jeremia. *KEHAT* 1: 203–20.
Gelin, A. 1959. *Le Livre de Baruch,* 2d ed. La Sainte Bible-Bible de Jérusalem 23. Paris.
Gifford, E. H. 1888a. Baruch. Pp. 213–86 of vol. 2 in *Apocrypha of the Speaker's Commentary* (= *ASC*), ed. H. Wace. London.
———. 1888b. The Epistle of Jeremy. *ASC* 2: 287–303.
Gilbert, M. 1972. La prière de Daniel, Dn 9, 4–19. *RTL* 3: 284–310.
Goettsberger, J. 1928. *Einleitung in das Alte Testament.* Freiburg.
Goldstein, J. A. 1979–80. The Apocryphal Book of I Baruch. *Jubilee Volume of the American Academy for Jewish Research Proceedings,* 46–47: 179–99.
Gunneweg, A. H. J. 1975. *Das Buch Baruch.* JSHRZ 3/2. Gütersloh.
Haenchen, E. 1965. Das Buch Baruch. Pp. 299–334 in *Gott und Mensch,* ed. E. Haenchen. Tübingen.
Harris, J. R. 1889. *The Rest of the Words of Baruch: A Christian Apocalypse of the Year 136 A.D.* London.
Harwell, R. R. 1915. *The Principal Versions of Baruch.* New Haven.
Heinisch, P. 1928. Zur Entstehung des Buches Baruch. *TG* 20: 696–710.
Hoberg, G. H. 1902. *Die älteste lateinsiche Übersetzung des Buches Baruch,* 2d ed. Freiburg.
Jones, E. W. 1968. The Prayer in Daniel ix. *VT* 18: 488–93.
Kahana, A. 1956. *Hassephārîm Haḥîṣônîm.* 2d ed. 2 vols. Tel Aviv (in Hebrew).
Kalt, E. 1932. *Das Buch Baruch.* HSAT 7/4. Bonn.
Kasser, R. 1964. *Papyrus Bodmer XXII.* Geneva.
Kneucker, J. J. 1879. *Das Buch Baruch.* Leipzig.
Lee, G. M. 1968. Apocryphal Cats: Baruch 6:21. *VT* 18: 488–93.
Mack, B. L., and Murphy, R. E. 1986. Wisdom Literature. Pp. 377–78 in *Early Judaism and Its Modern Interpreters,* ed. R. A. Kraft and G. W. E. Nickelsburg. Atlanta.
Martin, R. A. S. 1977. *Syntactical and Critical Concordance to the Greek Text of Baruch and the Epistle of Jeremiah.* The Computer Bible 12. Wooster, OH.
Mayer, R. 1967. *Einleitung in das Alte Testament.* Munich.
Metzger, B. 1957. *An Introduction to the Apocrypha.* Oxford.
Moore, C. A. 1974. Toward the Dating of the Book of Baruch. *CBQ* 36: 312–20.
———. 1977. *Daniel, Esther and Jeremiah: The Additions.* AB 44. Garden City, NY.
Moore, G. F. 1927. *Judaism in the First Centuries of the Christian Era.* 3 vols. Cambridge, MA.
Nauman, W. 1913. Untersuchungen über den apokryphen Jeremiasbrief. *BZAW* 25: 1–53.
Nickelsburg, G. W. E. 1981. *Jewish Literature between the Bible and the Mishnah.* Philadelphia.
Nickelsburg, G. W. E., and Stone, M. E. 1983. *Faith and Piety in Early Judaism.* Philadelphia.
Oesterley, W. O. E. 1914. *The Books of the Apocrypha.* New York.
———. 1935. *An Introduction to the Books of the Apocrypha.* New York.
Penna, A. 1956. Baruch. *La Sacra Bibbia* 11. Turin and Rome.
Pesch, W. 1955. Die Abhängigkeit des 11. salomonischen Psalms vom letzten Kapitel des Buches Baruch. *ZAW* 67: 251–63.
Pfeiffer, R. H. 1949. *History of NT Times.* New York.
Reusch, F. H. 1853. *Erklärung des Buches Baruch.* Freiburg.
Ringgren, H. 1947. *Word and Wisdom.* Lund.
Rost, L. 1976. *Judaism Outside the Hebrew Canon.* Trans. D. E. Green. Nashville.
Roth, W. M. W. 1975. For Life, He Appeals to Death (Wisd 13:18): A Study of Old Testament Idol Parodies. *CBQ* 37: 21–47.
Ryle, H. E. and James, R. M. 1891. *Psalms of the Pharisees, Commonly Called the Psalms of Solomon.* Cambridge.
Schüpphaus, J. 1977. *Die Psalmen Salomos.* ALGHJ 7. Leiden.
Stoderl, W. 1922. *Zur Echtsheitsfrage von Baruch 1–3, 8.* Münster.
Sundberg, A. 1958. *The OT of the Early Church.* HTS 20. Cambridge, MA.
Swete, H. B. 1984. Baruch; Epistle of Jeremiah. *The OT in Greek According to the Septuagint* 3. Cambridge.
Thackeray, H. St.J. 1903. Notes and Studies: The Greek Translators of Jeremiah. *JTS* 4: 245–66.
———. 1923. *The Septuagint and Jewish Worship.* 2d ed. Oxford.
———. 1927. *Some Aspects of the Greek OT.* London.
———. 1929. Baruch. *A New Commentary on Holy Scripture,* ed. C. G. Gore et al. New York.
Torrey, C. C. 1945. *The Apocryphal Literature.* New Haven.
Tov, E. 1975. *The Book of Baruch Also Called I Baruch.* SBLTT 8. Missoula, MT.
———. 1976a. The Relation between the Greek Versions of Baruch and Daniel. *Armenian and Biblical Studies,* ed. M. E. Stone. Jerusalem.
———. 1976b. *The Septuagint Translation of Jeremiah and Baruch.* HSM 8. Missoula, MT.
Vaux, R. de. 1956. Fouilles de Kirbet Qumrân. *RB* 63: 533–77.
Wambacq, B. N. 1957. *Jeremias, Klaagliederen, Baruch, Brief van Jeremias.* De Boeken van het Oude Testament. Roermond.
———. 1959a. Les prières de Baruch (i 15–11 19) et de Daniel (ix 5–19). *Biblica* 40: 463–75.
———. 1959b. L'unité litteraire de Baruch i–iii 8. *BETL* 12: 455–60.
———. 1966. L'unité de livre de Baruch. *Bib* 47: 574–76.
Weber, R. 1969. Baruch. Biblia Sacra: Iuxta Vulgatam Versionem 2. Stuttgart.
Ziegler, J. 1976. *Ieremias, Baruch, Threni, Epistula Ieremiae,* 2d ed. Göttingen. 1st ed. 1957.

CAREY A. MOORE

JEREMIAH, BOOK OF. The book of Jeremiah contains the legacy (Heb *dibrê* in 1:1 and 51:64 covers both "words" and "acts") of Jeremiah the prophet. The earliest record contained is of Jeremiah's boyhood call to be a prophet in the 13th year of King Josiah, i.e., 627 B.C. Jeremiah is last heard from in Egypt following the destruction of Jerusalem, i.e., sometime after 586 B.C. The collection of prophetic utterances, personal dialogues, autobiographical reports, and liturgical compositions, supplemented by a rich corpus of biographical and sermonic material written in another hand, combine to give us the most complete profile of any Hebrew prophet, also one of the best portraits of any known figure out of the ancient world. See JEREMIAH (PROPHET).

A. Canon
B. MT and LXX
C. Qumran Scrolls
D. Poetry and Prose
E. Literary Forms
F. Composition
G. Early Collections
   1. The Scroll of 605
   2. The First Edition of the Book of Jeremiah
   3. The Appendix on Kings and Prophets
   4. The Baruch Prose Collections
   5. The Book of Comfort
   6. The Foreign Nation Oracles
H. The Book of Books
I. Theology
   1. The Theology of the Prophet
   2. The Theology of the Book

A. Canon

Jeremiah is the largest of the three so-called Major Prophets in the Hebrew Scriptures. In our present canon the book is placed second—after Isaiah and before Ezekiel. The Talmud, however, preserves an older (pre-Masoretic) order in which Jeremiah is first immediately following Kings (*B. Bat.* 14b–15a). In the Talmud, notice is made of the duplicate accounts at the end of Kings and Jeremiah, and it assumes that both books derive from the same author, who is Jeremiah the prophet.

B. MT and LXX

The book has survived in two main versions from antiquity: the Hebrew Masoretic Text (MT) and the older Greek Septuagint (LXX). The two differ widely, more so than with any other Old Testament book. The Greek is one-eighth shorter than the Hebrew and after 25:13a the order of materials differs.

Because of the uncommonly large number of divergencies there has been considerable discussion over the years with regard to the transmission of the text, the basis of the Greek translation, and the question of which text is earlier and/or superior. This discussion has only intensified with the discovery of three partial Jeremiah manuscripts among the Dead Sea Scrolls of Cave 4. One is a short text and two are long. The long 4Q Jer[a] is dated ca. 200 B.C. and is proto-Masoretic. The short 4Q Jer[b] is dated in the 2d century B.C. and closely resembles the LXX, which, along with its *Vorlage* cannot be much older. (The LXX translation of the Prophets was done sometime between 250 and 150 B.C.; see SEPTUAGINT). The other long 4Q Jer[c] is no earlier than the 1st century B.C. (Cross).

The existence of a short Hebrew text of Jeremiah in the 2d century B.C. has given rise to the theory—now widely held—that the LXX translator or translators did not produce an abridgement but rather translated a Hebrew text of comparable length localized in Egypt where the translation was made. This Hebrew text is believed to have survived in comparative isolation from the proto-Masoretic text which originated in Babylon (Cross 1964). The high incidence of haplography in the Egyptian text results from an inactive history of transmission during which time omissions went undetected and uncorrected (Janzen 1967: 446–47). The proto-Masoretic text had a more active history of transmission and is therefore more developed, i.e., it contains more glosses and expansions. So on the whole it is more appropriate to speak about "additions" in the MT than about "omissions" in the LXX, even though, of course, important exceptions to the general rule do exist. One can be found in chap. 29 (LXX 36) where a rhetorical structure in the larger of two letters to the exiles argues for the originality of vv 16–20, which the LXX lacks (Lundbom 1975: 104–5).

Some MT additions are merely single words or phrases which provide embellishment but do not materially affect the sense, e.g., "thus says Yahweh" or "saith Yahweh"; "the prophet" attached to "Jeremiah" or "Hananiah" (28:5, 6, 10 [LXX 35:5, 6, 10]; etc.); "Nebuchadrezzar" (alt. "Nebuchadnezzar") where the LXX either does not mention the king or has only "King of Babylon" (21:2, 7; 22:25; 27:8, 20 [LXX 34:8, 20]; etc.); "Yahweh God of Israel" or "Yahweh of Hosts" where the LXX has only "Yahweh." Again there are exceptions, e.g., the LXX does name "Nebuchadnezzar" (24:1; 34:6 [MT 27:6]).

Certain additions in the MT do alter the message. In chap. 11, with its (exilic) addition of vv 7–8a,, the passage says that because previous generations were disobedient, Yahweh had no choice but to bring upon them the "words" (i.e., "curses") of the Deuteronomic covenant. In the LXX, where vv 7–8a are lacking, the passage says simply that the people did not heed Jeremiah's call for covenant obedience.

There are also passages which in the MT are duplicated but in the LXX are not, e.g., 6:13–15 = 8:10b–12 (Gk adds 8:10b–12); 30:10–11 = 46:27–28 (Gk adds the former in 37:10–11). Yet in some instances both duplicate in the same contexts: 10:12–16 = 51:15–19 [LXX 28:15–19]; 23:19–20 = 30:23–24 [LXX 37:23–24 with variations].

Occasionally one will find minor additions in the LXX, e.g., 2:28; 3:18; 9:13 [MT 9:14]; etc. Of a more substantive nature is the introduction of the term *pseudoprophētēs*, "false prophet," into the LXX, where it occurs a total of nine times (6:13; 33:7, 6, 11, 16 [MT 26:7, 8, 11, 16]; 34:9 [MT 27:9]; 35:1 [MT 28:1]; 36:1, 8 [MT 29:1, 8]). This term never appears in the MT.

Other variant LXX readings can be found in 10:5–10, where the shorter text with a different verse order is corroborated by 4Q Jer[b]; and in 45:9 where Ebed-melech faults King Zedekiah for leaving Jeremiah to die in the cistern, not "other men" as the MT has it (38:9).

The divergence after 25:13a results from different placements of the Oracles to Foreign Nations. In the Greek these come immediately after the words, "all that is written in this book" (13a), and fill up chaps. 25:14–31:44. This is roughly the center of the book. The location here has long been thought to be the earlier of the two (Eichhorn 1790: 120; deWette 1858). In the MT the foreign nation oracles are relocated to the end of the book, where they appear in chaps. 46–51. The original subscription to the collection remains in 25:13b [LXX 32:13]. The MT adds v 14 (not in the LXX), which makes a bridge to what follows. But it should be noted that the MT keeps the rest of the book intact. Baruch's expanded colophon—which closes the LXX book at 51:31:35—is chap. 45.

The foreign nation oracles are also in different sequences in the MT and LXX. The sequence in the LXX is Elam, Egypt, Babylon, Philistines, Edom, Ammon, Kedar, Damascus, and Moab. There is no apparent significance to this arrangement, except that Babylon is roughly in the center. The MT sequence is Egypt, Philistines, Moab, Ammon, Edom, Damascus, Kedar, Elam, and Babylon. Here we have geographical movement westward, beginning with Egypt and ending with Babylon. Babylon also occupies the climactic position at the end. Whether Babylon's position near the center in the LXX sequence is also meant to be climactic, one cannot say for certain.

The correspondence between the chaps. of the MT and those of the LXX are indicated in Table 1.

Table 1: Chapter Sequences of the Book of Jeremiah in the MT and LXX

MT	LXX
1–25:13a	1–25:13a
25:13b–38	32:13b–38*
26	33
27	34*
28	35
29	36*
30	37*
31	38
32	39
33	40*
34	41
35	42
36	43
37	44
38	45
39	46*
40	47
41	48
42	49
43	50
44	51:1–30
45	51:31–35
46:1–26 Egypt	26:2–25
46:27–28	26:27–28
47 Philistines	29
48 Moab	31*
49:1–6 Ammon	30:17–21/22
49:7–22 Edom	30:1–16
49:23–27 Damascus	30:29–33
49:28–33 Kedar	30:23–28
49:34–39 Elam	25:14–20**
50–51 Babylon	27–28**
52	52*
*vv lacking	**var. in order

The LXX translation of Jeremiah in its present state is not a unified piece. It has been observed, for example, that the same Hebrew words have different Greek equivalents in chaps. 1–28 and 29–51 (following the LXX numeration). This points to two different translators, and a third, perhaps, for chap. 52 (Thackeray 1902–3). The same data, however, have been used more recently to support a theory of one translator and a later reviser (Tov 1976; *IDBSup*, 807–11).

The quality and specific character of the LXX translation are variously assessed. S. R. Driver (1889: 333–36) concluded from a study of chaps. 2 and 7 that the translators rendered the Hebrew freely because they misread or misunderstood it. Therefore he took the LXX readings to be inferior to the Hebrew and judged the variations not to be recensional in character. Henry P. Smith (1887: 199) came to an opposite conclusion. He judged the LXX to be the superior text, and his sentiments have been echoed more recently by Cross and Janzen. Everyone, of course, recognizes that one's overall judgment must admit qualification when specific passages are analyzed. In poetry, for example, the LXX paraphrases when the Hebrew has a difficult expression, an archaic word form, or a syntactic structure that is not understood (8:18a; 9:2a—Eng 9:3a). But on the whole the LXX translation of Jeremiah is less "free" than, say, Job or Isaiah. Tov (1979: 75) believes the Jeremiah translator (he reckons only one) was generally faithful to his Hebrew *Vorlage,* and so far as the prose sections are concerned, his translation may even be considered literal.

The Greek contains scribal errors of the same sort as those found in the Hebrew text, e.g., homoioteleuton (34:5 [MT 27:5]; 46:4–13 [MT 39:4–13]) and homoioarcton (28:44b–49a [MT 51:44b–49a]). But in some cases it exposes MT errors, e.g., a wrong division of consonants in 23:33 (LXX presupposes *ʾtm hmśʾ* instead of MT's *ʾt mh mśʾ*). Here the LXX is supported by the Vulgate, and a reconstructed Hebrew reading was proposed already by J. D. Michaelis (1793: 200).

The LXX translates literally the Hebrew terms for God; it does not avoid anthropomorphisms as might be expected (Zlotowitz 1981: 183).

The relationship between the MT and the LXX is complex; therefore in textual criticism one must be cautious not to overgeneralize the tendentious qualities of each version.

C. Qumran Scrolls

Portions of at least four Jeremiah scrolls were among the finds in Caves 2 and 4 at Khirbet Qumran. In Cave 2 was one scroll (2QJer) consisting of fragments from chapters 42–44, 46–49 (Baillet 1962). These fragments consisted of 42:7–11, 14; 43:8–11; 44:1–3, 12–14; 46:27–47:7; 48:7, 25–39, 43–45; and 49:10 (?). On the basis of orthography, 2QJer is dated from "about the beginning of the Christian era, . . . from the last period of the occupation of the Qumran community" (Baillet 1962: 62). In the judgment of Tov this scroll was likely "copied by the Qumran covenanters, probably in Qumran itself" (Tov fc.a.). The scroll contains a number of small deviations from the MT, but it follows the MT order (where the foreign nation oracles come at the end of the book) and is judged on the whole to reflect the textual tradition of the MT.

The other Jeremiah scrolls come from Cave 4. 4QJer[a] is among the earliest of all the Qumran scrolls, dated on the basis of its orthography from 225–175 B.C., or roughly 200 B.C. (Cross *QBHT* 168, 202, 308; Freedman and Mathews 1985: 55). It is proto-Masoretic. 4QJer[a] first appeared in Janzen's 1963 Harvard dissertation on the text of Jeremiah, the results of which were published four years later (Janzen 1967). In 1973 most but not all of the fragments were published (without photos) when Janzen's dissertation was published (Janzen 1973: 173–181). The entire 4QJer[a] with photos is being prepared for publication by E. Tov. The fragments consist of 7:1–2, 15–19; 7:28–9:2 (>7:30–8:8); 9:7–15; 10:9–23; 11:3–20; 12:3–16; 12:17–13:7; 13:27–14:8; 15:1–2; 17:8–26; 18:15–19:1; 20:15–18; 22:3–16; and 26:10. Remnants of 15 columns have been preserved. The complete scroll is estimated at 54–58 columns where the average width of each column is 13.34 cm. The whole scroll would therefore have measured more than 8 m in length, longer than the great Isaiah scroll which was 7.3 meters. This scroll has an inordinate number of corrections, most all of which are in the direction of the MT. Corrections in some instances are made by supralinear additions; in other instances erasures have been made with a sharp instrument; in one case cancellation dots are used (Tov f.c.a.).

A partial scroll designated 4QJer[b] was also published without photos by Janzen (1973: 181–84). Cross (*QBHT* 308 and personal communication) dates this scroll in the mid-2d century B.C. It consists of three fragments: 9:22–10:18; 43:3–9; and 50:4–6. Of great importance are the fragments 9:22–10:18 and 43:3–9, which compare closely to the LXX. In 9:22–10:18 the short LXX text and LXX verse order are reflected. These fragments with photos will be published by Tov (f.c.c.). Tov does not believe, however, that the three fragments come from a single scroll but are rather from three separate scrolls. He therefore assigns different designations. The fragment 9:22–10:18 (Tov 9:21–10:22?) continues to have the designation 4QJer[b], while the fragment 43:3–9 (Tov 43:2–10) becomes 4QJer[d], and 50:4–6 becomes 4QJer[e].

The final scroll from Cave 4, 4QJer[c], is another long proto-Masoretic text in early Herodian script which dates from 30–1 B.C. (*QBHT* 308 and personal communication). The editio princeps will be published by Tov. From what originally was 25 columns of 18 lines per column the following fragments survive: 4:5, 13–16; 8:1–3; 8:20–9:5; 10:12–13; 19:8–9; 20:2–5, 7–8, 14–15; 21:6–10; 22:4–6, 10–28; 25:7–8, 15–17, 24–26; 26:10–13; 27:1–3, 14–15; 30:6–31:14; 31:16–26; 33:16–20. The writing on this scroll is less economical than on 4QJer[a], i.e., the margins are larger and the space between the lines is greater, which adds up to an estimated length for this scroll of twice the length of 4QJer[a].

The Qumran scrolls contain two types of paragraph divisions, open sections and closed ones. The sections in 4QJer[a] conform closely to Codex L; 4QJer[c] has more paragraph divisions than Codex L and also open sections where Codex L has closed sections (Tov f.c.a.).

D. Poetry and Prose

The book of Jeremiah contains a significant amount of poetry, that discovery having been made by Robert Lowth, who, in 1753, published his famous *Lectures on the Sacred Poetry of the Hebrews* (1815). Poetry was found also in other prophetic books (Lecture 18), and its dominant characteristic was said to be "parallelism" (Lecture 19). Lowth found poetry at the beginning and at the end of Jeremiah, and he judged the book to be about evenly divided between poetry and prose. The poetic sections were first delineated in Benjamin Blayney's Jeremiah commentary of 1784.

Poetry and prose were distinguished as separate sources by critics of the 19th and early 20th centuries, but no one contrasted the two forms of discourse as sharply as Bernhard Duhm in his commentary of 1901 (*Jeremia* KAC). Duhm believed that the poetry put us in direct contact with the prophet's *ipsissima verba;* however, because of a radical appropriation of the metrical theories of Julius Ley, Duhm concluded that Jeremiah wrote only in pentameter (or *kinah*) verse, which was the elegaic 3:2. This amounted to 280 verses of Masoretic text. Of the two prose sources in the book, one was Baruch's life of Jeremiah, which consisted of 220 verses, and the other derived from postexilic Deuteronomistic redactors, whose contribution totaled a grand 850 verses. This gradually emerging three-source theory adopted by Duhm reached classical formulation in the work of Mowinckel (1914). Source A was poetry which preserved the *ipsissima verba* of Jeremiah. Source B was biographical prose written by an admirer of the prophet. Mowinckel later (1946: 61–62) identified this admirer as Baruch. Source C was sermonic prose similar to that which is found in Deuteronomy and the Deuteronomistic History.

The strongest argument for two separate prose sources came from the double account of the Temple Sermon: chap. 26 was in biographical prose and chap. 7 in sermonic prose. Today, however, there is little inclination to distinguish between B and C prose. The stereotyped phrases characterizing C are found just as often in the speeches of B (Holladay 1960: 354). Also, the great bulk of C material, which includes the call passage in chap. 1, the Temple Sermon in chap. 7, and the New Covenant passage in chap. 31, is no longer believed by many scholars to be a retrojection of postexilic theology, but considered rather as a genuine reflection of Jeremiah's own preaching (Robinson 1924; Bright 1951; *Jeremiah* AB; Weippert 1973). In fact, the diction of C contains many striking affinities to the Jeremianic poetry (Bright 1951: 21; Holladay 1960; *Jeremiah* Hermenia). According to this view there is exilic prose in the book, but it is a relatively small amount which in most cases develops themes from Jeremiah's earliest preaching. Not all share this view, however. Some still believe that there is a considerable amount of exilic or postexilic prose in the book which comes from the hands of Deuteronomistic redactors (Thiel 1973; 1981; McKane *Jeremiah* vol. 1 ICC; Carroll 1981; *Jeremiah* OTL).

Holladay's work on poetic style and structure (1962; 1966a) enhances the earlier estimates of those who said that this discourse represents an advanced state of the art. One finds in the Jeremianic poetry an assortment of balancing techniques other than the common types of parallelism, varied rhythms of crescendo and diminution, wordplays on both sound and meaning, and a generous quantity of irony. Holladay also finds poetry hidden beneath some of the prose (1966b). While the book does appear to contain some poetry from other prophets or which is of unknown provenance, the vast majority is *sui generis* and a legacy of the Jeremianic preaching. Its diction shows influence from the poetry of Hosea, the Song of Moses (Deuteronomy 32), and certain psalms (e.g., 22; 31; 35; 69; 79). Though most scholars today do not credit the Lamentations to Jeremiah, one will find also in this poetry vocabulary and phraseology similar to that found in the Jeremianic poetry.

It was in Kittel's 1906 edition of *Biblia Hebraica* that the MT first appeared with poetry printed as poetry. Kittel himself edited the text of Jeremiah and is largely responsible for the way the poetry is read today. The larger reading public was first presented with Jeremiah's poetry—along with all the rest of the Old Testament poetry—when the complete RSV was published in 1952. Virtually all subsequent translations have translated poetry as poetry. They have also printed it as such. This has provided great assistance in the early work of delimiting Jeremiah's literary units, for in this book poetry and prose are interspersed. Some scholars have recently challenged the basis for making a prose-poetry distinction, one calling the idea of poetry a "Hellenistic imposition" on the Hebrew text (Kugel 1981: 85). But this is wide of the mark. Prose, of course, also has balance, rhythm, and distinct structural features—including parallelism—which suggests, at the very least, a common rhetorical base for poetry and prose. But poetic discourse in Jeremiah—and in the rest of the Old Testament—is well established, and further refinements of prose discourse will not alter that fact. The assumption that the book of Jeremiah contains an early substratum of poetry has been made by all critical methodologies of the past two centuries.

E. Literary Forms

Ancient discourse gives indications of having assumed conventionalized dress in the same way modern discourse does; in fact, some have maintained that ancient discourse is more conventionalized (Norden; Gunkel; see FORM CRITICISM [OT]. Yet when the Jeremiah material is compared to known literary genres of antiquity—both within the Bible and without—no "pure" genres emerge. Prose and poetry take a variety of forms, and although the forms in Jeremiah in some instances resemble forms appearing elsewhere, structures and stylistic features in both discourses owe their origin not to fixed genres but to canons established in ancient Hebrew rhetoric. Except for exilic and postexilic accretions, poetry and prose both bear the stamp of a particular rhetorical school, one existing most likely in Jerusalem during the 8th–6th centuries B.C. Speech forms have their own distinct character, and for this reason they do a better job of defining themselves than by having external genre criteria applied to them.

Divine oracles in the poetry may consist of a single verse (6:21; 14:10), but more commonly one finds speeches and reflective utterances of greater length which address Yahweh, kings, prophets, priests, the general population, and foreign nations of the world. The bulk of the speeches are those of a divine messenger who has been sent to announce Yahweh's judgment upon Judah. Some adopt legal language from the courtroom (2:5–9, 10–13), some are a watchman's warning of the approaching "foe from the north" (4:5–8), and some simply give vent to the divine and human pathos which disaster evokes (4:29–31; 15:5–9). But there are also speeches announcing a future salvation for Yahweh's people, including a return to Zion (chaps. 30–31). Speeches employ dialogue and trialogue with Yahweh, Jeremiah, the people, and even the enemy speaking in turn (4:19–22; 5:1–8; 6:1–7; 8:18–21). Now and then Jeremiah carries on a conversation with himself (4:19; 5:4–5). One speech is a devastating vision of cosmic destruction (4:23–26).

A significant amount of poetry in the book resembles the Psalms. Those passages of a more personal nature have been called Jeremiah's "confessions." These are individual laments, basically (Baumgartner 1987), some of which include a corrective answer from Yahweh (e.g., 15:15–21) or a joyful song of deliverance (e.g., 20:7–13). The brief personal lament in 10:23–25 requests divine correction. Whether these laments—which are unique in the prophetic corpus—found expression in public worship during Jeremiah's time is a much-debated question. They are so similar to individual laments of the Psalms for which a cultic setting is taken for granted. Communal laments, e.g., the drought liturgy of 14:1–9, would seem to be very much at home in preexilic temple worship. So also the laments made on behalf of exiled kings (22:10; 22:28–30), the slain of Judah (8:22–9:1—Eng 9:2), and all of creation (9:9–10—Eng 9:10–11). The wisdom psalm in 17:5–8 has a striking similarity to Psalm 1. Other liturgies in the book may well come from a source other than Jeremiah, e.g., 10:1–10 (MT only), which contrasts Yahweh to the false gods of the nations, or 10:12–16 (= 51:15–19), which praises Yahweh as both the creator of the world and the special portion of Jacob. In late prose, poetry is imported from the Psalms, e.g., 33:11b from Ps 106:1.

There is also wisdom material, e.g., the proverb in 31:29, the climactic rhetorical question which concludes prophetic speeches in 5:9, 29 and 9:8—Eng 9:9, and miscellaneous pieces such as those appearing in 17:9–10 and 11. The single Aramaic verse in the book (10:11) is a wisdom saying about the false gods of the nations.

Prose in the book divides into two basic styles which correspond more or less to the descriptions given for sources B and C. There is prose of a lighter sort, written in the third person, which basically narrates events in Jeremiah's life (e.g., chap. 26) and records the prophet's personal suffering (chaps. 37–44). This prose is "biographical" only in the sense that it is not "sermonic" prose (source C) and not "legendary" prose like the Elijah/Elisha stories. As remarkable as this prose is in the ancient world, it is not "biography" in the modern sense; we should call it rather "proto-biography." Yet it is the account of an eyewitness, and the supposition that Baruch stands behind it is well supported by evidence contained in the book.

The rest of the book's prose is an amorphous collection of prophetic preaching, moralizing about sin and judgment, and homiletical talk about future restoration and renewed covenants (chaps. 31–33). All is in heavy rhetorical style with accumulation of vocabulary and phraseology similar to what we find in Deuteronomy and the Deuteronomistic History. Some is written in the third person, but some is "autobiographical," being introduced by such first-person formulas as "And the word of Yahweh came to me (saying)" (1:4, 11, 13; 13:8; 16:1; 18:5; 24:4; 32:6), or

"And Yahweh said to me" (3:6; 11:6, 9; 14:11, 14; 15:1; 24:3), or "Thus Yahweh said to me" (13:1; 17:19; 27:2). There is also heavy prose which postdates the Jeremiah era, e.g., 3:15–18; 5:18–19; 9:11–15(—Eng 9:12–16); 9:22–23—Eng 9:23–24; etc.

In the heavy prose are a variety of literary forms. There are reports of visions (1; 24; 38:21–23), prayers to Yahweh which include also Yahweh's answers (32:16–44), and direct messages from Yahweh to Jeremiah (7:16–20; 11:14–17; 14:11–16; 15:1–4; etc.). The famous Temple Sermon (7:1–15) is heavy prose as are the sermons found in 11:1–8 and 34:12–22.

Prose of both types reports parables and object lessons (13:1–11; 18:1–12; 19; 27–28; 35). Chapter 29 is a letter (vv 4–23) to which the fragment of another letter (vv 24–28) has been attached. Expanded colophons are found in 36:1–8; 45; and 51:59–64 (Lundbom 1986), and perhaps also in 32:6–15 (Gevaryahu 1970: 370–72; 1973: 211–13).

F. Composition

The book of Jeremiah bears ample witness to the claim that people in antiquity compiled spoken and written discourse differently than we do today. The remark is frequently made that the book of Jeremiah is in great disarray (Bright 1951: 21; *Jeremiah* AB, lvi–lxiii). Materials are out of chronological sequence and in their compiled form seem to be without a coherent plan, something in modern compositions we come to take for granted. In order to understand not only the completed form of the book of Jeremiah, but also the process whereby the book was brought to its completion, the most important thing, perhaps, to realize at the outset is that chronology is but one criterion among a host of others which ancient scribes and other literary people used to order their materials. Second, ancient compositions do have coherence, but that coherence follows an inner logic which is still quite alien to the modern Western mind.

In the book of Jeremiah, as is true in other biblical books, we are confronted with a document that has undergone change. This introduces an element of complexity into the analysis that would not exist if our document had been composed at one point in time or had been preserved unaltered after leaving some author's hand. The turbulent effects of oral transmission have, of course, been greatly exaggerated. Some poetry in the book may have been subject to laws of oral transmission, but on the whole we have to do in Jeremiah with a written composition. Alterations, where they exist, are largely the work of scribes in charge of the compilation process—beginning in Jeremiah's lifetime and continuing for an unspecified number of years afterward.

The book has a certain chronological order. Jeremiah's call comes in chap. 1 (unlike that of Isaiah which comes in chap. 6 of his book), and the prophet's last recorded activities in Egypt are placed either near the end of the book (MT 44) or at the very end (LXX 51:1–30). Chapter 2 contains Jeremiah's earliest preaching, which precedes in time the confessions closing out the First Edition (20:7–18). All of chaps. 1–20, with only a few exceptions, are earlier than all the prose narratives of 24–29 and 34–44. Also, the account of Jeremiah's final suffering in 37–44 follows a chronological sequence with only a couple possible exceptions: chaps. 37 and 38 may be duplicate accounts of Jeremiah's imprisonment, and chaps. 39 and 40 duplicates of his release by the Babylonians. Attention then is paid to chronology, but the composition of the book consists of much, much more.

Material is brought together in some cases because of a common literary form, e.g., the substratum of confessions in 11–20. Literary form together with a common theme dictate the grouping in chaps. 2–3. Speeches here focus on the nation's religious harlotry, thus the designation "harlotry cycle." The group of speeches beginning at 4:5 is likewise the "foe cycle" because of a common theme running through about the foe from the north. Some conclude this cycle at 6:30 before the Temple Sermon and the added prose in 7:1–8:3; others extend the cycle into the poetry of chap. 8. Actually the cycle extends to the end of chap. 10 in order that the preaching about destruction by the foe might have along with it the necessary weeping and lamentation (see especially 8:18–9:10—Eng 9:11; 9:16–21—Eng 9:17–22). The theme of hope controls, though it does not exclusively dominate, the speeches in the so-called "Book of Comfort," both in its early (30–31) and in its late (30–33) editions.

Material in some cases is grouped on the basis of audience. We see this in chaps. 21–23 where varied utterances of Jeremiah have been brought together because they are directed toward kings (21:1–23:8) or prophets (23:9–40). The audience is also the controlling element in the Foreign Nation Oracles (chaps. 46–51).

Association techniques—a common possession, most likely, of the oral poet and the scribe—perform compositional functions. In the poetry are "catchwords," which may easily be identified once the literary units are delimited. The word "sons" links 3:14 with 3:19, thus setting off the prose in vv 15–18. The word "gather" (*ʾsp*) links 9:21—Eng 9:22 with 10:17, which suggests that the prose of 9:22–25—Eng 9:23–26 and the liturgical poetry of 10:1–16 are late additions. The word "know" (*ydʿ*) links 10:25 with 11:18, again showing that prose seems to have been inserted into what was originally a chain of poetic speeches. Three passages of poetry, 6:27–30; 7:29; and 8:4–9, were at one time another chain held together by the catchword "reject" (*mʾs*), which appears at the end of each poem:

6:30 *Reject* silver they are called
for Yahweh has *rejected* them.

7:29 For Yahweh has *rejected* and forsaken
the generation of his wrath.

8:9 Behold they have *rejected* the word of Yahweh
and what wisdom is in them?

This chain shows that the prose of 7:1–8:3 is a later insertion, perhaps made in order to embody 7:29 into sermonic material (Mowinckel 1946: 64). The foe cycle, therefore, does not conclude at 6:30.

The two poems in 22:20–23 and 23:9–11 were linked in an early chain by the catchword "broken" (*šbr*), which appears at the beginning of each poem:

22:20 Go up to Lebanon and cry out
and lift up your voice in Bashan
Cry from Abarim
for all your lovers are *broken.*

23:9 My heart is *broken* within me
all my bones shake

The Jehoiachin oracle and lament of 22:24–30—also the messianic prophecy of 23:1–8—are therefore later additions. Catchwords also link prose passages to adjacent poetry, e.g., "Terror on every side" in 20:3 and 10 (Bright *Jeremiah* AB, 134).

Material is compiled in some cases by means of rhetorical structures. Chapter 1, for example, is a chiasmus (abb'a') with two visions placed at the center and their respective articulations at the extremes:

a Articulation of the call vision (4–10)
b Vision of the call (11–12)
b′ Vision of the foe (13–14)
a′ Articulation of the foe vision (15–19)

Near the end of the foe cycle four originally separate utterances have been combined thematically into a chiasmus:

a Jeremiah *weeping* for the slain of Judah (8:22–9:1—Eng 9:2)
b Jeremiah warning about evil *tongues* (9:2–5—Eng 9:3–5)
b′ Jeremiah warning about evil *tongues* (9:6–8—Eng 9:7–9)
a′ Jeremiah *weeping* for all creation (9:9–10—Eng 9:10–11)

In chap. 29 a letter to the exiles and the fragment of another are combined in such a way that the opening words of one and the closing words of the other—which are the same—form an inclusion for the whole (vv 5, 28).

Some material in the book appears to have been structured for purposes of cultic recitation. In 14:1–15:4 two successive liturgies are sequenced form-critically in the same manner (Gerstenberger 1963):

a Lament over widespread destruction (14:2–6, 17–18)
b Communal complaint and supplication (14:7–9, 19–22)
c Judgment oracle from Yahweh and—in prose—the rejection of Jeremiah as mediator (14:10–16; 15:1–4)

Liturgical requirements may also offer an explanation for various lament and deliverance combinations, e.g., 20:7–13, and judgment and salvation combinations, e.g., chaps. 30–31 (see below).

Later material has been interspersed with earlier material at various points in the book. In chaps. 1–20 the inserted material is mostly prose, e.g., 7:1–8:3, although it can be poetry, e.g., 10:1–16. Prose comment on passages of poetry in some cases follows it (3:15–18, 24–25; 9:11–15—Eng 9:12–16; 22:11–12). In the King Collection (21:1–23:8) and in the early Book of Comfort (30–31), prose passages frame an earlier core of poetry (see below).

Finally, those compiling the book of Jeremiah had definite ideas about what made a suitable beginning and a suitable end. Visions were put at the beginning (chaps. 1; 24) and colophons at the end (45; 51:59–64; and originally 36:1–8) (Lundbom 1986).

G. Early Collections

The present book of Jeremiah was preceded by earlier compilations, some of which are still discernible within the larger collection. Recent studies done on rhetoric and composition indicate that these compilations were written documents from the very first, also that the bulk of the writing was done during Jeremiah's own lifetime.

1. The Scroll of 605. In chap. 36 we have an extraordinary account telling us how the first written collection came about. In the 4th year of Jehoiakim, i.e., 605, Yahweh told Jeremiah to prepare a scroll on which was to be written all that he had spoken concerning Israel, Judah, and the nations—from the time Yahweh's word first came to him until the present day. Jeremiah summoned for this task a certain Baruch ben Neriah, who was a scribe (v 32). A seal impression has been found with Baruch's name on it, followed by the title "scribe" (Avigad 1978). Baruch in all probability was the holder of some royal office in Jerusalem. After Baruch had written the scroll, he was to read it in the temple; Jeremiah could not do this because he was currently under a temple ban. Baruch did as he was told, probably the year following (MT 36:9), although there is some uncertainty about date because the LXX says it was four years later. In any case, the scroll was read three times, the third being before King Jehoiakim, who repaid the favor by casting it into the fire. The scroll was later rewritten and more material was added to it (v 32).

There has been much speculation about the contents of this 1st scroll. Most scholars have concluded that the scroll must lie within 1–25:13a, even if not all of the present material was included. According to this view, the words of 25:13a, "all that is written in this book," mark the scroll's conclusion (Muilenburg *IDB* 2: 823–35; Bright *Jeremiah* AB). But these same words make better sense when they are taken as a pointer to what originally lay ahead—and what in the LXX still does lie ahead—viz., the oracles against Babylon (cf. vv 12–13a).

The suggestion of Rietzschel (1966: 136) that the early scroll consisted of chaps. 1–6 must be rejected because the foe cycle does not end at 6:30. The only early material in the book which shows itself to be a self-contained collection is chaps. 1–20 (Lundbom 1975: 28–30). Whether 1–20 constitutes the scroll of 605 we cannot say for certain, but any discussion regarding the contents of this scroll ought to be focused on these chaps., not on 1–25:13a.

2. The First Edition of the Book of Jeremiah. The earliest book discernible within the present book consists of chaps. 1–20. These chaps. are held together by an inclusio made up of the final words from Jeremiah's last confession and the opening words of his call:

Jeremiah: Why *from the womb did I come forth*
to see trouble and sorrow
and end in shame my days?
(20:18)

Yahweh: Before I formed you in the belly I knew you
and before *you came forth from the womb*
I consecrated you
(1:5)

With the 1st scroll no longer extant, we can take chaps. 1–20 as the first edition of the book of Jeremiah. Rietzschel (1966) has suggested that chap. 45, which contains Jeremiah's personal word to Baruch at the time the scroll of 605 was written, originally stood at the end of chap. 20 being linked to it by the catchword "sorrow" (*yâgôn*; 20:18; 45:3). Chap. 45 is a scribal colophon written by Baruch (Lundbom 1986: 107), which provides some basis then for saying that Baruch is the one who wrote up the First Edition. It is not known who supplied the superscription in 1:1–3. Some have said that it was Baruch (Hyatt *IB* 5: 797–98), but others—those who believe the superscription is a composite (Budde 1921), as well as those who believe it is all one piece (Zalevski 1975)—say it dates from the exilic or postexilic periods.

The First Edition is introduced by the two visions in chap. 1. These credential Jeremiah for the preaching which follows, with the second vision on the foe from the north explaining why it is that Jeremiah composes laments for the nation and for himself. The first vision of the almond rod is associated with the prophet's call in 627 B.C. (1:4–12). The second vision of the boiling pot tipped away from the north carries with it the summons to begin his career (1:13–19), which dates not from 627 but rather 5 years later or so around 622. See JEREMIAH (PROPHET).

There are two major groupings following chap. 1, each containing its own type of material and having its own independent chronology. The division comes at the end of chap. 10. The 1st grouping ends with a psalm pleading for personal correction and for vengeance upon the enemy (10:23–25). The verb *klh* ("finish, consume") in 10:25 reinforces closure just as it does in 20:18 where the second grouping concludes.

The grouping of chaps. 2–10 is built upon a substratum of poetry, which comprise two cycles on "religious harlotry" and the "foe from the north." The fragment in 2:2–3 serves as an introductory foil for the two cycles, bringing to remembrance the time when Israel was faithful to Yahweh and in no danger of attack from external enemies (Holladay *Jeremiah* Hermeneia, 30–34). The cycle on harlotry consists of 2:4–3:5; 3:12–14, 19–23, the concluding verses of the latter being a liturgy of confession which is expanded in 3:24–25. The foe cycle consists of 4:5–5:17; 5:20–6:30; 8:4–9:10—Eng 9:11; 9:16–21—Eng 9:17–22; and 10:17–25. The laments of chaps. 8–9 belong to this cycle, so also 10:17–22, which is a word preparing people for the exile of 597. The mention of "the north" at the end of this lament (10:22) makes an inclusio with "the north" beginning the cycle (4:6). Here, too, we see that at the very end stands a confession (10:23–25).

The poetry in 4:1–4 is transitional: vv 1–2 conclude the preaching of chap. 3 directed at "faithless Israel"; vv 3–4 introduce judgment upon Judah, which begins in 4:5.

Two passages of prose in chaps. 2–10 preserve early traditions of Jeremianic preaching: 3:6–11, which is a 1st-person homily comparing Israel and Judah, and 7:1–8:3, which, except for 7:16–20, is a 3d-person account of sermons delivered in the temple. Included in the latter is the famous Temple Sermon of 609 (7:1–15). In 7:16–20 we have a personal word from Yahweh to Jeremiah. Other prose in 3:15–18; 5:18–19; 9:11–15—Eng 9:12–16; 9:22–23—Eng 9:23–24; and 9:24–25—Eng 9:25–26 is exilic. As for the poetic liturgies in 10:1–16, about all we can say is that they are later additions; we know neither their dates nor their provenance.

The substratum of poetry within chaps. 11–20 consists of Jeremiah's confessions in the main, but included also are speeches against Judah and Jerusalem, liturgies used in national emergencies, laments over the departure of Jehoiachin and the Queen Mother, and a handful of miscellaneous wisdom sayings. Interspersed are passages in prose which contain preaching, dialogues between Yahweh and Jeremiah, and reports about Jeremiah's prophetic activity.

It is not clear to what extent the poetry follows in chronological sequence. The confessions in 11:18–12:6 are thought by some to come from the beginning of Jeremiah's career when priestly kin at Anathoth turned against him for supporting Josiah's program of one sanctuary in Jerusalem. The confessions in 20:7–18 most likely come from ca. 605–604 B.C. when Jeremiah was being hunted by Jehoiakim. About the rest of the poetry there is uncertainty regarding date, except in the case of 13:15–27, which comes from just before the deportation of 597 and must be some of the "added words" on the rewritten scroll (36:32).

The prose at both ends of chaps. 11–20 gives evidence of at least some concern on the part of the compiler for establishing chronological sequence. The covenant preaching in 11:1–8 is best dated soon after 622, while the events recorded in 19:1–20:6 fit into the period between 609 and 605 (Bright *Jeremiah* AB, 174–75). Little more can be said about the dating of the prose, except that a few brief verses (11:7–8a; 16:14–15 [= 23:7–8]) come either from the end of Zedekiah's reign or else are exilic.

3. The Appendix on Kings and Prophets. Immediately following the First Edition is an appendix in chaps. 21–23 which contains preaching, laments, and narrative focusing on two groups: (a) Judah's royal house; and (b) Jerusalem's ministerium. Earlier there appears to have been two separate collections, for the text has retained introductory captions which read, "Concerning the house of the King of Judah" (21:11), and "Concerning the prophets" (23:9). Each collection has a core of poetry. At an earlier time the two compilations of poetry were linked together by the catchword "broken" (*šbr*) which begins the last "king poem" (22:20) and the first "prophet poem" (23:9).

The King Collection has expanded from the center out. At the core are three poems against Jehoiakim and his royal household (22:6–7, 13–17, 20–23) into which are interspersed a lament for Shallum (i.e., Jehoahaz; v 10) and a non-lament for Jehoiakim (vv 18–19). A rhetorical structure built on the key words "Lebanon" and "cedars" holds the Jehoiakim poems together (Lundbom 1975: 101–2). These key words highlight Jeremiah's basic criticism of Jehoiakim, i.e., that he was generous when it came to erecting cedar buildings in Jerusalem, but he cared nothing for the weightier matters of justice and righteousness.

After 597 this core was expanded to include the oracle and lament for young King Jehoiachin (22:24–30). Up front was placed more preaching against Jehoiakim (21:11–22:5) and the title in 21:11 was added. The prose of 22:8–9 and 11–12 may also be part of this expansion.

A second expansion occurred when the dated Zedekiah prose of 21:1–10 was added at the beginning, and the messianic prophecies of 23:1–8 were placed at the end. The Zedekiah prose belongs with chaps. 37–38, but here it functions to set up a contrast between Zedekiah, who is misnamed "Righteous of Yahweh" or "Righteous is Yahweh," and the future Davidic king whose name—and entire being—will be "Yahweh is our righteousness" (23:6). This second expansion dates from the very end of Zedekiah's reign or shortly after.

The core of poetry focused on the prophets consists of a lament over prophets—also priests—who are unfit for holy office (23:9–11), an oracle of judgment against the prophets of Jerusalem (vv 13–15), and a dialogue between Jeremiah and Yahweh about prophets who run but are not sent (23:18, 21–22). Into this dialogue has been inserted at a later time an independent judgment oracle (vv 19–20; it appears also in 30:23–24). The material in 23:12, 16–17, and 23–40—most of it prose—is also later expansion. Unlike the King Collection, there are no internal aids here which can help us with dating the core and its expansions. Probably what we have is preaching during the reigns of Jehoiakim and Zedekiah. We know that at the beginning of each king's reign Jeremiah sustained harsh attacks from other prophets (26:7–11; 28).

4. The Baruch Prose Collections. Within chaps. 24–45 are the prose passages said by many to come from the hand of Baruch, Jeremiah's close friend and colleague in the years subsequent to 605. They contain reports of divine revelations and record some of Jeremiah's late preaching, but for the most part are narratives describing the prophet's activities at the end of his early career and during the public years of his late career. The years covered are the first five of Jehoiakim's reign, i.e., 609–604, the first four of Zedekiah's reign, i.e., 597–594/3, and those immediately before and after Jerusalem's fall. Between 605 and 597, and between 594 and 588, Jeremiah is out of public view and not heard from.

One collection is particularly well intact. It is the so-called "Via Dolorosa" prose of chaps. 37–44. These chaps. describe Jeremiah's final sufferings from the point of view of one who observed them at close range. The collection is introduced by a superscription similar to those appearing in the Deuteronomistic History (37:1–2). From this collection may originally have come the prose accounts in 21:1–10; 32; and 34, for they, too, are about Judah's last days when Jerusalem was under siege.

The remaining chaps., viz., 24–29, 35–36, and 45, are not intact, lending support to the claim that the book of Jeremiah is in mass disarray. All contain dated superscriptions from which we can see that chronology has manifestly not been kept, at least not in the arrangement which now appears before us. Chapters 25–26, 35–36, and 45 are from the reign of Jehoiakim. Chapters 24 and 27–29 are from Zedekiah's reign. Chapter 45 is the easiest to account for. It is Baruch's colophon to the final book which comes from his hand (now only in the LXX at 51:31–35). However, when the two larger clusters of four chapters each from the respective reigns of Jehoiakim and Zedekiah are examined more closely, it will be seen that both have identical rhetorical (a b b′ a′) structures (Lundbom 1975: 107–11). This seems to indicate that originally they were two separate collections.

The present disarray is due to the breakup of these Jehoiakim and Zedekiah collections, although we do note that some passages, viz., 25–26, 27–29, and 35–36, did manage to stay together. The most plausible explanation for the breakup is that 24 was chosen to begin a larger composition being formed because it contained a revelatory vision. The present book now begins with two revelatory visions. Chapter 36 (originally only vv 1–8) was chosen to conclude this larger composition because it was Baruch's colophon (Lundbom 1986: 104–6). The present book also ends with a colophon.

Two interpolations were made into this larger composition between chaps. 29 and 35. One was the Book of Comfort (30–33), which is a separate collection (see section 5). It was inserted because its passages of hope were attracted by the hope expressed in Jeremiah's larger letter to the exiles (29). Chapter 34, which has two parts, vv 1–7 and 8–22, and which belongs with chap. 37, was the second interpolation. It was placed next to chap. 35 in order to set up a contrast between the obedient Rechabites and the disobedient Zedekiah.

5. The Book of Comfort. The present Book of Comfort comprises all of chaps. 30–33. At an earlier time, however, it consisted only of chaps. 30–31. The controlling theme of both editions is hope for national restoration through new and ongoing covenants.

The earlier edition of just 30–31 was built around a core of poetry. The prose frame is made up of sayings which begin with the words, "Behold the days are coming" (30:3; 31:27, 31, 38). Originally this collection was written up on a separate scroll (30:2).

The poetic passages comprising the core speak of hope and restoration in part, but actually the controlling theme is a more somber one about judgment and imminent exile. The whole is given a rhetorical structure in which judgment and hope oracles are combined, also laments with words of divine promise. Catchwords link up some of the paired passages. What we have here is a moving dialogue well suited for liturgical use:

a	Judgment (30:5–7) Hope (30:10–11)	*catchwords:* Jacob / save (*yšʿ*)
b	Judgment (30:12–15) Hope (30:16–17)	*catchwords:* wound (*mkh*) / heal (*rpʾ*)
c	Hope (30:18–21) Covenant Formula (30:22) Judgment (30:23–23) Covenant Formula (31:1) Hope (31:2–14)	

b′	Lament (31:15) Promise (31:16–17)	*catchwords:* weeping (*bky*) / children
a′	Lament (31:18–19) Promise (31:20–22)	*catchwords:* Ephraim / return (*šwb*)

The keystone of the arch is the judgment oracle of 30:23–24, which appears also in 23:19–20 where it has been editorially inserted. One will note how the covenant vows on either side of this judgment oracle are formulated in reverse order.

The concluding promise in 31:20–22 is bittersweet. Exile is ahead and Jeremiah expresses wonderment about how long this "changeable daughter" will change direction, also why now the females must give protection to the soldiers. With this final irony an inclusio is formed with another irony expressed at the beginning of the core: males there are said to be behaving like women in labor (30:6). Assuming exile to be imminent, the terminus a quo for the core would have to be 597 B.C. But those oracles which announce deliverance and a return to Zion are some of Jeremiah's earliest, coming from the beginning of his career when he anticipated the return of northern exiles who had been taken away to Assyria in 722.

The somber mood controlling the core gave way to a mood of joyful anticipation when the first Book of Comfort was compiled. One passage of the prose expansion announces a "new covenant" which will replace the Mosaic covenant now defunct. Another added fragment of poetry in 31:35–37 provides yet more assurance, stating that the unconditional covenant given to Abraham continues to be valid. We do not know when the first Book of Comfort was completed. It could have been at the time when the second expansion was made to the King Collection, for in 23:5–6 and 7–8 are two more "Behold the days are coming" promises. This would be at the very end of Zedekiah's reign, or shortly after.

Sometime later the Book of Comfort was enlarged by the addition of chaps. 32–33. This collection was tied together with an inclusio made up from the closing words of 33:26, "For I will restore their fortunes," and the opening words of 30:3, "And I will restore the fortunes of my people." The superscription to chap. 32 indicates that this passage belongs with the Zedekiah prose of 37–38; the same may apply to 33:1–13. The final material in 33:14–26 is lacking in the LXX and most likely represents an exilic addition. Its purpose is to reaffirm the covenants given to David and his royal line (2 Samuel 7) and to Levi's priestly line through Phinehas (Num 25:10–13). The prose insertion of 30:8–9 mentioning David is also late, though it does appear in the LXX.

6. The Foreign Nation Oracles. The book contains a separate collection of oracles which were spoken against nine foreign nations. In the LXX this collection follows 25:13a, while in the MT its placement is in chaps. 46–51 (see above). The location in the LXX is the earlier of the two, wherein one finds both superscription (25:13a) and subscription (LXX 32:13) supplied. In the MT these have been combined in 25:13. The MT has its own superscription to the collection in 46:1. Similar collections of foreign nation oracles are found in the books of Amos (1:3–2:3), Isaiah (chaps. 13–23) and Ezekiel (chaps. 25–32).

The inclusion of material in this collection has been determined by audience in the main, as is the case also in the King and Prophet Collections of chaps. 21–23. However, among the Babylon oracles is a liturgy which appears also earlier in the book (51:15–19; cf. 10:12–16). And at the end of the Egypt oracles the MT (only) duplicates an oracle addressed to Israel (46:27–28; cf. 30:10–11). The function here is to call home exiles who have gone away to Egypt.

The foreign nation collection has a complex history, one which may, for some oracles at least, include an early period of oral tradition. The different sequences within the LXX and MT suggest this, so also the time span over which these oracles were delivered. The first oracle against Egypt is dated in 605 (46:2), whereas the earliest date for the oracles against Edom, Ammon, and Moab is 590. This totals 15 years, and the time frame may be longer.

Jeremiah himself is said to have written a scroll of Babylon oracles (51:60). In 594/3 this scroll was given to Seraiah ben Neriah, the brother of Baruch, and he was instructed to take it with him on a trip he was making to Babylon. On arrival the prophecies were to be read aloud, after which Seraiah was to throw the scroll into the Euphrates, dramatizing Yahweh's curse on Babylon. This is related to us in Seraiah's colophon appended to the Babylon oracles (51:59–64 [LXX 28:59–64]; Lundbom 1986: 101–9). If Seraiah followed these instructions, then another early scroll has perished (cf. chap. 36). But a duplicate was made, to which Seraiah appended his colophon. A seal impression with Seraiah's name on it has been found (Avigad 1978), though it lacks the title "scribe." The biblical tradition says he held the office of "quartermaster" (51:59). We can assume, however, that like his brother, Seraiah had professional scribal training and was competent to perform a range of scribal functions.

There has been much discussion about whether the foreign nation oracles are genuinely Jeremianic. Most of the oracles are in poetry, but opinions about quality and style vary. Bright says the quality is high, with some oracles showing the same vividness as oracles addressed to Israel whose genuineness is not questioned (*Jeremiah* AB, 307–8). Also one finds in these oracles some of Jeremiah's most characteristic phrases, e.g., "terror on every side" (46:5; 49:29; cf. 6:25; 20:10); "faithless daughter" (49:4; cf. 31:22); "like a woman in labor" (49:24; 50:43; cf. 6:24; 22:23; 30:6); "haunt of jackals" (49:33; 51:37; cf. 9:10—Eng 9:11; 10:22); etc. So far as rhetorical structures are concerned, the speeches in 51:20–23 and 51:34–45 rank with the best of Jeremiah's speeches to Israel and Judah. In one instance a speech written for the "daughter of Zion" (6:22–24) is adapted for delivery to the "daughter of Babylon" (50:41–43).

Certain of the oracles do, however, contain portions which appear to be anonymous or from some other prophet. The Edom oracle has verses found also in Obadiah (49:7–16; cf. Obad 1–5), and verses in the Moab oracles (48:33–39) echo Isaiah 15–16. Other duplications or similar sounding verses: 48:43–44 (cf. Isa 24:17–18); 49:27 (cf. Amos 1:4, 14); 49:31 (cf. Ezek 38:11); 50:16b (cf. Isa 13:14b). The same oracle was also used in one case against two different nations, viz., the prose saying against Edom and Babylon (49:19–21; 50:44–46). The superscription to the Babylon oracles suggests that the tradition about Jeremiah's authorship of those oracles may be late, and may also be in some doubt. The Greek (27:1) makes no reference to Jeremiah, while in the Hebrew (50:1) "through Jeremiah the prophet" is tacked on at the end. The Foreign Nation Oracles, in any case, appear to be a mix of genuine and nongenuine sayings, and a blanket judgment either for or against Jeremianic authorship of the collection does not seem possible. Finally, as with the other poetic collections, so also here one finds prose insertions at various points.

H. The Book of Books

The present book of Jeremiah is really a "book of books." Though we may speak about oral composition and oral transmission for poetry within 1–20, 21–23, 30–31, and 46–51, the various collections and the completed book are written documents behind which stand Baruch, Seraiah, and other scribes who shared in the work. Jeremiah himself had a hand in the writing process (51:60). In Judah, as well as in the neighboring countries, it was a "scribal age" (Muilenburg 1970: 219). Asshurbanipal's huge library at Nineveh (650–630 B.C.) and the cache of 51 seal impressions from the early 6th century Jerusalem (Shiloh 1984: 19–20)—one of which has the name of Gemariah, son of Shaphan, on it (cf. 36:10–12, 25)—are just two of the more spectacular finds documenting this age.

The first book corresponding roughly to chaps. 1–51 was Baruch's compilation. In it the Foreign Nation Oracles followed 25:13a, and at the end was placed Baruch's colophon (LXX 51:31–35), which formerly concluded the First Edition. This book survives in the LXX version and in 4Q Jer[b] (though the latter is but a small fragment of it). Its provenance is Egypt where Baruch and Jeremiah were taken after 586 B.C. (43:5–7).

Another book corresponding roughly to chaps. 1–51 was completed in Babylon, though somewhat differently. In this version the Foreign Nation Oracles were relocated to the end, with those against Babylon appropriately being placed last. Seraiah's colophon concluded the book at 51:59–64. This book survives in the fragments 4Q Jer[a] and 4Q Jer[c] and in the MT. Seraiah, who went to Babylon in 594/3 and could have been exiled there ultimately, is possibly the compiler. In this version the final words of chap. 51, "thus far the words of Jeremiah"—which significantly are absent from the LXX—make an inclusion with "The words of Jeremiah . . ." beginning the book (1:1; 51:64). Two books then were completed in Egypt and Babylon respectively after the fall of Jerusalem, at roughly the same time the Deuteronomistic work was completed (Freedman 1963; 1983: 171–72).

Chapter 52 is a historical appendix derived for the most part from the Deuteronomistic History (2 Kgs 24:18–25:30). A historical appendix appears similarly at the end of 1 Isaiah (chaps. 36–39). The report of Gedaliah's governorship from 2 Kgs 25:22–26 is omitted, perhaps because it is covered extensively in Jeremiah 40–43. In its place is added—but only in the MT (52:28–30)—a summary of the various deportations to Babylon including the numbers of people taken. This fragment occurs nowhere else in the Bible. The final verses 31–34 recast slightly 2 Kgs 25:27–30, which is the concluding postscript to the Primary History (Genesis to 2 Kings). The date for this postscript is ca. 560 B.C. (Freedman 1983). By the middle of the 6th century, then, the tie was made between the completed book of Jeremiah and the completed Primary History. Verse 34 mentions Jehoiachin's death, which is not noted in 2 Kgs 25:30; however, from 2 Kings—in the MT only—is added "all the days of his life," which allows the book to conclude on a more positive note.

I. Theology

The theology in the book of Jeremiah is part subjective and part objective reflection. Ancient as well as current beliefs about Yahweh and his covenant people are refracted through the man Jeremiah, to which are added numerous witnesses to the life of faith which grow out of Jeremiah's own prophetic experience. The book also contains reflections by others who look at Jeremiah's life and preaching from a distance, and these form a second theological component no less important than the component of theology which derives from the prophet.

1. The Theology of the Prophet. We do not get from Jeremiah anything approaching a systematic theology. His preaching has a certain consistency to be sure, and thoughts of his are developed beyond the point of receiving merely passing mention. Nevertheless, ideas about Yahweh, Yahweh's word, the covenant, judgment, and salvation, etc., have their embodiment in rhetoric, i.e., in metaphors, argument, and ironic comment, in lyric poetry, and in impassioned preaching, not exactly the stuff of which systematic theology is made.

a. Sources for the Prophet's Theology. Traditions from the north, particularly those associated with Moses, predominate in the call and in the earliest preaching. Jeremiah reflects upon the Exodus, Wilderness Wanderings, and Settlement in 2:2–9, where his indebtedness to the Song of Moses is clear. From this song, which Cornill judged to be "a compendium of prophetic theology" (1891: 71), Jeremiah learned that Yahweh's grace toward Israel frames the entire sweep of world history. Within this frame, however, lie Israel's ingratitude, her corrupting ways with other gods, which result from settled and agrarian living, and Yahweh's punishment of Israel for what in his eyes is wrongdoing. Yahweh stays the hand of the enemy only as Israel is about to be completely destroyed. Then with a remnant Yahweh begins a new work of salvation, at which time the enemy is defeated. Jeremiah follows the Song of Moses in depicting the Mosaic Age as the idyllic period of national history, a time of purity when Israel was Yahweh's "devoted bride" or "first fruits" (2:2–3; cf. Deut 32:10–12). He also views Israel's settlement in the land as the time when things began to go bad (2:7; cf. 2:21; 8:13; Deut 32:13–18).

From Deuteronomy 1–28, which was originally a northern document, Jeremiah learned that the Mosaic covenant was conditional in nature, and that obedience to this covenant was the basis on which land tenure rested. The Mosaic covenant could be broken—as it repeatedly was by Israel—at the same time it could also be reconstituted. Jeremiah preached both messages—the brokenness of the covenant and Yahweh's decision to remake it—more clearly than any other prophet (2:20; 5:5; 7:5–10; 31:31–34; 32:37–41).

Jeremiah's preaching betrays indebtedness to the northern prophet Hosea. From Hosea, Jeremiah learned that the covenant is like a familial bond—between husband and wife or between father and son; that sin is rooted in a lack of the knowledge of Yahweh; and that a breach of covenant amounts to religious harlotry or adultery. Jeremiah follows Hosea in representing Yahweh as a deeply compassionate God, one who experiences personal hurt by having to vent his wrath, and one who wants, after the punishment is over, to receive his wayward child home again (31:16–20; cf. Hos 11:8–9).

During his long ministry in Jerusalem, Jeremiah appropriated theology from southern traditions associated with Abraham and David. One event associated with Abraham loomed very large for Jeremiah, as it did also for Isaiah and certain other prophets, and that was Sodom and Gomorrah's destruction (Genesis 18–19). From this, Jeremiah realized that Yahweh punishes entire cities for unrighteous living (5:1–8), and that a point can be reached where mediation for such cities is no longer possible (7:16–20; 11:14–17; 14:11–12; 15:1–2). Not only immoral prophets, but also seemingly innocent people, such as the man who brought the news of Jeremiah's birth to his father, are likened by Jeremiah to the inhabitants of these proverbial cities (23:14; 20:15–16) and must suffer a like fate when Jerusalem is destroyed. In his early preaching, Jeremiah stated that the blessings of the Abrahamic covenant were contingent upon Israel's repentance (4:1–2). But later he affirmed that Yahweh's covenants to Abraham and David were eternal and remained intact. Yahweh in future days would make good his promise to bless the nations through Israel, and Israel could count on David's royal line surviving, despite the nation's demise. This is fully in keeping with the basic tenets of southern theology.

It was perhaps from earlier prophetic preaching, most likely that of Micah, Isaiah, and also Amos—whose home was in the south—that Jeremiah learned of Yahweh's anger over urban injustice. In Jerusalem he discovered the rich exploiting the poor and wrongdoing going unpunished.

Wisdom materials too, collected at the Jerusalem court since the time of Solomon, had their impact upon the prophet. Jeremiah quotes proverbs and makes liberal use of wisdom themes, e.g., regularity and stability within the natural order (5:22, 24; 8:7). Jeremiah was much concerned with creation, but more over the threat of approaching chaos. Both creation accounts in Genesis 1–2 supply him with imagery in predicting the coming destruction (4:23–26; 18:1–11). Yahweh, for Jeremiah, is not simply God of the Exodus but God of the entire creation (10:12–16 [= 51:15–19]; 27:5; 32:17; 33:2), and at this point he anticipates the grand universalism of Second Isaiah. In the confessions, where Jeremiah's suffering finds such eloquent expression, indebtedness is to the Psalms and perhaps to an early edition of Job (Lundbom 1985: 600). About the only thing lacking in Jeremiah is priestly theology (33:17–22 is later), a fact which poses some interesting questions in that Jeremiah came from priestly stock.

On one occasion, northern and southern theologies came into direct conflict. This happened when Jeremiah gave his famous Temple Sermon and stated that land tenure and the temple's continued existence were contingent upon covenant obedience; further, that the nation was likely to lose both (7:1–15; 26:1–6). The people of Jerusalem, however, among whom were numbered not a few prophets and priests, had expanded the theology of Zion to the point where the eternal and unconditional covenant to David (2 Samuel 7) extended also to Jerusalem and the temple (Ps 132:11–18; Isa 31:4–5; 37:33–35). This precluded the destruction of either. Preaching northern theology on this occasion nearly cost Jeremiah his life, but in the end that is the theology which prevailed.

b. Theology and Time. The temple conflict of 609 shows that theology is time- and situation-bound. A century earlier, Isaiah preached that Zion was inviolable. Now Jeremiah considers this a false theology on which people are resting vain hopes. Von Rad has said, therefore, that the prophetic message is not timeless truth but a "particular word relevant to a particular hour in history" (*ROTT* 2: 129). At the same time, Jeremiah speaks also to the future—the immediate as well as the indefinite future—and here the prophetic word follows an uncertain course of fulfillment. Even within the prophet's own lifetime, early preaching about the future glory of Zion and the return of dispersed exiles was reappropriated from the exilic situation in Assyria to the newer situation which had developed in Babylon (3:12–14; 30:5–31:22). Thus, while theology in some instances may be time-bound, its life may also extend well beyond the hour of utterance and the particular situation at hand. The community of faith may even give a prophetic word its greatest prominence and its ultimate fulfillment at some later date. It could, for example, be argued that Jeremiah's vision of cosmic destruction (4:23–26) has more theological import for people in the nuclear age than for people in the late 7th and early 6th centuries B.C., who first heard it from his lips.

c. Yahweh. For Jeremiah, Yahweh most importantly is a living God, comparable to a natural supply of water (2:13; 17:7–8, 13). In a despondent mood he questions whether this can in fact be true, at least for him personally (15:18), but in better moments he knows that idols are the false resource; they cannot bring rain (14:22) nor have they power to save (2:27b–28; 11:12). Yahweh fills the creation (23:24); sends rain (5:24; 14:22b); controls the sea waters (5:22); and gives both lands and peoples into the hands of whomever he pleases (27:5–6). Yahweh is a God who "knows" (12:3; 15:15; 18:23; 29:23). He knows people and he knows events, not only those events which are current but also those planned for the future (1:5; 29:11; 33:3). Yahweh "remembers," too, both the good and the bad (2:2; 14:10), though in forgiveness he ceases to remember wrongdoing (31:34). He also has the capacity to "see" (12:3; 16:17; 32:24), even in the temple darkness or in secret places where evildoers imagine God cannot see (7:11; 23:24). More important, Yahweh is a God who acts. Many do not believe this (5:12), perhaps because Jeremiah has announced him to be the people's enemy. But to faithful individuals, such as Jeremiah, Baruch, and Ebed-melech the Ethiopian, protection and salvation are both promised and delivered (1:17–19; 45:5; 39:15–18; cf. 17:7–8). Yahweh is a righteous judge (11:20), although Jeremiah cannot understand why he allows the wicked to prosper (12:1–2). Yahweh will avenge himself eventually (5:9, 29; 9:8—Eng 9:9), and the humble can expect to receive mercy (3:12–13). Jeremiah discovers more than once that Yahweh can be overpowering, in some cases when he is suffering (1:6–8; 20:7; 32:25–26), but he is filled with rejoicing when his salvation comes (20:13).

d. Yahweh's Word. As a royal messenger, Jeremiah's job is to deliver the King's word—to Judah primarily, but also to foreign nations of the world. The divine word is central to Jeremiah's preaching; in fact, it is his preaching. In the capacity of royal messenger, Jeremiah also brings back messages to Yahweh and waits for him to respond. Yahweh's answer may take some time in coming; in one case, for example, it does not come for a full ten days (42:7). Jeremiah's dual role as spokesman for Yahweh and spokesman for the people makes him a mediator, and an active mediator he was, to judge from the many oracles and prayers surviving in his book.

Yahweh's word has enormous power—both creative as well as destructive power—and each is self-fulfilling (1:12, 4:28). Jeremiah stands in awe of its destructive power, comparing Yahweh's word to a consuming fire or a pounding hammer (23:29). No one can control it, least of all Jeremiah, who was overcome by it in his call, and later when he tried to hold it inside rather than proclaim it, he found he could not do so (20:8–9).

The divine word gives Jeremiah very serious problems. People will not listen when he speaks it (6:10, 19; 8:9); in fact they reproach him (17:15; 20:8; 38:4). This is particularly troubling when prophets opposing Jeremiah, who are also speaking in Yahweh's name, do not experience such difficulty. Jeremiah is thus led to reflect on true and false prophecy. The chief problem seems to be that he is delivering a word of judgment, and people do not want to hear that. They cannot believe judgment will come. Other prophets who are preaching peace and deliverance do not like hearing judgment either, particularly when Jeremiah preaches it "in Yahweh's name" (11:21; 26:9). And yet the trial of 609 showed that certain individuals did accept judgment preached in Yahweh's name, for it was on this basis that he was vindicated (26:16).

From Jeremiah's point of view, those prophets delivering a peaceful message had not stood in the divine council; they were running as messengers without having been sent (23:18, 21–22; 29:31). The word of Yahweh was not in them (5:13); in fact, their easy message was nothing but a vision of their own minds (23:16–17). These prophets were incapable of interceding for the people (27:18). A more serious charge made against them—also against certain priests—was that they were speaking lies (5:31; 14:14; 20:6; etc.). The lies multiplied and tended to become self-reinforcing because prophets were "stealing" oracles from one another (23:30). Prophets become false when they bear a false message from Yahweh (Overholt 1970). Time must pass before it becomes clear what truly is the word of Yahweh, who in fact has preached it, and which of two opposing words will stand (28:8–9; 44:28–30; cf. Deut 18:21–22). Jeremiah himself admits to having believed what the optimistic prophets, priests, and close friends of his were saying (4:10; 14:13; 20:7–10), which shows that this great man could at times be quite naive (cf. 11:18–19). Yet he is also very human. Yahweh notes his naiveté and calls it to the prophet's attention (12:6; 14:13–16).

e. Sin and Judgment. Behind all of Jeremiah's talk about sin and judgment lies a broken covenant. Jeremiah prayed that Yahweh on his part would not break the covenant (14:21); nevertheless it was broken and Israel bore the responsibility (2:20; 5:5; 11:10; etc.). Yahweh was innocent of any wrongdoing (2:5, 31). It is the people and the nation's leaders who no longer "know" Yahweh (2:8; 4:22; 9:2—Eng 9:3; 9:5—Eng 9:6; cf. Hos 4:1), where knowing Yahweh means "knowing his way" (5:4–5), "knowing his ordinances" (8:7), and doing justice to the poor and needy (22:16).

When Jeremiah talks then about the knowledge of Yahweh, he is talking about compliance with covenant stipulations. In the Temple Sermon five of the ten stipulations at the core of the Mosaic covenant are said to have been broken: stealing, murder, adultery, false oaths (lying), and going after Baal or other gods, which is the most serious infraction of all (7:9; cf. 2:8; 5:2; 9:1–5—Eng 9:2–6; 16:11; 18:15; Deut 32:16–17; Hos 4:2). Other broken commands are those pertaining to idols (8:19; cf. 10:14 [= 51:17]), the sabbath (17:19–27), and coveting the wife of one's neighbor (5:8). Jeremiah also echoes Deuteronomy's concern for justice and benevolence to the poor (2:34; 5:28; 7:5–7; etc.). These latter charges of inhumanity are leveled against Judah's kings, Jehoiakim in particular (21:12; 22:15–17). Prophets, meanwhile, are guilty of adultery and lying (23:14; 29:23).

Jeremiah has all these things in mind when he says the people have "forsaken Yahweh" (2:13; 16:11; 17:13; 19:4; cf. 2 Kgs 22:17), though "forsaking Yahweh" can also mean reliance upon foreign nations (2:14–19). Jeremiah says the people have "forgotten Yahweh" (2:32; 3:21; 13:25; 18:15; cf. Deut 32:18), which, in concrete terms, means they do not know the true source of their abundant crops. Having become overly sated, they lavish affection on "no gods" and indulge in fertility rites associated with them (5:7; cf. 22:20–21; Deut 32:13–15; Hos 2:10—Eng 2:8).

Jeremiah is sufficiently grounded in wisdom thought to realize that next to godlessness is foolishness, and the latter malady has contributed not a little to the nation's precarious condition (4:22; 5:21). He singles out foolish leaders for special mention (10:21; 14:18). If people have any skill, it is in doing evil (4:22).

Jeremiah emphasizes the human side of divine activity to an extent not found in other prophets (*ROTT* 2: 216–17). He is particularly reflective about the nature of sin and what impact it has both on the human condition and on the nation as a whole. The depths to which sin goes, also its range, taxes Jeremiah's understanding to the limits. Israel's abandonment of their God is something other nations would not think of (2:11); her rebellion is greater than chaotic sea waters (5:22–23). People are like instinct-driven animals (2:23–25; 5:7–8), teaching the most evil of women new things (2:33). Prophets keep pace by strengthening the hand of evildoers (23:14). Sin, however, is old, and extends back to Israel's earliest generations (2:20; 7:22–26; 22:21; 32:30; etc.). Yet if past generations were bad—and they were (2:5; 16:19)—sin's buildup over the years makes the present generation worse (16:12). A return to national health and well-being is now impossible (8:15, 22; 14:19; 30:12–15). Everyone is evil (5:4–5; 6:13 [= 8:10]; 9:3–4—Eng 9:4–5). Sin goes very deep (2:22; 17:1). "The heart," says Jeremiah, "is deceitful above all things" (17:9). Sinful people become hardened, intractable people; punishment has no effect on them; they are without shame, and he calls for their repentance to go unheeded (2:30; 3:3; 5:3; 6:15 [= 8:12]). Refining or winnowing the population as a whole proves to be impossible (6:27–30; 15:5–9; cf. Amos 4:6–11). Jeremiah says that people are unable to change their evil behavior (8:4–7; 13:23), which is to say that sin has an irreversible quality about it. Lustful urges cannot be given up (2:25), and people sink deeper into their sorry state of affairs; they keep going backward (15:6; cf. 7:24). In one of his confessions, Jeremiah says that people cannot direct themselves in the right way; correction, therefore, must come from Yahweh (10:23–24).

Those who are caught up in wrongdoing tend to be superficial and unknowing, both with respect to the intentions of others—including Yahweh—and about what they themselves are doing. They can be short-sighted too, not knowing what their end will be (5:31). Jeremiah notes how cavalier the wicked are, how they vacillate and wander about aimlessly (2:36; 4:1; 31:22; cf. Hos 7:11). They do not lay things to heart—not even their land which is ravaged by war (12:11). Women are superfluous in their dress, realizing not that the "lovers" they attract care nothing for them and would willingly kill them as not (4:30; 30:14). Prophets give a superficial message of "peace, peace, when there is no peace" (6:14 [= 8:11]). Kings spend lavishly on buildings while at the same time neglecting the weightier matters of justice and righteousness—a complete misunderstanding of their office and what it requires of them (22:13–17).

The people fail to perceive that their disregard of covenant obligations renders useless all the salvific liturgies recited in worship (7:8–10), and that Yahweh will not hear prayers when sacrifices are made to the Queen of Heaven (7:16–18) or other things are done to offend him (11:14–17). Even confessions of sin have no efficacy when real change does not occur (14:7–9, 20–22). The people know the ordinances of Yahweh but continue to break them (5:5); they talk of Yahweh even though he is distant from their hearts (12:2). Duplicity extends also to dealings with other people. All of this betrays on the part of the people acute unawareness or lack of understanding. The God of Israel has been reduced into another idol (Eichrodt 1950–51: 18). And the sin of Jerusalem's people contributes to Jeremiah's suffering, e.g., when he intercedes for the people they thank him with a curse (15:10–11; 18:20).

Fortunately evil cannot go on forever. Yahweh's anger is finally kindled to the point where he must avenge his name. Judgment is the result. The people have brought it upon themselves (2:17, 19; 4:18); it is "the fruit of (their) doings" (17:10). Jeremiah affirms in his early preaching the old theology that the father's sins are meted out upon the children and grandchildren (2:5–9). But later he states along with his younger contemporary Ezekiel that each person must die for his own sin (31:29–30; cf. Ezekiel 18; Deut 24:16). Yahweh's judgment in either case carries with it a reason, and that reason is sin (1:16; 4:17; 5:6; 8:14; 13:22; 30:14–15; etc.). This is in contrast to the reckless and arbitrary judgments of other ancient Near Eastern deities. It is also in contrast to the mindless judgments of evil people. Yahweh remains moral, however, even when his people are not.

Divine judgment affects the entire creation. The withholding of rain and its ruinous impact on the land (3:3; 5:24–25; 14:2–6) are portents of worse things to come. The final strike came when the Babylonian army brought down the nation in 587. Countless people died or were taken into exile, and the land was devastated.

Yahweh is the one who raised the question of pardon for Jerusalem (5:1–8), but his answer was negative because the city could not produce one righteous soul. Repentance would have made a difference (4:1–4), but the people refused. Pardon had to wait therefore until after the punishment was completed (31:34). Jeremiah was himself told on one occasion that he must repent for some worthless words he had uttered (15:19). This may have been when he called Yahweh a "dried-up brook" (v 18). Heschel, however, argues that the so-called worthless words are Jeremiah's call for Yahweh's vengeance upon those persecuting him (v 15). According to this view, Jeremiah has a case of "hypertrophic sympathy," i.e., an excessive amount of sympathy for the divine wrath (Heschel 1962: 126–27). Assuming Jeremiah did repent, he accomplished what the rest of the people could not. His pardon then would have consisted of being restored to the divine council and receiving once again from Yahweh a promise of salvation (15:20–21).

Because Yahweh is God over the whole earth, other nations cannot escape his punishment. Yahweh has no covenant with any of them; still, he must avenge himself for the evil done to his people and to Jerusalem (46:10; 51:35; cf. 10:25; Deut 32:34–43). But he also moves against them because they are wicked (25:31), proud (50:31–32), and trusting in their own gods (50:38; 51:47, 52).

f. Grace and Salvation. While sin and judgment form the bulk of Jeremiah's preaching, interwoven throughout are messages of grace and salvation. Even before he began preaching, Jeremiah was himself promised salvation (1:8), and that pledge was repeated (1:19; 15:20–21). Jeremiah prayed for his salvation, and when doubts gave way to belief and the crisis had passed, he expressed profound gratitude to Yahweh (17:14–18; 20:11–13).

Jeremiah's earliest preaching recalls Yahweh's prior grace to Israel (2:6–7). Most recently, Yahweh's grace was shown to the exiles who had survived the Assyrian wilderness (31:2), and these are now called to return to Zion (3:12–14; 31:4–6, 7–9; etc.). Salvation was even available to Jerusalem in the early days of the reform if the people had obeyed the covenant and repented of their wrongdoing.

During the dark days of 605 a salvific word was given to Baruch, and in 597 when Jerusalem surrendered, salvation was presented as an eschatological hope to exiles leaving for Babylon (30:5–31:22). Health would return (30:17; 33:6), but the exiles would have to settle down in Babylon, pray for that nation, and wait for Zion's restoration (29; cf. 24:4–7).

During Jehoiakim's and Zedekiah's reigns, Jeremiah announced Nebuchadnezzar as Yahweh's "servant," and proclaimed further that all nations—including Judah—must serve him (25:9; 27:6–7). Salvation would be realized through the exiles living in Babylon. In Jerusalem one person, however, did manage to get a salvific word from Jeremiah and that was Ebed-melech, who acted to save Jeremiah's life. The word came while Jeremiah was confined to the court of the guard. The nation, too, at this time, received some of its grandest eschatological promises, including the promise of a new covenant (31:23–33:13). Unlike judgment, divine grace and salvation do not require from Yahweh a reason; in fact, they most often come without a reason. It is entirely due to Yahweh's initiative that Israel can hope for national restoration, and also that a new covenant will be made where Yahweh's law will be written on people's hearts. See NEW COVENANT. This new act of grace will render unnecessary admonitions of one person to another to "know Yahweh" or "fear Yahweh" (31:31–34; 32:37–41; *ROTT* 2: 212–15). Yahweh at this future time will also forgive the people's sins.

The salvific word for the present, however, is a more modest one: Zedekiah, his house, and the city can be spared, but Zedekiah has to obey Yahweh's word and surrender (38:17–23). Even later people of the city are offered salvation, but they must desert to the enemy and surrender because the fate of Jerusalem is sealed (21:8–10). After Jerusalem is destroyed, Jeremiah speaks yet more words of hope and salvation to those allowed to remain in the land. They are to stay where they are, not go to Egypt as they plan to do (42:7–12).

Jeremiah then fulfills that part of his calling which was "to build and to plant" (1:10). And so far as the activity of Yahweh is concerned, he does not decide at any point to completely withhold his salvation. Salvation is continually in his mind; it is given simultaneously with judgment (e.g., 1:13–19; 21:8–10; etc.). Salvation is ever present as an option if only people will obey God's voice and repent of their evil (18:7–8).

2. The Theology of the Book. The theology of the book of Jeremiah supplements and expands the theology of Jeremiah by placing the latter in a wider context. This theology appears primarily in the prose material and in foreign nation poems of unknown provenance, but it is present as well in the book's compositional structures.

a. Theology in the Prose. The majority of the book's prose says little or nothing about causation or interconnections, as, for example, one finds in the Deuteronomistic History or in 2 Maccabees. The coming destruction is connected with the sins of Manasseh in 15:4, but this appears to be a late addition building on 2 Kgs 23:26 and 24:3. The summary notice in 37:1–2 also looks to be Deuteronomistic, though v 2 does codify an important theme of the Baruch prose, i.e., that people refused to listen to Jeremiah's word (11:6, 8b LXX; 13:11; 19:15; 36:31; 44:5, 16; etc.). In 25:3 the people are said not to have heeded Jeremiah for 23 years; this reflects more or less Jeremiah's own complaint in 6:16, 19. Theology in the book is on a continuum: There is a core of dynamic ideas which is Jeremianic; theological statements more or less explicit in nature come in the Baruch prose; and the most transparent theology giving causations or interconnections are to be found only in the latest additions to the book.

The Baruch prose has little explicit theology about the guiding hand of Yahweh. In 36:26, for example, it does say that "Yahweh hid them" (i.e., Jeremiah and Baruch). But most of the theology in this prose is subtle, indirect, and less than transparent. When it says in 36:24 that Jehoiakim and his servants did not "rend their garments" at the reading of Jeremiah's scroll, the unstated message is that Jehoiakim did not repent the way Josiah did when a scroll was read to him some years earlier (2 Kgs 22:11). In the notation of 28:17 that Hananiah died "in that same year, in the seventh month," what is implied is that Jeremiah's prophecy to Hananiah (v 16) was fulfilled, and thus Jeremiah was a true prophet according to the formula of Deut 18:21–22. A further theological conclusion which might also be drawn, given the conflict between the two prophets, is that Hananiah was a false prophet. This judgment is in fact made in the LXX in 35:1 [MT 28:1].

When Baruch records the release of Jeremiah by Nebuzaradan, he bears silent witness to Yahweh's fulfillment of earlier promises that Jeremiah would be saved. Therefore it should not be concluded that no good comes out of Jeremiah's final sufferings, nor should we say with von Rad (*ROTT* 2: 207) that "Jeremiah's path disappears in misery." The guiding hand of Yahweh is recognized throughout Jeremiah's *via dolorosa;* it is simply that this theology is not explicitly stated. Von Rad is correct, however, in saying that the Baruch prose does not make Jeremiah out to be a hero (*ROTT* 2: 207–8), i.e., the prophet is not glorified in his sufferings. It is generally thought that Baruch's explanation for Jeremiah's sufferings is that the sufferings were a consequence of his preaching about Jerusalem's capture and his call to surrender (*ROTT* 2: 207). But more broadly, the reason for his sufferings is that the people refused to listen to Yahweh's word, and this rejection manifested itself in anger toward the one who brought that word (1:18–19; cf. 20:15–16).

Prose of uncertain and exilic origin expands earlier theology. Exilic passages of hope and restoration, e.g., 3:15–18, develop Jeremiah's earliest preaching to northern Israel. The passage in 12:14–17 about the conversion of the nations to Yahweh expands upon Jeremiah's expressed universalism. Other passages repeat themes originating with Jeremiah and Baruch, only more transparently. One of the most common concerns Yahweh's reason for punishing the nations (5:19; 9:11–15—Eng 9:12–16; 11:7–8 MT; etc.).

b. Theology in the Foreign Nation Oracles. Although it is difficult in the foreign nation oracles to distinguish what comes from Jeremiah, what is imported from other prophets, and what is late theological expansionism, certain ideas seem not to emanate from Jeremiah. For example, Babylon is said to have "sinned" and "incurred guilt" against Yahweh (50:14 MT; 51:5). Also, Yahweh's vengeance on Babylon is to repay her for the destruction of the temple (50:28 MT; 51:11b). Yahweh is also said to reserve compassion and favor for the foreign nations (except Babylon) after their punishment is complete. The nations will be reinhabited (46:26), and their fortunes will be restored (48:47; 49:6, 39).

c. Theology in Compositional Structures. Compositional structures in the book are created with a liturgical purpose in mind, and frequently these structures embody a statement of implied theology. The two successive liturgies of lament, communal supplication, and rejection by Yahweh of Jeremiah's prayers in 14:1–15:4 explain why

Jeremiah was unsuccessful in his mediation on behalf of Jerusalem. The liturgical composition of 30:5–31:22 embodies a message which says that hope and divine promise will follow judgment and lamentation. This text also affirms that Yahweh will remake his covenant with Israel. The inclusion framing the two letters to the exiles in chap. 29 (vv 5, 28) emphasizes the need for people to settle down in Babylon so they may live and multiply. And the juxtaposition of narratives in 34–35 is a quiet homily on obedience and disobedience.

The inclusion which binds the First Edition (chaps. 1–20) together puts Jeremiah's cry of despair—which by itself says Jeremiah deserves to live no more than anyone else—into a larger context where Yahweh's call can affirm his birth and also his life (Lundbom 1975: 28–29; 1985: 600). This rhetorical structure also conveys the message that Yahweh's understanding exceeds Jeremiah's, which is another way of saying that Jeremiah does not really understand his own suffering (*ROTT* 2: 206). Finally, the inclusio framing the King Collection in 21:1–23:8, which repeats the play on names in 23:6 between Zedekiah and the future Davidic king, contrasts the righteousness of the future king with the unrighteousness of him who last sat on Jerusalem's throne. This is but a subtler version of that Deuteronomistic theology which sets up David as the model of the good king and Jeroboam as the model of the bad (2 Kgs 14:3, 24; etc.).

Bibliography

Avigad, N. 1978. Baruch the Scribe and Jerahmeel the King's Son. *IEJ* 28: 52–56 [reprinted in *BA* 42 (1979): 114–18].

Baillet, M. 1962. Jeremie. Pp. 62–69 in *Les 'Petites Grottes' de Qumran.* DJD 3. Ed. M. Baillet et al. Oxford.

Baumgartner, W. 1987. *Jeremiah's Poems of Lament.* Trans. by D. E. Orton. Sheffield.

Blayney, B. 1836. *Jeremiah and Lamentations.* 3d ed. London.

Bright, J. 1951. The Date of the Prose Sermons of Jeremiah. *JBL* 70: 15–29.

Budde, K. 1921. Über das erste Kapitel des Buches Jeremia. *JBL* 40: 23–37.

Carroll, R. P. 1981. *From Chaos to Covenant.* New York.

Cornill, C. H. 1891. *Einleitung in das Alte Testament.* Freiburg.

Cross, F. M. Jr. 1964. The History of the Biblical Text in the Light of Discoveries in the Judean Desert. *HTR* 57: 281–99.

Driver, S. R. 1889. The Double Text of Jeremiah. *Exp* 9: 321–37.

Eichhorn, J. G. 1790. *Einleitung ins Alte Testament.* Vol. 3. Reutlingen.

Eichrodt, W. 1950–51. The Right Interpretation of the Old Testament: A Study of Jeremiah 7:1–15. Trans. D. H. Gard. *TToday* 7: 15–25.

Freedman, D. N. 1963. The Law and the Prophets. *VT Sup* 9: 250–65.

———. 1983. The Earliest Bible. Pp. 167–75 in *The Bible and Its Traditions,* Michigan Quarterly Review 22:3, ed. M. P. O'Connor and D. N. Freedman. Ann Arbor, MI.

Freedman, D. N., and Mathews, K. A. 1985. *The Paleo-Hebrew Leviticus Scroll.* Winona Lake, IN.

Gerstenberger, E. 1963. Jeremiah's Complaints: Observations on Jer 15:10–21. *JBL* 82: 393–408.

Gevaryahu, H. 1970. Notes on Authors and Books in the Bible. *Beth Miqra* 43: 368–74 (in Hebrew).

———. 1973. Baruch ben Neriah the Scribe. Pp. 191–243 in *Zer Ligevurot* (Festschrift Zalman Shazar). Jerusalem (in Hebrew).

Heschel, A. J. 1962. *The Prophets.* New York and Evanston, IL.

Holladay, W. L. 1960. Prototypes and Copies: A New Approach to the Poetry-Prose Problem in the Book of Jeremiah. *JBL* 79: 351–67.

———. 1962. Style, Irony and Authenticity in Jeremiah. *JBL* 81: 44–54.

———. 1966a. Jeremiah and Moses. *JBL* 85: 17–27.

———. 1966b. The Recovery of Poetic Passages of Jeremiah. *JBL* 85: 401–35.

———. 1976. *The Architecture of Jeremiah 1–20.* Lewisburg, PA.

Janzen, J. G. 1967. Double Readings in the Text of Jeremiah. *HTR* 60: 433–47.

———. 1973. *Studies in the Text of Jeremiah.* Cambridge, MA.

Kugel, J. L. 1981. *The Idea of Biblical Poetry.* New Haven.

Lowth, R. 1815. *Lectures on the Sacred Poetry of the Hebrews.* Trans. by G. Gregory. Boston.

Lundbom, J. R. 1975. *Jeremiah: A Study in Ancient Hebrew Rhetoric.* SBLDS 18. Missoula, MT.

———. 1985. The Double Curse in Jeremiah 20:14–18. *JBL* 104: 589–600.

———. 1986. Baruch, Seraiah, and Expanded Colophons in the Book of Jeremiah. *JSOT* 36: 89–114.

Michaelis, J. D. 1793. *Observations Philologicae et Criticae in Jeremiae Vaticinia et Threnos.* Göttingen.

Mowinckel, S. 1914. *Zur Komposition des Buches Jeremia.* Oslo.

———. 1946. *Prophecy and Tradition.* Oslo.

Muilenburg, J. 1970. Baruch the Scribe. Pp. 215–38 in *Proclamation and Presence,* ed. J. I. Durham and J. R. Porter. Richmond.

Overholt, T. W. 1970. *The Threat of Falsehood.* Naperville, IL.

Rietzschel, C. 1966. *Das Problem der Urrolle.* Gütersloh.

Robinson, T. H. 1924. Baruch's Roll. *ZAW* 42: 209–21.

Shiloh, Y. 1984. *Excavations at the City of David.* Vol. 1, *1978–1982.* Qedem 19. Jerusalem.

Smith, H. P. 1887. The Text of Jeremiah. *Hebraica* 3: 193–200.

Thackeray, H. St.J. 1902–1903. The Greek Translators of Jeremiah. *JTS* 4: 245–66.

Thiel, W. 1973. *Die deuteronomistische Redaktion von Jeremia 1–25.* WMANT 41. Neukirchen-Vluyn.

———. 1981. *Die deuteronomistische Redaktion von Jeremia 26–45.* WMANT 52. Neukirchen-Vluyn.

Tov, E. 1976. *The Septuagint Translation of Jeremiah and Baruch.* HSM 8. Missoula, MT.

———. 1979. Exegetical Notes on the Hebrew Vorlage of the LXX of Jeremiah 27(34). *ZAW* 91: 73–93.

———. fc.a. The Jeremiah Scrolls from Qumran. In *The Texts of Qumran and the History of the Community.*

———. fc.b. Three Qumran Fragments of Jeremiah. *Textus.*

———. fc.c. 4Q Jer^{b}. *IEJ.*

Weippert, H. 1973. *Die Prosareden des Jeremiabuches.* BZAW 132. Berlin and New York.

Wette, W. M. L. de. 1858. *A Critical and Historical Introduction to the Canonical Scriptures of the Old Testament.* Vol. 2. 3d ed. Trans. T. Parker. Boston.

Zalevski, S. 1975. The Caption to the Book of Jeremiah. *Beth Miqra* 60: 26–62 (in Hebrew).

Zlotowitz, B. M. 1981. *The Septuagint Translation of the Hebrew Terms in Relation to God in the Book of Jeremiah.* New York.

JACK R. LUNDBOM

JEREMIAH, EPISTLE OF. The Epistle of Jeremiah is neither a letter nor was it written by Jeremiah the prophet. It has more the form of a homily against idolatry and idols. It is extant only in Greek and in several dependent versions. The placement of this epistle differs in various biblical mss. In codex Vaticanus as well as in Alexandrinus (and others), it stands after the book of Lamentations. In other Greek and Syriac mss, it comes after Baruch. This little book consists of 10 stanzas, each ending with a refrain. The same motif recurs throughout the book. In vv 1–7 the author says that the Jews whom Nebuchadnezzar will exile to Babylon will remain there for seven generations. In exile they must refrain from idolatry and worship God whose angel will be with them. Throughout vv 8–73 the author elaborates upon the folly of idolatry. In vv 8–16 he says that the Babylonian gods cannot speak and cannot dress. They can protect themselves neither from insults nor from rust and moths. Verses 17–23 deal with the insensate nature of the idols. Their eyes are filled with dust, they are locked in the temples for fear of robbers, and they are illuminated through lamps which they cannot see. They are incapable of recognizing that they are defiled by unclean animals. Verses 24–29 refer to the idols as being outwardly impressive (because they are expensively made), but they have no breath and cannot move or walk. The priests exploit them and impure women defile their offerings. Verses 30–40a elaborate even further on the worthlessness of the idols. Although they are defiled by priestesses, and priests take the idols' garments for their families, they cannot protect themselves. They can neither crown nor depose a king; they can neither give riches nor help those in need. Verses 40b–44 state that Bel and other idols are treated with disrespect by the Chaldeans themselves, a matter emphasized by the sacred prostitution enacted in the temples. Verses 45–52 add only the idea that idols are but the creation of men who will themselves perish at some point. Also, in times of war the idols are hidden because they are helpless. In vv 53–56 the author stresses once again that the idols are so helpless they cannot judge or redress a wrong; they cannot escape fire or war. Verses 57–65 propound the idea that idols are useless, because in contradistinction to a vessel or a door, which are useful, the idols are not. Moreover, the forces of nature fulfill divinely ordained functions, whereas idols can do nothing. In conclusion, vv 66–73 compare idols to a scarecrow, a thornbush, and a corpse. Thus, the righteous man who is free of idols will be far above reproach.

The author of the epistle was certainly not Jeremiah, but the text is dependent on both Jer 10:2–15 for the contents of the epistle and on Jeremiah 29 for its form (chap. 29 mentions a letter of Jeremiah to the exiles in Babylon). The epistle is dependent on the familiar *topoi* found in the Bible to describe the idols (cf. Jer 10:2–5, 8–11, 13b–15; Isa 44:9–20; 46:5–7; Ps 115:3–8; Deut 4:27–28). The epistle was most probably composed in Hebrew or Aramaic, and is very repetitive in its themes and phraseology. Two arguments for a Hebrew original are: (1) certain variant readings are best explained by positing a Hebrew original (vv 21, 54, 68); and (2) certain corrupt Greek readings seem to presuppose a Hebrew word (cf. vv 12, 72) or other Hebraism. The extant versions are the LXX and those based on it, such as the OL, Vulgate, and Syro-Hexaplar. There are no major differences between the various versions. The Arabic version is faithful to the LXX, while the Syriac is somewhat free.

The purpose of the epistle seems quite obvious. It is a vehement attack on idolatry, in particular on Babylonian idols, and is designed to protect Jews from idolatry in the Babylonian Diaspora and elsewhere. The exilic setting and the attack on Bel and other Babylonian idols is probably a literary fiction, for the author may have composed this document at the end of the 4th century B.C. This becomes clear from an allusion in the document itself (v 3) where it is said: "Once you have reached Babylon you will stay there for many years, for a long while, up to seven generations; but afterwards I will bring you away from there in peace." If we reckon from 587 (or 597), seven generations reaches 307 (or 317) B.C. Also, the epistle is probably mentioned in 2 Macc 2:1–4 (datable to the 1st century B.C.), and the earliest Greek translation derives from Qumran cave VII (which is dated ca. 100 B.C.). This gives us a *terminus ad quem* of the 1st century B.C., although it may have been composed as early as the end of the 4th century B.C. It may have been used by the author of the Wisdom of Solomon (cf. 13:10–15; 19) in the 1st century B.C. As evidenced by that text, idolatry was a central issue in the fight against Hellenism in Palestine from the time of the Diadochi through Roman times. It is therefore not altogether impossible that this document was used in Hellenistic Palestine (cf. *1 En.* 99:7, 9). There exists no reason to claim that the epistle was written outside Palestine, as some have suggested (Egypt, Babylonia, etc.), in particular when we take into consideration that our author most probably did not use the LXX, but a Hebrew recension.

The book was excluded from the Hebrew canon, but was accepted by Christians in Egypt. Christian writers do not mention the letter often; it was rejected by Protestants during the Reformation, but received by the Roman Catholics at the Council of Trent in 1546. In the Eastern church the epistle was accepted as canonical by some of the Church Fathers (Origen, Epiphanius, and others); in the West it appeared in the list of Hilary. See also JEREMIAH, ADDITIONS TO.

DORON MENDELS

JEREMIEL (ANGEL) [Lat *Hieremihel*]. The angelic name that appears in the Latin mss of 2 Esdr 4:36. The variant *remihel* is also attested, corresponding to *rmʾyl* in Syriac mss. The Latin transliteration *Hieremihel* is thought to correspond to Gk *yeremeēl* or *yeremiēl,* forms which appear in many mss of the LXX where the corresponding name in MT is *yĕraḥmĕʾēl* (RSV Jerahmeel: 1 Chr 2:25, 26, 27, 42; Jer 36:26 [—LXX 43:26]).

An apocalyptic tradition is cited in 2 Esdr 4:33–37 (cf. Rev 6:9–11) according to which this angel promised vindication to the souls of the righteous dead who asked, "How long?" The angel's name as reconstructed would interpret that vindication as an expression of God's compassion.

An alternative derivation is from a putative Hebrew **yārîmʾēl* involving the causative of the Hebrew or Aramaic verb *rwm* "to be high" and meaning "May El lift up/exalt" (cf. Isa 52:13; on the derivation, see *TPNAH,* 113–14. The verb *rwm* is not normally used to suggest resurrection.)

Other references to the angel occur, evidently, in the Greek version of *1 En.* 20:8, where the angel *Remeiēl* is "in charge of those who rise," and in *Apoc. Zeph.* 6:11–17, where *Eremiēl* (the text is Coptic) is set over the abyss and Hades. In *2 Baruch* the angel *rmʾyl* (Syr) interprets the vision in chaps. 53–74 (note 55:3; see Bogaert 1969: 1.428–37) and identifies himself as the destroyer of Sennacherib's army (63:6). In one Greek ms family of *Sib. Or.* 2:215, *eromiēl* is one of the four archangels.

Bibliography

Bogaert, P. 1969. *Apocalypse de Baruch.* SC 144. Paris.

GEORGE W. E. NICKELSBURG

JEREMOTH (PERSON) [Heb *yĕrēmôt*]. An alternate form of JERIMOTH.

JERIAH (PERSON) [Heb *yĕrîyāhû*]. A Kohathite, the first son of Hebron, whom, according to the 1 Chronicles, David appointed to service in the Temple and its cult (1 Chr 23:19). Jeriah appears nowhere else in the OT outside of 1 Chronicles. The Levitical genealogies of Exodus 6 and Numbers 3 do not include enumeration of the immediate descendants of Hebron. The source of the Chronicler's use of the name "Jeriah" remains uncertain. See JEKAMEAM. The style of the list, however, corresponds closely with the compositional techniques of the Chronicler. This suggests that Williamson (*1 and 2 Chronicles NCBC,* 161) may be correct in asserting that "the names of the heads of houses will then be current at the time of the list's composition." Jeriah's oversight of the Ruebenites, the Gadites, and the half-tribe of Manasseh in the "affairs of God and the affairs of the king" may represent either an ideal or real situation of a Hebronite family at the time of the composition of Chronicles (1 Chr 26:31–32).

Bibliography

Williamson, H. G. M. 1979. The Origins of the Twenty-four Priestly Courses, A Study of 1 Chronicles xxiii–xxvii. Pp. 251–68 in *Studies in the Historical Books of the Old Testament,* ed. J. A. Emerton. VTSup 30. Leiden.

JOHN W. WRIGHT

JERIBAI (PERSON) [Heb *yĕrîbay*]. A son of Elnaam and brother of Joshaviah (1 Chr 11:46), one of the Mighty Men of David's armies. These names appear in a list occasionally described as the "Additional" Mighty Men—sixteen in number (1 Chr 11:41b–47), since they are not included in the parallel list in 2 Sam 23:24–39 (= 1 Chr 11:26–41a). The origin of this additional list has been disputed: some have considered it a postexilic fabrication, yet the E Jordanian locale suggested by the names (e.g. all the known sites are E of the Jordan: Reuben, v 42; Ashteroth . . . Aroer, v 44; Moab, v 46) appears to be an unlikely invention, considering the suspicion regarded this area after the Exile. That David would have support from Moab is not surprising, considering (1) his Moabite ancestry (Ruth 4:18–22) and (2) the sequestering of his parents there (1 Sam 22:3–4). This list probably was an additional fragment available to the Chronicler (Williamson *1 and 2 Chronicles* NCBC, 104), so we may suggest that Jeribai was a Transjordanian war hero who joined David's forces.

JOHN C. ENDRES

JERICHO (PLACE) [Heb *yĕrîḥô*]. A town just NW of the Dead Sea which is best known as the site that Israel first conquered in their entrance into the land of Canaan. The Israelites encamped across the Jordan from Jericho (Num 22:1; 26:3), and from this camp, Joshua sent two spies to reconnoiter the city (Joshua 2), before undertaking a bizarre strategy of conquest (Josh 5:13–6:23). The city was later allotted to Benjamin (Josh 16:1, 7; 18:12, 21), but during the time of the Judges, became an outpost of Eglon of Moab ("the city of palm trees;" Judg 3:13). During the time of Elijah and Elisha, there was a school of prophets at Jericho (2 Kgs 2:4–5, 15). After the Babylonians had breached the wall of Jerusalem, Zedekiah attempted to escape the city under cover of darkness, but was captured near Jericho, from which he was delivered to Nebuchadnezzar, who forced him to witness the execution of his sons. Afterward Zedekiah was blinded (Jer 39:5–7). Most of the references to Jericho in the Apocryphal writings and the NT refer to the area of Jericho as it surrounded the Hasmonean/Herodian palace complex to the SW of the OT site (see E below).

A. Modern and Ancient Names of the Sites
B. Location and Topographical Description
C. History of Explorations and Excavations
D. History of Jericho (Tell es-Sultan)
   1. Mesolithic (ca. 9000–8700 B.C.)
   2. Proto-Neolithic (ca. 8700–8500 B.C.)
   3. Pre-Pottery Neolithic (ca. 8500–5200 B.C.)
   4. Pottery Neolithic A and B (ca. 5200–4000 B.C.)
   5. Early Bronze I (ca. 3300–3150 B.C.)
   6. Early Bronze II–III (ca. 3050–2300 B.C.)
   7. Early Bronze IV (ca. 2300–1950 B.C.)
   8. Middle Bronze Age (ca. 1950–1550 B.C.)
   9. Late Bronze Age (ca. 1550–1200 B.C.)
   10. Iron Age (ca. 1200–587 B.C.)
   11. Babylonian/Persian to Byzantine (587 B.C.–A.D. 636)
E. Roman Jericho (Tulul Abu el-ʿAlayiq)

A. Modern and Ancient Names of the Sites

The site of OT Jericho is situated on the mound of Tell es-Sultan (M.R. 192142), ca. 2 km NW of the modern oasis of Jericho known as er-Riḥa. The spring around which the ancient site grew is known as ʿAin es-Sultan or Elisha's Fountain, a name applied to the spring during the Middle Ages (Garstang and Garstang 1940: 30; cf. 2 Kgs 2:19–22). Occupational remains dated to the Hellenistic, Roman, and Islamic periods were found on the mounds of Tulul Abu el-ʿAlayiq (i.e., Roman Jericho, N.R. 191139; see E below), 2 km W of modern er-Riḥa (Kelso and Baramki 1955: 1–19; Pritchard 1958: 56–58).

B. Location and Topographical Description

Jericho (Tell es-Sultan) is located in the wide plain of the Jordan valley about 16 km NW of the N shore of the Dead

Sea and just to the E of the mountains of Judea. At its maximum height on the NW side, the mound rises 24 m, and its area is approximately 4 hectares. See Fig. JER.01. The fertile plain in which the site is situated is artificially irrigated by the spring of ʿAin es-Sultan, which is located on the E side of the ancient mound, and also by the spring of ʿAin Duq, located 3 km NW of Jericho. Since the site lies 825 ft. below sea level, the town has the distinction of being situated at the lowest spot in the world.

The topographical features which make Jericho a very fertile and ideal place for settlement have been discussed extensively by numerous authors. The first serious topographical survey was undertaken by Conder and Kitchner (*SWP* 3: 222–29). More recent discussions appear in Kenyon (1981: 1), Bartlett (1982b: 11–26), and Bienkowski (1986: 1).

C. History of Explorations and Excavations

The earliest known account of exploration pertaining to ancient Jericho dates to A.D. 333 and comes from the "pilgrim of Bordeaux" (Wilkinson, Hill, and Ryan 1988: 4). Although many other pilgrims and travelers visited the site thereafter, it was not until 1868 that the first preliminary excavation of Tell es-Sultan was undertaken by Charles Warren (Warren 1869: 14–16, Bliss 1894: 175–83). Warren cut E-W trenches across the mound with some 8 ft. square shafts sunk 20 ft. to bedrock. He cut through the EB town wall and just missed the famous Neolithic stone tower by less than 1 m. He concluded that

> Very little was found except pottery jars and stone mortars for grinding corn. The general impression given by the result of the excavations is that these

JER.01. Aerial view of Jericho from NE. *(Courtesy of T. A. Holland)*

mounds are formed by the gradual crumbling away of great towers or castles of sunburnt brick (1883: 225).

The first scientific excavations (1907–9 and 1911) were under the direction of Ernst Sellin and Carl Watzinger (1913). They excavated at Tell es-Sultan and also at the sites of Tulul and Abu el-ᶜAlayiq SW of Jericho.

Sellin and Watzinger excavated a considerable area of the tell (as is shown by the shaded area in Fig. JER.02). They found a large portion of the MB revetment glacis on the N, W, and E sides of the tell and also portions of the EB town walls. Their original interpretation of the revetment glacis was that it dated to the 9th century B.C. and that the EB walls belonged to the first half of the 2d millennium B.C., which appeared to confirm the biblical account of the capture of Jericho by Joshua (see below). However, Watzinger (1926: 131–36) rightly revised his dating and showed that the outer revetment was destroyed ca. 1600 B.C. and that the EB walls dated in fact to the 3d millennium B.C.

Above the spring, located on the SE side of the tell, the German excavators discovered houses belonging to the Israelite settlement which were dated fairly accurately from the 11th to the early 6th centuries B.C. They concluded that the town was destroyed by the Assyrians in 721 B.C. and 701 B.C., as well as by the Babylonians in 587 B.C., with a postexilic settlement which began in 539 B.C. upon the return of the Jews from Babylon (cf. Weippert and Weippert 1976: 145–47).

Since he disagreed with the results of the German excavations, John Garstang (1932–36) decided to undertake a new expedition to Jericho which lasted from 1930 to 1936 (for areas excavated on the tell see the composite sketch plan, Fig. JER.02). Garstang also excavated a number of MB and LB tombs (Garstang 1932: 18: 22, 41–54; 1933: 4–42; and Bienkowski 1986: 32–102). Owing to poor excavation techniques at the time, Garstang's stratigraphy and dating is partially unreliable, but he did break new ground in his discoveries relating to the Mesolithic and Neolithic periods at Jericho. Bienkowski (1986: 2–4) gives a good summary of Garstang's major finds in the publication based upon his doctoral dissertation (Holland 1988: 189–90).

With the advent of the greatly improved stratigraphical digging methods developed by Sir Mortimer Wheeler and Kathleen Kenyon (Kenyon/Wheeler Method) during the late 1940s and early 1950s, Kenyon embarked upon a fresh examination of Jericho in an effort to clarify her predecessor's results on the site. The excavations were conducted from 1952 to 1958 (Kenyon 1960; 1965; and 1981; Kenyon and Holland 1982 and 1983).

As Garstang did before her, Kenyon explored around the ancient tell and excavated numerous tombs ranging in date from the EB I (Kenyon's "Proto-Urban period") to the Roman period. The material from these tombs was extensively published in the first two volumes of the final Jericho reports (Kenyon 1960 and 1965). On the tell, Kenyon excavated three main trenches: Trench I, located in the middle of the W side of the mound; Trench II, situated on the NE end of the mound (note the misnumbering of Trenches I and II on the plan in Kenyon *EAEHL* 2:551); and Trench III, laid out on the S end of the mound. Various squares identified by letters also were sited on the tell and either partially or totally excavated to bedrock.

D. History of Jericho (Tell es-Sultan)

1. Mesolithic (ca. 9000–8700 B.C.). The earliest occupational remains discovered by Kenyon (table 1) come from the bottom of Squares EI, II, and V, which were excavated to bedrock, and are dated to the Mesolithic period, about 9000 B.C. (Kenyon 1981: pl. 144b). At the base of Square EI lay a natural oblong platform of clay over the bedrock which contained a group of three sockets for uprights, tentatively identified as supports for "totem poles" by Kenyon. The flint and bone tools associated with the structure are typologically akin to the Lower Natufian of Mount Carmel. The excavator suggests that the structure was some kind of shrine or sanctuary, probably set up by hunters who were camping around the original spring, probably located in the vicinity of Area H in ancient times. The finds associated with the Mesolithic levels consisted of a fairly large Natufian flint industry, bone tools, and stone vessels and tools.

The Natufian II (or Middle Natufian), microlithic, and other tools were found only in Squares EI, II, and V (Crowfoot Payne 1983: 624–29). However, on the evidence of a bone harpoon, also from Square EI, the earlier Natufian I period appears to be represented on the site. Other bone tools include an awl, a smoothing tool, and an unidentified object cut square at both ends and polished all over (Marshall 1982: fig. 230:1–2). Only four stone objects and one fragment are recorded from the Mesolithic levels in Squares EI, II, and V. The "socket" stones identified above as "totem poles" by Kenyon have been reclassified by Dorrell (1983: 489) as limestone mortars. Two polishing stones were also found.

2. Proto-Neolithic (ca. 8700–8500 B.C.). The Proto-Neolithic deposits excavated by Kenyon were encountered in three areas of the tell just above the natural huwwar bedrock in Squares FI, DI, and DII adjacent to Trench I, in Squares EI, II, V, and in Square MI. See Table 1.

The deepest Proto-Neolithic deposit was in Square MI with an accumulation of 4 m of occupation levels above bedrock (Kenyon 1981: pls. 129 and 295). Associated with these levels were one or more slight clayey humps which formed the boundary between a marked surface overlain by silty occupation levels. The humps, some of which were composed of defined "balls" of clay, forming elementary bricks, represented the bases of walls of slight shelters which probably had superstructures of branches and skins.

In Squares EI, II, and V, the Proto-Neolithic is represented by a very small deposit on the turf line which separates the lower Mesolithic level from the Proto-Neolithic level (Kenyon 1981: pls. 311 and 312). A series of post holes were found associated with the remains of huts and sandy floors. The two phases of occupation levels probably represent the very end of the period as they are immediately succeeded by the first Pre-Pottery Neolithic A house level, which suggests that the Proto-Neolithic settlement expanded from the nucleus tell, most probably the area around Square MI, just before the appearance of the

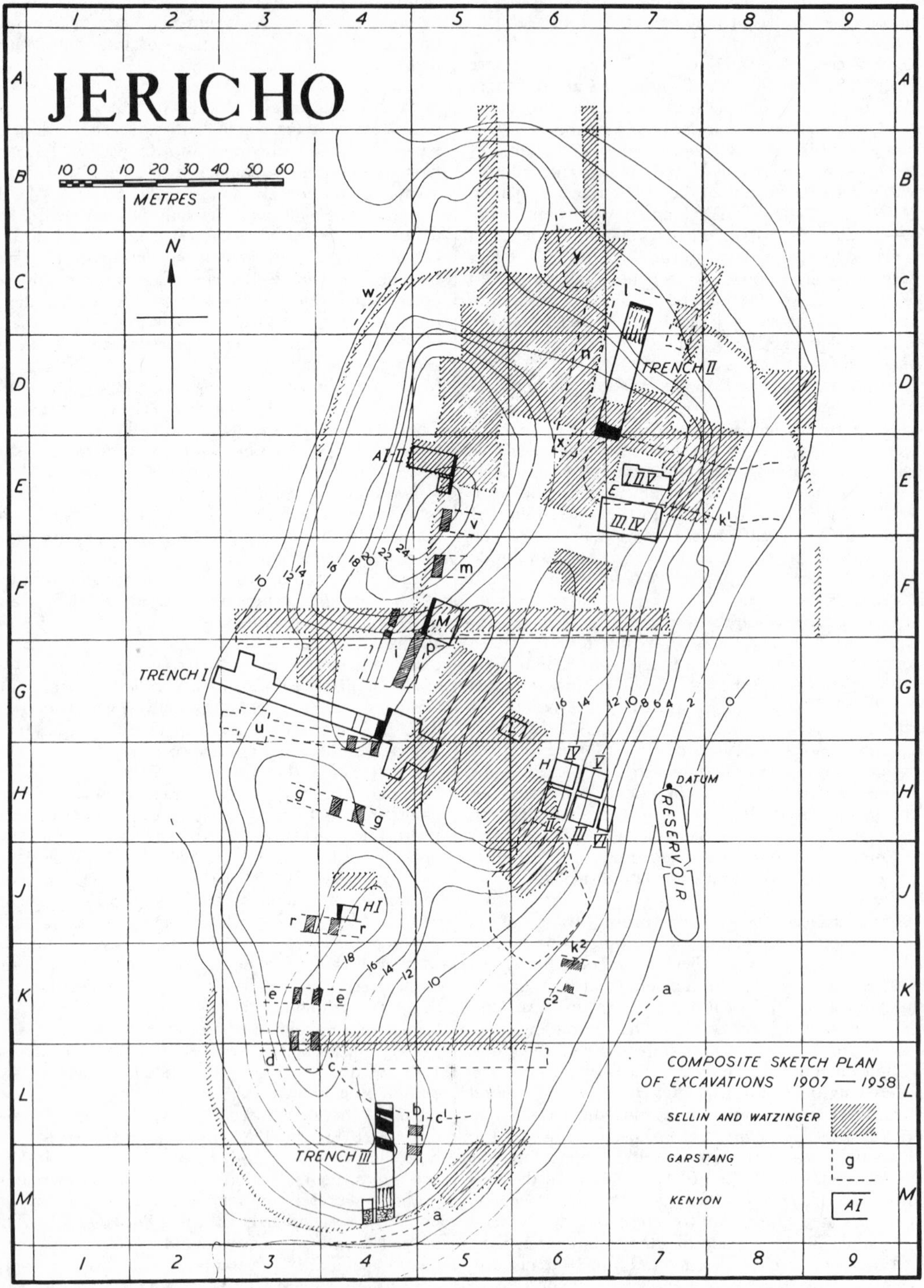

JER.02. Composite site plan of the Jericho excavations, 1907–58. *(Courtesy of T. A. Holland)*

round houses constructed during the Pre-Pottery Neolithic A period.

Very shallow deposits belonging to the Proto-Neolithic period were found in Squares FI, DI, and DII, an area 25 m S of Square MI and outside of the nucleus tell. The main characteristics of the deposit were black sticky layers, humps made of brick balls, and a few post holes.

The Proto-Neolithic flint industry from Jericho has been defined as Sultanian (meaning from Tell es-Sultan) by Crowfoot Payne (1983: 623, 629–30). The material discovered by Kenyon comes from Trench II and Squares DI, DII, EI, II, V, and MI. The flint was so fine-grained that it could be regarded as agate. A probable source of the flint was recently discovered by Noy in the Jordan Valley near Gilgal N of Jericho (Crowfoot Payne 1983: 629). One very interesting aspect of the flint industry of this period is the presence of pale gray obsidian tools. The analysis of a specimen from the lowest level on the site shows the source at Çiftlik in Anatolia, which confirms extensive trade relations at this period in the development of Jericho as an early center of civilization (Crowfoot Payne 1983: 638, n. 2).

Most of the Proto-Neolithic bone tools were found in Square MI, but a few fragments also came from Squares E and F (Marshall 1982: 584–86 and fig. 230).

Of the twenty-three Proto-Neolithic stones artifacts found, twenty were from Square MI, two from Square F, and one from Trench III (Dorrell 1983: 490 and fig. 218, pl. 1). The one limestone quern found is of special interest since the inside of the hollow used for grinding was stained red and may have been used to grind pigment rather than food grain.

3. Pre-Pottery Neolithic (ca. 8500–5200 B.C.). The Pre-Pottery Neolithic A (ca. 8500–700 B.C.) stages of occupation (table 1) and the areas of their discovery are further detailed in Kenyon (1981).

There was obviously an occupational gap between the Proto-Neolithic and the PPNA since in all the areas investigated, fully developed round houses, usually single-roomed, were found in contrast to the primitive huts constructed in previous periods. The houses were built with solid walls constructed with planoconvex mudbricks which, in many instances, had a hog-backed shape (Kenyon 1981: pls. 44a, 146a). The inward incline of the preserved portions of the walls and a considerable amount of brick debris in the collapse suggest that the roofs were domed, possibly similar to the so-called "beehive" houses still built in Syria and used for both storage and housing. The construction of these houses at Jericho indicates that the occupation had become sedentary. The areas covered by the houses was greater than the later Bronze Age town.

Whether for defense, protection from wild animals, or a natural rising of the level of the ground surrounding the settlement (Bar-Yosef 1986: 159–61), the PPN inhabitants soon found it necessary to construct a major, stone-built town wall (Fig. JER.03) of which Kenyon (1981: pls. 4, 6) found traces in all three of her main trenches. On the W side of the town in Trench I, the first town wall was associated with a large stone-built tower situated against its inner side, 8.5 m in diameter at the base with a surviving height of 7.75 m. The construction of the tower was solid except in the center, which had a staircase providing access to the top from the interior of the town. There were three further stages of the town wall which also made use of the tower. A rock-cut ditch which measured 9.5 m wide and 2.25 m deep (Kenyon 1981: pls. 4, 244) was cut on the W outer face of the wall during the second stage of its use.

The PPNA flint industry was so similar to that of the preceding Proto-Neolithic period that Crowfoot Payne (1983: 663–65) retained the name "Sultanian," which she coined to commemorate the importance of Jericho during these periods.

The large collection of PPNA stone vessels and tools included 171 vessels (bowls, platters, mortars, querns, etc.); 252 pestles; 174 polishing stones, 28 axes; 14 grooved stones (possibly used to straighten and smooth arrow-shafts); 21 flint hammerstones or nodules; 7 chisels or wedges; 2 hoe-shaped tools; and 15 miscellaneous objects, the purposes of which are unknown (Dorrell 1983: figs. 219–23 and pls. 1–11).

A total of 343 bone tool objects or fragments were found in the PPNA levels during Kenyon's excavations. There were many pins, awls, and pointed tools, probably used for skin working, as well as a shuttle for weaving (Marshall 1982: figs. 231–48 and pls. VIII–IX).

The PPNB (ca. 7000–5200 B.C.) stages of occupation and their areas of discovery (see table 1) are detailed in Kenyon (1981).

Architecturally, the houses of this period show a complete break in style from the round houses of the PPNA, and with no transitional structures. In all areas excavated, the house plans are rectilinear (a characteristic example is House B in Trench III, Phase xviii [see photograph and plan in Kenyon 1981: pls. 115 and 263c]). Wall NAD of House B is a typical example since it shows the characteristic bricks used in house construction. They are elongated with herringbone thumb impressions, usually laid as stretchers, but sometimes there is an occasional header, and they are all laid in a thick mudmortar (Kenyon 1981: pl. 116a and cf. pl. 138c). The mudmortar also was applied to the faces of walls and overlaid with a surface of burnished plaster which extended from the walls to form the floors.

Although constructed in the same manner as other PPNB houses found at Jericho, one partially excavated building in Trench I (Square XVIA, Phase xx) differs markedly in plan (Kenyon 1981: pls. 46b and 221). It consists of a rectangular room 6 m from E–W, and more than 5.50 m from N–S. A basin, carefully lined with plaster, is centrally situated on the E–W axis of the room, and associated with it are a series of pits. Adjoining the main room on both its E and W sides are enclosures with rounded walls. The inward curve of the eleven courses preserved of the E enclosure wall suggests that these rooms were domed. As this plan is unique among the houses excavated at Jericho, and the well-built and plastered basin plus the pits suggest ceremonial usage, Kenyon postulated that the building probably was a cult center or temple. However, the presence of bone tools may suggest an alternate hypothesis; the enclosures could have served as a skin working area or served as drying kilns, particularly since they were domed.

Further evidence for some kind of PPNB cult practice or possibly ancestor worship was the discovery of a number

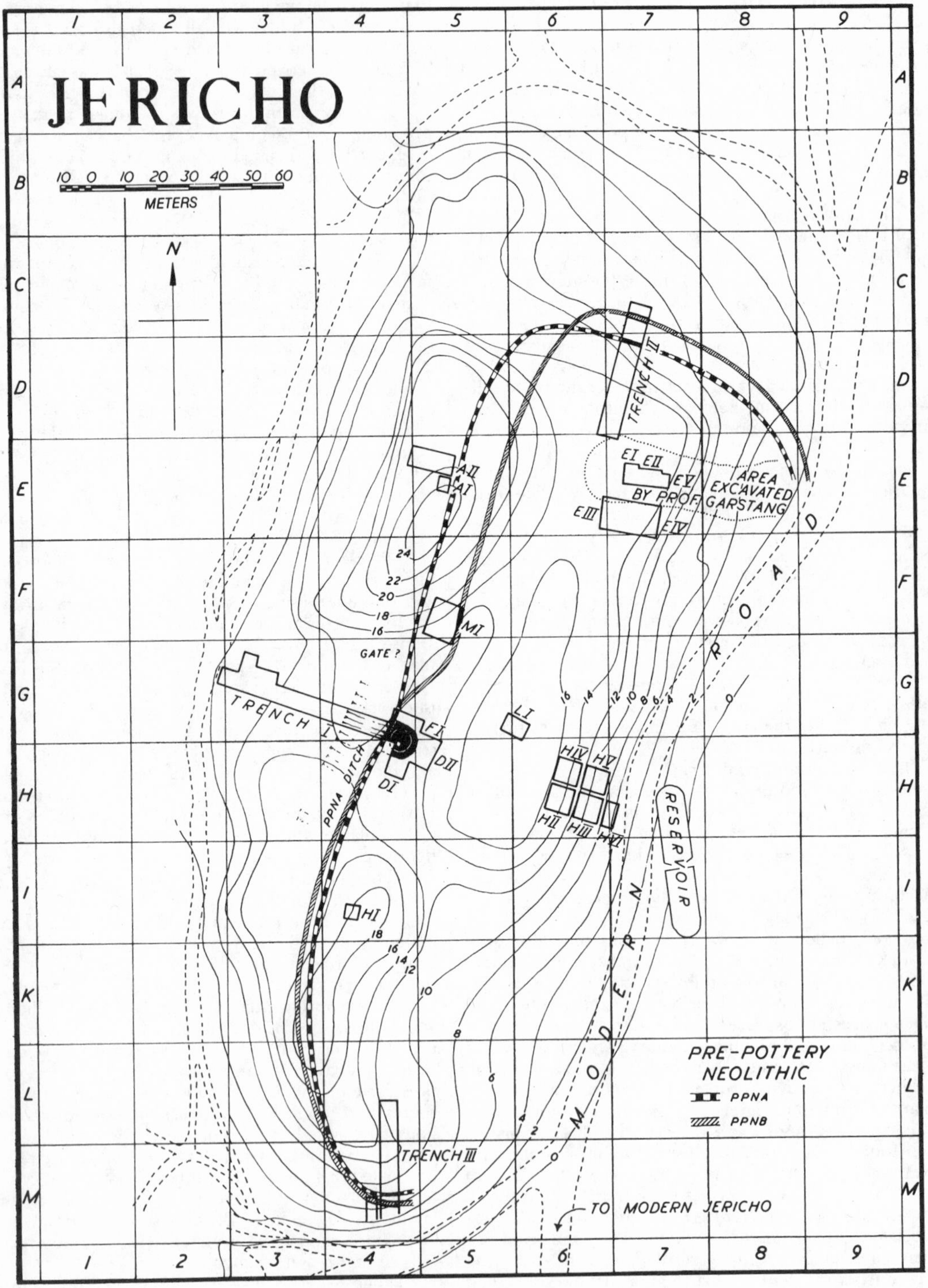

JER.03. Plan of Pre-Pottery Neolithic town walls at Jericho. *(Courtesy of T. A. Holland)*

of human skulls which had been molded over with plaster so that they resembled living heads (Kenyon 1981: pls. 50–59). Similar cult practices apparently existed at other sites during this period as similar plastered skulls have been found at ᶜAin Ghazal, NE of Amman (Rollefson 1983: 35, and pl. 4:1–2; 1985: 54–56, and fig. 6), at Beisamoun in N Israel (Ferembach and Lechevallier 1973: pls. 1, 2), and at Tell Ramad, near Damascus in Syria (Contenson and van Liere 1966: pls. 3c, 4c). Shells were inserted to represent eyes and traces of paint revealed that skin and hair also were portrayed in a lifelike image. The largest group found together consisted of nine examples buried in the fill below the plastered floor of a house in the SE corner of Square DI, belonging to Square XVII, Phase xliii (Kenyon 1981: 77 and pl. 220).

The latest PPNB level on the E side of Square DII (Stage XXVA-XXVI, Phase xxxviii–xxxix) above wall 140 contained a very simple clay stylized human bust which was part of a life-sized figure (Kenyon 1981: 531 and pls. 72, 242a), which also may indicate some cult practice as well as a development away from the practice of using human skulls for ritual purposes. The head of a more sophisticated life-sized clay stylized human figure, with inlaid shell eyes and painted features, was found by Garstang (1935: pl. 53) in Area 195, which he identified as coming from the "Upper Neolithic" (almost certainly PPNB according to Kenyon 1979: 36). The best and most recent examples of this early art form were discovered at the Neolithic site of ᶜAin Ghazal in Jordan (Rollefson 1983: 30–35). It is possible that the full-figure, stylized human statuettes may represent a transition between the practice of plastering human skulls and the making of a representation of a life-sized human figure which is almost totally stylized.

Kenyon's further excavations on the NE end of the tell, in the area previously excavated by Garstang, revealed a total of fifteen main PPNB building periods in Squares EI, II, and V, apart from at least two building periods removed by Garstang. All of the plans (Kenyon 1981: pls. 158–70 and 303–9) reveal that the houses were built around a courtyard which contained fireplaces. The equipment found is characteristic of all PPNB areas of the tell; it consists of many flint implements, fine stone bowls, bone tools, polishing stones, and querns (Kenyon 1957: pl. 16a and 1979: pl. 19). Also, many excellent examples of rush mats were found within the buildings (E. Crowfoot 1982: 546–50 and pls. 4–5).

4. Pottery Neolithic A and B (ca. 5200–4000 B.C.). The destruction of PPNB Jericho was followed by a considerable period of erosion, the exact time span of which has not been determined (table 1). The new settlers on the site had already developed the art of pottery making, although primitive, before their arrival; therefore this stage in the history of the tell is known as the Pottery Neolithic (PN). There were two groups of PN settlers: the first possessed fairly primitive pottery vessels made of coarse, straw-tempered wares as well as finely decorated wares with burnished, red-on-cream decoration; the second had more sophisticated pottery with more intricate shapes (i.e., vessels with inturned concave rims termed "bow rim" jars), many of which are decorated with a deep red slip, sometimes burnished, and bands of herringbone incisions (for PNA and PNB pottery shapes, see the Type Series in Kenyon and Holland 1982: figs. 1–19 and 21–33).

The Pottery Neolithic A people lived in pit dwellings which were cut into the PPNB ruins of the earlier town. The pits revealed a fairly long period of use since they contained a series of successively used floors. The edges of the pits always undercut the preceding levels (Kenyon 1981: pl. 118b) and sometimes are reveted by crude wall-like edges made of pisé and stones (see the oven and fire-pit in Trench II; Kenyon 1981: pl. 99). The stone and flint implements used by the PNA population were cruder than those found in the PPNB levels. The fine PPNB grinding querns, pestles, and stone bowls were succeeded by only crudely worked stone vessels and implements (Kenyon and Holland 1983: figs. 228: 11–26 and 229: 1–7). The most notable change in the flint industry was the appearance of coarsely denticulated sickle blades, which replaced the finely serrated edges of the PPNB blades (Crowfoot Payne 1983: figs. 313–15 and 335–37). That the coarser PNA-type sickle blade continued in use throughout the EB Age occupation of the tell suggests that a major portion of the EB Jerichoans were direct descendants of both the PNA and PNB populations.

On present evidence, the PNA people built no free-standing structures. Their PNB successors, although they initially built huts in the debris of the PNA pits, eventually began to construct free-standing houses having round and rectilinear walls, with stone foundations and a superstructure of handmade planoconvex ("bun-shaped") mudbricks (see Trench I building foundations in Kenyon 1981: pls. 74b, 75, and 228b). In Squares FI and DI, during the final Square XXXII of the PNB occupation, there is a large wall of bun bricks with stone foundations (Wall EO) which may represent a town wall (Kenyon 1981: pls. 77, 78, and 229).

The best evidence for the succession of the pottery Neolithic pits comes from Kenyon's Trench II, Stages X–XI (PNA) and Stage XII (PNB). The sequence of pits is illustrated in chart form (Kenyon 1981: pl. 257). On this evidence, Kenyon postulated that only PNA pottery occurred in the earlier pits of Stages X–XI and PNB pottery can be shown to have first appeared during Stage XII. However, PNA pottery does not entirely disappear during Stage XII. The continuing use of PNA vessels in Stage XII suggests that there was an intermingling of PNB newcomers with the PNA population.

The main flint assemblage during the PNA period has been identified as Yarmukian by Crowfoot Payne (1983: 706–16 and figs. 332–41). It includes axe/adze heads partly flaked and polished, bifacially flaked arrowheads, coarsely denticulated sickle blades, knives and scrapers of tabular flint, and flake knives with fine scale-flaking. The main deposit of PNB flints, identified as Ghassulian by Crowfoot Payne, were found in Garstang's layer VIII (J. Crowfoot 1937: 40–41 and pls. 7B:1 and 8A: 14–17). On the basis of the Garstang material and the sickle blades and derived adze heads excavated by Kenyon, Crowfoot Payne concluded there was a complete change in the flint industry from the PNA to PNB periods and that the new PNB people were part of the whole Ghassul-Beer-sheba civilization (Crowfoot Payne 1983: 718 and figs. 243–44). The small number of plant remains and the complete absence of charcoal retrieved from Kenyon's Pottery Neolithic levels supports Hopf's conclusion that the Jerichoans were herdsmen and hunters during this period (Hopf 1983: 578).

5. Early Bronze I (ca. 3300–3150 B.C.). On the evidence of a "turf" layer found in Trench I (Stage XXXIII) and in period MI (Stage XVIII), Kenyon concluded that Jericho was completely abandoned for approximately 300(?) years after the PNB period (table 1). The major evidence for the arrival of a new group of nomadic or seminomadic dwellers comes from a group of shaft tombs discovered by Kenyon which are numbered A94, A114, A13, K2, K1, A124, and A130 + A61. All these tombs contained multiple burials deposited during a long period of time (for pottery types, see Kenyon and Holland 1982: figs. 34–48). Most scholars have identified this period in Palestine as EB Age I and have divided the pottery into three main ware groups termed EB Ia (red-burnished), EB Ib (painted), and EB Ic (gray-burnished). At present, only the red-burnished and painted groups have been found on the ground and in the tombs at Jericho, which Kenyon designated Proto-Urban A and B on the basis of the tomb pottery.

Architecturally, the main evidence for the EB occupation of the tell comes from both Garstang's and Kenyon's excavations in Squares EIII–IV, located on the NE sector of the mound (grid E7, Fig. JER.04). The earliest excavated EB Ia house plans occur in Phases Q and P (Kenyon 1981: pls. 174 and 313b). The foundations of an apsidal-ended building are preserved along with the remains of a structure having three straight-sided walls, which also may be apsidal-ended, in the unexcavated NE portion of the area. The same type of house plan continues in Phase O, which ushers in the appearance of the distinctive EB Ib (Proto-Urban B) pottery decorated with painted red bands of grouped lines. EB Ib Phase N was completely destroyed and the succeeding rebuilt Phase M marked the end of the EB I occupation in Squares EIII–IV.

There is some evidence in Trench I to show that the EB occupants may have fortified their settlement. During Stage XXXIV, a town wall (A), associated with a semicircular tower, was built directly on the remains of the preceding Pottery Neolithic period Pit M (Kenyon 1981: pls. 79b and 240d). The pottery from Stage XXXIV (in the occupation and destruction Phases xxxviiia and xxxix–xl) is more closely aligned to EB forms than to the later fully developed EB pottery associated with the succeeding EB walls (C, D, F, and G) and the occupation layers above Wall A and its tower.

The main evidence concerning EB I religious customs and architecture at Jericho comes from Garstang's excavations in Area E, Level VII (= Kenyon's Squares EIII–IV, Phases M-L to DD), where he excavated a broad-roomed sanctuary, with its entrance facing E, designated Shrine 420 (Garstang 1936: 73–74 and pl. 41a). Several stone cult objects were found in the vicinity of the shrine and were thought to be associated with it. They included a small libation altar and a smoothed stone, oval-shaped in section, which was regarded as possibly a prototype of the *maṣṣebah* (Garstang 1936: 74 and pl. 41b).

The six EB I maceheads found in Kenyon's excavations (Trench II, Square M, and Squares EIII–IV; Holland 1983: 808–10 and fig. 365:2, 6) and the two found in Garstang's Level VII (Garstang 1936: pl. 36:24–25) may indicate either that they were employed for a ceremonial use or as weapons. No figures of a cult nature were found. Concerning the flint industry, Crowfoot Payne concluded that no distinction could be drawn between flints of the EB I period and those of the later EB periods, which are all classified as Cananean. However, the Cananean industry was certainly introduced at Jericho during the beginning of the EB I period and continued into the later EB periods as is illustrated in table 23 of the final report on the flint assemblage (Crowfoot Payne 1983: 750–51).

6. Early Bronze II–III (ca. 3050–2300 B.C.). Early Bronze II dates ca. 3100–2700 B.C. (called by Kenyon EB I–II, ca. 3050–2950 B.C., 2950–2700/2650 B.C. respectively [= 1st Egyptian Dyn. and into the 2d]) and EB III spans ca. 2700/2650–2300 B.C. (links with the 2d Egyptian Dyn.) and lasts until the beginning of the EB IV (Kenyon's "Intermediate Early Bronze-Middle Bronze Age" [EB-MB]).

EB II Jericho (table 1) appears to have evolved gradually from the EB I population, probably with an influx of new immigrants arriving from the N. However, the need for defensive walls was still of paramount concern throughout the EB and the settlement was completely surrounded by the large mudbrick Wall C during EB III, which had been constructed on top of the earlier town Wall B of the EB I period. For plan of the two inferred EB town walls, see Fig. JER.04. Kenyon's excavations also revealed that the later stages of the EB town wall had been protected by an external ditch enlarged at least four times; the recutting of the ditch may have removed artifactual evidence showing that the first wall also was associated with a ditch. The remains of a gateway were found in Trench II (Kenyon 1981: 148–49 and pls. 101b and 249c) as well as a probable gate by Garstang (described as a large oblong tower and assigned to Garstang's MBi period) in grid K6 on the E side of the mound, which probably enclosed the source of the spring (Garstang 1934: pl. 15). The town walls were built of unbaked rectangular mudbrick slabs, mold-made, measuring approximately 2 × 14 × 10 inches.

The earliest EB II houses contain rooms which are either oblong with one curved end or are completely circular (i.e., Trench III, Stage XV houses; Kenyon 1981: pl. 265c). The houses are irregularly positioned and reveal little evidence of town planning. The later EB II and III houses, on the other hand, in Squares EIII–IV for example, are rectangularly laid out and consistently orientated on a N-S axis (Kenyon 1981: pls. 317–20). A large number of brick-built silos were associated with these later houses. They were used for grain storage and testify to a flourishing agricultural community. Hopf (1983: 579) inferred that artificial irrigation was practiced from the presence of large quantities of carbonized naked, hexaploid bread-wheat remains found in the EB silos.

The EB cemetery in use during most of this period of occupation at Jericho testifies to some belief in a later life after death. Both Garstang and Kenyon excavated EB rock-cut chamber tombs containing multiple burials, about twenty in the earlier tombs and between fifty to one hundred in the later ones (Garstang 1932: 18–22, 38–41 and fig. 8, pls. 1–8; 1935: 155, 162–63 and pl. 34:1–40; Kenyon's EB Tomb Type Series [Kenyon and Holland 1982:

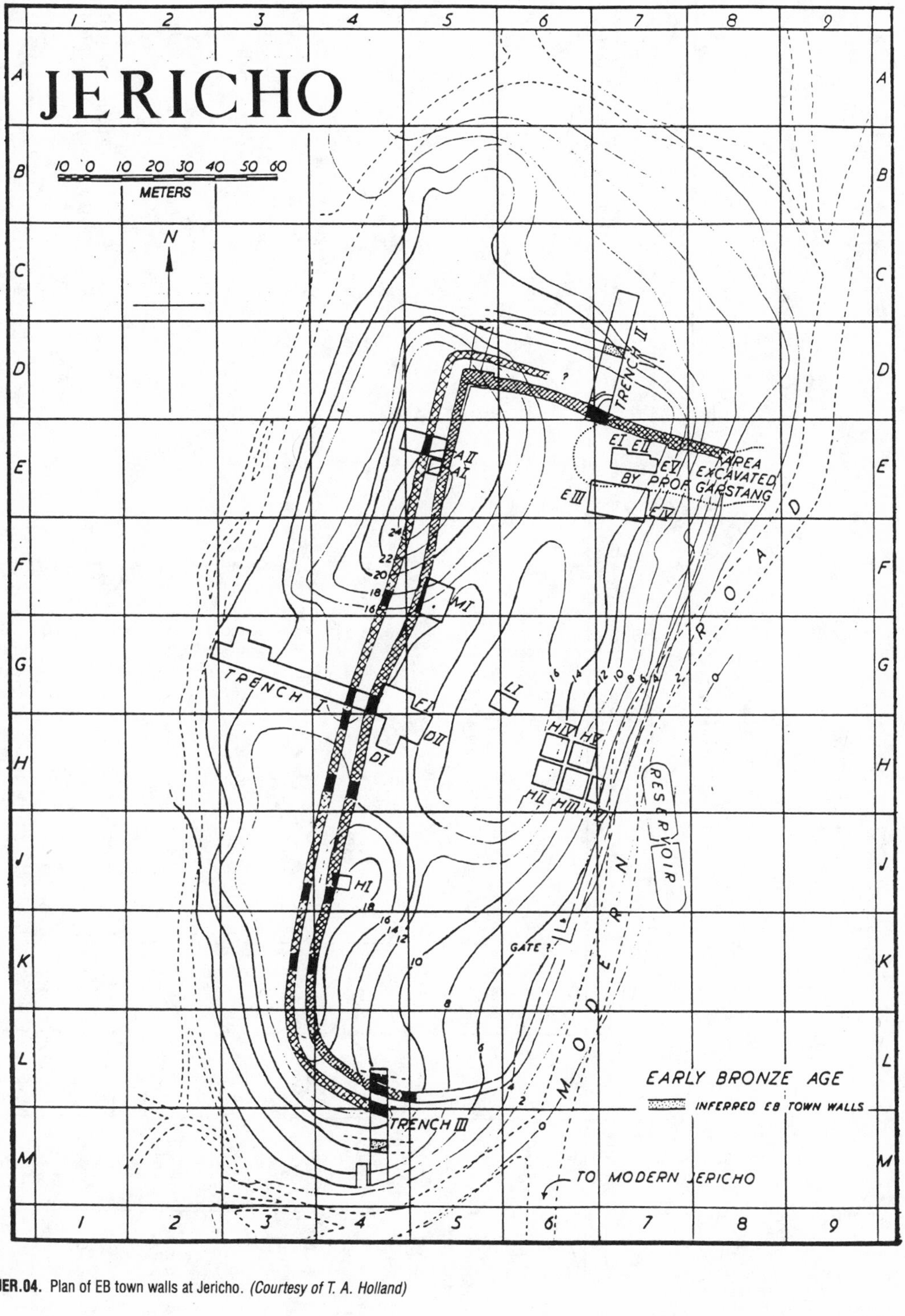

JER.04. Plan of EB town walls at Jericho. *(Courtesy of T. A. Holland)*

T.A. Holland—Jericho

Table 1. JERICHO CHRONOLOGICAL CHART

Period	Archaeological Dating	CORRELATION OF MAJOR EXCAVATIONS AT JERICHO														
				(Major Stages)												
		Sellin and Watzinger	*Garstang*	*Site A*	*Trench I*	*Square DI*	*Square DII*	*Square FI*	*Squares EI, II, V*	*Squares EIII–IV*	*Squares HII–VI*	*Site L*	*Square MI*	*Trench II*	*Trench III*	*Tombs (Selected exx.)*
Mesolithic	9000 B.C.	—	—	—	—	—	—	—	I, II	—	—	—	—	—	—	—
"Turf"	—	—	—	—	—	—	—	—	—	—	—	—	—	—	—	—
Proto-Neolithic	8700 B.C.	—	—	—	—	I	I	I	III	—	—	—	I to VI	—	—	—
Pre-Pottery Neolithic A	8500 B.C.	—	(?)	—	VA to XI–XII	II to XI	II to XI–XII	III to X	IV to IX	—	—	—	VII to IX–X	—	—	—
PPNA–PPNB	—	—	X to XVII	—	—	—	—	—	—	—	—	—	X	—	—	—
Pre-Pottery Neolithic B	7000 B.C.	—	(?)	—	XII to XXII	XII to XXVI	XII to XXVA–XXVI	XII to XXVI	IX–X to XV–XVI	—	—	—	XI to XV–XVI	—	—	—
"Gap"	—	—	—	—	—	—	—	—	—	—	—	—	—	—	—	—
Pottery Neolithic A	5200 B.C.	—	IX(?)	—	XXVII to XXIX	XXX	—	XXVII to XXIX	—	—	—	—	XVI, XVIA	X, XI	—	—
PNA + PNB	—	—	—	—	—	—	—	—	—	—	—	—	XVIB	—	—	—
Pottery Neolithic B	4700 B.C.	—	VII	—	XXX to XXXII	XXXI to XXXII–XXXIII	—	XXX to XXXII–XXXIII	—	MM to EE	—	—	XVII	XII	X	—
"Turf"	—	—	—	—	XXXIII	—	—	—	—	—	—	—	XVIII	—	—	—
Ghassulian/ Chalcolithic	4000 B.C.	—	—	—	—	—	—	—	—	—	—	—	—	—	—	—
Early Bronze I	3300 B.C.	—	VII	—	XXXIII to XXXVI–XXXVII	XXXIV	—	XXXIV, XXXV	—	DD to M–L	—	—	XIX to XXI	XIII to XV	XI.xxxvi, XI.xxxvi–xxxvii	A13, 84, 94, 114, 124, K1, K2
Early Bronze II	3050 B.C.	—	V, VI Tomb 24	—	XXXVII	—	—	—	—	L	I	G	XXI–XXII, XXII	XVI, XVI–XVII	XI.xxxix to XV–XVI	A108, 122, 127
	2850 B.C.	—	IV Tomb A	A, B	XXXVII–XXXVIII, XXXVIII	—	—	—	—	K to F	II	F to D	XXIII	XVII, XVII–XVIII	XVI	D12, F4

Early Bronze III	2650 B.C.	—	III Tombs A, 351	C to E	XXXVIII–XXXIX to XL–XLI	XXXV to XXXVIII	—	—	—	Fi to A	III to IV–V	C to A	—	XVIII to XX–XXI	XVII to XIX	A114, D12, F1, F3
"Gap"	(?)2500 B.C.	—	—	—	—	—	—	—	—	—	—	—	—	—	—	—
Early Bronze IV	2300 B.C.	—	I	—	XLI to XLII–XLIII	—	—	—	—	—	—	—	—	XXI, XXI–XXII	XX, XX–XXI	A86, 129, G28, H5, D1, O4, P24, K9, K27, L2, M17
Middle Bronze I–II	1950 B.C.	"Red City"	City C Storerooms Tombs 21, 30	—	XLIII, XLIV	—	—	—	—	—	V to XII–XIII	—	—	XXII, XXII–XXIII	XXI	B48, M11, B51, J45, A136
"Gap"	(?)1550 B.C.	—	—	—	—	—	—	—	—	—	XIII	—	—	—	—	—
Late Bronze II	1400 B.C.	—	City D Middle Bldg. Tombs 4, 5, 13	—	XLV	—	—	—	—	—	XIV	—	—	—	—	—
Destruction Debris	(?)1280 B.C.	—	—	—	—	—	—	—	—	—	—	—	—	—	XXI–XXII	—
"Gap"	—	—	—	—	—	—	—	—	—	—	—	—	—	—	—	—
Iron Age I	1200 B.C.	Quellhügel	City E Tomb II	—	—	—	—	—	—	—	—	—	—	—	—	—
Iron Age II	1000 B.C.	Quellhügel	Tomb 18	—	—	—	—	—	—	—	—	—	—	—	—	A85
	800 B.C.	Quellhügel 'Hilani' Bldg.	—	—	XLVI to XLVIII	—	—	—	—	—	—	—	—	XXII I, XXIII–XXIV	XXII	WH.1, 2
Babylonian/ Persian	587 B.C.	—	—	—	—	—	—	—	—	—	—	—	—	—	—	—
Hellenistic I and II	330 B.C.	—	—	—	—	—	—	—	—	—	—	—	—	—	—	—
Roman I (Herodian)	37 B.C.–A.D. 70	—	—	—	—	—	—	—	—	—	—	—	—	—	—	K23, G81, G66, D20, NS. 1
Roman II–III	A.D. 70–324	—	—	—	XLLX	—	—	—	—	—	—	—	—	XXIV	XXIII	—
Byzantine	A.D. 324–636	—	—	L	—	—	—	—	—	—	—	—	XXIV	—	—	—
Islamic/ Modern	A.D. 636—	—	—	LI, LII	—	—	—	—	—	—	—	—	—	XXV	—	—

217–43 and figs. 81–93]). That most of the bones were found completely disarticulated probably indicates that earlier burials were discarded, except for the skulls, to make room for further internments. The burial goods consisted of pottery vessels for holding food and drink as well as small juglets for oil or scent. The only personal ornaments were heads of carnelian, bone, shell, stone, and frit (for general bead types, see Talbot 1983: 796–98).

The EB was a period of international contacts. The pottery and other finds from Jericho reveal cultural contacts to the N with both Syria and NE Anatolia, and to the S with Egypt. The presence of KHIRBET KERAK WARE (originating in Anatolia), indicates either trade or the arrival of new immigrants at Jericho (Holland 1983: xxxiv–xxxv and xxxvii–xxxviii). Egyptian imports include both "Abydos" ware and a slate palette (Holland 1983: xxxiv; 1982a: 559 and fig. 226:16).

The violent destruction which brought about the end of EB Jericho was partially a result of the almost total deforestation of the area for building and fuel purposes. This certainly led to erosion during the end of the 3d millennium B.C., resulting in a weakening of the economy that left the inhabitants vulnerable to attack as well as to disease. The political events accompanying the fall of the EB population are unknown, but the archaeological finds show an absolute break in the occupation of Jericho for several hundred years until the tell was partially resettled by a group of Amorites around 2300 B.C.

7. Early Bronze IV (ca. 2300–1950 B.C.). Kenyon identified this period at Jericho as the "Intermediate Early Bronze–Middle Bronze Age," lasting about 350 years between 2300 and 1950 B.C. Albright and others dated this period to about 2400–2100 B.C. and labeled it either EB IV or EB IIIb. Whatever final dates and terminology may be assigned to this occupation, the one thing that is clear is that Jericho was frequented by newcomers who introduced a characteristic type of pottery related to N Syrian types (Kenyon 1981: fig. 12) and built individual rock-cut tombs entered by vertical shafts.

Kenyon found remains of EB IV houses, only in her Trenches I, II, and III, which were terraced into the underlying deposits on the W, N, and S slopes of the tell. In Trench I (Stage XLII, Phase liv), remains of two complexes of rooms were found. In the W complex were two solid clay blocks in adjacent rectangular rooms which were possibly altars (Kenyon 1981: 105–8 and pls. 86a and 231a). The discovery of an infant foundation burial below the dividing wall between the adjacent rooms and a bin containing a four-spouted lamp, which could have been used for offerings, may support Kenyon's suggestion that this might have been a cult center (Kenyon 1981: pls. 86b, 87a, b, and fig. 12:25).

The remains and contents of the three rooms found in Trench II, Stage XXI, Phase lxviii, indicate they were for domestic use since they contained mortars, a bin, and a number of crushed vessels (Kenyon 1981: 166–67 and fig. 12:2–5 and pl. 255a).

The house remains in Trench III (Stage XX, Phase lxxx) were so scanty that no plan was published, but a good assemblage of characteristic pottery was excavated (Kenyon and Holland 1983: 214 and figs. 104–5).

The evidence from the burial traditions of the EB IV people (Amorites?) indicates a tribal organization with each group maintaining its own burial customs since seven different classes of tombs were discovered by Kenyon. They were identified as the following types: Dagger, Pottery, Dagger/Pottery ("Square-Shaft"), Outsize, Bead, Composite, and Multiple Burial.

The Dagger type (e.g., Tomb A129; Kenyon 1965: fig. 23, plan and 1979: pl. 46, photograph) is usually small and, owing to its size, contains an intact skeleton in a crouched position on its side. If the burial is of a man, he is buried with a dagger, and if that of a woman, she is buried with a pin or beads. The prominence given to weapons in this type of tomb suggests a warrior class.

The Pottery-type tomb (e.g., Tomb G28, Kenyon 1960: fig. 96, plan and pl. 10:2, photograph) always contains only pottery and no weapons.

The Dagger/Pottery-type tomb (e.g., Tomb D1; Kenyon 1965: fig. 42, plan and pl. 4:1, photograph) shows a combination of features associated with the preceding two tomb types. A new feature associated with this type is that the weapons also may include a javelin. The main constructional difference of the shaft for this type is that it is square, rather than roughly and roundly cut, and is therefore also known as a "square-shaft" type.

The fourth type is termed "Outsize" (e.g., Tomb O4; Kenyon 1965; fig. 59, plan and pl. 5:1, photograph) since both the shafts and the chambers are considerably larger than those of the other tomb types and the funerary offerings are greater both in their numbers and size of the vessels (for example, compare Tomb O4 pottery with Pottery-type tomb vessels; Kenyon 1965: figs. 28 and 60–61). They are similar to the "square-shaft" tombs in that they also contain both pottery and weapons, and the skeleton is usually intact.

The fifth type, Bead tombs (e.g. Tomb K9; Kenyon 1965: fig. 40), has dismembered skeletons and few grave offerings apart from some beads, a pin, and sometimes fragments of bronze studs, possibly belonging to clothing items.

The sixth type, known as Composite tombs (e.g., Tomb L2; Kenyon 1965: fig. 79, plan) appears to combine some of the characteristics of the Dagger, Pottery, Dagger/Pottery, and Outsize types of tombs.

One seventh type of EB IV tomb, M17, is in a class by itself and is designated a Multiple-Burial type (Kenyon 1965: fig. 88, plan and pl. 10:1, photograph). It is distinguished from all the other tomb types in that it has three intact burials, whereas only two intact burials occasionally are found in the Dagger-type tombs.

8. Middle Bronze Age (ca. 1950–1550 B.C.). Kenyon found MB occupational remains (Table 1) in Trenches I, II, III (MB I/early MB II), and in Squares HII to VI (MB III). Owing to erosion, no domestic structures were found in Trenches I and II, but the extensive exposures extending W in Trench I and N in Trench II revealed MB remains of three successive and massive plastered ramparts which surrounded the MB town (see JER.05; also Kenyon 1981: Trench I, pls. 89b–92b, photographs, pl. 236, section; Trench II, pls. 108–10, photograph and pl. 259, section). The ramparts also were found in Trench III on the S of the mound (see Kenyon 1981: pls. 125b, 126a, and 127, photographs and pl. 273, section) as well as some house

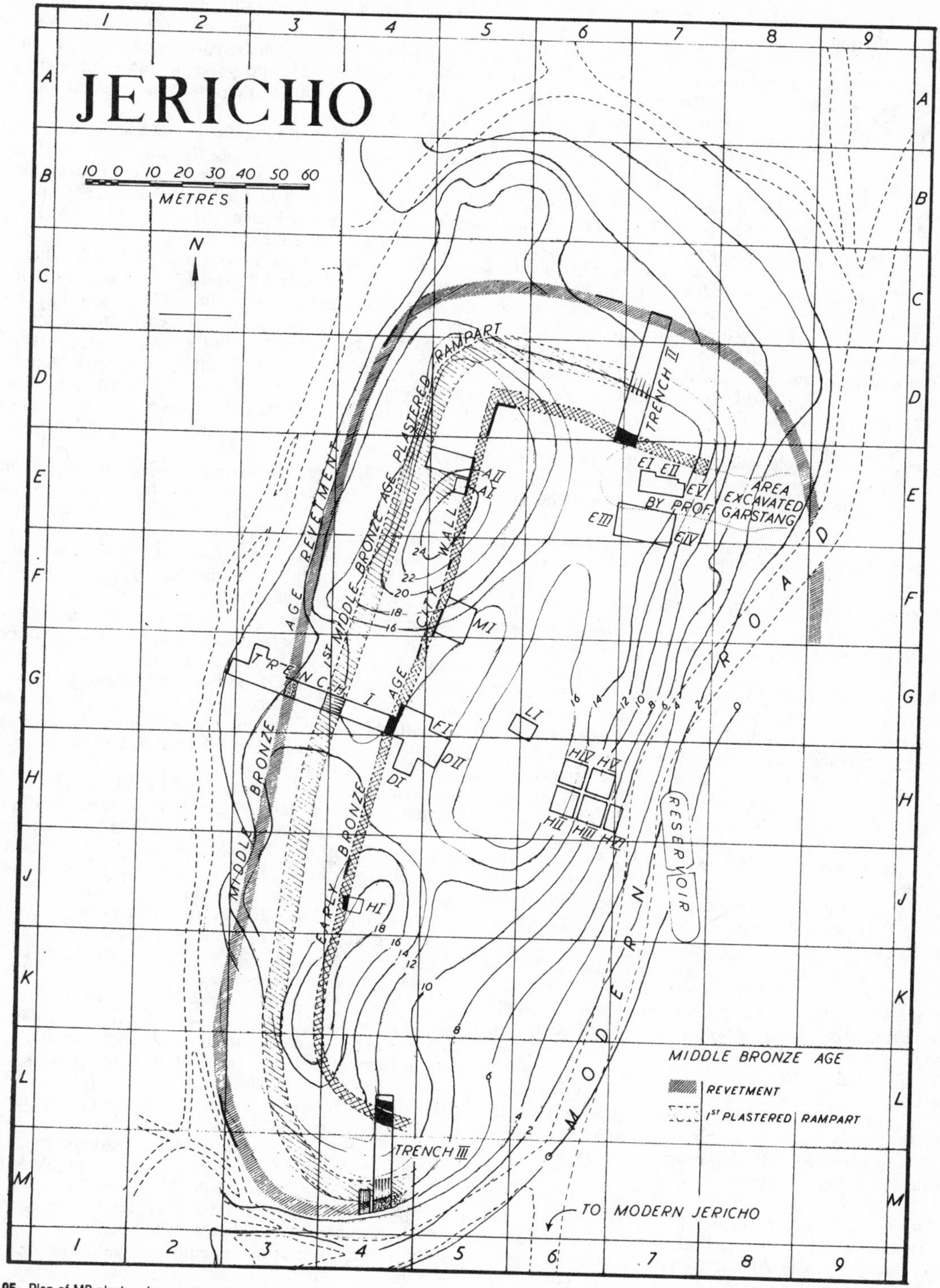

JER.05. Plan of MB plastered ramparts at Jericho. *(Courtesy of T. A. Holland)*

remains on the berm at the foot of the MB bank (Kenyon 1981: pls. 126b and 128a, photographs and pl. 272a, b, plans).

Although the few rooms excavated in Trench III (Stage XXI) were small and mostly irregular, a number of typical MB II vessels were found associated with the floor levels (Kenyon and Holland 1983: figs. 106: 1–30 and 108: 32–39).

The most complete MB II houses were excavated by Kenyon (1981: pl. 336a) in Area H (Stage XII) on the E side of the mound in grid squares H6–7 (Fig. JER.02) just NE of Garstang's so-called MB "palace storerooms" in grid squares H6, J5–6, and K5–6 (Garstang 1934: 118–30 and pls. 13–16). The combined Garstang/Kenyon sketch plan of this portion of the MB II city plan reveals an orderly layout of houses and two streets with drains oriented W–E, sloping down the mound to the water supply. A number of ground-floor rooms, particularly Garstang's room nos. 40–45 (1934: pls. 15, 16, and 41–42), and Kenyon's B and F (1981: 369, fig. 6 and pls. 198 and 336a), contained many large storage jars with carbonized grains, and also loomweights and saddle querns, which indicate that the street-level rooms served as working areas and possibly shops, while the second-story rooms were for living and bedrooms.

A 1988 revised radiocarbon determination of a charcoal sample (BM–1790R, 3300 ± 110 B.P.) from Kenyon's Area H rooms in Stage XII, Phase li, places this occupation within a calibrated date ranging from 1880–1390 B.C. (based on Stuiver and Reimer 1986). The carbonized plant remains from the storage jars in storerooms B and F, Stage XII, Phase lii–liii (Kenyon and Holland 1983: figs. 199: 4–6, 201: 1–4, and 202: 1–4), were analyzed by Hopf, who identified emmer, bread wheat, and barley in room F, and bread wheat, barley, lentil, field peas, vines, onions, oats, as well as grass and weed species in room B.

Some of the pottery found in the Area H rooms illustrates a high degree of artistic achievement—compare, for instance, the almost identical bird-shaped vases on pedestal stands from Garstang's room 73 (1934: pls. 26:8 and 44 top) and Kenyon's room A (Kenyon and Holland 1983: fig. 188: 5 and Kenyon 1957: pl. 48 top). Other fine vessels include Garstang's "snake" vase from room 68 and a rhyton from room 40 (Garstang 1934: pls. 25: 20; 43: 4; and 22: 21, 44).

The bulk of the evidence for everyday life at Jericho during the time of the MB comes, not from the sparse occupational remains, but from the large MB II multiple-burial tombs excavated by both Garstang and Kenyon in the necropolis N and NW of the tell (Garstang 1932: 41–54, 1933: 3–37; Kenyon 1960: 263–515, 1965: 167–478, particularly pottery Groups I–V as illustrated by the vessels in Tombs B48, B51, J45, and A136). Because of the excellent preservation of objects in the tombs, it is possible to reconstruct a typical living room at Jericho during this period with some degree of certainty.

All the MB buildings were violently destroyed by fire and their walls were covered with a thick layer of debris during the subsequent period of abandonment and erosion. On the basis of finding entire families buried together in some of the MB II tombs, Kenyon (1960: 267) postulated that disease was partially responsible for the demise of the population at this time. The heavy tilting of the Area H walls to the E (Kenyon 1981: pl 339, section) may indicate earthquake activity which may have resulted in sulfurous gases, fire, and possibly even some form of early plague, thus causing the total abandonment of the site at the end of the MB.

9. Late Bronze Age (ca. 1550–1200 B.C.). As already noted by Kenyon (1973: 527), the dating of the Late Bronze Age in Palestine is almost entirely dependent upon a study of the pottery from the key Palestinian sites of this period, those being Tell Beit Mirsim, Jericho, Megiddo, Hazor, Lachish, and Tell el-ʿAjjūl.

On the evidence of the Jericho pottery dated to the LB from the reused Tombs 4, 5, and 13 (Garstang 1933: 15–40 and pls. 4–26; Bienkowski 1986: 32–102 and figs. 27–51), it would appear that Jericho was reoccupied on a small scale in Area H on the E side of the tell during the second half of the 15th century B.C. (Table 1). Bienkowski suggests for Tomb 5 a late LB I/first half of LB IIa date (ca. 1425–1350 B.C. or slightly later) and for Tombs 4 and 13 a mid-LB IIa/early LB IIb date, ca. 1350–1275 B.C. (1986: 71, 90, and 102).

On the tell, the only building remains to survive erosion were Garstang's so-called "palace" and the Middle Building (1934: 105–8 and pl. 12), and the ruins of a house floor in Kenyon's Square Hill (Stage XIV, Phase liva) upon which were situated an oven and a LB IIb juglet (Kenyon 1981: 371 and fig. 14:6, pl. 199a, b) dated to the end of the 14th century B.C.

With regard to an LB fortification system at Jericho, there is no archaeological data to support the presence of a walled town. The so-called LB walls in Garstang's City D, which he associated with Joshua's destruction of Jericho (Josh 6:24), were misdated (Garstang and Garstang 1940: 129–40 and pls. 17–18) and later shown by Kenyon to be two successive phases of an EB town wall (Kenyon 1952: 64–72).

The meager material remains of LB Jericho, therefore, suggest that the settlement was relatively small and fairly poor (however, for a recent reevaluation of these remains, see Wood 1990). As Bienkowski (1986: 124) has shown, a study of the settlement patterns of the LB sites in Canaan shows that only eight of the seventy-six known settlements were fortified. This decline in the fortunes of Jericho and other sites in Canaan is the direct result of the establishment of the Egyptian 18th Dyn. and the expulsion of the Hyksos into Palestine (Kenyon 1973: 555–56).

10. Iron Age (ca. 1200–587 B.C.). After Jericho was abandoned during the early part of LB IIb, it was not thought to be reoccupied to any great extent until the 7th century B.C. However, a recent study of the pottery from the German excavations by the Weipperts (1976: 105–48) has revealed the presence of both Iron Age I and II forms. Garstang's "Cremation Pit" (Tomb 11) also may be dated to Iron Age I (1933: 36 and fig. 11) and the late 10th century B.C. Tomb A85 excavated by Kenyon (1965: 482–89 and figs. 252–53) was possibly in use until the early 9th century B.C. (Tushingham 1965: 487). The biblical account in 1 Kgs 16:34 suggests that the site was first reoccupied and fortified by Hiel the Bethelite during the time of Ahab (early 9th century B.C.).

The extensive 7th-century Iron Age occupation was

found by all three major expeditions to Jericho (Table 1). The German excavators Sellin and Watzinger (1913) uncovered the largest area in the uppermost strata of Jericho. See Fig. JER.02. Garstang recovered only one portion of an Iron Age II building in grid H6 and very few finds (1934: 102–4 and pls. 13, 15, and 24:2). Kenyon's Iron Age material from Jericho is now well documented both from the tell (Kenyon 1981: 111–13, 171–73, 219, and pls. 92b, 94, 232, and 255–56; Kenyon and Holland 1982: 455–536 and figs. 195–219; 1983: 58–84, 176 and figs. 23–31; Franken 1974) and tombs A85, WH.1, and WH.2 (Tushingham 1965: 479–515 and figs. 252–63).

The largest and most complete Iron Age II building excavated by Kenyon (in Stage XLVI, Phase lxix) was situated at the foot of Trench I on the W side of the tell, and was constructed in a tripartite plan typical of this period (Kenyon 1981: 111–12 and pls. 94, 232). Apart from the pottery, the most important find, slightly postdated to the aforementioned building, is that of a stamped storage jar handle from Trench I (Reg. YBT/42; Stage L, Phase lxxv) impressed with a two-winged "royal stamp" and two incised concentric circles around a deeply impressed central hole (Bartlett 1982a: 537 and fig. 220:1, pl. 3a). The presence of this handle probably indicates that Jericho was under the administration of Judah during this period. The pottery from even later phases on the mound strongly suggests that the site remained inhabited until the period of the Babylonian exile in 587 B.C.

11. Babylonian/Persian to Byzantine (587 B.C.–A.D. 636). Although there are no ancient building remains on the tell after the time of the Iron Age remains, ancient Jericho and the area in the immediate vicinity of modern Jericho was occupied during some, if not all, of the time between the Babylonian/Persian and Byzantine periods, particularly at the nearby site known today as Tulul Abu El-ʿAlayiq (Kelso and Baramki 1955: 1–19; and Pritchard 1958: 1–58).

The presence of an unstratified, barbed bronze arrowhead (Reg. 179; Kenyon and Holland 1982: 569 and fig. 229:18) from the W slope of the mound attests to the presence of Persian warriors or to their surrogates in the neighborhood.

Even later periods of encampment or temporary occupation on the mound are attested by epigraphic evidence in the form of another stamped jar handle. The upper arm of a Rhodian amphora (Reg. 199) bears a rectangular stamp which reads "In the term of Agestratos, in the month Agrianias" (May–June), dated to ca. 220–150 B.C. in the Hellenistic Period (Bartlett 1982a: 542 and fig. 220: 6).

During the course of Kenyon's excavations in the necropolis, Roman remains were found in seven tombs (table 1) and fourteen graves (Bennett 1965: 516–45 and figs. 264–81).

The sparce remains from the Byzantine period come from Kenyon's sites M and H on the tell. A pit dug into Square MI (Stage XXIV, Phase cxii) to a depth of over 14 m, probably to obtain brick material for building elsewhere, contained only one fragment of a fine Byzantine bowl (Kenyon 1981: 266; Kenyon and Holland 1983: 280 and fig. 119:14). An unstratified iron nail (Reg. 1907), possibly Byzantine, came from Site H (Holland 1982b: 569 and fig. 229:19).

Historically, Jericho was of great economic and military importance during the time of the Hellenistic and Roman periods. A perpetual source of fresh water from the spring of ʿAin es-Sultan and during later periods from the springs of ʿAin Dug, ʿAin Nureimah (Na'aran), and the Wadi Qelt brought to Jericho by aqueducts, gave Jericho its very existence from the time of trhe original settlement during the Mesolithic period until the present day. It served as an oasis providing food and more particularly the medicinal plants that were so prized by all powers who held sway over the site. Since Jericho was situated on the E flank of Judea, it remained militarily of great strategic importance. The continued settlement of the area until the present day and the existence of the modern town of Jericho testifies to its endurance and its unrivaled status as being the oldest continually inhabited oasis in the world.

T. A. HOLLAND

E. Roman Jericho (Tulul Abu el-ʿAlayiq)

Jericho of the Roman period is referred to in the Apocryphal writings and is where Bacchides is said to have built one of his fortresses (1 Macc 9:50). Later Ptolemy was made governor of the plain and the area was the scene of the massacre of Simon and his sons (1 Macc 16:11–17). The roses grown in Jericho must have been proverbial, since in Sirach 24:14 they are used as a metaphor for wisdom. In the NT, the most notable references to the city are as the site of the healing of two blind men (Matt 20:29–34) and as the home of Zacchaeus (Luke 19:1–10).

The most widespread remains from the Hasmonean and the Herodian periods were exposed in the W plain of Jericho, close to Wadi Qelt (the biblical Nahal Perat) at the site named Tulul Abu el-ʿAlayiq (M.R. 191139). The site, previously labeled by scholars as "Herodian" or "New Testament" Jericho (versus the older town mentioned in the OT, situated at Tell el-Sultan; see above) has proved to be a huge palace complex first built by the Hasmoneans and later rebuilt and expanded by Herod the Great. The palace was in close proximity to Jerusalem (only 20 km), and enjoyed an abundance of water, a pastoral landscape, and above all, mild winters in contrast to the cold winters of Jerusalem.

The first developments at Jericho, probably in the days of John Hyrcanus I (134–104 B.C.) included the construction of: (1) a long well-built water channel to carry water from the Wadi Qelt springs to the plain; (2) a royal estate; and (3) the first phase of a winter palace.

C. Warren (1869) was the first scholar to excavate at the site. He dug sections on top of the two tells which characterize this site, one to the S and the other to the N of the wadi. E Sellin and C. Watzinger followed Warren, and did additional minor work at the site. Larger excavations were conducted in 1950 (Kelso and Baramki) and 1951 (Pritchard). The most extensive excavations of the site have been directed by E. Netzer from 1973 to 1987.

1. The Hasmonean Period. The first palace built by Hyrcanus I, N of Wadi Qelt included a two story building, about 60 × 50 m, built on three sides of an inner courtyard. This building (only part of which has been exposed) included bath installations, a large ritual bath (*miqve,* two pools, one with and the other without steps), decorated rooms (with fresco and stucco), and at least one tower. This tower (13 × 13 m) at the SW corner, was built with ashlar stones in contrast to the rest of the walls which were of mudbrick.

Two swimming pools, one beside the other, were built W of the palace (each 8 × 9 m); perhaps they were separated to reserve one each for men and women. To the N of the palace was the large royal estate, at least 45 hectares of irrigated land, which was surrounded by a wall. Various agricultural installations (including many winepresses) were exposed close to this estate. The estate probably housed palm date trees (which were exploited mainly to produce date wine) and *opobalsamum* bushes (to produce perfumes and medicines). These remains accurately reflect Jericho's descriptions by Pliny, Strabo, Josephus, and others.

The first expansion of the palace was probably by Alexander Jannaeus (103–76 B.C.), who built a second long range water channel to carry water from Na'aran springs to the W plain of Jericho. Simultaneously, he added to the palace (to its E) a large luxurious complex with two large adjacent swimming pools in its center (each 18 × 13 m). The pools were surrounded by wide, paved platforms and gardens. This complex, built along one straight architectural axis also included a pavilion (21 × 17 m, surrounded by colonnades in the Doric style) at one edge and a large garden at the other edge (ca. 60 × 70 m, and probably also surrounded by colonnades).

The next massive addition to the palace complex was added by Jannaeus' widow, Queen Alexandra (76–67 B.C.). She constructed a pair of unique villas (the "twin palaces"), built one attached to the other in a *spiegel bilt* plan. Each of the houses (ca. 25 × 25 m) had a square courtyard in its center, a triclinium (open towards the courtyard through a *Distilos in antis*), bath installations, and various ritual baths. Each of these villas also had a neighboring garden with a small swimming pool in its center. Each of the villas and their gardens were terraced into the terrain's slope in order not to disturb the panoramic view from the above-mentioned "Doric" pavilion.

The twin palaces were probably built to house the two rival sons of the queen, of whom the oldest had served as the high priest since his father's death.

Only minor changes and additions were introduced into the palace during the 30 years between Alexandra and Herod the Great. They mainly included the introduction of more bath installations (both secular and ritual) and a large swimming pool (ca. 20 × 12.5 m).

2. The Herodian Period. During Herod's long reign (37–4 B.C.), he managed to build three independent palaces at the same site, which ultimately functioned as one. It seems that in Herod's early years (37–31 B.C.), the Hasmonean family continued to use its palace in Jericho. The dramatic murder of Aristobulus III in a swimming pool at Jericho, as told by Josephus, took place during a banquet organized by Herod's Hasmonean mother-in-law.

Herod built his first independent palace at Jericho (probably around 35 B.C.) not far from the Hasmonean one, S of Wadi Qelt. It was a large rectangular building (84 × 45 m), built on three sides of a peristyled courtyard. It included a large triclinium, various palatial and service rooms, a bathhouse in the Roman style, and a ritual bath. Although free-standing, it resembles an introverted city house similar to those at Pompeii. This design may reflect Herod's political insecurities (ca. 35–30 B.C.), when Jericho was officially taken from him and given to Egypt's queen, Cleopatra.

Herod's second palace at the site (built around 25 B.C.), was built as an open complex, exposed to the landscape around. It was built on top of the ruined Hasmonean complex, following the latter's destruction by the earthquake of 31 B.C. This palace's major wing (the E wing) was built NE of the ruined twin palaces. It comprised two levels: the upper one with various palatial and service rooms was built around a large peristyled courtyard; the lower one included the Hasmonean (20 × 12.5 m) swimming pool, a bathhouse in the Roman style, and various service rooms.

To the W, the two large Hasmonean swimming pools were combined into one large pool (32 × 18 m), surrounded by newly planted gardens. Perhaps another wing (perhaps a villa) was built on top of the Hasmonean artificial mound, but no evidence of this has been found.

The largest and most sophisticated palace built by Herod in Jericho, the Third Palace, was built around 15 B.C. on both sides of Wadi Qelt, N of the first palace and SE of the second one. Covering about 3 hectares, it was built following a grid system parallel to the wadi. Roman builders and artisans cooperated with the local artisans to use Roman concrete work, which was covered by small stones in the *opus reticulatum* and *opus quadratum* styles, side by side with the local mudbrick work.

The main wing of the palace was the N one. It included various palatial rooms, two small gardened peristyled courtyards, a relatively large bathhouse in the Roman style, and a huge triclinium. This outstanding triclinium (29 × 19 m) had rows of columns on three of its sides, similar in plan to the one in the first palace. Most of its floor was covered by an elaborate *opus sectile* floor (its tiles were looted in antiquity). The walls, like practically all the other walls in this wing, were covered with frescoes. The wing also included two long colonnades, built along the wadi, opposite the sunken garden. The ceilings of these colonnades, as well as those in other rooms, were decorated with elaborate stucco work.

The other three large wings of the third palace were built S of Wadi Qelt: the sunken garden, a huge pool, and an elaborate building. See Fig. JER.06.

The sunken garden, an elaborate formal garden (140 × 40 m), was flanked by two elevated colonnades on its short ends. The long S facade (Kelso and Baramki's "Grand Facade") was decorated with 48 niches, having a reflection water channel in front of them. The center of this facade was designed with a small semicircular garden, in the shape of a theater. The huge pool (90 × 42 m), probably served for swimming, boating, and water games.

Only foundations, a circle bounded by a square, have survived from the building which once stood on top of the artificial mound. There are good reasons to infer that above these foundations stood a round reception hall, 16 m in diameter, with four semicircular niches around it (a similar hall, 8 m in diameter, was integrated into the Roman-style bathhouse of the N wing). Following this

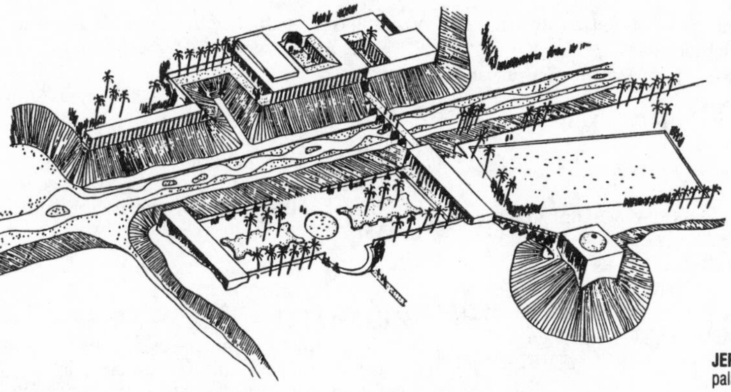

JER.06. Reconstruction of Herod's winter palace at Jericho. *(Courtesy of E. Netzer)*

reconstruction, this hall was similar in shape to the contemporaneous *Tempio di Merkuri* in *Baia.* This elevated hall was reached by a stair-bridge constructed upon a series of arches. A second bridge, of which we have no evidence, was probably built across Wadi Qelt, connecting the two parts of the palace.

The winter palace complex included also a series of structures built E of the Hasmonean palace. These structures (only partially excavated), were built along the fringe of the royal estate, perhaps to house the administrative staff. At their E edge, a small "industrial area" was exposed, probably to process some of the royal estate products (perhaps the *opobalsamum*).

Another important building project of Herod was revealed and excavated by Netzer (1975–76) at Tell el Samarat, S of Tell el-Sultan. This consists of the remains of a complex unique in the whole Greco-Roman world, which integrated a horse- and chariot-racing course, a theater's *cavea* 70 m wide, and an elaborate building (70 × 70 m) elevated on top of an artificial mound. Little more than the foundations have survived of this latter elevated building, which may have served as a reception area or a gymnasium.

This combined building project (which accommodated horse races, athletics, boxing, theater, and musical shows like the ones performed in the quinquennial games in honor of Augustus, which Herod established and maintained in Jerusalem and Caesarea) probably is that to which Josephus referred when he mentioned at Jericho a hippodrome, a theater, and an amphitheater.

Very few other Hasmonean or Herodian ruins are known in Jericho; however, there are a few independent dwellings. It can be assumed that Second Temple Jericho was spread over the plain's irrigated areas, probably in the character of a garden city, side by side with the royal estates.

Jericho as a whole functioned not only as an agricultural center and as a crossroad, but as a winter resort for Jerusalem's aristocracy. Indirect evidence of the extensive Jewish population in this period was found in the survey and excavations (Hachlili 1976–77) of a huge contemporary cemetery W of the plain and near the bottom of the mountains' slopes.

EHUD NETZER

Bibliography

Bartlett, J. R. 1982a. Iron Age and Hellenistic Stamped Jar Handles from Tell es-Sultan. Pp. 537–45 in Kenyon and Holland 1982.

———. 1982b. *Jericho.* Guildford, Surrey.

Bar-Yosef, O. 1986. The Walls of Jericho: An Alternative Interpretation. *Current Anthropology* 27: 157–62.

Bennett, C.-M. 1965. Tombs of the Roman Period. Pp. 516–45 in Kenyon 1965.

Bienkowski, P. 1986. *Jericho in the Late Bronze Age.* Warminster.

Bliss, F. J. 1894. Notes on the Plain of Jericho. *PEFQS,* 175–83.

Contenson, H. de, and van Liere, W. 1966. Seconde campagne à Tell Ramad, 1965: rapport préliminaire. *Annales Archaeologiques Arabes Syriennes* 16/2: 167–74.

Cook, S. A. 1910. The German Excavations at Jericho. *PEFQS,* 54–68.

Crowfoot, E. 1982. Textiles, Matting, and Basketry. Pp. 546–50 in Kenyon and Holland 1982.

Crowfoot, J. 1937. Notes on the Flint Implements of Jericho, 1936. *Liverpool Annals of Archaeology and Anthropology* 24: 35–50.

Crowfoot Payne, J. 1983. The Flint Industries of Jericho. Pp. 622–759 in Kenyon and Holland 1983.

Dorrell, P. 1983. Stone Vessels, Tools, and Objects. Pp. 485–575 in Kenyon and Holland 1983.

Ferembach, D., and Lechevallier, M. 1973. Découverte de deux crânes surmodelés dans une habitation du VIIme millénaire à Beisamoun, Israel. *Paléorient* 1/2: 223–30.

Franken, H. J. 1974. *In Search of the Jericho Potters.* Amsterdam.

Garstang, J. 1932. Jericho: City and Necropolis. *Liverpool Annals of Archaeology and Anthropology* 19: 3–22, 35–54.

———. 1933. Jericho: City and Necropolis. *Liverpool Annals of Archaeology and Anthropology* 20: 3–42.

———. 1934. Jericho: City and Necropolis. *Liverpool Annals of Archaeology and Anthropology* 21: 99–136.

———. 1935. Jericho: City and Necropolis. *Liverpool Annals of Archaeology and Anthropology* 22: 143–68.

———. 1936. Jericho: City and Necropolis. *Liverpool Annals of Archaeology and Anthropology* 23: 67–76.

Garstang, J., and Garstang, J. B. E. 1940. *The Story of Jericho.* London.

———. 1948. *The Story of Jericho.* rev. ed. London.

Hachlili, R. 1979. The Goliath Family in Jericho: Funerary Inscriptions from a First Century A.D. Jewish Monumental Tomb. *BASOR* 235: 31–65.

———. 1980. A Second Temple Period Jewish Necropolis in Jericho. *BA* 43/4: 235–40.

Holland, T. A. 1982a. Figurines and Miscellaneous Objects. Pp. 551–63 in Kenyon and Holland 1982.
———. 1982b. The Metal Objects. Pp. 564–69 in Kenyon and Holland 1982.
———. 1983. Stone Maceheads. Pp. 804–13 in Kenyon and Holland 1983.
———. 1988. Review of P. Bienkowski, *Jericho in the Late Bronze Age. JNES* 47: 189–90.
Hopf, M. 1983. Jericho Plant Remains. Pp. 576–621 in Kenyon and Holland 1983.
Kelso, J. L., and Baramki, D. C. 1955. The Excavation of New Testament Jericho (Tulul Abu el-ʿAliyiq). Pp. 1–19 in *Excavations at New Testament Jericho and Khirbet en-Nitla,* ed. W. F. Albright, and V. Winnett. AASOR 29–30. New Haven.
Kenyon, K. M. 1952. Excavations at Jericho, 1952. *PEQ,* 62–82.
———. 1957. *Digging Up Jericho.* London.
———. 1960. *Excavations at Jericho.* Vol. 1, *The Tombs Excavated in 1952–4.* London.
———. 1965. *Excavations at Jericho.* Vol. 2, *The Tombs Excavated in 1955–8.* London.
———. 1973. Palestine in the Time of the Eighteenth Dynasty. *CAH*³ 2/1: 526–56.
———. 1979. *Archaeology in the Holy Land.* 4th ed. London.
———. 1981. *Excavations at Jericho.* Vol. 3, *The Architecture and Stratigraphy of the Tell,* ed. T. A. Holland. London.
Kenyon, K. A., and Holland, T. A. 1982. *Excavations at Jericho.* Vol. 4, *The Pottery Type Series and Other Finds.* London.
———. 1983. *Excavations at Jericho.* Vol. 5, *The Pottery Phases of the Tell and Other Finds.* London.
Marshall, D. N. 1982. Jericho Bone Tools and Objects. Pp. 570–622 in Kenyon and Holland 1982.
Netzer, E. 1977. The Winter Palaces of the Judean Kings at Jericho at the End of the Second Temple Period. *BASOR* 228: 1–13.
———. 1982. Recent Discoveries in the Winter Palace of Second Temple Times at Jericho. *Qad* 15/1: 22–29 (in Hebrew).
Pritchard, J. B. 1958. *Excavations at Herodian Jericho, 1951.* AASOR 32–33. New Haven.
Riesner, R. 1983. Die Mauern von Jericho, Bibelwissenschaft zwischen Fundamentalismus und Kritizismus. *TBei* 14: 79–86.
Rollefson, G. O. 1983. Ritual and Ceremony at Neolithic Ain Ghazal (Jordan). *Paléorient* 9: 29–38.
———. 1985. The 1983 Season at the Early Neolithic Site of Ain Ghazal. *National Geographic Research* 1/1: 44–62.
Sellin, E., and Watzinger, C. 1913. *Jericho, die Ergebnisse der Ausgrabungen, 1913.* Leipzig.
Stuiver, M., and Reimer, P. J. 1986. A Computer Program for Radiocarbon Age Calibration. *Radiocarbon* 28, 2B: 1022–30.
Talbot, G. C. 1983. Beads and Pendants from the Tell and Tombs. Pp. 788–801 in Kenyon and Holland 1983.
Tushingham, A. D. 1965. Tombs of the Early Iron Age. Pp. 479–515 in Kenyon 1965.
Warren, C. 1869. Mounds at ʿAin es-Sultan. *PEFQS,* 14–16.
———. 1883. Tell es Sultân. *SWP* 3: 222–26.
Watzinger, C. 1926. Zur Chronologie der Schichten von Jericho. *ZDMG* 80: 131–36.
Weippert, H., and Weippert, M. 1976. Jericho in der Eisenzeit. *ZDPV* 92: 105–48.
Wilkinson, J.; Hill, J.; and Ryan, W. F. 1988. Jerusalem Pilgrims. P. 4 in *Jerusalem Pilgrimage 1099–1185.* The Hakluyt Society, Second Series, 167. London.
Wood, B. G. 1990. Did the Israelites Conquer Jericho? A New Look at the Archaeological Evidence. *BARev* 16/2: 44–58.

T. A. Holland
Ehud Netzer

JERIEL (PERSON) [Heb *yĕrîʾēl*]. A descendant, perhaps grandson, of Issachar according to the genealogy of 1 Chr 7:1–5. For a discussion of the list of Issachar's sons, see IBSAM.

M. Stephen Davis

JERIMOTH (PERSON) [Heb *yerîmôt*]. Var. JEREMOTH. Jerimoth appears as a proper name only in late biblical writings. Within Chronicles "Jerimoth" represents several different individuals contemporaneous with David, as well as several different Benjaminites. Those presented as David's peers seem retrojected anachronistically into preexilic Israel by the Chronicler. The name may have originated as the familial name of a Benjaminite clan in postexilic Jerusalem (see #3). The name also arises in an authentic source in Ezra 10:26–29, where it represents three different individuals. Jerimoth was most likely a common Judean name in the late 5th, early 4th century B.C.E. Its etymology, "exalted," reflects a theological tendency found in other names from this era (Silverman 1985: 283–85). The equivalence of the names "Jerimoth" and "Jeremoth" is best observed in 1 Chr 24:30 (= 1 Chr 23:23) and 1 Chr 25:4 (= 1 Chr 25:22) where the names are used for the one person in the same context.

1. The son of Bela and, according to 1 Chronicles, a military leader from the tribe of Benjamin during the reign of David (1 Chr 7:7). While it is possible that the Chronicler inserted Jerimoth into this passage from postexilic source material (Williamson *1 and 2 Chronicles* NCBC, 77–78), the stylistic characteristics of 1 Chr 7:6–12 suggest that the unit was composed by the Chronicler himself. Jerimoth here may represent a postexilic Benjaminite familial name (see #3) that the Chronicler retrojected into the time of David in order to establish impressive military support for David's rule.

2. The son of Becher, and according to 1 Chronicles, a military leader from the tribe of Benjamin during the reign of David (1 Chr 7:8). See #1.

3. A Benjaminite, the son of Shimei and inhabitant of Jerusalem (1 Chr 8:14). Geography seems to provide the organizing principle of the genealogical list in which Jerimoth appears. The name thereby provides important demographic evidence for the population of Jerusalem at some point in her history. Rudolph (*Chronikbücher* HAT, 77) has argued that either Josiah's reign or Nehemiah's governorship provides a suitable background for the appearance of Benjaminites in Jerusalem. The commonality of the names of the nine sons of Shimei with names recorded in elsewhere in Chronicles or in Ezra and Nehemiah (Curtis and Masden *The Books of Chronicles* ICC, 162), however, suggests that Jerimoth represents a segment of the postexilic, rather than the preexilic, population of Jerusalem.

4. A warrior, who, according to 1 Chronicles, joined David's revolt against Saul at Ziklag (1 Chr 12:5). 1 Chronicles 12 extends the list of David's warriors from the Chronicler's Deuteronomistic source (1 Samuel 31

[= 1 Chr 11:11–47]). The source of these warriors' names remains contested. Rudolph (*Chronikbücher* HAT, 103–7) argued that the names were later appended to the Chronicler's work in the 2d century B.C.E. Zeron (1974) has argued that Jerimoth and others in 1 Chronicles 12 represent an authentic preexilic source—a fragment of an otherwise lost genealogy of Absalom. Stylistic and structural indications, however, imply that this section was composed by the Chronicler (Williamson 1981). Jeremoth therefore represents the retrojection of a common name from the time of the Chronicler into David's military force to bolster further David's support in Israel.

5. The son of Azriel and the tribal leader of Naphtali at the close of the reign of David (1 Chr 27:19). Embedded within a list of the leaders of the twelve tribes of Israel (1 Chr 27:16–24), the reference to the "Chronicles of King David" (1 Chr 27:24) has spurred speculation concerning a source that the Chronicler used in his reworking of Samuel and Kings (Williamson *1 and 2 Chronicles* NCBC, 175–76). The passage's Chronistic style and the presence of Aaronides as an independent tribe, however, suggest that the Chronicler composed the passage. Jerimoth's presence most likely represents the retrojection of a name that was common in the early 4th century B.C.E. back into the time of the united monarchy.

6. A Merarite, the son of Mushi, whom, according to the 1 Chronicles, David appointed to service in the Temple and its cult (1 Chr 23:23). Jeremoth appears nowhere else as a Levite in the OT outside of 1 and 2 Chronicles. The Levitical genealogies of Exodus 6 and Numbers 3 do not extend this branch of the Levitical family beyond Jeremoth's father, Mushi. Although J. Liver (1968: 8.29–32) believes that Jeremoth and the other Levites in 1 Chronicles 23 may represent authentic persons contemporaneous with David or Solomon, Rudolph (*Chronikbücher* HAT, 154–55) argued that Jeremoth and the other Levites of 1 Chronicles 23 represent Levitical families after the time of the Chronicler. The style of the list, however, corresponds closely with the compositional techniques of the Chronicler. This suggests that Williamson (*1 and 2 Chronicles* NCBC, 160) may be correct in asserting that "the names of the heads of houses will then be current at the time of the list's composition"—the time of the composition of Chronicles (ca. 460 B.C.E.).

7. A son of Heman whom, according to the Chronicler, David and the Judean military leaders appointed as one of the leaders of the Levitical Temple instrumentalists (1 Chr 25:4). While the exact compositional history of the Levitical musicians in 1 Chronicles 25 remains contested, it is generally conceded that Jeremoth appears in a list of names that has been artificially constructed from a postexilic hymn (Williamson *1 and 2 Chronicles* NCBC, 167–68). The Chronicler anachronistically retrojected a common name that expressed the piety of his age into the founding establishment of Temple personnel during the reign of David.

8. A son of David, the father of Mahalath who, according to the Chronicler, married Rehoboam (2 Chr 11:18). The name "Jerimoth" is not attested elsewhere as a name for a son of David. Curtis and Madsen (369) raise the possibility that Jerimoth was therefore the son of one of David's concubines. Yet the late appearance of the name elsewhere and the Chronistic style of 2 Chr 11:18–23 suggest that the Chronicler borrowed the name from his day to produce artificially a son of David with an identical Levitical name, thereby relating two of his chief interests.

9. According to the Chronicler, a Levitical overseer of surplus Temple offerings gathered during Hezekiah's Temple reforms (2 Chr 31:13). The Chronistic style of the chapter clearly demarcates it as the Chronicler's own invention. Having already equated the name with a Levitical family (1 Chr 24:30), the Chronicler reuses "Jerimoth" to illustrate the propriety of Hezekiah's reforms.

10. A member of the family of Elam who lived in the Persian province of Judah during the mission of Ezra (Ezra 10:26). Jeremoth, a member of a family that had returned from exile with Zerubbabel, married a non-Judean wife. He consented to divorce her during the reforms of Ezra under the threat of complete ostracism from the Jerusalem temple-state. Through the list of Jeremoth's peers may be abbreviated (Rudolph *Esra und Nehemiah samt 3. Esra* HAT, 97–99), it is generally agreed that the names in the list of Ezra 10:18–43 authentically represent individuals from the Persian province of Judah during the mission of Ezra.

11. A member of the family of Zattu who lived in the Persian province of Judah during the mission of Ezra (Ezra 10:27). See #10.

12. A member of the family of Bani who lived in the Persian province of Judah during the mission of Ezra (Ezra 10:29).

Bibliography

Liver, J. 1968. *Chapters in the History of Priests and Levites.* Jerusalem (in Hebrew).

Silverman, M. H. 1985. *Religious Values in the Jewish Proper Names of Elephantine.* AOAT 217. Neukirchen-Vluyn.

Williamson, H. G. M. 1979. The Origins of the Twenty-four Priestly Courses: A Study of 1 Chronicles xxiii–xxvii. Pp. 251–68 in *Studies in the Historical Books of the Old Testament,* ed. J. A. Emerton. VTSup 30. Leiden.

———. 1981. "We Are Yours, O David": The Setting and Purpose of 1 Chronicles xii 1–23. *OTS* 21: 164–76.

Zeron, A. 1974. Tag für Tag kam zu David, um ihm zu helfen, 1. Chr. 12, 1–22. *TZ* 30: 257–61.

JOHN W. WRIGHT

JERIOTH (PERSON) [Heb *yĕrîʿôt*]. The daughter of Caleb and Azubah and the mother of Jesher, Shobab, and Ardon (1 Chr 2:18). This identification is admittedly merely the most probable among several alternatives (Braun *Chronicles* WBC, 39). The Vatican manuscript of the LXX represents not only Jerioth but also Azubah as the daughter of Caleb. However v 19 implies that Azubah was his wife. It is possible that the name "Jerioth" and the name "Azubah" both indicate the same person. In such a case the conjunction *waw* would be explicative and should be rendered something like "even." This suggestion actually fits Jerioth's being either Caleb's daughter or his wife. The latter proposal is precisely the understanding of the LXX's Alexandrian manuscript, though it keeps Jerioth and Azubah apart as two separate individuals—each a wife of Caleb. Textual emendation could make Jerioth the father of Azubah (Curtis and Madsen *Chronicles* ICC, 92) or a former husband of Azubah (Richter 1914: 110). On the absolute use thus required of the *Hipʿil* of *yld,* note Isa 66:9 where it has the force of "to cause to bear." The idea that Jerioth might have been a son of Caleb and Azubah hardly seems likely. Stamm (1967: 325) thinks the translation "(tent-)curtains" for Jerioth as a plural of *yĕrîʿâ* is unsatisfactory, and he assumes a connection with the verb *yrʿ*—"to tremble, to be faint-hearted" (cf. Ar *yariʿa*—"to be a coward"). Potentially either feminine or masculine in form, this short name lengthened by the hypocoristic element *-ôt* would then mean "(the) anxious or timid or fearful (one)." Neither Akkadian nor Egyptian appears to supply a parallel.

Bibliography

Richter, G. 1914. Untersuchungen zu den Geschlechtsregistern der Chronik. *ZAW* 34: 107–41.

Stamm, J. J. 1967. Hebräische Frauennamen. Pp. 301–39 in *Hebräische Wortforschung,* ed. B. Hartmann et al. VTSup 16. Leiden.

EDWIN C. HOSTETTER

JEROBOAM (PERSON) [Heb *yārobʿam*]. Two kings of N Israel bore this name, which means "may the people be great."

1. The son of Nebat, and the first king of the N kingdom of Israel (ca. 922–901 B.C.E.). Prior to his elevation to the N Israelite kingship, Jeroboam had served in Solomon's royal administration. He eventually opposed Solomon's policies and rebelled against the king. He fled to Egypt to escape Solomon's wrath and remained there until Solomon's death. Jeroboam subsequently returned home and was elevated to the kingship by the N Israelite tribes. He proceeded to develop a religiopolitical system for the new nation to establish its independence from the Davidic kingdom of Judah in the S. For this, Jeroboam is remembered in biblical tradition as the king who led Israel to sin, setting the new nation on its fateful course of decline and fall.

a. Sources. The main account of Jeroboam's rise to power and reign in 1 Kgs 11:26–14:20 is a compilation of several sources, but Cohn (1985) has called attention to the literary techniques by means of which the Deuteronomistic historian created a "unified story" out of his disparate sources. Even though this account of Jeroboam's career has been shaped to conform to the later perspectives of its author, most scholars believe that critical investigation of this complex—evidently drawn from archival texts, historical reports, prophetic oracles, and legends, etc.—can yield reliable information about the 10th-century situation.

As for other sources, the Chronicler presents with only slight variations parallel accounts of 1 Kgs 12:1–19 (cf. 2 Chr 10:1–19) and 1 Kgs 12:21–24 (cf. 2 Chr 11:1–4). In an account unparalleled in Kings, and of uncertain historical value, the Chronicler gives an account of the conflict between Jeroboam and the Judean king Abijah/Abijam (2 Chr 13:2–20). In addition, the LXX (Codex Vaticanus) preserves, as a supplement to its translation of the Hebrew account in Kings, an alternate version of Jeroboam's career (3 Kgdms 12:24a–z), but scholars are divided on the historical reliability of the additional details about Jeroboam that it provides (for a review and assessment of the various views, see Gordon 1975).

b. Rise to Power. Few details are known about Jeroboam's life before his rise to kingship. He is described in 1 Kgs 11:26 as an Ephraimite from the village of Zeredah, son of Nebat and the widowed Zeruah; the LXX supplement, however, fails to mention his father and identifies his mother as Sarira, a harlot—a note which is often dismissed as tendentious (for a contrary view, see Aberbach and Smolar 1969: 69–70).

Additional details provided by the LXX supplement claim that Jeroboam had 300 chariots prior to this escape to Egypt (v 24b) and that Pharaoh Shishak gave him an Egyptian princess in marriage (v 24e). This latter detail, however, may derive from confusion between Jeroboam and Hadad, an Edomite rebel against Solomon who, according to 1 Kgs 11:19, married Pharaoh's daughter.

According to 1 Kgs 11:26–28, Jeroboam was an official in Solomon's administration. His duties under Solomon included the oversight of the *sēbel* (v 28) in the district known as the "house of Joseph"—the tribal territory of Ephraim/Manasseh. The term *sēbel* is believed to refer to the temporary work forces drawn from the N Israelite tribes, not the *mas-ʿōbēd* "forced levy of slaves" (cf. 1 Kgs 9:21–22) which was the permanent, institutionalized force of corvée workers drawn from the Canaanite population (Mettinger 1971: 138).

While in this position of leadership, Jeroboam witnessed the oppressiveness of Solomon's administration and eventually revolted in an expression of solidarity with his N Israelite compatriots. It is generally agreed that Solomon's policies which alienated the northerners included heavy and inequitable taxation and the system of the *sēbel.* In addition, it has been suggested that Solomon's cession of N Israelite towns (1 Kgs 9:10–13) to the Phoenician king Hiram was the "last straw" which precipitated Jeroboam's revolt (Halpern 1974: 528). Miller has suggested further that cultic installations and personnel in the N may have been co-opted to support the "cultic primacy of Jerusalem" in the Davidic state (*HAIJ,* 230–31).

The account in 1 Kgs 11:29–39 claims that the Shilonite prophet Ahijah designated Jeroboam as the divinely chosen king of the N Israelite tribes, but the passage (especially vv 32–39) is so thoroughly laced with Deuteronomistic language and motifs that its historical value is suspect. Many scholars maintain, however, that vv 29–31(32) preserve a portion of an early tradition about the incident (Plein 1966: 18–20; Debus 1967: 80–87; Seebass 1967: 323–33; Gray, *1–2 Kings* OTL, 288; Weippert 1983: 346–50). Inasmuch as prophets frequently instigated political revolts in the N kingdom, there is good reason to suppose that Ahijah did encourage the rebellion. Caquot (1961: 25) has suggested that Ahijah was motivated by the hope that Jeroboam would select Shiloh for the religious center of his new kingdom.

Solomon responded to the rebellion by seeking to kill Jeroboam. Jeroboam fled to Egypt, where Shishak, king of Egypt, gave him asylum. Halpern (1974: 523–34) has suggested that Jeroboam hoped to win Egyptian support in his move against Solomon on the assumption that relations between Solomon and Egypt had shifted from cooperation to antagonism under the 22d Dyn. founded by

Shishak (Shoshenq I). Jeroboam remained in Egypt until Solomon died.

The sources do not agree on whether Jeroboam participated in the subsequent assembly at Shechem, the gathering at which the N Israelite leaders negotiated with Solomon's son Rehoboam to determine the future of their relationship to the house of David. According to 1 Kgs 12:1–19 and the parallel account in 2 Chr 10:1–19, Jeroboam was summoned from Egypt to the Shechemite assembly and participated in the proceedings (vv 3 and 12 of both accounts). 1 Kgs 12:20 suggests, however, that Jeroboam was summoned to Shechem and made king over Israel only after the discussions with Rehoboam had broken down and the decision had been made to break away from Davidic rule. Attempts to explain the inconsistencies, using the evidence of the LXX, have been vigorously debated (Gooding 1967; 1972; Klein 1970; 1973; McKenzie 1987).

c. Jeroboam and Rehoboam. The reasons for Rehoboam's involvement in the proceedings at Shechem are not specifically stated. Some have speculated that the N Israelites had a charismatic conception of kingship which gave them a natural reluctance to accept the regular dynastic succession when Solomon died, so Rehoboam went to Shechem to attempt to renew a personal union between N and S which supposedly had existed under his predecessors (Alt 1951: 4–9; Donner, *IJH*, 383–84); it has also been proposed that democratic tendencies existed in the N to which Rehoboam responded (Soggin 1984: 193). The uncertainties of a charismatic ideal of kingship or supposed democratic tendencies in the N aside, Miller justifiably suggests that urgent political realities prompted Rehoboam to go to Shechem to negotiate the matter of his kingship (*HAIJ*, 229–30).

1 Kgs 14:30 refers to continual conflict between Rehoboam and Jeroboam. This evidently refers to the skirmishes to determine the border which would separate the two kingdoms—essentially whether the territory of Benjamin would belong to Israel or Judah. In these struggles, Rehoboam succeeded in retaining control of most of the Benjaminite territory (cf. 1 Kgs 12:21), but he seems to have refrained from attempting to regain control of the rest of the N. According to 1 Kgs 12:22–24, the Judean prophet Shemaiah uttered an oracle against any such attempts on the grounds that what had happened was the will of Yahweh. This obviously reflects the Deuteronomistic historian's view of the course of events (cf. 1 Kgs 12:15), but the account may accurately recall a sentiment against exacerbating the difficult circumstances that had led to the schism.

d. Political Establishment. After Jeroboam was elevated to the kingship by the N Israelite tribes, he began the task of establishing a political and religious system for the new nation. According to 1 Kgs 12:25, he rebuilt Shechem and stayed there and then "went out" (*wayyēṣēʾ* often has the connotation of a military maneuver) and fortified Penuel. Whether this means that Jeroboam established Shechem as the first political capital of the new kingdom, followed by Penuel in Transjordan, is debated. Those who argue that this was the case attribute Jeroboam's supposed retreat from Shechem either to (1) Pharaoh Shishak's invasion in the fifth year of Jeroboam's reign (Mazar 1957; Ahlström 1982: 56–57) or (2) to religious opposition from within Shechem (Danelius 1967–68; Allan 1974). By the end of Jeroboam's reign, the capital was located at Tirzah (1 Kgs 14:17); Tirzah remained the N Israelite capital (cf. 1 Kgs 15:33; 16:8, 15, and 23) until Omri moved to Samaria. Miller (*HAIJ*, 244) suggests that Tirzah may have been the capital from the very beginning; according to this view, 1 Kgs 12:25 may only indicate that Jeroboam resided in Shechem and Penuel while state-sponsored construction work was underway in those cities.

The biblical texts provide no information about Jeroboam's administrative system. Given the urgent task of establishing a viable nation, however, it is reasonable to suppose that Jeroboam utilized Solomon's administrative apparatus with "perhaps some necessary adjustments" (Ahlström 1982: 63). No doubt the system of the *sēbel* was discontinued, and one must naturally suppose that officials who were loyalists of the Davidic state were removed from office. But the basic apparatus of the previous administration was no doubt kept in place. The Samaria ostraca of the 8th century B.C.E. provide evidence that the district system established by Solomon continued intact in the N kingdom with perhaps only slight modifications (Soggin 1984: 197).

e. Religious Establishment. Jeroboam's efforts to establish an independent religious system for the N Israelite kingdom are detailed in 1 Kgs 12:26–33. The account clearly serves the Deuteronomistic historian's polemical purposes against Jeroboam and the N kingdom. Its anachronistic and propagandistic elements suggest to Hoffmann (1980: 59–73) and Van Seters (1983: 313–14) that the entire account is a late invention without any historical basis. Others maintain that the account reliably reports the essential cultic measures undertaken by Jeroboam, despite the polemical judgments about them (Evans 1983: 120; Zevit 1985: 60–61). Donner (*IJH*, 383) and Zevit (1985: 61) identify the source from which the historical information was drawn as the annals of the kings of Israel mentioned in 1 Kgs 14:19.

According to 1 Kgs 12:26–33, Jeroboam's cultic measures included: (1) construction of two golden calves; (2) placement of the calves at cult centers in Bethel and Dan; (3) establishment of other sanctuaries; (4) appointment of non-Levitic priests; and (5) observance of the fall festival, the Feast of Ingathering, on the fifteenth day of the eighth month, at which time the king offered a sacrifice on the altar in Bethel. The Deuteronomistic historian viewed each of these measures as a violation of Deuteronomic law, explaining his negative judgments on Jeroboam and the N cultic establishment. But Jeroboam and his N Israelite contemporaries no doubt viewed these measures as a return to old traditions and practices, a departure from the alien Jerusalemite religion which had been imposed upon them by the Davidic state (Talmon 1958: 53–57; Ahlström 1982: 57–58; *HAIJ*, 242–43).

The reference to Jeroboam's choice of golden calf or bull images for the religious iconography of his new kingdom associates these images with Yahweh, the god of the exodus ("Behold your god, Israel, who brought you up from the land of Egypt"—1 Kgs 12:28) and recalls the golden calf episode in Exodus 32. These associations suggest that Jeroboam sought to revive an ancient cultic symbol of the divine presence of the Israelite deity Yahweh (Talmon 1958: 50; *CMHE,* 74–75; Ahlström 1982: 62, n. 91; *HAIJ,* 242). The calf images thus served as the N Israelite counterpart to the cherubim and Ark iconography in Solomon's Temple.

The installation of the golden calf images in Bethel and Dan further indicates the archaizing nature of Jeroboam's state religion. Bethel's Israelite associations are firmly anchored in the ancestral stories of Genesis (12:8; 13:3; 28:19; 31:13; 35:1–16) and Dan's priesthood claimed to have descended from Moses (Judg 18:30). Jeroboam chose Dan and Bethel for national sanctuaries to revive ancient Israelite traditions (*HAIJ,* 242), not to establish royal temples at strategic N and S border locations as Aharoni (1968: 28) has suggested.

Jeroboam's priesthood, according to 1 Kgs 12:31b, was non-Levitic. Cross (*CMHE,* 199) dismisses this claim because he thinks it belongs to the "Deuteronomistic polemic" against Jeroboam, and he argues that Jeroboam appointed two rival priesthoods of Levitic ancestry to serve at his two national sanctuaries—Aaronites at Bethel and Mushites at Dan. A modification of this view maintains that Jeroboam replaced the Aaronite priests at Bethel with Levites of Mushite ancestry (Halpern 1976: 38). Other scholars, however, think that 1 Kgs 12:31b and 2 Chr 11:13–17 accurately recall that Jeroboam dismissed Levites from priestly service, a move that Jeroboam would have found necessary because the Levites at the time, it is maintained, were priests and government employees of the Davidic state (Ahlström 1982: 57; *HAIJ,* 242). Given this understanding of Levites, Jeroboam naturally would have replaced the Davidic loyalists with his own cultic personnel.

The statement in 1 Kgs 12:31a that Jeroboam built holy shrines or sanctuaries can be taken as reliable, even though the expression used *(bêt [?] bāmôth)* reflects the Deuteronomistic historian's pejorative term *bāmôth* for these structures. But there is no reason to doubt that Jeroboam did engage in some such activity, inasmuch as kings in the ancient world typically built cities, fortresses, temples, etc., as "a political tool" in establishing a state administration (Ahlström 1982: 10–26).

As 1 Kgs 12:32–33 indicates, Jeroboam observed the Feast of Ingathering on the fifteenth day of the eighth month. The Deuteronomistic historian, who believed that the proper time to observe this festival was the fifteenth day of the *seventh* month (as was done in Jerusalem), says that Jeroboam set the date "in a month of his own choosing." This, again, reflects the pejorative judgment of the writer. Jeroboam's action is better understood as a reversion to an old agrarian calendar followed in the N which had been altered when a "full-scale synchronization" of divergent calendars was instituted by David or Solomon (Talmon 1958: 56–57). Jeroboam's choice of date for this festival was thus an integral part of his overall plan to restore traditional practices in the N.

f. Evaluation in Prophetic and Literary Tradition. The prophetic legend about the Judean man of God who denounced Jeroboam (1 Kgs 13:1–32) has been shaped by the Deuteronomistic historian into a prediction of Josiah's destruction of the altar in Bethel (cf. 13:1–3 and 2 Kgs 23:15). The legend, however, draws upon older prophetic traditions (Lemke 1976), indicating that the prophetic critique of the Bethelite cult preceded the work of the Deuteronomist.

Perhaps the earliest prophet to denounce Jeroboam was Ahijah. Ahijah had good reason to withdraw his support from Jeroboam, especially if he entertained hopes that Jeroboam would establish Shiloh as the religious center of the N Israelite nation. This loss of confidence in the new king underlies the account of Ahijah's condemnation of Jeroboam in 1 Kgs 14:1–18. The account in its present form, however, has been reworked and expanded by the Deuteronomistic historian, who uses the prophet's denunciation as the occasion to introduce the notion that because of Jeroboam's great sins which he "led Israel to commit" Yahweh would bring an end to the nation and scatter its people "beyond the Euphrates" (14:15–16; Evans 1983: 118–19).

The Deuteronomistic polemic against Jeroboam derives from Jeroboam's establishment of a state religion in the N—complete with iconography, priesthood, royal temples, and cultic calendar—which clashed with the Deuteronomistic historian's ideology. Measured by 10th-century N Israelite standards, Jeroboam's actions sought to restore N traditions and practices. But measured by the later standards of the Deuteronomist, Jeroboam's religious system represented a departure from true Yahwism. The Deuteronomist's literary framework, which is placed around the account of each king's reign, offers a grand redactional scheme by means of which nearly all N kings are charged with the perpetuation of Jeroboam's sins until all Israel had been seduced from allegiance to Yahweh (Mullen 1987). The end result was that Yahweh sent the nation into exile when it fell to the Assyrians (2 Kgs 17:21–23).

The portrayal of Jeroboam as the villain who set the N Israelite kingdom on its fateful course follows a typology of the *Unheilsherrscher,* which can be traced in the historiographic traditions about other ANE rulers—Naram-Sin most notably, but also Ibbi-Sin, Shulgi, and Nabonidus (Evans 1983). Manasseh, similarly, is presented by the Deuteronomist as the fateful ruler responsible for the fall of the S kingdom of Judah (2 Kgs 21:16; 23:26–27).

The tradition focusing on Jeroboam spanned a long history (Evans 1983: 114–18). Reflexes of a favorable assessment of Jeroboam can be found in the pre-Deuteronomistic traditions underlying 1 Kings 11 and 12, beginning with the oracle of his contemporary, Ahijah, and a related report of Jeroboam's rebellion against Solomon and rise to the kingship over N Israel. The annals of the kings of Israel recorded the information which underlies the account of Jeroboam's activity in establishing the N kingdom in 1 Kgs 12:25–33. These early traditions were subsequently reworked by the Deuteronomistic historian, who transformed Jeroboam into the arch-villain of the N kingdom. The positive portrait was not completely forgotten, however, as reflexes of it survive in the LXX's supplemental account. The interest in Jeroboam continued in the tradition of rabbinic interpretation, which has been studied by Aberbach and Smolar (1968).

Bibliography

Aberbach, M., and Smolar, L. 1968. Jeroboam and Solomon: Rabbinic Interpretations. *JQR* 59: 118–32.

———. 1969. Jeroboam's Rise to Power. *JBL* 88: 69–72.
Aharoni, Y. 1968. Arad: Its Inscriptions and Temple. *BA* 31: 2–32.
Ahlström, G. W. 1982. *Royal Administration and National Religion in Ancient Palestine.* Studies in the History of the Ancient Near East 1. Leiden.
Allan, N. 1974. Jeroboam and Shechem. *VT* 24: 353–57.
Alt, A. 1951. Das Königtum in den Reichen Israel und Juda. *VT* 1: 2–22.
Caquot, A. 1961. Aḥiyya de Silo et Jéroboam Ier. *Sem* 11: 17–27.
Cohn, R. 1985. Literary Techniques in the Jeroboam Narrative. *ZAW* 97: 23–35.
Danelius, E. 1967–68. The Sins of Jeroboam Ben-Nebat. *JQR* 58: 95–114, 204–23.
Debus, J. 1967. *Die Sünde Jerobeams.* FRLANT 93. Göttingen.
Evans, C. D. 1983. Naram-Sin and Jeroboam: The Archetypal *Unheilsherrscher* in Mesopotamian and Biblical Historiography. Pp. 97–125 in *Scripture in Context II: More Essays on the Comparative Method,* ed. W. W. Hallo, J. C. Moyer, and L. G. Perdue. Winona Lake, IN.
Gooding, D. W. 1967. The Septuagint's Rival Versions of Jeroboam's Rise to Power. *VT* 17: 173–89.
———. 1972. Jeroboam's Rise to Power: A Rejoinder. *JBL* 91: 529–33.
Gordon, R. P. 1975. The Second Septuagint Account of Jeroboam: History or Midrash? *VT* 25: 368–93.
Halpern, B. 1974. Sectionalism and Schism. *JBL* 93: 519–32.
———. 1976. Levitic Participation in the Reform Cult of Jeroboam I. *JBL* 95: 31–42.
Hoffmann, H.-D. 1980. *Reform und Reformen.* Zurich.
Klein, R. W. 1970. Jeroboam's Rise to Power. *JBL* 89: 217–18.
———. 1973. Once More: "Jeroboam's Rise to Power." *JBL* 92: 582–84.
Lemke, W. E. 1976. The Way of Obedience: I Kings 13 and the Structure of the Deuteronomistic History. Pp. 301–26 in *Magnalia Dei: The Mighty Acts of God,* ed. F. M. Cross, W. E. Lemke, and P. D. Miller, Jr. Garden City, NY.
Mazar, B. 1957. The Campaign of Pharaoh Shishak to Palestine. Pp. 57–66 in *Volume du Congrès, Strasbourg, 1956,* ed. G. W. Anderson et al. VTSup 4. Leiden.
McKenzie, S. L. 1987. The Source for Jeroboam's Role at Shechem (1 Kgs 11:43–12:3, 12, 20). *JBL* 106: 297–300.
Mettinger, T. N. D. 1971. *Solomonic State Officials.* ConBOT 5. Lund.
Mullen, E. T., Jr. 1987. The Sins of Jeroboam: A Redactional Assessment. *CBQ* 49: 212–32.
Plein, I. 1966. Erwägungen zur Überlieferung von I Reg. 11:26–14:20. *ZAW* 78: 8–24.
Seebass, H. 1967. Zur Königserhebung Jerobeams I. *VT* 17: 323–33.
Soggin, J. A. 1984. *A History of Ancient Israel.* Trans. J. Bowden. Philadelphia.
Talmon, S. 1958. Divergences in Calendar-Reckoning in Ephraim and Judah. *VT* 8: 48–74.
Van Seters, J. 1983. *In Search of History.* New Haven.
Weippert, H. 1983. Die Ätiologie des Nordreiches und seines Königshauses (I Reg 11:29–40). *ZAW* 95: 344–75.
Zevit, Z. 1985. Deuteronomistic Historiography in 1 Kings 12–2 Kings 17 and the Reinvestiture of the Israelian Cult. *JSOT* 32: 57–73.

CARL D. EVANS

2. A king of Israel, the son and successor of Joash (2 Kgs 14:23–29). He was the grandson of Jehu and a contemporary of Amaziah and Uzziah, kings of Judah (2 Kgs 14:23; 15:1). Jeroboam is said to have enjoyed a lengthy reign of forty-one years (ca. 786–746 B.C.E.). Gray (*I and II Kings* OTL, 72–73, 615) believes that 2 Kgs 14:23 confuses the date of Jeroboam's sole accession to the throne and the period of his coregency with his father, Joash.

The presentation of Jeroboam's reign in the Deuteronomistic history is illustrative of its selective and tendentious nature. Commentators and historians assess Jeroboam's reign as a marked political success and a period of prosperity for the N kingdom in the 8th century B.C.E. However the Deuteronomistic history dismisses the reign in a few verses (2 Kgs 14:23–29). The theological assessment of Jeroboam II is introduced and concluded in standard negative terms as continuing the apostasy of his namesake Jeroboam I (2 Kgs 14:23–24, 28–29). However, the report that he was able to extend the boundaries of the N kingdom and was successful in war is suprising. The most striking aspect is that Jeroboam is said to have been successful owing to Yahweh's compassion for Israel (2 Kgs 14:25–27). His expansionist policy is said to have been in accordance with the word of Yahweh delivered by the prophet Jonah. This oracle is not preserved elsewhere in the Hebrew Bible, although its nationalistic sentiments are in accord with the presentation of the figure Jonah in the book by that name. Clearly the Deuteronomistic history presents all aspects of the history of the N kingdom as part of divine providence. The scheme of affliction-compassion-restoration which is surprisingly applied to a N king is reminiscent of the major themes of the book of Judges.

The historical interpretation of these verses is particularly difficult. The extent of the expansion of the border is described as "from the entrance of Hamath as far as the Sea of Arabah" (2 Kgs 14:25). This is an expression that often refers to the ideal boundaries of Israel (Num 13:21; 34:8; Josh 13:5; Judg 3:3; 1 Kgs 8:65; Amos 6:14). The phrase "the entrance of Hamath" is often understood as a reference to a specific location, Lebo-Hamath, 70 k N of Damascus (*LBHG,* 65) or the S entrance to the Beqah valley, while "the Sea of Arabah" was the Dead Sea (Miller and Hayes *HAIJ,* 307–8). Most historians and commentators believe that Amos 6:13 provides confirmatory evidence for Jeroboam's territorial expansion into Transjordan (Wolff *Joel and Amos* Hermeneia, 288; *HAIJ,* 308). However, the pun based on the Hebrew place names Lodebar ("nothing") and Karnaim ("two horns" or "power") is a condemnation of the self-satisfaction of those who place their trust in human power or useless idols. It is doubtful then if this verse can be used as evidence for the expansionist policy of Jeroboam ben Joash, particularly since it is dependent upon the assumption that it is to be dated to the reign of Jeroboam II (Coote 1981: 88). The obscure reference in 1 Chr 5:17 to some kind of census in Transjordan during the reign of Jeroboam II is also cited as evidence of territorial gains in this area. 2 Kgs 14:28 adds further information on the expansionist policy of Jeroboam with the statement that "he recovered for Israel Damascus and Hamath, which had belonged to Judah." The MT is difficult to understand, particularly the prepositions before the names "Israel" and "Judah"; it reads literally "and how he restored Damascus and Hamath to Judah in Israel." The Syriac omits "to Judah" and emends "in Israel" to "to Israel." Gray (616–17) believes that the MT is indefensible and adopts an emendation proposed by Burney (1903: 320–21) "and his might in war with Damascus, and how he turned away the wrath of Yahweh from Israel." Apart from the textual problems, the verse is difficult to assess historically. Miller and Hayes (*HAIJ*, 308–9) are suspicious of the claim that Jeroboam captured Hamath and Damascus. They argue that it probably refers to the two cities either paying nominal tribute to the N kingdom or allowing Jeroboam commercial concessions. Haran (1967: 296), however, has argued that the verse indicates that Israel and Judah were allies and powerful enough to subdue Hamath and Damascus.

Although the historical details are extremely meager, most commentators present the reign of Jeroboam as a period of peace and prosperity for the N kingdom. It is assumed that he took advantage of the relative weakness of Assyria in implementing his expansionist policy. However, the precise timing of his expansion northward is debated. Haran (1967), who assumes the reliability of 2 Kgs 14:28, argues that Jeroboam's expansion was confined to the final years of his reign when Assur-nirari V was on the Assyrian throne (755–745 B.C.E.). Gray (617), who doubts the claim that Jeroboam actually captured Damascus and Hamath, thinks that the successful campaign against Damascus took place shortly after the campaign by Assurdan III (772) into Syria and before the decline of Assyrian power under Assur-nirari V when Damascus might have recovered.

Evidence for the prosperity of the N kingdom under Jeroboam II is based principally on material in the books of Amos and Hosea which is believed to provide background information on the economic and religious affairs of the N kingdom. Both prophets, according to the superscriptions of their books, were active in Israel during his reign (Amos 1:1; Hosea 1:1). They present a picture of a prosperous urban elite living in comparative luxury based on the social inequalities of the monarchic system through widespread exploitation. The standard view couples this rise in prosperity with a decline in ethical standards and widespread apostasy (*BHI*, 257–66). The oracles of these prophets also attack the religious apostasy of the N kingdom. Amos 7:10–14 provides a direct condemnation of Jeroboam pronounced at the royal shrine of Bethel in which Amos predicts the violent death of Jeroboam, the destruction of the dynasty, and the exile of the N kingdom. The passage is extremely complex and involves manifold literary and interpretative problems. It is usually seen as the culmination of Amos' rejection of the state religion of Jeroboam's reign, a cult which maintained the status quo of social and religious inequality (Wolff 308–10). De Geus (1982), however, has produced a different assessment of the nature of Jeroboam's reign with a study of archaeological data from the 10th century onward. He argues that the royal building programs of the 10th and 9th centuries imposed an increasing financial strain on the agrarian economy, which led to recession and stagnation in the 8th century. The architectural and pottery evidence, he argues, points to a period of decline following the 9th century. This economic analysis conflicts with the standard presentation of the reign of Jeroboam as a period of stability and economic prosperity.

Bibliography

Burney, C. F. 1903. *Notes on the Hebrew Text of the Books of Kings.* Oxford.

Coote, R. B. 1981. *Amos among the Prophets: Composition and Theology.* Philadelphia.

Geus, J. K. de. 1982. Die Gesellschaftskritik der Propheten und die Archäologie. *ZDPV* 98: 50–57.

Haran, M. 1967. The Empire of Jeroboam ben Joash. *VT* 17: 267–97.

KEITH W. WHITELAM

JEROHAM (PERSON) [Heb *yĕrōḥām*]. Name of seven individuals in the Hebrew Bible.

1. The grandfather of Samuel the prophet (1 Sam 1:1; 1 Chr 6:12, 19—Eng 6:27, 34). The two verses from Chronicles occur within variant genealogies for Kohath. They represent Jeroham as a Levite in the line of Korah because, in the Chronicler's view, Samuel's known priestly activities require that he be a Levite. The Chronicler may also have associated Samuel with the Korahites because "Elkanah" occurred both as the name of Samuel's father and as a descendant of Korah.

2. Father of Joelah and Zebadiah, two men who joined David at Ziklag, according to 1 Chr 12:8—Eng 12:7. This Jeroham is listed as "from Gedor," which is probably a dittography from the beginning of the next verse. There is no Gedar known in Benjaminite territory, and the introduction of the place name with the preposition *min,* "from," runs counter to the practice in the rest of the list. The name "Jeroham" occurs several times in Chronicles for Benjaminites. These occurrences of the name may be related, although their contexts are very different.

3. Father or ancestor of Ibneiah, who is listed among the Benjaminite residents of postexilic Jerusalem in 1 Chr 9:8. A parallel list of Benjaminite is given in Neh 11:7–9, but it does not mention either Ibneiah or Jeroham.

4. Ancestor of the Benjaminites mentioned in 1 Chr 8:27. The list of brothers in 8:12–14, which is expanded in vv 15–27, has Jeremoth (8:14) instead of Jeroham. Obviously, one of the two names is incorrect, but it is uncertain which one it is.

5. Father of Azarel, a chief officer (Heb *nāgîd*) over the tribe of Dan during David's reign according to 1 Chr 27:22.

6. Father of Azariah, one of the "commanders of hundreds" listed in 2 Chr 23:1 who conspired with Jehoiada to depose Athaliah.

7. A priest in postexilic Jerusalem who is listed as the father of Adaiah in 1 Chr 9:12 (= Neh 11:12).

STEVEN L. MCKENZIE

JERUBBAAL (PERSON) [Heb *yĕrūbbāᶜal*]. Var. JERUBBESHETH. Jerubbaal was the name given to Gideon after he destroyed his father's Baal altar (Judg 6:32). Some understand the references to this name in Judges 9 to be a different person from Gideon, two traditions being conflated (*NHI,* 152; *EHI,* 800–1). This makes Abimelech the son of Jerubbaal, not Gideon. The name has been variously translated as "Baal makes (himself) great" (deriving *yĕrūb* from the root *rbh; IPN,* 206; *ARI,* 112, 206; cf. *HALAT,* 414) or "Let Baal sue (his enemies)" (from the root *ryb;* Boling *Judges* AB, 144). There is also a possible word play on the assonance of the two roots (Soggin *Judges* OTL, 125). The name is changed significantly in 2 Sam 11:21, where the noun "shame" (Heb *bōšet*) is substituted for "Baal," Jerubbesheth. This change belongs to a class of similar names such as Ish-bosheth (2 Sam 2:8; = Eshbaal, 1 Chr 8:33; 9:39) and Mephibosheth (2 Sam 21:7, 8; = Meribaal, 1 Chr 8:34; 9:40). For later Israelites, the name "Baal" had become distasteful to pronounce and had lost its original meaning of "Lord," which earlier had been applied even to Yahweh (cf. Boling *Judges* AB, 135; Caspari 1915: 173–74; Moore *Judges* ICC, 195).

Bibliography

Boling, R. G. 1963. Who is Š-K-M? (Judges IX 28). *VT* 13: 479–82.
Caspari, W. 1915. Die kleineren Personenlisten in Samuelis. *ZAW* 35: 142–74.
Emerton, J. A. 1976. Gideon and Jerubbaal. *JTS* 27: 289–312.
Haag, H. 1967. Gideon-Jerubbaal-Abimelek. *ZAW* 79: 305–14.

KIRK E. LOWERY

JERUBBESHETH (PERSON) [Heb *yĕrubbešet*]. Var. JERUBBAAL. The father of Abimelech (2 Sam 11:21). A variant form, Jerubbaal, is mentioned in Judg 9:1. This variant form of the name replaces the reference to Baal, the Canaanite deity, found within the name, with Besheth, a form of the Hebrew word for "shame." In such a way the writer suggests that Baal worship was never seen as legitimate in Israel, which would appear to be the case by having Israelites hold names which would include references to this deity. This is similar to the name change found in 2 Sam 2:8 (MT "Ishbosheth"/LXX "Ishbaal"). Though Tsevat (1975) has argued against seeing this change as a "euphemistic substitution" by appealing to an Akkadian cognate, McCarter (*2 Samuel* AB) convincingly refutes such reinterpretation. This change in the form of the name from one which uses "baal" to one which uses "bosheth" is significant for two reasons. First, from the wording of the remainder of the verse it appears that the writer in 2 Sam 11:21 is not only making direct reference to the events described in Judg 9:50–55, but also copying from this early tradition. Second, however, this change of the name gives evidence that the David-Bathsheba-Uriah tale has been edited by a later, probably Deuteronomistic, editor, who would be likely to make such a substitution for theological reasons.

Bibliography

Tsevat, M. 1975. Ishbosheth and Congeners. *HUCA* 46: 71–87.

RANDALL C. BAILEY

JERUEL (PLACE) [Heb *yĕrûʾēl*]. A portion of the Wilderness of Judah which can be located probably to the SE of the Wilderness of Tekoa (2 Chr 20:20) and to the NW of the ascent of Ziz and En-gedi. The E side of this wilderness became the scene of Yahweh's defeat of the allied forces of Ammonites, Moabites, and Meunites (2 Chr 20:16; cf. vs. 1, 2, 20; 26:7). The meaning of Jeruel is probably either "City of God" from **Uru-ʾel,* like Jerusalem for *Uru-salim,* or "Founded by God." See also *MBA,* map no. 133.

YOSHITAKA KOBAYASHI

JERUSALEM (PLACE) [Heb *yĕrûšālayim*]. Pliny the Elder described Jerusalem as "by far the most renowned city of the ancient East" (*HN* V:14). Jerusalem is best known as the "holy city" (Isa 52:1), sacred to the three great monotheistic religions. Few subjects have generated so large a body of literature; the most recent comprehensive, but not exhaustive, bibliography on Jerusalem contains almost 6,000 titles (Purvis 1988).

A. Introduction
   1. State of Question
   2. Sources
B. Rediscovery of Jerusalem
   1. In the 19th Century
   2. In the 20th Century
   3. Since 1967
C. Background
   1. Names Associated with Jerusalem
   2. Geography and Topography
   3. Settlement
   4. Population, Size, Economy
D. United Kingdom
   1. Reign of David
   2. Reign of Solomon
E. Divided Kingdom
F. Second Temple Period
   1. Persian
   2. Hellenistic
   3. Hasmonean
   4. Herodian
   5. Roman
G. Postbiblical Period
   1. Aelia Capitolina
   2. Byzantine
   3. Early Arab
   4. Crusader
   5. Later Arab
   6. Ottoman
H. Theology
   1. Old Testament
   2. New Testament

A. Introduction

1. State of Question. There is much uncertainty about Jerusalem; many historical, archaeological, and topographical problems are unresolved. Jerusalem has played a prominent role in history, but the historical record is scant, and descriptions from literary sources are often imprecise. Despite Jerusalem's antiquity, archaeological remains are not so plentiful as in the case of other biblical sites such as Megiddo, Hazor, Dan, and Samaria. The archaeological data are frequently problematic, unassimilated, and unpublished. New questions continue to arise concerning earlier archaeological interpretations.

The fact that Jerusalem has been continuously and often densely inhabited for almost 6,000 years makes it difficult to excavate systematically. The accumulation of rubble from periodic destructions makes it hard to untangle Jerusalem's complex defense systems. Each time Jerusalem was rebuilt, stone robbers utilized masonry from previous occupations, thereby complicating the stratigraphy of the site.

Jerusalem's location on a mountain ridge is the source of severe topographical problems. Also, Jerusalem's contours have changed over the centuries; the Tyropoeon valley, for example, has now been practically filled in. On the other hand, the names of architectural features such as Jerusalem's gates have changed from time to time, just as the names of geographical areas such as Mount Zion have shifted location. All these problems give rise to controversy, making it almost impossible to advance conclusive answers about the history, archaeology, and topography of Jerusalem.

2. Sources. a. Written. The principal source for Jerusalem is the Bible, although it is quite imprecise about the topographical features of the city; nor is Jerusalem presented systematically. Jerusalem is the most prominent city in biblical literature; often, however, it is the eschatological, not the historical, Jerusalem that is being described.

The second major literary source for Jerusalem is Flavius Josephus' *The Antiquities of the Jews* and *The Jewish War,* the latter intended for Roman readers. Born in Jerusalem in C.E. 37, Josephus was an eyewitness for the period of the first Jewish revolt. Although he wrote from the Roman point of view, and despite some exaggerations (e.g., population figures) and inaccuracies, archaeology confirms in general his history and geography. Josephus is especially helpful in his detailed descriptions of Herodian monuments. He is the only source for the "three walls" of Jerusalem; unfortunately, his description of their alignment refers to several places unknown today.

b. Cartography. The traditional anti-iconographic attitude of Jews and Muslims accounts for the paucity of maps, portraits, and illustrations of Jerusalem. Maps of Jerusalem by Jewish cartographers did not exist before the 19th century. The earliest and most valuable nonliterary source for Jerusalem is the Madeba mosaic map of the 6th century C.E., portraying Byzantine Jerusalem. Indicative of Jerusalem's importance, it is the centerpiece of this map, and is depicted disproportionately large as an oval-shaped city surrounded by walls with six gates and twenty-one towers. Every feature of the Madeba map points to Jerusalem as the center of the world. Also, the Madeba map delineates Jerusalem's main colonnaded street, known as the *cardo maximus.* The caption on the map reads in Greek "Holy City of Jerusalem."

F. Sieber, an Austrian physician, produced the first modern, albeit primitive, map of Jerusalem in 1818. The outstanding cartographer in the first half of the 19th century was the British architect F. Catherwood. With a camera lucida he copied the outlines of the important buildings in Jerusalem, and also produced a panorama and map of the city.

Artistic records are also an important source of information about Jerusalem. D. Roberts and W. Bartlett, two well-known artists of 19th-century Jerusalem, not only reproduced the ancient sites but also generated a lively interest among Westerners in the Bible lands.

B. Rediscovery of Jerusalem

1. In the 19th Century. Despite Jerusalem's centrality in biblical history, the city was little known in modern times until the 19th century. As a consequence of Ibrahim Pasha's conquest of Jerusalem, Western travelers found it easier to visit Jerusalem with safety. Much of the credit for the rediscovery of Palestine, especially Jerusalem, in the 19th century belongs to the American biblical scholar, E. Robinson (1856). As the first scientific explorer of Palestine, he inaugurated a new era in the geographical study of the Holy Land. Robinson is associated especially with three monuments in Jerusalem: he was the first person in modern times to explore Hezekiah's tunnel; he discovered the remains of Jerusalem's reputed third wall, built but not completed by Herod Agrippa I; and he found the spring of an arch, bearing his name today, near the SW corner of the Temple platform. See Fig. JER.07.

One of the most significant steps in the rediscovery of Jerusalem was the establishment of the Palestine Exploration Fund (PEF) in 1865. Inspired by the achievements of Robinson, the PEF was formally organized in London to explore Palestine systematically, and specifically to promote the historical and archaeological research of Jerusalem. In the second half of the 19th century a contaminated water supply made Jerusalem an unsanitary city. As a preliminary step toward correcting the situation, the Royal Engineers under surveyor C. Wilson (Wilson and Warren 1871: 3–32) made, between 1864 and 1865, a historic ordnance survey, including a cartographic survey of Jerusalem, which produced the first modern scientific map of Palestine. Wilson's map of Jerusalem with its contour lines has been an indispensable tool for all later archaeologists. This ordnance survey also helped to launch the PEF.

From 1867 to 1870, C. Warren (1876) clarified the historical topography of Jerusalem by following the lines of the city walls and of the Temple Mount. He had set out to resolve two topographical problems: the exact location of the Temple, and the course of the three N walls of ancient Jerusalem. Around the four sides of the Temple enclosure he made soundings by an intricate series of shafts and tunnels, so as not to disturb existing structures or arouse the suspicions of the Turkish authorities in Jerusalem, who had forbidden him to excavate within 12 m of the walls. Despite the primitive methods imposed on him, Warren made accurate plans and measurements. He discovered in the SE corner of the Temple Mount a portion of the ancient city wall, still known as Warren's Ophel wall. He also investigated one of the ancient water systems, consisting of a vertical shaft and connecting tunnels, still known as Warren's shaft, near the Gihon spring. See Fig. DAV.03 and DAV.04. Warren's work marked the beginning of scientific archaeological research in Jerusalem.

From 1894 to 1897, an experienced American archaeologist, F. Bliss, and a British architect, A. Dickie (Bliss and Dickie 1898), continued Warren's work in Jerusalem, using the same system of shafts and tunnels. They excavated on both the W and the SE hill. Tracing the lines of the southernmost walls of ancient Jerusalem in successive periods was a vast project. Bliss and Dickie also explored the

Gihon channel. Although their dating of architectural features was unsatisfactory, Bliss and Dickie provided useful descriptions of architecture and masonry. It is disappointing that Bliss did not apply his knowledge of pottery to determine more accurately the chronology of ancient Jerusalem.

In the last quarter of the 19th century C. Clermont-Ganneau (1896) conducted additional investigations in the City of David, especially the course of the wall on the top of the E slope. Clermont-Ganneau also examined the area of the Antonia and the Ecce Homo arch.

2. In the 20th Century. Between 1909 and 1911 an Englishman, M. Parker, concentrating on the area of the Gihon spring and the slope above it, tried by furtive means to locate the treasury of Solomon's Temple, allegedly buried beneath the Temple Mount. In the course of his treasure hunt he cleared the subterranean tunnels and shafts of the Warren expedition, including Hezekiah's tunnel, with the hope they would lead to the Temple treasure. The only redeeming feature of this ill-conceived project was that Parker had enlisted L.-H. Vincent (1911), leading authority on the history and topography of Jerusalem, who recorded the expedition, mapping Jerusalem's ancient water system and replanning the accesses to the Gihon spring. Vincent determined on the basis of the water supply from the Gihon spring that ancient Jerusalem had been situated on the E, not the W, ridge.

As time passed, archaeological method slowly improved, although stratigraphy was still ignored. In 1913–1914 and 1923–1925 R. Weill (1920; 1947), French Egyptologist and historian, conducted the first Jewish expedition in Jerusalem. He concentrated on the S end of Jerusalem's E ridge where he cleared a large area in search of the tombs of David and the kings of Judah, uncovering sections of the City of David's E fortifications. During his excavation he was able to demonstrate that the SE hill of ancient Jerusalem was the site of the City of David, as well as of the pre-Israelite occupants, by finding indications of the early W fortifications to match chronologically those on the E side of the hill. Bliss and others had searched for this evidence, but were unable to find it.

Before World War I, archaeologists gave scant attention to ceramics as chronological indicators; their reliance on architectural features for dating was not decisive. From 1923 to 1925 R. A. S. Macalister and J. G. Duncan (1926) concentrated on the crest of the City of David's E slope, tracing the line of the fortification, which was the continuation of Warren's Ophel wall. They also excavated to bedrock a large area in the N section of the SE hill. Although Macalister, the excavator of Gezer, was an experienced archaeologist, he neglected stratigraphy. With the excavation of Macalister and Duncan on Ophel hill, it became certain that the City of David was situated on the E, not the W, hill.

When J. Crowfoot and G. FitzGerald (1929) continued in 1927 and 1928 the work of Macalister and Duncan on the SE ridge, instead of using the shaft-and-tunnel method of the pioneer excavators, they dug a trench from the summit of the W side of the E ridge down into the Tyropoeon valley. With their new method they discovered the City of David's W gate, known as the Valley Gate.

While rebuilding Jerusalem about 132 C.E., Hadrian erected a triple-arched entryway on the N side of the city (Magen 1988: 50). In 1931 and again in 1937–38, R. W. Hamilton (1940), trained in classical archaeology, excavated adjacent to the present N wall of the Old City, including the foundations of the Damascus gate. There, he found the facade of Hadrian's gate; but as a result of incomplete excavation, he misdated an earlier Herodian wall to the 2d century C.E.

From 1964 to 1966, J. B. Hennessy (1970) extended Hamilton's excavation beneath the Damascus gate, where he exposed the facade of the Crusader gate. He also redated to the Herodian period (pre-70 C.E.) the wall that Hamilton had misdated (Shanks 1987: 54); this wall was, in Hennessy's opinion, the third wall built by Herod Agrippa I.

For a decade beginning in 1934, C. N. Johns (1950), also a trained classical archaeologist, cleared the court of the Citadel, adjacent to the Jaffa gate on the W ridge, uncovering pottery from the late-Israelite period, but not prior to the 7th century B.C.E. When R. Amiran and A. Eitan (1970) continued work in the Citadel after 1967, they confirmed the conclusions of Johns.

Signaling a new era in the archaeology of Jerusalem, K. Kenyon (1974), a distinguished British archaeologist, excavated from 1961 to 1967 on Ophel hill. To reconstruct the history of Jerusalem, she was eager to date monumental structures, an objective that the inferior techniques of earlier excavators could not accomplish. She cut a deep trench down the entire E slope of the City of David, and then proceeded to carry out ceramic, stratigraphic, and architectural analyses. Among her significant contributions to the archaeology of Jerusalem, in addition to methodology, was her location of the Jebusite wall on the E ridge. She established that in the Canaanite and Israelite periods the wall line of the City of David was lower down the E slope, closer to the Gihon spring than previously thought. Situated 48 m down from the top of the ridge, the earliest fortification of Jerusalem dates to about 1800 B.C.E.; this MB II wall continued in use to the 8th century B.C.E.

Reviewing in detail the numerous independent excavations of Jerusalem's SE hill prior to Kenyon's dig, Simons (1952: 70) lamented the lack of methodological excavations. He concluded it would have been better had earlier excavators waited until more sophisticated methods had been developed, and more experience had been gained in digging Palestinian sites. For the earlier excavators, literary evidence alone was the basis of their investigations because they lacked Kenyon's expertise in stratigraphic digging and pottery analysis.

3. Since 1967. More digging has taken place in Jerusalem since 1967 than in all previous excavations combined. The reunification of the city as a result of the 1967 war has given Israeli archaeologists the opportunity to excavate the city intensively. There have been three major excavations and several limited ones. B. Mazar (1978), assisted by M. Ben-Dov (1985), directed the first of the major excavations between 1968 and 1978. He concentrated on the SW corner of the Temple Mount, and along the W and S walls of the Temple enclosure. See Fig. JER.07. Working adjacent to the retaining walls of the Temple Mount, Mazar recovered remains ranging from Iron Age II to Ottoman

JER.07. Excavations at SW Corner of Temple Mount in Jerusalem (El-Aqsa Mosque in upper right corner). Remains of "Robinson's Arch" can still be seen (left). In the foreground are the remains of Umayyad structures beneath which were found remains of the Herodian plaza leading up to the temple. See Fig. TEM.03. *(Photograph by Z. Radovan, by permission, Biblical Archaeology Society Jerusalem Archaeology Slide Set)*

times. (He found hardly any artifacts from the First-Temple period adjacent to the S wall of the Temple enclosure, which would have been the royal quarters.) The greatest concentration of finds belonged to the Herodian period. Mazar's dig confirmed Josephus' statement that, in preparation for the rebuilding the Temple, Herod doubled the size of the Temple Mount.

While Mazar was excavating adjacent to the Temple Mount, N. Avigad (1983) was digging in the center of the Jewish Quarter of the Old City, which is the E section of the W hill. Avigad's was the first dig ever to take place in the Jewish Quarter. Simultaneous with the reconstruction of the Jewish Quarter by the Jerusalem municipality, Avigad conducted his archaeological investigations, staying a few steps ahead of the construction crews. Avigad discovered remnants from the Hasmonean and Herodian periods, especially the latter. On the basis of the remains, it is clear that in the Herodian era some of the residents of Jerusalem lived in luxury.

In addition, Avigad's investigation of the Byzantine occupation of Jerusalem confirms the existence of the *cardo maximus* as portrayed in detail on the Madeba map. See Fig. JER.12. Laid out on a N–S axis, the *cardo* would have extended the entire length of the city, from the Damascus gate in the N almost to the Zion gate in the S.

Equally important, Avigad established that as early as the 8th century B.C.E. Jerusalem's W ridge—the "Second Quarter" (Heb *mišneh*) of 2 Kgs 22:14—had been first settled and later enclosed by a wall. In the 8th–7th centuries B.C.E. Jerusalem expanded to four times its previous size. Evidence for the foregoing hinges on Avigad's discovery of an Israelite wall, situated on the upper portion of the E slope of the W hill. See Fig. JER.10. The course of this broad defense is still uncertain, but it confirms Josephus' maximalist view about the size of the Jerusalem settlement in the preexilic period.

Between 1978 and 1984 Y. Shiloh (1981; 1984) continued the work of Kenyon and her predecessors in the City of David, on the SE hill above the Gihon spring, where settlement dates as early as the 4th millennium. Shiloh succeeded in identifying 25 occupational strata, extending from the Chalcolithic period to medieval times. He also reinvestigated Jerusalem's three complex water systems connected with the Gihon spring, including Warren's shaft (the earliest), the Siloam channel, and Hezekiah's tunnel (the latest) (Shiloh 1987). Shiloh also uncovered an impressive stepped stone structure, 18 m high and 16 m wide. Earlier excavators (Macalister, Kenyon) had exposed the upper courses of this monumental structure which, according to Shiloh, was erected in the 10th century B.C.E.

See Fig. DAV.01. He suggested that it may have served as a supporting rampart or podium for buildings on the royal acropolis. Shiloh's conclusions about the City of David may never be published completely because of his untimely death in 1987. See also DAVID, CITY OF.

Other important but limited projects conducted by Israeli archaeologists include that of D. Bahat and M. Broshi (1975), who continued A. D. Tushingham's (1968; 1985) excavations on Mount Zion and in the Armenian Quarter in an attempt to determine the extent and construction of Herod's palace. Also, S. Ben-Arieh and E. Netzer (1974) excavated N of the Old City.

C. Background

1. Names Associated with Jerusalem. A long history lies behind "Jerusalem"; it was the name of the city from early times. Jerusalem is mentioned for the first time in the Egyptian Execration Texts (19th–18th centuries B.C.E.), where the form of the name is probably to be read as Rušalimum. The name appears again in diplomatic correspondence: this time as Urušalim (Akk) in the Amarna letters (14th century B.C.E.). Abdi-Ḫiba, a vassal of Egypt who was reigning in Jerusalem at the time, sent letters to the Egyptian pharaoh Amenophis IV (Akhenaten), affirming his loyalty. Later Assyrian texts also refer to Jerusalem; for example, in the records of Sennacherib's siege of Jerusalem in 701 B.C.E. the form Ursalimmu (or variants) appears (*ANET,* 288).

The name "Jerusalem" (Heb *yĕrûšālayim*) is of uncertain etymology, although it is apparently of W Semitic (Canaanite) origin. It appears to be composed of the two elements: *yrw* "to establish" and *šlm,* the name of the W Semitic god Shalem, patron of the city. The meaning may be "foundation of (the god) Shalem," mentioned in a mythological text from Ugarit. Gen 14:18 refers to Melchizedek as king of Salem (Heb *śālēm*), likely Jerusalem. If so, this shortened form is the first biblical allusion to Jerusalem. In Psalm 76:3 (—Eng 76:2) Salem is used in synonymous parallelism to Zion, referring to the divine dwelling.

Josh 10:1–4 contains the first specific biblical reference to Jerusalem, whose inhabitants were Canaanites. There, it relates to Adoni-zedek, king of Jerusalem, formed a coalition with neighboring kings and attacked Gibeon. Joshua defeated them, but Jerusalem was not taken. According to Judg 1:8, the Judahites captured Jerusalem and destroyed it by fire. The text is historically unreliable; Jerusalem was not conquered until the time of David (2 Sam 5:6–7).

Some OT texts (Josh 15:8; 18:28; Judg 19:10; 1 Chr 11:4–5) equate "Jebus" (the name derived from the pre-Israelite inhabitants of Jerusalem) with Jerusalem, conveying the impression that Jebus (Heb *yĕbus*) was the pre-Davidic name for ancient Jerusalem. The city was never actually called Jebus, although it had been a Jebusite settlement. The Amarna Tablets attest that "Jerusalem," not "Jebus," was the name of the city; nor does "Jebus" appear in other ANE texts. Despite the lack of extrabiblical evidence, some would argue that Jebus and Jerusalem designate the same city. Others suggest that Jebus may be identified with Shaᶜfāṭ (M.R. 172136), situated slightly N of Jerusalem (Miller 1974: 126).

Zion (Heb *ṣîyôn*), another name for Jerusalem, is used more than 150 times in the OT. Its etymology is unclear, and its precise meaning is unknown. Zion is sometimes used metaphorically, at other times topographically, although the designation has changed across time. Originally, Zion was equated with the City of David, signifying the SE hill of Jerusalem (2 Sam 5:7). The Temple Mount to its N was also known as Zion. From the Byzantine period, Zion has been applied to the hill S of the SW corner of the present Old City. Zion may also designate Jerusalem as a religious capital.

2. Geography and Topography. Jerusalem, consisting of two ridges, is situated on a limestone plateau 800 m above sea level in the central hill country, bordering on the Judean desert, and removed from the major trade routes. To the W are the slopes of the Judean mountains; to the E the Judean desert, descending to the Dead Sea. Jerusalem's rugged terrain was a military advantage, making it easy to defend because it was hard to reach. At the same time, its location and natural features were a commercial disadvantage, since the commercial centers of Palestine were located on the coastal plain, not on the mountain ridge (Hopkins 1970: 11–12).

Jebusite Jerusalem and the later City of David were small settlements situated on the E hill of Jerusalem; they encompassed an area of only 10 to 15 acres at the SE corner of present-day Jerusalem, below the Temple Mount. This spur, completely outside the city walls since the 11th century C.E., is the smaller of two ridges lying below the present Old City. The topographic term for the crest of the SE hill is Ophel ("bulge," "projection"; Isa 32:14; Mic 4:8; 2 Kgs 5:24, and elsewhere), which may have designated the royal administrative area, or the higher part of a city enclosed with a wall. Ophel is also found at other royal centers of the Iron Age, such as Samaria and Dibon. For a long time the entire E spur of Jerusalem has been called Ophel.

Both eastern and western ridges are surrounded by precipitous valleys on three sides. See Fig. JER.08. It is bounded on the E and part of the N by the Kidron valley, and on the S and W by the Hinnom valley. The Tyropoeon, Josephus' term of uncertain origin which may be a corruption of a Heb name, translated "valley of the cheesemakers" (*JW* 5.4.1 §140), is the small N–S valley in the center, only a slight depression today. Also known as the central valley (in the Bible, simply "the valley"), the Tyropoeon divided the Ophel hill from the W ridge. The W ridge, lying between the Hinnom and Tyropoeon valleys, was broader than the E hill, and was the biblical equivalent of the suburbs. These two hills have been known by a variety of names in the history of Jerusalem; they have also expanded and contracted. The Ophel hill, together with the Temple Mount, composed the Lower City; the SW hill, named by Josephus the Upper City, covers the area of the present Jewish Quarter, the Armenian Quarter, the Citadel, and the traditional Mount Zion. The NE section of the Upper City has been designated as the Jewish Quarter since the 12th century C.E. Eventually, the Lower City was densely populated and became the area where the poor resided, whereas the more prosperous dwelt in the Upper City.

The decisive factor in the settlement of pre-Israelite Jerusalem, later the City of David, was access to a vital

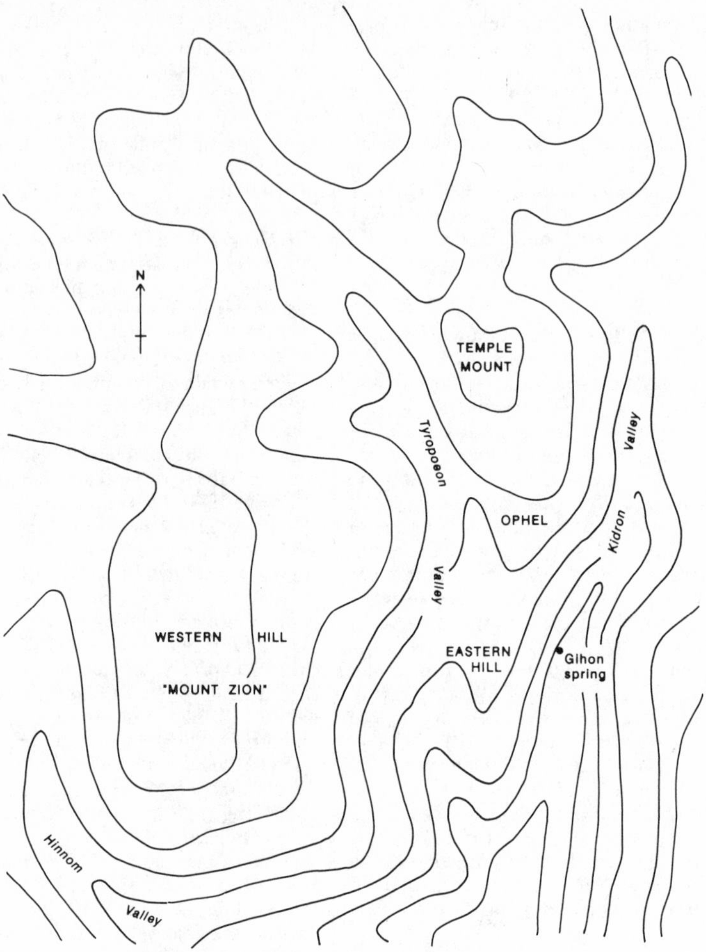

JER.08. Topographic map of Jerusalem.

water supply. The Gihon spring, situated at the foot of the SE ridge and flowing in the Kidron bed, was the perennial source of water. The minimum annual yield was 73,000 cubic meters (Wilkinson 1974: 33). Gihon, related to Heb *giḥa* ("a gushing forth") is so called because its water gushes intermittently. There was only a small yield from en-Rogel, the second source of water to the S of Gihon.

In the Iron II period the Gihon spring fed three interconnected water systems. The earliest water system, consisting of a shaft and connecting tunnels, is known as Warren's shaft. See Figs. DAV.03 and DAV.04. In time of siege it supplied water from the Gihon spring to the Jerusalem residents without the risk of their going outside the wall. The second of the water systems is the Siloam channel, 400 m long, a kind of aqueduct carrying water from the Gihon along the Kidron valley to a reservoir at the tip of the city. This water irrigated the fields through apertures in the channel wall. The third water system is Hezekiah's tunnel, an enclosed aqueduct diverting water from the Gihon spring to the Siloam pool at the SW corner of the city. See Fig. JER.09.

3. Settlement. Jerusalem was first settled on the Ophel, above the Gihon spring, where pottery, dating to the Chalcolithic period (3500 B.C.E.), and the remains of structures, dating to EB I and II (3000–2800 B.C.E.), were found. Kenyon's discovery of the Jebusite wall and adjacent tower halfway down the E slope indicated that the pre-Israelite city was larger than expected. Even though this fortification was low down, the Gihon spring still remained outside the city wall. Had it been located low enough to enclose the spring, the wall would have been vulnerable to attack. Apparently, the city wall was close enough to the Gihon spring to deter enemy access to the water supply.

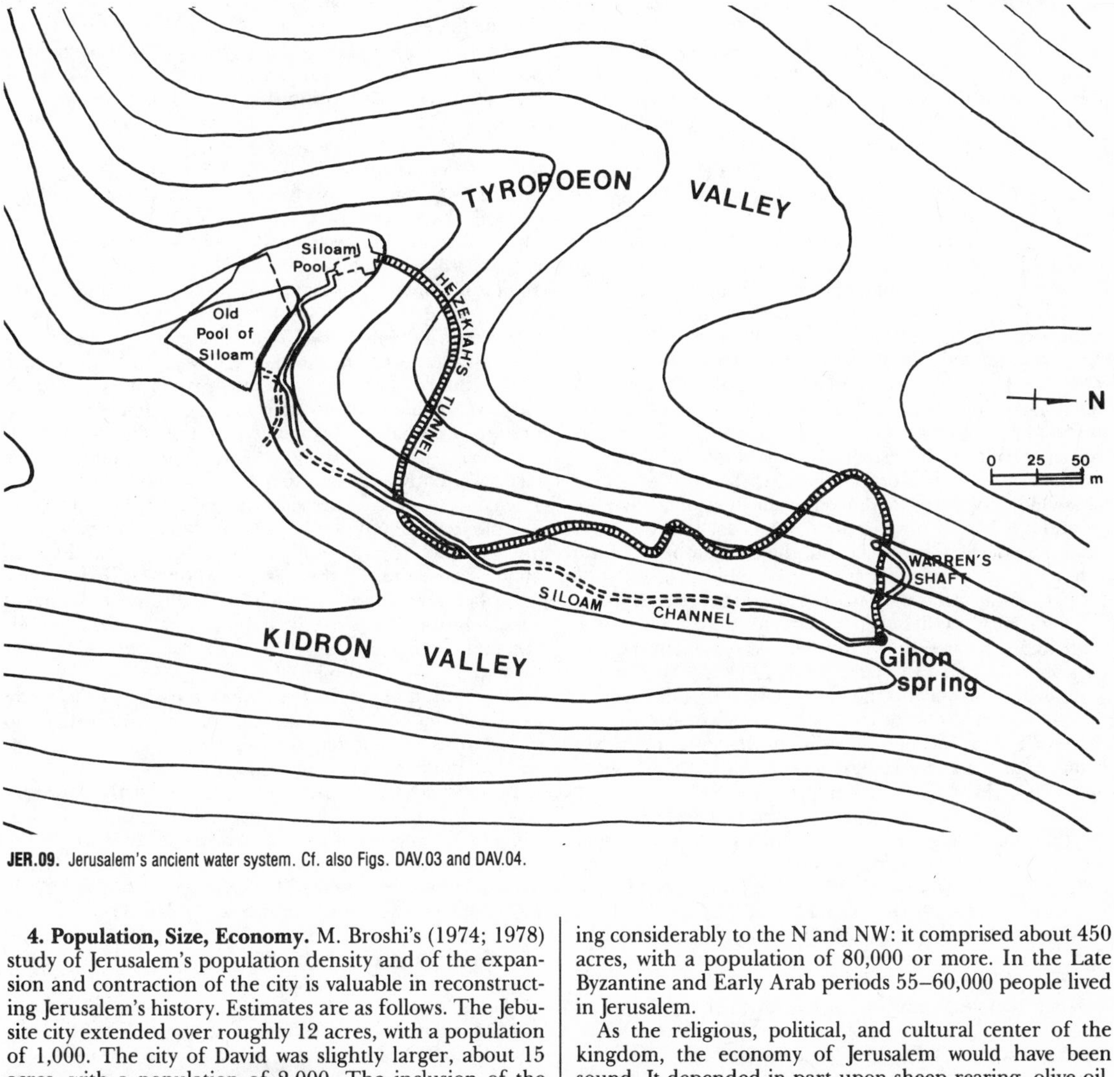

JER.09. Jerusalem's ancient water system. Cf. also Figs. DAV.03 and DAV.04.

4. Population, Size, Economy. M. Broshi's (1974; 1978) study of Jerusalem's population density and of the expansion and contraction of the city is valuable in reconstructing Jerusalem's history. Estimates are as follows. The Jebusite city extended over roughly 12 acres, with a population of 1,000. The city of David was slightly larger, about 15 acres, with a population of 2,000. The inclusion of the Temple Mount enlarged Solomon's city to 32 acres or more, with a population of 4,500–5,000. In Hezekiah's reign Jerusalem expanded considerably, extending to the W hill (Upper City); it may have been as large as 125 acres, with a population of 25,000, although some think that figure is inflated. Beginning in the latter part of the 8th century B.C.E., numbers were swelled by immigration from the N kingdom (after 721 B.C.E.) and from the provinces of Judah (after 701 B.C.E.), as Broshi points out. In Nehemiah's time Jerusalem shrank to about 30 acres, with a population of 4,500, although some would double that estimate. In the prosperous Hasmonean era Jerusalem expanded to 165 acres, with a population of 30–35,000. In Herod's reign 40,000 people occupied 230 acres. Jerusalem doubled in size during the Roman period, expanding considerably to the N and NW: it comprised about 450 acres, with a population of 80,000 or more. In the Late Byzantine and Early Arab periods 55–60,000 people lived in Jerusalem.

As the religious, political, and cultural center of the kingdom, the economy of Jerusalem would have been sound. It depended in part upon sheep rearing, olive oil, and fruit, not cereal crops. "Tyropoeon" (valley of the cheesemakers) suggests Jerusalem had a dairy industry. The quarrying of building stone was also an important industry. Pilgrims who came to Jerusalem three times a year would have generated income, but the main source of revenue was the Temple tax levied on every Jew living in Jerusalem and in the Diaspora. Also, the Temple supported a wide variety of craftsmen (Avi-Yonah 1966: 188–211).

D. United Kingdom

1. Reign of David. Jerusalem, the political, religious, and administrative center of David's kingdom, was so closely identified with him it was called the City of David. Jerusalem was his own city because he and his mercenaries had captured it. David was a diplomatic genius in establishing Jerusalem as the royal capital of the twelve-tribe federation. The city was both centrally-located and extraterritorial, ideal for consolidating the N and S tribes. It was also shrewd of David to transfer the ark, the symbol of the Mosaic tradition, to Jerusalem, thus making Jerusalem the national sanctuary in place of Shiloh. The priests and traditionalists were well-disposed by David's action. The presence of the ark in Jerusalem signified continuity between the Mosaic tradition and the Davidic dynasty.

Details about David's strategy for capturing the Jebusite stronghold are not clear, either textually or archaeologically. The pertinent biblical verses (2 Sam 5:6–8; 1 Chr 11:4–7) are difficult (McCarter, *2 Samuel* AB, 135–43). In reconstructing David's strategy, some suggest that Warren's shaft provided his warriors with access to the city. The Heb word *ṣinnor* (2 Sam 5:8) is thought to refer to Warren's shaft which the Jebusites had used as a safe access to the Gihon spring. Walking the length of the stepped tunnel, residents of Jerusalem could lower a container from the top of the vertical shaft (16 m deep and 2 m wide) and draw water conducted by the horizontal channel from the Gihon spring to a pool at the base of the vertical shaft. Mazar identifies *ṣinnor* with the conduit between the Gihon spring and the pool; several Israeli archaeologists (Mazar, Yadin, Aharoni, Shiloh) do not agree that *ṣinnor* refers to Warren's shaft. When Warren climbed the vertical shaft in 1867, some stated that he was repeating the feat of Joab, who scaled the water shaft to gain entrance into Jerusalem. However, on the basis of Warren's description of the difficulties associated with his own ascent, and inasmuch as Shiloh had to enlist professional mountain climbers to assist in investigating the shaft, it is questionable. Also, Shiloh (1987) found no evidence to support a pre-Davidic date for the shaft and tunnel. On the analogy of other hydraulic systems in ancient Israel, a 10th century B.C.E. date for the construction of the shaft is the earliest possibility, according to Shiloh, although the evidence is inconclusive. See also DAVID, CITY OF.

After capturing Jerusalem, David took up residence, fortified the city, and undertook a building program, extending the City of David in a N direction toward the present Temple Mount. According to 2 Sam 5:9, "David built the city round about from the Millo inward." This text is anachronistic with respect to the Millo: the Millo was built by Solomon and restored by Hezekiah. The Heb word *hamillo* is enigmatic and comes from a root meaning "fill"; it appears elsewhere in the OT (1 Kgs 9:15, 24; 11:27; 1 Chr 11:8; 2 Chr 32:5). It is subject to a variety of translations and interpretations: (a) a series of architectural terraces built by the Jebusites on the E slope of the E ridge, supporting houses and other structures (Kenyon); (b) an earth-fill S of the Temple Mount (Ben Dov); (c) the monumental stepped-stone structure near the crest of the hill, that may have been part of the defense system in the time of David and Solomon (Shiloh); and (d) the "fill" or land bridge joining the City of David with the royal acropolis to the N, known from the Solomonic era as the Temple Mount (Stager 1982: 121).

David's kingdom extended from Egypt to the Euphrates, with Jerusalem as its center. The list of administrators under David (2 Sam 8:15–18; 1 Chr 18:14–17) attests that he oversaw a well-organized administration in Jerusalem. Despite the economic prosperity realized from his military victories and other achievements, inevitable social changes brought resentment, alienation, and rebellion. His subjects resented taxes, conscription, and foreign influence; the tribes were alienated by their loss of traditional independence; ambitious and jealous members of the palace rebelled. Concern for succession to the throne led to palace intrigue throughout the history of the Davidic dynasty. Typical was Absalom's revolt which had the support of some of David's subjects (2 Samuel 13–20). After Absalom's death Adonijah became heir to the throne. When he apparently pressed his claim during the reign of Solomon he was executed.

2. Reign of Solomon. Under Solomon, Jerusalem enjoyed the status of an international capital. As the center of the empire, Jerusalem was a properous and cosmopolitan city. Solomon is best known for his extensive building projects, especially the Jerusalem Temple and the adjoining palace complex immediately S of the Temple, which incorporated residences, throne room, hall of justice, and arsenal (1 Kgs 7:1–12). His first undertaking was the Temple, which took seven years to build; the palace required 13 years to complete. Solomon accomplished his building program by the imposition of forced labor and heavy taxes, with the N tribes bearing the brunt. As well as alienating the N, his overly ambitious programs of building and expansion caused serious economic problems throughout the kingdom.

In preparation for the building of the Temple, Solomon extended the borders of the City of David northward to include the present-day Temple Mount—or Haram esh-Sharif ("the noble Sanctuary") as it is known in Islam. He undertook the actual construction in the fourth year of his reign. Although no archaeological evidence of the Temple remains, it is possible to reconstruct its plan from the biblical description (1 Kings 6), brief and ambiguous, as well as from comparison with extant temples of neighboring peoples. The actual edifice was relatively modest in size, measuring approximately 30 m long, 10 m wide, and 15 m high (Parrot 1957: 15–60).

A good parallel is an 8th century B.C.E. temple excavated in the 1930s at Tell Tainat in the Amuq valley of Syria; it was a long-room temple with a tripartite plan like the Solomonic Temple. All ancient temples in Syria were tripartite in structure. Although the number of rooms in Solomon's Temple may be open to question, more important is the fact that it was built on a long-room plan, with the entrance on the short side, and the shrine at the opposite end of the building.

The Temple, which was both a royal chapel and a national shrine, reflected foreign (especially Phoenician) influence, not only architecturally but also theologically. Without its own architectural tradition, Israel had to appeal to Hiram, king of Tyre, who supplied workers and materials to build the Temple (1 Kings 5; 2 Chronicles 2). Thirty thousand forced laborers, conscripted in Israel, assisted the Phoenician artisans. Sanctuaries to foreign gods of other nations were also located in Jerusalem.

The Temple, it had been assumed, stood where the Dome of the Rock stands today, an assumption that cannot be verified by archaeological excavation. On the basis of modern aerial maps, Jewish literature, and other sources, A. S. Kaufman (1983: 42) has suggested a slightly different location for the First and Second Temples: about 100 m to the NW of the Dome of the Rock. The site of the Temple is associated in popular tradition with the location of Araunah's threshing floor on Mount Moriah, where Abraham earlier had built an altar to sacrifice Isaac (Gen 22:1–19). Zerubbabel and Herod, in turn, built Temples on the same location. See also TEMPLE, JERUSALEM. The Dome of the Rock has marked the spot on the Temple Mount since the 7th century C.E.

The close physical association of the Temple and the palace in Jerusalem emphasized the religious, political, and cultural importance of Jerusalem as the capital. Together the Temple and the palace constituted the administrative center of the kingdom. In addition, the complex of Temple and palace underscored the connection between the religious and political life of the nation. Although the Temple was primarily a religious center, it also had a major role in the economic and political affairs of the kingdom. Ancient temples, it is said, were the first banks, conducting financial transactions and changing money.

As a financial center, the Temple had a significant treasury which the kings tapped when forced to pay tribute to foreign victors. During Rehoboam's reign, for example, Shishak (Shoshenq) attacked Jerusalem, but refrained from conquering the city, choosing instead to plunder the treasury of the Temple and the royal palace (1 Kgs 14:25–26). When Joash, king of Israel, defeated Amaziah of Judah, he also looted the Temple treasury, plundering the Temple and the palace (2 Kgs 14:8–14). The galleries or storerooms, standing three stories high and surrounding the Temple on three sides (1 Kgs 6:5–6), were used for storing weapons, cult objects, gifts, and booty.

The palace complex, immediately to the S of the Temple, was architecturally more impressive than the Temple. The palace enclosure consisted of the House of the Forest of Lebanon, so called from its adornment of columns in cedar resembling a forest, the Hall of Pillars, the Hall of the Throne (where Solomon rendered judgments), and the House of Pharaoh's Daughter.

E. Divided Kingdom

Generally speaking, Jerusalem declined in importance in this period. During his long reign Uzziah fortified Jerusalem, strengthening its walls with towers (2 Chr 26:9, 15). Jotham is credited with building the upper gate of the Temple (2 Chr 27:3) Uzziah and Jotham confined their building activities to Jerusalem proper, and did not undertake any expansion of the city to the W. Ahaz was judged harshly for having erected in the Temple an altar modeled on a pagan altar from Damascus.

In his excavation of the City of David, Shiloh recovered remains of anthropomorphic vessels and fertility figurines in the fill of an 8th century B.C.E. building, as well as zoomorphic figurines, all indicative of the diversity of religious practice in that period. The historians of Judah commended Hezekiah for his cultic reforms, which included purifying the Temple and centralizing worship in Jerusalem. His reform was religiously motivated (Cogan and Tadmor, *2 Kings* AB, 218–20); at the same time by centralizing the cult in Jerusalem, Hezekiah strengthened the Davidic dynasty, especially in its relations with other cities in the empire. When Samaria fell in 721 B.C.E., Jerusalem became the principal city of worship in Israel.

Hezekiah reinforced the Millo and the city wall with towers; he also built a new wall (2 Chr 32:5). The section of a massive fortification wall, 65 m long and 7 m thick, which Avigad (1983: 46–54) cleared in the middle of the Jewish Quarter, is associated with 8th and 7th century B.C.E. pottery, and may well be the fortification wall erected by Hezekiah. See Fig. JER.10. This was the first city wall ever built on the W hill. Running on a line almost identical with the later Hasmonean wall, this broad wall enclosed the Siloam pool located outside the MB II wall of the City of David. Avigad believes this wall surrounded the entire plateau of the W hill (perhaps the Mishnah and the Machtesh of Zeph 1:10–11) in the late monarchy. This wall was built over the ruins of Israelite houses, which date from the beginning of the 8th century B.C.E. The expansion to the unfortified W hill began, it appears, in the early 8th century B.C.E.; by the late 8th century B.C.E., this wall protected the W side of Jerusalem from Assyrian attack.

Hezekiah took additional steps to counter the imperialistic threats of Sennacherib. In preparation for the siege of 701 B.C.E., he constructed a new underground channel (2 Kgs 20:20; 2 Chr 32:2–4, 30; Isa 22:11) beneath the city to bring water from the Gihon spring outside the walls to the Siloam pool, which served as a large reservoir. According to the inscription found on the tunnel wall in 1880, two teams working from opposite directions performed an extraordinary engineering feat by cutting the tunnel through 533 m of bedrock beneath Ophel hill. Although the inscription does not mention Hezekiah's name, Hezekiah undoubtedly built this tunnel.

The kings of the late monarchy also had their roles to play in Jerusalem. Manasseh refortified Jerusalem, building a new outer wall (2 Chr 33:14). Jerusalem reached its zenith under Josiah. In addition to his religious reform which conferred special status on Jerusalem, making it the exclusive place of sacrifice, Josiah took advantage of Assyria's weakness to expand the territory of Judah.

Jerusalem was invaded when Jehoiakim rebelled against Babylon. When Jeremiah predicted the imminent Babylonian destruction of Jerusalem and Judah, Jehoiakim burned the prophet's scroll (Jer 36:20–26). This same chapter mentions a scribe, Gemariah, son of Shaphan (vv 10–12, 25), a supporter of Jeremiah who was in the court of Jehoiakim in his fifth year (604 B.C.E.). During the excavation of the City of David, Shiloh found on a plastered floor of a house (Area G, Stratum 10) more than 50 clay bullae bearing Heb seal impressions. Designating the find-spot the "bullae house," Shiloh speculated it may have been an official administrative archive. These bullae, yielding a corpus of more than 80 Heb names, were well preserved by the flames of the Babylonian destruction of Jerusalem. The name impressed on one of the bullae is "Gemariah ben-Shaphan," who may be the same scribe mentioned in Jeremiah 36.

Shiloh uncovered several other houses on the S area of the hill within the city walls. They were simple structures, square in shape, and built into the lower part of the stepped-stone structure. The Babylonians captured Jerusalem in 597 B.C.E., and then destroyed the city in 586

JER.10. Israelite city wall (8th century) uncovered in the Jewish Quarter on the hill W of the Tyropoeon Valley in Jerusalem. *(Photograph by N. Avigad, by permission, Biblical Archaeology Society Jerusalem Archaeology Slide Set)*

B.C.E. after a siege of 18 months (Lam 1:4; 2:2). Shiloh found evidence of the Babylonian destruction everywhere: thick layers of dark ash, scattered iron and bronze arrowheads, and collapsed structures.

After the destruction of Jerusalem in 586 B.C.E., Judah became part of the Neo-Babylonian Empire. There are many unanswered questions about what took place in Jerusalem between 586 and 538 B.C.E. Both Jerusalem and Judah, it appears, continued to be inhabited (2 Kgs 25:22–26; Jer 40:10; Ezek 33:21–27). Sacrificial worship apparently continued in Jerusalem during the exilic period since there is no reference to the destruction of the altar. Also, the fact that the Persians returned the Temple vessels to Jerusalem suggests a continuation of cult in the city (*HAIJ*, 426). Pilgrims continued to arrive in Jerusalem and to offer sacrifice at the Temple site (Jer 41:5).

F. Second Temple Period

1. Persian. After conquering Babylonia in 539 B.C.E., Cyrus II allowed the Jews to return to their homeland; he also authorized the rebuilding of the Temple. Judah became a Persian province with the name Yehud *(yhd)*. After the return from exile, Jerusalem ceased to be politically significant; emphasis was placed on the religious role, with the priesthood assuming prominence. The Persian period was a time of peace and prosperity, when Judah was allowed a great deal of administrative independence. However, Israelite society was badly divided, with deep antagonisms between the returning exiles and those who had remained in Judah during the exile. The rift was reflected, for example, in the rebuilding of the Temple: those engaged in the rebuilding, considering themselves the true Israelites, did not allow those who had remained in Jerusalem to participate in the religious life of the postexilic community.

With the encouragement of Haggai and Zechariah, and under the leadership of the governor Zerubbabel (a Davidic descendant) and the high priest Joshua, work began on the Temple in 520 B.C.E. Despite opposition from the Samaritans, who built their own temple on Mount Gerizim, the Second Temple was reconstructed, and then rededicated in 515 B.C.E. in the reign of Darius (Ezra 6:15–18). This more modest Temple did not compare in splendor with its predecessor, but it had the same basic architectural structure (Hag 2:3; Ezra 3:12).

In the time of Nehemiah Jerusalem once again became the administrative and religious capital of Judea. Appointed governor of Judea by Artaxerxes, Nehemiah arrived in Jerusalem in 445 B.C.E., and undertook the rebuilding of the city walls to provide security. Nehemiah was resented by Sanballat of Samaria, Tobiah of Ammon, and Geshem the Arab. Opposed to the refortification of Jerusalem, they harassed Nehemiah (Neh 2:19; 4:7). In rebuilding the walls Nehemiah divided the workers into groups, each responsible for a section of the wall (Nehemiah 3). According to Neh 6:15, the wall (perhaps a temporary filling of breeches) was restored in 52 days. Josephus, however, reports that it took two years and four months to complete the project (*Ant* 11.5.8 §179). The task of rebuilding the walls was an economic hardship on the people, preventing them from gainful employment elsewhere.

During this period the Upper City was not resettled; occupation was constricted to the area of the City of David and the Temple Mount. No archaeological remains from the Persian period have been found on the W hill: Avigad unearthed none in the Jewish Quarter, nor did Broshi recover any on Mount Zion (the W ridge below the present SW corner of the Old City). Kenyon discovered Nehemiah's E wall higher up on the E ridge than the Jebusite and Davidic wall, confirming that the city was more constricted in size during the Persian period than earlier (Williamson 1984). The E hill was adequate for the small number of people, mostly Israelites, in Jerusalem in Nehemiah's time. According to Neh 11:1–2, Nehemiah repopulated Jerusalem by requiring the nobility and a tenth of the rural residents to settle in the city.

In addition to Jerusalem's defense, Nehemiah was concerned with political and social reforms among the people. In trying to improve the economic condition of the needy, some of whom had been exploited by their own people, Nehemiah remitted taxes. The people had also grown careless about their religious obligations with regard to Sabbath observance (Neh 13:15–22) and mixed marriage (Neh 13:23–27), so Nehemiah addressed these issues. It was Ezra who reestablished the authority of the Mosaic Torah in this era.

2. Hellenistic. Persian rule came to an end in Judea when Alexander the Great captured Jerusalem in 332 B.C.E. Despite Josephus's statement (*Ant* 11.8.5 §336–39), it seems unlikely that Alexander entered Jerusalem, nor did he interfere with the administrative structures in Jerusalem. Alexander's victory marked the beginning of the Hellenistic period which was to last until 63 B.C.E. At this time, Jerusalem was confined to the Lower City, including the Temple Mount and the City of David. Shiloh's dig revealed evidence of dense settlement in the City of David. It is noteworthy that despite this dense settlement, the Jews of Jerusalem throughout the Hellenistic period were seriously at odds among themselves over religious matters (see below).

With the division of Alexander's vast empire among his generals at his death in 323 B.C.E., Judea, the frontier between the Ptolemies of Egypt and the Seleucids of Syria, came under the successive control of the Ptolemies and the Seleucids. Ptolemy I captured Jerusalem in 320 B.C.E., and by 301 B.C.E. Ptolemaic rule was stabilized. For roughly a century Palestine enjoyed a peaceful and prosperous era under the Ptolemies. Jerusalem's political role in this era was minor, although the city was the administrative center of Judea. The Jerusalem Temple and the priesthood played a prominent role in the Hellenistic period, with the Temple serving as the center of both religious and social life. The high priest oversaw both religious and administrative affairs. Otherwise, archaeological and literary sources provide little information concerning the Ptolemaic rule.

When Antiochus III (the Great) defeated the forces of Ptolemy V Epiphanes and annexed Palestine ca. 201–198 B.C.E., Seleucid rule over Judea began, lasting until 135 B.C.E. The Jews welcomed the Seleucids who showed them consideration. Among other things, the Seleucids provided financial assistance for the rebuilding of Jerusalem and for the repair of the damage to the Temple. The high priest continued to govern Jerusalem and Judea, and the people were subject to the Mosaic law. Among the privileges accorded to the Jews, taxes were remitted for a period of three years. Neither the Ptolemies nor the Seleucids forced the Jews to adopt the Greek way of life.

The Jews themselves were divided among Hellenists and anti-Hellenists, the former represented especially among the upper classes. The high priest Jason favored the Hellenizers, fostered Hellenization (1 Macc 1:11–15; 2 Macc 4:10–15), and transformed the Jewish city of Jerusalem into a Hellenistic *polis,* a Greek city-state, known as Antiochia, after Antiochus IV (2 Macc 4:9). It was situated on the E half of the W hill (Upper City), unsettled in the time of Nehemiah. This new Greek city-state signified a change in Jerusalem's juridical status rather than the construction of a new city (Tcherikover 1966: 165). As part of establishing Jerusalem as a Hellenistic *polis,* Jason built a *gymnasion* in the city under the patronage of Hermes and Hercules; the members of the *gymnasion* were called Antiochenes (2 Macc 4:9). The function of the *gymnasion* went beyond sporting events; pagan customs were introduced (1 Macc 1:11–15; 2 Macc 4:9–17), and it became a social center in competition with the Temple.

The Hellenistic reform enjoyed strong Jewish support, especially among the members of the Temple priesthood and the affluent upper class. Disdaining their own tradition these Hellenizing Jews, without outside coercion, fostered the introduction of Greek customs (Tcherikover 1966: 118, 140). The majority of Jews who were economically poor did not support Jason and the Hellenizers.

This Hellenistic reform took place in the reign of Antiochus IV, who had earlier been bribed to name Jason high priest in place of his brother Onias III. Antiochus IV (Epiphanes) was a strong patron of Hellenization, but the initiative to Hellenize Jerusalem came from the Jews themselves. His persecution of the Jews was not for the purpose of Hellenization, but was a response to the Maccabean revolt (Tcherikover 1966: 190–91). In his attempt to destroy Judaism, Antiochus IV desecrated the Temple, erecting an altar to Zeus, and dedicating the Temple to Olympian Zeus (1 Macc 1:41–63; 2 Macc 6:2–5).

In addition, Antiochus IV destroyed the walls of Jerusalem (1 Macc 1:31), and erected in 168 B.C.E. a Citadel for his garrison, called "Akra" by Josephus (*Ant* 12.5.4 §252; see also 1 Macc 1:29–36). The precise location of this Syrian fortress is uncertain because it has left no archaeological traces. Josephus located it in the Lower City, on the SE hill. Mazar would situate the Akra directly S of the Temple enclosure, adjacent to the Hulda gates. Others (Robinson, Warren, Vincent, Avi-Yonah) proposed locating it on the W hill, across the Tyropoeon valley, but Avigad found no significant artifacts from the early Hellenistic period in the Jewish Quarter. Housing Syrian troops as well as Jewish Hellenizers, the Akra was the symbol of foreign rule. Architecturally higher than the Temple, the Akra served the purpose of controlling the Temple, while keeping the Jews under surveillance.

Aided by his five sons, the Jewish priest Mattathias led a revolt against the Seleucid rule to curb the spread of Hellenistic culture and to gain Jewish independence. Judas Maccabee, one of Mattathias' sons, liberated Jerusalem from Antiochus IV in 164 B.C.E., with the exception of the Akra; thereupon the Temple was purified and rededicated (1 Macc 4:36–55). About 141 B.C.E. Simon, another son of Mattathias, captured the Akra and razed it. From the Maccabean defeat of the Seleucids until the Roman conquest under Pompey in 63 B.C.E., when Judea became part of the province of Syria, the Jews enjoyed a century of political independence, with Jerusalem serving as the capital of Judea, including Transjordan.

3. Hasmonean. When the Hasmoneans, a dynasty of Jewish high priests and kings descended from the family of Mattathias, ruled from 142 to 63 B.C.E., Jerusalem was their capital, the center of religious, political, and economic life until 63 B.C.E. Jerusalem enjoyed prosperity and was enclosed by new walls. It was a period of erecting monuments and tombs, and a time of expansion, as far as Transjordan. Hasmonean Jerusalem incorporated the Upper City and the City of David. The Upper City, in which was located the seat of Hasmonean government, was joined to the Temple Mount by a bridge spanning the Tyropoeon valley. Archaeologists discovered the remains of this bridge along the W wall of the Temple Mount in the form of an intact arch, which had served as a support for the bridge across the Tyropoeon valley. It was named "Wilson's arch" after Charles Wilson who investigated it in the 1860s. The city wall surrounded the W hill in its entirety. The Hasmoneans also built a fortress called Baris (not the same as the Akra) to defend the N side of the Temple. Baris was the forerunner of the fortress Antonia (Avi-Yonah *WHJP* 7: 228–31).

With Jerusalem as the capital of the kingdom, the Hasmoneans reached the height of their power under John Hyrcanus and his son Alexander Jannaeus, both serving successively as high priest and king of Judea. In 63 B.C.E. Pompey, putting an end to Hasmonean rule but retaining Hyrcanus as high priest, occupied the Upper City, attacked the Temple Mount, entered the Holy of Holies, and destroyed the walls of Jerusalem. From that time until the advent of Herod the Great in 37 B.C.E. the Hasmoneans ruled under the protection of Rome.

4. Herodian. When Jesus was born toward the end of Herod's reign, Jerusalem was the capital of Judea, which was part of the Roman province of Syria. Herod was a Hellenist, who ruled as a Roman vassal. The thirty-three years of Herod's rule (37–4 B.C.E.) constituted an era of economic prosperity, and the time when the Upper City attained the zenith of its development, with archaeology providing striking evidence of Jerusalem's splendor. Prosperity divided Jerusalem society, separating the rich from the poor. The economically deprived were relegated to the Lower City, where commerce was conducted; the affluent, including the king and the high priest, resided in the Upper City. Jerusalem's wealth was derived from Herod's building projects, as well as the half-shekel tax levied on Jewish communities around the world.

Avigad's excavations in the Upper City revealed a well-planned city whose residents lived an aristocratic lifestyle. There were remains of magnificent houses, some two or more stories high, built around a central court. Mosaic flooring, frescoes, and painted plaster adorned the homes of many Jerusalem residents. See Fig. JER.11. Painted pottery of superior quality, well-crafted furnishings, and beautiful stone objects, including tables, bowls, and purifi-

JER.11. Mosaic floor in aristocratic house of the Herodian period, excavated on hill W of the Temple Mount. *(Photograph by N. Avigad, by permission, Biblical Archaeology Society Jerusalem Archaeology Slide Set)*

cation jars, reflected the wealth of Jerusalem in the Herodian period.

a. Building Projects. Herod may be best remembered as a builder, especially for his military architecture; his name is synonymous with distinctive architecture and massive masonry (*WHJP* 7: 215). Remains of Herodian architecture can be found throughout Palestine. See also HEROD'S BUILDING PROGRAM. Among Herod's magnificent building projects was the Jerusalem Temple, entirely rebuilt to win the favor of the Jews who hated him. The Temple building was begun in 20 B.C.E. and dedicated 10 years later, although it was not completed until 63 C.E. This colossal Temple occupied an area 446 m N–S, and 296 m E–W. In preparation for the reconstruction of the Second Temple, Herod doubled the size of the Temple platform by filling in the surrounding valleys, especially to the S. The SE corner of the podium stood 45 m above the floor of the Kidron valley. The expanded area of the Temple esplanade measured 144,000 square meters; it was supported by massive retaining walls, still visible today. The best-known section of the remaining walls is called the *kotel* or "western wall" (formerly the "wailing wall"), the focus of Jewish prayer since the destruction of the Temple in 70 C.E. The Herodian walls were built "dry," that is, without cement or mortar between the ashlar stones which were quarried in Jerusalem. Today, the Muslim Haram esh-Sharif ("the noble Sanctuary") occupies the Herodian Temple Mount, easily identifiable by the Dome of the Rock.

Practically nothing remains of the Herodian Temple, but the ruins uncovered along the W and S walls of the Temple Mount, as well as details provided by Josephus, give some idea of the splendid architecture of Herodian Jerusalem. In addition to "Wilson's arch" along the W retaining wall, there was "Robinson's arch," assumed (wrongly) to have been an element of another bridge connecting the Temple Mount with the Upper City. Mazar established that this arch functioned as a span supporting a staircase descending from the Temple Mount to the Tyropoeon valley. On the S section of the Temple's outer court was the royal stoa or sheltered promenade; it was a rectangular hall, with four rows of columns, resembling a Roman basilica (*Ant* 15.11.5 §411–16). Along the S wall Mazar uncovered three gates for access to the Temple Mount. The single gate to the E dates to Crusader times; the double gate and triple gates which form the Hulda gates (possibly named after the 7th century B.C.E. prophet, or perhaps derived from the Heb word for "mole") date to the Herodian era, although the triple gate in its present form is Umayyad. In front of the Hulda gates was a monumental Herodian stairway, 61 m wide with 30 steps, leading up from the Ophel to the two main pilgrim entrances on the S side of the Temple Mount. See also TEMPLE, JERUSALEM.

In the NW corner of the Upper City near the present Jaffa Gate, Herod built a splendid, fortified palace to provide protection for the Upper City. Unfortunately, nothing remains of its superstructure. Like the Temple, the palace was constructed on a platform, 300–350 m N–S, and 60 m E–W. The palace was bounded on the N by the Citadel, on the W and S by the present Turkish city walls; the boundary on the E is unknown. The foundations of the palace have been uncovered in the court of the Citadel, and in the Armenian garden (Bahat and Broshi 1975) near the SW corner of the present city wall, and on Mount Zion, outside the wall of the Old City.

At the N side of the palace were three towers, named in memory of Phasael (Herod's brother), Hippicus (an unknown friend), and Miriamne (Herod's Hasmonean wife). The present-day Citadel (popularly called "David's Tower") adjacent to the Jaffa gate stands on the site of Herod's three towers; it is actually built on Phasael's tower. This fortress on the W side of the Old City guarded the royal palace and the W entrance of Jerusalem. Titus destroyed most of Jerusalem in 70 C.E., but he spared the Herodian fortress. The Crusaders built a fortress over Herod's, but the present architectural form of the Citadel was the work of Suleiman the Magnificent in the 16th century C.E. (Johns 1950; Amiran and Eitan 1970).

In 37–35 B.C.E. Herod rebuilt the Baris, situated at the NW corner of the Temple enclosure, enlarging it with towers. He named it Antonia in honor of his patron Mark Antony. The purpose of this huge fortress was to protect the Temple Mount; it also functioned as a palace and barracks. Titus destroyed the Antonia in 70 C.E. Although nothing remains of the Antonia fortress, it was a conjectured location of the Roman praetorium where Pontius Pilate judged Jesus (John 18:28–19:16). That the Via Dolorosa (Way of the Cross) begins at the Antonia is not compelling with respect to the location of the praetorium; the specific location of events in the life of Jesus was often determined by popular tradition. Some identified the broad stone pavement in the basement of the Sisters of Zion convent as the *lithostrothon* mentioned in John's account of the trial of Jesus before Pilate (19:13). However, P. Benoit (1952) demonstrated stratigraphically that this stone pavement and the contiguous "Ecce Homo" arch (John 19:5) were unrelated to the Antonia and to Jesus. Instead, they formed part of a small, E forum dating to Hadrian in 135 C.E. The praetorium of Jesus' trial was located at Herod's palace which served as the official residence of the Roman procurators when they came to Jerusalem during the major Jewish feasts (Benoit 1952: 550).

b. Josephus' Three Walls. In Herod's time the city walls surrounded Zion and Ophel hill, in addition to the S sector of the present-day Old City. The topography of Jerusalem's walls is controversial; Josephus refers to three successive walls which defended Jerusalem on the N (*JW* 5.4.1 §136). The first wall, the innermost, surrounding the entire city is least disputed; its date is uncertain, but it was the oldest of the walls. It is usually dated to the Hasmonean period, about 100 B.C.E. If Josephus' description of its 60 towers is to be accepted (*JW* 5.4.3 §158), the first wall must have been strong. Defending the NW edge of Jerusalem, it ran roughly S from the present-day Citadel (Jaffa Gate), around Mount Zion, along the Hinnom valley, to the Kidron valley; from the crest of the E hill, to the SE corner of the Temple Mount; then from Wilson's arch on the W wall of the Temple Mount back to the Phasael Tower (present-day Citadel). Johns discovered the NW corner of the first wall in the courtyard of the Citadel.

The exact course of the second wall is uncertain and controversial; related to this issue is the authenticity of the Church of the Holy Sepulchre (if it truly marks the place of Jesus' death and resurrection, it should be situated *outside* this second wall). Archaeological remains are sparse, and literary sources imprecise. The date of this wall is also in contention, having been ascribed to the Hasmonean and the Herodian periods, the latter being more probable. The second wall ran from the present-day Citadel, by way of the present-day Damascus gate, to the Antonia at the NW corner of the Temple. According to Josephus, this relatively short wall had 14 towers (*JW* 5.4.3 §158). It was also fortified by a quarry located in front of it which functioned as a defensive moat. Parts of this quarry have been uncovered in the recent excavation beneath the Lutheran Church of the Redeemer (Lux 1972). Because traces of this quarry were found here, 40 m *south* of the Church of the Holy Sepulchre, it is now fairly certain that this Church indeed marks a spot that was outside the second wall. The second wall as it appears on most maps is the alignment proposed by Vincent, who has now been proven wrong by the Lux excavations. The second wall of Vincent has been identified subsequently as a terrace wall of the Roman or Byzantine period. No part of the second wall itself, however, has yet been unearthed (Schein 1981: 23).

The alignment of the third, the outermost wall, remains a problem (Shanks 1987). Built to protect the N side of Jerusalem, it had 90 towers (*JW* 5.4.3 §158). The foundations of this wall, according to Josephus (*JW* 2.11.6 §218), date to the time of Herod Agrippa (41–44 C.E.), but it was completed only during the first revolt (66–70 C.E.). Some maintain that the third wall of Josephus followed the same course as the present-day N wall of the Old City (Vincent, Benoit, Simons, Kenyon, Hennessy, Hamrick); others, following Robinson, identify the third wall with an E–W wall 450 m further N (Sukenik, Mayer, Avi-Yonah, Ben-Arieh, Netzer, Broshi, Bahat). Kenyon considered the more northerly wall to be Titus' circumvallation rampart, intended to prevent Jews from leaving the city to obtain food, but it is too far N to have served that purpose. Hamrick (1977: 22) maintained that this northernmost wall was a defensive line built by Jewish insurgents about 68 C.E. to serve as a "barrier wall" against the attacking Roman army.

In their excavations between 1925 and 1927, E. L. Sukenik and L. A. Mayer (1930) concentrated on this northernmost wall, and they concurred with Robinson that it was the third wall referred to by Josephus. In their excavations of the same wall between 1972 and 1974, Ben-Arieh and Netzer (1974: 98–100) unearthed a continuous stretch of wall consisting of ashlars and fieldstones (measuring 45 m long and the width varying between 4.2 and 4.3 m), with towers, dating to the 1st century C.E. When J. B. Hennessy (1970) dug at the Damascus gate between 1964 and 1966, he was convinced he had uncovered the third wall of Agrippa I, maintaining that it followed the present line of the Old City's N wall. Archaeology cannot offer yet a conclusive answer because the evidence is ambiguous.

5. Roman. After Herod the Great, Jerusalem became a province of the Roman Empire, ruled by Roman prefects who resided in Caesarea. About 6 C.E. Caesarea became the capital, replacing Jerusalem. The high priest and Sanhedrin oversaw the government of Jerusalem, but their power was significantly reduced. The Jews in Jerusalem at that time were a disparate group of people, often at odds with themselves. Pontius Pilate, prefect of Judea (26–36 C.E.), is well-known to readers of the NT, but less known for having improved Jerusalem's water supply by constructing the first aqueduct, leading from "Solomon's pool" situated between Bethlehem and Hebron.

Gessius Florus, the last of the Roman prefects for Judea, provoked a Jewish rebellion against Rome in 66 C.E. by stealing funds from the Temple treasury. The Jews withstood the Romans temporarily; at that time the Christian community abandoned Jerusalem and fled to Pella. In 70 C.E. Titus attacked Jerusalem on the N side, always the most vulnerable, and built a siege wall around the city. Starvation prevented the defenders from resisting for long. The Temple area and the Lower City fell first; a month later, the Upper City met the same fate. The Temple platform remained standing, as did the three Herodian towers (Hippicus, Phasael, and Miriamne), and part of Jerusalem's western wall (*JW* 7.1.1 §1–2).

Evidence for Jewish presence in Jerusalem between 70 and 132 C.E. is only indirect; the archaeological and literary sources are scarce. The city was not entirely abandoned: the Tenth Legion was present, some Christians had returned from Pella, and Jews were still not forbidden to live in Jerusalem (Avi-Yonah 1973: 16; Peters 1985: 124–26). According to K. W. Clarke (1960: 273–74), a large Jewish population remained in Jerusalem after 70 C.E., and they continued to worship on the Temple Mount.

G. Postbiblical Period

1. Aelia Capitolina. Jewish Jerusalem was effectively finished when Hadrian established the Roman city of Jerusalem, limited to the W hill in the area of the modern Jewish Quarter. Hadrian visited Jerusalem in 129–30 C.E.; then he rebuilt the city, renaming it Aelia Capitolina. "Aelia" was derived from the emperor's second name; "Capitolina" recalled Jupiter, Juno, and Minerva, the deities of the Capitoline Triad in Rome, who became the patrons of Hadrian's new city. He also erected a Temple honoring Jupiter Capitolinus on the Temple Mount; on the present site of the Church of the Holy Sepulchre he built a temple to the Roman goddess Aphrodite.

This new, unwalled city of Hadrian was really a Roman colony, modeled on a Roman camp. Square in shape, as it remains today, it would have been divided into quarters by two streets. The main N–S street, the *cardo,* would have run from the Damascus gate to Zion gate. The main E–W street, the *decumanus,* would have extended from St. Stephen's gate (also called Lions' gate) to the Jaffa gate. A ceremonial tetrapylon, with remains still visible, was erected at the intersection of the streets. Hadrian also constructed a three-arched entryway (with towers on either side) into Aelia Capitolina, which Israeli archaeologists have recovered under the present Damascus gate (Magen 1988).

Hadrian's rebuilding and renaming of Jerusalem probably sparked the Second Jewish revolt under Bar Kokhba (Simeon Bar Koziba), which had begun in 132 and was crushed in 135 after the Jews had reoccupied Jerusalem (Avi-Yonah 1973: 16). Others attribute the revolt to Hadrian's failure to rebuild the Temple, and the fact that circumcision was forbidden. Nevertheless, after 135 C.E.,

Jews were forbidden by Hadrian's decree to live in Jerusalem, or even to visit the city under pain of death.

2. Byzantine. In 324, Constantine became the first Christian emperor to rule Palestine; shortly thereafter, the name Aelia Capitolina imposed by Hadrian was changed back to Jerusalem. The Byzantine period was a prosperous age, marked by intensive construction. Constantine is associated with three major building projects, each related to an aspect of Jesus' life: one in Bethlehem, another at Golgotha (the Church of the Holy Sepulchre), and the third on the Mount of Olives.

Consecrated in 335, the Church of the Holy Sepulchre (Anastasis) was razed in 614. Destroyed and rebuilt several times since, the most recent major restoration was undertaken in 1959. Although the present church stands on the original site in the NW quarter of Jerusalem, most of the structure visible today dates to the Crusader period in the 12th century. The Church of the Holy Sepulchre is divided basically into three parts: the basilica, the rock of Golgotha, and the tomb. The upper chapel adjacent to the principal entrance of the Church commemorates the location of Golgotha. Golgotha, translated "the place of a skull" (Matt 27:33 = Mark 15:22; Luke 23:33; John 19:17), is a name of uncertain origin; it is the traditional site of the crucifixion and the tomb of Jesus (John 19:41–42). See GOLGOTHA.

The tradition in the Jerusalem community regarding the Holy Sepulchre as the place of Jesus' burial goes back to the 4th century. In his 1838 visit to Jerusalem, Robinson questioned the authenticity of the Holy Sepulchre, which hinges on the location of Josephus' second wall (see above). Robinson assumed the sepulchre had also been inside the city wall in Jesus' time, whereas the crucifixion took place outside the city (Heb 13:12). The Garden Tomb, an alternative site, is situated outside the walled city, just N of the Damascus gate. Advanced by C. Gordon in 1883 as the true location of Golgotha on the basis of a fanciful rock formation, this site is unconvincing because of lack of evidence (Wilkinson 1978: 146, 198–200).

Avigad's excavations in the Jewish Quarter uncovered the Byzantine *cardo* measuring 12.5 m wide, paved with flagstones, and flanked on each side by colonnaded porticoes. See Fig. JER.12. Avigad, excavating only the S part of the street, found pottery sealed beneath the pavement as stratigraphic evidence for its Byzantine date. The Roman *cardo* has not been found, but it is assumed that the same street plan existed in Roman times. One day, there may be archaeological evidence that the N part of the street was constructed in the Roman period.

The numerous architectural remains uncovered by Avigad have been reconstructed and incorporated into the newly-rebuilt Jewish Quarter, destroyed between 1948 and 1967. The pattern of Byzantine Jerusalem as reconstructed by archaeology conforms well to the 6th century C.E. Madeba mosaic map depicting the arcaded *cardo* running from the Damascus gate S to the area of the Zion gate. The map also portrays several Byzantine churches, including the Church of the Holy Sepulchre and the Nea.

In the 5th century, Jerusalem expanded both to the N and S. The present-day St. Stephen's convent (Ecole Biblique et Archéologique Française), just N of the Damascus gate, marks the site of a church erected by the empress Eudocia in 460 as a repository for the relics of Stephen, the first Christian martyr. In 438, Empress Eudocia permitted Jews to live in Jerusalem.

In the 6th century the emperor Justinian, a great builder, erected the Nea (New Church). Dedicated in 543 to the Virgin Mary, it was destroyed by earthquake in 746, and never rebuilt. In 1970, Avigad uncovered the foundations of this church in the Jewish Quarter; he also discovered a Greek inscription mentioning Justinian and indicating the date of the church's consecration. In 614, the Persian army conquered Jerusalem, destroyed most of the churches, and expelled the Jews (Avi-Yonah 1976: 269).

3. Early Arab. From 638, when Byzantine Jerusalem surrendered to Caliph Omar, until the beginning of the Crusader period in 1099, Jerusalem was ruled by the Muslims. Jews were readmitted to Jerusalem and received favorable treatment, being permitted to build synagogues and religious schools (Peters 1985: 186). Jerusalem, known among Muslims as el-Quds, "the Holy" (Isa 52:1), ranks third, after Mecca and Medina, among the holiest cities in Islam. Jerusalem has never been the political or administrative capital of the Muslims; its importance for Islam is completely religious.

Although the Umayyad caliphs resided in Damascus, they supported an impressive building program in Jerusalem. Mazar uncovered the remains of a magnificent Umayyad palace S of the Temple enclosure. The complex consisted of six impressive buildings reflecting superior planning and architecture. The Umayyads established Jerusalem as a Muslim religious center. The Dome of the Rock (Qubbet es-Sahra), the octagonal shrine (not a mosque) on the Temple Mount, was completed in 691. Intended to instill pride in Muslims, it was built to protect the holy rock beneath, whence its name (Rosen-Ayalon 1975: 92). According to tradition, it is the rock where Abraham was prepared to sacrifice Isaac (Gen 22:1–19), the site of the threshing floor of Araunah where David built an altar (2 Sam 24:15–25), and the place from which Muhammad ascended to heaven on the steed Buraq. The silver-domed prayer mosque at the S edge of the Temple platform is the el-Aksa Mosque. Meaning "the furthermost," this mosque may have been intended to commemorate the farthest point of Muhammad's mystic "Night Journey" whence he ascended into heaven.

During the rule of the Abbasids, who were tolerant toward non-Muslims, Jerusalem declined. The Fatimid period, too, was a time of decline for Jerusalem. The eccentric Fatimid Caliph al-Hakim persecuted Jews and Christians, and ordered the destruction of Christian shrines, including the Church of the Holy Sepulchre.

4. Crusader. Jerusalem experienced a century of Crusader rule. After a five-week siege, including the massacre of Jews and Muslims, the Christians under Godfrey de Bouillon conquered Jerusalem in 1099. Jerusalem became the capital of the Crusader kingdom, called the Latin Kingdom of Jerusalem, until 1191 when it was replaced by Acco (Acre). The population was about 30,000, the vast majority Christian. Because most of the population was of French descent, the language of Jerusalem was French. Jews and Muslims were not permitted to reside in Jerusalem. The Crusader period was a time of intense building. The architectural style was Romanesque with some early

JER.12. Byzantine *cardo* in the Old City of Jerusalem. The man at the top of the photograph provides a useful scale. Column bases along the main N–S thoroughfare were found *in situ*. To the right can be seen doorways into the small shops along the street's edge. *(Photograph by Z. Radovan, by permission, Biblical Archaeology Society Jerusalem Archaeology Slide Set)*

Gothic elements. An excellent example of Crusader architecture is St. Anne's Church, inside St. Stephen's gate. The present white-stone church in Romanesque style was built in 1140. The Crusaders also refurbished the Church of the Holy Sepulchre, completing it in 1149. The present-day facade of this church is much the same as it was in the 12th century. The Crusaders, renaming the Dome of the Rock "Templum Domini," converted it into a Christian church, and affixed a cross on its dome.

The Citadel ("Tower of David") on the W side of the Old City near the Jaffa gate was Jerusalem's principal fortification in this period, and also served as the headquarters for government and military officials. The Crusader city wall followed for the most part the line of the present wall. Excavations at the Damascus gate uncovered foundations of a Crusader gate beneath the present Turkish structure.

5. Later Arab. In 1187, the Crusaders surrendered Jerusalem to the formidable Kurdish general Saladin (Salah ed-Din), founder of the Ayyubid dynasty. He impressed a distinctive Islamic character on Jerusalem, restoring the Dome of the Rock and the el-Aksa Mosque. Under Saladin, who was a cultured and humane ruler, Jews and Eastern Christians were allowed to reside in Jerusalem. In 1212, Saladin's nephew, al-Malik al-Muʾazzam, rebuilt the walls of Jerusalem, only to dismantle them seven years later, fearing the Crusaders were about to regain a well-fortified city.

The Mameluke sultans defeated the Ayyubids and ruled Jerusalem from 1244 to 1517. Great builders and skilled craftsmen, the Mamelukes left their mark on the architectural design of Jerusalem; the Muslim character of present-day Jerusalem is directly traceable to them. Their principal concern was the religious meaning of Jerusalem for Islam; for this reason they gave special attention to mosques and madrasas (Muslim theological schools). The Mamelukes made Jerusalem the center of Islamic studies; at the same time Jerusalem deteriorated economically, and the population dwindled to about 10,000.

6. Ottoman. From 1517, when the Ottoman Turks began to rule Jerusalem from Istanbul after a peaceful takeover, Jerusalem was on the decline, with the residents of Jerusalem living in acute poverty. Between 1537 and 1541 Suleiman I (the Magnificent) rewalled Jerusalem, unwalled since 1219, to protect it from bedouin incursion. The present Ottoman walls of the city follow the course of the Hasmonean walls, founded on bedrock, and utilize parts of them. Suleiman I also rebuilt the "Tower of David" and the aqueduct which brought water from "Solomon's pools." The Ottoman Turks constructed the present-day seven gates of Jerusalem, built for the most part over the gates of Roman times. The names of these gates have changed from time to time, and continue to do so. In 1542, Suleiman built the Damascus gate, a superb example of Ottoman architecture; known in Arabic as Bab el-Amud (gate of the column), it covered Hadrian's entryway of 135 C.E. After this flourish of building activity, Jerusalem underwent little development in the second half of the Ottoman Turkish era.

H. Theology

Jerusalem plays an important theological role in the OT and NT. The name Jerusalem occurs more than 650 times in the OT, especially in the historiographies (Samuel, Kings, Ezra-Nehemiah, Chronicles). With the exception of two possible references, it is absent from the Pentateuch, not having yet gained historical prominence in that period. Jerusalem appears frequently in the Psalms; also in the Prophets where there are some forty-nine occurrences in Isaiah, 102 in Jeremiah, twenty-six in Ezekiel, and eight in Micah. In the NT, Jerusalem appears more than 140 times, sixty-seven of which are in the Gospels, but never in the Catholic epistles.

1. Old Testament. The theological significance of Jerusalem in the OT is based on the divine presence symbolized in the ark of the covenant and the Temple. The holiness of the Temple and of Jerusalem rests on the presence of the ark; David's transfer of the ark inaugurated the cult of Yahweh in Jerusalem. By laying the foundation for the Temple, David made Jerusalem "the cornerstone of the religious and cultic unification of Israel" (Talmon 1974: 195).

The prophets, especially Isaiah, apply the name Zion to signify Jerusalem as the "City of Yahweh" (de Vaux 1969: 286). The uniqueness of Jerusalem can be summarized under the heading "Zion tradition," which comprises the following motifs: Yahweh, the great king, chooses Jerusalem as a permanent abode; Zion (not Sinai) as Yahweh's chosen mountain, located at the center of the world; the Gihon spring (Isa 41:17–18) as the miraculous stream flowing from the cosmic mountain; the pilgrimages of other nations to Jerusalem to acknowledge the sovereignty of Yahweh; and the inviolability of Jerusalem (Roberts 1973: 329). Jerusalem's deliverance from the siege of Sennacherib in 701 B.C.E. created the impression of the city's inviolability under all circumstances, thus reinforcing the Zion tradition.

Isaiah, vacillating between threat (1:7–9) and hope (2:2–4), believed that Jerusalem was inviolable because Yahweh dwelt in the city (de Vaux 1969: 292), but he modified this tradition by laying down conditions (1:19–20), requiring faith in Yahweh as a special condition for divine protection and salvation (7:9b). Nor did Isaiah hesitate to point out the sins of Jerusalem (3:8; 22:1–14; 28:14).

Micah and Jeremiah, convinced that Jerusalem would not be spared as a consequence of its sinfulness, denounced Judah's confidence in the inviolability of Zion. Micah's (3:12) shattering prediction that Jerusalem and the Temple would be reduced to rubble was repeated in substance a century later by Jeremiah, at the risk of his life (26:18–19), who opposed the belief that Jerusalem was invincible. Jeremiah also inveighed against the Judahites for considering the Temple an automatic assurance of divine protection, oblivious that such protection was contingent upon their own moral conduct (Jer 7:1–15).

Having indicted Jerusalem for apostasy, the prophets predicted that its inhabitants would be called to account. However, inasmuch as Yahweh's purpose is not to annihilate, Jerusalem was to be rebuilt on the faithful remnant. In contrast to the words of doom, the prophets of the exile proclaimed hope of restoration. Jeremiah described the rebuilding of Jerusalem and its walls (30:18–19; 31:38–39). Ezekiel, who considered Jerusalem the center of the nations (5:5; 38:12), saw the glory of Yahweh returning to the Jerusalem Temple. Deutero-Isaiah describes the "new Jerusalem" (40:1–2; 52:1, 7–8) in words of consolation and hope, reflecting belief in the future greatness of Jerusalem as the center of the nations (chaps. 60–62). For Haggai (2:6–8) and Zechariah (8:3–8), the rebuilding of the Temple was the fulfillment of this hope.

2. New Testament. Among the Synoptic Gospels, Luke gives far more prominence to Jerusalem than Matthew or Mark. The fact that geography plays an important role in Luke's theology may account for the gospel's preoccupation with Jerusalem (Fitzmyer, *Luke 1–9* AB, 163–69). Jerusalem is "the city of destiny for Jesus and the pivot for the salvation of mankind" (Fitzmyer, *Luke 1–9* AB, 164). Jesus has a special relationship to Jerusalem, which is the goal toward which he moves throughout the gospel.

Luke's gospel begins (1:9) and ends in the Temple of Jerusalem (24:53). Between these two Temple events, according to Luke, Jesus makes but one journey to Jerusalem, described in the so-called travel account (9:51–19:27). Within this account, there are several references to Jerusalem as the objective of the journey (9:51–53; 13:22; 17:11; 19:11). In the course of the journey, Jesus addresses an apostrophe to Jerusalem (Luke 13:34–35 = Matt 23:37–39), the place of the prophets' martyrdom, and where he, too, must suffer and die (Luke 13:33; Matt 16:21). Mark, too, describes only one journey to Jerusalem, whereas John mentions three. In Luke, the journey to Jerusalem assumes great importance by serving as the geographical framework for much of the material found only in this gospel; Luke alone, for example, recounts the story of the Good Samaritan (10:29–37). Appearing after the travel account, Jesus' prophecy concerning the destruction of Jerusalem (19:43–44), couched in the language of the prophets (Isa 29:3; Jer 6:6; Ezek 4:2), is exclusive to Luke.

The Jerusalem Temple, too, is prominent in Luke. Jesus is presented in the Temple (2:22–23), he makes his first pilgrimage to Jerusalem and the Temple at the age of twelve (2:41–50); Jesus cleanses the Temple (19:45–46), an event reported in the four Gospels (= Matt 21:12–13; Mark 11:15–17; John 2:14–16), whose purpose may have been to emphasize that the Temple was principally a place of prayer, and not a financial or economic institution (Wilkinson 1978: 117).

Jesus' mission, including the passion, resurrection and ascension, is brought to completion in Jerusalem (24:50). In contrast to Matthew, Luke locates all the appearances of the risen Christ to the disciples in the vicinity of Jerusalem (24:13–53); they are also instructed to remain in Jerusalem (Luke 24:49).

Mark's gospel can be divided into three geographical

sections: Galilee, the journey to Jerusalem, and Jerusalem itself. It is called the "Galilean gospel" because of Galilee's theological significance as the place of the imminent parousia. In Mark, Jerusalem is mentioned only a few times, outside the passion narrative. This gospel, often called the gospel of the passion, records several of Jesus' predictions of his death in Jerusalem (8:31; 9:31; 10:32–34).

Matthew's gospel, beginning with the infancy narrative, contains several references to Jerusalem. Jerusalem is called the "holy city" (4:5; 27:53); Jerusalem is also described as the "city of the great King" (5:35), given as the reason for not swearing by Jerusalem. Matthew (27:51 = Mark 15:38; Luke 23:45) refers to the curtain of the Jerusalem Temple being torn at the crucifixion, an indication of the new source of salvation in Jesus.

In John, the centers of Jesus' ministry are Galilee and especially Jerusalem, although Jerusalem is not mentioned in the passion narrative. John states explicitly that Jesus taught in the Temple (7:14). Jesus told the woman of Samaria, according to John, that the proper place of worship would be neither on Mount Gerizim nor in Jerusalem (4:21). In this gospel the glorified body of Jesus ultimately replaces the Temple.

John refers explicitly to two places in Jerusalem connected with Jesus' miraculous cures. One is a "pool, in Hebrew called Beth-zatha, which has five porticoes" (5:2), where Jesus cured a man who had been lame for thirty-eight years. Beth-zatha was a suburb immediately to the N of the Temple area, near the present-day Crusader church of St. Anne; there, a pool was discovered and excavated, and the five porticoes verified. Successive structures had been built over the ancient pool, including a pagan sanctuary after 135 C.E., a Byzantine church of the 5th century, as well as the Crusader church of the 12th century. On the combined basis of the NT, the ancient tradition, and the excavation, archaeologists attach a high degree of probability to the identity of the twin pool of St. Anne as the sheep pool of John 5:2 (Jeremias 1966: 38).

The second specific place in Jerusalem cited by John is the pool of Siloam (a later, Gk form of *šiloaḥ*), where Jesus instructed the blind man to wash (9:7). Mentioned also in Isa 8:6, *šiloaḥ* refers to a reservoir supplied with water from the Gihon spring by means of a canal. The pool of Siloam is located at the S end of the E hill, near where the Kidron and Tyropoeon valleys converge. In Isa 8:6, *šiloaḥ* refers to the aqueduct in use during Ahaz's reign, prior to the construction of Hezekiah's tunnel.

The geographical link between Luke and Acts is Jerusalem (Luke 24:47; Acts 1:8; 5:28; 6:7), whence the preachers of the gospel set out. Jerusalem is also the element unifying Jesus and the primitive community (Acts 10:39; 13:27, 31). According to Acts, the disciples remained in Jerusalem, as Jesus commanded (1:4, 12); there, they received the Spirit at Pentecost (2:1–47), and the preaching of the gospel begun in Jerusalem spread "to the end of the earth" (Acts 1:8). The church in Jerusalem assumed the leading role (8:14–16; 11:1–18) in the activities of the early church, and decisions were made in Jerusalem for the church at large (Acts 15:1–35; Gal 2:1–10).

Stephen's discourse on the differences between Judaism and Christianity, delivered in Jerusalem before the supreme council of the Jews (Acts 7), is the most negative passage in the NT on the religious practices associated with the Jerusalem Temple (6:11–15; 7:48). Christianity emerged only gradually from the matrix of Judaism; Stephen's speech, making him Christianity's first martyr, marked the emergence of Christianity as a distinctive sect.

In the context of Stephen's speech Paul, still named Saul, appears for the first time. Before his conversion he had persecuted the church in Jerusalem (Acts 9:13, 21). Afterwards, he acknowledged Jerusalem as the origin of the gospel (Rom 15:19). However, according to Gal 1:18–20, Paul went up to Jerusalem only three years after his conversion, and according to Acts (22:17–21), it was there, in the temple, that he received his commission to preach to the gentiles.

The eschatological expectations of Judaism and Christianity regarding Jerusalem and the Temple are quite different.

Both Jewish and Christian literature describe Jerusalem in metaphorical and eschatological terms. Some Jewish writers envisioned a new, restored, earthly Jerusalem in the end times (Tob 13:9–18; *2 Bar.* 32:2–4; *Test. Dan.* 5:12). Some Jewish and Christian apocalyptic texts looked forward to a new, perfect Jerusalem that would descend from heaven to earth (*4 Ezra* 7:26; 10:25–54; 13:36; Rev 3:12, 21:2–22:5). In Rev 3:12 "the new [transformed] Jerusalem which comes down from my God out of heaven," a metaphor for the Christian community, anticipates the more lengthy description in Rev 21:1–22:5.

Other Jewish and Christian literature utilize apocalyptic imagery to describe a perfect Jerusalem in heaven to which the just ascend (*2 Bar.* 4:1–7; *4 Ezra* 8:52; *4 Bar.* 5:35; Heb 12:22). In Heb 12:22–24 "the heavenly Jerusalem" is the place of the new covenant sealed through the blood of Jesus.

Allegorizing on the two sons of Abraham, Ishmael by the slave woman Hagar and Isaac (a type of the Christian) by the free woman Sarah (Gal 4:24–26), Paul contrasts sharply "the present Jerusalem" and "the Jerusalem above." He does not make the contrast between "the present Jerusalem" and "the future Jerusalem." In the allegory, the existing Jerusalem is equated with earthly Sinai, but then the earthly Jerusalem is transformed to the heavenly Jerusalem. Hagar symbolizes "the present Jerusalem," and Sarah symbolizes "the Jerusalem above." For the Christian, God's dwelling is no longer "the present Jerusalem," nor is "the present Jerusalem" the real mother; "but the Jerusalem above is free, and she is our mother" (Gal 4:26).

Bibliography

Amiran, R., and Eitan, A. 1970. Excavations in the Courtyard of the Citadel, Jerusalem, 1968–1969 (Preliminary Report). *IEJ* 20: 9–17.

Avi-Yonah, M. 1966. *The Holy Land from the Persian to the Arab Conquests.* Grand Rapids.

———. 1973. Building History from the Earliest Times to the Nineteenth Century. Pp. 13–19 in *Urban Geography of Jerusalem*, ed. D. Amiran. New York and Berlin.

———. 1976. *The Jews of Palestine: A Political History from the Bar Kokhba War to the Arab Conquest.* Oxford.

Avigad, N. 1983. *Discovering Jerusalem.* Nashville.

Bahat, D. 1983. *Carta's Historical Atlas of Jerusalem.* Jerusalem.

Bahat, D., and Broshi, M. 1975. Excavations in the Armenian Garden. Pp. 55–56 in Yadin 1975.
Ben-Arieh, S., and Netzer, E. 1974. Excavations Along the 'Third Wall' of Jerusalem, 1972–1974. *IEJ* 24: 97–107.
Ben-Arieh, Y. 1979. *The Rediscovery of the Holy Land in the Nineteenth Century.* Jerusalem.
Ben-Dov, M. 1985. *In the Shadow of the Temple.* New York.
Benoit, P. 1952. Prétoire, Lithostroton et Gabbatha. *RB* 59: 531–50.
Bliss, F. J., and Dickie, A. C. 1898. *Excavations at Jerusalem, 1894–1897.* London.
Broshi, M. 1974. The Expansion of Jerusalem in the Reigns of Hezekiah and Manasseh. *IEJ* 24: 21–26.
———. 1977. Along Jerusalem's Walls. *BA* 40: 11–17.
———. 1978. Estimating the Population of Ancient Jerusalem. *BARev* 4: 10–15.
Clarke, K. W. 1960. Worship in the Jerusalem Temple after A.D. 70. *NTS* 6: 269–80.
Clermont-Ganneau, C. 1896. *Archaeological Researches in Palestine during the Years 1873–1874.* Vol. I. Trans. A. Stewart. London.
Crowfoot, J. W., and FitzGerald, G. M. 1929. *Excavations in the Tyropoeon Valley, Jerusalem, 1927.* London.
Hamilton, R. W. 1940. Excavations Against the North Wall of Jerusalem, 1937–1938. *QDAP* 10: 1–53.
Hamrick, E. W. 1977. The Third Wall of Agrippa I. *BA* 40: 18–23.
Hennessy, J. B. 1970. Preliminary Report on Excavations at the Damascus Gate, Jerusalem, 1964–1966. *Levant* 2: 22–27.
Hopkins, I. W. J. 1970. *Jersualem: A Study in Urban Geography.* Grand Rapids.
Jeremias, J. 1966. *The Rediscovery of Bethesda.* Louisville, KY.
———. 1969. *Jerusalem in the Time of Jesus.* Trans. F. H. & C. H. Cave. Philadelphia.
Johns, C. N. 1950. The Citadel, Jerusalem. A Summary of Work since 1934. *QDAP* 14: 121–90.
Kaufman, A. S. 1983. Where the Ancient Temple of Jerusalem Stood. *BARev* 9: 40–59.
Kenyon, K. 1974. *Digging Up Jerusalem.* New York.
Lux, U. 1972. Vorläufiger Bericht über die Ausgrabung unter der Erlöserkirche im Muristan in der Altstadt von Jerusalem in den Jahren 1970 und 1971. *ZDPV* 88: 185–201.
Macalister, R. A. S., and Duncan, J. G. 1926. *Excavations on the Hill of Ophel, Jerusalem, 1923–1925.* London.
Magen, M. 1988. Recovering Roman Jerusalem—The Entryway Beneath Damascus Gate. *BARev* 15: 48–56.
Mazar, B. 1975. *The Mountain of the Lord.* Garden City, NY.
———. 1978. Herodian Jerusalem in the Light of the Excavations South and South-West of the Temple Mount. *IEJ* 28: 230–37.
Miller, J. M. 1974. Jebus and Jerusalem: A Case of Mistaken Identity. *ZDPV* 90: 115–27.
Murphy-O'Connor, J. 1986. *The Holy Land: An Archaeological Guide from Earliest Times to 1700.* 2d edition. New York.
Parrot, A. 1957. *The Temple of Jerusalem.* Trans. B. E. Hooke. London.
Peters, F. E. 1985. *Jerusalem: The Holy City in the Eyes of Chroniclers, Visitors, Pilgrims, and Prophets.* Princeton.
Purvis, J. D. 1988. *Jerusalem the Holy City: A Bibliography.* ATLA Bibliography Series 2. Metuchen, NJ.
Roberts, J. M. 1973. The Davidic Origin of the Zion Tradition. *JBL* 92: 329–44.
Robinson, E. 1856. *Biblical Researches in Palestine and the Adjacent Regions.* 3 vols. London.
Rosen-Ayalon, M. 1975. The Islamic Architecture of Jerusalem. Pp. 92–96 in Yadin 1975.
Schein, B. E. 1981. The Second Wall of Jerusalem. *BA* 44: 21–26.
Shanks, H. 1985. The City of David after Five Years of Digging. *BARev* 11: 22–38.
———. 1987. The Jerusalem Wall That Shouldn't Be There. *BARev* 13: 46–57.
Shiloh, Y. 1981. The City of David Archaeological Project: The Third Season, 1980. *BA* 44: 161–70.
———. 1984. *Excavations at the City of David, I, 1978–1982.* Qedem 19. Jerusalem.
———. 1987. Underground Water Systems in Eretz-Israel in the Iron Age. Pp. 203–44 in *Archaeology and Biblical Interpretation: Essays in Memory of D. Glenn Rose,* ed. L. Perdue, L. Toombs, and G. Johnson. Atlanta.
Simons, J. 1952. *Jerusalem in the Old Testament.* Leiden.
Stager, L. E. 1982. The Archaeology of the East Slope of Jerusalem and the Terraces of the Kidron. *JNES* 41: 111–21.
Sukenik, E. L., and Mayer, L. A. 1930. *The Third Wall of Jerusalem.* London.
Talmon, S. 1974. The Biblical Concept of Jerusalem. Pp. 189–203 in *Jerusalem,* eds. J. M. Oesterreicher and A. Sinai. New York.
Tcherikover, V. 1966. *Hellenistic Civilization and the Jews.* Trans. S. Applebaum. Philadelphia.
Tushingham, A. D. 1968. The Armenian Garden. *PEQ* 100: 109–11.
———. 1985. *Excavations in Jerusalem 1961–1967.* Vol. I. Toronto.
Vaux, R. de. 1969. Jerusalem and the Prophets. Pp. 275–300 in *Interpreting the Prophetic Tradition,* ed. H. M. Orlinsky. New York.
Vincent, L.-H. 1911. *Underground Jerusalem.* London.
Warren, C. 1876. *Underground Jerusalem.* London.
Weill, R. 1920. *La cité de David: Campagne de 1913–1914.* Vol. 1. Paris.
———. 1947. *La cité de David: Campagne de 1923–1925.* Paris.
Wilkinson, J. 1974. Ancient Jerusalem: Its Water Supply and Population. *PEQ* 106: 33–51.
———. 1978. *Jerusalem as Jesus Knew It.* London.
Williamson, H. G. M. 1984. Nehemiah's Walls Revisited. *PEQ* 116: 81–88.
Wilson, C., and Warren, C. 1871. *The Recovery of Jerusalem.* London.
Yadin, Y., ed. 1975. *Jerusalem Revealed: Archaeology in the Holy City, 1968–1974.* Trans. R. Grafman. Jerusalem.

PHILIP J. KING

JERUSALEM, COUNCIL OF. This conference (also called "the Apostolic Council") designates the meeting at Jerusalem of leaders of the early Church to discuss the implications of preaching a gospel of grace among the gentiles.

A. Historical Considerations

The historical questions surrounding the meeting are formidable. In Gal 2:1–10 Paul gives an account of the conference, which occurred on his second visit to Jerusalem following his "conversion." He, together with Barnabas and Titus, went "by revelation" to discuss the message he had been preaching among the gentiles. James, Peter, and John are the Jerusalem apostles specifically mentioned as present and in a private meeting "added nothing" to Paul's gospel. The Jerusalem apostles asked only that Paul and his colleagues "remember the poor," probably a reference to the offering Paul solicited for the Jerusalem saints. Another result of the meeting was an agreed-upon division of labor, which gave the Jerusalem leaders responsibility for the circumcised and Paul and his colleagues responsibility for the gentiles. Apparently, there was a third group present at Jerusalem (called by Paul "false brothers"), who tried unsuccessfully to force the circumcision of Titus.

The historical problems arise in the effort to connect Paul's account to the information found in Acts. Acts mentions five visits of Paul to Jerusalem (9:26–30; 11:27–30 and 12:25; 15:1–30; 18:22; 21:17–23:31). The question is: Which account (or accounts, if any) parallels Gal 2:1–10? A number of solutions have been proposed.

1. Acts 11:27–30; 12:25 Parallels Gal 2:1–10. Paul and Barnabas are commissioned by the Church at Antioch to carry the funds for famine relief, and while in Jerusalem, it is argued, they reach a private agreement with the leadership regarding the admission of gentiles to the church (Lake 1933: 445–74). Sometime after this meeting, the dispute between Peter and Paul over table-fellowship occurs at Antioch (Gal 2:11–14), precipitating a second, more public conference at Jerusalem (Acts 15:1–30). The major difficulties with this proposal are the silence of Acts regarding a private meeting at the time when the funds for famine relief are brought and the silence of Galatians regarding a third visit of Paul to Jerusalem.

2. Acts 15:1–30 Parallels Gal 2:1–10. This represents the most widely held proposal and rests on the fact that the persons, the locations, and the issues are the same in both accounts (Lightfoot 1914: 123–28; Hengel 1986: 111–26). The problem with this solution is the insistence on the so-called apostolic decree in the Acts account ("that you abstain from what has been sacrificed to idols and from blood and from what is strangled and from unchastity," 15:29), which, if actually agreed to by Paul, would invalidate his argument in Galatians. The decree may have come later, after the conference, as a compromise achieved without Paul to restore the broken fellowship between Jewish and gentile Christians.

3. Acts 15:1–4, 12 Parallels Gal 2:1–10. This proposal argues that Acts 15:1–30 actually reflects two conferences, which have been confusingly merged by the author into one. Acts 15:1–4, 12 reports a first conference to answer whether gentiles had to be circumcised to unite with the Church. Paul was present at this meeting and provided his account in Gal 2:1–10. A second conference was held at Jerusalem (Acts 15:5–11, 13–33) to deal with the issue of table-fellowship between Jewish and gentile Christians. Paul was absent from this second conference and thus was not a party to the "apostolic decree" (Weiss 1959: 259–73). The primary difficulty with this third proposal is that Acts 15 does not read like the confluence of two accounts of separate meetings.

4. Acts 18:22 Parallels Gal 2:1–10. The proposal is made that the meeting recorded in Acts 15:1–30 actually takes place later (at 18:22), when a brief note is made of Paul's greeting the church at Jerusalem. At this visit Paul is asked to "remember the poor," a request which he responds to not long after by soliciting gifts from Christians in Corinth and in Rome. The council must have immediately preceded the writing of 1 and 2 Corinthians and Romans (Knox 1950: 61–73; Lüdemann 1984: 149–57, 195–200). This explanation depends heavily on a Pauline chronology derived exclusively from his letters.

5. Acts 11:1–18 Parallels Gal 2:1–10. A recent proposal postulates the presence of Paul at the discussion recorded in Acts 11:1–18 when Peter silences the criticisms of "those of the circumcision." The writer of Acts is unaware that Paul and the Jerusalem leaders had a private meeting on this occasion, but the Pauline account is found in Gal 2:1–10. After Peter and Paul have left Jerusalem to engage in further missionary activity, James is pressured by the more conservative Jewish forces in the Church into a second conference at which time the "apostolic decree" is issued, representing a dramatic compromise. Acts 15:1–30 mistakenly records Peter and Paul as present at this second conference (Achtemeier 1987: 44–55). The obvious difficulty with this proposal lies in the speculative suggestion that Paul was present at the occasion of Peter's speech in Acts 11:1–18.

What can be said about the complexity of the historical problems surrounding the council and the variety of proposed solutions? Since Gal 2:1–10 represents the firsthand recollections of a participant at the conference and the Acts material is secondhand, historical priority must be given to Gal 2:1–10 as the normative account. Of the five visits to Jerusalem in Acts, the one mentioned in 15:1–30 seems to resemble most closely Gal 2:1–10 in personnel, structure, issues, and the basic agreement that circumcision is unnecessary for the admission of gentiles to the Church. Whether the visit should come later in the Acts chronology, perhaps at the time of the visit of 18:22, is beyond the scope of this study.

How then is one to explain the difficulties with the Acts 15:1–30 account, which represents sharp differences from the report in Gal 2:1–10? The Acts account is woven carefully into a larger narrative through which the writer addresses a prophetic word to the readers. The writer's intention (as revealed in the narrative) is not to chronicle historical events but to trace the activity of the divine Spirit in the life of the Church and the movement of the Church as a predominantly gentile group "to the end of the earth." Historicity is not the primary criterion by which the narrative is to be judged. Acts 15:1–30 seems to represent a critical reshaping of sources in order to support the theological purposes of the larger narrative, with its concern for the unity and mission of the Church.

B. Literary and Theological Considerations

Both Gal 2:1–10 and Acts 15:1–30 play crucial roles, respectively, in their literary contexts.

1. Gal 2:1–10. Paul argues at the beginning of Galatians that there is but one gospel, which exercises supreme authority in the life of the Church (1:6–9). The power of this gospel is evidenced in the remarkable transformation which it precipitated in Paul's own experience, a transformation confirmed by the testimony of the Judean Christians (1:22–24). Then comes the report of the Jerusalem Council (2:1–10) through which the Galatian readers discover that the gospel is not idiosyncratically Paul's, but is agreed to by the pillar apostles at Jerusalem. The mission to the gentiles in which the Christian message is offered free of the legal demands of circumcision is not to be seen as a sectarian movement. At the heart of the council's decisions is the mutual recognition of a mission to the gentiles and a mission to the Jews, both empowered by the one gospel of grace. The ensuing report of the conflict between Peter and Paul at Antioch (2:11–14), given of course from Paul's perspective, merely reiterates that the gospel alone can provide the bond for Christian unity. Readers in the Galatian communities learn that Peter's action in withdrawing from table-fellowship with gentiles *de facto* establishes something other than grace as the basis for unity. Later chapters elaborate the character of the gospel in terms of the righteousness of God manifested in the faithful death of Jesus Christ.

2. Acts 15:1–30. The Jerusalem Council is presented as a response to a dispute at Antioch, which takes place when visiting Judeans insist on circumcision as essential for salvation. Paul and Barnabas, as commissioners from Antioch, report on their mission among the gentiles and are opposed by believers from among the Pharisees. Two speeches are recorded. Peter's speech (15:5–11) serves to link the council to his previous vision at Joppa and his baptism of Cornelius (10:1–11:18) and to make him rather than Paul the precedent-setter for the mission to the gentiles. James' speech (15:13–21), citing Scripture, represents a compromise: no demand that gentiles be circumcised but adherence to the "apostolic decree." A letter embodying the compromise is then drafted for the church at Antioch, which in turn receives it with joy.

The council represents a critical turning point in the Acts narrative since the focus shifts from Peter to Paul, from Jerusalem to Ephesus, the Grecian cities, and Rome. The shift is a smooth, not an abrupt one. Continuity is maintained, and the compromise signals that the law continues to have significance for the lives of both Jewish and gentile Christians.

Bibliography

Achtemeier, P. J. 1987. *The Quest for Unity in the New Testament: A Study in Paul and Acts.* Philadelphia.

Caird, G. B. 1955. *The Apostolic Age.* London.

Haenchen, E. 1971. *The Acts of the Apostles: A Commentary.* Philadelphia.

Hengel, M. 1986. *Acts and the History of Earliest Christianity.* Philadelphia.

Jewett, R. 1979. *A Chronology of Paul's Life.* Philadelphia.

Knox, J. 1950. *Chapters in the Life of Paul.* New York.

Lake, K. 1933. The Chronology of Acts. Vol. 5, pp. 445–74 in *The Beginnings of Christianity.* London.

Lightfoot, J. B. 1914. *The Epistle to the Galatians.* London.

Lüdemann, G. 1984. *Paul, the Apostle: Studies in Chronology.* Philadelphia.

Weiss, J. 1959. *A History of the Period A.D. 30–150.* Vol. 1 in *Earliest Christianity.* Repr. New York.

CHARLES B. COUSAR

JERUSHA (PERSON) [Heb *yĕrûšāʾ*]. Var. JERUSHAH. Mother of Jotham, King of Judah (2 Kgs 15:33 = 2 Chr 27:1). Her name means "the inherited one" (Stamm 1967: 327). According to Jotham's regnal formula, Jerusha was the daughter of Zadok. Although the Lucianic text adds that she was "from Jerusalem," the Masoretic Text gives no place of origin for her father. This silence may indicate Zadok was well known to the readers (i.e., from the priestly line in Jerusalem). However, not all Judean regnal formulas identify the father's home (cf. Maacah, Azubah, and Abi). The absence of Zadok's home in the MT may simply reflect the writer's faulty source materials. The account in Chronicles preserves a variant spelling of Jerusha's name (Heb *yĕrûšâ*). See also JOTHAM; QUEEN; ZADOK.

Bibliography

Stamm, J. J. 1967. Hebräische Frauennamen. *VTSup* 16: 327.

LINDA S. SCHEARING

JESHAIAH (PERSON) [Heb *yĕšaʿyāh*]. Six individuals in the OT bear this name which may also be rendered "Isaiah" and means "Yahweh has saved." This name also appears in a Hebrew inscription from Palestine (Diringer 1934: 209), and it should be compared with *Ia-še-ʾ-ia-a-ma* (Tallqvist 1905: 68) from Babylon in the time of Cyrus (see Coogan 1976: 52–53 on *ia-a-ma* as the Babylonian equivalent of final *yhw* in Hebrew personal names). It is rendered variously in Gk: in 1 Esdr 8:33 (see #4 below) *Iesias* (LXX^{A} *Iessias*) and in 1 Esdr 8:47 (see #5 below) *Osaias.*

1. The second son of Hananiah the son of Zerubbabel named in 1 Chr 3:21 in a list of the descendants of David.

2. The third of six musicians of the family of Jeduthun named in 1 Chr 25:3 in the context of the Chronicler's presentation of the twenty-four divisions of the singers (1 Chr 25:1–8). In the subsequent list of the divisions by lot (1 Chr 25:9–31), Jeshaiah and his family are accorded the status of eighth among the twenty-four.

3. The son of Rehabiah (1 Chr 26:25) and a member of the levitical family responsible for the care of the "dedicated gifts"—here the spoils of war (see esp. vv 26–27)—in the temple treasuries.

4. Jeshaiah the son of Athaliah is named in Ezra 8:7 (= 1 Esdr 8:33) as the head of the lay family of Elam who returned from Babylon with Ezra. A considerably larger contingent of this family had returned earlier with Zerubbabel (cf. Ezra 2:7; Neh 7:12).

5. A Levite recruited from Casiphia to join Ezra in his return to Jerusalem (Ezra 8:19 = 1 Esdr 8:47). The designation "of the sons of Merari" is curious, since the Levites mentioned in the previous verse would also have been Merarites, as Mahli was a son of Merari (e.g., 1 Chr 6:4—Eng 6:19). Thus there is no evident distinction between these two groups in the text as it stands. 1 Esdr 8:47, however, reads *ʾek tōn uiōn Xanounaiou* which might represent Heb *kĕnānî,* Chenani of Neh 9:4 (Rudolph *Esra und Nehemia* HAT, 81).

6. An ancestor of Sallu, the head of a Benjaminite clan who lived in Jerusalem at the time of Nehemiah (Neh 11:7; he is not named in the parallel genealogy in 1 Chr 9:7–9, which is set in the time immediately following Zerubbabel's return). It may be that this genealogy derives from the time of Nehemiah (Clines *Ezra, Nehemiah, Esther* NCBC, 212, following Rudolph *Esra und Nehemia* HAT, 185), though it has also been proposed that it is preexilic (Kellermann 1966).

Bibliography

Coogan, M. D. 1976. *West Semitic Personal Names in the Murašû Documents.* HSM 7. Missoula, MT.

Diringer, D. 1934. *Le Iscrizioni antico-Ebraiche Palestinesi.* Florence.

Kellerman, U. 1966. Die Listen in Nehemia 11 eine Dokumentation aus den letzten Jahren des reiches Juda? *ZPDV* 82: 209ff.

Tallqvist, K. L. 1905. *Neubabylonisches Namenbuch zu den Geschaeftsurkunden aus der Zeit des Šamaššumukin bis Xerxes.* Acta Societatis Scientarum Fennicae 32/2. Leipzig.

J. S. Rogers

JESHANAH (PLACE) [Heb *yĕšānâ*]. A town named in the Chronicler's account of the defeat of the N Israelite king Jeroboam I by the S Judean king Abijah. Jeshanah is mentioned with Bethel and Ephron as cities which Abijah captured (2 Chr 13:19). Albright (1922: 125–26) identified the site as modern Burj el-Isāneh (M.R. 174156), near Bethel and 17 miles N of Jerusalem (McCarter *1 Samuel* AB, 146); that is, on the border between Israel and Judah following the division of the kingdom. The RSV emends the place called "Shen" (Heb "the Crag") in the MT of 1 Sam 7:12 to read "Jeshanah" on the basis of the Targum, which has *yšn,* and the LXX, which has *tēs palaias* (like the Heb *yĕšānâ,* a name meaning "the old [place]"). The story in 1 Samuel concerns the defeat of the Philistines at Mizpah and Ebenezer, both in this same area. Josephus (*Ant* 14.15.12) also mentions an "Isanas" as the headquarters of the general Pappas who was defeated there by Herod the Great.

Bibliography

Albright, W. F. 1922. Ophrah and Ephraim. *AASOR* 4: 124–33.

Jeffries M. Hamilton

JESHARELAH (PERSON) [Heb *yĕśar᾽ēlâ*]. See ASHARELAH (PERSON).

JESHEBEAB (PERSON) [Heb *yešebĕ᾽āb*]. A priest who received the fourteenth position in the priestly order of the Temple during David's reign (1 Chr 24:13). 1 Chronicles 24 is the only place where Jeshebeab appears in the OT. Therefore, an evaluation of the historical reliability of his appearance depends upon the literary context of 1 Chr 24:1–19. See GAMUL. However, the stylistic characteristics seem to link the list to the time of the composition of Chronicles. Jeshebeab may represent a Judean individual or priestly family in the late Persian period that the Chronicler has retrojected into the reign of David.

John W. Wright

JESHER (PERSON) [Heb *yēšer*]. A son of Caleb listed in the genealogy of Judah (1 Chr 2:18).

H. C. Lo

JESHIMON (PLACE) [Heb *yĕšîmôn*]. A "desert" or "wasteland"; used in the OT for both desert areas in general (Deut 32:10; Isa 43:19, 20; Psalms 68:7; 78:40; 106:14; 107:4) and specific locations (Num 21:20; 23:28; 1 Sam 23:19, 24; 26:1, 3).

1. The rugged barren band of land parallel to the Dead Sea in the E Judean hill country, also referred to as the Judean Wilderness (Baly and Tushingham 1971: 12, 112; Maps 20:E3, XIII:C6; *MABL:* 20, Map 3), though it has also been identified more specifically with the area NW of the Dead Sea (*IDB* 2: 245). OT sites near Jeshimon included the hill of Hachilah (1 Sam 23:19; 26:1, 3) and the wilderness of Maon (1 Sam 23:24). Because of the rapid descent to the Dead Sea and the extremely limited annual rainfall, Jeshimon was "a desolate and dangerous region" (Baly 1987: 52). This combination of characteristics also made it a place of refuge for those who sought protection: Jeshimon provided sanctuary for David as he attempted to evade Saul (1 Sam 23:19, 24; 26:1, 3).

2. A wasteland located N and E of the Dead Sea (*IDB* 2: 245) that could be seen from the top of Mt. Pisgah (Num 21:20) and Mt. Peor (Num 23:28). Beth-jeshimoth (Num 33:49), meaning "house of waste lands," was probably located in this region, since the name is descriptive of the type of soil in the area around the site (*LBHG,* 109). Jeshimon was perhaps traversed by "the way of Beth-jeshimoth" (Josh 12:3), one of three major roads that ascended out of the Jordan valley to the highlands of the Transjordan (*LBHG,* 61–62).

Bibliography

Baly, D. 1987. *Basic Biblical Geography.* Philadelphia.

Baly, D., and Tushingham, A. D. 1971. *Atlas of the Biblical World.* New York.

LaMoine F. DeVries

JESHISHAI (PERSON) [Heb *yĕšîšay*]. A Gadite mentioned only in 1 Chr 5:14. His name probably is cognate with the Hebrew adjective *yāšîš* ("aged, decrepit") and may have meant "venerable." Neither Jeshishai nor the others named in the Chronicler's genealogy for Gad (1 Chr 5:11–17) appear in other lists of Gadites (Gen 46:16; Num 26:15–18; 1 Chr 12:9–16—Eng 12:8–15).

M. Patrick Graham

JESHOHAIAH (PERSON) [Heb *yešôḥāyāh*]. A descendant of Simeon (1 Chr 4:36), described as one of the "princes in their families" (1 Chr 4:38). The name may mean "humbled by Yahweh." In the LXX the name appears as *Iasouia* (*Isuaia* in the Vg). The name Jeshohaiah, along with the names of the other Simeonite princes, is not found in any of the genealogies assigned to this patriarch. Nevertheless, in view of 1 Chr 4:42, Jeshohaiah and the others were probably part of the tribe of Simeon (Williamson *Chronicles* NCBC, 62).

Craig A. Evans

JESHUA (PERSON) [Heb *yēšûaᶜ*]. Var. JOSHUA. A common personal name associated with several figures, especially in the postexilic period.

1. A priest allotted the ninth priestly course at the time of David (1 Chr 24:11); possibly the ancestor of the house of Jeshua in Ezra 2:36 (= Neh 7:39 = 1 Esdr 5:24).

2. A priest or a Levite assisting a leading Levite with distributing temple offerings to priests in their towns in the aftermath of Hezekiah's Passover and reforms (2 Chr 31:15).

3. An alternate spelling for Joshua son of Nun in Neh 8:17. Neh 8:17 recalls this successor of Moses during the celebration of the Feast of Booths by the returning Judeans in Ezra-Nehemiah, possibly in order to link this occasion with the covenant renewal ceremony in Joshua 24 (Blenkinsopp *Ezra-Nehemiah* OTL, 292).

4. A name designating a family ("children of Jeshua") who returned from exile in the wave led by Zerubbabel and Jeshua son of Jehozadak (Ezra 2:6 = Neh 7:11 = 1 Esdr 5:11). Ezra-Nehemiah implies that this return followed directly Cyrus' declaration. Historical reconstruction indicates that the return occurred later, during Darius' reign (ca. 522 B.C.E.). This family is connected with another clan, Pahath-moab. Syntactical ambiguity in the text prevents one from ascertaining the precise nature of this connection. The RSV resolves the ambiguity by translating: "The sons of Pahath-moab, namely the sons of Jeshua and Joab" (Ezra 2:6). Jeshua is also related to Joab (Ezra 2:6 = Neh 7:11 = 1 Esdr 5:11). Together these families comprise the largest unit among the returning exiles (2812 according to Ezra 2:6 and 1 Esdr 5:11; 2818 according to Neh 7:11).

5. Head of a Levite family mentioned first among the few Levites (seventy-four) in the list of returned exiles (Ezra 2:40 = Neh 7:43 = 1 Esdr 5:26). He may be the Jeshua supervising the construction of the Temple (Ezra 3:9 = 1 Esdr 5:56—Eng 5:58). Presuming that the same individual is intended in a number of references, we can surmise that this Jeshua must have been prominent in the postexilic era. He appears in several significant events in Ezra-Nehemiah: as one of the Levites who help Ezra explicate the Torah during the great assembly (Neh 8:7 = 1 Esdr 9:48), as one of the leaders of community prayer (Neh 9:4–5), and as one of the signatories to the pledge (Neh 10:9, where he is identified as son of Azaniah). The name recurs also in the recapitulation of the names of leading Levites (Neh 12:8, 24).

Jeshua appears often with Kadmiel, Bani, and Hodaviah, although the nature of their relation remains unclear. A slight emendation of Neh 9:4 opens the possibility that the latter three were Jeshua's sons (see Williamson *Ezra, Nehemiah* WBC, 26). Possibly he was also the father of Ezer, a ruler of Mizpah, who helped build the wall (Neh 3:19).

6. Jeshua son of Jehozadak. The leading priest in the early Second Temple Period (especially 520–515 B.C.E.), who supervised the building of the temple and the reestablishment of religious and political life in Judah after the exile. Father of Joiakim (Neh 12:10).

Jeshua son of Jehozadak is named "Joshua" in Haggai and Zechariah (e.g., Hag 1:1) and "Jeshua" in Ezra-Nehemiah (e.g., Ezra 2:1). According to Haggai, he was instrumental in building the Second Temple (516 B.C.E.). Zechariah's visions describe ceremonies that purify Jeshua and empower him with certain emblems of authority and prerogatives previously reserved for kings. Ezra-Nehemiah and the parallels in 1 Esdras portray Jeshua as one of the leaders of the return from exile and attribute to him an important role in building the altar, restoring cultic practices, and initiating the building of the temple. Sir 49:12 also connects him with the restoration of the temple.

Surprisingly, given his outstanding priestly role, Jeshua never appears in any of Chronicles' genealogies. His father Jehozadak's genealogy (1 Chr 5:27–41—Eng 6:1–15), however, traces the prominent priestly line which includes Seriah (who was slaughtered by the Babylonians; see 2 Kgs 25:18–21), through Eleazar to Aaron. Jehozadak himself was exiled to Babylon by Nebuchadnezzar. Jeshua was presumably born in Babylon and came to Judah with Zerubbabel and a large contingent of Judeans (Ezra 2 = Neh 7 = 1 Esdr 5) shortly after Darius 1 ascended to the Persian throne (522 B.C.E.). The similarities between Jehozadak's genealogy (1 Chr 5:27–41—Eng 6:1–15) and Ezra's pedigree (Ezra 7:1–5) suggest that Jeshua and Ezra were close kinsmen, but extant biblical sources do not link their names (an omission especially striking in Ezra-Nehemiah).

a. Jeshua's Role. Haggai and Zechariah refer eight times to Jeshua son of Jehozadak the high priest (literally "the great priest")—a title relatively rare in the Hebrew Bible. References to (anonymous) high priests appear in Numbers and Joshua in connection with future cities of refuge. Only two individuals are so designated in preexilic Judah: Jehoiada (2 Kgs 12:11—Eng 12:10) and Hilkiah (2 Kings 22 and 2 Chronicles 34). Although Hilkiah was important and the one responsible for the discovery of the book of the Torah (621 B.C.E.), he nevertheless was subordinate to his king, Josiah.

Jeshua clearly exemplifies a new role for high priests. No preexilic high priest possesses his power and prominence. Biblical sources attach to Jeshua unprecedented religious and civil authority and signal a redefinition of spheres of control. With Jeshua, a diarchic structure of a (high) priest and (Davidic) governor replaces a preexilic subordination of priesthood to royalty. Jeshua's elevation initiates a theocratic authority that will continue to dominate much of the Second Temple period until 70 C.E.

Reasons for the extended powers of Jeshua as high priest can be sought in the radically changed conditions under Persian control. The Judean community urgently needed to restructure religious and political life. The trauma of captivity and the new circumstances of semi-autonomy without a local, indigenous monarchy called for new measures. It became necessary, for example, to reestablish a ritually proper cult after defilement by destruction and exile. Jeshua figures prominently in the resolution of these problems.

Jeshua, together with Zerubbabel, provided the necessary leadership for building the Temple in Jerusalem and restoring the cult (e.g., Ezra 3). The Temple in Jerusalem, no longer overshadowed by a local palace, became the economic—not merely cultic—center. It has been postulated therefore that Jeshua, as high priest, controlled internal fiscal matters for the province of Judah, whereas the governor Zerubbabel's role was more clearly defined by obligations to Persia (Meyers *Haggai, Zechariah* AB, 220–21).

b. Jeshua According to Haggai. Haggai presumes a pattern of diarchic leadership and addresses Jeshua and

Zerubbabel almost always together, each with his full title ("Joshua son of Jehozadak the high priest" Hag 1:1). He urges them (and the rest of the people) to build the Temple and have courage and notes their responsiveness. The address to Zerubbabel alone at the end of Haggai (Hag 2:21) could imply, however, that Haggai considered him relatively more important than Jeshua.

c. Jeshua According to Zechariah. Whereas Haggai presumes a diarchic structure, Zechariah articulates and grounds this new pattern theologically and pragmatically. Zechariah uses symbolism, visions, and oracles, some of which depict the purification and crowning of Jeshua. Zechariah 3 envisions Jeshua in a divine assembly where his filthy garments are replaced through divine command. Yahweh removes his transgression and a purified headgear is placed upon his head. This ceremony expresses a divine mechanism that permits the priesthood in general and Jeshua as high priest in particular to resume the functions of their holy office after the contamination of the exile (cf. a different process in Ezek 44:15, where some priests have remained faithful and hence ritually pure). Oracles develop the vision by bestowing upon the newly purified Jeshua further responsibilities, some of which had hitherto been royal prerogatives (e.g., an expanded role in administering justice, Zech 3:7). Jeshua and his fellow priests are also promised access to the heavenly court, a privilege normally associated with prophets (Meyers *Haggai-Zechariah* AB, 190–99). The Davidic ruler is not eliminated, but the power spheres have been redefined. Unprecedented authority is bestowed upon the priest and a theocratic form of government receives its imprimatur.

Another vision depicts two anointed (Zech 4:1–14, esp. 14), one of whom is presumably Jeshua and the other Zerubbabel, reiterating the diarchic pattern of Haggai.

Jeshua's investiture with royal emblems are proclaimed in an oracle. Zechariah is instructed by God to crown Jeshua (Zech 6:9–15) and to announce that the priest will have a seat besides that of a Davidic descendant. Royal imagery bestowed on Jeshua is so startling that many scholars have concluded that Zerubbabel, not Jeshua, had originally been named in the text to be replaced by Jeshua at a later point because of controversies concerning Zerubbabel. The received text, however, explicitly names Jeshua. Diarchic understanding of Judahite rule characterizes Zechariah. The fact that Jeshua is vested with great authority throughout this book eliminates the need to emend the text (Meyers *Haggai-Zechariah* AB, 351–52).

d. Jeshua According to Ezra-Nehemiah. Ezra-Nehemiah provides the most detailed narrative concerning actual (in contrast with Zechariah's symbolic) activities attributed to Jeshua. In Ezra-Nehemiah, Jeshua son of Jehozadak is a priest (not called high priest) who works in close partnership with Zerubbabel. Both men (together with nine others in Ezra 2:1 and ten in Neh 7:7) head the list of returnees. Together with members of the community they build the altar and establish the cult (Ezra 3). In the seventh month after their arrival (Ezra-Nehemiah does not specify the year), Jeshua and his brothers the priests and Zerubbabel and his brothers (presumably all nonpriestly returned exiles) build the altar and reestablish sacrifices and cultic procedures. This one occasion when Jeshua's name precedes Zerubbabel's in Ezra-Nehemiah suggests that Jeshua had the greater role in restoring the cult. In the second year after their arrival, Zerubbabel, Jeshua, and the rest of the community establish the foundations of the temple itself and celebrate the occasion (Ezra 3:8–13). Ezra-Nehemiah portrays Zerubbabel and Jeshua as co-workers, jointly involved in all subsequent activities, including the rejection of the adversaries' offer to help (Ezra 4:3). At a later point, both Zerubbabel and Jeshua respond to the exhortations of Haggai and Zechariah and resume building activities (Ezra 5:2). Neither is named in the subsequent dedication of the Temple.

e. Jeshua According to 1 Esdras. Although 1 Esdras does not differ markedly from Ezra-Nehemiah in its depiction of Jeshua, the great prominence accorded Zerubbabel in 1 Esdras serves to eclipse Jeshua's role in the events. By adding to Zerubbabel's role, 1 Esdras in fact diminishes Jeshua's importance in the restoration.

f. Conclusion. The biblical texts largely suggest parity in terms of significance between Jeshua the priest (or high priest) and Zerubbabel. A creative adaptation in the postexilic era has resulted in placing unprecedented power in the hands of the priests (or high priests). Jeshua seems to be the key figure in this transformation, having become an equal or perhaps even the superior partner in the actual leadership of the postexilic community.

Bibliography

Eskenazi, T. C. 1988. *In An Age of Prose: A Literary Approach to Ezra-Nehemiah.* SBLMS 36. Atlanta.

Japhet, S. 1982. Sheshbazzar and Zerubbabel—Against the Background of the Historical and Religious Tendencies of Ezra-Nehemiah. *ZAW* 94: 6–98.

TAMARA C. ESKENAZI

JESHUA (PLACE) [Heb *yēšûaʿ*]. A settlement in S Judah listed among the villages occupied by those returning from exile in Babylon (Neh 11:26). Its name appears to be related to the noun *yěšûʿāh* ("help," "salvation," "prosperity"), perhaps meaning "prosperous" town. There is general agreement that the list in Neh 11:25–36 is derived from an official document of the postexilic period (see Myers *Ezra, Nehemiah* AB, 187). If this list follows geographical order, Jeshua should be found in the vicinity of Ziklag and En-rimmon, both of which are located in the Negeb district of the tribal territory of Judah (Josh 15:31–32). This geographical hint and a similarity between the ancient and modern names has led to a tentative identification with Tell es-Saweh (Aharoni *LBHG,* 379), located approximately 19 km E and slightly N of Beer-sheba (M.R. 149076). However, it is not yet known whether this site was occupied during the postexilic period.

WADE R. KOTTER

JESHURUN [Heb *yešurûn*]. A poetic reference to Israel, either as people or place. In Deut 32:15, Jeshurun is the complacent people who provoke God to jealousy, in Deut 33:5 it is the place where the Lord becomes king before all the assembled tribes, and in Deut 33:26, it is used as a vocative to call the people of Israel to notice their God who "rides through the heavens" to their help. In

Isaiah 44:2 it is found in *parallelismus membrorum* to Jacob; both terms are used to refer to the servant chosen by God. Coming from the root *yšr* (be straight, right), the term is an ideal reference to Israel meaning "the upright one," although its form as either a diminutive or a denominative is uncertain. The relationship between the words Jeshurun and Israel is debated. Wächter (1971: 58–64) suggests that Jeshurun is a reminiscence of the name *yišarʾēl,* which he posits as the original form of *yiśrāʾēl* (Israel). With the domination of the Ephraimite tribes in the central-Palestinian highlands, the pronunciation of *yišarʾēl* was changed to *yiśrāʾēl* because the Ephraimites confused *šin* with *śin.* Seebass (1977: 161) argues that Jeshurun originally indicated a non-Israelite neighbor associated with Judah. Jeshurun was then incorporated into the tribal league as a substitute for the tribe of Simeon, a tribal name that does not appear in the Blessing of Moses in Deuteronomy 33. Mendenhall (*IDB* 2: 868) understands Jeshurun to be a hypocorism from the word Israel, a thesis supported by the LXX rendering *ēgapēmenos.* The MT references indicate that Jeshurun was acceptable as an alternative name for Jacob and Israel, but its infrequency, as well as the LXX translation with the participle instead of by transliteration, indicate that it was rare in popular usage.

Bibliography

Seebass, H. 1977. Die Stämmeliste von Dtn xxxiii. *VT* 27: 158–69.

Wächter, L. 1971. Israel und Jeschurun. Pp. 58–64 in *Schalom: Studien zu Glaube und Geschichte Israels,* ed. K.-H. Bernhardt. Arbeiten zur Theologie. Stuttgart.

SHARON PACE JEANSONNE

JESIMIEL (PERSON) [Heb *yĕśîmiʾēl*]. Descendant of Simon (1 Chr 4:36), described as one of the "princes in their families" (1 Chr 4:38). The name may mean "God sets." In the LXX, the name appears as *Ismael* (not to be confused with Ishmael). See Williamson *Chronicles* NCBC, 62.

CRAIG A. EVANS

JESSE (PERSON) [Heb *yišay*]. The father of David, a Bethlehemite from the tribe of Judah (1 Sam 16:1). The name is normally written as *yišay* except in 1 Chr 2:13 where it is inexplicably found in the form *ʾîšay.* Jesse was the son of Obed and grandson of Boaz (Ruth 4:17, 22; 1 Chr 2:12; Matt 1:5–6; Luke 3:32). In 1 Sam 16:1–23, Jesse is said to have had eight sons with David the youngest. 1 Sam 17:12 also explicitly states that there were eight sons of David. However, 1 Chr 2:13–16 only records seven sons and two daughters, Zeruiah and Abigail. The Syriac version of 1 Chr 2:14 inserts Elihu as the seventh son with David as the eighth. Elihu is not mentioned in the list of sons in 1 Sam 16:1–23, but is mentioned as a brother of David in 1 Chr 27:18 (LXX *Eliab*). There is also some confusion over the paternity of Abigail, who is described as the daughter of Nahash in 2 Sam 17:25. The position of David as the seventh son in Chronicles probably reflects the significance of David in the Chronicler's theology.

Jesse is portrayed mainly in a passive role as the father of the future king of Israel. He appears when Samuel visited Bethlehem to secretly anoint David as king in place of Saul but remains in the background except to send for David, who was among the sheep, after the other sons had been rejected (1 Sam 16:1–13). Immediately after this, Saul sent messengers to Jesse requesting that David be sent to the court to help control his fits of depression with music. Jesse then dispatched bread, wine, and a kid along with David to the king (1 Sam 16:14–23). It is again striking that Jesse does not directly reply in speech to Saul's request for David to remain permanently at the court. David's second introduction to the court of Saul comes when Jesse sent him to his three elder brothers who were serving with Saul's army in the valley of Elah against the Philistines (1 Sam 17:12–18). This second introduction of David to the court of Saul which appears to ignore the previous passage poses numerous difficulties. Furthermore, 1 Sam 17:12–31 is missing from LXXB but is found in LXXA. McCarter (*1 Samuel* AB) and Klein (*1 Samuel* WBC) believe that the shorter version of LXXB is original and has been expanded in the MT. Jesse is described in the MT with the peculiar expression *zāqēn bāʾ baʾ ănāšîm* "old and advanced in years" (RSV, 17:12). LXXL and Syriac presuppose *zāqēn bašānîm,* "old in years," which McCarter (*1 Samuel* AB, 301) prefers. Jesse is further described in MT as "this Ephrathite of Bethlehem in Judah" (RSV "an Ephrathite"). Ephrathah and Bethlehem are listed in the genealogy of Caleb (1 Chr 2:50–51). However, the phrase "an Ephrathite of Bethlehem in Judah" draws an important allusion to the book of Ruth and its Moabite connections (Ruth 1:2; 4:11). The Moabite ancestry of David is made explicit in Ruth 4:17–22 and 1 Chr 2:11–12. Interestingly, David is said to have taken his father and mother to Moab for safety while he is being pursued by Saul, although Jesse is not explicitly named (1 Sam 22:3–6).

The phrase "the son of Jesse" is used pejoratively on a number of occasions, particularly when Saul contemptuously refuses to name David explicitly as being disloyal (1 Sam 20:27, 30–31; 22:7–8), when Doeg the Edomite accuses Ahimelech of Nob of inquiring of Yahweh for him (1 Sam 22:9), when Nabal rejects the thinly veiled threat for protection money (1 Sam 25:10), or when the N tribes break from the S (1 Kgs 12:16). However, the theological centrality of David in the work of the Chronicler means that the phrase "David the son of Jesse" is used in a positive sense in 1 Chr 10:14 and 29:26 (cf. Acts 13:22).

The phrase "there shall come forth a shoot from the stump of Jesse" (Isa 11:1) is usually interpreted as a sign of hope that the Davidic dynasty will be restored. "The stump of Jesse" is taken to refer to the loss of the Davidic kingship in 587 B.C.E. rather than some previous military defeat (Clements 1980: 122; Kaiser 1983: 254). Although it is probable that the passage originally refers to the hope for a restitution of kingship, albeit in ideal terms, the phrase later is interpreted in a Messianic sense. The imagery may well derive from royal ideology in which the king was portrayed as the symbol of fertility (cf. Psalm 72). A similar image is contained in Isa 11:10 which offers "the root of Jesse" as a sign of universal hope (cf. Rom 15:12). Clements (1980: 125) interprets this verse as a postexilic addition which offers a new and different interpretation of 11:1. He also sees it as an attempt to link the promises of 11:1 and 11:12. Kaiser (1983: 262–63) leaves open the question of whether or not the phrase is a messianic designation or a reference to a new dynasty. Barth (1977: 59) argues that it is a collective term referring to the postexilic community.

Bibliography

Barth, H. 1977. *Die Jesaja-Worte der Josiazeit.* Neukirchen-Vluyn.
Clements, R. E. 1980. *Isaiah 1–39.* Grand Rapids.
Kaiser, O. 1983. *Isaiah 1–12. A Commentary.* London.

KEITH W. WHITELAM

JESUS (PERSON) [Gk *Iēsous*]. Several persons mentioned in the Bible bear this name, which is a Greek form of Joshua (Heb *yĕhôšûaʿ*; cf. the Gk of Luke 3:29; Acts 7:45; Heb 4:8). One of these is the son of Sirach, who wrote the deuterocanonical book of Ecclesiasticus; see WISDOM OF BEN-SIRA. The name "Jesus" also occurs as a surname of JUSTUS, a co-worker of Paul mentioned in Col 4:11. But, of course, by far the most frequent occurrence of the name is used in conjunction with Jesus of Nazareth, also known as Jesus Christ, who appears throughout the NT and is venerated as the central figure within Christianity. This entry discusses various aspects of this important biblical figure. It is comprised of five separate articles. The first is a broad overview of the figure of Jesus Christ, particularly assessing him as a historical figure who lived 2,000 years ago. The second explores an important issue within NT scholarship over the past two centuries: namely, the proper methodology to be used in attempting to recover this actual historical figure from the NT sources, whose interests were not entirely—or perhaps even primarily—historical. Related to this, the third article surveys scholarly attempts to cull from the NT the actual words (or *ipsissima verba*) spoken by the historical Jesus. The fourth article surveys broadly the teaching of Jesus of Nazareth, i.e. the message he proclaimed to his contemporaries. The fifth article focuses more on Jesus Christ as a religious figure, particularly on how he became the object of worship in the early Christian Church.

JESUS CHRIST

"Jesus Christ" is a composite name made up of the personal name "Jesus" (from Gk *Iēsous,* which transliterates Heb/Aram *yēšû(a)ʿ*, a late form of Hebrew *yĕhôšûaʿ*, the meaning of which is "YHWH is salvation" or "YHWH saves/has saved") and the title, assimilated in early Christianity to Jesus as a name, "Christ" (from Gk *Christos,* which translates Heb *māšîaḥ* and Aram *mĕšîḥāʾ*, signifying "anointed" and referring in the context of eschatological expectation to the royal "son of David"). The name "Jesus Christ" thus binds together the historic figure Jesus with the messianic role and status that early Christian faith attributed to him. In Jesus' own lifetime, his name, since it was common in Israel, called for a specifier: "Jesus the Galilean" (Matt 26:69; cf. 21:11), or, more often, "Jesus of Nazareth" or "Jesus the Nazarean."

This article treats Jesus of Nazareth as a figure of history, asking what can be known of his career, its purposes and outcome, by historical investigation. The question breaks down into parts. First, what are the available data on Jesus and what resources do we have for construing the data in an informed and reasonable way? Second, in what sociohistorical context did Jesus live and act? Third, what was the character of his encounter with the Israel of his time? What was the point of his proclamation of the reign of God, his preaching, and his symbolic actions? What provoked the conflicts that led to his arrest and execution? How did he himself understand and react to these conflicts? How and why did Jesus die? Fourth, what influence did Jesus have on the rise of the earliest Christian community and its life? These questions are the basis of the following outline:

A. Data on Jesus
   1. Canonical Gospels
   2. The Rest of the New Testament
   3. Data from Noncanonical Sources
   4. Indices to Historicity and to Nonhistoricity
B. Sociohistorical Context
C. The History of Jesus
   1. Beginnings
   2. The Proclamation and Its Meaning
   3. Jesus' Public Behavior
   4. The Teaching of Jesus
   5. The Identity and Destiny of Jesus
   6. Why and How Jesus Died
   7. The Easter Experience of the Disciples

A. Data on Jesus

1. Canonical Gospels. Jesus died *ca.* A.D. 30; the gospels of Matthew, Mark, Luke, and John came into being from 30 to 60 odd years later (i.e., from the '60s to the '90s of the 1st century). In the period before the finished composition of complete gospel narratives there certainly were oral traditions that were to provide the substance of the gospel literature, and perhaps some of these traditions circulated in written form as well. (See FORM CRITICISM; SOURCE CRITICISM.) Early practitioners of form criticism tended to attribute a direct and decisive relevance of their discipline to the historical appreciation of the data of oral tradition. More recently, sober critique has been brought to bear on classical NT form criticism, dismantling its ideological biases and salvaging its real analytic potential. Gradually the limited contribution of form criticism to judgments of historicity has found wide recognition.

The most basic and far-reaching issue connected with form criticism had been substantially acknowledged and clarified early in the 20th century; it came to be called the "kerygmatic" conditioning of both oral traditions and written gospels. *Kerygma* means "proclamation" and in the NT refers especially to the act of proclaiming salvation or to the content of the proclamation of salvation or to both. The context evoked by "kerygma" is accordingly the appeal for faith. The adjective "kerygmatic" has long been used in a wide sense to allude to the faith dimension that pervades the gospel literature. Born of faith, these writings solicited or supported faith and offered instruction in faith.

There is probably no non-kerygmatic writing in the gospels. In all probability, that is, nothing or virtually nothing in the gospel narratives was narrated merely because it happened, for the sole purpose of preserving the historical record. It is sometimes overlooked, however, that this negative ascertainment (gospel texts are not purely historical) by no means justifies the notion that a historical component is foreign to and excluded from the intentions of the originators, transmitters, and editors of the gospel literature. For example, the motive for recounting such symbolic actions of Jesus as the cures and exorcisms, the sending of the twelve, the dining with sinners, the solemn entry into Jerusalem, and the cleansing of the temple is irreducible to "community concerns" of a didactic and paraenetic sort. Other components in narrative intention are certainly discoverable, but these historic symbolic acts were all narrated also because they were acts that belonged in some significant way to the drama of Jesus' career (Trautmann 1980: 404–6). A like point must be made respecting conflict stories (Hultgren 1979: 72–75), Sabbath conflicts (Roloff 1970: 85), and other texts (Riesner 1981: 35–37).

It has often been urged that in earliest Christianity (apart from the composition of the passion story for cultic use) Jesus' career as a whole did not figure in Christian consciousness. The idea of a connected narrative about Jesus was thought to have come into being only with the project of composing the first gospel redaction, usually thought to be that of Mark. This supposition, however, proved liable to critique at three points. First, the memory of Jesus' career could not plausibly be limited to isolated anecdotes. Second, the passion story could not be reduced to an explanatory account of cultic practices (cultic etiology); stylistic analysis related the passion story, rather, to OT historical narratives. Finally, the supposed role of the Markan secrecy motif in bringing the gospel genre into being was entirely conjectural.

As for the story line finally to be found in the Synoptic Gospels, literary criticism (Jeremias 1966: 89–96) suggests that its main development took the form of pushing the beginning of the passion story further and further back. The story first began with the arrest of Jesus in Gethsemane; then, with the solemn entry into Jerusalem; then, with the confession of Jesus as Messiah in the region of Caesarea Philippi (Pesch *Markusevangelium 2* HTKNT, 1–27). This, to be sure, does not mean that the tradition of Jesus' baptism, for example, did not come into being until "the beginning of the story" had been pushed back to that point. What it does mean is that, though individual pericopes presented the whole gospel *in nuce,* the story of Jesus is unlikely ever to have been understood as isolated kerygmatic snapshots entirely unrelated to any story line.

Traditions relaying at least words of Jesus and perhaps also stories of Jesus may well go back to the pre-Easter days of Jesus' public career (Schürmann 1960). The concrete social situation and context *(Sitz im Leben)* for such a formation of tradition would have been the disciples' share in the public functions of Jesus as proclaimer of the reign of God. What was the corresponding social situation and context for the shaping and transmitting of traditions in the post-Easter Jerusalem community? The pioneers of NT form criticism answered by positing various distinct and independent social settings, e.g. baptismal liturgy, eucharistic worship, community instruction, community debates, etc. But the determination of a nexus between particular settings and the crystallization of particular speech forms rarely surpassed educated guesswork. On the other hand, definition of a single setting or *Sitz im Leben* for the Jesus tradition as a whole, though plausible, has proven thus far to be unverifiable.

To many scholars in the first half of the 20th century the systematic transmission of tradition in the earliest church appeared to be precluded by the expectation of an imminent end of history. But in fact there are solid indices in the earliest NT writings that the church was consciously engaged in the transmission of traditions (1 Cor 11:23—cf. 1 Thess 4:1; 1 Cor 11:3; 15:1–11). The tradition of Jesus' words, acts, and destiny appears to have constituted a distinct branch of teaching *(didachē)* parallel to but distinct from and supposed by the moral instruction *(paraenesis)* dispensed in the NT letters. Whether, like that moral instruction, it was authoritatively sponsored by leading figures in the earliest church remains an open question.

The only element of Synoptic criticism supposed here is the acknowledgment of four relatively independent lines of transmission: Markan tradition, logia tradition (Matthew and Luke), special Matthean tradition, and special Lukan tradition. Though the relative independence of Markan tradition and of the logia tradition is sometimes disputed, both appear to be probable (see Pesch *Markusevangelium 1* HTKNT, 63–67; Jeremias 1930 and Dupont 1954 on the Logia tradition).

Even if the relative antiquity of the several gospel redactions were known with certainty, this knowledge would leave still unanswered the question, "in what sequence did such-and-such parallel traditions come into being?" Again, even should literary-historical criticism establish the genetic sequence of parallel texts, this would still leave undecided the issue of historicity respecting the particular words and acts depicted in those texts. On the other hand, the question of the historicity of words and acts can sometimes be settled without a satisfactory prior settlement of any of the questions about the genetic order of the texts.

The origin and development of the Gospel of John poses special problems. This gospel concentrates its claim to authority in the witness of the "beloved disciple" (John 21:20–24; cf. 13:23; 19:26–27; 20:2–9), who is probably to be identified with the anonymous disciple of 1:35–42; 18:15–16. This anonymous disciple, in turn, is perhaps to be identified with John, the son of Zebedee. Beyond these variously probable though uncertain identifications, the origins of the Fourth Gospel remain historically mysterious.

Moreover, though the Johannine gospel tells the story of Jesus in distinctive fashion and affirms this story to be charged with historic truth, the key to the discourses of Jesus, to individual narrative units, and to the total sequence of events is not memory but sustained religious reflection of a high order. What the gospel affirms is not so much the actuality of remembered words and acts as it is the historic truth of Johannine theological themes. When applied to a work of this character, the standard indices to historicity turn out to yield relatively little. Nevertheless, on numerous matters (see below, C.1, 6, 7), the Fourth Gospel clearly seems to have retained significant historical data unavailable in the Synoptic tradition.

2. The Rest of the New Testament. The Acts of the Apostles, the NT letters, and the Johannine apocalypse all contain sayings of the risen Lord, and all these sources presuppose and allude to the story of the earthly Jesus. They nevertheless offer relatively few independent data on him. One saying (probably a Greco-Roman proverb) is attributed to Jesus in Acts 20:35. The other sayings attributed to him are known to us from parallels in the Synoptic Gospels (1 Cor 7:10 = Mark 10:9–12 = Matt 19:6–9; 1 Cor 9:14 = Matt 10:10; 1 Cor 11:24–25 = Luke 22:19–20; Rom 14:14 = Mark 7:15; somewhat less clearly and certainly, 1 Thess 4:16–17 = Matt 24:30–31).

The missionary speeches in Acts include a so-called "historical section" (Acts 2:22; 10:37–39; 13:23–25) in the kerygma. This correlates both with Peter's claim, "we are witnesses of everything he did in the country of the Jews and in Jerusalem" (Acts 10:39), and with the requisite qualification of a candidate to take the place of Judas among the twelve, namely, that he be "one of the men who have accompanied us during all the time that the Lord Jesus went in and out among us" (Acts 1:21). Salvation was seen to issue from the history of Jesus as attested both by the scriptures and by the testimony of eyewitnesses to that history. This view of salvation as coming from the history of Jesus is common also to the pre-Pauline faith formulas conserved in the letters of Paul (Phil 2:6–11; 1 Cor 11:23–25; 15:3–5; Gal 1:4; Rom 1:3–4; 3:25–26; 4:25; 8:34; 10:9).

Though the recounting of Jesus' words and acts is not to be expected in the diverse paraenetic genre of the NT letters, it is nonetheless worth noting that many letters abound with echoes of the gospel tradition.

Paul explicitly affirmed his inheriting of commands from the Lord (1 Cor 7:10); that this signifies his dependence on the Jesus tradition is confirmed by the fact that we find the command in question in Synoptic texts (Mark 10:9–12 = Matt 19:6–9). The attitude toward enemies and persecutors expressed in 1 Thess 5:15; 1 Cor 4:12–13; and Rom 12:14 should be related to Matt 5:10–12 = Luke 6:22–23 and to Matt 5:38–40 = Luke 6:29; for, apart from Jesus, Paul had no predecessor, source, or tradition to draw on for this theme (see, however, Exod 23:4–5 and Prov 25:21–22). Paul's claim to apostolic status (Gal 1:16–17) echoes the words of Jesus to Simon, the "rock" (Matt 16:17–19). Again, the Abba motif in Paul's references to community and personal prayer (Gal 4:6; Rom 8:15) reflects Jesus' distinctive address of God as *ʾabbāʾ* (Mark 14:36 = Matt 26:39, 42 = Luke 22:42; cf. Matt 6:9 = Luke 11:2; Matt 11:25–26 = Luke 10:21; Luke 23:34, 46; John 11:41; 12:27–28, etc.). The historicity of Jesus, born of woman (Gal 4:4), belonging to the race of Abraham (Gal 3:16; Rom 9:5) and the lineage of David (Rom 1:3), living under the Law (Gal 4:4), exercising a ministry to Israel in fulfillment of the promises to the patriarchs (Rom 15:8), and dying on a cross (*passim* in Paul) was as substantial to Pauline as it was to Markan or Lukan theology.

The Letter to the Hebrews repeatedly refers to the earthly Jesus, especially to his willing self-oblation as expiatory offering (Heb 2:15–18; 7:27; 9:14, 25–28). The resurrection was God's answer to Jesus' prayer in Gethsemane (5:7). Psalm 8 found fulfillment in Jesus' having been "for a short time"—i.e., between his coming into the world (10:5–7) and his exaltation (1:3, 13; 9:12)—"lower than the angels" (2:7, 9). The letter also alludes to the detail that Jesus' death took place "outside the gate" of the city (13:12).

In 1 Peter (Maier 1985) there are more than a dozen verbal and motif convergences not only with Synoptic tradition (e.g., the nexus between "seed" and "the word" in 1 Pet 1:23, as in the Synoptic interpretation of the parable of the Sower, Mark 4:14–20 = Matt 13:18–23 = Luke 8:11–15), but also with Johannine tradition (e.g., "believing" despite "not seeing" in 1 Pet 1:2 and John 20:29).

In the Letter of James (Davids 1985) there are roughly 20 probable allusions to sayings of Jesus. A dozen of them derive from the Sermon on the Mount (thus Jas 2:5, 13 reflect the beatitudes of Matt 5:3, 7). Though verbal and motif convergences are usually more suggestive than probative of literary dependence, the high incidence of convergence between the text of James and motifs gathered together in the Sermon on the Mount boosts the probability of the dependence of James on the Jesus tradition to the point of moral certainty.

It should be added that the First Letter of John presupposes the story of Jesus as we find it presented in the Gospel of John. Thus the writer urges without elaboration that his addressees are to live "just as he lived" (1 John 2:6). "Eternal life" is the heart of "what he promised us" (2:25). We know what love is from his laying down his life for us (3:16). He came "in water and in blood" (5:6; see John 19:34–35).

The positive yield of the non-gospel texts of the NT, then, is not a mass of independent data on Jesus, but an assurance that the Jesus tradition, so far from being alien to the other NT writers, was both congenial in principle and integral in fact to their faith. As sequel and support of the controlling proclamation of the kerygma, two branches of teaching took shape in early Christianity: the Jesus tradition and community paraenesis. From the NT letters it appears that from the outset the second of these found its ethos and nourishment in the first.

3. Data from Noncanonical Sources. The fallout in noncanonical tradition from the historic career of Jesus was enormous: gospels (mainly Jewish-Christian and gnostic), homilies, testimonies, liturgies, acts, apocalypses, rabbinic and Islamic traditions, texts in Hebrew, Aramaic, Syriac, Greek, Latin, Coptic, and other languages. Though this tradition is voluminous even in the fragmentary state in which it has survived, only a few short narratives and perhaps a dozen sayings have a serious claim to historical value. They include words such as the following (*Gos. Thom.* 82):

> He that is near me is near the fire;
> he that is far from me is far from the kingdom.

Study of the noncanonical traditions, which began in the late 19th century, gained momentum with the discovery at Nag Hammadi, Egypt, of a complete text of the *Gospel of Thomas,* 114 sayings in a 4th-century Coptic translation probably from Greek. But the hope of having found a mine of independent traditions as old and informative as those of the Synoptic Gospels proved on further analysis to be false.

Plausibly authentic anecdotes and sayings from the noncanonical tradition confirm and supplement historical data from the canonical gospels, but do not furnish good evidence for a different general view of Jesus. The Talmud (*b. Šabb.* 116b) offers a variant in Aramaic of the saying in Matt 5:17, which suggests that behind the Greek words *katalysai* ("to destroy") and *plērōsai* ("to fulfill") of the gospel saying stood the Aramaic words *pĕḥat* ("to diminish" or "take away") and *ʾôsîp* ("to add to"—i.e., "to bring to completion"). Otherwise Talmudic traditions on Jesus are probably late, some even as late as the early Middle Ages (Maier 1978: 127–28) and have no independent historical value.

4. Indices to Historicity and to Nonhistoricity. In forming historical judgments on the data of the gospels there are three possible verdicts: historical, nonhistorical, and suspended judgment. All these verdicts should turn not on general assumptions but on specific evidence. This means that the historian cannot do without concrete indices both to historicity and to nonhistoricity; it also means that the critic should acknowledge that in some instances the issue of historicity remains unresolved.

The indices to historicity are: discontinuity with early Christianity; originality vis-à-vis Palestinian Judaism; multiple attestation (i.e., attestation in relatively independent strands of tradition); multiform attestation (e.g., in narrative material and in sayings material); and correlation with modes of speech characteristic of Jesus (Jeremias 1971: 8–37). Such modes include the use of the divine passive (a circumlocution which for reverential reasons avoids naming God as the subject of an active verb; e.g., the second clause of the macarism "Happy the mourners, for they shall be comforted" is the equivalent of "for God is about to comfort them"); antithetical parallelism (Burney 1925: 83–85); rhythmic patterns in two-beat, three-beat, four-beat, and *qînâ* (dirge) meter (in Aramaic); alliteration, assonance, and play on words (in Aramaic); use of hyperbole and paradox; riddles and parables, especially as exhibiting stylistic and thematic features otherwise known to be characteristic of Jesus; new coinages in connection with "the reign of God"; a distinctive use of "amen" to introduce an emphatic statement; the use of *ʾabbāʾ* in addressing God.

All these indices operate independently of the recovery of historical intentions on the part of the narrator. On occasion, however, it may be possible to ascertain that a given writer means to affirm something precisely as having happened. If in addition it can be shown that the writer is knowledgeable on the matter and free of the intention to mislead, historicity may be inferred. An example is Paul's presentation of the eucharistic words of Jesus in 1 Cor 11:23–25.

Of the indices mentioned above, discontinuity with the transmitting church is regularly the most cogent. It was a clear tendency of the transmitting church to present Jesus as independent of John the Baptizer; therefore, it is highly probable that the tradition of Jesus' seeking the baptism of John is historical. Again, the index of originality vis-à-vis Palestinian Judaism is often cogent of itself, for we have far more extensive and persuasive evidence of Jesus' originality than we do of the originality of the post-Easter Christian community, especially that of the earliest and, in this context, most important community, Jerusalem. The other indices, though not independently cogent, are indispensable in marshaling cumulative and convergent evidence in favor of historicity. Increase in the probability of historicity accrues to data that are coherent with what has already been established as historical by appeal to discontinuity and originality. Here especially multiple attestation, multiform attestation, and stylistic indices are relevant confirmatory factors.

Before leaving the issue of historicity, we should distinguish two kinds of relations of accounts to events—namely, the one-to-one relation and what might be called the generic relation. In gospel reports of responses to Jesus, a solid case can occasionally be made for a one-to-one relation of text to event. In most cases, however, it is neither possible nor necessary to build a case for historicity. The widely varied responses to Jesus depicted in the gospel literature doubtless corresponded in general to the historical reality. It was to be expected in advance that responses to him would vary widely, and it must be assumed in retrospect that they did. The literature supports such expectations and assumptions.

The form critics were the first to recognize clearly that many Synoptic pericopes—especially those that failed to exhibit the inner coherence that would have typified a remembered event, but many other, quite coherent pericopes as well—were not, indeed, simply recorded memories and did not intend a one-to-one relation to a particular event. The gospel literature had been composed, and in this composition Jesus' career had been, in Bultmann's metaphor, "precipitated"—i.e., condensed and presented anew, in the pericopes (Bultmann 1963: 40). But the form critics failed, on the whole, to spell out clearly what this meant for historicity. Instead of fashioning a positive and supple conception of historicity adjusted to this literary insight, they left the impression that historicity itself, and not merely an excessively rigid conception of it, had thereby been put in doubt. A more apt and exact conclusion would be that besides the specific patterns of inference that followed on the indices to historicity, there were generic judgments supported by the typical character of numerous pericopes. The form-critical insight allowed the exegete to recognize that in a few strokes an individual pericope might present the gospel in a nutshell. It should also allow the historian to differentiate between the details, on the one hand, and generic or substantial historicity, on the other.

An example is the story of Zacchaeus the tax collector (Luke 19:1–10). Did there really exist a rich tax collector named Zacchaeus, who, being short, climbed a sycamore tree to catch a glimpse of the charismatic figure Jesus, as he walked along accompanied by a crowd? Did Jesus look up and address Zacchaeus by name and invite himself to table with him? The indices to historicity yield virtually nothing in response to these questions. Nevertheless we have solid evidence elsewhere (e.g., Mark 2:14–16 = Matt 9:9–10 = Luke 5:27–29) of Jesus' appeal to the ostracized tax collectors and publicans of the time. What the Zacchaeus episode adds to this is a further set of indications showing the early Christian community's understanding of how Jesus mounted his initiative toward sinners and of how the sinners reacted to it.

The commonest error respecting nonhistoricity turns on a false analogy. It is the assumption that since discontinuity with the transmitting church establishes historicity, continuity with the transmitting church establishes nonhistoricity. In fact, no conclusion can be legitimately drawn from the mere presence of such continuity. A true index to nonhistoricity is the incompatibility of data under examination either with data established as historical or with solidly grounded historical conclusions. If, for example, the historian were to succeed in recovering the eschatological scheme supposed by words of Jesus on the future, and if according to this scheme there was to be no interval between the vindication/glorification of Jesus and the consummation of history, then gospel tests positing such an interim would be nonhistorical.

Second, a positive index to nonhistoricity is attestation both as a post-Jesus development and as gospel datum. The Christian mission to gentile lands, for example, is attested as a post-Jesus development in Acts 13, but also as foretold by words of Jesus (Mark 13:10 = Matt 24:14; Mark 14:9 = Matt 26:13), foreshadowed by his travels (seemingly but not actually) outside lands inhabited by Jews (Mark 7:24, 31), and grounded on the explicitly universalist prophecy (Luke 24:47) or on the explicitly (Matt 28:19; cf. Acts 1:8; Mark 16:15) or implicitly (John 20:21–22) universalist mandate of the risen Christ. Why was the idea of the gentile mission converted into a gospel datum? It was a tendency of the early Christians to overlook what they did not have the resources to understand (namely, development and its legitimacy) and so to retroject developments to their origins.

Third, linguistic indices to nonhistoricity include the use of words having no Aramaic equivalents, or the use of a vocabulary attested for the early church but not otherwise attested for Jesus (e.g., in Jesus' "explanations" of his parables). This index, to be sure, is not cogent of itself.

If the hypothesis could actually be established, rather than merely posited, that early Christian prophets speaking in the name of the exalted Christ supplied the church with sayings that were finally assimilated to the Synoptic tradition, this might be made to generate concrete indices to nonhistoricity. Thus far, however, the case for this creative role on the part of Christian prophets has not been successfully made; hence, no conclusion along these lines appears to be justified (Hill 1979: 160–85; Aune 1983: 142–45).

B. Sociohistorical Context

Jesus of Nazareth entered upon his public career in the last quarter of a long period of decline in Jewish fortunes—i.e., from the triumph of the Maccabees when public plebiscite endorsed the pretentions to the high priesthood on the part of Simon and his sons (141 B.C.) to the fall of Jerusalem and destruction of the temple under Titus (A.D. 70). That from the Jewish standpoint this was a period of almost unrelieved decline is hardly open to doubt. Its halfway point was marked by the accession to power of Herod, a half-Jew and puppet of Rome, whose long and heartily detested reign was followed by the administrative division of Israel, and ten years thereafter by the imposition of direct Roman administration on Judea. Though initially welcomed, this last change eventually soured. Jerusalem had relapsed into the pre-Maccabean situation of rule by gentiles.

The administrative record of the Roman provincial governors of Judea varied from mediocre to atrocious. The heaviest burden on the Jews, however, was not inept or corrupt administration, but economic hardship and instability. Given a glaring inequality in the distribution of goods and a lack of agricultural land proportionate to a population of half a million, the combination of natural catastrophes (drought, earthquake, epidemic, famine—e.g., the great famine of A.D. 46–47) and oppressive taxation under competing tax systems, secular (Roman) and sacred (Jewish), was ruinous for the class of small landholders who constituted society's center of gravity, the marginal middle class. From this came periodic surges in the number of new poor, emigrants, revolutionaries, bandits, and beggars.

Socioeconomic instability characterized Palestine before, during, and after the time of Jesus. To lower the pressure of social unrest, the powers-that-be periodically lightened the tax burden (*Ant* 15.10.4 §365; 16.2.5 §64; 17.8.4 §205; 17.11.4 §319; 18.4.3 §90; 19.6.3 §299). Herod and his sons created work for the down-and-out by building new cities (*Ant* 18.2.3 §36–38). The basic socioeconomic structures, however, remained. Instability culminated in collapse—i.e., in the brief ascendancy of the socially rootless and the simultaneous outbreak of a disastrous revolt against Rome (A.D. 66–70).

The state of social crisis implicit in the data provided by Josephus is often mirrored in the gospel literature as well. Depressed classes figure prominently in the story. They include the socially insignificant, the poor and hungry, the physically or mentally disabled, and the socioreligious outcasts. Representatives of these groups hover on the edges or stand in the center of scene after scene. Jesus singled out as particularly favored beneficiaries of salvation the poor, the insignificant (including women and children), the heavily burdened, the possessed, the outcast, the blind, deaf, and dumb, the cripples and lepers.

Oppressive economic practices often figured in Jesus' parables, not as objects of reformist critique, but simply as matters of common knowledge, and so illustratively useful (Mark 12:1–11 = Matt 20:1–16 = Luke 16:1–8). Jesus' words and actions bore dramatically on the social scene, but inasmuch as they corresponded to none of the positions on the social order taken in the Israel of his time, they may well have seemed baffling or inadequate or offensive. On the religious parties and sects in the time of Jesus, see JUDAISM (GRECO-ROMAN PERIOD); PHARISEES; SADDUCEES; ESSENES.

C. The History of Jesus

1. Beginnings. Historically the most accessible data on Jesus' beginnings are not the infancy narratives (see MATTHEW, GOSPEL OF; LUKE, GOSPEL OF), but the ties between Jesus and the movement of John the Baptist (or "Baptizer"). John appeared in the wilderness north of the Dead Sea "in the fifteenth year of the reign of Tiberius Caesar" (Luke 3:1); i.e., not earlier than autumn, A.D. 27, nor later than midsummer, 29. His apparel (Mark 1:6 =

Matt 3:4), his manner of life (Matt 3:4b; Matt 11:18 = Luke 7:33), and his message to Israel all evoked the prophets of old (Mark 6:15 = Luke 9:8). John warned his contemporaries that definitive judgment was imminent (Matt 3:10 = Luke 3:9) and, in the face of imminent judgment, summoned them to repentance (Mark 1:4; Matt 3:7–10 = Luke 3:7–9), to the confession of sins (Mark 1:5 = Matt 3:6), and to a ritual act of washing meant to seal the repentance and mark the repentant for acquittal at the judgment about to break out (Mark 1:5 = Matt 3:6; Mark 1:8 = Matt 3:11–12 = Luke 3:16–17).

The mere phenomenon of the return of prophecy in the figure of John pointed, according to Judaic tradition, to the consummation of history. John's message, moreover, radicalized this eschatology, for it made clear that for John the standing religious resources of Israel, such as cultic means of expiation, were inadequate in the face of imminent judgment. God called for something beyond these standard means. He called, namely, for the repentance and the washing which were the main themes of John's prophetic summons to Israel.

In the face of judgment the election of Israel was itself at stake (Luke 3:8 = Matt 3:9). John's mission accordingly had an election-historical dimension to be construed from the field of meaning out of which he spoke and acted. Elements that define that field of meaning are the imminence of judgment and the deliberately chosen symbols of wilderness and water rite. If imminent judgment be taken as the matrix of John's field of meaning, the probable nexus binding all the motifs together was the well-established conception of Israel in the wilderness (Exodus to Deuteronomy) as the type of eschatological Israel. If the generation of the wilderness was made ready for salvation at Sinai by a bath of immersion (inferred from Exod 24:8 on the premise, *b. Yebam. 46b,* that there is no sprinkling without previous bath of immersion; cf. *Mek. Exod.* 13.21; 14:26; 1 Cor 10:1–2), it followed that Israel on the brink of judgment was similarly to be made ready for the judgment by being bathed and purified (Jeremias 1971: 42–49). The alternative was liability to the coming wrath (Matt 3:7 = Luke 3:7). "The coming one" (not God himself, but an apocalyptic figure not easily identifiable from biblical tradition) would wash "in the holy Spirit and in fire" precisely those whom John had washed in preparation for judgment (Matt 3:11 = Luke 3:16; cf. Mark 1:8). Refusal would mean exclusion from restored and saved Israel. Repentant Israel would be gathered like wheat into the barn, whereas unrepentant Israel would be burnt like chaff (Matt 3:12 = Luke 3:17). This grounds the inference that John conceived his prophetic task as that of assembling the remnant of Israel in the face of judgment. In and through this open, eschatological remnant of those destined for acquittal at the judgment, God would bring his holy people to restoration in the age to come (Meyer 1979: 115–28).

Among those who responded positively to John's call to baptism was Jesus of Nazareth. The Synoptic tradition is at one in affirming Jesus' participation in "the baptism of John" (Mark 1:9–11; Matt 3:13–17; Luke 3:21–22; John 1:32–33). The Synoptic Gospels date the start of Jesus' public career from the arrest of John (Mark 1:14 = Matt 4:12; Luke 3:19), leaving unexplained why Jesus had remained in Judea until John's arrest and why the arrest had had decisive personal meaning for Jesus (*paradothēnai* in Mark 1:14; Matt 4:12 probably signifies that in the arrest of John, Jesus saw a divine signal for himself; Luke 4:14). The Fourth Gospel fills this lacuna by representing Jesus as surrounded by his own disciples and sharing in the baptism movement apparently in alliance with but not alongside John (John 3:26, 4:1). In view of its discontinuity with the tendency of the tradition to accent the independence of Jesus, this Johannine tradition may well reflect the historic beginnings of Jesus' career.

Against the grain of competition between the movements inaugurated respectively by John and by Jesus, the gospel traditions are unanimous that Jesus all through his career maintained a positive attitude toward John and his mission. A saying of Jesus compares his generation to quarrelsome children, complaining,

> "We piped to you and you did not dance,
> we wailed and you mourned not"
> (Matt 11:17 = Luke 7:32).

A generation of sour critics piped and John did not dance; it wailed and Jesus did not mourn (Matt 11:18–19 = Luke 7:33–34). Both John and Jesus violated the sacred custom of fasting and feasting in accord with tradition, for both were signs of a break in the routines of ordinary history. For all the difference in style of life between John and himself, Jesus understood John to be allied with him in proclaiming the consummation of history and in being fatefully repudiated by those deaf to their proclamations.

In Jesus' view the baptism of John had been "from heaven" (Mark 11:30 = Matt 21:25 = Luke 20:4), i.e., authorized by God. John himself "came to you in [i.e., brought you] the way of righteousness" (Matt 21:32). In Jesus' phrase, John had been "more than a prophet" (Matt 11:9 = Luke 7:26). To define himself, John had invoked the Isaian cry to prepare "the way of the Lord" (Isa 40:3; Mark 1:3; Matt 3:3; Luke 3:4; John 1:23). This Isaian motif of preparation was the background of the later lines of Mal 3:23 (—Eng 4:5–6) on the sending of Elijah in advance of judgment to purify the priesthood (Mal 3:1–3) and to reconcile fathers and sons. In Sir 48:10 the task of Elijah included reestablishing "the tribes of Jacob" (cf. Isa 49:6). According to the Fourth Gospel, the Baptizer refused the title "Elijah" (John 1:21); according to the Synoptics, Jesus applied it to John (Matt 11:14; Mark 9:13 = Matt 17:12; Matt 11:10 = Luke 7:27). Hence, in the context of preparation for the reign of God, "no one greater has arisen among men than John"; when compared, however, with those who would see the arrival of what had been prepared: "the least in the reign of God [shall be] greater than he" (Matt 11:11 = Luke 7:28).

Jesus' unambiguous support for the mission of John throws light on how Jesus understood his own mission. John's task had been to alert Israel to the imminence of judgment and to assemble by baptism the remnant of Israel destined for cleansing, acquittal, and restoration. Jesus entered into and unreservedly affirmed this prophetic field of meaning. He not only endorsed John's mission as authentic, he aligned himself with that mission in the closest possible way. In the particulars of John's career he read divine signs bearing on himself. Jesus' acute awareness of how different the style of John's career was from his own only underscores his alliance with John's purposes. Like John, Jesus understood his own role as "preparationist." Other parties and sects had their own eschatological hopes and expectations, but only in the movements inaugurated by John and by Jesus was preparation for the eschaton the very *raison d'être* of the movement. Hence the closest analogy of John's movement was that of Jesus and vice versa. Jesus' role bore on the preparation of Israel for the definitive triumph of God. There remains the task of defining his understanding of how, concretely, this triumph was to be realized.

2. The Proclamation and Its Meaning. "Proclamation" in the sense of "the act of proclaiming" is a mode of speech; "proclamation" in the sense of "what is proclaimed" is a message. The Synoptic literature presents Jesus as adopting the proclamatory mode of speech (Mark 1:14–15 = Matt 4:17; cf. Luke 4:16–30); moreover, it repeatedly generalizes this datum (Mark 1:38 = Luke 4:43; Mark 1:39 = Matt 4:23 = Luke 4:44; Mark 1:45; the texts include redactional generalizations such as Matt 4:23; 9:15), depicting Jesus as proclaiming, especially in synagogues, the fulfillment of God's promises and Israel's hopes (Luke 4:16–30; Mark 1:39 = Matt 4:23; cf. Luke 4:44; see also Mark 1:21 = Luke 4:31; Mark 6:2; Matt 13:53).

As message, the proclamation of Jesus announced "the reign of God." This was not an unfamiliar theme. It was central, for example, to the *Qaddiš*, the synagogue prayer that regularly followed the Sabbath sermon:

> May he allow his great name to be glorified and hallowed in the world that he has created according to his will!
> May he allow his reign to reign in your lifetime and in your days and in the lifetime of all the house of Israel, speedily and soon!

In Jesus' message, as in the *Qaddiš*, the reign of God signified the triumph of God. In accord with the hope of Israel, it would be realized first of all in the climactic and definitive restoration of Israel, the primary object both of the promises of God and of the hopes of his people. Thus, Jesus proclaimed, not a reform, not a revolution, but a fulfillment—the imminent fulfillment of all God's promises to Israel.

These last words anticipate the survey of Jesus' teaching on the reign of God to be presented below. Jesus' proclamation presupposed God's effective governance of all creation and of all human history. The teaching of Jesus clarified the diverse meanings and referents of "the reign of God," namely: as a divine order or economy, as the triumph of God, as the vindication of his agents, as the condemnation of the hard-hearted, as the restoration of Israel, as the salvation of the nations, as still to come, and as disclosed in advance by present events intrinsically ordered to its coming. For all this richness of connotation and denotation, the reign of God (*hē basileia tou theou* in Gk; *malkûtāʾ dĕʾlāhāʾ* in Aramaic) primarily referred to the divine economy to be established by God's coming triumph. The most striking aspect of Jesus' usage, however, for in the whole tradition of ancient Judaism this was unique to him, was the affirmation that in his own mission the reign of God, God's climactic and definitive act of saving, had already begun. This message found repeated expression, for example, in parables responding to critics of Jesus' public career (see C.4 below).

The proclamation of Jesus kindled a blaze of new speech, much of it his own, but continuing far beyond him. He himself became a living font of *mĕšālîm:* aphorisms, parables, riddles, freshly minted and memorable. They presented new images from nature or from village life in the service of old themes such as imminent judgment or the challenge of present decision. Ancient Near Eastern symbols—reign, enthronement, wedding, harvest, vine and wine, the world-cloak, etc.—were honed and burnished in the service of Jesus' mission. He drew on the major resources of biblical rhetoric (parallelism, rhythm, rhyme, alliteration, assonance, word play), on its repertory of figurative forms (macarisms, proverbs, riddles, parables), and on its most powerful themes (election, judgment, and salvation) which he treated both in the mode of celebration and in that of lament.

The reign-of-God theme was vitalized by a profusion of new coinages. Well over half the words Jesus used of the reign of God had not previously been attested in connection with that theme. The reign "comes," "draws near," "overtakes you," "is among you"; one is "in" it or "not far from it," "enters into" it or is "cast out of" it. The language, moreover, discloses a consciousness of God's last and climactic intervention as already underway. Now is the time of the new wine and the new cloak (Mark 2:21–22 = Matt 9:16–17 = Luke 5:36–39). The fields are "white" (John 4:35), the harvest "great" (Matt 9:37 = Luke 10:2). The young man dead through sin "is alive again" (Luke 15:24, 32). The blind see, cripples walk, lepers are cleansed, the deaf hear, the dead are raised, good news is broken to the poor (Matt 11:5 = Luke 7:22). The function of these last phrases is twofold. The cascade of miracles is the sure sign of salvation; but, further, salvation itself is imaged in the miracles. That is, for Jesus and his hearers the reign of God was sight to the blind, mobility to cripples, life to the dead. The proper inference from Jesus' exorcisms was that the reign of God "has [already] overtaken you!" (Matt 12:28 = Luke 11:20); the annihilation of Satan and his power had already begun (see C.3 in this article). This was without precedent in biblical or postbiblical (e.g., Qumran) tradition.

In biblical precedent the reign of God connoted the long-awaited restoration of Israel: see Isa 24:23 on God's reign and Mount Zion; Isa 33:22 on Yahweh's reign and "our" salvation; Isa 52:7–10 on God's reign and the redemption of Israel; Zeph 3:14–20 on the reign of God and the rescue and restoration of the remnant of Israel. Intertestamental (e.g. *Ps. Sol.* 11:2; 17:3) and NT literature prolonged these ties. The reign of God evoked the banquet with Abraham, Isaac, and Jacob (Matt 8:11 = Luke 13:28), the twelve tribes gathered anew (Matt 19:28 = Luke 22:30), the new sanctuary to be built in three days (Mark 14:58 = Matt 26:61; John 2:19). The stubborn tendency of scholarship to dissociate the reign of God from the fortunes of Israel must accordingly be discounted as nonbiblical and ahistorical (Meyer 1979: 132–35).

Apposite here is J. L. Austin's (1962) analysis of speech as locutionary (the act of saying such-and-such), illocutionary (what one does in saying such-and-such), and perlocutionary (what one effects by saying such-and-such).

As a locutionary act, Jesus' proclamation evoked sharp and evocative images. The life of the age to come was riches for the poor, comfort for the mourners, a banquet for the hungry. This language echoed the prophets and the Psalms, but it designedly highlighted a particular perspective on fulfillment. It did not, for example, call to mind the countless biblical texts on the righteous (Heb *ṣaddîqîm*) and the upright (*yĕšārîm*), the holy (*qĕdôšîm*) and the pious (*ḥasîdîm*). Rather, it called to mind God's predilection for the poor or lowly (*ʿănāwîm*), for those brought low and afflicted (*ʿăniyyîm*). These were the favorites of God in the Psalms and in prophetic tradition from the time of Jeremiah and Zephaniah. Now, at last, the day would dawn for the poor and afflicted, the contrite and brokenhearted, the unimportant and unpretentious. They would not earn salvation. By counting on its promise, they would simply accept it.

In making his proclamation, then, Jesus was making promises. As an illocutionary act, the proclamation was accordingly not a threat but a pledge: its central term was not judgment but the reign of God. When proclamation and macarism were dramatized by symbolic acts such as dining with publicans and sinners (see below, C.3), this powerful dimension of promise, together with partial fulfillment in the present, was still more heavily underscored.

As a perlocutionary act, the proclamation was designed to elicit a believing acceptance of the promise and a corresponding celebration of God's goodness. When intended response and actual response are differentiated, however, diversity inevitably comes to light. The wise *(sophoi)* and intelligent *(synetoi)* were blind to the truth of the proclamation (Matt 11:25 = Luke 10:21). "This generation" of critics found fault equally with the severe style of John and the celebrative style of Jesus (Matt 11:18–19 = Luke 7:33–34). The correlation between Jesus' proclamation, his macarisms, and his initiative toward sinners was matched by his contemporaries' parallel responses to all three. Whereas few from the religious elite of scholars and the pious accepted him, the "simple" rejoiced in his proclamation as a revelation of divine goodness (Matt 11:25 = Luke 10:21). Like "the poor, the maimed, the blind, and the lame" who poured into the banquet hall in the parable (Luke 14:21), so the poor, the afflicted, the outcast accepted Jesus' invitation. The irreligious, in particular, responded to his initiative toward them with sheer delight (Luke 5:29; 19:9).

It is not easy to single out the particular scriptural sources of the central term in Jesus' proclamation, "the reign of God." The parallel between the *Qaddiš* and the Our Father (the "hallowing" of God's "name," as in Ezek 36:23, followed by the theme of God's eschatological "reign") seems not to provide helpful clues. The Psalms, to be sure, are a particularly rich, though by no means the sole, resource for the theme.

Gustaf Dalman (1902: 134) pointed out that in the NT, as in the whole of ancient Jewish literature, the Messiah may be enthroned and given "royal dignity" or "dominion," but "the reign of God" is never simply transferred to him. In two passages (Luke 12:32; 22:29) Jesus reveals God's intention to include Jesus' closest disciples in this royal dominion. In both texts the Gk word *basileia* reflects the Aramaic word *malkût(āʾ)* of Dan 7:18, 27. But given the distinction between the *malkût* (reign) of God and the *malkût* (royal dominion) that God would confer on the Messiah or on the Danielic "one like a son of man" and "the people of the saints of the Most High" and, in the gospel literature, on Jesus and his disciples, it is illegitimate to infer from Luke 12:32; 22:29 that the reign of God in Jesus' proclamation derived from Daniel 7. (On *basileia* made to refer to royal rank or dominion, see also Matt 16:28; 20:21; Luke 19:12; 22:30; 23:42).

In Luke's presentation of Jesus' own words (Luke 4:43; 16:16) and in other Synoptic texts (e.g. Matt 4:23; 9:35; cf. 11:5 = Luke 7:22), the proclamation of the reign of God is brought into relation with the proclamation of the herald (Heb *mĕbaśśēr*/Gk *euaggelizomenos*) of Isa 52:7–10; 61:1–2. In view of the burden of the herald's message to Israel, namely, "your God reigns!" (Isa 52: 7), this passage presents itself as a plausible source of Jesus' own proclamation. The fact that Isa 52:7–10 combines the motifs of the herald of good news, the reign of God, eschatological peace, and the restoration of Israel tends to fill out and confirm this hypothesis.

Again, Isa 61:1–3 takes up and carries forward themes from Isa 52:7–10 (the texts are associated in 11QMelch) and from the Isaian Servant songs. Now, Isa 61:1–3 resonates in several gospel passages (e.g., Luke 4:17–21; Matt 11:5 = Luke 7:22; Matt 5:3–4 = Luke 6:20–21). Three motifs—the reign of God (Isa 52:7), news of salvation (Isa 52:7, 61:1), the poor and the mourners as its destinataries (Isa 61:1–3)—are joined together in Jesus' proclamation (Luke 4:17–21; cf. Mark 1:15 = Matt 4:17), in his macarisms (Matt 5:3–4; Luke 6:20–21), and in the account that he gave of himself and his career (Matt 11:5 = Luke 7:22; Luke 16:16). This points to the combination of Isa 52:7–10 and 61:1–3 as not only a plausible but a probable source of his proclamation. The nexus between the two passages is the act of bringing news of salvation *(baśśēr)*.

From childhood on, Jesus had heard the targumic renderings of the Law and the Prophets in the synagogue. They naturally impinged on his thought and speech. There are a few instances in which targumic texts (despite the lateness of their redaction, long after the time of Jesus) are shown to have been ancient, for they are reflected in Jesus' words (e.g., Mark 4:11–12; Matt 26:52; possibly the parable in Mark 12:1–11 = Matt 21:33–44 = Luke 20:9–18; Chilton 1984: 98–101, 111–14). In the targums "the reign of God" was a frequent periphrasis designed to sidestep the idea that God should himself appear on earth. Hence, in place of "behold your God" (Isa 40:9) and in place of "your God reigns" (Isa 52:7), the targum has "the reign *(malkûtāʾ)* of your God has been made manifest" (*Tg. Isa.* 24:23; 31:4; *Tg. Neb.* Mic 4:7; Zech 14:9). On the one hand, there is very little reason to think that Jesus drew his distinctive thematization of the reign of God from some already fashioned "reign-of-God theology" in the targums; on the other hand, the frequency of *malkût* language in the synagogue may well have influenced his choice of the central term of his proclamation.

3. Jesus' Public Behavior. The principal public actions

of Jesus were symbolic and these symbolic acts were correlative to his proclamation. Proof of the latter point lies in the explicit or implicit reference of his public symbolic acts to the reign of God, a reference verifiable in each of three sets of texts considered in this section.

a. The Twelve. The discipleship that surrounded Jesus came into being through his personal call. The call was peremptory, admitting no delay in response (Mark 1:17, 20 = Matt 4:19, 22; Mark 2:15 = Matt 9:9 = Luke 5:28; Mark 10:21 = Matt 19:21 = Luke 18:22) and no competing claim, whether of Torah and custom (Matt 8:22 = Luke 9:60) or of family love (Luke 9:61–62; cf. Matt 10:37 = Luke 14:26). The key to this extreme rigor was the imminence—indeed, the advance presence—of the reign of God in the mission of Jesus and the priority of its demands over all other claims, even those of the Torah.

The historicity of the act of choosing twelve from among his disciples to participate most intimately in his mission (Mark 3:13–14 = Luke 6:13; Mark 6:7–13 = Matt 10:1, 9–14 = Luke 9:1–6; cf. Matt 19:28 = Luke 22:30) is beyond reasonable doubt. Historicity is assured, first of all, by two elements that go against the grain of post-Easter church tendencies: Judas Iscariot's membership in the twelve, and the passing over without mention of the status of the twelve in the interim between the career of Jesus and the last judgment; second, by multiple attestation (triple tradition, logia tradition, special traditions such as Luke 8:1–3; John 6:67–71; and the post-Easter pre-Pauline tradition transmitted by Paul in 1 Cor 15:5); third, by multiform attestation in story, logion, and faith formula.

The number twelve was symbolic; hence, the twelve were themselves a living symbol. The symbolic reference was to the twelve tribes of Israel. But inasmuch as the loss of the northern kingdom of Israel to the Assyrians in ages past had left only two and a half tribes (1QM 1:2; *2 Apoc. Bar.* 62:5; 77:19; 78:1; *Mart. Is.* 3:2), "twelve" in the eschatological context established by Jesus' proclamation could only signify "Israel restored." Jesus' appointment of the twelve accordingly signified that his mission and theirs bore on the restoration of Israel. Made up of notably disparate elements, the twelve were a reconciliatory sign. This intimates that the coming restoration itself would have an equally reconciliatory character.

Jesus, moreover, gave the twelve a role in the coming to be of this reconciliation and restoration by sending them (Mark 6:7 = Matt 10:5 = Luke 9:2) in groups of two (Mark 6:7; cf. Luke 10:1) to enlist Israel's welcome of the reign of God (Mark 3:14; Matt 10:7; Luke 9:2). They thereby participated in Jesus' own role as eschatological herald *(mĕbaśśēr/euaggelizomenos)*. This had been presaged by the word, "Come, follow me, and I will make you fishers of men" (Mark 1:17 = Matt 4:19), an image that, alluding to but modifying the sense of Jer 16:16, signified the task of "gathering" Israel in the sense of winning from Israel a common act of faith. The stakes were high, for acceptance would bring eschatological blessing, and refusal would bring eschatological condemnation (Mark 6:11 = Matt 10:12–15; cf. Luke 10:10–12).

b. Cures and Exorcisms. Jesus' equipping of the twelve for a mission that included the driving out of demons (Mark 6:7 = Matt 10:1 = Luke 9:1) presupposed his own career as an exorcist. At one point he even summed up his whole mission in these terms (Luke 13:32). Five texts with solid claims to historicity include reference to Jesus' career as exorcist and healer.

The double saying on Beelzebul and the advent of the reign of God (Matt 12:27–28 [= Luke 11:18–20]) reads:

> If I drive out demons by the power of Beelzebul,
> by whose power do your sons drive them out? . . .
> But if by the Spirit [Luke has "finger"] of God I drive
> out demons,
> then the reign of God has overtaken you.

The connecting of exorcisms with apocalyptic or absolute eschatology gives an entirely distinctive profile to this side of Jesus' career (Theissen 1983: 277–86). The accent on the correlation of Jesus' exorcisms with his proclamation is at once the main thrust of the text and an index (originality) to historicity. But the case for historicity is further supported by the sheer offensiveness to early Christian sensibility of the charge of sorcery; by the seeming or surface risk of relativizing the exorcisms of Jesus through reference to the exorcisms of others; and by the antithetical parallelism of question and statement—a trait distributed through all lines of Synoptic tradition and typical of the speech of Jesus (Mark 3:33–34 = Matt 12:48–49; Mark 8:12; 10:18 = Matt 19:17 = Luke 18:19; Mark 11:17; Matt 7:3–5 = Luke 6:41–42; Luke 12:51; 22:25).

The saying on the dynasty and the household divided against themselves (Mark 3:24–26 = Matt 12:25–26 = Luke 11:17) supposes the continuum of all evil and its solidarity with Satan (not a universal supposition in ancient Judaism) and affirms the decisiveness of his own attack on it (eschatology inaugurated and in process of realization). Indices to historicity are discontinuity (the offensiveness of the charge of sorcery) and originality (realized eschatology).

The saying on the binding of the strong man (Mark 3:27 = Matt 12:29 = Luke 11:21–22) is strikingly original, for the claim to have "bound" Satan in advance of the exorcisms is unparalleled. Jesus' giving the disciples a share in his power over the demons (Mark 3:14–15; 6:7; Matt 10:7–8; Luke 9:1–2) derives historical probability from other data, especially from the disciples' failure as exorcists (Mark 9:18, 28 = Matt 17:16, 19 = Luke 9:40). The historicity of Jesus' answer to the question of the Baptist (Matt 11:5 = Luke 7:22) is probable on the basis of the claim to absolute eschatology already underway. The text is a cry of joy at the launching of God's climactic and definitive saving act.

Finally, the solidly grounded historicity of Jesus' refusal of a demand for a "sign from heaven" (Mark 8:11–12 = Matt 16:1, 4; Matt 12:38–40 = Luke 11:29–30; Luke 11:16; John 4:48; 6:30–40) is by no means a counterindication putting the historicity of his exorcisms and cures in doubt. The demand was for a circus prodigy such as the parting of waters in imitation of the Moses tradition (*Ant* 20.5.1 §97) or the feat of floating down from "the pinnacle of the temple" sustained by angels (Matt 4:5–6 = Luke 4:9–10). Jesus' refusal to provide a flamboyant made-to-order "sign" of this kind, while it does not rule out exorcisms and cures, does sharply differentiate his intentions from those of the prophetic and messianic pretenders of whom we learn from Josephus.

The most distinctive feature of Jesus' cures and exorcisms derived from the context in which they were performed and which he himself repeatedly underscored: they pointed to the dawning reign of God. By his eschatological proclamation the exorcist had generated an all-commanding context for his encounter with the demons. Thanks to this context the exorcisms were sublated, promoted to the status of signs of the eschaton. Jesus' combat with Satan did not signal one moment among others in the endless seesaw of good and evil, but the decisive apocalyptic turning point. Furthermore, his cures and exorcisms went beyond symbolizing the restoration of Israel to the act of bringing it about. In the face of this momentous event, to which all Israel ought to have responded with faith, unbelieving Chorazin and Bethsaida and Capernaum were doomed (Matt 11:21–24 = Luke 10:13–15).

c. Fellowship with Sinners. If the cures and exorcisms of Jesus, besides eliciting faith, also provoked skepticism and malicious misconstrual, his initiative toward social outcasts, besides eliciting the joyous response of the outcasts, also provoked shock and resentment on the part of the learned and the pious. To his contemporaries it was a staggering phenomenon that Jesus did not shrink from dining with the irreligious (Mark 2:16–17 = Matt 9:11 = Luke 5:30; Matt 11:19 = Luke 7:34; Luke 15:1, 19:8). The intensity of the opposed reactions to this policy becomes intelligible in the light of two aspects of the social context. First, dining in common established among its participants a bond of fellowship, violation of which was rank betrayal. Second, it was through table fellowship that the ritual distinction between "the clean" and "the unclean" and the moral distinction between "the righteous" and "the sinners" found concrete social expression. Since gentiles were unclean (Deut 14:21) and uncleanness was contagious, Jews were not to eat with them (*Jub.* 22:16). But the rule applied by Jews to gentiles was also applied by religious Jews to irreligious Jews, especially to notorious "sinners" including heretics (Böcher 1972: 16–17), but often enough to the merely unobservant, who could not be counted on in matters of ritual purity. For at least some associations of the religious elite, probably including the Pharisees, this meant that table fellowship was virtually limited to their own membership.

To grasp the issue of Jesus' initiative toward and fellowship with "sinners," the first requisite is to define the term "sinners." The classic treatment of the issue is that of Joachim Jeremias. From 1931 (Jeremias 1931: 294) through publications over the following forty years (1969: 303–12; 1971: 108–21), he rightly maintained that "the sinners" in the gospels did not refer to the unobservant (the so-called "people of the land," *ʿam hāʾāreṣ*) but (a) to those who notoriously violated the commandments of God, and (b) to those engaged in universally despised trades (especially usurers, tax collectors, publicans, etc., *b. Sanh.* 25b), practitioners of which were deprived of civil and political rights. In attempting to recover the socioreligious situation in Palestine of the time of Jesus, one should neither identify these notorious sinners and outcasts (the *hamartōloi* of Mark 2:15–17 = Matt 9:10–13 = Luke 5:29–32, etc.) with the ordinary run of men, nor, on the other hand, disregard the continuity that the religious elite considered to exist between these diverse classes (see the reference to "other men"—literally, "the rest of men"—deprecated by the Pharisee of Luke 18:11; cf. John 7:49).

Repentance and conversion were cardinal themes in Judaism, richly represented in postexilic literature, regularly brought to mind by the synagogue, regularly finding cultic expression in the temple. The new element in the preaching of the Baptist had been his presupposition that at the threshold of judgment the ordinary Mosaic economy did not suffice. God called all the children of Israel to repent, to confess their sins, to seal their confession by a rite of washing as in the days of Sinai. The Baptist, to be sure, maintained the classic biblical structure of repentance: conversion first, communion second (Luke 3:7–14 = Matt 3:7–10; Josephus, *Ant* 18.5.2 §117). The daring of Jesus' initiative lay in its reversal of this structure: communion first, conversion second. In ancient Judaism "sinners" stood publicly and for the most part permanently condemned. Tax collectors and publicans, for example, had no way of knowing all whom they had robbed nor of how much, and so had no clear way to make the required "complete restitution plus a fifth." In this seemingly hopeless situation, Jesus' approach to the sinners proved to be irresistible. Contact prompted repentance; conversion flowered from communion.

In retrospect, Jesus' policy can nevertheless be seen to have had a profoundly traditional rationale, for the policy both envisaged and achieved traditional purposes: the conversion and forgiveness of sinners, their reconciliation with God and with Israel. That Jesus did in fact conceive his initiative toward sinners in terms of conversion and forgiveness is crystal clear from analysis of the many parables by which he defended his policy from its critics, e.g. the parable of the Laborers in the Vineyard (Matt 20:1–16), the parable of the Two Sons (Matt 21:28–32), the parable of the Two Debtors (Luke 7:41–43), the twin parables of the Lost Sheep and the Lost Coin (Luke 15:4–10), and the parable of the Prodigal Son (Luke 15:11–32).

The second aspect of Jesus' policy was the intent to win the sinner back not only to God but to his rightful family, Israel. Salvation belonged to Zacchaeus, said Jesus, "for he, too, is a son of Abraham" (Luke 19:9). Nothing could have been more fundamental to the eschatological restoration of Israel than the seemingly impossible feat of healing the division between the good and the wicked without forfeiting the claims of the moral order.

But the "Israel" to which the converted sinner was won back, was this the Israel of history prior to John the Baptist and to Jesus? Or was it the eschatological Israel coming into being through their work? The matter is clarified by consideration of the problem that followed upon Jesus' remarkable success in winning over sinners. This was the problem of winning over the righteous, as well. The parables listed above were without exception addressed to them. Collectively, these parables are the relics of a radical and poignant appeal. The appeal was radical, for it transcended the conventional grounds for the deep division between the righteous and the sinners. John the Baptist had relativized this division by calling the righteous, too, to repentance. Jesus fully agreed with and followed in this line. In and through a series of parables, he mounted an appeal to the righteous to enter with their brothers, the sinners, into a new fellowship of forgiveness, an eschatological covenant, a new and eschatological Israel. The story of the Prodigal Son ends on this note of poignant appeal, with the words of the father to the elder son: "But we had to celebrate and be glad, because your brother was dead and has come back to life; he was lost and is found" (Luke 15:32). The response of the elder son is left open and undecided. It would be settled only by the response that the hearer himself would make to Jesus' parable.

The three great symbolic acts reviewed here—the choice and sending of the twelve, the stream of exorcisms and cures, and the unprecedented initiative toward notorious sinners—perfectly translated Jesus' proclamation into action. The proclamation of the reign of God signified the long-promised and long-awaited restoration of Israel. Jesus' symbolic acts were bent on bringing it into being. His proclamation was to be no isolated word. It would be given mass and momentum in dramatic acts designed to signify and to realize a new Israel. The themes correlative to "the reign of God"—new people, new covenant, new code—began to emerge in the encounter between Jesus and his fellow Jews.

4. The Teaching of Jesus. The teaching of Jesus was less an initiative than the follow-through on an initiative. The initiative had been his proclamation and symbolic acts. These elicited responses were positive and negative. An important part of Jesus' teaching consisted in his response to the responses.

a. Jesus' Response to the Responses. A first response to him was puzzlement expressed as critique. Jesus' proclamation inescapably carried the claim that here at last God was speaking his climactic word to Israel. But how could that be? If the word of Jesus was the word of God, how could it have won so cool a reception in Israel? Was not the word of God like fire, like a hammer that shatters rock (Jer 23:29)? But the word spoken by Jesus was apparently returning to him empty. To this Jesus responded in a set of images as natural as they were compelling: Look at the sower. Some of the seed he sows falls on the path and is trampled; some is eaten by the birds; some falls on shallow ground, springs up early, and withers; some falls among thorns and is choked. Yet—harvest comes, the sheaves sway in the field, rich beyond measure (Mark 4:3–8 = Matt 13:3–8 = Luke 8:5–8). The listeners, in short, are told: do not judge so quickly or be misled by appearances. Harvest will come and it will be rich. Here "teaching" has become a renewed appeal for faith and confidence.

A second response to him was to hear his proclamation, perhaps with interest, but finally to dismiss it with a shrug. To this Jesus responded with vigor. The warnings and danger signals, the reproaches and rebukes that Jesus addressed to the dense (Luke 12:54–56), the deluded (Luke 23:31), and the perverse (Mark 3:6 = Matt 12:14 = Luke 6:11) drew on a wide variety of images and motifs and ranged over the scale of feeling from cool appeal for insight (Luke 13:6–9) through pathos and lament (Matt 23:37–39 = Luke 13:34–35) to angry indignation (Mark 3:5). The illusory supposition of life as usual, maintained in the teeth of the urgent proclamation, was like the calm before the deluge that wiped out mankind (Luke 17:26–27 = Matt 24:37–39). A crass and heedless Israel stood in imminent danger, like a bird about to be snared (Luke 21:34).

In the face of warning, what would happen to the fatuously unconcerned? Like salt that had lost its savor, they would be "thrown out" (Matt 5:13 = Luke 14:34; cf. Mark 9:50). Sometimes the warning was cool and dry: Israel was living on borrowed time, like a long-barren fig tree about to be cut down, for which the gardener has pleaded with the owner for a last chance (Luke 13:6–9). Sometimes, as in texts cast in dirge rhythm (Mark 4:24 = Matt 7:2 = Luke 6:38; Luke 13:24–27; Mark 9:50; Matt 20:16), warning was solemn. Elsewhere it was doleful and poignant (Matt 23:37–39 = Luke 13:34–35). At times Jesus' response was amazement (Mark 6:6), or anger (Mark 1:41) yielding to sorrow (Mark 3:5), or savagely bitter humor (Luke 13:33).

Exactly what was at stake in this set of texts on warnings to Israel? At stake were the status and destiny of individuals, of groups, of the entire nation. The alternatives were restoration and ruin, acquittal and condemnation, life and death. The danger was that of definitive condemnation at the judgment, which would come suddenly and soon. Suddenly: for it would come like lightning flashing from one end of the sky to the other (Luke 17:24). Soon: for the sign of its coming was "this present moment" (Luke 12:56). In a context of impending ruin (Luke 12:16–21, 58; 13:6–9; 21:34), the most urgent and immediate need was for awareness, alertness, insight. But the source of insight was the good, the generous heart; just so, Jesus warned the crowds, the source of blindness was the hardened heart: "See to it then that your [inner] light is not darkness!" (Luke 11:35 = Matt 6:23b).

The interactive sequence "prophecy/indifference/warning" was an age-old pattern, and this pattern is the clue to the depth-dimension of the texts. The seemingly impenetrable self-assurance that grounded Israel's indifference to prophetic warning appears as a radically continuous phenomenon throughout the history of the prophetic movement. It was the besetting temptation to take refuge in election. But election, said the prophets from Amos through Isaiah and Jeremiah and Zechariah down to the Baptist and Jesus, was two-edged. God's transactions with Israel, so far from guaranteeing unconditional protection, put his people in peril:

> Only for you have I cared
> out of all the earth's tribes;
> therefore will I punish you
> for all of your crimes (Amos 3:2).

It was pure illusion to affirm Yahweh's presence and infer from it that all was secure: "Is not Yahweh in our midst? No evil can come upon us!" (Mic 3:11). Because Israel clung to such illusions, Yahweh would "make this people wood"; his word would become fire in its mouth "and devour them" (Jer 5:14). It was utterly futile to call on "lying words" like the self-hypnotizing chant "the temple of Yahweh, the temple of Yahweh, the temple of Yahweh!" and to conclude "we are delivered!" (Jer 7:4, 10). If Israel regularly installed itself in this false consciousness, the prophets just as regularly made it their task to unmask and overturn it. The truth of election degenerated again and again into the dogma of unconditional blessings, but the Baptist resumed the whole prophetic tradition in his word:

> Do not begin to say to yourselves
> "We have Abraham for our father."
> I tell you: God can raise up sons to Abraham
> out of these stones (Luke 3:8 = Matt 3:9).

The election-historical aspect of Jesus' summons to Israel (maintenance of election in the sight of God hinged on response to the emissary of God) and its eschatological aspect (salvation at the judgment hinged on response to the selfsame emissary of God) both emerged directly from his proclamation insofar as it envisaged the definitive restoration of Israel. These aspects of his mission also emerged from the tone of his warnings to whoever ignored or rejected the proclamation. The election-historical and eschatological factors together offer the most adequate explanation of three hyperbolic features of Jesus' teaching: first, the distance between the terms in which questioners posed questions to him and the terms in which he cast his answers; second, the repeated warning that in the present situation the righteous were positioning themselves in greater danger of perdition than were the sinners; third, the Torah-transcendent character of Jesus' moral teachings in general.

Questions, whether prompted by shocked amazement (e.g., at Jesus' dining with sinners) or disappointment (e.g., at his reception by Israel), regularly bore on Jesus himself, his policies, and the way in which his career was unfolding. But often Jesus' answers to these questions took the form of descriptive figures imaging the way the reign of God comes (see the parables of the Sower, the Leaven, the Great Supper, the Good Employer, etc.). By correlating questions about himself with answers on the reign of God, Jesus repeatedly invited his interlocutors to find in him and in his mission an omega point: God's climactic and definitive revelation to Israel. This revelation said something new about the destiny of Israel. God meant his people to find their fulfillment through the mission of Jesus. Concrete acts—the breaking of news of salvation to the poor (Matt 11:4 = Luke 7:22; cf. Matt 5:3 = Luke 6:20), the bringing of sight to the blind, health to the lepers, life to the dead (Matt 11:5 = Luke 7:22), the seemingly scandalous initiatives toward notorious sinners (Mark 2:16–17 = Matt 9:11 = Luke 5:30; Matt 11:19 = Luke 7:34)—were mediating the advent of the reign of God. The clear implication was that a "reign of God" not correlative to the mission of Jesus was pure abstraction and illusion. Equally illusory and positively ruinous according to Jesus was the dismissal of his mission as irrelevant to Israel's status and destiny. On the contrary, his correlating of his own mission with the reign of God implied that everything hinged on response to him.

The sanction of this claim would be the coming judgment, a recurrent theme copiously attested by every line of transmission in the gospel literature. Entry into the reign of God was not guaranteed by election. Election itself was correlated with response to Jesus' summons. Election and entry into the reign of God made up a single issue to be resolved by human decision and divine judgment. For his hearers, then, the central issue at the judgment would be their response to Jesus and his proclamation (Mark 6:11 = Matt 10:14 = Luke 9:5; 10:10–11; Mark 8:38 = Matt 10:33; 16:27 = Luke 9:26; Matt 7:22–23 = Luke 13:26–27; Matt 7:24–27 = Luke 6:47–49; Matt 10:32–33 = Luke 12:8–9; Matt 12:41–42 = Luke 11:31–32). One should doubtless apply careful historical critique to all these texts; still, there is no plausibility in the view that they are *en bloc* unhistorical.

If the self-sufficiency of the righteous thwarted the response to Jesus, the self-effacement of the simple positively conditioned it; i.e., the response to Jesus was the act of one who humbled himself like a child (Matt 18:4). The full meaning of this act came to light in a judgment theme: the precise reference of the reversal imaged in "Whoever exalts himself will be humbled, whoever humbles himself will be exalted" (Matt 23:12; Luke 14:11; 18:14) was to the last judgment. ("Will be humbled/exalted" are divine passives; if parallels are consulted, the futures must be eschatological: see the many other generalizing conclusions of parables, such as Mark 4:25; 13:37; Matt 20:16; 21:44 = Luke 20:18; Matt 22:14; Luke 12:21; 13:30. The scriptural resource of this text, Ezek 21:31, also referred to reversal by God's judgment.)

The most disconcerting aspect of Jesus' teaching on the judgment was that, in view of their respective responses to John and to himself (Matt 11:18 = Luke 7:33–34), "sinners" were headed for salvation and the "righteous" for perdition. To say that "publicans and prostitutes will enter the reign of God ahead of you" (= the righteous) (Matt 21:31) might well be thought to have irritated the righteous; but the actual meaning of Jesus' words was much harsher: "they will enter and you will not!" The Aramaic substratum of "will enter . . . ahead" (Gk *proagousin*) is the *Hapᶜel* or *Paᶜel* participle of *qĕdam,* e.g. *mĕqaddĕmîn*; the reference of this atemporal participle was future; its sense was exclusive preference, not temporal precedence. Analogies include Luke 18:14, which in its originally intended sense reads: "this man, not the other, went down to his house having found God's favor." The motif of exclusion was also evoked by the image of exclusion from the banquet, referring to those who had refused the appeal of Jesus (Luke 14:24). To say that publicans and prostitutes would enter God's reign and that they, the righteous, would not, might have infuriated the righteous, but it meshed perfectly with the election-historical and eschatological claim of Jesus and with the divergent responses to it of many "sinners," on the one hand, and many righteous, on the other. Jesus' proclamation was divinely sanctioned; response was not optional but requisite; even the righteous risked ruin by turning it down.

Finally, these two distinct but inseparable aspects of Jesus' mission—its election-historical and its eschatological dimension—make intelligible the Torah-transcendent character of Jesus' moral teaching. The definitive restoration of Israel was coming to realization in those who accepted and rejoiced in his mission. The old order was obsolete; new wine called for new bottles (Mark 2:22 = Matt 9:17 = Luke 5:37).

b. Torah-Transcendent Teaching. Jesus declared the Deuteronomic legislation regulating divorce (Deut 24:1–

Deuteronomic legislation regulating divorce (Deut 24:1–4) to be henceforward irrelevant. Moses had allowed divorce as an accommodation to human frailty. The prescription of Genesis ("they shall be one flesh," Gen 2:24) specified the authentic will of God. Phrases such as "the Creator at the beginning" (Matt 19:4) or "from the beginning of the creation" (Mark 10:5) evoke the eschatological schema "as in the beginning, so in the end" (cf. *Barn* 6:13, *ta eschata hōs ta prōta,* "the last things [I shall make] like the first"). Following Ezekiel and Deutero-Isaiah, Jesus here and the NT writers elsewhere (Mark 1:13; Rom 5:17–19; 1 Cor 15:45) correlated the time of salvation with the restoration of Eden. As Israel's eschatological restoration came gradually to fulfillment, makeshift and provisional arrangements devised "in view of your hardness of heart" (Mark 10:5 = Matt 10:8) were rendered obsolete. The originality of Jesus' teaching on divorce, which may have provoked the later rabbinic ruling according to which anyone who said that this or that verse of the Torah was not from heaven but from Moses "by his own mouth" has "despised the word of the Lord" and should be "cut off" from among the people (*b. Sanh.* 99a Bar.), creates a strong presumption in favor of historicity.

Restoration of the norm of Paradise presupposed the advent of salvation, the time of eschatological espousals (Mark 2:19) when "good things" (Matt 7:11; cf. LXX Isa 52:7) were to be lavished on Israel. The disciple learned from experience that discipleship was transforming: the fruit was good because the tree was good (Matt 7:17–18 = Luke 6:43). Jesus' moral teaching was meant for and largely addressed to the graced and restored Israel that was coming into being in response to his word.

The transcending of the Torah might take the form of extreme radicalization of Torah prescriptions (Matt 5:22, 28, 34–37, 39, 44 [= Luke 6:27]). Given its remarkable originality, this profound transvaluation surely derived in substance from Jesus; its high point, the attitude toward enemies, is further supported by multiple attestation of nonresistance to injury and oppression (Matt 5:39b–41 = Luke 6:29), of rejoicing in persecution (Matt 5:10–12 = Luke 6:22–23), of love for enemies (Matt 5:46–47 = Luke 6:32, 35).

Jesus discriminated, in terms of relative weight, between the moral law and the ritual law. If he radicalized the first, he relativized the second. Moreover, he took every occasion to repudiate or relativize the scribal tradition *(hălākâ),* whether it bore on the moral or the ritual law. Thus the gospels contain not so much as a single word urging Sabbath observance, which had become the touchstone of Torah piety. Jesus attacked the *hălākâ* not only on divorce but on the magnification of Sabbath observances (Mark 2:27–28; cf. Matt 12:8 = Luke 6:5), food laws (Mark 7:15 = Matt 15:11), and fasting (Mark 2:18–19 = Matt 9:14–15 = Luke 5:33–34) and the relaxation of graver obligations such as to honor one's parents (Mark 7:10–13 = Matt 15:3–6) or to fulfill one's pledges (Matt 23:16–22). The logion in Mark 7:15–Matt 15:11 epitomized his perspectives:

> Nothing that goes into a man from outside can defile him,
> but only what comes out of a man defiles him.

The deepest and most authentic sense of the word "defile" belonged, not to the sphere of food laws, but to that of human speech. Tongue revealed heart, for "from the overflow of the heart the mouth speaks" (Matt 12:34 = Luke 6:45). In sins of speech, then, lay the real danger of defilement. Scribal tradition on food laws would not figure at all in God's judgment; by contrast,

> in accord with your words you will be acquitted
> and in accord with your words you will be condemned (Matt 12:37).

Jesus' commandments were essentially a code of discipleship. Was wealth what everyone wanted and could never get enough of? Then "sell what you have and give it to the poor" (Mark 10:21 = Matt 19:21 = Luke 18:22). But this summons to poverty, as the story of the rich man (Mark 10:17–22 = Matt 19:16–22 = Luke 18:18–23) shows, is ordered to discipleship. The sequence of Jesus' commands (Mark 10:21 = Matt 19:21 = Luke 18:22) is "(Go,) sell, give, and come follow." Detachment is for the sake of attachment.

Does everyone hanker to be first? Then be last. "If anyone would be first, he must be the last of all and the servant of all" (Mark 9:35; cf. Mark 10:43–44 = Matt 20:26–27; also Luke 22:26). Jesus applied this repudiation of the drive to prestige to the sphere of piety, above all. Piety should be secret, seen by God alone (Matt 6:3–4, 6, 17–18).

Even from so swift a survey as the above, it is evident that Jesus brought a new and independent vision of things and scale of values onto the scene of Palestinian Judaism. Without aspiring to comprehend all its aspects or to trace all its roots, scholarship should still be able to locate its principal perspectives and clarify them by contrast with those of Jesus' competitors for the allegiance of Israel.

c. Clarification by Contrast. The Jewish religious elite in the time of Jesus was reformist; it found the key to reform in the scriptures, especially in Exod 19:5–6 and numerous holiness texts of Leviticus (e.g. 20:26). In the first text, Judaic piety found the normative definition of the nation: Israel was called to "keep the covenant" by observing the Torah; it was called to be God's "own possession among all nations"; it was called to live a priestly life of holiness, for it was to be "a kingdom of priests and a holy people." In the second text (Lev 20:26) election, expressed in the idiom of separation, is offered, together with the holiness/separateness of the Lord himself, as the ground of a divine imperative: "you shall be holy."

Priestly theology lay at the foundations of Judaism. In accord with preexilic ideals accented now more heavily than ever, the exiles returning from Babylon made holiness—i.e. consecration, set-apartness—the central condition and sign of election. They defined themselves as the remnant of Israel and elect of God. "I have separated you from the nations" was the watchword of Ezra 9. Those who failed to separate themselves from (i.e., avoid intermarriage with) "the peoples of the land(s)" were outside the covenant (Ezra 9:1–2, 7–8, 11–15).

The ideology that bound up election with consecration and separation found full expression in the literature of the Essenes, which was obsessed with priestly ideals and concerns; CD 4:3–4 even defined "the elect of Israel," i.e., the whole sect, as priestly "sons of Zadok." Qumran was separatist in the maximal sense of claiming that the sect alone constituted the true Israel; it accordingly condemned all Jewish nonmembers as "sons of darkness," the great mass of whom were destined for ruin.

Probably the name "Pharisees" (Heb *pĕrûšîm*/Aram *pĕrîšîn*) signified "separated" and connoted "holy." It does not necessarily follow from this that the Pharisees equated "Israel" with their own fellowship. To be sure, they set themselves off from unobservant Jews as from "people(s) of the land" (*ʿammê hāʾāreṣ*); but Pharisaism was transformist, seeking to extend its own ideals and practices to all Jews. As the monastic movement was a leaven within early medieval Christianity, the Pharisees were a leaven within Second Temple Judaism. But unlike the monastic movement, the Pharisees claimed to be more than a leaven: the true vocation of all Israel without remainder lay, they claimed, precisely in Pharisaism. Under the rubric of "righteousness" they ranged through the moral heritage of the scriptures, interpreted and complemented by the specific differences of Pharisaic *hălākâ,* which focused on tithing and ritual purity. Their insistence on the latter ideal made them a table-fellowship party within Israel.

Individually and in the aggregate, Jesus' teachings suggest and, indeed, attest horizons altogether distinct from those of Torah piety. He himself was fully conscious of this; more, by his table fellowship with sinners, his Sabbath healings, and such parables as the Good Samaritan (Luke 10:29–37) and the Pharisee and the Publican (Luke 18:10–14), he mounted an attack on Judaism's reigning holiness-paradigm (Borg 1984: 102–9). On the positive side, his moral stance, though free-spirited and opposed to the punctilious attention to detail typical of scribal *hălākâ,* was in substance far more demanding and uncompromising than any scribal *hălākâ.* A prospective disciple learned—doubtless, with a shock—that he was to "let the dead bury the dead" (Matt 8:22 = Luke 9:60). Even Jesus' close disciples blanched at the seemingly utopian rigor of his exclusion of divorce (Matt 19:10; Mark 10:10 = Matt 19:9). The rich man, who had observed all the commandments from his youth, recoiled from the challenge of life without possessions (Mark 10:22 = Matt 19:22 = Luke 18:23). Jesus' radicalizations of the Torah (Matt 5:21–22, 27–28, 33–34, 38–39, 43–44) must have stunned and baffled as well as fascinated and inspired his first hearers just as they have had this effect on readers of the Sermon on the Mount across the centuries. Jesus overturned the whole mass of halakic accommodations to human frailty (e.g., Mark 10:2–12 = Matt 19:2–9; cf. Luke 16:18; Mark 7:6–7 = Matt 15:4–6). In what explanatory perspective could these views be seen to make sense?

The relevant considerations appear to be four. There was the election-historical factor: his teachings were meant for, and in the last analysis could only be meant for, restored Israel—followers summoned to be a community of the transformed. There was the eschatological factor: first, the reign of God took priority over every other consideration, even those of familial piety sanctified by the Torah; second, the time of fulfillment had arrived, bringing the reversals promised in the scriptures (Matt 5:3–6 = Luke 6:20–21) and the filling of all measures to the full (Matt 5:17; Luke 16:16). There was the prophetic factor: the code of the teacher and the taught was designed to accord with the tradition (Zeph 2:3; 3:11–13; Isa 57:15; 61:1–2) of the remnant of the poor (Matt 8:20 = Luke 9:58; Matt 11:28–30). Finally, there was a mystagogical factor: Jesus' followers were invited to enter into the mystery of his personal mission and destiny. Increasingly, this focused on the slowly crystallizing reality of rejection (Gk *apodokimasthēnai,* "to be rejected": Mark 8:31 = Luke 9:22; 17:25). After he had revealed this coming destiny to his appalled disciples (Mark 8:32 = Matt 16:22), he issued what amounted to a new call to discipleship: "If anyone wishes to follow me, let him deny himself and take up his cross[-bar] and *so* follow me" (Mark 8:34 = Matt 16:24 = Luke 9:23; cf. Matt 10:38 = Luke 14:27). In a word his teachings were unique because his mission and destiny were unique; so was the discipleship to which he summoned his followers.

5. The Identity and Destiny of Jesus: Traditions Public and Private. Interpretation of the words of Jesus has always taken some account of the factor of "audience," but T. W. Manson was the first to correlate diversity in Jesus' themes and vocabulary with his diverse audiences (Manson 1931: 320–29). The most important result was to draw attention to the existence of an esoteric tradition in the Synoptic Gospels, i.e., scenes depicting Jesus and his disciples alone and especially presenting instructions of Jesus reserved for them alone. Private or esoteric tradition, a many-sided phenomenon in the history of ancient philosophy and religion (Jeremias 1966: 125–32) and indisputably reflected in Synoptic texts, had as its principal themes in the gospel literature the identity and destiny of Jesus and the events of the eschatological crisis or "ordeal" and its resolution.

The public activity of Jesus as proclaimer and teacher, exorcist, wonderworker, and reconciler of notorious sinners inevitably prompted the question, "who is he?" (as in Mark 4:41 = Luke 8:25), i.e., "what kind of man is this?" (Matt 8:27) or, as in the questions posed to the Baptist (John 1:19–22), what role does this man play, or claim to play, in the scripturally attested scheme of the fulfillment to come?

a. The Messianic Connection. Though scholars addressing this issue have not reached consensus, there is one point at which agreement is all but unanimous: the post-Easter Christian community from virtually the outset of its existence confessed Jesus as the Messiah. Disagreement begins with the effort to say when the earliest followers of Jesus first predicated messiahship of him.

William Wrede (1901), followed by Rudolf Bultmann and his school, answered: "after the Easter experience of the disciples." N. A. Dahl (1974) modified this view by tracing the immediate roots of the Easter confession to the passion story. First, in response to the question of whether he was "the Messiah" (or "a king"), Jesus acknowledged, either by a word "extorted" from him, or at least by silence, that the answer was yes. Second, the *titulus* on the cross ("the king of the Jews") showed that this had figured in the accusations of which he had been found guilty and for which he was accordingly executed.

The views of Wrede and Bultmann, together with Dahl's minimal, if significant, modification of them, have had a wide following. It nevertheless remains a datum of the gospel story that Jesus' disciples through their spokesman Peter confessed him as Messiah during his public career (Mark 8:29 = Matt 16:16 = Luke 9:20; cf. John 1:40–42; 6:69). Why have scholars not accepted this gospel datum as historical? A major reason has been exegetical. Taking the Markan text to be the primitive account of the confession near Caesarea Philippi, many have interpreted the Markan Jesus to have rejected Peter's confession ("You are the Christ!" Mark 8:29) as "inadequate" or "wrong."

Several shortcomings of this reading, however, immediately present themselves. First, with reference to this particular pericope, the supposition of Markan priority is open to form-critical objection (Bultmann 1963: 258–59). Second, this reading of Mark contradicts the starting point of Mark's gospel (i.e., Jesus is indeed the Christ, Mark 1:1); moreover, it psychologizes the scene in a way congenial to modern but alien to Markan writing; finally, it mistakenly conceives the use of "Son of man" in the following pericope as an alternative to "Messiah." (The same error is not infrequently made respecting Mark 14:61–62.) Even if the question of historicity remains, recent critical literature has begun to change the state of the question.

The examination of popular messianic movements (Horsley and Hanson 1985) has shown the plausibility of a text like that of John 6:15, according to which a Galilean crowd "meant . . . to make him king." Again, a reconsideration of Markan materials and structure and of the use of "anointed" in contemporary Jewish sources has shown how the activity recounted in Mark 1–8 could very well have grounded the conclusion and confession of Peter (de Jonge 1986). If, moreover, the following words of Jesus and the exchange between Peter and Jesus (Mark 8:31–33 = Matt 16:21–23; cf. Luke 9:22) suppose the previous confession of Peter, as both the content of the text and its firm location in the Synoptic tradition suggest, historicity accrues to the confession from the historicity of the harsh rebuke addressed to Peter (discontinuity with the post-Easter status of Peter; coherence with evidence of Jesus' readiness to enter into "the ordeal" and the disciples' contrary dispositions of dismay and fear, Mark 10:32; their preferred concentration on glory and triumph, e.g., Mark 10:35–45 = Matt 20:20–28; their verbal readiness to suffer with Jesus, e.g., Mark 10:39 = Matt 20:22; Mark 14:29 = Matt 26:33 = Luke 22:33, but real unreadiness to do so, Mark 14:50 = Matt 26:56; Mark 14:71 = Matt 26:74 = Luke 22:60).

Factors relevant to the judgment of historicity respecting both Peter's confession and Jesus' self-understanding include the following. There was, first and foremost, the career structure based on Jesus' act of proclaiming the coming of the reign of God. This proclamation, since it bore on God's imminent and definitive saving act, presented itself as the climactic word of God to Israel. The role of eschatological proclaimer (Isa 52:7–10; cf. 61:1–3) had already been interpreted messianically in Qumran (11QMelch 18). It was certainly a role implying maximum authority, the authority not of the learned exegete but of the plenipotentiary envoy of God. Indices to just this consciousness on the part of Jesus are his distinctive use of "amen" to introduce authoritative statements and his use of the emphatic "I" in place of scriptural reference (Jeremias 1971: 35–36, 251–55). As accepters of the proclamation were destined for restoration, so its refusers were destined for ruin (Mark 6:10–11 = Matt 10:11–15 = Luke 9:4–5; cf. 10:4–12). Both in content and in style Jesus' teaching took full account of and repeatedly underscored the life-and-death character of the issue placed before Israel and the correlative fullness of authority on the part of the proclaimer and his word. Furthermore, this teaching presented the proclaimer of salvation as himself the author of its nascent realization in the present (e.g., Matt 12:28 = Luke 11:10; Mark 4:30–32 = Matt 13:31–32 = Luke 13:18–21).

Specific discrete data similarly relevant to the issue of messiahship include the following. First, in several probably authentic sayings, Jesus associated others with himself in scripturally grounded functions and dignity (Luke 12:32; 22:28–30 = Matt 19:28; cf. Mark 3:14–15 = Matt 10:1 = Luke 6:13; Mark 6:10–11 = Matt 10:11–15 = Luke 9:4–5; cf. 10:4–12). Second, in the historically authentic riddle on destroying the sanctuary and building another in (or after) three days (Mark 14:58 = Matt 26:61; John 2:19; cf. Mark 15:29 = Matt 27:40; Acts 6:14), Jesus attributed to himself a specifically royal (= messianic) task, namely, to build the house of God (Meyer 1981); this, in turn, heightens the probable historicity of the *kêpāʾ* (rock) word responding to Simon's confession of Jesus as Messiah (Matt 16:17–19; Meyer 1979: 185–97). Third, the symbolic acts of Jesus' entry into Jerusalem (Mark 11:1–10 = Matt 21:1–9 = Luke 19:29–38; John 2:13–18) and cleansing of the temple (Mark 11:15–17 = Matt 21:12–13 = Luke 19:45–46) were royal. Fourth, similarly indicative in their own way were the symbolic mockeries in the passion story such as the purple cloak and the crown of thorns (Mark 15:17–20 = Matt 27:28–31 = John 19:2–5; cf. Luke 23:11). These were complemented, fifth, by the explicit *titulus* on the cross (Mark 15:26 = Matt 27:37 = Luke 23:28 = John 19:19–22).

Whereas he accepted the messianic title in private, Jesus did not use "Messiah" of himself during his public career. This policy on self-disclosure apparently reflected a certain realism about the response of faith. Faith would not win out over unfaith if only the appeal to it were explicit and spectacular (cf. Luke 16:30–31). Jesus' policy was to set before Israel a proclamation and a sequence of acts charged with symbolic meaning; his teaching guided and encouraged a maximal interpretation of these events but refrained from spelling out this interpretation in determinate (e.g., titular) terms. Hence Jesus' refusal of the demand for a sign (Mark 8:11–12 = Matt 16:1–4 = Luke 11:16, 29; cf. Matt 12:38–39; John 6:30–36), the lack of public titles for himself or his following (e.g., Mark 3:33–34 = Matt 12:48–49 = Luke 8:21), the indirection of the response to the Baptist ("Tell John what you hear and see," Matt 11:4 = Luke 7:22), and the thanksgiving for revelation to the unlikely, "the simple" (Matt 11:25 = Luke 10:21), which exalted the divine over the human factor in positive responses to Jesus; compare the macarism on Peter (not "flesh and blood but my heavenly Father" has revealed [this] to you," Matt 16:17). If Jesus refused to set an explicit messianic claim before Israel, this reserve, which supposed that God's grace of "revelation" was ever operative (Matt 16:17; 11:25 = Luke 10:21), allowed the public to draw its own conclusion. Jesus' reserve did not in any case signify that the conclusion drawn by Peter was mistaken.

Even to recognize him as Messiah was only a first step in coming to know who he was, for the secret of his identity was bound up with the secret of his destiny. Jesus' messiahship was not simply definable in advance by messianic tradition. His identity would be defined by his destiny—a prophetic theme reserved for his disciples. The coming ordeal was, to be sure, a theme of public warning; that the ordeal would be launched by the repudiation, suffering, and death of Jesus, however, belonged to esoteric tradition. Hence, however public the imminence of eschatological crisis, the full scheme of Jesus' vision of the future was private.

b. Jesus' Scenario of the Future. Amid the chaos of scholarly opinion on Jesus' view of the future, the hypothesis of C. H. Dodd (1961: 21–84) offers an analysis having certain advantages, negative and positive. Among the negative advantages: the hypothesis did not attempt to transpose the time dimension of Jesus' scheme of the future into nontemporal categories (both this procedure and its product or result would have been alien to ancient Judaism); nor did the hypothesis attempt to retain the time dimension but to remove from it the pervasive note of imminence (for fear that Jesus' prophecy might otherwise be thought to have been mistaken). Among the positive advantages, Dodd's hypothesis took account not just of some "key data" but of all the data; better yet, it managed to make sense of all the data. Concretely, the main points of Jesus' view of the future included, first, an eschatology of woe bearing on the ordeal soon to break out. This would be fierce but brief. It would bring disaster to the Jewish people, capital, and temple. It would engulf Jesus and his disciples; indeed, it would be launched by Jesus' suffering and death. Second, the resolution of the ordeal was Jesus' eschatology of weal or bliss. It would be inaugurated by "the day of the Son of man." As the suffering of Jesus would launch the ordeal, so his vindication would bring it to an end. Jesus would be installed at the right hand of God for all to see. Images belonging to this resolution of the ordeal included the resurrection of the dead, the pilgrimage of the nations, the judgment, the banqueting of the saved with the patriarchs in the reign of God.

Dodd took "the day of the Son of man" to have originally signified both resurrection and second coming as a single event (Dodd 1961: 74–77). In fact, however, the Easter experience of the disciples had proved to comprehend only the resurrection of Jesus, not the consummation of history. Thus the differentiation of resurrection and parousia was effected *ex eventu* by the fact that Jesus' resurrection proved to be an isolated event. Once given this account of how the actual unfolding of events had separated elements originally conceived as a single event, it became possible for the critic to recover the original sense of parables (e.g., the Faithful and Unfaithful Servant, Matt 24:45–51 = Luke 12:42–46) that in their present state supposed an interim between resurrection and parousia.

c. The Son of Man. An important aspect of this reconstruction is the contextual and structural contribution that it makes to the much debated question of Jesus' use of the expression "the Son of man." Behind this phrase, so often found on the lips of Jesus in the gospels, there doubtless stood the Aramaic expression *bar ʾĕnāš(āʾ)*. This phrase could signify "man" (generic sense), "(some)one, a man" (indefinite sense), or "the man" (determinate sense). A translator into Greek had no idiomatic verbal resource capable of rendering the determinate sense to the exclusion of the generic sense. Both would be rendered by *ho anthrōpos* or (keeping the genetival locution) by *ho huios anthrōpou.* If (despite the limits of Greek idiom) the translator was bent on specifying the determinate to the exclusion of the generic sense, he might have recourse to the artificial strategem of doubling the Greek article; this would yield *ho huios tou anthrōpou.*

This appears to be just what the translators of the gospel tradition did. Their reason for wishing to specify the determinate sense is transparently theological: they intended it as a title, "the Son of man." This determinate, eschatological, titular sense was, no doubt, derivative from Dan 7:13–14, despite the fact that the Danielic phrase *kĕbar ʾenāš,* "one like a (son of) man," was in no sense titular. The translators and transmitters of the gospel tradition obviously rejoiced in the title, for even when *bar ʾĕnāš(āʾ)* bore a sense that was neither titular nor even determinate but generic or indefinite (especially if Jesus himself was the indirectly intended referent of the phrase), the early translators preferred to render it by "the Son of man." Their tendency was to maximize use of the title, preferring it to other renderings as often as possible, despite the inconcinnities that this practice entailed. So potent a bias in favor of the title on the part of the transmitters of the tradition is a factor to be kept in mind in dealing with the Son-of-man riddle in the gospels.

There is at present no sure evidence of the use of this eschatological title prior to the time of Jesus. True, the title occurs in the Similitudes of *1 Enoch* (37–71), but the attestation of this particular part of Enoch is late. In the Latin version of *4 Ezra* 13 (a work dating originally from A.D. 100) *ille homo* (that man), *ipse homo* (the same man, the man himself), and *vir* (a man, the man) is a supernatural figure derived from Daniel 7 and correlative to the Messiah found elsewhere in *4 Ezra.* God calls him "my Son" (13:32, 37, 52) and speaks of his "day" (13:52). The task of the Man is the judgment of the nations and the restoration of Israel. Christian influence on the text of *4 Ezra* 13 is improbable. Among the rabbis a messianic reading of Daniel 7 is attested for the 3d century (*b. Sanh.* 98a). It is possible, though at present uncertain, that prior to Jesus the "one like a man" in Daniel 7 had already been interpreted as it in fact came to be interpreted in *4 Ezra* 13, in the Similitudes of *Enoch,* and among the rabbis—namely, as an eschatological figure correlative to or coincidental with that of the Messiah. But, though this is a live possibility, it is still unattested for the pre-Jesus period.

On the supposition that the title had not been used prior to Jesus, the question is whether it was Jesus himself or the early Christian community that took the interpretative step of objectifying the "one like a man" as the bearer of a specific role to be played out in the eschatological scenario. The index of originality would heavily favor the first option. So striking a christological initiative on the part of the early post-Easter community would have no parallel in the gospel literature; as the creative adaptation of Jesus himself, it is paralleled by his transformation of messianic tradition. But is it possible to reconstruct Jesus' use of the title?

We begin by addressing the well-attested but anomalous phenomenon of texts paralleled except in their use of the Son-of-man title. It is a remarkable fact that such texts easily outnumber parallel texts in which all parallels exhibit the title (Jeremias 1967). Does the solution lie in positing an idiomatic usage in Aramaic according to which *bar (ʾĕ)nāš(āʾ)* is a straightforward periphrasis for the first-person personal pronoun (I/me) (Vermes 1967; 1978)? Possibly. The hypothesis is attractive in that it presents itself as a single complete solution of the problem it was designed to address. Its drawback is that the core of the solution, the idiomatic periphrasis in question, is unattested for middle Aramaic, 200 B.C. to A.D. 200 (Fitzmyer 1979: 58–60).

An alternative solution is to appeal to the bias in favor of the title on the part of the transmitters of the tradition. Inept use of the title to translate *bar ʾĕnāš(āʾ)* in the generic or indefinite sense with indirect self-reference may well have generated an entirely secondary imposition of the Greek title on texts that originally offered only the personal pronoun referring to Jesus. Son-of-man texts paralleled by texts without the title would accordingly drop from consideration as words of the historical Jesus (Jeremias 1967). There remain eleven Synoptic Son-of-man texts: two from the triple tradition (Mark 13:26 = Matt 24:30 = Luke 21:27; Mark 14:62 = Matt 26:64 = Luke 22:69), three from the logia tradition (Matt 8:20 = Luke 9:58; Matt 24:27, 37 = Luke 17:24, 26), two from the special Matthean tradition (Matt 10:23; 25:31), and four from the special Lukan tradition (Luke 17:22, 30; 18:8; 21:36). All but one of these texts (Matt 8:20 = Luke 9:58) bear on the parousiac Son of man. All but two of them belong to the esoteric tradition. The two exceptions are the anomalous text from the logia tradition (Matt 8:20 = Luke 9:58) and the response of Jesus to the high priest in the hearing before the Sanhedrin (Mark 14:62 = Matt 26:64 = Luke 22:69).

In the Synoptic gospels as they stand, texts on the Son of man break down into three main categories: those that directly apply the title to Jesus during his public career; those that use the title with reference to his suffering and/or glorification; and those that use the title with reference to the parousia/judgment. In terms of the present analysis, what is the status of these three sets of texts, and how did they come into being?

The Son-of-man title in the first set is in all probability entirely secondary, although this use has a perfectly intelligible point of departure. Jesus, no doubt, often used *bar ʾĕnāš(āʾ)* in a generic sense (e.g., Mark 2:27; Matt 4:4 = Luke 4:4); but when he did this with himself as indirectly signified referent, the translators into Greek converted *bar ʾĕnāš(āʾ)* into a title (Mark 2:20 = Matt 9:6 = Luke 5:24; cf. Matt 9:8). Similarly, Jesus, no doubt, often used *bar ʾĕnāš(āʾ)* in an indefinite sense (e.g., Matt 7:9; 8:9 = Luke 7:8); but when he did this with himself as an indirectly signified referent, the tradition again converted the expression into a title (Matt 11:19 = Luke 7:34). This predilection on the part of the translators obviously reflected the clear Easter equation of Jesus with the Son of man. This tendency of the tradition paved the way for an entirely secondary pre-redactional and even redactional imposition of the title on traditions, in Greek, that originally offered only the personal pronoun referring to Jesus. The result was a widespread, anomalous phenomenon: the use of the title in texts whose parallels lack it. That *both* of the parallel texts on Jesus' having nowhere to lay his head are outfitted with the title (Matt 8:20 = Luke 9:58) is perhaps attributable to sheer chance.

Use of the title in the second set of texts is either entirely secondary and explained in essentially the same way (Fitzmyer *Luke* AB, 210–11) or, more likely, it had a point of departure in a consciously ambiguous aphorism *(māšāl)* of Jesus, Mark 9:31 = Matt 17:22 = Luke 9:44, which in Aramaic retroversion would read:

> *mitmĕsar bar ʾĕnāšāʾ / lîdê bĕnê ʾĕnāšāʾ.*
> Man/the Man is [about to be] delivered [by God] into the hands of men.

"Man" is generic, the equivalent of mankind; "the Man" is determinate and titular. The hypothesis (Jeremias 1971: 281–86) is that Jesus intended the ambiguity. The ostensible sense was generic, a prophecy of human disaster at the hands of human beings; the subsurface sense was titular, a prophecy incorporating the coming suffering of Jesus into a divinely willed plan and identifying the Jesus about to suffer with the Son-of-man soon to be revealed in glory (Daniel 7). Such was the historical basis on which tradition (not Jesus) generated the second set of texts.

The third set of texts has a surer historical basis and a substantial historical development. Quite apart from the Son-of-man title, Daniel 7 figures in the words of Jesus (Matt 19:28 = Luke 22:28, 30b; Luke 12:32). Again, in the Son-of-man texts themselves the third-person use of the title, "the Son of man," since it maintains the duality of Jesus and the Son of man, is an index to pre-Easter tradition. The same is true of the fact that among the Son-of-man texts there is never any differentiation between resurrection and parousia.

It is not certain, as noted above, whether the Son of man was already an eschatological theme current in Judaism. If it was, Jesus could have evoked this theme in public preaching (Matt 12:40 = Luke 11:30; Luke 12:8). If it was not, Jesus' use of the Son-of-man title with reference to the consummation of history would in all probability have been limited to esoteric tradition—until the hearing before the Sanhedrin (Mark 14:62 = Matt 26:64 = Luke 22:69). The second possibility is highly probable, since nearly all the texts as they stand have the disciples alone for their audience.

The ultimate secret of Jesus' identity—his identity as the Son of man—was unambiguously revealed only with his resurrection from the dead. Prior to that it remained veiled, whether the veiled form functioned as promise (Matt 10:23) or as threat (Mart 14:62 = Matt 27:64 = Luke 22:69).

In the present prior to this revelation Jesus understood himself as the still hidden Messiah whose task was to win the heart of Israel. But the scenario of a prince sent to his people in the guise of a commoner to fire their allegiance in preparation for the day when he would be revealed as their king went dramatically awry. To depict aspects of his mission Jesus had drawn on the images of the physician (Mark 2:17 = Matt 9:13 = Luke 5:31) and of the messenger sent to announce that the banquet was ready (Mark 2:17 = Matt 9:13 = Luke 5:32; cf. Luke 14:16–17). But the physician was told to heal himself (Luke 4:23) and the messenger was sent back to his master with a set of refusals (cf. Luke 14:21). In dirge (mainly 3/2 beat) rhythm Jesus lamented the refusal:

O Jerusalem, Jerusalem, killer of prophets,
stoner of those sent to you,
how many times have I longed
to gather your children,
as a mother bird gathers her brood
under her wings—
but you would not have it!
(Matt 23:37 = Luke 13:34).

6. Why and How Jesus Died. The narrative scheme in the Synoptic gospels, insofar as it allows for only a single journey of Jesus to Jerusalem, was symbolic: he went to Jerusalem to die (Luke 13:33). The length of Jesus' public career according to the Fourth Gospel (ca. three years) probably approximated the historical reality. He must, then, have traveled to Jerusalem several times and stayed there at least for a few days at the yearly Passover and perhaps for other feasts as well.

Jesus experienced both success and failure in his mission. Two kinds of charisma were operative in bringing him a certain public success: "prophetic" charisma in his proclamation and "magic" charisma in his wonderworking. (These modern terms do not signify that Jesus was a prophet or a magician, though in point of fact he was the first and not the second.) The kind of popular success that was sometimes expressly noted in the tradition and more often was implicit in public scenes finds confirmation in the fact that, when planning to arrest him, his adversaries felt the need of stealth "lest there be a riot among the people" (Mark 14:2 = Matt 26:5).

Though Jesus addressed his proclamation to all Israel, there was a kind of popular success that he neither sought nor accepted, but repudiated. It is illustrated by his rejection of and flight from the attempt of a Galilean crowd "to make him king" (John 6:15). The success he rejected was the excitement of people at having found a champion of the depressed, a potential political and economic liberator who would free the nation and feed the hungry. The success that he sought was a positive response to his proclamation, to the teachings that explained it, and to the moral commands that accorded with it, as well as a positive response to his personal invitations to discipleship. This was, indeed, a response to a champion of the depressed, but one who offered neither a program for political independence nor any banquet in the present life. His following was not meant to look for revolution in the here and now. It was meant to look rather for the supreme revolution, the transcendent fulfillment that would be the consummation of history and the reign of God. Whatever the enthusiasm that his cures generated and however great the crowds that listened to him, Israel as a whole had not yet crystallized its response to his mission. Now he came to Jerusalem for Passover, determined to force the issue. He would place a public act dramatically epitomizing his mission and compelling the attention of Jerusalem. The way Jerusalem went the nation would go.

a. The Royal Entry and the Cleansing of the Temple. That Jesus did in fact place the act of cleansing the temple (i.e., driving money changers and merchants of sacrificial birds and animals from the temple court) is solidly probable in the light of the indices of discontinuity and originality. Respecting discontinuity with the early Church: even the most primitive account, that of Mark, has toned down a dangerous memory, probably for fear of otherwise allowing hearers to misconstrue Jesus' act as that of a revolutionary. Hence Jesus is depicted as acting alone, although the detail of Mark 11:16 implies the collaboration of his disciples in controlling the temple gates. (Whether the temple police intervened is unknown.) Matthew and Luke have carried the Markan tendency still further, offering jejune, gingerly accounts that reduce the dimensions of the event and obscure its causal relation to the conspiracy against and arrest of Jesus (contrast Mark 11:18). Finally, John has altogether removed the cleansing of the temple from the prologue to the passion story. Respecting originality vis-à-vis Judaism: in the history of the Herodian temple there is no real parallel to Jesus' act, although the story of Jesus, son of Ananias (*JW* 6.5.3 §300–9), illustrates how perilous it was for anyone to assume a public stance toward the temple that might be interpreted as negative. Thus what is distinctive about Jesus' act is first of all its sheer boldness.

What did the act mean? The answer depends especially on how its context is defined. The immediate context was Jesus' deliberately contrived solemn entry into the city and temple. Form-critically the entry narrative is a legend; stylistically it is overlaid with folkloric (Mark 11:1–6 = Matt 21:1–6 = Luke 19:28–34) and midrashic (Mark 11:9a = Matt 21:9a; John 12:13) motifs. Nevertheless historicity accrues to the substance of the entry account from the semantic bond uniting the entry with the cleansing. This bond could be severed, as the Gospel of John shows; but it is clear from the Synoptic tradition that the two events derive from one matrix and were originally elements of a single symbolic structure.

According to a fixed, age-old, Near Eastern structure of symbols, royal acclamation is followed by the new king's establishment or restoration of cult. In the gospel accounts the entry motifs were inescapably royal, for certain aspects of the procession from the Mount of Olives to the temple deliberately evoked the image of the king celebrated in Zech 9:9, "lowly and riding upon an ass." (Cited by Matthew and John, this text is implicitly referred to in the other accounts.) Though the cleansing scene offers no specifically messianic motif, there are reasons for relating it to messianism. Just as the task of temple building was specifically royal, so in classical biblical tradition, as in Mesopotamia, the tasks of establishing, maintaining, and restoring the cult were reserved to the king. As symbolic act, then, the cleansing belonged to the same royal or messianic thematic as the entry. Entry and cleansing together signaled the arrival of the time of fulfillment. The epiphany of the Son of David meant that "this age" had been overtaken by "the age to come." His visitation of the temple signified the end of the historic cult and the inauguration of eschatological cult. (This symbolism, to be sure, exhibits an open, unfinished structure, for it merely signifies an eschatological cult without specifying its character or content.)

It would be a mistake to infer from the symbolic character of the cleansing that Jesus did not intend a real critique of temple practice. Prophetic passion (John 2:17) powered the whole event and rightly gave it the name of a "cleansing." What provoked this passion is indicated both by Jesus' explanatory words (Mark 11:17 = Matt 21:13 = Luke 19:46; John 2:16), which, striking an eschatological note in the words "for all peoples" (Mark 11:17), contrasted the temple in God's holy intention with the temple in man's sinful history, and by the detail that Jesus "would not allow anyone to carry anything through the temple court" (Mark 11:16; cf. *m. Ber.* 9:5 on not using the temple court as a shortcut). What provoked this indignation was routine irreverence pragmatically sanctioned by authority. The record of his teaching shows that, so far from acquiescing in life's routine disorders, Jesus censured them and called for their reform. Thus he rigorously forbade the routine use of oaths (Matt 5:34–37), routine verbal abuse (Matt 5:22), routine concupiscence (Matt 5:28). He fiercely protested against the use of Torah and *hălākâ* to protect hardness of heart: the taken-for-granted practice of divorce (Mark 10:1–12 = Matt 19:1–12) and the spuriously pious refusal to help one's parents in need (Mark 7:10–12 = Matt 15:3–6). He warned that the heedlessly slanderous word would be remembered at the judgment (Matt 12:36–37) and he made sins of speech the epitome of uncleanness (Mark 7:15 = Matt 15:11). In short, he condemned all the shifts and dodges of "average carnal man" that Israel, like the world at large, simply assumed and accepted as part of the human condition. In full accord with this complex of views and commands, the cleansing of the temple was the fallout from a collision. Passion for the honor of God and the restoration of Israel collided with toleration of routine irreverence toward the temple, i.e., toleration of tables of money-changers (*m. Šeqal.* 1:3) and stalls of merchants (Zech 14:21) on the temple court, and the use of the court by water-carriers and others as a shortcut between Ophel and the eastern suburbs (*m. Ber.* 9:5).

In the Synoptic tradition the entry into Jerusalem and the cleansing of the temple are followed by the question about Jesus' authority (Mark 11:27–33 = Matt 21:23–27 = Luke 20:1–8; John 2:18–20), though none of the Synoptic Gospels connects it immediately with the cleansing. In the Gospel of John, on the other hand, the cleansing is immediately followed by the demand of "the Jews" for a sign justifying Jesus' pretention to superior authority. Though not provable, neither is it improbable that the original placement of the temple riddle (Mark 14:58 [= Matt 26:61]) was just where it is found now in John's gospel, namely, in an epilogue to the cleansing of the temple (John 2:18–20).

If such was the immediate demand of the authorities, it would clearly indicate that they had rightly interpreted Jesus' act as "prophetic" and perhaps as symbolic in intent. Jesus, however, refused to meet the demand except by the indirection of a riddle. To the Sanhedrists this response was pretentious and odious; probably caution in the face of Jesus' popular following and that alone (Mark 14:2 = Matt 26:5) postponed his arrest.

The original wording of the riddle is irrecoverable, but the subtraction of Markan redactional touches (Mark 14:58) would yield:

> I will destroy this sanctuary
> and in three days I will build another.

Behind such words stood the oracle of Nathan, the classic source of royal messianism (2 Sam 7:13–14), making the building of the sanctuary the task of David's son. A Qumran text (4QFlor 1–13) offers a messianic reading of the oracle (though without specifically referring this to the verses on the building of the sanctuary). The destruction of the sanctuary belonged, as we have seen (see C.5), to the eschatological ordeal. The three-days motif (cf. Luke 13:32–33) locates the building of the new sanctuary in the eschaton; it is the equivalent of the advent of the reign of God bringing the ordeal to an end.

In this reconstruction, the whole event takes on a peculiarly Zecharian allure: Jesus came to the temple "lowly and riding upon an ass" (Zech 9:9); he drove the buyers and sellers and money-changers from the courtyard, for "on that day there shall no longer be any merchant in the house of the LORD of hosts" (Zech 14:21); and, challenged to establish his authority by a "sign," he answered as "the man whose name is 'the Branch' " who would "build the temple of the LORD" (Zech 6:12).

The whole event triggered the conspiracy that led to Jesus' death (Mark 11:18 = Luke 19:47b–48). Judas Iscariot would become a linchpin of the conspiracy's success (Mark 14:10–11, 17–21 = Matt 26:14–16, 20–25 = Luke 22:3–6, 21–23; cf. John 13:21–30). But before it issued in his arrest (Mark 14:43–46 = Matt 26:47–50 = Luke 22:47–48; John 18:2–3), Jesus gathered with his disciples for the celebration of Passover.

b. Last Supper, Arrest, Trial, Execution. The Johannine account of the farewells of Jesus offers a chronology different from that of the Synoptic Gospels. All agree that Jesus died on a Friday. According to John, this was Nisan 14, whereas in the Synoptic Gospels it was Nisan 15. In John, then, there was no Passover meal on Jesus' last evening with his disciples; in the Synoptic Gospels the last supper was a Passover meal. Certainty about which of these chronologies is correct is beyond our reach, but probability on the basis of a mass of minute, circumstantial detail especially in the Synoptic accounts of the Last Supper favors their chronology.

Dominating the memory of what Jesus did and said at that meal were two sets of acts and words. First, there was Jesus' act of blessing, breaking, and distributing the unleavened bread; corresponding to the blessing customarily spoken over the bread, Jesus said: "This is my body" (Mark 14:22 [= Matt 26:26]; cf. Luke 22:19 [= 1 Cor 11:24]). Second, after the meal proper, Jesus distributed a single cup (the third cup or "cup of blessing" according to the Passover ritual) and, in accord with the blessing, bade his disciples to drink from it, saying: "This is my blood, covenant blood, (to be) poured out for many" (Mark 14:24 [= Matt 26:28]; cf. Luke 22:20 [= 1 Cor 11:25]). This scripturally charged language, by its allusions to Exod

24:8, Jer 31:31, and Isa 53:11–12, interpreted Jesus' imminent death as both an expiatory offering and a sacrifice sealing God's covenant with all who would enter the new Israel. If immediately following his words on the bread and, again, immediately following his words on the wine, Jesus gave the same bread and the same wine to his disciples to be eaten and drunk, this act of giving signified that by their eating and drinking they shared in the atoning power of his death and in the new covenant that his death would seal. The combination of these motifs thus defined his disciples as the nucleus of eschatological Israel. As the event of the cleansing of the temple brought into prominence a correlate of the reign of God (namely, the new people symbolized by the motif of the new sanctuary), so this complementary event, centered on the coming death of Jesus, highlighted another correlate of God's reign: the new covenant.

The historicity of the eucharistic acts and words of Jesus is commended by their distinctiveness and originality. Detailed linguistic analysis grounds an important conclusion on the genre of the Markan account: it is a historical report (Pesch 1978: 76–81). Also relevant to historicity is the fact that Paul by the phrase "from the Lord" (*apo tou Kuriou,* 1 Cor 11:23) designated the eucharistic words as a tradition that had originated with Jesus himself. See LAST SUPPER.

With the help of Judas, Jesus was arrested later on the same night in a garden on the Mount of Olives. In a trial before the hastily convened Sanhedrin, the riddle of the sanctuary was cited against him. The decisive moment, however, was his response, affirmative in content, to the high priest's question: "Are you the Messiah, the Son of the Blessed One?" (Mark 14:61 [= Matt 26:63]; cf. Luke 22:67, 70). Jesus was found guilty of blasphemy, which apparently lay in dishonoring the name of God by falsely claiming to be his "Son" (Blinzler 1969: 155–57). The condemnation for blasphemy was to death; since the Sanhedrin did not have jurisdiction in capital cases (the Romans reserved that to themselves), the case would be referred to the Roman Prefect temporarily in Jerusalem for the feast.

The following morning Jesus was tried before the Roman prefect, Pontius Pilate, on charges of sedition, the core element of which was the charge that he claimed to be a king (Luke 23:2). Found guilty by Pilate despite the political innocence implied in Jesus' answers and his silence, he was scourged and led to Golgotha, just outside the city gates, where Roman soldiers crucified him together with two brigands. If Mark 15:25 is an interpolation in the text (Blinzler 1969: 420–21), Jesus was crucified about noon and died some three hours later. By order of the prefect, the body of Jesus was taken down from the cross and buried in a nearby tomb provided by a disciple, Joseph of Arimathea (John 19:38–42).

Contributing to the irony and pathos of the passion story were the betrayal by Judas, the denials of Peter, the flight of the disciples, the presence (probably on the city wall) of the women, including the mother of Jesus, who had cared for him during his public career, the *titulus* on the cross ("the king of the Jews"), and the taunts of his enemies. The exact date of Jesus' death cannot be computed with certainty, but of the concrete possibilities the most likely is April 7 of the year 30.

c. The Why and the How of Jesus' Death. To sum up the why and the how of Jesus' death: What was it in him that provoked hostility on the part of the Jerusalem establishment? The answer probably lies in the extraordinary pretention to authority inherent in all that Jesus said and did throughout his public career. The supreme expression of this grandiose if implicit claim was his royal entry into Jerusalem, the cleansing of the temple, and the riddle imaging the destruction of the sanctuary and the building of a new one in, or after, three days. Had he not spoken words against and laid violent hands upon the untouchable? He had never taken care to reserve a place for the elite of scribes, elders, and priests in his scheme of the future. They repaid him in the same coin. In the tension-laden little world of Roman-dominated Israel there was not room enough for both this aristocracy and that incalculable popular figure and possible messianic pretender. The leaders of the Sanhedrin took the initiative and, with the help of a disaffected disciple of Jesus, they brought him down.

Was Jesus' will to specify his death as an expiatory offering coherent with his proclamation of God's gratuitous salvation even for notorious sinners? Some have thought not; they have accordingly dismissed as unhistorical the entire line of esoteric tradition bearing on Jesus' approaching destiny: his prophecy of rejection, death, and vindication; his word on giving his life as a ransom; the eucharistic words, especially on "covenant" and "for many."

This view, however, overlooks the context in which this esoteric tradition was not only intelligible but inevitable, namely, the dilemma which the prospect of Israel's rejection of his mission posed for Jesus. His offer of salvation was indeed free, but positive response to it was requisite, not optional. The prospect of rejection created an anomaly. The good news of the reign of God risked turning into a condemnation. Was the herald of Israel's restoration to become the instrument of its ruin? What could be done for the refuser in this situation of refusal?

Jesus found the solution in his own expiatory death. So far from responding to some unintelligible demand incompatible with grace, his expiatory death was an initiative of pure grace, meant above all for Israel (Pesch 1978: 105–9). Having willed his death for the forgiveness of the sins of Israel and the sins of the world, he took the decisive step toward this destiny when, in response to the authoritative question of the high priest, he explicitly affirmed in public, for the first and only time, his claim to be the messianic Son of God.

7. The Easter Experience of the Disciples. In the faith of Israel "resurrection" signified far more than the resuscitation of the dead. According to Dan 12:3 the risen shall shine "like the stars for ever and ever" (cf. the use of "stars" for angels in Dan 8:10). A like conclusion is attested by the words of Jesus to the Sadducees: "for when they rise from the dead, they neither marry nor are given in marriage, but are like angels in heaven" (Mark 12:25 [= Matt 22:30 = Luke 20:35]); the Lukan text continues: "for they cannot die any more . . ." (Luke 26:36).

Paul has furnished detailed and decisive evidence on

what "resurrection" meant to ancient Jews and Christians. In 1 Cor 15:50 he cited what was probably a pre-Pauline distich to the effect that neither the living nor the dead can enter the reign of God as they are (Jeremias 1955: 151–55); his resolution of this dilemma was that, just as the dead would be wholly transformed by resurrection (1 Cor 15:42–44), so the living would be simultaneously transformed at the parousia (1 Cor 15:51–52). The point is clear: the life of the age to come would differ radically from the conditions of present life. Though "resurrection" signified bodily life, the bodily life in question would be sublated, transformed, "pneumatic" (1 Cor 15:44). The leading theme of Paul's treatment of the nature of resurrection (1 Cor 15:35–58) was precisely the transformed corporeity of the resurrected dead (1 Cor 15:35–49), in accord with rabbinic conceptions and argumentation (Morissette 1972: 210–16), as well as of the living, once they were "changed" at the parousia (1 Cor 15:50–52).

Respecting the tradition of Easter texts in the NT, a few points may be noted from the start. The resurrection of Jesus is not depicted. Moreover, the original story of the discovery of the empty tomb has been nearly lost in an overlay of kerygmatic motifs. Again, what the tradition accounted as the first appearance of the risen Jesus, which was to "Simon" (Luke 24:34) or "Cephas" (1 Cor 15:5), has left no narrative depicting it. Further, the prehistory of the gospel texts can be penetrated only in part and that partial reconstruction is necessarily tentative. Finally, the accounts are unharmonizable among themselves. (On the resurrection texts in the gospels, see the *ABD* articles on each gospel.) However pertinent these observations, it nevertheless remains that testimony to the risen Jesus is early, firm, various but coherent, and acknowledged in all known currents of early Christian tradition as the foundation of the life of the church.

The following are seven positive ascertainments respecting the earliest stage of the tradition on "the Easter experience of the disciples." First, the Easter experience proper was not the discovery of an empty tomb; rather, it was the experience of appearances of Jesus.

Second, the sources depict the disciples' interpretation of these appearances as the realization, in the singular destiny of Jesus, of the eschatological resurrection of the dead. Simply put, the disciples explained their experience in the following terms: God had raised Jesus from the dead (1 Thess 1:10; 1 Cor 6:14; Rom 4:24; 8:11; 10:9; etc.).

Third, in this resurrection they saw the divine vindication of Jesus; hence they understood his exaltation as Messiah and Lord (1 Cor 8:6; 12:3; Rom 1:3–4; 8:34b; 10:9; Acts 2:36; 3:20–21; etc.) to be integral to his resurrection. The immediate consequence was an Easter explosion of christological speech.

Fourth, they understood themselves, correlatively, as the messianic community in which Israel had come to eschatological restoration.

Fifth, the Easter experience was an experience of forgiveness, for it effected reconciliation (Stuhlmacher 1986: 54)—the reconciliation to God through the communion offered by his glorified Son, of men who had earlier rejected this same Son (James), or abandoned him (the disciples in general), or "denied" him (Peter), or "persecuted" him (Paul).

Sixth, an integral element of the Easter experience was the missionary mandate of the risen Christ.

Seventh, Easter created a new situation with respect to the scheme of the future that Jesus had presented to his disciples (see above, C.5). If it had not been clear before, it was now clear that the Lord Jesus would himself come on clouds to signal the consummation of history (1 Thess 4:16–17 = Matt 24:30–31, etc.). A segment of time had now been inserted between the vindication of Jesus by resurrection and his parousia, which would mark the advent of the reign of God.

Each of these points calls for at least brief elaboration. We begin with the empty tomb. The primitive tradition on the empty tomb affirmed that early on the Sunday following the crucifixion some of the women associated with Jesus during his public career discovered that the tomb in which he had been buried was empty. They reported this to the disciples, who found that the story of the women was true.

Reduced to these terms, the tradition was a sober account of significant fact. It was not the ground of faith in the risen Jesus. Much less was it taken to be a proof that he had risen. It involved no angels and no proclamations. The unkerygmatic nature of the primitive tradition is indicated especially by Luke 24:24, "some of those who were with us went to the tomb and found it just as the women had said, but him they did not see." The account in John 20:1–2 (Benoit 1960) is comparable. Here Mary Magdalene discovered that the rock had been moved from the mouth of the tomb; she went to Simon Peter and "the other disciple, the one whom Jesus loved" with this perplexing piece of news. There was no angel on the scene. Mary acted on her own initiative. Her report was simply, "They have taken the Lord out of the tomb and we do not know where they have laid him" (John 20:2). (In this last line the plural "we" is possibly indicative of the tradition according to which Mary was accompanied by other women.) Such is the recovery of an originally pre-kerygmatic, pre-apologetic tradition on the tomb.

It follows that the Easter experience proper did not begin with the tomb but with the appearances of Jesus. The earliest text on the appearances is the pre-Pauline formula cited in 1 Cor 15:3–5.

> Christ died for our sins in accordance with the scriptures,
> and he was buried,
> and he was raised on the third day in accordance with the scriptures,
> and he appeared to Cephas, then to the twelve.

The formula moves from Jesus' death and burial (lines 1 and 2) to his resurrection and appearances (lines 3 and 4). The central affirmations are in the parallel lines 1 and 3; lines 2 and 4 functioned each as the warrant of the preceding statement. The result is that, as Harnack put it, "the burial authenticates the really occurring death and the vision authenticates the really occurring resurrection" (*SPAW*, 64). The whole formula therefore asserts: he really died and he really rose. As in all such formulas the accent falls on the resurrection. "He was buried" immediately attests the death, but it does so precisely in order to set up the climactic theme of resurrection. From this consciously fashioned transition it follows that the expression in line 3, "he was raised," is meant to comprehend the specifically corporeal dimension of "resurrection." The repeated motif of the advance testimony of the scriptures is a qualifier: Christ died for our sins, as the scriptures have prophetically attested that he would; and God raised him on the third day (cf. *Tg. Neb.* Hos 6:2), as the scriptures have prophetically attested that he would. Though the testimony of Cephas and "the twelve" is a most distinctive motif, it remains subordinate to the basic confession. (Inattention to the structure of the formula has repeatedly led to the mistaken supposition that the phrase "he was buried" attests the tradition of the empty tomb. It does not; the formula does, however, present a view of resurrection that coheres with and even entails the empty tomb.)

Second point: the disciples interpreted the appearances as evidence of Jesus' "resurrection"; that is, they understood an eschatological event, the resurrection of the dead, to have found unique advance realization in Jesus. This, of course, is inescapably implied in the formula we have already considered (1 Cor 15:3–5). In the career of Paul it is underscored as the revelation that reversed the direction of his life:

> You have heard of my former life in Judaism, how I persecuted the church of God violently and tried to destroy it . . . But [God] . . . was pleased to reveal his Son to me . . . (Gal 1:13, 15–16).

Furthermore, Paul clearly set this event apart from such ecstatic experiences as he recounted in 2 Cor 12:2–9, which, "whether in the body or out of it," comprehended being "caught up" into Paradise (2 Cor 12:2–3). It is not possible to specify what concrete experiential index led Paul to differentiate these experiences; in any case, he did differentiate them.

Third point: in the resurrection the disciples found the vindication of Jesus. Easter was the revelation that his historic claims, implicit and finally explicit, had been true and that they had now been stunningly established as true. Hence Jesus' exaltation as messianic Son and Lord was seen first of all as rooted in his history. Indeed, the resurrection brought the messianic history of Jesus to completion. Whether the text on the Messiah as both Son and Lord of David (Mark 12:35–37 = Matt 22:41–46 = Luke 20:41–44) derived from Jesus or from the early community, it makes this precise point. David (Ps 110:1) had himself called his son "Lord," for by the power of the Spirit (Mark 12:36 = Matt 22:43) he had heard God bid his (David's) son to sit at God's right hand, a newly anointed cosmic victor.

Jesus's exaltation, as the completion and vindication of this career, released an outpouring of christological speech that continued through the lifetime of the next two generations. Among the immediate sources of this phenomenon was the conviction that in Jesus the scriptures had come to plenary and convergent fulfillment. Soon the gentile world would come into view as a mission field and Jesus would be proclaimed as "Lord of all" (Rom 10:12; Acts 10:36; cf. 1 Cor 8:6), of Jew and Greek (Rom 10:12; Acts 20:21; cf. 11:20), the living and the dead (Rom 14:7–9; 2 Cor 5:15), the human and the spirit world (Phil 2:10–11). Henceforward the glorification of Jesus would prompt a gathering up of the hope motifs from the covenants, sagas, prophecies, and psalms of Israel and the poetry, philosophy, and mystery cults of Greece, to affirm that all human aspiration had come to realization in him.

Fourth point: the self-understanding of the disciples underwent a change correlative to the christology of Easter. The men and women who had been followers of Jesus now understood themselves as the messianic community of the new covenant. The promise of a new covenant (Jer 31:31–34) had been a key theme in nonrabbinic Judaism (Bar 2:35; CD 6:19; 8:21; 19:33–34; 20:12; 1QpHab 2:3); it arose among the disciples of Jesus as the Easter experience confirmed the Last Supper and the death of Jesus as covenant sacrifice. The community thus became the first fruits of messianic Israel, just a step ahead of its brethren. As the first fruits sanctify the whole harvest to come, so this new community on Zion sanctified all Israel on the point of entry into its true inheritance. Meantime, the community was the remnant of Israel (Rom 11:1–10; cf. remnant passages implicitly cited in Acts 2:21, 47, etc.), but, in accord with the scriptures on the remnant, it was destined to "strike root downward and bear fruit upward" (Isa 37:31), for the remnant on Mount Zion (Isa 37:32), made up of the *sōzomenoi* (Acts 2:47)—a remnant term (cf. LXX Isa 37:32) designating in Acts "those who would be saved," i.e., those destined for acquittal at the judgment—was the seed of national restoration.

Fifth point: Easter as reconciliation. It is a remarkable fact that Paul, addressing and arguing with Cephas, testified to the nonoriginality of the great Pauline theme of justification: "we [i.e., you as much as I] have come to know [by our encounter with the risen Christ] that man is made righteous not by works of the law but through faith in Christ" (Gal 2:15–16). Paul's main point was that the Easter experience had bypassed the Torah, neither comprehending nor entailing it; but in making this point he showed that he understood and counted on Cephas' having understood this normative experience as one of forgiveness and reconciliation. This corresponds to the plentifully attested Easter consciousness of the death of Jesus as expiatory offering (see the pre-Pauline formulas in 1 Cor 15:3–5; Rom 3:25–26; 4:25).

Sixth point: Easter as missionary mandate. Again, Paul was a privileged early witness to this dimension of the Easter experience. God "was pleased to reveal his Son to me, that I might proclaim him among the gentiles" (Gal 1:16). Paul supposes the same of the Easter experience of Cephas (Gal 2:7–9). Moreover, he inserted the Easter experience of the Apostles as a hinge moment in the three-step sequence that runs through the whole of his soteriology: (1) God's expiatory and redemptive act in Christ enacted in the world a universal economy of reconciliation (2) through the Easter appointment of ministers of the Spirit to proclaim "the gospel" and (3) through the acceptance of this gospel in "faith," making God's saving economy operative. If the third step in this sequence is a Pauline commonplace, it should be noted that the first two steps dominate the celebrated text of 2 Cor 5:18–21. As

Sinai "founded" the Law in Israel (LXX Ps 77:5), so the Easter revelation to those chosen as Apostles "founded" the gospel or "message of reconciliation" in the world (Hofius 1980: 11–16). Easter as missionary mandate would be retained and transformed in the later gospel tradition.

Seventh point: Easter inaugurated a new eschatological scenario. The variations among the NT writers on this theme are all held within the basic framework that emerged from the differentiation *ex eventu* of the Day of the Son of man. The resurrection of Jesus was not revealed to the whole world, so signaling its consummation. It was neither imposed on Jesus' judges (Mark 14:62 = Matt 26:64 = Luke 22:69) nor bestowed on "all the people" (Acts 10:41). Rather, it was reserved "to us who were chosen by God as witnesses" (Acts 10:41). In Jesus' original scheme of the future, the revelation of the Son of man would mark the end of the eschatological ordeal. In the actuality of events, Jesus' glorification, taking place long before the end of the ordeal and so of all history, apparently led the *hebraioi* (Cephas, the twelve, the Aramaic-speaking community of Jesus' followers in Jerusalem) to reduce to provisional status Jesus' eschatology of woe (the ruin of Israel, its capital, and temple). At the same time, it led the Greek-speaking Jewish converts of the Easter kerygma, the *hellēnistai* (Stephen and his followers) to conclude that Jesus' glorification vindicated and guaranteed his eschatology of woe—a view that made them pariahs in Jerusalem and led to their expulsion from the city. What all Christian parties held in common, however, was an interim between resurrection and parousia to be defined and dominated by the mission of the church.

From the foregoing account of the career of Jesus and of the Easter experience of his disciples, it follows that Jesus, as a historic figure and as an object of the Easter experience, was indeed the founder of Christianity. It further follows that Christianity had assumed its distinctive identity (though without yet arriving at thematic knowledge of that identity) in independence of gentile influence and prior to the mission to the gentile world.

Bibliography

Aune, D. 1983. *Prophecy in Early Christianity and the Ancient Mediterranean World.* Grand Rapids.

Austin, J. L. 1962. *How to Do Things with Words,* ed. J. O. Urmson. Cambridge, MA.

Barrett, C. K. 1968. *Jesus and the Gospel Tradition.* London.

Benoit, P. 1960. Marie-Madelaine et les disciples au tombeau selon Joh 20, 1–18. Pp. 141–52 in *Judentum—Urchristentum—Kirche,* ed. W. Eltester. BZNW 26. Berlin.

Betz, O. 1987. *Jesus: Der Messias Israels.* Tübingen.

Blinzler, J. 1969. *Der Prozess Jesu.* 4th rev. ed. Regensburg.

Böcher, O. 1972. *Das Neue Testament und die dämonisichen Mächte.* SBS 58. Stuttgart.

Borg, M. J. 1984. *Conflict, Holiness, and Politics in the Teachings of Jesus.* Studies in the Bible and Early Christianity 5. New York.

Bowker, J. 1973. *Jesus and the Pharisees.* Cambridge.

Bultmann, R. 1963. *The History of the Synoptic Tradition.* Trans. J. Marsh. Oxford.

Burney, C. F. 1925. *The Poetry of Our Lord.* Oxford.

Caird, G. B. 1965. *Jesus and the Jewish Nation.* London.

Chilton, B. 1984. *A Galilean Rabbi and His Bible.* Wilmington, DE.

———. 1985. The Gospel According to Thomas as a Source of Jesus' Teaching. Pp. 155–75 in Wenham 1985.

Dahl, N. A. 1974. The Crucified Messiah. Pp. 10–36 in *The Crucified Messiah and Other Essays.* Minneapolis.

Dalman, G. 1902. *The Words of Jesus.* Trans. D. M. Kay. Edinburgh.

Davids, P. H. 1985. James and Jesus. Pp. 63–84 in Wenham 1985.

Davies, W. D. 1974. *The Gospel and the Land.* Berkeley.

Dodd, C. H. 1961. *The Parables of the Kingdom.* 2d rev. ed. New York.

———. 1970. *The Founder of Christianity.* New York.

Dupont, J. 1954. *Les Béatitudes.* Louvain.

Farmer, W. R. 1982. *Jesus and the Gospel.* Philadelphia.

Fitzmyer, J. A. 1979. Another View of the "Son of Man" Debate. *JSNT* 4: 58–68.

Flusser, D. G. 1969. *Jesus.* New York.

Harvey, A. E. 1982. *Jesus and the Constraints of History.* Philadelphia.

Hengel, M. 1981. *The Charismatic Leader and His Followers.* Trans. J. C. G. Greig. Edinburgh and New York.

Hill, D. 1979. *New Testament Prophecy.* Atlanta.

Hofius, O. 1980. "Gott hat unter uns aufgerichtet das Wort von der Versöhnung" (2 Kor. 5.19). *ZNW* 71:3–20.

Horsley, R. A. 1987. *Jesus and the Spiral of Violence.* San Francisco.

Horsley, R. A., and Hanson, J. S. 1985. *Bandits, Prophets, and Messiahs.* Minneapolis.

Hultgren, A. J. 1979. *Jesus and His Adversaries.* Minneapolis.

Jeremias, J. 1930. Zur Hypothese einer schriftlichen Logienquelle Q. *ZNW* 29:147–49.

———. 1931. Zöllner und Sünder. *ZNW* 30: 293–300.

———. 1955. "Flesh and Blood cannot inherit the Kingdom of God" (I Cor. xv. 50). *NTS* 2: 151–59.

———. 1963. *The Parables of Jesus.* London.

———. 1964. *Unknown Sayings of Jesus.* 2d ed. Trans. R. H. Fuller. London.

———. 1966. *The Eucharistic Words of Jesus.* Trans. N. Perrin. London.

———. 1967. Die älteste Schicht der Menschensohn-Logien. *ZNW* 58: 159–72.

———. 1969. *Jerusalem in the Time of Jesus.* Trans. F. H. and C. H. Cave. Philadelphia.

———. 1971. *New Testament Theology.* Vol. 1, *The Proclamation of Jesus.* Trans. J. Bowden. New York.

Jonge, M. de. 1986. The Earliest Christian Use of *Christos:* Some Suggestions. *NTS* 32:321–43.

Maier, J. 1978. *Jesus von Nazareth in der talmudischen Überlieferung.* Darmstadt.

Maier, G. 1985. Jesus tradition im 1. Petrusbrief. Pp. 85–128 in Wenham 1985.

Manson, T. W. 1931. *The Teaching of Jesus.* Cambridge.

Meyer, B. F. 1979. *The Aims of Jesus.* London.

———. 1981. The "Inside" of the Jesus Event. Pp. 197–210 in *Creativity and Method: Essays in Honor of Bernard Lonergan,* ed. M. L. Lamb. Milwaukee.

Morissette, R. 1972. La condition de ressuscité. I Corinthiens 15, 35–49: structure littéraire de la péricope. *Bib* 53: 208–28.

Perrin, N. 1967. *Rediscovering the Teaching of Jesus.* London.

———. 1976. *Jesus and the Language of the Kingdom.* London and Philadelphia.

Pesch, R. 1978. *Das Abendmahl und Jesu Todesverständnis.* QD 80. Freiburg.

Riches, J. 1982. *Jesus and the Transformation of Judaism.* New York.

Riesner, R. 1981. *Jesus als Lehrer.* Tübingen.

Roloff, J. 1970. *Das Kerygma und der irdische Jesus.* Göttingen.

Sanders, E. P. 1985. *Jesus and Judaism.* London and Philadelphia.
Schürmann, H. 1960. Die vorösterlichen Anfänge der Logientradition. Pp. 342–70 in *Der historische Jesus und der kerygmatische Christus,* ed. H. Ristow and K. Matthiae. Berlin.
———. 1972. *Das Geheimnis Jesu.* Leipzig.
———. 1975. *Jesu ureigener Tod.* Freiburg.
Stuhlmacher, P. 1986. Jesus' Resurrection and the View of Righteousness in the Pre-Pauline Mission Congregations. Pp. 50–67 in *Reconciliation, Law, and Righteousness.* Trans. E. Kalin. Philadelphia.
Theissen, G. 1978. *Sociology of Early Palestinian Christianity.* Trans. J. Bowden. Philadelphia.
———. 1983. *The Miracle Stories of the Early Christian Tradition.* Trans. F. McDonagh. Edinburgh.
Trautmann, M. 1980. *Zeichenhafte Handlungen Jesu.* FB 37. Wurzburg.
Vermes, G. 1967. The Use of *bar naš/bar našāʾ* in Jewish Aramaic. Pp. 310–28 in M. Black, *An Aramaic Approach to the Gospels and Acts.* 3d ed. Oxford.
———. 1978. The "Son of Man" Debate. *JSNT* 1:19–32.
———. 1983. *Jesus and the World of Judaism.* London.
Wenham, D., ed. 1985. *The Jesus Tradition Outside the Gospels.* Gospel Perspectives 5. Sheffield.
Westerholm, S. 1978. *Jesus and Scribal Authority.* ConBNT 10. Lund.
Wrede, W. 1901. *Das Messiasgeheimnis in den Evangelien.* Göttingen. ET 1971.

BEN F. MEYER

QUEST FOR THE HISTORICAL JESUS

The phrase "quest for the historical Jesus" normally refers to a movement of scholarship that emerged with Reimarus in the 18th century and continues in various forms into the late 20th century. It is sometimes used in a broad sense to denote all historical research into the life and times of Jesus; sometimes it is used in a more narrow sense to denote only one branch of this, namely, revisionist theories linked to particular theological or political agendas. In this connection the term "the historical Jesus" is sometimes used to refer to Jesus as he actually was (whether or not we can know about him thus), and sometimes to refer to Jesus as he can be reconstructed by historians working within a particular frame of reference (whether or not this does justice to how Jesus actually was). The latter sense will be referred to below as "the historical Jesus."

A. Problems
B. Reimarus to Schweitzer
   1. Reimarus
   2. Strauss
   3. Renan
   4. Holtzmann
   5. Weiss
   6. Schweitzer
   7. The "Old Quest": Conclusion
C. Schweitzer to Käsemann
   1. Barth
   2. Bultmann
   3. Gospel Study
D. The "New Quest"
   1. Bornkamm
   2. Jeremias
   3. Schillebeeckx
   4. The "Jesus Seminar"
   5. Jesus the Cynic?
   6. Conclusion
E. The "Third Quest"
   1. Introduction
   2. Meyer
   3. Harvey
   4. Borg
   5. Sanders
   6. Others
   7. Unfinished Agendas
F. Conclusion

A. Problems

There are six commonly held but erroneous views about the quest. (1) Reimarus began it. In fact, Reimarus drew on the work of earlier writers, particularly English Deists (Brown 1985: 1–55). (2) All writers about Jesus have been trying to do the same thing, namely, to reconstruct his actual life and teaching. In fact, there have been several very different agendas informing writers, even within the same period. (3) Research into Jesus aims at an "objective" account. In fact, objectivity is now perceived to be a positivist myth, and historians need to take into account both the reality of external events and the point of view of all perceivers, themselves included (Meyer 1979: 76–110). (4) Twentieth century methods of gospel study—source, form, and redaction criticism—are part of the quest. They are not, or not particularly: They focus on the gospels and the communities behind them, and only tangentially on Jesus. (5) The quest has produced no useful results and should now be abandoned. Section E demonstrates the contrary. (6) The quest can be divided into discrete chronological sections. Though we follow this traditional outline, it is potentially misleading, since there is far more overlap and interplay between sections than can thus be indicated (e.g., the close links between Strauss and Bultmann, or between Schweitzer and Sanders).

B. Reimarus to Schweitzer

Schweitzer himself is responsible for the usual perception of the quest to that date and for drawing attention to it as a major theological phenomenon. His outline and angle of vision need to be supplemented by others (e.g., Meyer 1979: 25–59, Brown 1985) if a fair picture is to result. The first phase of the quest fell historically within a wider movement in which orthodox Christianity came under attack from rationalism, and he attempted to respond in various ways; the writers listed below belong on both sides of this divide and in various mediating positions. The rationale often given for the quest at this stage was that, since the Gospels disagreed about so many things, the historian had to enquire as to what exactly happened; in fact this was only one of many motivations, including the desire to discredit orthodox Christianity as a whole. A feature of this stage of the quest was the gradual concentration on the Synoptic Gospels, as the Gospel of John came to be seen as a secondary theological and nonhistorical account.

1. Reimarus. H.S. Reimarus (1694–1768) wrote a long criticism of Christianity which was published after his death by the philosopher G. Lessing. One section dealt with the aims of Jesus, arguing that he was a Jewish revolutionary whose disciples, after his failure and death, conceived the idea that he was divine. They stole his body and rewrote the story of his life in the light of an alternative Jewish expectation, not utilized by Jesus himself, according to which a divine being would appear on the clouds to end the world. The failure of this to happen discredits them, as Jesus' failure to bring about successful revolution had discredited him; Christianity as known subsequently is based therefore on a series of mistakes. Schweitzer praises Reimarus too much, but deserves credit for the bold and clear outlines of a historical hypothesis which continues to have successors (Brandon 1967: and see Bammel and Moule 1984).

2. Strauss. Reimarus' emphasis on the non-miraculous nature of Jesus' life was picked up by David Friedrich Strauss (1808–74), but whereas, for Reimarus, Jesus could be described thus in order to be dismissed, for Strauss the required rereading of the gospels meant that the truth of Jesus could be rescued in an ahistorical fashion. His massive book focused attention on the nature of the gospels (a question that has dominated much of 20th century research), arguing that they were mythical rather than historical. Neither the older orthodoxy nor the newer rationalism would do: On the one hand, supernatural and miraculous events do not and did not occur, while on the other hand, what seemed to be accounts of such happenings were in reality nonhistorical projections of early faith. Strauss' manifest unorthodoxy cost him his career, but arguably his questions still remain outstanding.

3. Renan. E. Renan (1823–92) typified a certain style of Jesus-research (see Schweitzer 1954: 180–92; Brown 1985: 233–38). Like Strauss, he achieved great notoriety from his book (1863), though his passage to skepticism had a different origin (French Roman Catholicism). With his treatment there came to prominence a theme that still dominates some accounts: the distinction between the early period of the ministry, in which Jesus won the hearts of all, and the later, when the high demands he made caused most to reject him. It is essentially a work of romantic fantasy, charming but cloying, and the great influence it has had on popular impressions of Jesus is in inverse proportion to its true worth as history.

4. Holtzmann. The second half of the 19th century saw the production, particularly in Germany, of a steady stream of lives of Jesus, of which probably the best known is that of H. J. Holtzmann (1832–1910). His book (1863) focused attention on the Synoptic Gospels, working on the assumption that to solve the problems they posed—their order of composition and mutual dependence—was to solve in principle the problem of Jesus. The earliest sources would give genuine access to history. The priority of Mark was a hypothesis designed to provide a straightforward (and essentially liberal) portrait of Jesus as the teacher of timeless ethical truths, whose ministry developed in clear-cut and comprehensible stages, with the decisive turning point at Caesarea Philippi (Mark 8:27–9:1). The two main aspects of Holtzmann's work—his portrait of the ministry, and his belief in source criticism as a means to historiography—have continued to exercise considerable influence.

5. Weiss. A decisive step towards a more accurate historical picture, and at the same time towards a continuing theological problem, was taken by Johannes Weiss (1863–1914). In focusing on the meaning of the "kingdom of God" in the teaching of Jesus, his book (1892; ET 1971) set its face against the liberalism of Ritschl (Weiss' father-in-law), and proposed instead a meaning based on a new awareness of Jewish apocalyptic: Jesus announced the imminent end of the world. Weiss still drew a psychologizing portrait of Jesus, but the emphasis now lay elsewhere, on a historical reconstruction which posed the same question as Reimarus, with the difference that it concerned Jesus and not merely his followers: The predicted end of the world did not materialize. Weiss was answered by various writers (Schweitzer 1954: 241–68), but he had set the question in the terms that would dominate Schweitzer's own work and, as a result, haunt the 20th century quest.

6. Schweitzer. The work of Albert Schweitzer (1875–1965) stands at the head of the present century like a colossus. To him belongs the credit for seeing the quite disparate "lives of Jesus" as, in a sense, a single movement, which in his own work he drew together and attempted to round off. In his thorough survey he built particularly on the work of Weiss; answering the thoroughgoing skepticism of William Wrede (whose work on Mark aimed to show that the apparently straightforward account of Jesus' ministry in that gospel was in fact a theological construct), he summarized the work of his predecessors in pithy prose, weighed them in the balance of his own rigorous analysis, found most of them sadly wanting, and offered his own fresh synthesis. In his "Sketch" (1901), and in the conclusion to the larger work (1954: 328–401), he argued that Jesus deliberately kept his Messiahship a secret, revealing it to the disciples in the Transfiguration and then commanding them to tell nobody, and that Judas betrayed this secret to the chief priests. He then goes on to argue that Jesus, who had begun by expecting the Son of man to appear during the course of his ministry, was disappointed, and went to his death in order to bring down the "Messianic woes" upon himself, so that his people might be delivered (1954: 368–69, 385–95; 1925: 234–36). The result is in one way purely negative: "The Jesus of Nazareth who . . . preached the ethic of the Kingdom of God, who founded the Kingdom of Heaven upon earth"—that is, "the historical Jesus" of most 19th century liberal "lives"—"never had any existence" (1954: 396). However, all is not lost for subsequent hermeneutics and theology: "Jesus means something to our world because a mighty spiritual force streams forth from Him and flows through our time also"; "not the historical Jesus, but the spirit which goes forth from Him and in the spirits of men strives for new influence and rule, is that which overcomes the world." The eschatological sayings, in their very oddity for modern humans, "raise the man who dares to meet their challenge . . . above his world and his time, making him inwardly free" (1954: 397, 399, 400). Schweitzer thus stands as the bridge between the centuries: summing up the 19th century, and pronouncing it a failure, he anticipates some of the major emphases of the 20th.

7. The "Old Quest": Conclusion. If there is a theme which unites the highly disparate writers between Reimarus and Schweitzer, it is their conviction that when a truly historical account of Jesus is arrived at it will be of vital importance for the Christian faith. For some, the importance was positive and immediate. Jesus, reconstructed in pious historiography, became the wise and gentle teacher of 19th century liberalism; Mark became the earliest gospel, a simple record of the Master's ministry. For others, the importance was largely negative. Reimarus, Strauss, and Schweitzer himself, in their different ways, undertook historical description in order to show that the traditional picture of Jesus could not be trusted. Reimarus went on to argue that Christianity as a whole was mistaken; Strauss, that its reality lay in the realm of timeless truth divorced from history; Schweitzer, that the new historical picture carried with it its own timeless imperatives ("He . . . sets us to the tasks which He has to fulfill for our time"; 1954: 401). The quest for "the historical Jesus", which had marginalized Jesus' eschatology in particular, had had its bluff called, and could not reply. There could be no doubt which of the two roads subsequent scholarship would have to take, and the subsequent story of the quest is not least the story of how the consequent hermeneutical challenge—how such a strange and remote Jesus could be relevant in a different culture and time—was variously met.

C. Schweitzer to Käsemann

Between Schweitzer's demolition of the 19th century quest in 1906 and Ernst Käsemann's lecture in 1953, new theological movements dominated European theology, most of which had only a small place for Jesus. This may be partly attributed to a failure of nerve after Schweitzer (How could a Jewish apocalyptic prophet be of use to theology today? How could one be sure of avoiding anachronism if one found an answer to the question?) and partly to the protest he himself mounted against the historical Jesus—though actually he was not the first to do so. One of the oddities of Schweitzer's book is his failure to mention M. Kähler, whose work gained in importance in the hands of Barth and Bultmann; and partly to the new agendas set for the Church by the convulsions through which the world passed during the period, to which the task of reconstructing the biography of Jesus seemed of comparatively little relevance. One of the significant trends during this period came in the reversal of an argument implicit in much of 19th century work: Instead of conceiving of Jesus as relevant, and therefore not particularly Jewish, scholarship after Schweitzer saw him as Jewish, and therefore not particularly relevant. The main reason for the new move, however, was profoundly theological, and found initial expression in Barth.

1. Barth. The second and subsequent editions of Karl Barth's *Commentary on Romans* includes a good deal of explicit criticism of the liberal "historical Jesus." The earthly Jesus, and all he represents in the way of religiousness and piety, ends on the cross, which thus stands as the judgment of God against all human piety. The meaning of Jesus, including the meaning of his life, is found in his death and there alone (Barth 1933: 160). His earthly life is necessarily irrelevant, and must for theological reasons be a stumbling block and not an open mirror to his theological significance (280). The early Barth thus anticipates a good deal of what subsequently came to be associated with Bultmann. Theology positively called for the collapse of the quest (Meyer 1979: 49).

2. Bultmann. Rudolf Bultmann (1884–1976), whose work dominates 20th century NT studies, is perhaps best known for two emphases (in some ways they go back to Strauss), both of which played an important negative role in Jesus-research. (a) He provided a detailed analysis of the literary forms of Synoptic material, arguing that in most cases these indicate an origin, not in the life of Jesus, but in the life of the early Church. (b) He argued that the gospels as they stand are mythical in various senses (not fully distinguished by Bultmann: see Thiselton 1980: 252–63), in particular in that they presuppose a prescientific worldview with which they clothe—and with which Jesus himself clothed—his essentially timeless message. The significance of Jesus could therefore be recaptured by translating-out the mythical language into that of existential decision (Bultmann 1958). Form criticism and demythologization were thus joint means towards a reading of the gospels which aimed *not* to find Jesus—lest, as has often been said within the Bultmann school, one should base one's faith on history and so turn it into a "work." Bultmann's own book on Jesus (1934) focuses principally on his teaching, interpreted as existentialist challenge to contemporary decision; the sayings are all that is left, and then only certain ones; it is both impossible and undesirable to try and discover the personality of Jesus himself. All that is needed is the bare fact that he died on a cross. In Bultmann's history-of-religious program, the main features of early Christianity were derived not from Jewish sources but from Hellenistic ones. The life and ministry of Jesus, firmly anchored in Judaism, were therefore only of tangential interest for Christian theology.

3. Gospel Study. Throughout this period the attention of Synoptic studies was focused more on the gospels themselves than on Jesus. Source criticism reached its peak in the work of Streeter (1924), with many still believing (like Holtzmann) that they would thus find secure historical grounding in the earliest sources, Mark and Q; this belief is still held by some who are trying to revive the Q hypothesis today (see Kloppenborg 1987). Some attempted to use form criticism in a similar fashion, not realizing that it was a tool designed to find the early Church, not Jesus. By the end of the period there had begun the serious study (sometimes called redaction criticism) of the gospels as wholes; again, this method was neither designed, nor particularly appropriate, for the task of discovering Jesus within his historical context. Some writers, including some Anglo-Saxons (e.g. Manson 1931, 1949) defied the moratorium, but in general attention was focused away from Jesus.

D. The "New Quest"

On 20 October 1953, Ernst Käsemann, then a professor in Göttingen and subsequently in Tübingen, delivered a lecture arguing that, though it is true that a "life of Jesus" cannot be written, one must be careful not to divorce

Christian faith altogether from its historical roots, lest it turn into a sort of docetism in which "Jesus" is simply a cipher, and the cross is robbed of its significance. If the earthly Jesus can only be understood in terms of Easter, Easter can only be understood in relation to Jesus (Käsemann 1964: 25). A "new quest," complete with careful theological rationale and motivation, was thus launched, which in certain respects still continues (see Robinson 1959; Meyer 1979: 51–54; Sanders 1985: 29–47). Within this movement there have developed certain criteria for assessing the probable historicity of individual sayings of Jesus: dissimilarity (if a saying is unlike both the Jewish background and the early Church; see Sanders 1985: 16–17; Hooker 1972); consistency (with other material known to be authentic); multiple attestation (if a saying appears in different layers of tradition); and linguistic or cultural tests (if the saying appears to fit with Palestinian Judaism of the time, not least in allowing a possible Aramaic basis). Mutual tension between these tests is quickly apparent, and it is not surprising that the results achieved on such a basis have not been particularly solid (see Barbour 1972).

1. Bornkamm. The first work to appear under this new look was that of G. Bornkamm. In many ways Bornkamm kept to the Bultmannian agenda: the miraculous was kept out of the picture, Jesus had no special foreknowledge of events to come, and he used no Messianic titles of himself. Nevertheless, some important changes were made. Bornkamm's Jesus speaks of an eschatological fulfillment in the present, as opposed to one located in the future. In several respects the gospels provide us with access to genuine historical happenings; the call of the twelve, for instance, need not (as with Bultmann) be attributed to the retrojecting tendency of the early Church. But still it is the message of Jesus, not the events in which he participated, that remains the focus of attention, and that, in the end, results in a summons to faith in the present as much as in the past (Bornkamm 1960: 188–91; see also Kümmel 1957, 1974, and Goppelt 1981).

2. Jeremias. The work of J. Jeremias, though recognizably Lutheran and thus falling within the post-Bultmannian mainstream, stands a little outside "new quest" research, looking from one point of view more like the pre-Schweitzer quest (in that Jeremias is clearly committed to finding in the gospels the Jesus who can be the basis for the Church's faith) and from another like the Third Quest (in that he insists on understanding Jesus within the matrix of his native Judaism, emphasizing especially the Aramaic base of several sayings). In various monographs (1958, 1963, and others), and above all in the first volume of his uncompleted *New Testament Theology* (1971), he presented a sustained account of Jesus' ministry and mission. Believing that the concrete historical setting of Jesus' work was vital for genuine Christian theology, and that the Jesus one discovered in that setting offered himself as the incarnation of the call of God to every generation, Jeremias painstakingly reconstructed an impressive collection of *ipsissima verba* (words most likely to be attributed to the historical Jesus) by means of linguistic and form-critical analysis. He argued in particular for a middle way between the imminent eschatology of Schweitzer (the end is near, but not yet) and the realized eschatology of C. H. Dodd (the kingdom is actually present in the ministry of Jesus: see, e.g., Dodd 1961), suggesting the cumbersome but more historically likely "eschatology in the process of being realized," or, as in the work of Ladd (1966), "inaugurated eschatology." There is a sense in which the kingdom is present, and another in which it is yet to come. Though in some ways this merely restates the problem, it avoids the false clarity of the alternatives.

3. Schillebeeckx. The Dutch Dominican Edward Schillebeeckx has produced one of the longest books (1979) on Jesus in this century, though the length owes a good deal to the protracted employment of detailed tradition criticism, resulting in portraits of various groups within early Christianity; through the gaps between them Jesus himself eventually appears. Schillebeeckx takes a position which is the mirror image of Bultmann in that he regards the resurrection appearances as stories from Jesus' lifetime read forward into the post-Easter appearances. His eventual leap from a purely historical Jesus to the incarnate Son of God is based on little or nothing within the body of the book. At the same time he has a wealth of insights into the philosophical context of scholarship on Jesus, and many of his sections—not least his discussion of Jesus' awareness of his own approaching death—are pregnant and fruitfully suggestive.

4. The "Jesus Seminar." In the last decade the post-Bultmannian movement has had a new focal point: the so-called "Jesus Seminar," an American group with its own journal *(Foundations and Facets Forum)* and regular meetings at which individual sayings are discussed, debated, and voted on according to a scale of probability. At one level these scholars (who include some of the best-known names in North American NT scholarship) are attempting to perform for their generation what Bultmann did for his: They hope to produce a more-thoroughgoing history of the Synoptic tradition, including extracanonical material. At another level, they are clearly convinced that such study, particularly if it demolishes the heroic Jesus beloved of some modern American Christianity, will be of great benefit to the world; so the seminar's results are announced in press conferences, and there is talk of a movie. At the same time, the seminar includes several scholars whose thought is running in a different direction, i.e., the Third Quest. This represents one of the major tensions within Jesus-research today.

5. Jesus the Cynic? It has commonly been assumed, at least since Schweitzer, that the more we put Jesus into his historical context the more he will turn out to be Jewish. This has been sharply challenged by two recent writers, who have suggested that the Jewish strands in the gospels are the accretions, and that the earlier we look the more we find Jesus to be much like the wandering Cynic preachers who were a familiar sight in the ancient Mediterranean world. First, there is B. H. Mack (1988), who argues that Jesus was not an apocalyptic prophet, but a popular sage, a wordsmith purveying aphoristic wisdom, one who shocked people into fresh thought for themselves about their social and personal situations, rather than teaching any particular doctrine. This bold line is backed up by a new history of gospel traditions in which what used to be thought the older layers—the more Jewish and apocalyptic strands—are argued to be later accretions, which culminated in a myth of Mark's making, a myth which has had

(Mack suggests) devastating effects on Western, particularly American, self-consciousness. Neither Mark's fiction of the first appearance of the man of power, nor his fantasy of the final appearance of the man of glory, fit the wisdom now required (Mack 1988: 376). In thus reversing what has been normal practice (going back behind the Hellenistic layers to find the original Jewish stratum), Mack is nevertheless very close to Bultmann and Wrede in his basic historical hypothesis and to many 19th century writers in his hermeneutical program: The original Jesus—Jesus as he really was, which turns out to be fairly un-Jewish—is what contemporary culture needs. The other writer is F. Gerald Downing, who has undertaken (1988) a large-scale collection of parallel sayings from the gospels and the Cynics. Despite the initial impression of parallelism, however, and the bracing hermeneutic wherein Downing challenges comfortable Western Christianity (1987), the case for a close link is weakened by the lack of evidence for any Cynic presence in Palestine, and by the fact that the sayings adduced as parallels come from a very wide geographical and chronological range. This movement of scholarship has, however, alerted Jesus-research to the dangers of assuming that Jesus' Jewishness—or anyone else's in the 1st century, for that matter—can be isolated from wider cultural influences and resonances.

6. Conclusion. The closer we get to our own day, the harder it is to plot patterns and movements. Yet it is undeniable that the so-called "new quest" has continued in various forms, without producing any solid results that have won wide scholarly approval (see Bowden 1988; and, for a recent exploration within the paradigm, Fredriksen 1988). In several ways it has been overtaken by a different movement, owing no allegiance to Bultmann, and producing quite different results. Although the debate between these two contemporary movements is often conducted in terms of method and historical analysis, it should be clear that differing implicit hermeneutical analyses and agendas are also playing a not-inconsiderable part.

E. The "Third Quest"

The current wave of books about Jesus offers a bewildering range of competing hypotheses. There is no unifying theological agenda; no final agreement about method; certainly no common set of results. But there are certain features which justify a unifying label. (On the distinction between this "third quest" and the previous "new quest," see Meyer 1979: 16–20; Charlesworth 1988: 26–28; and Neill and Wright 1988: 397–98.)

1. Introduction. The most obvious feature is that the massive recent researches into second Temple Judaism have forced scholars to rethink what might be involved in understanding Jesus within this background (as it is agreed, in this movement, that one must do: i.e., agreeing to that extent with Reimarus and Schweitzer against much of 19th century scholarship and the Bultmann school). First-century sources, particularly Josephus, are being studied seriously after generations of neglect by NT scholars. Serious, and in principle answerable, questions are being formulated, as for instance by Sanders (1985: 1): What was Jesus' intention, what was his relationship to his Jewish contemporaries, why did he die, and why did Christianity begin? The methods employed owe less to theological a prioris and more to the normal canons of historiography: hypothesis and verification, and testing of sources as part of that process (see Meyer 1979: 76–110; Sanders 1985: 3–22). The problem of the nature of the sources, particularly the Synoptic Gospels, has not been ignored, but neither is it now regarded as so difficult, even when modern literary approaches are taken seriously, as to forbid all serious historical research (see Freyne 1988; Sanders and Davies 1989: 335–44). Early "third quest" works include Brandon (1967) and Vermes (1973), portraying Jesus as revolutionary and a Galilean holy man respectively. The first option is now normally rejected (see Bammel and Moule 1984; though see Buchanan 1984 for a variant of the revolutionary theme). The second is taken up by Borg (1984: 229–63), though set in a different context. There are four outstanding works in the current literature.

2. Meyer. B. F. Meyer's book (1979) is the most learned and methodologically rigorous of the modern works. Basing his historical method on Lonergan's epistemology, he analyzes Jesus' aims, highlighting the restoration of Israel as the theme underlying the proclamation of the kingdom. He argues for the accuracy of the gospels' distinction between the public and private message of Jesus, such that the public actions (particularly table-fellowship with sinners) gained a depth of meaning through allowing the question of his identity to emerge. Jesus envisaged a new, reborn community, in which the covenant would be renewed and whose sins would be forgiven. The tradition generated by his life gives powerful clues to understanding why he did what he did (this, in opposition to some schemes [Vermes 1973, and most of the Bultmann school] which postulate a radical disjunction between Jesus and subsequent tradition).

3. Harvey. A. E. Harvey's Bampton Lectures (1982) are similarly adventurous in terms of method. Employing the notion of "historical constraint," Harvey argues that Jesus can and must be understood in terms of the constraints operating on anyone within the particular culture of the time. He begins with the crucifixion: What we know of Roman and Jewish practice indicates that the gospels are substantially correct in tracing the basic outline of events that led to Jesus' death. The constraint of Law enables us to plot Jesus' insistence that the urgency of the moment should override some legal provisions; that of Time, to understand the eschatological nature of his proclamation. What we know of Miracle in the ANE suggests that Jesus refused to work within normal categories. He was known as Messiah (though without "divine" overtones) during his lifetime: and, since the constraint of monotheism meant that no Jew could have thought of himself (or anyone else) as God Incarnate, we must think instead in terms of unique *agency* (on all this, see Neill and Wright 1988: 385–87, and Wright 1986).

4. Borg. M. J. Borg (1984) argues cogently that Jesus is to be seen as political, not in the sense that he was a revolutionary, but because he was actually perceived as a traitor to the nationalist cause. Into a situation of intense conflict, Jesus brought a summons to costly mercy and love, which cut across Israel's current expectations and badges of national identity. He warned Israel that resistance would lead to social and military disaster, which would have to be seen as divine judgment. The eschatological passages thus refer, not to a coming supernatural event, but to imminent national catastrophe (Borg 1987b). In this ministry, Jesus functioned as a sage or holy man, announcing the breaking in of the numinous into everyday reality (Borg 1987a). Many otherwise puzzling passages in the gospels come into fresh light within this context.

5. Sanders. E. P. Sanders (1985) gives a clear account of a Jesus seen without the spectacles of contemporary piety. He refuses to begin with the sayings, and starts instead his action against the Temple, understood within the framework of Jewish restoration eschatology, the hope that a new Temple would be built in the coming new age. Passages which speak of his conflict with Pharisees are mostly retrojections of later church-and-synagogue controversies; Jesus did challenge received wisdom in some ways, when his vision of a new age overrode Jewish custom ("leave the dead to bury their dead"; see Sanders 1985: 252–55). His attack on the Temple provoked reaction from the Jewish hierarchy, who handed him over to the Romans. He was not political in the sense of revolutionary, as witnessed by the fact that after his death his disciples were not also arrested. Sanders is arguably the clearest of the current writers on Jesus, and is candid about the issues (e.g., the "Son of man" question) which he leaves unsettled.

6. Others. Other works have appeared in the same vein, notably those of Caird (1965), Dodd (1971), France (1971), Yoder (1972), Riches (1980), Farmer (1982), Buchanan (1984), Lohfink (1984), Rivkin (1984), Segundo (1985), Lievestad (1987), Theissen (1987), Horsley (1987) and Freyne (1988). (See the survey in Charlesworth 1988: 9–29, 223–43.) Related studies include Derrett (1973), Bowker (1973), Chilton (1979; 1984), Lievestad (1987), Charlesworth (1988) and de Jonge (1988). All are exploring more or less the same issues, though with the same diversity of background and point of view.

7. Unfinished Agendas. Perhaps the most-striking feature of the third quest is its current open-endedness. There is some convergence on the question of appropriate method (see Meyer, Sanders), but further work needs to be done, not least in integrating the newer literary approaches to the gospels into the historical task (see now particularly Freyne 1988). The exact interrelation between Jesus and Judaism is extremely difficult to plot, and continual readjustments are to be expected for some time. So, too, the question of continuity and discontinuity between Jesus and the early Church is raised in new and acute forms by the current study, which so far has not taken on board the difficult, though clearly closely related, question of the resurrection. Theological questions, although quite properly bracketed off in many third quest writings, are never in fact far away, and the questions of the meaning of the cross, and the identity of Jesus (atonement and christology), are only two of many that could be explored. Many writers (not least those in the Third World., e.g., Segundo) imply a hermeneutic in which the Jesus (or the entire historical scenario) they rediscover can somehow be translated into contemporary relevance, but none so far has addressed the question head on, or in the necessary depth (though see Yoder 1972, and Hebblethwaite 1989).

F. Conclusion

The quest as normally conceived was born in an atmosphere of anti-Christian polemic (Reimarus) and has often continued to be seen in that light, whether by those who rejected the idea of "the historical Jesus" (Kähler etc.) or by those suspicious of the third quest for its sitting loose to theology. But any critique based on a theological a priori must take account of the fact that among orthodox theology's regular assertions is that of the full humanness of Jesus. Granted the contemporary puzzles over the meaning of the word "God" itself, it may seem on reflection quite proper for theology to give historical research its head. Not that historical research will wait for such permission. It deals, ultimately, with issues that lie in the public domain, not with matters that can only be discussed within the household of faith. The contemporary movements offer plenty of evidence that the quest for the historical Jesus is both as alive and as important now as it has ever been.

Bibliography

Bammel, E., and Moule, C. F. D., eds. 1984. *Jesus and the Politics of His Day.* Cambridge.

Barbour, R. S. 1972. *Traditio-Historical Criticism of the Gospels.* London.

Barth, K. 1933. *The Epistle to the Romans.* Trans. E. C. Hoskyns. London.

Betz, O. 1968. *What do we Know about Jesus?* Trans. M. Kohl. London.

Borg, M. J. 1984. *Conflict, Holiness and Politics in the Teachings of Jesus.* New York and Toronto.

———. 1987a. *Jesus: A New Vision.* San Francisco.

———. 1987b. An Orthodoxy Reconsidered: The "End-of-the-World Jesus". Pp. 207–17 in *The Glory of Christ in the New Testament,* ed. L. D. Hurst and N. T. Wright. Oxford.

Bornkamm, G. 1960. *Jesus of Nazareth.* Trans. I. and H. McLuskey with J. M. Robinson. New York.

Bowden, J. 1988. *Jesus: The Unanswered Questions.* London.

Bowker, J. W. 1973. *Jesus and the Pharisees.* Cambridge.

Brandon, S. G. F. 1967. *Jesus and the Zealots.* Manchester.

Brown, C. 1985. *Jesus in European Protestant Thought.* Grand Rapids.

Buchanan, G. W. 1984. *Jesus: The King and the Kingdom.* Macon, GA.

Bultmann, R. 1934. *Jesus and the Word.* Trans. L. P. Smith and E. H. Lantero. New York.

———. 1958. *Jesus Christ and Mythology.* New York.

Caird, G. B. 1965. *Jesus and the Jewish Nation.* London.

Charlesworth, J. H. 1988. *Jesus Within Judaism.* New York.

Chilton, B. D. 1979. *God in Strength: Jesus' Announcement of the Kingdom.* Freistadt.

———. 1984. *A Galilean Rabbi and His Bible.* Wilmington, DE.

Derrett, J. D. M. 1973. *Jesus's Audience: The Social and Psychological Environment in which He Worked.* New York.

Dodd, C. H. 1961. *The Parables of the Kingdom.* Rev. ed. London.

———. 1971. *The Founder of Christianity.* London.

Downing, F. G. 1987. *Jesus and the Threat of Freedom.* London.

———. 1988. *The Christ and the Cynics.* Sheffield.

Farmer, W. R. 1982. *Jesus and the Gospel.* Philadelphia.

France, R. T. 1971. *Jesus and the Old Testament.* London.

Fredriksen, P. 1988. *From Jesus to Christ.* New Haven.

Freyne, S. 1988. *Galilee, Jesus and the Gospels.* Philadelphia.

Goppelt, L. 1981. *The Ministry of Jesus in its Theological Significance.* Vol. 1 in *Theology of the New Testament.* Trans. J. Alsup. Grand Rapids.

Harvey, A. E. 1982. *Jesus and the Constraints of History.* London.

Hebblethwaite, B. L. 1989. The Jewishness of Jesus from the Perspective of Christian Doctrine. *SJT* 42: 27–44.
Hengel, M. 1974. *Judaism and Hellenism.* 2d. ed. London.
———. 1977. *Crucifixion.* Trans. J. Bowden. London.
———. 1981a. *The Charismatic Leader and His Followers.* Trans. J. C. G. Greig. Edinburgh.
———. 1981b. *The Atonement.* Trans. J. Bowden. London.
———. 1989. *The Zealots: Investigations into the Jewish Freedom Movement in the Period from Herod 1 until 70 A.D.* Trans. D. Smith. Edinburgh.
Holtzmann, H. J. 1863. *Die synoptischen Evangelien. Ihr Ursprung und geschichtlicher Charakter.* Leipzig.
Hooker, M. D. 1967. *The Son of Man in Mark.* London.
———. 1972. On Using the Wrong Tool. *Theology* 75: 570–81.
Horsley, R. A. 1987. *Jesus and the Spiral of Violence.* San Francisco.
Jeremias, J. 1958. *Jesus' Promise to the Nations.* SBT 24. Trans. S. H. Hooke. London.
———. 1963. *The Parables of Jesus.* Trans. S. H. Hooke. London.
———. 1971. *The Proclamation of Jesus.* Vol. 1 in *New Testament Theology.* Trans. J. Bowden. London.
Jonge, M. de. 1988. *Christology in Context.* Philadelphia.
Kähler, M. 1964. *The So-called Historical Jesus and the Historic, Biblical Christ.* Trans. C. E. Braaten. Philadelphia.
Käsemann, E. 1964. *Essays on New Testament Themes.* Trans. W. J. Montague. London.
Kloppenborg, J. S. 1987. *The Formation of Q.* Philadelphia.
Kümmel, W. G. 1957. *Promise and Fulfilment.* Trans. D. M. Barton. SBT 23. London.
———. 1974. *The Theology of the New Testament.* Trans. J. E. Steely. London.
Ladd, G. E. 1966. *Jesus and the Kingdom.* London.
Leivestad, R. 1987. *Jesus in His Own Perspective.* Trans. D. E. Aune. Minneapolis.
Lohfink, G. 1984. *Jesus and Community.* Trans. J. P. Galvin. Philadelphia and New York.
Mack, B. L. 1988. *A Myth of Innocence: Mark and Christian Origins.* Philadelphia.
Manson, T. W. 1931. *The Teaching of Jesus.* Cambridge.
———. 1949. *The Sayings of Jesus.* London.
Meyer, B. F. 1979. *The Aims of Jesus.* London.
Neill, S. C., and Wright, N. T. 1988. *The Interpretation of the New Testament, 1861–1986.* Oxford.
Reimarus, H. S. 1970. *Reimarus: Fragments,* ed. C. H. Talbert. Trans. R. S. Fraser. Philadelphia.
Renan, E. 1863. *La Vie de Jésus.* Paris.
Riches, J. R. 1980. *Jesus and the Transformation of Judaism.* London.
Robinson, J. M. 1959. *A New Quest of the Historical Jesus.* London.
Rivkin, E. 1984. *What Crucified Jesus?* London.
Sanders, E. P. 1985. *Jesus and Judaism.* Philadelphia.
Sanders, E. P., and Davies, M. 1989. *Studying the Synoptic Gospels.* London and Philadelphia.
Schillebeeckx, E. 1979. *Jesus: An Experiment in Christology.* Trans. H. Hoskins. London.
Schweitzer, A. 1901. *Das Messianitäts- und Leidengeheimnis: Eine Skizze des Lebens Jesu.* Tübingen.
———. 1925. *The Mystery of the Kingdom of God.* Trans. W. Lowrie. London.
———. 1954. *The Quest of the Historical Jesus.* 3d ed. Trans. W. Montgomery. London.
Segundo, J. L. 1985. *The Historical Jesus of the Synoptics.* London.
Strauss, D. F. 1972. *The Life of Jesus Critically Examined.* Trans. P. C. Hodgson. London.
Streeter, B. H. 1924. *The Four Gospels.* New York.
Theissen, G. 1987. *The Shadow of the Galilean.* Trans. J. Bowden. London.
Thiselton, A. C. 1980. *The Two Horizons.* Exeter.
Vermes, G. 1973. *Jesus the Jew.* London.
———. 1983. *Jesus and the World of Judaism.* London.
Weiss, J. 1971. *Jesus' Proclamation of the Kingdom of God.* Philadelphia.
Wright, N. T. 1986. 'Constraints' and the Jesus of History. *SJT* 39: 189–210.
Yoder, J. H. 1972. *The Politics of Jesus.* Grand Rapids.

N. T. Wright

THE ACTUAL WORDS OF JESUS

The actual words of Jesus—or *ipsissima verba*—refers to the words which Jesus actually spoke. This should be distinguished from the *ipsissima vox* (the very voice), a term which can be applied to sayings which give the sense but not the exact linguistic form of his actual utterances. In this sense, with a very few exceptions (words like *abba, ephphatha*) we simply do not have such *ipsissima verba* of Jesus. He spoke, in all probability, in Aramaic and the NT is written in Greek. Even if he understood and spoke some Greek he would scarcely have used it for his public utterances in the Galilean countryside. Greek was more at home in the towns and cities. Thus the Greek sayings attributed to Jesus in the gospels can at best give the sense of what he said, not the actual form of words. It is therefore convenient, as scholars more-frequently do, to speak of the authentic sayings of Jesus, referring to sayings which we have good reason to believe are "as close to something that Jesus said as we can reasonably hope for" (Sanders 1985: 357, n. 30). Discussion about what constitutes good reason for such belief usually focuses on two main areas: (a) how much trust we can place in the general accuracy of the relevant historical material; and (b) the means available for distinguishing within that material authentic from inauthentic sayings. Such means are often referred to as criteria, which might suggest objective tests which can be applied rigorously to individual sayings. If so, this is misleading.

A. Sources

While there are sayings of Jesus recorded in the Gospel of John and in the noncanonical gospels, as well as possible echoes of such sayings in the Pauline correspondence, it is clear that the main source of authentic sayings of Jesus is the Synoptic tradition which underlies the Synoptic Gospels. Little of the extracanonical material is likely to go back to Jesus, and where it does, it is frequently dependent on the Synoptic Gospels; the utterances of Jesus in the Gospel of John are so different from those of the Synoptic Gospels, both as to form and content, that they must be adjusted to be, largely the work of the early Church.

B. The Trustworthiness of the Synoptic Tradition

There is some confusion among scholars about who should bear the burden of proof: those who affirm the general trustworthiness of the synoptic tradition or those who adopt a more-sceptical attitude. This is misleading; scholars of either persuasion need to give an account of their *reasons* for their views.

The main grounds for caution about the trustworthiness

of the Synoptic tradition have been provided by form critics who have argued (a) that the forms in which the Synoptic sayings have come down to us are largely the work of the early Christian communities and relate to the typical situations in which they were communicated; (b) that in the process of communication the individual units of tradition have undergone a process of change. Others, notably Gerhardsson and, more recently, Riesner, have argued that contemporary techniques of memorizing and preserving sacred stories and sayings were essentially trustworthy and that at least some of the gospel material will have been passed on from an early date in this way. However, the variation between the Synoptic Gospels themselves shows the extent to which subsequent Christian writers felt at liberty to change their inherited texts. Moreover it is crucial to Gerhardsson's argument that he should be able confidently to distinguish the material which was thus passed on from the work of the evangelists, and this he does not do. Thus on either view scholars have to reckon with the possibility of accretions and alterations to the tradition and have therefore to distinguish carefully the work of the evangelists and of the Christian community from that which can be reasonably attributed to Jesus. Nevertheless, decisions about authenticity will be influenced by the extent to which the Synoptic tradition is seen either as "a folk tradition growing without constraints or as a consciously cultivated teaching tradition" (Riesner 1981: 502, whose confidence about the latter view is not altogether shared by Gerhardsson).

C. The Quest for Authentic Sayings

In their attempts to discern the authentic sayings of Jesus, scholars have appealed partly to general considerations of how formed units of tradition may develop: by additions, by fusing with other units, by being put into a particular framework, etc.; partly to certain tests of particular sayings. General formal considerations can suggest what the earliest forms of certain material were and also indicate in some cases relative dates for material contained within a particular complex (e.g., Jeremias' work on the parables). This is useful, but it does not prove whether the earliest form of early material in fact goes back to Jesus.

Thus certain tests have been proposed, principal among which is the dissimilarity test: A saying which is sufficiently distinct from known contemporary Jewish material and also from the later creations of the early Church may with certainty be attributed to Jesus. But what is meant by "sufficiently distinct"? If we mean, e.g., that it is quite unlike anything that we could conceive a Jew of the 1st century uttering, then clearly we should not attribute it to Jesus. Further, if we applied the test rigorously we would end up with very little material to consider, if any. And even if we had a small body of material which could thus with confidence be attributed to Jesus, it is likely that it would distort his teaching because we would have abandoned so much that united him with his fellow Jews. It is reasonable to assume however that Jesus did have a distinctive message, though not so distinctive as to be unintelligible to his contemporaries nor indeed wholly unrelated to their major concerns. What we therefore need to do is to identify a significant core of sayings within the tradition which is coherent within itself and at the same time constitutes a body of material that can be perceived as representing a significant development of contemporary Jewish thought.

While the dissimilarity test has attracted most attention, there are others: linguistic and stylistic tests, which falter on the simple fact that we have at best translations of Jesus' sayings, and tests of multiple attestation and of coherence, which at most represent pointers to or additional confirmation of a general hypothesis about where the central core of Jesus' proclamation lies.

By way of example we may consider Mark 7:15. A tradition historical analysis of Mark 7: 1–23 (Bultmann 1963: 74; Riches 1981: 136 and 217 n. 70) suggests that this was an independent logion around which other material in the section has subsequently clustered. This, while not providing proof of authenticity, nevertheless indicates an early date for the saying. Advocates of the dissimilarity test (Perrin 1976) have moreover claimed that it is a saying which meets all its requirements. It is certainly not a saying, with its apparent rejection of Levitical purity laws, which one could easily expect on the lips of a 1st century Jew. Nor indeed did such beliefs come easily to many early Christians. But here we encounter difficulties. If we take Mark 7:15 as an outright rejection of Levitical purity regulations, then we may want to question whether even Jesus, as a 1st century Jew, could have said and believed it. Equally, if it had been accepted as a saying of Jesus in the early Church, would the debates about table-fellowship with gentiles have raged as they did (Räisänen 1982)? Paul could have produced the saying and the debate would have been closed. However against this it can be argued that Paul did indeed know such a saying (Rom 14:14) but that it does not appear to have saved him trouble and anguish. So the debate remains inconclusive. If on the other hand one could make a link between the removal of cultic boundaries which seems to be advocated in Mark 7:15 and the advocacy of the removal of group boundaries in Matt 5:44, it would greatly strengthen the case for the authenticity of *both* sayings.

Lastly it has to be borne in mind that in applying a test like the dissimilarity test or indeed in searching for a central core of Jesus' sayings we are inevitably involved in making judgments about the *sense* of the Greek *sentences* the gospels attribute to Jesus. There is moreover an unavoidable element of circularity here. If we knew of a particular sentence that it conveyed adequately the sense of one of *Jesus'* sayings then we would be in a better position to conjecture what its sense was. However, to be in a position to attribute any sentence to Jesus we need first to be reasonably confident about its sense! This is merely to underline the point that we do not have hard and fast tests to enable us to establish what Jesus said. Rather we have to make reasonable conjectures on the basis of a Greek tradition of sayings of Jesus. In such conjectures we shall of course be guided by what we take to be the standard, contemporary sense of sayings attributed to Jesus, while being open to the possibilities of interesting shifts away from the standard, conventional sense (Riches and Millar 1985). We shall certainly learn what we can from his actions which, while by no means unproblematic as to their sense (Riches 1986) may still afford important clues about Jesus' intentions and beliefs. We shall, above all, be looking for those sayings which, taken together, can be seen to have a coherent sense and to offer an explanation both of Jesus' relationship to his contemporary world and its beliefs and to the subsequent history of the early Church and its beliefs.

Bibliography

Barbour, R. S. 1972. *Traditio-Historical Criticism of the Gospels.* London.

Bultmann, R. 1963. *The History of the Synoptic Tradition.* Trans. J. Marsh. Oxford. Repr. 1968.

Calvert, D. G. A. 1971. An examination of the criteria for distinguishing the authentic words of Jesus. *NTS* 18: 209–19.

Carlston, C. E. 1962. A positive criterion of authenticity. *BR* 33–44.

Catchpole, D. R. 1977. Tradition History. Pp. 165–80 in *New Testament Interpretation: Essays in Principles and Methods,* ed. I. H. Marshall. Exeter.

Conzelmann, H. 1959. Jesus Christus. *RGG* 3: 619–53.

Downing, F. G. 1968. *The Church and Jesus.* SBT, 2d ser. 10. London.

Gerhardsson, B. G. 1961. *Memory and Manuscript.* ASNU 22. Uppsala.

———. 1979. *The Origins of the Gospel Tradition.* Philadelphia.

Hahn, F. 1974. Methodologische Überlegungen zur Rückfrage nach Jesus. Pp. 11–74 in Kertelge 1974.

Hooker, M. D. 1970. Christology and Methodology. *NTS* 17: 480–87.

Jeremias, J. 1963. *The Parables of Jesus.* London.

———. 1971. *New Testament Theology.* London.

Käsemann, E. 1964. The Problem of the Historical Jesus. Pp. 15–47 in *Essays on New Testament Themes.* SBT 41. London.

Kertelge, K. 1974. *Ruckfrage nach Jesus.* QD 63. Freiburg.

Kümmel, W. G. 1974. *Jesu Antwort an Johannes den Täufer.* Wiesbaden.

Latourelle, R. 1974. Criterés d'authenticité historique des Evangiles. *Greg* 55: 609–38.

Lehmann, M. 1970. *Synoptische Quellenanalyse und die Frage nach dem historischen Jesus.* BZNW 38. Berlin.

Lentzen-Dies, F. 1974. Kriterien für die historische Beurteilung der Jesusüberlieferung in den Evangelien. Pp. 78–117 in Kertelge 1974.

Longenecker, R. 1975. Literary Criteria in Life of Jesus Research. Pp. 217–29 in *Current Issues in Biblical and Patristic Interpretation,* ed. G. F. Hawthorne. Grand Rapids.

McArthur, H. K. 1970. The Burden of Proof in Historical Jesus Research. *ExpTim* 82: 116–19.

McEleney, N. J. 1972. Authenticating Criteria and Mark 7.1–23. *CBQ* 34: 431–60.

Mealand, D. L. 1978. The Dissimilarity Test. *SJT* 31: 41–50.

Mussner, F. 1974. Methodologie der Frage nach dem historischen Jesus. Pp. 1128–47 in Kertelge 1974.

Perrin, N. 1976. *Rediscovering the Teaching of Jesus.* London.

Räisänen, H. 1982. Jesus and the Food Laws: Reflections on Mark 7.15. *JSNT* 16: 79–100.

Riches, J. 1981. *Jesus and the Transformation of Judaism.* New York.

———. 1986. Review of Sanders 1985. *HeyJ* 27/1: 53–62.

Riches, J., and Millar, A. 1985. Conceptual Change in the New Testament. Pp. 37–60 in *Alternative Approaches to New Testament Study,* ed. A. E. Harvey. London.

Riesner, R. 1981. *Jesus der Lehrer. Eine Untersuchung zum Ursprung der Evangelien-überlieferung.* WUNT 2/7. Tübingen.

Sanders, E. P. 1969. *The Tendencies of the Synoptic Tradition.* SNTSMS 9. Cambridge.

———. 1985. *Jesus and Judaism.* London.

Stein, R. H. 1980. The "Criteria" for Authenticity. Vol. 1, pp. 225–63 in *Gospel Perspectives: Studies of History and Tradition in the Four Gospels,* ed. R. T. France and D. Wenham. Sheffield.

Westerholm, S. 1978. *Jesus and Scribal Authority.* Lund.

Walker, W. O. 1969. The Quest for the Historical Jesus. *ATR* 51: 38–56.

JOHN RICHES

THE TEACHING OF JESUS CHRIST

The phrase "the teaching of Jesus" is used in a comprehensive sense to refer to the whole of Jesus' message, rather than in a more-restricted sense to refer to his "teaching" as a category distinct from his "preaching."

A. Introduction
  1. Modern Study
  2. Sources
  3. Using the Sources: Method
B. Important Preliminary Considerations
  1. Jesus' Message Not about Himself
  2. Eschatological Consensus in Question
  3. Relationship to Judaism
C. Jesus as Teacher of "Wisdom"
  1. Conventional Wisdom
  2. The Forms of Jesus' Wisdom Teaching
  3. The Subversive Wisdom of Jesus
  4. The Alternative Wisdom of Jesus
D. The Teaching of Jesus and Politics/Society
  1. Prophetic and Conflict Forms of Jesus' Teaching
  2. Criticism of Ruling Elites
  3. Challenge to the Core Value of Purity
  4. A Renewal Movement within Israel?
E. Jesus and the Future
  1. Eschatology
  2. Kingdom of God
  3. Sociohistorical Crisis
F. Conclusion

A. Introduction

1. Modern Study. The teaching of Jesus has been an object of study throughout Christian history, but especially so since the birth of modern biblical scholarship and the quest for the historical Jesus, beginning in the 18th century and burgeoning in the 19th century. Indeed, the modern study of Jesus' message is a central element in the quest for the historical Jesus.

Two factors accounted for the proliferation of studies of the teaching of Jesus in the 19th century. First, the new perception of the nature of the gospels that accompanied the birth of modern biblical scholarship meant that they were no longer seen as straightforward historical reports of what Jesus said and did. Rather, as documents written some 40 to 70 years after the life of Jesus, they came to be seen as the developing tradition of the early Church, containing (minimally) two levels of material: the convictions and perspectives of early Christian communities and the authors who wrote for them, plus material which may go back to Jesus himself. Thus the teaching of Jesus could no longer be seen as the sum total of all the words attributed to him by the evangelists, but had to be reconstructed through a historical-critical reading of the gospels, which distinguished between what goes back to Jesus and what must be viewed as the product of the early Church.

A second factor fueled the 19th century's focus on the teaching of Jesus: the Enlightenment suspicion of anything "supernatural" or "miraculous" or "doctrinal" in the gospels. With these elements set aside, what remained of the gospel portraits of Jesus was his teaching. Moreover, it was to his teaching that primary theological significance was assigned.

The legacy of the 19th century (perhaps best represented by the popular lectures given by Adolf von Harnack in Berlin in 1900, published as the best-seller *What is Christianity?*) stands in a relationship of continuity and discontinuity with 20th century scholarship. For the most part, this century's scholarship has been more skeptical about being able to recover the teaching of Jesus, and reluctant to ascribe much theological significance to historical reconstructions of Jesus' message. Nevertheless, major treatments of Jesus' teaching continued to appear: in English-language scholarship, especially Manson, Dodd, and Perrin; and in German-language scholarship, especially Bultmann, Bornkamm, and Jeremias. In the last 20 years, there has been a remarkable resurgence of studies of Jesus' teaching, including especially a refined awareness of the importance of the forms and functions of Jesus' message and of its relationship to his social world. What follows seeks to represent (except when otherwise noted) the consensus or near-consensus of mainstream Jesus scholarship as the 20th century nears its end.

2. Sources. Though a few early non-Christian documents mention Jesus, they say nothing about his message. All of the documentary evidence for reconstructing the message of Jesus is thus Christian, canonical and noncanonical. The meticulous study of these documents over the last two centuries has led to a number of widely shared conclusions about our sources for the teaching of Jesus.

First, within the NT the Synoptic Gospels (Matthew, Mark, and Luke) are the primary sources. John's gospel is not seen as a historical account of Jesus' message. Rather, John portrays what Jesus had become in the lives of post-Easter Christians; Jesus as a figure of history did not speak as he does in John's gospel. Second, within the Synoptic Gospels, the earliest layer of written tradition is known as "Q," defined as material found in both Matthew and Luke but not in Mark. Consisting of about 200 verses, Q is considered by most scholars to be the earliest collection of Jesus' teaching (50 C.E.?).

Third, Mark is the earliest of the canonical gospels (about 70 C.E.), and, along with Q, was used by the authors of both Matthew and Luke when they wrote their gospels some two decades later (for a minority position which argues against both Q and the priority of Mark, see Farmer 1982). Fourth, Matthew and Luke, in addition to containing much of Mark and Q, also contain material peculiar to each gospel (special Matthew and special Luke), some of which may go back to Jesus. Fifth and finally, the recently discovered (1945) *Gospel of Thomas* is the most important non-canonical source for the message of Jesus, containing some material which may be as old as anything found in the Synoptics. See THOMAS, GOSPEL OF. Though other early Christian documents both within the NT canon and outside of the canon contain echoes of Jesus' message, the primary sources are thus the Synoptic Gospels and Thomas.

3. Using the Sources: Method. Because even these primary sources are a mixture of traditions going back to Jesus and traditions which developed in the early Church, scholars have devised methods for sorting out this material in order to decide what is "historically authentic," i.e., what goes back to Jesus (Stein, Polkow, Boring, Crossan 1988, Evans). The methods are numerous and interrelated; rarely can a single one be used in isolation.

Six methods are commonly cited. First is multiple attestation: it counts in favor of the historical authenticity of a saying if it is found in more than one layer of early tradition. Second is the need to discount traditions which demonstrably reflect the developing tendencies of the early Church. Third is the environmental criterion: A saying must be "at home" in a Palestinian setting of the first third of the 1st century if it is to be regarded as authentic. Fourth is the criterion of distinctive "form" and "voice," especially as disclosed in the parables and aphorisms of Jesus. Fifth (and most controversial and thus disputed, at least in its strong form) is the criterion of "dissimilarity": if a saying is to be regarded as authentic, it must be dissimilar from both Jewish and early Christian material. Sixth is the criterion of coherence; namely, a saying, even if found in only one source (and even if that source is relatively late), may be regarded as authentic if it is consistent with an already well-established core of material.

Treating the teaching of the historical Jesus thus involves two steps: (1) the question of historical authenticity: deciding what parts of the material attributed to Jesus actually go back to him; and (2) the question of interpretation: deciding what those portions deemed to be authentic meant in the setting of 1st-century Jewish Palestine. In practice, the two steps are not always neatly sequential; sometimes a decision about the meaning of a saying affects the decision about whether it may be regarded as authentic.

B. Important Preliminary Considerations

Three general statements—two negative, and one positive—are important as prologue to an exposition of the teachings of Jesus.

1. Jesus' Message Not about Himself. The careful scholarly work on sources and methods in the last two centuries has led to a conclusion of the first importance: Jesus' message was not about himself. This conclusion is very different from the widespread popular image of Jesus' message, which sees it as largely about his own identity, his saving significance, and the importance of believing in him. But this image, based largely on John's gospel, is not an accurate image of Jesus' own message. Moreover, the relatively few sayings in the Synoptic Gospels where Jesus seems to speak of himself and his saving purpose reflect one of the tendencies of the developing tradition of the early Church: to ascribe to Jesus a set of convictions about his identity and purpose that emerged only after Easter. This conclusion engenders the question of Jesus' teaching afresh: If Jesus' message did not center on himself and his role in salvation, what was it about? It was, as we shall see, about God, the world of the everyday, and a way of transformation for both individual and social existence.

2. Eschatological Consensus in Question. Nor is it any longer taken for granted by scholars that his teaching was decisively shaped by the expectation of the end of the world. This represents a significant change from the consensus which dominated much of 20th century scholarship, which affirmed that Jesus' message centered on the imminent coming of the kingdom of God, understood as involving such eschatological (end-time) events as the resurrection of the dead, the last judgment, and the dawning of the everlasting kingdom, whether on this earth or in a "new" world. This eschatological understanding of the teaching of Jesus emerged near the beginning of the century in the work of J. Weiss and A. Schweitzer and became dominant by mid-century.

However, in the 1980's, it became clear that this was no longer a consensus, with perhaps a slight to substantial majority of scholars no longer holding it (see Borg 1986). A major paradigm shift away from an eschatological understanding of Jesus' teaching may be occurring, even though no replacement consensus has emerged. Thus, in what follows, neither an eschatological nor a non-eschatological framework for Jesus' message will be assumed, and we will return to the topic later (see E.1.).

3. Relationship to Judaism. Because of the mostly tragic history of Jewish-Christian relations, in which Jesus and "the Jews" have often been portrayed as bitter enemies, it is necessary at the outset to speak of the Jewishness of Jesus. This refers, first, to the obvious fact that Jesus' origins were Jewish: He was born a Jew, socialized as a Jew, and remained Jewish all his life. To be sure, he was not unaffected by other traditions. He lived in a cosmopolitan time and place. Hellenistic culture was present throughout Palestine (perhaps especially in Galilee), and Jesus almost certainly knew Greek as well as Aramaic.

Thus, second, it is important to add that to speak of Jesus' Jewishness is more than simply a reference to his origins: namely, the roots and focus of his message and mission were Jewish. There are strong continuities between his teachings and central elements of Jewish scripture and tradition. He restricted his teaching and activity to Jews (see Matt 10:5, 15:24). His concern was for the "shape" of his people's life. He did not seek to establish a new religion, but spoke about and sought the renewal of Judaism.

Yet there was tension and conflict between Jesus and some of his Jewish contemporaries, and it will be necessary to speak of that tension as we turn to an exposition of his teaching. As we do so, it is important to realize that the teaching of Jesus was initially part an intra-Jewish dialogue. The tension and conflict between Jesus and some of his Jewish contemporaries was an intra-Jewish dispute, analogous to (even though not exactly the same as) the tension between Jeremiah and his contemporaries in the 6th century B.C.E., or the tension between Israel's conventional wisdom and unconventional voices such as the authors of Ecclesiastes and Job. Jesus' voice is a Jewish voice, and what we shall call the alternative wisdom of Jesus is grounded in Judaism, in the "alternative consciousness of Moses" (Brueggemann) which resonates throughout the Jewish tradition.

C. Jesus as Teacher of "Wisdom"

The strongest consensus element of contemporary Jesus scholarship sees Jesus as a teacher of wisdom. "Wisdom," as a cross-cultural phenomenon and within the tradition of Israel, teaches a way of life. Grounded in a notion of "how things are" (an understanding of what is real, what is possible, what is important), it speaks of how one should live. Composed of a "worldview," a basic image of reality, and an "ethos," a way of life which is also a path through life, wisdom thus inculcates a way of seeing which is integrated with a way of living. Its "way" is most often contrasted to another way, so that teachers of wisdom ("sages") typically speak of two ways: the wise way and the foolish way, the righteous way and the wicked way, the way of life and the way of death.

The consensus that "teacher of wisdom" is a central category for understanding the teaching of Jesus is the result of two closely related developments in the last two decades. First, studies of Q (the earliest layer of the Synoptic tradition) have shown that it is dominated by wisdom forms of speech: beatitudes, parables, proverbs/aphorisms, and nature sayings. Thus the earliest stratum of the Jesus tradition is predominantly sapiential. Second, there has been intensive research on the forms themselves (especially parables and aphorisms) and their particular function in the message of Jesus.

1. Conventional Wisdom. In the history of religions, there are two main types of sages: teachers of "conventional wisdom" and teachers of "another way." The vast majority of sages are the former; Jesus was one of the latter, teaching an alternative wisdom. To understand this central claim, it is important to begin with the notion of conventional wisdom.

Conventional wisdom is the common or collective wisdom of a culture: It is "what everybody knows," the taken-for-granted understandings of "the way things are" and "how to live." Like wisdom itself, it is a cross-cultural phenomenon. Though its specific content varies from culture to culture, there are structural elements that are constant. First, it is practical; its very purpose is to provide guidance for the "wise" or "right" way of life, ranging from matters of etiquette to the central values of a culture. Second, its picture of the way to live is sanctioned by the notion of rewards and punishments. Its common theme is "Follow this way, and you will do well, or "You reap what you sow." Blessings and rewards, whether in this life or another, will follow its pursuit. This is true of both religious and secular forms of conventional wisdom: in Western religions, the notion of a last judgment; in Eastern religions, the notion of karma; in modern secular culture, the notion of success and prosperity as reward for hard work.

Third, conventional wisdom establishes boundaries and hierarchies: There are those who measure up to conventional wisdom's standards (achievement, propriety, gender, birth, etc.), and those who do not. The latter are the marginalized or even outcasts. Fourth, and cumulatively, conventional wisdom thus creates a world in which one lives, an ordering of reality which shapes perception, behavior, identity, and society.

These general features of conventional wisdom were found in particular form in the social world of 1st-century Jewish Palestine. It specific content was grounded in sacred tradition, especially the Torah, in which were found the stories of God's relationship to Israel and the laws by which Israel was to live. Thus it contained both Israel's image of reality, its picture of the way things were, and Israel's ethos, its way of life. Together with Israel's folk wisdom (found in part in the book of Proverbs), it defined the right way to live. Those who followed it were righteous and respectable and would be blessed, whether in this life or the life to come. Those who did not were regarded as on the margin or beyond the margin of the world created by conventional wisdom.

The "core value" (Neyrey 1986; 1988) or "paradigm" (Borg 1984; 1987) which gave shape to its conventional wisdom was purity. This was the product of a cultural dynamic expressed in the postexilic holiness code, "Say to all the people of Israel: 'You shall be holy; for I the Lord your God am holy' " (Lev 19:2; see also Lev 11:44, 20:26). Image of reality and ethos were linked together: God was holy, and Israel was to be holy. Holiness was understood as purity, which meant separation from all that was impure. Purity (and impurity) applied to people, places, and things. Though persons and groups within Israel argued about the precise meaning of holiness and purity, the concern for purity was not peculiar to a particular group, but was central to the dominant religious consciousness of the culture.

2. The Forms of Jesus' Wisdom Teaching. The last 20 years have seen major advances in our understanding of the forms of Jesus' wisdom teaching. Studies of the parables (Wilder, Funk, Via, Crossan 1973, Perrin 1976, McFague, Tolbert, Boucher, Scott) and aphorisms (Tannehill, Carlston, Williams, Crossan 1983, Perdue) have highlighted their function as forms of oral speech.

a. Parables. Though the word "parable" is used in the gospels to refer to many different forms of Jesus' sayings, it is most commonly used both in ordinary speech and by scholars to refer to a particular form, namely to the "short stories" which Jesus told. With their exact number dependent on definition and classification, there are about 30 parables attributed to Jesus in the Synoptic Gospels, and another 3 in the *Gospel of Thomas.* This is a remarkably large number, given the relatively small compass of Jesus' teaching. Though it is clear that the parables have undergone modifications in their transmission and application, a large majority are regarded by scholars as authentic; they are the bedrock of the Jesus tradition.

An understanding of Jesus' parables as metaphors has superceded the "single point" interpretation, with which Jülicher replaced their allegorical reading about 100 years ago and which dominated parable interpretation through the first two-thirds of this century. Under the "single point" interpretation, the parables were understood as stories illustrating a point or moral truth which could also be expressed in non-parabolic language: sacrifice everything for something of greater value; make the most use of what you have been given; small beginnings lead to great endings.

The metaphoric understanding of the parables sees their function in a very different light. The essence of metaphoric language is comparison: It understands one thing in terms of another. Metaphoric language thus does not make a point; rather, as comparison, metaphor invites the hearers to see something in the light of something else. Metaphor does not illustrate; it illuminates. When language functions metaphorically, it does not provide examples of something already known, but is an invitation to see something new or differently. Such are the parables of Jesus: They are short stories which invite a particular way of seeing.

b. Aphorisms. "Aphorisms" is here used comprehensively to refer to the short metaphorical sayings of Jesus, including beatitudes, nature sayings, and what are sometimes called proverbs. Compact, memorable, and evocative, they are crystallizations of insight. Even more numerous than the parables, there are over 100 of them, with the exact number again dependent on definition and classification. They are the most common form of Jesus' speech.

Aphorisms are both like and unlike proverbs. As literary forms, both are short pithy (and therefore) memorable sayings which crystallize insight. They differ, however, on the basis of "collective wisdom" versus "individual voice" (Williams, Crossan 1983). Proverbs are the former; generally anonymous, they are the voice of a culture's tradition, what everybody knows: "A stitch in time saves nine;" "Spare the rod and spoil the child." Proverbs are the folk wisdom of a culture made memorable. Aphorisms, on the other hand, are the product of an "individual voice," fresh creations which express the particular way of seeing of the speaker. As such, by their arresting or provocative quality, they invite the hearer to participate in that same way of seeing. Aphorisms not only crystallize insight, but invite further insight.

Some of Jesus' aphorisms are truisms, and their persuasive power depends upon their obvious truthfulness, which draws the hearers into agreement: "Figs are not gathered from thorns nor are grapes picked from a bramble bush" (Luke 6:44 = Matt 7:16); "No one can be a slave to two masters" (Matt 6:24 = Luke 16:13), "If a blind man leads a blind man, both will fall into a pit" (Matt 15:14 = Luke 6:39). Here the freshness of perception is not in the statement itself, but in the explicit or implicit application: the hearers are invited to see that something else is like that. Other aphorisms say something unexpected, reversing the normal understanding of things: "Blessed are the poor" (Luke 6:20 = Matt 5:3), or "The first shall be last" (Mark 10:31 par). Here they provoke a different way of seeing by jarring conventional perceptions.

Like the parables, Jesus' aphorisms are an invitational form of speech. They do not appeal directly to the will or intellect, as do statements of divine law or "doctrine"; rather, they appeal to the perception and imagination, inviting a particular way of seeing.

3. The Subversive Wisdom of Jesus. As a storyteller and an aphorist, Jesus used the traditional forms of wisdom to subvert and undermine the world of conventional wisdom.

As metaphoric narratives, Jesus' parables serve this purpose in different ways. Some are brief, arresting the imagination with compact and often surprising juxtapositions:

The kingdom of God is like leaven which a woman put into three measures of flour (Luke 13:20b–21 = Matt 13:33b = *Gos. Thom.* 96); the kingdom of God is like a grain of mustard seed which a man planted in a field (Mark 4:31–32 = Matt 13:31b–32 = Luke 13:19 = *Gos. Thom.* 20). In both instances, the kingdom of God (usually associated with greatness) is compared to something small and insignificant.

Most of the parables, however, are more extended narratives, and what we have in the gospels may be viewed as skeletal outlines or plot structures of an oral story which Jesus "performed" many times, and which he may have elaborated at length. In this case, the parables work differently: As extended stories, they create a world which the hearers are invited to enter. Entering the world of the story, the hearers are then invited to see something else in the light of the story.

Many of the most famous parables of Jesus work in this way. In "A Man Had Two Sons" (Luke 15:11–32, traditionally known as the Prodigal Son, though the climactic focus is really on the older son), the hearers are drawn into the story of a runaway son who had become as an outcast, the joy of his father upon his return, and the complaint of the older son about the father's generous treatment of the returned runaway. The voice of the older son is in fact the voice of conventional wisdom: The father's behavior violated the ordering of life on the basis of rewards and punishments, and the hearers are invited to see the tension between conventional wisdom and the father's gracious behavior. So also in the story of the vineyard owner hiring laborers to work in his vineyard (Matt 20:1–15): Those hired at the last hour are paid the same as those who labored all day. Not surprisingly, those hired first complain; like the older son, they are the voice of conventional wisdom, and their voice is contravened by the parable.

The subversion of conventional wisdom continues in other parables. Given the attitude toward Samaritans in 1st-century Jewish Palestine, the story of the Good Samaritan (Luke 10:30–35) puts together an impossible combination of words: good + Samaritan. Rather than it being an example story of neighborly behavior, the parable shatters the world of conventional wisdom. So also in the story of the Pharisee and tax collector (Luke 18:10–14): By reversing that culture's perception of Pharisees and tax collectors it thereby upsets the ordering of reality which pronounces the one righteous and the other an outcast.

The aphorisms work similarly. Some of them explicitly use the language of paradoxical polarity and reversal: first/last (Mark 10:31 par); humble/exalt (Luke 14:11, 18:14; Matt 18:4, 23:12); losing/finding (Mark 8:35 par, Matt 10:39 = Luke 17:33); relinquishing/receiving (Mark 10:21–30). Purity (and righteousness) is not a matter of conformity to the standards of a purity system; it is internal, a function of what is inside (Mark 7:15; Luke 6:43–45 = Matt 7:16–20, 12:33–35; Matt 5:8). There is a way of seeing which is not seeing, and a blindness which is metaphorical (Luke 6:39 = Matt 15:14; Luke 6:41–42 = Matt 7:3–5; Matt 6:22–23 = Luke 11:34–36).

Much of Jesus' wisdom teaching undermines the central focal points of the life of conventional wisdom: family, honor, wealth, and religion. These provided the primary basis for identity and security in his culture. Some of his most radical sayings called for leaving family or familial obligations (Luke 14:26 = Matt 10:37; Matt 10:34–36 = Luke 12:51–53; Luke 9:59–60; see also Mark 3:33–35). He spoke of wealth as a snare (Mark 10:23–25; Matt 6:19–21 = Luke 12:33–34; Matt 6:24 = Luke 16:13; see also Luke 6:24–26; 12:13–21; 16:19–31). He ridiculed the pursuit of honor (Luke 14:7–10; Mark 12:38–39; Luke 11:43 = Matt 23:6–7). Those who trusted in their own religious status or practice became object lessons of how not to live (Matt 6:1–6, 16–18; Luke 18:10–14; Luke 11:39–44 = Matt 23:23–27).

Like most teachers of wisdom, Jesus spoke of two ways. There is the wise way and the foolish way (Matt 7:24–27 = Luke 6:47–49), the narrow way and the broad way (Matt 7:13–14; see Luke 13:23–24). Strikingly, in the perception of Jesus, the broad way which leads to destruction is not the way of gross wickedness, but the way of conventional wisdom itself. As a sage, Jesus did not confirm the world of conventional wisdom, but challenged it.

4. The Alternative Wisdom of Jesus. The narrow way which leads to life is the alternative wisdom of Jesus. At its heart is an alternative image of reality, an alternative path, and an alternative paradigm for behavior.

Jesus imaged reality as gracious and generous rather than seeing it as ordered on the basis of rewards and punishments. In his nature sayings, he invited his hearers to see life as marked by a cosmic generosity: Consider the birds of the air, and the lilies of the field; they neither sow nor reap, nor toil nor spin, and yet God lavishes them with care (Matt 6:26–30 = Luke 12:24–28). So also the sun rises on the evil and the good, and rain falls on the just and the unjust (Matt 5:45). In these obvious facts, the hearers are invited to see pointers to the nature of God.

Similarly, the parables which subvert conventional wisdom's image of reality point to an alternative image of reality. The story of the overjoyed and gracious father in the parable of the Prodigal Son invites Jesus' hearers to image God as being like that. The story of the vineyard owner who paid all of his workers equally invites the same perception: God is like that. Reality—God—is not to be imaged as a judge who dispenses rewards in return for achievement, but as life-giving and nourishing. Consistent with the invitation to image God in this way is the term with which Jesus addressed God and which he apparently invited his hearers to use as well: *Abba* is the intimate and familiar term used by a very young child to address his or her father, much like the English "papa."

The alternative way or path of Jesus involves moving from a life centered in the standards, boundaries, and securities of conventional wisdom to a life centered in God. Jesus used a number of images to speak of this movement. What is needed is a new heart or a pure heart, that is, a transformation of the self at its deepest level, and not simply observance of the standards of conventional wisdom (Luke 6:43–45; Mark 7:6, 14–15; Matt 23:25–26 = Luke 11:37–41; Matt 5:8). What is called for is a radical centering in God, and not in the world: "No one can be a slave of two masters; you cannot be a slave of God and mammon" ("mammon" literally means "wealth," but metaphorically "worldly security"; Matt 6:24 = Luke 16:13; see Matt 6:19–21 = Luke 12:33–34). The way to this radical centering in God involves a metaphorical dying:

following the way or path of Jesus means taking up one's cross, a vivid image for death in Roman-occupied Palestine (Matt 10:38 = Luke 14:27; Mark 8:34). It is the same movement captured in Jesus' paradoxical aphorisms: Humbling leads to exalting, losing to finding, relinquishing to receiving (see C.3.). In quite traditional language, the alternative path of Jesus is thus a dying to the world of conventional wisdom as the basis of security and identity and a rebirth to a life centered in God.

The way of Jesus also led to a new paradigm for behavior. Whereas the conventional wisdom of his day spoke of purity or holiness as the dominant paradigm for behavior, Jesus consistently spoke of compassion: The father in the parable of the Prodigal "had compassion" (Luke 15:20), as did the good Samaritan (Luke 10:33); the unmerciful servant was the one who did not show compassion (Matt 18:23–35). Its centrality in his teaching is most compactly expressed in the climactic saying, "Be compassionate, even as God is compassionate" (Luke 6:36 = Matt 5:48; Matthew's "perfect" is redactional). The saying is an *imitatio dei,* connecting Jesus' image of reality with the alternative paradigm for behavior: Just as God is compassionate, so those who are followers of God are to be compassionate. Thus the fruit of the alternative way of Jesus, of a life centered in God and not in the world of conventional wisdom, is compassion. It is also captured in the familiar words of the "great commandment" (Mark 12:28–31 = Matt 22:34–40; see Luke 10:25–28): radical centering in God and love of neighbor go together, and are the summary of the way.

D. The Teaching of Jesus and Politics/Society

Though there is considerable scholarly agreement about Jesus as a teacher of subversive and alternative wisdom, there is less agreement about the extent to which his teaching directly concerned sociopolitical issues of his day, due largely to two factors. First is the legacy of the eschatological understanding of Jesus' message: If Jesus believed the world was soon to end, then he would hardly have been concerned about the sociopolitical structures and direction of an ongoing historical community. Second, there has been a tendency to understand Jesus' teaching in an individualistic mode, both in Christian piety throughout the centuries and in 20th century scholarly understandings of Jesus within an existentialist or (most recently) cynic framework.

There has consistently been a minority voice within scholarship challenging the apolitical understanding of Jesus. Sometimes this has taken the form of seeing Jesus as a political revolutionary over against Rome, a view that has never generated much assent (with some differences, Brandon and Buchanan). Recently, however, a number of studies have argued in various ways that Jesus was political in a different sense: not as a leader of a movement against Roman rule, but as one who sought a transformation of his own people's sociopolitical life (Gaston, Yoder, Stegemann, Lohfink, Borg, Herzog, Goergen, Oakman, Horsley).

Central to the question is how politics is defined. If politics is defined as "what political leaders do," then it is difficult to see a political thrust to Jesus' message and mission. But if "politics" is understood as concern for the shape of the city *(polis),* and by extension as concern for the shape of any historical community, there is considerable evidence of a strong sociopolitical component in Jesus' teaching.

1. Prophetic and Conflict Forms of Jesus' Teaching. First, in addition to wisdom forms of speech, there are prophetic forms of speech attributed to Jesus which link him to the classical prophets of Israel and their concern with justice, oppression, and the historical direction of their nation's life. These include "woes" (Luke 6:24–26; Luke 11:42–52, with parallels in Matthew 23), "threat oracles" (Luke 13:34–35 = Matt 23:37–39; Luke 19:41–44, Mark 13:2), and "indictments" too numerous to list. He also performed actions which recalled the symbolic acts of the prophets (Mark 11:1–10, 15–17). Moreover, the tradition refers to Jesus as a prophet, as he reportedly did himself (Mark 6:4; Luke 13:33). Second, there also is a very pronounced element of conflict in the teaching of Jesus. Controversy stories abound (all with various kinds of authorities), and many of the parables and aphorisms of Jesus reflect conflict settings. Some of his contemporaries seem to have found his message and activity to be threatening to the established ordering of life.

2. Criticism of Ruling Elites. The traditions about Jesus report harsh criticisms directed against the ruling elites of wealth, power, and righteousness. He spoke "woes" against the rich (Luke 6:24–26) and against the scribes who used the law for monetary gain (Mark 12:38–40). Stories which begin with "Once there was a rich man" consistently turn out badly (Luke 12:15–21; 16:19–31; see also Mark 10:17–25). He called Herod Antipas "that fox," a term of contempt (Luke 13:32), and criticized "the rulers of the gentiles" as models of how *not* to behave (Mark 10:42–43). According to Mark, he charged the wealthy religious elite who controlled the temple with having made it into a "den of robbers" (Mark 11:17), and accused them of being unfaithful murderous tenants of the vineyard of Israel (Mark 12:1–9).

3. Challenge to the Core Value of Purity. Purity (holiness) as the core value of Jewish conventional wisdom had produced a society ordered in accord with a "purity system" (Neyrey 1986, 1988). Among Jews, there were varying degrees of purity, determined not only by observance or non-observance of the law, but also by ancestry, gender, occupation, and physical wholeness. Genealogies were kept which determined what classes of Jews could intermarry. Though not intrinsically impure, women tended to be identified with the impure side of the spectrum; in a patriarchal and androcentric society, they were second-class citizens in the sense of being denied many of the prerogatives of men and were radically separated from men in public life. Certain occupations, notably those that involved suspicion of gross immorality or frequent contact with gentiles or women, rendered one impure and even "outcast" (beyond the purity system).

The poor were also associated with impurity, in part because their circumstances made following the life of conventional wisdom difficult, and in part because of the notion that prosperity was the reward for righteousness (poverty therefore was a sign that something was wrong). Persons with certain diseases or physical abnormalities were impure. Gentiles were by definition impure. Like outcasts, they were beyond the purity map, and therefore had no place in the "holy land," the boundaries of which were the outer limits of purity. Their very presence was polluting, yet they controlled the land of Israel. Not surprisingly, anti-Roman feelings were intense.

Thus the purity system generated a world with sharp social boundaries: between observant and nonobservant, men and women, prosperous and impoverished, whole and "impaired," Jew and gentile. As the core value, embedded within the conventional wisdom of Jesus' social world, the ethos of purity was thus also a politics of purity.

Within this background, Jesus' teaching about purity does not simply concern a matter of personal piety, but can be seen as a radical challenge to the politics of purity. His teaching that purity was not external but internal denied that purity was a product of observing external boundaries: "There is nothing outside a person which by going in can defile; but the things which come out of a person are what defile" (Mark 7:15; see also Luke 11:39–41 = Matt 23:25–26; Matt 5:8; Luke 6:43–45). He was often in conflict with the Pharisees (the group most committed to the extension of purity in public life), accusing them of being a source of defilement rather than purity (Luke 11:44 = Matt 23:27). He criticized the preoccupation with tithing and the sabbath, both central concerns of the purity system (Luke 11:42 = Matt 23:23; Mark 2:23–28, 3:1–6; Luke 13:10–17; 14:1–6). See UNCLEAN AND CLEAN (NT).

His behavior regularly transgressed the boundaries of the purity system. He was known for eating with "tax collectors and sinners," who were regarded as impure and outcasts. His entourage included women (Luke 8:1–3; Mark 14:40–41; see also Luke 23:55), and associations with women are reported in several stories shocking in their social context (Luke 7:36–50; 10:38–42; Mark 14:3–9). He touched and accepted persons whose physical condition (lepers, lame, maimed) made them unclean. He sided with the poor and marginalized. Luke's version of Jesus' inaugural address, whether it goes back to Jesus or is Luke's summary, catches this dimension very well: Jesus' message was good news to the poor, release to the captives, recovery of sight to the blind, liberty for those who are oppressed (Luke 4:18–19). He pronounced the poor "blessed" (Luke 6:20 = Matt 5:3), and many of the common people heard him gladly. Though his focus was on Israel, he was open to gentiles, and spoke of loving the gentile enemy (Matt 5:43–44 = Luke 6:27; see also Matt 5:38–41).

These traditions suggest that Jesus' message and activity had a boundary-shattering quality, radically calling into question the politics of purity which structured his own people's life. Moreover, seen in the context of the sociopolitical significance of purity, Jesus' alternative paradigm also has a sociopolitical meaning. As the "core value" involved in following the way of Jesus (see C.4 above), compassion leads to a vision of life very different from that generated by purity. Often contrasted to purity in the Jesus tradition, and etymologically related to "womb" (Trible), compassion is an inclusive image. Rather than establishing boundaries, compassion negates them; rather than dividing, it includes.

4. A Renewal Movement within Israel? One of the unresolved questions of contemporary scholarship is whether Jesus founded a movement whose purpose was the renewal of Israel. There are two issues: Did Jesus found a "movement"? If so, what was its purpose? Some have argued that a "movement" (as distinct from an "entourage" or "retinue" of followers) came into existence only after his death, and that all traces of "community formation" must be seen as a post-Easter development. Of those who think he did create a movement, some have seen it as an eschatological group preparing for the end (e.g., Schweitzer and Sanders), and thus unconcerned with the social world. Others have argued that Jesus founded a movement whose purpose was the renewal or revitalization of Israel (Dodd 1970, Stegemann, Schüssler Fiorenza, Lohfink, Borg, Horsley), citing as evidence the traditions that Jesus chose 12 disciples (symbolizing Israel), restricted his mission to Israel, and the analogies of other renewal movements within 1st-century Judaism (Theissen).

If Jesus did found a renewal movement, then it follows that his way was intended as a way for Israel. His emphasis upon compassion would then be seen not simply as an individual virtue, but as intended also as the core value for Israel. Just as the core value of purity generated a politics of purity, so also the core value of compassion generated a politics of compassion. Within this framework, the inclusiveness of the Jesus movement becomes an image of what Israel was to be. Both his message and movement disclose a concern for the historical "shape" and direction of Israel (see also E.3).

E. Jesus and the Future

A strong sense of crisis and urgency pervades the Jesus tradition, and this seems to have something to do with the future. Indeed, the future has played a large role in 20th century studies of the teaching of Jesus.

1. Eschatology. As noted earlier (see B.2.), the eschatological understanding of Jesus' message which dominated much of this century's scholarship is no longer a consensus. The collapse of the consensus is due to several factors: (1) A growing realization that the eschatological understanding of Jesus was based largely on the "coming Son of man" sayings, which the majority of scholars no longer see as authentic. (2) A refined understanding of Jewish apocalyptic material, including the realization that though some apocalyptic literature does speak of a coming end of the world, much does not (see, for example, Collins). (3) A reassessment of both the meaning and centrality of "kingdom of God." See KINGDOM OF GOD/HEAVEN.

At issue is not whether Jesus had an eschatology. He apparently spoke of a last judgment, though almost certainly not of his own second coming, or of his own return as judge or advocate. (For last judgment texts, see Luke 10:12 = Matt 10:15; Luke 10:13–14 = Matt 11:21–22; Luke 11:31 = Matt 12:42; Luke 11:32 = Matt 12:41. It is interesting that none of these speak of it as imminent; what they do have in common is a reversal of contemporary expectation, in keeping with the subversive wisdom of Jesus: In the judgment, when it comes, many of those who expected to be judged favorably will not be, and vice versa). He apparently affirmed an afterlife, though it was not a major theme of his teaching (see Mark 12:18–27, where he speaks about it in response to a challenge). He spoke of banqueting in the kingdom of God with Abraham, Isaac, and Jacob (Matt 8:11–12 = Luke 13:28–29).

These traditions indicate that there is a "cosmic" strain in Jesus' eschatology: Like many of his contemporaries, he apparently believed in the resurrection of the dead and saw history as having a final judgment at its boundary. The issue, however, is whether he thought all of this (judgment, resurrection, the messianic banquet) was to happen soon, and, if so, whether his message was pervaded by this expectation.

2. Kingdom of God. According to Mark's advance summary, the heart of Jesus' message concerned the kingdom of God: "The time is fulfilled, and the kingdom of God is at hand" (Mark 1:15). Twentieth century scholarship has generally accepted Mark's summary as historically accurate, and has spent considerable energy seeking the meaning of the phrase (for a dissenting view, which argues that Mark 1:15 is not only redactional but also misleading, see Mack). It has produced no consensus.

Since Weiss and Schweitzer, the understanding of the kingdom of God and the question of eschatology have been closely related, and the erosion of the eschatological consensus has been accompanied by a reassessment of the meaning of the phrase "kingdom of God." The key question is whether Jesus saw the kingdom as a future apocalyptic event or as a present mysterious reality. A majority of contemporary scholars hold a primarily or exclusively "present" view, emphasizing those traditions in the Synoptics (Matt 12:28 = Luke 11:20; Luke 17:20–21) and Thomas (*Gos. Thom.* 3, 113) which speak of a present kingdom, understood in either or both of the compatible senses of a mysterious presence pervading reality or as a power presently active in the world. A few hold a wholly or primarily future understanding, and the remainder maintain a "both/and" understanding. For those holding a partially or wholly future view, an important question is whether Jesus saw the future kingdom as coming in a dramatically objective and visible manner.

3. Sociohistorical Crisis. Yet another way of understanding the urgency associated with the future in the message of Jesus is to see the future crisis not as the imminent eschatological (final) judgment, but as a sociohistorical crisis flowing out of the historical direction of Jesus' social world (Gaston; Borg 1984, 1987; Goergen). The broad way leading to destruction then refers to the historical consequences of the path of conventional wisdom and its politics of purity; the crisis refers to the present as a time for radical change; and the threat includes the warnings of Jerusalem's and the temple's destruction, understood not as the vindicative act of an angry deity, but as the historical outcome of the present direction. This understanding is coherent with the understanding of Jesus' message as having a strong connection to politics and society (see D.). Jesus' message about the future would then be seen as a warning of contingent destruction, analogous to the prophets of Israel who were active before the destruction of the N and S kingdoms in the 8th and 6th centuries B.C.E.

F. Conclusion

A factor not often acknowledged in attempts to reconstruct the teaching of Jesus is the reciprocal relationship between an overall image of Jesus (a gestalt) and historical judgments about both the authenticity and meaning of the various traditions attributed to him. At some point, the study of individual traditions begins to generate a gestalt. In this respect, the process through which a historian of Jesus goes is analogous to that of a detective: out of the clues, a "hunch" arises. A hunch or gestalt, once generated, quite naturally begins to affect how the rest of the data are seen. In reconstructions of the teaching of Jesus, the eschatological gestalt leads to a denial or reinterpretation of traditions which suggest a historical future; the gestalt of Jesus as a Cynic leads to a denial of traditions which point to a concern with the community of Israel; and the gestalt of Jesus as concerned with the historical direction and future of Israel leads to a denial or reinterpretation of traditions which seem to point to the imminent end of history. There is no way to avoid this dialectic, and interpretations of the teaching of Jesus in the future will continue to work within it. However, one can be aware of the dialectic, and the effort can be made to seek gestalts which do not prematurely eliminate traditions which otherwise seem well-grounded.

Bibliography

Bailey, K. 1984. *Poet and Peasant and Through Peasant Eyes.* 2 vols. Grand Rapids.

Borg, M. 1984. *Conflict, Holiness and Politics in the Teaching of Jesus.* New York.

———. 1986. A Temperate Case for a Non-Eschatological Jesus. *Foundations and Facets Form* 2/3: 81–102.

———. 1987. *Jesus.* San Francisco.

Boring, M. E. 1988. The Historical-Critical Method's 'Criteria of Authenticity'. *Semeia* 44: 9–44.

Bornkamm, G. 1960. *Jesus of Nazareth.* Trans. I. and H. McLuskey with J. M. Robinson. New York.

Boucher, M. 1981. *The Parables.* Wilmington, DE.

Brandon, S. 1967. *Jesus and the Zealots.* New York.

Brueggemann, W. 1978. *The Prophetic Imagination.* Philadelphia.

Buchanan, G. 1984. *Jesus.* Macon, GA.

Bultmann, R. 1934. *Jesus and the Word.* Trans. L. P. Smith and E. H. Lantero. New York.

Carlston, C. E. 1980. Proverbs, Maxims, and the Historical Jesus. *JBL* 99: 87–105.

Charlesworth, J. 1988. *Jesus Within Judaism.* New York.

Chilton, B. 1979. *God in Strength: Jesus' Announcement of the Kingdom.* Freistadt.

———. 1984. *The Kingdom of God in the Teaching of Jesus.* Philadelphia.

Collins, J. 1984. *The Apocalyptic Imagination.* New York.

Crossan, J. D. 1973. *In Parables.* New York.

———. 1983. *In Fragments.* San Francisco.

———. 1988. Materials and Methods in Jesus Research. *Foundations and Facets Forum* 4/4: 3–24.

Davies, S. 1983. *The Gospel of Thomas and Christian Wisdom.* New York.

Dodd, C. H. 1961. *The Parables of the Kingdom.* New York.

———. 1970. *The Founder of Christianity.* New York.

Evans, C. A. 1989. Authenticity Criteria in Life of Jesus Research. *CSR* 19: 6–31.

Farmer, W. R. 1982. *Jesus and the Gospel.* Philadelphia.

Freyne, S. 1988. *Galilee, Jesus and the Gospels.* Philadelphia.

Funk, R. W. 1966. *Language, Hermeneutic and Word of God.* New York.
———. 1982. *Parables and Presence.* Philadelphia.
Funk, R. W.; Scott, B. B.; and Butts, J. R. 1988. *The Parables of Jesus.* Sonoma, CA.
Gaston, L. 1970. *No Stone on Another.* Leiden.
Goergen, D. 1986. *The Mission and Ministry of Jesus.* Wilmington.
Harnack, A. von. 1902. *What Is Christianity?* Trans. T. B. Saunders. New York.
Herzog, W. 1985. The Quest for the Historical Jesus and the Discovery of the Apocalyptic Jesus. *Pacific Theological Review* 19: 25–39.
Horsley, R. 1987. *Jesus and the Spiral of Violence.* San Francisco.
Jeremias, J. 1971. *New Testament Theology.* Trans. J. Bowden. New York.
———. 1972. *The Parables of Jesus.* 2d rev. ed. Trans. S. H. Hooke. New York.
Jülicher, A. 1888–89. *Die Gleichnisreden Jesu.* 2 vols. Tubingen.
Kloppenborg, J. 1987. *The Formation of Q.* Philadelphia.
Lohfink, G. 1984. *Jesus and Community.* Trans. J. P. Galvin. Philadelphia.
Mack, B. 1987. The Kingdom Sayings in Mark. *Foundations and Facets Forum* 3/1: 3–47.
Malina, B. 1981. *The New Testament World.* Atlanta.
Manson, T. W. 1931. *The Teaching of Jesus.* Cambridge.
———. 1949. *The Sayings of Jesus.* London.
McFague, S. 1975. *Speaking in Parables.* Philadelphia.
Neyrey, J. 1986. The Idea of Purity in Mark's Gospel. *Semeia* 35: 91–128.
———. 1988. A Symbolic Approach to Mark 7. *Foundations and Facets Forum* 4/3: 63–91.
Oakman, D. 1986. *Jesus and the Economic Questions of His Day.* Lewiston.
Perdue, L. 1986. The Wisdom Sayings of Jesus. *Foundations and Facets Forum* 2/3: 3–35.
Perrin, N. 1963. *The Kingdom of God in the Teaching of Jesus.* Philadelphia.
———. 1967. *Rediscovering the Teaching of Jesus.* New York.
———. 1976. *Jesus and the Language of the Kingdom.* Philadelphia.
Polkow, D. 1987. Method and Criteria for Historical Jesus Research. SBLSP, 336–56.
Riches, J. R. 1980. *Jesus and the Transformation of Judaism.* New York.
Ringe, S. 1985. *Jesus, Liberation, and The Biblical Jubilee.* Philadelphia.
Sanders, E. P. 1985. *Jesus and Judaism.* Philadelphia.
Schüssler Fiorenza, E. 1983. *In Memory of Her.* New York.
Schweitzer, A. 1950. *The Mystery of the Kingdom of God.* Trans. W. Lowrie. New York.
———. 1954. *The Quest of the Historical Jesus.* Trans. W. Montgomery. New York.
Scott, B. B. 1989. *Hear Then the Parable.* Minneapolis.
Stegemann, W. 1984. *The Gospel and the Poor.* Trans. D. Elliott. Philadelphia.
Stegemann, W., and Schottroff, L. 1986. *Jesus and the Hope of the Poor.* Trans. M. J. O'Connell. Maryknoll.
Stein, R. 1980. The Criteria for Authenticity. *Gospel Perspectives,* vol. 1. Ed. R. T. France and D. Wenham. Sheffield.
Tannehill, R. 1975. *The Sword of His Mouth.* Philadelphia.
Theissen, G. 1978. *Sociology of Early Palestinian Christianity.* Trans. J. Bowden. Philadelphia.
Tolbert, M. 1979. *Perspectives on the Parables.* Philadelphia.
Trible, P. 1978. *God and the Rhetoric of Sexuality.* Philadelphia.
Via, D. 1967. *The Parables.* Philadelphia.
Weiss, J. 1971. *Jesus' Proclamation of the Kingdom of God.* Trans. R. H. Hiers and D. L. Holland. Philadelphia.
Wilder, A. 1964. *The Language of the Gospel.* New York. (Reissued as *Early Christian Rhetoric.* Cambridge, MA. 1971.)
Williams, J. 1981. *Those Who Ponder Proverbs.* Sheffield.
Yoder, J. 1972. *The Politics of Jesus.* Grand Rapids.

MARCUS J. BORG

THE WORSHIP OF JESUS

The prevalence and centrality of the worship of Jesus in early Christianity from an early date has frequently been underestimated, as has its importance for understanding christological development. On the other hand, Johannes Weiss called the emergence of the worship of Jesus "the most significant step of all in the history of the origins of Christianity" (1937: 37). Since the major types of evidence for the worship of Jesus form a continuous tradition from the NT onwards, this article will treat ante-Nicene Christianity as a whole, and will conclude with the contribution which the tradition of worshipping Jesus eventually made to the trinitarian and christological developments of the 4th and 5th centuries.

A. Origins
B. Doxologies
C. Hymns
D. Pagan Perceptions of Christianity
E. Christian Adherence to Jewish Monotheism
   1. 1 Corinthians 8:6
   2. The Book of Revelation
   3. Missionary Christianity in the Apocryphal Acts
   4. Persecution and Martyrdom
F. Relationship to Patristic Christological Development

A. Origins

In the nature of the case, firm evidence of the point at which worship of Jesus began in early Christianity is unlikely to be available, but general considerations along with the available evidence point to the earliest Palestinian Jewish Christianity. In the earliest Christian community Jesus was already understood to be risen and exalted to God's right hand in heaven, active in the community by his Spirit, and coming in the future as ruler and judge of the world. As God's eschatological agent, he was the source of the experience of eschatological salvation and the enthusiasm of the Spirit which characterized Christian gatherings for worship, and he was the focus of all Christian relationship, through him, to God. Psalms and hymns celebrating his exaltation by God and God's work of salvation through him were probably sung and composed from the earliest times (Hengel 1983). To the living presence of a figure with this kind of religious role, thanksgiving and worship, naturally included within the worship of God, were the inevitable response. (For the very early origin of the worship of Jesus, see especially Hurtado 1988.)

Acclamations and prayers *addressed* to Jesus go back to the earliest times. The Aramaic cry *Maranatha* ("Our Lord, come!"; 1 Cor 16:22; *Did.* 10:6; cf. Rev 22:20), whose preservation in Aramaic in Greek-speaking churches indicates its very early origin, implies not only the expectation of the parousia, but present religious relationship with the one who is to come, whether or not it was associated with a eucharistic presence from the beginning. The NT evidence for personal prayer to Jesus as a regular feature of early Christianity has sometimes been underestimated. Paul (2 Cor 12:8; 1 Thess 3:11–13; 2 Thess 2:16–17; 3:5, 16; cf. Rom 16:20b; 1 Cor 16:23; Gal 6:18; Phil 4:23; 1 Thess 5:28; 2 Thess 3:18; Phlm 25) and Acts (1:24; 7:59–60; 13:2) take it for granted (cf. also 1 Tim 1:12; 2 Tim 1:16–18; 4:22). The dominant practice was undoubtedly prayer to God, but since Jesus was understood as the active mediator of grace from God (as in the epistolary formula, "Grace to you and peace from God our Father and the Lord Jesus Christ": Rom 1:7 and elsewhere) and as the Lord for whose service Christians lived, prayer addressed to him was natural. John 14:14 (where the correct reading is probably "if you ask *me*") makes prayer to Jesus a principle of regular petition.

Petitionary prayer to Jesus is not, as such, worship of Jesus. Two phrases drawn from the language of the OT cult, while they cannot be pressed to imply precisely the worship of Jesus, are nevertheless suggestive of the centrality of Jesus as object of religious devotion. In both Acts and Paul (whose usage here certainly reflects pre-Pauline Christian usage) Christians are those who "call on the name of our Lord Jesus Christ" (1 Cor 1:2; cf. Rom 10:12–14; Acts 9:14, 21; 22:16; 2 Tim 2:22; *Herm. Sim.* 9:14:3). The phrase, no doubt drawn into Christian usage especially from Joel 2:32 (Acts 2:21; Rom 10:13), regularly in the OT refers to the worship of God (e.g. Gen 4:26; 12:8; 13:4; Ps 105:1). Secondly, Acts 13:2 portrays the prophets and teachers at Antioch "worshipping *[leitourgountōn]* the Lord [Jesus]." The verb, which in Jewish usage referred to the cultic service of God, must here, in connection with "fasting," refer to prayer in the broadest sense with Jesus as its focus.

Since it was Jesus' functional divinity which made him the object of religious attention in Christian worship from the beginning, the transition from prayer, thanksgiving, and reverence to unambiguously divine worship of Jesus would not have been difficult or very self-conscious. It was a smooth process; there is no evidence that anyone contested or resisted it, even though the issues it raised for monotheistic faith and worship would soon have to be reflectively confronted. Certainly the view that the transition coincided with the movement of Christianity from a Jewish to a pagan Hellenistic environment (Bousset 1913: 92–125) is mistaken. Apart from involving an over-schematized division between Jewish and Hellenistic Christianity and neglecting the continuing dominance of Jewish Christian leadership in the churches of the gentile mission in the NT period, this view founders on the fact that two of the NT works in which the worship of Jesus is clearest—Matthew and Revelation—remain within a thoroughly Jewish framework of thought. That the worship of Jesus did not result from gentile neglect of Jewish monotheism, but originated within and had to be accommodated within a Jewish monotheistic faith, which passed into gentile Christianity along with it, is of the greatest importance for the course of later christological development.

The significance of Revelation, in which it is stressed that Jesus is worthy of explicitly divine worship, is discussed in section E.2. As for Matthew, the issue turns on his emphasis on *proskynēsis* (obeisance, prostration before someone as an expression of reverence or worship) paid to Jesus. Matthew uses the verb *proskynein* with Jesus as object 10 times (whereas Mark uses it in this way only twice, Luke only in 24:52 *v.l.*). On 5 of these 10 occasions there is no Synoptic parallel (Matt 2:2, 8, 11; 28:9, 17). On 3 of them, Matthew supplies the word *proskynein* where Mark has the gesture but not this word (Matt 8:2 = Mark 1:40; Matt 9:18 = Mark 5:22; Matt 15:25 = Mark 7:25). On the remaining 2 occasions Matthew supplies the word where the Markan parallel has not even the gesture (Matt 14:33 = Mark 6:51; Matt 20:20 = Mark 10:35). There are also 2 occasions where Mark has the word but Matthew omits even the gesture, and one where Mark has the gesture but Matthew omits it (Mark 5:6 = Matt 8:29; Mark 15:19 = Matt 27:30; Mark 10:17 = Matt 19:16). However, on these 3 occasions the worship (by demons, the mocking soldiers, the rich young man) would have been considered less than adequate by Matthew.

The evidence therefore suggests that Matthew uses *proskynein* in a semi-technical way for the obeisance which is due to Jesus and emphasizes that it expresses the proper response to Jesus. It is true that the word *proskynein* as well as the gesture it describes could be used of reverence for human beings, without any implication of idolatry (Matt 18:26; Rev 3:9; LXX Gen 18:2; 19:1; 23:7, 12; 33:6–7; 1 Kgdms 28:14; 3 Kgdms 2:19; Isa 45:14, etc.). But a large majority of Septuagintal uses of the word refer to the worship of God or false gods, and the gesture had become highly suspect to Jews in contexts where the idolatrous worship of a human being or an angel might be implied (Add Esth 13:12–14 [cf. Esth 3:2]; *Apoc. Zeph.* 6:14–15; Philo *Dec.* 64; *Gaium* 116; Matt 4:9; Luke 4:7; Acts 10:25–26; Rev 19:10; 22:8–9; cf. also *Mart. Pol.* 17:3). Thus, whereas in Mark and Luke the gesture of obeisance to Jesus is probably no more than a mark of respect for an honored teacher, Matthew's consistent use of the word *proskynein* and his emphasis on the point show that he intends a kind of reverence which, paid to any other human being, he would have regarded as idolatrous. This is reinforced by the fact that his unparalleled uses tend to be in epiphanic contexts (Matt 2:2, 8, 11; 14:33; 28:9, 17). Combined with his emphasis on the presence of the exalted Christ among his people (18:20; 28:20), Matthew's usage must reflect the practice of the worship of Jesus in his church.

In view of the origin of the worship of Jesus in Jewish Christianity, Hurtado (1988: 100) calls it "a significantly new but essentially internal development within the Jewish monotheistic tradition." That it constituted a new "mutation" (Hurtado) of Jewish monotheistic worship, rather than an abandonment of Jewish monotheism, become evident in section E below. Further evidence of the worship of Jesus throughout the whole ante-Nicene period permeates the following discussion.

B. Doxologies

The attribution of doxologies to Christ is particularly clear evidence of unambiguously divine worship, i.e., worship that is appropriately offered only to the One God. Moreover, an unbroken tradition of use of christological doxologies can be traced from the NT through the whole ante-Nicene period. We distinguish two types: the strict doxological form and the acclamatory doxology.

The basic structure of the strict doxological form, of which many variations and expansions are possible, is: "To whom/him/you (be/is) the glory for ever. Amen." Such doxologies are typically used by Jews and Christians as a conclusion to a prayer, a sermon, a letter, or a part of any of these. Though they are rare in extant Jewish literature, where the benediction (a different form with an equivalent function) is much more common, there is no doubt that the early Christian use of doxologies did derive from Judaism, where they were an expression of monotheistic worship. It is the One God of Israel to whom glory belongs eternally. There could be no more explicit way of expressing *divine* worship of Jesus than in the form of a doxology addressed to him.

A common early Christian way of christianizing the doxology without addressing it to Christ was by the addition of the phrase "through Jesus Christ" (Rom 16:27; Jude 25; *Did.* 9:4; *1 Clem.* 58:2; 61:3; 64; 65:2; *Mart. Pol.* 14:3; 20:2; cf. 2 Cor 1:20; 1 Pet 4:10; Justin *1 apol.* 65:3; 67:2; Origen *or.* 33:1, 6). But doxologies addressed to Christ also came into use. The commonest form was a doxology to Christ alone, of which three examples occur in the NT, though in relatively late NT documents (2 Tim 4:18; 2 Pet 3:18; Rev 1:5–6). Two other NT doxologies (Heb 13:21; 1 Pet 4:11) could but are not very likely to be addressed to Christ, and the same can be said for two doxologies in *1 Clement* (20:12; 50:7) which, if addressed to Christ, would be roughly contemporary with the three certain NT examples. However, the three clear NT examples are from different geographical areas and theological traditions and so presuppose a common Christian practice going back some time before the writing of these works.

Some examples of the strict doxological form addressed to Christ alone from the 2d and early 3d centuries are *Acts John* 77; *Acts Paul & Thecla* 42; *Acts Pet.* 20; 39; Mel. *Peri Pascha* 10, 45, 65, 105; *fr.* II 23 [Hall 1979: 94]; *M. Perp.* 1:6; Tert. *De orat.* 29; Hipp. *Dan.* 1:33; 4:60; Origen *princ.* 4.1.7; 4.3.14. Two special categories of further examples should be noted.

(1) The doxologies that end the homilies of Origen are characteristically addressed to Christ alone. Of 202 such doxologies, 181 are addressed to Christ (5 others may be addressed to Christ or to the Father; Crouzel 1980). This practice of Origen's is especially noteworthy since it contrasts with his own theory (*Or.* 14–15; cf. 33.1), and is likely therefore to be evidence not only of his own devotion to Christ but also of a normal practice of ending sermons in this way.

(2) The early Acts of the Christian martyrs seem always to have ended with a doxology to Christ alone (*Mart. Pol.* 21; *M. Carp.* Lat 7; *M. Pion.* 23; *M. Just.* Rec.B & C 6; *M. Perp.* 21:11; *M. Marcell.* Rec.N 5; *M. Irenaeus of Sirmium* 6; *M. Julius* 4:5; *M. Crispina* 4:2). In some cases, the later expansion of an original christological doxology into a later trinitarian form can be clearly seen (*M. Carp.* Gk 47; *M. Just.* Rec.A 6; *M. Das.* 12:2; *M. Agap.* 7:2; cf. *M. Eupl.* Gk 2:4). Here the trinitarian doxology is the post-Nicene development; the purely christological doxology is the early form. In many of these cases the christological doxology is attached to a standard form of reference to the reign of Christ (*Mart. Pol.* 21; *M. Carp.* Lat 7; *M. Pion.* 23; *M. Marcell.* Rec.N 5; *M. Irenaeus of Sirmium* 6; *M. Das.* 12:2; *M. Agap.* 7:2), so that the effect is to contrast the divine rule of Christ, to whom worship is due, with Caesar's idolatrous pretensions to divine worship. The doxology thus expresses precisely the issue of worship for which the martyrs died.

As well as the strict doxological form, acclamatory doxologies were also used with purely christological reference. Here the basic form is simply, "Glory to . . . ," with the object of praise expressed in the second or third person. Frequently a relative or casual clause follows, giving the reason for praise. This form is not normally a concluding formula (but see *Odes Sol.* 17:17), but forms an independent or even introductory ascription of praise. Its christological use in early Christianity seems to have been prevalent especially in Syria (*Odes Sol.* 17:17; *Acts John* 43; 78; *Acts Thom.* 59; 60; 80; 153), though not exclusively there (*M. Pion.* 11:6).

Besides its three purely christological doxologies, the NT also contains one doxology addressed to God and Christ together (Rev 5:13; cf. 7:10). This is the nearest the NT comes to later *trinitarian* doxologies in "coordinated" form, i.e., in which glory is ascribed to all three divine persons. They are less common in the pre-Nicene period than the doxology addressed to Christ alone, but are found. It is disputed whether this form of the doxology is original in *Mart. Pol.* 14:3 (see Jungmann 1965: 147 n. 4), but there seems to be a good case for claiming that it was regularly used by Hippolytus in the liturgy as well as in other works (Jungmann 1965: 5–8, 151–52, 152 n. 2, 155; Lebreton 1928: 622–25; but on the liturgy see also Hanssens 1959; 343–68), as it certainly was also in the Syriac liturgies from an early date (Jungmann 1965: 194–200). Other early doxologies to the trinity are in *Acts John* 94; 96; *Acts Thom.* 132 (all these in the acclamatory form); Dionysius of Alexandria (*ap.* Bas. *Spir.* 29).

C. Hymns

Hymns in praise of Christ are probably, as Martin Hengel has argued, "as old as the [Christian] community itself" (Hengel 1983: 93), and, like the doxology to Christ, can be traced in a continuous tradition through the early centuries. The singing of hymns "to the Lord" [i.e., to Christ] is already attested in Eph 5:19, then by Pliny's report (of Christians' own testimony) that Christians habitually, in their morning worship, sang a hymn to Christ as God (*carmen Christo quasi deo;* Pliny, *Ep.* 10.96.7). Ignatius' comment that by the concord and harmony of the Ephesian Christians the praise of Jesus Christ is being sung (*Iēsous Christos ąidetai:* Eph. 4:2; the following verse continues the thought in terms of singing through Christ to the Father) uses a metaphor which must reflect a practice of singing hymns in praise of Christ. Later evidence of the continuity of this tradition of christological liturgical hymns comes from the context of 3d-century christological debate. An anonymous early 3d-century writer, refuting the heretic Artemon who denied the deity of Christ, adduces as evidence of the antiquity of this belief the fact that "all the psalms and hymns *(ōdai)* written by believing brothers from the beginning hymn Christ as the Logos of God and speak of him as God *(ton logon tou theou ton christon hymnousin theologountes)*" (Eus. *Hist. Eccl.* 5.28.6). (In this text, as also in *Hist. Eccl.* 7.30.10, note the continuity with the early Christian terminology for such hymns in 1 Cor 14:26; Col 3:16; Eph 5:19: cf. Hengel 1983: 78–80.) Known hymns of some antiquity must be in the author's mind, since he also appeals quite accurately to named 2d-century writers who speak of Christ as God (*Hist. Eccl.* 5.28.4–5). Some years later, Paul of Samosata—the first Christian reformer who attempted to abolish the worship of Christ in the interests of a low christology—put a stop to psalms addressed to Jesus Christ, considering them to be modern compositions (*Hist. Eccl.* 7.30.10). (For the practice of singing hymns in praise of Christ, see also Or. *Cels.* 8.67; Porph. *ap.* Aug. *civ. Dei* 19.23.)

Those fragments of early Christian hymns which are preserved in the NT (and perhaps also in Ignatius) are not actually *addressed* to Christ, but are forms of "narrative praise" recounting the history of Jesus in the third person (especially Phil 2:6–11; 1 Tim 3:16). Like the narrative psalms of the OT, such hymns are praise of God for his saving acts in the history of Jesus, but they are at the same time also praise of Jesus the Savior, as Eph 5:19 makes plain, if it is to hymns of this type that it refers. Indeed, Phil 2:9–11 is virtually equivalent to a doxology addressed *to* Christ and *through* him to the Father. The tradition of hymns of narrative praise must have continued, because the hymnic elements in the work of Melito of Sardis seem clearly indebted to liturgical hymnody of this type. Melito makes the praise of Christ quite explicit by ending such compositions with formal christological doxologies (*Peri Pascha* 10, 45, 65, 105; *fr.* II 23 [Hall 1979: 94]). (Note also the combination of christological doxology and narrative praise in *Acts Thom.* 80, which may reflect a hymnic form.)

But hymns of praise actually addressed to Christ may also have originated at a very early date. A brief acclamation of praise to Christ, drawn from the messianic Psalm 118, is found in the context of the eucharistic liturgy in *Did.* 10:6: "Hosanna to the God of David!" ("Hosanna," originally a cry for divine help, had already in Jewish usage become a shout of praise to God: *TDNT* 9: 682–84; see HOSANNA.) Rev 5:9–10, which addresses praise to Christ in the second person, is not an actual hymn in Christian use: the seer has composed this heavenly liturgy for its context in his work. But it would be surprising if it did not reflect the use of hymns of this kind in John's churches. Moreover, Heb 1:8–12 understands Ps 45:6–7 and Ps 102:25–27 as *psalms addressed to Christ,* while Justin later attests a Christian exegesis of some psalms as addressed to Christ (*Dial.* 37–38; 63; 73–74; 126). In line with Hengel's argument that in the earliest Christian community the use of OT messianic psalms accompanied the composition of new songs (Hengel 1983: 92), this kind of christological exegesis of psalms could have inspired new Christian psalms addressed to Christ. So it may be to this type of hymn that Eph 5:19 and Pliny's report refer. Examples of such hymns which have survived from a later period are the lamp-lighting hymn *Phōs hilaron,* probably from the late 2d or early 3d century (see Tripolitis 1970), Clement of Alexandria's hymn to Christ the Savior in *paed.* 3:12, and probably the original ante-Nicene form of the *Gloria in excelsis.*

The special value of the hymns is that they help us much more than the doxologies to see how the worship of Jesus arose. As Hengel has shown in detail (1983; see also Stanley 1958), the earliest hymns celebrated the saving death and heavenly exaltation of Jesus as the one who now shares the divine throne and as God's plenipotentiary receives the homage of all creation. In offering praise to Christ they anticipate the eschatological consummation when all will acknowledge Christ's lordship and worship him. Thus the worship of Christ is the community's response to his eschatological history. It corresponds to the very high but still functional christology of the earliest Christian Church, according to which Jesus exercises all the functions of God in relation to the world, as Savior, Lord, and Judge, as well as to the same church's strong sense of the living reality of Jesus as the one who reigns now and is coming. The one who functions as God naturally receives divine worship, not of course as a competitor or supplanter of God in the community's worship, but as God's plenipotentiary whose praise redounds to God's glory (Phil 2:11; Rev 5:12–13).

What this shows, however, is that the role which Jesus played in the Christian religion from the beginning was such as to cause him to be treated as God in worship. But in a context of monotheistic worship, in which the uniqueness of God is defined by the restriction of worship to him, this had to be seen sooner or later to mean that Jesus belongs to the being of God. If functional Christology gave rise to the worship of Jesus then it had also to give rise to ontic Christology, as it did already in the NT period as well as subsequently. It is likely that it was the attribution of explicitly divine worship to Jesus which promoted the development of more explicit statements about his divine being.

D. Pagan Perceptions of Christianity

Interesting evidence that the worship of Jesus was the central distinguishing feature of early Christianity comes from pagan observers and critics. "To pagan observers . . . Christian identity centered on the worship of Christ" (Wilken 1980: 113; cf. Mühlenberg 1982: 144). Most 2d- and 3d-century pagan writers who discuss Christianity emphasize the worship of Jesus (Pliny *Ep.* 10.96.7); Lucian *Peregrinus* 13; Celsus *ap.* Or. *Cels.* 8.12, 14, 15; Porph. *ap.* Aug. *civ. Dei* 19:23; cf. *Mart. Pol.* 17:2). Also the 3d-century anti-Christian graffito from the Palatine hill depicts a man in prayer before a crucified man with the head of a donkey, and the inscription: "Alexamenos worships [his] God" (*Alexamenos sebete theon;* cf. Min. Fel. *Oct.* 9: 4; Tert. *Apol.* 16; *Ad Nat.* 1.14). See Fig. ART.48.

In a sense it was easy for pagans to see Christianity as a religious association devoted to the cult of Jesus, in the same way that other religious groups exalted particular teachers and heroes to divine or semi-divine status. But what set Christianity apart, in their eyes, was not only that Jesus was in fact unworthy of such a cult (as Celsus was at pains to argue), but also the *exclusivity* of Christian worship. They saw Christianity as having perverted the exclusive monotheism of the Jews, itself an objectionable superstition (Tac. *Hist.* 5.4–5), into the exclusive worship of Jesus as the only God. Mühlenberg persuasively interprets Pliny's report as implying this: "The skandalon, the fanatic obstinacy, as Pliny sees it, consists in the exclusivity of the divinity of Jesus" (1982: 139). According to Celsus, whose principal objection to Christians was their antisocial (indeed seditious) opting out of all religious practices except their own, Christians "want to worship only this Son of man, whom they put forward as leader under the pretense that he is a great God" (Or. *Cels.* 8.15). Celsus cannot understand how this can be compatible with the Jewish monotheistic tradition in which Christians claim to stand: "If these men worshipped no other God but one, perhaps they would have had a valid argument against the others. But in fact they worship to an extravagant degree this man who appeared recently, and yet think it is not inconsistent with monotheism if they also worship his servant" (Or. *Cels.* 8.12). In thus perceiving that Christians claimed an exclusive monotheism centered on the worship of Jesus, Celsus strikingly corroborates the accounts of the martyrs which are noted in E.4 below.

E. Christian Adherence to Jewish Monotheism

Before the advent of Christianity, Judaism was unique among the religions of the Roman world in demanding the *exclusive* worship of its God. It is not too much to say that Jewish monotheism was defined by its adherence to the first and second commandments. That the God of Israel was the one and only God meant not only that he was supreme, the Creator of heaven and earth, but also that he alone might be worshipped. By contrast, perhaps the principal religious feature of the rest of the Roman world was interreligious tolerance: One's participation in one cult did not imply that others or even oneself should not participate in other cults. Where a kind of monotheism was held by the more sophisticated—deriving from the Platonic tradition, for example—it denied the legitimacy of none of the existing forms of popular religion. Worship of the supreme transcendent God (in any case known by different names to different nations) was entirely compatible with also worshipping the lesser divine beings who were more immediately involved in affairs here on earth. The difference between Jewish and pagan monotheism did not, of course, turn on the *existence* of supernatural beings inferior to the supreme God, but on whether they might be worshipped.

It was this intolerant Jewish monotheism, with its condemnation of all other cults as idolatrous, which also made Christianity an objectionable oddity in the Roman world, with the additional scandal that Christianity somehow linked this exclusive monotheism to the cult of, not an ancient hero or a noble philosopher, but a recently crucified criminal. Intelligible as the thesis might seem—a priori—that Christianity adopted the worship of Jesus to the extent that it abandoned exclusive Jewish monotheism under the influence of the pagan environment, the evidence does not bear it out. On the contrary, it indicates that from the NT period onwards Christians held to exclusive monotheism as tenaciously as they did to the worship of Jesus, because both features were already definitive of Christian worship when it emerged from its original Jewish context into the pagan world.

The remainder of this article examines some of the evidence that the worship of Jesus was practiced in close conjunction with an adherence to Jewish monotheism.

1. 1 Corinthians 8:6. The worship of Jesus as Lord was undoubtedly practiced in the churches of the Pauline mission, but in combination with the exclusive monotheism of the parent religion. In 1 Cor 8:4–6, Paul takes up the issue of polytheistic and monotheistic worship by Christianizing the *šemaʿ*. In other words he aligns himself and his fellow Christians with the Jews in their rejection of the "many gods and many lords" of paganism, and does so by referring to the classic, constantly repeated declaration of Jewish exclusive monotheism in the *šemaʿ* (Deut 6:4). But he so expounds the *šemaʿ* as to include the lordship of Jesus within its terms, glossing its *theos* (God) with "Father" and its *kyrios* (Lord) with "Jesus Christ" (Wright 1986: 208; de Lacey 1982: 200–1).

2. The Book of Revelation. Revelation portrays the worship of Christ in heaven, quite explicitly as *divine* worship (5:8–12). The heavenly worship of God the Creator (4:9–11) is followed by the heavenly worship of the Lamb (5:8–12), and then, as the climax of the vision (5:13), the circle of worship expands to include the whole of creation addressing a doxology to God and the Lamb together. This very deliberate portrayal of the worship of Christ is noteworthy, not only because it occurs in a work whose thought-world is unquestionably thoroughly Jewish, but also because John shows himself quite aware of the issue of *monotheistic* worship. The whole book is much concerned with the question of true and false worship—with differentiating the true worship of God from the idolatrous worship of the beast. Moreover, the issue of worship is reinforced in the closing chapters of the work by the incident, included twice for strategic effect, in which John prostrates himself in worship before the angel who mediates the revelation to him. The angel explains that he is only a fellow-servant of God and directs John to worship God (19:10; 22:8–9). John is here making use of a traditional motif developed in apocalyptic literature precisely in order to protect monotheistic worship against the temptation of angelolatry (Bauckham 1981: 323–37). The point is that the angel is not the source of revelation, but only the instrument for communicating it to John. The source is God, who alone may be worshipped. But in the same passages Jesus is distinguished as source, not instrument, of revelation (19:10b; 21:16, 20). By implication he is not excluded like the angel from the strictly monotheistic worship, but included in it. It seems clear that in Revelation we have the deliberate treatment of Jesus as an object of worship *along with* a deliberate retention of the Jewish definition of monotheism by worship.

Because of this combination it seems that John is concerned not to represent Jesus as an alternative object of worship alongside God, but as one who shares in the glory due to God. He is worthy of divine worship because his worship can be included in the worship of the one God. Thus chapter 5 is structured so that the heavenly worship of the Lamb (5:8–12) leads to the worship of God and the Lamb together by the whole creation (5:13). It is probably the same concern which leads to a peculiar usage elsewhere in Revelation, where mention of God and Christ is followed by a singular verb (11:15) or singular pronouns (22:3–4; and 6:17, where the reading *autou* should be preferred). (Of these texts, 22:3 is particularly noteworthy as referring to worship.) Whether the singular in these passages refers to God alone or to God and Christ as a unity, John is evidently reluctant to speak of God and Christ together as a plurality.

3. Missionary Christianity in the Apocryphal Acts. The apocryphal Acts of the late 2d and early 3d centuries are much the best evidence of how conversion to Christianity was represented to outsiders. They should not be branded as gnostic, and their doctrinal peculiarities, with the exception of the *Acts of John,* are not likely to have seemed unorthodox at the time. They represent conversion to Christianity, again and again, as conversion from idolatry to the worship of the only true God *Jesus* (as well as references below, see *Acts John* 42; 44; 79). Admittedly, in the *Acts of John* this treatment of Jesus as the only God is combined with a consistent elimination of all distinction between Jesus and the Father (except in 93–102, 109, which Junod and Kaestli [1983: 581–89] show to be a secondary addition). But the other Acts are not really, as has been claimed, guilty of "naive modalism": they distinguish the Father and the Son as readily as they call Jesus the only God. In fact, they exhibit a relatively unreflective combination of monotheistic worship, worship of Jesus as God, and the trinitarian distinctions—a combination probably characteristic of much popular Christianity and capable, of course, of being condemned as modalism by more sophisticated trinitarian thinkers. (It seems, for example, much like the position of Pope Zephyrinus, quoted by Hipp. *haer.* 9:6, who condemns it as "ignorant and illiterate.")

What is particularly interesting, however, is the evidence that traditional Jewish monotheistic formulas, designed to assert monotheistic worship against paganism, are employed for the same purpose, but with reference to the worship of Jesus. For example, there seems to have been a form of the full doxology, attested only in early Christian literature (Rom 16:27; 1 Tim 1:17; 6:15–16; Jude 25; *1 Clem.* 43:6; *2 Clem.* 20:5) but surely of Jewish origin, in which glory is ascribed to the *only* God. This turns the doxology into an explicit assertion of *exclusive* monotheistic worship. In the apocryphal Acts this kind of doxology is addressed to Jesus (*Acts Pet.* 20; 39; *Acts John* 77; *Acts Paul* [PHeid p.6]; and acclamatory form in *Acts John* 43; and cf. the ascriptions of praise, not in strictly doxological form, in *Acts Pet.* 21; *Acts Thom.* 25; *Acts John* 85). Furthermore, in several of these cases, the words are: "you [Jesus] are the only God and there is no other" (or similar) (*Acts Pet.* 39; *Acts John* 77; *Acts Thom.* 25; *Acts Paul* [PHeid p.6]). This formula derives from Deutero-Isaiah's polemic against idolatry (Isa 43:11; 45:5, 11, 22; 46:9 etc.) and had already been taken up in Jewish propagandist literature in the Roman world (*Sib.Or.* 3:629, 760; *Ps.-Orph.* 16; cf. *Sib.Or.* 8:377, which is most likely Christian). It makes absolutely clear that in the apocryphal Acts, where the worship of Jesus is so prominent, it was conceived primarily in terms of Jewish monotheistic worship.

4. Persecution and Martyrdom. It was for their "atheism"—i.e., for their exclusive monotheistic worship—that Christians were persecuted and martyred. Probably they incurred a good deal of general dislike by their refusal to participate in what to their neighbors was ordinary social life but in their eyes would implicate them in idolatrous worship. Martyrdom resulted from refusal to worship the emperor or the traditional Roman state gods who were understood to guarantee the well-being of the empire.

In the conflict with the empire, which Christians saw as a conflict about monotheistic worship, they again took up traditional Jewish ways of asserting this. This is the case already in Revelation (14:7; 15:4; cf. the parody of a monotheistic formula in 13:4) and is also true of the Acts of the Martyrs (which, whether or not their records of the words of the martyrs are accurate, are evidence of Christian views on this issue). Repeatedly, under questioning, the martyrs claim to worship the One God who made heaven and earth (*M. Pion.* 8:3; 9:6; 16:3; 19:8, 11; *M. Fructuosus* 2:4; *M. Montanus & Lucius* 19:5; *M. Julius* 2:3; *M. Agap.* 5:2; *M. Crispina* 1:7; 2:3; *M. Phileas* Gk 9:10; Lat 3:4), call down destruction on the gods who did not make heaven and earth (Jer 10:11 LXX) (*M. Carp.* Gk 9; Lat 2; *M. Crispina* 2:3; *M. Eupl.* Lat 2:5), appeal to OT commandments prohibiting the worship of any but the one God (*M. Pion.* 3:3; *M. Montanus & Lucius* 14:1; *M. Julius* 2:1; *M. Irenaeus of Sirmium* 2:1; Phil. Thm. *ep.* 10 [*apud* Eus. *Hist. Eccl.* 8.10.10]; *M. Phileas* Lat 1:1), echo traditional Jewish polemic against idols (*M. Carp.* Gk 1:6–7; *M. Marcell.* Rec.M 1:1; *M. Irenaeus of Sirmium* 4:3; *M. Crispina* 3:2), and use other standard formula of Jewish monotheistic worship ("I know of no other God besides him": *M. Crispina* 1:4; cf. Dion. Al. *apud* Eus. *Hist. Eccl.* 7.11.5; "the living and true God": *M. Carp.* Lat 3:4; *M. Julius* 1:4; *M. Crispina* 1:6). But with no sense of incongruity the martyrs also speak of Christ—the crucified man—as God and of his worship (*M. Carp.* Gk 5; *M. Pion.* 9:8–9; 16:4–5; *M. Con.* 4:2; 6:4; *M. Maximilian* 2:4; *M. Julius* 3:4; *M. Felix* 30; *M. Phileas* Gk 5–6; *M. Eupl.* Lat 2:4), while their own prayers and worship as they approach and suffer martyrdom are usually to Christ (*M. Carp.* Gk 41; Lat 4:6; 5; 6:5; *M. Fructuosus* 4:3; *M. Con.* 6:4; *M. Julius* 4:4; *M. Felix* 30; *M. Irenaeus of Sirmium* 5:2, 4; *M. Eupl.* Lat 2:6; 3:3). We have already noticed (section B.) how the standard literary conclusion to the accounts of martyrdom sets the eternal divine kingship of *Christ* in implicit contrast to the pretended divinity of the emperor and the eternity of the empire.

F. Relationship to Patristic Christological Development

How could Jewish monotheism accommodate the worship of Jesus? It seems clear, from what we know of popular Christianity in the first three centuries, that for most Christians this was not a real problem. Worship of Jesus was worship of God. Jesus was not an alternative, competitive object of worship alongside the Father. His worship was included within the worship of the One God. In this way popular Christianity combined the exclusive monotheism of its parent religion with the worship of Jesus that the central datum of Christian faith and experience—the divine function of Jesus—required. However, in order to maintain and safeguard this position, it was necessary for reflective theology to reach a doctrinal understanding of the being of God and the being of Christ which could do justice to the two propositions: that only God may be worshipped, and that Jesus is such that he must be worshipped. The search for such an understanding, within the intellectual context of the time, occupied

Christian thinkers for the whole of the patristic period. The worship of Jesus was a major factor determining the result.

By means of a necessary oversimplification, we can identify two important trends in ante-Nicene Christianity's reflection on the relation of Jesus to God. One trend remained close to the worshipping life of the church *and* to Jewish monotheism; it reflects very faithfully the evidence just surveyed for the worship of Jesus and for the retention, in Christian witness, of exclusive monotheistic worship against the polytheistic worship of paganism. It is easy to see how this combination might lead in the direction of modalism, in which the distinction between the Father and the Son was simply denied. As we have already remarked in connection with the apocryphal Acts, by no means everything that, taken in isolation, sounds modalistic really is. But the danger was present. If only God may be worshipped and if Jesus may be worshipped, then the conclusion could be drawn that there can be no real distinction between God the Father and God as incarnate in Jesus.

Such a proposition was not likely to succeed in the long run. It neglected too much in the witness of the Bible and the tradition to the personal distinction between Jesus and his Father, and while doing justice to the worship of Jesus, abolished his mediatorial role, which was equally strong in the tradition, not least in the liturgy. But it is easy to see why it made an immediate appeal and was at first tolerated by the early 3d-century bishops of Rome. Noetus, defending his modalistic teaching against the elders of the church of Smyrna, asked: "What evil am I doing by giving glory *(doxazōn)* to Christ?" (Hipp. *Noët.* 1.6; the importance of the point is shown by the way Hippolytus takes it up in 9.2; 14.6–8; and concludes the work with his own doxology addressed to the Son along with the Father and the Holy Spirit: 18.2).

The other trend is represented by the tradition of intellectual theology, which was relatively more independent of the worship and witness of ordinary Christianity. This tradition begins in the Apologists of the 2d century and continues in the Alexandrians and the Origenist tradition. At first sight it may seem surprising that the danger of a paganizing of Christianity arose here rather than in popular Christianity, but there is a clear reason why this was in fact the case. Christianity had no difficulty in distinguishing itself from popular paganism towards which it was consistently intolerant, but the Christian intellectuals were engaged in a critical appropriation of pagan philosophy. The result was that they tended to use Platonic monotheism as the model for understanding the relation of Jesus to God. God the Father is the supreme God, while Christ, the Logos, is God in a subordinate and derivative sense. And just as the Platonist did not confine worship to the supreme God, but allowed the worship of lesser divinities to appropriate degrees, so the Christian practice of the worship of Jesus could be permissible as the relative worship of the principal divine intermediary, while absolute worship is reserved for the one who is God in the fullest sense. The danger in this Christian Platonism was the loss of monotheism in the Judeo-Christian sense.

In relation to worship we can see one possible effect in a suprising passage of Justin Martyr's first Apology, in which he defends Christians against the charge of atheism by claiming that in fact they worship a number of divine beings: not only God, but also "the Son who came from him . . . , and the host of other good angels who follow him and are made like him, and the prophetic Spirit, we worship and adore *(sebometha kai proskynoumen)*" (*1 Apol.* 6). The inclusion of the angels represents an attempt to assimilate the Christian view of the divine world as closely as possible to the Platonic hierarchy of divinity: first God, second God, and a multitude of lesser divine beings (cf. also Athenag. *Leg.* 10.5; Or. *Cels.* 8.13). This is apologetic and should not be taken as a serious claim that Christians worship angels, but it illustrates how Platonic influence could undermine the Jewish principle of monotheistic worship.

In Origen we see the growing gap between a platonically influenced intellectual theology and the popular faith and practice of the Church precisely in relation to this principle. Origen distinguishes four types of prayer and worship. Three of them (supplication, intercession, and thanksgiving) may quite properly be made to human beings as well as to God, but the fourth, which is prayer in the fullest sense of the word *(kyriolexia)* and is accompanied by praise, is properly offered only to the unoriginated God, not to any derived being and so *not even to Christ* (*Or.* 14–15; cf. *Cels.* 5.11; 8.26). Origen is conscious of how far this diverges from the practice of "uninstructed and simple" Christians (16.1), and the extent of the tension is indicated by his own divergent practice (see B. above) and even apparently divergent theory elsewhere (*Cels.* 8.67; cf. *Or.* 33.1). His ability elsewhere to accommodate actual Christian practice of worshipping Jesus is explained by *Cels.* 5.4: All types of prayer can be offered to the Logos, *provided* "we are capable of a clear understanding of the absolute and relative sense of prayer."

The absolute and relative sense of prayer correspond to Origen's hierarchical view of divinity, in which only the Father, the supreme God, is God in the absolute sense and the Son is divine in a relative sense, deriving his divinity from the supreme God and mediating between the supreme God and the rest of reality. Hence worship in the proper sense is due only to the supreme God, but must be offered through the mediation of the Son (*Or.* 15.1–2), who himself can be worshipped only *as an intermediary* who mediates our prayers to and himself prays to the Father (*Cels.* 8.13, 26). Thus Origen, constrained by, on the one hand, his platonically influenced doctrine of God and, on the other hand, the Christian practice of worshipping Jesus, halts between a rigorously monotheistic worship, which would allow only the one who is God in the fullest sense, the Father, to be addressed in worship, and a Platonic permission to worship, in appropriate degrees, all subordinate divinities (cf. *Cels.* 8.66–67).

Early Arianism was in one sense a reassertion of Judeo-Christian monotheism. Rejecting the notion of degrees of divinity, Arius drew an absolute distinction between the Creator and all creatures. Christ could not be a lesser divinity, and so he had to be in the last resort a creature. The effect was that Arius enabled the christological implications of the worship of Jesus to be clearly seen: Either Christians worship a creature, or Jesus belongs to the being of the One God who alone may be worshipped. If this was not at first fully recognized by the Arians, it was by Alexander of Alexandria (*Ep. Alex.* 31) and Athanasius, who continually accused the Arians of idolatry in worshipping Jesus whom they considered a creature (*Ep. Adelph.* 3; *Depos.* 2.23; 3.16). Arianism itself did not abolish the worship of the Son, but severely restricted it and understood it in a strongly Origenist way—as honoring the one who mediates worship to the Father who is the only proper object of worship (Theognis of Nicaea in *sermones Arianorum* fr. 16; Kopecek 1985: 170–72). The development of Nicene orthodoxy, on the other hand, was the attempt to do theological justice to the church's practice of worshipping Jesus with the worship due only to God. The achievement of the trinitarian doctrine which eventually emerged from the Arian controversies was to do this without lapsing into modalism. The triumph of Nicene orthodoxy at the fundamental level of acceptability to the Church at large was due to the justice it did to the place of Jesus in popular Christian faith, as expressed in the worship of Jesus.

Finally, the worship of Jesus again played a part as a christological principle in the christological debate which led to the Council of Chalcedon. It was the principle continually invoked by the Alexandrians, especially Cyril, against an extreme Antiochene Christology. If Jesus Christ is a man indwelt by God, a human subject alongside a divine subject in a relationship of grace, then the worship of Jesus is the worship of a man alongside the Logos (see Cyr. *Nest.* 2; and the 8th of the Twelve Anathemas in Cyr. *Nest.* 3, later adopted, in expanded form, as the 9th anathema of the Second Council of Constantinople in 553). Only if Jesus is the divine Logos incarnate is the worship of Jesus not idolatry but the worship of God incarnate. So the Council of Ephesus (431) decided.

Bibliography

Bauckham, R. J. 1981. The Worship of Jesus in Apocalyptic Christianity. *NTS* 27: 322–41.

Bousset, W. 1913. *Kyrios Christos: Geschichte des Christusglaube von den Anfängen des Christentums bis Irenaeus.* Göttingen.

Capelle, B. 1949. Le Texte du "Gloria in excelsis." *RHE* 44: 439–57.

Crouzel, H. 1980. Les doxologies finales des homélies d'Origène selon le texte grec et les versions latines. *Aug* 20: 95–107.

Deichgräber, R. 1967. *Gotteshymnus und Christushymnus in der frühen Christenheit.* SUNT 5. Göttingen.

Delay, E. 1949. A qui s'addresse la prière chrétienne? *RTP* 37: 189–201.

France, R. T. 1982. The Worship of Jesus: A Neglected Factor in Christological Debate? Pp. 17–36 in *Christ the Lord: Studies in Christology presented to Donald Guthrie,* ed. H. H. Rowdon. Leicester.

Hall, S. G. 1979. *Melito of Sardis: On Pascha and Fragments.* Oxford.

Hanssens, J. M. 1959. *La Liturgie d'Hippolyte: ses documents, son titulaire, ses origines et son caractère.* OCA 155. Rome.

Hengel, M. 1983. Hymns and Christology. Pp. 78–96 in *Between Jesus and Paul.* Trans. J. Bowden. London.

Hurtado, L. W. 1988. *One God, One Lord: Early Jewish Devotion and Ancient Jewish Monotheism.* Philadelphia.

Jungmann, J. 1965. *The Place of Christ in Liturgical Prayer.* 2d ed. Trans. A. Peeler. London.

Junod, E., and Kaestli, J.-D. 1983. *Acta Iohannis.* CChr Series Apocryphorum 1–2. Turnhout.

Klawek, A. 1921. *Das Gebet zu Jesus: Seine Berechtigung und Übung nach den Schriften des Neuen Testaments.* NTAbh 6/5. Münster.

Kopecek, T. A. 1985. Neo-Arian Religion: The Evidence of the *Apostolic Constitutions.* Pp. 153–179 in *Arianism: Historical and Theological Reassessments,* ed. R. C. Gregg. Philadelphia.

Lacey, D. R. de. 1982. "One Lord" in Pauline Christology. Pp. 191–203 in *Christ the Lord: Studies in Christology presented to Donald Guthrie,* ed. H. H. Rowdon. Leicester.

Lebreton, J. 1923–24. Le désaccord de la foi populaire et de théologie savante dans l'Église chrétienne du III- siècle. *RHE* 19: 481–506; 20: 5–37.

———. 1928. *Histoire de la Trinité des origines au concile de Nicée.* Vol. 2, 2d ed. Paris.

Mühlenberg, E. 1982. The Divinity of Jesus Christ in Early Christian Faith. Pp. 136–146 in *Studia Patristica XVII. Part One,* ed. E. A. Livingstone. Oxford.

Stanley, D. M. 1958. "Carmenque Christo Quasi Deo Dicere . . ." *CBQ* 20: 173–91.

Tripolitis, A. 1970. *Phōs Hilaron:* Ancient Hymn and Modern Enigma. *VC* 24: 189–96.

Wainwright, A. W. 1962. *The Trinity in the New Testament.* London.

Wainwright, G. 1982. "Son of God" in Liturgical Doxologies. Pp. 49–54 in *Jesus, Son of God?,* ed. E. Schillebeeckx and J. B. Metz. *Concilium* 153.

Weiss, J. 1937. *The History of Primitive Christianity.* Vol. 1. Trans. F. C. Grant. London.

Wiles, M. 1967. *The Making of Christian Doctrine.* Cambridge.

Wilken, R. L. 1980. The Christians as the Romans (and Greeks) Saw Them. Pp. 100–25 in *Jewish and Christian Self-Definition.* Vol. 1, *The Shaping of Christianity in the Second and Third Centuries,* ed. E. P. Sanders. London.

———. 1984. *The Christians as the Romans Saw Them.* New Haven.

Wright, N. T. 1986. "Constraints" and the Jesus of History. *SJT* 39: 189–210.

RICHARD BAUCKHAM

JESUS CHRIST, SOPHIA OF (NHC III,*4*). See EUGNOSTOS AND THE SOPHIA OF JESUS CHRIST.

JESUS, BROTHERS AND SISTERS OF. In the NT and in extracanonical literature there is mention of Jesus' brothers and sisters. The question of Jesus' brothers and sisters has been a point of controversy throughout church history.

A. NT Evidence

Several NT passages mention the brothers of Jesus (and his sisters in Mark 6:3 [= Matt 13:56] and Mark 3:32 according to some mss). In Mark 3:31–32 (= Matt 12:46 = Luke 8:19–20) Jesus' mother and his brothers try to separate him from a crowd that thought he was out of his mind. Jesus responds that whoever does the will of God is his true brother and sister and mother. Mark 6:3 (= Matt 13:55–56) records the judgment of people in Nazareth who questioned Jesus' wisdom by asking, "Is not this the carpenter, the son of Mary, the brother of James and Joses (Joseph in Matt) and Judas and Simon?" However, Mark 15:40 states that James the younger and Joses were the sons of another Mary, presumably not the mother of Jesus.

John 2:12 mentions that the brothers of Jesus accompanied him to Capernaum and they later tauntingly suggest that Jesus should publicly demonstrate his great deeds at the Feast of Tabernacles (7:3, 5, 10). John agrees with the Synoptics in having the brothers of Jesus refuse to believe in him during his lifetime.

Acts 1:14, on the other hand, includes the brothers of Jesus as part of a group praying together after the crucifixion with the 11 disciples and some women, including Jesus' mother Mary. Paul in 1 Cor 9:5 asks if he does not have the right to travel with a Christian woman (wife?) like the other apostles, the brothers of the Lord, and Cephas. And in Gal 1:19 Paul mentions James, "the brother of the Lord."

B. Evidence from ExtraCanonical Literature

Early church tradition associated with the historian Hegesippus and preserved by Eusebius in his *Ecclesiastical History* records the important role played by relatives of Jesus in the Jerusalem church. James is said to have been the first bishop of Jerusalem and after his martyrdom his brother Simeon succeeded him (*Hist. Eccl.* 2.1.10–17; 3.11).

A 2d-century pseudepigraphical work, *The Protevangelium of James,* is the earliest evidence for the view that Jesus' brothers were the children of Joseph from a previous marriage and that Mary remained a virgin after the birth of Jesus (*Prot. Jas.* 9:2; 19:1–20:3).

The gnostic writings from Nag Hammadi contain several references to brothers of Jesus, particularly James and Thomas. In one of 3 apocryphal writings attributed to James, the author states, "The one whom you hated and persecuted came to me. He said to me, 'Hail, my brother; my brother, hail!' As I looked up at him, the mother said to me, 'Do not be frightened, my son, because he said, 'My brother' to you. For you (pl.) were nourished with this same milk. Because of this he calls me 'My mother.' For he is not a stranger to us. He is a brother [by] your father" (*2 Apoc. Jas.* 50, 8–23). The revealer (Jesus) later says to James, "Your father is not my father, but my father has become a father to [you]" (51,19–22). Here James, whose father is presumably Joseph, is said to be a physical brother to Jesus as well as his spiritual brother.

Another Nag Hammadi text, *The Book of Thomas the Contender,* has the savior say to Thomas, "Now since it has been said that you are my twin and true companion, examine yourself. . . . Since you will be called my brother, it is not fitting that you be ignorant of yourself" (138,7–11). This apparently spiritualizes an alleged physical kinship. See THOMAS THE CONTENDER.

C. History of Interpretation

The ambiguity and brevity of the canonical references to Jesus' family led to three main interpretations. One view evidently supported by Tertullian among others, is named after a later proponent named Helvidius. According to this view, the brothers of Jesus were full blood brothers born to Mary and Joseph after the birth of Jesus.

Another view, defended by Origen, Eusebius, and Gregory of Nyssa, is identified with Epiphanius, Bishop of Salamis, whose *Against Heresies* includes the view that the brothers of Jesus were actually the sons of Joseph by a previous marriage.

A third understanding of the brothers of Jesus is found in the work of St. Jerome. Writing in opposition to Helvidius and the view that Mary and Joseph had other children after the birth of Jesus, Jerome argued on the basis of his interpretation of the canonical evidence that the brothers of Jesus were in fact his cousins. Their mother, Jerome argued, was the sister of Mary the mother of Jesus, who was herself named Mary and the wife of Clopas, who was also known as Alphaeus. Jerome's intent is clear from the title of his work, *Against Helvidius: The Perpetual Virginity of the Blessed Mary.*

D. Current Interpretation

Modern biblical scholarship has usually divided along confessional lines with regard to the brothers of Jesus. Protestant scholarship has generally understood the Gk term *adelphos* as referring to a physical brother, i.e., a biological descendant of the same mother and father. Roman Catholic and much of Orthodox scholarship, on the other hand, has generally interpreted *adelphos,* at least with reference to Jesus, as a kinsman or a cousin. This latter interpretation, based partly on the view that *adelphos* is the Gk equivalent of the broader Hebrew term *ʾaḥ,* accords with the views of St. Jerome and Epiphanius and is consistent with the doctrine of the perpetual virginity of Mary, the mother of Jesus. For classic discussions of these patristic views, consult the work of J. B. Lightfoot (1865) and Zahn (1900). More recent scholarship reviewing the history of interpretation can be found in the studies of Blinzler (1967), and McHugh (1975). The role of James the brother of Jesus is the topic of a recent study by Wilhelm Pratscher (1987) and recent scholarship is summarized in the commentary of R. Martin (*James* WBC).

An ecumenical taskforce concluded with regard to the brothers and sisters of Jesus, ". . . it cannot be said that the NT identifies them *without doubt* as blood brothers and sisters and hence as children of Mary. . . . The solution favored by scholars will in part depend on the authority they allot to later church insights" (Brown, Donfried, Fitzmyer and Reumann 1978: 72).

Bibliography

Blinzler, J. 1967. *Die Brüder und Schwestern Jesu.* 2d ed. Stuttgart.

Brown, R.; Donfried, K.; Fitzmyer, J.; and Reumann, J., eds. 1978. *Mary in the New Testament.* Philadelphia and New York.

Lightfoot, J. B. 1865. "The Brethren of the Lord." Pp. 252–91 in *The Epistle of St. Paul to the Galatians.* Grand Rapids. Repr. 1967.

McHugh, J. 1975. *The Mother of Jesus in the New Testament.* Garden City, NY.

Myer, A., and Bauer, W. 1963. "The Relatives of Jesus." *NTApocr* 1: 418–32.

Pratscher, W. 1987. Der Herrenbruder Jakobus und sein Kreis. *EvT* 47: 228–44.

Zahn, T. 1900. Brüder und Vettern Jesu. Vol. 6, pp. 225–364 in *Forschungen zur Geschichte des neutestamentlichen Kanons und der altkirchlichen Literatur.* Leipzig.

James A. Brashler

JETHER (PERSON) [Heb *yeter*]. **1.** The firstborn son of Gideon, who was asked by his father to execute the 2

Midianite kings, Zebah and Zalmunna, captured by Gideon (Judg 8:20). This is an act of bloody vengeance, for Zebah and Zalmunna had earlier killed the brothers of Gideon. However, Jether was not willing to perform the act.

2. The father of Amasa, a commander of David's army who was killed by Joab out of jealousy (1 Kgs 2:5, 32; 1 Chr 2:17). The name appears as Ithra (Heb *yitrāʾ*) in 2 Sam 17:25. Jether and Ithra are probably variants of the same name, and both are probably correct. He was probably of Ishmaelite origin (1 Chr 2:17) although 2 Sam 17:25 identifies him as an Israelite; the identification of 1 Chronicles has the support of the Codex Alexandrinus reading of the Samuel text. Recently, Levenson and Halpern (1980: 511–12) have put forward the suggestion that Jether may have been a Jezreelite, which has the support of another Septuagintal tradition, the Codex Coislinianus. Another problem is Jether's relationship to David's family. According to 2 Sam 17:25, his wife was Abigail the daughter of Nahash. However, in 1 Chr 2:17, Abigail was Jesse's daughter and so was David's sister. The 2 traditions are difficult to reconcile, although some scholars prefer the text of 1 Chronicles 2 over that of 2 Samuel (*NHT,* 326; McCarter *2 Samuel* AB, 393). McCarter (*2 Samuel* AB, 393) called attention to a peculiarity of the relationship between Jether and Abigail. Both texts of 2 Samuel and 1 Chronicles do not say explicitly that Abigail is the wife of Jether, so they were not married in the usual sense. Either Amasa was the fruit of an illicit relationship or, as McCarter has suggested as likely, theirs was a special type of relationship comparable to the *ṣadiqa* marriage of the ancient Arabs (*AncIsr* 29).

3. The son of Jada, a descendant of Jerahmeel (1 Chr 2:32). Jerahmeel is probably a clan in S Judah (1 Sam 27:10; 30:29) (Williamson *Chronicles* AB, 54).

4. The son of Ezrah, listed as a descendant of the tribe of Judah in 1 Chr 4:17. Myer (*1 Chronicles* AB, 29) suggests that Jether may be connected with Jattir, a town SE of Hebron.

5. A descendant of the tribe of Asher (1 Chr 7:38). He and Ithran of 1 Chr 7:37 are probably the same person (Curtis *Chronicles* ICC, 156).

Bibliography

Levenson, J. D., and Halpern, B. 1980. The Political Import of David's Marriages. *JBL* 99: 507–18.

H. C. Lo

JETHETH (PERSON) [Heb *yĕtēt*]. One of the 11 "tribal chiefs" (Heb *ʾallûpîm*) listed in Gen 36:40–43, a Priestly appendix to the Edomite material in Genesis 36, and in 1 Chr 1:51b–54, an abbreviated form of the appendix. The spelling is probably corrupt, and ought to be emended either to Jether *(yēter)* or to Ithran (*yitrān;* cf. 1 Chr 7: 36–37). See also JETHER; ITHRAN.

Ulrich Hübner

JETHRO (PERSON) [Heb *yitrô*]. Priest of Midian and father of Zipporah, Moses' wife. After Moses fled Egypt at the death of the Egyptian guard and subsequent Hebrew rejection, he came into the land of Midian in the Sinai wilderness. The Midianites lived in SE Sinai and NE Arabia on both sides of the Gulf of Aqaba. At a well, Moses came into contact with 7 shepherdesses and eventually their father, Jethro, priest of Midian. One of the shepherdesses, Zipporah, became wife to Moses and he remained in Jethro's employ until his call by Yahweh to return to Egypt. Scripture bears record that Jethro was a priest of Yahweh in a unique capacity (Exod 18:7–11).

One difficulty surrounding Jethro is the names that are given to him. He is called Reuel in 2 instances (Exod 2:18; Num 10:29). Apparently Jethro is called Hobab in Judg 4:11, although Num 10:29 indicates that Hobab is actually Jethro's son. The confusion of the names is not explained in Scripture. Several explanations have been offered. (1) The various names could have come from different sources of the original text, one source using Jethro and another using Reuel. (2) A misreading of the Numbers passage could have resulted in Jethro being called Hobab in Judges. (3) Jethro may have been known by various names and titles given to him by the various Midianite clans. Whatever the source of the names, it is clear that Jethro (Reuel) has a prominent place in Moses' life.

Another difficulty concerning the figure of Jethro has been the attempts to connect his priesthood with a pre-Mosaic Yahweh cult whose beliefs and rituals were transferred to Moses and Aaron (Exodus 18). This concept maintains that the Hebrew religion has Midianite roots. Using Exod 6:3 as a basis, some scholars insist that Yahweh was unknown to Israel until the time of Moses, who learned of Yahweh from Jethro, a Midianite Yahwistic priest. Though Moses and Aaron learned much from Jethro, it is doubtful that the concept of Yahwistic worship sprang from the Midianites. Judging from the Exod 18:11 statement, Jethro's conviction about Yahweh is confirmed when he hears of God's great deliverance of the Hebrews from Egypt. He blesses Israel's God by saying, "Now I know that the Lord (Yahweh) is greater than all gods." In fact, Jethro should be considered unique, for it is clear from other sources that generally the Midianites were idolaters (cf. Num 25:17–18; 31:16).

Moreover, Jethro contributed to Moses' ministry with some practical advice. When Jethro observed Moses trying to care for the civil matters of the nation, a job too great for one man, he advised a system whereby lesser problems could be handled by leaders of the people. The nation would be divided into units of thousands, hundreds, fifties, and tens with a leader over each unit. Moses would be then free to teach the people ordinances and laws and delegate the implementation of the law to able leadership.

Bibliography

Auerbach, E. 1953. *Moses.* Amsterdam.
Buber, M. 1946. *Moses.* Oxford.
Gressmann, H. 1913. *Mose und seine Zeit.* Göttingen.
Volz, P. 1932. *Mose und sein werk.* 2 vols. Tübingen.

Joel C. Slayton

JETUR (PERSON) [Heb *yĕṭûr*]. The tenth son of Ishmael (Gen 25:15: 1 Chr 1:31). With the exception of Kedemah, all sons of Ishmael were Arab tribes of the 7th through 5th centuries B.C. See also ISHMAELITES. As a tribe,

Jetur is mentioned in 1 Chr 5:19. See also ITURAEA for the history of this tribe.

A personal name *yṭwr*/*Iatouros* is attested in Nabatean and Gk inscriptions from the Ḥawrân area (Knauf 1989: 81); in Safaitic, i.e., Arabic, the name of the tribe is spelled *yẓr*. For its etymology, cf. Sabaic (and Proto-West Semitic) *ẓwr* "rock"; as a verb, "invest, besiege" (Beeston et al. 1982: 173); Safaitic *ẓrt*, Heb *ṭîrôt*, "corrals" (Knauf 1989: 60). Jetur, originally **yaẓûr*, may be translated "The one who builds stone fences," or "The one who besieges" (but whom?).

Orthographically, the Hebrew spelling *yṭwr* (instead of **yṣwr*) proves that this name entered the Hebrew tradition via (Official) Aramaic. The texts which refer to Jetur cannot, therefore, antedate the 7th century B.C.

Bibliography

Beeston, A. F. L.; Ghul, M. A.; Müller, W. W.; and Ryckmans, J. 1982. *Sabaic Dictionary*. Louvain-la-Neuve and Beirut.

Knauf, E. A. 1989. *Ismael*. 2d edition. ADPV. Wiesbaden.

ERNST AXEL KNAUF

JEUEL (PERSON) [Heb *yĕʿûʾēl*]. A personal name combining the theophoric element *ʾēl* with a component that cannot be determined with certainty. Rudolph (*Esra und Nehemia* HAT, 78), derives it from Ar *wʿj* which is used to describe the healing of broken bones or the closing of a wound and can also mean "save." Gehman (*WDB*, 441) suggests a derivation from Ar *waʿā* "keep in mind," "remember." Koehler (KB, 338) proposes a derivation from Heb *yʿh* "collect." An often found reading for the name is Heb *yĕʿîʾēl*. See JEIEL.

1. The head of a family from the sons of Zerah who is listed among the postexilic inhabitants of Jerusalem (1 Chr 9:6). The LXX records his name as *Iiēl* which corresponds to Heb *yĕʿîʾēl*. His name is absent from the list of family heads in Nehemiah 11. He and "their relatives" number 690.

2. A Levite of the sons of Elizaphan (2 Chr 29:13) who are listed as participating in the reform of Hezekiah by sanctifying themselves and cleansing the house of the Lord (29:15). Although his name is written in the MT as *wîʿîwʾēl*, it is to be read as *wîʿîʾēl* (LXX *Iiēl*).

3. One of 3 sons of Adonikam who were among those family leaders who returned from Babylonia during the reign of the Persian King Artaxerxes (Ezra 8:13; 1 Esdr 8:39). Ezra has Heb *yĕʿîʾēl* and records that he was accompanied by 60 males. 1 Esdras has Gk *Ieouēl* (Codex Alexandrinus) and *Geouēl* (Codex Vaticanus) while mentioning 70 males. Blenkinsopp (*Ezra-Nehemiah* OTL, 162–63) offers the various interpretations of the description of the Adonikam family as "those coming afterwards" (Heb *ʾaḥărōnîm*, Gk *eschatoi*).

RODNEY H. SHEARER

JEUSH (PERSON) [Heb *yeʿûš*]. Five persons in the Hebrew Bible bear this name, and the name also occurs in the Samaria ostraca (48:3; Lawton 1984: 340). As a name, Jeush is identical with *Yaġūt*, which is the name of a god (in classical Arabic) and of persons (in Safaitic and Palmyrene; Weippert 1971: 247). In Sabaic, the name is attested once as a cognomen (Harding 1971: 678). Whereas the name can be regarded as hypocoristic in Canaanite ("[God DN] helped"), in Arabic it is a descriptive imperfect-name ("He [i.e., the bearer of the name] is helping"; Knauf 1984: 468).

1. One of the sons of Esau (Gen 36:14, *qere* [*ketib* = *yʿys*]). This "son" represents a tribe of the Oholibamah-group, the smallest of the 3 Edomite tribal groups. The list of the Edomite tribes in Gen 36:10–14 may derive from a tradition that dates back to the 7th century B.C. (Knauf 1985a: 10, n. 45, 61–63; 1985b: 249 with n. 23). The names in this list were subsequently copied into Gen 36:18 and finally into Gen 36:5 (Weippert 1971: 437–46).

2. The son of Bilhan, and therefore the name of a family of Benjaminites (1 Chr 7:10).

3. The second son of Eshek, a Benjaminite (1 Chr 8:39).

4. The son of Shemei, a Levite (1 Chr 23:10ff.).

5. The son of the Judaean king Rehoboam and his wife Mahalath (2 Chr 11:19).

Bibliography

Harding, G. L. 1971. *An Index and Concordance of Pre-Islamic Arabian Names and Inscriptions*. Toronto.

Knauf, E. A. 1984. Yahweh. *VT* 34: 467–72.

———. 1985a. *Ismael*. Wiesbaden.

———. 1985b. Alter und Herkunft der edomitischen Königsliste Gen 36, 31–39. *ZAW* 97: 245–53.

Lawton, R. 1984. Israelite Personal Names on Pre-Exilic Hebrew Inscriptions. *Bib* 65: 330–46.

Weippert, M. 1971. *Edom: Studien und Materialien zur Geschichte der Edomiter auf Grund schriftlicher und archäologischer Quellen*. Diss., Tübingen.

ERNST AXEL KNAUF

JEUZ (PERSON) [Heb *yĕʿûz*]. A son of Shaharaim, a Benjaminite, mentioned in 1 Chr 8:10 in the detailed genealogy of Benjamin. This name occurs only here in the MT and is not found in the Apocrypha or the deuterocanonical literature. The name means "counselor." 1 Chr 8:9–10 indicates that Jeuz is one of 7 sons born to Hodesh. Shaharaim had already divorced Hushim and Baara (v 8) and was living in Moab. Rudolph (*Chronikbücher* HAT, 77) emphasizes that the structure of this extended genealogy rests in the geographical breaks which show parallel lists of Benjaminite families and their dwelling locations at a given time, probably either during Josiah's reign or the postexilic period. Williamson (*Chronicles* NCBC, 82) disagrees and sees no apparent structure whatever to this genealogy. However, the fact remains that there is a clear association of the family of Jeuz with Moab. This may hearken back to a relationship of earlier times. Ruth 1 and 1 Sam 22:34 clearly show that Israelites resided in Moab. This would have been more likely to have happened before Moabite independence from Israel. Jacob Myers (*1 Chronicles* AB, 60) sees a Benjaminite association with Moab to have been a more accurate reflection of a time when Moab was under Israelite control. Jeuz is said to be a *roʾšê ʾābôt*, which has clear implications of social, political, and military status. The role of Jeuz would have been much like the big men of anthropological terminology (Harmon

1983: 150). Orme (1981: 139) paints a picture of the big men which shows high visibility in community affairs and some judicial functions.

Bibliography

Harmon, G. E. 1983. *Floor Area and Population Determination.* Diss. Southern Baptist Theological Seminary.

Orme, B. 1981. *Anthropology for Archaeologists.* Ithaca, NY.

G. Edwin Harmon

JEWELRY, ANCIENT ISRAELITE. The study of jewelry in Bible times begins with a brief review of ancient manufacturing techniques, especially for metals, then moves to a summary of how metals are used in the Bible. The significance of a jewelry piece can be dependent on the valuation and association of the metal out of which it was made.

Most importantly, this summary takes into account archaeological finds dated by their contexts to the biblical period. Nevertheless, jewelry items can be treasured over long periods and ancient techniques can be employed in the same workroom with more modern ones. Even though dating for jewelry cannot be as accurate as for other artifacts, such as pottery, here archaeological finds are used with the study of Hebrew words to aid in understanding the meaning of biblical passages. The most striking jewelry mentioned in the Bible is undoubtedly those items belonging to the high priest's garb in Exodus 28 and 39. Although there is no present archaeological evidence for the jewelry, some suggestions are made below (E.1.d.).

Suggestions can be made with much more confidence for the wedding jewelry of Rebekah, the bride of Isaac, and Ezekiel's portrayal of Israel as bride and queen. For the catalogue in Isa 3:18–23 revised definitions of the vocabulary lead to a different interpretation of the passage. Lastly, more accurate knowledge of the booty and offering assemblages from the Exodus period and Midianite battles adds to the descriptive accuracy of the historical settings.

A. Manufacturing Techniques
B. How Metals Are Used in the Bible
   1. Gold
   2. Silver
   3. Copper/Bronze and Iron
C. Archaeological Finds of Iron Age Jewelry
D. Wedding Jewelry for the Queen
   1. Genesis 24
   2. Ezekiel 16
E. Symbols of Aristocratic Office
   1. The Signet
   2. The Catalogue of Isa 3:18–23
F. Booty and Offering Jewelry

A. Manufacturing Techniques

The most attractive and highly prized jewelry recovered from Bible lands was made from the precious metal gold. When other materials were used, the work had reminiscences of that first accomplished in gold. Important information about jewelry making comes from goldsmithing as depicted on wall paintings in Egypt. Gold can be worked effectively in the relatively pure state found in nature. Copper, silver, and other metals with which it is alloyed act to harden it since pure gold is quite soft. Gold in alloy with large amounts of silver is called "electrum." Silver occurs both in the pure state and combined with various ores from which it is recovered by refining. Silver is also soft and easily worked; usually it is alloyed with copper to harden it for making such items as coins and armaments.

Gold dust or ingots could be melted in a charcoal-fired furnace and poured onto a flat surface; or the ingot could be hammered out on an anvil with a stone tool. The jewelry pieces were made from flat sheets or bars. Scoring tools of bronze, wood, or horn would cut out the basic shape. The design could be worked from the back with a series of punches in *repoussé.* The metal would be placed over a bed of yielding but supportive warm pitch, resin, and wax. Blows from the hammer against the various sizes of punches projected the design in relief. When this procedure was done from the front it was called *chasing.* A similar effect was done by *stamping* when large punches had an entire design engraved on them. *Engraving* with a gouging tool was used infrequently because it wasted the precious metal.

Granulation, the most outstanding decorative process in ancient jewelry, formed rows of tiny gold spheres affixed to the sheet metal base, particularly in triangular patterns, with no trace of solder. After the 10th century of our era the technique was lost to jewelry smiths until 1933, when H. A. P. Littledale rediscovered the process which he named "colloid hard-soldering." Gum and a copper salt form an adhesive paste to affix the granules to the base after being placed on a transfer pattern. As the gold is heated in a crucible over a charcoal fire, an alloying process melts the gold and copper in a barely detectable join. The same method was used for *filigree* where gold wires were swirled and braided in patterns onto a background. The basic design of granulation could have come from bead work. The technique's origin is likely to have been in Mesopotamia at the beginning of the 2d millennium B.C. as a "dog collar" necklace from Ur suggests (Maxwell-Hyslop 1971: 6–7). Subsequently, the art of granulation moved to Byblos and S into Canaan; from there to Egypt and the Greek islands in the Middle to Late Bronze ages.

For basic structuring of a piece requiring a stronger bond, *hard soldering* used a flux and a solder alloy with a melting point lower than the metals to be joined. After cooling, the flux must be removed by scraping or "pickling" in a hot acid solution, as Egyptian reliefs depict.

Egyptians were masters in the art of *cloisonné* from early in the Old Kingdom through at least the LB Age. Here the concern was more with the artistic value of color than the rarity of the jewel; the goal was to present an array of reds and blues to articulate the design. Glass imitations of the intense colors of lapis lazuli, turquoise, and carnelian were a major artistic achievement of Egyptian jewelers. In pre-dynastic times they discovered how to make blue and green *faience* of soapstone or fired powdered quartz coated with vitreous glazes of copper compounds. *Frit* was a form of glass which, after light firing, was homogeneous throughout. Steatite and clay molds from Palestinian excavations were used for making faience and frit beads and amulets.

Casting by the *lost wax* process involved a wax model made in a stone mold. A clay outer cover made from the model could contain molten metal or glass after the wax was melted away. Then the clay could be broken to release the finished product.

Beadwork provided colorful variety and wearable flexibility. Beads occur by the dozens in archaeological excavations and are represented in wall painting and on statuary. In Egypt the common hieroglyph for gold was a collar of beads. Steps in manufacture from casting, piercing, and bow drilling of the individual beads are depicted as well as the complex art of stringing in the construction of broad collar necklaces. Hundreds of shapes of ancient beads have been classified. Shells, seeds, and attractive pebbles were readily available. Precious stones as well as their faience and glass imitations were abundantly used. Metal beads copied shapes of treasured stones, shells, seeds, buds, and blossoms. In Palestine the Egyptian patterns seem to be followed, and it is likely that their colors also symbolize aspects of nature. Dark blue lapis lazuli would be the color of the sky; turquoise of the water. Amethyst was used for the color of dawn and dusk in the desert; serpentine for vegetation. Carnelian probably was associated with blood, "blood-rich" (iron content) soil; gold, with the sun; silver with the moon.

B. How Metals Are Used in the Bible

The significance of a jewelry piece can be dependent on the valuation and association of the metal out of which it was made.

1. Gold. Although gold is the metal mentioned most frequently in the Bible, it is relatively rare among archaeological finds. Nevertheless, when found it tends to retain its original condition—shine, shape, and quality. Gold as used in the Bible represents wealth and leadership, but other associated items are silver, flocks and herds, jewelry, and special garments. The most lavish claims for the possession of gold are ascribed to Solomon. Spectacularly, he received 666 talents plus per year (1 Kgs 10:14–15). It has been estimated that a single talent weighed 75 pounds (Sellers *IDB* 4: 832). Solomon used gold for decorative armaments, his throne, vessels, etc. He instigated commercial enterprises to obtain gold and other products associated with royal riches from the mysterious land of Ophir. "The gold of Ophir" became a metaphor for opulence and was the symbol par excellence for Solomon's commercial acumen in the heyday of his empire.

The biblical emphasis is on Solomon's use of gold in the Jerusalem Temple. Passages describing the greatest amounts of gold used in ancient Israel and a significant majority of the occurrences of the main word for gold *(zāhāb)* in the Hebrew Bible are in association with the furnishings of the Temple. In light of passages such as 2 Kgs 24:13, there is not much hope for archaeological recovery of such items. The golden age which provides the standard descriptions and catalogues of the Temple furnishings is the Solomonic period. As the royal artisan of gold metallurgy and design, especially for the sacred equipment of worship for example, in overlay of cedar paneling, cherubim, doors, woodwork and utensils, Solomon stands without peer in the biblical tradition (1 Kings 6 and 7).

The main focal point of Solomon's wisdom is the building of the Temple, and the most striking aspect of that achievement is the procurement and utilization of gold. In Wisdom literature, gold is a metaphor for wisdom itself (Prov 25:11 suggests gold inlay in silver cloisonné); or the metal is associated with wisdom, but true wisdom is to be preferred over gold (Prov 3:13–14; 8:10; 16:16). The wise precepts of the Lord supercede gold (e.g., Pss 19:11—Eng. v 10; 119:127; Job 28:15, 16,19,23). In prophecy, idolatry is associated with the work of the goldsmith (Jer 10:3–5; Isa 2:7–8; 40:19). Idols of precious metals are presented frequently as the focus of alien and false cults (Deut 7:25; 29:16–18; Hos 2:8; 8:4; Isa 46:1, 6–7).

2. Silver. Silver is used in similar biblical contexts as gold and is paired with gold in catalogues of costly gifts, wealth, tribute, booty, tabernacle fittings, idol composition, and jewelry. Much silver is lost to archaeologists through corrosion in saline soils.

The most striking use of the metal in the Bible is the silver standard for commercial exchange—Heb *kesep* is often translated as "money" (Gen 23:16; 37:28; 42:28; Lev 27:2ff.,15,16ff.; Judg 16:5,18; 1 Kgs 21:2; 2 Kgs 12:10–11; Amos 2:6; Isa 55:1; Jer 32:9).

The most theologically significant to biblical studies and technically relevant to archaeological jewelry craft is reference to the silver-refining process to dramatize spiritual or religious purification (e.g., Mal 3:2–3). This involves crushing, washing, and straining of ore, followed by the cupellation process of heating and the production of "dross," i.e., what is left over of alloys after pure silver has been extracted (Ezek 22:18–22). Silver refining removes alloys of copper, tin, iron, and in the last stage, lead. God uses affliction for Israel's refining process as in Isa 48:10 where suffering points to a future hope.

3. Copper/Bronze and Iron. The terms for copper and iron appear much less frequently in the Bible than those relating to gold and silver. Archaeology has turned up many objects from biblical periods made of copper and iron. The overwhelming majority of jewelry items are in these metals from ancient Israel, but copper/bronze and iron jewelry are rarely mentioned in the Bible.

Israel first met up with metallurgical techniques in the Sinai with the people called "smiths," the Kenites (lit. "Cainites"). Tubal-cain in Gen 4:22 is referred to as the forger of all instruments of bronze and iron. Deuteronomy portrays the glorious bounty of the promised land in terms of metals as well as agricultural riches (viz. Deut 8:7–9).

The same word in Heb *nĕḥōšet* refers to both copper and bronze, an alloy of copper and tin. Malachite ore can contain naturally a small amount of tin, but more than 2 percent tin in copper is considered a deliberate attempt to produce the alloy that in Eng is "bronze." The addition of tin makes the metal stronger, harder, and more resistant to corrosion, and enables copper to have a lower melting point for the casting process when a cleaner, sharper result is required. Purer copper can be hammered into shape while cold, or can be heated slightly, for example by a torch flame, for the malleability appropriate to jewelry making. It is difficult with the naked eye to tell the difference between copper and copper alloyed with nearly 5 percent tin.

The most celebrated objects of cast bronze in the Bible are the Bronze Sea and the 2 pillars set in front of Solomon's Temple (1 Kgs 7:15–26). The Sea probably weighed 25 to 30 tons. Also, some of the Temple fixtures were in bronze, such as the clasps for draperies, pots, and altar grating. Other items in bronze are armaments (e.g., the probable composite bow in Ps 18:35—Eng v 34; Goliath's helmet and coat of mail, greaves, and javelin in 1 Sam 17:5–6; the shields made for the royal guard by order of King Rehoboam in 1 Kgs 14:26; and the fetters for Samson in Judg 16:21 and for King Zedekiah in 2 Kgs 25:7).

As gold and silver are paired in association with treasure and wealth, bronze and iron are paired in metaphor relating to strength, e.g., Behemoth in Job 40:18, and the warrior in Mic 4:13. Iron more frequently is used alone as a symbol of strength and this is surely due to the great variety of durable objects made of that metal, *barzel,* as mentioned in the biblical text. There is a close relationship between weapons and tools. The ability of iron to be shaped into strong instruments that can hit and cut is important in the destructiveness of war as well as the creative activities of peace. The threshing sledge as a weapon of Damascus against Gilead (Amos 1:3) is used in the violent process of making wheat into flour (Isa 41:15–16). Items crafted of iron in the biblical text, then, are heavy instruments for hitting such as rods, clubs, and hammers. Some are sharpened specifically for war, notably swords and spears, but others are crafted as tools: axes, plowpoints, pruning shears, and threshing blades for agriculture; masonry tools, the lapidary's stylus, yoke pieces, and gate bars. The details concerning these metal objects frequently emphasize salient aspects of narratives, laws, prophecies, traditions, epics, and events in the Bible. The strength of iron—its malleability under heat, its ability to be hardened, struck, and sharpened; its weight and durability—convey meanings beyond its immediate use in everyday life.

C. Archaeological Finds of Iron Age Jewelry

There are 2 primary groups of archaeological finds that can be classified as jewelry objects in the Iron Age biblical period, 12th to 6th centuries, in Palestine.

Group 1 contains finely crafted items made of precious metals that are usually found in association with each other. In gold, silver or electrum, they have designs skillfully molded, engraved or worked in repoussé. Generally, to this group belong a few bangle bracelets; some decorated rings including the ornate signet types; earrings, especially the lunate and penannular with various kinds of pendants; crescents, a few flat but most made of a thin wire body with a suspension loop; foil frontlets worn on the forehead and decorated with dots, crosshatchings, and rosettes; almost the whole class of items grouped together as star-disks, rectangular plaques, rosettes, and miscellaneous pieces, some in ivory and bone; a few outstanding fibulae and toggle pins; and decorated triangular plaques.

These are found hidden in hoards and sacred areas as part of obvious treasures of important buildings and carefully designed tombs. Many are illustrated on statues and figurines. Frequently they correspond to similar jewelry pieces in museum collections and those on pictorial representations from ancient Egypt, Mesopotamia, and the Mediterranean world. The closest Palestinian parallels are from the Bronze Age, and the Iron Age examples tend to be in the earliest strata (Iron I). They compare to insignia of office in Egypt, Greece, and Mediterranean countries and would belong to leaders in cult and politics.

Members of Group 2 are more humbly crafted and are found in greater numbers than those of Group 1. Findspots are humble graves, some mass burials and loci of everyday life on the mounds. The jewelry items are associated with other artifacts generally agreed to be of everyday or common use. Their materials are iron, bronze, and bone, made into simple basic shapes with little added design.

To this group belong simple bangle bracelets and anklets, solidly crafted or with 2 ends, of varying sizes and thicknesses; many simple rings similar in shape to bangles but much smaller; quite a number of earrings (lunate, balldrop, mulberry, and plain penannular ring); a few flat-type crescents; the majority of toggle pins and fibulae; and all the bone pendants.

The bone finger-shaped pendant may be the one uniquely Israelite jewelry piece as its existence presently seems to be limited to Iron Age Palestinian sites (Platt 1978: 23–8). The cylinder-like objects range from 5 to 9 cm in length. Their slightly narrower ends are pierced for suspension and they are decorated with rings, cross hatching, and ring-and-dot stamps placed in vertical rows of 3 to 9 designs. See Fig. JEW.01f. Because they are not found in pairs, they are probably not ear ornaments. Most likely they were worn on necklaces with amulets, scarabs, and beads, which are sometimes found in association with them.

The numbers of Group 2 items found in Iron II levels indicate that they belonged to the majority of the population. The design and craftsmanship develop their own styles from indigenous motifs rather than from outside sources. The fewer numbers of cult and political insignia in later periods may reflect the abolition of religious symbolism and imagery as prominent in biblical legislation. Iron II was poorer in traditional treasures but also freer from those traditions which had brought foreign styles and symbols with their accompanying powers. Palestine's jewelry in this period becomes less significant, yet more widespread, plentiful, and useful.

D. Wedding Jewelry for the Queen

1. Genesis 24. Rebekah's jewelry is referred to in Gen 24:22, 30, 47, with some general items of value given as wedding gifts to Rebekah, her mother and brothers in v 53. The narrator's style has provided 2 versions of the incident in which Abraham's servant has 2 kinds of jewelry items for Rebekah, plus a third description by Laban, her brother, saying that he saw her wearing the specific pieces. In the first account, v 22, the servant "took a gold ring weighing a half shekel" (RSV and Speiser *Genesis* AB), and "two bracelets (RSV)/bands (AB) for her arms weighing ten gold shekels." In the second account, v 47, the servant tells Laban that he "put the ring on her nose and the bracelet on her arms."

The words translated "bracelets" or "bands," *ṣĕmîdîm,* and worn in the area of (lit.) her hands probably refer to bangles as found abundantly by archaeology. In position on arms and wrists of female skeletons in burials and represented on Palestinian fertility plaques and Mesopotamian statuary in the Bronze Ages, these occur in pairs and can be worn in groups. A famous statue from Mari has in common with Rebekah in this chapter the association of a water jar (Frankfort 1963: pl. 62, p. 242, n. 47). The Mari statue holds a water jar in front of her with both hands and she has 3 bangles on each wrist. From the Middle Bronze Age at Tell el-Ajjul, 17th century B.C., and at Megiddo, Shechem, Beth-shan, and Gezer (16th, 15th, 13th centuries B.C.) are specific examples. Ajjul's "cenotaph" hoard, part of a queen's royal parure, had 2 sets of 5 bangles made of solid gold. The basic design is a round bangle with 2 ends, each of which is engraved with linear decorations marking in short cuts of 1 to 5 in number its designated place in 5 pairs. See Fig. JEW.01d. The 3 middle bracelets of each set are flattened slightly making 2 sides so that they can be positioned closely together. The others are flattened only on the one side touching the middle bangles. Interesting, in this Ajjul set there are 10 pieces, perhaps comparable to the 10-shekel weight mentioned for Rebekah's bracelets. The Iron Age has the same bangle style, especially in the metals of bronze and iron.

The Heb word *(ṣĕmîdîm)* is related to "couple" or "pair," with the verbal meaning of the act of joining two. Abraham's servant put on or over Rebekah's hands 2 objects making a pair, perhaps symbolizing the marriage bond.

The words translated "gold ring," *nezem zāhāb,* in v 47, put on the nose, refer in the Bible to a jewelry object worn either in the nose or ear. From Megiddo (Loud 1948: pl. 225:9, #a1102, "Remarks;" Tomb 2121 dated MB str. IX, 15th century?) came a typical small round tubular object with 2 overlapping ends, found "in position as a nose ring." Suspended from the ring and opposite the 2 ends is a drop made up of a cluster of little balls, giving the name of Mulberry Earring. See Fig. JEW.01b. From the Ajjul hoards were 3 singles and 8 pairs; they were also found at Lachish, Gezer, Beth-shan, Tell el Fara (S), and Gerar, and were quite popular during the Iron Age. The basic ring with 2 pointed ends is the most common form of Palestinian ear jewelry. The ends facilitate placement through holes pierced in the ear lobe or secondarily, in the nasal area.

From Tell Jemmeh, identified as Isaac's Gerar (Gen 26:6, etc.), a stone jewelry mold was found with a mulberry earring engraved on it (Petrie 1928: pl. XX:45, Aff 193, 9th century). Molds such as this were used by itinerant jewelry smiths from the EB at least, and especially in the MB. Use of them fit within the life-style of the biblical patriarchs (see bellows in luggage of Beni Hasan painting). The molds would cast beads, amulets, crescents, disks, rosettes, pendants, frontlets, pins, etc. These could possibly be the other kinds of ornaments associated in v 53.

In v 53, *kĕlî* translated "jewelry" (RSV)/"objects" (AB) of silver and gold means "things" or "items" in the majority of its many occurrences in the Bible. The noun is related to the verbal "finished, accomplished or completed" and is used with metals connoting that the material has been fabricated into a useful article. In light of its uses in Gen 31:37 and 45:20, Rebekah could have received various domestic utensils in silver and gold. Alternatively, in the booty passages of Exodus and Numbers, these items are specified as rings of gold in the ears of "wives, sons and daughters," and armlets, bracelets, signet rings, earrings, and beads, hence "jewelry."

The *migdānōt* "costly ornaments" (RSV)/"presents" (AB) given to mother and brother is less precise; no metal or material modifies the noun. In 2 Chr 21:3; 32:23 and Ezra 1:6 the reference is to valuable gifts, some in silver or gold, worthy of royalty or the Temple.

These general and collective terms witness to gifts completing the picture of a wedding agreement. They do not divert attention from the central point of the narrative. Rebekah of the "royal" line, after she has demonstrated her generous nature by watering the camels, receives specific jewelry items of paired bangles and nose ring to wear signifying that she is to be the wife of the wealthy patriarch Isaac, chosen by God.

2. Ezekiel 16. Besides Genesis 24, the narrative of the search for Rebekah as the wife for Isaac, Ezekiel 16 is striking in its use of marriage jewelry. Here more jewelry items are listed, and as if building upon the Rebekah sequence they are designated for particular parts of the body. In this instance characteristically, Ezekiel seems to speak out of knowledge of a long tradition and incorporates a wealth of detailed information. In the Babylonian Exile, 6th century B.C., the prophet knows Mesopotamian adornment styles and Israelite aristocratic costume. He depicts Jerusalem as an unwanted newborn child of mixed background whom God found still "weltering in her blood" of birth and whom he lovingly raised up to maidenhood as his bride and royal queen. The bestowal of fine garments and rich jewelry were the visible sign and pledge of his covenant.

The key passage is Ezek 16:11–13. It begins with two general terms for jewelry from the same root *ʿdh,* "and I *decked* you with *ornaments*" (RSV). The first designated items are "bracelets on your hands/arms" in a phrase reminiscent of Rebekah's wedding jewelry. These *ṣĕmîdîm* would be the bangle with 2 ends, and at this period could have had decorations of animal heads as finials or stylized representations of animal heads on each end. Possibly these finials (of snakes, lions, rams, etc.) could be links to the custom in the Bible of powerful rulers and nobles referred to as certain kinds of fierce animals (Ps 22:21–22—Eng vv 20–21; Jer 50:17; Ezek 22:25), and hence they are royal insignia. The next phrase *wĕrābîd ʿal gĕrônēk,* "and a chain on your neck," only occurs here and in Gen 41:42 (Joseph's necklace from Pharaoh). The reference is most likely not to a metal chain with interlocking loops, rare archaeologically (except in Greece). From Mesopotamia is the style of a single strand of beads worn as a choker high on the neck. The wife of Assurbanipal, on a 7th century B.C. relief from Kuyunjik (now in the British Museum, Maxwell-Hyslop 1971: 255, fig. 157), is seated on a throne at a banquet in a garden with the king. See Fig. JEW.01i. She has a single strand of choker beads and several other items suggested by the Ezekiel passage—bracelets, earrings, crown—and she is feasting. The Nimrud ivories from the palace of Assurbanipal show fashions of royal women from several parts of the empire. Some wear high chokers of beads in several strands. Joseph's neck jewelry is probably the Egyptian beaded broad collar.

It is placed on the *ṣawwāʿr,* a term usually stressing the back of the neck where the yoke is worn and where in this case the heavy falcon-spacer finials would be placed. Bronze Age Canaanite fertility figurines also have the intricately strung beaded broad collar. In the Ezekiel phrase *gārôn* has to do with the front of the neck or throat where the voice is located.

The third piece of jewelry is a ring, *nezem,* on the nose. Comparable to Rebekah's it is probably a small round ring with 2 ends for insertion and directly opposite, a tiny pendant with a mulberry (characteristically one cast in a steatite mold). The design had a long life in Palestine, especially popular during the Iron Age, and certainly a possibility in Ezekiel's time. The fourth set of jewelry is "earrings in your ears;" if *nezem* was a common designation for ear jewelry, Ezekiel takes particular care not to use it. He seems to be making specific reference to a style of jewelry particularly worn on the ears. The term *ʿăgîlîm* is used here and in Num 31:50 in the singular as an anonymous item in the booty list of Midianite gold articles. The use in Ezek 16:12 is suggested by a clear reference to ears and the fact that it is grouped with other items for the head—following nose ring and preceding crown. The noun is related to conjectured root *ʿgl* evidently meaning "to roll" (from round objects such as the Bronze Sea), but the overwhelming number of uses in the Bible of the root letters are with words relating to bovine animals such as *ʿēgel* = calf; *ʿeglâ* = heifer; *ʿăgālâ* = cart, the vehicle drawn by cattle.

The most common shape of gold earring in ancient Israel is an ovoid loop designated "lunate." The longer, narrower end of the loop goes through the pierced ear lobe in the front and bends downward to the back. The other end meets it just under the lobe. This end is thickened and forms the base of the earring. The graduated thickening thus resembles a crescent moon, hence the name "lunate." See Fig. JEW.01a. Because the crescent moon can look like the upturned horns of a bovine animal, there is a long association in the ANE of these 2 shapes. It is possible that lunate earrings are at home with the designation *ʿăgîlîm* relating to bovine horns. They were popular in the Iron Age and are found in many excavations from the 13th century at Tell el Fara (S) to the 6th century at Lachish. Spectacular examples come from Tell Jemmeh dated to the 10th century from the "goldsmith's house" (Petrie 1928: pl. 1:4–13). Some are quite long and some have the addition of a row of tiny balls. They also have a long history in Mesopotamia. The most elaborate come from Assyria in the 9th–7th centuries as shown on Assurbanipal's queen and Assyrian reliefs (Maxwell-Hyslop 1971: p. 255, fig. 157; pp. 254 & 237). Pendants suspended from the lunate base can represent 3 botannical stages of the pomegranate plant—the bud, the blossom, and the fruit. There is a bud pendant identified as coming from this type of earring found at Beth Shemesh (Maxwell-Hyslop 1971: 229).

The fifth reference is to a "crown" *ʿăṭārâ,* the primary piece of jewelry symbolizing leadership. Gold is mentioned as its composition in 2 Sam 12:30 (1 Chr 20:2) when David took the one belonging to the Ammonite king. In Prov 4:9 it is parallel to "fair garland." Well-known Egyptian crowns have a garland motif, some are in gold with flower medallions. The Nimrud ivories show possible metal crowns with a series of rosettes (Maxwell-Hyslop 1971: pl. 234 a & b). Assurbanipal's queen has a crown with battlements in the fortifications of the city wall. Isa 28:3–5 may have a picture with associations of a crown, flowers, and the city gate. From Palestinian excavations, such as Megiddo, Tell el Fara (S) in Bronze and Iron Ages, is a type of frontlet tied in back and having rosettes and pomegranates which could be a rendition in gold foil of a garland with flowers and fruit.

Enclosing the list of jewelry items is a second reference to the general word for jewelry *ʿdh* usually translated "ornament" (noun) and "to deck" (verb). Other associations with this term are bridal attire, for example in Isa 49:18; 61:10; Jer 2:32; 31:4. The most-lavish jewelry metaphor is in Song of Songs where parts of the body are compared to actual ornaments (Cant 1:9–11; 4:4,9; 5:10–16; etc.), and of course, the crown (Cant 3:11) with which his mother crowned him on the day of his wedding. These are strong associations of wedding and royalty. The Ezekiel 16 passage concludes in v 13 with "you succeeded to regal estate" *(limlûkâ).*

Coupled with the theme of royal wedding is a sad and devastating sequence when Ezekiel's queen became unfaithful and sank into the depths of harlotry, as chap. 16 continues. This is a prophetic image in Jer 2:2; 3:1; 4:30; Hos 2:5, etc., probably going back to Exod 32 and the Golden Calf. The vigorous tradition of the pejorative significance of jewelry from incidents such as these no doubt contributes to the noticeable lack (when compared with other ANE peoples) of gold and silver insignia and ornaments in our present Israelite archaeological assemblages.

The *ʿdh* jewelry becomes the badge of unfaithfulness in Ezek 23:40–42, etc. Because of her actions the prostitute will be given into the hands of her lovers who will take away her jewels and raiment, in contrast to the loving husband who clothes her. From these passages we learn what harlots wore. Especially enigmatic has been Ezek 16:36 (Platt 1975: 103–11). A more accurate translation probably is, "because *your triangular piece (nĕḥuštēk)* was shed" instead of the RSV "your shame was laid bare." "Triangular piece" is parallel in this poetic section to "genital area," "idols," and "blood of children" (RSV). There is a triangular jewelry piece of 3 recognized types that depict a Canaanite female figure with emphasis on the genital area. One exemplary gold foil plaque from Ugarit (Negbi 1970: pl. IV:17) has a female figure wearing a pelvic girdle with a triangle suspended from it at the pubic area. See Fig. JEW.01j. This would illustrate the wearing of the gold plaque or a garment, as other illustrations of the pelvic girdle show, perhaps the menstrual cloth, characteristic of a bovine economy where sexual intercourse during estrus was connected with conception. As polemic against this Canaanite religious practice is such legislation as Lev 18:19, "You shall not approach a woman to uncover her nakedness while she is in her menstrual uncleanness." Notable is the sequence of legislation against adultery (Lev 18:20) and sacrifice of children (Lev 18:21). This sequence was surely in the mind of Ezekiel as he could expect his hearers to make associations automatically. Lev 18:24 goes on to claim that these were the precise acts of the Canaan-

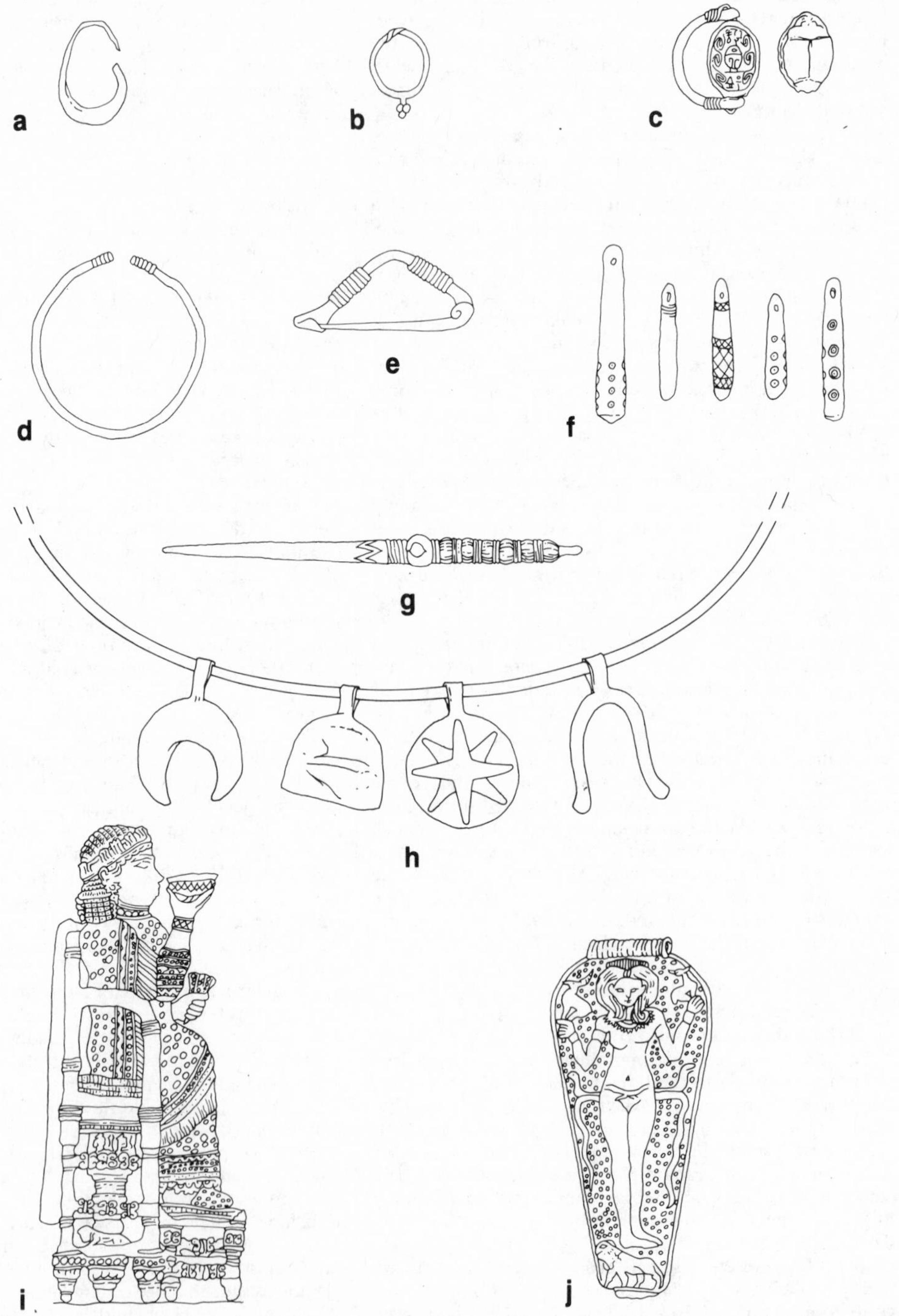

JEW.01. Samples of ancient Near Eastern jewelry. *a,* lunate earring; *b,* mulberry earring; *c,* Hyksos seal ring; *d,* bangle bracelet; *e,* fibula; *f,* bone pendants; *g,* toggle pin; *h,* Assyrian king's necklace; *i,* Kuyunjik relief depiction of Assurbanipal's wife; *j,* triangular plaque from Ugarit. *(Drawings by R. H. Brennecke, courtesy of E. Platt)*

ites who lost their land. Here is a vehicle used by Ezekiel, Jeremiah, and Hosea to express their prophetic messages for their times.

E. Symbols of Aristocratic Office

1. The Signet. a. Biblical Vocabulary. Two Heb nouns are translated "seal:" *ṭabaʿat* and *ḥōtām.* The first *(ṭabaʿat)* is associated with the verbal notion "to sink down" but the verb is not used with the noun, nor is there the logical association of a ring or seal "sinking down" into soft material as a stamp would. In Gen 41:42 and Esth 3:10, the object is put on the hand. In Isa 3:21; Num 31:50; and Exod 35:22, it is listed with other jewelry items. In the tabernacle sections of Exod (chaps. 25–31) the word is used for hardware fixtures of gold, usually translated "ring" (e.g., Exod 25:12).

In Esth 3:12 and 8:8, the verb *ḥtm* "to seal" is used with *ṭabaʿat.* The noun *ḥōtām* is used more often as "seal," e.g., Jer 22:24; Hag 2:23; Gen 38:18.

Lambdin sees *ṭabaʿat* as being of Egyptian origin, while *ḥtm* and its derivatives, used extensively throughout the Semitic languages, was borrowed in the earliest stages of Egyptian (Lambdin 1953: esp. p. 151). Hundreds of years before the biblical period both words were used in Egypt, at least, to refer to the same object or to objects with the same function.

Vergote sees the words referring to 2 different kinds of objects: *ḥtm* = cylinder seal, and Egyptian *dbʿt* = stamp seal ring, which developed later (Vergote 1959: 116f.).

b. History of the Seal. It is generally agreed that the cylinder seal originated in Mesopotamia at the end of the 4th millennium, probably during the "Uruk V" period in the S Euphrates area (Saggs 1962: 25–26). The typical thumb-sized cylinder-shaped object of semiprecious stone had a longitudinal perforation to be worn on a string or cord. Its surface was characteristically carved with a religious scene which when rolled over wet clay transferred the design to a sealed object. Saggs posits that in the 3d millennium exchanges between Mesopotamian and Egyptian merchants on the coast of South Arabia or Somaliland brought the cylinder seal to Egypt. The stamp seal may have had an Asiatic origin, but Hayes attests it in the Old Kingdom of Egypt, the 6th Dynasty, 25th–23d centuries B.C. (Hayes 1953–59: 1.141). It can be circular, rectangular, or oval with a flat side, carved with a design, and having a convex top.

c. The Scarab. The most well-known Egyptian seal is the scarab. Its origin is probably as simple as an ovoid bead strung on a cord, a bead of precious stone or metal fashioned to form an amulet. The ovoid shape occurs naturally among pebbles and could easily resemble the beetle with rounded wing case on the back and flat underside. The ordinary "dung beetle," *scarabaeus sacer,* makes a ball of dung around its food and rolls it with its legs. The Egyptians associated this activity with the globe of the sun rolling across the heavens on its daily journey, perhaps propelled by an invisible cosmic-sized scarab. The Egyptian words for "become" and "come into existence" and one of the sun god's names are from the same stem *(keper)* as the word for scarab beetle. These are written with a hieroglyph depicting the insect.

Scarabs are extremely popular in Egyptian jewelry and if related to bead design, the Egyptian jewelry craft par excellence, they are yet another of the several techniques that seem to be in adaptation, extension, or support of beadwork art. The favorite material is easily carved steatite (sometimes called "soapstone"), a form of talc, white or greenish-gray in color. Scarabs are also found in faience (ground quartz or clay cast into a mold and coated with vitreous glaze, especially in imitation of turquoise). Elegant scarabs were made in gold, silver, electrum, turquoise, lapis lazuli, carnelian, amethyst, jasper, onyx, hematite, feldspar, and glass.

The carved flat undersides make them significant: Their legends have names, titles, slogans, designs with animals, birds, and divine figures. The most familiar design is the cartouche or name plate with a rope at the outer edge lashed at one end, and hieroglyphs spelling the name or titles within. The seal does not necessarily bear the name of the owner but can indicate relationship such as subordinate officer or servant. Also, jewelry items can be heirlooms and their styles can be replicated in commemoration or in archaizing effect along with the modern and creatively contemporary in the same workroom. This is especially true for the most popular single kind of scarab in Palestine and Egypt: that with inscriptions relating to Thutmos III, the New Kingdom pharaoh during the greatest period of Egypt's empire, in LB I. His name was evidently regarded as potent centuries after his death and scarabs were treasured and made with his inscriptions for many years.

Aldred gives evidence that scarabs were worn as rings as early as the Middle Kingdom (Aldred 1971: 160). Originally tied to the finger with linen thread, gold wire came to replace the cord but the wire ends are coiled in imitation. This may be reminiscent of the "shenu" loop of the cartouche. Subsequently, a U-shaped ring base developed and the scarab gemstone was placed over the top with the wire ends wrapping around each side. This design enabled the seal to swivel; the flat surface turned up for sealing or rested against the finger for protection when not in use. During the 2d Intermediate Period (ca. 1630–1523) the ring base becomes heavier and has knobs capping each end of the "U." The knobs make the ring easier to hold in the stamp position. Another development was to mount the scarab in a gold or silver funda or base plate with holes or tubes to take the ends of the hoop, again aiding the swivel mechanism.

d. Seals of the Bible and Archaeological Finds. Gen 38:18 and 25, tribal chief Judah's signet with cord and staff are taken by Tamar in pledge. She speaks of them first, v 18, as "your signet *(ḥōtām)* and your cord and your staff which is in your hand." In both instances they are definite signs of Judah's identity. Speiser following Vergote identifies *ḥōtām* as a Mesopotamian-type cylinder seal; and he adds that "the inclusion of the cord is further proof that no signet ring was involved" (*Genesis* AB, 298). Following Lambdin's views on the words for seal and in light of archaeological evidence that scarab gemstones also occur in Palestine during the patriarchal period, a scarab signet could be suggested here. It is interesting to note that one of the earliest scarabs known comes from the Middle Kingdom in Egypt, Late 11th Dynasty, ca. 2000 B.C., from the burial of the estate manager Waḥ (Hayes 1953–59:

1.230; Aldred 1971: 184). A metal scarab composed of several layers of silver with a gold tube through the center was found with 2 large beads indicating that it was worn on a cord as a necklace or bracelet. In a humble grave from the burial complex of Hatshepsut, which Hayes dates 1489–1469 B.C., a scarab was found tied to the finger of an aged woman. This particular seal bears the name of Hatshepsut's daughter for whom the woman was probably a servant. Here the cord enables the scarab to serve as a ring, and it is important to note that this type of seal is in the possession of a woman.

Gen 41:42 lists 3 items the pharaoh conferred on Joseph: signet ring, garments of fine linen, and gold neck-jewelry. The necklace was most probably the gold-beaded broad collar with large (falcon?) finials as spacers and counterpoises. Vergote believes the reference is to *the* Gold Collar, the sign of the investiture of the Vizier (Vergote 1959: 134). King Tutankhamen conferred the gold signet ring as the sign of accession of Prince Huy as viceroy in Nubia (Mazar et al., eds. 1959: 1.106). Wilson notes that in the Old Kingdom the king's highest official "the Vizier was the Sealbearer of the King of Lower Egypt" (Wilson 1951: 80–81). By this office he was "authorized to supervise the movement of official parties or goods through Egypt," mainly as controller of Nile traffic *(ibid.)*. From the standpoint of the Bible, the ring as the first and most important of pharaoh's gifts is the sign par excellence of royal power. It heralded Joseph's climactic position in Egypt's government. From this position he was able to rescue and protect the house of Israel during famine and ultimately to bring the family to live in Egypt.

The historical period of the Joseph narratives is commonly understood to be at the time of the Hyksos, the Asiatic princes who became pharaohs at the end of the Middle Kingdom just before the end of the 18th century B.C. During the Hyksos period scarabs were produced prodigiously; they are one sign of the extent of the empire in Syria-Palestine. Their legends are difficult to decipher because the hieroglyphs and characteristic inscriptions, perhaps less familiar to them than to native Egyptians, are distorted. One popular feature, probably borrowed from earlier Egyptian design, is an interlocking spiral border. See Fig. JEW.01c. Hieroglyphs of life proclaiming abundant years for the pharaoh, Son of Rē, are also common.

Illustrative of the time of Joseph might be the New York Metropolitan Museum collection of 8 green-glazed steatite scarabs belonging to Ḥar with his titles as tax official for an important 15th Dynasty pharaoh (Hayes 1953–59: 2.8). Also from Palestine in MB II and III at Gezer and Megiddo are some fine examples (Guy and Engberg 1938: fig. 176:3 = pl. 107:19; Macalister 1912: vol. 3, pls. XXXI, XXXV; see Maxwell-Hyslop 1971: pl. 76).

A well-known passage relating to the study of scarab seals is Cant 8:6 which includes the phrases "set me as a seal upon your heart, as a seal upon your arm, for love is as strong as death." The Egyptian New Kingdom provenance for the royal wedding genre also has produced archaeologically heart-scarabs from 1 to 3 inches long. They were placed over the heart in the burial costume and the best examples are mounted in a gold funda and suspended from a cord. From the King Tut burial are also armlets and bracelets with large scarabs.

1 Kgs 21:8 tells how Queen Jezebel wrote letters in King Ahab's name and sealed *(ḥtm)* them with his seal *(ḥōtām)*, thus determining Naboth's fate. There is a famous purchased seal ring dated by the Hebrew paleography to the 9th or 8th century (Ben-Dor 1948). The sharp edges on the ring band made it unsuitable for wearing on the finger so it was probably strung on a cord. The finger inserted into the ring helped with exerting the required pressure for stamping.

Esth 3:10 refers to King Ahasuerus' promotion of Haman with the gift of his ring *(ṭabaʿat)*. From here Haman could effect a massive persecution of the Jews. Later in Esth 8:1–2, Queen Esther had successfully intervened on behalf of her people and Mordecai, her adoptive uncle, succeeded to Haman's position. Ahasuerus set Esther over the house of Haman and then gave Mordecai Haman's ring. Following this Esther set Mordecai over the house of Haman. Perhaps this sequence indicates that Esther is in a situation where as a woman she cannot own a seal of this designation. A stirrup seal-ring found at Persepolis has an antelope carving (Mazar, et al., eds. 1959: 4.194). It came from garrison quarters, near a wall and inside a baked-clay canteen. The stirrup seal type is probably a final stage of development for the signet ring. The entire ring was cast in a stirrup shape of one piece; it was non-swivel, and the seal was carved on the flat top surface. It was popular during the Iron Age in Israel and made its first appearance in Egypt at the beginning of the New Kingdom.

From the contexts of signets belonging to Judah, Pharaoh, and Joseph, Ahab, Ahasuerus, and Mordecai, this jewelry item can be a strong symbol of high office. Its use as a seal for documents, etc., is a significant means by which authority is expressed in the social setting. Seals and sealing with these and other meanings are also mentioned in such passages as Job 14:17; Isa 8:16; 29:11; Dan 6:17; 12:4; Jer 22:24–26; 32:14–15. In Hag 2:23, Zerubbabel, "governor of Judah," is proclaimed as a chosen signet ring on the Lord's hand, dramatically implying that he will be given authority as a precious royal jewel. The gemstones of the high priest's ephod, breastpiece, and crown may also carry these associations as they are to be carved with tribal names in the precious stones common to such royal rings "as a jeweler engraves signets," (RSV) Exod 28:11ff.; 39:6ff., 30. There are no extant archaeological illustrations for the high priest's gems.

2. The Catalogue of Isa 3:18–23. The passage has been enigmatic because in its catalogue are items that are little known. The vocabulary is problematic, this being the only place in the Hebrew Bible where the words for some of the items are used (for more on this problem, see HAPAX LEGOMENA). Important clues to their identity can be found in other biblical passages where these words or their relatives occur in explanatory contexts. Also, archaeological studies give some information about extant jewelry pieces to be matched up with the Hebrew words. For easy reference the list below (table 1) has the RSV translation for the numbered words in the first column, then Hebrew transliterations, and new suggestions (Platt 1979: 72). Of the 21 items, the first 13 are jewelry, and it is important to note their societal associations and who wears them. Not included in the list of 21 is the introductory word *tipʾeret* (v 18) which in the Hebrew Bible is primarily a collective term designating beautiful accoutrements belonging to an office of honored position, characteristically one that is indicated by a crown (e.g., Exod 28:2,40; Isa 28:1,4; 52:1; Jer 13:18,20; Ezek 16:17,39; Esth 1:4; Prov 4:9). Here this could be translated "insignia of office," appropriately summarizing the list that follows.

Table 1. The Jewelry Catalogue of Isaiah 3:18–23

RSV		Hebrew	Suggestions
Isa 3:			
v 18	In that day the Lord will take away the finery of	*tipʾeret*	the insignia of office:
	(1) the anklets,	*hāʿăkāsîm*	the ankle bangles,
	(2) the headbands,	*wĕhaššĕbîsîm*	and the sun- or star-disks,
	(3) and the crescents;	*wĕhaśśahărōnîm*	and the crescents,
v 19	(4) the pendants	*hannĕṭîpôt*	the drop pendants
	(5) the bracelets,	*wĕhaššērôt*	and the necklace cords,
	(6) and the scarfs;	*wĕhārĕʿālôt*	and the beads,
v 20	(7) the headdresses,	*happĕʾērîm*	the garland crowns,
	(8) the armlets,	*wĕhaṣṣĕʿādôt*	and the armlets (or foot jewelry),
	(9) the sashes,	*wĕhaqqiššurîm*	and the sashes (or girdles),
	(10) the perfume boxes,	*ûbātê hannepeš*	and the tubular "soul cases,"
	(11) and the amulets;	*wĕhallĕḥāšîm*	and the snake charms,
v 21	(12) the signet rings,	*haṭṭabbāʿôt*	the signet rings,
	(13) and the nose rings;	*wĕnizmê hāʾāp*	and the nose rings,
v 22	(14) the festal robes,	*hammaḥălāṣôt*	the loin cloths,
	(15) the mantles,	*wĕhammaʿăṭāpôt*	and the enveloping capes,
	(16) the cloaks,	*wĕhammiṭpāḥôt*	and the mantles,
	(17) and the handbags;	*wĕhāḥărîṭîm*	and the wallets,
v 23	(18) the garments of gauze,	*wĕhagilyōnîm*	and the thin garments,
	(19) the linen garments,	*wĕhassĕdînîm*	and the warriors' belts,
	(20) the turbans,	*wĕhaṣṣĕnîpôt*	and the turbans,
	(21) and the veils.	*wĕhārĕdîdîm*	and the outer cloaks.

(1) *"The ankle bangles."* This expression occurs here and in Isa 3:16 as a verb with more description: "mincing along as they go, *tinkling* with their feet" (RSV). No doubt these are the classic solid, round ankle-bangles worn in pairs as depicted on Late Bronze fertility plaques/figurines and found on female leg bones in burials. These are associated with women and could possibly be worn in imitation of the fertility figure. The word most likely is a technical term for bangles worn only on ankles and not on wrists and arms. The root also forms the name of a daughter of Caleb (Josh 15:16, and others).

(2) *"The sun- or star-disks."* This is the only time in the Hebrew Bible that the word and root occurs. Some linguists have seen a relation to "little suns." With (3) and (4) the designation would fit with associated pendants on the "Dilbat Necklace" (Maxwell-Hyslop 1971: 88–90). From Mesopotamia in the first half of the 2d millennium and now in the New York Metropolitan Museum, the necklace has a crescent moon (4), two sun-symbol rosettes and a star-disk. A 9th-century relief of King Assurnasirpal II shows the head and beard turned sideways to his right revealing a cord necklace with 4 pendants including an obvious crescent and a star-disk (Maxwell-Hyslop 1971: pl. 220). See Fig. JEW.01h. Rosettes perhaps representing the sun in gold, bronze, and bone occur in Palestinian Iron Age jewelry from Beth-shan, Gezer, Beth Shemesh, and Megiddo. Star-disks occur in silver, gold, ivory, and bone at Megiddo, Gezer, Beth-shan, and Hazor. Although the number of extant specimens is limited, star-disks, crescents, and rosettes were used in the time of Isaiah, who as a highly skilled political officer of the kingdom of Judah, prophesied during the second half of the 8th century concerning the Assyrian menace. The Mesopotamian evidence and assemblages of precious jewelry in Israelite sites indicate that these pendants could signify high office.

(3) *"The crescents."* The root having to do with the moon exists in several Semitic languages. In Judg 8:21,26, the plural refers to emblems designated as especially worn by kings of Midian and their camels. Archaeology has produced 2 types: one is flat with perforation in the tips; the other is a slender wire shaped like the letter *c* with the central metal loop for suspension.

(4) *"The pendants."* The root is associated with the dropping or dripping of liquid such as rain, honey, wine, and myrrh. A feminine plural noun is mentioned in Judg 8:26 with crescents and purple garments as belonging to Midianite kings. The obvious archaeological objects are bead-like pendants in drop shapes made in semiprecious stones—for example, turquoise, lapis lazuli, carnelian—as well as glass and faience. These would be strung with crescents and pendants in necklaces.

(5) *"The necklace cords."* This unusual term is probably related to the word for umbilical cord *(šōr)*, and the word for "chains" in Exod 28:14, "two chains of pure gold twisted like cords" to attach the high priest's ephod. In this case they might be the textile cords used for stringing beads and pendants in the ornate necklace styles.

(6) *"The beads."* From *rʿl*, to quiver, shake, reel, or dangle, would be beads in various shapes: seeds, blossoms, flower parts, etc., as well as geometric designs. Hundreds of bead-shapes have been classified in the materials of metals, semiprecious stones, and glass from the ANE.

(7) *"The garland crowns."* The noun is related to the introductory collective term and refers to an ornament worn on the head. In Isa 61:3,10, the bridegroom wears a garland or crown; in Ezek 24:17, there is a turban, perhaps like a bridegroom's crown; in Ezek 44:18, Levitical priests wear these turbans as do Aaron and his sons in Exod 39:28. Archaeological jewelry evidence suggests a frontlet made of a strip of metal foil with holes for ties to be placed across the forehead and knotted in the back. Several of these have flowers and rosettes in repoussé as well as places to attach pendant ornaments (see examples from Iron Age tombs at Megiddo). Palestinian frontlets are reminiscent of more elaborate Egyptian crowns worn by men and women where real flowers were imitated in metal, inlay, fabric, and leather.

(8) *"The armlets."* The word is used in the sing. in 2 Sam 1:10 with reference to Saul's "crown and *armlet* which was on his arm." The term also occurs in Num 31:50 where it is in a booty list coupled with "bangles" as in Rebekah's arm jewelry. From Assyrian reliefs a 2-ended metal bangle worn by royal men on the upper arm has animal-headed finials of rams, lions, etc., perhaps signifying a heraldic animal as used in Ps 22:21–22—Eng vv 20–21; Jer 50:17; Ezek 22:25.

(9) *"The girdles."* The term refers to ornamentation that is "bound on" from the verbal root. In Jer 2:32 the object is part of the queenly wedding dress with other ornaments (*ʿdh);* also the root is in a similar passage of Isa 49:18. If, with RSV, the term is related to a sash, it could be worn in the middle of the body such as the beaded girdles from Egypt worn on the hips (Wilkinson 1971: 264).

(10) *"The tubular 'soul' cases."* The unique phrase could refer to a type of pendant like the Egyptian cylinder amulets of the Middle Kingdom (Wilkinson 1971: 55), and represented later in a development like *tefillin.* These characteristically have papyrus or other rolls in them with writing having spiritual significance.

(11) *"The snake charms."* In Isa 3:3 the list of the men of high office includes "an expert in *charms*" from this root; in Jer 8:17 snakes and charms are associated. The uraeus snake is ubiquitous in Egyptian jewelry.

(12) *"The signet rings."* An example par excellence of jewelry used as insignia of office, Gen 41:42; Esth 8:2.

(13) *"The nose rings."* These are part of the bride-queen's jewelry in Ezek 16:12 with the example of the mulberry "earring" worn also in the nose.

Of these 13 jewelry items, 4 are associated in some way in the Bible with women, 8 more accurately relate to men of high rank. It is possible that women had versions of the items also, but at present the evidence is not convincing that these jewelry pieces were exclusively the property of women at any one historical period. A similar method of analysis applied to the 8 clothing items that follow in the catalogue (nos. 14–21) indicates at least 4 are associated with men of rank. Consequently, the interpretation of the passage must shift from a prophetic oracle denouncing women in general for the vain superficiality of extravagant fashions in dress and jewelry to a critique of persons in high office for their social injustice and misuse of power as is the topic of the entire collection of oracles in Isaiah 3.

F. Booty and Offering Jewelry

Two groups of passages are important for discussion of the types of jewelry items in booty and offering assemblages: (a) those in Exodus related to jewelry to be taken out of Egypt which very likely was part of the metal used for the Golden Calf, the acts of contrition that followed, and ultimately for the freewill tabernacle offering; and (b) the spoil from the defeat of Midian and their kings.

Exod 3:22 occurs in the early material about the Exodus, the most important event in the OT. Surprisingly, jewelry is mentioned as part of the command from God that Moses hears from the Burning Bush. The jewelry aspect must be significant if it is included at the critical time when God reveals himself to Moses and challenges the leader to the heroic task of bringing Israel out of slavery. The command is given initially to women, "each woman shall ask of her neighbor." The goods to be taken from Egypt are not more-usable and practical products for survival on the desert journey—such as grain, foodstuffs, domestic animals, and caravan equipment—but items of gold and silver (*kělê kesep ûkělê zāhāb),* with clothing mentioned somewhat secondarily in passing. Evidently these were not to be sizeable commodities, because the women, who were simply to ask for them peacefully in their own private domiciles, were directed to put them on their "sons and daughters," surely meaning their little children who had not come of age. Possibly this continues the mother-child theme of the opening chapters of Exodus (Exod 1:15ff.; 2:2; 2:10), but it may also serve to emphasize that these were not large amounts of gold and silver to be carried by adults for use in trade or commercial exchange. Since the items are associated with clothing to be worn, hence displayed openly, they are not secreted or hoarded away.

In Exod 11:1–2, in the midst of the Plague corpus just before the most significant plague (death of the firstborn), the *kělê* of both silver and gold is to be asked of Egyptian neighbors by women and this time also by men. In Exod 12:35 the same *kělê* is mentioned right after the unleavened bread saying that they had asked it of the Egyptians. Then v 36 serves to explain that this spoil is a special sign of God's favor rather than a valuable commodity in itself; it marks the ascendency of the Hebrews over the Egyptians by God's grace.

In Exod 32:2–3, when Aaron makes the Golden Calf, he asks for the "rings of gold" *(nizmê hazzāhāb)* which are "in the ears of *(bĕʾoznê)* your wives, sons and daughters." Aaron's request is directed to the male heads of households, but the wearers may be just women and children. Later in Exod 33:4 the penitent people mourned and "no man put on his ornaments (*ʿedyô*)." In v 5 God himself commands the stripping of ornaments as a sign that the people were removed from his favor because of the sin of the Golden Calf. Verse 6 makes the striking comment that from Mt. Horeb onward, the ornaments were not worn again.

In Exod 35:22 for the tabernacle offering the *kělî zāhāb* are specified; this catalogue gives insight as to the particular objects in the collective term. "So all who were of a willing heart brought brooches *(ḥāḥ)* and earrings *(nezem)* and signet rings *(ṭabaʿat)* and beads *(kûmāz),* all sorts of gold objects *(kělî zāhāb),* every man dedicating an offering of gold to the Lord."

Kělî is the general word for jewelry used most often in the booty and offering passages of Exodus. Its related verb means "to complete" and in the Bible the noun has many uses usually referring to a wrought or finished object, an article or utensil. The term particularly refers to something of value; in a plural, collective sense it means portable objects or precious goods that can be taken up when moving, traveling, or even going into exile. This can be baggage, furnishings, equipment, musical instruments, weapons, or simply implements and vessels.

In light of Exod 35:22, where the voluntary offering of gold is described, a list of jewelry objects precedes the use of *kělî* (of gold) indicating that the word means personal adornment, i.e., brooches, earrings, signet rings, beads, etc. Looking ahead to Num 31:50, the *kělî* of gold which "each man found" are specified as armlets and bracelets, signet rings, earrings, and beads. From the standpoint of archaeological finds, these would be the items often occurring together in the assemblages of precious jewelry in the LB and Early Iron Ages. Also, the objects associated under the general term *kělî* could be found grouped together in jewelry molds. These are carved stone (steatite, serpentine, etc.) rectangular objects, small enough to fit in the hand, from the Late Bronze and Iron I in Palestine and Egypt, and usually associated with itinerant smiths. They show a variety of objects which could be cast in gold, for example: beads, amulets, crescents, disks, rosettes, pendants, frontlets, pins, and earrings.

In the passage concerning the act of contrition (Exod 33:4), when "no man put on his ornaments," the noun *ʿadî* is probably synonymous with *kĕlî.* The noun is related to the verb "to deck oneself" and in other parts of the Bible the use is with the bride and bridegroom, the king and queen, then the harlot and citizens of high office who misuse their jewelry.

Earrings (*nezem* in the pl.) are the most frequently mentioned specific items of booty and offering (see Exod 32:3; 35:22; Num 31:50; Judg 8:24). In the sing. *nezem* can refer to nose ring, and the term probably means in its most basic sense an object in the shape of a ring used for a variety of purposes as specified. In extant Palestinian jewelry, examples of earrings, nose rings, and finger rings are composed of the same fundamental shape. Evidence from ancient Israel indicates a penchant for earrings with traditions going back to the MB. Elaborate examples occur in Mesopotamia during the 3d Dynasty of Ur, ca. 2100 B.C. In Egypt the style only becomes fashionable in the New Kingdom. Aldred believes that it was an Asiatic custom imported into Egypt during Hyksos times (Aldred 1971: 198). King Tut's elaborate examples are well-known. Dangles in Egyptian earrings tend to be separate and added as beads. In Palestine the pendant was cast with the ring as in the types known as mulberry, ball drop, tassel, and row of balls. The *ʿagîl* type is probably to be identified with the lunate earring. The lower part resembles a thickened crescent that can be associated with bovine horns.

The signet ring (the third term in the list of Exod 35:22) *ṭabaʿat,* is the swivel signet as described in the Joseph narratives, or the stirrup signet, cast in one piece sometimes with added bezel. Wilkinson sees the latter type appearing in Egypt at the beginning of the New Kingdom (Wilkinson 1971: 128–30); King Tut had several. It was popular in Palestine during the Iron Age.

The fourth item in the list is *kûmāz,* translated by the RSV as "armlets" here (Exod 35:22), but in Num 31:50 as "beads." Beads would be expected archaeologically with such items as mentioned in the list, and the related Arabic term means "bunch, heap" which fits well with the definition.

The first item in the list (Exod 35:22) is translated "brooches" (RSV), the only time the English word or its relatives are used in the Bible. Today the English definition is "large ornamental pin with clasp" but the Middle English forerunner of brooch includes pin, peg, spit, and skewer. The first archaeological association would be a fibula—an ornamental, bow-shaped, metal object with a pin for attachment and a clasp sometimes shaped like a human hand. See Fig. JEW.01e. Fibulae seem to have reached the Near East from Italy and Greece and are not generally common in Palestine until the 8th century, B.C. when they appear in overwhelming abundance. The predecessor of the fibula, used for the purpose of pinning the garment, is a straight stave like the Middle English definition. In Palestine it had a point at one end and a knob at the other.

This type of stave pin is found rather consistently in the jewelry of Mesopotamia even as far back into the 3d millennium as the Early Dynastic period in Ur. In MB and LB Palestine handsome gold examples occur at Tell el-ʿAjjul and Megiddo. A string would be tied to the stave under the knob and wound around both ends of the stave to secure the position of the pin in the cloth. As the design developed increasing elegance, more beads could be placed on top of each other with a knot in the cord to keep them from slipping down the stave. Designs in the metal could imitate the row of beads giving a baluster effect, or swirls and twists could decorate the part of the stave designed to remain outside the garment. For the cord attachment a ring was added just below the decoration and could even be worked into the center of the stave. See Fig. JEW.01g. The pierced hole in the center of the stave caused Egyptologist Sir Flinders Petrie to name this jewelry item "toggle pin." He imagined that it was fastened like a button to a garment by means of the hole and subsequently "passed through an eyelet in the other edge" of the garment (from his *Hyksos and Israelite Cities,* p. 12, and quoted in Henshel-Simon 1938: 169–70). It would demand a skilled tailor to make this an effective closing even for a garment of minimum bodily activity.

The decorations on the hafts of toggle pins are clues to their dates, and E. Henshel-Simon developed a typological scheme for identifying archaeological specimens. During the Iron Age, the decorated hafts became more elaborate making the pin top-heavy and awkward to use. When fibulae replaced them, the bead-like decoration was also the feature that distinguished and dated the fibula bow in typological sequence.

In Egypt toggle pins are associated with Hyksos, Asian, and N Mediterranean imports, so as in the case with earrings, it would not be unlikely for Hebrews coming out of Egypt to treasure toggle pins in their "all sorts of gold objects" (Exod 35:22).

The biblical term *ḥaḥ* seems to be related to brier or bramble indicating a sharp, pointed object to hook into something. It refers to an object put in the nose or jaws of a captive beast or person as a sign of subjection and desolation. If the piercing of 2 parts is indicated, it would be appropriate for this jewelry piece: The toggle pin is actually the "brier pin."

Another short catalogue of jewelry objects like that of Exod 35:22 occurs in Num 31:50 at the end of the Wilderness Wanderings when the Israelite soldiers bring a percentage of their spoil from the Midianite battle for "the Lord's offering" as commanded by Moses. Again the general phrase *kĕlî zāhāb,* "articles of gold," is used as a collective term with particular items in the singular in Hebrew but translated in the RSV as pl.: "armlets and bracelets," *ʾeṣʿādâ wĕṣāmîd;* the bangles for the wrists and upper arms, "signet rings," *ṭabaʿat;* lunate "earrings," *ʾagîl;* and "beads," *kûmāz.*

In Judges 8, jewelry items are mentioned again in connection with Midianite spoil but the particular items differ from the Num 31 passages. The Midianites and the Amalekites, ancient enemies from the Exodus-Wandering period, menace the agricultural economy aided by the now perfected technology of camel domestication. Gideon was sent and killed the kings Zebah and Zalmuna, then in Judg 8:21 "took the crescents *(haśśahărōnîm)* that were on the necks of their camels." He refused kingship but asked, "give me every man of you the earrings of his spoil *(nezem šĕlālô)*" (8:24). The weight came to "1,700 shekels of gold" (8:26), "besides the crescents *(haśśahărōnîm)* and the pendants *(wĕhannĕtipôt)* and the purple garments worn by the kings of Midian, and besides the collars that were about the necks of their camels." Gideon made an ephod of gold, perhaps following the precedent in Exod 25:7; 28; 29; 35; 39; but what that object was remains enigmatic.

The crescents worn by the Midianite kings and their camels were probably of 2 types, the flat and the suspension loop, as discussed above in Isaiah 3. The pendants worn with the crescents by the Midianite kings were probably of a "drop" shape, representing heavenly phenomena like stars or rain drops.

Bibliography

Aldred, C. 1971. *Jewels of the Pharaohs.* London.
Ben-Dor, I. 1948. Two Hebrew Seals. *QDAP* 6: 64–7.
Frankfort, H. 1963. *The Art and Architecture of the Ancient Orient.* Harmondsworth, Middlesex.
Guy, P. L. O., and Engberg, R. M. 1938. *Megiddo Tombs.* Chicago.
Hayes, W. C. 1953–59. *The Scepter of Egypt.* Pts. 1–2. Cambridge, MA.
Henshel-Simon, E. 1938. The Toggle-pins in the Palestine Archaeological Museum. *QDAP* 6: 169 ff.
Lambdin, T. O. 1953. Egyptian Loan Words in the Old Testament. *JAOS* 73: 145–55.
Loud, G. 1948. *Megiddo II. Seasons of 1935–1939.* Text Vol. and Plate Vol. OIP 62. Chicago.
Macalister, R. A. S. 1912. *The Excavation of Gezer.* Vols. 1–3. London.
Maxwell-Hyslop, K. R. 1971. *Western Asiatic Jewellery, c. 3000–612 B.C.* London.
Mazar, B. et al., eds. 1959. *Views of the Biblical World.* 4 vols. Ramat Gan, Israel.
Negbi, O. 1970. *The Hoards of Goldwork from Tell el-ᶜAjjul.* Göteborg.
Petrie, W. M. F. 1928. *Gerar.* London.
Platt, E. E. 1975. Triangular Jewelry Plaques. *BASOR* 221: 103–11.
———. 1978. Bone Pendants. *BA* 41: 23–28.
———. 1979. Jewelry of Bible Times and the Catalog of Isa 3: 18–23. *AUSS* 17: 71–84, 189–201.
Saggs, H. W. F. 1962. *The Greatness that Was Babylon.* New York.
Vergote, J. 1959. *Joseph en Egypte.* Louvain.
Wilkinson, A. 1971. *Ancient Egyptian Jewellery.* London.
Wilson, J. A. 1951. *The Burden of Egypt.* Chicago.

ELIZABETH E. PLATT

JEWISH CHRISTIANITY.
See CHRISTIANITY (EARLY JEWISH); EBIONITES; NAZARENES.

JEWISH VERSIONS OF THE BIBLE.
See VERSIONS, JEWISH.

JEWISH-CHRISTIAN RELATIONS 70–170 C.E.

The time between the Jewish War (ca. 70) and the age of Justin and Melito (ca. 170) was the crucial transition period for Jewish-Christian relations. Before this, Christianity was intimately, if uneasily, related to Judaism and in many ways was still a sectarian movement within it. By the late 2d century, Christian writings reveal a movement confident in its own identity as a gentile community distinct from, and generally hostile towards, Judaism, yet claiming the right to be called the New Israel. During the same period Judaism also underwent profound changes in the wake of 3 disastrous rebellions against Rome (66–70 C.E., 115–17 C.E., 132–35 C.E.). This century is thus one of the most important and intriguing for Jewish-Christian relations. It is also one of the most obscure. The extant evidence is widely scattered and rarely direct. It is also one-sided since most of it is Christian in origin, while Jewish sources are sparse and often embedded in later documents of the rabbinic tradition.

A. The Sociopolitical Setting
B. Jewish Christians
C. Yavnean Rabbis and their Successors
D. The Gospels and Acts
E. Judaizers
F. Marcion and the Gnostics
G. Justin and Melito
H. Festivals and Cult
I. Conclusion

A. The Sociopolitical Setting

The political and social status of Jews and Christians in the Roman empire and the effects of the Jewish rebellions against Rome are of considerable importance. The destruction of the Temple and much of Jerusalem in the war of 66–70 C.E. and the resulting ignominy of the Jews has been viewed as the crisis which precipitated the final breach between Christians and Jews (Harnack 1962: 63). Certainly for Judaism the consequences of the war were not insignificant—thousands dead or taken captive; economic chaos and the confiscation of property; increased taxation; the destruction of temple and city; and the disappearance of the sanhedrin. Yet the outcome was less devastating than appears at first sight: The final siege affected Jerusalem alone, the rest of Judea and the diaspora communities being hardly affected; the Jews' legal status was unaffected, and they continued to enjoy tolerance in religious matters; and the Yavnean sages founded their academy with Roman approval. These events may have strained Jewish-Christian relations and caused some Christians to distance themselves from Judaism, but they do not appear to have caused an immediate or final schism.

First-century Christian references to the war in fact concentrate mainly on the recalculation of eschatological beliefs (Mark 13:1–3,14–20 and parallels; Luke 19:41–4); it is only later and in retrospect that it is placed in the context of anti-Jewish polemic—for example, in the claim that the destruction of the Temple was a punishment for Jewish involvement in Jesus' death (Just. *Dial.* 16; *Gos. Pet.* 25). The Bar Kokhba rebellion in 132–35 C.E. had more significant consequences for Jewish-Christian relations. The intense messianism surrounding Bar Kokhba led to the harassment and execution of those who did not accede to it, including Christians (Just. *Apol.* 1.36.6). The severe repression which followed included the banning of Jews from Jerusalem, and this resulted in a definitive change in the Jerusalem Church which, from then on, came under gentile leadership (Eus. *Hist. Eccl.* 4.5). Further, this ban lived on in Christian memory and, together with the destruction of the temple, became in later writers the primary evidence of God's displeasure with the Jews (Just. *Apol.* 1.47; *Apos.Con.* 5.25) as well as the basis for the myth of the wandering Jew. It has also been suggested that a specific reference to Christians was added to the Jewish malediction against the heretics (see below) in the aftermath of the Bar Kokhba rebellion (Katz 1984: 72; Urbach 1981: 288). Thus the Bar Kokhba rebellion, more than the Jewish War, marked a decisive break between Jews and Christians though naturally things had not stood still in the interval.

Quite apart from these dramatic events the social and political standing of Jews and Christians was an important factor in their relationship. The Jews had been granted unusual privileges by the Romans—such as exemption from military duty and the emperor cult, the right to keep the Sabbath and to collect the temple tax—which allowed them to live according to their own customs and beliefs. They were viewed with suspicion and hostility by some and were occasionally subjected to outbreaks of violence, but the hostility was largely confined to a few of the Roman intelligentsia and the violence caused by localized tensions. More important, indeed one of the causes of Roman antipathy, was their success in attracting both converts and sympathizers (Gager 1983: 113–33). In general Jews thrived under the Romans and they were numerically superior to, and politically more secure than, the Christians.

While Christians still associated with Judaism they could share the privileges and the standing Jews enjoyed. Once separated, they faced a number of problems. They had to find their own niche in Roman society unprotected by the traditional rights of Jews, and it may be that one purpose of the book of Acts, for example, was precisely to support Christianity's claim to be a legal and respectable religion. They were accused of being a novel and upstart cult and were forced to explain their refusal to follow the religious practices of pagans and Jews (*Diogn.* 1–3; Or. *Cels.* 2.1, 2.4). Thus one motive for the claim that they, and not the Jews, were the true Israel was their need for a respectable and ancient pedigree. Christians also had to create a distinct sense of self-identity as well as compete with Jews for the attention of gentile sympathizers. The size and influence of Jewish communities made them powerful competitors and a potential embarrassment to Christian claims. In addition, as antipathy increased the more likely it was that Christians would be subject to Jewish harassment—the situation depicted throughout Acts and mentioned by Justin (*Apol.* 1.31.6), both probably with some exaggeration.

B. Jewish Christians

One group for whom the Jewish War was significant was the church in Jerusalem. Early tradition has it that they fled to Pella in the Transjordan before the final stages of the war (Eus. *Hist. Eccl.* 3.4.3.; Epiph. *Pan.* 29.7.7f.,30.2.7.). The same tradition suggests that they returned after the war and reestablished a somewhat depleted church under the leadership of Simeon, Jesus' cousin (Eus. *Hist. Eccl.* 4.22.4, 5.12; Epiph. *mens.* 15). This tradition has been challenged by the argument that the Jerusalem Christians allied themselves with the Jewish rebels and were slaughtered in the final siege, thus effectively marking the end of Jewish Christianity apart from a few scattered and insignificant survivors (Brandon 1968: 167–84). Alternatively it has been argued that the tradition of a wholesale flight to Pella is a legend designed to bolster the Jerusalem pedigree of the Pella church and that the war had no such dramatic effect on Jewish Christian fortunes (Lüdemann 1980: 161–73). The early tradition should not be too quickly dismissed but, whichever view we take, one stubborn fact remains—we hear little or nothing of the Jerusalem Christians after 70, and we must assume that they lost their previously preeminent position.

Of Jewish Christians in general we hear more but the evidence is obscure and tendentious and tells us more about the internecine disputes among Christians than about their relationship with Judaism. Later Church writers viewed them as heretics, and lumped them together into groups—e.g., Ebionites, Nazoreans, Elchasaites—but they had little first-hand information. Reliance on Jewish Christian sources reconstructed from the later Pseudo-Clementines is now rightly questioned. Justin may give us some information about the situation in the mid-2d century (*Dial.* 46–47), or he may simply be speaking hypothetically from his knowledge of apostolic documents.

About the relationship of Jewish Christian groups with Judaism after 70 we can make only a few generalizations. First, some of them (e.g., the Ebionites) were probably connected to pre-70 groups, but they rapidly became, if they were not already, a minority in the Christian movement, surviving longest in Transjordania and Syria. The mission to the Jews, which Paul already perceived to be largely a failure (Roman 9–11), had probably petered out by the end of the 1st century, and most Jewish Christians were henceforth probably descendants of Jewish Christian families rather than converts from Judaism. Second, in belief and practice they clung to their Jewish heritage, diverging mainly over christological/messianic claims (*Ps-Clem. Rec.* 1.43, 50). They probably attempted to maintain contact with, and where possible remain a part of, synagogue life. It was because they thought Paul chiefly responsible for the conflict with Judaism that they developed a frequently virulent anti-Pauline strain (*Ps-Clem. Rec.* 1:33–71; *Hom.* 11.35.3–6; *Epih.* 30.16.6–9). Third, some later sources express a remarkably irenic, two-covenant concept of salvation which accommodates both Jews and Christians (*Ps-Clem. Hom.* 8:6–7), a view which had earlier exponents too (*Ep. Barn.* 4:6). Fourth, Jewish Christians were ultimately marginalized as a result of their rejection by the two stronger groups, Judaism and gentile Christianity (see below on Matthew). Their fate in the first two centuries—from mother church, through marginal minority, to heretical outcasts—is indicative of the broader schism between Jews and Christians in this period.

C. Yavnean Rabbis and their Successors

The fate of Jewish Christianity immediately raises the issue of rabbinic actions taken at Yavneh. See JAMNIA (JABNEH), COUNCIL OF. It is generally agreed that the rabbis' task was to shore up and redefine Judaism in the wake of the disasters of the Jewish War. Some think that central to this process was a series of anti-Christian moves which had a profound effect upon the Jewish-Christian schism: the closure of the Jewish canon, the banning of heretical (i.e., Christian) books, the dissemination of anti-Christian propaganda, and above all the adoption of a malediction against the heretics *(birkat ha-minim)* into the synagogue liturgy (Davies 1963: 256–315). It is increasingly recognized, however, that Christians were not the sole, or in some cases not at all, the target of the Yavnean rabbis. The heretics and their works which the rabbis had to counter included far more groups than the Christians—Hellenizing Jews, Jewish Gnostics, indeed all non-Yavnean Jews. Jewish Christians, and later gentile Christians too, were at most only part of the problem. They may have been included in, but did not dominate, the ranks of rabbinic heretics. Further, it is clear that the influence of the rabbis spread only gradually in the first 2 centuries, especially among diaspora communities, so that their actions would have been neither immediately nor universally effective (Kimmelmann 1981: 226–44; Katz 1984: 43–76). Still, there may have been a disparity between rabbinic intent and Christian perception. Justin's frequent references to the cursing of Christians in the synagogues (*Dial.* 16, 35, 96, 107, 137) show that some Christians perceived themselves to be the primary target of Jewish antipathy. This would have been particularly true after 135 if at that time a specific reference to Christians *(noṣrim)* was added to the general malediction against heretics *(minim)*.

Apart from the specific question of Yavnean actions, what can we say more generally about Jewish reaction to Christianity? Unfortunately very little, for Jewish sources are largely silent on the matter. There may be a few scattered references in rabbinic literature to Jesus—portraying him as illegitimate, a magician, and a false teacher who was executed for leading the people astray—but the evidence is far from clear. Several persons named Jesus who lived at different times are confused with each other. Moreover, the evidence is mostly in texts of the 3d and 4th centuries and beyond and reflects the inner rabbinic debates of that time (Maier 1978; 1982). A more promising approach is to read the early rabbinic debate about "two powers in heaven" against the background of the Church's christological claims, though the role of Gnostics and other sectarians in both Judaism and Christianity has to be built into the picture too. It does, however, point to christology and the challenge to Jewish monotheism as a serious point of dispute (Segal 1986a: 133–62). In general, what rabbinic literature tells us about Jewish-Christian relations is slight and obscure. This is not surprising, since it is a literature which emerges from a closed, idealistic world and is notoriously silent about external events, even those that had a radical effect upon Judaism. Not all Jewish communities were like the rabbis, especially those in the Diaspora, but virtually no information about their reaction to Christianity has survived.

D. The Gospels and Acts

Yavnean opposition to Christianity, especially the malediction against the heretics, has often been used to reconstruct the *Sitz im Leben* of Matthew, Luke-Acts, and John. But the impact of Yavnean actions has been exaggerated and, at any rate, they do not fit the gospel evidence with precision. A troubled relationship with Judaism is nevertheless evident.

Matthew contains a curious tension between recognition of the favored position of Israel (Matt 10:5–6) with polemic against the Jews (Matt 8:11, 21:41) and commitment to a universal mission (Matt 28:19). Emphasis on Jesus' Jewishness—as messiah and upholder of the law, sent to redeem Israel—goes hand in hand with a slashing attack on the Pharisees (Matthew 23). Distance from the synagogue ("their synagogues" [Matt 4:23, 9:35, 10:17, 12:9, 13:54]; "their scribes" [Matt 7:29]; "the Jews to this day" [Matt 28:15]) goes along with an overwhelming concern with things Jewish. The work is almost certainly by and for Jewish Christians, recently and unhappily separated from the synagogue but also trying to come to terms with an increasingly dominant and successful gentile Christianity. They were thus an embattled minority vis à vis two majorities—non-Christian Judaism and gentile Christianity. The Judaism they knew bears many of the marks of the Yavnean academy (e.g., Matthew 23) and the gospel shares the Yavnean concern with law and commandments and the doing of God's will (e.g., Matthew 5–7). The Matthean relation to contemporary Judaism was full of tension, stress and hostility, yet relating to Jewish traditions and customs was essential for their own sense of identity.

The situation in John is not so different from Matthew, but the issues that divide Jews and Christians are solely matters of belief and we hear no echo in the Jewish opponents of the concerns of the Yavnean rabbis (Meeks 1985: 93–116). In the characteristic use of irony and misunderstanding it is almost always the Jews who are the foil and who thus misunderstand Jesus (John 5:39f., 7:14f., 8:17f.). Salvation is "from the Jews" (John 4:22) but apparently not now among them, for it comes exclusively through Jesus whom they reject (John 16:6). Indeed throughout John, christology is the main focus of disagreement. There are some clues to the situation at the time of writing: the persistent use of "the Jews" to denote those who oppose Jesus and his followers, most extremely in John 8 where the Jews are diabolized ("you are of your father, the devil," v 44); the references to believers being thrown out of the synagogue (*aposynagogos* John 9:22, 12:42–3, 16:1–4); and the possible inference that some Jews had believed in, but then rejected, Jesus (John 8:31). Not all references to the Jews are polemical, and being cast out of the synagogue cannot be tied directly to the Yavnean malediction against the heretics whose purpose was to curse and not to expel. Yet John indicates a situation of extreme hostility between the Johannine communities and the synagogue, with each side locked into its own position and no room for rapprochement.

Luke-Acts conveys a more distant relationship with Judaism partly because it was written by and for gentile Christians. Luke shares Matthew's concern to establish continuity with Judaism and to show Christianity to be the true inheritor of God's promises. But above all, Luke wishes to present the success of the gentile mission—the shift from Jerusalem to Rome—as central to God's eternal plan. The mission to the Jews has had its successes; but, by the end of Acts, the Church has turned its face towards the gentile world (Acts 28:16f.). Disputes with the Jews center on messiahship (the sermons of Acts) and resurrection (Acts 23), while the dispute with Jewish miracle workers (Acts 19:11–20) is an interesting illustration of conflict on a more popular level. In Luke, Jewish rejection of Jesus is viewed with pathos and the mitigating ignorance of the Jewish leaders in putting Jesus to death allows them a second chance (Acts 3:17; 13:27). But there is a darker side too, for the Jews are with few exceptions portrayed as the opponents of Jesus, of the early Church, and, especially, of Paul. Their actions are hostile and malicious, though often thwarted by Roman officialdom. This probably reflects the realities of Luke's own day: The Jews had had their chance but rejected it; they are now largely hostile towards Christianity; the future for Christianity lies in the gentile world.

There are similarities and differences between these 3 documents: Each reveals a church separate from the synagogue, but in Matthew there is a lingering sense of trauma and confusion; in John, bitter resentment of Jewish opposition but acceptance of a clean break; and in Luke-Acts, assumption of a separate identity and focus upon a gentile future.

E. Judaizers

"Judaizer" is a slippery term. Commonly it is used of Jewish Christians who encourage gentiles to adopt Jewish ways. Some use it to refer to Jewish Christians who retain, and gentile Christians who adopt, Jewish customs (Gager 1983: 35–36). In ancient texts it refers only to gentiles (Jos. *JW* 2.643; *Acts Pil.* 2:1) and some restrict the term to them (Gaston 1986: 35). It is at any rate clear that Judaizing in the Church was mostly found among gentile Christians, that it was fairly common, and that it provoked fear and alarm among ecclesiastical leaders. The motives for Judaizing probably varied. Justin implies that gentile Judaizers were enticed into the synagogue (*Dial.* 47) and Ignatius that they simply retained attachments that were formed when they were "godfearers" (*Ign. Phld.* 6:1; *Ign. Magn.* 8:1). "Those who call themselves Jews but are not" (Rev 2:9; 3:9) may be gentile Christians turning to the synagogue to avoid persecution. The existence of Judaizers and the reaction to them reveal 2 different but related things: first, that among ordinary Christians Judaism retained some attraction, in extreme cases enough to cause defection from church to synagogue (Just. *Dial.* 47); and second, that church leaders saw this as an alarming return to defunct traditions, a threat to Christian identity, and grounds for outspoken warnings in which opposition to the Judaizers readily spilled over into anti-Judaism.

F. Marcion and the Gnostics

Gnosticism may have originated among marginalized and disaffected Jews and, if not, certainly in close proximity to Judaism. In Christian gnostic writings there are a few neutral or even positive references to Judaism (*Exeg. Soul* NHC II,*6; Tri. Trac.* NHC I,*5*), occasional disparaging comments on Jews or Jewish practices (*Gos. Phil.* 52:1–3, 75:30–34) derived mainly from NT sources, and a considerable body of anti-Jewish material in which biblical themes, above all the biblical deity, are deliberately denigrated by reversing their value (thus the sect called the Cainites), or the demotion of Yahweh to the role of evil demiurge. In general, Gnostics were hostile to Jewish traditions and beliefs rather than to the Jewish people and, unlike most other Christians, they had no desire to claim for themselves the heritage and privileges of Israel (Gager 1983: 167–71).

Marcion's views were in some respects similar though more complex. See MARCION. His radical separation of the inferior though righteous God of Israel from the God of Love revealed by Jesus, and his rejection of the Jewish scriptures for his own Christian canon, might appear to be the most extreme expression of anti-Judaism in early Christianity. Yet his rejection of Judaism was rarely marked by hostility towards the Jews, and he conceded to them their God, their traditions, and their messiah (not identified with Jesus), even if they were considered inferior. As with the Gnostics, the absence of any desire to appropriate Jewish traditions seems to have allowed Marcion a more relaxed attitude towards the Jewish people. Marcion's radical separation of Judaism and Christianity, the most extreme of that time, probably had several causes—distorted Paulinism, Gnosticism, a rational and literal turn of mind—among which may have been a reaction to precisely those Christian Judaizers who confused and blurred the boundaries between them (Wilson 1986c: 45–58).

G. Justin and Melito

Justin's *Dialogue with Trypho the Jew* (ca. 165) conveys a remarkably irenic picture of Jewish-Christian interaction. Trypho may be a fictitious character and Justin, as the author, clearly controls both sides of the conversation. Yet Justin appears to be well-informed about contemporary Judaism, attributes believable opinions to Trypho, and, while naturally believing that he has won the day, presents the arguments of Trypho with sufficient fairness that a sympathetic reader may find them the more persuasive. The discussion, generally courteous and respectful in tone, ranges over 3 broad fields: the validity of the Mosaic law for Jews and Christians (*Dial.* 9–31); christology (*Dial.* 32–110); and the role of the gentiles as the children of God or True Israel (*Dial.* 111–42). Central to all 3 is the evidence of the Jewish scriptures, for even at this late date Justin does not call on the authority of Christian scriptures. We learn incidentally of other matters: disputes about the merits of the LXX as against the Hebrew version of scripture (*Dial.* 68–80) and of one version of the LXX as against another (*Dial.* 72–73); the ill-will aroused by Jewish persecution, especially during the Bar Kokhba uprising (*Dial.* 17, 33), and by the cursing of Christians in the synagogues; the existence of different groups of gentile and Jewish Christians and how they related to each other and to the Jews (*Dial.* 46–47).

Both the major issues and the incidental information provide rich insights into Jewish-Christian dialogue. There is every reason to think that they reflect the kinds of issues that divided (as well as some that united) Jews and Christians. Above all, the generally civil tone, despite occasional irritability and an overbearing self-assurance on Justin's part, and the fact that Trypho remains unconverted at the end, witness to a style of Jewish-Christian interaction all too rarely found elsewhere. The less sympathetic tone and the barely credible conversion of the Jew in two roughly contemporary dialogues—*The Dialogue of Athanasius and Zaccheus* and *The Dialogue of Timothy and Aquila*—make the evidence of Justin the more remarkable (Remus 1986: 59–80; Trakatellis 1986: 287–97).

The *Paschal Homily* of Melito of Sardis (also ca. 165) is strikingly different. Melito, a skilled rhetorician, covers 2 major themes in his overtly anti-Jewish sermon: first, that Judaism, its traditions, beliefs and attributes are defunct, superseded by and having their only continuing reality in Christianity (*Homily,* lines 224–44, 255–79, 280–300); second, that the Jews are solely responsible for the death of Jesus and thus the death of God—the first extant charge of deicide (*Homily,* lines 562–608, 693–716). Melito was a quartodeciman and thus particularly sensitive to the uncomfortable proximity of Jewish and Christian festivals. He was also conscious of the need to impress upon the Romans the respectable pedigree of Christianity. Above all, however, he was aware of the thriving and socially prominent Jewish community in Sardis which posed a constant threat to Christian claims and identity. His response to this situation reveals a level of antipathy and finality matched in early Christian literature only by the *Epistle of Barnabas* (Wilson 1986b: 81–102).

H. Festivals and Cult

In its early decades Christianity was heavily dependent on Jewish models for its organization and worship. Initially, for example, Christians celebrated the Sabbath like the Jews; only later, probably with the specific intent of dissociating Judaism and Christianity, was Sunday established (Bacchiochi 1977). The earliest celebration of Easter was probably no more than an adaptation of Passover, and one group, the "quartodecimans," continued to celebrate Easter on the same day as Passover well into the 3d century. The decision to introduce a distinctively Christian festival (Easter Sunday), which may go back to the gentile bishops who took over in Jerusalem after 135 C.E., was probably also a deliberate move of dissociation. Melito of Sardis, a quartodeciman, illustrates how a close association with Jewish festivals can, paradoxically, fuel strong anti-Jewish polemic.

The destruction of the Jerusalem Temple hit at the heart of the Jewish cult and, while the rabbis at Yavneh offered an alternative focus and took over some of the functions of the cultic personnel, hope for the rebuilding of the Temple was never entirely abandoned. Loss of the Temple could also have created uncertainty among Jewish Christians, while later proposals for its reconstruction could equally be seen by other Christians as a serious threat. The epistle to the Hebrews may illustrate the former. Its date and provenance remain obscure but it is probably of Jewish-Christian origin and written sometime after 70 C.E. partly in reaction to the events of the war. It is soaked in Jewish biblical and cultic traditions yet firm in its assertion of the superiority of the Christian over the Jewish reality. Whether it is covenant, hope, promises, law, or priesthood, the new is always superior to the old (Heb 7:18,22; 8:6; 9:11; 11:35; 12:24) for the old is impotent and imperfect (Heb 7:18,28; 8:7,13; 9:8–10; 10:1,2,9), indeed annulled (Heb 7:18; 10:9). The discarding of Judaism goes hand in hand with a form of self-definition which leans heavily upon it. Yet the argument is firm rather than shrill, marked by enthusiasm for the new rather than dislike for the old.

A quite different note is struck by the *Epistle of Barnabas.* It is best understood when located in Nerva's reign (96–98 C.E.), when Jewish fortunes underwent a brief revival. Nerva rescinded Domitian's extension of the Jewish tax, which had been much abused, and seems to have encouraged Jewish hopes for the reconstruction of the Jerusalem Temple. The strident tone, the note of urgency and anxiety in the letter are caused in part by the author's reaction to these events (Shukster and Richardson 1986: 17–32). The wholesale appropriation of Jewish traditions—properly, usually allegorically, understood—is more extensive, and the denial that the Jews are a covenant people is more explicit than in most other early Christian documents. Three things appear to have motivated the author: first, the tussle with Judaism over the proper interpretation of scripture, a theme which pervades the work and which probably reflects the author's own experiences with an increasingly confident rabbinic Judaism; second, the suggestion that the temple might be rebuilt, thus rejuvenating Judaism and making it an attractive alternative to Christianity, which evokes a passionate denunciation of Temple and cult (2:6–9; 5:1–3; 8:1–4; 16:1f.); and third, the confusion caused by those (Jews? Jewish Christians? Gentile Judaizers?) who claimed that the covenant privileges could be shared by both Jews and Christians—a view that the author adamantly opposes (4:11; 13:1; 14:1–2).

I. Conclusion

Two features of Jewish-Christian relations in this period stand out: their variety and their complexity.

"Variety" refers to the widely differing reaction of groups of Jews and Christians to each other, ranging on the Christian side from preservation or adoption of intimate ties with Judaism (Jewish Christians, Judaizers) to bitter and resolute rejection of it (Barnabas, Melito), and on the Jewish side from active persecution of Christians (Bar Kokhba) to an informed and civil dialogue with them (Trypho). Put simply, neither Judaism nor Christianity was a single, uniform entity. Each of them enveloped a wide variety of belief and practice. Different sorts of Jews met different sorts of Christians, and it is not surprising that they related differently to each other, too.

"Complexity" refers to the host of different factors which bred antipathy between Jews and Christians. *Political events:* the Jewish War and the Bar Kokhba rebellion, including their immediate effects and the subsequent use of them in anti-Jewish polemic. *Social standing:* the relative size, influence and official status of the 2 communities, generally favoring Jews, putting Christians on the defensive and sometimes involving persecution. *Territorial disputes:* common features and festivals, but above all competing claims to the Scriptures and heritage of Judaism which mark every document known to us in this period; in general, the greater the proximity the greater was the conflict. *Overlapping missions:* competition for the allegiance of the same group of interested gentiles, and disputed claims to magical and miraculous power. *Praxis:* reformation and selective adaptation of the Jewish law. *Continuity:* the existence of and the reaction to Jewish Christians, gentile Judaizers and exponents of the two-covenant theory. *Christology:* a crucial dividing line in almost all Christian documents, seen from the other side in the rabbinic discussion of "two powers in heaven." *Self-identity:* the reformulation of Judaism by the Yavnean sages and the Christian search for a distinctive identity as it went its separate way. *Hellenization:* the demise of the Christian mission to Jews and the shift to the gentile world.

The combined force of these factors eventually and inexorably drove the 2 communities apart. Jewish Christians resisted the trend and ended up in no-man's-land, while Christian Judaizers periodically attempted to reverse it. The Marcionites made a clean and fairly painless break, but for most Christians it was a separation which began in agony and ambiguity and ended in open and lasting hostility. In retrospect the period 70–170 C.E. can be seen to have been the crucial formative century for the essentially negative view of Judaism which was to dominate the Christian West.

Bibliography

Bacchiochi, S. 1977. *Anti-Judaism and the Origin of Sunday.* Rome.

Brandon, S. G. F. 1968. *The Fall of Jerusalem and the Christian Church.* London.

Davies, A. T., ed. 1979. *Anti-Semitism and the Foundations of Christianity.* New York.

Davies, W. D. 1963. *The Setting of the Sermon on the Mount.* Cambridge.

Gager, J. 1983. *The Origins of Anti-Semitism.* Oxford.

Gaston, L. 1986. Judaism of the Uncircumcized in Ignatius and Related Writers. Pp. 33–44 in Wilson 1986a.

Harnack, A. von. 1962. *The Mission and Expansion of Christianity in the First Three Centuries.* New York.

Harrington, D. J. 1983. *Gods's People in Christ.* Philadelphia.

Katz, S. T. 1984. Issues in the Separation of Judaism and Christianity after 70 C.E.: A Reconsideration. *JBL* 103: 43–76.

Kimmelmann, R. 1981. *Birkat ha-minim* and the Lack of Evidence for an anti-Christian Prayer in Late Antiquity. Pp. 226–44 in Sanders, Baumgarten, Mendelson 1981.

Lüdemann, G. 1980. The Successors of Pre-70 Jerusalem Christianity: A Critical Evaluation of the Tradition. Pp. 161–73 in Sanders 1980.

Maier, J. 1978. *Jesus von Nazareth in der talmudischen überlieferung.* Darmstadt.

———. 1982. *Jüdische Auseinandersetzung mit Christentum in der Antike.* Darmstadt.

Meeks, W. A. 1985. Breaking Away: Three New Testament Pictures of Christianity's Separation from the Jewish Communities. Pp. 93–115 in Neusner and Frerichs 1985.

Neusner, J. and Frerichs, E., eds. 1985. *'To See Ourselves as Others See Us': Christians, Jews, 'Others' in Late Antiquity.* Chico, CA.

Nickelsburg, G. W. and McCrae, G. W., eds. 1986. *Christians Among Jews and Gentiles.* Philadelphia.

Remus, H. 1986. Justin Martyr's Argument with Judaism. Pp. 59–80 in Wilson 1986a.

Richardson, P., and Granskou, D., eds. 1986. *Anti-Judaism in Early Christianity.* Vol. 1. Waterloo.

Ruether, R. 1975. *Faith and Fratricide.* New York.

Sanders, E. P., ed. 1980. *Jewish and Christian Self-Definition.* Vol. 1. Philadelphia.

Sanders, E. P. with Baumgarten, A. I. and Mendelson, A. eds. 1981. *Jewish and Christian Self-Definition.* Vol. 2. Philadelphia.

Sanders, E. P. and Meyer, B. F., eds. 1982. *Jewish and Christian Self-Definition.* Vol. 3. Philadelphia.

Sandmel, S. 1978. *Anti-Semitism in the New Testament.* Philadelphia.

Segal, A. 1986a. Judaism, Christianity and Gnosticism. Pp. 133–62 in Wilson 1986a.

———. 1986b. *Rebeccah's Children: Judaism and Christianity in the Roman World.* Cambridge.

Shukster, M., and Richardson, P. 1986. Temple and *Bet Ha-Midrash* in the Epistle of Barnabas. Pp. 17–37 in Wilson 1986a.

Simon, M. 1986. *Verus Israel.* Trans. H. McKeating. Oxford.

Trakatellis, D. 1986. Justin Martyr's Trypho. Pp. 287–97 in Nickelsburg and McCrae 1986.

Urbach, E. E. 1981. Self-Isolation or Self-Affirmation in Judaism in the first three centuries. Pp. 269–98 in Sanders, Baumgarten, Mendelson 1981.

Wilson, S. G., ed. 1986a. *Anti-Judaism in Early Christianity.* Vol. 2. Waterloo.

———. 1986b. Melito and Israel. Pp. 81–102 in Wilson 1986a.

———. 1986c. Marcion and the Jews. Pp. 45–58 in Wilson 1986a.

STEPHEN G. WILSON

JEWISH WAR (66–73 C.E.).

JEWISH WAR (66–73 C.E.). The name usually given by scholars to the uprising of the Jews against the Romans that took place between 66 and 73 C.E.

A. Causes and Factors
B. The Role of the Moderates and the Early Stages of Conflict
C. Preparations for War—Jerusalem and the Galilee
D. The Roman Campaign in Galilee and Judea
E. Anarchy in Jerusalem (67–70 C.E.)
F. The Siege and Fall of Jerusalem (70 C.E.)
G. The Capture of Masada (74 C.E.)

A. Causes and Factors

It is not difficult to find causes for the Jewish revolt against Rome. The primary sources suggest a number of very plausible ones, and modern scholars have offered other possibilities as well. Josephus, for example, focuses on a number of factors. For the most part he blames a small group of fanatical hotheads who utilized whatever means necessary (murder, pillage, burning homes, kidnapping) to foster rebellion (*JW* 1.1.4 §10). He also links the Jewish-pagan hostility which surfaced throughout Judea—especially in Caesarea—during the mid-1st century to the outbreak of the rebellion in Jerusalem (*Ant* 20.8.9 §184). Finally, he points an accusing finger at the corrupt and rapacious procurators whose ambitions, appetites, and incompetence contributed enormously to generating the final confrontation (*JW* 2.14.1 §272–76). Tacitus, too, implies that much responsibility for the war lies with the cruel and irresponsible behavior of governors such as Felix and Florus (*Hist.* 5.9.3–5; 5.10.1). Rabbinic literature, largely ignoring these kinds of historical factors, opts for moralistic considerations—social hostility, a breakdown of values, and overly materialistic concerns (*Tosefta Menaḥot* 13:22; *b. Git.* 55b–56a).

To these reasons modern scholars have added other, socioeconomic factors. The devastating famine of 48 C.E., when combined with the oppressive taxation by the procurators, impoverished the people. Little wonder that brigandage increased markedly in the 50s. The fact that the first act of the Jerusalem populace after the defeat of the Romans was the burning of the Jerusalem archives containing debt records indicates the role played by economic factors at the outbreak of the revolt. It has been suggested that the wealth pouring into Jerusalem from donations by Jews the world over heightened class tensions, making the rich richer and leaving others in even greater poverty.

Social conflicts within Jewish society at the time are also viewed by modern historians as an important factor that contributed to the revolt. The widening social rift within the city, together with rural disenfranchisement due to heavy taxation, population increase, and growing economic instability, added fuel to the fire of revolt.

Jewish-pagan tensions in late Second Temple Judea have likewise been singled out as a primary reason for the conflict with Rome. These tensions were exacerbated by the employment of local pagan inhabitants in Rome's auxiliary contingents stationed in Judea.

The existence of this wide range of theories regarding the causes for the revolt indicates the complexity of the problem. Our sources can substantiate each and every view, and there can be little doubt that many factors indeed contributed to the outbreak against Rome. The search for one basic cause, however, is misleading, for most if not all of the above factors were present in Jewish society, and each played a distinct role among one or more of the many groups involved in the events leading to the outbreak of the revolt. Divisions among the Jews were numerous. We know of the existence of moderate and radical camps among them. In the former were the high priestly families (undoubtedly Sadducees), some Pharisees, the Herodian family, the urban aristocracy, and others. The radical camp was comprised of a number of different groups that, even at the very beginning of hostilities, fought one another no less than they did the Romans and the moderates. By the end of the war, no less than five different revolutionary parties existed, and the tension and friction among them were devastating.

Compared to the later Jewish revolt under Bar Kokhba, or the previous one under Judah the Maccabee, the revolt of 66 C.E. was unique in its lack of overall organization, planning, and leadership. Given this chaotic situation, in which many different groups, each with its own ideology, leadership, and composition, were competing with one another, it is no wonder that to speak of an underlying cause of the revolt is misleading. The number of grievances were at least as numerous as the many different factions, and no doubt opinions and motivations differed even within any one group. For example, both Rabbi Simeon b. Gamaliel and Rabbi Yoḥanan b. Zakkai belonged to the Hillelite faction within Pharisaic circles. They even functioned together in a number of halakic matters. Nevertheless, their political paths (and presumably their attitudes toward the war as well) differed greatly: Rabbi Simeon, a leader of the moderate faction, stayed in Jerusalem until the bitter end (and probably died there during or soon after the end of the siege); Rabbi Yoḥanan fled the city at the height of the siege, seeking asylum with the Romans.

B. The Role of the Moderates and the Early Stages of Conflict

Judea's plunge into war was neither sudden nor total. Immediately after the cessation of the daily sacrifice on behalf of the emperor, and the capture of Masada in the fall of 66, the leading citizens of Jerusalem, together with the chief priests and Pharisees, tried—albeit unsuccessfully—to dissuade the people from embarking on a course of confrontation with Rome. They then attempted to crush the revolt by urging Florus and Agrippa to send troops to the city. The latter responded by dispatching 2,000 cavalrymen and, in alliance with the moderates, held the Upper City. The Lower City to the east, including the Temple Mount area, was in the hands of the revolutionaries; after a week of fighting the insurgents seized the Upper City as well.

The moderates were led by the wealthy aristocratic Jerusalemites, either of the priestly or lay variety. The Herodian family, the Sadducees, the Boethusians, and others of the priestly oligarchy were certainly foremost in these circles, tending to be more cosmopolitan and pro-Roman than others in the group, whether out of self-interest or because their political, social, and cultural perspectives demanded moderation and accommodation rather than confrontation and fanaticism.

What exactly did the moderates want? Some, indeed, were opposed to the revolt, as, for example, those who wished to avert hostilities by appealing to Agrippa and Florus. Others, however, do not seem to have been completely opposed to a revolutionary posture. Hatred for (or at least dislike of) Rome was probably widespread, even within the upper classes, both because of the desecration of the temple and appropriation of its money and because of Rome's curtailing of the authority of the aristocracy and high priests. Some may have shared in the apocalyptic fervor, while others may have feared the hostility of the urban poor and the rural peasants appealed to by the Sicarii. Some moderates may have wished to simply maintain their position of leadership in the community, even if this entailed a revolutionary stance with which they did not fully identify.

Other circumstances, however, may have been decisive. The anti-Jewish hostility which surfaced in many nearby Hellenistic cities at this moment of crisis, in addition to the threat of Roman retribution, served to unify disparate parts of the nation. Pro-Roman leaders then might have joined with the revolutionaries in self-defense. Undoubtedly, some of the more moderate leaders felt that by cooperating with the rebels they could more easily control the course of events, and perhaps even negotiate a settlement at an appropriate time. Even when the die was cast, there were those—and Josephus himself may have been one of them—who thought in terms of a limited conflict and the creation of a new modus vivendi with Rome, which would include curtailed procuratorial authority and, concomitantly, expanded Jewish autonomy. Preparations for war did not preclude suing for peace at the appropriate moment, as the city of Tiberias did in the spring of 67 (*JW* 3.9.8 §455). Finally, there appear to have been moderate leaders who felt that their cause might be supported—militarily or diplomatically—by fellow Jews throughout the empire.

The radical camp was at first spearheaded by two factions, one headed by a priest—Eleazar, son of Ananias—and the other by the Sicarii under Menachem, a descendant of Judas the Galilean. Eleazar had been the one primarily responsible for the decision to cancel the sacrifices on behalf of the emperor. He was supported by popular revolutionary leaders and led a coalition of lower priests and leaders of the populace in opposition to the traditional high priestly authorities. In the early days of the revolt Eleazar's group, composed primarily if not exclusively of Jerusalemites, occupied the temple and Lower City, thereby depriving their high priestly opponents of access to the temple (*JW* 2.17.6 §425). No doubt the conflict between these groups smacked of a class struggle as well.

During the course of their struggle, Eleazar and his followers were joined by the Sicarii and Menachem, who assumed control of the revolutionary forces in the siege of Herod's palace and the towers. Menachem entered Jerusalem fresh from the conquest of Masada and at the head of a band referred to by Josephus as "some of the most ardent promoters of hostilities" (*JW* 2.17.2 §408). Capturing the Roman garrison at Masada supplied Menachem and his followers with the weapons necessary to become a significant force in Jerusalem. He is described as having appeared "like a veritable king," and later on is said to have worn royal robes. Presumably, Menachem had regal pretensions, although it is far from clear whether he bore any messianic overtones.

After his victory in the Upper City, Menachem emerged as potentially the strongest leader in Jerusalem, arousing the jealousy of Eleazar's followers—despite their view of Menachem as being of inferior social rank. They thereupon attacked Menachem while he was at worship in the temple. Many were massacred on the spot; Eleazar b. Yaʾir and others escaped to Masada, where they remained for the duration of the revolt (*JW* 2.17.9 §447). Menachem himself took refuge in the Ophel in the Lower City, where he was caught, tortured, and finally put to death.

The Sicarii thus ceased to play any role in Jerusalem affairs. Josephus reports that the urban populace supported Eleazar in his confrontation with Menachem, assuming that the latter's death would end the revolt. This, however, was wishful thinking. A series of events unfolded in the coming months (August–November 66) which eliminated any hopes there might have been for rapprochement. According to Josephus, the same day the rebels decimated the Roman garrison in Jerusalem, the gentiles of Caesarea slaughtered some 20,000 local Jews. This set off a wave of Jewish reprisals throughout the country: Jews attacked their gentile neighbors in Syrian villages, in Philadelphia, Heshbon, Gerasa, Pella, Scythopolis, Gadara, Hippos, and the Golan, as well as in other places along the Phoenician coast from Tyre to Gaza. These were not coordinated attacks under a centralized leadership but rather local conflicts initiated by local leaders. Justus of Tiberias led the attack on Gadara and Hippos; John of Gischala, the one on the Tyrians. The gentiles, for their part, immediately sought vengeance, and many Jewish communities were adversely affected. Specifically mentioned are Scythopolis, Ascalon, Ptolemais, Hippos, Gadara, and Tyre. Even in the territory of Agrippa II, a Jewish delegation of 70 leaders was attacked and massacred.

Finally, and after much delay, the Roman governor of Syria, Cestius Gallus, decided to march on Jerusalem and put an end to the incipient rebellion (*JW* 2.18.9 §499–555). The time was October of the year 66. Gathering a large force of over 30,000 men in Antioch, Gallus passed through Ptolemais and Caesarea, put Lydda to the torch, and approached Jerusalem via Beth Horon. Repelling a Jewish attack in the Beth Horon area, Gallus then moved on Jerusalem and burned Bezetha, the northernmost suburb of the city. At first he tried to enter Jerusalem via Herod's palace, but altered his strategy five days later and decided to mount an assault on the N wall of the Temple Mount. Suddenly, however, Gallus withdrew from the city and headed toward the coast. The Jews, drawing courage from this surprising retreat, pursued the Romans. Apprehending them near Beth Horon, the rebels slew some 6,000 soldiers and captured a good deal of Roman equipment. Only by a deft stratagem was Gallus able to avert a complete and total defeat. The die thus had been cast. The Jewish victors returned to Jerusalem in joyous celebration, and many pro-Roman Jews left the city. The moderate elements united and succeeded in forming a provisional government which was to manage affairs in the city for over a year.

C. Preparations for War—Jerusalem and the Galilee

The defeat of Gallus ended any hopes of early negotiations, and the Jews were now irrevocably committed to war. The first act of the rebels was to set up a revolutionary government (*JW* 2.20.3 §562–68). The tasks of this group were formidable: new policy and strategy had to be formulated, reforms of existing institutions had to be made, and military preparation had to be undertaken. Joseph, son of Gorion, and Ananias, the former high priest, were selected to be supreme commanders in the city. Another member of the high priestly circles who played a prominent role in governmental affairs at the time was Joshua b. Gamla (*Life* 38 §193). Others were chosen to take charge of specific territories in the country: Joshua, son of Sapphas, a high priest, and Eleazar, son of the high priest Neus, were put in charge over Idumea; Joseph, son of Simon, over Jericho; Manasseh, over Perea; John the Essene, over Thamna, Lydda, Joppa, and Emmaus; John, son of Ananias, over Gophna and Acrabetta; and Josephus, over the Galilee, including Gamla (*JW* 2.20.3 §566–68).

We are particularly well informed about the preparations for war in the Galilee, for Josephus himself was central to these events. However, this abundance of information bears a price. Discrepancies and contradictions abound in his reports of the Galilee; his descriptions in *Jewish War* differ from those in the *Life*, and they were written some twenty years apart, each for its own purposes and each with its own tendentiousness.

One matter, however, is quite clear from Josephus' accounts. The Galilee was far from united on the question of war with Rome. Josephus found his greatest support among the "Galileans"—Jews from the countryside and villages. They were always found in his entourage, their leaders dined with him, and they were summoned to a conference, appointed to judicial-administrative positions, and served as emissaries to Jerusalem. These Galileans nurtured a deep hatred of the three largest Galilean cities—Sepphoris, Tiberias, and Gabara—and needed little excuse to attack them. Much of their animosity undoubtedly was linked to the age-old urban-rural tension, but some must have also related to differing views on the question of war with Rome. Of the larger cities, only Tarichaeae (Migdal) aligned itself with Josephus and was later joined by smaller towns like Jotaphata and Gamla. Tarichaeae's anti-Roman posture may have been influenced by its hostility to nearby Tiberias, which they understood as a direct result of Roman-Herodian rule. Tarichaeae was also a veteran Galilean settlement—in contrast to Tiberias, which had been settled in more recent years (19–20 C.E.) by a mixture of area residents and transferees from other places. Therefore, Tarichaeae's alliance with the rural Galileans against Tiberias reflected a complex set of issues: city versus city, an older settlement versus a newer one, an indigenous population versus foreigners.

When the Romans were finally ready to attack, the Galilee was prepared to offer little more than token resistance. Most were not inclined to fight; however, those who had a penchant for revolution were divided into numerous factions. The major city of Tiberias was torn asunder by rival claims. Josephus was thus able to accomplish very little. John sealed off the Upper Galilee, and the major urban centers turned their backs on revolution. With the arrival of the legions in the spring of 67, many of those whom Josephus had mustered to service had deserted, and Josephus was forced to take refuge in Jotapata, thus ensnaring himself in the Roman siege.

D. The Roman Campaign in the Galilee and Judea

Upon learning of the disastrous defeat of Cestius Gallus, Nero appointed one of his outstanding generals, Vespasian, to direct the campaign against the Jews. In the end, only a few places offered serious resistance to Rome: Jotapata, where a 47-day siege was required to subdue the city; Gamla, finally overrun after a vigorous resistance, triggering a mass suicide; and Tarichaeae, where rural Galileans played an active role in inciting the residents.

The Roman campaign of 67 ended with a quick foray into Judea and the capture of Jamnia and Azotus (*JW* 4.3.2 §130). Garrisons were placed there, and the legions spent the winter months in Caesarea and Scythopolis.

In the early months of 68, Roman strategy called for reducing all resistance in and around Judea, so that Jerusalem would be isolated. By late spring of 68, all Judea—including Perea and Idumea—had been subdued. Only Jerusalem stood alone and remained to be conquered.

At this moment, however, events in Rome caused all operations to be suspended for almost two years. On June 9, 68, Nero died and Vespasian's mandate to conduct the war likewise expired. He was forced to await fresh orders from the new emperor. The transfer of authority in Rome did not go smoothly. This year is known in Roman history as the Year of the Four Emperors. Galba was acknowledged as emperor but was soon followed by Otho; and he, in turn, by Vitellius. Rebellion and insurrection were the order of the day, and no one in the imperial city was interested or concerned enough to address himself to the question of Judea. After a year's waiting, and after having observed with consternation the increasing chaos engulfing Rome, Vespasian, on July 1, 69, staked a claim to become the new emperor of Rome. The road from declaration of intentions to final realization, however, was not altogether smooth, and another half year passed before Vespasian and Titus were able to validate that declaration. In December 69, Vespasian was acknowledged as Rome's new ruler. It was only then that the new emperor was prepared to realize his goals in Judea, but now he had to await the advent of spring, for it was a cardinal rule in the Roman army not to fight during the winter months.

E. Anarchy in Jerusalem (67–70 C.E.)

We know practically nothing about the events in Jerusalem during the year and a half in which the moderates ruled. Josephus' narrative for the year 67 focuses almost exclusively on the Galilee, and only toward the end does it mention Vespasian's campaign in Judea and Perea. Not only did the moderates enjoy supreme rule in Jerusalem but their influence on other areas was considerable as well. Josephus' reports from the Galilee of his contacts with the Jerusalem authorities during the early months of 67 are very important regarding this matter.

It was Vespasian's successes in the Galilee, and even more his incursions into the Judean countryside in late 67, that upset the balance of power in Jerusalem. Refugees poured into the city, and social, political, and religious strains soon became unbearable. One of the first to arrive in Jerusalem (around October 67) was John of Gischala.

Despite Josephus' attempts in *JW* to depict him as a wild-eyed radical, John appears to have adopted a rather cautious, moderate revolutionary posture in Gischala and the Upper Galilee. His political and military activity was spurred not so much by anti-Roman sentiments as by the need to defend his hometown from the raids of non-Jewish neighbors. His opposition to Josephus stemmed not from any radical proclivities but from the rivalry between two strong and moderate prorevolutionary leaders, each of whom aspired to control the Galilee. Nevertheless, John's identification with the moderate Jerusalemites was short-lived. Along with Jerusalem society in general, he, too, became radicalized, turning his back on his former allies and joining the newly emergent Zealot party. This took place during the winter of 67–68.

Josephus associates the Zealot party, which seems to have crystallized about this time, with the leadership of Eleazar b. Simon and Zecharias b. Amphicalleus. It was composed of two main elements—the lower-class priests, and refugees from the Judean countryside (referred to by Josephus as brigands). The formation of this party in the winter of 67–68 was no coincidence. The enormous increase in the population of Jerusalem and the presence among these refugees of disaffected revolutionary and brigand leaders, along with disillusionment with moderate leadership and the losses incurred the previous year, all contributed to an explosive atmosphere in the city. See ZEALOTS.

The Zealots unleashed a reign of terror throughout the city. They succeeded in taking over the temple precincts and fortified themselves against any popular reaction. This action, together with their selection of a nonqualified high priest, aroused public enmity against Zealot excesses. It was only then that the moderate leadership—Joseph, the son of Gorion, Rabbi Simeon b. Gamaliel, and the two priests, Ananus and Jesus b. Gamla, rallied to meet the challenge. Appeals to individuals and a mass move by the moderates was effected, and the Zealots feared an attack by the populace. The moderates then sent a delegation to negotiate with the Zealots. John was appointed but took this opportunity to change his allegiance (a step that he undoubtedly contemplated for some time) and side with the Zealots. He accused Ananus of betraying the city to the Romans and of preparing an attack on the Zealots scheduled for the next day (*JW* 4.3.14 §216–27). At his suggestion, the Zealots sent for the Jews of Idumea to aid them; with this invitation, yet another radical group was now to be introduced into the city.

Marshalling a large force under the command of four generals, the Idumeans marched to Jerusalem in a driving rainstorm only to find the gates barred. After a short delay the Zealots succeeded in evading the guards and opening the gates. The Idumeans, along with the Zealots, then conducted a purge of the populace, including the moderate leaders. After much plundering and killing, they tracked down the high priests, whom they considered arch-traitors. Ananus, the only moderate leader with sufficient stature to offer an alternative political course, was killed. Josephus claims that the capture of the city began with Ananus' death, its downfall with the sight of a high priest butchered in public (*JW* 4.5.2 §318). According to Josephus, at least, Ananus represented the one hope for a negotiated settlement with Rome. For their part, the Zealots hunted down other major figures. As a result of these acts, the number of people deserting Jerusalem increased dramatically; many of them urged Vespasian to overtake the city as soon as possible.

In the midst of such excesses, the Zealot coalition fell apart. John, who presumably had not taken part in the slaughter (perhaps out of attachment to his former allies), broke with them and was followed by some of the Idumeans. Other Idumeans left the city in disgust, and still others united with some of the priests and Jerusalem populace in order to confine both the Zealots and John within the temple area. Although he severed his ties with the Zealots, John never confronted them militarily. He was an ambitious, opportunistic, and charismatic leader. While he may not have engaged in the same bloody massacres as the Zealots, he was equally unable to unify the factious city.

In the spring of 69 John and the Zealots held the temple while the Idumeans, the remnants of the moderate party, and the Jerusalem populace laid siege to it. The latter groups, realizing they could never deliver the final blow by themselves, turned to another outside force, a move which only succeeded in further dividing the city.

It was at this point that Simon bar Giora was invited into Jerusalem. However, Simon and the Idumeans were unable to dislodge John and the Zealots from the temple area, and for over a year warfare ensued between the several factions. The Zealots were ensconced in the inner temple area, John in the outer temple precincts, and Simon, the Idumeans, and the Jerusalemites were in the Upper and Lower cities. Jerusalem continued to be ravaged throughout this period; murders and plundering were rampant, and vast stores of food were destroyed by both sides (*JW* 5.1.4 §21–6).

Thus, by the time Titus approached Jerusalem in the spring of 70 for his final assault, the city was teeming with rival revolutionary groups, each bearing its own distinct leadership, ideology, origin, and history. Leadership of the city had passed into the hands of Simon. According to Josephus, Simon commanded 10,000 of the 23,000 troops then in Jerusalem and was allied to a 5,000-strong Idumean contingent. John had 6,000 troops at his disposal, and the Zealots 2,400. These Jewish forces had fought one another for a year before they were able to forge some semblance of unity—but by then it was too late. Even if united, they could never have hoped to withstand the Roman onslaught. Sooner or later Jerusalem was doomed to fall. However, with the internal wounds still festering and the Jewish body politic so shredded, conquest by Rome came all the sooner.

F. The Siege and Fall of Jerusalem (70 C.E.)

Titus marched on Jerusalem at the head of four legions. At first the Jewish forces made a number of successful forays against the besiegers, as Titus initially concentrated his efforts on the northwestern section of the city just north of the Hippicus tower. Having successfully breached the outer two walls, the Romans found themselves in the narrow streets of the city. Utilizing their greater mobility and knowledge of the neighborhood, the Jews inflicted heavy casualties, and the Romans were forced to retreat. The respite, however, was brief. Four days later the Romans renewed their attack and, destroying a large section of the wall, took this part of the city. Now came the last and the most difficult stage of the siege—the assault on the Antonia fortress.

The Romans erected four ramparts against the Antonia fortress. Their advance was now much slower and more costly: They succeeded in breaking through the outer wall, only to find that the rebels had built another one directly behind it. Despondent because of the futility of their continual efforts, the Roman troops were given encouragement by Titus, and the siege work resumed. After repeated efforts, the Antonia was overrun, and the Romans continued on to the temple itself, where they were repelled by the forces of John and Simon. Josephus notes that it was at this point that the daily sacrifices at the temple were suspended, due to the lack of animals. With the Jewish forces ensconced within the temple precincts, Titus once again offered terms of peace. The appeal encouraged a number of people, particularly those from the upper classes and priestly families, to cross over to the Roman side. Titus sent them to Gophna, which was being used then as a refugee center.

Unable to dislodge the stones of the temple wall after using the battering ram for days, the Romans set fire to the gates and porticoes of the temple. Continuous fighting slowly forced the Jews back into the confines of the temple's inner court. It was at this point that Titus called a strategy meeting of his chief commanders to determine the fate of the temple: Should it be destroyed or spared? Overriding the advice of his advisers, Josephus reports, Titus decided that the edifice was not to be destroyed under any circumstances, as it would serve as an ornament to the Roman Empire. There is reason to doubt the accuracy of Josephus' narrative, since a 4th-century writer, Sulpicius Severus, reports that Titus himself decided to destroy the Jerusalem edifice. Destroying a temple could easily be construed as an act of impiety, and it is quite understandable that Josephus might have wanted to exonerate his friend and patron from having a hand in this act, if indeed he was responsible. The contradiction in our sources as to Titus' responsibility for the destruction of the Second Temple remains unresolved. Josephus reports that the temple was destroyed on August 30, the 10th of Ab, the same day the First Temple was destroyed by the Babylonians according to Jer 52:12 (2 Kgs 25:8 gives the dates as the 7th of Ab, and later rabbinic tradition settled on the 9th of Ab).

The Romans now proceeded to destroy the entire city. Rejecting Simon and John's suggestion to discuss terms of surrender, Titus had his troops burn large sections of Jerusalem. On the 20th of Ab, the Romans began their attack on the Upper City by constructing embankments in four places. At this point, the Idumeans sought to come to terms with Titus but were prevented from doing so by Simon. Completing the embankments in eighteen days, the Romans prepared for a final assault. Resistance was now slight; the remaining forces fled to underground passages or attempted to flee the city. The Romans quickly took the Upper City, and victory was complete; Jerusalem was in their hands. Following a mass slaughter, fire broke out and the city was entirely destroyed. John was sentenced to life imprisonment, and Simon was to be executed following the triumphant procession in Rome. Josephus estimates the number of those who perished in the siege at 1,100,000; Tacitus speaks of 600,000. Both numbers, however, appear to be exaggerated. The entire population of Jerusalem at the height of the siege probably never exceeded 250,000 (its 23,400 soldiers probably represented about 10 percent of the total population).

G. The Capture of Masada (74 C.E.)

Following the fall of Jerusalem, Jewish rebels continued to hold three fortresses: Herodium, Machaerus, and Masada. The first two were taken with relative ease by the new Roman legate, Lucilius Bassus.

In 73 C.E., Bassus died in office and was succeeded by Flavius Silva. The new governor turned his attentions to the last remaining Jewish stronghold at Masada (*JW* 7.8.2 §275–419). Only one spot—the western slope of the mountain—presented itself as an appropriate place for a ramp. The Romans proceeded to erect a 100-m-high embankment, on top of which large stones were placed to serve as a platform for the siege engines. They then threw their battering ram into action with devastating effectiveness, only to find that the Jews had erected a second wall behind the first. They set fire to this wall, but their plan at first appeared to have backfired as the wind blew the flames back in the face of the soldiers. However, a sudden wind change caused the flames to envelop the inner wall and set it ablaze.

The conquest of the fortress was imminent, and realizing that there was no hope of victory Eleazar gathered his comrades in an attempt to convince them that suicide was the only honorable course of action remaining. Josephus has left us a detailed account of what supposedly transpired. To be captured by the Romans would have meant torture, humiliation, and death. Eleazar is said to have reviewed some of the ideological tenets associated with the Fourth Philosophy (for instance, the recognition that there is but one God and that no Jew should become a slave) and finally argued that God had now turned against the Jews, dooming them to destruction. How else would He have let such wholesale destruction take place in Jerusalem or have allowed the city to fall into ruins? The misfortune which befell the entire Jewish nation was to be the lot of the Sicarii as well, but it should come at their own hands and not at the hands of the Romans; let them say, "We preferred death to slavery."

Realizing that not all were convinced by these arguments, Eleazar reportedly renewed his appeal. This time, however, the argument took a more philosophical bent. Its major themes were not Israel, God, and sin but rather soul, death, and suicide: Life, not death, is man's misfortune. Death liberates man's soul from the shackles of the body, from the miseries and pain of mortal life. Thus, the soul is restored to its pure sphere, unadulterated by things human. Eleazar then compared death to sleep in which the soul is liberated from the body to enjoy complete repose, holding conversation with God and foretelling things of the future. The example of Indian philosophers is invoked—people who hasten to release their souls from their bodies through immolation leave the soul as pure as possible. Moreover, God himself has decreed defeat; the Romans cannot claim this victory. To live and see the women and children desecrated, tortured, or sold as slaves is worse than death.

Subsequently, each of the defenders of Masada is said to have executed his own family; and each of these, in turn, was killed by ten men chosen by lot. These ten were then killed by the last survivor, who then committed suicide. Only two women and five children who had hidden in a cistern escaped this fate. The following day, upon entering the fortress, the Romans were astounded and dumbstruck by the mass suicide.

Despite its inherent drama and heroic grandeur, Josephus' account of the Masada episode is not without its problems. How is it that these pious Jews chose suicide? Did Eleazar really make such speeches? Is this story really based on the reports of two women and five children who had been hiding in a cistern? And even if plausible, Eleazar's second speech sounds more like the words of a Stoic philosopher than of a commander of a group of revolutionaries on an isolated mountain fortress in a remote province of the empire. If 960 people committed suicide, where are the remains of their bodies? And why would Josephus glorify a group of people whom he hated? Let us try to resolve at least some of these problems.

In the first place, similar mass suicides are well known in antiquity generally and in Jewish history in particular. Many Jews in Jotapata and Gamla preferred killing themselves to falling into Roman hands, and the actions of the Masada defenders are therefore quite plausible. Secondly, whether all the defenders of Masada died as described or whether some actually died fighting, the fact that so few bones have been found is surprising. No convincing explanation has heretofore been offered. Thirdly, Eleazar's speeches are almost definitely the product of Josephus' pen: he most probably attempted to put into the mouth of a hero what might or should have been said at that critical moment, an exercise that was universally practiced among ancient historians. Finally, it seems that Josephus' intent in telling the story was not so much to idealize the Sicarii as to fix the blame on this group of revolutionaries. He had Eleazar take responsibility for the war, admit that he was mistaken and had sinned, and that, in the end, God had rejected the Jews. The death of the Sicarii by their own hands was a dramatic statement of the futility and misguidance of those who dared to challenge Rome. Josephus remained the fierce opponent of Jewish revolutionaries to the very end. That he packaged all this in the dramatic account which lent an aura of heroism and even admiration to the victims was not his primary intention. At best, it was the price he was willing to pay to conclude his book on a heroic and dramatic note. (See the discussion in *HJP*^{2} 1: 484–513.)

Bibliography

Aberbach, M. 1966. *The Roman-Jewish War (66–70 A.D.): Its Origins and Consequences*. London.

Cohen, S. J. D. 1979. *Josephus in Galilee and Rome*. Columbia Studies in the Classical Tradition 8. Leiden.

Goodman, M. 1987. *The Ruling Class of Judaea*. Cambridge.

Horsley, R. A. 1979. The Sicarii: Ancient Jewish Terrorists. *JR* 52: 435–58.

———. 1981. Ancient Jewish Banditry and the Revolt Against Rome, A.D. 66–70. *CBQ* 43: 409–32.

Rajak, T. 1984. *Josephus: The Historian and His Society*. Philadelphia.

Rhoads, D. M. 1976. *Israel in Revolution: 66–74 C.E.* Philadelphia.

Smallwood, E. M. 1976. *The Jews Under Roman Rule*. SJLA 20. Leiden.

L. I. Levine

JEWS IN THE NT.

There are many references to "Jews" in the NT. The meaning and interpretation of these references is a matter of debate among scholars.

A. Historical Introduction
B. "The Jews" in Matthew
C. "The Jews" in Mark
D. "The Jews" in Luke
E. "The Jews" in Paul
F. "The Jews" in John
G. Conclusion

A. Historical Introduction

The English word "Jew" is related to *Iudaeus* in Latin and *Ioudaios* in Greek; *juif* in French and *Jude* in German represent similar borrowings. Current usage distinguishes between "Jewish," an ethnic designation, and "Judaic," to refer to the religious movement (especially in the ancient period), but etymologically the same word is in question. The entire complex of adjectives and nouns ("Jew," "Jewish," "Jewry," "Judaic," "Judaism") derives from "Judah," which became the most prominent of the twelve tribes of Israel during the monarchies of David and Solomon (ca. 1000–922 B.C.). Indeed, the consolidation of power in Jerusalem clearly aroused tribal jealousy; despite its theoretically neutral location, it represented the regnant influence of the Judeans (1 Kgs 11:26–40; *BHI* 178, 179; 207, 208). The ascendancy of Judean power therefore contributed to the division of Israel into northern and southern kingdoms at the end of Solomon's reign. Notably, the name "Israel" is appropriated by the northerners, and "Judah" is accepted as the designation of the southern kingdom. In 1 and 2 Kings, the stereotyped phrases, "the book of the chronicles of the kings of Israel," and "the book of the chronicles of the kings of Judah" appear very frequently; for example, in 1 Kgs 14:19; 15:7. When the Assyrians took Samaria (722/721 B.C.), the capital of Israel, and exiled thousands of its citizens (2 Kgs 17:1–6; *BHI* 257–58), the weakened kingdom of Judah—itself practically an Assyrian satellite (2 Kgs 16:5–16; *BHI* 259–61)—was all that survived of the nation. It has been observed that "Israel" is the natural designation of the chosen people of God in their discourse with one another, while "Jew(s)" (*Ioudaios*[*oi*]) is the normal reference of outsiders to the particular folk characterized by fidelity to the Hebrew Bible and its customs (*TDNT* 3: 360–61).

"Jews" might appropriately be used by the gentile Demetrius in respect of the nation (1 Macc 10:23), and—as the conventional designation—representatives of Israel might themselves use the term, especially in diplomatic contents (1 Macc 8:18, 20; *TDNT* 3: 360–61). The usage in the Diaspora appears to have been more common as a self-designation and may refer to the people of the covenant in any part of the world (2 Macc 1:1; *TDNT* 3: 363–65). If "Israel" remained the more proper name, God's own bestowal (Gen 32:28; *TDNT* 3: 362), "the Jews" was current, especially in the Diaspora, conforming with Hellenistic usage (*TDNT* 3: 369–71).

B. "The Jews" in Matthew

The distinction between "Israel" as the true name and "Jew(s)" as a common designation appears, at first sight, to be maintained in Matthew (*TDNT* 3: 376–77). Indeed, apart from one instance, every usage is within the phrase, "King of the Jews," and appears in the speech of gentiles: the three sages (2:2), Pilate (27:11), soldiers (27:29, 37). It has been argued (*TDNT* 3: 376) that Matthew is consistent with rabbinic usage, in that a preference for "Israel" as the correct designation is preserved (2:6, 20, 21; 10:6, 23; 15:24, 31; 19:28; 27:9, 42). But the last usage of "Jews," at 28:15, subverts any such consistency, when it refers to the false story of the theft of Jesus' corpse as ". . . spread among the Jews to this day." The reference not only assumes the same perspective upon people of the covenant as the earlier statements which gentiles make; it also associates "Jews" with a false account which is designed to undermine faith in Jesus' resurrection. For that reason, the usage assumes the division of the early Christian movement from Judaism (McNeile 1957: 434).

Attempts to dispense with the usage at 28:15, as a gloss (*TDNT* 3: 376), are understandable but doomed to failure. The evidence of manuscripts is quite straightforward, and Matthew otherwise manifests the conviction that belief in Jesus amounts to a transcendence of Judaism. The statement attributed to Jesus in 8:10, "Not even in Israel have I found such faith" (compare Luke 7:9), following as it does the Sermon on the Mount, uses precisely the designation ("Israel") which contrasts the centurion's faith to the very principle of Judaism, the election of Israel. When the crowds of 9:33 marvel, "Never was anything like this seen in Israel," the force of the statement is similar; taken together, 8:10 and 9:33 may also be said to shed new light on 15:31. Finally, the phrase "King of Israel" in 27:42

(compare Mark 15:32), a taunt in the mouths of Jesus' Jewish opponents, establishes that the conceptions of Judaism are profoundly at odds with the message to which Matthew is committed. But by this point, such ironies are anticlimactic: the Jewish people have already declared, "His blood be upon us and upon our children" (27:25).

The sources of the manifest anti-Judaism of Matthew are complex. "The Jews" to some extent represent those who reject Jesus and who therefore are themselves to be represented as liars (28:15) and willful murderers (27:25), in order to vindicate the christological claims of the Church (Ruether 1974: 94, 95). Then, too, Matthew—along with the other gospels—represents the Jewish leadership as primarily responsible for Jesus' death, although the method and agency of execution were inescapably Roman. That representation was convenient for apologetic purposes on two fronts. On one front, the Roman Imperium could be exculpated in the matter of the crucifixion: the message concerning Jesus could therefore be promulgated among gentiles without giving political offence (Ruether 1974: 88, 89). The uniquely Matthean episode of the dream of Pilate's wife (27:19) serves that purpose, as well as the people's response in 27:25. On the second front, the growing tension between followers of Jesus and the emerging authorities of synagogues after the destruction of the temple (A.D. 70) made it convenient to fasten guilt on the leaders of Judaism in Jesus' day (27:20; Mark 15:11; Ruether 1974: 87–89). Ruether has aptly referred to this complex of tendencies as the "anti-Judaic left hand" of christology (p. 95). In common with a recent convention, Ruether distinguishes the anti-Judaism of the early Church from the "racial anti-Semitism" of the modern period (pp. 220–21). But the Matthean prejudice against the Jews seems not only to be theological and apologetic (the gospel sets its face against the very people who tell false stories to confound faith in the risen Jesus [28:15], and even against their children [27:25]); but there also appears to be a rejection of "Jews" as such, not merely an argument with the theology and the leadership of Judaism.

The Matthean virulence concerning the Jews may, ironically, reflect the particularly close proximity of the gospel to the structures and authority of Judaism. As in all the gospels, no doubt is left as to the milieu of Jesus and his followers: they are Jewish, root and branch (Chilton 1984). Especially in Matthew, however, the connection between Jesus and Judaism is presented as inextricable to the point that there is no valid Judaism *apart* from Jesus. For example, the Matthean Jesus claims he has come to "fulfill" the law and the prophets (5:17), and even grants that the scribes and Pharisees he attacks "sit on Moses' seat" (23:2, 3). How scriptural fulfillment is to be reconciled with Jesus' formally antithetical attitude toward Scripture in the Sermon on the Mount (5:21–48), and how leaders can be obeyed whose teaching is—in violent terms—described as hypocritical (23:13–36), are matters which are left unresolved. No doubt, such tensions reflect the complex history of the composition of the document. Within that history, one of the axes of development is an ambivalent attitude toward the Jews and Judaism. But the inexorable tendency of that axis is one of an increasing hostility. The dark side of the movement from "the lost sheep of the house of Israel" (10:6; 15:24) to "all nations" (28:19) is a mounting intolerance—on an ethnic scale—of those who reject the message of Jesus.

C. "The Jews" in Mark

The tortured ambivalence of Matthew may be contrasted with the nearly studied restraint of Mark. All uses of the term "Jews" save one are in the phrase, "King of the Jews" (15:2, 9, 12, 18, 26), and do not present any significant novelty. The uses of "Israel" in Mark (12:29; 15:32) are similarly unremarkable, although the latter is as antagonistic to Judaism as its parallel in Matt 27:42. But a uniquely Markan parenthetical notice at 7:3, 4, is startling at two levels. First, the assumption that the reader needs to be informed that "the Pharisees and all the Jews" purify their hands and vessels manifests a greater distance from the institutions of Judaism than is the case in Matthew. Second, the Markan reference to "all the Jews" holding to practices of washing "cups and pots and copper vessels" is hyperbolic and implicitly condescending (Lane 1974: 245–47). The inference that Mark is written from the point of view of a Christianity which is essentially (and self-confidently) gentile, seems inescapable.

D. "The Jews" in Luke

A similarly detached attitude toward Judaism is manifest in Luke, where narrative asides extraneously refer to "elders of the Jews" (7:3) and to "Arimathea, a city of the Jews" (23:51). Obviously, great significance must not be read into such casual references, which are superimposed upon the by-now-familiar phrase, "King of the Jews" (23:3, 37, 38). In Acts, however, an apologetic usage of "the Jews" results in an explicit anti-Judaism, which, if less virulent than Matthew's, is nonetheless more direct (Ruether 1974: 88–90). The usages are ubiquitous (amounting to some seventy-eight instances), but their pattern is straightforward. "The Jews" can be regarded as pious, and to that extent susceptible of mission (2:5, 10, 14; 10:22; 16:1; 18:2, 24; 21:20, 21; 24:24). Mission, however, proves to be the primary occasion of statements against the Jews. The assertion that Jesus is Christ is assumed to be made in the face of Jewish opposition (9:22; 13:6; 18:5, 28) and sometimes of their deadly enmity (9:23; 12:3, 11). Nonetheless, Jesus is understood to have ministered in Judea (10:39), and despite the mortal opposition of Jews, strictures against associating with gentiles were observed (11:19; 16:3) until the full significance of Peter's vision (10:28) was grasped. The move to an explicit mission amongst the gentiles is accomplished, of course, by means of Paul. He preaches in synagogues, addressing Jews and their sympathizers (13:5, 13–16; 14:1; 17:1, 10, 17; 18:4, 19; 19:8–10; 20:21; 28:17), and the result is both success (13:43) and overt resistance (13:50; 14:2, 4, 5, 19; 19:9, the last a particularly evocative moment in the development of a predominantly gentile mission). Apostolic mission is therefore cast into an odd predicament: from the point of view of the Romans, it is Jewish (16:20; 18:14, 15; 19:33, 34; 24:5; 25:8, 10; 26:3), although its primary antagonists are Jews (14:2, 4, 19; 17:5, 13; 18:12; 19:33; 20:3, 19; 21:11, 27; 24:9, 18, 19, 27; 25:2, 7, 9, 15, 24; 26:2, 4, 7, 21; 28:19). That antagonism becomes the occasion on which Paul formally turns from the Jews to the gentiles (18:5, 6; 28:23–28). The last two passages cited manifest the apologetic device which informs the usage of Acts. To the very end, it is insisted upon that some Jews believed in the preaching of and about Jesus (28:24), and yet Jewish disbelief and violence—both legal and illegal—is taken as validating an explicit emphasis upon the mission amongst gentiles. So determined a pattern is in play that it even influences the presentation of the beginning of Jesus' ministry in Luke (4:14–30; Chilton 1987: 125–56).

E. "The Jews" in Paul

The pattern of Acts may be taken as a fulfillment of the Pauline typology, in which the gospel of Jesus and his judgment is to be announced first to Jews and then also to Greeks (Rom 1:16; 2:9, 10; 3:1–8; 9:24; 1 Cor 1:24). The point for Paul, however, is not that Jewish rejection occasions a definitive preference for gentiles, as in Luke—Acts; rather, Paul insists that there is, before the one and only Lord, fundamentally "no distinction between Jew and Greek" (Rom 10:12; 3:9, 29). For just that reason, Paul can refer to the salvation of "all Israel" when he has in mind both Jews and gentiles (Rom 11:25, 26; 1 Cor 12:13; Gal 3:28; Col 3:11). On the whole, Paul is not optimistic about the conversion of his own people (Rom 9:3); despite his best efforts to accommodate to them (1 Cor 9:20; 10:32), they offer only resistance (1 Cor 1:22, 23; 2 Cor 11:24; 1 Thess 2:14). In Galatians, the Pauline ambivalence is at its most tortured. His argument that he advanced in "Judaism" beyond many of his contemporaries (1:13, 14) is used to support the claim that Jewish practices are an illegitimate incursion into the gospel (2:11–21). The next chapter of Galatians attempts to justify that position by means of the argument that the law is but a guide to the covenant of Abraham, which is fulfilled in Christ. The use of the term "Judaism" appears to have been characteristic of Hellenistic Judaism (*4 Macc* 4:26 and *TDNT* 3: 365). In another respect, as well, Paul appears distant from the ethos of Palestinian Judaism. His argument for a "circumcision of the heart, in spirit, not letter" (Rom 2:17–29) as the qualification of a person who is a Jew secretly, is more reminiscent of Philo (*Quaes Gen* 3.46–52; *Quaes Ex* 2.2) than of the rabbis. Paul, then, is torn between rejecting Judaism and redefining it.

F. "The Jews" in John

No such doubt is evident in the gospel according to John, with its approximately sixty-seven references to "the Jews." Unless it is thought that the reader might forget where the events transpired, many of these identifying references, in narrative and even in sayings of Jesus, appear quite superfluous (1:19; 2:18, 20; 3:22, 25; 11:19, 31, 33, 36, 45; 12:9; 13:33; 18:12, 14, 20, 31, 36, 38; 19:7, 12, 14, 20, 31), and the stilted explanation of Jewish customs is reminiscent of Mark (2:6, 13; 4:9; 5:1; 6:4; 7:2; 11:55; 19:40, 42). In most of these instances, practically no useful information is conveyed: to say that Jews take part in debates in Judea, or that they keep a holiday called Passover, would not educate most of the intended readers of John. The point seems rather to typify Jewish reaction to Jesus. The gospel is so imbued with the notion that Jews reject Jesus, that Nicodemus, "a leader of the Jews" (3:1), is addressed by Jesus with a paradox which causes misunderstanding (v 3). When it is borne in mind that Nicodemus has just praised Jesus in remarkably unqualified terms and has apparently visited Jesus at some personal peril (v 2), the reaction seems strange. It is as if the Jewish rejection of Jesus was not only inevitable (1:11) but divinely intended. The dialogue between Jesus and the Samaritan woman (4:1–30) best represents the attitude toward Judaism in John's gospel. Notably, Jesus is in Samaria as a result of Pharisaic opposition in Judea (4:1–3), which is effectively the territory of conflict in John. Jesus addresses a paradox to the woman (4:10), but her perplexity leads to incipient faith (v 29), where in the case of Nicodemus, perplexity brought only doubt and rebuke (3:9, 10). Theoretically, Judaism is declared superior to the worship of Samaria, "for salvation is from the Jews" (4:22), but that statement does not ensure the salvation of any particular Jew. Judaism is the source, but no longer the boundary, of God's salvific activity in sending his son (cf. 3:16–21). It is therefore not surprising when conflict, misunderstanding, and mortal opposition characterize Jesus' relationship with his Jewish contemporaries (5:10, 15, 16, 18; 6:41, 52; 7:1, 11, 13, 15, 35; 8:22, 31–33, 48, 52, 57; 9:18, 22; 10:19, 24, 31, 33; 11:8, 54; 19:38; 20:19). The synoptic phrase, "King of the Jews," is also represented in John (18:33, 39; 19:3, 19, 21), but the most evident feature in the Fourth Gospel in respect of "the Jews" is anachronism. Jews are pictured as excluding followers of Jesus from synagogues during his lifetime (9:22; 12:42; 16:2), and both Jesus and his disciples refer to "the Jews" as if to an alien group (11:8; 13:33; 18:20, 36). There seems little doubt but that such anachronisms reflect the social experience of the community in which the gospel was produced. The attitude is not yet as harsh as in the Revelation, where Jews are called a "synagogue of Satan" (2:9; 3:9), but in the Johannine literature generally there seems to be no backward glance toward Judaism, not even out of sentimentality, as in Paul, or in respect of piety, as in Luke-Acts.

G. Conclusion

The division of Judaism and Christianity is one of the paramount religious developments of late antiquity, and yet the causes, the mechanisms, and the timing of that division are all matters of speculation and debate. That the central figure of the NT was regarded in his own time as a rabbi, and that his first disciples were Jewish, cannot reasonably be doubted; on the other hand, a definitive break with Judaism is reflected in Luke-Acts, John, and the Revelation, assumed in Mark, struggled for in Paul, and agonized over in Matthew. Of course, the use of the term "Jew(s)" is only one criterion of this development; documents such as Hebrews and 1 Peter obviously evidence a relationship with Judaism, although they make no reference to Jews as such. But the use of "Jew(s)" in the NT makes it obvious beyond any doubt that the division came about for social, not immediately ideological, reasons.

The simple fact that some Jews—indeed an eventual majority—did not accept the message concerning Jesus is a necessary, but not a sufficient, condition of the usage of the NT. The nature of that negative response, and of the reaction of early Christians, needs also to be taken into account. After the destruction of the temple, Judaism came increasingly to be a religion of Scripture and tradition, centered upon the Hebrew Bible and the Mishnah.

Jerusalem, the actual, urban, and cultic center could no longer serve as a cohesive focus, and religious authority came increasingly to be located in the expository functions of rabbis. Where the priestly hierarchy had concerned itself principally with what was done in association with sacrificial worship, rabbinic power influenced first of all what was said and thought; and only on that basis could it determine what was done. One index of that development is a Haggadah told of Rabbi Eliezer ben Hyrcanos, an ardent traditionalist who flourished at the end of the 1st century and the beginning of the 2d. Denounced before a Roman judge, Eliezer explained to his disciples that his condemnation was just, since he had once discussed a point of Scripture with a follower of Jesus (*Abodah Zarah* 16b, 17a). See GAMALIEL (PERSON). Apparently, what was once considered acceptable came to be seen as intolerable. Christianity, in the meantime, came more and more to be dominated by the perspective of gentiles, to whom Jewish customs had either laboriously to be explained or else simplistically to be derided. Within the movement of gentile Christianity, christology became the common denominator, rather than the kingdom of God, an explicitly early Jewish concept which Jesus himself had emphasized. The NT, in its reference to "the Jews," manifests various stages in the social interactions which produced, out of the ferment of early Judaism, two mutually hostile stepchildren: rabbinic Judaism, which sought the sanctification of life by means of Scripture and tradition, and Christianity, which anticipated the redemption of life by means of the messiah promised in Scripture (Neusner 1985).

Bibliography

Chilton, B. D. 1984. *A Galilean Rabbi and His Bible.* GNS 8. Wilmington, DE.

———. 1987. *God in Strength: Jesus' Announcement of the Kingdom.* The Biblical Seminar. Sheffield.

Lane, W. L. 1974. *The Gospel of Mark.* New London Commentary on the New Testament. London.

McNeile, A. D. 1957. *The Gospel According to St. Matthew.* London.

Neusner, J. N. 1985. The Jewish-Christian Argument in the First Century. *CC* 35: 148–58.

Richardson, P., and Grankou, D., eds. 1986. *Anti-Judaism in Early Christianity 1. Paul and the Gospels.* Studies in Christianity and Judaism 2. Waterloo.

Ruether, R. R. 1974. *Faith and Fratricide.* New York.

Wilson, S. G., ed. 1986. *Anti-Judaism in Early Christianity 2. Separation and Polemic.* Studies in Christianity and Judaism 2. Waterloo.

Bruce Chilton

JEZANIAH (PERSON) [Heb *yĕzanyāhû, yĕzanyāh*]. **1.** Son of the Maacathite and one of the troop commanders, who, following the destruction of Jerusalem in 587/586 B.C., chose to join Gedaliah, the ruler of Judah, at his administrative center at Mizpah (Jer 40:8; spelled "Jaazaniah" in some mss and in the parallel passage 2 Kgs 25:23). It is possible that he is to be identified with the Jaazaniah whose name appears on a contemporary seal from Tell en-Nasbeh. See JAAZANIAH (PERSON).

2. In the Hebrew text of Jer 42:1, reference is made to Jezaniah, son of Hoshaiah. However, this reading is clearly to be emended following the LXX (cf. also the MT of Jer 43:2) to read "Azariah son of Hoshaiah" (cf. RSV, JB, NAB, NEB). See AZARIAH (PERSON).

John M. Berridge

JEZEBEL (PERSON) [Heb *ʾîzebel*]. **1.** The daughter of Ethbaal, king of the Sidonians, and wife of Ahab the son of Omri and king of Israel (1 Kgs 16:29–31). As it is vocalized in the MT, the name Jezebel is probably a two-layered parody. The original name *ʾîzĕbūl* ("Where is the Prince?") first became *ʾî-zĕbūl* ("No nobility"). *Zĕbūl,* a title of Baal, was then distorted into *zebel* ("dung"; cf. 2 Kgs 9:37).

The biblical texts present a thoroughly negative picture of this undoubtedly powerful woman. Jezebel became the influential queen of the N kingdom as the foreign wife of Ahab. She fostered the worship of Canaanite fertility deities, supporting 450 prophets of Baal and 400 prophets of the goddess Asherah at her royal table (1 Kgs 18:19). In the meantime, she ruthlessly persecuted the rival prophets of Yahweh, causing them to go into hiding (1 Kgs 18:4). The great Elijah himself did not underestimate her death threats (19:1–3). Moreover, she contrived the legal death of Naboth the Jezreelite so that her husband could obtain his vineyard (1 Kings 21). Because of her so-called "harlotries and sorceries" (2 Kgs 9:22), she met her ignominious death at the hands of Jehu. But her death was not without dramatic flourish. Hearing the news of Jehu's massacre of the royal family, Jezebel "painted her eyes and adorned her hair." Looking down at her adversary from her window, she ridiculed Jehu as an upstart claimant to the throne like his predecessor, Zimri. Her harem eunuchs, sensing changes in power in Jehu's favor, flung her down from the window at Jehu's command. Jehu, whose appetite seemingly was not affected by the gruesome death ("he went in and ate and drank"), begrudgingly ordered a burial for the "cursed woman," since "she is a king's daughter." However, fulfilling Elijah's prophecy that "the dogs shall eat the flesh of Jezebel" (2 Kgs 9:30–37; cf. 1 Kgs 21:23), all that remained of Jezebel's body was her skull, feet, and hands.

In depicting her mainly as the unscrupulous foreign woman who illicitly intruded in affairs of her royal husband, the biblical texts gloss over the fact that Jezebel probably wielded considerable authority in her position as queen. According to Brenner (1985), Jezebel had two sources of power. The first was her status in her Phoenician homeland. As daughter of Ethbaal, king of the Sidonians, she was a princess by birth. According to Josephus (*Ant* 8.13.2), Ethbaal was also a priest in the Phoenician cult of the goddess Astarte (Ashtoreth). Brenner suggests that Phoenicia followed the Mesopotamian practice of appointing the king's daughter as the high priestess of the chief local god, in this case, Baal Melqart. With the king as high priest and his daughter serving as high priestess, links between the monarchy and the state religion were considerably strengthened. Together, the two were able to wield substantial political, economic, and religious power over the land. Hence, when Jezebel came to Israel she was accustomed to being an active participant in government. She promoted the cult of Baal, which had long enjoyed extensive support in Israel, since her status as the god's high priestess was integral to her authority as queen.

Another power base was derived from her husband, Ahab. In spite of the negative bias of the Deuteronomistic framework, the texts reveal that she was an active partner in her husband's rule. Her religious and political skills made her a natural colleague in his administration. She had enough material resources to support the 450 prophets of Baal and 400 prophets of Asherah at *her* table. Moreover, the Naboth story indicates that her letters written in Ahab's name and the use of the king's seal were routine acts on her part, rather than an illegitimate usurpation of authority. There is no suggestion that these exercises of power were restricted just to the Naboth episode. Brenner thinks that Ahab allowed Jezebel to carry on in her religious and political role because it strengthened his own rule more effectively. The biblical narrators would have suppressed information of Jezebel as high priestess of Baal, since they did not acknowledge the validity of a female priesthood and the authority inherent in it.

2. A prophetess in the church of Thyatira who, according to Rev 2:20–23, "beguiles" the congregation "to practice immorality and to eat food sacrificed to idols." Although she was probably a real person, her name Jezebel seems to be symbolic. It refers pejoratively to the "harlotries and sorceries" of the OT queen who supported the prophets of Baal and Asherah at her court (2 Kgs 9:22; 1 Kgs 18:19).

Bibliography

Ackroyd, P. R. 1983. Goddesses, Women and Jezebel. Pp. 245–59 in *Images of Women in Antiquity*, ed. A. Cameron and A. Kurht. Detroit.

Brenner, A. 1985. *The Israelite Woman*. Sheffield.

GALE A. YEE

JEZER (PERSON) [Heb *yēṣer*]. JEZERITES. The third of the four sons of Naphtali (Gen 46:24; 1 Chr 7:13). Jezer was the grandson of Jacob and Bilhah (Gen 30:7–8), the maid whom Rachel gave to her husband (Gen 30:3). At the time when Jacob descended into Egypt to visit Joseph, seven children and grandchildren of Jacob and Bilhah were mentioned in his genealogy (Gen 46:25). According to Westermann (1986: 153) and Noth (*IPN*, 172), Jezer's name was a short form of a theophoric name, probably meaning "Formed by God," following the idea present in Gen 2:7 and Jer 1:5. Jezer became the head of the Jezerites, one of the clans of Naphtali (Num 26:49). Jezer and his clan are not mentioned anywhere else in the OT outside of the genealogy of Naphtali.

Bibliography

Westermann, C. 1986. *Genesis 37–50*. Trans. J. J. Scullion. Minneapolis.

CLAUDE F. MARIOTTINI

JEZIEL (PERSON) [Heb *yĕzûʾēl* K; *yĕzîʾēl* Q]. One of the ambidextrous warriors from the tribe of Benjamin who joined David during the period of David's flight from Saul (1 Chr 12:3). He was a brother of Pelet and son of Azmaveth; Azmaveth should perhaps be identified with David's warriors in 11:33. In LXX^B,S^, his name was given as *ioel* (Joel), probably because a text was read without the letter *zayin* in the name. The Chronicler has doubled the list of warriors who supported David (1 Chr 11:41b–12:40) beyond what was contained in the parallel narrative (2 Sam 23:8–39 = 1 Chr 11:10–41a). The source for these additional lists can only be a matter of conjecture, though Williamson has provided a convincing argument for the structure of 1 Chronicles 11–12. The long list reflects the Chronicler's concern to show "all Israel" united in support of David, a characteristic theme of his history. Within the immediate context (1 Chr 12:1–8—Eng 12:1–7) the Chronicler is concerned with showing the support David enjoyed among Saul's kinsmen before Saul's death; the 23 Benjaminite warriors named here joined David while he was at Ziklag, the Philistine city given to David by Achish, king of Gath (1 Chr 12:1; 1 Sam 27:6). Ambidexterity or left-handedness among Benjaminites is also noted in Judg 3:15; 20:16.

Bibliography

Williamson, H. G. M. 1981. We Are Yours, O David. *OTS* 21: 164–76.

RAYMOND B. DILLARD

JEZRAHIAH (PERSON) [Heb *yizraḥyāh*]. Director of the choir at the dedication of the Jerusalem wall (Neh 12:42). His name is omitted in the LXX. The name, which means "Yahweh will shine forth," is the same as that of an Issacharite in 1 Chr 7:3 (RSV Izrahiah).

NORA A. WILLIAMS

JEZREEL (PERSON) [Heb *yizrĕʿeʾl*]. **1.** A descendant of Judah (1 Chr 4:3), usually understood as the eponymous ancestor or personification of the town of Jezreel in Judah (Josh 15:56). See JEZREEL (PLACE).

2. The symbolic name which the prophet Hosea gave, at God's command, to his oldest child, a son (Hos 1:4). In Hebrew, the name "Jezreel" (*yizrĕʿeʾl*) is very similar to "Israel" (*yiśrāʾēl*). The prophet plays on the similarity; Jezreel is a sign of Israel's fate.

The significance of "Jezreel" is twofold. In the first place, the name "Jezreel" recalls Jehu's bloodguilt and anticipates divine judgment against Jehu's dynasty (Hos 1:4–5). Jehu violently overthrew the Omride dynasty in the town of Jezreel, murdering King Joram, the queen mother Jezebel, their leading officials, and the Judean king Ahaziah (2 Kgs 9:1–10:11). Hosea announces that the house of Jehu will be punished with military defeat in the valley of Jezreel (Hos 1:4–5).

Secondly, "Jezreel" suggests divine beneficence. The Hebrew word means "God sows"; the valley of Jezreel is particularly fertile. In Hos 2:25—Eng 2:23, the prophet plays on the positive sense of the name to reverse the earlier word of judgment (cf. also 2:2; 2:24—Eng 1:11; 2:22). The precise meaning of the wordplay is disputed; it may be a promise to Israel of fertility, or it may mean that Israel will be firmly established in the land. In either case, the significance of the child's name is reversed and applied to the whole of Israel, becoming a sign of restoration and hope beyond judgment.

CAROLYN J. PRESSLER

JEZREEL (PLACE) [Heb *yizrĕʿeʾl*]. JEZREELITE. This toponym can be translated as "God sows" or "May God make fruitful." The name is associated with two distinct towns, as well as with a major geographical component of the Israelite kingdom.

1. A town in the tribal inheritance of Issachar (Josh 19:18), which scholars (*HGB*, 42) almost universally identify with Zerin/Tel Yizraʿal (M.R. 181218). The site is located at the E end of a fertile valley which shares the name Jezreel with the town. Jezreel is not mentioned in any ancient source prior to the Iron Age, so the site would seem to be an Iron Age foundation.

The first OT event associated with the site occurs during the preparations for Saul's battle at Gilboa, when the Israelite army camps at a spring near Jezreel (1 Sam 29:1). Under Solomon, Jezreel appears in the border description of the fifth district of the kingdom (1 Kgs 4:12), but serves to limit the district instead of being included within it. Jezreel was probably part of the tenth district of the kingdom (*LBHG*, 315). The town is absent from the list Shishak compiled of his conquests in Israel in the latter part of the 10th century B.C., so it is unlikely that the city was of much political importance at that time (*LBHG*, 327).

By the reign of Ahab (9th century B.C.), Jezreel had become the winter capital of the Israelite kingdom. As a political center, the town was the setting for a number of sanguinary events. Although the site has never been extensively excavated, the OT records that at the time of Ahab the city was defended by a city wall, which had at least one tall tower (2 Kgs 9:17). Ahab's palace was located in Jezreel and would seem to have had an upper story with windows (2 Kgs 9:32).

During Ahab's reign, a number of events occurred at Jezreel. Following the test between Elijah and the prophets of Baal and Asherah on the Carmel, Elijah is said to have run before Ahab's chariot when he returned to his palace in Jezreel (1 Kgs 18:46). A vineyard alongside the palace, belonging to Naboth the Jezreelite (1 Kgs 21:1), was coveted by Ahab and his queen Jezebel. When Naboth refused to sell his inheritance, Jezebel engineered his execution as a traitor (1 Kgs 21:10), so Ahab could acquire the property. Elijah cursed Ahab and his entire house for this crime (1 Kgs 21:23–24). See NABOTH (PERSON).

This curse was not carried out until the reign of Joram, Ahab's son. Jehu, commander of Joram's army, after being anointed by a disciple of Elijah, led a coup against Joram, killing him outside Jezreel and casting his corpse into Naboth's former vineyard (2 Kgs 9:25). On Jehu's order, Jezebel, Joram's mother, was thrown out of a palace window by palace eunuchs, and her corpse was trampled by Jehu's horses (2 Kgs 9:33). During the course of the coup, Jehu piled the heads of 70 sons of Ahab outside the gates of Jezreel, before killing all of Ahab's supporters within the city (2 Kgs 10:10).

As a part of this episode, the MT states (2 Kgs 10:1) that the elders of Jezreel were among the recipients of letters sent by Jehu concerning the fate of the sons of Ahab, who were living in Samaria. This passage is frequently emended (Cogan and Tadmor *2 Kings* AB, 113) on the grounds that since Jehu was in Jezreel at the time, the officials there would seem to have had little impact on the fate of the princes in Samaria.

By the time of Hosea (8th century B.C.), Jezreel had become a powerful symbol of the guilt of the Israelite kingdom, which was to be punished by destruction (Hos 1:4). The theological import of the prophetic passages referring to Jezreel in Hosea 1–2 is open to a number of interpretations (Andersen and Freedman *Hosea* AB, 172–86).

When the Assyrians destroyed the N kingdom of Israel, Jezreel lost its political importance, which was never regained. During the Hellenistic period the name of the town had become Esdraelon, the Greek version of Jezreel, from which the modern Zerin is derived.

In 2 Sam 2:9, Jezreel appears as part of a description of the kingdom of Ishbosheth, inherited from his father Saul. In this instance it seems clear that Jezreel represents a territory beyond that of the city itself, perhaps as large as the lands of Issachar and Naphtali (*HGB*, 31), although some doubt the ability of Ishbosheth actually to control the region following the defeat at Gilboa (McCarter *2 Samuel* AB, 87).

The use of Jezreel as a regional term leads to the question of the relationship of the town to the valley of the same name. Most scholars (cf. *LBHG*, 24) assume that the Jezreel valley stretched W from Jezreel to the plain of Acco and S to Ibleam (M.R. 177205). Some would extend the valley as far E as the Jordan (Pritchard 1987: 114), although most consider that region to be part of the valley of Beth-shean. A minority restrict the extent of the valley of Jezreel to the territory of the town itself (*GTTOT*, 31).

Whatever its exact extent, the Jezreel valley was a vital strategic link on the route between Egypt and Damascus. The valley was the scene of recorded conflict from the time of Thutmose III in the LB Age through the 1967 Arab-Israeli war. Its fertile land, which perhaps inspired the name "God sows," can make the valley an agricultural breadbasket, although neglect of drainage and conservation measures can turn much of it into an unhealthy marsh, as it was early in this century.

2. A town in the territorial inheritance of the tribe of Judah (Josh 15:56), as yet unidentified. Abel's (*GP* 2, 364) suggested identification with Kh. Terrama (M.R. 153098), although accepted by Rogerson (*RAB*, 94), should be rejected since the other towns mentioned in the passage are located to the SE of Hebron. This Jezreel would seem to have been the birthplace of Ahinoam (1 Sam 25:43), wife of David and the mother of his first son, Amnon, although Levenson and Halpern (1980: 513ff.) raise the possibility that Ahinoam came from the N Jezreel.

Bibliography

Levenson, J. D., and Halpern, B. 1980. The Political Import of David's Marriages. *JBL* 99: 507–18.

Pritchard, J. B. 1987. *The Harper Atlas of the Bible*. New York.

MELVIN HUNT

JIB, EL. See GIBEON (PLACE).

JIDLAPH (PERSON) [Heb *yidlāp*]. The seventh son of Abraham's brother Nahor and of Milcah (Gen 22:22). The name occurs here in a list made up mostly of personal names, and no evidence currently exists that it is also a name of a town or a region. In fact, it is otherwise unknown, and there is no ready explanation for it. Both "he weeps" and "he is sleepless" have been suggested as possible meanings. See *HALAT,* 214, 373, for the potential Hebrew root or roots and Semitic cognates and for citations of some literature which discusses them. Westermann (1985: 367) believes that the names among which Jidlaph appears do not make up a tribal enumeration. Rather, one has to reckon with a gradual development from a genealogical form still centered in the family to later tribal lists (cf. 25:13–16; 36:15–19). Kidner (*Genesis* TOTC, 144) considers the name to be of interest chiefly as an indication of Israel's consciousness of distant kinships.

Bibliography

Westermann, C. 1985. *Genesis 12–36.* Trans. J. J. Scullion. Minneapolis.

EDWIN C. HOSTETTER

JILAT, WADI AL-. A drainage catchment of about 160 km² at an altitude between 967 and 755 m, which lies in the SW portion of the AZRAQ basin on the Jordanian plateau.

Wadi al-Jilat is a tributary of the Wadi al-Dabi (Wadi Dhobai), which feeds into Qa al-Azraq. The area currently receives less than 100 mm of rainfall per year and lies vegetationally at the divide between steppe and desert. The surface geology comprises late Cretaceous and early Tertiary limestones, chalks, marls, and cherts, and there are more recent conglomerates and travertines in the valley floor. In an otherwise arid area, Wadi al-Jilat is attractive to settlement because the wadi has incised a shallow gorge in which water is often retained well after the end of the rainy season. Now, this is used on a seasonal basis by bedouin who pasture their sheep, goats, and camels on the sparse vegetation.

The Wadi al-Jilat was also attractive for settlement in the late Glacial and early post-Glacial periods (ca. 25,000–4500 B.C.). In the 1930s Waechter located and sounded a number of sites along the valley floor (Waechter et al. 1938) with flaked chert industries, which he described as "Aurignacian" and "Dhobaian" (he misidentified the location as Wadi Dhobai). More recently, Garrard has resurveyed the valley (Garrard et al. 1985) and located a total of twenty-six Stone Age sites. One of these is Upper Paleolithic (ca. 25,000–20,000 B.C.), at least four are late Epipaleolithic (ca. 12,000–7500 B.C.), and six are Neolithic (7500–4500 B.C.). The latter divide into Pre-Pottery Neolithic B and burin sites, and have stone structures visible on their surfaces. Five sites ranging from Upper Paleolithic to Neolithic were sounded by Garrard (Garrard et al. 1986).

In addition to the prehistoric sites, Glueck (1951), Field (1960), and King (King et al. 1983) have described two dams in the valley. The major dam is 28.85 m long and 5.80 m high, but only the downstream side is visible due to silting. This is faced with well-dressed ashlar masonry and is supported by three rectangular buttresses. It is also banked, with each succeeding stone course set slightly back from the lower one. It is covered with washum and graffiti, but no dating inscription exists. The ruin of a second smaller and more poorly built dam lies downstream, blocking a side wadi. Glueck (1951) suggested a Roman date for the main dam, but King (King et al. 1983) only found Byzantine and Umayyad sherds during his group's survey of the area. Since there are Umayyad parallels for such dams in the Hijaz, and there are a number of substantial Umayyad structures in the Jordan desert (castles and cisterns), the dam seems likely to date to this later period.

Bibliography

Field, H. 1960. North Arabian Desert Archaeological Survey 1925–1950. *Papers of Peabody Museum, Harvard* 45.

Garrard, A.; Byrd, B.; and Betts, A. 1986. Prehistoric Environment and Settlement in the Azraq Basin. *Levant* 18: 5–24.

Garrard, A.; Byrd, B.; Harvey, P.; and Hivernel, F. 1985. Prehistoric Environment and Settlement in the Azraq Basin. *Levant* 17: 1–28.

Glueck, N. 1951. *Explorations in Eastern Palestine, IV,* Pt. 1. AASOR 25–28. New Haven.

King, G.; Lenzen, C. J.; and Rollefson, G. O. 1983. Survey of Byzantine and Islamic Sites in Jordan. *ADAJ* 27: 385–436.

Waechter, J. d'A.; Seton-Williams, V. M.; Bate, D. A.; and Picard, L. 1938. The Excavations at Wadi Dhobai, 1937–38 and the Dhobaian Industry. *JPOS* 18: 172–86.

ANDREW N. GARRARD

JISR BANAT YAᶜAQUB (M.R. 209268). The Lower Paleolithic site of Jisr Banat Yaᶜaqub (Heb Gesher Bnot Yaacov) is located in the N sector of the Syrian/African Rift system, some 4 km S of the Huleh valley. Paleontological remains and lithic artifacts from the site were found in 1933 during the construction of a bridge over the Jordan river.

Between 1936 and 1951, M. Stekelis (1960) carried out a survey and excavations N and S of the bridge. It became evident that the site continues along the course of the Jordan below the present water level and was identifiable on both banks. These observations were corroborated by D. Gilead (1970) through an additional test pit. Proximity to the Syrian/Israeli border, the high-water level of the Jordan, and the various drainage activities have never enabled a thorough and prolonged field study at Jisr Banat Yaᶜaqub (J.B.Y.).

The prehistoric and paleontological finds are bedded in the Benot Yaacov Formation, which is exposed at the bridge and also known from bore holes drilled in the Huleh valley. The formation was initially described by Picard (1952) as the "Viviparus Beds," due to the dominance of this mollusk species in the sediment.

The Benot Yaacov Formation is bedded unconformably on the Yarda Basalt. This basalt flow yielded a radiometric age of 640,000 ± 120,000 years, and thus contributes indirectly toward dating the implentiferous beds.

Stekelis' observations at J.B.Y. resulted in a stratigraphic sequence of six strata. Layer V is characterized by a lithic assemblage shaped on basalt and is assigned to the Middle Acheulian. The biface component (cleavers and handaxes) was modified by the "bloc on bloc" technique. The typological proportions of handaxes and cleavers are 51 percent and 49 percent, respectively. The specific choice of basalt, the technique of manufacture, and the interbiface group frequencies are all unique to this layer and are not known elsewhere in Israel. These features are known from African sites; their presence at J.B.Y. might demonstrate the penetration of an African tradition into the Levant. The artifacts from Layers II–IV were modified on flint and manifest the earliest known appearance of the Levallois technique; the biface types/shapes are more evolved than those of Layer V, and the assemblage is assigned to the Upper Acheulian.

The uniqueness of the lithic assemblage, the paleontological assemblage, and the recent discovery of human paleontological remains, as well as the palynological analysis, all demonstrate the importance of the site to Pleistocene research in the Levant.

Bibliography

Bar-Yosef, O. 1975. Archaeological Occurrences in the Middle Pleistocene of Israel. Pp. 571–604 in *After the Australopithecines: Stratigraphy, Ecology and Culture Change in the Middle Pleistocene,* ed. K. W. Butzer and G. LL. Isaac. Chicago.

Geraads, D., and Tchernov, E. 1983. Femurs Humains du Pleistocene Moyen de Gesher Benot Ya'acov (Israel). *L'Anthropologie* 87/1: 138–41.

Gilead, D. 1970. Handaxe Industries in Israel and the Near East. *WoAr* 2: 1–11.

Goren, N. 1981. The Lower Palaeolithic in Israel and Adjacent Countries. In *Prehistoire du Levant,* ed. J. Cauvin and P. Sanlaville. Paris.

Hooijer, D. A. 1959. Fossil Mammals from Jisr Banat Yaqub. South of Lake Hula, Israel. *Bulletin Research Council of Israel* G8: 177–79.

Horowitz, A. 1973. Development of the Hula Basin, Israel. *Israel Journal of Earth Sciences* 22: 107–39.

———. 1979. *The Quaternary of Israel.* New York.

Horowitz, A.; Siedner, G.; and Bar-Yosef, O. 1973. Radiometric Dating of the Ubeidiya Formation, Jordan Valley, Israel. *Nature* 242: 186–87.

Picard, L. 1943. Structure and Evolution of Palestine. *Bulletin of the Geology Department, Hebrew University, Jerusalem* 4/2–4: 1–134.

———. 1952. The Pleistocene Peat of Lake Hula. *Bulletin of Research Council of Israel* G2/2: 147–56.

Stekelis, M. 1960. The Palaeolithic Deposits of Jisr Banat Yacub. *Bulletin of Research Council of Israel* G8: 61–89.

Tchernov, E. 1979. Quaternary Fauna. Pp. 259–90 in *The Quaternary of Israel,* ed. A. Horowitz. New York.

N. Goren-Inbar

JOAB (PERSON) [Heb *yôʾāb*]. Joab is a simple Hebrew name consisting of a theophoric element—*yô,* for "Yahweh"—in a nominal clause. Its meaning is "Yahweh is father"; hence, Joab is only formally different from Abijah.

1. In the Hebrew Bible, the name Joab is applied primarily to the commander in chief of David's army. This Joab was the son of David's sister, Zeruiah; he was one of three brothers—Joab, Abishai, and Asahel—who played a critical role in the establishment of David's military power. Abishai, at one time or another the commander of both the foreign mercenaries and the king's special corps of *šālišîm* (see DAVID'S CHAMPIONS), served as a kind of adjutant to Joab throughout David's reign (cf. 2 Sam 10:9–14; 20:4–22) and probably died sometime before Solomon's coup. Asahel was killed during the long war between the houses of David and Saul. Joab, the central figure of the three, was the commander of David's assembled armed forces, both the levies and the various components of the professional army. This view is in contrast to that usually expressed; namely, that Joab commanded the levies while Benaiah, the son of Jehoiada, commanded the professional soldiery. In fact, Joab is more often than not depicted as in command of the professional troops (cf. 2 Sam 10:7; the "mighty men" were elite troops and formed a separate category from both the levies and the regular professional soldiers—"the men of war" [cf. Schley *ISBE* 4: 564–65]; another category was the *šālišîm,* a small body of elite warriors loyal only to the king, as well as the foreign mercenaries and the bodyguard). Joab also appears to have had his own body of armor bearers (2 Sam 18:15) and his own following within the army (2 Sam 20:11). Even the doomed Uriah called Joab "my lord" to David, to whom he supposedly owed his highest loyalty (2 Sam 11:11). Joab is credited with taking the royal city of the Ammonites on his own (2 Sam 12:26–28) as well as defeating the Syrians (2 Sam 10:6–14) and Edomites (Ps 60:1—Eng superscript: Joab killed twelve thousand Edomites in the Valley of Salt; a similar feat is ascribed to Abishai in 1 Chr 18:12 and to David in 2 Sam 8:13–14). These are hardly the achievements of a commander of reserves. Joab was the leading military figure of David's reign, a professional soldier to whom all answered, a man who has been called "the gray eminence" of the Davidic era.

The testimony of the Davidic narratives carries a strange ambivalence toward Joab, depicting him both as the staunchest supporter of David, with no ambition for the throne himself, and as the Judean king's chief adversary at the court, at one point even threatening revolt (2 Sam 19:5–7). If the incidental evidence of the Davidic narratives is to be believed, Joab was the power behind David's throne, whether for good or for ill. To him are attributed the murders of the two commanders of the army of Israel, Abner the son of Ner (2 Sam 3:26–30) and Amasa the son of Jether (2 Sam 20:4–13). Joab is also reported to have had the rebel Absalom killed against the express orders of the king (2 Sam 18:1–15), a deliberate act for which he did not apologize and which appears to have cost him his high standing for a time (2 Sam 19:13). There are thus three clear instances in which Joab countermanded the king's wishes and slew, rightly or wrongly, persons in favor with David.

At the same time, Joab, along with his brother Abishai, was the trusted agent of David's policies. According to Chronicles, Joab achieved his leadership of the army when he led a daring raid up the watershaft to seize the city of the Jebusites for David (1 Chr 11:4–9; his name was not included in this tradition in the corresponding passage in 2 Sam 5:6–9). It was Joab who, with his brother Abishai, prosecuted the Ammonite and Syrian wars (2 Samuel 10–12) and yet gave the honor to David (2 Sam 12:26–30), though David had ceased to engage in direct military campaigns (2 Sam 21:15–17). Again, the two remaining sons of Zeruiah, along with the Philistine condottiere, Ittai of Gath, brought David the victory over Absalom (2 Sam 18:1–17) and put down the rebellion of Sheba, the son of Bichri (2 Sam 20:1–22). Joab elsewhere carried out David's cover-up of his affair with Uriah's wife (2 Sam 11:14–25) and interceded with David on behalf of Absalom (who had avenged the rape of his sister Tamar by slaying his brother Amnon—2 Sam 14:1–24). Conversely, Joab used harsh words to bring David to greet the troops after the death of Absalom and the dispersal of the rebel army (2 Sam 19:1–8b), and it was Joab who carried out David's ill-fated census of the people of Israel, though he had vehemently argued against the measure (2 Sam 24:1–14).

So great was Joab's influence in the Davidic court that he almost succeeded in putting Adonijah, Solomon's older brother, on the throne. Joab's support of Adonijah, in fact, seems to have divided the regime along the lines of the "old guard" and the "new men." The old priest Abiathar supported Adonijah, too, but Solomon found his support in the prophet Nathan, his mother Bathsheba, Benaiah, the son of Jehoiada, newly promoted to command the foreign mercenaries (probably following the death of Abishai), and the priest Zadok, probably a Jebusite, who founded the Zadokite line of priests in Jerusalem. The defeat of Adonijah's party may have been the result of a weakening of Joab's position on account of the absence of Abishai, Joab's brother and longtime adjutant. When Solomon's party came to power, the new king had Abiathar banished. Joab, however, he had killed, fulfilling his deathbed promise to his father to clear the family line of the bloodguilt of Abner and Amasa, whom Joab had slain. In a poignant scene, Joab clings to the horns of the altar for refuge and refuses to come out to die at the hands of Benaiah. "I will die here," he says, refusing either to apologize for his deeds or to seek clemency. In doing so, he embodies an ancient military tradition, that of making neither excuse nor apology for one's actions. If he is to be executed, he will force his enemies to violate the sanctity of the altar, under the protection of which he had so long fought for David, and the name of whose god he bore. That his overt religiosity was devoid of ethical content (Dalglish *IDB* 2: 908) is disputable today, and would have been challenged in his own day as well. After all, the views of Joab's political opponents prevailed in the matter and have guided the efforts to justify the old warrior's fate. In reality his execution was a judicial murder—the slaying of a loyal retainer out of political expedience. Certainly Solomon began his reign with a somewhat different "inner circle" of advisers from that of his father, one which was far more aloof from the ancient traditions and sentiments of the people than David's had been.

From a literary standpoint, the death of Joab served to bring to a close that haunting theme of the Davidic narratives—David's complicity in the deaths of Saul and his sons and successors, and the demise of his house. That Joab would be the final sacrifice in this saga is presaged in David's curse on Joab after the slaying of Abner—"May it [the blood of Abner] fall upon Joab, and upon all his father's house; and may the house of Joab never be without one who has a discharge, or who is leprous, or who holds a spindle, or who is slain by the sword, or who lacks bread!" (2 Sam 3:29; cf. Holloway 1987: 370–75). The way to his death, even at the hands of one who had served with him, is prepared by the rising crescendo of condemnation of the sons of Zeruiah by David (usually in response to Abishai's ruthlessness: cf. 2 Sam 3:39; 16:5–14; 19:16–23). This theme culminates in the infamous scene where the dying monarch names to his son and successor the unsettled scores his heir must even (1 Kgs 2:1–9). David's orders include the command to kill Joab through treachery ("use your wisdom [i.e., cunning], but do not let his gray hairs go down to Sheol in peace"). David reasons that Joab's slaying of Abner and Amasa has brought bloodguilt upon him and his house (a serious concern in ancient times), and that Joab must be slain to cleanse the stain from David's line. Thus, Joab is made to bear the bloodguilt for David's treatment of Saul and his family, a bloodguilt which, in the minds of most Israelites, probably extended far beyond the deaths of Abner and Amasa (see the curse of Shimei, 2 Sam 16:7–8, and the proscription of Saul's remaining sons in 2 Sam 21:1–6). Joab thus serves as the scapegoat for David's own bloody treatment of his political opponents. With Abishai, he also provides a violent foil for the depiction of David as a man of suffering renunciation, a motif which is used to exculpate David in the very matters in which Joab is to be blamed.

The Joab of history and literature is a complex figure, a man of shrewd judgment, ruthless energy, and potentially great treachery, who nonetheless sought no more than to look out for his own interests in the context of his greater service to his king. Joab seems in many respects to have functioned almost independently of David; at least he was willing to act on his own judgment when a weak and injudicious king threatened the longevity of the kingdom, as in Absalom's revolt. One suspects that David both depended upon and resented Joab's autonomy. Joab, for his part, seems to have remained content to let the military power of the kingdom accrue to himself (a significant portion of royal authority in the ANE), while leaving to his uncle, David, the public honor. Joab's career cannot be understood apart from his strong family and party ties to David's cause, probably from the time of David's exile in the wilderness (1 Sam 22:1–2): family loyalties tied Joab's career inextricably to that of David, and Joab, better than anyone, would have grasped and exploited this connection. At the end of his life he was probably a man of unequaled public esteem; for his military exploits alone, he may have enjoyed a popularity far wider than David's, at least among the soldiery. The effort expended to condemn him is the best measure of his stature in the kingdom.

2. One of the descendants of the house of Kenaz, a family of craftsmen (better, smiths) in the tribe of Judah, who dwelt in the "valley of smiths" (1 Chr 4:14).

3. The eponymous ancestor of a Judean clan which returned from the Babylonian exile with Zerubbabel. The clan is regularly listed as "the sons of Pahath-moab, namely, the sons of Jeshua and Joab" (Ezra 2:6; Neh 7:11). This family was still on hand in the time of Ezra the scribe, when it was headed by Obadiah, the son of Jehiel (Ezra 8:9; 1 Esdr 8:35).

Bibliography

Alt, A. 1930. *Die Staatenbildung der Israeliten in Palästina.* Leipzig. Repr. 1960. The Formation of the Israelite State in Palestine.

Pp. 171–237 in *Essays in Old Testament History and Religion.* Trans. R. A. Wilson. Oxford.
———. 1950. Das Grossreich Davids. *TLZ* 75: 213–20. Repr. 1953. *KlSchr* 2: 66–75.
Holloway, S. W. 1987. Distaff, Crutch or Chain Gang: The Curse of the House of Joab in 2 Sam 3:29. *VT* 37: 370–75.

D. G. SCHLEY

JOAH (PERSON) [Heb *yôʾāḥ*]. Four individuals in the OT bear this name, which means "Yahweh is brother."

1. Joah the son of Asaph was an official under Hezekiah, king of Judah (2 Kgs 18:18, 26, 37; Isa 36:3, 11, 32). The responsibilities of his office as *hammazkîr* ("the remembrancer," often translated as "recorder") are nowhere defined in the OT and remain somewhat uncertain. Recent opinion has gravitated toward "herald" or official spokesperson (*AncIsr* 1: 132; Mettinger 1971: 52–54), even "chief of protocol" (Williams 1975: 235–37). Joah served as one of three representatives of Hezekiah in negotiations with the Rabshakeh of Sennacherib, king of Assyria.

2. Joah, the son of Zimmah, is named as the fourth of seven generations of Levites of the family of Gershom through Gershom's oldest son Libnah in 1 Chr 6:6—Eng 6:21 in the Chronicler's artful schematization of the tribe of Levi in 1 Chr 5:27–6:66—Eng 6:1–81 (see Williamson *Chronicles* NCBC, 68–70).

3. The third son of Obed-Edom (1 Chr 26:4) in the schematization offered by a reviser of the Chronicler's organization of the gatekeepers in the temple at Jerusalem (Williamson *Chronicles* NCBC, 169; Rudolph *Chronikbücher* HAT, 173).

4. Joah, the son of Zimmah, and, apparently, the father of Eden (1 Chr 29:12), is named as one of the Gershonite Levites who rallied to the cause of Hezekiah's call for reform. Any attempt to identify this figure with one or more of the preceding is hazardous (Williamson *Chronicles* NCBC, 354). It is entirely possible that the list of good levitical names in which this Joah appears had nothing to do with the time of Hezekiah (Rudolph *Chronikbücher* HAT, 295–96).

Bibliography

Mettinger, T. N. D. 1971. *Solomonic State Officials.* ConBOT 5. Lund.
Williams, R. J. 1975. A People Come out of Egypt. An Egyptologist Looks at the Old Testament. VTSup 28: 231–52.

J. S. ROGERS

JOAKIM (PERSON) [Gk *Iōakim*]. **1.** Described as a son of Zerubbabel, a priest, and a leader of returning exiles (1 Esdr 5:5). The reference to Joakim as a son of Zerubbabel conflicts with the information provided in 1 Chr 3:19, where the only sons of Zerubbabel mentioned are Meshullam, Hananiah, Hashubah, Ohel, Berechiah, Hasadiah, and Jushab-hesed; nor is there any reference to a Joakim among the priests of the Davidic line (Myers *1 and 2 Esdras* AB, 66). Accordingly, Torrey has suggested that the Hebrew text may have originally read *wyqm bw zrbbl,* "and Zerubbabel arose with him" (Torrey 1945: 404; cf. Myers, 66).

2. Described in the book of Judith as the high priest, functioning as both religious and military leader, who ordered the residents of Bethulia and Bethomesthaim to deny the Assyrian general Holofernes access to Jerusalem from the north (4:6–7; cf. 4:8, 14; 15:8). Joakim is referred to in both the Latin and Syriac versions of the story as Eliachim, where the prefix *Jeho,* meaning "Yahu," has been replaced by the prefix, *Eli,* meaning "God" (Moore *Judith* AB, 150). The historicity of Joakim's priesthood is in doubt, as are many other ostensibly historical details recounted in the book (Nickelsburg 1981: 106ff.). The name Joakim recalls a postexilic setting and the name of the high priest, Joiakim, son of Jeshua, mentioned in Neh 12:26 (cf. 1 Esdr 5:5 and Jos. *Ant* 20.102 §234), but there is no evidence to suggest that, at the time, the high priest exercised such a wide range of powers (Moore *Judith* AB, 150). For these and other reasons, some scholars have argued that the names used in the book of Judith are pseudonyms for historical figures of other periods. Assigning the composition of Judith to A.D. 117, Volkmar (1863) identifies Joakim with the Judeans who returned to Jerusalem under the reign of either Trajan or Hadrian. Gaster, believing the book to have been written around A.D. 63, identifies Joakim with the Pharisee Onias (*EncBib* cols. 2644–46). And Ball, dating the book to the Hasmonean period, identifies Joakim with the Hellenist Alcimus (Ball 1888; also Steinmann 1953: 23–34, esp. 32). Moore points out, however, that each of these theories is plagued with difficulties that make them less than tenable (Moore, 53–54). It may be that, as Montague argues, Joakim is instead "a representative figure of the priesthood in general" (Montague 1973: 16).

3. Described as the husband of Susanna (Sus 4, 6, 28f., 63).

Bibliography

Ball, C. 1888. *Judith.* Apocrypha of the Speaker's Commentary. London.
Montague, G. 1973. *The Books of Esther and Judith.* New York.
Nickelsburg, G. 1981. *Jewish Literature Between the Bible and the Mishnah.* Philadelphia.
Steinmann, J. 1953. *Lecture de Judith.* Paris.
Torrey, C. 1945. A Revised View of First Esdras. Pp. 395–410 in *Louis Ginzberg Jubilee Volume.* New York.
Volkmar, G. 1863. *Handbuch der Einleitung in die Apokryphen.* Vol. 1. Tübingen.

FREDERICK W. SCHMIDT

JOANAN (PERSON) [Gk *Iōanan*]. The father of Joda and son of Rhesa, according to Luke's genealogy tying Joseph, the "supposed father" of Jesus, to descent from Adam and God (Luke 3:27). Gk *Iōanna* is read in some later texts, including the Vulgate and TR, while D omits it, substituting a genealogy adapted from Matt 1:6–15 for Luke 3:23–31. The name Joanan falls within a list of seventeen ancestors of Jesus who are otherwise unknown in the biblical documents, including Matthew's genealogy (Fitzmyer *Luke 1–9* AB, 500), although Marshall (*Luke* NIGTC, 163), following the suggestions of Hervey (1853: 111–12, 145–46) and some earlier scholars (see RHESA), makes an interesting proposal. This proposal states that, although Joanan appears to be equivalent to Heb *yhwhnn*

(2 Esdr 10:6; 2 Chr 23:1; et al.), with the divine name used as prefix, the Hebrew name has the same meaning as Heb *whnny* (Gk *Hanania;* 1 Chr 3:19; cf. 3:24 with Gk *Iōanan*), with the divine name used as suffix. Thus, Joanan in Luke could be one of Zerubbabel's sons, if Rhesa, which intervenes, is not a proper name (unknown as a son of Zerubbabel) but a transcription of Aram *rys,* meaning "prince," standing in apposition to Zerubbabel. This solution indicates the possibility that Luke was using here an originally Aramaic genealogy in reverse order not dependent upon the LXX. The strength of this position rises or falls upon how Rhesa is interpreted, although there also is the question of the relation of Luke's genealogy to Matthew's, which would still diverge in tracing the line of Zerubbabel.

Bibliography

Hervey, A. 1853. *The Genealogies of Our Lord and Saviour Jesus Christ.* Cambridge.

STANLEY E. PORTER

JOANNA (PERSON) [Gk *Ioanna*]. One of the female followers of Jesus during his earthly ministry listed with Mary Magdalene and Susanna in Luke 8:2–3. Joanna was one of the women who provided monetary or material aid out of their own pockets and efforts to help Jesus' band of disciples. Later, Joanna was a witness to the empty tomb who reported what she saw to the apostles (Luke 24:10). Thus, her name is probably preserved because she was known to the post-Easter community as a witness to the life, death, and empty tomb of Jesus. That only Luke ever mentions Joanna may be because she was one of his sources for the uniquely Lukan material in his gospel.

Joanna is also notable because she was the wife of Chuza, one of Herod Antipas' estate managers. Thus, she is an example of how the gospel affected people connected with the established authorities, people who were financially comfortable compared to most of the Galilean populace. We are led to believe that this rather prominent woman left her family and home to travel with Jesus and to provide assistance for his itinerant band of disciples. We may also see here an example of how the gospel breaks down class barriers and nullifies social taboos, for in the Jewish society of Jesus' day women were not allowed to be disciples of a prominent Jewish teacher, much less to be part of his traveling entourage (Witherington 1984: 6–10, 116–18). In 1st-century Judaism, such behavior would have been considered scandalous for any woman but especially for a married woman. Thus, to some degree Jesus presents both a religious and a social threat to the structure of early Judaism, for he gave both men and women the opportunity to be full-fledged disciples.

Bibliography

Witherington, B. 1979. On the Road with Mary Magdalene, Joanna, Susanna, and other Disciples: Luke 8.1–3. *ZNW* 70: 242–48.
———. 1984. *Women in the Ministry of Jesus.* Cambridge.

BEN WITHERINGTON III

JOARIB (PERSON) [Gk *Iōarib*]. The name of the priestly clan of Mattathias, the original leader of the Jewish resistance against the Hellenizing activities of Antiochus Epiphanes and the father of five sons who aided him (1 Macc 2:1; 14:29). The Heb name *yĕhôyārîb* or *yôyārîb* means "Yahweh contends." It appears as a clan name five times in the OT (Neh 11:10; 12:6, 19; 1 Chr 9:10; 24:7). In 1 Chr 24:7, it is reported that Jehoiarib was made the head of the first of twenty-four divisions of priests by David himself, but the verse probably reflects the Chronicler's view of how the priesthood was or should have been organized in his own day (*Oxford Annotated Bible,* 522). Scholars have sometimes suggested that the list in 24:7–18 derived from the Maccabean period, since the name Jehoiarib replaced the name Jedaiah at the head of the list (cf. 9:10), but Myers (*Chronicles* AB, 165) rejects this view on the grounds that there is a tendency toward the elevation of Jehoiarib in the lists taken as a whole. The other references to Jehoiarib list the clan among those having members return from Exile.

In 1 Macc 2:1 and 14:29, Mattathias is pointedly traced to this clan, which stood at the head of the priestly divisions. Goldstein (*1 Maccabees* AB, 17) suggests that 14:29 belonged to a dynastic document and that the Hasmoneans wished to emphasize their legitimacy as well as God's contending on behalf of Jehoiarib's descendants. Of course, the name itself was subject to derogatory inversion; namely, that God contends for their opponents (cf. *1 Maccabees* AB, 200).

The list of priestly divisions with Jehoiarib at the head was set up on stone in Palestinian synagogues after the second revolt against Rome, apparently in hopes that one day the temple and its priesthood would be restored.

PAUL L. REDDITT

JOASH (PERSON) [Heb *yôʾāš*]. Var. JEHOASH. **1.** Father of Gideon; from the family of Abiezer of Manasseh (Judg 6:11, 25–32). His name appears in the narrative describing Gideon's heroic deeds (Judg 6:1–8:35). The account connects Joash with three cultic objects—an oak associated with oracles (the "oak at Ophrah," v 11), an altar to Baal, and an Asherah (v 25). Although Gideon complained that his family was the weakest in Manasseh (v 15), the text portrays his father as wealthy and influential. Joash owned property in Ophrah (v 11) and commanded the respect of Ophrah's citizenry. After Gideon destroyed the altar of Baal, Joash spoke to the city's outraged inhabitants in his son's defense (vv 30–31). See also GIDEON (PERSON).

2. The son of Shelah; a Judahite (1 Chr 4:22). His name appears fourth in the list of Shelah's five sons (1 Chr 4:21–23) that concludes the Chronicler's genealogy of Judah (1 Chr 4:1–23). The LXX B reads *Joada* in v 22.

3. The son of Becher; a Benjaminite (1 Chr 7:8). His name appears second in the list of Becher's nine sons (1 Chr 7:6–12).

4. A "mighty man"; the son of Shemaah of Gibeah; a Benjaminite (1 Chr 12:3). He was second-in-command of the ambidextrous warriors who joined David at Ziklag. By juxtaposing Saul's enmity to David (1 Chr 12:1) with the phrase identifying the warriors as "Saul's kinsmen" (1 Chr 12:2), a sense of irony is created. While Saul is David's enemy, Saul's family are David's friends.

5. The steward in charge of David's "stores of oil"

(1 Chr 27:28). His name appears in a list of officers who manage David's property (1 Chr 27:25–31).

6. A "son" of Ahab (1 Kgs 22:26 = 2 Chr 18:25). According to the text, Joash and Amon (the governor of Samaria) were given custody of the prophet Micaiah after Micaiah prophesied failure for Ahab's Ramoth-gilead campaign (1 Kings 22 = 2 Chronicles 18). If the text is accepted literally, then Joash was an otherwise unknown son of Ahab, king of Israel. Two alternatives have been proposed, however, which challenge this identification. The term "king's son" is used in other passages to designate an official (cf. Jer 36:26; 38:6; 2 Chr 28:7). If the phrase in 1 Kgs 22:26 (= 2 Chr 18:25) is understood in this manner, then Joash was Ahab's officer, not literally his son (Jones, *1–2 Kings* NCBC, 369). The title may have originated with the practice (which was later discontinued) of filling the post with one of the king's sons (de Vaux, *Anc Isr,* 119ff.). A more complicated identification of the Joash mentioned in 2 Kgs 22:25 is based on the assumption that 1 Kings 20 and 22 are out of place. J. M. Miller (1966) argued that the battle accounts in chaps. 20 and 22 originally pertained to the Jehu period. Later, the kings mentioned in the accounts became associated with Ahab of Israel and Jehoshaphat of Judah. The Joash of 1 Kgs 22:26, therefore, is not the son of Ahab but the son of Jehoahaz, king of Israel (2 Kgs 13:10).

7. The ninth king of Judah; son(?) of Ahaziah and Zibiah of Beer-sheba (2 Kings 11–12; 2 Chr 22:10–24:27). Although 2 Kgs 12:2 (—Eng 12:1) states that Joash reigned forty years, scholars vary in their chronology of his reign: 837–800 B.C.E. (Albright 1945: 470); 835–796 (Thiele 1977: 75); or 832–803 [793] (Hayes and Hooker 1988: 38–40). Joash's account can be divided into two sections: his early life and coronation (2 Kings 11; 2 Chr 22:10–23:21) and his reign (2 Kings 12; 2 Chronicles 24).

Joash is first mentioned in reference to the massacre in 2 Kgs 11:1–2. When Athaliah heard of the death of her son (Ahaziah), she ordered the deaths of the Davidic heirs and installed herself as queen of Judah (v 1). According to vv 2–3, Joash, an infant son of Ahaziah, escaped the purge. His aunt (Jehosheba) hid him in the house of the Lord for six years while Athaliah reigned over Judah. In the seventh year, a priest (Jehoiada) presented the seven-year-old Joash to the guards as the legitimate king (v 4).

The report of Joash's escape in vv 1–3 is curious. Why would Athaliah kill Joash when she could have ruled as his regent? How could Joash have escaped her notice for six years? To answer these questions scholars either explain how the escape might have been possible (i.e., Joash posed as a priest's child and thus escaped detection [Gray, *1–2 Kings* OTL, 570]) or challenge the historicity of the massacre and/or Joash's escape (Ginsberg 1967: 91–93; *HAIJ,* 302–5). Ginsberg argued that the massacre (as described in vv 2–3) never took place: Athaliah would not have ordered Joash's death because (1) he was her grandchild; (2) he was an infant and therefore no threat; and (3) Athaliah (being a woman and an Omride) was hated while Joash (being a Davidide) was her only claim to legitimacy. Thus, Ginsberg concluded the account in vv 1–3 arose out of confusion with a prior slaughter, or from a very selective slaughter aimed at protecting Joash from ambitious relatives. While Ginsberg challenged the massacre's historicity, a more radical proposal by Miller and Hayes has challenged the escape's historicity. Perhaps the massacre was more successful than vv 2–3 allows, and *all* the heirs were killed. If this happened, then the child Jehoiada presented to the guards in v 4 was not Ahaziah's son, but a pretender foisted on the people by the priesthood (*HAIJ,* 303–5).

Liverani's literary analysis of Joash's escape and coronation reveals interesting similarities between 2 Kings 11 and other ANE accounts of royal escapes and coups (Liverani 1974: 438–53). All provide dramatically persuasive accounts (with common plot elements) of how a recent usurpation is justified by a former one. The accounts thus function to legitimate the current ruling family and to serve as propaganda.

The report of the coup is found in vv 4ff. After Jehoiada instructed the guards (vv 4–8), Joash was brought to the temple where he was crowned, given the testimony, proclaimed king, and anointed (vv 9–12). When Athaliah investigated the clapping and shouting, Jehoiada ordered the guards to seize and kill her (vv 13–16). Although two covenants are mentioned in v 17 (v 17a—Lord/king/people; v 17b—king/people), this may be due to a case of dittography. Verse 17b is missing from both 2 Chr 23:16 and Lucianic LXX.

The Chronicler both supplements and contradicts the Kings account of the coup. Supplementary material includes the names and lineage of the commanders of the guards (2 Chr 23:1), reference to singers and musical instruments at Joash's coronation (2 Chr 23:13), and mention of Jehoiada's sons at Joash's anointing (2 Chr 23:11). Contradictory material focuses on the coup's participants: for the Chronicler, the Levites and "all Judah" supported the coup, while three groups not mentioned in Kings—the captains, nobles, and governors of the people—rejoice at Joash's enthronement (2 Chr 23:20). The Chronicler mentions only one covenant (between the priest/people/king) after Athaliah's death (2 Chr 23:16).

Was the coup which placed Joash on the throne a popular uprising or a palace conspiracy? Stade (1885) suggested that 2 Kings 11 contains two accounts of the coup, a priestly account (vv 4–12; 18b–20) and a popular account (vv 13–18a) in which the people or the priests play respectively significant roles. However, even in Stade's "popular" source (vv 13–18a), the "people of the land" do little besides ratifying the actions of the priests and guards. Reviv (1986) argued that the priesthood functioned as a "political pressure group" in this period. If so, then the coup may have resulted from strained relations between palace and temple rather than from a surge of nationalism.

The report of Joash's reign is found in 2 Kings 12 and 2 Chronicles 24. Joash's introductory regnal formula is contained in 2 Kgs 12:1–4 (—Eng 11:21–12:3). In the seventh year of Jehu (king of Israel), Joash (son of Zibiah of Beer-sheba) began to reign. Although Joash does "right" in Yahweh's eyes (for Jehoiada is his teacher), he is nevertheless criticized for allowing the high places to continue. Only two events of Joash's reign are recorded—the repair of the temple and an incursion by the Syrians into Judean territory. Both deal with temple finances.

Although the general concern of 2 Kgs 12:5–17 (—Eng

4–16) is the temple's repair, the account focuses more on describing its financial arrangements than on the repair itself. This falls into two narrative sections: the first attempt (vv 5–9 [—Eng 4–8]) and the second attempt (vv 10–17 [—Eng 9–16]). Joash's initial orders to repair the temple are ignored. Only the second attempt (organized and implemented by Jehoiada, the priest) is successful.

Whereas vv 5–17 (—Eng 4–16) deal with the allocation of monies for repairs, vv 18–19 (—Eng 17–18) focus on the role temple finances played in Joash's international affairs. Hazael, king of Syria, captured Gath and made plans to move toward Jerusalem. According to v 19 (11Eng v 18), Joash "persuaded" Hazael to spare Jerusalem by offering tribute from royal votive offerings.

The report of Joash's reign concludes with the account of his death in vv 20–22 (—Eng 19–21). Verse 20 and the latter part of 22 (—Eng 19, 21) contain the usual concluding formula for Judean kings. The intervening verses, however, describe a conspiracy by Joash's servants (Jozacar, the son of Shimeath, and Jehozabad, the son of Shomer) which resulted in Joash's death. No motivation is given for the assassination.

Once again, the Chronicler's account supplements and contradicts the material in Kings. Supplementary material includes the account of Jehoiada's death (2 Chr 24:15–16), Joash's subsequent worship of idols (vv 17–19), and the murder of Jehoiada's son, Zechariah (vv 20–22). In 2 Chronicles 24, however, the report in Kings is contradicted at four main points. First, the writer's positive evaluation of Joash is limited to "all the days of Jehoiada the priest" (2 Chr 24:2) rather than "all his (Joash's) days" (2 Kgs 12:4 [—Eng 12:3]). Second, the details of the temple's repairs differ as to who is responsible for the repair (the priests and Levites), for its initial failure (Levites), for the source of its financing (Mosaic tax), and for the making of utensils of silver and gold for service in the temple. Third, the conflict with the Syrians is portrayed as an actual military engagement rather than an adverted threat (2 Chr 24:23–25). The Syrians "came up against" Joash and killed the princes of the people (v 23). Because of Joash's apostasy, he was wounded and his army "delivered" into the hands of the Syrians. Fourth, the servants named in the conspiracy are different. In Chronicles it is two men of foreign origin—Zabad, the son of Shimeath the Ammonitess, and Jehozabad, the son of Shimrith the Moabitess—who kill the wounded Joash (v 26).

Though it is impossible to say with certainty what motivated the assassination of Joash, it is important to note the relationship between the palace and the temple during this period. Joash was placed on the throne by a coup organized by the priests. In all probability, a priest (Jehoiada) served as regent during the king's childhood. Joash came into conflict with the priests over financing temple repairs and later stripped the temple of its treasures to pay off Hazael. If the account of Zechariah's execution in the temple precinct is true (2 Chr 24:20–22), then this may have further exacerbated relations between the priests and the king. It is very possible that the priesthood which helped put Joash on the throne also had a hand in his death.

8. The twelfth king of Israel; son of Jehoahaz (2 Kgs 13:10–25; 14:8–16 = 2 Chr 25:17–24). According to 2 Kgs 13:10, Joash reigned for sixteen years. Although Albright (1945: 16–22) dates Joash's kingship from 801 to 786 B.C.E., Thiele (1977: 75) places it three years later (798–782 B.C.E.), while Hayes and Hooker (1988: 47–48) date it three years earlier (804–789 B.C.E.). Joash's reign was the third of four generations of the Jehu dynasty in Israel (Jehu, Jehoahaz, Joash, and Uzziah/Jeroboam II).

The introductory regnal formula for Joash (2 Kgs 13:10–11) is immediately followed by a concluding formula (vv 12–13). This leaves the events of Joash's reign (his encounter with Elisha, 2 Kgs 13:14–19; Elisha's death, vv 20–21; Joash's subsequent victories over Ben-hadad, vv 22–25; and Joash's victory over Amaziah of Judah, 2 Kgs 14:8–16 = 2 Chr 25:17–24) standing outside the book's normal framework for each king. Since there is a parallel version of vv 12–13 in 2 Kgs 14:15–16, vv 12–13 are often thought to be secondary. Lucian places vv 12–13 after v 25 and omits 14:15.

In 2 Kgs 13:14–19 is a prophetic tale describing a deathbed encounter between Joash and Elisha. When Joash went to Elisha (who was fatally ill), Elisha commanded him to draw his bow (v 16), shoot an arrow toward Aram (v 17), and strike the ground with the remaining arrows (v 18). When Joash stopped after three strikes, Elisha became angry and revealed that each strike stood for an Israelite victory over Syria. Although Joash could have put an end to the Syrian threat, he would now enjoy only three victories (vv 18–19).

After Elisha's death (vv 20–21), the narrative shifts to Syrian relations with Israel (vv 22–25). Hazael reportedly oppressed Israel during the time of Jehoahaz (vv 22–23) and succeeded in capturing some Israelite territory (v 25). When Ben-hadad (Hazael's son) became king (v 24), Joash is credited with winning three battles and recovering the cities lost during his father's reign. Although no reference is made in vv 22–25 to the words of Elisha (v 19), the placement of vv 22–25 (with the mention of three victories in v 25) gives a "prophecy-fulfillment" structure to these narratives.

At least two epigraphical discoveries—the Rimah Stela and the Zakir Inscription—provide background data for this period. According to the Rimah Stela (see Cody 1970), Adad-nirari III of Assyria campaigned westward, subjugated western kings, and received tribute from Damascus, Tyre, Sidon, and Joash of Samaria. Although the campaign's date is unknown, scholars usually associate it with the last westward campaign made by Adad-nirari III in 796 B.C.E. (Millard and Tadmor 1973: 64; cf. Shea 1978: 101–13 for an opposing viewpoint, i.e., Adad-nirari's first campaign in 805 B.C.E.). The defeat of Damascus by Adad-nirari III may have paved the way for the warfare reflected in the Zakir Inscription (*ANET,* 655–56). Ben-hadad (son of Hazael) formed a coalition of Aramean kings, laid siege to Hatarikka, and was defeated by Zakir, king of Hamath and Laʾash. The defeat of Damascus by Adad-nirari III and the internal fighting between Aramean kings reflected in the Zakir Inscription help explain why the Israelite victories mentioned in 2 Kgs 13:25 may have been possible.

Miller argued that the Elisha narrative and the victories reported in v 25 should be associated with Jehoahaz, instead of Joash. Miller's theory is based on the association of the three Israelite/Syrian battles in 1 Kings 20 and 22 with the battles mentioned in 2 Kgs 13:25. According to Miller (1966; 1968), it was Jehu who lost territory to Hazael (cf. 2 Kgs 10:32–33 with 1 Kgs 20:34), and it was Jehu's son (Jehoahaz) who successfully challenged Ben-hadad II. Israel's victories were limited to three due to Jehoahaz's untimely death at the battle at Ramoth-gilead.

In 2 Kgs 14:8–14, Joash's victory over Amaziah of Judah at Bethshemesh is recorded. When Amaziah asked to look Joash "in the face," Joash responded with a fable and a warning (vv 8–10). Amaziah did not listen and engaged Joash's troops at Bethshemesh. Joash's victory cost Judah all the treasures of the temple and palace, a 400-cubit stretch of Jerusalem's walls, and the indignation of hostages (vv 11–14).

Bibliography

Albright, W. F. 1945. The Chronology of the Divided Monarchy of Israel. *BASOR* 100: 16–22.

Cody, A. 1970. A New Inscription from Tell Rimah and King Jehoash of Israel. *CBQ* 32: 325–40.

Ginsberg, H. L. 1967. The Omride-Davidid Alliance and Its Consequences. *PWCJS* 4: 91–93.

Hayes, J. H., and Hooker, P. K. 1988. *A New Chronology for the Kings of Israel and Judah.* Atlanta.

Liverani, M. 1974. L'histoire de Joas. *VT* 24: 438–53.

Millard, A. R., and Tadmor, H. 1973. Adad-Nirari in Syria. *Iraq* 35: 57–64.

Miller, J. M. 1966. The Elisha Cycle and the Accounts of the Omride Wars. *JBL* 85: 441–54.

———. 1968. The Rest of the Acts of Jehoahaz (1 Kings 20; 22:1–38). *ZAW* 80: 337–42.

Page, S. 1968. A Stela of Adad-nirari III and Nergal-Eres from Tel al-Rimah. *Iraq* 35: 139–53.

Reviv, H. 1986. The Priesthood as a Political Pressure Group in Judah. Pp. 205–10 in *Matthias Augustin Klaus-Dietrich Schunck (Hrsg).* Frankfurt.

Shea, W. H. 1978. Adad-Nirari III and Jehoash of Israel. *JCS* 30: 101–13.

Stade, B. 1885. Anmerkungen zu 2 Ko. 10–14. *ZAW* 5: 275–97.

Thiele, E. R. 1977. *A Chronology of the Hebrew Kings.* Grand Rapids.

LINDA S. SCHEARING

JOB, BOOK OF. A book in the third division of the Hebrew Bible (the "Writings") that recounts the story of Job, a righteous man whose motives for being righteous are tested through a series of personal tragedies and sufferings. When three old friends arrive to condole him, they all engage in a dialogue focusing not only on the cause of Job's personal misfortune but also more generally on the problem of evil. Their dialogue (or, more properly, "dispute"), in which Job sharply questions the nature of divine justice, ends without resolution, whereupon yet another character, the young Elihu, appears to offer his own observations on the nature of Job's predicament. Eventually God appears on the scene to upbraid Job for complaining, and to restore Job's family, property, and health.

A. Contents
B. Structure
  1. On the Basis of Diction
  2. On the Basis of Dramatic Movement
  3. On the Basis of Individual Components
C. Scholarly Issues
D. Competing Arguments
E. Composition
F. Date and Language
G. Related Works in the Ancient World
H. Canon and Text
I. History of Interpretation

A. Contents

The book of Job consists of a narrative framework and a poetic core. The prose section is divided into a prologue (1:1–2:13) and an epilogue (42:7–17); the poetry is embedded between these two. Together prose and poetry examine the possibility of being good without thought of either reward or punishment and explore the nature of innocent suffering; whether or not it exists, how one ought to act in the presence of misery, and why such injustice occurs. The prose framework deals with loss and eventual restoration without so much as a raised voice, and in its simplicity embraces and makes possible the eruption of volcanic emotions in the poetry.

Emphasizing the historical gap between the time of the hero and the subsequent narrating of the events, the narrative sets the action in (pre-)patriarchal times. Job's possessions, like those of the patriarchs, consist of cattle and servants; not only his three friends but also his enemies (nomadic Sabeans and Chaldeans) come from the greater environment associated with Abraham's wanderings; the monetary unit, *qeśiṭāh* (42:11) belongs to that ancient era (cf. Gen 33:19); Job's life span exceeds that of the patriarchs; and his sacrifice of animals corresponds to the practice prior to official priests. The name Job recalls a folk hero associated in Ezek 14:14, 20 with Noah and Daniel, probably the Dan'el of Canaanite epic texts. Although the meaning of Job's name is uncertain, similar forms are attested from early times in Egypt and Mesopotamia with the meanings "Where is the divine father?" and "Inveterate Foe/Hated One." In accord with the universality typical of early wisdom, the hero seems to have been an Edomite, famous for the wisdom of its inhabitants, and the setting in the land of Uz echoes the noun *ʿeṣāh* (counsel).

The action of the prologue (1:1–2:13) alternates between earth and heaven, the events of the latter hidden from Job. The hero, perfect outwardly and inwardly according to irrefutable testimony (1:3, 8), enjoys the fruits of virtue—until God directs the Adversary's attention to him, eliciting suspicion of Job's motive for being good and provoking a test to determine the truth. Calamity befalls Job without warning, intruding on a serene setting of festivity. Marauding Sabeans strike Job's property, then fire continues the destruction; Chaldeans wield the penultimate stroke, and a fierce windstorm levels the house in which Job's children are eating and drinking. Messengers convey the news, their formulaic expressions heightening the pain. This narrative strategy informs readers of these events at the same time it informs Job (Weiss 1983). Having lost his children and possessions, Job blesses the Lord as source of good and ill (1:21). A second heavenly scene ensues, with God's "I told you so" and the Adversary's insistence that a real test must touch the actual person (2:3–5). God accedes once more, insisting that Job's life must not be taken. The final scene depicts a sorely afflicted Job, but one who retains his integrity despite his wife's urging to curse God and die (2:9–10). This time Job's confession takes interrogative form, but he does not curse God. Having heard of Job's misfortune, three of Job's friends, Eliphaz, Bildad, and Zophar, journey from their homes in Teman, Shuah, and Naaman respectively to offer comfort in adversity. Twice the narrator enters the story to pronounce the obvious judgment that in all this Job did not sin, adding "with his lips" the second time. The slight alteration suggests, at least to some people, a gulf between outward expression and inward resentment (*Baba Bathra* 16b). A *Leitwort* (leading, or theme, word) in 1:9 and 2:3 (*ḥinnam,* for nothing, without cause) links the prologue with the poetry (cf. 9:17; 22:6).

The poetic dialogue consists of three distinct units: Job versus Eliphaz, Bildad, and Zophar (chaps. 3–31), Elihu's attack on Job's friends and on Job (chaps. 32–37), and God's lectures to Job (38:1–42:6, with brief responses by Job in 40:3–5 and 42:1–6). Job opens the dispute with a curse, but not against God except indirectly as creator of the birthday Job damns (chap. 3). He invokes uninterrupted darkness on that day, preferring that his mother had remained in a state of perpetual pregnancy or that he had died at birth, finding rest and equality in Sheol. His hidden fear that calamity might befall him had prompted excessive religious scrupulosity in the story (1:5) and erupts again in 3:25. From here on, each friend in turn responds to Job. This alternation of speakers occurs in three cycles, with the order of the friends being Eliphaz (chaps. 4–5, 15, 22), Bildad (chaps. 8, 18, 25), and Zophar (chaps. 11, 20—note that Zophar has no response in the third cycle). Job answers each of them in turn (chaps. 6–7, 9–10, 12–14, 16–17, 19, 21, 23–24, 26–27). Once the friends are reduced to silence, Job contrasts his former happiness (chap. 29) with his present misery (chap. 30) and utters an oath of innocence designed to force God's hand (chap. 31). Unlike most oaths in the Bible, Job's imprecations actually state the penalty that will beset the guilty person. He disavows, among other things, idolatry, lying, adultery, lust, greed, abuse of power, lack of concern for the poor, and misuse of land.

Surprisingly, Job's extreme action yields an unexpected interlocutor (chaps. 32–37), the youthful Elihu, whose name means "He is my God." Having stood by silently while Job's friends tried to answer his arguments, Elihu can contain his words no longer. Lashing out at the comforters-turned-accusers, he then turns against Job with comparable contempt, claiming that God speaks through nocturnal experiences (33:15–16) and disciplines by means of adversity, both to elicit repentance (33:19–30). Citing Job's own words (e.g., 33:33 and 6:25; 33:24 and 6:23; 33:22 and 6:29), Elihu endeavors to overwhelm him with his own "perfect knowledge," a characteristic of his God as well. Elihu denies that one who hates justice will govern, and notes that God's all-encompassing power rules out any need for partiality (34:17–20). Like Zophar, Elihu exalts God to the point of rendering human deeds worthless insofar as God is concerned: good and evil affect human beings but do not touch God in any way. Such thinking naturally issues in majestic praise of the creator (chaps. 36–37), who now speaks from a storm (38:1). God asks Job question after question, forcing him to recognize that he knows very little about the mysteries of the universe (chaps. 38–39). The heavenly teacher lectures Job on the wonders of nature and calls to mind wild animals who live outside the human domain. God parades these creatures before Job: lion, mountain goat, wild ass, wild ox, ostrich, horse, hawk and eagle (chap. 39).

Not content with Job's initial repentance (40:3–5), God boasts about two special creatures, Behemoth and Leviathan (chaps. 40–41). In introducing them, God seems to concede that human pride and wickedness in general present a challenge even to the creator (40:10–14). Although God transforms the mighty Behemoth and Leviathan into innocuous playthings for the deity's amusement, the puny Job is no match for their strength. Realizing that his earlier Titanism was ludicrous, Job relents (42:1–6). The dispute has not been a total disaster, for Job's secondhand knowledge of God vanishes before the immediacy of sight. Hearing gives way to seeing, which enables Job to gain a proper perspective on his place in the universe. Complaint also acquiesces to profound silence. No longer does Job claim to be the measure of all things.

The epilogue (42:7–17) ties up all loose ends. Having repented, of what is unclear, Job intercedes on behalf of the three friends, at whom God is angry because they did not speak truth about God *as Job did.* A temporal connection between prayer and restoration occurs, and Job returns to his previous state, with one bonus: his three daughters possess unsurpassed beauty, besides an inheritance. Seven times the verb *brk* occurs in the story (1:5, 10, 11, 21; 2:5, 9; 42:12), alternating between the meanings "curse" and "bless" except the last two, which are reversed.

B. Structure

To some extent the shape of the book depends on one's predisposition, but three different ways of viewing the structure commend themselves. Readers may emphasize (1) the diction, (2) the dramatic movement, and (3) the individual components in outline form. By discounting brief prosaic introductions and observations, the 1st approach yields two parts, prose and poetry. The 2d perspective uses narrative introductions—and to some extent conclusions—to distinguish three divisions, specifically 1:1–2:10; 2:11–31:40; and 32:1–42:17. The 3d approach divides the book into five discrete sections: chaps. 1–2; 3–31; 32–37; 38:1–42:6; and 42:7–17.

1. On the Basis of Diction. Perhaps the most noticeable feature of the book is its use of a story to enclose a poetic center. This device was widely employed among sages of the ANE to provide a specific historical framework within which to interpret teachings that had broad application, whether philosophical ruminations about innocent suffering and the governance of the universe or collections of aphorisms to enable others to make wise decisions. For example, Ahiqar and Anksheshankh have left significant proverbial sayings for posterity, but in each instance an account of the teacher's personal adversity encloses the collection of maxims. See also AHIQAR. Little effort to connect this prose framework with the poetic teachings is evident, so that both story and poetry stand on their own. Nevertheless, the juxtaposition of the two parts of the book offers a way of understanding the teaching that would otherwise not occur. Just as a simple frame enhances a painting, delineating its original features and drawing attention away from itself to the art, so these brief biographies give vital data about the hero's words and character.

In a sense, the Joban poetry interrupts the story, which suspends Job's destiny in midair until the poetry has reached its goal; only then does the tale resume and achieve closure. The narrator of the story, who freely intrudes twice to pass independent judgment on the hero (1:22; 2:10), recedes in the poetry so that other voices may be heard. The lyrical poetry of Job, whose threatened ego fights for survival against overwhelming odds, the confident assurances of Eliphaz and his companions, Elihu's brash rebuttal of all four, and the divine interrogation—all this takes place while the narrator creates a story within an earlier story, the folktale. The narrator's resumption of the tale after Job's claim to have seen the deity gives the impression of returning to reality, at least a realm that ordinary people comprehend. *Do ut des* (I give in order to receive) still functions in this land of Uz, for divine anger departs as a result of Job's obedient deed, and God restores Job at this time. Prologue elicits dialogue, and epilogue terminates it. The epilogue does more than end the dialogue, for the force of "anti-wisdom" within the poetry evaporates under the heavy hand of the narrator. Viewpoints collide everywhere, not just in the dialogue. The prose framework and that in the poetic core speak opposing views: the former ultimately seems to affirm the reward of the innocent (Job is at least compensated for his suffering, if not rewarded for his virtue) while the latter proclaims most persuasively that the innocent are not rewarded. To this day no satisfactory harmonization has been found.

2. On the Basis of Dramatic Movement. Introductions at 1:1–5, 2:11–13, and 32:1–5 suggest another way of dividing the book. The first introduces Job and gives essential insights into his character, which will soon be assailed mightily. The second introduction identifies Job's three friends and sets up expectations about their role as comforters, whereas the third introduction describes Elihu's boldness in venturing to address his elders without their consent and justifies his fury at the level of discourse so far. Thus understood, the book of Job becomes a drama consisting of three episodes: God afflicts Job, Job challenges God, God challenges Job. Another way of stating the drama is the hidden conflict, the conflict explored, and the conflict resolved (Habel 1985). This interpretation depends on an understanding of narration through dialogue, so that the fundamental category of the book is said to be prose with the poetic dialogues retarding the movement of plot and heightening the emotional pitch.

This approach encounters difficulties other than the brevity of the first part, since Job's laconic confessions in this section differ from his outpouring of resentment in the second unit, although his two repentant statements in part three balance the shorter confessions nicely. More to the point, the narrator's commendation of Job's conduct (1:22; 2:10) marks two closures, and although section two ends appropriately (31:40, "The words of Job are ended"), the third section concludes reluctantly. God's first speech evokes Job's final words, or so he says (40:4–5), only to give way to a second divine speech and an additional response from Job (42:2–6). Each indecision necessitates further brief introductions of speakers, but these comments play no role in the suggested structuring of the book. The description of plot development also presents difficulty, for Elihu's speeches hardly contribute to resolving the conflict between Job and God. Actually, the epilogue alone describes the resolution, the divine speeches functioning as disciplinary chastening of the hero.

3. On the Basis of Individual Components. Yet another means of structuring the book derives its clues from the distinctive components in it: (1) a story about Job's affliction, (2) a dispute between him and three friends, (3) the speeches of Elihu, (4) divine speeches punctuated by Job's submission, and (5) a story about Job's restoration. The second division fails to qualify as a consistent dispute, since the 3d cycle breaks off without Zophar's final speech and thereafter Job appears either to address the divine enemy or to enter into nostalgic monologue. This approach does not disparage the dialogue by labeling it an almost interminable retardation of the plot, since the poetic speeches possess value in their own right apart from any progress they may signal toward some unspoken telos. Because the action moves toward a divine pronunciation of Job's innocence in the debate between Job and his friends, the dialogue gives an impression of progress, particularly the emergence of references to the figure of an "advocate" or "redeemer." Emotional changes and high points mark still another kind of movement in the poetry, indicating that progress does occur even when opposing intellectual positions come no closer together than at the beginning.

C. Scholarly Issues

More critical problems surround the book of Job than perhaps any other book of the OT. Many of these problems relate to the structure of the book itself.

Perhaps the most obvious problem concerns the composition of the book, more specifically the relationship of the prose framework to the poetic core (see E below). Even though prose and poetry can be intermixed with great literary effect (e.g., Jonah), a number of apparent inconsistencies are associated with this prose/poetry distinction. The patient Job of the prose framework contrasts with the defiant Job of the poetic core; and the God who is proud of Job and commends him in the prologue/epilogue rebukes him in the dialogue. However, these contrasts can be an understandable function of the plot development. More seriously, the "happy ending" effected by God (42:10–17) seems to undermine the integrity and force of Job's penetrating argument as presented in the dialogue (i.e., that God does not guarantee "happy endings"). Thus, some questions have been raised about the literary relationship between the prose framework and the poetic dialogue: initially the framework was thought to be secondary, although the dominant hypothesis now is that this framework reflects an original folktale that was subsequently embellished by the poetic dialogue.

Indeed, some tension seems to exist between the prose prologue and epilogue. The Satan—whose penetrating questions about the ultimate motives for human righteousness precipitated the "testing" of Job in the prologue—is never mentioned in the epilogue. Moreover, the epilogue does not even return to the issue of the "test."

In the poetic dialogue itself, the most noticeable structural feature is the predictable "round-table" cycle of the debate, with each friend speaking in turn. Yet in the 3d cycle of the debate (esp. chaps. 25–28) this symmetry dissolves: Bildad's 3d speech is surprisingly brief (chap. 25), Zophar has no 3d speech, Job paradoxically seems to express sentiments that previously have been found only on the lips of his three friends (26:5–14), and there are literary clues that several "Job speeches" may have been spliced together (e.g., 27:1; 29:1). Some scholars have attempted to reconstruct a 3d speech for Zophar out of Job's paradoxical statements, while others hold that the hymnic reflections on wisdom (chap. 28) are secondary.

The nature and function of the Elihu speeches (chaps. 32–37) are problematic. Are these speeches secondary or original? Most scholars opt for the former, pointing out that their appearance breaks an otherwise clear pattern: Job never replies to Elihu, and in the epilogue neither God nor the narrator acknowledges his presence and participation in the dialogue (as they do Eliphaz, Bildad, and Zophar; 42:7–9). Indeed, the speeches seem intrusive—something even Elihu must apologetically admit (32:6–22): they delay the smooth movement from Job's plea that God appear and respond (chap. 31) to God's actual appearance and response (chap. 38). However, Elihu's speeches fail to provide the anticipated "breakthrough solution." Is the resultant sense of disappointment unintended (i.e., does the text of Job preserve the remains of a clumsy author [or secondary redactor?] who, like Elihu, tried unsuccessfully to steer the issue to a clear resolution)? Or does the author have some specific reason for introducing Elihu and having his arguments prove so noticeably inadequate; and if so, what is that reason?

Similarly, the nature and function of the theophany (chaps. 38–40) have presented other problems. Was it original, and why are there *two* divine speeches (38:1ff.; 40:6ff.), each ending with a capitulation by Job? Does Yahweh "contaminate" the test of Job's character by appearing in this manner, or has the test already been decisively resolved? Does Yahweh not attempt to "bully" Job into submission just as Job had cynically predicted (i.e., Yahweh forces the issue back to the question of his power, not his justice)?

Other "historical" questions have centered on the time and circumstance of the writing (see F below) and possible connections with other ANE writings (see G below). The more "philosophical" questions, however, have centered on the various "answers" that are (or are not) given for the "problem of human suffering" (see G below). The quest for such "answers" is an understandable human desire, but it may be unfair to expect the book of Job to answer these questions.

However, if he had wanted to, the author undoubtedly *could* have provided some (perhaps even satisfactory) resolution to the story. If he wished to retain the dialogue, the author could have explicitly addressed its point (or its pointlessness?) and the ambiguity of Job's final reaction, explicitly telling the reader whether or not the test was resolved, and if so, how it was resolved. The author similarly could have had God more explicitly underscore the fact that no human being (neither Job nor the reader) can know or understand why the world operates the way it does (i.e., have God exercise his "power play" more obviously and directly on the reader). Indeed, to some extent the author seems to permit the plot to devolve toward this insight.

If he eliminated (or ignored) the dialogue altogether, the author *literarily* could have resolved some aspects of the narrative. For example, he could have portrayed a resolute Job who never complained and who made a complete *and unselfish* submission to God. He could even have depicted this Job continually suffering and eventually dying in pain. In this scenario, Satan would lose the wager, but the narrative could have still ended on the upbeat note that God still retained pride in (the now-deceased) Job (assuming the author cannot portray Job being resurrected from the dead). The reader would at least still be left with a moral example (Job), and whatever vague hopes might be associated with the notion of retaining divine favor posthumously.

Or the author could have depicted Job finally and decisively cursing God and having Satan thereby win the wager. Such a scenario conceding the truth of the Satan's claim could have itself constituted not only a profound anthropological lesson into human motivation (that even the best of human intentions *are* colored by self-interest) but also a touching theological lesson about the predicament of God (who, despite the unconditional love shown for humans, can only be loved conditionally for the benefits rendered, not unconditionally for God's sake).

It is of course unfair to expect an ancient author to write a literary piece to provide satisfying answers to the questions raised by subsequent generations of readers. Nevertheless, many readers have wished that the author could have explicitly cited the "Fall" and "Original Sin" (Genesis 3–4) to explain human suffering, more explicitly drawing the conclusion that (for the time being?) the world does not operate according to God's original intent at Creation. Again, some readers have wished that the author could have developed the figure of a more diabolical "Satan," thereby portraying a sort of cosmic dualism that explains suffering as caused by an evil presence actively working to undo God's otherwise harmonious and just creation.

Regardless of how satisfying or unsatisfying they may be to subsequent readers, all these hypothetical resolutions would at least represent clear and deliberate attempts to resolve the profound problem of human suffering. The fact that the author of the finished book seems not to make such an explicit attempt perhaps reveals an awareness of how intractable the problem is. Perhaps the author was content merely to raise the issues, knowing from experience, reflection, and realization that any answer that human beings can articulate and comprehend is necessarily inadequate.

D. Competing Arguments

In a book that features a deity who asks copious questions, it occasions little surprise that the central theme of the book is stated interrogatively: does anyone serve God for nothing (1:9)? Society seems to take for granted the principle of retribution, the reaping of what one sows, despite occasional exceptions. Job's case stretches the belief to the limit, and in doing so the book probes an even profounder mystery: can religious trust survive every eventuality? The author recognizes that religion cannot endure unless its adherents transcend self-interest and reject all relationships grounded in the hope of reward for service duly rendered or fear of punishment for failing to meet expected standards of belief or practice.

As one might expect, an ambiguous answer rises above the heat of conflict, and the ambiguity penetrates to the very core of the story as well as the poetic dispute. On the surface, it appears that Job utterly rejects every semblance of a magical concept of reality whereby human beings manipulate deity for their benefit. After all, he retains his loyalty to God in the face of extreme adversity, explaining that we ought to accept weal and woe as equally sent by God. Still, the story endorses the principle of reward and retribution in subtle ways (Job is supremely virtuous and rich) as well as not so subtle (Job offers sacrifices to propitiate deity, and God seems to reward Job in the end for faithfulness). Despite its radical challenge to dogma, especially in the undeserved fate of Job's children, the story ultimately bows to tradition.

The center of gravity shifts in the poetic dispute, where the fundamental order of the universe comes under attack. Job questions the moral underpinnings of human existence, for he no longer receives appropriate dividends from above. Ironically, his complaint presupposes the very principle that he denies, else he would have no basis for dispute with God. The question, "Does God rule justly?" alternates with another, "How should a person respond to undeserved suffering?" Like the Mesopotamian *I Will Praise the Lord of Wisdom,* the book of Job functions as a paradigm of an answered lament, a model for those undergoing present suffering. The model consists of four movements: undeserved affliction, complaint, hearkening, restoration (Gese 1958). It gives free rein to the expression of anger, while at the same time urging the individual to submit humbly to the mystery and majesty of creation. The book offers no satisfactory answer to the agonizing query, the shortest question of all, "Why?" Even if the arrangement between God and the Adversary does not really constitute a wager, the idea of testing a faithful servant is only slightly more palpable, at least to modern consciences.

The book of Job addresses more than one question and proposes several competing answers. Presumably, the author's answer, insofar as one option takes precedence over all opposing views, is hidden within the divine speeches. These lectures on the wonders of nature argue for a morality that transcends human values and contend that God governs the universe wisely. The frightening monsters, described in language that conjures up images of crocodiles and hippopotami, posed a threat to order in Egyptian mythology but yielded to divine domestication according to this astonishing text (Keel 1978). The deity's activity in providing for the needs of wild animals and in causing rain to fall beyond the regions of human habitation implies that caprice does not speak the final word. Saadia Gaon makes the argument more explicit: the gift of life satisfies the issue of divine justice, and anything beyond that falls into the category of mercy. Owing their very existence to the creator, human beings have no claim on God.

This line of reasoning comes closest to Eliphaz' insistence that human deeds have no effect on God, who does not even trust holy ones. For Eliphaz, the basic issue becomes clear in a terrifying revelation: "Can a mortal be more righteous than God? Can a man be purer than his Maker?" (4:17). Not content to rest his case on a word from God, he appeals to proverbial wisdom (reaping and sowing) and to ancestral teaching ("We are older than you"). At first gentle toward Job and holding out hope of eventual restoration as a result of submission, Eliphaz becomes increasingly less patient, accusing Job of heinous crimes. In doing so, Eliphaz fails to see the inconsistency with his earlier insistence that God derives no pleasure from human morality.

Although Eliphaz alludes to human existence as drinking iniquity like water, Bildad extends this point to include the birth process itself. He also expresses an exceedingly low estimate of human worth. Matters lack any ambiguity whatsoever for Bildad; Job's children sinned and paid for it, for God does not pervert justice. It follows that Job's repentance will accomplish restoration. Zophar's contribution to the argument skirts the issue of justice altogether: God takes mercy into account, punishing less than people deserve. Moreover, Zophar bears witness to an inner voice that announces the brevity of ill-gotten wages.

Elihu plows the same furrow that Job's three friends have opened, as if youth inevitably do so. Like Eliphaz, he thinks God warns mortals by means of frightening dreams and visions; Elihu also questions the effect of virtue or wickedness on God, concluding that morality concerns human beings only (35:8). Like Bildad, Elihu cannot even imagine the possibility that God rules unjustly. Like Zophar, Elihu thinks favored persons escape penalty for their sins. His arguments lay greater stress on educative discipline and the role of a mediator in moving the deity to compassion.

Job also entertains thoughts about an advocate who will plead his case and press for vindication. This daring concept (9:33) disappears almost as abruptly as it occurs, only to return a second (16:19) and third time (19:25) with greater tenacity. Job remains adamant in his protests of innocence, and this unyielding stance obliges him to attribute fault to God. Failing to obtain a hearing in the divine court, Job concludes that God has abandoned justice altogether. Because Job believes in the unlimited power of God, he naturally assumes that the problem belongs to the realm of will. The deity clearly does not want to execute justice throughout the land, Job charges, and with this concession Job broadens his scope to include the miserable wretches of society who know nothing but deprivation from birth to death. Fleeting thoughts about survival beyond the grave only distress Job, who denies the likelihood itself. He soon realizes that his only hope consists in a formal pronouncement of innocence within a court of law. To this end he pleads with God to write out the crimes for which he now suffers, vowing to parade the charges for all to see. In desperation, he enters into an oath of innocence, a self-imprecation designed to force God to answer. Confused to the end, Job forgets that human action has no control over arbitrary deities—or free ones (Hempel 1961). Readers forget this point too, frequently remarking that such action forced God to respond. Even Israel's sages knew better; neither curses nor oaths automatically move from word to deed.

E. Composition

A noticeable lack of coherence within the book implies that more than one author contributed to its final form. Differences between framework and core suggest that the author of the poetry used a popular folktale to pose the religious problem to be examined in the dispute. The depiction of the hero differs sharply in the two parts, a model of patience in the story, a defiant rebel in the poetry. The names for God differ, Yahweh in the prose, El, Eloah, Shaddai in the dispute (with one exception). The story endorses the principle of reward and retribution, despite Job's temporary misfortune, but neither Job nor God subscribes to the theory. Job rejects it outright and God ignores it completely. The epilogue has God condemn the friends for speaking lies about the creator and praise Job for telling the truth, whereas the divine speeches adopt quite a different attitude toward Job's attempt to justify himself at God's expense.

Confusion also exists within the poetic section. The 3d cycle of speeches breaks off prematurely with no response by Zophar; furthermore, Job's arguments at this point become wholly out of character. He seems to surrender to the friends' understanding of things, which contradicts everything he has said previously and makes nonsense of what follows. Various rearrangements of chaps. 24–27 restore Zophar's last speech; perhaps Job's final remarks to the friends were so blasphemous that later readers replaced them with Zophar's sentiments. Chapter 29 presents a problem, for it interprets the argument and offers a feeble rationale for religion. The poem pronounces wisdom off limits for humans (Job seeks God, not wisdom!) but then concedes that God has made it accessible to everyone who is religious and moral, a conclusion Job only reaches after God's speeches. Furthermore, wisdom has two different meanings; practical knowledge in the dialogue, the nature of the universe in the poem. Elihu appears without advance warning and cites previous material with great familiarity. He may represent the later Jewish community's dissatisfaction with the divine speeches. Both God and the narrator in the epilogue ignore Elihu, as does Job. Moreover, the oath in chap. 31 arouses expectation of a divine visitor, which Elihu delays interminably. The divine speeches also seem to suggest supplementation. The primary problem extends beyond particular sections that differ markedly from the rest, especially the descriptions of horse and ostrich, to the simple fact that God speaks twice and elicits two submissions from Job. The second speech has struck many readers as excessive browbeating.

Literary unity within the dialogue has its defenders, who offer various justifications for rejecting a theory of textual accretion. The breakdown of the 3d cycle is a subtle way of declaring Job the victor (but why does Job endorse their view of retribution?). Job 28 functions as an interlude, retarding the action of the drama and assuaging human emotions. Elihu serves as an ironic foil to the deity, and the citation of earlier speeches constitutes instances of literary anticipation or foreshadowing. Variety in style and vocabulary is a mark of literary craft, and God's two speeches address Job's dual charges. Stylistic affinities between the hymn on wisdom's inaccessibility and the Elihu narratives, on the one hand, and the rest of the poetry, on the other hand, have led some interpreters to posit common authorship over a long period of time. The silence about Elihu in the epilogue baffles critics of all persuasions.

The folktale may have developed by stages, with the wife and friends playing somewhat different roles from the ones in the present book (Vermeylen 1986). The three friends may once have functioned in the way the Adversary does now. Inasmuch as these verses featuring "the Satan" can be omitted without serious loss, the story in all essentials probably existed long before the addition of the motif of a heavenly adversary. The story manifests exquisite style, causing one interpreter to question the appropriateness of using the term folktale (Good 1988) and leading another to postulate an epic substratum (Sarna 1957).

F. Date and Language

Although the book is set in pre-Mosaic times, the actual time of composition is much later. Linguistic evidence seems to indicate a date in the 6th century or later (Hurvitz 1974), despite the complete silence about the national calamity in 587 B.C.E. Specific indicators for dating the book are exceedingly rare. Job's powerful outcry about the desirability of incising his testimony on a rock with lead inlay may allude to the Behistun Rock on which the Persian King Darius proclaimed his accomplishments to all passers-by. Mention of caravans from Teman and Sheba (6:19) and the nomenclature of officials (kings, counselors, princes) in 3:14–15 corresponds to Persian hierarchy. The use of the definite article *ha-* with *Śaṭan* suggests a stage in the development of the figure prior to the Chronicler and parallel to Zechariah. The abundance of Aramaisms, while problematic, may indicate a date in the late 6th or 5th century. The relationship between Job and comparable laments or lyrical texts in Jeremiah and Deutero-Isaiah is difficult to assess, but priority may go to the latter books. Similarities between Job and theological probings within the Psalter (37, 49, 73) certainly exist, but the uncertain dates of these psalms render them dubious witnesses about the actual date of the book of Job. The possible allusion to Job in Qoheleth 6:10–11 may echo familiarity with the folktale, and the recently discovered Targum of Job from Qumran, dating from the 2d or 3d century B.C.E., suggests a considerably earlier date for the book of Job.

An attempt to provide a specific historical setting for the book in Teman lacks cogency. According to this hypothesis, the book was written between 552 and 542 B.C.E., when Nabonidus conquered Tema and marauding soldiers took Job's possessions, forcing him to ransom his life (Guillaume 1968). Likewise, an effort to understand the book as a paracultic tragedy intended for use at the New Year Festival (Terrien) has failed to persuade many readers. Two astonishing features of the book remain unresolved: why did the author choose an Edomite for its hero, and why did the analogy between Job's affliction and Israel's defeat by Babylon and enforced exile not affect the depiction of the hero? Given the hostile sentiments toward Edom in prophetic texts from the exilic and postexilic period, the identification of the perfectly righteous man as an Edomite, made explicit in an appendix to the book in the LXX, seems strange until one recognizes the universalism of wisdom literature. Moreover, having set the story in (pre-)patriarchal times, the author could not have introduced an Israelite, for the nation did not appear on the historical scene until centuries later.

Two other factors, sometimes thought to indicate a late date for Job, alter the situation little: the emergence of monotheism and monogamy. The heavenly Adversary can act only insofar as God allows it to do so, and the divine speeches also insist on the creator's authority over the entire cosmos. Such "modified monotheism" still employs mythic language about antagonists over whom the creator exercises control. Moreover, Job imagines the possibility of a mediator's forcing a guilty deity to acknowledge Job's innocence. One hesitates to label such thinking "monotheism," although it resolutely refuses to exonerate God by positing a rival deity. The noteworthy assumption that a wealthy man like Job in patriarchal times had only one wife may suggest that monogamy had become the rule rather than the exception when the author composed the folktale.

The language of the book contains more rare words than any other biblical work, Hosea being its nearest rival. The linguistic forms have caused interpreters to posit theories of composition in another language, primarily Aramaic. Much clarity of language and syntax comes from Northwest Semitic, so that theories of translation into Hebrew from another language seem superfluous. Nevertheless, the rare dialect of the book often defies understanding, and the frequent references to obscure animals and natural objects do not help matters. A single example illustrates the problem. In 4:10–11 five different words for lion stretch modern translators' wits to the breaking point.

G. Related Works in the Ancient World

Belief in the moral governance of the universe was widespread in the ancient world. Gradually this conviction gave rise to confidence that certain actions ensured well-being most of the time. By behaving in specific ways, individuals controlled the gods, who also benefitted from human attention to the cult and to ethics. During periods of social turmoil, doubt about the deity's benevolence became prevalent and produced literary texts resembling the book of Job in some ways. From Egypt come three works of this nature: *The Admonitions of Ipuwer, The Dispute Between a Man and His Ba,* and *The Eloquent Peasant* (*ANET,* 441–44, 405–10), all dating from the 12th Dynasty (1990–1785 B.C.E.).

A section of *The Admonitions of Ipuwer* cites conventional belief ("He [God] is the herdsman of all; there is no evil in his heart. His herds are few, but he spends the days herding them") only to lament the wickedness that the deity allowed to stand. Because of social upheaval, the author denies the existence of a providential deity guiding human affairs. He asks: "Where is he today? Is he asleep?" and insists that "his power is not seen." Although the god possesses authority, knowledge, and truth, "turmoil is what you let happen in the land, and the noise of strife." Death naturally follows, and the poet entertains the possibility that the divine herdsman loves death. *The Dispute Between a Man and His Ba* (*ANET,* 405–7) describes a miserable person who tries to persuade his soul to join him in a pact to commit suicide, primarily because his name reeks and he lacks companions who act virtuously. The man longs for death, which is "like a sick man's recovery," "like the fragrance of myrrh (and lotus)," "like a well-trodden way," "like the clearing of the sky," "like a man's longing to see his home." *The Eloquent Peasant* (*ANET,* 407–10) complains bitterly to a government official, Rensi, son of Meru, about a lesser functionary who robbed him. Because of his rhetoric, the peasant is imprisoned and encouraged to plead his case; unknown to him, scribes record his speeches for the entertainment of the court. The peasant speaks nine petitions, becoming more exasperated over time and threatening to appeal to Anubis. When servants come from Rensi to reward the peasant, he mistakes their purpose and welcomes death with the words: "A thirsty man's approach to water, an infant's mouth reaching for milk, thus is a longed-for death seen coming, thus does his death arrive at last." Like the book of Job, these texts have prose frameworks enclosing poetic complaints.

From Mesopotamia come at least four texts that explore the problem of unjust suffering: *Man and his God, I Will Praise the Lord of Wisdom, The Babylonian Theodicy,* and *A Dialogue Between a Master and his Slave.* In the Sumerian *Man and his God* (2d millennium; *ANET,* 589–91), a sufferer complains to the gods but confesses guilt and is restored. He accuses the deity, here called a "righteous shepherd," of becoming angry, thereby encouraging human enemies to conspire against the sufferer without fear of divine retaliation. Appealing to the intimate relationship of father and son, the sufferer asks how long the deity will leave him unprotected. Nevertheless, he surrenders all right to protest divine conduct and subscribes to conventional wisdom: "Never has a sinless child been born to its mother; a sinless workman has not existed from of old." *I Will Praise the Lord of Wisdom* (*ANET,* 434–37) discovers a solution in the inscrutability of the gods and the necessity for human beings to perform proper cultic acts. The sufferer believes in divine compassion ("I will praise the Lord of wisdom . . . whose heart is merciful . . . whose gentle hand sustains the dying . . .") despite his own wretched state. Contrasting his earlier prestige with his present dishonor, he complains about inability to discover the face of the one to whom he prays. Circumstances compel him to conclude that the gods may have a different value system from the one constructed by human beings. This concession leads him to ask: "Who can know the will of the gods in heaven? Who can understand the plans of the underworld gods? Where have humans learned the way of a god?"

The Babylonian Theodicy (ca. 1100 B.C.E.; *ANET,* 601–4) resembles Job in that a sufferer engages in a dispute with a learned friend. An acrostic poem of 27 stanzas with 11 lines each, this dispute entertains the possibility of divine culpability ("Narru king of the gods, who created mankind, and majestic Zulummar, who pinched off the clay for them, and goddess Mami, the queen who fashioned them, gave twisted speech to the human race. With lies, and not truth, they endowed them forever"). The sufferer complains of having been orphaned early, and his friend reminds him that we all die. When told that wild asses trample fields and lions kill, the friend points out that the wild animals pay with their lives and that the plan of the gods is remote. The sufferer insists that his good deeds have not brought favorable response from the gods, and this remark arouses the friend's anger over such blasphemy. The friend does concede that the one who bears the god's yoke may have sparse food, but this situation can change for the better in a moment. The sufferer lingers on the notion that morality yields no profit. In the end, the complainant prays that the shepherd (i.e., god) who abandoned him will yet "pasture his flock as a god should."

The Dialogue Between a Master and his Slave (*ANET,* 437–38) resembles Ecclesiastes more than the book of Job, but some features of the Dialogue echo the conditions underlying Job's distress. A master determines to pursue a course of action and his servant, the proverbial aye-sayer, encourages him. The master changes his mind and the slave defends this decision. Nothing commends itself to the master—not dining, marrying, hunting, philanthropy, or anything else—except suicide, better still, murdering the slave. This poor wretch, caught in his rhetoric, seems to say that the master would gladly join him in death within three days.

The Canaanite epic of Keret (*ANET,* 142–49) bears some resemblance to the book of Job. The hero loses his wife and sons but eventually finds favor with the gods and acquires a new wife and additional children. More remote parallels such as Prometheus Bound have been compared with Job, but differences stand out (Prometheus was a Titan, not a human being, and he suffered the wrath of Zeus through wilful conduct). An Indian tale about a discussion among the gods over the existence of pure goodness among earthly creatures singles out a certain Harischandra, whom the god Shiva submits to a test that demonstrates his incredible virtue.

The author of the book of Job may have known about the Mesopotamian (and Egyptian?) prototypes, but the biblical text cannot be explained solely on the basis of earlier parallels. These explorations of the governance of the universe and unjust suffering may have provided an intellectual stimulus, but the biblical author has produced something that stands alone as *sui generis.* Still, structural similarities (framework enclosing poetic disputes) and common ideas place the biblical work in the wider context of intellectual and religious foment. This observation also extends to specific units within the book of Job, for example, the oath of innocence in chap. 31, for which Egyptian execration oaths offer a close parallel (Fohrer *Job* KAT).

The claim that the book of Job is *sui generis* does not imply originality for everything in Job. In fact, striking similarities exist between elements within this book and other biblical material: the laments in Jeremiah (chaps. 3 and 20) and in the Psalms, hymnic passages in Amos (4:13; 5:8–9; 9:5–6) and Deutero-Isaiah, the book of Ruth, prophetic lawsuits, and proverbial wisdom. Sometimes the author seems to offer a parody of biblical texts (e.g., Job 3 and Genesis 1; Job 7:17–21 and Psalm 8). Occasionally Job shares expressions in common with another textual unit (e.g., 38:5 with Ps 30:4, "Surely you know"; and 13:20 with Prov 30:7, "Two things"—but the connection between these texts is unclear).

The book of Job is usually discussed in connection with Proverbs, Ecclesiastes, Sirach, Wisdom of Solomon, and a few Psalms (e.g., 37, 49, 73). Modern scholars call these works "wisdom literature" and consider their closest parallels to be in Egypt and Mesopotamia rather than in the rest of the biblical canon. In some ways Job resists inclusion in this corpus, primarily because of the dominance of the lament genre and the theophany. Nevertheless, it seems best to designate the book "wisdom" and to recognize that, like Sirach some years later, the author of Job begins to widen the scope of traditions accessible to the sages.

On the basis of the texts to which modern critics have given the title wisdom literature, four quite distinct types are discernible: proverbial sayings, religious or philosophical reflections in discourse form, nature wisdom, and mantic revelation. The book of Job lacks the last of these types. Collections of aphorisms from the 3d millennium to the 3d century B.C.E. have survived in Egypt, and Mesopotamian proverbs date from the 3d and 2d millennium. The philosophical probings from both areas rival the proverbial sayings in antiquity. The book of Job unites these two types of wisdom—the brief saying and reflective discourse—while restricting nature wisdom to a discrete unit, specifically chaps. 38–40. In general, the aphorisms present a positive view of reality, resting on belief in a reliable order and in the capacity of the human intellect to control one's actions and thus to promote well-being.

On the other hand, the intellectual reflection about the problem of suffering and the meaning of life is markedly less optimistic. The former type of thinking, by means of aphorisms, has a decidedly practical purpose, although its utilitarianism possessed a profound religious grounding: because right conduct sustained the order of the universe, the gods reward appropriate behavior. The reflective discourses question such certainty as found in these brief aphorisms, comprising a sort of "anti-wisdom." The sages therefore demonstrate unusual willingness to examine their presuppositions and to criticize themselves. The author of Psalm 37 affirms traditional belief in the face of all evidence that seems to indicate otherwise, but Psalm 49 takes human frailty much more seriously, and Psalm 73 probes deeply into the nature of the relationships between worshipper and deity. Here the assurance that God is good to the upright appears dubious when taking into account the prosperity of evildoers, until the psalmist goes to the holy place and reflects on the destiny of the evil ones. Then the intimacy with God becomes a source of unsurpassed joy and divine presence more precious than anything else in all creation.

Although the nature wisdom in the book of Job resembles lists of flora and fauna from onomastica in ancient Egypt—where encyclopedic knowledge of different subjects seems to have served to train young courtiers (von Rad 1972)—decisive differences make the identification of Job 38–40 as lists highly doubtful (Fox 1986). Ancient sages study nature as a means of learning more about human beings through analogy, for the wise assume that the same laws govern the universe, animals, and humans.

Because undeserved suffering posed an immense intellectual and religious problem for the sages, they sought arduously for a satisfactory answer. Their most common understanding, the *retributive,* is grounded in the order of the universe and the will of its creator. A second explanation, the *disciplinary,* derives from the context of the family, where well-intentioned parents punish their children as an act of love, hoping thus to shape character and to protect the young ones from harm. In time, the school also endorses this method of controlling the actions of youth. A third approach to suffering, the *probative,* bears impressive witness to the disinterested nature of religion. God tests human hearts to ascertain whether or not religion is pure, and in doing so replaces human self-interest with the centrality of holiness. A fourth interpretation, the *eschatological,* contrasts present discomfort with future restoration, indicating that hope springs eternal in the human breast. A fifth suggestion, the *redemptive,* derives from the sacrificial system and the idea that the spilling of blood alone makes atonement. A sixth response, the *revelatory,* takes suffering as an occasion for divine disclosure of previously hidden truth, both human pride and the mystery of the living God. A seventh understanding of suffering, the *ineffable,* is a humble admission of ignorance before unspeakable mystery, one so profound that a self-revealing deity in the book of Job remains silent about the reason for Job's suffering and fails to affirm meaning behind such agony. An eighth explanation for suffering, the *incidental,* implies that an indifferent deity stands by and thereby encourages evil, which seems trivial to the High God who fashioned mortals to be subject to suffering as the human condition. All these understandings of suffering in one way or another find expression in the book of Job.

H. Canon and Text

As in the case of Qoheleth (Ecclesiastes), the disturbing thoughts of Job did not prevent its acceptance in the biblical canon. An occasional rabbinic dissent against the historicity of the character Job has survived (*Baba Bathra* 15a), and one Christian thinker, Theodore of Mopsuestia, questioned the book's sacred authority. The sequence of writings varied at first, Job being placed between Psalms and Proverbs in the Talmud, and in Codex Alexandrinus, but preceding Psalms and Proverbs in Cyril of Jerusalem, Epiphanius, Jerome, Rufinus, and the Apostolic Canons. Jewish tradition designates the two different sequences by the acrostic abbreviations *ʾmt* ("truth") for Job (*ʾiyob*), Proverbs (*mišlê*), and Psalms (*tehillîm*), and *tʾm* ("twin") for Psalms, Job, and Proverbs. The Council of Trent fixed the order with Job in the initial position.

Textual problems abound in the book, and the much shorter Greek versions seldom resolve the difficulties. Often merely a paraphrase, the Greek text sometimes elucidates a theological bias in the present MT, for example the repointing of a negative particle in 13:15 to affirm trust in God even when faced with the prospect of death at the deity's hand (Pope, *Job* AB, 95–96). The Syriac Peshitta assists in clarifying obscure meanings of the Hebrew text. Enough of the Targum from Qumran has survived to confirm the same disorder in chaps. 24–27 as that in the Hebrew. One surprising feature of the Targum is its termination at 42:11 instead of 42:17. See also JOB, TARGUMS OF. Jerome's Latin translation of the Hebrew text of Job was influenced by the Greek translations of Aquila, Theodotion, Symmachus, and the Alexandrian version as mediated by Origen's Hexapla.

I. History of Interpretation

The *Testament of Job,* the oldest surviving interpretation of the book of Job, probably comes from Alexandria in the 1st century B.C.E. See also JOB, TESTAMENT OF. One of many such "last words" of a famous person, it is characterized by zeal against idols, extensive speculation about Satan, cosmological dualism, interest in women, burial customs, magic, merkabah mysticism, angelic glossolalia, and patience. The *Testament of Job* differs considerably from the biblical story. The essential variations are that (1) Job destroys Satan's idol, incurring wrath, but an angel reveals Satan's identity to Job; (2) Job's possessions and good works are magnified in haggadic fashion; (3) Job's devoted wife, Sitis, begs for bread and eventually sells her hair to enable them to survive; (4) Satan concedes defeat in wrestling with Job; (5) Baldad poses "difficult questions" and Zophar offers royal physicians, but Job relies on the one who created physicians; (6) Sitis refuses to die until she knows that her children receive proper burial, and Job assures her that their creator and king has already taken them up; (7) God condemns the friends for not speaking truth *about Job;* (8) Job's daughters inherit magical items, enabling them to speak ecstatically; and (9) chariots take Job into heaven.

Unlike the Epistle of James (5:11), early opinions about Job's character did not always emphasize his patient endurance. The *Abot de Rabbi-Nathan* accuses Job of sinning with his heart and in this way defends divine justice. Rashi faults Job for talking too much. According to Glatzer (1966), later interpreters went beyond calling Job a saint or an imperfectly pious man to quite different categories: a rebel (Ibn Ezra, Nachmanides), a dualist (Sforno), a pious man searching for truth (Saadia Gaon), one who lacked the love of God (Maimonides), an Aristotelian denier of providence (Gersonides), one who confused the work of God and Satan (Simeon ben Semah Duran), a determinist (Joseph Albo), one who failed to pacify Satan, a scapegoat, and isolationist (the Zohar), one who suffered as a sign of divine love (the Zohar, Moses ben Hayyim). In Jewish legend, God turned Job over to Samael (Satan) to keep him occupied while the Jewish people escaping from Egypt crossed the Red Sea, then God rescued Job from the enemy power at the last moment.

The early church stressed Job's suffering as a lesson in living and had readings from Job in the liturgy of the dead. Gregory the Great wrote thirty-five books of Sermons on Job, and Augustine read the book as an example of divine grace. Thomas Aquinas saw the book of Job as the starting point for discussing the metaphysical problem of divine providence (Damico and Yaffe 1989). Calvin wrote 159 sermons on Job, mostly polemical defenses of providence (Dekker 1952). This early Christian concentration on the suffering hero of faith gave way in the 17th and 18th centuries to an emphasis on Job as a rebel. For instance, Voltaire saw Job as a representative of the universal human condition (Hausen 1972).

Modern critics continue the tendency to understand Job in the light of prevailing intellectual or religious sentiments. For Carl Jung, psychological insights provide the key to understanding Job. Jung emphasizes the importance of a marriage between an unreflective but powerful deity, Job's afflicter, and *Ḥokmāh* (wisdom), who taught

God that the Cross, not abusive force, was the answer to Job. Jack Kahn draws on modern psychiatry to understand the grief process through which Job passed. Two literary treatments of Job have greatly influenced Western thinking about the problem of evil, Goethe's *Faust* and Archibald MacLeish's *J.B.* An anthropological approach to the book of Job emphasizes the people's desire to establish order by sacrificing Job as a scapegoat (Girard 1987), and a liberation theologian stresses Job's identification with the causes of the poor (Gutiérrez 1987). A philosopher explains Job's offense as ingratitude, a bitterness of spirit that harbors resentment toward God for allowing affliction to strike a heavy blow against Job's security (Wilcox 1989). Artists depict Job's suffering in the light of Greek mythology (William Blake) and the Holocaust (Hans Fronius). A Yiddish interpreter uses Goethe's *Faust* as a lens through which to view Job positively (Chaim Zhitlowsky 1919); a contemporary novelist likens the Jewish fate under Hitler to Job's affliction (Elie Wiesel) and is opposed by a humanist who contrasts Job's survival with the victims of Auschwitz and Dachau (Rubenstein). Some existentialist writers seem to have used Job as an example of the human situation (Camus, Kafka), and at least one Marxist philosopher thinks of Job as an exemplary rebel against theism and abusive power that religion fosters in the western world (Ernst Bloch).

The current fascination with literary theory has produced several different understandings of the book of Job. In one instance, readings are offered from the perspective of feminism, vegetarianism, materialism, and NT ideology (Clines 1989). An older reading of the book as drama has been revitalized (Alonso-Schökel 1977), and a shift from viewing Job as tragedy to comedy has occurred. In this view, Job's final restoration qualifies the book as a comedy in the classical sense of the word (Whedbee 1970). Attention has come to the ways modern interpreters silence the shrill voice of dissent, whether in the revised Roman Catholic liturgy (Rouillard 1983) or in the act of interpretation itself (Tilley 1989). In providing a fresh translation, a contemporary poet (Stephen Mitchell) has taken great license and removed the sting of Job's *cri de coeur* by omitting crucial verses.

Specialists in Hebrew Bible continue to wrestle with the meaning of key texts in the book of Job, particularly 19:23–27 and 42:6. Confronted with several possible translations (and probable textual confusion in 19:23–27), interpreters concede the impossibility of certainty. A parallel in the Canaanite epic of Baal and Anat may explain Job's daring thought that extends the concept of a *gōʾēl* to the realm of the gods, but the matter is complicated by the two previous allusions to an umpire (*mōkîah,* 9:33) and a witness (*ʿēdî // sahadî,* 16:19, 21). Such foreshadowing occurs throughout the book of Job: 9:17 and 38:1–42:6; 11:5–6 and 38:1–42:6; 13:7–12 and 42:7–9; 22:30 and 42:10; 9:32–35 and 32–37 (ironically); 8:6–7 and 42:10–17 (Habel 1985). Moreover, the ambiguity of Job's remarks in 19:23–26 leaves unclear Job's personal circumstances at the time of seeing God. Does Job expect vindication before death, or is his expectation considerably more bold? With respect to the missing object in 42:6, the suggestions are varied: Job repents of his finitude, he rejects (drops) his anticipated lawsuit, he falls down to the earth in shame, he only pretends to repent, knowing how to manipulate an unjust ruler, he rejects God, he recants his earlier words. Less likely, the verb *mʾs* is understood reflexively (I loathe myself, I melt away, I abase myself).

One conclusion seems to force itself on readers: the author of the book does not believe that the natural order is moral (Tsevat 1966). The God whom Job worships and accuses of injustice transcends morality. Consequently, this book does not present a comforting deity nor a particularly accommodating universe. Perhaps that attitude is appropriate in an examination of the possibility of disinterested goodness. Nevertheless, the evocative power of this book "crashes into the abyss of radical aloneness" (Susman 1969) and arouses high praise in many readers, for example: "Here, in our view, is the most sublime monument in literature, not only of written language, nor of philosophy and poetry, but the most sublime monument of the human soul. Here is the great eternal drama with three actors who embody everything: but what actors! God, humankind, and Destiny" (Alphonse de Lamartine, cited in Hausen 1972: 145).

Bibliography

Alonso-Schökel, L. 1977. Toward a Dramatic Reading of the Book of Job. *Semeia* 7: 45–59.

Aufrecht, W. E., ed. 1985. *Studies in the Book of Job.* SR Sup 16. Waterloo, Ontario.

Barr, J. 1971–72. The Book of Job and Its Modern Interpreters. *BJRL* 54: 28–46.

Ceresko, A. R. 1980. *Job in the Light of Northwest Semitic.* Rome.

Clines, D. J. A. 1989. Job. Pp. 181–201 in *The Books of the Bible,* ed. B. W. Anderson. New York.

Crenshaw, J. L. 1981. *Old Testament Wisdom.* Atlanta.

———. 1983 (ed.). *Theodicy in the Old Testament.* Philadelphia and London.

———. 1984. *A Whirlpool of Torment.* Philadelphia.

Crossan, J. D., ed. 1981. *The Book of Job and Ricoeur's Hermeneutics.* Semeia 19. Chico, CA.

Curtis, J. B. 1983. On Job's Witness in Heaven. *JBL* 102: 549–62.

Damico, A., and Yaffe, M. D., eds. 1989. *Thomas Aquinas: The Literal Exposition on Job.* Atlanta.

Damon, S. F. 1966. *Blake's Job.* New York.

Dekker, H., ed. 1952. *Sermons from Job: John Calvin.* Grand Rapids.

Dick, M. B. 1979. The Legal Metaphor in Job 31. *CBQ* 41: 37–50.

Duquoc, C., and Floristan, C. 1983. *Job and the Silence of God.* Concilium 169. New York.

Fohrer, G. 1983. *Studien zum Buche Hiob (1956–1979).* BZAW 159. Berlin and New York.

Fox, M. V. 1986. Egyptian Onomastica and Biblical Wisdom. *VT* 36: 302–10.

Freedman, D. N. 1968. The Elihu Speeches in the Book of Job. *HTR* 61: 51–59.

———. 1968. The Structure of Job 3. *Bib* 49: 503–8.

Gese, H. 1958. *Lehre und Wirklichkeit in der Alten Weisheit.* Tübingen.

Girard, R. 1987. *Job: The Victim of his People.* Stanford.

Glatzer, N. N. 1966. The Book of Job and Its Interpreters. Pp. 197–220 in *Biblical Motifs,* ed. A. Altmann. Cambridge, MA.

Glatzer, N. N., ed. 1969. *The Dimensions of Job.* New York.

Good, E. M. 1988. Job. *HBC,* 407–32.

Goodman, L. E., trans. 1988. *The Book of Theodicy: Translation and Commentary on the Book of Job by Saadiah Ben Joseph Al-Fayyumi.* YJS 25. New Haven.

Gordis, R. 1978. *The Book of Job.* New York.
Guillaume, A. 1968. *Studies in the Book of Job, with a New Translation.* Leiden.
Gutiérrez, G. 1987. *On Job: God Talk and the Suffering of the Innocent.* Maryknoll, NY.
Habel, N. C. 1985. *The Book of Job.* Philadelphia.
Hausen, A. 1972. *Hiob in der französischen Literatur.* Bern and Frankfurt.
Hempel, J. 1961. *Apoxysmata.* BZAW 81. Berlin.
Hurvitz, A. 1974. The Date of the Prose Tale of Job Linguistically Reconsidered. *HTR* 67: 17–34.
Janzen, J. G. 1985. *Job.* Atlanta.
Kahn, J. H. 1975. *Job's Illness: Loss, Grief, and Integration.* Oxford.
Keel, O. 1978. *Jahwes Entgegnung an Ijob.* FRLANT 121. Göttingen.
Kegler, J. 1977. Hauptlinien der Hiobforschung seit 1956. Pp. 9–25 in *Der Aufbau des Buches Hiob,* ed. C. Westermann. Stuttgart.
Kubina, V. 1979. *Die Gottesreden im Buche Hiob.* Freiburg.
Lévêque, J. 1970. *Job et son Dieu.* Paris.
Matenko, P. 1968. *Two Studies in Yiddish Culture.* Leiden.
Mettinger, T. N. D. 1988. *In Search of God.* Philadelphia.
Michel, W. L. 1987. *Job in the Light of Northwest Semitic.* Vol. 1. BeO 42. Rome.
Muenchow, C. 1989. Dust and Dirt in Job 42:6. *JBL* 108: 597–611.
Müller, H. P. 1970. *Hiob und seine Freunde.* Zurich.
———. 1977. Alt und Neues zum Buch Hiob. *EvT* 37: 284–304.
———. 1978. *Das Hiobproblem.* Darmstadt.
Oorschot, J. V. 1987. *Gott als Grenze.* BZAW 170. Berlin and New York.
Ploeg, J. P. M. van der, and Woude, A. S. van der, eds. 1972. *Le Targum de Job de la Grotte XI de Qumran.* Leiden.
Rad, G. von. 1972. *Wisdom in Israel.* Nashville.
Roberts, J. J. M. 1977. Job and the Israelite Tradition. *ZAW* 89: 107–14.
Rouillard, P. 1983. The Figure of Job in the Liturgy: Indignation, Resignation, or Silence? Pp. 8–12 in Duquoc and Floristan 1983.
Sanders, P. S., ed. 1968. *Twentieth Century Interpretations of the Book of Job.* Englewood Cliffs, NJ.
Sarna, N. M. 1957. Epic Substratum in the Prose of Job. *JBL* 76: 13–25.
Schmid, H. H. 1966. *Wesen und Geschichte der Weisheit.* BZAW 101. Berlin.
Schmidt, L. 1976. *De Deo.* BZAW 143. Berlin.
Susman, M. 1969. God the Creator. Pp. 86–92 in Glatzer 1969.
Terrien, S. 1957. *Job: Poet of Existence.* Indianapolis.
———. 1965. Quelques remarques sur les affinites de Job avec la Deutero-Esaie. Pp. 295–310 in *Volume du Congres: Geneve, 1965.* VTSup 15. Leiden.
Tilley, T. W. 1989. God and the Silencing of Job. *Modern Theology* 5: 257–70.
Tsevat, M. 1966. The Meaning of the Book of Job. *HUCA* 37: 73–106.
Van Selms, A. 1985. *Job.* Grand Rapids.
Vawter, B. 1983. *Job and Jonah: Questioning the Hidden God.* New York.
Vermeylen, J. 1986. *Job, ses Amis et son Dieu.* Leiden.
Weiss, M. 1983. *The Story of Job's Beginning.* Jerusalem.
Westermann, C. 1981. *The Structure of the Book of Job.* Philadelphia.
Whedbee, W. 1970. The Comedy of Job. *Semeia* 7: 1–39.
Wilcox, J. T. 1989. *The Bitterness of Job: A Philosophical Reading.* Ann Arbor.
Wilde, A. de. 1981. *Das Buch Hiob.* OTS 22. Leiden.
Zerafa, P. P. 1978. *The Wisdom of God in the Book of Job.* Rome.
Zhitlowsky, C. 1919. Job and Faust. Pp. 75–162 in *Two Studies in Yiddish Culture,* ed. P. Matenko. Leiden.

JAMES L. CRENSHAW

JOB, TARGUMS OF. There are two mss of targums (Aramaic translations) to the book of Job among the Dead Sea Scrolls found at Wadi Qumran: a substantial text found in Cave 11, consisting of about 20 percent of the book in 38 fragmentary cols (11QtgJob); and two small ms fragments from Cave 4, essentially comprising about a dozen fragmentary lines from two cols (4QtgJob). The ms do not overlap; the Cave 4 fragments preserve text from chaps. 3–5, while the Cave 11 material preserves intermittent text from 17:14 to the end of the book. Because of the lack of common text and, even more, because the Cave 4 Targum is so little preserved, it is an open question as to whether these two texts preserve the same or distinct Aramaic versions of Job. In any case, neither of these targums appears to show any direct relationship to the standard targum found in the Rabbinical Bible and available, for example, in the edition of Lagarde (cf. Fitzmyer 1974).

The larger targum from Cave 11 was published by van der Ploeg, van der Woude and Jongeling in 1971, and there followed an edition by Sokoloff in 1974, which is now considered the standard reference on the text. Major studies of 11QtgJob include Beyer 1984: 280–298; Jongeling et al 1976: 1–73; and Sokoloff 1974). The targum fragments from Cave 4 were published by Milik in 1977 (DJD vol. 6).

These two targums, especially the Cave 11 targum, are of considerable importance for the study of the book of Job, for the study of targumic traditions, and for the study of Aramaic during the Hellenistic and Roman periods. They constitute the earliest mss of Job translations in existence and 11QtgJob is the earliest known ms of Job of any significant length. It is also the only lengthy targum known from so early a period. (There exists another Qumran targum, a translation of Leviticus, but like 4QtgJob it is fragmentary.) Paleographical considerations suggest that both existing Qumran Job targum mss were copied during the 1st century C.E. The original editors proposed that 11QtgJob was actually composed in the latter half of the 2d century B.C.E.; more recently a later date has been proposed, namely, the 1st century B.C.E. (Kaufman 1973; Zuckerman 1987).

By and large, the Cave 11 Targum seems to adhere to its Heb *Vorlage* quite closely, certainly far more closely than targums of the Palestinian tradition preserved by the early rabbis. (The Cave 4 targum seems to be fairly literal as well, although it is simply too small to allow for reasonable judgment as to characteristics of this sort.) Where there appear on occasion to be editorial alterations in 11QtgJob, they tend to be focused upon avoiding implicit disrespect for the Deity, upgrading the image of Job, and perhaps downgrading the image of the friends, especially Elihu (cf. Tuinstra 1970; Zuckerman 1980). In this respect the sentiments of the translator seem to fall somewhat in line with the view of Job found in the pseudepigraphical *Testament of Job.*

The targum also appears to preserve the famous rereading of the phrase in Job 13:15, *lw ʾyḥl,* traditionally translated, ("though He [i.e., God] slay me, yet will I trust in Him") instead of *lʾ ʾyḥl* ("if He slays me, I have no hope"). Although a direct translation of Job 13:15 is not preserved in the existing 11QtgJob, the phrase appears to be quoted in 11QtgJob 25:7 = Job 34:31. The translator also shows some indication of exemplifying the rabbinical rule of scriptural interpretation, exposition by means of another similar passage (Zuckerman 1978).

It may be more than simply a coincidence that two out of the three clearly targumic texts found among the Dead Sea Scrolls are targums of Job. Moreover, in the most prominent discussion of targums in the early rabbinical literature (*t. Šabb.* 13:2; cf. *b. Šabb.* 115a; *j. Šabb.* 16:1), the particular targum under discussion is also a targum of Job. In that instance, Rabban Gamaliel (80–110 C.E.) is said to have been reading a targum of Job, which reminded R. Halafta that Gamaliel's grandfather, Gamaliel the Elder (30–70 C.E.) had once been brought a targum which he subsequently ordered to be hidden. In this latter instance the targum in question was, once again, a targum of Job.

We can only wonder why a good deal of the specific evidence we have of written targums from the period of the early rabbis centers upon targums of Job? One probable reason is that the Hebrew of Job, even at this early time, must have been recognized as being notoriously difficult to read and comprehend. Hence, if any biblical text cried out for a popular translation so that it would be more widely accessible in the vernacular of the day, Aramaic, it would certainly have been Job. Moreover, it would not only be because of the difficult nature of the language that targumic renditions of Job were called for. In all likelihood the controversial issues raised in Job were also deemed to require special handling, especially in more popular translations that would make Job more broadly available to the Jewish community in rabbinical times. We might suspect that it was in translations of this nature that various small adjustments were often made in order to conform the text to pietistic standards.

On the other hand, it is also quite likely that more straightforward renderings of Job were made in targumic form. After all, 11QtgJob and 4QtgJob, insofar as they are preserved, are fairly accurate renderings which contain relatively limited editorial adjustments. In fact, it may even be partly for this reason that Gamaliel the Elder wished to hide away the targum that was brought before him. That is, he may have deemed the targum too correct to be exposed to the uninitiated (note in this respect *b. Meg.* 3a). It is also likely that Gamaliel did not like the idea that any biblical text should be committed to writing in the vulgar language of the time and that this also prompted his suppression of the targum brought to his attention.

Regardless, it does seem fairly reasonable to assume that when the rabbis thought of a biblical targum around the beginning of the Common Era, the stereotypical example would seem to have been a targum of Job. And this at least supports the assumption that the Job known to the popular audience of that time was likely Job in translation as opposed to Job in the hard-to-read original Hebrew.

Bibliography

Beyer, K. 1984. *Die Aramaischen Texte vom Toten Meer.* Göttingen.
Caquot, A. 1974. Un écrit sectair de Qoumrân: le "Targum de Job." *RHR* 185: 9–27.
Delcor, M. 1973. Le targum de Job et l'araméen du temps de Jésus. Pp. 78–107 in *Exégèse biblique et judaïsme,* ed. J.-E. Menard. Strassburg (also in *RSR* 47: 232–61).
Fitzmyer, J. 1974. Some Observations on the Targum of Job from Qumran Cave 11. *CBQ* 36: 503–24.
———. 1978. The Targum of Leviticus from Qumran Cave 4. *Maarav* 1: 5–23.
Gray, J. 1974. The Massoretic Text of the Book of Job, the Targum and the Septuagint Version in the Light of the Qumran Targum (11QtgJob). *ZAW* 86: 331–50.
Jongeling, B. 1972. Contributions of the Qumran Job Targum to the Aramaic Vocabulary. *JSS* 17: 191–97.
———. 1975. The Job Targum from Qumran Cave 11 (11QtgJob). *Folia Orientalia* 15: 181–86.
Jongeling, B.; Labuschagne, C.; and Woude, A. van der, eds. 1976. *Aramaic Texts from Qumran.* Leiden.
Kaufman, S. 1973. The Job Targum from Qumran. *JAOS* 93: 317–27.
Morrow, F. 1973. 11Q Targum Job and the Massoretic Text. *RQ* 8: 253–56.
Muraoka, T. 1974. The Aramaic of the Old Targum of Job from Qumran Cave XI. *JJS* 25: 425–43.
———. 1977. Notes on the Old Targum of Job from Qumran Cave XI. *RQ* 9: 117–25.
Ploeg, J., van der; Woude, A. van der; and Jongeling, D., eds. 1971. *Le Targum de Job de la Grotte XI de Qumrân.* Leiden.
Ringgren, H. 1978. Some Observations on the Qumran Targum of Job. *ASTI* 11: 117–26.
Sokoloff, M. 1974. *The Targum to Job from Qumran Cave XI.* Ramat-Gan.
Tuinstra, E. W. 1970. Hermeneutische Aspecten van de Targum van Job uit Grot XI van Qumrân. Ph.D. diss., Groningen.
Woude, A. van der. 1969. Das Hiobtargum aus Qumran Höhle XI. (English version in *AJBA* 1: 19–29.)
York, A. 1974. *Zrʿ rwmʾh* as an Indication of the Date of 11QtgJob? *JBL* 93: 13–18.
Zuckerman, B. 1978. Two Examples of Editorial Modification in 11QtgJob. Pp. 269–75 in *Biblical and Near Eastern Studies: Essays in Honor of W. S. LaSor,* ed. G. Tuttle. Grand Rapids.
———. 1980. The Process of Translation in 11QtgJob. Ph.D. diss., Yale.
———. 1983. "For Your Sake . . .": A Case Study in Aramaic Semantics. *JANES* 15: 119–29.
———. 1987. The Date of 11Q Targum Job: A Paleographic Consideration of Its *Vorlage. JSP* 1: 57–78.

Bruce Zuckerman

JOB, TESTAMENT OF. Slightly shorter than the NT book of Romans, the *Testament of Job* embellishes the biblical story of Job in praise of the virtue of patience (*hypomonē*). The prosaic and occasionally humorous composition shows characteristics of similar works such as the *Testaments of the Twelve Patriarchs* and the *Testaments of Abra-*

ham, Isaac, and *Jacob.* Though listed among non-canonical works in the 6th-century Gelasian Decree (5.6.4), the *Testament of Job* is otherwise unmentioned until the 19th century, when its first modern edition was edited by Cardinal Mai (1833), who took the work to be Christian. Migne's French translation, a quarter century later (1858), provided the first translation into a modern European language.

Flanked by a prologue (*Testament of Job* 1) and an epilogue (chaps. 51–53), the bulk of the *Testament* (chaps. 2–50) engages Job first with a revealing angel (chaps. 2–5), then with Satan (chaps. 6–27), next with the three kings ("friends" in the biblical book of Job; chaps. 28–45), and finally with his three daughters (chaps. 46–50). Five poetic passages appear at *T. Job* 25:1–8; 32:1–12; 33:3–9; 43:1–17; and 53:2–4. The *Testament of Job* locates the cause of Job's illness in his destruction of an idol's temple. Job's wife Sitis—and indeed female slaves, widows, and daughters—all figure prominently in this curious text. Jewish burial interests abound. But the principal moral point of the work is captured in the sentence, "Patience is better than anything" (27:7).

The text exits in 4 Gk mss dated from the 11th to the 16th centuries. In addition 3 mss, only one of which is complete, survive from a translation into Old Church Slavonic done around the 11th century (three other Old Church Slavonic mss may exist: Schaller 1979: 317, n. 134). Since 1968, fragments of a 5th century Coptic version (P. Köln 3221) have been known. The impending publication of these will make possible the publication of a critical edition of the text of the *Testament of Job.*

The *Testament of Job* clearly draws from the LXX (Schaller 1980), especially Job 29–31. Septuagintal phrases, and in a few cases apparent direct quotations, have been taken into the *Testament.* Scholars are divided on the unity of the book, but a strong case in its favor has been made by Schaller (1979: 304–6).

The origin and purpose of the work have been variously assessed. M. R. James (1897), who first extensively studied the *Testament,* proposed a Jewish Christian origin in Egypt. K. Kohler (1898) conjectured, mainly from the hymnic sections of the document, an origin among the Therapeutae—a Jewish contemplative sect described by Philo in *De contemplativa.* Spitta (1907) concluded the writing to be pre-Christian but unrelated to the Essenes or to the Therapeutae. Later scholarship has come to favor the Jewish origins of the *Testament of Job* (Rahnenführer 1971; Schaller 1979). Similarities to Jewish merkabah mysticism—speculations about the divine chariot—have been noticed (Urbach 1967; Kee 1974). Jacobs (1970) views the *Testament* as a sample of Jewish martyrdom literature, while Rahnenführer (1971) sees the text as a piece of Jewish missionary propaganda. A proposal has been made that an original Jewish testament was edited by 2d-century Montanists to argue precedent for female prophecy (Spittler 1971), but this view has not found wide acceptance.

It seems best to regard the text as one of unclear origin within sectarian Judaism, mingling interests in magic, merkabah mysticism, standard Jewish features such as burial proprieties and opposition to idolatry along with the care of the poor and female prophetic utterance. Neither a specific origin nor a date more precise than 100 B.C.E.–200 C.E. can be determined.

Two eras in modern times reflect scholarly interest in the *Testament of Job.* A 15-year period at the turn of the century (1897–1911) yielded the first modern edition of the text (James 1897), the first English translation (Kohler 1898), and the first major study (Spitta 1907). With the publication by Philonenko (1958) of a French translation, with introduction and notes, a generation of renewed study began. This period gained impetus from S. Brock's publication (1967) of a new edition of the text, saw the emergence of several doctoral dissertations (Carstensen 1960; Spittler 1971; Nicholls 1982), and witnessed additional translations into German (Schaller 1979; before him, Riessler 1928), English (Spittler, *OTP* 1: 829–68; Thornhill 1984), modern Hebrew (Hartom 1965). During the thirty year period of 1958–1988, the *Testament of Job* increasingly appeared in introductions to pseudepigraphic literature and achieved deserved recognition as an exemplar of the mingled diversity of Hellenistic Judaic spirituality.

Bibliography

Brock, S. P. 1967. *Testamentum Iobi,* with J.-C. Picard, *Apocalypsis Baruchi graece.* Pseudepigrapha Veteris Testamenti graece 2. Leiden.

Carstensen, R. 1960. The Persistence of the Elihu Point of View in Later Jewish Literature. Ph.D. diss., Vanderbilt (summarized in *LTQ* 2[1967]: 37–46).

Collins, J. J. 1974. Structure and Meaning in the Testament of Job. *SBLSP,* pp. 35–52. ed. G. MacRae. Cambridge, MA.

Hartom, A. S. 1965. *hassᵉparîm hahysônîm,* 6.1–42. Tel Aviv.

Jacobs, I. 1970. Literary Motifs in the Testament of Job. *JJS* 21: 1–10.

James, M. R. 1897. *Apocrypha anecdota 2.* Texts and Studies 5/1. Cambridge.

Kee, H. C. 1974. Satan, Magic, and Salvation in the Testament of Job. *SBLSP,* pp. 53–76.

Kohler, K. 1898. The Testament of Job. Pp. 264–338 in *Semitic Studies in Memory of A. Kohut,* ed. G. A. Kohut. Berlin.

Kraft, R. A.; Attridge, H.; Spittler, R.; and Timbie, J. 1974. *The Testament of Job According to the SV Text.* SBLTT 5, Pseudepigrapha Series 4. Missoula, MT.

Mai, A. 1833. *Scriptorum veterum nova collectio e Vaticanis codicibus,* 7.180–91. Rome.

Migne, J. P. 1858. *Dictionnaire des apocryphes* 2[=24]: 401–20. Troisième et dernière encyclopédie théologique 23–24. Paris.

Nicholls, P. H. 1982. The Structure and Purpose of the Testament of Job. Ph.D. diss., Hebrew University.

Philonenko, M. 1958. Le Testament de Job et les Therapeutes. *Semitica* 8: 41–53.

Rahnenführer, D. 1971. Das Testament des Hiob und das Neue Testament. *ZNW* 62: 68–93.

Reissler, P. 1928. *Altjüdisches Schrifttum ausserhalb der Bibel.* Augsburg.

Schaller, B. 1979. *Das Testament Hiobs.* JSHRZ 3/3. Gütersloh.

———. 1980. Das Testament Hiobs und die Septuaginta-Übersetzung des Buches Hiob. *Bib* 61: 377–406.

Spitta, F. 1907. Das Testament Hiobs und das Neue Testament. Pp. 139–206 in his *Zur Geschichte und Literatur des Urchristentums* 3/2. Göttingen.

Spittler, R. 1971. The Testament of Job. Ph.D. diss., Harvard.

Thornhill, R. 1984. The Testament of Job. Pp. 617–48 in *The Apocryphal Old Testament,* ed. H. F. D. Sparks. New York.
Urbach, E. 1967. The Traditions about Merkabah Mysticism in the Tannaitic Period. Pp. 1–28 in *Studies in Mysticism and Religion* (Festschrift for G. Sholem), ed. E. Urbach et al. Jerusalem (in Hebrew).

RUSSELL P. SPITTLER

JOBAB (PERSON) [Heb *yôbāb*]. Five individuals in the Bible bear this name. The name has been compared with the Sabaean tribal name *yhybb,* probably to be vocalized *yuhaybab,* by J. Halevy and E. Glaser (1890: 303, see Jobab no. 1 below). The difference between the Sabaean name and its Heb rendering (one would perhaps expect Heb *yêbāb*) may be explained by the fact that the form of the foreign name was assimilated to the NW Sem name *yôbāb* (see *IPN,* 226, n. 3). The identification of the biblical *yôbāb* with the Gk *Iōbaritai* mentioned by Ptol. (*Geog.* 6.7.24), first proposed by S. Bochart (*Geographia sacra* 1: 190), is not acceptable. On the one hand, the Gk rendering would have to be altered in an inadmissible way to *Iōbabitae;* on the other hand, that tribal name mentioned in SE Arabia beside the Gk *Sachalitai* (= Sabaean *sʾkln*) is to be identified with the legendary place name Wabār in the sands of the large Arabian desert. According to its formation, the name *yhybb* is an imperfect form of the causative stem, since it is found occasionally in Sabaean names of tribes or clans (e.g. *yhblḥ, yhśḥm,* etc.). The meaning of the name is not known, since it remains uncertain whether the root *ybb* is to be connected with Ar *yabāb,* "waste, deserted."

1. The last of thirteen sons of Joktan (Gen 10:29; 1 Chr 1:23). This name occurs in the so-called "Table of Nations" (Genesis 10) where it is a tribal rather than personal name associated with the progenitor of Arabic tribes, Joktan (Westermann 1984: 526). The Sabaean tribe with a similar name *(yhybb)* was one of the three old tribal federations of the ancient country of Sumʿay in the central highland of Yemen. This tribe or its tribal leaders are mentioned in several inscriptions from the same region (CIS IV 37.6; RES 4176.5, 8, 9; 4231.2; Gl 1378.2). The text of RES 4176 was engraved into a large rock near the mountain of Riyām in Arḥab during the first quarter of the 3d cent. B.C. and contains the statute of the god Taʾlab for his worshippers from Sumʿay. In these regulations it was ordained that the leader of the tribe *Yuhaybab* was placed in charge of the property of the god and that he had to organize a banquet for the pilgrims during the annual pilgrimage to the sanctuary of Taʾlab.

Bibliography

Glaser, E. 1890. *Skizze der Geschichte und Geographie Arabiens.* Vol. 2. Berlin.
Westermann, C. 1984. *Genesis 1–11.* Trans. J. J. Scullion. Minneapolis.

W. W. MÜLLER

2. The son of Zerah from Bozrah, and the king who ruled in Edom after Bela (Gen 36:33–34 = 1 Chr 1:44–45). The name occurs in parallel lists (Gen 36:29–39 = 1 Chr 1:43–50) which utilize a formula found elsewhere in the Bible (1 Kgs 16:22; 2 Kgs 1:17; 8:15; 12:22; 13:24) to recount the succession of kings (in Edom and Israel). The formula is "King X reigned. He died and King Y reigned in his stead." The LXX associates this Jobab with the main character of the book of Job in its enlargement of the final chapter of the book (see Pope *Job* AB, 354).

3. The king of Madon summoned by Jabin king of Hazor to fight against the invading Israelites (Josh 11:1). He is also counted among the kings defeated by Joshua W of the Jordan (Josh 12:29), although in this list he is not mentioned by name.

4. The first son born in Moab to Shaharaim and his wife Hodesh (1 Chr 8:9). The name appears twice in this genealogy of Benjamin (1 Chronicles 8); once as a son (v 9), and the other time as a grandson of Shaharaim (v 18, see below). As with several names that recur in the Chronicler's genealogies (cf. e.g. CALEB, GERA), it is difficult to identify each Jobab.

5. A son of the Benjaminite Elpaal, son of Shaharaim and his wife Hushim (1 Chr 8:18). After Shaharaim sent Hushim and another wife, Baara, away he had offspring by Hodesh in Moab. Elpaal's sons appear in two sections (1 Chr 8:12–15, 17–18), and Jobab is the last son in the second segment.

MARK J. FRETZ

JOCHEBED (PERSON) [Heb *yôkebed*]. A Levite woman, wife of Amram, mother of Aaron, Moses, and Miriam (Num 26:59). Jochebed is mentioned by name only in the Levitical genealogies of Exodus 6 and Numbers 26 (cf. Exod 2:1–10). The writer of Exod 6:20 introduces her as Amram's wife and aunt (*dōdātô;* RSV "his father's sister") and mother of Aaron and Moses. Num 26:59 omits the information that she was Amram's aunt, describing her instead as "the daughter of Levi, who was born to Levi in Egypt." Numbers 26 adds that she was mother of Miriam as well as Moses and Aaron.

Exod 6:20 describes Jochebed as Amram's *dōdātô,* a word which means "uncle's wife" in Lev 20:20 (cf. Lev 18:14). The RSV of Exod 6:20 translates *dōdātô* as "father's sister," probably on the basis of Num 26:59, which calls Jochebed "the daughter of Levi," that is, sister of Amram's father, Kohath. However the relationship is to be understood, the marriage of Amram and Jochebed seems to run contrary to priestly laws which prohibit sexual relations between a man and his "uncle's wife" (Lev 18:14; 20:20) and between a man and his "father's sister" (Lev 18:12). This may be the reason that the LXX of Exod 6:20 presents Jochebed as Amram's cousin, "daughter of his father's brother." In referring to Jochebed as "the daughter of Levi," the genealogist of Num 26:59 underscores the relationship between the family of Jacob and later generations of Israelites. See Burns (1987: 85–90).

In including Jochebed as the first of three women in the family line of Aaron, the genealogist of Exod 6:20–25 reflects the postexilic community's interest in the pedigree of priests' mothers and wives. See Johnson (1969: 87–99). Although Jochebed is the only wife and mother to be included in the genealogy of Numbers 26, her appearance there, together with her ancestral lineage, likewise establishes the full legitimacy of Aaron as priest in the family of Levi. In fact, according to Num 26:59 Aaron (who is the focus of vv 58b–61) is more closely linked with Levi through Jochebed than through Amram.

Bibliography

Burns, R. J. 1987. *Has the Lord Indeed Spoken Only through Moses?: A Study of the Biblical Portrait of Miriam.* SBLDS 84. Atlanta.

Johnson, M. D. 1969. *The Purpose of Biblical Genealogies.* SNTSMS 8. Cambridge.

Wilson, R. R. 1977. *Genealogy and History in the Biblical World.* YNER 7. New Haven.

RITA J. BURNS

JODA (PERSON) [Gk *Iōda*]. Var. HODAVIAH; HODIAH. **1.** Son of Iliadun and one of the Levites over twenty years old appointed under Zerubbabel to oversee the reconstruction of the temple (1 Esdr 5:58). An LXX variant substitutes "Judah" (Gk *Iouda*), which also appears in the Ezra 3:9 parallel of this passage where the MT reads Heb *yĕhûdâ*. However, instead of "Joda," other parallel lists of Levites mention either Hodaviah (Ezra 2:40 = Neh 7:43 = 1 Esdr 5:26), or Hodiah (Neh 9:5; 10:10–11—Eng 10:9–10) along with Jeshua and Kadmiel. Therefore, it is difficult to be certain whether to identify LXX *iōda* with Heb *yĕhûdâ,* Heb *hôdawyāh,* or Heb *hôdîyāh;* although Joda might be considered a separate person altogether.

2. The son of Joanan and father of Josech in Luke's genealogy of Joseph, the husband of Mary (3:26). Since Joda and sixteen other names in vv 24–27 appear nowhere else in the Bible, it is wise not to attempt identification with OT persons (Fitzmyer *Luke* AB, 500). However, Kuhn (1923: 212) maintains that Luke's *iōda* results from an incorrect spelling of LXX *ōdia* (or *ōdouia*) in 1 Chr 3:24 (Heb *hôdawyāhû,* "Hodaviah"). He concludes that even though the position of Joda in Luke's genealogy does not correspond to his position in 1 Chronicles 3, the frequent confusion of *iōda* and *ōdia* in the LXX justifies the identification of Luke's Joda with Hodaviah/Hodiah of 1 Chr 3:24. Consequently, in Matthew's parallel genealogy (1:13), Abiud may represent Luke's Joda. See ABIUD.

Bibliography

Kuhn, G. 1923. Die Geschlechtsregister Jesu bei Lukas und Matthäus, nach ihrer Herkunft untersucht. *ZNW* 22: 206–28.

MARK J. FRETZ

JODAN (PERSON) [Gk *Iōdanos*]. One of four priestly descendants of Jozadak who divorced their foreign wives during Ezra's reform (1 Esdr 9:19). The parallel in Ezra 10:18 also lists four descendants of Jozadak through Jeshua, but in the place of Jodan it records Gedaliah. The difficulties of identifying individuals such as Jodan raise questions about the sources of and literary relationships among Ezra, Nehemiah, and 1 Esdras.

MICHAEL DAVID MCGEHEE

JOED (PERSON) [Heb *yôʿēd*]. The father of Meshullam and an ancestor of Sallu, a Benjaminite and provincial leader who agreed to settle in Jerusalem (Neh 11:7). Although Sallu's line is referred to in both the list in Nehemiah 11 and 1 Chronicles 9 (cf. v 7), Joed is not mentioned. This, like other differences in the two lists, suggest that there is no direct literary relationship between the two lists (contra Kellermann 1966: 208–27 and Mowinckel 1964: 146–47). Some, however, have conjectured that both writers were dependent upon common archival materials (Schneider *Esra und Nehemiah* HSAT, 42–43; Brockington *Ezra, Nehemiah and Esther* NCBC, 187; cf. Myers *Ezra, Nehemiah* AB, 185). In any event, the presence of Joed in the list provides no further evidence of use in resolving the problem. Apart from the probable significance of the name itself ("Yahweh is witness"), nothing is known about this Benjaminite patriarch (Brockington, 189).

Bibliography

Kellermann, U. 1966. Die Listen in Nehemia 11 eine Dokummentation aus den letzten Jahren des Reiches Juda? *ZDPV* 82: 209–27.

Mowinckel, S. 1964. *Studien zu dem Buche Ezra-Nehemia I: Die nachchronistische Redaktion des Buches. Des Listen.* Skrifter utgitt av Det Norske Videnskaps-Akademii Oslo. Oslo.

FREDERICK W. SCHMIDT

JOEL (PERSON) [Heb *yôʾēl*]. Relatively common name in ancient Israel. As Dahlberg (*IDB* 2: 925) points out, the wide distribution of the name among the tribes of Israel is theologically significant in view of its meaning: "Yaw (Yahweh) is God."

1. A prince (Heb *nāśîʾ*) in the tribe of Simeon who is listed in 1 Chr 4:35 in the context of two accounts (4:39–41 and 42–43) about territorial expansions of the Simeonites in the time of Hezekiah. The list of princes in 4:34–37 may have been independent at one time. Its connections with the surrounding passages are not strong. This is particularly true with regard to the lists which precede it. None of the names in 4:34–37 is directly related to the descendants of Simeon in 4:24–26. No other information is given in the Bible about this Joel or any of the other individuals listed in 4:34–37.

2. A Reubenite listed in 1 Chr 5:4. The section of genealogy which Joel heads (5:4–6) is probably a fragment. It is not at all connected with the beginning of the Reubenites in 5:3. Also, while some of the names in 5:3 are found in other Reubenite genealogies (Gen 46:9; Exod 6:14; Num 26:5–6), the names in 5:4–6 are not found elsewhere in the OT as Reubenites. Certain variant readings in the versions (LXX^{L}—"Joel his son," Syriac—"Joel son of Carmi") reflect attempts to integrate Joel into Reuben's line (Braun *1 Chronicles* WBC, 70). The occurrence of the name Baal in 5:6 may indicate the presence of authentic and early N tradition in the fragment, as Williamson (*Chronicles* NCBC, 64) suggests. The lack of connection between 5:3 and 5:4–6 means that the reference in v 6 to exile under Tiglath-Pileser III cannot be used to interpret 5:1–2 as an allusion to the transfer of Reuben's birthright to Joseph (*contra* Myers *1 Chronicles* AB, 35–36).

In 5:8 the name Joel is found again. However, 5:7–10 may be another fragment. The editor of the passage apparently makes Beerah the antecedent of *ʾehāyw* and sees 5:7–10 as the continuation of 5:4–6. But this connection is not strong and does not seem original. In addition, the different titles for Beerah *(nāśîʾ)* and Jeiel *(rōʾš)* suggest that 5:4–6 and 5:7–10 are two separate groups of Reubenites from two different time periods. Hence, the identification of the Joel in 5:4 with the one in 5:8 is probably secondary.

3. Reubenite listed in 1 Chr 5:8 who has been identified secondarily with the Joel in 5:4 (see above). That the Joel in 5:8 was a Reubenite is suggested by the references in that verse to Aroer, Nebo, and Baalmeon which are found in earlier Reubenite settlement lists (Num 32:34, 38; Judg 13:9) and on the Mesha stele (lines 9, 14, 26, 30) as part of the territory taken from Israel under Omri's son.

4. Chief (Heb *rōʾš*) of the tribe of Gad mentioned in 1 Chr 5:12. The entire genealogy in 5:11–17 is distinctive in that it contains no material from elsewhere in the OT (Williamson NCBC, 65).

5. Kohathite Levite and ancestor of Samuel the prophet according to 1 Chr 6:21—Eng 6:33. This Joel, however, does not appear in the parallel genealogy in 6:7–13—Eng 6:22–28. Instead, one finds the name Shaul, although Williamson (NCBC, 71) sees these as distinct, albeit related, genealogies. The Chronicler has apparently incorporated Samuel into the Kohathite line in order to legitimize his activities as a priest.

6. The older son of Samuel the prophet (1 Sam 8:2) and according to 1 Chr 6:18—Eng 6:33; 15:17 the father of Heman, the chief singer of the Kohathite Levites under David and Solomon. The name Joel has been lost from the MT at 1 Chr 6:13—Eng 6:28 but can be restored, as in the RSV, on the basis of the passages just cited and of the readings of the versions (LXX, Syriac) for 6:13.

7. Man of Issachar whose name occurs in 1 Chr 7:3 in the context of a military census list now in genealogical form (7:2–5). Only 7:1 has parallels elsewhere in the OT (Gen 46:13; Num 26:23–25).

8. One of David's "mighty men" according to 1 Chr 11:38. In the parallel list 2 Sam 23:36 has Igal *(yigʾāl)*. The variant names obviously reflect a *g*/*w* confusion, though it is not clear which is original. Chronicles also refers to Joel as the brother of Nathan, while Samuel has "son of Nathan." See DAVID'S CHAMPIONS.

9. A chief (Heb *śār*) of the Gershomite Levites at the time when David brought the ark up to Jerusalem (1 Chr 15:7, 11). Dahlberg (*IDB* 2: 925) assumes that this Joel is the same as the one in 1 Chr 23:8; 26:22 (see item no. 10 below), although the texts themselves do not explicitly indicate this.

10. Gershonite listed among the Levites whom David organizes in preparation for Solomon's building the temple in 1 Chr 23:8; 26:22. (On the form "Gershon" instead of "Gershom" see Braun WBC, 82). In 1 Chr 23:8 this Joel is the son of Ladan and the brother of Jehiel, while in 26:22 he is the brother of Jehiel and the grandson of Ladan. (Ladan is elsewhere called Libni (1 Chr 6:3—Eng 6:17; Exod 6:17; Num 3:21.) Also, in 26:22 Joel and Zetham are described as being in charge of the temple treasuries.

11. A chief (Heb *śār*) of Ephraim, included in 1 Chr 27:20, in the Chronicler's list of chiefs (27:16–22) in connection with David's census described in 1 Chronicles 21. In 27:23–24, the Chronicler not only explains why the census was sinful ("Yahweh had promised to make Israel as many as the stars of the sky") but also mitigates David's offense by explaining that he neither included those below twenty years of age nor completed the census.

12. Kohathite, called the son of Azariah, whom Chronicles (2 Chr 29:12) lists among the first Levites to respond to Hezekiah's orders to cleanse the temple. The passage as a whole is a stylized presentation of how all Levitical branches participated with equal enthusiasm in Hezekiah's reform movement.

13. Son of Pethuel and prophet. See JOEL, BOOK OF.

14. Member of the family of Nebo (Gk *Nooma*) who is listed in Ezra 10:43 (= 1 Esdr 9:35) among those in postexilic Judah who divorced their foreign wives and children at Ezra's bidding. Several differences occur between the lists in Ezra 10:43 and 1 Esdr 9:35, but Joel is found in both. Cogan (1979: 37–39) cites similarities between these two verses and the Reubenite list in 1 Chr 5:4–8 (see nos. 2 and 3 above) in support of his suggestion that the names in Ezra 10:43 (= 1 Esdr 9:35) refer to Reubenites who resettled their homeland E of the Jordan following the exile. He thinks that it was these repatriated Reubenites who were the Chronicler's source for his Reubenite genealogies.

15. Overseer (Heb *pāqîd*) of postexilic Jerusalem according to Neh 11:9. The verse raises several intriguing questions. It is not clear, first of all, whether Joel was considered a member of the tribe of Judah or of Benjamin. The fact that his second in command is named Judah suggests the former, but certainty is not possible. Secondly, the precise function of the office of *paqid* remains obscure, though it seems to be a title for a lay leader as opposed to a priestly (*nāgîd* 11:11) or a military title (*śār* 7:2).

Bibliography

Cogan, M. 1979. The Men of Nebo—Repatriated Reubenites. *IEJ* 29: 37–39.

STEVEN L. MCKENZIE

JOEL, BOOK OF.

In the MT, Joel is the second of the twelve so-called Minor Prophets, and one of the shortest prophetic books in the Hebrew Bible.

A. Unity

Underlying all aspects of the study of Joel is the fundamental issue of the book's unity. Though one of the shortest prophetic books in the canon, Joel contains two distinct parts. The opening chapters describe a natural disaster resulting from a locust plague (chaps. 1–2 [—Eng 1:1–2:27]), while the concluding chapters predict the restoration of exilic Israel after an apocalyptic war with the nations (chaps. 3–4 [—Eng 2:28–3:21]; on the different versification in Hebrew and English Bibles, see E below). Since these two sections of Joel are unified by certain obvious similarities of language and thought and at the same time set apart by clear differences, an ongoing debate exists among scholars about their relationship. Do the two parts of Joel represent two distinct messages which have been subsequently combined into one prophetic collection, or are they elements of a single prophetic proclamation?

The traditional view that the book of Joel contains a unified message from a single prophetic figure is still the most popular among modern commentators (e.g., Kapelrud 1948; Ahlström 1971; Rudolph *Joel* . . . KAT; Wolff, *Joel and Amos* Hermeneia; Prinsloo 1985). According to this view, the two parts of Joel form a coherent whole in which the locust plague (chaps. 1–2 [—Eng 1:1–2:27]) signifies the approaching apocalypse (chaps. 3–4 [—Eng 2:28–3:21]). As the armies of locusts have invaded Judah and will be destroyed, so the armies of the nations will gather against Judah to be judged and defeated. The identification of both events with the day of Yahweh (1:15; 2:1, 11; 3:4 [—Eng 2:31]; 4:14 [—Eng 3:14]) links them together under a single concern: the ultimate vindication of Judah.

Since Vernes (1872) first questioned the unity of Joel in the last century, an alternative interpretation of the relationship between the two parts of Joel has become widely accepted. According to this view, put into its classical form by Duhm (1911: 184–88), the two parts of Joel are too distinct to represent a unified language or point of view. Whereas chaps. 1–2 [—Eng 1:1–2:27] describe a locust plague which has already happened and which has brought divine judgment on Judah in the form of an agricultural catastrophe, chaps. 3–4 [—Eng 2:28–3:21] do not mention locusts, Judah's agricultural catastrophe, or divine judgment on Judah at all. Instead these chapters predict a future cosmic battle in which the destruction of Jerusalem and the Diaspora will be avenged on the nations in order to restore the political fortunes of Judah. Two different authors seem to be present: a prophetic figure interpreting a massive locust outbreak as divine judgment, and a later apocalyptic writer anticipating the culmination of human history and the exaltation of Judah in a great cosmic conflict. Thus, Joel is a collection of diverse traditions rather than a unified composition.

The lack of a consensus about the unity of Joel illustrates the difficulty of interpreting the relationship between two parts of the same corpus which have similarities and differences, both of which are rather striking. Each position must account for conspicuous evidence to the contrary. A. Weiser (*Der Zwölf kleinen Propheten* ATD) has tried to avoid the difficulties of both positions by suggesting that the two sections of Joel were written by the same author in two different times and situations, but Weiser's view has not been adopted by many. In spite of the fact that many recent commentators are persuaded by the similarities between the parts of Joel to regard the book as a unity, the differences are more significant. The stronger arguments support a modified version of the two-stage interpretation of the book of Joel, a view which will be presented together with the prevailing alternatives in the analysis of Joel which follows.

B. Literary Structure

1. The Book. While the book of Joel contains a variety of literary forms, those who regard Joel as a unity see in it a literary architecture which unites these forms in a coherent whole. Two of the more thorough and influential presentations of the structure of the book of Joel as a unity are those by Kapelrud (1948: 3–9) and Wolff (*Joel and Amos* Hermeneia, 6–12).

Kapelrud sees in Joel a single liturgy, designed for a ritual of repentance at the temple, which begins with a psalm of lamentation (1:2–2:18) that includes a community lament (1:2–12), a description of distress (2:1–11), and calls to repentance (1:13–20, 2:12–18). The liturgy concludes with a divine oracle (2:19–4:21 [—Eng 2:19–3:21]) delivered in response to the lament and containing three subsections (2:19–27; 3:1–5 [—Eng 2:28–32]; 4:1–21 [—Eng 3:1–21]). Wolff recognizes similar basic subdivisions within Joel but considers them linked by the symmetry of a literary parallelism rather than by a liturgical structure. A lament over scarcity (1:1–20), an announcement of catastrophe (2:1–11), and a call to repentance (2:12–17) in the first part of the book are balanced and reversed respectively by a promise of economic restoration (2:21–27), a promise of Jerusalem's salvation (4:1–3, 9–17 [—Eng 3:1–3, 9–17]), and a promise of the spirit (3:1–5 [—Eng 2:28–32]).

According to these analyses, the center of Joel is to be found at 2:17, 18. Speeches before this midpoint describe disaster, those after it salvation. Calls to lamentation and repentance before this point are followed by oracles assuring a divine response and restoration. This two-part structure is not uncommon in prophetic books which usually begin with oracles of judgment and conclude with oracles of salvation.

Even for those who regard Joel as a compilation of the works of different authors, Joel 2:17, 18 is generally recognized as the center of the book, in this case marking off the oracles of judgment of the original prophet from those of a later apocalyptic editor predicting salvation. Duhm (1911: 184–88), for example, sees in 1:1–2:17 a series of prophetic speeches concerning various disasters—military invasion, locust plague, drought—composed in poetry. He then understands Joel 2:18–4:21 (—Eng 2:18–3:21) as an addition written in prose by a synagogue preacher with an apocalyptic ideology.

2. Community Lamentations and Prophetic Response (Chaps. 1–2 [—Eng 1:1–2:27]). The language and literary forms Joel uses to deliver his response to the locust plague are indebted to the speech forms of Joel's own prophetic tradition as well as to the forms developed by temple personnel for the religious liturgies used in public worship.

The title of the book of Joel (1:1), as is customary for prophetic books, names the author of the book, his family, and identifies his speeches as divine rather than human utterance. Unfortunately for a determination of Joel's historical setting, the title does not list the reigning monarch as prophetic titles frequently do.

The speeches of Joel actually begin with a summons to listen (2:2–4), a conventional form used by prophets to gain the attention of their audience and alert it to the delivery of a solemn proclamation (cf. Isa 1:2; Mic 1:2; Jer 2:4; Amos 8:4). This summons includes a brief description of the disaster, which will be the focus of the prophetic message, and an admonition to recall it in future generations.

The opening summons is followed by a series of speeches delivered to various sectors of society: consumers (drinkers of wine; 1:5–10), farmers (1:11–12), and priests (1:13–18). Using elements of the lament genre, a prayer employed in temple liturgy to appeal to God for assistance in a crisis, Joel urges each group to declare its distress to God and appeal for divine aid. The opening two lines of each speech begin with imperative verbs, the second of which is always *hêlîlû,* "wail!", a term used frequently in the Bible in descriptions of ceremonies of lamentation (e.g., Jer 4:8; Amos 8:3). The first two elements in the lament genre, a cry to God followed by a description of the nature of the distress, are recognizable in these speeches. Concluding the series of speeches is the prophet's own prayer of lament (1:19–20).

The description of the locust infestation embedded in these calls to lamentation is concluded in a poem about the day of Yahweh (2:1–11). The unity of this poem is indicated by the use of inclusion in which references to the day of Yahweh and the darkness which accompanies it (2:1–2, 10–11) enclose the description of the locust plague in 2:3–9. In this poem and throughout the preceding speeches the prophet employs highly figurative language to convey the terror of the massive infestation of the locust. The insect hordes are described as a populous nation occupying the land (1:6), as brush fires crackling through the stubble (2:3, 5), as lions with fearsome teeth (1:6), as thieves who steal through the windows (2:19), and as thunderclouds darkening the sky (2:2, 10). But the most prominent metaphor for the locust is the invading army (1:6; 2:4–9). Contrary to some who wish to reverse the last image and see human or apocalyptic armies described with the image of locusts in chaps. 1–2, the structure of the simile in 2:4–9 clearly indicates that locusts are described using the image of human armies (Thompson 1955; see further C.2 below).

The culmination of Joel's appeals to society is found in a call to repentance (2:12–17). The call reflects both prophetic and priestly perspectives. In the prophetic tradition, this call emphasizes that true repentance is an inner reorientation and commitment: "Rend your hearts, not your garments" (2:13). At the same time, Joel insists that regular cultic rituals be observed, and he calls the priests to gather the entire community for a public ceremony in order to grieve for its sins and appeal for God's compassion and assistance.

Joel 2:18–27 is a prophetic oracle conveying the divine response to the lamentations prescribed in the previous speeches. Since the oracle promises salvation, as do those following in 3:1–4:21 (—Eng 2:28–3:21), it has been widely regarded as the beginning of the second half of the book of Joel. There is no doubt that in its focus on salvation Joel 2:18–27 resembles the speeches following it, but when its language is examined in detail, its closest ties are with the speeches which precede it.

The language of the salvation oracle in Joel 2:18–27 is directly based on the description of the locust plague in 1:2–2:17 and systematically reverses the previous images of devastation. God answers the cry for compassion and promises mercy (2:18–27; cf. 2:17). Grain, wine, and olive oil will be restored (2:19; cf. 1:10) and Judah's reproach removed (2:19; cf. 2:17). The invading locusts will be driven out into lands as desolate as those it brought into being in Judah (2:20; cf. 2:3). The land which mourned is told to rejoice (2:21; cf. 1:10). The animals longing for pasture will again graze (2:22; cf. 1:19–20). Orchards, trees and vineyards stripped of fruit and foilage will again produce (2:22; cf. 1:12). Everything devoured by the locust will be restored (2:25; cf. 1:4). A people summoned to wail *(hêlîlû)* will again praise *(hillaltem)* God (2:26; cf. 1:5, 11, 13).

Since the linguistic connections between Joel 2:18–27 and the preceding sections are so numerous and carefully constructed, and since neither the locust nor the images of ecological disaster it caused are mentioned in Joel 3:4 (—Eng 2:28–3:21), this salvation oracle is better understood as the conclusion to the 1st part of Joel rather than the introduction to the 2d part.

3. Hymns of the Apocalypse (Chaps. 3–4 [—Eng 2:28–3:21]). Two oracles proclaiming God's future activity make up the concluding section of Joel. Both are joined to the preceding chapters by conventional editorial phrases employed to append supplemental material: "After this" (3:1 [—Eng 2:28]) and "In those days, in that time" (4:1 [—Eng 3:1], cf. Amos 9:11). Both of these oracles describe an apocalyptic conflict as a result of which Jerusalem will be vindicated and restored.

The second oracle (4:1–21 [—Eng 3:1–21]) is the most elaborate. It is generally understood to be a continuation of the preceding prophetic oracles (2:18–3:5 [—Eng 2:18–2:32]) which answer the prayers of lamentation in the first part of Joel (e.g., Kapelrud 1948: 7–8, Wolff, *Joel and Amos* Hermeneia, 73–75). In most cases the chapter is viewed as a composite work and divided into at least four sub-units, vv 1–3, 4–8, 7–17, 18–21, the second of which is frequently considered a later addition (Wolff, *Joel and Amos* Hermeneia, 74).

The literary form which throws most light on the structure and function of Joel 4 (—Eng 3), and suggests that the chapter may in fact represent a more unified composition than generally believed, is the divine warrior hymn. Hymns celebrating divine victories over Israel's enemies are among the oldest poems in the Bible (e.g., Exod 15:1–18, Judges 5) and are common during the Israelite monarchy (e.g., Psalms 2, 24, 29, 68, 89, 97). In the postexilic period, this hymnic form was revived by apocalyptic writers to describe the divine warrior's final vindication of Judah and defeat of its enemies (Isa 59:15b–20, 66:14b–16, 22–23; Zech 14:1–21, Ezekiel 38–39; see Hanson 1975: 123–34). Based on an ANE mythic pattern of divine combat, reflected in such ANE works as the Baal Cycle and Enuma Elish, these hymns describe the deity challenged by an enemy, marching out to battle while the cosmos shakes, defeating the enemy, returning victoriously to the mountain sanctuary to be enthroned king, and finally bestowing fertility and plenty on the world.

Such is the pattern which underlies Joel 4 (—Eng 3). The hymn opens with the description of the challenge to the sovereignty of the divine warrior by the nations who have exiled God's people, sacked the divine sanctuary, and seized the land (4:1–8 [—Eng 3:1–8]). In response, the divine warrior declares war and goes into combat to destroy the nations (4:9–14 [—Eng 3:9–14]). The cosmos is shaken during God's march (4:15–16 [—Eng 3:15–16]). Victorious in battle, the divine warrior is enthroned on the holy mountain (4:17 [—Eng 3:17]). Fertility and well-being are bestowed on all creation (4:18 [—Eng 3:18]). Finally, the salvation of God's people is proclaimed (4:19–21 [—Eng 3:19–21]).

Preceding this divine warrior hymn is a shorter composition, Joel 3:1–5 (—Eng 2:28–32), which anticipates the same events described in more detail in Joel 4 (—Eng 3): the salvation of God's people in an apocalyptic conflict (3:3–5 [—Eng 2:30–32]). Rather than detailing the conflict which will usher in the new era, this brief eschatological oracle describes the egalitarian character of the community which will emerge (3:1–2—Eng 2:28–29).

C. Theological Themes

Joel has not always been held in high regard as a major contributor to prophetic thought (e.g., J. M. P. Smith et al., *Micah* . . . ICC, 67–68). The locust plague has been viewed as a less significant crisis than the great political developments to which such prophets as Isaiah and Jeremiah addressed themselves (Duhm 1916: 398–99). The book lacks the hard hitting social criticism of other prophets. And the eschatological hymns in chaps. 3–4 (—Eng 2:28–3:21) detailing the divine judgment on Israel's neighbors have been seen as representing the narrow exclusivism of postexilic Judaism (Wood *JBC,* 442).

In spite of this assessment, the book of Joel is a fine example in many respects of both prophetic and apocalyptic thought, and such images in Joel as the rending of the heart (2:13) and the pouring out of the spirit (3:1–2 [—Eng 2:28–29]) have enjoyed a lively history in later generations. In Joel's response to the ecological crisis precipitated by the locust infestation, Joel may in fact have a unique contribution to make among Israel's prophets to a vision of the integrity of creation—the interrelatedness between human society and its environment—in biblical religion. Of all the themes in Joel, the one most widely recognized and discussed as a controlling topic in the book is the "Day of Yahweh." This is indeed a useful topic on which to center a discussion of the themes of Joel since it ties together the major concerns of Joel and at the same time is a crucial topic in the debate on the unity of the book.

1. The Day of Yahweh. The day of Yahweh is referred to five times at significant points in the corpus of Joel (1:15; 2:1, 11; 3:4 [—Eng 2:31]; 4:14 [—Eng 3:14]). Its precise meaning in Joel is not completely obvious, however, since the concept of the day of Yahweh is put to a variety of uses in biblical literature as a whole.

In general, the day of Yahweh is used by biblical writers for a decisive divine intervention in human affairs (Everson 1974: 335–37). In the earliest actual occurrence of the phrase, Amos 5:18–20, the prophet Amos employs it for an act of divine judgment when Israel will experience defeat and disaster (cf. Ezek 7:1–20; 13:1–5, Zephaniah 1). Amos implies, however, that his audience thinks of the day of Yahweh as a day of salvation and good fortune rather than a day of punishment, a fact which has led scholars to the conclusion that the phrase traditionally had a positive meaning, describing either the victory of Yahweh on Israel's behalf in a holy war (von Rad 1959) or the enthronement of Yahweh in Israel's cult (Mowinckel 1961: 2.229). This positive use of the concept is in fact revived among apocalyptic authors following the exile who apply it to the anticipated restoration of Judah and judgment of its enemies (e.g., Zech 14:1–9, Obad 15–21, Isa 63:1–4). Which of these conceptions is intended in the use of the day of Yahweh in Joel is dependent on a closer examination of the contexts in which the phrase occurs.

2. The Day of Judgment: The Locust Plague. The concern of the first half of Joel is a massive outbreak of the desert locust which has plagued human society in the Middle East since the earliest human records (Thompson 1955). Traditionally designated *Schistocerca gregaria,* the desert locust of North Africa and the Middle East has, since V. M. Dirsh's reclassification of locusts in 1974, been recognized as a subspecies of *Schistocerea americana,* a species of locust at home in North America. It is now classified *Schistocerca americana, subspecies gregaria.* Known popularly as the desert locust, *Schistocerea americana, subspecies gregaria* inhabits and breeds in the immense desert stretching from Saharan Africa through the Arabian Peninsula and into W India, an area including the Sinai Peninsula and Judean desert. In the right combination of circumstances, still not completely understood by scientists, but involving climate as well as biological and behavioral changes in the insect itself, the desert locust multiplies rapidly, crowds together into dense, gregarious swarms, and migrates in large bands borne on wind currents into neighboring fertile areas in search of food (Krebs 1978: 302–16).

The effect of such a swarming of the desert locust can be catastrophic. Locusts eat their own weight in green food each day. An invasion of Somaliland in 1957 was estimated to include 1.6×10^{10} locusts and weighed 50,000 tons. Observers have left reports of the kind of devastation this swarming caused in the last great infestation of Jerusalem and its environs (Whiting 1915), an account highly reminiscent—down to such images as darkening skies and whitened tendrils of the fig tree—of Joel's description of the plague he experienced (1:7; 2:2). Though partially controlled in the modern era by insecticides sprayed from the air on breeding areas, the desert locust remains a serious threat and is monitored constantly by the United Nations Food and Agriculture Organization's Emergency Center for Locust Operations. As contemporary experience illustrates, the swarming of the desert locust described by Joel represents no mere inconvenience nor mundane difficulty for human society. With its spectre of malnutrition, starvation, and loss of life the locust plague poses a threat to human society every bit as serious as a military invasion, to which it is in fact compared (1:6; 2:1–11).

Joel's perception of the life-threatening character of the ecological crisis and of the extent to which the fate of human life is linked to the fate of the earth is illustrated by his repeated use of the same terms and images to describe the responses of humanity and nature to the locust infestation. As the priests mourn so does the land (1:9–10). As the vines wither and dry up so do the farmers and so does the joy of the people (1:11–12). As Joel cries out to God so do the animals in the barren pastures (1:19–20). Assurances of restoration are directed to the land, animals, and people (2:18, 21, 22). Within these images lies a profound appreciation for the interrelatedness of a people and its environment and for the crucial significance of this relationship for human survival.

Because descriptions of the locust plague are followed in Joel by the great apocalyptic hymns in chaps. 3–4 (—Eng 2:28–3:21), scholars have customarily interpreted the plague as a sign of and prelude to these coming events rather than as a crisis with its own independent significance. This interpretation of the locusts is closely related to a particular view of the day of Yahweh in Joel. According to this view, the day of Yahweh refers to a single event, the day of apocalyptic salvation with which it is associated in Joel 3:4 (—Eng 3:14). References to the day of Yahweh in the context of the plague (1:15; 2:1, 11) link the locusts to this coming conflict and restoration.

A recent illustration of this common understanding of the day of Yahweh in Joel is found in Wolff's designation for Joel 1:1–20, "Locusts as Forerunners of the Day of Yahweh," and in his interpretation of the great day of Yahweh poem in 2:1–11 as a hymn in which locusts are only a metaphor for the invasion of apocalyptic armies (*Joel and Amos* Hermeneia, 17, 37–48). Even those who believe the two parts of Joel come from different authors tend to see a single, apocalyptic meaning for the day of Yahweh in Joel. They differ from such scholars as Wolff who defend the integrity of Joel, however, in that they understand the references to the day of Yahweh in 1:15 and 2:1, 11 as interpolations made by an editor responsible for chaps. 3–4—Eng 2:28–3:21 in order to unite the older material about the locust plague with the newer apocalyptic additions (Duhm 1911: 184–88; J. M. P. Smith et al., *Micah* . . . ICC, 50–51).

Though adopted by only a few scholars (e.g., Bourke 1959), the interpretation of the day of Yahweh in Joel 1:15 and 2:1, 11 as a day of divine judgment distinct from the apocalyptic salvation described in Joel 3–4 (—Eng 2:28–3:21) is a reasonable alternative. The appeal to the priests to lament the day of Yahweh in 1:15 connects this day directly to the current disaster. Likewise, the use of the day of Yahweh as an inclusive device to frame the vivid picture of the locust hordes in 2:1–11 also unites the day to the plague. A close connection appears to be drawn in this poem between the conventional language of darkness accompanying Yahweh's judgment day and the dark clouds of invading locusts (2:2, 10; cf. Amos 5:18–20 and Zeph 1:14–16). The interpretation of the day of Yahweh as judgment is particularly compelling if Joel 1–2 (—Eng 1:1–2:27) is seen as an original whole, not to be understood through the interpretive lens of Joel 3–4 (—Eng 2:28–3:21). According to this point of view, Joel, in the tradition of the classical prophets Amos and Zephaniah, saw in Israel's reversals the day of Yahweh's judgment and seized the opportunity to call for repentance and renewal.

In his calls to remorse (1:5–20) and repentance (2:12–17) in the day of divine judgment, Joel stands firmly at the center of Israel's prophetic tradition. While he does not, in this brief account of the locust plague detail social injustice, Joel does reflect the fundamental prophetic insight that ritual activity without genuine inner renewal will not avert the disintegration of the society. "Turn to me with your entire heart (self)," writes Joel, "rend your hearts, not your garments" (2:12–13).

3. The Day of Salvation: The Apocalypse. The meaning of the Day of Yahweh in chaps. 3–4 (—Eng 2:28–3:21) is seldom debated. Here it clearly designates a day of salvation: a climactic war in which the nations that have occupied Judah and exiled the Jews will be judged and defeated and in which Judah's political and economic fortunes will be restored. This understanding of the day of Yahweh places Joel 3–4 (—Eng 2:28–3:21) within the apocalyptic movement which developed in the postexilic era.

The development of apocalyptic thought among prophetic schools in the postexilic period has been described by such scholars as Plöger (1968) and Hanson (1975). A key feature of this apocalyptic movement was a vision of salvation conceived less and less in terms of the actual political and religious institutions of Israel and the Near East, and more and more in terms of a cosmic intervention in human affairs and a radical alteration of the status quo. Oracles and hymns describing these expectations were composed and appended to such prophetic collections as Isaiah (chaps. 56–66) and Zechariah (chaps. 9–14) to give them an apocalyptic cast.

The divine warrior hymn in Joel 4 (—Eng 3) reflects this apocalyptic mentality. The war it describes is not one in the flow of ordinary history but a cosmic conflict which will usher in a new era of world politics. All of Israel's past enemies will be defeated in a single stroke of divine combat. The nations actually singled out—Tyre, Sidon, Philistia, Egypt, Edom—are Israel's traditional enemies and are symbolic of all hostile powers rather than allies in an actual war. The location of the battle—the Valley of Jehoshaphat—is not an actual place but a symbolic name, "Yahweh has judged," which described the character of the war. The images of the fertility and abundance accompanying a restored Judah are so excessive that they suggest a recreation of the natural order. The possession of the spirit by all flesh described in Joel 3:1–2 (—Eng 2:28–29) reflects a reality beyond the experience of postexilic Jews. These apocalyptic images reach beyond current events and political structures to describe a future salvation in ultimate terms.

The apocalyptic mentality which dominates Joel 3–4 (—Eng 2:28–3:21) has been faulted for its otherworldly orientation, its violent resolution to the predicament of postexilic Israel, and its exclusiveness which reserves salvation only to the community on Mount Zion. Indeed, when the author of 4:10 (—Eng 3:10) calls for the nations to beat their plowshares into swords, he reverses a traditional prophetic image (Isa 2:4, Micah 4:3) which anticipated the resolution of Israel's relations with the nations in more peaceful and inclusive terms.

While these characteristics of the apocalyptic vision in Joel 3–4 (—Eng 2:28–3:21) cannot be denied, they should be understood as elements of a world view uniquely capable of sustaining the faith and life of a community marginalized by present power structures (see D.2 below). Such groups—among them the group which likely produced Joel 3–4 (—Eng 2:28–3:21)—often perceive most clearly the violence and corruption within powerful human institutions and their need of divine judgment (4:1–8 [—Eng 3:1–8]). The judgment envisioned, however, is not something such a community has in its power to accomplish, but rather a judgment which it leaves to divine prerogatives (4:11–12 [—Eng 3:11–12]). These groups often find the will to survive in the interim by visions of cosmic renewal (4:18–21 [—Eng 3:18–21]) and of egalitarian societies undivided by traditional categories of age, gender, family, and class (3:1–2 [—Eng 2:28–29]). The apocalyptic vision of Joel thus represents powerful images for survival in a situation in which the status quo offers little well-being or hope for change.

D. Author

1. Name. Joel is a sentence name composed of a shortened form of the divine name Yahweh (*yô*-[Jo-]) and the word *ʾel* (-el), "God." It means Yahweh is God. The name Joel was not uncommon in ancient Israel. It appears, for example, as Samuel's oldest son (1 Sam 8:2) and as one of David's heroes (1 Chr 11:38). The occurrence of the name Joel chiefly in the Chronicler's History is regarded by Wolff (*Joel and Amos* Hermeneia, 24–25) as evidence of its popularity in the postexilic period, and an indication of the postexilic date of the prophet. Its use in the Deuteronomistic History, however, makes this argument inconclusive (1 Sam 8:2).

2. Social Role. Since neither the superscription (1:1) nor the speeches of Joel provide more information about the prophet than his and his father's names, nothing certain can be said about his occupation or position in Israelite society. A popular theory, however, describes Joel as a cult prophet, an official related to the temple in Jerusalem. Especially prominent among Scandinavian scholars (Kapelrud 1948: 176; Ahlström 1971: 130–37), this theory is based on the fact that Joel calls the people to a community ceremony of repentance at the Temple (2:15–17) and employs features of temple prayers to call the people to lament (1:5–10; see B.2 above). In fact, Kapelrud has argued that the book of Joel represents a unified Temple liturgy designed for communal worship (1948: 3–9).

While Joel was certainly familiar with temple worship and its forms, and considered participation in communal ceremonies of repentance crucial, no firm evidence confers on Joel's cultic status. Many features of the book, however, argue to the contrary: Joel's authority and stance toward society derived not from his official status in the cult but from the personal reception of divine revelation which marked out prophetic figures in Israel (1:1a). Prophets in Israel commonly delivered speeches at religious sanctuaries (e.g., Jeremiah 7; Amos 7:10–17) and even came from priestly families (e.g., Jeremiah 1:1; Ezekiel 1:3), yet they do not appear to be professional members of Israel's religious institutions. They spoke on the basis of their own charismatic gifts (e.g., Amos 7:14–15). Joel addresses the priests not as part of his own social group, but as one sector of society which must respond to the crisis. Furthermore, his own words heavily reflect prophetic forms of speech (1:1–4; 2:18–27; see B.2 above), and his language makes use of traditional prophetic phraseology (e.g., 1:5 and Isa 13:6; 2:2 and Zeph 1:15–16). Thus the common characterization of Joel as a cult prophet is by no means assured. He may well have found his place among prophetic circles who represented an institution in Israelite society distinct from the cult (Wolff *Joel and Amos* Hermeneia, 11–12).

If Joel 3–4 (—Eng 2:28–3:21) is a later addition to the prophetic response to the locust plague, then the question must be raised about the author of this material and his social setting. As has already been noted in the treatment of the themes of these chapters (C.2), they appear to represent the new apocalyptic orientation of the postexilic era. The apocalyptic orientation seems to arise especially among members of prophetic schools who have been excluded from current power structures and have lost hope of achieving salvation within the status quo. The loss of status, power, and wealth was a common experience of Jews following the destruction of Jerusalem and the fall of the monarchy. The experience of disenfranchisement may have been even more acute, as Hanson (1975) has argued, among particular groups within postexilic society who found themselves outside the restructured temple hierarchy and its vision for a restored Judah. Within such a precarious social position, the apocalyptic vision of radical renewal by cosmic intervention has great power. It is likely that groups in just this social situation, as Plöger (1968: 96–105) and Hanson (1986: 313–14) have argued, composed the hymns in Joel 3–4 (—Eng 2:28–3:21) and appended them to the Joel corpus.

3. Date. The brief superscription (1:1) of Joel contains no historical data, unlike many of the prophetic books which date the prophecy to the reign of a particular king. As a result, the historical setting of the author and the date of the book of Joel must be inferred from references in the text of the book itself. This inductive task is made particularly difficult because the first part of the book centers on an ecological catastrophe rather than a historical crisis and the second part of the book mentions neighboring countries in highly symbolic fashion. Joel thus contains few references to Israelite or ANE politics which might help to locate the book within a definite historical period. Scholarly estimates of the date of Joel have consequently ranged widely from preexilic to postexilic times.

The placement of Joel together with the 8th century prophets near the beginning of the Book of the Twelve in both the Hebrew and Greek canons (see F below) reflects a traditional understanding of Joel as preexilic prophet. This view is still common with estimates of Joel's preexilic date ranging from the late 9th century (Bič 1960) to the early 6th century just before the fall of Jerusalem (Rudolph, *Joel . . .* KAT). Most scholars, however, now place Joel in the postexilic period, somewhere between the late 6th (Ahlström 1971: 129) and the early 4th centuries (Wolff *Joel and Amos* Hermeneia, 4–6).

The issue of Joel's unity has a direct bearing on the question of date, since a two-stage development of the book, which appears likely, would involve two different historical settings for the two parts of the collection. A judgment about the date of the second part of Joel is much easier to make in this regard than a judgment about the first part. References in Joel 3–4 (—Eng 2:28–3:21) to the fall of Judah, the dispersion of the Jews, and the return of the exiles (4:2, 7 [—Eng 3:2, 7]) all point to a postexilic political scene. Furthermore, the apocalyptic vision expressed in the form of a divine warrior hymn reflects the perspective and literary activity which provided eschatological additions in the postexilic period to such other prophetic collections as Isaiah, Zechariah (Hanson 1975) and Habakkuk (Hiebert 1986: 136–43). References to the Greeks (4:6 [—Eng 3:6]), and quotations of earlier prophetic literature (e.g., 4:10—Eng 3:10 = Isa 2:4; 4:16 [—Eng 3:16] = Amos 1:2) may be further evidence for the postexilic period.

The first part of Joel is much more difficult to place. In its view of the locusts as God's judgment and its call to repentance and inner renewal, Joel reflects the major concerns of preexilic prophecy. Its language of the day of Yahweh is remarkably similar to that of the 7th century prophet Zephaniah (1:14–16), and similarities have also been noted with Jeremiah's speech (Kapelrud 1948: 179–80, 189–90). Other characteristics, however, may point to the postexilic period. Lack of reference to a king, frequent references to the priests, and a positive view of cultic ritual have been taken to reflect the priestly theocracy described in such postexilic prophets as Haggai, Zechariah, and Malachi. Furthermore, such expressions as "gracious and compassionate," (*ḥannûn wĕraḥûm;* 2:13) and "house of our God" (*bêt ʾĕlōhênû;* 1:16) have been judged to reflect postexilic Hebrew conventions (Hurvitz 1966: 95, 172). It is difficult to know which of these data to weigh more heavily in determining the actual date of the original speeches of Joel to which the apocalyptic visions were later added.

E. Text and Versions

The textual witnesses to Joel and the rest of the twelve Minor Prophets derive from the same basic tradition of textual transmission. No major textual traditions or families can be distinguished in Joel and the Minor Prophets, as can be identified, for example, in such other sections of the Hebrew Scriptures as the Pentateuch and some of the historical books (Former Prophets). Yet the various witnesses do preserve variant readings and are useful in establishing the text of Joel.

The MT is, in general, well preserved. An early witness to the textual tradition preserved by the Masoretes is a scroll of the Minor Prophets from the era of the Second Jewish Revolt which has been recovered from the Wadi Murabba'at (DJD 2). It contains portions of Joel 2:20–4:21 (—Eng 2:20–3:21). Fragments of the Hebrew text of Joel are now available from an even earlier manuscript of the Minor Prophets (75 B.C.E.) discovered among the Qumran Scrolls (4QXII^c; DJD 11: 54–99). This manuscript, which contains portions of Joel 1:10–2:1, 2:8–23, and 4:6–21 [—Eng 3:6–21], stands in the same textual tradition as the MT and the versions. Its relative affiliation with MT or OG cannot be determined.

A unique feature of the Greek versions is their division of Joel into only three chapters instead of the four of the MT, a division followed in modern English Bibles. Joel 3:1–5 of the MT is affixed by G to Joel 2 as vv 28–32. Joel 4:1–21 of the MT thus becomes Joel 3:1–21 in G. Among the Greek translations extant for Joel, the OG is the most significant. It is a literal translation on the whole and is close to MT in character. A scroll of the Minor Prophets from Nahal Heber contains portions of Joel and is a recension of the OG which aims to bring the OG into harmony with proto-Rabbinic texts (Barthélemy 1963). The Targum Jonathan to the Prophets and the Vulgate both presume the MT and present few independent readings.

F. Canonical Position

Joel appears in the biblical canon among the twelve shorter prophetic books often referred to as the Book of the Twelve or the Minor Prophets because of their brief length. An important principle determining the order of the twelve in both the Masoretic Text and the Septuagint appears to be their relative chronology, established by their superscriptions or historical allusions within the book themselves. In both collections, the 8th century prophets (Hosea, Amos, Micah) appear at the beginning, while the late preexilic (Nahum, Habakkuk, Zephaniah) and postexilic (Haggai, Zechariah, Malachi) prophets appear at the end. The books for which a date is difficult to determine—Joel, Obadiah, and Jonah—are scattered among the 8th century prophets in the MT and grouped after them in the LXX.

In the MT, Joel is located second, after Hosea and before Amos. This position seems to have been determined by parallels in content between the last chapter of Joel and the book of Amos which follows (Wolff, *Joel and Amos* Hermeneia, 3–4). The bicolon "Yahweh roars from Zion/ And from Jerusalem utters his voice: is found verbatim at the end of Joel (4:16 [—Eng 3:16]) and at the beginning of Amos (1:2). Joel 4:18a (—Eng 3:18a) has a close parallel in Amos 9:13b. In addition, three of the nations Joel refers to in the final chapter—Tyre, Philistia, and Edom—are also singled out by Amos in the oracles against the nations which introduce his prophecy. The editors of the Minor Prophets in the MT may in fact have wished the reader to interpret Amos' critique of the nations in light of Joel's vision of their universal judgment (chap. 4 [—Eng chap. 3]).

In the LXX, Joel is located fourth among the Minor Prophets, after the three 8th century prophets Hosea, Amos, and Micah, and together with the undated books Obadiah and Jonah. The editors of the LXX thus appear to have been somewhat more interested in chronological categories than the editors of the MT. While the occurrence of Joel with the 8th century prophets and before the later preexilic prophets in both the MT and LXX has been taken into consideration at times in the dating of Joel (D.3), Joel's canonical position is no more decisive for its date than the position of its companions Obadiah and Jonah, both of which are now widely considered late.

Bibliography

Ahlström, G. W. 1971. *Joel and the Temple Cult of Jerusalem.* Leiden.
Barthélemy, D. 1963. *Les devanciers d'Aquila.* VTSup 10. Leiden.
Bergler, S. 1988. *Joel als Schriftinterpret.* Frankfurt am Main.
Bič, M. 1960. *Das Buch Joel.* Berlin.

Bourke, J. 1959. Le Jour de Yahve dans Joël. *RB* 66: 5–31, 190–212.
Dirsh, V. M. 1974. *Genus Schistocerca.* The Hague.
Duhm, B. 1911. Anmerkungun zu den Zwölf Propheten. *ZAW* 31: 1–43, 81–110, 161–204.
———. 1916. *Israel's Propheten.* Tübingen.
Everson, A. J. 1974. The Days of Yahweh. *JBL* 93: 329–37.
Hanson, P. D. 1975. *The Dawn of Apocalyptic.* Philadelphia.
———. 1986. *The People Called.* New York.
Hiebert, T. 1986. *God of My Victory: The Ancient Hymn in Habakkuk 3.* HSM 38. Atlanta.
Hurvitz, A. 1966. The Identification of Post-Exilic Psalms by Means of Linguistic Criteria. Ph.D. Diss. Hebrew University (in Heb).
Johnson, A. R. 1962. *The Cultic Prophet in Ancient Israel.* Cardiff.
Kapelrud, A. S. 1948. *Joel Studies.* Uppsala.
Krebs, C. J. 1978. *Ecology: The Experimental Analysis of Distribution and Abundance.* New York.
Kutsch, E. 1962. Heuschreckenplage und Tag Jahwes in Joel 1 und 2. *TZ* 18: 81–94.
Loretz, O. 1986. *Regenritual und Jahwetag im Joelbuch.* Altenberge.
Mowinckel, S. 1961. *Psalmstudien.* 2 vols. Amsterdam.
Myers, J. M. 1962. Some Considerations Bearing on the Date of Joel. *ZAW* 714: 177–95.
Ogden, G. S. 1983. Joel 4 and Prophetic Responses to National Laments. *JSOT* 26: 97–106.
Plöger, O. 1968. *Theocracy and Eschatology.* Trans. S. Rudman. Richmond.
Prinsloo, W. S. 1985. *The Theology of the Book of Joel.* BZAW 163. New York.
Rad, G. von. 1959. The Origin of the Concept of the Day of Yahweh. *JSS* 4: 97–108.
Sellers, O. R. 1935–36. Stages of Locusts in Joel. *AJSL* 52: 81–85.
Stephensen, F. R. 1969. The Date of the Book of Joel. *VT* 19: 224–29.
Thompson, J. A. 1955. Joel's Locusts in the Light of Near Eastern Parallels. *JNES* 14: 52–55.
Vernes, M. 1872. *Le peuple d'Israël et ses espérances relatives à son avenir depuis les origines jusqu' à l'époque persane (Ve siècle avant J.C.).* Paris.
Whiting, J. D. 1915. Jerusalem's Locust Plague. *National Geographic* 28: 511–50.

THEODORE HIEBERT

JOELAH (PERSON) [Heb *yôʿēʾlâ*]. Brother of Zebadiah and son of Jeroham from Gedor, one of the ambidextrous warriors from the tribe of Benjamin who joined David during the period of his fleeing from Saul (1 Chr 12:8—Eng 12:7). While many of the cities mentioned in 1 Chr 12:1–8—Eng 12:1–7 can be located within the borders of Benjamin, the location of Gedor is not certain. Curtis (*Chronicles* ICC, 196) argued that the towns in 12:5–8—Eng 12:4–7 were in Judah rather than in Benjamin (1 Chr 4:4) and that two lists had been combined here as coming from Benjamin alone. The Chronicler has doubled the list of warriors who supported David (1 Chr 11:41b–12:40) beyond what was contained in the parallel narrative (2 Sam 23:8–39 = 1 Chr 11:10–41a). The source for these additional lists can only be a matter of conjecture, though Williamson has provided a convincing argument for the structure of 1 Chronicles 11–12. The long list reflects the Chronicler's concern to show "all Israel" united in support for David, a characteristic theme of his history. Within the immediate context (1 Chr 12:1–8—Eng 12:1–7) the Chronicler is concerned to show the support David enjoyed among Saul's kinsmen before Saul's death; the twenty-three Benjaminite warriors named here joined David while he was at Ziklag, the Philistine city given to David by Achish, King of Gath (1 Chr 12:1; 1 Sam 27:6). Ambidexterity or lefthandedness among Benjamites is also noted in Judg 3:15; 20:16.

Bibliography

Williamson, H. G. M. 1981. We Are Yours, O David. *OTS* 21: 164–76.

RAYMOND B. DILLARD

JOEZER (PERSON) [Heb *yôʿezer*]. One of the ambidextrous warriors from Benjamin who joined David during his time at Ziklag (1 Chr 12:7—Eng 12:6). He and four others are designated Korahites. Korah is probably intended as the name of an otherwise unknown locality in Benjamin, though some have thought it was a town in Judah (1 Chr 2:43). Alternatively Korah could be an ancestor, possibly identified with one of the other individuals known by that name in the Bible. See also JOELAH.

RAYMOND B. DILLARD

JOGBEHAH (PLACE) [Heb *yogbŏhâ*]. A fortress town built by the sons of Gad in the kingdom of Sihon, which was given by Moses (Num 32:35). It is identified near the caravan route which led the three hundred men of Gideon to victory over the armies of Midian (Judg 8:11).

Wüst (1975), Kallai (*HGB*, 296–97) and many others locate Jogbehah, an Ammonite frontier fortress, at *Ruǧm ʾal-Gubēḥah* (M.R. 231159), where an Ammonite military tower is found. Along with Jazer, Jogbehah is the easternmost boundary between Gad and Reuben. Tel Ṣāfūṭ (32°3′N, 35°49′E) is occasionally mentioned as the location because *Gubēḥah* is outside of known Ammonite territory.

The LXX mistakenly reads at Num 32:35 *kai hupsosan autas* ("and they elevated them") because this is the only city in the list that is missing the *nota acusativi* in Hebrew.

Bibliography

Wüst, M. 1975. *Untersuchungen zu den siedlungsgeographischen Texten des Alten Testaments.* Vol. 1. Wiesbaden.

PAUL NIMRAH FRANKLYN

JOGLI (PERSON) [Heb *yoglî*]. The father of Bukki, who was selected to oversee the distribution of the land of Canaan (Num 34:22). Neither the derivation nor the meaning of the name is clear. It is generally analyzed as a *Qal* (not *Hopʿal*) imperfect from the root *glh* "reveal, be manifest" (*TPNAH*, 164). It falls in the class of abbreviated names for which no theophoric element is attested (*TPNAH*, 169).

RAPHAEL I. PANITZ

JOHA (PERSON) [Heb *yôḥāʾ; yōḥāʾ*]. **1.** A Benjaminite, the son of Beriah (1 Chr 8:16). His father and uncle Shema (= Shimei? 1 Chr 8:21) are named as the heads of families which once lived in Aijalon, who put to flight the inhabitants of Gath (1 Chr 8:13), an incident otherwise unknown. He is attributed five brothers, if one understands (with the RSV) the names in 1 Chr 8:14 as referring to additional brothers of his father and uncle (contra the NEB!). His name occurs in the 2d of two Benjaminite lists in 1 Chronicles (1 Chr 7:6–12; 8:1–40), each reflecting a different tradition and time period. According to 1 Chr 8:28, Joha and his Benjaminite contemporaries apparently lived now in postexilic Jerusalem, although this impression may have been secondarily imposed from 1 Chr 9:34 upon material originally supportive of contemporary Benjaminite locations outside Jerusalem. At any rate, the Chronicler's interest in the tribe of Benjamin for his day is self-evident.

2. A Tizite, the son of Shimri and brother of Jediael, and one of David's mighty men (1 Chr 11:45). In the LXX mss Vaticanus and Alexandrinus he is called "Joazae." His name is one of sixteen names listed in the unparalleled supplement (1 Chr 11:41b–47) to the larger synoptic list (2 Sam 23:8–39 = 1 Chr 11:10–41a) of notable men of war who supported David in his rise to power (1 Chr 11:10). As numerous other gentilic names in this supplement appear to refer to Transjordanian locations, this individual too must have hailed from a place E of the Jordan. See TIZITE.

Roger W. Uitti

JOHANAN (PERSON) [Heb *yôḥānān*]. A relatively common name in the Hebrew Bible meaning "Yahweh is or has been gracious."

1. One of the Benjaminites who joined David's forces at Ziklag when he was fleeing from Saul according to 1 Chr 12:5—Eng 12:4. By means of this list the Chronicler makes the point that some of Saul's fellow tribesmen like Johanan supported David from the beginning.

2. Eighth name in the list of the mighty Gadite officers who also joined David at Ziklag according to 1 Chr 12:13—Eng 12:12.

3. One of those listed in the high priestly genealogy in 1 Chr 5:27–41—Eng 6:1–15. He was the son (or descendant) of Azariah, the priest at the time of Solomon, according to 5:35–36—Eng 6:9–10. (The parenthesis describing Azariah should be read with 6:35 [—Eng 6:9] and not with 5:36 [—Eng 6:10] as it stands in the MT [*IDB* 2: 929]).

4. Ephraimite whose name is incorrectly transliterated as Johanan by the RSV in 2 Chr 28:12. It should be "Jehohanan" instead. See JEHOHANAN.

5. Oldest son of king Josiah according to 1 Chr 3:15. He may have died at an early age since he did not succeed his father and nothing else is known about him.

Steven L. McKenzie

6. The son of Kareah, and one of the Judean troop commanders who, following the destruction of Jerusalem in 587/6, chose to join Gedaliah, the ruler of Judah, at his administrative center at Mizpah (Jer 40:7–8; 2 Kgs 25:23). Following the assassination of Gedaliah, Johanan emerges as the leader of "all the remnant of Judah," a community which he then leads to Egypt.

The OT does not provide a date for these events. However, the fact that the text states only that Gedaliah's assassination took place "in the seventh month" (Jer 41:1; 2 Kgs 25:25) appears to imply that this occurred in the same year as the fall of Jerusalem ("in the fourth month" [Jer 39:2]). But it is also possible that the assassination took place some years later, and that it was this that led to the deportation which, according to Jer 52:30 (cf. Josephus, *Ant* 10.9 §7), occurred in Nebuchadrezzar's twenty-third year (582/581).

Whereas 2 Kgs 25:22–26 gives only a brief description of the appointment and assassination of Gedaliah and the flight to Egypt (the Chronicler makes no mention of this period), a full account of these events is contained in Jer 40:7–43:7. Without addressing ourselves to the question of the historicity of the events relating to Johanan, son of Kareah, we may take note of these events as they are narrated in the book of Jeremiah. Although told by Johanan of the plot against his life, Gedaliah chose not to believe this warning; he also rejected Johanan's offer to kill Ishmael secretly (40:13–16). Following the assassination of Gedaliah and others (41:1–3, 4–7), Ishmael sought to escape to Ammon, taking as hostages the daughters of the king (entrusted to Gedaliah) and "all the people who were left at Mizpah" (41:10). His plans were foiled when he was intercepted at Gibeon by Johanan and his allies. Although Ishmael escaped, his hostages were able to join Johanan (41:11–16). Fearing Babylonian reprisals for the assassination of Gedaliah, Johanan and the people made their way to a place near Bethlehem, intending to go to Egypt (41:17–18). Here they consulted the prophet Jeremiah (42:1–6; although 40:6 informs us that Jeremiah opted to remain in Judah with Gedaliah, it is noteworthy that he plays no role in 40:7–41:18). In the prose sermon delivered by Jeremiah (42:9–22), a choice is laid before the people: if they remain in the land of Judah, there is the promise of restoration; but if they persist in their plan to go to Egypt, each and every one will perish "by the sword, by famine, and by pestilence" (42:17 [15–17], 22). Accusing Jeremiah of having spoken falsely (43:2–3), Johanan and "all the remnant of Judah" (43:5; cf. 40:15; 42:2, 15, 19) depart for Egypt, taking Jeremiah and Baruch with them (43:4–7).

Both Jer 40:7–43:7 and 2 Kgs 25:22–26 underscore the view that hope for the future lies not with those who were left in the land of Judah (this was forfeited when Johanan and "all the remnant of Judah" chose to go to Egypt), but with the exiles in Babylon.

Bibliography

Ackroyd, P. R. 1971. Aspects of the Jeremiah Tradition. *IJT* 20: 1–12.

Baltzer, K. 1961. Das Ende des Staates Juda und die Messias Frage. Pp. 33–43 in *Studien zur Theologie der alttestamentlichen Überlieferungen,* ed. R. Rendtorff and K. Koch. Neukirchen-Vluyn.

Lohfink, N. 1978. Die Gattung der "Historischen Kurzgeschichte" in den letzten Jahren von Juda und in der Zeit des Babylonischen Exils. *ZAW* 90: 319–47.

Pohlmann, K.-F. 1978. *Studien zum Jeremiabuch.* FRLANT 118. Göttingen.

Seitz, C. R. 1985. The Crisis of Interpretation over the Meaning and Purpose of the Exile: A Redactional Study of Jeremiah xxi–xliii. *VT* 25: 78–97.
Wanke, G. 1971. *Untersuchungen zur sogenannten Baruchschrift.* BZAW 112. Berlin.

JOHN M. BERRIDGE

7. Son of Elioenai (1 Chr 3:24) and a member of the last generation of the Davidic line recorded in the genealogy for David in 1 Chronicles 3.

8. One of those who returned from Babylon with Ezra according to Ezra 8:12 (= 1 Esdr 8:38). He is called the son of Hakkatan, but Dahlberg (*IDB* 2: 930) may be correct in suggesting that one should read *haqqaton* as an epithet for Johanan: "Johanan the younger."

9. High priest after the return from exile listed in Neh 12:22–23. These two verses are apparently an editorial note about the chronology and method of recording the heads of Levitical families. Verse 22 contains later additions ("and Jaddua" and "and the priests in the reign of Darius the Persian") which have made it difficult. Williamson (*Ezra, Nehemiah* WBC, 357–65) summarizes proposed solutions and offers a compelling one of his own.

The relationship of the Johanan and Eliashib mentioned in 12:22–23 to each other and to others of similar names is extremely important for the thorny issue of the date of the return of Ezra. Eliashib in these two verses and elsewhere (12:10–11; 13:28) was the high priest in Nehemiah's day (Neh 3:1). Johanan the high priest in 12:22 should be identified with Jehohanan the high priest referred to in one of the Elephantine papyri (30:18 in *CAP*). This Johanan is called the son of Eliashib in Neh 12:23 and is listed following Eliashib and Joiada in 12:22. Most scholars have concluded, therefore, that Johanan was the grandson of Eliashib. In 12:11 the name Jonathan for the grandson of Eliashib and son of Joiada may be an error for Johanan. The Jehohanan son of Eliashib in whose chamber Ezra fasted according to Ezra 10:6 is also frequently identified with Johanan the high priest of Neh 12:22–23 and elsewhere. Josephus' reference to Johanan (*Iōannēs*) the high priest (*Ant* 11.297–301) is often cited as further information about this individual (e.g., *IDB* 2: 930) but should probably be disqualified from consideration for it would appear to describe an individual who lived much later (Williamson 1977).

If these identifications (except for the one by Josephus) are correct they provide an important argument for dating Ezra after Nehemiah. Ezra fasted in the room of Jehohanan (Ezra 10:6) who is identified as the grandson of Eliashib who served as high priest during Nehemiah's reforms. In addition to variations on this argument (Williamson *Ezra, Nehemiah* WBC, 152–53), however, there are at least two important perspectives that make it far from conclusive. Williamson's own view is that the identifications above are dubious (WBC, 153–54). He points out that both Eliashib and Johanan are common names. He further suggests that the reference in Neh 13:4 to Eliashib the priest who was over the chamber of the temple both distinguishes this Eliashib from the high priest and relates to the chamber in Ezra 10:6, so that Jehohanan in the latter verse should not be identified with Johanan the high priest of Neh 12:22–23. While the identification of Johanan the high priest (Neh 12:22–23) as the grandson of Eliashib the high priest seems well founded, Williamson's caution is well taken, particularly as it applies to Ezra 10:6.

Another important proposal relating to the identification of Eliashib and Johanan in these passages has been made by Cross (1975). The list of priests in Nehemiah 12 is too brief for the period of time it is meant to fill and is almost certainly defective. On the basis of the attested practice of papponymy (naming a son after his grandfather) in the high priestly line and of evidence from the Samaria papyri, Cross restored two generations at two different places in that genealogy. The names had been lost from the genealogy as a result of haplography. One of his restorations involved the inclusion of an Eliashib and a Johanan before the Eliashib who was a contemporary of Nehemiah. It was the earlier (restored) Johanan referred to in Ezra 10:6. Cross' proposal is based on sound arguments and must be given very serious consideration.

Bibliography

Cross, F. M. 1975. A Reconstruction of the Judean Restoration. *Int* 29: 187–203 = *JBL* 94: 4–18.
Williamson, H. G. M. 1977. The Historical Value of Josephus' *Jewish Antiquities* XI. 297–301. *JTS* n.s. 28: 49–66.

STEVEN L. MCKENZIE

JOHANNINE COMMA.

In the Clementine edition of the Vg and in the Textus Receptus, 1 John 5:7–8 reads:

> For there are three who bear witness *[in heaven, the Father, the Word and the Holy Spirit; and these three are one. And there are three who bear witness in earth]*, the spirit and the water and the blood; and these three are one.

The bracketed words constitute the so-called "Johannine Comma," a reading which has been the object of considerable controversy in NT textual criticism.

Support for the reading in Gk manuscripts is meager, occurring only in 61, 629, 918, and 2318, as well as in varying forms by later hands in the margins of five others (88, 221, 429, 635, and 636), and none of these can be dated earlier than the 14th century. In ancient versions other than the Lat, the Comma is noticeably absent from all pre-14th century manuscripts of the Copt, Syr, Eth, Arm, Ar, and Slav translations of the NT. It does not occur in the Gk Fathers, who would certainly have used it to their advantage in the trinitarian controversies if only they had known it. Even in the Lat version, the Comma does not appear in OL manuscripts until after A.D. 600, nor in the Vg until after A.D. 750, and even then it is geographically limited to texts of Spanish origin or influence until the 10th century.

The tripartite reading of spirit, water, and blood in 1 John 5:7–8 was the subject of trinitarian reflection in North Africa in Cyprian, *De eccl. cath. unit.* 6 and *Epist.* 73.12, but with no certain reference to the Comma. Facundus, a 6th century bishop from N. Africa, cites the text without the Comma (*Pro Def. Tri. Cap. Iust.* 1.3.9) and quotes Cyprian as giving a trinitarian understanding of the shorter text. The earliest uncontested use of the Comma is the *Liber Apologeticus* (1.4) of Priscillian, a 4th century bishop in Spain. It occurs in the 5th century *Contra Varimadum* (1.5), a trinitarian treatise of N. African provenance, and in the *Hist. persec. Afr. Prov.* (2.82) of Victor, bishop of Vita, as well as in *De Trinitate* (1.4.1) of Fulgentius, 6th century bishop of Ruspe, both in N. Africa. In Italy, Cassiodorus quotes the Comma in *Epist. S. Joannis ad Parthos* (10.5.1) and in Spain, Isidore of Seville, who died A.D. 636, has awareness of it in *Test. div. Script.* 2. So, certain Latin Fathers from N. Africa and Spain from A.D. 400–650 evidence knowledge of the Comma and about A.D. 600 the reading begins to surface in some Lat manuscripts of the NT of Spanish origin. It must be remembered, however, that the Comma does not appear in Tertullian, Hilary of Poitiers (treatise on the Trinity), Ambrose, Augustine, Bede, and other major Latin Fathers, nor does it occur in the Vg of Jerome.

The Comma, which interrupts the thought of the passage, is an interpolation originating in the 3d or 4th century as a trinitarian explanation of 1 John 5:7–8. What was likely a marginal gloss was incorporated into certain Lat texts and eventually translated back into Gk in some late Gk manuscripts.

In view of the paucity of external evidence and the transcriptional probability that the Comma arose due to theological reasons, this reading would have been relegated to a historical footnote had it not been for certain events in the 16th century. Observing that the Comma occurred only in the Lat version and not in any Gk manuscript known to him, Erasmus omitted it from his editions of the Gk testament in 1516 and 1519. Stunica, editor of the Complutensian Polyglott (printed 1514; published 1522), assailed Erasmus for omitting the Comma and included it in his own text, translated from the Lat. In response to a wider outcry, Erasmus maintained that he had searched many Gk manuscripts, failing to find even one which contained the Comma. Ms. 61, containing the Comma and apparently produced at the time for that very purpose, was brought to Erasmus' attention and, fearing a negative response to his edition, he included the Comma in his 3d edition of 1522, but not without suspicion that 61 had been revised according to the Lat. The reading was accepted into Stephanus' 3d edition of 1550 and the Elzevir text of 1633, later known as the Textus Receptus. It then achieved wider currency in the Clementine Vg in 1592, which became the official Bible of the Roman Catholic Church, and in the Rheims edition. Not originally in Luther's Bible, later editors added it to his text beginning in 1582. Although earlier bracketed by Tyndale as questionable, the reading was adopted in the KJV. Thus the Comma gained widespread acceptance in the 16th and 17th centuries.

However, since Lachman in 1831, the Comma has been rejected from critical editions of the Gk text as a dogmatic expansion of the text in the Latin tradition.

Bibliography

Ayuso, T. 1947–48. Nuevo Estudio sobre el "Comma Ioanneum." *Bib* 28: 83–112, 216–35; 29: 52–76.

Bludau, A. 1903. Das Comma Johanneum (1 Io. 5, 7) im 16. Jahrhundert. *BZ* 1: 280–302, 378–407.

———. 1915. Das Comma Johanneum bei den Griechen. *BZ* 13: 26–50, 130–62, 222–43.

———. 1920. Das "Comma Johanneum" bei Tertullian und Cyprian. *TQ* 101: 1–28.

Jonge, H. de. 1980. Erasmus and the Comma Johanneum. *ETL* 56: 381–89.

Künstle, K. 1905. *Das Comma Johanneum auf seine Herkunft untersucht.* Freiburg.

Metzger, B. M. 1975. *A Textual Commentary on the Greek New Testament,* corr. ed. New York.

CARROLL D. OSBURN

JOHN (DISCIPLE) [Gk *Iōannēs*]. The name of John, the son of Zebedee and the brother of James, occurs thirty times in the Synoptic Gospels, Acts, and Galatians. These NT texts are the best sources for accurate information about this disciple of Jesus. Without his name having been specifically cited, John is mentioned in the epilogue to the Fourth Gospel (John 21:2). As one of the sons of Zebedee, he belonged to a group of seven disciples who witnessed an apparition of the risen Lord.

A. General
B. The Synoptic Gospels
C. Acts
D. The Gospel of John
E. Ecclesiastical Tradition

A. General

The Gospels are less clear about the name of John's mother than they are about the name of his father. Mark indicates that a woman named Salome was a bystander at the crucifixion of Jesus (Mark 15:40) and Matthew tells that the mother of the sons of Zebedee was one of the onlookers (Matt 27:56), leading to the plausible suggestion that Salome was the name of John's mother. By trade John was a fisherman (Matt 4:21; Mark 1:19; Luke 5:10; cf. John 21:3), the trade of his father. The family business was moderately successful and the family seems to have been of some means because they had hired servants (Mark 1:20). From Mark 1:21 it would appear that they lived near Capernaum, on the N shore of the Sea of Galilee.

Within the Gospels, John is clearly portrayed as a disciple of Jesus (Matt 10:1; Mark 14:32; Luke 6:13; 9:54; John 21:1), that is, as one who followed after Jesus, the itinerant and charismatic preacher (Matt 4:22; Mark 1:20; 5:37; Luke 5:11). He was chosen as one of the twelve (Matt 10:2; Mark 3:17; Luke 6:14) and is called an apostle (Matt 10:2; Mark 3:14; Luke 6:13).

Since John's name appears after James' on all three Synoptic lists of the twelve and since James is twice identified as Zebedee's son, while John is identified as his brother (Matt 4:21; 10:2; Mark 1:19; 3:17; cf. Matt 17:1), it is likely that John was younger than James.

B. The Synoptic Gospels

John appears most frequently (ten times) in Mark, the earliest of the Synoptics. On Mark's list of the twelve chosen by Jesus, John and his brother James are cited immediately after Simon Peter (Mark 3:16–17). Their position on the list is indicative not only of the earliness of their call, but also of the importance which they enjoyed among the Twelve.

Mark emphasizes their importance by indicating that the pair of brothers, like Simon, received a special name from Jesus. John and James were called *Boanerges,* which Mark translates as "sons of thunder" (Mark 3:17). Apart from this translation, Mark offers no explanation of the epithet—just as he offers no explanation of the name Peter (Mark 3:16; cf. Matt 10:2; 16:18). Perhaps the name is indicative of the brothers' impetuosity (Mark 9:38–41; 10:35–45; Matt 20:20–28; Luke 9:49–50; 52–56). The more recent Synoptic Gospels, Matthew and Luke, avoid the epithet. They also cite Andrew, Simon's brother, before citing the names of James and John on the list of the Twelve (Matt 10:2; Luke 6:14).

John and James were among the first disciples called by Jesus during the Galilean ministry (Mark 1:19–20; Matt 4:21–22). Like the other pair of brothers among the Twelve, Simon and Andrew (Mark 1:16–18; Matt 4:18–20), John and James were called by Jesus while they were at work. They were mending their nets at the time that they received the invitation. Matthew and Mark emphasize the radical nature of their decision to follow Jesus, the itinerant preacher, by citing its immediacy and the fact that it entailed the abandonment of their work.

Luke has combined the tradition of the call of John and James with a tradition about a miraculous catch of fish (Luke 5:1–11). James and John, identified as the sons of Zebedee, are presented as partners with Simon. The three partners were so amazed at the miraculous catch of fish, and Jesus' words to Simon, that upon their return to shore they abandoned everything in order to follow Jesus. Since it is quite unlikely that James and John were business partners of Peter (compare *metochoi,* "partners" of v 7 with *koinōnoi,* "partners" in v 10), it is reasonable to assume that the Lukan narrative reflects the special association of the triumvirate of Simon, James, and John in the ministry of Jesus.

James and John were with Jesus when he entered the house of Simon and Andrew on the occasion of the cure of Simon's mother-in-law (Mark 1:29). Peter, James, and John were the only three disciples whom Jesus allowed to accompany him when he raised the daughter of Jairus from the dead (Mark 5:37; Luke 8:51). The three were chosen by Jesus to ascend the mountain where Jesus was transfigured and to witness the transfiguration (Mark 9:2–4; Matt 17:2–3; Luke 9:28, 31). Enveloped by a cloud, they heard the heavenly voice which identified Jesus as the Son. Luke adds the detail that they had been overcome by sleep prior to the vision (Luke 9:32), while Matthew adds that they were overcome by awe at the sound of the voice (Matt 17:6). All three accounts suggest that John and the others remained silent about their experience until after Jesus' resurrection from the dead (Mark 9:9–10; Matt 17:9; Luke 9:36).

The intimacy that the group of three enjoyed with Jesus continued until the time of his passion. Peter, James, and John, accompanied by Andrew, whose name is listed in last place among the group, privately asked Jesus about the final times as they were sitting on the Mount of Olives opposite the city of Jerusalem (Mark 13:3). Jesus' eschatological discourse (Mark 13:5–37; par.) was addressed to them. Peter, James, and John were again selected by Jesus to be with him at the time of the agony in the garden (Mark 14:33; Matt 26:37). In their account of the scene, as in their accounts of the raising of Jairus' daughter and the transfiguration, the Synoptics generally highlight the initiative of Jesus in choosing the three to accompany him.

Although John was one of the privileged three chosen to accompany Jesus on these significant occasions, Mark tells that John was twice rebuked by Jesus. Once John, serving as a spokesman for the disciples, reported that they had forbidden an exorcist who did not belong to their company to expel demons in the name of Jesus (Mark 9:38–41; Luke 9:49–50). Jesus ordered the disciples to desist "for he that is not against us is for us," but Luke notes that this order (phrased in the plural, and therefore intended for all the disciples) was specifically directed to John.

Another incident serves to highlight John's lack of real understanding of the significance of Jesus' ministry (Mark 10:35–45; Matt 20:20–28). Inappropriately, James and John asked Jesus for a favor, which they specified as the privilege of being seated beside him when he entered into his glory. Apparently they had understood the kingdom preached by Jesus according to the nationalist and militaristic views popular among many contemporaries with an apocalyptic outlook. Their self-serving request prompted the indignation of the ten others in the group of twelve. Jesus asked James and John whether they were ready to drink his cup and to be baptized with his baptism, apparently a reference to Jesus' imminent suffering and the disciples' future martyrdom. While assuring the sons of Zebedee that they would have opportunity to suffer for his sake, he told them that it was beyond his power to give them a privileged place in the kindom. Jesus profited from the occasion to speak to the group of disciples about the quality of leadership expected from them.

Matthew who tends to idealize the disciples and, consequently tends to improve upon the somewhat negative portrayal of the disciples in Mark (e.g., by dropping Jesus' reproach of John in Mark 9:38–41), attributes the importunate question to the mother of the sons of Zebedee (Matt 20:20–21), but implies that the brothers were associated with her in the request (Matt 20:22–24).

Matthew seems to have been impressed that Jesus had called two sets of brothers (Matt 4:21; 20:24; cf. Mark 10:41). Twice he refers to James and John as the (two) sons of Zebedee without mentioning their names (Matt 20:20; 26:27). On the other hand, he seems not to have given as much emphasis to the association of the three privileged disciples in Jesus' ministry as did Mark. Matthew does not mention that James and John accompanied Jesus to Peter's house (Matt 8:14; cf. Mark 1:29) nor that the three went with Jesus to Jairus' house (Matt 9:22–23; cf. Mark 5:37). He omits the specific reference to the four disciples gathered on the Mount of Olives for the eschatological discourse (Matt 24:3; cf. Mark 13:3).

Luke tells a story about John and his brother (Luke 9:52–56) that is found in neither of the other two Synoptics. After making the decision to move towards Jerusalem, Jesus sent two of his disciples into a Samaritan town to prepare the way. Because of Jesus' intention to go to Jerusalem, the townspeople refuse to accept Jesus. The brothers want to call divine vengeance upon the town in the form of a destructive fire, but Jesus impedes them with a rebuke. All told, this is the third reproach addressed to John in the Synoptic tradition.

On the other hand, Luke seems occasionally to intimate that John had a more important role in the early Church than did his older brother. He specifies that Peter and John were the two disciples sent into the city to prepare for Jesus' final passover (Luke 22:8; cf. Mark 14:13). When describing the presence of the privileged three in the home of Jairus (Luke 8:51) and on the mountain of transfiguration (Luke 9:28), Luke cites the name of John before that of James. This is consistent with the sequence of the names (John followed by James) found on the list of the eleven in Acts 1:13.

C. Acts

When James was killed by Herod Agrippa I in 43 A.D., prior to the arrest of Peter, James is identified as having been "the brother of John" (Acts 12:2). This is another indication of Luke's according a greater role to John than to James.

Acts does not ascribe any particular role to John at the so-called Council of Jerusalem (Acts 15:4–30). Nonetheless, in what appears to be a reference to those events, Paul (Gal 2:9–10) mentions John, along with James (the brother of the Lord) and Cephas as one of the pillars *(styloi)* of the community of Christians in Jerusalem. The pillars not only extended a gesture of fellowship to Paul and Barnabas but also, according to Paul's say-so, recognized the legitimacy of the latter's mission to the gentiles.

Paul's linking of Cephas and John, indicating the authority enjoyed by these two in Jerusalem, concurs with the traditions cited in Acts which, apart from Acts 12:2, always links John with Peter (cf. Luke 22:8). Neither John's father nor his brother is mentioned in the three accounts of Acts where John appears with Peter (Acts 3:1–11; 4:1–22; 8:14–25). In all three accounts the principal role is ascribed to Peter; John has nothing specific to do or say (despite the defense attributed to both Peter and John in Acts 4:19–20 and the retrospective attribution of the speech in Acts 3:12–26 to both Peter and John in Acts 4:1).

In the first account (Acts 3:1–11), John is with Peter as they go to the temple to pray at the ninth hour. They (cf. v 11) were the means of the cure of the lame man brought about in Jesus' name. A second account (Acts 4:1–22) describes the arrest, scrutiny, and release of Peter and John who had proclaimed Jesus' resurrection from the dead. They were perceived as having been disciples of Jesus (v 13: "with Jesus"; cf. Mark 3:14) and as being bold in their proclamation (cf. Acts 4:31) despite the fact that they were incapable of writing and that they were just "ordinary" people (*idiotai,* either as an affirmation of their lack of expertise or as a repeated reference to their apparent illiteracy). In their rebuttal, Peter and John spoke of their role as witnesses (v 20). In Acts 8:14–25, Peter and John again appear as leaders of the Jerusalem church, this time delegated to go to Samaria to oversee the evangelization of that area by Philip. On that occasion they prayed for and laid hands upon those whom Philip had baptized.

D. The Gospel of John

John is never mentioned by name in the Fourth Gospel. Under the rubric of the "sons of Zebedee" his presence at the fishing incident connected with an appearance of the risen Jesus is cited in the epilogue to the gospel (John 21:2).

Ecclesiastical tradition has commonly associated the Fourth Gospel's BELOVED DISCIPLE (John 13:23–26; 19:26–27, 35; 20:2–10; 21: 20–24; cf. 1:35–40; 18:15–16), presumed to be the author of the gospel (John 21:24), with John, the son of Zebedee. If the identification is correct—as some scholars continue to maintain—the Fourth Gospel provides additional information about John: his intimacy with Jesus, his acquaintance with the high priest, his presence at the foot of the cross, his inspection of the empty tomb, and so forth.

There are, however, weighty arguments against the identification. The weightiest may be the affirmation that John, the Galilean fisherman, was unable to write (Acts 4:13). Another serious argument is the tradition about the death of John. Although Mark 10:39 may well be a *vaticinium ex eventu* (prophecy after the event), it probably indicates that John had died before the gospel of Mark was written, that is, sometime before the Fourth Gospel was composed.

E. Ecclesiastical Tradition

The common tradition of the Church affirmed that, after his leadership role in the church of Jerusalem, John moved to Ephesus, where he lived to an old age and died a natural death. The tradition is summarized by Eusebius (*Hist. Eccl.* 3.18.1; 23.3–4; 39.3–4; 4.18.6–8; 5.8.4; 18.14; 20.6; *PG* 20.252, 255–64, 296–98, 376, 449, 479–82, 486) who appeals to Irenaeus (3.18.1; 39, 3–4), Justin (4.18.6–8), Clement of Alexandria (3.39.3–4), Apollonius (5.18.14) and Polycrates (5.24.3) as early witnesses to the tradition.

The testimony of Irenaeus (*Haer.* 2.22.3.5; 3.1.2; 3.4; *PG* 7.783–85, 845), Justin (*Dial.* 81.4; PG 6.669) and Clement of Alexandria (*q.d.s.,* 42; *PG* 9.648–50) about John is known from extant sources, but the pertinent texts from Apollonius and Polycrates are extant only in the portions cited by Eusebius. Irenaeus claimed that he had reports on John's Ephesian ministry coming from Polycarp and Papias.

The mid-2d century apocryphal *Acts of John* is another early witness to an Ephesian residency by John. Among the Latin Fathers, Tertullian tells of John's death at a late age (*De anima.* 50; *PL* 2).

The tradition maintained that John was once banished to the island of Patmos, an island not far off the coast of Asia Minor relatively near Ephesus, but that he later returned to Ephesus where he lived until the time of Trajan. Since the tradition ascribed all five books in the NT's Johannine corpus (John, 1-2-3 John, Revelation) to John, the Patmos exile allowed for John's presumed composition of Revelation (Rev 1:9). Historical criticism has, however, convincingly shown that all five works could not have been written by the same author and that it is highly unlikely that John, the son of Zebedee, was the author of any one of them.

Making use of his several sources, Eusebius narrated a number of stories about John, including his raising a man from the dead at Ephesus (*Hist. Eccl.* 5.18.14; *PG* 20; 479–

82) and his regaining a robber and murderer for Christ (3.39, 3–4; *PG* 20.296–98). Irenaeus tells of his having opposed the heretic Cerinthus (*Haer.* 3.3.4; *PG* 7.853). Later, Jerome told the story of John, feeble and quite old, being carried to gatherings of Christians, for whom he had but a single message: "Little children, love one another" (*Commentary on Galatians* 6,10; *PL* 26, 433).

The Patristic tradition about John is, however, not entirely consistent. The Muratorian fragment suggests that John was with the other apostles when the gospel was written, a version of the tradition that would preclude the late date suggested by other Patristic witnesses for the gospel's composition. Heracleon (cf. Clement of Alexandria, *Strom.* 4.9; *PG* 8.1281), and later authors like Philip of Side (5th century) and George the Sinner (9th century) intimate that John died a martyr's death.

Bibliography

Kügler, J. 1988. *Der Jünger, den Jesus liebte.* SBB 16. Stuttgart.
Parker, P. 1962. John the son of Zebedee and the Fourth Gospel. *JBL* 81: 35–43.
Schnackenburg, R. 1975. *Das Johannes Evangelium.* Vol. 3. HTKNT 4. Freiburg.

RAYMOND F. COLLINS

JOHN (PERSON) [Gk *Iōannēs*]. John was a common Jewish name during the Hellenistic age and was especially popular among the priesthood.

1. The son of a priest named Simeon, from the clan of Joarib. He was the father of Mattathias and the grandfather of Judas Maccabeus (1 Macc 2:1; cf. 14:29 and Josephus *Ant* 12.6.1 §265). The Joarib clan had an illustrious ancestry (1 Chr 24:7; Josephus *Life* 11). Some scholars maintain, however, that the importance of the clan in Chronicles, Ezra, and Nehemiah was a result of Hasmonean interpolations (opposing this viewpoint are Liver 1968: 33–52 and Grintz 1972: 155–56). The family had long resided in Jerusalem (1 Macc 2:70; 9:19; 12:25; see also *Ant* 12.6.1 §265).

2. The eldest of the five sons of Mattathias and the brother of Judas Maccabeus (1 Macc 2:2; *Ant* 12.6.1 §266). His nickname (or *cognomen*) "Gaddi" was used to distinguish one bearer of a common name from another. A nickname was formed by shortening or altering an existing name (see *IPN,* 36–41) or by a descriptive (or derogatory) epithet. In the case of Gaddi, the nickname has been transliterated from Hebrew or Aramaic *(gaddî)* into Greek *(Gaddi).* Some scholars have suggested that Gaddi is formed with the DN Gad, the Semitic god of fortune, and therefore might have had the meaning "my fortune" (on this question, see Fowler *TPNAH,* 157, 340); however, the exact meaning remains uncertain.

When Bacchides determined to move against the Maccabeans, Jonathan sent his brother John with a convoy of goods to the Nabateans, perhaps as a bribe for their support (1 Macc 9:32–42; *Ant* 13.1.2, 10–11; 13.1.4, 19–21; Goldstein *I Maccabees* AB, 380–83). A marauding tribe called the Jambrites from Medeba ambushed the convoy, plundered the goods, and killed John and his companions. Josephus called the tribe *Amaraioi,* perhaps indicating the Semitic *ʾmry.* The personal name *yʾmrw* is attested in a Nabatean inscription (*CIS* II 195; dated 39 C.E., from Umm-er-Resas, 16 miles SE of Medeba), which might indicate that the Jambrites were a Nabatean tribe (see Clermont-Ganneau 1898: 185). Jonathan's band avenged John's murder by devastating the Jambrites and their allies the Nadabites at an important wedding ceremony.

Bibliography

Clermont-Ganneau, C. 1898. *Recueil d'archaeologie orientale.* Vol. 2. Paris.
Grintz, J. M. 1972. From Zerubbabel to Nehemiah. *Zion* 37: 125–82 (in Hebrew).
Liver, J. 1968. *Chapters in the History of the Priests and Levites.* Jerusalem.

SCOTT T. CARROLL

3. The "son of Acco" and father of Eupolemus; Eupolemus was one of the men selected by Judas Maccabeus to head the Jewish delegation to Rome (1 Macc 8:17). The phrase "son of Acco" probably denotes John as a member of the priestly clan of Hakkoz (1 Chr 24:10). This John is remembered for having earlier negotiated certain concessions from Antiochus III, concessions that were beneficial to the Jews but that were rescinded when the pro-Hellenizing Jason, aided by Antiochus IV Epiphanes, supplanted Onias III as high priest in Jerusalem (2 Macc 4:11; see Goldstein *II Maccabees* AB, 228–29). The rescinding of these policies was one of the factors that led to war between the anti-Hellenizing Jews led by Judas Maccabeus and the Seleucid forces of Antiochus IV.

4. An envoy whom the Jews sent to Lysias, a general of Antiochus IV attempting to end the war between the Jews and the Seleucids (2 Macc 11:17). John and Absalom are mentioned as Jewish envoys in a letter Lysias addresses to "the community of the Jews" (vv 16–21). The author of 2 Maccabees depicts Lysias as negotiating with Judas Maccabeus, the leader of the anti-Hellenizing Jews; however, because the pro-Hellenizing Jewish high-priest Menelaus is mentioned twice in another letter preserved in 2 Maccabees 11 (vv 27–33), it has been argued that Lysias actually negotiated with Menelaeus, and that John and Absalom were envoys who served his faction, not that of Judas Maccabeus—a claim Goldstein originally supported (*I Maccabees* AB, 271) but subsequently opposed (see *II Maccabees* AB, 409–10).

5. See JOHN THE BAPTIST.
6. See JOHN (DISCIPLE).
7. See MARK, JOHN (PERSON).

GARY A. HERION

8. The father of Simon Peter (John 1:42; 21:15–17). Matt 16:17 describes Simon as Bar-Jona *(Bariōna),* that is, "son of Jonah," not John. The familiarity of the Matthean text led to a reading "Jona" (*Iōna; Iōanna* in Codex Koridethi) in some majuscule and most of the minuscule mss of John 1:42. The most important witnesses of John 1:42, including the early papyri (P^{66} and P^{75}), read "son of John" *(ho huios Iōannou).* An elliptical "of John" (only *Iōannou*) appears in John 21:15–17, where some mss also have a variant reading under the influence of Matt 16:17. Greek-language Christians may have regarded *Iona* as a diminutive of *Iōanes,* but the Hebrew clearly distinguishes Jonah *(yônâ)* from John *(yôḥānān)*. Since nothing is known about the man except that he was the father of Simon Peter, it may be that there were two different traditions about his name.

9. A member of the high priestly family (Acts 4:6). Nothing further is known about this John and his relative Alexander (Acts 4:6). Luke's text suggests that the high priest then in office was Annas, who was in office from 6 to 16, but who continued to be influential during the term (17–36) of his son-in-law, Joseph-Caiaphas (John 18:13). A Western reading of Acts 4:6 substitutes "Jonathan" (*Iōnathas* in Codex Bezae and many Old Latin mss.) for "John," apparently identifying the individual as the son of Annas who succeeded Caiaphas in the office of high priest (Josephus, *Ant* 20.8.5; *JW* 2.13.3).

Raymond F. Collins

JOHN THE BAPTIST. A 1st-century Jewish oracular prophet significant in the NT as a precursor of Jesus. John the Baptist was an ascetic, and conducted a ministry in the Judean wilderness that involved preaching and baptism. His popularity and the revolutionary possibilities of his message of social justice led to his arrest, imprisonment, and execution by Herod Antipas, probably in A.D. 28 or 29.

A. The Sources, Their Character, and Their Use
   1. Josephus
   2. Mark
   3. Matthew
   4. Luke-Acts
   5. John
B. A Reconstruction of John's Mission
   1. The Origin of John the Baptizer
   2. John's Prophetic Mission
C. Summary

A. The Sources, Their Character, and Their Use

There are two forms of John's title in the NT: *ho baptistēs* "the baptist" is a formal title; *ho baptizōn* "the baptizer" is an epithet. Grammatically, the latter form is a present active participal in which the verbal meaning of habitual behavior rings strongly; it most likely was the earlier form, historically speaking.

The primary sources for determining the history of John the Baptist are the NT and Josephus. In the NT John is referred to in all four gospels and in the book of Acts, while in Josephus there is one short but suggestive passage. This passage is especially important because it is the only extrabiblical source. However, we cannot use either of these sources without weighing their historical reliability. All ancient historical documents are biased in one way or another by special interests and apologetic concerns. This judgment applies to Josephus as well as to the NT. The distinctive character and perspectives of each of the gospels and Acts have been greatly illuminated through tradition criticism, redaction criticism, the new literary criticism, and social science criticism. Likewise the interests (both social and personal) that govern Josephus' histories have come under closer scrutiny. All of this newer understanding (as well as older methods of scholarship) must be considered as we try to determine the history of John the Baptizer.

How does John appear in each of the sources? The sources will be examined in the order Josephus, Mark, Matthew, Luke-Acts, John. (Neither at this point, nor elsewhere in this study, is any single theory of gospel origins assumed.)

1. Josephus. Josephus' *Jewish Antiquities* is a work of 20 books relating the history of the Jews from creation to the Jewish-Roman war of 66–70 C.E. The immediate context of Josephus' report about John is an account of events during the early 1st century C.E., beginning with the assessment of property in Judea by the governor of Syria, QUIRINIUS (see also CENSUS, ROMAN). This occasioned an uprising under Judas the Galilean, the narrating of which leads Josephus to describe the three "philosophies" of Judaism (the PHARISEES, SADDUCEES, and ESSENES), as well as the "fourth philosophy" (the ZEALOTS) started by Judas. He reports among other events the building of Tiberias by Herod Antipas and various indiscretions by Pilate, who was procurator of Judea. Especially important is the report of Jesus' life and death in a paragraph (*Ant* 18.3.3) a bit shorter than the one about John, a paragraph whose authenticity has been hotly disputed in modern times.

The paragraph about John the Baptist is immediately preceded by an account of Herod's divorce from the daughter of Aretas, king of Petra, and of the latter's retaliation by making war on Herod. Aretas defeated Herod, and the paragraph on John picks up from that defeat, which some Jews believed was caused by God as just vengeance on Herod for his execution of John. He had executed John even though the latter was said to be a good man who exhorted his fellow Jews to live righteously and practice justice and piety. Josephus observes that John baptized people as bodily parallel to inward cleansing. But the size of John's movement frightened Herod and so he struck preemptively by executing John at the fortress of Machaerus. The text of Josephus' account of John the Baptist follows:

> But to some of the Jews the destruction of Herod's army seemed to be divine vengeance, and certainly a just vengeance, for his treatment of John, surnamed the Baptist. For Herod had put him to death, though he was a good man and had exhorted the Jews to lead righteous lives, to practice justice toward their fellows and piety towards God, and so doing join in baptism. In his view this was a necessary preliminary if baptism was to be acceptable to God. They must not employ it to gain pardon for whatever sins they committed, but as a consecration of the body implying that the soul was already thoroughly cleansed by right behavior. When others too joined the crowds about him, because they were aroused to the highest degree by his sermons, Herod became alarmed. Eloquence that had so great an effect on mankind might lead to some form of sedition, for it looked as if they would be guided by John in everything that they did. Herod decided therefore that it would be much better to strike first and be rid of him before his work led to an uprising, than to wait for an upheaval, get involved in a difficult situation and see his mistake.

Though John, because of Herod's suspicions, was brought in chains to Machaerus, the stronghold that we have previously mentioned, and there put to death, yet the verdict of the Jews was that the destruction visited upon Herod's army was a vindication of John, since God saw fit to inflict such a blow on Herod. (Josephus *Ant* 18.5.2 §116–19)

The following observations concern this report. Points 1–3 concern Josephus as an author; points 4–7 are about John's life.

1. Josephus did not have to report the connection between John and Herod's death in order to tell the history of Herod. Why did he report it?
2. Josephus judged John favorably as a good man. (Thus John was good grist for Josephus' apologetic mill.)
3. Josephus knew John's "theology." Baptism was a bodily action parallel to and expressive of soul cleansing and righteous behavior.
4. John exhorted people to live uprightly and to practice just acts toward others and piety toward God.
5. John baptized people who responded to his exhortations.
6. John was popularly known after his death to the degree that people could connect him with Herod's defeat by Aretas, king of Petra. John had a high degree of prominence.
7. Herod killed John preemptively because he became suspicious of and alarmed by the size and enthusiasm of John's following.

2. Mark. At the beginning of Mark's story of Jesus, John appears prominently as a preacher and baptizer to whom many people—including Jesus of Nazareth—responded. As Jesus is baptized, God tells him that he is his son. After John is arrested, Jesus begins his own preaching mission in Galilee. However, the narrative of John's arrest and execution (6:14–29) is held until about one-third of the way through the gospel. A previous narrative concerns John's disciples' practice of fasting as the Pharisees did, in contrast to the practice of Jesus' disciples, who didn't fast (2:18–22). John the Baptist next appears in the middle of the gospel, at the point where Jesus asks his disciples who people say he is; some answer that he is John (8:28). Finally, when Jesus is in Jerusalem, and the Jewish leaders ask Jesus about his authority, he evades answering directly by asking them whether they believe John's baptism was from God or not (11:27–33).

The following observations may be made about how John the Baptist fits into Mark as a story, and about what we learn concerning John beyond what is found in Josephus. First, regarding Mark as a story, Mark tells us very little about John. This gospel seems to have no interest in John for his own sake. Second, Mark's interest is in Jesus; consequently, all of the material about John is subordinated to this interest. John's preaching and baptizing mission gives Mark the opportunity to emphasize that the missions of both John and Jesus are the fulfillment of prophecy (1:2–3). John is seen obliquely as Elijah (1:6; 9:11–13), who prepares the way for Jesus and announces his arrival as the one mightier than John: Jesus will baptize with the Holy Spirit rather than with water (1:1–8). The fasting of John's disciples gives Mark a chance to portray Jesus and his disciples as the new, to be contrasted with the old (2:18–22). John's death becomes an opportunity for Mark to emphasize that Jesus and his true disciples must also face death if they are to remain faithful (6:7–44; 8:34; 9:13; 13:9–13). Finally, John's popularity makes possible Mark's portrayal of Jesus as superior to the Jerusalem authorities (11:27–33).

Regarding John's life, it can be observed that:

1. John was a prophet (1:6–8; 11:32) who lived an ascetic life (1:6; 2:18) in the wilderness (1:4).
2. He preached that people should repent and be baptized for the forgiveness of one's sins. Those to whom he preached included Herod Antipas (6:18).
3. He also predicted that a person far mightier than himself would come and baptize with the Holy Spirit those whom he had baptized with water (1:7–8).
4. Many people responded to his preaching and were baptized (1:5). They took him for a prophet (11:32); some of them remained with him as his disciples (2:18; 6:29); they fasted as the Pharisees did (2:18); and some of them buried John (6:29). John's movement was of a magnitude similar to that of Jesus' (6:14–16; 8:28).
5. One of those baptized by John was Jesus, who believed that John was Elijah (9:11–13); Jesus' disciples did not fast (2:18).
6. The Jerusalem authorities knew John well and were aware of his reputation as a prophet (11:30–33).
7. Herod arrested and killed John for personal reasons, because John criticized him for marrying his sister-in-law, Herodias (6:17–18). Herod killed John because of pressure from Herodias (6:19). He himself didn't want to kill John because he also regarded him as a righteous and holy man (6:20).
8. Jesus began his preaching mission in Galilee after John had been arrested (1:14).

3. Matthew. Matthew's distinctive use of traditions about John the Baptist is evident from deviations from Mark both in material with parallels in Mark and in additional material. After Matthew's story of Jesus' birth, John appears in the wilderness preaching not (as in Mark 1:4) a "baptism of repentance for the forgiveness of sins," but rather repentance, "for the kingdom of heaven is at hand" (Matt 3:2). This is exactly the same message that Jesus preached in his own mission (4:17), and is just one of many ways in which Matthew ties John and Jesus together. Other links are the story of children sitting in the market, in which John and Jesus are portrayed equally as messengers from God who are rejected by their generation (11:16–19), and the ignoble death meted out to both (17:9–13).

Whereas Mark's ordering of material implies that John is the forerunner of the Messiah, Matthew makes this point explicitly through the formula he uses eleven times to introduce fulfilled prophecy: "For this is he who was spoken of by the prophet" (3:3). (This proof from prophecy is only one example of the generally argumentative character of Matthew.) Matthew's emphasis on prophecy fulfillment probably accounts for his placement of the description of John's way of life next (3:4–6). Matthew means to say here (as he makes explicit later on [17:9–13]) that John is Elijah, who must precede the Messiah, who is Jesus.

Another of Matthew's major themes appears in John's extremely harsh preaching against the Pharisees and the Sadducees (3:7–10, 12). They are declared by John to be presumptuous hypocrites who have to be with obvious insincerity (3:7). This theme of insincerity is developed with respect to the Pharisees in Matthew 23. The character of the Jewish leaders in Jerusalem is likewise portrayed in the question about Jesus' authority (21:23–27), as well as in the parable of the two sons that follows (21:28–32). In both cases the leaders refuse to believe that John the Baptist is a prophet of God (referred to euphemistically as "heaven," "righteousness," 21:26, 32), which makes them worse than the lowest members of society, "tax collectors and harlots," who did believe John (21:32).

The next section, found exclusively in Matthew, contains a conversation between Jesus and John (3:14–15). It indicates that John knew Jesus, and implies that he knew Jesus to be the sinless Messiah. This episode has two Matthean emphases: how close John and Jesus are, and how wrong John's followers are when they do not turn to follow Jesus after Jesus' baptism by John.

In Mark, the entire populace asks Jesus why John's disciples fast, unlike Jesus' disciples; in Matthew (9:14) by contrast, John's disciples themselves ask the question, and thereby condemn themselves through the implicit association with unbelieving Pharisees. They are the "old" in contrast to John and Jesus who are the "new" (9:16–17).

It is in this light that we can understand John the Baptist's question to Jesus as Matthew intends it (11:2–6). John of course clearly knows that Jesus is "he who is to come" (3:1–17). This episode is told by Matthew for the benefit of John's disciples, who have not yet become Christians. "And blessed is he who takes no offense at me" (11:6), i.e., you people who in the late 1st century still remain followers of John instead of Jesus, whom John declared mightier than himself (3:11).

This message is additionally emphasized in the next section (Matt 11:7–15). John is praised as the prophet Elijah, as "more than a prophet," as the messenger of the Messiah, as the greatest of humans (11:9, 10, 11, 14); at the same time it is Matthew's belief that the least Christian is greater than John (11:11), even though Christians suffer violence as John and Jesus did (11:12). That John suffered violence is shown by the story of his death (14:1–12). This tale, as well as the report that some thought that Jesus *was* John the Baptist (16:14), again shows the close connection between prophet and Messiah. Indeed, John and Jesus are united in a common liquidation at the hands of the powerful (17:9–13), whose antagonism to both prophet and Messiah (in contrast to Jesus' high regard for John) is seen once more in the passage where the Jerusalem officials question Jesus' authority (Matt 21:23–27).

Matthew has used John the Baptist traditions with distinctive aims and purposes, among which the following are prominent:

1. John is the prophet (Elijah) of Jesus (the Messiah). John knowingly prepares for Jesus' coming as Messiah, while Jesus knowingly regards John as Elijah, the greatest of humans before Jesus.
2. John and Jesus are equally men of God. All righteous people (Jesus' disciples, Christians) will believe their messages, while the unrighteous (John's disciples, Pharisees, Herod, Jewish leaders) disbelieve and even kill them.
3. Despite Jesus' high regard for John, even the least Christian is greater than John.

What historical material beyond that found in Josephus and Mark is present in Matthew?

1. There is an additional reference to John's asceticism (11:18).
2. John harshly attacked the Pharisees and Sadducees (3:7–10), Herod (14:4), and the Jewish leaders in Jerusalem (21:32). These people did not believe in John, but outcasts such as tax collectors and harlots did (21:32).
3. John preached the same message as Jesus (3:2; 4:17).
4. John knew of Jesus and regarded him as the sinless Messiah before he baptized him (3:14–15). Jesus regarded John very highly (11:9–14), but he regarded his own followers even more highly (11:11).
5. While John was in prison he had doubts about whether Jesus really was the Messiah (11:2–6). These doubts evidently rested on the unexpected character of Jesus' activity and message (11:5–6).

4. Luke-Acts. As in the case of Mark and Matthew, the author of Luke-Acts also has a distinctive portrayal of John the Baptizer. This is seen most readily and fully in the birth story of John and Jesus (Luke 1 and 2), and the account of John's appearance as a baptizer and Jesus' baptism (3:1–22). Luke's perspective is succinctly summed up by Jesus himself in 16:16: "The law and the prophets were until John; since then the good news of the kingdom of God is preached." Thus, Luke fits John into his historical scheme: Israel (law and prophets including John), Jesus, and the Christian Church.

Most distinctive in Luke is the opening tale, which interweaves the stories of the birth of John and Jesus. The scheme can be set out as follows:

The announcement of *John's* birth (1:5–25)
The announcement of *Jesus'* birth (1:26–35)
The two mothers meet (1:36–45)
Mary praises God for *Jesus* (1:46–56)
Zechariah praises God for *John* (1:57–80)

Thus we have the chiastic pattern A, B, A + B, B, A. In this way Luke makes the basic two-sided point: John the Baptist and Jesus are closely allied in the scheme of salvation, but John is subordinate to Jesus.

John and Jesus are allied through Luke's stories of their births, which are united together because their mothers are relatives (1:36); both births are miraculous and thus merit special praise to God. Yet John is subordinated to Jesus in several ways: Elizabeth is barren and both she and her husband are very old, yet she conceives in the normal manner (1:24), while Mary conceives by the Holy Spirit when she is still unmarried (1:34–35); when Mary greets Elizabeth, the fetus (the future John) leaps in her womb for joy in the presence of the mother of her Lord, i.e., Jesus the Messiah (1:41, 44). Finally, and most importantly, John is clearly only a prophet (1:76) like Elijah (1:17), while Jesus is the Son of God and Messiah (1:32–35).

Perhaps most significant for our analysis is that after the birth story there follows the story of John's appearance and Jesus' baptism (chap. 3). The same themes of alliance between John the Baptist and Jesus, with the subordination of the former to the latter, are again present. Essentially, John is the prophet of Jesus the Messiah. Apparently, John does not even baptize Jesus, since he is already imprisoned when Jesus is baptized (3:20, 21; cf. 4:14 with Mark 1:14). John's prophetic status is emphasized by the inclusion of his prophetic preaching to the wealthy, tax collectors and soldiers (3:10–14), as well as by the note about reproval of Herod for his marriage to Herodias and "for all the evil things that Herod had done" (3:1, 9–20). The implied antipathy between John and Herod is echoed later by Herod's wish to kill Jesus and the latter's defiant response (13:31–33). This reference reminds us that Luke omitted the story of John's execution by Herod (after 9:7–9), and this omission expresses Jesus' distinctive superiority to John, for it is the Messiah who must die in a special way (24:26). In the baptism story it is made explicit that Jesus—not John—is the Messiah (3:15–17).

Luke elaborates the distinction between John's and Jesus' disciples. Along with fasting he adds prayer as another difference between them (5:33; 11:1) and he molds the "parable" of the garment so as to emphasize the rejection of Jesus by John's (and the Pharisees') disciples: they say "The old is good" (5:39, 36). Furthermore, Luke emphasizes more than the other gospels the difference between positive and negative responses of various groups to John and so to Jesus. This difference is not only present in the tales about Jesus' authority (20:1–8) and John's question to Jesus (7:18–23), but is made even more fully in Jesus' comments on John, which set out the different responses to John's preaching. Luke's Jesus declares that "all the people and the tax collectors" accepted baptism by John while the "Pharisees and the lawyers" did not, and they thereby rejected the "purpose of God for themselves" (7:29–30).

Thus, in various ways John the Baptist is the transitional figure between "the law and the prophets" and Jesus the Christ, the Son of God. This view is confirmed by all seven references to John the Baptist in Luke's second volume, the book of Acts.

5. John. The picture of John the Baptizer in the gospel of John is very clearly focused, and as in Luke's case it may be summed up in one of the gospel's pungent statements: "He was not the light, but came to bear witness to the light" (1:8). In accordance with this gospel's outlook, John the Baptist is not seen in strictly historical terms. Rather, the terminology is abstract and especially legal: John is essentially a witness sent by God (1:6) to tell the truth about Jesus (5:33, 35; 10:41). This basic theme is sustained by two subthemes; John is not the light, rather Jesus is the light; since Jesus is the light he ranks before John and must increase in stature, while John must decrease.

Apart from brief references to John the Baptist in chaps. 5 and 10, all of the material about the Baptizer is found in chaps. 1 and 3. The opening of the gospel presents Jesus as the true light of the world and John as the true witness to that light. The basis for the truth of John's witness is that he was "sent from God" (1:6). But that he was really sent from God and that he speaks the truth is shown substantively by his exaltation of Jesus over himself (1:15), and by his denial before Jews sent from Jerusalem that he has any status as Messiah, as Elijah, or as the prophet (1:19–28). As a witness John is simply the voice announcing the coming of Jesus as Lord and Son of God (1:23, 34), who was revealed to him and Israel as the "Lamb of God, who takes away the sin of the world" (1:29, 36) during his baptizing mission (1:30, 33). Moreover, John baptizes only with water (1:26, 31) while Jesus "baptizes with the Holy Spirit" (1:33). Finally, John's disciples turn to Jesus because they too see him as the Messiah (1:35–41).

After Jesus performs various signs which manifest his glory (2:11), all of these basic themes are reemphasized in the second half of chap. 3 (including 4:1). Prior to John's imprisonment (3:24), he and Jesus are carrying on parallel baptizing missions. However, Jesus and his disciples are "making and baptizing more disciples than John" (3:26; 4:1). When John's disciples report this to him, he is not chagrined at all; rather he is filled with joy because these developments conform to his true testimony that he must decrease while Jesus the Christ must increase (3:26–30).

These, then, are the sources at our disposal. They must be used critically in any attempt to describe the life of John the Baptist and his following. Scholars who focus on the history of the Christian groups that produced the gospels try also to ascertain the relation of these groups to followers of John the Baptist as this is reflected in the gospels. For example, gospel materials that emphasize John's allegiance and subordination to Jesus are seen as evidence for (1) the existence of discrete groups of John's followers in the late 1st century and (2) the Christians' efforts to convert them to Jesus as the Christ. Here we will focus only on an attempt to reconstruct the career of John.

B. A Reconstruction of John's Mission

Historical reconstruction requires critical methodology in at least two areas: (1) the development and use of criteria to judge the historical reliability of evidence, and (2) the development and use of appropriate models for locating biblical persons and groups in settings which are understandable to modern readers. The former requirement has engaged scholarship for generations, and some degree of consensus has been reached (Boring 1985; Oakman 1986, Appendix 1). Yet scholars always vary in their application of various criteria. In the present reconstruction the "environmental criterion" is seen as of primary importance. This criterion states that evidence must fit the situation of the persons or groups being studied.

The latter requirement is quite new in scholarship because the social sciences, from which appropriate models are derived, have not been used much until recently. This has been the case not only in biblical studies (Hollenback 1983) but also in all historical scholarship on the ancient world. However, now scholars have demonstrated that researchers must develop and use appropriate models if they are to avoid ethnocentric and anachronistic reconstructions. (For biblical studies see especially the work of Malina; for the ancient world in general see especially Carney 1975 and Kautsky 1982.)

Briefly, for our immediate purposes, the studies of Richard A. Horsley (1984; 1985) are especially helpful. As we reconstruct the "historical John the Baptist," it will be seen that he fits quite well the type "oracular prophet," which Horsley distinguishes from the "action prophet." These in turn he distinguishes from "social bandits" and "popular kings" as well as sicarii and zealots. These types must be seen in two primary settings: (1) the specific socioeconomic conditions of 1st-century Palestine and (2) the specific cultural traditions of Israel. The essence of the former is the aristocratic-peasant social structure while the essence of the latter are the traditions derived from the Hebrew scriptures that remain popular in the oral traditions of the non-literate population.

The aristocratic-peasant social structure is characterized primarily by exploitation of the latter by the former through heavy taxation and brutal treatment. These conditions were perennial, but they were exacerbated in times of devastating crises such as famines and wars. Thus varieties of social disturbance were the result. This was especially the case at the time of Herod's death in 4 B.C.E., Pontius Pilate's rule (26–36 C.E.), and just before and during the great revolt (66–70 C.E.).

The cultural traditions of Israel help us to grasp the various social types present in 1st-century Palestine. We are especially interested in the prophetic types (Horsley and Hanson 1985; Horsley 1985). The "action prophet" both announced the messages of God and led a popular movement with the expectation that God would intervene in liberating action. The prototype of the tradition was the Exodus from Egypt. Moses, Joshua and the Judges were the main prototypes, as on a lesser scale perhaps were Elijah and Elisha. In the 1st century there was the unnamed prophetic leader of the Samaritans who led a movement to restore the temple on Mt. Gerizim, a movement which was ruthlessly crushed by Pilate (*Ant* 18.4.1 §85–87). Around 45 C.E. Theudas led a movement to the Jordan River in apparent imitation of the Exodus, but he and his followers were also crushed by the Judean governor Fadus (*Ant* 20.5.1 §97–98). Finally, about 56 C.E., a Jewish prophet from Egypt led a movement to capture Jerusalem by commanding the walls to fall down in apparent imitation of Joshua at Jericho. In this case the leader escaped but many of his followers were killed by the governor Felix (*Ant* 20.8.6 §168–71; *JW* 2.13.5 §261–63).

Josephus' accounts of these and other similar prophetic movements establish a distinctive pattern: a popular prophet preaches a message of liberation that captures the imagination of the common people, who then march out en masse to a holy site expecting a miraculous deliverance from God as in the days of old.

The "oracular prophet" did not lead such a movement, but rather only pronounced words of judgment or redemption, as did the classical prophets of the 8th and 7th centuries. The two cases in the 1st century about whom we have some information are John the Baptizer and Jesus son of Ananias. We shall note the case of the latter in order to see the pattern of the oracular prophet, and then test whether John the Baptizer fits the category as far as we can determine from our sources. The following is Josephus' narrative concerning Jesus son of Ananias:

> But a further portent was even more alarming. Four years before the war [62 C.E.], when the city was enjoying profound peace and prosperity, there came to the feast at which it is the custom of all Jews to erect tabernacles to God, one Jesus, son of Ananias, a rude peasant, who, standing in the temple, suddenly began to cry out, "A voice from the east, a voice from the west, a voice from the four winds; a voice against Jerusalem and the sanctuary, a voice against the bridegroom and the bride, a voice against all the people." Day and night he went about all the alleys with this cry on his lips. Some of the leading citizens, incensed at these ill-omened words, arrested the fellow and severely chastised him. But he, without a word on his own behalf or for the private ear of those who smote him, only continued his cries as before. Thereupon, the magistrates, supposing, as was indeed the case, that the man was under some supernatural impulse, brought him before the Roman governor; there, although flayed to the bone with scourges, he neither sued for mercy nor shed a tear, but, merely introducing the most mournful of variations into his ejaculation, responded to each stroke with "Woe to Jerusalem!". When Albinus, the governor, asked him who and whence he was and why he uttered these cries, he answered him never a word, but unceasingly reiterated his dirge over the city, until Albinus pronounced him a maniac and let him go. During the whole period up to the outbreak of war he neither approached nor was seen talking to any of the citizens, but daily, like a prayer that he had conned, repeated his lament, "Woe to Jerusalem!". He neither cursed any of those who beat him from day to day, nor blessed those who offered him food: to all men that melancholy presage was his one reply. His cries were loudest at the festivals. So for seven years and five months he continued his wail, his voice never flagging nor his strength exhausted, until in the siege, having seen his presage verified, he found his rest. For, while going his round and shouting in piercing tones from the wall, "Woe once more to the city and to the people and to the temple," as he added a last word, "and woe to me also," a stone hurled from the ballista struck and killed him on the spot. So with those ominous words still upon his lips he passed away (*JW* 6.5.3 §300–9).

There were many other prophets besides Jesus son of Ananias, to whom Josephus refers only in general terms. For example, Josephus refers to "numerous prophets" who called on the people in the midst of crises during the great revolt, to "await help from God" for their deliverance (*JW* 6.5.2 §286). These prophets also follow a distinctive pattern: an oracular prophet preaches a message either of judgment on the powerful (e.g., Jesus son of Ananias), or of deliverance for the suffering masses in the midst of crises when apocalyptic hope is at fever pitch among the common people (e.g., the "numerous prophets" in Jerusalem during the war). They are regarded by the "upper-class Roman collaborators" either as threats to political stability or as raving madmen, so the authorities try to silence or even kill them. "Oh Jerusalem, Jerusalem, killing the prophets and stoning those who are sent to you!" (Matt 23:37; Luke 13:34). Now our question is whether John the Baptist was one of these oracular prophets.

1. The Origin of John the Baptizer. Since Josephus says nothing about John's origin, we must depend on the gospels. The case for understanding Luke's birth story of John as legendary no longer needs demonstration (R. E. Brown 1977). Yet, whether or not Luke 1 and 2 reflect a Baptist source (Wink 1968, Dodd 1963), there seems to be no good reason to doubt that, as this story indicates (Luke 1:5), John was a descendant of devout rural priests. Indeed, other sections of the gospels confirm that John had priestly concerns. He engaged in the rituals of baptism, fasting, and prayer (Luke 5:33; 11:1).

Yet John comes on the scene as more than simply a rural priest. He appears in the wilderness of Judea as a radically alienated person. In addition to the wilderness habitation itself, his alienation is indicated not least by his food and clothing: "Now John was clothed with camel's hair, and had a leather girdle around his waist, and ate locusts and wild honey" (Mark 1:6). This asceticism became proverbial: "For John came neither eating nor drinking" (Matt 11:18). Most of all, he scathingly attacked the Jerusalem establishment for its impiety and injustice (Matt 3:7–10).

How can we account for John's Jeremiah-like separation from the normal securities and meanings of traditional life? First, John's general cultural setting is significant. There was a long-standing tradition of alienation among the prophets of ancient Israel. Jeremiah has already come to mind: "I did not sit in the company of merrymakers, nor did I rejoice; I sat alone" (Jer 15:17). Then, in exilic and postexilic Judaism various groups of alienated priests appear on the scene. P. D. Hanson sees the "dawn of apocalyptic" taking place among groups of alienated visionary priests as early as the 6th–5th centuries B.C.E. (1975: 209–28, 280–86, 389–401). Moreover, in the middle of the 2d century B.C.E. there was a sharp revulsion against the Maccabees which nourished, among others, the Qumran community, a group that consisted largely of lower rural priests alienated from the aristocratic urban priests of Jerusalem (Cross 1958: 95–119; 1973: 332–42). Among the important statements from the Dead Sea Scrolls which express this rift is the following interpretation of Hab 2:8a ("Because you have plundered many nations, all the remnant of the people shall plunder you."): "This refers to the final priests of Jerusalem who will amass for themselves wealth and gain by plundering the people" (1QpHab 2:8; Gaster 1964: 249). The case of Qumran is especially significant because John was like the people of Qumran in many respects; he may even have been a member of that group or a similar group (Davies 1983; Betz 1985). Josephus supports this statement by his references to the great social and economic gulf that existed between the aristocratic priests and the large mass of lower clergy that developed just before the great revolt in the 60s C.E.

> There now was enkindled mutual enmity and class warfare between the high priests, on the one hand, and the priests and leaders of the populace of Jerusalem, on the other. Each of the factions formed and collected for itself a band of the most reckless revolutionaries and acted as their leader. And when they clashed, they used abusive language and pelted each other with stones . . . Such was the shamelessness and effrontery which possessed the high priests that they actually were so brazen as to send slaves to the threshing floors to receive the tithes that were due to the priests, with the result that the poorer priests starved to death (*Ant* 20.8.8 §180–81; also 29.9.2 §205–7; further details in Stern 1976: 561–700).

More broadly-based alienation is indicated by the first revolt of the Jews against the Romans upon the death of Herod the Great in 4 B.C.E. (*JW* 2.1.1–6.2 §1–92; *Ant* 17.9.1–11.3 §206–314; Farmer 1958; Horsley and Hanson 1985: 111–17).

A striking confirmation of the luxury of the Jerusalem (probably priestly) aristocracy has come to light in the recent excavations in the "Jewish Quarter of the Old City" of Jerusalem (Avigad 1976: 1.23–35). In this "fashionable and wealthy residential section overlooking the Holy Temple" a Herodian house of 2,000 square feet was unearthed, as well as a larger one the archaeologists dubbed "The Mansion." On a stone weight found in "The Mansion" was inscribed "Bar Kathros," the name of one of four priestly families mentioned in the Talmud (*Pesaḥ* 57a) as exploiting the people and beating them with rods. "Our Bar Kathros was probably of this family," conjectures Avigad (1976: 29; see also Mazar 1980). These houses with their varied contents demonstrate the luxury of the aristocracy in Jerusalem just before the time of John the Baptist.

Thus John was surrounded by a pervasive climate of alienation; one scholar (Ford 1976) argues that this probably reached into his own family. It was from this urban setting that John retreated to the wilderness, a location of profound symbolic significance as the place of death, purification and rebirth (Hollenbach 1974; W. D. Davies 1974: 75–104). These meanings are reflected at Qumran, where those who joined the community separated themselves from the wicked "to the end that they may indeed 'go into the wilderness to prepare the way,' i.e., do what Scripture enjoins when it says, 'Prepare in the wilderness the way . . . make straight in the desert a highway for our God' [Isa. 40:3]" (1QS 8:12–16; Gaster 1964: 64). That going into the wilderness sometimes had even messianic significance is indicated by Matt 24:26a: "So, if they say to you, 'Lo, he [the Messiah] is in the wilderness,' do not go out."

This is as far as a quest for the origin of John can take us. We may conclude, despite the paucity of particulars about John before his public appearance, that he came from a family of radicalized rural priests. This direction was most likely the result of the alienation the lower rural priesthood generally felt toward the Jerusalem aristocracy. At some point John left his family and took up a prophetic desert existence. (Zech 13:4 shows that John adopted clothing of a type worn by other alienated prophets, not only Elijah [as in 2 Kgs 1:8].) Finally he appeared in public as an apocalyptic prophet.

2. John's Prophetic Mission. A basic problem in determining the meaning of John's prophetic-baptizing mission is the question of the audience to which his various proclamations and judgments are addressed. Scholars often make no distinctions in this respect. Scobie (1964: 62–73) is typical when he speaks vaguely of "people" or of the "wicked" in contrast to the "righteous" without inquiring into the socioeconomic class structure of Palestine. Kraeling (1951: 49–59) is of the exceptional opinion that the "brood of vipers" saying was addressed to the priestly aristocracy. Horsley and Hanson (1985: 177–80) carry this further: there is evidence of "class conflict in John's message" in that he announces "God's imminent overthrow of the established order as headed by the sacerdotal aristocracy and Herod Antipas."

Who was John's first audience? It may be that he never preached a general message to the nation at large. If he did, it is now difficult to determine what the message was. What would it mean for him to preach such a general message anyway? Preaching to the nation "as a whole" (Kraeling 1951: 49) is a vague notion hard to pin down. Of course his particular proclamations undoubtedly had import for the Jewish people at large, and perhaps even for the Diaspora; but he, like Amos at Bethel and other OT prophets in their particular places, must have spoken specific messages at specific times and places to specific groups. Even if we accept Mark's statement that "all the country of Judea and all the people of Jerusalem went out to him" (1:5), nevertheless, before that occurred, John must have preached something to someone that attracted other people's attention.

a. John's Opening Salvo. (1) His Audience. If John was an alienated rural priest who was compelled to take up the role of an apocalyptic prophet, then it is reasonable to assume that his first and major proclamation was an attack on the powerful Jerusalem establishment (Matt 3:7) and other associated powerful social groups (Luke 3:10–14). We have good indirect evidence for this, while we have no evidence at all for his preaching to the powerless. We cannot use Matt 21:32 as evidence because it is another case of Matthew making John like Jesus (21:31). John, like other oracular prophets, may have been a "spokesperson for the common people" (Horsley and Hanson 1985: 179), but this is very different from the idea that he had a "ministry to the poor" (Wink 1968: 20). Rather, his message of judgment was to the powerful, as Luke 7:30 indicates: "Pharisees and lawyers."

(2) His Message. What was John's message to these powerful ones? It can be inferred only from what he says to those who come to him for baptism, for we do not have accounts of any of his words spoken to persons in other settings except his attack on Herod Antipas (Mark 6:17–18; Luke 3:19). Considering the OT prophetic tradition, John's message must have been that the wrath of God was coming on them as faithless Israelites (Matt 3:7). Only if they repented of their apostasy, gave up their presumption (Matt 3:9), and instead did works fit for repentance (Matt 3:8), both works of ritual purification (John 3:25; Dodd 1963: 281; Kysar 1975: 63) and works of social justice (Luke 3:10–14), would they escape God's wrath. Apocalyptic emphasis on God's imminent intervention against them must also have been strong (Matt 3:10).

Most distinctive was John's call for the repentant ones to come to the Jordan to be baptized as an action symbolic of their return to God. The fact that he was labelled "the baptizer" indicates the emphasis he must have put on this ritual. Both Mark (1:4) and Luke (3:3) say that he preached "a baptism of repentance for the forgiveness of sins," and this fits his initial message. That was the meaning of his baptism as he proclaimed it to the powerful apostate. However, at the time that he actually baptized some of them, he added a further component to his ritual: it anticipated the coming of one who would bring a radical purification to the repentant ones (Luke 3:16–17).

This means that we have no evidence that John initially proclaimed the coming of a messianic figure, let alone the kingdom of God. It is doubtful that John preached about the one to come except to the repentant individuals who came for baptism. He seems not to have mentioned the coming one even to the unrepentant ones who desired baptism (Matt 3:7–10). Moreover, it is also likely that John's ethical preaching (Luke 3:10–14) was addressed only to persons who actually came to him for baptism. In other words, John's opening salvo was a stark message of doom familiar from portions of the OT prophets, except that he added the possibility of escape through the baptism of repentance.

(3) His Location. If this was John's message, where did he deliver it? It is almost impossible to believe that he was "preaching" (it) in the wilderness of Judea" alone (Matt 3:1). Luke (3:2–3) says only that the "word of God came to John . . . in the wilderness" but that he called for people to be baptized in "all the region about the Jordan." In this respect Luke differs from Mark and Matthew who say that people from Judea, Jerusalem (Mark, Matthew), and the region of the Jordan (Matthew) went out to John. While the gospels (especially Luke) tend to generalize, one wonders whether all the people who came from as far away as Jerusalem and beyond (Jesus evidently came all the way from Galilee!) responded to hearsay reports alone. Is it not more probable that John had previously preached his message in populated places, in the villages and cities, even in Jerusalem itself? Kraeling (1951: 64) raises this issue and suggests that John went to the highways to preach, while W. R. Brownlee (1957: 36) suggested that John "found places in the wilderness where he could meet people" in villages and towns. It would be in such places that he could address directly those for whom his message was intended. That he traveled about considerably is supported by the claim that he went as far away from Judea as Aenon-at-Salim, which is at least 30, if not 70 kilometers N of the Dead Sea and Jerusalem (John 3:23; Brown *John* AB, 151). This coheres with what we know about prophets in general, namely, they went to the people to whom their messages applied.

Why don't we hear more about John's travels? Because the gospel writers weren't interested in that sort of thing. They don't tell us very much about John at all, and while they tell us a lot about Jesus, we learn little from them about his movements. Consider the following: if not for the gospel of John we would never know that John went as far N as Aenon-at-Salim, or that Jesus baptized and had disciples while John was still carrying on his own public mission. Besides all this the gospels are interested not in John's mission itself, but rather in proving that John "appeared in the wilderness" as the forerunner of Jesus in fulfillment of Isa 40:3 (Mark 1:2–4).

We are left then with the following picture: John the Baptizer originates as a wilderness character who emerges as a prophet in populated places, proclaiming to powerful sinners a prophetic-apocalyptic message of imminent doom on them because of their impurity and injustice, and calling upon them to come to the Jordan and be baptized as a sign of their repentance and a pledge of their renewed faithfulness to God.

b. John's Message to Those Coming for Baptism. In the gospel accounts all of John's words (except the word against Antipas) are spoken to persons seeking baptism. These words show that John was hostile to those whom he judged to have bad faith, while he was friendly to those who were truly repentant. To the former he repeated threats and warnings and perhaps added new ones, while to the latter he gave hope for further dramatic renewal of their lives as well as ethical guidance relevant to their particular vocations.

(1) To the Unrepentant Powerful. (a) The Priestly Aristocracy in Jerusalem. That Matthew (3:7–10) and Luke (3:7–9) differ with regard to John's audience is of little consequence in determining its identity since the "brood of vipers" speech itself shows the audience's character clearly enough. This speech is his "most contemptuous saying" (Kraeling 1951: 49), but except for the Antipas saying, it is his only thoroughly negative one. Indeed, all of his other sayings are wholly positive, spoken to repentant sinners. To say that "John concentrated by far the greater part of his attention on stern warnings of future punishment . . ." (Scobie 1964: 62) is at best misleading.

The "brood of vipers" saying is consistent with numerous doom sayings that OT prophets commonly spoke against the unrepentant powerful of the nation, a likeness apparent first in the epithet, for to accuse someone of being a viper was "to castigate him as evil in his inmost being" (Kraeling 1951: 48). Thus, and second, the following query must be bitter and sarcastic irony, especially since the verb "show" *(hypodeiknymi)* is normally used for special or divine revelation (Acts 9:16). Third, the sarcasm is occasioned by the fact that the addressees are hypocrites in that they do not practice deeds to match their sham repentance (Luke 3:8a) and by the fact of their arrogant and complacent presumption about their standing with God (3:8b). John then rounds off his castigation with the warning, doubtless repeated from earlier occasions, that in "the coming wrath" which is already appearing (3:9a) these arrogant hypocrites will be destroyed (3:9).

It is important to note that John does not say anything here about repentant ones escaping the coming doom. It needs to be emphasized that in this saying he pronounces doom for a specific group of unrepentant persons because the specificity of the particular group he is addressing makes superfluous a reference to repentant ones. The failure to notice the particularity of John's message to specific groups has caused the unwarranted generalizing of his message. Kraeling (1951: 49) is thus correct that this denunciation is "too bitter to be addressed to the nation as a whole." There is only one group that it fits well and that is the ruling priestly aristocracy in Jerusalem, which perpetrated the most heinous social injustices.

If the view just adumbrated is accepted, an interesting question naturally arises: why did those aristocrats come at all to be baptized, especially since they were apparently insincere? Did they come simply to observe or even to interrogate John? John 1:19–25 supports this view, and Josephus (*Ant* 15.10.4 §365–69) shows that political leaders such as Herod the Great spied on various persons and groups. Or did John act ironically, as if they came to be baptized, in order to shame them further? Maybe the statement that they were coming for baptism is erroneous. But John's opening question could mean at least that the addressees were coming with some kind of positive intentions if not for baptism itself. Or perhaps, upon encountering the audacious prophet again in person, some of these authorities thought it wise to make a kind of Pascalian wager and so sought baptism without concern about the "good fruit" it presupposed, simply to be on the safe side. (Gamaliel later suggested a similar wager to the Jerusalem authorities, Acts 5:33–39.)

Probably this question cannot be answered. But it seems certain that in John's mind his addressees were another group of complacent authorities who were perpetrating injustice. These authorities in particular have it in their power to "bear fruits" of piety and justice, and John directs his harshest words (as far as we know) to those who would make a charade of even the sacred ritual of baptism. There is no evidence that any of these most powerful ones responded positively to John's preaching, and one passage appears to indicate that they did not (Matt 21:32a: "For John came to you ["chief priests and elders," 21:23a] in the way of righteousness, and you did not believe him").

(b) Herod Antipas. In connection with John's attack on the unrepentant powerful who came to him, it is appropriate to include his denunciation of Herod Antipas, even though we have no record that the latter ever came to him for baptism or for any other purpose. Antipas is the only named individual who is said to have been denounced by John. Despite the fact that gospel materials about John and Antipas have been the subject of legendary elaboration, there is good reason to accept the historicity of John's attack on Antipas, as both Kraeling (1951: 83–88) and Scobie (1964: 179–86) do.

This denunciation is especially remarkable because Antipas was a political figure of some stature. John's attack and the revolutionary potential of his movement were apparently what caused Antipas to arrest and execute him. What caused John to denounce Antipas? An attempt has been made above to explain his attack on the Jerusalem authorities. Can this attack on Antipas also be explained? Was there some occasion in John's career that made it appropriate for him to express such a negative judgment? Was it made at a face to face meeting either when Antipas sought out John or when John sought out Antipas in his palace in Tiberias or elsewhere?

A comparison of three related texts makes the following picture plausible: at a later time, when Jesus had gained some notoriety, which included having crowds follow him and sending his disciples out on a preaching mission, Jesus looked like John to Antipas (Mark 6:14–16) and Antipas became intent on arresting and killing him (Luke 13:31–33). But Jesus left his territory and frustrated this intention. This analogy between Jesus' movement and John's is confirmed by Josephus in that he also attributes Antipas' attention to John to the fact that he was leading a mass movement that was seen by Antipas as a political threat (*Ant* 18.5.2 §118). It is interesting to notice that when Jesus was warned about Antipas' evil intention, he let loose against him one of the most severe verbal attacks recorded of Jesus. He called Antipas a "fox" (a cunning destroyer) (Luke 13:32). Is it not likely that when John became aware of Antipas' interest in him, he similarly let loose a verbal attack on him? This kind of an occasion is all the more likely when it is considered that John had no vocational or social connection with Antipas as he had with the Jerusalem aristocracy. If this suggestion has merit, it also indicates something of the range as well as the size of John's movement; it must have spread far beyond Judea into Antipas' territory. It is significant in this connection also that John was not liquidated by the Jerusalem authorities as was Jesus but by the ruler of Galilee and Perea.

Whatever may have been the occasion for John's attack it needs to be stressed that his attack had legal, moral, and political significance. It probably was much more wide ranging than simply a criticism of Antipas' marriage. Luke 3:19 has John reprove him also "for all the evil things that Herod had done." The marriage was a legal issue because it contravened Lev 20:21: "If a man takes his brother's wife, it is impurity"; this aspect is stressed in the gospels. It was a moral issue because the divorce shamed Antipas' first wife, the Nabatean king Aretas' daughter, whom Antipas put away in order to marry Herodias; this aspect is found neither in the gospels nor in Josephus. Finally, it had political significance because it threatened to further destabilize an already unstable political situation caused by the divorce of king Aretas' daughter, whom he had originally married for political reasons. As a matter of fact, this issue seems to have been a prominent cause of the later war (in 36 C.E.) between Aretas and Antipas in which Herod was defeated (and which is the context of Josephus' story of John's arrest and liquidation [*Ant* 18.5.1 §109–15]). In view of these many factors the conclusion is likely that John's criticism was a massive attack on the integrity of Antipas as a person and as a ruler. That is why Antipas had him eliminated but did not destroy Jesus, who escaped for the moment.

Thus, the view of those scholars who seek to prove "that John's Messianic preaching must have been completely non-political" (Scobie 1964: 184) must be rejected. In the first place, this part of John's preaching is not messianic. In the second place, it is historically inappropriate to separate so sharply John's "religious" from his "political" message. While it is possible to distinguish politics from religion, especially for 20th century people, nevertheless, at no time is it possible to separate them, and in 1st century Palestine, as social scientists have shown, it would not be possible even to distinguish them (Carney 1975; Malina 1986b). Thus only one conclusion is possible, namely, that John was calling on Antipas to change himself, his politics, and his policies. He must have also called on him and the Jerusalem authorities to practice piety and justice. See also HEROD ANTIPAS.

(2) To the Repentant Powerful. John the Baptist addressed two different kinds of words to the truly repentant powerful who came to be baptized. Again, chronology is uncertain but it is logical to examine them in the order that follows.

(a) The Second Baptism. If we are to interpret this section (Luke 3:16b–17; Matt 3:11–12; Mark 1:7–8) adequately, it is essential to observe two factors in the texts not usually taken into account. First, John addresses in this particular case those whom he is in the process of baptizing. He is not speaking to others, such as those who are seeking baptism in bad faith, let alone to people in general. Rather, he is speaking only to those who are seeking baptism in good faith. His first words, "I baptize you with water" (Matt 3:11a; Luke 3:16a) have almost the character of a baptismal formula and can be seen as an analogue of the Christian formula, "I baptize you in the name of the Lord Jesus" (Acts 19:5). He tells those he is baptizing that their present baptism is to be succeeded by a second and much greater baptism performed by a much greater person than he.

Second, John's emphasis falls not on the fact that one mightier than he is coming, but rather on the fact that his baptism will be succeeded by another, greater baptism. By making the announcement during the very act of baptizing, John radically depreciates his own rite. His baptism will be superceded by a second baptism because the latter will effect a result that John's baptism is incapable of performing. He says in effect: "There is one coming after me who is mightier than I because he has to do a mightier deed than I, namely, baptize with Holy Spirit and fire." The second baptism, thus, is the really important one, while his first baptism is but a preliminary to it. To be sure, the self-depreciation of John the Baptist in the gospel of John is exaggerated and related to the ministry of Jesus, but as Dodd (1963: 256–59) argues, apart from that it is essentially historical. John understood his work to be inadequate compared to what he evidently saw that needed to be done.

This understanding of second baptism as John the Baptist expressed it was very soon supplanted by the early Christians' identification of the "coming one" as Jesus. The process can be seen in Paul's first sermon in Acts (13:16–47), where John's baptism is no longer connected to the coming one's baptism (Acts 13:24–25). In fact, baptism is not even mentioned in connection with the coming one, and even the announcement of his coming is separated from John's baptism: "Before his [Jesus'] coming John had preached a baptism of repentance to all the people of Israel. And as John was finishing his course, he said, 'What do you suppose that I am? I am not he. No, but after me one is coming, the sandals of whose feet I am not worthy to untie' " (Acts 13:24–25). This separation of John's baptism from the second baptism of the coming one has prevailed in Christian thought and even in modern scholarship up to the present time.

What John meant by his baptismal statement must be determined in the light of these two factors. The focus thus should be not on identifying the character of some "coming one" but on the contrast between John's water baptism and another's "holy spirit and fire" baptism. Those who focus on the coming one as a "transcendent" messiah (Kraeling 1951: 63; Scobie 1964: 66) go beyond the evidence. The fluidity of messianic ideas in John's day is ignored as well (de Jonge 1966; *IDBSup,* 588–91; see also MESSIAH). What John meant by his water baptism is clear enough even without referring to the Christian summaries of it ("a baptism of repentance for the forgiveness of sins"), for his speech to the unrepentant powerful strongly implies that it had to do with repentance and commitment to new acts of righteousness which are the fruits of repentance (Matt 3:8).

The important and more problematic matters are determining the original words describing the second baptism and establishing their meaning. The phrase "Holy Spirit and fire" has received most scholarly attention. What is its meaning? Since John is addressing repentant sinners coming for baptism, they are doing a positive act to which one would expect him to respond positively. Just as he responded negatively to those who came for baptism in bad faith, so one would expect him to respond positively to those who came in good faith. Hence, "Holy Spirit and fire" must have a positive meaning. Negative meanings involving judgment and destruction can be eliminated from consideration so the question that remains is, What positive meaning is intended?

A significant possibility is purification. Purification is linked with an anticipated messenger in Mal 3:1–3: "the messenger of the covenant in whom you delight, behold, he is coming. . . . For he is like a refiner's fire and like fuller's soap; he will sit as a refiner and purifier of silver, and he will purify the sons of Levi and refine them like gold and silver . . ." The Rule of the Community from Qumran proclaims that at the time of God's visitation he will "purge all the acts of man in the crucible of his truth, and refine for Himself all the fabric of man, destroying every spirit of perversity from within his flesh and cleansing him by the holy spirit from all the effects of wickedness. Like waters of purification He will sprinkle upon him the spirit of truth, to cleanse him of all the abominations of falsehood and of all pollution through the spirit of filth . . ." (1QS 4:20, 21; Gaster 1964: 53). Notice especially the analogy between "waters of purification" and cleansing by the "holy spirit" and the "spirit of truth." Note also Ezek 36:25–26: "I will sprinkle clean water upon you, and you shall be clean from all your uncleannesses . . . A new heart I will give you and a new spirit I will put within you . . ."

Fire is a traditional symbol of judgmental destruction. The prophet Malachi (3:18–19—Eng 3:18–4:1) envisions the day when God acts as "burning like an oven" and destroying the arrogant and evildoers. A strikingly vivid image from one Qumran hymn foresees the "rivers of Belial" (1QH 3:28) overflowing "like a fire consuming all . . ." (1QH 3:29). But destruction is not the only meaning of fire imagery, and cannot be its meaning in John the Baptist's preaching. That John was particularly interested in purification coheres with his priestly background and also with his interest in religious-ascetic practices, such as fasting and prayer (Luke 5:33; 11:1; Acts 14:23; *Gospel of Thomas* 104). Hence, it may be concluded that John told those he was baptizing that his baptism of repentance would be followed soon by a second, radical cleansing of them from all evil. In this regard John is in full accord with the OT prophetic emphasis on the need for radical renewal, a perspective seen, for example, in the call for a new covenant by Hosea (1–3) and Jeremiah (31).

There is one major problem with this line of interpretation. Luke 3:17 appears not to fit the meaning we argue for 3:16. The imagery of Luke 3:17 seems to represent the separation of the righteous from the wicked in a metaphor of winnowing; grain is separated from chaff, which is burned with "unquenchable fire." The analogy with purification is strong: purification involves the removal of impurity from a valued substance; so winnowing removes the impurity, the chaff, from the valued grain. However Luke 3:17 is interpreted, 3:16 must be taken to mean that John looked for an eschatological purification of his repentant baptized ones.

John the Baptist's message can be summarized thus: Now is the time of repentance in view of the imminent execution of God's wrath on unrepentant powerful sinners. Those that do not repent will be destroyed by God's wrath, while those who do will receive an additional second baptism greater than John's that will bestow on them a final and perfect purification. In the meantime, they are to do ritual and moral acts that befit their repentance and that anticipate the final purification.

(b) Ethical Criticism and Obligation. Among those who came to be baptized by John were at least three distinct social or vocational groups. There seems to be no good reason to doubt the historical authenticity of John's baptism of persons from these groups even though we have no other supporting evidence except Luke 7:29 and Matt 21:32. However, we cannot accept as historical Luke's statement (3:10) that "multitudes asked" John, "What then shall we do?" For not only is "multitudes" a favorite Lukan editorial term (see 3:7), but it does not appropriately describe the specific groups mentioned, namely the tax collectors and soldiers. Therefore, the likely addressees must be deduced from John's answer; the Baptist's response targets those who have more than the minimum of food and clothing, the relatively wealthy. The questions asked of John indicate that the relatively wealthy have responded positively to his message. Part of that response would be their baptism and further instruction. John addresses appropriately specific demands to each group. The relatively wealthy are to share their clothing and food with the destitute. Tax collectors are not to extort but are to follow the exact demands of their superiors. And soldiers are to quit taking advantage of their possession of the force of arms and their social position (which gave them judicial advantage) in order to rob others; and they should not agitate for salary increases.

Several things are noteworthy about John's ethical criticism, but the most important is that every one of these three cases of criticism has to do with economic matters. Each case assumes the distinction between a relatively wealthy class and a very poor class that suffers oppression by the wealthy. In line with the OT prophets, John asks the oppressors, as part of their baptism of repentance, to cease their oppression of the poor who are powerless against them. Their changed practices will constitute "fruits that befit repentance."

(i) Tax Collectors. The case of the tax collectors is particularly clear and helps in understanding the other cases. There were a variety of ways in which the local Jewish authorities as well as the Romans extracted money from the populace. Stern (1976: 330–36) lists no less than five Roman forms alone: poll-tax (census tax), agricultural tax, customs, confiscation (especially of Temple funds), and the *angria,* a type of corvée. In addition to these Roman taxes, there were the Jewish religious taxes, the Temple tax and the tithes. See also CENSUS, ROMAN; TAX COLLECTOR.

But it was in connection with collecting customs on transported goods and various other government revenues that the specific kind of official referred to in Luke 3:12 figures, for the collection of such duties was farmed out to local Jews by the Romans. There was a hierarchy of such officials. Zacchaeus, for example (Luke 19:1–9), was the "head of a society of publicans" (Stern 1974: 333) who were subordinate to him. Tax collectors (called publicans) could grow rich through collecting "more than [was] appointed" them (Luke 3:12), i.e., more than they had contracted with and paid their superior for. Zacchaeus, for example, had paid some official (probably a Roman) for his office, which gave him tax collecting privileges at Jericho. He in turn was paid by others for the privilege of collecting certain of those taxes. At each of these levels a tax collector could earn his own livelihood and usually also gain his relative wealth by collecting more than he paid for his office (Herrenbruck 1981; Oakman 1986).

That some publicans grew very rich is seen in the case of Zacchaeus. Zacchaeus could give away half his income and restore fourfold any fraudulent acquisitions and still be a rich man. In 66 C.E. at Caesarea, "the Jewish notables, with John the tax collector . . . offered Florus eight talents of silver" as a bribe in order to get him to stop undesirable building activities next to the synagogue (*JW* 2.14.4 §284–88).

The point is that publicans were not only quislings contaminated by contact with Gentiles, and sometimes robbers, but were also part of the wealthy oppressing establishment. For such persons to heed John's call to repentance with its accompanying demand of good works would entail a total rejection of their former way of life with its class involvement and class consciousness. When John the Baptist demanded that they should not collect funds beyond what they had contracted for, he was striking at the root of the tax-farming system. That this was the case, and the possibility that John had repentant tax-collectors among his followers as well as numbers of poor tax-payers who had felt their oppression and were glad to hear John denounce the oppressive system, may have been the major reason that Antipas finally took notice of John. Note that upon the death of Herod the Great, the requests made of the new ruler, Archelaus, are the following: "that he should lighten the yearly payments," that he "release . . . the prisoners," and that he remove the taxes "levied upon public purchases and sale" that "had been ruthlessly exacted" (*Ant* 17.8.4 204–5). It is also generally accepted that taxes were a contributing factor in causing the Great War of 66–70 C.E. (Rhoads 1976: 80–81).

(ii) Soldiers. There is a connection between tax collectors and soldiers in the sense that people like Zacchaeus and Joseph, as indicated above, could "avail themselves of the assistance of military forces" (Stern 1974: 333; Gibson 1981). Alliances between tax collectors and the military were common in ancient societies. Kautsky (1982) has shown that the two main functions of ancient aristocratic governments were taxation and warfare. The point is that they, like all military and police forces, served the needs of those who ruled. They may have been direct supporters of the tax collectors, as the Greek phrase *kai hymeis* "and we" (Luke 3:14) suggests. Or they could have been supporters of the Jerusalem establishment. In the course of military service soldiers might commit various deeds of oppression, motivated in part by their aspiration to rise above the mediocrity of their social situation compared with those whom they served.

Upon these soldiers John lays radical ethical demands. If the soldiers heeded these demands, just as in the case of the tax-collectors, it would have meant a radical revision of their private conduct, and might also have challenged the very foundations of the social order. For example, John asked them not to request a raise in pay (suggesting personal sacrifice) because their wages were already being taken out of the hides of the powerless poor. In addition, soldiers attempting to implement John the Baptist's reforms risked being guilty of insubordination, because they might have had to disobey the orders of superiors to enforce their demands against the populace, who had limited means to resist official predation.

(iii) The Relatively Wealthy. In the case of the first group whom John the Baptist addresses (tax collectors), economic matters are at the forefront and the distinction between the destitute and the relatively wealthy is prominent. The very wealthy were not necessarily directly enjoined. John asks the relatively wealthy to share their moderate wealth with the destitute.

If we connect the image of social stratification indicated by John's words with the fact that at his time Palestine was relatively prosperous compared to the period just after Herod's death and just before the great revolt, we arrive at a significant observation regarding the context of John the Baptist's ethical criticism. Like the period of Jeroboam II in which Amos prophesied (ca. 750 B.C.E.), the Herodian era was a period characterized by relative prosperity along with "the impoverishment of the masses" (Stern 1976: 577; see further chaps. 11–12, esp. pp. 691–92). In other words, it was a classic case of social and economic oppression and John puts the burden of justice directly on the bureaucracy and indirectly on their superiors, the ruling elite.

(iv) Social Justice. In every case of John's ethical criticism he strikes at structural injustice. He directly addresses the relatively privileged and powerful groups in society who perpetrate injustices. It is notable in this connection that he does not ask those who are repenting to fast and pray. Evidently, these specifically religious practices were reserved for his more immediate followers. Presumably John's assumption is that these people will return to society and play their normal vocational roles. Thus, John's baptism is nowhere exclusively connected with fasting and prayer but is directly connected with social justice. He asked the baptized to forsake the normal socially accepted ways of acting and living and to take up new ways. In this sense, then, it is necessary to call John the Baptist a social rebel (Hobsbawn 1971; Kautsky 1982). John is a rebel insofar as he leads a movement which sharply attacks the legitimacy of the current social structures. His movement has not yet spilled over into overt disruption of society (he has not yet become an "action prophet"), though it is clear that his movement has that potential (and Antipas apparently saw it that way); but he certainly is fomenting social unrest. And for him the restructuring of society begins not with the "common people," nor with the very wealthy, but with the relatively privileged bureaucratic groups who have some power to change affairs. Evidently at John's time there were at least a few members of these classes who still had some sensitivity to injustice and were vulnerable to his eschatological-apocalyptic message. While undoubtedly some of his following, maybe even most of them, were the destitute masses, it remains true that not one word in the NT is addressed to them. John the Baptist's criticism of the powerful, of course, implies concern for the weak. Like the classical prophets he addresses only those responsible for and likely to change the sorry state of affairs reigning in his society. Thus it is misleading to say "that John's converts were drawn from the common people" (Manson 1949: 39), and it is pertinent to observe that "it is prosperity, not poverty, that causes social criticism and, ultimately, revolution" (Schneidau 1976: 38).

C. Summary

The preceding analysis seems to justify the following picture of John the Baptist's career. Having suffered the outrages perpetrated on the lower country clergy by the urban priestly aristocracy of Jerusalem, John the Baptist also suffered profound alienation from the status quo and left society for the real and spiritual wilderness of Judea. Perhaps he was at Qumran or some such place for a while. Then there explodes in him and from him a radical prophetic-apocalyptic vision that brings him back to attack society at its heart, its powerful ones. He proclaims an imminent day of wrath for the unrepentant perpetrators of impiety and injustice unless they are baptized in repentance and begin to do deeds of justice that ultimately entail the radical revision of the social system of his day. As might be expected, most of the powerful respond to him negatively and eventually facilitate his liquidation.

Surprisingly enough, however, some of them responded positively. Sensing perhaps that he has asked the impossible of them, as he baptizes them he promises that they will soon be baptized in a new way by a greater one who will be able to cleanse them of evil in radical eschatological fashion. With this cleansing they will be up to following the ethical standards that he has demanded of them. Meanwhile, they are to return to their former social roles and begin to practice the new vision of social justice they have gotten from him. Some of them, however, stay with him, practicing forms of piety such as fasting and prayer that were seen perhaps to anticipate that final cleansing. These disciples formed a distinct group, one of many such groups that sprang up at that time. This group, however, was distinguished from others by its unique prophetic-social vision and practices, at least as long as it remained under the inspiration of its founder, John the Baptist.

Thus, John the Baptist fits the model of an oracular prophet very well, with the proviso that he adds uniquely to that model his practices of baptism, fasting, and prayer.

Bibliography

Avigad, N. 1976. How the Wealthy Lived in Herodian Jerusalem. *BARev* 2/1: 23–35.

Badia, L. F. 1980. *The Qumran Baptism and John the Baptist's Baptism.* Lanham, MD.

Bammel, E. 1971–72. John the Baptist in Early Christian Tradition. *NTS* 18: 95–128.

Betz, O. 1985. Die Bedeutung der Qumran-schriften für die Evangelien des Neuen Testaments. *BK* 40: 54–64.

Böcher, O. 1979. Lukas und Johannes der Täufer. *Studien zum Neuen Testament und seiner Umwelt* 4: 27–44.

Boring, M. E. 1985. Criteria of Authenticity: The Lucan Beatitudes as a Test Case. *Forum* 1: 3–38.

Brown, R. E. 1977. *The Birth of the Messiah.* Garden City, NY.

Brownlee, W. H. 1957. John the Baptist in the Light of Ancient Scrolls. Pp. 33–53 in *The Scrolls and the New Testament,* ed. K. Stendahl. New York.

Carney, T. F. 1975. *The Shape of the Past: Models and Antiquity.* Lawrence, KS.

Cross, F. M. 1958. *The Ancient Library of Qumran and Modern Biblical Studies.* Garden City, NY.

———. 1973. *Canaanite Myth and Hebrew Epic.* Cambridge, MA.

Davies, S. L. 1983. John the Baptist and Essene Kashruth. *NTS* 29: 569–71.

Davies, W. D. 1974. *The Gospel and the Land.* Berkeley.

Dodd, C. H. 1963. *Historical Tradition in the Fourth Gospel.* Cambridge.

Farmer, W. R. 1958. Judas, Simon, and Athronges. *NTS* 4: 147–55.

Fleddermann, H. 1984. John and the Coming One (Matt 3:11–12/Luke 3:16–17). *SBLSP* pp. 377–84.

Ford, J. M. 1976. Zealotism and the Lukan Infancy Narratives. *NovT* 18: 280–92.

Gaster, T. H. 1964. *The Dead Sea Scriptures.* Rev. ed. Garden City, NY.

Gibson, J. 1981. Hai Telonai kai hai Pornai. *JTS* 32: 429–33.

Hanson, P. D. 1975. *The Dawn of Apocalyptic.* Philadelphia.

Herrenbrück, F. 1981. Wer waren die "Zöllner"? *ZNW* 72: 178–94.

Hobsbawn, E. J. 1971. *Primitive Rebels: Studies in Archaic Forms of Social Movement in the 19th and 20th Centuries.* Manchester.

———. 1973. "Peasants and Politics." *Journal of Peasant Studies* 1: 3–22.

Hollenbach, P. 1974. The Meaning of Desert Symbolism for Civilization in Ancient Israel. *Iowa State Journal of Research* 49: 169–79.

———. 1979. Social Aspects of John the Baptizer's Preaching Mission in the Context of Palestinian Judaism. *ANRW* 2/19/2: 850–75.

———. 1982. The Conversion of Jesus: From Jesus the Baptizer to Jesus the Healer. *ANRW* 2/25/1: 196–219.

———. 1983. Recent Historical Jesus Studies and the Social Sciences. *SBLSP* pp. 61–78.

Horsley, R. A. 1984. Popular Messianic Movements around the Time of Jesus. *CBQ* 46: 471–95.

———. 1985. "Like One of the Prophets of Old": "Two Types of Popular Prophets at the Time of Jesus. *CBQ* 47: 435–63.

Horsley, R., and Hanson, J. 1985. *Bandits, Prophets, and Messiahs.* New York.

Jonge, M. de. 1966. The Use of the Word 'Anointed' in the Time of Jesus. *NovT* 8: 132–48.

Kautsky, J. H. 1982. *The Politics of Aristocratic Empires.* Chapel Hill, NC.

Kraeling, C. H. 1951. *John the Baptist.* New York.

Kysar, R. 1975. *The Fourth Evangelist and His Gospel.* Minneapolis.

Lindeskog, G. 1983. Johannes der Täufer: Einige Randbemerkungen zum heutigen Stand der Forschung. *ASTI* 12: 55–83.

Malina, B. 1981. *The New Testament World: Insights from Cultural Anthropology.* Atlanta.
———. 1983. The Social Sciences and Biblical Interpretation. Pp. 11–25 in *The Bible and Liberation,* ed. N. K. Gottwald. Maryknoll, NY. Repr. *Int* 36 (1982): 229–42.
———. 1986a. *Christian Origins and Cultural Anthropology.* Atlanta.
———. 1986b. "Religion" in the World of Paul. *BTB* 16: 92–101.
Manson, T. W. 1949. *The Sayings of Jesus.* London.
Mazar, B. 1980. Excavations Near Temple Mount Reveal Splendors of Herodian Jerusalem. *BARev* 6: 44–59.
Meier, J. P. 1980. John the Baptist in Matthew's Gospel. *JBL* 99: 383–405.
Merklein, H. 1981. Die Umkehrpredigt bei Johannes dem Täufer und Jesus von Nazaret. *BZ* 25: 29–46.
Nepper-Christensen, P. 1985. Die Taufe im Matthäusevangelium in Lichte der Traditionen über Johannes der Täufer. *NTS* 31: 189–207.
Nodet, E. 1985. Jésus et Jean-Baptiste selon Josèphe. *RB* 92: 321–48; 497–524.
Oakman, D. 1986. *Jesus and the Economic Questions of His Day.* Lewiston, NY.
Parker, P. 1981. Jesus, John the Baptist, and the Herods. *PRS* 8: 4–11.
Reumann, J. 1972. The Quest for the Historical Baptist. Pp. 181–99 in *Understanding The Sacred Text,* ed. J. Reumann. Valley Forge, PA.
Rhoads, D. M. 1976. *Israel in Revolution, 6–74 C.E.* Philadelphia.
Schneidau, H. 1976. *Sacred Discontent.* Baton Rouge, LA.
Scobie, C. H. H. 1964. *John the Baptist.* Philadelphia.
Smith, D. 1982. Jewish Proselyte Baptism and the Baptism of John. *ResQ* 25: 13–32.
Stern, M. 1974. The Province of Judaea. Vol. 1, pp. 308–76 in *The Jewish People in the First Century,* ed. S. Safrai and M. Stern. CRINT. Assen and Philadelphia.
———. 1976. Aspects of Jewish Society: The Priesthood and other Classes. Vol. 2, pp. 561–630 in *The Jewish People in the First Century,* ed. S. Safrai and M. Stern. CRINT. Assen and Philadelphia.
Wink, W. 1968. *John the Baptist in the Gospel Tradition.* SNTSMS 7. Cambridge.

PAUL W. HOLLENBACH

JOHN THE DIVINE, DISCOURSE OF.

See VIRGIN, ASSUMPTION OF THE.

JOHN, ACTS OF (BY PROCHORUS).

A 5th-century Greek romance that primarily describes the miraculous activities of John on Patmos. It must be distinguished from the earlier *Acts of John* ascribed to Leucius, to whom five 2d and 3d century Apocryphal Acts are attributed: the Acts of John, Peter, Paul, Andrew, and Thomas. These early acts provided impetus and served as models for a number of later writings that are sometimes called "secondary Acts" (See *IDB* 1: 167; *NTApocr* 571–78). The *Acts of John by Prochorus* belongs to this later collection of Acts. The author used the earlier *Acts of John,* but he modified the material rather extensively (*NTApocr* 575). Prochorus, the legendary author, appears in Acts 6:5.

In addition to the Greek text, manuscripts exist in Latin, Coptic, Ethiopic, Arabic, Armenian, and Old Slavonic (*IDB* 1: 932; Zahn 1880: iii). A complete Greek text may be found in Zahn, and a summary of the work is provided by Lipsius. No English translation is available at this time.

The *Acts of John by Prochorus* begins with the disciples meeting in Gethsemane after the ascension. Peter informs them of their mission to travel, teach, and baptize. John is selected to go to Asia, and Prochorus is to accompany him. Like the other Apocryphal Acts, this work is structured around a series of journeys. It contains the typical earthquakes, stays in prison, storms at sea, and a shipwreck. The journeys provide the occasions for John to perform many miracles, such as casting out demons, healing the sick, bringing the dead back to life, and changing sea water into drinking water. Sometimes those who learn of John's activities are offended and attempt to kill him or exile him. On one occasion John is killed by an angry mob; but he returns to life. However, these miraculous activities most often result in the conversion and baptism of those who witness them.

Bibliography

Lipsius, R. E. 1883. *Die Apokryphen Apostelgeschichten und Apostellegenden.* Vol. 1. Braunschweig.
Zahn, T. 1880. *Acta Joannis.* Erlangen.

DANA ANDREW THOMASON

JOHN, APOCRYPHON OF

(NHC II,*1;* III,*1;* IV,*1;* and BG 8502,2). This is the clearest and therefore the most important text representing mythological Gnosticism. The tractate was originally written in Gk and survives in three independent translations into Coptic. BG 8502,2 and NHC III,*1* represent a short recension of the work, while II,*1* and IV,*1* are copies of the same Coptic translation of a long recension.

Most the scholarly discussion of *Ap. John* has been based on BG 8502,2 which was published earlier (Till 1955) than the copies in the Nag Hammadi codices (Krause 1962) and is also better preserved. It occupies pp. 19,6 to 77,7 in the Papyrus Berolinensis 8502 with only pp. 21–22 having suffered serious loss. The other representative of the short recension NHC III,*1*, originally comprised pp. 1 to 40,11 but of these pp. 19–20 are missing, only a small fragment survives of pp. 1–2 and 3–4, and pp. 5–8 and 21–40 show serious lacunae in the text. Of the long recension NHC II,*1* is found on pp. 1,1 to 32,9 and IV,*2* occupied pp. 1,1–49,28. II,*1* is relatively well preserved with serious loss of text limited to pp. 1–4. IV,*1* is in an extremely fragmentary state. Its value lies in supplementing II,*1* where it suffered lacunae or scribal error. Thanks to the presence of parallel versions the Coptic text of both the short and long recension can be determined with a high degree of accuracy except for a few words and phrases.

All four copies of *Ap. John* are written in Sahidic with IV,*1* conforming more closely to the standardized spelling of this Upper Egyptian dialect. In spite of the presence of three independent translations of the Gk, it is often difficult if not impossible to determine from the original reading where they differ. It appears that all three translators had serious difficulties understanding and/or rendering the complexities of the Gk text. Thus a dependable critical edition that reflects the original Gk seems out of reach.

The title *Apocryphon of John* is found as a subscript to all four copies. It reflects the Christian framework of the revelation found at the beginning and end of the tractate (II *1,5–2,26* and *31,25–32,5*) in which John, the son of Zebedee, receives a revelation from the resurrected Christ in response to questions about the Savior, his Father and "that aeon to which we shall go." Afterwards the savior instructs John to write the mysteries down and give them secretly to his fellow spirits.

The revelation itself is only marginally Christian and does not directly deal with John's questions. Rather it presents a description of the ineffable Spirit, the divine realm of light, the origin of the evil Creator Yaldabaoth, the creation of the spiritual world rulers and of man, and the rescue of the immovable race from the imprisonment in the body and material world. Christ and Sophia are part of the light world. The Fall occurred when Sophia desired to bring forth a being without the consent of the great Spirit and her consort. She produced Yaldabaoth who possesses some of her light power. He created angels to rule over the world and together they fashioned man in the image of the perfect Father. Yaldabaoth is tricked to breathe the light power of his mother into Adam. The evil powers created woman and sexual desire to spread the light particles, and to make escape more difficult. The savior was sent down to rescue those who possess the light sparks by reminding them of their heavenly origin.

It is clear that the cosmological section of *Ap. John* was already known to the Christian heresiologist Irenaeus in about 185 C.E. He assumed that the writing available to him represented the teachings of certain Gnostics (*Haer.* I.29). It appears that Irenaeus knew only a literary source or an early form of *Ap. John* without the Christian framework, the latter part of the revelation, and the present title. The long recension is most likely an expanded form of the short one. It adds, apart from minor details, a descriptive title at the beginning (II *1,1–4*), a lengthy enumeration of the powers who rule over the different parts of the human body (II *15,29–19,12*), and a remarkable section at the end of the revelation spoken in the first person by the perfect Pronoia relating three descents into the world (II *30,12–31,25*).

Ap. John shares a number of themes and mythologumena with such other representatives of mythological Gnosticism as *The Hypostasis of the Archons* (NHC II,*4*), *On the Origin of the World* (NHC II,*5*), *The Gospel of the Egyptians* (NHC III,*2* and IV,*2*), *The Sophia of Jesus Christ* (NHC III,*4* and BG 8502,3), *The Three Steles of Seth* (NHC VII,*5*) and *Trimorphic Protennoia* (NHC XIII,*1*). In view of the important differences between these writings, it is unlikely that they come from the same sectarian background. Literary borrowing would explain both the common traditions and the different uses to which these are put. There is no basis to assume with Irenaeus and other opponents of Gnosticism that such writings represented the teaching of distinct sects. The fact that the details of the myths proved to be very unstable and were readily corrupted in the translation and copying process indicates that they were not intended as object of belief and held little importance in themselves.

The importance of *Ap. John* lies in the insight it gives into esoteric, speculative thought and biblical interpretation found on the heterodox fringes of 2d and 3d century Christianity. Secondly, the short and long recension of *Ap. John* present a good example of the way such texts were sometimes augmented and changed in the process of transmission. Furthermore, the two copies of the long recension show how Coptic orthographic conventions evolved in the 4th century C.E.

The two recensions of *Ap. John* appear to be 3d century creations based, at least in part, on a 2d century antecedent. The text has left no hints about the identity of the original author, the redactors, or their provenance.

Bibliography

Krause, M., and Labib, P. 1962. *Die drei Versionen des Apokryphon des Johannes im koptischen Museum zu Alt-Kairo.* ADAIK, koptische Reihe 1. Wiesbaden.

Layton, B. 1987. *The Gnostic Scriptures.* Garden City, NY.

Schenke, H.-M. 1962. Das literarische Problem des Apokryphon Johannis. *ZRGG* 14: 57–63.

Schmidt, C. 1907. Irenaeus und seine Quelle in adv. haer. I,29. Pp. 315–36 in *Philotesia. Paul Kleinert zum LXX. Geburtstag dargebracht,* ed. A. von Harnack et al. Berlin.

Till, W. 1955. *Die gnostische Schriften des koptischen Papyrus Berolinensis 8502.* 2d ed. rev. by H.-M. Schenke. Berlin. 1972.

Wisse, F. 1971. The Nag Hammadi Library and the Heresiologists. *VC* 25: 205–23.

———. 1988. The Apocryphon of John (II,1; III,1; IV,1; and BG 8502,2). *NHL,* pp. 104–23.

FREDERIK WISSE

JOHN, EPISTLES OF. The three documents in the NT traditionally known as the Johannine epistles are not in each case epistles in the strict sense of the word, nor are they necessarily the work of an individual named John. 1 John (1 Jn) does not name its author, and 2 John (2 Jn) and 3 John (3 Jn) are the work of one identified in the letters as "the Elder." While 2 and 3 Jn clearly are epistles in the ancient sense of that classification, the literary form of 1 Jn is quite different and problematic. Their place in the Christian canon results from several factors, not least of all is their traditional association with the fourth evangelist. But they won their canonical status also by their relevance to the ongoing struggles of the Church to maintain its identity and order.

There are apparent allusions to these documents in the writings of church leaders by the middle of the 2d century (*Ep. Barn.* 5:9–11). Some claim that these allusions are closer to actual citations (Polyc. *ep.* 7), although such claims are debated. The first unquestionable citations appear in Irenaeus toward the end of the 2d century, demonstrating that the author knew 1 and 2 Jn (*haer.* 1.16.3; 3.16.5). The Muratorian fragment, which lists the documents generally accepted as authoritative, seems to refer to two epistles and attributes them to John, the fourth evangelist. Unfortunately, scholars are still divided as to whether the fragment should be dated at the end of the 2d or 4th centuries. Other citations toward the end of the 2d century and fragments of Clement's commentary on the NT books (*Adumbrationes*) affirm the recognition of 1 and 2 John.

3 Jn is attested by the middle of the 3d century (Euseb. *Hist. Eccl.* 6.25.10), but along with 2 Jn appears to be among the disputed books by the time of Eusebius. The

more ready acceptance of 1 Jn seems to have been based on its association with the thought and language of the Fourth Gospel. That the author of 2 and 3 Jn is "the Elder" cast doubt on their authenticity as apostolic writings. Origen acknowledges the doubt of the Johannine authenticity of 2 and 3 Jn (*Jo.* 5.3). Jerome in the 5th century still questioned a common authorship of the three writings.

However, all three were generally accepted and associated with the fourth evangelist by the late 4th century in the western church. The eastern church was slower in recognizing the documents. 1 John is found in the *Syrian Peshitta* (5th century) and 2 and 3 John only later in the *Philoxenian Version* (ca. 500).

It is sometimes proposed that 1 Jn was valued by the early Church because it represented an acceptable treatment of the thought of the Fourth Gospel over against the gnostic interpretation of the Gospel of John. It contributed, therefore, to the effort to the Church to seize the Fourth Gospel as an "orthodox" writing. 2 John likewise treats the reaction of the Church to a schismatic movement similar to the one found in 1 John (supposed to be gnostic) and hence won its way into the accepted writings of the Church. Its common authorship with 2 John ("the Elder"), plus the fact that it strove to secure order for the Church, succeeded in finally bringing about the acceptance of 3 John.

Many of the questions which emerged in the early evaluation of these three writings continue to be central issues in the critical study of them. Who was their author? What is their relationship with the Fourth Gospel? What is the nature of their response to the separatist of which they speak? This article will attempt to suggest the contours of the contemporary discussion of 1, 2, 3 John and to pose a viable approach to them. Our discussion will move through the following topics:

A. Textual Considerations

The texts of 1, 2, and 3 Jn are well preserved. They are not strongly attested in the Greek mss although eighty-one such witnesses are preserved. The Latin witnesses contain a number of readings not attested in the Greek. It has been argued both that this fact renders the Latin witnesses of little value and that it hints at the existence of Greek mss which have not survived.

The textual problems in the three writings are fewer in number than is the case in many other NT books. Still, there are a few which merit attention.

1 Jn 1:4 contains the problem of whether "our" or "your joy" was intended. The textual evidence itself is almost equally divided. That the writing completes the writer's joy seems the more difficult reading which copyists might have attempted to resolve. The "your" may also reflect the influence of John 15:11 on copyists.

1 Jn 2:20 reads "you all *(pantes)* know" and "you know all things *(panta)*" in various manuscripts. The textual evidence itself is indecisive and so the issue must be determined on the basis of the sense of the context. Does the author intend to affirm the knowledge the readers have or to declare that as a result of their anointing they need no further knowledge? The former seems the more likely, and the latter an effort of copyists to supply an object for the verb "know."

1 Jn 3:14 is represented without "the brethren" as well as with it and with "our brethren". The importance of this variation has to do with the author's concept of the community's love. Many prefer the shorter reading and argue that there was a tendency for copyists to add direct objects to verbs.

1 Jn 5:6 is found in two different forms. In some "spirit" is substituted for "blood" after "came by water and". In others "spirit" is added either before or after "water". The textual decision is important in this problematic verse for what it tells us about the author's central affirmation of the historical Jesus. Most, however, agree that the efforts to introduce the spirit here are efforts to imitate John 3:5.

The famous "Johannine Comma" after 1 Jn 5:7 is found in the Latin textual tradition and a very few Greek witnesses. The addition reads, "in heaven: Father, Word, and Holy Spirit; and these three are one; and there are three who testify on earth": (continues with v 8). There is near unanimity that this is an addition which arose from the trinitarian controversies of the later church during the 4th century.

2 Jn 8 presents the reader with a series of personal pronouns, "your . . . you . . . you" in the RSV (*apolesēte . . . eirgasametha . . . apolabēte*). Textual witnesses suggest two alternative readings: "your . . . we . . . you" and "we . . . we . . . we." The reading, "your . . . we . . . you," appeals to many critics in spite of the fact that it is the most weakly attested of the alternatives. This preference is due to two reasons: it represents the most difficult of the three and it is likely to have invited scribal correction for the sake of smoothness.

3 Jn 9 implies a previous letter of some kind written by the author to Gaius ("I have written something" *egraspa ti*). Textual witnesses in some cases add *an* after the verb, which introduces a subjunctive mood ("I would have written"), and others lack "something" *(ti)*. Most accept the

NovTG[26] and UBSGNT readings (RSV translation) as the best and argue that a tendency to avoid an implicit depreciation of an apostolic letter, as well as common error, caused the variant readings.

B. Literary Genre

While the three documents have been labeled "epistles" the question of the literary genre is problematic in the case of 1 John. There is little doubt that 2 and 3 John are representative of the epistolary form of the Greco-Roman world. They have formal affinities with certain of the letters of the NT (Philemon, Titus) and extant secular Hellenistic correspondence.

The case is not as clear with 1 Jn. On the one hand, there are the recurring allusions to the writing of the document, "I am (we are) writing" or "I write" (1:4; 2:1, 7, 8, 12, 13, 14, 21, 26; 5:13). But the document lacks the usual epistolary features as a comparison with 2 and 3 John shows. There is no addressee or author named (2 Jn 1 and 3 Jn 1), greeting or prayer (2 Jn 3, 3 Jn 2), thanksgiving (2 Jn 4, 3 Jn 3–4), closing and greetings to others (2 Jn 12–13 and 3 Jn 13–15). Its content lacks what has been called the "conversational" quality of an epistle (1 Corinthians). The problem is further aggravated by the somewhat disconnected nature of the structure of the writing (cf. D.1 below).

Efforts to isolate the precise literary genre of 1 John have produced a variety of suggestions. Among the most prominent of the proposals is that 1 Jn should be read as a "general epistle" intended to be passed among a number of groups much as Galatians might have been intended for a number of Christian communities in the region of Galatia. Others find it helpful to think of it as a "tractate" or an "instructional booklet" produced for general reading by Christians, even if an immediate group was in the author's mind. A comparison with a document such as 1 Timothy leads some to argue that a category like "pastoral epistle" is the best way to understand the author's work. That 1 John is a homily has been proposed. It has been called a "manifesto" in that it is intended to make public a particular point of view.

A number of features of 1 John help to shape the literary form in which it needs to be read. First, it is obviously a written communication intended for those affected by a rather specific set of circumstances (cf. E.1 below). Second, it is comprised of a series of rather loosely related subsections which have a homiletical quality about them. The repetitious style of the book (cf. C.1 below) betrays the origin of much of its content in oral communication. Third, the document has a "pastoral flavor" about it. That is to say, the efforts of the author demonstrate a deep concern for the readers and an attempt to address their needs, emotional as well as moral and creedal. Fourth, the author assumes a posture of authority with regard to the readers which influences the reception of the writing.

These features dictate certain conclusions regarding 1 John. One cannot take it to be a general letter of some sort given the specificity of the situation addressed therein. The author certainly has a particular community of readers in mind. But it cannot be assumed that the document does not have its roots in homilies simply because it is presently in written form. The work is profitably read with attention to the pastoral stance of its author and the function the work was designed to play in the lives of the first readers. The author was known to the first readers and was accepted as one who spoke from the vantage point of some authority or privilege.

It may, therefore, be useful to imagine that the present form of 1 John is the result of the author's effort to draw together bits and pieces of several homilies, link them loosely together, give the whole a general unity by means of thematic links among sections, and supply a written tone by the use of frequent references to "I write" or "I am writing". The effort would have been to bring together homilectical pieces directed to the critical situation facing the community as a pastoral attempt to reassure and strengthen the faith of some of the segments of a community schism. The disparate portions of the document were drawn from different homilies delivered at different times and perhaps different locations amid the emerging crisis. They were pulled together and published as an effort to make a more concerted response to that crisis and to make the response more widely available. This view is reflected in the proposed structure of the document (cf. D.1 below) and is made more feasible by an understanding of the situation facing the first readers (cf. E.1 below).

C. Style

1. 1 John. The style of 1 John has long been recognized as one of its unique and problematic features. It is commonly acknowledged that the progression of thought in 1 John is not a simple linear development. The classical view is that the document moves in what has been called a "spiral" development. That is to say, the author tends to repeat certain themes and to advance similar themes in different parts of the writing. Characteristic of the spiral is that it moves forward but only by returning to one of its original points in the process of that advance. The readers feel as if they are being brought back to a point made earlier while the recurrence of the theme provides a slightly different perspective or association. This feature has been only somewhat differently characterized by speaking of "cycles" of argument or of "recapitulation". A simple example of this spiral logic is found in the antichrist theme in 2:18–23 and 4:2–3. An appreciation of the author's style allows the reader to see that the return to this theme is to further its explication by making more specific the nature of the doctrinal position of the opponents under attack. While the recognition of such a spiral development is helpful, it does not entirely account for the repetitious quality of the writing.

That repetition has both a thematic and a linguistic dimension. Themes are repeated as the example given above and the recurrence of the theme of the "world" (2:15; 3:13; 4:5; 5:4) illustrate. But the repetitious quality of the author's style is reflected in stereotypical expressions as well as in major themes. Examples abound: "born of God" (2:29; 3:9; 4:7; 5:4, 18), "little children" (2:1, 12, 28; 3:7, 18; 4:4; 5:21), "beloved" (2:7; 3:2, 21; 4:1, 7, 11), "abides" (*menein,* e.g., 2:6; 3:6; 4:12), and "walk" (1:6, 7; 2:6, 11).

The literary function of both repetition and spiral-like progression seems clear. It has the effect of reinforcing certain themes and of fixing certain images in the readers' minds. Its purpose seems clearly to be didactic since it strengthens the author's communication of fundamental points. It also gives a somewhat disjointed document a stylistic unity.

Another feature of the style of 1 John is the use of various kinds of parallelism. Parallelism in this case refers to the pattern which states a proposition in one sentence or clause and then either repeats it in different words in the next (synonymous parallelism), or states the opposite of the proposition in the next sentence or clause (antithetical parallelism). It is not too much to say that this is the manner in which the author's logic works: to state one proposition and to draw from it still another which may be the opposite of the first or another affirmation drawn from the positive side of the first. In either case, in the second half of the parallelism the author draws out an implication of the first half. An instance of this kind of logic appears in 4:7. The equation of loving and knowing God is first stated. From that proposition arises its opposite: one who does not love does not know God.

Examples of synonymous parallelism appear in 2:11, 27; 3:6; and 5:2–3. Examples of the antithetical parallelism are found in 1:5b, 6–7, 8–9, 4–5; 2:9–10, 23; 3:7b–6a, 14; and 4:6.

A perusal of these examples makes a number of things clear about the author's style. This author uses parallelism loosely and freely, so that the pairs of propositions need not be strict parallels. Obviously the author is more fond of antithetical than synonymous parallelism for the examples of the former are more easily found than those of the latter. Further, there is a certain poetic quality about the author's argumentative style. In the parallelism there is a sound and resonance which, although short of strict poetry, nonetheless has a poetic quality, especially when read aloud. The repetitious quality of the use of parallelism implies that this material may have been written to be heard rather than read or that oral-homiletic sources are at its base.

Moreover, the use of antithetical parallelism suggests the dialectical style of this author. By this is meant that the author exploits the way a proposition generates an opposite proposition. The technique is to use one statement as the ground from which to derive a contradictory statement. The author then explores the relationship between the opposing assertions. This is typical not only of the argument throughout the writing but also of the structure of the work as a whole (cf. D.1 below).

Finally, and closely related to the dialectical style of the author, antithetical parallelism exemplifies a dualistic style. The author is prone to draw distinctions in sharp contrast, e.g., one is either a child of God or of the devil (3:10). But the contrasting style in which the text is written suggests a dualistic mode of thought as well. The author tends to contrast opposites, to use opposing terms, and to state the negative and positive side by side. The dualism of the thought of the document joins forces with the dualistic style to stress the limitation of choices for the reader—alignment with one or the other side without recourse to a moderate position.

Another stylistic feature has been called "variation". This refers to the way in which the author uses an expression a number of times and then varies it slightly in other uses. The use of familial language illustrates this point. The author refers to Christians as "children of God" (e.g., 5:2), "little children" (e.g., 5:21), "born of God" (e.g., 3:9), "fathers" (2:13–14), and "brothers" (e.g., 3:13). Another example is the language the author uses for the relationship a Christian has with God. It is spoken of as "knowing" God (2:3), "seeing" God (3:6), "abiding" in God (4:13), "have fellowship" with God (1:6), being "in the light" (2:9), and being "of God" (3:10). With this technique of variation the author states the matter in such a range of ways that the reader cannot help but understand one or the other of them. Furthermore, the author simply avoids boredom through variation.

Another stylistic feature is the use of catch-words, or the association of thoughts through single words or phrases. The outline of the structure given below (D.1) suggests that the major segments of the document find their relationship through the association of words or phrases. But often, too, the argument within any given segment proceeds on the basis of word association. The course of the argument within 3:4–18 exemplifies this practice. The author uses the word "deceive" in v 7 which seems to spark the idea of the "devil" in v 8. To "love his brother" in v 10 calls to mind the negation of brotherly love, namely Cain (v 12). "Murder" (v 15) brings to mind the free giving of life in the crucifixion (v 16), which in turns initiates the thought on the free surrender of worldly goods in v 17.

This is not to say that the author's thought wanders aimlessly in a kind of stream of consciousness, although that may sometimes appear to be the case. More accurately, the way in which the author makes a point is often through the association of words and phrases. If some would characterize the structure of the thought of 1 Jn in terms of a spiraling of thought, others could just as successfully argue that it is through the associative relationship of words and expressions.

The final stylistic feature of 1 Jn to be noted may be appropriately labeled "pastoral". What is meant by this expression is that the author seems to possess a concern for the total condition of the readers and to address them in a way that nurtures their whole life of faith. It is instructive, for instance, the way in which this author combines and alternates between exhortation and comfort or assurance. Seldom do you find exhortation in 1 Jn far from some assuring word of comfort. Two examples must suffice. Note the relationship of 4:1–3 and 4:4–6. Contrast 2:7–11 and 2:15–17 with 2:12–14.

The author is skillful enough as a pastor (or simply as a teacher) to know that the readers must be affirmed in their present condition and feel secure there if they are to be able to respond to exhortations to do more. This is a mark of one sensitive to the human condition and effective in motivating the reader.

All in all, while the style of 1 Jn is problematic in many ways, it shows signs of considerable skill and effectiveness.

2. 2 and 3 John. The rhetorical style of the two shorter letters may be characterized as epistolary exhortation. But the style is far more subtle than the simple announcement of injunctions. Both letters reflect a careful design to ingratiate the author with the reader before stating the exhortation. The first four verses of each of the letters serve to establish a cordial relationship with the reader in the context of which the exhortations are announced. The hope of the author to see the reader personally in each case (2 Jn 12 and 3 Jn 14) has the effect both of reminding the reader of that personal relationship with which the letters began and subtly to suggest that the reader will be held accountable to the author.

The logic of these letters is much more straightforward and clear than that of 1 Jn. In 2 Jn the author establishes the general principle of communal love (5–6), then describes the dangers of the "deceivers" (7–9), and finally exhorts an exception to the principle of communal love (10–11)—it is not to be applied to the deceivers. In 3 John the pattern is even clearer. The general principle of hospitality is announced (5–8). It is then applied to Diotrephes to show him in violation of it (9–10). Then appeal to an even more general principle is made—imitating good (11–12). The pattern is that of the positive, the negative, and again the positive. In both cases the logic is simple and appealing.

Both arguments, however, contain still further subtle tones. In 2 Jn, for instance, a careful use of warning is found in v 8—not overstated but clearly articulated. In 3 Jn the use of example is effective. The negative example of Diotrephes, who refuses hospitality (9–10), is contrasted with Demetrius (11–12), whose exemplary Christian life need only be mentioned, not detailed.

Short as they are, these two letters show signs of having been thoughtfully conceived and executed. They are examples of skillful persuasion.

D. Structure and Contents

1. 1 John. To discern a clear and logical structure to the contents of 1 Jn is very difficult. This is due in no small way to the fragmentary nature of the document the author has produced and the author's unusual logic (cf. C.1 above). It is further due to the nature of the document, its literary form, and its compositional history.

A variety of structures have been proposed. They range all the way from very simple to vastly complex. Simple structures have been proposed: A prologue with three "cycles" of argument; three major parts, introduced by an "exordium" or prologue and concluded with a postscript. More complex structures include these proposals: Two major sections in parallel structure (e.g., within the first part 2:12–17 parallels 1:8–2:2); fourteen units linked together; five divisions with a total of 196 cola.

Essential to the discernment of the structure of 1 Jn is the detection of a central theme or themes. This involves the decision as to what message is central to the author's intent and how subordinate themes are used to further the main argument. Again, there is a variety of views. Some proposals include (1) the description of the Christian life, (2) the essence of Christianity and the community of faith, (3) criteria for the new covenant communion with God, (4) exploration of fundamental affirmations about God, and (5) applications of the certain Christian principles to the crisis brought about by the schism in the community.

It has been proposed, too, that the structure is best understood in relationship to the structure of the Fourth Gospel. Attempts are made to see the major sections of 1 Jn as elucidations of the major sections of the gospel of John. Each of the writings has a prologue, two main parts and an epilogue. 1 Jn 1:1–4 parallels John 1:1–18. 1 Jn 1:5–3:10 is a kind of commentary on John 1:19–12:50, and 1 Jn 3:11–5:12 a commentary on John 13:1–20:29. 1 Jn 5:13–21 parallels John 21:1–25.

A further effort to understand the structure (or lack of it) in 1 Jn has turned to theories of sources and rearrangement. It has been proposed that the apparent lack of clear order is due to the none too careful use of a written source or sources by the author. Furthermore, might it be that the original order of the document was disrupted by some disarrangement and that the writing must be reordered if one is to discover the author's own structure?

In some of these cases the ingenuity of the critic seems to exceed that of the author of the document. It may be better to recognize and take more seriously the fragmentary nature of the writing, but even then one is not clear where one fragment concludes and another begins. Clearly the author of 1 John worked out of a logic which is quite different from that of the modern critic.

Still, the following proposed structure is a basis upon which to try to discern the major movements of thought in 1 John. It is proposed that nine discrete segments are detectable. These are perhaps fragments of homilies originating in the Johannine community. Each of the segments is dialectical in its internal structure, that is, each poses two topics and explores the relationship between the two. The outline given below further suggests the possibility that each of the major units has a triadic structure, i.e., three subdivisions. The five major units are linked together by means of one of the author's favorite stylistic techniques, the use of word or phrase association (cf. C.1 above). These individual units are: (1) Introduction: Christian Life and Fellowship (1:1–4); (2) Light and Darkness (1:5–2:11); (3) Believers and the World (2:12–17); (4) Truth and Lie (2:18–29); (5) the Children of God and the Children of the Devil; (6) the Spirit of Truth and the Spirit of Error; (7) God's Love and the Believer's Love; (8) the Son and Witnesses to the Son; and (9) Conclusion: Knowing and Doing.

The interrelatedness of these disparate units is found in links between a section and the preceding one made through words or phrases. This linking technique is part of the author's way of moving the argument through word and phrase association (cf. C.1 above). The following connections between the major sections and the words or phrases which bind the connection may be no accident: 1:1–4 to 1:5–2:11 by "proclaim," (1:3 and 5); 1:5–2:11 to 2:12–17 by "walks in darkness" (2:11) and "sin" (2:12); 2:12–17 to 2:18–29 by "world passes away" (2:17) and "last hour" (2:18); 2:18–29 to 3:1–24 by "born of God" (2:29) and "children of God" (3:1); 3:1–24 to 4:1–6 by "the Spirit" (3:24) and "every spirit" (4:1); 4:1–6 to 4:7–5:5 by "we know the spirit of truth" (4:6) and "knows God" (4:7); 4:7–5:5 to 5:6–12 by "Jesus . . . the Son of God" (5:5) and "Jesus Christ" (5:6); and 5:6–12 to 5:13–21 by "life" and "Son of God" (5:12) and "eternal life" and "Son of God" (5:13).

Such a structure as proposed here, along with the means of tying the units together through word or phrase association, emphasizes the role of homiletical pieces in the composition of 1 John and the style of the author.

2. 2 and 3 John. The content and structure of the two short epistles is far less difficult to describe than is the case with 1 John. 2 and 3 John clearly follow an epistolary form at the heart of which are a series of exhortations. Scholars have seen the relationship among the exhortations in different ways, but there is general agreement that some such exhortations form the core of the letters.

2 John is addressed to a community of Christians—"children of the Elect Lady". The letter is comprised of six parts: (1) salutation (vv 1–2); (2) apostolic greeting (v 3); (3) thanksgiving (v 4); (4) exhortations (vv 5–11); (5) closing (v 12); and greetings (v 13). 3 John is structured in a very similar manner, but it is addressed to an individual—Gaius. The letter has seven parts: (1) salutation (v 1); (2) prayer (v 2); (3) thanksgiving (v 3); (4) exhortations (vv 5–11); (5) commendation (v 12); (6) closing (vv 13–14); and (7) peace and greetings (v 15).

Several observations are appropriate. First, the letters are in epistolary form but reflect a peculiar Johannine flavor, e.g., the use of "truth" (2 Jn 1; 3 Jn 12). Second, they are very similar in structure with conclusions that are almost identical in content. Third, 3 Jn is far more specific, naming three different individuals, while 2 Jn is more general without mention of individuals.

E. Setting and Purpose

1. 1 John. There is universal agreement that this writing was produced to address a situation brought on by a schism within a Christian community. It has been argued, however, that some of the references to the dissenting group are purely rhetorical and should be taken as little more than an inner-family disagreement. Still, 2:19 unquestionably refers to a group which seems to have separated itself from the community addressed in the document. Exegetes have attempted to discern in this verse whether the separatists left voluntarily or were expelled. The sense of the verb *(exerchesthai)* is usually taken to mean that this group has by its own will separated itself from the body addressed by the author.

From 1 Jn we gain some impressions of the nature of the separatist group. A conservative reading of the document suggests that they are charged by the author with a number of things: (1) They do not practice love in their relationships with the readers (2:9–11; 4:20–21). (2) They do not acknowledge the humanity of the Christ (4:2–3; cf. 2:22; 5:5–6). (3) They have aligned themselves with those forces which are opposed to faith, i.e., "the world" (4:5–6; 2:15–15). (4) As a consequence of the above, the author views them as instruments of evil (3:8) and actors in the last days, i.e., antichrists (2:18–23). Such a drastic assessment of former colleagues in the faith suggests the seriousness with which the author understands the situation. (5) They were never authentic Christians, i.e., truly members of the confessing community addressed by the author (2:19).

From these explicit references other of the author's statements may be seen as allusions to the views of the separatists. (1) They do not adhere to the teachings of the author and/or the general community (4:6). (2) They falsely claim to know and love God (2:4; 4:20) and to be "in the light" (1:6; 2:9). (3) They are guilty of "mortal" sin (5:16). (4) They falsely regard themselves free of sin (1:6–10; 3:3–6). (5) They are without moral restrictions in their behavior (3:4–10).

Efforts abound to identify the separatists with a specific group known to us elsewhere in the NT or in early church history. Some have argued that they are Jews, but most seek their identity among Christian groups. It is clear that the author has a christological difference with the separatists. It has been advanced both that the dissenters held a view of Christ which stressed his humanness and that they emphasized his divinity to an excess unacceptable by the author. It is clear too that the author has a moral quarrel with the separatists. But as to whether they embraced a total amorality or simply a more liberal morality is not clear. The separatists have been grouped with the NT forms of proto-gnosticism attacked in Colossians (2:8) and 1 Timothy (6:20), the libertines inferred from 1 Corinthians 8–9, and followers of John the Baptizer. Likewise, there are those who see a direct line of descent between these separatists and the docetists and gnostics attack in early church writers, e.g., Irenaeus. It has also been proposed that the dissenting group was comprised of gentiles who had not experienced the expulsion of the Johannine Christians from the synagogue (see JOHN, GOSPEL OF) and who shared a different religious background from the formative group of Johannine Christians.

The nature of the evidence about the separatists seriously qualifies our ability to identify them with other groups. These dissenters are known only indirectly through the author's polemic against them, and wisdom leads us to be careful about defining a group too precisely from the words of an antagonist. A more cautious description admits only a sketch of the views of the separatist group. They probably held a view of Christ which was conservative in its attribution of human characteristics to the Messiah. They did not practice a strict morality which evoked the charge that they did not love others in the community as they should. That they were pure docetists and/or antinomianists pushes the evidence too far. But that they were predecessors of a later gnostic Christianity and even that their descendants found a comfortable church home among such a group is very likely.

From this evidence arises a scenario which may have produced the setting for the writing of 1 John. Within a community which stood in the tradition of that one responsible for the Fourth Gospel (cf. F.1 below) there arose a tension between two groups. It is likely that the single community to which we refer was comprised of a number of congregations associated with one another by a common origin and tradition. It may be that we should imagine a parent body with a number of smaller gatherings of Christians (perhaps "house churches"). One of the two groups held to a view of Christ and a morality which gradually alienated them from their brothers and sisters in the church until that group eventually withdrew from the community. On the basis of the evidence for the relationship between 1 John and the Gospel of John it may be surmised that the dispute centered in the interpretation of the tradition of the community, known to us in the Fourth Gospel. Specifically, the dispute centered in the understanding of the christology and moral teachings of the Gospel of John.

The schism produced anxiety and anger within the remaining community. On the one hand, there were those who viewed the separatists as apostates from the true faith. Most likely the leaders of the community, including the author of 1 John, took this posture toward the separatists. On the other hand, there were those who were confused and troubled by the schism, unsure of the correct stand on the central issues. We may surmise that a majority of the community found themselves in this situation. To address the latter group, the author of the document again and again directed portions of homilies toward the situation, seeking to reassure the "faithful" that the dissenters were guilty. Finally, to share that view with a wider segment of the community the author published a collection of fragments of those homilies for circulation.

The general purpose of 1 John, then, was to preserve a Christian community from dissolution, to protect the identity and composition of that community, and to arrest a movement which threatened the very heart of what the author understood to be a genuine faith and life.

The specific purposes of 1 John were twofold: First, it sought to show convincingly that the Christian commitment of the separatists was doubtful and that their views did violence to a proper understanding of the faith. Second, it sought to assure the remaining community that they stood within the fold of the truth faith and to reinforce their position in order to prevent further disintegration.

2. 2 John. This epistle seems to share a concern for the influence of another group of Christians whose views the Elder finds threatening. The exhortations contained in the letter address two issues which stand at the center of the view of the separatists in 1 John. First, the readers are exhorted to remain faithful to a morality which, it is charged in 1 John, the separatists have violated (5–6, compare 1 Jn 2:7–11). Further, the readers are urged to resist the views of those who advocate a christology which does not stress "the coming of Jesus Christ in the flesh" (7, compare 1 Jn 4:2). They are exhorted to protect "the doctrine of Christ" by denying hospitality to any who seem to compromise it (9). For good reason, therefore, most critics understand that 2 John was written amid a stage of the same crisis discernible in 1 John.

It would appear that 2 John was evoked to protect individual congregations from the threat posed by the separatists more fully described in 1 John. It was written because those separatists were being received by the congregations in the name of Christian hospitality and were hence able to exert the influence of their views. The purpose of 2 John is to suggest that the preservation of "true Christian doctrine" is a higher value than the extension of hospitality to all who claim Christian commitment.

3. 3 John. The situation is not so clear in the case of the last of the epistles. Here a certain Diotrephes is charged by the Elder with four offenses. First, he is asserting authority and importance for himself (9a). Second, he refuses to acknowledge the authority of the Elder and perpetuates gossip about the author (9). Third, he refuses hospitality to "the brethren" (10). Finally, he ejects from the church those who will not abide by his view (10). Gaius, the recipient of the letter, is subtly urged to side with the Elder against Diotrephes and to offer hospitality to other Christians (5–8). The letter has the obvious purpose to enlist the loyalty of Gaius for the author and to strengthen the Elder's influence in a congregation in which Diotrephes threatens it.

But the picture is clouded. Among the issues involved in determining the situation and purpose of 3 John are these questions: Are Gaius and Diotrephes leaders in one congregation or separate ones? Is Diotrephes himself a member of the separatist group? Is the situation of 3 John related in any way to the schism which seems to have occasioned 1 and 2 John? What is the authority of the Elder? Scholars differ in their answers to these questions.

Still, a viable picture arises. It is most likely that Gaius and Diotrephes are leaders in a single congregation, hence the Elder hopes to preserve his influence there by winning Gaius' support. That Diotrephes was a separatist seems unlikely. While the charge that he challenges the authority of the Elder fits the image of the view of the separatists, the charge that he denies hospitality makes little sense unless he is a member of the same community over which the Elder has some authority. Care must be taken not to read the situation of 1 and 2 John into 3 John, but the common authorship of 2 and 3 John ("the Elder") suggests the possibility that a similar situation is obtained for both. The likelihood of that possibility depends upon whether or not the evidence of 3 John can be reasonably fitted within the picture of the situation proposed above for 1 and 2 John.

What may have been the case is that Diotrephes is one who has tried to preserve his segment of the community (a satellite or house church) from the schism troubling other segments. He has done so by advocating that his congregation become independent of the influence of the parent body and simply refuse to receive representatives of either of the two positions in the schism. "The brethren" to whom Diotrephes refuses hospitality may well have been representatives of the Elder and of the parent body which was trying to hold firm against the action of the separatists. Hence, the congregation represented by Gaius and Diotrephes, in the Elder's view, stands a chance of drifting away from the position of the parent body. The letter is written to try to protect such further disintegration of the total community.

But in trying to prevent the alienation of this segment of the community the author clashes with the authority of one of the leaders of the congregation in question. The Elder challenges the authority of Diotrephes and hence raises the question of the structure of authority in the community. 3 John has often been compared with other early Christian literature (e.g., 1 Tim 3:1–16 and *Didachē*) as evidence for the emergence of church order. While it is true that some order of authority is implicit in the letter and that there is an effort on the part of the Elder to firm up that order, the epistle is too brief for us to surmise from it the exact structure of the Johannine church at the time of its writing.

Hence, it does appear that the crisis of the schism is the occasion for all three of the writings. But that such was the case poses further questions of the authorship of 1, 2, and 3 John, as well as the sequence of their composition.

F. Authorship, Date, Locale, and Sequence

The theories of authorship, date, locale, and sequence are premised on views of certain related issues. Only after dealing with those can one suggest possible solutions to these four puzzles.

1. The Johannine Epistles and the Gospel of John. The first of the cluster of issues involves the relationship between these writings and the Fourth Gospel. There is common acknowledgment of similarities between the Johannine gospel and 1, 2, and 3 John.

Between 1 John and the Gospel of John there are numerous common features and themes. Among the most important are these: Life (e.g., John 1:4)—1:2; 4:9; 5:11–12, 16. Eternal Life (e.g., John 3:16)—1:2; 2:25; 3:15; 5:11, 13, 20. Light and Darkness (e.g., John 8:32)—1:5; 2:8. Truth (e.g., John 8:32)—2:21; 3:18; 5:7. Father/Son (e.g., John 3:35)—2:22, 23; 4:14. Son, used as title for Christ (e.g., John 5:23)—1:7; 2:24; 3:23; 4:9, 10, 14; 5:9, 10, 11, 12, 20. Abide in (e.g., John 15:5)—2:24, 27, 28; 3:15, 24; 4:13, 15, 16. New Commandment (e.g., John 13:34)—2:7–8.

Between 2 John and the Gospel of John there are fewer common features or themes: Truth—1, 2, 3, 4. Abide in—2, 9 (twice). Father/Son—3, 9. New Commandment—5.

3 John and the Fourth Gospel share one common theme, namely, truth—1, 3 (twice), 4, 8, 12.

Still, there are important differences between the Gospel of John and each of the Johannine epistles which are equally important. Examples of the uniqueness of 1 Jn when compared with the Fourth Gospel include the following themes: imminent "last hour" (2:18), expiation (2:1; 4:10), anointing of believers (2:20, 27), lust (2:16–17), antichrists (2:18; 22; 4:3), lawlessness (3:4), false prophets (4:1), spirit of error (4:6), day of judgment (4:17), mortal and nonmortal sins (5:16–17), and ethical considerations (3:4; 4:20).

Concepts articulated in 2 John but notably absent from the Fourth Gospel include these: doctrine (9–10), the church as "lady" (1, 5), antichrist (7), and reward (8). In 3 John the following are found but missing in the Gospel of John: church (6, 9, 10), heathen (7), and authority (9).

The similarities and differences are enough to have evoked theories both that the fourth evangelist was the author of all the Johannine epistles and that that evangelist authored none of the other Johannine writings. The assessment of the evidence must be done with attention to the facts that we are dealing in 1, 2, and 3 Jn with different genre than gospel, that clearly a different situation obtains between the writing of the gospel and the epistles, and that the relative lengths of the gospel and epistles seriously affect their comparison. Each of the epistles must be evaluated individually.

The similarities between the Fourth Gospel and 1 John are the most impressive. But the differences are so significant as to weigh against the tradition that equates the fourth evangelist with the author of 1 John. For instance, the careful articulation of the present and future eschatologies of the Fourth Gospel is entirely lost in 1 Jn with its view of the imminent end (cf. G.5 below). It might be argued, however, that the evangelist wrote 1 Jn at a time when the author embraced a different eschatology. This means that 1 Jn might have been written before the Fourth Gospel at a time when the evangelist held strictly to a futuristic eschatology. But the situation implicit in 1 John argues decisively against a pre-gospel date. Could it then be that the evangelist wrote 1 John a decade or more after penning the gospel and at that time conceived of eschatology quite differently?

A simpler solution seems to be that the author of 1 John was a student of the Fourth Gospel and lived in a community which cherished that gospel as its primary tradition. The community had, however, undergone changes since the writing of the gospel, so that its views were no longer identical to those articulated by the fourth evangelist. In particular it may be that the differences between 1 John and the Gospel of John could be the result of the influence of other Christian traditions on the community. Particularly that seems to have been the case with regard to the soteriology of 1 John, which is markedly different from that of the gospel (cf. G.2 below). Hence, it is most likely that 1 John arose within a community descended from the community behind the Fourth Gospel but was written by one other than the fourth evangelist. This view accounts for both the similarities and the differences between the two writings.

That proposal is equally effective in dealing with 2 and 3 John. The evidence in each case is, of course, limited, since these two epistles are so very brief. But the similarities with the Gospel of John dictate nothing more than a Christian orientation influenced by the tradition which arose out of the Fourth Gospel. The presence of such concepts as "doctrine" in 2 John and the "church" in 3 John suggests significant developments beyond the conceptuality of the Gospel of John.

Hence, while sharing a tradition rooted in the Gospel of John, 1, 2, and 3 John do not evidence a common authorship with the gospel.

2. The Relationship among 1, 2, and 3 John. The next seminal question is whether one author is responsible for all three of the writings. That 2 and 3 John both claim to come from the hand of one identified as "the Elder" argues for their common authorship, as do marked similarities among these two epistles (2 Jn 12 and 3 Jn 13–14) and the fact that they are nearly of identical length. It is possible that one or the other was written by someone attempting to mimic an original, but the differences between the two (the absence from 3 John of any reference to the christological issue of 2 John) argue against such a view.

1 John shows impressive similarities with 2 and 3 John. The vocabulary is strikingly similar (86 percent of the words in 2 John and 70 percent of those in 3 John are found in 1 John). But the differences are notable. 1 John does not identify its author as "the Elder," betrays a different and far more poetic style, and demonstrates nothing of the more developed view of the church and its authority structure found either implicitly or explicitly in 2 and 3 John. But again the evidence is slim, given the reduced size of 2 and 3 John, and the literary genre of 1 John is distinctively different from that of its companions.

The question of the identity of the Elder responsible for 2 and 3 John must be addressed. While it is sometimes claimed that the Elder assumes some official status in those epistles which bear this title, such a view is questionable. It is to be noted that in neither 2 nor 3 Jn does the author threaten any sort of "official" action against the disobedient. To the contrary, the Elder seems intent upon eliciting some respect by virtue of persuasion and appeal to sound doctrine (2 Jn 9). The manner in which the Elder attempts to win the favor of the reader (cf. C.2 above) counts against the view that the author speaks from any position of official authority. Clearly the Elder is a revered leader of some sort, but that does not presuppose a position of official authority. Hence, the Elder speaks with authority not unlike that of the author of 1 John who appeals to his/her role in the preservation of the tradition of the community (1:1–4).

Nonetheless, given all of these considerations, it is the wiser choice to conclude that the evidence for common authorship is not convincing. But, on the other hand, the similarities are enough to argue for the three having originated in a single community. Furthermore, the situation implied by the three is sufficiently similar to suggest that, not only were they all written for segments of the same community, but that they represent efforts to address portions of that community in a relatively common period of time.

3. The Sequence of the Composition of 1, 2, and 3 John. If it is the case that these three writings come from at least two different hands (none of which is the fourth evangelist) out of a community which embraces the Johannine tradition shaped by the Fourth Gospel and address a common situation (if at different points in time), can one discern their chronological order with any greater exactness?

A variety of views have been proposed, ranging all the way from the theory that the canonical order reflects their chronological order to the exact opposite. The similarities between the content of 1 and 2 John tie them closely together. But the nature of 1 John makes it difficult to determine precisely what stage the schism had reached at the time the document was published. This is due in part to its fragmentary nature (cf. D.1 above) and its genre (cf. B above). Still, it is clear that 2:19 was written after the separatists had left the community addressed in 1 John. It has been proposed that 2 John was written while the separatists were still exerting influence within the community before their withdrawal. But that view supposes that the separatists did not continue to try to influence satellite congregations after terminating relationships with the parent body of the community.

It is impossible to demarcate exactly the order of 1 and 2 John, and far better to suppose that they were written at nearly the same time and at the same stage in the schism of the church. Perhaps 2 John was written by the Elder to alert the satellite congregations of the dangers of extending hospitality to the separatists at the very time the author of 1 John was publishing the collection of homiletical fragments as a way of bolstering the entire community (parent and satellite congregations) amid the crisis.

3 John represents another kind of a problem. On the one hand, the Elder's attack upon Diotrephes for not offering hospitality to some seems strange, if the congregation has just received a letter from the same author warning against indiscriminate hospitality. On the other hand, could Diotrephes be one of the dissenters still in the community before the schism mentioned in 1 John 2:19 has taken place? Some would, of course, cut 3 John free of the situation implied in 1 and 2 John and propose that it comes either significantly before the surfacing of any dissension in the community or long after the schism has been survived.

It has been proposed above (E.3) that Diotrephes was attempting to preserve his satellite church from the schism disrupting the entire community. If that indeed was the case, it is likely that 3 John was written after its two companions and reflects the ongoing problems brought about by the schism in the near past. That is, 3 John reflects the efforts of some in satellite congregations to try to deal with the situation brought about by the schism. Diotrephes was simply endeavoring to free his congregation of any involvement in the issue. The Elder, in this case, is trying to modify an earlier injunction against the extension of hospitality to the separatists by saying that the congregation should receive "the brethren" (5, 10), i.e., the representatives of the parent body of the community. The indications are that 3 John was written after 2 John to correct, among other things, an overzealous reaction to the first of the letters from the Elder.

Therefore, there is some chronological sense to the canonical order of these three documents, even if such a correspondence occurred as much by accident as by design.

4. Date and Locale. The dates of the three documents can be fixed only approximately. The dating of each depends, of course, on the conclusion one has reached with regard to its relationship with the Gospel of John and the other two writings. While some would contend that one or more of the epistles predates the gospel, most would locate them in time after the writing of the Fourth Gospel. If the theory advanced above is sound, a number of considerations enter into the process of determining the date to be assigned.

The first issue regards the dating of the Gospel of John itself. Many would date the Johannine epistles at least a decade later than the gospel, although that period of time is little more than an informed guess. How long a period of time might have elapsed between the writing of the gospel and the publication of the epistles? Several things seem to have occurred in the intervening period of time. First, the Johannine community has recovered from the trauma of the expulsion from the synagogue which occasioned the production of the gospel. See JOHN, GOSPEL OF. The issue is no longer the relationship of the community to the synagogue and external opponents, but now an internal matter. Second, it would appear that the Johannine community has come under the influence of other Christian perspectives and to some degree integrated those perspectives within their own view of Christian life and faith (and death of Jesus understood as expiation, 1 Jn 2:2). Third, the tendency of the community to understand faith in terms of proper doctrine (2 Jn 9) has developed beyond the hints of that view found in the Gospel of John. Fourth, some unofficial organizational structure has emerged in the Johannine church to replace the informal, spirit-led authority implied in the Gospel of

John, with the consequences that the terms, "church" (3 Jn 6, 9, 10) and "Elder" have become commonplace.

It is feasible that such changes might occur within the course of a decade in a body which is still in the process of finalizing its form and nature. Therefore, if one dates the Gospel of John 90–95, as do many, the Johannine epistles could be assigned dates of 100–5. If one is inclined to date the gospel a decade earlier, the Johannine epistles could well have been written by 90–95.

Little can be said with certainty about the locale of the Johannine community. Tradition has placed it in Ephesus, and many would still argue for that tradition. Recent developments in Johannine scholarship, however, have been inclined to locate that community in closer proximity to Palestine. Hence, a theory that the community was in Syria is feasible, if unprovable. Such a theory arises from speculation concerning the character of the synagogue which it is supposed was the original home of the Johannine Christians. Assuming that the locale of the Fourth Gospel is the same locale in which 1, 2, 3 John were written, the theory might also be a reasonable hypothesis for the Johannine epistles.

G. Theology

1. The View of Christ. The nucleus of the teachings of 1 and 2 John is the view of Christ. No other NT writing stresses the importance of the humanity of Jesus for Christian faith as do these two documents. It is doubtless that this insistence arose in response to the views of the separatists who seem to have qualified the humanity of Christ (cf. E.1 and 2 above). Hence the christology of these two writings is expressed in a polemic tone.

The author of 1 John stresses that Christ "has come in the flesh" (*en sarki,* 4:2) and the Elder echoes that the "deceivers" are those "who will not acknowledge the coming of Jesus Christ in the flesh" 2 Jn 7). The insistence that Jesus is the Christ in 1 John (e.g., 4:15; 5:1) seems to arise from a desire to equate the messianic agent of God with the human, Jesus. The meaning of 1 Jn 5:6 is often debated, but generally exegetes agree that it has to do with this central motif of the humanity of Christ. It is feasible that "water" represents either the human birth of the Christ or his baptism and that "blood" is a cipher for the reality of his death. The denial that Jesus came "not with the water only" may be a refutation of a view which attempted to limit the association of the Christ with the human Jesus to a period after his baptism but short of his death.

The theological contribution of 1 and 2 John is not only that they affirm the importance of the affirmation of the humanity of Jesus but, as well, the fact that they position this view so that it becomes the focal point of the whole of Christian faith. In 2 John this view of the human, historical appearance of the Messiah is elevated to the status of "the doctrine *(didachē)* of Christ". This is a way of saying that such a view of Christ is the "proper" understanding of Christ. With this perspective the epistle contributes toward the emergence of an "orthodoxy" within the Church, especially as it has to do with the correct understanding of Christ. The Elder identifies those who would qualify this proper doctrine as "the antichrist" and "deceivers" (*planos,* 7), a probable reference to the apocalyptic view that the last days would see the emergence of agents of evil who would try to seduce the true believers into falsity (e.g., Rev 13:14; cf. 5 below).

2 John simply summarizes what is affirmed in 1 John in this regard, for the author of 1 John claims that failure to believe in the humanity of Christ has dire consequences for the faith. The failure to identify Christ with Jesus is equated with the eschatological "lie" (cf. Rev 14:5), and one who holds this view is among the dreaded "antichrists" of the last time. Such a faulty view of Christ is a denial, not only of the messianic agent, but of God as well (2:22). The "spirit" which inspires persons to deny that Jesus came in fleshly form is "not of God" (4:3), and such persons are part of the realm of unbelief, i.e., "of the world" (4:5). The appearance of Christ in the human Jesus is the witness of God; consequently those who deny that appearance do not believe God but make God out to be a "liar" (*pseustēs,* 5:10), thus equating God with the Devil (John 8:44). By implication, one who embraces the view of the fleshliness of the Christ has the Son and hence "life," and one who does not is denied a relationship with Christ and its benefits, namely, salvation (5:12).

This emphasis upon the humanity of the appearance of Christ is surely rooted in the Johannine tradition. "In the flesh" of 1 Jn 4:2 and 2 Jn 7 is reminiscent of John 1:14. At the same time, it is a decision to stress that dimension of the Fourth Gospel over those indications in the Johannine view of Christ which minimize his human qualities (in John 19:30 Jesus does not die but "gave up his spirit"). 1 and 2 John reflect an interpretation of the Johannine tradition which allows it to be read in harmony with the emerging "orthodoxy" of the Church, as opposed to the separatists from the community who interpreted the same tradition along lines more compatible with what was to become the gnostic heresy.

2. The Saving Work of Christ. 1 John teaches a soteriology which goes beyond the tradition rooted in the Fourth Gospel. That gospel gives expression to an understanding of the death of Jesus which never uses metaphors of a sacrificial death drawn from Jewish cultic practices. See JOHN, GOSPEL OF. The soteriology of 1 John, on the other hand, betrays a quite different understanding of the saving work of Christ.

Christ appeared, it is affirmed in 3:8, in order to destroy the power of evil. The death of Jesus is spoken of as an "expiation" (*hilasmos,* 2:2; 4:10). The word is unique to this writing, but its root is present in words used in Rom 3:25 and Heb 2:17 to articulate the meaning of the cross. Its basic meaning is a making of appeasement and is used in the Septuagint of a sacrificial "covering over" in cultic practices. It expresses an effort to alleviate the cause of the alienation between the divine and humans.

Other images called forth to speak of the meaning of the death of Jesus include that of the "cleansing" of sin by his blood (1:7b, 9). The verb, *katharizō,* has the sense of a freeing of contamination and has roots in the concept of the sin offering in the Hebrew Scriptures (Lev 4:1–12). That Jesus himself was free of sin (3:3 and 5) also relates to the cultic images employed, since the atoning sacrifice offered to God for sin must itself be free of sin (Leviticus 4 and 1 Pet 1:19). The work of Christ is characterized as "forgiveness," which is used in synonymous parallelism with "cleansing" (cf. 1:9 and 2:12). A similar expression is found in 3:5 where it is declared that Jesus "appeared to take away *(airein)* sins". With regard to the overcoming of sin Jesus is called an "advocate" *(paraklētos)* in 2:1. It is a Johannine word (John 15:26) which means "one called to the side of another" for the purposes of defense and aid.

It is clear that the author of 1 John was free to use a number of different metaphors in the effort to express the significance of the death of Jesus. But it is also clear that metaphors drawn from the sacrificial cultic practices of Judaism figured prominently in those efforts.

That the saving work of Christ has universal effect is affirmed in 2:2 with the expression, "the sins of the whole world". The efficacy of the death of Jesus is suggested by the use of the word "all" *(pas)* in 1:7 and 9.

Associated with the appropriation of the benefits of the work of Christ in 1 John is the "anointing" (*chrisma,* 2:20 and 27). This unction is by "the Holy One" and yields confidence in the faith (2:20). It teaches the Christian what is necessary and "abides" with the believer (2:27). Commentators disagree as to what practice lies behind these references. Some argue that it is an allusion to baptism; others claim that it has to do with an initiatory anointing with oil. Whichever view one adopts, the anointing seems to have been a cultic practice in the Johannine church by means of which the new believer appropriated for her/himself the benefits of Christ's work.

The result is that one who embraces the benefits of Christ's death is freed of sin and its influence (3:5). But therein lies a problem in understanding the theology of 1 John.

3. The Understandings of Sin. The author of 1 John uses the noun, sin *(hamartia),* no less than seventeen times. Six of those uses are in the plural and eleven in the singular, which suggests that the author was not careful to distinguish between the state of sinfulness and its expression in specific acts. In addition, the verbal form is used nine times. Obviously sin is synonymous with a condition alienated from God and unbelief, aligned with the forces of evil (3:8), and given to behavior which violates the will of God. The author equates sin with "lawlessness" (*anomia,* 3:4). The separatists are labeled as victims of sin (3:9) who "walk in darkness" (1:6), an allusion to a lifestyle disengaged from the Creator.

But a serious contradiction arises within the treatment of sin in the first of the writings. The author claims, on the one hand, that the Christian is guilty of sin (1:8, 10). On the other hand, there is the absolute assertion that the Christian does not sin (3:6, 9). This contradiction is resolved by interpreters in a number of ways. One such effort is to argue that the author intended to contrast sin as a way of life, which the Christian has repudiated, and sin as an occasional lapse in behavior of which the Christian is guilty. Such a view is made more attractive when one understands 1 Jn as a series of homiletical fragments loosely linked together. It is feasible that one homily stressed the sense in which the Christian has been removed from a lifestyle characterized by alienation from God, while another emphasized the inevitable failure of Christians to live out what they have become in Christ.

Still another approach to this contradiction is to contrast two different views of sin. The claim that the Christian is free to sin builds upon the view of sin in the Gospel of John which understands it basically not as a matter of immoral life but rejection of the revelation of God in Christ (e.g., John 15:22; 16:8). Sin is the opposite of belief, in this case. That the Christian is guilty of sin presupposes a different view of sin, namely, that of immoral behavior. Such a view is also rooted in the Gospel of John (John 8:46).

Some have proposed that the separatists held to a pre-gnostic view of perfectionism, which claimed that the believers were those whose origin was "born of God"—the true Creator God—and hence they could not sin and were free of any moral law. (Hence they are characterized as "lawless," 3:4.) The author of 1 John, however, attacks such a view and advocates instead a "Johannine perfectionism," which holds that unbelief is the only sin in the ultimate sense. In the author's attack upon the opponents, the reality of Christian sin is stressed; in the advocacy of the community's position, the freedom from sin is affirmed.

Yet another important element in the view of sin in 1 John is encountered in 5:16–17. There the author makes a distinction between "mortal" and "nonmortal" sin (*hamartia pros thanaton* and *hamartia mē pros thanaton*). It is this distinction which has led the Church at times to try to classify specific immoral acts in these two ways, and which has caused exegetes to struggle with the distinction for centuries. Again it may be helpful to read 1 John in the light of the Johannine tradition. What the author chooses to call "mortal sin" is unbelief. Failure to believe costs one "life" in the Johannine sense of salvation. Unbelief leads inescapably to the opposite of life, "death". "Nonmortal sin" is simple human failure to live the will of God within the context of faith. The author's concern for the quality of the Christians' moral lives and the development of ethics beyond the confines of what is found in the Fourth Gospel leads to the distinction made in this passage.

4. Morality. The authors of these writings are all concerned with nurturing a proper Christian moral life. This is doubtless the case, in part at least, because of the threat posed by the separatists, whose moral perspective was liberal at best. 1 John in particular stresses the centrality of morality for the Christian, and the Elder builds a moral appeal into both of the epistles (2 John 5–6, 3 John 11).

In 1 Jn the morality of the Christian is characterized as "walking in the light" (1:7), "keeping his commandments" (2:3), and being "in the truth" (2:4). It is in righteous living that Christians express the fact that they are "born of God" (e.g., 3:9), "children of God" (e.g., 3:1), and "abide in" God or Christ (e.g., 2:6, 24). Loving others is the sign that Christians that have passed from death to life (3:14). Indeed, one who loves is "born of" and "knows" God (4:7). In 3 John the readers are exhorted to imitate good and assured that one who "does good" is "of God" (11).

But righteousness is understood as concrete behavior, not some internal state of the soul. Righteousness is doing the right or just thing (*ho poiōn tēn dikaiosynēn dikaios estin,* 3:7). "Doing good" is the comparable expression used in 2 John (11). The moral life involves separation from the "world," which is the symbol of unrighteousness (4:5), and overcoming the "lust" and "pride" of the world (2:16).

The moral life is rooted in love, and it is for its clear articulation of the centrality of love that 1 Jn has rightly become best known. Love has its origin in God, for "God is love" (4:16), and "love is of God" (4:7). The divine love is expressed in Christ (4:9), and hence God took the initiative in loving humans (4:10). But that expression of divine love is what evokes and even creates the possibility of love among humans (4:11, 19). God, who is unseen, abides among humans as love (4:12) so that abiding in love is abiding in God (4:16). Human love for God is appropriately expressed in loving others (4:20; 5:1).

The commandment of the Johannine Jesus to "love one another" (John 13:34) is repeated five times in the course of 1 John (3:11, 23; 4:7, 11, 12) and once in 2 John (5). Paraphrases of that commandment ("love his brother/the brethren/the children of God") occur six times in 1 John (2:10; 3:10, 14; 4:20, 21; 5:2). That this injunction is stated in the restricted form of loving other Christians of the community, rather than all humans, is troublesome to some. Some arguments have been advanced which favor interpreting the commandment in terms of a universal love. Those efforts, however, may not be entirely honest with the limited vision of the Johannine community. However, given the discussion of the divine nature of human love, it is clear that the logic of the Johannine position moves toward the universal character of the Christians' responsibility to love, even if that view is not explicitly expressed in the formulas of 1 and 2 John.

But like being righteous, loving is a matter of concrete behavior. It is not enough to speak about love, but love must be executed in deeds (3:18). In 3 John love is executed specifically in the extension of hospitality and the support of other Christians (5–8). In 1 John love means sacrificially giving of one's worldly goods to others in need (3:17). Such giving is modeled after Jesus' act of sacrificing his life. That model dictates that Christians, too, must be willing to "lay down our lives for the brethren" (3:16).

The eschatological view of the author of 1 John motivates moral purification (3:3). But a faithful response to the injunction to love eliminates any fear of facing the judgment of that last day (4:18).

5. The View of the End Times. Eschatology is not a peripheral issue in 1 John. The "last hour" is present, the author asserts, because the "antichrists" of the end times are present (2:18). This single verse raises two questions relevant to the eschatology of the document. First, why does the author use the expression, "the last hour," instead of the more standardized, "last days" (John 6:40)? It has been proposed that the imminence of the final acts of God led the author to use "hour" rather than "day." It has also been argued that the expression is shaped by the references to Jesus' "hour" in the Fourth Gospel (John 2:4).

Even more perplexing in 2:18 is the word "antichrist" *(antichristos)* which is used four times in 1 John (2:18—twice, 22; 4:3) and once in 2 John (7). These are the only uses of this word in the NT. It is not found in the Jewish intertestamental literature, the Midrashim, nor the Talmud. It seems that the Johannine community, by the time of the writing of 1 and 2 John, had devised this title as part of its apocalyptic expectation. That the author of 1 John can use the term in both the singular and plural (2:18) is an indication that the concept was pliable. It seems to symbolize the final assertion of evil at the end time, an idea expressed in other imagery in NT apocalypticism (e.g., 1 Thess 2:1–12). It may be that the title was conceived amid the Johannine crisis, since the view of Christ was a central issue in the debate with the separatists.

In the view of the author of 1 Jn the end time involves the appearance of the antichrist(s), as well as the power of lie (2:22) and deceit (2:26, cf. 2 Jn 7). Christians are protected against these mighty evil forces by their anointing (2:27, cf. 2 above). The expectation of the parousia of Christ is expressed in 2:28. That event will bring a transformation of the Christians, in which they will become "like him" (3:2). The last day will include a final judgment (4:17) in the face of which Christians need have no fear, if they have been faithful in their love (4:18). That some reward awaits Christians is suggested by 2 Jn 8. The moral implication of this hope is the call for purification (3:3).

It is interesting that 1 and 2 John give expression to an eschatology which is of an apocalyptic kind. While some features of a futuristic and even apocalyptic eschatology are found in the Gospel of John (resurrection, 6:40), such features are not the most distinguishing mark of Johannine eschatology. The views of 1 and 2 John are evidence that the Johannine community had been influenced by other Christian beliefs about the end time. But they may also reflect the way in which the crisis of the schism in the community aroused apocalyptic expectation.

H. Value

The value of these three documents resides in four interrelated areas. The first is the contribution they make to an understanding of the emerging church at the end of the 1st century. They exemplify the way in which the Church found it necessary to begin to draw more clear lines between what constituted an authentic Christian faith and what needed to be deemed an aberration of that faith. The Church thought it important to develop an orthodoxy in the light of which claims of truth could be evaluated. While such a development is unfortunate in some ways, it provided the Church with a clear identity by which to preserve itself in the future. 1 and 2 John contribute two vital aspects of that emerging orthodoxy. The first is the centrality of the humanity of Christ, and the second is the importance of the moral dimension of Christian life. Around these two themes a good deal of what is essential to historic Christianity could be summarized.

More specifically, in 1, 2, and 3 John one witnesses the Christian community struggling to rescue itself from an annihilation resulting from a schismatic movement. The writings are a glimpse into the heart of a religious community attempting to contend with a diversity of views and beliefs. The glimpse informs the readers of the traumatic nature of schism and the array of emotions which arise as a consequence of the tearing asunder of what once had been a single religious body. The defensive and polemical stance of the authors does not exemplify the best response to diversity—indeed, one would hope that there are more creative possibilities. But still the authors show us what is at risk in diversity and what the tragic results of different fundamental orientations can be for the solidarity of a community.

The second contribution is the way in which 3 John promotes the emergence of a clear structure of authority in the Church. While that structure is not specifically defined in 3 John, directions for its development are obvious. For its identity and preservation the Church thought it necessary to have, not only a clear orthodoxy, but also to be able to manage itself in the face of the improper assertions of power on the part of persons such as Diotrephes. With that development of authority there came some new dangers. But in 3 John we see none of the absoluteness and inflexibility of ecclesiastical authority characteristic of later periods in the history of the Church. What we do see is the effort to establish legitimate authority to preserve good order for the sake of the community.

Third, the three writings suggest a pastoral sensitivity and mode of operation which has value for today. The writers in each case were acutely aware of the human condition and ways by which humans may be nurtured to deal with that condition. In 1 John there is evidence of a concern to balance exhortation with affirmation. In 2 and 3 John there is evidence of an awareness of what motivates humans to change their behavior and a high degree of importance attached to personal relationships.

Finally, the value of the so-called Johannine epistles cannot be discussed without mention of the view of Christianity as rooted and centered in love. If there is one single ingredient which characterizes the core of the Christian gospel and its moral imperative, it is surely love. 1 and 2 John give expression to that fact with a clarity unsurpassed in the NT literature. For that contribution alone the writings merit preservation and appreciation.

Bibliography

Bogart, J. 1977. *Orthodox and Heretical Perfectionism in the Johannine Community as Evident in the First Epistle of John.* SBLDS 33. Missoula, MT.

Brown, R. E. 1979. *The Community of the Beloved Disciple.* New York.

Burge, G. M. 1987. *The Anointed Community: The Holy Spirit in the Johannine Tradition.* Grand Rapids.

du Rand, J. A.; Coetzee, J. C.; Kotze, P. P. A.; and du Toit, B. A. 1979. *Studies in the Johannine Letters. Neot* 13. Bloemfontein, South Africa.

Haas, C.; Jonge, M. de; and Swellebgrebel, J. L. 1972. *A Translator's Handbook on the Letters of John.* Helps for Translators. New York.

Lieu, J. 1986. *The Second and Third Epistles of John,* Edinburgh.

Malatesta, E. 1978. *Interiority and Covenant: A Study of einai en and menein en in the First Letter of Saint John.* AnBib 69. Rome.

Segovia, F. F. 1982. *Love Relationships in the Johannine Tradition.* SBLDS 58. Chico, CA.

Whitacre, R. A. 1982. *Johannine Polemic: The Role of Tradition and Theology.* SBLDS 67. Chico, CA.

Robert Kysar

JOHN, THE GOSPEL OF.

The fourth of what are now the canonical gospels was attributed to John, a disciple of Jesus, as early as the last quarter of the 2d century. Irenaeus clearly identifies the "disciple whom Jesus loved" with the author of the Fourth Gospel (*haer.* 3.1.2), and the Muratorian Canon speaks of a disciple, John, as responsible for the fourth of the gospels. The traditional association of the gospel with the disciple, John, Son of Zebedee, was firmly embedded by the 4th century.

There is textual evidence of the existence of the Gospel of John early in the 2d century, but its inclusion in the canon was not without difficulty. Its use in the writings of the earliest Church Fathers is not prominent, although it is argued that allusions to the gospel are discernible. It is perhaps only the prominence of John in gnostic Christian circles which brought it center stage for the Church as a whole. Its role in Valentinian Gnosticism has been long recognized. More recently, its affinities with the library discovered at Nag-Hammadi further document the popularity of the gospel among gnostic Christians. It was the gnostic, Heracleon, who wrote the first commentary on the Gospel of John.

In its defense against Gnosticism the Church embraced the Gospel of John and attempted to demonstrate that the gospel affirmed the "orthodox Christian faith". The affiliation of the gospel with gnostic Christian beliefs led some, however, to reject it along with Revelation, as Irenaeus witnesses (*haer.* 3.2.12). There ensued a struggle between those who favored the gospel and those who believed its gnostic associations barred it from a place among the books of the Church. The naming of John among the accepted writings in the Muratorian Canon may be evidence of such a struggle. Origen sought to wrest John from the grip of gnostic interpreters. By the end of the 4th century it was clear that John's place in the canon was secured.

The storm of controversy around the gospel in the nascent centuries of Christianity continues in recent times, and the question of its interpretation is still not settled. This article will attempt to characterize the current status of that debate and delineate what seem to be the major lines of interpretation today.

A. Textual Considerations
B. Structure and Distinctiveness
  1. Structure and Contents
  2. Distinctive Features
C. Literary Features
  1. Style
  2. Drama
  3. Narrative and Discourse
  4. Irony and Double Entendre
  5. Symbolism
  6. Characters
D. Purpose and Historical Origin
  1. Purpose
  2. Historical Origin
E. Date and Authorship
  1. Date
  2. Authorship
F. Sources and Composition
  1. Relationship with the Synoptic Gospels
  2. Source Theories
  3. Theories of Composition and Redaction
G. Theology
  1. Christ
  2. The Cross
  3. Dualism
  4. Faith
  5. Eschatology
  6. The Spirit
  7. The Sacraments
  8. The Church
H. Value
  1. The Historical Jesus
  2. Religious Value

A. Textual Considerations

The oldest extant portion of NT writings is a papyrus fragment (P^{52}) containing bits of John 18 and dating from the first half of the 2d century. John is well represented in other papyri, including such witnesses as P^{66} and P^{75}. Many conclude from this strong witness the importance of John in a so-called "Egyptian" text which existed as early as, if not prior to, the "Western" text. Among the important uncial codices and versions John is equally well represented. The significance of patristic citations has been a point of recent controversy, but there, too, the text of John is suitably established. Origen's text of the gospel exhibits great affinities with the "Caesarean" text and the Vaticanus and Sinaiticus codices.

However, the gospel has its share of disputed passages. Only a few of those which are particularly significant and in some cases controversial can be mentioned here.

7:52–8:12 has been decisively shown not to have been a part of the original gospel. The oldest Greek witnesses do not include it (e.g., P^{66} and P^{75}). In other mss the section is located elsewhere or missing entirely.

1:3–4 may be punctuated several different ways. Should "that which was made" (*ho gegonen*) be taken with the conclusion of v 3 or the beginning of v 4? A quotation in Tatian lends weight to beginning a new sentence with *ho gegonen,* as does the omission of *en* in v 4 by P^{66}.

1:18 contains the unresolved question whether to read *ho monogenēs theos* or *ho monogenēs huios.* The attestation of $P^{66\ 75}$ for the former leads many to prefer it.

7:39 may be read "For as yet the Spirit had not been given" or "For as yet the Spirit was not". The first is supported by Latin and Syriac versions, while the second is attested in Greek mss and is the more likely.

7:52 raises the problem of whether or not "the prophet" was used here as a messianic title. The definite article, "the," is missing in the majority of witnesses, but present in P^{66}. The latter is increasingly gaining acceptance as the preferred reading.

20:31 holds the difficult question of whether an aorist ("may come to believe") or a present subjunctive ("may go on believing") was intended. Both have strong early support (cf. D.1 below).

B. Structure and Distinctiveness

Studies of the structure of the gospel and its distinctiveness stress both the problematic character of the work of the evangelist and its artistic quality.

1. Structure and Contents. The structure of the gospel presents the reader with a number of difficulties. Among these is the geographical locale of Jesus in chaps. 5 and 6. The setting for chap. 5 is Jerusalem (v 1), and the reader is never told of a movement to Galilee in the course of the chap. But the next chap. opens with Jesus in Galilee (6:1). Some have proposed that chap. 6 belonged originally after chap. 4 and that the order of the chaps. suffered disarrangement. 14:31 is another anomaly. It would seem to indicate a conclusion to the final discourses, even though they continue in the succeeding chaps.

A period of Johannine scholarship was marked by the effort to restore the structure of the gospel to a better and proposed original order. Those efforts met with little consensus among scholars and today have for the most part given way to an effort to see purpose in the present order. While the recent appreciation of the present order has succeeded where theories of rearrangement failed, the reader is still left with the impression that the fourth evangelist did not always smooth over transitional points in the narrative. It must be said that while the structure of the gospel exhibits considerable skill, it is not without its faults. A common view is that the evangelist has incorporated and redacted traditional materials without always covering the "seams" between the traditional and redactional materials. Moreover, one must conclude that, in spite of arguments to the contrary, geographical movements were not central to the author's purpose.

The structure of the gospel has most frequently been viewed in two major parts. The first, sometimes called the "Book of Signs," covers chaps. 1–12 and the second, labeled the "Book of Glory," chaps. 13–20. There is ample justification for such a division, even though the titles may not be as descriptive as they might. The first section, 1–12, depicts Jesus' public ministry. There he performs a number of wondrous deeds, engages in discussion with opponents and the crowds, and moves freely between Galilee and Judea. In chaps. 13–20 Jesus is restricted to discussions with his disciples alone (13–17) and to the passion experience (18–21). The theme suggested by the text itself pivots around "the hour"—the death and resurrection. In chaps. 1–11 it is declared on several occasions that Jesus' "hour has not come" (2:4; 7:30; 8:20). 12:23 announces the advent of the crucial time of revelation, and throughout chaps. 13–20 the presence of the "hour" is affirmed (13:1; 17:1). The first major part of the gospel is preparation for the "hour," the second the depiction of the "hour" itself.

Another pivotal theme in the relationship of the two major parts of the gospel is conceptually synonymous with the "hour" but employs the language of "glorification" (17:1). In the first section the "glorification" is spoken of as a future event (7:39; 12:16). In chaps. 13–21 the time of glorification is present (13:31; 17:5). Chap. 12 is clearly intended in this structure as the transitional bridge between the two.

The narrative of Jesus' ministry is prefaced with a hymn (1:1–18) which celebrates the salvific work of God through the Word *(logos).* Here the author alerts the reader to the identity of Jesus and his place in the divine plan. The reader thus knows from the first chap. the issue which is central to the entire gospel and the resolution of the discussions which transpire through the course of the story, namely, who is this man Jesus.

1:19–51 briefly establishes the relationship between Jesus and the immediate circle of disciples and provides a historical beginning for the ministry of Jesus. Included in this section is the first of the several witnesses of John, the Baptizer.

2:1–5:47 includes the narration of three wondrous acts (signs) and a series of discussion/dialogues. It begins with the Cana sign (2:11) and moves immediately to the cleansing of the Temple which announces Jesus' relationship with the Judaism of his day (2:19). The Nicodemus discourse is followed by another testimony of the Baptizer and then by the story of the faith of the Samaritans. Two healings—the royal official's son and the man with the thirty-eight year illness—are back to back in 4:43–5:18. Speeches on the subject of the relationship of the Father and the Son's activity and the witnesses to Jesus conclude the section. The section climaxes with the accusation of unbelief (5:19–47).

That accusation of unbelief begins the steady crescendo of opposition to Jesus which is sharply heightened in chap. 6. The chap. begins with three wondrous deeds—the feeding of the multitude, the walking on the sea, and the wondrous landing of the boat (6:1–21). There follows the lengthy bread of life discourse. Here Jesus makes the high claims for himself consistent with the announcement of the prologue of the gospel. The response is a schism among his hearers which finds many who had believed now leaving him (6:22–71).

In dramatic fashion the evangelist portrays the degree of opposition to Jesus' claims at the end of chap. 6 and then brings him to the locale where that opposition is the strongest (7:1–9). 7:10–10:42 has Jesus in Jerusalem, the center of the opposition and unbelief. A series of addresses in the Temple (7:10–52; 8:12–59) clarify the nature of the opposition. Chap. 9 is the skillful story of the possibilities of faith told through the giving of sight to the blind man and the resultant blindness of the religious leaders. Chap. 10 further explores that opposition in contrast to the relationship of believers with Jesus.

The opposition reaches its peak in chap. 11, when in response to the wondrous act of raising Lazarus to life the plot on Jesus' life is set in motion. The inevitability of that plot is confirmed in the anointing of Jesus' body for burial (12:1–11). There follows the entry into Jerusalem which suggests the nature of Jesus' kingship and the arrival of the Greeks which signals the advent of the "hour" (12:12–36). Significantly the first major portion of the gospel concludes with the statement of the unbelief of the religious leaders, its meaning in terms of OT prophecy, and a final public word of Jesus concerning the division among humans caused by his presence (12:37–50).

The second major portion of the gospel is prefaced by the foot washing and the commandment to love one another. These acts and words of love, however, are set over against the prediction of Judas' betrayal and Peter's denial (13:1–38).

Chaps. 14–17 are comprised of three clusters of final instructions to his disciples and a prayer for them and their glorification in Jesus' glorification. The so-called "farewell discourses" are a mosaic of themes introduced, explored, dropped, and reintroduced. They address the loss of the disciples in the death of Jesus in contrast to their gain, the intimacy they have with Christ, and the assurance that is theirs in tribulation. Woven into these themes is the promise and the role of the "Counselor" who comes to continue Jesus' ministry. The prayer of chap. 17 focuses on Jesus' concern for his disciples and his imminent fate.

The passion narrative is the story of the exaltation and glorification of Jesus (18:1–20:29). Judas' betrayal and Peter's denial are told now as they were predicted. The religious trial is narrated with the greatest of brevity. The political trial before Pilate, however, is given detailed attention and focuses upon the nature of the kingship that is bestowed upon Jesus in the cross (18:28–19:16). The royal disposition of Jesus which marks the whole of the passion story is maintained as he dies on the cross and is buried in a tomb fit for a king (19:17–42—cf. G.2 below).

The discovery of the empty tomb is told but with attention to the possibilities for faith it offers (20:1–10). Three resurrection appearances bring the story to its final climax. First, the risen Christ appears to Mary Magdalene (20:11–18); second, he presents himself to the disciples with Thomas absent (20:19–23); and finally, to Thomas and the other disciples (20:24–29). The final words of Jesus in the gospel are an invitation to belief and a beatitude for those who believe without seeing. The final words of a human actor in the gospel are an affirmation of the assertions with which the gospel began—"My Lord and my God!" (20:27–29). Against the opposition which tried its best to turn its back on Jesus, God in the cross and resurrection reveals that man's status as the king of humanity.

The evangelist's own conclusion recognizes the limitations of the gospel but declares it has been written to evoke faith in Jesus as the Christ and Son of God (20:30–31).

Chap. 21 is clearly an appendix, added after the completion of the first 20 chaps. But it appropriately concludes some issues of importance left unresolved in the earlier chaps., namely, Peter's reinstatement and commissioning, as well as the role of the beloved disciple.

2. Distinctive Features. This gospel is marked by a series of features which are distinctive when compared with the first three gospels of the canon. Those features may be summarized in three general categories.

a. Vocabulary and Style. Many of the most frequent expressions found in the Synoptic Gospels are rare or missing entirely from the Gospel of John (e.g., "Kingdom of God/Heaven," "Sadducees," "scribes," "forgive," "demons," "tax collectors"). In contrast there is an almost unique Johannine vocabulary which makes use of such expressions as "life," "light," "darkness," "truth," "world," "the Jews," "know," "Counselor" and "Son" as a title for Jesus. While not absent from the synoptics, the term "Father" used of God appears with common regularity in John, as does the expression, "him who sent me," a rare synoptic reference to God. The double "amen" (e.g., 1:51; 10:1; 12:24) is unique to the Fourth Gospel. The "I am" formula in its various forms, so frequent in John (e.g., 6:20, 35, 51; 8:24; 15:5) is seldom encountered in the first three gospels.

The style of the Fourth Gospel also sets it apart from the other gospels (cf. C.1 below). Most notable is the style of the Johannine Jesus' discourses. In contrast to the economy of the words of Jesus as they are found in the first three gospels, the Johannine Jesus is made to speak at great length and repetitiously. Even the so-called sermons in the Synoptic Gospels are comprised of short, distinct sayings as opposed to the longer and often rambling discourses of the fourth evangelist's Jesus (compare Matthew 5–7 with John 14–16).

b. Order and Content. One striking difference between the synoptics and the Fourth Gospel is that the latter narrates the ministry of Jesus within a framework of three Passovers (2:13; 6:4; 13:1), while the synoptics have only one Passover (e.g., Mark 14:1). The result for the Johannine story is that Jesus' Judean ministry is much more lengthy than is the case in the synoptic accounts.

The order of events is often different in John, for example, the place of the Temple cleansing (contrast John 2:13–20 and Mark 11:11–17). While the synoptics agree that the crucifixion took place on the day of Passover (e.g., Mark 14:12; 15:42), the fourth evangelist takes care to say that Jesus died one day earlier on Passover eve (e.g., 18:28; 19:14). Unlike the Synoptic Gospels, the fourth evangelist narrates concurrent ministries of Jesus and John, the Baptizer (e.g., 3:23).

Equally important are the major synoptic narratives which are missing from the Johannine account, such as the baptism and temptation of Jesus (e.g., Mark 1:9–13), the confession at Caesarea Philippi (e.g., Mark 8:27–30), the transfiguration (e.g., Mark 9:2–10), the Garden of Gethsemane story (e.g., Mark 14:32–42), and the institution of the eucharist (e.g., Mark 14:22–25). Certain kinds of narratives and discourses, such as exorcisms and narrative parables, are missing in John, although abundant in the synoptics.

On the other side, the Johannine gospel includes a significant number of narratives unique to itself. Among them are the wonder at Cana (2:1–11), the conversations with Nicodemus (3:1–13) and the Samaritan woman (4:1–42), the raising of Lazarus (11:1–44), the foot washing (13:1–20), the conversation with Pilate (18:28–19:16), and three resurrection stories unknown outside of John (20:11–29).

The Johannine discourses are equally unique in kind and content. Among the "I am" sayings are the distinctive "allegorical sayings" such as 10:1–16 and 15:1–10. As well there are the so-called "farewell discourses" of chaps. 14–16 which include the Paraclete ("Counselor") sayings (14:15–17, 26; 15:26–27; and 16:7–14) and which conclude with the unique prayer of chap. 17.

c. The Portrayal of Jesus. The most evident distinction in the presentation of the figure of Jesus is the fact that the Johannine Jesus is made constantly to speak of himself and his unique identity, while the Synoptic Gospels most often have Jesus speaking about the kingdom of God/Heaven. When, for example, Jesus is challenged for having performed a healing on the Sabbath, he defends his action by appealing to his unique status (5:19–23). While the synoptic Jesus is frequently found in a rabbinical form of dialogue with others (e.g., Matt 22:23–33), the Johannine Jesus is more often proclaiming his unique relationship with God. The commands to keep silence with regard to who Jesus is or what he does found scattered throughout the synoptics (e.g., Mark 8:30) are conspicuous by their absence in the Fourth Gospel.

The Johannine Jesus is given an aura of divine foreignness with the result that he is described with greater emphasis upon his divine nature than is the case in the synoptics. He knows the thoughts of others before they are expressed (e.g., 2:24–25); he has no need to pray, because of his unique relationship with the Father (11:42); and he is rescued from the hostile intent of a crowd simply because "his hour had not come" (7:30). Such a presentation is captured in the christological title the fourth evangelist uses four times, "only *(monogenēs)* Son" (1:14, 18; 3:16, 18).

The wonder stories of the Fourth Gospel contribute to this unique presentation of Jesus. They are called, "signs" (*sēmeia,* e.g., 2:11; 4:54; 20:30). The Synoptic Gospels use this term in reference to wonders only to suggest an illegitimate request for a demonstration of power (e.g., Luke 11:29, but cf. Acts 2:22 and 2:43). The wondrous deeds of Jesus are conceived by the fourth evangelist in a way quite distinct from the Synoptic Gospels. In the first three gospels the wonders are expressions of the inbreaking of the reign of God announced by Jesus (e.g., Luke 11:20). In John the wonders are indications of the identity of the person of Jesus and point to the "bringer" rather than that which is brought. The manner in which the symbolic meaning of the signs is exploited by the fourth evangelist (cf. C.5 below) is still another distinctive quality in the portrayal of the wonders of Jesus.

John contains only seven or eight wonder stories (depending on whether one understands 6:16–21 as one or two signs), but the wondrous character is often more emphasized. The healing is done at a distance (4:43–53). The dead one who is raised has been buried four days (11:39, contrast Mark 5:35–42). Jesus not only walks on the water but immediately effects the landing of the boat (6:16–21, contrast Mark 6:45–52). He changes ordinary water into the finest wine of the wedding party (2:1–11). Such an accenting of the wondrous quality contributes to the portrayal of the uniqueness of the man Jesus.

These three types of unique differences between John and the Synoptic Gospels set it off from its canonical colleagues. They suggest some of the unique literary features of the document as well.

C. Literary Features

It is clear that the structure of the gospel, viewed as a literary creation, is deliberate and effective. Such is only one example of what scholars are more and more seeing as evidence of the literary skill of the fourth evangelist.

1. Style. The vocabulary and grammar of the gospel is deceptively simple in its appearance. The vocabulary is relatively limited and the grammar lacks many of the complexities of other Hellenistic writings. It has been argued that the style reflects Semitic influences and may even be a translation from Aramaic. Original Semitic expressions dot the pages of the document, e.g., *messias* (Messiah, 1:41 and 4:25) which is unique to John among the NT writings. Other phrases have a Semitic coloring to them, e.g., "doing the truth" (*poiein tēn alētheian,* 3:21). Modern scholarship has shown little interest in the proposal that the gospel was originally written in Aramaic and then translated into Greek but has tended to believe that the evangelist's Greek was strongly influenced by a Jewish background.

The style also exhibits a poetic quality, which is evident especially in the speech materials. Examples abound, but chap. 17 certainly betrays the signs of balance, rhythm, parallelism, and resonance. The repetition which is so prominent in the speeches of Jesus suggests poetic redundancy and indicates that the material may have been written to be read aloud. That this poetic style reflects a meditative quality has long been acknowledged. Stereotyped expressions (e.g., "I have come" 5:43; 12:46; 18:37) expose didactic and reflective purpose. Recent studies have proposed numerous chiastic structures in both the speech and narrative sections (e.g., 6:36–40). In a similar manner the use of inclusion is more and more recognized. The subunit, 6:51–58, begins and concludes with the statement that one who eats the bread from heaven "will live for ever". On a larger scale the prologue concludes by using the term, God, to describe the Word (1:18), and Thomas' words in 20:28 confess Jesus to be God.

2. Drama. The narratives of the gospel are often told in a dramatic style. They progress in deliberate stages which constitute scenes and evoke a sense of suspense as the narrative moves forward. Such dramatic structure is typical of a series of longer narratives within the gospel. Among these are 4:1–42; 6:1–71; 9:1–41; 11:1–44 and 18:28–19:16.

In 9:1–41 the author has constructed a dramatic story comprised of seven scenes (vv 1–7, 8–12, 13–17, 18–23, 24–34, 35–38, and 39–41). With those scenes the evangelist gradually shifts the attention of the reader from the physical healing of the blind man to the spiritual insight concerning Jesus' identity. The result is that the man is healed not alone of his physical ailment but his spiritual blindness as well, and the lack of sight is revealed to be the ailment of the religious leaders. Similarly one is treated to the progressive faith of the man healed of blindness and the progressive unbelief of the religious leaders. 18:28–19:16 is another prime example of a longer narrative structured with dramatic skill.

The narratives, however, are not exclusively of this longer variety. Punctuating the story are much shorter tales told with economy and clarity (e.g., 2:1–11; 2:12–25; 4:43–54; 12:1–11; 13:1–30). The author has skillfully alternated the style of the stories to keep the reader off guard. Nor is drama the exclusive property of the longer narratives. In 4:43–54 the reader's suspense is piqued by Jesus' implication that he will not perform the healing (v 48), then by the question of whether or not the healing has actually been effected (v 51). The shorter narratives are told with as much care and skill as are the longer ones.

3. Narrative and Discourse. More briefly it should be noted the way in which the gospel moves back and forth between narrative and discourse. The Fourth Gospel contains more discourse materials than do the Synoptic Gospels, but not at the expense of narrative. The interrelationship between narrative and discourse is a feature of the literary skill of the author.

In many cases the author attaches to a narrative discourse material which explores the meaning of the story just related. This is most obviously the case in chap. 6 in which the bread of life discourse is clearly intended to be the elucidation of the meaning of the feeding of the multitude. Such a pattern is discernible in 5:1–47; 9:1–10:42; and 13:1–38 as well.

However, the author is equally satisfied to allow narratives to stand by themselves and speak for themselves (e.g., 2:1–11; 4:43–54; 12:12–19; and 18:1–19:42). Sometimes speech material is unaccompanied by narrative setting of any significance (e.g., 7:10–52; 8:12–59; 14:1–17:26). Sometimes the discourse illuminating the narrative is integrated into the story itself, as is the case with 4:1–42 and 11:1–44.

The evangelist saw both discourse and narrative as important to the purpose of the work, but varied the relationship between the two in a provocative and unmonotonous way.

4. Irony and Double Entendre. Irony is an important feature in this gospel. The author is fond of setting up situations in which the reader knows something important that some of the actors/speakers in the narrative do not know. In that situation the actors are made to say something of far greater significance than they know. Examples include 4:12; 7:27, 35–36; 8:22; 11:50; 12:12–15, 19; 13:37; 19:19.

But irony is more than an occasional technique found in individual sayings. The whole gospel is framed in irony. The opening verses of the gospel inform the reader of the identity of Jesus, while individual characters throughout the narrative struggle to make this discovery for themselves (e.g., 1:43–51; 6:30–31; 14:8; 18:33, 37). Irony is essential to the author's presentation of the crucifixion. Pilate mockingly calls Jesus the king (19:14), places the sign on the cross declaring Jesus to be king (19:19), and puts Jesus to death for having claimed to be king of the Jews (19:12). Ironically, Jesus is king (19:36), and the crucifixion is his enthronement in the view of the evangelist (cf. G.2 below). While the actors believe that they are ridding their society of a troublesome false claimant to royalty, they are actually enthroning him in his rightful office. This author captures and articulates the ironic quality of the Christian view of the cross.

The author's fondness for the use of words with multiple meanings is closely related to irony. This pattern in the discourse materials is frequent: Jesus uses an ambiguous word or an expression which is misunderstood by his listeners and occasions a continuation of his speech. The best known example of this is found in the use of the word *anōthen* (3:1–13) which means "again," "from above," or "from the beginning". While Jesus intends the second or third meaning, Nicodemus understands the word in terms of its first meaning and is puzzled; Jesus must then go on to explicate his meaning. Such misunderstanding occurs in a number of other conversations (e.g., 2:19–20; 4:7–16, 31–34; 6:41–43, 52; 7:52; 8:22; 12:32–36; 18:33–38 and possibly 5:18 and 10:33). In most of these cases Jesus speaks on a spiritual or intangible level while his listeners understand his words on a physical or tangible level of reality.

The functions of such misunderstanding are several. In some cases they produce a humorous situation (e.g., 4:15). Often they occasion Jesus' continuation of his speech and hence move the conversation forward (e.g., 3:5–13). The reader gradually gains an impression after several occurrences of this pattern. Humans are attached to the physical, mundane reality of their existence in such a way as to be blinded to the spiritual dimension of life and, more importantly, the revelation of God in Christ.

The double entendre, however, is also a means by which the author communicates a profound depth of meaning. The author may have intended several of the meanings embedded in the ambiguous language attributed to Jesus. This is to suggest that *anōthen* is intentionally used to imply that the Christian experience of faith is both a birth "from above" (from God) and a re-birth. *Pneuma* used in 3:8 becomes a condensed analogy in which the Spirit is compared to the wind. On three occasions Jesus is made to speak of his being "lifted up" (*hyspoō,* 3:14; 8:28; and 12:32). It is clear that this is Johannine language for the cross. The verb had two distinct meanings in Hellenistic Greek: To be lifted up on a cross and to be exalted to high office (as in the enthronement of a king). The evangelist's view of the cross as the enthronement of Jesus as king leads one to conclude that both meanings of the word are appropriate.

Such rich, ambiguous language teases the reader into contemplation of the meaning of the Christ revelation for human existence. It is a poetic kind of use of language in which words are made to say all that custom takes them to mean and even more.

5. Symbolism. The centrality and power of the symbolism of the Fourth Gospel is a long acknowledged feature of the work. This constitutes still another instance of the poetic quality of the author's style.

Three kinds of symbolism are apparent in the gospel. The first are the metaphorical speeches of Jesus in which he is made to identify himself with another reality. This kind of symbolism is found in 4:13–14; 6:35–65; 8:12; 10:1–16; 15:1–10, as well as elsewhere. The reader is invited to reflect on the way in which Jesus is comparable to such realities as light, water, bread, a shepherd, a vine, resurrection and life, and the way.

Another kind of imagery is found in the dualistic symbols of the gospel. They are a variety of means of speaking of the contrast between the life of faith and of unbelief (cf. G.3 below). Such symbols are found in abundance in the hymnic prologue to the gospel (e.g., light and darkness in 1:5, but cf. 1:4, 10–12). Another instance of dualistic symbols is "above and below" (e.g., 8:23). The religious background of such a dualism is often debated, but its literary significance seems clear: The reader is made to sense that one must decide between the poles of the dualism—one either accepts or rejects the revelation of God, and there is no middle option.

Finally, there is a symbolic dimension to the narratives of Jesus' actions in the gospel. That symbolic dimension is articulated in a number of cases (e.g., chaps. 6, 9, and 11). In others it is left to the reader to exploit the full meaning of the action of Jesus. Hence, the narrative of the cleansing of the Temple is thought to be a representation of the manner in which the revelation of God in Christ cleanses and replaces contemporary Judaism. Other narrated actions of Jesus (and others) are rich with symbolic possibilities—2:1–11; 6:16–21; 12:1–11, 12–19, 20–22; 20:1–10; 21:1–14.

As powerful as the symbolism of the gospel is, it has become a problem for interpreters of the text. Implicit symbolic meaning opens the door for speculative proposals. Furthermore, it may lead the interpreter to seek additional meaning where none may have been intended. But such is the nature of the reading of a poetic gospel—meaning is constituted not alone by the writer's intention but also by the reader's own dialogue with the text. There is, consequently, a certain open-endedness to the meaning of the Gospel of John, which can only be credited to the skill of the author.

6. Characters. There is no modern sense of characterization in the figures presented in the gospel, but they are used effectively by the author in the task of proclamation. In general one may say that the characters of the gospel are models of faith or unbelief. The opponents of Jesus serve as models of what it means to reject the revelation in Christ, while the disciples are models of acceptance.

Believers are, however, representations of faith at different levels of maturation. There are characters who model the transition from unbelief to the beginning stages of faith (e.g., Nicodemus, 3:1–13; 7:50–51; 19:39, the Samaritan woman, 4:1–30, 29–42, and the blind man, 9:1–41). There are characters who model the failure to come to faith (e.g., the man with the thirty-eight year illness, 5:1–18, and "many disciples," 6:60–71). The royal official represents a profound faith which believes on the basis of Jesus' word without evidence of the success of the wondrous healing of his son (4:43–54). Martha models growth in faith (11:1–44), and Mary the gratitude and love of faith (12:1–8). Thomas demonstrates the way in which faith is born from doubt (20:24–28). In the tale of the discovery of the empty tomb the evangelist represents three different kinds of faith in the three characters involved (20:1–10).

Some persons are passed over with little or no interest (e.g., Annas, 18:19–24, Joseph, 19:38–42), while others are more developed (e.g., Pilate, 18:28–19:16). But in each case they invite the process of identification by the reader. Thereby, the evangelist has enticed the readers to examine their own posture in relationship to the revelation of God as they contemplate each of the characters depicted in the pages of the gospel.

D. Purpose and Historical Origin

The purpose of the document and theories of its origin are closely interrelated. The first can only be discovered through the process of exploring the second.

1. Purpose. The purpose of the gospel is explicitly stated in what was most likely the original ending of the document, 20:31. The author declares that the gospel has the purpose of nurturing the faith of the readers in Jesus as the Christ and Son of God, in order that they might gain "life". Such a purpose is clearly evident throughout the document.

But 20:31 is plagued by a textual problem which hampers a more precise understanding of the purpose of the gospel. Is the faith it seeks to nurture an initial acceptance of Christ, or the strengthening of Christian life? Was the gospel a missionary document written for evangelistic purposes, or was it written for a community of faith in order to advance the maturation of faith? The key verb in the verse is "believe," but the textual witnesses are divided over whether the form of the verb is an aorist *(pisteusēte)* or a present subjunctive *(pisteuēte)*. Both have impressive attestation, making any textual decision tenuous at best. But further, did the author use the tenses of the subjunctive mood carefully and deliberately? Consequently, the verse does not help us to decide if the purpose of the gospel was missionary or maturational.

The decision must be determined on the impression gained from the reading of the whole document rather than on the basis of the statement in 20:31. While contemporary scholarship is not unanimous in its view, there is a clear preference for the view that the gospel was addressed to members of a Christian community in order to strengthen their faith in the midst of a critical situation. Such a view is admittedly somewhat impressionistic. Still, the attention to the nurturing of faith in the farewell discourses (chaps. 14–17), the concern for apostasy (e.g., 6:60–69), and attention to the theme of the quality of sound faith (e.g., 4:43–53; 6:25–27; 20:29) contribute decisively to that impression.

2. Historical Origin. Equally significant in determining the precise purpose of the gospel is the supposed situation out of which and for which it was written. A variety of options have been proposed. The setting has been reconstructed in terms of a conflict over authority in the community, the crisis of martyrdom in the midst of evangelistic endeavors, the threat of docetism, and a mission to the Samaritans, to mention only a few.

But another reconstruction has gained considerable prominence in recent decades. That hypothesis holds that the gospel was written to a Christian community which had only recently suffered expulsion from its synagogue home. The evangelist's purpose, it is proposed, was to nurture faith in the crisis brought on by that experience. On three occasions the word, *aposynagōgos* ("put out of the synagogue"), appears in the gospel (9:22; 12:42; and 16:2). The proposal is that such references reflect the time and situation of the author and his community and not that of the historical Jesus. Other evidence of a similar kind supports such conjecture. The high claims Jesus makes for his own authority and the response that he thus made "himself equal to God" (5:18) fit more likely within a context of a Christian-Jewish dialogue than within the context of Jesus' own ministry. Chap. 9 seems to reflect the experience of the Johannine community laid over the tale of healing. It is conjectured that the Jesus story has been reinterpreted and told now with an eye to the situation of a band of Christians who were struggling to come to grips with their identity as a community isolated from their previous religious home in the synagogue and now set in conflict with those who had until only recently been colleagues in faith.

Such a hypothesis for the setting of the gospel gains credibility by virtue of the fact that it offers feasible explanations for a number of features of the writing. It makes understandable, for instance, the reasons for the apparent anti-Jewish polemic evident throughout the work. The term, "the Jews," is used in a pejorative way in such passages as 9:18; 10:31; 18:12, 36–38; and 19:12. Jesus is made to attack the Jews and declare that they are unfaithful to their heritage in refusing to believe in him (e.g., 8:42–44) and speaks as if he himself were not a Jew (e.g., 7:19; 8:17; 10:34). The superiority of the Christian to the Hebraic revelation is asserted a number of times (e.g., 1:18; 6:49–50; 8:58; cf. 2:1–22). Such a stance in relationship toward Judaism is made understandable, if the Johannine community stood in opposition to the synagogue from which it had been expelled.

But the thought of the gospel betrays, at the same time, a clearly Jewish quality. While the religious setting for Johannine thought has long been debated, there is increasing acknowledgment of its Jewish character. Not least among the factors which precipitated this acknowledgment are the allusions to the Passover (e.g., 2:13; 6:4; 11:55; 13:1), to Gen. 1:1 in the prologue, and the frequent use of OT images (e.g., 10:11; 15:1–4; 6:51). If the Johannine community had its origins in Jewish Christianity within the structure of the synagogue, such a Jewish interpretation of Christian faith would be only natural.

Other features of the gospel are also illumined by the proposal of an expulsion from the synagogue. Existing as a newly independent religious community set over against Judaism would account for the radical exclusivism of the gospel (e.g., 14:6), for the "sectarian" quality of the self-perception of the community as set in opposition to the "world" (e.g., 16:33), for the dualistic scheme which construes reality in terms of either one or the other allegiance (e.g., 1:5), and for the tendency to see Jesus in terms of a foreigner in this earthly realm (e.g., 8:23).

What was the event which occasioned the expulsion of the Johannine Christians from the synagogue? Some would argue that it was the introduction of another group of Christians into the community—a group which held to a christology intolerable to the Jews of the synagogue. Others suggest the occasion for the fracture was the enforcement of a formal benediction against the heretics (the *Birkath ha-Minim*) propagated, it is proposed, by the Council of Jamnia (ca. 90–95 C.E.). Still others would argue that it is more likely the expulsion took place earlier, in part as a result of the destruction of the Temple in 70 C.E. and the quest for a new Jewish identity brought about by that tragic event.

Although the details of the reconstruction remain controversial, there is a wide acceptance of the hypothesis in its general form. This proposed setting predisposes the reader to see the gospel as an effort to address the crisis resulting from the expulsion and the ensuing controversy with the synagogue. The evangelist attempted, it is thought, an interpretation of the Jesus tradition which helped the community deal with the issues involved in their situation, most especially with the relationship to Judaism, with questions of self-identity, and with Christian life in a situation of minority status and some oppression. Contemporary efforts to date the writing of the gospel depend heavily upon conjectures as to when such a situation might have existed.

E. Date and Authorship

1. Date. The gospel has been dated as early as 40 and as late as 110 C.E. But the latest possible date has been fixed by the discovery in Egypt of the Rylands Papyrus 457 (P^{52}) which contains 18:31–33, 37–38. This ms is usually dated between 125 and 150. Other textual finds make it undeniable that the gospel circulated in Egypt in numerous copies in the middle and last half of the 2d century. No one, therefore, is inclined to propose a date later than 100–10.

The earliest date for the gospel hinges upon the question of whether or not it presupposes the destruction of the Temple in 70 C.E. Most agree that it does, although there have been persistent attempts to argue otherwise. The reasons for positing a post-70 date include the view of the Temple implicit in 2:13–22. Most would argue that the passage attempts to present Christ as the replacement of the Temple that has been destroyed.

The argument that John is to be dated late in the 1st century has often invoked the high christology of the evangelist. The contention is that such a lofty view of Christ necessitates an extensive period of time. Such a view has, however, increasingly lost credibility among scholars, since it is clear that such a perspective imposes an evolutionary schema upon the development of early Christian thought. Moreover, recent investigations of the christology of the NT have demonstrated the existence of a variety of views as early as the time of Paul (e.g., Rom 1:3–6, Phil 2:5–11). Therefore, the christology of the gospel does not dictate a late 1st century date.

The relationship of John and the Synoptics has significance for the dating of the Fourth Gospel. If it is supposed that the fourth evangelist employed the synoptics in the composition of the gospel, it then becomes necessary to date the Gospel of John after the writing of the synoptics (i.e., after 85). Unfortunately the issue of the fourth evangelist's knowledge and use of the synoptics is unsettled at the present (cf. F.1 below). However, a slim majority of scholars still maintain that there is not sufficient evidence in the gospel to hold that the evangelist knew or used any one of the synoptics. If such was the case, the gospel could have been composed before or contemporaneously with the composition of the synoptics.

Another issue in the dating of the gospel has to do with the nature of the tradition it contains. It is supposed that the tradition is a highly developed one and that the differences between the Johannine and synoptic materials are due to that tradition which has been carefully shaped in the Johannine community. How long a period of time would such a process of formulation take? The answer to that question influences the date one is compelled to assign to the gospel. But perhaps it is not so much the length of time a community has to shape a tradition in its own language and concepts as the character of the community. Therefore, the Johannine community with its peculiar circumstances and constituency might have formulated the Jesus tradition rather quickly into its own liking. Consequently, the quality of the distinctive Johannine tradition does not readily yield itself to use in the task of determining a date of origin for the gospel.

Of greatest importance to the dating of the gospel is the speculation as to what date is suggested by the setting proposed for the document. However, those who propose that the setting of the gospel was the experience of the expulsion from the synagogue (cf. D.2 above) cannot agree on a date when such a situation might have existed, for there is no agreement as to what caused the expelling of the Christians. Those who relate the expulsion to a formal effort on the part of Judaism to purge itself of Christian believers link the composition of the gospel with a date soon after the Council of Jamnia, which is supposed to have promulgated such an action. Hence, these scholars would date John after 90. Those inclined to see the expulsion more in terms of an informal action on the part of a local synagogue are free to propose an earlier date.

Given all these considerations most often the gospel is assigned a date of 90–95, which continues the inclination of previous decades of scholarship to conclude that John is the last of the four gospels to be written. There are others, however, who argue that the date might well have been as early as 80–85.

2. Authorship. The authorship of the gospel is no less easy to determine. Many are willing simply to plead ignorance on this question and confess that there is too little data upon which to build a viable thesis. And that conclusion proves to be the most prudent. Tradition has given us the handy name, "John," but the document itself is silent about its author's identity. Tradition has further linked the fourth evangelist with John, son of Zebedee, but again the internal evidence for such an association is slim (e.g., the fact that the sons of Zebedee are not mentioned in the gospel, except in the appendix at 21:2, while they figure so prominently in the synoptic accounts). Other candidates include John, the Elder, the supposed author of 2 and 3 John.

Intertwined with the question of authorship is the mysterious disciple "whom Jesus loved". This anonymous beloved disciple poses two related questions: Who was he/she, and is it possible that this is the author's way of referring to himself? The beloved disciple appears five times in the narrative of the gospel (13:23; 19:26–27; 20:1–8; 21:7; and 21:20–24) and is sometimes found in two references to "another disciple" who remains nameless (18:15–16 and 19:35). John, son of Zebedee, is most often nominated for the unique status of the one "whom Jesus loved," but other proposals include Nicodemus and Lazarus, among others.

Two interesting facts are worthy of note. First, the beloved disciple does not appear in the narrative until 13:23. Second, Peter appears in all but one (19:26) of the narratives in which the beloved disciple is mentioned. The first fact has been used to argue against the effort to identify the beloved disciple with John, Son of Zebedee (and sometimes for an identification with Lazarus, who appears in the narrative for the first time in chap. 11). The second fact has been employed to argue that some kind of contrast between the beloved disciple and Peter is suggested by the author.

Honesty dictates that the identity of this mysterious figure must remain unknown and that speculations are finally fruitless. The evidence is not sufficient to identify him with any of the popular candidates, nor are there enough hints to suggest just how the author might have wanted the reader to construe the relationship between the beloved disciple and Peter. However, it might be that this figure is intended to represent the Johannine community's founder, well known to the evangelist's first readers. As such the author may have wanted to show that the Johannine community was founded on the witness of one as close to Jesus and as reliable as Peter. It seems likely that the beloved disciple is appealed to as the source of the tradition upon which the community and the gospel were founded. This may be the most one can claim to know about the identity of the disciple for whom Jesus is said to have had a special affection.

Was the beloved disciple the fourth evangelist? Such an argument is still common in some circles of scholarship, but remains unlikely. It would seem presumptuous of the author to have claimed that special status for himself and far more likely that it is a status given to the revered founder of the community. See also BELOVED DISCIPLE.

Connected with this question is the query as to whether or not the author was an eyewitness to the historical Jesus. The supposition that the author was one and the same with the beloved disciple is often advanced as a means of insuring that the evangelist did witness Jesus' ministry. Two other passages are advanced as evidence of the same—19:35 and 21:24. But both falter under close scrutiny. 19:35 does not claim that the author was the one who witnessed the scene but only that the scene is related on the sound basis of eyewitness. 21:24 is part of the appendix of the gospel and should not be assumed to have come from the same hand as that responsible for the body of the gospel. Neither of these passages, therefore, persuades many Johannine scholars that the author claims eyewitness status.

The most that can be concluded about the author is that he (or she) was a prominent and respected figure in the Johannine community who assumed sufficient authority to undertake the task of reinterpreting the tradition in the light of the crisis facing the Church. This figure was no doubt trained to some undetermined degree in Jewish thought while not ignorant of the Greek mentality, was a sophisticated thinker, and was a skillful writer. That Greek was a second language for the author is entirely possible, although efforts to prove that the gospel was first written in Aramaic are not convincing nor widely held today. It is likely, however, that the author was versed in Aramaic.

F. Sources and Composition

The gospel poses serious questions for the critical scholar. It presents itself as a careful and deliberate composition, yet not without serious flaws. For example, compare 3:22 and 4:2 (cf. B.1 above). It seems to give expression to a thoughtful and even sophisticated theological stance, yet not without serious contradictions. For example compare 3:17 and 9:39. Both in terms of its literary features and its content the gospel puzzles the careful reader. Efforts to solve those puzzles have in large part centered in a cluster of questions related to the composition of the gospel, namely, the sources used by the author and the process by which the gospel came into existence.

1. Relationship with the Synoptic Gospels. The question of the sources employed by the fourth evangelist has intrigued scholars for centuries. Foremost among the questions posed by the gospel is the literary relationship between it and the Synoptic Gospels. Were all or any of the Synoptic Gospels among the sources utilized in the composition of the Fourth Gospel? The answer is made difficult, if not impossible, by two contrasting features of the Fourth Gospel. On the one hand is the fact that there are clear similarities and parallels between Johannine materials and those which can be found in other gospels. On the other hand stands the fact that there are so many points at which the Fourth Gospel seems to depart from any synoptic materials and exhibits such striking features peculiar to itself.

The first fact can be illustrated by a number of narratives which are clearly parallels to synoptic stories. These include a passion narrative which, while clearly distinct, nonetheless follows a pattern found in the Synoptic Gospels. Moreover, narratives such as the entry into Jerusalem (12:12–19; compare Matt 21:1–9 = Mark 11:1–10, Luke 19:28–40), the cleansing of the Temple (2:13–22; compare Matt 21:10–17 = Mark 11:11–17, Luke 19:45–46), the feeding of the multitude (6:1–15; compare Matt 14:13–21 = Mark 6:32–44, Luke 9:10–17), and the wonder of Jesus' walking on the sea (6:16–21; compare Matt 14:22–33 = Mark 6:45–52) seem to betray a literary dependence of the fourth evangelist on the synoptics. Even when the parallels are not strict there appear to be resemblances between the Johannine and synoptic materials. Examples include several of the healing stories told by the fourth evangelist (e.g., 4:46–53; 5:1–9; 9:1–7) which have many features of synoptic healing stories.

Sayings material in John also occasionally has close affinities with that found in the synoptics. The best examples include 12:25 (cf. Mark 8:35 and parallels), 12:27 (cf. Mark 14:34–36 and parallels), 13:20 (cf. Matt 10:40) and 16:24 (cf. 14:13–14; 15:7 and Matt 7:7; Luke 11:9). The metaphor of the grain of wheat in 12:24 cannot help but call to mind Mark 4:30–32 or Mark 4:1–9, 26–29.

Still other similarities are less exact but hint at some relationship between the fourth and first three gospels. The Johannine anointing story has been seen as a conflation of the similar story in Mark 14:3–9 (and/or its parallels) and Luke 7:36–50. Jesus' identification with the "good shepherd" (10:11) and "the vine" (15:1) are sometimes seen in relation to the synoptic parables of the shepherd (e.g., Matt 18:10–14) and the vineyard (Matt 20:1–16).

These similarities provide evidence of a literary relationship of some kind among John and the synoptics. But the distinctive features of the Fourth Gospel pose a difficulty for evidencing such a relationship (cf. B.2 above). Those distinctive features demonstrate that, if there was a literary use of one or more of the Synoptic Gospels in the composition of the Fourth Gospel, the synoptic presentations have undergone drastic and thorough transformation in John. The distinctiveness of John does not in itself prove that the fourth evangelist wrote independently of the Synoptic Gospels. It does, however, demand an explanation from one who would argue that the fourth evangelist was indebted to one or more of the synoptics.

Those who argue for one or more of the synoptics as a source(s) employed by the fourth evangelist draw attention to the similarities between John and the first three gospels and emphasize that the fourth evangelist transformed the material at his disposal in the process of composition. Those who deny such a view contend that the distinctiveness of the Fourth Gospel is better explained by a theory of independence from the synoptics. They attribute the similarities to common traditions residing behind the literary forms of all of the gospels.

The debate over the question of the fourth evangelist's knowledge and use of one or more of the Synoptic Gospels as a source has swung back and forth. Within the period of modern critical scholarship consensus has moved from an assumption that the fourth evangelist knew and used the synoptics in the composition process to a widespread view that such was not the case. Most recently the discussion has become more heated with a significant number of scholars once again advancing the hypothesis that the relationship between John and the synoptics is best explained by reference to some form of literary dependence. Their argument has been strengthened by some success in showing that the incidents of contact between John and one or more of the synoptics are precisely at the points at which critics have been able to demonstrate evidence of redactional themes in the synoptics. If the synoptic passage can be shown to reflect the peculiar redactional features of the evangelist, its presence in John cannot be explained as having been founded on common preliterary tradition. Efforts in accomplishing this complicated task have been, at this stage, only partially successful.

Until some greater degree of evidence of the presence of synoptic redactional features in John is forthcoming, the issue remains at a stalemate. Most of the parallels between Johannine and synoptic passages can be explained equally well by appeal to literary dependence or to common preliterary tradition. The decision hinges on the intrinsic appeal of one theory or the other and how well the theory coheres with other views one holds of the Fourth Gospel and its origin.

2. Source Theories. Other sources for the composition of the gospel in addition to or instead of the Synoptic Gospels are sometimes proposed. Most frequently it is those who hold that the fourth evangelist did not use the synoptics in the writing of the gospel who are interested in proposing other sources. This group is concerned to understand the nature of the tradition which rests behind the gospel, since it is often their view that it was in the development of that tradition that the similarities and differences between John and the synoptics were shaped. There is considerable consensus today that the fourth evangelist employed tradition in the production of the gospel, but beyond that general agreement there is little in common among the various views proposed.

Some would contend that any source analysis of the gospel is, however, impossible. This is so, they maintain, because of the peculiar nature of the Fourth Gospel. First, apart from those passages in which there seems to be some contact with synoptic passages, the source critic has nothing with which to compare the Johannine material. The source analysis of the Synoptic Gospels has been fruitful because a source methodology could work with the comparison of the three synoptics. Such is not the case with the Fourth Gospel, leaving the source critic without a fundamental basis for a credible method. Second, it is observed that, whatever sources the fourth evangelist used, the content of those sources has been thoroughly integrated with the Johannine literary style and theological perspective. The effect is that the evangelist has concealed the sources within the document, thus making it impossible to detect their influence upon the work.

Finally, there is no accepted method for source analysis of the Fourth Gospel. It is the method for detecting evidence of the use of sources which is crucial for the defense of any source analysis of the Fourth Gospel. What shall count as evidence that a source was employed in the composition of any given passage?

The criteria for source detection are usually of four kinds. First, stylistic features figure prominently in some methods. Variations from what is taken to be the general style of the gospel may signal the intrusion of source material (e.g., the use of different words for "boat" in 6:17 and 6:22). Once a source has been reconstructed, it is necessary to show that it has some stylistic unity. Second, *aporia* ("a difficulty") in the text may be an indication of the use of a source. That is, when there seems to be a break in the flow of the narrative or discourse, it may be due to the inclusion of a source. A classic example is 14:31, followed as it is by two additional chaps. of discourse. Third, form criticism has been invoked as a means of identifying sources. This method calls for the establishment, first, of the normative Johannine forms (e.g., the long narrative followed by a discourse in which the narrative is interpreted) and, second, the identification of passages which depart from those normal forms (e.g., the short healing narratives such as 4:46–53). The variant forms, it is argued, were drawn from a source. Finally, content or ideological tension may be taken as evidence of the use of a source. When a passage expresses an idea which contradicts another idea widely expressed in the gospel, one might assume that this passage has been included in the gospel from a source which taught a view different from the one advocated by the evangelist. A proposed example of such is in the positive view of signs expressed in 2:11 contrasted with 20:29. There is, unfortunately, no agreement on the relative validity of these criteria, and they are used in varying degrees and roles in source analyses.

It is seldom denied, however, that behind the Fourth Gospel resides an *oral* tradition which was rooted in pre-Johannine Christian history and then preserved and shaped by the Johannine community itself. Those not inclined to find evidence of a literary dependence on the Synoptic Gospels would contend that the synoptic contacts in the Fourth Gospel are due to the roots of the Johannine tradition in a common Christian tradition. In the process of the preservation and nurturing of that tradition, the Johannine community gave the Jesus material a peculiar interpretation and translated it into its own unique imagery and language. Thus, for instance, the saying attributed to Jesus in 12:25 demonstrates by its similarity with Mark 8:35 (and parallels) its basis in a common tradition shared by both the synoptic and Johannine communities. But the peculiar language (e.g., "loves-hates") and concepts (e.g., "world" and "eternal life") of 12:25 reflect the manner in which the saying has been preserved within the Johannine thought world.

It is sometimes argued that the fourth evangelist wrote the gospel directly from such oral tradition. Thus the author gave literary expression for the 1st time to a tradition that had before been only oral. But it might also be the case that the Johannine oral tradition had taken various written forms before the composition of the Fourth Gospel, and the evangelist may have used those written pieces in the production of the gospel along with oral traditions. Whether or not evidence of such written sources can be discerned in the gospel is a debated point.

The most widely held proposal for a literary source is that of a *signs source.* A number of things in the gospel contribute to the effort to reconstruct such a source: The presence of the series of wonder stories in the narrative, the unique use of the word, *sēmeia* ("signs"), to designate such wonders, the numbering of the signs in 2:11 and 4:54, and the reference to signs in the conclusion of the gospel. It is further proposed that the delicate and complicated attitude toward the role of signs in nurturing faith found throughout the gospel is explained by the fact that the evangelist was using a collection of wonder stories which purported a view of signs about which there was some reservation on the part of the author of the gospel. What is proposed is that there was a collection of the wonders of Jesus circulating within the Johannine community prior to the writing of the gospel. That collection was absorbed in part into the content of the gospel. Efforts to reconstruct such a signs source from the gospel vary. At one extreme is the argument that it contained not only the wonders narrated in the gospel, but also the calling of the disciples in 1:19–51 and a passion story. At the other extreme is the suggestion that the collection was little more than seven wonder stories told consecutively. Some such thesis is embraced by a large number of Johannine scholars, but by no means has agreement been reached on such a proposal. See also SIGNS/SEMEIA SOURCE.

A second hypothesis is that a *saying source* was employed by the fourth evangelist. However, discourse has proven to be even more difficult for the source critic than narrative material. This is due, in large part, to the homogeneous style and content of the discourses. Still, at least two efforts are worthy of mention here. The first is Rudolf Bultmann's famous "Revelation Discourses" hypothesis in which he argued that the fourth evangelist employed a collection of sayings which originated in a pre-Christian gnostic community. The second is a less developed theory which argues that the discourses in part stem from homilies originating in the Johannine community which were collected and then incorporated into the gospel. One clue to such homilies in the Johannine discourses has been their midrashic quality, that is, the way in which they often elucidated an OT passage (e.g. 6:25–59). The effort to delineate a sayings source has not only been difficult; it has been rare. When it has been undertaken, it has been met with little scholarly acceptance.

Finally, many would agree that, if the evangelist was not dependent upon the Synoptic Gospels, the passion narrative reflects the influence of a source. Efforts to reconstruct such a *passion source* are seldom attempted. It is, nonetheless, widely assumed that some such source of a passion narrative was at the evangelist's disposal.

In general it must be concluded that the source analysis of the Fourth Gospel has been unsuccessful in delineating clear blocks of material which have been incorporated into the gospel from earlier documents. The enterprise has failed to influence scholarly treatment of the gospel in any comprehensive way.

3. Theories of Composition and Redaction. The solution to the difficulties of the Fourth Gospel may reside less in the question of the sources employed by the fourth evangelist than in the process by which the document was composed. Those difficulties often cited by source critics as the criteria for the isolation and reconstruction of the sources adapted by the author may better be explained by the process by which the gospel was written. What is proposed is that the gospel was not written in its entirety by its author in one single, short period of time. Rather, it is the result of a process which may have involved several editions of the gospel, plus revision at the hand of still another or several authors. Such "developmental" theories of composition have become widely discussed and embraced in scholarly circles.

For purposes of summary it may be said that these theories of composition fall into two types. The first emphasizes that the composition process involved a number of stages in which the gospel was gradually expanded into its present form. The earliest stage might have entailed the production of a "pre-gospel" out of oral tradition (and perhaps on the basis of some early literary source). That pre-gospel was then edited and expanded on a number of occasions until it reached a completed form. Often it is argued that there is no reason to think that a single author was not responsible for this whole of the process. The completed gospel then underwent some final revisions, most likely at the hand of another author (the redactor).

Less influential has been the proposals which suggest that the process involved a "basic gospel" which has been revised a number of times. The "basic gospel" hypothesis imagines a less evolutionary emergence of the present gospel and is less inclined to attribute so much of the process to a single author. A foundational and complete gospel was produced. That document was then radically revised once or twice at the hands of several persons and finally (perhaps) revised in minor ways to produce the present gospel. It is usually argued that the extensive revisions involved reordering of the basic gospel. For instance, the narrative of the cleansing of the Temple was placed toward the close of the ministry of Jesus in the basic gospel and moved in one of the subsequent revisions; and the three Passover structures of the present gospel were imposed upon the basic gospel in a later revision.

It is generally recognized that some revision-redaction of the gospel did take place, regardless of how one views the process of composition. Chap. 21 is almost universally acknowledged as a later addition to the gospel which ended at 20:31. Such testimony to the work of a redactor has encouraged scholars to look for redaction elsewhere in the gospel. Some understand that the completed gospel underwent extensive redaction with numerous additions, others that the final redaction was minimal (e.g., only the addition of chap. 21). The passages which seem to address the sacraments are sometimes thought to be redactional. Some maintain that "water and" in 3:5 and the discourse in 6:51–59 are insertions of a later hand by one interested in strengthening the explicit sacramental teachings of the gospel. It has been recently argued that portions of chaps. 13–17 come from a redactor at the time of the writing of the Johannine epistles some ten years or more after the completion of the gospel. While it has often been maintained that the prologue in 1:1–18 was a hymn incorporated into the gospel, it has also been argued that this passage was added to the gospel after its completion.

While none of these theories—a literary dependence upon one or more of the Synoptic Gospels, the use of other sources, or the process of composition—adequately solves all of the problems posed by the Fourth Gospel, they each make contributions toward a better way of reading the document. While often these three distinct approaches to the composition of the gospel are set in opposition to each other, there is no reason to view them as exclusive of one another. That is to say that the author of the gospel may have used one or more of the synoptics along with other sources in a lengthy process of composition.

G. Theology

The theological nature of the Fourth Gospel has long been recognized. It is clear that the fourth evangelist was concerned to nurture the readers through the explication of a number of theological themes important to the Johannine community. It is clear, too, that the evangelist possessed a certain theological acumen. Therefore, the analysis of the gospel in terms of its religious teachings has persistently been one of the major efforts of the scholarly enterprise.

But it has not been an easy task, for the gospel evades systematic and clear elucidation. Among the significant tasks for the theological critic are these: First, some religious-philosophical setting must be established for the concepts used in the gospel. This has not been easy, and efforts to focus the religious background of the thought of the gospel have run the gamut of the options in the 1st century Greco-Roman world. Increasingly, however, a strong case has emerged for looking first of all to the Hebraic tradition and Judaism for the conceptuality which most influenced the fourth evangelist. Second, the theological critic must employ conceptual patterns which convey the thought of the author without doing violence to them. In particular this has involved the task of suspending, insofar as possible, modern conceptuality to allow the concepts of the gospel to speak for themselves. Third, the theological critic must come to grips with the conceptual tensions (or "paradoxes") expressed in the gospel and try to understand the theological method of a writer who employed such tensions. Fourth, the theological critic must contend with the fact that theological themes are hopelessly intertwined with one another in the Fourth Gospel, so that it is nearly impossible to isolate one theme for elucidation without thereby being forced to treat a number of related themes.

Notwithstanding such difficulties in the task, there is much to be learned from John with regard to the view of one segment of early Christianity.

1. Christ. At the heart of the theological concern of the fourth evangelist stands a view of Christ and everything else seems inseparably tied into that view. But typical of the mind(s) represented in the gospel that the singularly significant view is marvelously complex and is comprised of a series of motifs. The gospel explores a variety of images as means of expressing the relationship between Jesus and God and between Jesus and humanity.

While one may be suspicious that any distinction between "person" (or "nature") and "function" (or "work") is a modern and not a Johannine one, it appears to be the case that the evangelist strove to articulate the unique function and identity of Jesus. The gospel accomplishes this task by means of a number of images used of Christ.

a. God and the Word of God. Among the images employed to express the identity of Jesus are two which make the bold assertion that Jesus is God. The first of these is the use of the title, *logos* (Word), for Jesus in 1:1–18. The search for the religious and philosophical background out of which this title was drawn has led only to the recognition of the enormous breadth of meaning the word carried in 1st century Greek. It had associations with the creative and prophetic work of God in the OT and had become identified with both Torah and Wisdom in Jewish thought. Among Hellenists the word had a philosophical heritage which equated it, among other things, with the rational center of being itself. Very likely the word was chosen for its wide meaning, encompassing as it did both Hellenistic and Hebraic shades of meaning. Typical of the evangelist's love of words with multiple meanings, it engages the reader—regardless of his or her background—on the very first page of the gospel. It is clear, however, that the evangelist meant to claim that Jesus was the self-expression of God—the revealed, public side of the divine being. By claiming that Jesus is the Word of God the author supposes that Jesus is the divine medium of communication with humanity.

The Word is said both to be God and to be with *(pros)* God (1:1). The language suggests both identification with God and distinctive individuality—a paradoxical relationship typical of Johannine christological reflection. The existence of the Word precedes creation, and it is through the Word that creation is accomplished (1:2–3). The Word, therefore, is the "life" and "light" of humanity, i.e., the source of authentic and meaningful existence. Through the Word God sought to restore the divine human relationship, empowering humans to become "children of God," although such efforts were rejected (1:10–12). In Jesus the Word became incarnate and manifested the identity and nature of God (1:14).

As the prologue began with the assertion that Jesus (the Word) is God, so it would appear to end. 1:18 is marred by a textual problem but may have originally spoken of Jesus as the "only God" *(monogenēs theos)*. As the gospel began with the assertion that Jesus is God, so the gospel concludes with the confession of Thomas, "My Lord and my God" (20:28). Thus by identifying Jesus with the Word and attributing to him the title, God, the fourth evangelist boldly claims the divine identity of the central figure of the gospel. This is reinforced by the fact that Jesus is made to claim that to know and to see him is to know and see the Father (8:19; 14:9), a further articulation of 1:18.

Several additional suggestions have been offered with regard to the meaning of the confession, "Lord and God," in 20:28. The first is that the two titles encompass both the common name for the deity in Hellenistic and Jewish thought of the 1st century. Consequently, Thomas' confession makes a universal claim for the divinity of Christ. The second suggestion is that in Hellenistic Judaism the title, God, represented the creative power of the deity, and the title, Lord, the eschatological power of the deity. Thus, Thomas' confession is understood to attribute the two definitive divine powers to Christ.

It should be noted that pre-existence is claimed for Jesus in 17:24 as well as 1:1. (8:58 may also imply such a view.) While such a claim is not unique to the Fourth Gospel (cf., e.g., Col 1:15–16), nowhere else is it accompanied with such a clear identification of Christ with God.

This high and unequaled NT assertion regarding Jesus demonstrates the author's concern to say that Jesus is the one in whom humans encounter the true revelation of God. That concern is manifested in the other images used of Jesus. But associated with it is the necessity to claim that Jesus is related to the One he reveals. In this case, the claim is made that he is fully identified with the God whom he reveals.

b. The "I Am". Another image of Jesus, equally bold, may also address the concern to proclaim Jesus' identification with the One he reveals. One of the unique features of the gospel is the frequent appearance of the emphatic "I am" *(egō eimi)* on the lips of Jesus. These are of three types. The first is the formula with a predicate (e.g., 11:25). Although this formula has been discussed in terms of a peculiar revelatory expression of a revealer god, it may be explained as a simple emphatic assertion. The second appearance of the formula is with an implied predicate (e.g., 6:20). But it is the third type which is most provocative. It is the use of the absolute "I am" without either an explicit or implicit predicate. Such expressions occur at least four times (8:24, 28, 58; 13:19).

There is common agreement that the use of the bare "I am" suggests at least a claim for divine authority, if not divine identity. There is less agreement as to the religious setting from which such a formula was drawn. The Hermetic writings, for instance, provide ample evidence of the propensity for the god to speak with the "I am" expression. Still, evidence for the absolute use of the formula is not readily found in Hellenistic literature. It seems clear that the usage is drawn from the OT tradition and suggests the sacred name of God in Exod 3:14. The LXX employs the "I am" in Isa 41:4; 43:10; 46:4 in rendering the speech of Yahweh.

The absolute formula implies Jesus' self-claim of divine identity and authority. This is borne out in a number of passages in the gospel. With the utterance of the *egō eimi* in 6:20 the boat wondrously reaches land immediately. In 8:58 the expression evokes the effort to stone Jesus. In the story of the arrest of Jesus the simple, "I am," in reply to the guards' inquiry causes them to fall back upon the ground (18:6). Such a use of the absolute formula suggests that the formula accompanied with a predicate is no less a revelatory expression.

The sacred name for God is placed on the lips of Jesus as a means by which the evangelist claims divine status for the main character of the story. In effect, the evangelist has employed another means of suggesting the divine identity and function of Jesus.

c. Son Titles. One of the most frequent titles for Jesus in the Gospel of John is "son." "The Son" is used seventeen times. "Son of man" is found thirteen times; "Son of God" eight times; "only Son" three times; and "only Son of God" once. It is clear that the son titles represented an important image in the thought of the fourth evangelist and one by which special claims for the identity and function of Jesus are made.

The simple title, "son," suggests an intimate relationship between God and Christ. It is said that the Father loves the Son (3:35), gives him authority (17:2), and bestows on him the power of judgment (5:22, 27). The Son does nothing on his own but only imitates the Father (6:38) and teaches only what has been given to him to say (8:28, 40; 12:49–50; 17:8, 14, 16–18). While the Father and the Son are said to be one (10:30; 17:11, 22), the Son is dependent on the Father (5:30, 36) and obeys the Father (8:25; 10:15; 15:10, 15). The Father is greater than the Son (14:28). Significantly, it is claimed that a response to the Son constitutes a response to God (3:18; 12:47–48). Divine functions are assigned to the Son, e.g., to bestow life and eternal life (6:44; 3:36).

As if to underline the uniqueness of the relationship implied in sonship, the evangelist four times uses the expression, "only" *(monogenēs)* to modify a son title (1:14; 3:16, 18; and possibly 1:18). This would seem to guard against any tendency to reduce the significance of the title to that which might be claimed by a human who stands in relationship with God as a "son".

Whether the son title was intended to suggest function exclusively is frequently debated. It is clear that, as the Father's Son, Jesus is given functions preserved elsewhere for God only (e.g., judgment, 8:16, resurrection of the dead, 6:39–40, and bestowal of life, 10:28; 11:25–26). But function here seems to make a correlative claim for divine identity. The son title connotes a unique bond of both identity and function between Jesus and God.

The titles, Son and only Son, are unique to the Fourth Gospel and its christology (cf., however, Matt 11:27). But the evangelist also employs the two more traditional son titles, "Son of man" and "Son of God". The first is used in two associations it has in the Synoptic Gospels, namely, with the cross and eschatological themes. The Johannine Son of man appears in conjunction with the expressions "lifted up" (3:14; 8:28; 12:34), "glorified" (12:23, 34; 13:31, 32), and "ascending" (3:13; 6:62)—all Johannine articulations of the meaning of the cross (cf. 2 below). 1:51 is still another use of the Son of man title which some argue is associated with the cross. The evangelist also uses the title to speak of the benefits of the crucifixion (6:27, 53). But it further appears in conjunction with judgment, which is said to be both present (9:39) and at the end of the age (5:27).

The less frequent title, Son of God, appears most often in its traditional role as a messianic designation (1:34, 49; 10:36; 11:27; 19:7; 20:31). It is likewise used in connection with eschatological themes, namely, judgment (3:18) and resurrection (5:25).

It is clear that the evangelist has employed the "Son of man" and "Son of God" titles from Christian tradition, but modified them in accord with the peculiar Johannine perspective. The traditional use of the "Son of man" title in association with the cross and eschatology is preserved but not without the special Johannine view of the two themes. The "Son of God" title is continued as a messianic claim but is set within the context of the Johannine understanding of what he is and does (e.g., he bestows "life," 20:31).

Most significantly the evangelist and/or the community fashioned the titles, Son and only Son, as a means to express all that was preserved in the two older son titles and perhaps even more. Through their unique son titles they sought to explore the relationship between Christ and God and to bring to a bolder and more radical affirmation the claim of absolute identity between the two without sacrificing the unique individuality of each.

d. The One Sent. Perhaps the most prominent of the images employed for Jesus in the gospel is that of one who has been sent (e.g., 5:24, 30; 10:36; 11:42; 12:44–45; 17:8; 20:21). The verbs employed in these statements alternate between *apostellō* and *pempō*. Efforts to discern some nuance of difference between the meaning of the two verbs with regard to the sending of Jesus have been attempted but with little success. It appears, rather, that the evangelist varies the verb as a means of stylistic richness and nothing more.

Christ here is conceived of as a special envoy of God

within the conceptuality of the 1st century Greco-Roman world. It has been suggested that the formula of being a "sent one" is investiture language whereby the envoy was given the authority of the sender and should, therefore, be accorded the same dignity as the sender. But the language also recalls the ancient Hebraic notion of the prophet of God, sent with the "Word of the Lord".

The result of this sort of language is to say once again that a response to Christ constitutes a response to God, which is perhaps the central theme of Jesus christological thought. It suggests that Jesus is one given a divine commission and standing in a special relationship with the divine Sender. Above all, however, it constitutes the christological credentials of the Johannine Jesus—his mission from the Father is what validates his claims (17:21).

e. Origin and Destiny. Being sent connotes origin and that image is tied with the picture of the Johannine Jesus as one who has come into this world from another realm and will eventually depart again to return to his original home. This picture is comprised of a number of metaphors for the origin and destiny of Jesus.

Jesus does not belong to this world but to some heavenly realm (8:23; 17:16; 18:36). He is then from "above" (*anō,* 8:23; *epanō,* 3:31), as opposed to others who are from "below" *(katō).* Jesus' origin is unknown to those who do not believe and is crucial knowledge for a proper understanding of his identity (8:14).

So Jesus is said to have descended (*katabainō,* 3:13; 6:33, 38, 41, 42, 50, 51, 58) and will once again ascend (*anabainō,* 3:13; 6:62; 20:17). The same language of movement is used of Jesus' return to the Father—he is said "to go away" (*hypagō,* 7:33; 8:14, 21, 22; 13:3, 33, 36; 14:4, 5; 16:5, 10, 17). The metaphor uses space to speak of the unique origin and destiny of Jesus.

Such images of the origin and destiny of Jesus fit the christology of the gospel within the dualistic structure of the evangelist's thought (cf. 3 below) and present Jesus as a "foreigner" in this worldly realm. As such Jesus is portrayed as one who comes from the divine into the human realm there to reveal that which humans must know about God and themselves to live an authentic life as it was intended by the Creator. This image seems to say in different words what is suggested by the image of Jesus as God's special envoy.

Through use of these five images, along with less frequent ones, the fourth evangelist has attempted to structure a claim for the absolute uniqueness of Jesus. Jesus is, above all, one who reveals God and the salvific intent of God. But such a revelation is possible only for one who participates in a special relationship with God. That relationship, the evangelist claims, is of a such a kind that Christ may be given the titles and functions of divinity.

But we miss the point of Johannine christology if we fail to see the evangelist's purpose is this portrayal. It is not simply to present a case for the divinity of Christ. That may have been one of the issues pressed upon the Johannine Christians by the dialogue with the synagogue. The purpose of the evangelist was not without an apologetic dimension. But it is the kerygmatic dimension which surfaces as central. The evangelist wants to say through the christological images that it is alone in the revelation of God in Christ that humans gain access to the benefits of a proper relationship with their Creator. The purpose of the christology of the gospel is to say that one's relationship with Christ is determinative of one's relationship with God. That kerygmatic purpose, too, has its roots in the relationship of the Johannine community with the synagogue, for it is the Christians' affirmation of Christ which gives them their essential identity over against their Jewish opponents.

2. The Cross. Soteriology is hardly separable from christology in the Fourth Gospel, since it is the view of Christ as the revealer of the Father which constitutes the salvific opportunity for humanity. Revelation comprises the central soteriological theme. The revelation is in itself saving (e.g., 14:7). But at the heart of the revelation is the cross and resurrection, and the Johannine view of the cross is like none other in the NT. Through a variety of themes the evangelist describes of the meaning of Jesus' death.

a. Enthronement. The cross is viewed in the Fourth Gospel as the enthronement of Jesus as king. This is evident in a number of ways. First, the expression, "lifted up" *(hypsoō)* is used four times to refer to the crucifixion (3:14; 8:28; 12:32, 34). These passages have been said to function in a manner similar to the three passion predictions of the synoptic tradition (e.g., Mark 8:31; 9:12; 10:33–34). As noted above (C.4), the Greek verb was used of both the lifting up of one on a cross and the enthronement of a royal figure. With this verb the evangelist expresses the enigma of the cross—it is both a scandalous death and the act by which Christ assumes his rightful position as king of humanity.

Second, the enthronement motif is expressed in the ironic title placed on the cross by Pilate, "Jesus of Nazareth, the King of the Jews" (19:19), as well as by the discussion of kingship in the trial of Jesus before Pilate. It is in that discussion that the essential question emerges—is it Caesar or Christ who is the authentic king (18:33; 19:15)? There, too, the true nature of Christ's kingship is articulated (18:36).

Third, it is the kingly posture of Jesus throughout the trial and crucifixion which underlines the meaning of the cross as an enthronement. Jesus is never really a victim throughout this ordeal but is always in control of the situation. He allows himself to be arrested (18:1–11) and is able to alter the course of events should he choose to do so (19:11). His death is a voluntary act in which he hands over his spirit (19:30). He is buried in a virgin tomb, as a king would be buried (19:41).

It is in the cross, then, that the true identity of Jesus is declared, as he is elevated to his status as the rightful ruler of creation.

b. Glorification and Ascension. The fourth evangelist understands the cross as a "glorification" of Jesus—the act by which divine presence is poured out upon Jesus. "Glory" *(doxa)* in Johannine theology seems to mean the revelation of God's presence. In Christ the divine reality is perceived through the eyes of faith (1:14; 2:11). "Glorification," therefore, is the manifestation of that divine presence.

Jesus is made to speak of the cross as his glorification (e.g., 12:23; 17:1, 5). The evangelist uses the expression almost as a synonym for crucifixion (e.g., 7:39; 12:16). The glorification of Christ is the glorification of God (13:31–32; 17:1). Consequently, as the cross reveals the true identity of Son, it reveals the presence and identity of the Father. It is in the cross that God makes the divine presence known to the world. This is to say that the cross is salvific in that the cross is the revelation of God.

Closely aligned with the theme of glorification is that of ascension. The cross is viewed as part of the process by which Jesus returns to his divine origin. It is closely tied to the resurrection as a part of the ascending process, since Jesus ascends to his Father in the act of rising from the dead after having laid down his life (20:17). The cross and the resurrection are the means by which Jesus departs ("goes away," *hypagō,* 16:7). It is the completion of the sojourn of the revealer of God in this human realm (19:30).

It is evident that the evangelist saw the crucifixion, resurrection, and ascension as a single event in which time distinctions were transcended. Consequently, the cross is not viewed as the tragedy overcome in the resurrection, as much as it is taken to be the first stage of a revelatory occurrence. The cross cannot be separated from the resurrection, nor the resurrection from the cross. Both are dimensions of the manifestation of the divine presence in connection with the person and ministry of Jesus.

Again, the ascension-return theme is understood as revelation of God, and revelation is understood to have salvific effect.

c. The New Passover. The Passover pervades the entirety of the ministry of Jesus (2:13; 6:4; 11:55). The fourth evangelist obviously wanted to set the Christ event within the framework of the Exodus-Passover theme (cf., 6:1–59). In the passion story this is equally clear. Jesus is made to die at the very time the lambs are being slaughtered in preparation for the Passover meal that same evening (19:14—cf. B.2 above). The symbolism suggests that Christ is to be viewed as the new Passover lamb by which God liberates humanity from oppression, just as Israel was freed from slavery in Egypt with the first Passover. The point would seem to be that the cross is the revelation of God which unleashes a power to free humans from oppressive forces which hamper their being children of God (1:12). The title, "lamb of God," in 1:29 and 36 may mean the Passover lamb, although it has also been understood to refer to the sacrificial lamb or the apocalyptic lamb of Revelation.

This poses the question of whether one is to find in the Fourth Gospel the understanding of the cross as cultic sacrifice, as this is expressed, for instance, in 1 John 2:2. While Jesus' death is clearly viewed as an act of sacrifice (e.g., 15:13), the effort to explicate this theme in terms of analogies drawn from sacrificial cultic worship are notably absent. That the killing of the lambs for the Passover meal was regarded as a sacrifice by 1st century Judaism is uncertain. The lamb of God is said to "take away the sins of the world" (1:29), and that may be the one clear fragment of a cultic analogy for the death of Jesus to be found in the gospel. However, given the meaning of the passion narrative, it is safer to assume that the evangelist understood Jesus as the Passover lamb who removed sin by virtue of the revelation that frees humans from sin.

d. The Supreme Act of Divine Love. Jesus interprets his death as the supreme act of love (15:13)—an act which transforms the relationship of the believers to him from that of servants to "friends". The cross, therefore, emerges as the model of divine love.

Recognizing the cross as the revelation of God's love for humanity sheds light upon five other significant passages. First, the cross is spoken of as the divine "drawing" *(helkō)* of humans to God (12:32). If the cross is the supreme act of divine love, the drawing power is the power of love. Second, the cross is presented in parabolic form in 12:24. It is a death which yields results, as the planting of a seed produces growth. The death of Jesus is understood as the sprouting of divine love—the revelation of that love which saves humans from their predicament.

Third, the cross is presented in an acted parable in the foot washing. The washing of the disciples' feet is interpreted as a cleansing. The cleansing is a washing in the love mentioned in 3:16. Fourth, in 11:50 the cross is declared to be the death of one person on behalf of the whole people. It is an act of self-giving love for the sake of the results it yields for others.

Finally, the cross creates a new family of God (19:26–27). This is an often debated passage, but the proposal is that it be seen as the closure of the theme introduced in 1:12. By the cross the believers, represented by the beloved disciple, are brought into Jesus' family, represented by the mother of Jesus. It is an expression of love which draws humans together into a new family grouping (cf. 11:52).

Again, the meaning of the cross is found in its revelatory character. As it reveals the love of God for humans, it saves them from life in alienated lovelessness.

3. Dualism. The readers of the Fourth Gospel are made to feel that they stand in the midst of a divided reality. The entire thought of the gospel is framed within the bounds of a dualism between that which represents authentic life in relationship with God and that which represents inauthentic life without relationship with God.

The dualism is presented in the gospel with a series of symbolic polarities: Light and darkness (e.g., 1:5), above and below (e.g., 8:23), life and death (e.g., 3:36), truth and falsehood or lie (e.g., 8:44–45), heaven and earth (e.g., 3:31), God and the devil (8:42–44). In every case Christ is the representative of the positive pole, and believers are aligned with that pole. Opponents are, on the other hand, affiliated with the negative pole—that which opposes God, Christ, and the believer.

Two other dualistic symbols dominate the gospel. The first is the pejorative use of the word, "world" *(kosmos).* In some cases, the world is used in a neutral sense to describe the realm of human life and activity (e.g., 1:9; 16:21). But more often the word seems to stand for the realm of evil set over against the revelation. The world hates the believer but embraces the unbeliever (7:7; 15:18). Christ and the believers are not of the world, while unbelievers are (8:23; 15:19; 17:14). The "ruler" of the world is the satanic figure (12:31; 14:30). The world cannot receive the Spirit (14:17) and rejoices in Jesus' suffering (16:20). The world produces tribulation for the believers (16:33).

It is obvious that "world" is sometimes used to represent one of the negative poles of the Johannine dualism as a cipher for that which is opposed to Christ and the revelation.

Another dualistic symbol employed by the evangelist is the negative references to "the Jews". There is a variety of uses of this term in the gospel, to be sure. In some cases it is used in a purely descriptive sense of the Jewish people and their heritage (e.g., 4:22). Other times it is used of a crowd of people, and there seems to be no negative flavor to the expression (e.g., 11:19). The Jews are sometimes said to be among those who believe in Jesus (e.g., 8:31).

But more often the term designates opponents of Jesus who are hostile to him and his message. Examples include 5:16, 18; 6:41; 7:1; 9:18, 22; 10:31; 11:8; 18:12; 19:14–15. Many efforts have been made to explain these pejorative uses of the expression. It has been proposed that "the Jews" means Judeans, as opposed to Galileans, and that sometimes does appear to be the case (e.g., 11:19). It is also clear that the term functions to designate the religious leaders, so that it may be used interchangeably with "the Pharisees" (e.g., 9:13 and 18) and the "chief priests" (19:14 and 15). But often "the Jews" stands for those who are unbelievers, hostile to Jesus and the revelation.

What is the reason for this dualistic scheme? It is one of the features of Johannine theology best understood in terms of the setting of the gospel (cf. D.2 above). The Johannine community expelled from the synagogue has a sense of themselves as an enclave of believers in a hostile world. The mentality has been described as "sectarian," meaning that they conceived of themselves as the possessors of the truth while all those around them live in error. Because of this dualistic social reality, the community imposed such a dualistic scheme upon the cosmos. They experienced their own fellowship as "light" over against the "darkness" of unbelief, and hence understood the whole of reality in this manner. The pejorative use of the term "the world" reflects their sense that the majority in their environment were hostile to them and their beliefs. Because their primary opponents were the Jews of the synagogue, the major opponents of Jesus are spoken of as "the Jews". It is clear that the evangelist had no interest in condemning the Jewish people as a whole and that the pejorative use of "the Jews" only reflects the concrete situation in which the community lived.

The degree to which the evangelist understood this dualism as cosmic is often discussed. In some sense it is surely the case that the whole of reality was conceived of as divided between truth and falsehood. But more important is the fact that the dualism of the gospel presents the readers with two alternatives by which they may live their lives—by faith or by unbelief. The primary function of the dualism is then "existential". That is to say, the impact of the dualistic language is to lead the readers to the point of decision with regard to Christ, i.e., the revelation. By the use of this scheme the evangelist wanted to reinforce the community in their unpopular stand in favor of Christ. But it is their faith in particular which marks them off from the others in their community.

4. Faith. It is through the acceptance of Christ and the revelation that one affiliates with the realm of the "light," "truth," and the "world above". It is by faith that persons move from out of the "world" to become part of the community of God's children. Faith is, then, the positive human response to the revelatory act of God in Christ. It is the personal appropriation of the revelation and its benefits.

The object of the verb "believe" *(pisteuein)* is almost without exception Jesus (cf. 14:1 for a rare exception). The most common constructions with the verb are three in number. The most frequent is "believe in," using the preposition *eis* (e.g. 1:12; 3:18; 12:46). This construction seems to denote a personal allegiance to Jesus. The second construction is the verb with Jesus or his words and works as objects (e.g., 2:22; 4:21; 8:46; 10:37–38; 14:11). Simple trust of Jesus and his message is suggested by this use of the verb. Something quite different is implied by the third construction, the use of the verb with "that" *(hoti)*. In this case, belief has as its object a statement about Jesus (e.g., 8:24; 14:10; 16:30; 17:8).

So, faith is a personal alignment of oneself with Jesus and entrusting him with confidence. But it is also a willingness to accept certain doctrinal statements about Jesus' identity and mission. For the evangelist all of this was part of the process of the faith acceptance of the revelation. It is instructive that for the Johannine community the personal trust of Jesus could not be separated from, but flowed into, the acceptance of creedal statements concerning him. In the Fourth Gospel one witnesses the movement of the understanding of faith toward an intellectual consent to certain propositions about Jesus.

The basis or ground of faith in the Fourth Gospel varies as well. In some cases it is the words of Jesus which become the foundation of faith (e.g., 4:50), in others the works of Jesus (e.g., 10:38; 14:11). Somewhat confusing is the role of the signs as the basis of faith. In a number of passages it is affirmed that the signs do evoke faith and that they are intended to do so (e.g., 2:11, 23; 6:26; 20:30–31). Elsewhere the impression is given that signs are less than a desirable basis of faith (e.g., 4:48; 6:14–15, 30; 10:41). 20:29 may be a clue to the Johannine understanding of signs in relation to faith. Faith is nurtured by the experience of signs and wonders, but the most mature faith does not depend upon "seeing signs" or marvels (cf. 14:11).

Believing is connected with "seeing" and "hearing" Jesus. To "see" Jesus holds within itself the possibility of seeing God (14:8–9), and to "hear" him is an invitation to hear the Father (5:24). By this association it is suggested that faith involves a willingness to perceive beyond the historical Jesus the One whom he reveals. Likewise, faith is associated with knowing (e.g., 8:31–32; 10:38; 6:69; 17:8). Faith as trust involves the intimate relationship between persons and Jesus implied in the Hebraic sense of "know" *(yādaʿ)* and produces a certain confidence in the believer.

The noun, faith *(pistis),* never appears in the Fourth Gospel but the verb always does. This suggests the dynamic character of the act of believing, as the evangelist understood it. Faith is conceived not as a static possession but as a process of trust.

One further characteristic of faith in the Fourth Gospel is on the surface confusing. The evangelist alternates between speaking of faith as if it were an act for which humans are responsible and as if it were a gift for which God alone is responsible. Examples of the first are found in the invitation to believe (e.g., 12:44; 19:35; 20:31) and the command to believe (12:36; 14:11). It is also expressed in the narrative of 6:66–69 in which the freedom to withdraw faith is presumed.

But examples of the second are numerous. Believers are those "given" *(didōmi)* to Jesus (e.g., 6:37; 17:2). They are "drawn" *(helkō)* by the Father (6:44). Believers are determined by their affiliation—whether they are "hearers" of God (8:47), children of God or of the Devil (8:44), "sheep" of Jesus (10:3), or "of the world" (14:17). Other passages which suggest the dominant role of God in determining faith are 12:39–40 and 15:16.

This apparent contradiction is resolved in several different ways by interpreters. Some stress one or the other of the two views represented in the gospel, while others suggest that the contradictory views constitute an intentional paradox.

It may be that this is an instance of a tension between tradition and the evangelist's redaction, supposing that one view is traditional and the other redactional. Whether or not that is the case, the result is that the evangelist holds in tension two quite contradictory thoughts, namely, that humans are free either to believe or not and belief is wholly determined by God's gift of faith. The thought of the gospel balances these two truths with the result that humans are not allowed to credit their faith to their own will but still are responsible for the absence of faith. Faith is ultimately a gift of God, but it is a gift for which humans alone are responsible to accept or reject. The relationship with God offered to humans in Christ is entirely a gift for which humans can take no credit but for the rejection of which they must bear responsibility.

5. Eschatology. The classical ideological tension in the Fourth Gospel is encountered when one attempts an analysis of what the evangelist teaches with regard to the acts of God at the end time. It has long been recognized that the fourth evangelist claims that the ultimate gifts of God, usually associated with the end times of history, are already accessible to the believer in Christ. This claim is made, however, without compromising the future dimension of those gifts. In effect there are two types of eschatological thought in the Fourth Gospel.

The first is the classical futuristic eschatology in which the events of the end times are spoken of as standing out in a future time—resurrection (e.g., 6:39–40, 54), judgment (e.g., 12:48), and eternal life (e.g., 12:25). The promised return of Jesus is mentioned in 14:3, 18, 28, and the intervening time is conceived as a period of tribulation (chaps. 15 and 16) in typical eschatological fashion.

But a present, realized eschatology stands alongside of the futuristic one. Resurrection is conceived as the experience of coming to faith in Jesus (e.g., 5:24) and is a present reality in Christ (11:25–26). Judgment is a present reality for believers (e.g., 3:18), and along with it eternal life is already a possession of—and not simply a promise to—the believers (e.g., 5:24). It is implied that the parousia has occurred in the giving of the Spirit (e.g., 14:3; 16:7).

These apparently contradictory views are not found, as one might suspect, in different parts of the gospel, but rather in close proximity to one another. For instance, in 5:24–26 a present eschatology is asserted and in 5:27–29 a futuristic one. The promise of a future resurrection of the dead is declared in 6:39, 40b, 44b, and 54b; but the believer is said to already have eternal life in 6:40a, 47, 51, 54a, and 58.

Again interpreters are divided on the solution to the juxtaposing of these views. It is suggested that one was the evangelist's view and that the other was the view of a redactor. It is argued that the evangelist intended one as the primary view, and the other to be interpreted in the light of the first. The fact that the views are found side by side in the gospel suggests, however, that here again the evangelist employed a tradition which had one eschatological view and supplemented it with the other view.

It has been proposed that still a third view of eschatology may be present in chaps. 14 and 17. In the first of these chaps. the heavenly home awaiting believers is discussed. It appears to some that the evangelist has in mind the access to this heavenly abode immediately upon death (e.g., 14:3). Chap. 17 speaks of the heavenly perfection and unity the believers will be accorded (e.g., 17:11, 23). However, such an interpretation remains uncertain.

The evangelist seemed to want to say that these eschatological realities are present in the life of the believer, although there is still a future and unfulfilled quality to them. The result of the evangelist's view is that believers are invited to turn their attention from the future to appreciate the quality of Christian existence in the present. But part of that Christian life style is to stand suspended between the present and the future. The evangelist may have wanted to correct an excessively future orientation without dispensing with the value of the future for the believer.

6. The Spirit. Surely one basis for the affirmation of the present eschatological realities in the Christian community is the way in which the evangelist conceived of the presence of the Spirit of God. Because of the presence of the Spirit, eternal life and resurrection are likewise present. The pneumatology of the gospel is rich and intriguing. It is comprised of two components.

The first is the role of the Spirit presented in the major part of the gospel. In many of these passages the Spirit is thought of in a manner not unlike that found elsewhere in the NT. The Spirit is the presence of God (4:24), and the power and character of God given to Jesus (1:32, 33; 3:34). The Spirit provides new life for believers and is the power which moves one into a new existence (3:5–8; 4:23; 6:63). These ideas are found expressed in the unique Johannine style, of course, but they are similar to views of the Spirit expressed in other early Christian literature.

The second dimension of the Johannine pneumatology is, however, unique to the Fourth Gospel, namely, the concept of the Spirit as the Paraclete ("Counselor," *paraklētos*). This view is found exclusively in a series of four passages within the farewell discourses—14:15–17, 26; 15:26–27; 16:7–11, 12–14. Here the Spirit is called the Paraclete. The word had associations with two different environments in Hellenistic Greek. It was a common forensic term, meaning one who speaks on behalf of another, supports, and intercedes for another in a legal setting. However, it was also used in the religious realm of one who brought words of eschatological comfort to the afflicted. It was also used of the proclaimer of religious truth. The Greek word is found only in the Fourth Gospel and in 1 John 2:1 in the NT. See also PARACLETE.

The religious background of the concept of the Paraclete has been explored with several different conclusions. One influential view suggests that the concept came to the Johannine community out of Jewish angelology of the intertestamental period.

The word may have been chosen for its rich and multiple meanings in a manner similar to the use of the word *logos* in 1:1–18. The evangelist (and/or the Johannine community) sought to enliven and enrich the meaning of the Spirit by designating it with this new word—a word which captured and articulated more of the Christian conviction about the identity and work of the Spirit than was possible in more traditional language. In typical Johannine fashion language is used to break open new meaning.

In the Paraclete passages it is said that the origin of the Spirit is divine. It is sent by the Father at the request of the Son (14:16) and in Jesus' name (14:26), or is sent by Jesus himself from the Father (15:26; 16:13). The Paraclete is termed "another Paraclete" (14:16), "the Spirit of Truth" (14:17; 15:26; 16:13), and "the Holy Spirit" (14:26). It comes only as a result of Jesus' departure (16:7, 8, 13). The function of the Paraclete has to do primarily with the believers' life together. The believers alone recognize the Paraclete (14:17), and it dwells within them (14:16–17). For the believers the Paraclete does a number of things. It teaches them (16:13), announces what will happen in the future (16:13), declares what belongs to Christ and what does not (16:14), glorifies (16:14) and witnesses to Christ (15:26), reminds persons of what Jesus said (14:26), and speaks only what it hears and not out of itself (16:13). With regard to those outside the community of faith the Paraclete is unknown and unrecognized (14:17). Consequently the Paraclete functions as a judge of the world (16:8–11).

The Spirit conceived as Paraclete accomplishes a number of things for the fourth evangelist and the Johannine community. (1) It makes Christ present to compensate for what was experienced as abandonment and loss by his departure. (2) It may have answered the doubt caused by the delay of the parousia. (3) It provided a divine strength for the community amid its crisis of isolation from the synagogue. (4) It provided a means by which persons separated by time from the historical revelation in Christ could avail themselves of its benefits. (5) It brought assurance of knowing that the community of faith was correct and the world wrong as to the identity of Christ. (6) It made present the benefits of the Christian life, including eternal life, resurrection, and release from judgment. (7) It provided divine guidance for the interpretation of the Johannine tradition in the light of the crisis caused by the expulsion from the synagogue.

The view of the Spirit in the gospel revises a traditional understanding of the Spirit with a new dimension and new meaning. In particular, it elucidates the role of the Spirit in making the revelation of God in Christ present for the believer.

7. The Sacraments. No other issue so divides modern scholarship as that of the view of the sacraments in the Gospel of John. The debate centers around several facts about the gospel: (1) the apparent silence of the gospel regarding baptism and eucharist, and (2) the way in which some passages seem to speak of those sacramental acts in a veiled or symbolic manner.

The first fact is that the Fourth Gospel presents the reader with no institution of the eucharist. In the place where the synoptics narrate the origin of the eucharist stands the account of the foot washing (13:1–10). The last meal Jesus celebrates with his disciples before his passion is not a Passover meal at all. Thus one of the basic features of the institution scenes in the synoptics is missing. Furthermore, there is no account of the baptism of Jesus, and there is confusion about whether or not Jesus practiced baptism (compare 3:22 and 4:2). Water baptism is treated critically and assigned strictly to the Baptizer in contrast with Spirit baptism (1:26, 31, 33). One is left with the impression that the sacraments of baptism and eucharist did not figure in the theology of the fourth evangelist.

The second fact with which we must contend, however, is that the gospel employs a number of symbols which, at least to the modern readers, call to mind these two sacraments. Many interpreters take the mention of water in 3:5 as a reference to baptismal water and understand 2:1–11 as a veiled allusion to baptism. Most would read 6:51–59 eucharistically. It has been proposed that the foot washing is a symbolic reference to one of the sacraments. 19:34 is also taken by some to mean that the water of baptism and the blood of the eucharist come from the side of Jesus as a result of his death. Still other passages suggest the sacraments to other interpreters (e.g., 15:1–10).

Efforts to understand these two disconcerting facts range widely. Some understand the evangelist to have been a profound sacramentarian who sought to explicate the meaning of the sacraments rather than to narrate their founding. It is thought that the evangelist may have taken the institutional accounts for granted and saw no reason to retell them. The feeding of the multitude and the bread of life discourse in chap. 6, it is proposed, is an effort to read the eucharist back into the ministry of Jesus, thus making any account of an institution of the meal redundant. The discourse in chap. 3 really has to do with the way in which baptism is the means by which the Spirit brings its gift of new life, contend some.

At the other extreme are those who would argue that the evangelist was either an antisacramentarian or else ignorant of the sacraments. They would argue that there is an effort to direct the attention of the readers away from such physical signs as sacraments. It has been proposed that the sacramental passages of the gospel ("water and" at 3:5 and the discourse in 6:51–59) are the results of efforts of a later redactor to write the sacraments into the original gospel which made no mention of them.

Midway between the two extremes are interpreters who proffer that the evangelist sought to revise a view of baptism and the eucharist. For instance, it is argued that the effort was to direct attention to the spiritual meaning of these rites and away from the physical elements involved in them (as in the insistence that Jesus baptizes with the Spirit and not with water—1:26, 33).

The problem is a difficult one, but one might conclude that there is little in the gospel which must be taken as reference to the sacraments. If the gospel did go through a process of composition in which additional materials were added to the document in the light of new experiences in the Johannine community, it may be that the baptismal and eucharistic hints are additions made at a later stage in the composition process. It may be that the community upon its expulsion from the synagogue did not know or practice the sacraments. This would have been the case as a result of their thoroughly Jewish/Christian orientation. Later, however, baptism and the eucharist were introduced or reemphasized as part of their new identity as Christians separated from Judaism. This would account for the fact that the eucharistic section of the bread of life discourse (6:51–59) seems to stand out as a secondary revision of the earlier discourse. It would also explain why there is fleeting reference to water in 3:5. The result is that in the final form of the gospel, as we know it, the sacraments have only begun to emerge as significant. Perhaps in that final stage of composition some of the narratives and sayings of Jesus were beginning to be understood in terms of their sacramental importance.

8. The Church. If little can be said with confidence about the role of the sacraments in the Johannine community, little more can be said with regard to its own ecclesiological self-understanding. Interpreters have asserted that there is no developed doctrine of the Church in the gospel. But others have found extensive reference to a view of the Church in the same document. There are a number of important features of the self-understanding of the community which are ecclesiological in nature, even if one cannot justifiably claim on their basis a full Johannine doctrine of the Church.

First, the Johannine community understood itself as living under the influence of the Paraclete through whom the presence of Christ was made real (cf. 6 above). It is not far from the truth to characterize the Johannine church as charismatic (or, better, pneumatic) insofar as it gained its life and existence from the gift of the Spirit. The second thing which can be said of the Johannine community is that it conceived itself as the enclave of the children of God within a world that shared a far different orientation (1:12; cf. 3 above). To a large degree these two characteristics give the Johannine church its definitive shape.

Third, however, it must be said that the Johannine church understood itself as wedded inseparably to Christ. This is evident in the figure of the vine and branches (15:1–7), as well as in the recurrence of the concept of the mutual indwelling of Christ in the believers and believers in Christ (e.g., 6:56; 17:21, 26). The self-understanding of the Johannine community is christocentric.

Fourth, the Johannine community understood itself as a body sent in mission (4:35–38). Their mission is understood once again on a christocentric model. They are sent, even as Christ was sent (e.g., 17:18; 20:21).

Finally, the Church as it is presented to us in the gospel is a diverse and inclusive community. The mission to the Samaritans suggested by 4:1–42 implies that the community may have contained Samaritans and perhaps others of a diverse background. The tension between the Jewish and Hellenistic features of the gospel may be explained by the fact that persons of both backgrounds were part of the community. Furthermore, the prominence of women in the Gospel of John suggests that the community was inclusive in membership and leadership. Mary Magdalene is honored as the first to meet the resurrected Christ and to be sent forth with the news of the resurrection (20:11–18), and other women are portrayed in a positive manner (e.g., 4:1–42; 12:1–8).

H. Value

The value of the Fourth Gospel was debated in the early Church and continues to be a controversial subject. However, a number of clear contributions are made by this gospel. Not least among them is its literary quality (cf. C above). But two other kinds of contributions may be narrowed out for further discussion.

1. The Historical Jesus. In past decades the Fourth Gospel has been dismissed as valueless when it came to the investigation of the historical Jesus. It was thought that John was the "spiritual" or theological gospel that had little interest in the history of the founder of Christianity. More recently, however, that view has been shown to be false for several reasons. First, redaction criticism has demonstrated that the Synoptic Gospels are equally as interested in advancing certain theological ideas as is the fourth. The synoptics as well as John put history to the service of proclamation. Second, the study of the Fourth Gospel has opened avenues for a different assessment of its historical basis. It is rooted in a primitive tradition, just as are the synoptics. It is not necessarily dated as late as some would have thought a century ago (cf. E.1 above). Traditional words and acts of Jesus may in principle be presented in the Fourth Gospel.

In particular there is something to be said for the historicity of the three year ministry of Jesus, as presented in the Fourth Gospel. To be sure, the threefold Passover scheme may be present for theological reasons, but it may nonetheless reflect historical reality. Furthermore, there is no reason to doubt in principle that some of the unique narratives of the Fourth Gospel may have historical roots (e.g., a mission to the Samaritans, 4:1–42). Nor are the words of Jesus necessarily only the product of the mind of the fourth evangelist or the Johannine community. It has been proposed that the discourses may have been a form of midrash of traditional sayings of Jesus. It is possible, therefore, that in the discourse passages there resides authentic words of Jesus which have been reinterpreted in the light of the situation of the community.

This is not to argue that the Johannine gospel presents us with a faithful portrayal of the historical Jesus. Clearly that portrayal is thoroughly filtered through Johannine conceptuality and concerns, and the theological interests of the evangelist figure far more prominently than does the representation of history. But the point is that the value of the Fourth Gospel as a source for understanding the historical Jesus is in general no different than that of the other gospels. It must be critically mined for what might be historical, and each individual saying and each feature of every narrative must be evaluated. It may well be that something of the historical Jesus can be discerned amid the Johannine narratives and discourses.

2. Religious Value. Clearly the greatest contribution of the Fourth Gospel lies in its theological teachings. The Christian church has in practice made the Fourth Gospel definitive for a number of its doctrines, in particular the views of Christ, the Spirit, and the Trinity. But it may be that the religious value of the document lies as much in what it exemplifies theologically as what it specifically teaches.

The gospel represents the results of the efforts of a religious community to define its identity amid a life-threatening situation. In doing that the fourth evangelist invoked the tradition of the community and, so far as we can detect, presented that tradition as one of the resources by which the community could survive its situation. The Fourth Gospel exemplifies, first of all, the way in which critical situations necessitate the redefinition of identity and the use of religious tradition for that purpose.

But the evangelist was not content simply to repeat the traditional as an answer to the question of Christian identity. There is ample evidence that the tradition of the Church was reinterpreted, expanded, and reshaped in an effort to make it useful to the Christians in the midst of their crisis. The methodology of the evangelist was to interpret tradition in the light of experience. The implication is that tradition is valuable not in and of itself but only as it is interpreted in the light of contemporary experience and need.

The value of this methodology is that it teaches the contemporary religious community that its traditions must always be read and reread in the light of experience. The value of tradition is lost if it is only propagated for its own sake—repeated as a static content to be received and recited generation after generation. Rather, the value of tradition is found in its very dynamic quality whereby it is subjected to new study and new interpretation within a specific, concrete historical situation.

Bibliography

Ashton, J. ed. 1986. *The Interpretation of John. IRT* 6. Philadelphia and London.

Barrett, C. K. 1975. *The Gospel of John and Judaism.* Trans. D. M. Smith. Philadelphia.

———. 1978. *The Gospel According to St. John.* 2d ed. Philadelphia.

———. 1982. *Essays on John.* Philadelphia.

Beutler, J. 1984. *Habt keine Angst.* SBS 116. Stuttgart.

Borgen, P. 1965. *Bread from Heaven.* NovTSup 10. Leiden.

Bruce, F. F. 1983. *The Gospel of John.* Grand Rapids.

Bultmann, R. 1971. *The Gospel of John.* Trans. G. R. Beasely-Murray. Philadelphia.

Burge, G. M. 1987. *The Anointed Community.* Grand Rapids.

Cullmann, O. 1976. *The Johannine Circle.* Trans. J. Bowden. Philadelphia.

Culpepper, R. A. 1975. *The Johannine School.* SBLDS 26. Missoula, MT.

———. 1983. *The Anatomy of the Fourth Gospel.* Philadelphia.

Dauer, A. 1984. *Johannes und Lukas.* FB 50. Würzburg.

Dodd, C. H. 1953. *The Interpretation of the Fourth Gospel.* Cambridge.

———. 1963. *Historical Tradition in the Fourth Gospel.* Cambridge.

Duke, P. D. 1985. *Irony in the Fourth Gospel.* Atlanta.

Forestell, J. T. 1974. *The Word of the Cross.* AnBib 57. Rome.

Fortna, R. T. 1970. *The Gospel of Signs.* SNTSMS 11. Cambridge.

Howard, W. F. 1955. *The Fourth Gospel in Recent Criticism and Interpretation.* Rev. by C. K. Barrett. London.

Johnston, G. 1970. *The Spirit-Paraclete in the Gospel of John.* SNTSMS 12. Cambridge.

Jonge, M. de. 1977. *Jesus: Stranger from heaven and Son of God.* SBLSBS 11. Missoula, MT.

Käsemann, E. 1968. *The Testament of Jesus.* Trans. G. Krodel. Philadelphia.

Kysar, R. 1975. *The Fourth Evangelist and His Gospel.* Minneapolis.

———. 1976. *John, the Maverick Gospel.* Atlanta.

Martyn, J. L. 1978. *The Gospel of John in Christian History.* New York.

———. 1979. *History and Theology in the Fourth Gospel.* Rev. ed. Nashville.

Meeks, W. A. 1967. *The Prophet-King.* NovTSup 14. Leiden.

Minear, P. S. 1984. *John, the Martyrs' Gospel.* New York.

Nicol, W. 1972. *The Semeia in the Fourth Gospel.* NovTSup 14. Leiden.

Nicholson, G. C. 1983. *Death as Departure.* SBLDS 63. Chico, CA.

O'Day, G. R. 1987. *Revelation in the Fourth Gospel.* Philadelphia.

Reim, G. 1974. *Studien zum Alttestamentlichen Hintergrund des Johannesevangeliums.* SNTSMS 22. Cambridge.

Robinson, J. A. T. 1985. *The Priority of John,* ed. J. F. Coakley. London.

Schnackenburg, R. 1968–82. *The Gospel According to St. John.* 3 vols. Trans. K. Smyth. New York.

Segovia, F. F. 1982. *Love Relationships in the Johannine Tradition.* SBLDS 58. Chico, CA.

Smith, D. M. 1965. *The Composition and Order of the Fourth Gospel.* New Haven.

———. 1984. *Johannine Christianity.* Columbia, SC.

Wengst, K. 1981. *Bedrängte Gemeinde und verherrlichter Christus.* BibS (N) 5. Neukirchen-Vluyn.

Whitacre, R. A. 1982. *Jesus Polemic.* SBLDS 67. Chico, CA.

Woll, D. B. 1981. *Johannine Christianity in Conflict.* SBLDS 60. Chico, CA.

ROBERT KYSAR

JOIADA (PERSON) [Heb *yôyādāᶜ*]. Var. JEHOIADA. A name which means "Yahu knows". Joiada (LXX *Iōdae, Iōada*) is the contracted form of Jehoiada found elsewhere in the OT and used alternately in English versions (Neh 13:28; Neh 3:6 KJV).

1. A son of Paseah who worked with Messullam to repair the "Old Gate" on the Wall of Jerusalem under Nehemiah (Neh 3:6).

2. A postexilic high priest listed in genealogies as the son of Eliashib (Neh 12:10–11, 22; 13:38). There are two problems with these chronologies. First, there is some confusion concerning the listing of Joiada father of Jonathan (Neh 12:11) and Eliashib, Joiada, Johanan as the succession of high priests (Neh 12:22). Other passages (Ezra 2:43; Neh 12:23) designate Eliashib as the father of Johanan. Williamson (*Ezra, Nehemiah* WBC) notes that these two passages (Ezra 2:43; Neh 12:23) are related and may refer to another Eliashib and Johanan since they were common names. Also in the chronologies of the high priests (Neh 12:10–11; 22), the use of the word, son, does not necessarily mean father and son relationship. Joiada could be Johanan's brother or he could be Eliashib's grandson. Second, there is a problem with the time span of the list given. The list Eliashib to Joiada to Jonathan to Jaddua suggests a time span of 150 years. Williamson (1977) proposes that it is likely that some of the names of high priests have not been included.

Joiada's son who married the daughter of Sanballat the Horonite (Neh 13:28) is used to describe the enforcement of Nehemiah's ban on foreign marriages. The son was banished from Judah but there is no evidence that Joiada's family was punished in any other way.

Bibliography

Williamson, H. G. M. 1977. The Historical Value of Josephus' *Jewish Antiquities XI. 297–301. JTS* 28: 49–66.

GARY C. AUGUSTIN

JOIAKIM (PERSON) [Heb *yôyāqîm*]. A son of Jeshua, the high priest and father of Eliashib (Neh 12:10, 12, 16). His name means "Yahweh raises up" and is a variation of Jehoiakim. His name also occurs in Josephus's *Antiquities*, where he is noted as having died during the Feast of Tabernacles. Because his son Eliashib served as high priest during the time of Nehemiah, his tenure of office can be dated roughly to the early 5th century B.C.

James M. Kennedy

JOIARIB (PERSON) [Heb *yôyārîb*]. Var. JEHOIARIB. A personal name formed with the theophoric element *yô* (an alternate form uses *yĕhô*) and the imperfect of the Hebrew verb *rîb* which means "Yahweh will contend," "Yahweh contends," or "may Yahweh contend" in the sense of conducting a lawsuit or legal case on behalf of someone (*IPN*, 201, 245). The variety of forms of the name and the question whether, in certain instances, it is patronymic makes uncertain a determination of the number of individuals who bear it.

1. One of eleven (Ezra 8:16) sent by Ezra to Iddo at "Casiphia the place" with a request for "ministers for the house of our God" (v 17). He and another—Elnathan—are described as "men of understanding." It has been suggested that both names should be deleted (as does 1 Esdr 8:42–43—Eng 8:43–44) as a marginal gloss (Rudolph *Esra und Nehemia* HAT, 80; Williamson *Ezra-Nehemiah* WBC, 113); that the name may be a longer form of the previously listed Jarib (see Noth *IPN*, 201). This person's name appears in the LXX as *Iōarib* which is also the Greek spelling (RSV Joarib) of the ancestral head of the priestly family from which the family of Mattathias claimed descent (1 Macc 2:1 Codex Vaticanus; 14:29; Jos *Ant* 12.6.1 = *Iōaribos* where the name describes a priestly "division").

2. The son of Zechariah and father of Adaiah (Neh 11:5) who is listed in a linear genealogy of Maaseiah, one of the sons of Judah, who lived in Jerusalem following the return from Exile. His name in the LXX appears variously as *Iōiarib* (Codex Alexandrinus), *Iōreim* (original reading of Codex Sinaiticus) and *Iōrib* (Codex Vaticanus and the corrector of Codex Sinaiticus).

3. One whose name appears in several lists of priests who returned from the Babylonian exile. In the list preserved in Neh 11:10–13, *yôyārîb* (*Iōrib* = codices Vaticanus and Alexandrinus; *Iōreim* = Codex Sinaiticus) is described as the father of Jedaiah (11:10) who is the first-listed of six (Blenkinsopp *Ezra-Nehemiah* OTL, 322, 325), five (Myers *Ezra-Nehemiah* AB, 187, 236) or four (Rudolph *Esra und Nehemia* HAT, 184, who believes *yākîn* is an error for *ben* thus making *yôyārîb* the "son of" Seraiah) houses or groupings of priests whose number totals 1,192. The list in Neh 12:1–7 numbers twenty-two "heads of the priests and of their relatives in the days of Jeshua" the high priest. *Yôyārîb* (LXX = *Iōiarib*) is listed seventeenth (12:6) of those who came up from Babylon with Zerubbabel the governor and Jeshua. In this list, which Williamson (*Ezra, Nehemiah* WBC, 360) and Blenkinsopp (*Ezra-Nehemiah* OTL, 334) believe depends upon the Joiakim list (Neh 12:12–21), the priestly patronymics are represented as actual immigrants. The "master list" (Blenkinsopp *Ezra-Nehemiah* OTL, 335) in Neh 12:12–21 numbers twenty-one priestly "fathers' houses" with their corresponding "heads" during the time of the high priest Joiakim, the son of Jeshua (Neh 12:10), thus representing the generation after the return. The house or family of *yôyārîb* (LXX = *Iōiarib*) is positioned sixteenth in this list with Mattenai as its head (12:19).

There are two lists in 1 Chronicles where the name of *yĕhôyārîb* (see JEHOIARIB), a "head of a house of a father" of priests (24:4, 6), appears and is assumed to be identical to the *yôyārîb* mentioned in #3 above. The list in 1 Chr 24:7–18 numbers twenty-four divisions of Aaronide priests. This, according to Winter (1956: 216), was sufficient for each division to officiate in the Temple twice a year for a turn of one week according to the lunar calendar (48 seven-day-weeks). The Chronicler attributes this priestly organization of his own day to David (*HJP*^{2} 2: 247) who acted concurrently with representatives of the two recognized branches of the Aaronic priesthood (vv 1–3). This "procedure" (*mišpāṭ*) rested on divine command given to Aaron (v 19). The entire context, suggests Welch (1939: 86–87), reflects an impasse on the constitution of the higher clergy during the period of the Return which required resolution by appeal to a higher (and more revered) authority. The final development of priestly organization in the Hebrew Bible appears to have been reached with this enumeration (Rudolph *Chronikbücher* HAT, 162; Braun *1 Chronicles* WBC, 239) although attempts to date it vary. The method of organization was that of lots (vv 5, 7) and the first lot fell to *yĕhôyārîb* (*Iarib;* Codex Vaticanus = *Iareim*) (24:7). Rudolph (*Chronikbücher* HAT, 161–62) attributes this primary positioning to a genealogical connection with the Hasmoneans (see #1 above) during whose time the redaction of 1 Chronicles 24 occurred. The list in 1 Chr 9:10–13 numbers six priestly "heads of their fathers' houses." Here *yĕhôyārîb* (Codex Vaticanus = *Iōarim*, Codex Alexandrinus = *Iōareib*) is listed second following Jedaiah, a positioning which Rothstein (*Chronik* KAT, 436) attributes to listing the sequence from the standpoint of the Eleazar line rather than from the line of Ithamar to which he believes *yĕhôyārîb* belongs. Because Jedaiah precedes *yĕhôyārîb* here and *yôyārîb* in Neh 11:10 (where the former is called the son of the latter) and because Jedaiah follows *yĕhôyārîb* in 1 Chr 24:7 and *yôyārîb* in Neh 12:6, 19, it has been assumed that *yĕhôyārîb* and *yôyārîb* are variant spellings of the same patronymic.

Yĕhôyārîb is also mentioned in the Talmudic literature: *b. Taᶜan.* 29a, where the priestly division so named is described as being on duty when the temple was destroyed; *m. Baba Qamma* 9:12 with corresponding Gemara (*b. Baba Qamma* 111a), where payments and offerings to priestly divisions related to committed robberies are regulated.

Bibliography

Welch, A. C. 1939. *The Work Of The Chronicler: Its Purpose and Date.* London.

Winter, P. 1956. Twenty-six Priestly Courses. *VT* 6: 215–17.

Rodney H. Shearer

JOKDEAM (PLACE) [Heb *yoqdĕᶜām*]. A town situated in the south-central hill country of Judah (Josh 15:56), within the same district as Maon. This settlement is listed among the towns within the tribal allotment of Judah (Josh 15:21–

62). One common, but very tentative, suggestion places the ancient town at modern Khirbet er-Raqqa (M.R. 160096), located approximately 7 km S of Hebron (Boling and Wright *Joshua* AB, 389). LXX B provides the alternative reading *iorkeam,* suggesting a possible relationship between this settlement and a place known as Jorkeam, which appears as a metaphorical descendent of Hebron in 1 Chr 2:44.

WADE R. KOTTER

JOKIM (PERSON) [Heb *yôqîm*]. An individual of Judah, son of Shelah (1 Chr 4:22). The Vulgate seems to reflect a Rabbinic tradition linking Jokim with Elimelech of the book of Ruth. This passage reflects a partial or total conquest of Moab of which Jokim may have taken part.

DAVID CHANNING SMITH

JOKMEAM (PLACE) [Heb *yoqmŏʿām* or *yoqmĕʿām*]. A levitical city of the Kohathites in Ephraim (1 Chr 6:53—Eng 6:68). In Josh 21:22, the corresponding place in the parallel list is taken by KIBZAIM. According to 1 Chr 23:19 and 24:23, a Hebronite levitical family bore the similar name Jekameam (Heb *yĕqamʿām*), and one could conjecture that since David assigned Hebronite levites to duties on the west side of the Jordan (according to 1 Chr 26:30) perhaps the family of Jekameam should be associated with the levitical city Jokmeam.

Jokmeam also appears as one of the cities in Solomon's fifth administrative district (1 Kgs 4:12). Judging from its placement after Abelmeholah and its placement at the end of the list of towns in that district, some have sought its location on the Ephraimite side in the Jordan valley and have suggested an identification with Tell el-Mazâr (M.R. 195171). According to this perspective, Jokmeam of 1 Kgs 4:12 is the same as the levitical city in 1 Chr 6:53—Eng 6:68. Alternatively, some scholars consider the elements in 1 Kgs 4:12b to be out of order or that some of the elements are explanatory additions, and they interpret that the verse describes the territory of Solomon's fifth district first from W to E from Taanach to Bethshean, and then from S to N extending as far as Jokmeam. According to this perspective, Jokmeam is an alternative spelling or a corruption for Jokneam of Zebulun (Josh 12:22, 19:11, 21:34). See also Aharoni *LBHG,* p. 313; Gray *I and II Kings* OTL, p. 134.

WESLEY I. TOEWS

JOKNEAM (PLACE) [Heb *yoqnĕʿām*]. A city in the Jezreel valley, mentioned in connection with the borders of the tribe of Zebulun and as a Levitical city (Josh 19:11; 21:34). Its king is mentioned in the list of rulers defeated by Joshua (Josh 12:22). The many LXX variants *(iek[o]nam, iekman, iekommam)* indicate some confusion of the labials. The place may be referred to in Judith (7:3) as Cyamon. Eusebius mentions a Kammona (which Jerome rendered as Cimona) located on the road from Legio (near Megiddo) to Ptolemais (= Acco), six miles from the former (*Onomast.* 116.21), which is precisely where Tel Yoqneam lies (M.R. 160229). In the Crusader period this site was called Caymont or Mons-Cain, from which derived the Arabic name of the site, Tell Qeimun.

A. Description of the Site

Tell Qeimun (or Tel Yoqneam) dominates the exit of Wadi Milḥ in the Jezreel valley, hence its strategic importance throughout history. The site is first mentioned in a topographical list of sites in Asia conquered by Thutmoses III: number 113 on this list, *ʿn qnʿm,* should most probably be read *ʿn (y)qnʿm,* "the spring of Jokneam." Numbers 112 and 114 on that list are *ḥrqt* (Helkath) and *kbʿ* (Gaba), identified respectively with Tel Qashish and Tel Shush to the N and S of Qeimun/Yoqneam. The tell itself measures some 40 dunams as it rises steeply to a height of 60 m above its surroundings. The highest point of the site is in its SW corner, from which the surface of the site more gradually slopes to the N and E. Due to the sloping terrain, the buildings of all periods were built upon, and supported by, a series of terraces.

B. The Excavation

The excavation of Tel Yoqneam is the focus of a regional archaeological research project, the Yoqneam Regional Project. See Fig. JOK.01. See also QASHISH, TEL; QIRI, TEL. The site has been excavated since 1977; nine seasons have so far been carried out, and one or two additional seasons are planned in order to reach the earliest (EB) levels of occupation. Several areas have so far been tested, but the main effort was focused in area A (and B) in the N and NW of the site, where an area of about 2 dunams (ca. 5 percent of the site's surface) is being investigated. Twenty-three layers of occupation have been encountered so far spanning MB I through the Ottoman period. Pottery found out of context indicates occupation at the site also during MB I and the EB Age. Such a long time span of ca. 4500 years is very unusual, and is so far unattested at any other site in Palestine, except Jerusalem. Neighboring Megiddo, for example, was abandoned 2000 years before Yoqneam. Not in all periods, however, did the occupation extend over the entire site: during the Mamluk, Byzantine, and Roman periods, for example, occupation was limited to the southern, high part of the site.

1. Bronze Age. The MB and LB strata so far have been unearthed only in two deep sections, located in the NW part of the Tel. During MB I, Yoqneam was fortified by a 3 m wide mudbrick wall, which was substituted in MB II by another fortification wall, only the inner face of its lowest course has been preserved in the area thus far excavated. No trace of any LB fortification has, however, been encountered, and it seems that the site was unfortified. The transition between MB and LB appears to have been peaceful since no sign of destruction between strata XXI and XX was noted. The ceramic assemblages of both periods are varied. An impression of a scarab on a bowl found out of context should be attributed to Amenemhet III (stratum XXIII). The practice of infant burials in jars under the house floors is characteristic of strata XXI–XX. The LB settlement ended in a great disaster evidenced by a 1.5 m thick destruction layer.

2. Iron Age. After the LB destruction, which occurred probably in the second half of the 13th century B.C., the site was abandoned for a period of time, and was reoccu-

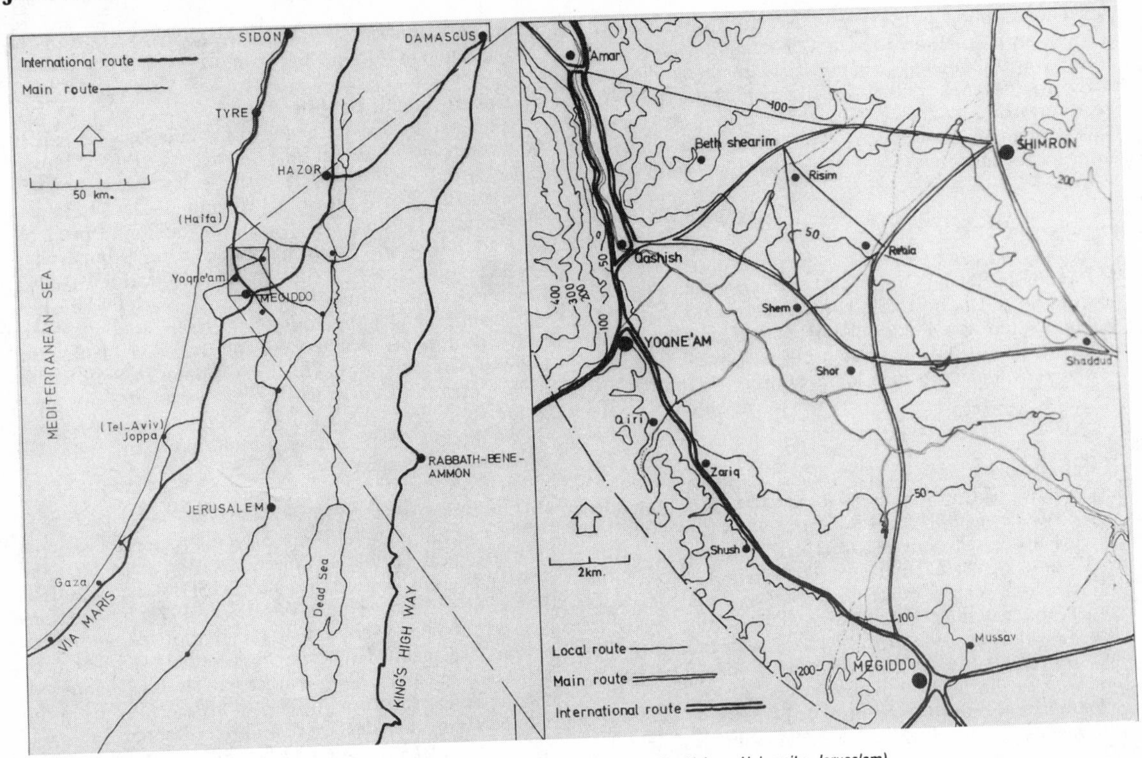

JOK.01. Area map of the Jokneam Regional Project. *(Courtesy of the Institute of Archaeology, The Hebrew University, Jerusalem)*

pied towards the end of the 12th or early 11th century B.C. This settlement was unfortified, however; the houses situated at the edge of the site were built so that they formed a continuous defensive line. There are no clear cut criteria by which we can identify the ethnicity of the inhabitants of the site at the time (strata XVIII–XVII). It should be noted that Philistine pottery is extremely rare. By the end of the 11th century B.C. Yoqneam was violently destroyed (stratum XVII). In one of the buildings consumed by the conflagration, two installations designed for the production of olive oil were uncovered. Also found was a large amount of pottery, some of which was clearly imported from the Phoenician coast. Two knives and a sickle blade, all made of iron, are noteworthy. The entire assemblage shows a very close affinity to that of Megiddo VI A, which was also destroyed in a large conflagration at that time. The cause of this destruction is not yet clear: it could have been military (the Israelite conquest of the Canaanite enclaves in the valleys during the time of David?) or natural (the shattered nature of some of the walls suggests that the site was destroyed by an earthquake).

A very massive casemate wall was erected in Yoqneam in the 10th century, which in turn was substituted in the 9th century by an equally massive double wall. These two fortification systems, exposed over a length of ca. 60 m, are very impressive insofar as they were carefully planned and constructed, and accompanied by fine drainage systems. The city's water system should be dated to that period: it has not yet been entirely excavated, but its location (inside the defenses on the NW corner of the tower) has clearly been established. Strata XIV–XII represent a well-fortified Israelite town situated on the NW border of the kingdom facing Phoenicia. Indeed, a large part of the ceramic assemblage as well as other finds attributable to these strata exhibit a distinctively "Phoenician flavor."

Stratum XI reflects a rather limited occupation of the site, in part reusing houses of the previous stratum and partly built on top of the defenses (which were then no longer in use). This settlement probably represents the Assyrian control of the region following the campaign of Tiglath-pileser III in 733/2. No trace of destruction was noted between Strata XII–XI.

3. Persian and Hellenistic Periods. It appears that Yoqneam was rather intensively occupied during the Persian period (6th–4th centuries B.C.) even though it is not mentioned in the records of that time. The architectural features as well as several characteristics of the ceramic assemblage clearly indicate close contacts with the Phoenician coast. An ostracon on which were inscribed Hebrew, Phoenician, and Persian names was discovered, clearly demonstrating the "cosmopolitan" nature of Yoqneam (undoubtedly due to its location on an important international route). The remains of the Hellenistic period are rather scanty, including mainly an isolated watchtower on the N side of the site, several coins, and a ceramic assemblage including simple local ware, megarian bowls, terra sigilata, and wine jars imported from the island of Rhodes.

4. Later Periods. The early Islamic settlement (stratum IV: Late 9th/Early 10th century C.E.) is not known from any record of the time. This is a well-planned urban settlement, as evidenced by the regular layout of the streets and by the uniform planning and construction of the houses. Among the ceramic finds were some Egyptian imports. In the Crusader period, Yoqneam was encircled by a defensive wall. A square fortress with corner towers was built on the SW acropolis, and to its E was a church. Although its construction is massive, several features seem to indicate that the church was built in haste, and probably was never completed. The written records indicate that in 1139 Yoqneᶜam/Caymont became the administrative center of the region. The site is last mentioned in the Crusader period in a contract dated 1283.

During the Mamluk period (14th–15th centuries) the settlement was confined to the S, higher part of the site: several phases of construction were distinguished in houses which were built over the ruined church and in its vicinity. A violent transition between the Crusader and Mamluk settlements is indicated. Literary sources mention a caravanserai built on the summit of the site by Dahir al-ᶜUmar, the Bedouin ruler of the Galilee in the 18th century. This structure was apparently incorporated into the remains of the Crusader fortress, and its remains—which cover the entire area of the acropolis—are still noticeable above ground.

Bibliography

Ben-Tor, A. 1978. Yoqneᶜam et Environs (Chronique Archeologique). *RB* 85: 96–102.

———. 1980. The Regional Study: A New Approach to Archaeological Investigation. *BARev* 6: 30–44.

Ben-Tor, A., and Rosenthal, R. 1977. The First Season of Excavations at Tel Yoqneᶜam. *IEJ* 28: 57–82.

Ben-Tor, A.; Portugali, Y.; and Avissar, M. 1978. The Second Season of Excavations at Tel Yoqneᶜam. *IEJ* 29: 65–83.

———. 1983. The Third and Fourth Seasons of Excavations at Tel Yoqneᶜam. 1983. *IEJ* 33: 30–54.

Ben-Tor, A. et. al. 1987. A Regional Study of Tel-Yoqneᶜam and its Vicinity. *Qad* 20: 2–17 (in Hebrew).

AMNON BEN-TOR

JOKSHAN (PERSON) [Heb *yoqšān*]. A clan name in the genealogy of Abraham by his wife Keturah in Gen 25:2. Jokshan is the second of seven sons born to Keturah. He is described in 25:3 as the father of Sheba and Dedan. This designation is problematic because of two statements in the genealogies in Genesis 10. In the Cushite genealogy of Gen 10:7 Sheba and Dedan are listed as the sons of Raamah. Then, in Gen 10:28, Sheba is described as one of the Arabian tribes descended from Joktan. Winnett (1970: 189) rejects the equation of Jokshan with Joktan on etymological grounds. He suggests that the people of the city of Raamah considered themselves to be descendants of an "eponymous ancestor" named Jokshan. The Dedanites and Sabeans, who later lived in Raamah, simply took up this ancestral line as well.

Like the other sons of Keturah, Jokshan is described as receiving gifts from his father Abraham. However, he was not to share in the inheritance of the land of Canaan and was sent "eastward to the east country" (Gen 10:6).

Bibliography

Winnett, F. V. 1970. The Arabian Genealogies in Genesis. Pp. 171–96 in *Translating and Understanding the Old Testament,* ed. H. T. Frank and W. L. Reed. Nashville.

VICTOR H. MATTHEWS

JOKTAN (PERSON) [Heb *yoqṭān*]. Son of Eber, brother of Peleg, and father of thirteen descendants, whose settlements ranged from Mesha to Sephar, in the hill country to the east (Gen 10: 25–30). As a descendant of Shem, Joktan represents that part of the line which, in the Table of Nations, is found in SW Arabia. There is a possible relationship between the name and a figure remembered as the ancestor of the S Arabs, *Qaḥṭān* (Winnett 1970: 181; Simons *GTTOT*, 48–49).

Although it is unclear whether Joktan is a prefixed verbal form of the Sabaean root *qtn* (cf. Ryckmans 1934 1: 190; Biella 1982: 452), its meaning, "to be small," is associated with this root in West Semitic and appears in geographic names such as Qatna. Its possible appearance here as the last named figure of the Table of Nations to have descendants listed, raises the question of a word play between Joktan and Jepheth, the first named figure in the Table. Jepheth's name is related to the concept of enlarging *(ptḥ)* in the word play of Gen 9:27, and is also a prefixed verbal form.

The relationship of Joktan to Jokshan, the son of Abraham and Keturah, in Gen 25:2, 3, is not clear. Despite the fact that both figures have "sons" named Sheba and Dedan, the equation of the two names is linguistically implausible, and all ancient versions follow the Hebrew in distinguishing the two. Further, since both are geographic names, the different ancestry in the two chapters may reflect distinct peoples among the inhabitants of both Sheba and Dedan.

Bibliography

Biella, J. C. 1982. *Dictionary of Old South Arabic. Sabaean Dialect.* HSS 25. Chico, CA.

Ryckmans, G. 1934–35. *Les noms propres sud-sémitiques.* 3 vol. Louvain.

Winnett, F. V. 1970. The Arabian Genealogies in the Book of Genesis. Pp. 171–96 in *Translating & Understanding the Old Testament,* ed. H. T. Frank and W. L. Reed. Nashville.

RICHARD S. HESS

JOKTHEEL (PLACE) [Heb *yoqtĕʾēl*]. **1.** A town situated in the Shephelah, or low-lands, of Judah (Jos 15:38), within the same district as Lachish. This settlement is listed among the towns within the tribal allotment of Judah (Josh 15:21–62). It has been suggested (Boling and Wright *Joshua* AB, 386) that Joktheel may be the same place as Jekuthiel, a place name which appears in 1 Chr 4:18 as the "father" of Zanoah and the "uncle" of Socoh. If this is the case, then a location in the vicinity of Zanoah and Socoh seems likely, although it is not possible at the present time to provide a more precise identification.

2. New name given to the Edomite stronghold Sela (modern Petra) after its capture by Amaziah (2 Kgs 14:7).

WADE R. KOTTER

JONADAB (PERSON) [Heb *yonādāb*]. Var. JEHONADAB. The name of two men in the OT. The name may mean "Yahu is liberal," ". . . is noble," and it has been found on an ancient Heb seal (*TPNAH,* 82, 351).

1. The son of Shimeah, David's brother. He is a friend of Amnon, and advises Amnon how to seduce his sister Tamar (2 Sam 13:3–5). Two years later, it is Jonadab who reassures David that only Amnon has been killed by Absalom, and not all of David's sons (13:32–35). 2 Sam 13:5 has the variant *yĕhônādāb* in all mss. Several mss of the LXX (codices Vaticanus, Alexandrinus, Coisilianus, and Basiliano-Vaticanus) have *iōnadam/b* in 2 Sam 13:3a, however. The Gk Lucian recension and 4QSam[a] read *(yĕ)hônātōn* in 2 Sam 13:3a, confusing Jonadab with Jonathon (see below).

The RSV renders the description of Jonadab in v 3 as "a crafty man". This is misleading, since the Heb literally means "wise". The rabbis elaborated this as "wise for doing evil" (*Sanh.* 21a). McCarter believes that the word "friend" used to describe Jonadab's relationship to Amnon is a technical term for a routine matchmaker, with parallels in Akk terms for a best man (*2 Samuel* AB, 321). The "King's Friend" may have been an actual official; and if part of Amnon's motivation for raping his sister was to succeed to the throne through a matrilineal claim (*ISBE* 2: 977), then Jonadab may have intended to raise himself to this office by helping Amnon. Certainly Jonadab's cool reaction to the news of Amnon's death seems to rule against a true friendship (McCarter *2 Samuel* AB, 333).

Jonadab may be the same as the Jonathan, also son of David's brother Shimeah (or SHIMEI), who slew a Gittite giant in 2 Sam 21:21 and 1 Chr 20:7. See JONATHAN (PERSON) #5; *IDB* 2: 964. In 2 Sam 21:21, most Gk uncials and many cursive mss, as well as the Syr, have *Iōnadab.* In 1 Chr 20:7, the Syr has Jonadab. This and the confusion of Jonadab and Jonathan in some mss of 2 Sam 13:3a make equating the two possible. McCarter, however, believes that Jonathan and Jonadab were brothers, and there was an ancient tendency to identify them (*2 Samuel* AB, 451).

ROBERT D. MILLER II

2. The son of Rechab and the founder of the Rechabite community (2 Kgs 10:15–28, Jer 35:6–7, 1 Chr 2:55) during the reign of Jehu (842–815 B.C.E.). In 2 Kgs 10:15–20, Jonadab accompanies Jehu during his massacre of the followers of Baal. The participation of Jonadab in the revolt of Jehu and zealous purge of the worshippers of Baal are indications of the fanatical devotion to Yahweh of Jonadab and his Rechabite followers.

Jeremiah's dealings with Rechabites in Jeremiah 35 provide further insight into Jonadab and the Rechabites. When Jeremiah offers the Rechabites wine during their visit to the temple, the Rechabites respond quoting the command of Jonadab: "You shall not drink wine, neither you nor your sons; you shall not build a house; you shall not sow seed; you shall not plant or have a vineyard, but you shall live in tents all your days, that you may live long days in the land where you sojourn" (Jer 35:6–7).

While the historical accuracy of the quotation is impossible to verify, it is the only clue available apart from 2 Kings 10 about the possible perspective of Jonadab and the Rechabite community. The quotation suggests that Jonadab and the Rechabites expressed Yahwistic faith by shunning settled life, rejecting agriculture, and holding to some form of pastoralist ideal (cf. Carroll *Jeremiah* OTL, 653; Bright *Jeremiah* AB, 190). Such expression of Yahwism would certainly be consistent with the fervid anti-Baalist crusade in which Jonadab participated with Jehu. 2 Chr 2:55 associates Rechab, Jonadab's father, with the Kenites. See KENITES. If authentic, this connection could support the pastoralist ideal suggested by Jer 35:6–7 (cf. Gottwald 1979: 577).

Bibliography

Gottwald, N. K. 1979. *The Tribes of Yahweh.* Maryknoll, NY.

J. M. BRACKE

JONAH (PERSON) [Heb *yônâ*]. **1.** Jonah, son of Amittai. See JONAH, BOOK OF.

2. One of six Levites who divorced their foreign wives during Ezra's reform (1 Esdr 9:23; Gk *iōanes*). The parallel account in Ezra 10:23 also lists six Levites but differs from 1 Esdras in that it records the name "Eliezer" instead of "Jonah". The difficulties of identifying individuals such as Jonah raise questions about the sources of and literary relationships among Ezra, Nehemiah, and 1 Esdras.

MICHAEL DAVID MCGEHEE

JONAH, BOOK OF. A book of the OT/Hebrew Bible, the fifth in the collection of "Minor Prophets," recounting the story of Jonah, son of Amittai, who was called by God to prophesy against Nineveh.

The book of Jonah is one of the most familiar and popular in the Bible, yet it contains many puzzles. It is difficult to classify and to date. Its precise message is hard to determine. On the face of it it is a very simple, direct narrative, yet it has produced a wide variety of interpretations. The number of questions it raises can be multiplied: Is it "history" or a "story"? What could it have meant to those who included it in the Biblical canon? Is it a unity or the work of various hands? For example, does Jonah's long, psalm-like prayer in chapter 2 belong to the original book or was it added later? Is the book in the "right" place in the Bible? It is located among the prophetic writings but is the only one which consists solely of a story about the prophet, and the only "prophecy" it contains consists of five words in the Hebrew. What connection, if any, is there between the Jonah of the Book and the person of the same name in 2 Kgs 14:25?

To these, and many other questions, there are no simple answers and much critical debate. Furthermore any evaluation should also recognize the remarkable power of the book to move, stimulate, and challenge readers of different religious traditions for over two millennia.

A. Content and Structure
B. Literary Character
  1. Poetry and Prose
  2. Narrative Devices
  3. Genre
C. Date and Authorship
D. Status of Text and Canonical Position
E. Theological Ideas and Motifs

A. Content and Structure

The book of Jonah, like any composition or work of art, is a self-contained world, one that works by its own rules and logic. Some rules it shares with the rest of the Bible, others are unique. So it is valuable to gain some understanding of how the book is constructed and what methods the author employs, its "internal" system, before asking "external" questions about the authorship, dating, and place in the Bible.

The book divides neatly into two parallel sections of two chapters each (Lohfink 1961; Landes 1967; Cohn 1969; Magonet 1976). Both sections contain certain "key words" whose recurrence highlights the comparison between them. Chapter 1 begins with God telling Jonah to *"arise"* and *"go"* to Nineveh and *"call out"* against it. When Jonah does indeed *"arise"* (1:3), as we would expect of an obedient prophet, it is, however, to flee in the opposite direction, to Tarshish, probably S Spain, at the other end of the world. In response, God unleashes the powers of nature to force him back. On the ship is a pagan crew of sailors who try to understand what is happening to them. They identify Jonah as the cause, seek to discover why and recognize the hand of God in the storm. They do their best to save Jonah. His invitation to them to throw him overboard may be seen as an exercise in self-sacrifice on their behalf or a manifestation of his own death wish—though his "correct" answer would have been a request to be taken back to Jaffa. However, by asking them to throw him overboard, rather than merely jumping himself, he brings them into another difficulty. Trapped between doing nothing, and thus drowning, or throwing him overboard, and thus being punished by death for shedding innocent blood, they pray to God who alone can resolve this "double-bind": "let us not *perish*" (1:14). They throw Jonah overboard and the storm abates. The sailors offer sacrifices and make vows to Israel's God and perhaps, as later Jewish tradition suggests, "convert" thereby to Israel's faith.

Chapter 2 sees Jonah saved from drowning by a "great fish" and praying to God from its belly. God responds and the fish vomits him out.

Chapter 3 introduces a second call, in almost identical language to that of chapter One, utilizing the same three terms: *"arise," "go"* and *"call out"*. This time Jonah obeys completely, he *"arises"* and *"goes"* to Nineveh (3:3) and *"calls out"* (3:4). His few words to the Ninevites, another pagan community equivalent to the sailors, lead them to repent. Even though Jonah's decree offers no hope, their king argues that God might change His mind in response to their change in behavior, if they turn aside from their evil way and their violence. His hope is expressed using the same term that the captain and sailors had: "that we *perish* not" (3:6, 9). God sees how they turn from evil and does not destroy them.

Chapter 4 finds an angry Jonah again praying to God, as in Chapter Two, though here God's response is given in more detail as a dialogue, expressed in words and actions, ensues between them. God "appoints" three more natural agencies to act upon Jonah. As a result, Jonah's desire to die because of his "ideological" distress at the forgiving of Nineveh is replaced by a desire to die because of physical distress (compare 4:3–4 and 4:8–9). In a final question God suggests that Jonah felt "pity" for the plant that gave him shade, something never formerly said about Jonah's actual feelings, surely he could see by analogy why God should have pity on Nineveh with its myriad citizens and animals. The book ends with this question and challenge.

In very general terms chapters 1 and 3 put Jonah in the context of the outer "pagan" world. In both cases the leader of the pagans (the captain, the king) acknowledges that there is a single divine power to whom they turn. It is important to note that two different terms for "God" are used here in quite specific ways. The Heb *ʾelōhîm,* usually translated as "God," is a general term for God (and also divine beings, "other gods," "angels" and powerful human beings)—it is used here as the supreme divine power. The *tetragrammaton, YHWH,* is Israel's name for the supreme God of the world, but with whom Israel has a special covenantal relationship. Whereas the sailors identify the "God" *(ʾelōhîm)* who saves them as Israel's God, and thus make vows to *YHWH,* the Ninevites make an act of repentance before "God" *(ʾelōhîm)* but do not make that step of acknowledging *YHWH.*

Chapters 2 and 4 contain the inner discussion between Jonah and God represented in the language of prayer, of divine responses in words and actions, and some physical activity directed against Jonah's body. The two parts of the Book can be represented in the following table:

Table 1: Structure of the Book of Jonah

CHAPTER ONE	*CHAPTER THREE*
Call (Arise, Go, Call) (v 2)	Call (Arise, Go, Call) (v 2)
Jonah arises—flees to Tarshish (v 3)	Jonah arises—goes to Nineveh (v 3)
God acts—storm (v 4)	Jonah acts—prophesies destruction (v 4)
Sailors call to their gods (v 5)	Ninevites believe, fast, and don sackcloth (v 5)
Captain identifies *ʾelōhîm*'s power behind the storm (v 6)	King dons sackcloth, issues decree, seeks *ʾelōhîm*'s will (vv 6–8)
Sailors seek *YHWH's* will (vv 7–13)	
Sailors pray to *YHWH:* "let us not perish" (v 14)	King orders Ninevites to pray to *ʾelōhîm:* "lest we perish" (v 9)
Storm abates (v 15)	God "relents" (v 10)
CHAPTER TWO	*CHAPTER FOUR*
Jonah saved	Jonah angry
Jonah prays	Jonah prays
God responds	God responds

The symmetry of this structure helps us recognize certain elements of the story that we might otherwise overlook. The parallels between the sailors with their captain and the Ninevites with their king indicate that the former are not merely an accidental background against the story of Jonah's flight. Like the Ninevites they are representatives of the "pagan" world. Like them, they too acknowledge the hand of God in the world, but unlike them they go further in identifying that universal "God" through the name that Israel uses and may indeed come to join Israel. There is therefore a graded universalism within the book. Jonah becomes an instrument for spreading divine knowledge in the world whether consciously obedient or not.

B. Literary Character

1. Poetry and Prose. The book is for the most part a narrative. The "Psalm" in chapter 2 interrupts the story and is a different literary genre. This, among other factors, has led scholars to assume it is an addition. However, there is no *a priori* reason why a biblical book should not contain a mixture of genres or why the same author should not be capable of varying style to suit the point that is to be made. Moreover, recent work suggests that there is no hard and fast line of division between "poetry" and "prose" within the Bible, and that in the case of "poetry" it is more accurate to speak of "heightened language" within Hebrew texts, most of which have some sort of metrical component (Kugel 1981; Christensen 1987).

2. Narrative Devices. a. Word Repetitions. We have already noted that the repetition of the words associated with Jonah's "call" provide a method for comparing the two sections of the book, or, in terms of the narrative itself, comparing the consequences of Jonah's disobedience and ultimate obedience to God's word. This feature of word repetition is particularly common within the book and allows for "subliminal" messages to be conveyed to the reader. A few examples illustrate the effect:

(1) "Go down." The Hebrew root *yārad* occurs three times in the first chapter: Jonah "goes down" to Jaffa and "goes down" into the ship (1:3), during the storm he "goes down" into the inner part of the ship (1:5). In the "Psalm" in chapter 2 he says that he "went down" to the bottoms of the mountains (2:7). In addition there is a word play in 1:5, only recognizable in the Hebrew, where the statement that he "fell into a deep sleep" is expressed as *wayyērādam* in which *yārad* can clearly be heard. There is thus a continuous hint that Jonah's flight from God is not merely "horizontal" to another part of the world, but actually a "descent," ultimately into death and the underworld.

(2) "Great." One of the most frequently repeated words in the book is the term *gādôl,* meaning "great." Among those so designated are: Nineveh (1:2; 3:2, 3; 4:11); the storm wind (1:4) and the storm (1:4, 12); the fear of the sailors (1:10, 16); the fish (2:1); the "great ones" of Nineveh (3:5, 7); and Jonah's anger (4:1). It is also present as a verb meaning to "raise a child," but here in terms of Jonah not "raising" (growing) the plant (4:10). When one remembers that biblical Hebrew uses adjectives very sparingly and that this repetition is quite obtrusive, some explanation is demanded. It may imply that all the events in the story are "larger than life" and suggest that for the author and initial audience this was perceived as a sort of parable rather than true history. Other explanations are possible, but it is a factor that must be taken into account in any evaluation of the story.

(3) "Appointing." In the same vein it is very obvious that four "miraculous" events in the book are introduced by the same verbal root *mānāh,* "to count, number, reckon" and here "appoint": the great fish (2:1); the "plant" (4:6); the worm (4:7); and the wind (4:8). When we couple this information with the awareness that in each case a different divine name *ʾelōhîm* (sometimes with the definite article—*haʾelōhîm* or *YHWH*), or a combination of the two, is used, the reader becomes aware that something more is being conveyed.

Again, the precise nuance, is a matter of interpretation, but such features require careful consideration. In this particular case the repetition of the same verbal form with a different subject each time forces the reader to examine the implications of the different usage of divine names on each occasion and suggests that they are not random changes. Whereas in chapters 1 and 3 the use of names is related to the religious perceptions of the "pagan world," the use in chapters 2 and 4 seems to relate to the "private" internal dialogue between Jonah and God. Thus the fish that saves Jonah is "appointed" by *YHWH,* whereas the worm and the wind are "appointed" by variants of the name *ʾelōhîm.* The plant itself, which has a twofold purpose—expressed as a powerful word-play in the Hebrew "to be a shade" over Jonah *(lihyôt ṣēl),* but also to "rescue him" *(lĕhaṣṣîl lô)* from his anger/evil (4:6)—is introduced by both divine names in combination *(YHWH-ʾelōhîm).* Though many commentators assume this division of names is arbitrary, given the general precision with which words are used throughout the book, this seems unlikely. A possible explanation is that for these two chapters a different system of interpreting the names is in operation, a prefiguration of the later Rabbinic view that they represented two different divine attributes—*ʾelōhîm* suggesting God's attribute of justice, *YHWH,* God's attribute of mercy (Strikowsky 1976). Thus the fish that saves Jonah is a "merciful" act, the worm and wind are part of the process of educating Jonah on his own physical person, and the plant, with its double function, to save and to instruct, serves both purposes. Again, other explanations may be possible, but the precision of the utilization of the names must be taken into account.

(4) "Evil." One final example is also highly suggestive, particularly because it shows the variety of meanings contained within the individual Heb root. Thus the word *rāʿâ* refers to the "evil" of the Ninevites that has risen up to God (1:2); the "great evil" of the storm according to the sailors (1:7, 8); and the "evil way" from which the king of Nineveh asks his citizens to turn back (3:8). It is this latter that introduces the most striking sequence utilizing this word. In 3:10, God sees that they turn from their "evil" way, and repents of the "evil" (i.e. punishment) that He had intended to do to them. But this will be experienced by Jonah as "a great evil" (4:1), a phrase usually translated in terms of Jonah being "displeased." Again, the significance of this is subject to a variety of interpretations, but the "evil" that shifts between the Ninevites, God, and Jonah within the space of two verses, binds the three "characters" of the story together at this crucial moment.

b. Use of Quotations. A feature of the book is the presence of a number of sentences and phrases that resemble passages from elsewhere in the Bible (Feuillet 1947; Fränkel 1967; Ackerman 1981). There is a relationship between 4:2 and Exodus 34:6–7 and other passages which we will explore further in the next section. The "Psalm" contains apparent "quotes" from other Psalms—compare 2:4 with Ps 42:8; Jonah 4:5 and 4:9 with Ps 31:23 and 31:7 respectively (see further below). The argument of the king of Nineveh that God might repent if they "turn from their evil way" reflects Jer 18:7, 8, 11; 26:3, 13, 19. Other statements (including the miraculous interventions and his request to die) reflect the episode of Elijah's flight from Jezebel into the desert (compare Jonah 4:8 with 1 Kgs 19:4). Jonah's argument with God (4:2) echoes the language of the children of Israel confronted by the Red Sea on escaping from Egypt (Exod 14:12).

When such parallel passages occur in different parts of the Bible, a number of possible explanations exist: that A quotes B; that B quotes A; that both have a common source; that both were edited in later; that it is purely a coincidence. The relatively large number of such apparent "quotations" and allusions in Jonah is suggestive of a conscious literary ploy by the author, though each case must be argued on its own merits. Nevertheless the contrast between the behavior of Jonah and that of Elijah, the irony of the king of Nineveh quoting Jeremiah's theology back at Jonah, as well as Jonah's use of God's "attributes," all complement the narrative and seem to conform with the author's overall strategy of reversing expectations and conventions.

c. Ironic Inversion. There is one major narrative device that runs throughout the book. We noted above that when God tells Jonah to "arise" and "go," our conditioning as readers of the Bible is to anticipate an obedient response—but our expectations are subverted when Jonah indeed arises, but to go in the opposite direction. The "hero," with whom we would expect to identify, acts in an inexcusable way. Conversely, in the same general way, the sailors, and more shockingly the "evil" Ninevites, behave in exemplary fashion: the former trying to save Jonah and displaying piety and integrity; the latter, in the person of the king, taking the mechanical responses of fasting and sackcloth into the higher dimension of turning away from evil and violence. In short the author reverses the conventions of biblical narrative in terms of the encounter between a prophet and the people, and between Israel and the outside world.

(1) Jonah Prays—Chapter 4. This technique of challenging the reader's natural identification with Jonah recurs in the presentation of Jonah's various statements throughout the book. The most shocking occurs in his prayer to God in the final chapter. What begins as a standard prayer formula "Please Lord" (4:2) (compare the identical opening words of the captain of the sailors, 1:14) concludes with the standard formula used in petitionary prayer, though somewhat disturbing in its content: "now, Lord, take, *please*, my soul from me. . . ." (Compare the negative formula of the captain in his petition: "*please* let us not perish. . . ."). But Jonah's prayerful opening is interrupted as his anger bursts through (4:2): "Is that not my word when I was back on my own land. . . ." But the reader is further shocked when Jonah quotes against God as an accusation the time-honored formula of God's "attributes" of mercy and compassion—"I knew you were a God who is gracious and compassionate, slow to anger and great in mercy and repenting of evil." This formula, expressed in its fullest form as God's response to Moses' request to learn about God's glory (Exod 34:6–7), recurs or is echoed in numerous variations (Num 14:18; Ps 103:8–13; Nah 1:3; Joel 2:13–14). Only here is it thrown back at God as an accusation, when God extends this compassion and willingness to forgive Nineveh. Thus Jonah's prayer, though it utilizes the correct opening and closing terminology, is quite inappropriate.

(2) Jonah Prays—Chapter 2. This device may also be operating in the case of the "Psalm" of chapter 2, which has been identified as a later addition, one of the grounds being its apparent inappropriateness—Jonah giving a psalm of thanksgiving when he is not yet saved (although he has been saved from drowning). Another problem is the absence of any reference in the "Psalm" to his mission or any acknowledgment that he was wrong in fleeing from God. If the author tends to put "inappropriate" prayers into the mouth of Jonah, these absences become quite significant. Jonah is willing to thank God for getting him out of trouble, but not to acknowledge his own responsibility in getting into trouble in the first place. Compare (2:4) "You cast me in . . ." and the concluding "You brought me up . . ." (2:7).

Arguments about the "genuineness" of the "Psalm" fall into two general categories: psychological or stylistic. The former include the suggestions given above that it is inappropriate. Since the "Psalm" does suggest that Jonah is capable of some degree of personal repentance and piety, those who wish to paint him as particularly unredeemable argue that it portrays a Jonah different from the rest of the book. However, since their case depends on excluding the "Psalm" from consideration, their argument is circular. (Incidently, that Jonah could compose a "psalm" while in the belly of a fish is no more absurd than the notion that he could survive in one for three days. Attempts to collect cases of sailors who underwent such an experience are unconvincing.)

Among the "stylistic" arguments, the one that the rest of the book is "prose" and this "poetry" is weak, considering the mixture of poetry and prose in other biblical books. The similarity of the "Psalm" to other "thanksgiving psalms," particularly in its opening and closing sentences, has reinforced the view that it belonged originally to such a collection and was edited into the book. Since the narrative part invokes the cultic area of sacrifices and vows (1:16), it is not inappropriate to have Jonah compose a typical cultic thanksgiving psalm to express his gratitude. More to the point, Jonah's "Psalm" differs significantly from others in the Psalter by maintaining the narrative form in the way it organizes the terminology of the "underworld," so that Jonah's descent is presented as a geographical sequence.

Furthermore, the "Psalm" contains two instances of a key word or phrase being repeated in a strategic manner. Twice Jonah is "surrounded" (the identical form of the Hebrew verb appearing both times)—by the "streams" (surface currents) in v 4 and by the "deep" in v 6; twice he invokes "Your holy temple"—he looks to it (v 5); his prayer reaches it (v 8). Thus, his physical descent is contrasted with his "spiritual" ascent. This technique of repeating a word or phrase accompanied each time by additional words is also used in the narrative sections of the Book, which would again suggest a common author.

Whereas the opening and closing verses of the "Psalm" and the initial description of the stages of his descent echo similar phrases in other "Psalms" (compare 2:4 with Ps 42:8), during the second phase where he sinks into the very depths, the language is uniquely that of Jonah with no echo elsewhere. Jonah's descent from conventional experience is matched by a move beyond conventional language. The use of phrases from elsewhere in the Bible, with a strong possibility of deliberate borrowing, echoes the technique apparently used in the narrative parts of the book and again points to a common authorship.

A different approach to the authenticity of the "Psalm" is in terms of the structure of the book as a whole, whereby Jonah's "descent" is seen as the mirror-image of the "ascent" of the Ninevites in chapter 3 (Magonet 1976: 60–63).

All the above views can be argued in various ways; however, it is also evident that the narrative part of the book does seem to be dependent on the actual content of the "Psalm" itself (Ackerman 1981). The "Psalm" might be there precisely to indicate the inappropriateness of Jonah's response, in line with other similar inadequacies he has shown. This might explain the comic touch of the fish "vomiting" him out—the word used being particularly strong and implying some disgust. But more specifically, Jonah's closing words include the promise to make a major sacrifice of thanksgiving to God and pay his vows—the language being virtually identical to that of the sailors. Presumably this can only be done in the Temple. Jonah is thus ready to return to Jerusalem and make the appropriate pious gesture in gratitude for being saved. That is why God has to call him "a second time" at the beginning of chapter 3. This repetition of the call is not merely a stylistic device but, in terms of the story, is a necessary reminder to Jonah that he still has an unfulfilled task to complete.

3. Genre. Until the modern period, the historicity of the book, with a few exceptions, seems to have been taken for granted. Thus the references to the sign of Jonah in the Gospels (Matt 12:38–41; Luke 11:29–32) have been important for establishing the "truth" of the book for Christians. Likewise the reading of the book on the Jewish Day of Atonement *(Yom Kippur)*, the most solemn day of the Jewish calendar, has given it considerable educational and moral force within the Jewish tradition.

With the rise of historical criticism came the search for sources, as well as scepticism about the miraculous elements and the lack of evidence in external sources of a massive act of "repentance" in Nineveh. This led, in turn, to conservative attempts to "prove" its historical truth. This concern has waned, at least in scholarly circles, and has been replaced with an attempt to identify the precise "genre" of the book: Is it a parable or legend, a folk tale or didactic story? Is it a "satire," or is the humor better defined as "irony" (Good 1965; Rauber 1970; Holbert 1981; Ackerman 1981; Golka 1986)? Should one avoid Western categories altogether and turn instead to biblical or rabbinic terminology in trying to define it—is it thus a *mashal* (a term used of proverbial and parabolic materials) or a *midrash* (a category of Rabbinic exegesis that also includes short parables)? Certainly the book is closer in tone to individual tales about Elijah or Elisha, or to the story of Balaam (Numbers 22–24) than to the historical books as a whole or the historical anecdotes within Isaiah and Jeremiah.

To a large extent these attempts reflect a scientific interest in precise definition and categorization of the biblical materials. However, on another level they may nevertheless indicate a concern with preserving the "religious truth" of the book in an age when its "historical truth" can no longer be assumed. The absence of consensus on an appropriate descriptive term reflects the difficulty of such an exercise given the limited amount of biblical and extra-biblical materials with which to compare it and the unique character of the book itself.

C. Date and Authorship

Dating the book is problematic because there is virtually no direct information and everything has to be derived by internal evidence of varying degrees of trustworthiness (see Wolff, *Dodekapropheton* BK; Allen; *Joel, Obadiah . . .* NICOT).

It is notable that there is no time signature to the book itself, listing the kings during whose reign he prophesied, unlike the majority of the prophetic books. Even if these are late editorial additions, they give a starting point for investigation. The absence of a date may be because the author, and subsequently the editors, assumed that the reader would identify the Jonah of the book as the Jonah of 2 Kgs 14:25, in which case no such additional information was needed. However, it must also be noted that the absence of a time may accord with other features of the author's literary technique. For example, Jonah is not referred to as a prophet throughout the book. This could also be because of assuming the Kings reference, but its effect is to make Jonah an anonymous individual, out of time, struggling with an unacceptable word of God.

Given the lack of direct evidence, scholars have had to work with a variety of factors, linguistic and historical, to determine the date.

The use of words and phrases that reflect Aramaic usage has been seen as pointing to a late date for the book. However, some of the words relating to the sea voyage may be technical maritime terms, possibly Phoenician in origin, which could have been available at any period. Other grammatical constructions may reflect the earlier influence of Aramaic in the N kingdom. In general, the number of such forms is suggestive of a post-exilic date, but there is no conclusive evidence.

The statement in 3:3 that Nineveh "was" a great city, suggests that it was no longer in existence at the time of composition, i.e., after 612 B.C.

Earlier assumptions that the "universalism" of the book reflect a protest against the strong particularistic attitudes of the returning exiles cannot be proven, and universalistic views may be found in earlier biblical materials.

We have already noted above the possible presence of "quotations" from other parts of the Bible, both within the narrative and "Psalm" section of the book. If these are accepted as deliberate utilizations of material from elsewhere in the Bible, they are again suggestive of a relatively late date of composition.

In general the nature of the book and the various considerations given above suggest that it is not the work of the 8th century prophet Jonah mentioned in Kings, and that the book is a much later composition, though suggested dates range from the 6th to the 4th century. The same dating problems make it impossible to determine the authorship, once the prophet himself has been excluded.

D. Status of Text and Canonical Position

The text of the book has been remarkably well preserved. The most thorough recent study (Trible 1963: 1–65) indicates the presence and absence of a number of *matres lectionis* which affect the spelling of the words, but not their meaning. The genuineness of a couple of words is questioned because of their unusual form or on metrical grounds, but none of these have major consequences. Similarly the ancient versions raise no significant questions about the MT.

No record is preserved of any dispute about its place in the canon among the Twelve "Minor Prophets," despite its major difference in style to the others. It may owe its place there to the identification of Jonah with the prophet in 2 Kings 14. This would account for its location in the first half of the collection, which is probably based upon the chronological view held at the time of compilation (Wolff, *Dodekapropheton* BK, 53).

E. Theological Issues and Motifs

The use of a narrative form affects the way the book is perceived and received. The onus is placed very firmly upon the reader to interpret the events described. For example, no reason is given in the opening chapter for Jonah's flight from God. This leaves the reader with the responsibility of "gap-filling" about this crucial question. Given the role of Nineveh in Israelite history (the capital of the Assyrian Empire that destroyed the N Kingdom), the reader may well sympathize with an Israelite prophet who refused to go there to preach. But this brings the reader, like Jonah himself, into direct conflict with God's express command, so that the reader is forced to identify with, and even share, the tension experienced by the "hero." Even the explanation offered by Jonah in chapter 4 does not resolve the initial question. Jonah quotes good religious traditions about God being "compassionate and merciful" (see discussion above) but it is still not clear to what he is actually objecting. This leads inevitably to a whole range of possible interpretations, all of which have surfaced in classical religious traditions and modern scholarship (Bickerman 1967; Allen, *Joel, Obadiah* . . . NICOT, 188–191). For example, Jonah was jealous that God's special love for Israel was here being extended to those he considered as Israel's enemies—the particularistic/universalistic conflict; Jonah was committed to a God of strict justice and was scandalized by God's compassion for those he considered to be wicked and due for severe punishment—the justice/mercy conflict. These and other interpretations may be argued out and different weight may be given to the various viewpoints depending on the reader's own concerns or interests.

The significance of this is not that one or the other view is right or wrong, but rather that it is in the nature of "narrative" to be suggestive and allusive in this way rather than to be assertive or dogmatic. The exercise of exploring the possible reasons is as much a part of the "message" of the book as the story itself because it, too, demands that the reader continually reassess his or her view of events and motivations. The reader, like Jonah, is forced to reevaluate an understanding of the world and of God's will. It is therefore erroneous to focus solely on the character of Jonah and condemn him as a "narrow, chauvinistic, hater of Gentiles" as some extreme interpretations with anti-Jewish overtones have suggested (Golka 1986); it is equally erroneous to identify totally with the author as a sublime, universalistic, almost "pre-Christian Christian" as have others for whom the Hebrew Bible is read in the light of the Christian canon. The narrator who "knows" what is going on, the characters who appear in the story, and the reader who encounters the book, all play their part in a process of interpretation. Thus the nature of the book and the awareness of these implications is vital for an attempt to understand and evaluate it.

We began by listing a series of questions raised by the book and it is worth remembering that it concludes with a question. "If you (Jonah) can have pity . . . should not I (God) have pity. . . ." No answer is offered by the text but various exegetical and liturgical traditions have tended to assume that Jonah said "yes," and was suitably repentant. This need not be the case, and given the frequency with which the author breaks conventions, it is probably best to leave the matter open—or, as the whole thrust of the narrative has been, to leave it to the reader to respond to the challenge posed equally to Jonah and the reader. For that, after all, is the culminating effect of the narrator's strategy of demanding the reader's engagement. The book is subversive in its inversion of conventions and challenging of stereotypes and prejudices. Thus, despite its unconventional narrative form, its place among the prophetic books is ultimately appropriate. It clearly addresses the issue of the relationship of Israel to the outside world, represented as two major tendencies. Yet the polemic does not overwhelm its artistic values. Most strikingly a relatively small vocabulary (for example, the repetition of two verbs alone creates the vivid effect of the storm) is used to considerable effect and creates multiple dimensions of meaning. The significant echoes of other biblical events or narratives provide reference points that lead to startling new understandings, both of the event cited and of the character of Jonah himself. In this, at least, the Book seems to stand within the tradition of interpretation through parable that was to become Rabbinic *midrash*.

Bibliography

Ackerman, J. S. 1981. Satire and Symbolism in the Song of Jonah. Pp. 213–46 in *Traditions in Transformation: Turning Points in Biblical Faith*, ed. B. Halpern and J. D. Levenson. Winona Lake, IN.

Bickerman, E. J. 1967. *Four Strange Books of the Bible*. New York.

Christensen, D. L. 1987. Narrative Poetics and the Interpretation of the Book of Jonah. Pp. 29–48 in *Directions in Biblical Hebrew Poetry*, ed. E. R. Follis. JSOTSup 40. Sheffield.

Cohn, G. H. 1969. *Das Buch Jona im Lichte der biblischen Erzählkunst.* SSN 12. Assen.
Feuillet, A. 1947a. Les sources du livre de Jonas. *RB* 54: 161-86.
———. 1947b. Le sens du livre de Jonas. *RB* 54: 340–61.
Fränkel, L. 1967. *weraḥamāyw ʿal kōl maʿaśāyw. Maʿānôt* 9: 193–207 (in Hebrew).
———. 1972. *Haʾantitezah keyesōd siprûti bemiqrāʾ.* Pp. 129–46 in *hammiqrāʾ wetôldôt yiśrāʾēl.* Jerusalem (in Hebrew).
Golka, F. W. 1986. Jonaexegese und Antijudaismus. *Kirche und Israel* 1: 51–61.
———. 1988. Divine Repentance: A Commentary on the Book of Jonah. In *Divine Revelation,* ed. G. A. F. Knight and F. W. Golka. Grand Rapids.
Good, E. M. 1965. *Irony in the Old Testament.* Philadelphia.
Holbert, J. C. 1981. Deliverance Belongs to Yahweh: Satire in the Book of Jonah. *JSOT* 21: 59–81.
Kugel, J. L. 1981. *The Idea of Biblical Poetry.* New Haven.
Landes, G. M. 1967. The Kerygma of the Book of Jonah. *Int* 21: 3–31.
Lohfink, N. 1961. Und Jona ging zur Stadt hinaus (Jona 4:5). *BZ* 5: 185–203.
Magonet, J. D. 1976. *Form and Meaning: Studies in Literary Techniques in the Book of Jonah.* Bern.
Rauber, D. F. 1970. Jonah—The Prophet as Shlemiel. *BToday* 49: 29–37.
Strikowsky, A. 1976. Divine Nomenclature in Jonah. *Niv: A Journal Devoted to Halacha, Jewish Thought and Education.* Friends of the Midrashia in Israel.
Trible, P. L. 1963. *Studies in the Book of Jonah.* Diss. New York.

JONATHAN MAGONET

JONAM (PERSON) [Gk *Iōnam*]. The father of Joseph (not the "supposed father" of Jesus) and son of Eliakim, according to Luke's genealogy tying Joseph, the "supposed father" of Jesus, to descent from Adam and God (Luke 3:30). Gk *Iōnam* is read in B, Leningrad and Oxford, and most of the versions, but there is a significant variant Gk *Iōnan,* found in A, G, H, L, and Vulgate. D omits the name, substituting a genealogy adapted from Matt 1:6–15 for Luke 3:23–31. The name Jonam occurs nowhere else in the biblical documents, including Matthew's genealogy, and falls within a list of eighteen otherwise unknown descendants of David's son Nathan (Fitzmyer *Luke I–IX* AB, 501). Kuhn (1923: 208–9) argues that two seemingly parallel lists of names—Luke 3:23–26 (Jesus to Mattathias) and 3:29–31 (Joshua/Jesus to Mattatha)—were originally identical, the first perhaps reflecting a Hebrew context and the second, in an Aramaic context, tracing Mary's line of descent (since it does not mention Joseph as Jesus' father). Jonam, in the 2d list, corresponds to Nahum, in the 1st list. According to Kuhn, Gk *Naoum* representing Heb *nḥwm* was corrupted to Gk *Anoum* representing Heb *ḥnw* or *ḥnn* (cf. Neh 3:30 in LXX B). Gk *Iōnam,* Kuhn believes, is itself a corruption of Gk *Iōanam,* found for Gk *Iōanan* in 1 Chr 3:24a. (Gk *Iōnan* is also found in variants for Gk *Iōanan.*) With no textual variants for Jonah and Nahum to support confusion of the two in the NT, Kuhn's theory has little plausibility.

Bibliography

Kuhn, G. 1923. Die Geschlectsregister Jesu bei Lukas und Matthäus, nach ihrer Herkunft untersucht. *ZNW* 22: 206–28.

STANLEY E. PORTER

JONATHAN (PERSON) [Heb *yônātān; yĕhônātān*]. The names Jonathan and Jehonathan (Heb "Yahweh has given") appear to be used interchangeably.

1. A Levite from the town of Bethlehem in Judah, who, according to Judges 17–18, founded a priesthood at Laish (later called Dan). This Levite, whose name (Jonathan) is provided only at the close of the narrative (Judg 18:30), was hired by the Ephraimite Micah to serve as priest in his private shrine (17:7–13). The Danites, searching for new territory, received a favorable oracle from Jonathan as they journeyed northward. The narrative relates that Jonathan was later persuaded by the Danites to serve as the first priest at the new sanctuary at Dan. The image taken from Micah's shrine was housed in this Danite tribal sanctuary (18:11–31). The priesthood founded by Jonathan is said to have continued until the people went into captivity (734 or 722/1 B.C.E.; 18:30).

Jonathan is reported to be a direct descendant of Moses through Gershom (18:30). The MT, however, through the addition of the letter *nun* to the name of Moses (rather than being incorporated into the text, this has been suspended above the line and inserted between the first two consonants of the name Moses), has altered the name of Moses (cf. the versions) to that of Manasseh (the apostate king).

2. See JONATHAN SON OF SAUL.

3. Son of Abiathar, who, together with Zadok, served as priest during the reign of king David (2 Sam 15:36; 1 Kgs 1:42). Stationed at En-rogel at the time of Absalom's revolt, Jonathan and Zadok's son Ahimaaz acted as couriers, conveying to David information pertaining to Absalom's plans which was supplied by the spy Hushai. Upon being discovered and forced to flee, they were assisted in escaping from Absalom's men by a woman at Bahurim, who hid them in a well (2 Sam 15:24–29, 32–37; 17:17–22). It was Jonathan who later brought to Adonijah the news that Solomon had been anointed king (1 Kgs 1:41–48). Solomon removed Abiathar from his office of priest and banished him to Anathoth (2 Kgs 2:26–27). Since Jonathan was also an active supporter of Adonijah, it can be assumed that he shared the fate of his father.

4. King David's uncle (Heb *dôd;* so RSV, JB, NAB; NEB reads "nephew" [cf. 1 Chr 20:7]) and a member of his personal staff (1 Chr 27:32). As usually translated, 27:32 states that Jonathan shared with Jehiel son of Hachmoni the task of tutoring David's sons (see RSV). However, a preferred translation of 27:32 is probably one which does not take Heb *hûʾ* ("he") with v 32b. The text thus names only Jehiel as the one responsible for such tutoring of David's sons (cf. LXX). Jonathan, who is referred to as a man of understanding and learning, was David's counselor.

5. Son of Shimei or Shimea, David's brother. He slew a Philistine giant at Gath (1 Sam 21:20–21; 1 Chr 20:6–7). His name is given as Jonadab in some mss of the LXX (cf. 1 Sam 13:3). The Philistine slain by Jonathan is one of four warriors identified in 2 Sam 21:15–22 as being among the *yĕlîdê hārāpâ.* As traditionally understood, this designation refers to those who were descendants of Raphah, eponymous ancestor of the Rephaim, a legendary race of giants (RSV translates "descended from the giants"). More recently, however, it has been argued that the Philistine *yĕlîdê hārāpâ* was an elite corps of warriors dedicated to a deity. The corps was so designated either because of its emblem, the scimitar, or because *rp*ʾ (a divine epithet) was the patron deity of the corps (see the discussions in L'Heureux and Willesen).

6. One of David's thirty mighty men (2 Sam 23:32; 1 Chr 11:34; see DAVID'S CHAMPIONS). For the MT's "the sons of Jashen, Jonathan, Shammah the Hararite" in 2 Sam 23:32–33 (see RSV), a suggested reading is "Hashem the Gizonite; Jonathan son of (cf. some mss of LXX) Shammah the Hararite" (see, e.g., NEB; cf. 1 Chr 11:34). In 1 Chr 11:34 Jonathan is identified as the son of Shagee rather than as the son of Shammah (1 Sam 23:32; cf. also 23:11).

7. Son of Uzziah. He was in charge of the royal supplies in the provincial towns, villages, and fortresses during the reign of David (1 Chr 27:25).

8. One of the Levites who formed part of a commission sent by Jehoshaphat to teach the law in the cities of Judah (2 Chr 17:8; Jehonathan in RSV and other English translations).

9. A high-ranking government official who held the position of *sōpēr* during the reign of Jehoiakim (Jer 37:15, 20; 38:26). It is probable that Jonathan's office was that of state or royal secretary. He was preceded in this office by Elishama (Jer 36:12, 20–21). The prophet Jeremiah, accused of having deserted to the Babylonians (Jer 37:11–16), was imprisoned in the house of Jonathan, which had been made into a prison.

10. One of the two sons of Kareah who, following the destruction of Jerusalem in 587/6 B.C.E., chose to join Gedaliah, the ruler of Judah, at his administrative center at Mizpah (Jer 40:8 in the MT). However, as is indicated by the LXX and the parallel passage in 2 Kgs 25:23, the MT's "and Johanan and Jonathan sons of Kareah" is to be emended to read "and Johanan son of Kareah" (see RSV, JB, NAB; the NEB follows the MT).

11. The father of Ebed, one of the "heads of their fathers' houses" who returned from exile with Ezra (Ezra 8:1, 6). Ebed, a member of the Adin phratry *(mišpāḥâ),* was accompanied by the 50 male members of his extended family (Ezra 8:6; 1 Esdr 8:32 has Obed and 250 men).

12. A priest named as one of those who were heads of priestly families in the time of the high priest Joiakim (Neh 12:12–21). He is the head of the family of Malluch (12:14; the MT reads "Malluchi" [cf. however Neh 12:2]).

13. Another priest named in the list of those who were heads of priestly families in the time of the high priest Joiakim (Neh 12:12–21). He is the head of the family of Shemaiah (12:18; JEHONATHAN in RSV and other English translations).

14. A high priest who held office in the post-exilic period. He was the son of Joiada and the father of Jaddua (Neh 12:10–11). The name Jonathan, however, is undoubtedly a scribal error for Johanan (cf. the list of high priests in Neh 12:22; also Neh 12:23). It is known that the high priest during the time of Nehemiah was Eliashib (Neh 3:1, 20). Johanan is identified as the grandson of Eliashib in Neh 12:10, but as the son of Eliashib in Neh 12:23 (although it is possible that Heb *ben* is to be translated as "grandson" in Neh 12:23; cf. NEB, JB). Further, according to Ezra 10:6 (1 Esdr 9:1), Ezra retired to the temple chamber of Jehohanan (Johanan) son of Eliashib. While it is possible that the Jehohanan (Johanan) of Ezra 10:6 is to be identified with the high priest Johanan mentioned in Nehemiah 12 (cf., e.g., the NEB's translation of Heb *ben* as "grandson" in Ezra 10:6), this is far from certain. Such an identification would lend support to the view that a late date for Ezra is to be preferred (from the Elephantine papyri [*CAP,* 30.18, 31.17], we know that a Johanan served as high priest during the reign of Darius II). However, with respect to the high priestly genealogy in Neh 12:10–11, it has recently been suggested that one of the occurrences of the two names Eliashib and Johanan has fallen out of the text by haplography (Cross 1975: 10). According to this hypothesis, the sequence of high priests is as follows: Eliashib I, Johanan I (b. ca. 520 and a contemporary of Ezra), Eliashib II (b. ca. 495 and a contemporary of Nehemiah), Joiada, Johanan II (b. ca. 445; it is this Johanan whose name appears in the Elephantine papyri).

15. The father of Zechariah, one of the Levites who participated in the dedication of the rebuilt walls of Jerusalem in the time of Nehemiah (Neh 12:35; the reference to the priests at the beginning of v 35 [MT reads "of the sons of the priests"] is probably to be taken with vv 33–34). In Neh 12:35, the ancestry of Zechariah and Jonathan is traced back to Asaph, the founder of a guild of temple musicians.

16. A priest who is reported to have led the prayers at a sacrifice during the time of Nehemiah (2 Macc 1:23).

17. Son of Asahel. One of four men who, according to Ezra 10:15 in the MT, stood opposed to either Ezra's reform measures relating to the putting away of foreign wives, or (and this is probably how 10:15 is to be understood) the procedure by which these measures were to be carried out. The ambiguity of the Hebrew text is reflected in most English translations (cf. however the JB, which reads "were opposed to this procedure"). The LXX reads "only Jonathan . . . and Jazias . . . were with me in this" for the MT's "were opposed to this."

18. A Jerahmeelite. Son of Jada, brother of Jethen, and father of Peleth and Zaza (1 Chr 2:32–33).

19. Son of Mattathias and leader of the Maccabeans 160–143 B.C.E. Mattathias, who belonged to the priestly family of Joarib (alternately Jehoiarib; cf. 1 Chr 24:7), was a native of Jerusalem who later settled with his family in Modein (1 Macc 2:1). Following the death of his brother Judas in 160 B.C.E., Jonathan, who was nicknamed Apphus (2:2), was quickly recognized as military leader by his own people (9:28–31). Jonathan later attained a position of considerable power and influence when he was able to take advantage of the unstable political situation within the Seleucid empire. Rival claimants to the throne sought Jonathan's support. In order to secure such support, Alexander Balas, a pretender to the throne, appointed Jonathan high priest in 152 B.C.E. (10:15–21). Alexander also appointed Jonathan general and governor of a province (10:65). When Demetrius II Nicator came to power, the privileges extended to Jonathan by Alexander were confirmed. But when Demetrius refused to remove a Syrian garrison from the Acra in Jerusalem, Jonathan threw in his lot with Antiochus, the son of Alexander Balas. Antiochus was supported in his bid for the throne by the general Trypho. Trypho, however, though ostensibly championing the cause of Antiochus, was in fact seeking to secure the kingdom for himself. In the belief that his own ambitions were threatened by Jonathan, Trypho, through an act of deception, had Jonathan imprisoned in Ptolemais. Jonathan was executed by Trypho and buried near Baskama in Gilead in 143 B.C.E. (12:39–48; 13:12–23). The bones of Jonathan were later taken by Simon and placed in a family grave in Modein (13:25–30). Jonathan was succeeded by his brother Simon. With his assumption of both religious and civil power, Jonathan may be regarded as the one who laid the foundations for the later Hasmonean dynasty (142–63 B.C.E.).

20. A general, who, in 142 B.C.E., was sent by Simon Maccabeus with a large army to fortify the garrison established a year earlier in the coastal port of Joppa (cf. 1 Macc 12:33–34; 14:5) and to expel the occupants from the city (1 Macc 13:11). He was the son of Absalom (who is possibly to be identified with Absalom father of Mattathias [1 Macc 11:70]).

Bibliography

Cross, F. M. 1975. A Reconstruction of the Judean Restoration. *JBL* 94: 4–18.

L'Heureux, C. E. 1976. The *yelîdê hārāpāʾ*—A Cultic Association of Warriors. *BASOR* 221: 83–85.

Willesen, F. 1958. The Philistine Corps of the Scimitar from Gath. *JSS* 3: 327–35.

JOHN M. BERRIDGE

JONATHAN SON OF SAUL. Jonathan was the oldest son of Saul, son of Kish, and his wife Ahinoam, daughter of Ahimaaz. He was the heir to the Saulide throne of Israel before his untimely death at Mt. Gilboa. The throne eventually passed on to David, who is portrayed as having been a very close personal friend of Jonathan.

A. Jonathan from a Literary Perspective

Most of the passages that involve Jonathan appear to have been written to justify David's replacement of the Saulide house on the throne of Israel. Their literary dimension must accordingly be examined fully before any judgment can be made concerning their underlying historical veracity.

Jonathan's opening appearance in the Bible is in 1 Sam 13:2–3, when, as commander of one of Israel's battalions during a planned campaign against the Philistine garrisons controlling the Michmash pass, he is depicted as attacking the Philistine garrison at Gibeah/Geba prematurely, instead of waiting for his father to launch a simultaneous attack against the Philistine garrison at Michmash, on the other side of the wadi, with the remaining Israelite forces. This initial victory forces Saul to have to retreat to Gibeah/Geba, leaving the Michmash outpost intact, and to draw up a new strategy to cope with the Philistine retaliation, which would now include reinforcement troops from the Philistine plain. Needing his own reinforcements, Saul leaves Jonathan at Gibeah/Geba with some troops and goes to Gilgal to muster additional men. While Saul is at Gilgal, Yahweh rejects him as king over Israel for disobeying a divine command, in favor of a new candidate, who is "a man after His own heart" (13:14).

1 Samuel 14 implies that Jonathan, the heir-elect, is the new candidate for king in its recounting of how Jonathan puts his trust in the Lord by following his heart and bravely venturing across the wadi with his weapons bearer, gains access to the Philistine outpost by being mistaken as an Israelite deserter, and slays 20 enemy soldiers, thereby throwing the Philistine forces into chaos and launching what becomes a victorious battle for Israel (14:1–23). Yet Jonathan inadvertently breaks a divinely invoked food ban that his father had imposed on the troops in his absence and fails to repent when he learns the truth (14:24–30). His deed is discovered by oracular consultation with Yahweh through the Urim and Thummim, who declares him to be guilty (14:36–44). Although the troops ransom Jonathan, believing that he has had Yahweh's favor that day in battle (14:45), it is revealed, after the confirmation that Saul has been irrevocably rejected by Yahweh (1 Samuel 15) that David, not Jonathan, is the new candidate whom Yahweh has chosen. Jonathan, the heir to the throne, has been rejected from the kingship because of his insubordination. David is secretly anointed by Samuel to confirm his designation as king-elect (16:1–14).

1 Samuel 13–14 play the dual role of depicting Saul's rejection from the kingship for disobedience to prophetically mediated divine command and of depicting Jonathan's rejection from the role of king-elect for insubordination. The account of Jonathan's rejection appears to have been structured by using the tripartite kingship ritual pattern—the designation of the king-elect, his testing through a military deed, and his subsequent confirmation by coronation after his successful completion of the military deed (Halpern 1981: 125–48; Edelman 1984: 197–99). The first step is presumed because of Jonathan's status as heir-elect by birth. It is also hinted at by Samuel's going, immediately after Saul's rejection at Gilgal (13:15), to Gibeah, where Jonathan is stationed. The second step is represented by the episode in 14:1–23, where Jonathan follows the inclinations of "his heart" by trusting in Yahweh. The third step is aborted because of Jonathan's failure in his testing after his breaking of the divinely imposed food ban (14:24–44). The same pattern can be seen to have been used to structure the account of Saul's rise to the kingship and of David's succession to the throne of Israel. See SAUL.

Jonathan's next appearance is immediately after David's slaying of Goliath, where he is said to have "loved" David as his own soul and to have made a covenant with David, giving him his (royal) robe, his armor, his sword, his bow, and his girdle (1 Sam 18:1–4). At this point David replaces Jonathan as military commander and is reported to have been successful wherever Saul sent him and to have gained the support of all the people and Saul's servants (18:5). The verb *love* in Hebrew can have political overtones, referring to a treaty relationship, and appears to be used in this way in the Jonathan passages (Thompson 1974). These narratives seem to be intended to demonstrate Jonathan's acceptance of Yahweh's earlier negative judgment of him in chaps. 13–14 and his willingness to recognize David as Yahweh's new candidate to succeed Saul on the throne of Israel. He does this by formally binding himself to David in a covenant and by passing his weapons to David, an act which is a gesture of political surrender (2 Sam 8:7, 11, 12; 2 Kgs 11:10).

Most of the remaining scenes in 1 Samuel in which Jonathan appears stress his covenant relationship with David and affirm his knowledge and acceptance of David's status as king-elect, while simultaneously revealing Saul's progressive acquiescence in Yahweh's choice. In 1 Sam 19:1–7 Saul becomes jealous of David's military success and esteem and orders Jonathan and his servants to kill David. It is stated in this context that "Jonathan delighted much in David." Because of their covenant Jonathan warns David to hide, argues on David's behalf before his father, and persuades him to remove his death sentence against David. He then restores David to the court.

After another attempt on his life by Saul, David goes to Jonathan and asks why Saul seeks his life (20:1–42). Jonathan agrees to help David in any way possible (v 4) and swears to apprise David of his father's intention, whether good or evil, saying "may Yahweh be with you as he has been with my father." In the revealing speech in vv 14–17, Jonathan asks David not to cut off his loyalty to Jonathan's house forever and not to let the name of Jonathan be cut off from the house of David in the future, when Yahweh will cut off all of David's enemies from the face of the earth. Jonathan has him swear to keep this promise "by his love for him," i.e., on the basis of their existing covenant relationship (v 17). When Saul learns that Jonathan has excused David from the New Moon feast, he curses him and orders him to send for David so that he can be killed, in order to enable Jonathan's kingdom to be established (vv 30–31). Jonathan questions why David should be put to death (v 32), thereby emphasizing his acceptance of David as the new king-elect of Israel, in contrast to Saul's refusal to accept the divine plan. The chapter ends with Jonathan's warning David of Saul's intention to kill him and with another reference to the covenant entered into by Jonathan and David and the oath sworn in the name of Yahweh to maintain peaceful relations between David's and Jonathan's descendants forever.

In the subsequent accounts of Saul's pursuit of David through the Wilderness of Judah, Saul's explicit knowledge of the covenant between Jonathan and David is revealed (22:7–8), after which Jonathan is reported to go to David while he is in hiding at Horesh in the Wilderness of Ziph to strengthen David's hand in God (23:17). The two then renew their covenant before Yahweh, after which Jonathan returns home (23:17–18). In this final scene between Jonathan and David, the narrator's message is completely revealed in Jonathan's direct confession that David, not he, will be the next king over Israel and that Saul also knows this fact. Jonathan's death at Gilboa is briefly reported in 31:2.

There is an allusion to the covenant between Jonathan and David toward the end of the lament over Saul and Jonathan, quoted from the Book of Jashar in 2 Sam 1:19–27. In v 26 David is quoted as saying, "I am distressed for you, my brother Jonathan; very pleasant have you been to me; your love to me was beautiful, surpassing the love of women." It should be noted that this is the only statement in the first person in the lament and that it is placed almost as a superscript and introduced by a statement that refers back to v 19. In addition, it is framed by parallel phrases in vv 25 and 27. Although David is said in v 17 to have written the lament personally, his authorship may be questioned and, along with it, the originality of v 26 (Edelman 1988). In view of the use of the covenant theme and the related verb *love* to describe the covenant relationship as a literary device to portray Jonathan's acceptance of David as the divinely chosen heir to Saul, the secondary introduction of the theme into the lament would be a logical way to give the theme an air of authenticity.

The theme of the covenant between Jonathan and David continues in 2 Samuel in connection with David's actions on behalf of Meribaal, Jonathan's young, crippled son. In 2 Sam 9:1 David is portrayed as asking, "Is there still anyone left of the house of Saul, that I may show him kindness for Jonathan's sake?" Upon learning from a former servant of the Saulide house of Meribaal's existence, David has him brought to the court and restores to him the Saulide family estates, "For I will show you kindness for the sake of your father Jonathan" (9:7). In a related incident David is said to have spared Meribaal from being one of the seven Saulides sacrificed by the Gibeonites to end a three-year famine, "Because of the oath of Yahweh that was between them, between David and Jonathan, the son of Saul" (21:7). It is generally recognized that historically, Meribaal's escape from sacrifice was almost certainly due to David's ignorance of his existence and that his subsequent discovery led to his becoming a mandatory member of the king's table, so that he could be constantly scrutinized by David's servants. See MERIB-BAAL.

A slightly different approach to the Jonathan narratives suggests that Jonathan should be understood to function on a literary level as a mediator between Saul and David and as a king-elect who abdicates his throne to David. This proposal is based on a structural analysis of 1 Samuel 13–31, in which it is discerned that narrative sections concerning Jonathan (18:1–5; 19:1–7; 20:1–21:1—Eng 20:1–42; 23:15b–18) have been artfully alternated with sections involving Saul and David (16:14–17:58; 18:6–30; 19:8–25; 21:2–23:15a [with other material]; 23:19 ff. [with much other material]). The resulting narrative is seen to be introduced by a preamble recounting Saul's rejection (chaps. 13–15) and a focal scene recounting David's anointing (16:1–13). According to this understanding of the narrative structure, the theme of the covenant between David and Jonathan functions literarily as a means of identifying the two, while Jonathan's conveyance of his royal armor and sword to David (18:1–5) is Jonathan's symbolic abdication as heir-elect in favor of David (Jobling 1976).

B. The Historical Jonathan

Very little is known about Jonathan after one removes the literary patterning outlined above and seeks for information about his career. Both 1 Sam 14:49 and 1 Chr 8:33; 9:39 name him as the eldest son of Saul, a relationship which would have made him the heir to the Saulide throne. He died alongside his father and two of his younger brothers, Abinadab and Malchishua, at Mt. Gilboa, during the unsuccessful Israelite campaign against Beth-shan. At the time of his death, he had a young son, Meribaal, who was probably an infant or toddler. This suggests that he was perhaps 30 or 31 years old when he died, assuming that comparative figures for marriage ages for males in the ANE, 27 through 31, were applicable to ancient Israel and to royalty (Roth 1987). No figures are given in the Bible.

It is unlikely that Jonathan fought at the battle of the Michmash pass, as currently portrayed in 1 Samuel 13–14. If one presumes that the corrupted regnal figure for Saul in 1 Sam 13:1 was 22 years old, Jonathan would probably have only been an 8–10-year-old child at the time of the battle; and the legal age for military service was 20 (Num 26:2, 4). The location of the two Philistine outposts in E Benjamin and Mt. Ephraim on opposite sides of the Wâdī Suweinit would have required their elimination during the early years of Saul's reign, so that he could secure his E flank and prevent periodic Philistine incursion through his territory to man the garrisons. In addition, his victory would have given him control over the E half of one of the main E-W routes from the Philistine plain to the Jordan valley. It appears that the biblical narrator has used a Saulide-era battle as the backdrop for his theological portrayal of Jonathan's rejection as king-elect in favor of David; but, perhaps unknowingly, he has chosen one that Jonathan could not possibly have participated in.

The historicity of the covenant between David and Jonathan is difficult to judge but probably also has been developed by the biblical narrator in order to convey his message. While Jonathan may have been good friends with David while he was at the Saulide court, subsequent historical developments weigh against their having entered into a covenant in which Jonathan would have recognized the divine choice of David as Saul's successor to the Israelite throne. After Saul and Jonathan both died at Gilboa, Saul's youngest son, Eshbaal, acceded to the throne, indicating the acceptance of the principle of dynastic succession from the founding of the Israelite monarchy. It was only in the wake of Eshbaal's murder, which David may have arranged (see ESHBAAL), that David gained the Saulide throne in place of another inexperienced Saulide, possibly claiming to be a legitimate candidate on the basis of optative affiliation, because of his marriage to Saul's daughter Merab (Tsevat 1958). The theme of the covenant and "love" between David and Jonathan seems to ignore the actual course of history, a disregard which suggests in turn its literary origin.

Bibliography

Edelman, D. 1984. Saul's Rescue of Jabesh-Gilead (1 Sam 11:1–11): Sorting Story from History. *ZAW* 96: 195–209.

———. 1988. 2 Sam 1:26 in Light of the Historicity of David's Covenant with Jonathan. *SJOT* 4: 66–75.

Halpern, B. 1981. *The Constitution of the Monarchy in Israel.* HSM 25. Ann Arbor.

Jobling, D. 1976. Saul's Fall and Jonathan's Rise: Tradition and Redaction in 1 Samuel 14:1–46. *JBL* 95: 367–76.

———. 1978. Jonathan: A Structural Study in 1 Samuel. Pp. 4–25 in *The Sense of Biblical Narrative.* JSOTSup 7. Sheffield.

Morgenstern, J. 1959. David and Jonathan. *JBL* 78: 322–35.

Roth, M. 1987. Age at Marriage and the Household: A Study of Neo-Assyrian and Neo-Babylonian Forms. *Comparative Studies in Society and History* 29: 715–47.

Thompson, J. A. 1974. The Significance of the Verb *Love* in the David-Jonathan Narratives in 1 Samuel. *VT* 24: 334–38.

Tsevat, M. 1958. Marriage and Monarchical Legitimacy in Ugarit and Israel. *JSS* 3: 237–43.

DIANA V. EDELMAN

JOPPA (PLACE) [Heb *yāpô*]. A town on the coast of the Mediterranean Sea mentioned in connection with the original tribal territory of Dan (Josh 19:46). When Solomon built the Jerusalem temple—and again when the temple was rebuilt in the postexilic period—timbers from Lebanon were shipped to Joppa, where they were unloaded and carried overland to Jerusalem (2 Chr 2:15—Eng 2:16; Ezra 3:7). It was in Joppa that Jonah hired a ship to carry him to Tarshish "away from the presence of the Lord" (1:3). In the NT Joppa is mentioned in connection with Peter's missionary activity (Acts 9:36ff.).

A. Identification and History

Biblical Joppa can be securely identified with modern Jaffa (M.R. 126162), a city situated on the top of a high hill just S of Tel Aviv. Since antiquity the city has been a way station for conquerors traveling from Egypt northward or from the N countries southward. It was also the first stop for pilgrims on their way to Jerusalem. It is not surprising therefore that Joppa is frequently mentioned in the Bible and in numerous ancient records.

The name Joppa is derived from the Phoenician word meaning "the beautiful"; in Greek the town was called *Ioppe* and in Arabic *Yâfâ el-ʿAtiqa*, "ancient Jaffa." The earliest mention of Joppa is in connection with its capture by Thutmose III in the 15th century B.C. (*ANET,* 242). It is mentioned again in the Harris papyrus, which is a folktale describing the capture of Joppa by a strategy reminiscent of the story of Ali Baba and the 40 thieves and the legend of the Trojan horse (*ANET,* 22–23). Joppa is mentioned subsequently in two of the Amarna Letters, which inform us that in the 14th century the city was an Egyptian stronghold containing royal granaries. In papyrus Anastasi I, a satiric letter apparently of the 13th century, an Egyptian royal official gives an account of his experience in Joppa (*ANET,* 475ff., esp. 478). The name of Joppa is inscribed on the "prism stele" of King Sennacherib of Assyria, found in his palace at Nineveh; it relates that on his way to fight King Hezekiah of Judah he took Joppa and a number of towns in its vicinity, an event which occurred about 700 B.C. (*ANET,* 287).

The inscription of Eshmunezer, king of Sidon (dated probably to the 6th century B.C.), relates that as an expression of gratitude from the "Lord of Kings" (king of Persia), he received two harbor towns on the Palestinian coast, Joppa and Dor (*ANET,* 662). The Sidonian occupation of Joppa in the Persian period is also known from the description of the coastal towns of Syria and Palestine attributed to the Greek voyager Scylax. In the Hellenistic period Joppa was colonized by Greeks. The papyri of Zenon, an Egyptian treasury official who visited the country in 259/258 B.C. during the reign of Ptolemy II, shed some light on the history of the city in his time. In the Hasmonean period the city was captured from the Seleucids and became the port of Judea. During the war with the Romans, it was destroyed first by Cestius Gallus and then by Vespasian but was quickly rebuilt. From this period onward Joppa is frequently mentioned by Greek and Roman historians.

B. Excavations

From 1948 to 1950 P. L. O. Guy carried out the first exploratory excavations in Joppa. In 1952 Guy's excavations were continued down to virgin soil (Bowman, Isserlin, and Row 1955). The excavators established that the earliest remains at that spot were sherds dating from the 5th century B.C. and that the site was uninhabited prior to that date. They also discovered a structure from the 4th or 3d century B.C. of which only the floor of one of the rooms was preserved. The walls of the building were repaired in the 2d century B.C., and in the following century the level of the floor was raised. During the Byzantine period the area was settled anew.

In 1955 J. Kaplan undertook a systematic excavation of ancient Joppa. By 1964 three areas (A, B, C) in different sections of the mound had been excavated during six seasons of excavations. Limited soundings were also carried out in the clock square of Joppa, in which was discovered part of the cemetery of the gentile population of Joppa, dated to the Late Hellenistic and Roman periods.

1. Area A. Seven occupation levels, the latest dating from the 1st century B.C., were excavated here; and the following stratification was established.

Level I, just beneath the surface, was dated to the Hellenistic period. This level is divided into two sublevels, I-A and I-B. Level I-A contained a section of a wall of dressed stone, 2.2 m wide, with a casemate construction adjoining it. They date from the 1st century B.C., i.e., from the Hasmonean period. In level I-B the corner of a square fortress, also built of dressed stone, was uncovered, with a wall 2.5 m wide. The fortress was dated to the 3d century B.C. To this level was also assigned a group of five round, stone floors, 0.8–1.2 m in diameter, each with a small, stone basin. These floors were found in the S section of the excavation and had no connection with the walls. Level II here was dated to the Persian period. A section of a dressed stone wall, 2.5 m wide, and some adjacent structures were cleared. The wall dates from the second half of the 5th century B.C. and was apparently built by the Sidonians.

Level III, dating to the Iron Age, was also divided into two sublevels. Remains of sublevel III-A, preserved at the E edge of the excavation, contained a rough stone wall, approximately 0.8 m thick, adjoining a stone floor sloping eastward. These structures were assigned to the 8th century B.C. Level III-B, found at the W edge of the excavation, contained a section of a courtyard with a floor of beaten earth and an ash pit nearby, with Philistine sherds of the 11th century B.C.

Likewise, level IV (LB IIB) also consists of two sublevels. Sublevel IV-A contained the threshold of the citadel gate and two entrance walls, 18 m long and 4 m apart, built of gray mud bricks. The walls run in an E-W direction from the gate into the citadel. The passageway between the walls was paved with stone and pebbles. The walls and gate were destroyed by fire, apparently late in the 13th century B.C. The bronze hinge of the gate was discovered in situ near the bottom of the left jamb. Beneath these structures were the remains of sublevel IV-B, which included the lower part of an earlier gate, fallen stone doorjambs, and two entrance walls, all of which followed the same line as the structures of sublevel IV-A. It is clear that sublevel IV-A had been built on the ruins of a previous occupation level, IV-B, which had also been burned, apparently earlier in the 13th century (in the published interim reports, sublevel IV-B appears as level V). Inscribed upon four of the stone jambs were the five titles of Rameses II and part of his name, and it appears that the inscriptions were originally set symmetrically on both sides of the gateway. The gate and the entrance walls dating from the time of Rameses had been dug deep into the E part of the ruined citadel of Joppa. As a result, remains from the 18th to 14th centuries B.C. situated to the N and S of the entrance walls lay at a higher level than the threshold of Rameses' gate. These strata were only partially cleared.

In level V (LB IIA) some building remains were found, as well as a small silo built of rough stones set between the S entrance wall of Rameses' gate and parts of the structures of level VI S of it. Quantities of potsherds of the 14th century B.C. were found in the silo and its vicinity.

Level VI (LB I) contained some remains of mud-brick buildings on stone foundations. North of the N entrance wall a locus of pottery vessels was uncovered, including bichrome and gray-burnished ware. South of the entrance wall was a heap of sherds probably thrown there when the inhabitants had cleared an adjacent area. These broken vessels are of Cypriot origin and include base ring and monochrome type wares. Level VI is dated from the second half of the 16th century to the second half of the 15th century B.C.

The lowest level excavated (VII) was dated to the MB III period. Sections of two brick walls were found at the N and S edges of the excavated area. It seems that subsequently occupation levels VI–IV were concentrated in the space between these two walls. The outer face of the N wall did not adjoin any visible glacis, while the S wall was set on a rampart of beaten earth and kurkar. This rampart belongs to an earlier, unexcavated layer, probably level VIII. Level VII is tentatively dated to the period between the second half of the 17th century and the first half of the 16th century B.C.

The excavations in area A were resumed in 1970, and the area was extended on the S and W sides. Here, too, as in the excavations in the 1950s, settlement strata of the Early Arabic, Byzantine, and Roman periods were missing. Some scattered remains attest the destruction and damage caused to these strata in the past century. The same is true for the remains from the late Second Temple and Hasmonean periods found in Joppa. In these new excavations in area A, once again reasonably well-preserved strata begin in the early part of the Hellenistic period (level I). The remains consisted mainly of sections of walls built of brick-shaped ashlar blocks set on their narrow end. These walls were often constructed on top of the Persian period walls. A fieldstone altar (2.4 × 2.4 m) was uncovered in square L-4, standing in a room the measurements of which were only 3.9 × 5.3 m. This type of cult hall is also known from the same period in Cyprus.

Persian period remains (level II) covered almost the

entire excavated area, dating from the second half of the 5th century to the Macedonian conquest, i.e., to the period in which the Sidonians held Joppa. Several building stages of that period were discovered, notably sections of walls of a large store building for keeping imported goods and Attic vessels, extending from E to W across the entire area. In its W part were found fragments of mud-brick floor and the entrance was paved with large stones. The walls were built of regularly spaced ashlar pilasters with a fill of fieldstones between them, and several coins of Straton I were found among the stones. In the excavations in the 1950s, great heaps of blacksmith's waste had been discovered in various places apparently above the Persian stratum; this waste was also found in the subsequent excavations, along with part of a forge. Two coins of Alexander the Great were found in one heap of the waste. The floor of the forge, black from the soot mixed into it, was cleared near W.800 of the store building; a container was set against the wall, an iron sickle lay on its bottom, and a knife lay nearby. It was apparently the remains of a furnace for heating the metal to be worked. All evidence suggests that this iron smithy was in use when the large store building was already in ruins. In square K-3, an early Persian stratum, the foundations of a pre-5th-century building were discovered under the ashlar walls. This stratum was designated stratum II-B, and that of the ashlar structures stratum II-A.

In the new excavations in level III, the Israelite period (Iron Age II) contained no building remains, only layers of earth mixed with ashes. At the bottom of this stratum were found two cattle burials dug into the Iron I stratum, with stone markers nearby. The burial of the cattle whole clearly points to some religious ritual; and indeed, it appears that this had been a sacred site hundreds of years earlier (see below). A different picture emerged under the ashlar blocks of the Persian stratum in squares I_2–I_3. Here an Iron II stratum was found, and underneath it was an Iron I stratum. In depressions and pits belonging to this last level was found Philistine pottery of the 11th century B.C. The pits and depressions were partly dug into a layer of rubble and clay bricks fallen from a nearby structure.

Under these strata were cleared the foundations of a long hall. A citadel with mud-brick walls was attached to it on the S side. The hall measured 4.4 m × 5.8 m and was entered from the N. The floor was covered with a coat of white plaster, and on it were two round, stone bases of wooden columns which had supported the beams of the roof. The pottery finds were meager; however, the skull of a lion, with half of a scarab seal near its teeth, was found on the floor, suggesting that the building was a temple where a lion cult was practiced. Despite the paucity of the pottery finds, the building could be dated from the end of the 13th century to the beginning of the 12th century B.C. The N temple at Beth-shean from the time of Rameses III, which is identical in plan with this Joppa structure, also supports this date. The inscription on the half scarab found near the lion's teeth contained the name of Queen Tiy, wife of Amenhotep III; but it should be remembered that scarabs of kings of the 18th and 19th Dynasties continued to be used as talismans or jewelry for generations afterward (therefore they cannot serve as conclusive evidence for dating remains).

2. Area B. Excavations in this area were concentrated in the premises of the Ḥammam building adjoining the Jaffa Museum and on the slope to the W of it. In the Ḥammam a sandwich-built glacis sloping from W to E was uncovered. The external revetment was made of thin stone slabs which rested on layers of sandy soil. Beneath them were courses of mud bricks laid in a layer of gray soil. The potsherds unearthed in this layer indicated that the glacis is not later than the 8th century B.C., making it contemporary with level III-A in area A.

Beneath the brick and gray layer, the excavation revealed a thick layer of kurkar, indicating that there must have been an earlier glacis here. Indeed, layers of beaten earth and kurkar were found also on the slope of the Ḥammam, situated at a lower level than the 8th century glacis and resting on the E slope of a rampart of beaten earth. This rampart dates to the 18th century B.C., i.e., to the beginning of the Hyksos period. It probably enclosed Joppa in a square area.

3. Area C. The excavation of this area revealed six occupation levels and a catacomb built of dressed stone. The levels of this area are later than those excavated in area A and in effect represent a continuity of them.

The first (upper) level contained a rough mosaic floor from the 6th–7th centuries A.D. The second level had structures from the 5th century A.D., situated immediately beneath the mosaic floor. In the third level was found a section of a large 4th-century A.D. building built on thick rubble foundations and containing a floor made of large stone slabs. The fourth level, dating from the 3d century A.D., contained a section of foundations lying under the stone floor slabs of the large building of the previous occupation level. That previous building was a two-room structure in the fifth level (dating to the beginning of the 2d century); its foundations were sunk deep into the earlier levels. In this level were found pottery, a stone bowl, a bronze jug, and a hoard of bronze and silver coins, all not later than the reign of Trajan. The sixth level contained a section of a private dwelling from the 1st century A.D. with a courtyard and cistern. A doorway, approximately 2 m high, of which two jambs had survived, was situated in the wall facing the courtyard. Numerous pottery vessels and lamps were found on the floor of the courtyard. Behind the E wall of the fifth occupation level was uncovered part of the courtyard of a burial cave of extremely fine construction—with ashlar blocks laid as headers and stretchers. The catacomb consisted of three chambers. The first was damaged by the collapse of the ceiling, and its entrance was blocked with ashlar stones, and the ceiling of the second chamber was also destroyed. The third, the front chamber, had been reconstructed after the collapse of its ceiling; it was fitted with a new roof supported by arches of ashlar stone. These supported stone slabs that formed the floor of a private dwelling erected above the chamber.

Among the artifacts found in area C were two Greek inscriptions. One of them, engraved on limestone, reports (in three identical versions) that during the reign of Trajan a man named Judah was the *agoranomos* of Joppa. The second is a fragment of a votive inscription from the 3d century B.C. which mentions Ptolemy IV Philopator. Many jar handles with Greek and Latin stamps were also found, as well as a tile fragment with the stamp of the Tenth Legion and a pyramidal seal engraved with the name "Ariston."

4. Area Y. Area Y, located near St. Peter's Church at the intersection of Mifratz Shlomo Street and the Ring road, was first excavated in August 1964 and again in May 1968. Some remains were found beneath the square in front of the church. The site is located W of the W glacis of the Joppa citadel. The area was not inhabited prior to the Persian period, and its finds consisted mainly of tombs and various installations (see above, the results of the excavation carried out nearby by the Leeds Expedition). Two strata of settlement—a Hellenistic and a Persian—were uncovered in area Y; beneath the latter was virgin clay soil containing tombs and other MB installations.

Hellenistic remains were found immediately below the ruins of modern buildings. In the S part of the area, a section of an ashlar structure was uncovered with walls preserved to a height of 1 m. The N part of the area contained the corner of a large building, also built of ashlar, in which were several square rooms side by side. This building may have been part of the Joppa agora. The Persian period is represented only by layers of ashes. There were no building remains, although many fragments of Attic pottery were found. An infant burial in a jar, dating from the 17th century B.C., was discovered in the virgin soil. In addition to the remains of the body, it contained a red-burnished juglet, and outside near the burial was a scarab seal of the Hyksos type. In the N part of the site, two furnaces dug into the loam were discovered. One furnace was almost intact, except for its vaulted roof. It was constructed over a MB tomb containing funerary offerings and a scarab seal. A bed of ashes and pits dug into the loam in the E part of the area were found filled with ashes and animal bones. These remains date from LB I. In one of the pits were found full-length bones of domestic animals preserved from the upper end to the hoof. These finds suggest that a cult place was located close by.

Bibliography

Bowman, J.; Isserlin, B.; and Row, K. 1955. The Expedition to Jaffa. *Proceedings of the Leeds Philosophical Society* 7: 231–50.

Kaplan, H. 1982. The Ties between Sidonian Jaffa and Greece in the Light of Excavations. *Qadmoniot* 15: 64–68.

JACOB KAPLAN
HAYA RITTER KAPLAN

JORAH (PERSON) [Heb *yôrâ*]. Var. HARIPH. Head of a family of Babylonian exiles who are listed as returnees under the leadership of Zerubbabel and others (Ezra 2:18). In the parallel lists (Neh 7:24 = 1 Esdr 5:16) the name is Hariph. Since Jorah carries the meaning of "autumn rain" and Hariph also refers to "autumn," these are apparently two forms of the same family name. The leader of this clan affixed the family name Hariph to the covenant document of Nehemiah in Neh 10:20—Eng 10:19. The absence of Sheshbazzar's name from the list of Ezra 2 raises questions about its connection with the preceding chapter and about the relationship between Sheshbazzar and Zerubbabel. For discussion of this problem, see AKKUB.

Many do not regard the list and covenant of Nehemiah 10 as belonging originally in this context. Williamson (*Ezra, Nehemiah* WBC, 325–30) surveys various views about the origins of this list. He concludes that it was compiled from other lists in Ezra and Nehemiah in order to be attached to the terms of an agreement drawn up by Nehemiah following his reforms of Nehemiah 13. This document was then kept in the temple archives until being inserted into its present position. (See also Clines *Ezra, Nehemiah, Esther* NCBC, 199–200; Myers *Ezra-Nehemiah* AB, 174–75; Jepsen 1954: 87–106.)

Bibliography

Galling, K. 1951. The Gōlā-List according to Ezra 2 and Nehemiah 7. *JBL* 70: 149–58.

———. 1964. Die Liste der aus dem Exil Heimgekehrten. Pp. 89–108 in *Studien zur Geschichte Israels im persischen Zeitalter*. Tübingen.

Jepsen, A. 1954. Nehemia 10. *ZAW* 66: 87–106.

CHANEY R. BERGDALL

JORAI (PERSON) [Heb *yôray*]. A Gadite who was a son of Abihail and one of seven kinsmen who are named alongside four (or three; see SHAPHAT) tribal leaders (1 Chr 5:13). "Jorai" is possibly the abbreviated form of a longer name that meant "Yahu has seen." Jorai and his kinsmen lived opposite the Reubenites in "Bashan as far as Salecah" and "in Gilead, in Bashan . . . and in all the pasture lands of Sharon to their limits" (1 Chr 5:11, 17). Neither Jorai nor the others named in the Chronicler's genealogy for Gad (1 Chr 5:11–17) appear in other lists of Gadites (Gen 46:16; Num 26:15–18; 1 Chr 12:9–16—Eng 12:8–15). See also JACAN.

M. PATRICK GRAHAM

JORAM (PERSON) [Heb *yôrām*]. Var. JEHORAM. **1.** King of Judah, son and successor of Jehoshaphat. The years of his reign are variously reckoned as (852) 847–845 B.C.E. (Begrich 1929; and Jepsen 1979), (853) 848–841 B.C.E. (Thiele 1965), or 850–843 B.C.E. (Andersen 1969).

Information concerning the reign of Joram is found in 1 Kgs 22:51—Eng 22:50; 2 Kgs 8:16–24; 2 Chronicles 21. In addition, his name appears in synchronistic dating lists and truncated genealogies in 2 Kgs 1:17; 8:25; 8:29 (= 2 Chr 22:6); 2 Kgs 11:2 (= 2 Chr 22:11); 2 Kgs 12:19—Eng 12:18; 1 Chr 3:11; 2 Chr 22:1. The reports concerning Joram in the books of Kings rest to a large extent upon traditional material that goes back to the annals of the Judean kings and that was taken over by the Deuteronomistic redactors when they composed these books. In contrast to the brief survey of the reign of Joram given by the Deuteronomistic redactors (2 Kgs 8:16–24), the Chronicler devoted a whole chapter to Joram (2 Chronicles 21).

The chronological statements concerning the time when Joram ascended to the throne are contradictory. According to 2 Kgs 8:16 he began to rule in the fifth year of Joram of Israel. Conversely, 2 Kgs 1:17 says that the

Israelite Joram became king in the second year of the reign of Joram of Judah. The discrepancy between these two statements is obvious. This discrepancy is the likely reason why the statement in 2 Kgs 1:17 was simply left out of the LXX translation. The discrepancy can be explained by assuming that Joram took over a regency for his father, Jehoshaphat, while the latter was still alive. For reasons unknown to us (illness? cf. 1 Kgs 15:23; 2 Kgs 15:5), Jehoshaphat transferred the affairs of government to his son Joram in 852 B.C.E. (following Jepsen). The synchronism in 1 Kgs 1:17 must then refer to the time when Joram's regency began. Following the death of his father, Jehoshaphat, in 847 B.C.E. (again following Jepsen), Joram then reigned as sole monarch. It is this latter date which is in mind in 1 Kgs 22:51—Eng 22:50 and 2 Kgs 8:16. The *wîhôšāpāṭ melek yĕhûdāh* of 8:16 ("and Jehoshaphat, king of Judah"—often understood to mean "Jehoshaphat was yet king of Judah") goes back to a scribal error and is to be expunged; it allows the false impression that the numerical statements in the verse refer to a time when Jehoshaphat was still alive. According to 2 Kgs 8:17 Joram was 32 years old when he began his reign, and he reigned for eight years. These statements should rather be taken as referring to the total length of time that Joram exercised ruling powers, beginning from the start of his regency. He ruled as sole monarch for hardly more than two years.

Both as regent and as king Joram most likely continued the policy of alliance with the Omride royal house of the N kingdom, a policy which his father, Jehoshaphat, had already pursued successfully. In the year 867 B.C.E. (following the chronology of Jepsen), while he was still the crown prince, Joram had married the Omride princess Athaliah. This had been a diplomatic marriage, a security for the policies of peace and cooperation that had recently arisen in the wake of the rapprochement between the two neighboring states that had gone through a protracted period of hostile relations following the breakup of the United Kingdom (926 B.C.E.). Athaliah was not actually a daughter of Ahab, as 2 Kgs 8:18 (which does not identify her by name) indicates; rather, following the Hebrew text of 2 Kgs 8:26, she was a daughter of Omri *(bat-ʿomrî)* and a sister of Ahab.

Historical information relating to the time of Joram's reign is scanty. According to 2 Kgs 8:20–22 the Edomites shook off Judean overlordship at this time and gained their independence. This tidbit of information agrees with what is said back in 1 Kgs 22:48–49—Eng 22:47–48, where it is presupposed that the territory of Edom was being administered by a Judean governor. However, the reference to the Edomite revolt pays no attention to 2 Kgs 3:4–27, with its mention of an Edomite king whose existence at this time is in any case a matter of dispute.

According to 2 Kgs 8:21–22 Joram led a campaign against the rebellious Edomites but, despite a victory in the field, could not subdue the rebellion. The biblical text here creates a very confused picture; one suspects that, in reality, Judah experienced a defeat at the hands of the Edomites. This rebellion marked the effective end of Judean hegemony over Edom; further attempts to subdue this neighboring folk to the S (cf. 2 Kgs 14:7) were unsuccessful.

Finally, during the reign of Joram the city of Libnah (Tell Bornat, in the W hill country) also declared its independence. The political background to this event remains unclear, and whatever effect it had seems to have been only temporary.

The Deuteronomistic redactors of the books of Kings, in their theological estimation of Joram, reproach him for religious misbehavior, although they do not more precisely specify the nature of that misbehavior. In the opinion of the Deuteronomists, it was Joram's marriage to Athaliah that was ultimately responsible for his errant religious behavior; for she led Joram along the "way of the house of Ahab" (2 Kgs 8:18). This remark insinuates that Joram had an inclination toward veneration of Baal. It remains questionable, however, whether this remark also indicates that the king took steps in the direction of official toleration of cultic activities in honor of that Canaanite deity.

The Chronicler, building on the Deuteronomistic representation of the history of Joram, constructs out of the reports in the books of Kings and various other sources a depiction of Joram which is still more condemnatory (2 Chronicles 21). Along with the core tradition concerning Joram in the books of Kings (2 Chr 21:1 = 1 Kgs 22:51—Eng 22:50; 2 Chr 21:5–10 = 2 Kgs 8:17–22), the Chronicler also takes over the Deuteronomistic judgment concerning him (2 Chr 21:6 = 2 Kgs 8:18). Indeed, the Chronicler sharpens that judgment through the added accusation that Joram fostered the cult of the high places and led his subjects astray into the practice of idolatry (2 Chr 21:11). In his material which is not found in the Deuteronomistic History the Chronicler ascribes to Joram a terrible and bloody crime: he had his brothers, whom their father, Jehoshaphat, had provided with riches and had endowed with fortified cities, slain without exception (2 Chr 21:2–4). Beyond that the Chronicler cites from a legendary letter of the prophet Elijah (a letter which the prophet could only have dictated proleptically before his death) in which divine punishment is proclaimed upon Joram for his crimes against both humanity and Yahweh—a punishment which is to befall not only Joram himself but also his children, his wives, and his possessions (2 Chr 21:12–15). The carrying out of the predicted punishment is then reported without delay. Bands of Philistines and Arabs fall upon Judah and carry off not only the treasures of the royal palace, but also the wives of the king and all of his sons except for the youngest, Ahaziah (2 Chr 21:16–17; note the text-critical apparatus in *BHS* on MT's *yĕhôʾāhāz* in v 17b; in 22:1 it is reported that the sons were slain by the band of raiders). Joram himself died in agony of an illness of the bowels. The populace refused to mark his passing with the appropriate funerary ceremonies and denied him burial in the tombs of the kings (2 Chr 21:18–20). The whole of 1 Chronicles 21 is thus stamped by the pattern: guilt–prophetic pronouncement of judgment–fulfillment of prophetic pronouncement. Even though the Chronicler might have reached back to previously existent traditions in his own material, still these traditions exhibit characteristics suggesting a relatively late time of origin. They contribute hardly anything to the reconstruction of the historical Joram, but they do show how the theologically negative picture of him was sharpened with the passage of time.

Joram is also mentioned in the NT. Since the family tree

of Jesus as given by Matthew includes the kings of the Davidic lineage among the forebears of Jesus, Joram occupies a place in that genealogical succession (Matt 1:8).

2. King of Israel, son of Ahab, the successor to his brother Ahaziah. The determinations of the years of his reign show only modest differences: 851–845 B.C.E. (Begrich 1929; and Jepsen 1979), 852–841 B.C.E. (Thiele 1965), and 853–842 B.C.E. (Andersen 1969).

The block of material from 2 Kgs 1:17 to 9:26 is assigned to the time of Joram. In addition, Joram is mentioned again in 2 Kgs 9:29 and is referred to in 2 Chr 22:5–7. In actuality, however, the textual material relating to Joram is considerably less than all this: 2 Kgs 8:16–24 concerns the roughly contemporary Judean king Joram; 2 Kings 2, 2 Kings 4, 2 Kgs 6:1–7, and 2 Kgs 8:7–15 are exclusively traditions about prophets, although they do demonstrate that the prophetic groups which gathered about Elisha belong to the time of Joram's reign. Moreover, even the texts which speak of the battles with the Syrians (2 Kgs 6:8–7:20) or presuppose some sort of subjection to the Aramean state of Damascus (2 Kings 5) hardly stem from the time of Joram's rule. These narratives nowhere mention the name of Joram; they speak only of the "king of Israel." It is possible that these anonymous traditions, which came out of the circles of the prophetic groups, have been arranged in a chronologically inappropriate place. Their historical statements fit in much better with the constellation of political realities at the time of the Jehu dynasty, especially under the kings Jehoahaz and Joash.

Finally, the historical background to the narrative in 2 Kgs 3:5–27 is also not immune to questioning. This narrative reports on a campaign which Joram carried out against the Moabites in conjunction with Jehoshaphat of Judah and with the king of Edom. At the very least the reference to a king of Edom, who is not here named, is an anachronism at the time of Joram and Jehoshaphat (cf. 1 Kgs 22:48–49—Eng 22:47–48—along with 2 Kgs 8:20–22). It is not impossible that the text of 2 Kgs 3:5–27 was originally transmitted without the name of the king to whom it historically belonged and was transmitted anonymously for a time. If this is so, then it is quite possible that it applies to some other historical situation, namely, to one during the era of the Jehu dynasty. To be sure, the probability of such dislocation is not so strong for the text at hand as it is for the traditions transmitted by 2 Kgs 6:8–7:20. In any case the material relating to the end of Joram in 2 Kgs 8:28–9:26 is historically reliable.

Joram ascended the throne after the brief reign of his brother Ahaziah, who died as the result of an accident and did not leave behind a son (2 Kgs 1:2, 17). Joram undoubtedly held fast to an external policy of peaceful alliances with the neighboring states and a domestic policy of equal treatment of both the Canaanite and the Israelite elements of the population. Such policies had been inaugurated already in the time of Omri, had been practiced in exemplary fashion by Ahab, and had certainly been continued by Ahaziah. The statement, which apparently goes back to the annals of the Israelite kings, to the effect that Joram removed the cultic pillar of Baal that his father, Ahab, had set up (2 Kgs 3:2), could indicate that in his religious policy Joram struck some sort of compromise with the Yahwistic circles that had taken up a position of opposition to the Omride ruling house. However, it would be difficult to see in this gesture any fundamental altering of the principle of equal treatment in matters pertaining to religion, since the Baal temple in Samaria continued to stand and was only done away with by Jehu (2 Kgs 10:25–27). A traditio-historical perspective upon the Elijah traditions even gives the impression that the influence of Jezebel upon the administering of governmental affairs considerably increased after the death of Ahab during the reigns of Ahaziah and Joram. After the accession of Ahaziah to the throne, Jezebel entered upon the rank of "queen mother" (*gĕbîrâ,* 2 Kgs 10:13), a position which granted her considerable opportunities for influencing policies dealing with domestic and religious matters. Possibly Jezebel used the dignity of her office as "queen mother" to counteract the inclinations of Joram in the direction of an easing of tensions with the Yahwistic factions; she may well have been active in promoting Canaanite ways in socio-cultural and religious matters, in furthering syncretistic practices and the veneration of Baal, and in generally suppressing the influence of genuinely Israelite traditions. However, her efforts actually led to a heightening of tensions within the populace. Finally, in the revolution of Jehu, these tensions exploded and cost Joram and Jezebel their lives.

In his foreign policy Joram nurtured a good relationship with the small neighboring state of Judah and its kings Jehoshaphat, Joram, and Ahaziah. Athaliah, the sister of Joram's father (2 Kgs 8:26), had married into the Judean royal house and, from her base in Jerusalem, certainly served as a guarantee of friendly relations. Further evidence of these friendly relations is the visit of Ahaziah of Judah to the wounded Joram in Jezreel (2 Kgs 8:29; 9:16, 21–29) and the sojourn in the N kingdom of members of the Davidic ruling house at the same time (2 Kgs 10:12–14). Although it is not expressly so stated, one can reliably assume that the treaty-based relationship with the Phoenicians, which had been set up earlier by Omri through the marriage of Ahab and Jezebel, also was maintained under Joram.

On the basis of the historical circumstances at the time, it does not seem at all improbable that Joram militarily confronted the growing Moabite threat upon the Israelite settlement region in the vicinity N of Seil Heidan. On his victory stele the Moabite king Mesha reports having enjoyed considerable successes in Israelite territory (*ANET,* 320–21), such that the settlements of the tribe of Gad were severely oppressed. So it is not difficult to imagine that Joram reacted to the expansion by the Moabites with a military campaign (2 Kgs 3:4–27), one which he carried out in alliance with Jehoshaphat—but not with a king of Edom, since at the time none such yet existed. (The references to a king of Edom in vv 9, 12, and 26 are to be regarded as secondary additions to the text.) If there was such a campaign, it finally terminated without definitive success for Israel. While such a campaign is historically probable in itself, it is not easy to explain why the allies attacked Moab from the S, across Judean and Edomite territory, instead of going by way of the Israelite settlements in the N part of the Moabite sphere of influence. The fact that the stele of the Moabite king Mesha—erected only some time later—makes no mention of this campaign also complicates matters.

Because of the lack of any clear information in the sources, it is difficult to evaluate the relationship of Joram to the Arameans and the Assyrians. Under the impact of the increasing Assyrian drive toward expansion, Joram's father, Ahab, had set aside the latent animosities with the Aramean state of Damascus and had, in alliance with Hadadezer of Damascus and Irḫuleni of Hamath, put an end to the advance into Syria of the Assyrian king Shalmaneser III at the Battle of Qarqar (853 B.C.E.). Three other campaigns which Shalmaneser III led into Syria fell during the reign of Joram, namely, the campaigns in the 10th, 11th, and 14th years of Shalmaneser's reign (849, 848, and 845 B.C.E.).

On each of these occasions, Shalmaneser was confronted by a coalition of Syrian and Palestinian states under the leadership of Hadadezer of Damascus. Even though the Assyrian inscriptions claim that this coalition suffered defeat every time, nonetheless the Assyrian army was each time compelled to turn back. In other words the alliance functioned for as long as Hadadezer was alive; and he did indeed succeed in repulsing the Assyrian invasion into Syria—though certainly at a heavy cost. The Assyrian sources (*ANET,* 279–80) never mention the name of Joram of Israel, nor do they in any other fashion clearly confirm the participation of Israelite contingents in the battles. This silence in the Assyrian sources gives the impression that Joram had backed out of the anti-Assyrian coalition. Such a conclusion is not to be ruled out. Given the way in which the Assyrian inscriptions are worded, however, this conclusion is also not probable. Already in the texts which refer to the first campaign of Shalmaneser III and the Battle of Qarqar, Ahab of Israel is explicitly mentioned only in a single version, the so-called Monolith inscription (col. ii, lines 90–102; *ANET,* 278–79). In the other copies of this annalistic text, the name of Ahab does not appear (*ANET,* 279; cf. Timm 1982: 185–89). One can therefore assume that reference to the participation of Israel is included in the summarizing phrases to be found in the increasingly stereotyped reports concerning the later campaigns of Shalmaneser. If that is so, then Joram did hold fast to the policy of alliance with Aram-Damascus, Aram-Hamath, and the other small Syro-Palestinian states and did indeed contribute to the resistance against the Assyrian advance. Under these circumstances it is very unlikely that he would have gotten involved in a battle with the Arameans of Damascus, a battle of such proportions that the very existence of Israel was threatened, as is presupposed in 2 Kgs 6:8–7:20.

The end of the anti-Assyrian coalition and therewith also of the alliance between Israel and Aram came about through a change of ruling power in Damascus. Hadadezer, the king who had been at the head of the alliance, died. The accession of Hazael to the throne led to the collapse of the united front that had up to this point protected both Syria and Palestine from Assyrian hegemony. The old animosities between the former allies apparently resurfaced. According to 2 Kgs 8:28–29 and 9:14–15 Joram led the Israelite army to the defense of the Transjordanian border town of Ramoth-gilead, which was being attacked by the Arameans under Hazael. Joram was wounded in this conflict and returned to Jezreel to recuperate. During his absence the field commander Jehu was anointed as monarch in Ramoth-gilead by a disciple of the prophet Elisha and then proclaimed as king by the officers (2 Kgs 9:1–14). Before news of all of this could spread, Jehu hastened back to Jezreel and there killed the unsuspecting king Joram, who had actually gone out to meet Jehu (2 Kgs 9:15–24). The site of the bloody deed is identified as the piece of property which had belonged to Naboth of Jezreel (2 Kgs 9:25–26), whom Ahab had had killed. Thus the death of Joram appears as the fulfillment of a divine oracle which had once proclaimed retribution for Ahab on precisely this spot, even though it is upon Joram that the retribution actually falls. After he had dispatched the king, Jehu also had the queen mother, Jezebel, thrown out of a window of the palace (2 Kgs 9:30–37). Then, following the traditional practice of usurpers (cf. 1 Kgs 15:29; 16:11), he had the remaining members of the "house of Ahab" slain (2 Kgs 10:1–11, 17). This slaughter not only put an end to the Omride dynasty, which had ruled in Israel for more than three decades (882–845 B.C.E., following the chronology of Jepsen); but it also obliterated the whole royal line that stemmed from Omri. Jehu established a new dynasty, one which was to rule over Israel for nearly a century.

In their introduction (2 Kgs 3:2–3) the Deuteronomistic redactors give Joram the same negative evaluation that they give to the other kings of the N kingdom, although they ameliorate it somewhat in comparison to their evaluation of Joram's parents, Ahab and Jezebel—this because Joram had removed the cultic pillar of Baal. In the work of the Chronicler, which mentions the kings of N Israel only tangentially, Joram appears in conjunction with Ahaziah of Judah. The Chronicler's material consists of an excerpt from 2 Kings 8 (2 Chr 22:5–6 = 2 Kgs 8:28–29) and of a summary of an episode from 2 Kings 9 to which the Chronicler has added theological commentary (2 Chr 22:7 = 2 Kgs 9:21–23). The broader context (2 Chr 22:4–9) clarifies the Chronicler's intention, which is to show that Ahaziah of Judah opened himself to the pernicious influence of Joram and his family and was punished by God for having done so. The punishment fell when Ahaziah got entangled in the revolution of Jehu and the downfall of Joram and met his own end in the process. The Chronicler's interest thus rests totally on the fate of the Judean king, while Joram serves only as a background figure.

3. A Levite, a member of the house of Amram, and a descendant of Moses' son Eliezer (1 Chr 26:25; cf. 23:6–24). He appears in a list of Levites to whom have been entrusted the oversight of the temple treasures, which is to say of the implements pertaining to the sacrifices and the other cultic activities as well as of the dedicated gifts (1 Chr 26:20–28). While the text is set in the time of David, it more likely reflects arrangements in the postexilic Jerusalem temple. Joram belongs to that particular group which has the responsibility of administering the dedicated gifts.

4. A priest from the time of Jehoshaphat (2 Chr 17:8) who was sent out along with another priest, eight Levites, and five high officials in order to instruct the people in the Book of the Law of God. It is unlikely that any older tradition lies behind this notice about instructing the people, in contrast to what one reads in 2 Chr 19:4–11.

5. An Aramean prince, son of King Toi of Hamath (2 Sam 8:10). After David's victory over the Aramean king Hadadezer of Zobah, who had been in conflict with Hamath, Toi sent his son to David at Jerusalem with costly gifts (8:9–12). The real name of this Aramean prince was almost certainly Hadoram, as given in the parallel passage in 1 Chr 18:10. For an Aramean to be named Joram would be most surprising, since this form of the name contains the theophoric element *Ya[hweh]*. The appearance of the name Joram for an Aramean prince has been taken as evidence for a subjection of Hamath to the overlordship of David, an event which led to changing the name of the successor to the throne of Hamath (Malamat 1963: 6–8; 1983: 18, 39–42). However, it is more likely that in 2 Sam 8:10 we are dealing with a scribal error, since the LXX here attests essentially the same form of the name as appears in 1 Chr 18:10.

6. A brother of Tibni, the individual who briefly contested Omri for the throne of Israel (1 Kgs 16:21–22). The reference has it that both Tibni and Joram died and thereby cleared the way for Omri to become king. To be sure, the phrase "Joram, his brother" does not appear in the Hebrew text of v 22; it is to be found only in the LXX version. Since the origin of this additional phrase in the LXX cannot be explained, a strong claim is made for its originality; for unknown reasons, it must have fallen out of the Hebrew text. This state of affairs has certain consequences for the interpretation of the verse. If the death of both brothers can be related in one breath, then the supposition lies close at hand that these brothers met some sort of violent end rather than natural deaths.

Bibliography

Andersen, K. T. 1969. Die Chronologie der Könige von Israel und Juda. *ST* 23: 69–114.

Bartlett, J. R. 1983. The "United" Campaign against Moab in 2 Kings 3:4–27. Pp. 135–46 in *Midian, Moab and Edom,* ed. J. F. A. Sawyer and D. J. A. Clines. JSOTSup 24. Sheffield.

Begrich, J. 1929. *Die Chronologie der Könige von Israel und Juda.* BHT 3. Tübingen.

Bernhardt, K.-H. 1971. Der Feldzug der drei Könige. Pp. 11–22 in *Schalom: Studien zu Glaube und Geschichte Israels A. Jepsen zum 70. Geburtstag dargebracht,* ed. K.-H. Bernhardt. Aufsätze und Vorträge zur Theologie und Religionswissenschaft 51. Stuttgart.

Davies, C. G. 1979. *The Aramean Influence upon Ancient Israel to 732 B.C.* Th.D. diss., Southern Baptist Theological Seminary.

Hallo, W. W. 1960. From Qarqar to Charchemish: Assyria and Israel in the Light of New Discoveries. *BA* 23: 34–61.

Jepsen, A. 1941–44. Israel und Damaskus. *AfO* 14: 153–72.

———, ed. 1979. Pp. 204–18 (chronological table) in *Von Sinuhe bis Nebukadnezar.* 3d ed. Berlin.

Jepsen, A., and Hanhart, R. 1964. Pp. 1–48 in *Untersuchungen zur israelitisch-jüdischen Chronologie.* BZAW 88. Berlin.

Lipiński, E. 1978. Aramäer und Israel. *TRE* 3: 590–99.

Malamat, A. 1963. Aspects of the Foreign Policies of David and Solomon. *JNES* 18: 1–17.

———. 1983. *Das davidische und salomonische Königreich und seine Beziehungen zu Ägypten und Syrien.* Vienna.

McCarter, P. K. 1974. "Yaw, Son of ʿOmri": A Philological Note on Israelite Chronology. *BASOR* 216: 5–7.

Miller, J. M. 1964. The Omride Dynasty in the Light of Recent Literary and Archaeological Research. Ph.D. diss., Emory University.

———. 1967. The Fall of the House of Ahab. *VT* 17: 307–24.

Napier, B. C. 1959. The Omrides of Jezreel. *VT* 9: 366–78.

Schweizer, H. 1974. Pp. 17–210 in *Elischa in den Kriegen.* SANT 37. Munich.

Steck, O. H. 1968. *Überlieferung und Zeitgeschichte in den Elia-Erzählungen.* WMANT 26. Neukirchen-Vluyn.

Strange, J. 1975. Joram, King of Israel and Judah. *VT* 25: 191–201.

Tadmor, H. 1975. Assyria and the West: The Ninth Century and Its Aftermath. Pp. 36–48 in *Unity and Diversity,* ed. H. Goedicke and J. J. M. Roberts. Baltimore.

Thiele, E. R. 1965. *The Mysterious Numbers of the Hebrew Kings.* Rev. ed. Grand Rapids.

———. 1976. An Additional Chronological Note on "Yaw, Son of ʿOmri." *BASOR* 222: 19–23.

Timm, S. 1982. *Die Dynastie Omri.* FRLANT 124. Göttingen.

Unger, M. F. 1957. *Israel and the Arameans of Damascus.* Grand Rapids.

Weippert, M. 1971. *Edom.* Diss., Tübingen.

———. 1978. Jau(a) mār Ḫumrî—Joram oder Jehu von Israel? *VT* 28: 113–18.

WINFRIED THIEL
Trans. Charles Muenchow

JORDAN RIVER [Heb *yardēn*]. The river that runs from Mt. Hermon S to the Dead Sea, thus separating the W part of ancient Palestine (Cisjordan, West Jordan, "Canaan," "the promised land" [Num 34:10–12; Josh 22:35]) from the E part (Transjordan, East Jordan, "East Palestine" [Glueck 1968]). It is common to differentiate between the Upper Jordan river (N of the Sea of Galilee) and the Lower Jordan river (S of the Sea of Galilee). The Lower Jordan river was the dividing line between the two halves of the tribe of Manasseh (Josh 16:7), and it also constituted the W boundary of the tribes of Reuben and Gad (Numbers 32); thus two and one-half of the Israelite tribes resided outside the "promised land." It also constituted the W boundary of the earlier kingdoms of Sihon and Og (Deut 1:4). The Upper Jordan was the E boundary of the tribe of Naphtali (Josh 19:33–34), while the Lower Jordan was the E boundary of the tribes of Issachar (Josh 19:22), Ephraim (16:7), Benjamin (18:2), and Judah (15:5).

A. "Jordan" in Ancient Texts
B. The Name
C. Geological History
D. The Upper Jordan River
  1. The Sources of the Jordan
  2. The Huleh Basin Area
  3. The Sea of Galilee
E. The Lower Jordan River
  1. South of Galilee
  2. The River's Course
  3. Tributaries
  4. Fords and Bridges
F. The Jordan River as Religious Symbol

A. "Jordan" in Ancient Texts

The Heb *yardēn* appears 181 times in the OT, mostly (165 times) with the definite article; so it is usually "the Jordan." Most references are in the historical narratives of Genesis–Kings and Chronicles, with only 10 references appearing elsewhere. The LXX, the Apocrypha, and NT (15 references) use *Iordanēs.* The oldest references to the Jordan, however, appear in 19th Dyn. Egyptian records as *ya-ar-du-na* (see *ANET,* 242), one of which (*ANET,* 477) addresses the important question of how best to cross the river. The first biblical reference is in the story of Abram and Lot (Gen 13:10), in which Lot chooses the plain or circle (Heb *kkr*) of the Jordan for his flocks. The location is uncertain. Elsewhere the word is used for the S Jordan valley around Jericho (Deut 34:3) and also for the middle Jordan valley around Succoth and Zarethan (1 Kgs 7:46). Glueck (1968: 79) claims that *kkr* is the *ghor* (see C below), and only secondarily applies to separate locales. Since Lot ends up in Sodom (usually located at the S end of the Dead Sea), it is possible that the plain there was fertile and therefore considered a *ghor (kkr).*

The Jordan river figures prominently in the story of the Israelites' entrance into the promised land (Joshua 1–4). Moses was not permitted to cross it with the other Israelites (Deuteronomy 34; cf. Num 20:10–13; Deut 32:48–52), and the Jordan was a clear natural landmark for establishing tribal boundaries (see above). In fact 117 of the biblical references to the Jordan river mention it in connection either with this crossing or with these boundaries. Indeed, it is in this context (of crossing and boundary) that the Jordan river continues to stand as a powerful theological symbol or metaphor within both Judaism and Christianity (see F below).

Various judges and their troops fought back and forth and beside this boundary line (e.g., Judg 3:28; 6:33; 7:24; 8:4; 12:5–6; cf. 1 Sam 13:5–7); David likewise crossed and recrossed it both in victory and in defeat (2 Sam 10:17; 16:14; 17:22–24; 19:15–18, 31–41; etc.). Elijah and Elisha repeated Joshua's feat of stopping or splitting the water's flow (2 Kings 2; 6:1–7); and Elisha told Naaman the Syrian to bathe in its waters to cure himself of leprosy (2 Kgs 5:12). Isa 9:1 foretells of a new glory for Galilee beside the Jordan, and the "jungle of the Jordan" figures in the prophecies of Jeremiah (12:5; 49:19; 50:44) and Zechariah (11:3). In the NT Jesus and many other Jews were baptized by John the Baptist in the Jordan (Mark 1:1–11 and parallels).

B. The Name

There is some debate on the meaning of the name of the river, Heb *yardēn.* Some translate it as "the descender," from the Semitic *yrd,* "to descend"; thus it is "the river that comes down" (BDB, 432–34). McKenzie (1965), however, thinks this is improbable; and Gehman (*WDB* [1970 ed.] "Jordan") calls this a popular etymology.

Cohen (*IDB* 2: 973–78) thinks the name is Aramaic; it may even ultimately be non-Semitic. He notes that *-dn* may reflect the Indo-Aryan *don,* "river"; cf. Danube, Don, Dniester), while *yr-* could be Indo-European for "year"; thus *yrdn* could mean "perennial river" (see Aharoni *LBHG,* 111). It is also called the river of Dan. Alden (1975) translates *yardēn* as "water judges." The "water" is derived from the Hurrian *iar,* "water," and in Heb *dan* means "judges"; thus *yardēn* means "the water (or river) of Dan."

Kenyon (*HDB* rev. ed., "Jordan") notes as fanciful Jerome's derivation of the name Jordan from the names of two rivers, the "Jor" and the "Dan." Smick says that Jerome's "jor" is derived from *yĕʾōr,* "stream" (equivalent to Gk *hreithron*); thus *yrdn* represents "the stream of Dan." Smick (1973: 26–31), following Gordon (1959: 122, n. 19), argues persuasively that *yardēn* simply means "river": the Hebrew use of the definite article along with it suggests that it is a common noun, not a proper name. For example, in the works of Homer, Nestor refers to the Celadon in Elis of the Peloponnisos as *Iardanou amphi hreethra* (*Il.* 7.135), and Menelaus came to Crete, where the Cydonians dwelt *Iardano amphi hreethra* (*Od.* 3.292). Smick translates this phrase (used for two different rivers) as "on both sides of the streams of the river"; thus *Iardanos* is an old E Mediterranean word for "river."

Another term for the Jordan in Arabic is *esh-Sheri'a,* "the watering place" or *esh-Sheri'a el-Kebireh,* "the big water." Some call the entire river *el-Urdan/Urdunn,* "Jordan," others use this term only to refer to the Lower Jordan river, while still others use the term to refer only to the Upper Jordan river, calling the lower Jordan *esh-Shriat* (pl. of *sheri'a*), "the fords." Har-el (1978: 65, quoting Horowitz), says the upper Jordan was called *el-kabir,* while the lower Jordan was the "Lesser" *(el-Urdun es-saghir).*

C. Geological History

The Jordan river runs through 124 miles of the Great Rift valley, a 4000-mile-long tectonic fault zone stretching from Turkey to E Africa. Some 20 million years ago a shift begun in the subsurface plates beneath the continents created a massive fracture in the earth's surface. Two faults in the earth's crust run parallel from Mozambique and Lake Nyasa N through Ethiopia, the Red Sea, Aqaba, the Wâdī el-Arabah, the Dead Sea, and the Jordan river. The edges of the two continental plates are clearly visible on maps as the two sides of the Red Sea and of the Jordan valley. Further N there is a single fault through the Bekaa valley of Lebanon and the Ghab marshes of Syria. This fault divides the Lebanon mountain range (Jebel Libnan) from the Anti-lebanon. The latter includes the biblical Mt. Amana (Cant 4:8; Jebel Zebadani) in the central region and Mt. Hermon at the S end. A ridge, the Jebel Bir ed-Dahr, separates the Jordan river from the Litani (Leontes) river in Lebanon.

The Lower Jordan valley portion of the Great Rift was formed by further faulting over 2 million years ago. It is the lowest spot on earth, reaching 2570 ft below sea level at the bottom of the Dead Sea. Between ca. 70,000 and 14,000 B.P. the area from Galilee to the Dead Sea was a single body of water, which has been called the Lisan Lake. In the following post-pluvial period, the Lisan Lake dried up, leaving the Sea of Galilee and the Dead Sea, with the Lower Jordan river gradually eroding its way between the two across this old lake bed.

The Rift valley averages 6 miles wide, but it is only 1.5 miles wide at Marj 'Ayoun in the extreme N, 4 miles wide at the Sea of Galilee, 7 miles wide at Beth-shan, and 15 miles wide at Jericho. Cretaceous (65–136 million years ago) limestone, dolomite, and chalk are found along the edges of the Great Rift. The Rift valley has several levels. One level, ca. 650 feet above the river, is geologically Pliocene (2–13 million years ago). Lower down, about 150 feet above the Jordan's waters, is the *ghor* ("bottom" or "depression") of the Quaternary period (2 million years ago to the present). The river area itself (i.e., the floodplain) is called the *zor* (Arabic for "thicket"). Between the *zor* and the *ghor* are some eroded marl hills called *katar* which, together with the *ghor,* once constituted the bottom of the ancient Lisan Lake.

In biblical times the *zor* was called "the jungle (Heb *gāʾôn*) of the Jordan" (Jer 12:5; 49:19; 50:44; Zech 11:3). Here *gāʾôn* (lit. "pride") may mean "swelling up" in the spring flood. Hebrew *gāʾôn* also means "luxuriant growth," so "pride" could be an anthropomorphism of the river's "pride" in its vegetation. The salt-tolerant Euphrates poplar and the Jordan tamarisk are characteristic of the Jordan's banks. There are also willows, acacia, Dead Sea "apples of Sodom" (a wild grape), oleander, thistles, reeds, broom plant, and underbrush. In earlier times this "jungle" of trees and brush was between 200 yards to a mile wide and was the home of lions (which became extinct there in the 19th century), leopards, boars, ibex (all three still present ca. 1900). Foxes, hyenas, and jackals are still present in the *zor,* as are 100 species of birds (23 of which are unique to the Jordan valley and 45 of which use the valley as a migration route). With the advent of modern drainage and the extension of cultivation into the area, the *zor* had begun to diminish.

Except for the river itself and its tributaries, the valley is rather dry. Rainfall in the Huleh basin is ca. 22 inches a year, while at Jericho it is less than 3.5 inches a year. The summers are hot, averaging 80°F at Huleh and 90°F at Jericho (even reaching 130°F on occasion). The winters, however, are mild, averaging between 52 and 57°F in the Huleh and at Jericho.

D. The Upper Jordan River

1. The Sources of the Jordan. There are four sources for the Jordan, fed by the melting snows on Mt. Hermon (ca. 9232 ft above sea level). The westernmost source is the Bareighit ('Iyon/'Ayoun), a stream beginning in a short valley at the S end of the Jebel Bir ed-Dahr. There are springs at Marj 'Ayoun (Jdeidah), 1650 ft above sea level, S of Ijon (M.R. 205308) and N of modern Metullah (at the N tip of modern Israel's border with Lebanon). About 1.5 miles S of Metullah the stream flows past Abel-beth-maacah (M.R. 204296). There are spectacular 60-foot falls at et-Tannur. Several maps show the Bareighit flowing into the Huleh swamp (*GP,* 192; Smick 1973: 192), but others show it joining the 24-mile-long Hasbani less than 1 mile before the latter joins the remaining sources (the text of *GP,* 192 says that the Bareighit joins the Hasbani just before the marshes). See Fig. JOR.01.

The Hasbani is the next westernmost source of the Jordan river, beginning halfway between Damascus and Sidon (1800 ft above sea level) on the W slope of Mt. Hermon near Hasbaya (Baal-gad) in Lebanon. It crosses the modern Lebanon-Israel border at Jisr al-Gharje (ca. 400 ft above sea level). The third source of the Jordan river is the Leddan, which starts at the S end of Mt. Hermon in the springs of ʿAin Leddan (altitude of ca. 500 ft), W and SW of Dan (Tell el-Qadi; M.R. 211294). The Leddan runs only 4 miles before joining the Banias.

The Banias is the fourth and easternmost source of the Jordan river. It is 6 miles long, and starts 2 miles further E of the Leddan in a large cave 1200 ft above sea level at the base of Mt. Hermon. The cave was considered the home of a god, which the Greeks identified as Pan (giving the name Paneas to the city and district, whence the modern Banias). Herod the Great built a temple here to Augustus Caesar. His son, Philip the Tetrarch, added to the site and called it Caesarea Philippi after Tiberius Caesar and himself (see also Matt 16:13–20; Mark 8:27). The Banias joins the Leddan at Sede Nehemiya (M.R. 208288), and a half mile further the Hasbani joins them. The mingled waters split a few miles further and at one time flowed on in separate channels as the Jordan and the Turan (Tara?) through the marshes and into old Lake Huleh.

2. The Huleh Basin Area. The Huleh basin or depression (ca. 14 miles long by ca. 5 miles wide) is about 15 miles N of the Sea of Galilee. At the S end of the basin is the former Lake Huleh (perhaps Meron; Josh 11:5–7; Josephus' Semechonitis). The marsh may have been a source of reeds for the papyrus manufactured in ancient Phoenicia. In the 1950s both the marsh and the lake were drained (except for an 800-acre wildlife preserve at the S end of the old lake), providing 15,000 acres of new farmland. Today, Israel's W canal drains the Jordan section, and the E canal the Turan flow. The triangular-shaped Lake Huleh was originally 2 miles wide by 3 miles long, and from 9 to 17 feet deep. In the hills W of the former marsh is Kedesh (M.R. 200279).

On the W edge is Einan (ʿAin Mallaha), found in 1954 during the drainage operations. Several strata of round houses and numerous burials were found dating from the Natufian culture of the Mesolithic (ca. 14,000 B.C.; Pritchard [1987: 16] dates it ca. 10,300–8500 B.C.). The people had sickle blades, but it is not clear whether these were used in harvesting wild grain or if it is possible that they already had some domesticated grain. In any event this marks the beginning of an agricultural tradition around the Jordan river that extends through the biblical period into the present. Beisamun is also located on the W side of Huleh (Pritchard [1987: 26] shows it SW of Huleh). Here a Pre-Pottery Neolithic culture from ca. 7000 B.C. preserved the skulls of their dead and remolded the features in plaster (a number of these have also been found further S at Jericho).

Jisr Banat Yaʿaqub (Heb Gesher Benot Yaʿakob, "Bridge of the Daughters of Jacob") is 2.5 miles S of Huleh (before it was drained). The name is derived from the Crusader convent of the Daughters of St. James (Jacob) located there. To its W were found Pleistocene deposits (2 million to 10 thousand B.C.; Pritchard [1987: 16] says 1.5 million to 90 thousand B.C.), including elephant, deer, horse, bison, pig, and rhinoceros remains, along with flint and basalt bifacial axes dating ca. from 300,000 to 100,000 B.P. (Anati 1963: 67).

3. The Sea of Galilee. Below the Jisr Banat Yaʿaqub the Jordan river flows 7.5 miles through a gorge as much as 1000 feet deep, cut through Pleistocene basalt. It enters a plain about a mile N of the Sea of Galilee. The Sea of Galilee is 12 miles long and 7 miles wide, reaching as deep

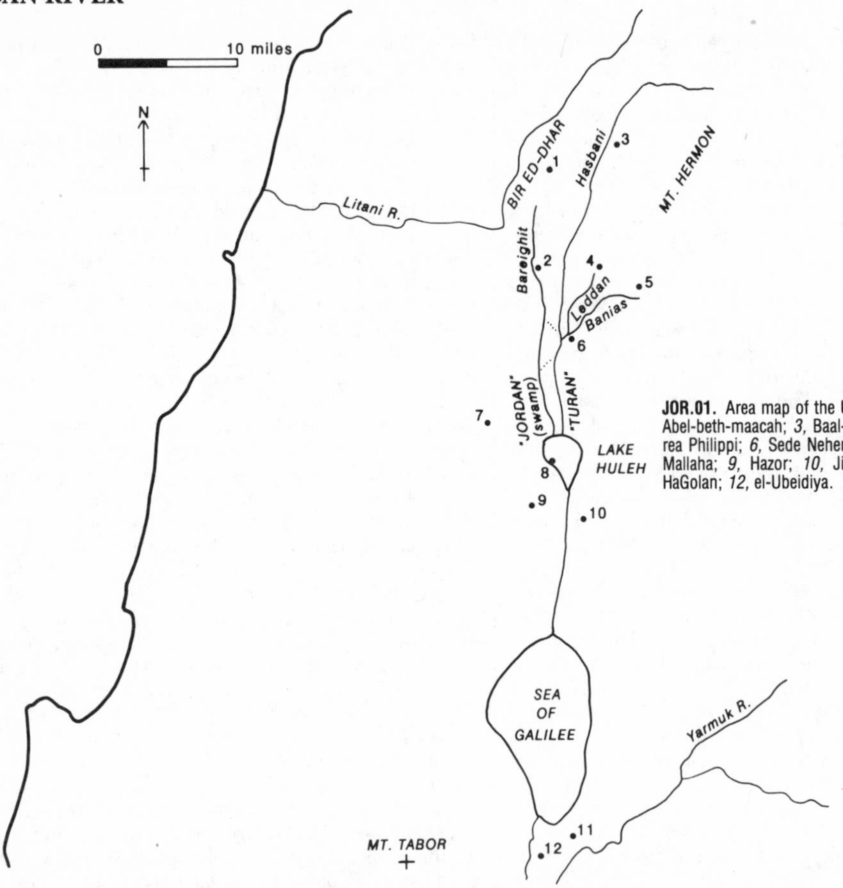

JOR.01. Area map of the Upper Jordan River. *1,* Ijon; *2,* Abel-beth-maacah; *3,* Baal-gad; *4,* Dan; *5,* Banias/Caesarea Philippi; *6,* Sede Nehemiya; *7,* Kedesh; *8,* Einan/ᶜAin Mallaha; *9,* Hazor; *10,* Jisr Banat Yaᶜaqub; *11,* Shaar HaGolan; *12,* el-Ubeidiya.

as 150 feet in one place. It is the lowest freshwater lake in the world and is an important fishing area. There are 35 species of fish in the Jordan river, 16 of which are unique to the Jordan. In Greco-Roman times the fish were salted for export at Magdala, one of several settlements around Galilee.

E. The Lower Jordan River

1. South of Galilee. The Jordan river flows out of the S end of the Sea of Galilee. A mile S is Tell Ali, a Neolithic site with some remains like Beismun and Jericho. A similar culture is found further S at Munhata. East of the Jordan and N of the Yarmūk is the site of Shaar HaGolan (M.R. 208233), where the Neolithic Yarmūkian culture was first discovered in 1943, dating from ca. 5000 B.C. (Pritchard says 6000–5000 B.C. for both Munhata and Shaar HaGolan). It is significant both for its more than 100 "art" pieces (including human figurines carved in pebbles and molded in clay) and for its pottery decorated in a herringbone pattern.

Two miles S of Galilee are the mounds of Maskana and el-Ubeidiya (M.R. 205232), where excavators have found evidence of the Pebble Culture (ca. 600,000–300,000 B.P.; Aharoni [1978: 13] says 900,000–700,000 B.P.; Pritchard [1987: 16] says 1.5 million–90 thousand B.P.). At Ubeidiya skull fragments from this culture were found (Anati 1963: 31, 59–60), and animal remains included alligator, elephant, hippopotamus, and rhinoceros.

2. The River's Course. The Lower Jordan river flows S to the Dead Sea, which is ca. 50 miles long, 10 miles wide, 1285 feet below sea level, and (in places) another 1285 feet deep. Any fish still in the Jordan river of course die when they reach the 35 percent salt water of the Dead Sea. On a map the Jordan runs 124 miles, but the actual course of the river is actually twice that long because it twists and turns so much. This is especially true of the Lower Jordan river, which is 65 miles long when measured in a straight line between the Sea of Galilee and the Dead Sea, but actually winds on for 135 miles. It ranges from 2 to 10 feet deep and is ca. 100 feet wide. Its shallowness, swiftness, and tortuous course make it unnavigable, although U.S. Navy Lt. W. F. Lynch (1849: 265) floated two flat-bottomed boats from the Sea of Galilee to the Dead Sea in 1848 and reported 27 threatening rapids and many lesser ones. Anati (1963: 15), however, claims it is navigable in most parts and affords easy communication throughout the valley, although he may have meant that it could be easily crossed.

3. Tributaries. The Jordan river traditionally flooded in the spring (Josh 3:15), when its rushing waters carried a great deal of silt downstream, forming deltas at the Sea of Galilee and the Dead Sea. Lynch (1849: 267) measured the waters as 11 feet deep in April. According to the Bible the Israelites walked across the Jordan river during the spring flood (Josh 3:10–17; 4:1–24; cf. Ps 114:3, 5), when the waters were miraculously parted or stopped. The latter (an actual blockage in the flow of the Jordan river) is attested on several occasions in the recent past. It was blocked at Damiyah for 16 hours in A.D. 1267 and again in 1907. In 1927 it was blocked for more than 21 hours. Schattner (1962: 54) reports several stoppages lasting for a few hours, such as one at Kefar Ruppin (between Beth-shan and Pella) in 1956.

Part of the flood and perennial waters comes from springs and tributaries along the way. Because of the rain-shadow effect on the E slopes of the Cisjordanian hill country, there are fewer tributaries feeding into the Jordan river from the W. However, because rainfall is often abundant in the hills of Transjordan, the tributaries flowing into the Jordan river from the E are more numerous and more voluminous. The more abundant water from the E tributaries helps explain why there were more settlements on the E side of the Jordan valley than on the W side. See also JORDAN VALLEY.

The northernmost tributary flowing from the E is the Yarmūk, which flows out of ancient Bashan and Gilead. It is not mentioned in the Bible, but today it forms part of the boundary between Syria and the Hashemite kingdom of Jordan. The Yarmūk enters the Jordan 5 miles S of the Sea of Galilee, almost doubling the water volume of the Jordan. Among the other wadis flowing into the Jordan from the E are the Arab (which joins the Jordan about 4 miles below the Yarmūk), the Taiyiba, the Ziqlab, the Jurm, the Yabis (perhaps the Cherith of 1 Kgs 17:3), the Kufrinja (draining the Ajlun area), the Rajib, the Zerqa (biblical Jabbok, Gen 32:22), the Shuᶜeib (the biblical "waters of Nimrin," Isa 15:6), the Kafrein, and the Hisban (Wâdī Rama, which joins the Kafrein before entering the Jordan; together they are sometimes called the Wâdī Abu-Gharaba). These last three tributaries form the plains of Moab (Num 22:1).

The fewer W tributaries of the Jordan river are also important. In the N the Wâdī Bireh (Naḥal Tabor) flows from the vicinity of Nazareth and enters the Jordan just below the Yarmūk and above the Arab. The Wâdī el-Jalud (Naḥal Harod; Judg 7:1ff.) flows from Gilboa, the Jezreel valley, and the Beth-shan area. The Wâdī Fariᶜah is fed by ᶜAin Fariᶜah (biblical Tirzah) and enters the Jordan below the Zerqa. At the S end of the valley, the strong springs at Jericho compensate for this area's lack of rainfall and made the large oasis there attractive for settlement as early as the Natufian period (Mesolithic, ca. 12,000–10,000 B.P.). Carbon 14 tests suggest the first settlement at Jericho was ca. 8000 B.C. Jericho also receives some water from Wâdī Qilt, another candidate for the Cherith (1 Kgs 17:3).

Whereas the four sources of the Upper Jordan river (see D.1 above) drain an area of 2735 km^2 (17 percent of the total area that feeds into the Jordan river), the tributaries of the Lower Jordan river drain 13,600 km^2. Of this, 2000 km^2 represent ancient Samaria and Judea (12 percent of the total area feeding into the Jordan), while the remaining 11,600 km^2 (71 percent) constitute ancient Bashan, Gilead, and Ammon. The flow of the Jordan has ranged from 8 to 35 billion cubic feet per year, with an average of 20 billion cubic feet per year above the Galilee. Below the Galilee the Yarmāk adds ca. 17 billion cubic feet per year, and the Zerqa adds ca. 1.6 billion cubic feet per year (although the flow is irregular). (The Jordanian E Ghor Canal today diverts part of the Yarmāk's waters away from the Jordan river, while the Israeli canal from Huleh to Beth-shan diverts 11 billion cubic feet per year into the water-supply grid of Israel.)

4. Fords and Bridges. Fords build up wherever tributaries deposit enough silt to create sandbars. Condor counted 60 fords, one of the northernmost fords of the lower Jordan being the Makhadat Umm es-Sisan at the Wâdī Arab (ca. 8.5 miles S of the Sea of Galilee). Another ford is the one at Beth-barah (Judg 7:24) below Beth-shan. The Damiya ford (at the Wâdī Zerqa) was at the biblical site of Adam (M.R. 201167), while the Roranije ford was at the mouth of the Wâdī Shuᶜeib (M.R. 201143). There are two fords within 8 miles of Jericho: al-Maghtas (at the end of the Wâdī Qilt) and the el-Henu (half a mile to its S). The former (M.R. 202137) has been a favorite pilgrimage spot as the supposed location of Bethany beyond the Jordan, the site of Jesus' baptism. Lynch (1849: 255) and Brown (*John 1–12* AB, 44) record a tradition that this was also the place where Joshua and the Israelites crossed (cf. Boling *Joshua* AB, 170, also map p. 137).

The Jordan was first bridged by the Romans. Roman remains are found in several places: (1) just below Galilee; (2) 5 miles S at the mouth of the Wâdī Yarmūk; and (3) at Damiyah. In more recent times the main bridge over the Upper Jordan has been the Jisr Banat Yaᶜaqub (M.R. 209268). The main bridges over the Lower Jordan include the Degania and Ashdot-Yaᶜacob (M.R. 204229); the Jisr el-Majami (at the Wâdīs Arab and Bireh/Tabor); the Sheikh Hussein (M.R. 205211); the Damiya (M.R. 201167); the Allenby over the Roranije ford E of Jericho (M.R. 201143); and the Abdallah SE of Jericho (M.R. 201135) on a road opened in 1958 from Amman to Jerusalem.

F. The Jordan River as Religious Symbol

Most pilgrims to the Jordan river experience at least a slight disappointment that results when its relatively small physical size fails to measure up to their prior mental image of it. Indeed, because so many of the biblical references to the Jordan appear in connection with boundaries and crossings and because notions of "boundary crossings" are often laden with symbolic and metaphoric connotations of a religious nature, it is not surprising that the Jordan river has become a significant *metaphysical* reality within Judaism and Christianity.

Such a use of the Jordan river as religious metaphor may even have begun in biblical times. Indeed, in Psalm 42 "land of Jordan" (v 7) seems to be a poetic name for the netherworld (Dahood *Psalms I* AB, 258; Smick 1973: 101). The Jordan as a symbol of crossing from life to death (or from this world to heaven) seems to underlie Heb 3:17–19, and it continues to find expression in numerous Christian hymns ("Roll, Jordan, Roll"; "Jordan River is Deep and Wide"; "On Jordan's Stormy Banks I Stand"; and "I Won't Have to Cross Jordan Alone"). Glueck's statement that the river is "of limitless sanctity to many millions of people" (1968: 19) perhaps overstates the case, but its importance is extended as a symbol or a metaphor of momentous, climactic, and often miraculous events.

Bibliography

Aharoni, Y. *The Archaeology of the Land of Israel.* Philadelphia.
Alden, R. 1975. Jordan. Vol. 3, pp. 684–92 in *Zondervan Pictorial Encyclopedia of the Bible.* Grand Rapids.
Anati, E. 1963. *Palestine before the Hebrews.* New York.
Brinton, J. 1967. The Crookedest River What Is. *Aramco Magazine* 18/2: 14–21.
Geraty, L., and Herr, L., eds. 1986. *The Archaeology of Jordan and Other Studies.* Berrien Springs, MI.
Glueck, N. 1968. *The River Jordan.* New York.
Gordon, C. 1959. *The World of the OT.* New York.
Har-el, M. 1978. The Pride of the Jordan: The Jungle of the Jordan. *BA* 41: 65–75.
Hopkins, I. 1983. "Captain" MacGregor and the Exploration of the Upper Jordan. *PEQ* 115: 55–59.
Lynch, W. 1849. *Narrative of the U.S. Expedition to the River Jordan and the Dead Sea.* Philadelphia.
McKenzie, J. 1965. Jordan. Pp. 453–54 in *Dictionary of the Bible.* New York.
Pritchard, J. 1987. *The Times Atlas of the Bible.* London.
Schattner, I. 1962. *The Lower Jordan Valley.* ScrHier 11. Jerusalem.
Smick, E. 1973. *Archaeology of the Jordan Valley.* Grand Rapids.
Thompson, H. O. 1987. *Biblical Archaeology.* New York.
Yassine, K.; Ibrahim, M.; and Sauer, J. 1988. The East Jordan Valley Survey. Pp. 157–207 in *Archaeology of Jordan,* ed. K. Yassine. Amman.

HENRY O. THOMPSON

JORDAN VALLEY. The Jordan valley, part of the huge Miocene rift which extends from N Syria to Central Africa, in the section between Lake Tiberias (= Sea of Galilee) and Aqaba, is entirely below sea level. From the freshwater Lake Tiberias (ca. 212 m below sea level), the Jordan river meanders S and empties into the salty, sterile Dead Sea (ca. 394 m below sea level). From here the valley broadens into the Wâdī Araba to Aqaba. The total length from Tiberias to Aqaba is ca. 380 km, while from Tiberias to the Dead Sea is 105 km. The levels of both Tiberias and the Dead Sea fluctuate greatly, but the level of the Dead Sea is consistently dropping and its salinity is increasing.

A. Geography

The relatively flat floor of the valley is called the *ghor* and in the N is 3.5 km wide (almost all of which is on the E side), whereas closer to the Dead Sea it widens to ca. 10 to 13 km. The Jordan river meanders through a small secondary valley, about 30 to 60 m deep, called the *zor.* Along the edge of the *zor* rising up to the *ghor* proper are the barren, generally uncultivable, marl hills of the *katar.*

On the E and W sides of the valley are hills which rise to 600–1200 m above sea level. These enclose the valley for its entire length and help to keep temperatures mild during the winter. The valley floor formed slowly from the continuous erosion of soil from the hills, mainly via the 14 major and secondary wadis which flow into the Jordan and the Dead Sea. The main tributary into the Jordan river is the Yarmūk river, with the second being the river Zerqa (Jabbok). Nine other wadis flow from the E hills—Wâdīs Arab, Ziqlab, Jurm, Yabis, Kufrinja, Rajib, Shuʿeib, Kafrein, and Hisban.

Rainfall occurs only between October and May, with an annual mean of 380 mm in the N and 164 mm in the Wâdī Araba. Temperatures also vary, with the S generally a few degrees warmer all year-round than the N. The mean summer temperature is 30.5°C (86.9°F), with mean extreme at 41.5°C (106.7°F); and the mean winter temperature is 14°C (57.2°F), with mean extreme at 5.3°C (41.5°F).

Population and settlement have varied throughout the valley's history, though it is likely there has always been a nomadic population, a fact which makes the extent of settlement difficult to estimate. Today, more than 70,000 people live in the valley, encouraged by extensive government projects for rehabitation and development of the some 360,000 dunams of cultivable land between the Yarmūk river and the Dead Sea.

B. Exploration

In the 19th century travelers to the area without exception reported nomadic occupation and some degree of cultivation. In 1811 the explorer Burckhardt observed a combination of "luxuriant growth" and some "parched desert" with some cultivation by the nomadic settlers.

In the 1840s several small surveys were conducted by the British and American navies. In 1847 the British made a five-week boat trip down the Jordan river into the Dead Sea. The following year saw the American exploration. Between 1875 and 1877 an American archaeologist with the American-Palestine Exploration Society, S. Merrill, explored the area E of the river.

However, not until the 1920s were any archaeological surveys conducted in the area. The first of these was by W. F. Albright (Albright 1926). In the 1930s N. Glueck made the first detailed survey of the E half of the valley between Tiberias and Aqaba. He discovered a total of 90 sites, observing that they were mainly in the *ghor* area rather than *zor.*

In 1953 DeContenson and Mellaart surveyed the area between Tiberias and the Dead Sea, the same area surveyed in detail by the 1975–76 survey project. This latter project, directed by M. Ibrahim, K. Yassine, and J. Sauer, sought to provide a comprehensive examination of this area, to visit already known sites, and to locate new ones. The survey found a total of 224 sites and confirmed that most sites (representing all periods from Neolithic to Ottoman) were located near wadis and springs. One quarter of the sites were between the Wâdīs Kufrinja and Zerqa, probably the best irrigated and most fertile region and the most extensively used throughout history. This contrasts with the 23-km stretch between the Wâdīs Zerqa and Shuʿeib, where the *katar* is extensive and there are no perennial streams.

In 1985 an intensive survey of the E foothills between Sweimeh, near the Dead Sea, and the Wâdī Jurm was directed by M. Muheisen. The survey sought to locate Paleolithic settlements and cave shelters. More than 100 such sites were recorded, the most important of which was Abu Habil.

In 1973 a survey of the E foothills of the S *ghor* between the Dead Sea and the Red Sea also revealed extensive occupation, notably in the EB, such as Bâb edh Dhrâᶜ, Numeira, and Tell el Khalifeh. This survey was complemented by the Bergmuseum metallurgical survey of metal mining and smelting sites in the S *ghor.*

The early archaeological, historical, and anthropological heritage of the Jordan valley is now threatened by its development for farming, irrigation, housing, and roadworks in addition to the effects of ongoing military activity. These facts led to the establishment by the Institute of Archaeology and Anthropology of the Yarmūk University of the "Jordan Valley Project," a long-range and broadscope plan to document the social history of the valley through collations of bibliographies, atlases, photographs, and videos. This is complemented by fieldwork, including selecting MA theses, on aspects of the Jordan valley and currently the study of irrigation systems (ancient and modern), forms of housing and shelter, village plans, and settlement patterns.

All these surveys have revealed constant occupation in various regions of the valley from the Neolithic to Mamluk periods. This evidence is supported by an increasing amount of excavation work being conducted in the valley. Upwards of some 20 sites have been or are being excavated between Tiberias and the Dead Sea. Sites like Pella and the Wâdī Hammeh, Tell el-Hayyat, Tell es-Saᶜidiyeh, Tell Abu Hamid, Tell DeirᶜAlla, and Tell Mazar are all multiperiod tell sites and, except for Pella, which is located in the foothills, are easily identified mounds in the central valley floor. Other sites of only one or a few occupation periods that have had major excavations include Tell Shuneh North, Kataret es-Samra, Tell Umm Hammad, Tiwal esh-Sharqi, and Tuleilat Ghassul. However, much more work remains to be done, especially since so much rich archaeological evidence is being threatened by the development of the valley.

The following summary of settlement periods is based largely on surveys and evidence supplied by these excavations. The archaeological evidence of the valley dates to about 10,000 B.C., with evidence from the foothills dating to ca. 400,000 B.C. and still-earlier material from the highlands and deserts.

The valley seems often to have experienced changes in climate and settlement, though a nomadic presence has probably always existed. After about 5000 B.C., coincidental with a drying phase, the population apparently shifted northward. The Wâdī Kafrein area was much wetter even as recently as five centuries ago—possibly swampy and malarial—whereas the Wâdī Yabis region was much cooler and drier.

Surveys and excavations have shown the E Bank historically to be more settled than the W because of more numerous and consistent water sources. However, the E and W were clearly linked by trade routes to the Mediterranean from centers in central Jordan and Damascus. A relatively easy E–W route through Beth-shan to Haifa avoided travel through the hills of Lebanon. There were also secondary Roman roads linking Amman to Damiya via Salt and the Decapolis centers of Gerasa and Gadara to the Jordan valley.

C. Through the Chalcolithic

All Pre-Pottery flint sites found in the 1975–76 survey were near or on the first rise of the E foothills, usually near wadis. The Muheisen survey revealed Paleolithic occupation in rock-shelters and caves up in the foothills.

The Neolithic/Chalcolithic evidence shows extensive occupation in the E foothills near wadis, on the valley floor, on the edge of the *katar* hills, and in the *zor.* Most sites were concentrated along primary wadis and near water sources and appear to have been open agricultural settlements. The evidence of the first settlement sites between ca. 10,000 and 6000 B.C. is from the S area in the Wâdīs Nimrin and Shuᶜeib across the valley from Jericho. After 6000 B.C. domesticated agriculture was established in the valley, with evidence from Jericho and Ghassul of wheat and barley cultivation and sheep and goat domestication. Significant architectural features of this period are the stone dolmens in the foothills about 50 to 100 m above the valley floor overlooking Ghassul and Damiyeh. In the S *ghor* the farming community of Bâb edh Dhrâᶜ has yielded pottery from ca. 4500 B.C.

D. The Early Bronze Age

Early Bronze sites, generally more defined than earlier Neolithic-Chalcolithic sites, seem to have been mostly fortified villages or cities. Generally they are located along the E foothills, sometimes on the edge of the *katar,* and particularly on isolated foothills overlooking the valley floor. EB I pottery was found at sites over the entire valley, but later EB II–III material was detected only in the area just N of the Dead Sea.

The EB IV (2300–1950 B.C.) is well represented in the valley in settlement sites and tombs. Located again near wadis, most communities were unfortified farming communities—their proliferation implies an increase in population. Located across the valley in the foothills, along the valley floor, and on the edge of the *katar* hills, many sites reveal an abundance of basalt saddle querns suggesting agricultural communities. One of the largest of these is Tell Umm Hammad, near the Wâdī Zerqa. Tombs were usually cut into the *katar* hills, with narrow shafts leading into single, oval-shaped chambers.

E. The Middle Bronze Age

Some MB I–III (1950–1550 B.C.) sites were rebuilt over earlier ruins, though most were founded *de novo.* The number of sites is less than the EB, with most of the settlements in the central and N parts of the valley; no clear evidence emerges from the S region near the Dead Sea. Some sites have evidence of minor stone structures and probably represent small to medium-sized villages. They are distributed in the lower E foothills, the valley floor, the edge of the *katar,* and the *zor* itself.

F. The Late Bronze Age

The LB Age (1550–1200 B.C.) is less well represented than many other periods. The sites are concentrated between the Wâdīs Yabis and Zerqa, in the foothills (e.g., Pella), the valley floor (e.g., Tell Deir ᶜAlla and Mazar), and near the *katar* (Tell es-Saᶜidiyeh). Deir ᶜAlla appears to have been the most prominent of these and probably served as a religious center. Most LB sites were reoccupied in the Iron Age and later, some becoming very large settlements.

G. The Iron Age

Iron I (1200–918 B.C.) sites usually were located in already developed areas and continued to be occupied into the Iron II period. One small site has been identified in the S (Rashidiyeh West), and several large sites in the N, (e.g., Tell Deir ʿAlla, Pella, Tell Al-Maʿajajeh, and Tell Mazar).

While there was some continued occupation from Iron Age I into Iron Age II, most sites seem to have been abandoned until the Hellenistic, Roman-Byzantine, or Islamic periods. Some, however, show evidence of Persian settlement (e.g., Tell el-Maʿajajeh, Tell Mazar, and Tell ʿAmmata).

H. Hellenistic Through Byzantine Periods

Hellenistic settlements are found across the valley from the foothills to the *zor* and usually on sites with evidence of earlier occupation. Most reveal habitation into the Early Roman period.

The Roman-Nabatean era (63 B.C.–A.D. 324) saw the formation of the Decapolis, which included the valley sites of Pella and Beth-shan.

In the S *ghor* the Nabateans constructed an impressive irrigation system at Wâdī Telah, S of the Dead Sea. The dam directed water through a 500-m stone canal to a large pool in the hills. From there it was diverted into irrigation channels to irrigate a large area on the valley floor.

Early Roman sites are well represented throughout the valley, usually on the ruins of earlier occupation. Most were continuously occupied, but some were temporarily abandoned until later Byzantine and Islamic periods. The population density apparently increased from the Hellenistic phase, with better-developed and larger-scale Roman agricultural systems.

The Late Roman phase is less well represented, mostly on sites occupied from the Early Roman period, with no new major sites established. Road milestones have been found near the main Jordan valley road close to Khirbet Sleikhat, Keraymeh South, and El-Hamra.

The increase in population and site density in the Byzantine era shows settlement expansion into the barren area between the Wâdīs Zerqa and Nimrin, with evidence of cisterns to store water. The Late Byzantine period shows the same density with apparently agricultural communities located throughout the valley, especially on the valley floor.

I. The Umayyad Period

The Umayyad occupation (ca. A.D. 630–730) reveals a less extensive occupation with settlement declining sharply, probably reflecting the move of the capital from Damascus to Baghdad. Irrigation systems and agricultural settlements continue, with the area S of the Wâdī Zerqa showing large reservoirs and connected canal systems.

Bibliography

Albright, W. F. 1926. The Jordan Valley in the Bronze Age. AASOR 6: 13–74.

DeContenson, H. 1964. The 1953 Survey in the Yarmouk and Jordan Valleys. *ADAJ* 8–9: 30–46.

Glueck, N. 1934. Explorations in Eastern Palestine I. AASOR 14: 1–113.

———. 1935. *Explorations in Eastern Palestine, II.* AASOR 15. Philadelphia.

———. 1939. *Explorations in Eastern Palestine, III.* AASOR 18–19. New Haven.

———. 1951. *Explorations in Eastern Palestine, IV.* Pts. 1 and 2. AASOR 25–28. New Haven.

Ibrahim, M.; Sauer, J.; and Yassine, K. 1976. The East Jordan Valley Survey, 1975. *BASOR* 222: 41–66.

Jordan Valley Commission, The. 1972. *Rehabilitation and Development Plan of the Jordan Valley (East Bank) 1973–75.* Amman.

Khouri, R. G. 1981. *The Jordan Valley.* Amman.

Lynch, W. F. 1849. *Narrative of the U.S. Expedition to the River Jordan and the Dead Sea.* Philadelphia.

Mavromatis, E. 1922. *Irrigation of the Jordan Valley.* London.

Mellaart, J. 1962. Preliminary Report of the Archaeological Survey in the Yarmouk and Jordan Valleys for the Point Four Irrigation Scheme, 1953. *ADAJ* 6–7: 126–57.

Merrill, S. 1881. *East of the Jordan.* Repr. 1986. London.

Rast, W. E., and Schaub, R. T. 1974. Survey of the Southeastern Plain of the Dead Sea, 1973. *ADAJ* 19: 5–53.

Moawiyah M. Ibrahim

JORDAN, JUNGLE OF (PLACE) [Heb *gāʾôn hayyardēn*].

The vegetative growth along the river bed as the Lower (Galilee to Dead Sea) Jordan river winds its way through the floodplain called the *zor* 20 to 150 feet below the valley floor called the *ghor.*

The *zor* ranges from 200 yards to a mile across. *Zor* has been translated "thicket." The tropical heat and spring floods have produced a tangled thicket of vines, the Jordan tamarisk, willow, the Euphrates poplar, oleander, reeds, thorns, thistles, and other plants. Har-el (1978: 71) notes the reeds in the water, the cane, strip bushes (especially the wild orache, genus *Atriplex*), the trees plus bramble, asparagus, licorice, etc. The willow is characteristic of the N section of the river. The oleander flourishes in gravel and large stones.

The jungle provided cover for wild animals, including lions (Jer 49:19; 50:44; Zech 11:3). In 1848 Lynch (1849: 212, 226) saw "tiger" (leopard; Har-el 1978: 72) tracks and wild boar. There were jackals, hyenas, desert rats, otters, and as recently as 1898, bears. This may have made it a place of danger (Jer 12:5) though in this passage (5d) the contrast to running on safe ground (5c) may refer to stumbling in the tangle. While the tangle has receded somewhat in the face of modern agriculture, there are still some animals. Glueck (1968: 78) refers to jackals and wolves. To this wild life one should add many species of birds. Lynch (1849: 267) sighted wild ducks, herons, snipes, gulls, pigeons, partridges, hawks, storks, and swallows.

The Heb word *gāʾôn* comes from the root *gʾh,* which means "to rise up" and hence the nouns "pride" and "exaltation." The KJV translates Zech 11:3 as the "pride of the Jordan," which BDB (145) takes as majesty (Job 38:11, "majesty of thy waves"), referring to the green and shady banks. BDB notes a variant of "swelling" as referring to the agitated waters of the river, which is how the KJV translates the three Jeremiah references. Holladay (*CHAL,* 52) suggests "height" of the waves for Job 38:11 and for the thicket of the Jordan of Jer 12:5. Glueck (1968: 78) says the thorns and thistles grow shoulder high. Lynch (1849: 227) described thorn bushes so large and abundant they looked like apple orchards, and there were 5-foot-high *kelakh* with up to 35 stamen each 10 inches long. He also noted deadwood caught in the branches of trees 15 feet above the ground, suggesting the depth of the spring floods (1849: 217, 246–48).

The LXX for Jer 12:5 and Zech 11:3 translates *gā'ôn* with *phryagma,* which Liddell and Scott render as the neighing of a spirited horse, and hence they metaphorically apply it to arrogance (LSJM, 1958). This supports the KJV translation "pride," but it anthropomorphizes the Jordan; "jungle" makes sense in our terms today.

Glueck (1968: 77) and Schattner (1962) claim the Jordan floodwaters deposit no silt like the Nile, while Har-el (1978: 71) claims the fertile soil which settles at the pride of the Jordan contributes to its fertility and its lush plant life.

Bibliography

Glueck, N. 1968. *River Jordan.* New York.

Har-el, M. 1978. The Pride of the Jordan: The Jungle of the Jordan. *BA* 41/2: 65–75.

Lynch, W. F. 1849. *Narrative of the United States Expedition to the River Jordan and the Dead Sea.* Philadelphia.

Schattner, I. 1962. *Lower Jordan Valley: A Study in the Fluviomorphology of an Arid Region.* ScrHier 11. Jerusalem.

HENRY O. THOMPSON

JORDAN, PREHISTORY OF. Interest in the prehistoric archaeology of Jordan might be traced back to the late 19th century, when Doughty remarked on several "flint instruments" that must have represented "an human labour . . . [by an] old human kindred which inhabited the land so long before the Semitic race" (Doughty 1921: 74, 76–77). Doughty's astonishment (1921: 74) at these obviously ancient products of humanity was not widely shared by his contemporaries passing through the land E of the Jordan river, nor were the immediately succeeding generations of travelers and pilgrims much interested in these old relics from a time that preceded biblical accounts of human history in the region. Nevertheless, shortly after the turn of the century several surveys had revealed the wealth of Stone Age human presence in this largely unexplored and poorly described area (e.g., Field 1960; Rhotert 1938; Zeuner 1957).

Despite a handful of concerted archaeological excavations and explorations (e.g., Kirkbride 1958, 1966; Waechter and Seton-Williams 1938; Huckriede and Wiesemann 1968) in the 2d and 3d quarters of the 20th century, it has been only within the last 10 to 15 years that the pace of prehistoric research in Jordan has accelerated. As a consequence, only the general outlines of Jordan's Stone Age past have emerged with any systematic clarity, and detailed reconstructions of lifeways in extreme antiquity cannot yet match the results obtained elsewhere in the Levant, such as Palestine, Lebanon, and Syria, where fieldwork has had a long and intensive history. Nevertheless, recent campaigns in Jordan have demonstrated that although overall trends common to the greater Levant are paralleled in the mountains, valleys, high plateaus, and deserts of Jordan, the region also demonstrates some remarkable aspects of local innovation and influence.

A. Lower Paleolithic
   1. Early Acheulean
   2. Middle Acheulean
   3. Late Acheulean
B. Middle Paleolithic
C. Upper Paleolithic
D. Epipaleolithic Period
E. Neolithic Period
   1. PPNA Phase
   2. PPNB Phase
   3. PPNC Phase
   4. Pottery Neolithic A Phase
   5. Pottery Neolithic B Phase

A. Lower Paleolithic (ca. 1,000,000–100,000 B.P.)

1. Early Acheulean (ca. 1,000,000–500,000 B.P.). Early evidence for human occupation is rare in Jordan, as it is elsewhere in the Near East, for a combination of reasons. Because these early ancestors lived in small groups that rarely stayed at one location for an appreciable amount of time, the accumulation of artifacts (principally chipped stone tools and debris) left for later archaeological discovery was numerically small and sparsely distributed over the landscape. The extreme age also allowed a long period of time for erosive forces to destroy Lower Paleolithic sites or to cover them from view by increasing depths of sedimentary deposits.

Despite these limitations, one site in Jordan appears to be an extremely ancient campsite. Located on a high terrace near Pella, the site of Abu Khas (Villiers 1983) overlooks the deep Jordan valley to the W. Hundreds of tools and thousands of flakes lie in a slightly disturbed sedimentary complex. The exclusive use of stone hammers (or hard hammer technique) to fashion the tools resulted in relatively crude specimens with distinctively sinuous cutting edges. Both technologically and typologically, the artifacts from Abu Khas resemble the stone tool industry from ʿUbeidiya, a site on the W bank at the S tip of Lake Tiberias that has been dated to more than 680,000 B.P. (Bar Yosef 1975: 574–75, 589). No animal remains were found at Abu Khas, but the variety of stone tools indicates that the inhabitants found the site to be a lucrative hunting location to which they returned frequently. No human fossils have been discovered either, although it is assumed that, as was the case at ʿUbeidiya (Tobias 1966), the inhabitants belonged to *Homo erectus.*

2. Middle Acheulean (ca. 500,000–250,000 B.P.). As was the case for the Early Acheulean, sites that can be ascribed to the Middle Acheulean period are also rare in Jordan and the rest of the Levant. Although lifestyles of the two periods were essentially similar, a distinction is seen in how the later *Homo erectus* hunters made their tools. The principal innovation was the use of "soft hammers" (animal bone, antler, or wood) to finish the process of implement manufacture, resulting in tools with straighter and more efficient cutting edges. In addition, small flakes of chert and flint became more important elements in the tool kits in the forms of knives, scrapers, and other "light-duty" implements.

In a small wadi along the S edge of Jebel Uweinid, near Azraq in the E desert, a heavily eroded series of hand axes, cleavers, and a few flakes that have been assigned to the Middle Acheulean were discovered in 1981 (Rollefson 1984). The location of the site suggests that it may have been selected because it was on a natural animal track between the springs and lake shores of Azraq and the grazing afforded in the hilly country to the SW.

3. Late Acheulean (ca. 250,000–100,000 B.P.). In definite contrast to the previous stages of the Lower Paleolithic, the Late Acheulean period is well represented throughout the region. The techniques used to make stone tools were refined to the extent that implements were often shaped to an elegance and symmetry that did not relate only to the utility of the artifacts. Heavy butchering tools became smaller and more easily manipulated, and the light-duty flake tools became an elaborate component of the tool kit. One particular method of tool manufacture, the Levalloisian techniques, began to assume great importance among the Neanderthal groups that now occupied the countryside, and well-formed spear points and knives appeared with consistent frequency.

The small Neanderthal hunting groups maintained the economic patterns of their forebears; their movements from one hunting location to another were dictated by the availability of game, plant resources, and water. Some sites appear to have been very favorable to the Late Acheulean people in Jordan, for artifact layers contain dense accumulations of stone tools at several oasis locations in the Azraq basin such as ʿAin el-Assad (Harding 1967: 155; Rollefson 1983a) and C-Spring (Garrard et al. 1987; Copeland fc.). On the other hand, the vast majority of Late Acheulean sites throughout the land were small in size; and the few numbers of artifacts at each indicate the short duration of occupation.

One outstanding Late Acheulean site in S Jordan offers a clear glimpse of a particular Neanderthal strategy of timing the hunt with the seasonal migration of game from winter grazing grounds deep in the Wâdī Araba to spring and summer vegetation in the highlands. This site, Fjaje, is actually a complex of Late Acheulean sites that extends 15 to 20 km along the semicircular rim of the Wâdī Araba escarpment, near Shobak. In the S section of this extensive distribution of hand axes and flake tools is the main campsite, a large (ca. 15 acres) area where a variety of different artifact types are concentrated (Rollefson 1981, 1985). The location of the Fjaje complex astride a major animal migration route is interpreted as a seasonal (springtime) meeting place where a relatively large number of Neanderthal hunting bands came to cooperate in a temporarily abundant "harvest" of animals that were concentrated in the wadi system on their way back to highland pasturage.

B. Middle Paleolithic (ca. 100,000–40,000 B.C.)

Many prehistoric archaeological surveys have revealed that Middle Paleolithic sites are more numerous than for any other period in the prehistoric past (e.g., MacDonald et al. 1983; Rollefson fc. a, b). The mobile hunting and gathering mode of life common to the Lower Paleolithic was maintained throughout the Middle Paleolithic period, although Neanderthals of the latter period developed a different approach to acquire and process organic and inorganic resources necessary for their survival. This cultural development is most clearly seen in the chipped-stone tool kit, where the large and relatively complex Acheulean hand axes and cleavers were replaced by smaller and more diversified Mousterian flake tools. Levalloisian techniques that were popular in many Late Acheulean sites became a prominent method of tool manufacture in almost all Middle Paleolithic camps, prompting the term *Levalloiso-Mousterian* for the material culture of the later Neanderthals (cf. Garrod and Bate 1937). A second cultural manifestation that used the Levalloisian techniques, called the Yabrudian, is known from restricted locations in Syria, Lebanon, and Palestine (e.g., Jelinek 1982), but with the possible exception of the far NE section of Jordan (Copeland and Hours 1981), the Levantine Mousterian, dominated by the Levalloisian techniques of tool manufacture, is characteristic of the area E of the Jordan Rift valley system.

Most of the known Middle Paleolithic assemblages in Jordan come from eroded or wind-deflated surface sites, and the rarity of in situ sites has greatly hindered detailed interpretations of the daily lives of Mousterian Neanderthals in Jordan. Nevertheless, a small protected rock-shelter in the Wâdī el-Ali between Tafila and el-Hasa (Clark et al. 1988) contains undisturbed stone tools, debris, and animal remains that will enhance the reconstruction of Neanderthal lifeways. Another rock-shelter in the Ras en-Naqb region of S Jordan also appears to contain undisturbed Middle Paleolithic deposits that promise to expand our understanding of Middle Paleolithic strategies and adaptations (Henry et al. 1983).

C. Upper Paleolithic (ca. 40,000–17,000 B.C.)

Recent archaeological surveys have shown a dramatic decrease in the number of sites attributable to the appearance of modern *Homo sapiens* hunters in Jordan (e.g., MacDonald, Rollefson, and Roller 1982; MacDonald et al. 1983; Rollefson fc. a, b). Comparable decreases in site numbers elsewhere in the Levant were shown to be correlated with paleoclimatic data that portrayed a colder and increasingly more desertified landscape throughout the Near East (Bar Yosef 1981), and the combination of the desiccation and the reduced Upper Paleolithic evidence was often interpreted as reflecting a starkly reduced population. But when one compares the number of sites per thousand years, the figures for the longer-lasting Middle Paleolithic are comparable in magnitude to those of the briefer Upper Paleolithic. The relatively larger size of some of the Upper Paleolithic sites further suggests that the population of the region may actually have increased despite a deterioration of the environment (cf. Rollefson fc. a).

Recent publications on Upper Paleolithic sites in Palestine have argued that two distinct cultural traditions occur near the coast and in the Negeb desert (Gilead 1981; Marks 1981). One of these, the Ahmarian, is characterized by large numbers of small blades, bladelets, and points but few end scrapers and burins. The other tradition is called the Levantine Aurignacian, which is dominated by end scrapers and burins made on sizable blades and flakes, while more diminutive elements are rare. The Ahmarian appears to span the entirety of the Upper Paleolithic time period, although no absolute dates older than ca. 27,000 B.C. are known for the Levantine Aurignacian.

Currently the information from Jordanian in situ Upper Paleolithic sites is scanty, but it appears from preliminary excavation reports that the Upper Paleolithic dichotomy of Palestine is also present in Jordan. Two sites investigated by Henry in the Wâdī Rum region indicate Levantine Aurignacian affiliations (Henry 1982: 430), and the huge Site 618 at the head of the Wâdī el-Hasa drainage is evidently Ahmarian (Clark et al. 1988). The case for Upper Paleolithic traditions in the greater Azraq basin remains open to interpretation (cf. Garrard et al. 1985; Garrard, Byrd, and Betts 1986). Few details are yet available from anywhere in Jordan to flesh out the skeletal framework of this long but poorly known period of human development.

D. Epipaleolithic Period (ca. 17,000–8,500 B.C.)

The closing millennia of the Pleistocene epoch witnessed considerable variation in terms of climate change, subsistence economy, settlement patterns, and stone tool production.

The *Kebaran complex* is a generic term that covers marked regional variability in the Sinai, Palestine, and Jordan in terms of the presence and relative frequencies of specific stone tool types and the techniques used to produce them. Nevertheless, this geographic cultural diversity is loosely linked together by the dominance of microlithic tools (made on bladelets less than 50 mm long and 10 mm wide) that are supplemented by end scrapers and burins of larger dimensions. Ground-stone implements (mortars, pestles, and "bowls") appear in some quantity in Palestinian Kebaran sites (Bar Yosef 1981: 395), although such indicators of the intensive collection of wild plant resources have not been reported from Jordan. Here, Kebaran period sites (ca. 17,000–12,500 B.C.) have been found principally in the modern desert regions of the country, such as near Ras en-Naqb (Henry 1982, 1983), the E desert/steppe (Muheisen 1983; Garrard, Byrd, and Betts 1986), and the Wâdī el-Hasa drainage of W central Jordan (Clark et al. 1988; Clark, Majchrowicz, and Coinman fc.; cf. MacDonald et al. 1983). Since it appears that the climate of this period may have been even drier than at present (Garrard et al. 1987), it is not surprising that grinding stones are absent at Jordanian Kebaran sites.

Beginning at about 12,500 B.C. the environment throughout the Near East appears to have become somewhat cooler and moister than in the Kebaran period. Following the climatic change, possibly reflecting increasingly available plant and animal resources, human exploitation of modern desert regions became intensified. A palpable change in chipped-stone tools is also evident, for microliths took on regular shapes such as rectangles, trapeziums, and triangles, giving rise to the term *Geometric Kebaran* for the cultural period. Numerous sites from the Geometric Kebaran phase are known from Palestine and Sinai (Bar Yosef 1981), although known sites in Jordan from this time remain relatively scarce (Henry 1983; cf. Muheisen 1983). Ground-stone artifacts occur only sporadically, and it appears that seed or nut processing, if practiced at all, followed other methods not preserved in the archaeological record.

Throughout the Kebaran and Geometric Kebaran phases, the settlement pattern of Epipaleolithic hunting-and-gathering groups appears to have consisted of base camps that were occupied for several weeks or more at a time, while smaller sites reflect temporary specialized activities such as hunting camps or transient stations. The location of small sites in the highland zones and larger, probably more permanent sites at lower elevations suggests a transhumant pattern of settlement (Henry 1983: 135; Bar Yosef 1981: 395).

The last phase of the Epipaleolithic lasts from ca. 10,000–8,500 B.C. and signals a growing momentum in socio-economic aspects that, by the end of the phase, become virtually indistinguishable from the succeeding Early Neolithic period. Like the preceding Kebaran and Geometric Kebaran stone tool industries, this period exhibits marked geographic variation in tools and technologies (e.g., Henry 1983; Clark 1984; Byrd 1987) which have prompted a growing number of named variants that tend to add unnecessary complexity for a summary of developments. Since *the Natufian* is a term that has specific meanings for several prehistorians, for the sake of convenience all of the Late Epipaleolithic manifestations in Jordan will be subsumed under this Natufian label (cf. discussion in Bar Yosef 1981: 398; Henry 1983: 136).

Known settlements of the Natufian period are relatively numerous in Jordan; and as the result of several recent intensive surveys, they have been found in extremely diverse environments, including the Jordan valley (Edwards in McNicoll et al. 1984), the arid and semiarid sections of the Wâdī el-Hasa drainage (MacDonald et al. 1983; Byrd and Rollefson 1984; Clark et al. 1988), the arid and semiarid Transjordanian plateau (Kirkbride 1966; Byrd 1987; Henry and Turnbull 1985), and the bleak E basalt desert (Betts 1982). Site sizes range from small camps of several hundred m^2 in Wâdī Judayid in the Ras en-Naqb region (Henry and Turnbull 1985) or even smaller at Site 14/7, NE of Azraq (Betts 1982), up to several thousand m^2 at Tabaqa (Byrd and Rollefson 1984) and in the Wâdī Hammeh (Edwards in McNicoll et al. 1984; Edwards et al. 1988). The larger sites probably reflect a considerable degree of residential permanence that was made possible as the consequence of intensive plant collection, especially cereal grains. The crescent-shaped lunate microlith is the "hallmark" of the Natufian tool assemblage; but the presence of grinding stones, mortars, and tools with sickle sheen indicates a growing dependence on those plant resources that would become domesticated by the close of this period. Indeed, suggestions that Natufian groups had initiated the process of human control over cereal crops (Gebel 1984: 7) seem well-founded.

At the present time the elaborate artwork and burial practices known from Palestinian Natufian sites such as 'Ain Mallaha (*DBSup* 8: 372–81) and el-Wad (Garrod and Bate 1937: 9–19) are not well represented in Jordan, but the carved stone "wall" decorations at Wâdī Hammeh 27 (Edwards et al. 1988) and a possible Natufian cemetery near Tabaqa along the Wâdī el-Hasa (Rollefson in MacDonald et al. 1983: 316) offer promise for similar artistic and ritual parallels.

E. Neolithic Period (ca. 8500–4000 B.C.)

The Neolithic developments in the Near East represent a continuation of Late Epipaleolithic trends in increasing cultural control of wild resources. This relatively long period of economic and social transformations has been subdivided into five phases: the aceramic Neolithic consists of Pre-Pottery Neolithic A or PPNA (ca. 8500–7500 B.C., the Pre-Pottery Neolithic B or PPNB (ca. 7500–6000 B.C.) (Kenyon 1979; cf. Moore 1982), and the Pre-Pottery Neolithic C or PPNC (ca. 6000–5750 B.C.). Pottery manufacture became established in the 6th millennium and characterizes Pottery Neolithic A or PNA (ca. 5500–4750 B.C.) and Pottery Neolithic B or PNB (ca. 4750–4000 B.C.). These dates are tentative, however, since very few reliable absolute dates are available for ceramic Neolithic developments (cf. Weinstein 1984: 304–5).

1. PPNA Phase (ca. 8500–7500 B.C.). The earliest Neolithic phase has been tentatively identified at only one site in Jordan, at Sabra 1 near Petra (Gebel 1983). By contrast, Syria (Moore 1975) and Palestine have a considerable number of PPNA sites (e.g., Kenyon 1979; Bar Yosef, Gopher, and Goring-Morris 1980; Noy, Friedman, and Burian 1981; Ronen and Lechevallier 1985). During this period sites reflect a great degree of variation in size and inferred population, and permanent village settlement was made possible by the agricultural contributions of wheat and barley species. No definite indications of animal husbandry are known from PPNA sites, for animal bone reflects only hunted species.

2. PPNB Phase (ca. 7500–6000 B.C.). In contrast to the relative scarcity of PPNA sites in the Near East, permanent villages of the PPNB period are numerous throughout the area; and Jordan reflects this regional growth very well. Farming settlements range in size from only a few acres at the hamlet of Khirbet Hammam (Rollefson and Kafafi 1985), to medium-sized villages at Beidha (Kirkbride 1966) near Petra and Shuᶜeib (Rollefson fc. c), above the Jordan valley, to enormous townlike expanses of 30 acres or more at Basta in S Jordan (Gebel et al. 1988) and ᶜAin Ghazal near Amman (Rollefson and Simmons 1986). Permanent settlements were founded in areas with sufficient rainfall to support farming, and the domestication of goats contributed to the animal protein in the diet of PPNB peoples (e.g., Köhler-Rollefson and Rollefson 1987). Smaller temporary camps and settlements were scattered in large numbers throughout the more arid parts of Jordan, including the S steppes and plateaus (MacDonald et al. 1983; Rollefson fc. a) and E steppes and deserts (Betts 1986; Waechter and Seton-Williams 1938; Garrard, Byrd, and Betts 1986).

PPNB architecture was solid, roomy, and sophisticated (Banning and Byrd 1984, fc.). Burial practices are well documented at Beidha (Kirkbride 1966), Basta (Gebel et al. 1988), and especially at ᶜAin Ghazal (Rolston in Rollefson et al. 1985; Rollefson 1983b, 1986). The plastered-skull cult manifested so dramatically at Jericho (Kenyon 1979: 34–36) is known in Jordan only at ᶜAin Ghazal (Rollefson 1983b). Small clay figurines of humans and animals are numerous in PPNB sites; and they appear to have fertility and "luck" connotations in many cases, although there is strong evidence that a "cattle cult" may have had important religious significance (Köhler-Rollefson 1985; McAdam pers. com.; Rollefson 1986: 50).

Perhaps the most impressive feature of the PPNB period is the elaborate human statuary found at Jericho (Garstang 1935: 166–67) and more recently at ᶜAin Ghazal (Tubb 1985; Rollefson and Simmons 1988). It is likely that the statuary is connected with ancestor worship, although on a larger scale than the family orientation suggested for the plastered-skull cult (Tubb and Rollefson fc.).

The closing centuries of the PPNB period have posed a major problem to scholars interested in the Neolithic of the Levant. Throughout S Lebanon, S Syria, Palestine, and Jordan there was a consistent abandonment of farming villages by the end of the 7th millennium; some of the villages had been continuously occupied for more than 2000 years. Although some pollen evidence had supported the interpretation of a regional decrease in rainfall, recent research has strongly challenged this conclusion (van Zeist 1985: 201). Furthermore, ᶜAin Ghazal did not suffer this fate until well into the 6th millennium (ca. 5750 B.C.), and the site's location at the border of rainfall farming indicates that climatic patterns did not deteriorate to levels incapable of sustaining dry farming.

An alternative hypothesis has been developed that entails the basic incompatibility of agriculture and goat herding (Köhler-Rollefson 1985) and the added impact of systematic deforestation for architectural requirements (Rollefson fc. d; Köhler-Rollefson and Rollefson 1987): in essence, PPNB populations simply degraded the environment around permanent settlements (and attendant sources of water) to such an extent that permanent occupation by even relatively small populations was no longer possible.

3. PPNC Phase (ca. 6000–5750 B.C.). While all of the known PPNB villages in the S Levant became deserted by ca. 6000 B.C., with the possible exception of Tell Ramad, near Damascus (de Contenson and van Liere 1966), the settlement at ᶜAin Ghazal continued to prosper and even grow for another few centuries. But the ecological pressures suffered by its sister settlements were also felt at ᶜAin Ghazal; and major changes in architecture, subsistence economy, lithic technology, and ritual all reflect a distinctive cultural character that has been called the PPNC phase (Rollefson and Simmons 1988; Köhler-Rollefson and Rollefson 1987). Evidence of agricultural practices was poorly preserved, but there are clear indications that expanded animal husbandry (including goats, cattle, pigs, dogs, and perhaps sheep) was supplemented by hunting expeditions into nearby steppe and desert regions to the E. Although ᶜAin Ghazal remained a huge permanent settlement, there are suggestions that a sizable proportion of the population may have lived there on a seasonal basis in cadence with the development of seminomadic pastoralism (Köhler-Rollefson 1985).

4. Pottery Neolithic A Phase (ca. 5500–4750 B.C.). The absence of permanent settlements in Palestine, S Syria, and Jordan (except ᶜAin Ghazal) appears to have lasted until sometime in the latter half of the 6th millennium, when some sites were eventually resettled on a permanent basis (e.g., Jericho [Kenyon 1979] and Munhata [Perrot 1966]) and new ones were established. In Jordan several new permanent villages or hamlets of small size were founded in the N (Kafafi 1985; Gebel and Muheisen 1985) and S (Bennett 1980). ᶜAin Ghazal also witnessed resettlement, but in view of the unsubstantial architecture, habitation appears to have been only on a temporary, probably seasonal basis that coincided with nomadic pastoralism (Rollefson and Simmons 1986; Köhler-Rollefson and Rollefson 1987). The known permanent settlements in Jordan are near small-flow springs outside the traditional PPNB area, and farming and hunting appear to have been the mainstays of these hamlets. The production of well-made pottery, with characteristic Yarmoukian features (Stekelis 1972), is found on all W Jordanian sites of this period. Overall, the absolute population of the region seems to have declined markedly, although activity in the steppes and deserts of E Jordan may have supported considerable populations of nomadic and seminomadic pastoralists and hunters (Betts 1986). Many of the enigmatic "burin sites" of E and S Jordan may date from this period of increased exploitation of arid lands, but little reliable dating evidence is available to substantiate this interpretation (but see Rollefson 1988).

5. Pottery Neolithic B Phase (ca. 4750–4000 B.C.). This period of Neolithic development is known from several sites in Palestine, including Jericho (Kenyon 1979); but to date no parallels have been found in Jordan. Ceramic innovations and the reestablishment of substantial architecture set this phase apart from the PNA at Jericho, and the phase appears to merge into later Chalcolithic developments. Indeed, it may be the case that Tuleilat Ghassul (cf. Hennessy 1969), a substantial village across the Jordan valley from Jericho, may include a transition from the final Neolithic to earliest Chalcolithic phase. Other PNB sites may exist in Jordan, but if this is the case, they may be buried beneath some of the larger tells in the N part of the country such as Pella (cf. Rollefson fc. e) and Tell Husn, near Irbid (C. Johnson, pers. com.).

Bibliography

Banning, E., and Byrd, B. 1984. The Architecture of PPNB ʿAin Ghazal, Jordan. *BASOR* 255: 15–20.

———. fc. Houses and the Changing Residential Unit: Domestic Architecture at PPNB ʿAin Ghazal, Jordan. *Proceedings of the Prehistoric Society.*

Bar Yosef, O. 1975. Archaeological Occurrences in the Middle Pleistocene of Israel. Pp. 571–604 in *After the Australopithecines,* ed. K. Butzer and G. Isaac. The Hague.

———. 1981. The Epi-Paleolithic Complexes in the Southern Levant. Pp. 389–408 in *Prehistoire du Levant,* ed. J. Cauvin and P. Sanlaville. Paris.

Bar Yosef, O.; Gopher, A.; and Goring-Morris, A. 1980. Netiv Hagdud: A "Sultanian" Mound in the Lower Jordan Valley. *Paleorient* 6: 201–6.

Bennett, C. M. 1980. Soundings at Dhra, Jordan. *Levant* 12: 30–39.

Betts, A. 1982. A Natufian Site in the Black Desert, Eastern Jordan. *Paleorient* 8/2: 79–82.

———. 1986. *The Prehistory of the Basalt Desert, Transjordan: An Analysis.* London.

Byrd, B. 1987. *Beidha and the Natufian: Variability in Levantine Settlement and Subsistence.* Ann Arbor.

Byrd, B., and Rollefson, G. 1984. Natufian Occupation in the Wadi el-Hasa, Southern Jordan. *ADAJ* 28: 143–50.

Clark, G. 1984. The Negev Model for Paleoclimatic Change and Human Adaptation in the Levant and Its Relevance for the Paleolithic of the Wadi el-Hasa (West Central Jordan). *ADAJ* 28: 225–48.

Clark, G.; Majchrowicz, D.; and Coinman, N. fc. A Typological and Technological Study of Upper Paleolithic Collections from the Wadi el-Hasa Survey with Observations on Adjacent Time-Stratigraphic Units. In *The Wadi el-Hasa Project Final Report,* ed. B. MacDonald.

Clark, G., et al. 1988. Excavations at Middle, Upper, and Epipaleolithic Sites in the Wadi Hasa, West-Central Jordan. In Garrard and Gebel 1988.

Contenson, H. de, and van Liere, W. 1966. Seconde campagne a Tell Ramad, 1965. *Annales Archaeologiques Arabes Syriennes* 16: 167–74.

Copeland, L. fc. Analysis of the Paleolithic Artifacts from the Sounding of A. Garrard at C-Spring, 1985 Season. In *The Hammer on the Rock: Studies on the Paleolithic of Eastern Jordan,* ed. L. Copeland and F. Hours. BARIS.

Copeland, L., and Hours, F. 1981. La fin de L'Acheuleen et l'Avenement du Paleolithique Moyen en Syrie. Pp. 225–38 in *Prehistoire du Levant,* ed. J. Cauvin and P. Sanlaville. Paris.

Doughty, C. 1921. *Travels in Arabia Deserta.* 3d ed. New York.

Edwards, P.; Colledge, S.; Macumber, P.; and Bourke, S. 1988. Late Pleistocene Prehistory in the Wadi al-Hammeh, Jordan Valley. In Garrard and Gebel 1988.

Field, H. 1960. *North Arabian Desert Archaeological Survey, 1925–1950.* Papers of the Peabody Museum of Archaeology and Ethnology, Harvard University 45/2.

Garrard, A., and Gebel, H. 1988. *The Prehistory of Jordan.* BARIS 396. Oxford.

Garrard, A.; Betts, A.; Byrd, B.; and Hunt, C. 1987. Prehistoric Environment and Settlement in the Azraq Basin: An Interim Report on the 1985 Season. *Levant* 19: 5–25.

Garrard, A.; Byrd, B.; and Betts, A. 1986. Prehistoric Environment and Settlement in the Azraq Basin: An Interim Report on the 1984 Excavation Season. *Levant* 18: 5–24.

Garrard, A.; Byrd, B.; Harvey, P.; and Hivernel, F. 1985. Prehistoric Environment and Settlement in the Azraq Basin: Preliminary Report on the 1982 Survey Season. *Levant* 17: 1–28.

Garrod, D., and Bate, D. 1937. *The Stone Age of Mount Carmel.* Vol. 1. Oxford.

Garstang, J. 1935. Jericho: City and Necropolis, Fifth Report. *Annals of Archaeology and Anthropology* 23: 143–84.

Gebel, H. 1983. Sabra I und die Wadi-Systeme um Petra. *AfO* 29–30: 282–84.

———. 1984. *Das Akeramische Neolithikum Vorderasiens.* BTAVO B 52. Tübingen.

Gebel, H., and Muheisen, M. 1985. Note on ʿAin Rahub, a New Late Natufian Site near Irbid, Jordan. *Paleorient* 11/1: 107–10.

Gebel, H., et al. 1988. Preliminary Report on the First Season of Excavations at the Late Aceramic Neolithic Site of Basta. In Garrard and Gebel 1988.

Gilead, I. 1981. Upper Paleolithic Tool Assemblages from the Negev and Sinai. Pp. 331–42 in *Prehistoire du Levant,* ed. J. Cauvin and P. Sanlaville. Paris.

Harding, G. 1967. *The Antiquities of Jordan.* Amman.

Hennessy, J. 1969. Preliminary Report on a First Season of Excavations at Teleilat Ghassul. *Levant* 1: 1–24.

Henry, D. 1982. The Prehistory of Southern Jordan and Relationships with the Levant. *JFA* 9: 417–44.

———. 1983. Adaptive Evolution Within the Epipaleolithic of the Near East. Vol. 2, pp. 90–160 in *Advances in World Archaeology,* ed. F. Wendorf and A. Close. New York.

Henry, D.; Hassan, F.; Henry, K.; and Jones, M. 1983. An Investigation of the Prehistory of Southern Jordan. *PEQ* 115: 1–24.

Henry, D., and Turnbull, P. 1985. Archaeological, Faunal and Pollen Evidence from Natufian and Timnian Sites in Southern Jordan. *BASOR* 257: 45–64.

Huckriede, R., and Wiesemann, G. 1968. Der jungpleistozäne Pluvial-See von el Jafr und weitere Daten zum Quartär Jordaniens. *Geologica et Palaeontologica* 2: 73–95.

Jelinek, A. 1982. The Tabun Cave and Paleolithic Man in the Levant. *Science* 216: 1369–75.

Kafafi, Z. 1985. Late Neolithic Architecture from Jebel Abu Thawwab, Jordan. *Paleorient* 11/1: 125–27.

Kenyon, K. 1979. *Archaeology in the Holy Land.* 4th ed. London.

Kirkbride, D. 1958. Notes on a Survey of Pre-Roman Archaeological Sites near Jerash. *Bulletin of the Institute of Archaeology* 1: 9–20.

———. 1966. Five Seasons at the Pre-Pottery Neolithic Village of Beidha in Jordan. *PEQ* 98: 8–72.

———. 1986. Resolving the Revolution: Late Neolithic Refinements of Economic Strategies in the Eastern Levant. Paper presented to the ICAZ Conference, Bordeaux, August 1986.

———. 1988. The Fauna from Neolithic ᶜAin Ghazal. In Garrard and Gebel 1988.

Köhler-Rollefson, I. 1985. Cattle Cult and Domestication in the Neolithic of the Near East. Paper presented to the Annual Meeting of the American Schools of Oriental Research, Anaheim, November 1985.

Köhler-Rollefson, I., and Rollefson, G. 1987. Cultural Degradation of the Environment during the Neolithic (6500–5000 B.C.): Faunal Evidence from ᶜAin Ghazal, Jordan. Paper presented at the XII INQUA Congress, Ottawa, July 1987.

MacDonald, B.; Rollefson, G.; Banning, E.; Byrd, B.; and D'Aniebele, C. 1983. The Wadi el-Hasa Survey 1982: A Preliminary Report. *ADAJ* 27: 311–23.

MacDonald, B.; Rollefson, G.; and Roller, D. 1982. The Wadi el-Hasa Survey 1981: A Preliminary Report. *ADAJ* 26: 117–32.

Marks, A. 1981. The Upper Paleolithic of the Negev. Pp. 343–52 in *Prehistoire du Levant,* ed. J. Cauvin and P. Sanlaville. Paris.

McNicoll, A., et al. 1984. Preliminary Report on the University of Sydney's Fifth Season of Excavation at Pella in Jordan. *ADAJ* 28: 55–86.

Moore, A. 1975. The Excavation at Tell Abu Hureyra in Syria: A Preliminary Report. *Proceedings of the Prehistoric Society* 41: 50–77.

———. 1982. Four Sequence for the Levantine Neolithic, ca. 8500–3750 B.C. *BASOR* 246: 1–34.

Muheisen, M. 1983. La prehistoire en Jordanie: Recherches sur l'epipaleolithique: l'example du Gisement de Kharaneh IV. Diss., Bordeaux.

Noy, T.; Friedman, E.; and Burian, F. 1981. Naḥal Lavan 108: A Pre-Pottery Neolithic A Site in the Western Negev, Israel. *PEQ:* 81–88.

Perrot, J. 1966. Troisième campagne de fouilles a Munhata (1964). *Syria* 43: 49–63.

Rhotert, H. 1938. *Transjordanien: Vorgeschichtliche Forschungen.* Stuttgart.

Rollefson, G. 1981. The Late Acheulian Site at Fjaje, Wadi el-Bustan, Southern Jordan. *Paleorient* 7/1: 5–21.

———. 1983a. Two Seasons of Excavations at ᶜAin el-Assad, Near Azraq, Eastern Jordan. *BASOR* 252: 25–34.

———. 1983b. Ritual and Ceremony at Neolithic ᶜAin Ghazal. *Paleorient* 9/2: 29–38.

———. 1984. A Middle Acheulian Surface Site from Wadi Uweinid, Eastern Jordan. *Paleorient* 10/1: 127–33.

———. 1985. Late Pleistocene Environments and Seasonal Hunting Strategies: A Case Study from Fjaje, near Shobak, Southern Jordan. Pp. 103–7 in *Studies in the History and Archaeology of Jordan II,* ed. A. Hadidi. Amman.

———. 1986. Neolithic ᶜAin Ghazal: Ritual and Ceremony II. *Paleorient* 12/1: 45–52.

———. 1988. Stratified Burin Classes at ᶜAin Ghazal: Implications for the Desert Neolithic of Jordan. In Garrard and Gebel 1988.

———. fc. a. Chipped Stone Artifacts from the Limes Arabicus Survey. In *Interim Report on the Limes Arabicus Project, 1980–1985,* ed. S. Parker. BARIS.

———. fc. b. The Lithics Collections from the 1983 Sahab Area Survey. In *The Sahab Countryside,* ed. M. Ibrahim, et al. Monographs of the Institute of Archaeology and Anthropology (Yarmouk).

———. fc. c. Observations on the Neolithic Village in Wadi Shuᶜeib. *ADAJ.*

———. fc. d. ᶜAin Ghazal: Emergence and Consequences of Early Neolithic Population Aggregation. In *Occasional Papers of the Museum of Anthropology.* California State University, Fullerton.

———. fc. e. The Chipped Stone Tools from Pella.

Rollefson, G., and Kafafi, Z. 1985. Khirbet Hammam: A PPNB Village in the Wadi el-Hasa, Southern Jordan. *BASOR* 258: 63–69.

Rollefson, G., and Simmons, A. 1986. The Neolithic Village of ᶜAin Ghazal, Jordan: Preliminary Report on the 1984 Season. *BASORSup* 24: 147–64.

———. 1988. The Neolithic Settlement at ᶜAin Ghazal. In Garrard and Gebel 1988.

———. fc. The Neolithic Village of ᶜAin Ghazal, Jordan: Preliminary Report on the 1985 Season. *BASORSup* 25.

Rollefson, G., et al. 1985. Excavation at the Pre-Pottery Neolithic N (PPNB) Village of ᶜAin Ghazal (Jordan), 1983. *MDOG* 117: 69–116.

Ronen, A., and Lechevallier, M. 1985. The Natufian-Early Neolithic Site at Hatula, Near Latrun, Israel. *Quartär* 35–36: 141–64.

Stekelis, M. 1972. *The Yarmoukian Culture of the Neolithic Period.* Jerusalem.

Tobias, P. 1966. *A Member of the Genus Homo from ᶜUbeidiya.* Jerusalem.

Tubb, K. 1985. Preliminary Report on the ᶜAin Ghazal Statues. *MDOG* 117: 117–34.

Tubb, K., and Rollefson, G. fc. Plaster Statues from ᶜAin Ghazal. *Antiquity.*

Villiers, L. 1983. Final Report on Paleolithic Sampling at Abu el Khas, Northern Jordan. *ADAJ* 27: 27–44.

Waechter, J., and Seton-Williams, V. 1938. The Excavations at Wadi Dhobai 1937–1938 and the Dhobaian Industry. *JPOS* 18: 172–86.

Weinstein, J. 1984. Radiocarbon Dating in the Southern Levant. *Radiocarbon* 26/3: 297–366.

Zeist, W. van. 1985. Past and Present Environments of the Jordan Valley. Pp. 199–204 in *Studies in the History and Archaeology of Jordan II,* ed. A. Hadidi. Amman.

Zeuner, F. 1957. Stone Age Exploration in Jordan, I. *PEQ* 89: 17–54.

GARY O. ROLLEFSON

JORIM (PERSON) [Gk *Iōrim*]. The father of Eliezer and son of Matthat according to Luke's genealogy tying Joseph, the "supposed father" of Jesus, to descent from Adam and God (Luke 3:29). Jorim is omitted in D, which substitutes a genealogy adapted from Matt 1:6–15 for Luke 3:23–31; and 2 Esdr 10:18 B reads Gk *Iōreim,* as one of the sons of the priests who married foreign women, in proximity to Gk *Eliezer.* The name Jorim occurs nowhere else in the biblical documents, including Matthew's genealogy, and falls within a list of 18 otherwise unknown descendants of David's son Nathan (Fitzmyer *Luke 1–9* AB, 501). Kuhn (1923: 208–9) argues that two seemingly parallel lists of names—Luke 3:23–26 (Jesus to Mattathias) and 3:29–31 (Joshua/Jesus to Mattatha)—were originally identical, the first perhaps reflecting a Hebrew context and the second, in an Aramaic context, tracing Mary's line of descent (since it does not mention Joseph as Jesus' father). However, Jorim, in the second list, does not have a corresponding name in the first list.

Bibliography

Kuhn, G. 1923. Die Geschlechtsregister Jesu bei Lukas und Matthäus, nach ihrer Herkunft untersucht. *ZNW* 22: 206–28.

STANLEY E. PORTER

JORKEAM (PLACE) [Heb *yorqāᶜām*]. A village in Judah occupied by the Hebronite clan of Caleb (1 Chr 2:44). The formula "x the father of y," used throughout the list in which this name appears, leaves the impression that the names are those of persons, though here the Chronicler uses it to denote places (y founded by x). The LXX^{B} is quite possibly correct in reading Jokdeam in place of Jorkeam, so linking the place with the Jokdeam of Josh 15:56. The location, in either case, is set in the hill country of Judah, quite near Hebron.

ELMER H. DYCK

JOSECH (PERSON) [Gk *Iōsēch*]. The father of Semein and son of Joda according to Luke's genealogy tying Joseph, the "supposed father" of Jesus, to descent from Adam and God (Luke 3:26). There is some textual uncertainty here. Greek *Iōsēch* is read in numerous Gk mss and several early versions, but Gk *Iōsēph* is read in other mss, the Vulgate, and the TR (Tischendorf). Josech is omitted in D, which substitutes a genealogy adapted from Matt 1:6–15 for Luke 3:23–31. The name Josech falls within a list of 17 ancestors of Jesus who are otherwise unknown in the biblical documents, including Matthew's genealogy (Fitzmyer *Luke 1–9* AB, 500); and is not remotely similar to any of the names in 1 Chr 3:19–20.

STANLEY E. PORTER

JOSEPH (PERSON) [Heb *yôsēp*]. Several persons in the OT, Apocrypha, and NT bear this name.

1. See JOSEPH, SON OF JACOB.

2. The father of Igal, the individual selected from the tribe of Issachar to spy out the land of Canaan (Num 13:7).

3. A Levite who was one of the "sons of Asaph" (1 Chr 25:2, 9).

4. One of the Israelites who, at the time of Ezra, had married a foreign wife (Ezra 10:42 = 1 Esdr 9:34).

5. A priest during the postexilic period, at the time when Joiakim was high priest (Neh 12:14).

6. Ancestor of Judith, who is the heroine of the deuterocanonical book of Judith (Jdt 8:1). The heroine is introduced immediately with what the writer considers most important, that is, her Jewish lineage. With a list of at least 16 ancestors, this genealogy is the longest for all women given in the Bible. Of the Hebrew names mentioned, only the three most distant, Salamiel, Sarasadai, and Israel, may likely refer to well-known historical persons. There is no specific information about the identity of the others listed. If the genealogy is authentic, there are obviously many omissions; but since the book of Judith is generally considered to be a novelette, the genealogy may well be fictitious. However, the use of a genealogy in introducing a significant person in salvation history is consistent with biblical tradition and emphasizes the importance in the mind of the writer of belonging to this people. There are various scholarly opinions about this genealogy, but none establishes certainty (Moore *Judith* AB, 185–88).

7. Son of Zechariah and a commander in Judea (1 Macc 5:18) during the period when Judas Maccabeus was in control of the territory (164–161 B.C.E.). Reports of repression of Jews by Gentiles in Gilead and Galilee brought Judas and Jonathan to march on Gilead with a force of 8000 and their brother Simon with 3000 to Galilee (5:20). Joseph, son of Zechariah, and Azariah, a leader of the people, were left in Judea with the rest of the forces to guard it. They were expressly instructed not to engage in battle with the gentiles until the return of Judas and Simon (5:18–19). When the Maccabee brothers were known to have subdued the territories and brought the oppressed Jews to Judea for safety, Joseph and Azariah ignored orders and launched a campaign against Jamnia, where they were severely routed and suffered great losses (5:55–62). The writer of the account uses the opportunity to indicate that deliverance was to come through the family of the Maccabees (*HJP*^{2} 1: 164–65).

8. One of the Maccabee brothers in the epitome of Jason of Cyrene (2 Macc 8:22). The five-volume history, which was the work of Jason, is now lost; but his abridgment of it is available to us as 2 Maccabees. This parallels 1 Maccabees 1:10–7:50. The writer of 1 Maccabees names the sons of Mattathias as John, Simon, Judas, Eleazar, and Jonathan (1 Macc 2:2). Jason of Cyrene speaks of "Joseph" instead of "John" among the five brothers (2 Macc 8:22). The passage in 2 Maccabees is difficult for at least two reasons. The army is divided into four parts, leaving Eleazar without forces. Also, the transferral of the name "Joseph" for "John" raises questions. Goldstein attempts an understanding of the text which could see Joseph, son of Zechariah, and also Azariah (1 Macc 5:18) as half-brothers of the five sons of Mattathias (*2 Maccabees* AB, 299–300). See #7. Thus Joseph and John would be two different persons, and there would be seven brothers in all. Others simply see Joseph as a variant for John, and thus the number of brothers would remain at five (RSV 2 Macc 8:22 n.).

BETTY JANE LILLIE

9. See JOSEPH, HUSBAND OF MARY.

10. The reported "brother" of James, and Simon, and

Judas, and Jesus and possibly the son of Mary, the mother of Jesus (Matt 13:55). There is much textual variance at this point, although Gk *Iōsēph* receives a B rating in *UBSGNT* (for variant readings see *NovTG*[26]). Mark 6:3 in a similar list (cf. 15:40, 47; see below #11) has Gk *Iōsētos,* though with significant textual variants, for Gk *Iosē* and a few for *Iōsēph* (again see *NovTG*[26]). If it is true, as many scholars believe, that Gk *Iosēs* follows the Galilean pronunciation of the Heb *ywsp,* then, on the basis of this factor and other significant contextual features, Matt 13:55 and Mark 6:3 may be parallels at this point (see e.g., Swete 1898: 107). There are three major views about the status of Joseph and the others as "brothers" of Jesus. The Hebrew or Aramaic word for "brother" has a wide enough semantic range to allow that these may be half-brothers of Jesus by way of a previous marriage for Joseph, Jesus' "supposed father" ("Epiphanian" view, now rarely held); or they may be cousins of Jesus as sons of Mary's sister, possibly named Mary wife of Clopas ("Hieronymian" view); or they may be the actual physical brothers of Jesus and sons of Mary by Joseph ("Helvidian" view). The first view is often associated with an Orthodox perspective; the second with a Roman Catholic perspective (e.g., McHugh [1975: 200–253], who gives a thorough treatment of the issues, although he proposes a fourth solution with three different Marys); and the third with a Protestant perspective (e.g., Mayor 1897: v–vlvii), although this is not always the case (cf. Lightfoot 1856: 256–91, who was an Epiphanian). In light of other references to Jesus' brothers, especially in the Greek-language environments of 1 Cor 9:5; Gal 1:19; Acts 1:14; and John 2:12; 7:2–8, and on biblical rather than problematic theological criteria, it is most plausible to see Joseph here as an actual brother of Jesus and the son of Mary by Joseph (e.g., Hill *Matthew* NCB, 222). Regardless of his familial relations, nothing more is known of this Joseph than his possible citation in Matt 27:56 (#11 below).

11. The reported "brother" of James and son of a woman named Mary, one of the three women watching the crucifixion (Matt 27:56). There is much variance in the Greek mss. Some mss read *Iōsēph* while others read *Iōsē;* and there are slight variations in syntax, including a reading which adds another Mary. At Mark 15:40 and 47 there are variants for Gk *Iōsētos* and *Iōsē,* and a few for *Iōsēph* (cf. Mark 6:3 in #10 above). Whereas most scholars are agreed that Mark 15:40 and 47 refer to another Mary (probably the wife of Clopas) and her son, on the basis of citation of James as "the younger" and the unclear means of reference concerning whether it is Mary the mother of Jesus (contra Gundry 1982: 579), the major question is whether the Joseph of Matt 27:56 is the same Joseph as the one in Matt 13:55. Some believe that Matt 27:56 refers to an undetermined Mary with two otherwise unknown children (Hill, 356); others assert that this Mary is the "other Mary" of Matt 27:61 and 28:1 (Schnackenburg 1987: 282); others equate this Mary with Mary the wife of Clopas in John 19:25 (McNeile 1915: 425; Brown 1978: 69); and still others believe that this Mary, James, and Joseph are the same as in Matt 13:55 (McHugh 1975: 241), although it does not necessarily follow that Joseph is a son of Mary the mother of Jesus. Regardless of his familial relations, nothing more is known of this Joseph than his possible citation in Matt 13:55 (#10 above).

12. The father of Jannai and son of Mattathias according to Luke's genealogy tying Joseph, the "supposed father" of Jesus, to descent from Adam and God (Luke 3:24). This Joseph is omitted by D, which substitutes a genealogy adapted from Matt 1:6–15 for Luke 3:23–31. This Joseph falls within a list of 17 ancestors of Jesus who are otherwise unknown in the biblical documents, including Matthew's genealogy (Fitzmyer *Luke 1–9* AB, 500), except for Luke 3:30 and reference to Joseph, the "supposed father" of Jesus. Kuhn (1923: 208–9) believes that the two Josephs of Luke 3:24 and 30 were originally identical, both derived from a common list that subsequently formed the basis for two parallel lists in Luke's genealogy: 3:26–29, Jesus to Mattathias; and 3:29–31, Joshua/Jesus to Mattatha; the first perhaps reflecting a Hebrew context and the second, in an Aramaic context, tracing Mary's line of descent (since it does not mention Joseph as Jesus' father). This proposal has not proved convincing to most scholars.

13. The father of Judah and son of Jonam according to Luke's genealogy tying Joseph, the "supposed father" of Jesus, to descent from Adam and God (Luke 3:30). This Joseph is omitted by D, which substitutes a genealogy adapted from Matt 1:6–15 for Luke 3:23–31. This Joseph falls within a list of 18 ancestors of Jesus who are otherwise unknown in the biblical documents, including Matthew's genealogy (Fitzmyer, 501), except for Luke 3:24 and reference to Joseph, the "supposed father" of Jesus. Although Jeremias (1969: 296) believes that it is anachronistic for Luke to include this name here, since it first appears as a personal name in the postexilic period (e.g., Ezra 10:42; Neh 12:14; 1 Chr 25:2, 9), caution must be exercised in light of the limited nature of the available evidence and the possibility that 1 Chronicles is historically reliable at this point. See above (#12) on Kuhn's proposal.

14. See JOSEPH OF ARIMATHEA.

15. The unsuccessful of two followers of Jesus, the other being Matthias, from whom the replacement apostle for Judas was chosen, also called Barsabbas and surnamed Justus (Acts 1:23). This Joseph is distinguished from others named Joseph by his patronymic in Aramaic meaning either "son of the Sabbath" or "son of the elder" (D pc read Gk *Barnaban,* obviously confused with Joseph called Barnabas in Acts 4:36; see #16 below). Following the custom of many Jews of the time, he also had a Latin name, Justus, resembling his Jewish name (cf. Matt 16:17; Acts 13:9; 17:5), probably used in his dealings with gentiles. This Joseph is not the Judas Barsabbas of Acts 15:22. Nothing further is known of him, except that Eusebius (*Hist. Eccl.* 3.39.9–10) records a legend of Papias from the daughters of Philip that Joseph "drank poison but by the Lord's grace suffered no harm."

16. A Levite from Cyprus and member of the Church of Acts who sold a field and brought the proceeds to the apostles; also known as Barnabas, which is said to mean "son of encouragement" (Acts 4:36). Greek *Iōsēs* is read in C Majority and syr^{h}, but Gk *Iōsēph* is clearly the correct reading. There have been various explanations of how "son of encouragement" is derived from Barnabas (see Brock 1974). This significant individual in the history of the Church (not to be confused with Joseph Barsabbas in

Acts 1:23; see #15 above) is known by the name Barnabas elsewhere in the NT. See also BARNABAS.

Bibliography

Brock, S. 1974. Barnabas: Huios Para Klēseōs. *JTS* n.s. 25: 95–98.
Brown, R. E., et al. 1978. *Mary in the NT.* Philadelphia.
Gundry, R. H. 1982. *Matthew: A Commentary on His Literary and Theological Art.* Grand Rapids.
Jeremias, J. 1969. *Jerusalem in the Time of Jesus.* Philadelphia.
Kuhn, G. 1923. Die Geschlechtsregister Jesu bei Lukas und Matthäus, nach ihrer Herkunft untersucht. *ZNW* 22: 206–28.
Lightfoot, J. B. 1865. *The Epistle of St. Paul to the Galatians.* Repr. Grand Rapids.
McHugh, J. 1975. *The Mother of Jesus in the NT.* Garden City.
McNeile, A. H. 1915. *The Gospel according to St. Matthew.* London.
Mayor, J. B. 1897. *The Epistle of St. James.* Repr. Grand Rapids.
Schnackenburg, R. 1987. *Matthäusevangelium 16:21–28:20.* Neue Echter Bibel. Würzburg.
Swete, H. B. 1898. *The Gospel according to St. Mark.* London.

STANLEY E. PORTER

JOSEPH AND ASENETH. An apocryphal Jewish romance which recounts the conversion of the gentile Aseneth to the God of Israel, her marriage to the patriarch Joseph, and the conflicts surrounding that conversion and marriage. The story is a midrashic elaboration of Gen 41:45, 50–52; and 46:20, which briefly mention Joseph's marriage to Asenath (LXX Aseneth), daughter of Potiphera (LXX Pentephres), priest of On (Heliopolis).

After much neglect by biblical scholars because of the 5th-century date and the Christian character assigned to the apocryphon in several early publications (Batiffol 1889–90: 7–18, 30–37), *Joseph and Aseneth* is now recognized to be a Jewish composition from around the turn of the eras (Burchard 1965: 99–106, 143–51). For this reason it is often included in the OT Pseudepigrapha and is considered significant for the study of early Judaism and Christian origins.

A. Contents

The story falls into two parts. The first, chaps. 1–21, begins with Aseneth, the exceptionally beautiful virgin daughter of Pentephres, priest of Heliopolis and chief nobleman of pharaoh, voluntarily secluded in her ornate quarters in order to avoid the many suitors who seek her hand in marriage. When Joseph, who is touring Egypt to gather grain, announces plans to dine in the house of Pentephres, Aseneth arrogantly refuses her father's suggestion that she be given to Joseph in marriage. When Joseph arrives, she is so impressed with his beauty that she changes her mind and falls madly in love with him. However, Joseph spurns her because, in his words:

> It is not proper for a man who worships God, who blesses with his mouth the living God and eats blessed bread of life and drinks a blessed cup of immortality and is anointed with blessed ointment of incorruption, to kiss a strange woman, who blesses with her mouth dead and dumb idols and eats from their table bread of strangling and drinks from their libation a cup of deceit and is anointed with ointment of destruction. (8:5)

After praying for Aseneth's conversion, Joseph leaves, promising to return in a week. In the meantime Aseneth repudiates her idols and penitently turns to the God of Israel. She is then visited by a "man from heaven," who announces the heavenly acknowledgment of her conversion and describes the blessings that now accrue to her. Foremost among these are life and immortality, in which Aseneth participates symbolically by eating a mysterious honeycomb, which is said to be the same immortal food as that eaten by the angels in paradise. When Joseph returns, he greets and kisses the gloriously transfigured Aseneth. The couple is married by pharaoh amid elaborate festivities, and from their union are born Manasseh and Ephraim.

In the second part of the story, chaps. 22–29, pharaoh's son becomes jealous of Joseph and enlists the aid of Joseph's brothers, Dan, Gad, Naphtali, and Asher, to murder Joseph and abduct Aseneth. The plot fails because of timely divine intervention and the efforts of some of Joseph's other brothers, especially Simeon, Levi, and Benjamin. Pharaoh's son is mortally wounded during the conflict; and when the grief-stricken pharaoh also dies, Joseph becomes king of Egypt.

B. Text

Joseph and Aseneth is extant in 16 Greek manuscripts and numerous versional witnesses. Of the two principal forms of the story, one about two-thirds as long as the other, the longer form lies closer to the original in the judgment of most specialists (Burchard 1970: 3–34), although a number of modern studies and translations have been based on the short recension (Philonenko 1968: 125–226) because of the lack of a critical edition of the long text.

C. Original Language

Joseph and Aseneth was almost certainly composed in Greek. Semitisms abound, but these reflect strong Septuagintal influence and are no more than should be expected from Greek-speaking Hellenistic Judaism. The significance of the word play on the name Aseneth in 15:7 is not apparent in Greek, but attempts to explain this word play in Hebrew and Aramaic are themselves problematic and would not in any case prove the existence of a Semitic original. Frequently used words which have no Semitic equivalents, such as *athanasia,* "immortality" and *aphtharsia,* "incorruption" are among the compelling evidences for a Gk original.

D. Religious Character

The once-predominant view that *Joseph and Aseneth* is a Christian composition has given way to the consensus that the work is Jewish. Although some scholars maintain that there are a few Christian interpolations (Holtz 1968: 482–97), the work is devoid of any distinctively Christian traits while being replete with elements which have strong affinities in Hellenistic Judaism.

In spite of the consensus that *Joseph and Aseneth* is Jewish, attempts to relate the Judaism reflected in the work to one of the known Jewish groups of the time have been unsuccessful. Alleged points of contact with the Essenes, Therapeutae, Merkabah mystics, and gnostic groups are overshadowed by more fundamental differences. Similarly, the superficial parallels which some have noted between Aseneth's conversion and mystery initiation do not justify the claim that the Judaism represented in the work was shaped appreciably by the mystery religions.

The type of Judaism represented in *Joseph and Aseneth* existed in dynamic tension with gentiles and struggled to maintain a distinctive Jewish identity. Table fellowship and intermarriage with gentiles, including the marriage of a convert and a born Jew, were live issues. Conversion to Judaism carried the possibility of ostracism from former gentile family and associates. The story seems also to reflect considerable discord within the Jewish community centering on the perception of the convert. Since it is these sociological dimensions of conversion to Judaism that are central and determinative in shaping the narrative, it is more difficult than many have supposed to extrapolate the ritual formalities and theological understanding of conversion for purposes of history-of-religions comparisons (Chesnutt 1988: 21–48). The curious juxtaposition of blatant syncretism with an explicit concern to resist assimilation compounds the problem of characterizing the Judaism reflected in *Joseph and Aseneth.*

E. Provenance

The apocryphon seems to have been composed in Egypt. The pervasive tension between Jews and Egyptians and between the God of Israel and the Egyptian gods is developed in such a way as to suggest that the Egyptian setting of the story was dictated not merely by the biblical framework, but also by the milieu in which the author and his community actually lived. In addition, Egyptian elements are discernible in various individual motifs. For example, contemporaneous perceptions of the Egyptian goddess Neith seem to have influenced the portrayal of Aseneth at some points.

F. Date

The extensive dependence of *Joseph and Aseneth* on the various parts of the LXX (Delling 1978: 29–56) indicates a date of composition no earlier than ca. 100 B.C. Since the story reflects a time when there was concern about and a realistic possibility of gentile conversions to Judaism, it must have been written before the measures against Judaism which Hadrian imposed at the time of the Second Revolt in A.D. 132–35. If an Egyptian provenance is assumed, *Joseph and Aseneth* must have been written prior to the period A.D. 115–17, during which the Jewish pogrom under Trajan resulted in the virtual annihilation of Egyptian Jewry. A more specific date within these broad limits is difficult to determine, but the conciliatory attitude toward gentiles fits better before than after A.D. 70, and in Egypt such an outlook fits better before than after the pogrom against Alexandrian Jews in A.D. 38. The absence of reference to the Romans and the depiction of Egypt as an independent country with rulers favorably disposed toward Jews may reflect the Ptolemaic period in Egypt before the Roman takeover in 30 B.C., but this is by no means certain.

G. Readership and Purpose

Although some have understood *Joseph and Aseneth* as missionary propaganda designed to win gentiles to the Jewish faith, the author's assumption that his readers are familiar with the patriarchal narratives and can understand other allusions to Scripture makes it more likely that he envisioned a readership primarily Jewish or at least of those who already stood very close to Judaism. Moreover, his repeated use of the formula "it is not proper for a man (woman) who worships God to . . ." (8:5, 7; 21:1; 23:9, 12; 29:3) and his other ways of defining the conduct befitting "those who worship God" (23:10; 28:5, 7) are clearly directed inward, to Jews, and not outward.

Not even the polemic against idolatry indicates that the work was written for gentiles. Jews themselves needed to be reminded of their distinctiveness vis à vis gentiles and of the danger of assimilation to gentile religion and culture. Moreover, Jews who were less than accommodating toward gentile converts and who doubted the propriety of marriage to converts needed reassurance that true conversion entailed the utter repudiation of idols and therefore that marriage to a convert was no concession to idolatry. Such intramural concerns seem best to account for the detailed narrative of Aseneth's renunciation of idolatry and everything associated with it. There is no indication that this critique of idolatry is calculated to attract outsiders.

The exalted estimation of the convert in *Joseph and Aseneth* suggests that one of the primary purposes of the work was to enhance the status of converts within the Jewish community (Chesnutt 1988: 37–43). Through the story the author shows that converts to Judaism are beneficiaries of all the blessings and privileges of the people of God and that as such they are to be received fully into the community of Israel and are suitable mates for Jews. The author even has God's own chief angel appear in the story to provide heavenly endorsement of the conversion and marriage of the prototypical proselyte.

At the same time the author is obviously concerned to extol Jewish life and religion and to warn against exogamy and idolatry, perhaps in order to show that the openness to gentile converts is no concession to pagan idolatry and its corrupting effect and no threat to a distinctive Jewish self-identity. Since Aseneth was unacceptable as a wife for Joseph until she renounced her idols, her story entails no concession to idolatry. Similarly, opposition to exogamy is not abandoned but confirmed in the story; Aseneth could marry a "son of God" only because she had become a "daughter of the Most High" (6:3, 5; 18:11; 21:4). Neither does full acceptance of the convert entail any diminution of the blessed status enjoyed by Jews as the people of God; these blessings are in fact affirmed and articulated at great length in *Joseph and Aseneth,* but with the emphasis that the Jew by conversion participates in them every bit as fully as the Jew by birth. Membership in the people of God according to this apocryphon is not even determined by ethnic descent but by acknowledgment of the true God and is characterized by "proper" conduct. Thus the true convert is on equal footing with the Jew by birth, and the latter must avoid the contamination of idols and engage in "proper" conduct in order to retain God's favor. "Proper" conduct is defined to include not only the avoidance of gentile impurity but also the treatment of both Jews and gentiles with magnanimity and respect in situations of conflict (8:5; 21:1; 23:9, 12; 29:3; see also 28:5, 14).

H. Special Problems

Among the most interesting and problematic features of *Joseph and Aseneth* are the formulaic references to the bread of life, cup of immortality, and ointment of incorruption (8:5–7, 9; 15:5; 16:16; 19:5; 21:21). These have most commonly been supposed to reflect some sort of sacred meal, perhaps related to the sacred meals attested in other ancient sources. A minority view is that the reference is not to a ritual meal at all but to the everyday Jewish meal, which itself had a solemn religious character, or to the entire Jewish way of life. Aseneth never actually receives any bread, cup, or ointment anywhere in the narrative; instead, she eats a piece of honeycomb and is then said to have eaten bread of life, drunk a cup of immortality, and been anointed with ointment of incorruption. The honeycomb probably represents manna; in any case both the honeycomb and the triadic formula with which it is equated symbolize the access to life which is the unique privilege of those who worship the God of Israel.

The triad of bread, cup, and ointment is reminiscent of the biblical formula "grain, wine, and oil" and, like that formula, summarizes the staples of Jewish life. Moreover, food, drink, and oil are precisely those items regarded in Jewish tradition as most susceptible to impurity by association with idolatry. Therefore whether the triadic formula in *Joseph and Aseneth* echoes some special Jewish ritual which is set over against pagan rites or simply originated in the peculiarly Jewish use of the staple commodities of life in contrast to the defiling food, drink, and oil of the gentile world, it certainly functions as a representative expression for Jewish life in a gentile environment.

The episode involving the bees in 16:17–23 is notoriously enigmatic. The incident serves to accentuate the importance of the honeycomb as a symbol of life and immortality, and the miraculous appearance and disappearance of the comb and the bees at the command of the man from heaven function to confirm the veracity of this heavenly visitor's pronouncements to Aseneth, but the symbolism in the description of the bees and their strange behavior has defied explanation.

Investigation into the history-of-religions affinities of this apocryphon and its significance for the study of Christian origins continues. Expressions such as "son of God," "bread of life" (cf. John 6), and "cup of blessing" (cf. 1 Cor 10:16); theological ideas such as the conceptions of God, sin, repentance, and salvation; images of conversion such as new creation and emergence from death to life; and liturgical and paraenetic patterns such as the prayers and the "then-now" paradigm illustrate the significance of *Joseph and Aseneth* for the study of the NT and Christian origins.

Bibliography

Aptowitzer, V. 1924. Aseneth, the Wife of Joseph. *HUCA* 1: 239–306.

Batiffol, P. 1889–90. *Le Livre de la Prière d'Aseneth.* Pp. 1–115 in Studia Patristica: Études d'ancienne littérature chrétienne 1–2. Paris.

Brooks, E. W. 1918. *Joseph and Asenath.* Translations of Early Documents, Series 2. London.

Burchard, C. 1965. *Untersuchungen zu Joseph und Aseneth: Überlieferung-Ortsbestimmung.* WUNT 8. Tübingen.

———. 1970. Zum Text von "Joseph und Aseneth." *JSJ* 1: 3–34.

———. 1979. Ein vorläufiger griechischer Text von Joseph und Aseneth. *DBAT* 14: 2–53.

———. 1987a. Der jüdische Asenethroman und seine Nachwirkung: Von Egeria zu Anna Katharina Emmerick oder von Moses aus Aggel zu Karl Kerényi. *ANRW* 2/20/1: 543–667.

———. 1987b. The Present State of Research on Joseph and Aseneth. Vol. 2, pp. 31–52 in *Religion, Literature, and Society in Ancient Israel, Formative Christianity and Judaism,* ed. J. Neusner et al. Langham, MD.

———. 1987c. The Importance of Joseph and Aseneth for the Study of the NT. *NTS* 33: 102–34.

Chesnutt, R. D. 1988. The Social Setting and Purpose of Joseph and Aseneth. *JSP* 2: 21–48.

Collins, J. J. 1983. Pp. 89–91, 211–18 in *Between Athens and Jerusalem: Jewish Identity in the Hellenistic Diaspora.* New York.

Cook, D. 1984. Joseph and Aseneth. Pp. 465–503 in *The Apocryphal OT,* ed. H. F. D. Sparks. Oxford.

Delling, G. 1978. Einwirkungen der Sprache der Septuaginta in 'Joseph und Aseneth'. *JSJ* 9: 29–56.

Doran, R. 1986. Pp. 290–93 in *Early Judaism and Its Modern Interpreters.* Ed. R. A. Kraft and G. W. E. Nickelsburg. Atlanta.

Goodman, M. 1986. Joseph and Aseneth. *HJP²* 3/1: 546–52.

Holtz, T. 1968. Christliche Interpolationen in 'Joseph und Aseneth'. *NTS* 14: 482–97.

Kee, H. C. 1983. The Socio-Cultural Setting of Joseph and Aseneth. *NTS* 29: 394–413.

Lindars, B. 1987. 'Joseph and Asenath' and the Eucharist. Pp. 181–99 in *Scripture: Meaning and Method,* ed. B. P. Thompson. Hull, England.

Nickelsburg, G. W. E. 1981. Pp. 258–63 in *Jewish Literature between the Bible and the Mishnah.* Philadelphia.

Philonenko, M. 1968. *Joseph et Aséneth.* SPB 13. Leiden.

Sänger, D. 1979. Bekehrung und Exodus: Zum jüdischen Traditionshintergrund von 'Joseph und Aseneth.' *JSJ* 10: 11–36.

———. 1980. *Antikes Judentum und die Mysterien: Religionsgeschichtliche Untersuchungen zu Joseph und Aseneth.* WUNT 2/5. Tübingen.

———. 1985. Erwägungen zur historischen Einordnung und zur Datierung von 'Joseph und Aseneth.' *ZNW* 76: 86–106.

Schwartz, J. 1984. Recherches sur l'évolution du roman de Joseph et Aséneth. *REJ* 143: 273–85.

West, S. 1974. Joseph and Aseneth. *Classical Quarterly* 24: 70–81.

RANDALL D. CHESNUTT

JOSEPH OF ARIMATHEA. A reportedly good, righteous, and rich member of the Sanhedrin, who was expecting the kingdom of God and had become a follower of Jesus and who received from Pilate the body of Jesus for burial in his own tomb (Mark 15:43, 45; Matt 27:57, 59; Luke 23:50–51; John 19:38).

Two issues arise when discussing Joseph of Arimathea. First is the location of Arimathea. New Testament Arimathea is probably to be identified with the Judean city W of the hill country of Ephraim and NW of Jerusalem known in Hebrew as Ramah, Ramathaim-zophim, or Rathamin (see Rogerson NAB, 148; Fitzmyer *Luke 10–24* AB, 1526), although Eusebius places it near Lydda to the SW (*Onomast.* 144.28; cf. 1 Macc 11:34; Josephus *Ant* 13.127). This city, which played a part in the life of Samuel and his parents (1 Sam 1:1, 19; 2:11; 7:17; 8:4), is specified as a "Jewish town" by Luke (23:50), possibly to help non-Jewish readers (Marshall *Luke* NIGTC, 880). The Greek text at Mark 15:43 and John 19:38 allows the interpretation that when Jesus' crucifixion took place, Joseph came directly "from Arimathea" to participate in the events surrounding it (if the prepositional phrase modifies the verb of motion) or, more likely, that he was originally from the city of Arimathea and presumably now living elsewhere, probably in Jerusalem (if the prepositional phrase modifies the name Joseph). The textual variant in Mark 15:43 and John 19:38, with the word *the* before the prepositional phrase *from Arimathea* (see NovTG[26]) argues for the latter interpretation.

The second and more important issue regarding Joseph of Arimathea is the motivation for his act of burial (see Broer 1972: 175–83, 190–98; esp. Brown 1988). Schreiber (1981) has recently focused upon the redactional differences among the gospel accounts with Mark emphasizing Joseph as the renowned leader of the Jews, Matthew as the disciple of Jesus, Luke as the Sanhedrin member, and John as a disciple fearful of the Jews. This description raises several crucial questions which must be decided before Joseph's motivation can be determined. First, there is the question of whether Joseph was a member of his local village council or whether he was a member of the Jerusalem Sanhedrin. According to Mark 15:43 he was a "respected" (see Swete 1898: 369 on *euskēmōn*) or possibly "rich" member of a council, and according to Luke 23:50 he was a good and just man. Although the term used for "council" in Mark 15:43 and Luke 23:50 was probably not a technical term at this stage in its usage (see Taylor 1959: 600; followed by Broer, 1972: 175–77, who states that even though Luke believes Joseph was a member of the Sanhedrin, Mark does not make this indication; cf. Lührmann *Markusevangelium* HNT, 267), four facts argue that he was a member of the Jerusalem council: (1) he appears to have been a wealthy landowner (Matt 27:57; Jeremias 1969: 96; some scholars think Matthew inserted this on the assumption that such an important figure would have to be wealthy; McNeile 1915: 426; cf. Barrick 1977); (2) he reportedly did not consent in the decisions or actions regarding Jesus (Luke 23:51; see Fitzmyer, 1526); (3) the word for council, used with reference to the Sanhedrin by Josephus (*JW* 2.405), is not modified to specify any other than the one in Jerusalem (see Marshall, 879); and (4) he is associated with Nicodemus, a member of the Jerusalem Sanhedrin (John 19:39; Brown *John 13–21* AB, 939).

The second factor is Joseph's relation to Jesus. Mark 15:43 and Luke 23:50 say that he was looking forward to the kingdom of God, which would not distinguish him from many other Jews of the time, especially the Pharisees. Matthew (27:57) goes further and specifies that he "was a follower" of Jesus (there is a textual variant here which does not affect this point), although possibly a secret one (see John 19:38, with the term *disciple,* although on the basis of textual variants regarding who came to take the body, Murphy-O'Connor [1974: 266–67] believes that Joseph is a later interpolation in the story; contra Brown *John 13–21* AB, 938; cf. Curtis 1972: 442–43). The facts that Joseph reportedly was involved in Jesus' burial, that Matthew does not limit discipleship exclusively to the Twelve, and that instruction of the disciple probably entailed acceptance of the coming kingdom give witness to his being more than a passive observer of Jesus (Wilkins 1988: 160–67; contra Bonnard *Matthieu* CNT, 408–9; cf. Brown [1988: 240–44], who believes that Joseph could have acted simply out of pious motives as a faithful member of the Sanhedrin).

A third factor is the prescriptions in Jewish law regarding the burial of bodies. According to Roman law execution signaled the sacrifice of all of the victim's earthly possessions and left the right of burial only to the good favor of the magistrate, although the body was often released to relatives. Jewish law on the contrary held that burial was a duty to be performed even for enemies (Jos. *JW* 3.361ff.), and according to Deut 21:23 and rabbinic law the body was not to hang on a cross after sundown (see Lane *Mark* NICNT, 577–78; Brown 1988: 234–38 for details). Joseph, as a leader of the Jews, and out of respect for Jewish law, especially in light of his apparent dissent from the voting for Jesus' execution (Luke 23:51), and possibly as a favor to Jesus' followers and as a friend of Pilate (*Gospel of Peter* 2.3), felt compelled to request from Pilate the right to bury him. But this motive faces the difficulty of why Joseph would have risked ceremonial uncleanness (*ISBE* 2: 1131; perhaps servants helped him; see Brown *John 13–21* AB, 940), to say nothing of his political and religious careers (John 19:38; cf. Mark 15:43, where Joseph "took courage" to go to Pilate), for such a criminal as Jesus. As depicted in the Gospels, Joseph at the least probably felt that Jesus' message of the coming of the kingdom warranted this one final act of devotion (Gould *Mark* ICC, 297–98), with Matthew seeing this as a further sign of Joseph's being a follower. The NT documents agree that Joseph, with help from others (though no family members), prepared and laid Jesus' body in a tomb and rolled a stone across the opening. John 19:41 states that the new tomb was in a garden near the place of crucifixion. The fact that the tomb was unused by members of his family may indicate that Joseph had recently come from Arimathea and possibly had made his fortune in Jerusalem, with his family tomb still in his village of origin, although the special circumstances of Jesus' death as a criminal may have required a special tomb (see Kee *IDB* 3: 980).

Bibliography

Barrick, W. B. 1977. The Rich Man from Arimathea (Matt 27:57–60) and 1QIsa[a]. *JBL* 96: 235–39.

Broer, I. 1972. *Die Urgemeinde und das Grab Jesu.* SANT. Munich.

Brown, R. E. 1988. The Burial of Jesus (Mark 15:42–47). *CBQ* 50: 233–45.

Curtis, K. P. G. 1972. Three Points of Contact between Matthew and John in the Burial and Resurrection Narratives. *JTS* n.s. 23: 440–44.

Jeremias, J. 1969. *Jerusalem in the Time of Jesus.* Philadelphia.

McNeile, A. H. 1915. *The Gospel according to St. Matthew.* Repr. Grand Rapids, 1980.

Murphy-O'Connor, J. 1974. Review of Broer 1972. *RB* 81: 266–69.

Schreiber, J. 1981. Die Bestattung Jesu: Redaktionsgeschichtliche Beobachtungen zu Mk 15:42–47 par. *ZNW* 72: 141–77.

Swete, H. B. 1898. *The Gospel according to St. Mark.* London.

Taylor, V. 1959. *The Gospel according to St. Mark.* London.

Wilkins, M. J. 1988. *The Concept of Disciple in Matthew's Gospel.* NovTSup. Leiden.

Stanley E. Porter

JOSEPH OF ARIMATHEA, NARRATIVE BY.

See VIRGIN, ASSUMPTION OF THE; PILATE, ACTS OF.

JOSEPH, HISTORY OF. The document known as the *History of Joseph* is extant in six Greek papyrus fragments, three of which are housed in the Bodleian Library at Oxford (Lindsay 1885: 304), two in the British Museum (Milne 1927: 187–90; Denis 1970: 235–36; Kenyon 1893: 225, 227), and one in the Louvre (Ricci 1902: 431). The Bodleian fragments appear to be written in the same 6th- or 7th-century hand as those of the British Museum and thus probably originated from the same manuscript. The single fragment which is preserved in the Louvre is written in a different hand and duplicates part of the text contained in the fragments belonging to the British Museum. The Louvre fragment therefore represents a second manuscript copy of the *History of Joseph.*

The extremely fragmentary nature of the text which has survived on papyrus allows very little to be known about the document itself. The title, *History of Joseph,* is artificial, having been arbitrarily assigned to this text by H. J. M. Milne, who edited the fragments belonging to the British Museum (Milne 1927: 187). This appellation is due to the repeated occurrence of the names of the Hebrew patriarch Joseph and his father, Jacob, within the legible lines of the papyrus fragments. Mention is made also of a pharaoh, and of Joseph's brothers Reuben and Simeon, and of ten brothers collectively. Apart from such proper names and titles, the fragments of the *History of Joseph* consist of disjointed letters, words, and phrases representing a minimum of continuous text.

More information concerning the nature of this document may be deduced, however, from a comparison of the extant text of the *History of Joseph* with the corresponding passages of the biblical book of Genesis. A number of apparent points of contact between these two texts suggest that the *History of Joseph* does generally follow the story line of the biblical account of the patriarch Joseph. Discernible among the surviving fragments of the *History of Joseph* are possible references to Joseph's appointment by pharaoh to a position of authority over Egypt and his handling of the available grain before and during the famine, the confrontation between Joseph as a ruler of Egypt and his ten brothers who had come to him from Canaan to buy grain, the discussion between the brothers while in prison acknowledging the consequences of their former mistreatment of their brother Joseph, the return of nine of the brothers to Canaan and their report to their father, Jacob, concerning what had transpired in Egypt, and Jacob's lamentation about losing his son Simeon as he had formerly lost Joseph (*OTP* 2: 467).

A more precise assessment of the relationship between the biblical text and the *History of Joseph* may be obtained by closer scrutiny of the lines of the recto of fragment 227 in the British Museum (*OTP* 2: 469–70). A single biblical verse (Gen 42:29) describing the return of Joseph's brothers to Canaan and their report to their father appears to be somewhat embellished in the *History of Joseph* by the inclusion of details of a dialogue between Jacob and his sons and the emotion expressed by the father after seeing only nine sons return without Simeon. Such liberal treatment of the biblical text by the author of this pseudepigraphon and the absence of verbal agreements with the text of Genesis would seem to characterize this document as a paraphrase of the biblical story of Joseph. This would allow the *History of Joseph* to be categorized tentatively as a midrashic expansion of at least part of the OT book of Genesis.

In spite of the extreme paucity of actual text which is available for study, certain elements can be identified in the *History of Joseph* which may provide clues as to the theological orientation of this document. One of the principal themes of the surviving parts of the *History of Joseph* seems to be a tendency to elevate and thus exemplify the person of Joseph. This is demonstrated by several instances in the text where Joseph is referred to as "king of the people," "one who feeds the Egyptians," and "savior of Egypt" (*OTP* 2: 469). This observation is further supported by references to the God of Israel as the "God of Joseph," even within a context in which Joseph's father, the patriarch Jacob, is present.

Perhaps the single most distinctive characteristic of the extant text of the *History of Joseph* is the phrase "Joseph, remembering Jacob," which occurs partially at least 11 times among the surviving fragments of this document. Such an excessively high proportion of repetitions of a single phrase within so limited an amount of text indicates that this phrase must have been a central theme of at least the segment of text represented among the extant papyri of the present pseudepigraphon. It is perhaps significant that the two occurrences of the phrase "Joseph, remembering Jacob" on the recto of the Louvre fragment are immediately followed by a vacant space deliberately created by the scribe in the text of the papyrus; this could indicate a liturgical use for this document. It has been suggested that the emphasis apparently placed upon the remembrance of his father, Jacob, by Joseph might betray a Sitz im Leben in which oppression of the Jews would necessitate a stricter observance of their national and religious traditions (*OTP* 2: 469).

The parameters for dating the *History of Joseph* are established by the date of the papyri themselves and by certain affinities with earlier documents. On paleographic grounds the 6th- or 7th-century date of the papyri containing the *History of Joseph* defines the terminus ad quem for this document. Parallels with such early pseudepigrapha as the *Testaments of the Twelve Patriarchs* and *Joseph and Aseneth* raise the possibility that the *History of Joseph* may have originated at least several centuries earlier.

The *History of Joseph* shares its central theme of "Joseph, remembering Jacob" with the *Testament of Joseph* (3:3), where Joseph intimates that he was able to resist the advances of the Egyptian Potiphar's wife by remembering the words of his father, Jacob. The exaltation of Joseph, which was described above as one of the prominent themes of the *History of Joseph,* also appears to be one of the identifying characteristics of the pseudepigraphon *Joseph and Aseneth* (*OTP* 2: 469). Further indication of a possible connection between these two documents perhaps may be seen in *Joseph and Aseneth* (25:6), where Joseph is described as king, giver of food, and savior, roles which coincide with the three principal concepts of Joseph projected in the *History of Joseph.*

Bibliography

Denis, A.-M. 1970a. *Fragmenta Pseudepigraphorum quae supersunt Graeca.* PVTG 3. Leiden.

———. 1970b. *Introduction aux pseudépigraphes grecs d'Ancien Testament.* SVTP 1. Leiden.

Kenyon, F. G. 1893. *Greek Papyri in the British Museum.* Vol. 1. London.

Lindsay, W. M. 1885. The Fayoum Papyri in the Bodleian Library. *The Athenaeum* 3019: 304.

Milne, H. J. M. 1927. *Catalogue of the Literary Papyri in the British Museum.* London.

Ricci, S. de. 1902. Bulletin Papyrologique. *Revue des études grecques* 15: 431.

George T. Zervos

JOSEPH, HUSBAND OF MARY (PERSON) [Gk *Iōsēph*]. The supposed father of Jesus and husband of Mary the mother of Jesus (Luke 3:23; Matt 1:16).

There are several important issues to discuss regarding Joseph, the husband of Mary. First, Joseph is mentioned in Matthew, Luke, and John but does not appear in Mark, except indirectly at 6:3 in a few manuscripts (see *NovTG*[26]), which read "the son of the carpenter." Apart from John (1:45; 6:42), where Jesus is twice referred to as the "son of Joseph" (see Sproston 1985), Joseph is only mentioned in the birth and childhood stories about Jesus. Matthew gives the most detailed information, recounting that when Mary was betrothed to Joseph (1:18), she was found to be pregnant, and Joseph, being a "just man and unwilling to put her to shame," was going to divorce her (1:19), when an angel appeared and told him that the child was conceived of the Holy Spirit (1:20). When Joseph awoke, he took Mary as his wife (1:24). After the visit of the wise men, Joseph was again warned in a dream about a plot by Herod against his child and was commanded to take him to Egypt (2:13), where the parents and child remained until after Herod's death (2:19). Luke also mentions that Mary was betrothed to Joseph when she was told that she would conceive a son, recording that Joseph went up from Galilee with Mary to Bethlehem, "because he was of the house and lineage of David" (2:4), during Quirinius' enrollment, where the family was later visited by shepherds after the birth of the child (2:16).

The limitation of the Joseph material to Matthew and Luke has led some scholars to speculate that Joseph, possibly significantly older than Mary at the time of their marriage, died sometime after Jesus' 12th year (Luke 2:41–50) and before the beginning of his ministry. This hypothesis gains strength from the fact that Mark, mentioning nothing of Jesus' life before his baptism, nowhere mentions Joseph. The apocryphal NT documents contain other Joseph traditions which are compatible with this scenario. For example, *Prot. Jas.* 9.2 says that Joseph was an old man who already had children; and the *History of Joseph the Carpenter* records in some detail that Joseph lived to be 111 years old, having married at 40, and having been married for 49 years, and producing six children before his first wife died. He then lived with Mary for two years before Jesus' birth and would have died during Jesus' twenties.

A second issue surrounds Joseph's origin. Matthew does not mention Joseph's hometown, but Luke states (2:4) that "Joseph also went up from Galilee, from the city of Nazareth, to Judea, to the city of David, which is called Bethlehem." Matthew only mentions that Jesus was born in Bethlehem but that when Joseph brought his family back from Egypt, he was afraid to return to Judea because of the reign of Archelaus; and having been warned in a dream, he went to Nazareth in Galilee. Whereas some scholars find a persistent tension in these accounts (e.g., Fitzmyer *Luke 1–9* AB, 406), choosing instead to focus exclusively on the centrality of Bethlehem, they are not inherently incompatible. It is plausible that Joseph was originally from Bethlehem, but that something, possibly his business or a family migration years earlier, resulted in his or his family's residing in Nazareth for an extended period of time, before he returned to Bethlehem for the enrollment under Quirinius (cf. *IDB* 2: 979; *ISBE* 2: 1130).

A third issue is the character of Joseph and his response to learning that Mary was pregnant. Matt 1:19 describes Joseph as "being a just man and unwilling to put [Mary] to shame," when he learned of her pregnancy. Before using this verse to comment upon Joseph's character, it is important to mention the status of Mary and Joseph's relationship when Joseph learned of her pregnancy. Matt 1:18 says that "before they [Mary and Joseph] came together," Mary was found to be pregnant. Traditionally this verse has been interpreted as supporting the concept of the virgin birth, with the verb "come together" understood as referring to sexual intercourse. Some more recent commentators have suggested that the verb refers to living together, with no reference to sexual intercourse. The customs of betrothal in Palestine during this time probably entailed a legal arrangement whereby the intent of a complete marriage between two partners was arranged by the man and a representative of the woman. Whereas there is some evidence that sexual intercourse was involved in effecting the betrothal (much of the evidence appears to be later), usually this involved monetary payment, with the betrothed couple refraining from sexual intercourse until the formal marriage. There is a large quantity of evidence which shows that the virginity of the bride was to be desired. See VIRGIN. In any case if the woman was found to have had sexual intercourse with anyone other than her betrothed husband, a divorce or annulment could be effected if she was at fault. That Mary was a virgin during the time she was betrothed to Joseph is indicated by Matt 1:25, which says that Joseph did not know Mary until after the birth of Jesus (McHugh 1975: 157–63).

The cause of Joseph's wanting to divorce Mary secretly upon learning that she was pregnant has led to the following interpretations: Joseph suspected that Mary had been sexually unfaithful and possibly was preserving his own reputation; he was completely bewildered at this development because of her supposed virginity; he had a legal, if not moral, obligation to divorce a woman who was to bear the child of another man, though he desired to preserve her reputation; Joseph, being a compassionate man, desired to spare Mary shame; and a recently revived proposal that Joseph knew of the virgin conception and felt inadequate to be involved with such a marvelous act or to expose Mary to possible ridicule (McHugh 1975: 164–72; Bulbeck 1948; cf. Cantwell 1982: 305–12). Before any of these solutions can be adopted, it is necessary to understand what it means that Joseph was "just" in light of his not being willing to expose Mary publicly. Some of the views are that Joseph was discreet in not wanting to expose her publicly (Spicq 1964: 207); that Joseph was kind or merciful and therefore unwilling to expose Mary publicly; that Joseph had respect or awe for God's plan and therefore was unwilling to expose her publicly; and that Joseph was obedient to the OT law but unwilling to expose her publicly (Brown 1977: 125–27). Although Brown argues for the fourth position, the linkage by "and" of the participle with "just" and the negated participle "not willing" makes a more likely understanding that Joseph, a man devoted to the righteous standards of the OT and thus within his rights to divorce Mary publicly, chose a less public or even more lenient divorce, rather than a public accusation, when it became obvious in her physical appearance that she was pregnant (see Carson 1984: 74–75, 81; following Hill 1964–65; cf. Brown 1977: 128; Tosato 1979; Gundry 1982: 21–22; Pesch 1967: 83). Joseph's high moral standards and his desire not to bring undue infamy on his betrothed, Mary, are in keeping with his character as elsewhere exemplified in the biblical account. He is recorded as taking Mary with him to Bethlehem for the enrollment even though women did not need to be present, as being responsive to the several dreams which informed him about the special nature of Mary's child, and as taking special care to preserve the child's life by fleeing to Egypt, besides fulfilling necessary purification rites after birth of the child. Brown (1977: 228–29) sees Matthew as rewriting "a pre-Matthean narrative associating the birth of Jesus, son of Joseph, with the patriarch Joseph and the birth of Moses," while Carson (1984: 90–91) suggests a parallel with Jacob's fleeing the famine in Canaan (Genesis 46). Joseph was apparently regarded by Mary as holding authority in her son's life when in speaking to Jesus she refers to Joseph as "your father" (Luke 2:48). Note however that Joseph is not called the "father" of Jesus in Matthew 2 (Machen 1930: 175–76), even though it is arguably true that Matthew's account of Jesus' infancy is presented from Joseph's perspective, as opposed to Mary's perspective in Luke (see Stendahl 1983: 57). Davies and Allison (*Matthew* ICC, 182; cf. Brown, 1977: 111–12) note that Joseph, Jesus' father, like OT Joseph had a father named Jacob, went to Egypt, had dreams about the future, was chaste, and was disinclined to shame others, thus pointing to the possibility of a Joseph typology in Luke 1–2.

The fourth issue concerns reference to Joseph in the genealogies of Matthew (1:16) and Luke (3:23). One of the first noticeable differences between the two is that in Matthew's genealogy Jacob is the father of Joseph, the husband of Mary, but in Luke's genealogy Joseph is the son of Heli. This issue is of less concern here than it is in relation to Heli, Matthat, and Matthan. See MATTHAT; GENEALOGY. Matthew's and Luke's genealogies follow the line of Joseph, who is apparently designated as Jesus' legal father and a descendant in the line of David (Luke 2:4; 3:23; see Cranfield 1988: 180; cf. Matt 1:1; Luke 1:27, where "of the house of David" refers to Joseph; the badly attested textual variant in Matt 1:16, which reads that "Joseph . . . was the father of Jesus," is undoubtedly to be rejected; see *TCGNT,* 2–7). More significant for discussion of Joseph is the parenthetical phrase in Luke 3:23, "as was supposed," with reference to Jesus being the son of Joseph (a textual variant places "son" after the phrase, but this does not affect interpretation). Some scholars have taken the article following Joseph, *tou,* as referring to "son," making the parenthetical comment read "of Joseph as was supposed" (Godet 1890: 143). This supposedly alleviates the problem with the variants in the genealogies, with Heli the father of Mary, but this understanding is to be rejected. First it is based on a change of punctuation added by later editors. Second it requires an unnatural relationship between *tou* and what is its normal appositional antecedent, the preceding name (see Machen 1930: 203–4; Marshall *Luke* NIGTC, 162). The best understanding is "being a son, as was supposed, of Joseph, the son of . . ." There are two major interpretations of the phrase. The first is that Luke was uncertain about the historical accuracy of the entire genealogy, or he realized that Jesus' descent had already become a matter of polemical dispute (Johnson 1969: 230–31). A second alternative, more likely in light of the statements mentioned above regarding Joseph's response to Mary's becoming pregnant, is that the gospel writer knew that in fact Joseph was not the physical father of Jesus and that the phrase was added possibly to avoid misunderstanding in relation to Luke 1–2 (Marshall, 162).

Bibliography

Brown, R. 1977. *The Birth of the Messiah.* Garden City.

Bulbeck, R. 1948. The Doubt of St. Joseph. *CBQ* 10: 296–309.

Cantwell, L. 1982. The Parentage of Jesus Mt 1:18–21. *NovT* 24: 304–15.

Carson, D. A. 1984. Matthew. Vol. 8, pp. 1–599 in *The Expositor's Bible Commentary,* ed. F. E. Gaebelein. Grand Rapids.

Cranfield, C. E. B. 1988. Some Reflections on the Subject of the Virgin Birth. *SJT* 41: 177–89.

Globe, A. 1980. Some Doctrinal Variants in Matthew 1 and Luke 2, and the Authority of the Neutral Text. *CBQ* 42: 52–72.

Godet, F. 1890. *Kommentar zu dem Evangelium des Lukas.* 2d ed. Hannover.

Gundry, R. H. 1982. *Matthew: A Commentary on His Literary and Theological Art.* Grand Rapids.

Hill, D. 1964–65. A Note on Matthew 1:19. *ExpTim* 76: 133–34.

Johnson, M. D. 1969. *The Purpose of the Biblical Genealogies, with Special Reference to the Setting of the Genealogies of Jesus.* SNTSMS 8. Cambridge.

Machen, J. G. 1930. *The Virgin Birth of Christ.* New York.

McHugh, J. 1975. *The Mother of Jesus in the NT.* Garden City.

Pesch, R. 1967. Eine alttestamentliche Ausführungsformel im Matthäusevangelium. *BZ* 11: 79–95.

Spicq, C. 1964. "Joseph, son Mari, étant juste . . ." (Mt. I, 19). *RB* 71: 206–14.

Sproston, W. E. 1985. 'Is not this Jesus, the son of Joseph . . . ?' (John 6:42). Johannine Christology as a Challenge to Faith. *JSNT* 24: 77–97.

Stendahl, K. 1983. Quis et Unde? An Analysis of Matthew 1–2. Pp. 56–66 in *The Interpretation of Matthew,* ed. G. Stanton. Philadelphia.

Tosato, A. 1979. Joseph, Being a Just Man (Matt 1:19). *CBQ* 41: 547–51.

Stanley E. Porter

JOSEPH, PRAYER OF. The pseudepigraphon known as the *Prayer of Joseph* has survived only in three fragments preserved in the writings of the Christian Father Origen and in references to Origen in Gregory, Basil, Eusebius, and Procopius. Fragment A, the largest of the three, is only nine sentences long and is quoted in Origen's *Commentary on John* 2.31 [25]. Fragment B, which is only one sentence, comes to us from Origen's *Philocalia* (23.15) compiled by Saints Gregory and Basil. It is also cited in Eusebius' *Preparation for the Gospel* 6.2 and in Procopius' *On Genesis.* Fragment C, also one sentence, similarly comes to us from Origen's *Philocalia* through Gregory and Basil. Thus only eleven sentences out of eleven hundred lines, the original length of the document according to Nicephorus, have survived. However, the Prayer is named in several of the ancient lists besides Nicephorus, such as the Sixty Books and the canon lists of Mechitar of Ayrivank and Pseudo-Athanasius. Clearly the Prayer had a wide circulation in antiquity.

With such a small sample of the text surviving, it is hazardous to conclude too much about the character of the original. Mutually exclusive hypotheses have been proposed on the questions of date, original language, and provenance. However, in recent scholarship a slight preference is perhaps discernible for the *Prayer of Joseph*'s being understood as a product of the 1st century C.E. originally written either in Aramaic or Greek by a Jewish author.

In fragment A Jacob describes events associated with his wrestling with the angel at Peniel (Genesis 32). Fragment B suggests that Jacob is addressing his account to Joseph; and this, of course, raises the possibility that the document properly belongs to the genre of testamentary literature. Jacob reveals that in a preexistence, before he entered into mortality, he was one of the chief angels of God, a ruling spirit, and that his name in this preexistent state was *Israel,* which he interprets as meaning "man seeing God." Jacob further explains that in his angelic preexistence he was "the archangel of the power of the Lord," "the chief captain among the sons of God," and the "firstborn of every living thing."

Jacob identifies the angel with whom he wrestled as Uriel and describes the contest in distinctly negative terms. Apparently Uriel, described here as the eighth in rank after Israel among the ruling angels of God, was attempting to establish preeminence over his superior by attacking him in his mortal condition. Jacob's victory seems based upon his knowing the name of his attacker and his own angel name and rank and his calling upon God "by the inextinguishable name," likely some esoteric name of Yahweh. The emphasis on the power of names, the preexistence of Jacob as the ruling angel Israel, and the identification of a hostile Uriel as the angelic antagonist of Genesis 32 are the remarkable theological features of the *Prayer of Joseph.*

In the second fragment Jacob seems to be addressing Joseph and perhaps also his grandsons Ephraim and Manasseh. He explains that he has "read in the tablets of heaven all that shall befall you and your sons." The heavenly tablets are known from *Jubilees* and the Enoch literature; the vision of the future and its transmission by the seer to his posterity are commonplaces in the Pseudepigrapha and other literature of the period and are elsewhere attributed to Adam, Enoch, and Moses.

The third fragment reiterates the identity of Jacob as the preexistent angel Israel, "a chief captain of the power of the Lord." It further adds that Jacob was reminded of his preexistent identity by his encounter with the angel Uriel.

Bibliography

Denis, A.-M. 1970. *Introduction aux pseudépigraphes grecs d'Ancien Testament.* Leiden.

James, M. R. 1920. *The Lost Apocrypha of the OT.* New York.

Smith, J. Z. 1968. The Prayer of Joseph. Pp. 253–94 in *Religions in Antiquity: Essays in Memory of Erwin Ramsdell Goodenough.* Leiden.

———. 1985. Prayer of Joseph. *OTP* 2: 699–714.

STEPHEN E. ROBINSON

JOSEPH, SON OF JACOB. The 11th son of the patriarch Jacob, and the principal character in the biblical narrative of Genesis 37–50.

A. The Name
B. The Tribe
C. The Story
   1. Theme: Familial Strife
   2. Plot
   3. Theological Concerns
D. Sources
E. Genres
   1. Sitz im Leben
   2. Dating
F. Purpose of the Story

A. The Name

The name itself derives from the Hebrew verb *ysp.* It maintains its verbal form with an appropriate meaning: "He adds." The popular etymology for the name in Gen 30:24 suggests that the divine name was the subject of the verb and that the meaning of the name is: "May the Lord add (to me another son)." Indeed, it is clear that names of this type commonly employed an additional element, the name of the deity who would underwrite the power of the name given to a human. From extrabiblical sources, for example, the name "Jacob-El" illustrates the form. That combination is implied by the explanation of the name Joseph. But this hypothetical long form is not attested in the OT traditions about Joseph.

B. The Tribe

The OT tradition about Joseph does not include him in the list of Israel's patriarchs, instead listing these as Abraham, Isaac, and Jacob (Exod 2:24; 3:6, 15; 4:5; etc.). Joseph belongs to the next generation, as one of the eponymic "fathers" of the twelve tribes of Israel (so, Josh 18:11; Judg 1:22; 2 Sam 19:21; 1 Kgs 11:28).

The tradition remembers that the tribe of Joseph was divided, perhaps at the time in the history of the tradition when Levi ceased functioning as a secular tribe: the subdivision of Joseph yielded two tribes, Ephraim and Manasseh, incidentally preserving the number twelve, a structural constant in the political organization. This division appears in the narrative concerning the Joseph tradition in Gen 48:1–12 and in the report of the patriarchal blessing in vv 13–20. The same tradition is reflected in Josh 14:4; 16:4; 17:17, and in the Blessing of Moses in Deuteronomy 33. In Deut 33:13–17 Moses blesses the tribe of Joseph. But the final line, v 17b, recognizes the split in the structure of the Joseph tribe between Ephraim and Manasseh. Moreover, the Joseph unit becomes a symbol for the N kingdom, the nation of Israel, in contrast to the S kingdom, the nation of Judah (Ezek 5:6; 37:19; Obad 18; Zech 10:6).

C. The Story

For the OT tradition it is important to note not only that Joseph is the son of Jacob, one of a group of brothers who give their names to the twelve-tribe union that comprises Israel, but also that Joseph is the son of Rachel, the favorite wife of Jacob. The birth story sets the Joseph tradition into the form of a popular tale. Rachel, the favorite wife, had been barren. Leah, the sister of Rachel and the second wife of Jacob, had given birth to Reuben and Simeon. Rachel had adopted the son of her servant, Bilhah, and named him Naphtali. But only after the competition had taken Leah through six sons did Rachel finally break free from her barren status. The text makes the event explicitly an act of intervention from God: "God remembered Rachel . . . and opened her womb." Thus, just as in the Abraham saga, where Sarah had been barren and in competition with Hagar, so in the Jacob saga, Rachel, who once was barren, gives birth to a son in the midst of family competition, indeed, family strife. That son is Joseph.

1. Theme: Familial Strife. Moreover, the birth story for Joseph has as its context other traditions surrounding strife in the family. The strife theme belongs to the complex of narrative motifs developed throughout the range of the Abraham saga and the Jacob saga. Indeed, the position of the death report for Jacob in Genesis 49 suggests that the Joseph tradition has been bound into the structure of the Jacob saga. From its larger context the Joseph story inherits a milieu of strife.

The position of the Joseph death report in Gen 50:22–26, an element which forms a counterpoint to the Joseph birth story, suggests that the patterns of a Joseph saga can still be seen in the Genesis narrative. Moreover, immediately preceding the Joseph death report, a recapitulation of motifs from earlier stages of the Joseph narrative suggests that at Joseph's death, the family so marked by strife has still found no reconciliation. In this small segment of narrative, the brothers approach Joseph, who holds the power of life and death over them, and weave a tale about Jacob's last wishes for reconciliation between the brothers and Joseph. Joseph responds favorably and grants his forgiveness to his brothers and, through that act, makes his contribution to reconciliation for the family. But the storyteller suggests by the particular construction of the scene that the reconciliation achieved is in fact a sham. The brothers' story about Jacob's last wish has no parallel in the preceding narratives. The brothers apparently intended to deceive Joseph in order to gain asylum. And with that act of deception, the story of a broken and suspicious family comes to an end.

2. Plot. A carefully constructed narrative about Joseph appears in the middle of the larger saga about Jacob with its emphasis on strife that breaks a family apart. This narrative about Joseph stands within the limits of the hypothetical Joseph saga, which is framed by a birth report and a death report. This narrative is different from the surrounding stories about Jacob and his family. It is not a collection of individual tales constructed into a family saga. It is a unit from the first scene to the last. It begins in 37:1 with a notation that "Jacob dwelt in the land of his father's sojournings, in the land of Canaan." And it ends in 47:27 with an exact parallel to its beginnings, the only two changes reflecting the consequence of the long, connected story: "Israel dwelt in the land of Egypt, in the land of Goshen."

The structure of the story framed by these two parallel sentences reveals a clearly constructed plot: (1) exposition (Gen 37:1–4); (2) complication (Gen 37:5–36); (3) digression (Genesis 39–41); (4) complication (Genesis 42–44); (5) denouement (Genesis 45); and (6) conclusion (Gen 46:1–47:27). Moreover, the unifying theme for the development of this plot is the same as the one that dominates the Abraham saga and the Jacob saga: strife in the family. Some indication of a critical role for the promise theme in the patriarchal traditions appears here. For example, in Joseph's speech, 45:4b–13, Joseph avers that "God sent me before you to preserve life. . . . God sent me before you to preserve for you a remnant on earth and to keep alive for you many survivors. So it was not you who sent me here, but God. . . ." The many survivors fulfill the promise for great posterity, the promise that descendants would become a great nation. But the dominant theme in the Joseph story is strife in a family, broken family structures, and eventually, reconciliation that restores the family to a position of unity. The nature of that reconciliation is a key for the Joseph traditions in the Pentateuch, indeed, for the theological structure of the Pentateuch itself.

In the middle of the rather tight structure for the Joseph story, Genesis 39–41 represents a discrete, perhaps originally independent story about Joseph. The story has been used by the author of the larger narrative about Joseph. But in the present position as digression in the movement of narrative about Joseph and his brothers, this unit reveals its character as a story within a story, a story with its own independent structure, genre, and intention. The structure of the independent story comprises three distinct scenes, each designed to depict Joseph as the ideal administrator. The first scene, chap. 39, sets Joseph in Potiphar's house. Finding favor in Potiphar's sight because of his skill as administrator in the house, Joseph rises to the position of overseer in the house. When Potiphar's wife attempts to seduce him, he refuses, not only because to submit would be a "sin against God," but also because it would violate the responsibility he carried as administrator of Potiphar's house. His refusal brought false accusation from the woman and prison from Potiphar, but clearly that fate occurs with Joseph's integrity intact. In prison he rises to a position of trust in the eyes of the captain of the guard, receiving responsibility for two of the pharaoh's servants jailed when they had fallen from the pharaoh's favor. The servants dream prophetic dreams, report them to Joseph, and despite the negative meaning of one, receive interpretations from Joseph. Forgotten by the fortunate servant restored to the pharaoh's favor, Joseph waits in prison until the pharaoh dreams a dream. When none of the pharaoh's professional wise men could interpret it, the servant from the prison recalls Joseph's abilities and recommends him to the pharaoh. Called to the royal chambers, Joseph interprets the royal dream. The pharaoh heeds Joseph's suggestion to appoint a steward for the grain collected during the years of plenty. That steward should be wise and perceptive (the virtues characteristic for an administrator of skill); and since Joseph meets those virtues, he is appointed to the post.

As a complete story, this depiction of Joseph shows a pattern of virtue for all administrators to imitate. But in the larger Joseph story, the digression serves the narrative function of transition. It transports Joseph, the brash but abused brother in Jacob's family, from his position in Canaan to his position in Egypt, where, in his new position of power, he may in turn choose to be brash and abusive.

The second complication in the structure of the Joseph story reverses the role of the principals as they appeared in the first complication. In the first complication Joseph is brash but at the mercy of his brothers. Indeed, the brothers manufacture a story to deceive the old father and set the stage for the broken family. In the second complication Joseph is still brash. But in this case, the unsuspecting brothers are at the mercy of the strange Egyptian who controls the food reserves. Joseph toys with them before he breaks the tension of the scene. First, he accuses them of spying. In order to prove their innocence, the brothers must return to their homes in order to bring the youngest son of Jacob and Rachel to the mysterious vizier. But in the process, they must leave a brother in Egypt, in prison, to await their return with proof of their true identity.

The brothers delay their return to Egypt, however, until the food bought in their first trip had been consumed. The reason for the delay rests with the father's reluctance to send the youngest son of Rachel to such an uncertain fate. But in addition, the narrator heightens the sense of fate hanging over the brothers: when they had arrived at a resting-place on the journey to their homes after the first trip to Egypt, they discovered their money hidden in the sacks of grain. Without their knowledge Joseph had ordered the money be hidden in their sacks, but the discovery brought no joy. It does not disclose an act of reconciliation offered by Joseph to his brothers. It brought fear. "At this their hearts failed them. . . . 'What is this that God has done to us?' " With fate so mysterious, the brothers leave a brother in prison. When necessity finally weighed more heavily than their reluctance to return, they petitioned their father for permission to take Benjamin, the youngest son of Rachel, and return for a new round of provisions. With great fear and only after the strongest possible guarantee from Judah, Jacob agreed. And the brothers set out for Egypt again. In Egypt they gain an audience with the mysterious vizier, only to learn that no charge of theft lies against them. Their anxiety had had no ground in reality. They introduce their younger brother, arrange for the grain, and set out with all of the brothers in the company. All appears to be in order.

At this point Joseph springs the final trap. A servant overtakes the brothers' caravan and accuses them of stealing the divining cup of the Egyptian. Protesting their innocence, the brothers submit to a search with a vow that any guilty brother found with the cup would die and the others would become slaves to the mysterious vizier. The storyteller's skill holds the audience in suspense while he depicts the Egyptian searching each bag from the oldest brother to the youngest. (A similar technique for maintaining suspense appears in Genesis 31.) And again, the storyteller (or Joseph) springs his trap. The object of the search had been hidden in Benjamin's bag. Benjamin would have to die, and the other brothers would become slaves. In that dire crisis the brothers return to Egypt in order to appear before the Egyptian.

The tension in the scene builds to a climax as the brothers present themselves to the Egyptian. The brothers expect to hear the judgment pronounced against them in accord with the oath. But in that setting, Judah offers himself in the place of the younger brother (cf. Moses in Exod 32:32). At the highest point of tension, Joseph breaks the charade and identifies himself as Joseph to his brothers (45:1–3). The revelation might have been depicted as good news. The brothers might assume that now they would be free of the judgment against them. But the storyteller controls the scene by observing that the brothers were dismayed when they learned Joseph's identity. Joseph, even as brother, had the power of life and death over the guilty group. He could now openly seek his revenge. But the story moves in the opposite direction. Instead of death for the guilty brothers, Joseph "fell on his brother Benjamin's neck and wept (cf. Gen 33:4) . . . and he kissed all of his brothers and wept on them, and after that his brothers talked to him." The reconciliation among the brothers contrasts with the negative image in 37:4.

The conclusion carries the dramatic turning point in the story to a smooth ending. Joseph makes arrangements with his brothers for transporting the families still at home in Canaan, including the father, Jacob, to Egypt. The point is, of course, that in Egypt Jacob and the family (the children of Israel) would be under Joseph's protection. But against the backdrop of the larger narrative, the transportation of the family to Egypt represents the reconciliation of a family broken apart by the strife among the brothers.

3. Theological Concerns. The theological character of that reconciliation is important to note. (1) Joseph avers that his own move to Egypt was the result, not of the evil intended against him by the brothers, but of the good intended for him and for many survivors (the descendants of Jacob/Israel or perhaps all the families of the world who eat from the bounty stored by Joseph in Egypt) from the hand of God. (2) But the story is not primarily about God's intervention to save the day; it is also about Joseph's initiative, even in the face of hostility, to save the day for all the people of the world. It is also about Joseph's initiative to save the day for his brothers and his father. To be sure, he sports with them; there is no reconciliation in that. But finally, he welcomes his family to Egypt and shows them how to prepare for their future. The family disregarded a tragic past and committed themselves to one another in a common future. As a result, the reconciliation that appeared elusive for the patriarchal generation came to some fruition through Joseph. (3) Joseph's wisdom and perception influence not only the story within the story (Genesis 39–41), but also the entire structure of the narrative.

Joseph's integrity as administrator facilitates reconciliation of the family.

D. Sources

The Joseph story has served OT scholars as a showcase for evidence that can be used to support identification of the classical pentateuchal sources. The Priestly source does not appear in the narrative to any significant extent. Indeed, even the few fragments defined by source critics as a part of P can be understood more adequately as intrinsic parts of the whole. Gen 37:1–2, for example, serves as a key in the parallel that marks the beginning and ending of the story and cannot be explained as an imitation of the Priestly formula about the generations of Israel.

The more important argument about sources in the Joseph story asserts that in the middle of the predominantly J narrative fragments of the E source appear and that this can be detected by the significant presence of repetitions and duplications of material. For example, the brothers of Joseph appear as the sons of Israel (J) or the sons of Jacob (E). A compassionate brother, at first Judah (J), then Reuben (E), defends Joseph against the plan to sell him to the Ishmaelites (J) or simply to let him fall into the hands of the Midianites (E). Joseph becomes the slave of an unnamed Egyptian whose wife attempts to seduce him (J) or the slave of Potiphar, the captain of the prison (E). Joseph becomes the administrator of the land of Egypt (J), but he has responsibility for the pharaoh's household (E). The sons of Israel (J) or of Jacob (E) come to Egypt. Joseph accuses them of seeking advantage in Egypt (J) or of being spies (E). On their return they find their money hidden in their sacks of grain at an inn on the way to their home (J) and the rest of the money when they arrive at home (E). On the second journey they are invited to settle in Egypt by Joseph (E) and by the pharaoh (J).

Yet, more recent examination of the story softens the argument for two sources by suggesting that one author can use repetition as a narrative technique for emphasis, perhaps simply for variety. Perhaps two brothers could be depicted as compassionate by a single source. Perhaps the mysterious Egyptian could accuse the sons of Jacob of general exploration seeking advantage, then of a more specific act, spying for military advantage. The strongest argument for two sources in the Joseph story is the doublet represented by the reference in 37:25 to the Ishmaelites, then the reference in 37:27 to the Midianites. The doublet is compounded in 37:36 with a note that the Midianites sold Joseph in Egypt to Potiphar, while 39:1 notes that Potiphar had bought Joseph from the Ishmaelites. This apparent doublet disappears, however, if one recognizes that the words "Midianite traders passed by" in 37:28 are a gloss. If these words were not in the text, then the brothers would be the subject of the verbs in v 28: "They drew Joseph up and lifted him out of the pit and sold him to the Ishmaelites for twenty shekels of silver and they (the Ishmaelites) took Joseph to Egypt." The gloss could have arisen to shield the other sons of Israel against the charge of selling a brother into slavery, a crime punishable by death (Deut 24:7). Moreover, to treat the reference to the Midianites in vv 28 and 36 as glosses removes the obvious contradiction in the story. Verse 28 reports that the Midianites sold Joseph to the Ishmaelites, while verse 36 reports that they sold him to Potiphar.

These observations support more recent analysis of the Joseph story that concludes that the story is fundamentally a unit, the work of one hand. It is easy to argue that that hand belongs to the Yahwist (J). The Joseph story fits appropriately in the larger structure of the Yahwist. The Yahwist has used the Joseph story to bridge the gap between patriarchs in Canaan and Israelites in Egypt. But there is no clear evidence that the author who constructed the lengthy narrative, the Joseph story, was the Yahwist. The appropriate conclusion seems to be that the Yahwist has used a carefully constructed, distinct story about Joseph as the structural bridge for the larger narrative about Israel's early history. While the Yahwist might have been the author, this conclusion cannot be firmly supported.

Questions about sources for the Joseph story must move the reader not only through observations about the classical sources for the Pentateuch as they might or might not appear in the Joseph story, but also through observations about other sources employed in the construction of the story. For example, the story within the story (Genesis 39–41) represents a distinct element in the structure of the Joseph story as it now appears. What can be said about the tradition preserved in that story? An Egyptian narrative, commonly called the "Tale of the Two Brothers," describes the events in the relationship of two brothers. The younger brother lived with his older brother and his wife. It was his duty to work in the older brother's fields; and in return the older brother provided food, shelter, and clothes for the younger brother. The younger brother was highly successful in his work, producing a good return from the cattle in his care. On one trip from the field to the older brother's house in order to obtain seed for planting, the younger brother encountered the seductive invitation of the elder brother's wife. The younger brother refused the invitation. But the woman manufactured false evidence and accused him of an attack. Her husband then created a plan to kill his younger brother. Saved by a message from a cow in his care, the younger brother fled. The story continues beyond its parallel with Joseph. But the pattern at the beginning of the tale suggests a plot in common with the account of Joseph in the house of Potiphar.

A second Egyptian story relevant for understanding the Joseph traditions is the "Tale of Sinuhe." This story enlarges the picture of relationships between Palestine and Egypt. Sinuhe, an Egyptian official who left his homeland in voluntary exile, met hospitality in the various stages of his journey. Indeed, the ideal relationships developed by the young man in foreign courts suggest that, like Joseph, Sinuhe served as a model for a courtier in a period of relative prosperity. And he carries that model back to his home and his own people.

It is possible that these Egyptian stories undergird the Joseph story, particularly the story within the story. This observation does not suggest that the author of the Joseph story has used the Egyptian parallels in the same way that he used the story within the story to build his narrative; rather it suggests only that the narrative motifs were part of the culture that gave rise to the Joseph story.

The pattern of the Joseph story puts greater weight on the creativity of the author. To be sure, the author used traditions of storytelling such as the "Tale of the Two Brothers" in the construction of the Joseph story. And the traditions of the promise to the fathers or the strife within the family represent building blocks for the narrative. The Joseph story does reveal its position in the history of Israel's tradition and, indeed, in the tradition of storytelling in the ANE world. Yet, the significance of the Joseph story lies in its own unique construction with its own unique functions and intention.

E. Genres

The genre of the Joseph story supports this description of the constructional uniqueness in the structure of its narration. A consensus is that the Joseph story is a novella, a genre category that facilitates the original conceptions of an artist rather than the patterns of a traditional folk story handed down from one generation to the next. It may be the case that a tale lies behind this extended story of Joseph, a brief story that would have concentrated on the event that broke the unity of Jacob's family and then the event that would have brought them together again. A novella is a creative construction by the author, designed to meet the author's distinctive goals. The author presents not simply what happened long ago and far away, but rather what happened and continues to happen so that the traditions carried by the plot structure capture each new audience. Historical figures and events are caught up into an imaginative fabric produced by the creative activity of the author. Its concern is not to report historical events; it is to build a plot that will hold the audience through its development to a point of climax. And in its development, it reflects the process of life that can give identity to its audience. Indeed, the genre facilitates construction of the plot so that particular facets in the process of life can have an impact on the audience as forceful influences in that quest for identity.

The story within the story (chaps. 39–41) can be isolated from the longer novella and analyzed for itself. The patterns of three scenes in this story depict the ideal shape of the administrator in a household, in a prison, and finally in the royal court. As ideal administrator, the hero emerges as a figure whose virtues can be imitated by all subsequent administrators. Joseph sets the pace for all who exercise responsibility in the organization of a superior. As the ideal whose virtues can be imitated by future generations, this figure functions as the hero of a legend. The story about Joseph, who rises from rags to riches, is a legend designed to show courtiers what responsibility in their profession looks like. It should be clear that classification of this story, so similar to narratives from Egypt, does not define historicity in the Joseph story. The rise from rags to riches may be accurate history describing how one of Israel's ancestors in fact rose to power in Egypt. It may be a story of magnificent imagination, influenced by similar tales and legends from Egypt. To define the story as legend does not establish or deny historicity for the tradition that Joseph was an Egyptian vizier. It shows simply that the story depicts Joseph as the administrator whose virtues should be imitated by all subsequent administrators.

1. Sitz im Leben. The question about setting for these levels of tradition in the Joseph story is more difficult. The legend shows evidence of setting in the circles of ANE wisdom. The hero at the center of the legend depicts the virtues of *wisdom* and *perception,* virtues that enable any person to function as administrator in a royal court, a prison, a complex household (cf. 1 Kgs 3:3–15). That wisdom legend influences the larger novella. Yet, it does not necessitate the conclusion that the novella is also a wisdom story. The setting for the novella is a literary one, the productivity of the author who imposes his own mark onto the shape of the story. That the author knows the cultural constructions of Egypt reveals a cosmopolitan milieu. It might be reasonable to imagine that the author was at home in the enlightenment supported by the royal court, perhaps even the cultural activity of the Solomonic court. That the author had access to a wisdom legend suggests familiarity with wisdom resources. But with the same manner of caution that guards against identification of the author of the story as the Yahwist, so caution guards against ready identification of the setting for the story as a whole as wisdom. At most it can be said that it is a carefully constructed artwork from the hand of an author.

2. Dating. The question of the historical situation for the Joseph novella hides two questions: (1) when did the author of the novella compose the story? and (2) what is the period in which the Joseph story is set? If the Sitz im Leben defined above (the enlightenment of the royal court) has any merit, then the time for the construction of the novella might be set in the Solomonic court or some period shortly after that time when the patronage of the king could have supported such artistic composition. That time, roughly the 10th century B.C., would correspond to the period traditionally identified as the time for the origin of the Yahwist's production of the whole narrative tradition.

At least two important pieces of extrabiblical evidence have been appealed to in order to date the era in which the Joseph novella is set. A number of documents (most notably, the Amarna Letters) attest to the LB period. These were rootless people living on the fringe of society. It is possible that the OT term *Hebrew* is related to this widespread term. See HABIRU, HAPIRU. When Potiphar's wife accuses Joseph of an attack to her husband, she calls him a *Hebrew,* as if the term were derogatory. One might inquire whether the *habiru* might have been involved among the people noted by an Egyptian frontier official in a report about passage of people in and out of Egypt during periods of famine. Other documents attest to the invasions of the Hyksos, a Semitic people who usurped political control in Egypt during a period from 1700 to 1550 B.C. See HYKSOS. It is possible that these people were more favorable to people like Joseph and his family, and it is also possible that the reference to a pharaoh "who did not know Joseph" (Exod 1:8) recalls a period when the Hyksos leadership in Egypt was rejected in favor of a new dynasty of native Egyptian kings.

Yet, it is important to note that none of the documents from the 2d millennium mention Joseph and his brothers by name. The documents serve only to establish that the Joseph story builds its plot with careful attention to cultural detail from a particular period. The story employs historical verisimilitude effectively. But the effective description of a culture that did in fact exist does not establish the historicity of the events and personalities set out in the Joseph novella, nor does it deny it. The story has value *as a story,* not as an object that leads its audience behind the story to some other reality such as the factual, historical events involving Joseph, his brothers, and his father. The same point can be made about the definition of the genre for the story. To define the story as novella does not mean that the description of the events in the plot is simply fiction. Nothing in the designation of the genre denies the possibility that the plot structure reflects historical events. But the designation of the genre does not enable the critic to move behind the story to reconstruct the process of history.

F. Purpose of the Story

The Joseph novella has at least two significant intentions. (1) It intends to depict the ideal power figure. Joseph, the vizier of Egypt, uses his power not only to facilitate the reconciliation of his family and their security during devastating years of famine, but also to preserve people from all the neighboring world who come to him for food. He administers the grain reserves in Egypt without prejudice for one group of people or another. The twin virtues of wisdom and perception become the virtues that all persons in positions of power should have (1 Kgs 3:12; cf. also Ps 105:16–22). (2) The novella also bridges the OT traditions about the patriarchal fathers in Canaan (Genesis 11–38) and those about the Israelites in Egypt (Exodus). One should not conclude from this observation that the Joseph novella has no value in and of itself. Its value within its own construct comes to light particularly in the second stage of its account of movement from Canaan to Egypt. Reconciliation comes to a family torn apart by strife by moving beyond contention to consider prospects for the future. The death report about Joseph, with its bond concerning Joseph's bones as part of the move back to Canaan (cf. Exod 13:19; Josh 24:32), expands the Joseph tradition into the future stages of Israel's life on the land. At this point of transition, the Joseph story plays an essential role in the shape of Israel's traditions. The structure of the Pentateuch/Hexateuch shows a problem not only in the position of the Sinai traditions within the framework of the whole, but also in the relationship between the patriarchal theme and the Exodus theme. What kind of relationship did the patriarchal traditions, with their focus on strife/promise have with the Exodus tradition, with its focus on redemption from oppression? The Joseph novella answers the question. But the answer lies not simply in having Jacob in Canaan become Israel in Egypt. The promise theme from Gen 12:1–3 finds no explicit point of contact here; implicitly it appears in the act of God through Joseph to save a remnant of Jacob's people. But promise language does not appear.

In place of the promise language, the content of the entire Joseph story revolves around the issue of strife that breaks a family apart. And as a story about strife, the Joseph novella fits the context in the patriarchal theme generally; and the Joseph novella in particular is focused upon that strife. How can a family torn apart by strife be reconciled? Or, more to the point of the theology reflected in Gen 12:1–3, how can a family broken apart by strife serve as a vehicle for God's blessing? The answer to the question posed for the entire patriarchal theme is that given by Joseph's leadership: the family turns from the strife in the past to a commitment to each other for a common future. That intimacy is secured in the symbol of the Joseph tradition with the oath to bury Joseph's bones with the family in Canaan. The familial intimacy lost in the Garden and in the struggles among people during the periods of the Flood and the Tower of Babel could be restored among the descendants of Abraham, Isaac, and Jacob through their mutual commitment to a common future. Moreover, the power exercised by Joseph over the Egyptians but also over the family facilitates reconciliation. The Joseph story ends on a note of common hope, indeed, a note of union for the future.

Yet, the Joseph tradition does not end uniformly on a note of reconciliation. The death report for Jacob illustrates the continued break in the family and suggests that the final reconciliation in the people of God is projected beyond the patriarchal people to the next generation. The question posed (by the Yahwist?) in the Joseph narrative is thus: Will a reconciliation restore the intimacy of God's people in the next generation? That facet of manipulation, that ploy of deception, in contrast to the Joseph novella recalls the negative element in the patriarchal sagas and anticipates the negative element in the Moses saga. God acts for the sake of the people. But the people show tragically a negative, rebellious side. In what manner can reconciliation for these people ever occur? For further discussion, see commentaries on Genesis in AB, OTL, BKAT, IBC, and FOTL.

Bibliography

Coats, G. W. 1975. *From Canaan to Egypt: Structural and Theological Context for the Joseph Story.* CBQMS 4. Washington.

Humphreys, W. L. 1970. *The Motif of the Wise Courtier in the OT.* Diss., Union Theological Seminary.

Rad, G. von. 1971. The Joseph Narrative and Ancient Wisdom. Pp. 292–300 in *PHOE.*

Seybold, D. A. 1974. Paradox and Symmetry in the Joseph Narrative. Pp. 59–73 in *Literary Interpretations of Biblical Narratives,* ed. K. R. R. Gros-Louis, J. S. Ackerman and T. S. Warshaw. Nashville.

GEORGE W. COATS

JOSEPHUS (PERSON). A 1st-century Jewish politician, soldier, and historian, whose writings constitute important sources for our understanding of biblical history and of the political history of Roman Palestine in the 1st century C.E.

Josephus was born in 37 C.E. and was given the Hebrew name Joseph ben Mattathias. His mother was a descendant of the Hasmonean family that had ruled Jerusalem a century earlier, and by birthright he was a priest. In Jerusalem he received a superb education, and at the age of 27 (in 64 C.E.) he led a delegation to the court of the Roman emperor Nero. Two years later he was pressed to serve as the general of the Jewish forces in Galilee in the revolt against Rome. He was captured and afterwards became a Roman citizen and pensioner of the Flavian emperors Vespasian, Titus, and Domitian. He is most widely known by the Roman name he then acquired, Flavius Josephus (or simply "Josephus").

In Rome Josephus resided in an apartment within the emperor's house and devoted much of his time to writing. In part his works were addressed to his fellow Jews, justifying to them not only Roman conduct during the Jewish War, but also his own personal conduct in switching loyalties. However, his writings were also designed to justify Jewish culture and religion to an interested and sometimes sympathetic Roman audience. The earliest of his extant writings is the *Bellum Judaicarum* (or *Jewish War*), which was apparently drafted initially in Aramaic and then translated into Greek 5 to 10 years after the 70 C.E. destruction of Jerusalem. His second work, *Antiquitates Judaicae* (or *Jewish Antiquities*), was published more than a decade later; it was much longer, and recounts Jewish history from creation to the Jewish War, and contains some valuable historical information. His last two works, probably published shortly before his death, include the *Vita* (or *Life*), an autobiography intended primarily to defend his conduct during the Jewish War 30 years earlier, and *Contra Apionem* (or *Against Apion*), an apologetic defense of Judaism against a wave of anti-Semitism emanating from Alexandria. Josephus probably died ca. 100 C.E., several years after Trajan had become emperor in Rome. His writings, while generally ignored by fellow Jews, were preserved by Christians not only because they chronicled generally and so well the "time between the testaments," but also because they contained specific references to John the Baptist, Jesus of Nazareth, and Jesus' brother James.

A. *Life*
B. Other Works
  1. *The Jewish War*
  2. *The Jewish Antiquities*
  3. *Against Apion*
C. Josephus on Jewish Law
D. Language and Style of Josephus
E. Josephus' Influence
F. The Text of Josephus
G. Paraphrases and Translations
H. Scholarship on Josephus

A. *Life*

Josephus is the author of the first autobiography that has come down to us from antiquity, but this work *(Life)* is for the most part a defense of his mission as a general in Galilee and contains few other details about his life. Some scholars believe that the bulk of its content was actually written shortly after the war itself—prior to the publication of his *Jewish War* (ca. 75–79 C.E.)—but that it was revised, supplemented, and updated prior to its publication ca. 95 C.E. The only pagan writers who do refer to events in the life of Josephus—the 2d-century Suetonius (*Vespasian* 5.6) and Appian (fragment 17) and the 3d-century Dio Cassius (66.1)—mention only his prediction that the Flavian Vespasian would become emperor (though there are slight discrepancies in these accounts). Josephus is never mentioned in the Talmudic corpus, unless he is the anonymous philosopher in Rome whose aid was solicited by four rabbis intent on persuading Domitian to annul his earlier decision to exterminate the Jews of the Roman Empire (*Der. Er. Rab.* 5).

Josephus (*Life* 1 §5) indicates that he was born in the first year of the reign of Gaius Caligula (37 C.E.). He also says that he was descended on both his parents' sides from the first of the 24 courses of priests and, on his mother's side, from the royal Hasmoneans (*Life* 1 §2). Consequently, it has even been suggested that Josephus may have had ambitions to be not only high priest, but also king of Judea, though the fact that his opponents apparently never mentioned such ambitions militates against such a view.

The first event which Josephus mentions about his life occurred when, at the age of 14 (*Life* 2 §9), the chief priests and leaders of Jerusalem constantly came to him for information about the laws. The motif of the precocious youngster who amazes his teachers is, however, commonplace, being found also in the biographies of Moses, Homer, Aeschines, Alexander the Great, Apollonius of Rhodes, Augustus, Ovid, Nicolaus of Damascus, Apollonius of Tyana, and Jesus. Likewise, the statement (*Life* 2 §10–12) that Josephus spent time (from the ages of 16 to 19) with the various sects of Jews (Pharisees, Sadducees, and Essenes) in order to select the best is similar to the motif found in the lives of Nicolaus of Damascus, Apollonius of Tyana, Justin, and Galen. Josephus also says that he spent three years with an otherwise unknown hermit named Bannus, but there is a problem in the text, since Josephus says that he was 19 when he completed both his experimentation with the sects and his sojourn with Bannus. Josephus then decided to join the Pharisees, though one would have expected him to favor the Sadducees, who were more closely affiliated with the priests and were more conservative than the Pharisees. But apparently Josephus realized that his ambitions would be better served by joining the Pharisees, since they were more popular with the masses (*Ant* 18.1.3 §15).

Josephus is silent about his activities between the ages of 19 and 26, but we may conjecture that it was particularly during these years that he made great progress in the study of Greek language and literature. In the year 64, when he was only 27, he was entrusted with the very delicate mission of securing the release of some priests who were imprisoned in Rome (*Life* 3 §13). Josephus' success was due to his resourcefulness in obtaining the help both of Aliturus, a Jewish actor in Nero's court, and of Nero's mistress, Poppaea Sabina, who was a "sympathizer" with Judaism (perhaps a so-called "semi-proselyte"). The fact that the emperor gave some gifts to Josephus (whereas we would have expected Josephus to send gifts to the emperor) could be explained most readily if we assume that Nero hoped thereby to persuade Josephus to use his influence to defuse the impending Jewish revolt against Rome. We do not know whether Josephus attempted such a mission, but in any case the revolt did break out two years later.

When the revolt did occur, the revolutionary council appointed Josephus to serve as general in Galilee, clearly the most important theater of the war since the Romans, who were based in Syria, were almost certain to strike there first in their march toward Jerusalem. It is remarkable that Josephus should have been chosen when he was a mere 29 years old and (as far as we know) without any military experience. Indeed, Josephus himself apparently has two contradictory accounts of this appointment. In the first (*JW* 2.20.3 §562–68), written apparently sometime between 75 and 79 (i.e., within a decade of the revolt), he indicates that he was named to conduct the war by the revolutionaries after they had won over to their side the moderates, whether by persuasion or by force. In the *Life* (4 §17), published approximately two decades later, Josephus declares that the coalition of Jewish leaders, who favored pacification, appointed him with the intention that he would try to induce the rebels to fight only in self-defense, whereas actually they hoped that the Roman general, Cestius Gallus, would prevail. Especially incriminating is Josephus' statement that he declined to give grain to the revolutionary leader John of Gischala since he intended to keep it either for his own use or *for the Romans* (*Life* 13 §72). If Josephus had really been sincere in opposing the Romans, we may suggest that he should have followed the model of the Maccabees in their war against the Syrian Greeks two centuries earlier and fought like a guerrilla. His decision instead to remain in Jotapata played to the Romans' strength, which was siege warfare. Moreover, if and when things seemed hopeless, he should have retreated toward Jerusalem and joined his forces with those defending that city, which was much better fortified than Jotapata.

The later account (in the *Life*) would appear to correct the earlier one (in *JW*); and Josephus could afford to tell the truth, since now he was famous and honored. In defecting to the Romans, he was merely following the wishes of the council which had appointed him. One possible way of reconciling the two versions is to say that initially Josephus sincerely attempted to fight against Rome, but that when he saw that it was hopeless, he went over to the Roman side. The fact that upon his surrender to the Romans at Jotapata he received a tract of land outside Jerusalem, some sacred books (presumably Torah scrolls), the liberation of some friends, Roman citizenship, lodging in the former palace of the Roman general Vespasian, and a pension would indicate that he had done something significant to ingratiate himself with the Romans. His prediction that Vespasian would become emperor has often been compared with that of Rabbi Johanan ben Zakkai's prediction (*Giṭ.* 56a–b); however, the two should be differentiated, since Johanan asked and received nothing for himself. That two people independently might have made the same prediction does not seem implausible in view of the fact that Vespasian was clearly the most experienced Roman general of the time; indeed, Josephus (*JW* 6.5.4 §312), Suetonius (*Vespasian* 4), and Tacitus (*Hist.* 5.13) all indicate that there was a prediction in the air that someone from Judea would become ruler of the world at that time.

Moreover, it is hard to believe that it was by mere chance that Josephus and another of his men were the last two who survived the suicide pact at Jotapata; it seems more likely, as the Slavonic version of *JW* (3.8.7 §391) would have it, that Josephus had carefully manipulated the lots. His action is hardly excused by the fact that Josephus was not alone in siding with the Romans (the Jewish king Agrippa II also did so) or that he felt that he had to survive in order to write the history of the period and in order to defend the Jews against anti-Semitic attacks. On the other hand, Josephus may have been sincerely convinced first, that the war was a terrible mistake, since an independent state was hardly a sine qua non for Judaism; second, that the Jews had been given considerable privileges by the Romans; and, third, that they were well on their way to converting the Empire to Judaism. If the revolutionary council had indeed been sincere in prosecuting the war, it should have made a greater effort to enlist the support of Jewish communities outside Palestine, especially in Asia Minor, Syria, Egypt, and Babylonia (each of which had an estimated million Jews). It should also have attempted to entice the Parthians, the traditional and often successful opponent of the Romans, to coordinate the attack and to induce various other discontented rebel tribes to coordinate their revolts. However, the fact that we do not have the accounts of Josephus and his opponents, such as Justus of Tiberias, means that we have a one-sided view; yet the fact that Josephus himself did not destroy his own self-incriminating record leads us to believe in its essential truthfulness. And even if we did have Justus' work, there is no guarantee that it would be more reliable than that of Josephus; after all, Justus could hardly have served for so many years as court secretary to Agrippa II, a puppet of the Romans, unless he, too, had been a lackey of the Romans. Indeed, Josephus and Justus seem to have been rivals precisely because they were so similar in their outlook.

B. Other Works

1. *The Jewish War.* In the introduction to his *Jewish War* (= *JW*), Josephus, following the example of his model, Thucydides, presents a raison d'être for his work by vehemently criticizing his predecessors (none of whom is extant) for their inaccuracies, their bloated rhetoric, and their prejudice. He declares that he composed his work originally in his ancestral language—presumably Aramaic (though some have suggested that it was in Hebrew)—to be sent to the barbarians of the upper country (Babylonia and Parthia) apparently as a warning for them not to repeat the mistake of clashing with the Roman Empire (*JW* 1. Proem 1 §3). Not a single fragment of this Aramaic/Hebrew version has come down to us, presumably because of the bitterness felt by the Jews toward Josephus, whom they regarded as a despicable traitor. But the very title of his work, "Concerning the Jewish War," betrays that it was written from the point of view of the Romans (cf. other Roman works such as "Concerning the Punic War" and "Concerning the Gallic War"). Josephus himself, with the help of assistants, then proceeded to translate it into Greek. This help must have been considerable since very few Aramaisms or Hebraisms remain in our Greek text (which is written in an excellent Greek style, far superior to that of *Ant,* which was completed more than a decade later).

The date of the composition of *JW* has usually been given as the end of Vespasian's reign or the beginning of Titus' reign (ca. 79), since it has a negative attitude toward Alienus Caecina, who, after originally deserting to Vespasian, was put to death by Titus for conspiracy (*JW* 4.11.2–3 §634–44). There seems reason to believe, however, that the 7th and last book of *JW* was composed toward the end of the century during the reign of Domitian, inasmuch as it shows adulation for Domitian (7.4.2 §85–88; there is almost total disregard for him in the first six books) and inasmuch as the rate of elision of final vowels is also markedly different. The book is decidedly incoherent, and parts of it may even have been written in the reign of Nerva or in the early years of Trajan's reign at the end of the century. Moreover, Book 6, culminating in the poignant account of the destruction of the temple, provides an admirable close to the work.

As sources, Josephus, of course, drew upon his own experience as a general in Galilee and later as an adviser to Titus. He also utilized the memoirs of Vespasian and Titus (*Life* 65 §342, 358); it is perhaps to these that Josephus owes his generally accurate topographical information. In addition, Josephus indicates that King Agrippa II orally had provided additional information. Though Josephus agrees with the Talmudic rabbis in condemning the revolutionaries, in stressing the internal division among the Jews, and in describing the terrible famine that afflicted the inhabitants of Jerusalem, he mentions by name only one of them, Rabban Gamaliel; and there is no direct indication of his indebtedness to Talmudic tradition concerning the war. In particular, he disagrees with the rabbis when he omits their mention of the courage of the Jewish captives and when he declares that Titus urged that the temple be spared (*JW* 6.4.3 §241); whereas the rabbis (in agreement with the 4th-century Christian historian Sulpicius Severus) declare that Titus favored its destruction. Josephus' bias may be indicated by the fact that he ignores altogether the fact that during the war many Romans sided with the Jewish revolutionaries (a fact even the Roman historian Dio Cassius noted).

As to the causes of the war, Josephus completely neglects the messianic element (as he does the messianic prophecies in Daniel), broad hints of which are to be found in Tacitus (*Hist.* 5.13) and Suetonius (*Vespasian* 4). Moreover, inasmuch as the other two great revolts against Rome (115–117 and 132–135) were messianic and inasmuch as even Josephus himself describes the appearance of Menahem, the rebel leader, as resembling that of a king (*JW* 2.17.8 §434)—hence like a political messiah—we may guess that there was indeed a messianic aspect to the revolt.

Josephus neglected two other causes of the war. One was the increasing power within Rome of anti-Semitic freedmen of Greek origin who resented the idea of a Jewish "nation within a nation." The second was the pagan resentment of the tremendous Jewish success in winning converts to Judaism, which seemed well on its way to becoming the major religion of the Empire. We may also guess that Josephus, in his eagerness to be apologetic, chose to de-emphasize as a factor the dissension between Jews and non-Jews in Palestine. It has also been suggested that Josephus, who was himself descended from the Hasmoneans, suppressed the connection between them and the revolutionaries he despised. Moreover, like most ancient historians, Josephus pays little attention to the social and economic causes of the war, such as overpopulation, uneven distribution of land, and heavy taxation. In addition, Josephus assigns the blame for the war to one sect, the Fourth Philosophy; whereas the Jerusalem Talmud (*Šabb.* 10.5.29b) ascribes the fall of the temple to the existence of no fewer than 24 sects. Finally, to judge from Josephus, the revolt was foolhardy; whereas actually it would have had a good chance of success if it had enlisted more support among Jews throughout the Empire and in Babylonia and had coordinated its efforts with those of the Parthians and various barbarian tribes.

The turning point of the war was the siege of Jerusalem and the destruction of the temple in 70 C.E. According to Josephus (*JW* 6.4.3 §241) Titus, in a meeting with his staff, urged that the temple be spared. However, although the 4th-century Christian historian Sulpicius Severus was clearly aware of Josephus' account, he, nevertheless, states that Titus decreed the destruction of the temple (*Chronica* 2.30.6–7). Inasmuch as Sulpicius Severus used Tacitus in the chapter just before this, it has been suggested that his source was a lost part of Tacitus' *Hist.* and that this, in turn, was based on a lost work of Antonius Julianus, who was actually present at Titus' council (*JW* 6.4.3 §238). Both the Talmud (*Giṭ.* 56b) and Dio Cassius (6.65) support Josephus' account; and the proem to the poem of Valerius Flaccus likewise seems to accord with it, since it speaks of Titus' conquest of Jerusalem "as he hurls the brands and spreads havoc in every tower," the most prominent building in Jerusalem being the temple. Moreover, Josephus seems to contradict himself when he states that it was Titus who ordered the city and the temple to be burned (*JW* 7.1.1 §1) and when he likewise declares that Titus captured and set fire to the temple (*Ant* 20.10.5 §250). One cannot therefore avoid the conclusion that in his main account of the destruction of the temple in *JW* Josephus attempted to whitewash Titus by stressing his clemency.

Josephus' spectacular account of the capture of Masada has been the subject of much scholarly debate. The recent excavations of the site by Yadin have, on the whole, confirmed Josephus' reliability; indeed, the very name of the Sicarii leader who defended the fortress, Ben-Jair, has been found inscribed on a potsherd. There are some discrepancies, however: (1) Josephus says that Herod's palace was on the W slope, whereas actually it is on the N slope; (2) he says that the columns of the palace were monolithic, whereas in actuality they were made up of several sections; (3) the Roman siege works are much more complicated than those mentioned by Josephus; (4) the fact that some of the casement apartments were found burned while others were not contradicts Josephus' statement that all of them were burned; (5) Josephus says that the food of the defenders had been burned, whereas Yadin found that some of it had been preserved; (6) Josephus says that there were 960 who committed suicide, whereas Yadin found only 25 skeletons; (7) Yadin found 11 ostraca with names inscribed on them, whereas Josephus (*JW* 7.9.1 §395) says that 10 were chosen by lot for the gruesome task of killing the rest; and (8) Josephus makes no mention at all of the connection between the Sicarii of Masada and the Dead Sea sect, whereas the discovery of a scroll of liturgies based on the peculiar calendar of the Qumran sect strongly indicates a connection.

Of course, Josephus was not present at Masada; and he admits that his account is based on the evidence of a single woman who had managed to hide and thus to survive (*JW* 7.9.2 §404). We may also note that Josephus, who hardly admired the intellectual power of women, describes her as "superior in sagacity and training to most of her sex." Moreover, Josephus was so fiercely hated that he had to be careful of what he wrote. In addition, there must have been many Romans (and Jewish captives who had assisted them) who had participated in the siege who could challenge any misrepresentation made by Josephus. If in this account Josephus intended to raise the stature of the Roman commander, Flavius Silva, a member of the same imperial family which had adopted him, he could have done so much more effectively by depicting the Jewish defenders as fighting to the last man instead of committing suicide. Finally, Josephus declares that the Romans, upon entering Masada, acknowledged the greatness of the daring of the Sicarii, the nobility of their resolve, and their contempt for death (*JW* 7.9.2 §405–6). Josephus would have been loath to make such a statement in view of his negative evaluation of the Sicarii as among the most despicable of the five revolutionary groups (*JW* 7.8.1 §262). Therefore his account of the fall of Masada is all the more likely to be true.

Of course, the two speeches which Josephus puts into the mouth of Eleazar ben-Jair are artificial and belong to the tradition of most classical historians. In ben-Jair's second speech the presence of passages closely corresponding to Posidonius, Euripides, and particularly Plato (e.g., on the relationship of body and soul and on the nature of immortality, especially as couched in Platonic and Stoic phraseology) support the view that these speeches were penned in Josephus' scriptorium, presumably with the help of his Greek assistants. It would seem unusual for Eleazar ben-Jair, a member of a sect known for its extreme piety, to have such an intimate knowledge of Plato, especially since, as Josephus says, pious Jews were utterly antipathetic toward the study of other languages and literatures (*Ant* 20.12.1 §264). The propriety of suicide was much debated at this very time in Greek and Roman philosophical circles; and Josephus' discussion may well be directed toward this audience.

As to whether the suicide itself actually took place, it has been objected that the Sicarii, as pious Jews, must have realized that suicide would be a terrible sin according to Jewish law—technically, no less than murder—and that it could only be justified when one was certain that he would be forced to worship idols, commit murder, or engage in an illicit sexual act (all this was later codified in Jewish law, but none of it applied at Masada). As guerrillas, moreover, the Jews should have fought to the last man, especially since they were well armed and had plenty of water and food. However, we should note that the number of defenders could hardly have exceeded 200 to 300 (since the 967 people at Masada included women and children) and that the Sicarii were pious in their own peculiar way and followed their own Halakah, just as they did when they engaged in a raid on Passover (*JW* 4.7.2 §402), when such attacks would normally be prohibited. There was, moreover, a precedent for the mass suicide, namely, that at Gamala (*JW* 4.1.10 §79–81), where more than 5000 took their own lives. Finally, we must remember that the Sicarii were fanatics who were no longer acting rationally. It has been suggested that perhaps the Romans murdered the defenders and that Josephus attempted to cover up for them as he did for Titus in connection with the burning of the temple. But the fact that the Sicarii were admired by the Romans—a statement one would never expect from Josephus—would seem to militate against such a theory.

2. *The Jewish Antiquities.* Written about a decade after *JW,* Josephus' *Jewish Antiquities* (= *Ant*) sets out to survey the history of the Hebrew people from their biblical beginnings up to the time of the Jewish War of 66–70 C.E. Josephus' treatment of biblical episodes is noteworthy insofar as it raises questions about the type of biblical text he used and the type of interpretation he practiced. His treatment of postbiblical events is noteworthy because it sheds some light on an otherwise poorly attested period. His treatment of 1st-century events is noteworthy because in some places it overlaps with the early chapters of *JW* and because it provides independent testimony to important NT persons and events.

a. The Biblical Period. Josephus' opening statement, that he will set forth the "precise details" of what is written in the Scriptures, "neither adding nor omitting anything," (*Ant* 1. Proem 2 §5) has occasioned much amazement, since he has modified the Bible, sometimes drastically, on almost every page. The question of the meaning of Josephus' statement is of great importance, since it involves the issue of how much liberty one was permitted in interpreting the Bible during this period. It is unsatisfactory to say that Josephus was counting on the ignorance of his readers since the Jews of the Diaspora certainly knew the LXX, which they believed to be divinely inspired and which differs drastically in many places from Josephus' paraphrase. Moreover, Pseudo-Longinus' (9.9) highly laudatory—and casual—paraphrase of Gen 1:3, 9, 10 in a work of literary criticism dating presumably from the 1st century C.E., shows that the LXX was well-known; the vast number of converts to Judaism during the two centuries before Josephus would seem to indicate that it was widely used by Jewish missionaries.

Others have suggested that the phrase "neither adding nor omitting anything" is a traditional and meaningless way of affirming one's accuracy, as may be seen by its use by Dionysius of Halicarnassus in the 1st century and by Lucian in the 2d century. That Josephus' phrase is not necessarily to be taken literally would seem to be indicated by the fact that the gospel of Matthew uses similar language (in 5:17–18), even though portions of the law *were* in fact abolished by Jesus' disciples in his own lifetime.

Actually the phrase is taken from Deut 4:2: "You shall not add to the word which I command you, neither shall you diminish from it, that you may keep the commandments of the Lord your God which I command you." Josephus understood the phrase in the sense which is apparent from this verse and which accords with rabbinic exegesis; namely, that one is not permitted to add to or subtract from the *commandments* and that one is permitted latitude in interpreting only the narrative portions of the Pentateuch. An alternative suggestion is that Josephus included in "Scriptures" not only the written Bible but also Jewish tradition generally. This would imply that some of the midrashic interpretation of the Bible had been committed to writing by Josephus' time, since we find midrashic materials in such Hellenistic Jewish writers as Artapanus, Eupolemus, Ezekiel the tragedian, and Philo. While such a statement four decades ago would have been considered most unlikely (inasmuch as the earliest rabbinic midrashic commentaries on the Bible date from a century after Josephus', we now have midrashim among the Dead Sea Scrolls dating from the century *before* Josephus which he parallels at several points. To this may be added the midrashim in the work ascribed to Philo entitled *Biblical Antiquities,* which is apparently contemporaneous with *Ant.*

Moreover, there would seem to be a precedent for modifying the sacred LXX text which Josephus (*Ant* 1. Proem 3 §10) cites as justifying his presentation of biblical history to gentiles. Even the rabbis (*Meg.* 9a), in obvious praise, refer to the miraculous way in which the translation was accomplished, despite the fact that deliberate changes were made in the process of translation. The fact that three major recensions had emerged by the time of Jerome, despite the curse placed on those who ventured to add, or transpose, or subtract (*Let. Aris.* 306), shows that the curse was not taken too seriously.

When we examine how Josephus handles the actual biblical narrative, we find that he had two audiences in mind. The fact that he cited the LXX as a precedent for his work shows that he was directing his work to gentiles with apologetic intent, since that translation originally had been commissioned by King Ptolemy Philadelphus. Indeed, he specifically declares (*Ant* 1. Proem 2 §5) that his work was undertaken in the belief that the whole Greek world would find it worthy of attention. Again, at the very end of the work, he boasts that no one else would have been equal to the task of issuing so accurate a treatise for the Greeks (*Ant* 20.12.1 §262). On the other hand, we should also expect that Josephus would seek a Jewish audience for his work, since it would seem that the majority of the Jews in the Mediterranean world were Greek speaking; hence they would be a natural audience for his work. Indeed, that Josephus has a Jewish audiences in mind for his treatise is indicated by the fact that he highlights certain episodes—notably the incident of Israel's sin with the Midianite women (Num 25:1–9), which he expands greatly (*Ant* 4.6.7–12 §§131–35), and Samson's relations with foreign women (Judg 14:1–16; *Ant* 5.8.5–12 §§285–317)—in order to combat the increasing assimilation of Jews with gentiles.

In this portion of his narrative, there are many details shared with his presumed contemporary Pseudo-Philo, apparently indicating a common source used by both (whether written or, more probably, oral). Josephus' tendency to give names and other such details which are missing in the Bible (e.g., the name of the man who inspired the building of the Tower of Babel [Nimrod], and the name of Pharaoh's daughter who adopted Moses [Thermuthis]) may be due to the influence of rabbinic midrashim. The same details are sometimes found in certain pseudepigraphic works such as *Jub.* and *L.A.B.* and in such sectarian works as the Samaritan Asatir and 1QapGen. In addition, Josephus seems to have employed a Hellenistic Jewish tradition. In particular the Hellenistic Jewish writers might have provided Josephus both with an excellent precedent for rewriting the Bible and with a stylistic model (though he does not cite their works as a forerunner for his own). This would have been especially true of Philo, who writes such excellent Greek. However, Josephus mentions Philo only once (*Ant* 18.8.1 §259–60) and refers to other Jewish writers on only one other occasion (and even then he refers to them as if they were pagans; *AgAp* 1.23 §218). Nevertheless, it is noteworthy that Philo's question as to why the Torah begins with creation rather than with the laws (*Op* 1.1–3) is paralleled in *Ant* 1. Proem 4 §21 and also that Philo's description of Abraham's attack on the Assyrians (*Abr* 40.230–35) is paralleled in *Ant* 1.10.1 §177. Furthermore, Philo's interpretation of the names Abel and Ishmael (*Migr* 13.74; *Mut* 37.202) is paralleled in *Ant* 1.2.1 §52 and 1.10.4 §190, while Philo's allegorical interpretation of the tabernacle and priestly garments (*Vita Mos* II.18, 21, 24) is closely paralleled in *Ant* 3.7.7 §179–87. Hölscher (PW 9) held that Josephus' single source was a Hellenistic Jewish midrash, a claim that seems extreme, especially since we have no trace of such a work.

We must not, however, exclude the possibility that Josephus introduced details of his own, particularly for apologetic reasons. In particular the fact that his portraits of such biblical personalities as Abraham, Moses, Samson, Saul, David, and Solomon are consistent in emphasizing their cardinal virtues (as well as the dramatic and erotic elements) and in de-emphasizing theological and magical elements would seem to indicate a personal imprint rather than a stage in the development of the midrashic tradition. In view of the fact that during the many years he lived in Rome Josephus apparently had no occupation other than writing and that he apparently composed an average of only about ten lines a day, we should expect a careful and consistent composition. We may also discern the influence of contemporary events upon Josephus' reconstruction of the biblical past. For example, his elaboration of the sacrifice of Isaac seems to have been influenced by the martyrdom during the Maccabean revolt. In his elaboration of the story of his namesake, Joseph, who likewise was accused falsely, Josephus seems to have portrayed himself. He likewise appears to have identified personally with the prophet Jeremiah, who also suffered at the hands of his fellow Jews, as well as with Daniel, Esther, and Mordecai, who suffered for their convictions. Moreover, he seems to have identified himself with King Saul, whom he viewed as a martyred general like himself.

An important question centers around the issue of the biblical text that Josephus had at his disposal. It is important because the answer would help shed significant light on the state of the text in 1st-century Palestine, almost a millennium before our first extant complete Hebrew manuscript. Josephus seems to have had in his possession texts in Hebrew, Aramaic, and Greek; and he varied in his use of them from biblical book to book. In view of the fact that in Josephus' time there were a number of divergent Hebrew and Greek texts of the Bible, we cannot be sure which version he used at any given time, especially since he usually paraphrased and elaborated rather than translated. Nor must we discount the possibility that Josephus followed a tradition independent of both the MT and the LXX, as may be seen from the fact that he agrees with Pseudo-Philo in some places that diverge from both the MT and the LXX.

The fact that Josephus was himself writing in Greek would make it seem likely that his chief textual source was the LXX, especially since he cited it as a precedent for presenting the history of the Jews to a non-Jewish audience (*Ant* 1. Proem 3 §10–12) and since he devoted so much space paraphrasing the account of the translation given in *Let. Aris.* (*Ant* 12.2.1–15 §11–118), hardly what one would expect in a work which is essentially a political and military rather than a cultural and religious history of the Jews. And yet, the very fact that he paraphrased the Bible in Greek would seem to indicate that he hoped to improve on that rendering, since there would hardly be much point otherwise in a new version. Hence it is not surprising that where the style of the LXX is more polished, as in the Additions to Esther or in 1 Esdras, he adheres more closely to its text. And yet, to have ignored the LXX, in view of the tremendous regard in which that version was held, would have been looked upon as an attempt to hide something. Nevertheless, even when Josephus agrees with the LXX, this is not necessarily an indication that he had the LXX text before him, since he may have incorporated an exegetical tradition which had been known earlier to the translators of the LXX. Finally, the biblical texts found at Qumran indicate that the differences between the Hebrew and the Greek texts were not so great as had been previously thought.

As to Josephus' possible use of an Aramaic Targum, we must not forget that Aramaic was Josephus' mother tongue, as it was for Jews generally in Palestine at that time. While it is true that the earliest Targum, that of Onkelos, dates from the 2d century C.E., no doubt the practice of translating the Bible into Aramaic was much older; indeed, the fact that its origin is attributed to Ezra in the 5th century B.C.E. (*Meg.* 3a) meant that it had the sanctity and the authority associated with the great Ezra, the second Moses (*t. Sanh.* 4.7). The very fact that the Targums, at least as we know them, permit themselves considerable latitude in paraphrasing the text must have attracted Josephus to them. If Josephus is indeed much freer in vocabulary, style, order, and content in his rendering of biblical material in the first five books of *Antiquities* than in Books 6–11 (as seems to be the case), it may well be that the reason for this is the availability of Targums for these earlier books. Josephus probably utilized a Hebrew text and/or an Aramaic Targum as a basis for his elaboration of the books of the Pentateuch, especially since Josephus probably heard a portion of the Pentateuch read weekly in the synagogue, along with a Targum. And yet, where he seems to be following the Hebrew, this may be due merely to an attempt to avoid using the same word as the LXX (cf. his paraphrase of *Let. Aris.*, where he is almost pathological in avoiding the same language).

In the book of Joshua, Josephus seems closer to the MT; whereas for Judges and Ruth he is relatively free, perhaps because he was using a Targum. The most interesting case is that of the book of Samuel, where, to judge from the Dead Sea fragments, Josephus favored a Greek text in a Proto-Lucianic version, though not to the total exclusion of the Hebrew, since, at the very least, he heard portions from Samuel during readings of the *haftaroth* in the synagogue on seven Sabbaths and holy days. To say, as does Kahle (1959: 229–37), that Josephus agrees with Proto-Lucian because Christian copyists modified his text (as they presumably did Philo's quotations from the Bible) is to fail to explain why these copyists restricted their revisions to only certain books of the Bible. For Ezra, Josephus particularly (but not exclusively) employed the apocryphal book of Esdras because of its superior Greek style, its elimination of some chronological difficulties, and its romantic interest in the debate as to whether wine, the king, or a woman is most powerful. For Esther, Josephus used a Greek text, notably because he found it to be stylistically more polished than the rest of the Greek Bible.

As to the changes which Josephus made in his version of the biblical narrative, Josephus declares in his preface that he proposes to set forth the details in their proper order *(taxin),* using a military term implying a battle array (as if he were about to marshal troops in literary battle, presumably against anti-Semites). Whereas Moses, he says, had left his writings in disarray, just as he had received them from God (*Ant* 4.8.4 §197), we see that Josephus rearranged them following the "thematic" school of a number of Hellenistic historians, thus juxtaposing those items which belonged together on the basis of subject, regardless of chronology and source, and removing theological difficulties and contradictions inherent in the narrative. For example, he substitutes the verb *ektisen,* "founded" for the LXX's *epoiēsen,* "made" to avoid the impression that God created the world out of preexistent matter (*Ant* 1.1.1 §27). Similarly, he omits the plural verb in "let us make man in our image," since it would seem from this that God was a plurality of powers or had assistants (*Ant* 1.1.1 §32). Again, when he deals with chronological difficulties in the biblical ascription of unusual longevity to the patriarchs, he cites precedents in Greek and non-Greek literature and furthermore rationalizes by noting other factors, such as their diet, which contributed to their long life spans (*Ant* 1.3.9 §107–8); yet even here he closes as do Herodotus and other ancient historians, with the formula, "On these matters let everyone decide according to his fancy." Again, he often seeks to avoid anthropomorphisms, such as the one implied in the Hebrew word *mĕraḥepet,* "moving" (Gen 1:2; cf. *Ant* 1.1.1 §27). Sometimes his goal is to provide better motivation or to eliminate obscurity, as in his explanation of the "strange" fire (Lev 10:1) which Nadab and Abihu brought (*Ant* 3.1.7 §209). Sometimes he is concerned with how his work will sound to the ear; hence, for example, he says that he is inclined to omit the names of the 70 descendants of Jacob who went down to Egypt because they would sound strange to a Greek ear but that he includes them, nonetheless, only in order to refute the anti-Semitic charge that the Israelites were of Egyptian rather than of Mesopotamian origin (*Ant* 2.7.4 §176–77). Another goal is to enhance the sense of drama, so that, for example, he adds that Samuel was tossing with sleeplessness the night God instructed him to select a king (*Ant* 6.3.3 §37). Moreover, Josephus increases the irony, for example, by using the word for happiness on five occasions in the brief pericope describing Abraham's intended sacrifice of Isaac (*Ant* 1.13.1–4 §222–36). Josephus uses allegory only occasionally, perhaps in reaction to Philo; one case, however, where he does appeal to allegory is in explaining various articles in the temple (*Ant* 3.7.7 §179–87). Finally, Josephus, in reformulating the biblical narrative, focuses to an even greater degree on certain key personalities, such as Abraham, Joseph, Moses, Samson, Saul, David, and Solomon.

As to Hellenizations in *Ant,* Thackeray (1929: 100–124) devised a kind of Documentary Hypothesis for the later books, postulating that for Books 15 and 16 Josephus had an assistant who had a particular love of Greek poetry, especially Sophocles, and for Books 17 through 19 another assistant who had a penchant for Thucydides. The truth is, however, that there are many Sophoclean and Thucydidean elements in the earlier books as well. Moreover, while Josephus (*AgAp* 1.9 §50) admits that he had helpers for *JW* (presumably his first published work), he says nothing about such for *Ant.* Indeed, many of the Sophoclean and Thucydidean phrases may have come to him through other writers he knew, notably Dionysius of Halicarnassus. Finally, whereas he may have needed assistants to help him with the Greek of *JW,* which he wrote shortly after his arrival in Rome, he must have improved his knowledge of Greek during the intervening years preceding his completion of *Ant.*

In his rewriting of the Bible, Josephus is clearly indebted to the Greek tragedians. Thus the paradoxical juxtaposition of *apora* and *porima* (*Ant* 1.14 Proem 3 §14) is found in only one other ancient author (Aesch. *PV* 904). Josephus' indebtedness to Sophocles is seen in his extrabiblical statement, so reminiscent of *Oedipus the King,* that all were mentally blinded as by a riddle in finding a solution to the problem confronting King Solomon. We may add that especially in the account of the binding of Isaac (*Ant* 1.13.1–4 §222–36) there are many reminiscences of Euripides (esp. Eur. *IA*), who was the most popular dramatist of the Hellenistic period.

Josephus' developed picture of the original bliss of mankind (*Ant* 1.1.4 §46) is clearly indebted to Homer and Hesiod, as is the phrase that Isaac was born on the threshold of Abraham's old age (*epi gērōs oudōi; Ant* 1.13.1 §222). The concept of a periodic destruction of the earth alternately by fire and water has its parallel in Plato (*Ti.* 22C), though it is found in rabbinic sources as well. Josephus' indebtedness to Herodotus (2.75) is manifest in his description of the ibis that helped put to flight the winged serpents encountered on the march through the desert to Ethiopia (*Ant* 2.10.2 §247). Occasionally direct comparisons with pagan sources are possible. Thus Josephus would have his readers compare Noah's Flood with that of Deucalion, implied by the fact that he used the same word for God's giving of advice to Noah (*hypothemenou; Ant* 1.3.2 §76) as is employed for Prometheus' giving of advice to Deucalion (Apollodorus 1.7.2); this is confirmed by the fact that instead of LXX *kibōtos,* Josephus uses the word *larnax* for Noah's ark, the same word Apollodorus used for Deucalion's ark.

The most striking form of Hellenization occurs in Josephus' description of biblical heroes (Abraham, Joseph, Moses, Samson, Saul, David, Solomon, Esther) in terms of the four cardinal virtues, the external qualities such as good birth and handsome stature, and the spiritual attribute of piety. Josephus' motives may well have been apologetic since the Jews had been accused of being misanthropic and of having failed to produce marvelous men (*AgAp* 2.12 §135). Thus, for example, Josephus omits the scene where Hagar weeps after having been cast out by Sarah (Gen 21:16; cf. *Ant* 1.12.3 §218), since such a scene might support the charge that Abraham lacked piety. In response to the blood libel with which the Jews had been charged (*AgAp* 2.8 §91–96), Josephus inserts a speech wherein God declares that he does not crave human blood, in direct contrast to Artemis, who rejoices in human sacrifice (Eur. *IA* 1524–25).

Moreover, in his biblical modifications, Josephus appeals to political, military, and geographic interests. Thus, in his version of the rebellion of Korah (*Ant* 4.2.1 §12), he stresses the theme of civil strife *(stasis),* so familiar to readers of Thucydides (3.82–84). Likewise, Josephus' graphic description of the sequence of luxury, voluptuousness, love of gain, gross recklessness, disdain for order and for the laws, and grave sedition corrupting the aristocracy (*Ant* 5.2.7 §132–35) is one familiar to readers of Polybius and Livy.

Josephus likewise appeals to the philosophical interests of his readers by comparing the religious groups of the Jews to the Greek philosophical schools (*Life* 2 §12; *Ant* 15.10.4 §371). In particular, since Stoicism was the favorite philosophy of Hellenistic intellectuals, he frequently employs Stoic terminology; thus the key Stoic word *pronoia,* "providence," appears no fewer than 74 times in the first half of *Ant.* Moreover, Josephus goes out of his way in his paraphrase of the book of Daniel to note how mistaken are the Epicureans, who exclude providence *(pronoian)* from human life (*Ant* 10.11.7 §278).

Josephus also introduces a number of typical dramatic motifs, in particular the concept of *hubris* ("insolence," "overweening pride") and its consequences. For example, he describes the generation of the Tower of Babel in terms of the typical tragic sequence of prosperity, insolence, and punishment (*Ant* 1.4.2 §113). Likewise, he condemns Haman for not bearing his good fortune wisely and for not making the best use of his prosperity with prudent reason (*Ant* 11.6.12 §277), terms familiar to Greek tragedy. An indication that Josephus is thinking of the language of tragedy may be seen in his comment (in connection with Saul's slaughter of the priests of Nob) that it is characteristic of men, when they attain power, to lay aside their moderate and just ways "as if they were stage-masks" (*Ant* 6.12.7 §264).

Finally, to make his narrative more appealing, Josephus introduces romantic motifs reminiscent of Homer, Herodotus, Xenophon, and Hellenistic novels. The erotic motif is particularly evident in Pharaoh's meeting with Sarah (*Ant* 1.8.1 §165), in the infatuation of Potiphar's wife with Joseph (*Ant* 2.4.2–5 §41–59), in Moses' marriage to the Ethiopian princess (*Ant* 2.10.2 §252–53), and in the account of Ahasuerus' actually falling in love with Esther (*Ant* 11.6.2 §202).

On the other hand, despite the fact that Josephus admits his theological and moralistic purpose in his preface, he actually downplays the theological element in *Ant.* Thus he gives a purely practical reason for circumcision—namely, the desire to prevent assimilation—rather than the connection with the covenant between God and Abraham (Gen 17:10–11; cf. *Ant* 1.10.5 §192). Again, whereas the rabbis have Abraham appeal to Isaac to sacrifice himself for the sanctification of God's name, in Josephus Abraham makes no such appeal (*Ant* 1.13.3 §228–31). Moreover, in his version of Samson, Josephus omits miraculous details and thus diminishes the role of God. In addition, most strikingly, in his entire adaptation of the narrative of Ruth, Josephus nowhere mentions God, whereas there are 17 references to God in the biblical story. That Josephus does not de-emphasize the role of God in his account of Moses may be due to the fact that the Greeks believed that great leaders, such as the Spartan Lycurgus, had to be divinely directed. Again, whereas in the book of Esther there is not a single reference to God, the LXX and Josephus, for apologetic reasons, supply this lack in several places. As to miracles, Josephus frequently tells his readers to make up their own minds—a formula found in Herodotus, Thucydides, and many other ancient historians.

b. The Postbiblical Period. Josephus' account of the postbiblical period is very uneven. There are some figures (such as Herod) or events (such as the accession of the Roman emperor Claudius) for which he provides extraordinary detail; there are others—e.g., the period from Ezra to Alexander—for which he is extraordinarily skimpy. This brevity may be explained most simply by postulating that Josephus had few sources for this period; but two other factors may have been at work: (1) the Jews had achieved almost nothing of importance; and (2) Josephus, bearing in mind that his history would consist of only 20 books, sought to emphasize the period of the Hasmoneans, his ancestral family, and their rivals, the Herodians.

As for Alexander, the fact that Josephus' account of Alexander's meeting with the high priest (*Ant* 11.8.5 §329–39) is closely paralleled by the account in the Samaritan. Second Chronicle of the meeting between Alexander and the Samaritan high priest would seem to confirm its historicity. The notion that Jerusalem was at that time hardly worth visiting is not convincing; the fact that the oldest Gk and Lat sources do not mention such a visit and the suggestion that Josephus introduced it for merely apologetic reasons are hardly conclusive, since the Talmud and Samaritan sources quite independently have a similar tradition.

Josephus' extensive summary of *Let. Aris.* is remarkable for the fact that although it closely adheres to the content of the original, it constantly modifies the language, particularly with Stoic terminology, so that there is only one instance where as many as 12 words of the original have been retained. We may wonder why Josephus, in a history of the Jews, devotes such an inordinately long space to what is, at best, a peripheral historical incident; but Josephus' aim may well have been to provide a precedent for an appeal to the Flavians to allow the Jews to practice their ancestral religion (this time after the disastrous revolt against Rome). The changes that are made are intended primarily to render the account less offensive to non-Jews.

Josephus likewise closely parallels 1 Maccabees (*Ant* 12.5.2–13.6.6). Differences may be explained either by the hypothesis that Josephus had both a Hebrew and a Greek text, or that he had only a Greek text, probably in a more accurate and full form than ours, which he adapted for his Greco-Roman readers. In addition, however, as a descendant of the Hasmoneans, Josephus must have had access to oral traditions and was, at times, more objective than the author of 1 Maccabees, who was closer in point of time to the events themselves. Josephus' additions are generally geographical and topographical; and they supply the names of participants, the number of casualties, and motives, perhaps obtaining this information from a Hellenistic historian (presumably Nicolaus of Damascus). Josephus has also increased admiration for his ancestors Mattathias and Judas. Finally, Josephus, in his attempt to differentiate between the Maccabees and the revolutionaries of his own day, has emphasized the ideal of martyrdom; whereas 1 Maccabees attributes the victory to God, Josephus attributes it to the piety of the soldiers. One mystery is Josephus' failure to use the last three chapters of 1 Maccabees, whether because they were missing from Josephus' copy or because Josephus viewed Nicolaus of Damascus as a superior source from that point on. And yet, it is surprising that Josephus used Nicolaus as much as he did, since the latter (as Herod's secretary) was presumably opposed to Josephus' Hasmonean ancestors. To say, as some scholars have, that Josephus has no independent value for this period is to deny what seems most reasonable, namely that Josephus, as a direct descendant of the Hasmoneans, had oral traditions from his family.

Among Josephus' major sources for the Roman period were the decrees apparently available either from the imperial archives in Rome, or through Nicolaus of Damascus, or through Josephus' close friend Agrippa II. Most scholars accept their authenticity, even though Josephus' version often does not correspond with the style known to us from inscriptions and despite the invitation to the reader to check their accuracy (this is a mere formality, since in antiquity it was very difficult to locate any given piece of information because of inadequate filing systems).

There is no figure in all antiquity about whom we have more detailed information than Herod; and by far our chief authority is Josephus, whose main source was Nicolaus of Damascus. Josephus himself, as a Hasmonean, is clearly prejudiced against Herod, particularly in *Ant*, basing himself perhaps on oral traditions derived from his Hasmonean ancestors, Herod's bitter opponents. Most studies have confirmed the disparaging picture rendered by Josephus; but the recent magisterial work by Schalit (1968) attempts to rehabilitate him as one who sincerely believed that the Jews could attain peace and prosperity only through cooperating with the Pax Romana. However, despite Josephus' judicious comments, we may question whether or not the Jews were, in fact, far more prosperous at the end of Herod's reign (4 B.C.E.) than they were at the beginning (37 B.C.E.) and whether or not his vast building program solved the problem of unemployment. If Herod was really well-disposed toward Rome, we may well ask why Josephus, who was similarly so loyal, should have been so negative toward him. Also if Herod claimed to be the Messiah, as seems clear from Epiphanius, we may ask why Josephus, in his bitter and exhaustive account, did not mention this, since a political messiah by definition would be a rebel against the Roman Empire, and this would have defamed Herod's reputation completely. Yet we would seem to be justified in viewing skeptically Herod's account of how Cleopatra had attempted to seduce him and how he was dissuaded only with difficulty from killing her (cited in *Ant* 15.4.2 §97–103). Such a story may well have arisen when Herod attempted to enter the good graces of Octavian, who had come to power after defeating Antony and Cleopatra.

Occasionally we are fortunate enough to be able to check

Josephus' account of specific incidents. One example is in connection with the expulsion of the Jews from Rome in 19 C.E. (*Ant* 18.3.5 §81–84). Josephus would have us believe that the Jews were expelled because four Jewish scoundrels pocketed for themselves the gifts for the Jerusalem temple which a certain noble Roman proselyte named Fulvia had entrusted to them. It seems hard to believe that Tiberius, who was the emperor at this time and who was noted for his strict adherence to legal procedure, would have expelled all the Jews without a trial because of the misdeeds of a few. More credible is the account of Dio Cassius (57.18.5a) that the Jews were expelled because of their success in converting to Judaism so many Romans, including some of high birth. In view of the offense, Tacitus (*Ann.* 2.85) seems to imply more plausibly that the expulsion was restricted to proselytes—those "tainted with this superstition." In view of the fact that the Jews had on an earlier occasion (139 B.C.E.) likewise been expelled from the city because of proselyting activities (Val. Max. 1.33), Dio's account seems preferable to that of Josephus; thus the key to the incident is what Josephus mentions only incidentally—the fact that Fulvia was a proselyte.

As for the period of the procurators (1st century C.E.), we are fortunate to have another account with which to check Josephus' report of an incident associated with Pontius Pilate (*Ant* 18.3.1 §55–59; *JW* 2.9.2–3 §169–74). However, this second account (Philo *Gaium* 18 §299–305) is so different that the question has been raised as to whether it refers to the same incident as Josephus. In Philo, Pilate brings into Jerusalem shields without images; whereas in Josephus he brings in standards with images. In Philo the incident occurs after several years of misrule by Pilate, whereas in Josephus it comes at the beginning of his procuratorship. In Philo the people appeal unsuccessfully to Pilate, apparently in Jerusalem; whereas in Josephus they appeal successfully in Caesarea. In this case, though Philo is contemporary with Pilate and less involved, he is probably less reliable than Josephus, since he is writing, presumably from hearsay, an apologetic work about events which occurred some distance from his home.

We may well wonder why Josephus devoted so much space to an account of the assassination of the emperor Caligula and the accession of Claudius (*Ant* 19.1.1–4.6 §1–273), events only tangentially related to Jewish history, especially in light of the fact that there is not much of a parallel account in *JW* (2.11.1–5 §204–14; there are usually extensive parallels to almost all other incidents). We may suggest that the key is Josephus' friendship with Agrippa II, the son of the man (Agrippa I) who, according to Josephus, was responsible for Claudius' assumption of the throne. To some degree the length of the narrative may be due simply to the availability of an extensive narrative, whether by Cluvius Rufus, as Mommsen (1870) conjectured, or in other sources, notably details derived orally from Agrippa II.

c. Josephus and Christian History. The chief reason why Josephus' works have survived in their entirety is that they contain references to John the Baptist, to James the brother of Jesus, and, above all, to Jesus himself (the so-called *Testimonium Flavianum;* see below).

There can be little doubt as to the authenticity of Josephus' reference to John the Baptist (*Ant* 18 §116–19), especially since the language is particularly typical of this part of *Ant,* since it contains two different forms of the word *baptism* (which an interpolator would almost certainly have avoided), since it is approximately twice as long as the Jesus passage and yet has no reference to the connection between John and Jesus, and, above all, since the reason given for John's death contradicts the Gospels. Moreover, the 3d-century Origen, who explicitly states that Josephus did not believe in Jesus as Christ, cites this passage. As to the relative lengths of the passages about John and Jesus, it may be that John was originally the more important of the two or that Josephus was wary of speaking about messianic movements, such as the one connected with the name of Jesus, inasmuch as this ipso facto involved revolt against Rome. As to the discrepancy between Josephus and the Gospels, one possible solution is to suggest that the two accounts supplement one another: the Christians, as moralists, emphasized that John had provoked Herod Antipas with his moral rebuke (Mark 6:17–18); but Josephus, as a political historian, stressed that John had been executed because it was feared that, with his ability to attract crowds, he would lead a revolt. In any case if the passage about John had been interpolated by a Christian, we would have expected some reference to John's connection with Jesus. Finally, Josephus' account seems to be historically valid; since he praises him as a "good man," we should have expected Josephus to agree with the Gospels in giving the cause of John's death; whereas the political charge against John clearly embarrassed Josephus, who so fiercely opposed all revolutionary stirrings.

Most scholars have regarded the so-called *Testimonium Flavianum*—Josephus' reference to Jesus Christ—as interpolated, at least in part. In this passage (*Ant* 18.3.3 §63–64) Josephus notes that during the procuratorship of Pontius Pilate "there lived Jesus, a wise man, if indeed one ought to call him a man." He reports that he accomplished surprising feats, and taught many people, and "won over many Jews and many Greeks." The text then baldly claims that "he was the Messiah" and reports how Pilate had him crucified and how, on the third day, he appeared alive to those who loved him, as had been previously prophesied. We should note, however, that aside from this passage and possibly those about John and James, there are no other passages in Josephus the authenticity of which has been questioned; therefore the burden of proof rests upon anyone who argues that these are later interpolations.

Though this passage is found in all the Gk mss of Josephus (the earliest of which, to be sure, dates from the 11th century) and in all the versions (including the Lat translation of Cassiodorus, which dates from the 6th century), Origen, who cites five passages also from Book 18 of *Ant,* expresses wonder that Josephus did not admit "Jesus to be the Christ" (*comm. in Mt.* 10.17) and elsewhere states that Josephus "disbelieved in Jesus as Christ" (*Cels.* 1.47). The implication of these statements is that in the 3d century Origen could find in *Ant* some passage about Jesus but that it was basically neutral (if it had been negative, Origen probably would have attacked Josephus sharply instead of merely expressing wonder). Moreover, the fact that Josephus refers to Jesus in his reference to James the brother of "the aforementioned Christ" (*Ant* 20.9.1 §200)—a passage the authenticity of which has been almost universally acknowledged—indicates that Jesus had been mentioned previously.

The fact that there are no fewer than 11 Christian writers prior to the 4th-century Eusebius (who quotes it in three different forms) and no fewer than 5 between Eusebius and Jerome, all of whom knew Josephus' works and yet did not refer to the *Testimonium,* constitutes a strong argument that the passage originally did not exist in its present form. If it had been original, it would have been a powerful argument in polemics against the Jews, especially since one charge (as early as the middle of the 2d century) was that Jesus had never lived at all and was, in fact, a figment of Christian imagination (Just. *dial.* 8). The fact that there was a passage about Jesus in *Ant* may help to explain the Talmud's silence about Josephus, since the very mention of Jesus in a neutral sense would most probably have been frowned upon by the rabbis. Further indications that the original version of the *Testimonium* was different from its present form come from Agapius, a 10th-century Christian Arab, whose version of the *Testimonium* does not read "if indeed we ought to call him a man," omits references to Jesus' miracles and to the role of Jewish leaders in accusing Jesus, states not that Jesus appeared to his disciples on the third day but that his disciples reported this, and (most important) that he was "perhaps the Messiah," rather than "he was the Messiah." This is further reinforced by the fact that another Christian, Michael the Syrian, says, in his (12th-century) version of the *Testimonium,* that Jesus "was thought to be the Messiah" (so also Jerome, *De Viris Illustribus* 13; though one wonders how a believing Christian could have cited such a text without recording a strong reaction against it).

Furthermore, we may note that the passages about John, Jesus, and James (see below) do not appear in the parallel passages in *JW;* and we may therefore be suspicious that the lines about them in *Ant* were interpolated. However, this may be due to the fact that the Christians had become more important in the interval between the publication of the two works. As to the language of the *Testimonium,* Thackeray (1929: 141) has noted the remarkable fact that the phrase "such people as accept the truth gladly" *(hēdonēi)* is characteristic of precisely this portion of *Ant* since we find it eight times in Books 17–19 (allegedly the work of Josephus' Thucydidean assistant) and nowhere else in Josephus. The word *hēdonēi* could hardly have been interpolated by a Christian, since it has a pejorative connotation, though we must be careful not to impute too much significance to the choice of individual words in a passage which consists of two short paragraphs (there are also other places in the *Testimonium* which are characteristic not of Josephus but of Eusebius).

However, if Josephus did insert a passage of some sort about Jesus, we may well ask what his motive was. Laqueur suggested that, having alienated the Jews by his behavior in the war against Rome and by his use of the LXX, Josephus turned to the Christians, who had not participated in the rebellion against Rome and who believed that the LXX was divinely inspired, in the hope that they would purchase his work (1920: 274ff.). But there is no evidence that Josephus needed any further financial support, since he apparently had a very comfortable imperial pension. Furthermore, it seems unlikely that Josephus would have sought to gain the very small Christian audience when it would probably have meant alienating the much larger potential audience of Hellenistic Jews (who also regarded the LXX as authoritative).

As a Jew, Josephus might well have acknowledged someone to be the Messiah without necessarily being excluded from the Jewish fold; but since the concept of messiah at this time had definite overtones of revolution and political independence, Josephus, as a loyal member of the Roman royal family, could hardly have recognized Jesus as such. Indeed, Josephus avoids the use of the term *messiah,* except here and in *Ant* 20.9.1 §200 (also in connection with Jesus).

The passage about the death of James the brother of Jesus (*Ant* 20.9.1) has been regarded as authentic by almost all scholars, since the language is thoroughly Josephan; yet it sharply diverges from the eulogy of the high priest Ananus, as found in *JW* 4.5.2 §319–20. But there are numerous contradictions between the *JW* and the *Ant* passages; and, in any case, Origen in the 3d century did have a text about James, since he explicitly says (*comm. in Mt.* 10.7) that Josephus bore witness to so much righteousness in James (though our *Ant* text has no such direct encomium).

A word may be said about several other passages in Josephus which are paralleled by the NT. Josephus speaks of a census by Quirinius, governor of Syria, at the time when Archelaus was removed from his position as ethnarch in 6 or 7 C.E. (*Ant* 17.13.5–18.1.1); whereas Luke 2:1–5 speaks of the census as taking place at the time of Jesus' birth, near the end of the reign of Herod (4 B.C.E.). It seems hard to believe that there had been an earlier census under Quirinius, since Quirinius is not listed in any source as one of the governors of Syria during the reign of Herod and since, moreover, Josephus (*Ant* 18.1.1 §3) declares that the census shocked the Jews (this implies that it was unprecedented). Moreover, if there had been an earlier census, Josephus would most probably, in accordance with his custom, have made a cross-reference to it.

Furthermore, Josephus mentions a certain Theudas, an impostor who persuaded the masses to follow him in the expectation that he would fulfill his promise that the Jordan river would part at his command but who, together with many followers, was slain by the armed forces of the procurator Fadus (*Ant* 20.5.1 §97–98). Luke likewise mentions a Theudas who was slain and whose followers were dispersed, presumably after attempting a revolutionary movement (Acts 5:36). Despite the chronological discrepancy (Acts sets it before Judas' revolt in 6 C.E., while Josephus sets it ca. 44 C.E.), it is tempting, especially in view of the unusual nature of the name Theudas, to identify the two. Another parallel occurs in connection with the false prophet from Egypt (*JW* 2.13.5 §261–63; *Ant* 20.8.6 §169–72), 400 of whose followers were killed by the soldiers of the procurator Felix (the passage in *JW* gives the number of his followers as 30,000); Acts 21:38 speaks of the Egyptian revolutionary but gives the number of his followers as 4000. See EGYPTIAN, THE.

3. *Against Apion.* In writing his work *Against Apion* (= *AgAp*), published in the last years of his life, Josephus followed the precedent of other Greek apologists. A work attacking the Greeks might well have made a positive impression upon chauvinistic Romans, since Roman intellectuals had ambivalent feelings toward the Greeks, who had been their mentors in almost every field. It has also been conjectured that Josephus was particularly eager to defend his Jewish countrymen against anti-Semitic movements in order to win his way back into their good graces after his disgraceful surrender to the Romans. A third purpose may have been to supply a handbook to Jewish missionaries and propagandists in their efforts, which in Josephus' day were notably successful, though there was no way in antiquity for books to be produced in large numbers.

Josephus was not the only Jewish apologist of his day, as is clear from the fact that Philo wrote similar works (*In Flaccum* and *Hypothetica*); indeed, the latter work, in its brief summary of Jewish law, seems to have served as a model for the second part of *AgAp* (2.14 §145–41, §295). In addition to Philo, another forerunner of Josephus was Dionysius of Halicarnassus, whose *Roman Antiquities*—especially its encomium of Rome (Dion. Hal. *Ant. Rom.* 1.4–2.29)—apparently served as a model for *Ant* (at least in title and in number of books). Both Dionysius and Josephus, in turn, follow the standard rhetorical pattern for such encomiums as described later and more fully in a handbook by Menander of Laodicea (3d century). Inasmuch as this handbook prescribes the same order of topics in both encomiums and invectives, Josephus is apparently following the order of topics which his opponent Apion, who was a grammarian, presumably adopted.

One of the charges of the anti-Semites was that the Jews had come late to civilized life. Josephus, like other Oriental intellectuals and like the Greco-Jewish historian Demetrius in the 3d century B.C.E., challenges this hypothesis by modifying biblical chronology so as to make the Jews contemporary with personalities and events of Greek history. It has been debated whether Josephus actually found the selections which he cites from numerous Greek authors or whether he invented them. However, we must assume that the citations are authentic unless proven otherwise, not only because it would have been difficult, with Josephus' admittedly limited knowledge of Greek, to forge passages in various styles, but also because he himself was under constant attack from his numerous enemies and therefore had to take precautions to avoid the damning charge of falsifying his sources.

C. Josephus on Jewish Law

Inasmuch as Josephus' works were issued more than a century before the codification of the Mishnah by Rabbi Judah the Prince, they, together with the works of his older contemporary Philo, are a most important source for our knowledge of the state of Jewish law in the 1st century. Moreover, since Josephus was born in Jerusalem and, according to his own report, had such an excellent education in Halakah (Jewish law) that by the age of 14 he was constantly consulted about the laws by the chief priests and the leaders of Jerusalem (see above), he is a much more valuable source than Philo, who lived in Alexandria, who (so far as we can tell) possessed a minimal knowledge of Hebrew, and who apparently never studied with the great sages of his era, such as Shemaiah, Abtalyon, Hillel, and Shammai. Josephus' knowledge of Jewish law was apparently acknowledged by the other Pharisees, since they comment that if the Galileans' devotion to him was due to his expert knowledge of Pharisaic laws they, too, were learned (*Life* 39 §198). Likewise, Josephus boasts (*Ant* 20.12.1 §263) that his fellow Jews admit that he far excelled them in Jewish learning, the most important component of which was clearly law. Finally, the fact that he indicates his intention to write a work on the laws (*Ant* 20.12.1 §268) in which he proposes also to explain the reasons for the laws (*Ant* 1. Proem 4 §25) further indicates how well versed in law he considered himself to be. The very fact that he included a long summary of the laws in Books 3 and 4 of *Ant,* which is a historical work (whereas other historians, such as Dion. Hal. and Livy, did not) is an indication that he was directing his survey to non-Jewish readers for apologetic purposes (since, as he self-consciously says [*Ant* 4.8.4 §196], the survey is consonant with Moses' reputation for virtue). We may also suggest that his summary might have proved useful to Jewish missionaries. Indeed, if we are to take Josephus at all seriously when he promises neither to add to nor to subtract from Scripture, which certainly includes Jewish law, his presentation should be of great value.

There are many instances in *Ant* where Josephus agrees with the system of Jewish law as we have it codified in later rabbinic writings. A few of the many examples are: (1) he agrees with *m. Para* 5.3 that a lamb to be offered for sacrifice should be one year old (3.9.1 §226); (2) he agrees with *m. Sanh.* that blasphemers are not merely to be stoned (Lev 24:14–16) but also to be hanged (4.8.6 §202); (3) he agrees with *Ber.* 27b that there are two required daily prayers (4.8.13 §212); (4) he declares (with *Sipre* 109b) that women's testimony is unacceptable (4.8.15 §219); (5) he concurs with *Sanh.* 2a, 20b that a king must consult the Sanhedrin of 71 before entering upon a voluntary war (4.8.17 §224); (6) like *Mak.* 22a he states that the number of lashes to be inflicted upon a lawbreaker is not 40 but 39 (4.8.21 §238); (7) like *Giṭ.* 90a he believes that divorce is permissible for any reason whatsoever (4.8.23 §253); and (8) he states (4.8.27 §271) that one must pay double not only for the theft of animals but also for the theft of money (*B. Qam.* 64b). Concerning lost property, Josephus differentiates on the basis of whether the object is found in a private or public place (4.8.29 §274) and indicates that one must proclaim publicly where the object has been found (cf. *m. B. Meṣ.* 2.1). Also, one should not be punished if the person he injured lives for several days before dying (*Ant* 4.8.33 §277; cf. *t. B. Qam.* 9.5–6). Josephus opposes costly shrouds (*AgAp* 2.26 §205; cf. *Moʿed Qaṭ.* 27b; *Ketub.* 8b), and he even agrees with the oral tradition (*t. B. Meṣ.* 2.29) in placing the law concerning pointing out the road to a lost traveler immediately after the law concerning lost objects (*Ant* 4.8.29, 31 §274, 276).

There are, however, a number of places where Josephus disagrees with the rabbis; and this raises the question whether Josephus reflects an earlier stage of the oral law. Such an hypothesis would apparently be supported by the fact that Philo (*Spec Leg* I–IV), CD, and especially 11QTemple likewise record laws, including much oral law, in a systematic way. Indeed, the newly discovered manuscript of the Talmud (*ʿAbod. Zar.* 8b) states that Rabbi Judah ben-Baba, a younger contemporary of Josephus, records laws of fines. Again, the fact that Josephus breaks down each biblical law into more precisely defined cases would seem to reflect a written legal code.

There are a number of possible explanations for Josephus' deviations from the rabbinic formulation of the oral law. In the first place, since Josephus wrote *Ant* in Rome many years after his departure from Jerusalem and had little or no contact with Talmudic rabbis there, he may have forgotten what he had learned; but this seems unlikely because memories were so carefully cultivated in those days and because Josephus had so many enemies that he had to be careful not to give occasion for a charge of heresy. Apologetic reasons seem to lie behind many of Josephus' revisions of Jewish law, just as they lie behind his recasting of the biblical narratives. Thus, whereas the Bible (Lev 19:14; Deut 27:18) declares that one must not put a stumbling block in front of the blind, Josephus extends this by declaring that one must point out the road to those who are ignorant of it (*Ant* 4.8.31 §276). Here Josephus would seem to be responding to the charge of those anti-Semites, such as Juvenal (*Satires* 14.103), who had accused the Jews of failing to point out the road to non-Jews. Similarly, by adding the detail that those who dig wells must cover them not to prevent others from drawing water but rather to protect passersby from falling into them (*Ant* 4.8.37 §283), he is answering the charge of those—such as Juvenal (14.104)—who had declared that Jews direct "none but the circumcised to the desired fountain."

Apologetic motives likewise seem to lie behind Josephus' nonbiblical and non-Talmudic equation of abortion with infanticide (*AgAp* 2.24 §202), since otherwise the law applicable to Jews would appear to be more lenient than the Noachian law applicable to gentiles, which (*Sanh.* 57b), through an interpretation of Gen 9:6, forbids killing a fetus in utero. In particular, Josephus must have felt uneasy that Jewish law on this subject was more lenient than that of Plato (*Ap.;* Plutarch, *De Placitis Philosophorum* 5.15), who states that a fetus is a living being (the rabbis [*Sanh.* 72b] declared that an abortion is permissible if the fetus is endangering the life of the mother).

Likewise, Josephus may have had an apologetic motive both in stating that the law with regard to the rebellious child applied to daughters no less than to sons (*Ant* 4.8.24 §263; the rabbis [*m. Sanh.* 8:1] restrict the law to sons alone) and in declaring that the mere intention of doing wrong to one's parents is subject to immediate punishment by death (*AgAp* 2.30 §217). Here his motive may have been to show that the Jews were no more permissive toward children than were the Romans, who were noted for their strictness. Josephus' statement (*AgAp* 2.27 §207) that it is a capital crime for a judge to accept bribes (there is no such law in the Talmud) similarly was occasioned apparently by the fact that it might appear that Jewish law was less severe than both Noachide law, which required the death penalty, and Roman law (*Lex Cornelia testimentaria,* 81 B.C.E.), which inflicted the penalty of exile upon such a judge.

Again, especially in light of the very successful Jewish missionary movement, Josephus' omission of the prohibition of converting Ammonites and Moabites to Judaism until the tenth generation (Deut 23:4) and Edomites and Egyptians until the third generation (Deut 23:7–8) may be explained by Josephus' eagerness to answer the anti-Semitic charge that the Jews were exclusivistic and misanthropic. If, indeed, Josephus also omits the child sacrifice to Moloch (Lev 18:21)—whereas one would expect him to mention this in order to contrast it with the Jewish opposition to human sacrifice—this may be due to the fact that it was no longer being practiced. Likewise, if Josephus does not omit the seemingly embarrassing law that one may charge interest from a non-Jew but not from a Jew (Deut 23:21; cf. *Ant* 4.8.25 §266), which would appear to play into the hands of anti-Semites, the reason may be that he was eager to attract non-Jews to Judaism; and interest-free loans may well have proved a major attraction.

Another possible explanation for Josephus' deviations is that he had sectarian leanings. Indeed, Yadin has noted that there are parallels between Josephus' classification of the laws and that of the author of 11QTemple and recalls that Josephus himself stated that he had spent several years with the Essenes and with a hermit named Bannus (*Life* 2 §9–12). Indeed, there are even parallels in detail: e.g., both 11QTemple (63.5) and Josephus (*Ant* 4.8.16 §222) declare that the public officers of the nearest town are to wash their hands in holy water over the head of a heifer in expiation for an undetected murderer, whereas the Bible (Deut 21:6) does not specify the head. Again, whereas the Bible (1 Kgs 21:13) says that there were two false witnesses against Naboth, Josephus (*Ant* 8.8.8 §358) mentions three, apparently in accord with CD (9.17, 22), which likewise requires three witnesses in capital cases.

Still another explanation for Josephus' version of Jewish law is that he may be following Philo. Indeed, there are no fewer than four instances where Josephus' interpretation of law agrees with that of Philo in the latter's *Hypothetica* (even though so little of this work has survived): (1) the public reading of the Torah on the Sabbath (*AgAp* 2.17 §175), (2) the death penalty for abortion (*AgAp* 2.24 §202), (3) the prohibition of concealing anything from friends (*AgAp* 2.27 §207), and (4) the prohibition of killing animals that have taken refuge in one's home (*AgAp* 2.29 §213). While it is true that these are also paralleled in rabbinic sources, the rabbinic parallels are not quite so precise as those in Philo. In particular we may cite the striking parallel in language between Philo (*Hypothetica* 7.9) and Josephus (*AgAp* 2.29 §213) in the statement of the law concerning the animal that has taken refuge in one's home as a suppliant.

As we have suggested above, Josephus may likewise have been influenced by Roman law in an effort to smooth his way with his Roman audience, though admittedly he nowhere indicates that he had studied or admired Roman law and, indeed, insists on the unique excellence of Jewish law (*Ant* 1. Proem 4 §22–23; *AgAp* 2.16 §163). We may, however, note that Josephus' statement that a thief, if unable to pay the penalty imposed upon him, is to become the slave of the aggrieved party (*Ant* 4.8.27 §272) is paralleled neither in the Bible nor in the Talmud, but rather in Roman law.

Another explanation of Josephus' deviations may be that he confuses commands with advice. Thus his statement, which is without parallel, that the law commands *(keleuei)* that in seeking a spouse one should not be influenced by a dowry (*AgAp* 2.24 §200) may be mere advice, since the verb *keleuei* (like the Latin *iubeo* to which it corresponds) may mean "recommends" or "advises," as indeed it seems to mean in *Life* 75 §414. The Talmud (*Qidd.* 70a) has similar advice, that one should not choose a wife for the sake of her money.

We may be surprised that Josephus is occasionally less liberal than the rabbis, notably in his attitude toward artistic representation. Thus he is ready to lead the Jews of Galilee to destroy the palace of Herod the Tetrarch because it had been decorated with images of animals (*Life* 12 §65); and he condemns King Solomon for placing the images of bulls and lions in the temple (*Ant* 8.7.5 §195), whereas even the Bible itself (1 Kgs 7:25; 10:20) contains no such rebuke and the rabbis actually state that all faces are permissible except that of a human (*ʿAbod. Zar.* 43b). The explanation here may be that the rabbis were realistic enough to perceive that the masses of the people were liberal in their interpretation of the laws concerning art work, as indicated by the artistic representation that has come down to us; hence they made no attempt to stop them. Josephus, on the other hand, had no "constituency" and hence felt that he could afford to maintain an unyielding posture; indeed, he may have felt a necessity to do so while among the Galileans, who were known for their religious zealotry.

D. Language and Style of Josephus

With the completion of K. H. Rengstorf's (1973–83) concordance of Josephus (except for the small portion of *AgAp* [2.5–9 §51–113] which is extant only in Latin), we are now in a position to examine Josephus' language against the backdrop of that of his predecessors and contemporaries. This concordance, we may remark, lists every occurrence of every word (with the exception of a very few common words), has a very high degree of accuracy, is very generous in quoting lemmas, lists noteworthy textual variants, and often cites the Latin translation of Josephus. Unfortunately, unlike the truncated dictionary of Josephus by Thackeray and Marcus (1930–55), it usually does not give the meaning of the word in a given passage but merely lists all the meanings at the beginning of the entry. Moreover, it omits the context for prepositions, conjunctions, pronouns, numbers, and particles, though it is precisely such words that are often the key to the appreciation of the author's style; and it is not sufficiently analytical with regard to Josephus' grammar.

Ladouceur (1977) has demonstrated that in declensional and conjugational forms, Josephus, far from being dependent upon any single author, such as Dionysius of Halicarnassus, fluctuates freely between classical and post-classical usage; and much of his grammatical usage is paralleled in Polybius and in Attic inscriptions of the first century B.C.E.

As to Josephus' employment of assistants, it is ironic that no one has been able to pinpoint the influence of assistants in *JW*, Josephus' earliest work, in which he himself says he received such help (*AgAp* 1.9 §50); but while Josephus says nothing of obtaining such assistance for *Ant,* Thackeray (1929: 115) claims to have found signs of it in *Ant* 15 and 16 (an assistant well versed in Sophocles) and 17–19 (an assistant steeped in Thucydides). Moreover, there is no indication of the work of assistants in *AgAp*, Josephus' final and most polished work. In addition, the influence of Sophocles and of Thucydides was so pervasive in other Greek writers of this period, notably Dionysius of Halicarnassus, that it is at least as likely that Josephus' language was influenced directly by those writers as indirectly through the alleged assistants. The fact that Josephus used Strabo as a major source in *Ant* 13–15 shows that there is no sharp dividing line at the beginning of Book 15, as Thackeray claims. In addition, we may note that Nicolaus of Damascus, who was Josephus' main source for *Ant* 14–17, was steeped in Sophocles and thus may have been a source of the Sophoclean element in Josephus. Inasmuch as Josephus wrote *Ant* after spending over 20 years in Rome in a Greek-speaking environment, we may suppose that during this interval he perfected his knowledge of Greek to the point where assistants were not needed; in any case if he needed assistants for *Ant,* he should have required them also for the *Life* and *AgAp,* which were written immediately thereafter. As to the occurrence of poetic words and Ionic prose forms in Josephus, they may simply represent a non-Attic dialectical contribution to the *koine,* as seen in the papyri, and should not be used as unambiguous evidence of the literary influence.

In his narrative style Josephus appears to have followed the pattern of his Greek predecessors. Thus his use of double narrative—i.e., two stories on the same theme (e.g., *Ant* 18.3.4 §66–80; and 18.3.5 §81–84)—is in accord with the literary technique of the tragic school of Hellenistic historians. Again, in his suicide narratives, he follows the pattern found in many Greek and Roman writers; and this, we may suggest, would tend to impugn the historical value of such accounts.

Book 7 of *JW* presents a special problem. On the basis of a study of crasis and elision, Morton and Michaelson (1973) have concluded that there is a marked difference between Book 7 and the other books of *JW,* though, of course, this may indicate only that Book 7 did not benefit from the careful editing that the other books received. Moreover, there are sharply different rates of elision for the various parts of *AgAp,* whereas no one has seriously doubted the unity of that work. In the most recent study of Book 7, Schwartz (1985) concludes, on the basis of content rather than of style, that the book consists of three strands, the first composed in 79–81 C.E. (the date usually assigned to the whole work), the second in 82–83 C.E., and the third early in Trajan's reign (ca. 100 C.E.). One other interesting result of the work of Morton and Michaelson is that *Life* and *JW* have a definite stylistic relationship and presumably a common source; this would appear to suggest an answer to a persistent question in Josephan scholarship, namely, whether the *Life* is largely based upon a work which was utilized by Josephus for *JW* many years earlier.

As we have noted, we do not have a single fragment of any Aramaic version of *JW;* and there is no evidence that the Slavonic version is dependent on it. Indeed, despite Josephus' statement (*JW* 1. Proem 1 §3) that he originally composed the work for the benefit of the Jews of the "upper country" (presumably in Aramaic, the language of the Babylonian Jews), doubt has been expressed that he composed such a version at all. But Josephus seems to have been fully at home in Aramaic, since he apparently used a source in that language (presumably in the Babylonian dialect) for his extended account of Asinaeus and Anilaeus (Schalit 1965).

Despite his long residence in Rome, there is no conclusive evidence that Josephus knew Latin. Indeed, since such a large percentage of the intellectuals there were fully conversant in Greek, he probably saw no need to learn Latin. The only Roman writer he mentions by name is Livy (*Ant* 14.4.3 §68). Mommsen (1870) suggested that Josephus' source for the lengthy account of the assassination of Caligula and the accession of Claudius was a Latin history by Cluvius Rufus, since Cluvius (according to an emendation, *Ant* 19.1.13 §91–92) is said to have given an apt quotation from Homer, an anecdote which would seem to be derived from Cluvius himself. It has also been noted that Josephus' style in Book 19 is more metaphoric and more highly colored than is usual for him. But aside from the fact that there is no indication that Cluvius' history (which is now lost) covered the period of Caligula and Claudius, the rhetorical style may have come from another writer within the same rhetorical tradition; and the fact that Josephus' account places such stress on the role of Agrippa I in these events would seem to indicate the likelihood that his source (or one of his major sources) was an oral tradition from the family of Agrippa, with which Josephus was very close.

E. Josephus' Influence

Josephus seems to have been ignored by classical writers; indeed, the only pagan writer who definitely knows the works of Josephus is the 3d-century Porphyry, who (*De Abstinentia ab Esu Animalium* 4.11) refers (*Abst.* 4.11) to Josephus' discussion of the Essenes in *JW, Ant,* and *AgAp* (there is no allusion to them in our text of *AgAp,* however).

Josephus' influence becomes most noticeable in the Church Fathers. In particular we may cite his influence upon the Greek Hegesippus, Hippolytus, Origen, Theophilus, Eusebius, John Chrysostom, and Pseudo-Kaisarios, as well as upon the Latin Minucius Felix, Tertullian, Jerome, and Augustine. Indeed, for writers such as Origen, Eusebius, and Jerome, Josephus was the most useful source for confirming the Bible. Jerome (*Epistula ad Eustochium* 22.35 = *Patrologia Latina* 22.421) praises Josephus as a second Livy; and, in fact, so marked was his favor for Josephus that during his lifetime it was thought that he had translated *JW* into Latin. Indeed, the Church Fathers found in *JW* a strong affinity with NT themes, especially the significance of the destruction of the temple and its connection with the passion of Jesus.

During the Middle Ages Josephus was regarded as an authority in such diverse fields as biblical exegesis, allegory, chronology, arithmetic, astronomy, natural history, geography, military tactics, grammar, etymology, and theology. For Christians who were cut off from the direct Jewish tradition, it was Josephus who supplied pilgrims with their knowledge of the Holy Land. In catalogues of medieval libraries his works commonly appear with the Church Fathers. In the monastery of Cluny, Josephus is listed as one of the authors whose works were read during Lent. His influence was even greater then than it has been in modern times because he was said to have written certain works which are generally regarded as spurious, notably *4 Maccabees* and *Hegesippus,* as well as, of course, the paragraphs about Jesus in *Ant.* We may note, in particular, the influence of Josephus upon such medieval Latin authors as Bede, Rabanus Maurus, Fulcher of Chartres, and, above all, Peter Comestor, whose *Historia Scholastica,* written in the 12th century, soon became the most popular book in Europe. An indication of Josephus' influence upon this work is the fact that Comestor is often a clue to restoring the original text of the Latin translation of Josephus, and vice versa. Josephus' influence may also be seen in the popularity of the legend of Josephus the physician who cured Titus of a swollen leg (cited in Landolfus Sagax's *Historia miscella* [ca. 1000] and in the 13th-century *Sachsenspiegel*).

Among Byzantine Greek authors whom Josephus influenced we may cite George Hamartolos, Malalas, Zonaras, the anonymous author of *De obsidione toleranda,* Nikephoros Kallistos Xanthopoulos, and the anonymous author of *Palaea Historica.* Josephus was unknown among Jewish writers during the Middle Ages; but the influence of Josippon (see below) was profound on such Jewish commentators as Rashi in the 11th century and the Franco-German Tosafists in the two centuries thereafter.

During the Renaissance the enormous popularity of Josephus may be gauged from the fact that between 1450 and 1700 there were more editions of *Ant* (73) and of *JW* (68) than of any other historical work in Greek. The 14th-century Nicolas of Lyre was greatly indebted to Josephus in his biblical commentary. During this period, as in the Middle Ages, Josephus was ignored by Jewish writers, with the notable exception of Abrabanel in the 15th century and Azariah dei Rossi in the 16th century. As to the popularity of Josippon, it has even been suggested that this paraphrase was a link in the chain of events which culminated in the readmission of the Jews to England by Cromwell.

The influence of Josephus upon modern literature has been profound but has been documented fully only for Spanish literature (in an unpublished study). Until our own days a common sight in many homes was a copy of Josephus alongside the Christian Bible since his works bridged the chronological gap between the OT and NT. Among strict English Protestants only Josephus and the Bible were permitted to be read on Sunday. The growing sanctity of the Hebrew Scriptures in England by the end of the 16th century led playwrights to turn to the Apocrypha and Josephus for source material, in particular for plays about Herod. In the period before the American Revolution, the earliest book by a Jewish author (other than the Bible) printed in America was L'Estrange's 1719 translation of *JW.* The second book of Jewish authorship printed in America was Morvvyne's 1722 translation of Josippon.

In French literature we may note Josephus' influence on Corneille, Racine, and Voltaire. In Italian he was particularly influential on Petrarch. In Spanish literature he especially influenced such writers as Alfonso the Learned, Lope de Vega, and Tirso de Molina. Josephus' popularity was particularly great among Spanish Conversos (the so-called Marranos), who practiced their Judaism secretly after their conversion to Christianity in the 14th and 15th centuries and who found in Josephus an author who was both accepted by the Church (because of the *Testimonium*

Flavianum) and proud of his Jewish heritage and faith. In German literature his influence is particularly to be seen in the 20th-century Lion Feuchtwanger's very popular, and largely autobiographical, trilogy about him (1932, 1936, 1942).

F. The Text of Josephus

So far as we can tell, all the writings of Josephus have been preserved, thanks to the interest of the Christian Church. There are 133 manuscripts of some or all of his works; but the earliest of these dates from the 11th century; and the text, especially of *Ant,* is often in doubt. Only one papyrus fragment of his works has been found (of *JW* 2.20.6–7 §576–79; and 2.20.7–8 §582–84), but it consists of only 38 complete words and 74 words in part. The fact, however, that there are no fewer than nine places (several of them, to be sure, based on somewhat shaky conjectures deriving from the number of letters in a line) where the fragment differs from known manuscripts leads one to think that the text of *JW,* which is in much better shape than that of *Ant,* is even less secure than has been supposed. The fact that the papyrus agrees now with one group of our extant manuscripts and now with another leads one to suggest that a century ago the editor of the definitive text of Josephus, Benedictus Niese, relied excessively on one family of manuscripts. Hence, for example, in the famous episode at Masada (in *JW* 7), we should now have less confidence in the reliability of the text. Another clue to the unreliability of the text that we possess may be found in the fact that the Church Fathers of the 3d and 4th centuries (Origen, Eusebius, and Jerome) declare that, according to Josephus, Jerusalem was destroyed because of the murder of James the Just, a statement nowhere to be found in our present text of Josephus. While such statements may represent tendentious writing, they may also reflect a text different from ours. Similarly, as Shlomo Pines has noted, there are statements in the 10th-century Arabic historian Agapius allegedly drawn from Josephus which are not in our texts (1971: 49–63).

The best modern edition of the Gk text remains the *editio maior* of Niese (7 vols., 1885–95), which has a much more conservative and full apparatus criticus than his *editio minor* (6 vols., 1888–95). Of the complete or partial Gk mss mentioned by Schreckenberg (1972), 50 were unknown to Niese, though only 2 of these are apparently of any major significance. Naber's edition (1888–96), which appeared almost simultaneously with that of Niese, has a smoother and more readable text than that of Niese but is too free with emendations and has numerous errors in the apparatus criticus.

G. Paraphrases and Translations

There are two translations into Latin, the first a free paraphrase of *JW* dating from the 4th century and ascribed to a certain Hegesippus, and the second a more literal translation of the works (with the exception of *Life*) made under the direction of Cassiodorus in the 6th century. Inasmuch as our earliest Greek mss date from the 11th century, these Latin versions, especially that ascribed to Cassiodorus, are of considerable value for the reconstruction of the text; they have not been fully exploited hitherto for this purpose, partly because we have critical editions solely for *AgAp* and the first five books of *Ant* (the latter, moreover, is based on only a few of the 171 manuscripts, its stemma is less than careful, and manuscripts are cited irregularly and inconsistently).

We have a Syriac version of Book 6 of *JW.* Its editor, Heimann Kottek (1886), has conjectured that the translator had before him a portion of the Aramaic original; but inasmuch as that original is completely lost, it is difficult to substantiate this claim.

A Hebrew paraphrase of *JW* was apparently prepared in S Italy in the 10th century (though Zeitlin [1962–63] has dated it as early as the 3d or 4th century). Its author is known as Josippon, and this paraphrase has come down to us in three very different recensions; the work has now, for the first time, been scientifically edited by D. Flusser. See JOSIPPON. Josippon's chief source was, it seems, Hegesippus, though he also shows knowledge of the Apocrypha and of the Latin translation of the first 16 books of *Ant.* In terms of purpose, whereas Josephus views the war between the Jews and the Romans as one for national liberty, Josippon looks upon it as a holy war. He thus emphasizes two opposite trends—submission to the Romans and willingness to suffer martyrdom. The sole translation of this work into English is that of Peter Morvvyne in 1558, but it was based upon an abbreviated Latin version. A translation of the full text from the original Hebrew is now being prepared by Steven Bowman of the University of Cincinnati.

Another paraphrase, dating from the 11th century, was made into Old Russian, the definitive edition of which has been issued by Meščerskij (1958). Eisler (1929–30) suggested that this version is at least partially based on Josephus' original Aramaic version of *JW,* but this is problematic since its grammatical constructions only occasionally deviate from the Greek text. There are translations of this version into French and German, but not into English. It has been suggested, though hardly conclusively, that this version was used in the ideological struggle against the Khazars, who had been converted to Judaism in the 8th century.

What is of particular interest in the Slavonic text is the additions pertaining to John the Baptist and Jesus, though, curiously, neither of them is mentioned by name. It seems hardly likely that a Jew (i.e., Josephus) could have written "according to the law of *their* fathers" or "they [i.e., the Jews] crucified him," as we find in the Slavonic text. (An English translation of the passages pertaining to John and Jesus is to be found at the end of the 3d volume of the Loeb Library translation of Josephus.)

For many years the standard translation of Josephus' works into English was that of William Whiston in 1737, which has been reprinted at least 217 times. The translation has undoubted virility, but is based on Haverkamp's inferior 1726 text, is full of outright errors, and in its notes has such strange notions as that Josephus was an Ebionite Christian and a bishop of Jerusalem.

The Loeb Classical Library edition, by Henry St. J. Thackeray et al. (originally in nine volumes, now reprinted in ten volumes [London, 1926–65]) contains an eclectic Greek text which is dependent on Niese and Naber, with relatively few original emendations. The translation is often rather free, the commentary (frequently indebted to

Reinach's French edition) is increasingly full, and there are a number of useful appendixes, especially bibliographical, in the last four volumes. Geoffrey A. Williamson's 1959 translation of *JW* (revised by E. Mary Smallwood in 1981) is popular and readable, having removed passages which appear to interrupt the narrative. Gaalya Cornfeld's 1982 translation of *JW* is often closely related to Thackeray's Loeb version; it has an extensive commentary and lavish illustrations but contains many errors.

H. Scholarship on Josephus

There is no classical or Jewish author for whom we have more complete or more fully annotated bibliographies than Josephus. Schreckenberg (1968), covering the period from the appearance of the editio princeps of the Latin translation in 1470 to 1965, lists 2207 entries; but the arrangement is year by year instead of by subject matter; there are numerous omissions; summaries are missing from a large number of items; and there are many errors, as is inevitable in this kind of work. His supplement (1979), arranged alphabetically by author, in which he attempts to be complete through 1975, has 1453 entries. Feldman (1986) has approximately 2600 entries, arranged alphabetically by author, of which about 900 cover the period from 1976 through 1984, while approximately 1900 are items that Schreckenberg missed, and the remainder contain summaries where Schreckenberg lacked them. This work also supplies indexes of citations and of Gk words in Josephus, both of which are missing from Schreckenberg's second volume. It also lists nearly 300 corrigenda for Schreckenberg's first volume and about 200 for his second volume.

Feldman (1984) also lists 5543 entries, arranging the subject matter according to 29 major topics and 428 subtopics and presenting not only summaries but, in most cases, criticisms, often at length, of the various items and, for all major problems, an evaluation of the state of the question. He also gives a list of desideratums in the field and the reasons why such works are needed. (Corrigenda to this volume will be found in Feldman 1986.) The most recent critical bibliographies of Josephus are those by Bilde (1988) and Feldman (in Feldman and Hata 1989: 330–448).

As to works about Josephus, Hölscher (PW 9: 1934–2000) has written the most influential general survey, in which he deals especially with Josephus' sources. His theory that for *Ant* Josephus made uncritical use of an intermediate lost Hellenistic midrash is based on the hypothesis, popular with scholars of his era, that ancient authors would have found it most difficult to consult more than one source at a time; this is largely contested today.

The most original and most challenging work on Josephus remains that by Laqueur (1920), who concludes that Josephus' works reflect the circumstances of the time when he wrote, a point that has now been further developed by Schwartz (1985). The fairest and most comprehensive overall survey remains the semipopular series of lectures delivered by Henry St. J. Thackeray (1929). His most original theory, developed at some length in the work, that Josephus employed an assistant who was well versed in Sophocles for Books 15 and 16 of *Ant* and another assistant who was well acquainted with Thucydides for Books 17 through 19, has been challenged, since Sophoclean and Thucydidean words appear throughout Josephus' works (see above). Moreover, in his chapter on the *Testimonium Flavianum,* Thackeray was unduly influenced by the irrepressible Eisler (1929–30).

Shutt (1961) is concerned primarily with the relationship between Josephus' language and style and those of Nicolaus of Damascus, Dionysius of Halicarnassus, Polybius, and Strabo. His conclusions are hardly convincing, however, since many of the words cited are hardly unique with those authors.

Cohen (1979) has written the most challenging and most influential book since Laqueur (1920), to whom he is much indebted. Cohen suggests that Josephus used a preliminary draft for both *JW* and *Life* but that he modified it less in *Life;* however, such a theory is hard to substantiate, since we do not have a single fragment of the memoir; and we may well ask why Josephus did not use such a document for all the material common to *JW* and *Life.* Moreover, Cohen is hypercritical of Josephus' credibility except when it fits into his own theory that Josephus indeed originally backed the revolt against the Romans as he admits. Cohen argues that after Josephus surrendered, he invented a moderate faction to make it appear that he had not been alone in his defection.

Rajak (1983) in a useful, if less challenging, corrective to Cohen, interprets Josephus' social, educational, and linguistic background in the light of what can be known of his contemporaries and their attitudes. The book focuses on the Jewish revolt against the Romans, which the author interprets in the comparative light of other revolutions. Two collections of essays by various scholars have also appeared (Feldman and Hata 1987, 1989).

Bibliography

Bilde, P. 1988. *Flavius Josephus between Jerusalem and Rome.* Sheffield.

Cohen, S. J. D. 1979. *Josephus in Galilee and Rome.* Leiden.

Eisler, R. 1929–30. *Iesous Basileus ou Basileusas.* 2 vols. Heidelberg.

Feldman, L. 1984. *Josephus and Modern Scholarship (1937–1980).* Berlin.

———. 1986. *Josephus: A Supplementary Bibliography.* New York.

Feldman, L., and Hata, G., eds. 1987. *Josephus, Judaism, and Christianity.* Detroit.

———. 1989. *Josephus, the Bible, and History.* Detroit.

Feuchtwanger, L. 1932. *Der jüdische Krieg.* Berlin.

———. 1936. *The Jew of Rome.* Trans. W. and E. Muir. New York.

———. 1942. *Josephus and the Emperor.* Trans. C. Oram. New York.

Kahle, P. 1959. *The Cairo Geniza.* 2d ed. Oxford.

Kottek, H. 1886. *Das sechste Buch des Bellum Judaicum.* Diss., Leipzig and Berlin.

Ladouceur, D. J. 1977. Studies in the Language and Historiography of Flavius Josephus. Ph.D. diss., Brown University.

Laqueur, R. 1920. *Der jüdische Historiker Flavius Josephus.* Geissen.

Meščerskij, N. 1958. *History of the War of the Jews of Flavius Josephus in Old Russian.* Moscow and Leningrad (in Russian).

Mommsen, T. 1870. Cornelius Tacitus and Cluvius Rufus. *Hermes* 4: 295–335.

Morton, A. Q., and Michaelson, S. 1973. Elision as an Indicator of Authorship in Greek Writers. *Revue de l'Organisation Internationale pour l'Etude des Langues Anciennes par Ordinateur* 3: 33–56.

Pines, S. 1971. *An Arabic Version of the Testimonium Flavianum and Its Implications.* Jerusalem.
Rajak, T. 1983. *Josephus: The Historian and His Society.* London.
Rengstorf, K. H. 1973–83. *A Complete Concordance to Flavius Josephus.* 4 vols. Leiden.
Schalit, A. 1965. Evidence of an Aramaic Source in Josephus' "Antiquities of the Jews." *ASTI* 4: 163–85.
———. 1968. *König Herodes.* Berlin.
Schreckenberg, H. 1968. *Bibliographie zu Flavius-Josephus.* Leiden. Supplementary volume, 1979.
———. 1972. *Die Flavius-Josephus-Tradition in Antike und Mittelalter.* Leiden.
Schwartz, S. 1985. Josephus and Judaism from 70 to 100 of the Common Era. Diss., Columbia University.
Shutt, R. J. H. 1961. *Studies in Josephus.* London.
Thackeray, H. St. J. 1929. *Josephus the Man and the Historian.* New York. Repr. 1967.
Thackeray, H. St. J., and Marcus, R. 1930–55. *A Lexicon to Josephus.* 4 fascicles. Paris.
Zeitlin, S. 1962–63. Josippon. *JQR* 53: 277–97.

LOUIS H. FELDMAN

JOSES (PERSON) [Gk *Iōsēs*]. Greek equivalent of the Hebrew Joseph (Mark 6:3 = Matt 13:55; Mark 15:40 = Matt 27:56).

1. Brother of Jesus (Mark 6:3). The meaning of the word *brother* is uncertain. It is simplest to understand Jesus' brothers as the sons of Joseph and Mary born after Jesus. In general the early Church Fathers understood them to be the children of Joseph by a previous marriage. Beginning with Jerome, many have held that they were Jesus' cousins, the children of Mary's sister. See JESUS, BROTHERS AND SISTERS OF.

2. Son of one of the women named Mary who witnessed Jesus' crucifixion (Mark 15:40) and burial (Mark 15:47). Some argue that this Mary was the sister of Jesus' mother (John 19:25); and thus Joses was Jesus' cousin, to be identified with the Joses in #1 above. Both Joseses listed above probably needed no further identification because they were well-known to the first readers of the gospel. In Acts 4:36 some manuscripts read Joses for Joseph, the given name of Barnabas, Paul's companion.

GARETH LEE COCKERILL

JOSHAH (PERSON) [Heb *yôshâ*]. A descendant of Simeon (1 Chr 4:34), described as one of the "princes in their families" (1 Chr 4:38). The name may mean "Yahweh is a gift." In the LXX the name appears as *Ios[e]ia.* (Lucian reads *Ioas;* the Vg *Iosa.*) See Williamson *Chronicles* NCBC, 62.

CRAIG A. EVANS

JOSHAPHAT (PERSON) [Heb *yôšāpāṭ*]. **1.** A Mithnite, one of David's warriors, a member of "the Thirty" (1 Chr 11:43). The addition in Chronicles (1 Chr 11:41b–47) to the list in 2 Sam 23:8–39 (= 1 Chr 11:8–41a) contains several references to cities or regions in Transjordan (Reuben, Ashteroth, Aroer, Moab), and it is possible that "Mithnite" (LXX^{B,S} "Bethanite"), the descriptive adjective applied to Joshaphat, refers to an otherwise unknown locality in that region (along with other terms in the list: Mahavite, Mezobaite; see Williamson *Chronicles* NCBC, 103–4). The total number of names in the list exceeds 30; by reading *šālîšîm,* "officers" instead of *šĕlōšîm,* "thirty" this list would name members of David's officer corps rather than a distinctive military unit called "the Thirty." The Chronicler has doubled the list of warriors who supported David (1 Chr 11:41b–12:40) beyond that contained in the parallel narrative (2 Sam 23:8–39 = 1 Chr 11:10–41a); the source for these additional lists can only be a matter of conjecture. The long list reflects his concern to show "all Israel" united in support for David, a characteristic theme of the Chronicler's history.

2. One of the priests appointed by David to blow trumpets during the transfer of the ark from the house of Obed-edom to Jerusalem (1 Chr 15:24).

Bibliography

Mazar, B. 1963. The Military Elite of King David. *VT* 13: 310–20.
Na᾽aman, N. 1988. The List of David's Officers (SALISIM). *VT* 38: 71–79.
Williamson, H. G. M. 1981. We Are Yours, O David. *OTS* 21: 164–76.

RAYMOND B. DILLARD

JOSHAVIAH (PERSON) [Heb *yôšawyāh*]. A son of Elnaam and brother of Jeribai (1 Chr 11:46), one of the mighty men of David's armies (1 Chr 11:46). These names appear in a list occasionally described as the "additional" mighty men—16 in number (1 Chr 11:41b–47)—since they are not included in the parallel list in 2 Sam 23:24–39 (= 1 Chr 11:26–41a). The origin of this additional list has been disputed: some consider it a postexilic fabrication, yet the E Jordanian locale suggested by the names (e.g., all the known sites are E of the Jordan: Reuben, v 42; Ashteroth . . . Aroer, v 44; Moab, v 46) appears to be an unlikely invention, considering the suspicion regarding this area after the Exile. That David would have support from Moab is not surprising, considering (1) his Moabite ancestry (Ruth 4:18–22) and (2) the sequestering of his parents there (1 Sam 22:3–4). This list probably was an additional fragment available to the Chronicler (Williamson *1 and 2 Chronicles* NCBC, 104), so we suggest that Joshaviah was a Transjordanian war hero who joined David's forces. See also DAVID'S CHAMPIONS.

JOHN C. ENDRES

JOSHBEKASHAH (PERSON) [Heb *yošbĕqāšâ*]. One of the 14 sons of Heman who were appointed to prophesy with musical instruments under the direction of their father and the king (1 Chr 25:4). Joshbekashah received the 17th lot cast to determine duties (1 Chr 25:24). Scholars have long suggested that the final nine names in 1 Chr 25:4 can be read as a liturgical prayer. For instance, Joshbekashah could be understood as a participial form of the verb *yšb* followed by the word *qāšâ,* a feminine adjective which is used elsewhere as a noun (Ps 60:5—Eng 60:3). The resulting translation would be "sitting (in) adversity," and the phrase would form part of the fourth line of the liturgical prayer reconstructed by scholars. For a reconstruction and translation of the prayer, a summary of interpretative possibilities, and bibliography, see ELIATHAH.

J. CLINTON MCCANN, JR.

JOSHEB-BASSHEBETH (PERSON) [Heb *yōšeb baššebet*]. Found only at 2 Sam 23:8, the name belongs to one of David's mighty men. See DAVID'S CHAMPIONS. The name is unusual in form in the Hebrew onomasticon; the name Jashobeam at the corresponding point in 1 Chr 11:11 has led to explanation of Josheb-basshebeth as a corruption of an original **yišbaʿal* (so *IPN,* 247). The name was perhaps first altered by dysphemic pronunciation of the theophoric element as *bōšet* (see also ISH-BOSHETH).

PHILIP C. SCHMITZ

JOSHIBIAH (PERSON) [Heb *yôšibyāh*]. Son of Seriah, a descendant of Simeon (1 Chr 4:35), described as one of the "princes in their families" (1 Chr 4:38). The name probably means "Yahweh causes to dwell." In the LXX the name appears as *Isabia.* See Williamson *Chronicles* NCBC, 62.

CRAIG A. EVANS

JOSHUA (PERSON) [Heb *yĕhôšûaʿ*]. Var. JESHUA. Five persons in the Bible bear this name. Outside the biblical corpus, Joshua ben Hananiah was an important early rabbinic sage (#6 below).

1. The man who served as Moses' "servant"/"minister" (Heb *mĕšārēt:* Exod 24:13; Josh 1:1) during the wilderness period, and subsequently led the Israelite entry into Canaan, and apportioned the land to the respective tribes. Joshua's territorial inheritance (Josh 19:49–50), his burial site (Josh 24:30), and the genealogical note in 1 Chr 7:27 all indicate that he belonged to the tribe of Ephraim. Num 13:16 reports that Moses renamed Hoshea as Joshua ("Yahweh is salvation"), apparently to explain why a person living in a generation born before the sacred Tetragrammaton was revealed (Exod 6:3) was given a "Yahweh" name.

Joshua first appeared in the Bible as a warrior who fought, at Moses' command, against the Amalekites (Exod 17:9–13). As a sort of cultic apprentice, he accompanied Moses onto Mt. Sinai (Exod 24:13; 32:15–18); and he served at the tent of meeting (Exod 33:11; cf. Acts 7:44–45). Among the 12 spies sent to reconnoiter Canaan (Numbers 13–14), only Joshua and Caleb trusted that Yahweh could lead Israel to victory in the promised land.

As Moses approached the time of his death, the Lord instructed him to designate Joshua as his successor (Num 27:12–23; Deut 3:23–28); and the book of Joshua relates how Joshua faithfully carried out the commands of Moses as he executed the double task of leading the Israelites into the promised land and putting them in possession of it (cf. Lohfink 1962). Following Israel's settlement in Canaan, Joshua led the gathered Israelites in a renewal of the covenant with Yahweh (Joshua 24).

Efforts to reconstruct the history of the traditions underlying the Joshua stories have usually concluded that most of the references to Joshua in the Pentateuch are secondary insertions (Möhlenbrink 1943; Noth *HPT,* 175–77) and therefore do not reflect historical reality. For example, a critical reading of Num 13:30–31; Deut 1:34–37; and Josh 14:6–8 suggests that there was a preliminary stage of the spy story of Numbers 13–14 in which there was only one spy—Caleb—who exhibited appropriate faith in Yahweh. See CALEB. Because tradition assigns Moses and Joshua to tribes (Levi and Ephraim) which probably had different historical origins and settlement histories (cf. Ramsey 1981: 65–68, 84–88), there is some question as to whether the two men were historically associated with each other.

According to a widely held thesis, the entire block of material from Joshua through 2 Kings in the Hebrew Bible was composed by an individual or a school, the Deuteronomistic Historian(s) (Dtr), who lived in the late 7th to mid-6th century B.C. (Noth *NDH;* cf. Cross *CMHE,* 274–89) and utilized a variety of sources, of varying historical value. Some tradition critics have concluded that the sources for Joshua 2–9 belonged to the genre of *etiological sagas* and have minimal historical value (Alt *KlSchr,* 176–92; Noth *Josua* HAT, 11–12; Fohrer 1968: 200–201). In any case it is frequently questioned whether the Ephraimite Joshua would likely have been a central figure in events leading to occupation of Benjaminite territory (Joshua 2–9). Some historians (e.g., Alt *KlSchr,* 176–92; Gottwald 1979: 153) theorize that Joshua established a reputation as a warrior in the battle of Beth-horon (Josh 10:1–15), a site on Ephraimite soil. This reputation, plus his decisive role in the Shechem assembly (Joshua 24) led to his name's being incorporated into other stories of neighboring regions. Noth (*Josua* HAT, 61, 139) acknowledged Joshua's role in the Shechem assembly but believed that the original hero of the battle of Beth-horon was a now-unknown Benjaminite hero whom Joshua displaced as the account was transmitted. Another proposal (Weinfeld 1988: 329–32) is that it was Joshua's settlement of Timnath-serah (Josh 19:50) that established his military reputation and eventually led to a magnified role. Yet another theory is that virtually the entire body of Joshua material is fiction created by Dtr and even later writers (Van Seters 1983: 322–37).

A different group of scholars has argued that etiology can be shown not to have been a controlling motive in the Conquest stories and that the testimony of archaeological evidence generally confirms the historicity of these narratives (cf. Albright 1963: 24–34). Consequently, while acknowledging that the settlement in Canaan was more complicated than the account in Joshua implies, they have credited to Joshua a historical role which is much closer to that reported in the OT (cf. *IDB* 2: 546–48; *BHI,* 129–43; de Vaux *EHI,* 593–680; Boling and Wright *Joshua* AB, 72; but see 212 and 243–44).

The sources underlying the accounts of the territorial assignments (Joshua 13–21) are dated to the period of the Monarchy by most scholars (Soggin *Joshua* OTL, 11–14; Gottwald 1979: 155–63) and therefore cannot be taken as reflecting actual events from Joshua's day. Bright (*IDB* 2: 545) and Gottwald (1979: 160), who may be taken as representatives of the conservative and the revisionist wings of critical historical scholarship, respectively, concur that it was Dtr who introduced the motif of Joshua presiding over the allotment of the promised land.

The historical reconstructions just mentioned all rely to a considerable degree on inferences about stages of the traditions' development prior to the final form of the narrative. Another approach to the Joshua material, less interested in recovering the historical facts, examines the literary or theological characterization of Joshua in the canonical text. What understandings of Joshua are proffered by the narrative now before us (which is the one stage of the tradition of whose shape we can be certain)?

Close reading reveals that the biblical narrative portrays Joshua as more than just a successor to Moses. Numerous passages seem consciously to portray him as an antitype of Moses (cf. Wenham 1971: 145–46; Childs *IOTS*, 245). The Lord assures Joshua that the divine presence will accompany him as it did Moses (Josh 1:5; 3:7; cf. 4:14). The crossing of the Jordan, led by Joshua, is described as analogous to the crossing of the Red Sea (Josh 4:23). Joshua's encounter with the commander of the army of Yahweh (Josh 5:13–15) exhibits a striking resemblance to Moses' encounter with the angel of Yahweh at the burning bush (Exod 3:2–5). Joshua exercises the authority to reinterpret or even suspend divine commands spoken to Moses (Josh 6:17; 8:27; cf. Polzin 1980: 73–145). Joshua 12 juxtaposes a summary of Joshua's military feats (vv 7–24) to those of Moses (vv 1–6). Joshua's assignment of the inheritances for nine and one-half tribes W of the Jordan is paralleled to the similar work by Moses for the Transjordanian tribes (Josh 13:8–33 = 14:1–19:51). Joshua's function as covenant mediator in Joshua 24 resembles that of Moses at Sinai (Exodus 20–24). The note of Joshua's death (Josh 24:29) assigns to him the epithet "servant of Yahweh," which was frequently used of Moses (e.g., Josh 1:1; 8:31).

The canonical tradition, of course, does not grant Joshua status fully equal with that of Moses. A few passages explicitly assign Joshua a role inferior to that of Moses (Num 11:26–29; 27:20–21). Also, the deeds of Moses outstrip those of Joshua; and the signs and wonders performed by Moses are much more numerous (e.g., Exodus 7–11; 14:21–31; 15:22–25; 17:1–7; Num 20:2–13). Joshua functions occasionally as an intercessor for the people (cf. Josh 7:6–9), but not nearly so often as Moses (e.g., see Exod 32:11–14; Num 11:2; 12:13; 14:13–19; 21:7). In addition, Joshua's speaking for the Lord (see further below) is not nearly so extensive as is Moses' (cf. numerous passages in Deuteronomy); and the teaching and law giving of Moses are normative for both Joshua and the Israelites (e.g., Josh 1:7–8, 13; 4:10; 8:30–35; 11:12–15; 22:2; 23:6). Finally, the NT contains a scant 3 references to Joshua, in contrast to around 80 for Moses.

The portrait of Joshua contains a number of elements which elsewhere appear in connection with kings. The commissioning episode in Num 27:15–23 speaks of Joshua as one who will "go out and come in" before the people of Israel, that they may not be as "sheep which have no shepherd." This terminology refers to leadership in battle, usually associated with a royal figure (e.g., 2 Sam 5:2; 1 Kgs 22:17; 2 Kgs 11:8). The charge to Joshua in Josh 1:2–9 utilizes language associated with the installation of monarchs (cf. Deut 17:18–20; 1 Kgs 2:1–5; Porter 1970). Nelson (1981) submits that the parallels between Joshua and King Josiah (in whose time Dtr likely lived and wrote) are especially notable and that the Joshua story provided historical precedent for Josiah's revolutionary reforms. The description of faithful Josiah in 2 Kgs 22:2 is the only text besides Josh 1:7 and 23:6 to express total obedience to the law by the phrase borrowed from Deut 17:20, "turning not from it to the right hand or to the left." Both Joshua and Josiah gathered everyone to hear the Book of the Law and renew the covenant (Josh 8:30–35; 2 Kgs 23:2–3). The Passover celebration in Josh 5:10–12 may be seen as a model for Josiah's observance (2 Kgs 23:21–23).

Later Jewish traditions referred to Joshua as a prophet (Sir 46:1; *Eup.* [Eus. *Praep. Evang.* 9.30.1]; Jos. *Ant* 4.7.2; 4.8.46), and this characterization is not without foundation in the biblical narratives. It is true that certain Priestly texts imply that, unlike Moses, Joshua needed priestly mediation (Num 27:15–23; Josh 14:1; 19:51). But in the book of Joshua, the Lord often speaks directly to Joshua (e.g., Josh 1:1; 3:7; 4:1, 15; 8:18; 20:1). Joshua uses the prophetic formula, "Thus says Yahweh" (Josh 7:13; 24:2). 1 Kgs 16:34, in an allusion to Josh 6:26, reports the fulfillment of "the word of Yahweh, which he spoke by Joshua the son of Nun." As did the later prophets, Joshua exercises the intercessory function (Josh 7:6–9; cf. 2 Esdr 7:107) in a fashion similar to Moses (Exod 32:11–13; Num 14:13–19). It is not entirely impossible that the author considered Joshua to be the "prophet like Moses" referred to in Deut 18:15–19.

Bibliography

Albright, W. F. 1963. *The Biblical Period from Abraham to Ezra.* New York.

Fohrer, G. 1968. *Introduction to the OT.* Trans. D. Green. Nashville.

Gottwald, N. K. 1979. *The Tribes of Yahweh.* Maryknoll, NY.

Lohfink, N. 1962. Die deuteronomische Darstellung des Übergangs der Führung Israels von Moses auf Josue. *Scholastik* 37: 32–44.

Möhlenbrink, K. 1943. Josua im Pentateuch. *ZAW* 59: 14–58.

Nelson, R. D. 1981. Josiah in the Book of Joshua. *JBL* 100: 531–40.

Polzin, R. 1980. *Moses and the Deuteronomist.* New York.

Porter, J. R. 1970. The Succession of Joshua. Pp. 102–32 in *Proclamation and Presence,* ed. J. I. Durham and J. R. Porter. Richmond.

Ramsey, G. W. 1981. *The Quest for the Historical Israel.* Atlanta.

Van Seters, J. 1983. *In Search of History.* New Haven.

Weinfeld, M. 1988. Historical Facts behind the Israelite Settlement Pattern. *VT* 38: 324–32.

Wenham, G. J. 1971. The Deuteronomic Theology of the Book of Joshua. *JBL* 90: 140–48.

George W. Ramsey

2. The reputed governor of Jerusalem during the reign of King Josiah (2 Kgs 23:8). He is linked, probably on the basis of his position as governor, with the high places of the "gates" (or, following other pointings, "satyrs" or "genii"; see Jones *Kings* NCBC, 621), which high places were destroyed at the entrance of the city. Although the exact location of the two gates referred to is unknown (Robinson *2 Kings* CBC, 220), it is probable that one standing in the city gate had the door to Joshua's home on his left (Rehm

Kings EB, 215). Yadin thinks that the reference in the verse is not to a gate in Jerusalem but to a gate in Beer-sheba which was near the governor's house. He believes that he has found the *bāmôt* (the word for "high places" may be translated as a singular item) referred to (see Shanks 1977: 4–12; contra Rainey 1977, who sees the altar as dismantled probably by Hezekiah before 701 B.C.). There is no further biblical or extrabiblical record of this Joshua (Rehm *Kings* EB, 223).

3. A son of Jehozadak, and the high priest and consequently religious leader to whom the 6th-century prophet Haggai delivered his message, along with Zerubbabel, governor of Judah (Hag 1:1; 2:2). Jehozadak was son of Seraiah (1 Chr 6:14–15), the chief priest killed by Nebuchadnezzar at Riblah after the destruction of Jerusalem (cf. 2 Kgs 25:18ff.; Jer 52:24ff.), and brother of Ezra the scribe (Ezra 7:1). Joshua and his brother were apparently born and reared in Babylon and were among the earliest to return from Exile. This description has been questioned by many scholars, especially in relation to the faithfulness of the Chronicler's account and the succession of the priesthood (see Mitchell, et al. *Haggai, Zechariah, Malachi and Jonah* ICC, 44). The book of Haggai records that Joshua was receptive to Haggai's exhortation regarding the condition of the temple (Hag 2:4) and that he, along with the remnant of the people, obeyed the voice of God and worked at rebuilding it (Hag 1:12, 14). Zechariah (6:11) says that when a group of exiles returned from Babylon, Zechariah was instructed by God to take their silver and gold and make a crown to put upon the head of Joshua, calling him Branch, as a symbol of his rebuilding the temple. But Mitchell et al. question whether this was the original reading, since this command contradicts other teaching in Zechariah and Haggai which says that Zerubbabel fulfilled the messianic prophecies. Thus Zerubbabel's name may have been used here and corrected by a later scribe who wanted to align this account with history, since no descendant of Zerubbabel is recorded as becoming high priest of the entire community (Mitchell et al., 185–86). Other scholars posit that both were crowned, and some that the text is correct as it stands (see Barker 1977). This person is probably the same one known in Ezra and Nehemiah as JESHUA, son of Jozadak, in which case the only other pertinent information about this Joshua is that some of his descendants married foreign women (Ezra 10:18; Baldwin *Haggai, Zechariah, Malachi* TOTC, 39).

4. A man from Beth-shemesh who owned a field in which the ark of the covenant stopped on its return from the Philistines to the people of Israel in Kiriath-jearim (1 Sam 6:14). Possibly reference is to the man who owned the field during the time of the narrator of the account (McCarter (*1 Samuel* AB, 136). The ark is recorded as being placed upon or beside a stone in his field (the stone did not serve as an altar, as v 14 might imply—see Gordon 1986: 102; contra Rehm *Samuel* EB, 19, n. 14), while the cart on which the ark was riding was split up so that a sacrifice of the milch cows pulling it could be made (1 Sam 6:18). McCarter *1 Samuel* AB, 137) contends that reference to the stone adds verisimilitude to the story, and Klein (*1 Samuel* WBC, 59) notes that the narrator does not recognize the apparent conflict of this sacrifice of cows with the OT law which mandated unblemished males (Lev 1:3; 22:19), possibly evidencing the antiquity of the elements in the account. There is no other record of this Joshua.

5. The father of Er and son of Eliezer according to Luke's genealogy tying Joseph, the "supposed father" of Jesus, to descent from Adam and God (Luke 3:29). Joshua is omitted in D, which substitutes a genealogy adapted from Matt 1:6–15 for Luke 3:23–31. The name Joshua as an ancestor of Jesus occurs nowhere else in the biblical documents, including Matthew's genealogy, and falls within a list of 18 otherwise unknown descendants of David's son Nathan (Fitzmyer *Luke 1–9* AB, 501). Joshua is not included in Kuhn's (1923: 207–11) discussion of the supposed parallel lists of names in Luke 3:23–26 and 29–31.

Bibliography

Barker, M. 1977. The Two Figures in Zechariah. *HeyJ* 18: 38–46.

Gordon, R. P. 1986. *1 and 2 Samuel.* Exeter.

Kuhn, G. 1923. Die Geschlechtsregister Jesu bei Lukas und Matthäus. *ZNW* 22: 206–28.

Rainey, A. F. 1977. Beer-Sheva Excavator Blasts Yadin—No Bama at Beer-Sheva. *BARev* 3: 18–20, 56.

Shanks, H. 1977. Yigael Yadin Finds a Bama at Beer-sheva. *BARev* 3: 3–12.

STANLEY E. PORTER

6. Joshua ben Hananiah was a Palestinian rabbinic sage active during the early period of Yavneh (Jamnia), from the destruction of the temple in 70 to before the Bar Kokhba rebellion. *M. ʾAbot* 2:8 lists him as a disciple of Yohanan ben Zakkai, the putative founder of rabbinism. No ancient source outside of rabbinic literature attests to Joshua's existence.

The earliest and most historically useful materials about Joshua are halakic opinions that first appear in the Mishnah, ca. A.D. 200, perhaps 75 years after his death. These materials, nearly one-third of which are in the order of Purities (*Ṭohorot*), were not redacted independently; and Joshua rarely appears alone in them. In over three-quarters of them his teaching is reported with that of sages or a named master, and nearly half of the earliest materials are disputes with Eliezer ben Hyrcanus. Akiba appears to have been a major tradent of Joshua's opinions.

Because Joshua's early teachings are so integrated with those of other masters and so shaped by the redaction of the Mishnah, they do not display a distinctive religious philosophy. However, in a set of disputes with Eliezer (*m. Ter.* 8:1–3; *Pesaḥ.* 6:5; *Šabb.* 19:4), Joshua rules that if a person performs a forbidden act under the assumption that it is permitted, he/she should not be penalized for the improper behavior. This view of the importance of intention in determining liability, particularly for handling heave offering, is important in teachings assigned to Ushan masters but not Yavneans; and it appears to be the dominant view of the Mishnah as a whole. Joshua's teaching may have played a role in the development of early rabbinism's position on the question of intention, especially in matters pertaining to the cult.

The early materials contain little biographical information about Joshua. *M. Maʿas. Š.* 5:9 implies that he was a Levite, and a long narrative at *m. Roš Haš.* 2:8–9 depicts him in opposition to Gamaliel II's declaration of the new moon and thus in conflict with the Yavnean patriarchate.

Later materials also depict Joshua as an opponent of the patriarchate (*y. Ber.* 4:1 7c–d; *Taᶜan.* 4:1 67d; *b. Ber.* 27b–28a). Other traditions place him in Peqiᵓin (*b. Sanh.* 32a) and allege that he was a poor needle maker or blacksmith (*y. Ber.* 4:1 7d; *b. Ber.* 28a).

Joshua is perhaps best known because of the story of the oven of Akhnai (*b. B. Meṣ.* 59b), in which, by quoting Deut 30:12 ("It [the Torah] is not in heaven"), he in principle rejects divine intervention in the interpretation of Scripture. He is alleged to have joined Eliezer in effecting Yohanan ben Zakkai's escape from Jerusalem in 70 (*ᵓAbot R. Nat.* A, chap. 4, B; chap. 6; *b. Giṭ.* 56a; *Lam. Rab.* 1.5.31) and to have opposed a Jewish rebellion against Hadrian (*Gen. Rab.* 64:10). The provenance and historicity of these later, mostly legendary, materials are difficult to determine. See also *EncJud* 10: 279–81; Avery-Peck 1985: 272–73.

Bibliography

Avery-Peck, A. J. 1985. *Mishnah's Division of Agriculture.* Chico, CA.
Eilberg-Schwartz, H. 1986. *The Human Will in Judaism.* Atlanta, GA.
Green, W. S. 1981. *The Traditions of Joshua ben Hananiah.* Leiden.

WILLIAM SCOTT GREEN

JOSHUA, BOOK OF. The sixth book of the Hebrew Bible and first book of the Former Prophets in the OT canon. It describes the Israelite invasion of Canaan, followed by division of the land into territories assigned by sacred lot to the tribes of Israel. It is titled after the central figure in the book, Joshua son of Nun.

A. Outline of Contents
B. Context and Canonical Form
 1. Classic Theme of Biblical Tradition
 2. Stories and Lists in Editorial Frameworks
C. The Book of Joshua in Modern Study
 1. The Primary History: Tetrateuch and Deuteronomistic Corpus
 2. History of Traditions
 3. Archaeology and Social World
 4. Elohistic Israel and Yahwistic Israel
 5. Levitical Sponsorship: Dtn, Dtr 1, Dtr 2

A. Outline of Contents

The canonical book of Joshua follows a roughly sequential pattern. There are five major parts to the book: (1) theological moblization and entrance into the land (1:1–5:12); (2) the warfare in Canaan (5:13–11:23); (3) the inheritance (12:1–19:51); (4) provisions for keeping the peace and the teaching (20:1–21:45); (5) threat of civil war and how to avoid it (22:1–34); and (6) end of the era (23:1–24:33). Each of these, in turn, can be subdivided into smaller parts.

1. Theological Moblization and Entrance into the Land (1:1–5:12)
 a. Marching Orders (1:1–18)
 b. Reconnaissance of Jericho (2:1–24)
 c. Crossing the Jordan (3:1–4:18)
 d. Encampment at Gilgal (4:19–5:12)
  (1) Ecumenical Rationale and Royal Reaction (4:19–5:1)
  (2) Resumption of Circumcision (5:2–9)
  (3) Resumption of Passover (5:10–12)
2. Warfare in Canaan (5:13–11:23)
 a. First Phase: South and Central Hills (5:13–10:43)
  (1) The Angelic Commander (5:13–15)
  (2) Jericho: Destruction and Curse (6:1–27)
  (3) Ai ("The Ruin"): Two Battles (7:1–8:29)
  (4) Shechem Covenant (8:30–35)
  (5) South-central Canaan (9:1–10:39)
  (6) Summary of the First Phase (10:40–43)
 b. Second Phase: Hazor and the Far North (11:1–15)
 c. Summary of Conquest (11:16–23)
3. The Inheritance (12:1–19:51)
 a. List of the Former Kingdoms (12:1–24)
 b. Redistribution of the Land (13:1–19:51)
  (1) Land that Remained to Be Taken (13:1–7)
  (2) Retrospect: Moses and Transjordanian Territories (13:8–33)
  (3) Cisjordanian Territories: Early Phase (14:1–17:18)
  (4) Cisjordanian Territories: Shiloh Phase (18:1–19:51)
4. Provisions for Keeping the Peace and the Teaching (20:1–21:45)
 a. Cities of Refuge, to Counter Blood Feud (20:1–9)
 b. Residential and Pasture Rights for the Levites (21:1–42)
 c. Summary: Yahweh True to His Word (21:43–45)
5. Threat of Civil War and How to Avoid It (22:1–34)
 a. Transjordanian Tribes: Exhortation, Blessing, Dismissal (22:1–8)
 b. Religious Strife and Resolution without Joshua (22:9–34)
6. End of the Era (23:1–24:33)
 a. Joshua's Farewell Address; Ending in Threat (23:1–16)
 b. The Shechem Covenant; Beginning with Promise (24:1–28)
 c. Various Burial Notices (24:29–33)

B. Context and Canonical Form

1. Classic Theme of Biblical Tradition. The book of Joshua—which presupposes and continues a story line that begins in the book of Exodus (how Yahweh liberated a group of state slaves in Egypt and reconstituted them, by covenant in the Sinai Wilderness, to be a special possession of Yahweh, who claims ownership of all the earth) and continues through Numbers (a generation spent wandering in the wilderness) and Deuteronomy (renewal of covenant on Moab)—recounts a classic theme in biblical tradition: how Israel came to be established in the land of Canaan. Yahweh gave Israel a land on which to live, astride the Jordan, with Yahweh as their only sovereign. Many city-kingdoms had been destroyed (Joshua 1–12), the redistributed land generally pacified (chaps. 13–22), and the covenant renewed yet again (chaps. 23–24).

The "Conquest" as Yahweh's gift, a supreme example of divine grace, was a recurring motif in stories told for both edification and entertainment, in which parents and teacher-priests explained to children and worshippers the meaning of their life together as Israelites (Joshua 2–11). It was a theme regularly sung in worship, exalting Yahweh as the ultimate power at work in the world—protecting the weak and breaking the chains of bondage—so that in the Bible love and justice became virtual synonyms, also known as righteousness (see for example, Pss 44:1–8; 78:54–55; 80:8–9, 11; 105:43–45; 106:34–38; 114:1–8; 135:10–12; 136:17–22).

Prophets in Israel and Judah used the same theme, in many of the same ways, but more frequently as expressions of God's prior beneficence, forming the background to the Sovereign's indictment for breach of covenant (see for example Hosea 11; 13:4–6; Amos 2:9–10; Micah 4–6; Jer 2:6–7; 32:20–23; Ezek 20:5–6).

It is a curious fact, however, that in their allusions to the "Conquest" era, psalmists and prophets make only generalized references to the takeover of W Palestine (recounted at length in Joshua), while frequently making specific reference to the prior era, the movement into Transjordan under leadership of Moses (stories in Numbers 21–35, which are only summarized briefly in Joshua through a flashback in 13:8–33). Thus the book of Joshua reflects a complicated process of tradition formation and literary composition, extending from experiences which early generated nuclear stories to the time of the final editors, reflecting both the spectacular rise and tragic fall of the N and S monarchies (Wright *Joshua* AB, 5–27). It is the long history of some 600 years subsequent to the career of Joshua that will explain the didactic arrangement and rhetorical structure of the finished book, incorporating complementary perspectives from the end of the monarchic era. The old story of victorious entrance into the land that was God's gift was edited for the last time not long before or after the Babylonian invasions of 598 and 587 B.C.E. It is less widely recognized, perhaps, that the idealized story of Joshua as military commander par excellence was finally told with a lively sense of humor and priestly self-irony, of a sort rarely encountered outside the ancient Scriptures.

2. Stories and Lists in Editorial Frameworks. While mere mention of Joshua may evoke mental images of massive invasion by a unified national army, proceeding to victories of something like genocidal proportions (an image which indeed seems to be mirrored in a number of editorial passages of Joshua), the arrangement of the book and close reading evoke a different image; but one not so quick to come to sharp focus. Fully one-fifth of the total book is devoted to the crossing of the Jordan and preparations for the first battle, at the choice oasis of Jericho. Following the introduction of Joshua as commander who is to be strictly obedient to Yahweh's *tôrâ* in chap. 1, incongruities abound. Spies sent from Shittim to reconnoiter "all the land," proceed only as far as Jericho and the house of Rahab the harlot, who speaks as though she had been intently studying the book of Deuteronomy. Thus the spies, providentially, learn all that they need to know concerning "all the land."

After the elaborately detailed, ritually ordered crossing of the Jordan from Shittim to Gilgal (3:1–4:18), again providentially facilitated, the army encamped at Gilgal allows itself to be temporarily incapacitated by undergoing the ritual surgery of circumcision and then celebrates the Passover. Neither circumcision nor Passover was observed during the wilderness period according to the text, but both would become indispensable marks of Jewish identity after the Babylonian invasions and deportations. Their resumption has high didactic value at just this point in the story line.

The second major segment of the book tells a mere handful of warfare stories, beginning abruptly with an obscure pericope announcing the arrival of a heavenly warrior on holy ground (5:13–15). The unit makes sure in any case that we know who was ultimately and truly in command at the fall of Jericho, and it was not Joshua.

The victory at Jericho in chap. 6 similarly shows timely collaboration of (1) strict obedience to Yahweh's command and (2) Providence, when the walls tumble down. And yet, after all their obedient efforts, the Israelites would not be allowed to enjoy the fruits of victory. Jericho is cursed by Joshua for some unspecified reason and placed forever off-limits to Israelite settlement. Furthermore, Joshua had specified that no booty for private gain was to be taken from Jericho.

While the performance of Joshua and Israel at Jericho is presented as nearly flawless, it is just the opposite at Ai (or, more precisely Ha-Ai, "The Ruin") in the second warfare story (chap. 7). Here a serious miscalculation of opposing strength (and, it may be implied, failure to consult the oracle) led to a nearly disastrous defeat. An elaborate accounting for the defeat is given in the story of Achan's violation of the booty decree *(ḥerem)* at Jericho. In the sequel to this defeat, victory is providentially assured as Yahweh takes direct command, ordering an ambush behind the town and then drawing defenders out of "The Ruin." Scholars regularly note literary affinities with the strategy for final victory of "Israel," after two resounding defeats, in the civil war with Benjamin which concludes the wider era (Judges 20).

In Joshua the story line takes us next, for a brief interlude, to the north-central hill country, the Shechem valley, flanked by Mt. Gerizim and Mt. Ebal. On the latter Joshua built an altar. He wrote on the stones a copy of Yahweh's *tôrâ* (cf. chap. 1) and read it all, "the blessing and the curse," to the people assembled before the levitical priests charged with protective custody of Yahweh's covenant ark. In the LXX this note about the Shechem assembly is placed *after* the general Canaanite reaction, which is described next in MT.

In chap. 9 the story line returns, as abruptly as it had digressed in 8:30, to the south-central highlands, where a summit gathering of Canaanite kings is underway, while Joshua and the fighting force are to be found at Gilgal. The Hivite residents of Gibeon, speaking for a tetrapolis of villages on the N flank of Jerusalem and claiming to be, like Joshua and his followers, brand-new immigrants, trick the leaders of Israel into a defensive alliance. It is specified that Israelite leaders failed to consult the oracle. The Gibeonite embassy is familiar with the Exodus and Transjordanian conquest tradition (9:9–10), as well as Deuteronomic teaching regarding relations with distant and nearby towns (Deuteronomy 20), but makes no reference to anything that has happened thus far in Joshua 1–8. When the ruse is discovered, "the leaders of the Israelite congregation" propose a solution that assigns lowest social status (temple slaves) to the Gibeonites, which they readily accept; and Joshua is relieved of direct responsibility for the beginning of the affair. Scholars regularly note literary affinities with the tragicomic sequel to the Benjaminite civil war (Judges 21), where the "elders" similarly find an ingenious, if considerably less than admirable, way to maintain a distinctive, twelve-tribe Israelite identity.

In chap. 10 the Israelite-Gibeonite treaty triggers a coalescence of Gibeon's nearby S kingly neighbors: Adonizedek (of Jerusalem), Hoham (Hebron), Piram (Jarmuth), Japhia (Lachish), and Debir (Eglon). Joshua and the force are summoned from Gilgal, and Gibeon is spared because Yahweh providentially marshals heavenly forces (sun and moon) to participate in the right cause, that is, keeping treaty faith (10:1–14). Then, as though unaware of v 15, where Joshua and all Israel return to Gilgal, the chapter continues with another preformed story (vv 16–27) about Joshua's pursuit and capture of the five kings in a cave at Makkedah, followed by their execution and exposure of the corpses. The chapter continues with yet another distinct unit (vv 28–39) reporting successes against seven opponents as sequel to the defense of Gibeon. The list begins with Makkedah and proceeds to Libnah. In addition to Lachish and Hebron from the preceding units, it includes Eglon and Debir (both now as *town* names) and centers in a reference to Horam of Gezer, whose forces this unit understands were also involved in the Canaanite muster.

Nothing more is said, whether in narrative or archival form, in the second major segment of Joshua about warfare in the center and the S, which is hyperbolically summarized to include the Negeb (10:40–42). Except for digression to the Shechem neighborhood (8:30–35) and the sequel to the defense of Gibeon (10:16–39), all the action occurs in the narrowly restricted area that will be inherited by Benjamin (assigned and occupied, 18:11–23) and Dan (assigned but not successfully settled, 19:40–48; cf. Judg 1:34; 18:1–31).

If the convocation between Ebal and Gerizim (8:30–35) is somehow supposed to account for "all the land" between the latitude of Gibeon and the Esdraelon, then one brief story alone (11:1–23) is told to account for the entire N third of the Cisjordanian territorial claims (Esdraelon and Galilee). The victory against a mighty coalition of kings headed by Jabin of Hazor was accomplished by a strategem (hamstringing the chariot horses) considered by the narrator to be truly inspired. And it was followed through to a genocidal conclusion, down the chain of command: Yahweh to Moses, Moses to Joshua, Joshua to the Israelite forces (11:14–15). This is clearly rhetorical exaggeration, as indicated by a general summary statement (11:16–22), before we read that Joshua gave it for an inheritance to Israel "and the land was at rest from warfare" (v 23). At this point there is an abrupt transition in chap. 12; and the reader moves onto very different literary terrain, the description of territorial allotments to the tribes.

After devoting a mere one-fourth of the book to "Conquest" (chaps. 6–11, 16 columns in RSV format) but appearing to leave large geographic gaps, the finished book devotes equal space (16 columns in RSV) to redistribution of the land, leaving no gaps. Without prejudging questions of historicity (to which we shall return below), the reader encounters a mixture of idealization and redactional corrective which together yield a bifocal perspective on the entire era. In the remainder of this description it will be necessary, here and there, to include additional critical commentary.

Chapter 12 serves as a retrospective introduction to the land division, listing 31 kings on both sides of the Jordan who had been defeated by the people of Israel and had their land repossessed. The chapter has long been recognized as, in some way, secondary to the story line because it includes a number of kings and towns not mentioned anywhere else in the book.

Chapter 13, where Joshua has attained a ripe old age, begins with Yahweh reminding the aged commander of all the land that yet remained to be conquered (13:1–6), thus providing an expansive corrective to the preceding hyperbolic summaries. Then, instead of Joshua's proceeding directly to allotments for the nine and one-half tribes in Cisjordan, as he is commanded to do in v 7, narrative action is suspended for a lengthy review of the Transjordanian territories previously assigned by Moses. The section is replete with references to the narrative tradition of Numbers 21ff., takes special notice of arrested developments in central and N Transjordan (Geshur and Maacath, v 13), and twice emphasizes exceptional status for Levites (vv 14 and 33).

Chapter 14 begins as though the assignment of land to the Cisjordanian tribes is, at last, about to begin. The place of assembly is not specified; and it is now Eleazar the priest and Joshua (in that order) who preside over the sacred lot, as they do also in the summary to the section (19:51); and Shiloh (after 18:1) is specified as the place of assembly. In chap. 14, however, after a brief summary of Moses' assignment by lot to the Transjordanian tribes we read how Joshua at Gilgal (sic) receives an embassy from Judah pressing the specific claim of Caleb's clan to Hebron, promised by Moses and now honored by Joshua (14:6–15a). The unit is perhaps to be read as a flashback, although the syntax in v 6 is not disjunctive. In any case with Caleb's capture of Hebron (specifically offsetting the earlier, generalized claim to capture of Hebron by Joshua and all Israel) another Conquest story was preserved, after which we read again and for the last time that "the land was at rest from warfare" (14:15b). The repetition of this formula looks like a standard framing device, enclosing material and interests which have been either presupposed or overlooked thus far and providing the division of Cisjordan with a new introduction. The new introduction gives a priority to the priestly role in events and decision making that is otherwise played down in Joshua, except for the ritual processions, the passing references to the oracle before battle, and two appearances of the Levites as custodians of the ark of the covenant. With this "corrective," description of Cisjordanian allotments will, at last, begin.

Chapter 15 (3 of the 16 columns for the "inheritance" in RSV) is all about Judah. A description of borders (vv 1–12) and a list of towns which are readily but variously grouped by scholars into twelve districts (vv 20–62) frame another story of conquest by clans, not tribes or "all Israel" (Caleb at Hebron again and Othniel at Debir). The second is a doublet of Judg 1:11–15. While scholars generally suspect that the description of borders for Judah, and the remaining tribes, reflects a complicated history beginning in the premonarchic era, there is general agreement that the segmented list of cities in Judah reflects administrative organization from the time of David or later. The list includes a number of towns which are not otherwise mentioned in the early tradition and/or appear from archaeology to have been first settled in the 10th century or later.

Chapters 16 and 17 are all about the sons of Joseph. There is more than likely some historical connection between tribal alignments known from 18th-century Mari texts ("sons of the left [the north]" and "yaminites [southerners]") and the biblical Rachel tribes (Joseph and Benjamin). Here, however, Joseph is counted as two tribes, Ephraim and Manasseh, with the latter already partly settled E of the Jordan. The S border of "Joseph," shared with Benjamin and Dan, is sketchily described (16:1–3), before the specific description of Ephraim begins, giving a more detailed description of its border with W Manasseh (16:5–8). We also learn that there are Ephraimite towns which lie entirely within the territory of Manasseh (v 16), while Canaanites survive in Gezer "to this day" (v 10) when the redactor was living.

The inheritance of Manasseh (17:1–13) shows a distinctive form. After a general introduction (v 1), this section falls into two parts concerned with subgroups (vv 2–6) and borders (vv 7–13). First mentioned is allotment of Gilead and Bashan, in N Transjordan, to Machir, here described as the firstborn of Manasseh and "father" of Gilead. Machir (simply "son of Manasseh" in 13:31) appears to be a constituency originally concentrated in Cisjordan, where an element of it persists effectively as late as the Song of Deborah (Judg 5:14), but eventually shifted in part to Transjordan. At the outset of chap. 17 there is no hint that this assignment in Transjordan happened in the Mosaic era (thus reinforcing the scholarly hunch that chap. 13 belongs to a secondary or "corrective" stratum). Next comes a list of the rest of Manasseh's clans (a number of which do double-duty as place names in north-central Cisjordan): Abiezer, Helek, Asriel, Shechem, Hepher, and Shemida (v 2). Two of the six, Helek and Shemida, also appear as prominent locales in the Samaria ostraca.

The distinctive description of Manasseh's inheritance continues, with allotment to daughters of Zelophehad (of the clan of "Hepher" in v 2) because he had no male heirs (vv 3–6). That is, the territory of Hepher is subdivided as inheritance for the five daughters (Mahlah, Noah, Hoglah, Milcah, and Tirzah), where again the personal name, e.g., Tirzah, may also appear as a prominent place name. The result is a total of ten shares for W Manasseh. Here again, what looks like a supplementary and exceptional insertion has the priest Eleazar and Joshua, in that order, presiding.

Finally the territory of W Manasseh is described (17:7–13) in a form that intersperses border description and town list. For description of the N territories there was apparently no archival source comparable to that in the S for Judah and, as we shall see, Benjamin.

Chapter 17 concludes with yet another story where Joshua alone presides as judge (as with Caleb's petition in 14:6–15). At issue now is Ephraim's complaint about receiving only one portion (as compared, by implication, with W Manasseh's ten). Joshua's solution is to direct Ephraim to the forested hill country, with instructions to clear it and thus expand Ephraim's inhabitable terrain.

With all of chaps. 14–17 devoted to Judah and the Joseph tribes, allotments for the remaining seven Cisjordanian tribes are briefly reported, without narrative interruption. These allotments are made on the basis of an extensive land description ordered by Joshua, who alone is mentioned as presiding, in an expansive introduction to the section (18:1–10). The place of assembly is now specified as Shiloh, as in the stories of Samuel at the end of the premonarchic era.

For Benjamin the description returns to the pattern displayed for Judah, its neighbor on the S: borders (18:11–20) and segmented town list (18:21–28). The towns are numerous and close together, clustered in two groups. The E cluster (vv 21–24) includes a portion of territory extending considerably N of the border with Joseph. Here it is not a matter of making exceptions for residential, farming, or grazing rights of one tribe within territory of another (as in 16:9; 17:8; and passages pertaining to Levites). Rather, the description seems to reflect a time after the split of the monarchy when Benjamin and SE Ephraim were both administered from Jerusalem. It is probable that in a much earlier period Benjamin had ranged much farther S of its "border" with Judah, since the names of groups best known among the "Benjaminites" at Mari in the 17th century survive as extinct clans (Er and Onan, Genesis 38) in Judahite traditions (Albright 1973: 7–8). "Biblical" Benjamin was at last crowded into a narrow corridor stretching across the watershed and down to the Jordan.

Simeon's towns (19:1–9), with no trace of boundary description, fall entirely within the larger territory of Judah. It appears from the story in Genesis 34, at Shechem, that Simeon (together with Levi) had at an early period ranged much farther N.

Zebulun's inheritance (19:10–16) was a part of the poorer S extremity of the Galilee mountains and a contiguous wedge out into the Jezreel plain.

For Issachar (19:17–23) there is even less attempt to trace a border. Three fixed reference points are given (Jezreel, Tabor, Jordan river) with two segments of a town listed interspersed. Issachar, whose name means "hired man," would be the center of continuing struggle to control the fertile fields and strategic crossroads in the Jezreel, not finally won for Israel until the days of Deborah and Barak (Judges 4–5).

To Asher (19:24–31) fell one of the most prosperous areas in the land, the lush plain of Acco and its narrow N reaches as far as Rosh ha-Niqra (ancient "Ladder of Tyre"), together with territory inland from the great Canaanite cities farther N along the modern Lebanese coast. It is not clear, however, that Tyre and Sidon were considered part of Israelite territory. Again, the description is not highly unified. A fabled man named "Qazardi, chief of Aser" in papyrus Anastasi I (*ANET,* 477) may belong to the pre-Yahwist constituency called Asher. No doubt the earlier concentration of Asherites was on the W slopes of lower Galilee. Qazardi's territory has deep ravines.

Naphtali's description, borders and town list, is more coherent (19:32–39). Controlling the major trade routes connecting the coastal plain and port of Acco with all points N and NE, Naphtali enjoyed the heartland of Galilee.

Finally, Dan's entry (19:40–48) has two parts. The first (vv 40–47a) describes Dan's original allotment on the coastal plain (where its neighbors were Judah, Benjamin, and Ephraim), resembling the general form variously employed throughout these chaps.: here a few elements of border description, but mostly towns listed without directional connectives. The second part (vv 47b–48) reports continued local resistance to Dan's claim and the tribe's relocation in the far N (see Judges 17–18). In the earliest period the people of Dan may have been known as seafarers (Judg 5:17). The name is plausibly connected with one of the Sea Peoples, the Dananu, and the move to relocate in the N may well be related to events represented by destruction of Tel Qasile (founded by Sea Peoples) and its resettlement by another such group, most likely the Shardan (Yadin 1968: 9–23).

The conclusion to this third major segment of the book (19:49–51) is also in two parts. The first reports that Joshua's request for the town of Timnath-serah in the Ephraimite highlands as his personal inheritance was answered affirmatively by Yahweh and granted by the assembly. This rounds off the second phase of land division, which began in 18:1 at Shiloh, with Joshua alone named in the text. It is followed by another note in v 51, where the priest Eleazar and Joshua (in that order) have completed the task they began in 14:1.

At the end of chap. 19, with the story of Conquest told (chaps. 1–11) and redistribution of land by sacred lot completed (chaps. 12–19), the reader is left to wonder perhaps about the tribe of Levi, whose place among the "twelve tribes" seems to have been filled by division of the great N tribe of Joseph (Ephraim and Manasseh). Or, if one were not inclined to wonder about Levi, one might proceed directly to Joshua's farewell address (chap. 23) and the "all Israel" covenant at Shechem (chap. 24), with no sense of a gap but a sure sense of redundancy in the final chapters.

Chapters 20–22 must therefore be of high rhetorical significance in the canonical book. Two social institutions are here singled out for special attention before proceeding in chap. 22 to the story of Israel's life on the land, astride the Jordan river, as Yahweh's gracious gift.

The cities of refuge (chap. 20) are a special group of six towns (which also appear in the following list of levitical towns (chap. 21). There are three on each side of the Jordan (N, central, and S), designated to provide protective asylum for one who might otherwise become the innocent target of private vengeance. The plan is announced by Moses (Num 35:9–34), and the three Transjordanian towns are so designated by Moses (Deut 4:41–43), leaving appointment of three in Cisjordan as a matter for exhortation by Moses (Deut 19:1–13). While it has been argued that the system is a late (7th-century) development (McKeating 1975: 53–55), there is no reference to the institution in the historical books of 1 and 2 Samuel, 1 and 2 Kings, and 1 and 2 Chronicles; and nowhere after establishment of monarchy and strong central government are they presupposed (they were no longer needed). They are either historical (and early) or utopian, much more likely the former; for there are remarkably few examples of private vengeance in the Bible. Classic examples are seen in the stories of Gideon (Judges 8) and the anonymous N Levite (Judges 19–20), both of whom are presented in scathing caricature, probably for this reason. Cain is the exception, the guilty one who is, nevertheless, protected by deity. But Cain was not Israelite; he lived, as it were, in prehistory, as part of the universal human problem, in early Yahwist perspective. That problem is only compounded when human "vengeance" acquires rival religious sponsorship, as will nearly happen in Joshua 22.

Chapter 21 at last accounts for the Dispersion of Levites, who are to have residential and grazing rights at specified towns, 48 in all, in each of the 12 territories. Three questions persist in critical study: (1) the origin and purpose of the system, (2) the background of the surviving list (with parallels in 1 Chr 6:39–66—Eng 54–81, and (3) the effect of redactional use in Joshua 21 (see below, especially C.1 and C.5).

The summary which follows this section (Josh 21:43–45) makes no reference, direct or otherwise, to the refuge cities and levitical towns of chaps. 20–21 but follows coherently the end of chap. 19, from which it has been detached for insertion of these two key institutions. At last all is in readiness for the story of Israel's life in Transjordan and Canaan.

After Joshua's blessing and dismissal of the Transjordanian tribes at Shiloh (22:1–9), we plunge abruptly into a story of near civil war on the E-W axis. At issue is an altar near the Jordan (on which side is not clear), built by the E tribes to the alarm of the W tribes. Outright warfare is only averted by lengthy negotiation (the logic of the arguments unfathomable). The only hero is the head of the W embassy Phinehas ben Eleazar the priest. Joshua is not mentioned in the story. Another incongruity: this Phinehas, here presiding at Shiloh, is apparently a predecessor of the ranking Aaronite priest at Bethel, whom the Israelites will tardily consult in the warfare with Benjamin at the end of the wider era (Judg 20:27–29), there at last to receive another reliable oracle. The story here has a happy ending. The W tribes are satisfied and the E tribes give a confessional sentence name to their altar: "There is a witness between us / Yahweh is truly God!" (22:34). It is impossible to suppress the rhetorical relationship between the stories in Josh 22:10–34 and Judg 19–20; the first a close brush with civil war on the E-W axis (early in the era), the other a tragically costly civil war on the N-S axis of Cisjordan (at the end of the era).

Joshua's farewell address in chap. 23 (place unspecified), returns to the subject of an unfinished conquest. Further success, we read, will depend upon following most scrupulously "all that is written in the book of the law of Moses" (v 6), so as to maintain Israel's Yahwist identity. The summary command is "to love Yahweh your God" (v 11), after which the speech spirals downward to end in a bone-jarring warning: threat of exile and total national destruction, disappearance from among the family of nations.

The book concludes in chap. 24 with an expansive description of the covenant of all the tribes at Shechem, where Joshua presides (vv 1–28, 31). The narrative is interrupted in vv 29–30 for the notice of Joshua's death and burial at Timnath-serah, together with the flint knives used in the circumcision at Gilgal (according to LXX). Also buried at Shechem were the bones of Joseph, in a burial plot legally purchased by his father Jacob. Eleazar also died, to be buried in "the Gibeah" ("the hill?" See LXX) belonging to Phinehas his son. Thus, among the worthies of the era, it is Eleazar who gets the last word in the MT. The LXX continues, describing apostasy that introduces the following era of the judges.

In both LXX and MT the book of Joshua appears to end twice: once with Joshua's threatening exhortation (at Shiloh, if we take a lead from preceding context), and again with the people-forming promises at Shechem.

C. The Book of Joshua in Modern Study

As the preceding review of contents suggests, the book of Joshua raises many and complicated questions for the interpreter. How should one understand the evidence for a process preserving stories over a span of centuries but also reflecting historical developments during the interim between original event and final telling? What should one make of the obvious interest in certain towns and not others as places of assembly and the role of Yahweh's portable throne (ark of the covenant)? How does archaeology, especially with a rising interest in ancient Israel's social world, contribute to understanding of the text? What about the still-earlier beginning of the story line in Genesis 12–50, which is also in the background of the classic theme of new constitution at Sinai? Who were the traditionalists who contributed to the bifocal perspective in the canonical book, and what was their social location down the centuries?

1. The Primary History: Tetrateuch and Deuteronomistic Corpus. There is now a broad scholarly consensus that Joshua is, in some sense, a "Deuteronomistic" book. Deuteronomy presents itself as a collection of farewell speeches by Moses, given as he presides over a renewal of the Sinai covenant, with the people of Israel poised for invasion from a base in the "plains of Moab." The latter topographical term refers to the location of repeated Moabite incursions on the W edge of the Transjordanian plateau near the escarpment and N of the recognized political border of Moab at the Arnon. Deuteronomy, it is agreed on all hands, shows a pattern for the organization and governance of Israel, and for the role of Moses, that is modeled on forms and practices of international diplomacy. Moses is ambassador-mediator between God and the people as subjects of sworn allegiance to Yahweh—the only Sovereign of the universe.

Yahweh as Divine Warrior and Israel's Commander in Chief will redistribute the land as tribal "inheritances." The Heb term *naḥălâ*, "inheritance" stands for the suzerain's grant of a plot of ground (hence a "fief" or "estate") in exchange for the promise of military service upon call.

With Ten Commandments describing binding basic policy of the realm (Deuteronomy 5) and with lengthy exhortation effectively obliterating any distinction between loyalty and love in relationship to Yahweh (chaps. 6–11), Deuteronomy sets forth the conditions upon which alone the Conquest will succeed and endure (chaps. 12–26), with alternatives clear: blessing or curse (chaps. 27–28). Glimpses of a preexilic process toward "canonization" of Deuteronomic teaching are seen in the accounts of reforms sponsored by the Jerusalem kings: Hezekiah (2 Kgs 18:1–3; 2 Chronicles 29–31) and Josiah (2 Kings 22–23; 2 Chronicles 34–35), where details of the reforms look like mirror images, only occasionally blurred, of the Deuteronomic "legislation."

The book of Joshua belongs therefore, together with Deuteronomy, as a confessional introduction to the generally unified story of Israel's life on the land astride the Jordan that unfolds from Joshua through 2 Kings (Wright *Joshua* AB, 41–66). Deuteronomistic influence in Joshua is seen most directly in the framework which underscores the field commander's dependence upon the book of the Torah, that is, the "treaty teaching" (Josh 1:7–8; 23:6), and Joshua's attentiveness to the word of Yahweh as Commander in Chief (throughout).

Yet the book also displays the sorts of structural and linguistic disjunctures (doublets, contradictions, lexical and stylistic variations which appear to cluster) that have encouraged attempts to trace the narrative sources of Genesis–Numbers (J, E, P) into the book of Joshua and beyond. Such source criticism has generally attributed the bulk of chaps. 1–11 to E, with the qualification that D has recast stories to such an extent that J is almost entirely suppressed and little survives of E that is unrevised. The P source is not present as a narrative source except perhaps in chap. 22 (which, however, is most unlike P stories in the books preceding Deuteronomy). On the other hand, it was P, as argued by many scholars, that provided archival material for the bulk of the chapters on land division. But if so, there are surprisingly scant traces of specifically "Priestly" editing, if the concerns of the latter are characteristically represented by such material as Leviticus and Ezekiel. Joshua's farewell address is widely recognized by source critics as a Deuteronomistic composition, while chap. 24 stems from a Deuteronomistic rewrite of E. In all this one encounters an influence of D so pervasive in narratives (with corresponding absence of P) that there is little to sustain further search for tetrateuchal sources in Joshua, along the older lines. The quest has been mostly abandoned. Scholars now posit a Primary History comprised of: (1) a Tetrateuch, book of Genesis–Numbers (epic sources of the peoples' origins framing large blocks of "Priestly" materials), introducing (2) a "Deuteronomistic History" in Joshua–2 Kings (Freedman, *IDB* 3: 711–27).

By far the clearest rhetorical connections of Deuteronomy are with the books which follow it. In addition to the framework passages in Joshua, noted above, compare the speeches of chief protagonists in Joshua, beginning with the speeches of Yahweh (1:2–9; also 3:7–8; 6:2; 7:10–15; 8:1, 18; 11:6; 13:1–7; 20:2) and Joshua (1:10–11, 13–15; also 3:5–6, 9–10; 4:21–24; 19:20, 23; 23:2–16; 24:1–15).

Deuteronomistic influence is also found within stories. In the spy story it is notably Rahab the non-Israelite who uses Deuteronomic reasoning (2:1–11). The embassy from Gibeon depends on a knowledge of Deuteronomic regulations for different approaches to near and distant cities (Deuteronomy 20) in its negotiations with Israelite leaders (9:7–10), whereas the latter can find no such precedent in order to undo the problematic covenant (9:16–25). In these stories we note a sharp contrast with signs of Deuteronomistic influence in stories of the later premonarchic period. In the book of Judges, the marks of Deuteronomistic rhetoric are largely confined to framework passages, and the old stories are left unrevised because they illustrate subsequent hard times that led to the establishment of monarchy. In Joshua, however, the old stories are retold in such a way as to present the leadership of Joshua as ideal, yet not itself adequate without timely collaboration of Yahweh and the cosmic army.

The two Shechem scenes (8:30–35 and chap. 24) proceed from direct command of Moses in Deuteronomy 27. The chain of command is emphasized (1:7–8) and reemphasized (4:10; 11:11–14, 20, 23): Yahweh to Moses, Moses' *tôrâ* to Joshua, Joshua to the people.

2. History of Traditions. More productive than the older approach via literary source documents has been the recent half century of efforts to reconstruct the origins of narrative and archival materials taken up in Joshua in relation to various tribal constituencies that formed Israel in the pre-state period and their major religious centers.

Both the arrangements at the crossing of the Jordan to set up 12 stones at Gilgal as a memorial of the miraculous event (chaps. 3–4) and the proceedings at the capture of Jericho (chap. 6) read like accounts of liturgical happenings. Together they frame the notices about circumcision and Passover at Gilgal. From this point on, Joshua and the people are found frequently at Gilgal (9:6; 10:6, 15, 43; 14:6). At the end of the wider era, the Benjaminite Saul will become king at Gilgal (1 Sam 11:12–15; cf. 13:2–15a) in one stratum of the text.

It is a credible conclusion that nearly one-fourth of the book of Joshua reflects the story-telling and liturgical reenactment of "conquest" at a Gilgal sanctuary, which continued to flourish (2 Kgs 2:1; 4–38) long after the legitimating role had been taken over by royal sanctuaries: Jerusalem in the S, Bethel and Dan in the N. Thereafter Gilgal is denounced by prophets from both the N and the S (Hos 4:15; 9:15; 12:11; Amos 4:14; 5:15).

It is possible to make out broad lines of the "ritual conquest" formerly celebrated at Gilgal, as worked out originally by Kraus (1951) and others (esp. Soggin 1966), later appropriated in the Jerusalem cultus and postmonarchic circles (Cross *CMHE*, 103–11):

1. The people sanctify themselves as for a divinely sanctioned war, or to approach a sanctuary (Josh 3:5).
2. The covenant ark, throne of the deity and war palladium, is carried in solemn procession (= battle array) to the Gilgal sanctuary.
3. The Jordan, temporarily dammed, plays the role of the Red Sea.
4. Twelve stones are set up at the sanctuary (cf. Exod 24:4), symbolic of the covenanted tribes.
5. The fighting force is circumcised and the Passover celebrated.
6. The angelic general of Yahweh's army appears at the holy place.

Within this configuration, however, it is the interlude for resumption of circumcision and Passover that present serious disjunctions in the progress of the narrative, where, like the angelic commander, they are never again echoed in the book. It is more likely that the notices about circumcision and Passover are secondary in the story line and that the arrival of the commander launches the second large segment of the book.

With the exception of (1) Achan's execution and burial (at a site presumably in Judah), (2) the diversion to Shechem (in the heartland of "Joseph"), and (3) the S campaign as sequel to defense of Gibeon (backbone of Judah), all of the action in chaps. 2–10 takes place in territory that will be finally assigned to Benjamin (18:11–28). If the narrative configuration of these chapters reflects the compilers' indebtedness to an early Gilgal version of the crossing plus a handful of more narrowly "Benjaminite" stories, it will explain the absence of specific allusions to the Transjordanian conquest led by Moses, except in disjunctive and supplementary contexts (e.g., 1:12–18; 13:1–14:15; 17:3–6).

Apart from the story of the victory against Jabin's forces in Galilee, with no clear signs of place attachment in this case (and considerable debate about the story's relationship to tradition represented in Judges 4–5), N tradition in the narratives of Joshua is confined to the two scenes at Shechem (8:30–35; and 24:1–28). The two units represent at least a chronological disagreement: did the Shechem assembly precede or follow the redistribution of the land? It is the first of these scenes that is most often regarded by critics as secondary, on stylistic grounds. If it therefore serves as chronological corrective to chap. 24, then there is no clear indication of where the first phase of land reform in Cisjordan (chaps. 14–17) occurs. The MT has Joshua presiding at Gilgal in the Gibeon story (9:6; 10:6, 15) and returning there after the S campaign (10:43). The LXX, however, lacking 10:15 and 43, may be the better text. The one remaining reference to Joshua at Gilgal (14:6) may be read as flashback (reading the converted imperfect Heb verb as a pluperfect). In other words it appears that there was a strong tradition according to which the Shechem assembly was presupposition, not consequence, of the warfare outside of "Benjamin." This leaves a strong presumption that the center for the first phase of land division in Cisjordan (chaps. 14–17) was at Shechem. Those chapters in fact deal only with the most extensive tribal territories, Judah and the Joseph tribes, using lists, to be sure, which in present form are not earlier than the period of the divided monarchy. Thus it is not surprising that elsewhere the clearest evidence of a more extensive document describing borders and listing towns enclosed thereby is confined to Benjamin, narrowly confined between Judah and Joseph at the beginning of the Shiloh-phase allotments (18:11–28). This use of an archive from the period of the Monarchy tallies well with the claims of the warfare stories. We may suspect that Benjamin's turf was so war torn that the tribe was unable to consolidate its own territorial claim until the Shiloh phase.

The genesis of Shiloh tradition is obscure. Shiloh is abruptly mentioned for the first time in 18:1 as the starting point for a survey of Cisjordan, to provide the basis for territories of the seven remaining constituencies. Shiloh elsewhere plays a prominent role only late in the wider era, when Gilgal is once again prominent. It may be that the eclipse of Shechem and the shift to Shiloh were historically related to the aspirations of Gideon and the sequel, counterrevolution at Shechem, represented by the story of

Abimelech (Judges 8–9), which is reasonably correlated with a massive destruction stratum at the site (Tell Balata) from the third quarter of the 12th century (give or take a decade). If the shift to Shiloh occurred early in the movement to restore a monarchy in the central highlands, Joshua's presence in chapters 18–19 is entirely plausible. The stories of Gideon and Abimelech would seriously blur the idealized Conquest picture and were appropriately reserved for "Book Two" of Israel's life in the land. The subsequent eclipse of Shiloh, surely due to Philistine offensives into the highlands, left Gilgal in the Jordan valley as the place of the muster at the end of the wider era (as it had been in the beginning) and the elevation of Saul.

Turning from Benjamin to the remaining territorial description (chap. 19), debate continues as to whether the borders are "ideal" or "real" and, in either case, how old in formulation. With the evidence that Solomon's administrative districts (1 Kings 4) would render the Joshua borders dysfunctional, it is likely that chap. 19 is a mixture of reality and ideality, with memory and resources both fragmentary.

3. Archaeology and Social World. Energy recently spent in debating the pertinence of archaeology for interpretation of Joshua (Wright *Joshua* AB, 74–80) is as nothing compared to the pace of exploration and excavation on both sides of the Jordan in the same period (Boling 1988). Here it will be better to reserve judgment about what archaeology can and cannot do, while describing what archaeologists have found that may be pertinent.

A 13th-century setting for the Exodus and career of Moses (toward the end of the century, better than early) is holding well. A recent attempt to lower the end of the MB (ca. 1500 B.C.E.) so as to accommodate a 15th-century date for Moses (Bimson 1981) encounters awesome head winds from experienced field archaeologists. At the same time the data that confound do not go away.

The site of Jericho (Tell es-Sultan), once a strongly fortified city with an urban tradition going back to a Pre-Pottery Neolithic era, appears to have been little, if anything, more than the residence of a local strongman at a defunct town site in the 14th century, with no surviving evidence of occupation in the 13th century. A variation on the theory that Jericho was scene of a "ritual conquest" combines evidence from archaeology and medical history (Hulse 1971), reading the story of Jericho as the ritual cursing of a disease-ridden oasis. If so, the unique treatment of Jericho as manifesting public health policy will make sense, as well as the execution of Achan and family together with contaminated objects in an effort at control of pestilential disease (Boling, *Joshua* AB, 214–15; 1983). There are indications that the "ban" (Heb *ḥerem*) improbably generalized to virtually genocidal proportions by the Deuteronomistic Historians, originated in such ad hoc degrees (Meyers 1978). For yet another possible explanation of the gap between narrative and strata at Jericho, see below.

The site of Ha-Ai, if identified with et-Tell (which also means "The Ruin"), had been a massive walled city in the EB but was virtually uninhabited throughout most of the 2d millennium, until a small unwalled village is found nestled within the remnants of defense walls already a thousand years old, early in Iron I. It has often been assumed therefore that while the battle of Jericho is mostly liturgical (Soggin, *Joshua* OTL, 83–88), the story of The Ruin is entirely etiological. Alternatively it has been argued that the name Ha-Ai is secondary, in a story that originally recounted the capture of nearby Bethel (Judg 1:22–26), which was destroyed and soon reoccupied, as known from excavations (*IB* 2: 583–84). Yet another proposal sees incoming Israelites finally retelling far older Conquest stories, from the expulsion of the Hyksos and earlier (Jericho and The Ruin), in stereotypical form, but with Joshua as military hero.

No such ready rationalizations are available to account for the shape and content of the Gibeon story, where LB evidence at the site of el-Jib is confined to tombs, and the town site, if occupied, was another unwalled village, like Ha-Ai, at the end of the 13th century, and a number of others in the vicinity.

It is with the diversion to Shechem (8:30–35) and the S sequel to the defense of Gibeon (chap. 10) and then Hazor in Galilee that the correlation of stories and stratigraphy improves. There was a late 14th-century destruction of Shechem, whether accidental or otherwise is, of course, not known from excavation. If that destruction of Shechem may be related to the tradition about Jacob's claim to the area by right of conquest (Gen 48:22, in contrast to the legal purchase of a burial plot, according to Josh 24:32), then it appears to have been followed by a generally peaceful period of nearly 200 years, until the third quarter of the 12th century, with a massive destruction sealing Abimelech's local reversion to monarchy at Shechem. Excavations reveal that it was at some time during this period that an altar and sacred area, without any nearby settlement, were flourishing on Mt. Ebal (Zertal 1985). See also EBAL, MOUNT.

A roll call of the S opposition is inconclusive. According to biblical tradition Jerusalem remained a small but strongly fortified Canaanite highland city until it was taken by David. Nothing from extensive excavations on the S spur of Jerusalem ("City of David") suggests otherwise.

Evidence from Hebron is minimal (because of restricted access for excavations of an area of continuous occupation to the present) and unpublished. Jarmuth, if located at Tell Yarmuth, had meager LB presence; it was a small hamlet or burial ground. Lachish was destroyed ca. 1160 B.C.E. Eglon, with Tell el-Hesi now ruled out, is unknown archaeologically; likewise Makkedah. Libnah, best identified with Tell Bornat, has yet to be extensively uncovered. Debir, if located at Tell Beit-Mirsim, was destroyed in the late 13th century. If identified with Khirbet Rabud, which now appears best on general topographical grounds, there is no evidence of destruction within the era.

The possible correlations between narrative claims and excavated strata thus appear minimal. On the other hand, the idioms "put to the sword" or "put under the ban" (*ḥerem),* used formulaically in the material, may not mean total destruction, if the purpose was the elimination of royal opposition in order to take over habitable towns and if the *ḥerem* was originally an ad hoc decree regarding the taking of booty or protection against epidemic and the like.

Finally, to complete the roll call, if the destruction of Canaanite Hazor is correctly dated to the second quarter of the 13th century, then the chronological range appears too broad for one commander's lifetime. Yet it is spacious enough to include many other sites, especially in the S hills, which suffered destruction (some of them more than once) in the last phase of the LB and beginning of the Iron I period. Excavations attest to an exceedingly turbulent scene up and down the Canaanite corridor throughout the period. Much of the turbulence seems, however, to have been avoided for the better part of 200 years by the population centering in Shechem. How many of the destruction levels were due to natural causes, how many reflect inter–city-state warfare, and the extent to which Joshua 2–12 represents either cause or response are now unanswered questions calling forth new approaches. Especially helpful is the recent escalation of surface surveys on both sides of the Jordan, when combined with results of controlled excavations and subjected to queries and investigative methods originally at home in the social sciences.

Archaeological surveys in recent years have shown that, in the same 200 years framed by destruction layers at Shechem, the hill country to the N of Shechem and to the S as far as the latitude of Hebron saw a blossoming of small unwalled settlements for the first time in history, with a parallel development in upper Galilee. Between Hebron and Shechem alone the number of villages in a 4200 km^2 area surveyed increased from 23 in LB to 114 in Iron I (Stager 1981). The settlements were occupied by families practicing a subsistence agricultural economy based on dry farming (Hopkins 1985). Development of the settlements required enormous investments of labor to construct the necessary agricultural terraces. The villagers were considerably poorer than the higher social strata that lived inside the great walled cities of the plains, but without any marks of distinctiveness in their material culture that are not subject to continuing intense debate. Some of these highland families were probably newcomers from N and E. Many were surely refugees or pioneers, retreating from the intercity warfare, subscription, taxation, and exploitative demands for agricultural surplus in the old city-state centers, much of which is vividly illustrated, for the 14th century, in the Amarna Letters. Still others of these farming families must represent an outward spread of population from the Shechem vale, where the settlement of new villages begins in the 14th century (Campbell 1968), when Labayu and sons clearly care little about Egyptian sovereignty and are accused of having given Shechem over to the *habiru.* The latter term (like biblical "Hebrew") is a general label for societal marginals and not a synonym for Israelite, although many early Israelites were, or had been, "Hebrews." This looks like a strong link between a destruction level, on the one hand, and Amarna and the Bible, on the other.

Data for the study of demographic patterns and urbanization on both sides of the Jordan are now massive. In a control sample of 77 excavated sites (Gonen 1984) the transition from MB to the first phase of the LB saw a reduction in number of towns by more than half (from 54 to 24). Town life picked up again in the 14th century, and by the 13th century the number of occupied sites in the sample was back to the MB levels (56 sites). When results of regional surface surveys were added to the picture, the disruption at the MB/LB transition in Cisjordan is even sharper; evidence for LB is only 37 percent of the total for MB. Furthermore, the LB settlements in the sample were greatly reduced in size and most often unwalled. There was an early shift of concentration to the coastal plain and important communication routes. The highlands suffered initially from a process of desertion. However, as the highlands were resettled throughout LB, the percentage of small (11 to 50 dunams) and medium-sized (51–100 dunams) settlements remained rather constant; but the number of tiny settlements (10 dunams or less) increased fourfold by the end of the LB. Finally, it appears that the total area occupied by the 13th-century sites was, nevertheless, only about 45 percent of the area for the MB II settlements.

Comparison with the E Jordan valley, always ideally suited for the most intensive agriculture, is instructive. In the N half of the valley alone (between the Yarmūk and the W Rajib), a recent survey recorded 106 sites, 52 of them new additions to the archaeological map (Ibrahim, Sauer, and Yassine 1976). There the reduction in number of sites from MB II (25 sites) to LB (13 sites) and the situation in Iron I (23 sites) are amazingly close to the Cisjordanian sample. Again, the earlier transition was far more disruptive than the later one, as 8 of the 13 LB sites continued into Iron I (Boling 1988).

The pattern on the Transjordanian plateau is different but not unrelated. Survey of 346 sites between the Yarmūk and the Zarqa (biblical Jabbok) produced evidence for MB II at 21 sites, LB at 23 sites, and Iron I at 77 sites (Mittman 1970). However, only 4 of the MB II sites continued into LB, while 19 of the LB sites continued into Iron I. Again, the earlier transition was far more turbulent.

In contrast to the picture previously drawn on the basis of N. Glueck's pioneering survey work, there is now abundant evidence for settled LB population in central Transjordan (from the Zarqa to the Mujib, biblical Arnon), especially in the upper bend of the Zarqa. However, the settled LB population, at about the same level as in MB II, is found in obviously new alignments at widely scattered sites throughout LB until a veritable explosion of new settlements occurs in Iron I (Boling 1988).

Survey on the "Moab" plateau (585 sites) between the two grand canyons (Mujib and Hasa, biblical Zered) shows a distribution of sedentary population in MB II, ca. 5.3 percent of all sites in the survey (Miller 1979a, 1979b; Mattingly 1983), approximating the situation in the N (6.1 percent of the 346 sites in the N Jordan survey). Here the major difference in MB II is a number of walled towns in the N but a total absence of such sites on the S plateau between EB and Iron I. In the N there developed much earlier a tradition of city-state polity, which is reflected in both the biblical and extrabiblical references. Most striking, however, is a sharp increase in the number of sites in "Moab" (up from 31 sites in MB II to 75 sites in LB), still unwalled. In other words while the density of settlements declined by half in the N Jordan valley and while population was regrouping throughout N Jordan, the percentage of LB settlements reflected in the surveys more than doubled on the S plateau (up from 5.3 percent for MB II "Moab," to 12.8 percent in LB) and nearly doubled that in the N. The territorial state of Moab, snugly situated between the two grand canyons, had thus emerged, with a much smaller state, Ammon, at the desert fringe lagging not far behind.

To summarize the picture on the E-W axis as currently reflected in archaeological evidence, we see widespread political chaos and social disintegration at the end of the MB period, the decades when Egypt was successful in expelling the Hyksos and in reclaiming the cities of Canaan and Transjordan for a native Egyptian dynasty. Initial decline of the few power centers in the Cisjordanian highlands was followed by gradual resettlement of the hill country from within and without the land. Refugees and/or dropouts from the old power centers of the plains and valleys moved into the empty highlands and onto the Transjordanian plateau, where there were few fortified towns S of the Yarmūk and none S of the Mujib. In both areas, W highlands and E plateau, they could practice a subsistence agriculture without also having to support an urban elite.

The other increment to the populations E and W came from the widespread collapse of the international peace. The initial desertion of the highlands and fragility of new LB alignments in N and central Transjordan made them also a happy hunting ground for other newcomers from the N and NE, such as the Amorite kingdoms of Sihon and Og, as well as from the S.

The biblical conquest of Transjordan came from the S, where the picture is still far from clear. Excavations in the heartland of "Edom" (at Umm el-Biyarah, Tawilan, and Buseirah) produced no evidence for a wide-ranging territorial state until well into Iron II, 8th to 6th centuries B.C.E. More recently, a survey of over 1000 sites on the S bank of the Wâdī el-Hasa and tributaries (thus only the N extremity of "Edom") found no definite MB pottery; and LB evidence was almost nonexistent. There appear to have been a series of small but permanent settlements along the S bank of the Wâdī el-Hasa by the early 12th century (MacDonald 1982, 1983a, 1983b, 1984), which now look like spillover from the burgeoning population on the "Moab" plateau just to the N. Thus the kings of Edom, who ruled a territorial state from Bosrah in the 8th century and later, may well have had lesser and local predecessors here and there, even contemporaries, each claiming locally the prerogatives of *mlk,* "king".

While the formation of a major territorial kingdom of Edom was long preceded by Moab's head start in the N, it also lagged behind a flourishing network of settlements to the S, in the coastal wadis of the N Hejaz from the end of the LB (Ingraham et al. 1981). This was the heartland of biblical Midian. The far-flung commercial reach of this culture is now well documented in the distribution of the so-called "Midianite" pottery, which emanates chiefly from two sites, Tayma and Qurayya; the latter is also the best candidate for the place name (Beth)-Yhwh in Egyptian topographical lists of Amenhotep (Gk Amenophis) III (1386–1349) and Rameses II (1279–1213; Kitchen 1982: 238–39).

There is therefore much to be said for the biblical story line, recounting "conquest" in Transjordan led by Moses, where especially Moab and Midianites pose the opposition, separately or together, in the region immediately N of the Arnon. If the stories in Numbers 21ff. are judged on source-critical grounds to be a late monarchic (or even postexilic) redaction, we may observe that another set of stories, with action centering in the same places, will be needed to comprehend the shifting demographic patterns, at the LB–Iron I transition, which are emerging with ever greater clarity (Boling 1988).

From another angle of vision, researches into modern *segmentary societies,* especially as correlated with lineage systems, are directly pertinent to study of Joshua and the tribal organization of ancient Israel (Wilson 1984; Frick 1985). In societies which display segmentary lineage systems, political organization is regularly based on genealogical reckoning and operative descent rules. As societal segments move from one place to another, experience expansion, or decline because of whatever circumstances, new alignments result and genealogy in time adjusts to affirm the newer arrangements, which will be widely accepted as the way it has always been. That ancient Israel in the pre-state period was in many respects comparable to such lineage-based societies is a hunch now energetically pursued. When the lineage-based society develops into a state, the "official" genealogy will prefer the lineal form, while various societal segments will continue to tell their own stories. As a result, we have, finally, the complementary perspectives within the finished book of Joshua. The final edition, we have suggested, was designed to be supportive of life in the postmonarchic situation. It draws deeply on traditionary roots going back not only to the post-Mosaic followers of Joshua, but all the way to a pre-Mosaic "Israel." That early "prehistory" is equally important for critical interpretation of Joshua.

4. Elohistic Israel and Yahwistic Israel. The clearest sources for history of the normative twelve-tribe system are the lengthy poems incorporated in Genesis–Judges, five in particular, to which may be applied the principles of sequence dating originally at home in archaeology. The five major units comprising the corpus may be understood on stylistic and historico-linguistic grounds as premonarchic in all essentials. The poems may be arranged in chronological sequence, either in order of composition or in order of content. An earlier date of composition is no guarantee of higher historicity; a later composition may in fact reflect accurately a considerably earlier situation. The proposed sequence (Freedman 1979, 1980) followed in Table 1 has turned out to be remarkably in phase with the shifting demographic pattern outlined above.

Table 1: Early Hebrew Poems

Poem	Content	Composition
Genesis 49	14th–13th	11th
Exodus 15	13th–12th	12th
Numbers 23–24	12th	11th
Deuteronomy 33	12th	11th
Judges 5	12th	12th

In the Testaments of Jacob (Genesis 49), twelve tribes are named in the clearest compact witness to earliest Israel. Several of the testaments are worth noting in particular. Though Reuben is "firstborn" (on which side of the Jordan Reuben lives is not clear), Judah has the most exalted status (vv 9–12), with no compelling reason to regard that status as anachronistic. Joseph is one tribe which may have ranged on both sides of the Jordan (as reflected in the later prose narratives of the patriarchs), N and S of the Jabbok, in a period prior to formation of the Amorite kingdoms (which in turn probably postdates destruction of Ugarit; ca. 1200) and long before the Yahwist organization under Eleazar and Joshua redefined old "tribal" areas. Simeon and Levi are denounced for their violence (vv 5–7) in terms which indicate that they are being evicted from the Israel organization. What is said of Gad, who apart from Joseph may alone represent a Transjordanian constituency in Genesis 49, fits very well with the demographic patterns and the suggestion that the Amorite kingdoms were recent newcomers to the region flanking the Jabbok. The defeat of Sihon, when it came, would be greatly facilitated by Israelites already, and for a long time, in residence there as part of a variegated sedentary population. Thus we may understand King Mesha's 9th-century claim that "the people of Gad had lived *mᶜlm*" (from ancient times) in the land of Moab's recent expansion, N of the Arnon. And if Jephthah's career falls in the 11th century, his argument that Israel had lived alongside Ammonite territory for "three hundred years" would be an approximately accurate round number. Genesis 49 thus describes pre-Yahwistic Israel in a poem where other divine names are preferred: El, Shaddai, and probably ᶜAli. This earliest Israel had its center for some time in an El-berit sanctuary at Shechem in the early post-Amarna period. Earliest Israel was crushed by Merneptah roughly a century later, so decisively that in the second major poem of the corpus the name Israel does not occur.

In the Song of the Sea (Exodus 15), there is no hint of a lineage system, no connection with patriarchal traditions or promises about the land of Canaan. The horizon of the poem is limited to the S wilderness, traditional home of Yahweh (see above, on the LB settlements in N Hejaz). The Song of the Sea links the tradition of the Exodus from Egypt with the crossing of the sea and march through the wilderness to the sacred mountain, holy habitation of Yahweh, somewhere in Sinai. The four peoples who are struck dumb with terror at Yahweh's redemptive activity (Philistia, Edom, Moab, Canaan) can only have coexisted in their traditionally assigned territories during the 12th century B.C.E.

The Oracles of Balaam in Numbers 23–24 concern "Israel" in Transjordan, but there is no tribal roster. The poet's concern does not yet include Canaan. Moabite "occupation forces" N of the Arnon are confronted, we suggest, with elements of Yahwistic Israel and Elohistic Israel now making common cause: tent-dwelling newcomers (more to the S and E?) and village-farmer sympathizers (surely more on the N = Gad). We must, apparently, understand that the dismantling of Sihon's kingdom had only cleared the way for an early attempt at Moabite expansion N of the Arnon, in a region yet to be consolidated as "Reuben" (Boling 1988: 30–35, 60–61). Such a reading helps to account for the collaboration of the "elders of Midian" (Num 22:7) on Moab's side in the affair. It is likely that Midianite commercial interests were by this time counting on Moabite "protection" against the mounting resistance of an expanding Yahwist movement, with nascent disruption of the caravan trade, soon to be celebrated at length in the Song of Deborah, from the highlands of Cisjordan (Chaney 1983). That Midianites were now to be found in considerable strength N of the Arnon is clear from the story of Beth-peor (Numbers 25).

In the Testaments of Moses (Deuteronomy 33) the tribal roster reappears. Here Judah has fallen on hard times (v 7). The eclipse of Judah may be connected with the Egyptian ruler Merneptah's campaign (ca. 1235 B.C.), if we are not already into the Philistine period. Reuben, wherever situated, seems to be in equally dire straits (v 6). Simeon appears to have withdrawn from central Cisjordan to the N Negeb (Josh 19:1–9) after its ouster in Genesis 49. If so, it has now gone under, passed over in silence; it will only retain a place in idealized prose genealogies. Simeon's slot is here filled by division of a greatly expanded Joseph, who gets the most expansive treatment (vv 13–17). Levi appears to have undergone a transformation. Evicted for its violence in Genesis 49, Levi is now the zealous keeper of the oracle and instructor in how to keep Yahweh's covenant. If the name refers to elements of a single tribe (which is easier to comprehend than the disappearance of a "secular" Levi to be replaced by a "sacral" tribe of the same name), then it is reasonable to think that some of the levitical families made their way to Egypt, after banishment in Genesis 49, there to undergo religious conversion, thanks to Moses, and emerge as a "palace guard" in the newly constituted alternative kingdom. The revival of Levi led at last to rival priestly houses, deeply entrenched in both the N and S kingdoms after Solomon, as cultivators of the prose tradition.

Finally, in the Song of Deborah (Judges 5), the organization "Israel" appears to consist of ten territorially based tribes. Here again it is Judah that is most conspicuous for its absence, and we are deep into the Philistine period. Judah has joined Simeon; but unlike Simeon, Judah will revive to engulf the territory where Simeon had sought to relocate (Josh 15:20–63). Two Transjordanian constituencies are faulted for not answering the call to arms: Gilead (= E Manasseh) and Reuben. That there is no mention of Gad suggests that Moab has once again expanded N of the Arnon (cf. the story of Ehud vs. Eglon in Judg 3:12–30), so that Gad's earlier residence there is receding into the "ancient times" to which Mesha refers in the 9th century B.C.E. Lack of any mention or allusion to Levi in Judges 5 has always been a major crux. But the omission is not very surprising in a roll call of *territorially-based* tribes. If Deuteronomy 33 represents an earlier situation, with Levi already elevated as teacher and oracle keeper for "Yahwist Israel" on the move, the levitical families are now already dispersed. Levi comes in for neither praise nor blame in Judges 5, we may suspect, because its members are functioning, in effect, as muster officers in every other tribe on both sides of the Jordan and with very mixed success.

The transition from Elohistic Israel to Yahwistic Israel had far-reaching political implications (Mendenhall 1962, 1973) working for societal transformation (Gottwald 1979): governance by God and the rule of ethic. Effective first in Transjordan, the reform movement centered for a period at Shechem (Josh 8:30–35), which because of its revolutionary implications was at least played down in circles close to the Jerusalem throne (in favor of Shiloh).

There it was emphasized that Joshua's covenanting came at the end, after conquest and land division were complete (chap. 24).

5. Levitical Sponsorship: Dtn, Dtr 1, Dtr 2. While the pioneering study of the "Deuteronomistic" work regarded it as a product of the Exile or later (Noth *ÜgS*), interpretation which regards the work as merely etiology of national destruction is inadequate. In the canonical book of Joshua (and throughout the Former Prophets) we recognize signs of at least two major "editions," both of them making use of older stories and both of them shaped by a rediscovered book of Mosaic Torah. We have adopted the symbols *Dtr 1, Dtr 2,* and *Dtn* as convenient shorthand.

Dtr 1 stands for the major portion of the books Joshua–2 Kings. It represents a late preexilic enterprise, from the time of the reforming king Josiah. The work was clearly designed to be supportive of life under a reformed Davidic monarchy, and the figure of Joshua is presented as an ideal for the Jerusalem king in matters military, legitimating Josiah's reconquest of Cisjordan in a period of Assyrian weakness. While the battles in Joshua 6–11 are presented as examples of properly holy warfare, they are also the last such prior to Josiah. For Judges 2 begins with announcement that Yahweh will no longer participate in expansionist warfare against Canaanites.

Dtr 2 stands for a subsequent edition, addressed to a drastically altered situation. The bulk of Dtr 2 may be exilic, but it need be only post-Josianic to make sense. There is thus an unresolved tension running throughout the Dtr corpus.

Dtn stands for the bulk of Deut 4:44–28:68, an old Book of the Law of Moses which so effectively accounted for demise of the N kingdom that it became in Josiah's day, with a new introduction, theological preface to the entire story from Moses to Mosaic revival in the late 7th century B.C.E. Without the explicit regulation of kingship in Deut 17:14–20, Dtn is neither promonarchic nor antimonarchic. It is simply amonarchic and stems from no "royal" sanctuary. The best guess is that Dtn comes from certain levitical circles claiming premonarchic legitimacy, concentrated mostly in the N originally and calling for a grass-roots renewal of covenant on the Sinai/Moab/Shechem pattern. It is a reasonable working hypothesis that the tradition is rooted in the experience of some levitical families left stranded in Egypt, after events reflected in the story of Genesis 34 and the poetry of Gen 49:5–7, while other levitical families acquired legitimacy with the Yahwist takeover and reform (to various degrees) at sanctuaries of the older Israelite lineage system. Sociologically the Levites in the lineage-based society may be understood as a quasi-guild structure, a professional "caste," which one might enter by choice or appointment, not alone by heredity (Polk 1979; Gottwald 1979). Dispersal of the levitical carriers of militant Yahwism throughout the territory of the other "tribes" was institutionalized in the system of levitical towns (Joshua 21). This probably began, indeed, in the premonarchic period; for subsequent levitical history was very different in the N and S kingdoms; and there is nowhere any hint of a functioning system of levitical towns anywhere in the books of Samuel and Kings, except most indirectly.

The alienation of many N Levites must have begun as early as Solomon's reign, with exploitative fiscal policies draining the N, to the economic and military advantage of the S. The list of towns in Joshua 21 reflects a series of monarchic adaptations. The Gershonites (21:27–33) were consigned en masse to the distant N. The name Gershon/m—first son of Levi in the standard genealogy of Exod 6:16–19—also appears as a patronymic of Moses' grandson Jonathan, founder of the priesthood at Dan (Judg 18:30). It is likely that Gershon/m was the name of a major division of Levi alternatively called "Mushites" in the fragmentary genealogy of Num 26:58a (Cross *CMHE,* 197–98). The Gershonites/Mushites, claiming Moses as their priestly progenitor, functioned in N towns, a number of which first became "Israelite," it appears, thanks to David's conquests. After banishment of the Mushite priest Abiathar (originally of Shiloh) from Jerusalem early in Solomon's reign, priesthood in Jerusalem became the exclusive prerogative of the Zadokites, whose Aaronite legitimacy was rooted in David's early power base at Hebron (Cross *CMHE,* 207–15).

It is descendants of those N Levites at premonarchic sanctuaries (predominantly Mushite) that are the best candidates for producers of nuclear Dtn. They were spurred on by such actions as Solomon's sale of the Cabul district, which contained three or four "Gershonite" towns (Abdon, Rehob, Mishal, and possibly Helkath), to Hiram of Tyre (Halpern 1974: 523). Nor did the N administration do anything to heal the breach, which was doubtless widened by early relocation of the N capital away from Shechem and by Jeroboam's priestly appointments at Bethel (originally Aaronite; Judg 20:26–28) and at the high places (non-levitical; 1 Kgs 12:31). The Chronicler reports that Rehoboam was able for three years to exploit a newfound support among the victims of Jeroboam's priestly assignments (2 Chr 11:13–14, 17). From such a milieu, out and away from the great royal sanctuaries, Dtn took documentary shape (and likely also the specific contents of the town lists in Joshua 21) in relation to the late 8th-century reform of Hezekiah, after the fall of the N kingdom (2 Kings 18 = 2 Chronicles 29). There must have been a major flight from the N after the fall of Samaria (721 B.C.E.), when Jerusalem saw enormous expansion, exploding onto the W ridge. Thus it is not surprising to find evidence of rival priestly houses both drawing upon Dtn, with one of them closer to the Jerusalem throne and dominating formation of the literature until the untimely death of Josiah.

Further evidence of the unresolved tension is the use of a distinctive formula in the numerous references to levitical personnel. There are "the priests the Levites" (Deut 18:1); and there is "the Levite" or "all the tribe of Levi" (Deut 12:12, 18; 16:11, 14; 26:11, 13). "The priests the Levites" are the most prestigious; in Joshua they carry and guard the ark of Yahweh's covenant (Josh 3:3; 8:33). But when Deuteronomy refers to "the Levite" or "all the tribe of Levi" (persons in need of special benevolence, along with other unlanded persons: aliens, widows, orphans), context generally indicates client priests in much larger numbers. It was for them, as the teachers of Israel, that provisions had been made in the institution of levitical towns. Thus Dtn was careful to stipulate that every Levite shall have the same prerogatives of priesthood at the most prestigious of sanctuaries, the one especially distinguished by Yahweh's choice (Deut 18:6). In Deut 18:1, where "the priests the Levites" is immediately explained appositionally (but without a conjunction) as "all the tribe of Levi," we may thus have a gloss claiming for all levitical males the same prestigious status of "the priests the Levites," status stemming from the very early period.

In summary, we may recognize in Dtr 1 the penultimate product of a long experience and process of tradition formation in the land, telling the story from Moses to Josiah (2 Kgs 22–23), and from a predominantly S Aaronite perspective. Joshua is presented as military commander par excellence and as such a model for Jerusalem kings, who may use the power of the throne to implement the teaching of Moses. But the effort died with Josiah. We may recognize in Dtr 2 the contributions of other levitical families, fleeing S after 721 B.C.E., with their own "Mushite" and "N Aaronite" memories of the way it had been and with Dtn's promise of full priestly status at "the place which Yahweh shall choose," only to be outmaneuvered there (2 Kgs 23:9, which puts it in the best possible light: it was their own fault). The book of Joshua ends therefore on a different note; for Dtr 2 supplies the only cracks discernible in the portrait of Joshua, displays an interest in an Israel much more extensive than Josiah's Cisjordan kingdom, recalls the important role of N priesthoods in the premonarchic decision making, and in general commends a way of looking at the past that will be positively supportive of life in Exile. For Israel the postmonarchic "congregation" is direct descendant of Israel the premonarchic "assembly." Joshua's farewell address unmistakably anticipates exile, but the two chapters framing it are entirely upbeat, making the point that in order to maintain identity as Israel it will be better to keep talking (chap. 22) and renewing promises to God and to one another (chap. 24).

The structure of the book of Joshua in final form is integrally related to the book of Judges. This is evident in Table 2. See JUDGES, BOOK OF. In this arrangement pericopes represented by the first column (the "Josianic" edition) make virtually continuous reading, with rarely any noticeable gaps. Not so the second column, which in a variety of ways annotates and supplements the first edition, with scant indication of overwriting it. The result is a sobering reminder of how impossible it is for one historian to know all of the truth and how difficult it is indeed to tell all the truth that one knows.

Table 2: Book of Joshua

	Dtr 1		*Dtr 2*
	I. Mobilization and Entrance		
	Yahweh, Joshua, and Israel	1:1–11	
		1:13–18	E Jordanian tribes
		2:1–24	Rehab's house
	Opening the river	3:1–16	
		3:17–4:8	Twelve stones
		(4:9)	Twelve other (LXX) stones
	Crossing the river	4:10–11	
		4:12–13	E Jordanian tribes
	Closing the river	4:19–5:12	Cultic encampment
	II. Warfare		
	The commander	5:13–15	
	Intervention I: Jericho	6:1–21	
		6:22–25	The Rahab splice
	The curse on Jericho	6:26–27	
	Defeat at The Ruin	7:1–26	
	Second attack on The Ruin	8:1–2	
		8:3–11	Judges 20 prefigured: part I
	Intervention II: The Ruin	8:12–19	
		8:20–25	Judges 20 prefigured: part II
	The sign	8:26–29	
		8:30–35	Shechem: chronological corrective
	Gibeon treaty	9:1–15	
		9:16–27	Judges 21 prefigured
	Intervention III: Keeping faith	10:1–11	
		10:12–15	Sun and Moon (cf. Joshua at The Ruin)
	Sequel	10:16–43	
	A N coalition	11:1–15	
	Concluding summary	11:16–23	
	III. Inheritance of Land		
SHECHEM phase		12:1–21	Former lords
		13:1–23	Transjordanian flashback
		14:1–15	Special introduction to Judah
	Judah and Ephraim	15:1–16:10	
	Manasseh, E. and W.	17:1–2	
		17:3–6	Daughters of Zelophehad
	W Manasseh	17:7–13	
	Joshua as judge	17:14–18	
SHILOH phase	Seven more estates	18:1–19:48	
	Joshua's estate	19:49–50	
		19:51	Conclusion to Part III
	IV. Two Key Institutions		
		20:1–9	Asylum towns
		21:1–42	Levitical towns
	Conclusion to Parts I–III	21:43–45	
	V. How to Avoid Civil War		
		22:1–34	Phinehas ben Eleazar
		23:1–16	Final warning
	Shechem covenant	24:1–28	

Bibliography

Albright, W. F. 1973. From the Patriarchs to Moses: I, From Abraham to Joseph. *BA* 36: 5–33.

Bimson, J. J. 1981. *Redating the Exodus and Conquest.* JSOTSup 5. Sheffield.

Boling, R. G. 1982. Levitical History and the Role of Joshua. Pp. 241–61 in *WLSGF*.

———. 1988. *The Early Biblical Community in Transjordan.* Sheffield.

Campbell, E. F. 1968. The Shechem Area Survey. *BASOR* 190: 19–41.

Chaney, M. L. 1983. Ancient Palestinian Peasant Movement and

the Formation of Premonarchic Israel. Pp. 39–90 in *Palestine in Transition,* ed. D. N. Freedman and D. F. Graf. Sheffield.
Freedman, D. N. 1979. Early Israelite Poetry and Historical Reconstructions. Pp. 89–96 in *Symposia,* ed. F. M. Cross. Cambridge, MA. Repr. in Freedman 1980: 167–78.
———. 1980. *Pottery, Poetry, and Prophecy.* Winona Lake, IN.
Frick, F. S. 1985. *The Formation of the State in Ancient Israel.* SWBA 4. Sheffield.
Gonen, R. 1984. Urban Canaan in the Late Bronze Period. *BASOR* 253: 61–73.
Gottwald, N. K. 1979. *The Tribes of Yahweh.* Maryknoll, NY.
Halpern, B. 1974. Sectionalism and the Schism. *JBL* 93: 519–32.
———. 1983. *The Emergence of Israel in Canaan.* Chico, CA.
Hopkins, D. C. 1985. *The Highlands of Canaan.* Sheffield.
Hulse, E. V. 1971. Joshua's Curse and the Abandonment of Ancient Jericho: Schistosomiasis as a Possible Medical Explanation. *Medical History* 15: 376–86.
Ibrahim, M.; Sauer, J.; and Yassine, K. 1976. The East Jordan Valley Survey, 1975. *BASOR* 222: 41–66.
Ingraham, J. L., et al. 1981. Preliminary Report on a Reconnaissance Survey of the Northwestern Province. *Atlal* 5: 59–84.
Kitchen, K. A. 1982. *Pharaoh Triumphant.* Warminster.
Kraus, H.-J. 1951. Gilgal. Ein Beitrag zur Kulturgeschichte Israels. *VT* 1: 181–99.
Mattingly, G. L. 1983. The Exodus-Conquest and the Archaeology of Transjordan: New Light and an Old Problem. *GTJ* 4: 245–62.
McDonald, B. 1982. The Wadi el-Hasa Survey 1979 and Previous Archaeological Work in Southern Jordan. *BASOR* 245: 35–52.
———. 1983a. The Wadi el-Hasa Archaeological Survey, 1982: Phase III. *ASOR Newsletter* (January 1983): 5–8.
———. 1983b. The Late Bronze and Iron Age Sites of the Wadi el-Hasa Survey, 1979. Pp. 18–28 in *Midian, Moab, and Edom,* ed. J. F. A. Sawyer and D. J. A. Clines. JSOTSup 24. Sheffield.
———. 1984. The Wadi el-Hasa Archaeological Survey. Pp. 113–28 in *The Answers Lie Below,* ed. H. O. Thompson. New York.
McKeating, H. 1975. The Development of the Law on Homicide in Ancient Israel. *VT* 25: 46–68.
Mendenhall, G. E. 1962. The Hebrew Conquest of Palestine. *BA* 25: 66–87 (= *BAR* 3: 100–20).
———. 1973. *The Tenth Generation.* Baltimore.
Meyers, C. 1978. The Roots of Restriction: Women in Early Israel. *BA* 41: 91–103.
Miller, J. M. 1979a. Archaeological Survey South of the Wady Mujib. *ADAJ* 23: 79–92.
———. 1979b. Archaeological Survey of Central Moab: 1978. *BASOR* 234: 43–52.
Mittmann, S. 1970. *Beitrage zur Siedlungs- und Territorialgeschichte des nördlichen Ostjordanlandes.* Weisbaden.
Polk, T. 1979. The Levites in the Davidic-Solomonic Empire. *StudBT* 9: 3–22.
Soggin, J. A. 1966. Gilgal, Passah und Landnahme. VTSup 15: 263–77.
Stager, L. E. 1981. Highland Village Life in Palestine Some Three Thousand Years Ago. *The Oriental Institute News and Notes* 69: 1.
Wilson, R. 1984. *Sociological Approaches to the OT.* Philadelphia.
Yadin, Y. 1968. And Dan, Why Did He Remain with the Ships? *AJBA* 1: 9–23.
Zertal, A. 1985. Has Joshua's Altar Been Found on Mt. Ebal? *BARev* 11: 126–43.

ROBERT G. BOLING

JOSHUA, PSALMS OF (*4Q378–379*). Two highly fragmentary manuscripts from Qumran Cave 4 (*4Q378* and 4Q*379*) contain an otherwise unknown work which has come to be known as the *Psalms of Joshua.* The text had a narrative framework that followed the outline of events in the biblical book of Joshua. The death of Moses, the succession of Joshua, the crossing of the Jordan, and the destruction of Jericho are all referred to. In contrast to the canonical Joshua, however, much of the material preserved in the *Psalms of Joshua* consists of admonitory speeches, prayers, songs, and curses. The style is strongly biblicizing, with occasional quotations from the biblical text (esp. Deuteronomy and Joshua). Where identifiable, the biblical text type is Septuagintal.

It is unlikely that the document was composed by the Qumran community. Neither the content nor the diction shows any affinity with the distinctive theology or terminology of Qumran sectarian writings (e.g., the *Rule of the Community* or the *Thanksgiving Hymns*). The *Psalms of Joshua* uses divine names avoided in Qumran compositions *(yhwh, ʾĕlōhîm, ʾĕlôah)* and does not use the term favored at Qumran *(ʾēl).* Moreover, the *Psalms of Joshua* is cited as an authoritative text in a Qumran composition *(4QTestimonia).* The only clue to a more specific provenance is the reference to the date of the crossing of the Jordan that identifies it as a jubilee year. The same calculation is implied by *Jub.* 50:4.

The date of composition is extremely difficult to fix. An expanded form of the curse of Josh 6:26 on the one who rebuilds Jericho may contain a historical allusion to the activity of the Hasmonean ruler Simon (reigned 142–134 B.C.E.), but the case is not conclusive. The expanded curse is quoted in the *Testimonia.* That text consists of a series of four quotations. The first three are from the Pentateuch and were apparently understood as prophecies of an eschatological prophet, a royal messiah, and a priestly messiah. The fourth is the curse from the *Psalms of Joshua,* which was apparently also given eschatological significance.

Bibliography

Newsom, C. A. 1988. The 'Psalms of Joshua' from Qumran Cave 4. *JJS* 39: 56–73.

CAROL A. NEWSOM

JOSIAH (PERSON) [Heb *yōʾšiyyāh(û)*]. The root of the name is probably *ʾwš,* "to give" (Gordon *UT,* 354a, no. 117); compare also *yōʾwšiyyāhû* (Jer 27:1), Joash, and *yāʾûš* of the Lachish Letters (from *yāhûyāʾûš* or *ʾelyāʾûš,* "Yahweh/God shall grant" [Gibson *TSSI* 1: 37]), and Ug *ʾušn,* "gift". The root may, however, be *yšy,* "Yahweh brings forth" (Bauer 1930: 77), or Arabic *ʾasā,* "to heal" (Noth *IPN,* 212; 1956: 326).

1. King of Judah ca. 640–609 B.C.E.; son and successor of Amon. Josiah after his father's murder was made king by the "people of the land" (2 Kgs 21:24; 2 Chr 33:25), designating especially the Judean landowners enjoying full citizen rights (*THAT* 2: 299–300). He came to the throne at the age of eight and reigned for 31 years (2 Kgs 22:1; 2 Chr 34:1). His mother was Jedidah, daughter of Adaiah of Bozkath (cf. Josh 15:39).

a. Josiah's Reform in the Sources. The early years of Josiah's reign are presented in different ways by the sources. Chronicles records that in the 8th year of his reign (ca. 632 B.C.E.) Josiah began to seek the God of David his father (2 Chr 34:3a). This indicates an "inner attitude of loyalty towards God" (Williamson *Chronicles* NCBC, 95). In the 12th year of his reign (628/627 B.C.E.), he began to purge Judah and Jerusalem of the high places with their attendant cult objects (vv 3b–5) and then extended his efforts to Manasseh, Ephraim, and Simeon, as far as Naphtali (vv 6–7). In the 18th year of his reign (622/621 B.C.E.), after the finding of the Book of the Law in the temple, he carried out a great reform program (34:8–35:19).

But the author of Kings mentions only the reform in the 18th year of Josiah (2 Kgs 22:3), though this too extended beyond the borders of Judah and included the "cities of Samaria" (23:19), that is, the territory of the former N kingdom.

Another difference between the biblical sources concerns the reform of the cult. According to 2 Kings 23 Josiah removed both the Canaanite cult and the foreign emblems of worship. According to Chronicles only the Canaanite cult was removed. Manasseh had already purged the foreign idols (2 Chr 33:15). Chronicles' picture in 34:3b–7 is, however, essentially dependent on 2 Kings 23 (Williamson *Chronicles,* 397–99).

b. Civil War in Assyria and the Reform. For Chronicles, Josiah's reform begin in 628/627 B.C.E., coinciding with the beginning of civil war in Assyria (Cross and Freedman 1953: 56–58; Cazelles 1981: 25, n. 17). According to the Babylonian Chronicle (Wiseman 1956), Sin-shar-ishkun and Sin-shum-lishir revolted against Assur-etel-ilani in 627 B.C.E. By 626 Nabopolassar, king of the Babylonian marshland, had joined the war. In the same year he and Sin-shar-ishkun, when Assur-etel-ilani's army posed a serious threat to them both, appear to have agreed to recognize each other as kings of Babylon and Assyria respectively (Reade 1970: 4). These events allowed Josiah gradually to assert his independence and extend the reform into the former territory of the kingdom of Israel. Political objectives influenced the move into the N provinces (Nelson 1983: 183–84). Both Egypt and Judah wished to avoid a concentration of power in Asia and consequently supported the weaker party, Assyria. It is conceivable that Josiah remained a nominal vassal of Assyria right up to the end. But the call to reform was primarily religious, being voiced above all by those responsible for the law book (McKay 1973: 43).

c. The Law Book and the Reform. The account in Kings indeed considers the reform entirely a consequence of the law book's discovery; and it may be that Chronicles, if it is not drawing on a separate tradition (Cross and Freedman 1953: 57), prefers to spread out the reform in order to illustrate the theme of righteousness rewarded (Williamson *Chronicles,* 401–2). The piety of Josiah is shown earlier than in Kings; and the repairs to the temple, which in Kings were the occasion for the finding of the law book, now become an integral part of the reform.

The law book itself functions as a reward for Josiah's faithfulness as well as an encouragement to further obedience. In addition, because Josiah responds to the book's demands, he is told by the prophetess Huldah that he will not witness the destruction of Jerusalem but will die "in peace" (2 Chr 34:28), perhaps with the sense that the state will still be intact (Gray *1–2 Kings* OTL, 727).

d. Elements in the Reform. McKay (1973: 28–29) points out that Kings distinguishes three main aspects in Josiah's reform: the purge of the temple and its precincts, the destruction of the high places in Jerusalem and Judah, and the desecration of the sanctuaries in the old N kingdom (2 Kgs 23:4–20, 24). Chronicles provides a similar structure, but the purge of the temple is ascribed to Manasseh (2 Chr 33:15–16)—a notice which is quite possibly historical but probably marks a very limited action (Williamson *Chronicles,* 394–95). The reform may well have begun before the discovery of the law book, though this early stage was not confined to removing foreign cults (McKay 1973: 28–44) and the waning of Assyrian influence will have been a contributory factor (Cross and Freedman 1953; Rose 1977: 52, n. 15; Mayes 1978); but the Chronicler's account does not prove that its author has preserved an independent record of it (Williamson *Chronicles,* 398).

The territorial extent of Josiah's reform in the former N kingdom has been questioned (Rose 1977: 61, n. 49; Nelson 1981: 537–38), but the Meṣad Ḥashavyahu (Yabneh-Yam) inscriptions seem to show that N Philistia was under Josiah's control (Naveh 1960; Christensen 1984: 678), so that a substantial advance into the N territory would appear to have been feasible. Josiah and Pharaoh Psamtik I (ca. 664–609 B.C.E.) were probably allies, and Egypt will have been able to use the coastal route for its military operations in the N (Cazelles 1981: 31; Nelson 1983: 183–89).

e. The Finding of the Law Book. The law book which influenced Josiah's reform was found in the temple according to the account in 2 Kings 22, but when and by whom it was composed remain obscure. The narrative of repairs to the temple, which forms the context for the discovery of the law book, strongly resembles the story of King Joash's temple restoration in 2 Kings 12 and is therefore sometimes judged to be an invention of a Deuteronomistic Historian (Dietrich 1977: 18–22; Mayes *Deuteronomy* NCBC, 90–91). The account of the discovery of the law book has also been thought unhistorical (Mayes *Deuteronomy,* 85–103), even a "discovery legend" *(Auffindungslegende)* with the aim of legitimating the reform (Diebner and Nauerth 1984). While one may accept Deuteronomistic influence on the portrayal of these matters, to regard their substance as fiction seems to allow the historian a greater measure of freedom in respect of his sources than he is likely to have enjoyed (*NDH,* 84–88). It is preferable to follow the common opinion that the document existed and forms at least part of our book of Deuteronomy (Lundbom 1976; Dietrich 1977; Scharbert 1981: 45, n. 21).

f. Josiah in the Deuteronomistic History. Josiah plays an important role in the Deuteronomistic History. When Jeroboam I established a countercultus to Jerusalem in Bethel and Dan, his great sin (1 Kgs 12:26–33), an unnamed prophet foretold Josiah's destruction of Bethel (13:2). Josiah alone of the kings, not excepting David, escaped all criticism (2 Kgs 22:2) and gave his full attention to fulfilling the law of Moses (23:25a; see Cross *CMHE,*

283). The cultus was centralized according to the ancient law of the sanctuary; no doubt this move was influenced at least in part by a desire to possess the dues going to the Levites who controlled the country sanctuaries (Claburn 1973) and to ensure that royal control of all public worship, which had existed since Sennacherib left Hezekiah little more than Jerusalem, should continue (Levin 1984: 352).

g. The Passover. The climax of the reform was the celebration of the Passover (2 Kgs 23:21–23; 2 Chr 35:1–19). The narrative in Kings has been judged to be the work of a postexilic redactor (Levin 1984: 353–54, 371), but the Passover may have been removed from the family circle and centralized at the temple as a Yahwistic response to the child sacrifice practiced in the vicinity (Delcor 1982). Josiah's work for the true God reaches a climax in covenant renewal (Nelson 1981: 536). 2 Chronicles 35 offers a more detailed description of the Passover feast (vv 1–19) with emphasis on the role of the priests, Levites, and singers.

h. The Fall of the Assyrian Empire. Outside events do not appear in the biblical record until 609 B.C.E., but the Assyrian kings' grip on their own empire was growing steadily weaker (Garelli and Nikiprowetzky 1974: 125–28). In 623 Assur-etel-ilani died at Nippur while besieging Sin-shar-ishkun, who then marched on Nineveh and mounted the Assyrian throne. Meanwhile Cyaxares, a Mede who had succeeded in imposing his authority over Scythian and Persian tribes, proceeded to attack the E Assyrian provinces. By 616 Nabopolassar controlled all Babylonia. In 614 Assur fell to Cyaxares, and in 612 the Medes and Babylonians captured Nineveh, and the last Assyrian king, Assur-uballit II, withdrew to Haran. Meanwhile Egypt had been trying to help Assyria since at least 616—the Babylonian Chronicle features a gap between 623 and 616—when Nabopolassar encountered the army of Psamtik I (ca. 664–609 B.C.E.) on the Euphrates. Nevertheless, Nabopolassar captured Haran in 610 and in roughly the same year Psamtik I died.

i. Josiah's Death. The new pharaoh, Neco II (ca. 609–594 B.C.E.), continuing his father's policy, quickly marched N to help the Assyrians. At Megiddo he killed Josiah, whose body was then taken to Jerusalem for burial (2 Kgs 23:29–30). Chronicles provides a reason for his early and violent death by stating that he went to fight Neco, disobeying the word of God spoken by the pharaoh, "I am not coming against you this day, but against the house with which I am at war; and God has commanded me to make haste. Cease opposing God, who is with me, lest he destroy you" (2 Chr 35:21). Josiah was mortally wounded in the ensuing battle, but died in Jerusalem, and was mourned by Jerusalem and Judah (vv 20–24). This account may, however, depend on a revised and expanded form of that in Kings (Williamson 1982, 1987), or it may represent the Chronicler's own reworking of Kings (Begg 1987).

It is generally thought (e.g., Malamat 1973) that Josiah died trying to stop Neco, though he had apparently not interfered in 616 or 610. More attractive is the view (Nelson 1983: 188) that Josiah went out from Megiddo, a Judean fortress, as was Meṣad Ḥashavyahu much farther S, to welcome his ally Neco, intending to open the pass for the Egyptian forces. But Neco wanted the strategically placed Megiddo, which controlled his communications with Egypt, for himself. Unwilling to allow an ally who might change sides the opportunity of blocking his retreat before a victorious army, he killed Josiah by treachery, putting into Megiddo an Egyptian garrison. Judah will have been demoralized and unable to make an effective response.

j. Jeremiah on Josiah. For the Deuteronomistic Historian, Josiah was an outstanding king (2 Kgs 23:25), perhaps even Judah's most perfect ruler (Nelson 1981: 540). Yet Jeremiah took little notice of him. It has been argued by supporters of a low chronology that Jeremiah's prophetic career began only after the death of Josiah (Whitley 1968; Holladay 1980, 1981, 1983; Levin 1981); but although caution is necessary in linking Jeremiah's oracles with what we know of the sequence of historical events (Ackroyd 1984: 50), the evidence adduced for a low chronology is not conclusive (Scharbert 1981: 41, 46).

Jeremiah compares Josiah favorably with Jehoiakim: "Did not your father eat and drink and do justice and righteousness" (Jer 22:15). The precise force of the expression "eat and drink" is obscure, but it may simply mean that, although he kept a royal court and enjoyed life, he still practiced justice (Smend 1977: 452–54).

Josiah's motives for cultic reform were not purely religious, and it is likely that even in his lifetime its limited effect on the people was perceptible. He met his death in a political dispute. This Jeremiah saw, and his cool appraisal of Josiah furnishes a corrective to the enthusiasm of the Deuteronomistic Historian.

2. Son of Zephaniah, to whose house three Jews from the Exile bring gifts (Zech 6:10). It is not certain whether or not he should be identified with the son of Zephaniah in v 14.

Bibliography

Ackroyd, P. R. 1984. The Book of Jeremiah—Some Recent Studies. *JSOT* 28: 47–59.

Bauer, H. 1930. Die hebräischen Eigennamen als sprachliche Erkenntnisquelle. *ZAW* 48: 73–80.

Begg, C. T. 1987. The Death of Josiah in Chronicles: Another View. *VT* 37: 1–8.

Bogaert, P.-M., ed. 1981. *Le Livre de Jeremie.* BETL 54. Louvain.

Cazelles, H. 1981. La vie de Jérémie dans son contexte national et international. Pp. 21–39 in Bogaert 1981.

Christensen, D. L. 1984. Zephaniah 2:4–15: A Theological Basis for Josiah's Program of Political Expansion. *CBQ* 46: 669–82.

Claburn, W. E. 1973. The Fiscal Basis of Josiah's Reforms. *JBL* 92: 11–22.

Cross, F. M., and Freedman, D. N. 1953. Josiah's Revolt against Assyria. *JNES* 12: 56–58.

Delcor, M. 1982. Réflexions sur la Pâque du temps de Josias d'après 2 Rois 23, 21–23. *Henoch* 4: 205–19.

Diebner, B. J., and Nauerth, C. 1984. Die Inventio des sefaer hattôrāh in 2 Kön 22. *DBAT* 18: 95–118.

Dietrich, W. 1977. Josia und das Gesetzbuch (2 Reg. XXII). *VT* 27: 13–35.

Garelli, P., and Nikiprowetzky, V. 1974. *Le Proche-orient asiatique: Les empires mésopotamiens: Israël.* La Nouvelle Clio 2 bis. Paris.

Holladay, W. L. 1980. The Identification of the Two Scrolls of Jeremiah. *VT* 30: 452–67.

———. 1981. A Coherent Chronology of Jeremiah's Early Career. Pp. 58–73 in Bogaert 1981.

———. 1983. The Years of Jeremiah's Preaching. *Int* 37: 146–59.

Hollenstein, H. 1977. Literarkritische Erwägungen zum Bericht über die Reformmassnahmen Josias 2 Kön. 4ff. *VT* 27: 321–36.
Levin, C. 1981. Noch einmal: die Anfänge des Propheten Jeremia. *VT* 31: 428–40.
———. 1984. Joschija im deuteronomistischen Geschichtswerk. *ZAW* 96: 351–71.
Lundbom, J. R. 1976. The Law Book of the Josian Reform. *CBQ* 38: 293–302.
Malamat, A. 1973. Josiah's Bid for Armageddon: The Background of the Judean-Egyptian Encounter in 609 B.C. *JANES* 5: 267–80 (Gaster Festschrift).
Mayes, A. D. H. 1978. King and Covenant: A Study of 2 Kings Chs 22–23. *Herm* 125: 34–47.
McKay, J. W. 1973. *Religion in Judah under the Assyrians 732–609 B.C.* SBT n.s. 26. London.
Naveh, J. 1960. A Hebrew Letter from the Seventh Century B.C. *IEJ* 10: 129–39.
Nelson, R. D. 1981. Josiah in the Book of Joshua. *JBL* 100: 531–40.
———. 1983. *Realpolitik* in Judah (687–609 B.C.E.). Pp. 177–89 in *Scripture in Context II,* ed. W. W. Hallo, J. C. Moyer, and L. C. Perdue. Winona Lake, IN.
Noth, M. 1956. Remarks on the Sixth Volume of Mari Texts. *JSS* 1: 322–33.
Reade, J. 1970. The Accession of Sinsharishkun. *JCS* 28: 1–9.
Rose, M. 1977. Bemerkungen zum historischen Fundament des Josia-Bildes in II Reg. 22f. *ZAW* 89: 50–63.
Scharbert, J. 1981. Jeremia und die Reform des Joschija. Pp. 40–57 in Bogaert 1981.
Smend, R. 1977. Essen und Trinken—ein Stück Weltlichkeit des Alten Testaments. Pp. 446–59 in *Beiträge zur Alttestamentlichen Theologie: Festschrift für Walther Zimmerli zum 70. Geburtstag,* ed. H. Donner, R. Hanhart, and R. Smend. Göttingen.
Whitley, C. F. 1968. Carchemish and Jeremiah. *ZAW* 80: 38–49.
Williamson, H. G. M. 1982. The Death of Josiah and the Continuing Development of the Deuteronomic History. *VT* 32: 242–48.
———. 1987. Reliving the Death of Josiah: A Reply to C. T. Begg. *VT* 37: 9–15.
Wiseman, D. J. 1956. *Chronicles of Chaldaean Kings (626–556 B.C.) in the British Museum.* London.
Würthwein, E. 1976. Die josianische Reform und das Deuteronomium. *ZTK* 73: 395–423.

ROBERT ALTHANN

JOSIPHIAH (PERSON) [Heb *yôsipyāh*]. The father of one of the family heads—Shelomith—who, with 160 males, returned with Ezra from exile in Babylon during the reign of the Persian king Artaxerxes (Ezra 8:10; 1 Esdr 8:36). His inclusion among the sons of Bani is supplied by the LXX (but not Codex Vaticanus) of Ezra and by 1 Esdras. His theophoric name, with an imperfect form of Heb *ysp* followed by the contracted proper name of the deity, gives expression, according to Noth (*IPN,* 212), to the wish for additional children—"may Yahweh add to (those children already born)."

RODNEY H. SHEARER

JOSIPPON, BOOK OF. A version of the writings of Flavius JOSEPHUS dating to the medieval period and written in a superb biblical Hebrew style. The book begins with the list of Japheth's descendants (Gen 10:2–5), which the author identifies with existing nations of his own day. A fabulous history of ancient Italy follows (based on unhistorical sources from the early Middle Ages). Then the book proceeds to its real aim: the presentation of the history of the Second Temple period, ending with the fall of Masada.

A. Introduction

For the past 500 years this book has been available in two different forms, each reflected in a different printed edition. The older of these editions (the editio princeps), based on a condensed and carelessly restyled form of the original, was published in Mantua around 1480 and has had little influence on modern scholarship. The second printed edition, based on an expanded and rewritten form of the original, was published in Constantinople in 1510 and became the source of all subsequent printings (most recently reedited by H. Huminer [1971]). Until recently the Constantinople edition was the form of Josippon most familiar to both scholars and other interested readers, and it is properly regarded as a pseudepigraphon (a writing falsely attributed to Josephus).

However, a third critical edition of Josippon has recently been prepared (Flusser 1978–80), based not on these printed editions but rather on the original manuscript evidence itself; and it now appears that originally the book of Josippon was not intended to be a pseudepigraphon. Consequently, we are now in a position to make some confident claims about the original form and to understand how the two printed editions came to depart from it.

B. The Original Form

1. Authorship. Among the extant mss of Josippon are three based on a manuscript copied by Rabbi Gershom ben-Judah (ca. A.D. 960–1028), who probably made his copy to use as a textbook on Second Temple history. One of these three mss preserves the original author's note that he wrote and translated "from the book of Joseph (i.e., Josephus) ben-Gurion the priest in the year 885 from the destruction." Since it was customary then to reckon the destruction of the temple from the year A.D. 68, we can conclude that the book was written in A.D. 953. This accords well with the up-to-date description of Japheth's descendants that begins the book. There, the author states that the Hungarians were already settled along the river Danube, a situation that did not exist prior to A.D. 895–899. Similarly, he refers to the Muslim conquest of Tarsus (in Asia Minor) and to the ongoing Muslim-Byzantine conflict, yet he is still unaware of the Byzantine recapture of Tarsus in 965. This is exactly the perspective of an author writing in the middle of the 10th century.

The author was self-conscious of his work as a historian, and states: "I have collected stories from the book of Joseph ben-Gurion and from the books of other authors who wrote down the deeds of our ancestors, and I compiled them in one scroll." The name of this author, however, did not appear on the work itself and was soon forgotten; consequently, the book became known simply as the "Book of Joseph ben-Gurion" or, in Latin, "Josephus Gorionides" (a confused reference to Flavius Josephus; see

B.2 below). Since Josephus was quoted therein as the main source for the book, it erroneously came to be ascribed to this 1st-century writer himself (a mistake that was deliberately compounded by the person who prepared the version on which the Constantinople edition was based; see C below). Thus the book also came to be known generally as *Sefer Josippon* ("Josippon" being the Judeo-Greek form for Josephus), although the name Josippon itself does not appear in the original texts of the book. The fact that the book was known by this Judeo-Greek title indicates that its first readers were Byzantine Jews.

The anonymous author of this medieval book apparently lived in S Italy, which at that time was a center of Jewish culture and of Hebrew literary activity. This S Italian provenance is reflected not only by some Italian words which crept into the text, but also by the author's familiarity with the region, including his firsthand knowledge of the environs of Naples, the town in which he presumably lived and wrote.

2. Sources. Although the book was written in biblical Hebrew, the anonymous author was far better versed in Latin literature than in postbiblical Hebrew rabbinic sources. And even though S Italy at the time was under the sway of Byzantine civilization, where the official language was Greek, the author was apparently unable to utilize sources written in Greek. Thus, in examining the sources used in the writing of this book, we must appreciate the importance of the author's background education in Latin.

Two main sources were utilized in the composition of the main part of the book dealing with the Second Temple period. The first was a Latin mss containing 16 of the 20 books of Josephus' *Ant* and a paraphrase of Josephus' *JW.* This Latin paraphrase, commonly called *Hegesippus,* was written around A.D. 370; and it is noteworthy that the four extant Latin mss of this paraphrase were all written in Italy, where the author of Josippon lived and wrote. Like *Hegesippus,* the book of Josippon ends with the fall of Masada. Although it is not certain, it also appears that the author of Josippon knew some scattered bits of information from *JW* itself; and he also refers to Josephus' *AgAp.* The author's second main source for Second Temple history was the Apocrypha (in the Vulgate). In his description of the Maccabean period, the author depends on 1–2 Maccabees, which he combined in order to present a clearer picture of the events. From 1 Esdras 3–4 he based his description of the contest of the three young men, in which Zerubbabel was victorious. His stories about Daniel's victory over Bel and the dragon and about Esther and Mordecai are recounted according to the apocryphal additions to Daniel and Esther. An additional source for Esther's prayer is the prayer of Aseneth as it appeared in one of the Latin translations of *Joseph and Aseneth,* a Jewish romance originally written in Greek (Flusser 1985).

In composing that portion of the book dealing with the history of ancient Italy and the founding of Rome, the author drew upon various legends contained in early medieval Latin sources, which themselves were obscure and have not been preserved. However, it is possible to detect some of the more reliable roots of these sources; e.g., there is a later elaboration of the chronicle by the Church Father Jerome, a reference to Cyrus' death from the patristic historian Orosius (ca. 400), a reference to the beginning of Roman history from the Roman poet Virgil, and a reference to the war with Hannibal from Titus Livius.

Thus, when following his main historical sources, the original author of the book of Josippon was a responsible historian with excellent historical insight, whose integrity as a historian shaped his use of sources and limited his use of fables and other fantastic stories. This is in marked contrast with the person who prepared the pseudepigraphic version on which the Constantinople edition was based (see C below).

3. Impact. Because it was directed to readers unfamiliar with Latin and Greek, the book of Josippon quickly became a first-rate source of information about the Second Temple period for both Jews and Arabs—an Arabic translation had been completed by the time of the Arab scholar Ibn-Hazm (ca. 1063), who referred to the book by name (see Wellhausen 1897; Pines 1985). Jewish biblical and Talmudic scholars who did not know the OT Apocrypha and believed that the book was written by Josephus himself (including such famous commentators as Rashi [ca. 1100]), all used the book of Josippon in their treatises and commentaries.

However, the book of Josippon did not satisfy those Christians (and Muslims) who thought that from it they could learn what Josephus had recorded about Jesus and the rise of Christianity. Because the last four books of Josephus' *Ant* were not accessible to him, the author of Josippon himself was unaware of the passages about Jesus (*Ant* 18.3.3 §63–64), about his brother James' martyrdom (20.9.1 §200), and about John the Baptist (18 §116–19). However, because he utilized *Hegesippus,* he was familiar with its passages alluding to Christian subjects; but with the exception of a reference to John the Baptist, he omitted these passages altogether. Thus the original author of Josippon wrote nothing about Jesus.

Nonetheless, in two extant mss of Josippon (and partially in a third) a small text, written in imitation of Josippon's style, was interpolated (see Levi 1932; Flusser 1978–80: 1, appendix). Written sometime before 1150, this interpolation contains a confused and polemical story about Jesus and the beginnings of Christianity along with a story about Susanna (derived from the OT Apocrypha). The stories are set during the reign of the emperor Caligula (A.D. 37–41); thus the hero of the Susanna story is renamed from Daniel to Nahman. In this text Jesus' claims are connected with those of the insane Caligula, showing that this interpolation was influenced by the earlier (Aramaic) form of the medieval Jewish story *Toledot Yeshu* ("The History of Jesus"), which was blatantly anti-Christian. This interpolation was subsequently condensed into a note of only a few lines. Only vestiges of this note appear in the Mantua printed edition of 1480, probably the result of censorship. This brief note about Jesus is also preserved in only one of the two mss on which the 1510 Constantinople edition was based; in the other it was deleted by an ecclesiastical censor. It was then omitted in all subsequent printed editions, from the first Constantinople print (1510) on.

C. Subsequent (Constantinople) Form

As noted above, from the recent study of the mss evidence, we now know that the original author of the book of Josippon was a learned Jew keenly aware of his responsibilities as a historian. He did not pretend that his work was written by Josephus, but rather cited Josephus as his main source. On the whole his references to Josephus are basically correct; however, he refers to Josephus incorrectly as "Joseph ben-Gurion," when in fact his real Hebrew name was "Joseph ben-Matthias." Here the original author of Josippon was simply misled by his Latin source (*Heges.* III.3.27, based upon *JW* 2 §253), where "Joseph the son of Gorion" is named first among the Jewish leaders of the war.

However, no one can claim that the subsequent author of the expanded form of the book of Josippon—the form underlying the Constantinople printed edition—was a responsible historian. Although he himself did not lack Jewish or secular knowledge, his secondary reformulation of the book of Josippon was written in the spirit of unrestrained medieval fantasy, incorporating a number of fictitious elements. For example, he invented an imaginary description of the crowning of Vespasian in Rome (by a Pope!), patterned according to the custom of crowning medieval emperors.

This author made one other change that had a significant impact on how the book of Josippon would be viewed in the centuries following: he converted it into a pseudepigraphon. He took advantage of three things to create a book that no longer simply cited Josephus as a main source but actually now claimed to have been written by Josephus himself. The first of these was the fact that the name of the original author had been forgotten, and thus, since Josephus is often expressly quoted in the book, it was—from the 11th century on—commonly ascribed to Josephus himself. The second was the title that had come to be associated with the book—*Sefer Josippon,* "the book *of* Josippus/Josephus." The third was the knowledge that, before writing *JW* in Greek for his Roman audience, the 1st-century Josephus composed it in his native language (*JW* 1. Proem 1 §3), a version of *JW* that has not survived. See JOSEPHUS. Thus he cast his revision of Josippon in such a way as to portray Josephus speaking in the first person about himself and about the purpose of his book, giving the false impression that this expanded form of the Hebrew Josippon was the lost original that Josephus had initially written for fellow Jews. This, of course, greatly enhanced the reputation of this work, since many medieval Jews, Christians, and Muslims believed this false ascription of authorship to Flavius Josephus.

It appears that this recasting of the original Josippon occurred during the first half of the 12th century, and no later than ca. 1160. Sometime in the 14th century it was edited by Judah Leon Mosconi, whose edition became the basis of the Constantinople printed edition of 1510. This edition immediately became the standard; and from the 16th century on it was translated into Yiddish, Ladino, Latin, German, English, Czech, and Polish. Thus, until the recent preparation of a new critical edition, only this secondary revision of Josippon was known. Modern scholars were quick to recognize its pseudepigraphic character but to view it, nevertheless, as an important source of medieval Jewish folklore containing vestiges of ancient Jewish sources and legends.

Bibliography

Flusser, D. 1974. Der lateinische Josephus under der hebräische Josippon. Pp. 122–32 in *Josephus Studien,* ed. O. Betz. Göttingen.

———. 1978–80. *The Josippon.* 2 vols. Jerusalem (in Hebrew).

———. 1985. Joseph and Asenath. Pp. 77–78 in *Dappim: Research in Literature,* ed. S. Yaniv. Haifa (in Hebrew).

Huminer, H., ed. 1971. *Josiphon.* Jerusalem.

Levi, I. 1932. Jesus Caligula et Claude dans une interpolation du Josippon. *REJ* 91: 139–41.

Pines, S. 1985. A Preliminary Note. *Jerusalem Studies in Arabic and Islam* 6: 145–61.

Wellhausen, J. 1897. *Der arabische Josippon.* Berlin.

DAVID FLUSSER

JOTAPATA (PLACE). See IOTAPE (PLACE).

JOTBAH (PLACE) [Heb *yoṭbâ*]. The hometown of Haruz, whose daughter Meshullemeth married Manasseh, king of Judah, and gave birth to his son and heir Amon (2 Kgs 21:19). Forrer (1920: 61) has suggested that the place name *[ ]-at-bi-ta* that appears in the annals of Tiglath-pileser III, describing his 732 B.C.E. campaign to Galilee (*ANET,* 283), be restored to *ia-at-bi-te* and be identified with biblical Jotbah. According to the annals 650 prisoners were exiled from this place.

It has also been suggested that Jotbah be identified with "Jotapata," the fortress where Josephus was besieged by Vespasian (*JW* 3.141–334), with "Yŏdpat" (*M.* ʿ*Arak.* 9:6; Klein 1939: 163), and with "Yōṭbat" of Talmudic literature (*t. Nida* 3:11; *b. Nida* 20A). All four have been identified with Khirbet Shifăt (M.R. 176248) N of the Beth Netofa valley. The finds from this site and its situation conform to Josephus' very dramatic description of Jotapata. See also IOTAPE (PLACE). However, in recent surveys (Meyers, et al. 1978: 6) Iron Age finds have not been found at the site; Gal (1982: 22, 117) therefore suggests that the biblical Jotbah be identified with Kerem el-Ras (M.R. 181239). The land adjoining this ten acre site is called Jifat, and the pottery collected there dates from the 10th to the 8th century B.C.E.

It is significant that the grandson of MESHULLEMETH of Jotbah, King Josiah, married Zebudah, a woman from the town of Rumah (2 Kgs 23: 36). Rumah is either identified with Khirbet Ruma (M.R. 177243) or is located in its vicinity. This site is near both proposed locations of Jotbah, 6 km NE of Kerem el-Ras and 10 km S of Khirbet Shifăt.

Bibliography

Forrer, E. 1920. *Die Provinzeinteilung des Assyrischen Reiches.* Leipzig.

Gal, Z. 1982. The Lower Galilee in the Iron Age. Diss., Tel Aviv (in Hebrew).

Klein, S. 1939. *Sefer Ha Yišub.* Repr. Jerusalem, 1977 (in Hebrew).

Meyers, E. M., et al. 1978. The Meiron Excavation Project. *BASOR* 230: 1–24.

RAFAEL FRANKEL

JOTBATHAH (PLACE) [Heb *yoṭbātâ*]. The 18th encampment of the Israelites, after leaving the Wilderness of Sinai, as listed in Num 33:33–34, where it is placed between Hor-haggidgad and Abronah. In Deut 10:7 it is listed as the station after Gudgodah. The Deuteronomy passage also relates that the area was well supplied with water, which probably is the basis for its name: "Pleasantness." Suggested locations include et-Taba, the source of a marshy winter lake near the Wâdī Ghadhaghed (Abel *GP,* 216; Simons *GTTOT,* 259, and map IIIc; M.R. 153922), and the vicinity of Tabeh, about 11 km SW of Eilat (Aharoni *LBHG,* 199–200; Rothenberg 1961: 163–64; M.R. 139878). Robinson visited the latter area but did not mention it in connection with the biblical site (1856: 160–61). For a discussion of the location of any of the places associated with the journey of the Israelites from Egypt through Sinai, see DOPHKAH.

Bibliography

Beit-Arieh, I. 1988. The Route through Sinai—Why the Israelites Fleeing Egypt Went South. *BARev* 15/3: 28–37.

Robinson, E. 1856. *Biblical Researches in Palestine.* Boston.

Rothenberg, B. 1961. *God's Wilderness.* New York.

JEFFREY R. ZORN

JOTHAM (PERSON) [Heb *yôtām*]. **1.** The son of Jahdai, a Judahite who belonged to the clan of Caleb (1 Chr 2:47).

2. The youngest of the 70 sons of Jerubbaal, who was also known as Gideon (Judg 9:5; cf. 8:30). By hiding himself, Jotham escaped the fury of his half-brother Abimelech who, with the help of hired rascals, murdered the remaining sons of Jerubbaal. With these rivals eliminated, the citizens of Shechem made Abimelech their king (Judg 9:6). Once informed about Abimelech's investiture, Jotham went to the top of Mt. Gerizim overlooking Shechem and projected his voice to those standing in the valley below. By means of a powerful fable (Judg 9:8–15), Jotham rebuked the men of Shechem who had supported Abimelech's conspiracy. This intricately structured fable discloses that when the trees sought for a king to rule over them, they were turned down by the olive, the fig, and the vine, which were thoroughly committed to their ordinary and useful functions. But when the bramble was offered the kingship, it accepted. The irony is powerful. If the olive, the fig, and the vine are understood agricultural symbols of goodness, it follows that the bramble would be an easily recognized symbol of uselessness.

In the ensuing application (Judg 9:16–20), the fable is interpreted against Abimelech's supporters, who have not acted "in good faith and honor" (vv 16, 19). Having forgotten the risks that Jerubbaal had taken in their behalf, they sponsored the slaying of his legitimate sons and rallied around a scoundrel of their own clan. Jotham concluded his speech with a curse against Shechem and its king that was fulfilled three years later when the city was demolished and Abimelech was struck by a lethal millstone hurled by a nameless woman (Judg 9:53–54). Lindars (1973: 361) argues that by speaking a fable, Jotham chose to express his criticism obliquely. His listeners were induced to ponder their role in making Abimelech king. But whatever the style of his critique, Jotham was required to flee for his life. In this deftly framed attack, Jotham articulated an antimonarchic sentiment that was popular among the more conservative members of the Israelite tribal confederacy.

3. The son of Uzziah (presumably the throne name for Azariah; 2 Kgs 15:32; 1 Chr 3:12) who first served as regent (ca. 750–742 B.C.E.) before succeeding his father as king of Judah (ca. 742–735 B.C.E.). His mother was Jerusha, "the daughter of Zadok" (2 Kgs 15:33), likely "the hereditary priest in Jerusalem" (Gray *1 and 2 Kings* OTL, 629). Though neither 2 Kings 15 nor 2 Chronicles 27 provides more than a cursory treatment of Jotham's reign, both sources report that he ascended to the Jerusalem throne at the age of 25 and ruled for 16 years (2 Kgs 15:33; 2 Chr 27:1). After a consideration of Jotham's historical context, which is partially clouded by perplexing chronological references, we shall note how this Judean king is respectively treated by the Deuteronomistic Historian and the Chronicler.

a. Jotham's Historical Context. Though on occasion Judah was required to acknowledge the supremacy of Israel under Jeroboam II (ca. 786–746 B.C.E.), the reigns of Uzziah (ca. 783–742 B.C.E.) and Jotham constituted a period of prosperity for Judah. Having mended Jerusalem's defenses, reorganized its army, and restored the distant Edomite site of Elath (Ezion-geber?) as a Judean seaport (2 Kgs 14:22), Uzziah bequeathed a sturdy kingdom to his son. Whereas Uzziah undoubtedly retained the title of king as long as he lived, the leprosy that he suffered toward the end of his regal tenure rendered him incapable of performing the duties of his office. Thus Jotham, as the crown prince, took charge of the affairs of state (2 Kgs 15:5–6; 2 Chr 26:21). The discovery of a signet ring with a seal bearing the Hebrew inscription *lytm,* "Belonging to Jotham" in the period III city at Tell el-Kheleifeh (possibly Ezion-geber) seems to buttress the biblical witness that during the 8th century B.C.E. Judah's monarchs extended their influence into Edom. While the matter is less than unequivocal, the lack of any additional title (e.g., "of the king") makes Uzziah's son Jotham a likely referent. Glueck (1959: 167–68) perceives this ring to be the badge of office of the person who was appointed to govern this region in Jotham's behalf.

It is impossible to establish a precise chronology for Jotham. According to 2 Kgs 15:30 Hoshea became king of Israel during "the twentieth year of Jotham the son of Uzziah." This synchronism is contradicted by 2 Kgs 17:1, which links Hoshea's arrival on the Israelite throne with the rule of Jotham's son Ahaz. Nor can 2 Kgs 15:30 be reconciled with the notation in 2 Kgs 16:33 that Jotham's rule spanned 16 years, unless his period as regent of Judah is to be added to 16 years of independent rule. It is more likely, however, that the 16-year figure encompasses Jotham's functions as both regent and king. Given the credibility of the synchronism in 2 Kgs 15:32, which links the advent of Jotham's rule with the second year of Pekah's tenure as king of Israel, perhaps Jotham's role as regent began in ca. 750 B.C.E.; and with Uzziah's death in ca. 742 B.C.E., his status shifted from regent to monarch (Albright 1945: 21). Since certain knowledge about the length of Jotham's tenure is beyond our reach, Gray (70, 628) advances the reasonable proposal that Pekah's second year as

Israel's sovereign may signal Jotham's assumption of duties as regent and that 2 Kgs 15:33 credits Jotham with a six-year reign (perhaps "when cyphers instead of words were used," Heb *šēš* [six] was misread as *šēš ʿeśrē* [sixteen]). Finally, the Chronicler's presentation of Jotham of Judah and Jeroboam II of Israel as contemporaries (1 Chr 5:17) poses no problem so long as the former is understood to have the status of regent.

b. Jotham in the Deuteronomistic History. Jotham is introduced as the one who governed "the people of the land" once his father Azariah (Uzziah) had become divinely stricken with leprosy (2 Kgs 15:5). In his ritually unclean condition, Uzziah would be dependent on his son for the execution of regal functions. In 2 Kgs 15:32–38 the focus narrows on Jotham himself. Following mention of his age when he entered the regal office, length of tenure, and mother's name (2 Kgs 15:33), a formulaic phrase assesses Jotham in an approving manner. As had Uzziah before him (2 Kgs 15:3), Jotham "did what was right in the eyes of the Lord" (2 Kgs 15:34). Even so, since Jotham failed to demolish the "high places" (Heb *bāmôt*), his people persisted in their religious apostasy (2 Kgs 15:35a—the wording replicates that used in the presentations of Amaziah's reign in 14:4 and Uzziah's in 15:4). Prior to mention of Jotham's death, burial, and replacement on the throne by his son Ahaz (2 Kgs 15:38), two more distinctive disclosures are made about his reign. First, Jotham is credited with having constructed "the upper gate of the house of the Lord" (2 Kgs 15:35b). Presumably this is the N gate within the Jerusalem temple compound to which Jer 20:2 and Ezek 9:2 allude. Second, the Syro-Ephraimite coalition involving two staunch anti-Assyrian monarchs, Pekah, king of Israel and Rezin, king of Aram, is depicted as emerging during Jotham's period of rule; and the havoc it played with Judah is perceived as divinely instigated (2 Kgs 15:37). Though the crisis would escalate during the reign of Ahaz (see Isa 7:1–8:15), Judah felt discomfort even as Jotham governed.

c. Jotham in Chronicles. Though the Chronicler's portrayal of Jotham (2 Chr 27:1–9) shares much in common with its Deuteronomistic antecedent, one noteworthy deletion and several new particulars serve to intensify this monarch's virtue and competence. On the one hand, the impact of the Syro-Ephraimite coalition on Judah is not even hinted. On the other, Jotham is presented as a devout man of faith, master builder, and triumphant leader in the battlefield. As one who "ordered his ways" before the deity (2 Chr 27:6), Jotham's righteousness is set, in general terms, over against his people's proclivity for "corrupt practices," and, in specific terms, over against his father Uzziah's intrusion as a lay person into the sacred precincts of the Jerusalem temple which brought on his leprosy (2 Chr 27:2; cf. 26:16–21). The king's building program extended well beyond the "upper gate" of the temple complex. Concentrating on "the wall of Ophel" (2 Chr 27:3) to the S, Jotham seems to have augmented Uzziah's earlier efforts at strengthening Jerusalem's defenses (an activity in which Hezekiah [2 Chr 32:5] and Manasseh [2 Chr 33:14] would later engage; see Simons 1952: 330–31). Moreover, Jotham improved Judah's position by constructing cities in the Judean highlands and erecting "forts and towers" in the wooded regions (2 Chr 27:4). The superlative aspect of the Chronicler's report, however, is discernible in his disclosure regarding Jotham's triumph over the nomadic Meunites, who infiltrated Judah—here we accept the conjecture of Miller and Hayes (*HAIJ,* 311) that "Ammonites" in the Heb text (2 Chr 27:5) should be corrected to "Meunites." The amount of tribute that the enemy rendered to Jotham (27:5), estimated by Myers (*2 Chronicles* AB, 156) as 3.25 tons of silver and 65,000 bushels each of wheat and flour, is manifestly exaggerated. Though the Chronicler does not present Jotham's accomplishments in a dispassionate manner, the impression he gives that this Judean king was skilled in matters of national defense has an authentic ring to it.

Bibliography

Albright, W. F. 1945. The Chronology of the Divided Monarchy of Israel. *BASOR* 100: 16–22.

Glueck, N. 1959. *Rivers in the Desert.* New York.

Lindars, B. 1973. Jotham's Fable—A New Form-critical Analysis. *JTS* n.s. 24: 355–66.

Simons, J. 1952. *Jerusalem in the OT.* Leiden.

J. Kenneth Kuntz

JOY. The experience of deliverance and the anticipation of salvation provide the most significant occasions for rejoicing among the people of God in the OT. The coming of the Messiah, who delivers his people and brings salvation becomes the basis for rejoicing in the NT. The response of joy, gladness, or happiness is not only a deep inward feeling, but is expressed in celebration when God's people gather together.

The idea of joy is most commonly expressed in the OT by *śimḥâ/śamaḥ* and in the NT by *chara/chairō.* Among the other 12 Hebrew roots used for some aspect of joy, the most frequent are *gyl, rnn, śwś,* and *ʿlz.* The LXX prefers the Gk word *euphrainō* to translate *śamaḥ* and inclines toward *agalliaō* (its first occurrence in Greek literature) to translate *gyl,* the latter expressions more commonly used of exultant joy. Although *chara/chairō* are not the prominent words for joy in the LXX, they become so in the NT perhaps because of their common use during the time of the NT. They are found, for instance, in a papyrus expressing the joy of friends on the occasion of a marriage (*P. Oxy.* 3313.4, 20). In addition to the terms *euphrainō* and *agalliaō,* the NT also employs *makarios/makarizo,* commonly translated "blessed" or "happy," and *kauchasthai/kauchēma,* "boast."

In the OT rejoicing is frequently expressed in connection with the feasts; in fact, they are called "times of rejoicing" (Num 10:10). Recalling God's marvelous act of delivering Israel from bondage, the Feasts of Passover and Unleavened Bread were occasions of great joy (2 Chr 30:21–27; Ezra 6:22; cf. also Psalms 95 and 98). Communal exultation also characterized the Feasts of Pentecost and Tabernacles (Deut 16:11, 14, 15; Lev 23:40) at which times the people of Israel were enjoined to remember that they were once slaves in Egypt (Deut 16:12). Similarly, the Feast of Purim was celebrated with joy and gladness to celebrate divine deliverance from potential annihilation under Persian rule (Esth 8:17).

Yahweh's effective help in battle gave occasion for expressing joy (2 Chr 20:27) as so often illustrated in the Psalms (Pss 9:2; 13:7; 21:1; 109:28). The knowledge of the nearness and protection of God in times of need and distress brought joy (Ps 16:9). One could find joy in sensing God's presence at any time as in Ps 16:11: "You fill me with joy in your presence" (cf. Ps 21:6).

Past deliverance gave Israel hope for the future. In particular the Prophets point to the joy yet to be experienced, an eschatological joy. This can be seen especially in Isaiah 40–66, where there are numerous references to joy and rejoicing. This celebration is connected not only with the salvation of Israel (Isa 44:23; 65:14–19; cf. also Zeph 3:14–17; Zech 2:10), but with the gift of salvation God is preparing for all humankind (Isa 56:7). The righteous will ultimately experience everlasting joy (Isa 51:11).

Israel's corporate joy was commonly expressed in great celebration. Musical instruments often accompanied singing and dancing (1 Sam 18:6). David had in fact appointed the Levites "to sing joyful songs" to the accompaniment of musical instruments such as lyres, harps, and cymbals (1 Chr 15:17). The intensity of celebration was sometimes quite high as illustrated by the account of the anointing of Solomon as king of Israel: "And all the people went up after him, playing on pipes, and rejoicing with great joy, so that the earth was split by their noise" (1 Kgs 1:40; RSV). The book of Psalms gives numerous examples of the joyous songs of praise, or victory, sung by the people of God (e.g., Psalms 33 and 95).

Not only do God's people rejoice, but God himself is represented as rejoicing "in his works" (Ps 104:31) and in his people (Deut 30:9; Pss 147:11; 149:4; Zeph 3:17). Joy does not always have religious connotations in the OT. Good wine can bring joy (Ps 104:15; Judg 9:13), and so also should a birthday (Job 3:7), and the years of one's youth or old age (Eccl 11:8–9).

The NT era was inaugurated by the cry of the angel of the Lord: "Do not be afraid; for behold, I bring you good news of a great joy which will come to all the people; for to you is born this day in the city of David a Savior, who is Christ the Lord" (Luke 2:10–11). The appearance of the Messiah providing salvation for all humankind permeates every NT book with the mood of joy. Schramm thus aptly observes, "this cry of joy is a fitting title for the whole NT" (Otto and Schramm 1980: 94).

Among the first three gospels Luke especially highlights the soteriological aspect of joy (Gulin 1932–36, 1: 99). The parables of the lost sheep, the lost coin, and the prodigal son reveal the joyous response of the father (and the angels) when one sinner repents and is saved (Luke 15, esp. vv 5, 6, 7, 9, 10, 32). Conversely, there is joy for the one who receives salvation (Luke 19:6; cf. Matt 13:44). The progress of the salvation of God extending to the gentiles becomes a significant occasion of joy in the book of Acts (Acts 11:23; 13:48; 15:3). The gentiles who are saved are filled with joy (8:8, 39).

All the redeemed are brought into a close union with Christ, where they experience great joy. Abiding in Christ brings "fullness of joy," according to John (John 15:11). Paul likewise finds the ultimate source of the believer's joy stemming from being "in Christ" (Phil 4:4; 3:1). It is upon this premise that he encourages his readers to let joyfulness be a constant characteristic of their daily lives (cf. also 1 Thess 5:16). Paul also sees the experience of joy as a result of the indwelling of the spirit (1 Thess 1:6; Rom 14:17; cf. also Acts 8:39). He in fact describes joy as a "fruit" of the Spirit's presence (Gal 5:22).

The life of discipleship is a life of increasing joy—joy not only in growing in the faith (e.g., Phil 1:25), but in helping others grow in the faith. The NT is replete with references to the joy of those involved in the mission of the Church and the edification of its members. Paul rejoiced when he saw the successful spread of the gospel (Phil 1:18) and on occasions when he had indication of spiritual growth among the members of the churches (e.g., Phlm 7; 1 Thess 3:9; Rom 16:19; Col 2:5). When Paul discerned a positive response on the part of the Corinthians to his tearful visit and sorrowful letter, he told them of his great joy (2 Chr 7:4, 7, 9, 13, 16). John likewise rejoiced in the obedience of his community (2 John 4; 3 John 3, 4).

The NT is much less explicit than the OT about the manner in which joy is expressed. There is no doubt that joy was understood in terms of a deep inward experience, but this inner disposition likely found tangible expression in the Christian communities when they gathered. It would probably be safe to assume that the OT concept of joyous celebration with jubilant singing and praise to God provided a model for the NT congregations. The NT does stress that joy is to be shared (Rom 12:12; 2 Cor 7:13) and even employs a word *(sugchairō)* that emphasizes the shared nature of joy (1 Cor 12:26; Phil 2:17–18; Luke 15:6, 9).

The deep-rooted joy of the Christian is not abated when the circumstances of daily life are adverse. Joy is experienced in suffering and even persecution. This was the teaching of the Sermon on the Mount (Matt 5:11–12) and the experience of the early Church (Acts 5:41; cf. 1 Thess 1:6). Paul exemplified this possibility of joy in suffering in his own life (2 Cor 7:4; Col 1:24) and encouraged his churches to follow suit (Phil 2:17–18). Suffering is prominent in the background to the statements concerning joy in 1 Peter and Hebrews. Eschatological anticipation, however, provided incentive for rejoicing even when one's personal property was plundered (Heb 10:34) or when one faced persecution (1 Pet 4:13). The early Church looked forward to the second advent of Christ as a time of joy (Matt 25:21, 23). The ultimate triumph of God and "the marriage of the Lamb" will consummate the joy of God and all his people (19:7) and result in cries of "Hallelujah!" (Rev 19:1, 3, 4, 6).

Bibliography

Gulin, E. G. 1932–36. *Die Freude im Neuen Testament.* 2 vols. AASF 24, 37. Helsinki.

Morrice, W. 1984. *Joy in the NT.* Grand Rapids.

Nauck, W. 1955. Freude im Leiden. *ZNW* 46: 68–80.

Otto, E., and Schramm, T. 1980. *Festival and Joy.* Nashville.

CLINTON E. ARNOLD

JOZABAD (PERSON) [Heb *yôzābād*]. Jozabad occurs only in postexilic biblical writings. While it was quite possibly a common Judean name in the Persian period, the Chronicler seems to have retrojected anachronistically the name of a levitical treasurer from the time of Ezra and

Nehemiah (#6) to legitimate his portrayal of the reigns of Hezekiah (#3) and Josiah (#4).

1. A Benjaminite warrior, who, according to the Chronicler, joined David's forces at Ziklag before David became king (1 Chr 12:5—Eng 12:4). See JERIMOTH. The Chronicler associates Jozabad with Gedar, a town in S Judah.

2. Two Manassites, who, according to the Chronicler, deserted their kinsman Saul to join the forces of David at Ziklag (1 Chr 12:21—Eng 12:20).

3. According to the Chronicler a levitical overseer of surplus temple offerings gathered during Hezekiah's temple reforms (2 Chr 31:13). The Chronistic style of the chapter clearly demarcates it as the Chronicler's own invention. The Chronicler seems to have taken the name of a levitical overseer of temple revenues from the time of Ezra and Nehemiah (see #6) and applied it anachronistically to legitimate his portrayal of the reforms of Hezekiah.

4. A levitical prince who donated sacrificial animals for Josiah's Passover (2 Chr 35:9). As Josiah's Passover evidences the Chronicler's style, Jozabad represents the Chronicler's use of a levitical name from his own day to legitimate his narrative of an earlier period. Given substantial onomastic overlap with 2 Chronicles 31, the Chronicler uses the name Jozabad to show continuity between Josiah's Passover and Hezekiah's reforms. 1 Esdr 1:9 reads "Joram" rather than "Jozabad."

5. A member of the priestly family of Passhur who lived in the Persian province of Judea during the mission of Ezra (Ezra 10:22). Jozabad's family, the family of Passhur, composed the largest priestly clan to return from Exile with Zerubbabel (Ezra 2:38), though it ultimately disappeared from the Second Temple priestly houses. Despite, or perhaps on account of, his priestly lineage, this Jozabad had married a non-Judean wife. He consented to divorce her during the reforms of Ezra under the threat of complete ostracism from the Jerusalem temple state. For the authenticity of the list of Ezra 10, see JERIMOTH. 1 Esdr 9:22 reads Gedaliah instead of Jozabad.

6. A prominent levitical temple official in the Jerusalem temple during the mission of Ezra (Ezra 8:33). From the brief description of his duties in Ezra 8:34, Jozabad aided in the administration of temple treasuries (see 1 Chr 26:20–28). Jozabad's family had returned to Judah from Babylon with Zerubbabel (Ezra 2:40). Their prominence among the levitical families may help explain his important social position within the Judean temple state (see also Ezra 3:9; Neh 9:4–5; 10:10–11—Eng 9–10; 12:8). See JESHUA (PERSON). While certainty is not possible, this Jozabad most likely married a non-Judean wife and consented to divorce her under the threat of complete ostracism from the Jerusalem temple state (Ezra 10:23). He later was among the levitical teachers who interpreted the Torah to the people at Ezra's public reading (Neh 8:7). It is also possible that this same levitical Jozabad appears again during Nehemiah's governorship as an administrator of the outside work of the temple (Neh 11:16), a duty seemingly associated with the temple treasuries (see 1 Chr 26:20–32). The precise attribution is difficult, however, because of the contested date of Nehemiah 11. Kellermann (1966: 209–27) argues that the list reveals the inhabitants of Jerusalem in the years immediately before Exile, while Blenkinsopp (*Ezra-Nehemiah* OTL, 322–27) argues that the list reflects the years subsequent to Nehemiah, to which Jozabad may represent a later addition to fill out the lists. Williamson's hypothesis (*Ezra, Nehemiah* WBC, 344–49) that Nehemiah 11 reflects another account of Nehemiah's repopulation of Jerusalem (see Nehemiah 7), however, seems to account best for the available data. If so, in Jozabad we have a brief example of a levitical temple official whose career spanned the missions of both Ezra and Nehemiah.

Bibliography

Kellermann, U. 1966. Die Listen in Nehemia 11 eine Dokumentation aus den letzten Jahren des Reiches Juda? *ZDPV* 82: 209–27.

JOHN W. WRIGHT

JOZACAR (PERSON) [Heb *yôzākār*]. A servant of Joash, king of Judah, who, with Jehozabad, conspired against the king and killed him (2 Kgs 12:22—Eng 12:21). In some mss he is called Jozabad, instead of Jozacar. This variation can be accounted for as a copyist's error wherein the *bet* is read as a *qop* and the *dalet* as a *reš*. In 2 Chr 24:26 he is named Zabad, a shortened form of Jozabad.

PAULINE A. VIVIANO

JOZADAK (PERSON) [Heb *yôṣādāq*]. Var. JEHOZADAK. The father of Jeshua, a priest contemporary with Zerubbabel (Ezra 3:2, 8; 5:2; 10:18; 1 Esdr 5:5, 48, 56; 6:2; 9:19; Sir 49:12), and the grandfather of Joiakim, a priest contemporary with Nehemiah (Neh 12:26). The name is a shortened form of Jehozadak, which means "Yahweh is righteous." The shortened form is used for this individual in Ezra-Nehemiah along with Jeshua *(yēšûaᶜ)*, a shortened form of Joshua *(yĕhôšūaᶜ)*. The longer forms for these two individuals are preserved in 1 Chronicles, Haggai, and Zechariah. For a full discussion of this variant, see JEHOZADAK.

JEFFREY A. FAGER

JUBAL (PERSON) [Heb *yûbāl*]. Son of Lamech and Adah and the brother of Jabal, a descendant of Cain (Gen 4:21). Jubal is described as the father of lyre and pipe players. Jubal's association with the pipe and his relation to Jabal, who may have been associated with nomadic shepherding, have led to comparisons between him and the Greek shepherd god Pan, inventor of the lyre (Westermann 1984: 331); Wenham *Genesis 1–15* WBC, 113). Two other possible connections with music include (1) the name of Jubal's half-sister, Naamah, which may suggest the playing of music (cf. Ug *nᶜm*); and (2) the similarity between the name Jubal and the Hebrew word for the ram's horn (Heb *yôbēl*), which was blown to proclaim special days and seasons (*EncMiqr* 3:582; Gabriel 1959: 417). As a passive participle derived from the root *ybl* (see JABAL), Jubal may mean something like "brought in the procession," possibly reflecting the appearance of this root in the *yôbēl*, the jubilee year (North 1964: 380).

Bibliography

Gabriel, J. 1959. Die Kainitengenealogie. Gen 4, 17–24. *Bib* 40: 409–27.

North, R. 1964. The Cain Music. *JBL* 83: 373–89.

Westermann, C. 1984. *Genesis 1–11: A Commentary.* Minneapolis.

RICHARD S. HESS

JUBILEE, YEAR OF. Leviticus 25 details the biblical system of jubilee. The Hebrew term at the center of this system, *yôbēl,* "jubilee" has an uncertain etymology. The most common view is that *yôbēl* means "ram" (cf. Phoen *ybl*), since ram's horn was used for trumpets and the year of jubilee was announced by the blowing of the trumpet. But the word used in the instructions of Lev 25:9 is the more common *šôpar.* Elsewhere, however, *yôbēl* or *qeren hayyôbēl,* "the horn of the ram" or *šôpěrôt hayyôbēlîm,* "trumpets of rams" are expressions used for trumpets (e.g., Exod 19:13; Josh 6:4–8, 13). The word *jubilee,* derived from *yôbēl,* is etymologically unconnected with Lat *jubilare* and its English derivative "jubilation."

The year of jubilee came at the end of the cycle of 7 Sabbatical Years. Lev 25:8–10 specifies it as the 50th year, though some scholars believe it may have been actually the 49th—i.e., the 7th Sabbatical Year. In this year there was a proclamation of liberty to Israelites who had become enslaved for debt, and a restoration of land to families who had been compelled to sell it out of economic need in the previous 50 years. Instructions concerning the jubilee and its relation to the procedures of land and slave redemption are found entirely in Leviticus 25. But it is also referred to in Leviticus 26 and 27 in other contexts.

A. Socioeconomic Background
   1. Israelite Kinship Structure
   2. Israelite Land Tenure
B. Theological Basis
   1. The Theology of Land
   2. The Status of the Israelites
C. Exegetical Outline
   1. Detailed Analysis of Leviticus 25
   2. Summary
D. Historical Question
E. Ethical Development
   1. In the OT
   2. In the NT
   3. Contemporary Application

A. Socioeconomic Background

The jubilee was in essence an economic institution. It had two main points of concern: the family and the land. It was rooted therefore in the kinship structure of Israelite society and the system of land tenure that was based upon it.

1. Israelite Kinship Structure. Israel had a three-tier pattern of kinship, comprising the tribe, the clan, and the household. Gideon's modest reply to his angelic visitor shows us all three: "Look at my clan—it is the weakest in the tribe of Manasseh; and I am the least in my father's house" (Judg 6:15). The last two smaller units had greater social and economic importance than the tribe in terms of benefits and responsibilities relating to individual Israelites. The father's house (Heb *bêt ʾāb*) was a place of authority, even for married adults like Gideon (Judg 6:27; 8:20). It was also the place of security and protection (Judg 6:30–32). The clan was a larger grouping of a number of fathers' houses and an important subsection of the tribe (Heb *mišpāḥâ*). The clans were named after the grandsons of Jacob or other members of the patriarchal family tree (see Numbers 26 and 1 Chronicles 4–8), thereby acknowledging that they were units of recognizable kinship (see Kartveit 1989). But sometimes the clan name was attached to the territorial area of its settlement, such as a village or group of villages. The clan had important responsibility in the preservation of the land allotted to its constituent households. The jubilee was primarily for the economic protection of the smallest of these units—the father's house. However, in Leviticus 25, it is interwoven with the economic practice of the redemption of land and persons; and those redemption procedures were primarily for the protection of, and the responsibility of, the clan. The two sets of provision were complementary, as we shall see. See FAMILY for full description of Israel's kinship terminology and structure.

2. Israelite Land Tenure. Whatever may have been the process by which the Israelites emerged in Canaan, once they were able to establish control over most of the land, they operated a system of land tenure that was based on these kinship units. Thus the territory was allotted to tribes, "according to their clans," and within the clans each household had its portion or "heritage." Judges 21:24 describes the Israelite soldiers returning each to his tribe, to his clan, and to his (household) inheritance. This system had two features that stand in complete contrast to the preceding pattern of Canaanite economic structure as described from the biblical perspective.

a. Equitable Distribution. In Canaan the land was owned by city-state kings and their nobles, with the bulk of the population as taxpaying tenant farmers. In Israel the initial division of the land was explicitly to the clans and households within the tribes, under the general rubric that each receive land according to size and need. The documentary evidence for this is to be found in the tribal lists of Numbers 26 (especially vv 52–56) and in the detailed territorial division of land recorded in Joshua 13–21, where the repetition of the phrase "according to their clans" indicates the intention that the land should be distributed throughout the whole kinship system as widely as possible.

b. Inalienability. In order to protect this system of kinship distribution, family land was made inalienable. That is, it was not to be bought and sold as a commercial asset, but was to remain as far as possible within the extended family or at least within the circle of families in the clan. It was this principle which lay behind Naboth's refusal to sell his patrimony to Ahab (1 Kings 21), and it is most explicit in the economic regulations of Leviticus 25.

B. Theological Basis

Lev 25:23 can be translated as follows: "The land shall not be sold permanently, for the land belongs to me; for you are 'guests' and 'residents' with me." This statement, at the heart of the chapter describing the jubilee, provides the hinge between the social and economic system described above and its theological rationale. Following the inalienability rule, the chapter presents the two theological factors upon which the jubilee and related laws are based: the theology of the land and the status of the Israelites.

1. The Theology of Land. One of the central pillars of the faith of the Israelites was that the land they inhabited was Yahweh's land. It had been his even before Israel entered it (Exod 15:13, 17). This theme is found often in the Prophets and Psalms, as part of Israel's cultic tradition. At the same time, although ultimately owned by Yahweh, the land had been promised and then given to Israel in the course of the redemptive history. It was their "inheritance" (Deuteronomy passim), a kinship term appointing Israel as heir of Yahweh.

This dual tradition of the land—divine ownership and divine gift—was associated in some way with every major thread in Israel's theology. The promise of land was an essential part of the patriarchal election tradition. The land was the goal of the Exodus redemption tradition. The maintenance of the covenant relationship and the security of life in the land were bound together. Divine judgment eventually meant expulsion from the land, until the restored relationship was symbolized in the return to the land.

The land, then, stood like a fulcrum in the relationship between God and Israel (cf. its position in Lev 26:40–45). It was a monumental, tangible witness both to that divine control of history within which the relationship had been established and also to the moral and practical demands entailed by that relationship. For the Israelite, living as his family on his allotted share of Yahweh's land was proof of his membership in God's "family" and became the focus of his practical response to God's grace. Nothing that concerned the land was free from theological and ethical dimensions—as every harvest reminded him (Deuteronomy 26).

2. The Status of the Israelites. The Israelites are described in two ways in Leviticus 25.

a. Guests and Residents. "You are guests and residents [RSV; "aliens and tenants" in NIV] with me" (v 23). These terms, *gērîm wĕtôšābîm,* describe a class of people who resided among the Israelites in Canaan, but were not ethnic Israelites. They may have been descendants of the dispossessed Canaanites, or immigrants. They had no stake in the tenure of the land, but survived by hiring out their services as residential employees (laborers, craftsmen, etc.) for Israelite landowning households. Provided the household remained economically viable, its resident alien employees enjoyed both protection and security. But otherwise, their position could be perilous. Hence they are frequently mentioned in Israel's law as the objects of particular concern for justice because of their vulnerability.

The Israelites were to regard their status before God as analogous to that of their own residential dependents to themselves. Thus they had no ultimate title to the land—it was owned by God. Nevertheless, they could enjoy secure benefits of it under his protection and in dependence on him. So the terms are not a denial of rights, but rather an identification of specific classes of people as having a relationship of protected dependency.

The practical effect of this model for Israel's relationship with God is seen in vv 35, 40, and 53. If all Israelites share this status before God, then the impoverished or indebted sibling is to be regarded and treated in the same way as God regards and treats all Israel.

b. Slaves. "They are my slaves whom I brought forth out of the land of Egypt" (vv 42, 55). Three times in this chapter the Exodus is mentioned, twice more in the following chapter (26:13, 45). It was regarded as an act of redemption in which God had "bought" Israel for himself. Freed from slavery to Egypt, they were now slaves of God himself. Therefore nobody could now claim as his own private property a fellow Israelite, who belonged by right of purchase to God alone. The Exodus redemption thus provided the historical and theological model for the social and economic practice of redemption and jubilee. Those who are God's freed slaves are not to make slaves of one another (25:39, 42). This weight of theological tradition concentrated into 25:23 gives a seriousness to the economic measures outlined in the rest of the chapter.

C. Exegetical Outline

1. Detailed Analysis of Leviticus 25. Leviticus 25 is a complex chapter in which several different economic practices have been thrown closely together, along with parenthetic sections and exceptive clauses. Source critics have come to no kind of consensus over alleged documentary division of the material, and the multiplicity of theories is little help in understanding the chapter. However, in its present form, the text has some definable paragraphs that guide us through its provisions.

a. Vv 1–7. The chapter opens with the law of the SABBATICAL YEAR on the land. This is an expansion of the fallow year law of Exod 23:10–11, which was also further developed in Deut 15:1–2 into a year in which debts (or more probably the pledges given for loans) were to be remitted.

b. Vv 8–12. The jubilee is then introduced as the 50th year to follow the 7th Sabbatical Year. Verse 10 presents the twin concepts that are fundamental to the whole institution, namely, liberty and return: liberty—from the burden of debt and the bondage it may have entailed; return—both to the ancestral property if it had been mortgaged to a creditor, and to the family which may have been split up through debt servitude. It was these two components of the jubilee, freedom and restoration, that entered into the metaphoric and eschatological use of the jubilee in prophetic and later NT thought.

c. Vv 13–17. The financial implications of a recurring jubilee are then spelled out. The apparent sale of a piece of land really amounted only to a sale of the use of the land. So an approaching jubilee diminished the cost for the purchaser, inasmuch as he was buying the number of harvests until the jubilee restored the land to its original owner.

d. Vv 18–22. At this point some exhortation is inserted to encourage the observance of the sabbatical regulations, by promising special blessing in the preceding year. The theological principle was that obedience to the economic legislation of Israel would require, not prudential calculations, but faith in the ability of Yahweh to provide through his control of nature as well as history.

e. Vv 23–24. These central verses in the chapter constitute a heading to the remaining paragraphs, which are primarily concerned with the economic redemption of land and persons, interwoven with the jubilee. We have already noted the major theological traditions embodied in them.

f. Vv 25–55. We come now to the practical details of redemption and jubilee. In these verses there are three descending stages of poverty with required responses, interrupted by parenthetic sections dealing with houses in cities, and Levite properties (29–34), and non-Israelite slaves (44–46). The stages are marked off by the introductory phrase, "If your brother becomes poor" (25, 35, 39, 47). Probably this phrase introduced an original series of redemption procedures, unconnected with the jubilee. The addition of jubilee regulations complicates matters in places but functions as a necessary complement to the effects of redemption.

(1) Stage 1 (25–28). Initially, having fallen on hard times (for any reason—none is specified), the Israelite landowner sells, or offers to sell, some of his land. To keep it within the family, in line with the inalienability principle, it was first of all the duty of the nearest kinsman (the *gōʾēl*) either to preempt it (if it was still on offer) or to redeem it (if it had been sold). Second, the seller himself retained the right to redeem it for himself, if he later recovered the means to do so. Third, in any case, the property, whether sold or redeemed by a kinsman, reverted to the original family in the year of jubilee.

(2) Exception (i): (29–31). The above rules did not apply to dwelling places in the walled cities. This was probably because the primary intention of the redemption and jubilee provisions was to preserve the economic viability of families through the secure possession of their inherited land. City houses were not part of that productive economic base, and so did not need to be subject to indefinite redemption rights or jubilee return to seller. However, village dwellings were treated as part of the rural scene and therefore were included.

(3) Exception (ii): (32–34). This is a rider to exception (i). Since the Levites as a tribe had no inherited share in the land but were allotted certain towns, their dwellings in them were to be subject to normal redemption and jubilee provisions.

(4) Stage 2 (35–38). If the poorer brother's plight worsens and he still cannot stay solvent, presumably even after several such sales, it then becomes the duty of the kinsman to maintain him as a dependent laborer by means of interest-free loans.

(5) Stage 3a (39–43). In the event of a total economic collapse, such that the poorer kinsman has no more land left to sell or pledge for loans, he and his whole family sell themselves to—enter the bonded service of—the wealthier kinsman. The latter, however, is commanded in strong and repeated terms, not to treat the debtor Israelite like a slave, but rather as a resident employee. This undesirable state of affairs is to continue only until the next jubilee—i.e., not more than one more generation. Then the debtor and/or his children (the original debtor may have died, but the next generation were to benefit from the jubilee, vv 41, 54), were to recover their original patrimony of land and be enabled to make a fresh start.

(6) Exception (iii) (44–46). This is a reminder that the redemption and jubilee provisions applied to Israelites and not to foreign slaves or resident aliens. This reinforces the point that they were primarily concerned with the distribution of land and the viability of Israelite families, neither of which applied to the nonlandowning population.

(7) Stage 3b (47–55). If a man had entered this debt bondage outside the clan, then an obligation lay on the whole clan to prevent this loss of a whole family by exercising their duty to redeem him. The list of potential kinsman-redeemers in vv 48–49 shows how the responsibility moved outward from the nearest kinsman to the extent of the clan itself ("family" in RSV v 49 is a misleading translation for Heb *mišpāḥâ,* "clan"). The whole clan had the duty of preserving its constituent families and their inherited land. It also had the duty to see that a non-Israelite creditor behaved as an Israelite should toward an Israelite debtor and that the jubilee provision was adhered to eventually.

2. Summary. From this analysis of the chapter, it can be seen that there were two main differences between the redemption and jubilee provisions. (1) Timing. Redemption was a duty that could be exercised at any time, locally, as circumstances required, whereas jubilee was twice a century as a national event. (2) Purpose. The main aim of redemption was the preservation of the land and persons of the clan, whereas the main beneficiary of the jubilee was the extended family, or "father's house." The jubilee therefore functioned as a necessary override to the practice of redemption. The regular operation of redemption over a period could result in the whole territory of a clan coming into the hands of a few wealthier families, with the rest of the families in the clan in a kind of debt servitude, living as dependent tenants of the wealthy—i.e., precisely the kind of land-tenure system that Israel had overturned. The jubilee was thus a mechanism to prevent this and to preserve the socioeconomic fabric of multiple household land tenure with the comparative equality and independent viability of the smallest family-plus-land units.

Now these household units held a central place in the experience and expression of Israel's covenant relationship with God, as can be seen from their role in social, military, judicial, cultic, and educational spheres. See FAMILY. In the light of this centrality of the family, the jubilee can be seen as more than merely an economic regulator (and certainly more than the utopian measure of social justice it is sometimes portrayed as). In attempting to maintain or restore the viability of such households, it was in fact aimed at preserving a fundamental dimension of Israel's relationship with Yahweh. We noticed this already in considering the weight of theological tradition packed into v 23. Three reminders of the Exodus and its implications (38, 42, 55) reinforce the point. This in turn explains why the neglect of these institutions, bemoaned in the following chapter (Leviticus 26) led not merely to economic distress but also to a broken relationship and eventual Exile—a connection also very clearly perceived by the Prophets.

D. Historical Question

But did it ever happen? Were the jubilee regulations real and practicable legislation, or were they academic and utopian? While there is evidence that kinship redemption was practiced (Jeremiah 32, Ruth 4), there is simply no evidence of a national jubilee in the extant historical documents of Israel (though some would discern an allusion to a jubilee year in Isa 37:30, where a double year of fallow seems to be envisaged; but it may refer merely to the disastrous effect of invasion). This silence does not, of course, prove that it never did happen. Nor can we say that it was economically impossible and so could not have happened, because there is evidence from other ANE civilizations of periodic nationwide remissions of debt in connection with the accession of a new king. However this ANE evidence comes from centuries earlier than the origins of OT Israel (Gordon 1953; Finkelstein 1961; Lewy 1958).

Nevertheless, scholars are divided: some see the law as a late, idealistic, formulation from the same period as the Holiness Code within the Priestly compilation to which this part of Leviticus is usually assigned (Ginzberg 1932; *AncIsr;* Westbrook 1971). Others regard the jubilee as part of Israel's earliest, premonarchic, laws, which fell into disuse. This latter position is more commonly held by those scholars who have done most research into the ANE parallels and the sociological background (Schaeffer 1922; Jirku 1929; van der Ploeg 1972; Stein 1953; North 1954; Wildberger 1956; *IDBSup,* 496–98. Gottwald regards the redemption provisions, but not the jubilee, as reflecting "old conditions" [1979: 264]).

We have seen that the aim of the jubilee was to maintain or restore the socioeconomic basis of the nation's covenant relationship with God. This would reduce the likelihood of its being an exilic invention in view of evidence that there developed in the later period a loosening of the ancient family-land basis in the future vision of an expanded people of God that would include foreigners and eunuchs, (Isa 54:1; 56:3–7). Israel's identity and relationship with God would no longer be so closely tied to a social system in which kinship and land ownership were determinative of one's standing within the religious community. It is hard to see what purpose would have been served by framing new idealistic legislation designed to preserve those very things. Conversely, it makes sense to see the jubilee as a very ancient law which fell into neglect during Israel's history in the land, not so much because it was economically impossible, as because it became irrelevant to the scale of social disruption. The jubilee presupposes a situation where a man, though in severe debt, still technically holds the title to his family's land and could be restored to full ownership of it. But from the time of Solomon on this must have become meaningless for growing numbers of families as they fell victim to the acids of debt, slavery, royal intrusion and confiscation, and total dispossession. Many were uprooted and pushed off their ancestral land altogether. After a few generations they had nothing to be restored to in any practicable sense (Mic 2:2, 9; Isa 5:8). This would explain why the jubilee is never appealed to by any of the prophets as an economic proposal (though its ideals are reflected metaphorically). In the only occasion when a slave release is mentioned by a prophet (Jeremiah 34) the law appealed to was the Sabbatical Year release of Hebrew slaves (Exod 21:1–7; Deut 15:12–18)—not the jubilee. The people in question were fellow Judeans, but they were effectively landless (a distinctive feature of the "Hebrew" class), not mortgaged debtors who could be restored to their property. The story shows how fragile and transient their actual release was.

E. Ethical Development

1. In the OT. We have seen that the jubilee had two major thrusts: release/liberty and return/restoration. Both of these lent themselves readily to the process of transfer from the strictly economic provision of the jubilee itself to a wider metaphoric application. There are allusive echoes of the jubilee particularly in later Isaiah. The mission of the Servant of Yahweh in Deutero-Isaiah has strong elements of the restorative plan of God for his people, aimed specifically at the weak and oppressed (Isa 42:1–7). Isaiah 58 is an attack on cultic observance without social justice and calls for liberation of the oppressed (v 6), specifically focusing on one's own kinship obligations (v 7). Most clearly of all, Isaiah 61 uses jubilee images to portray the one anointed as the herald of Yahweh to "evangelize" the poor, to proclaim liberty to the captives—using the word *dĕrôr* which is the explicitly jubilary word for release—and to announce the year of Yahweh's favor, almost certainly an allusion to a jubilee year. The ideas of redemption and return are combined in the future vision of Isaiah 35 and put alongside a transformation of nature itself. Thus in the OT the jubilee attracted an eschatological imagery while maintaining an ethical application in the present. Therefore it could be used to portray God's final intervention for messianic redemption and restoration; but it could also support ethical challenge for justice to the oppressed in contemporary history.

2. In the NT. Jesus announced the inbreaking of the eschatological reign of God. He claimed that the hopes of restoration and messianic reversal were being fulfilled in his own ministry. The "Nazareth manifesto" (Luke 4:16–30) is the clearest, programmatic statement of this and quotes directly from Isaiah 61, which is strongly influenced by jubilee concepts. Scholars are agreed that Jesus made use of jubilary imagery, though there is division over exactly what he meant by it. Some have argued that Jesus called for a literal enactment of the levitical jubilee (Trocmé 1961; Yoder 1972). Others, noting that Jesus used the prophetic texts and not the levitical law, argue that he was merely using jubilary language as a way of showing the kind of response required by the arrival of the kingdom of God, without intending an actual national jubilee. Sloan (1977) notes that Jesus' use of *aphēsis* carries both the sense of spiritual forgiveness of sin and also literal and financial remission of actual debts. Thus, the original background of economic *dĕrôr* has been preserved in Jesus' challenge concerning ethical response to the kingdom of God. Ringe (1985) traces the interweaving of major jubilee images into various parts of the gospel narratives and the teaching of Jesus (e.g., the beatitudes, the response to John the Baptist [Matt 11:2–6], the parable of the banquet [Luke 14:12–24], various episodes of forgiveness, teaching on debts [Matt 18:21–35], etc.). The evidence is broad and conforms to the pattern already set in the OT—namely, the jubilee as a model or image for the kingdom of God embodies both eschatological affirmation and ethical demand. Likewise in Acts the jubilary concept of eschatological restoration is found in the otherwise unique idea of *apokatastasis*. It occurs in Acts 1:6 and 3:21, related to God's final restoration of Israel and all things. Significantly, the early Church responded to this hope at the level of economic mutual help—thus fulfilling the sabbatical hopes of Deuteronomy 15 (Acts 4:34 is virtually a quotation of Deut 15:4).

3. Contemporary Application. Without envisaging any literal enactment of its provisions, the jubilee still remains a powerful model in formulating Christian biblical ethics. Its primary assumptions and objectives can be distilled and used as a guide and critique for our own ethical agenda in the modern world.

a. Economically. The jubilee existed to protect a form of land tenure that was based on an equitable and widespread distribution of the land and to prevent the accumulation of ownership in the hands of a wealthy few. This echoes the creation principle that the whole earth is given by God to all humanity, who act as co-stewards of its resources. There is a parallel between the affirmation of Lev 25:23, in respect of Israel, that "the land is mine," and the affirmation of Psalm 24, in respect of humanity as a whole, that "the earth is the Lord's and everything in it, the world and all who live in it." The moral principles of the jubilee are therefore universalizable on the basis of the moral consistency of God. What he required of Israel reflects what in principle he desires for humanity—namely broadly equitable distribution of the resources of the earth, especially land, and a curb on the tendency to accumulation with its inevitable oppression and alienation. The jubilee thus stands as a critique not only of massive private accumulation of land and related wealth, but also of large-scale forms of collectivism or nationalization which destroy any meaningful sense of personal or family ownership.

b. Socially. The jubilee embodied a practical concern for the family unit. In Israel's case this meant the extended family, the "father's house," which was a sizable group of related nuclear families descended in the male line from a living progenitor, including up to three or four generations. This was the smallest unit in Israel's kinship structure; and it was the focus of identity, status, responsibility, and security for the individual Israelite. It was this that the jubilee aimed to protect and periodically to restore if necessary. Notably, it did so, not by merely "moral" means—i.e., appealing for greater family cohesion or admonishing parents and children—but by legislating for specific structural mechanisms to regulate the economic effects of debt. Family morality was meaningless if families were being split up and dispossessed by economic forces that rendered them powerless (Neh 5:1–5). The jubilee aimed to restore social dignity and participation to families through maintaining or restoring their economic viability. The economic collapse of a family in one generation was not to condemn all future generations to the bondage of perpetual indebtedness. Such principles and objectives are certainly not irrelevant to welfare legislation or indeed any legislation with socioeconomic implications.

c. Theologically. The jubilee was based upon several central affirmations of Israel's faith, and the importance of these should not be overlooked when assessing its relevance to Christian ethic and mission. Like the rest of the sabbatical provisions, the jubilee proclaimed the sovereignty of God over time and nature; and obedience to it would require submission to that sovereignty; hence the year is dubbed "holy," "a Sabbath to Yahweh," to be observed out of the "fear of Yahweh." Furthermore, observing the fallow year dimension would also require faith in God's providence as the one who could command blessing in the natural order. Additional motivation for the law is provided by repeated appeals to the knowledge of God's historical act of redemption, the Exodus and all it had meant for Israel. And to this historical dimension was added the cultic and "present" experience of forgiveness in the fact that the jubilee was proclaimed on the Day of Atonement. To know yourself forgiven by God was to issue in practical remission of debts and bondages for fellow Israelites. And, as we have seen, the inbuilt future hope of the literal jubilee blended with an eschatological hope of God's final restoration of humanity and nature to his original purpose. To apply the jubilee model, then, requires that people face the sovereignty of God, trust his providence, know his redemptive action, experience his atonement, practice his justice, and hope in his promise. The wholeness of the model embraces the Church's evangelistic mission, its personal and social ethics, and its future hope.

Bibliography

Ellison, H. L. 1973. The Hebrew Slave: A Study in Early Israelite Society. *EvQ* 45: 275–302.

Finkelstein, J. J. 1961. Ammisaduqa's Edict and the Babylonian "Law Codes." *JCS* 15: 91–104.

———. 1965. Some New Misharum Material and Its Implications. *AS* 16: 233–46.

Ginzberg, E. 1932. Studies in the Economics of the Bible. *JQR* n.s. 22: 343–408.

Gordon, C. H. 1953. Sabbatical Cycle or Seasonal Pattern. *Or* n.s. 22: 79–81.

Gottwald, N. K. 1979. *The Tribes of Yahweh.* Maryknoll, NY.

Hoenig, S. B. 1969. Sabbath Years and the Year of Jubilee. *JQR* 59: 222–36.

Jirku, A. 1929. Das israelitische Jobeljahr. Vol. 2 of *Reinhold-Seeberg-Festschrift,* ed. W. Koepp. Leipzig.

Kartveit, Magnar. 1989. *Motive und Schichten der Landtheologie I Chronik 1–9.* Stockholm.

Leggett, D. A. 1974. *The Levirate and Goel Institutions in the OT with Special Attention to the Book of Ruth.*

Lemche, N. P. 1976. The Manumission of Slaves—the Fallow Year—the Sabbatical Year—the Jobel year. *VT* 26: 38–59.

Lewy, J. 1958. The Biblical Institution of *dĕrôr* in the Light of Akkadian Documents. *EI* 5: 21–31.

Lewy, J., and Lewy, H. 1942–43. The Origin of the Week and the Oldest West Asiatic Calendar. *HUCA* 17: 1–152.

Massynbaerde Ford, J. 1984. *My Enemy is My Guest: Jesus and Violence in Luke.* Maryknoll, NY.

Neufeld, E. 1958. Socio-Economic Background of *yōbēl* and *šᶜmiṭṭa.* *RSO* 33: 53–124.

North, R. 1954. *Sociology of the Biblical Jubilee.* Rome.

Ploeg, J. van der. 1972. Slavery in the OT. *VTSup* 22: 72–87.

Ringe, S. H. 1985. *Jesus, Liberation, and the Biblical Jubilee: Images for Ethics and Christology.* Philadelphia.

Schaeffer, H. 1922. *Hebrew Tribal Economy and the Jubilee as Illustrated in Semitic and Indo-European Village Communities.* Leipzig.

Sloan, R. B., Jr. 1977. *The Favorable Year of the Lord.* Austin, TX.

Stein, S. 1953. The Laws on Interest in the OT. *JTS* n.s. 4: 161–70.
Trocmé, A. 1961. *Jésus-Christ et la revolution non-violente.* Geneva.
Vaux, R. de. 1961. *Ancient Israel: Its Life and Institutions.* London.
Westbrook, R. 1971. Jubilee Laws. *Israel Law Review* 6: 209–26.
Wildberger, H. 1956. Israel und sein Land. *EvT* 16: 404–22.
Wright, C. J. H. What Happened Every Seven Years in Israel? OT Sabbatical Institutions for Land, Debts and Slaves. *EvQ* 56: 129–38, 193–201.
Yoder, J. H. 1972. *The Politics of Jesus.* Grand Rapids.

CHRISTOPHER J. H. WRIGHT

JUBILEES, BOOK OF. *Jubilees* presents itself as the account of a revelation which was disclosed to Moses on Mt. Sinai. After a prefatory chapter in which the Lord tells Moses in advance about Israel's apostasies and eventual repentance, the book takes the form of a first-person narrative recited by an "angel of the presence" whom the deity had instructed to tell Moses about everything "from the beginning of creation till My sanctuary has been built among them for all eternity" (1:27 [quotations from *Jubilees* are from Charles 1902]). The revelation proves to be a heavily edited rehearsal of the material from Genesis 1 to Exodus 20, all of which is encased in a chronology which divides time into units of 49 years (= jubilees), each of which consists of seven "weeks of years." The author does not include all of the biblical text, but he does follow the story line of Genesis–Exodus and often augments his base with additional details and at times with entirely new accounts (e.g., the war between Esau and Jacob [37:1–38:14]).

A. Texts and Titles

The commonly accepted theory about the textual evolution of *Jubilees* is that it was written in Hebrew, translated from Hebrew into Greek and possibly into Syriac, and rendered from Greek into Latin and Ethiopic. The Hebrew original and the Greek version were lost long ago; in fact, Western scholars had no text of the book until the 19th century, when Ethiopic and Latin copies first became available. Today, the entire text is preserved only in Ethiopic (the book enjoyed canonical status in the Abyssinian church); 27 copies of this granddaughter version have been identified to date. The Latin translation exists now in one manuscript (a palimpsest) which contains more than one-fourth of the text. The Greek version remains lost; only citations of it in some Greek and Latin writings from the patristic and Byzantine periods have survived. The Syriac version, if there ever was one, is visible presently only through 29 citations which have been found in an anonymous chronicle and which reproduce all, or more frequently parts, of about 137 verses. Fragments from 12 manuscripts of the original Hebrew version have been discovered among the Dead Sea Scrolls; nevertheless, only a few of these have been published. Though a fragment of another copy was reportedly found at Masada, this now appears not to be part of a Hebrew text of *Jubilees*.

The book received different names throughout its long textual journey. Its Hebrew title (if that is the proper word) is apparently given in CD 16:2–3, where it is cited and called "the book of the Divisions of the Times for Their Jubilees and Weeks." In Greek it circulated under several names: *Jubilees* (also attested in Syriac), the Little Genesis (seemingly the more common designation; the reason for the adjective is unknown), or, among other possibilities, the *Apocalypse of Moses*. The Ethiopic title is the same as the one in CD 16:2–3: the book of the Division(s) of the Times, or simply Division(s).

B. Date and Authorship

From the time that *Jubilees* became known in Europe until the end of the 19th century, scholars generally dated it to the 1st century C.E. The work of Bohn and Charles around the turn of the century led to a new agreement (apart from a few wildly divergent views, such as that of Zeitlin) that the book was composed at some point in the 2d century B.C.E. Bohn placed it in the middle of the century, Charles at the end. Since the discovery of the Dead Sea Scrolls and of fragments of *Jubilees* among them, the question of date has been approached from new angles. The paleographically determined date of some of the Hebrew fragments (4Qm 16 Jub[a] and 4Qm 17 Jub[a]) is ca. 100 B.C.E.—a date which virtually requires that one adopt an earlier time of composition than the one Charles defended. It seems clear that the book, which neither commands nor reflects separation from the remainder of the Jewish population but which manifests striking similarities with important teachings of the Scrolls, was written before the Qumran community was formed. There is no consensus about when this group exiled itself from the rest of the nation, but most scholars would now agree that the exodus to Qumran transpired during the high priestly tenure of either Jonathan (152–142) or Simon (142–134). This would imply that *Jubilees* was written no later than ca. 150–140 B.C.E. Several students of the book have found in it allusions to Maccabean wars; if they are correct, the book could not antedate ca. 166. However, others have argued that these allusions are open to other interpretations and that the apocalyptic passage in *Jubilees* 23 makes no reference to either the decrees of Antiochus IV forbidding the practice of Judaism (167) nor to the Maccabean response to these edicts. Nickelsburg and Goldstein have inferred from these circumstances that the book was written before 167. It should be added, though, that *Jubilees* 23 shares the standard opaqueness of apocalyptic language and that some passages in it have been interpreted by Charles and Davenport as references to the Maccabean uprising (e.g., v 20). Moreover, 4:19 may allude to *1 Enoch* 83–90, which was written, it seems, after ca. 164 B.C.E. In general one may say that the book was probably written at some point between 170 and 140.

There is strong reason to believe that *Jubilees* was written by a priest. This follows from the nature of the book with its heavy emphasis on priestly concerns, from the special attention devoted to the line of righteous men through whom the sacerdotal legislation was transmitted from earliest times, and from the extraordinary status of Levi among the sons of Jacob.

In addition to repeating and often expanding many passages which modern scholars assign to the priestly editor of the Pentateuch (e.g., creation according to Genesis 1, circumcision in Genesis 17), *Jubilees* adds numerous sections which betray the writer's priestly bent. Sections about sabbath laws, which appear in chaps. 2 (vv 1, 17–33) and 50 (vv 6–13), form a kind of *inclusio* around the narratives of the book. The sacred calendar exercises the author frequently: it was revealed to Enoch (4:17–18); some features of it were clarified by the events of the Flood (6:23–38); and festivals were celebrated properly by the patriarchs on the exact dates for them (Weeks: 6:17–22; 15:1–2; 44:1–4; cf. 22:1–6; Tabernacles: 16:20–31; 32:4–7, 27–29; Unleavened Bread: 18:18–19; 49:22–23; Atonement: 34:18–19; for Passover, see 49:1–22a). The writer also deals regularly with sacrifices: Adam offered one upon leaving Eden (3:27); Enoch burns incense on the mount in Eden (4:25); Noah makes atonement for the earth (6:1–4; cf. 7:3–5; and Gen 8:20); Abraham provides extensive instructions about procedures and the woods which may be used in sacrifice (21:7–16); and the descriptions of festival celebrations include notices about the offerings presented (e.g., 15:1–2; 16:20–31). Among other priestly concerns, mention should be made of the prohibition of consuming blood (6:7–14 [cf. Gen 9:6]; 7:31–32; 21:6, 17–18); tithes (13:25–27; 32:2, 5, 8–15); circumcision (15:25–34; 20:3); separation of the holy race from the nations (22:16–18; 25:4–10; cf. 27:10; 30:6–16; see also 16:17–18; 22:12); and avoidance of impurity and uncleanness (e.g., 3:8–14; 6:37; 7:20–21; 11:17; 16:5–6; 20:3–7; 21:21–23; 22:16–23; 23:14, 17, 21; etc.). In view of all this, it comes as no surprise to learn that the descendants of Isaac are to become "a kingdom and priests and a holy nation" (16:18).

These and other priestly laws were transmitted in writing by a line of righteous heroes from earliest times. Enoch, who was the first to learn how to write (4:17), passed along teachings to Methuselah, who in turn transmitted them to Lamech, from whom Noah received them (7:38–39; the context deals with firstfruits and the year of release). Noah gave to his son Shem his book about medicines (a priestly domain) for combating the effects of the evil spirits (10:14). Later, Abraham learned to read the books of his fathers (12:27; cf. 21:10, where Enoch and Noah are mentioned), and he handed this lore to Jacob (12:27; cf. 21:10, where Enoch and Noah are mentioned), and he handed this lore to Jacob (39:6–7). Finally, the writer notes that Jacob gave all of his books and those of his ancestors to Levi "that he might preserve them and renew them for his children until this day" (45:16).

Levi, the third son of Jacob, lent his name to the tribe of Levites and thus was the titular ancestor of Israel's priests according to the Bible. Yet nothing is said there about his actually functioning as a priest. In *Jubilees,* however, Levi himself becomes the divinely ordained priest who begins serving in this capacity at an early age. In Gen 49:5–7 Jacob criticized Levi and Simeon for their massacre of the Shechemites, but the author of *Jubilees* claims that the two brothers were regarded as righteous for their act and that Levi's descendants were eternally chosen for the priesthood on the basis of what their ancestor had done in Shechem (30:17–20). When Jacob brought his sons Levi and Judah to see his aged parents, Isaac took Levi (the older of the two) by his right hand and blessed him first (31:12–17). He prophesied that he and his descendants would forever be priests, princes, judges, and chiefs of the nation, that they would teach, and bless, and eat at the divine table. Only later did Isaac bless Judah, whom he had taken by his left hand (vv 18–20). In chap. 32 Jacob is pictured as counting his sons backward and thus arriving at Levi as the tenth (he was the third oldest of the 12). To him there fell the "portion of the Lord, and his father clothed him in the garments of the priesthood and filled his hands" (i.e., he ordained him [32:3]). In this context, which speaks of tithing, one reads that Levi presided as priest at Bethel (v 9). Jacob, just before his death, delivered all of his books and those of his fathers to Levi (45:16).

This strong sacerdotal emphasis in the book probably reflects the office of the author, while the prominence of Levi mirrors the lofty status of the high priest in Second Temple Judaism. Students of the legal material in *Jubilees* have recognized that it does not correspond with the traditions of either the Pharisees or the Sadducees, but that it stands closer to what is known of Essene halakah. The Qumran literature has documented their thesis; the 364-day solar calendar is just one fundamental point on which *Jubilees* and the scrolls (including now the Temple Scroll) agree. It is likely, then, that the priestly author belonged to the movement that was later called Essene, whatever may have been its original name.

C. Theology

The first chapter of *Jubilees* places the narrative of chaps. 2–50 in a new context compared with Genesis–Exodus. The Lord, who reveals to Moses "the earlier and the later history of the division of all the days of the law and of the testimony" (1:4), informs him that he is to record the revelation "in a book in order that their generations may see how I have not forsaken them for all the evil which they have wrought in transgressing the covenant which I establish between Me and thee for their generations this day on Mt. Sinai. And thus it will come to pass when all these things come upon them, that they will recognise that I am more righteous than they in all their judgments and in all their actions, and they will recognise that I have been truly with them" (vv 5–6). The audience for whom the book is intended clearly lives long after Moses' time, and it must be convinced of divine fidelity and the urgency of maintaining the covenant. After Israel's apostasy in the land (vv 7–12) and subsequent captivity (vv 13–14) are predicted, the Lord informs Moses that the exiles will repent (v 15) and that he will shower his favors upon them—including the building of his eternal sanctuary among them (vv 16–18). Moses intercedes for the people unsuccessfully (vv 19–21), but God reiterates that only after confession of sin and repentance will a new time dawn—a time when they shall never again turn from the Lord (vv 22–25). Some future generation, presumably that of the author, must receive this message of God's faithfulness, Israel's infidelity, and the power of confession, repentance, and obedience to the covenantal stipulations to open a new day in the covenantal relationship between the Lord and his holy people.

One should view the author's eschatological teachings in the context of the Law and Israel's future. Israel, which had received the covenant, had failed to obey its stipulations (cf. 23:16, 19; 15:33–34; etc.). Both chaps. 1 and 23 survey the great difficulties which will beset the apostate nation because it has violated covenant and command; but both also point toward a change and the way in which it is to be accomplished and picture the contours of a new, ideal age (for chap. 1, see above). Here again the legal focus is transparent. After depicting the punishments which Israel will endure (23:22–25), the author writes (v 26):

And in those days the children will begin to study the laws,
And to seek the commandments,
And to return to the path of righteousness.

Then the span of human life, which had been shortened because of evil, will be lengthened until it approaches 1000 years. (vv 27–28)

And all their days they will complete and live in peace and in joy,
And there will be no Satan nor any evil destroyer;
For all their days will be days of blessing and healing. (v 29)

The writer envisages neither a messiah (though Levi and Judah and their descendants are at the center of his interests [see especially 31:12–20]) nor a resurrection of the dead. A messiah is never mentioned, and the phrase "rise up" in 23:30 almost certainly has a different meaning in its context. Rather, of the departed righteous the author says:

And their bones will rest in the earth,
And their spirits will have much joy. (v 31ab)

But of those who will live in the new age he writes: "And their souls will cleave to Me and to all My commandments, and they will fulfil My commandments, and I shall be their Father and they will be My children" (1:24). At that time the Lord will live forever with Israel in his sanctuary on Mt. Zion (1:17, 27–29; cf. 4:26).

The author's teachings about the centrality of the Law and its importance for the future also allow one to place in context his practice of founding essential legal practices in the time of the ancients of Genesis rather than in the age of Moses. For example, the different periods of impurity for a woman after bearing a male or female child are based on the time Adam and Eve spent outside the Garden before being led into it (3:8–14; see Lev 12:2–5). The lex talionis harks back to Cain, who killed Abel with a stone and was himself killed by one when his house collapsed on him (4:31–32; cf. Exod 21:24; Lev 24:19–20; Deut 19:21). Noah first celebrated the Festival of Weeks (see 6:17–22) and later Abraham, too, observed this holiday, which became the anniversary of the Noahic, Abrahamic, and Mosaic covenants (6:17–22; 15:1–2). The Festivals of Tabernacles (16:20–23; 32:4–9, 27–29) and Unleavened Bread (18:18–19) and the Day of Atonement (34:17–19, which commemorates Jacob's torment on learning of Joseph's "death") also were introduced in the age of the fathers. The author's reason for antedating these practices can only be surmised, but it is clear that he wished to impress upon his audience that these essential acts of obedience to the covenant were not the innovations of a later age that were imposed upon the religion of the patriarchs. They had been in force since earliest times, were inscribed immutably and eternally on the heavenly tablets (of the numerous cases, see, for example, 3:10, 31; 6:17; 15:25; 16:28–29; etc.), and in some instances were practiced in heaven (Sabbath [2:30]; Festival of Weeks [6:18]; circumcision [15:27]). These provisions were to be observed scrupulously in the present if the ideal future was to be realized.

Bibliography

Albeck, C. 1930. *Das Buch der Jubiläen und die Halacha.* Sieben und vierzigster Bericht der Hochschule für die Wissenschaft des Judentums in Berlin. Berlin-Schöneberg.

Baars, W., and Zuurmond, R. 1964. The Project for a New Edition of the Ethiopic Book of Jubilees. *JSS* 9: 67–74.

Baumgarten, J. 1977. The Calendar of the Book of Jubilees. Pp. 101–14 in *Studies in Qumran Law.* SJLA 24. Leiden.

Berger, K. 1981. *Das Buch der Jubiläen.* JSHRZ 2/3. Gütersloh.

Bohn, F. 1900. Die Bedeutung des Buches der Jubiläen. *TSK* 73: 167–84.

Charles, R. H. 1895. Maṣḥafa kufālē *or the Ethiopic Version of the Hebrew Book of Jubilees.* Anecdota Oxoniensia. Oxford.

———. 1902. *The Book of Jubilees or the Little Genesis.* London.

Davenport, G. L. 1971. *The Eschatology of the Book of Jubilees.* SPB 20. Leiden.

Goldstein, J. 1983. The Date of the Book of Jubilees. *PAAJR* 50: 63–86.

Littmann, E. 1900. Das Buch der Jubiläen. Pp. 31–119 in vol. 2 of *Die Apokryphen und Pseudepigraphen des Alten Testaments,* ed. E. Kautzsch. Tübingen.

Nickelsburg, G. W. E. 1981. The Book of Jubilees. Pp. 73–80 in *Jewish Literature Between the Bible and the Mishnah.* Philadelphia.

Rabin, C. 1984. Jubilees. Pp. 1–139 in *The Apocryphal OT,* ed. H. F. D. Sparks. Oxford.

Testuz, M. 1960. *Les idées religieuses du Livre des Jubilés.* Geneva and Paris.

VanderKam, J. 1977. *Textual and Historical Studies in the Book of Jubilees.* HSM 14. Missoula, MT.

———. 1981. The Putative Author of the Book of Jubilees. *JSS* 26: 209–17.

———. 1989. *A Critical Text and English Translation of the Ethiopic Book of Jubilees.* CSCO. Leuven.

Wiesenberg, E. 1961–62. The Jubilee of Jubilees. *RevQ* 3: 3–40.

Zeitlin, S. 1939–40. The Book of Jubilees, Its Character and Its Significance. *JQR* 30: 1–31.

———. 1957. The Book of 'Jubilees' and the Pentateuch. *JQR* 48: 218–35.

JAMES C. VANDERKAM

JUCAL (PERSON) [Heb *yûkal*]. See JEHUCAL (PERSON).

JUDAH (PERSON) [Heb *yĕhûdâ*]. The name of several individuals mentioned in the Bible.

1. The fourth son of Jacob and eponymous ancestor of the tribe of Judah. See JUDAH (PLACE).

2. A Levite in the postexilic period, an ancestor of Kadmiel, who heads one of three families charged with the oversight of the rebuilding and repairing of the temple (Ezra 3:9). Evidently Judah represents a leading family, for his family and offspring supervised this momentous reconstruction project. The term "workmen" (RSV, i.e., those whom Judah's family supervised), may refer either to the levitical foremen or to the common laborers. The "work" which is supervised represents the Heb word *mĕlāʾkâ* rather than *ʿăbōdâ*. It has been convincingly demonstrated that *mĕlāʾkâ* refers expressly to an enterprise calling for skill and workmanship, while *ʿăbōdâ* refers to raw or unskilled labor (Milgrom 1970). It is thus an appropriate term to use to describe a project as sacred and demanding such dexterity as temple repairs.

A problem appears when Ezra 3:9 is compared with Ezra 2:40. In the latter, Kadmiel is listed as one of the two branches of the family of Hodaviah (or Hodevah in Neh 7:43), not of Judah as in 3:9. This suggests that Hodaviah/Hodevah and Judah are probably the same person. While the meaning of "Judah" still remains uncertain, that of "Hodaviah" appears quite transparent—"Give praise/thanks to Yahweh." Nevertheless, "Judah" more than likely has some connection with the Heb verb *yādâ* (*Hipʿil,* "give thanks," "praise"), as Hodaviah clearly has. Given then that both names are built from the same verb, it is quite possible that Hodaviah is the more correct of the two, but that the more familiar "Judah" slipped into the text.

It is not uncommon for a Hebrew name to be borne by several persons throughout the OT. Surprisingly, the names of Abraham, Isaac, and Jacob appear only in connection with the patriarchs. No father or mother named a son after one of these legends, as we do with a George Washington Carver or a Martin Luther King. It is with the fourth generation of the patriarchs, Judah, that others bear a patriarchal name; and all are in the postexilic period; and most are Levites. If the name has something to do with praise or giving thanks, it is an appropriate one to have, given the release by Cyrus, the return to Canaan, the rebuilding of the temple, and the opportunity of a fresh start.

3. One of ten Levites who during the postexilic period had taken a foreign wife and at the urging of Ezra divorced her (Ezra 10:23, LXX *Iodom/Ioydas*). Nothing is said here of what happened to his foreign wife and other divorcées after the divorces were finalized. In addition to Judah, other culprits with ancient names guilty of indiscreet marriages include a Benjamin in v 32 and an Amram in v 34.

It is interesting that Ezra 10:13 identifies the ceremony of marriage dissolution as a "work" *(mĕlāʾkâ),* the same word used for the work on the temple (see above). This is clearly a temporary project, but the nuance of "skilled" work is palpably absent this time.

4. One of the Benjaminites (maybe) who lived in Jerusalem in the days of Nehemiah and whose father's name was Hassenuah (Neh 11:9). His office was that of "second over the city." His colleague, Joel, was chief administrator of the city. It is not totally clear whether or not these two were also Benjaminites (as are those named in vv 7–8). Perhaps they were Judeans. Would two Benjaminites occupy the two top administrative positions in rebuilt Jerusalem?

His father's name—Hassenuah—is interesting. It means "the hated/unloved one" if one allows the interchangeability of the sibilants *śin* and *samek* (cf. Gen 29:31, Leah was "hated" [*śĕnûʾâ*]). On the other hand, Ezra 2:35 mentions the large family (3630) of Senaah [a place name?]; and this may be the origin of Hassenuah.

5. A Levite who, along with seven other Levites, returned with Zerubbabel from Exile (Neh 12:8). More than likely he is the same as the Hodaviah of Ezra 2:40 (or the Judah of Ezra 3:9). See #2 above.

6. Prince of Judah who took part in the dedication of the wall of Jerusalem (Neh 12:34). However, it is possible that the seven names listed in Neh 12:33–34 (of which our Judah is one) are in fact priests and not laity. One reason for opting for this is that v 41 lists seven priests who accompanied the other half of the twin procession. Thus the seven names of vv 33–34 balance the seven names of v 41 (and these latter are clearly sacerdotal people).

7. Priest and a musician who took part in the dedication of the wall of Jerusalem, specifically in the processional embrace of the city and its walls (Neh 12:36). He is possibly a descendant of the Levite musician mentioned in #5.

Bibliography

Milgrom, J. 1970. *Studies In Levitical Terminology, I.* UCPNES 14. Berkeley, CA.

VICTOR P. HAMILTON

8. The father of Simeon and son of Joseph (not the "supposed father" of Jesus) according to Luke's genealogy tying Joseph, the "supposed father" of Jesus, to descent from Adam and God (Luke 3:30). Judah is omitted in D, which substitutes a genealogy adapted from Matt 1:6–15 for Luke 3:23–31. Apart from the patriarch Judah mentioned in Luke 3:33, this name appears in a list of 18 otherwise unknown descendants of David's son Nathan (Fitzmyer *Luke 1–9* AB, 501). Although Jeremias (1969: 296) believes that it is anachronistic for Luke to include this name here, since it first appears as a personal name in the postexilic period (e.g., Ezra 3:9; 10:23; Neh 11:9), caution must be exercised in light of the limited nature of the available evidence. Kuhn (1923: 208–9) argues that two seemingly parallel lists of names—Luke 3:23–26 (Jesus to Mattathias) and 3:29–31 (Joshua/Jesus to Mattatha)—were originally identical, the first perhaps reflecting a Hebrew context and the second, in an Aramaic context, tracing Mary's line of descent (since it does not mention Joseph as Jesus' father). Judah (Gk *Iouda*), in the second list, corresponds to Jannai, in the first list. With no textual variants for either name to support confusion of the two, Kuhn's theory has little plausibility.

Bibliography

Jeremias, J. 1969. *Jerusalem in the Time of Jesus.* Philadelphia.
Kuhn, G. 1923. Die Geschlechtsregister Jesu bei Lukas und Matthäus, nach ihrer Herkunft untersucht. *ZNW* 22: 206–28.

STANLEY E. PORTER

JUDAH (PLACE) [Heb *yĕhûdâ*]. Var. JUDEA. The name of an Israelite tribe in S Cisjordan, as well as the name of the territory associated with that tribe and the name of the kingdom that, after the death of Solomon, controlled that territory. See also JUDAH, HILL COUNTRY OF.

A. Judah, Son of Jacob

The eponym of the tribe of Judah was born to Jacob as his fourth son by his wife Leah (Gen 29:35). In Akkadian sources we find the name forms *ya-á-du, ya-a-ḫu-du* and *ya-ku-du.* This is similar to the *yĕhûd* or *yahûd* from the Persian period. An inscription found in a rock-cut tomb in W Judah, that most probably dates back to the 7th or 6th century B.C.E., has *hry yhd,* "the mountains of Judah." On Arad Ostracon 40 the text is unfortunately damaged after *yĕhûd* (l.13); it is therefore not certain that *-āh* followed, as is often assumed.

Both the etymology and the original meaning are disputed. There is, however, a growing consensus that the original meaning was geographic: Mt. Judah. Compare expressions such as *ʾereṣ yĕhûdâ* (Amos 7:12), *midbar yĕhûdâ* (Judg 1:16), *negeb yĕhûdâ* (1 Sam 27:10). Consequently, the main tribe of this area was called after its territory. The last step was the name *yĕhûdâ* as the name of a state.

Apart from the eponym, the use of *yĕhûdâ* as a personal name seems to be postexilic. It is a striking fact that a name *yĕhûdâ* until now has not been found among the hundreds of extrabiblical personal names discovered on ostraca and seals. This could speak in favor of Lipínski's hypothesis that the name is related to Arabic *wahda/yahda,* "ravine"/"canyon." But a derivation of the root *yhd (Hopʿal)* is more probable, as was suggested by W. F. Albright as early as 1927. This was recently defended again by A. R. Millard (1974). The ending *-āh* could be a shortening of a theophoric element (see *TPNAH,* 165).

B. The Place of Judah in the System of Twelve Tribes

There is not one system of twelve tribes in the OT, but two. See GAD (PERSON). Judah has a prominent place in both systems. But this is also due to the fact that both systems follow an ancient tradition of border description: starting in the SE and moving clockwise. This tradition is already found in the old border description of Canaan (cf. Num 34:1–12).

Already in the last century many historians found the appearance of Judah in the twelve-tribe system suspicious. The old Song of Deborah (Judges 5) does not mention a tribe of Judah. This tribe is not even blamed for its absence. This must mean that the author did not even expect Judeans to fight with "all-Israel" in this very important battle. The questions arose whether Judah was a part of premonarchic "Israel," or whether there was a tribe of Judah at all before the time of David (for the history of this discussion see de Geus 1976: chap. 1). In general there were and still are the following possibilities.

1. A tribe of Judah never existed. "Judah" was the name of the state that was created by David in the mountains of Judah (territory). It consisted from the start of several different groups. Hebron was the center of this state.

2.a. There did exist a "Judah" in the time of the judges. But it was rather a "Greater Judah"; from the start it was a confederation of several different groups. German scholars like Noth spoke of a S six-tribe amphictyony around Hebron, consisting of Judah, Simeon, Levi, Calebites, Kenites, and Jerahmeelites. This S confederation originally had nothing to do with the N amphictyony, called "Israel." Only after David became king also over the N tribes did Judah (with Levi and Simeon) become included in the system. Some even thought that the twelve-tribe system was especially created to defend the admission of the S groups into "Israel."

2.b. There did indeed exist a Greater Judah in the S. But this Judah was completely independent of the N. At the same time, however, the S and the much larger N group had so much in common that they considered each other as brothers (cf. 2 Sam 19:40–44).

3. There existed during the period of the judges an "Israel" of which also the S tribes Judah, Simeon, and Levi (but not the other three) were always a part. The separate developments in the N and in the S are to be explained from the geographic isolation of the S groups.

When trying to reconstruct the early history of the tribe of Judah, one should remember three important facts. The first is that later sources describe former Judah with the later state of Judah in mind. The second is that our most important source for premonarchic Israel, the book of Judges, has in general a N outlook. The role of Judah in Judges is only marginal. But this does not mean that Judah did not exist. The third fact is the geographic isolation of the S tribes because of the Hivite-Jebusite enclaves along the line Gezer-Jerusalem. Jerusalem was only integrated into Israel by David, and Gezer became Israelite as a gift from pharaoh to Solomon (1 Kgs 9:16).

C. Settlement

Until very recently the prevailing opinion among OT scholars was that the tribe of Judah had been far more successful in its settlement than the N tribes. The fact that we find hardly any settlement traditions about Judah should mean that this was a peaceful process in the S, without any great conflicts like those that were "remembered" much later (Auld 1975: 285; de Vaux 1970: 125). As a result of this absence of great conflicts, the relations of the ancient Judeans with the peoples surrounding them were much more relaxed than was the case in the N. Compare the case in which a Bethlehemite family sought refuge in Moab, and the way the Moabite Ruth was absorbed, or the relations with the Philistines in the time of Samson. Even the eponym of the tribe sees no objection to marrying a Canaanite woman (Gen 38:2). His friend Hirah from Adullam, too, is often considered as being a Canaanite. Also the cooperation with other groups, some of them non-Israelites, such as Kenites and Calebites, illustrates this typical Judean quality. In 1 Samuel 25 we hear of the Calebite Nabal, who has his business among Judeans but who lives in his own Calebite village of Maon.

Literary research has long been undecided as to whether the settlement of the Judeans (with the Simeonites) occurred from the S and was therefore separate from that of the N tribes, or whether for Judah and other tribes the movement was from N to S, with Judah being part of a greater movement. Memories of a settlement from the S are the originally Simeonite and Calebite traditions about Hormah, Hebron, and Arad (Numbers 13–14, 20; Joshua 14–15; Judges 1). Hesitatingly de Vaux (1970: 131) concludes that it is more probable that all six groups that were to form Greater Judah came from the S. This, of course, is consistent with the first possibility mentioned above.

Judges 1, on the other hand, tells us how Judah and Simeon set off to conquer their inheritance from the N.

This relies on the N location of Bezek (Judg 1:4) and its identification with Khirbet Ibziq (M.R. 187197). In all traditions Judah is closely connected with Simeon. In Genesis 34 we find a connection between Simeon and Levi with Shechem. Another argument for the N origin of Judah is that one of their leading clans, that of Ephrath, came from the N. Ephrath settled in or around Bethlehem (de Vaux 1970; Demsky 1986–87). Such a N origin for the Judeans is more consistent with possibility 3, and to a lesser degree, with possibility 2.b.

Modern archaeological research has eliminated two of the three popular "models" for the Israelite settlement (Lemche 1985; Finkelstein *AIS*). The first model, that of a military conquest by intruding foreign tribes, finds no archaeological support whatever. The second, of a revolt of peasants and slaves against the Canaanite LB city-states, is at least very improbable for Judah: there were very few LB towns. The only towns that existed at the end of the LB were Tell Beit Mirsim, Debir (= Khirbet Rabud), and Jerusalem. Bethlehem existed in the Amarna Age, as "a town in the land of Jerusalem" (EA 290). During the 14th or 13th century it became uninhabited. Hebron also existed in the Amarna Age as a residence of a chieftain. But also here we have to suppose a hiatus in habitation at the end of the LB. (Other possibilities of LB towns that continue into the Early Iron Age are Beth-zur and Khirbet Jedur [*AIS*, 52].) This leaves at the moment only the third model, that of gradual sedentarization involving only smaller and local conflicts with indigenous pastoral groups (*AIS*, 351; de Geus 1976; 164–71). Archaeological research has also shown that there were only very few Iron Age I sites in Judah. Up until now intensive surveys have resulted in only ten such sites (*AIS*, 353). And the material culture of these sites is best explained from the N, where Iron Age I settlement was much denser. See MANASSEH (PLACE). Therefore it seems certain that the Iron Age settlers, who were to become the tribe of Judah, were emigrants from the central Ephraimite hills. The above mentioned "wedge" of Hivite and Canaanite towns separated them from their N kinsmen at the time when they became fully sedentary. A separate development in the material culture, especially in ceramics, between N and S becomes visible early in the Iron Age I. Also this testifies to the isolation of the S groups.

D. Territory

The core of the Judahite territory was the mountain ridge between Bethlehem and Hebron. In the N the territory was confined by the Benjaminites and the possessions of the Jebusites. To the E lay the desert of Judah. In the S, around Hebron and toward the desert of the Negeb, lay the territories of allied groups. We know almost nothing about the extension of the tribal territory to the W. One can suspect that any expansion went in that direction and that this brought about the conflicts with the Philistines. In the 11th century B.C. the Philistines were involved in a process of expansion to the E and NE. There are possibly some indications for a Judean expansion toward the NW (Miller and Hayes *HAIJ*, 106). The OT gives us no information on the original tribal area of Judah. No tribal borders are given. The border description we find now in Joshua 15 is in fact a part of the old border description of Canaan. The N border is simply the S border of Benjamin in reversed order. The town list of Josh 15:21–62 contains a document from the later Monarchy (Aharoni *LBHG*, 87, 248–53, 347).

E. Greater Judah

An essential feature of all old traditions about the tribe of Judah is that the tribe rarely operated alone. It was probably too small to do so. From the earliest times it cooperated with Simeon. For later generations these two tribes were regarded more or less as one and the same tribe. Most of the villages assigned to Simeon are also assigned to Judah. And all of them are situated within the boundaries designated for Judah (*HAIJ*, 103). Calebites, Othnielites, Kenites, Jerahmielites, and possibly Levites were also confederates of the Judeans. Thanks to the analysis of 1 Sam 30:27–31 by Zobel (1975: 253–77) we know more about this ancient confederation. In view of the unimportant settlement period of the Judeans, one suspects that this confederation around Hebron already existed when the Judeans (and Simeonites?) joined it. Zobel showed convincingly that this confederation was not the work of David himself. It existed before him. We do not know what brought these groups together. Was it the continuing importance of Hebron as cultic center of the S? Or do we have to think of a more or less automatic development into larger units as a result of population expansion and increasing production? Did Hebron, as the central marketplace, in this way become the center of an early state? Or do we have to reckon with external factors? Outside pressure could have come from the Philistines; but one could also think of the Amalekites, who seem to have been the most important threat in earlier times.

Bibliography

Anderson, G. W. 1970. Israel: Amphictyony: ʿAM; ḲĀHĀL; ʿĒḎÂH. Pp. 135–51 in *Translating & Understanding the OT*, ed. H. T. Frank and W. L. Reed. Nashville.

Auld, A. G. 1975. Judges 1 and History: A Reconsideration. *VT* 25: 261–85.

Coote, R. B., and Whitelam, K. W. 1987. *The Emergence of Early Israel in Historical Perspective*. SWBA 4. Sheffield.

Danell, G. A. 1946. *Studies in the Name Israel in the OT*. Uppsala.

Demsky, A. 1986–87. The Clans of Ephrath: Their Territory and History. *TA* 13–14: 46–60.

Geus, C. H. J. de. 1976. *The Tribes of Israel*. Assen and Amsterdam.

———. 1983. Agrarian Communities in Biblical Times: 12th to 10th Centuries B.C.E. *Recueils de la Societié Jean Bodin* 41: 207–38.

———. 1988. The New City in Ancient Israel. Two Questions concerning the Reurbanisation of ʾEreṣ Yiśraʾel in the Tenth Century B.C.E. Pp. 105–15 in *"Wünschet Jerusalem Frieden." IOSOT Congress 1986*, ed. M. Augustin and K.-D. Schunck. BEATAJ 13. Frankfurt.

Gottwald, N. K. 1979. *The Tribes of Yahweh*. Maryknoll, NY.

Halpern, B. 1983. *The Emergence of Israel in Canaan*. Chico, CA.

Lemche, N. P. 1985. *Early Israel*. VTSup 37. Leiden.

Lindars, B. 1979. The Israelite Tribes in Judges. Pp. 95–112 in *Studies in the Historical Books of the OT*, ed. J. A. Emerton. VTSup 30. Leiden.

Lipínski, E. 1973. L'étymologie de "Juda". *VT* 23: 380–81.

Mazar, A. 1982. Iron Age Fortresses in the Judean Hills. *PEQ* 114: 87–109.
Millard, A. R. 1974. The Meaning of the Name Judah. *ZAW* 86: 216–18.
Smend, R. 1967. Gehörte Juda zum vorstaatlichen Israel? Pp. 200–210 in *Zur ältesten Geschichte Israels,* ed. R. Smend. Ges. Studien 2. Munich.
Vaux, R. de. 1970. The Settlement of the Israelites in Southern Palestine and the Origins of the Tribe of Judah. Pp. 108–34 in *Translating & Understanding the OT,* ed. H. T. Frank and W. L. Reed. Nashville.
Zobel, H. J. 1965. *Stammesspruch und Geschichte.* BZAW 95. Berlin.
———. 1975. Beiträge zur Geschichte Gross-Judas in früh- und vordavidischer Zeit. Pp. 253–77 in *Congress Volume, Edinburgh 1974.* VTSup 28. Leiden.

C. H. J. de Geus

JUDAH THE MACCABEE. See JUDAS MACCABEUS (PERSON).

JUDAH THE PRINCE, RABBI. Rabbinic leader and patriarch *(nāśîʾ)* during the late 2d century C.E. Judah's great accomplishment was to consolidate the hegemony of the rabbinic movement—with the patriarch at its head—over the organized Jewish community of Palestine. His patriarchate represents the end of all challenge to his family's right to that office; and during his lifetime the descent of the patriarchal dynasty from Hillel the Elder was finally accepted as historical fact (see Levi 1895); at his death, Judah explicitly bequeathed the title of *nāśîʾ* to one of his sons (*b. Ketub.* 103b).

Judah's success is reflected in the numerous legends that make him the intimate personal friend of the Roman emperor, always called Antoninus in these stories but in fact (if there is any historical kernel to them at all) probably one of the Severan dynasty. His wealth also was legendary (*b. B. Meṣ.* 85a), and one of his strategies for achieving political stabilization after the wars of the previous century was to bring about an alliance between the patriarchate and the remaining wealthy Jewish families of the land. This strategy provoked resentment (*b. Erub.* 86a), some of which was directed at his own uneducated sons-in-law (*j. Moʿed Qaṭ.* 3.1, 81c; *b. Ned.* 51a), but achieved success when the Roman authorities confirmed patriarchal control over the autonomous Jewish judiciary in Palestine (see Alon 1977: 401–2, 411–12, 428–29). Judah's relationship with the Roman authorities is also reflected in several legal innovations attempted by him that would have had the effect of softening continued Jewish hatred of Rome for having destroyed Jerusalem and its temple. Into this category can be placed Judah's proposal to eliminate the annual fast commemorating the destruction (*b. Meg.* 5b) and possibly as well his willingness to exempt several important centers outside Judea proper from the obligation to tithe agricultural produce (*j. Dem.* 2.1 22c; *b. Ḥul.* 6b). In the latter case Judah is reported to have defended his action with the claim that every generation's leadership is expected to institute some alteration in the received tradition. During Judah's lifetime the practice of dividing leadership over the rabbinate among several individuals was apparently temporarily suspended; and after his death his successors retained the power to grant rabbinic ordination, a power previously held by all rabbis with respect to their own disciples (*j. Sanh.* 1.2 19a). In the end Judah was remembered as the first since Moses who had "combined Torah and [political] greatness in one place" (*b. Giṭ.* 59a; see also *t. Sanh.* 11.8).

Judah's best-known achievement is that the Mishnah was compiled under his leadership and then circulated under his name. There is no consensus among modern scholars as to the intended function of the Mishnah, the actual method by which it was put together, or Judah's own role in this process (see Neusner 1973); but this text resembling a kind of legal syllabus rapidly became the main focus of rabbinic study of oral Torah both in Israel and in Babylonia; and the Talmud which eventually emerged as the fundamental document of rabbinic Judaism took the form of an elaborate commentary on the Mishnah.

Bibliography

Alon, G. 1977. Those Appointed for Money. Pp. 374–435 in *Jews, Judaism and the Classical World.* Trans. I. Abrahams. Jerusalem.
Levi, I. 1895. De l'origine davidique de Hillel. *REJ* 31: 202–11; 32: 143–46.
Neusner, J. 1973. *The Modern Study of the Mishnah.* Leiden.

Robert Goldenberg

JUDAH, ADMINISTRATION OF (POSTEXILE). See PALESTINE, ADMINISTRATION OF (POSTEXILIC JUDEAN OFFICIALS).

JUDAH, HILL COUNTRY OF (PLACE) [Heb *har yĕhûdâ*]. Named by association with the territory allotted to the tribe whose eponymous ancestor was Judah, the fourth son of Jacob and Leah (Gen 29:35; 49:2–4, 8–12).

The hill country of Judah formed the core of what at first was a tribal territory, then in the time of David a state the capital of which was at Hebron, and again after the civil war between Rehoboam and Jeroboam and later the province of a foreign government. The hill country of Judah is located in the S part of the mountain ridge which extends from the Jezreel valley in the N to the Negeb. The expression "hill country of Judah" is used only twice in the Bible: Josh 21:11 and Luke 1:65. However, the physical setting is well understood. Judah is situated S of a line drawn due W from the N shore of the Dead Sea to the Mediterranean. As distinct from the Wilderness of Judah and the Shephelah, the hill country encompasses approximately 250 square miles (ca. 640 km^2)—slightly less than the land area of New York City.

The S border of the tribal territory of Judah is described in Josh 15:1–5 as extending S from the Dead Sea to the Wilderness of Zin, then turning W to a point S of Kadesh-Barnea, then curving NW to the brook of Egypt (Wâdī el-Arish) and the Mediterranean. On the E Judah is bounded by the Dead Sea, and on the W, the Mediterranean. On the N Judah shares a border with Benjamin (NE) and Dan (NW) (Josh 15:5–12; cf. 18:11–20).

The hill country of Judah is caused by an arching of the earth's crust (anticline) in which the hard Cenomanian limestone is exposed along the top of the ridge and the W slopes of the arch. The ridge of the Judean arch lies roughly NNE by SSW, paralleling the Mediterranean shore and reaching an elevation of ca. 3350 feet at Hebron; Jerusalem is at ca. 2700 feet. This hard limestone is bedded in layers which create natural terracing and which erode into deep v-shaped canyons. This limestone weathers to form a rich, fertile, reddish soil called terra rossa, which is excellent for vineyards and fruit trees (esp. olive and almond). This is the land of terraced farming.

The hill country presently receives 16″–30″ (400mm–750mm) annual rainfall depending on location. As weather patterns move in from the W over the Mediterranean and drop most of their precipitation on the W side of the ridge, the runoff water has eroded deep v-shaped canyons into the hard-bedded limestone as it flows from the watershed back toward the Mediterranean Sea. Topography seems to have made the area somewhat "closed" and provincial. The deep E-W canyons make travel from N to S in Judah most difficult if not impossible except along the ridge. These canyons also make it very difficult to ascend into the hill country from the coastal plain to the W, thereby providing some measure of protection for the people in the hill country as well as causing a degree of isolation in certain periods of history. To the W at ca. 1050 feet a relatively thin layer of soft Senonian chalk is exposed, having been weathered into a narrow "chalk moat" lying virtually N-S and providing a natural line of communication as well as separating the hill country of Judah from the Shephelah or foot hills to the W. The Shephelah provided a natural buffer between the wide-open coastal plain and the hill country of Judah. To the E lies the Wilderness of Judah.

PAUL WAYNE FERRIS JR.

JUDAH, WILDERNESS OF (PLACE) [Heb *midbar yĕhûdâ*]. The Wilderness of Judah is an area roughly 10 miles (16 km) wide by 30 miles (50 km) long located E of a line rising out of the Jordan valley from the Wâdī Auja, ca. 4.5 miles (7km) N of Jericho, passing within a half mile to the E of Jerusalem and Bethlehem. The specific name Wilderness of Judah is used only twice in biblical narrative (Judg 1:16; Matt 3:1) and once in the title of a psalm (Ps 63). Most commonly it is simply referred to as "the wilderness." The Wilderness of Judah is bounded on the E by the Dead Sea and the sheer cliffs jutting up to 1300 feet (400 m), delimiting the Rift valley; on the N by the hill country of Ephraim; on the S by the Negeb; and on the W by the rather visible demarcation between the hard Cenomanian limestone of the hill country of Judah and the softer Senonian chalk of the Wilderness of Judah.

The Wilderness of Judah makes up the E slope of the Judean arch. Its soft Senonian chalky limestone and clay weathers into a light brown, less fertile rendzina soil, which will support grasses and grains when there is sufficient moisture. Situated on the lee side of the central hill country, the Wilderness of Judah receives only 4″–12″ (100 mm–300 mm) annual rainfall, far less than locations only a few thousand yards to the W.

Although the soft chalky limestone erodes into more rolling terrain, and because it erodes more easily, the wadis cut through into the underlying hard Cenomanian limestone and form deep E-W canyons as they cut their way E to the Rift valley below. This makes N-S travel in the Wilderness of Judah as impossible as it is on the W of the Judean arch.

Because it is on the edge of the arable land, this is the "pasture" land where shepherds graze their flocks and herds. The scarcity of water, the meager fertility, and the difficulty of travel combine to make the Wilderness of Judah a place of severity and testing and a place of refuge (e.g., 1 Sam 22:4; 23:29; 24:1, 22; cf. Psalm 57; 2 Samuel 15–16; Psalm 63; Jeremiah 9; Matthew 3–4; *JW* 6.326, 351, 366). It also figures significantly in prophetic imagery (e.g., Isa 32:15–16; 35; 40). It was to the Wilderness of Judah that John the Baptist had withdrawn, preaching the gospel of the kingdom (Matthew 3), when he introduced Jesus' public ministry. It was in the Wilderness of Judah that Jesus faced his threefold temptation (Matthew 4). It was to the Wilderness of Judah that many of the early Church retired to a hermitic or monastic pursuit of holiness.

PAUL WAYNE FERRIS JR.

JUDAISM. This entry consists of 7 articles surveying Judaism from the time of the Babylonian exile (586 B.C.E.) to the Mishnaic period and beyond (ca. 3d century C.E.). The 1st article provides a broad survey of the diversity of Judaism*s* that flourished in the Greco-Roman period, both in Palestine and throughout the larger Mediterranean world. The 2d article focuses particularly on diverse forms of Judaism within Palestine. The 3d and 4th articles respectively survey Judaism in Egypt and North Africa, while the 5th examines Judaism in the ancient city of Rome. The 6th article covers Judaism in Babylonia, while the 7th surveys Judaism in the Mishnaic period.

JUDAISM IN THE GRECO-ROMAN PERIOD

The purpose of this article is to provide an overview of Judaism in the period between 63 B.C.E. and 200 C.E.

A. Introduction
B. The Temple
  1. The Temple in Palestinian Judaisms Before 70 C.E.
  2. The Temple in Diaspora Judaisms
  3. The Temple After 70 C.E.
C. The Pharisees
D. The Sadducees
E. The Essenes
F. Josephus
G. The "Fourth Philosophy" and Other Popular Movements
H. Jesus-Centered Judaism
I. The Samaritans
J. Early Rabbinic Judaism
K. Judaism and the Attraction of Judaism in the Diaspora
L. Philo
M. The Bible Rewritten
N. Testaments and Apocalypses
O. The LXX and the Role of Scripture

A. Introduction

During the decade of the 1980s the study of early Judaism reached a watershed. The longstanding assumption that Jewish religious belief and practice were largely uniform and consistent throughout the ancient Mediterranean was abandoned. The evidence of archaeology, particularly synagogue art, made untenable George Foot Moore's notion of rabbinic Judaism as "normative Judaism"—the dominant and legitimate form of Jewish religion—against which variants could be judged inauthentic or heretical. When studied critically and inductively, the major written sources—Ben Sira, the Apocrypha and Pseudepigrapha, the works of Josephus and of Philo, the Dead Sea Scrolls, and the Mishna—appeared to reinforce one another only very generally and sometimes very little. It became clear that no single set of data, either from literature or archaeology, could characterize the varied expressions of Jewish religious life and belief in the ancient world. The consensus that Jewish religion from ca. 330 B.C.E. to 200 C.E. exhibited an "almost unlimited diversity and variety" (Kraft and Nickelsburg 1986: 2) found full expression in the model of multiple Judaisms, each representing a discrete system and program. The aim of this entry is to describe important aspects of this diversity.

The model of multiple Judaisms depicts them as distinct but not disparate. It suggests that they are too divergent to be seen as simply variations of a single pattern. Rather, like offspring from the same parents, the different Judaisms possess aspects of a common legacy, but not necessarily the same aspects, or in the same way, or in the same proportion. For example, Jewish writings from both Palestine and the diaspora exhibit diverse understandings of common religious rituals and concepts. Even so basic a rite as circumcision is used and interpreted differently in the Hebrew Bible, Paul, 1 Maccabees, Josephus, and Philo (Smith 1982). Likewise, the concept of the messiah, long thought essential to all forms of Jewish religion, is in fact employed only in some texts of this period and then inconsistently (Neusner, et al. 1987). These examples illustrate the complexity of the data and justify the model of multiple Judaisms.

Because it attempts to preserve diversity and avoid harmonization, the model of multiple Judaisms raises anew the problems of definition and classification. The model requires a theoretical framework that justifies classifying the varied Judaisms together, that explains their commonalities. But that framework cannot suppress the differences between and among the Judaisms, and it must supply the means to separate one Judaism from another. The framework for multiple Judaisms must simultaneously distinguish Judaism from not-Judaism and avoid collapsing the diverse Judaisms to a single Judaism.

For these purposes, two standard ways of defining early Judaism will not serve. The conventional theological definition, which presents Judaism as essentially a religion of covenant-maintenance with Yahweh, who is understood to be the one real god, is too monolithic to capture adequately the diversity the model proposes. The standard ethnic definition—which presents Judaism as the religious behavior of all groups identified, by themselves or by others, as Jews—fails to supply any larger category at all.

Constructing an appropriate framework within which to situate the diverse Judaisms is complicated by the character of the data. A proper definition of any Judaism should describe "a worldview and a way of life that together come to expression in the social world of a group of Jews" (Neusner et al. 1987: ix). Despite recent archaeological discoveries, particularly in the state of Israel, most of the evidence for ancient Jewish religious life is literary. Although most Jewish documents illustrate a worldview and recommend at least aspects of a way of life, the relationships of the texts to concrete social groups is neither clear nor certain. For example, the collective character of the Mishna suggests that a specific community stands behind it and was shaped by it. But the same cannot be said for all the Jewish writings of the Greco-Roman period. For instance, the mere presence of a document at Qumran does not tell how it was regarded by the Dead Sea community. The problem is even more acute with anonymous or pseudepigraphic works and those authored by individuals. It often is impossible to show that the worldview and way of life promulgated by an important Jewish text ever affected a group of Jews. Thus, description of the varied Judaisms of the ancient Mediterranean is necessarily partial, and much of it is limited to worldview.

Moreover, the conventional challenges of literary evidence to any historical research apply fully to the study of early Judaism. No author is disinterested, and separating a text's biases and interests from the historical information it supplies is never simple. Flavius Josephus has reasons for presenting Jewish religion as he does, and in some instances scholarship is unable to penetrate beneath them. Likewise, on the basis of its redaction, the Mishna can only be supposed to supply a highly particular 3d century perspective on 1st century Palestinian Jewish religion.

Although the multiplicity of Judaisms emerges clearly in the Hellenistic period and obviously was accelerated by the impact of Hellenistic culture, the ingredients of these divisions are already evident in the Persian period. The transformation of Israelite religion caused by the destruction of Jerusalem in 587 B.C., the cessation of the sacrificial cult, and the Babylonian Exile supplies the contours of the larger Judaic framework within which the various Judaisms developed.

That framework consists of 4 components: (1) the Temple, (2) Israelite scripture, (3) nonscriptural or extrascriptural tradition, and (4) apocalypticism. These components are all, to some degree, scholarly constructions, but each, except apocalypticism, corresponds to a category or term in the written sources themselves. All the Judaisms of the Greco-Roman period drew on a transformed Israelite legacy comprised of these 4 components. But they did not draw on it in the same way nor from each of the 4 in equal measure, nor in most cases even from all of them. Each Judaism can be analytically described and distinguished from others in terms of these components.

In reality, of course, none of these components existed in isolation. Indeed, all, in different ways, are implicated in one another. Moreover, each of them, if taken as the final locus of authority of a Judaism, has the capacity to absorb or even nullify the other 3 components. For instance, an apocalyptic Judaism could, and did, negate the importance of the Temple and levitical conduct; and a Judaism based on a levitical tradition, as was early rabbinism, could surpass the meaning of scripture's words and suppress the supernaturalism and eschatology of apocalyptic speculation.

It also is important to note that the components *temple, scripture,* and *tradition* are empty categories that were filled in differently by different Judaisms. In some Judaisms the temple was a concrete reality; for others it was a metaphor or an idealization. Likewise scripture. It is not only that different Judaisms focused on different parts of scripture or interpreted the same parts in conflicting ways. Rather, there was no single scripture that all Judaisms employed. Greek-speaking Jews, primarily but not exclusively in the diaspora, rarely resorted to a Hebrew text but instead used the Septuagint (LXX). Although the LXX was known to be a translation, the Judaisms that used it accorded it the de facto status of an original; as in the case of Paul and Philo, they used its language, syntax, etc. as the basis of interpretation. The *Letter of Aristeas* legitimated the status of the LXX with the suggestion that it was divinely inspired. By contrast, in Rabbinic Judaism the Targums—translations of the Hebrew Bible into Aramaic (usually dated after 200)—were always treated as interpretations, never as scripture. Hence, different Judaisms not only read scripture differently; textually and linguistically, they read different scriptures.

The component of nonscriptural or extrascriptural tradition also varied from Judaism to Judaism. Some Judaisms appear to have been heirs to distinctive levitical traditions that supplemented and complemented, but sometimes contradicted, scripture. Others drew on nonscriptural versions of scriptural materials, which made minor biblical figures and themes objects of great interest.

This article examines the nature of the diverse early Judaisms in three ways. First it examines one major component of the larger framework, the Temple, to illustrate the varied ways it was understood and appropriated in different Judaisms of the period (see B. below). Next it reviews the data about the major Judaisms of this period both within Israel and in the diaspora, with a brief excursus on Josephus, a key source for many of them (see C.-L. below). In the last 3 sections (M.-O.) it briefly considers some of the varieties of the treatment of scripture and scriptural traditions.

B. The Temple

The Temple in Jerusalem was a central feature for a number of Judaisms in the Greco-Roman period. Following the return to Jerusalem from exile in Babylon (ca. 535 B.C.E.), the Temple was rebuilt under Zerubbabel. Cyrus, the king of Persia, had both encouraged the rebuilding of the Temple and provided funds for the construction (Josephus, *Ant* 11.1–3). The Temple was rebuilt once again and expanded under King Herod toward the end of the 1st century B.C.E. The importance of the Temple for the Jewish people and for certain Judaisms can be seen not only in this persistence in maintaining and rebuilding the Temple, but also in the prominent place the Temple holds in the Jewish literature of the Greco-Roman period.

The Temple was the symbolic center for a number of Judaisms until after its destruction by the Romans in 70 C.E. Even in the Mishna, the first collection of writings produced by rabbinic Judaism (edited ca. 200 C.E.), the Temple, though destroyed, continued as an essential, symbolic institution and structure for that Judaism. The desecrations of the Temple under Antiochus Epiphanes (165 B.C.E.) and under Pompey (65 B.C.E.) are recorded respectively, in the book of Daniel and the *Psalms of Solomon.* Offenses against the Temple contributed to Jewish revolts against foreign domination in the case of the Maccabean revolt (165 B.C.E.), the first revolt against Rome in 66 C.E., and the Bar Kokhba rebellion of 133 C.E.

1. The Temple in Palestinian Judaisms Before 70 C.E. The Temple in Jerusalem was the most prominent institution in Judea. As the center of the cult of Yahweh and the seat of native Jewish, as opposed to Roman, rule, it represented both the forgiveness of sins and the hope for national sovereignty. Its grandeur and massive size suggest that considerable resources were required for its maintenance, which evidently was a national priority (Strange, *ANRW* 2/19/1: 655). Despite the Temple's imposing physical presence and undeniable cultural centrality, most of the surviving written evidence reflects the views of its critics rather than of the Judaism represented by its personnel and administration.

Differences of opinion about how the Temple should be run and who should perform the cultic rites are important factors in distinguishing the various Palestinian Judaisms from one another. For example, the Temple was an essential feature of the religion of the Qumran community. The rank or order (Heb *serek*) of the community members was organized according to levels of purity or holiness which approximated those of the Temple in Jerusalem. In its organization and self-understanding, Qumran replicated the Temple (Schiffman 1975: 60ff.).

The Damascus Document (CD) from Qumran is explicit about the priests who profane the Temple and fail to observe the distinction between clean and unclean (CD 5.2ff.). These so-called false priests "teach lies," "prophesy falsely," and lead the people to exchange the "law engraved on their hearts for the *smooth things* they speak" (1QH 4). The War Scroll, which describes the final battle between the sons of light and the sons of darkness, reveals the community's belief that after this holy war they would reconstitute the Temple in its pure and true form (Vermes 1980: 122–23). The extreme concern with purity and matters of inclusion and exclusion from the community at Qumran are derived primarily from the levitical codes in Leviticus 13 and 21, which deal with the disqualification of priests from Temple service (Schiffman 1989: 69). In the Dead Sea Scrolls these levitical regulations, which originally pertained only to the priests and their service in the Temple, are applied to the entire Qumran community. Qumran idealized the Temple in its community structure. The community understood itself as the *true* Temple, and ordered its life to accord with its tradition of how the Temple in Jerusalem should be run. In the view of the Qumran community, false priests now control the Temple; but soon God would intervene and restore the true priests, and "true People of God" (cf. War Scroll 3)—the Qumran community itself—to the Temple in Jerusalem.

Fragments of *Jubilees,* a book that records the things revealed to Moses during his 40 days spent on Mt. Sinai, were found at Qumran (see CD 16.2–4). *Jubilees* is concerned with ritual purity, Sabbath laws, tithes, circumcision, incest, calendrical issues, and sacrifice. Obedience to these laws is its central message. The book, which dates from between 161–140 B.C.E., is "a primitive history rewritten from the standpoint of ritual law" (Charlesworth, *OTP* 2: 35–46). The author appears to be from priestly circles. Unlike other texts at Qumran, *Jubilees* lacks evidence of a break or hostility toward the Temple in Jerusalem. While the Temple is central in both *Jubilees* and the Dead Sea Scrolls, *Jubilees* appears to represent a period prior to the decisive break between the Qumran sectarians and the priests and Temple in Jerusalem.

The attack almost certainly on the leadership in the Jerusalem Temple is particularly strident in the mid-1st century B.C.E. *Psalms of Solomon.* The "sinners" are repeatedly described as *anomia,* or lawless (*Pss. Sol.* 1:8; 2:3, 12; 4:1, 8, 12). They are profaners who live in hypocrisy and strive to impress others (chap. 4). They have stolen from the Temple's sanctuary, and have no regard for the distinction between pure and impure (2:3–13; 8:11ff.). Similarly, two documents from the so-called Pseudepigrapha, the *Testament of Levi* and *The Lives of the Prophets,* say that the priests of the Temple have profaned the priesthood, defiled the altar of the sanctuary, and behaved shamefully behind the veil (Heb *dabir*) of the Temple (*T. Levi* 16:2–4; 14:4–6; *Liv. Pro.* 3:15ff.). The *dabir* of the Temple is torn in *T. Levi* 10:3 to expose the deeds of the priests on the other side.

It appears that the 1st century C.E. Jewish popular movement centered on Jesus of Nazareth was also at points hostile toward the Temple. In Mark, the earliest Gospel, Jesus responds negatively to a disciple's comment about the beauty of the Temple: "Do you see these great buildings? Not one stone will be left upon another which will not be torn down" (Mark 13:2). In Mark 14:58 and 15:29 it is charged that Jesus meant (in 13:2) he would tear the Temple down, though in 14:56 the narrator claims this is not what Jesus said. Also, the Synoptics report that when Jesus died the veil of the Temple was torn in two. While the precise meaning of this symbolic act is debated, some have understood this as a devaluation of the Temple.

The Samaritans constituted an important pre-70 Palestinian Jewish group which was essentially Temple-based. The Samaritans were in competition and conflict with the Temple in Jerusalem and claimed that the true center of Yahweh's cult was ancient Shechem and Mt. Gerizim, not Zion. This naturally met with opposition from the Jerusalem priests. However the Temple looms large also in the life of the Samaritans and the history of the Samaritan schism and debate. They too made Temple and Temple traditions central to their religious life and behavior.

The symbol and the system of the Temple informed the debates among the Judaisms of pre-70 Palestine (Blenkinsopp 1981). Those debates were not only theoretical; they convey the sense of a real place that varied groups sought to control and, in some cases, perhaps to supplant.

2. The Temple in Diaspora Judaisms. Even outside the land of Israel, where travel to Jerusalem was difficult and rare, differences among Judaisms can be understood in terms of the Temple. For example, the evidence of the Jews in Egypt presents three distinct perspectives on the Temple.

Despite Deuteronomy's stricture that Yahweh has only one valid sanctuary—"the place God will choose as a dwelling for God's name," widely assumed to be Jerusalem—Jewish sacrificial worship administered by priests and levites was carried out in Egypt. A temple was built at Leontopolis, by the priest Onias (either III or IV), sometime in the 2d century B.C.E. and was closed by the Romans in 74 C.E. (Hayward 1982). Josephus (*JW* 7.436) claims that it functioned for 343 years. It may have influenced the author of the Third Sibyl (Collins 1983: 63, 71, 95). The 1st century B.C.E. work known as *3 Maccabees* offers a different view; it reveres the Jerusalem Temple (Anderson, *OTP* 2: 509–64). A third perspective on the Temple, one typical of diaspora Jews shaped by Hellenistic philosophy, appears in the works of Philo of Alexandria. Philo devotes a large portion of *Special Laws* I to a discussion and description of the Temple, the priests in the Temple, their vestments, the qualifications for the priests and high priest, the animals used for sacrifice, and the requirements of the worshipper in the Temple.

For an audience that clearly knows little about Temple worship and sacrifice, Philo explains that among the 12 tribes of Israel one was selected, on its special merit, for the priestly office. There are tithes and revenues collected for the Temple, which are to continue eternally. The priests must have no deformity, bodily imperfection, or skin disorder. They are to symbolize perfection of the soul (*Spec Leg* I.80). In *Spec Leg* I. 83ff. Philo describes the vestments of the priests in great detail. These vestments symbolize the cosmos (the heavens, stars, and "sublunar" regions). As he does to the levitical rules and the Decalogue throughout *Special Laws*, Philo allegorizes the Temple, the priests, and the legislation associated with the cult to represent platonic types imbedded in the very structure of the cosmos. The Temple in Jerusalem, for Philo's audience, is treated as a "cosmic mystery" (Goodenough 1940: 208), and described as a representation of the eternal virtues and *logos* of the cosmos.

A similar transformation takes place in the NT epistle to the Hebrews, which speaks symbolically, or typologically about the Temple. There Jesus is spoken of both as the *perfect* high priest and *perfect* sacrifice. In heaven is the "true tabernacle which the Lord has pitched" (Heb 8:2). Those who are priests on earth "serve a copy, a mere shadow of the heavenly" (8:5). As with Philo, the images and symbols of the Temple remain central for the author of Hebrews. However, the meaning of these symbols, and of the Temple itself has been transformed. The Temple, its priests, laws, and sacrifices, are earthly, imperfect types for perfect and abiding cosmic mysteries and truths.

Another figure associated with the Jewish diaspora is Paul of Tarsus. The Temple was important to Paul, but only as an image and only when understood to represent the community. "Do you not know you are the Temple of God? If any man destroys the Temple of God, God will destroy him, for the Temple of God is holy, and that is what you are" (1 Cor 3:16). For Paul the community becomes the locus of holiness and sanctity. In this vein, though in a somewhat allegorical manner, he applies levitical legislation and the notion of sacrifice to a man corrupting the community with impure behavior (Gk *porneia*; 1 Corinthians 5).

Though often transformed and reappropriated, the

structure, function, and legal framework of the Temple supplied the fundamental model for religious activity and self-understanding for varied diaspora Judaisms. Despite the divergent understandings of the Temple and its meanings—understandings that range from the strongly literal to the extremely figurative—few Jewish groups before 70 appear to have anticipated having a religion with no Temple at all. The intense disagreement about the operation and significance of the institution attests to its widespread importance.

3. The Temple After 70 C.E. The Temple's destruction necessitated the development of strategies of reinterpretation, even for those pre-70 Judaisms that in effect had bypassed the Temple in their religious practice. Even Pharisees and those who came to be called Christians, who fared well in the post-70 period and whose systems did not require a literal Temple, still laid claim to traditions that produced the Temple, and each had to account for its significance.

Following the destruction of the Temple, various Judaisms turned to other aspects of their heritages to adapt to the changed reality in the post-70 period. All of them, to be sure, turned to scripture, which had been a basic component of the Jewish cultural framework since the Persian period. In addition, texts such as *2 Baruch, 4 Baruch,* and *4 Ezra* reflect the increasing emergence of what they call "the law" as a response to the Temple's loss.

The Temple's destruction appears to have created a religious and cultural upheaval. Several documents from the post-70 period, assigned to the Pseudepigrapha, explicitly reflect on the destruction of the Temple and its meaning. Many attempt to trace this event to some injustice or "faithlessness." The *Apocalypse of Abraham* 27 describes the destruction of the Temple, which it claims is a result of "evil works" (*OTP* 1: 702).

The 587 B.C.E. destruction of the Temple is depicted allegorically in *2 Baruch* in order to address the destruction of the Temple in the time of the author. In *2 Baruch* 6 the Temple is destroyed and the veil, the mercy seat, the tables, the vestments, and the vessels are all taken away. These items are stored in the earth, "until the last times," "until the moment that it will be said that it will be restored forever." In *2 Bar.* 10:18 the priests of the Temple take the keys to the sanctuary and cast them into heaven saying, "take these keys, guard your house yourself, for we have been found false stewards." Essentially the same passage is contained in *4 Bar.* 4:4, and a similar passage can be found in *ʾAbot R. Nat.* 4 (Goldin 1955: 37).

After the destruction, all that Israel has left is God and God's "law" which will last forever (*2 Bar.* 77:5; 85:3). The righteous are those who keep "the law." "The law" is God's gift to Israel (*4 Ezra* 3:19; 7:22ff.; 8:28). The importance of the scribe, and the renaissance of figures like Baruch and Ezra, support the role of the law in the post-70 period.

This "law" is thought to derive largely from behavioral regulations that initially supposed and were intended for the Temple system and service. In certain respects, the continuation (and in some cases the intensification) of "legal" issues and concerns in the post-70 period testifies to the importance of the Temple even after its destruction. For a number of groups within Judaism in the post-70 period, the levitical system persisted long after the institution for which it was designed had disappeared. This is dramatically evident in the Mishna, the first collection of the teachings of the rabbis.

Although the Temple had been destroyed for over a century, the Mishna discusses the Temple and Temple issues as if the building were still standing. Over half of the tractates of the Mishna, in fact, pertain to the Temple. Tractate *Qodašim,* for example, contains discussions about issues central to the Temple, such as sacrifices and vows. Although the Mishna's treatment of the Temple may be a utopian fantasy or a hope for the cult's future restoration (Neusner 1989), the document provides a strategy and a means for the adaptation and continuity of the levitical religion the Temple had represented and promulgated.

C. The Pharisees

Of the pre-70 Jewish groups, the Pharisees are perhaps the best known, because of their role as Jesus' principal opponents in some gospel narratives. But Josephus and early rabbinic literature also provide information about them (Neusner 1971). Indeed, Josephus claims to have been a Pharisee (*Life* 9–12), and Paul's enigmatic assertion that he was a Pharisee "as to law" (Phil 3:4–6) is often taken as a claim of membership in the Pharisaic group.

Josephus (*JW* 2.8.2–14; *Ant* 18.1.2–6) lists the Pharisees as one of the three sects or philosophical schools (Gk *hairesis*) among the Jews. The others are the Sadducees and the Essenes. In Josephus, the Pharisees appear primarily as a political interest group. In modern sociological terms, they were from the retainer class (Saldarini 1988). With no political power of their own, the Pharisees depended on good relations with the ruling class to achieve their goals for Jewish society. Josephus reports that the Pharisees gained and then lost the support of John Hyrcanus, who ruled the Hasmonean kingdom from 134–104 B.C.E. (cf. *b. Qid.* 66a).

A similar story (*JW* 1.5.2) describes how the Pharisees gained the favor of Queen Alexandra, widow and successor of Hyrcanus' son, Alexander Janneaus, who had succeeded his father after a futile struggle for power between his brothers Aristobulus and Antigonus. According to Josephus, during Alexandra's rule (76–67 B.C.E.) the Pharisees became the real administrators of the state, with the power "to bind and to loose," and enjoyed royal authority. *Ant* 13.15.5ff. recounts Alexander's deathbed advice to Alexandra to work with the Pharisees to ensure her successful reign. Because the Pharisees are the "most accurate interpreters of the law," they are respected by and popular with the people, who do whatever the Pharisees say. The Gospels' highly stylized conflict stories, which ally the Pharisees with the Herodians against Jesus, suggest continued Pharisaic collaboration with political powers during the reign of Herod (37–4 B.C.E.). These stories depict the Pharisees as a political interest group, but they do not reveal a political program or the focus of the Pharisees' interests.

Josephus' reports about the Pharisees' beliefs address general philosophical matters, not matters of Jewish communal practice. In *Jewish War* (2.8.14) and *Antiquities* (18.1.3–4) he describes the positions of the Pharisees and Sadducees on such issues as fate, free will, the immortality of the soul, and reward and punishment. The Pharisees, he says, believe that the soul is imperishable, and that the souls of the wicked are punished eternally. They believe in fate, free will, and God. They make no concession to luxury, show respect for their elders, and follow the guidance of reason and what is good. Worship is conducted according to their views, which are influential among the people. They cultivate harmonious relationships with one another and with the community. In *Life* he compares the Pharisees to Stoics. Taken together, these statements do not constitute a program for reforming Palestinian Jewish society and do not suggest what might have been at stake in the Pharisees' political activity.

A hint about the Pharisees' goals may appear in Josephus' claim (*Ant* 13.10.6) that the Pharisees observe "traditions of the fathers" not recorded in the law of Moses, traditions the Sadducees reject (Baumgarten 1987). Regrettably, Josephus does not discuss the content of these traditions, which can only be conjectured on the basis of the NT and early rabbinic literature.

The Gospels depict the Pharisees primarily as debate partners for Jesus and report almost nothing of their role in larger Palestinian society. A few positive pictures notwithstanding (John 3; Acts 5), the Gospels usually present the Pharisees negatively, as a religious type antithetical to Jesus and his teaching. The contention between the Pharisees and Jesus tends to be about issues of purity, Sabbath observance, fasting, and tithing. The dispute between Jesus and the Pharisees about eating with unclean hands becomes the occasion to contrast the Pharisees' "traditions of the elders" with the commandments of God (Mark 7:1–23 and Matt 15:1–20). The Gospel stories depict the Pharisees at least as a lay group concerned with applying its own tradition of levitical piety to the context of everyday life and commerce (Neusner 1973).

Although the use of rabbinic materials for the study of the Pharisees is complicated by problems of redaction and dating, it is widely assumed that early rabbinism either derived from or appropriated much of the pre-70 Pharisaic agenda. Seven disputes between Pharisees and Sadducees from the Mishna and Tosefta focus largely on issues of purity. Moreover, if the earliest stratum of the Mishna is assumed to reflect Pharisaic concerns, then there is clear overlap between the rabbinic picture of the Pharisees and that of the Gospels (Neusner 1971).

The character of the sources permits only a schematic picture of the Pharisees; a nuanced description is not possible. On the basis of the way those sources reinforce one another, the Pharisees appear as a lay group that drew on a discrete, nonscriptural tradition of levitical piety and attempted through political means to reform Palestinian Jewish society to conform to that tradition.

D. The Sadducees

Information about the Sadducees is both more sparse and more questionable than what is known of the Pharisees. No Jewish source was composed from the Sadducean point of view: no figure from antiquity identifies as a Sadducee; no Jewish movement or group claims Sadducean descent. In the sources that mention them—Josephus, the Gospels, and rabbinic literature—the Sadducees tend to be coupled with the Pharisees and rarely appear alone. Josephus claims to have been a Pharisee, and the Pharisees may have been gaining power and acceptance in Palestine after the Temple's destruction, when he wrote. Thus, his description of the Sadducees may be biased against them (Cohen 1979). In rabbinic literature, the Sadducees are treated almost as outsiders (Saldarini 1988: 301).

Because they are so often coupled with the Pharisees, in Josephus the Sadducees resemble a political interest group, and in the Gospels they appear as opponents of the Jesus movement. Likewise, in rabbinic literature their disputes with the Pharisees follow the Pharisaic agenda and focus mainly on issues of purity.

Materials in all three sources agree that the Sadducees deny resurrection of the dead (*Ant* 18.1.4; Mark 12:18; *b. Sanh.* 90b, *ʾAbot R. Nat.* A, 5). Josephus adds that they do not believe in fate, accept no observance "apart from the laws" (*Ant* 18.1.4), and reject traditions of the Pharisees (*Ant* 13.10.6). These scant reports cannot justify a judgment that the Saducees were scriptural literalists or had no traditions of their own. Sadducees may have been a part of the ruling elite, but they cannot be identified with it (Saldarini 1988). On the basis of the sources, it is difficult to say much about the kind of Judaism the Sadducees represent.

E. The Essenes

The third of Josephus' three *haireseis* are the Essenes. Philo (ca. 40 C.E.), in *Every Good Man is Free* (12–13; 75–91), and *Hypothetica* 11.1–18 (preserved in Eusebius, *Praeparatio evangelica*), and Pliny the Elder, in *Natural History* 5.15.73, ca. 77 C.E., also mention the Essenes, but their accounts are of slight historical importance (Beall 1988). The contents of the Dead Sea Scrolls (DSS), discovered in caves along wadi Qumran in 1947, and the descriptions of Josephus provide the most information about the Essenes. Although the issue is still debated, the DSS are almost universally regarded as documents from a monastic-like Essene community that lived near the shores of the Dead Sea (Cross 1980). The scrolls cover a period approximately from Hasmonean expansion (ca. 150–120 B.C.E.) to the destruction of the community by the Romans (ca. 70–72 C.E.), and they describe the beliefs, order, construction, theology, and some of the history of the community (Cross 1969; Charlesworth 1979–81). Certain scrolls, as in the case of the Damascus Document, seem to have been written outside of Qumran and may even pre-date the Qumran community. The scrolls are not monolithic. They were written over a substantial period of time, and their views on issues of the Temple, law, the Romans, and communal order suggest some variety even within the broad rubric of Essene Judaism (Davies 1982; Murphy-O'Connor 1974).

The most widely accepted theory of the origins of the Qumran community assumes that these Essenes withdrew to the desert to protest what they regarded as the illegitimate Hasmonean claim to the high priesthood. The Essenes' hostility to the Temple's leadership surfaces in several sources, including Josephus. The literature of Qumran denounces the priesthood in Jerusalem as false and profaners (cf. CD 1; 1 QS 7,11). The centerpiece of Qumran ideology is the expectation that God will soon act, judge, and condemn these false leaders and priests, and will restore the Qumran community to the Temple in

Jerusalem and the high priesthood. The so-called Teacher of Righteousness, whom the scrolls depict as the founder of the community, may have been deposed as high priest and exiled when the Hasmoneans assumed control of the Temple.

According to Josephus, the Essenes are Jews by birth and have more "mutual affection" than other groups (*JW* 2.8.2–13). They turn aside from pleasures as evil and regard as a virtue self-control and not succumbing to passions. They "despise riches," transfer their property to the sect upon joining, and hold all things in common. Josephus says the Essenes regard marriage with contempt and will adopt other people's children as if they were their own. They dress simply, avoid all kinds of "defilements," and have no city of their own.

The Essenes apparently had pockets in many cities, and offered hospitality and support to other members who were passing through. They rigorously avoided contact with outsiders and were strictly warned about speaking ill of the group. The community had a series of strict punishments for violations of purity regulations, for failure to abide the rules of the community, or for denegrating the community in either language or action (Forkman 1972). The community ordered itself along the lines of the Temple in Jerusalem. The various members and initiates were organized in order of their standing in the community, the number of years they had been members, and the degree of purity they had achieved (Schiffman 1975). In their life, actions, and self-understanding the Essenes sought to replicate the Temple.

The Qumran community also valued the role and authority of scripture. The DSS evidence a distinctive type of exegesis referred to as *pesher.* The stories and passages from scripture were understood strictly in terms of the history and destiny of the community (Fitzmyer 1974). Some of the prophetic literature, especially Habakkuk and the Psalms, figure prominently in Qumran's distinctive scriptural interpretation. The recently published Temple Scroll details the community's eschatological hopes about the Temple in Jerusalem, and the War Scroll depicts the holy war waged by God on behalf of the community against the wicked priests and the *kittim,* the term the community seems to have applied to the Romans (Vermes 1980).

The doctrine of the Essenes, Josephus writes in *Ant* 18.1.2, 5 (11, 18–22), is to leave all things to God. They regard souls as immortal and strive to fulfill paths of righteousness. He claims the Essenes are more virtuous than either Greeks or barbarians. Their wisdom is, to those who have experienced it, "inescapable bait." This description—typical of Jewish apologetic literature of this period—is designed to appeal to non-Jewish, Greco-Roman readers. By emphasizing the Essenes' asceticism, the wisdom of their teaching, and their dedication to their beliefs and lifestyle, Josephus aims to make their religious practices appear admirable, virtuous, and worthy of emulation.

The Judaism of the Essenes, as represented in the DSS, exhibits the components of the Judaic framework that emerged during the Persian period. Though withdrawn from the Temple and disapproving of its current leadership, the Qumran community clearly expected to gain control of the institution and the administration of its rites. Qumran Judaism, therefore, was Temple-centered in a concrete, this-worldly sense. The community expected to achieve victory as the result of an eschatological war, which among other things would bring a definitive end to the present political order. Thus, the Qumran worldview had a pronounced apocalyptic element.

As a virtual community in exile, Qumran had to devise rules for behavior both to maintain the community's distinctive life in the present and to prepare for the new order of the future. In so doing, it devised a "unique system of Jewish law," some of which was based on biblical exegesis and some not (Schiffman 1983: xi). Although the DSS do not claim the community's practice as inherited tradition, the duration of the community and its likely origin as the result of intra-priestly conflict suggest that it may have followed nonscriptural levitical traditions different from those applied by the Jerusalem priesthood.

Finally, the Qumran community justified its apocalyptic vision and its distinctive levitical practices with interpretation of scripture, and it is obvious that scripture was an important source of religious authority and legitimation. In contrast to other Judaisms, the evidence for the Essene Judaism of Qumran displays the components of Temple, tradition, scripture, and apocalyptic with unusual definition and balance.

The Essenes are not mentioned in the NT or rabbinic literature, and there is no trace of their Judaism after 70 C.E. Because of the discovery of the Dead Sea Scrolls, we know more about the Essenes than the other *haireseis* Josephus mentions. But there is little evidence that their Judaism had a significant impact on ancient Palestinian Jewish society.

F. Josephus

Because so much information about the Judaisms in the Greco-Roman period comes from Josephus, he deserves brief consideration on his own. The sheer amount of his writing and its impact on the history of Judaism sets Josephus apart from other writers of this period.

Josephus was born ca. 37 C.E. into a priestly family. Though he claims to have chosen the way of the Pharisees after studying several Jewish philosophies, no clear Pharisaic tendency is evident in his interpretation of Judaism. However, his writing does exhibit sympathy toward the Judean ruling classes and their attempts to retain control of Jewish society and suppress the popular movements that challenged Roman rule (Saldarini 1988: 81; Rajak 1984). Whether or not this thoroughgoing prejudice renders his history too biased to be useful continues to be discussed (Cohen 1979; compare Moehring, *ANRW* 2/21/2: 864–944 and Saldarini).

Josephus commanded rebel troops in Galilee during the first revolt against Rome, perhaps because he, like others of the Judean ruling class, anticipated the loss of Roman support and opted for popularity with the Jewish masses (Goodman 1987). Sensing defeat, Josephus surrendered to Rome and sided with Vespasian and his son Titus. Josephus' prediction that Vespasian would become Emperor (*JW* 3.3.9) helped endear him to the *Caesarea familia.* Josephus went to Rome as a client of the Flavians and wrote *The Jewish War.* Sponsored by others he wrote *Antiquities of the Jews* which included, as an appendix, his *Life.*

Josephus wrote *Jewish War* sometime during the reign of Titus (ca. 80), and *Antiquities* later (ca. 94). Later still he produced a short apologetic work, entitled *Contra Apion,* defending Judaism against a variety of charges. Josephus used several sources for his history, including Nicolaus of Damascus, other popular traditions, and the Bible (Schwartz 1983; Attridge 1986). His narrative of the politics and struggle for power in Roman Palestine exhibits a primary interest in the relation of the Jewish state and religion, and the Jewish ruling class, to the empires and powers that surround it. Josephus writes from the perspective of the upper class and balances a loyalty (perhaps resigned) to Rome with a dedication and loyalty to the Jewish people and religion. He speaks positively of rulers and groups who bring order and criticizes those who are destabilizing.

Throughout this political history the reader is given substantial information about the religious practices and convictions of the Jewish people. Loyalty to Torah, to the Temple, to the learned and disciplined nature of many Jewish groups are all features regularly encountered in Josephus' descriptions of Judaism(s). Josephus is an apologist for Jewish religion in the Roman world, and he addressed a largely Roman audience. He describes the history and beliefs of the Jewish people in a manner both understandable and appealing to his audience. Josephus is an invaluable source for the history of the Judaisms of Palestine, and his writings constitute a significant chapter in the embrace of and interest in Judaism by the wider Greco-Roman world.

G. The "Fourth Philosophy" and Other Popular Movements

In addition to the three *haireseis,* Josephus also refers to a variety of other 1st century Palestinian Jewish groups that scholarship now classifies as popular movements. The best known of these is the "Fourth Philosophy," but the list also includes the Zealots, the *Sicarii,* various prophetic, messianic, or royal groups, and even social bandits. All of these played a role in the rebellion against Rome, which is their common trait in Josephus' account of them.

Josephus' hostility to such rebel groups is well known, and not surprisingly his descriptions of them are truncated and focus almost exclusively on political or military matters. But many of these movements, according to Josephus, justified their action in religious terms, as expressions of loyalty or obedience to Israel's God. Thus, there may have been Palestinian Judaisms in which piety could lead to revolution. On the basis of what is known of the Bar Kokhba rebellion (132–35 C.E.), this option retained considerable appeal and resilience through the reigns of both Trajan and Hadrian (*m. Sota* 9.14). However, for various political purposes, the preserved literary sources—from Ben Sira to the Mishna—discourage revolution as a legitimate expression of devotion to the God of Israel. Thus, although the popular movements merit treatment in this overview, a secure interpretation of any of them as a Judaism is impossible to attain.

In Josephus' account, the Fourth Philosophy appears primarily as a tax-resistance movement. The Romans had deposed Herod's son Archelaus, imposed their own direct rule in Judea, and charged Quirinius, a Syrian legate, to conduct an assessment of how much tax could be extracted from the territories (Horsley and Hanson 1985: 190ff.). Josephus writes that "a Galilean named Judas was urging his countrymen to resist (the assessment), reproaching them should they submit to paying taxes to the Romans and tolerate human masters after serving God alone. Judas was a teacher [Gk *sophistes*], with his own party, in no way similar to others" (*JW* 2.118).

In *Antiquities* 18 Josephus writes that Judas was from Gamala, in Gaulanitis (actually not Galilee), and that he was "in league" with Zaddok the Pharisee and had pressed hard for the resistance to the assessment. Judas claimed these taxes were nothing short of slavery and urged the nation to "claim its freedom." If they would succeed in their resistance, said Judas, "the Jews would pave the way for good fortune; if they fail, they would at least obtain glory and honor for their high ideals." Of course, they could be confident that God would join them in their fight. Josephus writes that the people listened to this "with relish," and that Judas and Zaddok succeeded in establishing "an alien fourth philosophy" among the Jews. "When their numbers grew they filled the nation with unrest, and were at the root of the afflictions which ultimately enveloped it."

Josephus stresses that the Fourth Philosophy was formed in response to unjust rules and inept local Roman governors and legates. But in his account, the burden of new taxes and fidelity to the traditions and laws of the Jews provoked the formation of this revolutionary movement and drove it to rebellion. He says (*Antiquities* 18) that the beliefs and behavior of the Fourth Philosophy closely resembled those of the Pharisees, except for their unusual commitment to freedom.

The tensions related to the formation and rise of the Fourth Philosophy are responsible for a variety of anti-Roman movements between the death of Herod the Great and the Bar-Kokhba revolt in 133 C.E. Syrian domination, which lead to the Maccabean revolt, and subsequent Roman domination from 66 B.C.E. on, frequently resulted in irreconcilable choices for Jews between their loyalty to their beliefs and nation and their service to foreign rulers. While there were periods of relative calm and cooperation between Romans and Jews in Palestine, the imposition of taxes, expansive building projects (especially under Herod), conflicting foreign beliefs, and insensitivity to native Jewish religion provoked unrest and resistance.

One example of such social unrest and resistance has recently been referred to as "social banditry" (Horsley and Hanson 1985). The socioeconomic inequities in Palestine under Roman rule resulted in a rather widespread robbing of the rich (or whoever had resources) by the peasantry of Palestine. Both in *Life* 77 and *JW* 4.84 Josephus describes groups of brigands (Gk *lestai*), and he mentions in particular that Gischala (in upper Galilee) had been "infiltrated by a sizable gang of brigands." Other incidents involving brigands are found in *JW* 3.434; 2.541ff., and elsewhere. The reality of brigandry points to the breakdown of Palestinian society and widespread dissatisfaction with Roman rule. The brigands represent the beginning of fairly comprehensive resistance to Roman domination in the pre-66 period.

This period of unrest in Palestine also provoked a number of popular or charismatic leaders. Some were referred to as "king," others "prophets," and others "messiah." In the Galilean city of Sepphoris Judas, the son of Ezekias, a well-known brigand chief, led a raid and revolt at the death of Herod ca. 4 B.C.E. (*Ant* 17.271ff.). A servant of King Herod named Simon, "spurred on by chaotic social conditions, dared to don the diadem, and was proclaimed king by some fanatical men, because he thought himself more worthy of this than any other" (*Ant* 17.273). This Simon led a popular revolt, plundering royal palaces throughout the land, until captured and beheaded. In *Antiquities* 17 Josephus also describes Anthronges, a man of renown, who aspired to be king. He and his 4 brothers each had followers, and were not afraid to die. They fought hard against Roman and Herodian troops. "Whenever seditious bands came across someone suitable," writes Josephus, "that person could be set up as king" (*Ant* 17.278–85). Indeed, Judas the Galileans' son, Menachem, was a leader in the first revolt and was hailed in Jerusalem as a king (*JW* 2.433ff.).

Several literate groups employed the term "messiah" for a leader, or expected leader. The mid-1st century B.C.E. *Psalms of Solomon* (17:32), the DSS (Vermes 1980: 118ff.), and some strands of the Jesus tradition within Palestine used this term to describe their leader. When discussing popular movements, however, Josephus assiduously avoids the term "messiah." The emergence of the figure Menachem in 66 C.E. among the popular resistance group the Sicarii—the "dagger men"—has been viewed by some as a brief episode of messianism among this group, and the Bar Kokhba revolt of 133 is treated in later rabbinic tradition as a "Messianic movement" (Horsley and Hanson 1985: 118; 127ff.).

There were also several "prophetic movements" in the 1st century. These leaders attempted to identify with the Israelite prophets of old and reiterated their message of a nation that had strayed from the commands of God, impending judgment, and the hope of vindication and restoration. Josephus describes in some detail one Theudas who persuaded most of the "common people" to take their possessions and follow him to the river Jordan. He said he was a prophet, and that at his command he could divide the river (*Ant* 20.97–98). Fadus, the governor of Judea, had Theudas captured and beheaded. Josephus also describes an Egyptian Jewish prophet who, though a charlatan, was credible enough to rally about 30,000 "dupes," and to incite them to try to storm Jerusalem. Many were killed or captured, but the Egyptian escaped (*JW* 2.261ff.). John the Baptist, mentioned in the Gospels as related ideologically, if not by kinship, to Jesus of Nazareth, is depicted as a prophetic leader in the tradition of Isaiah or Elijah. There were others, including the Zealots and various resistance groups which coalesced after the start of the 66 revolt to fight against Rome.

"Charismatic Judaism" is a modern scholarly term that identifies a supposed popular form of piety, primarily centered in Galilee. This scholarly construction would also qualify as a "popular movement." The figures usually associated with this putative Judaism are Honi the Circlemaker (*m. Taᶜan.* 3.8; *b. Taᶜan.* 23a; *j. Taᶜan.* 81d), Haninah ben Dosa (*m. Ber.* 5.5; *t. Ber.* 3.20; *m. Soṭa* 9.15; *ᵓAbot* 9–10), and Jesus of Nazareth.

In the primary passage about Honi, Honi prays unsuccessfully for rain, and then draws a circle, stands inside it, and refuses to move until God makes it rain. His actions appear to be a version of a magical rite. After the rain falls, Simeon b. Shetah rebukes Honi's behavior but declines to excommunicate him. Josephus also refers to a certain Onias who once prayed successfully for rain to end a drought during the time of Hyrcanus II, but was stoned to death for refusing to issue a curse on Hyrcanus' brother and rival Aristobulus II (*Ant* 1.22–25).

The passage about Haninah in *m. Ber.* claims that, when he prayed for the sick, he knew by the fluency of his prayer who would live or die (5.5). Tosefta *Ber.* 3.3 assigns a nearly identical saying to Akiba, so there is no way securely to attribute either saying to Haninah. The Babylonian and Palestinian Talmuds (*Ber.* 34b and 9d respectively), contain stories of Haninah's successful prayer for healing of Rabban Gamaliel's son. Thus, Haninah is celebrated in rabbinic tradition primarily for the efficacy of his prayer, not for a distinctive kind of Judaism.

A fundamental problem with the classification "charismatic Judaism" is that it is based on biographical information about a few figures, mostly from a handful of late rabbinic passages. But rabbinic documents are dominated by consensus, and their sense of the individual—of separate existences—is minimal. The documents do not lend themselves easily to biographical reconstruction (Green 1981: 18–19). The scholarly category of charismatic Judaism also relies on strained analogies with Jesus of Nazareth (Vermes 1983: 42, 49). Rabbinic traditions about such figures do not provide evidence for a distinctive Galilean Judaism.

The many popular movements in this period resulted from social unrest, a failure of the ruling class, and Roman maladministration. The religious aspirations and traditions of Israel supported the hope of freedom from foreign domination and/or the social ills that plagued society. The identification with these religious traditions and hopes were the means by which many popular leaders gathered support and a substantial following.

H. Jesus-Centered Judaism

The beginning and early stages of the Jesus movement are depicted in the four NT Gospels written 40–70 years after Jesus' death in 33 C.E. These Gospels are stylized narratives which purport to tell the story of the life of Jesus, but do so with a focus on the issues confronting the people by or for whom the Gospels were written.

It is anachronistic, though still commonplace, to identify the Jesus movement of 1st century Palestine as "Christianity." In its historical and religious context and in its varied forms, the Jesus movement was a type of *Judaism* and was viewed as such by non-Jews. The classification "Christianity" sets the Jesus movement over against Judaism and also obscures important differences within this Judaism. Jesus-centered Judaism was not monolithic. The internal differences within this Judaism parallel those that distinguished other Judaisms from one another. Some variants of this Judaism stressed scripture, tradition, and aspects of levitical piety, while others were dominated by apocalypticism.

Mark's gospel, for example, is thoroughly apocalyptic in orientation (Mack 1988; Kee 1977). The day of the Son of

Man, the woes and birth pangs which precede the end of the age, the arrival of the kingdom of God, and the struggle with evil powers are central features of Mark. These apocalyptic themes are highlighted in Mark 13, but in fact run throughout the gospel. The apocalyptic nature of Jesus-centered Judaism fits well into the volatile and fragmented milieu of Palestine in the 1st century (Horsley 1987). Matthew, on the other hand, while still maintaining an apocalyptic component, stresses issues of law, tradition, and levitical piety.

Where Mark does not engage issues of Sabbath observance (Mark 2) or food laws (Mark 7), Matthew enters into lengthy debate on the validity of his community's interpretation of these laws (Overman 1990). Both Matthew and Mark develop traditions grounded within Israelite history which are meant to support their respective versions of Jesus-centered Judaism. The popular, traditional figures of Moses, Isaiah, or one of the prophets are used in support of the portrayal of Jesus and the sort of Judaism the writers wished to present. In the so-called Q source common to Matthew and Luke, popular oral sayings about Israelite heroes and traditions combine with an apocalypticism in order to present this particular form of Jesus-centered Judaism (Mack 1988; Kloppenborg 1989).

A central feature of the Gospels is the hostility between Jesus and the Jewish religious authorities. The so-called conflict stories in the Gospels usually concern a dispute over some aspect of Jewish law or tradition (Hultgren 1979). A stock feature of all the gospels is Jesus healing on the Sabbath, or his followers violating purity regulations. These acts lead to an encounter between Jesus and the Jewish authorities who are described somewhat indiscriminately as scribes, Pharisees, chief priests, Sadducees, the elders of the people, or some combination of these groups. By whatever name, these groups are intended to represent the opposition to the Jesus movement in 1st century Palestine.

In the conflict stories Jesus and his followers are accused by the religious authorities of violating the laws and traditions of Israel. This provides an occasion for Jesus to introduce his interpretation of scripture and enter into debate with these authorities over the role and meaning of scripture, tradition, and religious practice. Jesus is frequently portrayed as citing scripture, alluding to a famous Israelite prophet, or telling a story or parable that can be related to Israelite tradition and history.

The relationship between the Jesus movement and the Temple in Jerusalem remains a matter of considerable debate (Sanders 1985). Jesus goes up to the Temple when in Jerusalem, and his act of driving out the money changers is depicted as a defense of the purpose and role of the Temple in Jewish religious life (Mark 11:15–18). However, Jesus' threat against the Temple, saying he would destroy it and build another, emerges clearly in the Gospel trial scenes, and plays a significant role in Jesus' death (Juel 1977). At his death the Temple veil is torn in two. Whether this should be read as a denunciation of the Temple as an institution or just the current Temple personnel (or something else altogether) is a debated question.

There were varieties of Jesus-centered Judaism. What these disparate groups held in common was their allegiance to the person of Jesus, which distinguished them collectively from all other Judaisms. However, each Jesus-centered Jewish community portrayed and described him in its own way. Otherwise, Jesus-centered Judaisms reflected the diversity found among the other Judaisms of this period.

I. The Samaritans

In terms of the larger Judaic framework, Samaritanism (though often called a sect) constituted a Judaism during the Greco-Roman period. The Samaritans claimed Shechem and the adjacent Mt. Gerizim as their historic cultural and religio-cultic center. They claimed to be the descendants of the tribes of Ephraim, Manasseh, and Levi, and to represent faithful, continuous worship of Yahweh from the time of the Israelite conquest of Canaan. What finally separated the Samaritans from the Jews who were loyal to the cult in Judah was the question of which was the true holy place, Jerusalem or Shechem (Purvis, *CHJ* 2: 591–613). Samaritans condemned the leadership in Jerusalem and its Temple cult as an aberration.

Those loyal to the Jerusalem Temple tended to charge that Samaritans were not Jews but syncretistic in life and belief, in some sense half-Yahwistic and half-pagan. This claim goes back to 2 Kings 17, and persisted as late as the writings of Josephus (*Ant* 9.288) and the NT gospels of Matthew, Luke, and John. In Luke and John, Samaritans represent in a novel way the inclusion of the other or outsider into true Israel. These stories in Luke or John, along with Matt 10:5, represent some animosity between Samaritans and the Judaism centered on the Jerusalem cult in the Hellenistic and Roman periods. Originally, worship of the God of Israel took place near Shechem, on Gerizim, long before a cult was established in Jerusalem. For various reasons, as Israelite history progressed Jerusalem became more and more the exclusive sacred center of the Israelites.

Samaritanism represents a clear objection to this development. This tension developed following the return of the exiles from Babylon and is apparent in the postexilic documents of Ezra, Nehemiah, and 1 Esdras. While friction between the two groups is demonstrable during the Persian period, the tension between Samaritan Judaism and Jerusalem-based Judaism was most pronounced in the Hellenistic period. The temple on Mt. Gerizim, according to both literary and archaeological record, was built around the time of Alexander the Great (*Ant* 11.302ff.). The sanctuary on Mt. Gerizim was destroyed by the Hasmonean leader John Hyrcanus ca. 128 B.C.E., and some 20 years later Shechem was razed. Excavations have shown that the Temple was rebuilt during the reign of Hadrian (Purvis 1986: 88).

Samaritan Judaism was clearly Temple oriented and centered. Like other Judaisms, Samaritanism also had a dispersion. There were Samaritan diaspora communities as far away as Rome, Thessalonica, and the island of Delos. Two inscriptions from Delos clarify the importance of the Temple and cultic worship for the Samaritans, even when far removed from Mt. Gerizim (Kraabel 1984).

The second important component of Samaritan Judaism is the Samaritan Pentateuch, written after the destruction of the Temple on Gerizim during the reign of John Hyrcanus. Samaritans responded to this crisis by reaffirming their claim to be the true carriers of faith in Yahweh, and their conviction that Gerizim, though now in ruins, remained the true place for worship of God, and not Jerusalem. The edition of the Pentateuch drafted by the Samaritans promoted this claim. The ideology of the Samaritan Pentateuch is evident in its emphasis on Gerizim and Shechem and its downplaying of Jerusalem and Zion. Certain lengthy interpolations in Deuteronomy and at the end of the 10 commandments in Exodus seek to establish the position that God already established Shechem and Gerizim as the true place of worship and that Jerusalem and its priesthood were the latecomers (Purvis, *CHJ* 2: 612). In the view of the Samaritans, the Jerusalemites were inauthentic. These differences about both Temple and scripture distinguish Samaritan Judaism from other Judaisms.

J. Early Rabbinic Judaism

The principal source of information about early rabbinic Judaism is the Mishna, a philosophical legal treatise written in Hebrew and produced in Palestine about 200 C.E. under the auspices of the Patriarch Judah I, known familiarly as Rabbi. The Mishna is the first collection of the rabbis' own tradition and teaching, primarily on matters of *halakhah* (religious law and practice). Much of the Mishna is anonymous—so that the document often seems to speak for itself. However, it also contains opinions, disputes, and occasionally stories about or in the names of approximately 150 sages, who are dated from the 2d century B.C.E. to the beginning of the 3d century C.E. The bulk of the attributed material is reported in the names of fewer than 20 rabbis, primarily from 3 generations (roughly from the destruction of the Temple in 70 to the aftermath of the Bar Kokhba rebellion in 132–35).

The Mishna does not follow scripture's organization and does not present itself as an interpretation of scripture, which it cites with relative infrequency. Rather, the document is divided into 6 large sections or orders—*Zeraᶜim* ("seeds," agriculture), *Moᶜed* ("appointed times," festivals), *Našim* ("women," marriage and family law), *Neziqin* ("damages," civil law), *Qodašim* ("holy things," the rules of the Temple cult), and *Tohorot* ("purities," uncleanness taboos)—that together constitute 63 tractates. The Mishna is the foundation document of rabbinic Judaism. The rest of rabbinic writings, including the collections of scriptural exegesis called *midrash,* are now thought to postdate the Mishna. The Tosefta and the Palestinian and Babylonian Talmuds, the major collections of halakhic teaching, assume the Mishna and follow its organization.

The entire Mishna appears to have been redacted at once and according to a strict literary agenda. The sayings of discrete sages appear in a limited set of highly disciplined rhetorical forms that distinguish neither individual nor generation but are ubiquitous throughout the document. Moreover, rabbinic literature in general is collective, avoids biography as a genre, and fabricates tales about sages to illustrate idealized rabbinic values. Stories about early rabbis in later rabbinic literature cannot be supposed to have historical verisimilitude or reliability. Thus, it is impossible responsibly to present the story of early rabbinism in terms of the teachings and deeds of discrete rabbinic teachers. Rather, the history of rabbinism is best told in terms of the documents the rabbis produced.

The Mishna's Judaism emerged in the aftermath of the Temple's destruction in 70 and addressed the problem of how to sanctify the life of the people Israel in the absence of a cult. The Mishnaic answer is the promulgation of a levitical religion, which transformed priestly behavior and extended it to the life of the entire people in the natural and social world. The Mishna's piety consisted of a host of behaviors—food, purity, and kinship taboos; observance of Sabbath, holy days, and festivals; prayer—that promulgated levitical categories.

Jacob Neusner's revolutionary work shows that the earliest stratum of the Mishna's ideas, from before 70, deals with special laws of marriage, rules about when sexual relations may take place, and eating domestic meals in a state of purity, as if one were a priest. These concerns, along with the Mishna's assumptions about tithing and distinctive Sabbath observance, appear central to the agenda of the Pharisees, from whom rabbinic Judaism is thought to derive.

The next layer of the Mishna's ideas, from 70–135, focuses on taxes paid to the poor and the priests and on the conduct of the Temple cult itself. It also addresses taboos affecting the production of crops and on the ritual of the red cow, which raises the question of how to achieve purity outside of the Temple. The final layer of Mishnaic teachings constitutes a "range of topics so expanded that laws came to full expression to govern not merely the collective life of a small group but the political and social affairs of a whole nation" (Neusner 1989: 51). It includes civil and criminal law, the conduct of the cult, the documents necessary for the transfer of property, and the relationship between those expert in rabbinic teaching and those who are not.

It is important to note that more than half of the Mishna's contents pertain to matters of the cult—an astonishing trait of a document allegedly completed nearly 130 years after sacrifices had ceased and the Temple destroyed. Thus, in addition to its concern for the achievement of holiness in the realm of the everyday, the Mishna also has a strong utopian element (Neusner 1988: 48).

The shift in the Mishna's Judaism from a focus on the Temple to the entire nation of Israel as the locus of holiness was accompanied by the key and distinctive Mishnaic doctrine that the human being is the center of creation and has "the power, effected through an act of sheer human will or intentionality, to inaugurate and initiate those corresponding processes—sanctification and uncleanness—which play so critical a role in the Mishnah's account of reality. The will of the human being, expressed through the deed of the human being, is the active power in the world" (Neusner 1989: 199).

The Judaism of the Mishna draws on scripture but does not present itself as scriptural. It is surely Temple-oriented, but it treats the Temple as part of an idealized vision of a world to be achieved. Though utopian, the Mishna's Judaism eschews apocalyptic and supernaturalism. Much of the halakhic teaching in the Mishna draws on and elaborates rabbinic tradition, which may have its origins with the Pharisees.

The well-known rabbinic doctrines of the dual Torah

(oral and written) and of the study of Torah as an act of piety, though sometimes implicit in the Mishna's passages, receive their fullest expression in the post-Mishnaic tractate ʾ*Abot* and in later rabbinic literature.

K. Judaism and the Attraction of Judaism in the Diaspora

As in Palestine, Jewish religion in the diaspora was diverse. The evidence precludes any claims for a monolithic diaspora Judaism. The highly philosophical writings of Philo express a diaspora Judaism certainly different from that practiced by the Jews in Egypt whose worship centered on the temple in Leontopolis. Josephus' historiography and his version of Jewish history in *Antiquities* reflects another Judaism informed by issues of Roman influence and domination. Paul's letter to the Romans or Juvenal's *Satire* 14 both reflect the involvement of gentiles in the Jewish community in Rome, which left a distinctive mark on Judaism there, and the city of Sardis reflects still another expression of Judaism in a thriving Jewish community in Asia Minor. The identity and nature of Judaism in the diaspora varied from locale to locale, from community to community. Three distinct communities help illustrate the strength and diversity of the Judaisms in the diaspora.

A large Jewish community existed in Rome from at least the 2d century B.C.E. By the turn of the eras there were 20,000–50,000 Jews in Rome (Penna 1982: 328). The Jewish community in Rome was sizable and at times worrisome to the Romans. Both the emperors Tiberius and later Claudius cracked down on the Jews. The so-called Claudian edict is reported by Suetonius (*Claudius* 25.4) and Dio Cassius 60.6.6. The Dio Cassius text states the Jews were forbidden to assemble in Rome, while the Suetonius text claims they were expelled. Dio's report probably represents an initial restriction against assembling ca. 41 which was followed by an expulsion under Claudius in 49 C.E. (Smallwood 1976: 215). Despite occasional political confrontations, the Jews in Rome continued to grow in number and influence. In the early 2d century Juvenal's *Satires* 14 relates with obvious consternation the inroads the Jewish religion was making into Roman society.

Alexandria was another Roman center with a large Jewish population. Jews in and around Alexandria produced a number of literate and prolific authors. Figures such as Aristobulus and Philo, and such documents as the *Sibylline Oracles* Book 3, the LXX, and the *Letter of Aristeas* are examples of the literature and *litterati* generated by the Jewish culture in this city. The Jewish community in Alexandria can be traced back at least until the 3d–4th century B.C.E. A number of scholars hold that the synagogue had its origin in Egypt, perhaps in Alexandrian Jewry (Hengel 1975). The literature from Alexandria provides an important example of the life and worldview of some diaspora Jews.

A third significant Jewish center was that of Sardis. Jews had settled in Sardis from the 3d century B.C.E., and the size and influence of this diaspora community continued to grow, as the epigraphical and archaeological evidence from Sardis shows (Kraabel 1978; 1982). Josephus mentions Sardis and the Jewish community in *Ant* 16.171; 14.259, and several times in *Antiquities* 11. The Jewish community in Sardis played an important role in the larger life and culture of the city as well as that part of Asia Minor. The Sardis synagogue in particular, an enormous and striking building, given to the Jewish community by the city *boule,* symbolizes the presence and impact of the Jewish community on the city. The synagogue occupies a central and prominent place in the layout and structure of the city (Kraabel 1978). The Sardis diaspora community has come to symbolize the success, so to speak, of diaspora Judaism in the Greco-Roman period throughout the Greek East. While there were certainly periods of persecution and stress, many diaspora communities sunk roots into the Greco-Roman culture, making a sizable impact on the life and culture of the cities and settings where these Jewish communities flourished.

In the diaspora (and in Palestine as well), Jewish communities gathered together in local or domestic settings, such as a home or a generic public building (White 1990). Scholars have tended to suppose that the formal, developed, and elaborate character of 3d to 5th century synagogues also applied to the gathering places of the earlier Greco-Roman period. But the common buildings that have been excavated at Gamala or Magdala in Palestine or at Delos or Ostia in the diaspora—which have been identified as "synagogues"—are small, simple structures that lack the traits of the later synagogues. In the period 63 B.C.E.–200 C.E., whether in inscriptions, the NT, or Josephus, it is better to understand the term "synagogue" to mean a public gathering or town hall rather than as a technical term for a religious institution specifically for Jewish worship (Meyers and Kraabel 1986: 175–210; Overman 1990: 56–61). During the 2d or 3d centuries, the elaborate synagogue building began to develop. By the late Roman period, such synagogues were scattered throughout the Greco-Roman world. Often, as in the cases of Sardis, Ostia, or Stobi, these were significant (even magnificent) buildings. Whether in the more refined and replete synagogues that appeared after 200, or in the plain and often domestic setting of the earlier Greco-Roman period, most Judaisms of the diaspora were in some sense synagogue-based (Kee 1990).

So far as we know, diaspora Jews understood themselves as part of historic Israel, albeit separated by an expanse of miles and culture. They made use of many of the traditions, rituals, and above all scriptures common to Israel. Yet Jews in the diaspora did develop a variety of distinctive traits when compared with their Palestinian counterparts. By all accounts, diaspora Judaism, as a result of the role of the synagogue, dispensed with a priesthood. Synagogue gatherings were administered by lay people. Also, the sacrifices performed by the priests in Jerusalem were not replicated in the diaspora synagogues. Diaspora Jews retained the scriptures and provided a prominent place for them in their life and worship. This was the Greek Bible or LXX. The Jewish writers of the diaspora were thoroughly steeped in the LXX, as well as in Hellenistic philosophy, literature, and historiography. The LXX became a vital vehicle for diaspora Jews to create a religious and cultural discourse that was both traditional and accessible to the broader Greco-Roman world (Kraabel 1987).

Both Philo and Josephus represent examples of diaspora Jews who use elements and traditions common to many

Judaisms in Palestine, yet adapt them to the culture and audience for which their writings were intended. Josephus likens the three *haireseis* in Palestine to Greek philosophy. He stresses in particular their view of fate and free will. When retelling the history of the Jews in *Antiquities,* he relates the great traditions and heroes of Israel's history in language and terms familiar to his Greco-Roman, largely non-Jewish readers. This is particularly true with his portrayal of Moses as the perfect lawgiver (Tiede 1972).

Philo also stresses scripture. He interprets Jewish history and religion using allegorical exegesis informed by Platonic and Stoic principles. The categories and figures of historic Israel are transformed by Philo. Moses, the patriarchs, the historic traditions, sources of authority, and myths of Israel merge with the dominant philosophies and influences of his culture. The result is a striking synthesis of historic Jewish traditions and beliefs and Greco-Roman philosophy and culture.

The interplay between these two vast categories was carried on throughout the diaspora. The result was a diversity of Judaisms, all of which put their own distinctive stamp on the process of this dynamic cultural synthesis.

Exponents of Jesus-centered Judaism in the diaspora, such as Paul or Luke, faced many of the same issues that confronted Josephus or Philo. Both Luke and Paul draw repeatedly from the scriptures, traditions, and heroes of Israel. Yet this is done with an eye toward the life and questions faced by their respective diaspora communities. For example, along with the scriptures, Luke reflects the influence of Stoic philosophy. Typical of the cultural diversity characteristic of diaspora Jews, Luke's highly stylized portrait of Paul in Acts depicts a cosmopolitan man who is equally at home in the Jewish synagogue, among the Greek philosophers, or holding forth in the Roman court. These were the cultural arenas that were part of the world of diaspora Jews.

The writings of Paul reflect issues which confronted many diaspora Jews when encountering the gentile world. The letters to the Romans and Galatians take up questions about the role of traditional Jewish practices, such as circumcision and dietary laws, in the urban centers of the Greco-Roman world. Paul spoke within Judaism. He said he was a Jew, of the tribe of Benjamin, and unto the law a Pharisee (Phil 3:5). The history and heroes of Israelite tradition and religion provide much of the framework for Paul's explanation of Judaism. The figure of Abraham is central to Paul's interpretation of Judaism in the diaspora for both Jews and gentiles (Romans 4; Galatians 3). Paul frequently takes up issues of law and scriptural debate, drawing heavily from the LXX; his view of history and the future is informed by an apocalyptic worldview similar to many Jews in Palestine. In the face of opposing views and factions, Paul also claims his interpretation of Judaism is authentic (Georgi 1985; Luedemann 1989). The challenge that faced Paul, like many other diaspora Jews, was how historic Judaism, as he understood it, related to gentiles who were increasingly becoming a part of the life of Jewish communities in the diaspora.

Diaspora Jews did tend to retain certain cultic practices; modified food laws, circumcision, and Sabbath observance. But in general it was the task of diaspora communities to fashion and appropriate Judaism in cultural and religious contexts quite different from those of Palestine. However well accepted, Jews were still minorities in these great urban centers, and the Jews of the diaspora were daily confronted with philosophies, political realities, and religions that constituted in some manner a challenge, if not a threat, to their religion. Judaisms in the diaspora cultivated a dynamic interaction with the elements of the Greco-Roman world which surrounded it.

Some of the events that shaped Jewish identity and religion in Palestine were not part of the experience of many diaspora Jews. The Babylonian exile, Seleucid domination, the Maccabean revolt and expansionism, Roman occupation of Palestine in 63, or even the destruction of the Temple in 70 C.E. may have only been stories diaspora Jews heard but were not part of their own diaspora experience. These critical historical events in Palestine, then, would have played a much smaller role in shaping Jewish religion in the diaspora. As a result of these and other differences, the varieties of religious expression within diaspora Judaism tended to vary from traditional "Palestinian Judaism" in some significant respects. For example they made important aspects of traditional Judaism portable or symbolic; the scriptures, the Temple, the land, even the synagogue community itself. Many Jews outside of Palestine grafted a Jewish theology of diaspora onto the Greco-Roman culture and social structure (Kraabel 1987: 58). The literature, philosophy, and at points the religions of the broader Greco-Roman world influenced and coalesced with traditional aspects of Judaism.

As Judaism in the diaspora transformed and appropriated aspects of the culture around it, many in the broader Greco-Roman world found themselves attracted to Judaism. This dynamic between diaspora Jews and Greco-Roman culture is an important chapter in the story of Jewish religion in the diaspora. The influence of many diaspora communities can be seen in the attraction it held for many in the gentile world. The celebrated case of the Roman family in Juvenal's 14th Satire has already been mentioned, however this is by no means an unusual case. Josephus throughout his works mentions many cases of gentile respect and enthusiasm for Judaism. *Antiquities* records at least 7 instances of conversion to Judaism by a gentile (Cohen 1987: 419). *Antiquities* also talks about adherants, and not only those who become circumcised and convert to Judaism. *Contra Apion* 2.282 mentions Greeks who respect and emulate the Jewish religion. Speaking of the Jews of Antioch, Josephus writes, "they were constantly attracting to their religious ceremonies many Greeks, and these they had incorporated in some measure with themselves" (*JW* 7.3.3).

Further, the life of the synagogues of some of these diaspora communities reveal more evidence for the appeal of diaspora Judaism to non-Jews. Acomonea in Asia Minor, for example, had a gentile benefactor, Julia Severa. Sardis itself is evidence of the popularity of Judaism, at least in that city. Also, the NT, particularly the Acts of the Apostles, speaks of a class or group of gentiles, called "Godfearers," who can be found in and around the diaspora synagogues. While there has been some debate about the existence of such a group this does accurately reflect the interest Judaism had in the diaspora setting among non-Jews (Overman 1988). An inscription from Aphrodisias which mentions certain "God-fearers" (Gk *Theosebes*) may in fact represent a group of gentile sympathizers. However the inscription was not found *in situ,* and a number of other questions remain (Reynolds and Tannenbaum 1987; Gager 1986).

The presence of "God-fearers" of "proselytes" around the synagogue does not suggest, as Martin Hengel claimed in an astonishing sentence, that Judaism "had to stoop to constant and ultimately untenable compromises" (1974, 1: 313). On the contrary, diaspora Judaism and Greco-Roman culture engaged in a lively exchange and religious and cultural give-and-take for a number of centuries. The attraction and on occasion conversion of many in the gentile world to Judaism is proof of the vitality and strength of Judaism in the diaspora. Further, it demonstrates how well these diaspora communities engaged, adopted, and transformed certain elements of the broader Greco-Roman world, in order to forge a resilient and diversified Judaism in the great cities and centers of the diaspora.

L. Philo

One of the primary sources for Jewish life in the diaspora is Philo Judeus. Philo was a wealthy and influential Jew of Alexandria who left an extensive body of literature. Much of Philo's work is devoted to explaining Judaism to a gentile audience. In this regard Philo faced the same essential task faced by most diaspora communities. In his treatment of the Jerusalem Temple Philo not only spiritualized and placed the Temple in a neo-platonic framework, but he explained the Temple as if he were addressing an audience which had little or no knowledge of it. This theme is carried throughout most of Philo's work. According to E. R. Goodenough, Philo's *Embassy to Gaius* and *Against Flaccus* comprise part of Philo's apologetic literature. It has been suggested that in these two documents we find more autobiographical material concerning Philo, and they are thus a source for understanding Philo the man, as well as the philosopher and statesman (Goodenough 1940: 34ff.).

As the title indicates, his *Apology for the Jews* also falls into this category of apologetic material, as does his short essay on the *Contemplative Life.* An important document in the Philonic corpus that intended to introduce a gentile audience to the substance of the Jewish faith and life is Philo's *Life of Moses.* In this work Moses emerges as the ideal figure, prophet or hero. It is worth bearing in mind that simply because Moses is defined in "Hellenistic" terms and depicted in so-called Hellenistic guise, even to the point of being called a "divine man," this does not suggest that this work is intended strictly for a non-Jewish audience (Tiede 1972: 107ff.). Philo's language and thought also provide insight into the nature and philosophical worldview of diaspora Jews as well as gentiles in Alexandria.

Philo treats Moses and Israel's patriarchs in such a way as to stress their virtue *(arete),* in accordance with the dominant ethics and values of Hellenistic Stoic philosophy. In his treatment of the great men of the Jewish tradition, Philo appeals to the widely accepted and reiterated paradigm of Cynic-Stoic ethics and ideals. It is the virtue and wisdom of Moses, and then of Abraham, Isaac and Jacob, which elevate them to the level of ideal men. Similarly, Moses is portrayed as the ideal lawgiver, priest, king, or *man of God.*

Philo's ideal treatment of the patriarchs can be seen in the second major division of his work, the *Exposition of the Law.* This division of Philo's work comprises at least 9 treatises; *On the Creation of the World, On Abraham, On Isaac, On Jacob, On Joseph, On the Decalogue, Special Laws* (in 4 books), *On Virtues,* and *Rewards and Punishments.* This is the major portion of Philo's work, and it is his distinctive treatment of the law and related themes and heroes which has in many circles become the hallmark of Philo's work. Throughout this multi-volume work Philo tries to align the history, heroes, and laws of Israel with the widely accepted laws and philosophy of the broader Greco-Roman culture. *On the Creation of the World,* for example, appears to be patterned on Plato's *Timaeus,* and utilizes such venerable Greek philosophical notions as the *logos,* natural law, and Platonic forms. Similarly, *On Virtues* provides a general summary of Jewish legal principles according to classical Greek virtues.

In *Special Laws,* Philo takes up specific issues relating to Jewish law. These four books follow the *Decalogue,* where Philo has said all other laws follow from these ten. Concerning Jewish law, Philo's treatment of circumcision is of particular interest. In *Special laws* I Philo, as is characteristic of his work throughout, allegorizes Jewish circumcision in a way which diverts attention from the act of circumcision itself and focuses instead on the symbolic value of the act. Philo writes that circumcision is "the excision of pleasures which bewitch the mind. . . . The legislators thought it good to dock the organ which ministers to such intercourse, thus making circumcision the figure of the excision of the excessive and superfluous pleasure, not only of one pleasure, but of all the other pleasures signified by one, and that the most imperious." Throughout his work Philo allegorizes the command and act of circumcision, characterizing circumcision as a nearly, but not quite, symbolic circumcision of one's ethics, if not one's heart; (*Spec Leg* I.305; *Migr.* 92; Borgen 1987). Indeed for Philo, the symbols and traditions of historic Judaism, whether the Temple, scripture, or levitical rules, are almost always transformed into symbolic categories that appeal to both Jews and gentiles in his Alexandrian setting.

Philo represents the fusion of Hellenistic philosophy, notably Stoicism and Neoplatonism, with the historic faith and figures of Israel. In the hands of Philo, the religion of the Jews becomes an *oikoumene,* a monotheistic religion that can embrace and contain the religions and philosophies of the world. The timeless truths, precepts, and virtues of the cosmos are contained in the traditions and religion of the Jews. Philo brought profound expression to this claim in his corpus. A primary vehicle for promoting and explaining Judaism, whether to Jews or non-Jews, was his treatment and exposition of scripture. *On Virtues, On Special Laws, Questions and Answers to Exodus, The Life of Moses* and more reveal that scripture, in the form of the LXX, was a central source of authority for Philo and the window through which he could, with the help of his creative, allegorical, and symbolic exegesis, reach his audience.

M. The Bible Rewritten

An important and widespread phenomenon within Judaism in the Greco-Roman period was the appearance of a number of documents that retold the stories and history of the Bible. Sometimes this reiteration of biblical stories and heroes took the form of copying a genre derived from the Bible (Psalms, Apocalypses, histories), or these stories and figures were passed on in the form of narratives that constituted a cross between biblical histories and ancient romances. *Joseph and Asneth, 3* and *4 Maccabees* and the *Testament of the 12 Patriarchs* are examples of the latter. These are Jewish narrative writings which are supported and inspired by canonical stories and figures.

The Jews of the postbiblical era were not the first to engage in this work. Within the Hebrew Bible, Chronicles is the first book to draft a rewritten history of Israel. This type of literary activity flourished in the Greco-Roman period. Much of this vast body of material has been collected and edited by J. Charlesworth in *OTP.* This literature comes forth with such force that one would be remiss not to represent it as a significant aspect of Jewish religion and life in the Greco-Roman period. Documents such as *Pseudo-Philo, Jubilees, Paralipomena of Jeremiah,* the *Ascension of Isaiah,* and Josephus' multivolume *Antiquities of the Jews,* along with many others can all be classified as literature which retells the biblical story in the postbiblical period. Because there is a great deal of biblical material and important interpretation of biblical figures and history in *1 Enoch, 2 Baruch, 4 Ezra,* and of course Philo, these can also be included in this category.

Interpretation of scripture, response to the destruction of the Temple in 70, the casting of Jewish history and heroes in Hellenistic terms, and issues related to eschatology and authority are just some of the themes these documents take up. Some of these works were originally written in Greek, while others reveal they are Greek translations of an earlier Hebrew version. Some works focus on a specific part of the Bible. *Jubilees* retells material from Gen 1:1 through Exod 12:50. *The Assumption of Moses* is a valediction by Moses based on Deuteronomy 31–34; *Pseudo-Philo* is an expansion of accounts in the Pentateuch, Joshua-Judges, and 1 and 2 Samuel; the last 15 columns of the Temple Scroll from Qumran retell a section of Deuteronomy (Harrington 1986).

The 1st century B.C.E. *Psalms of Solomon,* and the 1st century *Odes of Solomon* are both examples of Jewish literature from this period which emulate a genre from the Bible itself. Related to this, many documents from this period seize upon biblical heroes and figures to tell their story, and invest their message with an authority they otherwise would lack. The biblical figure of Jeremiah is such a person in this period, as is his scribe Baruch. The same can be said for Ezra the scribe, Moses, and many of the patriarchs. The message and authority of these texts and stories were supported by appeal to the great figures and stories of Israel's biblical history. The authors and people behind these many texts were clearly biblically centered, though naturally their interpretations varied from text to text and place to place.

The phenomenon of retelling the biblical story, and reiterating and fashioning stories about biblical heroes served a variety of purposes. Each text, and each story from the respective documents, must be examined on its own terms to decipher the purpose and message of this retold history. The books of *2 Baruch, 4 Ezra,* or the *Assumption of Isaiah* are all different with distinct messages. However, within this category of rewritten biblical history and legend, some general comments can be made. First, the retelling of Israel's history was certainly educational (it reminded people of what they might otherwise forget). But more importantly, this phenomenon points to the issues of self-definition and understanding. The widespread phenomenon of rewriting the Bible in this period was a result of the need on the part of Jews both at home and in the diaspora to clarify who they were, whose they were, and what the future held for them. One understands oneself primarily through the past in which one places oneself. This is clearly the case with many Jewish communities in this period. By appeal to the past, and the recasting of scriptural history and Israel's biblical heroes, a variety of Jewish communities were able to redefine and redirect themselves.

N. Testaments and Apocalypses

Related to the phenomenon of rewriting the Bible, or retelling Israel's history, is the growth of two similar types of literature in the Greco-Roman period, one commonly called "Testaments" and the other "Apocalypses." These categories are somewhat artificial. Some "Apocalypses" are not technically apocalypses, and some "Testaments" are not testaments as such (Kolenkow 1986). Most of this, however, is essentially the result of scholarly debates over names and genres that historically have been rather arbitrarily assigned to this literature. The literature of Enoch; the *Sybylline Oracles;* the *Testament of Moses;* the *Apocalypse of Abraham;* certain literature from Qumran and from Paul (1 Thessalonians); and the early Jesus tradition (Q; the Gospel of Mark) are among the many documents which represent this social and literary development within the Judaisms of this period. Along with the new edition of much of this literature edited by Charlesworth, there has recently been a renewed interest in the scholarship and study of many of these documents (see Collins 1987).

In addition to being in some sense scripturally oriented this literature also reflects the importance and persistence of apocalypticism within several of the Judaisms of the Greco-Roman period. Most of these texts, *2 Baruch, 4 Ezra,* the Apocalypses and Testaments mentioned above, and many more documents reveal the prominence and importance of apocalyptic. In addition to the long-held connection between wisdom literature and apocalyptic, some of the basic traits of apocalyptic are a highly developed eschatology, belief in heavenly visits, revelations, and the tenaciously held belief in the in-breaking of God in the near future. God's action is usually expected to amend the difficulties of the present, judge the offenders of the author and community, and vindicate the "righteous." Apocalypticism usually envisions a decisive end to the present order, and it is compatible with both a levitical system such as Qumran, or an antinomian Judaism such as Paul's.

Recently scholarship has come to recognize the role political oppression and struggle played in many of the apocalyptic documents and movements (Horsley 1987). The role of political domination and the impact of Roman imperial power and rule should not be underestimated in evaluating the shape and nature of various Jewish movements and literature in this period. The Testaments and Apocalypses, along with several of the groups mentioned above, are powerful testimony to this reality within Judaism in the Greco-Roman period.

The final throes of apocalypticism can be seen early in the 2d century C.E. *The Apocalypse of Abraham,* the Book of Revelation, *2 Baruch,* or *4 Ezra*—and in a more overtly political sense, the Bar-Kokhba revolt—represent the final act of apocalypticism within Judaism. By the second half of the 2d century and the dawn of the rabbinic period, documents with an apocalyptic orientation all but disappear. While there is a small amount of evidence of apocalyptic in rabbinic literature, rabbinism generally avoided apocalypticism (Saldarini 1975). As a major tendency in Jewish religion, the apocalyptic worldview did not survive the 2d century, at least in the literature, and can be restricted to having played a role—a major role—within Judaism of this formative and fluid period, but not beyond.

O. The LXX and the Role of Scripture

Among the contributions made by the many different forms and varieties of Judaism in this period, one of the most enduring was the translation and interpretation of the Hebrew Bible into Greek; the so-called Septuagint (LXX). The translation and origin of the LXX is related in the highly stylized work, *The Letter of Aristeas.* Aristeas tells the story of the request by Demetrius, head of the library at Alexandria, to Ptolemy II (285–246 B.C.E.) to send a delegation to Jerusalem asking that the High Priest Eleazar appoint 6 elders from each of the 12 tribes, "who possess skill in the law and ability to translate," in order to render the Hebrew text of the Bible into Greek (39) (Orlinsky, *CHJ* 2: 534–62). This translation was to be deposited in the royal library.

The letter goes on to tell about the translation itself and the enthusiastic reception it received from "all the people" when it was read aloud. *Aristeas* 308–11 claims that the translation received a great ovation, and the priests and elders declared that it was so good (accurate) that no revision of any sort should take place: the text should stand as is. The section concludes by noting that this work "should be preserved imperishable and unchanged forever." The repeated claims of authority and authenticity concerning the translation suggest that the LXX did not receive an immediate and ubiquitous reception. Clearly the author of the *Letter of Aristeas* offers an apology for the LXX and its inspired, accurate, and abiding status. The author hopes the translation will be viewed by Alexandrian Jews as their inspired holy writ.

It is undeniable, however, that the LXX quickly became the Bible of diaspora Jews. The authors of the NT use the LXX. Paul and Luke, for example, make extensive use of it and demonstrate far more than a passing acquaintance with it.

To speak of *the* LXX (i.e., in the singular) is misleading for it suggests that there was *one* LXX which came into being at a particular point in time and in one place. The LXX, despite the myth recorded in *Aristeas,* was not a single, fixed document in the mid-3d century B.C.E. There were many manuscripts and transmissions, and certain books were rendered into Greek at different times by different people. Isaiah, for example, may be 100 to 150 years later than the Pentateuch. The various authors, translations, and versions of the LXX, or parts thereof, are expressions, or *interpretations* of a type of Judaism in a diaspora setting.

Josephus' use of scripture is an interesting case in point. Which text and language(s) Josephus used when referring to biblical passages is still contested among scholars (Feldman 1984: 130ff.). At points, apparently, Josephus used some form of a Greek translation of the Hebrew, some version of the LXX. Philo used the LXX extensively, but rewrote it freely and continued to provide new formulations and emphases (Collins 1983: 12). Authors from this period who refer to biblical passages in the Greek do not often agree on the content, let alone the message or interpretation of the text.

According to Philo, by the mid-1st century C.E. in Alexandria, there was a holiday that celebrated the translation of the LXX, in which both Jews and Greeks participated (*Vita Mos* II.41). Given this claim, even if exaggerated, and given the extensive use of the LXX by Philo and others throughout the Greek-speaking world, it is plausible to conclude that the LXX was read and received throughout the diaspora as the diaspora Jewish Bible or "holy writ." As V. Tcherikover (1958) observed, the *Letter of Aristeas* stands near the beginning of a long process of cultural and religious development within diaspora communities. Philo, on the other hand, may well stand at the apex of this historical and theological development within diaspora Judaisms. That development was Judaism, in varying forms and shades in the diaspora, presenting traditional Jewish monotheism combined with a universal philosophy inherited from the Greco-Roman world. For these communities, the Greek Bible was their centerpiece. Interpretation, allegorization, and the integration of these scriptures with the dominant philosophies of the day became the hallmark of diaspora literature. While Jews in the diaspora laid claim to the scriptures and stories of Jews in Palestine, they were not finally reading, or hearing, the same Bible. The LXX is related to the Hebrew text(s), but it is not the same. Any translation is by necessity an *interpretation,* and the LXX is no exception.

While the tendencies of the LXX interpreters are still not fully understood, the work done on LXX Isaiah provides an example of this broader point concerning the LXX. The agenda of LXX Isaiah included advocacy for the inclusion of non-Jews and the consistent expansion of the Greek concept of *nomos* to include certain connotations which were part of the language and ethos of Hellenistic philosophy and religion (Seeligmann 1948; Olley 1978). The translator(s) of Isaiah emphasized the importance of constructive interaction with non-Jews. Therefore it is not surprising that LXX Isaiah provides a prominent place for the central Greek notion and term *oikoumene.* In the hands of the translators, LXX Isaiah articulates a worldwide monotheistic religion that combines traditional Hebrew stories and belief with Greek philosophy and religion. In order to accomplish this the translators had to transform salient notions and terms from the Hebrew text to better fit the message and the world in which the message was to be conveyed. While LXX Isaiah is clearly related to its Hebrew antecedent, it provides an interpretation, not simply a reiteration, of the religion and life of that Hebrew text. The LXX is not the same Bible as its Hebrew counterpart, but rather provides an *interpretation* of it.

The importance of the translation and impact of the LXX is difficult to overstate. The literature, holy writ, and traditions of Judaism(s) which were historically tied to Palestine became easily accessible, and in many places were enthusiastically received in the broader Greco-Roman world due to the Greek Bible. Moreover, the LXX also signals the emergence of the importance of scripture generally within many Judaisms during this period (regardless of whether those scriptures were in Greek or Hebrew). In the Greek-speaking world the importance of scripture for Philo, Paul, Luke, or a host of Hellenistic Jewish authors is unmistakable (Holladay 1983; Collins 1983). For Qumran, *2 Baruch, 4 Ezra,* and Josephus, the importance of scripture and the scriptural tradition emerges with force. While not always citing scripture explicitly, it is clear these authors, and whoever it is they address or represent, assign significant importance and authority to these scriptural traditions.

The emergence of the role of scripture for apologetic and polemical reasons, as well as for the purposes of self-definition and education is an important feature of many Judaisms in this period (Overman 1990: 23–30). The precise meaning and use of the notions of "scripture," "law," and the "traditions" about scripture and law vary from place to place and from author to author. These are not static or fixed ideas and categories. Various Judaisms naturally understood and interpreted these concepts, texts, and traditions differently. However, they all assign authority and prominence to this scriptural tradition with Jewish history and culture, however they understood it, and they all use that tradition to define, defend, and articulate *Judaism* as they understood it and practiced it.

Bibliography

Attridge, H. 1976. *The Interpretation of Biblical History in the Antiquitates Judaicae of Flavius Josephus.* HDR 7. Missoula.

———. 1986. Jewish Historiography. Pp. 311–44 in Kraft and Nickelsburg 1986.

Baumgarten, A. 1987. The Pharisaic *Paradosis. HTR* 80: 63–78.

Beall, T. 1988. *Josephus' Description of the Essenes Illustrated by the Dead Sea Scrolls.* SNTSMS 58. Cambridge.

Blenkinsopp, J. 1981. Interpretation and Sectarian Tendencies: An Aspect of Second Temple History. Vol. 2, pp. 1–26 in *Jewish and Christian Self-Definition,* ed. E. P. Sanders. Philadelphia.

Borgen, P. 1987. *Philo, John, and Paul.* Atlanta.

Charlesworth, J. 1979–81. The Origin and Subsequent History of the Authors of the Dead Sea Scrolls: Four Transitional Phases Among the Qumran Essenes. *RQ* 10: 213–23.

Cohen, S. 1979. *Josephus in Galilee and Rome: His Vita and Development as a Historian.* Leiden.

———. 1987. Respect for Judaism By Gentiles According to Josephus. *HTR* 80: 409–30.

Collins, J. 1983. *Between Athens and Jerusalem.* New York.

———. 1987. *The Apocalyptic Imagination.* New York.

Cross, F. 1969. The Early History of the Qumran Community. Pp. 63–79 in *New Directions in Biblical Archaeology,* ed. D. N. Freedman and J. C. Greenfield. Garden City.

———. 1980. *The Ancient Library of Qumran and Modern Biblical Studies.* Grand Rapids.

Davies, P. R. 1982. The Ideology of the Temple in the Damascus Document. *JJS* 33: 287–301.

Davies, W. D., and Finkelstein, L. 1989. *The Cambridge History of Judaism.* Vol. 2. Cambridge.

Edwards, R. 1971. *The Sign of Jonah in the Theology of the Evangelists and Q.* London.

Feldman, L. 1984. *Josephus and Modern Scholarship 1937–1980.* New York and Berlin.

Fitzmyer, J. 1974. *Essays on The Semitic Background of the New Testament.* Missoula.

Forkman, G. 1972. *The Limits of Religious Community.* Lund.

Freyne, S. 1980. *Galilee: From Alexander the Great to Hadrian.* Wilmington.

———. 1987. Galilee-Jerusalem Relations According to Josephus' *Life. NTS* 33: 600–9.

Gager, J. 1986. Jews, Gentiles, and Synagogues in the Book of Acts. *HTR* 79: 91–99.

Georgi, D. 1985. *The Opponents of Paul in Second Corinthians.* Philadelphia.

Goldin, J. 1955. *The Fathers According to Rabbi Nathan.* New Haven.

Goodenough, E. R. 1940. *An Introduction to Philo Judaeus.* New Haven.

Goodman, M. 1987. *The Ruling Class of Judea: The Origins of the Revolt Against Rome A.D. 66–70.* Cambridge.

Green, W. S. 1981. *The Traditions of Joshua Ben Hananiah: The Early Legal Traditions.* Leiden.

Harrington, D. 1986. The Bible Rewritten. Pp. 239–46 in Kraft and Nickelsburg 1986.

Hayward, R. 1982. The Jewish Temple at Leontopolis: A Reconsideration. *JJS* 33: 429–44.

Hengel, M. 1974. *Judaism and Hellenism.* 2 vols. Philadelphia.

———. 1975. Prosuche und Synagoge: Judische Gemeinde, Gotteshaus und Gottesdienst in der Diaspora und in Palestinea. Pp. 157–84 in *The Synagogue: Studies in the Origins, Archeology, and Architecture,* ed. J. Gutmann. New York.

Holladay, C. 1983. *Fragments From Hellenistic Jewish Authors.* Vol. 1. Chico, CA.

Horsley, R. 1987. *Jesus and the Spiral of Violence.* San Francisco.

Horsley, R., and Hanson, J. 1985. *Bandits, Prophets, and Messiahs: Popular Movements at the Time of Jesus.* Minneapolis.

Hultgren, A. 1979. *Jesus and His Adversaries.* Minneapolis.

Juel, D. 1977. *Messiah and Temple: The Trial of Jesus in the Gospel of Mark.* SBLDS 31. Missoula.

Kee, H. 1977. *The Community of the New Age.* London.

———. 1990. The Transformation of the Synagogue after 70 C.E.: Its Import for Early Christianity. *NTS* 36: 1–24.

Kloppenborg, J. 1987. *The Formation of Q.* Philadelphia.

———. 1989. The Formation of Q Revisited. SBLSP, pp. 204–15.

Kolenkow, A. 1986. The Literary Genre *Testament.* Pp. 259–67 in Kraft and Nickelsburg 1986.

Kraabel, A. T. 1978. Paganism and Judaism: The Sardis Evidence. In *Paganisme, Judaisme, Christianisme: Melanges offerts a Marcel Simon,* ed. A. Benoit and M. Philonenko. Paris.

———. 1979. The Diaspora Synagogue. *ANRW* 2/19/1: 477–510.

———. 1982. The Roman Diaspora: Six Questionable Assumptions. *JJS* 33: 445–64.

———. 1984. New Evidence of Samaritan Diaspora has been Found at Delos. *BA* 47: 44–46.

———. 1987. Unity and Diversity Among Diaspora Synagogues. Pp. 49–60 in *The Synagogue in Late Antiquity,* ed. L. Levine. Philadelphia.

Kraft, R., and Nickelsburg, G., eds. 1986. *Early Judaism and Its Modern Interpreters.* Philadelphia and Atlanta.
Lampe, P. 1987. *Die stadtromischen Christen.* Tubingen.
LeMoyne, J. 1972. *Les Sadduceens.* Paris.
Luedemann, G. 1989. *Opposition to Paul in Jewish Christianity.* Trans. E. Boring. Philadelphia.
Mack, B. 1988. *A Myth of Innocence.* Philadelphia.
Markus, R. 1974. *Christianity in the Roman World.* New York.
Meyers, E., and Kraabel, A. T. 1986. Archaeology, Iconography, and Nonliterary Remains. Pp. 175–210 in Kraft and Nickelsburg 1986.
Moehring, H. 1979. Joseph ben Matthia and Flavius Josephus. *ANRW* 2/21/2: 864–944.
Murphy-O'Connor, J. 1974. The Essenes and their History. *RB* 81: 215–44.
Neusner, J. 1971. *The Rabbinic Traditions About the Pharisees Before 70.* Leiden.
———. 1973. *From Politics to Piety: The Emergence of Pharisaic Judaism.* Englewood Cliffs.
———. 1979. The Formation of Rabbinic Judaism: Yavneh (Jamnia) from A.D. 70–100. *ANRW* 2/19/2: 3–42.
———. 1988. *From Testament to Torah: An Introduction to Judaism in Its Formative Age.* Englewood Cliffs.
———. 1989. *The Mishna: An Introduction.* Northvale, NJ.
Neusner, J.; Green, W. S.; and Frerichs, E., eds. 1987. *Judaisms and Their Messiahs at the Turn of the Christian Era.* Cambridge.
Olley, J. 1978. *Righteousness in the Septuagint of Isaiah: A Contextual Study.* Missoula.
Overman, J. A. 1988. The God-Fearers: Some Neglected Features. *JSNT* 32: 17–26.
———. 1990. *Matthew's Gospel and Formative Judaism: The Social World of the Matthean Community.* Minneapolis.
Penna, R. 1982. Les Juifs a Rome au temps de l'apôtre Paul. *NTS* 28: 321–47.
Purvis, J. 1986. The Samaritans and Judaism. Pp. 81–98 in Kraft and Nickelsburg 1986.
Rajak, T. 1984. *Josephus: The Historian and His Society.* Philadelphia.
Reynolds, J., and Tannenbaum, R. 1987. *Jews and Godfearers at Aphrodisias.* Cambridge Philological Society Supplementary 12. Cambridge.
Saldarini, A. 1975. Apocalyptic and Rabbinic Literature. *CBQ* 37: 348–58.
———. 1988. *Pharisees, Scribes, and Sadducees in Palestinian Society.* Wilmington.
Sanders, E. P. 1985. *Jesus and Judaism.* Philadelphia.
Schiffman, L. 1975. *The Halakha at Qumran.* Leiden.
———. 1983. *Sectarian Law in the Dead Sea Scrolls, Courts, Testimony, and the Penal Code.* Brown Judaic Studies 33. Chico, CA.
———. 1989. *The Eschatological Community of the Dead Sea Scrolls.* SBLMS 38. Atlanta.
Schwartz, D. 1983. Josephus and Nicolaus on the Pharisees. *JSJ* 14: 157–71.
Seeligmann, I. 1948. *The Septuagint Version of Isaiah: A Discussion of Its Problems.* Leiden.
Smallwood, M. 1976. *The Jews Under Roman Rule.* Leiden.
Smith, J. 1982. *Imagining Religion: From Babylon to Jonestown.* Chicago.
Strange, J. 1979. Archaeology and the Religion of Judaism in Palestine. *ANRW* 2/19/1: 646–85.
Tcherikover, V. 1958. The Ideology of the Letter of Aristeas. *HTR* 51: 59–85.
Tiede, D. 1972. *The Charismatic Figure as Miracle Worker.* SBLDS 1. Missoula.
Vermes, G. 1974. *Jesus the Jew.* New York.
———. 1980. *The Dead Sea Scrolls in English.* Hammondsworth.
———. 1983. *Jesus and the World of Judaism.* London.
Walasky, P. 1983. *"And So We Came to Rome": The Political Perspective of St. Luke.* SNTSMS 49. Cambridge.
White, L. M. 1990. *Building God's House: Aspects of Architectural Adaptation Among Pagans, Jews, and Christians.* Baltimore.

J. ANDREW OVERMAN
WILLIAM SCOTT GREEN

PALESTINIAN JUDAISM

Judaism emerged in Palestine during the period following the return from Babylonian exile in 538 B.C.E., and Palestine remained a center of the reigious, cultural, and intellectual development of Judaism for centuries. The chronology of Judaism's development in Palestine can be broadly outlined. The textual sources for emerging and developing Judaism can be categorized by type. And the major issues which united and divided Jews in this period can be examined as evidence of the unity and diversity of Palestinian Judaism.

A. Chronology
1. Where to Begin
2. Where to End
3. Some Important Midpoints
B. Nature of the Extant Sources
1. Individually Authored Writings
2. Writings of an Identifiable Group
3. Pseudepigraphic Writings
4. Rabbinic Writings
5. Nonliterary Sources and Non-Jewish Writings
C. Issues Which United and Divided
1. The Temple and Its Priesthood
2. Scripture and Its Interpretation
3. Foreign Domination and Its Termination

A. Chronology

1. Where to Begin. While the idea of "Judaism" as denoting the way of life of the Jewish people or a portion thereof is *traditionally* traced back to the revelation of the Torah to the Israelites at Mt. Sinai in the time of Moses, historically it can be traced back only to the period following the return from the Babylonian Exile in 538 B.C.E., commonly referred to as the Second Temple period. While the Gk term *ioudaioi* for Jews (rather than simply Judeans) is first attested in inscriptions from the 3d century B.C. in Ptolemaic Egypt, the Gk term *ioudaïsmos,* from which the English "Judaism" derives and for which there is no ancient Hebrew or Aramaic equivalent, is not attested until the 2d century B.C.E. Then it first appears in the context of recounting the struggle, internal as well as external, between Judaism and Hellenism during the Maccabean Revolt of 167–164 (2 Macc 2:21; 8:1; 14:38). Although the history of Judaism is very much rooted in the Hebrew Bible, it is neither synonymous nor simply continuous with that text. Rather, the matrix of beliefs, practices, and institutions that comes to define the subsequent history of Judaism in all its diversity may be said first to take recognizable shape in the context and as a consequence of the extended and complex encounter between Israelite society and the broader international cultural matrix we call Hellenism.

That encounter was to have a deep impact on virtually every aspect of Israelite society and culture, albeit to varying extents in different locations and at different socioeconomic strata. Its beginnings may be dated roughly to the conquest by Alexander the Great in 331 B.C.E. of Palestine and the surrounding Mediterranean lands in which Israelite diasporan communities were already found or soon to be established. That historical juncture, more simply denoted as the beginning of the 3d century B.C.E., marks therefore the opening bracket of the present survey, even though the preceding period will be regarded as its backdrop.

2. Where to End. The concluding historical bracket for present purposes is more difficult to determine. Postbiblical Judaism was not consolidated, in relative terms to be sure, until the emergence of the rabbinic movement as the dominant religious force in Jewish society in the centuries following the destruction of the Second Temple in 70 C.E. That process of transformation had roots in the period preceding the destruction and was accelerated as one of its consequences; but it only comes to literary expression in the 3d century C.E., starting at the beginning of that century with the "publication" by Rabbi Judah the Patriarch of the Mishnah, a pedagogic digest of rabbinic rules *(halakhah)* accompanied at times by exemplifying narratives *(aggadah).* While both those rules and narratives may derive from the actual teachings and deeds of sages of the preceding centuries, in their present rhetorical refiguration they attest most directly to the social and intellectual agenda of the early 3d century patriarchate in its program of solidifying the rabbinic class and extending its influence into the larger Jewish society of Palestine. To a lesser extent, they attest to the Jewish diaspora, notwithstanding resistance from within and without rabbinic circles.

The ancillary, less-tightly structured Tosephta, or supplement, to the Mishnah not only gives us a sense of the Mishnah's high degree of rhetorical redaction, but also of the extent to which its succinct laws and narratives required the amplification of interpretation. In other words, most of what we think we know of the lives and teachings of the mishnaic sages known as the *tanna'im* (first 2 centuries C.E.) has been filtered through the works of the post-mishnaic *amora'im* (3d through 4th centuries C.E. in Palestine). The same can be said for the other major rabbinic constructions of the 3d century, those being the earliest collections of rabbinic scriptural commentary or midrash (the Mekiltas, the Sifra, and the Sifres); while incorporating traditional raw materials with long prehistories, they configure them according to the pedagogical plans and purposes of those 3d-century documents.

We therefore have virtually no internal or external direct witnesses to Judaism of Palestine between the year 90 C.E. and the early 3d century (the major exception being the letters and other archaeological finds associated with the rebel leader Bar Kokhba/Kosiba from around 132–135 C.E.). If we wish to look critically at post-Temple Judaism we must extend our sights into the early and mid 3d century C.E., from whence our first literary evidence derives. It is also then that the important institution of the synagogue, having had a history extending at least as far back as the 3d century B.C.E. (but in Ptolemaic Egypt), now emerges into clear archaeological view on Palestinian soil. But there is another reason for including the 3d century within our historical brackets, and that has to do with the ascension of Christianity in the late 3d and especially early 4th centuries, boosted by its new toleration, then advocation, by the Roman empire initiated by the Emperor Constantine (d. 337). For it is around then that Palestinian Judaism's continuing transformation has to be seen no longer mainly in terms of its encounter with the high culture of pagan Hellenism (first Greek and then Roman), but in its encounter with an increasingly self-confident and assertive Hellenistic Christianity—which had appropriated for its own elect self-understanding the very symbols and scriptures that Judaism had once thought were its alone.

3. Some Important Midpoints. If the 3d century B.C.E. marks the beginnings of an intensive encounter between Judaism and Hellenism, and the 3d century C.E. marks a relative solidification of that transformation as it prepared to face a new (and in many ways more serious) challenge, then this crucial 600-year period in the history of Judaism may be divided virtually in half by the destruction of the Jerusalem Temple by Rome in 70 C.E. Before that date, the many varieties of Judaism defined themselves, whether positively or negatively, in relation to the paramountcy—religious, social, and political—of the Temple. After that date, the single variety of Judaism that eventually survived the Temple's loss did so in part by providing compelling alternatives to its priestly functions and functionaries, even while preserving the symbolic power of its memory in new or refigured forms of religious enactment. Once again, notwithstanding rabbinic Judaism's important roots in and similarities to at least some varieties of late Second Temple Judaism, it is neither synonymous nor simply continuous with any of them.

Finally, two other watershed events, already mentioned, subdivide the two halves of our story, with each event centering on the Jerusalem Temple, in the first instance as a presence to be contested and in the second as an absence to be restored: the Maccabean Revolt in 167–164 B.C.E. and the Bar Kokhba Revolt of 132–35 C.E. The Maccabean Revolt can be seen with hindsight as a successful struggle to prevent the complete Hellenization, voluntarily from within and under compulsion from without, of Judaism as centered in the Temple and its city of Jerusalem. However, the revolt's larger goals of a complete end to foreign domination and the restoration of Israelite sovereignty were only briefly to be achieved; they were frustrated by Rome's conquest of Palestine in 63 B.C.E., when the Hasmonean descendants of the Maccabees were effectively removed from power and replaced by Rome with the Idumaean Herod and his incompetent and insensitive Roman successors. But the hopes engendered by the Maccabean Revolt of a complete national and religious redemption yet to come remained very much alive, albeit in a variety of forms, contributing to the sequence of events that led to the Great Revolt against Rome in 66–74 C.E.

The Bar Kokhba revolt, some 60 years later, can be seen not only as a military failure to restore the ravaged Temple and its city to their former states of glory. More important, it was a shocking repudiation of the very hope that an end to the present order of foreign domination could be expected soon or could be hastened by human acts on the political plane of history. The tragic consequences of the Bar Kokhba revolt were to be a major contributing factor in the full-fledged emergence of rabbinic Judaism, both socially and literarily, during the next century.

B. Nature of the Extant Sources

Our ability to describe ancient Judaism of Palestine, both in its overall character and in its more specific varieties, is severely hampered by the nature of our ancient sources. The difficulties of using rabbinic writings, the earliest of which can be dated in the 3d century C.E., to reconstruct the history of Judaism in the period of the Second Temple have already been noted. In the Second Temple period itself, there is a rich abundance of Jewish sources of diverse types and from a variety of socioreligious perspectives, yet these do not make historical reconstructions less complex: These very differences in perspective produce pictures that are often in discord with one another when they overlap and that leave gaping holes when they do not. These sources are mainly literary and can be divided among 3 types of "authorship": (1) works of named individuals, (2) ideological expressions of an identifiable group, and (3) writings pseudepigraphically attributed to a biblical seer.

1. Individually Authored Writings. In the first category are works by only two known Palestinian Jewish authors: the early 3d century B.C.E. wisdom collection of Yeshua Ben Sira (included in the Apocrypha), and the late 1st century C.E. Jewish history *(Antiquitates Judaicae),* account of the revolt of 70 C.E. *(Bello Judaico),* defense of Judaism *(Contra Apionem),* and autobiography *(Vita)* of Flavius Josephus (37–ca. 100 C.E.). Josephus, although he lived most of his life in Palestine, produced all of his works in Rome, in part under Roman patronage and largely as apologia, whether for Rome's conduct in the war, for his own conduct in the same, or for Judaism against pagan vilification.

These two writers, while having lived in very different times and having produced very different types of writings, had much in common: They were both members of a priestly, aristocratic, significantly Hellenized, and politically active Jewish intelligentsia, and considered themselves to have been divinely inspired mediators of Israel's scriptures, teachings, and history to their respective times of transition. Ben Sira gives a firsthand view of Hellenized scribal wisdom during the seeming calm before the Maccabean storm. Josephus provides the sole continuous narrative history of postbiblical Judaism, drawing upon extensive Jewish and Roman sources as well as personal experience. In seeking to extend the story of Israel from its biblical beginnings into his own stormy time, Josephus draws his models from the conventions of non-Jewish Greco-Roman historiography. In the course, however, he provides extensive descriptions of the major varieties of Judaism of the period between the Maccabean Revolt and the destruction of the Temple.

For both Ben Sira and Josephus, it is difficult to determine to what extent their writings are broadly representative of Jewish society and culture of their times, or to what degree they are limited by the skewed vantage of their particular personal, political, or social circumstances. For example, when Ben Sira (38:24–39:11) provides a glowing encomium to the sagely Jewish scribe (our only such ancient description) as one who is financially independent enough to devote himself to piety, learning, worldliness, and political influence, is he describing himself; the scribal class of his time; or some ideal type? Similarly, given Ben Sira's strong priestly proclivities, are we to assume a close if not inseparable link between Jewish scribalism and the priesthood in his time or only in himself?

Likewise with respect to Josephus, on whom modern historians are so dependent in reconstructing so many aspects of Jewish history and Judaism of late Second Temple times: To what extent are his schematic portrayals of Judaism's 3 or 4 "philosophies" or "schools" *(hairēseis),* as he calls them (*JW* 2.119–66; *Ant* 13.171–73; 18:11–25; *Life* 10–12), colored by his desire to present Judaism in philosophical terms attractive to a Hellenized audience (whether Jewish or non-Jewish)? Does he wish to suggest apologetically that all of the respectable Greco-Roman philosophical currents of his time can be found among this one people, or to argue polemically on behalf of one of those philosophies, namely the Pharisees, as the most attractive and responsible occupiers of the moderate middle way? Similarly, to what extent may Josephus' portrayals of the various Jewish nationalist insurrectionists of the 1st century C.E.—groups for whom we have hardly any other sources—be taken at face value? This applies especially to those involved in the revolt of 70 C.E. To what extent should Josephus' views be tempered in light of his desire to remove blame for the failed revolt and its disastrous consequences from Rome, from the Jews as a whole, or from himself, and place it squarely on these irrational hotheads?

2. Writings of an Identifiable Group. If in the first category there are only two named Jewish individuals whose works have been preserved, in the second category there is only one Second Temple Jewish group whose own writings have survived. That is the community at Qumran, usually identified with, or at least thought to be a part of, the Essene movement, long known secondarily from ancient sources (Josephus, Philo of Alexandria, and Pliny), but whose own writings, included among the Dead Sea Scrolls, have only recently come to the light of scholarship and publication. Which of these scrolls are the product of, and therefore directly reflective of, this community, its history, practices, and ideology, and which were simply preserved in their library, the products of different times or groups? Turning to these scrolls for which there is a consensus that they are indeed "sectarian," to what extent are their representations of the past events and present practices of the Qumran community to be trusted, and to what extent are they idealized or stylized projections either from present self-understandings to past origins, or from future expectations to present circumstances?

The difficulties in employing the specifically "sectarian" Dead Sea Scrolls for historiographic purposes apply not only to our reconstruction of the Judaism of the Qumran community itself and its satellite "camps," but also to our understanding of Second Temple Judaism more generally. Since the Qumran community is the *only* Second Temple group from which we have substantial firsthand data, it is tempting (indeed often necessary) to extrapolate from it to other varieties of ancient Judaism, or to the overall character of Jewish life and institutions, about which we have much less direct evidence. Yet given the highly rhetorical and introverted nature of these writings, such extrapolation poses great difficulties. To what extent should we presume that this group defines the nature of Jewish "sectarianism" more generally? For example, might we surmise that other such groups (Pharisees and early followers of Jesus) were similarly organized or similarly viewed themselves in absolute distinction from those outside their community and from the institutions centered in the Temple? To what extent can we use these scrolls' denigrative symbolic allusions to other groups (perhaps the Pharisees and the Sadducees) to inform us of the nature of those groups? To what extent can we infer the nature of "normative" Jewish practice (to the extent that such existed, at least in the Temple and under the influence of its priesthood) from the community's self-defining repudiation of those practices?

3. Pseudepigraphic Writings. The third type of literary sources, of which we have the largest number, are those that are attributed to a venerated biblical authority (e.g., Enoch, Abraham, the 12 patriarchs, Moses, Solomon, Baruch, Daniel, Ezra). Such a pseudepigraphic writing may convey an account of a heavenly vision (apocalypse) or divine revelation which was vouchsafed to a biblical seer, perhaps hinted at but never fully recorded in what came to be considered canonical Scriptures. Or it may convey the concealed final words (testament) of exhortation and prediction of a biblical patriarch to his biological or spiritual progeny. For these works, we know the identities neither of their historical authors nor of their historical communities of "readers." To the extent that some of them were preserved among the Dead Sea Scrolls or at Masada, we can connect them, indirectly at least, with a known group which considered them to be sufficiently consistent with their own self-understandings to warrant their copying and safekeeping.

Like the writings of Ben Sira and Josephus, the many pseudepigraphic writings from the period 300 B.C.E.–100 C.E. were preserved by various Christian churches, who considered their hortatory or predictive messages to be particularly appropriate to *their* own self-understandings, often with the added assistance of editorial glosses or reframings. Aside from the Dead Sea Scrolls, archaeological remains, and the sparse ancient testimonies of Greco-Roman pagans, most extant sources for Second Temple Judaism were preserved because they suited the needs of later Christian churches. Presumably much more was written, perhaps of very different nature from what has survived, but was not preserved because it did not suit the canonical tastes of the post-70 C.E. rabbinic and early Christian "victors."

This is not to deny the immense importance of the extensive pseudepigraphic literature that has survived, but to recall how few pieces of the puzzle of ancient Judaism are available with which to reconstruct its picture. The surviving texts often seem to have been produced by, or at least for, small groups that considered themselves to be part of a covenantal elect, notwithstanding their seeming pariah status vis-à-vis the larger Jewish society and its central institutions. Such groups probably sought and found in these pseudepigraphic writings confirmation of their socioreligious self-understandings in terms of a formerly revealed but presently concealed larger divine plan, both moral and historical, whose realization, often thought to be imminent, would redress the present imbalance of power and vindicate their readers' sufferings. The specific literary conceits of such texts were part of their rhetorical message: Their privileged readers could experience being exhorted by ancient covenantal patriarchs and seers, or could gain visionary access to a heavenly, undefiled holy realm, in either case fortifying through the experience of such knowledge their elect self-understandings in the midst of discordant historical circumstances.

But who were such groups? How large or widespread might they have been? What would have been their socioreligious profiles? Might they together have constituted a movement, or should they be differentiated more precisely one from the other? How might they have been related to named groups or individuals known to us from other sources? Or might we be mistaken in thinking in terms of coherent groups at all? Do these writings denote the mood of the time, or reactions to it?

4. Rabbinic Writings. Having previously noted the difficulties of employing rabbinic texts, all edited in their present forms no earlier than the early 3d century C.E., for reconstructing pre-70 C.E. Judaism, let us now stress that even for the period after 90 C.E., for which historiography is largely dependent on rabbinic sources, their historiographic employment is still fraught with problems. Like the Dead Sea Scrolls (from which rabbinic texts obviously differ in many significant ways), we are dealing with a collective, intramural literature that is not the simple product of a single author. Rabbinic texts sometimes explicitly and otherwise implicitly claim to be transmitting an ancestral heritage that goes back ultimately to the revelation at Sinai. However, they are also texts that subtly yet radically transform received traditions so as to attune them rhetorically to the rabbinic movement's program of training new disciples and socializing them through the very dialectic of their Torah studies into a cohesive class which would be confident in its self-understanding as Israel's divinely authorized teachers, judges, and leaders. In so doing, 3d century rabbinic texts may be expected to project such self-empowering rabbinic self-images back—not only onto their considered biblical antecedents, but also onto the rabbinic founding figures (e.g., Hillel, Rabban Yoḥanan Ben Zakkai, Rabbi Akiba) of earlier generations. Notwithstanding this primary, introverted nature and function of early rabbinic texts, they emerge at precisely the time when the rabbinic class itself emerges as a major force in broader Jewish society, largely through the strengthening of the Patriarchate under Judah the Patriarch at the beginning of the 3d century C.E. Under the leadership of Judah and his successors, the newly expanded and solidified class of sages sought to position themselves so as to transform Israel's practices, institutions, and self-understandings along rabbinic lines.

Thus, there are two intertwined transformations underway that not only are reflected in the earliest rabbinic texts but to which those texts discursively contribute: the transformation of rabbinic society itself and that of its relation with Jewish society more broadly. For this reason, both legal (halakhic) and narrative (aggadic) texts cannot be assumed to be representational of their own historical settings, whether rabbinic or extra-rabbinic, in any simple way. For example, we cannot assume that stories about rabbinic sages happened as told; or that rabbinic rules were broadly normative at the time of their formulation. Rather, such rabbinic representations have to be evaluated in complex relation to the rhetorical nature of their discursive contexts, and wherever possible to the sparse but significant contemporary evidence of extra-rabbinical sources. Only by such critical analysis can historians understand the relation of these texts to the sociohistorical contexts and emerging religious system of which they are to some extent symptomatic, and which they are yet in the process of transforming.

5. Nonliterary Sources and Non-Jewish Writings. The above concentration on Jewish literary sources should not be taken to minimize the importance of our nonliterary sources for Judaism of Palestine of the same period. For the most part, however, nonliterary sources from this period must also be interpreted before they can be employed, and it is usually necessary to interpret them in relation to our known literary sources. Often the pictures derived from nonliterary sources enable us to complement or supplement those derived from literary sources, but just as often they force us to reconsider our accustomed ways of reading and interpreting those literary sources.

For the late Second Temple period, recent nonliterary discoveries of particular significance derive from excavations along the W and S walls of the Jerusalem Temple, from the discovery of Herodian priestly villas nearby, from the Qumran encampment, and from Herod's fortress and palace and the remains of Masada. From the period between the fall of the Temple and the 3d century C.E. there is very little archaeological evidence, except for the important letters, writs, coins, and other finds from the so-called Bar Kokhba caves of Wadi Murabbaʿat and Naḥal Ḥever. In the 3d century this relative archaeological silence comes to an end with the proliferation of Galilean synagogue remains, coinciding with the emergence of rabbinic literature. Also significant for the period of rabbinic emergence are the archaeological remains of the catacombs at Beth Shearim, and more recently those of the urban centers of Caesarea, Sepphoris, and Beth Shean (Scythopolis). Another important ancillary source, but once again literary, are the scattered references to Jews and Judaism in non-Jewish Greek and Latin writers, both Christian and pagan, although most of these derive from outside of Palestine.

C. Issues Which United and Divided

In light of the above, it is impossible to paint a single picture of Judaism in Palestine in late antiquity. Our sources, for the most part rhetorically written from some partisan position or another, do not permit a simple description of what Jews in general (the man or woman "in the street") of that time believed or practiced. Those common characteristics of Judaism which from an "outside" perspective may be said (and were said) to have distinguished the Jews as a group from the surrounding Greco-Roman cultures and religions (e.g., Sabbath and festival observances, Temple rites, dietary and purity rules, sexual modesty), when viewed from an "inside" perspective may be said to have been precisely the issues which deeply divided the Jews (and hence Judaism) of antiquity. Rather than smoothing over these differences and divisions in order to obtain some composite picture of how ancient Judaism might have looked from an undifferentiating distance, it is preferable to delineate those issues which define both the common concerns and the differing responses that repeatedly recur in our extant sources in all of their diversity of perspective. For the sake of convenience, they may be grouped under three headings.

1. The Temple and Its Priesthood. At the center of Judaism of the Second Temple period was the Jerusalem Temple itself, rebuilt after the destruction of 586 B.C.E. in 515 B.C.E. But this rebuilt Temple was not simply a restoration of what had previously been. Sacrificial worship was now for the first time centralized in one place, even though there were those who thought that cultic centralization need not preclude the establishment of sites of worship and the application of purity strictures elsewhere in Israel. The centralization of sacrificial worship in Second Temple times was in part due to the strictures of the book of Deuteronomy, newly incorporated into a Torah canon, and in part due to the desire of the ruling Persian empire and its successors to locate local political and religious authority in one place and under one leadership, that leadership (with some notable exceptions) having been the Temple's priesthood (see Ezra 1:3–4; 7:13–24). But if the Temple and priesthood benefited from the political and economic backing of the empire, it also functioned at its will. While in covenantal terms the priesthood and their service mediated between God and Israel, maintaining the equilibrium of that tipsy balance, then in Second Temple times they similarly served as mediators between Israel's foreign rulers and its local populace.

Thus, the Temple was now the national center not only of worship, both daily and festival, but also of political and judicial authority—and controversy. It is not surprising therefore that virtually every major conflict, both internal—whether deriving from differences regarding Israel's covenantal duties or from tensions between its socioeconomic strata—and external—between the local populace and its foreign rulers—repeatedly centered on the Temple and its priesthood. Notwithstanding the unifying role of the Temple, to which all Jews were expected to contribute and to which very large numbers flocked for the 3 annual pilgrimage festivals, it was also a source and focus of deep divisions from the very time of its rebuilding. In fact, it may be said that precisely because of its centrality, as the primary national institution and symbol, the Temple was a magnet for national and religious tensions.

From the time of the Maccabean Revolt in particular, Temple-centered tensions intensified: Not all were happy with the Hellenization of its wealthy upper priesthood; not all recognized the genealogical legitimacy of its High Priests; not all considered its practices to be in compliance with proper standards of levitical purity. Some even questioned whether such a Temple, built at the direction of a foreign empire rather than a truly anointed Israelite leader, was a proper divine abode at all. Some participated fully in the Temple services notwithstanding their discontents; others sought to reform it; others attempted to wrest control from the reigning priesthood. Still others declared their alienation and exile from it, developing alternative forms of worship, alternative purity realms and priestly hierarchies, and even alternative routes of access to a heavenly Temple unsullied by the worldly forces of evil and pollution.

The very centralization of religious worship and authority in the Second Temple necessitated, for some at least, the need for decentralized complements (e.g., the synagogue and Pharisaic fellowship) or alternatives (e.g., the Qumran camp), even while the Temple was still standing. But once it was destroyed, the need to create or locate alternative media of worship and atonement, alternative loci for human access to the divine presence, became even more pressing. In short, how would Israel become a "kingdom of Priests and a holy nation" (Exod 19:6) without its priestly, holy center? The rabbinic response to this crisis was not to discredit the destroyed Temple or its priesthood—quite to the contrary, they kept Temple and priesthood symbolically and intellectually alive—but to shift Judaism's primary focus from Temple to Torah and from priests to sages, and to make of Torah study and practice (including the study of priestly matters and the practice of ritual purity) the central religious acts of which they themselves would be the officiants. Rabbinic Judaism, like that of the Qumran community before it (see 1QS 9:3–6; 4QFlor 1:7), viewed Torah deeds as occupying the central religious place once held by the performance of Temple sacrifices. Even without a sanctuary, Israel could sanctify God's name and their collective life through prayer and the study and practice of His Torah (for examples from early rabbinic literature, see Fraade 1990).

2. Scripture and Its Interpretation. The "returnees" from the Babylonian Exile introduced another change that was to be central in defining and dividing Judaism of the Second Temple period: the establishment of the "Torah of Moses" as Israel's commonly held canonical charter around 450 B.C.E. (Nehemiah 8). Again, this was the consequence not only of internal needs: interpreting their Exile and Return in prophetic covenantal terms, the restored Judean community required the establishment of a commonly acknowledged expression of those terms. It was the consequence also of external, imperial dictates. The Persian empire and its successors (with some notable exceptions) sought to rule its subject peoples by allowing them autonomy of local rule under their own laws and legal authorities, to which the empire would lend its authoritative backing in return for payment of taxes and peaceful conduct (see Ezra 7:25–26; and the "Passover Papyrus" from Elephantine).

But the composite and didactic nature of this Torah text, with its many repetitions and gaps, required that it be interpreted and amplified before it could be societally implemented in any systematic way. Most immediately such interpretation was required to set the Temple and its priesthood on their properly functioning courses: the Temple's plan, the sacrificial procedures, the priestly rotations, the cultic-festal calendar, purity strictures, etc. But other areas of Israel's covenantal obligations also needed to be regularized to the extent possible: Sabbath, diet, tithing, marriage and divorce, etc. The authority to interpret and adjudicate Torah law rested with professional scribes closely associated with the priesthood.

Naturally, those groups that questioned the central priesthood's legitimacy or conduct also questioned the authority and interpretations of their allied scribes. They propounded and practiced alternative rules (to them they were not the alternatives but the originals), and would justify their rules through the citation or rephrasing of Scripture. But often they simply claimed that their rules had been divinely conveyed through a prophetic teacher; or through a long-hidden revelatory writing by an ancient biblical seer which they were now privileged to possess, to read, and to follow.

Such disaffected groups would also comment upon, but more often simply "rewrite," biblical narratives, poems, and prophecies in such a way as to justify their self-understandings as the true inheritors of Israel's covenantal code—the central actors in Israel's sacred history. That history they might interpret, not simply as a continuous line from the biblical past to the historical present, but as a prologue to the imminent consummation of history by a reenactment of the primeval cataclysm in which God vanquished the forces of evil and vindicated the persevering righteous few.

How precisely such rewritten scriptures were understood in relation to what came to be considered canonical Scripture is not always clear: Were they complements, supplements, or substitutes? The Qumran community in some writings seems to have distinguished between Scripture and its commentary or interpretation (e.g., the *pesharim,* and the scriptural citations of the Damascus Document), while in others it seems to have substituted rewritten Torah for Torah (e.g., the Temple Scroll). The Pharisees, according to Josephus and the NT, viewed the nonscriptural legal traditions of which they were the self-proclaimed advocates and authorities as the inherited "traditions/laws of the elders/ancestors" (*Ant* 13.297, 408; 17.41; Matt 15:2; Mark 7:3, 5), for which they claimed divine authorization (*Ant* 17.41). Later rabbinic writings, beginning in the 3d century C.E., redrew this distinction as being one between written Torah and oral Torah. *Both* were revealed by God to Moses and Israel at Mt. Sinai, and the two together constituted the complementary totality of revelation: Written Torah was closed and forever immutable, while its oral (rabbinic) amplification was open and forever fluid. Implicit in these differences in approach to Scripture and its supplementation was the question of the continuity of revelation: How and by whom was new knowledge—whether of correct conduct, of the cosmos and humanity's place therein, of divine justice, or of Israel's sacred history—to be revealed? And what was the relation of such newly revealed or discovered knowledge to that which was commonly acknowledged as Israel's Torah?

But another important development, evidenced already in the Dead Sea Scrolls (1QS 6:6–8; 8:12–16), comes to full expression in early rabbinic literature: The very engagement in study, whether of the Torah itself or of its authoritative amplifications, could itself be experienced as a redemptive act of divine service—an enactment of the covenant rather than simply the means toward its fulfillment—and this, ideally at least, for a society as a whole and not just for its scribal virtuosi.

3. Foreign Domination and Its Termination. With the help of the classical prophets, the Babylonian returnees and their descendants interpreted their Exile and Return in positive covenantal terms: God had not only punished Israel for its infidelity, but had demonstrated His own fidelity by employing the Persian king Cyrus to redeem a righteous remnant and reestablish both them and His house in Jerusalem. But these very same prophetic understandings engendered the expectation that foreign rule, like foreign exile, would soon come to an end and Davidic rule be restored (e.g., Amos 9:11; Isa 11:1), thereby completing the redemptive plan whose beginning had been so dramatically experienced. As time dragged on, and as one ruling empire was succeeded by another (Persian, Macedonian, Ptolemaic, Seleucid, and eventually Roman), the question "How much longer?" grew all the more urgent. When prophecies seem to fail, or at least to be delayed, the first response is to reinterpret them. Thus, when the Seleucid Antiochus IV upset the equilibrium of Jewish religious and political autonomy, the consequent tumult had to be placed within the received prophetic scheme: Jeremiah's predicted 70 years between Israel's exile and final vindication (Jer 25:11–14; 29:10) had been divinely decoded as 70 weeks of years for the exilic seer Daniel (Dan 9:24–27) so as to point roughly to the time of the Maccabean Revolt. Then Syrian rule, itself encoded as the final horn of the last of four beasts (Daniel 7), would fall, after which Israel's salvation would immediately follow (for similar calculations see CD 1:3–12; *1 En.* 93:9–10).

Even so, what was to be Israel's role in this divine drama now entering its final act? For those who rejected the Hellenizing reforms forced upon them from within and without, there were essentially two alternatives: armed revolt against the Hellenizers and Syrian forces (emphasized in 1 Maccabees), or passive resistance and martyrdom in the face of their edicts (emphasized in 2 Maccabees). But behind this choice lay a more fundamental question: Was Israel's sacred history totally in divine hands—He alone bringing it to its redemptive end, both employing and terminating foreign rule according to His plan? Or did it require some human assistance—a demonstration of the readiness of Israel's pious to rid themselves of the defiling foreign influences in their midst? The Maccabean Revolt, in the context of the most acute encounter between Judaism and Hellenism, brought this dilemma to its first clear expression. Both responses presumed that *divine* intervention would be required to bring the events to their redemptive consummation; the question was the required *human* role in a sacred history that was rapidly approaching its long-anticipated climax.

But once again that climax was delayed, and its delay became even more irksome with the rule of Rome beginning in 63 B.C.E. Although Rome preserved the rudiments of local autonomy, the disintegration of Hasmonean rule meant that Roman rule pressed harder and closer to home in its administrative and military presence in Palestine, and especially in Jerusalem. And since the Roman emperor was regarded as a deity, the presence of his image on coins, statues, and military standards meant that subservience to Rome added religious insult to political injury. A series of skirmishes and insurrections, beginning under Herod's rule (37–4 B.C.E.) and extending through the period of Roman governors and procurators ensued. These stemmed in part from the incompetency and insensitivity of Roman rulers and their agents, and in part from a growing irritability and impatience of the local population. But also to be figured into the volatile situation were growing internal Jewish socioeconomic and religious cleavages and tensions, which often became interlaced with resentment against Roman rule and anticipation of its end.

Many self-proclaimed prophets, miracle workers, and would-be kings (some examples, about whom we know only from Josephus, being the "sophists" Judas and Matthias, Judah the Galilean who founded the "Fourth Philosophy," and a prophetic miracle worker named Theudas) appeared on the scene; they tapped into such popular anti-Roman sentiments only to be cut down, thereby frustrating the expectations that had been placed in them. One such figure may have been Jesus of Nazareth, whose followers, however, maintained and transformed their faith in him after his crucifixion by Rome.

The ignominy of Roman rule, the unrelenting pressures of socioeconomic cleavage, and the intensification of internal religious conflict led many to reflect upon the nature and origins of evil in a world they had been taught was created and guided by an omnipotent and benevolent God. The Deuteronomic scheme of reward and punishment no longer provided an adequate explanation. The sacrificial immune system was no longer up to the job. More radical diagnoses and cures were sought. For those to whom Rome itself epitomized the very force of evil and darkness which ruled the world and under which they suffered, the elimination of that rule would represent much more than just a political release. Jeremiah's 70 years of Babylonian rule, reinterpreted by Daniel to extend to Syria as the last of the wicked beasts, was now reinterpreted to extend to and hopefully terminate with Rome's rule (*2 Baruch* 38).

Once again three alternatives of human response presented themselves: accommodation, passive resistance, and active revolt. According to Josephus, these three paths were followed respectively by, among others, the Pharisees, the Essenes, and the Zealots. With the cessation of the Temple sacrifices on behalf of the Roman emperor in 66 C.E., the political, socioeconomic, and religious combustibles ignited, both in war with Rome and in equally violent internal fighting, resulting after 4 years in the destruction of the Temple and the ravaging of its city, and after another 4 years in the elimination of the last remaining Jewish resistance at Masada.

Once again, some Jews interpreted the catastrophe as an immediate prelude to the end, which would soon come if only Israel returned to the terms of the Torah *(2 Baruch)*, while others counseled that the righteous should simply sit tight while God's inscrutable plan ran its course *(4 Ezra)*. For yet others, the utter failure of the revolt and the dashing of its engendered expectations, the loss of Israel's atoning center, and the intensification of Roman rule with its consequent economic burdens—these were too much to bear. Some were led to apostasy and others to a dualistic renunciation of this world so as to pursue personal salvation in otherworldly realms.

But for many, the hope for the overthrow of Rome on the plane of history, to be followed by the restoration of Jerusalem, the Temple, and Davidic messianic rule, remained very much alive, albeit temporarily deferred. That deferral seemed to some to be coming to an end in 132, when once again the violation by the Roman emperor Hadrian of Jewish religious and political sensitivities sparked a major Jewish revolt under the religio-military charge of Simon Bar Kokhba (actually, Kosiba, his messianic nom de guerre being an interpretation of Num 24:17), whose leadership and possible early successes were understood in redemptive terms. The disastrous consequences of this failed revolt—the building of a pagan Roman temple on the site of the former Jewish temple, the de-Judaizing of Jerusalem and its surrounding Judea, tremendous loss of life, and severe economic hardship—resulted not only in a major (but by no means complete) population shift to the Galilee. It led also, under eventual rabbinic leadership, to an equally significant shift in attitude toward foreign rule and Israel's human role in history.

The post-Bar Kokhba rabbinic sages despised Rome and what it represented, even as they accommodated to the reality of its rule. If, in biblical terms, Israel was Jacob and Rome was Esau, then their struggle in the womb of history would continue, but as one between competing cultures and not armies. That struggle would eventually end with Jacob succeeding on the heels of Esau, but the time for that succession would be determined by God and not humans.

It was not that Israel had no role to play toward that end, but rather that its role was now conceived to lie on the inner rather than outer plane of history. Its internal life, both social and religious, required a radical restructuring and redirecting in accord with the divine plan of Torah (as rabbinically construed). Even while accommodating to the brute realities of the Roman kingdom, Israel could experience the joys of the heavenly kingdom by attuning its collective life to the laws and narratives of the written Torah as interpreted in the oral. Israel's task now was not to rid itself of Roman rule but to bring its collective life under heavenly rule; not to rebuild the centralized Temple but to fashion and frequent decentralized institutions (such as the synagogue) for worship and the experience of God's transcending presence in the midst of historical exile. While Rome was evil and would eventually be removed, battle needed to be waged more immediately with the inclination to do evil within each person. The weapons necessary for bringing that inner evil under control were to be brandished in the communal life of Torah study and practice. As the Roman empire declined and was Christianized, the terms of the struggle and the hope for its eventual termination remained essentially the same, but with Esau reinterpreted—as Jeremiah's 70 years had once been—to refer now to Christendom.

Bibliography

Avi-Yonah, M. 1976. *The Jews of Palestine.* Oxford.

Cohen, S. J. D. 1987. *From the Maccabees to the Mishnah.* Library of Early Christianity 7. Philadelphia.

Collins, J. J. 1984. *The Apocalyptic Imagination.* New York.

Fraade, S. D. 1990. *From Tradition to Commentary.* Albany.

———. fc. Of Priests, Scribes, and Sages in Second Temple Times. *JBL.*

Hengel, M. 1974. *Judaism and Hellenism.* 2 vols. Philadelphia.

Horsley, R. A., and Hanson, J. S. 1985. *Bandits, Prophets, and Messiahs.* Minneapolis.

Knibb, M. A. 1987. *The Qumran Community.* Cambridge.

Levine, L. I. 1985. *The Rabbinic Class in Palestine during the Talmudic Period.* Jerusalem (in Hebrew).

Levine, L. I., ed. 1987. *The Synagogue in Late Antiquity.* Philadelphia.

Maccoby, H. 1988. *Early Rabbinic Writings.* Cambridge.

Neusner, J. 1981. *Judaism: The Evidence of the Mishnah.* Chicago.

Nickelsburg, G. W. E. 1981. *Jewish Literature Between the Bible and the Mishnah.* Philadelphia.

Smallwood, E. M. 1981. *The Jews Under Roman Rule.* Leiden.

Stern, M. 1976–84. *Greek and Latin Authors on Jews and Judaism.* 3 vols. Jerusalem.

Stone, M. E. 1980. *Scriptures, Sects and Visions.* Philadelphia.

Stone, M. E., ed. 1984. *Jewish Writings of the Second Temple Period.* CRINT 2. Assen and Philadelphia.

Stone, M. E., and Satran, D., ed. 1989. *Emerging Judaism.* Minneapolis.

Steven D. Fraade

JUDAISM IN EGYPT

The connection of the Jews with Egypt goes back into the distant past of the 2d millennium B.C. The memory of the captivity and the Exodus has been central to the Jews throughout the centuries and has contributed much to the identity of the people. Evidence of Jewish settlement in Egypt comes from a later time, however (Davies and Finkelstein *CHJ* 1: 375–76). Emigration took place around 600 B.C., increased by the capture of Jerusalem and the destruction of the First Temple by the Babylonians in 587. Documentation for this emigration is found in Jer 44:11: "The word came to Jeremiah concerning all the Jews that dwelt in the land of Egypt, at Migdol, at Tah'panhes, at Memphis, and in the land of Pathros . . ."

A. Preludes
B. The Hellenistic Period
  1. From Alexander to Ptolemy VI
  2. From Ptolemy VI to the Roman Conquest
C. The Roman Period
D. Status of the Jews

A. Preludes

A series of Aramaic papyri of the 5th century found at Elephantine Island, opposite Aswan in S Egypt, has revealed that there was a military colony of Jews on the island (Davies and Finkelstein *CHJ* 1: 376–400; Sayce and Cowley 1906; Sachau 1911; Porten 1986). They had a temple with pillars of stone and 5 stone gateways. There was an altar for sacrifices to their god Yahu. In addition there are other gods, such as Anath and Bethel. Thus, the religion of these Jews tended to be syncretistic, such as presupposed by Jeremiah in the word of God addressed against the Egyptian Jews: "Why do you provoke me to anger with the works of your hands, turning incense to other gods in the land of Egypt" (44:8). The temple at Elephantine existed before the Persian king Cambyses invaded Egypt in 525 B.C.

An order issued by the authority of Darius II in 419 B.C. instructs the colony to celebrate the Feast of Unleavened Bread and probably the Passover. There are also probably references on the ostraca found to the Day of Preparation and the Sabbath. The relations between these Jews and their neighbors worsened, and in the year 410 B.C. the priest of the Egyptian god Khnum, the patron god of Elephantine, with the aid of the local Persian commander, Waidrang, stirred up the Egyptians to attack the Jews, destroy their temple, and stop all sacrifice. The Jews wrote to Bagohi, the Persian governor of Judea, and to others, such as the high priest in Jerusalem, Joḥanan. Another copy went to the Samarian governor's two sons, Delaiah and Shelemiah. In these letters they tried to enlist support for the restoration of the temple. The authorization was given that the "altar house of the God of Heaven" should be rebuilt so that "the meal-offering and incense" may again be offered. Thus no permission of animal sacrifices was given.

In 404 B.C., Egypt revolted against the Persians and won independence. A letter reporting the accession of the Egyptian King Nepherites, written in 399 B.C., is the latest dated document. The earliest dated document was written in 495 B.C. Thus these papyri give direct information covering about a century of the life of this Jewish community, which was founded at an even earlier date.

The Jews were organized as a combined temple community and a sociomilitary community. As members of the military garrison the Jews served together with non-Jews in the same detachment, but the leaders were non-Jews, Persian, and other nationals. The governor and the garrison commander exercised both civil-judicial and military functions. These seem to have been Persian, and so also the police. A person with a Hebrew name was 'Anani the Scribe (and) chancellor at the court of satrap Arsames in Memphis. Although the leaders at Elephantine seem to have been non-Jews, the garrison as such must have been predominantly Jewish, since it was known as "the Jewish force." The Jews had their own priests and other leaders who represented them. One of the leaders had the name of Jedaniah, who was in charge of the communal archives and the temple treasures. Intermarriage with non-Jews is documented, and there was also participation in Jewish observance on the Sabbath by non-Jews who either had become proselytes or were active symphathizers.

The existence of the Jewish temple at Elephantine in Egypt, as well as the Samaritan temple on Mount Gerizim, the temple at Araq el-Emir in Transjordan, and Onias' temple at Leontopolis in Egypt show that the Deuteronomic program of centralized and exclusive worship in the Jerusalem temple was not put into effect among Jews everywhere. The temple and the Jewish military colony at Elephantine testify to a rich variety within Jewish religion and life at the time of Ezra and Nehemiah. Its origin has been connected with the statement in the *Letter of Aristeas* that Jews went as auxiliaries to fight in the army of the Egyptian king Psammetichus against the king of the Ethiopians. The ruler referred to is probably Psammetichus I, who largely relied on foreign mercenaries in his fight for uniting Egypt as an independent kingdom. Some of the Jews who took part in the campaign against the Ethiopians might then have been stationed at Elephantine.

No corresponding line can be drawn of the history of the Elephantine Jewish community after the latest datable document from 399 B.C. No traceable evidence for its continued existence has been found. The community might have been removed from the island. In any case, it disappears from the scene of history.

B. The Hellenistic Period

1. From Alexander to Ptolemy VI (332–181 B.C.). The history of the Jews under Macedonian/Ptolemaic rule falls into two sub-periods, the reign of Ptolemy VI Philometor serving as a dividing line. During the period before the reign of Ptolemy VI Philometor (181–45 B.C.) the Jews settled in towns and in the country and gradually grew in sufficient number to form communities of their own within the general structure of the Ptolemaic society. The period from the beginning of Ptolemy VI Philometor until the Roman conquest (181–30 B.C.) was the time in which the Jews in Egypt fully flourished (*CPJ* 1: 189).

As background, the general political context needs be sketched. Alexander the Great conquered Egypt in 332 B.C., and after his death in 323 B.C. his senior generals, the Diadochi, formed a collective group of rulers. One of the generals, Ptolemy, was satrap of Egypt. When the collective leadership broke up, the empire was divided into 3 main parts: the kingdom of Antigonid Macedonia, the Seleucid kingdom in W Asia, and the Ptolemaic kingdom in Egypt.

Ptolemy I, called Soter, managed to defend his position in Egypt and founded the Ptolemaic dynasty. Egypt became an independent "Macedonian" kingdom, engaged in hard struggle to maintain its independence and to play a leading role in the affairs of the Hellenistic world. Alexandria, the city founded by Alexander, became the capital, and from this N center of Egypt, in close approximity to the other centers of Greek civilization, the Ptolemies ruled over the long and narrow country created by the river Nile. Since the native Egyptians regarded the Ptolemies as an alien government—in spite of all the Egyptian traditions taken over by these rulers—the Ptolemies employed Macedonians, Greeks, and people from other non-Egyptian nations in their administration and army. Moreover, many prisoners of war from various nations were brought to Egypt as slaves (Rostovtzeff 1941, 1: 1–43, 255–422).

In the Seleucid realm, a decentralized administrative system prevailed, built on a reorganization of the old Persian satrapies. The government of Ptolemaic Egypt, on the other hand, became a highly centralized and more ruthlessly efficient version of the ancient Pharaonic system. This reorganization took mainly place during Ptolemy I Soter ([323] 304–284 B.C.) and Ptolemy II Philadelphus (284–246 B.C.). The whole land was the personal possession, the "house," of the king. The first man in the state beside the king was the *dioketes,* who bore responsibility for the entire possessions and income of the king. Egypt had of old been divided into *nomes,* and these into *toparchies.* The local administrative unit was the village. The chief officials were the military *strategos,* and the *oikonomos* for economic matters. The leading officials were usually Greeks and Macedonians (Hengel 1974: 1.18–9).

The encounter of the Jews with Hellenistic Egypt, therefore, took place within the framework of the Ptolemies' military and economic expansions. According to Josephus (*JW* 2 §487; *AgAp* 2 §35) Alexander the Great gave the Jews permission to settle in Alexandria on a basis of equal rights with the Greeks. They received this favor from

Alexander in return for their loyalty to him. Josephus' reports on this do not appear to be credible. They have a clear apologetic motive, and seem to be composed with the aim of ascribing the privileges accorded the Jews of Alexandria to Alexander the Great himself. Josephus' statement about the equal rights of Jews and the Greek full citizens of Alexandria is very much debated in recent research (Tcherikover 1966: 272; Kasher 1985: 2; *CPJ* 1, 1957: 1–3).

Josephus has more reliable information on the immigration of Jews from Palestine to Egypt during the interim period of Alexander's successors, the Diadochi (323–301 B.C.). Ptolemy I Soter conquered Palestine for the first time in 320 B.C.; he conquered it again in 312 B.C., 302 B.C., and finally in 301 B.C. It is probable that in the course of these wars numerous Jewish prisoners were taken into Egypt, as also is told in the *Letter of Aristeas* (12–14). According to Aristeas (12–27, 37), 100,000 Jewish captives were brought to Egypt, of whom 30,000 were placed in fortresses, and the rest, i.e., old men and children, Ptolemy gave to his soldiers as slaves. Ptolemy II Philadelphus (284–246 B.C.) gave amnesty and freedom to the slaves.

Some Jews seemed to follow Ptolemy I voluntarily, as exemplified by the high priest Hezekiah and some of his friends who followed him. Josephus, drawing on material from Hecataeus of Abdera, tells that Hezekiah and the other Jews following the battle of Gaza, 312 B.C., received in writing the conditions attaching to their settlement and political status, and emmigrated (*AgAp* 1 §186–89). The historical value of Josephus' report is disputed among scholars. Recent research has shown, however, that the sections in Josephus, *AgAp* 1 §183–204, do not render material from a Jewish forger but information derived from the work of the authentic Hecataeus, a contemporarian of Alexander and Ptolemy I (Kasher 1985: 2–3; Tcherikover 1966: 272–73 and 426–27). In another passage Josephus (*AgAp* 1 §194) reports that after Alexander's death myriads of Jews migrated to Egypt and Phoenicia in consequence of the disturbed condition of Syria.

The Jews settled all over Egypt, in the towns and in the country. Although living in Egypt, their ties with Jerusalem and Palestine remained strong and communication was made the easier by the fact that for about 100 years (301–198 B.C.) Palestine was one of the Ptolemies' foreign possessions.

Some places, such as in Migdol, Tahpanhes, Noph/Memphis, and the land of Pathros (i.e. the S country) were inhabited by Jews already from the time of the prophet Jeremiah (Jer 44:1). The settlement in various places in Lower Egypt is attested by inscriptions, some of which come from the 3d century. Numerous papyri from the middle of the 3d century and later, give evidence of Jewish population in the villages and towns of the Fayûm (*CPJ* 1: 3). The evidence for Jewish presence in Upper Egypt during the 3d century is meager. The existence of a Jewish community at Elephantine in Upper Egypt until about 400 B.C., Jeremiah's reference to the land of Pathros, and the attestation of ostraca of Jewish settlements in the 2d century B.C. indicate that some Jews lived also in that part of the country during the 3d century B.C. This conclusion is supported by evidence for the existence of a synagogue in Upper Egypt already in the 3d century B.C. (*CPJ* 1: 3–4.8).

Besides this synagogue at an unknown place in Upper Egypt, 3d century synagogues are known to have existed in Schedia, Crocodilopolis-Arsinoe, and Alexandrou-Nesos. Since the synagogues were centers of Jewish religious, political, and cultural life, the reference to a synagogue indicates that there was an organized Jewish community at that place.

The inscription at Schedia (Kafr ed Dauwar, 20 km SE of Alexandria) contains the dedication of a synagogue: "in honor of King Ptolemy and Queen Berenice his sister and wife and their children, the Jews built the *proseuche*." A similar inscription has been found in Crocodilopolis-Arsinoe, the main city, the metropolis, of the Fayûm district (about 100 km S of Cairo): "in honor of King Ptolemy, son of Ptolemy and Queen Berenice, his wife and sister and their children, the Jews in Crocodilopolis (dedicated) the *proseuche*." In Alexandou-Nesos, another town in the Fayûm district, a juridical papyri dated 218 B.C., contains a petition of an unnamed woman, complaining that a local Jew, Dorotheos, had stolen her cloak. She reports that Dorotheos fled to the synagogue holding the cloak. By the intervention of a person by the name of Lezelmis the cloak was deposited with the synagogue verger, Nikomachos, to keep till the case was tried (*CPJ* 1: 8, 239–41; *CPJ* 3: 141, 164; Kasher 1985: 138, 144–46).

What was the nature of these communities? The dedication of the synagogues to the king show that the Jewish communities recognized the king and were recognized by him. The dedications are on behalf of the reigning sovereign in the same way as are the pagan dedications, but direct ruler worship was avoided by the Jews (Fraser 1972, 1: 226–27, 282–83, 298–99, cf. Philo, *Gaium* 137–38, 141–42, 356–57; Jos. *Ant* 12 §67; Kasher 1985: 30, 257, n. 92). The recognition of the synagogue by the king implied that he had given the Jews a legal status as a community, most probably in the form of a *politeuma*.

The settlers from various ethnic groups were in many places organized as such *politeumata*. Such communities in Egypt were the politeumata of Idumaeans, Phrygians, Cretans, Lycians, Cilicians, and Boeotians. The legal status of such a *politeuma* has not been clarified at every point, but basically it was the confirmation by the king that an ethnic community was permitted—within limits—to live in accordance with its ancestral laws. In the case of the Jews, this meant the right to live according to the Laws of Moses (*CPJ* 1: 6–8; Tcherikover 1966: 299–301; Kasher 1985: 30, 41). It is probable that the high priest Hezekiah, who joined Ptolemy in 312 B.C., received the charter of such a *politeuma*, an event which Josephus cited Hecataeus as relating: that Ptolemy I gathered Jews who were prepared to follow him to Egypt and read to them a document: "For he possessed (the conditions) of their settlement and their political constitution (drawn up) in writing" (*AgAp* 1 §189). A variant of the formula 'to live according to their ancestral laws' was also used by the Seleucid King Antiochus III on the occasion of his conquest of Jerusalem in 198 B.C. (*CPJ* 1: 7 and note 19; *Ant* 12 §142). Moreover, in the *Letter of Aristeas* 310 the Jewish community of Alexandria is called *politeuma*.

The largest Jewish community in Egypt was this one in Alexandria. The first authentic evidence of the presence of Jews in Alexandria is given by Aramaic and Greek inscriptions from the necropolis of Ibrahamiya in the environs of the town, probably of the reign of Ptolemy I or II (*CPJ* 1: 3, n. 8 and *CPJ* 3: 138–39). The Alexandrian literature, especially the translation of the Bible into Greek, testifies to the strength and vitality of the Jewish community of Alexandria already from the 3d century B.C.

The main occupations for the Jews in Egypt were military service and agriculture. Although the Ptolemies identified themselves with Pharaonic and other Egyptian traditions, they were aliens among the native Egyptians. As noted earlier, they depended therefore upon Macedonian and other non-Egyptian military personnel for their power. Accordingly numerous Jews served in the army as soldiers on duty or as soldiers of the reserves. To lessen the cost of maintaining an army, and to make the military forces identify themselves with the government, the Ptolemies adopted the policy of settling large number of soldiers in special military colonies, where in return for a plot of farmland they were obliged to return to active service upon call. This plot of land was liable to be withdrawn and restored to the king's possession, yet, in the process of time, it became gradually a permanent possession and could as such be inherited by the leaseholder's (the *cleruch's*) children. The terms used to designate such a military colony was *katoikiai* or *cleruchies*. (*CPJ* 1: 11–15).

There is no evidence for self-contained Jewish military units in the 3d century B.C. Josephus (JW 2 §487) reports that Alexandrian Jews were permitted to take the title of Macedonians, which probably meant that some Jews served in the Macedonian unit. The possibility should not be excluded, however, that there were separate Jewish units or sub-units at places where the Jews were numerous enough to form fairly large communities, such as in the Fayûm. (Kasher 1985: 40–48). Some Jews served as officers, such as Eleazar, son of Nicolaus, who, according to an inscription at the Fayûm, served as *hegemon*. This term generally designated a high officer next in the rank to the *strategos* (*CPJ* 3: 163; Kasher 1985: 46).

The other main occupation for Jews in the 3d century B.C. was agriculture. Having received allotments from the king, many soldiers were at the same time farmers. Other Jews were lease-holders, "king's peasants," field hands, vine-dressers, shepherds, and so on. Jews also held positions in the police and in the governmental administration. A renegade Jew, Dositheos, son of Drimylos, served as one of the 2 heads of the royal secretariate; later he was called to the highest priestly office in Egypt—that of being priest in the ruler-cult as the eponymous priest of Alexander and the deified Ptolemies. He served during the reigns of Ptolemy III Euergetes I (246–21 B.C.) and Ptolemy IV Philopator (221–204 B.C.), (*CPJ* 1: 230–36; Kasher 1985: 60).

As the Jews penetrated into Ptolemaic Egypt, Hebrew and Aramaic gradually ceased to serve as spoken and literary languages, especially in Alexandria, but also increasingly in other parts of Egypt, as seen from inscriptions and papyri written in Greek. Since the Jewish communities within limits were permitted to follow the ancestral laws, the knowledge of the laws of Moses was a fundamental need for the Jews themselves, and to a varying degree also for their sovereigns and employers, the different levels of the Ptolemaic administration (cf. Kasher 1985: 5; *CPJ* 1: 31; Tcherikover 1966: 348).

The Gk translation of the Hebrew Bible, the Septuagint (the Translation of the Seventy), probably was initiated during the reign of Ptolemy II Philadelphus (284–246 B.C.) and was (with the exception of the book of Daniel) completed towards the mid-2d century B.C. The Greek spoken and written by the Jews reflected their background. The Septuagint (LXX) contains many Hebraisms; and a learned Greek, Cleomedes, gibes at the rude folk dialect used in the synagogues. The translators to some extent modified the Hebrew text, at times drawing on some of the current exegetical traditions (*CPJ* 1: 30–32; Tcherikover 1966: 348; Fraser 1972, 1: 689–90). The legendary story about the translation as recorded in the *Letter of Aristeas* is discussed below.

The LXX served as basis for the Jewish Alexandrian literature. The pieces preserved of this literature from the 3d century are largely found in Eusebius, *Preparatio Evangelica*. Eusebius had 5 fragments of Demetrius, and Clement of Alexandria preserves still another fragment. Demetrius wrote in the 3d century B.C. under Ptolemy IV Philopator (221–204 B.C.), probably in Alexandria. His work was apparently called *On the Kings of Judaea*. The fragments mainly concerned the patriarchal history of the LXX Pentateuch and were probably part of the preface to an account of the Judaean monarchy. He formulates the biblical history in the form of Greek chronological historiography, corresponding to the chronological presentation of Egyptian history by the Egyptian priest Manetho, who also lived in the 3d century B.C. The goal which Demetrius and Manetho had in common was to demonstrate the considerable age of the respective national traditions (Hengel 1974, 1: 69; Fraser 1972, 1: 690–94; Attridge 1984: 246–97; *ANRW* 2/20/1: 248–51). Demetrius is also an exegete. He builds his book on the LXX and raises exegetical problems and gives answers (cf. the exegetical form of *quaestiones et solutiones*).

Eusebius has also preserved parts of the drama *The Exodus* written in Greek iambic trimeter by one Ezekiel, otherwise unknown. The tragedy covered most of the life of Moses in a version which for the most part followed the Septuagint translation quite closely, from Moses' birth to the Exodus with the crossing of the Red Sea, the destruction of the Egyptians, and closing with a description of the oasis Elim. A remarkable departure from the LXX text is found in a dialogue between Moses and his father-in-law, in which Moses describes a dream. In his dream Moses is conveyed to Sinai's peak, where he sees a gigantic throne and upon it, God himself in human semblance. God bids him approach the throne, gives him the sceptre, seats him on the throne, and crowns him. From the throne, Moses beholds the whole universe. According to the interpretation, Moses will cause a great throne to arise, and he himself will rule over mortals. Morever, he will see all things in the present, past, and future.

The fragments place emphasis on the Passover, and they express a cosmic understanding of Jewish existence. Moses' cosmic kingship implies a claim by the Jewish nation to be the ruler of the world. Accordingly, the opposing Egyptians who fought against the Jews, were destroyed. The tragedy shows how an Egyptian Jew employs Greek literary form to interpret Jewish self-understanding. The tragedy was written during the second half of the 3d century or the first half of the 2d century B.C. (Nickelsburg 1984: 125–30; Fraser 1972, 1: 707–8; Cf. Borgen 1984: 267–68). See EZEKIEL THE TRAGEDIAN.

The Egyptian priest Manetho counselled Ptolemy I Soter on native religion, and in his history of Egypt he also interpreted the Exodus of the Hebrew people. He represented them as mixed up with a crowd of Egyptian lepers and others, who for various maladies were condemned to banishment from Egypt. Manetho's work reflects the hostility of Egyptians to foreigners, and especially to Jews (*AgAp* 1 §229; 2 §1–15; *ANRW* 2/20/2: 41–52; Fraser 1972, 1: 508–9). At the same time his polemic against the Jews testifies to the fact that they represented an important factor in Egyptian society already.

2. From Ptolemy VI to the Roman Conquest (181–30 B.C.). The Jews of Egypt not only consolidated their positions during the period from Ptolemy VI Philometor (181–145 B.C.) to the Roman conquest in 30 B.C., but they became a considerable military and political force. The background was the weakening of the Ptolemaic government since the mismanagement of the Egyptian economy by Ptolemy IV Philopator and Ptolemy V Epiphanes (204–181 B.C.). The Ptolemaic relationships with the native Egyptians deteriorated, fomenting local revolts. Moreover, the foreign policy of the Seleucids in Antioch grew more aggressive, and they consistently were on the military offensive. Family quarrels and court intrigues drained the strength of the Ptolemaic dynasty from the inside. When the Ptolemaic kings called for assistance from Rome, the new power in the West, Egypt became almost a client of Rome. In 198 B.C. Antiochus III (222–187 B.C.) conquered Palestine, and in 170 B.C. Antiochus IV Epiphanes (175–164 B.C.) invaded Egypt, but had to withdraw upon the ultimatum given him by the Roman envoy Popilius Laenas (Tcherikover 1966: 73–89; Rostovtzeff 1941, 2: 705 and 871; Wilson *IDB* 2: 55–56; Fraser 1972, 1: 119–20).

When the relation between Jerusalem and the Seleucid occupants grew tense, pro-Ptolemaic sympathies developed in the city, and shortly before the Maccabean revolt in 167, many Jews emigrated to Egypt. Of special importance is the emigration of Onias of the Jerusalem high priestly family.

According to Josephus (*JW* 1 §33 and 7 §423), the high priest of Jerusalem, Onias III, fled to Egypt during the persecution by Antiochus IV Epiphanes (175–164 B.C.) in 175 B.C. Conversely, Josephus presented another version (*Ant* 13 §62 and 12 §387) in which he connected the emigration to Egypt with the appointment of Alcimus to the high priesthood in Jerusalem, about 162–160 B.C. When Onias IV realized that the Seleucid authorities had managed to abolish his family's claim to the high priesthood, he left for Egypt. In Egypt he found an ally in Ptolemy VI Philometer. V. A. Tcherikover, after having analyzed the passages in detail, reached the conclusion that the account in Josephus' *Antiquities* is the more reliable one (Tcherikover 1966: 228–31; 276–77; Kasher 1985: 7).

Onias IV and his sons Helkias and Hananiah had a remarkable career in Egypt. Onias was priest and warrior and was given an important role to play in Ptolemy VI's counter-move against the threatening power of the Seleucids. Onias and his Jewish followers formed a military force of some size, and they were settled in the Leontopolis district about 190 kilometers SE of Alexandria. The settlement is today identified as Tel el-Yehoudieh, 3 km S of present-day Shibin el Qanatir. Onias built a temple, and the area along the E branches of the Nile Delta was called "the Land of Onias." The settlement and the temple were probably built some years after Onias and his followers had emigrated to Egypt; that is, when Onias had gained a reputation as a good general and had organized around him a Jewish force of military value. V. A. Tcherikover suggests that the date of the founding of the military settlement *(katoikia)* might have been some time before the death of Ptolemy VI Philometor in 145 B.C. (Tcherikover 1966: 277–80; *CPJ* 1: 2 and 19–21). The location of this military center was strategically important, and the fact that the Jews were assigned the defense of such a sensitive area for about 100 years indicates their strong position in Ptolemaic politics (Kasher 1985: 7–8). Their alliance with the Ptolemaic rulers also proved that they favored a centralized government and wanted to mark themselves off from the native Egyptians.

The many intrigues and conflicts within the weakened Ptolemaic dynasty caused problems, however. In the conflict between Ptolemy VI Philometor and his younger brother, Ptolemy VII Euergetes II (Physcon), the power of the population increased, and for a century populace, especially in Alexandria, played a decisive and disastrous part in Egyptian politics. The death of Ptolemy VI Philometor in 145 left Queen Cleopatra II and her son to face Ptolemy VII, who ruled Cyrene. Onias, his friend Dositheus, and the Jewish soldiers were the leading force in support of Cleopatra. The Queen could not withstand Ptolemy VII Euergetes II, however, and she was forced to marry him. He then ruled as king from 145–116 B.C. Ptolemy VII turned against the supporters of the late Philometor. Accordingly, he persecuted the Jews. Josephus tells that when preparing to attack Onias, Ptolemy VII decided to exterminate the Jews of the country and ordered that they should be thrown naked and fettered at the feet of drunken elephants. The elephants, however, left the Jews untouched and attacked the king's men, killing many of them. When the king saw that the Jews were not hurt, he repented of his evil intent. The Jews instituted a festival in memory of this day of salvation (*AgAp* 2 §53–55). The story, although legendary, is probably based on a version of some actual danger (Fraser 1972, 1: 1 and 121; Tcherikover 1966: 282; *CPJ* 1: 21–22).

The relationship between Ptolemy VII and the Jews was normalized, as seen by the fact that synagogues were dedicated to him. Such a move from the king might have been furthered by the native Egyptians' numerous revolts, and an unrest in the Greek population of Alexandria.

When Ptolemy VII died, his niece-wife, Cleopatra III reigned from 116 to 101 B.C. Cleopatra chose her younger son Ptolemy X Alexander I to be co-regent. The Alexandrians compelled her to depose him and allow the older son, Ptolemy IX Lathyrus, to share her throne. In the subsequent tension and conflicts between the Queen, her sons, and the population, the Queen's control of the capital and the country was largely built on the loyal support of the Jews. The sons of Onias IV, Helkias and Hananiah, were appointed high officers in the Queen's army. Josephus tells that Cleopatra appointed the two Jewish generals "at the head of the whole army." Although probably an exaggeration, the statement testifies to their leading position in the army also beyond the Jewish units (Ant 13 §349). When Ptolemy IX Lathyrus, having fled to Cyprus, conducted a campaign against his mother with Seleucid help, Cleopatra entered into an alliance with the Hasmonean king Alexander Janneus (*CPJ* 1: 23, and *CJP* 3: 141–42; Tcherikover 1966: 283).

The Jewish leaders were not simply military supporters of the Queen, they also influenced her in her political decisions. When Cleopatra went to Palestine in the years 104–102 B.C. against the Seleucids and Ptolemy IX Lathyrus, some of her advisers recommended her to betray her ally, King Janneus, and seize the country for herself. Hananiah said, "I would have you know, that this wrong to the king will turn all the Jews who dwell in your kingdom into your foes" (*Ant* 13 §354). Moreover, this incident shows that Hananiah, although of high priestly family from Jerusalem, recognized the Hasmonean government and did not try to return to Jerusalem and its temple. Hananiah's brother, Helkias, had been killed in one of the battles fought in Palestine (Tcherikover 1966: 283–84; Kasher 1985: 11).

Cleopatra's younger son, Ptolemy X Alexander I had been recalled to Alexandria in 107 B.C. and was her coregent, until he murdered her in 101 B.C. Ptolemy X Alexander I was expelled in 89 B.C. by the Alexandrian populace, the army, and his older brother, Ptolemy IX Lathyrus, known as Soter II, who gained the support of the Alexandrians due to the popularity of his wife, Berenice IV. In 88 B.C. there seems to have been a persecution of the Jews in Alexandria, but further details are not known (Kasher 1985: 12; Fraser 1972, 1: 123–24).

During the half of the century from Ptolemy IX Lathyrus' (Soter II) death in 80 B.C. to the death of Cleopatra VII in 30 B.C., the conflicts between the Alexandrians and the Ptolemies continued almost without interruption. Josephus tells of two incidents in which the Jews were directly involved. The first took place during the turbulent reign of the Roman "puppet," Ptolemy XI Auletes. In 58 B.C. he was forced to leave the city, and in 55 B.C. the Roman proconsul of Syria, Gabinus, whose cavalry was commanded by Marc Antony, marched to Egypt to restore Ptolemy XI Auletes to the throne. The guarding of Pelusium in NE Egypt was in Jewish hands, and through the interference of Rome's friend Antipater, the strong man in Jerusalem, the Jews allowed the Romans to pass through Pelusium without any hindrance and to enter Egypt (Tcherikover 1966: 284; Kasher 1985: 12–13).

In a similar way, the Jewish garrison at Pelusium yielded to pressure from Jerusalem in 48 B.C., when Julius Caesar was at Alexandria in a very unfavorable situation. When King Mithridates of Pergamum went with auxiliary troops to extricate him, he at first met opposition from the Jewish garrison at Pelusium. Antipater showed the Jews a letter from the high priest, Hyrcanus II, and persuaded them to change their allegiance and even to provide Mithridates with supplies needed for the journey (Tcherikover 1966: 284; Smallwood 1976: 37–38).

Although the Egyptian Queen Cleopatra VII had outstanding leadership abilities, the reign of the Ptolemaic dynasty was approaching its end. The Roman Antony and the Egyptian Queen were defeated by Octavian in the battle at Actium in 31 B.C., and Antony and Cleopatra ended their lives subsequently. The Romans annexed Egypt in 30 B.C. and made it into a province. A new era had begun.

In this most-glorious period of the Egyptian Jews insofar as political history is concerned, what is known about their religious and cultural life?

Various synagogues are referred to in inscriptions from this period (*CPJ* 1: 139–40; Schürer *HJP* 3/1: 47–50):

(a.) Two synagogues in Alexandria are referred to: one from Hadra, dated to the 2d century B.C. ("to God, the Highest . . . the sacred precinct and the *proseuche* and its appurtenances"); and one from the Gabbary quarter of SW Alexandria, dated to 37 B.C. ("In honor of the queen and the king, to the great God who listens to prayer, Alypos made the *proseuche* in the 15th year, Mecheir . . .").

(b.) Two inscriptions in Athribis in the S part of the Delta are probably to be dated to the 2d century B.C. ("In honor of King Ptolemy and Queen Cleopatra, Ptolemaios son of Epikydes chief of police and the Jews in Athribis (dedicated) the *proseuche* to the supreme God," and "In honor of King Ptolemy and Queen Cleopatra and their children, Hermeas and his wife Philotera and their children (gave) this place for sitting for the *proseuche*").

(c.) Two inscriptions attest the presence of synagogues in the W Delta, both dated between 143 and 117 B.C. One is in Xenephyris ("In honor of King Ptolemy and Queen Cleopatra his sister and Queen Cleopatra his wife, the Jews of Xenephyris (built) the gateway of the *proseuche* when Theodoros and Achillion were *prostatai*), the other is in Nitriai ("In honor of King Ptolemy and Queen Cleopatra his sister and Queen Cleopatra his wife, the benefactors, the Jews in Nitriai (dedicated) the *proseuche* and its appurtenances").

(d.) As for upper Egypt, a large number of ostraca have been found in the vicinity of Thebes with Hebrew names inscribed on them. Most of these ostraca refer to the reigns of Ptolemy VI Philometor (181–45 B.C.) and Ptolemy Euergetes II (145–16 B.C.) (*CPJ* 1: 194–226).

Thus the Jewish population was spread out over all of Egypt. Usually the synagogues served as the community centers. An exception of special interest is Onias' temple and the Land of Onias. At Leontopolis (Tell el-Yehoudieh) in the nome of Heliopolis, an extensive number of Jewish epitaphs has been found. The remains of Onias' temple are thought to have been identified in the same Tell. Originally it was probably meant to compete with Jerusalem Temple, and to express rejection of its high priest. Later this claim seems to have been modified, so that the Jewish garrison at Pelusium in 48 B.C. complied to the letter from the high priest in Jerusalem, Hyrcanus II, and let the army of Mithridates pass through the town (*JW* 1 §33; 7 §436; Schürer *HJP* 3/1: 145–47; Tcherikover 1966: 275–84; Kasher 1985: 119–35; *CPJ* 3: 145–63). For Egyptian Jews in general, there is no evidence that Onias' temple became a serious alternative to the Temple in Jerusalem (*CPJ* 1: 45).

Josephus tells that Onias asked Ptolemy to build a temple to make it possible for him to worship God after the manner of his fathers. The temple was built on the pattern of the Temple in Jerusalem. Thus Onias' temple shows that those who belonged to it stressed the continuity with the traditions from Jerusalem (*JW* 1 §33; *Ant* 12 §389, in contradiction with *JW* 7 §425–32; see also Kasher 1985: 132–35; Hayward 1982: 429–43). Josephus likewise conveys their need for legitimation for having a temple in Egypt. They based it on a prediction by the prophet Isaiah, as stated in a letter purported by Josephus to have been written by Onias: "For this is indeed what the prophet Isaiah foretold, 'There shall be an altar in Egypt to the Lord God,' and many other such things did he prophesy concerning this place." The reference is to Isa 19:18–19. Onias was both high priest and warrior, and the Jewish community on the Land of Onias was a military settlement. They had a temple and a fortress, and they received help from God in their military activity (*Ant* 13 §65 and 68).

The main Jewish community in Egypt, the one in Alexandria, continued to express its religious convictions in literary forms. *Aristobulus,* the *Letter of Aristeas,* and the *Sibylline Oracles* 3, belong to this period. Aristobulus came from a high-priestly family and lived at the time of Ptolemy VI Philometor (181–145). His work has the form of an exegetical dialogue, where he answers questions raised by the Ptolemaic king (Borgen 1984: 274–79; 1987a: 8–9). See also ARISTOBULUS.

The author of the *Letter of Aristeas,* addressed to Aristeas' brother Philocrates, presents himself as a Greek courtier of Ptolemy II Philadelphus. He tells about a series of events connected with the Gk translation of the Torah. According to *Let. Aris.* the translation took place during the early part of the reign of Ptolemy II Philadelphus, and was done by 70 Jewish scholars sent from the high priest in Jerusalem upon request from King Ptolemy. The date when the letter was written is uncertain, but it presupposes the existence of the LXX translation. A date in the middle or second half of the 2d century B.C. is probable, and in spite of its own claim to have been written by a non-Jew, a Jew must have been the real author (*ANRW* 2/20/1: 83–85; Fraser 1972, 1: 698–704; Kasher 1985: 208–11). See also ARISTEAS, LETTER OF. The *Sibylline Oracles* also use a pagan figure as medium, the prophetess named Sibyl. *Sib.Or.* 3 in the standard collection is Jewish. Its main corpus has been dated to the time of Ptolemy VI Philometor (181–145 B.C.) (Collins 1984: 365–71).

These books have several features in common. They all express a positive attitude to the Ptolemaic rulers: *Aristob.* has an exegetical dialogue with King Ptolemy. *Aristeas* tells how King Ptolemy II Philadelphus wants copies of Jewish books for his library, and how he entertains the Jewish scholars. In *Sib. Or.* 3 a Ptolemaic king, probably Ptolemy VI Philometor or his anticipated successor, is endorsed as a virtual Messiah (3:162–95, 652–56; Collins 1984: 366–67). See also SIBYLLINE ORACLES.

All 3 books place emphasis on what Jews and gentiles have in common. Both Aristobulus and Aristeas agree that when the Greek poets and philosophers speak of "Zeus," they mean the true God whom the Jews worship. Similarly, in 2 Jewish inscriptions from Ptolemaic times found in Upper Egypt, Pan, as the universal god, seems to be identified with the God of the Jews (Hengel 1974, 1: 264). The Sibyl (3: 97–161) draws on myths and legends which were familiar to the gentiles. At the same time, all 3 books exalt the Jews, their philosophy, and religion and express a feeling of Jewish superiority. Aristobulus states that Jewish philosophy, found in the laws of Moses, has many points of agreement with the Greeks, whose philosophers and legislators learned from Moses. The pagan Aristeas makes King Ptolemy to express admiration of the Jewish Temple, worship, wisdom and laws; the Jewish sages exceed the philosophers in their wisdom. The Sibyl appeals to the Greeks to refrain from idolatry and adultery, and prophesies that people from all countries will send gifts and worship in the Temple in Jerusalem. The Jews carry the moral leadership of the human race.

Let. Aris. and especially the *Sibylline Oracles* level criticism against idolatry. *Let. Aris.* contrasts the one God, the Creator, with the idols and idolatry of the Egyptians. The Sibyl offers very sharp criticism of Romans and Greeks for their idolatry and adultery. Also in the fragments of *Aristob.* there is a similar statement: Orpheus and Aretus, in quotations given, had no holy concepts of God since they used polytheistic names of the One God. Both *Let. Aris.* and *Sib. Or.* 3 present the views of Jewish communities for whom Jerusalem and its Temple were the center. Aristeas describes the Temple and its cult, the city and the country, and tells about the gifts to the Temple from King Ptolemy. *Sib. Or.* 3 shows great interest in the Jerusalem Temple. The Greeks can avoid disaster by sending sacrifices to the Jewish Temple. The people from all countries will come confessing their sins and acknowledge the God who is worshipped in the Jerusalem Temple.

Both *Let. Aris.* and *Sib. Or.* 3 deal with politics. Aristeas pictures the ideal kingship and the ideals of his rule. The Sibyl idealizes Ptolemy VI Philometor, and throughout the book emphasizes warfare. The Jews play a role in some of the military actions, although the hope is expressed of a life of peace around the Temple in Jerusalem.

In different ways the writings take up a position in 2 fronts. On the one hand they go against Jewish isolationists, on the other hand they avoid assimilation and apostasy by stressing allegiance to some distinctive marks of Judaism, such as the Temple of Jerusalem and Jewish standards. Moreover, Aristeas defends Jewish observances, such as the dietary laws; Aristobulus glorifies the Sabbath and discusses the celebration of the Passover.

Another book from this period, *On The Jews* by the historian Artapanus, is more syncretistic (Fraser 1972: 1. 704–6; Attridge 1984: 166–68). Artapanus probably wrote his book in Alexandria in the 2d century B.C. The fragments preserved by Eusebius and Clement tell about Abraham, Joseph, and Moses. His concern is similar to that of Aristobulus, Aristeas, and the Sibyl: He weaves Jewish and non-Jewish elements together, so as to glorify the Jewish people. He reflects an Egyptian environment outside the Hellenistic circles connected with the Ptolemaic administration. Artapanus pictures Moses as the father of Egyptian civilization including the political organization of the country. Moses is even seen as father of Egyptian polytheistic religion, and the Egyptian priests bestow on him semi-divine honors. He is called Hermes (= Thoth) because he has interpreted the sacred letters of the hieroglyphic script. Moses is moreover pictured as a successful warrior against the Ethiopians, in command of a peasant army. Even in this role he ends up being loved by the Ethiopians so that they submit to circumcision, as also do some of the priests.

Artapanus shows kinship with Ezekiel the Tragedian in giving Moses divine attributes, but he does it in a syncretistic way. In his glorification of Moses and in his version of the salvation of the Jews in the Exodus, Artapanus is in direct opposition to the anti-Jewish account of Moses given by the Egyptian priest Manetho.

Thus, the literature from the period between Ptolemy VI Philometor and the Roman conquest reflects the tension within the Jewish communities with a wide range of attitudes from assimilation to separation. Typical for the literature is the attempt to combine distinctive Jewish observances with a fusion of Jewish and Greek ideas or Jewish and Egyptian ideas. The superiority of the Jewish religion is stressed, and in the end time the Jewish nation will play an exalted role among the nations.

C. The Roman Period

In many respects the transfer into Roman rule meant discontinuity with the Ptolemaic past (*CPJ* 1: 55–65; Tcherikover 1963: 1–8; Kasher 1985: 18–20). The Ptolemaic capital had become a provincial city in the Roman Empire. The Roman prefect in the *praetorium* replaced the Ptolemy and his court in the palace. The Roman legions replaced the multi-ethnic Ptolemaic army. From now on, the resources of Egypt and Alexandria had to serve the needs and aims of the new rulers and their home base, Rome. Nevertheless, the victory of Augustus had brought to an end the Ptolemaic dynasty which had proved itself unable to rule effectively. At first, therefore, the Roman conquest meant fresh life into a decaying administration. The result was economic progress. Apart from the appointment of the prefect, Augustus and his early successors only changed so much as was necessary to control the bureaucracy and make it more efficient.

Philo tells that Augustus confirmed the rights of the Jewish community to live in accordance with their ancestral laws (*Flacc* 50 and *Gaium* 152–58). Nevertheless, they entered into a new situation in important areas. They were eliminated as a military factor along with the Ptolemaic army as a whole, even though their realization of being dependent on the central government had caused them to change their allegiance from the Ptolemaic dynasty to the Romans. Nevertheless, it was the Greeks that the Romans used in their administration and to whom they gave privileges. The problem was how to distinguish Greek from non-Greek among the rather mixed population of Egypt. In 4–5 B.C. it was decided that the criterion was to be gymnasium education.

A few Jews continued the tradition of Dositheus, Onias, Helkias, and Hananiah and had high posts in the government of the country, now in the Roman administration. The most prominent examples were Philo's brother Alexander and his son Tiberius Alexander. Alexander was *alabarch,* which probably meant that he was custom superintendent on the E side of the Nile. He was also steward of the property of Antonia, mother of the emperor Claudius. Tiberius Alexander attained the high offices of procurator of Palestine, prefect of Egypt, highest ranking officer in Titus' army in the Jewish war, and probably prefect of the guard in Rome. Alexander remained faithful to Judaism, and donated the gold plating of the 9 gates of the Temple court in Jerusalem. His son, Tiberius Alexander, left his ancestral religion, as had Dositheus, son of Drimylos, in the 3d century B.C. (*CPJ* 1: 49, n. 4; *CPJ* 2: 188–90; Smallwood 1976: 257–59; Kasher 1985: 347).

On the whole it proved more difficult for Jews to meet the requirements for entering governmental posts, although Philo indicates that it still was possible, since he admonishes Jews who pursue education with no motive higher than from desire of an office under the rulers (Tcherikover 1963: 14–15; Borgen 1981: 122–29; Mendelson 1982: 44–46; Borgen 1984: 254–56; *ANRW* 2/21/1: 115–17).

During the period between 30 B.C. and A.D. 117, three armed uprisings and revolts demonstrate that the situation of the Egyptian Jews was deteriorating and moving towards their extermination: the armed uprising at the death of emperor Gaius Caligula in A.D. 41; the impact of the Jewish war in Palestine on the tensions in Egypt, 66 and 70–73 A.D.; and the suicidal messianic revolution of Jews in Cyrene and Egypt in the years A.D. 115–17.

What were the causes and circumstances for these tragic events to take place? The main reason for the crisis in 38–41 A.D. was the growing conflict between the Jews and the Greeks, and Gaius Caligula's enforcement of the emperor worship (Philo, *Flacc; Gaium;* Bell 1926: 14–30; Smallwood 1976: 237–50; *CPJ* 1, 1957: 65–74; *ANRW* 2/21/1: 429–36). The Greeks wanted a ruling from the prefect Flaccus on the constitutional question of Jewish status in the city, and they succeeded in getting Flaccus to issue an edict making the Jews to be "foreigners and aliens." They were now aliens without the right of domicile, and without the rights to have an administration of their own under the leadership of the council of elders.

Flaccus issued this edict after the anti-Jewish forces exploited the visit of the Jewish King Agrippa by setting up a lunatic named Carabas in royal robes in the gymnasium and saluting him as king in a mocking scene. Then the crowd clamored for the installation of images of the emperor in the synagogues. A cruel pogrom followed. The Jews were driven together into a ghetto, and members of the Jewish council of elders were arrested and tortured so severely that some died. An embassy of 5 persons, headed by Philo, was sent to Rome for the purpose of explaining to Gaius Caligula the traditional rights of the Jewish community. The Greeks sent a counter-embassy, headed by the anti-Jewish writer Apion. Philo's mission was a complete failure.

Suddenly the situation changed. In A.D. 41, Gaius Caligula was assassinated and Claudius succeeded him. The Alexandrian Jews started an armed uprising against the Greeks, and they received help by Jews from Egypt and from Palestine. Roman intervention put an end to the conflict, and Claudius issued an edict giving back to the Jews the rights held before the pogrom started, reinstating the *politeuma* and protecting the synagogues. The struggle before the emperor continued. Finally he settled the questions in a letter (*CPJ* 2: 36–55; Bell 1976: 1–37). He confirmed the rights of the Jews, chastised both ethnic groups for their share in the disturbances in Alexandria, and forbade Jews to participate in the activities in the gymnasium and to take gymnasium education. Claudius stated explicitly that the Jews lived "in a city not their own."

In A.D. 66 the Alexandrian Greek polis wanted the emperor Nero to cancel the Jews' rights in the city. In the same year Nero decided to recognize the exclusive sovereignty of the Greek polis in Caesarea Maritima over all residents in the city, thereby cancelling the rights of the Jewish community. According to Josephus a number of Jews entered the amphitheatre in Alexandria where the members of the polis were deliberating on the subject of an embassy to be sent to Nero. The Greeks tried to capture the Jews, got hold of three of them, and took them away to be burned alive. This aroused the whole Jewish community who attempted to set fire to the amphitheatre. The Roman Prefect, Philo's nephew Tiberius Alexander, crushed the Jewish revolt. The soldiers killed the Jews, burned and plundered their houses. The Jews tried to oppose the Roman troops with arms, but they were totally routed. According to Josephus 50,000 Jews were killed (*CPJ* 1: 78–79).

The Jewish community structure was not abolished, however. The council of elders as institution remained intact. In A.D. 73 some Jewish guerrilla fighters, the Sicarii, fled from Palestine to Egypt, and instigated the Egyptian Jews to revolt under the slogan "No lord but God." After the Sicarii had killed some of the moderate Jews of rank, the leaders of the council of elders in Alexandria called a general assembly and charged the Sicarii for causing dangerous trouble. The assembly seized 600 Sicarii on the spot. The Sicarii who escaped farther into Egypt were arrested and brought back to Alexandria. All were put to death by the Romans. Moreover, the Romans, fearing that the Jews might again join together in revolutionary actions, demolished Onias' temple. This indicates that this temple was still a center of militant Judaism (*JW* 7 §409–20 and 433–36).

The suicidal revolution in A.D. 115–17 involved the Jews in Alexandria and Egypt, in Cyrene, and on Cyprus (*CPJ* 1: 89–90; Tcherikover 1963: 28–32; Hengel 1983: 655–86; Smallwood 1976: 397). The Jews "as if shaken by a strong rebellious spirit," attacked their Greek and Egyptian neighbors. At first the Jews were victorious, but then began to suffer defeats; when it developed into a war with the Romans they were crushed. All who participated in the war fought to exterminate the enemy.

The Jewish revolt was messianic in character. Its aim was to destroy pagans and their polytheistic temples and to establish Jewish control of the whole area, probably also with the final aim of delivering Judea and Jerusalem from Roman occupation. The aim was the liquidation of the Roman regime and the setting up of a new Jewish commonwealth, whose task was to inaugurate the messianic era. In Cyrene a Jewish messiah appeared, King Loukuas-Andreas (Hengel 1983: 655–86).

The revolution was crushed by the Roman legions. In many places the Jewish population was almost totally annihilated. The great synagogue as well as other synagogues and buildings in Alexandria and in all of Egypt were demolished. Some Jews, mainly in Alexandria it seems, survived, but the strength of Egyptian Jews had been broken forever. In this way the more than 700 years of Jewish settlement and history in Egypt had virtually come to an end, and it took more than a century for Jewish life in Egypt to reawaken.

D. Status of the Jews

After this historical survey some further comments should be made with regard to the status of the Jewish communities.

Philo declares that there were a million Jews resident in Alexandria and the country from the slope into Libya to the boundaries of Ethiopia (*Flacc* 43). They worked in many professions (*CPJ* 1: 48–55). In Alexandria there were many synagogues scattered all over the city. One of the synagogues was larger and more beautiful than the others (*Gaium* 134–35; cf *t. Sukk.* 4:6; *b. Sukk.* 516; *j. Sukk.* 5:55a; Kasher 1985: 349–51). Of the 5 quarters of Alexandria, 2 were called Jewish because most of the Jews inhabited them. In the other sections of the city there were many Jews scattered about (Philo *Flacc* 55). Papyri, ostraca, and inscriptions also testify to the Jewish habitation all over Egypt in the later Ptolemaic and early Roman periods (*CPJ* 3: 197–209).

The organization of the Jewish communities varied in different places. In Alexandria there was a united corporation of the large Jewish community. According to the *Letter of Aristeas,* the Jewish community formed a *politeuma* at whose head stood elders and leaders. From the time of Strabo (about 63 B.C. to some time after A.D. 21) there was an *ethnarch* at the head. Strabo defines his function: He "governs the people and adjudicates suits and supervises contracts and ordinances just as if he were head *(archon)* of a sovereign state" (Stern 1976: 278). According to Philo (*Flacc* 74), a *genarch,* who was presumably identical with the *ethnarch,* died when Magius Maximus was to become prefect of Egypt for the second time in A.D. 11–12. At that time Augustus reintroduced a council of elders, the *gerusia,* who assumed the leadership, although the office of *ethnarch* does not seem to have been abolished. The degree of autonomy of Alexandrian Jewry may have been made possible by the fact that Alexandria from Augustus had no city council (Stern 1976: 280; Kasher 1985: 254–55).

Similar forms of organization probably existed in the places of Egypt where the Jewish communities were of sufficient size. Thus, the Jewish *politarch* at Leontopolis may have been the equivalent of the *ethnarch* in Alexandria (Kasher 1985: 127). Of course, the priestly military leadership of the Land of Onias gave this community a distinction of its own during the time of Onias IV and his sons.

Both in the Ptolemaic period and the Roman period the rights of the Jews of Egypt were generally, as already shown, based on the formula that they were permitted to live and have government according to their ancestral laws and customs. The implications and applications of this formula depended, however, on the interplay among the Jewish communities, the political authorities, and the other groups in the country.

Certain rights were commonly recognized: to worship their God; to own and gather in synagogues as community property; to keep the Sabbath and celebrate the feasts of the New Moon, of Passover/Unleavened Bread, of the Weeks, the Day of atonement, the feast of Tabernacles, etc. (Philo *Spec Leg* II:39–222; cf *Gaium* 116–18). The celebration of the other feasts, such as the celebration of the

Septuagint at Pharos (Philo *Vita Mos* II:41–42) and the celebration of the feast in memory of their deliverance when Ptolemy VII Euergetes II (Physeon) wished to have them killed by elephants (Schürer *HJP*² 3/1: 145).

Tensions existed at some of these points, however. Philo refers to a Roman prefect who attempted to compel Jews to do service to him on the Sabbath and in this way do away with the law of the seventh day and other laws (*Somn* 2 §123–32). On the other hand there were Jews who internalized the meaning of the observances to such a degree that they did not comply to the external customs and regulations (Philo *Migr* 89–93; Borgen 1984: 260–61; 1987b).

One specific point in their laws which the Romans permitted them to follow was the right to pay the tax to be transmitted to the Temple in Jerusalem (*Gaium* 311–17; *Ant* 14 §216 and 16 §160–66; Rajak 1985: 23). Strabo, the Talmud, and a papyrus testify to the existence of Jewish legal institutions in Egypt, based on the office of *ethnarch* and/or the council of elders. According to Strabo, the *ethnarch* presided over the courts and supervised contracts. The supervision of contracts is indirectly confirmed by the papyrus recording the registration of a loan contract between two Jews of Alexandria in 13 B.C. at the Jewish records office (Stern 1976: 280–82; *t. Peʿa* 4:6; *t. Ketub.* 3:1; *CPJ* 2: 8–10). Finally, the *ethnarch* supervised the implementation of the edicts of the Roman authorities (Applebaum 1984: 474).

Against this background it is a problem that according to papyri found at Abusir el-Meleq (approximately 130 km SE of Alexandria) the Jews to a large extent resorted to non-Jewish tribunals both in the Ptolemaic and Roman times. The reason seems to be that the jurisdiction of the Jewish court was not compulsory, at least not in cases of general nature. Moreover, legal documents from Fayûm in the 3d and 2d centuries B.C. show that the Jews freely used the Hellenistic laws of Ptolemaic Egypt. M. Stern supposes that Jewish organization and law were not yet established in those military settlements at that time (*CPJ* 1: 32–36; *CPJ* 2: 1–24; Stern 1976: 280–82).

In some respects the Jews had a more-favorable or at least equal status to that of the "Greek" citizens of Alexandria. The Jews were permitted to have their own council of elders, while the Greek citizens were denied a corresponding council (Lewis 1985: 29). In case of corporal punishment, the Jews were punished with the same kind of flogging as the Greek citizens (Philo *Flacc* 78–80).

In other areas the situation of the Jews was less favorable. Augustus introduced a capitation tax, the *laographia*, payable by the male population of Egypt between the ages of 14 and 60 or 62 (*CPJ* 1: 59–65; Smallwood 1976: 231–34). The Greek citizens of Alexandria were exempted, while the Greek members of the capitals, the *metropoleis*, of the *nomes*, paid a reduced rate. The criterion for this concession was the Greek education, and from A.D. 4/5 the "members of the gymnasium" were recognized as a class. The Jews in Egypt in general were classified as non-Greeks and made liable for the tax. Those who could prove that they met the criterion for Greek citizenship were treated as the Greeks. This increased the tension between the Greeks and the Jews, and was one of the causes of the conflict in Alexandria in A.D. 38.

After the destruction of the Temple of Jerusalem in A.D. 70 and the victory of the Romans in the Jewish War, the Jewish tax, *fiscus Judaicus*, was founded. The Jews had to pay the tax previously paid to the Temple of Jerusalem to the Templa of Jupiter Capitolinus. This tax was an additional burden beyond the other taxes levied on the Jews in Egypt (*CPJ* 1: 80–82). All through the Ptolemaic and Roman periods a delicate balance existed between the Jews' refusal to recognize divine attributes of the political heads of state and their expression of loyal acceptance of their rule. The dedication of the synagogues to the political head of state is documented by archaeological findings for members of the Ptolemaic dynasty, but not for the Roman emperors, as far as Egypt is concerned. Philo, in *Gaium* 133, tells, however, that honorific inscriptions and emblems in honor of the emperors were placed in the synagogues (cf. *Flacc* 48–49; Smallwood 1970: 220–21). Upon the accession of Gaius Caligula, the Jewish community of Alexandria expressed their loyalty by passing a resolution in Gaius' honor. Flaccus did not forward this resolution to Gaius Caligula, however (*Flacc* 97–103). Philo praises Augustus for ordering sacrifices of whole burnt offerings to be carried out daily at his expense in the Temple of Jerusalem as a tribute to the most high God (*Gaium* 157–317). This delicate balance between the political authority of the emperors and the exclusive claim of the monotheistic worship of the Jewish nation was upset when Gaius Caligula demanded that images of the emperor be placed in the synagogues and in the Temple of Jerusalem (*Flacc* 41–50; *Gaium* 134–35, 188, 203, 346).

During the late Ptolemaic and the early Roman periods the literary output of Egyptian Jews reached its height. In addition to the monumental works of Philo, the Wisdom of Solomon, the *Third Book of Maccabees* and *Sibylline Oracles* 5 seem to belong to these 200 years.

The Wisdom of Solomon was probably written sometime between 200 B.C. and A.D. 50, most probably during the 1st century B.C. (Schürer *HJP*² 3/1: 568–79; Nickelsburg 1981: 175–85). The central theme is the view that God's cosmic Wisdom is sought and made known to the King of Israel, Solomon, and is seen to be at work in the history of Israel and its worship of the One God. God's deliverance of the righteous and his warfare against the ungodly is the subject of the first part (Wis 1:1–6:11). This "book of eschatology" is framed by exhortations addressed to rulers, kings, and judges. In the second part, "the book of wisdom" (Wis 6:12–9:18) the king, writing in the first person, directs the attention of his royal colleagues to his own example, as seekers of God's wisdom. In the third part, Wisdom of Solomon 10–19, the blessings of godliness and the curse of ungodliness is seen in the different fates of the Israelites and the Egyptians in the biblical story. A lengthy and sharp attack on idolatry occurs in Wisdom 13–15.

The book Wisdom of Solomon outlines the cosmic significance of Jewish existence; interprets the universal role of Israel, represented here by the king, presumably Solomon; and attacks Egyptian idolatry on the basis of Israel's monotheism. Some Greek philosophical concepts have been "conquered" and made to serve Jewish self-understanding and Jewish imperial ideology.

The *Third Book of Maccabees* is an aetiological romance

probably written at the beginning of the Roman period to explain an already existing festival, and to provide the Jews of Alexandria with ammunition in their struggle against the resident Greeks (Schürer *HJP*² 3/1: 537–42 with criticism of Kasher 1985: 211–32; Nickelsburg 1981: 169–72). The main basis for the book seems to have been an older aetiological legend, recorded by Josephus in *AgAp* 2 §5. As already stated earlier, according to this legend Ptolemy VII Physcon cast the Jews, who supported Cleopatra, before drunken elephants. These turned instead against the king's friends, and the king changed his plans.

In *3 Maccabees* this story seems to have been transferred back to the time of Ptolemy IV Philopator and woven together with the problems the Jews faced when that king wanted the Jews and others to worship Dionysus as condition for giving them full citizenship. The book offers support to the view that the Jews had an intermediate status higher than the native Egyptians, but lower than the full citizens of Alexandria. The king removed the privileges of the Jews and degraded them to the rank of natives. Their previous state was that of an ethnic *politeuma* in exile "worshipping God, and living according to his law they held themselves apart in the matter of food." They had the Jerusalem Temple as their religious center. On the condition that they entered into the royal cult of Dionysus they could obtain full citizenship. The end result was that the king issued a letter of protection for the Jews to all the governors in the provinces and permitted the Jews to put to death apostates among their own people.

Philo's numerous works bring together many of the elements found in earlier literature (Borgen 1984: 233–82; *ANRW* 2/21/1: 98–154):

(1) The positive evaluation of the Ptolemaic rulers, found in the *Letter of Aristeas,* in *Aristobulus,* and the *Sibylline Oracles* 3, is also expressed by Philo in his praise of King Ptolemy II Philadelphus (*Vita Mos* II:28–31) and his positive evaluation of the Ptolemaic kings in *Gaium* 138–39. He extends this positive view to the Roman rulers Augustus and Tiberius (*Gaium* 141–61). This positive attitude is conditioned upon their recognition of the rights of the Jews to live in accordance with the laws of their ancestors and to worship the One God. Accordingly, Gaius Caligula and the prefect Flaccus are under the judgment of God for their removal of the privileges of the Jews and their attempt to force them to worship the emperor (Stemberger 1983: 43–48; Borgen 1987b: 275–76).

(2) Philo continues the approach seen especially in the *Letter of Aristeas,* in *Aristobulus,* and the Wisdom of Solomon to interpret the laws of Moses and Jewish existence in general by means of Greek ideas and religious traditions. According to Philo, the authentic philosophy is formulated by Moses, and Greek philosophy contains elements of this true philosophy and is at some points derived from the teachings of Moses.

(3) The sharp polemic against polytheistic cult expressed in writings such as the *Sibylline Oracles* 3, the Wisdom of Solomon, and *3 Maccabees* is also found in Philo's writings. Philo even advocates death penalty for renegades to be executed on the spot, corresponding to the killing of Jewish apostates according to *3 Macc.* (*Spec Leg* I:54–55 and 315–16; Alon 1977: 112–24).

(4) The universal role of the Jewish people is a central theme in Jewish literature in Egypt. According to Philo, Moses was appointed king of a nation destined to offer prayer forever on behalf of the human race (*Vita Mos* I:149; cf. *Spec Leg* I:97; *Gaium* 3–4). The translation of the laws of Moses into Greek made God's cosmic laws known to the Greek-speaking world. Other peoples have begun to honor these laws, and Philo expresses the wish and hope that the time will come when all nations will cast aside their ancestral customs and honor the laws of Moses alone (*Vita Mos* II:43–44).

The quality of the life of the Jewish nation when they adhere to the cosmic principles given them in the Laws of Moses will bring victory over their enemies, and the Jewish nation will be the head of all nations (*Praem* 79–172). Philo favors the achievement of this aim by peaceful means, but he does not exclude the possibility of military warfare (*Virt* 22–50; *Praem* 93–95). He even draws on the expectation of an eschatological warrior-king, who will be a Jewish world emperor (*Praem* 95 and *Vita Mos* 1 §290, based on LXX Num 24:7). Moreover, the diaspora Jews will return to their home land (*Praem* 164–65). Philo himself oscillates between military and spiritual warfare, but he testifies to the existence of a militant eschatology in the Jewish community, ideas which probably inspired the Jews to take up arms at the death of Gaius Caligula in A.D. 41, and in the revolts of A.D. 66 and A.D. 115–17.

(5) Philo continues the tendency found in the earlier writings to stress the superiority of the Jewish nation. Philo's emphasis of the God-given role of the Jewish nation suggests that he did not only fight for equal rights for the Jews, but claimed that the call of the Jews was to be the head nation with other nations as their vassals (*ANRW* 2/21/1: 109–11).

(6) Philo testifies to the continuation of ideological attacks of the Jews from the non-Jews. His treatises *De confusione linguarum* and *De mutatione nominum* defend the Laws of Moses and Jewish institutions against apostates who are inclined to mock. And in *Apologia pra Iudaeis* he defends the Jews against attacks and criticism akin to the negative interpretation of Moses by the Egyptian historian Manetho and others. Thus, Philo tells that there were people who abused Moses as an impostor and prating mountebank (*Apol. Jud.* 6:2).

In this connection it should be mentioned that Josephus *Against Apion,* the anti-Jewish *Acts of the Alexandrian Martyrs,* and Gnostic writings prove that there was a broad stream of anti-Semitic tradition, attitudes, and literature in Egypt. The Jewish polemic against aspects of pagan culture and against some of the other ethnic groups, such as the Egyptians, was at times as pointed. Thus, the *Sib.Or.* 5, written towards the end of the 1st century A.D., is openly hostile to the gentiles in Egypt and Rome (Schürer *HJP*² 3/1: 595–608; Kasher 1985: 327–45; *ANRW* 2/21/1: 340–41; Collins *ANRW* 2/20/1: 436–38; Tcherikover 1963: 1–32; Hengel 1983: 655–85). An eschatological savior will appear, the adversaries will be destroyed, and a glorious Jerusalem will appear.

The Jewish expansion by ideological and peaceful means was defeated by the persecution of Alexandrian Jews in A.D. 38 and the subsequent edict by Claudius: the Jews were to be content with their established privileges in a city which was not their own (*CPJ* 1: 69–74; *CPJ* 2: 36–55; Smallwood 1976: 246–50).

Accordingly, the God-given universal calling of the Jewish nation could not be fulfilled by peaceful means. The militaristic eschatology was the alternative, and the fierce revolution in A.D. 115 was a logical result. The establishment of a Jewish empire by military means failed, however, and led instead to disastrous destruction in A.D. 117 rather than to a new age with the Jewish nation as the head.

Bibliography

Alon, G. 1977. *Jews, Judaism and the Classical World.* Jerusalem.

Applebaum, S. 1974. The Organization of the Jewish Communities in the Diaspora. Pp. 464–503 in *The Jewish People in the First Century,* ed. S. Safrai and M. Stern. *CRINT* 1/1. Assen.

Attridge, H. W. 1984. Historiography. Pp. 157–84 in Stone 1984.

Bell, H. I. 1926. *Juden und Griechen im Römischen Alexandreia.* BAO 9. Leipzig.

———. 1976. *Jews and Christians in Egypt.* Westport, CT.

Borgen, P. 1981. *Bread from Heaven.* NovTSup 10. Leiden.

———. 1984. Philo of Alexandria. Pp. 233–82 in Stone 1984.

———. 1987a. Aristobulus and Philo. Pp. 7–16 in *Philo, John and Paul: New Perspectives on Judaism and Early Christianity,* ed. P. Borgen. BJS 131. Atlanta.

———. 1987b. Philo, Luke and Geography. Pp. 273–85 in *Philo, John and Paul: New Perspectives on Judaism and Early Christianity,* ed. P. Borgen. BJS 131. Atlanta.

Collins, J. J. 1984. The Sibylline Oracles. Pp. 357–81 in Stone 1984.

Fraser, P. M. 1972. *Ptolemaic Alexandria.* 3 vols. Oxford.

Hayward, R. 1982. The Jewish Temple at Leontopolis. *JJS* 33: 429–43.

Hengel, M. 1974. *Judaism and Hellenism.* 2 vols. London.

———. 1983. Messianische Hoffnung und politischer "Radikalismus" in der "Jüdisch-hellenistischen Diaspora." Pp. 655–86 in *Apocalypticism in the Mediterranean World and the Near East,* ed. D. Hellholm. Tübingen.

Kasher, A. 1985. *The Jews in Hellenistic and Roman Egypt.* Tübingen.

Lewis, N. 1985. *Life in Egypt under Roman Rule.* Oxford.

Mendelson, A. 1982. *Secular Education in Philo of Alexandria.* Vol. 7 in *Monographs of the Hebrew Union College.* Cincinnati.

Nickelsburgh, G. W. E. 1981. *Jewish Literature Between the Bible and the Mishnah.* Philadelphia.

———. 1984. The Bible Rewritten and Expanded. Pp. 89–156 in Stone 1984.

Porten, B. 1968. *Archives from Elephantine.* Los Angeles.

Rajak, T. 1985. Jewish Rights in the Greek Cities under Roman Rule. Pp. 19–35 in *Approaches to Ancient Judaism 5: Studies in Judaism and its Graeco-Roman Context,* ed. W. S. Green. BJS 32. Atlanta.

Rostovtzeff, M. 1941. *The Social and Economic History of the Hellenistic World.* 2 vols. Oxford.

Sachau, E. 1911. *Aramäische Papyrus und Ostraka aus einer jüdischen Miltitärkolonie zu Elephantine.* 2 vols. Leipzig.

Sayce, A. H., and Cowley, A. E. 1906. *Aramaic Papyri Discovered at Assuan.* London.

Smallwood, E. M. 1970. *Philonis Alexandrini Legatio ad Gaium.* 2d ed. Leiden.

———. 1976. *The Jews under Roman Rule.* Leiden.

Stemberger, G. 1983. *Die Römische Herrschaft im Urteil der Juden.* Erträge der Forschung 195. Darmstadt.

Stern, M. 1976. *From Herodotus to Plutarch.* Vol. 1 of *Greek and Latin Authors on Jews and Judaism.* Jerusalem.

Stone, M., ed. 1984. *Jewish Writings of the Second Temple Period.* CRINT 2/2. Assen.

Tcherikover, V. 1963. The Decline of the Jewish Diaspora in Egypt in the Roman Period. *JJS* 14: 1–32.

———. 1966. *Hellenistic Civilization and the Jews.* Philadelphia.

PEDER BORGEN

JEWS IN NORTH AFRICA

Pre-Hellenistic Hebrew seals found at Zliten (Tripolitania in W Libya) and at Cyrene (E Libya), also an amphora inscribed with Hebrew letters at Busetta (Tripolitania) suggest the presence of Jews in N Africa before the Ptolemaic conquest of Cyrenaica. The Jews of Jerba and Boreion, indeed, claimed settlement from the time of Solomon. Jews, probably military colonists, were introduced into N Africa by Ptolemy Lagos in the late 4th century B.C.E., occupying the royal reserves. One of the new Jewish villages may have been Kafarodis (Heb "new village"). A Jewish paramilitary settlement has been identified at Ein Targhuna. The Jewish element in Cyrene was influenced by the Hasmonean revolt in Judea; the book *2 Maccabees,* of which only an abridgment remains, was the work of the Cyrenean Jason. In the 2d century B.C.E., when N Africa was reunited with Ptolemaic Egypt (145 B.C.E.), a fresh wave of Jews entered the region.

In the early 1st century B.C.E. the 5 cities of Cyrenaica (Cyrene, Barka, Berenice, Teucheira, Ptolemais) became independent, and Roman contractors took over the royal lands as sheep runs. The expansion S under the Ptolemies had caused a decline in agriculture, as the Libyans of the S could no longer move N in the summer with their flocks, whose manure was lost to the agriculture of the fertile mountains. The Roman contractors' flocks further restricted the Libyan cultivators, and the Jewish settlers of the royal lands suffered and were probably evicted.

A considerable part of the Jewish population lived in Cyrene, Berenice (Benghazi), Apollonia, Ptolemaiṣ, Barka, and Teucheira. There is evidence of the existence of synagogues at Cyrene, Berenice, and Boreion; the affluent community of Berenice also owned an amphitheatre for assembly, and the community was administered by a board of archons. Apollonia and Ptolemais have yielded Jewish funerary inscriptions. A number of Jewish tombs with Gk inscriptions have been studied at Teucheira, revealing a poor community of low cultural level, which also suffered a high infant mortality rate. A few of the inhabitants possessed Roman citizenship, and some Libyan influence was perceptible. This community may have reached Teucheira from Egypt in the late 2d century B.C.E., when a small group appears to have been educated in the city's gymnasium. The known inscriptions cease in 94 C.E. Some young Jews were admitted to the gymnasia of Cyrene and Ptolemais at the end of the 1st century B.C.E., and one Elazaros son of Jason held an important post in the administration of Cyrene during Nero's reign.

In the late 1st century B.C.E. the Cyreneans endeavored to prevent the Jews from transmitting the half-shekel tax due to the Temple of Jerusalem. The Roman government overruled the city's opposition, and from the proceedings it is evident that the Jews of Cyrene were privileged noncitizens exempt from the tax normally paid by that class. In the year 73 C.E. an extreme activist, Jonathan, who had fled from Judea, appeared at Cyrene and initiated an anti-Roman movement. The richer Jews warned the governor and the movement was suppressed, but the governor seized the opportunity to execute 3,000 wealthy Jews and to confiscate their property. This act paved the way for revolt; in 115 C.E. there broke out the great Jewish rising which lasted 3 years and raged through Cyrene, Egypt, Cyprus, and Mesopotamia. The destruction in Cyrene has been amply revealed by archaeology, and other places damaged were Balagrae, Teucheira, and probably Berenice. Marmarica also suffered heavily. It would seem that Jews returned to Cyrenaica only at the end of the 2d century.

Jewish communities in the W countries of N Africa do not seem to have been influenced by the revolt. A large number of Jews from Judea are thought to have been resettled in the Syrtis in central Libya (*Iscina Locus Augusti Iudaeorum*—Medinet e-Sultan), others in Carthage. It is unknown when the first Jewish communities reached NW Africa (Tunis, Numidia, Algeria, Morocco). Rabbi Akiba visited the country in the early 2d century; Volubilis has yielded an inscription of Mishnaic date. Judah the Prince (late 2d century C.E.) said that Judaism extended from Tyre to Carthage, where several mishnaic scholars were active. For the Jews of Africa the later 2d century initiated a period of prosperity which lasted until the end of the 3d century. Both proselytes and gentiles practicing Jewish rites began to appear. Something is known of the Jewish cemetery at Gamart near Carthage. Synagogues are known in Tunis at Carthage, Hamam Lif, Utica, Tozar, Henshir Dju'ana, Qirwan, Yehudiyah, Sidi Brahim, and Sousse; in Numidia at Hippo, Simitu, Henshir Fuara, Kesur al Halphun, and Tipasa; in Mauritania at Sitifis, Oziah, Aumale, Cherchel, Volubilis, and Constantine. A synagogue certainly existed at Oea (Tripolitania), and another at Boreion in the same region. The organization of the synagogues probably derived from Roman influence: The posts of archisynagogos, archon, grammateus, and gerusiarch are known among the synagogue officials.

The emperor Constantine's Edict of Toleration in 313 presaged the end of the toleration of Judaism. Christianity had spread throughout N Africa in the course of the 4th century. Largely due to the pressure of the Christian church an increasing number of laws progressively restricted Jewish rights and reduced their communities to an oppressed minority.

A highly controversial question is that of Judaism and its influence on the Berbers, the original natives of N Africa who spoke a Semitic language. The Greeks and others claimed that they were Canaanites who had been expelled from Palestine by Joshua, but this was a politically inspired invention. Ibn Khaldun, writing in the 12th century, was the first to record (with due caution) the possible existence of judaizing Berbers in the Aures mountains (Numidia), in W Tripolitania, and in Mauretania. As Jewish proselytization was impossible under Byzantine and Islamic rule, any such activity would have belonged at the latest to the 3d century C.E.; it has been pointed out that traditions of Judaeo-Berbers are found in areas which had been inhabited by Jews in the Roman period. Further, Libyan proselytes were known to R. Hoshayah, Tertullian, and Saint Augustine. Libyan influences were present at Teucheira; there were Libyan converts in Cyrene, in E Cyrenaica, and even in Jaffa. The Jewish Berber queen Dahya el-Kahina, who gallantly fought the Muslim invaders in the Aures, may therefore be something more than a myth.

Bibliography

Applebaum, S. 1979. *Jews and Greeks in Ancient Cyrene.* Leiden.

Hirschberg, H. Z. 1959. Judaizing Berbers in North Africa. *Zion* 22: 10–20 (in Hebrew).

———. 1965. *A History of the Jews of North Africa.* Jerusalem (in Hebrew).

Pucci, M. 1981. *La rivolta ebraica al tempo di Traiano.* Pisa.

Simon, M. 1962. *Recherches d'histoire Judeo-Chretienne.* Paris.

Stern, M. 1974. The Jewish Diaspora. Pp. 117–83 in *The Jewish People in the First Century,* ed. S. Safrai, M. Stern. CRINT 1/1. Assen.

SHIMON APPLEBAUM

JUDAISM IN ROME

Paul's epistle to the Romans and the book of Acts inform us about the presence of Jews at Rome in the 1st century. The information they supply is indirect and within a theological context; nevertheless, they are sufficient for us to realize that the Christian community of Rome, both in its historical origin and in its internal structure, was closely bound to the Judaism of the capital of the empire (see *StadtrChr*). Consequently, in order to know about the church of Rome it is absolutely necessary to know about the life of the Jews. The Letter to the Romans clearly presupposes a substantial Jewish component of that Christian community, as can be deduced both from the terminology used ("Jewish" and "Israel" occur 11 times; see especially Rom 2:17, but also 1:16, 2:9, 10, 28, 29; etc.) as well as from the themes treated (e.g., the value of the Mosaic law and the salvation of the people of Israel). The Acts of the Apostles in its concluding chapter mentions two meetings Paul had in Rome with the Jews of the city, first with the "most important ones" (28:17) and then with "many" others (28:23). Even if these meetings did not produce great results, their positioning at the climax of the book emphasizes the importance which Luke attached to them. Also, the writer devotes a much greater attention to the Jews of Rome than that which he gives to the members of the Roman church itself (both groups, however, are described as "brothers"; 28:15, 17). These two sources attest to the period ca. A.D. 50–60. But the history of the Jews at Rome begins much earlier, and it extends beyond into the following centuries.

A. History of Jewish Presence at Rome
B. Internal Organization of the Jewish Community
C. Size of the Jewish Community
D. Location in the City
E. Social Status
F. Typical Religious Beliefs

A. History of Jewish Presence at Rome

A number of sources, some of which have the advantage of being contemporaneous with the information supplied, provide us with data about the history of Jews in Rome. Valerius Maximus (writing at the time of Tiberius) provides an historical note about the earliest presence of the Jews at Rome. Referring to events of 139 B.C., he notes that in this year the *Praetor Peregrinus* (the municipal authority in charge of foreigners) expelled from Rome the astrologers and the Caldeans; besides that, he "forced the Jews to head back to their homes, who had tried to spoil Roman customs with the religious cult of Jupiter Sabazius" (*Facta ac Dicta Memorabilia* 1.3.3). According to the literary sources, the only historical possiblity for the first arrival of the Jews in Rome coincides with one or more of the three delegations sent from Palestine at the time of the Maccabee brothers ca. mid-2d cent B.C.: Judas (1 Macc 8:17–32), Jonathan (1 Macc 12:1–4), and Simon (1 Macc 14:24). It is unclear just what the "cult of Jupiter Sabazius" was. This could be a corruption for *YHWH ṣĕbāʾôt.*, an allusion to the feast of the sabbath, or a witness to a syncretistic form of Judaism from Asia Minor (which was the native land of god Sabazius).

A more certain date for Jewish arrival in Rome coincides with Pompey's conquest of Palestine and Jerusalem in 63 B.C., a conquest which consisted of forced importation (see Philo *Gaium* 155; Josephus *Ant* 14.71.120; *JW* 1.154.180). We do not know the extent to which commercial motivations may have influenced this policy (in contrast, probably, to the Jewish communities in the port cities of Pozzuoli and Ostia). In any case, already in October of 59 B.C. Marcus Tullius Cicero referred to a crowd *(turba)* of Roman Jews that was present during his speech defending the governor of Asia, who had been accused of extorting from the Jews of that province (*Flacc.* 66). Likewise, in the 1st century B.C. we have statements alluding especially to the Jews' zeal in winning converts (see Hor. *Sat.* 1.4.138–44 [esp. 142–143]; 1.5.97–104; 1.9.60–73; see also Ov. *Ars Am.* 1.76).

The more-extensive information we have comes from the 1st century A.D. While Augustus was generous in their regard (see *Gaium* 154–58), the emperor Tiberius (14–37) in the year 19 had a certain number of Jews deported to Sardinia (Josephus *Ant* 18.81–84; Suet. *Tib.* 36; Tac. *Ann.* 11.28; Dio Cassius *Hist.* 57.18). There is also the much-discussed decree of the emperor Claudius (41–54), which can be dated to A.D. 49 or even earlier to 41. According to the famous text of Suetonius, Claudius "expelled from Rome Jews continually causing disturbance, Chrestus being the instigator" (*Claud.* 25); but on the other hand, according to another text "He did not expel them, but ordered them not to hold meetings while still continuing in their traditional way of life" (Dio Cass. *Hist.* 60.6.6). It is possible to harmonize the two accounts by suggesting that Claudius did not drive from Rome *all* the Jews, but only those involved in a riot (and thus the statement of Acts 18:2 would have to be judged exaggerated). Under the emperor Nero (54–68) Jews must have enjoyed complete freedom; indeed, even Nero's second wife, Poppaea Sabina, was at least sympathetic toward Judaism, if not in fact a proselyte (*Ant* 20.195 describes her as "God-fearing"). The situation worsened under Vespasian (69–79) who, after the conquest of Jerusalem in A.D. 70, turned the annual tax for the Temple of Jerusalem, now destroyed, into a tax for the temple of Jupiter Capitolinus: (Josephus *JW* 7.218; Dio Cass. *Hist.* 66.7.2; we also know that Domitian was later extremely rigorous in collecting it [Suet. *Dom.* 12]).

The presence and life of the Roman Jews in the 2d–4th centuries is abundantly and directly documented in the burial inscriptions of the 6 or 7 Jewish catacombs (similar to those of the Christians) thus far uncovered near some of the roads leading out from Rome (1 near the Via Portuensis; 3 next to the Via Appia; 1 along the Via Labicana; 1 double catacomb close to the Via Nomentana); these served as cemeteries for the different Jewish communities of the city. Taken together they have provided us with about 580 inscriptions, of which 75 percent are in Greek, while the remainder are mostly in Latin (only 3 are in Hebrew, 1 is in Aramaic, and 2 are bilingual, of which 1 is Greek-Latin and the other Aramaic-Greek). The oldest of these cemeteries was certainly the so-called Catacombs of Monteverde close to the Via Portuensis (today it no longer exists because of a cave-in during the 1920s). It served the Jews of the Trastevere Quarter, who according to Philo made up the oldest Jewish settlement in Rome.

B. Internal Organization of the Jewish Community

These catacomb inscriptions provide important information about the internal organization of the different groups of Roman Jews. Roman Jews, as opposed to those of Alexandria (see *Ant* 12.108; 14.117; Philo *Flacc.* 74), were not grouped together in a single social entity; they did not form a true and properly called *politeuma.* Rather, they were subdivided into various communities designated by the term *synagogē* (this title never indicates a place of worship, which instead was called *proseucha,* from its use as a place for "prayer" [see *CIL* VI: 9821; *Gaium* 156; Juv. *Satira* 3.296]; besides, archeology has not yet brought to light any remains of such buildings, while the beautiful ruins of the synagogue of nearby Ostia are well known).

At present, 11 Jewish communities have been documented (2 others are under discussion). In all probability 5 of these preceded Paul's arrival in Rome. The oldest could possibly be the one named "of the Hebrews" (set up when it was the only one in existence), followed by the one of the *Vernaculi* (constituted, in contrast to the preceding one, by the Jews already born in Rome). There follow 3 others, distinguished by the name of their respective benefactors, all of the Augustan period: those of the *Augustenses,* of the *Agrippenses,* and of the *Volumnenses.* The remaining 6, certainly of later date, bear the following names: *Campenses, Suburenses, Calcarenses,* "Tripolitani," "of Elaias," and "of Scina."

There is no documentation for a higher administrative body which might have presided over all these groups. Only in the 4th century do we know of the title *archigerousiarchēs* (from the Villa Torlonia catacomb in the Via Nomentana), but it is possible that here we are dealing with an honorific title restricted to only one "synagogue." The internal structure of the different communities consisted of a number of offices attested on burial inscriptions. They can be listed as follows according to the order of their importance:

First were the *gerousiarchēs,* who presided over the council of the elders in charge of the administration of each community and the safeguarding of its religious, judicial, and financial interests (in fact the members of the council were called "presbyters").

Second were the *archontes,* who made up the executive committee of the individual councils; elected for a year, they could be re-elected and in practice held the effective control of the community (there also existed the position of "archon designate," inasmuch as the title is also assigned to children).

Third was the *grammateus,* who acted not only as a "Doctor of the Law" but also as secretary or chancellor.

Finally, there were also a "general collector" in charge of gathering funds destined for the common coffer; an administrator of the common goods; an attorney (i.e., the legal protector of the community); the *archisynagogus,* who concerned himself with the place of worship and presided over the religious assemblies (the title often appears even among pagan communities of the Greek world); and a minister, similar to a sacristan for the service of the synagogue. Other honorific titles included "father/mother of the synagogue" (reserved for men/women of special merit) and "priest" (indicating only levitical ancestry, since outside Jerusalem there was no priestly ministry either after or before A.D. 70).

Apart from the disputed ordinance of Claudius mentioned above, these communities must have enjoyed guaranteed juridical security. In fact, Julius Caesar's legislation in favor of the Jews is well-known, and it was substantially retained in force all the way to Constantine (the package of laws is found in *Ant* 14.185–246). It comprised 3 principal privileges: full freedom of association and worship, exemption from military service, and the power to constitute separate tribunals. In particular, the Jews of Rome—like all Jews in the Empire—were exempted from all the religious cults of the state, including that of the emperor. Consequently, scholars have noted some problems with Dio Cassius' note that the emperor Domitian in A.D. 95 executed the consul Flavius Clemens and "many others who were deviating toward Jewish customs: of them only some were put to death, others were deprived of their goods" (*Hist.* 67.14). The same historian reports that Domitian's successor, Nerva, forbade accusing anyone "neither of ungodliness nor of Jewish way of life" (*Hist.* 68.1.2). Inasmuch as Judaism was a *religio licita,* it is possible that we have here a veiled allusion to Christianity, even if it had a distinctively Jewish stamp (that is already understood in Eus. *Hist. Eccl.* 3.18.4).

C. Size of the Jewish Community

The number of Jews in Rome must have varied according to the historical periods. Since Cicero's type of literary oration tends to amplify the colorings of his discourse, we should be cautious in interpreting his comments about a Jewish *turba* ("crowd"; see above). The first certain information concerns the year 4 B.C., when up to 8,000 Roman Jews accompanied a delegation from Palestine requesting Augustus to unify Palestine with the province of Syria after the death of Herod the Great (*Ant* 17.300). In addition, we know that in A.D. 19 Tiberius exiled to Sardinia 4,000 Jewish youths old enough to bear arms (Tac. *Ann.* 11.85.4; Suet. *Tib.* 36). If we take into account the relationship between these youths and their respective families, we can legitimately deduce that at the time of St. Paul the Jews at Rome numbered around 20,000 (out of a total population of nearly 1,000,000). The circumstances probably changed as a result of the Jewish war. In fact, according to Josephus, 100,000 Jewish slaves were sold in A.D. 70 at a low price (*JW* 6.420); it is quite reasonable to suppose that a large part of this human merchandise ended up in the capital of the empire (Martialis also refers to Jews who had come to Rome from Jerusalem after its destruction; *Epigr.* 7.55). Both Martialis and Juvenal provide us with interesting details about their impoverished condition between the end of the 1st century and the beginning of the 2d century (see E. below).

D. Location in the City

In contrast to Alexandria, where the Jews occupied 2 out of the 5 quarters of the city (*Flacc.* 55), at Rome they were distributed in various areas. However, in all probability, they were more numerous and resided for longer periods of time in the Trastevere section of the city; indeed, that is the only section Philo recounts for the time of Augustus (*Gaium* 155), which is confirmed by the relative antiquity of the Jewish catacomb of Monteverde (see above). But the Jews were also present in at least 4 other parts of the city. One was the popular and ill-famed quarter of the Subura, from which one of the Roman "synagogues" takes its name (see above). The same must be said for the Campus Martius (the name of another of the "synagogues"; see above), while the location of the *Calcarenses* "synagogue" is uncertain (it comes from *calcaria* = lime-kiln). Perhaps it was located in the neighborhood of the place where Diocletian later built his baths (in front of the modern Stazione Termini). Another area of Jewish settlement was in the vicinity of the *Porta Capena,* opposite the Circus Maximus (see Juvenal's *Satira* 3.11–14); but here settlement seems to have been a matter of almost gypsy-like encampments. We also know that a Jew lived near the *macellum* (= market), probably on the Caelian hill (see Frey *CII,* 210).

E. Social Status

The Jews of Rome must have had a middle-low tenor of life. Certainly no conclusion can be drawn from the presence in Rome of the Herodian family members Agrippa I (friend of Caligula and of Claudius) and of his daughter Berenice (paramour of Titus; Suet. *Tit.* 7; Dio Cass. *Hist.* 66.15.3–4). Already the very beginnings of the Jewish presence at Rome were due to a small nucleus of "prisoners of war later freed by their masters" (*Gaium* 155; see above). Explicit references to Jewish slaves are very rare (a woman by the name of *Acme* was in the service of Livia, the wife of Augustus, *Ant* 17.134, 141; a circumcised slave was in the service of Trimalchio in the *Satyricon* (68.6) of Petronius Arbiter; on the other hand, the obscene verse of Mart. *Epigr.* 7.35.4 has metaphorical meaning). Jewish mercantile activities are not attested, but we are informed about handicraft works (see Acts 18:2) and activities associated with the theater (see Josephus, *Life* 3; Mart. *Epigr.* 7.82; 11.94). We also know about a Jewish dealer in brimstone matches (Mart. *Epigr.* 1.41), about a woman who foretold the future and "for a few coins sells all the dreams you want" (Juvenal, *Satira* 6.543, 546f), and about a young beggar (Mart. *Epigr.* 12.57.13).

The Jewish catacombs provide other pieces of evidence, which generally reveal a prevalent condition of poverty. The family burial rooms are very few, and even fewer are those decorated with paintings. Likewise, the sarcophagi are rare and not very elaborate; many tombs are completely without any epitaph; and even the inscriptions are more often than not rudimentary, containing evident grammatical mistakes. This source mentions a painter (*CII,* 109), a butcher (*CII,* 210), and a teacher (*CII,* 133; see also 201 and 508). It is not clear whether any socially prestigeous persons came from the "synagogues" of Rome; the case of Josephus cannot be cited as evidence for Roman Judaism, since his education and status were achieved prior to his stay in Rome. An exception could be Caecilius of Calacte, literary critic of the Augustan period (and probably a Jew), against whom the anonymous author of *On the Sublime* (see 1.1f; 4.2; 8.4; 32.1, 8) argues. In any case, no comparison is possible between the Jews of Rome and those of Alexandria.

F. Typical Religious Beliefs

Pagan literary sources (including Horatius, Ovid, Seneca, Persius, Martial, Juvenal) attest to two typical Jewish practices which apparently particularly impressed the citizens of Rome: circumcision and observance of the Sabbath (see especially Pers. *Satira* 5.179–88). But there is also reference to abstinence from pork and to fasting in general. Likewise the Romans were surprised by the concept of a divinity not capable of being represented artistically (see Juv., *Satira* 14.97; Petronius, Fr. 37; Lucanus, *Pharsalia* 11.593), which could be viewed as a contempt for the gods (see Tac. *Hist.* 5.13).

On the tombstones of the Jewish catacombs there often appear decorations which represent typical objects of worship: the *menorah* (7-branched candlestick), the *aron* (synagogue shrine for the Torah scrolls), the *shofar* (ram's horn trumpet which sounded the beginning of the New Year), the *etrog* (citrus fruit for the feast of the Tabernacles), and the *lulab* (small branch for the same feast). The catacomb of the Randanini Vineyard (on the Via Appia) also exhibits wall paintings of obvious pagan origin, such as the goddess Fortuna crowning a young naked man (perhaps evidence of syncretism?).

One would expect the inscriptions to emphasize the typical Jewish (i.e., Pharisaical) hope in the resurrection, inasmuch as they deal with death; however, such a hope has very little documentation. The longest and most important text relating to resurrection-belief is that of *Regina,* from the name of the deceased, datable in the 2d century (see *CII,* 476, line 6: *Nam sperare potest ideo quod surgat in aevom promissum,* "One is able to hope, because he/she will rise in the promised age"). This perhaps attests to a syncretistic adaptation to the religious concepts of the pagan surroundings, even if one must consider the stereotyped repetition of the epigraphic formulae (which can also reflect more the thought of the marble worker than of the one commissioning the inscription). For example, quite often there recurs the formula of probable pagan origin: "Take courage, no one is immortal!" (*CII,* 314, 335, 380, 401, 450) and "Friends, I am waiting for you here!" (*CII,* 32). We would say that in addition to containing a good wish for peace, these inscriptions generally limited themselves to underlining the moral qualities of the deceased, such as marital fidelity (*CII,* 457), pious observance of the Law (*CII,* I 72, 111, 132, 509), and regular attendance at the synagogue (*CII,* 321); once the deceased is designated as a "singer of the psalms" (Fasola 1976: 19–20). About one dead person we read simply: *bene vixit in judaismo* ("he lived well in Judaism" *CII,* 537); perhaps that was the best praise.

Bibliography

Fasola, U. 1976. Le due catacombe ebraiche di Villa Torlonia. *RivArCr* 52: 7–62.

Frey, J. B. 1930–31. Les communautes juives a Rome aux premiers temps de l'Eglise. *RSR* 20: 269–297; 21: 129–68.

Leon, H. J. 1960. *The Jews of Ancient Rome.* Philadelphia.

Penna, R. 1982. Les Juifs a Rome au temps de l'apôtre Paul. *NTS* 28: 321–47.

Smallwood, E. M. 1981. *The Jews Under Roman Rule.* 2d ed. SJLA 20. Leiden.

Stern, M. 1974–80. *Greek and Latin Authors on Jews and Judaism.* 2 vols. Leiden.

Vogelstein, H., and Rieger, P. 1895–96. *Geschichte der Juden in Rom.* 2 vols. Berlin.

Wieffel, W. 1977. The Jewish Community in Ancient Rome and the Origins of Roman Christianity. Pp. 100–19 in *The Roman Debate,* ed. K. P. Donfried. Minneapolis.

ROMANO PENNA

BABYLONIAN JUDAISM

The Babylonian exile may have begun in the days of King Jehoiakim (609–598 B.C.E.) as implied in Dan 1:1; 2 Chr 36:6–7 and by Josephus (*AgAp* 1:19). Evidently this exile was only of limited extent. But in the spring of 598 B.C.E., Nebuchadnezzar exiled Jehoiachin the king of Judah to Babylon, together with a considerable segment of the upper class of Judean society. Among the exiles were government authorities (2 Kgs 24:14–15; Jer 24:1; 29:2), the nobility of Judah and Jerusalem (Jer 27:2), lords of estates, and the "men of might" who were subject to military conscription (2 Kgs 24:15–16). Also exiled were the priests and prophets (Jer 29:1), the craftsmen and smiths (Jer 29:1–2), and many residents of the coastal plain and the S (Negeb) of Palestine (Jer 13:18–19).

The deportation of the government and the religious leadership helped maintain the Judean national and religious distinctiveness in the midst of a pagan population whose external ritual was magnificent and whose monumental temples seemed exotic and impressive. This situation challenged the leaders, who labored to prevent the absorption of the exiles into their alien surroundings. Indeed, the fact that the Babylonian exile has continued to exist down to our generation is proof of its having maintained to a great degree its religious and ethnic distinctiveness.

The Babylonian exile is called *haggôlâ* or *gôlâ* ("the exile" or simply "exile") in the Bible (Ezra 1:1) as well as in the literature of the Mishnaic period, (*m. Šeqal.* 2.4) and the literature of the Talmudic sages (*b. Roš Haš.* 23b). This appelation may derive from the perception of the high qualitative level of the exiles to Babylon, or perhaps is an allusion to their large population which expanded over the course of time.

A. Economic Status
B. Civil and Legal Standing
C. Leaders and Leadership
D. Intellectual and Religious Life

A. Economic Status

We cannot learn much about the economic status of the exiles from the books of Ezekiel, Jeremiah, Second Isaiah, or Daniel. From Ezekiel (1:1) we learn that the exiles were settled near the river Chebar by their captors. This region is well-watered, and it is very fertile. The prophet Ezekiel himself evidently lived in Tel-abib (Ezek 3:15); his activities extended from 593 to 571 B.C.E.

From the books of Ezra and Nehemiah we learn that some of the exiles became wealthy. They assisted their fellow Jews who went on pilgrimages to Jerusalem and sent with them expensive gifts for the building of the Temple (Ezra 1:4–6; 8:25–32). It is said of the "heads of fathers' houses" who made the pilgrimage to Jerusalem that "They gave after their ability into the treasury of the work three score and one thousand darics of gold, and five thousand pounds of silver, and one hundred priests' tunics" (Ezra 2:69). We also learn of pilgrims to Jerusalem who brought with them servants and assorted pack animals (Ezra 2:65–66; Neh 7:67–68).

More details concerning the economic status of the exiles can be learned from tablets unearthed in Babylonian excavations and published by E. F. Weidner (1939). From them we learn of Jewish craftsmen employed in the large construction projects of Nebuchadnezzar. They were brought to the city of Babylon together with many other craftsmen from Tyre, Byblos, and Aradus. We also learn that Judean exiles of good family, headed by King Jehoiachin, his family, and his nobles, were maintained by special allocations from the royal treasury. This substantiates the biblical account of the release and the provisions for King Jehoiachin (2 Kgs 25:27–30).

We glean additional details from the archives of the house of Murašu which dated back to 455–403 B.C.E. The house of Murašu was located in Nippur, 90 km SW of Babylon. The documents deal with moneylenders, hirers and leasers of lands, tax collectors, and people who served as middlemen between landowners and agricultural workers. From them we learn of Jewish workers whose task it was to irrigate fields, Jewish fishermen, and a Jewish shepherd. Of the more than 150 officials mentioned in these documents, 13 of them were Jews. See also MURASHÛ, ARCHIVE OF.

The caravan trade in Babylon expanded during this period, and the demand for merchandise was increasing. The prices of many consumer goods rose, especially the prices of food commodities. We may assume that the Jewish farmers, along with the others, reaped economic benefits from this development. Josephus (*Ant* 11.3) reports that many of the exiles did not return to Judea after the declaration of Cyrus, because they did not want to abandon their possessions. The exiles evidently felt quite content to remain in the foreign country of Babylon, following the advice of the prophet Jeremiah (29:5–7).

In the Seleucid Period, local agriculture made great strides forward. It became diversified through the introduction of new varieties of crops, which were brought from countries lying to the west. Naturally, agriculture flourished, demand increased, and prices rose. Jewish farmers excelled, and we find interesting evidence of this in documents from the end of the 3d century B.C.E. Antiochus III, the king of Seleucia (223–187 B.C.E.), was in the E part of his kingdom subduing an uprising against his authority. While there he heard about revolts against his rule in Lydia and Phrygia. He wrote the following to Zeuxis, the head of the satrapy of Lydia (according to Polybius 16.1, 8), approximately in the year 201: "I determined to transport 2,000 Jewish families with their effects from Mesopotamia and Babylonia to the fortresses and most important places. For I am convinced that they will be loyal guardians of our interests because of their piety to [their] God, and I know that they have had the testimony of my forefathers to their good faith and eagerness to do as they are asked . . . and since I have promised it, use their own laws. And when you have brought them to the places mentioned, you shall give each of them a place to build a house and cultivate and plant with vines, etc." (*Ant* 12.149–52).

Many researchers have dealt with the disputed authenticity of this letter. However, when it is linked with other evidence, we can see that the letter as a whole is historical, although perhaps not in every detail (Marcus 1957).

The Mishnah tells us about a Jewish farmer from Babylon: "Ben Antinus brought up first fruits from Babylon and they would not accept them . . . lest it should be established as an obligation" (*m. Ḥal* 4.11). The man was "an important man" *(Midr. Tan.),* the owner of an agricultural estate. To judge by his Hellenistic name (according to some mss his name was Titus), it is possible that he lived and was active in the Seleucid period. This Mishnah continues: "Joseph the priest brought the first fruits of his wine and oil, and they did not accept them from him." Since the 2 occurrences are related in one continuous passage, we may assume that the farmer, as well, came up from Babylon, bringing with him wine from his vineyard and oil from his olive orchard.

We are not well enough informed about the Parthian period to know much about the economic activities of the Jews of Babylon at that time. However, we can accept the assumption that no great occupational changes took place, since in the ancient world it was customary for sons to continue in their fathers' vocation. We learn of the wealth of the Jews of Babylon and of their generosity from a tradition that deals with the bringing of the shekel tax from the lands of the diaspora to the Temple. It tells of the offerings made to the priests by the Jews of Babylon and Media: "This was the richest [fund] of all of them, for in it were golden istras and golden darics" (*t. Šeqal.* 2.4). Josephus tells how the Jews of Babylon gathered and kept in the city of Nisibis the pledged donations and the half-shekels they paid, and that from there they brought them up to Jerusalem, tens of thousands of Jews traveling together, because of the fear of highwaymen (*Ant* 18.312). King Herod (37–4 B.C.E.) was anxious to protect the pilgrims from Babylon. He learned that Zamaris, a military commander, had left Babylon leading 500 soldiers, including cavalry and archers, and had arrived in Syria. Herod convinced them to settle in the toparchy of Batanaea, and there he built them a settlement called Bathyra, so that they would maintain the security of the Jews coming up to Jerusalem.

Josephus also tells us of Jewish merchants in royal courts who employed their influence to convert royalty to Judaism in Adiabene, including Izates I (35–60 C.E.), Queen Helena, her brother, and her husband Monobazus I. Also, Josephus writes at great length about a merchant named Ananias who had access to the court of Abennerigus the king of Charax Spasinu (lies between the mouths of the Tigris and the Euphrates). Izates, who was staying at Abennerigus's court in keeping with his father's command, there converted to Judaism under the influence of Ananias and with the mediation of the ladies of the court (*Ant* 20.17–35). Josephus also tells of another Jew, Eleazar, who came from Galilee and urged Izates to be circumcised (*Ant* 20.43).

We do not know where these first merchants came from. In any case, their presence and their religious influence in royal courts is important information, because we cannot assume that they carried on their activities only through contacts with non-Jews, without any personal contact with local Jews.

We also learn of Abba Bar Abba, who lived at the end of the 2d century C.E. and who is referred to in the Talmud and in midrash as Abuha Deshmuel ("The Father of Shmuel," his illustrious son). He dealt in silks and fabrics, often far from his city of Nehardea. He became a wealthy merchant and was also the owner of a large estate (Beer 1982).

From Josephus we also learn about the poorer Jews of Babylon. He tells us about an insurrection led by two brothers, Anilaeus and Assinaeus. Their father died, and their mother turned them over to a weaver so that they would learn his trade (which was not very respectable in middle class circles at that time and place). Other poor young people rallied around them. (For more on this insurrection, see below).

B. Civil and Legal Standing

According to later rabbinic tradition, Nebuchadnezzar treated the prisoner exiles very cruelly (*Midr. Pss.*, Psalm 137). But evidently the reference is to the brutal treatment of the Jewish prisoners from Palestine by the Romans after the destruction of the Second Temple. From the book of Daniel we learn that Nebuchadnezzar issued an order to bring to his court some "of the children of Israel, and of the seed royal, and of the nobles . . . to stand in the king's palace" (Dan 1:3–4). However, Josephus tells us that King Darius gave much exceptional honor to Daniel (*Ant* 10.263–264). According to the LXX, Daniel was appointed to a very high post in the kingdom. As is well known, Cyrus showed tolerance to many religions in his kingdom. He restored ruined temples and ritual sites destroyed by his predecessors, and he actively supported them with money and various ritual necessities (*ANET,* 316–17). This was also true of the destroyed temple in Jerusalem (Ezra 1:5–11). We have no knowledge of the treatment of the Jews in his kingdom by Cambyses (530–522 B.C.E.), who was Cyrus's successor. However, concerning their treatment by Cambyses's successor, Darius I, it is said in the book of Ezra (6:8–12) that he approved the construction of the temple in Jerusalem, despite the opposition of various ethnic groups.

The historical truth of the book of Esther is questionable, but in any case we do not find in it information concerning an anti-Jewish government policy. We learn that Ahasuerus (perhaps Xerxes I, 486–465 B.C.E.), his nobles, and his advisors were frivolous and hedonistic. This is corroborated by other sources. R. G. Kent (1953: 150) reports an inscription bearing the king's declaration that he had destroyed the temples of foreign gods and had forbade their worship. From the book of Esther we learn of competition and jealousy among nobles and officials in the king's court. The book of Daniel (6:4–9) tells how nobles and advisors became jealous of Daniel and tried to destroy his status in the royal court. They also denounced the three young men—Shadrach, Meshach and Abednego—to the king, and they were consequently thrown into the fiery furnace (Dan 3:8–12). In short, these were common intrigues, not an expression of deliberate policy. Thus it is possible to sum up the religious policies of the Achaemenian kings in the words of Ghirshman: ". . . the Achaemenians were particularly well-disposed towards monotheistic peoples, above all the Jews."

In the beginning of the Seleucid period, Alexander the Great promised freedom of religion in Palestine to the high priest in Jerusalem, as well as exemption from payment of taxes every sabbatical year. The high priest requested the king to grant freedom of worship to the Jews of Babylon as well, and the king agreed. He also asked Jewish soldiers to enlist in his army (*Ant* 11.338–39). Many researchers have investigated the authenticity of this meeting between Alexander and the high priest (Marcus 1951). In any case, further on we see that Alexander's relationship with the Jews of Babylon was marked by understanding for their religious precepts.

Seleucus Nicator (312–281/280 B.C.E.) granted the Jews equal civil rights, similar to those granted the Macedonians and the Greeks in the new cities established by him throughout his empire and in Syria, including Antioch the capital (*Ant* 12.119). According to Josephus, this was not temporary policy. He tells us that the attitude of Antiochus II (262–247/6 B.C.E.) to the Jews was tolerant (*Ant* 12.125), as well. Furthermore, Antiochus III (223–187 B.C.E.), whom the Jews of Palestine aided in his war against the Ptolemaians (*Ant* 12.134, 138, 142) granted the Jews the right to maintain the purity and holiness of Jerusalem, and he levied heavy fines on those who did not abide by the law. We cannot assume that the king dealt with Jews according to a double standard, that he was partial to the Jews of Palestine but treated the Jews of Babylonia differently, unless we find that he had some special reason to do so. We know of a case of a double standard of this type in the time of Antiochus IV Epiphanes (175–164 B.C.E.), who employed extremely harsh measures against the Jews of Palestine, out of urgent economic necessity and because of internal struggles in Jerusalem between Hellenists and their antagonists.

As for the military service of the Jews of the Seleucid empire, it should be borne in mind that the rulers had an army of mercenaries from Macedonia and Greece. However, an urgent need to suppress rebellious ethnic groups brought about the necessity for a vigorous conscription. In the reign of Seleucis I and Antiochus I, the kings drafted young men of the generation born in the Macedonian and Greek settlements established under royal sponsorship. But this did not satisfy their needs, so they were forced to mobilize auxiliary forces from among various peoples in their kingdom, including Jews (Stern 1974: 43 n. 200).

The rise of a new dynasty that had a cultural and religious policy of a different character than that of the Seleucids, was of great importance for the Jews of Babylon. The change began in the middle of the 3d century B.C.E. At that time, a number of states in E Seleucia rebelled, including Bactria, Parthia, Armenia, and others. The leader most dangerous to the future of the Seleucid kingdom was Arsakes, the first king of Parthia. The dynasty destined to conquer Seleucia and to rule over it until 224/226 was named after him. It was then conquered by Ardashir I, the founder of the new Sassanian empire; this occupation of course lasted a long time. Between 160–140 B.C.E. Mithridates I (171–137), the king of Parthia, successfully conquered Elymais, Media, Persis, Characene, Babylonia, and Assyria and became the founder of the kingdom of Parthia, although he still had many battles to fight in Iran.

Many Jews lived in those countries, and we do not know what became of them. In any case, it is worth mentioning the relationship of Antiochus Sidates (138–129 B.C.E.) to the Jews. As he was besieging Jerusalem, John Hyrcanus requested of him a cessation of hostilities for the 7 days of the Feast of Tabernacles. The king agreed, and in addition he sent presents for the sacred worship and the treasury (*Ant* 13.242–44). Nicolas of Damascus says of this king: "After defeating Indates, the Parthian general . . . Antiochus remained there two days at the request of the Jew Hyrcanus because of a festival of his nation on which it was not customary for Jews to march out." And Josephus continues and explains: "Nor does he speak falsely in saying this; for the festival of Pentecost had come around, following the Sabbath, and we are not permitted to march either on the Sabbath or on a festival" (*Ant* 13.251–52).

In summing up this study of the civil and legal standing of the Jews of Babylon in the days of the Seleucids, it can be said that as a rule the relationship of the Seleucid kings to the Jews was tolerant. Further on we deal with the influence of their Hellenistic culture on the Jews in their kingdom. In any case, we are told of priests from Babylon who stayed in the Temple in Jerusalem on the Day of Atonement (*m. Yoma* 6.4) and even took an active part in the worship (*m. Menaḥ* 11.7). As has already been noted, many Jews went up to Jerusalem from Babylon. Out of consideration for them a number of religious laws were established, for example: "They intercalate the year only when . . . and because of the residents of the exilic communities, who have not been able to go forth from their homes" (*t. Sanh.* 2.12), or a different formulation: "They intercalate the year only when . . . and because of the residents of the exilic communities who have left their homes and could not otherwise reach [Jerusalem] in time" (*Sanh.* 11a). The lawmakers were also concerned about the pilgrims' peaceful return to Babylon after the Feast of Tabernacles, so they postponed the prayers for rain until "fifteen days after the Feast, to give time for the last of the Israelites to reach the Euphrates" (*m. Taʿan.* 1.3). It is extremely difficult to determine just when these laws were enacted, whether in Seleucid or in Parthian times, in the days of the descendants of Arsakes.

We also learn of dignitaries from Persia who ate at the table of Alexander Janneus (103–76 B.C.E.). The visitors reminded the king that in their last visit they had met a man who addressed them with "words of wisdom." They were referring to Simon ben Shetach, the king's brother-in-law, who was forced by him to run away to Egypt (*Gen. Rab.* 91:3). And Josephus tells us that Herod appointed Ananel of Babylon to the position of high priest in Jerusalem (*Ant* 15.22, 39). Josephus supplies us with additional instructive information on the Parthians who invaded Syria in 40 B.C.E. and enthroned Antigonus, the last of the Hasmoneans, who was the enemy of Rome and the lackey of Parthia. Antigonus issued an order to cut off an ear of John Hyrcanus, so that as a deformed person he would not be able to officiate as high priest (*Ant* 14.366). The Parthians took Hyrcanus with them as a prisoner to Babylon. He was received there with great honor by the local Jews and by Jews from nearby countries, and the Parthian King Phraates IV (approximately 40–3/2 B.C.E.) freed him from his chains and allowed him to live among his people in Babylon. They saw in him a king and a high priest, and they honored him accordingly (*Ant* 15.12–15).

The Parthian kingdom is not notable for having had a centralized government. It was a quasi-feudal state that suffered from internal disputes between various vassals and rival candidates for the throne, because the throne was not hereditary but elected (i.e., it was elected by or subject to confirmation by a majority of the nobility). So it is not surprising that in the days of King Artabanus III (38–12), when dissension increased in his kingdom, 2 young men from Nehardea, Asinaeus and Anilaeus, rebelled against him. Other young people rallied around them. They acquired arms and built themselves a fortress. They proceeded to intimidate their neighbors, to rob cattle from the herds in their vicinity, and to broaden the scope of their authority over their surroundings. At first the authorities were unable to suppress them, and their rule lasted from 20 to 35 C.E. They lost control due to an internal dispute over the marriage of Anilaeus to a non-Jewish woman (see below). The alien woman put poison in Asinaeus's food because she feared that he would convince his brother to banish her from his house, since their marriage was not in keeping with Jewish law. Anilaeus was left alone at the head of his men. He fought against villages ruled by Mithridates, who was the son-in-law of King Artabanus. Mithridates was defeated, and he became Anilaeus's prisoner, but Analaeus freed him in order to forestall the king's intervention. After some time, Anilaeus was killed, and with his death the rebellion of the 2 brothers came to an end (*Ant* 18.314–70). Josephus describes the aftermath of the rebellion in these words: "The Babylonians were now rid of the pressure imposed by Anilaeus, which had curbed their hatred against the Jews—for in general they always quarreled with them because of the contrariety of their laws, and whichever party happened to feel more self-confident would initiate an attack on the other. Accordingly, now that Anilaeus and his men were no more, the Babylonians began to attack the Jews" (*Ant* 18.371).

Josephus continues with the tale of the Jews' flight to the city of Seleucia, where they took refuge from their attackers. There were many Macedonian residents in the city, which had a Greek majority, and many Syrians who had citizenship rights. For 5 years, until approximately 40/41, none of these groups harmed the Jewish residents. But the ethnic groups were continuously involved in conflicts, especially the Greeks and the Syrians. In one of the quarrels, the Jews allied themselves with the Syrians against the Greeks. The Greeks were reluctant to give up their dominant position in the city, and little by little they managed to win the Syrians over to their side. As a sign of the bond of fidelity and friendship that now united the former enemies, they fell upon the Jews and slaughtered 50,000 of them or more. Only a small number of Jews managed to escape to Ctesiphon, which was situated near Seleucia. Josephus continues: "All the Jewish people in this region now became terrified of both the Babylonians and the Seleucians since all the Syrians who were citizens of these places fell in line with the Seleucians and made war against the Jews their policy. Most of the Jews flocked to Neardea and Nisibis, where they were safe because these cities were fortified and were furthermore populated by men who were valiant fighters every one" (*Ant* 18.378–79).

At the beginning of the 2d century C.E., Marcus Ulpius Traianus, the emperor of Rome (98–117 C.E.), conquered Ctesiphon, the capital of Parthia, and advanced into Babylon. Behind his back a great part of the population of Mesopotamia, including Jews, rose up against the Roman armies. This uprising and the great Jewish insurrection against the Romans (ca. 114–117), which broke out in Cyrene and spread from there to Egypt, Cyprus and, finally, to Mesopotamia, forced the Romans to retreat (*CAH* 9: 236–52). The Jews' participation in the insurrection is an indication of the Babylonian Jews' hatred toward the Romans, "the destroyers of the Temple," and of their preference for the Parthian authorities, the descendants of "the builders of the Temple" (Cyrus). This empathy for the Parthians was widespread in Palestine, as well. Rabbi Judah the Prince exchanged presents with King Artabanus V of Parthia (*j. Peʾa* 1.1). Some researchers do not identify Artabanus with the king himself (Dinari 1978). Rabbi Judah the Prince, upon learning of this Parthian king's defeat at the hands of Ardashir I (which brought the Parthian regime to an end), said, "The bond has been sundered" (*m. ʿAbod. Zar.* 10b–11a).

C. Leaders and Leadership

In a later chronicle, *Seder ʿOlam Zuta* (composed circa the 8th century), the anonymous author presents a list of exhilarchs. The list is headed by Jehoiachin the king of Judah. A listing of the entire dynasty follows (Neubauer 1895: 74–77). However, it is apparent that the compiler copied the earliest names from the listing in 1 Chr 3:18ff., and that he did not have before him a tradition concerning the later exhilarchs who held the office until the 3d century C.E. The author's tendency is clear; he wanted to show the ancient origins of the institution and the genealogy of the exhilarchs of his time, starting with the house of David. In the Talmud we hear for the first time of the son of the exhilarch Rabbi Nathan who, according to the commentaries of Gaonim (Heads of Academies), went up to Palestine in the third or fourth decade of the 2d century (Beer 1976). Nevertheless, we cannot rule out the possibility that among the heads of Babylonian Jewry were descendants of Jehoiachin. It is unthinkable that the Jews of Babylon, whose numbers increased greatly over the generations and whose places of residence were spread out over a large area, could continue to exist as a socioreligious formation without centralized leadership, which was recognized by the authorities and whose task it was to look after their political and religious needs.

The descendants of Jehoiachin, who were recognized leaders in both Babylon and Palestine, included Zerubbabel the son of Shealtiel, "governor of Judah" (Hag 1:1), and Sheshbazzar, "the prince of Judah" (Ezra 1:8). Some scholars maintain that Sheshbazzar is in fact identical to Zerubbabel. As already noted, we cannot rule out the possibility that there were other leaders in Babylon who were descendants of Jehoiachin, but whose names were not preserved. We cannot compare the fate of the sons of David in Palestine to that of their relatives in Babylon, because in Palestine the sons of David were pushed aside by the high priesthood following the renewal of the divine service in the Temple. Of course, no such situation existed in Babylon. Perhaps those priests who did not go up to Palestine and continued to live in Babylon became nothing more than teachers of the law. Note Ezra's title as it is referred to in the letter of Artaxerxes: "the priest, the scribe of the Law of the God of heaven" (Ezra 7:21) or "a ready scribe in the Law of Moses" (Ezra 7:6) or "the priest, the scribe, even the scribe of the commandments of the Lord, and of his statutes to Israel" (v 11). The aspect of the law is strongly stressed, not the aspect of the priesthood or the ritual.

Other leaders of the Jewish community in Babylon should not be overlooked, including Ezekiel the son of Buzi, Ahab the son of Kolaiah, and Zedekiah the son of Maaseiah (Jer 29:21–23). We have no information concerning the genealogy of Nehemiah the son of Hacaliah (Neh i:1). Similarly, his duties as the chief cupbearer of King Artaxerxes I (464–424 B.C.E.) and his appellation, "Tirshatha" (Neh 7:65), have not been sufficiently clarified. Mordecai should also be mentioned here. According to the book of Esther, he was of the lineage of Kish (Esth 2:5), and it is not clear if the reference is to Kish, the father of King Saul. The young men Daniel, Hananiah, Mishael, and Azariah filled unclearly defined positions in the court of Nebuchadnezzar. "The elders" should also be included in this list of leaders. Theirs was a very ancient institution in Israel. In Babylon the elders may have carried on most of their activities on a local level (Jer 29:1; Ezek 8:1).

Knowledge concerning Jewish leadership in Babylon during the Seleucid Period is unclear. But since we are dealing with a very traditional society, it cannot be assumed that the leadership underwent revolutionary changes, except that prophecy probably ceased to function in Babylon but continued in its Palestinian counterpart. Since we do not find evidence from that period concerning scholars who taught the law to individuals and the public, we may assume that the priests filled the role of "maintainers of the law." It is instructive to note that similar processes took place in Palestine and Babylon: the circle of students and teachers of the law, outside the priesthood, slowly widened. We hear of men learned in the law in Babylon of the Parthian period, such as Hillel the Elder and Nahum the Mede. Both of them resettled in Palestine. On the other hand, Rabbi Judah the son of Bathyra lived in Nisibis and maintained contact with those in charge of the Temple in Jerusalem (*j. Pesaḥ.* 3b). Acts 2:9 mentions pilgrimages to Jerusalem during this period. However, after the destruction of the Second Temple there was an increase in the number of Jews who left Palestine and went down to Babylon, and their numbers increased after the Bar Kokhba war. The most famous wise man forced to leave Palestine, because he was influenced by heretical ideas, was Hananiah the nephew of Rabbi Joshua. His religious activities in Babylon caused negative reactions in Palestine (Neusner 1969).

D. Intellectual and Religious Life

The biblical text provides little information about either the intellectual or religious life of Babylonian Jewry. In the book of Ezekiel there is no evidence of the exiles observing practical religious precepts. There is some mention of them in the books of Daniel and Esther: piety and devotion, attention to the ritual propriety of food and drink, attention to three prayers a day in the direction of Jerusalem, fasts, and customs related to mourning. Also, in the book of Tobit we find mention of knowledge of the Pentateuch and the words of the prophets, the giving of charity, the observance of the Feast of Weeks, and strict observance of burial according to the law.

We do not have any evidence concerning when and where synagogues were first founded. Were they a creation of the Babylonian exile? Perhaps the exiles brought with them the custom to pray in public. Furthermore, we have no evidence of the existence of schools for children or adults among the Jews of Babylon. We do have knowledge of the existence of such institutions among the general Babylonian population. The Babylonians in high social circles conducted a lively intellectual life (*CHJ* 1: 342–58; Bickerman 1988: 51–65, 91–100). Presumably this atmosphere influenced certain Jewish groups in Babylon. However, the Jews' objective need to maintain their distinctiveness had a decisive influence on them with regard to their study and the observance of their religious duties in their pagan surroundings.

More information can be gleaned from what is *not* mentioned in the Murašu tablets: none of the documents containing Jewish names was signed on the Sabbath or on a Feast Day (Zadok 1976). This is a very significant fact for scholars studying the religious situation of the lower strata of Jewish society at that time because, for the most part, the documents deal with that segment of society. It is more difficult to draw conclusions concerning the relationship of the people mentioned in the texts to the Jewish religion. Many of the names listed were common among various Semitic peoples. Even names of clearly Jewish origin, such as "Shabtai" or "Haggai," are not necessarily names belonging to Jews. These names appear in pagan Phoenician and Palmyran sources. Bickerman (*CHJ* 1: 342–58) pointed out the informative phenomenon of fathers whose names were definitely pagan, but who gave their children theophoric names containing components such as *-yahu* or *-yah.* He explains this phenomenon in the following manner: the parents were given pagan names when the belief in YHWH weakened, before the return to Zion. However, after the return to Zion, the rebuilding of the temple, and the renewal of the divine service, the religious faith in God became stronger, and children were again given names having the divine name as components. Indeed, names such as Benaiah, Benael, Pedaiah, and Menachem refer to the return to Zion, the rebuilding of the Temple, and the renewal of the ritual. Although among those going up with Ezra to Jerusalem we also find—alongside names such as Obadiah, Shechaniah, and Johanan—W Semitic names (e.g., Daniel, Jahaziel, and Michael), as well as Babylonian and Iranian names (e.g., Hattush, Bigvai, and Azgad; Ezra 8:2–19; Neh 7:7–62) and even clearly pagan theophoric names (e.g., Mordecai, Esther, and Zerubbabel), this cannot be viewed as proof of the Jews' assimilation by choice into their surroundings. It is possible that the names of functionaries or officials were changed by their superiors into names common in the general society. The most well-known case of this type is the one involving Daniel, Hananiah, Mishael, and Azariah, whose names were changed by official decree to Belteshazzar, Shadrach, Meshach, and Abed-nego (Dan 1:6–7).

A very important influence of the environment on the Jews of Babylon was their acceptance of the Aramaic language, which was the *lingua franca* in the Persian kingdom from the 5th century B.C.E. onward. At the same time, the Aramaic script replaced the ancient Hebrew script. Another important change was the one that took place in the Hebrew calendar. The months were now referred to by their Babylonian names, even though some of them were named after pagan gods. It seems that these influences in Achaemenian times did not adversely affect the Jews' essential belief in One God, the creator of the world and its administrator, who commanded Israel to observe his precepts, especially to observe the Sabbath. Sabbath observance caused the Jews of Babylon to become a distinct ethnic and religious body. Second Isaiah mentions several times the importance of this religious obligation (Isa 56:2, 4, 6; 58:13).

The Jews of Babylon possessed an alert historical consciousness, which was manifested in many ways. From the sources we learn of prayer in the direction of Jerusalem (Dan 6:11); of the observance of four fasts, accompanied by weeping and mourning, related to the events of the destruction of the Jerusalem Temple (Zech 7:3, 5; 8:19); of fasts accompanied by the spreading of sackcloth and ashes (Isaiah 58:5; Esth 4:13); of confession of sins; and of prayer for redemption. More strictly observant Jews of Babylon put into practice the procedures of mourning, because of the destruction of the Temple and the Exile, and they are known as "mourners of Zion" (Isa 61:3). According to Josephus, some Jews of Babylon did not use the oil of aliens (*Ant* 12.120; *Life* 74).

The words of Hecataeus of Abdera (4th and 3d centuries B.C.E.) may be accepted as a summary of the situation: "neither the slander of their neighbors . . . nor the frequent outrages of Persian kings and satraps can shake their determination; for these laws, naked and defenseless, they face tortures and death in its most terrible form, rather than repudiate the faith of their forefathers" (*AgAp* 1.191). Josephus then brings a number of examples to verify his statement. According to one of them, Alexander the Great was once in Babylon. There he commanded his soldiers to rebuild the destroyed temple of Bel. The Jews among them refused to take part in the reconstruction of a pagan temple, and they were punished with flogging and heavy fines for refusing an order. However, finally, perhaps after their refusal was explained to the king, he freed them and exempted them from participating in the reconstruction (*AgAp* 1.191). This incident is indicative of Alexander's treatment of the Jews, and it is in keeping with his promise to the high priest, as mentioned earlier. This was probably the attitude of the Seleucid kings toward the Jews, as long as they were not beset with economic difficulties (Rostovtzeff 1964, 1: 507; 2: 695–96, 1282; 3: 1427 n. 234). But when they were in financial straits, especially in order to meet payments to the Romans, they would loot the treasures concealed in various temples, including the one in Jerusalem, and this finally brought about the Maccabean insurrection (2 Macc 3:3–15).

As a rule, the Parthians were indifferent in their relationships to the various religions in their kingdom. However, in connection with the Asinaeus and Anilaeus affair we learn of a case in which Sabbath observance played a role. Josephus tells us that the satrap of Babylon planned to attack the camp of the two brothers on the Sabbath, because he knew that on that day they do not conduct war (*Ant* 18.318–19). This is an indication that non-Jews were aware of the Babylonian Jews' observance of the Sabbath. However, Asinaeus did fight on the Sabbath, despite the protests of his soldiers. Josephus also tells us of another case concerning Mithridates, the son-in-law of King Artabanus, who also wanted to fight the two brothers on the Sabbath (*Ant* 18.354). This is important evidence of the religious level of the Babylonian Jewish public with regard to Sabbath observance. Also instructive is this community's abstention from intermarriage. According to Josephus, Asinaeus married a non-Jewish woman, and in so doing he aroused the anger of his men. They considered this marriage to be a sin that might cause a great calamity to befall them (*Ant* 18.340, 349–52). These two fundamentals—Sabbath observance and abstention from intermarriage by the lower social strata—are in themselves enough to explain the Babylonian Jews' maintenance of their distinctiveness for generations in a pagan environment. But in order to observe these fundamentals to the point of self-sacrifice, in cases such as those indicated by Josephus, they must have had some sort of education for religious duties.

The first learned men, "scholars of the Law," of whom we hear in Babylon and its environs date back to the Parthian Period. We do not know if these scholars studied in Jerusalem or in Babylon. Hillel the Elder studied in Palestine under Shemaiah and Abtalion (*j. Pesaḥ.* 66a), and even though the Palestinians diparaged him ("What can be expected from a Babylonian?" *j. Pesaḥ* 6:1), they nevertheless admitted that he had learned the whole body of Jewish learning in Babylon. They said: "For three reasons did Hillel come up from Babylon," and the Jerusalem Talmud (*Pesaḥ* 6:1) sums up, "He expounded and he consented and he went up and he accepted the law." In other words, the law or laws that he expounded in Babylon were accepted in Jerusalem (Ginzberg 1976: 356 n. 4). We have no knowledge from sources in the Second Temple period of study of the law in Babylon. Rabbi Simon ben Lakish, who lived in the 3d century C.E. and who lived and was active mostly in Tiberias, asserted that three people who came up (to Palestine) brought with them from Babylon "learning and established it in Palestine. They are Ezra, Hillel, and Rabbi Hiyya the Great" (*m. Sukk.* 20.6a). Rabbi Akiba met in Nehardea a scholar named Nehemiah who passed on to him a law in the name of Rabban Gamaliel the Elder (*m. Yebam.* 16.7).

We have more evidence of relations between the Jews of Babylon and the Jews of Palestine in the Parthian Period. Queen Helena went up to Jerusalem in the 1st century C.E. (*Nazir* 3.6) to pray there and to sacrifice thank-offerings (*Ant* 20.49). She donated a golden candelabrum to the Temple and "a golden tablet on which was written the [Num 5:12–28] passage concerning the suspected adulteress" (*Yoma* 3.10). Also "Monobazus the King would make all the handles of the utensils of the Day of Atonement out of gold (*Yoma* 3.10). When Helena came to Jerusalem she found that there was a great famine in the land. She sent emissaries at her expense to Alexandria in Egypt to buy grain, and to Cyprus to buy cakes of dried figs to distribute to the needy. It is also said that upon his hearing of the famine in Jerusalem, Izates the son of Queen Helena sent large sums of money to the heads of the city (*Ant* 20.51–53). It is said of King Monobazus that "he arose and wasted his treasures in two droughts" (*t. Peʾa* 4:18). A relative of the kings of Adiabene, whose name was also Monobazus, fought alongside the Jewish combatants against the Romans in the war of the destruction (*JW* 2.520). But not only Jews and proselytes made pilgrimages to Jerusalem. A non-Jew joined a caravan of pilgrims, and upon his return to Nisibis he told Rabbi Judah ben Bathyra about his trip (*b. Pesah.* 3b).

King Herod's appointment of Ananel from Babylon to the high priesthood in Jerusalem (*Ant* 15.39, 41) throws interesting light on Herod's policies. If this information is true, we have important evidence of relations between priests in Babylon and their colleagues in Palestine, as already pointed out. Indirectly we learn from Josephus of the maintenance of genealogical records of the priests in Babylon. Indeed, in another passage Josephus tells us of the archives in Jerusalem in which the genealogical records of the priests—from Egypt and Babylon as well as those from Palestine—were kept (*AgAp* 1.33). One of the foundations upon which Babylonian Jewry maintained itself as an independent religious formation and as a part of the entire community of Israel was the Hebrew calendar. In order to keep the festivals at a single, fixed time, messengers went from Palestine to Babylon or bonfires were lit on mountaintops so that they could be seen in Babylon, thus informing the Jews of Babylon when the new moon appeared and enabling them to calculate the dates of the festivals (*m. Roš Haš.* 2.4). When it was decided to intercalate a year, the Sanhedrin in Jerusalem notified the Diaspora, including Babylon and Media, to that effect (*t. Sanh.* 2.6, 7). We also know of Rabbi Akiba, who lived in the first half of the 2d century C.E., who proclaimed a leap year in Nehardea (*b. Yebam.* 16.7).

After the destruction of the Second Temple in 70 C.E., and especially after the war of Bar Kokhba (132–35 C.E.), some scholars went down from Palestine to Babylon. The arrival of "Abba the Tall," Rab, in approximately 219, brought about a period of prosperity in the study of the Law in Babylon. Rab in Sura and Shmuel in Nehardea gave public instruction in the Law and trained many pupils. In this period academies were established, and they continued to exert an influence on Jews, not only in Babylon but throughout all the lands of their dispersion, as late as the 12th century.

Bibliography

Alon, G. 1952. *The Jews in Their Land in the Talmudic Age.* Trans. G. Levi. Jerusalem.

Beer, M. 1976. The Babylonian Exilarchate in the Arsacid and Sasanian Periods. *TA* 3: 11–32.

———. 1982. *The Babylonian Amoriam: Aspects of Economic Life.* Ramat Gan (in Hebrew).

Bickerman, E. J. 1988. *The Jews in the Greek Age.* London.

Debevoise, N. C. A. 1938. *Political History of Parthia.* Chicago.

Dinari, Y. 1978. Rabbi Sent a Mezuzah to Artaban. Pp. 86–105 in *Michtam Le David,* ed. Y. Gilat and E. Stern. Ramat-Gan.

Ghirshman, R. 1954. *Iran.* New York (esp. pp. 132–204).

Ginzberg, L. 1976. *An Unknown Jewish Sect.* New York.

Kent, R. G. 1953. *Old Persian.* New Haven.

Marcus, R. 1951. *Josephus, Jewish Antiquities. Books 9–11.* LCL. Cambridge, MA.

———. 1957. *Josephus, Jewish Antiquities. Books 12–14.* LCL. Cambridge, MA.

Neubauer, A. 1895. *Mediaeval Jewish Chronicles.* Vol. 2. Oxford.

Neusner, J. 1969. *A History of the Jews in Babylonia: The Parthian Period.* Leiden.

Oppenheimer, A., et al. 1983. *Babylonia Judaica in the Talmudic Period.* Wiesbaden.

Rostovtzeff, M. 1964. *Social and Economic History of the Hellenistic World.* 3 vols. Oxford.

Shaked, S. 1984. Iranian Influence on Judaism. *CHJ* 1: 308–25.

Stern, M. 1966. The Politics of Herod and Jewish Society Towards The End of the Second Commonwealth. *Tarbiz* 35: 245–6, 251–3.

———. 1974. *Greek and Latin Authors on Jews and Judaism.* Jerusalem.

Weidner, E. F. 1939. Jojachin, König von Juda. *Mélanges Syriens* 2: 923–35.

Zadok, R. 1976. *The Jews in Babylonia in the Chaldean and Achaemenian Periods in the Light of the Babylonian Sources.* Tel-Aviv.

MOSHE BEER
Trans. Menahem Erez

JUDAISM IN THE MISHNAIC PERIOD

The early 1st through 3d centuries C.E. are commonly referred to as the Mishnaic period, a recognition of the centrality of the corpus of the Mishna (a 3d century Hebrew compilation of traditions, see below) within rabbinic Judaism, the dominant religious system of the Jews from the 3d century up to the modern period. These years are also known as the late Hellenistic, or the Roman, or the Early Christian period, depending on the context of the reference. In this complex and turbulent transitional era new systems replaced the Temple-centered Israelite religious and political structures that had endured during the previous millennium.

A. Continuity with Israelite Religion
B. Historical Discontinuities and Developments
C. Religious Systems
D. Clerical Leadership
E. At Yavneh
F. At Usha
G. The Role of Women
H. Textual Production and Advances
I. Revision of Theology
J. Revision of Ritual
K. Establishment of Rabbinic Culture and Continuity with Subsequent Forms of Judaism

---

A. Continuity with Israelite Religion

In many respects Judaism of this period perpetuates major elements of the myth and ritual of ancient Israel. The idea of the centrality and sacrality of the territory of Israel and of Jerusalem derive from Israelite antecedents. The period witnessed the canonization of biblical literature under rabbinic sponsorship, and with it the acceptance of theological ideas and frameworks of Israelite origin within rabbinic communities. One focus was the emphasis on Torah and scribal ideals. Other influences included the use of the Hebrew language for sacred writing and prayer (though Aramaic was the common language of the market place and Greek was used in official communications) and the continued espousal of many symbols out of Israelite culture. The rabbinic calendar was built directly upon the Israelite model, with a few notable additions and modifications. Dietary regulations in rabbinism drew heavily on antecedents from older Israelite practice and the cult, but the destruction of the Temple in 70 C.E. by Rome necessitated significant modifications.

Obviously, the forced cessation of the cult led to the abandonment of the rituals of sacrifice, though the details of past practices were subjects of much concern in rabbinic literature. The practice of the earlier Israelite system of purity and uncleanness also was suspended with the demise of the Temple, though rabbinic teachers maintained an active interest in debating and delineating the rules for cultic purity. Together, rules for sacrifice and purity occupy about one-third of the Mishnaic corpus. The remainder deals with agricultural, festival, familial, and civil matters.

B. Historical Discontinuities and Developments

Several key historical and social forces shaped Judaism in this period. The destruction of the Temple and the subsequent Roman imperial domination of Israel deprived Jewish leaders of meaningful political power and forced them to turn inward for fresh expressions of Jewish identity. The failure of a messianic rebellion against Rome under the leadership of Simeon bar Kokhba with support from leading rabbis in 132–35 C.E. left little doubt of the futility of hope for the restoration of political independence under the Judaic leadership of that age. In this period the influence of quasi-governmental Jewish authorities, such as the patriarchate, declined and the authority of the rabbinate, internal to the Jewish communities of the

Near East (Israel and Babylonia), increased. The rise and spread of Christianity and other serious competing religious systems in the area in this epoch demanded that Judaic religious leaders articulate new understandings of Israelite destiny.

The irrepressible hope for redemption from political subjugation led to complex speculation on the nature of the promise of messianic redemption, a subject of Israelite contemplation in earlier ages (cf. biblical depictions in Isaiah and Micah). Overall, the rabbinic emphasis on Torah overshadowed and even eclipsed many of the major themes of alternative theological world views inherent in the received Israelite heritage.

C. Religious Systems

The amalgam constituting rabbinic Judaism which took shape in the Mishnaic period drew on the contributions of several immediate Jewish predecessor and contemporaneous groups and ignored or rejected others. The rabbis themselves claimed to be heirs of the Pharisees, a group of politically active Judean pietists of the 1st century. Mainly concerned with the Sabbath, agricultural taboos, and rules of purity, this society established a model of table fellowship and religious literacy emulated within later rabbinic circles. By way of contrast, the authors of the NT Gospels adopted a caricatured and stylized view of the Pharisees and typecast them as the opponents of Jesus.

The integration of an apocalyptic perspective is less apparent within the later rabbinic synthesis of Judean religious attitudes of the 1st century. Recent theories argue that apocalyptic speculation is a mode of expressing alienation from the corridors of political power and social resistance to external control. As rabbinic views evolved they tended tacitly to condone national powerlessness, dismissing it as irrelevant to the present and ultimate reality they envisioned; in the process they thereby devalued apocalyptic expressions, which loomed as threats to the stability of rabbinic society. Likewise they rejected miracle-working charismatic holy men (cf. the story of Honi the Circle Drawer, *m. Taᶜan.* 3:8).

Rabbinic synthesizers correspondingly downplayed the major dimensions of other Judaic systems which did not express values and concerns sympathetic to their social condition and philosophical tendencies. The Sadducees, about whom we possess little systematic evidence, appear within rabbinic traditions as adversaries whose theological views were rejected. We also have incomplete data concerning early communities of mystics, though many scholars assume that merkabah (chariot-throne) and other forms of Jewish mysticism have their roots in the Mishnaic period.

The Dead Sea community serves as an informative example of an intermediary system of Judaism of the early part of this era. The residents of the village of Qumran left ample evidence of their apocalyptic-messianic theology and social organization and ritual, locating this community on a historical continuum between Israelite and early Hellenistic forms of religion on the one hand, and early Christian communal patterns on the other. Although small in number and insignificant in cultural influence, the Qumran example illustrates a stage of Judaic development prior to the incipient rabbinic and early Christian alternatives.

Major communities of diaspora Judaism (i.e. outside the Land of Israel) in this age were located in Alexandria, Babylonia, and in Asia Minor. The writings of Philo illustrate the philosophical literacy achieved by the Greek-speaking Jews of Alexandria and, according to some interpretations, they demonstrate the emergence of a cosmic-mystical form of Judaic speculation. The Jewish community of Babylonia shows signs of growth in this time but takes a position of leadership only after the transition to Sassanian rule (226 C.E.) and the decline of the community in Israel in the 3d and 4th centuries. In Asia Minor, archaeological evidence substantiates the existence and influence of Jews within communities like Sardis and indicates the central positions they occupied within the social structures of the towns of the area.

D. Clerical Leadership

In this era, the axis of Judaic leadership shifted from national political figures associated with the Temple in Jerusalem, provincial princes and hereditary priests, to local authority vested in rabbinic scribal holy men in villages and towns. Imperial Roman authorities encouraged similar transfers of prerogative throughout the Near East to better facilitate the ultimate arrogation of dominance and control within the empire. These historical developments are echoed in the internal rabbinic traditions themselves. The narrative account for instance of the founding of the first rabbinic academy at Yavneh by Rabban Yohanan ben Zakkai portrays the master emerging from a besieged Jerusalem, obtaining the sanction of Roman authority, and establishing an authorized center of Torah study at the defenseless coastal town (*ᵓAbot R. Nat.* 4).

The rapid rise of rabbinism may be associated in part with the sanctioned ascendence of local holy men, ascetics, miracle workers, dream interpreters, and magicians throughout the area. Consequently, factors including changes in patterns of leadership, the greater literacy of the age attributable to minor technological advances in writing (such as the adoption of the codex for publication and dissemination of knowledge), and the breakdown of priestly custody over the authorized canon all contributed to the successful expansion of the influence of the rabbinic class.

As other forms of local authority lost influence, rabbis increased their political engagement with governmental forces; they became adept at balancing their need to hold sway within their communities and at the same time to refrain from challenging the external forces which governed their land and lives from without. The Judaic system they established, with adaptation and accretion along the way, provided for centuries a viable set of social, political, and philosophical structures for the Jewish community in the subsequent historical settings under Roman, Babylonian, Islamic, and medieval Christian European domination. We know of the life and teachings of hundreds of rabbinic figures. The following mention of the activities of a few illustrates the character of rabbinic leadership in this era.

E. At Yavneh

The period ensuing upon the destruction of the Temple and founding of the Yavnean center was a time of internal conflict, self-definition, and transition. See JAMNIA (JABNEH), COUNCIL OF. Influential leaders of the epoch included Rabbis Yohanan ben Zakkai and his disciples, Joshua, and Eliezer *(m. Abot 2:8),* and numerous others such as Akiba, Ishmael, Gamaliel, and Eleazar ben Azariah.

Akiba ben Joseph was among the best known sages of this time. His extensive ventures included engagement in rabbinic legislation, biblical exegesis, mystical speculation, and (ill-fated) political activism and martyrdom in support of the Bar Kokhba revolt.

His contemporary, Joshua ben Hananiah was rabbi in Jerusalem and later at Yavneh and Pekiʾin in Israel (1st and 2d centuries C.E.). As a Levite, it is assumed that he sang in the Temple before it was destroyed. He then took up the trade of needle maker or blacksmith.

With Eliezer ben Hyrcanus, Joshua is said to have carried Yohanan ben Zakkai out of Jerusalem in a coffin during the siege of the city (*b. Giṭ.* 56a). During his later career he was the center of some contention within rabbinic circles. Several sources recount his humiliation by the Patriarch, Gamaliel (*b. Roš Haš.* 25a). Joshua's dispute with Gamaliel over the requirement to recite the evening prayer brought about the events which lead to the deposition of Gamaliel and ascension of Eleazar ben Azariah to the patriarchate (*b. Ber.* 28a). Eleazar exemplified the wealthy adherent of the rabbinic movement, a man of prominent ancestry who sought conciliation between the contending factions of the sages and those who supported the interests of the priestly and patriarchal followers.

Joshua is also associated with a dispute with Eliezer ben Hyrcanus over the ritual cleanness of the tiled ovens of Akhnai. Joshua ruled that these ovens were unclean; Eliezer said they were clean. Eliezer invoked a heavenly voice on his own behalf to prove his position correct. Joshua responded with the famous declaration: "The Law is not in heaven" (a reference to Deut 30:12), i.e., the rabbis alone have the authority to decide matters of the law, not some supernatural voice, or even a direct revelation. Many other legal disputes between Joshua and Eliezer ben Hyrcanus appear in rabbinic sources. According to tradition he engaged in discourses with political figures and various groups: the Roman emperor Hadrian; with the elders of Athens; with the Jews of Alexandria.

F. At Usha

The generation following in the aftermath of the failed revolt (132–135 C.E.) was a time of systematization and standardization within Judaic thought and practice. Judah, Meir, Simeon ben Gamaliel, and Simeon bar Yohai are representative of this generation's central rabbinic authorities.

Judah bar Ilai was a Rabbi of the 2d century C.E. in Usha, in the lower Galilee in Israel. He was a student of Akiba and Tarfon, was ordained by Judah ben Baba, and survived the Hadrianic persecutions. Numerous traditions attributed to Judah and his contemporaries Meir, Simeon, and Yose are preserved in rabbinic literature.

Judah's legal sayings illustrate some of the concerns and activities of the rabbis of his generation. Several of his rulings, for example, deal with the standardization of rabbinic liturgy (*m. Ber.* 4:1) and the regulation of prayer (*m. Ber.* 4:7, *t. Ber.* 1:9, *t. Ber.* 3:5) and daily liturgical blessings (*t. Ber.* 6:18). Other rules ascribed to Judah emphasize the importance of concentration and intention during the performance of rituals (*t. Ber.* 2:2), or with the importance of maintaining the proper frame of mind during recitation of prayers (*m. Ber.* 2:2). Judah also is associated with legislation concerning the recitation of blessings over foods (*m. Ber.* 6:4, *t. Ber.* 4:4–5), with blessings over natural wonders, both those for which one is permitted to recite blessings (*m. Ber.* 9:2) and those for which one is forbidden to recite because it would appear to be a form of idolatry (*t. Ber.* 6:6).

Judah's contemporary, Meir was a descendant of a family of proselytes which traced its line back to the Roman emperor Nero. He was a student of both Akiba and Ishmael and is listed as one of the 7 disciples of Akiba who issued a famous edict concerning the calendar. He also was one of the 5 rabbis ordained by Judah ben Baba during the Hadrianic persecutions. He was married to Beruryah, one of the few learned women mentioned in the Talmud. Meir was thus involved in her tragic life (discussed below) and in the events of the Bar Kokhba war.

Meir was associated with the legendary Elisha ben Abuya, the well-known heretic of his time, known also as Aher (the "other"). Some rabbinic sources depict Meir as Aher's would-be disciple and is also said to have been called after Elisha's death to extinguish the fire of his burning tomb.

Meir is prominently linked to the major rabbinic legislative and political activities of his generation. He is said to have served as *ḥākām,* sage, in the Ushan court. His technical ability to defend both sides of opposing legal viewpoints was greatly extolled. Ultimately, his opposition to the patriarch Simeon ben Gamaliel, is said to have been the basis for his exile from Israel.

Legal rulings ascribed to Meir comprise an important part of the earliest rabbinic compilations, Mishna and Tosefta. His role in these works is so important that the Talmud stipulates that any anonymous ruling in the Mishna is to be attributed to Meir; hence the corpus of his traditions was one of the primary documents used in its redaction.

Meir's dicta deal with most of the central values of rabbinic Judaism in its period of systematization in the latter half of the 2d century. An illustration of a tradition attributed to him indicates his understanding of rabbinic ritual as a coherent system of practice:

> R. Meir used to say, "There is no man in Israel who does not perform one hundred commandments each day [and recite over them one hundred blessings] . . . And there is no man in Israel who is not surrounded by [reminders of the] commandments: [Every person wears] phylacteries on his head, phylacteries on his arm, has a mezuzah on his doorpost and four fringes on his garment around him . . ." [*t. Ber.* 6:24–25].

Simeon ben Gamaliel (II), another Rabbi of this period held the hereditary office of patriarch or president. He studied Greek and supported a policy of peace with Rome. According to one Talmudic source, two of his rabbinic colleagues, Meir and Nathan, sought to oust Simeon from his position as patriarch during a struggle for power within the ranks of rabbinic leadership. In the Talmudic account of the political tension, the 2 masters became angry when Simeon decreed that the students in the academy should not stand in their honor when they entered the college. They then conspired to test Simeon on an obscure tractate of the law in order to bring him to disgrace. One of Simeon's supporters prepared him in the laws of this tractate and he was able to pass the test. He then banished Meir and Nathan from the academy. Nonetheless they continued to send messages with legal problems to the college. The leaders of the academy then recognized that they should readmit the two, and did so (*b. Hor.* 13b). The account demonstrates how one episode of internal strife was brought to resolution through compromise.

Among the other rules attributed to Simeon was his statement that not all who wish to recite God's name in the prayers may do so (*m. Ber.* 4:8), showing a restrictive view regarding the use of divine names for liturgical purposes. Simeon's legal views were almost always decisive. The Talmud declares that the law follows in accordance with Simeon Ben Gamaliel in all instances except for three (*b. Ketub.* 77a).

Another prototype of rabbinic leadership was Simeon bar Yohai, a 2d century C.E. rabbinic leader, mystic, and ascetic of the generation of rabbinic activity at Usha in the Galilee. Simeon was one of the two most prominent students of Akiba (with Meir), another of the five rabbis ordained during the Hadrianic persecutions following the Bar Kokhba revolt. According to the version of the incident in the Babylonian Talmud (*Ber.* 28a), he was the student who provoked the deposition of Gamaliel from the position of patriarch of Israel by bringing up in the academy the issue of whether the recitation of the evening prayer was obligatory or optional.

Simeon is the subject of many rabbinic legends. Best known is the story of his hiding in a cave with his son after having been sentenced to death by the Romans. According to some versions of the story when he emerged from the cave after 12 years and saw that people were not engaged solely in the study of Torah, his mystical gaze set the world afire with only a glance (*b. Šabb.* 33b), and a heavenly voice reprimanded him and sent him back to the cave for another year.

Simeon's rulings cover most of the major topics taken up in rabbinic sources. On the importance of the study of the Torah for instance, he says, "If I had been at Mt. Sinai at the time the Torah was given to Israel, I would have asked God to endow man with two mouths, one to talk of the Torah and one to attend to his other needs." On further reflection, he retracted this saying, "But the world can barely withstand the slander of [persons with] one [mouth]. It would be all the worse if [each individual] had two [mouths] (*j. Ber.* 3b)."

The Talmud uses Simeon as the paradigm of a scholar totally immersed in the study of the Torah. Accordingly a rabbi of his caliber would not be required to interrupt his study even for the important and timely daily recitation of the *šĕmaᶜ* (Deut 6:4) (*j. Ber.* i.3b).

Medieval Jewish mystics identified him as the (pseudonymous) author of the Zohar, one of the most important rabbinic mystical compilations. He was also associated with the day of *lag bĕᶜomer,* the 18th of Iyar, a mystical festival celebrated to this day at the traditional place of his burial in Meron in the Galilee in Israel.

One of the more famous messianic sayings attributed to him declares that if the Jews properly observed 2 consecutive Sabbaths, they would be redeemed (*b. Šabb.* 118b). He is assigned authorship of the Midrashic compilations of Sifre Numbers and Deuteronomy (*b. San.* 86a) and of the Mekhilta of R. Simeon Bar Yohai to the book of Exodus. Several short apocalyptic mystical compilations are also linked with his name.

G. The Role of Women

Beruryah (2d century C.E.) was one of the few famous women in rabbinic Judaism of late antiquity, a rare woman scholar in that male-dominated culture. She was the daughter of Hananyah ben Teradyon and was wife of Meir. Rabbinic traditions portrayed Beruryah as a sensitive yet assertive figure. The Talmud recounted anecdotes illustrating Beruryah's piety, compassion, and wit. In one source she admonished her husband Meir not to be angry at his enemies and not to pray for their death. She suggested that instead he pray that their sins cease and that they repent (*b. Ber.* 10a).

When two of her sons died one Sabbath day, a story in the Midrash reported that she delayed telling her husband until Saturday night when he had finished observing the Sabbath in peace (Midrash to Proverbs 31:10). The Talmud also narrated anecdotes of Beruryah's sharp wit. When Yose the Galilean asked her for directions on the road, she derided him for speaking too much with a woman (*b. ᶜErub.* 53b).

The folklore surrounding Beruryah was extensive and poignant. Accounts which weave together the rabbinic sources retold the tragic events of Beruryah's life and the life of her family. According to tradition, not only did two of her sons die suddenly on a Sabbath day, but her father was martyred in the Bar Kokhba rebellion, her sister was taken captive to Rome, and her brother became a brigand (possibly an anti-Roman terrorist) and was murdered. The drama of her life climaxed in the so-called Beruryah incident. She was said in an 11th century tradition preserved by Rashi (commentary to *b. ᶜAbod. Zar.* 18b) to have mocked a misogynistic rabbinic tradition which labelled women as flighty. Meir was said to have sent a student to tempt her to discredit her criticism. Tragically, she was thought to have committed suicide after submitting to the advances of her husband's disciple.

Beruryah's public involvement in rabbinic affairs and instruction was clearly an exception to the prevailing propensities and expectations of that society. Contemporary study reveals the ambivalence toward women within this era of rabbinism. Mishna's framers regarded women alternatively in some circumstances as possessors of legal rights and duties, in others as chattels subservient to men. Mainly in matters pertaining to sexual and reproductive function, Mishna treated wives, levirate widows, and minors as property. Divorcees and widows in Mishnaic law controlled their own sexuality and property. However, critical analysis of the evidence confirms that women were deemed nonentities in almost all public social circumstances, and were denied access to most forms of intellectual and political pursuits and achievements.

H. Textual Production and Advances

The Mishna, published after the turn of the 3d century, stood as the single most authoritative compilation of the early rabbinic estate. It was a composite of the religious statements of rabbis from prior to the destruction of the Temple to the time of its publication. Mishna appears to be a legal code. More precisely it is a study book of legal statements, disputes, lists, and anecdotes detailing the views of hundreds of named rabbinic authorities and containing accompanying anonymous statements—assumed by some to stem from Hellenistic or ancient Israelite times—on various practical and theoretical subjects of concern to the early rabbis. It is a unique compilation in style and content whose influence extends far beyond its time and place.

Recent critical analysis has delineated the specifics of Mishnaic literary form and diction, the contributions of rabbinic masters of each of 4 generations, and the theological assumptions and creative contributions of each tractate as coherent expressions of rabbinic worldviews. A rabbi of the Mishnaic period is called a *tannāʾ* (pl. *tannāʾîm,* teacher), to distinguish him from a rabbi of the later Talmudic era, designated an *ʾămôrāʾ* (pl. *ʾamôrāʾîm*).

The Tosefta is a companion document and a systematic appendix to Mishna. Though the date of its publication is not certain, analysis has shown it to be a composite, in part Mishna commentary, in part supplementary to Mishna, and in part a repository of independent rabbinic teachings.

The collections of rabbinic scriptural interpretations, the books of midrash, frequently cite the authorities of the Mishnaic age, thus ostensibly serving as a major source of data for the period. Current advances in the study of major works of rabbinic midrash have better described the composite nature of that literature and confirmed the post-Mishnaic date of some of those collections. Contemporary research on Sifra (a midrash on the book of Leviticus), Sifre to Numbers and to Deuteronomy, Mekhilta to Exodus, Genesis Rabbah, and Leviticus Rabbah has shown that early midrash compilations rest on distinctive conceptual foundations meant to articulate coherent theological postures and to justify social and political contexts to communities of Jews of late antiquity of the time of their redaction.

The post-Mishnaic rabbinic collective literature in the Babylonian Talmud and the Talmud of the land of Israel are both dependent for their organizational structure, content and authority, on the development, publication and dominance of Mishna in the prior age. The Talmuds contain a fair amount of baraita traditions, traditions thought to be from Mishnaic times, often concerning or attributed to the rabbis of the Mishnaic period.

Recent scholarship has tended to critically limit the value of discrete traditions within Mishna and other early rabbinic texts as sources of evidence for the historical reconstruction of the period, emphasizing the distorting influence of the *tendenz* of the documents' editors and their complex redactional histories. Apart from highlighting these problems and pitfalls for using the early texts, great advances have been made in the past two decades in understanding the underlying rabbinic religious system the documents as a whole express. The previously prevailing view that treated the evidence of rabbinic literature as disconnected and anecdotal has been superseded by recent more critically integrative and analytically sophisticated assessment of the evidence within its cultural context, illustrated best by the work of Jacob Neusner and his students.

I. Revision of Theology

The most consequential advance for the history of Judaism during this era within rabbinism is the establishment of a Torah-dominated theology. Rabbinic claims to authority rested on their asserted association with the revelation at Mt. Sinai through the concept of the dual Torah. This ideology postulated that Moses received as divine revelation both the written Torah (i.e. the Pentateuch) and a concomitant oral Torah. The latter was memorized and passed from teacher to student for generations and constitutes the substance of the rabbinic teachings finally set down in writing in Mishna. The rabbis did not specify all those elements of their teachings which go back to Sinai, nor did they claim to present the divinely revealed *ipsissima verba* of such traditions. The sages of the early age also did not adequately account for the nature of Mishna, replete with its disputed rules and statements and direct attributions to late antique authorities, in light of their implicit claim that it represented the revealed instruction of a millennium earlier.

The theological underpinnings of the rabbinic system relied more for their potency on the authority of the personality of the rabbi who represented an embodiment of the Torah, and accordingly of divine revelation, than on a tight, internal and deductive, philosophical logic.

The basic theological postulates and practices of the rabbinic system sustained the centrality of the concept and symbol of Torah. The rabbis asserted that the study of Torah was the central ritual act of Judaism, equivalent to all other obligatory actions combined. Accompanying doctrine urging restraint against the abuses of power was present within the system's assertions, for instance, that Torah had to be studied for its own sake, not as a tool for political or economic gain.

The rabbis began in this era to transform or "rabbinize" Israelite heritage based on their values and priorities. They reexamined Israelite myth, affixing a rabbinic veneer to its narrative. In their complex recasting of traditions, the sages imputed rabbinic traits to the heroes of ancient Israel, from the patriarchs to Moses (called *rabbēnu,* "our rabbi"), David, and other major figures; like the later masters, they studied Torah and kept the commandments. Rabbinic literary expressions depicted God himself as supreme rabbi with personality traits closely akin to the sages.

The rabbinic Judaism of this period enunciated a stable religious system, defiant of the vicissitudes of historical change. Within rabbinic Torah-centered theology, apocalyptic attitudes played a peripheral role. Depiction of and retreat from evil as a main form of expressing a social basis of intensified passive-aggressive, retreat-engagement with political challenge was basically uncharacteristic of the mainstream of rabbinic conceptualization. Instead rabbis institutionalized a view of messianism promising salvation without emphasizing immediate deliverance. Rabbinic limitations on and utilizations of the messianic idea vary in later ages usually intensifying subsequent to periods of persecution.

J. Revision of Ritual

Within Judaism of the Mishnaic period, the process of the "rabbinization" of Israelite festivals engendered revision of numerous rituals and restatement of the mythic basis for cyclical celebrations. Passover was formerly a springtime festival of rebirth with connections to the biblical accounts of the exodus from Egypt and was centered on the ritual offering and consumption of the paschal lamb. The rabbis established the *sēder,* a structured fellowship meal, as the primary festive ritual and mandated the recitation of a *hāggādâ,* rabbinic expositions of scriptural passages combined with liturgical recitations and songs and the manipulation of special foods and objects. This mode of celebration downplayed references to the preceding cultic forms of celebration, and focused instead on the Israelite narrative roots as subjects for rabbinic exposition.

The feast of *Šabûᶜôt* (Pentecost) also took on new meaning as a celebration of the revelation of the Torah on Mt. Sinai, in contrast to its prior central purpose as a feast of the first fruits brought to the temple in Jerusalem. In later times the revision of the pilgrimage festivals led to such additional changes as the establishment of *Śīmḥat tôrâ* (the festival of rejoicing for the Torah) on the last day of *sûkkôt* (Tabernacles).

Rabbinic scribal values made study of the Torah the central ritual, as noted. In the synagogue the scroll itself was utilized as a symbol and object in worship. It was housed in a prominent niche in synagogues and used for the periodic readings throughout the year. In this era the Jews employed a cycle for reading the Torah on sabbaths in public on a triennial basis, as well as readings on Mondays and Thursdays, fast days, and new moons; there was a special sequence of readings for the festivals.

Earliest inscriptions in synagogues, such as the Theodotus inscription (1st century C.E.), refer to the "purposes of reciting the law and studying the commandments." However, the equivocal implications of limited material evidence of synagogues from the first 2 centuries C.E. make it difficult to ascertain whether the rabbis as a group had significant influence in the institutions or even to what degree synagogues predominated as central religious structures. Evidence from subsequent periods in Israel and the Diaspora (4th to 6th centuries C.E.) suggests that later rabbis did not play a dominant role in the construction or administration of these assembly halls.

Whatever their role in public synagogues may have been, rabbis did undertake to institutionalize the rituals of prayer during the Mishnaic era. The two major liturgies were the *šĕmaᶜ*, a litany of earlier scribal origins, and the Prayer of Eighteen Blessings (the *ᶜamîdâ*), a priestly and patriarchal liturgy, incorporated into rabbinic ritual at Yavneh.

The *šĕmaᶜ* consisted of biblical verses which emphasized the theological themes such as the unity of God, the need to love God, to keep the commandments, and references to reward and punishment, alongside of supporting rabbinic liturgy, which made reference to the classical mythic themes of creation and redemption and emphasized the virtues of Torah study.

By contrast, the Prayer of Eighteen Blessings made overt entreaty for the messianic redemption, the restoration of Davidic kingship, and condemnation of the heretics; for independent legal authority; and for the rebuilding of the Temple; it included the priestly benediction.

The ultimate regularization of these liturgies and their forms and the integration of the components of prayer into composite services resulted from historical and social processes of conflict between factions supporting patriarchal and priestly authority within the community and groups representing the ascent of rabbinic influence.

One perspective on the stages of conflict and compromise, resulting in the conflation of interests and texts is compressed and dramatically recounted in the narrative of the deposition of Gamaliel II (*b. Ber.* 27b–28a, *j. Ber.* 4:1) mentioned above. In that account the rabbis unseated the patriarch after a dispute over a liturgical issue: the obligation to recite the prayer in the evening. Major shifts in the control of the academy ensued and the patriarch ultimately was forced to accept a diminished role in the governance of the community.

K. Establishment of Rabbinic Culture and Continuity with Subsequent Forms of Judaism

By the close of the Mishnaic period rabbinic myth, ritual, and social patterns pervaded the Jewish populations of Israel and Babylonia and constituted a dominant cultural force. Subsequently, Jewish intellectuals developed a philosophical rabbinism in the Middle Ages under the influence of classical traditions, originally preserved within Islamic culture.

Other Jewish thinkers developed mystical forms of rabbinic expression which became widespread within the popular culture of the Jews. Although competing forms of non-rabbinic Judaism arose regularly (such as Karaism in the early Middle Ages), the Judaic system which took initial shape in the Mishnaic era dominated until the modern age. Modern Orthodox Judaism perpetuates forms of Torah-centered rabbinism. Even those new Judaic systems which developed after the enlightenment and reformation of Judaism in early 19th century Europe, maintained some continuities with the rabbinic heritage. Reform Judaism rejected rabbinism, but developed its own form of rabbinate. And modern Zionism, as complex as it was, drew heavily on previous Judaic symbolic expression. The flag of the state of Israel, for example, according to a principal interpretation, recalls in its design the stripes of the sages' prayer shawl, of antecedent ages going back through the Mishnaic period; the chief rabbinate of the state of Israel derives its authority from the Judaic world views of the dual Torah which took shape in the formative Mishnaic era.

Bibliography

Avi-Yonah, M. 1976. *The Jews of Palestine.* Oxford.

Brown, P. 1971. *The World of Late Antiquity: From Marcus Aurelius to Mohammed.* London.

Goodenough, E. R. 1935. *By Light, Light: The Mystic Gospel of Hellenistic Judaism.* New Haven.
Hanson, P. D. 1975. *The Dawn of Apocalyptic.* Philadelphia.
Heinemann, J. 1977. *Prayer in the Talmud.* Berlin.
Hoffman, L. 1987. *Beyond the Text: A Holistic Approach to Liturgy.* Bloomington, IN.
Kraabel, A. T. 1982. The Roman Diaspora: Six Questionable Assumptions. *JJS* 33: 445–64.
Levine, L. I. 1981. *Ancient Synagogues Revealed.* Jerusalem.
Moore, G. F. 1954. *Judaism in the First Centuries of the Christian Era: The Age of the Tannaim.* Cambridge, MA.
Neusner, J. 1981. *Judaism: The Evidence of the Mishnah.* Chicago.
———. 1983. *Judaism in Society: The Evidence of the Yerushalmi.* Chicago.
———. 1986. *Judaism: The Classical Statement. The Evidence of the Bavli.* Chicago.
———. 1986a. *Judaism and Scripture: The Evidence of Leviticus Rabbah.* Chicago.
Scholem, G. 1961. *Major Trends in Jewish Mysticism.* New York.
Wegner, J. R. 1988. *Chattel or Person? The Status of Women in the Mishnah.* New York.
Zahavy, T. 1977. *The Traditions of Eleazar Ben Azariah.* Missoula, MT.
———. 1987. *The Mishnaic Law of Blessings and Prayers: Tractate Berakhot.* Atlanta.

TZVEE ZAHAVY

JUDAIZING. In the ancient sources, the noun "Judaizer" and the verb "to Judaize" refer primarily to the actions of gentiles. While the verb can be used to designate the forced conversion of gentiles to Judaism, it normally refers to the taking over of Jewish customs by gentiles without conversion. Gaston argues that those who encourage others "to Judaize" may be either Jews, Christian Jews, or Gentiles and for the sake of terminological precision should never be referred to specifically as "Judaizers" (1986: 35–36).

The Greek verb "to Judaize" is found only in the NT in Gal 2:14. In this text, Paul confronts Cephas: "If you, though a Jew, live as a Gentile and not as a Jew, how can you compel the Gentiles to live as Jews?" The clear implication is that gentiles are being compelled to live according to Jewish customs. Moreover, Paul argues in Galatians that for gentiles to be required to assume the obligations of the Mosaic law threatens the integrity of the gospel. At issue for Paul is the manner in which gentiles lay claim to righteousness. The controversy in Galatians is not with Judaism as such but with those who argue that the gentiles must be circumcised and assume the obligations of the Mosaic law (Sandmel 1979: 112; see also Betz *Galatians* Hermeneia).

Outside of the NT, Esther 8:17 (LXX) recounts that many gentiles declared themselves to be Jews because they feared the Jews. Plutarch (*Cic.* 7:6) also states that a freed slave named Caecilius was said to be given to Jewish practices. Josephus tells of a certain Metilus who spared his life by promising to become a Jew, even to the point of circumcision (*JW* 2.17.10). He also writes of a time in Syria when the Syrians thought "they had rid themselves of the Jews, still each city had its Judaizers, who aroused suspicion" (*JW* 2.18.2). Ignatius denounces those who are Christians and yet live according to Judaism (*Magn.* 8:1). In their case, they have not received grace. Moreover, according to Ignatius, it is "monstrous" to speak of Christ and to practice Judaism (*Magn.* 10:3). What Ignatius means by the term "Judaism" is a matter of debate (Gaston 1986: 36–38), but that there is some connection between the condemned practice and Judaism is evident. In the *Acts of Pilate* 2:1, we read that Pilate's wife feared God and favored the customs of the Jews. Finally, in Canon 29 of the Council of Laodicea, those who "Judaize" are strongly condemned (Mansi 1759: cols. 563–604, Canon 29).

These sources indicate that either because of fear or genuine attraction there were those who embraced Jewish practices. This also suggestes that Judaism was a dynamic religious phenomenon. Moreover, the authors of these writings were apparently compelled to acknowledge the tendency "to Judaize." The respective authors' motives in mentioning "Judaizers" may not always be evident, but that does not refute the clear indication that there were non-Jews who embraced Jewish customs.

Bibliography

Bornkamm, G. 1971. *Paul.* Trans. D. M. G. Stalker. New York.
Gaston, L. 1986. Judaism of the Uncircumcised in Ignatius and Related Writers. Vol. 2, pp. 33–44 in *Anti-Judaism in Early Christianity,* ed. Stephen G. Wilson. Waterloo, Ontario.
Mansi, J. D. 1759. *Sacrorum Conciliorum Nova et Amplissima Collectio.* Vol. 2. Florence. Repr. Paris, 1901.
Sandmel, S. 1979. *The Genius of Paul.* Philadelphia.

JAMES W. AAGESON

JUDAS (PERSON) [Gk *Ioudas*]. Greek form of the Hebrew name Judah.

1. See JUDAS MACCABEUS.

2. Son of Chalphi, and a commander of the army of Jonathan, who along with Mattathias the son of Absalom, remained faithful to Jonathan when the rest of his army deserted him (1 Macc 11:70). At the outset of his reign Demetrius II Nicator (Seleucid ruler 145–139 and 129–125 B.C.) repeated the promises of his father to Jonathan to grant favors to the Jews (cf. 1 Macc 10:25–45) in exchange for Jonathan's help in fighting Trypho, a former supporter of Alexander Balas. Demetrius II sent officers with a large army to intercept Jonathan, who was gathering troops throughout Palestine. The opposition set an ambush for Jonathan and his army at Hazor, causing all of his men to flee except for the two commanders. According to 1 Macc 11:72, Jonathan attacked, apparently single-handedly, and put the enemy to flight, causing his soldiers to rejoin him for the battle. Pointing to Josephus (*Ant* 13.5.7 §161), who reports that about fifty men remained loyal to Jonathan, Goldstein (*1 Maccabees* AB, 442–43) surmises that the commanders were named in order to flatter their families, and that some subordinates of the commanders must also have remained loyal.

3. Son of Simon, the younger brother of Judas Maccabeus. In 138 B.C. Simon dispatched his two sons Judas and John (1 Macc 16:2) to fight against Cendebeus, commander of Seleucid forces along the coast of Judah, quartered at the newly fortified city of Kedron (1 Macc 15:41). John called out an army of 20,000 and advanced on Cendebeus. They met in a plain outside Modein, where

John's forces defeated the enemy and Judas was wounded (16:4–9). Four years later Simon took his sons Mattathias and Judas with him on their final tour of the area around Jericho. At a banquet held in the fortress at the town of Dok, all three men were ambushed by Simon's ambitious son-in-law Ptolemy, who hoped to gain favor with the Seleucid ruler Antiochus VII Sidetes by killing Simon.

4. Coauthor of a letter purportedly sent to Aristobulus and other Jews in Egypt (2 Macc 1:10). This Judas is not identified further, but scholars often assume that reference is to Judas Maccabeus. If this assumption is correct, the author perhaps placed Judas's name in the letter in order to connect more closely the introductory letters (1:1–9 and 1:10–2:18) of 2 Maccabees to the story of Judas which follows. In any case, the letter is possibly spurious and the inclusion of the single name "Judas" seems out of place.

5. The brother of Jesus, mentioned by Jesus' townspeople (Mark 6:3 = Matt 13:55). Jesus had come to his own part of the country or hometown (Gk *patris*), but was unable to perform many miracles there. The townspeople were offended by his works and wisdom and sneered that they knew his father, mother, and brothers James, Joses, Judas, and Simon. Scholars generally assume that the town in question was Nazareth, though neither Mark nor Matthew identifies it and Mark had previously (2:1) reported that Jesus was at his house *(oikos)* in Capernaum. The reference to Judas as Jesus' brother most naturally suggests common parentage, though some early Church fathers thought Judas and the others were sons of Joseph by a previous marriage, and Jerome contended that the Gk word *adelphai* meant "cousins."

Early tradition ascribed the book of Jude (a shortened form of the name Judas) to this brother. Scholars are divided over the matter. On the one hand, the book is generally dated around the end of the 1st century, too late for even a younger brother of Jesus, and it seems to look back upon the time of the apostles (v 17). On the other hand, it is difficult to understand why someone would choose as a pseudonym the name of so obscure a person. (See JUDE, EPISTLE OF; also *Mark* NCBC).

Bibliography

Beare, F. W. 1981. *The Gospel according to Matthew.* Oxford.

PAUL L. REDDITT

6. The disciple who betrayed Jesus. See JUDAS ISCARIOT.

7. Another of the twelve disciples, other than Judas Iscariot. In Luke 6:14–16 and in Acts 1:13 he is described as Judas *iakōbou,* "son of James" (not "brother" as in several versions). The James intended here has not been conclusively identified. In John 14:22 Judas is mentioned as "Judas (not Iscariot)," although Brown maintains that this refers to yet another Judas (*John* AB, 641).

This Judas is usually identified with the Thaddeus mentioned in the lists of Matt 10:3 and Mark 3:18. Brown believes that this equation is a mistaken tradition based on attempted gospel harmonies (*John* AB, 641; also Barrett 1956: 388). If Judas and Thaddeus are the same person, then Thaddeus and Lebbaeus, the equivalent found in some mss, were likely hypocoristic names used to avoid confusion with Judas Iscariot. Brown (*John* AB, 641) believes that the "(not Iscariot)" in John 14:22 is a later scribal addition, and the 5th century OL codex Veronensis reads "Judas *sed alius*" ("the other") in John 14:22; thus the earliest text may have read simply "Judas," with later changes being made to distinguish him from Judas Iscariot (Barrett 1956: 388).

Judas is not to be equated with Judas the brother of Jesus (#5 above; *ISBE* 2: 1115; cf. Koester 1965: 296–97). Neither is he the same as the author of the book of Jude, as was maintained by Tertullian (Barclay 1960: 198). The identity of Judas is further confused by a variety of other ms readings for John 14:22. In the Curetonian Syr Gospels (2d–7th centuries) he is "(Judas) Thomas" = Judas the Twin (*Acts* NICNT, 44, n. 46). In the Sinaitic Syr (2d–7th centuries) only "Thomas" is present. This is part of the Syriac tradition that Judas and Thomas are the same person (*Gos. Thom.* 80:10). In the Coptic Sahidic (3d–6th centuries), however, he is "Judas the Cananean," intended to equate him with the apostle Simon the Cananean (*John* AB, 641). The OL codices Vercellinis, Veronensis, Sangermanensis, and Claromontanus (all 4th–9th centuries) all read "Judas Zealotes" for the name in the list of Acts 1:13, as does the *Epistola Apostolorum* (before 150 A.D.; Lake and Cadbury 1932: 14).

Whatever his identity, the only event the Gospels record of his career is John 14:22, where he asks Jesus, "Lord, how is it that you will manifest yourself to us, and not to the world?"

8. Judas Barsabbas. See BARSABBAS (PERSON).

9. The owner of a home in Damascus where Paul stayed before his baptism by Ananias (Acts 9:11). Judas may have been a Christian; if not, he was not hostile to the movement. The Gk text reads *iouda,* not *ioudas* (Bruce *Acts* NIGTC, 201). The home of Judas is said to have been on the "street called Straight." This would have been either the decumanas or the cardo, the two perpendicular main roads of every Roman town. Tradition has identified the road of Acts 9:11 with the E-W Darb el-Mostakim, and has placed Judas's house near the W end (Bruce *Acts* NICNT, 199). Outside of the NT, reference has been found of two theaters in Damascus located on a street "called Straight" (Negev 1972: 88).

It may be that Luke included the name of Judas either because of his interest in people who hosted early Christians (Williams *Acts* BHNTC, 123: cf. Simon the tanner in Acts 10:6 and Mnason in Acts 21:16), or because such details are characteristic of visions such as Ananias' (Lake and Cadbury 1932: 102).

Bibliography

Barclay, W. 1960. *The Letters of John and Jude.* Edinburgh.
Barrett, C. K. 1956. *John.* London.
Koester, H. 1965. *"Gnōmai Diaphoroi." HTR* 58: 279–318.
Lake, K., and Cadbury, H. J. 1932. *The Beginnings of Christianity.* Vol. 1, pt. 5. New York. Repr. Grand Rapids, 1979.
Negev, A. 1972. *Archaeological Encyclopedia of the Holy Land.* Jerusalem.

ROBERT D. MILLER II

10. A Jew from Galilee who led a rebellion against Roman authority in A.D. 6. In Acts 5:37 Gamaliel mentions

Judas of Galilee and Theudas as leaders of movements that failed because they were not of God. The Jewish historian Josephus is our main source of information about him (*Ant* 18.1.1–6; *JW* 2.8.1). He calls him Judas the Galilean, but says that he was born in Gaulonitis E of the Sea of Galilee. Judas may have been called "the Galilean" because Galilee was the center of his rebellion or because nearby Gaulonitis was associated with Galilee.

Josephus accuses Judas of sowing the seeds of rebellion that led to the Jewish war of independence in A.D. 66 and to the destruction of the Temple in A.D. 70. Judas and a Pharisee named Zaddok formed a Jewish sect that Josephus compares to the Pharisees, Sadducees, and Essenes. The members of this sect were in agreement with the Pharisees except in their passionate belief that the Jews should submit to the rule of God alone. For this belief they were willing to suffer hardship and death. Although Josephus does not give a name for Judas' followers many scholars have identified them with the Zealots.

The census of A.D. 6 was the occasion of Judas' rebellion. In that year, at the request of the Jews, Archelaus, son of Herod the Great, was deposed as tetrarch of Judea and Samaria. Archelaus had been a client of Rome, but now the area he had ruled came under direct Roman control as part of the province of Syria. In order to establish a basis for taxation, Quirinius, the governor of Syria, held a census of the population and property of this territory now under his supervision.

Many pious Jews probably saw this census as an encroachment on God's right to number His people and on His ownership of their land. The high priest was able to convince most people to go along with the new order. Judas, however, taught that only God could be called "master" (Gk *despotēs*) and that to submit to the census was to deny His lordship. God would deliver His people only when they rose up in armed rebellion against this outrage.

Judas' sons followed the example of their father. Menahem was a leader of the rebellion in Jerusalem shortly before the war with Rome (*JW* 2.17.8–9). Two more of his sons, James and Simon, were crucified by the Romans (*Ant* 20.5.2). Eleazar, probably Judas' grandson, led the defense of the fortress at Masada after the fall of Jerusalem (*JW* 7.8.1). See Hengel (1989: 76–145) for further information.

Bibliography

Hengel, M. 1989. *The Zealots*. Edinburgh.

GARETH LEE COCKERILL

JUDAS ISCARIOT. One of the twelve disciples of Jesus, possibly from Judea, who served as treasurer of the itinerant group. His name always appears last in the lists of the Twelve and he is described as assisting the authorities in capturing Jesus. Judas Iscariot is mentioned twenty times in the four gospels and twice in Acts. Although he is designated as "one of the Twelve" in Matthew (26:14, 47) and Mark (14:10), and listed among them in Luke (6:16) as well as in Mark (3:19) and Matthew (10:4), he is not a central figure in the events portrayed.

A. The Name
B. The Act of Judas
C. Judas as One of the Twelve
D. Judas in the Four Gospels
  1. Mark
  2. Matthew
  3. Lukan Tradition
  4. The Gospel of John
E. Judas in Later Christian Tradition
  1. The Apostolic Fathers
  2. NT Apocrypha
F. Judas in Recent Discussion

A. The Name

Judas Iscariot appears in five different forms: (a) the original name, *Judas*, the Hellenized form of the Hebrew name *Yĕhûdâ* (Mark 14:43; Matt 26:25, 47; 27:3; Luke 22:47f; Acts 1:16, 25; John 13:29; 18:2f, 5); (b) *Judas Iscarioth* (Mark 3:19; 14:10; Luke 6:16; and as v 1 Matt 10:4 and Luke 22:47), which is the Semitic form of Iscariot; (c) *Judas Iscariot*, the Greek form (Matt 10:3; 26:14; Luke 22:3; John 6:71; 12:4; 13:2, 26; 14:22; and as variant readings in Mark 3:19; 14:10, 43; Luke 6:16); (d) *Judas, the one called Judas Iscariot* (Matt 26:14; Luke 22:3; John 6:71); and (e) *Judas, son of Simon Iscariot* (John 6:71; 13:2, 26).

The term "Iscariot" did not belong, at first, to the name itself but emerged to distinguish this Judas from many others of that name (cf. Luke 6:16; Acts 1:13; John 14:22). Schwarz lists nine interpretations of the term "Iscariot" and adds another of his own (Schwarz 1988). These fall into four main groups:

(i) Some hold that the term "Iscariot" indicates that Judas belonged to the group of the Sicarii: dagger-wielding assassins (Cullmann 1956: 15; 1970: 21–23; 1966); and thus they concluded Judas was a member of the Zealot party.

(ii) Others suggest that the term is derived from the Heb *šāqar* and designates the "false one." This highlights the character of Judas by alluding in his surname to his act of deception and betrayal (Torrey 1943; Gärtner 1971).

(iii) Others believe that the word designates his deed. He was a "deliverer" (root *škr*), and thus *ho paradidous* is a simple translation of (I)Skariot(h). It has been noted that the LXX of Isa 19:4 translates the *Piʿel* of *škr* ("capture and hand over") with Gk *paradidomi*, the same word used in Mark 3:19 to designate Judas (*ho paradidous*, "the one who betrayed him"). Morin (1973) takes the Markan designation to be a literal translation of *(i)skariot*, "the one handing over." Still others suggest that it refers to what Judas did for a living, concluding that he was a red dyer (Ehrman 1978; Arbeitman 1980) or a fruit grower (Krauss 1902).

(iv) Some believe that the name Iscariot indicates hometown. Was Judas perhaps the only one of the Twelve from Judea, from the village of Kerioth (Josh 15:25)? Billerbeck gives many cases where the Heb *ʾîš* is connected with a hometown and calls this "the right explanation" (1922: 537; so also Haugg 1930: 76 and Dalman 1929: 28–29). Askaroth or Askar, near Shechem, has also been suggested (Dalman 1935: 213). Schwarz (1988) proposes that the original Aramaic yields the translation "the man from the city" = Jerusalem. This is supported by evidence from the Targums where the formula appears frequently at least in the plural, "men from the city," and the word *keriotha* is often used to mean Jerusalem. If those who suggest that the term "Iscariot" came into use only after Judas' death are correct (Torrey 1943; Vogler 1985) then it is also possible that not even the evangelists knew what it meant (Dalman 1902: 51–52).

Although it seems plausible (Klauck 1987) to interpret "Iscariot" as designating place of origin there is no consensus on this or on the place designated.

B. The Act of Judas

The usual word for the deed of Judas is *paradidonai,* which occurs 122 times in the NT, 57 times in connection with the capture of Jesus. It appears 18 times in the Gospels in the general sense; e.g., "It is necessary for the Son of Man to be handed over." The verb is connected directly with Judas 44 times. The word is many-layered, appearing often in the NT without reference to Judas (Popkes 1967).

For example, it is used of the chief priests who deliver Jesus to Pilate (Mark 15:1, 10; Matt 27:2, 18; Luke 24:20; John 18:30, 35); to describe his being delivered over to the "Jews" (John 18:36), or by the contemporaries of the apostles (Acts 3:13). Pilate "hands [Jesus] over" to be crucified (Matt 27:26; Mark 15:15; Luke 23:25; John 19:16). It is striking that Judas is never mentioned without some reference to this act; apart from it Judas has no recognizable identity in any of the Gospels.

In Luke 6:16 the noun *prodotes* (traitor) stands in its place, and in Acts 1:16 Judas is designated as the *hodegos,* the one who pointed the way to those who sought to take Jesus captive. However, most often Judas is simply noted as the "one who handed him over."

Judas is never mentioned by Paul, although Paul repeats the tradition of Jesus being handed over without specifying who did it (1 Cor 11:27). The same verb is used by Paul in theological contexts as in Rom 4:25: "Jesus was delivered to death for our misdeeds." In Rom 8:32 it is God who delivers his own son, and in Gal 2:20 Jesus delivers himself to death (so also Eph 5:2, 25). This widespread variation in usage of the term suggests caution in translating *paradidonai* as "betray." That translation is, in fact, quite peripheral in biblical literature (Klauck 1987: 45). The oldest occurrence of the word in connection with Jesus' capture occurs in 1 Cor 11:23b, where Judas is not mentioned by name. The tradition of *Judas* as betrayer was not found in Paul or in the earliest layers of the tradition.

Recent studies (Klauck 1987; Vogler 1985) of the pre-Synoptic layers of the tradition have led to two important conclusions. First, Judas was neither a symbolic figure nor a product of kerygmatic imagination, but a clearly recognizable historical figure, i.e., an actual disciple of Jesus. His designated name, Iscariot, comes from a Semitic milieu; and our knowledge that he belongs to the circle of the Twelve also rests on tradition which comes from the Aramaic-speaking Church. Missing from the earliest traditions are any aspects of the paid informant who, in remorse, later commits suicide. We have portrayed rather a man who is no worse than his colleagues in the circle of the disciples and who received as much recognition from Jesus as did the rest and may have been honored by Jesus in this singular mission. The subsequent understanding of his action as a "betrayal" may come from the Aramaic-speaking Church, which later felt compelled to make Judas at least partially responsible for the death of Jesus. It was covered up with a theological rationalization of the death of Jesus in which Judas became a villain.

Second, the interpretation of the deed of Judas was soon changed, for as the Church began to interpret the death of Jesus, an increasingly larger degree of blame was placed on Judas. He was initially remembered only as the first who had parted company with Jesus even though all the other disciples likewise had occasion to abandon Jesus, leaving him dying on the cross attended only by a few female followers. However, Judas' initial abandonment was eventually seen as a betrayal, and, eventually, the Church used the term "betrayer" to designate his deed, at times (Mark 14:21) avoiding the use of his name (Vogler 1985: 37; cf. Klauck 1987: 48–76).

C. Judas as One of the Twelve

The term "the Twelve" designates the inner circle of the disciples of Jesus. It occurs once in Paul, eleven times in Mark, eight times in Matthew, nine times in Luke–Acts, and four times in John. Judas' attachment to this group has posed theological problems since antiquity. These problems are even more acute if Jesus himself established this group and chose Judas to be a part of it.

The earliest reference to the Twelve is found in 1 Cor 15:5. As the negative tradition about Judas formed, it mentioned only eleven disciples at the post-resurrection appearances (Matt 28:16; Luke 24:9, 33; Mark 16:14; Acts 1:26; cf. 1:13). Given the theological difficulties of including Judas among the Twelve, it seems highly likely that the tradition of his attachment to the Twelve rests on historical fact. The more the community reflected on the capture and trial of Jesus and on Judas' role, the more critically they judged Judas' actions. They were, however, unable to conceal his place among the Twelve.

D. Judas in the Four Gospels

The negative portrayal of Judas can be seen by examining the evidence from the Gospels, written a generation or two after the events.

1. Mark. Mark says very little about Judas, and attributes his action to no particular motive. He is simply the one who handed Jesus over (3:19; 14:10, 44). Three parts of the Judas tradition that Mark appropriated from an earlier source are traceable:

a. In 14:43, 46, perhaps the oldest layer of redaction, it is simply reported that while Jesus was speaking, Judas, one of the Twelve, appeared with an armed crowd sent by the chief priests, lawyers, and elders, who seized Jesus and held him fast. The designation "Iscariot" is missing, and the verb *paradidonai* is not attached directly to Judas, attesting to the antiquity of the tradition.

b. Slightly more recent are the two reports in 14:18 and 14:21. The first states that as they sat at supper Jesus predicted that one of them, now eating with them, would hand him over. The second states that while Jesus' death is necessary, it is too bad for the person who will hand him over. This tradition is promoting the view that the death of Jesus was no accident, that Jesus had a premonition of it, and that, indeed, it was according to the divine plan revealed in Scripture (Gerhardsson 1981).

c. A later development is evident in 14:10, where mention is made of a financial reward offered by the leaders.

According to Vogler (1985: 55–56), the final redaction of Mark reflects the following concerns:

(1) Judas was not just any false brother who had smuggled himself into the inner circle of the Twelve but was "chosen of God and of Jesus Christ." Judas had a place in the community, even participating in the Last Supper. He belonged to the core of the Church (cf. Klauck 1987: 63).

(2) Just as Jesus and his circle of disciples could not protect themselves from the defection of Judas, neither can the Church protect itself from defectors.

(3) Just as the Church is not certain that there will be no defectors, so the individual believer is never certain whether he/she may not ultimately become a defector. The question "Not I, surely?" (14:19) leads the readers of Mark to ask this critical question of themselves.

(4) Defection means not only changing one's loyalty but also brings a curse, or at least a woe (14:21). Perhaps it can even be connected with the anathema of the early Church, and in the later Church the term "kiss of Judas" refers to any act of defection.

2. Matthew. Matthew offers nothing by way of tradition that is not found in Mark, but the redactional development is notable. Three texts (26:15, 25, 50) are taken over from Mark but developed. In one of them Matthew quotes Judas directly (26:15), thus livening up the narrative and providing Judas with some new features. To each of the three texts he has added new materials (Vogler 1985: 71).

(a) In 26:14–16 Matthew adds the detail that Judas received money for turning Jesus in. There is no explanation of the reason for this. In the anointing story Matthew states that "the *disciples*" were indignant at the waste (26:8), while Mark has *"certain of those present"* (but Mark escalates their anger by mentioning it twice [14:4, 5], and gives no indication that Judas might be driven by love for money).

(b) In Matt 26:20–25 Judas is portrayed as an unscrupulous man. Although he has already put into action his plan to betray Jesus (26:14) and should not even be there eating with them, still in the hearing of the others he asks: "Could it be I?"

(c) Matt 26:47–50 highlights this character trait when Judas brazenly meets Jesus in the garden with a kiss and the appellation: "Hail, Rabbi." In Mark he greets him with the words "Rabbi, Rabbi," and in all three Synoptic Gospels he kisses (in Luke he is about to kiss) Jesus. In Matthew the ruthless Judas of questionable moral background carries out his act, seeks repentance by trying to return the money (Matt 27:3–5), throws it down in the Temple, and goes out and hangs himself (27:5).

To heighten this dark picture of Judas, Matthew draws sharp contrasts between Judas' behavior and that of others around him: the woman who anoints Jesus' feet (26:6–13), the disciples at the table (26:20–35), and finally between Judas and Jesus himself (26:47–56).

Matthew's account stands alone in describing Judas' remorse and even his confession of guilt (27:3–10). The account is unlike that of Luke, but at no point does Matthew pass judgment on Judas or ascribe any ulterior motive to his deed.

In Matthew, Jesus relates to Judas in all gentleness during those last days, as seen especially from his greeting in the garden. According to Luke, Jesus addressed him by name, saying: "Judas, do you hand over the Son of Man with a kiss?" (Luke 22:48). But Matthew has Jesus using a word he uses for no other person in direct address: "Friend, what are you here for?" (Matt 26:50). The Greek word *hetairos* ("friend") occurs only in Matthew and each time as direct address; twice in parables (20:13; 22:12) and once here. In all cases the one addressed is committing an ungrateful action against the one who has been generous. Here it highlights the very important relationship of trust which exists between Jesus and Judas.

Matthew's portrait of Judas is based on traditions found in Mark's gospel, except for the account of his death preserved in 27:3–10. Matthew's redaction of the Markan materials is noteworthy. The narrative becomes more lively by the introduction of direct address in 26:15, 25, 50. More important, Matthew has added new dimensions to the portrait of Judas. In 26:14–16 he provides additional information about the amount of money Judas received. In another passage (26:20–25) Jesus traces Judas' deed back to the inherent nature of Judas: "It would have been better for that man if he had never been born" (24, cf. Mark 14:20–21; Luke 22:22). In Matthew's account the perversity of Judas is heightened by the fact that he has already taken steps, as one of the Twelve, to betray Jesus (26:14–16), and despite this joined the others in the final meal.

It is hardly correct that "seen from a purely human standpoint, [Jesus] must have hated Judas like poison" (Guardini 1964: 416). Rather, Matthew's portrait of Judas serves as an example to the community. The transgressor, or the betrayer, is openly exposed. Peter, from Galilee, finds his way to genuine repentance, whereas Judas, from Judea, in spite of his remorse exercises the final judgment on himself. This represents a considerable escalation of the debt laid on Judas.

3. Lukan Tradition. In the Lukan writings there are four separate pieces of tradition dealing with Judas:

a. Luke 22:1–6. While Matthew suggests that Judas acted because of love for money, Luke goes considerably beyond that and attributes it to the entrance of Satan into Judas (22:3). This fits with Luke's notion that the devil left Jesus for a season (Luke 4:13) now to return, and through one of the Twelve, Satan will now bring the conflict between God and Satan to a decisive stage. Luke does not, like Mark and Matthew, have Jesus rebuke Peter with the words: "Get you behind me Satan" (Mark 8:33; Matt 16:23). Only in Luke does Satan enter Judas. Luke, furthermore, sets Judas on equal footing with the chief priests and officers of the Temple because he goes to negotiate with them. They want to take Jesus into captivity but cannot because of the crowds (19:47; 20:19). Luke provides a reason for Judas' deed and also prepares for the act that made it possible to capture Jesus. Just as Ananias is possessed by Satan in Acts 5:3, so here Satan takes over Judas and sets the execution of Jesus into motion. But Luke also portrays Judas as acting in partnership with the upper levels of authority in Judaism.

b. Luke 22:21–23. It is remarkable that in Luke's description of the Last Supper Judas stays until the very end; indeed, he is not even exposed as a traitor at this meal. If Matthew and Mark have avoided the problem of having Judas participate in this most intimate meal with Jesus by exposing him at the outset, Luke introduces a different problem: How can the betrayer, possessed as he is of Satan, participate in the inner circle of the Twelve with Jesus? Luke affirms that even in this intimate circle a betrayer, indeed one possessed of Satan, can be present. He is known to Jesus (22:21–23) but not exposed. Instead, in Luke's narrative the disciples break out into a jealous dispute about who among them ranks the highest. Perhaps it is Luke's way of saying that the act of betrayal is not restricted to one person alone, and although Judas' act is singular, there is in this context also a reminder that Peter will deny his Lord three times, in spite of his assurances that he will not.

c. Luke 22:47–53. The words "with . . . Judas . . . at their head" (v 47) are Luke's own, stressing Judas' leadership role. He does not actually depict Judas kissing Jesus, although it is clear that he intends to do so. Jesus addresses Judas by name with no qualifiers, signifying an early tradition. Most striking is also the way in which Judas is interrogated by Jesus (v 48); "the hour of darkness may now reign" (v 53), but ultimately Jesus is in charge. As Grundmann (*Luke* THKNT) has said: "The One who has come to free those sitting in darkness . . . came under their power himself through those who served it. Their hour will however be ended by his hour and the power of darkness will be overcome through his victory."

d. Acts 1:16–20. At the center of this narrative stands Peter, acting as an interpreter of the act of Judas. Missing is any reference to Satan; instead, Peter (through Luke's redaction) speaks of the way in which Scripture was fulfilled through the deeds of Judas. Nothing is said of a betrayal, rather, his deed is described as "acting as a guide to those who arrested Jesus" (Acts 1:16). To be sure, as Lüthi (1955: 113) has noted, while Matthew attributes an immoral dimension to Judas' financial negotiations, here it is explicitly described as "the price of his villainy" or unrighteousness. Luke sees *adikia* as related to *mamona* (16:8), and while his account of the death of Judas is clearly secondary to that of Matthew, neither one necessarily reflects historical reality. Luke tied it to two OT texts: Pss 69:26 and 109:8.

As for elements of the tradition, Luke offers little information about Judas that is not found elsewhere in the NT. Yet the shape and form which he gives it is uniquely his own, directed no doubt to his own community. By now it is clear that a supernatural element is needed to explain his action, and thus Satan is introduced for the first time. By having Judas at the Last Supper throughout the evening, Luke shows that satanic powers can permeate the very inner circle of believers when they meet with their Lord. His Judas does not seek repentance. He ends his own life even though "he had this ministry with us" (Acts 1:17). But Luke's understanding of salvation history also includes the victory of Jesus over Judas, the victory of good over evil, of light over darkness.

4. The Gospel of John. There are a total of five references to Judas Iscariot in the Fourth Gospel.

a. John 6:64–71. Unique is the introduction of Judas' unbelief so early in the ministry of Jesus. While the Synoptic Gospels have also introduced Judas when naming the Twelve, they have only identified him further with the words "the one who handed him over." John, however, introduces Judas here to show that Jesus is aware that, although he chose Twelve, "yet one of you is a devil" (v 70). Later, of "the Jews" Jesus says that their "father is the devil" (8:44). Here John's concern is to affirm that Jesus knew everything: "Jesus knew from the first who those were that did not believe and who it was that would betray him" (6:64). Where Luke speaks of Satan entering into Judas, John states flatly: "One of you is a devil" (6:70). John's gloss explains that "he meant Judas, son of Simon Iscariot."

b. John 12:1–8. John's editing of the anointing story builds on certain traditional materials, e.g., only here does John refer to Judas as "Iscariot" and only here does he use the expression *heis tōn mathētōn,* "one of the disciples." He prefers the term *ek tōn mathētōn,* and he uses the traditional formula "the one who was to betray him." What is new in this story is the notice that Judas served as treasurer and, secondly, that he was a thief who used to pilfer the money put into the common purse. Since the narrative reads well without any reference to Judas whatever, this could well be a later Johannine redactional addition. Since no group can long survive without confidence in its treasurer, and since the other gospels do not mention it, we may assume that John is here adding later gossip for which there is no historical evidence. It does, however, fit into his overall attempt to demonize Judas.

c. John 13:2–30. The context is the footwashing and the Last Supper. Judas serves as the backdrop of the footwashing, for having spoken of his willingness to demonstrate the love Jesus had for his own, the narrative abruptly jars us with: "The devil had already put it into the mind of Judas . . . to betray him." We are led to believe that Judas participates in the washing of the feet without objection. The gloss in v 10 addresses the matter; Jesus was aware of who would betray him. He also knows whom he has chosen, but one of them is excluded from this choice, "the one who eats bread with me has lifted his heel against me." Jesus is then described as being in "deep agitation of spirit" (v 21) because of the betrayal. The scene is similar to that of the Synoptics: the disciples ask who is it, and finally by dipping bread in the dish and giving it to Judas the secret is revealed. "As soon as Judas had received it, Satan entered him." When Jesus tells him, "Do quickly what you have to do," no one at the table understood what he meant. The perplexity of the disciples also indicates that Judas was not an "outsider" from the start. Rather, the reference to Satan entering him after he ate the bread indicates that Judas was a believer like the other disciples. He fully participated in their common life with Jesus. Twice John says that he received the bread (v 27, 30). But for John light and darkness are essential parts of moral reality, and when Judas departs he takes leave of the light and goes out into the darkness.

d. John 17:12. Even in the great prayer of Jesus recorded in chap. 17, the discordant note of Judas is sounded, although he is not named. "Not one of them is lost except the son of perdition who must be lost, for

Scripture has to be fulfilled." The divine will is here applied to Judas, and he is called something similar to the son of iniquity (2 Thess 2:3), i.e., someone born from and destined for iniquity. Judas appears here more like an automaton than a free, willing person.

e. John 18:1–11. What is striking here is the mechanical behavior Judas displays. Described only as "Judas, the betrayer" he appears as the leader of the contingent of soldiers and police provided by the chief priests and the Pharisees, equipped with torches, weapons, and lanterns. John confines himself simply to saying that after Jesus had come forward to ask them whom they were seeking and had identified himself, "there stood Judas the traitor with them" (v 5).

For John there is no genuine interaction between Jesus and Judas. The latter represents the evil darkness and he comes across the stage as an actor merely playing his part. Jesus can only rebuke him for murmuring about the waste of money at the anointing. John blames that solely on Judas and for the worst of motives.

In the final scene in Gethsemane in John's account Jesus says nothing to Judas. Luke leaves open the question whether Judas kissed Jesus in the garden, but John portrays no interaction at all between the two. For him the realm of darkness cannot touch the Lord of Light, and he damns Judas into darkness. It may make good drama, but we have moved far from a description of the actual historical situation.

E. Judas in Later Christian Tradition

1. The Apostolic Fathers. The *Shepherd of Hermas* alludes to betrayers in *Herm. Sim.* viii.6.4 who cannot escape death. Although Judas is not named, he could be in mind. In *Herm. Sim.* ix.19.1–2 there is an allusion to Judas, since all betrayers are condemned to death with no hope of repentance. In the *Martyrdom of Polycarp* (#6) it is said that those who betrayed Polycarp will receive the same punishment as Judas. In the Fragment of Papias transmitted by Irenaeus (*Haer.* 5.33.3f.) it is said that Jesus met unbelief in Judas, and that he had been told he would not see the Kingdom of Heaven (Hennecke 1963–65, 2: 62–63). Papias shared the Fourth Gospel's assessment of Judas. In the Papias fragment transmitted by Apollinaris of Laodicea (about 310–390), there is a gruesome and detailed account of Judas' death. Although it takes some elements from Luke's account, it goes much beyond it, presenting Judas as "a model of great ungodliness" (cf. Gk *mega de asebeias hypodeigma*) to terrorize the reader and to prevent others from taking the path of betrayal.

2. NT Apocrypha. The *Gospel of the Ebionites* (first half of 2d century) mentions Judas (the) Iscariot as the twelfth disciple (1) with no reference to the betrayal. The *Gospel of Peter,* the earliest noncanonical account of the passion (dated about 150), also has no reference to Judas or to his deed or his fate (14:59). In the *Acts of Peter,* Peter, smitten with sharp affliction, complains about the devil and his manifold artistries, mentioning in particular his influence on Judas: "You forced Judas, my fellow-disciple and fellow-apostle, to act in a godless manner, so that he delivered up our Lord Jesus Christ, who shall punish you for it" (8). In the *Acts of John* appears the following: "I am your God, but not the God of the Traitor" (96). The radical dualism is evident.

In the *Acts of Thomas* (3d century, E Syria) the devil brags, "I am the one who stirred up Judas and bribed him to deliver up the Christ" (32). A later reference in the same work warns the reader: "Abstain . . . from thievery, which enticed Judas Iscariot and brought him to hanging" (84).

The *Acts of Pilate* (latter half of 4th century) contains an extensive legend about the death of Judas, meant to fit in between Matt 27:5a and 27:6. In this episode, Judas goes home and discusses his plan with his wife, who tries to dissuade him, but through a miracle he is proved right that Jesus will be raised up in three days (*Acts Pilate* pt. I; James 1955: 116). The *Arabic Infancy Gospel* presents a legend which shows that already in early childhood Judas was possessed of the devil (35).

The Coptic *Book of the Resurrection of Christ by Bartholomew* describes Jesus' encounter with Judas in hell: "he turned to Judas Iscariot and uttered a long rebuke, and described the sufferings which he must endure. Thirty names of sins are given, which are the snakes which were sent to devour him." After the harrowing of hell, only three souls are found there: Herod, Judas, and Cain (James 1955: 183). One fragment states that the reason Judas could not be redeemed from hell is that before his hanging he had worshipped the devil in the form of a snake (Vogler 1985: 130). A further Coptic fragment deals with a miracle of feeding in which Judas, even before he had decided to betray Jesus, remained aloof from the other disciples and did not receive bread to distribute to the crowd (Vogler 1985: 131).

Against this strong tide of rejection of Judas, it is interesting to note that according to Irenaeus, Theodoret, and Epiphanius there existed a *Gospel of Judas.* Unfortunately, nothing remains of it, but it would appear to have emerged from a group of gnostics who did not concur in the wholesale condemnation of Judas. Instead they celebrated the mystery of his betrayal and read the *Gospel of Judas* as holy writing (Hennecke 1963–65, 1: 313–14), as suggested by Irenaeus: "Others again allow Cain to be born of higher power and confess Esau, Korah, the Sodomites, and others as their relatives, which although they are hated by their creator, yet he did them no great harm. For the Sophia took from them what belonged to them as her own. The betrayer Judas knew this, he alone recognized the truth and completed the mystery of betrayal; he separated all earthly and heavenly matters. This composition they call the Gospel of Judas" (*Haer.* 1.31.1). Apparently this group felt that Judas rendered a great service by handing Jesus over to his enemies, thus bringing about the salvation of humanity. Above all, it is clear from the discoveries at Nag Hammadi that there still remained people within the early Church who could treat Judas without polemic as a human being, not as a demonic creature. In the Dialogue of the Savior he appears as a normal, inquisitive disciple alongside Matthew and Mariam (Robinson 1977: 229–38).

The evidence for this positive interest in Judas is remarkable. It could well be the forerunner of the positive interest many Jews displayed in Judas, and indeed may be inherent in the early gospel accounts. Any attempts, however, to allow the historical Judas to emerge were in time overshadowed by a reading of the gospel in which people are divided into good people and bad people, and according to which bad people have no hope of redemption. It is hard to find support in the texts for such an attitude on the part of Jesus toward Judas.

F. Judas in Recent Discussion

The numerous novels about Judas in the 20th century, and their revisions of the traditional point of view (not to mention contemporary movies or musicals in which he figures) signals the continuing search for the Judas of history. From a theological perspective, the carefully nuanced discussion of Judas by Karl Barth (1957: 458–507) indicates that the issue is more complex than either the gnostic gospels of the 2d century or the canonical gospels of the 1st century admit.

The dilemma which the NT texts pose is that Judas is clearly a disciple of Jesus from early on. He enjoyed the trust of Jesus and the respect and confidence of the group. The paltry sum for which he allegedly "betrays" Jesus is hardly an adequate motive to account for the action. It is impossible to ascertain what is being betrayed. Certainly if Jesus did not want to allow himself to be captured on that night he had plenty of opportunity to flee. Is it possible that Judas did not so much betray Jesus as was betrayed by him, i.e., that the hopes and wishes of Judas, along with those of the other disciples, were dashed when Jesus had his opportunity to confront the powers? Was Judas in fact selected by Jesus personally to be the agent who would make contact with the authorities to avoid tumult or a riot, and that the remorse of Judas came only as it became clear to him that Jesus, too, would die and not establish his kingdom?

The sources do not reveal answers to these questions, but there has been much discussion of this issue from at least the time of Origen, who first posed the theological questions (Laeuchli 1953). As Origen already noted, the discrepant accounts of the various Gospels create the historical problem, which precedes the theological problem. Thus the gospel writers have, in their own way, contributed to the enigma of the life and work of Judas Iscariot, an enigma which defies easy solution. In no other person do the elements of free will and divine providence come together so ambiguously. No doubt this is the reason why Judas has held such a compelling attraction for theologians and artists over the centuries and does even now. In a study of Judas, history and theology came together. But even more directly, ethics as well, for those who condemn Judas, and especially those who use him to fuel the fires of anti-Semitism, have not learned the meaning of Christ's death, which was meant to put an end to all judgment and condemnation. Is it too much to suggest that whatever Judas did, he too was covered by the intercessory prayer of Jesus from the cross: "Father, forgive them for they know not what they do"?

Bibliography

Arbeitman, Y. 1980. The Suffix of Iscariot. *JBL* 99: 122–24.
Barth, K. 1957. *Church Dogmatics*. Vol. 2. Grand Rapids, MI.
Billerbeck, P. 1922. *Kommentar zum NT.* Vol. 1. Munich.
Bosch, J. 1955. *Judas Iscariote el calumniado.* Santiago, Chile.
Cullmann, O. 1956. *The State in the NT.* New York.
———. 1966. Der zwolfte Apostel. Pp. 214–22 in *Vortrage und Aufsatze, 1925–1962,* ed. K. Fröhlich. Tübingen-Zürich.
———. 1970. *Jesus und die Revolutionaren seiner Zeit.* Tübingen.
Dalman, G. 1902. *The Words of Jesus.* Edinburgh.
———. 1929. *Jesus-Jeshua.* Studies in the Gospels. London.
———. 1935. *Sacred Sites and Ways: Studies in the Topography of the Gospels.* London.
Ehrman, A. 1978. Judas Iscariot and Abba Saqqara. *JBL* 97: 572–73.
Gärtner, B. 1971. *Iscariot.* Philadelphia.
Gerhardsson, B. 1981. Jesus, Ausgeliefert und Verlassen—Nach dem Passionsbericht des Matthausevangeliums. Pp. 262–91 in *Redaktion und Theologie des Passionsberichtes nach den Synoptikern,* ed. M. Limbeck. Darmstadt.
Goldschmidt, H. L., and Limbeck, M. 1976. *Heilvoller Verrat? Judas im Neuen Testament.* Stuttgart.
Guardini, R. 1964. *Der Herr: Betrachtungen über die Person und das Leben Jesus Christi.* 13th ed. Würburg.
Halas, R. B. 1946. *Judas Iscariot: A Scriptural and Theological Study of His Person, His Deeds, and His Eternal Lot.* Washington, DC.
Harris, J. R. 1900. Did Judas Really Commit Suicide? *AJTh* 4: 490–513.
Haugg, D. 1930. *Judas Iskarioth in den neutestamentlichen Berichten.* Freiburg.
Hennecke, E. 1963–65. *NT Apocrypha.* 2 vols. Trans. by R. McL. Wilson. London.
Ingholt, H. 1953. The Surname of Judas Iscariot. Pp. 152–62 in *Studia Orientalia Ioanni Pedersen dicata.* Hauniae.
James, M. R. 1955. *The Apocryphal NT.* Oxford.
Jens, W. 1975. *Der Fall Judas.* Stuttgart.
Klauck, H.-J. 1987. *Judas—Ein Jünger des Herrn.* Freiburg.
Krauss, S. 1902. *Das Leben Jesu nach judischen Quellen.* Berlin.
Laeuchli, S. 1953. Origen's Interpretation of Judas Iscariot. *ChHist* 22: 253–68.
Lüthi, K. 1955. *Judas Iskarioth in der Geschichte der Auslegung.* Zurich.
Morin, J. 1973. Les deux derniers des douze: Simon le Zelote et Judas Iskarioth. *RB* 80: 332–58.
Nunes, D. 1968. *Judas, Traidor ou Traido?* Rio de Janeiro.
Popkes, W. 1967. *Christus Traditus: Eine Untersuchung der Dahingabe im Neuen Testament.* Zurich.
Robinson, J. M. 1977. *The Nag Hammadi Library.* New York.
Schwarz, G. 1988. *Jesus und Judas.* BWANT 123. Stuttgart.
Smith, W. B. 1911. Judas Iscariot. *HibJ* 9: 532–35.
Torrey, C. C. 1943. The Name "Iscarioth." *HTR* 36: 51–62.
Vogler, W. 1985. *Judas Iskarioth.* 2d ed. Theologische Arbeiten 42. Berlin.
Wagner, H., ed. 1985. *Judas Iskariot: Menschliches oder Heilsgeschichtliches Drama?.* Frankfurt.

William Klassen

JUDAS MACCABEUS.

The leader of the Jewish revolt against the religious persecutions of Antiochus IV Epiphanes. He was of a priestly family of the *mišmar* (tribe) of Jehoiarib (1 Chr 24:7). His family home was the village of Modiin, on the western slopes of the Judean hill country. He was the third son among five (1 Macc 2:2) of his father Mattathias.

Judas Maccabeus became the leader of the revolt after his father died, at about the end of 166 B.C.E. He led it from guerrilla warfare into a full-fledged revolt against Seleucid rule and he won some battles of great military importance, showing an outstanding military talent. He also took the warfare beyond the borders of Judea and entered into diplomatic relations with Rome. These two activities became major lines of policy in the development of the Hasmonean house later on.

We may assume that he was chosen to be the leader of the revolt after Mattathias' death, though he was not his eldest son, either because of some former military experience or because of the talent he showed in the exploits during the earlier stages of the revolt. Regardless, he was not a village boy or a farmer who became a military leader, but a son of an important family, which opposed the Hellenization and its supporters. According to 2 Maccabees he was forced to leave Jerusalem at the beginning of the persecution, which indicates that he was staying there at that time (1 Macc 5:27) and was not in his hometown of Modiin.

Judas' military career is covered by our two principal sources, 1 Maccabees and 2 Maccabees. We will list below his battles and military exploits. Judas' first known battle was against Apollonius, who came from Samaria (1 Macc 3:10), where he was probably a governor. Apollonius was defeated somewhere on his way toward Jerusalem, and fell on the battlefield. The battle took place probably toward the end of 166. Shortly afterward Judas defeated Seron at Beth-Horon (1 Maccabees 3:13–26). Seron was probably an officer at the coastal region.

Judas' third and most important battle was at Emmaus. In this battle he was forced to use new tactics because his opponent, Gorgias, was a better commander and had under his command a bigger army. Judas indeed used more complicated maneuvers and counter-movements than before. Intelligence, ruse, night march, moral exhortation, consideration of topographical conditions, and discipline—all were used in Emmaus. The Syrian forces were defeated and retreated to the coastal plain, in about the first half of 165 B.C.E.

In the battle of Beth-Zur, the Syrian commander was Lysias, the regent of the W part of the Seleucid Empire. Lysias tried to invade Judea from the S, but was stopped by Judas at Beth-Zur. Scholars think that he was not defeated by Judas, but left the country for political reasons.

After Lysias' retreat, Judas Maccabeus took over the Temple Mount and cleansed the Temple of the impurities caused by the Hellenizers and the Seleucid garrison (December, 164 B.C.E.). The following year (163 B.C.E.) saw the expeditions of the Maccabees to save Jews in Galilee and Transjordan, who were threatened by their enemies.

Encouraged by these successful exploits, Judas attacked Akra, the fortress of the Seleucid garrison and the shelter of the Hellenizers, his internal enemies. To this attack on the most vital base of the Seleucid suzerainty in Judea, Lysias, now the regent of the new boy-king Antiochus V, reacted forcefully by a second expedition led by himself and accompanied by the king (spring 162 B.C.E.).

Lysias had with him a greater army than ever before, including elephants. He invaded Judea again from the S and put a siege on Beth-Zur, which surrendered to him. Then he beat off Judas at Beth-Zecharia and followed him to Jerusalem, where he besieged him in the Temple Mount. It looked as if the revolt had come to its end, and it would only be a matter of time till the besieged would surrender. But Judas Maccabeus and his followers defended themselves courageously and before being able to take the place, Lysias was forced to return to Antiochia because of internal problems. He raised the siege and made a treaty with the insurgents.

Whatever the situation in Judea at that time, Judas did not acquiesce to it. Yet the new Seleucid king, Demetrius I, was not ready to let Judas be active in Judea or to change the arrangements made by the Seleucid government.

At first Nicanor, who was appointed *Strategos* (military governor) of Judea, negotiated with Judas (*mala fide* according to 1 Macc 7:27–30; *bona fide* according to 2 Macc 14:18–28), but when this failed they met on the battlefield. First in Kefar Salma, where Nicanor was repulsed and retreated to the Akra, and later at Adasa, where he was killed and his army dispersed (on the 13th of Adar, 161 B.C.E.).

At this juncture, before the battle of Adasa, when Judas Maccabeus was in all probability awaiting a new expedition to be sent by Demetrius to retaliate and to crush the revolt, he sent an ambassador to Rome to seek support against this impending threat. The result was a treaty between the Romans and the Jews (1 Macc 8:23–32). But this treaty did not prevent Demetrius from sending Bacchides to Judea. Bacchides' army met Judas at Elasa. The Jewish forces were defeated and Judas Maccabeus fell on the battlefield (160 B.C.E.).

A list of battles is not enough to estimate Judas' generalship, statesmanship, and leadership. We have to estimate his achievements within the context of that period. Judas is the person who contributed most to the repel of the persecution, decreed by Antiochus IV and instigated by the Hellenizers. This achievement was a direct result of the inability of the Hellenizers to rule Judea and the incessant demand on the Seleucid government to allocate armies to support them and to pursue the religious persecution ordered by the king. Judas Maccabeus is the person under whose leadership the rebels made this policy untenable and instead of settling the situation to the benefit of the Seleucid government turned it into an unsustainable expense.

Using the Jewish potential power to the utmost, Judas Maccabeus caused not only a change of Seleucid policy, but also the dimunition of the influence of the Hellenized nobility in Judea with the Seleucid government. This was a beginning of a change in Jewish society, which ended in it expelling the Hellenized component and rebuilding on new foundations.

Judas' activity was not limited to Judea alone, and his succor expeditions paved the way for the conquest of Israel and the foundation of a Jewish state all over the country.

Though mainly a warrior, Judas Maccabeus was well aware of the importance of diplomacy for the achievement of his aims. These aims were beyond the immediate war against Antiochus' policy, and they were, so it seems, national and political, and perhaps also dynastic. Judas took the important step toward involving Rome in the struggle against the Seleucids and was also involved in negotiations with the Seleucid authorities. Although Judas' diplomatic activity was futile, it showed the way to his followers.

His most impressive achievements were military. His leadership attracted his people and he made of his supporters an army. He knew the means to win on the battlefield, but he could not (or it was premature at the time) turn his military achievements into political gains. This was done by his brothers.

Judas Maccabeus is admired in 2 Maccabees, he is highly appreciated in 1 Maccabees, and he is critically or skeptically viewed in the book of Daniel, where he is called (according to most commentators) "a little help" (Dan 11:34). Historically, his achievements were tremendous, though they may have sown seeds of future problems.

URIEL RAPPAPORT

JUDE, EPISTLE OF. The Epistle of Jude was written to warn against false teachers and is found as the 26th book in the NT canon.

A. Form and Structure
B. Literary Relationships
C. Theological Character
D. The Opponents
E. Date
F. Authorship
G. Destination
H. Message

A. Form and Structure

A careful analysis of the structure of Jude is essential to an adequate understanding of it:

1–2	Address and Greeting	
3–4	Occasion and Theme	
3	A.	The Appeal to Contend for the Faith
4	B.	The Background to the Appeal: The False Teachers, Their Character and Judgment (forming Introductory Statement of Theme for B[1])
5–23	Body of the Letter	
5–19	B[1].	The Background: A Midrash on Four Prophecies of the Doom of the Ungodly
5–7		*"Text" 1: Three Old Testament Types*
8–10		+ interpretation
(9)		including secondary "text" 1a: Michael and the Devil
11		*"Text" 2: Three More Old Testament Types*
12–13		+ interpretation
(12–13)		including secondary allusions
14–15		*"Text" 3: A Very Ancient Prophecy*
16		+ interpretation
17–18		*"Text" 4: A Very Modern Prophecy*
19		+ interpretation
20–23	A[1].	The Appeal
24–25	Concluding Doxology	

This analysis should make clear that in form Jude is a letter which contains (in vv 4–19) a "midrash" or section of formal exegesis. It is important to notice how the initial statement of the theme of the letter (vv 3–4) contains two parts (A and B) which correspond, in reverse order, to the two parts of the body of the letter (B[1] and A[1]). The main purpose of the letter is the appeal "to contend for the faith" which is announced in v 3 and spelled out in vv 20–23. But v 4 explains that this appeal is needed because the readers are in danger of being seriously misled by certain false teachers. The claim made in v 4 that these teachers are people whose ungodly behavior has already been condemned by God is then substantiated by the exegetical section (vv 5–19) which argues that they are the ungodly people of the last days to whom many scriptural types and prophecies of judgment refer. Despite its length and central position, the discussion of the false teachers (vv 4–19) is not the main object of the letter. It establishes the danger in which the readers are placed by the influence of the false teachers and so performs an essential role as background to the appeal, but the real climax of the letter is reached only in the exhortations of vv 20–23. In vv 4–19 Jude establishes the need for his readers to "contend for the faith," but only in vv 20–23 does he explain what "contending for the faith" involves. Thus his negative polemic against the false teachers is subordinate to the positive Christian teaching of vv 20–23.

Further explanation of the structure of the "midrash" (vv 4–19) is needed. This is a very carefully composed piece of scriptural commentary which argues for the statement made in v 4. Though the form of argument will be strange to modern readers, its hermeneutical presuppositions and exegetical methods were widely accepted in contemporary Judaism and can be paralleled especially from the Qumran commentaries on Scripture (the *pešārîm*), as well as from some other parts of the NT (e.g. 1 Pet 2:4–10).

There are four main "texts" (vv 5–7, 11, 14–15, 17–18), each followed by a section of interpretation (vv 8–10, 12–13, 16, 19). These "texts" *function* as texts in the midrash, but are not all scriptural quotations: in fact, none is an actual quotation from our canonical OT. The first pair of "texts" (1 and 2) are summaries of Scripture: three groups of people (in text 1) and three individuals (in text 2) who were famous scriptural examples of divine judgment and here function as types of the false teachers who are similarly doomed to judgment. "Texts" 3 and 4 form a second pair, this time of verbal prophecies of the false teachers. "Text" 3 is quoted from *1 En.* 1:9 and "text" 4 from oral tradition of the apocalyptic teaching of the apostles: they show that the false teachers and their doom have been prophesied from the very earliest times up to the most recent times.

Despite the somewhat anomalous nature of the "texts," the midrashic structure of texts followed by interpretations is clear, since the distinction between text and interpretation is marked in three ways: (1) The tense of the verbs in the "texts" is past or future, referring to types in the past or prophesying the future (in "texts" 2 and 3 the aorists are prophetic past tenses), whereas the interpretations use present tenses, referring to the fulfillment of the types and prophecies at the present time, i.e. in the form of

Jude's opponents. (2) Phrases with *houtoi* ("these people") are used in a formulaic way to introduce each section of interpretation. These resemble similar formulae used in the Qumran commentaries (4QFlor 1:2, 3, 11, 12, 17; 4QpIsa 3:7, 9, 10, 12; 4QpIsa^b 2:6–7, 10) and occasionally elsewhere (Gal 4:24; 2 Tim 3:8). In Jude they serve to identify the false teachers as the people to whom the prophecies refer, and so make the transition from the prophecy to its application to the false teachers. In each case the interpretation then describes the false teachers in a way which conforms to the prophecy. (3) Introductory formulae introduce "texts" 1, 3 and 4, and distinguish "texts" 3 and 4 from the preceding sections of interpretation. "Text" 2 lacks an introductory formula, but is sufficiently marked out by its form as a prophetic woe-oracle.

In addition to the four main "texts," there is a secondary "text" (1a), which is introduced in v 9 to help the interpretation of "text" 1. This is a summary of an apocryphal account of the death of Moses. The use of such a secondary text in the course of the interpretation of another text can be paralleled in the Qumran commentaries, as can the incorporation of implicit allusions to other texts in the course of the interpretation of a given text, a practice which Jude adopts in vv 12–13, where there are allusions to Ezek 34:2; Prov 25:14; Isa 57:20; *1 En.* 80:6.

Exegetical techniques used in the midrash include the lavish use of catchword connections. Words from the same stem are used to link "texts" together (the practice known by the rabbis as *gezera sawa*), to link a "text" to its interpretation, and to link the introductory statement of theme (v 4) to the "texts." For example, the catchword "ungodly" links "texts" 3 and 4 (vv 15, 18), and both these "texts" to v 4. But not all the catchword connections are visible in English translations. Again, such use of catchword connections can be amply paralleled at Qumran and elsewhere (e.g. 1 Pet 2:4–10).

Thus Jude's midrash resembles the Qumran commentaries in its use of exegetical formulas (especially the *houtoi* phrases) and exegetical methods (especially catchword connections). In form it resembles especially the so-called "thematic *pešārîm*" (such as 4QFlor). It also shares with the Qumran commentaries, as also with much early Christian exegesis, the hermeneutical presupposition that Scripture is prophetic of the last times in which the interpreter and his community are living, and indeed actually refers to themselves and their enemies. It seems that Jude's midrash is an unusually sustained and elaborate exercise in the kind of scriptural exegesis which must have been typical of the early Church from an early date and declined to the extent that Christianity moved away from its Palestinian Jewish origins.

B. Literary Relationships

Many of Jude's pervasive allusions to the OT have already been noticed in section A. Scholars have often supposed that Jude, like most NT writers, used the LXX version, but the evidence is in fact against this. He uses some standard items of Jewish Greek vocabulary and idiom, which are found in the LXX, but none of his many allusions to specific verses of the OT echoes the language of the LXX. Moreover, some of his allusions depend on a meaning of the Hebrew text which is not rendered in the LXX. In two cases (Prov 25:14: Jude 12; Isa 57:20: Jude 13) the LXX gives a quite different sense from that of the Hebrew, and Jude is plainly following the Hebrew. In a third case (Ezek 34:2: Jude 12), while Jude's dependence on the LXX is not impossible, his allusion is closer to the Hebrew. It seems, therefore, that it was with the Hebrew Bible that Jude was really familiar. When he wished to allude to it, he did not stop to find the LXX translation, but made his own translation, in terms appropriate to the style and content of his work.

Jude evidently set high value not only on Jewish Scriptures which are now canonical, but also on apocryphal works. Besides his explicit quotation from *1 Enoch* in vv 14–15 (*1 En.* 1:9), there are further allusions in v 6 (cf. *1 En.* 10:4–6, 12; 12:4; 15:3; 15:7; and perhaps also *2 En.* 7:2; 18:4–6) and in v 13 (*1 En.* 80:6), while the scheme of four metaphors from nature in vv 12b–13 seems to relate to *1 En.* 2:1–5:4; 80:2–7. We cannot be sure of the extent of the Enochic corpus he knew, but he was evidently very familiar with parts of our *1 Enoch.* He treats Enoch, whose prestige he indicates in the phrase "the seventh from Adam" (Jude 14; cf. *1 En.* 60:8; 93:5; *Jub.* 7:39), as an authoritative prophet. Since he also treats an oral prophecy of the apostles (v 18) as authoritative prophecy, we do not have to conclude that he had a canon of Scripture which included the Enoch literature along with OT books. He may (like the author of *4 Ezra* 14) have treated apocalypses such as *1 Enoch* as authoritative literature alongside the OT canon. The evidence is not sufficient to determine the exact status the Enoch literature held for Jude. As for his text of Enoch, there are some indications in v 6 and vv 14–15 that he knew the Aramaic original rather than, or as well as, the Greek version, though since the relevant chapters of *1 Enoch* in Greek are extant only in one manuscript, we cannot be entirely sure that he did not know a form of the Greek text closer to the Aramaic than ours.

Another apocryphal work was the source of Jude's reference to the dispute over the body of Moses (v 9). This story is no longer extant in the form Jude knew it, but from various sources it can be reconstructed with high probability and in some detail (see Bauckham, *Jude, 2 Peter* WBC, 47–48, 65–76), as follows:

> Joshua accompanied Moses up Mount Nebo, where God showed Moses the land of promise. Moses then sent Joshua back, saying, "Go down to the people and tell them that Moses is dead." When Joshua had gone down to the people, Moses died. God sent the archangel Michael to remove the body of Moses to another place and to bury it there, but Samma᾿el, the devil, opposed him, disputing Moses' right to honorable burial. [The text may also have said that the devil wished to take the body down to the people, so that they would make it an object of worship.] Michael and the devil engaged in a dispute over the body. The devil slandered Moses, charging him with murder, because he slew the Egyptian and hid his body in the sand. But Michael, not tolerating the slander against Moses, said, "May the Lord rebuke you, devil!" At that the devil took flight, and Michael removed the body to the place commanded by God. Thus no one saw the burial-place of Moses.

This story may have been known to Jude as the ending of the *Testament of Moses,* whose extant Latin text breaks off before the end. The probability of this would be increased if, as some scholars have thought, there are allusions elsewhere in Jude to the extant text of the *Testament of Moses* (Jude 16: cf. *T. Mos.* 7:7, 9; 5:5; Jude 3: cf. *T. Mos.* 4:8), but these alleged allusions are far from certain.

That there is a close relationship between Jude and 2 Peter is obvious to any careful reader. The resemblances are largely between Jude 4–13, 16–18, and 2 Pet 2:1–18; 3:1–3. Almost all scholars have agreed that in view of the degree of close verbal resemblance the relationship must be a literary one. The view that Jude is dependent on 2 Peter was once common, but in the last half-century has received almost no support from scholars. A few recent writers have postulated a common source used by Jude and 2 Peter, but by far the most widely accepted view is that 2 Peter is dependent on Jude. A strong reason to prefer this view is that while much of the content and some of the words of Jude 4–19 reappear in 2 Peter, Jude's elaborate midrashic structure and exegetical techniques do not. It is much more difficult to imagine Jude constructing his complex midrash from the material in 2 Peter than to imagine the author of 2 Peter discarding the midrashic features of Jude's work as he reused some of the material for other purposes.

It has sometimes been claimed that Jude shows acquaintance with the Pauline literature, but the terminology Jude shares with Paul is really no more than the common vocabulary of the early Church.

C. Theological Character

In much recent scholarship Jude has been placed, along with other "late" NT writings, under the general umbrella of "early Catholicism." In part, this is a result of associating Jude closely with 2 Peter, which is generally classified as "early Catholic." However, it is a mistake to suppose that because material from Jude has been taken over by 2 Peter, the context and character of the two letters are similar. Careful redaction-critical study of 2 Peter's use of Jude shows that the author has adapted the material he borrowed from Jude for a different context and a different purpose.

Jude's language about "the faith" in vv 3 and 20 also contributes to the judgment that the work is "early Catholic." Jude is supposed to view the Christian message as a fixed body of credal belief which is authoritatively transmitted from the apostolic age. However, the objective use of *pistis* ("faith") to mean "what is believed" can be paralleled in Paul (Gal 1:23), where it refers simply to the gospel. The notion of a body of orthodox doctrine needs no more to be read into Jude's use of the term than it does into Paul's. The concept of tradition in Jude 3 can also be amply paralleled in Paul, who frequently refers his readers back to the traditions he delivered to them when he founded their churches as an unalterable standard of Christian truth (e.g. 1 Cor 11:2, 23; 15:3; 2 Cor 11:4; Gal 1:8–9).

Two further features, in addition to the development of fixed credal orthodoxy, which are usually considered characteristic of "early Catholicism" are the fading of the imminent eschatological expectation and the growth of institutionalized office in the Church. In Jude, however, the Parousia hope is lively and pervades the letter (vv 1, 14, 21, 24). The whole argument of the midrash (vv 4–19) hinges on the expectation that Jude's opponents are to be judged by the Lord at his Parousia and so presupposes an imminent Parousia. As for ecclesiastical officials, they are not so much as mentioned in Jude. Jude's opponents were evidently charismatics who claimed prophetic revelations, but his response is not the "early Catholic" one of restricting charismatic activity to ecclesiastical officials or subjecting it to their control. He addresses not officials but the whole community, who all enjoy the inspiration of the Spirit in charismatic prayer (v 20) and are all responsible for upholding the gospel (v 3). The usefulness of the general concept of "early Catholicism" is in any case beginning to be seriously questioned, but it should at least be quite clear that it is inapplicable to Jude.

The evidence points rather to Palestinian apocalyptic Jewish Christianity as the milieu to which Jude belongs. We have seen (in section A) that the midrash section (vv 4–19) shows the author to be an accomplished practitioner of Jewish exegesis of a kind which can be most closely paralleled in the Qumran literature and is not typical of the literature of Diaspora Judaism. His use of the Enoch literature and the apocryphal account of the death of Moses point in the same direction, as does his dependence on the Hebrew Bible (see section B above).

D. The Opponents

The opponents against whom Jude warns his readers have usually been thought to be gnostics. Few modern scholars are willing to identify them with a specific gnostic sect, and many speak cautiously only of "incipient Gnosticism," such as may also be characteristic of Paul's opponents in Corinth or the Nicolaitans in Revelation. However, secure exegetical evidence for specifically gnostic teachings cannot be found in Jude. His polemic seems entirely aimed against the opponents' practice and advocacy of immorality: they must, therefore, have been people who were *in principle* libertines. Their immorality must have been real, not a polemical slur, since it is the sole reason for Jude's attack on them. He is not casting aspersions on the morality of people he really disagrees with for other reasons. Everything he says about them can be directly related to their antinomianism. This antinomianism could have been one of the streams which flowed into later Gnosticism, but it is not itself distinctively gnostic.

The opponents were evidently itinerant charismatics who had arrived in the church or churches to which Jude writes. They reject all moral authority, whether that of the law of Moses (vv 8–10) or that of Christ himself (vv 4, 8). Their denial of Christ as Master and Lord (v 4) is not to be understood as a doctrinal error, but as rejection of his moral demands: by their immoral practice they in effect disown him as Master and repudiate his authority as Lord. Evidently they understood the grace of God in Christ (v 4) as a deliverance from all external moral constraint, so that the man who possesses the Spirit (v 19 is Jude's response to this claim) becomes the only judge of his own actions, subject to no other authority. Like the Corinthians, whose slogan was "All things are lawful for me" (1 Cor 6:12; 10:23), they take Christian freedom to mean that the really spiritual person is free from the constraints of conventional morality. In their indulgence in sexual misconduct (vv 6–8, 10), they may have been deliberately flouting accepted standards of Jewish morality and conforming to the greater permissiveness of pagan society. For their authority to behave in this way, they appealed to their charismatic inspiration, manifested in prophetic visions ("dreaming," v 8, is a pejorative reference to these), in which perhaps they received revelations of the heavenly world and their own exalted status in it.

The most puzzling feature of the opponents, their attitude to angels (vv 8–10), is probably to be understood with reference to angels as guardians of the Law and of the moral order of the world. When accused of sin by the standard of the law of Moses or of the order of creation, they spoke disparagingly of the angels who gave the Law and administered the moral order of the world, alleging that these angels were motivated by ill-will toward humanity. Such an attitude to the angels of the Law does resemble the views of many later gnostics, but it stops far short of the cosmological dualism characteristic of these gnostics, for whom the hostile angels were the creators and lords of the material world.

Jude's opponents were not simply members of the Church, but teachers: vv 11–13 portray them, with appropriate OT types, as people who lead others astray and, notably, as shepherds who feed themselves instead of the flock. They were present at the Church's fellowship meals (v 12), where no doubt they imparted their prophecies and teachings to the Church. They gathered their own faction of followers, who considered themselves truly in possession of the Spirit (v 19).

It is possible, though by no means certain, that Pauline teaching may have had some influence on the opponents. They could have been taking to an extreme and misinterpreting Paul's teaching about grace and the Law. Not only did Paul himself recognize and oppose the danger of an antinomian distortion of his teaching on Christian freedom (Rom 3:8; 6:1, 15; Gal 5:13), but also the blaspheming of angels, so distinctive of Jude's opponents (vv 8–10), is not too distant from some of Paul's treatment of the angels of the Law and "the elemental spirits of the world" (Gal 3:20; 4:3; 8–9; Col 2:8–23; Rom 8:33–39).

E. Date

In the history of scholarship Jude has been assigned to a very wide range of dates, from the 50s to the late 2d century. Recent scholars are not inclined to date the work very far into the 2d century, but many consider a date relatively late in the 1st century to be probable. However, the most important factor in this opinion is the classification of Jude as an "early Catholic" work, which we have already seen to be unjustified (section C above). Nor does the character of the opponents' teaching (see section D above) require a late date, since it is not developed Gnosticism.

A late date has also been deduced from v 17, in which the author is often thought to be looking back on the apostolic age as an era now past. However, this is by no means a necessary understanding of the verse and is probably a mistaken one. It is not the apostles themselves, but their predictions, which belong to the past. As in vv 3 and 5, Jude is recalling his readers to the instruction they received at their conversion, from the apostles who founded their churches. The apocalyptic prophecy of v 17 formed part of the initial Christian teaching which was given to these churches at their foundation. Understood in this way, Jude's statement is parallel to many of Paul's in which he refers his readers back to the teaching he gave them when he established their churches (1 Cor 15:1–3; Gal 1:9; 1 Thess 4:1–2; 2 Thess 2:5), with the one difference that, since Jude is evidently writing to churches he did not found himself, he speaks of the apostles' teaching rather than his own (but cf. Rom 6:7; 16:17). If v 18 ("they said to *you*") means that Jude's readers themselves had heard the apostles' preaching at the time of the founding of their churches, then the passage suggests an earlier rather than a later date for the letter.

If 2 Peter is dependent on Jude (see section B above), then the date of 2 Peter is a *terminus ad quem* for Jude, but scholarly opinions on the date of 2 Peter differ almost as much as do those on the date of Jude. Perhaps all that can be said, in general, is that the letter of Jude gives a general impression of primitiveness and contains nothing that requires a late date. It could very plausibly be dated in the 50s, and might be one of the earliest of the NT writings.

F. Authorship

The letter is attributed to "Judas, a servant of Jesus Christ and brother of James" (v 1). This Judas (traditionally in English "Jude") has usually been identified as Judas the brother of Jesus, who is mentioned in Matt 13:55; Mark 6:3; and Hegesippus (*apud* Euseb. *Hist. Eccl.* 3.19.1–20.6). Other identifications have occasionally been suggested, but are implausible because they do not satisfactorily account for "brother of James." Since for purposes of identification reference would normally be made to one's father, not one's brother, the James in question must have been very well-known. The only man in the early Church who could be called simply James without risk of ambiguity was James the Lord's brother.

However, the question arises whether the letter was really written by Judas the brother of Jesus or is a pseudepigraphal work attributed to Jude by a later writer. There is no scholarly consensus on this point. Against the pseudepigraphal hypothesis, it has sometimes been argued that Jude was too obscure a figure in the early Church for a later writer to adopt him as a pseudonym that would lend authority to his work. Though this may be true of large parts of the early Church, it would not be true of Palestinian Jewish-Christian circles, where the blood relations of Jesus were prominent in the leadership of the churches until well into the 2d century, or in East Syrian Christianity, whose favorite apostle, Judas Thomas, came to be considered the twin brother of Jesus and thereby identified with Judas the brother of Jesus. However, it is unlikely that a pseudepigraphal work from either of these contexts would have described Jude in the way he is identified in v 1. A Syrian writer would certainly have called his pseudonym Judas *Thomas* (or Didymus), as Syrian Christian literature always does. A Jewish-Christian writer would surely have given Jude his common title "brother of the Lord," which, in such circles, would not only distinguish him from other Judases, but would indicate his authoritative status. That this title is not used is much more easily explained if the letter is authentic. Not wishing to claim an authority based on mere blood-relationship to Jesus, Jude avoids calling himself "brother of the Lord," which readers would have taken (especially in a letter opening) as his claim to authority. Instead, he bases his authority to address his readers on his being "a servant of Jesus Christ" (cf. Phil 1:1).

Of Judas the brother of Jesus, we know little. One of the four brothers, probably younger than James (Matt 13:55; Mark 6:3), he was presumably, like the other brothers, not a follower of Jesus during his ministry (Mark 3:21, 31), but became a believer after the resurrection (Acts 1:14). According to 1 Cor 9:5, Jesus' brothers became traveling missionaries, and this general reference probably includes Jude, especially as it most likely does not include James, who seems to have remained in Jerusalem. Jude's missionary labors would most probably be among Jews, but not necessarily in Palestine: he could have gone to the Diaspora. Julius Africanus (*apud* Euseb. *Hist. Eccl.* 1.7.14) says that the family of Jesus spread the gospel throughout Palestine, starting from Nazareth and Cochaba (most likely Kaukab in Galilee, northwest of Sepphoris, rather than Kaukab in Transjordan): this confirms both the missionary role and other indications that the family remained based in Galilee.

The only other possibly reliable information is Hegesippus' story (*apud* Euseb. *Hist. Eccl.,* 3.19.1–20.8) about the grandsons of Jude (whose names are given in another fragment as Zechariah and James). As descendants of David and related to Jesus the Messiah, they were denounced as politically dangerous and brought before the emperor Domitian. But when they explained that they were only poor farmers, working with their own calloused hands, and that the messianic kingdom they expected was heavenly and eschatological, the emperor dismissed them as harmless and ordered the persecution of the Church to stop. Hegesippus adds that they became leaders of the churches and survived until the reign of Trajan. No doubt the story preserves some historical memory, but it has a clearly apologetic thrust in showing that the emperor himself had recognized that Jewish Christianity was not a political danger, while the trial before Domitian himself and especially his ordering persecution to cease as a result are improbable. Thus it would be unwise to trust the chronological implications of the story: that Jude had grandsons who were adult in the reign of Domitian and (even less trustworthy because not stated by Hegesippus) that Jude himself was then dead. But if Jude, as one of the younger brothers of Jesus, were born ca. A.D. 10, he could have had grandsons aged thirty in A.D. 90, when he himself would be eighty. Thus, even if the letter had to be dated fairly late in the 1st century, it could still be an authentic letter of Jude. But, as we have seen (section E), there is no reason to date it so late.

A late dating of Jude is the major reason why many scholars have concluded it must be pseudepigraphal. If we reject that reason, there remains only one obstacle to its authenticity: the language of the letter, which has often been said to be Greek too good to be attributable to a Galilean Jew of peasant stock. Although the author was certainly a Semitic speaker who habitually used the OT in Hebrew and probably read the book of Enoch in Aramaic (see section B), his command of literary Greek is quite impressive. However, this should not be exaggerated. A wide vocabulary, which Jude has, is easier to acquire than skills in grammar and style, which are adequate but not remarkable in Jude. The kind of skills he shows (see Bauckham *Jude, 2 Peter* WBC, 6–7) are the rhetorical skills which a Jewish preacher in Greek would need to acquire and which he could acquire from familiarity with Jewish literature in Greek and from much listening to Jewish and Christian sermons. It is not easy to estimate how competent in Greek a Galilean Jew would have been, but in Jude's case, if his missionary career took him among Greek-speaking Jews, there seems no reason why he should not have acquired the degree of competence displayed in this letter.

Finally, it should be noted that the character of the letter—its exegetical methods (section A above), its indebtedness to Palestinian Jewish literature (section B above) and haggadic traditions, its apocalyptic perspective (section C above)—is entirely consistent with authorship by a Palestinian Jewish-Christian leader of the first generation, as Judas the brother of Jesus was. The preservation of this short letter in the NT therefore affords us a rare glimpse into those early Palestinian Christian circles in which Jesus' own blood relations were leaders.

G. Destination

Little can be said about the destination of the letter. The formal opening (vv 1–2) identifies it as a real letter, and, as the specific occasion for writing (v 4: itinerant teachers from elsewhere have been misleading the readers) and the particular characteristics of the opponents (section D above) indicate, it is not a general letter to all Christians, but an occasional letter to a specific church or group of churches. The latter possibility might explain the failure to specify a place in v 1, but specific destinations were sometimes omitted when letters were later copied for the benefit of a wider readership.

Both the identity of the author and the Jewishness of his letter suggest that the recipients would probably be Jewish Christians. On the other hand, although antinomianism was not unknown in 1st-century Judaism, the antinomian teaching of the opponents points most plausibly to a gentile environment (as with the antinomian problems in Paul's Corinth and in the churches of the book of Revelation). Perhaps we should think of a predominantly, but not exclusively, Jewish-Christian community in a gentile environment.

H. Message

In appreciating the message of Jude, it is important to bear in mind the structure explained in section A above. The purpose of the letter, to urge the readers "to carry on the fight for the faith" (v 3), is really only fulfilled in vv 20–23. The exegetical section (vv 4–19) about the false teachers establishes the danger they pose to the readers, while vv 20–23 explain how the readers should respond to this danger, or, more positively, how, in the light of this danger, they are "to carry on the fight for the faith." The danger is antinomianism, the claim that the gospel frees Christians from moral obligation. Such teaching and the immoral behavior which follows from it incur divine judgment: this point is made by identifying the opponents as the sinners of the last days whose judgment has been predicted all along. The true gospel, on the other hand, which Jude's readers must maintain in the face of antinomian teaching is a gospel with necessary moral implications. It must be lived out in a way of Christian life which Jude summarizes in four injunctions in vv 21–22: (1) the gospel ("your most holy faith") received from the apostles, with its clear moral implications, must be the foundation on which the Christian community is to be built; (2) prayer under the inspiration of the Spirit shows a reliance on God to be distinguished from the prophetic inspiration claimed by the opponents; (3) the readers must maintain their place in God's love by obeying his will; (4) they must live in expectation of the Lord's coming, when he will show mercy to those who remain faithful to him. Thus obedient discipleship leads to eschatological salvation, by contrast with the path of immorality, which is leading the antinomians to eschatological judgment.

Jude's denunciation of the opponents, because of the serious danger they pose to his readers, is accompanied by a genuine pastoral concern not only for those they have led astray but even for the opponents themselves. Although the text of vv 22–23, which advises the readers on how to deal with the opponents and their followers, is uncertain, the general advice is clear: to exercise Christian love, but in connection with great care to avoid the contaminating effect of the opponents' influence.

The doxology (vv 24–25), which has often been admired, depends on liturgical tradition, but is nevertheless framed to conclude the message of the book. It is in effect a confident prayer that God will preserve the readers from the spiritual disaster with which the false teaching threatens them, and bring them to the destiny he intends for them, when they will be presented as perfect sacrifices in his heavenly temple. All the concerns of the letter are finally aimed at this goal: that the Church should be fit to be offered to God's glory.

Bibliography

Albin, C. A. 1962. *Judasbrevet: Traditionen Texten Tolkningen.* Natur och Kultur. Stockholm.

Bauckham, R. J. 1988. The Letter of Jude: An Account of Research. *ANRW* 2/25/5: 3791–826.

———. 1990. *Jude and the Relatives of Jesus in the Early Church.* Edinburgh.

Busto Saiz, J. R. 1981. La carta de Judas a la luz de algunas escritos judios. *EBib* 39: 83–105.

Cantinat, J. 1973. *Les Epîtres de Saint Jacques et de Saint Jude.* SB. Paris.

Chaine, J. 1939. *Les épîtres catholiques.* 2d ed. EBib. Paris.

Ellis, E. E. 1978. Prophecy and Hermeneutic in Jude. Pp. 221–36 in *Prophecy and Hermeneutic in Early Christianity,* ed. E. E. Ellis. WUNT 18. Tübingen.

Eybers, I. H. 1975. Aspects of the Background of the Letter of Jude. *Neot* 9: 113–23.

Gunther, J. J. 1984. The Alexandrian Epistle of Jude. *NTS* 30: 549–62.

Hahn, F. 1981. Randbemerkungen zum Judasbrief. *TZ* 37: 209–18.

Heiligenthal, R. 1986. Der Judasbrief: Aspekte der Forschung in den letzten Jahrzehnten. *TRu* 51: 117–29.

Maier, F. 1906. *Der Judasbrief.* BibS(F) 11/1–2. Freiburg.

Mayor, J. B. 1907. *The Epistle of St. Jude and the Second Epistle of St. Peter.* London.

Osburn, C. D. 1976–77. The Christological Use of I Enoch i.9 in Jude 14, 15. *NTS* 23: 334–41.

———. 1985. 1 Enoch 80:2–8 (67:5–7) and Jude 11–12. *CBQ* 47: 296–303.

Rowston, D. J. 1974–75. The Most Neglected Book in the New Testament. *NTS* 21: 554–63.

Seethaler, P. A. 1987. Kleine Bemerkungen zum Judasbrief. *BZ* 31: 261–64.

Seller, G. 1986. Die Häretiker des Judasbriefes. *ZNW* 77: 206–25.

Spitta, F. 1885. *Die Zweite Brief des Petrus und der Brief des Judas.* Halle.

Werdermann, H. 1913. *Die Irrlehrer des Judas- und 2. Petrusbriefes.* BFCT 17/6. Gütersloh.

Wisse, F. 1972. The Epistle of Jude in the History of Heresiology. Pp. 133–43 in *Essays on the Nag Hammadi Texts in Honour of Alexander Böhlig,* ed. M. Krause. NHS 3. Leiden.

Wolthius, W. 1987. Jude and Jewish Traditions. *Calvin Theological Journal* 22: 21–41.

RICHARD BAUCKHAM

JUDEA (PLACE) [Heb *yĕhûdâ*]. See JUDAH (PLACE).

JUDEA, RIDGE OF. See RIDGE OF JUDEA (PLACE).

JUDEIDEH, TELL (M.R. 141115). An ancient site in the Shephelah, about 2 km N of Beth-govrin, situated 398 m above sea level.

It is generally agreed that the site is to be identified with Moresheth-gath—the birthplace of the prophet Micah (Mic 1:1; Jer 26:18), and was one of the cities captured by Sennacherib in his campaign against Judah in 701 B.C. (Mic 1:14). The book of Micah places Moresheth-gath in the vicinity of Lachish and Mareshah (Mic 1:13–15). Eusebius (*Onomast.* 134.10), Hieronymus, and the Medeba Map locate the site N of Beth-govrin. The city is to be reckoned among those which Rehoboam fortified, if the reading "Moresheth-gath and Mareshah" is accepted for "and Gath and Mareshah" in 2 Chr 11:8.

The ancient settlement was spread over the natural hill, an elongated rectangular area about 580 m long. Excavations have concentrated on the S part of the hill at the site of the walled citadel.

Little was uncovered from the Bronze Age, apart from a few graves. From the scanty material published in the excavators' report (Bliss and Macalister 1902), it is difficult to assign exact dates to this material. The excavators were of the opinion that the site was abandoned at the end of the Bronze Age and remained unoccupied until the end of the Judean kingdom.

Three main periods are distinguishable in the Iron Age: (1) Pre-Israelite (i.e., Canaanite); (2) Jewish (Israelite II); and (3) Hellenistic-Roman. In the vicinity of the mound, graves belonging to the Iron Age and the Roman period

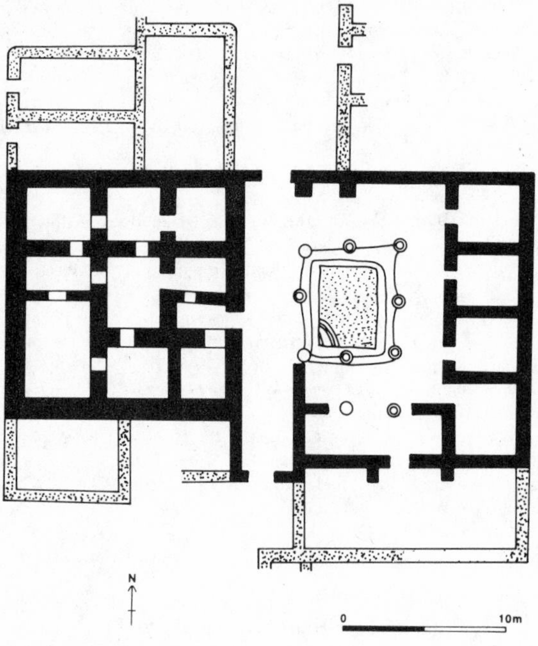

JUD.01. Plan of military headquarters at Tell Judeideh, Herodian Period. *(Redrawn from* EAEHL *3: 695)*

were found. From the Iron Age II, 37 handles stamped with *lmlk* seals were discovered. The handles include the two- and four-winged types as well as reference to the four cities (Ziph, Hebron, Socoh, *mmšt*). Building remains were also found.

The main finds belong to the Roman period. In the Early Roman period, there was a military enclosure on the S part of the hill. The enclosure was surrounded by a wall which had four double-winged gates flanked by square internal towers. The main streets passed through the gates and crossed at right angles in the center of the enclosure in a manner typical of military camps. The headquarters in the center consisted of two buildings. The W building was square and had eight rooms arranged around a courtyard. The E building was Hellenistic in plan with rooms arranged around an enclosed courtyard, having a peristyle of eight columns and a pool in the center. See Fig. JUD.01. Nothing was found in the buildings to indicate their dates, but on the basis of their style the buildings should be assigned to the time of the Herodian dynasty.

Bibliography

Bliss, F. J., and Macalister, R. A. S. 1902. *Excavations in Palestine 1898–1900*. London.

Broshi, M. 1977. Judeideh, Tell. *EAEHL* 3: 694–96

M. Broshi

JUDGE, JUDGING.

JUDGE, JUDGING. The OT uses several different terms to express the idea of "judge" or "judging." These occur both as nouns and as verbs.

A. The Noun "Judge"
   1. The Root *Špṭ* in Akkadian Literature
   2. The *Šāpiṭum,* "Judge," in Extrabiblical Literature
   3. The Usage of the Root *Špṭ* in the OT
   4. The Role of the *Šôpēṭ* in the OT
   5. The Usage of *Dyn* in Extrabiblical Literature
   6. The Root *Dyn* in the OT
   7. Others Who Judged in Israel
B. Judging (Verb)
C. Judging and Ruling
   1. Synonyms
   2. God Judges the Whole Earth

A. The Noun "Judge"

Although the roots *špṭ* and *dyn* are often used in parallel in the OT and in the literature of the ANE, there is evidence suggesting that originally they were not synonymous in meaning. The *šôpēṭ,* unlike the *dayyān,* was an undifferentiated executive appointed to play several administrative roles which included deciding cases. The translation of *šôpēṭ* to mean "undifferentiated executive" is comprehensive and more apt than "judge" (*CMHE* 219 no. 3).

1. The Root *Špṭ* in Akkadian Literature. In Akkadian there are two homonymous roots: *špṭ* I and *špṭ* II. *Špṭ* I is often used in parallel with *dyn* when used in connection with legal matters. *Špṭ* II, on the other hand, means "to threaten" or "to warn." It is significant that when it refers to "threat," or "warning," *špṭ* appears only in the OB period as attested in the Mari texts. The substantive *šāpiṭum,* "judge," is not attested until after the OB period (ca. 2000–1600 B.C.). This strongly suggests that the agent *šāpiṭum* was originally West Semitic and was introduced into the Akkadian language and administrative system by the Amorites. Prior to their arrival, the title for "judge" was *dayyānu(m),* an official who decided cases like a modern law-court judge or magistrate. This fact is supported by the fact that the root *dyn* is used forensically in all Semitic languages. While the *dayyānu(m),* "law-court judge," only decided cases which the litigants brought to him, the *šāpiṭum,* "judge," as an undifferentiated executive, performed many other functions which included deciding cases of litigants under his jurisdiction.

2. The *Šāpiṭum,* "Judge," in Extrabiblical Literature. In the Mari documents, the agent *šāpiṭum* was a person whom the king *(šarrum)* appointed to perform some special tasks. His authority was delegated to him in order that he might assist in the administration of a territory or in conducting military campaigns (cf. *ARM* 1, 73: 45–53). The functions of the *šāpiṭum* included that of "arbitrating" in domestic affairs of litigants within his jurisdiction (*ARM* 8, 84: 1–10). He was also appointed by the *šarrum* to act as a territorial governor (cf. Kupper 1957; *ARM* 2, 98: 7–14).

3. The Usage of the Root *Špṭ* in the OT. The term *šôpēṭ* is a participle of the verb *šāpaṭ* which, because it is multifarious in meaning, is translated "decide," "judge," "rule," "govern," "vindicate," "deliver," etc. In the English versions of the Bible, it is uniformly and erroneously translated "judge." This universal rendering of *šāpaṭ* is very unfortunate because it conceals other meanings which elucidate the appointment and function of the *šôpēṭ* in

Israel. Whereas the root *dyn* occurs only 25 times, the root *špṭ* is attested in 180 references in the *Qal.* To distinguish between *dyn* and *špṭ* as used in the OT, close attention should be paid to their contexts. Extrabiblical literatures, which are older than the OT, should also be consulted to elucidate the original usage and to realize the changes which may have taken place in the usage of *špṭ* diachronically. The fact that among the Semitic people *dyn* is overwhelmingly used in legal documents and in reports of legal decisions suggests that it was the original forensic term denoting "to judge." It is also significant that when the root *špṭ* is used with *bên . . . ûbên,* ("between . . .") it generally refers to the restoration of *šālôm* which prevailed prior to the prevailing strife or dispute (Gen 16:5; Judg 16:27).

4. The Role of the *Šôpēṭ* in the OT. The substantive *šôpēṭ* is used with reference to both God and humans. This is similar to the usage of *šāpiṭum* in Akkadian literature. Just as the *šāpiṭum* exercised authority delegated to him by the *šarrum* or by the deity, similarly the *šôpēṭ* of the book of Judges exercised authority delegated to him by Yahweh, the *šôpēṭ kol hāʾāreṣ,* "the Judge of all the earth," (Gen 18:25). That one was chosen by God to function as *šôpēṭ* was signified by the spirit of God which descended upon that person (Judg 2:16; 3:9, etc.). Yahweh had the authority to appoint and depose a *šôpēṭ,* "judge" (cf. Ps 82:1–8). The role of Yahweh as *šôpēṭ par excellence* compares to that of the Canaanite patron deity 'El who appointed the gods Baʿl, Yamm, and Mot to function as judges, under his authority (cf. *CTA* 6.VI.28–29).

The main task for which the judges were appointed was to maintain harmonious relations among the Israelites. The judge made legal decisions in civil disputes (Judg 4:5; 1 Sam 7:15; cf. 2 Sam 15:4). Most of the disputes which related to the *šôpēṭ* were those which concerned the welfare of the poor, the widow, the orphan, and the stranger (Psalm 82; Jer 5:28–29; 22:15; Deut 1:16–17, etc.). In this function the judges did not always pass a verdict which justified the plaintiff and condemned the defendant. The judges often acted as arbitrators, i.e., restorers of *šālôm* which prevailed before the onset of strife or hostilities (Gen 16:5; 19:9; Judg 11:27). For this reason, if those who were wronged failed to acquire justice from human judges, they summoned Yahweh, the Judge preeminent, to intervene (Ps 6:7–9; Ps 82:8). Because Yahweh was considered righteous in all his judgments, an innocent person who felt he had been judged unjustly directly appealed to Yahweh to judge (*špṭ*) him, that is, "to deliver," "to vindicate," or "to reward" him according to God's criterion of retribution (Ps 26:1; cf. Judg 11:27). The root *špṭ* in both Akkadian and Hebrew usage also referred to the "administering," "ruling," or "governing" of a territory. This is the general meaning of *špṭ* in the book of Judges (Judg 3:10; 4:4; 1 Sam 7:6; cf. *ARM* 1, 73: 45–53).

In the Akkadian texts of Mari, apart from governing a territory, a *šāpiṭum,* "judge," also commanded armies against enemies of the king (*ARM* 2, 98: 7–14). This compares very closely to the roles played by the judges in premonarchical Israel: they led armies and delivered the Israelites from their oppressors and enemies, e.g., Judg 1:16, "The Lord raised up judges, who saved them . . ."; Judg 3:10, ". . . he judged Israel; he went out to war." In this usage, the term *špṭ* refers to "delivering" or "saving," (Heb *yšʿ*).

5. The Usage of *Dyn* in Extrabiblical Literature. The root generally used in legal decision-making in Semitic languages is *dyn.* This is evidenced in the Akkadian texts, e.g., the Code of Hammurabi in which the legal term for making a decision or judgment on a case is *dyn,* "to judge" in a forensic sense (*AHW* p. 171). The term *dyn* is also found in Arabic, Aramaic, and Syriac bearing the same legal meanings. Thus in Akkadian the term *dînum* refers to the verdict passed by the *dayyānu(m),* "law-court judge," or by the *šāpiṭu(m),* "judge," i.e., "undifferentiated executive" (cf. *ARM* 8, 83 and 87). In Ugaritic, on the other hand, the root *dyn* is used in parallel with *ṯpṭ,* e.g., *ydn dn ʾlmnt, yṯpṭ ṯpṭ ytm,* "He [Dan'il] judged the cases of the widow, he presided over the orphans' lawsuits" (*CTA* 17.V.6–8 cf. *CTA* 16.IV.45–47). The Ugaritic usage compares to Hebrew where *špṭ* and *dyn* are also used in parallel (Ps 9:5; Isa 3:13–14; Jer 5:28). This wide usage indicates that the root has a very long history.

6. The Root *Dyn* in the OT. The usage of the root *dyn* in the OT is similar to its use in Ugaritic texts. In both literatures, the roots *dyn* and *špṭ* are used in parallel in a way which suggests close similarity in meaning, though not necessarily implying synonymy. The root *dyn* is sparsely used in Hebrew and Aramaic and only accounts for twenty-five occurrences. Besides 2 Sam 19:10—Eng 19:9 where the root *dyn* is in the *Nipʿal* form, all other usages are in the *Qal* form. The substantive *dyn* is attested in twenty-four references which generally bear the meaning "judgment" in a juridical sense. In Prov 22:10, the root *dyn* in the term *mādôn,* "strife," appears in parallel use with *qālôn,* "abuse." In this reference, *dyn* has lost its juridical meaning and may be translated "quarreling" (cf. 2 Sam 19:10—Eng 19:9; Eccl 6:10).

7. Others Who Judged in Israel. As Judge *par excellence* and king (Jer 21:12; 22:16; Ps 72:2; Prov 31:5, 8, 9) God appointed human judges who deputized for him in the administration of justice. In many ancient communities, advanced age was a status position, which symbolized one's authority reflected in his wisdom based on his experience with life. Thus a tribal leader (Gen 49:16), or a high priest (Zech 3:7) or one who achieved the status of leadership by virtue of military valor, e.g., a premonarchical judge, was expected also to decide cases as a judge. Similarly, by virtue of his position, the king was expected to judge *(špṭ),* i.e., dispense justice *(mišpāṭ)* by protecting the poor, the widow, the orphan, and the stranger against exploitation by the rich or the strong. Thus the phrase *ʿāsāh mišpāṭ ûṣĕdāqāh,* "to execute justice and righteousness," refers to the maintenance or restoration of justice and equity among the citizens of his state.

B. Judging (Verb)

In the OT as well as in the ANE in general, the root *špṭ* referred both to the judging of the people and to the ruling or governing of a territory. Because it is multifarious in meaning the root *špṭ* can only be translated correctly by paying close attention to the context in which it is used. Thus in Zech 7:9 *špṭ* can best be translated "to render judgment" or "to condemn" (Ezek 23:45). In Deut 1:16–17, *mišpāṭ* refers to "deciding a case" but in 1 Kgs 7:7 it means "the place of judgment." At Mari, the *šāpiṭum,* as ruler of a territory, also acted as a judge who settled disputes in the area of his jurisdiction. Similarly, in premonarchical Israel, the *šôpēṭ* decided cases just like the *dayyānu(m)* of the ANE. A king also acted as a judge (cf. 2 Sam 8:15). Because to rule or govern a territory also implied maintaining peace by preventing situations which disturbed *šālôm,* it is from the root *špṭ* that the terms for judging and ruling are derived. In several other contexts, the Hebrew term *mišpāṭ* refers to "judgment," "custom," "right," and "statute." When the term *mišpāṭ* is used with *ʿāsāh,* it is best rendered by the meaning "to execute judgment/justice" (Ezek 39:21). In Amos 5:24 and Mic 6:8 *mišpāṭ* means "justice." The term *šĕpāṭîm,* which always appears in the plural, as well as *šĕpôṭ* (2 Chr 20:9 and Ezek 23:10), is rendered by the meaning "acts of judgment." When used with *ʿāsāh, šĕpāṭîm,* it refers to the infliction of punishment (Exod 12:12; Num 33:4; Ezek 5:10, *passim*).

In the OT the root *dyn* is not widely attested even though its parallel usage suggests that it was used as a synonym of *špṭ*. In some contexts, the root *dyn,* like *špṭ,* also bears the meaning "to govern" or "to judge." While *mišpāṭ* refers to justice as the rendering of judgment, the Heb term *dîn* refers solely to "decision" or "judgment" in a juridical sense.

Since peace was the main concern of justice in Israel, there are other terms which, according to the context, can be best translated "judgment"; e.g., in the RSV *taʿam* (Ps 119:66) is translated "taste," "judgment," as referring to discernment granted by Yahweh. The other term, *pāqad ʿal,* "to visit upon," strictly means "to punish," i.e., "to execute judgment." In several contexts the Hebrew verb *rîb* is to be rendered "to contend," "to strive" (Judg 11:25; 1 Sam 25:29). There are some words which seem to be derived from the root *dyn,* which are uncertain in meaning, e.g., *šaddîn* in Job 19:29; (Pope *Job* AB, 147–48).

C. Judging and Ruling

The Mari texts evince that judging and ruling could be performed by the same person, the *šāpiṭum.* The *šāpiṭum* was appointed to administer a territory in the absence of the *šarrum* (cf. Kupper 1957: 581; *"Baḫdin-Lim . . ."*). He was also appointed as a commander during a military campaign (cf. *ARM* 1, 73: 45–53). Because of his prominent position in the community the *šāpiṭum* also judged the people in their domestic quarrels (*ARM* 8, 84: 1–11). In the Ugaritic literature, Dan'il as king was also expected to judge or administer justice for defenseless people such as the widow, the orphan, and the sojourner (*CTA* 16.IV.45–54). The OT shows that the premonarchical rulers (*šôpĕṭîm*) conducted military campaigns (Judg 2:16; 3:10), governed the state (Judg 10:3; 12:7), and also administered justice (Judg 4:4). The root *špṭ* is therefore multifarious in meaning in both the Akkadian and the OT. The best meaning of the term in every usage is determined only by paying close attention to the context in which *špṭ* is used.

In the OT, which is written primarily for teaching the way of the Lord to the people of Israel, the term *špṭ* ("to judge") was not used forensically in the administration of civil law. Judging was a divine role delegated by Yahweh himself to those he anointed to become leaders in politics as well as to those he appointed judges in judicial affairs. Judges were therefore strictly required to judge impartially irrespective of the statuses of the litigants (Exod 23:26; Deut 1:16–17). To maintain pure justice in settling disputes, the judges were admonished not to accept bribes because bribes blind the eyes of judges (Deut 23:2–3; Isa 1:23; 5:23; 10:1; Amos 5:12; 6:12; Mic 3:11; 7:3; Prov 6:19; 12:17; 18:15).

1. Synonyms. The term *šāpaṭ* is synonymous with *dyn* particularly in its wider meaning of "judging" or "the administration of justice." Though *dyn* is sparsely used in the OT, its synonymity with *špṭ* is indicated by their parallel use. At all events, *dyn,* as attested in extrabiblical literature, was the term used in legal decision-making processes. Only the context in which *dyn* is used will determine its best nuance. In Jer 21:12, for lack of the most appropriate word, the RSV has correctly rendered *dinû . . . mišpāṭ* as "Execute . . . justice." That *dyn* is used forensically is elucidated by the context which shows that the oppressed person wants justice because he has been robbed by wicked people whom, apparently, he knew. Similarly, in Jer 22:16 the fact that *dān* and *dîn* are used in connection with the needy and the poor, people who were defenseless (cf. Ps 72:2; Prov 20:8; 31:5–9), implies that the root *dyn* is used in connection with the execution of justice. The root *špṭ,* though used synonymously with *dyn,* is normally a special term which implies righteousness and holiness on the part of the people who judge (*špṭ*). Because Yahweh was originally regarded as the sole Judge of the whole world (Gen 8:25), *špṭ* as well as its derivative *mšpṭ* implies a morally good character on the part of those who judge (*špṭ*). In general, however, the root *dyn* should be rendered synonymously with *špṭ,* particularly when it is used in the OT without contextual hints. The substantive *dîn* could therefore refer to "justice" and "legal rights" whereas the verbal form referred to "judging," that is "rendering justice [to]."

2. God Judges the Whole Earth. In the OT Yahweh is regarded as the just Judge of the whole world—an attribute which is also affirmed of Shamash in Mesopotamia. According to Ecclesiastes and Job and from the complaint of the prophets, for example, Jeremiah, the justice of God's judgment was not always clear. From the experience of those who were unjustly treated by the wicked, people realized that God either delayed to act or even deceived them (Jer 20:17). For this reason those wronged by evil people had to demand God's hearing or judgment (Ps 17:12; 26:1–12; 43:1, etc.). Because, as Creator of the world, God is universal, it is he who judges the nations with justice, requiting every person justly (Gen 15:14; 1 Sam 2:10; Ps 76:89; 110:6).

Bibliography

Fensham, C. F. 1959. The Judges and Israelite Jurisprudence. Pp. 15–22 in *Ou testamentiese werkgemeenskap in Suid Afrika.*

———. 1984. The Ugaritic Root Tpṭ. *JNES* 12: 63–69.

Fergusson, H. 1888. The Verb *Špṭ*. *JBL* 8: 130–36.

Kupper, J. K. 1957. *Les nomades des en Mésopotamie au temps des rois de Mari.* Bibliothéque de la Faculte de philosophie et lettres de l'Universite de Liège 142. Paris.

Marzal, A. 1971. The Provincial Governor at Mari: His Title and Appointment. *JNES* 30: 186–217.

Stol, M. 1972. Akkadisches *šāpiṭum, šāpaṭum* und westsemitisches *špṭ*. *BiOr* 29: 276–77.

Temba L. J. Mafico

JUDGES, BOOK OF. The seventh book of the Hebrew Bible and second book of the Former Prophets in the Jewish canon of Scripture adopted by the early Christian church as the OT. Judges is a collection of stories about persons and events of the premonarchy period in ancient Israel, arranged to present an edifying history of the period extending from the death of Joshua to the establishment of monarchy as told in 1 Samuel. The historiography of Judges is essentially religious, displaying various qualities of leadership along with problematics of Yahwist peoplehood, when "there was no king in Israel," and each one "did what was right, as he saw it" (17:6; 21:25). The title "Judges" reflects a public activity and/or office of the leaders, especially in times of hardship and oppression, about whom the stories were told. The authority of the leaders is dependent upon Yahweh, whose role as divine warrior is subordinated to his role as divine judge (11:27) and subject to the general duty of law, whether local or international, to conform with standards of justice (Good 1985: 399).

A. Outline of Judges
B. Context and Canonical Form
  1. A Persistent Problematic
  2. Stories in Didactic Editorial Framework
C. The Book of Judges in Modern Study
  1. Judges as Narrative Art
  2. Judges as Historiography
  3. Archaeology and Social World
  4. Levitical Sponsorship? Dtn, Dtr 1, Dtr 2

A. Outline of Judges

The present book of Judges is composed of three parts. The first is an introduction summarizing the Conquest and the final settlement in Canaan (Judg 1:1–3:6). The second part is the history of the judges proper (3:7–15:20), which is itself composed of two subsections: one treating an initial phase of judges' activities (Othniel, Ehud, Deborah and Barak, and Gideon, culminating in the account of two "minor" judges; 10:1–5); and the other treating a subsequent phase of judges' activities, beginning with 10:6–16, and then reviewing the exploits of Jephthah, three "minor" judges, and finally Samson (ending in 15:1–20). The third part is a series of supplementary stories, including another story about Samson (chap. 16), about Micah's shrine and Micah's Levite (chaps. 17–18), and about the rape and murder of a Levite's concubine (chap. 19) and the civil war that followed (chaps. 20–21).

B. Context and Canonical Form

1. A Persistent Problematic. The book of Judges, which presupposes and continues the story line that began in the book of Exodus and came to a climax in the book of Joshua, deals with a fundamental problematic of biblical religion; that of living a life of faithful obedience to the expressed will of Yahweh. Exodus recounts how Yahweh liberated a group of state slaves in Egypt and reconstituted them by covenant in the Sinai wilderness to be his own special possession governed directly by Yahweh through the mediation of Moses. After a generation of moving about Sinai and S Transjordan (Numbers), and a renewal of the covenant in Moab (Deuteronomy), the book of Joshua tells of Israel's entry and settlement in Canaan. The book of Joshua ends with yet another renewal of covenant, this time at Shechem, and with the notice of Joshua's death.

In picking up the story at this point, the book of Judges must deal with a pair of implicit questions: (1) How will reconstituted Israel now conduct its affairs as the people of Yahweh settled in their God-given home? and (2) How will Israel be governed now that there is no Moses or Joshua to exercise leadership?

It is a curious fact that those who are remembered as leaders in the book of Judges are rarely mentioned elsewhere in the Hebrew Bible. Apart from a doublet (cf. Judg 1:11–15 and Josh 15:13–19) and a brief genealogical interest in Othniel (1 Chr 4:13) and Ehud (1 Chr 7:10; 8:6), the list of echoes is limited to Jerubbaal (Gideon) in 1 Sam 12:11 (cf. 2 Sam 11:21), Jephthah in 1 Sam 12:11, Bedan (Abdon?) in 1 Sam 12:11, and Jair (where interest centers, however, in Jair's villages: Num 32:41; Deut 3:14; Josh 13:30; 1 Kgs 4:13; 1 Chr 2:22–23). The prophet-king-maker Samuel at the outset of the following era was also remembered as the last of the judges (1 Sam 7:15–8:3), but the memory was rarely evoked.

The opposition in the era gets nearly equal attention elsewhere: Sisera (1 Sam 13:9) together with Jabin (Ps 83:9), Zeba and Zalmunnah (Ps 83:11, cf. "day of Midian" in Isa 9:4 and defeat of Midian at Oreb in Isa 8:1–3). Also see reference to the demise of Abimelech (2 Sam 11:21).

In a pair of deuterocanonical and NT writings (Sir 46:11–12 and Heb 11:32) the interest is entirely on the leaders, praised as a group in the former, and with names specified in the latter (Gideon, Barak, Samson, Jephthah—in that "uncanonical" order). That the list in Heb 11:32 is out of phase with the canonical book and mentions only half of the Deborah-Barak team combines with other indicators of theological perspective to suggest that rhetorical and didactic-ethical concerns outweighed strict chronological sequence (if it was accurately remembered) in the organization of the book of Judges.

2. Stories in Didactic Editorial Framework. a. The Outer Framework. The canonical book is framed by a question-and-answer repeated from chap. 1, and a generalization echoing throughout the final chapters. At the outset, sometime after the death of Joshua, the Israelites make inquiry: "Who shall go up first for us to do battle" against the Canaanites? Whether the anticipated warfare is, from Israel's side, offensive or defensive as sequel to Joshua is unclear. In any case, the oracle answers: "Judah shall go up" (1:1–2). After initial successes in the S (1:3–19) qualified by corrective notices about Caleb at Hebron (1:20), Jebusites in Jerusalem (1:21), and Joseph's takeover of Bethel in the near N (1:22–26), the progress of land settlement deteriorates so that by the end of the chapter Israel is in nearly disastrous straits. The beginning of chap. 2 finds "all the Israelites" at Bochim (= Bethel?) weeping (Heb *bōkîm*) before Yahweh, in response to which the oracle brings bad news: because of Israel's covenant breaking, Yahweh will no longer evict Canaanites (2:1–5).

Late in the judges era, after recounting a civil war that would have obliterated Benjamin (chap. 20), except for a punitive raid on Jabesh-gilead and the premeditated abduction of women at a Shiloh vintage festival (chap. 21), the book concludes with a sweeping but ambiguous generalization providing a rationale for monarchy: "In those days there was no king in Israel; every man did what was right, as he saw it" (21:25). Out of context that statement might describe either a bad scene (anarchy) or a good one (governance by internalized ethic).

The same generalization and the same question-and-answer have already occurred in close proximity (but in reverse sequence) in the concluding chapters (chaps. 17–20). Here, however, Israel would be mobilized for civil, not offensive or defensive, warfare. The stage is set by two stories in chap. 17, concerning a northerner, Micah an Ephraimite. In the first story Micah acquires a molten image for divinatory purposes (17:1–5), and in the second hires a young Levite from Bethlehem in Judah to be his priest and thus secure Yahweh's favor (17:7–13). As connective between stories we read the identical statement (17:6) with which the book ends: "In those days . . . no king . . ." Here the cliché unquestionably describes a bad scene, where the target of polemic is a N sanctuary, and not "all Israel." In the body of the book "all Israel" is in fact mentioned explicitly only once (8:27), specifically as "playing the harlot" with Gideon's ephod (another divinatory object).

The stories of Micah's free-lance N establishment are in turn followed by a grim account of conquest at Dan, where Micah's Levite (hired out from under Micah) founds a priestly house tracing descent from Moses (18:30), "throughout the period that the House of God was at Shiloh" (18:31).

Juxtaposed with these stories about the corrupting exploitation of a young Levite from the S is the account in chap. 19 of a well-established Levite from the N who journeys S to Bethlehem to reclaim his runaway concubine-wife. Despite his own implication in permitting the subsequent rape and murder of the woman, at Gibeah in Benjamin en route home, this Levite as self-designated leader rallies the Israelite militia for private vengeance. With the forces mustered and ready at Mizpah, we hear the same questions as at the outset of the era: "Who shall go up first for us?" And the same oracular answer: "Judah will go first" (20:18). But there would be two resounding defeats before the Israelites inquire, at last, at Bethel (where the ark of the covenant was then to be found), and receive a reliable oracle (20:26)!

From this description of the outer framework it should be clear that the book of Judges displays a clash of perspectives and tensions within its organization which are deeply rooted in the different histories of northern and southern, eastern and western constituencies of Israel from very early times. The storytellers and redactors thus reflect the tug of competing loyalties to various sanctuary sites and the teaching of their personnel, down the years.

b. Introduction (1:1–3:6). The book's introduction is complex. All of 1:1–2:5, as described above, is prologue, summary recapitulation at the outset of the era following Joshua's death and burial which is now told again (2:6–10 read as past perfect: "Joshua had died . . .") in a text strikingly similar to Josh 24:28–31, but with the sequence appropriately revised for introduction to the new era.

The next segment (2:11–23) sets forth the pattern of the period, beginning with a formula that regularly introduces each of the "savior" judges: "Israelites did what was evil in Yahweh's sight" (2:11; 3:2; 4:1; 6:1; 10:6; 13:1), "they prostrated themselves to other gods," the Baals and the Ashtaroth. Such behavior was followed invariably by the victory of oppressors, as Yahweh had promised (2:11–15). It was, equally, an era which also experienced the compassion of Yahweh, who raised up a leader to rescue them. Yahweh was motivated to do so by the sound of their suffering. Yet at the death of the leader, they "turned and behaved more corruptly than their fathers, following other gods," so that at last Yahweh let the enemies remain "without evicting them at once" (2:16–23).

Chap. 3 begins with the ironic explanation that the peoples which Yahweh allowed to remain (Philistines, Canaanites, Sidonians, Hivites, Hittites, Amorites, Perizzites, and Jebusites) were to be there for one purpose: that the future generations of Israelites might have direct experience of warfare and thus be covenantally tested (3:1–4). An ominous side effect, however, was intermarriage and apostasy (3:5–6).

Thus ends the introduction to the era. In the stories which follow, relief at any pressure point, whether from invasion or from resident enclaves within the land, is understood as deliverance for "Israel," no matter how local the threat and the organized resistance. The body of the book is in two parts, as signaled by a special introduction to Jephthah in chap. 11.

c. History with the Judges, Part One. (1) Othniel (3:7–11). The story of Othniel ben Kenaz versus the oppressor Cushan-rishathaim comes first and is most obscure. Othniel's origin is in the S hills around Hebron. Cushan's base was probably Armon-harim ("Hill-country Fortress") not Aram-naharaim (Mesopotamia); the latter would result from a common scribal lapse, with the introduction of word-dividers and spacing in written texts. The story displays the exemplary relationship between a local leader activated to display Yahweh's spirit and a populace petitioning Yahweh for collective relief. "Yahweh's spirit" will only next be mentioned in 6:34. In this example story, "to judge" is to mobilize and successfully lead the people in defensive warfare, which in this case produced "40 years" of pacification, till Othniel died.

(2) Ehud (3:12–30). The second of the savior judges is a left-handed Benjaminite. The name Benjaminite means "son of the right hand [the south]," but there is more than wordplay involved. Left-handedness, considered peculiar and unnatural, was notably frequent in this tribe (see Judg 20:16; and cf. 1 Chr 12:2). The left-handedness may have been artificially induced (binding the right arms of the young children) so as to produce superior warriors. Left-handed persons have a distinct advantage in physical combat, especially in regard to ancient armaments and defenses (Halpern 1988: 40–43). Ehud is activated by Yahweh in response to the Moabite incursion and oppression from field headquarters at the City of Palms (probably the Jericho oasis). Eglon ("young bull") was famed for his obesity, and is slain by Ehud in a single-handed act of diplomatic treachery. Eglon's forces were stampeded and men from the highlands of Mount Ephraim joined in the pursuit. The result was "80 years" of peace.

(3) Shamgar was another single-handed deliverer, versus an entire Philistine brigade (3:31). That he was an

Anathite may point to a hometown Beth-Anath in Galilee. More likely the label identifies Shamgar as a (former?) mercenary, relating his background to a military contingent under tutelage of the fertility/warrior goddess Anath. Defeat of the Philistines was deliverance for the Israelites. No specifically Yahwist claims are made for Shamgar.

(4) Deborah and Barak, that is, "Honey Bee" and "Lightning" (4:1–24) display collaboration of a "judge" (Barak, Heb 11:32) and a prophetess, the wife of Lappidoth (that is, "Flashes"). Deborah's oracular activity and leadership of the militia makes her the heroic one, in a story told at the expense of Barak. Oppression is blamed on "Jabin, king of Canaan," mentioned as such only in the introductory and concluding verses. Verse 17 refers in a flashback to "Jabin, King of Hazor," thus recalling an older treaty which explains the presence of Heber's Kenite clan in the far N and the setting for Heber's wife, Jael. Opposition in the field is headed by Sisera who commands 900 especially sturdy chariots constructed with iron fittings. Sisera's name is non-Semitic, probably of Anatolian origin, as was the knowledge of iron technology. Prodded and accompanied by Deborah, Barak musters forces from Naphtali and Zebulun at a northern Kedesh, and on Mount Tabor, while Sisera's force assembles near Tabor, at the Kishon river. Yahweh confounds the opposition (the narrative does not say how), and Sisera flees N on foot, with Barak in hot pursuit. If the narrative implies that Heber's clan had changed sides (4:17), Jael was an exception. She slays Sisera while he is enjoying her hospitality; and so Deborah's taunting prophecy (4:9) is fulfilled. Barak arrives at the scene too late to take any credit, but returns in time for the celebration.

(5) The Song of Deborah and Barak (5:1–31) is a priceless piece of archaic Hebrew poetry which offers direct access to religion and polity of the Yahwist organization in the late 12th–early 11th centuries B.C.E. In the form of a victory hymn, the song celebrates the theophany of Yahweh as experienced by those who participated at the rout of Sisera's chariotry, thanks to a timely cloudburst and flash flood. For "the stars in their courses" (source of rain?) "fought against Sisera" (5:20).

It was a battle for control of the broad and fertile Esdraelon plain, pegged to the time of Shamgar and Jael (5:6a), spurred on by Israel's successful control of the caravan routes through the highlands of Ephraim and Galilee (5:6b–7), interrupted only by Canaanite control of the intervening plain. In this far older song it is a coalition of "kings of Canaan" whose forces Sisera commands.

While the prose story highlights *dramatis personnae* and mentions only the tribes of Zebulun and Naphtali, the older song calls the tribal roll, for praise or blame as appropriate. Six of the W tribes are variously lauded for responding to the muster: Ephraim, Benjamin, Machir (= W Manasseh?), Zebulun, Issachar, and Naphtali. Two coastal tribes, Asher and Dan, are faulted for what sounds like subservience to Sea Peoples. Two Transjordan constituencies are faulted for staying at home: Reuben and Gilead (= E Manasseh?). Two territorial tribes are treated with silence: Judah and Gad. There is similarly no mention of Levi, which, however, is not surprising in a roster of territorially based units.

Absence of Judah suggests that the events occurred well along in the Philistine period, which rendered Judah totally ineffectual and posed a threat of complete encirclement for the Joseph tribes. Silence concerning Gad in Transjordan most likely reflects one of Moab's incursions into the territory N of its recognized border at the Arnon. Such incursions happened frequently enough that Gad's territory, near the Transjordan escarpment, is known elsewhere in scripture as "plains of Moab."

The song has the highland peasantry pitted against the professional soldiery of the feudal elite from older city-state centers of the plains and the Galilean crossroads at Hazor. After lauding Deborah as a "mother in Israel" (for giving the right oracular answer?), the song turns at last to imagining the scene at Harosheth-haggoim, where Sisera's mother is inquiring anxiously about the tardiness of her son's return, only to be ironically reassured by "the wisest of her captains' ladies" that they are surely enjoying the spoils of war. Verse 31 is a chiastic couplet, quite distinct from the sort of repetitive and seconding patterns that occur throughout the song, and probably represents what Deborah and Barak sang in the prose narrative tradition, prior to incorporation of the archaic victory hymn. Again the land was pacified, for 40 years.

(6) Gideon, that is, "Hacker," gets proportionately far more attention than any other figure in the book (6:1–8:35). He was a savior who nearly became king. The crisis surmounted by this man from the Abiezrite clan of W Manasseh, depradations by Midianites and other easterners at harvesttime, was an annually recurring one, which left the Israelite peasantry desolate after pillaging that ranged as far S as Gaza. These Midianites probably represent a later wave of immigration from E Anatolia (as distinct from the earlier Midianites of Mosaic tradition, most likely also from the N), who brought with them the domesticated camels which made them such effective tax collectors. Description of the Midianite oppressors as Yahweh's response to Israel's relapse (6:1–6) is the most elaborate thus far and will be matched only by the introduction of Jephthah (10:6–9). When the people petition Yahweh for relief, Yahweh sends a prophet, the only one to be mentioned in the book, who brings Yahweh's indictment, a warning for breach of covenant (Heb *rîb,* verbal element in the name Jerubbaal).

Similarly, the stories of Gideon's authentication as leader are without close parallel. A recruiting angel appears in human form to confront Gideon under an oak (sacred tree?) at Ophrah which belongs to his father Joash (note Yahwist name), while Gideon is beating out wheat in a winepress so as to conceal his activity from Midianites in the neighborhood. In the interview which follows, Gideon demands a sign that he is in fact dealing with Yahweh, and is convinced by the sign that he must soon die! Reassured to the contrary by Yahweh, Gideon promptly builds an altar for Yahweh at Ophrah (still there in the narrator's day) and sacrifices a bull upon it, according to Yahweh's instructions. He names the altar: "He Creates Peace/Well-Being" (6:11–24). The socioreligious practice is illustrated by the "Bull site" in Manasseh, an open Iron Age I cult place (Mazar 1982; Kochavi 1985).

Only now does the reason for Gideon's initial reluctance, and his nickname "Hacker," become clear. He is to be a reformer, charged with dismantling his father's Baal-altar and chopping down the Asherah alongside it. When the townsmen object after the fact, Joash the apostate advises it will be better to let Baal press his own case, thus ironically legitimating the given name of his son, Jerubbaal, "Let Baal Sue" (6:25–32). The reader is thus reminded of Yahweh's indictment brought by a prophet at the beginning of the Gideon stories. This story explains how Judge Hacker, son of the apostate Joash, could properly wear a Baal-name, which occurs with increasing frequency in chaps. 7 and 8.

The remainder of chap. 6 describes the opposing forces: Midianites, Amalekites, and easterners versus the peasants' militia from Manasseh, Asher, Zebulun, and Naphtali, mustered by Gideon, who is now clothed with Yahweh's spirit (6:33–35). But Gideon will hold out for another confirmatory sign. The fleece test, when Yahweh is also able to do it in reverse, convinces Gideon that God has told him the truth (6:36–40).

In chap. 7, "Jerubbaal" (that is, Gideon), according to the text, stations the troops, and Yahweh readies his force by drastically reducing their numbers. Now it is Yahweh who tests the warriors, selecting from the 22 muster units 300 of the less alert, those who incautiously lap at the water like dogs. The initial victory will be Yahweh's alone (7:1–8). With the force thus drastically reduced, Gideon is advised by Yahweh to conduct a nighttime reconnaissance, from which Gideon learns that the outcome of battle is adequately foreseen in the Midianite camp (7:8–15). The 300 men are divided into three units, for a nighttime surprise attack from the camp's perimeter. Each warrior is heavily laden with a trumpet in one hand and a flaming torch inside a heavy ceramic jar in the other. With simultaneous blowing of trumpets and shattering of jars, the opposition is stampeded by the sound and light terror, turning first upon one another and then to disorganized flight. Gideon and the militia had not yet done any fighting, and Yahweh had won, as promised (7:16–22).

Israelites rallied from Naphtali, Asher, and Manasseh give chase. Gideon now sends "envoys" (plural of "angel" in 6:11) throughout all of Mount Ephraim. The tardily mustered Ephraimites capture and execute two Midianite kings, Oreb and Zeeb, bring their amputated heads to Gideon in Transjordan, and voice their indignation at not being summoned at the outset. They are appeased by Gideon's explanation that it was Yahweh's prerogative to give them Oreb and Zeeb (7:23–8:3), for Gideon is on the trail of two others.

The bulk of chap. 8 concerns Gideon in Transjordan. The men of Succoth and Penuel are not persuaded that Gideon's business deserves their provisioning; and Gideon, notably, makes no reference to Yahweh's legitimation. This is Gideon's war; the victory this time will be Gideon's (8:4–9). And so it happens. The two kings Zebah and Zalmunna are taken alive at Karkor and brought to Succoth and Penuel which are, as Gideon had promised, terrorized before the kings are executed. The narrator has withheld until now information that goes a long way toward explaining the caricature of Gideon as savior-judge throughout these chapters. Whereas it was a prime concern of the early Yahwist movement to curtail the vendetta (cf. Deut 32:35 and the institution of cities of refuge), Gideon had taken the Israelite militia into Transjordan in pursuit of blood vengeance. There was also rich booty (8:4–21).

The final narrative segment tells how Gideon, for a good Israelite reason, declined the offer of dynastic rule. He requested instead contributions of the valuables taken as booty, out of which he made an ephod, an elaborate priestly vestment worn (or displayed to be consulted) as having divinatory value. "And all Israel" [its only occurrence in the body of the book] "prostituted themselves there." Still, the land had been pacified for 40 years (8:22–28).

In a few compact editorial verses which make a rough transition (8:29–32), the reader is introduced to the house of Jerubbaal: numerous wives and 70 sons plus Abimelech, whose mother was a slave-wife from Shechem. Finally we read that Gideon died at a ripe old age, to be buried in the tomb of his father. With Gideon dead, the good that he had done was quickly forgotten, along with Yahweh's acts of salvation. Israelites prostituted themselves to a deity called "Baal of the covenant" (alternatively "El of the covenant"), and worshiped at Shechem in the stories which follow.

(7) Abimelech's Career is the organizational midpoint of the book. Archaeological evidence will be assessed below which strongly suggests that the careers of Deborah and Barak were roughly contemporary or slightly later than Abimelech. In any case, considerations of space suggest that the stories in Judges are arranged so as to center rhetorically in the abortive experiment with monarchy at Shechem, where covenant renewal had climaxed the preceding era. In BHS 10 pages are required for chaps. 1–5, 11 pages are given over to Gideon and Abimelech alone (chaps. 6–9), and 20 pages suffice for all that follows (chaps. 10–21).

Unlike the achievements of his father Gideon, which are entertainingly narrated with sustained tension between favorable and unfavorable valuations, Abimelech's story is told by an extremely hostile narrator. The name Abimelech, "My Father is King," is ambiguous, the referent of "Father" being either Gideon or the God of Israel. The name recurs with unparalleled frequency (39 times in 57 verses).

Abimelech's path to power as king of the Shechem city-state, which is reverting to Bronze Age governance in the story, is rapidly recounted: negotiations through his mother's connections with the Shechem elite, appropriation of funds from the Shechem temple in order to hire mercenaries, liquidation of the 70 brothers with the exception of Jotham, the youngest, who hid away, and coronation near a (sacred?) oak at the Shechem fortress (9:1–6).

Jotham's fable addressed to the Shechem elite, telling about the trees who set forth to anoint a king over them but who could only persuade the worthless bramble to accept the office (9:7–15a) is followed by Jotham's statement of readiness to let the rightness of their action be proved or disproved by appropriate blessing or curse (i.e., historical process), whereupon Jotham flees, not to be mentioned again in Scripture outside the chapter (9:15b–21).

In addition to being king at Shechem (never explicitly king "in Israel"), Abimelech also became, like his father, field commander (Heb *śar*) of the Israel militia, for three years. The split loyalty is presented as his undoing: God sends an evil spirit between Abimelech and the Shechem elite. The mention of "God" in v 23 will be echoed twice in vv 56–57 (the name Yahweh is totally absent), signaling the narrator's theological valuation, which otherwise is left to the tone of the narrative plus Jotham's pronouncement.

Gaal ben Ebed ("Loathsome, son of Slave"), a full-blooded Shechemite, undermines Abimelech's kingship, objecting to Abimelech's half-Shechemite genealogy. The coup is thwarted when Abimelech's appointee as Shechem commandant, Zebul ("Big Shot"), gets wind of the matter and sends word to Abimelech. Gaal is enticed out of the city for open combat and Gaal escapes, but there are many casualties (9:26–41).

Abimelech retaliates for the Shechemite support of Gaal by ambushing and slaughtering Shechem's peasants in the fields, following up the slaughter by seizing the city, razing it, and sowing it with salt, presumably thus laying it under another curse (9:42–45).

Probably v 45 refers only to the poorer quarters of the lower city, as known from excavations. For the next scene has the Shechem elite crowding into the "stronghold of covenant-El's temple." Abimelech's force sets fire to the place and the elite perish in the building's destruction (9:46–49).

There was a similar structure at Thebez called "Strong's Tower," where Abimelech fought his final campaign and died an ignominious death—he drew too close to the structure and "a certain woman" threw down an upper millstone which crushed his skull (9:50–54).

The summary is brief. Seeing that Abimelech was dead, the Israelites "went away, each to his own place" (9:55), a statement adumbrating the disbanding of the militia at the end of the era (21:24). Abimelech had experienced justice, as had the Shechem elite; Jotham's invocation of historical process had been the right word at the right time (9:57).

(8) Two "Minor" Judges follow Abimelech. First, "in order to save [salvage?] Israel" arose Tola ("Worm"?), a man of Issachar who lived (presumably as "resident alien") at Shamir in the hill country of Ephraim. Tola is the first of five who are said to have "judged" Israel, but about whom very little information and no warfare stories survive. Was their activity strictly local? Were they also saviors? Perhaps Tola was thought to have saved Israel by presiding over disputes in such a way that violence was mostly avoided. The list of five is broken open and used to frame the stories about Jephthah, presumably because Jephthah was remembered in both ways: presiding over both internal and external relations, and resorting to military force only when diplomatic recourse was exhausted (see below). Jephthah's name may well have occurred in the same archive as the other five.

With Jair the Gileadite, second in the minor-judge sequence, the center of attention shifts to N Transjordan. The political effectiveness of Jair is represented in genealogical metaphor: he had 30 sons in 30 towns, still called "villages of Jair" at the time of composition and redaction. That Tola judged for "23 years" and Jair for "22 years" (not round numbers) suggests an archival source concerning local or regional administration.

d. History with the Judges, Part Two. (1) Introduction (10:6–16). These verses ironically echo the first introduction (esp. 2:11–3:6), listing all the oppressors of part one, with whose deities Israelites had become entangled, and including Ammonites who will next become the chief oppressors. This time, however, crying out to Yahweh is inadequate. The gods must go. Upon their removal, the plight of Israel becomes intolerable to Yahweh.

(2) Jephthah. His story unfolds with inverted rhetorical relationship to those whose stories are told in part one. Jephthah's family is well-to-do (cf. Gideon) but he is the son of a prostitute, driven out by the sons of his father's wife. His military prowess comes to be certified by activity of a mercenary band which rallies around him at Tob, near the modern border between Syria and Jordan (11:1–3). Ammonite expansion in central Transjordan mounts to the point where Jephthah is summoned by the elders to take charge of the militia as *qāṣîn* (a ranking officer in Joshua's organization, Josh 10:24). Jephthah, however, holds out for highest rank, in covenanting at Mizpah, a Yahwist sanctuary in central Transjordan, location uncertain (11:4–11).

Jephthah first acts vis-à-vis the Ammonites (like Moses before him and prophets after him) as ambassador of Yahweh to earthly courts, in this case a foreign court under the supposed sovereignty of Chemosh, who elsewhere is god of Moab (not Ammon). The dispute is over territory N of the recognized Moabite border at the Arnon, territory with a long history of rival Ammonite/Moabite/Israelite claims. In two embassies Jephthah is presented as making every effort to settle the matter by diplomacy before taking to the field, where Yahweh would be the judge (11:12–28). Only now, in relation to Jephthah's tour to muster the militia, is there reference to Jephthah's manifestation of Yahweh's spirit (11:29). Jephthah seems thus to be presented at the outset of "part 2" as an exemplary leader, apparently the best since Deborah in chaps. 5 and 6.

But Jephthah was not flawless. The sacrifice of Jephthah's daughter in literal fulfillment of a vow (whether hastily worded in reference to livestock or implying a state of desperation before the battle) shows Jephthah and his family marked for tragedy. The cultural background of the women's annual lamentation on the hills, legitimated by the story, remains obscure.

As the next and final Jephthah units show, the tragic dimension of Jephthah's career was not confined to his family. Here there is a brief account of intertribal war, Jephthah's force versus Ephraimites west of the Jordan, precipitated by jealousy of Jephthah's Transjordanian achievements, to which the Ephraimites claim not to have been invited. Negotiations quickly evolve into violence, with heavy Ephraimite casualties (12:1–4), followed by the execution of Ephraimite fugitives at the Jordan crossings, fugitives recognized by a dialect difference: Ephraimites cannot produce the sibilant in "Shibboleth" to the satisfaction of the Gileadite sentries. Jephthah is not mentioned in this final unit, however (12:5–6). The long section closes with a rubric familiar from the "minor judge" list, according to which Jephthah had "judged Israel six years."

(3) Three More "Minor Judges" exercise leadership west of the Jordan river: Ibzan of Bethlehem (most likely in Zebulun) for 7 years, Elon of Aijalon (specifically in Zebulun) for 10 years, and Abdon of Pirathon (in

Ephraim) for 8 years (12:8–15). No warfare stories are told.

(4) Samson ("Little Sun") belongs to a Danite family living in the region flanked by Judah and the Philistine frontier. Concluding formulas in 15:20 and 16:31, familiar from each of the minor-judges and Jephthah materials, are a distinct redactional signal to two blocks of material.

One group of stories (13:1–15:20) explain and display Samson's prodigious strength, recounting the young man's exploits on the western frontier, thus legitimating the claim in 15:20, where "judged Israel" refers to defeated Philistines. There is no indication that in Samson's case it had anything to do with management of intertribal conflict.

In chap. 13, after the notice about the resumption of doing evil and the consequent 40 years of Philistine oppression, Samson's surpassing physical strength is explained as the result of a prenatal agreement between his mother and an angelic ambassador of Yahweh (cf. recruitment of Gideon in chap. 6). The envoy gave her the news that she was bearing a son. The son would be a Nazirite (Num 6:13–21) from birth, who would begin the liberation of Israel from the Philistines; she was to begin at once observing the Nazirite vow. Here the unnamed mother is much quicker to get the message than is the father, Manoah, ponderous head of the house who is presented as something of an isolationist in face of the prolonged Philistine threat.

Chaps. 14 and 15 show Samuel's strength and virility as sadly subversive of the charismatic promise while also legitimating the assertion that he "judged Israel." First there is the eye-catching Philistine woman whom he wheedles his parents into visiting as prospective daughter-in-law, "for she is the right one in my eyes" (14:1–3). This anticipates the formulaic cliché which echoes at the end of the era (17:6; 21:25). En route to Timnah for the parental negotiations, Samson slays a young lion barehanded; and on a subsequent visit he finds the carcass full of bees—and honey. It was widely understood that honey held enlightening and courage-producing potential (1 Sam 14:24–30). Thus it might have been a sign which Samson either failed to recognize or else suppressed by not telling his parents where he found the honey. The story sets the stage for a seven-day wedding feast at Timnah, where Samson propounds a riddle and makes a wager with his "thirty friends" (public functionaries?). They, however, cheat by threatening the bride to extract the answer to the riddle. Their breach of faith brings on Samson a manifestation of Yahweh's spirit, so that the problematic marriage is providentially annulled, but not without the death of 30 other Philistines with whose garments and gear Samson pays his wager obligation. The bride, unbeknownst to Samson, becomes the wife of Samson's best man. The chapter makes it clear that Samson has the requisite physical prowess to be a deliverer; it is lack of civic commitment that will make him a tragic figure.

In chap. 15 Samson returns sometime later to visit his "bride," and is so enraged by the alternative offer of her younger sister that his fury is unleashed (no mention of Yahweh's spirit this time). He captures 300 jackals, ties them tail to tail with a torch between each pair, and turns them loose in fields, vineyards, and orchards. Philistines retaliate by executing the bride and her father, to which Samson responds by smiting Philistines "leg on thigh." Having in effect just announced his retirement, Samson retreats to Judah and hides out in a cave at Etam, location uncertain (15:1–8).

But his retirement was not to last. Philistines deploy themselves against Lehi ("Jawbone") in Judah, demanding Samson's extradition, to which Samson agrees, provided that the Judahites themselves do not try to harm him. As Yahweh's spirit empowers him, Samson promptly breaks free of the new ropes with which he is bound, picks up a donkey jawbone, lays low a whole contingent of Philistines, composes a brief poetic couplet on the subject, and is about to die of thirst when, at last, he addresses Yahweh directly in 15:18, and his prayer is answered. There are clearly etiological elements in the chapter, all subordinate or secondary to the characterization of "Little Sun," of whom it could at last be said that he "judged Israel" (15:9–20).

Chapter 16 adds two stories which underscore the tragic element: first a brief unit about a one-night visit to a prostitute in Gaza (16:1–3), followed by a prolonged love affair with Delilah ("Flirty") of Vineyard Valley (RSV "Valley of Sorek"; Nahal Sarar, which begins about 13 miles SW of Jerusalem, guarded in ancient times by the town of Beth-shemesh). The stories are shaped by tradition's uniform characterization of Samson, but they are not two versions of the same story. It is implied that Judge Samson learned nothing from the near-fatal Gaza escapade, and nearly destroyed Israel as a result of the Delilah affair.

The cutting of the Nazirite's hair was public recognition of release from a vow (which in this case had been made for him) and discharge from active duty (Num 6:13–20). Thus Israel was left for a while without the Nazirite judge during the Philistine crisis. But Samson's hair would grow again, and Samson could voluntarily reenlist, to achieve a momentary settling of accounts with Philistines. Samson is thus presented as a tragicomic figure. While he ran afoul through his lusty self-interest, consequent suffering evoked a new confession, and he died honorably while effecting Yahweh's justice toward Philistine terror. The concluding formula in 16:31 ("He had judged . . ."), repeated from 15:20 but in perfect tense and disjunctive syntax, strongly suggests a second compiler. Chaps. 14 and 15 answer the question: Whatever became of "Little Sun," prodigal son of Manoah? He judged Israel. Chap. 16 answers the question: What became of Judge Samson?

(5) Micah's Place. The S Danite setting of the Samson stories formed a natural bridge to the concluding framework stories described briefly above (B.2). These stories begin in chap. 17, with the blossoming of Micah's religious establishment in the near N (probably early Bethel). Micah ("Who is like Yahweh?") is another prodigal, but one whose doting mother is a sponsor of divinatory equipment for Micah's shrine (17:1–5). In the sequel, Micah employs as his priest a young itinerant Levite from Bethlehem in Judah (17:7–13). The connective hetween stories is the first full statement of the assertion with which the book will end: "In those days, there was no king in Israel. Each one did what was right in his own eyes" (17:6). Here the assertion clearly describes a bad scene; it is S polemic aimed at a N sanctuary.

(6) The Migration of Dan. The polemic intensifies in chap. 18, which begins with a partial echo: "no king in Israel." Here Micah's place is "providentially" deprived of its divinatory equipment and priest, stolen and hired away by the Danites who, because of continued resistance to their settlement along the coast, are moving to the far N. The town of Laish, peaceably isolated, is an unsuspecting sitting duck for the Danites, who promptly rebuild and rename it ("Dan") and install there Micah's image and the young Levite who is at last identified as Jonathan, grandson of Moses! Here ends a S version of the founding of what would become the other infamous northern royal sanctuary, controlled by a rival branch of the Mosaic priesthood throughout the period that the "House of God" (i.e., the legitimate one, with another branch of Mosaic family) was at Shiloh (18:1–31).

(7) The Anonymous Levite and the Gibeah Outrage. Chapter 19 begins with an echo of the anarchy formula "no king in Israel," but in syntactical form that suggests yet another block of preformed narrative to follow. This story too unfolds on the N-S axis, with strongly inverted rhetorical relation to the preceding chaps. 17 and 18. Here it is a prosperous Levite from Ephraim, whose troubles begin when his concubine-wife becomes angry and runs off S to the home of her father at Bethlehem in Judah. When the Levite follows to reclaim her, he is feasted by her father for the better part of a week. Getting a late start for home on the fifth day, they are able to proceed only as far as Gibeah in Benjamin, where once again the Levite enjoys lavish hospitality as a sojourner, but thanks only to another prosperous Ephraimite who is likewise a "resident alien" in Benjamin. In a scene which echoes the story of Lot at Sodom (Genesis 19), protection of the stranger does not here extend to the concubine-wife, who is offered by the Levite to local hooligans who are terrorizing the place. The woman is found by the offended Levite next morning, raped and dead at the door. He transports the body home to Ephraim, carves the corpse into twelve pieces (cf. 1 Sam 11:7 and 1 Kgs 11:30–39) and sends them off to all the tribes with the call to muster. He has in effect set himself up as "judge"—for civil war in pursuit of private vengeance (cf. Gideon in Transjordan, chap. 8). But it will get worse before it gets better.

(8) The "Unholy" War (chap. 20). The warfare against Benjamin, it is specified, involved "all Israel" (20:1) for the first time since a similar specification about the harlotry at Gideon's ephod (8:27). In chaps. 20–21 Israel is distinctively the *qāhāl,* "assembly" (21:5) or *ʿēdâ,* "congregation" (21:10, 13, 16); this is genuinely early usage and not itself a sign of postexilic editing in priestly circles (Anderson 1970; Hurvitz 1972; 1974; Boling 1983). The story perhaps originated in the suppression of a Benjaminite independence movement (Schunk 1963: 69–70). Here the bitterly ironic caricature of institutional life savagely turned toward "national" self-destruction continues. Two calamitous defeats by those who represent "Israel" come on the heels of oracular advice received at W Mizpah, specifying that Judah should go first to battle, as in 1:2. Only upon the third muster and inquiry, at Bethel while the ark of Yahweh's covenant is there, is the oracle reliable and victory achieved. Here, in contrast to 2:1–5 and chapter 17, the attitude toward Bethel is not polemical. The warfare left only 500 survivors hiding out, all males.

(9) Resolution (chap. 21). When at the outset of the final scenes, the people inquire at Bethel to learn why it has come about that one tribe is nearly extinct, the oracle is silent. They are thrown back upon their own devices and conclude that another small civil war will be advisable, to slaughter the men of Jabesh-gilead, who had not rallied against Benjamin (the E-W axis again), and to capture virgins for the 500 Benjaminites. The expeditionary force returns, however, with only 400 women. Another 100 are secured by the Benjaminites, thanks to the reasoning of Israel's elders, who propose a Benjaminite raid on Shiloh at festival time and offer a theologically foolproof rationale. If Shiloh's fathers and brothers come to complain, the elders will be able to say: "We did them a gracious deed. For we [the elders] did not take them; neither did you give in to them." And so it happened in the story. In response to the picture of tragic anarchy leading to the brink of national suicide, the final chapter of Judges draws upon the comic vision: "In those days there was no king in Israel" (except Yahweh, that is); "every man did what was right, as he saw it" (governed by internalized ethic, that is). Lamenting the atrocious behaviors, the book concludes by commending an enduring principle for decision-making in the maintenance of community for the well-being of every family.

C. The Book of Judges in Modern Study

Judges poses many and complicated questions. How to understand the evidence for a process preserving stories over a span of centuries and for editorial activity which reflects historical developments between original event and final telling? What to make of the narrators' and redactors' interest in certain towns and not others as places of assembly and oracular inquiry? How to correlate results of archaeological exploration, and critical study of ancient Israel's social world, with literary criticism? Who were the traditionists who generated the stories and what can be said of their social location down the centuries to the final compilation and redaction?

1. Judges as Narrative Art. The structure of Judges is distinctive, with indications of successive editing throughout introductory and concluding chapters, but much less frequently in the connections between stories that make up the body of the book. Rarely did the redactional activity in the body of the book invade essential contents of narratives. This is in striking contrast to the preceding book, where the model leadership of Joshua is displayed in highly stylized narrative. Thus early Israel's narrative art survives in its purest form in Judges. An appropriate label for such stories is "historical romance," a category better known from the classical world where they appear regularly in one of two genres: ideal and comic. The ideal genre tells of a well-known figure in popular language for popular delight as well as edification. The comic genre is a more sophisticated one, appearing less frequently, and intended for more discriminating attention. Stories that comprise the body of Judges correspond mainly to the "ideal" genre, that is, stories of leaders whose varying Yahwistic effectiveness is evaluated in the telling. The outer framework gives abundant evidence of the comic vision.

2. Judges as Historiography. The first products of Israelite history-writing do not appear until the 10th century B.C.E., when historiography answered a new need for the Davidic empire's self-understanding. Two major works stem from the Solomonic era and/or its immediate sequel. One is the "Court History of David" (2 Sam 9:20) or "Succession Document" (if it continues in 1 Kings 1–2). To the same period belongs the essential compilation of old materials that form the epic core of Genesis through Numbers. The main story line of the epic core is identified by the symbol "J," as it represents a version of origins which attained favored status in Jerusalem and Judah and notably uses the divine name Yahweh in stories referring to periods long preceding Moses. Other lexical and stylistic contrasts, as well as theological ones, distinguish the J material from its originally N (Ephraimite) counterpart, committed to writing perhaps a century later, after the split at the death of Solomon. The northern or "E" version prefers the generic noun Elohim and avoids use of the proper name Yahweh until the latter is revealed to Moses in Exodus 3. In general, material in Genesis-Numbers displays a simpler, earthier, livelier account than does E. The latter has its own theological perspective, with concentration upon angelic messengers, miracles, and related concerns. At Sinai, for example, J revels in the splendor of Yahweh's theophany (Exodus 19), while it is E that contributes the revelation of the divine will (Exodus 20), according to most critics. In general we may say that while J was not uncritically supportive of the Davidic establishment, E sought to undergird a Mosaic revival in the north. It is generally agreed that J and E were brought together in the S after the destruction of the N kingdom had shown that Moses and the prophets spoke the truth. Finally the corpus was supplemented and reedited in the 6th century B.C.E. by priests who were in exile in Babylonia.

It is not clear how far the epic core told the story after Moses. After a long interruption by the bulk of Deuteronomy, the JE material resurfaces in Deuteronomy 34, reporting the death and burial of Moses. Attempts to trace the JE story line into Joshua–Judges (see the classic commentaries of Burney [1970] and Moore [*Judges* ICC]) and beyond have met with little agreement among critics. It is often suspected that Judges 1 is J's account of conquest, at last yielding pride of place to an E account (the bulk of Joshua 1–11), but if so the trail then peters out.

More persuasive and productive than the older approach to literary source-strata has been the recent half-century of efforts to reconstruct the origins of stories and archival materials in relation to the various tribal constituencies that comprised Israel in the pre-state period. At the same time a broad consensus has formed around the relation of Joshua–2 Kings to the preceding book of Deuteronomy. The result is a Primary History comprised of (1) the Tetrateuch (Genesis–Numbers), and (2) a Deuteronomic corpus (Deuteronomy–2 Kings) which did not undergo a priestly redaction. The two have been dovetailed together so that the lengthy speeches of Moses (Deuteronomy 1–33) precede the old narrative account of his death and burial.

The core of Deuteronomy (essentially 4:44–27:26) presents itself as the farewell speech of Moses, delivered in the plains of Moab as he presides over renewal of the Sinai covenant, with the people poised for entry into the land of promise. Deuteronomy displays a pattern for the organization and governance of the tribal league, and for the role of Moses thus far as well as prophets in the future, in analogy to forms and practices of international diplomacy. Israel is the Kingdom of Yahweh, formed and ever reformable, thanks to the Sovereign's stipulation of binding basic policy (Decalog) for the development of legal tradition.

With the core of Deuteronomy given a new frame (1st and 3d speeches) to serve as introduction, the books of Joshua–2 Kings follow as the result of a full-scale chronicling project, mainly completed in the period of Judahite revival under King Josiah (ca. 640–609). Deuteronomy is the basis for one of two themes pervading the corpus: ancient covenantal curses account for the demise of the N kingdom. That disaster of 721 B.C.E. only heightened one of Deuteronomy's enduring concerns, to find provision for jobless Levites at the central Yahwist sanctuary (Deut 18:1–8). Provision for such teacher-priests, in turn, presents the most notable discrepancy between Deuteronomic platform and Josianic policy (2 Kgs 23:9).

The second recurring theme of Samuel and Kings—God's promises to David—was undergirded by Judah's experience: nearly 400 years with a single dynasty in power. With the destruction of Jerusalem and Judah (587) the corpus underwent a final editing, ending with release of the Davidic king Jehoiachin from a Babylonian prison (2 Kgs 25:27–30).

Evidence for the growth of the book of Judges corresponds in general to the foregoing description of the larger corpus: an old didactic collection of preformed narrative units was redacted in two major stages, Josianic and post-Josianic.

Traditions taken up in the book of Judges are thus neither so much promonarchical or antimonarchical as they are amonarchical and pro-Mosaic, with the rule of ethic and governance by Yahweh alone making the difference between anarchy and community well-being, i.e., premonarchic memories are adapted for the postmonarchic era.

3. Archaeology and Social World. For a 13th-century setting of the exodus and career of Moses (better later in the century than earlier) and for the problematics of reading archaeological data alongside biblical texts, see JOSHUA, BOOK OF, section C.3.

If Judges 1 is read as a flashback, then despite Joshua's achievement there was a period after his death when the situation deteriorated to the point where many towns and regions had in effect to be "conquered" all over again. On any reading of the chapter it is impossible to square the stories entirely with evidence from excavations and surveys. On the one hand, archaeology in the Judahite hill country and Shephelah has documented widespread upheaval in the period ca. 1250–1150 B.C.E. On the other hand, a number of plausibly identified biblical sites in the far S, towns which are said to have been conquered or settled in Joshua–Judges, were not actually founded until the 10th century when Israel had become, under David, a territorial state, controlling a small empire. Given the frequency and ease with which an ancient population (and its town name) could relocate after major destruction (with often a natural cause) to a promising nearby site, it is probably futile to seek one-for-one correlations with the brief notices brought together in Judges 1.

Of the major places of assembly in Judges only the location of Gilgal (2:1), somewhere near Jericho and, in any case, not a sizable "ruin," is uncertain.

Recent excavations at Tell Dan point to mid–12th century for its takeover. Bethel (modern Beitin), figuring prominently in the outer framework of Judges (1:22–26; 20:18; 21:2) is probably identical with Bochim in 2:1–5, as well as the target of polemic in the Micah stories (chap. 17). The site shows a 13th-century destruction followed almost at once by resettlement.

Bethel is also a point of reference for locating the sacred tree where Deborah held forth (4:5), in whose story "Jabin King of Canaan who reigned in Hazor" is at the root of resistance to the Israelite caravan trade through the plain of Esdraelon. Hazor (Tell el-Qedah) saw a destruction of the LB city in the second quarter of the 13th century. But in the earliest Iron Age town (presumably "Israelite") there is a characteristic Canaanite temple with corresponding furnishings. It was in this period that N Galilee saw a rapid spread of new, unwalled, upland settlements, and terrace farming, for the first time in history. The data thus attest to shifting demographic patterns in the far north providing a plausible setting for the flashback to the era of the Jabin (Joshua 11) whose policy at Hazor explains the subsequent move of a Kenite clan to the far N, and Jael's presence in Judges 4 and 5, which celebrate victory "at Taanach by Megiddo's stream." Extensive excavations at Megiddo and Taanach show a significant occupational gap at the former. Megiddo was abandoned or lightly occupied from ca. 1125 to the beginning of the first Iron Age town there, ca. 1100–1050. Taanach in the 12th century was, like Hazor, not extensively occupied, and was destroyed ca. 1125. The team of Deborah and Barak may thus plausibly be located in the second half of the 12th century.

Likewise Abimelech at Shechem. There was a destruction of the LB city in the 14th century (cause unknown), but it was soon reoccupied and followed by an interlude of roughly 200 years before it was destroyed again, in the middle to late 12th century. The latter destruction may reasonably be correlated with the story of Abimelech in chap. 9.

The same long interlude at Shechem saw a blossoming of unwalled settlements, for the first time in history, throughout the hill country to the N of Shechem and to the S as far as Hebron. Like the roughly contemporary phenomenon in N Galilee, these settlements were occupied by families practicing a subsistence agricultural economy based on construction of terraces for dry-farming (see JOSHUA, BOOK OF, section C.3; and Stager 1985).

These developments centering in the Shechem area may in turn be viewed against the background of Shechem's pragmatic stance vis-à-vis Egyptian administration in the 14th century, as seen in the activities and attitudes of Labayu and his sons, in the Amarna correspondence (Campbell 1960). Whatever the cause of the 14th-century destruction of Shechem, it did not curtail a movement toward functional independence in the wider area.

Shiloh and the W Mizpah figure only in the outer framework, and both may well have emerged as prominent in the wake of Shechem's destruction. Mizpah (probably Tell en-Nasbeh) was one of the many new settlements atop the hill country in the late 13th–early 12th centuries. Shiloh was an out-of-the-way rallying point, a town site which had lain in ruins largely uninhabited throughout the LB Age. It became another of the flourishing farming settlements and probably had a small temple in the prestate period. With subsequent destruction of Shiloh by the Philistines, the place of Israelite muster once again became Gilgal, in the days of Samuel and Saul.

The Philistine crisis which generated the Samson stories was not finally surmounted until the establishment of monarchy with Saul and the transformation of Israel into a territorial state centered in W Palestine under David and Solomon. In this respect, Israel lagged some two centuries behind developments in Transjordan where a strong territorial state, Moab, was already in place on the plateau S of the Arnon, with a smaller Ammonite state at the desert fringe of Gilead, in the era of Moses (see Sauer 1986). In the case of Israel it was not so much cultural lag as it was communal preference and sworn allegiance to a divine Sovereign which undergirded resistance and rebellion. Conflicting Ammonite, Moabite, and Israelite claims N of the Arnon, and Jephthah's negotiations in chap. 11, now make sense in view of shifting demographic patterns as reconstructed from excavations and surveys in Transjordan. See also JOSHUA, BOOK OF, section C.3. The reemergence of Israel as an effective tribal organization happened first in Transjordan, to which point it was nearly pushed back by the time of Samuel.

Early Israel was, in many respects, what anthropologists call a segmented society with correlated lineage systems. In such societies political organization is regularly based on genealogical reckoning and operative descent rules. As segments move from one place to another, undergo expansion or decline due to whatever circumstances, new adjustments result and genealogy, in time, adjusts to affirm the new arrangements, which come to be widely accepted as the way it has always been. Something similar happens with chronology. The large round numbers assigned to careers of savior-judges, and the more plausible shorter careers of "minor judges" (with some in both categories very likely contemporaries), are arranged end-to-end for an improbable lengthy era.

The hypothesis that early Israel was such a segmented society helps to understand the tensions which pervade the book of Judges, on both the N-S axis and the E-W axis. Some of these roots go deep, not only to the post-Joshua constituencies and their leaders in times of crisis, but on into the pre-Mosaic and pre-Yahwistic period of "Elohistic" Israel (see also JOSHUA, BOOK OF, section C.4).

4. Levitical Sponsorship? Dtn, Dtr 1, Dtr 2. While it is clear that the finished book of Judges shortly foresees or soon follows the dismantling of state and temple in 587, interpretation is inadequate which regards the book and the larger corpus as mainly an etiology of national destruction. Throughout the Former Prophets are signs of at least two major "editions," both of them making use of older units and large blocks of material, and both of them shaped by a book of Mosaic Torah. Dtn, Dtr 1, and Dtr 2 are convenient shorthand for this sequence of editions.

Dtr 1 forms the major portion of the Former Prophets, a late preexilic product probably from the reign of the reforming King Josiah. Designed to be supportive of life under a monarchy reformed according to the law of Moses, it presents Joshua as an ideal for the king in matters military, while the stories of Judges are left unrevised to display the problematics of life without monarchy.

Dtr 2 is a subsequent edition. It may be exilic, but need only be post-Josianic to account for the editorial editions.

Dtn is the bulk of Deut 4:44–28:68, an old Book of the Law of Moses, rediscovered in Josiah's day, which effectively accounted for the demise of the N kingdom. Given a new introduction, it became a theological preface to the story unfolding from the era of Moses to the Mosaic revival, late 7th century B.C.E. *Dtn* is neither promonarchical nor antimonarchical, without the explicit regulation of kingship in Deut 17:14–20, which therefore appears to be secondary. Clearly *Dtn* stems from no "royal" sanctuary. It most likely stems from levitical circles claiming premonarchical legitimacy, mostly in the N, and calling for grassroots covenant renewal on the Sinai/Moab/Shechem pattern. Continuing rivalry of levitical-priestly families claiming descent from Aaron (Jerusalem, Bethel, Hebron) or Moses (Dan, Shiloh, and probably Shechem) explains many tensions in the traditions. See also JOSHUA, BOOK OF, section C.5.

With the collapse of the N kingdom and a flooding of refugees and immigrants into the S, and with Josiah's closure of sanctuaries a century later but without adequate provision for unemployed priests, the constituencies would be in place in Jerusalem to account for the contrasts between *Dtr 1* and *Dtr 2*. The former (mainly Aaronite) frames a collection of stories with polemic against Bethel and Dan, and centers in the demolition of Shechem. *Dtr 2* (mainly Mushite) is clearest in the tragicomic frame around the entire era: united in chap. 1 for offensive war but on the ropes by the end of the chapter, reunited at last but for civil war which nearly eliminates a tribe at the end of the era.

The main configuration of the structure of Judges may thus be presented in schematic outline:

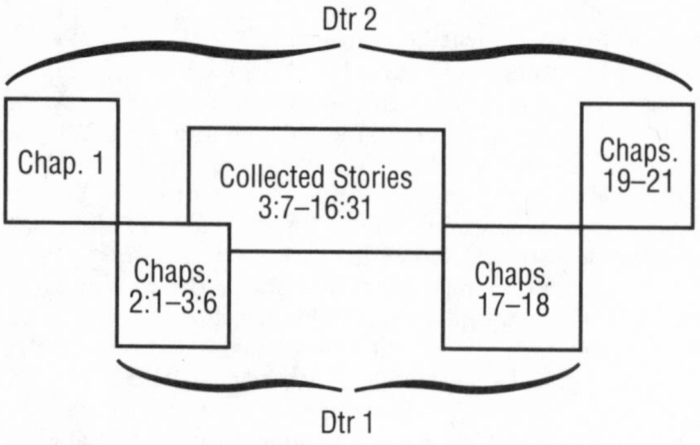

JUD.02. Structure of the book of Judges.

Slavish reliance upon archaic institutions which had displaced Yahweh's governance (i.e., "going by the book") is consigned to the past. The chaos and despair that descended on Judah in the wake of Josiah's death is countered by a comic vision that has rediscovered an enduring center of religious faith in public life. For commentaries, see Boling *Judges* and *Joshua* in AB, Hoppe *Joshua Judges* OTM, commentaries on Joshua/Judges/Ruth in NCBC (Gray) and ATD (Hertzberg), and commentaries on Judges in CBC (Martin), OTGuides (Mayes), IB (Myers), and OTL (Soggin). For further discussion, see *CMHE;* Freedman *IDB* 3: 711–27; and *WHJP* 3/2: 23–38, 3/7: 129–63.

Bibliography

Anderson, G. W. 1970. Israel: ʿAm, Kahal; ʿEdah. Pp. 135–51 in *Translating and Understanding the Old Testament,* ed. H. T. Frank and W. L. Reed. New York and Nashville.

Auld, A. G. 1984. *Joshua, Judges, and Ruth.* Philadelphia.

Boling, R. G. 1983. Levitical History and the Role of Joshua. Pp. 241–61 in *WLSGF.*

———. 1987. *The Early Biblical Community in Transjordan.* Sheffield.

Burney, C. F. 1970. *The Book of Judges.* 2d ed. New York.

Campbell, E. F. 1960. The Amarna Letters and the Amarna Period. *BA* 23: 2–22. Repr. in *BAR* 3: 54–75.

Chaney, M. L. 1983. Ancient Palestinian Peasant Movements and the Formation of Premonarchic Israel. Pp. 36–90 in *Palestine in Transition,* ed. D. N. Freedman and D. F. Graf. Sheffield.

Crenshaw, J. L. 1978. *Samson: A Secret Betrayed, A Vow Ignored.* Atlanta.

Dumbrell, W. J. 1983. "In Those Days There Was No King in Israel . . .": The Purpose of the Book of Judges Reconsidered. *JSOT* 25: 23–33.

Frick, F. S. 1985. *The Formation of the State in Israel.* Sheffield.

Geus, C. H. J. de. 1976. *The Tribes of Israel.* Amsterdam.

Good, R. M. 1985. The Just War in Ancient Israel. *JBL* 104: 385–400.

Gottwald, N. K. 1979. *The Tribes of Yahweh.* Maryknoll, NY.

Halpern, B. 1983. *The Emergence of Israel in Canaan.* Chico, CA.

———. 1988. *The First Historians.* San Francisco.

Hopkins, D. C. 1985. *The Highlands of Canaan.* Sheffield.

Hurvitz, A. 1972. Linguistic Observations on the Priestly Term *ʿEdah* and the Language of P. *Imm* 1: 21–23.

———. 1974. The Evidence of Language in Dating the Priestly Code. *RB* 81: 24–56.

Kochavi, M. 1985. The Israelite Settlement in Canaan in the Light of Archaeological Surveys. Pp. 54–60 in *BibAT.* Jerusalem.

Mayes, A. D. H. 1974. *Israel in the Period of the Judges.* SBT n.s. 29. London.

Mazar, A. 1982. The Bull Site—An Iron Age I Open Cult Place. *BASOR* 247: 27–42.

McKenzie, J. L. 1966. *The World of the Judges.* Englewood Cliffs, NJ.

Mendenhall, G. E. 1962. The Hebrew Conquest of Palestine. *BA* 25: 66–87. Repr. in *BAR* 3: 100–20.

———. 1973. *The Tenth Generation.* Baltimore.

Richter, W. 1963. *Traditionsgeschichtliche Untersuchungen zum Richterbuch.* Bonn.

———. 1964. *Die Beiarbeitungen des "Retterbuches" in der deuteronomischen Epoche.* Bonn.

Sauer, J. 1986. Transjordan in the Bronze and Iron Ages. *BASOR* 263: 1–26.

Schunk, K.-D. 1963. *Benjamin, Untersuchungen zur Enstehung und Geschichte eines israelitischen Stammes.* BZAW 86. Berlin.

Stager, L. E. 1985. The Archaeology of the Family in Ancient Israel. *BASOR* 206: 1–35.

Wilson, R. 1984. *Sociological Approaches to the Old Testament.* Philadelphia.
Wright, G. E. 1965. *Shechem: Biography of a Biblical City.* New York.
Yadin, Y. 1968. And Dan, Why Did He Remain in Ships? *AJBA* 1: 9–23.

ROBERT G. BOLING

JUDGMENT, DAY OF. See DAY OF JUDGMENT.

JUDGMENT, HALL OF (PLACE) [Heb *ʾulām hammišpāṭ*]. One of the buildings associated with Solomon's palace complex (1 Kgs 7:7). The context of the passage suggests that this was another name for the main ceremonial hall, or "Hall of the Throne" (throne room), where one might have an official audience with the king. The text seems to list the major compartments of the palace complex as one would logically encounter them moving from the (public) entrance to the (private) living quarters: one first had to pass through the Hall of Pillars to reach the Hall of Judgment. Assuming that Solomon's palace was constructed along the typical lines of the Syro-Phoenician *bīt hilāni,* the "Hall of Pillars" would correspond to the portico and front hall of the typical *bīt hilāni,* while the "Hall of Judgment" would be the large room behind it. Not only was this room equipped with a dais for the throne, it seems to have been furnished with either an open hearth or a portable brazier (Jer 36:22), as attested in other *bīt hilānis* (see Ussishkin 1973).

Bibliography

Ussishkin, D. 1973. King Solomon's Palaces. *BA* 36: 78–105.

GARY A. HERION

JUDITH (PERSON) [Heb *yĕhûdît*]. **1.** The wife of Esau and daughter of Beeri the Hittite (Gen 26:34). Hoffner (1969: 32) has shown that the names of persons called "Hittites" in the OT are almost all good Semitic names, e.g., Ephron, Gen 23:8; Adah, Gen 36:2; Ahimelech, I Sam 26:6; etc. Judith is a good Semitic name from Heb *yĕhûd* (plus the feminine gentilic suffix), meaning "Jewess." Therefore, it is most likely that Judith is part of a group of Canaanites living in the hills near Hebron and not a Hittite from Anatolia. This conclusion is also supported by Gen 36:2 where Esau took wives from the Canaanites, including Adah the daughter of Elon the Hittite, and by Gen 28:1 where Isaac charges Jacob not to marry one of the Canaanite women (as Esau had done, cf. Gen 27:46).

2. Heroine of the book of Judith (Gk *Ioudith*), daughter of Merari and widow of Manasseh (Jdt 8:1–2). Her genealogy, extending back 16 generations, is one of the longest in the OT and indicates her importance. Using her beauty and courage she enticed Holofernes, general of Nebuchadnezzar, and cut off his head. This enabled her to deliver the Hebrew people from a seemingly invincible foe. In addition, her piety and patriotism are models for emulation.

Bibliography

Hoffner, H. A. 1969. "Some Contributions of Hittitology to Old Testament Study." *TynBul* 20: 27–55.

JAMES C. MOYER

JUDITH, BOOK OF. Named after its heroine (Gk *Ioudith* = Heb *yhwdyt,* "Jewess"), this book, whose central theme is "The Omnipotent Lord has foiled them by the hand of a female" (Jdt 16:5), is regarded by Jews and Protestants as apocryphal, and by Roman Catholics since the decrees of the Council of Trent in 1546 as deuterocanonical.

A. Summary
B. Historicity
C. "Explanations" for the Book's Errors
D. The So-Called "Imbalance" of the Book
E. The Prose and Poetic (16:1–17) Accounts
F. Genre
G. Irony: The Key to the Book
H. Religious Views and Values
  1. In Speeches, Prayers, and Conversations
  2. The Heroine's Character
I. Original Language
J. Author and Place of Composition
K. Date of Book
L. Canonicity
  1. Among Jews
  2. Among Christians
M. The LXX of Judith
N. Other Ancient Versions

A. Summary

The content of the book may be summarized as follows. In the twelfth year of his reign Nebuchadnezzar, king of the Assyrians, left his capital Nineveh to wage war against the Median king, Arphaxad. While many of Nebuchadnezzar's subjects in the east rallied to his aid, those in the west, from Cilicia in the north to Ethiopia in the south, scoffed at his appeal for help. Unable to do anything about it at the time, he swore that some day he would punish them for it. Finally, in his 18th year (the year after he had destroyed Arphaxad and his "invincible" city, Ecbatana) Nebuchadnezzar decided to avenge himself on the west (chap. 1).

Summoning Holofernes, his greatest general, Nebuchadnezzar spelled out his plans for revenge: those nations who would submit to Holofernes by offering tokens of earth and water Nebuchadnezzar would personally deal with later; meanwhile those refusing to submit to Holofernes were to be slaughtered and looted without mercy.

So Holofernes marshaled an enormous army of 120,000 choice infantrymen, 12,000 mounted bowmen, as well as the support people and supplies needed for such an army. Starting out from Nineveh, they made the trek to Bectileth in N Cilicia in just three days. Then the army hacked its way through Put and Lud, plundering Rassisites and Ishmaelites in the process. Crossing the Euphrates River and proceeding through Mesopotamia, Holofernes' army then razed the walled towns along Wadi Abron and occupied Cilicia. Many people and towns were destroyed by him, including Midianites and peoples in the plain. Seacoast towns such as Sidon, Tyre, Okina, Azotus, and Ascalon (chap. 2) threw themselves upon his mercy, saying, "Come and treat us as you see fit." Holofernes not only tore down their sanctuaries and sacred poles, but even commanded that everyone should worship Nebuchadnezzar as god—and him only!

Holofernes' army then advanced toward Esdraelon and camped between Geba and Scythopolis (chap. 3). The Israelites in Judea, who only a short time before had returned from exile and had just recently rededicated their Temple at Jerusalem, were terrified. The territory of Samaria and cities like Kona, Beth-horon, Belmain, and Jericho secured their hilltops and prepared for war. Joakim, the high priest in Jerusalem at the time, specifically ordered Bethulia and Bethomesthaim, near Dothan, to secure the passes (since access to Judea and Jerusalem was through a narrow pass wide enough for only two men at a time to pass).

Israelites throughout Judea—priests, men, women, children, even animals—wore sackcloth, and were fasting and praying for themselves and especially for their Temple at Jerusalem (chap 4).

When Holofernes learned of this resistance, he was both surprised and angered. Demanding information on the Israelites, he got a full report from one Achior, leader of the Ammonites. Achior told how the Israelites had lived first in Chaldea, next in Mesopotamia, and then in Canaan. There they grew rich until a terrible famine forced them to Egypt, where they were ultimately enslaved by Pharaoh. Through the intervention of their god, they left Egypt, their god even drying up the Red Sea for them. They lived in the Sinai for a while, but then invaded the land of the Amorites, driving out its inhabitants. "And as long as they did not sin against their god," Achior said, "they prospered." But the Israelites sinned so much that finally their god allowed them to be conquered and exiled to a foreign land, from which they had just recently returned. If these people were sinning now, Achior was certain, their god would let the Assyrians conquer them. But if not, then the Assyrians could not defeat them (chap. 5).

Holofernes and his staff scoffed at Achior's counsel. He "rewarded" Achior by setting him in a place where the Israelites might find him and adopt him as a friend. Thus, Achior would share their fate, death at the hands of the Assyrians.

Once the Bethulians found Achior and heard his story, they renewed their prayers while Uzziah, their chief magistrate, took Achior into his own home (chap. 6).

Holofernes, on the advice of the leaders of Esau and Moab, seized the water sources of Bethulia, thereby assuring that the town would die either of starvation or thirst. And indeed after thirty-four days of siege, the cisterns of Bethulia were going dry and its people were collapsing in the streets. The situation was so desperate that its citizens demanded that their magistrates surrender the city, arguing that it was better to be living Assyrian slaves than "free" Israelite corpses. Uzziah offered them a compromise: if there was no relief from God within the next five days, then they would surrender the city (chap. 7).

Everyone in Bethulia accepted the compromise except one person, Judith, daughter of Merari. This beautiful and wealthy young widow of Manasseh was best known for her piety (since the untimely death of her husband almost three and a half years earlier, she had devoted herself to prayer and to fasting on all days except when they were prohibited). No one ever spoke ill of her. She summoned the three magistrates to her place and upbraided them, scolding them for trying to put God to the test. She insisted that God will do as he pleases, unmoved by the ploys of men. God might very well be testing his people in the present crisis, for, unlike some earlier occasions, he was not punishing them now inasmuch as they had not sinned against him. To Uzziah's snide suggestion that she, being such a righteous woman, should intercede for the people, Judith offered a counterproposal: she and her maid would leave town that night, and within five days the Lord would deliver Israel by her hand. The magistrates promptly gave her their blessing (chap. 8).

But first Judith, covered with sackcloth and ashes, prayed to the Lord, begging him for the same support he had granted her ancestor Simeon when he avenged Hamor's rape of Dinah. She begged God to crush the Assyrian forces threatening Jerusalem and its Temple. She also prayed for a beguiling tongue and a strong hand to overthrow her enemy (chap. 9).

Her spiritual preparation completed, Judith bathed and put on her most fetching attire, so that every male who saw her, be he Israelite or Gentile, was struck by her beauty. Then, with the blessing of the town fathers, she and her maidservant left Bethulia, taking with them only enough kosher rations for a few days.

As the two made their way through the valley, they were arrested by an Assyrian patrol, who, captivated by Judith's beauty, ended up personally escorting them to Holofernes' tent (chap. 10).

Holofernes' efforts to reassure Judith were clearly unnecessary, for she immediately took charge. She shamelessly flattered him on his accomplishments, assuring him, "I will say nothing false to 'my lord' this night" and "If you follow the advice of your maidservant, God will accomplish something through you, and 'my lord' will not fail to achieve his ends." She told Holofernes about what had transpired between Achior and the Bethulians. Moreover, Judith confirmed Achior's words to the Assyrians: Israel could not fall to the Assyrians unless it had sinned against God—and, Israel was about to do exactly that! The siege of Bethulia would shortly prompt its citizens to eat and drink things forbidden by their God. When they did that, they would deserve to die at Assyrian hands. Therefore she would remain in camp, leaving it only at night with her maid to pray. When God revealed to her that the impending sacrilege had occurred, then she herself would guide Holofernes' army to Jerusalem without loss of life or limb.

Delighted by her information and beauty, Holofernes believed her every word (chap. 11). To his invitation that she share his dinner, Judith declined, insisting that "Your servant will not exhaust her [kosher] supplies before the Lord God accomplishes by my hand what he has planned."

Until late that night and for the next three days Judith stayed in her own tent, leaving the Assyrian camp only at night to bathe and then pray, after which she would eat her one meal of the day. But on the fourth day Holofernes, intent on seducing her, invited her to a small dinner party in his tent. "Dressed to kill," Judith accepted his invitation, saying, "I will do whatever 'my lord' desires right away, and it will be something to boast of until my dying day."

His lust welling up within him, Holofernes drank so much wine (chap. 12) that by the time everyone but Judith had tactfully withdrawn for the evening, he was sprawled on his couch, dead drunk. Judith, taking his sword and praying for strength, struck Holofernes' neck twice, chopping his head off and then rolling his body onto the floor. Next she grabbed his canopy and had her maid drop the head into her sack. The two of them then, as usual, left the camp "to pray."

Arriving in Bethulia, Judith told everyone what God had done, how he had shattered the enemy by the hand of a mere female. As she offered Holofernes' head as evidence, she assured them that her "honor" was still intact (chap. 13).

Judith then mapped out the strategy for the next day. The Bethulians were to act as if they were coming down to fight, whereupon the Assyrians would alert their general, only to find him and themselves headless. *Then* the Israelites would attack.

That settled, Judith had Achior brought to her. On seeing the severed head, Achior collapsed. After hearing her story, Achior firmly believed in Israel's God, to the extent of his being circumcised and becoming a Jew, as are his descendants to this day.

The next day it all happened exactly as Judith had planned. The Assyrians panicked when they learned about Holofernes (chap. 14). Not only did the Bethulians attack them, but so did Israelites from all their cities far and wide, pursuing the Assyrians as far as Damascus. Looting the Assyrian camp took an entire month, during which time the high priest Joakim and the Jewish Council came down from Jerusalem to visit the scene and congratulate Judith. Then she and the people gradually worked their way toward Jerusalem, the women dancing along the route and the warriors, armed and garlanded, marching behind them (chap. 15).

Along the way Judith sang a psalm that told of the murderous boasts of the Assyrians, how "the Omnipotent Lord had foiled them by the hand of a female," and how "Her sandal ravished his eyes; her beauty captivated his mind; and the sword slashed through his neck!" She also insisted that burnt offerings were of little significance to God; rather, he was impressed by a person's fear of him.

Once back home, Judith remained there for the rest of her life. Although many men wanted her, she remained a celibate. Before dying at the ripe old age of 105, she manumitted her faithful maidservant and distributed her property among her closest relatives on both sides of the family. For the rest of Judith's life—and for a long time afterward—no one dared to threaten her people (chap. 16).

The preceding summary has been unusually detailed so as to enable the reader to perceive some of the book's strengths and weaknesses. The story, at least as presented in the Greek, is well told, especially chapters 10–13, which are a masterpiece of irony. The character and personality of both Judith and Holofernes are most vividly drawn. (Even supporting characters like Nebuchadnezzar, Uzziah, and Achior seem to have a life of their own.) And whether or not one agrees with the book's theology and ethics, its religious concerns and values are effectively expressed in the story's plot, speeches, and prayers. Nonetheless, the book bristles with problems.

B. Historicity

The story purports to be a historical account, and indeed it has many of the outward trappings of one, including various kinds of dates and numerous well-known and unknown (but not improbable) ethnic, personal, and place names. Even more important perhaps, apart from a few improbable details and obvious embellishments for literary effect, such as the Palestinian "Thermopylae" in Jdt 4:7 (see Momigliano 1982: 227–28), the story has a quite believable plot. Divine or miraculous intervention is virtually absent, the book's frequent allusions to praying and fasting notwithstanding. It is Judith and her courageous people who destroy the enemy. Thus a present-day scholar like Montague (1973: 8) can conclude that the author of Judith

> reworked . . . a story whose historical nucleus went back two centuries to the Persian period . . . there is a historical nucleus which gave rise to the Judith tradition, though this nucleus is now difficult to recover.

But as long ago as 1689, when Capellus characterized the book as "a most silly fable" (*Commentarii et notae criticae in Vet. Test.*, p. 575), scholars have questioned the story's historicity because of its shocking carelessness with well-established historical and geographical facts: "The use by its author of Jewish history from the Bible is marked by either freedom or recklessness about such matters as chronology" (Sandmel 1978: 62). The most flagrant "errors" are, of course, those in the opening verse: "It was in the *twelfth* year of the reign of Nebuchadnezzar, who ruled over the *Assyrians* from his capital *Nineveh* . . . ," because, as most students of the Bible know, Nebuchadnezzar was king of Babylonia, not Assyria, and Nineveh was destroyed in 612 B.C., that is, several years *before* Nebuchadnezzar came to the throne. Finally, the twelfth year of Nebuchadnezzar would have been the fourth year of the reign of Zedekiah (cf. Jer 32:1), Judah's last king in the *pre*exilic period; yet elsewhere in Judith the story is set in the *post*exilic period (cf. 4:3, 6; 5:18–19). These are but the story's most egregious historical "blunders."

As for the book's geographical errors, Holofernes' enormous army accomplished the 300-mile trek from Nineveh to N Cilicia in *three days* (2:21), then fought its way through Put and Lud ([2:23], countries usually identified by scholars as Libya in Africa and Lydia in Asia Minor), only to find itself crossing the Euphrates and going west *through Mesopotamia* (2:24) to Cilicia (2:25)! Even though Holofernes' itinerary along the Palestinian coast appears more geographically correct, his attack against Bethulia and Judea seems to come from the north (cf. 4:6; 8:21; 11:14, 19); yet 7:17–18 suggests that his attack came from the south, the latter view being also that of the Vulgate and its Aramaic source (see below).

With 4:6, geographical errors give place to geographical ignorance and uncertainty, for five of the eight Israelite cities mentioned there are unidentifiable. Worst of all, the location of Bethulia, which is mentioned 19 times in the text (but nowhere else in the Bible!) and whose setting includes a number of geographical and topographical clues (cf. 3:10; 4:6; 6:11; 7:12–13; 10:10–11; 11:19) is *totally unknown.* See BETHULIA (PLACE). Nonetheless, some historical atlases (e.g., *MBA,* 132) "locate" it on one of their maps.

All this being the case, it is perhaps a bit surprising that Achior's summary of Israel's history is (given, of course, its brevity and purpose) a reasonably accurate one, albeit from a Deuteronomistic point of view.

C. "Explanations" for the Book's Errors

Scholarly efforts over the past century to preserve some semblance of historicity for the Judith story have taken three major tacks, each with a number of "minor" variations supplied by its later proponents.

Steinmetzer (1907) proposed the "evolving text" theory. The original story, Steinmetzer argued, concerned events in the days of Ashurbanipal of Assyria (668–627 B.C.) but was later given a new setting in the days of Cyrus the Great of Persia (550–530 B.C.), and still later, of Artaxerxes I Longimanus (465–424 B.C.), also of Persia; the narrative was finally adapted to the events and atmosphere of the days of the infamous Antiochus IV Epiphanes of Syria (175–163 B.C.). Thus, the theory "explained" the various elements in the Judith story that were appropriate for a particular historical time and place.

The second theory was the "pseudonym hypothesis," according to which, for one reason or another, all the characters in Judith were deliberately disguised historical personages. Thus, for example, Judith's "Nebuchadnezzar" and "Holofernes" actually represented the Emperor Trajan and Lusius Quietus or Pompey and his general Scaurus or Antiochus IV Epiphanes and his general Nicanor. But even though the pseudonym theory now looks better, especially in light of the Essene practice in the Dead Sea literature of giving well-known persons a disguised name, the theory fails insofar as full and exact parallels for all the characters within a particular scenario or historical period seem lacking.

The third, and probably the most popular hypothesis, is the "two-accounts theory," in which the Judith story (chaps. 4–16) was combined with the "historical" account of a pagan king's war in the east and west (chaps. 1–3). On the basis of internal onomastic and historical clues, scholars have variously identified Judith's "Nebuchadnezzar" as Ashurbanipal of Assyria; Artaxerxes III Ochus of Persia (358–338 B.C.)—who actually had a general named Holofernes and an advisor named Bagoas; Antiochus IV Epiphanes of Syria; or Demetrius I Soter of Syria (162–150 B.C.), not to mention "Nebuchadnezzar IV" and others. (For details, see Pfeiffer 1949: 295–96; and Soubigiou *Judith* SBJ 4: 490.)

The postexilic setting of the story (cf. 4:3; 5:19), the presence of Persian terms (e.g., *kidaris,* "turban," in 4:14; and *akinakēs,* "sword," in 13:6) and practices ("to prepare earth and water" in 2:7) as well as authentic names of that period (e.g., Judith [see Heltzer 1980], Holofernes, Bagoas, and Joakim), plus (with the exception of "Scythopolis" in 3:10 and "Azotus" in 3:28) the absence of Greek personal and place names—all make it quite likely that the storyteller utilized information, possibly oral in form, from the time of Artaxerxes III (*HJP*[2] 3/1: 218). But if so, the story in its present form was written much later.

D. The So-Called "Imbalance" of the Book

The oft-cited charge that chaps. 1–7 (i.e., the story prior to Judith's appearance) are detractive and peripheral to the "real" story (i.e., Judith 8–16) has been refuted, hopefully once and for all, by Craven (1977; 1983). She has shown that chaps. 1–7, in a number of ways and on a variety of levels, serve as an effective and indispensable foil for chaps. 8–16. In the first half of Judith, Nebuchadnezzar and Holofernes, resorting to fear and brute, masculine force, won many battles; but Judith, with her "soft" feminine beauty and wiles, reinforced by her religious faith, won the war. Israelite men hid behind their city walls (Judith 4–6) while Judith and her maid went out to meet the enemy face-to-face (Judith 10–13).

Craven's compositional analysis proves that the book is made of a whole cloth and was intended from the beginning as a balanced and proportional narrative. As shown in Fig. JUD.03 (see Craven 1977: 60, 87–88), each half of the book has a threefold chiastic structure and a distinctive thematic repetition, namely, *fear* or its denial in Judith 1–7, and *beauty* and its effects in 8–16. In terms of both content and form, then, Section D (Judith's triumph over Holofernes) is the heart of the story as well as the center of the chiastic structure.

In some respects, the book of Judith is misnamed. Its message and structure would have been more clearly perceived if down through the ages it had had a more appropriate title, such as "Beast and the Beauty."

E. The Prose and Poetic (16:1–17) Accounts

Like the story of the Canaanite oppression in Judges 4 and 5, the tale of Judith has both a prose (Judith 1–15) and a poetic version (16:1–17).

Although scholars debate whether the poetic version in Judith was composed before, after, or at the same time as the prose narrative, Jansen (1936: 63–71) and others (Dancy, *Judith* CBC; and Moore, *Judith* AB, 252–57) maintain that the author of the prose account adopted a synagogal psalm—one patterned after the song of triumph par excellence, namely, the Song of the Sea in Exodus 15 (see Skehan 1963)—and adapted it; i.e., substituted what is now 16:5–10 (a masterpiece of irony) for the "incident" originally recounted in the synagogal hymn. If so, then it is likely that 16:13–17 are, even as they claim to be, "a new song" (16:13), that is, they represent an even later addition. In comparison with the rest of the song and the prose account, vv 13–17 are inferior in literary style and theologically different, in that they contain "apocalyptic/eschatological" elements (16:15, 17) and deemphasize the cultus (16:16).

F. Genre

If Judith is not history, then what is it? Over the past century three general types of answers have been given, each having a number of variations. Many students of the book have agreed that it is a *novel,* but they have disagreed as to the particular type. Is it "a Jewish novel" (Altheim and Stiehl 1963: 200–1), "a Jewish-Hellenistic novel"

Chapters 1–7

1. Introduction to Nebuchadnezzar and his campaign against Arphaxad (1:1–16).
2. Nebuchadnezzar commissions Holofernes to take vengeance on disobedient vassal nations (2:1–13).
3. Development:
   - A. The campaign against the disobedient nations; the people surrender (2:14–3:10).
     - B. Israel hears and is "greatly terrified"; Joakim orders war preparations (4:1–15).
       - C. Holofernes talks with Achior. Achior is expelled from the Assyrian camp (5:1–6:11).
       - C' Achior is received into Bethulia; he talks with the people of Israel (6:12–21).
     - B' Holofernes orders war preparations; Israel sees and is "greatly terrified" (7:1–5).
   - A' The campaign against Bethulia; the people want to surrender (7:6–32).

Chapters 8–16

- A. Introduction of Judith (8:1–8).
  - B. Judith plans to save Israel (8:9–10:9a).
    - C. Judith and her maid leave Bethulia (10:9b–10).
      - D. Judith overcomes Holofernes (10:11–13:10a).
    - C' Judith and her maid return to Bethulia (13:10b–11).
  - B' Judith plans the destruction of Israel's enemy (13:12–16:20).
- A' Conclusion about Judith (16:21–25).

JUD. 03. Chiastic structure in the book of Judith.

(Zenger 1981: 437), "a religious novel" (Andrews 1954: 35), "a short historical novel which carries a strong religious message" (Dancy *Judith* CBC, 67), or "a quasi-historical novel" (Metzger 1957: 51)?

Others have maintained that Judith is some type of *folktale:* "an epic rescue story" combining the themes of the Faithful Wife and the Female Warrior (so Coote in Alonso-Schökel 1974: 21–26; Thompson 1955–58, type 888), or a tale exemplifying "the perennial battle of the sexes" (so Dundes in Alonso-Schökel 1974: 28–29), or "an example narrative," with suprahistorical or metahistorical dimensions in which Nebuchadnezzar is a type of Anti-Yahweh (Haag 1963: 38–42).

Still other scholars have characterized the book as an *apocalypse:* one with eschatological aspects (so Scholz 1885), or "an apocalyptic parable" (Lefèvre, *SDB* 4: 1315–21), or an expression of *Heilsgeschichte* ("Salvation History") portraying a battle essentially between Yahweh and Anti-Yahweh (Dreissen 1953: 81), or a synthesis of two genres, the haggadic and the apocalyptic (Steinmann 1953: 129; Delcor 1967).

Doran (1986: 304) rightly cautions against reading Judith "in too allegorical a manner." It may be that those who subscribe to the apocalyptic/eschatological interpretation have put an undue emphasis on Jdt 16:15a and 17, neither of which need necessarily be interpreted in an apocalyptic or eschatological sense and, in any case, may not have been part of the text originally (so Jansen 1936; Moore, *Judith* AB, 251–52, 253–57). It should also be noted that Holofernes, not Nebuchadnezzar, is the villain who gets his deserved punishment.

All things considered, the book of Judith is best regarded as a folktale which offers an example story of a pious widow who, strengthened by her religious faith, courageously took matters into her own hands and defeated the enemy.

G. Irony: The Key to the Book

No biblical book is so quintessentially ironic as Judith. Failure to recognize this fact has been a primary reason for a number of misinterpretations of the book. The author of Judith was an ironist *extraordinaire* who, because he often meant the opposite of what he said, was sometimes misunderstood. A perfect case in point is the very first verse of Judith. Torrey (1945: 89) rightly maintained that Judith's ancient audience would have understood that verse as ironic, even as a modern reader would understand a story which began, "It happened at the time when Napoleon Bonaparte was king of England, and Otto von Bismarck was on the throne in Mexico." The storyteller, speculated Torrey, might even have given his listeners "a solemn wink" as he delivered his opening sentence.

Judith herself is certainly an ironic figure: a beautiful and desirable widow, she lived the life of a celibate after her husband's death; a childless widow, she gave spiritual and political rebirth to her people; a wealthy woman, she spent most of her life fasting; very feminine in appearance, she brutally murdered Holofernes with her own two hands.

Holofernes, too, is an ironic figure: able to conquer the entire west, he was unable to conquer Bethulia; intending to master Judith, he was mastered by her—by the very sword with which he himself had used to claim the lives of so many others.

Even the minor characters are ironic. Achior, a seasoned warrior, fainted upon seeing the decapitated head. A man of action, Achior was also a wise man, almost an Ahikar *redivivus* (Cazelles 1951). See ACHIOR (PERSON). A pagan Ammonite, Achior from the beginning showed more faith in Israel's God than did the Israelite magistrate of Bethulia, Uzziah (= "God is my strength"), who in "womanly" fashion hid behind the safety of high walls while Judith, in "manly" fashion, went out to meet the enemy face-to-face. (On the "serial androgyny" of Judith, see Montley 1978.) King Nebuchadnezzar, "Lord of the whole world" (2:5) could not conquer Israel. The Assyrian soldiers who arrested Judith ended up escorting her to Holofernes' quarters, a perfect example of the captive taking captive the captors.

Good (1965: 81–82) has shown that there are several forms of irony in the OT, including

> *punctual* irony, the use of words and expressions of ironic intention . . . at, more or less isolated, "points" . . . *episodic* irony . . . an entire episode with an ironic aim or intent . . . [and] *thematic* irony, the conjunction of a number of episodes all of which point to an ironic theme or motif.

All three types of irony abound in Judith. Of the numerous examples of *punctual* irony, one might note the following: "So who are you, Achior, . . . that *you play the prophet,* . . . advising us not to make war against the people of Israel because their god will protect them? *Who is god except Nebuchadnezzar? He will send his forces and wipe them off the face of the earth! Their god won't save them.*" (6:2); "*My servants will now 'deliver' you* to the hill country . . . *You will not die—until you are destroyed with them!*" (6:6–7); "*God did well to send you* [said Holofernes to Judith] . . . to give strength to our hands and destruction to those who insulted my lord . . . If you do as you have promised, . . . *you shall . . . be famous throughout the world*" (11:22–23).

As for *episodic* irony, the punctual ironic statements taken together in the exchange between Holofernes and Achior (e.g., 5:5, 20–21, 23–24; 6:2, 3, 5, 7–9) or those in the exchanges between Holofernes and Judith (e.g., 11:1, 5–6, 16, 22, 23; 12:4, 14, 18) constitute splendid examples. Moreover, when these two episodes are taken together, *thematic* irony is created, i.e., Achior spoke the truth and was *not* believed while Judith dissimulated, equivocated, and outright lied—and was believed!

The heroine's relationship with all the males in the story—the elders, the Assyrian soldiers, Achior—is ironic, but especially so with Holofernes. For as Winter so nicely put it, "Holofernes, on seeing Judith, loses his head before it has been cut off" (*IDB* 2: 1024). For the brutal murder itself, the author uses most erotic terms: "Her sandal *ravished* his eyes; her beauty *captivated* his mind; and the sword *slashed through* his neck!" (16:9). Given the patriarchal character of Judith's day, one can scarcely imagine a more ironic theme than the book's central one: "The Omnipotent Lord has foiled them by the hand of a female" (16:5). (For a more detailed analysis of irony in Judith, see *Judith* AB, 78–85.)

H. Religious Views and Values

The theological views and values of the author are skillfully conveyed in two ways: (1) explicitly by the speeches, prayers, and conversations of the characters; and (2) implicitly by the actions of the characters, especially Judith.

1. In Speeches, Prayers, and Conversations. In Judith, neither God's various titles (4:2, 11; 5:8; 6:19, 21; 7:28; 8:11; 9:2, 7, 11, 12; 13:18) nor his attributes (see 4:13; 8:14, 20; 9:2, 11, 12; 16:13, 15) are in any way unusual or noteworthy. As in other postexilic books, Yahweh is the Creator of the Universe and the Lord of History (see 9:5, 13; 13:18) who has guided Israel from the days of the patriarchs (5:26; 8:26; 9:2–4) down through the postexilic period (5:17–19; 8:18–20), and will continue to do so until the very end (16:17).

God's covenant with Israel is interpreted largely in Deuteronomistic terms (5:17–18, 20–21; 8:20; 11:10). Consequently, there is a very strong emphasis on the importance of Jerusalem (4:2; 10:8; 11:19; 15:9; 16:18), its Temple (4:2–3, 12; 8:21, 24; 9:8, 13; 16:20), and everything associated with it, including its altar and utensils (4:14–15), high priest (4:6), the priests and Levites (4:14–15), and various kinds of sacrifices and offerings (4:14; 9:1; 11:13; 16:18 [16:16 notwithstanding]). The efficacy of prayer, fasting, and wearing sackcloth (4:11–15; 8:5–6; 9:1) is unquestioned. Judith's concerns for *kašrût* are central to her character as well as to the plot (10:5; 11:11–15; 12:4, 19).

With the exception of almsgiving and the baptizing of gentile converts to Judaism (14:10), virtually all the traditional Jewish practices of Maccabean Pharisaism are mentioned. Were it not for the sweeping authority of the high priest (4:6) and the very strenuous fasting of Judith herself (8:6), a much earlier date could be assigned Judith's Pharisaism.

2. The Heroine's Character. As for religious values expressed by *the actions* of Judith, the storyteller obviously subscribed, without any reservations, to two very popular but highly debatable aphorisms, namely, "All's fair in love and war" and "The end justifies the means." He was also clearly suggesting that courage and cleverness, Pharasaic piety and ardent patriotism, undergirded by a strong faith in Yahweh, held not only Judith in fine stead but would do the same for other Jews in any time or place. Such a message helps to explain the story's popularity among Jews despite its omission from the Jewish canon.

No one doubts Judith's cleverness or courage. But many have questioned her character and conduct. To be sure, she prayed constantly and fasted frequently (8:4–8); she ate only kosher foods even in the crises of life (12:1–2, 19); she honored the memory of her deceased husband by never remarrying; and she did all the proper things right before she died (16:22–24). But in her dealings with Holofernes she was a shameless flatterer (11:7–8), a bold-faced liar (11:12–14, 18–19), and a ruthless assassin (13:7–8; "a clever and resourceful assassin" [Nickelsburg 1981: 106]).

While Bissell's indictment (1886: 163) of her is obviously expressed in Victorian language and reflects a clearly Victorian sexual morality, it still expresses adequately the thoughts and feelings of many who have either rejected the book or accepted it, albeit with reservations:

> The character [of Judith] . . . is objectionable . . . from a moral standpoint . . . Her way is strewn with deception from first to last . . . she would have been willing even to have yielded her body to this lascivious Assyrian for the sake of accomplishing her purpose . . . That God in his providence interposed to prevent such a crime, cannot relieve her of the odium attaching to her conduct . . . there are elements of moral turpitude . . .

Nonetheless, by the standards of *her* day and *her* people, Judith *was* deeply religious (8:8), one who prayed to God even as she chopped off Holofernes' head (13:7). In fact, the author of Judith could very well have described her as "the saint who murdered for her people." (The word "saint" is used here not in the sense of one who is morally "perfect" but, rather, of one who is totally dedicated to one's God.)

I. Original Language

Even if Aramaic was the original language of the Judith story (so Bruns 1954: 12–14), the LXX gives every indication of being a translation of a Hebrew text. Variant readings in the LXX point in this direction (see 8:21; 10:3; 12:16; 16:11, 15) as do certain awkward words and phrases which are best explained by positing the misreading of a Hebrew word which resembles in appearance the one presupposed by the extant Greek rendering (see 1:8; 2:2; 3:9; 12:7; see especially Zimmermann 1938).

Then, too, a number of Hebrew idioms are rendered quite literally by the Greek, e.g., "all flesh" (2:3); "on the left," i.e., north (2:21); "a month of days" (3:10); "generation after generation" (8:32); and "to speak peace" (15:8). Finally, the ubiquitous paratactic construction (i.e., "and" followed by the verb); the infinitive absolute construction (2:13; 6:4; 7:15; 9:4); the abundance of resumptive pronouns (10:2; 16:3, 5); the superabundance of *spodra* (Gk for Heb *mʾd,* "very"); instances of hendiadys (2:12; 7:18; 8:5; 9:8; 10:3; 14:10; 16:1)—these and other features regularly remind a reader that Judith is a translation from the Hebrew. (For further details, see Cowley, *APOT* 1: 244; Enslin 1972: 40–41.)

J. Author and Place of Composition

Several lines of evidence suggest that the author of Judith was a Palestinian Jew (although Luria [1975: 328–41] argues for a Syrian provenance) and probably an early Pharisee. First, the *Vorlage* of the Greek Judith was Hebrew. Second, the central events of the story (i.e., chaps. 4–16) take place in Palestine itself, where the author evidenced a better grasp of geography than he did in those areas outside Palestine (i.e., in chaps. 1–3). Third, the religious ideas of the book are Palestinian and Pharisaic, with no traces of either Sadducean (Craven 1983: 118–21; but see Mantel 1976: 60–80) or Alexandrian influence.

K. Date of Book

Judith contains basic and unmistakable Hellenistic elements. There are, for example, "details of fact" characteristic of that period, including the wearing of garlands (Jdt 3:7), the use of olive wreaths (15:13), reclining while eating (12:15), and, most important of all for the Judith story, worshiping a king as god (3:8). Institutional arrangements first characteristic of the Maccabean/Hasmonean periods are also present in the book, namely, the sweeping political and military powers of the high priest (4:6) and the supremacy of the Jerusalem Council over other Jewish councils (4:6, 8; 11:14).

Even more significant, a number of items in the Judith story are reminiscent of the general "plot," spirit, terminology, and traditions of the days of Judas Maccabeus (167–161 B.C.), who fought at Jamnia, Azotus, and Beth-horon as well as at other prominent towns mentioned in Judith. Especially striking are the parallels between the Judith story and the defeat of Nicanor, a general of Antiochus IV Epiphanes, as narrated in 1 Macc 7:43–50:

> So the armies met in battle on the thirteenth day of the month of Adar. *The army of Nicanor was crushed, and he himself was the first to fall in battle. When his army saw that Nicanor had fallen, they threw down their arms and fled. The Jews pursued them a day's journey* . . . *And men came out of all the villages of Judea round about, and* . . . drove them back to their pursuers . . . *Then the Jews seized the spoils and the plunder, and they cut off Nicanor's head* . . . *and brought them and displayed them just outside Jerusalem. The people rejoiced and celebrated that day* as a day of great gladness. And they decreed that this day should be celebrated each year on the fourteenth of Adar. *So the land of Judah had rest for a few days.* (italics added)

The central threat in the book of Judith (i.e., that a mortal king had to be worshiped as god [3:8]) is identical with that of another book composed in the days of Judas Maccabeus, namely, the book of Daniel, where in chap. 3, for instance, Antiochus IV Epiphanes, thinly veiled as "Nebuchadnezzar," demands that he be worshiped as a god.

But some other evidence in Judith suggests an even later date for the book, one in the Hasmonean period (135–63 B.C.). Inasmuch as Azotus, Scythopolis, Mount Gerizim, Shechem, and all the territory of Samaria were independent of Israel until conquered by John Hyrcanus I (135–104 B.C.), the very open and friendly attitude of Jerusalem toward Samaria and its territories (so Jdt 4:4, 6) as well as the total absence of idolatry throughout the land (so Jdt 8:18–20) strongly suggests that the Judith story received its final form sometime after 107 B.C., i.e., after the Samaritan Temple of Mount Gerizim had been destroyed and Samaritan territory had been "integrated" into the Judean state.

While one might argue that because the above-mentioned places were also part of the even larger kingdom of Alexander Janneus (103–78 B.C.) and therefore Judith could have been written in his day (so *HJP*² 3/1: 218–19), it should be noted that the book does not reflect the very devisive and vicious sectarianism of Janneus' day when Pharisees and Sadducees persecuted and killed one another in great numbers. Thus, the religious views of Judith are more appropriate for the days of Hyrcanus than for those of Janneus; for they are essentially those of early Pharisaism, and they are not belligerently sectarian in character, that is, they are not anti-Sadducee or anti-Essene in emphasis.

L. Canonicity

1. Among Jews. The books of Esther and Judith each feature a beautiful Jewess whose courage and wiles save her people from certain destruction. The book of Esther mentions neither God nor any religious institutions or practices except fasting, while the book of Judith, filled as it is with allusions to God and numerous religious beliefs and practices, pulsates with the blood and spirit of Pharisaic piety. Yet it was the book of Esther, admittedly only after a long debate, that ultimately became part of the Jewish canon. For details, see ESTHER, BOOK OF.

In spite of the fact that Judith was part of the "Alexandrian Canon" (i.e., biblical and apocryphal works translated into Greek for those Jews who could not read Hebrew), there is no evidence that in Palestine Judith was ever regarded as canonical. Evidently it was not used by the Essenes at Qumran, or at least no trace of it has been found there among the Dead Sea Scrolls. The rabbis at Jamnia who established the canon of the Hebrew Bible around A.D. 90 may have rejected the book because, contrary to the prohibition in Deut 23:3, Achior, an *Ammonite,* was accepted into the Jewish religion (so Steinmann 1953: 61–62); or possibly Judith represented too "liberated" a woman for the rabbis to memorialize (so Craven 1983: 117–18); but most likely, the book ran counter to Halakah (i.e., Talmudic Law), whereby a gentile convert to Judaism had to be circumcised *and baptized* in order to become a Jew, and Achior was not baptized (so Orlinsky 1974: 218). In any event, the story of Judith, or of a woman who did something comparable to what Judith did, has remained a popular story among Jews for the last two thousand years, as the existence of numerous Midrashim attest (see below).

2. Among Christians. Although some Greek Fathers in the Eastern Church accepted Judith as canonical (e.g., Clement of Alexandria [A.D. 150?–?215], the Council of Nicaea [325], and Junilius [fl. ca. 542]), more did not. Judith was rejected by Melito of Sardis (fl. ca. 167), Origen (185?–254), Athanasius of Alexandria (293?–373), Cyril of Jerusalem (315?–386), and a host of others. (For details on these Church Fathers, see Altaner 1960; *HJP*^{2} 3/1: 220.) In the West the situation was quite different. Apart from Jerome (A.D. 340?–420), who evidently spoke approvingly of the fact that the Jews of his day did not regard the book as canonical, western Church Fathers routinely accepted it, including Hilary of Poitiers (315?–?367), Augustine (354–430), the Council of Carthage (397), and others.

Appreciated more by those Fathers who put a high premium on celibacy (see Moore, *Judith* AB, 64), Judith did not have a book-length commentary written on it until that of Rhabanus Maurus (780?–856). The book's canonicity was not again questioned until the time of the Protestant and Catholic reformations of the 16th century. Then, following the lead of both the Jews and Martin Luther (the latter viewing it as an allegorical passion play), Protestants came to regard the book as apocryphal, while the Roman Catholic Church in its decrees at the Council of Trent in 1546 called Judith, along with other "apocryphal" books, deuterocanonical.

M. The LXX of Judith

Despite the absence of a Hebrew *Vorlage* with which to compare it, the LXX of Judith appears to be a very literal rendering of the Hebrew syntax and idiom. Then, too, many of the niceties of "good" (i.e., classical) Greek are either lacking or underrepresented. Genitive absolutes, subordinate clauses, and Greek particles are especially underused (for details, see Cowley, *APOT* 1: 244). Paradoxically, the book evidences a rich and flexible Greek vocabulary, especially in those areas of great interest to its translator, notably military terms and words for "sin" and "the Temple" (for further details, see Enslin 1972: 41). The translation was made no later than the 1st century A.D., since Clement of Rome (30?–?99) alluded to Judith in *1 Clem* 55:4–5.

N. Other Ancient Versions

The Old Latin (OL) of Judith, like other books of the apocrypha, is a translation of the LXX rather than of a Semitic text. By contrast, Jerome's Latin Vulgate (or Vg) is a paraphrase of a then-current Aramaic text and attempts to bring the OL into closer conformity with it (see Voigt 1925). His translation varies considerably from the text of the LXX. Of the 340 verses in the LXX, the Vg omits 43 verses entirely and omits large parts of 45 more. It also adds 32 verses which have no counterpart in either the LXX or the OL. Some of these variants clearly reflect Jerome's Aramaic *Vorlage* (see Moore, *Judith* AB, 95–97, 100–1). Whether that Aramaic text was based upon an older Hebrew account or upon the LXX is unclear.

The so-called ancient "Hebrew versions" of Judith are actually medieval Hebrew translations of the Latin (see Meyer 1922; Grintz 1957), not independent witnesses to another and older Semitic tradition of the Judith story (but so Dubarle 1958; 1961; 1966; 1969; 1975). Likewise, the dozen or so Midrashim ("expositions") dating to the Middle Ages (Gaster 1893–94; Dubarle 1966), seem closely related to the LXX and/or the Vg. (so *HJP*^{2} 3/1: 219ff.). The Syriac, Coptic, and Ethiopic versions of Judith, as with other books of the apocrypha, are literal translations of the LXX. Unfortunately, only the Greek (*OTG* 3/1; Hanhart 1979) and the Vulgate (*Librae Iudith,* 1950) have scientific editions of Judith.

Taken together, the preceding evidence indicates that the ancient versions of Judith, including the usually helpful Vulgate, are of little help in establishing the original text of the LXX.

Bibliography

Alonso-Schökel, L. 1974. Narrative Structure in the Book of Judith. *Protocol Series of the Colloquies of the Center for Hermeneutical Studies in Hellenistic and Modern Culture,* 12/17.

Altaner, B. 1960. *Patrology.* Tr. by H. C. Graef. Edinburgh and London.

Altheim, F., and Stiehl, R. 1963. Esther, Judith, und Daniel. Vol. 1, pp. 195–213 in *Die aramäische Sprache unter den Achaemeniden.* Frankfurt am Main.

Andrews, H. T. 1954. *An Introduction to the Apocryphal Books of the Old and New Testaments,* 5th ed., rev. by C. H. Pfeiffer. Grand Rapids.

Bissell, E. C. 1886. The Book of Judith. *The Apocrypha of the Old Testament.* New York.

Bruns, E. J. 1954. Judith or Jael? *CBQ* 16: 12–14.

Cazelles, H. A. 1951. Le Personnage d'Achior dans le livre de Judith. *RSR* 39: 125–37, 324–27.

Craven, T. 1977. Artistry and Faith in the Book of Judith. *Semeia* 8: 75–101.

———. 1983. *Artistry and Faith in the Book of Judith.* SBLDS 70. Chico, CA.

Delcor, M. 1967. Le livre de Judith et l'époque grecque. *Klio* 49: 151–79.

Doran, R. 1986. Narrative Literature. Pp. 287–310 in *Early Judaism and Its Modern Interpreters,* ed. R. A. Kraft and G. W. E. Nickelsburg. Atlanta.

Dreissen, J. 1953. *Ruth, Esther, Judith in Heilsgeschichte.* Paderborn.

Dubarle, A. M. 1958. Les Textes divers du livre de Judith: À propos d'un ouvrage récent. *VT* 8: 344–73.

———. 1959. La Mention de Judith dans la littérature ancienne, juive et chrétienne. *RB* 66: 514–49.

———. 1961. Rectification: Sur un text hébreu de Judith. *VT* 11: 86–87.

———. 1966. *Judith: Formes et sens des diverses traditions.* AnBib 24. Rome.

———. 1969. L'Authenticité des textes hébreux de Judith. *Biblica* 50: 187–211.

———. 1975. Les Textes hébreux de Judith: Un nouveau signe d'originalíte. *Biblica* 56: 503–11.

Enslin, M. S., ed. 1972. *The Book of Judith.* Leiden.

Gaster, M. 1893–94. An Unknown Hebrew Version of the History of Judith. *PSBA* 16: 156–63.

Good, E. M. 1965. *Irony in the Old Testament.* Philadelphia.
Grintz, J. M. 1957. *The Book of Judith.* Jerusalem (in Hebrew with English summary).
Haag, E. 1963. *Studien zum Buche Judith.* TTS 16. Trier.
Hanhart, R. 1979. *Iudith.* Septuaginta, Vetus Testamentum graecum, 8/4. Göttingen.
Heltzer, M. 1980. Eine neue Quelle zur Bestimmung der Abfassungszeit des Judithbuches. *ZAW* 92: 437.
Jansen, H. L. 1936. La Composition du chant de Judith. *AcOr* 15: 63–71.
Luria, B. Z. 1975. Jews of Syria in the Days of Antiochus Epiphanes and the Book of Judith. *Beth Miqra* 62: 328–41.
Mantel, H. 1976. Ancient Hasidim. *Studies in Judaism* 60–80 (in Hebrew).
Metzger, B. 1957. *An Introduction to the Apocrypha.* Oxford.
Meyer, C. 1922. Zur Enstehungsgeschichte des Buches Judith. *Bib* 3: 193–203.
Momigliano, A. 1982. Biblical Studies and Classical Studies: Simple Reflections about Historical Method. *BA* 45: 224–28.
Montague, G. T. 1973. *The Books of Esther and Judith.* Pamphlet Bible Series 21. New York.
Montley, P. 1978. Judith in the Fine Arts: The Appeal of the Archetypal Androgyne. *Anima* 4: 37–42.
Nickelsburg, G. 1981. The Hasmoneans and Their Opponents. Pp. 101–60 in *Jewish Literature between the Bible and the Mishnah.* Philadelphia.
Orlinsky, H. M. 1974. *Essays in Biblical Culture and Bible Translation.* New York.
Pfeiffer, R. H. 1949. *History of New Testament Times.* New York.
Sandmel, S. 1978. Judith. Pp. 62–65 in *Judaism and Christian Beginnings.* New York.
Scholz, A. 1885. *Das Buch Judith, eine Prophetie.* Würzburg.
Skehan, P. W. 1963. The Hand of Judith. *CBQ* 25: 94–110.
Steinmann, J. 1953. *Lecture de Judith.* Paris.
Steinmetzer, F. 1907. *Neue Untersuchung über Geschichtlichkeit der Judith-erzählung.* Leipzig.
Thompson, S. 1955–58. *Motif-Index of Folk-Literature.* Rev. ed. 6 vols. Bloomington, IN.
Torrey, C. C. 1945. *The Apocryphal Literature: A Brief Introduction.* New Haven.
Voigt, E. E. 1925. *The Latin Versions of Judith.* Leipzig.
Volkmar, G. 1863. *Handbuch der Einleitung in die Apokryphen.* Vol. 1. Tübingen.
Zenger, E. 1981. Das Buch Judith. Pp. 428–534 in *Historische und legendarische Erzählungen.* JSHRZ 1/6. Gütersloh.
Zimmermann, F. 1938. Aids for the Recovery of the Hebrew Original of Judith. *JBL* 57: 67–74.

CAREY A. MOORE

JULIA (PERSON) [Gk *Ioulia*]. A Roman Christian who received greetings from Paul in Rom 16:15. That Julia was the wife (or sister) of Philologus because she is coupled with him in v 15 is only a possibility. She was probably a gentile Christian. See NEREUS (PERSON). "Julia" was the Lat name of the *gens Julia* (Lampe *StadtrChr,* 66–67, 146, 152–53, 296). Women were often called by the name of their *gens* without cognomen. Three groups carried the name "Julius/Julia": the noble members of the famous *gens;* the provincials who had received Roman citizenship from Caesar or Augustus (and these provincials' descendants); and the numerous freed(wo)men of the *gens* with their descendants. The third group outnumbered the members of the first two. It is most likely, therefore, that the Christian Julia was a freed slave of the *gens Julia* or a descendant of a freed slave of this *gens.* Either way, she probably had Roman citizenship: slave masters with famous *gens* names like "Julius/ia" possessed Roman citizenship and in most cases passed it on to their slaves on the occasion of their release; the freed slaves bequeathed the citizenship and the *gens* name to their freeborn children. Slave masters of the *gens Julia* were the emperors Augustus, Tiberius, and Caligula, but many other patrons also carried the *gens* name and passed it on to their freed(wo)men (cf. e.g., Tacitus *Hist.* 1.76, *Ann.* 3.40; 15.50; 13.10). That Julia was an imperial freedwoman (cf. Phil 4:22; Christians in the emperor's household) is therefore one possibility among others.

PETER LAMPE

JULIUS (PERSON) [Gk *Ioulios*]. A centurion of the Augustan cohort who guarded Paul on his sea voyage from Caesarea to Rome (Acts 27:1–44). Julius was a common Roman name, made famous by Julius Caesar. Yet the centurion was probably not a Roman citizen, since his unit was an auxiliary cohort whose men did not receive citizenship until the completion of their 25 years' service (Webster 1985: 142–43).

During his trial before Governor Porcius Festus, Paul had appealed to Caesar, so the governor sent him to Rome under the guard of Julius and some of his soldiers. Julius treated Paul kindly on the journey, allowing him to visit friends when the ship stopped at the port of Sidon (27:3). After the vessel reached Myra, the centurion transferred Paul to another ship bound for Rome. He disregarded Paul's warning against further sailing as the dangerous winter season approached, agreeing with the ship's captain and owner to continue the voyage (27:9–11). As they sailed past Crete, a severe storm struck the ship, pummeling it for 14 days. When the ship finally ran aground on a shoal just off Malta, the soldiers planned to kill Paul and the other prisoners to keep them from escaping. But Julius stopped them, thus saving Paul's life (27:41–43). He also ordered all 276 passengers and crew to swim or float on wooden planks to shore, a plan which enabled every person aboard to be saved from drowning (27:43–44).

Scholars have questioned the historicity of various aspects of Julius' role in the entire travel narrative. Broughton (1933: 443–44) expressed surprise that a prisoner as important as Paul was not entrusted to a higher-ranking officer. Ramsay hypothesized that Julius might have been one of the *frumentarii,* a special corps of officer-couriers who acted as secret police, and could well have escorted a prisoner bound for Rome (1925: 314–15). But Sherwin-White has shown that the *frumentarii* did not begin functioning as secret police until early in the 2d century C.E.; in Paul's time they merely supervised grain shipments (1963: 109). More likely possibilities are that Julius served in a police role as a *praepositus* (chief of detachment) or else was assigned to escort Paul to Rome as part of his duties on Festus' administrative staff (Watson 1969: 145; Webster 1985: 270).

According to Conzelmann, an army centurion such as

Julius would have had little voice in the seafaring decisions affecting the ship (*Acts* Hermeneia, 216), whereas Luke portrays him conferring as an equal with the ship's captain and owner (27:9–12). Haenchen likewise discounts the possibility that Julius would have paid any attention to the opinions of one of his own prisoners such as Paul (*Acts* MeyerK, 708–11). More conservative scholars such as Marshall defend the historicity of Luke's portrayal of both Julius and Paul (*Acts* TNTC).

Julius' role in Lucan theology has not received due attention. Luke focuses more attention on Julius than any other person except Paul in the long travel narrative in Acts 27–28. While Julius does not become a Christian as does the more famous centurion Cornelius in Acts 10, he does act as the friendly gentile par excellence. By allowing Paul to visit friends in Sidon and by saving him from the threatening soldiers, Julius shows how gentiles and Christians can treat each other with mutual respect. That mutual respect pays off too, as God works through Paul's prophecy (27:21–26, 31) and Julius' commands (27:42–44) to save both the gentiles and Christians after the shipwreck. Surely Luke intends Julius' relationship with Paul to be a model for friendly, mutually beneficial relationships between gentiles and Christians.

Bibliography

Broughton, T. R. S. 1933. The Roman Army. Pp. 427–45 in *The Beginnings of Christianity*. Pt. I, vol. 5. Ed. F. J. Foakes-Jackson and K. Lake. London.

Ramsay, W. M. 1925. *St. Paul the Traveller and Roman Citizen*. 15th ed. London.

Sherwin-White, A. N. 1963. *Roman Society and Roman Law in the New Testament*. Oxford.

Watson, G. R. 1969. *The Roman Soldier*. Ithaca, NY.

Webster, G. 1985. *The Roman Imperial Army of the First and Second Centuries A.D.* Totowa, NJ.

MARK J. OLSON

JULIUS CAESAR. Perhaps the most celebrated personality of ancient Rome, Gaius Julius Caesar, as the first Roman emperor, laid the foundations of the aristocratic Roman Empire that ruled the Mediterranean area and much of Europe. The principal connected sources, apart from Caesar's own writings, are Suetonius' *Life of Julius Caesar* and Plutarch's *Life of Caesar,* though there are numerous references in contemporary and later ancient authors, since even in the ancient world Caesar was a historically fascinating figure who was seen to have instituted a major change in the Roman world. Born in 100 B.C. (or perhaps 102) of a patrician family already developing the myth of a divine origin, Caesar followed a typical "public" career in order to become involved in politics. His progress through the various positions normally held was quite regular: military and diplomatic service in the late 80s and in the 70s, quaestor (financial assistant) in 69 or 68, aedile (superintendent of public buildings and works) in 65, and praetor (administrator of justice) in 62. In addition, in 63 he was elected by popular vote to the life position of *pontifex maximus.* At the same time he was building his political influence, becoming involved in a number of schemes (including suspicion of involvement in the "conspiracy" led by Catiline). In some of these he was linked with the rich and powerful senator M. Licinius Crassus, while his political activity showed an increasingly popular line. Following his praetorship, Caesar was made governor of the province of Further Spain where he first displayed his skill as a military commander.

On his return from Spain Caesar joined an informal political alliance (the so-called "First Triumvirate") with Pompey and Crassus (since all three were having requests blocked by a group of conservatives in the senate) to secure the consulship of 59. Caesar's daughter Julia was married to Pompey to cement the alliance. Their opponents got Bibulus in as Caesar's colleague, and Caesar had to use force to push through legislation to satisfy the coalition's various requests. Caesar received a special command of several provinces with a large army for 5 years, but it was mainly in Transalpine Gaul that he spent the next 9 years (58–50) adding large areas to the Roman empire. The campaigning was sometimes difficult, and occasional atrocities were committed against defeated native tribes, but in the end Caesar achieved an important conquest. The campaign also secured for him a loyal and seasoned army and a large amount of booty (which he used to pay off his enormous debts and to distribute as bribes in order to broaden his political influence).

Toward the end of his command in Gaul, the die-hard conservatives in the senate, afraid of Caesar's rising power, threatened to prosecute him for the illegalities of his first consulship and so bring about his political extinction. They won Pompey over to their side, even though he had renewed his political alliance with Caesar in 56. The ambition for power which each had meant that they would almost inevitably come into collision; the deaths of Julia in 54 and Crassus in 53 widened the breach. To protect his own position, Caesar crossed the river Rubicon (the border of his province) and invaded Italy on January 10, 49.

With his more seasoned army Caesar soon gained control of Italy, leading Pompey to withdraw to Greece with many of the senators. Caesar turned first to defeating forces loyal to Pompey in Spain, before crossing to Greece where he eventually defeated Pompey at Pharsalus in August 48. He pursued Pompey to Egypt but arrived to find his opponent had already been murdered by the local ruling dynasty in an attempt to gain his favor. With some difficulty due to lack of troops, Caesar then spent the winter extricating himself from a domestic quarrel in Egypt which ended with the establishment of Cleopatra, now his mistress, on the throne. He then defeated a Pontic army, which had invaded Asia Minor, at Zela in August 47. He returned to Rome but in January 46 had to go to N Africa where he conducted a 4-month campaign against the Pompeian forces assembled there, which ended with a major battle at Thapsus. The wars now seemed over and Caesar returned to Rome to celebrate a fourfold triumph for his Gallic, Alexandrian, Pontic, and African victories. But in 45 he had to fight his hardest campaign against the remnants of the Pompeian forces led by Pompey's sons in Spain, culminating in victory at Munda.

During these years Caesar sponsored an extensive and diverse range of legislation, but it is not clear whether this program was merely haphazard and incomplete, or whether Caesar had some long-term plan to alter the whole face of the Roman constitution. There is controversy too over Caesar's personal intentions. He continued to use the titles and powers of the republican constitution, since they cast a veil of legality over his position and actions. However, there was an unusual accumulation of offices, the dictatorship particularly being used in new and abnormal ways (culminating in the grant to him of the dictatorship for life early in 44). In combination with unprecedented and highly extravagant honors, these offices showed that Caesar was concentrating power in his own hands, perhaps because his desire and flair for administrative efficiency saw some sort of monarchy as the only practical solution to the problems which had faced the republican form of government for the last 100 years. At the time of his death Caesar was planning campaigns against Parthia and Dacia; they may have been partly an excuse to avoid a decision about what to do with the state.

Caesar also received emblems of royalty: a purple robe, statues, a gilt chair in the senate. There were some abortive attempts to offer him a crown, but these were not pressed due to the unpopularity of the idea of monarchy among the Romans. Allied to the question of monarchy is the question whether Caesar wished to be deified. There were some signs, including a senatorial decree for a temple and *flamen* (priest) for him. This suggests that full deification was planned, but the decree was not implemented until after his death.

Caesar's often-publicized "clemency" did much to conciliate the aristocracy. But his unusual powers and excessive honors, his disregard for republican procedure, the suspicion that he wished to be *rex* (king), alienated even men of his own party and he was assassinated on the Ides (15th) of March 44 in a conspiracy led by Brutus and Cassius. His death left a vacuum until his grandnephew Octavian, adopted as his son in his will, emerged to take up where his adoptive father had left off.

Caesar was married three times, but there were scandals throughout his life linking him with persons of both sexes; of his numerous mistresses the most famous were Servilia, the half-sister of Cato and mother of Brutus, and Cleopatra. As a person Caesar was extravagant, versatile, affable, and highly cultured. As a commander he had the ability to grasp the right moment for action and to gain the loyalty of his men. As an orator he was reputed to be second only to the great Cicero. As a writer his style was lucid and compressed, free of rhetoric, with simple but well-chosen vocabulary. His writings, in the new genre known as *commentarii,* include seven books on his Gallic campaigns, and three books on the civil wars; while they are masterly descriptions of warfare, they also served the purpose of propaganda for Caesar's achievements.

Bibliography

Gelzer, M. 1968. *Caesar: Politician and Statesman.* 6th ed. Trans. P. Needham. Oxford.

Bruce A. Marshall

JUNIAS (PERSON) [Gk *Iounia*]. The only woman who is called an "apostle" in the NT (Rom 16:7). She was born a Jew, and is closely associated to Andronicus. Her name was the Lat name of the *gens Junia* (see the material in Lampe 1985 and *StadtrChr,* 66–67, 146–47, 152–53, 296). Women were often called by the name of their *gens* without cognomen (similar examples are Mary [Rom 16:6] and Julia [Rom 16:15]). Two groups carried the name of the *gens Junia:* the noble members of the famous *gens,* and the freed(wo)men of the *gens* with their descendants. The second group outnumbered the first. The chances therefore are that the Christian Junia was a freed slave of the *gens.* Either way, she probably had Roman citizenship: slave masters with famous *gens* names like "Junius/ia" possessed Roman citizenship and in most cases passed it on to their slaves on the occasion of their emancipation; the freed slaves bequeathed the *gens* name and the citizenship to their freeborn children. Without exception, the Church Fathers in late antiquity identified Andronicus' partner in Rom 16:7 as a woman, as did minuscule 33 in the 9th century which records *iounia* with an acute accent. Only later medieval copyists of Rom 16:7 could not imagine a woman being an apostle and wrote the masculine name "Junias." This latter name did not exist in antiquity; its explanation as a Greek abbreviation of the Latin name "Junianus" is unlikely.

Bibliography

Brooten, B. 1978. "Junia . . . hervorragend unter den Aposteln" (Röm 16,7). Pp. 148–51 in *Frauenbefreiung: Biblische und theologische Argumente,* ed. E. Moltmann-Wendel. Munich.
Fàbrega, V. 1984–85. War Junia(s), der hervorragende Apostel (Röm. 16,7), eine Frau? *JAC* 27–28: 47–64.
Lampe, P. 1985. Iunia/Iunias: Sklavenherkunft im Kreise der vorpaulinischen Apostel (Röm 16,7). *ZNW* 76: 132–34.
Lüdemann, G. 1987. *Das Frühe Christentum nach den Traditionen der Apostelgeschichte.* Göttingen.
Schüssler Fiorenza, E. 1976. Die Rolle der Frau in der urchristlichen Bewegung. *Concilium* 12: 3–9.

Peter Lampe

JUSHAB-HESED (PERSON) [Heb *yûšab ḥesed*]. A son of Zerubbabel (1 Chr 3:20). The verse here preserves a second group of Zerubbabel's offspring, distinct from those in v 19. It has been suggested that this group of children was listed separately because they were born after the return to Palestine (Williamson *Chronicles* NCBC, 57; Rudolph *Chronicles* HAT, 29). The name, which may reflect the hopes of the time, means, "kindness will be returned." The Greek codex Alexandrinus renders the name *Asobaesd* (= Heb *yāšôb (ha)ḥesed*).

Russell Fuller

JUST, JUSTICE. The English language does not distinguish between the two Hebrew terms *mišpāṭ,* "justice," and *dîn,* "judgment." The substantive *mišpāṭ,* like the root *špṭ* from which it is derived, is multifarious in meaning. In the Mari documents, the meanings of the root *špṭ,* according to various contexts, include "to rule," "to govern," "to command [an army]," "to judge [in a forensic sense]," "to arbitrate [in a dispute]," "to warn," "to punish," and "to vindicate." Consequently, the substantive *mišpāṭ* yields a variety of meanings such as "justice," "judgment," "rights," "vindication," "deliverance," "custom," "norm." Although some contexts of *mišpāṭ* show that the root *špṭ* and the substantive *mišpāṭ* were also used in a forensic sense, there is strong evidence that attests that originally the substantive *mišpāṭ* referred to the restoration of a situation or environment which promoted equity and harmony *(šālôm)* in a community. When referring to purely legal matters, the Semitic root normally used is *dyn* ("to judge") and the substantive *dîn* referred to a decision reached in a legal court. In several biblical passages, however, both *dyn* and *špṭ* are used in parallel contexts which present them as synonyms (1 Sam 24:15; Jer 5:28; 21:12; Isa 3:13–14; Prov 31:9; Ps 7:9; 72:1–4). Similar usage of *špṭ* is also reflected in the Ugaritic literature with reference to the gods Baal, Yamm, and Mot, and to the legendary kings Kirta and Aqhat. The usage of the root *špṭ* in the OT is therefore greatly elucidated by a comparison with other Semitic languages. To arrive at the best meaning of justice in the OT, it is therefore important to pay close attention to every context in which it is used.

A. God as Judge and Guardian of Justice

The Israelites, like other Semitic people in the ANE, regarded the deity as the Judge of the whole earth (Gen 18:25). God's universal judgeship was based on the fact that it was He who created the world and established equity and justice (Ps 99:1–4). He was thus regarded as the source and guardian of justice because justice and righteousness are his very nature and attributes (Ps 97:2). In several biblical passages, the two terms "righteousness" *(ṣĕdāqâ)* and "justice" *(mišpāṭ)* are used synonymously (Amos 5:24; Gen 18:19). Justice was central among the Israelites because they were very much concerned with social relationships among themselves as a people covenanted to God and also among the nations surrounding them. In this connection, as Judge *(šôpēṭ)*, God would administer justice by punishing those whose conduct made the lives of others very difficult in the world (Ps 94:2–4). God was thus summoned to judge the nations for their disregard of justice in their social dealings with other people (Ps 9:7–9). It is not piety which God required of humans, but the practicing of justice and righteousness (Amos 5:21–24; Mic 6:6–8). In the OT, God's justice is manifested in his retribution to all people and nations according to their just deserts. Those who felt unjustly treated by others in social, economic, and political relationships summoned God to judge them, that is, to do them justice by saving them from their enemies or oppressors (Ps 7:6–11). In several other texts in the book of Psalms, when the Israelites summoned God to judge *(špṭ)* them, they were calling him to avenge them of their enemies simply as vindication for their own uprightness (Ps 17:2; 26:1–3; 28:3–4). It appears that the Israelites based God's retributive justice on the principle of judgment by ordeal. In this type of judgment, the innocent, that is, the righteous *(ṣaddîq)*, would be vindicated while the wicked would be requited according to their unrighteousness. This is best illustrated in the quarrel between the Israelites and the Ammonites. Jephthah, as judge of Israel, tried to prove the Israelites' innocence to the king of the Ammonites. When his explanation of the situation failed to convince the king of the Ammonites, Jephthah summoned Yahweh, the Judge *(haššôpēṭ)*, to decide the case between the Israelites and the Ammonites. Military victory by the Israelites was construed to mean vindication for the Israelites' innocence while a decisive defeat inflicted on the Ammonites was seen as God's judgment *(mišpâṭ)* and punishment for the Ammonites' unprovoked aggression (Judg 11:27; cf. Gen 16:5).

B. Fairness of God's Justice

The Israelites expected God's justice to be fair because it issued from God who was a righteous Judge (Ps 7:11; 9:8; 119:137; 145:17). Those who were appointed to the office of judge *(dayyān* or *šôpēṭ)* or magistrate were expected to reflect God's holy nature (Exod 18:21). Consequently, when executing justice, the judges *(šôpĕṭîm)* were to be absolutely fair, realizing that they were acting as agents or deputies of the holy God (Deut 1:16–17; cf. Exod 18:21–23). In this light, the so-called judges *(šôpĕṭîm)* of the book of Judges were appointed by God to act for him as administrators of justice in two ways. In a military emergency, they liberated the Israelites by commanding military campaigns against the aggressive enemies who threatened their freedom and peace *(šālôm)*. In peacetime, the judges administered justice by deciding disputes arising among their people (Judg 4:4–5). That these judges were just and righteous people is implied in the Deuteronomistic summary statement that when they died, the children of Israel forgot the way of the Lord (Judg 2:17–19).

C. God's Justice in Relation to the Poor

In several biblical passages, particularly in the Psalms and the Prophets, God is portrayed as having a special concern for the poor, particularly the widow, the fatherless, and the oppressed (Ps 10:17–18; 82:1–8; cf. 109:16). When they summoned God to judge them, the poor and oppressed did not expect him to reward them with material benefits beyond those they were normally entitled to in order to lead a normal good life. When they sold their produce and services, they expected a fair deal from the merchants (Amos 2:6–7). Ownership of land and property, freedom and security, constituted their inalienable human rights endowed upon them by God, their creator. For this reason, passages which refer to justice *(mišpāṭ)* of the poor are in actual fact referring to the rights of the poor (Jer 5:28). Therefore, justice *(mišpāṭ)* does not solely refer to moral norm, but also refers to basic human rights. For this reason, when the prophet Amos refers to the poor as the righteous *(ṣaddîq)*, he is referring to their being on the right with respect to their dispute with the oppressors over the infringement of their basic rights. It was therefore natural that the people oppressed by the economic, social, and political systems and others, such as the sojourners, who experienced some injustices, should appeal to God to intervene in order that their rights *(mišpāṭ)* might be restored (Ps 146:7–9; cf. 119:153–59). Since God requites all people according to their just deserts, those who felt innocent of any wrongdoing against other people, and who had not transgressed God's law, summoned God to test, try, or examine them to verify their uprightness in order that he might judge *(špṭ)* them accordingly (Ps 139:23–24). In making this summons, God was invoked to reward the wicked according to their wickedness and the upright in heart according to their righteousness (Ps 94:

1–3). God judges in order to restore the lost rights of the oppressed (Ps 76:9). He establishes justice in the world by eliminating inequalities (Ps 113:4–9). God's justice aims at creating an egalitarian community in which all classes of people maintain their basic human rights. See also JUDGE, JUDGING; POOR, POVERTY.

Bibliography

Adamiak, R. 1982. *Justice and History in the Old Testament.* Cleveland.
Boecker, H. J. 1980. *Law and the Administration of Justice in the Old Testament and in the Ancient Near East.* Minneapolis.
Whitelam, K. W. 1979. *The Just King: Monarchical Judicial Authority in Ancient Israel.* JSOTSup 12. Sheffield.

TEMBA L. J. MAFICO

JUSTIFICATION. A term that describes the event whereby persons are set or declared to be in right relation to God. The word is often used to summarize the central message of the gospel proclaimed by Paul. Despite its historic importance in Christian dogmatic tradition, however, especially in Protestantism, the noun "justification" rarely appears in the Bible. The classic Pauline statements concerning the justification of human beings (e.g., Gal 2:15–16; Rom 5:1) characteristically employ forms of the verb *dikaioun* ("to justify"). The noun *dikaiosynē,* which appears frequently in Paul and elsewhere in the NT, is more appropriately translated by the word "righteousness" or, as in common classical and Hellenistic usage, "justice." Strictly speaking, only in Rom 4:25 and 5:18 does the word *dikaiōsis* ("justification") appear. In Rom 5:16 the noun *dikaiōma,* here set in opposition to *katakrima* ("condemnation"), probably means "pronouncement of acquittal." See also the RIGHTEOUSNESS articles.

A. Terminology
B. Hebrew Scriptures and LXX
C. Qumran
D. Early Christian Traditions
E. Paul
F. Other NT Writings
G. Conclusion

A. Terminology

Both in the OT and in the NT the terms "just, justification, justify" usually translate exactly the same linguistic stock represented elsewhere in English translation by "righteous, righteousness." The English language regrettably lacks a verb etymologically akin to "righteousness." (Scholars such as Grobel and Sanders have sought to remedy the deficiency by exhuming an old Anglo-Saxon verb, "to rightwise" [= to justify, set right], but this proposal has not elicited enthusiastic acceptance.) Consequently, English translations of the Bible are generally unable to convey the close linguistic linkage between "the righteousness of God" and the justification of persons. The difficulty is illustrated by the RSV translation of Rom 3:26: "It was to prove at the present time that he [God] himself is righteous [*dikaion*] and that he justifies [*dikaiounta*] him who has faith in Jesus." This is not merely a Pauline pun; the verbal connection reflects an underlying theological coherence. In order to grasp this coherence and to appreciate the distinctive early Christian development of this complex of ideas, it is necessary to trace the functions of "righteousness/justification" language in the OT and in Jewish tradition.

B. Hebrew Scriptures and LXX

"Justification" as a theological concept has its metaphorical roots in legal language. To be "justified" is to be proved right or innocent before the bar. In the world portrayed by Israel's Scriptures, legal judgment is executed within the framework of the covenant with Yahweh; consequently, "righteousness" (*ṣĕdāqâ,* rendered by the LXX as *dikaiosynē*) in this context is a relational term which means faithful adherence to the structure of obligations established by the covenant. An excellent illustration of this is provided by Gen 38:1–26: Tamar, pretending to be a prostitute, tricks Judah into fathering her sons, but is pronounced "more righteous" than he, because he has defaulted on his obligation to her (cf. Deut 25:5–10). The oblique phrasing of Gen 15:6 (Abraham's trust in God's promise was "reckoned" as righteousness) may reflect the writer's sensitivity to the anomaly here: despite the absence of any explicit covenant relationship at that point in the narrative, Abraham is granted a standing before God normally ascribed only to participants in the Mosaic covenant. (Paul was later to capitalize upon the scrupulous turn of phrase: see Rom 4:3–8.)

Of course, precisely because "righteousness" characterizes faithful adherence to the covenant relationship, the term can be predicated of Yahweh no less than of the human covenant partners. God's righteousness is manifest in his resolute faithfulness to the covenant with Israel. Indeed, in the lament Psalms, the psalmist can frequently appeal to God's righteousness as a way of invoking the Deuteronomic covenant promises: if God is truly righteous, he will surely confer the promised deliverance and blessing (cf. Ps 31:1; 71:2). In some cases, as in Psalm 143, it is suggested that God, in his righteousness, will (or should) come to the aid of Israel on the grounds of the covenant relationship, apart from any consideration of Israel's worthiness (see esp. vv 2, 11–12); because the honor of God's name is at stake, he will not only judge and punish but also "vindicate his people" (Ps 135:13–14; cf. Ps 43:1). Both in intercession and in praise, *ṣĕdāqâ/dikaiosynē* can become a summary description of God's mighty salvific deeds on Israel's behalf (Ps 71:15–19; 98:2). Thus, the term characterizes not merely an abstract attribute of God but an aspect of the divine character made manifest in the action of claiming and delivering Israel.

Under the circumstances of the Exile, however, claims concerning God's unwavering faithfulness to the covenant became intensely problematical. How can God be described as righteous if he abandons Israel to her enemies? Particularly in Deutero-Isaiah, God's righteousness becomes the ground and content of an eschatological hope for the setting right of human historical experience: despite present appearances to the contrary, God will reveal his righteousness in a way which will vindicate Israel's trust in him, thus leading all nations to acknowledge his cosmic lordship. (Cf. Isa 51:4b–5 [LXX]: "For the Law will go forth from me, / And my judgment will go forth as a light to the nations. / My righteousness draws near quickly, /

And my salvation will go forth as a light, / And in my arm will nations hope.") In contexts such as these, the idea of God's righteousness becomes strongly associated with the ideas of deliverance and *vindication;* the latter notion is further reinforced by the LXX rendering of *ṣedeq/ṣĕdāqâ* as *dikaiosynē.* In Isa 50:7–9, for example, a passage full of legal imagery, the prophet describes God as "he who vindicates me" *(ho dikaiōsas me)* before all accusers and adversaries.

C. Qumran

The Qumran literature provides evidence for the further development of the concept of God's righteousness/justification within an apocalyptic sectarian form of Judaism. A much-discussed passage from the community's Manual of Discipline describes the hope of God's righteousness in terms reminiscent of the canonical Psalms but with heightened emphasis on the idea that God's righteousness will effect forgiveness and cleansing of sins.

> As for me, my judgment [*mišpāṭî*] is with God.
> In his hand are the perfection of my way
> and the uprightness of my heart.
> He will wipe out my transgression through his righteousness [*ṣidqôtāw*] . . .
> As for me, if I stumble, the mercies of God shall be my eternal salvation.
> If I stagger because of the sin of flesh,
> my judgment [*mišpāṭî*] shall be
> by the righteousness of God [*ṣidqat ʾēl*] which endures for ever.
>
> (1QS 11:2–3,12)

Some translations of this text have attempted to underscore its "Pauline" flavor by translating *mišpāṭî* as "my justification." This interpretation is probably slightly misleading: more to the point is the recognition that the passage portrays God's righteousness as the ground of hope for a speaker who acknowledges his own sinfulness. There is no reason to suppose that this Qumran conception had a direct influence on the formation of early Christian teaching about justification; rather, 1QS bears witness to the ongoing vitality within Judaism of the belief in God's righteousness as the basis for Israel's hope of vindication. Here again the expectation of justification is closely bound to the idea of covenant. The people of Qumran anticipate justification precisely because they participate in a community which seeks to live in faithful adherence to a particular understanding of God's covenant with Israel; consequently, they expect the God of the covenant to vindicate them in the final judgment.

D. Early Christian Traditions

The earliest Christians formulated their teaching about justification and about the righteousness of God in a linguistic and theological environment conditioned decisively by Jewish scripture and tradition. Consequently, the Christian understanding of justification represents a development of Jewish tradition rather than an innovation. Indeed, the traditions of Jesus' teaching preserved in the Synoptic Gospels use the language of justification infrequently; where these traditions do speak of "being justified," they typically carry the basic sense of being "proved right," as in the proverbial saying, "Wisdom is justified by her children" (Luke 7:35; cf. Matt 11:19: ". . . by her works"!). Two Lukan passages (Luke 10:29; 16:15) portray the desire for justification as a superficial seeking for human approval. In the parable of the Pharisee and the tax collector, on the other hand, Luke uses "justification" language with something of its characteristic OT covenant resonance: the tax collector "went down to his house justified" in the sense that he stood in right relation to God. Matthew 12:37 offers the single instance in the Gospels of an eschatological referent for justification language: "I tell you, on the day of judgment men will render account for every careless word they utter; for by your words you will be justified, and by your words you will be condemned." Here the root imagery of the law court is projected into a vision of final divine judgment (cf. Matt 25:31–46). In none of this material does "justification" receive an interpretation different from conventional Jewish usage.

Arguably the earliest distinctively Christian usage of language about justification centers on Jesus as "the Righteous One" *(ho dikaios),* the messianic figure who is unjustly rejected and killed (Acts 3:14; 7:52) but subsequently vindicated *(edikaiōthē)* by God (1 Tim 3:16) through the resurrection. Such christological conceptions are a natural outgrowth of the earliest Church's hermeneutical convention of interpreting the lament Psalms as prophetic prefigurations of the Christ's passion; the result is that the traditional hope for God's vindication of Israel becomes focused upon and enacted through the cross and resurrection. Within this framework of thought, Jesus' death was interpreted as having a vicarious sacrificial significance: "For Christ also died for sins once for all, the Righteous One for the unrighteous [*dikaios hyper adikōn*]" (1 Peter 3:18). While these formulations appear in texts written later than the Pauline epistles, in each case there is good reason to think that they preserve common early Christian tradition. (For discussion of the idea of Jesus' death as saving event in the context of Jewish thought, especially *4 Maccabees,* see Williams 1975.)

E. Paul

In the Pauline letters, there are a number of passages often regarded as citations of pre-Pauline liturgical or confessional traditions that refer to Christ as "our righteousness" (1 Cor 1:30) or to his death as a vicariously efficacious one whereby "we might become the righteousness of God" (2 Cor 5:21) or to baptism as the instrumentality through which "you were washed, you were sanctified, you were justified [*edikaiōthēte*] in the name of the Lord Jesus Christ and in the Spirit of our God" (1 Cor 6:11). Whether these formulations are pre-Pauline or not, they bear witness to the same sphere of Jewish-Christian theological conceptualities reflected in other NT writings: justification is interpreted as God's act of deliverance wrought through Jesus Christ, the Righteous One, whose sacrificial death avails for the salvation of the covenant people. This tradition is epitomized in the confessional formula of Rom 4:25, which (probably echoing Isaiah 53) acclaims "Jesus our Lord, who was put to death for our trespasses and raised for our justification [*dikaiōsis*]." This formula, by connecting justification with resurrection, underscores the connotation of "vindication" present in the terminology. None of these passages makes the characteristically Pauline linkage between justification and faith, nor is there any polemical antithesis here between Christ and the Torah.

Even the doctrine of justification by faith is presented by Paul as a commonly held conviction of early Jewish Christianity. In his account of the confrontation at Antioch, Paul represents himself as having said to Peter, "We ourselves, who are Jews by birth and not gentile sinners, since we know that a person is not justified by works of the Law but through the faith of Jesus Christ, even we have put our trust in Christ Jesus in order that we might be justified out of the faith of Christ and not out of works of the Law, because out of works of the Law 'no one shall be justified' " (Gal 2:15–16, citing Ps 143:2). According to Paul's account of the matter, all parties were agreed on the affirmation that persons are justified *dia pisteōs Iēsou Christou* ("through the faith of Jesus Christ": on the translation of this phrase, see below); the controversy at Antioch concerned the social and ritual implications of this confession. Whether Paul's claim is in fact true or whether it is a rhetorical tactic is difficult to say. Early Christians would generally have shared Paul's belief that Christ's death and resurrection were the basis for justification (see the discussion of pre-Pauline formulations above); it seems likely, then, that Paul's original contribution to the discussion was his inference that this truth now abrogated any necessity for gentile converts to be circumcised and to obey the Jewish dietary laws. Consequently, the doctrine of justification by faith became Paul's theological warrant for an understanding of the Church as a new people of God in which Jews and gentiles could be united in table fellowship (cf. Dahl 1977).

The precise relation between faith and justification is a difficult exegetical issue. Traditionally, Paul's expression *dia/ek pisteōs Iēsou Christou* in Gal 2:16 (cf. 3:22; Rom 3:22, 26) has been understood to mean "through believing in Jesus Christ" (objective genitive). The texts would then establish a dichotomy between two different modes of human religious disposition: seeking justification through "works of the Law" versus through believing in Jesus Christ (cf. also Rom 4:1–8 for the antithesis between "works" and "faith"; the dichotomy would have appeared odd to Jewish Christians, as attested by James 2:18–26). A number of recent studies (Williams 1980; 1987; Johnson 1982; Hays 1983; 1987) have argued instead for an interpretation of *dia/ek pisteōs Iēsou Christou* as "through Jesus Christ's faithfulness" (subjective genitive). On this reading, texts such as Gal 2:16 would juxtapose human striving to Christ's accomplished act of obedient self-sacrifice. This interpretation would be consistent with the view of justification articulated in Rom 5:18–19: "Then as the trespass of one [Adam] led to condemnation for all, so also the righteous act [*dikaiōma*] of one [Christ] leads to the justification [*dikaiōsis*] of life for all. For just as by the disobedience of one [Adam] many were made sinners, so also by the obedience of one [Christ] will many be made righteous [*dikaioi*]." Here Christ's act of obedience is explicitly interpreted as vicariously efficacious for the justification of "many." The differences between these interpretations of "faith of Jesus Christ" should not be exaggerated: both stress the death and resurrection of Jesus as the decisive act of God upon which justification depends, and both agree in regarding trust/faith as the appropriate response to this divine act. Furthermore, on either reading, Paul emphatically dissociates justification from the Law, which finally has no power to give life (Gal 3:21), and associates it with a relation to Jesus Christ. To do otherwise, in Paul's view, would be to deny the efficacy or necessity of Christ's death, and thus to "nullify the grace of God; for if righteousness [*dikaiosynē*] were through the Law, then Christ died to no purpose" (Gal 2:21).

In Galatians, confronting an acute pastoral crisis, Paul pushes this line of theological reflection to radical conclusions about the incompatibility of Torah and Christ: ". . . if you receive circumcision, Christ will be of no advantage to you . . . You are severed from Christ, you who would be justified by the Law; you have fallen away from grace" (Gal 5:2, 4). In the subsequent letter to the Romans, however, he steers a more moderate course, developing other lines of thought already foreshadowed in Galatians (cf. Gal 3:8–9; 3:23–25; 4:21): though the Law has no power to accomplish the justification of the ungodly, it already points toward God's ultimate purpose, which has now been fully revealed in the gospel. The Law bears witness that God always intended to reveal his righteousness through Jesus Christ in such a way that Jews and gentiles alike will experience salvation, just as Isaiah prophesied (Rom 1:16–17, 15:8–12). Thus, Paul's development of "the righteousness of God" in Romans deliberately picks up motifs from Deutero-Isaiah, portraying God's righteousness as his covenant-faithfulness, which manifests itself in the act of eschatological deliverance. This is the meaning of Paul's claim that although "the righteousness of God has been manifested apart from Law" (i.e., in Jesus Christ), nonetheless "the Law and the prophets bear witness to it" (Rom 3:21–22), as the story of Abraham illustrates (Romans 4).

Once it is recognized that "the righteousness of God" in Romans is deliberately explicated in terms of this OT covenant conceptuality, it becomes apparent that the term refers neither to an abstract ideal of divine distributive justice nor to a legal status or moral character imputed or conveyed by God to human beings. It refers rather to God's own unshakable faithfulness. (Piper [1983: 203] interprets God's righteousness as an "unswerving commitment always to preserve the honor of his name and display his glory.") Insofar as "righteousness" may be ascribed to the human beneficiaries of God's grace (cf. passages such as Phil 3:9; Rom 9:30–10:4), this righteousness should be interpreted primarily in terms of the covenant relationship to God and membership within the covenant community.

In view of these exegetical observations, the traditional debate in Christian theology over whether justification is "forensic" or "ethical" demands reformulation. "Righteousness" refers to God's covenant-faithfulness which declares persons full participants in the community of God's people. This declaration has a quasi-legal dimension, but there is no question here of a legal fiction whereby God juggles his heavenly account books and pretends not to notice human sin. The legal language points rather to the formal inclusion of those who once were "not my people" in a concrete historical community of the "sons of the living God" (Rom 9:25–26). (Justification is only one of the metaphors that Paul can use to describe this act of inclusion by grace; elsewhere he can speak, for example, of "adoption," as in Gal 4:5 and Rom 8:15.) On the other hand, though the gift of incorporation into this community neither presupposes a prerequisite moral uprightness on the part of the recipients (Rom 5:6–11) nor offers a magical transformation of moral character, participation in the covenant community carries with it a very definite normative demand for radical obedience to God (Rom 6:1–19; 12:1–2), because the very purpose of the covenant community is to manifest God's righteous design for his human creatures.

This interpretation of justification as God's act of claiming and vindicating a covenant community also precludes the individualistic error of treating justification as the believer's personal experience of forgiveness and deliverance from a subjective sense of guilt (Stendahl [1976] has stressed the absence of these categories in Paul). Paul, in Romans, does not begin with a human predicament and then present justification as the solution to it (cf. Sanders 1977; 1983). Rather, he assumes as a starting point the kerygmatic proclamation that God has acted to justify Jews and gentiles alike on the same ground. This proclamation raises the issue of God's righteousness as a theological problem. If God justifies people apart from Torah, does that mean he has capriciously abandoned his special covenant relationship with Israel? The problem is one of theodicy: "What shall we say, then? Is there injustice on God's part?" (Rom 9:14). The bulk of Romans then is a defense of God's righteousness, as assertion that God is faithful to his promises precisely in the act of justifying people through Jesus rather than through Torah. Thus, Romans deals with "justification" on two levels: (1) the "justification" of persons who are placed in right covenant relation to God through God's act in Christ and their response to it in faith; and (2) the "justification" of God's integrity in so acting.

F. Other NT Writings

In the rest of the NT, "justification" plays a relatively minor role. As the brief survey (above) of justification in the traditions of Jesus' teaching suggests, none of the gospel writers emphasizes justification as a major theological motif. The vocabulary of righteousness/justification is negligible in John (cf. John 16:8, 10 for the only instances) and altogether absent from Mark. Matthew has several sayings, especially in the Sermon on the Mount, that portray righteousness *(dikaiosynē)* as the goal of human hope or conduct (5:6, 10, 20; 6:1, 33; cf. 3:15). Some of these texts, in which righteousness is closely identified with "the kingdom of God" (5:6, 10; 6:33), might plausibly be interpreted in a manner consistent with Paul's understanding of the eschatological manifestation of the righteousness of God, but others (5:20 and 6:1) clearly refer to human moral performance. Luke's parable of the Pharisee and the tax collector (18:9–14) appears to reflect a "Pauline" understanding of justification, but Luke's failure to develop this theme in Acts suggests that the real point of the parable is the contrast between pride and repentance rather than between "justification by works" and "justification by faith." The only reference in Acts to justification appears in Paul's synagogue speech in 13:38–39: "Through this man forgiveness of sins is proclaimed to you, and by him every one that believes is freed [*dikaioutai*] from everything from which you could not be freed [*dikaiōthēnai*] by the Law of Moses." Here the connection with belief and the antithesis to the Law are faithful echoes of Pauline theology, but the use of *dikaioun* with *apo* (literally "justified from") is peculiar, and the link with "forgiveness of sins" is characteristically Lukan. The effect of this single, rather awkward, reference is simply to highlight the complete absence of justification as a theme of Christian proclamation elsewhere in Acts.

In the later NT epistles, there are two important passages that reflect a continuing concern about the Pauline formulation of the doctrine of justification. Titus 3:5–7 is a full and emphatic restatement of the doctrine, linking justification more directly with baptism than Paul did (but cf. 1 Cor 6:11) and reaffirming the Pauline denial of works as the means of justification: ". . . not because of deeds done by us in righteousness, but in virtue of his own mercy . . . which he poured out upon us richly through Jesus Christ our Savior, so that we might be justified by his grace and become heirs in hope of eternal life." The diction is more inflated than Paul's, and nothing is said here about faith, but the overall position is clearly a deft summary and extension of Paul's characteristic teaching on justification, preserving the Pauline heritage in a later historical setting.

The Letter of James, on the other hand, contains a notorious passage (2:14–26) which has often been read as a frontal assault on the Pauline doctrine of justification by faith: "You see that a person is justified by works and not by faith alone" (2:24). Briefly, it must be maintained that the understanding of "justification by faith alone" against which this polemic is aimed represents a caricature of the Pauline position (cf. Reumann 1982). Paul, like James, was insistent that faith is manifest in active obedience, and (interestingly) Paul never uses the expression "justification by faith *alone*" (*sola fide* is a slogan of the Reformation, not of Paul). The teaching of James is a corrective against a distortion that Paul himself vehemently forswore (Rom 3:8; 6:1–2). We will probably never know whether such a position was actually championed by a "hyper-Pauline" antinomian wing of the Pauline school (certainly the Pastorals represent a quite different direction of development of the Pauline tradition) or whether James has constructed a rhetorical "straw man," representing his own misinterpretation of the Pauline tradition. In either case, the conflict between James and Paul on "faith and works" is more a matter of terminology than of theological substance. If there is a material difference between the two writers, it is to be found rather in the fact that James' remarks never in any way link justification to God's redemptive act in Christ. See also JAMES, EPISTLE OF.

G. Conclusion

"Justification" has its roots in prophetic interpretation of God's covenant with Israel. Particularly in Deutero-Isaiah, God's righteousness provides the grounding for the hope of a future event whereby God will not only demonstrate his faithfulness to Israel but also extend salvation to the gentiles. Though Jesus apparently did not adopt this motif as a central theme of his preaching, the early Jewish-

Christian communities began to interpret Jesus' death and resurrection as the event through which this eschatological covenant promise was brought to fulfillment. Paul placed the idea of the righteousness of God near the center of his own theological reflection and stressed its inclusive dimension: God's eschatological righteousness revealed in Jesus Christ necessarily entails the justification of Jew and gentile on equal terms. Justification, consequently, cannot be abstracted from the formation of the "Israel of God" (Gal 6:16), a palpable historical community in which Jews and gentiles bear witness together to the grace of God. Whatever the reason (and many have been suggested), Paul's powerful and highly nuanced understanding of justification does not appear to have been widely influential in the early Church. Only much later was it "rediscovered" through hermeneutical innovations that allowed Augustine and Luther to reinterpret it for their own times as an antidote to Pelagianism and as a word of reassurance to the terrified introspective conscience (cf. Stendahl 1976). Historical criticism suggests, however, that Paul's understanding of justification must be interpreted resolutely in terms of OT affirmations of God's faithfulness to the covenant, a faithfulness surprisingly but definitively confirmed through Christ's death and resurrection (Rom 15:8). This reading of justification in Paul opens the possibility of new hermeneutical applications in a century haunted anew by questions of theodicy.

Bibliography

Barth, M. 1968. Jews and Gentiles: The Social Character of Justification in Paul. *JES* 5: 241–67.

———. 1971. *Justification.* Grand Rapids.

Beker, J. C. 1980. *Paul the Apostle.* Philadelphia.

Brauch, M. T. 1977. Perspectives on "God's Righteousness." Pp. 523–42 in E. P. Sanders, *Paul and Palestinian Judaism.* Philadelphia.

Bultmann, R. 1964. *Dikaiosyne Theou. JBL* 83: 12–16.

Conzelmann, H. 1968. Die Rechtfertigungslehre des Paulus. *EvT* 28: 389–404.

Dahl, N. A. 1977. The Doctrine of Justification. Pp. 95–120 in *Studies in Paul.* Minneapolis.

Friedrich, J.; Pöhlmann, W.; and Stuhlmacher, P., eds. 1976. *Rechfertigung: Festschrift für Ernst Kasemann.* Tübingen.

Furnish, V. P. 1968. *Theology and Ethics in Paul.* Nashville.

Gyllenberg, R. 1973. *Rechtfertigung und Altes Testament bei Paulus.* Stuttgart.

Hays, R. B. 1983. *The Faith of Jesus Christ.* SBLDS 56. Chico, CA.

———. 1985. Have We Found Abraham to Be Our Forefather according to the Flesh? *NovT* 27: 76–98.

———. 1987. Christology and Ethics in Galatians: The Law of Christ. *CBQ* 49: 268–90.

Hübner, H. 1974–75. Existentiale Interpretation der paulinischen Gerechtigkeit Gottes. *NTS* 21: 462–88.

Johnson, L. T. 1982. Romans 3:21–26 and the Faith of Jesus. *CBQ* 44: 77–90.

Käsemann, E. 1969. The Righteousness of God in Paul. Pp. 168–82 in *New Testament Questions of Today.* Philadelphia.

———. 1971. Justification and Salvation History in the Epistle to the Romans. Pp. 60–78 in *Perspectives on Paul.* Philadelphia.

Kertelge, K. 1967. *"Rechtfertigung" bei Paulus.* Münster.

Klaiber, W. 1982. *Rechtfertigung und Gemeinde.* FRLANT 127. Göttingen.

Küng, H. 1964. *Justification.* London.

Müller, C. 1964. *Gottes Gerechtigkeit und Gottes Volk.* FRLANT 86. Göttingen.

Piper, J. 1983. *The Justification of God.* Grand Rapids.

Reumann, J. 1982. *Righteousness in the NT,* with responses by J. A. Fitzmyer and J. D. Quinn. Philadelphia and New York.

Sanders, E. P. 1977. *Paul and Palestinian Judaism.* Philadelphia.

———. 1983. *Paul, the Law, and the Jewish People.* Philadelphia.

Stendahl, K. 1976. *Paul among Jews and Gentiles.* Philadelphia.

Stuhlmacher, P. 1965. *Gerechtigkeit Gottes bei Paulus.* FRLANT 87. Göttingen.

Williams, S. K. 1975. *Jesus' Death as Saving Event.* HDR 2. Missoula, MT.

———. 1980. The "Righteousness of God" in Romans. *JBL* 99: 241–90.

———. 1987. Again *Pistis Christou. CBQ* 49: 431–47.

Ziesler, J. A. 1972. *The Meaning of Righteousness in Paul.* SNTSMS 20. Cambridge.

RICHARD B. HAYS

JUSTIN MARTYR (PERSON). Justin Martyr was the most significant of the 2d-century apologists for Christianity. He was born in Samaria, lived for a time at Ephesus, and finally conducted a training school for Christians at Rome until his martyrdom about 165. His most famous pupil was the Syrian Tatian, who later modified his teaching and left the Church.

Justin's first work seems to have been his treatise *Against All Heresies,* opposed to the Samaritans Simon Magus (Acts 8?) and Menander, as well as Marcion. See MARCION, GOSPEL OF. Later he composed his *Apology* now divided into two parts. The work is addressed to Antoninus Pius and his two adopted sons. Its date may be given by Justin's insistence on eternal fire for the wicked, for in the year 156 Polycarp of Smyrna, favorably received at Rome the year before, was burned alive after threatening his judge with "eternal fire." Justin's essay begins with the demand to investigate accusations and explains what Christians believe and do. The so-called "second apology" looks like a continuation of the first, perhaps with more emphasis on the philosophy espoused by the future emperor Marcus Aurelius.

The *Apology* begins with a refutation of anti-Christian slanders and a description of Christian moral teaching. It continues with a lengthy discussion of OT prophecy as fulfilled in Christ, with remarks about philosophy along the way. It ends with fairly full and important descriptions of baptism and eucharist (filling in the gap between the *Didache* and Hippolytus) and a quotation of a letter from Hadrian against informers. The second part asks the emperor to "subscribe" to Justin's petition.

Later he wrote his *Dialogue with the Jew Trypho,* in which texts like those in the *Apology* are given more complete exegesis and Trypho presents Jewish interpretations. The most important features are (1) the OT text(s) used by Justin, and (2) his picture of the nascent New Testament:

(1) In the OT exegesis of the *Apology,* Justin used "testimony sources" with texts already chosen by Christians, whereas in the *Dialogue* he used texts transmitted by Jews. He thought that the testimony texts were authentic, while the other version(s) had been corrupted. When he claimed

in the *Dialogue* that Jews had cut predictions of Christ out of their text he was comparing their version(s) with his own Christian book (Skarsaune 1987).

(2) The "New Testament" of Justin is especially interesting because he certainly knew the major Pauline epistles but never quoted from them, presumably because of the confusion over the epistles caused by Marcion's radical revisions. He knew and referred to the Apocalypse of John. He also knew several Gospels, which he sometimes identified for Greek readers as "memorabilia of the apostles" somewhat like the *Memorabilia of Socrates* by Xenophon. In his christological exegesis of Psalm 21 (22) (*Dial.* 99–107) he refers to the "memorabilia" 13 times, including one reference to the "memorabilia of Peter" for information found only in Mark 3:16–17 (partly Luke 6:14 D). This seems to show he knows Mark as a book, just as *Apol.* 61.4 reflects John 3:3, 5. He thus uses "the memorabilia compiled by the apostles and those who followed them" (*Dial.* 103.8). Other passages, however, are based on mixtures of texts which may well go back to traditions or anthologies before Justin's time (Bellinzoni 1967). This is not to say that he knew a pre-Tatianic *Diatessaron.* Both kinds of quotations are obviously opposed to Marcion's special edition. There seem to be no traces of Hebrews, the Pastoral Epistles, or the Catholic or General Epistles in Justin's writings.

His theology also deserves attention, for in regard to Christ he has taken the Logos doctrine developed in Hellenistic Judaism after Philo and combined it with a picture of prophecy fulfilled as set forth in his testimony book(s). What holds the two together is insistence upon the incarnation of the Logos, even though he never cites John 1:14.

Bibliography

Bellinzoni, A. J. 1967. *The Sayings of Jesus in the Writings of Justin Martyr.* NovTSup 17. Leiden.

Grant, R. M. 1988. *Greek Apologists of the Second Century.* Philadelphia.

Skarsaune, O. 1987. *The Proof from Prophecy: A Study in Justin Martyr's Proof-Text Tradition.* NovTSup 66. Leiden.

ROBERT M. GRANT

JUSTUS (PERSON) [Gk *Iustos*]. **1.** The surname of Joseph, also called Barsabbas, a person put forward by the apostles along with Matthias as a candidate to replace Judas (Acts 1:23). Matthias and not Joseph Justus was the person on whom the lot fell and who was subsequently enrolled with the eleven apostles (1:26). Based on the criteria given for the candidates, Joseph Justus would have been one of those who accompanied the apostles "during all the time that the Lord Jesus went in and out among us, beginning from the baptism of John until the day when he was taken up from us" (1:21–22). The name Justus (righteousness) was not uncommon among Jews and proselytes living in the Greco-Roman world. This epithet, implying obedience and devotion to the Jewish Law, was perhaps given to him by other Jews.

2. Titius Justus, a Corinthian "worshipper of God" whose house was next to the synagogue (Acts 18:7). As a "worshipper of God" (Gk *sebomenos ton theon*), this gentile must have heard Paul speak about Jesus during Paul's stay in Corinth in the early 50s on his second journey. When Paul angrily separated himself from the synagogue, stating, according to Luke, "from now on I will go to the gentiles" (18:6), it was to the house of Titius Justus he went. Presumably Paul used this man's house for teaching and church meetings, although he probably continued to live with Prisca and Aquila (cf. 18:3). Acts does not say explicitly whether Titius Justus actually became a Christian. During Paul's Corinthian visit on his third journey (with Prisca and Aquila no longer living in Corinth) his, as well as the Church's, host was a certain Gaius (Rom 16:23), leading some commentators to harmonize Acts 18:7 and Rom 16:23. They have proposed that Titius Justus and Gaius, because each was Paul's host, were thus the same person whose full Roman *tria nomina* would have been Gaius Titius Justus (Goodspeed 1950: 382–83). The manuscript readings for Acts 18:7 offer the following variations: rather than "Titius Justus" (e.g., as in mss p. 74, B), some have "Titus Justus" (e.g., Sinaiticus, E); a few have only "Justus" (e.g., A); and a very few read only "Titus" (e.g., some Vg mss). The second and fourth readings have led some to guess that this Corinthian was the Titus of Paul's letters, but there is nothing further to support that proposal.

Acts locates the house of Titius Justus in Corinth next to the synagogue. In 1898 a heavy stone, a fragmented plinth once part of the lintel of a doorway, was found on the Lechaion Road in Corinth bearing the inscription in Greek "Synagogue of the Hebrews" (Finegan 1981: 152). Because of the style of the lettering, it has been dated after the time of Paul. The synagogue it marked was probably the successor to the one in which Paul preached, probably on the same site. The inscription is poorly cut, suggesting that the synagogue members were not wealthy (cf. Paul's characterization of the Corinthians in 1 Cor 1:26). Because the stone is quite heavy, it probably lies close to the synagogue site. On that assumption, archaeologists point out that the synagogue was not far from the marketplace, on the east side of the Lechaion Road and in a predominantly residential district. The same description would thus hold for the house of Titius Justus if Acts is correct in locating it "next door" (18:7).

3. Jesus Justus, a Jewish Christian who sent greetings to the Colossians along with Paul from his place of imprisonment (Col 4:11). Jesus (the Greek form of Joshua or Jeshua) was his Jewish name. It was common for Jews to have this name (cf. Acts 13:6) up until the 2d cent. C.E. Justus was his Latin surname, which denoted loyal observance of the law, and was probably given to him because of his reputation. He is named along with Aristarchus and Mark as being the only "men of the circumcision" among Paul's "fellow workers for the kingdom of God" who were with Paul during his imprisonment. The presence of these Jewish-Christian missionaries was comforting to Paul (Col 4:11). This would be particularly the case in light of the earlier crisis at Antioch (Gal 2:11–12), and its aftereffects (cf. Gal; Phil 3) when Paul was opposed by many Jewish-Christian missionaries.

Bibliography

Finegan, J. 1981. *The Archaeology of the New Testament.* Boulder, CO.

Goodspeed, E. J. 1950. Gaius Titius Justus. *JBL* 69: 382–83.

Haenchen, E. 1971. *The Acts of the Apostles.* Trans. B. Noble and G. Shinn. Oxford.

Lightfoot, J. B. 1879. *St. Paul's Epistles to the Colossians and to Philemon.* London.

JOHN GILLMAN

JUTTAH (PLACE) [Heb *yuṭṭâ*]. A levitical city assigned to the tribe of Judah which appears in Josh 21:16, but omitted from the Chronicle's Hebrew text although found in some LXX versions of the Chronicler. Besides being mentioned in the Joshua levitical city list, Juttah appears in only one other OT text, the allotment lists of Judah in Josh 15:55. It is described as being in the SE hill country district of Maon along with Carmel and Ziph.

The first geographer to describe Juttah was Eusebius (*Onomast.* 108: 8–10). Eusebius wrote that *Iettan* was a very large Jewish village 18 Roman miles from Eleutheropolis in the middle of Darome in the Negeb. The site is not mentioned again until 1714 when Relandi (1714: 870) quoted the two Joshua texts and Eusebius. He suggested that Juttah was the birthplace of John the Baptist and the home of Zachariah and Elizabeth. Relandi argued that *polis Iouda* (city of Judah) of Luke 1:39 should read *polis Iouta* (city of Juttah). As with most of Relandi's commentaries, no identification is made.

It was E. Robinson (1841: 190) who made the first positive association of biblical Juttah with the village Yaṭṭā (M.R. 158095). Located in the Ziph district, just E of Hebron at the edge of the Judean wilderness, Yaṭṭā has been identified with biblical Juttah by Guérin (1869: 205–6), Wright (*WHAB,* 125) Aharoni (*LBHG,* 379), and Boling (1985: 25). The strategic location of this ancient city is important because of the watershed road that passes Yaṭṭā. This road extends N to Hebron, Jerusalem, and Shechem, and S to Eshtemoaʿ, Arad, and Mormah. There have been very few archaeological surveys conducted at Yaṭṭā and no excavations. The only historical period that has been identified is Byzantine, although the occupation of the site is obviously much older. Today a large Palestinian village which holds the biblical name sits on the site. Until an excavation is done, the ancient occupation of Yaṭṭā will be unknown. See Peterson 1977: 551–56.

Bibliography

Boling, R. 1985. Levitical Cities: Archaeology and Texts. Pp. 23–32 in *Biblical and Related Studies Presented to Samuel Iwry.* Winona Lake, IN.

Cross, F. M., and Wright, G. E. 1956. The Boundary and Province Lists of the Kingdom of Judah. *JBL* 75: 202–26.

Guérin, M. V. 1869. *Description Géographie Historique et Archéologique de la Palestine.* Vol. 3: *Judée.* Paris.

Peterson, J. L. 1977. *A Topographical Surface Survey of the Levitical "Cities" of Joshua 21 and I Chronicles 6.* Diss. Seabury-Western Theological Seminary.

Relandi, H. 1714. *Palaestina ex Monumentis Veteribus Illustrata.* Vol. 2. Trajecti Butavorum.

Robinson, E. 1841. *Biblical Researches in Palestine.* Vol. 2. Boston.

JOHN L. PETERSON

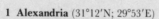

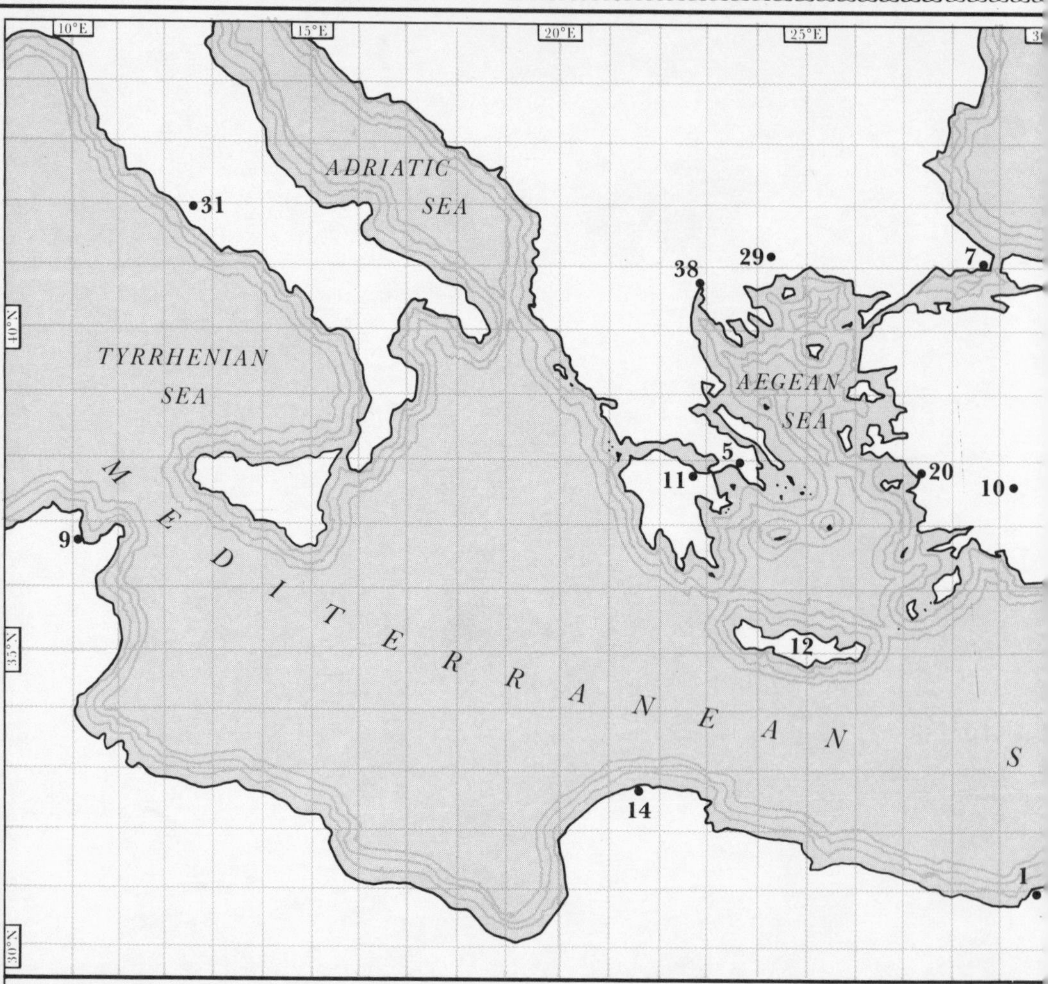

1 Alexandria (31°12′N; 29°53′E)
2 Amarna, Tell el- (27°38′N; 30°52′E)
3 Antioch (36°12′N; 36°10′E)
4 Assur (35°27′N; 43°16′E)
5 Athens (37°58′N; 23°43′E)
6 Babylon (32°33′N; 44°24′E)
7 Byzantium/Constantinople (41°01′N; 28°58′E)
8 Carchemish (36°49′N; 38°01′E)
9 Carthage (36°54′N; 10°16′E)
10 Colossae (37°46′N; 29°15′E)
11 Corinth (37°56′N; 22°56′E)
12 Crete
13 Cyprus
14 Cyrene (32°48′N; 21°54′E)
15 Damascus (33°30′N; 36°18′E)
16 Dumah/al-Djawf (Jauf) (29°48′N; 39°52′E)
17 Dura-Europus (34°46′N; 40°46′E)
18 Ebla/Tell Mardikh (35°48′N; 36°45′E)
19 Elephantine (24°05′N; 32°53′E)
20 Ephesus (37°55′N; 27°17′E)
21 Haran (36°51′N; 39°00′E)
22 Hattusas/Boghazköy (40°02′N; 34°37′E)
23 Mari (34°33′N; 40°53′E)
24 Memphis (29°51′N; 31°15′E)
25 Nag Hammadi (26°04′N; 32°13′E)
26 Nineveh (36°25′N; 43°10′E)
27 Nuzi (35°22′N; 44°18′E)
28 Persepolis (29°57′N; 52°52′E)
29 Philippi (41°05′N; 24°19′E)
30 Qurayya (28°47′N; 36°00′E)
31 Rome (41°53′N; 12°30′E)
32 Seleucia (33°05′N; 44°35′E)
33 Sidon (33°33′N; 35°22′E)
34 Susa (32°11′N; 48°15′E)
35 Tadmor/Palmyra (34°36′N; 38°15′E)
36 Tarsus (36°52′N; 34°52′E)
37 Thebes/Luxor (25°42′N; 32°38′
38 Thessalonica (40°38′N; 22°58′E)
39 Ugarit/Ras Shamra (35°35′N; 35°45′E)
40 Ur (30°56′N; 46°08′E)
41 Uruk (31°18′N; 45°40′E)